ALL YOU NEED TO KNOW ABOUT...

Knights and Castles

Illustrated by **Charles Dutertre**

CHERRYTREE BOOKS

The castle

Castles were usually built on top of a hill
or rocky slope, where they were difficult to attack.
The castle protected the land around it.

The castle was where a lord,
his lady and his knights lived.
It was their home.

The castle was surrounded by thick walls and lookout towers.

Outside the walls there was a moat – a deep ditch full of water.

Inside the walls

Castles were well protected. It was difficult to get in.

First you had to cross the drawbridge. Guards could raise it with heavy chains to keep the enemy out.

Armed soldiers stood guard on the wall-walks and turrets.

drawbridge

The main courtyard was like a busy village, filled with people and animals.

keep

There was even a vegetable plot.

main courtyard

turret

9

Inside the keep

The lord and his family lived in the keep, which was the safest part of the castle. Everyone hid there if the castle was under attack.

On the first floor was the great hall, where everyone ate, and where the lord held court.

Food and drink were stored on the ground floor.

The soldiers kept their weapons in the guard room, at the top of the keep. They all slept here too.

Only the lord and his family had their own bedrooms. There was not much furniture, and it was very cold in winter.

Minstrels went from castle to castle to play music.

The ladder to the keep could be pulled inside in times of danger.

Who **lived** in a castle?

A castle was home
to many people.

Soldiers guarded
the castle.

The
falconer
trained
birds of
prey for
hunting.

Servants cleaned
and cooked.

A nurse
looked after
the lord's
children.

Knights from nearby
castles came to visit.

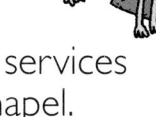

The chaplain held services
in the castle chapel.

Joiners, carpenters and stonemasons built and repaired the buildings.

The blacksmith made shoes
for the horses, and tools.

Cooks prepared the food
in the large kitchen.

A day begins...

The lord gets dressed in his fine clothes –
with help from a servant.

The bath water takes a
long time to heat up...

...which is
why...

The lady of the castle is woken and her lady-in-waiting helps her to dress.

Her hair is plaited, and covered in a wimple and a veil.

...several people bath at the same time in a big wooden barrel.

Flowers help to make the water smell sweet.

15

A feast!

Banquets were held in the great hall.

The knights' food was served on thick slices of bread, called trenchers. They ate with knives and spoons — there were no forks.

Musicians played to announce each new course.

The lord and lady, and their guests, sat at the table of honour. They ate off silver plates.

Players entertained the diners.

17

Pastimes

A favourite pastime for the lord was hunting deer and wild boar.

Falcons were used to hunt small animals.

The knights liked to play ball games…

…and chess.

Children played
with hoops and
other toys.

The ladies embroidered,
while listening to music.

Training a knight

A knight's job was to fight wars.
His training started when he was still a child.

At about seven, a lord's son was
sent to train with another lord.

He became a page. He learned
how to look after horses…

…and how to ride them.

He also learned about
hunting and good manners.

When he was fourteen,
he became a squire.

He looked after the knights'
weapons and armour.

He learned how to use a lance. If he missed the target,
a heavy bag of sand swung round and hit him on the head!

He practised fighting…

…and using a sword.

The big day

When he was twenty-one, the apprentice prepared for a big ceremony, the dubbing, at which he would become a knight.

The dubbing was a religious ceremony. The knight-to-be spent the night before in prayer.

In the morning, squires helped him to put on his coat of mail…

his tunic…

and his helmet.

When he was ready, he would kneel
before the lord. The lord placed his sword on
the young man's shoulders, to show that he was now a knight.

He was given his
sword and spurs.

For the rest of his life,
a knight had to be brave and
loyal, and defend the weak.

Weapons and armour

The first knights wore long coats of mail, which were made up of tiny iron loops.

Later, when weapons had become even more dangerous, knights needed more protection. They wore a solid coat of armour that covered the whole body. It was very heavy.

The club was a heavy ball of metal with spikes.

Shields, decorated with coats-of-arms, gave extra protection.

Knights were equipped with a sword and crossbow.

The long lance was used to pierce the enemy's armour and to push him off his horse.

The knight's horse also wore protective armour.

25

A tournament

To practise for battle, and to show off their skills,
knights took part in tournaments.

Knights on horseback fought in teams, or one-to-one.

The herald would announce the names of the knights taking part.

The winners won the horses and armour of the losers.

One-to-one fighting was called jousting. It was exciting to watch. Two knights charged at each other and tried to push each other off their horses. They used blunt lances so that it was not so dangerous.

27

Off to War

Knights fought on horseback, with their lance and sword. Just before the battle, the herald would sound his trumpet.

The knights spurred on their horses and charged at the enemy. Their armour was very heavy — if they fell, they couldn't get up, so the enemy could take them prisoner.

Crossbows fired
short arrows.
They took a long
time to reload.

Archers, on foot,
shot long arrows
from their bows.

Attacking **a** castle

The attackers used a big catapult to hurl stone balls against the castle walls.

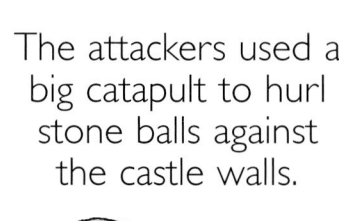

They pushed huge wooden towers full of soldiers up to the outer wall.

Archers fired burning arrows to set light to any wooden structures.

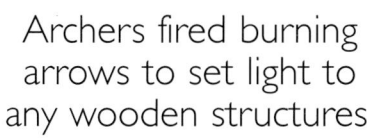

Other soldiers used a battering ram to try to break in.

Defending a castle

Hiding behind the ramparts,
archers shot arrows at the enemy.
Crossbows were fired through narrow slits.

The defenders threw all kinds of things at the enemy:
boiling water, stones, hot sand…

Castles were very
difficult to capture.

Sometimes, the enemy simply
waited until those inside gave in
because they were starving.

Outside the castle walls

All around the castle, local peasants farmed the land.
The land belonged to the lord. The peasants had to give part
of their harvest to the lord to feed the people in the castle.
In return, the lord had to protect the peasants.

The animals provided meat, wool and leather.

The windmill belonged to the lord. The peasants ground their corn there.

Find out more...

Bows and arrows

Longbows could send arrows
300 metres or more.

Marriage

Young noblemen got married very
young, at about fourteen or fifteen
years old, and they usually
had many children.

Sharing a bed

Castles were not very comfortable.
They were cold and dark.
In the early castles, people slept on
straw mattresses on the floor.
Later, they slept in groups in big beds.

Built to last

The early castles were built of earth and wood. Later castles had thick stone walls, which were difficult to destroy.

Throwing stones

The trebuchet was used to sling large stones over the top of the castle walls.

Caerphilly Castle

Caerphilly Castle in Wales was a very strong castle, with many towers, moats, ditches and tunnels within the outer walls.

Coats-of-arms

Every lord had his own family arms, with its own colours and shapes.

Index

animals 9, 18, 35
apprentices 22
archers 29, 32
armour 21, 24, 25, 27, 28
arrows 29, 31, 32, 36
attack 10, 30, 31
ball games 19
banquets 16
bathing 14, 15
battering ram 31
battles 26, 28
bedrooms 11, 36
birds of prey 12
blacksmiths 13
bows 29, 36
bravery 23
Caerphilly Castle 37
carpenters 13
castles
    attacking 30, 31
    buildings 7, 8, 9, 37
    defending 32, 33
    inhabitants 12, 13
    inside 10, 11, 36
    outside 34
    situation 6
catapults 31
chapel 12
chaplain 12
chess 19
children 12, 19, 20, 36
cleaning 12
clothes 14, 15
clubs 25
coats of mail 22, 23
coats-of-arms 25, 37
cooking 12, 13
corn 35
courtyard 9
crossbows 25, 29, 32
deer 18
drawbridge 8
dubbing ceremony 22, 23

embroidery 19
enemies 8, 25, 28, 32, 33
falconers 12, 18
fighting 20, 21, 27
food 10, 11, 13, 16
forks 16
furniture 11
great hall 10, 16
guard room 11
guards 8
harvest 34
helmet 22
heralds 27, 28
horses 13, 20, 25, 26, 27, 28
hunting 12, 18, 20
joiners 13
jousting 27
keep 9, 10, 11
kitchen 13
knights 6, 12
    dubbing ceremony 22, 23
    eating 16
    fighting 28
    pastimes 19
    tournaments 26, 27
    training 20, 21
    weapons and armour 24, 25
knives 16
ladies 6, 15, 17, 19
lady-in-waiting 15
lances 21, 25, 27, 28
land 6, 34
leather 35
longbows 36
lord's family 10, 11, 12, 20
lords 6, 10, 11, 14, 17, 18, 23, 34, 35, 37
manners 20
marriage 36
meat 35
minstrels 11
moats 7, 37
music and musicians 11, 17, 19
nurses 12

pages 20
pastimes 18-19
peasants 34, 35
players 17
playing 19
prayer 22
prisoners 28
protection 6, 8, 24, 25, 34
riding 20
servants 12, 14
shields 25
skills 26
sleeping 11
soldiers 8, 11, 12, 31
spoons 16
spurs 23
squires 21, 22
stonemasons 13
swords 21, 22, 25, 28
tools 13
tournaments 26-27
towers 7, 31, 37
toys 19
training 20, 21
trebuchet 37
tunic 22
tunnels 37
turrets 8, 9
vegetable plot 9
veil 15
village 9
walls 7, 8, 31, 34, 37
wall-walks 8, 9
wars 20, 28
weapons 11, 21, 24-25
wild boar 18
wimple 15
windmill 35
winter 11
wood 37
wool 35

Volume 1

THIRD EDITION

PATHOLOGY OF THE SKIN

WITH CLINICAL CORRELATIONS

ELSEVIER CD-ROM LICENCE AGREEMENT

Volume 1

THIRD EDITION

PATHOLOGY OF THE SKIN

WITH CLINICAL CORRELATIONS

Phillip H McKee MD FRCPath
Formerly Associate Professor of Pathology and
Director, Division of Dermatopathology
Department of Surgical Pathology
Brigham and Women's Hospital and Harvard Medical School
Boston MA
USA

Eduardo Calonje MD DipRCPath
Director of Diagnostic Dermatopathology
Department of Dermato-Histopathology
St John's Institute of Dermatology
St Thomas's Hospital
London
UK

Scott R Granter MD
Associate Professor of Pathology
Harvard Medical School
Associate Pathologist
Brigham and Women's Hospital
Boston MA
USA

ELSEVIER
MOSBY

ELSEVIER
MOSBY

An imprint of Elsevier Limited

First published 1989
Second edition 1996
Third edition 2005
   Reprinted 2005, 2006

ISBN 0 323 03672 4

British Library Cataloguing in Publication Data
A catalogue record for this book is available from the British Library

Library of Congress Cataloging in Publication Data
A catalog record for this book is available from the Library of Congress

Notice
Medical knowledge is constantly changing. Standard safety precautions must be followed, but as new research and clinical experience broaden our knowledge, changes in treatment and drug therapy may become necessary r appropriate. Readers are advised to check the most current product information provided by the manufacatctureer of each drug to be administered to verify the recommended dose, the method and duration of administration, and contraindications. It is the responsibility of the practitioner, relying on experience and knowledge of the patient, to determine dosages and the best treatment for each individual patient. Neither the Publisher nor the editors assume any liability for any injury and/or damage to persons or property arising from this publication.

The Publisher

ELSEVIER
your source for books,
journals and multimedia
in the health sciences

www.elsevierhealth.com

Working together to grow
libraries in developing countries

www.elsevier.com | www.bookaid.org | www.sabre.org

ELSEVIER   BOOK AID International   Sabre Foundation

Commissioning Editor: Michael Houston
Project Development Manager: Sheila Black
Editorial Assistant: Kathryn Mason
Project Manager: Naughton Project Managemen, Aoibhe O'Shea
Design Manager: Sarah Russel
Copyeditor: Isobel Black
Marketing Managers: Jemma Zighed (UK), Ethel Cathers (USA)

Printed in China
Last digit is the print number: 9 8 7 6 5 4 3

The publisher's policy is to use **paper manufactured from sustainable forests**

Contents

List of Contributors   vi
Preface   vii
Acknowledgements   viii
Dedications   x

Volume 1

1   The structure and function of skin   1
2   Disorders of keratinization   37
3   Inherited and autoimmune subepidermal blistering diseases   81
4   Acantholytic disorders   139
5   Spongiotic, psoriasiform and pustular dermatoses   171
6   Lichenoid and interface dermatoses   217
7   Superficial and deep perivascular inflammatory dermatoses   261
8   Granulomatous, necrobiotic and perforating dermatoses   287
9   Inflammatory diseases of the subcutaneous fat   341
10 Diseases of the oral mucosa   385
11 Diseases of the genital skin   473
12 Degenerative and metabolic diseases   539
13 Cutaneous adverse reactions to drugs   623
14 Neutrophilic and eosinophilic dermatoses   673
15 Vascular diseases   709
16 Idiopathic connective tissue disorders   775
17 Infectious diseases of the skin   837

Volume 2

18 Disorders of pigmentation   993
19 Diseases of collagen and elastic tissue   1023
20 Diseases of the hair   1061
21 Diseases of the nails   1127
22 Tumors of the surface epithelium   1153
23 Melanocytic nevi   1241
24 Melanoma   1309
25 Cutaneous lymphoproliferative diseases and related disorders   1357
26 Cutaneous metastases and Paget's disease of the skin   1497
27 Tumors of the hair follicle   1519
28 Tumors and related lesions of the sebaceous glands   1565
29 Tumors of the sweat glands   1589
30 Cutaneous cysts   1663
31 Connective tissue tumors   1683

Glossary   G1
Index   I1

Contributors

Thomas Brenn MD PhD

Assistant Professor of Pathology
Harvard Medical School
Associate Pathologist
Brigham and Women's Hospital
Boston, MA
USA

Tumors of the surface epithelium *with Phillip H McKee*
Tumors of the hair follicle *with Phillip H McKee*
Tumors of the sweat glands *with Phillip H McKee*

Wayne Grayson MBChB(UFS) PhD FCPath(SA)

Associate Professor of Pathology and Principal Pathologist
Division of Anatomical Pathology
National Health Laboratory Service
University of the Witwatersrand
Johannesburg
South Africa

Infectious diseases of the skin
with Phillip H McKee and Eduardo Calonje

Alexander JF Lazar MD PhD

Assistant Professor of Pathology and Dermatology
University of Texas MD Anderson Cancer Center
Houston, TX
USA

Tumors and related lesions of the sebaceous glands
with Phillip H McKee

B Jack Longley MD

Professor
Department of Dermatology
University of Wisconsin Health
Madison, WI
USA

Diseases of the nails *with Richard K Scher*

Sallie Neill MB ChB FRCP

Consultant Dermatologist
St John's Institute of Dermatology
St Thomas's Hospital
London
UK

Diseases of the genital skin *with Eduardo Calonje*

Rodrigo Restrepo MD

Director, Laboratory of Pathology
Clinica Medellin
Associate Professor of Pathology and Dermatopathology
Department of Surgical Pathology
Universidad Pontificia Bolivariana
Medellin
Colombia

Diseases of the hair *with Phillip H McKee and Eduardo Calonje*

Richard K Scher MD FACP

Professor of Clinical Dermatology
College of Physicians and Surgeons
Columbia University
New York, NY
USA

Diseases of the nails *with B Jack Longley*

Sook-Bin Woo DMD MMSc

Assistant Professor
Harvard School of Dental Medicine
Attending Dentist and Consultant Pathologist
Brigham and Women's Hospital
Boston, MA
Staff Pathologist, Pathology Services Inc.
Cambridge, MA
USA

Diseases of the oral mucosa

Preface

Dermatopathology, in company with all other branches of medicine, is undergoing a unique revolution as a result of the advances brought about by the molecular era in our understanding of the etiology and pathogenesis of disease. Newer classifications and treatment regimens have a solid scientific basis rather than mere gestalt or idiosyncratic views. Having said that, the basis for all therapeutic measures and clinically directed research programs remains completely dependent upon diagnostic accuracy.

Dermatopathology is a unique branch of pathology, since it enables the clinician to directly view the patient's gross pathology and, as a result, the success of the specialty often depends as much upon careful clinicopathological correlation as it does upon histological features particularly, for example, in the context of the inflammatory dermatoses. The third edition has been completely re-written and re-organized while at the same time retaining clinicopathological correlation as its basis. Innumerable new entities have been included and, in recognition of their particular importance, new chapters discussing diseases of the hair follicle, nail, external genitalia and oral mucosa have been added. In addition a chapter has been devoted to the cutaneous manifestations of adverse drug reactions. The illustrations, which now number in excess of 5000, are mostly new, largely representing replacement photographs or pictures of new entities. With the passing of each year new variants of well recognized conditions are described with astounding frequency and the number of newly described entities expands exponentially. As a result, increasing numbers of pictures have been necessary to ensure that the reader has as wide a spectrum of illustrations as possible to facilitate accurate histological diagnosis.

Writing the third edition has been an enormous challenge to all involved. We, the authors, have learnt much from the literature and from our peers, fellows and residents and sincerely hope that you, the readers, gain as much from reading this text as we have gained from writing it.

PH McKee
E Calonje
SR Granter

Acknowledgements

The third edition has taken five years to write. It became very clear at an early stage that it was not possible to undertake the immense job of writing and illustrating this new edition while concurrently working full time as dermatopathologist and Director of Service at Brigham and Women's Hospital in Boston. As a result, two very close friends and colleagues, Eduardo Calonje and Scott Granter came on board to help. Their contribution has been immeasurable and is very much appreciated. In addition, two wonderful friends in the Division of Dermatopathology at Brigham and Women's Hospital, Thomas Brenn and Alex Lazar, are first authors on the chapters dealing with epidermal and appendage tumors. I am also indebted to Wayne Grayson, a close friend for many years, Sook Bin-Woo, who gently corrected all of my oral pathology misdiagnoses, and Rodrigo Restrepo for his fabulous hair disease chapter. Other important contributors whom I thank for their great help and enthusiasm include Sallie Neill, Jack Longley and Richard Scher. I also thank Jo-Anne Vergilio for her helpful advice and useful criticism of the cutaneous lymphoma chapter and Pratista K Ramdial for her valuable editorial assistance.

Over the past 5 years I have been extremely fortunate to have had the help and support of my secretary and friend Carol Foss. She has uncomplainingly devoted more hours than I can imagine, dealing with many of the administrative details and referencing aspects relating to the book. Her help has been tremendous and her kindness very much appreciated. Without her, the book would undoubtedly have been delayed for many additional years.

One of the great difficulties in writing a book as comprehensive as this is obtaining high quality examples of many of the rarer entities that are included. I am indebted to many of my clinical colleagues and friends for their kindness in lending me so many precious slides to photograph and clinical images to use. I must also make reference to my friend Alan Marsden, MD from St George's Hospital in London, who provided the majority of clinical images included in the first and second editions and more recently, to the Institute of Dermatology in London which supplied the majority of clinical illustrations in the third edition. Without their generosity, it would not have been possible to properly illustrate the clinical aspect of this book. I am also particularly grateful to NC Dlova, MD of the Nelson R Mandela School of Medicine, Natal, South Africa for so kindly supplying numerous beautiful clinical photographs for the infectious diseases chapter.

I also want to take this opportunity to thank the many people who in various ways have contributed to my career in dermatopathology: firstly my aunts Kathleen and Norah (now deceased), who brought me up and propelled me into medical school to follow the family tradition; Professor Florence McKeown and the late Martin Beare, MD of the Royal Victoria Hospital in Belfast, who kindly informed me one day that I was going to train as a dermatopathologist whether I liked it or not! Professor John Tighe MD, who was Head of the Department of Pathology at St Thomas' Hospital in London, where I was a member of faculty, offered me every encouragement and helped keep me on the straight and narrow! My great friend Anthony du Vivier from King's College Hospital in London gave me considerable support and encouragement when I first moved to London and introduced me to Tim Hailstone and Yitek Tracz of Gower Medical Publishing when the concept of *Pathology of the Skin with Clinical Correlations* was first broached. Fiona Foley, now Executive Vice President of Elsevier's Global Medicine Division, has been a friend and given her support and encouragement for more years than she would care to remember. Chris Fletcher deserves special mention. In addition to being a wonderful and extremely loyal friend, he has been a source of great support for very many years and, in combination with the late Ramzi Cotran, was responsible for giving me the wonderful opportunity of running the Division of Dermatopathology at Brigham and Women's Hospital, Harvard Medical School, until I took early retirement.

The third edition is very much a team effort and we have been helped by an amazing group of people from Elsevier without whom this book would never have happened. They are a truly remarkable team and include Michael Houston (Executive Publisher), Sheila Black (Project Development Manager), Isobel Black (Copy Editor), Sarah Russell (Designer), Nora Naughton (Project Manager), Sarah Abel (Production Controller) and Kathryn Mason (Editorial Assistant). Michael, in addition to being an old friend, offered continuous encouragement and wined me and dined me as and when he thought it was necessary! Sheila Black had very many roles in addition to her official one. Most importantly she acted as a therapist and mediator and as a result became a great friend of us all. Isobel Black is a very remarkable woman. Her skill at copyediting is such that she could easily have become one of the editors of this book. We are very grateful for the kindness shown to us by the Naughton Project Management team and for the design skills of Sarah Russell.

Last, but by no means least, my gratitude goes to our children (now grown up), Andrea, Kathryn, Sharon and Stephen, who continue to dismiss dermatopathology as most certainly not for them but all of whom, to their great credit, are now wonderfully successful in the careers of their choosing. I thank them all for their love and the immense pleasure they have given me over the past years.

Phillip H McKee

I want to thank the following colleagues for their continuous encouragement and friendship: Pratista Ramdial, Bong Kim, Anne Stewart, Luisa Fernanda Motta, José María Rodenas, Mario Dueñas, Mar Blanes Martínez, Ana Cristina Ruiz, Esmeralda Vale, Isabel Viana and Nora Mendez.

Eduardo Calonje

I am indebted to my teachers and mentors who patiently taught me the art and science of pathology. The late Dr Ramzi Cotran supported me throughout training and as a faculty member in his department. I am one of the truly fortunate to have been mentored by this great man. I am also indebted to Dr Joseph "Mac" Corson, a genuine gentleman and scholar, who taught me the principles of diagnostic pathology by example. I wish also to thank Dr Martin Mihm, Jr for his support and encouragement.

Scott R Granter

Dedications

Writing the third edition has been an immense undertaking, which has occupied every free waking moment and more throughout the past 5 years. Without the complete and wholehearted encouragement of my wonderful wife and best friend Gracie, the book would never have been finished. How she coped with me continuously working on the book, let alone my unpredictable moods and passionate rages is a source of great mystery to me. Her help has been truly immeasurable and completion of this book with an intact marriage reflects the degree of her support.

Phillip H McKee

To my parents Julio and Alicia who have given me so much.

To my wife Claudia and children Mateo and Isabella. This work will not have come to fruition without their continuous support and love. This effort is more theirs than mine.

Eduardo Calonje

For Bethany, Walter and Joan.

Scott R Granter

In memoriam

The late Neil Smith MD was a wonderful friend and colleague and a superb dermatopathologist. His breadth of knowledge and insightful diagnoses were a source of inspiration to innumerable residents, fellows and peers. He had a unique ability to get to the heart of a problem and his opinion was very widely sought throughout the world. Tragically, Neil died at an early age. It was a great pleasure to have worked with him, albeit for only a brief time. He is very much missed. This edition is a tribute to his memory.

Phillip H McKee

The structure and function of skin

Epidermis   1
Ultrastructure and composition   4
Epidermal dendritic cells   13
Merkel cells   18
Epidermal appendages   20

Dermis   28

Blood supply   32

Nervous system   35

Subcutaneous fat   36

The skin or integument is a double-layered membrane covering the exterior of the body and is continuous with the mucous membranes lining the body's orifices. It shows a marked variation in thickness, measuring from less than 1 mm (on the eyelid) to more than 4 mm (on the back). The wide range of properties of the skin is summarized in *Table 1.1*.[1,2]

The skin can be divided into two parts:
- an outer layer, the epidermis (Gr. *epi*, on; *derma*, skin)
- an inner layer, the dermis, which rests on and is attached to the subcutaneous fat (hypodermis, panniculus adiposus).

There are two further subdivisions:
- glabrous (smooth) skin, which is typified by a thick keratin layer and is found on the palms and soles
- hair-bearing (thin) skin, which covers the rest of the body.

There is considerable regional variation in structure, making knowledge of the normal anatomy of the skin at its varying sites essential for the accurate diagnosis of skin biopsies (*Figs 1.1–1.15*).

References

1.   Goldsmith, L.A. (ed.) (1991) Physiology, biochemistry and molecular biology of the skin, 2nd edn. New York: Oxford University Press.
2.   Freinkel, R.K., Woodley, D.T. (eds) (2001) The biology of the skin. New York: Parthenon Publishing.

Epidermis

The epidermis, derived from ectoderm, is a keratinizing stratified squamous epithelium from which arises the cutaneous appendages, namely the pilosebaceous follicles, nails, and apocrine, eccrine and apoeccrine sweat glands. In addition to keratinocytes there is a 'clear' cell population, which includes melanocytes and Langerhans' cells. Merkel cells are also present although these are difficult to identify in hematoxylin and eosin stained sections. The epidermis comprises four clearly defined layers or strata:
- basal cell (stratum basale, stratum germinativum)
- prickle cell (stratum spinosum)
- granular cell (stratum granulosum)
- keratin (stratum corneum) (*Fig. 1.16*).

Table 1.1
Properties of the skin

• Maintains integrity of the body
• Protects from injurious stimuli
• Absorbs and excretes liquids
• Regulates temperature
• Waterproofs
• Absorbs ultraviolet light
• Metabolizes vitamin D
• Detects sensory stimuli
• Provides cosmetic functions
• Acts as a barrier against microorganisms

The epidermis continuously renews itself. It is divided functionally into four compartments: stem cell, transit amplifying cell, differentiating cell and functional cell.[1]

The site and source of the epidermal stem cells has long been a cause of controversy. Although in hair-bearing skin, the follicular bulge is thought to represent a major source of the epidermal stem cells, particularly in regenerating skin following trauma, there is considerable evidence to support the concept of an epidermis-based subpopulation of stem cells especially in glabrous skin where, by definition, hairs are absent. Thus cell kinetic studies demonstrate that the basal cells of the epidermis include three populations: stem cells, transit-amplifying cells (which remain in the basal layer until they become committed) and committed cells (which following cell division rapidly ascend into the suprabasal epithelium to undergo terminal differentiation).[2]

- *Stem cells*, by definition, are relatively undifferentiated, are physically protected and have unlimited capacity for cell division but do so very slowly (slow-cycling stem cells).[3] They may be identified in vivo by their long-term retention of tritiated thymidine, high level of expression of β1 and α6 integrins, and diminished expression of transferrin receptor.[1,4] Stem cells have tremendous proliferative potential, the epidermis being renewed every 2 weeks throughout life.[5]
- *Transit-amplifying cells* have only a limited capacity for mitosis (four or five divisions) before becoming committed to terminal differentiation.
- *Committed cells* have irreversibly lost the capacity to divide and inevitably progress along keratinization pathways. Loss of α6β4 integrin and expression of keratin 1 are characteristics of committed cells.[4]

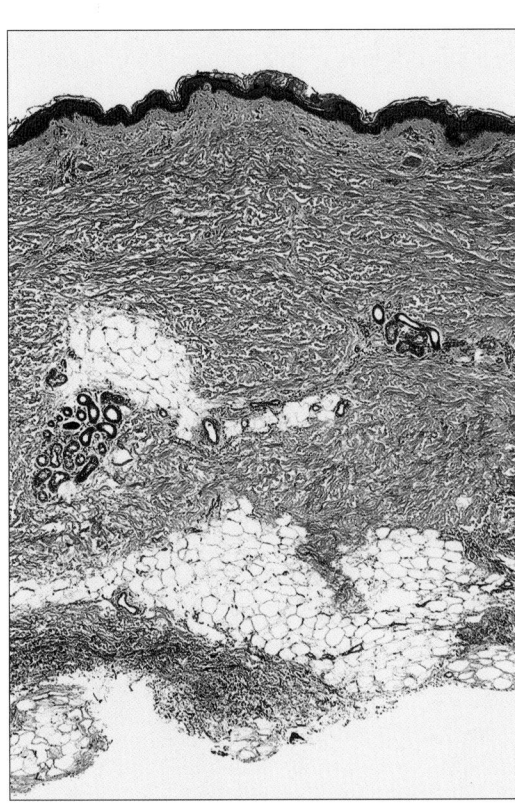

Fig. 1.1
Skin from forearm showing a fairly thin epidermis. Compare the thickness of the dermis with that from the back. Two eccrine sweat glands are present.

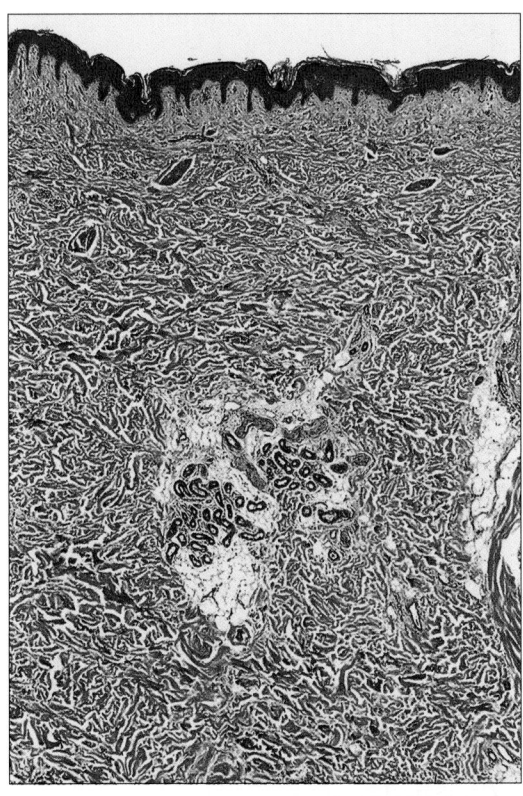

Fig. 1.2
Skin from the lower back: at this site the dermis is very thick and is characterized by broad parallel fascicles of collagen.

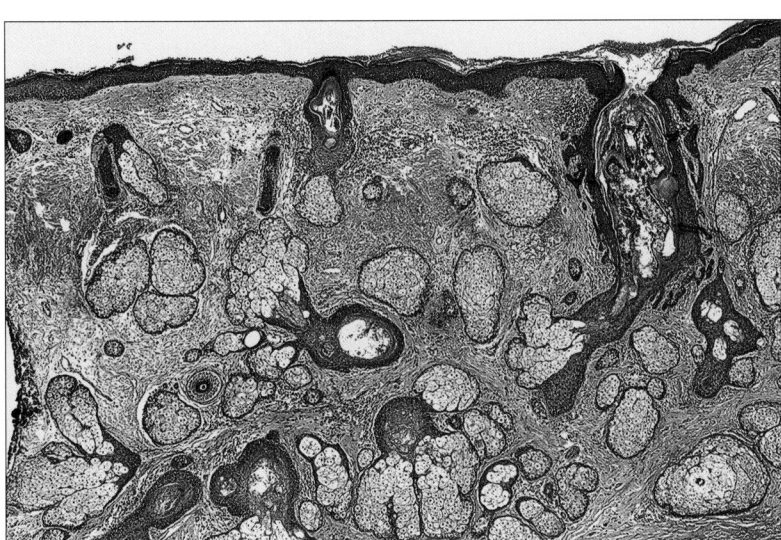

Fig. 1.3
Skin of the nose showing conspicuous sebaceous glands: at this site, they often drain directly onto the skin surface. These appearances should not be confused with sebaceous hyperplasia.

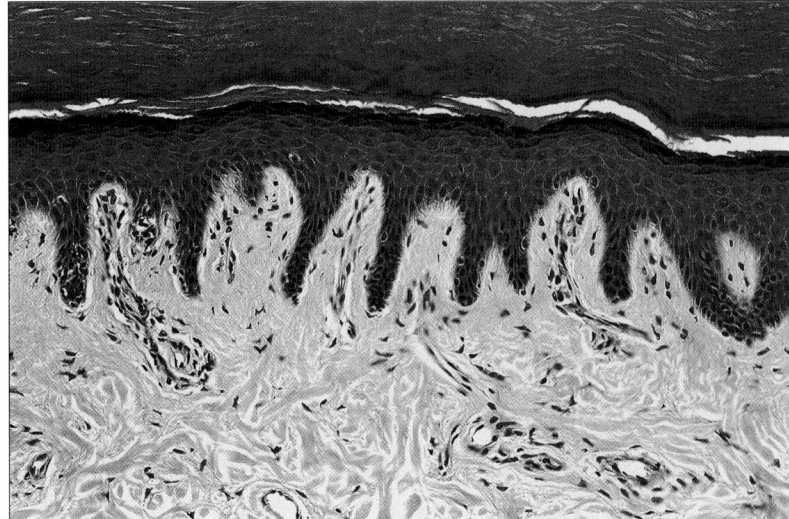

Fig. 1.4
Skin from the sole of the foot is typified by a thickened stratum corneum and prominent epidermal ridge pattern. The dermis is relatively dense at this site. Similar features are seen on the palms and ventral aspects of the fingers and toes.

The follicular bulge is discussed in Chapter 20.

Basal cells are cuboidal or columnar with a large nucleus typically containing a conspicuous nucleolus. Small numbers of mitoses may be evident. Clear cells are also present in the basal layer of the epidermis. These represent melanocytes. Very occasional Merkel cells may also be present but these are not easily identified in hematoxylin and eosin stained sections.

Histologically, prickle cells are polygonal in outline, have abundant eosinophilic cytoplasm and oval vesicular nuclei, often with conspicuous nucleoli.

Keratohyalin granules typify the granular cell layer (*Fig. 1.17*). Further maturation leads to loss of nuclei and flattening of the keratinocytes to form the plates of the keratin layer (stratum corneum).

Adjacent cells are united at their free borders by intercellular bridges (prickles or desmosomes), which are most clearly identifiable in the prickle cell layer and in disease states of the skin where there is marked intercellular edema (spongiosis) (*Fig. 1.18*). Uniting the epidermis with the dermis is the basement membrane region, easily identified by periodic acid–Schiff (PAS) staining and type IV collagen immunohistochemistry (*Figs 1.19, 1.20*).

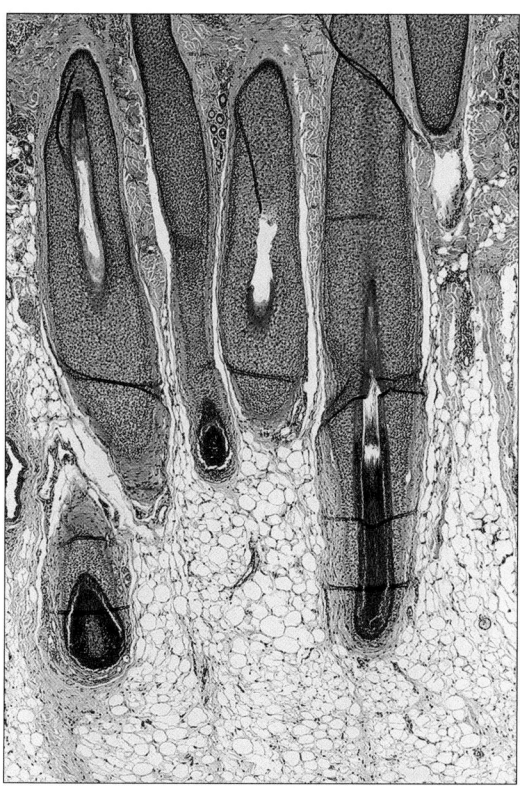

Fig. 1.5
Skin from the scalp characterized by numerous terminal hair follicles with many of the bulbs in the subcutaneous fat.

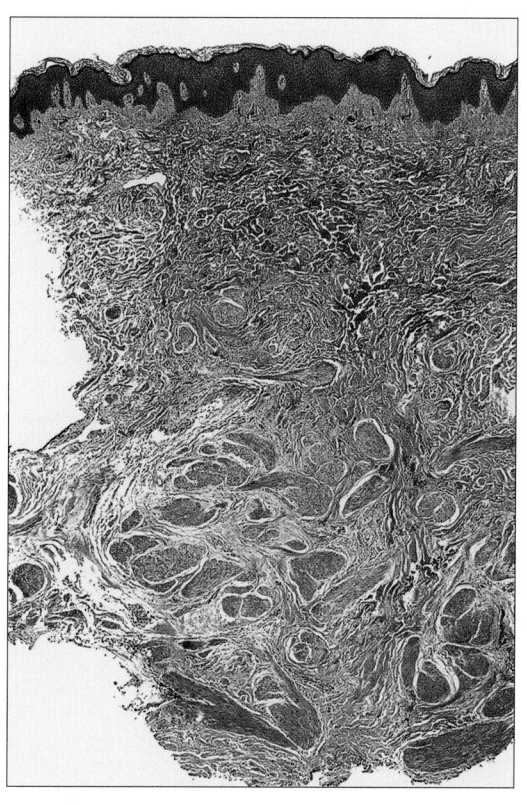

Fig. 1.6
Skin of areola showing abundant smooth muscle fibers: lactiferous ducts may also sometimes be present (not shown).

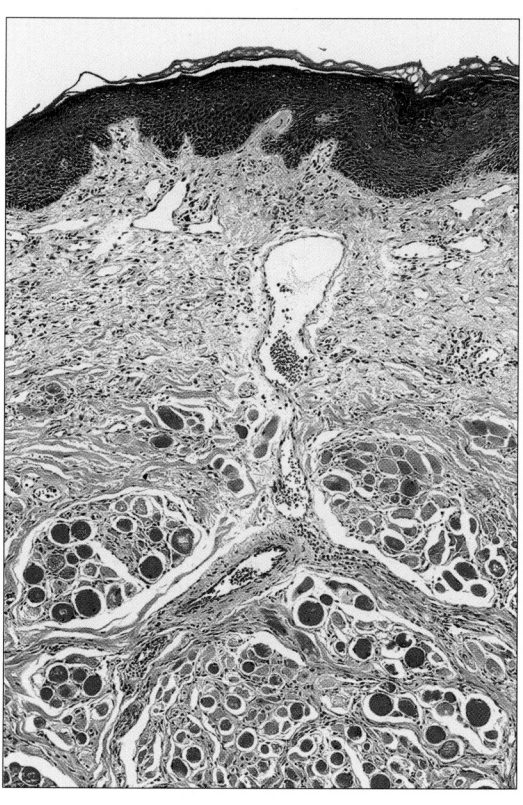

Fig. 1.7
Skin from the outer aspect of the lip: note the keratinizing stratified squamous epithelium and skeletal muscle fibers.

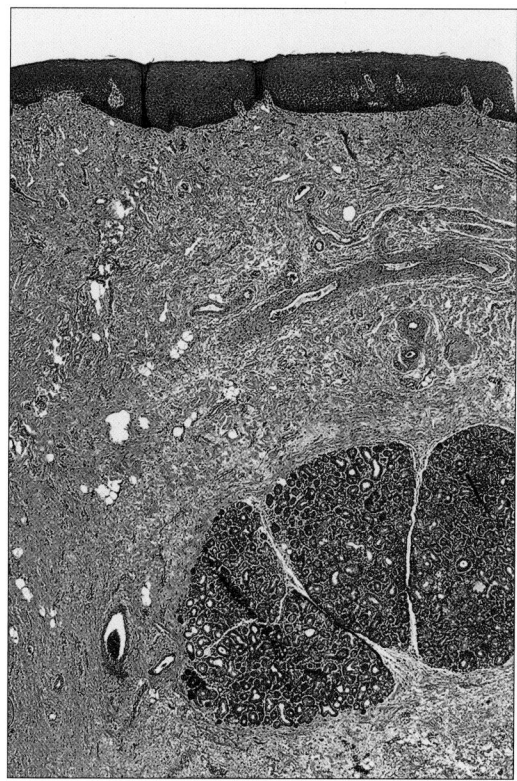

Fig. 1.8
Mucosal aspect of lip: at this site the squamous epithelium does not normally keratinize. Minor salivary glands as shown in this field are not uncommonly present.

Toker cells represent an additional clear cell population, which may be found in nipple epidermis of both sexes in up to 10% of the population.[6] The cells are large, polygonal or oval and have abundant pale staining or clear cytoplasm with vesicular nuclei often containing prominent, albeit small, nucleoli. The cytoplasm is mucicarmine and PAS negative.[6] The cells may be distributed singly but more often they are found as small clusters, not uncommonly forming single layered ductules.[6] They are located along the basal layer of the epidermis or suprabasally and are also sometimes seen within the epithelium of the terminal lactiferous duct.

Toker cells are of particular importance as they may be mistaken by the unwary as Paget cells. They are thought to be the source of mammary

Paget's disease in those exceptional cases where an underlying ductal carcinoma is absent.[7] Toker cells express CK7, AE1, CAM 5.2, epithelial membrane antigen (EMA) and cerbB2 and occasionally estrogen receptor.[8] Carcinoembryonic antigen (CEA) may also be present albeit weakly.[8] They are thus indistinguishable from Paget cells by immunohistochemistry.

Ultrastructure and composition

By electron microscopy, the basement membrane region (*Fig. 1.21*) conveniently divides into four zones,[9–11] namely:

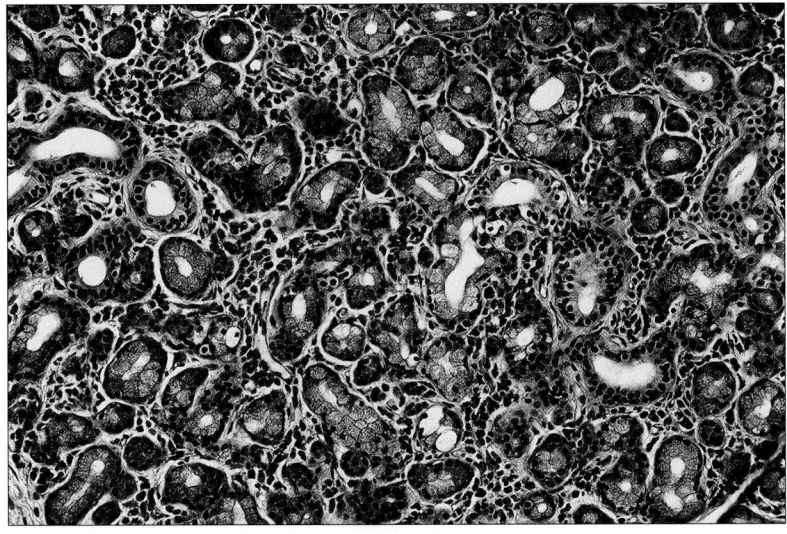

Fig. 1.9
Mucosal aspect of lip: close-up view of the salivary gland shown in *Fig. 1.8*.

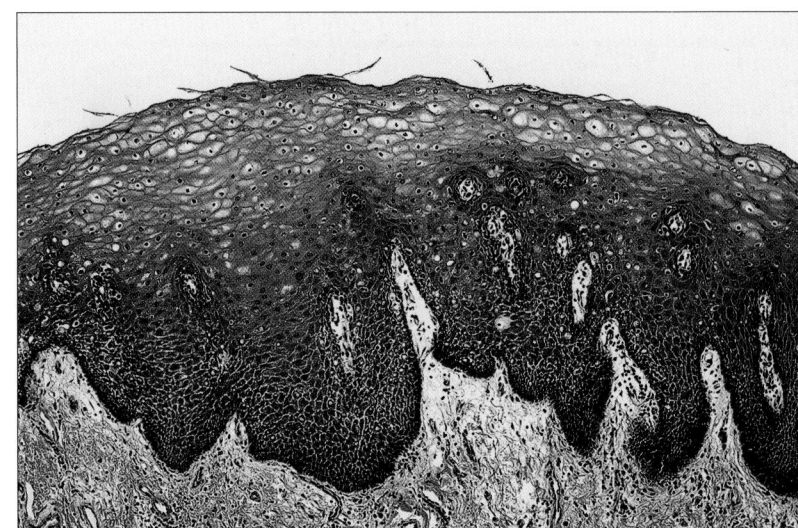

Fig. 1.10
Mucosal aspect of lip: the cytoplasm of the keratinocytes is often rich in glycogen.

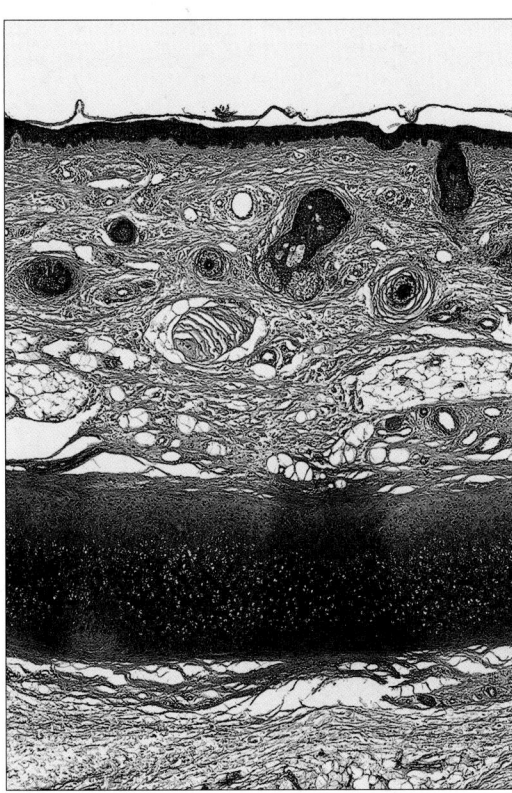

Fig. 1.11
Skin from the ear showing vellus hairs, and a fairly thin dermis overlying the auricular cartilage.

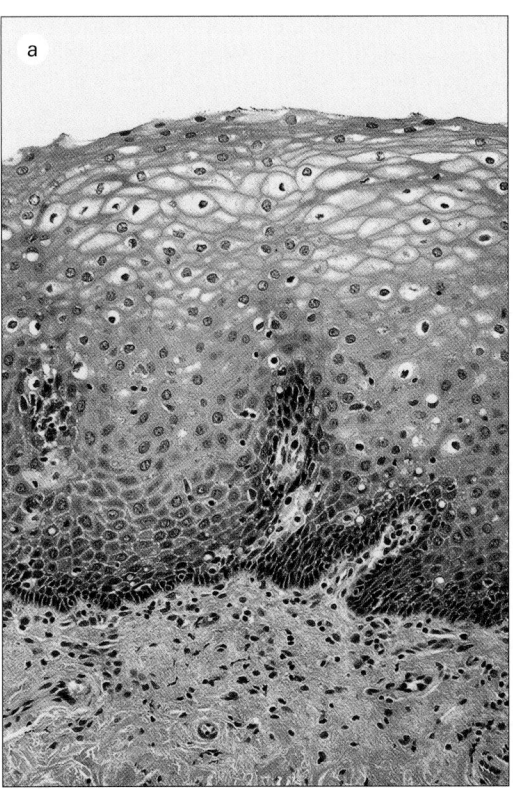
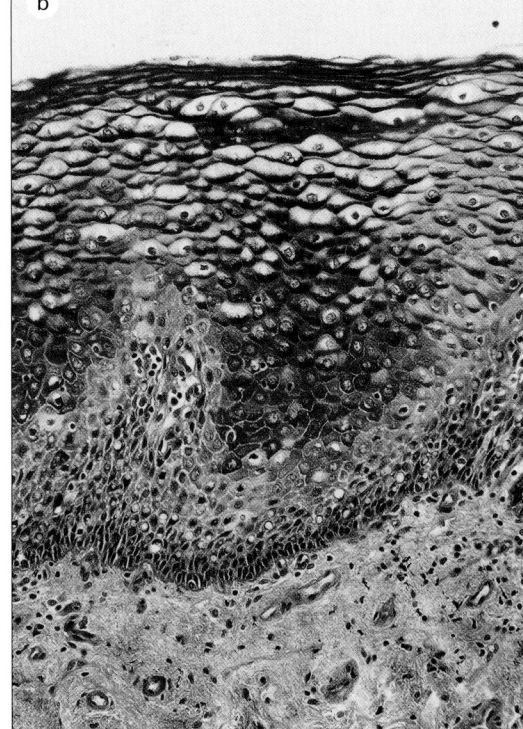

Fig. 1.12
(a, b) Vulval vestibule: at this site the stratum corneum is absent and there is no granular cell layer. The suprabasal keratinocytes have clear cytoplasm due to abundant glycogen and revealed by the periodic acid–Schiff reaction.

- the cell membrane and the hemidesmosomes of the basal keratinocyte
- the lamina lucida (approximately 35-40 nm wide)
- the lamina densa (approximately 30–50 nm wide)
- the sub-basal lamina fibrillar zone (fibroreticular network).[12–16]

At a molecular level, an interconnecting network of intermediate (keratin) filaments extends from the nuclear membrane and via connecting fibrils establishes contact with both desmosomes and hemidesmosomes (*Fig. 1.22*). From the former, cadherins establish contact with adjacent keratinocytes while from the latter, transmembranous integrin fibrils extend through the lamina lucida to the lamina densa. Intermediate filaments also interact with microfilaments and microtubules.[16] In addition to providing mechanical stability to the cell and the epidermis, there is evidence to suggest that the filament network is important in signal transduction and possibly intracytoplasmic transport mechanisms.[17] The following description places the molecular structure of the basement membrane into an anatomical and functional context (*Table 1.2*).

Situated at regular intervals along the plasma membrane of the basal keratinocytes are the hemidesmosomes, so-called because of their morphological resemblance to desmosomes (*Fig. 1.23*). It should be noted, however, that at a molecular level they are quite different. Hemidesmosomes anchor the epidermis through anchoring filaments to the underlying lamina densa, which is itself attached to the immediately adjacent dermis by means of the anchoring fibrils (*Fig. 1.24*).[18,19] The hemidesmosomes are approximately 500–1000 nm in diameter and provide a site of attachment for the basal keratin filaments. They are constant in number (1.8/nm of basal keratinocyte cell membrane)

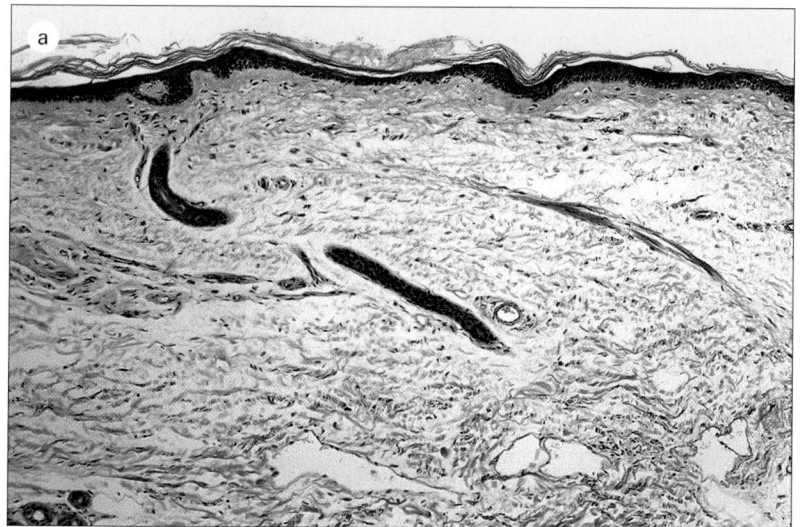

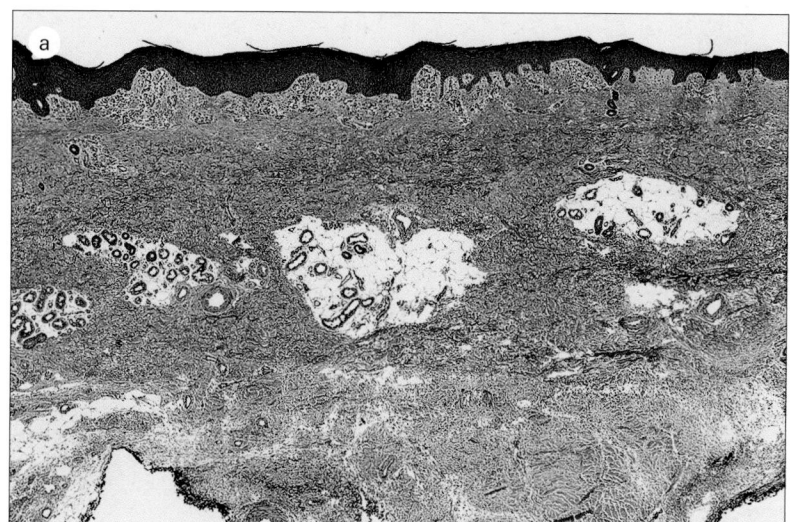

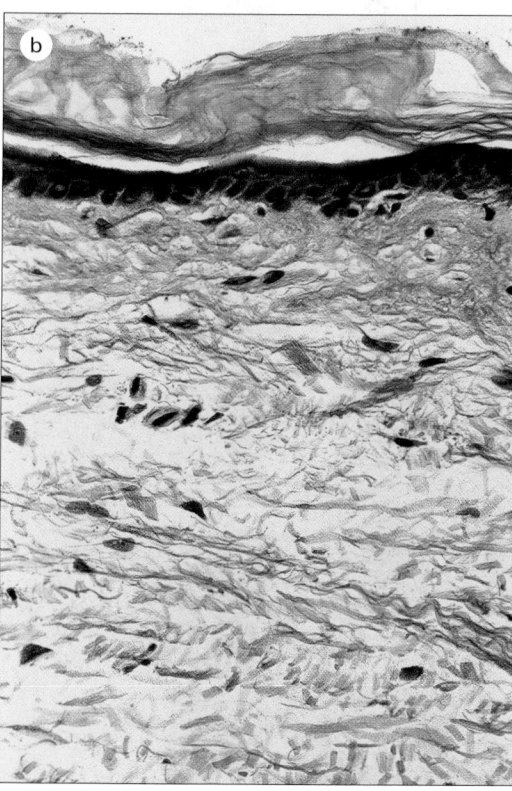

Fig. 1.13
Variation of skin: (a) sample of skin from the forearm of a 92-year-old female. Note the epidermal thinning and dermal atrophy; (b) high power view.

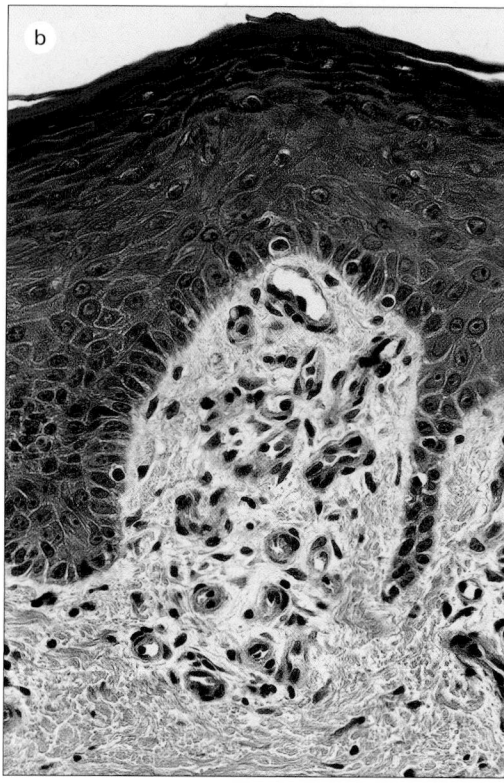

Fig. 1.14
Stasis change: (a) skin from the lower leg. Although abnormal, the presence of stasis change characterized in this example by papillary dermal lobular capillary proliferation is a very common feature at this site; (b) high power view.

irrespective of site, sex and age.[20] They are composed of an intracellular inner plaque to which keratin filaments are associated, an intracellular outer plaque which is attached to the cell membrane of the basal keratinocyte and an extracellular sub-basal dense plate which is of importance in anchoring filament adhesion.

Hemidesmosomal constituents consist of:

- transmembranous proteins mediating cell-matrix adhesion including $\alpha_6\beta_4$ integrin, $\alpha_3\beta_1$ integrin, $\alpha_2\beta_1$ integrin and bullous pemphigoid 180 kD antigen (BPAG2)
- plaque proteins involved in intermediate filament anchorage including bullous pemphigoid 230 kD antigen (BPAG1) and plectin[16]
- additional components of the hemidesmosomal region include IFAP300 and p200.

$\alpha_6\beta_4$ integrin is a transmembrane protein that mediates cell-matrix adhesion, hemidesmosomal stability and epidermal signal transduction.[21,22] Integrins are surface proteins, which bind to extracellular matrix proteins including laminin, collagen, fibronectin and vitronectin.[23] They are also of importance in signaling mechanisms via tyrosine kinases, initiating and regulating cytoskeleton organization, keratinocyte proliferation, apoptosis and differentiation pathways.[23,24] The β_4 component of $\alpha_6\beta_4$ integrin has a long intracytoplasmic tail (of approxi-

mately 1000 amino acids) by which it is linked to the keratin intermediate filaments through the intermediate filament associated protein IFAP300.[16,23] The extracellular components bind to laminin-5 and laminin-1 within the lamina lucida.[16] $\alpha_6\beta_4$ integrin is also of paramount importance in hemidesmosome assembly. Antibodies to $\alpha_6\beta_4$ integrin added to epithelial cells in tissue culture result in impaired assembly of hemidesmosomes.[25] Mutation of the β_4 integrin gene results in defective hemidesmosomes and is found in the pyloric atresia-associated variant of hemidesmosomal epidermolysis bullosa.[26] $\alpha_3\beta_1$ integrin is expressed on the cell surface at focal adhesion sites around basal and suprabasal cells in addition to

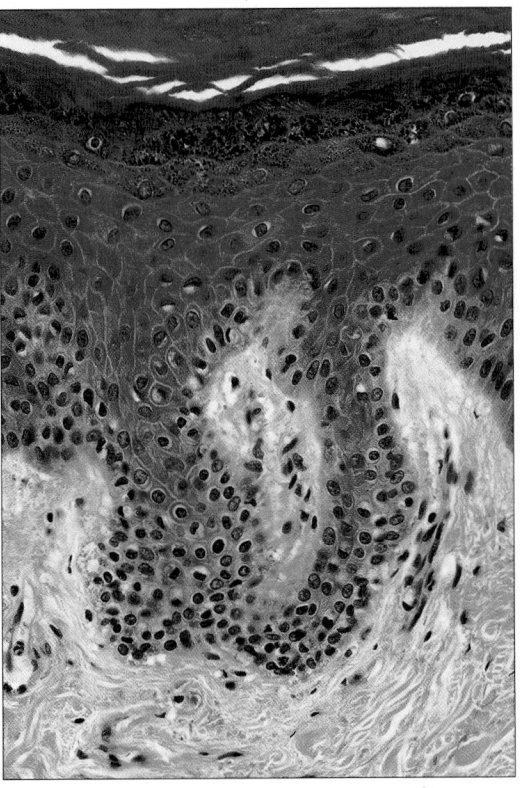

Fig. 1.17
Normal epidermis: prickle cells have abundant eosinophilic cytoplasm and contain vesicular nuclei with conspicuous nucleoli. Note the conspicuous basophilic keratohyalin of the granular cell layer.

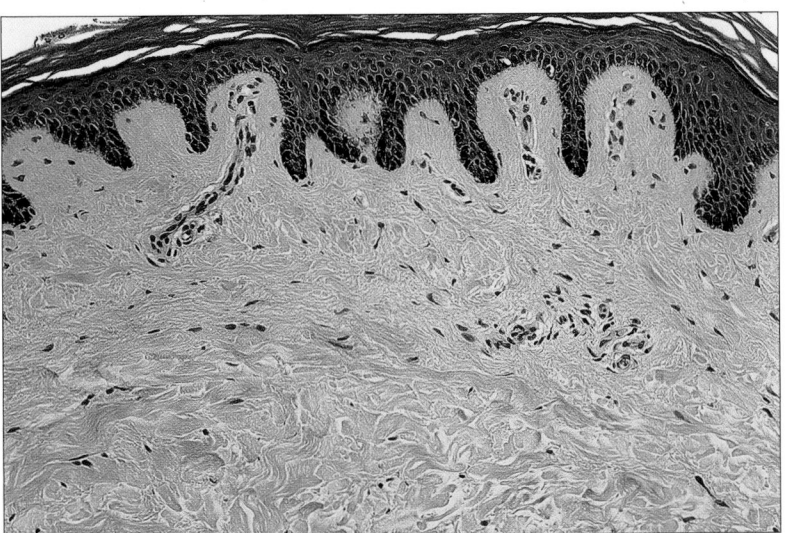

Fig. 1.15
Variation of normal skin: in dark-skinned races, the presence of intense basal cell melanin pigmentation is a normal histological finding.

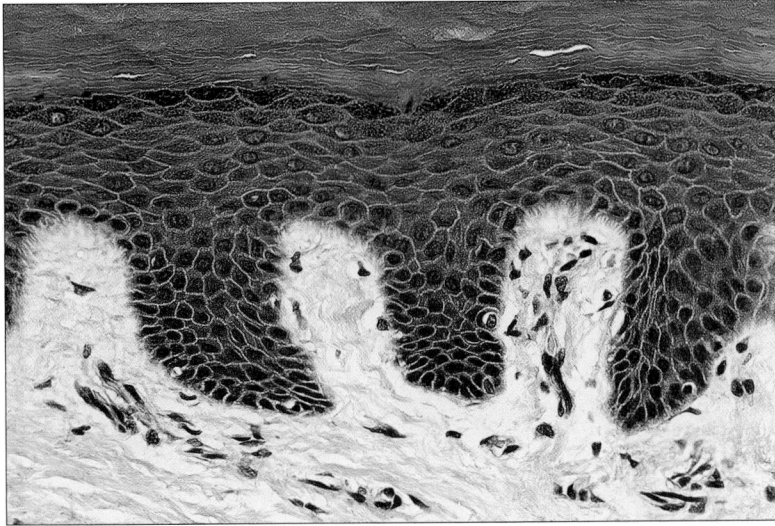

Fig. 1.16
Normal skin from the fingertip showing the clearly defined layers of the epidermis.

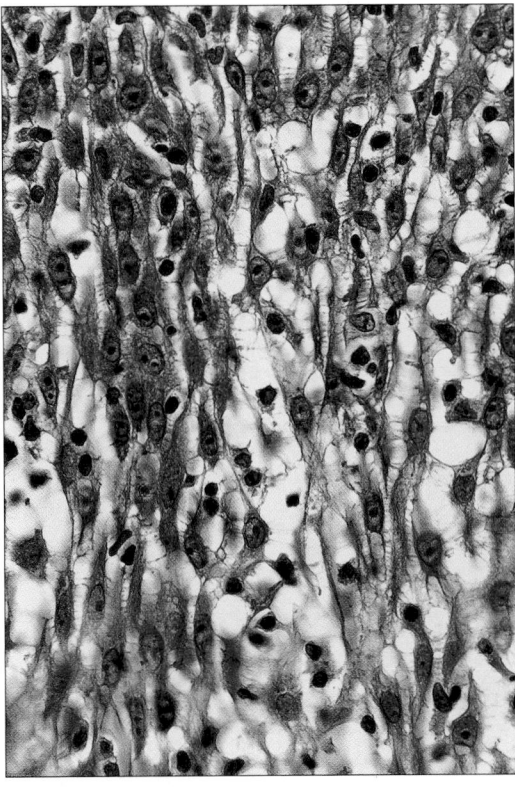

Fig. 1.18
Spongiotic epidermis showing distinct intercellular bridges (prickles, desmosomes).

being present along the base of the cell, indicating that it is of importance in both cell–cell and cell matrix adhesion.[4] It is however linked to the actin cytoskeleton and is believed to play a role in extracellular matrix organization.[5]

Bullous pemphigoid 180 kD antigen (BP180, BPAG2, type XVII collagen) is a 155 kD transmembrane protein with a collagenous carboxyl terminal extracytoplasmic domain (hence its alternative designation type XVII collagen) and a non-collagenous intracytoplasmic amino-terminal cytoplasmic domain.[27] It is thought to associate with α_6 integrin via its intracytoplasmic tail.[28] The extracellular domain lies within the lamina lucida and it is likely that this component forms part of the anchoring filament.[16] The gene for BP180 has been localized to 10q24.3.[29,30] Mutation of the BP180 gene results in defective or absent hemidesmosomes and is the molecular basis for hemidesmosomal generalized atrophic benign epidermolysis bullosa (GABEB).[31] Antibodies against this same antigen are responsible for the autoimmune dermatoses, bullous pemphigoid, pemphigoid gestationis, lichen planus pemphigoides, one variant of linear IgA disease, and some cases of cicatricial pemphigoid.[32–34]

Bullous pemphigoid 230 kD antigen (BP230, BPAG1) is a member of the plakin family, which also includes plectin, envoplakin, periplakin and desmoplakin.[35] These are all characterized by a dumbbell-like structure with a central parallel helical coiled-coil rod flanked by globular N- and

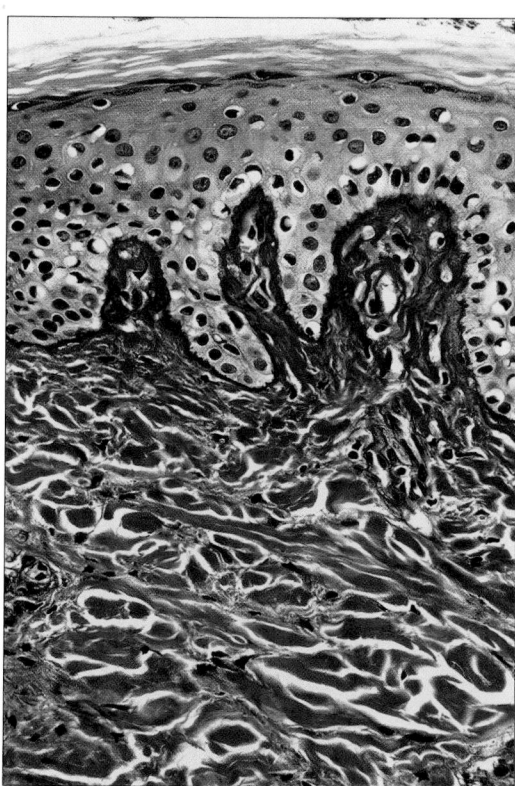

Fig. 1.19
Palmar skin showing a well-defined pink-staining basement membrane. Periodic acid–Schiff reaction.

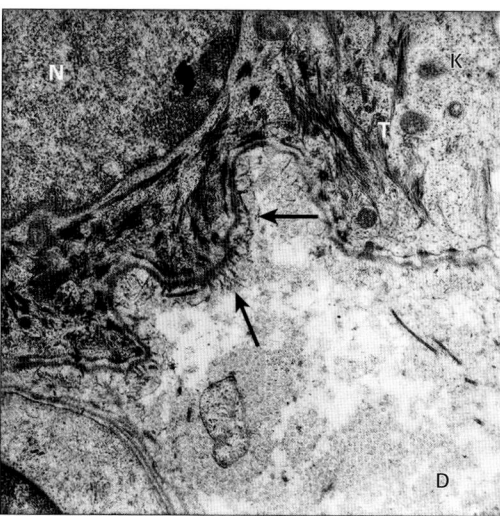

Fig. 1.21
Basement membrane region of normal epidermis: electron micrograph showing epidermodermal junction. Note the conspicuous basal keratinocyte hemidesmosomes, the lamina lucida and lamina densa. (D, dermis; K, keratinocyte; N, nucleus; T, tonofilament; arrows, anchoring fibrils.)

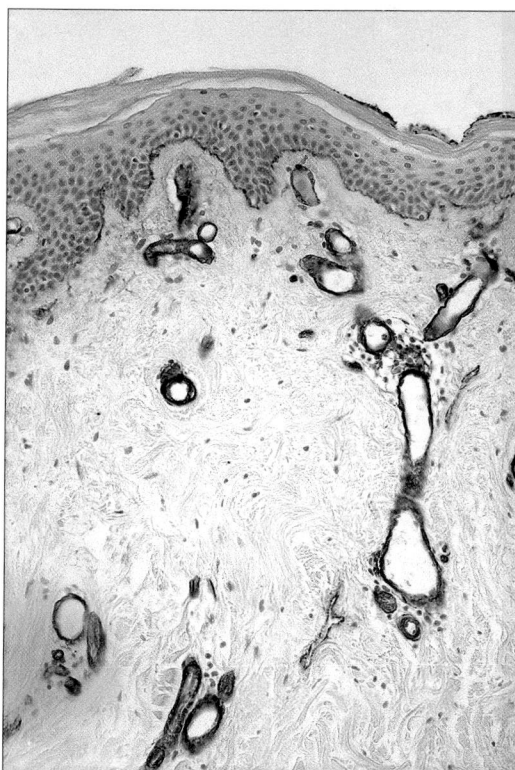

Fig. 1.20
The basement membrane of the epidermis and vasculature is outlined with type IV collagen immunohistochemistry.

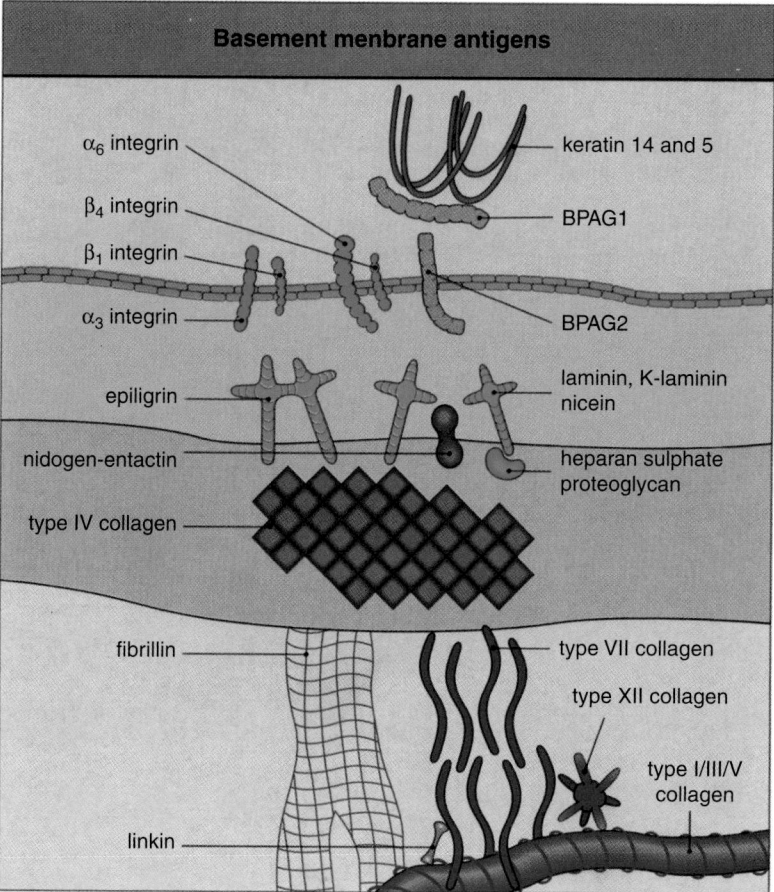

Basement menbrane antigens

α_6 integrin — keratin 14 and 5
β_4 integrin — BPAG1
β_1 integrin
α_3 integrin — BPAG2
epiligrin — laminin, K-laminin nicein
nidogen-entactin — heparan sulphate proteoglycan
type IV collagen
fibrillin — type VII collagen
type XII collagen
type I/III/V collagen
linkin

Fig. 1.22
Basement membrane antigens. By courtesy of J.A. McGrath, MD, St John's Institute of Dermatology, London, UK.

C-domains. It is wholly intracytoplasmic and localizes to the innermost aspect of the hemidesmosomal plaque and thereby functions in keratin intermediate filament anchorage.[36] Antibodies to BP230 are regularly present in bullous pemphigoid although they do not appear to play a pathogenic role.[37] BPAG1 has been localized to chromosome 6p11–12.[38]

Plectin is an intracytoplasmic protein present in many tissues. As with BP230, it also localizes to the innermost aspect of the hemidesmosome and is of major importance in keratin intermediate filament anchorage. It is a dumbbell-shaped homodimer, which comprises a central α-helical coiled-coil rod domain flanked by globular domains.[39] The C-terminal domain interacts with intermediate (keratin) filaments and can bind to β_4 integrin; the N-terminal domain interacts with actin and offers an

Table 1.2
Basement membrane antigens

Constituent	Location	Genodermatosis	Autoimmune bullous disease
Keratins 5 and 14	Basal keratinocyte	EB simplex	None
Keratins 1 and 10	Suprabasal keratinocytes	Epidermolytic hyperkeratosis	None
Keratin 9	Nails and hair	Pachyonychia congenita	None
$\alpha_6\beta_4$ integrin	Epidermal–dermal junction	JEB–pyloric atresia	None
BP180	Epidermal–dermal junction	GABEB	BP, CP, HG, LPP
Plectin	Hemidesmosome	EBS–MD	BP
BP230	Hemidesmosome		BP
Laminin 5	Lamina lucida	Junctional EB	CP
Type VII collagen	Sub-lamina densa	Dystrophic EB	EBA, BSLE, LAD

BP, bullous pemphigoid; BSLE, bullous systemic lupus erythematosus, CP, cicatricial pemphigoid; EB, epidermolysis bullosa; EBA, epidermolysis bullosa acquisita; EBS–MD, epidermolytic EB with muscular dystrophy; GABEB, generalized atrophic benign epidermolysis bullosa; HG, herpes gestationis; JEB, junctional EB; LAD, linear IgA disease; LPP, lichen planus pemphigoides.

alternative binding site for β_4 integrin.[39,40] The gene has been localized to 8q24.13.[41] Intermediate filament associated protein (IFAP300) is a related if not identical protein. Some patients with bullous pemphigoid have antibodies to plectin.[42] Mutation of the plectin gene presents as epidermolysis bullosa associated with muscular dystrophy.[43] The association results from the additional role of plectin anchoring the actin filaments to the cell membrane of muscle cells.

Anchoring filaments (2–4 nm in diameter) pass through the sub-basal dense plaque in the lamina lucida before entering the lamina densa.[9,18] The lamina lucida constituents include the extracellular domain of BP180 and laminins-1, -5 and -6.[16]

Laminin-1 is a non-collagenous glycoprotein, which mediates keratinocyte attachment and binds with type IV collagen, entactin (nidogen) and basement membrane heparin sulfate proteoglycan.[16]

Laminin-5 (epiligrin, kalinin, nicein), a non-collagenous glycoprotein, is a major constituent of the anchoring filaments and is therefore of particular importance in basement membrane adhesion.[16,44,45] It is composed of three chains known as α_3, β_3, and γ_2: α_3 has been mapped to 18q11.2, β_3 to 1q32 and γ_2 to 1q25–31.[44] Mutations in any of the three laminin-5 genes results in absence of hemidesmosomes and presents as junctional epidermolysis bullosa.[46] Antibodies against laminin-5 also account for some cases of cicatricial pemphigoid.[47]

Laminin-6 is an additional component of the anchoring filament.[16]

The lamina densa is 30–50 nm thick and consists of fine filamentous material. Its constituents include type IV collagen, entactin (nidogen) and heparin sulfate proteoglycan.[16]

Type IV collagen is present in all basement membranes as a lattice structure and provides structural stability.[16]

Entactin is a sulfated non-collagenous glycoprotein.[9,48] Its suggested function is to bind laminin-1, heparin sulfate proteoglycan and type IV collagen.[16]

Heparin sulfate proteoglycan is predominantly a lamina densa constituent, although it may also be present within the lamina lucida and sub-lamina densa connective tissue.[9,49] It is responsible for the negative charge of the basement membrane and is thought to be at least in part responsible for the selective permeability of the basement membrane.[16]

Chondroitin-6-sulfate proteoglycan represents an epidermal lamina densa constituent.[50] It is also present within the lamina densa of the adnexae and the vasculature.

Deep to the lamina densa is the fibrillar zone, composed of individual collagen fibers, microthread-like fibrils, elastic microfibrils (oxytalin

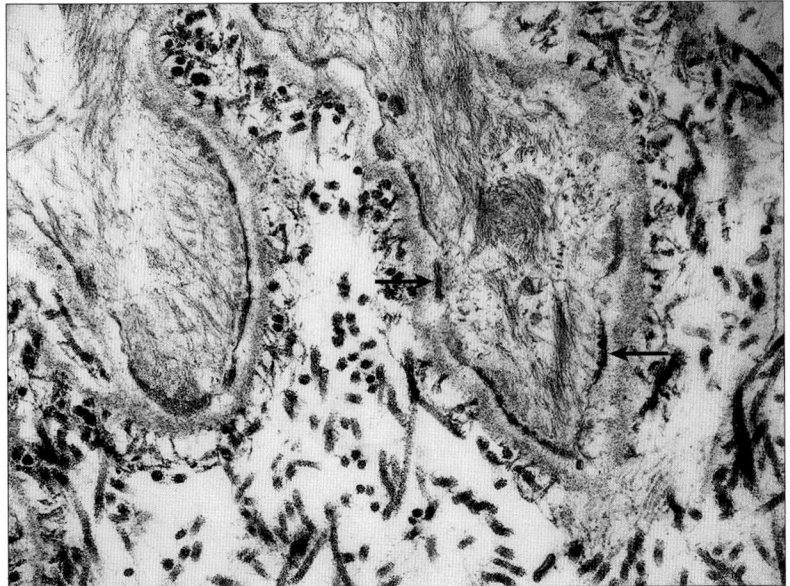

Fig. 1.23
Basement membrane region showing conspicuous hemidesmosomes (arrowed).

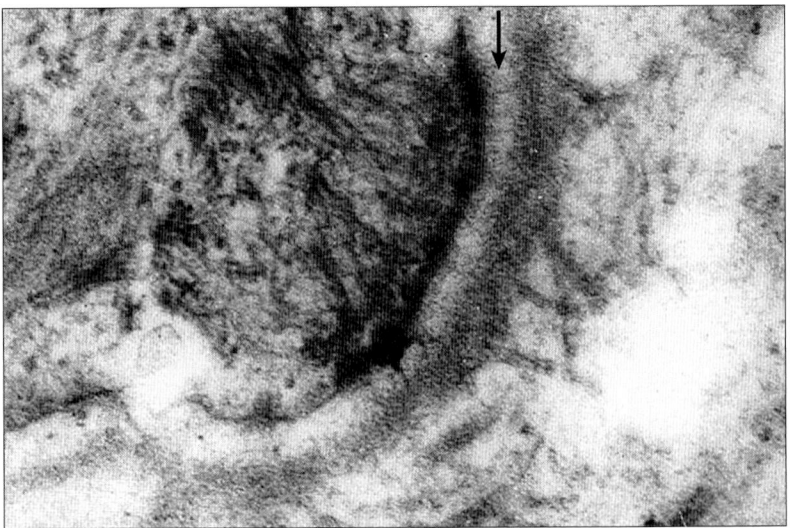

Fig. 1.24
Epidermodermal junction showing anchoring filaments (arrowed) extending from the hemidesmosome to the lamina densa.

fibers) and 800 nm long cross-banded anchoring fibrils, which appear to connect the lamina densa to underlying 200×170 nm type IV collagen-rich globular anchoring plaques.[16]

The anchoring fibrils are generally believed to form loops slung from the lamina densa, in addition to a more vertically orientated component.[9,51] It is thought that the former are of particular importance in maintaining adhesion. The fibrils are intimately associated with types I, III and V collagen fibers adding to the structural integrity of the basement membrane region. Although it has been thought that anchoring fibrils are inserted into anchoring plaques in the upper papillary dermis, this view has been recently challenged and it is now suggested that most fibrils arise and terminate within the lamina densa.[51]

Anchoring fibrils have characteristic irregular cross-banding and show fan-like projections at both ends. They are composed of type VII collagen (molecular weight 290 kD) (*Fig. 1.25*) which consists of three α-chains comprising straight helical collagenous rod domains flanked by non-collagenous globular amino and carboxyl termini. Anchoring fibrils are composed of multiple type VII collagen molecule pairs united at their carboxyl termini.[16] The amino terminals are inserted into the lamina densa and anchoring plaques respectively.[16] Type VII collagen has a high affinity for fibronectin, and it is thought that this is an important mechanism of attachment of the lamina densa to the underlying dermis.[52-55] The type VII collagen gene has been localized to the short arm of chromosome 3 (3p21).[56]

Antibodies against the amino non-collagenous terminus are responsible for epidermolysis bullosa acquisita, bullous systemic lupus erythematosus and some cases of linear IgA disease (sub-lamina densa variant).[57,58] Mutations of the type VII collagen gene result in the various subtypes of dominant and recessive dystrophic epidermolysis bullosa.[59,60]

Elastic microfibrils are present within the fibroreticular network and are responsible for tissue flexibility and stretching. They are complex structures composed of a number of microfibrillar proteins and glycoproteins, including the 350 kD fibrillin.[61,62] Fibrillin-containing microfibrils may exist as a fibrillar mantle surrounding an elastin core or be found independently as elastin-free microfibrils. The latter, located beneath the lamina densa, are known as the dermal microfibril bundles (*Fig. 1.26*).[9]

These are believed to represent the terminal arborizations of the dermal elastic tissue system. Several other structural glycoproteins that may be associated with the elastic microfibrils include serum amyloid P component, vitronectin and some orcein-stainable components, but only fibrillin is thought to extend to the lamina densa.[62]

Sub-lamina densa fibrillar zone constituents include types I, III, V and VII collagen, fibrillin and linkin.[63]

Basal cells contain tonofilaments aggregated into bundles or tonofibrils. Tonofilaments are composed of the 8–10 nm diameter keratin intermediate filament. This is an α-helical protein, responsible for cytoplasmic skeletal structure, and present in all epithelial cells.[17,64] Keratin consists of a group of over 30 antigenically different subtypes (including more than 10 hair keratins). Epidermal keratins are divided into two main groups:

- small acidic keratins (type I): K10–K20
- larger neutral–basic keratins (type II): K1–K9.[65-70]

In vivo keratins exist as pairs, one being contributed from each group (e.g. basal keratins contain types 5 and 14; suprabasal, types 1 and 10, *Fig. 1.27*).[67] The flattened, fully differentiated keratinocytes of the stratum corneum consists predominantly (85%) of keratins 1 and 10.[69] The upper epidermis also contains keratin 2, which is synthesized during terminal differentiation.[71] Plantar and palmar epidermis is characterized by suprabasal keratin 9 synthesis.[72] Hair shaft and nail plate keratins are not discussed in this section. Hyperproliferative states, as for example in wound healing, are associated with keratins 6 and 16.[70] Type I keratins are encoded on chromosome 17q12–21, while type II keratins are encoded on chromosome 12q11–12.[73]

Keratins form a 310 amino acid α-helical coil with an amino terminal non-helical head and a carboxyl terminal tail domain. Types I and II keratins unite to form rod-like coiled-coil heterodimers, two of which are aligned to form stable heterotetramers.[70] More than 5000 heterotetramers form a solitary 10 nm diameter keratin filament 20–30 μm long.[65]

Keratin filaments form a cage around the nucleus and course throughout the cytoplasm before being inserted laterally into the cytoplasmic facet of the desmosome and basally into the hemidesmosome.[69] In association with the actin microfilaments and microtubules, they represent

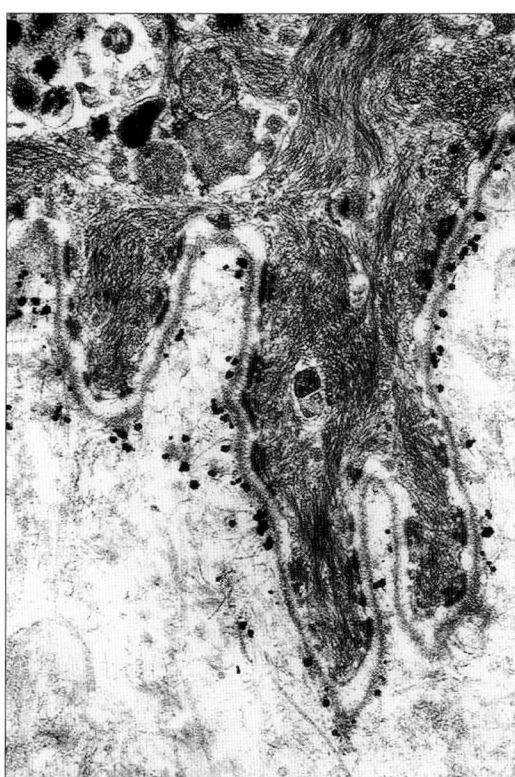

Fig. 1.25
Anchoring fibrils are composed predominantly of type VII collagen as shown in this immunogold electron microscopic preparation. By courtesy of J.A. McGrath, MD, St John's Institute of Dermatology, London, UK.

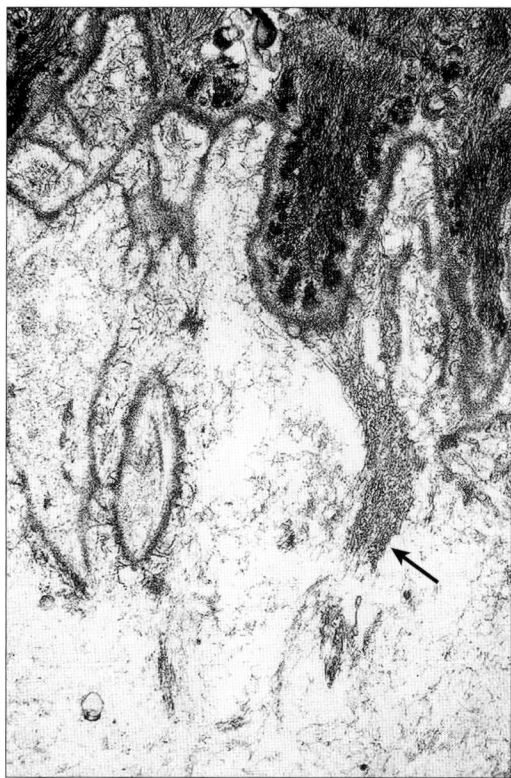

Fig. 1.26
Dermoepidermal junction of normal skin showing a well-formed dermal microfibril bundle (arrowed). Courtesy of J.A. McGrath, MD, St John's Institute of Dermatology, London, UK.

a flexible cytoplasmic 'scaffolding' and are of major importance in maintaining the structural integrity of both the keratinocyte and of the epidermis.[74] Ultrastructurally, they are particularly conspicuous in the prickle cell layer (*Figs 1.28, 1.29*).

Mutations in the keratin genes result in perturbations in keratin assembly with consequent mechanical fragility.[75] Thus mutations in keratin 5 and 14 genes are associated with epidermolysis bullosa simplex variants.[76] Mutations of keratin 1 and 10 genes are responsible for bullous ichthyosiform erythroderma.[77,78] Mutations in keratin 2 gene are responsible for bullous ichthyosis of Siemens while mutations in keratin 9 gene result in epidermolytic palmoplantar keratoderma.[79]

Electron microscopy shows that the cell membranes of adjacent cells interdigitate freely and form numerous 0.1–0.5 μm diameter intercellular junctions called desmosomes (*Fig. 1.30*), consisting of two dense plaques 10–15 nm thick on adjacent cell membranes with a multilayered zone (30 nm wide) in between (*Fig. 1.31*).[80,81] The desmosome is composed of membranous and inner plaque proteins, responsible for intercellular adhesion. The former is represented by the calcium dependent desmosome-specific cadherin molecules, desmocollin and desmogleins 1 and 3.[82] These are glycosylated transmembrane proteins. Their amino

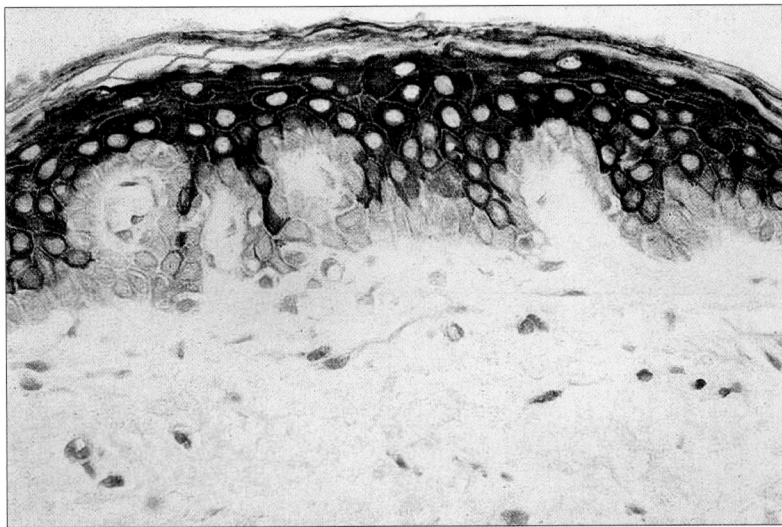

Fig. 1.27
In normal skin suprabasal keratinocytes preferentially express keratins 1 and 10 as shown in this picture. Antibody courtesy of I.M. Leigh, MD, Royal London Hospital Trust, London, UK.

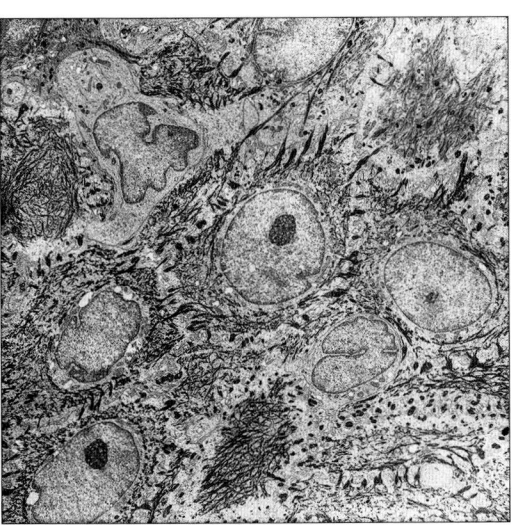

Fig. 1.28
Mid-prickle cell layer of normal epidermis: the abundant tonofibrils form a distinct interlacing lattice within the cytoplasm of the keratinocytes.

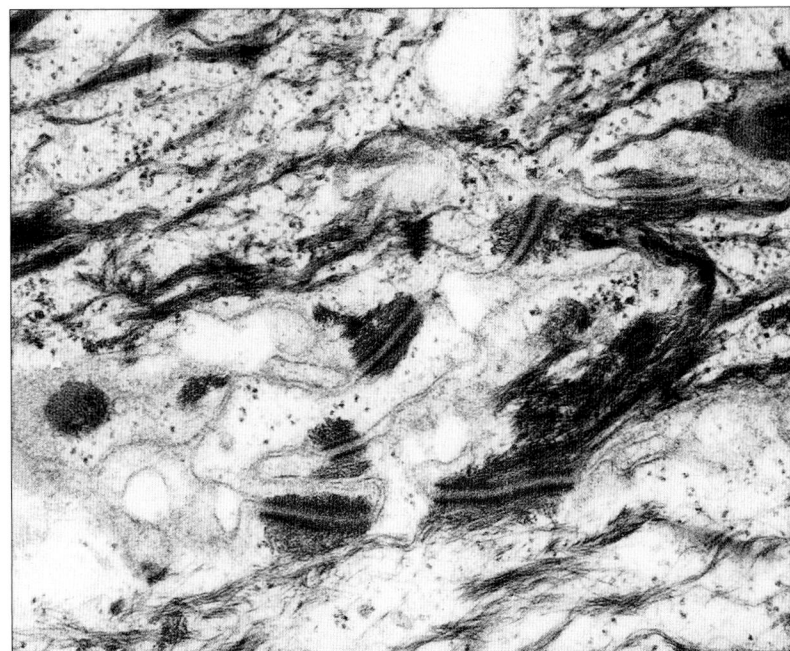

Fig. 1.30
Mid-prickle cell layer of normal epidermis: there are complex interdigitations between adjacent cell membranes with numerous desmosomal junctions.

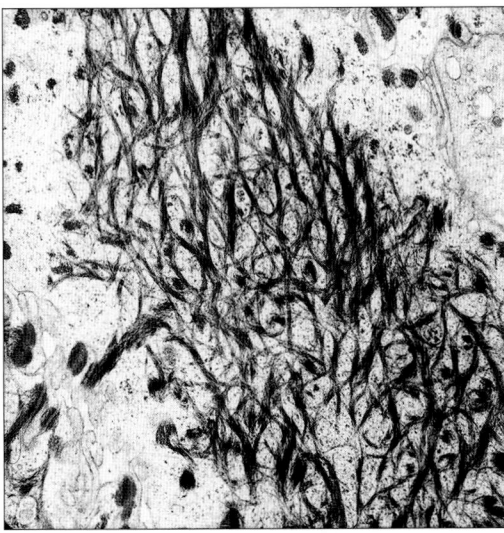

Fig. 1.29
Mid-prickle cell layer of normal epidermis: tonofibrils are composed of aggregates of tonofilaments (keratin).

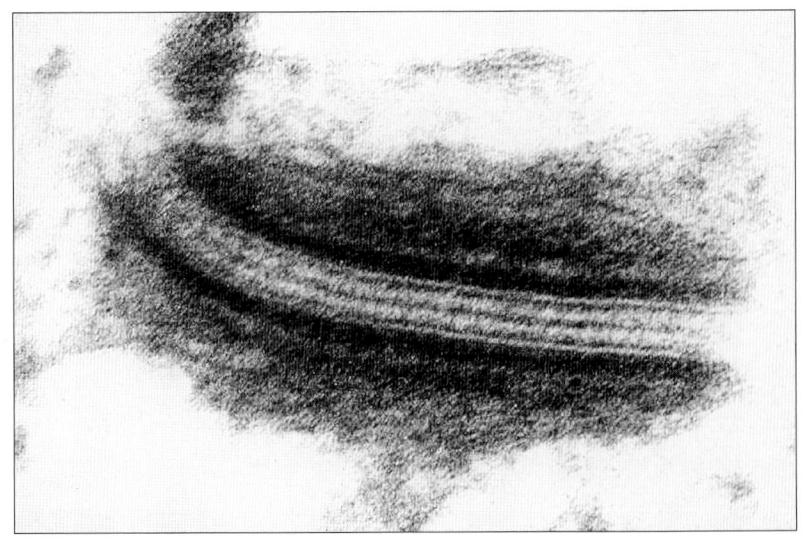

Fig. 1.31
Mid-prickle cell layer of normal epidermis showing the stratified nature of the desmosome.

terminal domains form dimers within the plane of the membrane and unite adjacent cell membranes.[83–85] The intracytoplasmic (carboxyl terminal) domains bind to plakoglobin, which is a member of the cadherin-associated family of proteins.[19,81,86] In addition, desmocollins bind to desmoplakin.[83] The desmosomal cadherins are coded for by three desmoglein and three desmocollin genes located at 18q21.[87]

The inner plaque proteins include plakoglobin, plakophilin (band 6) and desmoplakin.[19] In addition to filament interactions, it is thought that plakoglobin may be involved in cell growth control regulation.[19] Plakophilin is a plakoglobin-like molecule and has signaling in addition to anchorage functions.[19,88] Mutations of plakophilin gene are associated with skin fragility and ectodermal dysplasia.[89] Desmoplakin, for which there are at least two isoforms, also has important intermediate filament anchorage functions, which are mediated by its carboxyl terminus.[19,90] Abnormal desmosomal function with acantholysis is seen in Darier's disease due to a mutation in the ATP2A2 gene localized to 12q23–24.1.[91] Epidermal junctions also include E-cadherin mediated links to the actin cytoskeleton through β- and α-catenins.[5]

The prickle cells and, to a greater extent, the cells of the granular layer, contain lamellated oval membrane-coating granules, also known as Odland bodies, which measure approximately 100×500 nm. They are bound by a double-layered membrane and contain parallel lamellae (resembling stacks of coins) measuring about 2 nm thick.[92] Membrane-coating granules may be found anywhere in the cytoplasm, but are particularly conspicuous adjacent to the plasma membrane (*Fig. 1.32*). They contain a mixture of lipids including phospholipids, sphingolipids and cholesterol.

Membrane-coating granules release their lipid contents by exocytosis into the intercellular space of the stratum corneum.[93] This forms a highly efficient water barrier.[94] Inherited abnormalities of the epidermal lipid barrier have been described in X-linked ichthyosis.[95] Membrane-coating granules have also been shown to contain a mixture of hydrolytic enzymes, including acid phosphatase, glycosidases, proteases and lipases.[96] It is likely that activity of these enzymes on the lipids and desmosomal proteins within the extracellular milieu is important in barrier formation and natural desquamation.[96]

The cells of the granular layer also contain keratohyaline granules, which are not membrane bound and consist of irregular amorphous aggregates of approximately 2 nm electron-dense particles (*Figs 1.33, 1.34*). Keratohyaline granules are intimately associated with tonofibrils.[97]

The cells of the keratin layer consist mainly of abundant aggregated tonofibrils embedded in keratohyalin granules surrounded by a characteristic thick (15–20 nm) cornified cell envelope, deep to the cell membrane (*Fig. 1.35*). The development of the cell envelope is in part dictated by the activity of the membrane-associated epidermal transglutaminases 1 and 3, which cross-link precursor proteins via Nε-(γ-glutamyl)-lysine isopeptide bonds resulting in the precipitation of insoluble polymers that form much of the cell envelope.[98,99] The major constituents of the cell envelope include involucrin, cystatin A, elafin, small proline rich proteins/cornifins (SPRRs), annexin I, envoplakin, plasminogen activator type 2, cystatin-α, desmosomal proteins, keratins

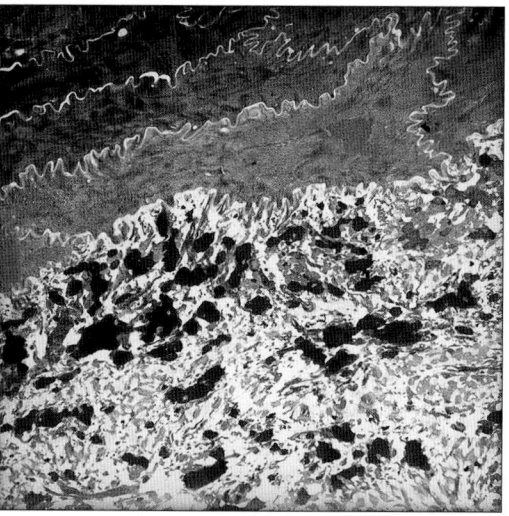

Fig. 1.33
Granular cell layer: non-membrane-bound keratohyalin granules are conspicuous beneath the lamellae of the stratum corneum.

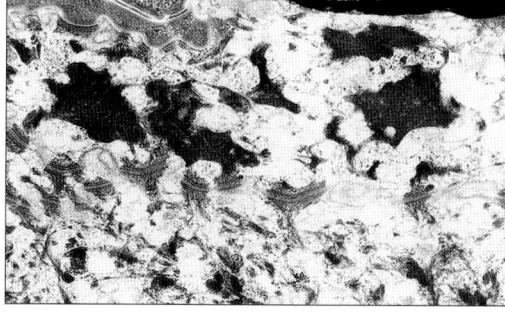

Fig. 1.34
Granular cell layer: the keratohyalin granules are composed of aggregates of electron-dense granules.

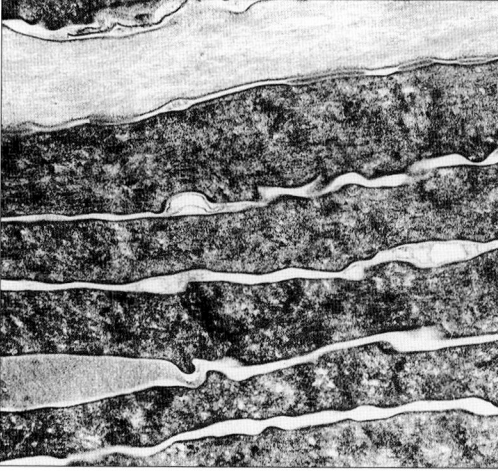

Fig. 1.35
Stratum corneum of normal epidermis: the superficial aspect of the epidermis consists of flattened, anucleate keratinized squames. The spaces between individual cells are artifactual. The intercellular particulate material is believed to be derived from membrane-coating granules.

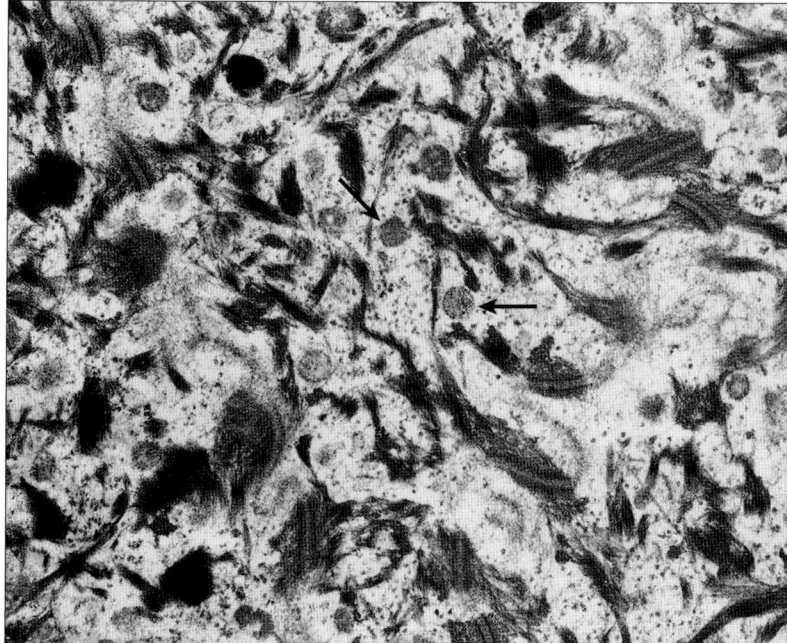

Fig. 1.32
Keratohyalin and membrane-coating granules (arrowed) are present in the granular cell layer.

and loricrin (the major constituent) (*Fig. 1.36*).[100,101] The genes coding for involucrin, profilaggrin, trichohyalin, SPRRs and loricrin have been mapped to the epidermal differentiation complex on 1q21.[81] Cell envelope formation represents an expression of terminal differentiation of the keratinocyte.[99] Although the cell membrane persists in the stratum corneum, it is lost as the keratinocytes move more superficially. Mutations in a number of genes have been documented correlating with abnormalities of envelope formation. For example, mutation of the transglutaminase type 1 gene results in lamellar ichthyosis and mutation in the loricrin gene causes Vohwinkel's syndrome.[102,103]

Keratohyalin contains large quantities of the precursor molecule profilaggrin.[104] Profilaggrin undergoes proteolysis and dephosphorylation to form the active molecule in the stratum corneum.[105] Filaggrin is believed to function as a transient cross-linking protein that induces disulfide bonding between adjacent keratin filaments, thereby inducing correct alignment.[106] Degradation of filaggrin by proteolytic enzymes is thought to release free amino acids – pyrrolidonecarboxylic acid and urocanic acid.[105] The former is believed to help maintain the stratum corneum, while the latter plays a role in ultraviolet B (UVB) absorption.[105,107] The active molecule filaggrin is largely responsible for keratin filament aggregation and constitutes a transient matrix protein within the stratum corneum.[108] The gene for profilaggrin has been mapped to 1q21.[3]

Maturation of the epidermis is expressed in the form of keratinization, the undifferentiated basal cells being transformed into the terminally differentiated, albeit dead cells of the stratum corneum composed almost entirely of keratin fibers.

The precise mechanism of keratinization is incompletely understood, but depends on a complex interrelationship between irreversible growth arrest at the level of the suprabasal keratinocytes and the activation of differentiation genes controlling keratinization and the formation of the cornified cell envelope.[23] It involves interplay between keratin filaments and the products of keratohyalin granules and membrane-coating granules.

The horny layer forms a tough and flexible membrane, which sheds its superficial aspect continuously as large clusters of fully keratinized squamous cells. It consists of protein rich keratinocytes embedded in a lipid-rich intercellular matrix, which has been likened to bricks and mortar.[109] It prevents the loss of body fluids and influx of water into the skin by means of the lipid deposits between the cornified cells. The epidermal lipids consist mainly of equal quantities of ceramides, cholesterol and free fatty acids, and are largely but not exclusively of lamellar body derivation.[110] They are covalently linked to the cornified envelope.[23] The stability and integrity of the horny layer is believed to be due to disulfide cross-linkages between adjacent keratin molecules.

Keratinocytes, in addition to the functions outlined in *Table 1.1*, have an immune function as demonstrated by their ability to synthesize and release a very wide range of cytokines including interleukin (IL)-1, IL-6, tumor necrosis factor alpha (TNF-α), granulocyte–macrophage colony stimulating factor (GM-CSF), macrophage colony stimulating factor (M-CSF), basic fibroblast growth factor (B-FGF), transforming growth factor alpha (TGF-α) and TGF-β (*Fig. 1.37*).[111]

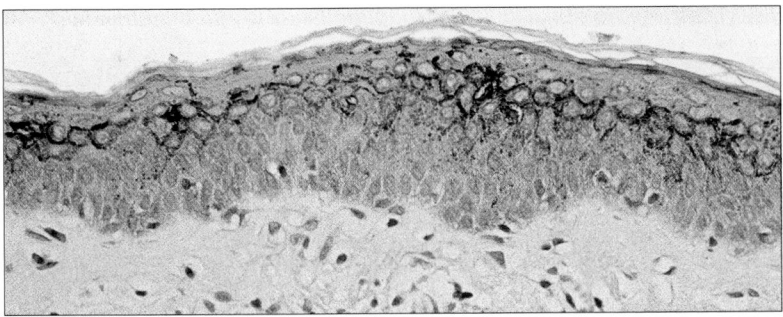

Fig. 1.36
Normal epidermis: involucrin is expressed by the keratinocytes of the granular layer and stratum corneum. Antibody courtesy of F. Watt, MD, ICRF, London, UK.

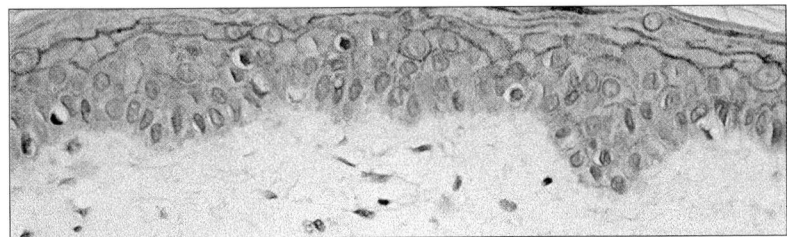

Fig. 1.37
Normal epidermis synthesizes a large number of cytokines and growth factors. In this field normal expression of TGF-α is shown.

References

1. Janes, S.M., Lowell, S., Hutter, C. (2002) Epidermal stem cells. *J Pathol*, **197**, 479–491.
2. Potten, C.S., Morris, R.J. (1988) Epidermal stem cells in vitro. *J Cell Sci* (Suppl.), **10**, 45–62.
3. Lavker, R.M., Sun, T-T. (2000) Epidermal stem cells: properties, markers and location. *Proc Natl Acad Sci USA*, **97**, 13473–13475.
4. Jones, P.H., Harper, S., Watt, F.M. (1995) Stem cell patterning and fate in human epidermis. *Cell*, **80**, 83–93.
5. Fuchs, E. (2001) Beauty is skin deep: the fascinating biology of the epidermis and its appendages. *Harvey Lectures Series*, **94**, 47–77.
6. Toker, C. (1970) Clear cells of the nipple epidermis. *Cancer*, **25**, 601–610.
7. Lundquist, K., Kohler, S., Rouse, R.V. (1999) Intraepidermal cytokeratin 7 expression is not restricted to Paget cells but is also seen in Toker cells and Merkel cells. *Am J Surg Pathol*, **23**, 212–219.
8. Van der Putte, S.C., Toonstra, J., Hennipman, A. (1995) Mammary Paget's disease confined to the areola and associated with multifocal Toker cell hyperplasia. *Am J Dermatopathol*, **17**, 487–493.
9. Uitto, J., Baver, E.A., Moshell, A.N. (1992) Symposium on epidermolysis bullosa: molecular biology and pathology of the cutaneous basement membrane zone. *J Invest Dermatol*, **98**, 391–395.
10. Stanley, J.R., Woodley, D.T., Katz, S.I. et al (1982) The structure and function of basement membrane. *J Invest Dermatol*, **79**, 69–72.
11. Woodley, D.T., McNutt, S. (1992) The basement membrane zone at the dermal–epidermal junction of human skin. In: Lin, A.N., Carter, D.M. (eds) Epidermolysis bullosa: basic and clinical aspects. New York: Springer-Verlag, pp 19–36.
12. Briggaman, R.A., Wheeler, C.E. (1975) The epidermal–dermal junction. *J Invest Dermatol*, **65**, 71–84.
13. Eady, R.A.J. (1988) The basement membrane. Interface between the epithelium and the dermis: structural features. *Arch Dermatol*, **124**, 709–712.
14. Woodley, D.T., Sarret, Y., Briggaman, R.A. (1991) Autoimmunity to type VII collagen. *Semin Dermatol*, **10**, 232–239.
15. Fine, J.D. (1991) Structure and antigenicity of the skin basement membrane zone. *J Cutaneous Pathol*, **18**, 401–409.
16. Woodley, D.T., Chen, M. (2001) The basement membrane zone. In: Frienkel, R.K., Woodley, D.T. (eds) The biology of the skin. New York: Parthenon Publishing, pp 133–152.
17. Djabali, K. (1999) Cytoskeletal proteins connecting intermediate filaments to cytoplasmic and nuclear periphery. *Histol Histopathol*, **14**, 501–509.
18. Uitto, J., Christiano, A.M. (1992) Molecular genetics of the cutaneous basement membrane zone: perspectives on epidermolysis bullosa and other blistering skin diseases. *J Clin Invest*, **90**, 687–692.
19. Green, K.J., Jones, J.C.R. (1996) Desmosomes and hemidesmosomes: structure and function of molecular components. *FASEB*, **10**, 671–681.
20. Tidman, M.J., Eady, R.A.J. (1984) Ultrastructural morphometry of normal human dermal–epidermal junction: the influence of age, sex and body region of laminar and non-laminar components. *J Invest Dermatol*, **83**, 448–453.
21. Clark, E.A., Brugge, J.S. (1995) Integrins and signal transduction pathways: the road taken. *Science*, **268**, 233–239.
22. Stepp, M.A., Spurr-Michaud, S., Tisdale, A. et al (1990). α6β4-integrin heterodimer is a component of hemidesmosomes. *Proc Natl Acad Sci USA*, **87**, 8970–8974.
23. Jetten, A.M., Harvat, B.L. (1997) Epidermal differentiation and squamous metaplasia: from stem cell to cell death. *J Dermatol*, **24**, 711–725.
24. Spinardi, L., Ren, Y.L., Sanders, R. et al (1993) The β4 subunit cytoplasmic domain mediates the interaction of α6β4 integrin with the cytoskeleton of hemidesmosomes. *Mol Biol Cell*, **4**, 871–884.
25. Borradori, L., Sonnenberg, A. (1999) Structure and function of hemidesmosomes: more than simple adhesion complexes. *J Invest Dermatol*, **112**, 411–418.
26. Vidal, F., Aberdam, D., Miquel, C. et al (1995) Integrin β4 mutations associated with junctional epidermolysis bullosa with pyloric atresia. *Nat Genet*, **10**, 229–234.
27. Hirako, Y., Owaribe, K. (1998) Hemidesmosomes and their unique transmembrane protein BP180. *Microsc Res Tech*, **43**, 207–217.
28. Hopkinson, S.B., Baker, S.E., James, J.C.R. (1995) Molecular genetic studies of a human epidermal autoantigen (the 180-kD bullous pemphigoid antigen/BP180): identification of functionally important sequences within the BP180 molecule and evidence for an interaction between BP180 and α6 integrin. *J Cell Biol*, **130**, 117–125.
29. Li, K., Sawamura, D., Guidice, G.J. et al (1991) Genomic organization of collagenous domains and chromosomal assignment of human 180 kD bullous pemphigoid antigen (BPAG2), a novel collagen of stratified squamous epithelium. *J Biol Chem*, **266**, 24064–24069.
30. Sawamura, D., Normura, K., Sugita, Y. et al (1990) The 2300kDa and 180kDa bullous pemphigoid antigens are distinct gene products. *J Invest Dermatol*, **98**, 942–943.
31. McGrath, J.A., Gatalica, B., Christiano, A.M. et al (1995) Mutations in the 180kD bullous pemphigoid antigen (BPAG2), a hemidesmosomal transmembrane collagen (COL17A1), in generalized atrophic benign epidermolysis bullosa. *Nat Genet*, **11**, 83–86.
32. Zillikens, D., Giudice, G.J. (1999) BP180/type XVII collagen: its role in acquired and inherited disorders of the dermal–epidermal junction. *Arch Dermatol Res*, **291**, 187–194.
33. Giudice, G.J., Emery, D.J., Zelickson, B.D. et al (1993) Bullous pemphigoid and herpes gestationis autoantibodies recognize a common non-collagenous site on the BP 180 domain. *J Immunol*, **151**, 5742–5750.
34. Kawahara, Y., Amagai, M., Ohata, Y. et al (1998) A case of cicatricial pemphigoid with simultaneous IgG autoantibodies against the 180 kD bullous pemphigoid antigen and laminin 5. *J Am Acad Dermatol*, **38**, 624–627.
35. Ruhrberg, C., Watt, F.M. (1997) The plakin family: versatile organizers of cytoskeletal architecture. *Curr Opin Genet Dev*, **7**, 392–397.
36. Guo, L., Degenstein, L., Dowling, J. et al (1995) Gene targeting of BPAG1: abnormalities in mechanical strength and cell migration in stratified epithelia and neurologic degeneration. *Cell*, **81**, 233–243.

37. Skaria, M., Jaunin, F., Hunziker, T. et al (2000) IgG autoantibodies from bullous pemphigoid patients recognize multiple reactive antigenic sites located predominantly within the B and C subdomains of the COOH-terminus of Bp230. *J Invest Dermatol*, **114**, 998–1004.

38. Sawamura, D., Nomura, K., Sugita, Y. et al (1990) Bullous pemphigoid antigen: cDNA cloning and mapping of the gene to the short arm of chromosome 6. *Genomics*, **8**, 722–726.

39. Steinbock, F.A., Wiche, G. (1999) Plectin: a cytolinker by design. *Biol Chem*, **380**, 151–158.

40. Wiche, G. (1998) Role of plectin in cytoskeletal organization and dynamics. *J Cell Sci*, **111**, 2477–2486.

41. Liu, C.G., Maercker, C., Castonon, M.J. et al (1996) Human plectin: organization of the gene, sequence analysis and chromosome localization (8q24). *Proc Natl Acad Sci USA*, **93**, 4278–4283.

42. Laffite, E., Favre, B., Fontao, L. et al (2001) Plectin, an unusual target antigen in bullous pemphigoid. *Br J Dermatol*, **144**, 136–138.

43. Gache, Y., Chavanas, S., Lacour, J.P. et al (1996) Defective expression of plectin/HD1 in epidermolysis bullosa simplex with muscular dystrophy. *J Clin Invest*, **97**, 2289–2298.

44. Burgeson, R.E., Chiquet, N., Deutzmann, R. et al (1994) A new nomenclature for laminins. *Matrix Biol*, **14**, 209–211.

45. Tryggvason, K. (1993) The laminin family. *Curr Opin Cell Biol*, **5**, 877–882.

46. Kivirikko, S., McGrath, J.A., Baudoin, C. et al (1995) A homozygous nonsense mutation in the α3 chain gene of laminin-5 (LAMA3) in lethal (Herlitz) junctional epidermolysis bullosa. *Hum Mol Genet*, **4**, 959–962.

47. Seo, S.H., Kye, Y. C., Kim, S.N. et al (2001) Antiepiligrin cicatricial pemphigoid with autoantibodies to the beta subunit of laminin 5 and associated with severe laryngeal involvement necessitating tracheostomy. *Dermatology*, **202**, 63–66.

48. Carlin, B., Jaffe, R., Binder, B. (1981) Entactin, a novel basal lamina-associated sulfated glycoprotein. *J Biol Chem*, **256**, 5209–5214.

49. Caughman, S.W., Krieg, T., Timple, R. et al (1987) Nidogen and heparin sulfate proteoglycan: detection of newly isolated basement membrane components in normal and epidermolysis bullosa skin. *J Invest Dermatol*, **89**, 547–550.

50. Fine, J.D., Couchman, J.R. (1988) Chondroitin-6-sulphate containing proteoglycan: a new component of human skin dermoepidermal junction. *J Invest Dermatol*, **90**, 283–288.

51. Uitto, J., Pulkkinen, L. (1996) Molecular complexity of the cutaneous basement membrane zone. *Mol Biol Rep*, **23**, 35–46.

52. Woodley, D.T., Wynn, K.C., O'Keefe, E.J. (1990) Type IV collagen and fibronectin enhance human keratinocyte thymidine incorporation and spreading in the absence of soluble growth factors. *J Invest Dermatol*, **94**, 130–143.

53. Burgeson, R.E., Lunstrum, G. P., Rokosova, B. et al. (1990) The structure and function of type VII collagen. *Ann N Y Acad Sci*, **580**, 32–43.

54. Woodley, D.T., O'Keefe, E.J., McDonald, J.A. et al (1987) Specific affinity between fibronectin and the epidermolysis bullosa acquisita antigen. *J Clin Invest*, **79**, 1826–1830.

55. Yamada, K.M. (1983) Fibronectin and other structural proteins. In: Hay, E.D. (ed.) Cell biology of extracellular matrix. New York: Plenum Press, pp 95–110.

56. Parente, M.G., Chung, L.C., Ryynänen, J. et al (1991) Human type VII collagen: cDNA cloning and chromosomal mapping of the gene. *Proc Natl Acad Sci USA*, **88**, 6931–6935.

57. Tanaka, T., Furukawa, F., Imamura, S. (1994) Epitope mapping for epidermolysis bullosa acquisita autoantibody by molecularly cloned cDNA for type VII collagen. *J Invest Dermatol*, **102**, 706–709.

58. Shirahama, S., Furukawa, F., Yagi, H. et al. (1998) Bullous systemic lupus erythematosus: detection of antibodies against the non-collagenous domain of type VII collagen. *J Am Acad Dermatol*, **38**, 844–848.

59. Wessagowit, V., Ashton, G.H., Mohammedi, R. et al (2001) Three cases of de novo dominant dystrophic epidermolysis bullosa associated with mutation G2043R in COL7A1. *Clin Exp Dermatol*, **26**, 97–99.

60. Christiano, A.M., Anhalt, G., Gibbons, S. et al (1994) Premature termination codons in the type VII collagen gene (COL7A1) underlie severe, mutilating recessive dystrophic epidermolysis bullosa. *Genomics*, **21**, 160–168.

61. Sakai, L.Y., Keene, D.R., Engvall, E. (1986) Fibrillin, a new 350 kD glycoprotein is a component of extracellular microfibrils. *J Cell Biol*, **103**, 2499–2509.

62. Dahlback, K., Ljungquist, A., Lofberg, H. et al (1990) Fibrillin immunoreactive fibers constitute a unique network in the human dermis: immunohistochemical comparison of the distribution of fibrillin, vitronectin, amyloid P component and orcein stainable structures in normal skin and elastosis. *J Invest Dermatol*, **94**, 284–291.

63. Briggaman, R.A., Yoshiike, T., Woodley, D.T. et al (1988) Linkin, a newly recognized component of extracellular matrix associated with microthread-like filamentous network beneath stratified squamous epithelium. *J Cell Biol*, **107**, 590A.

64. Steinert, P.M., Freedberg, I.M. (1991) Molecular and cellular biology of keratins. In: Goldsmith, L.A. (ed.) Physiology, biochemistry and molecular biology of the skin, 2nd edn. New York: Oxford University Press, pp 113–147.

65. Fuchs, E. (1992) Genetic skin disorders of keratin. *J Invest Dermatol*, **99**, 671–674.

66. Moll, R., Franke, W.W., Schiller, D.L. et al (1982) The catalogue of human cytokeratins: patterns of expression in normal epithelia, tumors and cultured cells. *Cell*, **31**, 11–24.

67. Albers, K., Fuchs, E. (1992) The molecular biology of intermediate filament proteins. *Int Rev Cytol*, **134**, 243–279.

68. Steinert, P.M., Steven, A.C., Roop, D.R. (1985) The molecular biology of intermediate filaments. *Cell*, **42**, 411–420.

69. Steinert, P.M., Roop, D.R. (1988) The molecular and cellular biology of intermediate filaments. *Ann Rev Biochem*, **57**, 593–625.

70. Smack, D.P., Korge, B.P., James, W.D. (1994) Keratin and keratinization. *J Am Acad Dermatol*, **30**, 85–102.

71. Collin, C., Moll, R., Kubicka, S. et al (1992) Characterization of human cytokeratins 2, an epidermal cytoskeletal protein synthesized during differentiation. *Exp Cell Res*, **202**, 132–141.

72. Langbein, L., Heid, H.W., Moll, I. et al (1993) Molecular characterization of the body site-specific human epidermal cytokeratins 9: cDNA cloning, amino acid sequence, and tissue specificity of gene expression. *Differentiation*, **55**, 57–71.

73. Milisavljevic, V., Freedberg, I.M., Blumenberg, M. (1996) Close linkage of the two-keratin gene clusters in the human genome. *Genomics*, **34**, 134–138.

74. Fuchs, E., Cleveland, D. (1998) A structural scaffolding of intermediate filaments in health and disease. *Science*, **279**, 514–519.

75. McGrath, J.A., Ishida-Yamamoto, A., Eady, R.A.J. (1993) Keratin abnormalities in genetic skin disease. *Retinoids Today and Tomorrow*, **31**, 4–7.

76. Coulombe, P.A., Hutton, M.E., Letai, A. et al (1991) Point mutations in human keratin 14 genes of epidermolysis bullosa simplex patients: genetic and functional analysis. *Cell*, **66**, 1301–1311.

77. Fuchs, E., Esteves, R.A., Coulombe, P.A. (1992) Transgenic mice expressing a mutant keratin 10 gene reveal the likely genetic basis for epidermolytic hyperkeratosis. *Proc Natl Acad Sci USA*, **89**, 6906–6910.

78. Rothnagel, J.A., Dominey, A.M., Dempsey, L.D. et al (1992) Mutations in the rod domain of keratins 1 and 10 in epidermolytic hyperkeratosis. *Science*, **257**, 1128–1130.

79. Reis, A., Hennies, H.C., Langbein, L. et al (1994) Keratin 9 gene mutations in epidermolytic palmoplantar keratoderma (EPPK). *Nat Genet*, **6**, 174–179.

80. Garrod, D.R. (1993) Desmosomes and hemidesmosomes. *Curr Opin Cell Biol*, **5**, 30–40.

81. Haake, A., Scott, G.A., Holbrook, K.A. (2001) Structure and function of the skin: overview of the epidermis and dermis. In: Freinkel, R.K., Woodley, D.T. (eds) The biology of the skin. New York: Parthenon Publishing, pp 19–46.

82. Koch, P.J., Franke, W.W. (1994) Desmosomal cadherins: another growing multigene family of adhesion molecules. *Curr Opin Cell Biol*, **6**, 682–687.

83. Shapiro, L., Fannon, A.M., Kwong, P.D. et al (1995) Structural basis of cell–cell adhesion by cadherins. *Nature*, **374**, 327–336.

84. King, I.A., Sullivan, K.H., Bennett, R. et al (1995) The desmocollins of human foreskin epidermis: identification and chromosomal assignment of a third gene and expression pattern of three isoforms. *J Invest Dermatol*, **105**, 314–321.

85. Yue, K.K.M., Holton, J.L., Clarke, J.P. et al (1995) Characterization of a desmocollin isoform (bovine DSC3) exclusively expressed in lower layers of stratified epithelia. *J Cell Sci*, **108**, 2163–2173.

86. Troyanovsky, S.M., Troyanovsky, R.B., Eshkind, L.G. et al (1994) Identification of the plakoglobin-binding domain in desmoglein and its role on plaque assembly and intermediate filament anchorage. *J Cell Biol*, **127**, 151–160.

87. Simrak, D., Cowley, C.M.E., Buxton, R.S. et al (1995) Tandem arrangement of the closely linked desmoglein genes on human chromosome 18. *Genomics*, **25**, 591–594.

88. Heid, H.W., Schmidt, A., Zimbelmann, R. et al (1994) Cell type-specific desmosomal plaque proteins of the plakoglobin family: plakophilin 1 (band 6 protein). *Differentiation*, **58**, 113–131.

89. McGrath, J.A. (1999) A novel genodermatosis caused by mutations in plakophilin 1, a structural component of desmosomes. *J Dermatol*, **26**, 764–769.

90. Kouklis, P.D., Hutton, E., Fuchs, E. (1994) Making a connection: direct binding between keratin intermediate filaments and desmosomal proteins. *J Cell Biol*, **127**, 1049–1060.

91. Sakuntabhai, A., Ruiz-Perez, V., Carter, S. et al (1999) Mutations in ATP2A2, encoding a Ca2+ pump, cause Darier's disease. *Nat Genet*, **21**, 252–253.

92. Landman, L. (1986) Epidermal permeability barrier: transformation of lamellar granule-disks into intercellular sheets by a membrane fusion process, a freeze fracture study. *J Invest Dermatol*, **87**, 202–209.

93. Freinkel, R.K., Traczyk, T.N. (1985) Lipid composition and acid hydrolase content of lamellar granules of fetal rat epidermis. *J Invest Dermatol*, **85**, 295–298.

94. Elias, P.M., Goerke, J., Friend, D.S. (1977) Mammalian epidermal barrier layer lipids: composition and influence on structure. *J Invest Dermatol*, **69**, 535–546.

95. Ballabio, A., Parenti, G., Garrozzo, R. et al (1987) Isolation and characterization of a steroid sulfatase cDNA clone: genomic deletions in patients with X-chromosome-linked ichthyosis. *Proc Natl Acad Sci USA*, **84**, 4519–4523.

96. Menon, G.K., Ghadially, R., Williams, M.L. et al (1992) Lamellar bodies as delivery systems of hydrolytic enzymes: implications for normal and abnormal desquamation. *Br J Dermatol*, **126**, 337–345.

97. Fukuyama, K., Kakimi, S., Epstein, W.L. (1980) Detection of a fibrous component in keratohyalin granules of newborn rat epidermis. *J Invest Dermatol*, **174**, 174–180.

98. Polakowska, R.R., Goldsmith, L.A. (1991) The cell envelope and transglutaminases. In: Goldsmith, L.A. (ed.) Physiology, biochemistry and molecular biology of the skin, 2nd edn. New York: Oxford University Press, pp 168–201.

99. Michel, S., Schmidt, R., Shroot, B. et al (1988) Morphological and biochemical characterization of the cornified envelopes from human epidermal keratinocytes of different origin. *J Invest Dermatol*, **91**, 11–15.

100. Ishida-Yamamoto, A., Takahasi, H., Lizuka, H. (1998) Loricrin and human skin diseases: molecular basis of loricrin keratodermas. *Histol Histopathol*, **13**, 819–826.

101. Steinert, P.M., Marekov, L.N. (1995) The proteins elafin, filaggrin, keratin intermediate filaments, loricrin, and small proline rich proteins 1 and 2 are isodipeptide cross-linked components of the human cornified cell envelope. *J Biol Chem*, **270**, 17702–17711.

102. Russell, L.J., Digiovanna, I.J., Rogers, G.R. et al (1995) Mutations in the gene for TGase 1 in autosomal recessive lamellar ichthyosis. *Nat Genet*, **9**, 279–283.

103. Korge, B.P., Ishida-Yamamoto, A., Pünter, C. et al (1997) Loricrin mutation in Vohwinkel's keratoderma is unique to the variant with ichthyosis. *J Invest Dermatol*, **109**, 604–610.

104. Fleckman, P., Dale, B.A., Holbrook, K.A. (1985) Profilaggrin, a high-molecular-weight precursor of filaggrin in human epidermis and cultured keratinocytes. *J Invest Dermatol*, **85**, 507–512.

105. Vigneswaran, N., Hanake, E., Hornstein, O.P. (1989) Are differences in filaggrin expression suitable for discriminating benign, pre-malignant and malignant skin lesions? An immunohistochemical study. *Pathol Res Pract*, **184**, 402–409.

106. Dale, B.A., Resing, K.A., Lansdale Bacles, J.D. (1985) Filaggrin: a keratin filament associated protein. *Ann N Y Acad Sci*, **455**, 330–342.

107. Scott, I.R., Harding, C.R. (1986) Filaggrin breakdown to water binding compounds during development of the rat stratum corneum is controlled by the water activity of the environment. *Dev Biol*, **115**, 84–92.

108. Resing, K.A., Dale, B.A. (1991) Proteins of keratohyalin. In: Goldsmith, L.A. (ed.) Physiology, biochemistry and molecular biology of the skin, 2nd edn. New York: Oxford University Press, pp 148–167.

109. Elias, P.M. (1996) The stratum corneum revisited. *J Dermatol*, **23**, 756–768.

110. Harris, I.R., Farrell, A.M., Grunfeld, C. et al (1997) Permeability barrier disruption coordinately regulates mRNA levels for key enzymes of cholesterol, fatty acid, and ceramide synthesis in the epidermis. *J Invest Dermatol*, **109**, 783–787.

111. Luger, T.A., Schwartz, T., Krutmann, J. et al (1990) Cytokines and the skin. In: van Vloten, W.A., Willemze, R., Lange Vejlsgaard, G. et al (eds) Cutaneous lymphoma. Current problems in dermatology. Basel: Karger, vol. 19, pp 35–49.

Epidermal dendritic cells

The epidermis contains two types of dendritic cell: melanocytes and Langerhans' cells.

Melanocytes

Melanocytes, of neural crest origin, are usually located along the basal layer of the epidermis and in the hair bulb. They are also present within the eye, ears and meninges. They are normally first detected by the fiftieth day of intrauterine life.[1–4] Melanocyte migration to the epidermis and survival is dependent upon the tyrosine kinase receptor c-Kit and its ligand, stem cell factor.[4] Piebaldism, characterized by localized hypopigmented patches as a result of lack of melanocyte migration, is due to mutation in the c-Kit gene (*Fig. 1.38*).[5] The ratio of melanocytes to basal cells ranges from approximately 1:4 on the cheek to 1:10 on the limbs. They appear as vacuolated cells in hematoxylin and eosin stained sections (*Fig. 1.39*).

The function of melanocytes is the production of melanin, a pigment that varies in color from yellow to brown or black and accounts for the various skin colors within and among races.[6]

Melanin is thought to protect the mitotically active basal epidermal cells from the injurious effects of ultraviolet light (UVL) (*Fig. 1.40*). This may account for individuals with less pigmentation (fair-haired and light-skinned) having a much greater risk of sunburn and developing cutaneous malignancies (squamous cell and basal cell carcinomas, and melanoma) when exposed to excessive UVL than those who are naturally heavily pigmented.[7] On the basis of initial responses to sunlight (i.e. three minimum erythema doses for about 45–60 minutes of noon exposure in northern (20–45°) latitudes in early summer), people may be classified into six clinical subtypes, and these have a considerable bearing on their likelihood to develop skin cancer (*Table 1.3*).[8]

Melanin is formed by a series of enzymatically controlled reactions from the substrate tyrosine via dopa and dopaquinone.[9,10] Recent work suggests that the melanin concentration in UVL-stimulated melanocytes is not controlled by transcriptional mechanisms but depends on activation of a pre-existing reservoir of tyrosinase.[11] The latter enzyme forms the basis of the dopa reaction (*Fig. 1.41*). Melanin can also be identified by silver techniques such as the Masson–Fontana reaction (*Fig. 1.42*).

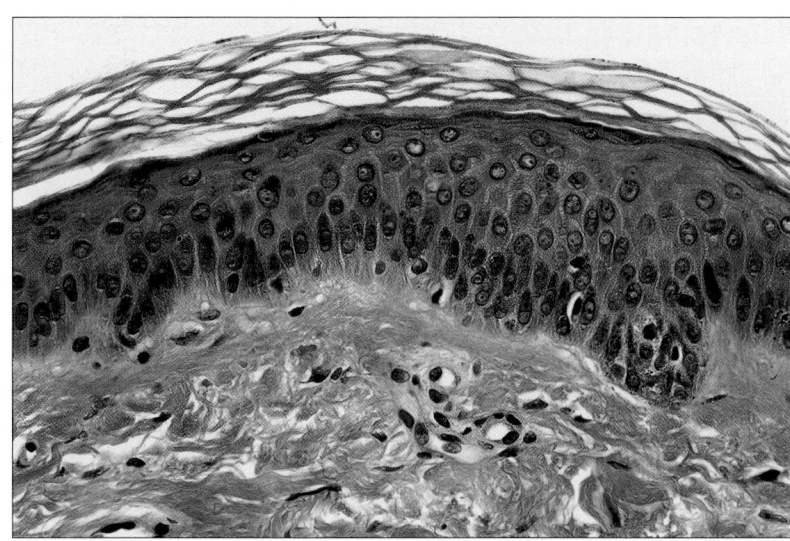

Fig. 1.40
Melanin pigment: actinically damaged skin. Note that the melanin pigment is located in a 'cap' overlying the keratinocyte nuclei.

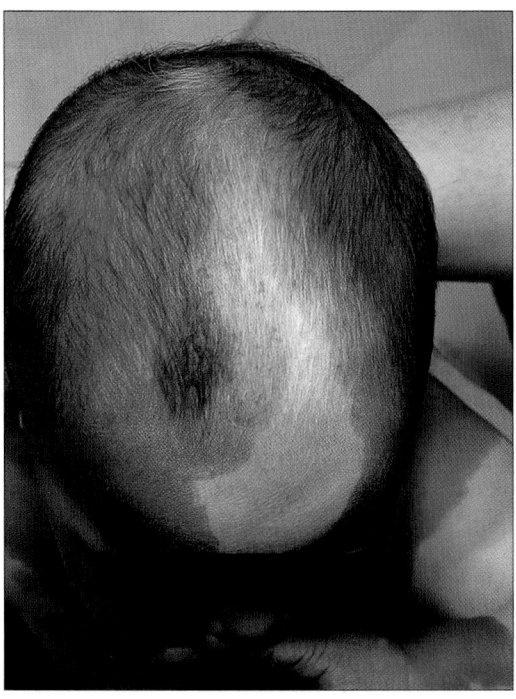

Fig. 1.38
Piebaldism: note the localized non-pigmented lesions. By courtesy of the Institute of Dermatology, London, UK.

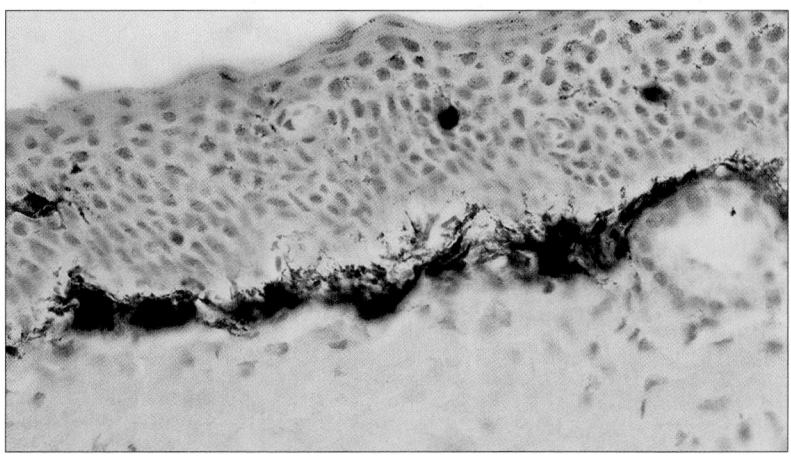

Fig. 1.41
Positive dopa reaction. By courtesy of R.J. Francis, FIMLS, Department of Morbid Anatomy, London Hospital, London, UK.

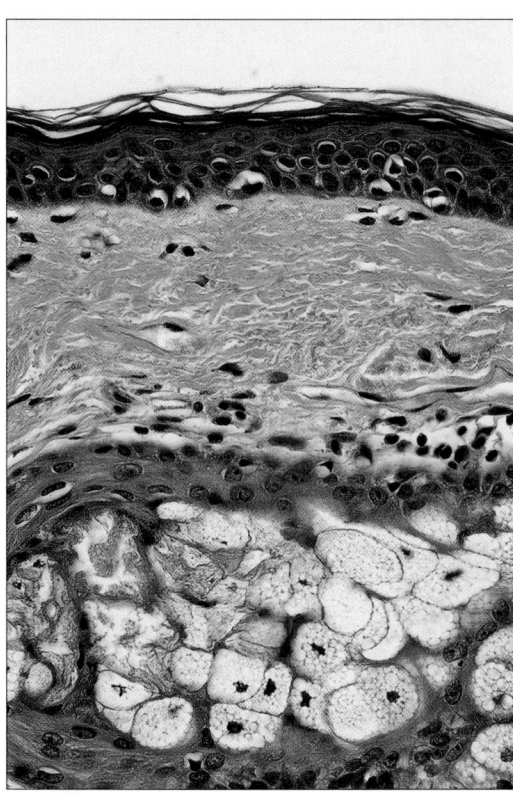

Fig. 1.39
Normal epidermis: melanocytes are seen along the basal layer of the epidermis. They have a round-to-oval vesicular nucleus. The cytoplasmic vacuolation is a fixation artifact.

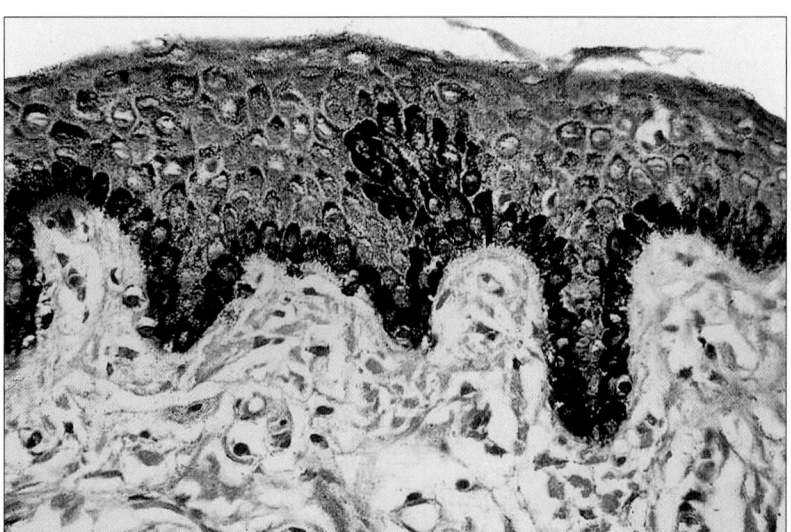

Fig. 1.42
Normal epidermis: this section of black skin has been stained by the Masson–Fontana reaction for melanin. Note the heavy pigmentation, which is present in both melanocytes and keratinocytes.

Ultrastructurally melanocytes have pale cytoplasm and are devoid of tonofilaments and desmosomes (*Fig. 1.43*). They are easily recognized by their specific cytoplasmic organelles (melanosomes) derived from the smooth endoplasmic reticulum (*Fig. 1.44*).[12,13] Melanosomes are believed to represent a specialized variant of lysosome.[14]

Table 1.3
Classification of normal skin types on the basis of response to sunlight

Skin colour (unexposed skin)	Skin type	Sunburn	Tan
White	I	Yes	No
	II	Yes	Minimal
	III	Yes	Yes
	IV	No	Yes
Brown	V	No	Yes
Black	VI	No	Yes

Reproduced with permission from Fitzpatrick, T.B. (1988) *Archives of Dermatology*, **124**, 869–871. Copyright 1988, American Medical Association.

There are two subtypes of melanin in human skin, one of which typically predominates:[3]

- *eumelanin* is a brown or black pigment and is synthesized from tyrosine; it is particularly found in African–Americans and other dark-colored races
- *phaeomelanin* has a yellow–red color and is synthesized from tyrosine and cysteine;[3] it predominates in Caucasian skin.

Mature melanosomes of eumelanin are ellipsoidal in shape, while phaeomelanin-producing melanosomes are spherical.[7] Four stages in the development of melanosomes are recognized.[12] Stage 1 eumelanosomes are spherical and non-lamellated (tyrosinase negative), but progressive lamellation (10 nm periodicity) and melanization accompanied by vesiculoglobular body development results in the densely pigmented stage 4, 400 nm long, ellipsoidal melanosomes.[12] Phaeomelanosomes remain spherical and pigmentation is centered on the vesiculoglobular bodies, tyrosinase-containing lamellae not being evident.[12] Melanosomes in dark-skinned races are larger and present in greater numbers than those in white skin races.[3]

Melanocytes are the only cells (with the possible exception of Schwann cells) capable of producing melanosomes. These are transported along the dendritic processes of the melanocytes (*Fig. 1.45*) and are engulfed as membrane-bound (lysosomal) single or compound melanosomes by a group of adjacent largely basally located keratinocytes (epidermal melanin unit) where they are typically seen in an umbrella-like distribution over the outer aspect of the nucleus (*Figs 1.46, 1.47*).[14,15] A

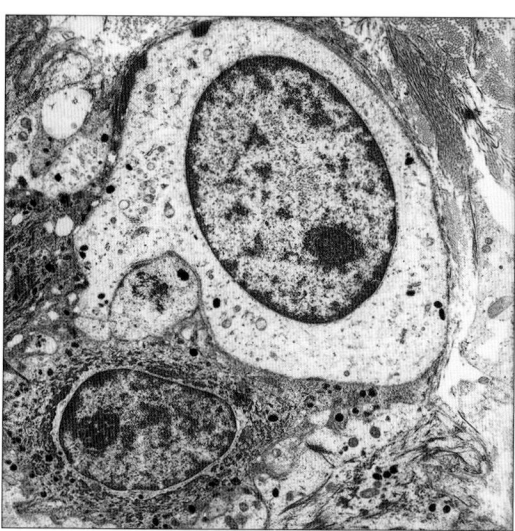

Fig. 1.43
Melanocyte characterized by abundant pale cytoplasm and scattered solitary melanosomes. Note the absence of tonofibrils and desmosomes.

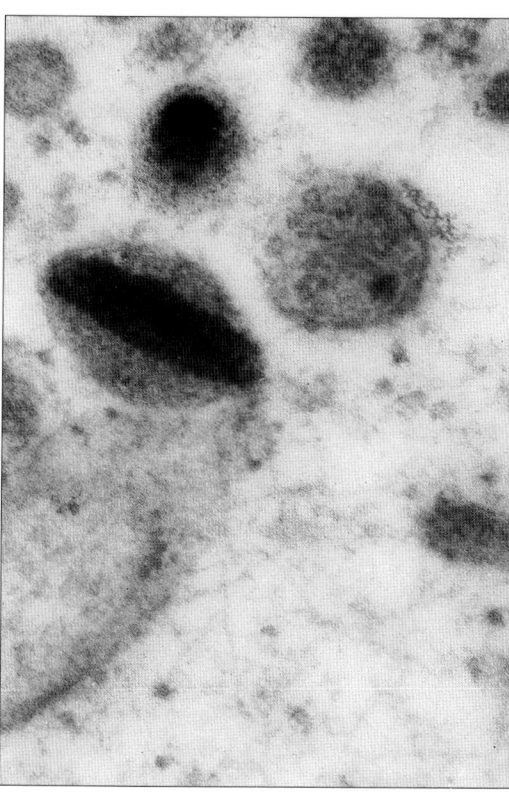

Fig. 1.44
Solitary melanosome showing the typical striated internal structure.

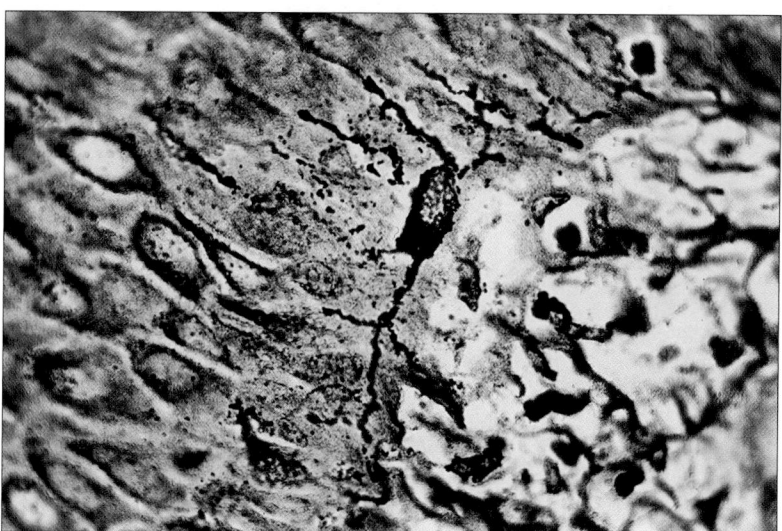

Fig. 1.45
Normal skin stained by the Warthin–Starry technique. The melanocytic dendritic processes are clearly outlined.

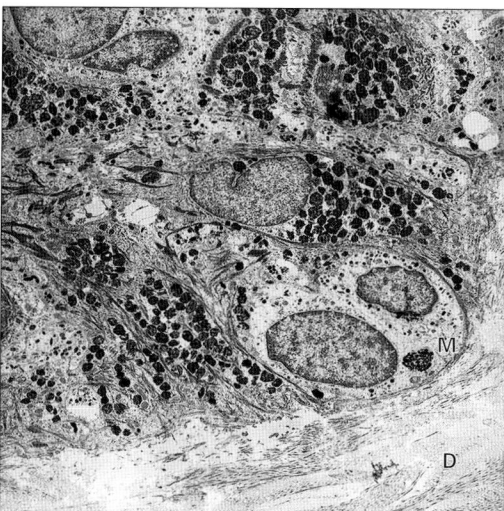

Fig. 1.46
Lower prickle cell layer of normal epidermis: compound melanosomes are present within the cytoplasm of keratinocytes. Two melanocytes (M) are also present. (D, dermis.)

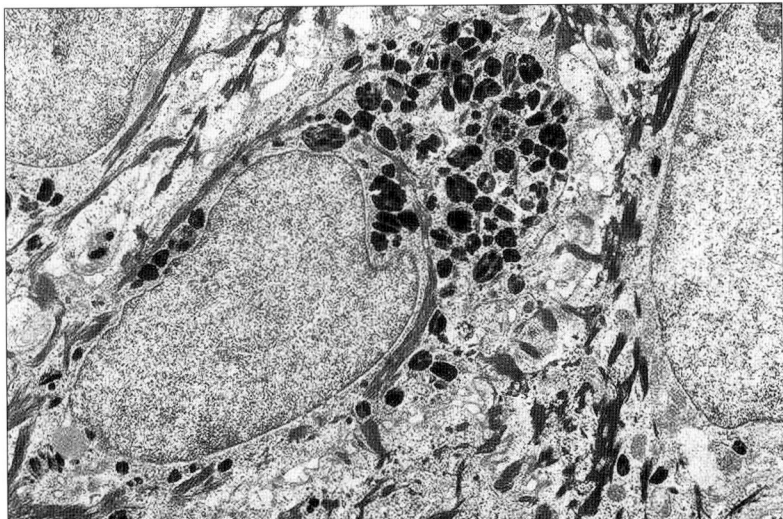

Fig. 1.47
Compound melanosomes form a protective shield overlying the keratinocyte nucleus.

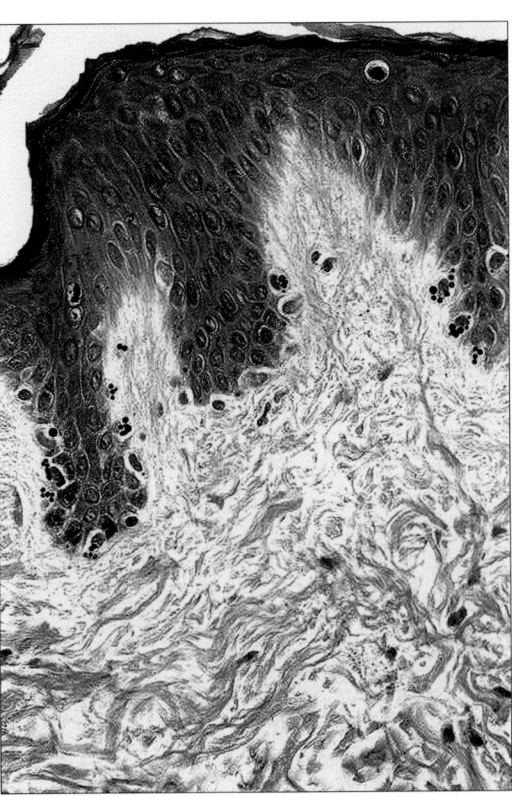

Fig. 1.49
Macromelanosomes: note the large spherical melanosomes in the cytoplasm of the melanocytes.

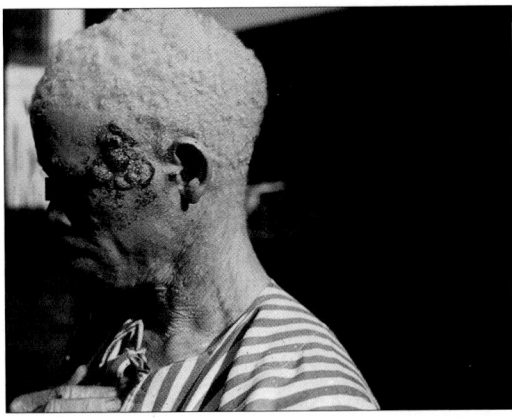

Fig. 1.48
Squamous cell carcinoma: multiple tumors on the face of an African albino highlight the risk of skin cancer in persons with this disease. By courtesy of the late M.S.R. Hutt, MD, St Thomas' Hospital Medical School, London, UK.

5. Fleischman, R.A., Saltman, D.L., Stastny, V. et al (1991) Deletion of the c-kit proto-oncogene in the human developmental defect piebald trait. *Proc Natl Acad Sci USA*, **88**, 10885–10889.
6. Jimbow, K., Fitzpatrick, T.B., Wick, M.M. (1991) Biochemistry and physiology of melanin pigmentation. In: Goldsmith, L.A. (ed.) Physiology, biochemistry and molecular biology of the skin, 2nd edn. New York: Oxford University Press, pp 873–909.
7. Fitzpatrick, T.B. (1986) Ultraviolet-induced pigmentary changes: benefits and hazards. *Curr Probl Dermatol*, **15**, 25–38.
8. Fitzpatrick, T.B. (1988) The validity and practicality of sun-reactive skin types I through VI. *Arch Dermatol*, **124**, 869–871.
9. Hearing, V.J., Jiménez, M. (1989) Analysis of mammalian pigmentation at the molecular level. *Pigment Cell Res*, **2**, 75–85.
10. Naeyart, J.M., Eller, M., Gordon, P.R. et al (1991) Pigment content of cultured human melanocytes does not correlate with tyrosinase level. *Br J Dermatol*, **125**, 297–303.
11. Jimbow, K., Quevedo, W.C. Jr, Fitzpatrick, T.B. et al (1976) Some aspects of melanin biology: 1950–1975. *J Invest Biol*, **67**, 72–89.
12. Breathnach, A.S. (1971) An atlas of the ultrastructure of human skin. London: Churchill.
13. Jimbow, K., Fitzpatrick, T.B., Quevedo, W.C. Jr (1986) Formation, chemical compositions and functions of melanin pigments in mammals. In: Matoltsy, A.G. (ed.) Biology of the integument. New York: Springer-Verlag, vol. 2, pp 278–296.
14. Orlow, S.J. (1995) Melanosomes are specialized members of the lysosomal lineage of organelles. *J Invest Dermatol*, **105**, 3–7.
15. Kobayashi, N., Nakagawa, A., Muramatsu, T. et al (1998) Supranuclear melanin caps reduce ultraviolet induced DNA photoproducts in human epidermis. *J Invest Dermatol*, **110**, 806–810.
16. Sakamoto, F., Ito, M., Sato, Y. (1987) Ultrastructural study of macromelanosomes in a unique case of spindle and epithelioid cell nevus. *J Cutan Pathol*, **14**, 59–64.
17. Beitner, H., Nakatani, T., Hedblad, M.A. (1990) A transmission electron microscopic study of dysplastic nevi. *Acta Derm Venereol*, **70**, 411–416.
18. Alvarez-Franco, N., Reyes-Mugica, M., Ruiz-Maldonado, R. et al (1991) Macromelanosomes as morphologic markers in childhood neurofibromatosis. *Pediatr Dermatol*, **8**, 91–93.
19. Schiaffino, M.V., Baschirotto, C., Pellegrini, G. et al (1996) The ocular albinism type 1 gene is a membrane glycoprotein localized to melanosomes. *Proc Natl Acad Sci USA*, **93**, 9055–9060.

compound melanosome typically contains from three to six single melanosomes.[3] The precise method of transfer of melanosome to keratinocyte is unknown. In heavily pigmented skin and dark hair, melanosomes remain solitary and are longer than those seen in melanogenesis in paler races.[7] Other cells that may contain compound melanosomes include macrophages (melanophages), melanoma cells and, occasionally, Langerhans' cells, the other type of epidermal dendritic cell.

The functions of the melanin pigments include resistance to the effects of UVL, control of vitamin D_3 synthesis, and local thermoregulation.[13] Melanocyte numbers increase as a response to ultraviolet irradiation.[11] Albinos who are deficient in melanin develop premature actinic skin damage and cancer (*Fig. 1.48*).[10]

Macromelanosomes (giant melanosomes) measure several microns in diameter and therefore are readily visible in hematoxylin and eosin stained sections. They may be encountered in normal skin, in lentigines, dysplastic nevi, Spitz nevi, in the café-au-lait macules of neurofibromatosis and in albinism (*Fig. 1.49*).[16–19]

References

1. Holbrook, K.A. (1998) Melanocytes in human embryonic skin and fetal skin: review and new findings. *Pigment Cell Res*, **1** (Suppl.), 6–17.
2. Fitzpatrick, T.B. (1971) The biology of pigmentation. *Birth Defects Orig Art Ser*, **7**, 5–12.
3. Nordlund, J.J., Boissy, R.E. (2001) The biology of melanocytes. In: Freinkel, R.K., Woodley, D.T. (eds) The biology of the skin. New York: Parthenon Publishing, pp 113–131.
4. Haake, A., Scott, G.A., Holbrook, K.A. (2001) Structure and function of the skin: overview of the epidermis and dermis. In: Freinkel, R.K., Woodley, D.T. (eds) The biology of the skin. New York: Parthenon Publishing, pp 19–46.

Langerhans' cells

Langerhans' cells, first described by the medical student Paul Langerhans in 1868, are intraepidermal antigen-processing cells responsible for the development of cutaneous contact allergic hypersensitivity reactions.[1,2] They represent potent stimulators of a wide range of T-cell-mediated immunoreactions.[3] They are therefore the primary cellular intraepidermal response to tumor antigens and microorganisms and they play a major role in skin graft rejection.[4,5]

Langerhans' cells are found within the suprabasal layers of the epidermis and also in the dermis, but are difficult to identify with confidence using standard histological techniques. Cells showing striking cytoplasmic vacuolation in the upper reaches of the epidermis are likely to be Langerhans' cells (*Fig. 1.50*). They can be demonstrated more readily, however, by a variety of methods, including supravital reactions such as methylene blue, enzymatically using adenosine triphosphatase, and immunohistochemically using a range of monoclonal antibodies.[3] Langerhans' cells may also be identified in the squamous epithelium of the oral cavity, esophagus, anus, cervix and vagina.

Langerhans' cells express a number of leukocyte and macrophage antigens including major histocompatibility complex (MHC) class I (HLA-A, B, C), MHC class II (HLA-D), CD1a, CD1b, CD18 (β_2 integrin), CD29 (β_1 integrin), CD45 (CLA), Lag and Fc-IgG receptor II and – when activated – Ig-Fc receptor, interleukin-2 receptor (CD25) and CD4 (*Fig. 1.41*).[3,6–11] They also express S-100 protein, vimentin, E-cadherin and intercellular adhesion molecule 1 (ICAM-1) (*Figs 1.51, 1.52*).[11,12] In the human, anti-CD1a antibody is the most specific for identifying Langerhans' cells in tissue sections.[3]

Langerhans' cells are characterized by their dendritic processes, which extend upwards between the keratinocytes as far as the granular cell layer and downwards to the epidermal–dermal junction.

Ultrastructurally, Langerhans' cells are distinguished from keratinocytes by an absence of desmosomes and tonofilaments, and while they may occasionally contain compound melanosomes, they never have solitary melanosomes or premelanosomes within their cytoplasm.

The Langerhans' cell typically has a lobulated nucleus (*Fig. 1.53*) and clear cytoplasm containing the characteristic Langerhans' (Birbeck) granules (rod or racquet inclusions, *Fig. 1.54*). As far as is known these are a specific ultrastructural feature.[3,6,13] The granules are believed to play an important role in antigen presentation because their number increases during contact sensitivity reactions.[4,5] Continuity with the cell

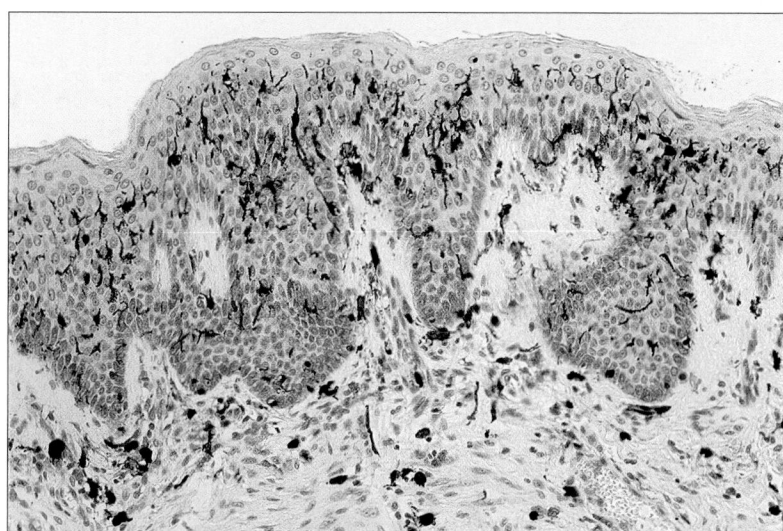

Fig. 1.52
Contact dermatitis: Langerhans' cells are found in large numbers in allergic contact dermatitis.

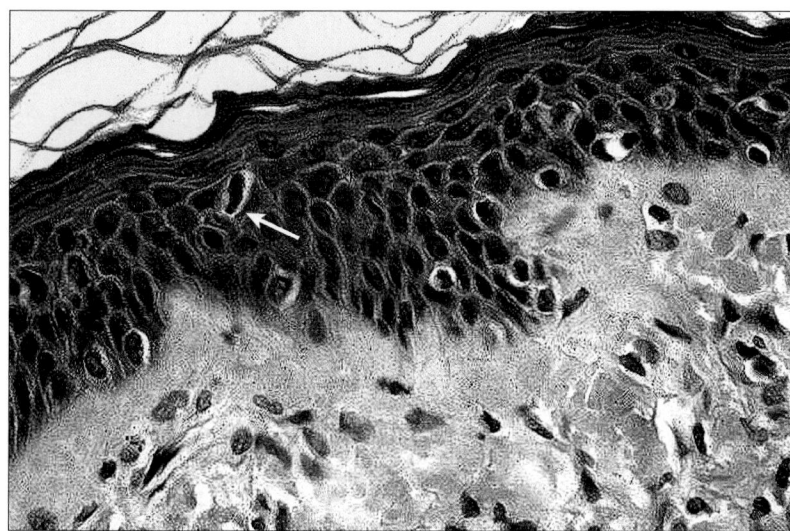

Fig. 1.50
Normal skin: the cell in the mid epidermis is a Langerhans' cell (arrowed). Note the vacuolated cytoplasm.

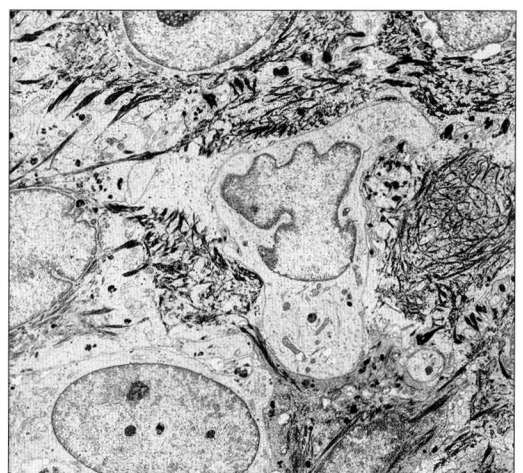

Fig. 1.53
Langerhans' cell: note the characteristic lobulated nucleus. Dendritic processes are evident.

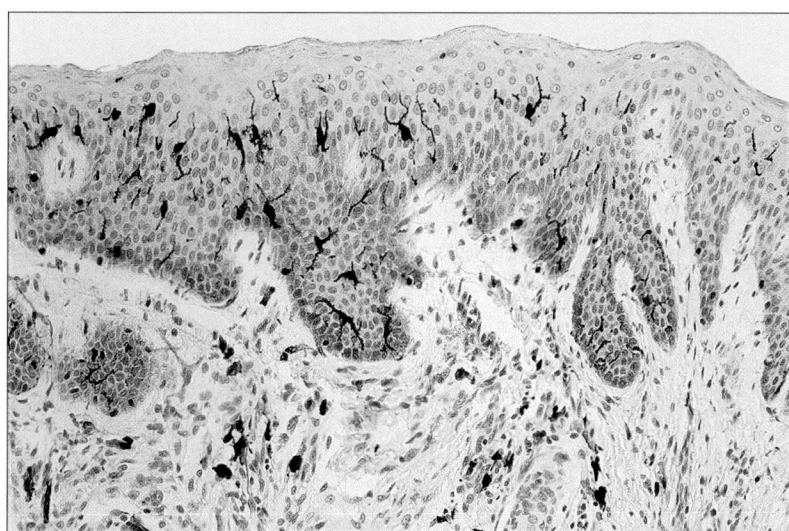

Fig. 1.51
Langerhans' cells express S-100 protein: note the conspicuous dendritic processes.

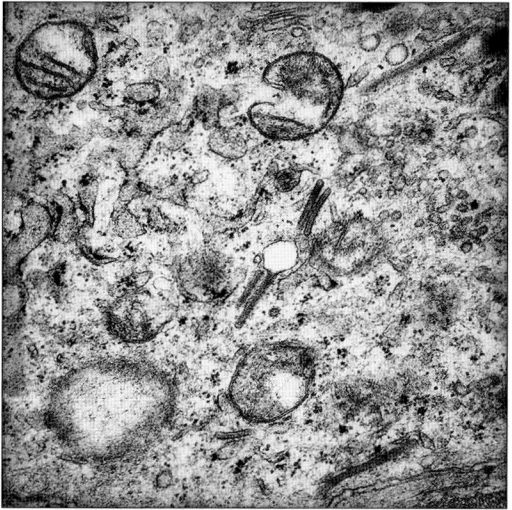

Fig. 1.54
Langerhans' granules: typical rod and racquet forms with the characteristic trilaminar structure.

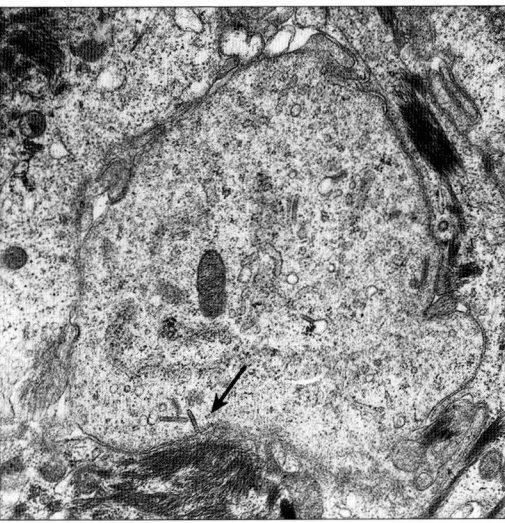

Fig. 1.55
High power view of a Langerhans' cell dendritic process: a Langerhans' granule can be seen in continuity with the plasma membrane (arrowed).

membrane has been demonstrated (*Fig. 1.55*) and it is thought that they form from fusion of cell membrane-derived components with endosomes and lysosomes.[11] Their main function is to render foreign proteins into immunogenic peptides (linear oligopeptides) for presentation to effector T-cells.[11]

At one time the Langerhans' cell was believed to represent a 'worn out' melanocyte, but is now known to be derived from bone marrow[14] and functions as an immunocompetent cell participating in delayed hypersensitivity and skin allograft reactions. It therefore plays an important role as an antigen-presenting cell in T-lymphocyte-dependent immune responses.[11,15,16] Following antigen stimulation, sensitized Langerhans' cells migrate to the paracortical zone of the lymph node under the influence of TNF-α and α_6 integrin, in close apposition to, and stimulating, T-lymphocytes.[17–19] It is then thought that the resultant antigen-specific T-cells return to the epidermis to effect the immune reaction against the sensitizing antigen.[3]

In addition to mediating T-cell responses, it has been suggested that Langerhans' cells may play a role in extrathymic T-lymphocyte maturation and intraepidermal differentiation.[15]

Langerhans' cell responses are important in the development of cutaneous neoplasms and dysplasias.[20] It has been shown that a reduction in their number or antigen-presenting function, as can be induced by UVL or chemical carcinogens, may play an important role in the earlier stages of development of experimental and naturally occurring epidermal tumor.[21]

References

1. Langerhans, P. (1886) Über die nerven der menschlichen haut. *Virch Arch Pathol Anat*, **44**, 325–337.
2. Toews, G.B., Bergstresser, P.R., Streilein, J.W. et al (1979) Epidermal Langerhans' cell density determines whether contact hypersensitivity or unresponsiveness follows skin painting with DNFB. *J Immunol*, **124**, 445–453.
3. Hauser, C., Elbe, A., Stingl, E. (1991) The Langerhans' cell. In: Goldsmith, L.A. (ed.) Physiology, biochemistry and molecular biology of the skin, 2nd edn. New York: Oxford University Press, pp 144–163.
4. Williams, I.R., Kupper, T.S. (1996) Immunity at the surface: homeostatic mechanisms of the skin immune system. *Life Sci*, **58**, 1485–1507.
5. Streilein, J.W., Lonsberry, L.W., Bergstresser, P.R. (1979) Corneal allografts fail to express Ia antigens. *Nature*, **282**, 326–327.
6. Krall, G. (1991) Monoclonal antibodies to Langerhans' cells in man and experimental animals. In: Becker, Y. (ed.) Skin Langerhans' (dendritic) cells in virus infections and AIDS. Dordrecht: Kluwer Academic, pp 25–38.
7. Kashihara-Sawami, M., Imamura, S. (1991) Detection of Langerhans' cells with monoclonal antibodies. In: Becker, Y. (ed.) Skin Langerhans' (dendritic) cells in virus infections and AIDS. Dordrecht: Kluwer Academic, pp 39–58.
8. Stingl, G., Katz, S.I., Clement, L. et al (1978) Immunologic functions of Ia-bearing epidermal Langerhans' cells. *J Immunol*, **121**, 2005–2013.
9. Stingl, G., Wolff-Schreiner, E.C., Pinchler, W.J. et al (1977) Epidermal Langerhans' cell bear Fc and C3 receptors. *Nature*, **268**, 245–246.
10. Kashihara, M., Ueda, M., Horiguchi, Y. et al (1986) A monoclonal antibody specifically reactive to human Langerhans' cells. *J Invest Dermatol*, **87**, 602–607.
11. Cruz, P.D. (2001) The epidermis: an outpost of the immune system. In: Frienkel, R.K., Woodley, D.T. (eds) The biology of the skin. New York: Parthenon Publishing, pp 255–263.
12. Udey, M.C. (1997) Cadherins and Langerhans' cell immunobiology. *Clin Exp Immunol*, **107** (Suppl.), 6–8.
13. Birbeck, M.S., Breathnach, A.S., Everall, J.D. (1961) An electron microscopic study of basal melanocyte and high level clear cell (Langerhans' cell) in vitiligo. *J Invest Dermatol*, **37**, 51–63.

14. Katz, S.I., Tamaki, K., Sachs, D.H. (1979) Epidermal Langerhans' cells are derived from cells originating in bone marrow. *Nature*, **282**, 324–326.
15. Sprecher, E., Becker, Y. (1991) Dendritic cells in the epidermis and the lymph nodes – a review. In: Becker, Y. (ed.) Skin Langerhans' (dendritic) cells in virus infections and AIDS. Dordrecht: Kluwer Academic, pp 3–23.
16. Kripke, M.L., Munn, C.G., Jeevan, A. et al (1990) Evidence that cutaneous antigen-presenting cells migrate to regional lymph nodes during contact sensitization. *J Immunol*, **145**, 2833–2838.
17. Cumberbatch, M., Kimber, I. (1992) Dermal tumor necrosis factor-α induces dendritic cell migration to draining lymph nodes, and possibly provides one stimulus for Langerhans' cell migration. *Immunology*, **75**, 257–263.
18. Price, A.A., Cumberbatch, M., Kimber, I. et al (1997) α_6 integrins are required for Langerhans' cell migration from the epidermis. *J Exp Med*, **186**, 1725–1735.
19. Haake, A., Scott, G.A., Holbrook, K.A. (2001) Structure and function of the skin: overview of the epidermis and dermis. In: Frienkel, R.K., Woodley, D.T. (eds) The biology of the skin. New York: Parthenon Publishing, pp 19–46.
20. Muller, H.K., Halliday, G.M. (1991) Langerhans' cells in tumor development and regression. In: Becker, Y. (ed.) Skin Langerhans' (dendritic) cells in virus infections and AIDS. Dordrecht: Kluwer Academic, pp 79–97.
21. Obata, M., Tagami, H.J. (1985) Alteration in murine epidermal Langerhans' cell population by various UV irradiations, quantitative and morphologic studies on the effects of various wavelengths of monochromatic radiation on Ia-bearing cells. *J Invest Dermatol*, **84**, 139–145.

Merkel cells

Merkel cells, which were first described in 1875, represent part of the affector limb in cutaneous slowly adapting type-1 (SA1) mechano-receptors and are therefore particularly concerned with touch sensation.[1,2] It is thought likely that this function is mediated through release of neuromodulatory chemicals rather than by direct mechanical transduction.[1] These cells are widely dispersed in the epidermis, hair follicular epithelium and mucous membranes of mammals (*Fig. 1.56*), and have also been described in fish, amphibians and reptiles.[3] They are present in adult humans, and show maximum distribution on the lips, hard palate, palms, finger pads, proximal nail folds and dorsum of the feet (*Fig. 1.57*).[4,5] Elsewhere they are more frequent on sun-exposed skin than on non-sun-exposed skin.[3] They appear to be particularly numerous in actinic keratoses.[6]

The precise origin of Merkel cells remains unknown. Two hypotheses have been proposed: either they represent a modified keratinocyte with neuroendocrine features or, alternatively, they are derived from the neural crest.[1,2] The former is favored as a consequence of developmental, immunocytochemical and ultrastructural considerations.[1] Fetal epidermis grafted onto denervated dermis of nude mice has been shown to develop Merkel cells.[7] By immunocytochemistry, fetal Merkel cells are first identified within the epidermis rather than the dermis.[8] Merkel cells express epithelial keratins and ultrastructurally they share features in common with keratinocytes (see below).

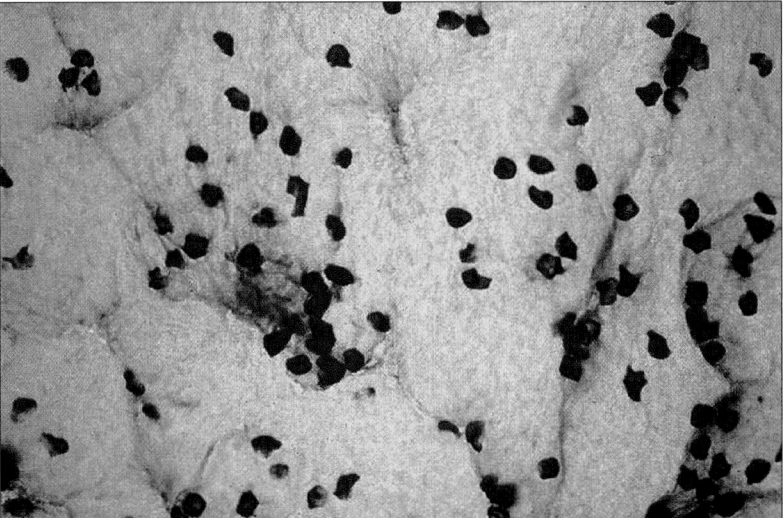

Fig. 1.56
Merkel cells: large numbers are normally found in the epithelium of the rabbit lip (troma-1 antibody). By courtesy of J.P. Lacour, MD, and J.P. Ortonne, MD, University of Nice, France.

Immunocytochemically human Merkel cells express neuropeptides including synaptophysin, vasoactive intestinal peptide (VIP) and calcitonin gene-related polypeptide (CGRP).[9–11] They contain neuron-specific proteins including neuron-specific enolase (NSE) and protein gene product (PGP) 9.5.[12,13] In addition, Merkel cells express desmosomal proteins, membranous neural cell adhesion molecule and nerve growth factor receptor.[14–16] Merkel cells show a positive uranaffin reaction.[17]

Merkel cells contain keratin filaments, particularly keratin filament types 8, 18, 19 and 20, which are characteristic of simple epithelium and fetal epidermis.[14,18,19]

Under normal circumstances Merkel cells do not appear to divide.[20] This presumably relates to their forming synapses with intraepidermal nerve endings, a circumstance when mitosis would not usually occur.[20] Merkel cells have, however, been shown to increase in number in sun-damaged skin.[3,21]

Merkel cells cannot be recognized in conventional hematoxylin and eosin stained sections. Rather, immunocytochemistry, particularly using antikeratin antibodies (*Fig. 1.58*), or electron microscopy, is necessary for their identification. They are located within the lower epidermis or the follicular external root sheath.[22]

Within the epidermis Merkel cells are located suprabasally and make synaptic junctions with myelinated type I sensory neurons (*Fig. 1.59*).[23,24] Ultrastructurally (*Figs 1.60, 1.61*), the Merkel cell is characterized by the presence of cytoplasmic spines, membrane-bound dense core granules (80–120 nm diameter) and synaptic junctions.[5,24] Intermediate filaments are present in the cytoplasm. The nucleus is lobulated and sometimes contains rod-like inclusions.[1] Although Merkel

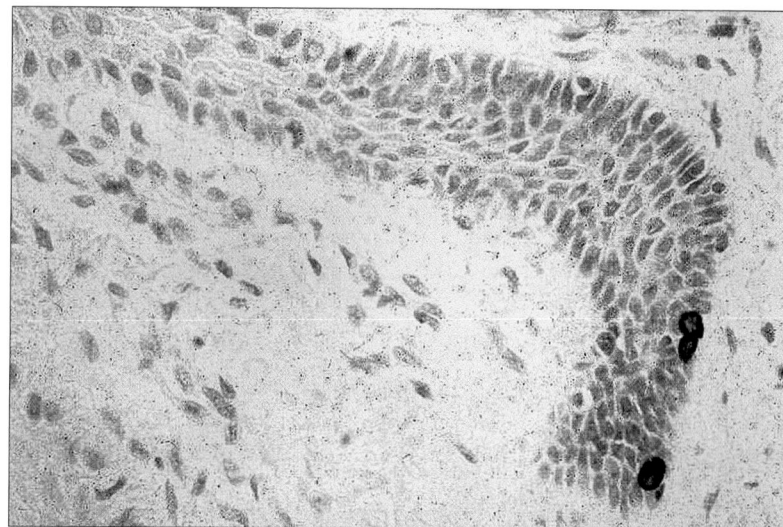

Fig. 1.58
Positive labeling for CAM 5.2 identifies Merkel cells in this obliquely sectioned epidermal ridge.

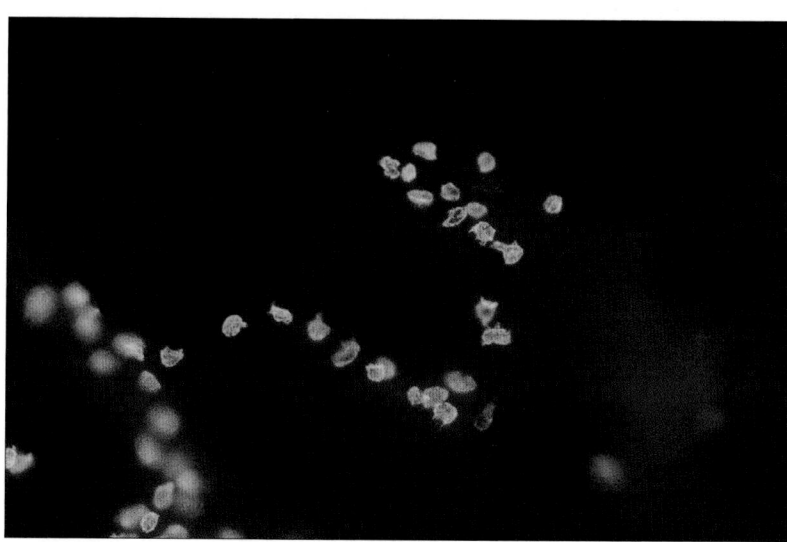

Fig. 1.57
Merkel cells: separated human epidermis showing a striking linear arrangement (troma-1 antibody). By courtesy of J.P. Lacour, MD, and J.P. Ortonne, MD, University of Nice, France.

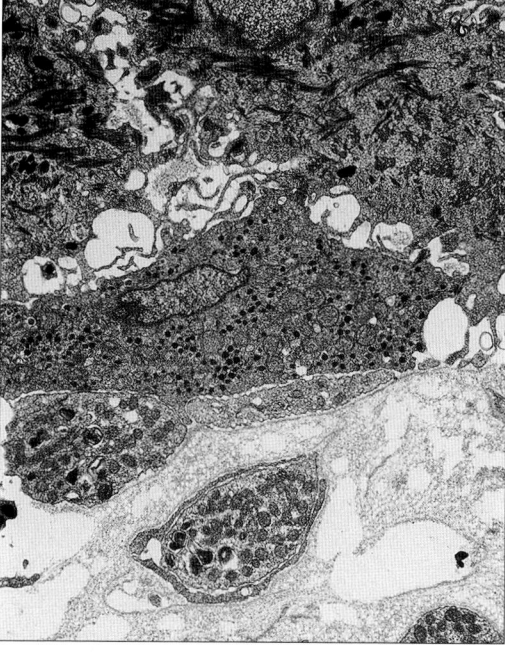

Fig. 1.59
A heavily granulated Merkel cell is present in the midfield. This is located immediately adjacent to a small nerve fiber. By courtesy J.A. McGrath, MD, St John's Institute of Dermatology, London, UK.

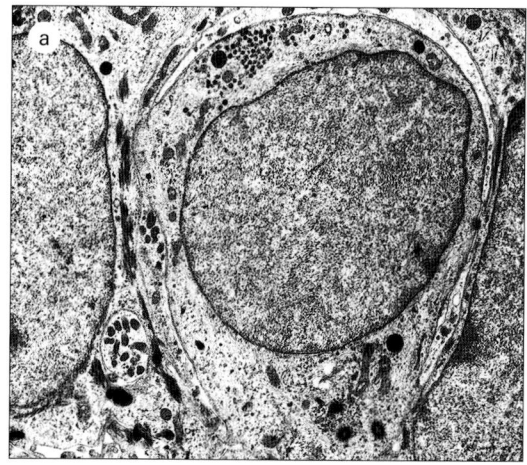
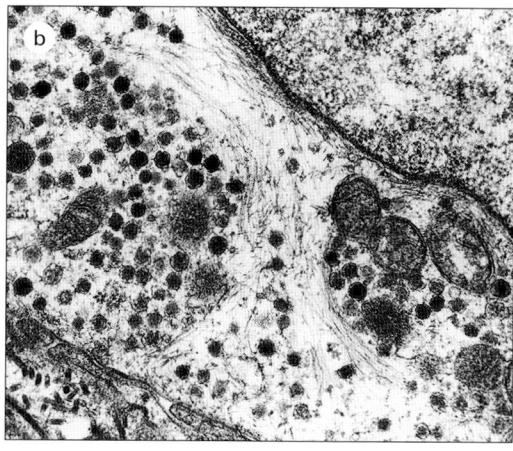

Fig. 1.60
(a, b) The Merkel cell is typified by intracytoplasmic membrane-bound granules. By courtesy of A.S. Breathnach, MD (1977) Electron microscopy of cutaneous nerves and receptors. *Journal of Investigative Dermatology* **69**, 8–26. Blackwell Publishing Inc., USA.

cells do form desmosomal attachments with neighboring keratinocytes, they do not form hemidesmosomal attachments to the basement membrane region. The granules are principally located on the basal side of the nucleus in close proximity to the synaptic junction.[3] The Golgi apparatus is typically sited on the opposite side of the nucleus.

Although solitary Merkel cells are occasionally seen, they are more often aggregated at the bases of epidermal ridges in glabrous skin, or associated with follicles in hairy skin.[25] At the latter site they are described as tactile corpuscles or touch domes of Pinkus (Haarscheiben) (*Fig. 1.62*). Typically the overlying epidermis is acanthotic and the lateral margins bounded by an inverted collarette. Merkel cells are conspicuous and the papillary dermis contains a rich vascular and abundant nerve supply.

In addition to their mechanoreceptor function, it has recently been suggested that Merkel cells may play a primary role in the induction of subepidermal and perifollicular nerve plexuses.[18] It is also postulated that they are of importance in epidermal development and maintenance and that their paracrine function may influence dermal connective tissue cells, nerves and blood vessels.[1]

References

1. Tachibana, T. (1995) The Merkel cell: recent findings and unresolved problems. *Arch Histol Cytol*, **58**, 379–396.
2. Munger, B.L. (1991) The biology of Merkel cells. In: Goldsmith L.A. (ed.) Physiology, biochemistry and molecular biology of the skin, 2nd edn. New York: Oxford University Press, pp 836–856.
3. Moll, I., Bladt, U., Jung, E.G. (1990). Presence of Merkel cells in sun-exposed and not sun-exposed skin: a quantitative study. *Arch Dermatol Res*, **282**, 213–216.
4. Lacour, J.P., Dubois, D., Pisani, A. et al (1991) Anatomical mapping of Merkel cells in normal human adult epidermis. *Br J Dermatol*, **125**, 535–542.
5. Winkelmann, R.K., Breathnach, A.S. (1973) The Merkel cell. *J Invest Dermatol*, **60**, 2–15.
6. Merot, Y., Mooy, A. (1989) Merkel cell hyperplasia in hypertrophic varieties of actinic keratoses. *Dermatologica*, **178**, 189–193.
7. Moll, I., Lane, A.T., Franke, W.W. et al (1990) Intraepidermal formation of Merkel cells in xenografts of human fetal skin. *J Invest Dermatol*, **94**, 359–364.
8. Moll, I., Moll, R. (1993) Merkel cells in ontogenesis of human nails. *Arch Dermatol Res*, **285**, 366–371.
9. Hartschuh, W., Weihe, E., Yanaihara, N. et al (1983) Immunohistochemical localization of vasoactive intestinal polypeptide (VIP) in Merkel cells of various mammals: evidence for a neuromodulator function of the Merkel cell. *J Invest Dermatol*, **81**, 361–364.
10. Ortonne, J.P., Petchot-Bacque, J.P., Verrando, P. et al (1988) Normal Merkel cells express a synaptophysin-like immunoreactivity. *Dermatologica*, **177**, 1–10.
11. Garcia-Caballero, T.G.R., Gallego, E., Rosón, M. et al (1989) Calcitonin gene-related peptide (CGRP) in the neuroendocrine Merkel cells and nerve fibers of pig and human skin. *Histochemistry*, **92**, 127–132.
12. Gu, J., Polak, J.M., Tapia, F.J. et al (1981) Neuron-specific enolase in the Merkel cells of mammalian skin. *Am J Pathol*, **104**, 63–68.
13. Dalsgaard, C-J., Rydh, M., Haegerstrand, A. (1989) Cutaneous innervation in man visualized with protein gene product 9.5 (PGP 9.5) antibodies. *Histochemistry*, **92**, 385–389.
14. Ortonne, J.P., Darmon, M. (1985) Merkel cells express desmosomal proteins and cytokeratins. *Acta Derm Venereol*, **65**, 161–164.
15. Gallego, R., Garcia-Caballero, M., Fraga, A. et al (1995) Neural cell adhesion molecule in Merkel cells and Merkel cell tumors. *Virchows Arch*, **426**, 317–321.
16. Narisawa, Y., Hashimoto, K., Nihei, Y. et al (1992) Biological significance of dermal Merkel cells in the development of cutaneous nerves in human fetal skin. *J Histochem Cytochem*, **40**, 65–71.
17. Beiras, A., Garcia-Caballero, T., Espinosa, J. et al (1986) Staining of Merkel cells of pig snout epidermis using the uranaffin reaction: morphometric analysis of neuroendocrine granules. *Differentiation*, **28**, 136–154.
18. Moll, R., Moll, I., Franke, W.W. (1984) Identification of Merkel cells in human skin by specific cytokeratin antibodies: changes of cell density and distribution in fetal and adult plantar epidermis. *Differentiation*, **28**, 136–154.
19. Saurat, J.H., Didierjean, L., Skalli, O. et al (1984) The intermediate filament proteins of rabbit normal epidermal Merkel cells are cytokeratins. *J Invest Dermatol*, **83**, 431–435.
20. Vaigot, P., Pisani, A., Darmon, Y.M. et al (1987) The majority of epidermal Merkel cells are non-proliferative: a quantitative immunofluorescence analysis. *Acta Derm Venereol*, **67**, 517–520.
21. Gould, V.E., Moll, R., Moll, I. et al (1985) Neuroendocrine (Merkel) cells of the skin: hyperplasias, dysplasias and neoplasms. *Lab Invest*, **52**, 334–353.
22. Munger, B.L., Ide, C. (1988) The structure and function of cutaneous sensory receptors. *Arch Histol Cytolol*, **51**, 1–34.
23. Breathnach, A.S. (1979). The mammalian and avian Merkel cell. In: Spearman, R.I.C., Riley, P.A. (eds) The skin of vertebrates. Dorchester, Dorset: Henry Ling Ltd, Dorset Press, vol. 9, pp 283–291.
24. Hartschuh, W., Weihe, E. (1980) Fine structural analysis of the synaptic junction of Merkel cell–axon complexes. *J Invest Dermatol*, **75**, 159–165.
25. Smith, K.R. Jr (1970) The ultrastructure of the human Haarscheibe and Merkel cell. *J Invest Dermatol*, **54**, 150–159.

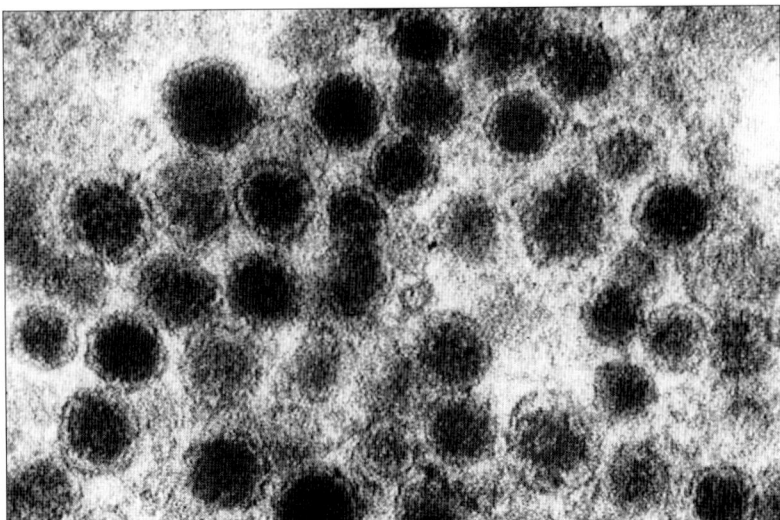

Fig. 1.61
Merkel cell granules are membrane bound and measure approximately 150 nm in diameter. By courtesy of A.S. Breathnach, MD (1977) Electron microscopy of cutaneous nerves and receptors. *Journal of Investigative Dermatology* **69**, 8–26. Blackwell Publishing Inc., USA.

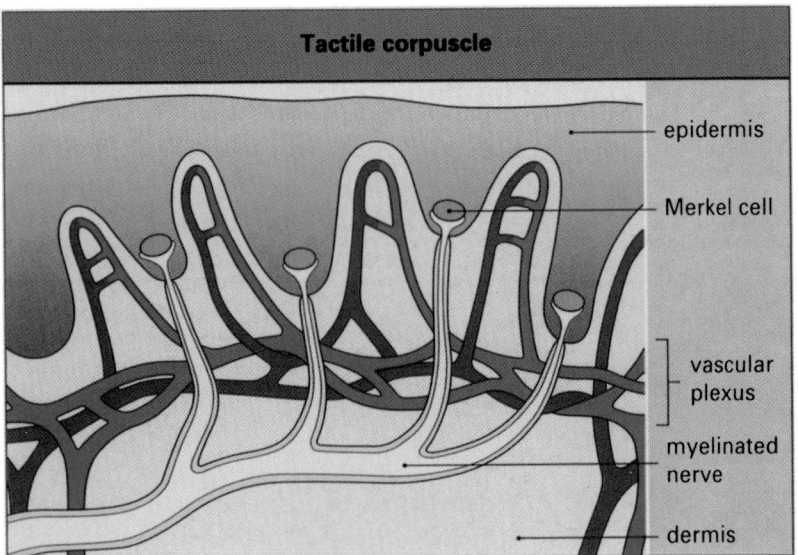

Tactile corpuscle

— epidermis

— Merkel cell

vascular plexus

myelinated nerve

— dermis

Fig. 1.62
Tactile corpuscle (hair disc). Modified from Camisa, C. and Weissmann, A. (1982) *American Journal of Dermatopathology* **4**, 527–535. Masson Publishing USA, New York.

Epidermal appendages

Sebaceous glands

Sebaceous glands usually develop as lateral protrusions from the outer root sheath of hair follicles, but at certain sites, such as the eyelids, lips, areolae, nipples and labia minora, they appear to arise independently and drain directly onto the skin's surface (*Figs 1.63, 1.64*).[1,2] They are widespread in distribution, being found everywhere on the body except on the palms and soles. They are particularly abundant on the face and scalp, in the midline of the back and about the perineum, and are concentrated around the orifices of the body. Those of the eyelid are known as the glands of Zeis and the Meibomian glands. Sebaceous glands within the areolae are known as Montgomery's tubercles.

The largest sebaceous glands are associated with small vellus hairs in specialized pilosebaceous units known as sebaceous follicles (the so-called pores of the face). Sebaceous glands consist of several lipid-containing lobules, usually connected to a hair follicle (*Fig. 1.65*). Each lobule is composed of an outer layer of small cuboidal or flattened basophilic germinative cells, from which arises the inner zone of lipid-laden vacuolated cells with characteristic crenated nuclei (*Fig. 1.66*). The secretions drain into the sebaceous duct, which joins the hair follicle at the level of the infundibulum (*Fig. 1.67*). The duct is lined by keratinizing stratified squamous epithelium and is continuous with the external root sheath. The glands are known as holocrine glands because their secretions depend on complete degeneration of the acini, with release of all the cells' lipid contents to become sebum.[3]

Immunochistochemically, the sebaceous cells label strongly for EMA (*Fig. 1.68*). They neither contain CEA or low molecular weight keratin (CAM 5.2), nor express S-100 protein.

Ultrastructurally, the mature sebaceous gland shows gradual accumulation of variably sized, non-membrane-bound, lipid inclusions in differentiating cells (*Fig. 1.69*). Numerous mitochondria, ribosomes and membrane-bound vesicles may also be evident.[4,5] As the cells mature before their disintegration, the lipid droplets completely fill the cytoplasm and compress the centrally located nucleus (*Fig. 1.70*).

Sebaceous glands are largely inactive during prepubertal life, but enlarge and become functionally active during and after puberty.[3] The mechanism of control of sebaceous activity is incompletely understood.

Secretion appears to have a circadian rhythm, largely under the control of androgens (testosterone) and probably inhibited by estrogens.[1,6,7] It therefore comes as no surprise that sebaceous glands of males are larger and more functionally active than those of females.

The secretion of sebaceous glands is called sebum, an exceedingly complicated lipid mixture that includes triglycerides (57%), wax esters (26%) and squalene (12%).[8] Its function in man, although uncertain, possibly includes waterproofing, control of epidermal water loss, and a protective function, inhibiting the growth of fungi and bacteria. Secreted sebum undergoes significant changes due to the presence of

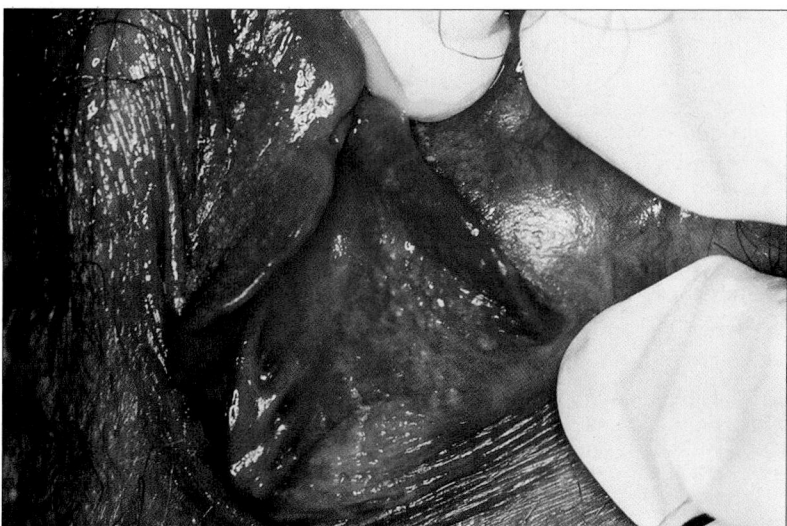

Fig. 1.63
Sebaceous glands: on the inner aspect of the labia these appear as tiny yellow papules (Fordyce spots). By courtesy of S.M. Neill, MD, Institute of Dermatology, London, UK.

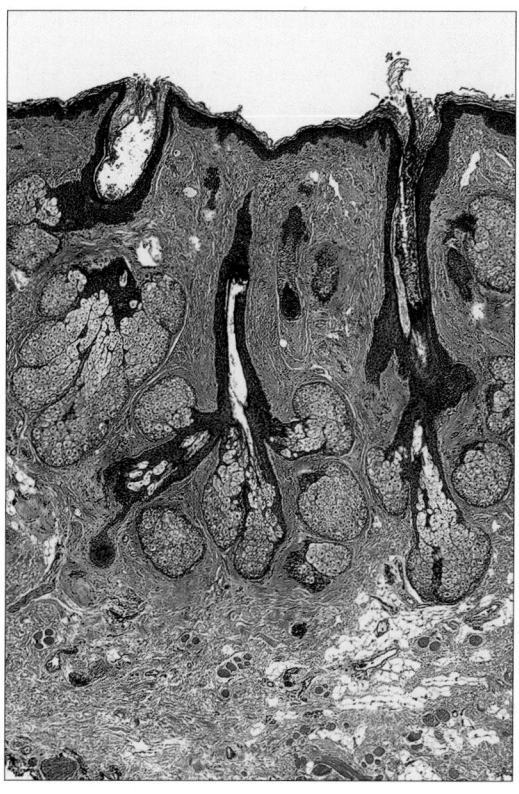

Fig. 1.65
Section of skin from the nose showing multiple sebaceous glands.

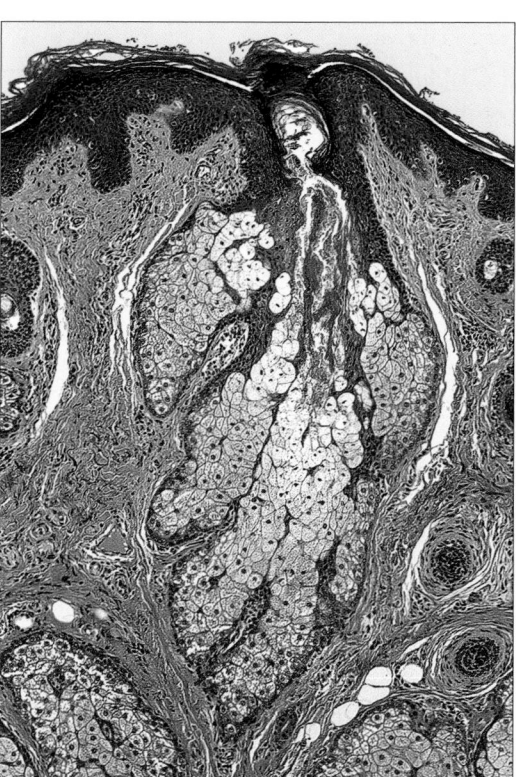

Fig. 1.64
On the vulval mucosa sebaceous glands are conspicuous, but arise independently of a hair follicle and open directly onto the surface epithelium.[3]

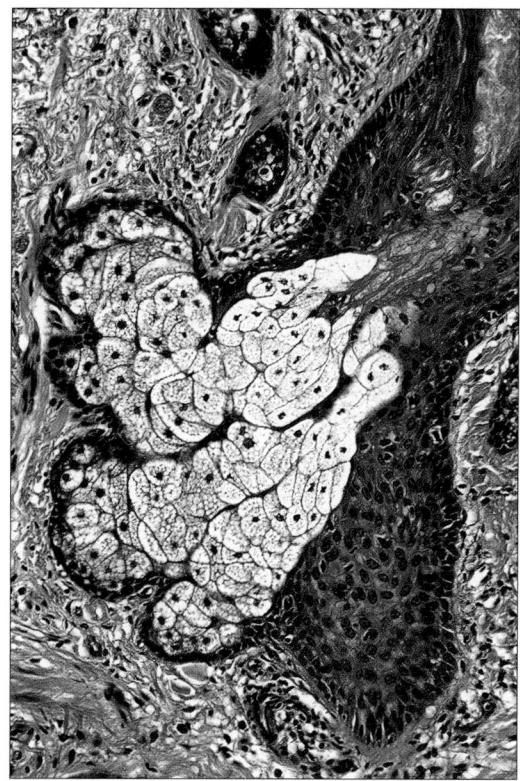

Fig. 1.66
Sebaceous lobule: germinative cells are basophilic and flattened. With maturation the cells acquire their characteristic 'bubbly' cytoplasm.

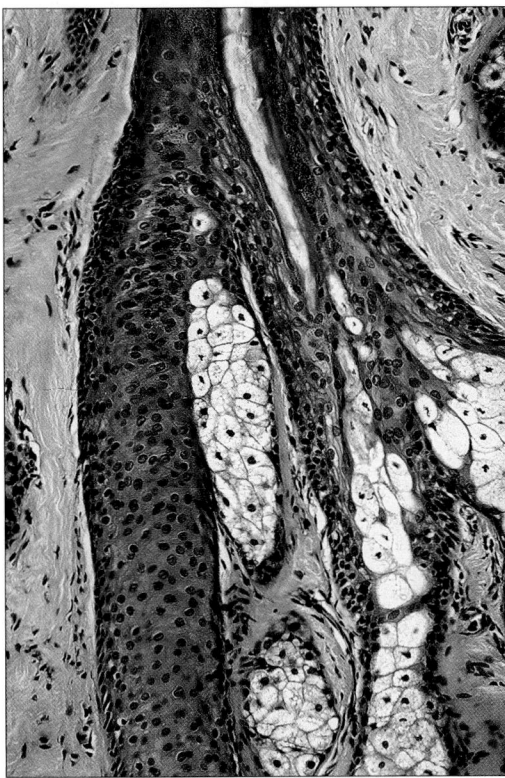

Fig. 1.67
Sebaceous duct lined by keratinizing stratified squamous epithelium; it is continuous with the external root sheath.

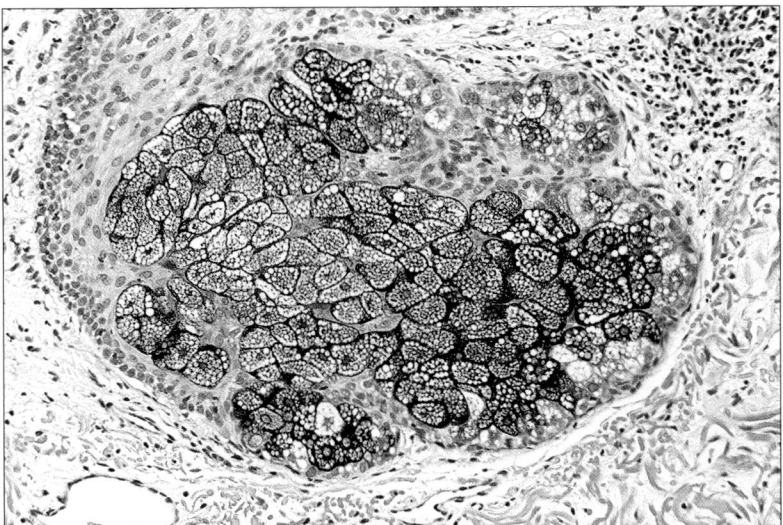

Fig. 1.68
Sebaceous epithelial cells normally strongly express EMA.

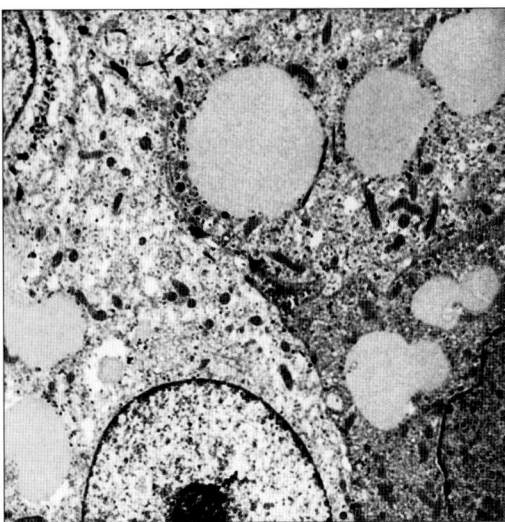

Fig. 1.69
Electron micrograph of the periphery of a normal sebaceous gland showing small, discrete, intracytoplasmic lipid inclusions.

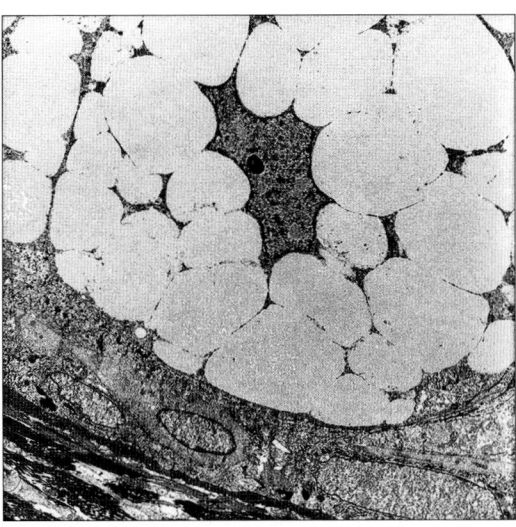

Fig. 1.70
In this field from the centre of a sebaceous lobule, the cytoplasm is completely distended with lipid droplets. Germinative cells are evident in the left lower quadrant.

Propionibacterium acnes (triglyceride hydrolysis) within the pilosebaceous canal and *Staphylococcus epidermidis* (cholesterol ester formation) on the perifollicular skin.[1,9,10] Skin surface lipid is composed of a mixture of sebum and epidermal lipids. The latter is of greater significance on sites with fewer sebaceous glands (e.g. lateral trunk and limbs).[8]

References

1. Strauss, J.S., Downing, D.T., Ebling, F.J. et al (1991) Sebaceous glands. In: Goldsmith, L.A. (ed.) Physiology, biochemistry and molecular biology of the skin, 2nd edn. New York: Oxford University Press, pp 712–740.
2. Botek, A.A., Lookingbill, D.P. (2001) The structure and function of sebaceous glands. In: Freinkel, R.K., Woodley, D.T. (eds) The biology of the skin. New York: Parthenon Publishing, pp 87–100.
3. Stewart, M.E., Steele, W.A., Downing, D.T. (1989) Changes in the relative amounts of endogenous and exogenous fatty acids in sebaceous lipids during early adolescence. *J Invest Dermatol*, **92**, 371–378.
4. Bell, M. (1974) A comparative study of the ultrastructure of the sebaceous glands of man and other primates. *J Invest Dermatol*, **62**, 132–143.
5. Breathnach, A.S. (1971) Ultrastructure of human skin. London: Churchill, pp 335–352.
6. Strauss, J.S., Kligman, A.M., Pochi, P.E. (1962) The effect of androgens and estrogens on human sebaceous glands. *J Invest Dermatol*, **39**, 139–155.
7. Pochi, P.E. (1982) Commentary: androgen effects on sebaceous glands. *Arch Dermatol*, **118**, 803–804.
8. Greene, R.S., Downing, D.T., Pochi, P.E. et al (1970) Anatomical variation in the amount and composition of human skin surface lipids. *J Invest Dermatol*, **54**, 240–247.
9. Marples, R.R., Leyden, J.J., Steward, R.N. et al (1974) The skin microflora in acne vulgaris. *J Invest Dermatol*, **62**, 37–41.
10. Eichenfield, L.F., Leyden, J.J. (1991) Acne: current concepts of pathogenesis and approach to rational treatment. *Pediatrician*, **18**, 218–223.

Apocrine glands

Apocrine glands are found predominantly in the anogenital and axillary regions, but are also located in the external auditory meatus (ceruminous glands), the eyelid (Moll's gland), and within the areola.[1–3] They are derived from the epidermis, and develop as an outgrowth of the follicular epithelium. They first appear during the fourth to fifth month of gestation. Their function in man is unknown, but in other mammals they are responsible for scent production and have importance in sexual attraction. As with sebaceous glands, they are smaller in childhood, becoming larger and functionally active at puberty. The secretions of the ceruminous glands are believed to lubricate, clean and protect the external ear from bacterial and fungal infections.[4]

Apocrine glands include two distinct components:

- a complex secretory component situated in the lower reticular dermis or subcutaneous fat (*Fig. 1.71*)
- a tubular duct linking the gland with the pilosebaceous follicle at a site above the sebaceous duct.

Microscopically the secretory portion comprises an outer discontinuous layer of myoepithelial cells and an inner layer of cuboidal to columnar eosinophilic cells (*Fig. 1.72*). Although a histological artifact, secretory droplets, which appear to be pinched off from the superficial aspect of the columnar cells (decapitation secretion), can be seen on light microscopy. The duct portion is formed by a double layer of cuboidal epithelium. It is morphologically indistinguishable from the eccrine duct.

Immunohistochemically, the secretory unit shows very strong labeling with the antibody CAM 5.2 (both cytoplasmic and membranous), and there is luminal accentuation (*Fig. 1.73*).[5] The apocrine duct is negative. EMA labels the cytoplasm of the secretory cells, and is accentuated along the luminal border (*Fig. 1.74*). It is also present along the luminal aspect of the apocrine duct. With CEA, there is faint, focal staining of the secretory epithelium. The luminal aspect of the duct is strongly outlined. Cytoplasmic granules express epidermal growth factor.[6] The myoepithelial cells of the secretory unit are reactive for S-100 protein and smooth muscle actin (*Figs 1.75, 1.76*).

The apocrine secretory epithelium strongly expresses the enzymes NADH diaphorase, esterase, acid phosphatase and β-glucuronidase.[2] It shows weak reactivity or fails to express amylophosphorylase, leucine aminopeptidase, succinic dehydrogenase and cytochrome oxidase. The apocrine gland also can be stained with cationic colloidal gold at pH 2.0.[6]

Ultrastructure of the apocrine reveals cuboidal to columnar secretory cells containing numerous osmiophilic secretory vacuoles (*Figs 1.77, 1.78*).[6-9] Mitochondria are present in large numbers. While some show obvious double cristae, others are so electron dense that the internal structure is obscured.[9] The Golgi is conspicuous. The luminal border is

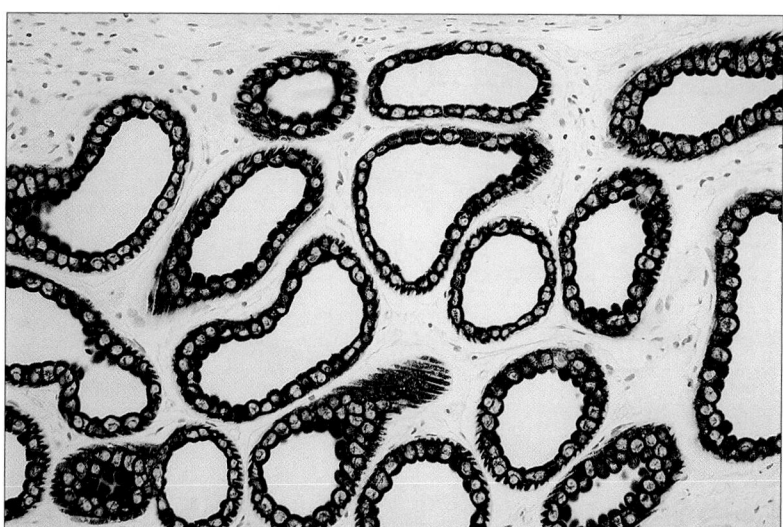

Fig. 1.73
The secretory unit (but not the duct) strongly expresses CAM 5.2.

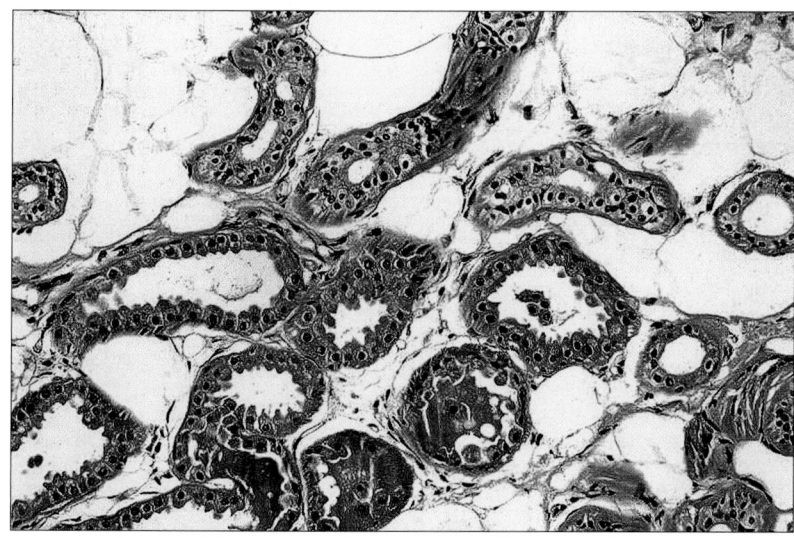

Fig. 1.71
This specimen from normal axillary skin shows apocrine secretory lobules in the subcutaneous fat. Ducts are present in the upper half of the field.

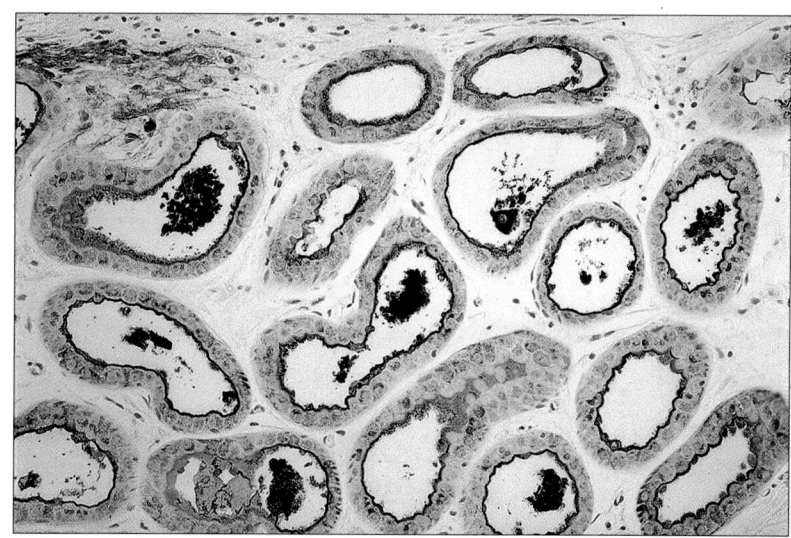

Fig. 1.74
The apocrine gland labeled for EMA: note the marked luminal accentuation.

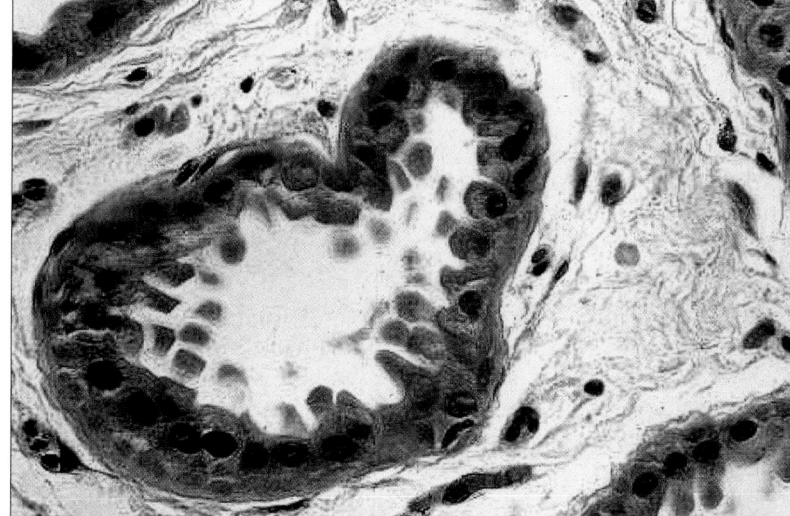

Fig. 1.72
Apocrine gland: lobules are lined by tall columnar cells with intensely eosinophilic cytoplasm. 'Decapitation secretion' is conspicuous.

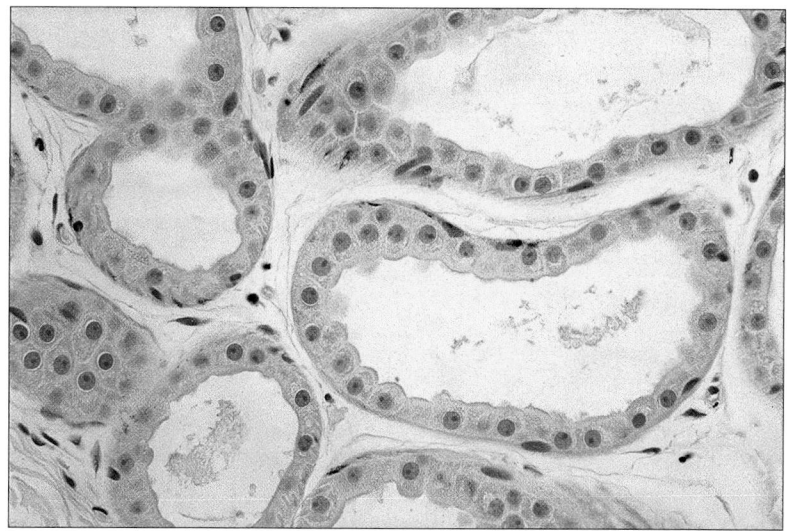

Fig. 1.75
S-100 protein labeling of the apocrine gland: note the expression of this antigen by the myoepithelial cells.

lined by prominent microvilli (*Fig. 1.79*). There is no ultrastructural evidence of decapitation secretion. The secretory cells lie adjacent to longitudinally orientated myoepithelial cells resting on the basement membrane.[9]

The mechanism of apocrine secretion and control of apocrine glands is uncertain, but they do receive adrenergic sympathetic innervation, and

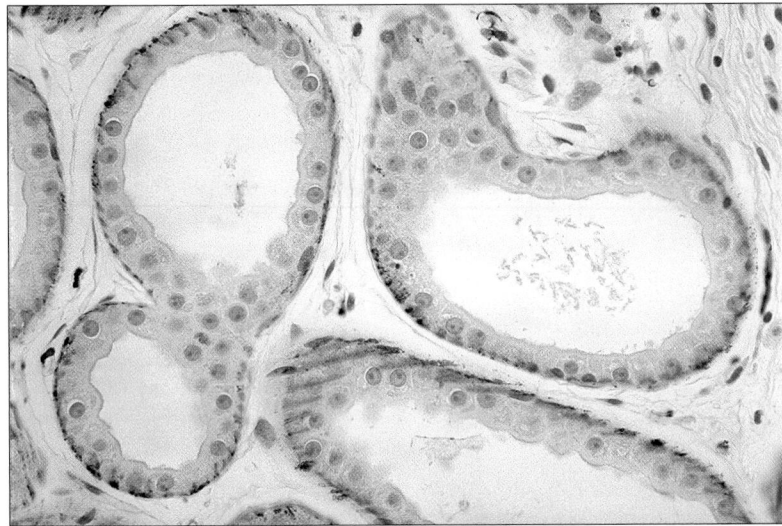

Fig. 1.76
The myoepithelial cells show strong labeling for smooth muscle actin.

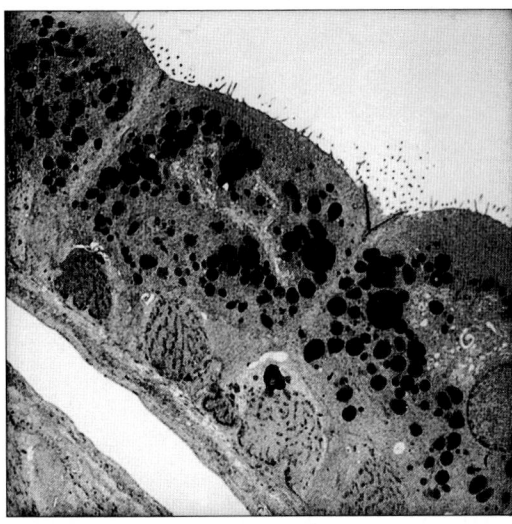

Fig. 1.77
Apocrine gland: note the electron-dense secretory vacuoles and luminal microvilli. Myoepithelial cells ensheath the secretory epithelium.

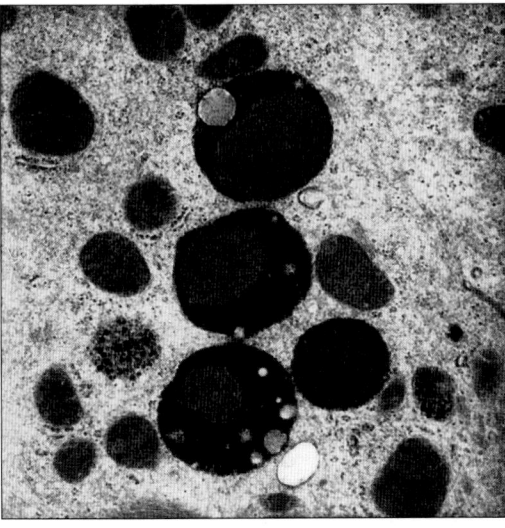

Fig. 1.78
Apocrine gland: close-up view of secretory vacuoles.

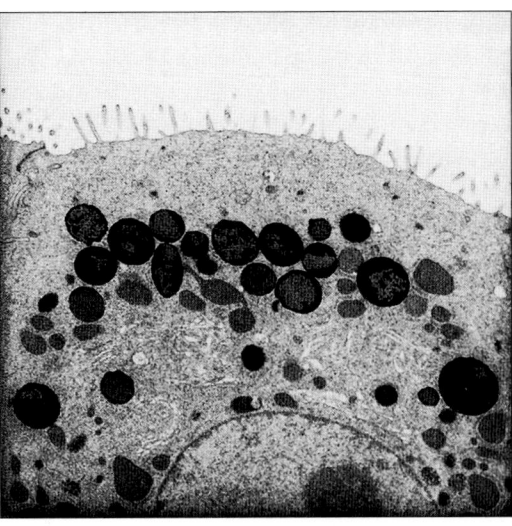

Fig. 1.79
Apocrine gland: close-up view of microvilli.

secretion is provoked by external stimuli such as excitement or fear. The unpleasant odor of apocrine secretion, which is odorless in itself, is due to breakdown products produced by cutaneous bacterial flora.

References

1. Ebling, F.J. (1989) Apocrine glands in health and disease. *Int J Dermatol*, **28**, 508–511.
2. Robertshaw, D. (1991) Apocrine sweat glands. In: Goldsmith, L.A. (ed.) Physiology, biochemistry and molecular biology of the skin, 2nd edn. New York: Oxford University Press, pp 763–775.
3. Scrivener, Y., Cribier, B. (2002) Morphology of sweat glands. *Morphologie*, **86**, 5–17.
4. Roeser, R.J., Ballachanda, B.B. (1997) Physiology, pathophysiology, and anthropology/epidemiology of human ear canal secretions. *J Am Acad Audiol*, **8**, 391–400.
5. Guarner, J., Cohen, C., DeRose, P.B. (1989) Histogenesis of extramammary and mammary Paget's cells: immunohistochemical study. *Am J Dermatopathol*, **11**, 313–318.
6. Saga, K. (2001) Histochemical and immunohistochemical markers for human eccrine and apocrine sweat glands: an aid for histopathologic differentiation of sweat gland tumors. *J Invest Dermatol Symp Proc*, **6**, 49–53.
7. Hibbs, R.G. (1962) Electron microscopy of human apocrine glands. *J Invest Dermatol*, **38**, 77–84.
8. Bell, M. (1974) The ultrastructure of human axillary apocrine glands after epinephrine injection. *J Invest Dermatol*, **63**, 147–159.
9. Hashimoto, K., Gross, B.G., Lever, W.F. (1966) Electron microscopy of human apocrine glands. *J Invest Dermatol*, **46**, 378–390.

Eccrine sweat glands

Eccrine sweat glands are derived from a specialized downgrowth of the epidermis at about the third to fifth month of intrauterine life. Their main function is heat control when the body is exposed to a warm environment or during heavy exercise.[1–3] They are found everywhere on the skin, but are not present in the mucous membranes. Their sites of maximum concentration are the palms, soles, axillae and forehead. They measure from 0.05 to 0.1 mm in diameter; those on the palms and soles are the largest.[3]

Histologically, eccrine sweat glands are divided into four subunits:

- a highly vascularized coiled secretory gland
- a coiled dermal duct
- a straight dermal duct
- a coiled intraepidermal duct (the acrosyringium).

The secretory component lies in the lower reaches of the reticular dermis or around the interface between the dermis and subcutaneous fat (*Fig. 1.80*) and is surrounded by a thick basement membrane and loose connective tissue often rich in mucin. It embodies an outer discontinuous layer of contractile myoepithelial cells and an inner layer of secretory cells (*Fig. 1.81*) comprising two cell types: large clear pyramidal cells, which appear to be responsible for water secretion, and smaller, darkly staining mucopolysaccharide-containing cells (probably secreting a glycoprotein), which are much less commonly seen. The latter autofluoresce and may be identified by the PAS reaction (*Fig. 1.82*). Between adjacent cells are canaliculi, which open into the lumen of the tubule (*Fig. 1.83*).[4] Sometimes the secretory lobules show striking clear cell change due to glycogen accumulation (*Fig. 1.84*).

The myoepithelial cells contract in response to cholinergic stimuli.[5] They have a spindle cell morphology and are distributed in a spiral, parallel array along the long axis of the secretory tubule.[6] On the basis of their keratin intermediate filament expression, they appear to be of ectodermal rather than mesenchymal derivation.[6] They do not label for vimentin. Myoepithelial cells develop from the epithelial cells of the tip of the secretory coil and not as might be expected from adjacent mesenchymal cells.[6] Whether they have contractile properties, in addition to providing structural support, is unknown although it would seem likely.

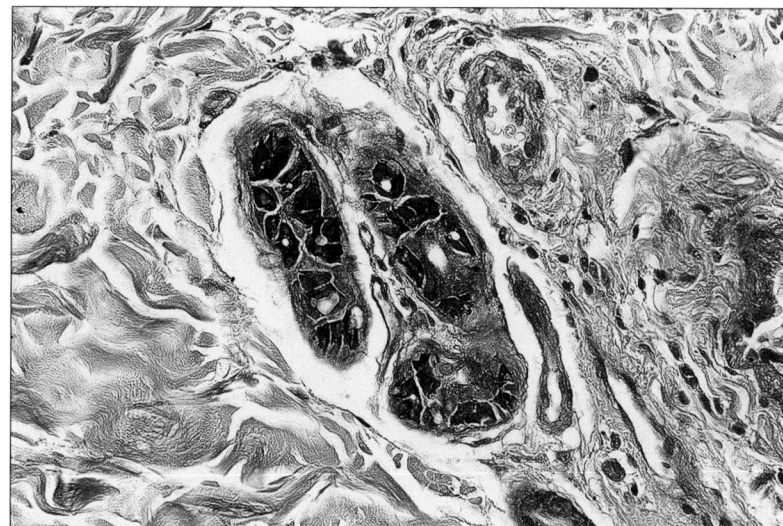

Fig. 1.82
Normal eccrine gland: the dark cells contain diastase-resistant PAS-positive granules.

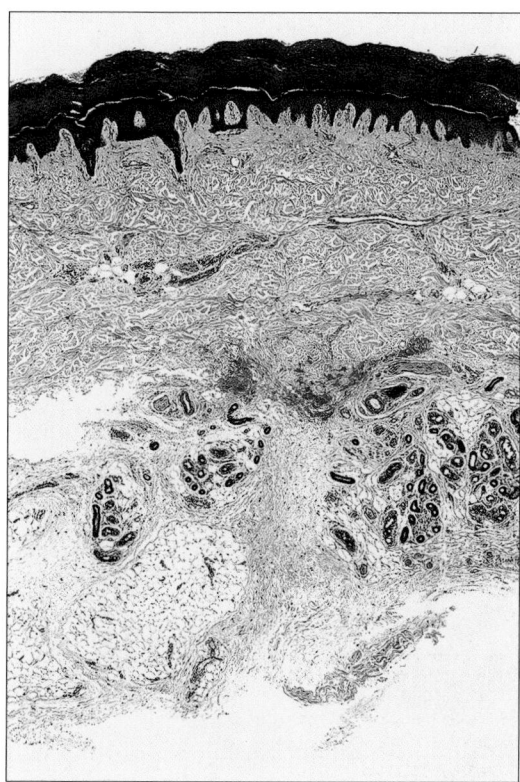

Fig. 1.80
Palmar skin: eccrine glands are numerous at this site and are located in the deep reticular dermis and subcutaneous fat.

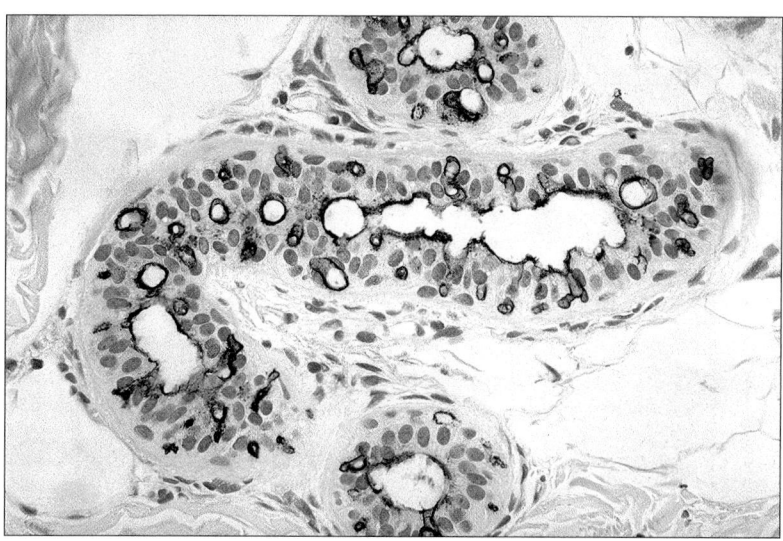

Fig. 1.83
Normal eccrine sweat gland: intercellular canaliculi are clearly demonstrated using peroxidase-labeled anti-EMA.

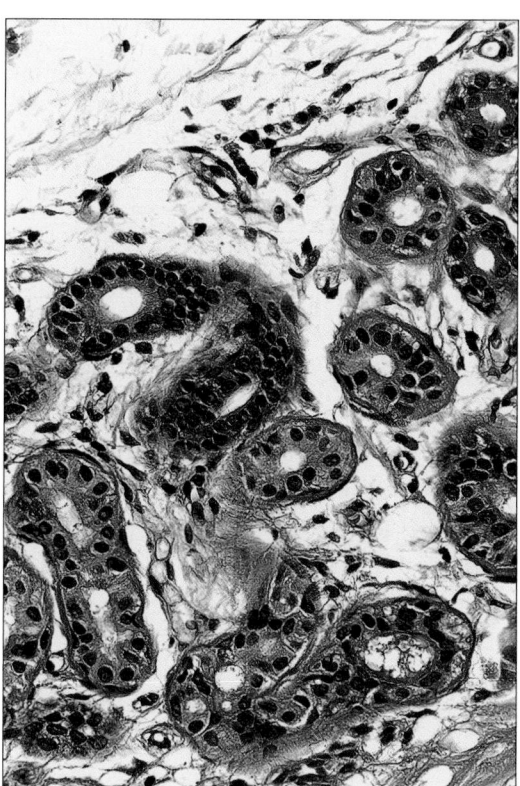

Fig. 1.81
Section through an eccrine gland: the secretory unit is in the lower field. Sections through the coiled duct are evident in the upper field. The epithelium of the duct is more darkly stained than that of the glandular component.

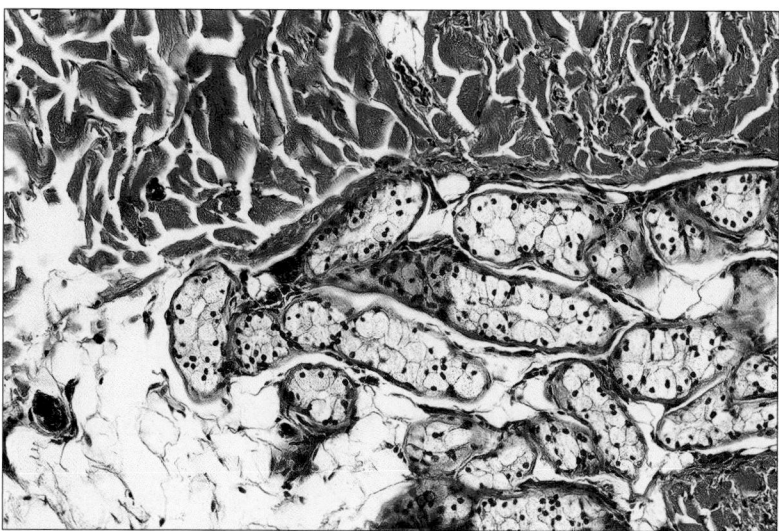

Fig. 1.84
In this eccrine gland excessive glycogen has resulted in vacuolated epithelium.

The dermal duct components consist of a double layer of cuboidal basophilic cells (*Fig. 1.85*). The duct is not merely a conduit, but has a biologically active function, modifying the composition of eccrine secretion and, particularly, the reabsorption of water. The intraepidermal portion of the sweat duct opens directly onto the surface of the skin (*Fig. 1.86*). A myoepithelial layer is absent. Morphologically, the apocrine duct is identical.

The secretory unit is strongly labeled by the antibody CAM 5.2 (both cytoplasmic and membranous) and there is luminal accentuation (*Fig. 1.87*). The ductal component is completely negative. EMA can be detected along the luminal aspect of the secretory unit and outlining the intercellular canaliculi (see *Fig. 1.83*). It is also present around the luminal border of the duct, and is often present in large quantities within the lumen. CEA is present in a similar distribution to EMA although secretory labeling tends to be rather focal and somewhat weaker while the ductal lumen is more strongly outlined (*Fig. 1.88*). The myoepithelial cells can be identified by antibodies to S-100 protein, desmin and smooth muscle actin (*Fig. 1.89*).[7]

The eccrine glands show strong activity for the enzymes amylophosphorylase, leucine aminopeptidase, succinic dehydrogenase and cytochrome oxidase (*Fig. 1.90*).[8,9] Weak or no activity is seen for NADH diaphorase, esterase and acid phosphatase.

With electron microscopy, the serous cells are characterized by abundant intracytoplasmic glycogen granules and numerous mitochondria (*Figs 1.91–1.93*).[2] Adjacent cell membranes, which show marked interdigitations, may separate to form microvilli-lined intercellular canaliculi (*Fig. 1.94*). The mucous cells contain numerous electron-dense lipid droplets and lysozymes (*Fig. 1.95*). Myoepithelial cells are present at the periphery of the secretory coil within the eccrine basal lamina (lamina densa) and contain abundant myofilaments with characteristic dense bodies. The sweat duct lumen is bordered by conspicuous

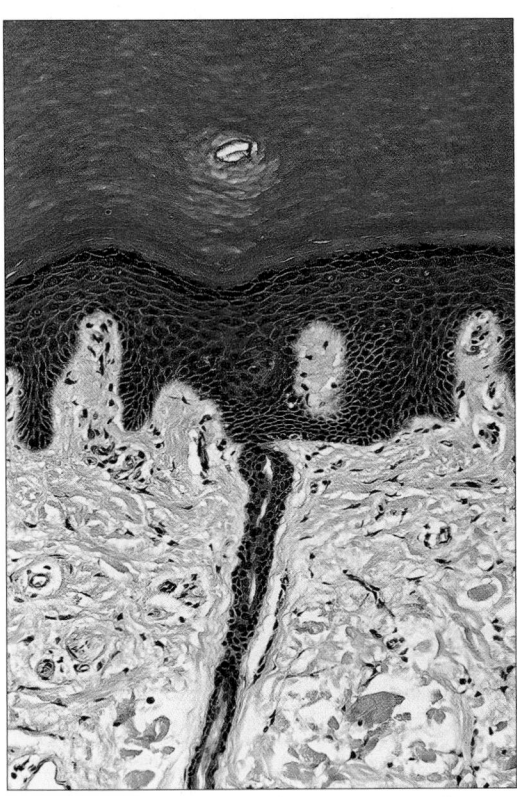

Fig. 1.85
The straight dermal eccrine duct.

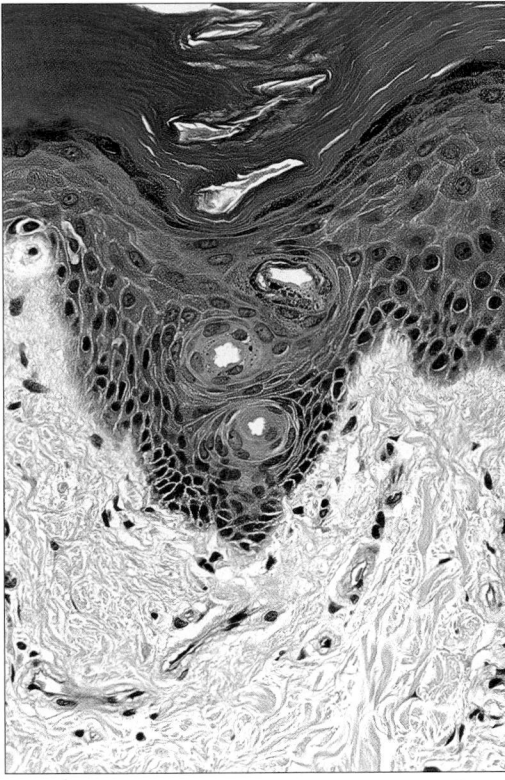

Fig. 1.86
Normal coiled intraepidermal eccrine sweat duct (acrosyringium).

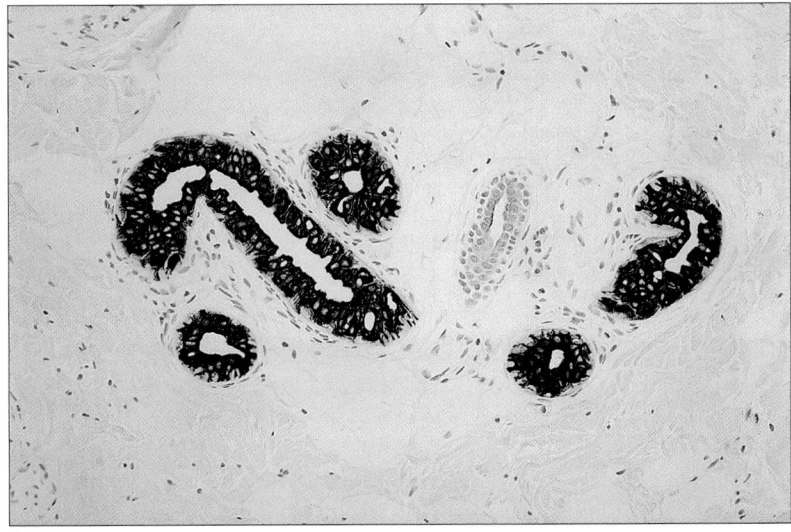

Fig. 1.87
The eccrine gland (but not the duct) labels strongly for CAM 5.2.

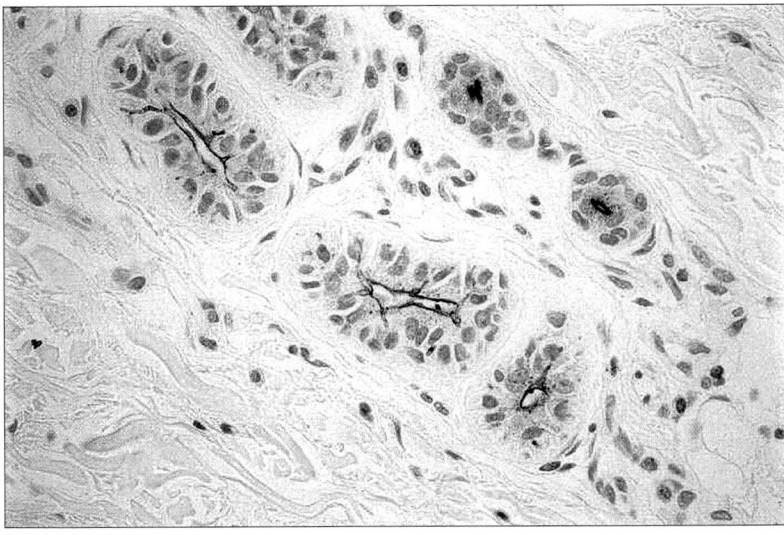

Fig. 1.88
The luminal border of the eccrine sweat gland labels positively for CEA.

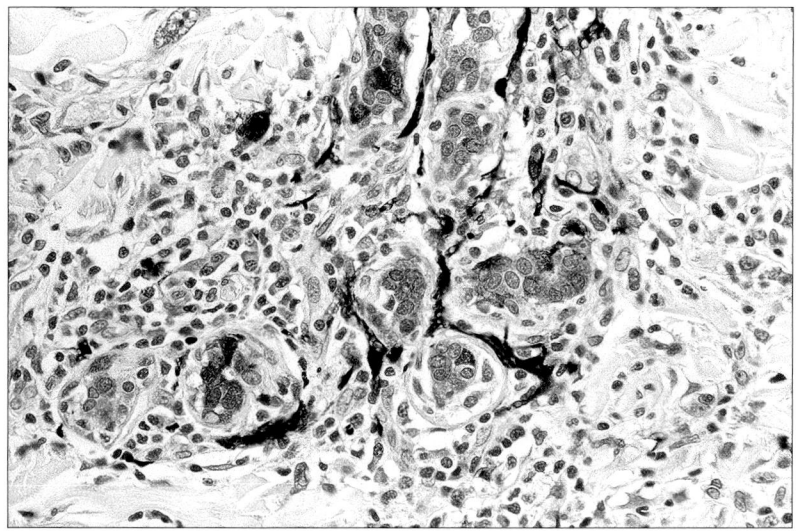

Fig. 1.89
Eccrine gland: secretory epithelium and myoepithelial cells may be labeled for S-100 protein.

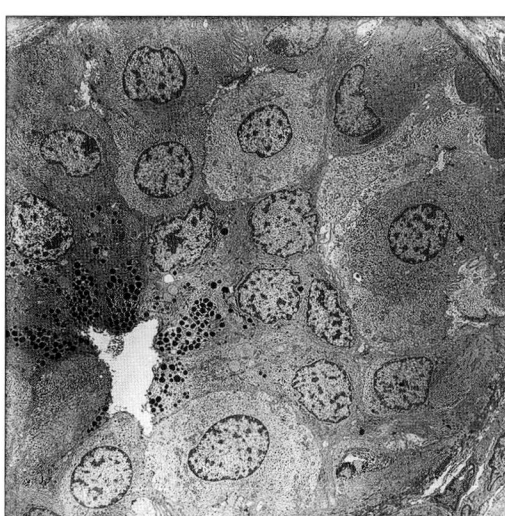

Fig. 1.91
Eccrine gland: low power electron micrograph showing the lumen in the lower left quadrant, granular mucous-secreting cells and serous cells. An intercellular canaliculus is present in the upper left quadrant.

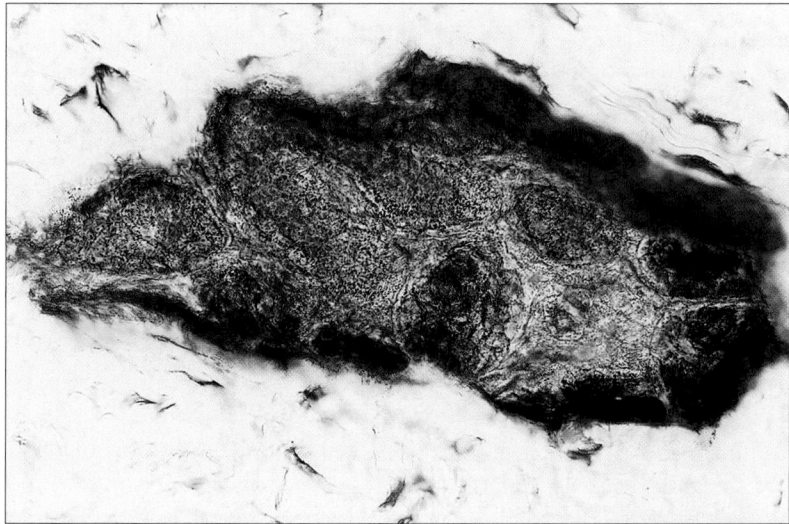

Fig. 1.90
The eccrine secretory epithelium contains abundant succinic dehydrogenase. By courtesy of N. Ramnarain, FIMLS, Institute of Dermatology, London, UK.

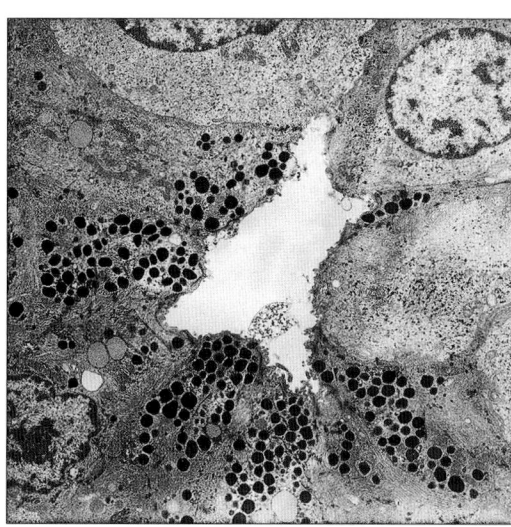

Fig. 1.92
Eccrine gland: note the conspicuous mucus cells.

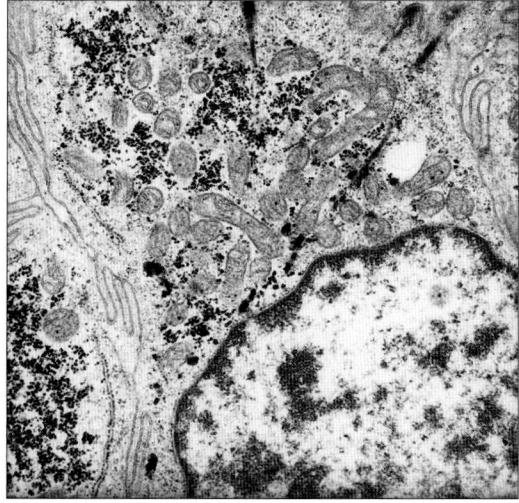

Fig. 1.93
Eccrine gland: the clear cells contain aggregates of tiny, electron-dense glycogen granules. Numerous mitochondria are present. Note the complex interdigitating cell membranes.

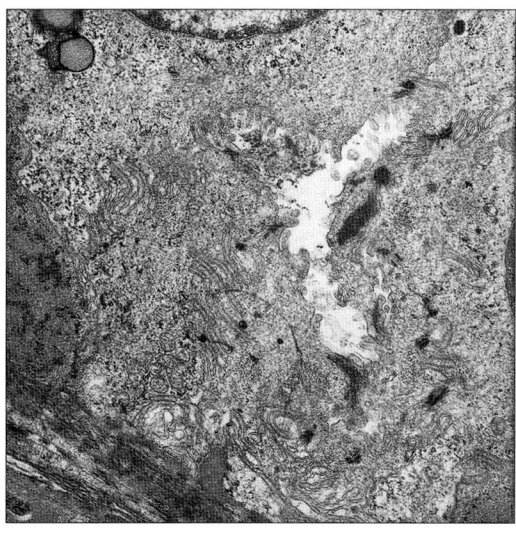

Fig. 1.94
Intercellular canaliculus between two eccrine clear cells.

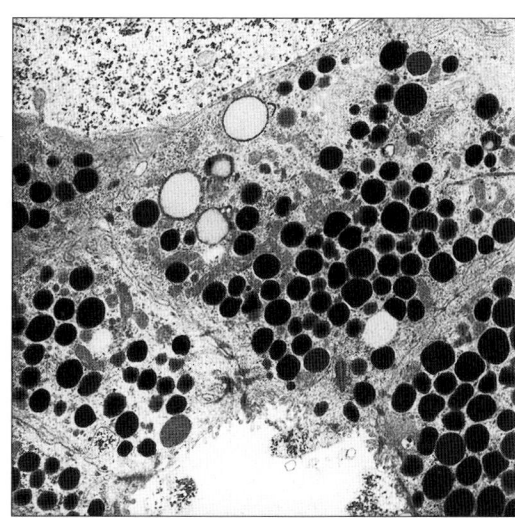

Fig. 1.95
Eccrine gland showing dark cells with numerous electron-dense secretory granules.

microvilli (*Fig. 1.96*).[10] The cytoplasm contains numerous clear vesicles. Tonofilaments are characteristically orientated in a circumferential manner deep to the plasma membrane, the so-called cuticle of light microscopy (*Fig. 1.97*). This is particularly well developed in the acrosyringium.

Function of the eccrine gland is under the control of cholinergic postganglionic sympathetic nerve fibers. The activity of the secretory component is stimulated by thermal, emotional and gustatory functions. Thermal sweating is dependent on an intact hypothalamus, which is activated by temperature changes of its perfusing blood, and is considered further in the section on cutaneous vasculature (see page 32). Thermoregulatory sweating occurs, especially on the face and upper trunk. Emotional sweating presumably is under the control of the limbic lobe. This induces particularly palmar sweating. Gustatory sweating of the lips, forehead and nose occurs after a hot spicy meal and is of uncertain function or central control.

Eccrine sweat is secreted as a slightly hypertonic solution, reabsorption of sodium chloride occurring in the ductal system.[3] It has a basic similarity to the plasma from which it is derived, the duct appearing to be largely responsible for the additional modifications that occur. It is a clear hypotonic solution with a pH of 4–6.8. In addition to water, it contains sodium, chloride, potassium, urea and lactate.

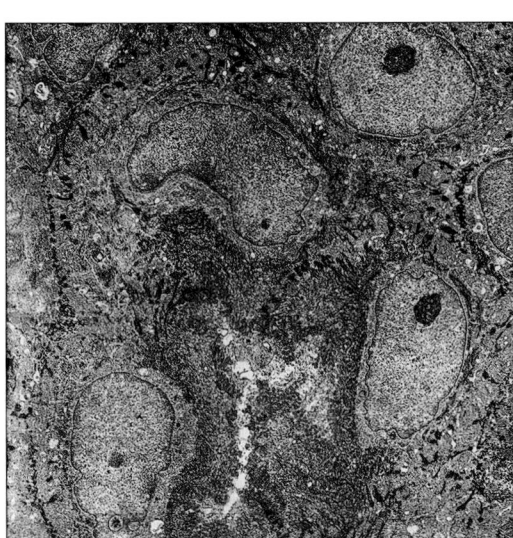

Fig. 1.96
Lumen of the eccrine dermal duct lined by conspicuous microvilli.

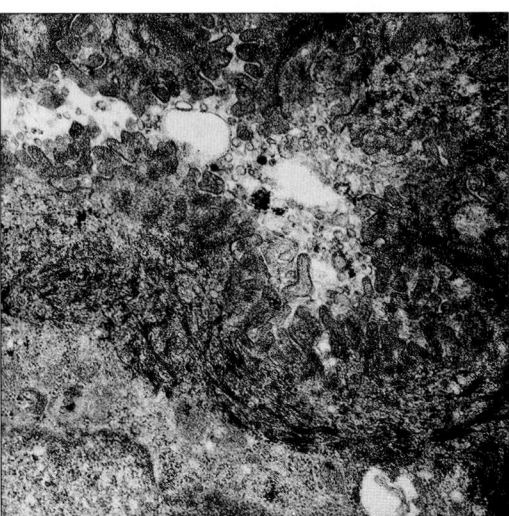

Fig. 1.97
High power view of eccrine dermal duct showing microvilli and circumferentially orientated tonofilaments.

References

1. Sato, K., Kang, W.H., Saga, K. et al (1989) Biology of sweat glands and their disorders. I. Normal sweat gland function. *J Am Acad Dermatol*, **20**, 537–563.
2. Sato, K., Kang, W.H., Sato, F. (1991) Eccrine sweat glands. In: Goldsmith, L.A. (ed.) Physiology, biochemistry and molecular biology of the skin, 2nd edn. New York: Oxford University Press, pp 41–762.
3. Hurley, H.J. (2001) The eccrine sweat glands: structure and function. In: Freinkel, R.K., Woodley, D.T. (eds.) The biology of the skin. New York: Parthenon Publishing, pp 47–76.
4. Sato, K., Kang, W.H., Saga, K. et al (1989) Biology of sweat glands and their disorders. II. Disorders of sweat gland function. *J Am Acad Dermatol*, **20**, 713–726.
5. Sato, K., Nishiyama, A., Kobayashi, M. (1986) Mechanical properties and functions of the myoepithelium in the eccrine sweat gland. *Am J Physiol*, **237**, C177–184.
6. Hori, K., Hashimoto, K., Eto, H. et al (1985) Keratin type intermediate filaments in sweat gland myoepithelial cells. *J Invest Dermatol*, **85**, 453–459.
7. Seidal, T. (1991) Immunoreactivity to desmin in secretory epithelium of eccrine sweat glands. *Histopathology*, **18**, 89–91.
8. Guarner, J., Cohen, C., DeRose, P.B. (1989) Histogenesis of extramammary and mammary Paget cells: an immunohistochemical study. *Am J Dermatopathol*, **11**, 313–318.
9. Saga, K., Morimoto, Y. (1995) The localization of alkaline phosphatase activity in human eccrine and apocrine sweat glands. *J Histochem Cytochem*, **43**, 927–932.
10. Hashimoto, K., Gross, B.G., Lever, W.F. (1966) Electron microscopic study of the human eccrine gland I. The duct. *J Invest Dermatol*, **46**, 172–185.

Apoeccrine glands

Recently, Sato and colleagues have described the presence of axillary glands in adults having the morphology of both apocrine and eccrine epithelium.[1–3] The duct opens directly onto the skin surface. The secretory component comprises a dilated apocrine segment, while proximally the epithelium is compatible with an eccrine derivation showing intercellular canaliculi and dark cells. Similar glands have not been identified within the upper arm nor in the inguinal region.[1] The apoeccrine gland is similar to the eccrine gland in terms of pharmacology and secretory activity.[2]

References

1. Sato, K., Leidal, R., Sato, F. (1987) Morphology and development of an apoeccrine sweat gland in human axillae. *Am J Physiol*, **252**, R166–180.
2. Sato, K., Sato, F. (1987) Sweat secretion by human axillary apoeccrine sweat glands *in vitro*. *Am J Physiol*, **252**, R181–187.
3. Scrivener, Y., Cribier, B. (2002) Morphology of sweat glands. *Morphologie*, **86**, 5–17.

Hair

The normal structure and function of the hair is discussed in Chapter 20.

The nail apparatus

The normal structure and function of the nail is discussed in Chapter 21.

Dermis

The dermis or corium (L. *corium*, leather) supports the epidermis and is composed of a fibrous connective tissue component (collagen and elastic fibers) in intimate association with ground substance. Within the dermis are the epidermal appendages (surrounded by a connective tissue sheath), blood vessels and nerves, and a cellular component including mast cells, fibroblasts, myofibroblasts and macrophages. Smooth muscle is also represented in the arrector pili muscles. There is marked regional variation in the thickness of the dermis, which is especially marked on the palms and soles, and much thicker on the back of the body than on the front.

The dermis is divided into papillary and reticular layers:
- *Papillary dermis* is bounded superiorly by the epidermis, laterally by the epidermal ridges, and inferiorly by the superficial vascular plexus and reticular dermis. It is highly irregular and accounts for the complex arrangement of whorls, loops and arches that constitute fingerprints.
- *Reticular dermis* lies between the papillary dermis and the subcutaneous fat. Collagen fibers within the reticular dermis have a parallel orientation, which accounts for the lines of cleavage of the skin.

Collagen

Collagen is a complex protein synthesized within a variety of cells including fibroblasts, myofibroblasts, osteoblasts, chondroblasts, smooth muscle cells, endothelial cells and various epithelial cells.[1] At least 20 antigenically different types are recognized.[2] Collagen genes comprise at least 20 types coded for on more than seven chromosomes.[3,4]

Collagens are exceedingly complex proteins, their coding being distributed between at least 50 separate exons.[3] The synthesis of collagen requires at least 20 different specific enzymes (*Fig. 1.98, Table 1.4*). The basic molecule of collagen is the monomer tropocollagen, which has a molecular weight of approximately 300,000 daltons and is composed of three α-chains (approximately 1000 amino acids) of molecular weight 95,000 daltons. Each α-chain is a left-handed helix, but the three chains are interwoven around a central axis to form a right-handed superhelical molecule. The chains are arranged in peptide units of three, with the amino acid glycine occupying every third position.[5,6] The other two sites, the X and Y positions, may be occupied by a variety of other amino acids, frequently proline in the X position and hydroxyproline in the Y position. The presence of these three particular amino acids appears to maintain the structural integrity of the collagen molecule.

A variety of collagen molecules exist, depending on the occupants of the X and Y positions.[6] Synthesis of collagen depends on the production of an insoluble precursor molecule, procollagen, which is secreted into the intercellular milieu and degraded by enzymes into the soluble adult protein.

Procollagen is synthesized on membrane-bound ribosomes and secreted into the cistern of the rough endoplasmic reticulum. It consists of three pro-α-chains, which differ from the α-chains of collagen because they contain additional polypeptide residues at both the amino and carboxyl terminals.[6]

A variety of steps follow the synthesis of the pro-α-chains. Collagen characteristically contains hydroxylysine and hydroxyproline, the latter being of particular value to helical stability by forming intermolecular hydrogen bonds. Hydroxylation of the prolyl residues by the enzyme prolyl hydroxylase and hydroxylation of lysyl residues by lysyl hydroxylase occurs in the presence of oxygen, ferrous iron and vitamin

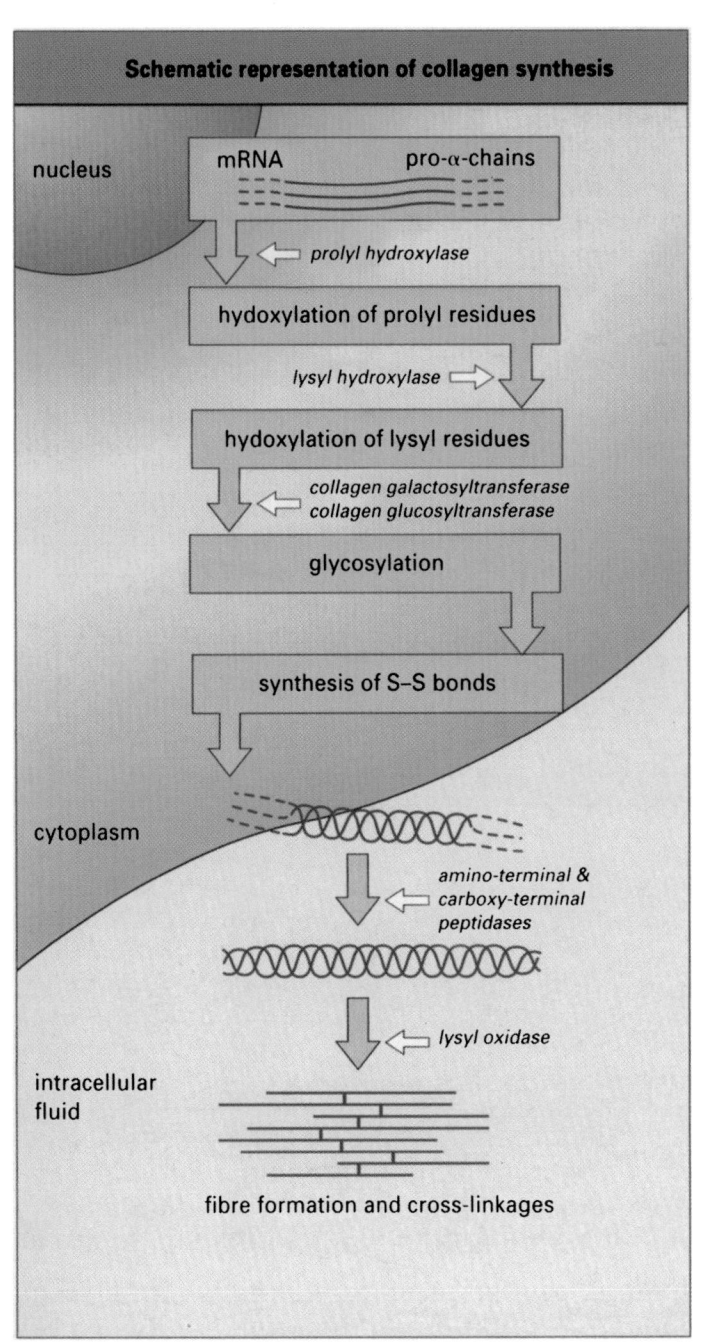

Fig. 1.98
Schematic representation of collagen synthesis.

Table 1.4
Enzymes involved in collagen biosynthesis; nature and location of events

Event	Enzyme	Location
Transcription	Many	Nucleus
splicing	'Splicesome-complex'	Nucleus
Transport	Unknown	Nucleus–cytoplasm
Translation	Many	Cytoplasm/RER
Signal cleavage	Signal peptidase	RER membrane
Prolyl hydroxylation	Proline 4-hydroxylase	RER lumen
	proline 3-hydroxylase	RER lumen
Lysyl hydroxylation	Lysyl hydroxylase	RER lumen
Hydroxylysyl glycosylation	Collagen glucosyl transferase	RER lumen
	collagen galactosyl transferase	RER lumen
Heterosaccharide addition and modification	Many	RER lumen
Intrachain disulfide bond formation	Disulfide isomerase	RER lumen
Chain assembly	Not known	RER lumen
Interchain disulfide bond formation	Disulfide isomerase	RER lumen
Triple helix propagation	Prolyl *cis trans* isomerase	RER lumen
Transport to Golgi	Many (unknown)	RER/Golgi
Modification of heterosaccharide	Many	Golgi
Sulfation	Sulfotransferase	Golgi
Exocytosis	Many	Cell surface
Amino terminal processing	Procollagen aminoprotease	ECM
Carboxyl terminal processing	Procollagen carboxyl protease	ECM
Fibril formation	Non-enzymatic	ECM
Cross-link formation	Lysyl oxidase	ECM

ECM, extracellular membrane; RER, rough endoplasmic reticulum. Reproduced with permission from Byers, P.H. (1989) *American Journal of Medical Genetics*, **34**, 72–80. Wiley-Liss, Inc., a subsidiary of John Wiley & Sons, Inc.

C.[6] Galactose and glycose attach to the collagen molecule via the hydroxyl group of hydroxylysine, though the precise function of the incorporation of these sugar residues is unknown. Pro-α-chain association follows, with the development of the triple helix configuration (beginning at the carboxyl terminus) and disulfide bonding at the amino and carboxyl extensions within the Golgi.[3] The fully formed procollagen molecule is secreted in vesicles at the cell surface into the intercellular fluid where the amino acid extensions are cleaved via the amino and carboxyl terminal peptidases, producing the collagen molecule.[3] Deletion of peptidase cleavage sites from proα1 or proα2[1] results in abnormal collagen formation and forms the basis of type VII Ehlers–Danlos syndrome.[2]

The collagen molecules have a rod-shaped appearance and measure approximately 1.5×300 nm.[6] They are further strengthened by the development of covalent cross-linkages (including side to side, end to end and overlapping types) depending, at least in part, on the enzyme lysyl oxidase.[5] Deficiency of the latter is associated with type VI Ehlers–Danlos syndrome. Collagen molecules intertwine to form microfibrils, which in turn form a tight network of collagen fibrils. Interweaving of the fibrils results in the mature collagen fiber.

Collagen is not a homogenous entity, but consists of a variety of genetically distinct subtypes, designated types I–XX according to morphology, amino acid composition and physical properties. The dermis contains predominantly type I collagen (85–90%), type III collagen (8–11%), and type V collagen (2–4%).[6] In the dermis the broad bands of reticular collagen (*Fig. 1.99*) are type I, while the finer fibers (also known as reticulin) of the papillary dermis (*Fig. 1.100*) are type III. Type IV collagen is present within the lamina densa of the basement membrane region. Type V collagen is present throughout the dermis and also in the lamina lucida, and type VI collagen surrounds the dermal nerves and blood vessels. As discussed on page 9, type VII collagen is a major constituent of the anchoring fibril.

When longitudinal sections of collagen are examined electron microscopically they show cross-striations (D-spacing) with a periodicity of approximately 64 nm (*Fig. 1.101*). The cross-striations are seen

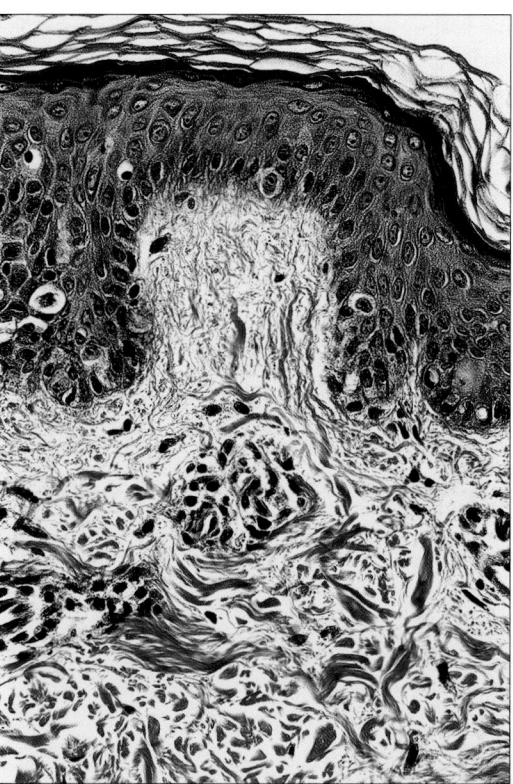

Fig. 1.100
Normal skin of forearm: in the papillary dermis the collagen fibers are much finer and sometimes have a vertical orientation. Trichrome.

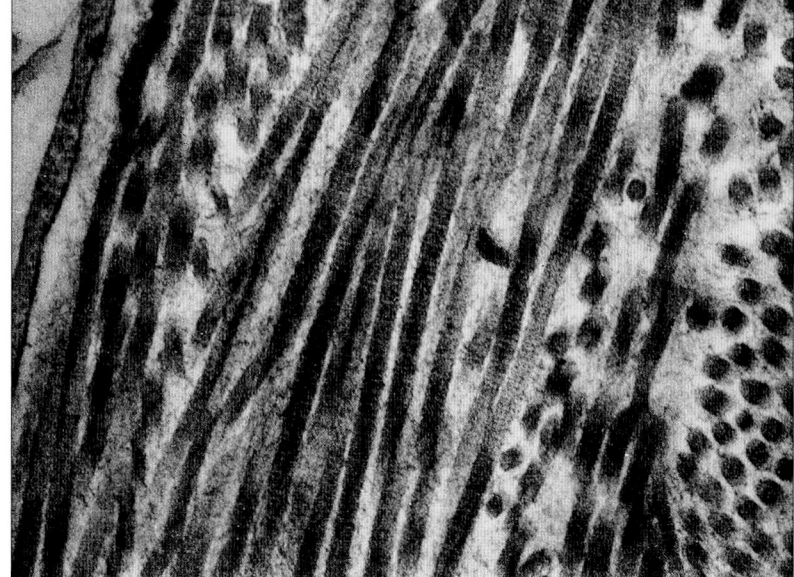

Fig. 1.101
Collagen has cross-striations with a periodicity of 64 nm.

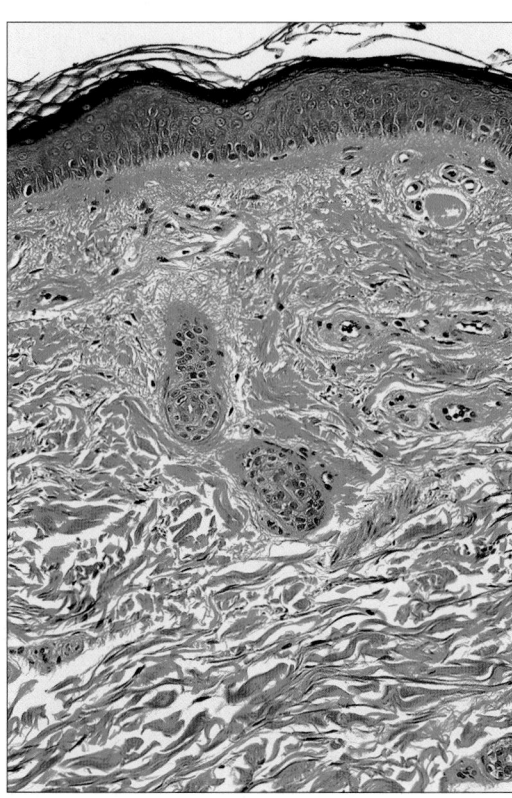

Fig. 1.99
Normal skin of back: broad bundles of collagen typify the reticular dermis. Masson's trichrome.

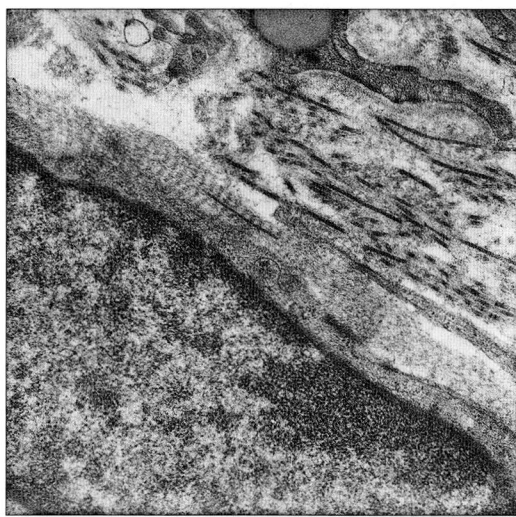

Fig. 1.102
Fibrous long-spacing collagen: compare with the adjacent conventional collagen fibers. There is a very different periodicity.

because of the longitudinal overlap of individual collagen molecules, which occurs during assembly of the mature fibril.[6] Fibrous long-spacing collagen is a variant with a periodicity of 90–120 nm (*Fig. 1.102*). It is characteristically seen in peripheral nerve and central nervous system tumors. Collagen bundles exhibit anisotropy and are therefore birefringent when viewed with polarized light (*Fig. 1.103*).

Elastic tissue

Elastic fibers are essentially responsible for the retractile properties of skin.[7] In normal dermis they comprise a very minor constituent (2–4%).[8] They are intimately associated with collagen, but cannot be easily seen with hematoxylin and eosin staining. Their structure, however, is readily apparent using special stains such as elastic–van Gieson.

In the papillary dermis the elastic fibers are thin and tend to run at right angles to the skin surface, while those in the reticular dermis are thicker and often orientated parallel to the skin surface (*Figs 1.104, 1.105*). Elastic fibers are synthesized by fibroblasts and possibly smooth muscle cells.

Electron microscopically, elastic fibers are composed of approximately 11 nm diameter microfibrils (composed of elastic tissue microfibrillar protein) embedded in an amorphous electron-dense compound consisting of a complex protein called elastin (*Fig. 1.106*).[8–10] This is a polypeptide of 800 amino acids with an approximate molecular weight of 72,000 daltons.[9] Elastic tissue microfibrillar protein is composed of fibrillin. There are at least three types of fibrillin, which is a high molecular weight protein rich in cysteine and containing epidermal growth factor-like regions that are of particular importance in calcium binding.[11,12]

Unique to elastin are the amino acids desmosine and isodesmosine, which help (by forming covalent cross-links) to maintain the structural integrity of the fibers. During synthesis of the elastic fiber the microfibrillary component is first formed and then embedded in elastin. While elastic fibers account for cutaneous elasticity they are also thought (in combination with ground substance) to be responsible for prevention of overextension.

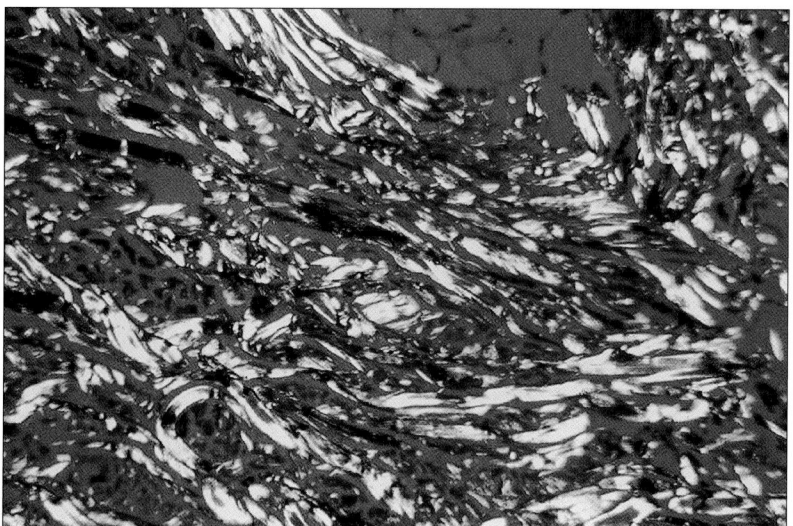

Fig. 1.103
Collagen of the reticular dermis shows birefringence when viewed with polarized light. Masson's trichrome.

Fig. 1.105
Reticular dermis: the elastic fibers are long and fairly thick and tend to run parallel to the surface epithelium.

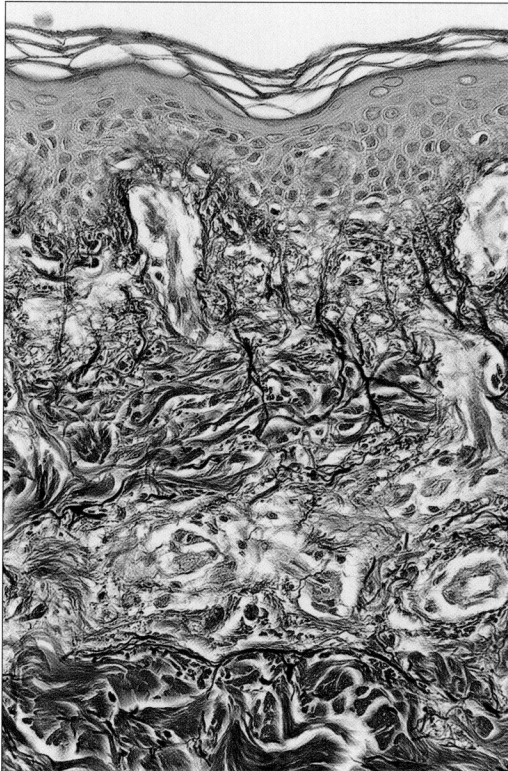

Fig. 1.104
Papillary dermis: the elastic fibers are delicate and orientated perpendicular to the epithelial surface. Weigert–van Gieson stain.

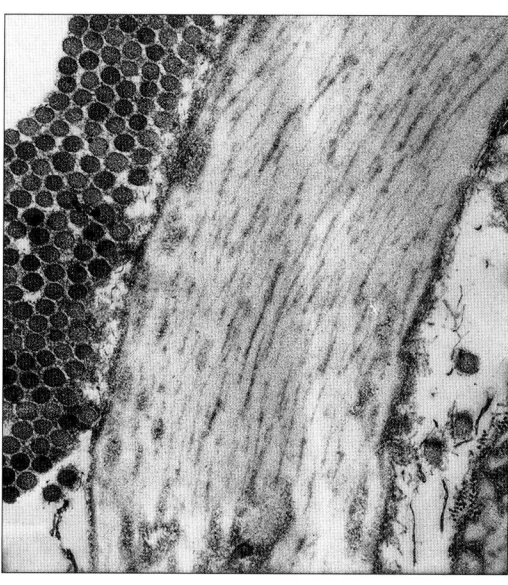

Fig. 1.106
The elastic fiber consists of microfibrils embedded in an electron-dense matrix called elastin.

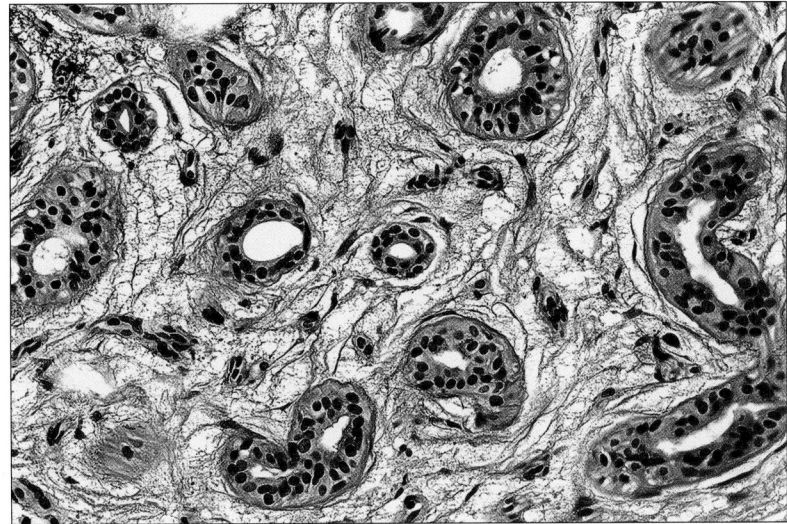

Fig. 1.107
Ground substance: an eccrine gland from the sole of the foot shows an abundance of glycosaminoglycans. Alcian blue stain, pH 2.5.

Ground substance

Ground substance is ubiquitous to all tissues of the body, forming the milieu for the cellular and fibrous constituents. It consists predominantly of fibronectin and the glycosaminoglycans, which are hyaluronic acid, chondroitin-4-sulfate and dermatan sulfate.[12] These are synthesized in the skin by fibroblasts, and possibly by smooth muscle cells and mast cells.

Except when present in very large amounts, ground substance cannot be easily detected by routine hematoxylin and eosin staining (*Fig. 1.107*). Cationic dyes, such as alcian blue at appropriate pH and electrolyte concentration, are usually necessary for its demonstration.

Ground substance should not be regarded as merely the embedding medium for cellular and fibrous components of the dermis. It has other functions, including the transportation of water and electrolytes, and is intimately concerned with the permeability and osmolarity of interstitial fluids.

References

1. Wenstrup, R.J., Murad, S., Pinnell, S.R. (1991) Collagen. In: Goldsmith, L.A. (ed.) Physiology, biochemistry and molecular biology of the skin, 2nd edn. New York: Oxford University Press, pp 481–508.
2. Kadler, K.E., Holmes, D.F., Trotter, J.A. et al (1996) Collagen fibril formation. *J Biochem*, **316**, 1–11.
3. Byers, P.H. (1989) Inherited disorders of collagen gene structure and expression. *Am J Med Genet*, **34**, 72–80.
4. Uitto, J., Shamban, A. (1987) Heritable skin diseases with molecular defects in collagen or elastin. *Dermatol Clin*, **5**, 63–84.
5. Byers, P.H., Wenstrup, R.J., Bonadio, J.F. et al (1987) Molecular basis of inherited disorders of collagen biosynthesis: implications for prenatal diagnosis. *Curr Prob Dermatol*, **16**, 158–174.
6. Prockop, D.J., Kivirikko, K.I., Tuderman, L. et al (1979) The biosynthesis of collagen and its disorders. Part I. *New Engl J Med*, **301**, 13–23.
7. Uitto, J., Fazio, M., Bashir, M. et al (1991) Elastic fibers of the connective tissue. In: Goldsmith, L.A. (ed.) Physiology, biochemistry and molecular biology of the skin, 2nd edn. New York: Oxford University Press, pp 530–557.
8. Uitto, J., Paul, J.L., Brockley, K. et al (1983) Elastic fibers in human skin: quantitation of elastic fibers by computerized digital image analyses and determination of elastin by a radioimmunoassay of desmosine. *Lab Invest*, **49**, 499–505.
9. Uitto, J., Shamban, A. (1987) Heritable skin diseases with molecular defects in collagen or elastin. *Dermatol Clin*, **5**, 63–84.
10. Christiano, A.M., Lebwohl, M.G., Boyd, C.D. et al (1992) Workshop on pseudoxanthoma elasticum: molecular biology and pathology of the elastic fibers. *J Invest Dermatol*, **99**, 660–663.
11. Uitto, J., Christiano, A.M., Kähäri, V-M. et al (1991) Molecular biology and pathology of human elastin. *Trans Biochem Soc*, **19**, 824–829.
12. Goetinck, P.F., Winterbottom, N. (1991) Proteoglycans: modular macromolecules of the extracellular matrix. In: Goldsmith, L.A. (ed.) Physiology, biochemistry and molecular biology of the skin, 2nd edn. New York: Oxford University Press, pp 558–575.

Blood supply

The skin receives a rich blood supply from perforating vessels within the skeletal muscle and subcutaneous fat.[1] Most of the blood flow is directed toward the more metabolically active constituents of the skin, namely the epidermis, hair papillae and the adnexal structures. While the dermal papillae are richly vascularized, no capillaries actually enter the epidermis, which receives its nutrition by diffusion.

From the subcutaneous vessels arise two vascular plexuses linked by intercommunicating vessels (*Fig. 1.108*):

- the deep vascular plexus lies in the region of the interface between the dermis and subcutaneous fat
- the superficial vascular plexus lies in the superficial aspects of the reticular dermis and supplies the papillary dermis with a candelabra-like capillary loop system.[2]

Each loop consists of an ascending arterial limb and a descending venous limb. The vessels of the dermal papillae comprise terminal arterioles, arterial and venous capillaries, and postcapillary venules, with the last predominating.[2] Within the deep vascular plexus are small muscular arteries, which give rise to the arterioles that supply the superficial vascular plexus (*Fig. 1.109*).

The histology of these plexuses is similar, the difference being one of size rather than structure (arterioles have a diameter of less than 0.3 mm). From the lumen outwards the arteriole consists of a very thin intima resting against a conspicuous internal elastic lamina. Next to this is the media, consisting of two layers of smooth muscle, which constitutes the bulk of the vessel.[2] The adventitia surrounding the media

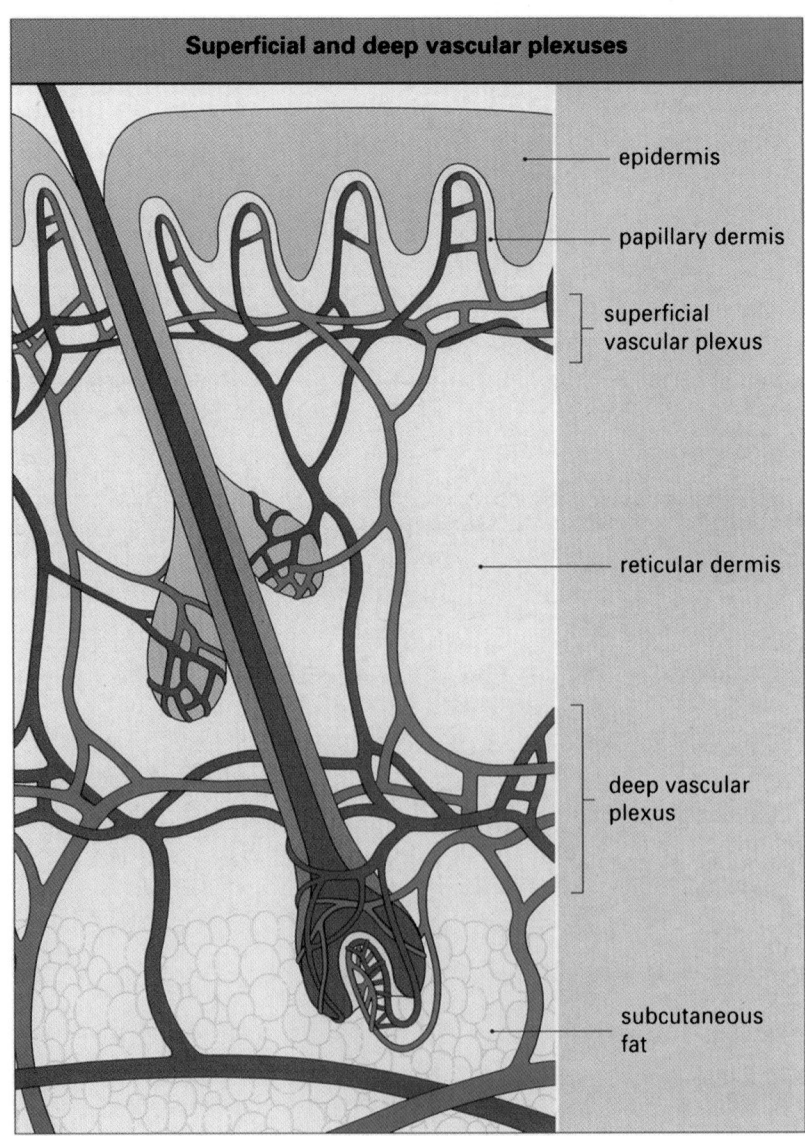

Superficial and deep vascular plexuses

epidermis

papillary dermis

superficial vascular plexus

reticular dermis

deep vascular plexus

subcutaneous fat

Fig. 1.108
Relationship of the superficial and deep vascular plexuses.

is composed of loose connective tissue. In small muscular arteries (but not arterioles), the adventitia often contains elastic fibers constituting the external elastic lamina. Small arterioles have an endothelium surrounded by a single layer of smooth muscle.

Capillaries consist of a single layer of endothelial cells, but may have adjacent pericytes, which have less well developed dense bodies and fewer filaments than smooth muscle cells. Endothelial cells and pericytes form tight junctions.[2] Venous capillaries have numerous pericytes and a multilayered basement membrane in contrast to arterial vessels where the basement membrane is solitary and homogenous.[2] Each dermal papilla is supplied by a single capillary loop. Endothelial cells contain vimentin filaments, Weibel–Palade bodies measuring approximately 0.1×3 μm (containing factor VIII) and numerous pinocytotic vesicles (*Figs 1.110, 1.111*).

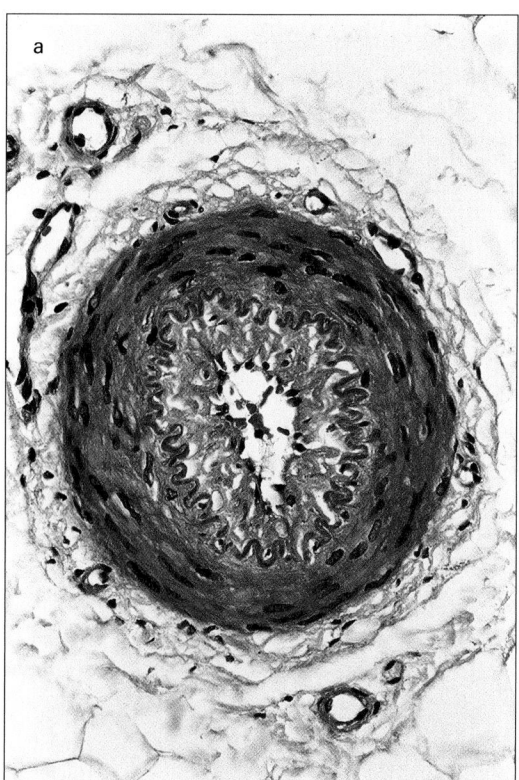
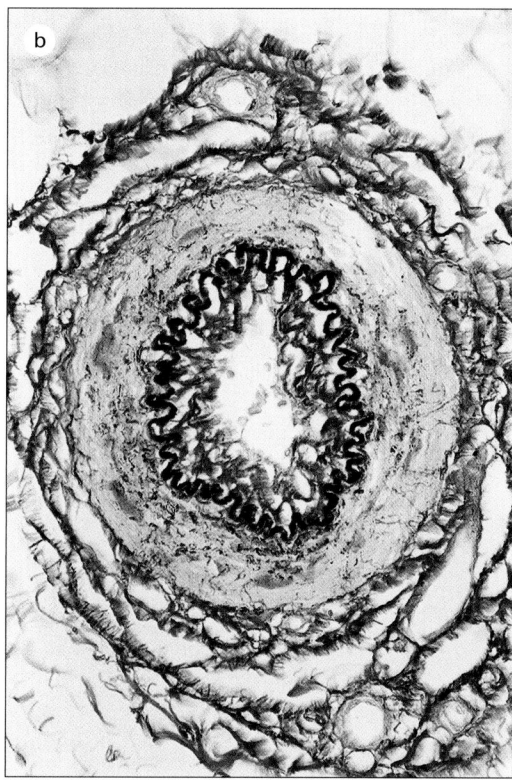

Fig. 1.109
Small muscular artery from the deep vascular plexus from the lower leg of an elderly man with endarteritis (intimal thickening). Note the thick muscle coat and conspicuous internal elastic lamina, the latter accentuated by the Weigert–van Gieson reaction. (**a**) Hematoxylin and eosin; (**b**) Weigert–van Gieson.

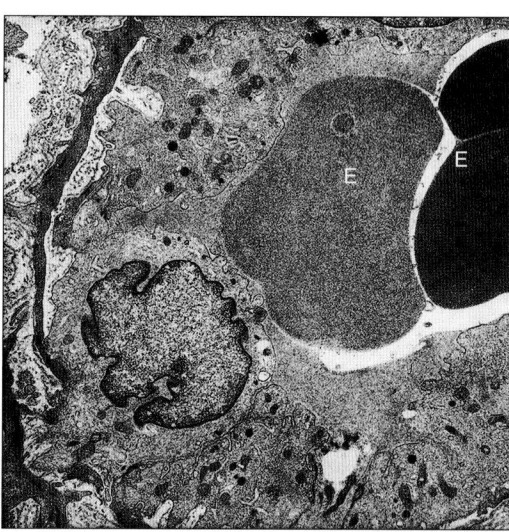

Fig. 1.110
Normal dermal capillary: note the lining of endothelial cells surrounded by a pericyte cell process and adjacent basal lamina. The lumen contains erythrocytes (E).

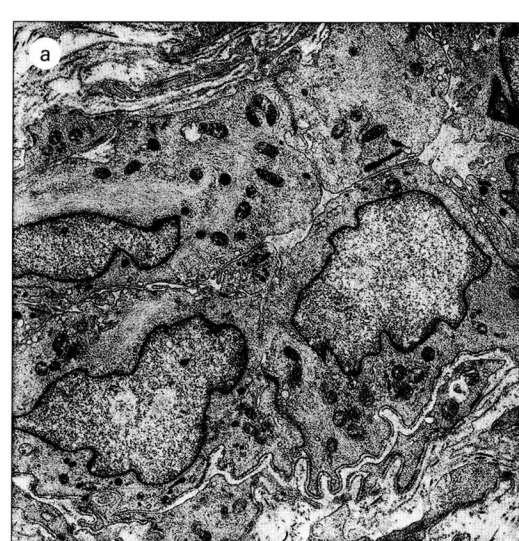
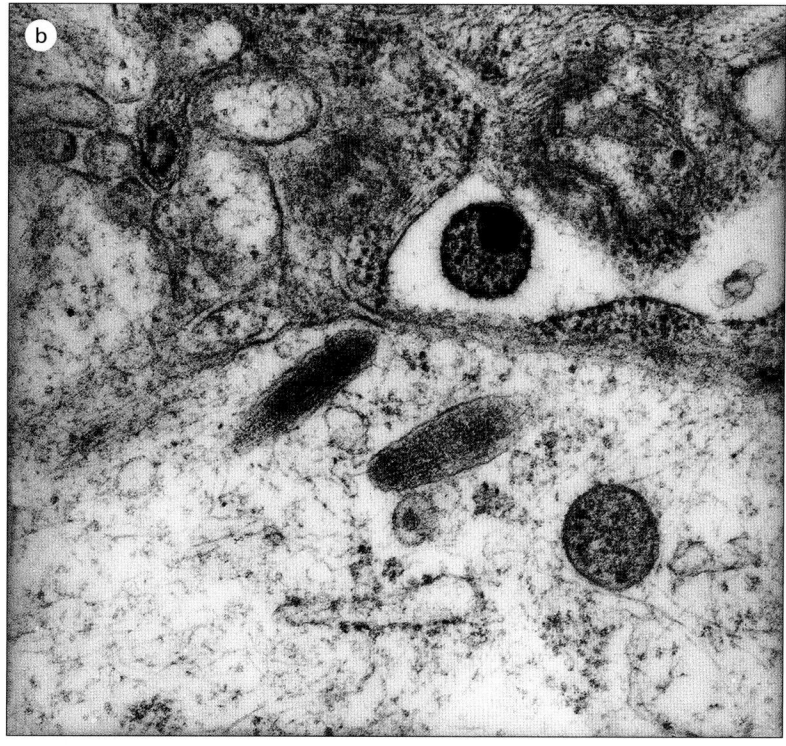

Fig. 1.111
(a) Small dermal arteriole: the lumen is compressed to a narrow slit-like space; (b) high power view of typical Weibel–Palade bodies. These are characteristic of blood vessel endothelium.

Postcapillary venules are larger, but have the same basic structure as capillaries. Their wall is devoid of smooth muscle. The small muscular venules into which the postcapillary venules drain have an intima made up of flattened endothelial cells surrounded by a smooth muscle layer one or two cells thick. They are therefore similar to small arterioles, but with much wider lumina.

Veins are composed of an endothelium surrounded by a muscle coat several layers thick. Typically an internal elastic lamina is poorly represented. There is usually a thick connective tissue adventitia, but elastic fibers are absent (*Fig. 1.112*); only very large muscular veins have elastic tissue.

Also present in the dermis are veil cells, which surround all the microvessels and separate them from the adjacent connective tissue.[3] Their function is unknown.

The capillary loop in the dermal papilla has an ascending arterial component and an intrapapillary segment, which is characterized by a hairpin turn and a descending venous capillary segment.[4] Capillary loops run perpendicular to the skin surface, except in the nail where they have a parallel orientation.

The dermis is richly supplied with arteriovenous anastomoses. Specialized shunts (glomus bodies), found primarily in the dermis of the fingertips, consist of an arterial segment (Sucquet–Hoyer canal), which connects directly to the venous limb (*Fig. 1.113*). The canal is surrounded by several layers of modified smooth muscle cells (glomus cells) with a particularly rich nerve supply. Glomus bodies function as sphincters, allowing the capillaries of the superficial dermis to be bypassed, therefore increasing the venous return from the extremities.

Cutaneous blood flow (under hypothalamic control) is of extreme importance in thermoregulation.[5] Mediated by the autonomic nervous system, heat loss can be increased or decreased by varying the blood flow to the superficial vascular plexuses. If the environmental temperature exceeds that of the body, then the blood flow to the papillary dermis increases. A concomitant increase in eccrine sweat gland secretion, evaporation of which cools the outer parts of the body, lowers the temperature of the circulating blood and maintains a stable core temperature. Temperature control therefore depends on a delicate interplay between both vascular and sweat gland function.

The dermis also contains an extensive lymphatic system, which is closely associated with the vascular plexuses. Although largely disregarded except for their role in tumor spread, lymphatics are of major importance in removing the debris of daily wear and tear including fluid, cells and macromolecules (*Fig. 1.114*).[6] They also represent the primary disposal mechanism for contaminating microorganisms.[6] Lymphatics

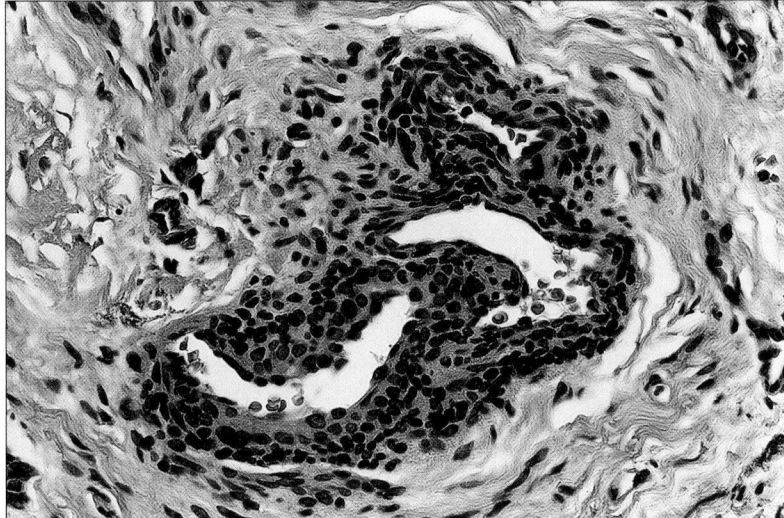

Fig. 1.113
Glomus body: note the arterial and venous limbs connected by a vascular channel rich in glomus cells.

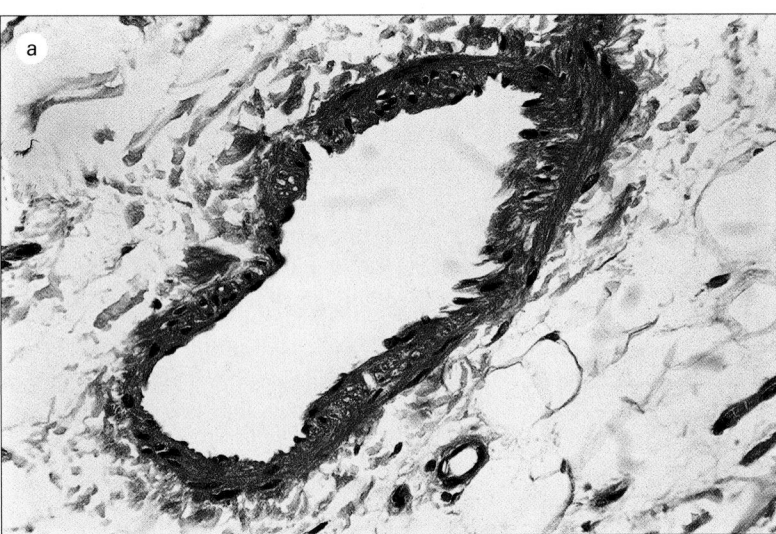

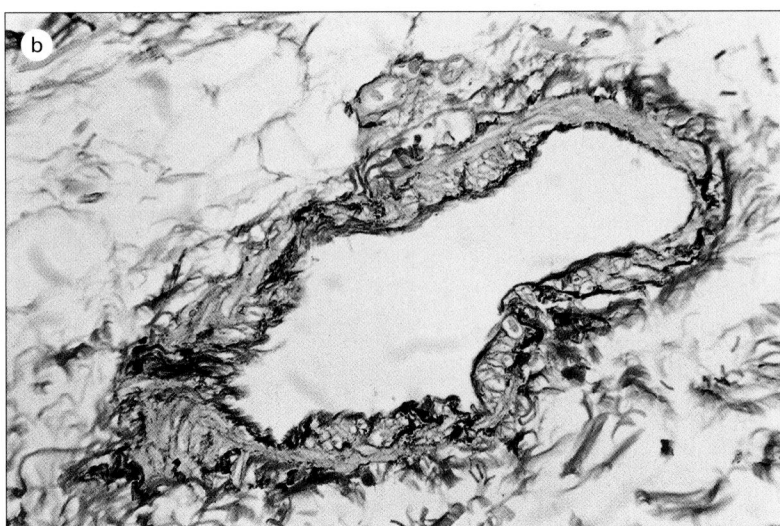

Fig. 1.112
Companion vein to *Fig. 1.109*: note the wide diameter of the lumen in comparison to the relatively thin muscle coat. There is a little elastic tissue but no discernible internal elastic lamina. (**a**) Hematoxylin and eosin; (**b**) Weigert–van Gieson.

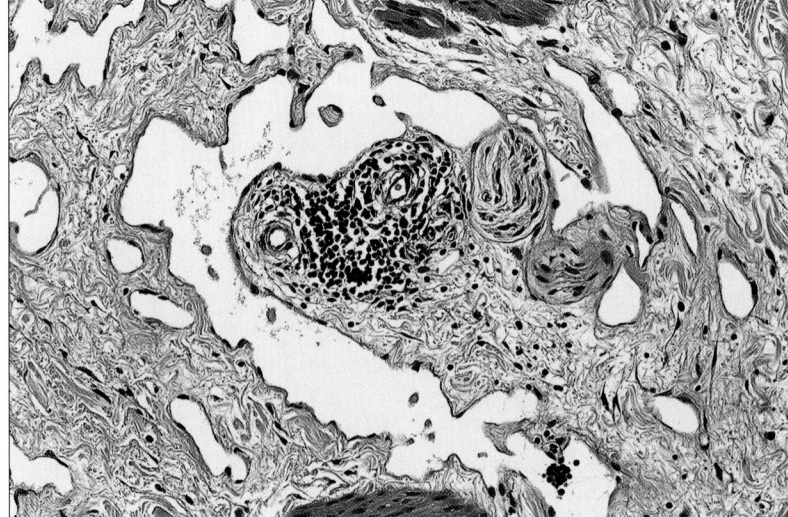

Fig. 1.114
Lymphatics: these exceedingly thin-walled channels are normally not visible in the dermis. They are readily apparent, however, when obstructed as in this patient with lymphedema following radiotherapy for breast carcinoma.

have been shown to supply the major route for epidermal Langerhans' cells to reach the regional lymph node following antigen stimulation.[7] Under normal circumstances these delicate vessels are collapsed and are difficult to detect. They are supported by a delicate elastic tissue scaffolding and consist of a large thin-walled collapsed vessel lined by attenuated endothelium and characterized by the presence of multiple valves.[6] Their presence is much more obvious in obstructive situations (e.g. lymphedema or due to the presence of metastases). Dermal lymphatics are loosely aggregated into a superficial and deep plexus, which drain into muscularized lymphatic trunks.[6] In the lower limbs the lymphatic trunks are very thick and muscular and can be confused with an artery. The absence of an internal elastic lamina readily allows their distinction.

Vascular endothelial cells may be identified by the monoclonal antibody CD31 or by an anti-von Willebrand factor antibody. Vascular endothelial growth factor receptor 3 (VEGFR-3) has not lived up to its promise to be a useful lymphatic endothelial cell marker. Lymphatic vessel endothelial hyaluronan receptor 1 (LYVE-1), Prox-1 and podoplanin may be more useful.[8,9]

References

1. Ryan, T.J. (1991) Cutaneous circulation. In: Goldsmith, L.A. (ed.) Physiology, biochemistry and molecular biology of the skin, 2nd edn. New York: Oxford University Press, pp 1019–1084.
2. Braverman, I.M. (1989) Ultrastructure and organization of the cutaneous microvasculature in normal and pathologic states. *J Invest Dermatol*, **93**, 2S–9S.
3. Yen, A., Braverman, I.M. (1976) Ultrastructure of the human dermal microcirculation: the horizontal plexus of the papillary dermis. *J Invest Dermatol*, **66**, 131–142.
4. Higgins, J.C., Eady, R.A.J. (1981) Human dermal vasculature. I. Its segmental differentiation. Light and electron microscopic study. *Br J Dermatol*, **104**, 116–130.
5. Kranning, K.K. (1991) Temperature regulation and the skin. In: Goldsmith, L.A. (ed.) Physiology, biochemistry and molecular biology of the skin, 2nd edn. New York: Oxford University Press, pp 1085–1098.
6. Ryan, T.J. (1989) Structure and function of lymphatics. *J Invest Dermatol*, **93**, 18S–24S.
7. Silberberg-Sinakin, I., Thorbecke, G. J. (1980) Contact hypersensitivity and Langerhans' cells. *J Invest Dermatol*, **75**, 61–67.
8. Cumick, G.H., Jiang, W.G., Gomez, K.F. et al (2002) Lymphangiogenesis and breast cancer metastasis. *Histol Histopathol*, **17**, 863–870.
9. Karkkainen, M.T., Alitalo, K. (2002) Lymphatic endothelial regulation, lymphedema, and lymph node metastasis. *Semin Cell Dev Biol*, **13**, 9–18.

Nervous system

The skin is richly innervated, rendering it highly susceptible to the myriad sensory stimuli that continually bombard the exterior of the body.[1,2]

The innervation comprises:

- an efferent non-myelinated system, responsible for the function of the cutaneous vasculature and skin appendages and derived from the sympathetic division of the autonomic nervous system
- an afferent myelinated and non-myelinated system responsible for the appreciation of cutaneous sensation.

The cutaneous nerves therefore supply the skin appendages and form prominent plexuses around the hair bulbs and the papillary dermis. The afferent receptors consist of free nerve endings, nerve endings in relation to hair, and encapsulated nerve endings. Free nerve endings, of both myelinated and non-myelinated types and with a low conduction speed, are mainly responsible for the appreciation of temperature, itch and pain.

Hair follicles are supplied by an intricate network of myelinated fibers, some of which ramify as free nerve endings in the periadnexal fibrous tissue sheath, while others enter the epidermis to terminate as expansions in intimate association with Merkel cells in the external root sheath. The hair disc is a complex structure consisting of basally situated Merkel cells and an associated myelinated peripheral nerve fiber (see *Fig 1.62*). Despite the name it has an inconstant association with hair follicles. Hair discs are slowly adapting mechanoreceptors.

There are various types of encapsulated nerve endings, including the specialized corpuscles of Pacini and Meissner.

- *Pacinian corpuscles* are responsible for the appreciation of deep pressure and vibration and are found predominantly in the subcutaneous fat of the palms and soles, dorsal surfaces of the digits, around the genitalia, and in ligaments and joint capsules.[2] They are round to oval and quite large, measuring up to 0.5×2 mm. They consist of a central core of packed lamellae, which enclose a nerve terminal and are surrounded by a cellular layer, within a laminated capsule (*Fig. 1.115*). Each corpuscle is therefore supplied with a single myelinated nerve ending.
- *Meissner's corpuscles* are involved in the appreciation of touch sensation (rapidly adapting mechanoreceptors) and are found predominantly in the dermal papillae of the hands and feet, the lips, and on the front of the forearm.[2] Oval in shape and measuring about 80×30 μm, they comprise a perineural-derived lamellated capsule surrounding a core of cells and nerve fibers, and are supplied by myelinated and non-myelinated nerve fibers (*Fig. 1.116*). They make intimate contact with the basal keratinocytes.[2] Meissner's corpuscles have a multiple nerve supply and each nerve may also supply multiple corpuscles.

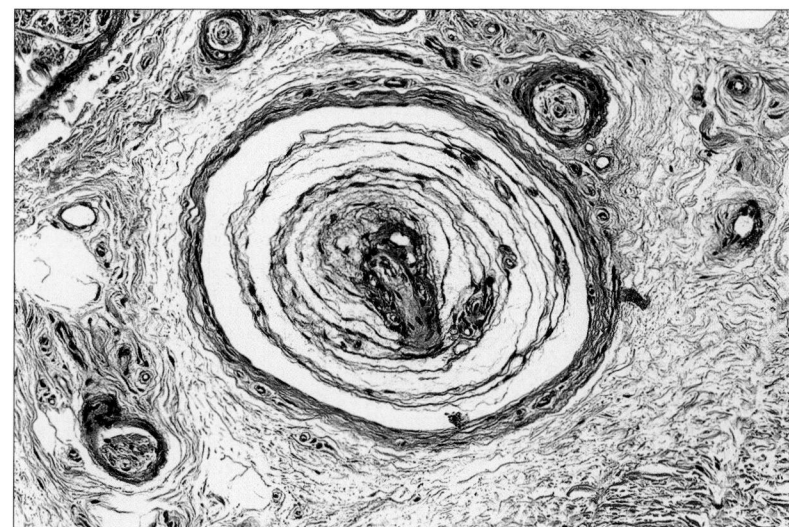

Fig. 1.115
Pacinian corpuscles showing their characteristic lamellar internal structure.

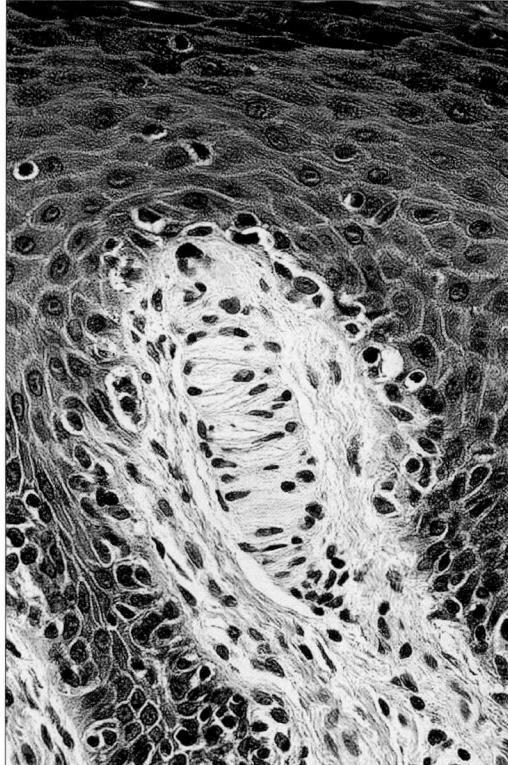

Fig. 1.116
Meissner's corpuscle within a dermal papilla: with hematoxylin and eosin staining it appears as perpendicularly orientated lamellae of Schwann cells.

References

1. Munger, B.L., Ide, C. (1988) The structure and function of cutaneous sensory receptors. *Arch Histol Cytol,* 51, 1–34.
2. Lynn, B. (1991) Cutaneous sensation. In: Goldsmith, L.A. (ed.) Physiology, biochemistry and molecular biology of the skin, 2nd edn. New York: Oxford University Press, pp 779–815.

Subcutaneous fat

The subcutaneous fat is divided into lobules by vascular fibrous septa, and its cells are characterized by the presence of a large single globule of lipid, which compresses the cytoplasm and nucleus against the plasma membrane (*Fig. 1.117*).

The adipocyte is large, measuring up to 100 μm in diameter.[1] The cytoplasm contains numerous mitochondria. Smooth endoplasmic reticulum is prominent and a Golgi is often conspicuous.[2] Processing for routine histological preparation dissolves the lipid, but the use of special stains on frozen sections will reveal its presence (*Fig. 1.118*).

The subcutaneous fat may contain large numbers of mast cells. Deposits of brown fat may be seen in the newborn and occasionally in adults, particularly in the interscapular region, the back, thorax and mediastinum.[2] The brown coloration is due to the high cytochrome content.[2] The brown fat cytoplasm contains numerous, somewhat pleomorphic, mitochondria. Endoplasmic reticulum and a Golgi apparatus are not usually visible.[2] The adipocytes have a bubbly appearance with the nucleus located towards the center of the cell (*Fig. 1.119*).

The subcutaneous fat is involved in thermoregulation, insulation, provision of energy, protection and support, has a cosmetic role, and functions as a nutritional store.[1,2]

References

1. Ryan, T.J., Currie, S.B. (1989) Cutaneous adipose tissue. In: Ryan, T.J., Currie, S.B. (eds) Clinics in dermatology. London: Lippincott, pp 37–47.
2. Spearman, R.I.C. (1982) Structure and function of subcutaneous tissue. *Physiol Pathophysiol Skin,* 7, 2252–2281.

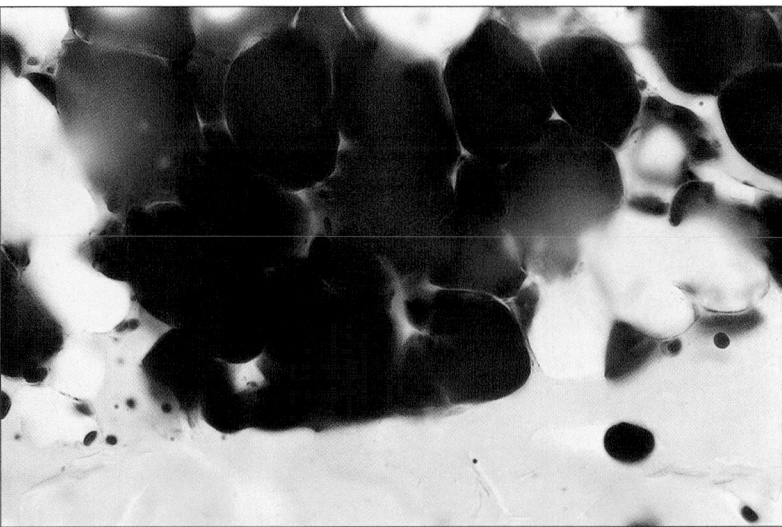

Fig. 1.118
Adult fat in frozen section stained by the Sudan IV technique.

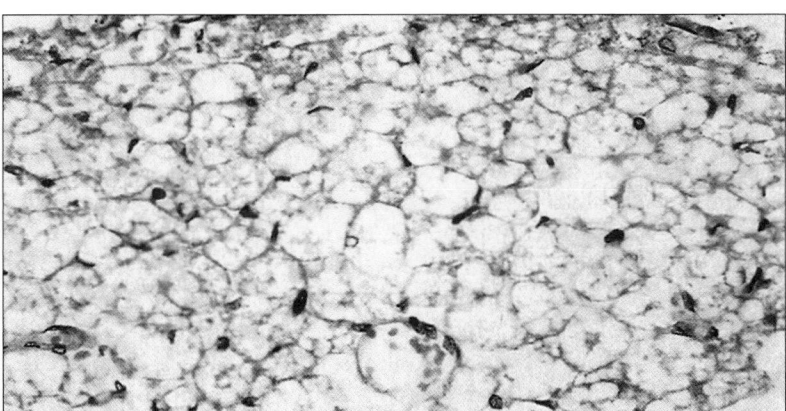

Fig. 1.119
Typical brown fat showing pink granular cytoplasm.

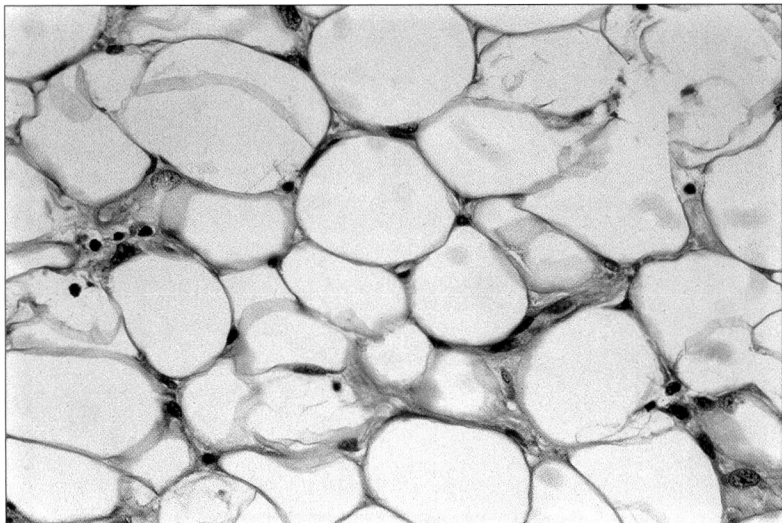

Fig. 1.117
The lipid contents of fat cells are dissolved during processing using conventional (paraffin-embedding) techniques. The cells therefore appear empty and have peripheral compressed nuclei.

Ichthyosis 37
Ichthyosis vulgaris 37
Sex-linked ichthyosis 39
Autosomal recessive congenital ichthyosis 42
Lamellar ichthyosis 42
Congenital ichthyosiform erythroderma 43
Congenital bullous ichthyosiform erythroderma 45
Ichthyosis bullosa of Siemens 48
Linear epidermolytic epidermal nevus 49
Epidermolytic acanthoma 49
Focal epidermolytic hyperkeratosis 49
Ichthyosis fetalis 50
Netherton's syndrome 51
Sjögren–Larsson syndrome 52

Pityriasis rotunda 54

Follicular ichthyosis 54

Lichen spinulosus 55

Phrynoderma 55

Ichthyosis follicularis with alopecia and photophobia 56

Keratosis pilaris 56
Keratosis pilaris atrophicans 57

Acquired ichthyosis 58

Palmoplantar keratoderma 59
Epidermolytic palmoplantar keratoderma 59
Diffuse palmoplantar keratoderma 60
Erythrokeratoderma variabilis 61
Progressive symmetric erythrokeratodermia 62
Striate palmoplantar keratoderma 62
Punctate palmoplantar keratoderma 63
Keratosis punctata of the palmar creases 64
Marginal papular acrokeratoderma 64
Keratoderma climactericum 65

Palmoplantar ectodermal dysplasias 66
Focal palmoplantar keratoderma with oral hyperkeratosis 66
Pachyonychia congenita type II 67
Focal non-epidermolytic palmoplantar keratoderma with esophageal squamous carcinoma 67
Acquired palmoplantar keratoderma and internal malignancy 68
Palmoplantar keratoderma with periodontopathia 69
Vohwinkel's syndrome 70
Hidrotic ectodermal dysplasia 71
Keratitis–ichthyosis–deafness syndrome 72

Olmsted syndrome 73

Acrokeratosis verruciformis of Hopf 74

Clavus 74

Callus 74

Porokeratosis 74

Hyperkeratosis lenticularis perstans 78

Granular parakeratosis 79

Ichthyosis

The term ichthyosis (Gr. *ichthys*, fish) is applied to a number of conditions characterized by abnormal keratinization.[1,2] The clinical features range from mild involvement, often passed off as 'dry skin' (xerosis), through to severe widespread scaly lesions causing much discomfort and social embarrassment (*Fig. 2.1*). The scales are often shed as clusters rather than as single cells as is the norm.[1] The pathogenesis of the ichthyoses is very complex but ultimately depends upon two distinct final common pathways: one relates to retention of corneocytes (e.g. ichthyosis vulgaris, recessive X-linked ichthyosis), the other involves epidermal hyperproliferation (e.g. congenital ichthyosiform erythroderma, bullous ichthyosis, Sjögren–Larsson syndrome and Refsum's disease).[3]

Ichthyosiform dermatoses are classified into the following groups:
- congenital diseases in which the cutaneous manifestations are the major features (*Table 2.1*)
- variants in which the skin lesions are but one facet of a more sinister systemic illness (*Table 2.2*)
- a heterogeneous acquired variant (*Table 2.3*).[4]

References

1. Rand, R.E., Baden, H.P. (1983) The ichthyoses – a review. *J Am Acad Dermatol*, **8**, 285–305.
2. Williams, M.L. (1992) Epidermal lipids and scaling diseases of the skin. *Semin Dermatol*, **11**, 169–175.
3. Shwayder, T., Ott, F. (1991) All about ichthyosis. *Pediatr Clin North Am*, **38**, 835–857.
4. Dykes, P.J., Marks, R. (1977) Acquired ichthyosis: multiple causes for an acquired generalized disturbance in desquamation. *Br J Dermatol*, **97**, 327–334.

Ichthyosis vulgaris

Clinical features

This relatively common disorder (incidence of 1:250 to 1:1000 births) has an autosomal dominant mode of inheritance.[1,2] It may present initially as keratosis pilaris (follicular hyperkeratosis) on the arms, buttocks and thighs. The disease is usually fairly mild and apparent within the first few months or years of life. It affects the sexes equally and presents as dryness (xerosis) and slight to moderate fine white fish-like scaling, particularly involving the arms and legs and characteristically sparing the flexures (*Fig. 2.2*). The trunk may be affected. The face is uninvolved (possibly due to the effect of increased sebaceous secretions) and the neck is often spared.[3] The scalp, however, is frequently affected.[2] There is seasonal variation, with improvement of the condition in the summer months, particularly in humid climates.[2] The palms and soles show increased palmar and plantar markings in contradistinction to sex-linked ichthyosis and may show mild hyperkeratosis.[3] An association with keratosis punctata of the palms and soles has also been documented.[4] Chapping of the hands and feet can be a problem.[5] There is no evidence of hair, nail or teeth involvement. There is an increased incidence of atopic disorders.[5] Serum lipids are normal.[3]

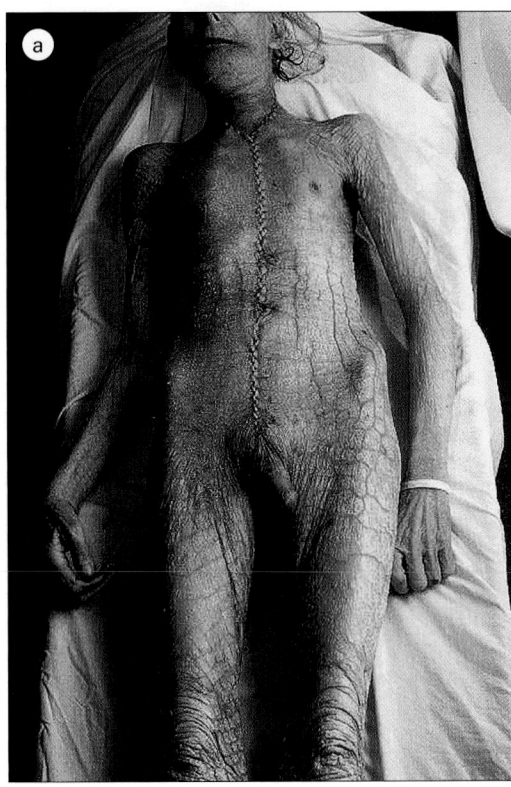

Fig. 2.1

(a, b) Severe generalized ichthyosis: this was an incidental finding at postmortem. Ichthyosis can be very disfiguring and a considerable social disadvantage.

Table 2.1

Ichthyosis: classification of the major ichthyosiform dermatoses

Condition	Mode of inheritance	Defect	Age of onset	Clinical appearances	Associated features	Histological features
Ichthyosis vulgaris	Autosomal dominant	Profilaggrin deficiency	Childhood	Fine, light scales; flexures spared; increased palmar/plantar markings; keratosis pilaris	Atopy	Decreased to absent granular layer
X-linked ichthyosis	X-linked recessive	Steroid sulfatase deficiency	Birth or infancy	Large dark scales; lateral face and neck commonly involved; flexures variably involved; palms and soles normal	Corneal opacification; steroid sulfatase deficiency	Normal or increased granular layer
Lamellar ichthyosis	Autosomal recessive	Heterogeneous; defective transglutaminase 1	Birth	Large thick scales; uniform generalized involvement; flexures affected; hyperkeratotic palms and soles	Ectropion, prematurity common	Normal or thickened granular layer
Congenital ichthyosiform erythroderma	Autosomal recessive	Heterogeneous; defective lipoxygenase; ? defective loricrin	Birth	Collodion membrane; intense erythroderma; variable fine to plate-like scaling	Mild ectropion; mild eclabion; palmoplantar keratoderma	Normal or increased granular layer
Epidermolytic hyperkeratosis	Autosomal dominant	Defective keratins 1 and 10	Birth	Coarse, verrucous scales, particularly in flexures; bullae especially in infancy or childhood	Offensive odor; frequent cutaneous infections; prenatal diagnosis possible	Vacuolization of granular and malpighian layers

Adapted with permission from Rand, R.E., Baden, H.P. (1983) *Journal of the American Academy of Dermatology*, **8**, 285–305.

Table 2.2

Ichthyosis: systemic variants

Condition	Mode of inheritance	Age of onset	Clinical appearances	Associated features
Refsum's disease	Autosomal recessive	Childhood	Mild, variable ichthyosis	Polyneuritis; nerve deafness improves with dietary restriction of phytanic acid
Sjögren–Larsson syndrome	Autosomal recessive	Birth	Mild lamellar ichthyosis	Spastic paralysis; mental retardation; macular retinal degeneration
Rud's syndrome	Probable autosomal	Infancy	Lamellar ichthyosis	Dwarfism; mental deficiency; hypogonadism; epilepsy
KID syndrome	Autosomal dominant and recessive	Birth or childhood	Dry, scaly, erythema; verrucous plaques; progeria appearance	Keratitis; neurosensory deafness; squamous carcinoma
Northerton's syndrome	Autosomal recessive	Birth or infancy	Ichthyosis linearis circumflexa; trichorrhexis invaginata	Stunted growth; mental retardation

Adapted with permission from Rand, R.E., Baden, H.P. (1983) *Journal of the American Academy of Dermatology*, **8**, 285–305.

Table 2.3
Diseases associated with acquired ichthyosis

- Lymphoma (especially Hodgkin's lymphoma)
- Carcinoma of bronchus, breast and cervix
- Sarcoidosis
- Lupus erythematosus
- Drugs: nicotinic acid

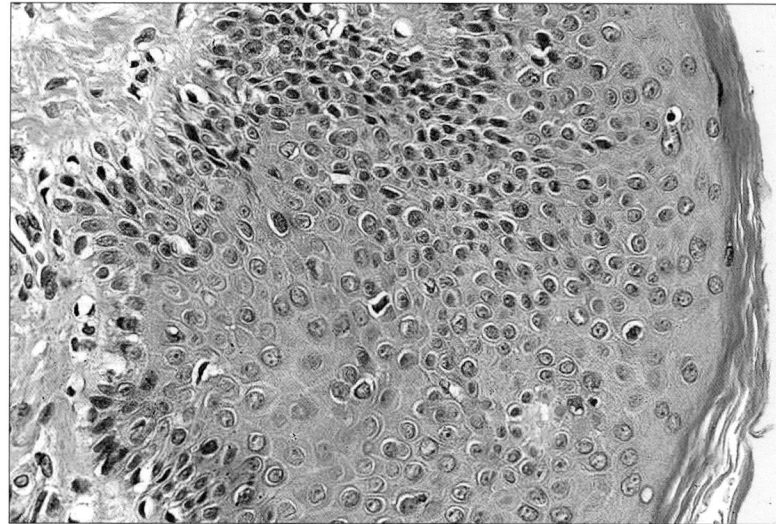

Fig. 2.3
Ichthyosis vulgaris: there is hyperkeratosis. The granular cell layer is absent.

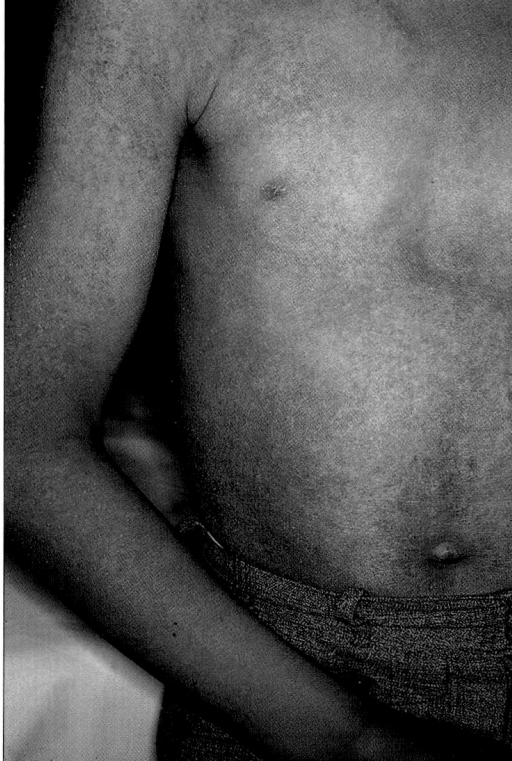

Fig. 2.2
Ichthyosis vulgaris: abdominal involvement is most noticeable in this patient. Sparing of the flexures is characteristic of this variant of ichthyosis. By courtesy of W.A.D. Griffiths, MD, Institute of Dermatology, London, UK.

3. Shwayder, T., Ott, F. (1991) All about ichthyosis. *Pediatr Clin North Am*, **38**, 835–857.
4. Just, M., Ribera, M., Bielsa, I. et al (1999) Keratosis punctata of the palmar creases: report of two cases associated with ichthyosis vulgaris. *Br J Dermatol*, **141**, 551–553.
5. Rabinowitz, L.G., Esterly, N.B. (1994) Atopic dermatitis and ichthyosis vulgaris. *Pediatr Rev*, **15**, 220–226.
6. Nirinsuksiri, W., Presland, R.B., Brumbaugh, S.G. et al (1995) Decreased profilaggrin expression in ichthyosis vulgaris is a result of selectively impaired post-transcriptional control. *J Biol Chem*, **270**, 871–876.
7. Nirunsuksiri, W., Zhang, S.H., Fleckman, P. (1998) Reduced stability and bi-allelic, co-equal expression of profilaggrin mRNA in keratinocytes cultured from subjects with ichthyosis vulgaris. *J Invest Dermatol*, **110**, 854–861.
8. Presland, R.B., Boggess, D., Lewis, S.P. et al (2000) Loss of normal profilaggrin and filaggrin in flaky tail (ft/ft) mice: an animal model for the filaggrin-deficient skin disease ichthyosis vulgaris. *J Invest Dermatol*, **115**, 1072–1081.
9. Anton-Lamprecht, I., Hafbrauer, M. (1972) Ultrastructural distinction of autosomal dominant ichthyosis vulgaris and X-linked recessive ichthyosis. *Humangenetik*, **15**, 261–264.
10. Michel, S., Juhlin, L. (1990) Cornified envelopes in congenital disorders of keratinization. *Br J Dermatol*, **122**, 15–21.
11. Marks, R., Barton, S.P. (1983) The significance of the size and shape of corneocytes. In: Marks, R., Plewig, G. (eds) Stratum corneum. Berlin: Springer-Verlag, pp 161–170.
12. Wells, R.S., Kerr, C.B. (1966) The histology of ichthyosis. *J Invest Dermatol*, **46**, 530–535.
13. Feinstein, A., Ackerman, A.B., Ziprkowski, L. (1970) Histology of autosomal dominant ichthyosis vulgaris and X-linked ichthyosis. *Arch Dermatol*, **101**, 524–527.

Pathogenesis and histological features

Icthyosis vulgaris is characterized by deficiency of profilaggrin, a major constituent of the keratohyalin granules.[6] It is thought that this occurs as a consequence of defective posttranscriptional control mechanisms associated with mRNA instability.[6,7] Flaky tail mice, which represent an animal model of ichthyosis vulgaris, produce defective profilaggrin with resultant absence of filaggrin.[8] Ultrastructurally, the keratohyalin granules are abnormal and associated with decreased amounts of filaggrin.[9] Although the precise pathogenesis of scale production is unknown, it is probably related to increased adhesiveness of the keratin lamellae. There is no evidence of increased epidermopoiesis.[3] The profile of the cornified envelopes is abnormal, there being increased numbers combined with a diminished size as compared to normal skin.[10] This correlates with diminished size of the stratum corneum keratinocytes in icthyosis vulgaris.[11]

Ichthyosis vulgaris is characterized by mild to moderate hyperkeratosis associated with an atrophic or normal epidermis and a thin or absent granular cell layer (*Fig. 2.3*).[12,13] Occasionally parakeratosis is evident.

The lesions of keratosis pilaris show dilated follicles containing large keratin plugs. In the upper dermis a mild chronic inflammatory cell infiltrate may be present. Specimens taken from the front of the lower legs often show the most characteristic features. Specimens of the upper arms may often appear histologically near normal.

References

1. Bousema, M., van Diggelen, O., van Joost, T. et al (1989) Ichthyosis: reliability of clinical signs in the differentiation between autosomal dominant and sex-linked forms. *Int J Dermatol*, **28**, 240–242.
2. Rand, R.E., Baden, H.P. (1983) The ichthyoses – a review. *J Am Acad Dermatol*, **8**, 285–305.

Sex-linked ichthyosis

Clinical features

Also known as steroid sulfatase deficiency and ichthyosis nigricans, this X-linked, recessively inherited disorder has an incidence of 1:6000 male births; lesions may be present at birth.[1–3] The disease is exceedingly rarely expressed in females.[4] Cutaneous lesions tend to be more conspicuous and severe than in the autosomal dominant variant.[2] The scales are large and dark and are seen particularly on the trunk, the extensor surface of the extremities, the scalp, the preauricular region and the neck (*Figs 2.4–2.7*).[2] Involvement of the flexures is also sometimes present (*Fig. 2.8*).[1] The palms and soles are usually unaffected and keratosis pilaris is not a feature. Involvement of the trunk and neck often gives the skin a dirty appearance. Lesions may improve or disappear in warm weather.[2] The hair, nails and teeth are not affected.

Corneal opacities due to comma-shaped deposits in the posterior capsule of Descemet's membrane or corneal stroma, visible with slit-lamp examination (*Figs 2.9, 2.10*), are characteristic and may be detected in female carriers.[5] Undescended testes may be a feature in as many as 25% of affected patients.[6–8] Rarely testicular cancer has been documented.[6]

Pathogenesis and histological features

The disease is associated with a deficiency of the microsomal enzyme, steroid sulfatase/STS (sterol sulfate sulfohydrolase/arylsulphatase C).[9] This is a membrane-bound enzyme, which hydrolyses the 3-β-sulfate esters of cholesterol and the sulfated steroid hormones.[10] Absence of this hormone is associated with persistence of the sulfate moiety on a number of sulfated steroid hormones and cholesterol sulfate.[3]

Recessive X-linked ichthyosis is characterized by a raised serum cholesterol sulfate.[10] The corneocytes contain excess cholesterol 3-sulfate and diminished free sterol.[11] Steroid sulfatase deficiency possibly results therefore in persistence of the lipid contents of the membrane-coating granules and hence increased or persistent adhesion between adjacent keratin plates in the stratum corneum. Steroid sulfatase deficiency can be detected using the patient's peripheral leukocytes and cultured skin fibroblasts. Diagnosis may also be affected by lipoprotein electrophoresis, which shows increased mobility of low density and very low density lipoprotein in addition to the steroid sulfatase deficiency.[12,13]

The gene locus for recessive X-linked ichthyosis is within the Xp22.3 region of the X chromosome.[14,15] The gene, which has been cloned and characterized, is located adjacent to the boundary of the X unique and pseudoautosomal regions.[16] Recently indirect genotypic analysis using polymorphic DNA markers closely linked to the STS gene has been shown to be a reliable method of detection of the carrier status.[14,17] Complete deletions of structural STS gene have been reported in 90% of patients with sex-linked ichthyosis;[14,16–19] the other 10% show partial deletions or point mutations.[1] Carrier status can also be confirmed by fluorescent in situ hybridization (FISH) analysis.[19] Recently, rapid diagnosis and differentiation from ichthyosis vulgaris using polymerase chain reaction (PCR) has been documented.[20]

Lesions show non-specific features of compact hyperkeratosis associated with a granular cell layer, which may be normal or increased in thickness (*Fig. 2.11*).[21,22] Follicular plugging is not a feature. Occasionally thinning of the granular layer is seen, causing confusion with the auto-

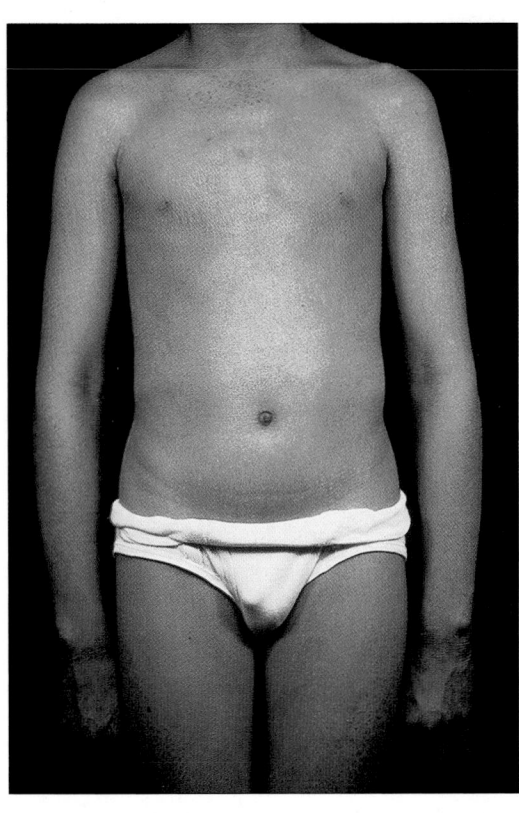

Fig. 2.4
Sex-linked ichthyosis: although only mildly affected, this child shows widespread scaling. By courtesy of the Institute of Dermatology, London, UK.

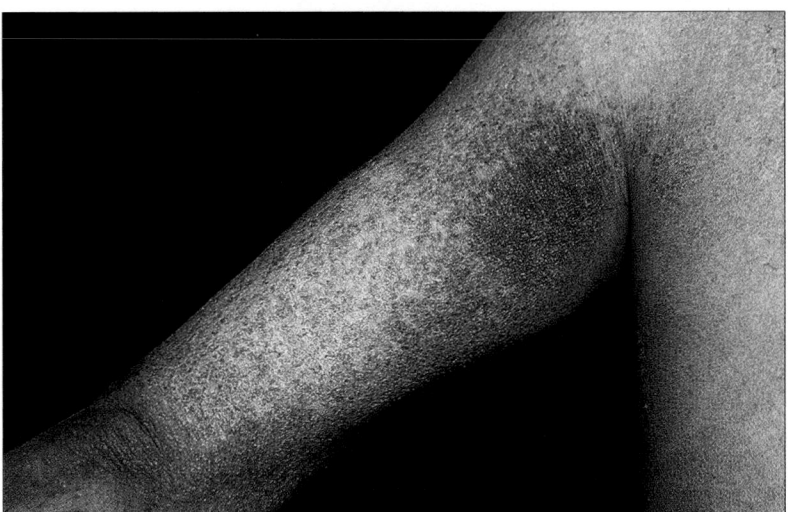

Fig. 2.6
Sex-linked ichthyosis: the scales are large and disfiguring. By courtesy of R.A. Marsden, MD, St George's Hospital, London, UK.

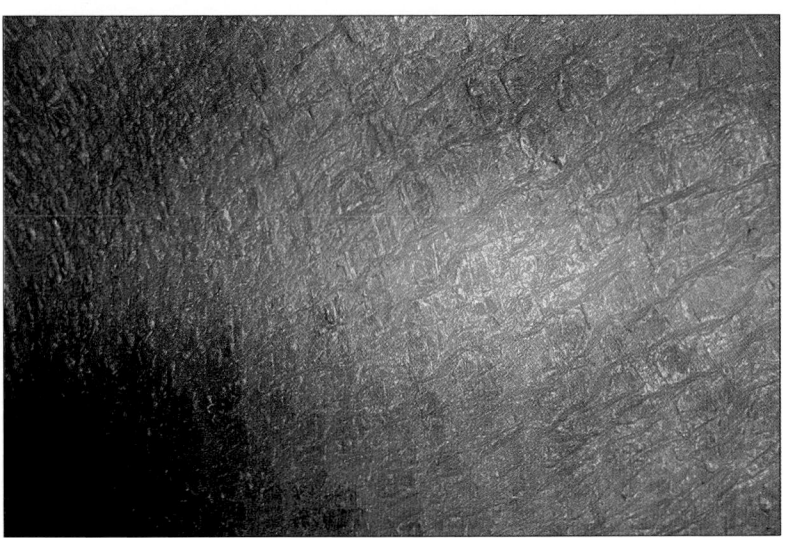

Fig. 2.5
Sex-linked ichthyosis: the scale is coarser than that seen in ichthyosis vulgaris. By courtesy of the Institute of Dermatology, London, UK.

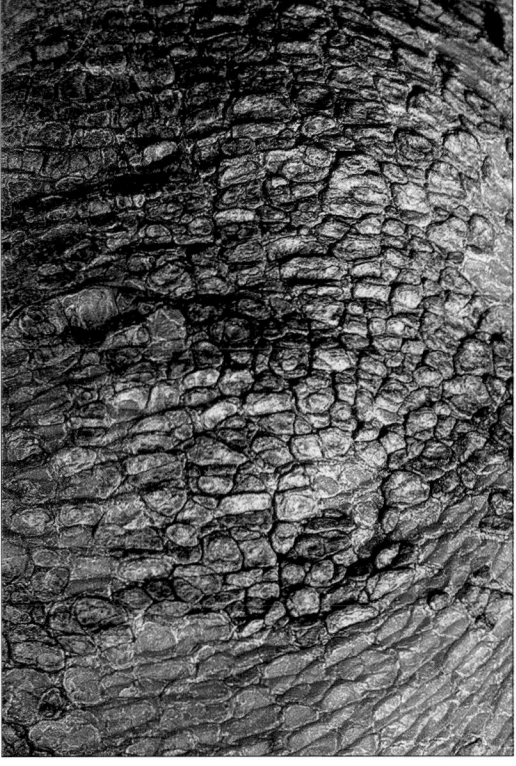

Fig. 2.7
Sex-linked ichthyosis: in this example the scales appear dirty. This can be an extremely embarrassing condition. By courtesy of the Institute of Dermatology, London, UK.

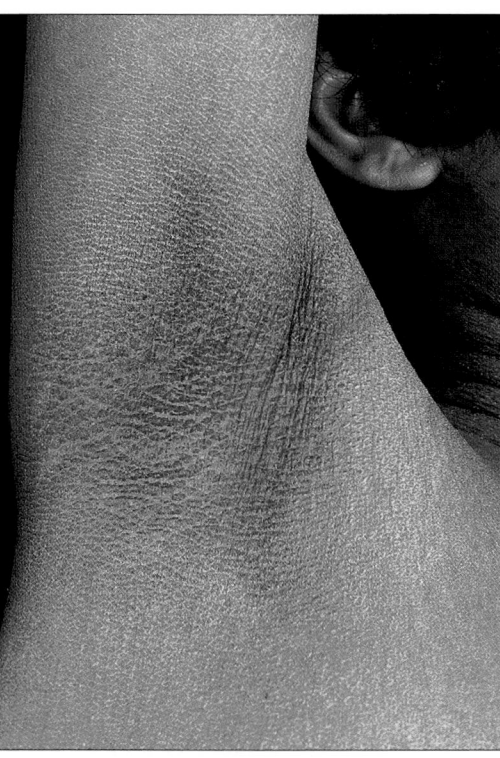

Fig. 2.8
Sex-linked ichthyosis: involvement of the flexures is sometimes a feature of this variant. By courtesy of the Institute of Dermatology, London, UK.

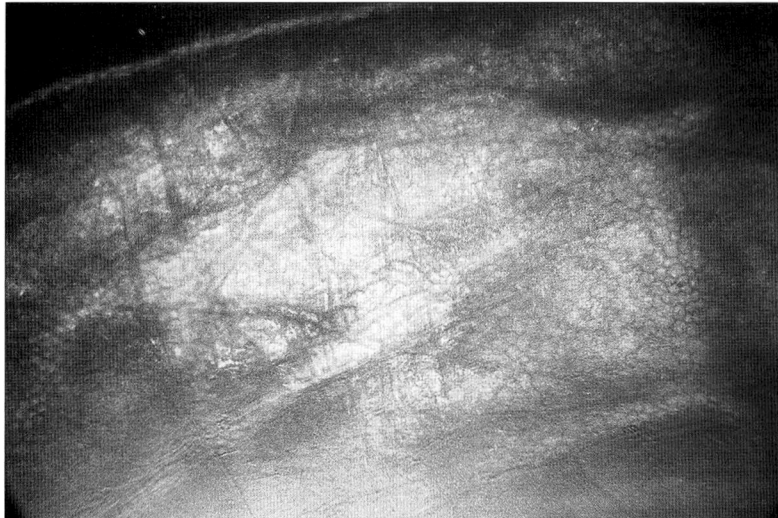

Fig. 2.10
Sex-linked ichthyosis: same lesion as in *Fig. 2.9* viewed by specular microscopy. By courtesy of R.J. Buckley, MD, Moorfield's Eye Hospital, London, UK.

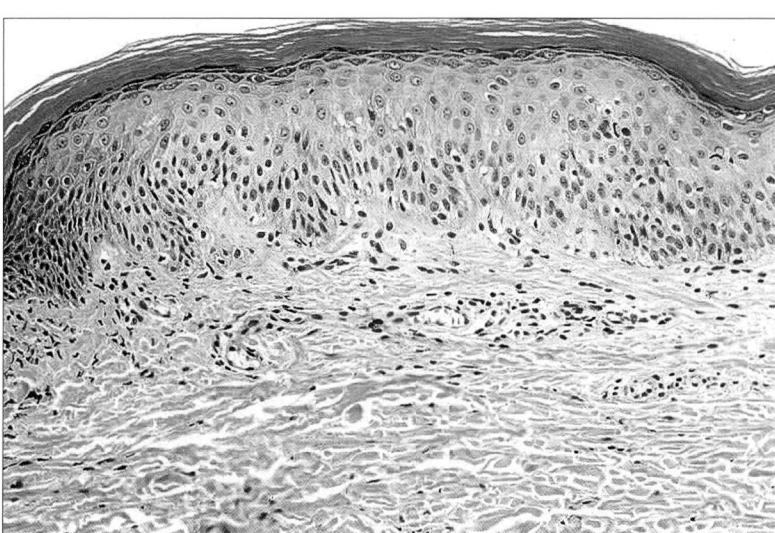

Fig. 2.11
Sex-linked ichthyosis: there is hyperkeratosis and mild acanthosis. The granular cell layer is normal. A mild perivascular lymphocytic infiltrate is present in the superficial dermis.

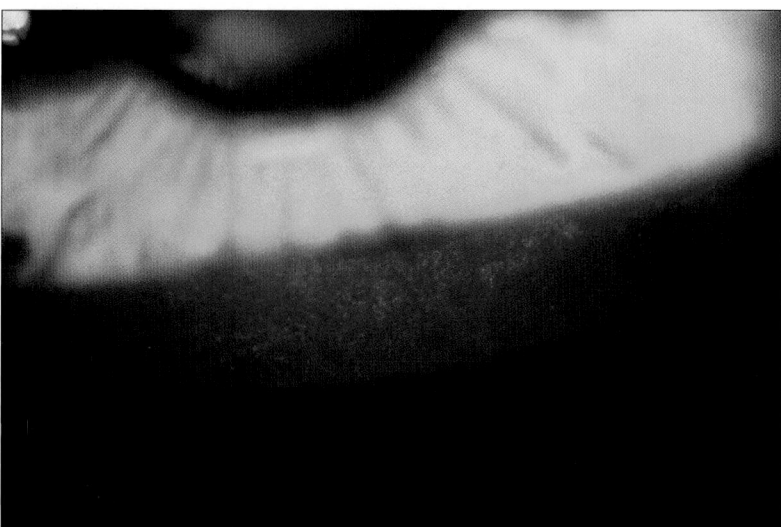

Fig. 2.9
Sex-linked ichthyosis: characteristic linear opacities at the level of Descemet's membrane. Slit-lamp photograph. By courtesy of R.J. Buckley, MD, Moorfield's Eye Hospital, London, UK.

somal dominant variant. Slight acanthosis and a lymphocytic perivascular inflammatory cell infiltrate may be evident. Keratohyalin granules show no abnormality.

X-linked ichthyosis is characterized by a normal proliferation rate.[1]

References

1. Hernández-Marin, A., González-Sarmiento, R., De Unamuno, P. (1999) X-linked ichthyosis: an update. *Br J Dermatol*, **141**, 617–627.
2. Mevorah, B., Krayenbuhl, A., Bovey, E.H. et al (1991) Autosomal dominant ichthyosis and X-linked ichthyosis. *Acta Derm Venereol*, **71**, 431–434.
3. Shwayder, T., Ott, F. (1991) All about ichthyosis. *Pediatr Clin North Am*, **38**, 835–857.
4. Mevorah, B., Frenk, E., Müller, C.R. et al (1981) X-linked recessive ichthyosis in three sisters: evidence for homozygosity. *Br J Dermatol*, **105**, 711–715.
5. Haritoglou, C., Ugele, B., Kenyon, K.R. et al (2000) Corneal manifestations of X-linked ichthyosis in two brothers. *Cornea*, **19**, 861–863.
6. Lykkesfeldt, G., Hoyer, H., Lykkesfeldt, A.E. et al (1983) Steroid sulphatase deficiency associated with testicular cancer. *Lancet*, **2**, 1456.
7. Ghadially, R., Chong, L.P. (1992) Ichthyoses and hyperkeratotic disorders. *Dermatol Clin*, **10**, 597–607.
8. Sever, R.J., Frost, P., Weinstein, G. (1968) Eye changes in ichthyosis. *JAMA*, **206**, 2283–2286.
9. Shapiro, L.J., Buxmann, M.M., Weiss, R. et al (1978) Enzymatic basis of typical X-linked ichthyosis. *Lancet*, **II**, 756–757.
10. Williams, M.L. (1992) Epidermal lipids and scaling diseases of the skin. *Semin Dermatol*, **11**, 169–175.
11. Williams, M.L., Elias, P.M. (1981) Stratum corneum lipids in disorders of cornification. I. Increased cholesterol sulphate content of stratum corneum in recessive X-linked ichthyosis. *J Clin Invest*, **68**, 1404–1410.
12. Arndt, T., Pelzer, M., Nenoff, P. et al (2000) Lipoprotein and apolipoprotein electrophoresis in X-chromosome recessive ichthyosis. *Hautarzt*, **51**, 490–495.
13. Epstein, E.H., Krauss, R.M., Shackleton, C.H.L. (1981) X-linked ichthyosis: increased blood cholesterol sulphate and electrophoretic mobility of low-density lipoprotein. *Science*, **214**, 659–660.
14. Gillard, E.F., Affara, N.A., Yates, J.R. et al (1987) Deletion of a sequence in eight of nine families with X-linked ichthyosis (steroid sulphatase deficiency). *Nucleic Acids Res*, **15**, 3977–3985.
15. Tiepolo, L., Zuffardi, O., Fraccaro, M. et al (1980) Assignment by deletion mapping of the steroid sulphatase X-linked ichthyosis locus to Xp 22.3. *Hum Genet*, **54**, 205–206.
16. Shapiro, L.J., Yen, P., Pomerantz, D. et al (1989) Molecular studies of deletions at the human steroid sulphatase locus. *Proc Natl Acad Sci USA*, **86**, 8477–8481.
17. Herrmann, F.H., Wirth, B., Wulff, K. et al (1989) Gene diagnosis in X-linked ichthyosis. *Arch Dermatol Res*, **280**, 457–461.
18. Aviram-Goldring, A., Goldman, B., Netanelov-Shapira, I. et al (2000) Deletion patterns of STS gene and flanking sequences in Israeli X-linked ichthyosis patients and carriers: analysis by polymerase chain reaction and fluorescence in situ hybridization techniques. *Int J Dermatol*, **39**, 182–187.
19. Valdes-Flores, M., Kofman-Alfaro, S.H., Jimenez-Vaca, A.L. et al (2001) Carrier identification by FISH analysis in isolated cases of X-linked ichthyosis. *Am J Med Genet*, **102**, 146–148.
20. Nomura, K., Nakano, H., Umeki, K. et al (1995) A study of the steroid sulfatase gene in families with X-linked ichthyosis using polymerase chain reaction. *Acta Derm Venereol*, **75**, 340–342.
21. Wells, R.S., Kerr, C.B. (1966) The histology of ichthyosis. *J Invest Dermatol*, **46**, 530–535.
22. Feinstein, A., Ackerman, A.B., Ziprkowski, L. (1970) Histology of autosomal dominant ichthyosis vulgaris and X-linked ichthyosis. *Arch Dermatol*, **101**, 524–527.

Autosomal recessive congenital ichthyosis

Autosomal recessive congenital ichthyosis (ichthyosis congenita) includes lamellar ichthyosis and congenital ichthyosiform erythroderma (congenital non-bullous ichthyosiform erythroderma).[1] Although these variants are clinically and histologically distinct, they represent ends of a spectrum, patients sometimes presenting with lamellar ichthyosis but later showing features of congenital ichthyosiform erythroderma.[2]

References

1. Williams, M.L., Elias, P.M. (1985) Heterogeneity in autosomal recessive lamellar ichthyosis. Clinical and biochemical differentiation of lamellar ichthyosis and non-bullous congenital ichthyosiform erythroderma. *Arch Dermatol*, **121**, 477–488.
2. Bernhardt, M., Baden, H.P. (1986) Report of a family with an unusual expression of recessive ichthyosis. Review of 42 cases. *Arch Dermatol*, **122**, 428–433.

Lamellar ichthyosis

Clinical features

This is a very rare variant (approximately 1:300,000 live births) with an autosomal recessive mode of inheritance.[1] Recently the possibility of an autosomal dominant variant has been raised.[2] The sexes are equally affected. The infant is often born encased in a thick 'collodion' plate-like shell of keratin (*Figs 2.12, 2.13*), and while the term 'collodion baby' is most often applied to cases of lamellar ichthyosis, similar appearances are sometimes found in a number of other disorders such as congenital ichthyosiform erythroderma, Netherton's syndrome, Sjögren–Larsson syndrome and trichothiodystrophy. Within a few days the shell is shed to reveal a mild erythroderma with generalized scaling (*Fig. 2.14*). The scales are large, dark and plate-like and cover the entire body including the palms, soles, scalp and flexures (*Fig. 2.15*).[3,4] Fissuring of the hands and feet occurs and the skin around the joints may become verrucous.[1] There is often associated difficulty with sweating and hyperpyrexia may be a feature.[5] There is nail dystrophy and hair involvement (scarring alopecia), and severe ectropion (up to 80% of patients) and eclabium are characteristic (*Fig. 2.16*).[6] The ectropion is of the cicatricial type and develops as a consequence of excessive dryness and associated contracture of the anterior lamella of the eyelid.[6] Complications include corneal ulceration, vascularization and corneal scarring with eventual blindness.

Primary conjunctival lesions have also been described including ichthyosis, keratinization, hyper- and parakeratosis and papilla development. The teeth are not affected.

Pathogenesis and histological features

Epidermopoiesis is normal or marginally increased.[7] Mutations, deletions and insertions in the transglutaminase 1 gene (*TGM 1*) (with resultant defective attachment and cross-linking of cell envelope proteins), mapped to 14q.11, have been identified in a subgroup of patients with lamellar ichthyosis.[8–14] The condition however is heterogeneous.[15,16] The lamellar ichthyosis phenotype has thus also been mapped to multiple other sites including chromosomes 2q33–35, 3p21 and 19p12–q12.[17–19]

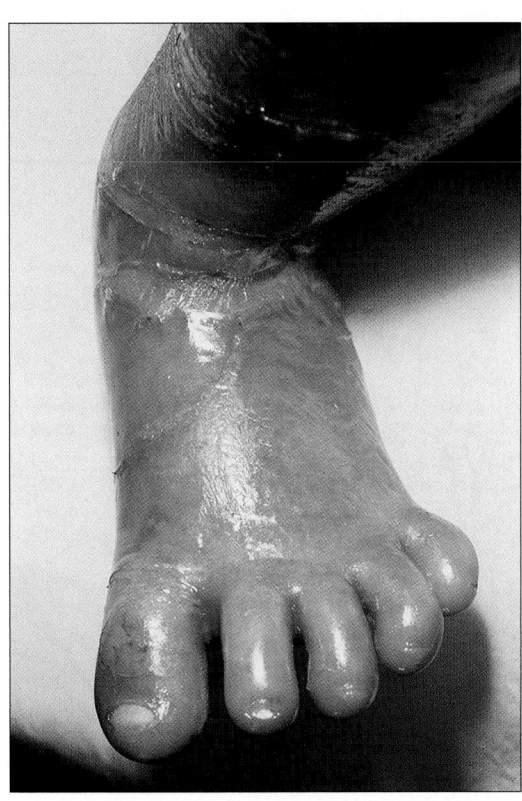

Fig. 2.13
Lamellar ichthyosis: note the erythema. The skin is shiny, taut and shows fissuring around the anterior aspect of the ankle. By courtesy of D. Atherton, MD, Children's Hospital at Great Ormond Street, London, UK.

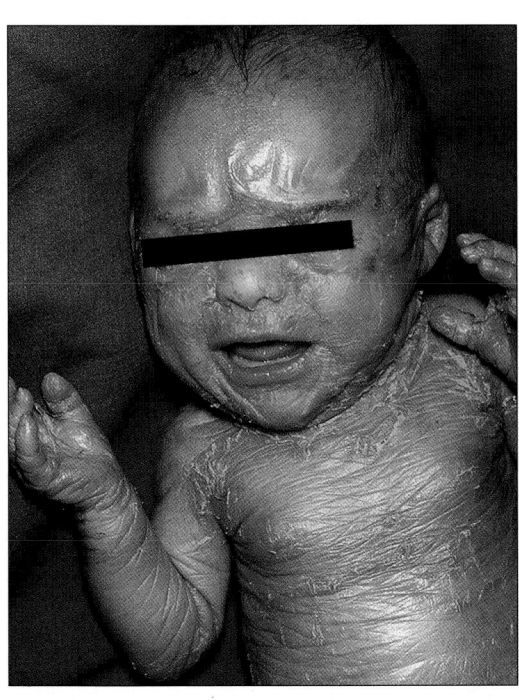

Fig. 2.12
Lamellar ichthyosis: the collodion membrane is best seen on the forehead. There is scaling and erythema on the trunk. By courtesy of R.A. Marsden, MD, St George's Hospital, London, UK.

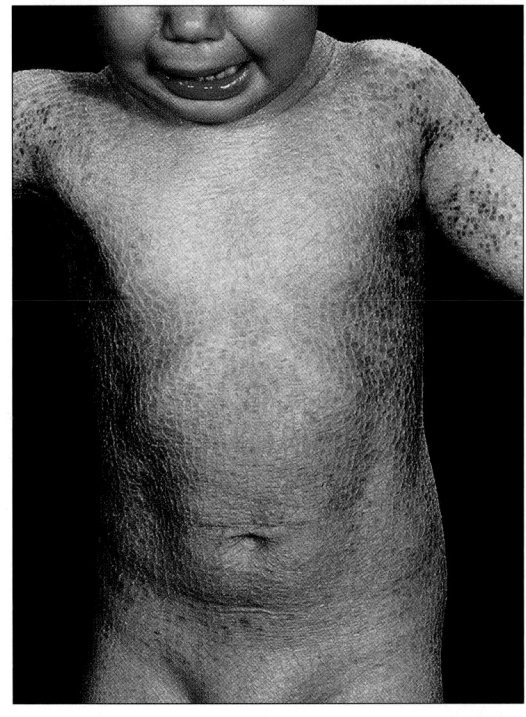

Fig. 2.14
Lamellar ichthyosis: note the widespread and prominent large dark brown scales. By courtesy of D. Atherton, MD, Children's Hospital at Great Ormond Street, London, UK.

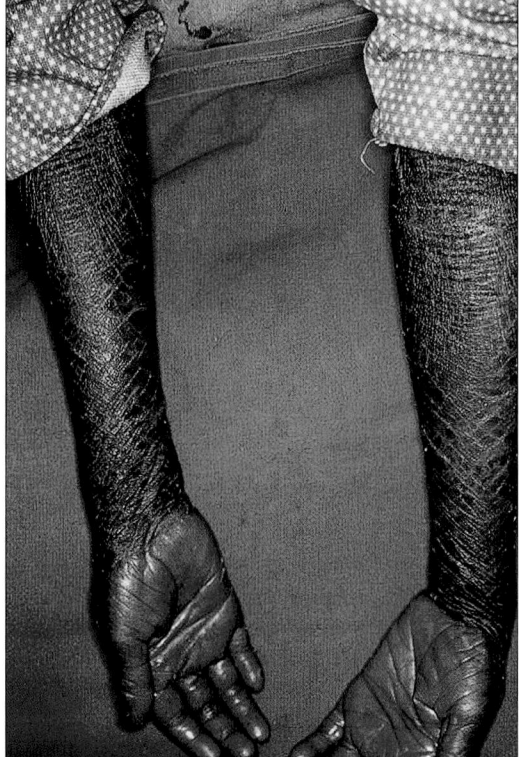

Fig. 2.15
Lamellar ichthyosis: in this adult patient, the scales are large and plate-like. By courtesy of W.A.D. Griffiths, MD, Institute of Dermatology, London, UK.

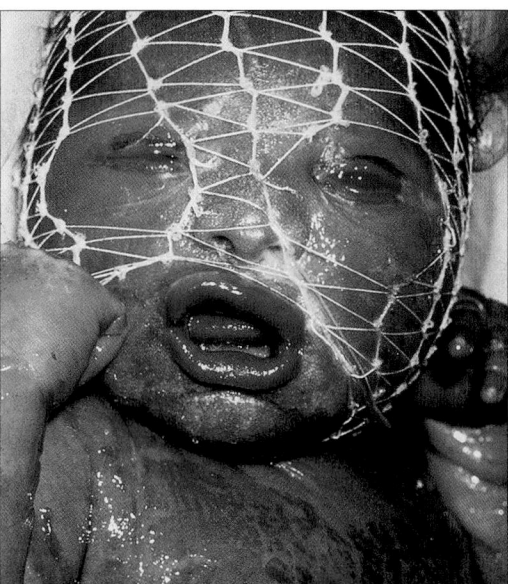

Fig. 2.16
Lamellar ichthyosis: in this infant, there is gross ectropion and eclabion. By courtesy of D. Atherton, MD, Children's Hospital at Great Ormond Street, London, UK.

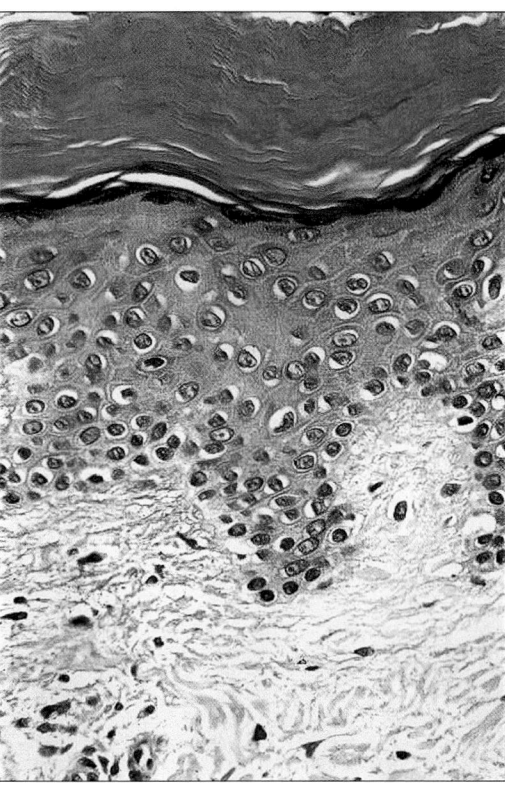

Fig. 2.17
Lamellar ichthyosis: there is very marked compact hyperkeratosis with a conspicuous granular cell layer.

Lesions show marked hyperkeratosis (which may be extreme in the collodion baby) and mild acanthosis with a normal or thickened granular cell layer (*Fig. 2.17*). Epidermal papillomatosis associated with a psoriasiform appearance has also been documented.[4] Dilatation and tortuosity of the dermal capillaries is sometimes evident. Follicular hyperkeratosis may occasionally be a feature.

Ultrastructural studies show defective development of the cornified cell envelopes and electron-dense debris adjacent to the plasma membranes.[14]

Prenatal diagnosis of lamellar ichthyosis can be achieved by fetoscopy and biopsy.[20]

References

1. Rand, R.E., Baden, H.P. (1983) The ichthyoses – a review. *J Am Acad Dermatol*, **8**, 285–305.
2. Traupe, H., Kolde, G., Happle, R. (1984) Autosomal dominant lamellar ichthyosis: a new skin disorder. *Clin Genet*, **26**, 457–461.
3. Williams, M.L., Elias, P.M. (1985) Heterogeneity in autosomal recessive lamellar ichthyosis. Clinical and biochemical differentiation of lamellar ichthyosis and non-bullous congenital ichthyosiform erythroderma. *Arch Dermatol*, **121**, 477–488.
4. Shwayder, T., Ott, F. (1991) All about ichthyosis. *Pediatr Clin North Am*, **38**, 835–857.
5. Ghadially, R. (1992) Ichthyoses and hyperkeratotic disorders. *Dermatol Clin*, **10**, 597–607.
6. Cruz, A.A., Menezes, F.A., Chaves, R. et al (2000) Eyelid abnormalities in lamellar ichthyosis. *Ophthalmology*, **107**, 1895–1898.
7. Hazell, M., Marks, R. (1985) Clinical, histologic and cell kinetic discriminants between lamellar ichthyosis and nonbullous congenital ichthyosiform erythroderma. *Arch Dermatol*, **121**, 489–493.
8. Candida, A., van Hooijdonk, E.M., Steijlen, P.M. et al (1991) Epidermal transglutaminase in the ichthyoses. *Acta Derm Venereol*, **71**, 173–175.
9. Laiho, E., Ignatius, J., Mikkola, H. et al (1997) Transglutaminase 1 mutations in autosomal recessive congenital ichthyosis: private and recurrent mutations in an isolated population. *Am J Hum Genet*, **61**, 529–538.
10. Huber, M., Rettler, I., Bernasconi, K. et al (1995) Mutations of keratinocyte transglutaminase in lamellar ichthyosis. *Science*, **267**, 525–528.
11. Russell, L.J., DiGiovanna, J.J., Rogers, G.R. et al (1995) Mutations in the gene for transglutaminase 1 in autosomal recessive lamellar ichthyosis. *Nat Genet*, **9**, 279–283.
12. Yang, J.M., Ahn, K.S., Cho, M.O. et al (2001) Novel mutations of the transglutaminase 1 gene in lamellar ichthyosis. *J Invest Dermatol*, **117**, 214–218.
13. Esposito, G., Auricchio, L., Rescigno, G. et al (2001) Transglutaminase 1 gene mutations in Italian patients with autosomal recessive lamellar ichthyosis. *J Invest Dermatol*, **116**, 809–812.
14. Yotsumoto, Y., Akiyama, M., Yoneda, K. et al (2000) Analysis of the transglutaminase gene mutation and ultrastructural characteristics in a Japanese patient with lamellar ichthyosis. *J Dermatol Sci*, **24**, 119–125.
15. Huber, M., Rettler, I., Bernasconi, R. et al (1995) Lamellar ichthyosis is genetically heterogeneous – cases with normal keratinocyte transglutaminase. *J Invest Dermatol*, **105**, 653–654.
16. Bale, S.J., Russell, L.J., Lee, M.L. et al (1996) Congenital recessive ichthyosis unlinked to loci for epidermal transglutaminases. *J Invest Dermatol*, **107**, 808–811.
17. Parmentier, L., Lakhdar, H. Blanchet-Bardon, C. et al (1996) Mapping for a second locus for lamellar ichthyosis to chromosome 2q33–35. *Hum Mol Genet*, **5**, 555–559.
18. Parmentier, L., Clepet, C., Boughdene-Stambouli, O. et al (1999) Lamellar ichthyosis: further narrowing, physical expression mapping of the chromosome 2 candidate locus. *Eur J Hum Genet*, **7**, 77–87.
19. Fischer, J., Faure, A., Bouadjar, B. et al (2000) Two new loci for autosomal recessive ichthyosis on chromosome 3p21 and 19p12–q12 and evidence for further genetic heterogeneity. *Am J Hum Genet*, **66**, 904–913.
20. Perry, T.B., Holbrook, K., Hoff, M.S. et al (1987) Prenatal diagnosis of congenital nonbullous ichthyosiform erythroderma (lamellar ichthyosis). *Prenat Diagn*, **7**, 145–155.

Congenital ichthyosiform erythroderma

Clinical features

This also has an autosomal recessive mode of inheritance. A collodion membrane is often present at birth.[1] After shedding, the infant typically presents with an intense generalized erythroderma.[2] While plate-like scales may be seen on the extensor surfaces of the legs, the scalp, face, upper extremities and trunk are covered with fine white scaling (*Figs 2.18–2.23*).[1,3] Mild ectropion and eclabium may be complications and palmoplantar keratoderma is sometimes evident. Exceptionally, congenital ichthyosiform erythroderma has been associated with retinitis pigmentosa.[4] There is an increased risk of developing skin cancer including basal and squamous cell carcinomas.[5]

Pathogenesis and histological features

Congenital ichthyosiform erythroderma is associated with increased epidermopoiesis.[3,6] Mutations in lipoxygenase-3 (ALOXE3) and 12(R)-lipoxygenase (ALOX12B) have been identified in a kindred of six families.[7] A loricrin gene mutation has been identified in another family presenting with this phenotype although the subsequent clinical manifestations became more suggestive of a palmoplantar keratoderma variant.[8] The pathogenesis is at least in part mediated by defective and irregularly distributed lamellar granules showing intracytoplasmic accumulation of transglutaminase 1.[9]

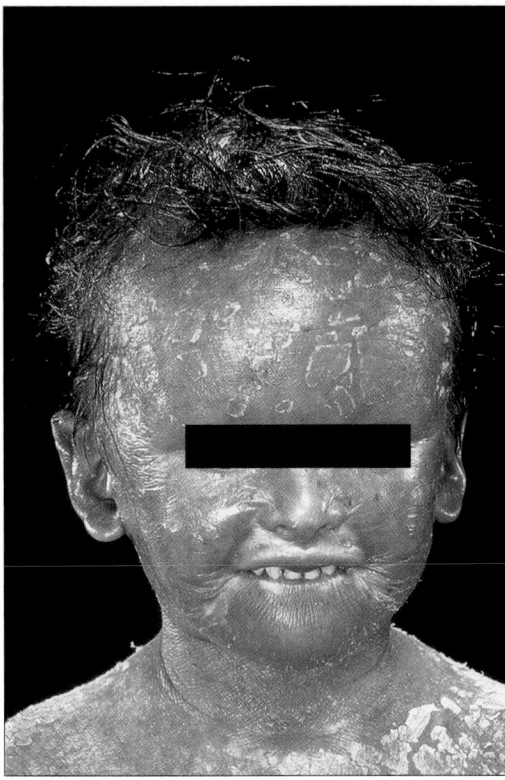

Fig. 2.18
Congenital ichthyosiform erythroderma: there is intense erythema and fine scaling is also present. The scalp hair is sparse and the eyebrows are absent. By courtesy of D. Atherton, MD, Children's Hospital at Great Ormond Street, London, UK.

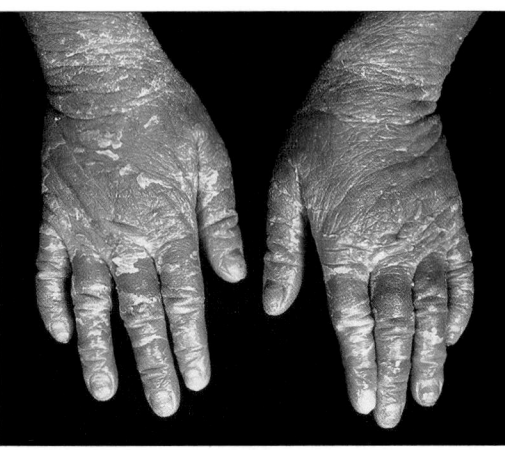

Fig. 2.19
Congenital ichthyosiform erythroderma: there is marked erythema with severe scaling. Blistering is not seen in this variant of ichthyosis. By courtesy of D. Atherton, MD, Children's Hospital at Great Ormond Street, London, UK.

This variant is characterized by hyperkeratosis, focal parakeratosis and acanthosis.[2,3] The granular cell layer may be normal or increased in thickness. The hyperkeratosis is much less marked than that seen in lamellar ichthyosis.[2]

Ultrastructurally, there are conspicuous lipid droplets and increased numbers of small and dysmorphic lamellar bodies.[8,10]

References

1. Shwayder, T., Ott, F. (1991) All about ichthyosis. *Pediatr Clin North Am*, **38**, 835–857.
2. Williams, M.L., Elias, P.M. (1985) Heterogeneity in autosomal recessive lamellar ichthyosis. Clinical and biochemical differentiation of lamellar ichthyosis and non-bullous congenital ichthyosiform erythroderma. *Arch Dermatol*, **121**, 477–488.
3. Hazell, M., Marks, R. (1985) Clinical, histologic, and cell kinetic discriminants between lamellar ichthyosis and non-bullous congenital ichthyosiform erythroderma. *Arch Dermatol*, **121**, 489–493.
4. Rajagopalan, B. (2001) Non-bullous ichthyosiform erythroderma associated with retinitis pigmentosa. *Am J Med Genet*, **15**, 181–184.

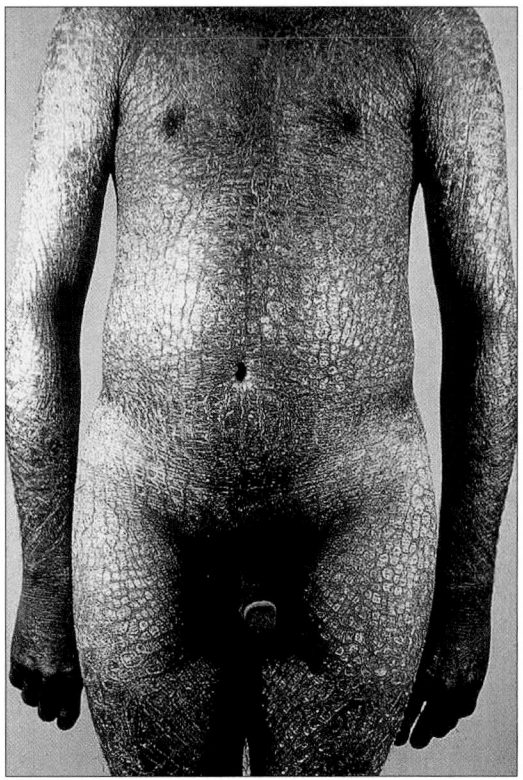

Fig. 2.21
Congenital ichthyosiform erythroderma: there is generalized plate-like scaling. By courtesy of the Institute of Dermatology, London, UK.

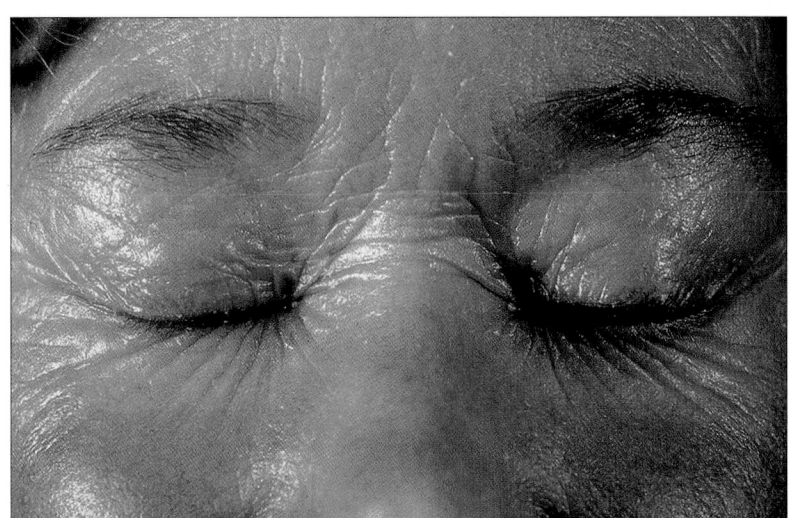

Fig. 2.20
Congenital ichthyosiform erythroderma: there is intensive erythema and fine scaling. By courtesy of the Institute of Dermatology, London, UK.

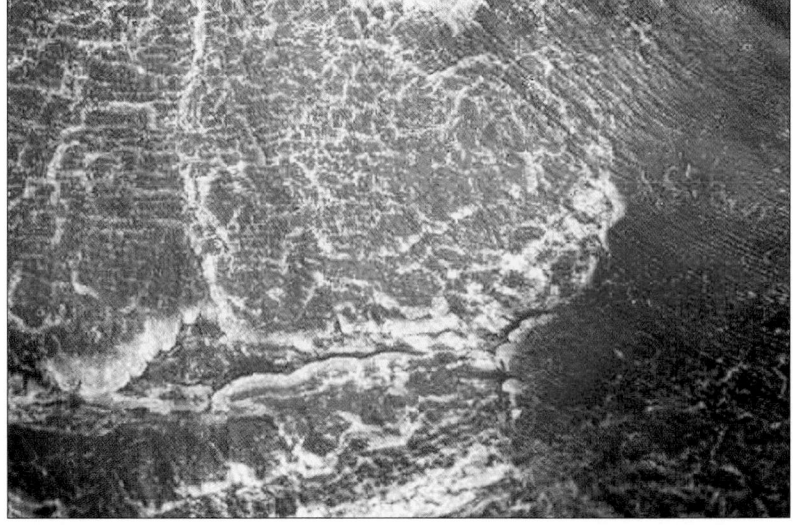

Fig. 2.22
Congenital ichthyosiform erythroderma: the scales are large, thick and white. By courtesy of the Institute of Dermatology, London, UK.

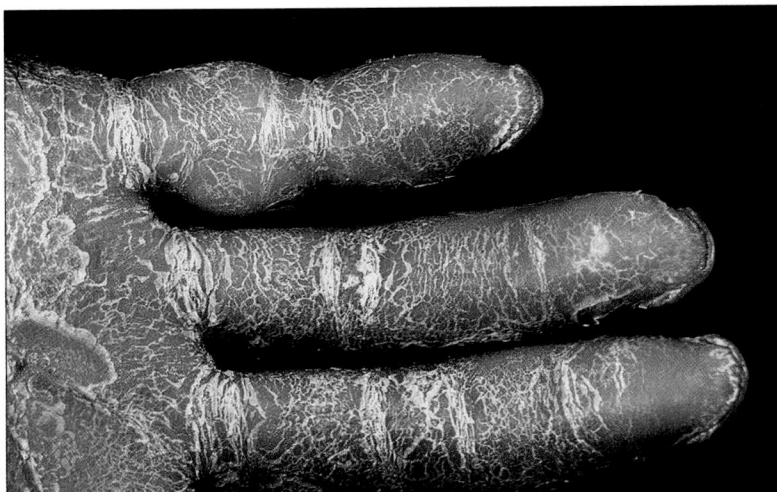

Fig. 2.23
Congenital ichthyosiform erythroderma: there is severe palmar involvement and constriction bands are evident. By courtesy of the Institute of Dermatology, London, UK.

5. Elbaum, D.J., Kurz, G., MacDuff, M. (1995) Increased incidence of cutaneous carcinomas in patients with congenital ichthyosis. *J Am Acad Dermatol*, **33**, 884–886.
6. Dover, R., Burge, S., Ralfs, I. et al (1986) Congenital non-bullous ichthyosiform erythroderma – cell kinetics before and after treatment with etretinate. *Clin Exp Dermatol*, **11**, 431–435.
7. Jobard, F., Lefèvre, C., Karaduman, A. et al (2002) Lipoxygenase-3 (ALOXE3) and 12(R)-lipoxygenase (ALOX12B) are mutated in non-bullous congenital ichthyosiform erythroderma (NCIE) linked to chromosome 17p13.1. *Hum Mol Genet*, **11**, 107–113.
8. Matsumoto, K., Muto, M., Seki, S. et al (2001) Loricrin keratoderma: a cause of congenital ichthyosiform erythroderma and collodion baby. *Br J Dermatol*, **145**, 657–660.
9. Ammirati, C.T., Mallory, S.B. (1988) The major inherited disorders of cornification: new advances in pathogenesis. *Dermatol Clin*, **16**, 497–508.
10. Ghadially, R., Williams, M.L., Hou, S.Y.E. et al (1992) Membrane structure abnormalities in the stratum corneum of the autosomal recessive ichthyoses. *J Invest Dermatol*, **99**, 755–763.

Congenital bullous ichthyosiform erythroderma

Clinical features

Congenital bullous ichthyosiform erythroderma (also known as epidermolytic hyperkeratosis, bullous ichthyosis, bullous erythroderma ichthyosiformis congenita of Brocq) is a very rare disease (incidence of 1:300,000 births) and, although sometimes inherited by an autosomal dominant mode, it more often appears to arise by spontaneous mutation. At birth the infant may show marked hyperkeratosis, erythroderma, or even present as a collodion baby. Although the scales are soon lost, leaving a generalized moist, tender erythroderma, re-epithelialization leads to further scale production followed by the development of widespread blistering (*Figs 2.24, 2.25*) which heals without scarring. As the patient becomes older, the erythema and blistering become less apparent and, later, the disease is complicated by the development of verrucous hyperkeratosis, especially in the flexures (*Figs 2.26–2.30*). The scales have been said to assume a porcupine quill-like appearance (ichthyosis hystrix) and scalp involvement may simulate tinea capitis.[1] Nail dystrophy may sometimes be a feature. Congenital bullous ichthyosiform erythroderma is associated with considerable morbidity and significant mortality due to sepsis, fluid loss and electrolyte imbalance.[1]

A nevoid variant in which the lesions follow Blaschko's lines is also recognized.[2] In the past such lesions may have been mistaken for epidermal nevi showing epidermolytic hyperkeratosis. Offspring of affected patients with the nevoid variant may show the features of generalized congenital bullous ichthyosiform erythroderma. Exceptionally, an annular variant may also be encountered.[3]

Pathogenesis and histological features

This condition is associated with markedly increased epidermopoiesis.[4] There is considerable evidence in the recent literature confirming that congenital bullous ichthyosiform erythroderma represents a genetic disorder of keratin expression.[5] Transgenic mouse studies using a truncated human keratin 10 gene have been shown to result in the pathobiological and biochemical phenotype of epidermolytic hyperkeratosis.[6] Epidermolytic hyperkeratosis shows linkage to the type II keratin gene cluster on chromosome 12q.[7,8] Direct sequencing of keratin 1 and 10 genes have identified point mutations in a number of affected families.[9–15] Interestingly, keratin 1 mutations are associated with severe palmoplantar hyperkeratosis while keratin 10 mutations are not.[13] A heterozygous point mutation in the keratin 10 gene has also been

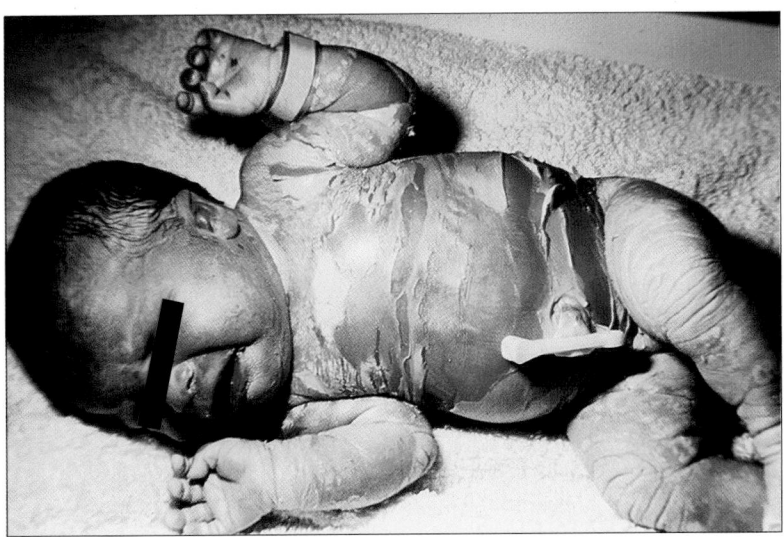

Fig. 2.24
Congenital bullous ichthyosiform erythroderma: newborn infant with widespread blistering involving the torso. The arms display more obvious ichthyotic features. By courtesy of the late M. Beare, MD, Royal Victoria Hospital, Belfast, N. Ireland.

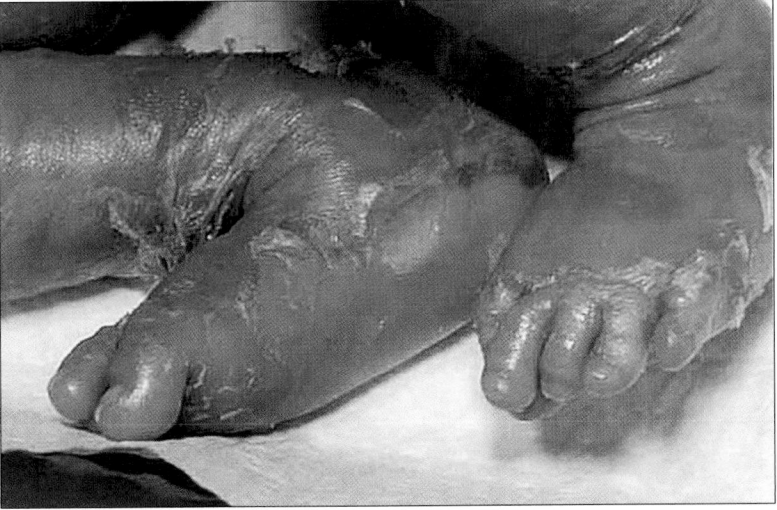

Fig. 2.25
Congenital bullous ichthyosiform erythroderma: close-up view showing intense erythema and blistering. By courtesy of M. Liang, MD, The Children's Hospital, Boston, USA.

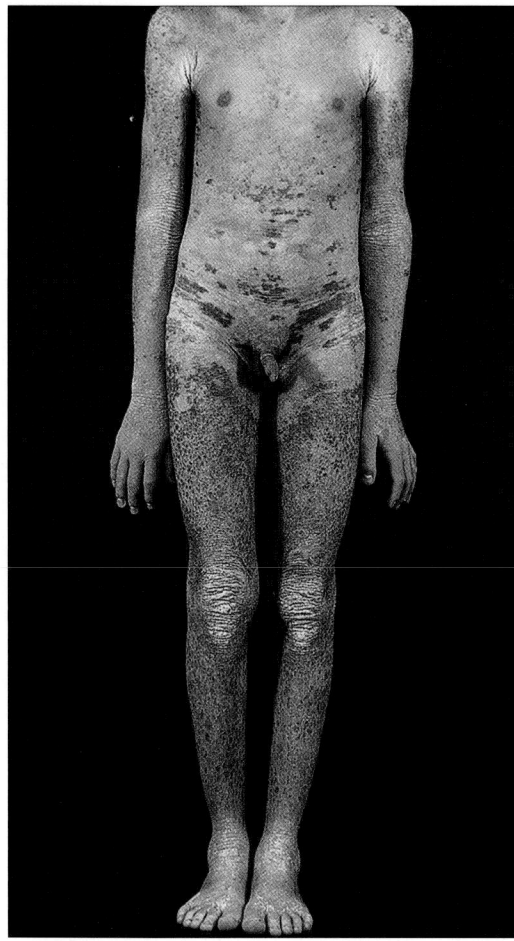

Fig. 2.26
Congenital bullous ichthyosiform erythroderma: adult showing very generalized scaling, particularly severe on the legs. By courtesy of the Institute of Dermatology, London, UK.

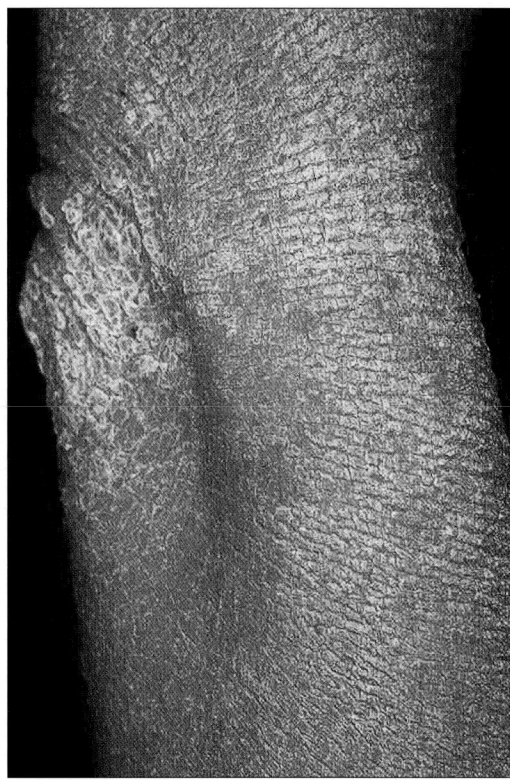

Fig. 2.27
Congenital bullous ichthyosiform erythroderma: same patient as *Fig. 2.26* showing elbow involvement. By courtesy of the Institute of Dermatology, London, UK.

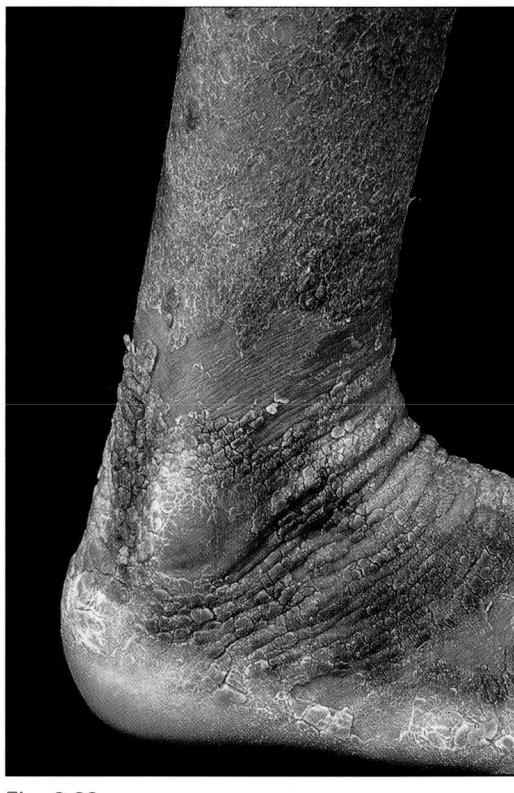

Fig. 2.29
Congenital bullous ichthyosiform erythroderma: blistering may sometimes be seen in adulthood. By courtesy of the Institute of Dermatology, London, UK.

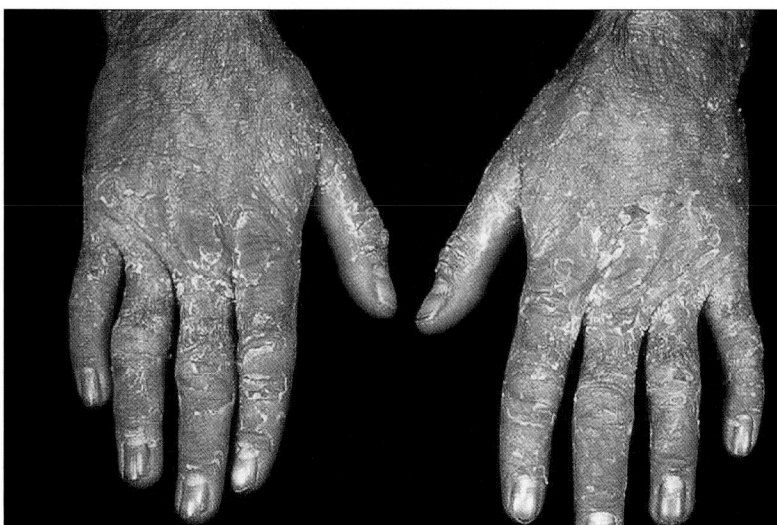

Fig. 2.28
Congenital bullous ichthyosiform erythroderma: the hands are particularly affected. By courtesy of the Institute of Dermatology, London, UK.

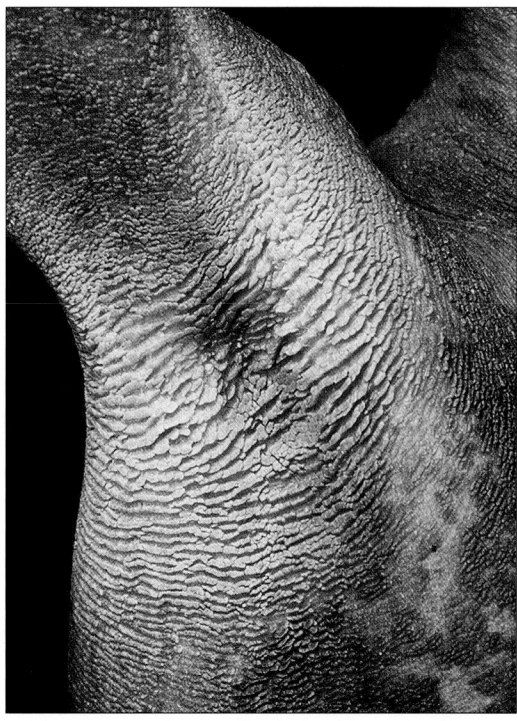

Fig. 2.30
Congenital bullous ichthyosiform erythroderma: adult showing very severe verrucous flexural scaling. By courtesy of R.A.J. Eady, MD, Institute of Dermatology, London, UK.

identified in the nevoid variant of congenital bullous ichthyosiform erythroderma.[16,17]

The histological features are known as epidermolytic hyperkeratosis or granular degeneration and are very striking.[18,19] There is massive hyperkeratosis, papillomatosis and acanthosis associated with a greatly thickened and abnormal granular cell layer, which typically contains irregular, enlarged and intensely eosinophilic intracytoplasmic inclusions (*Figs 2.31–2.33*). Suprabasal keratinocytes show marked intracellular edema (cytolysis), which eventually results in breakdown and intraepidermal blister formation.

By immunocytochemistry epidermolytic hyperkeratosis shows a normal distribution pattern of keratins 5/14 and 1/10, but in addition there is overexpression of keratin 14 in the suprabasal epithelium accompanied by quite marked labeling of the upper epithelial layers by keratin 16, as would be expected in a hyperproliferative state.[20]

Ultrastructural studies have shown that the intracytoplasmic inclusions seen on light microscopy are composed of both abnormally aggregated keratin filaments, and enlarged, often smooth-edged, electron-dense keratohyalin granules (*Fig. 2.34*).[18] While basal keratinocytes appear normal, the abnormal keratin is distributed throughout the entire suprabasal thickness of the epithelium. These changes, which appear to precede cytolysis, may form the basis of prenatal diagnosis including amniotic fluid squame analysis.[18,19]

Immunoelectron microscopy has identified that the keratin filaments are composed of keratins 1 and 10.[20]

Differential diagnosis

In the correct context, the features of congenital bullous ichthyosiform erythroderma are diagnostic. However, the changes of epidermolytic hyperkeratosis may be associated with a variety of other lesions, including linear verrucous epidermal nevus, epidermolytic keratoderma and epidermolytic acanthoma. It may also represent an incidental finding in seborrheic keratosis, actinic keratosis, in situ squamous cell carcinoma, invasive squamous cell carcinoma, nevi, epidermal and pilar cysts.[21] Epidermolytic hyperkeratosis may also be seen in normal, particularly actinically damaged skin. In such incidental lesions, the changes are limited to the epidermis overlying just one or two dermal papillae in contrast to the much more extensive involvement of the other conditions mentioned above. Therefore, accurate clinical information is necessary to avoid diagnostic confusion.

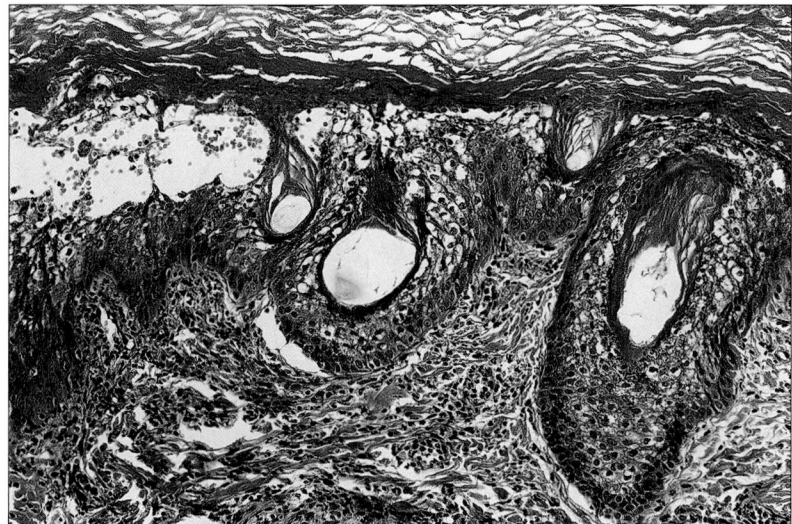

Fig. 2.31
Congenital bullous ichthyosiform erythroderma: there is massive hyperkeratosis and acanthosis. The epidermis shows conspicuous superficial vacuolation which has resulted in vesiculation.

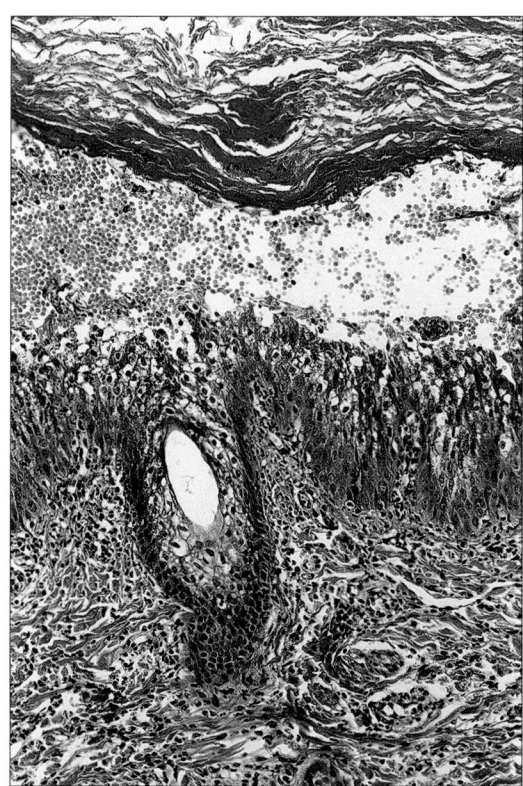

Fig. 2.32
Congenital bullous ichthyosiform erythroderma: close-up view showing vacuolation.

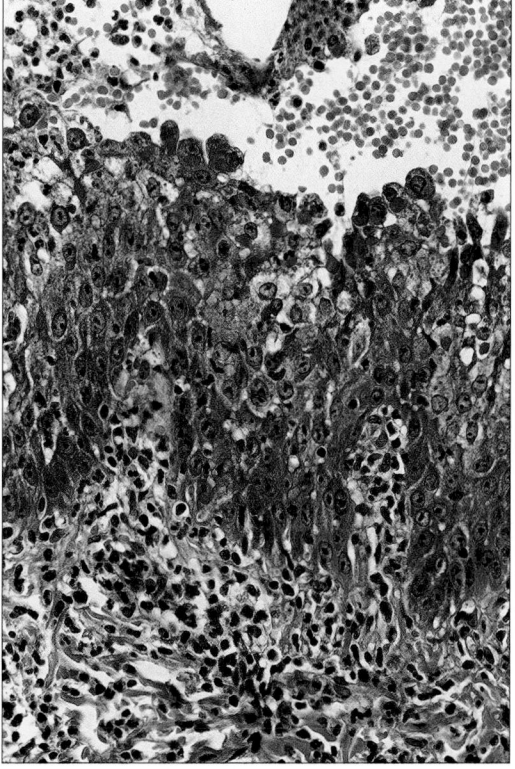

Fig. 2.33
Congenital bullous ichthyosiform erythroderma: there is intracellular edema, and irregular eosinophilic granules (representing dense abnormal aggregates of keratin filaments) are present in the superficial layers of the epidermis.

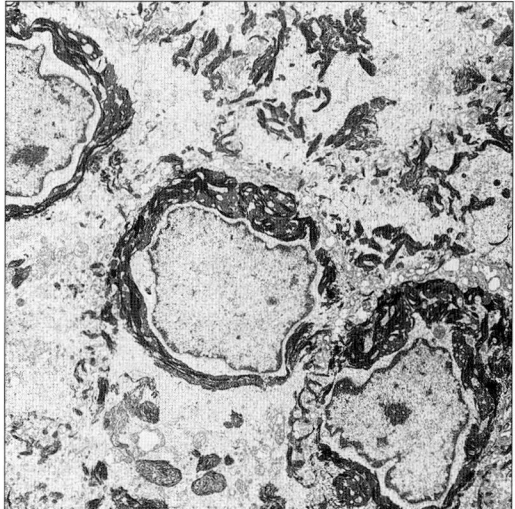

Fig. 2.34
Congenital bullous ichthyosiform erythroderma: striking perinuclear keratin clumping is evident. By courtesy of R.A.J. Eady, MD, Institute of Dermatology, London, UK.

References

1. Shwayder, T., Ott, F. (1991) All about ichthyosis. *Pediatr Clin North Am* **38**, 835–857.
2. Irvine A.D., McLean W.H.I. (1999) Human keratin diseases: the increasing spectrum of disease and subtlety of the phenotype–genotype correlation. *Br J Dermatol*, **140**, 815–828.
3. Yoneda, K., Morita, E., Akiyama, M. et al (1999) Annular epidermolytic ichthyosis. *Br J Dermatol*, **141**, 748–750.
4. Frost, P., Weinstein, G.D., Van Scott, E.J. (1966) The ichthyosiform dermatoses II. Autoradiographic studies of epidermal proliferation. *J Invest Dermatol*, **47**, 561–567.
5. Fuchs, E. (1992) Genetic skin disorders of keratin. *J Invest Dermatol*, **99**, 671–674.
6. Fuchs, E., Esteves, R.A., Coulombe, P.A. (1992) Transgenic mice expressing a mutant keratin 10 gene reveal the likely genetic basis for epidermolytic hyperkeratosis. *Proc Natl Acad Sci USA*, **89**, 6906–6910.
7. Compton, J.G., Digiovanna, J.J., Santucci, S.K. et al (1992) Linkage of epidermolytic hyperkeratosis to the type II keratin gene cluster on chromosome 12q. *Nat Genet*, **1**, 301–305.
8. Bonifas, J.M., Bare, J.W., Chen, M.A. et al (1992) Linkage of the epidermolytic hyperkeratosis phenotype and the region of the type II keratin gene cluster on chromosome 12. *J Invest Dermatol*, **99**, 524–527.
9. Cheng, J., Syder, A.J., Yu, Q-C. et al (1992) The genetic basis of epidermolytic hyperkeratosis: a disorder of differentiation – specific epidermal keratin genes. *Cell*, **70**, 811–819.
10. Chipev, C.C., Korge, B.P., Markova, N. et al (1992) A leucine–proline mutation in the H1 subdomain of keratin 1 causes epidermolytic hyperkeratosis. *Cell*, **70**, 821–828.
11. Rothnagel, J.A., Dominey, A.M., Dempsey, L.D. et al (1992) Mutations in the rod domains of keratins 1 and 10 in epidermolytic hyperkeratosis. *Science*, **257**, 1128–1130.
12. Whittock, N.V., Ashton, G.H., Griffiths, W.A. et al (2001) New mutations in keratin 1 that cause bullous congenital ichthyosiform erythroderma and keratin 2e that cause ichthyosis bullosa of Siemens. *Br J Dermatol*, **145**, 330–335.
13. DiCiovanna, J.J., Bale, S.J. (1994) Clinical heterogeneity in epidermolytic hyperkeratosis. *Arch Dermatol*, **130**, 1026–1035.
14. Mayuzumi, N., Shigihara, T., Ikeda, S. et al (2000) Recurrent R156H mutation in a Japanese family with bullous congenital ichthyosiform erythroderma. *J Eur Acad Dermatol Venereol*, **14**, 304–306.
15. Arin, M.J., Longley, M.A., Epstein, E.H. Jr et al (2000) Identification of a novel mutation in keratin 1 in a family with epidermolytic hyperkeratosis. *Exp Dermatol*, **9**, 16–19.
16. Paller, A.S., Syder, A.J., Chan, Y.M. et al (1994) Genetic and clinical mosaicism in a type of epidermal nevus. *N Engl J Med*, **331**, 1408–1415.
17. Moss, C., Jones, D.O., Blight, A. et al (1995) Birthmark due to cutaneous mosaicism for keratin 10 mutation. *Lancet*, **345**, 596.
18. Holbrook, K.A., Dale, B.A., Sybert, V.P. et al (1983) Epidermolytic hyperkeratosis: ultrastructure and biochemistry of skin and amniotic fluid cells from two affected fetuses and a newborn infant. *J Invest Dermatol*, **80**, 222–227.
19. Anton-Lamprecht, I. (1983) Genetically induced abnormalities of epidermal differentiation and ultrastructure in ichthyoses and epidermolyses: pathogenesis, heterogeneity, fetal manifestation and pre-natal diagnosis. *J Invest Dermatol*, **81**, 149S–156S.
20. Ishida-Yamamoto, A., McGrath, J.A., Judge, M.R. et al (1992) Selective involvement of keratins K1 and K10 in the cytoskeletal abnormality of epidermolytic hyperkeratosis (bullous congenital ichthyosiform erythroderma). *J Invest Dermatol*, **99**, 19–26.
21. Ackerman, A.B. (1970) Histopathologic concept of epidermolytic hyperkeratosis. *Arch Dermatol*, **102**, 253–259.

5. Rothnagel, J.A., Traupe, H., Wojcik, S. et al (1994) Mutations in the rod domain of keratin 2e in patients with ichthyosis bullosa of Siemens. *Nat Genet*, **7**, 485–490.
6. McLean, W.H.I., Morley, S.M., Lane, E.B. et al (1994) Ichthyosis bullosa of Siemens – a disease involving keratin 2e. *J Invest Dermatol*, **103**, 277–281.
7. Steijlen, P., Kremer, H., Vakkilzadeh, F. et al (1994) Genetic linkage of the keratin type II gene cluster with ichthyosis bullosa of Siemens and with autosomal dominant ichthyosis exfoliativa. *J Invest Dermatol*, **103**, 282–285.
8. Irvine, A.D., Smith, F.J., Shum, K.W. et al (2000) A novel mutation in the 2B domain of keratin 2e causing ichthyosis bullosa of Siemens. *Clin Exp Dermatol*, **25**, 648–651.
9. Whittock, N.V., Ashton, G.H., Griffiths, W.A. et al (2001) New mutations in keratin 1 that cause bullous congenital ichthyosiform erythroderma and keratin 2e that cause ichthyosis bullosa of Siemens. *Br J Dermatol*, **145**, 330–335.

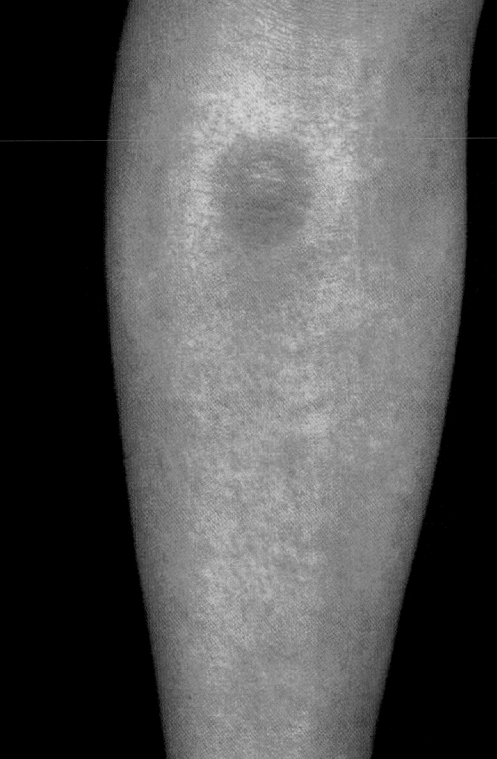

Fig. 2.35
Bullous ichthyosis Siemens: flexural hyperkeratosis with early blister formation. By courtesy of W.A.D. Griffiths, MD, Institute of Dermatology, London, UK.

Ichthyosis bullosa of Siemens

Clinical features

Ichthyosis bullosa of Siemens is inherited as an autosomal dominant. The condition, which is milder than congenital bullous ichthyosiform erythroderma, presents at birth with blistering subsequently replaced by lichenified hyperkeratosis of the limbs, predominantly affecting the flexures and shins (*Fig. 2.35*).[1,2] The skin remains fragile and blisters on mild trauma, giving rise to characteristic superficial peeling with a molting-like appearance (Mauserung phenomenon) (*Fig. 2.36*).[2,3] Symptoms usually improve with age. Erythroderma is typically absent. Rarely pustulation and hypertrichosis may be additional features.[3,4] There is considerable clinical overlap between ichthyosis bullosa of Siemens and congenital bullous ichthyosiform erythroderma and their distinction can best be achieved by molecular genetic analysis.

Pathogenesis and histological features

Bullous ichthyosis is associated with a point mutation in the keratin 2e gene.[4–9]

Histologically and by electron microscopy, the features are indistinguishable from congenital bullous ichthyosiform erythroderma except that they are milder and the epidermolysis and cytoplasmic inclusions are restricted to the more superficial prickle and granular cell layers as opposed to involving almost the entire epidermis as is typical of the latter condition. Subcorneal separation may be evident.

References

1. Traupe, H., Kolde, G., Hamm, H. et al (1986) Ichthyosis bullosa of Siemens: a unique type of epidermolytic hyperkeratosis. *J Am Acad Dermatol*, **14**, 1000–1005.
2. Murdoch, M.E., Leigh, I.M. (1990) Ichthyosis bullosa of Siemens and bullous ichthyosiform erythroderma – variants of the same disease? *Clin Exp Dermatol*, **15**, 53–56.
3. Steijlen, P.M., Perret, C.M., Schuurmans Stekhoven, J.H. et al (1990) Ichthyosis bullosa of Siemens: further delineation of the phenotype. *Arch Dermatol Res*, **282**, 1–5.
4. Basarab, T., Smith, F.J., Jolliffe, V.M. et al (1999) Ichthyosis bullosa of Siemens: report of a family with evidence of a keratin 2e mutation and a review of the literature. *Br J Dermatol*, **140**, 689–695.

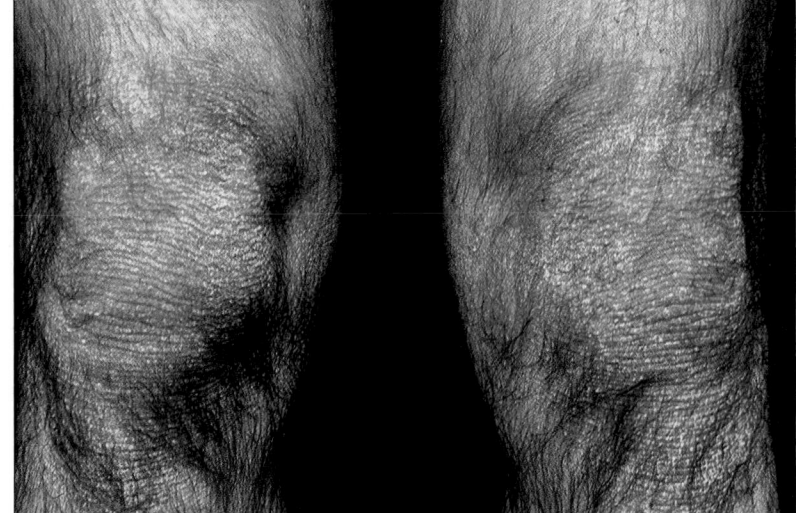

Fig. 2.36
Bullous ichthyosis Siemens: marked hyperkeratosis is present over the knees and extending onto the shins. By courtesy of W.A.D. Griffiths, MD, Institute of Dermatology, London, UK.

Linear epidermolytic epidermal nevus

Linear verrucous epidermal nevi occasionally show the features of epidermolytic hyperkeratosis. Some patients with such a lesion, although by no means all, in reality suffer from the nevoid variant of congenital bullous ichthyosiform erythroderma.[1–4] It is therefore important that patients with apparent epidermolytic epidermal nevi are offered genetic counseling. This topic is considered in more depth on page 45.

References

1. Paller, A.S., Syder, A.J., Chan, Y.M. et al (1994) Genetic and clinical mosaicism in a type of epidermal nevus. *N Engl J Med*, **331**, 1408–1415.
2. Moss, C., Jones, D.O., Blight, A. et al (1995) Birthmark due to cutaneous mosaicism for keratin 10 mutation. *Lancet*, **345**, 596.
3. Ang, P., Tay, Y.K. (1998) Linear epidermolytic epidermal nevus – a case report. *Singapore Med J*, **39**, 220–221.
4. Irvine, A.D., McLean, W.H.I. (1999) Human keratin diseases: the increasing spectrum of disease and subtlety of the phenotype–genotype correlation. *Br J Dermatol*, **140**, 815–828.

Epidermolytic acanthoma

Clinical features

Isolated epidermolytic acanthoma (also termed disseminated epidermolytic acanthoma) is an acquired lesion that presents as a verrucous papule or plaque approximately 1.0 cm in diameter and sometimes resembling a viral wart, nevus or seborrheic keratosis.[1–3] Lesions may present at any site, but the scrotum, head, neck and leg are particularly affected.[2,3] Although usually solitary, occasional patients may present with multiple localized or disseminated lesions.[4–8] Variants affecting the mucosae of the oral cavity and female genital tract have also been documented.[9,10] Caucasians and the Japanese are predominantly affected.[3]

Pathogenesis and histological features

Although not proven, it has been suggested that epidermolytic acanthoma develops as a consequence of keratin 1 and 10 gene mutation.[3]

The lesion is characterized by hyperkeratosis, parakeratosis, acanthosis and papillomatosis (*Fig. 2.37*).[1,2] The upper prickle cell and granular cell layers show features of epidermolytic hyperkeratosis (i.e. severe reticular degeneration accompanied by eosinophilic keratin inclusions) (*Fig. 2.38*).

Epidermolytic acanthoma displays diminished expression of keratins 1 and 10 and increased expression of the hyperproliferative keratins 6 and 16.[3]

Differential diagnosis

Identical histological changes are seen in congenital bullous ichthyosiform erythroderma, linear epidermolytic epidermal nevus, epidermolytic palmoplantar keratoderma and in focal epidermolytic hyperkeratosis. Clinical information is usually necessary to avoid diagnostic confusion.

References

1. Shapiro, L., Baraf, C.S. (1970) Isolated epidermolytic acanthoma. A solitary tumor showing granular degeneration. *Arch Dermatol*, **101**, 220–223.
2. Cohen, P.R., Ulmer, R., Theriault, A. et al (1997) Epidermolytic acanthomas: clinical characteristics and immunohistochemical features. *Am J Dermatopathol*, **19**, 232–241.
3. Leonardi, C., Zhu, W., Kinsey, W. et al. (1991) Epidermolytic acanthoma does not contain human papillomavirus DNA. *J Cutan Pathol*, **18**, 103–105.
4. Miyamoto, Y., Ueda, K., Sato, M. et al. (1979) Disseminated epidermolytic acanthoma. *J Cutan Pathol*, **6**, 272–279.
5. Hirone, T., Fukushiro, R. (1973) Disseminated epidermolytic acanthoma. *Acta Derm Venereol*, **53**, 393–402.
6. Chun, S.I., Lee, J.S., Kim, N.S. et al (1995) Disseminated epidermolytic acanthoma with disseminated superficial porokeratosis and verruca vulgaris in an immunosuppressed patient. *J Dermatol*, **22**, 690–692.
7. Metzler, G., Sonnichsen, K. (1997) Disseminated epidermolytic acanthoma. *Hautarzt*, **48**, 740–742.
8. Sanchez-Carpintero, I., Espana, A., Idoate, M.A. (1999) Disseminated epidermolytic acanthoma probably related to trauma. *Br J Dermatol*, **141**, 728–730.
9. Quinn, T.R., Young, R.H. (1997) Epidermolytic hyperkeratosis in the lower female genital tract: an uncommon simulant of mucocutaneous papillomavirus infection – a report of two cases. *Int J Gynecol Pathol*, **16**, 163–168.
10. Aloi, F.G., Molinero, A. (1988) White sponge nevus with epidermolytic changes. *Dermatologica*, **177**, 323–326.

Fig. 2.37
Epidermolytic acanthoma: the lesion is papillomatous with hyperkeratosis and a lateral collarette.

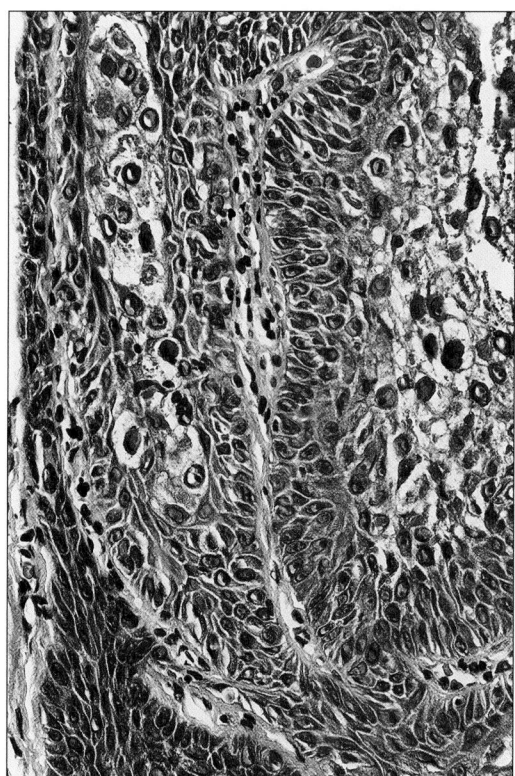

Fig. 2.38
Epidermolytic acanthoma: there is cytoplasmic vacuolation and eosinophilic inclusions are conspicuous.

Focal epidermolytic hyperkeratosis

Focal epidermolytic hyperkeratosis (incidental epidermolytic hyperkeratosis) represents a non-specific finding of epidermolytic hyperkeratosis in the epidermis overlying or adjacent to an unrelated lesion. It is very common and has been described, for example, in seborrheic keratoses, overlying scars and fibrous histiocytoma, in banal and dysplastic nevi, actinic keratosis, squamous cell carcinoma in situ and melanoma.[1–5] It may also be seen in normal skin.

References

1. Ackerman, A.B. (1970) Histopathologic concept of epidermolytic hyperkeratosis. *Arch Dermatol*, **102**, 253–259.
2. Mahaisavariya, P., Cohen, P.R., Rapini, R.P. (1995) Incidental epidermolytic hyperkeratosis. *Am J Dermatopathol*, **17**, 23–28.
3. Williams, B.T., Barr, R.J. (1996) Epidermolytic hyperkeratosis in nevi. A possible marker for atypia. *Am J Dermatopathol*, **18**, 156–158.

4. Sanchez, Y.E., Martin-Dorado, M.M., Lopez-Negrette, E. et al (2000) Incidental epidermolytic hyperkeratosis (IEH): an epidemiological study. *Am J Dermatopathol*, **22**, 352 (letter).
5. Conlin, P.A., Rapini, R.P. (2002) Epidermolytic hyperkeratosis associated with melanocytic nevi. *Am J Dermatopathol*, **24**, 23–25.

Ichthyosis fetalis

Clinical features

Ichthyosis fetalis (harlequin fetus, harlequin ichthyosis, ichthyosis congenita) is an extreme and rapidly fatal subtype, where babies are born with a fissured 'armor-plated' skin (*Figs 2.39, 2.40*).[1–4] It probably

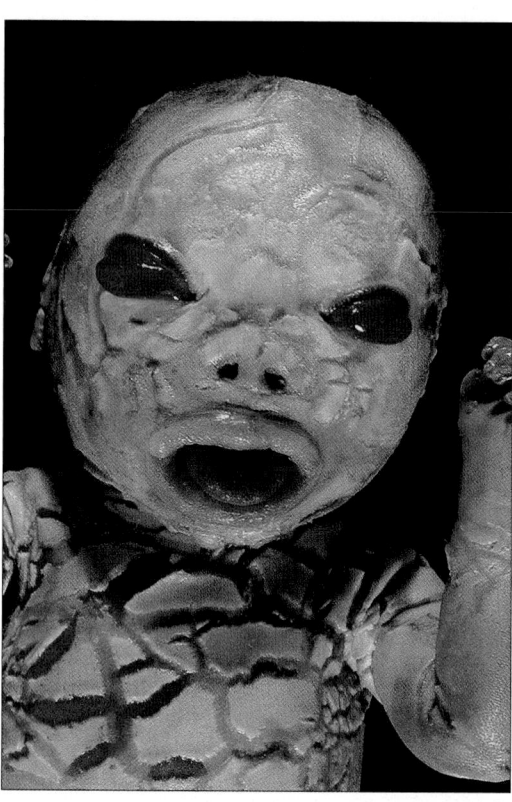

Fig. 2.39
Ichthyosis fetalis: the most extreme form of congenital ichthyosis. There is an exceedingly high mortality.

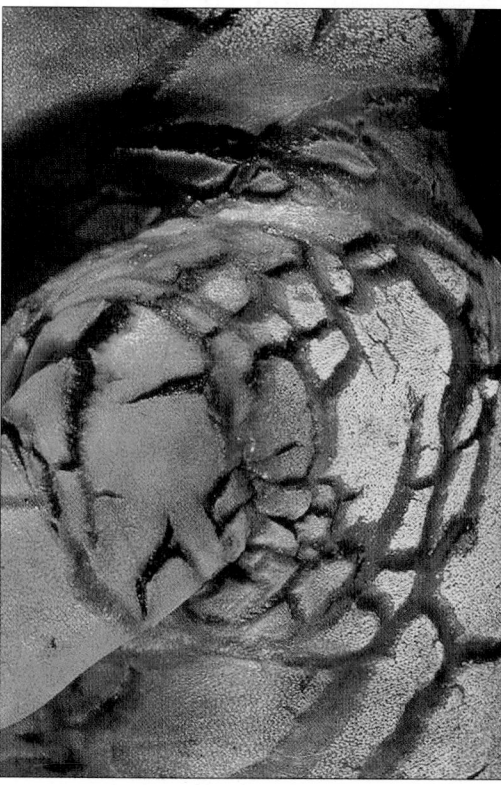

Fig. 2.40
Ichthyosis fetalis: the scales are very thick and are often referred to as armor-plating.

represents a heterogeneous group of diseases with a usually autosomal recessive mode of inheritance.[1] An autosomal dominant variant has also been documented.[2] Ectropion and eclabium are frequent complications, and the ears and nose are often malformed.[2] Harlequin fetus has a very high mortality due to respiratory and feeding difficulties accompanied by excessive fluid loss.[3] In rare long-term survivors, following shedding of the scales, a severe erythroderma reminiscent of non-bullous ichthyosiform erythroderma develops.[5] Fortunately antenatal diagnosis is possible.[6,7]

Pathogenesis and histological features

The locus for harlequin fetus has not yet been identified. In one patient, the disease was associated with a de novo deletion of chromosome 18q.[8] Calpain 1 expression is diminished in harlequin fetus. This may result in aberrant calcium-mediated signaling in epidermal differentiation.[9]

The lesions are characterized by massive hyperkeratosis (sometimes with lipid deposits) associated with a normal or absent granular cell layer (*Fig. 2.41*). The hair follicles are usually affected first, during the second trimester.[2,7] Parakeratosis may also sometimes be evident.[10] Acanthosis is often marked and papillomatosis is sometimes a feature. The adnexae appear normal. A sparse mixed inflammatory cell infiltrate may be present in the superficial dermis.[7]

Ultrastructurally the harlequin fetus has recently been shown to be associated with deficient or morphologically abnormal lamellar body formation (including concentrically lamellated forms) and deficient intercellular lipid lamellae within the stratum corneum.[1,2,10] Small vesicles, devoid of internal lamellation, may be present in the granular cell layer (and retained in the stratum corneum), but show no association with the keratinocyte cell membranes as is typical of normal lamellar bodies.[1,10] Recent immunocytochemical evidence suggests that these vesicles represent abnormal lamellar bodies characterized by an inability to discharge their lipid contents into the intercellular space. Keratin and filaggrin expression have also been shown to be defective.[2] In the harlequin fetus, the keratinocytes may display the hyperproliferative keratins K6 and K16 and show an inability to convert profilaggrin to filaggrin.[2] The results of ultrastructural and biochemical analyses also suggest that the harlequin fetus is a heterogeneous condition.

References

1. Milner, M.E., O'Guin, W.M., Holbrook, K.A. et al (1992) Abnormal lamellar granules in harlequin ichthyosis. *J Invest Dermatol*, **99**, 824–829.

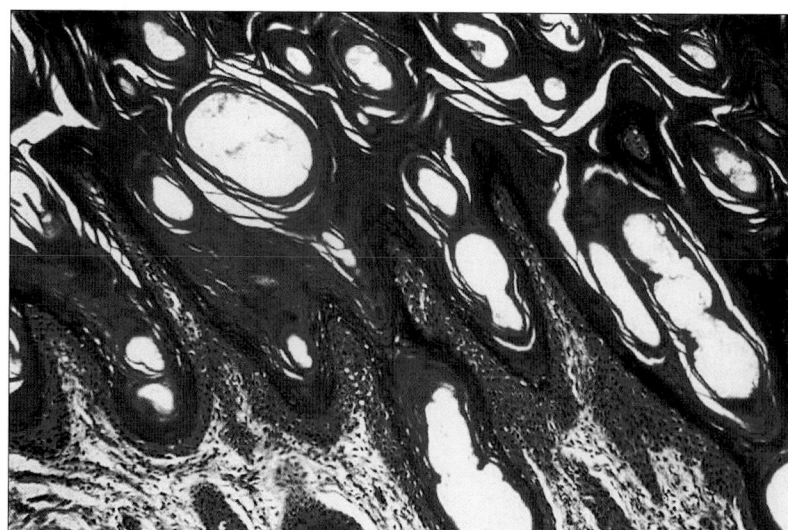

Fig. 2.41
Ichthyosis letalis: there is massive hyperkeratosis associated with a conspicuous granular cell layer and a papillomatous epithelium. The dilated spaces in the stratum corneum represent dilated ostial of eccrine ducts. By courtesy of M.M. Black, MD, Institute of Dermatology, London, UK.

2. Dale, B.A., Holbrook, K.A., Fleckman, P. et al (1990) Heterogeneity in harlequin ichthyosis, an inborn error of epidermal keratinization: variable morphology and structural protein expression and a defect in lamellar granules. *J Invest Dermatol*, **94**, 6–18.

3. Shwayder, T., Ott, F. (1991) All about ichthyosis. *Pediatr Clin North Am*, **38**, 835–857.

4. Williams, M.L. (1992) Epidermal lipids and scaling diseases of the skin. *Semin Dermatol*, **11**, 169–175.

5. Haftek, M., Cambazard, F., Dhouailly, D. et al (1996) A longitudinal study of a harlequin infant presenting clinically as non-bullous congenital ichthyosiform erythroderma. *Br J Dermatol*, **135**, 448–453.

6. Blanchet-Bardon, S., Dumez, Y., Labbe, F. et al (1983) Prenatal diagnosis of a harlequin fetus using EM. *Ann Pathol*, **3**, 321–325.

7. Akiyama, M., Suzumori, K., Shimizu, H. (1999) Prenatal diagnosis of harlequin fetus by the examination of keratinized hair canals and amniotic fluid at 19 weeks estimated gestational age. *Prenat Diagn*, **19**, 167–171.

8. Stewart, H., Smith, P.T., Gaunt, L. et al (2001) De novo deletion of chromosome 18q in a baby with harlequin ichthyosis. *Am J Med Genet*, **102**, 342–345.

9. Michel, M., Fleckman, P., Smith, L.T. et al (1999) The calcium-activated neutral protease calpain 1 is present in normal fetal skin and is decreased in neonatal harlequin ichthyosis. *Br J Dermatol*, **141**, 1017–1026.

10. Fleck, R.M., Barnadas, M., Schulz, W.W. et al (1989) Harlequin ichthyosis: an ultrastructural study. *J Am Acad Dermatol*, **21**, 991–1006.

Netherton's syndrome

Clinical features

Netherton's syndrome is a rare genodermatosis inherited as an autosomal recessive. It combines the features of ichthyosis, most often icthyosis linearis circumflexa, occasionally congenital non-bullous ichthyosiform erythroderma (lamellar ichthyosis), trichorrhexis invaginata (bamboo hair) and an atopic predisposition.[1] It is believed to affect approximately 1:200,000 of the population.[2] Ichthyosis linearis circumflexa consists of an erythematous, scaly rash predominantly affecting the trunk and limbs.[3] It is composed of polycyclic, migratory, annular and serpiginous lesions with a characteristic double-edged scale (*Figs 2.42–2.45*). In infancy, erythema and scaling may be widespread, but later the face is often predominantly affected (particularly marked around the mouth and eyes), along with the perineum,[4] and as such the eruption can be mistaken for acrodermatitis enteropathica (*Fig. 2.46*).[1] Later the scalp, face and eyebrows may show a yellowish scaling.[5] Ichthyosis linearis circumflexa is typically non-pruritic,[5] and the nails and teeth are not involved.[3] Rarely, infants may also show palmoplantar hyperkeratosis.[6]

Trichorrhexis invaginata (due to a transient and repeated defect of keratinization, with resultant hair shaft intussusception)[7] presents clinically as coarse and lusterless hair, which is short, brittle and fragile (*Fig. 2.47*). Pili torti and trichorrhexis may also be evident (*Fig. 2.48*).[5]

Patients with Netherton's syndrome may in addition suffer from failure to thrive with hypernatremia,[4,8,9] aminoaciduria,[5] mental retardation,[5,7] immune defects and frequent infections.[1,5]

Pathogenesis and histological features

Netherton's syndrome results from mutations in the SPINK5 gene which has been localized to 5q32.[10,11] Nonsense, frameshift deletions and insertions and splice site defects resulting in premature termination codons and a defective serine protease inhibitor have been identified.[11–13]

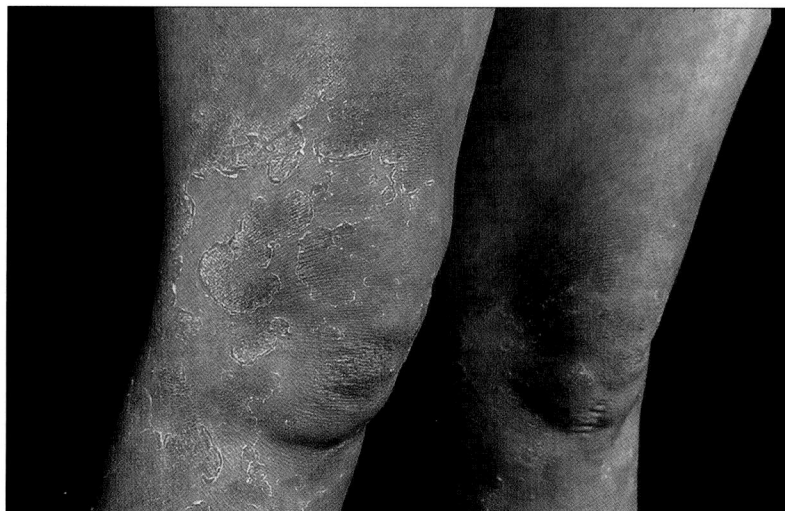

Fig. 2.42
Netherton's syndrome: ichthyosis linearis circumflexa. Note the serpiginous lesions with characteristic double border. By courtesy of M. Judge, MD, Institute of Dermatology, London, UK.

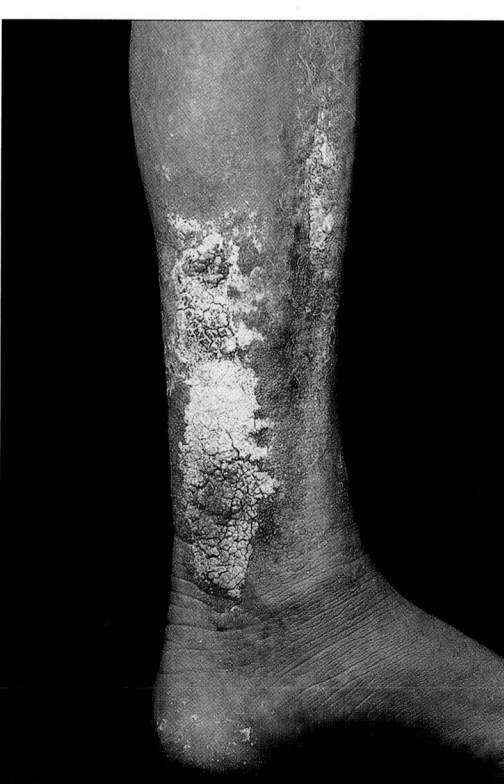

Fig. 2.43
Netherton's syndrome: hyperkeratotic lesions may be prominent.

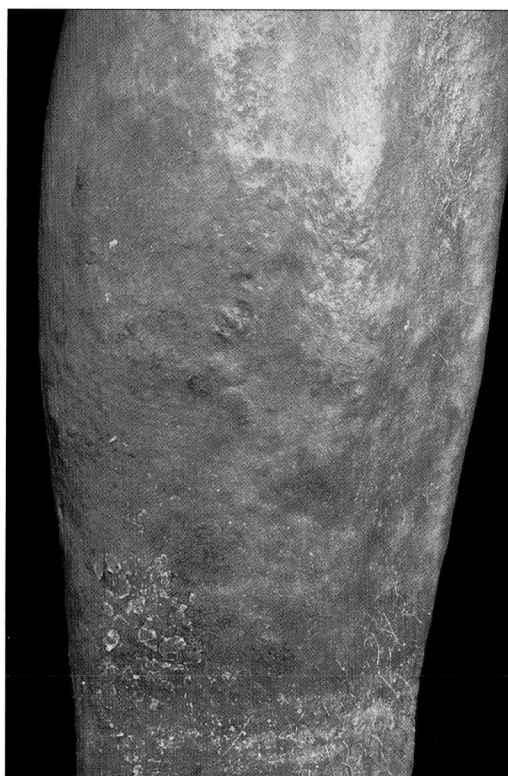

Fig. 2.44
Netherton's syndrome: focal loss of the polycyclic pattern.

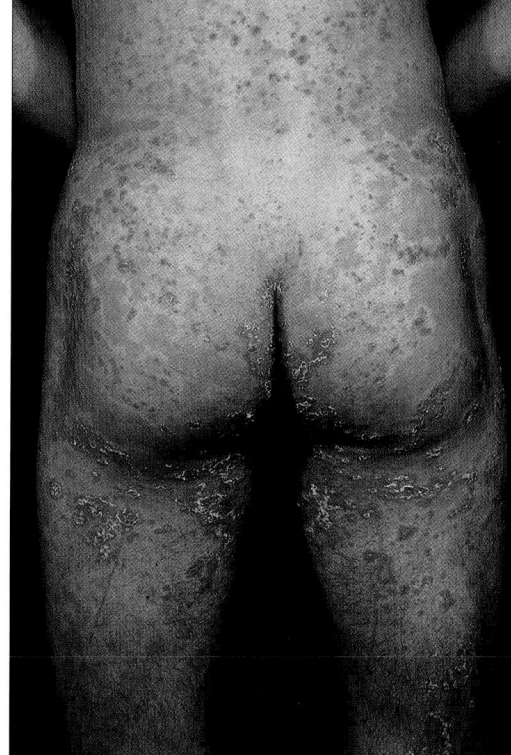

Fig. 2.45
Netherton's syndrome: prominent involvement of the trunk and limbs.

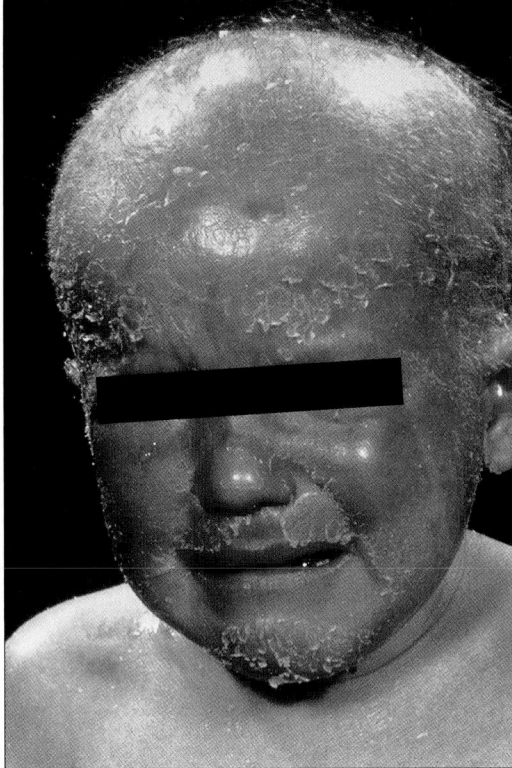

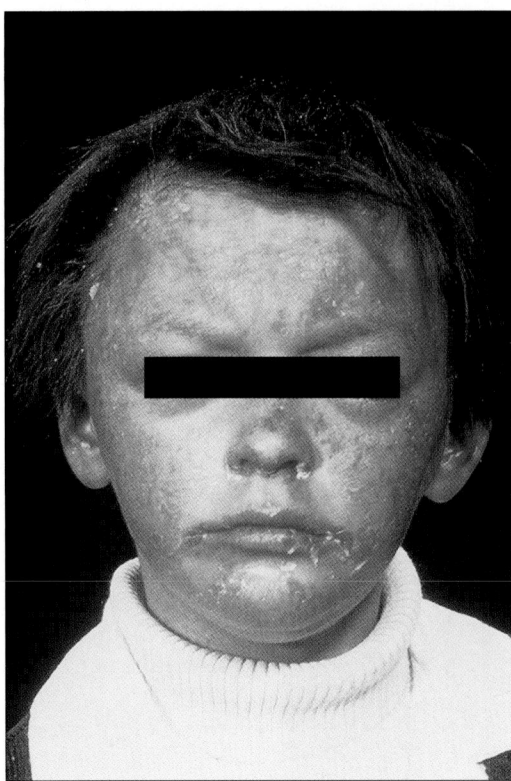

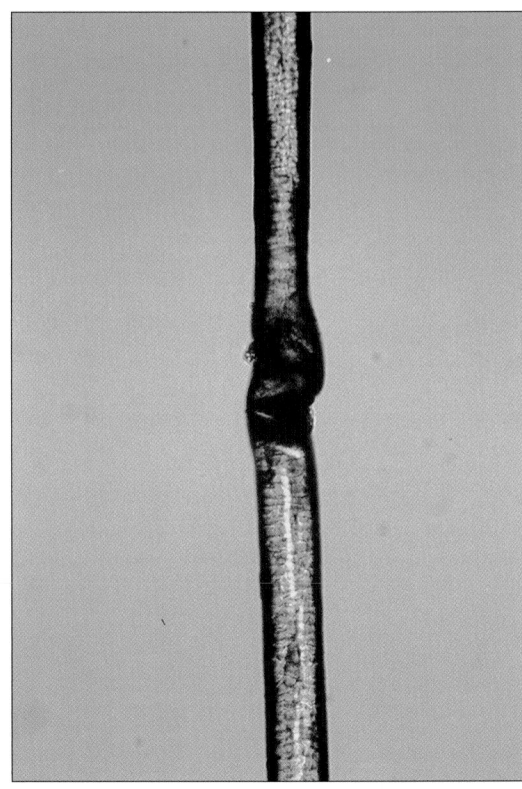

Fig. 2.46
Netherton's syndrome: there is profound erythema with scaling. By courtesy of M. Judge, MD, Institute of Dermatology, London, UK.

Fig. 2.47
Netherton's syndrome: the hair is dull and appears short and thin. The eyebrows are deficient. By courtesy of A. Griffiths, MD, Institute of Dermatology, London, UK.

Fig. 2.48
Netherton's syndrome: bamboo hair (trichorrhexis invaginata). By courtesy of M. Judge, MD, Institute of Dermatology, London, UK.

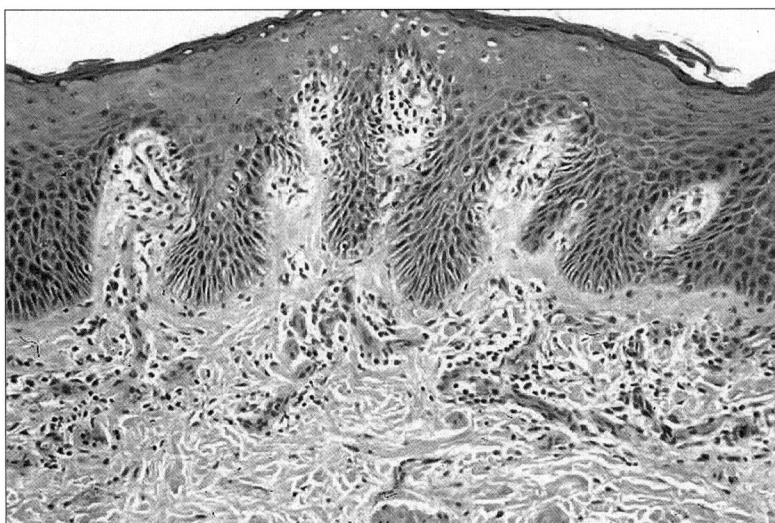

Fig. 2.49
Netherton's syndrome: there is slight parakeratosis associated with psoriasiform epidermal hyperplasia. A mild chronic inflammatory cell infiltrate surrounds the superficial vasculature. By courtesy of M. Judge, MD, Institute of Dermatology, London, UK.

For diagnostic features, the biopsy must be taken from skin just preceding the lesion's scaly margin (*Fig. 2.49*).[14,15] In this region the epidermis may show psoriasiform hyperplasia with associated spongiosis. There is a thick adherent parakeratotic scale. Small, dark, round or oval granules may be identified within the stratum granulosum. These are diastase-resistant, PAS and Sudan black positive and are thought to represent an influx of serum exudates resulting from the accompanying dermal inflammation.[4] Similar 'inclusions' have been described in psoriasis and atopic eczema[16] and as such are not specific. Rarely, the parakeratotic

scale may be associated with the presence of Munro microabscesses making distinction from psoriasis histologically extremely difficult (if not impossible) in the absence of clinical information.[6]

References

1. Greene, S.L., Muller, S.A. (1985) Netherton's syndrome: report of a case and review of the literature. *J Am Acad Dermatol*, **13**, 329–337.
2. Pruszkowski, A., Bodemer, C., Fraitag, S. et al (2000) Neonatal and infantile erythrodermas: a retrospective study of 51 patients. *Arch Dermatol*, **136**, 875–880.
3. Murphy, G.M., Griffiths, W.A.D. (1989) Netherton's syndrome. *J R Soc Med*, **82**, 683–684.
4. Krafchik, B.R. (1992) What syndrome is this? *Pediatr Dermatol*, **9**, 157–160.
5. Krafchik, B.R., Toole, J.W.P. (1983) What is Netherton's syndrome? *Int J Dermatol*, **22**, 459–462.
6. Shwayder, T., Banerjee, S. (1997) Netherton syndrome presenting as congenital psoriasis. *Pediatr Dermatol* **14**, 473–476.
7. Pinkus, H. In: Comments, Wilkjinson, R.D., Curtis, G.H., Hawk, W.A. (1964) Netherton's disease. *Arch Dermatol*, **89**, 46–54.
8. Plantin, P., Delaire, P., Guillet, M.H. et al (1991) Syndrome de Netherton, aspects actuels: a propos de neuf cas. *Ann Dermatol Venereol*, **118**, 525–530.
9. Judge, M.R., Morgan, G., Harper, J. (1994) A clinical and immunological study of Netherton's syndrome. *Br J Dermatol*, **131**, 615–621.
10. Mägert, H-J., Standker, L., Kreutzmann, P. et al (1999) LEKT1, a novel 15-domain type of serine protease inhibitor. *Biol Chem*, **274**, 21499–21502.
11. Chavanas, S., Garner, C., Mohsin, A. et al (2000) Localization of the Netherton syndrome gene to chromosome 5q32, by linkage analysis and homozygosity mapping. *Am J Hum Genet*, **66**, 914–921.
12. Chavanas, S., Bodemer, C., Rochat, A. et al (2000) Mutations in *SPINK5*, encoding a serine protease inhibitor, cause Netherton's syndrome. *Nat Genet*, **25**, 133–136.
13. Bitoun, E., Chavanas, S., Irvine, A.D. et al (2001) Netherton syndrome: disease expression and spectrum of SPINK5 mutations in 21 families. *J Invest Dermatol*, **118**, 352–361.
14. Hauser, I., Anton-Lamprecht, I., Hartschuh, W. et al (1989) Netherton's syndrome: ultrastructure of the active lesion under retinoid therapy. *Arch Dermatol Res*, **281**, 165–172.
15. Hauser, I., Anton-Lamprecht, I. (1996) Severe congenital generalized exfoliative erythroderma in newborns and infants: a possible sign of Netherton's syndrome. *Pediatr Dermatol*, **13**, 183–199.
16. Zina, A.M., Bundino, S. (1979) Ichthyosis linearis circumflexa Cornel and Netherton's syndrome: an ultrastructural study. *Dermatologica*, **158**, 404–412.

Sjögren–Larsson syndrome

Clinical features

This autosomal recessive inherited disorder combines the features of ichthyosis, spastic bi- or quadriplegia and mental retardation.[1–5] It is rare, with an incidence of 0.4 per 100,000 of the population.[4] Although the disease may be encountered worldwide, the prevalence is particularly high in Northern Sweden.[2]

The ichthyosis, which develops in the first year of life, affects the entire body with the exception of the central face and is typically intensely pruritic (*Fig. 2.50*).[3,5] The skin has a brownish-yellow color and appears wrinkled.[4] Hyperkeratosis around the umbilicus is said to be characteristic.[5] Erythroderma is not a feature and the hair, nails and sweat glands are unaffected.[3,4]

The spasticity, which presents in early childhood, predominantly affects the legs and is often associated with contractures. The majority of patients are wheelchair bound.[4] Kyphoscoliosis may also be present.[3]

Mental retardation is typically present but is not invariable (*Fig. 2.51*).[1] Epilepsy is sometimes a feature.[3]

Visual acuity is often impaired and photophobia is a frequent complaint. Macular degeneration associated with crystal deposition is characteristic (*Fig. 2.52*).[6]

Pathogenesis and histological features

Sjögren–Larsson syndrome results from deficiency of microsomal fatty aldehyde dehydrogenase.[7] The gene has been mapped to 17p11.2 and multiple mutations including missense mutations, deletions and insertions have been identified.[8–10] Epidermal hyperproliferation has been demonstrated in Sjögren–Larsson syndrome.[11]

Histologically, there is papillomatosis, basket-weave hyperkeratosis and acanthosis (*Fig. 2.53*).[12] The granular layer may be slightly thickened. A light lymphohistiocytic infiltrate is sometimes present around the superficial dermal vasculature.

Ultrastructurally, there are lamellar inclusions in the prickle and granular cell layers.[12] Lipid inclusions are not a feature.

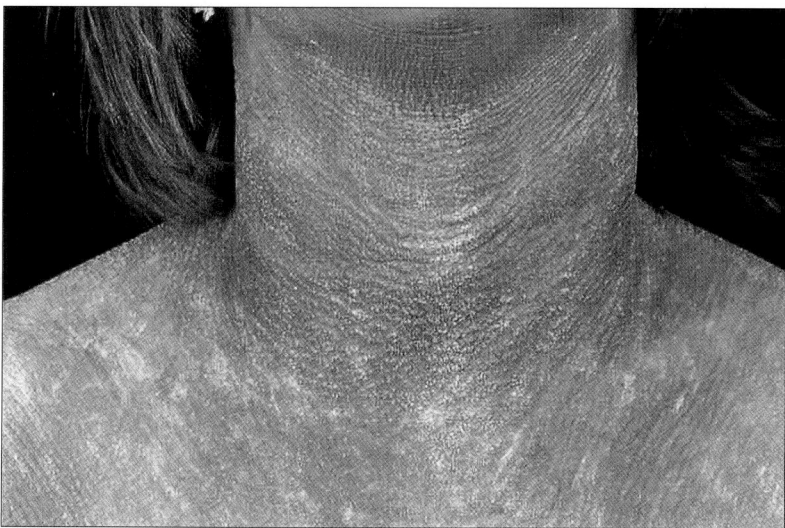

Fig. 2.50
Sjögren–Larsson syndrome: there is severe scaling and the skin has a yellowish-brown color. By courtesy of M. Willemsen, MD, University Medical Center, Nijmegen, Belgium.

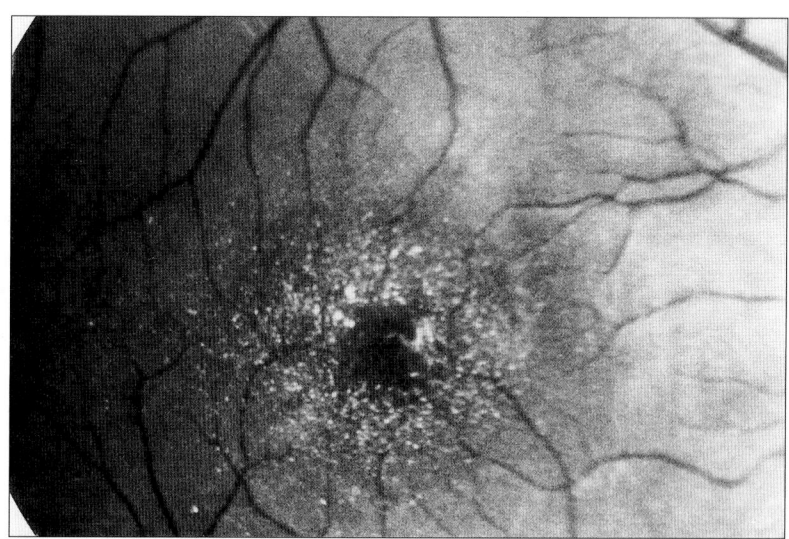

Fig. 2.52
Sjögren–Larsson syndrome: characteristic macular crystals. By courtesy of M. Willemsen, MD, University Medical Center, Nijmegen, Belgium.

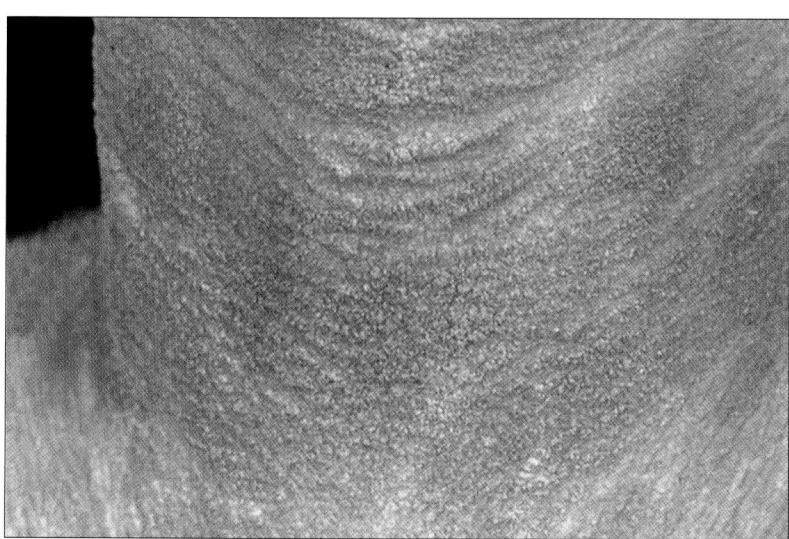

Fig. 2.51
Sjögren–Larsson syndrome: close up view of Fig. 2.50. By courtesy of M. Willemsen, MD, University Medical Center, Nijmegen, Belgium.

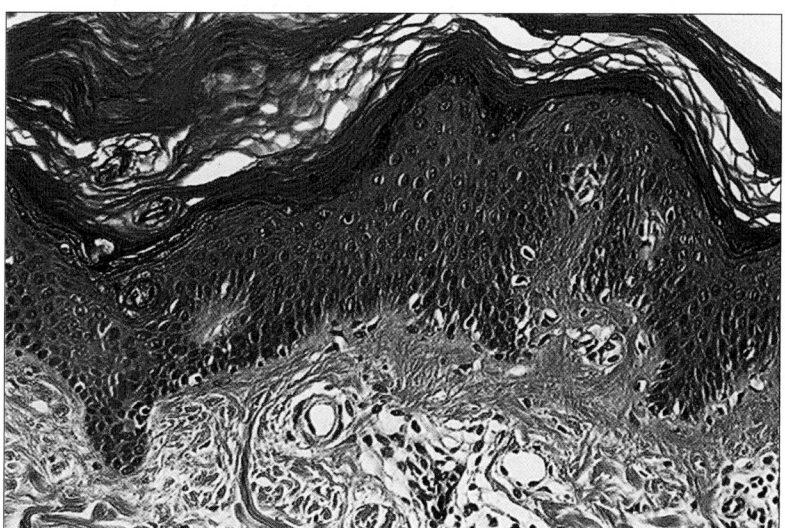

Fig. 2.53
Sjögren–Larsson syndrome: there is hyperkeratosis, hypergranulosis and mild papillomatosis. A light superficial perivascular lymphocytic infiltrate is present. By courtesy of M. Willemsen, MD, University Medical Center, Nijmegen, Belgium.

References

1. Sjögren, T., Larsson, T. (1957) Oligophrenia in combination with congenital ichthyosis and spastic disorders. *Acta Psychiat Neurol Scand*, **32** (Suppl. 113), 1–113.
2. Jagell, S., Gustavson, K-H., Holmgren, G. (1981) Sjögren–Larsson syndrome in Sweden. A clinical genetic and epidemiological study. *Clin Genet*, **19**, 233–236.
3. Rizzo, W.B. (1993) Sjögren–Larsson syndrome. *Semin Dermatol*, **12**, 210–218.
4. Lacour, M. (1996) Update on Sjögren–Larsson syndrome. *Dermatology*, **193**, 77–82.
5. Willemsen, M.A.A.P., Ijlst, L., Steijlen, P.M. et al (2001) Clinical, biochemical and molecular genetic characteristics of 19 patients with the Sjögren–Larsson syndrome. *Brain*, **124**, 1426–1437.
6. Willemsen, M.A., Cruysberg, J.R., Rotteveel, J.J. et al (2000) Juvenile macular dystrophy associated with deficient activation of fatty aldehyde dehydrogenase in Sjögren–Larsson syndrome. *Am J Ophthalmol*, **130**, 782–789.
7. Rizzo, W.B., Dammann, A.L., Craft, D.A. (1988) Sjögren–Larsson syndrome. Impaired fatty alcohol oxidation in cultured fibroblasts due to deficient fatty alcohol: nicotinamide adenine dinucleotide oxidoreductase activity. *J Clin Invest*, **81**, 738–744.
8. Rizzo, W.B., Carney, G., De Laurenzi, V. (1997) A common deletion mutation in European patients with Sjögren–Larsson syndrome. *Biochem Mol Med*, **62**, 178–181.
9. Rizzo, W.B., Carney, G., Lin, Z. (1999) The molecular basis of Sjögren–Larsson syndrome: mutation analysis of the fatty aldehyde dehydrogenase gene. *Am J Hum Genet*, **65**, 1547–1560.
10. Sillén, A., Anton-Lamprecht, I., Braun-Quentin, C. et al (1998) Spectrum of mutations and sequence variants in the FALDH gene in patients with Sjögren–Larsson syndrome. *Hum Mutat*, **12**, 377–384.
11. Jagell, S., Linden S. (1982) Ichthyosis in the Sjögren–Larsson syndrome. *Clin Genet*, **21**, 243–252.
12. Ito, M., Oguro, K., Sato, Y. (1991) Ultrastructural study of the skin in Sjögren–Larsson syndrome. *Arch Dermatol Res*, **283**, 141–148.

Pityriasis rotunda

Clinical features

Also known as pityriasis circinata, this acquired disorder of keratinization was originally described in the Japanese.[1] It is also not uncommon in South Africans (Bantu) and West Indian blacks,[2,3] but has only rarely been reported in Caucasians with the exception of a subpopulation of Italians in Sardinia.[4-7]

Patients present with persistent, very sharply defined, circular or oval areas of hyper- or hypopigmentation associated with a fine scale (*Fig. 2.54*). Lesions, which are usually multiple and frequently numerous, are characteristically non-inflammatory and asymptomatic. Often they are confluent. They measure 0.5–28 cm in diameter and are particularly located on the trunk and limbs. The sex incidence is equal. Lesions are sometimes associated with gradual remission during the summer months and relapse in winter.[6] The maximum incidence is in the third to fifth decades. There is often a family history of ichthyosis vulgaris.[8] It may occasionally be associated with a familial incidence.[8,9]

Pityriasis rotunda sometimes appears to be a cutaneous marker of severe internal disease including tuberculosis,[1] cancer (particularly hepatoma),[10,11] leukemia,[12] cirrhosis,[6] ovarian and uterine disease,[13] undernutrition and favism.[8] Pityriasis rotunda might best be regarded as an acquired circumscribed variant of ichthyosis.[12]

Histological features

The histological features are subtle and comprise hyperkeratosis with a diminished or absent granular cell layer and loss of the epidermal ridge pattern. Increased pigmentation of the basal keratinocytes may be evident. A mild perivascular chronic inflammatory cell infiltrate is sometimes present in the superficial dermis. A superficial fungal infection, for example tinea (pityriasis) versicolor, should always be excluded by a PAS reaction or silver stain.[14]

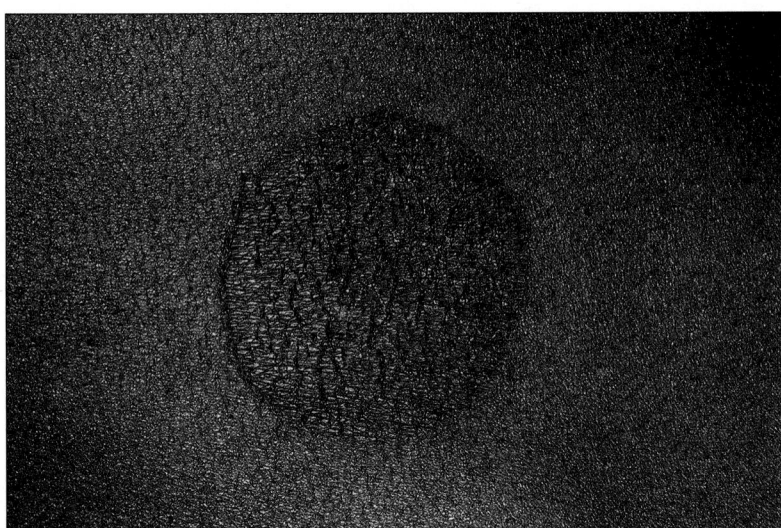

Fig. 2.54
Pityriasis rotunda: characteristic lesion showing circumscription, scaling and hyperpigmentation. By courtesy of R.A. Marsden, MD, St George's Hospital, London, UK.

References

1. Ito, M., Tanaka, T. (1960) Pseudo-ichthyose acquise en taches circularies: pityriasis rotunda. *Ann Dermatol Syphilol*, **87**, 26–37.
2. Findlay, G.H. (1955) Pityriasis in the South African Bantu. *Br J Dermatol*, **77**, 63–64.
3. Sarkany, I., Hare, P.J. (1964) Pityriasis rotunda (pityriasis circinata). *Br J Dermatol*, **77**, 63–64.
4. Kahana, M., Lew, A., Ronnen, M. et al (1986) Pityriasis rotunda in a white patient. *J Am Acad Dermatol*, **15**, 362–365.
5. El-Hefnawi, H., Rasheed, A. (1966) Pityriasis rotunda. 'Pseudo-ichtyose acquise en taches circulaires': report and study of first case in UAR. *Arch Dermatol*, **93**, 84–86.
6. Segal, R., Hodak, E., Sandbank, M. (1989) Pityriasis rotunda in a Caucasian woman from the Mediterranean area. *Clin Exp Dermatol*, **14**, 325–327.
7. Aste, N., Pau, M., Aste, N. et al (1997) Pityriasis rotunda: a survey of 42 cases observed in Sardinia, Italy. *Dermatology*, **194**, 32–35.
8. Lodi, A., Betti, R., Chiarelli, G. et al (1990) Familial pityriasis rotunda. *Int J Dermatol*, **29**, 483–485.
9. Guberman, D., Lichtenstein, D.A., Gilead, L. et al (1997) Familial pityriasis rotunda. *Acta Derm Venereol*, **77**, 162.
10. Zina, A.M., Ubertalli, S., Bundino, S. (1986) Pityriasis rotunda. *Int J Dermatol*, **25**, 56–57.
11. Berkowitz, I., Hodkinson, H.J., Kew, M.C. et al (1989) Pityriasis rotunda as a cutaneous marker of hepatocellular carcinoma: a comparison with its prevalence in other diseases. *Br J Dermatol*, **120**, 545–549.
12. Lewibowitz, M.R., Weiss, R., Smith, E.H. (1983) Pityriasis rotunda. A cutaneous sign of malignant disease in two patients. *Arch Dermatol*, **119**, 607–609.
13. Waishan, M. (1986) Pityriasis rotunda. *Cutis*, **38**, 247–248.
14. Gupta, S. (2001) Pityriasis rotunda mimicking tinea cruris/corporis and erythrasma in an Indian patient. *J Dermatol*, **28**, 50–53.

Follicular ichthyosis

Clinical features

Follicular ichthyosis (ichthyosis follicularis) is a poorly documented entity in which patients present with horny, follicular lesions which although usually generalized, show a predilection for the head and neck (*Figs 2.55, 2.56*).[1,2] In the report by Hazell and Marks, associated clinical findings included pseudoacanthosis nigricans affecting the axillae, comedones on the cheeks and fingers and dental malocclusion.[2] Literature subsequent to these two papers has focused on the association of ichthyosis follicularis with alopecia and photophobia (see below).

Histological features

The lesions are characterized by compact follicular orthohyperkeratosis with hypergranulosis extending into the deeper reaches of the hair follicle and associated with normal interfollicular epithelium. Inflammatory changes are absent.

Differential diagnosis

Follicular ichthyosis is histologically indistinguishable from keratosis pilaris and lichen spinulosus.

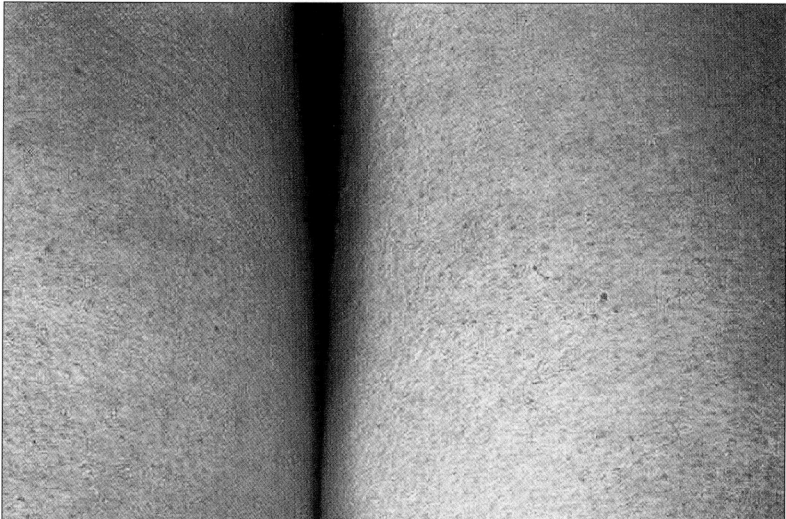

Fig. 2.55
Follicular ichthyosis: bilateral follicular lesions. By courtesy of the Institute of Dermatology, London, UK.

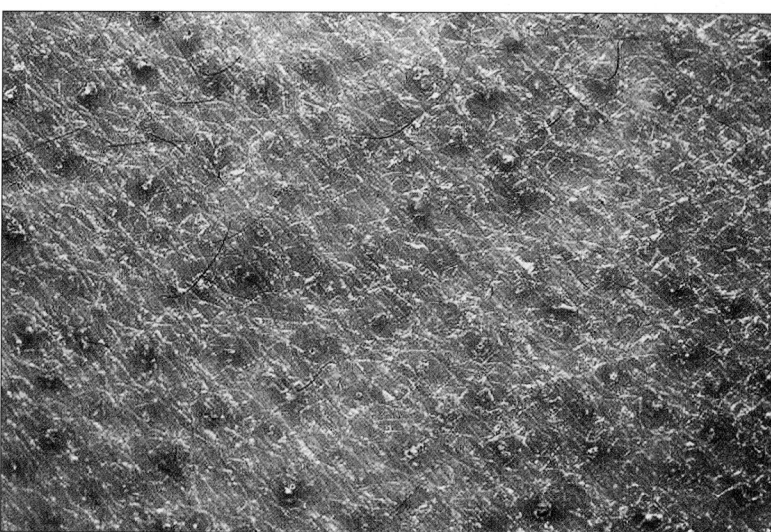

Fig. 2.56
Follicular ichthyosis: the follicles are plugged with thorn-like scale. By courtesy of the Institute of Dermatology, London, UK.

References

1. Waddington, E., Marks, R. (1978) Follicular ichthyosiform disorders. In: Marks, R., Dykes, P.J. (eds) The ichthyoses. Lancaster: MTP Press.
2. Hazell, M., Marks, R. (1984) Follicular ichthyosis. *Br J Dermatol*, **111**, 101–109.

Lichen spinulosus

Clinical features

Lichen spinulosus is a rare dermatosis of unknown etiology which particularly affects the extensor surfaces of the arms and legs, back, chest, buttocks, face and neck.[1] Occasionally lesions are generalized. Lesions present in the second and third decades as round to oval, 2–6 cm flesh-colored and sometimes pruritic, symmetric plaques composed of multiple 1–3 mm thorny grouped follicular papules which protrude above the surface of the skin.[1–3] The texture has been likened to a nutmeg grater. Males are affected more often than females. There is no racial predilection.[2] Other than a cosmetic nuisance the condition is of no clinical significance. Lichen spinulosus has been described in association with Crohn's disease, human immunodeficiency virus (HIV) infection and as an adverse drug reaction.[4–7]

Histological features

Lichen spinulosus is characterized by keratotic plugging of dilated follicular infundibula and a perivascular and perifollicular lympho-histiocytic infiltrate.[1] Sebaceous glands may be atrophic or absent. Perforating folliculitis-like features may be superimposed.

Differential diagnosis

There is considerable histological overlap with keratosis pilaris and the follicular lesions of pityriasis rubra pilaris. The distinction is best made clinically.

References

1. Friedman, S.J. (1990) Lichen spinulosus: clinicopathologic review of thirty-five cases. *J Am Acad Dermatol*, **22**, 261–264.
2. Boyd, A.S. (1989) Lichen spinulosus: case report and overview. *Cutis*, **43**, 557–560.
3. Strickling, W.A., Norton, S.A. (2000) Spiny eruption on the neck. Diagnosis: lichen spinulosus (LS). *Arch Dermatol*, **136**, 1165–1170.
4. Kano, Y., Orihara, M., Yagita, A. et al (1995) Lichen spinulosus in a patient with Crohn's disease. *Int J Dermatol*, **34**, 670–671.
5. Cohen, S.J., Dicken, C.H. (1991) Generalized lichen spinulosus in an HIV-positive man. *J Am Acad Dermatol*, **25**, 116–118.
6. Resnick, S.D., Murrell, D.F., Woosley, J. (1992) Acne conglobata and a generalized lichen spinulosus-like eruption in a man seropositive for human immunodeficiency virus. *J Am Acad Dermatol*, **26**, 1013–1014.
7. Lee, M.L., Piper, D.W., Fischer, G.O. et al (1989) Lichen spinulosus after the ingestion of omeprazole. *Med J Aust*, **150**, 410.

Phrynoderma

Clinical features

Phrynoderma (toad skin) most often develops as a consequence of vitamin A deficiency.[1–4] Other proposed etiological factors include deficiencies of the vitamin B complex, riboflavin, vitamin C, vitamin E and essential fatty acids.[4] In Western countries most cases develop as a result of malabsorption.[4,5] Patients present with xerosis, hyperpigmentation and multiple 2–6 mm, red–brown, dome-shaped papules with a central folliculocentric crater filled with laminated keratinous debris.[1,4] The elbows and knees are predominantly affected but lesions may extend to involve the thighs, upper arms and buttocks.[1]

Histological features

The papules consist of a cystically dilated follicular infundibulum filled with keratinous debris.[4]

References

1. Pettit, J.H.S. (1984) Phrynoderma. *Int J Dermatol*, **22**, 117–119.
2. Neill, S.M., Pembroke, A.C., du Vivier, A.W. et al (1988) Phrynoderma and perforating folliculitis due to vitamin A deficiency in a diabetic. *J R Soc Med*, **81**, 171–172.
3. Nakjang, Y., Yuttanavivat, T. (1988) Phrynoderma: a review of 105 cases. *J Dermatol*, **15**, 531–534.
4. Bleasel, N.R., Stapleton, K.M., Lee, M.S. et al (1999) Vitamin A deficiency phrynoderma: due to malabsorption and inadequate diet. *J Am Acad Dermatol*, **41**, 322–324.
5. Barr, D.J., Riley, R.J., Greco, D.J. (1984) Bypass phrynoderma. Vitamin A deficiency associated with bowel-bypass surgery. *Arch Dermatol*, **120**, 919–921.

Ichthyosis follicularis with alopecia and photophobia

Clinical features

Ichthyosis follicularis with alopecia (atrichia) and photophobia (IFAP syndrome) is an exceedingly rare disorder characterized by the presence of non-inflammatory thorn-like (filiform) follicular hyperkeratoses resembling a nutmeg grater, ichthyosiform dry skin, generalized complete non-scarring alopecia (with absence of eyelashes and eyebrows) and severe photophobia.[1–6] Ocular findings may include corneal deformity and opacity with surface vascularization.[6] Angular cheilitis, keratotic psoriasiform plaques on the extensor surfaces of the extremities and nail dystrophy with chronic infection may also be present.[2,6] Sweating and dentition are normal.[5]

Pathogenesis and histological features

The mode of inheritance and pathogenesis of this disorder is unknown although autosomal dominant and X-linked recessive forms have been described.[2,5]

The follicular lesions are characterized by projecting hyperkeratotic plugs showing focal parakeratosis and associated hypergranulosis.[6] Hair shafts and sebaceous glands are absent.[1] Sweat glands are normal.[5]

The psoriasiform plaques show hyperkeratosis with parakeratosis, acanthosis, spongiosis and a band-like upper dermal lymphohistiocytic infiltrate.[6]

References

1. Eramo, L.R., Esterly, N.B., Zieserl, E.J. et al (1985) Ichthyosis follicularis with alopecia and photophobia. *Arch Dermatol*, **121**, 1167–1174.
2. Rothe, M.J., Weiss, D.S., Dubner, B.H. et al (1990) Ichthyosis follicularis in two girls: an autosomal dominant disorder. *Pediatr Dermatol*, 7, 287–292.
3. Hamm, H., Meinecke, P., Traupe, H. (1991) Further delineation of the ichthyosis follicularis, atrichia, and photophobia syndrome. *Eur J Pediatr*, **150**, 627–629.
4. Martino, F., D'Eufemia, P., Pergola, M.S. et al (1992) Child with manifestations of dermotrichic syndrome and ichthyosis follicularis–alopecia–photophobia (IFAP) syndrome. *Am J Med Genet*, **44**, 233–236.
5. König, A., Happle, R. (1999) Linear lesions reflecting lyonization in women heterozygous for IFAP syndrome (ichthyosis follicularis with atrichia and photophobia). *Am J Med Genet*, **85**, 365–368.
6. Sato-Matsumura, K.C., Matsumura, T., Kumakiri, M. et al (2000) Ichthyosis follicularis with alopecia and photophobia in a mother and daughter. *Br J Dermatol*, **142**, 157–162.

Keratosis pilaris

Clinical features

This fairly common condition, which has an autosomal dominant mode of inheritance, is probably a follicular variant of ichthyosis and, indeed, frequently accompanies ichthyosis vulgaris.[1–3] The age at presentation is most often in the first two decades with a peak during adolescence.[2] Up to 40% of adults may be affected.[2] There is no racial predilection. There is an apparent increased incidence in females and lesions present as pruritic small follicular keratoses, sometimes containing small distorted hairs. They are most often found on the lateral aspects of the arms and thighs, although the face, trunk and buttocks may also be affected (*Figs 2.57, 2.58*).[2] Seasonal variation with lesions being much more severe in winter is often documented.[2] There is an increased incidence of atopy.[2]

Keratosis pilaris atrophicans is a rare variant that shows a predilection for the face and is accompanied by inflammatory changes followed by atrophy, scaring and alopecia (see below).[3,4]

Although keratosis pilaris most often presents as an isolated phenomenon, occasionally it may develop in association with systemic disease including Hodgkin's lymphoma, vitamins B12 and C deficiency, hypothyroidism, Cushing's disease and treatment with adrenocorticotropic hormone.[3,5,6]

Histological features

Keratosis pilaris is characterized by follicular dilatation and keratin plugs, which may contain a single or several distorted hair shafts (*Figs 2.59, 2.60*).[5] A mild, non-specific chronic inflammatory cell infiltrate surrounds the dermal blood vessels and sometimes involves the hair follicles themselves.

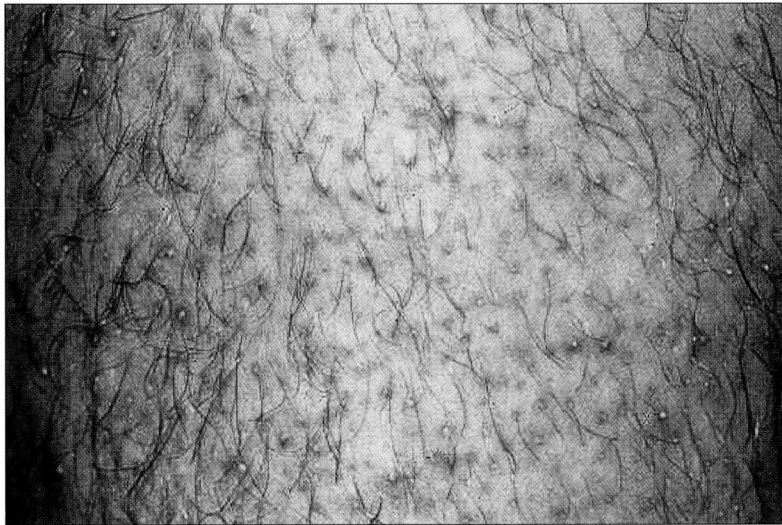

Fig. 2.57
Keratosis pilaris: typical follicular papules and pustules on the thigh. By courtesy of R.A. Marsden, MD, St George's Hospital, London, UK.

Fig. 2.58
Keratosis pilaris: note the conspicuous plugged follicles. By courtesy of the Institute of Dermatology, London, UK.

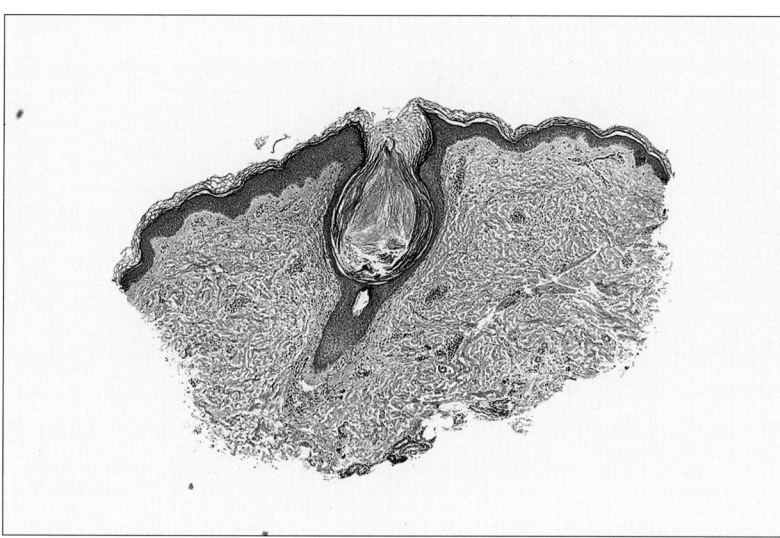

Fig. 2.59
Keratosis pilaris: there is follicular dilatation and plugging.

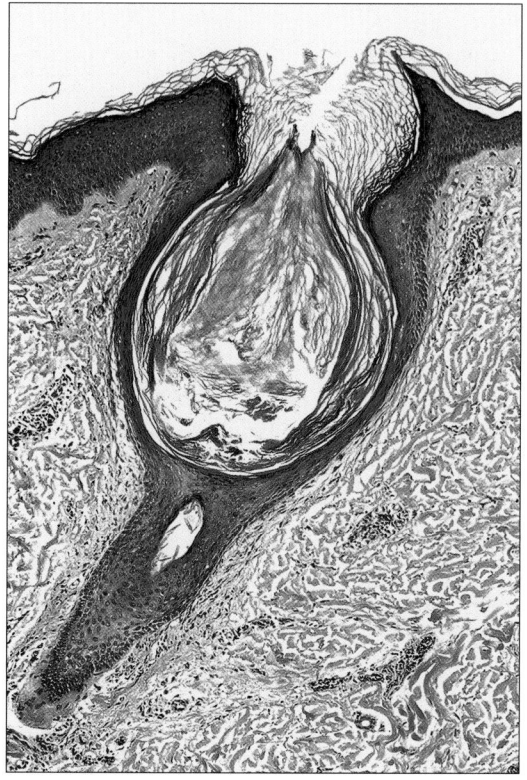

Fig. 2.60
Keratosis pilaris: note the atrophy of the infundibular epithelium.

References

1. Mevorah, B., Marazzi, A., Frenk, E. (1985) The prevalence of accentuated palmoplantar markings and keratosis pilaris in atopic dermatitis, autosomal dominant ichthyosis and control dermatological patients. *Br J Dermatol*, **112**, 679–685.
2. Poskitt, L., Wilkinson, J.D. (1994) Natural history of keratosis pilaris. *Br J Dermatol*, **130**, 711–713.
3. Lateef, A., Schwartz, R.A. (1999) Keratosis pilaris. *Cutis*, **63**, 205–207.
4. Baden, H.P., Byers, H.R. (1994) Clinical findings, cutaneous pathology, and response to therapy in 21 patients with keratosis pilaris atrophicans. *Arch Dermatol*, **130**, 469–473.
5. Sallakachart, P., Nakjang, Y. (1987) Keratosis pilaris: a clinico-histopathologic study. *J Med Assoc Thailand*, **70**, 386–389.
6. Thomsen, K., Nyfors, A. (1973) Keratosis pilaris: skin marker of Hodgkin's lymphoma? *Arch Dermatol*, **107**, 629–630.

Keratosis pilaris atrophicans

Clinical features

Keratosis pilaris atrophicans combines the features of follicular hyperkeratosis and scarring.[1] Although some authors believe this to represent a single disease entity, others prefer to subdivide into a number of categories including ulerythema ophryogenes, atrophoderma vermiculata and keratosis follicularis spinulosa decalvans.[2] Evidence of different modes of inheritance, clinical differences and variable associations supports the latter.[2]

Follicular keratoses may also be seen in a number of other dermatoses including follicular ichthyosis, ichthyosis vulgaris, lichen spinulosus, phrynoderma, erythrokeratoderma, pityriasis rubra pilaris and Jadassohn–Lewandowsky's syndrome.[3]

Ulerythema ophryogenes (keratosis pilaris atrophicans facei, KPAF) presents at birth or in early infancy with follicular papules and surrounding erythema followed by atrophic scarring affecting the lateral aspect of the eyebrows (*Fig. 2.61*).[3–5] The cheeks, forehead, temples and neck may also be involved (*Fig. 2.62*). Later on, the entire eyebrow may be lost. Keratosis pilaris affecting the extensor aspects of the arms and thighs is also sometimes present.[3] It is believed to be inherited as an autosomal dominant.

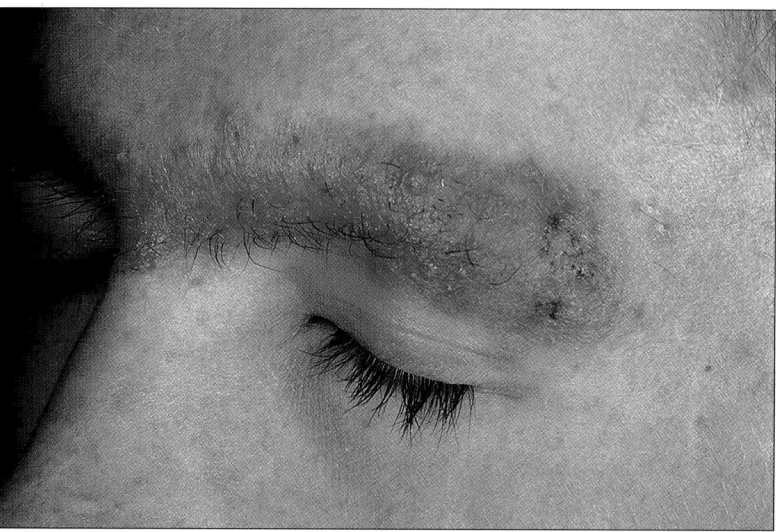

Fig. 2.61
Ulerythema ophryogenes: there is intense erythema with loss of follicles. The eyebrow is a commonly affected site. By courtesy of the Institute of Dermatology, London, UK.

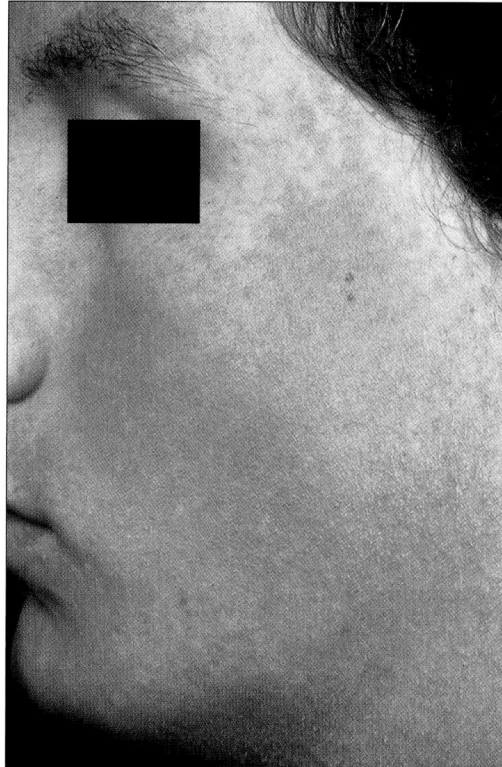

Fig. 2.62
Ulerythema ophryogenes: the cheek is also frequently involved. By courtesy of the Institute of Dermatology, London, UK.

The condition may be associated with a number of other inherited conditions including Noonan's syndrome, wooly hair, cardiofaciocutaneous syndrome, Cornelia de Lange syndrome, Rubinstein–Taybi syndrome and partial monosomy 18.[3,6–12] The association with Noonan's syndrome is of particular importance since such patients suffer from potentially life-threatening congenital pulmonary stenosis. Ulerythema ophryogenes is also associated with atopy.[13]

Atrophoderma vermiculata (ulerythema acneiforme, atrophoderma vermiculatum, atrophoderma reticulata, acne vermoulante, folliculitis ulerythema reticulata, folliculitis ulerythematosa, honeycomb atrophy) is an exceedingly rare form of atrophic keratosis pilaris thought to be inherited as an autosomal dominant. Patients present with follicular keratoses and pitted depressions separated by normal skin (worm-eaten appearance) affecting the cheeks, ears and forehead (honeycomb atrophy).[2,14,17] The disorder presents in patients after 5 years of age.[2] Unilateral nevoid variants following Blaschko's lines have been documented.[15–17]

Keratosis follicularis spinulosa decalvans is characterized by diffuse atrophic keratosis pilaris associated with scarring alopecia affecting the scalp.[18–20] Other conditions sometimes present include atopy, palmoplantar hyperkeratosis, photophobia and punctate keratitis.[18] In some patients it is inherited as an X-linked recessive disorder which has been mapped to Xp21.13–p22.2.[21,22] X-linked dominant and autosomal dominant variants have also been proposed.[19]

Pathogenesis and histological features

The pathogenesis of keratosis pilaris atrophicans is unknown although it involves blockage of the follicular ostium by a keratinous plug.

It is characterized by follicular hyperkeratosis with ostial dilatation, atrophy of the sebaceous gland and a scanty perifollicular or perivascular lymphohistiocytic infiltrate.[3,11,12,16]

References

1. Baden, H.P., Byers, R. (1994) Clinical findings, cutaneous pathology, and response to therapy in 21 patients with keratosis pilaris atrophicans. *Arch Dermatol*, **130**, 469–475.
2. Oranje, A.P., van Osch, L.D.M., Oosterwijk, J.C. (1994) Keratosis pilaris atrophicans: one heterogeneous disease or a symptom in different clinical entities? *Arch Dermatol*, **130**, 500–502.
3. Pierini, D.O., Pierini, A.M. (1979) Keratosis pilaris atrophicans facei (ulerythema ophryogenes): a cutaneous marker in the Noonan syndrome. *Br J Dermatol*, **100**, 409–416.
4. Zakon, S.J., Goldberg, A.L. (1951) Ulerythema ophryogenes (Unna–Taenzer). *Arch Dermatol*, **64**, 785–787.
5. Davenport, D.D. (1964) Ulerythema ophryogenes: review and report of a case: discussion of relationship to certain other skin disorders and association with internal abnormalities. *Arch Dermatol*, **89**, 74–80.
6. Neild, V.S., Pegum, J.S., Wells, R.S. (1984) The association of keratosis pilaris atrophicans and woolly hair, with and without Noonan's syndrome. *Br J Dermatol*, **110**, 357–362.
7. Mallory, S.B., Krafchik, B.R. (1990) Ulerythema ophryogenes in Noonan syndrome. *Pediatr Dermatol*, **7**, 77–78.
8. Güleç, A.T., Karaduman, A., Seçkin, D. (2000) Noonan syndrome: a case with recurrent keloid formation. *Cutis*, **67**, 315–316.
9. Reynolds, J.F., Neri, G., Herrmann, J.P. et al (1986) New multiple congenital anomalies/mental retardation syndrome with cardio-facio-cutaneous involvement: the CFC syndrome. *Am J Med Genet*, **25**, 413–426.
10. Zoulis, C.C., Stratakis, C.A., Rinck, G. et al (1994) Ulerythema ophryogenes and keratosis pilaris in a child with trisomy 18p. *Pediatr Dermatol*, **11**, 172–175.
11. Centeno, P.G., Rosón, E., Peteiro, C. et al (1999) Rubinstein–Taybi syndrome and ulerythema ophryogenes in a 9-year-old boy. *Pediatr Dermatol*, **16**, 134–136.
12. Flóres, A., Fernández-Redondo, V., Toribio, J. (2002) Ulerythema ophryogenes in Cornelia de Lange syndrome. *Pediatr Dermatol*, **19**, 42–45.
13. Mertens, R.L.J. (1968) Ulerythema ophryogenes and atopy. *Arch Dermatol*, **97**, 662–663.
14. Frosch, P.J., Brumage, M.R., Schuster-Pavlovic, C. et al (1988) Atrophoderma vermiculatum: case reports and review. *J Am Acad Dermatol*, **18**, 538–542.
15. Rozum, L.T., Mehregan, A.H., Johnson, S.A.M. (1972) Folliculitis ulerythematosa reticulata: a case with unilateral lesions. *Arch Dermatol*, **106**, 388–389.
16. Arrieta, E., Milgram-Sternberg, Y. (1988) Honeycomb atrophy on the right cheek. *Arch Dermatol*, **124**, 1101–1104.
17. Nico, M.M.S., Valente, N.Y.S., Sotto, M.N. (1998) Folliculitis ulerythematosa reticulata (atrophoderma vermiculata): early detection of a case with unilateral lesions. *Pediatr Dermatol*, **15**, 285–286.
18. Rand, R.E., Baden, H.P. (1983) Keratosis follicularis spinulosa decalvans: report of two cases and literature review. *Arch Dermatol*, **119**, 22–26.
19. Maroon, M., Tyler, W.B., Marks, V.J. (1992) Keratosis pilaris and scarring alopecia. Keratosis follicularis spinulosa decalvans. *Arch Dermatol*, **128**, 397, 400.
20. Romine, K.A., Rothschild, J.G., Hansen, R.C. (1997) Cicatricial alopecia and keratosis pilaris. Keratosis follicularis spinulosa decalvans. *Arch Dermatol*, **133**, 381, 384.
21. Oosterwijk, J.C., Nelen, M., van Zanwoort, P.M. et al (1992) Linkage analysis of keratosis follicularis spinulosa decalvans and regional assignment to human chromosome Xp21.2-p22.2. *Am J Hum Genet*, **50**, 801–807.
22. Oosterwijk, J.C., van der Wielen, M.J., van de Vosse, E. et al (1995) Refinement of the localization of the X-linked keratosis follicularis spinulosa decalvans (KFSD) gene in Xp22.13-p22.2. *J Med Genet*, **32**, 736–739.

Acquired ichthyosis

Acquired icthyosis is an important paraneoplastic manifestation of a number of malignancies. Hodgkin's lymphoma is most often encountered, but non-Hodgkin's lymphoma and a range of carcinomas have all been associated.[1–8] Acquired ichthyosis may also accompany HIV infection, sarcoidosis, connective tissue diseases including dermatomyositis and systemic lupus erythematosus, celiac disease and graft-versus-host disease.[4,9–12] Acquired ichthyosis following administration of lipid-lowering agents, including triparanol and diazacholesterol, and kava consumption has been documented.[13,14] The features of acquired ichthyosis most resemble those of icthyosis vulgaris both clinically and histologically (*Figs 2.63–2.65*).

References

1. Kurzrock, R., Cohen, P.R. (1995) Cutaneous paraneoplastic syndromes in solid tumors. *Am J Med*, **99**, 662–671.
2. Pagliaro, J.A., White, S.L. (1999) Specific skin lesions occurring in a patient with Hodgkin's lymphoma. *Australas J Dermatol*, **40**, 41–43.
3. Ameen, M., Chopra, S., Darvay, A. et al (2001) Erythema gyratum repens and acquired ichthyosis associated with transitional cell carcinoma. *Clin Exp Dermatol*, **26**, 510–512.
4. Inuzuka, M., Tomita, K., Tokura, Y. et al (2001) Acquired ichthyosis associated with dermatomyositis in a patient with hepatocellular carcinoma. *Br J Dermatol*, **144**, 416–417.
5. Yeh, J.S.M., Munn, S.E., Plunkett, T.A. et al (2000) Coexistence of acanthosis nigricans and the sign of Lesser–Trélat in a patient with gastric adenocarcinoma: a case report and review of the literature. *J Am Acad Dermatol*, **42**, 357–362.
6. Yokote, R., Iwatsuki, K., Hashizume, H. et al (1994) Lymphomatoid papulosis associated with acquired ichthyosis. *J Am Acad Dermatol*, **30**, 889–892.
7. Estines, O., Grosieux-Dauger, C., Derancourt, C. et al (2001) Paraneoplastic acquired ichthyosis revealing non-Hodgkin's lymphoma. *Ann Dermatol Venereol*, **128**, 31–34.
8. Kato, N., Yasukawa, K., Kimura, K. et al (2000) Anaplastic large cell lymphoma associated with acquired ichthyosis. *J Am Acad kermatol*, **42**, 914–920.
9. Singh, A., Thappa, D.M., Hamide, A. (1999) The spectrum of mucocutaneous manifestations during the evolutionary phases of HIV disease: an emerging Indian scenario. *J Dermatol*, **26**, 294–304.
10. Menni, S., Boccardi, D., Brusasco, A. (2000) Ichthyosis revealing celiac disease. *Eur J Dermatol*, **10**, 398–399.
11. Cather, J.C., Cohen, P.R. (1999) Ichthyosiform sarcoidosis. *J Am Acad Dermatol*, **40**, 862–865.
12. Dilek, I., Demirer, T., Ustun, C. et al (1998) Acquired ichthyosis associated with chronic graft-versus-host disease following allogeneic peripheral blood stem cell transplantation in a patient with chronic myelogenous leukemia. *Bone Marrow Transplant*, **21**, 1159–1161.
13. Proksch, E. (1995) Antilipemic drug-induced skin manifestations. *Hautarzt*, **46**, 76–80.
14. Ruze, P. (1990) Kava-induced dermopathy – a niacin deficiency? *Lancet*, **335**, 1442–1445.

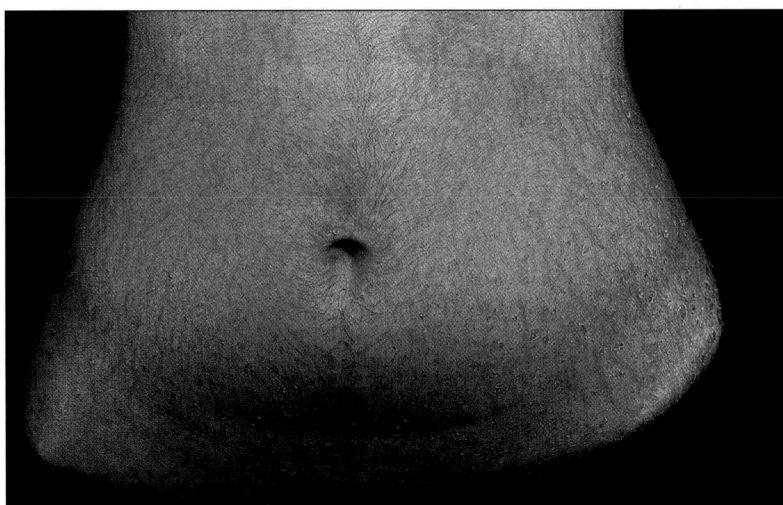

Fig. 2.63
Acquired ichthyosis: cutaneous manifestations most often resemble ichthyosis vulgaris. By courtesy of the Institute of Dermatology, London, UK.

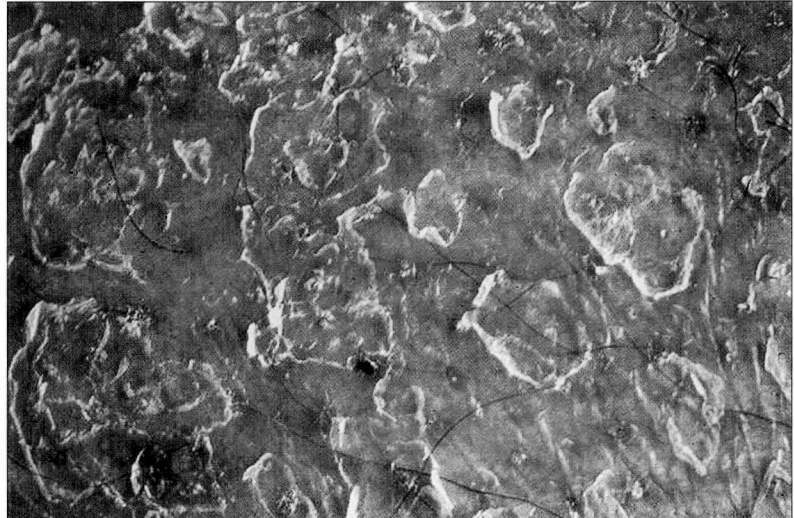

Fig. 2.64
Acquired ichthyosis: close-up view of the scale in *Fig. 2.63*. By courtesy of the Institute of Dermatology, London, UK.

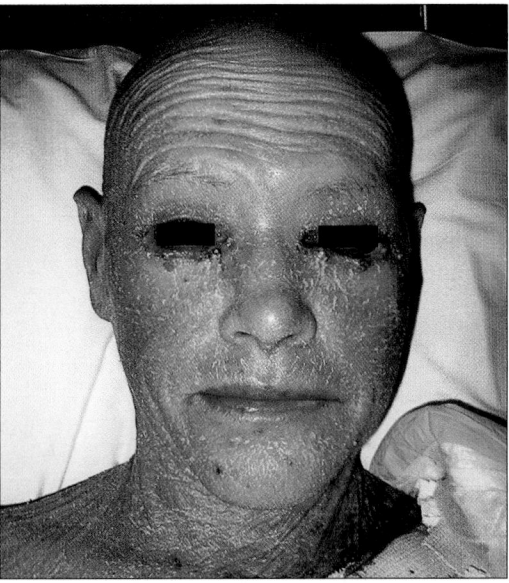

Fig. 2.65
Acquired ichthyosis: there is intense erythema and scaling. This patient also suffered from graft-versus-host disease. By courtesy of B. Solky, MD, Department of Dermatology, Brigham and Women's Hospital and Harvard Medical School, Boston, USA.

Palmoplantar keratoderma

The palmoplantar keratodermas (PPK) consist of a large heterogeneous group of conditions, including keratoderma palmaris et plantaris and palmoplantar ectodermal dysplasia, all showing hyperkeratosis of the palms and soles and classified on the basis of mode of inheritance, distribution of lesions, additional clinical features and associated abnormalities.[1–5] At least 30 subtypes are recognized and subdivided into two broad subtypes, one in which lesions are restricted to the skin and the other in which there is a much broader spectrum of ectodermal defects (palmoplantar ectodermal dysplasias) affecting skin, mucosae, nails, hair, teeth and neurological abnormalities.[5]

There are three major clinical categories: diffuse, focal, and punctate.[5] In many subtypes, the underlying molecular defect has been identified.[5] Histologically, they are characterized by orthohyperkeratosis, hypergranulosis and acanthosis.

References

1. Sybert, V.P., Dale, B.A., Holbrook, K.A. (1988) Palmar–plantar keratoderma: a clinical, ultrastructural and biochemical study. *J Am Acad Dermatol*, 18, 75–86.
2. Bergfeld, W.F., Derbes, V.J., Elias, P.M. et al (1982) The treatment of keratosis palmaris et plantaris with isotretinoin. *J Am Acad Dermatol*, 6, 727–731.
3. Lucker, G.P.H., van de Kerkhof, P.C.M., Steijlen, P.M. (1994) The hereditary palmoplantar keratoses: an updated review and classification. *Br J Dermatol*, 131, 1–14.
4. Stevens, H.P., Kelsell, D.P., Bryant, S.P. et al (1996) Linkage of an American pedigree with palmoplantar keratoderma and malignancy (palmoplantar ectodermal dysplasia type III) to 17q24. Literature survey and proposed updated classification of the keratodermas. *Arch Dermatol*, 132, 640–651.
5. Kelsell, D.P., Stevens, H.P. (1999) The palmoplantar keratodermas: much more than palms and soles. *Mol Med Today*, 5, 107–113.

Epidermolytic palmoplantar keratoderma

Clinical features

Also known as Vorner's disease, this variant is one of the more commonly encountered forms of palmoplantar keratoderma. It is inherited as an autosomal dominant and usually presents in the first few weeks or months of life.[1–5] Patients present with symmetrical well-demarcated yellowish keratoderma diffusely affecting the palms and soles and bordered by an erythematous margin.[1] Hyperhidrosis may sometimes be present and painful blisters are not uncommon.[2,5] Rarely, associated knuckle pads have been documented.[6]

Pathogenesis and histological features

Epidermolytic palmoplantar keratoderma (EPPK) results from keratin 9 gene mutations.[7] This variant of palmoplantar keratoderma is not associated with malignancy. Patients in one large kindred showed a high incidence of breast and ovarian cancer.[8,9] It is now believed that this represented a coincidental co-segregation of a keratin 9 mutation with a BRCA1 mutation on 17q21.[1]

Histologically, there is hyperkeratosis, papillomatosis, hypergranulosis, and acanthosis accompanied by the features of epidermolytic hyperkeratosis, namely, perinuclear cytoplasmic vacuolation (cytolysis) affecting the upper prickle and the granular cell layers with eosinophilic intracytoplasmic inclusion-like keratin aggregates (*Fig. 2.66*). A superficial dermal perivascular lymphohistiocytic infiltrate may sometimes be present.

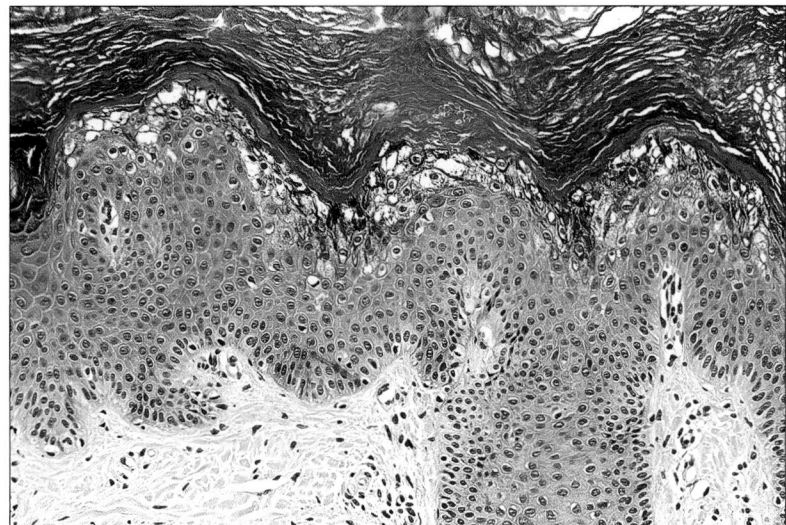

Fig. 2.66
Epidermolytic palmoplantar keratoderma: there is hyperkeratosis, papillomatosis, cytoplasmic vacuolation and conspicuous intracytoplasmic inclusions – the features of epidermolytic hyperkeratosis.

Electron microscopy confirms the perinuclear keratin aggregates and cytoplasmic vacuolation.[7]

References

1. Stevens, H.P., Kelsell, D.P., Bryant, S.P. et al (1996) Linkage of an American pedigree with palmoplantar keratoderma and malignancy (palmoplantar ectodermal dysplasia type II) to 17q24. Literature survey and proposed updated classification of the keratodermas. *Arch Dermatol*, **132**, 640–651.
2. Thomas, J.R. III, Greene, S.L., Su, W.P.D. (1984) Epidermolytic palmoplantar keratoderma. *Int J Dermatol*, **23**, 652–655.
3. Camisa, C., Williams, H. (1985) Epidermolytic variant of hereditary palmo-plantar keratoderma. *Br J Dermatol*, **112**, 221–225.
4. Moriwaki, S-I., Tanaka, T., Horiguchi, Y. et al (1988) Epidermolytic hereditary palmoplantar keratoderma. *Arch Dermatol*, **124**, 555–559.
5. Berth-Jones, J., Hutchinson, P.E. (1989) A family with palmoplantar epidermolytic hyperkeratosis. *Clin Exp Dermatol*, **14**, 313–316.
6. Nogita, T., Nakagawa, H., Ishibashi, Y. (1991) Hereditary epidermolytic palmoplantar keratoderma with knuckle pad-like lesions over the finger joints. *Br J Dermatol*, **125**, 496.
7. Reis, A., Hennies, H-C., Langbein, L. et al (1994) Keratin 9 gene mutations in epidermolytic palmoplantar keratoderma (EPPK). *Nat Genet*, **6**, 174–179.
8. Blanchet-Bardon, C., Nazzaro, V., Chevrant-Breton, J. et al (1987) Hereditary epidermolytic palmoplantar keratoderma associated with breast and ovarian cancer in a large kindred. *Br J Dermatol*, **117**, 363–370.
9. Torchard, D., Blanchet-Bardon, C., Serova, O. et al (1994) Epidermolytic palmoplantar keratoderma cosegregates with a keratin 9 mutation in a pedigree with breast and ovarian cancer. *Nat Genet*, **6**, 106–110.

Diffuse palmoplantar keratoderma

Clinical features

Diffuse palmoplantar keratoderma (Unna–Thost, tylosis) is an autosomal dominant disorder characterized by a diffuse, smooth hyperkeratosis involving the palms and soles as well as the ventral surfaces of the fingers and toes (*Figs 2.67–2.69*).[1] An autosomal recessive variant (mal de Meleda) has also been described.[1] Reported incidences have ranged from 1:12,000 to 1:40,000 and there appears to be a particularly high incidence in some parts of Sweden.[1–3] Symptoms usually present in the first 3 years of life.[1] Many patients suffer from increased sweating and, therefore, maceration is common. There is a greatly increased risk of dermatophyte infections.[1] Patients with this variant may also show axillary and groin involvement, subungual hyperkeratosis, onychodystrophy and central facial lesions.[4]

Although diffuse palmoplantar keratoderma was originally believed to be associated with esophageal carcinoma (Howell-Evans syndrome), re-examination of the affected kindreds disclosed that the keratoderma would better be classified as focal (see focal non-epidermolytic palmoplantar keratoderma with esophageal squamous carcinoma, p. 67).[5] There are, however, rare instances of diffuse palmoplantar keratoderma associated with cutaneous squamous cell carcinoma, for example Huriez syndrome (palmoplantar keratoderma with sclerodactyly) and Schöpf–Schulz–Passarge syndrome (palmoplantar keratoderma with squamous carcinoma arising in the areas affected by keratoderma).[6,7] Acquired diffuse palmoplantar keratoderma may also be associated with malignancy.[8]

Pathogenesis and histological features

Diffuse palmoplantar keratoderma has been mapped to 12q11–13, the site of the keratin II genes.[9,10] There is however evidence for genetic heterogeneity. Thus a mutation in keratin I has been identified in one family but not in others.[11,12]

This disorder is characterized by marked hyperkeratosis, hypergranulosis, acanthosis and an exaggerated epidermal ridge pattern (*Fig. 2.70*). A chronic inflammatory cell infiltrate is sometimes evident in the

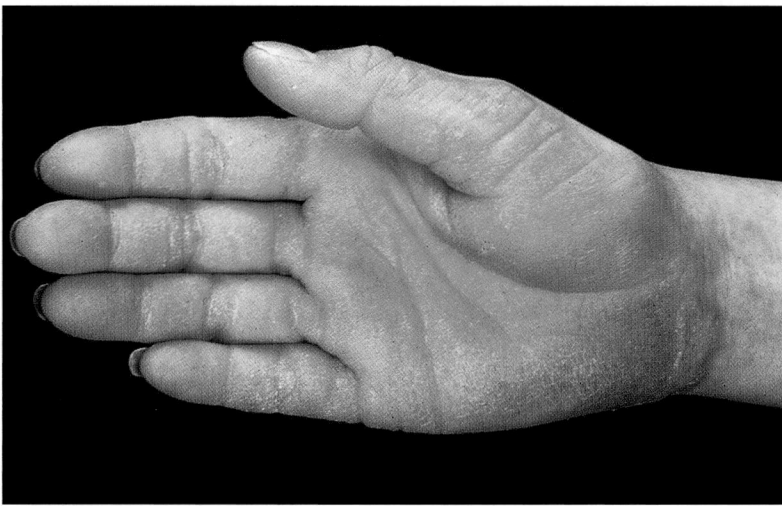

Fig. 2.68
Diffuse palmoplantar keratoderma: in this patient the palms of the hands were also affected. By courtesy of W.A.D. Griffiths, MD, Institute of Dermatology, London, UK.

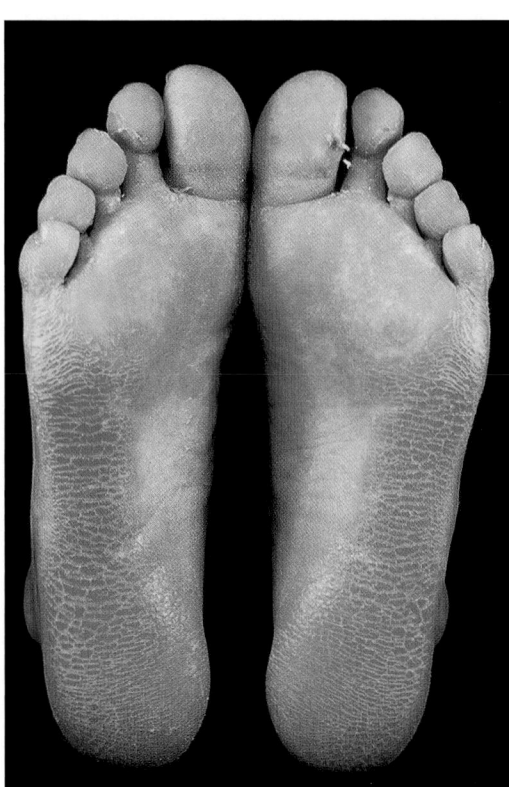

Fig. 2.67
Diffuse palmoplantar keratoderma: there is hyperkeratosis affecting the entire sole of the foot. By courtesy of W.A.D. Griffiths, MD, Institute of Dermatology, London, UK.

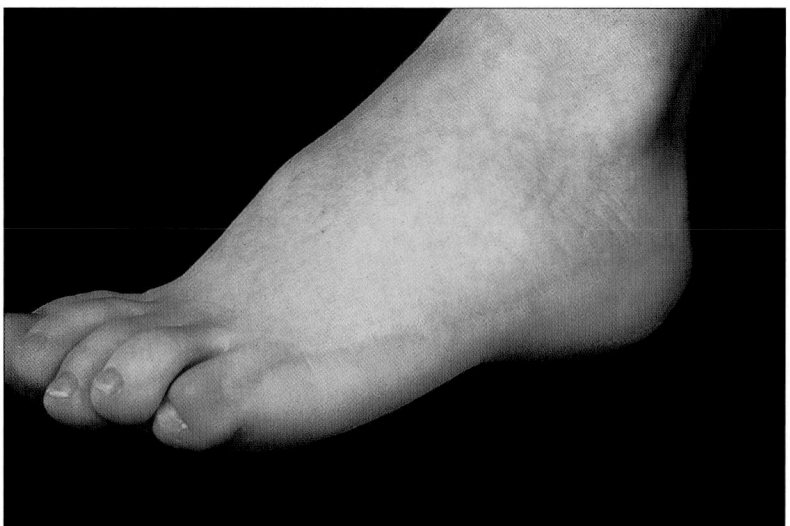

Fig. 2.69
Diffuse palmoplantar keratoderma: the border of the lesion is marked by a linear zone of erythema. By courtesy of W.A.D. Griffiths, MD, Institute of Dermatology, London, UK.

superficial dermis. The presence of spongiosis and vesiculation should suggest a concomitant dermatophyte infection and prompt evaluation of a PAS or silver stained section.[1] In the diffuse recessive variant, the hyperkeratosis is even more marked than in the dominant form and the epidermis shows prominent psoriasiform hyperplasia.[1]

References

1. Nielsen, P.G. (1988) Hereditary palmoplantar keratoderma and dermatophytosis. *Int J Dermatol*, **27**, 223–231.
2. Kansky, A., Durinovic-Bello, S., de Jongh, B.M. et al (1982) HLA antigens in Yugoslav patients with palmoplantar keratoderma, type Unna–Thost: a family study. *Acta Derm Venereol*, **62**, 313–316.
3. Rook, A., Wilkinson, D.S., Ebling, F.J.G. (1979) Textbook of dermatology, 3rd edn. Oxford: Blackwell, vol. 2, pp 1300–1302.
4. Bergfeld, W.F., Derbes, V.J., Elias, P.M. et al (1982) The treatment of keratosis palmaris et plantaris with isotretinoin. *J Am Acad Dermatol*, **6**, 727–731.
5. Ellis, A., Field, E.A., Field, J.K. et al (1994) Tylosis associated with carcinoma of the esophagus in a large Liverpool family – a review of six generations. *Eur J Cancer B Oral Oncol*, **30B**, 102–112.
6. Huriez, C.L., Deminati, M., Agache, P. et al (1969) Génodermatose scléroatrophiante et kératodermique des extrémités. *Ann Dermatol Syphiligr*, **96**, 135–146.
7. Stevens, H.P., Kelsell, D.P., Leigh, I.M. et al (1996) Punctate palmoplantar keratoderma and malignancy in a four-generation family. *Br J Dermatol*, **134**, 720–726.
8. Murata, Y., Mumano, K., Tani, M. (1988) Acquired diffuse keratoderma of the palms and soles with bronchial carcinoma: report of a case and review of the literature. *Arch Dermatol*, **124**, 497–498.
9. Lind, L., Lundström, A., Hofer, P.A. et al (1994) The gene for diffuse palmoplantar keratoderma of the type found in Northern Sweden is localized to chromosome 12q11-q13. *Hum Mol Genet*, **3**, 1789–1793.
10. Kelsell, D.P., Stevens, H.P., Ratnavel, R. et al (1995) Genetic linkage studies in non-epidermolytic keratoderma: evidence of heterogeneity. *Hum Mol Genet*, **4**, 1021–1025.
11. Kimonis, V., DiGiovanna, J. J., Yang, J.M. et al (1994) A mutation in the VI end domain of keratin I causes non-epidermotropic palmar–plantar keratoderma. *J Invest Dermatol*, **103**, 764–769.
12. Kelsell, D.P., Stevens, H.P. (1999) The palmoplantar keratodermas: much more than palms and soles. *Mol Med Today*, **5**, 107–113.

Erythrokeratoderma variabilis

Clinical features

This rare ichthyosiform dermatosis generally has an autosomal dominant mode of inheritance although an autosomal recessive variant has recently been described.[1–5] Lesions usually present soon after birth or during the first year of life and are of two types:

- In type 1, there may be symmetrically distributed, discrete figurate and often bizarre patches of erythema, which vary in size, shape, number and location over periods of hours and days (*Fig. 2.71*).[3] These are sometimes temperature or stress related.[1,6]

- In addition to the features found in type 1, also present in type 2 are well-defined geographical, reddish-yellow-brown greasy, hyperkeratotic plaques arising either within the erythematous lesions or, more often, independently (*Fig. 2.72*). Lesions are usually asymptomatic although occasionally mild pruritus is a feature.[4]

The condition particularly affects the face, buttocks and extensor surfaces of the extremities.[7] While cold weather in winter and emotional problems may sometimes exacerbate the condition, the symptoms often improve in the summer months.[4] Erythrokeratoderma variabilis is occasionally associated with high estrogen levels and symptoms may worsen with estrogen-containing oral contraceptive therapy.[1,2,4] Hypertrichosis (of vellus hairs) and mild keratoderma of the palms and soles may additionally be evident.[3,6] The mucous membranes, hair, teeth and nails are unaffected and there are no associated systemic manifestations.[4]

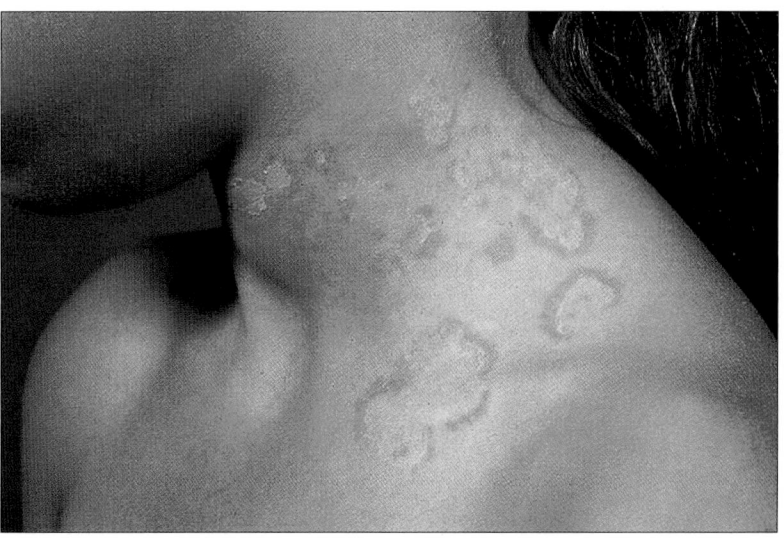

Fig. 2.71
Erythrokeratoderma variabilis: annular and serpiginous erythematous lesions showing scaling and the characteristic railing edge. By courtesy of R.A. Marsden, MD, St George's Hospital, London, UK.

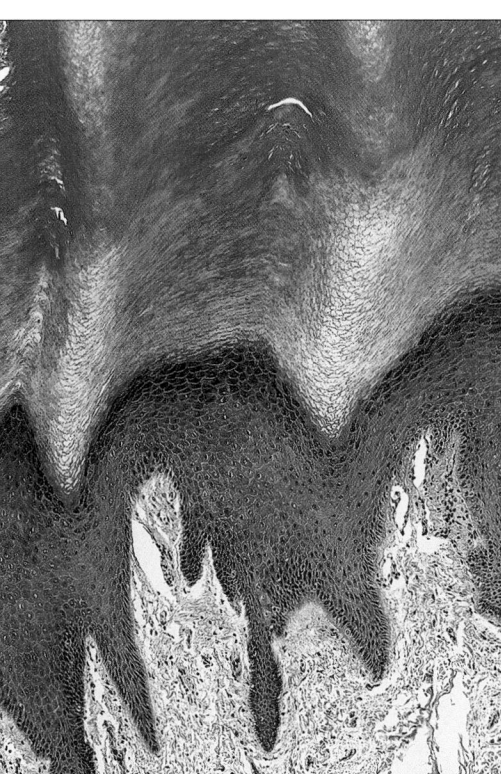

Fig. 2.70
Diffuse palmoplantar keratoderma: there is massive hyperkeratosis, hypergranulosis and acanthosis.

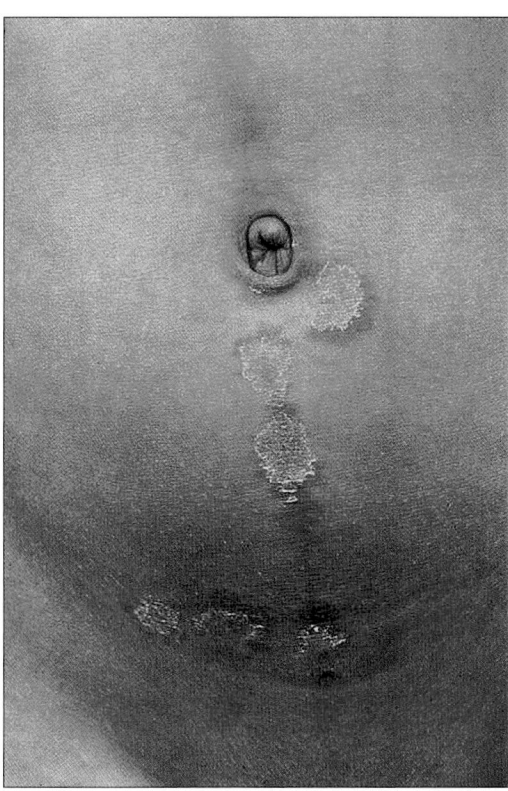

Fig. 2.72
Erythrokeratoderma variabilis: in these lesions there is more pronounced scaling.

Pathogenesis and histological features

Initially linked to the RH1 locus on 1p, erythrokeratoderma variabilis has been mapped to 1p34–p35, which includes GJB3.[7,8] Germline mutations of the genes, which code for the connexins Cx31 and Cx30.3, have been identified in a number of families with this disorder.[8–10]

The histopathological features of this disease are not specific, consisting of marked orthohyperkeratosis, irregular acanthosis and variable papillomatosis, which may resemble church spires.[3,11] Dyskeratotic cells with pyknotic nuclei reminiscent of the grains of Darier have been described in one case.[6] The granular cell layer appears normal. A perivascular lymphohistiocytic inflammatory cell infiltrate may be present in the superficial dermis. Pilosebaceous follicles and sweat glands are normal.[11] Immunocytochemistry has shown persistence of basal keratinocyte keratin within the stratum corneum but the significance of this is uncertain.[12]

Ultrastructural studies have revealed markedly diminished numbers of Odland bodies in the granular cell layer.[6,11] Conspicuous non-myelinated nerve fibers and Schwann cells have been described in the papillary dermis.[6,11] These, however, are not consistent findings.[12] Nuclear encirclement by condensed keratin filaments and keratohyalin has also been recorded.[12]

References

1. Rand, R.E., Baden, H.P. (1983) The ichthyoses – a review. *J Am Acad Dermatol*, 8, 285–305.
2. Gewirtzman, G.B., Winkler, N.M., Dobson, R.L. (1978) Erythrokeratoderma variabilis: a family study. *Arch Dermatol*, 114, 259–261.
3. Schellander, F.G., Fritsch, P.O. (1969) Variable erythrokeratoderma. *Arch Dermatol*, 100, 744–748.
4. Armstrong, D.K.B., Hutchinson, T.H., Walsh, M.Y. et al (1997) Autosomal recessive inheritance of erythrokeratoderma variabilis. *Pediatr Dermatol*, 14, 355–358.
5. Knipe, R.C., Flowers, F.P., Johnson, F.R. et al (1995) Erythrokeratoderma variabilis: case report and review of the literature. *Pediatr Dermatol*, 12, 21–23.
6. Rappaport, I.P., Goldes, J.A., Goltz, R.W. (1986) Erythrokeratoderma variabilis treated with isotretinoin. A clinical, histologic and ultrastructural study. *Arch Dermatol*, 122, 441–445.
7. Van der Schroeff, J.G., van Leeuwen-Cornelisse, I., van Haeringen, A. et al (1988) Further evidence for localization of the gene of erythrokeratoderma variabilis. *Hum Genet*, 80, 97–98.
8. Richard, G., Smith, L.E., Bailer, R.A. (1998) Mutations in the human connexin gene GJB3 cause erythrokeratoderma variabilis. *Nat Genet*, 20, 366–369.
9. Di, W.L., Rugg, E.L., Leigh, I.M. et al (2001) Multiple epidermal connexins are expressed in different keratinocyte subpopulations including connexin 31. *J Invest Dermatol*, 117, 958–964.
10. Wilgoss, A., Leigh, I.M., Barnes, M.R. et al (1999) Identification of a novel mutation R42P in the gap junction protein beta-3 associated with autosomal dominant erythrokeratoderma variabilis. *J Invest Dermatol*, 113, 1119–1122.
11. Vandersteen, P.R., Muller, S.A. (1971) Erythrokeratoderma variabilis: an enzyme histochemical and ultrastructural study. *Arch Dermatol*, 103, 362–370.
12. McFadden, N., Oppedal, B.R., Ree, K. et al (1987) Erythrokeratoderma variabilis: immunohistochemical and ultrastructural studies of the epidermis. *Acta Derm Venereol*, 67, 284–288.

Progressive symmetric erythrokeratodermia

Clinical features

Also known as erythrokeratodermia progressiva symmetrica, this condition is inherited as an autosomal dominant with incomplete penetrance, although sporadic cases may also be encountered.[1,2] It usually presents in the first year of life with fixed, symmetrical and sometimes pruritic, erythematous scaly plaques on the extensor surfaces including the elbows, knees, buttocks, dorsal surfaces of the feet and hands and head.[1–5] The face, chest and abdomen are typically unaffected.[2] The plaques gradually extend during the first few years and then become static.[3] Additional features include palmoplantar keratoderma and pseudoainhum (constriction bands on the fingers and toes). The sex incidence is equal.[2] There is clinical overlap with erythrokeratoderma variabilis and indeed patients may present with features of both diseases. However progressive symmetric erythrokeratoderma lacks transient migratory erythema.[1]

Pathogenesis and histological features

A mutation in the loricrin gene on chromosome 1q21 has been identified in one family with progressive symmetric erythrokeratoderma.[6]

Histologically, there is marked basket-weave hyperkeratosis with focal parakeratosis, hypergranulosis and psoriasiform hyperplasia.[2,3] Paranuclear vacuolation may be evident in the granular cell layer.[3,7] A perivascular lymphocytic infiltrate is present in the superficial dermis.[5]

Ultrastructurally, characteristic loricrin-rich intranuclear granules are seen in the granular cell layer.[6] Lamellar granules are increased in number and lipid droplets may be evident in the cornified cells.[3] The cornified cell envelopes show greatly reduced staining for loricrin with immunohistochemistry.[6] Swollen mitochondria in the granular cell layer are said to be a helpful ultrastructural diagnostic pointer.[3–5,7]

Differential diagnosis

Progressive symmetric erythrokeratodermia can be distinguished from psoriasis by the absence of suprapapillary plate thinning, neutrophil infiltration and Munro microabscesses.[2] In addition the parakeratosis tends to be very focal and hypergranulosis is usually present.

References

1. McGrath, J.A., Eady, R.A.J. (2001) Recent advances in the molecular basis of inherited skin diseases. *Adv Genet*, 43, 1–32.
2. Ruiz-Maldonado, R., Tamayo, L., del Castillo, V. et al (1982) Erythrokeratoderma progressiva symmetrica: report of 10 cases. *Dermatologica*, 164, 133–141.
3. Nazzaro, V., Blanchet-Bardon, C. (1986) Progressive symmetrical erythrokeratoderma: histological and ultrastructural study of a patient before and after treatment with etretinate. *Arch Dermatol*, 122, 434–440.
4. Kudsi, S., Naeyaert, J.M. (1990) Progressive symmetric erythrokeratoderma of Darier Gottron. *Dermatologica*, 180, 196–197.
5. Gray, L.C., Davis, L.S., Guill, M.A. (1996) Progressive symmetric erythrokeratoderma. *J Am Acad Dermatol*, 34, 858–859.
6. Ishida-Yamamoto, A., McGrath, J.A., Lam, H. et al (1997) The molecular pathology of progressive symmetric erythrokeratodermia: a frameshift mutation in the loricrin gene and perturbations in the cornified cell envelope. *Am J Hum Genet*, 61, 581–589.
7. Niemi, K-M., Kanerva, L. (1993) Histological and ultrastructural study of a family with erythrokeratoderma progressiva symmetrica. *J Cutan Pathol*, 20, 242–249.

Striate palmoplantar keratoderma

Clinical features

Striate palmoplantar keratoderma (Brünauer–Fuhs–Siemens syndrome, acral keratoderma, keratosis palmoplantaris striata) is an autosomal dominant disorder characterized by linear bands of keratoderma affecting the palmar aspects of the palms and fingers (*Fig. 2.73*) accompanied by

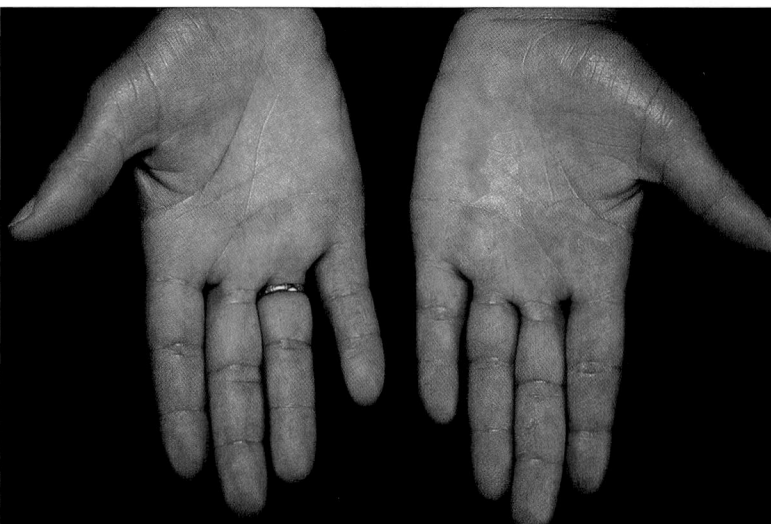

Fig. 2.73
Striate palmoplantar keratoderma: linear hyperkeratotic bands are present best seen along the ulnar border of the palm. By courtesy of the Institute of Dermatology, London, UK.

keratoelastoidosis marginalis of the hands.[1] All present with frequently crateriform, keratotic papules along the borders of the hands and feet (*Fig. 2.79*).[1] Although usually discrete, in some patients the papules may coalesce into plaques.

Acrokeratoelastoidosis presents in childhood and adolescence with yellowish, warty and crateriform keratotic or pearly papules predominantly affecting the sides of the hands, wrists, fingers and feet.[2–5] There is no racial predilection and the sexes are affected equally. Patients may also develop circumscribed keratodermatous knuckle pad-like lesions, palmoplantar hyperkeratosis and hyperhidrosis (*Fig. 2.80*).[1,3] Sporadic and autosomal dominant variants have been described. The disorder may be linked to chromosome 2.[6] Repeated trauma is believed to be of etiological importance.

Focal acral hyperkeratosis is clinically identical to acrokeratoelastoidosis, patients presenting with keratotic papules along the sides of the hands, fingers and feet.[7,8] It has also been designated acrokeratoelastoidosis without elastorrhexis.[9] Other reported cases have been mistakenly documented as acrokeratoelastoidosis.[10] Females are affected more often than males. Although originally thought to be a disorder of black children, more recently it has been described in whites.[11]

Mosaic acral keratosis is similar if not identical to focal acral hyperkeratosis, being characterized by keratotic papules distributed in a mosaic or jigsaw-puzzle pattern along dorsal aspects of the feet and adjacent lower legs.[12] Hyperkeratosis may be seen on the palms and soles.[1] Only females, predominantly black, are affected.[1]

Degenerative collagenous plaques of the hands affect the sun-damaged skin of the elderly and present as symmetrical yellowish, keratotic or smooth papules and plaques affecting the thumb, first web and side of the index finger.[4,13–18] The ulnar border of the hand and volar aspect of the wrist may also be involved. Keratoelastoidosis marginalis of the hands is a similar condition described in Australians in which keratotic papules develop at sites of trauma along the index finger and thumb.[19] The skin is typically grossly sun damaged. Calcified variants of degenerative collagenous plaques are known as digital papular calcific elastosis.[20,21]

Histological features

Acrokeratoelastoidosis is characterized by massive orthohyperkeratosis overlying a crateriform dell lined by acanthotic epidermis. Hypergranulosis may be present. The dermis shows fragmentation and loss of the elastic tissue (elastorrhexis). Collagen may be disorganized or appear homogenized or pale staining.[2,3]

Focal acral hyperkeratosis and mosaic acral keratosis are histologically identical with the exception that the elastic tissue appears normal.[7–12]

Degenerative collagenous plaques of the hands are characterized by a dense zone of thickened and distorted collagen with fragmentation of elastic fibers and overlying hyperkeratosis and acanthosis.[4,13–18] The papillary dermis is spared. Calcification is sometimes a feature (digital papular calcific elastosis).[19–21] Telangiectatic vessels may also be seen and increased dermal mucin has been described.[19]

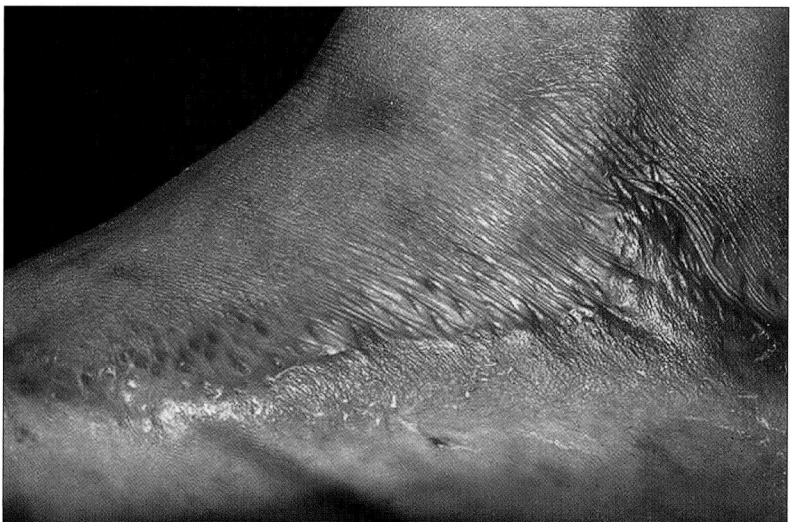

Fig. 2.79
Marginal papular acrokeratoderma: there is a linear band of scaling along the border of the foot. By courtesy of the Institute of Dermatology, London, UK.

References

1. Rongioletti, F., Betti, R., Crosti, C. et al (1994) Marginal papular acrokeratodermas: a unified nosography for focal acral hyperkeratosis, acrokeratoelastoidosis and related disorders. *Dermatology*, **188**, 28–31.
2. Costa, O.G. (1954) Acrokeratoelastoidosis. *Arch Dermatol Syphilol*, **70**, 228–231.
3. Rubegni, P., Aloe, G. De, Romano, C. et al (1997) Acrokeratoelastoidosis: a report of two sporadic cases. *Clin Exp Dermatol*, **22**, 62–64.
4. Shbaklo, Z., Jamaleddine, N.F., Kibbi, A-G. et al (1990) Acrokeratoelastoidosis. *Int J Dermatol*, **29**, 333–336.
5. Dyall-Smith, D. (1996) Acrokeratoelastoidosis. *Australas J Dermatol*, **37**, 213–214.
6. Greiner, J., Kruger, J., Palden, L. et al (1983) A linkage study of acrokeratoelastoidosis: possible mapping to chromosome 2. *Hum Genet*, **63**, 222–227.
7. Dowd, P.M., Harmann, R.R.M., Black, M.M. (1983) Focal acral hyperkeratosis. *Br J Dermatol*, **109**, 97–103.
8. Blum, S.L., Cruz, P.D., Siegel, D.M. et al (1987) Hyperkeratotic papules on the hands and feet. *Arch Dermatol*, **123**, 1225–1230.
9. Matthews, C.N.A., Harmann, R.R.M. (1974) Acrokeratoelastoidosis (without elastorrhexis). *Proc R Soc Med*, **67**, 1237.
10. Handfield-Jones, S., Kennedy, C.T.C. (1987) Acrokeratoelastoidosis treated with etretinate. *J Am Acad Dermatol*, **17**, 881–882.
11. Richey, T.K., Fitzpatrick, J.E. (1996) Yellowish papules on lateral aspect of palms. *Arch Dermatol*, **132**, 1365, 1368.
12. Jacyk, J., Smith, A. (1990) Mosaic acral keratosis. *Clin Exp Dermatol*, **15**, 361–362.
13. Burks, J.W., Wise, L.S. Jr, Clark, W.H. (1959) Degenerative collagenous plaques of the hands. *Arch Dermatol*, **82**, 362–366.
14. Mehregan, A.H. (1966) Degenerative collagenous plaques of the hands. *Arch Dermatol*, **93**, 633.
15. Ritchie, E.B., Williams, M.H. (1966) Degenerative collagenous plaques of the hands. *Arch Dermatol*, **93**, 202–203.
16. Sehgal, V.N., Singh, M., Korrane, R.V. et al (1980) Degenerative collagenous plaque of the hand (linear keratoelastoidosis of the hands). A variant of acrokeratoelastoidosis. *Dermatologica*, **161**, 200–204.
17. Abulafia, J., Vignale, R.A. (2000) Degenerative collagenous plaques of the hands and acrokeratoelastoidosis: pathogenesis and relationship with knuckle pads. *Int J Dermatol*, **39**, 424–432.
18. Mortimore, R.J., Conrad, R.J. (2001) Collagenous and elastic marginal plaques of the hands. *Australas J Dermatol*, **42**, 211–213.
19. Kocsard, E. (1964) Keratoelastoidosis marginalis of the hands. *Dermatologica*, **131**, 169–175.
20. Jordaan, H.F., Rossouw, D.J. (1991) Digital papular calcific elastosis: a histopathological, histochemical and ultrastructural study of 20 patients. *J Cutan Pathol*, **17**, 358–370.
21. Rahbari, H. (1991) Collagenous and elastic marginal plaques of the hands. *J Cutan Pathol*, **18**, 358–370.

Keratoderma climactericum

Clinical features

Keratoderma climactericum (Haxthausen's disease, climacteric keratoderma) is an acquired disorder which is restricted to menopausal

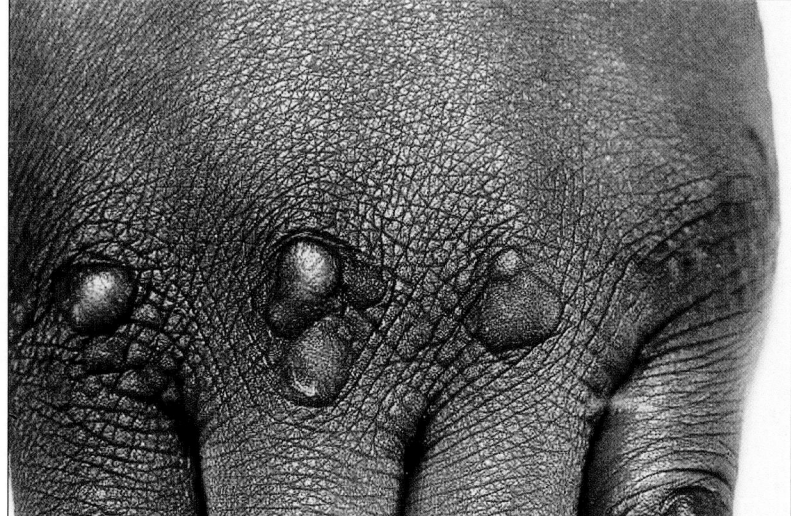

Fig. 2.80
Acrokeratoelastoidosis: knuckle pads are conspicuous in this patient. By courtesy of the Institute of Dermatology, London, UK.

women.[1,2] Lesions present on the weight-bearing surfaces of the sole of the foot as erythematous hyperkeratotic and fissured plaques and then spread to involve the rest of the plantar skin (*Fig. 2.81*). Patients are often overweight. Palmar involvement is sometimes seen with lesions affecting the area between the thenar and hypothenar eminences.[2] Similar lesions have been documented in younger women who have undergone bilateral oophorectomy.[3] The condition is distinguished from congenital palmoplantar keratoderma by its late onset.

Histological features

The plantar skin shows massive hyperkeratosis, hypergranulosis, acanthosis and spongiosis with lymphocytic exocytosis.[2] A superficial perivascular dermal lymphohistiocytic infiltrate is present and vertically orientated dermal collagen associated with atypical myofibroblasts is often seen.[2]

References

1. Haxthausen, H. (1934) Keratoderma climactericum. *Br J Dermatol*, **46**, 161–167.
2. Deschamps, P., Leroy, D., Pedailles, S. et al (1986) Keratoderma climactericum (Haxthausen's disease): clinical signs, laboratory findings and etretinate treatment in 10 patients. *Dermatologica*, **172**, 258–262.
3. Wachtel, T.J. (1981) Plantar and palmar hyperkeratosis in young castrated women. *Int J Dermatol*, **20**, 270–271.

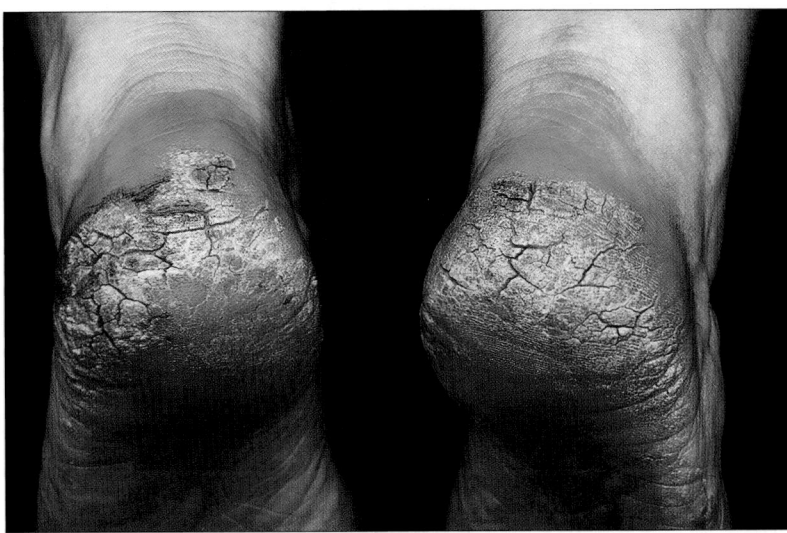

Fig. 2.81
Keratoderma climactericum: there is massive hyperkeratosis with fissuring over the heels. By courtesy of the Institute of Dermatology, London, UK.

Palmoplantar ectodermal dysplasias

Focal palmoplantar keratoderma with oral hyperkeratosis

Clinical features

Focal (non-epidermolytic) palmoplantar keratoderma with oral hyperkeratosis (Jadassohn–Lewandowsky syndrome, pachyonychia type I, palmoplantar ectodermal dysplasia type I) is usually associated with an autosomal dominant mode of inheritance although an autosomal recessive variant has been described.[1,2] It has a high incidence in Croatia and Slovenia and also appears to be more commonly seen in Jews.[3,4] Clinical features may be present at birth or appear within the first 6 months of life.[1,5] The sex incidence is equal.

The features include massive hyperkeratosis of the distal nail beds of the fingers and toes, resulting in elevation and apparent thickening of the nail plate (*Figs 2.82, 2.83*). Nail infections are a frequent complication.[5] Also present are palmoplantar keratoderma, hyperhidrosis and follicular keratosis, xerosis and verrucous lesions, which most often arise on the elbows, knees and lower legs (*Fig. 2.84*). Patients also develop alopecia, nail bed infections and show premature eruption of the teeth.[1,6] Erythema and blistering of the soles of the feet, and to a lesser extent on the palms of the hands, are sometimes present; leukokeratosis oris is almost invariably evident (*Fig. 2.85*).[1,6,7] Laryngeal involvement has also been documented.[8]

Pathogenesis and histological features

This variant of focal palmoplantar keratoderma is heterogeneous. Mutations have been described in keratin K16 and K6a genes.[9–14]

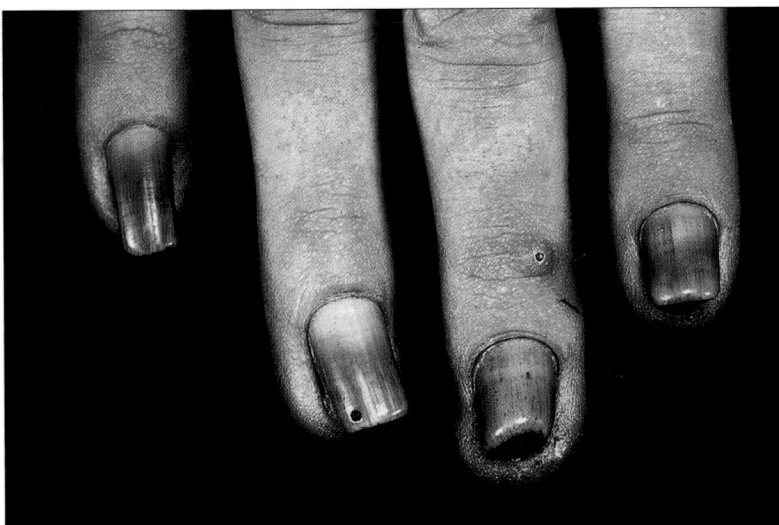

Fig. 2.82
Pachyonychia congenita: there is gross nail deformity with transverse arching of the distal portion. Although the nail plate appears to be thickened, most of the changes are, in fact, due to massive hyperkeratosis of the nail bed, resulting in elevation and bending of the nail plate. By courtesy of R.A. Marsden, MD, St George's Hospital, London, UK.

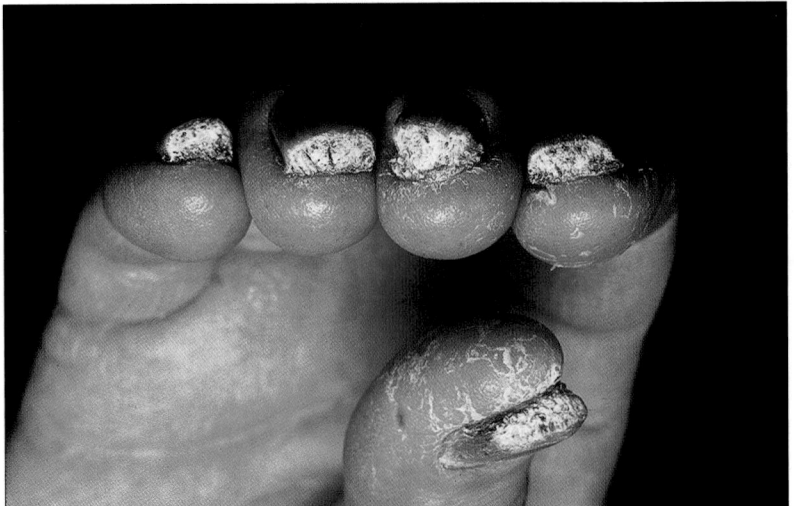

Fig. 2.83
Pachyonychia congenita: in this view, the subungual hyperkeratosis is more obvious. By courtesy of W.A.D. Griffiths, MD, Institute of Dermatology, London, UK.

The nail beds show massive hyperkeratosis.[1] The palmoplantar lesions are characterized by hyperkeratosis, hypergranulosis and acanthosis.[1] Round to oval darkly staining perinuclear inclusions representing densely aggregated keratin filaments in the prickle cell layer have been described.[11] The follicular lesions show plugging of the ostia with surrounding hyperkeratosis, parakeratosis and acanthosis.[6] A mononuclear perivascular chronic inflammatory cell infiltrate may be present in the superficial dermis. The oral lesions are indistinguishable from those of the white sponge nevus, consisting of parakeratosis, acanthosis and epithelial vacuolation. No evidence of dysplasia is seen.

References

1. Daniel Su, W.P., Chun, S.I., Hammond, D.E. et al (1990) Pachyonychia congenita: a clinical study of 12 cases and review of the literature. *Pediatr Dermatol*, **7**, 33–38.
2. Haber, R.M., Rose, T.H. (1986) Autosomal recessive pachyonychia congenita. *Arch Dermatol*, **122**, 919–923.
3. Videnic, N., Kansky, A., Basta-Juzbasic, A. (1991) Pachyonychia congenita (Jadassohn–Lewandowsky syndrome): a review of 25 cases in Croatia. *Acta Dermatol*, **18**, 173–180.
4. Franzot, J., Kansky, A., Kavcic, S. (1981) Pachyonychia congenita (Jadassohn–Lewandowsky syndrome): a review of 14 cases in Slovenia. *Dermatologica*, **160**, 462–472.
5. Kansky, A., Basta-Juzbasic, A., Ivankovic, D. et al (1993) Pachyonychia congenita (Jadassohn–Lewandowsky syndrome) – evaluation of symptoms in 36 patients. *Arch Dermatol Res*, **285**, 36–37.
6. Feinstein, A., Friesman, J., Schewach-Miller, M. (1988) Pachyonychia congenita. *J Am Acad Dermatol*, **19**, 705–711.
7. Stevens, H.P., Kelsell, D.P., Bryant, S.P. et al (1996) Linkage of an American pedigree with palmoplantar keratoderma and malignancy (palmoplantar ectodermal dysplasia type III) to 17q24. Literature survey and proposed updated classification of the keratodermas. *Arch Dermatol*, **132**, 640–651.
8. Cohn, A.M., McFarlane, J.R., Knox, J. (1976) Pachyonychia congenita with involvement of the larynx. *Arch Otolaryngol*, **102**, 233–235.
9. Shamsher, M., Navsaria, H.A., Stevens, H.P. et al (1995) Novel mutations in keratin 16 gene underlie focal non-epidermolytic palmoplantar keratoderma (NEPPK) in two families. *J Invest Dermatol*, **4**, 1875–1881.
10. Kelsell, D.P., Stevens, H.P., Ratnavel, R. et al (1995) Genetic linkage studies in non-epidermolytic palmoplantar keratoderma: evidence for heterogeneity. *Hum Mol Genet*, **4**, 1021–1025.
11. McLean, W.H.I., Rugg, E.L., Lunny, D.P. et al (1995) Keratin 16 and keratin 17 mutations cause pachyonychia congenita. *Nat Genet*, **9**, 273–278.
12. Smith, F.J.D., McKusick, V.A., Nielsen, K. et al (1999) Cloning of multiple keratin 16 genes facilitates prenatal diagnosis of pachyonychia type I. *Prenat Diagn*, **19**, 941–946.
13. Smith, F.J.D., McKenna, K.E., Irvine, A.D. et al (1999) A mutation detection strategy for the human K6A gene and novel mutations in two cases of pachyonychia congenita type I. *Exp Dermatol*, **8**, 109–114.
14. Bowden, P.E., Haley, J.L., Kansky, A. et al (1995) Mutation of a type II keratin gene (K6a) in pachyonychia congenita. *Nat Genet*, **10**, 363–365.

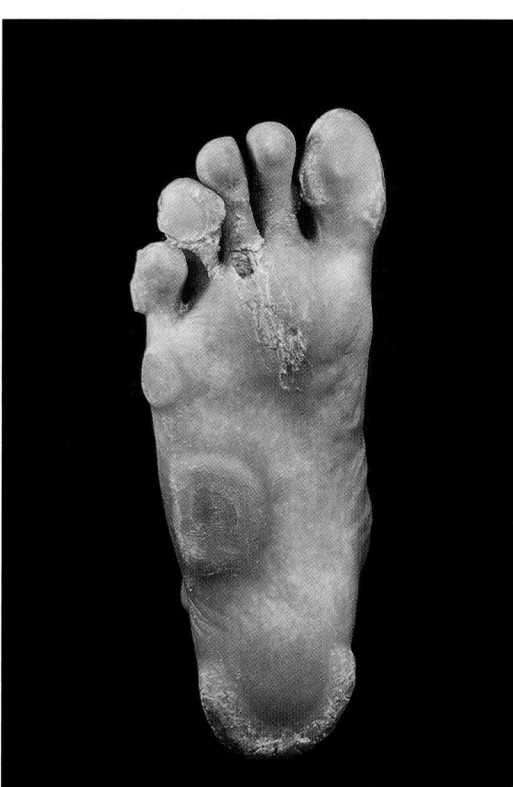

Fig. 2.84
Pachyonychia congenita: discrete, yellow, hyperkeratotic plaques on the soles of the feet are a common manifestation. By courtesy of R.A. Marsden, MD, St George's Hospital, London, UK.

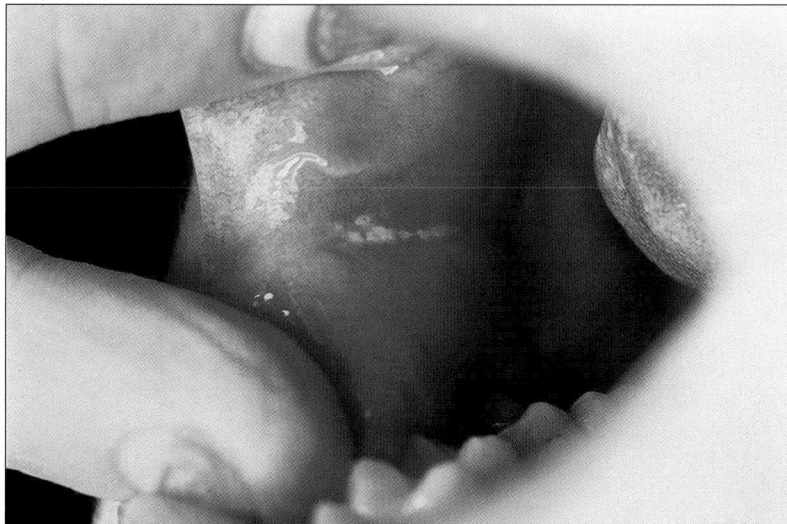

Fig. 2.85
Pachyonychia congenita: leukoplakia of the buccal mucosa is a frequent accompanying feature. By courtesy of R.A. Marsden, MD, St George's Hospital, London, UK.

Pachyonychia congenita type II

Clinical features

Pachyonychia congenita type II (palmoplantar ectodermal dysplasia type II, Jackson–Lawler syndrome, Jackson–Sertoli syndrome) is inherited as an autosomal dominant. It is characterized by limited and usually mild, focal palmoplantar keratoderma over pressure areas, subungual hyperkeratosis, epidermal cysts, steatocystoma multiplex, abnormal eyebrows and body hair (pili torti), natal teeth, angular cheilosis and hoarseness.[1,2] Plantar lesions may be delayed until late childhood. In contrast to pachyonychia congenita type I, patients do not develop leukokeratosis oris. This palmoplantar ectodermal dysplasia has no known association with malignancy.

Pathogenesis and histological features

Pachyonychia congenita type II results from mutations in keratin 17 and keratin 6b genes.[3–6] Interestingly, mutations in keratin 17 may also result in steatocystoma multiplex in isolation.[3]

Histologically the subungual changes and keratoderma are similar to those described in the type I variant, although milder. The epidermoid cysts and steatocystomata show typical features.

References

1. Gorlin, R.J., Pindborg, J.J., Cohen, M.M. Jr (1976) Syndromes of the head and neck. New York: McGraw-Hill.
2. Stevens, H.P., Kelsell, D.P., Bryant, S.P. et al (1996) Linkage of an American pedigree with palmoplantar keratoderma and malignancy (palmoplantar ectodermal dysplasia type III) to 17q24. Literature survey and proposed updated classification of the keratodermas. *Arch Dermatol*, **132**, 640–651.
3. Covello, S.P., Smith, F.J.D., Sillevis Smitt, J.H. et al (1998) Keratin 17 mutations cause either steatocystoma multiplex or pachyonychia type 2. *Br J Dermatol*, **139**, 475–480.
4. McLean, W.H.I., Rugg, E.L., Lunny, D.P. et al (1995) Keratin 16 and keratin 17 mutations cause pachyonychia congenita. *Nat Genet*, **9**, 273–278.
5. Smith, F.J.D., Corden, L.D., Rugg, E.L. et al (1997) Missense mutations in keratin 17 cause either pachyonychia congenita type 2 or a phenotype resembling steatocystoma multiplex. *J Invest Dermatol*, **108**, 220–223.
6. Smith, F.J.D., Jonkman, M.F., van Goor, H. et al (1998) A mutation in human keratin K6b produces a phenocopy of the keratin 17 disorder pachyonychia congenita type 2. *Hum Mol Genet*, **7**, 1143–1148.

Focal non-epidermolytic palmoplantar keratoderma with esophageal squamous carcinoma

Clinical features

The combination of autosomal dominant palmoplantar keratoderma and esophageal squamous carcinoma was first recognized in 1958 and subsequently termed the Howell-Evans syndrome.[1–5] Although initially regarded as a diffuse keratoderma, a subsequent clinical re-evaluation determined that the lesions were focal, sparing non-traumatized areas (*Figs 2.86, 2.87*).[4] The condition typically presents between 6 and 15 years of age (late-onset), patients developing sometimes painful hyperkeratoses on the pressure areas, which disappear with prolonged bed-rest.[5] Palmar involvement may be seen in manual workers. This syndrome, also termed palmoplantar ectodermal dysplasia type III, includes keratosis pilaris particularly affecting the upper arms and thighs, multiple epithelial cysts and gray–white buccal mucosal hyperkeratosis (this last feature typically predates the onset of keratoderma and may therefore represent a clinical diagnostic clue of early involvement in family members of a pedigree).[5–9] Nails are unaffected.[6] In the largest kindred reported to date, 28% developed esophageal squamous carcinoma (89 affected members) of whom 84% died of their tumor.[4]

Pathogenesis and histological features

The condition has been mapped to 17q23-qter region (*TEC* locus) distal to the keratin gene cluster, thereby excluding a keratin gene mutation.[10–12]

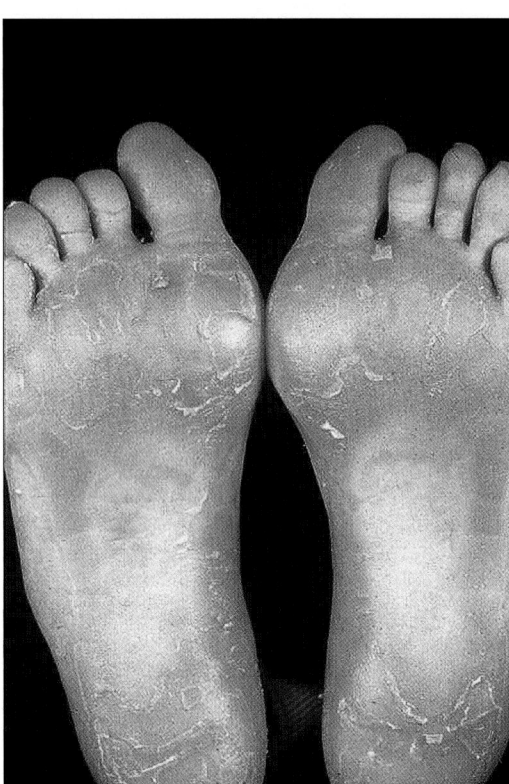

Fig. 2.86
Focal non-epidermolytic palmoplantar keratoderma: focal autosomal dominant palmoplantar keratoderma is associated with an increased risk of esophageal squamous carcinoma. By courtesy of the Institute of Dermatology, London, UK.

The cutaneous lesions are characterized by hyperkeratosis, hypergranulosis and acanthosis. Epidermolysis is absent.

The buccal mucosal lesions are characterized by parakeratosis, acanthosis and spongiosis accompanied by cytoplasmic vacuolation of the prickle cell layer.[4]

References

1. Howell-Evans, W., McConnell, R.B., Clarke, C.A. et al (1958) Carcinoma of the esophagus with keratosis palmaris et plantaris (tylosis): a study of 2 families. *QJM*, 27, 413–429.
2. O'Mahony, M.Y., Hellier, M., Huddy, P. et al (1984) Familial tylosis and carcinoma of the esophagus. *J R Soc Med*, 77, 514–517.
3. Marger, R.S., Marger, D. (1993) Carcinoma of the esophagus and tylosis: a lethal genetic combination. *Cancer*, 72, 17–19.
4. Ellis, A., Field, E.A., Field, J.K. et al (1994) Tylosis associated with carcinoma of the esophagus in a large Liverpool family – a review of six generations. *Eur J Cancer B Oral Oncol*, 30B, 102–112.
5. Stevens, H.P., Kelsell, D.P., Bryant, S.P. et al (1996) Linkage of an American pedigree with palmoplantar keratoderma and malignancy (palmoplantar ectodermal dysplasia type III) to 17q24. Literature survey and proposed updated classification of the keratodermas. *Arch Dermatol*, 132, 640–651.
6. Tyldesley, W.R. (1973) Tylosis, leukoplakia, and esophageal carcinoma. *BMJ*, 4, 427–431.
7. Tyldesley, W.R. (1974) Oral leukoplakia associated with tylosis and esophageal carcinoma. *J Oral Pathol*, 3, 62–70.
8. Ritter, S.B., Peterson, G. (1976) Esophageal cancer, hyperkeratosis, and oral leukoplakia. Occurrence in a 25-year-old woman. *JAMA*, 235, 1723.
9. Ritter, S.B., Peterson, G. (1976) Esophageal cancer, hyperkeratosis, and oral leukoplakia: follow-up family study. *JAMA*, 236, 1844–1845.
10. Risk, J.M., Field, J.R., Whittaker, J. et al (1994) Tylosis esophageal cancer mapped. *Nat Genet*, 8, 319–321.
11. Hennies, H-C., Hagedorn, M., Reis, A. (1995) Palmoplantar keratoderma in association with carcinoma of the esophagus maps to chromosome 17q distal to the keratin gene cluster. *Genomics*, 29, 537–540.
12. Kelsell, D.P., Risk, J.M., Leigh, I.M. et al (1996) Close mapping of focal non-epidermolytic palmoplantar keratoderma (PPK) locus associated with oesophageal cancer (TOC). *Hum Mol Genet*, 5, 857–860.

Acquired palmoplantar keratoderma and internal malignancy

Acquired diffuse palmoplantar keratoderma may represent a paraneoplastic phenomenon associated with a number of internal malignancies including carcinoma of the bronchus, esophagus, stomach, urinary bladder and myeloma (*Fig. 2.88*).[1–6] There are also reports of acquired filiform (filiform palmoplantar keratoderma) and punctate (punctate porokeratotic keratoderma) variants associated with a range of visceral cancers including breast, kidney, colon and lung.[7,8]

References

1. Parnell, D.A., Johnson, S.A.M. (1969) Tylosis palmaris et plantaris: its occurrence with internal malignancy. *Arch Dermatol*, 100, 7–9.
2. Millard, L.G., Gould, D.J. (1976) Hyperkeratosis of the palms and soles associated with internal malignancy and elevated levels of immunoreactive human growth hormone. *Clin Exp Dermatol*, 1, 363–368.
3. Murata, I., Ogami, Y., Nagai, Y. et al (1998) Carcinoma of the stomach with hyperkeratosis palmaris et plantaris and acanthosis of the esophagus. *Am J Gastroenterol*, 93, 449–451.
4. Smith, C.H., Barker, J.N., Hay, R.J. (1995) Diffuse plane xanthomatosis and acquired palmoplantar keratoderma in association with myeloma. *Br J Dermatol*, 132, 286–289.
5. Murata, Y., Kumano, K., Tani, M. et al (1988) Acquired diffuse keratoderma of the palms and soles with bronchial carcinoma: report of a case and review of the literature. *Arch Dermatol*, 124, 497–498.

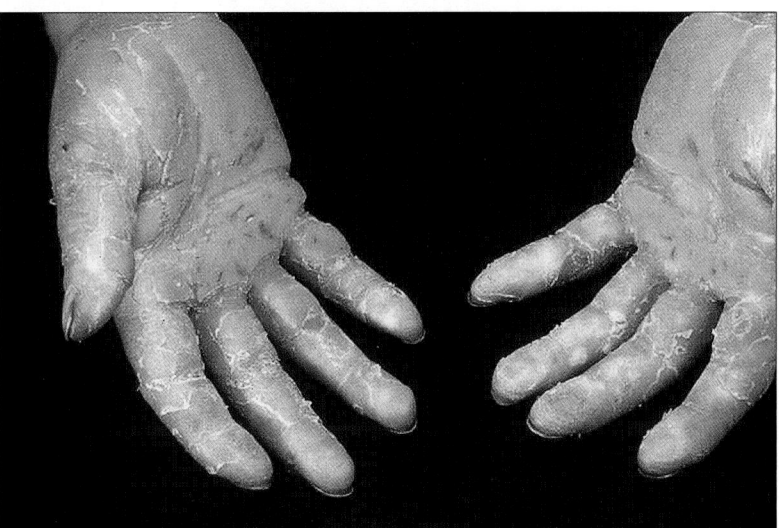

Fig. 2.87
Focal non-epidermolytic palmoplantar keratoderma: in this patient, the palms were also severely affected. By courtesy of the Institute of Dermatology, London, UK.

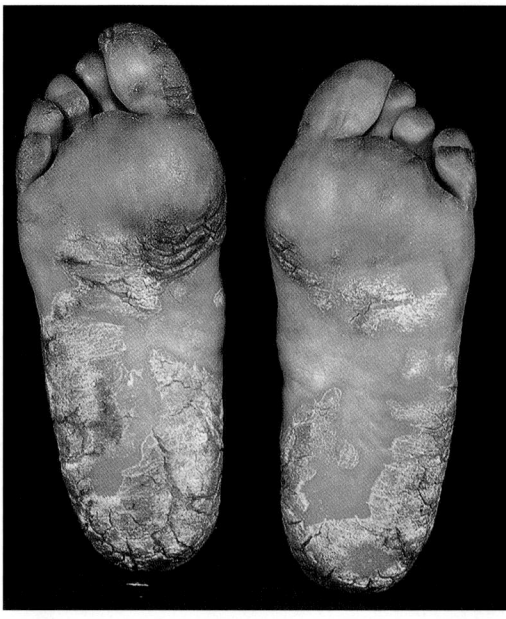

Fig. 2.88
Acquired palmoplantar keratoderma: acquired disease may be a manifestation of underlying malignancy. By courtesy of the Institute of Dermatology, London, UK.

6.   Kuchmeister, B., Rasokat, H. (1984) Acquired disseminated papulous palmar keratoses – a paraneoplastic syndrome in cancers of the urinary bladder and lung? *Z Hautkr*, **59**, 1123–1124.
7.   Fegueux, S., Bilet, S., Crickx, B. et al (1988) Hyperkératose palmo-plantaire filiforme et cancer recto-sigmoïdien. *Ann Dermatol Venereol*, **115**, 1145–1146.
8.   Herman, P.S. (1973) Punctate porokeratotic keratoderma. *Dermatologica*, **147**, 206–213.

Palmoplantar keratoderma with periodontopathia

Clinical features

Palmoplantar keratoderma with periodontopathia (Papillon–Lefèvre syndrome, palmoplantar ectodermal dysplasia type IV) is rare and has an autosomal recessive mode of inheritance.[1] The incidence is 1–4 per million of the population.[2] There is an equal sex incidence and onset is usually in the first decade. It is characterized by symmetrical and marked palmoplantar keratoderma sometimes affecting the dorsal aspects of the hands and feet (*Figs 2.89, 2.90*).[3] Hyperhidrosis may also be present, associated with gingivitis and marked periodontosis involving both deciduous and permanent teeth.[4,5] Periodontosis is unrelated to oral hygiene and results in loss of attachment of teeth to the periodontal ligament (*Fig. 2.91*) and atrophy of the alveolar processes (maxillar and mandibular) with eventual loss of teeth. The periodontal ligament, which is a dense fibrous band, attaches the tooth to the alveolar bone and carries the blood vessels, lymphatics and nerves.[6] Psoriasiform lesions may be evident on the knees and elbows and onychogryphosis has been documented (*Fig. 2.92*).[3] The adnexae are not usually affected. Presentation is usually in the early years of life (2–4 years of age).

There is sometimes associated calcification of the falx cerebri and choroid plexus.[6] Other features, which may sometimes be present, include deafness, deformity of the terminal phalanx, follicular hyperkeratosis and mental retardation. Patients show an increased risk of infection, particularly furunculosis; this has been associated with defective neutrophil chemotaxis and phagocytosis and impaired B- and T-cell mitogenic responses.[7]

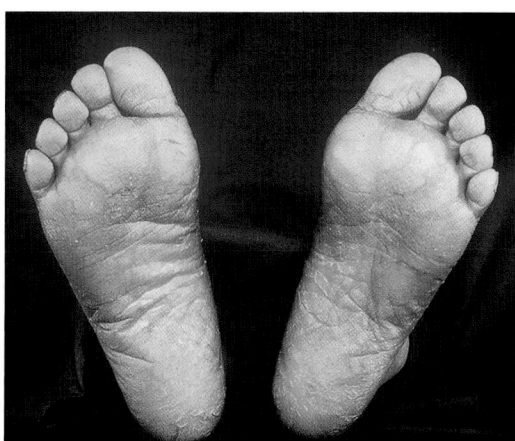

Fig. 2.89
Papillon–Lefèvre syndrome: there is marked hyperkeratosis affecting the soles of the feet. By courtesy of W.A.D. Griffiths, MD, Institute of Dermatology, London, UK.

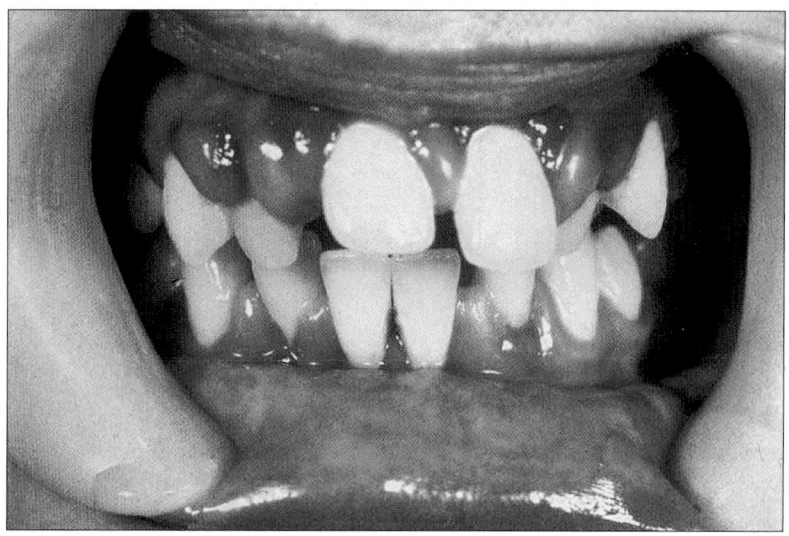

Fig. 2.91
Papillon–Lefèvre syndrome: gingival inflammation and swelling with the particularly characteristic irregular positions of the teeth which, as a result of destruction of supporting tissues, have shifted under the forces of mastication. This patient is a 12-year-old child, but the severity of the periodontal destruction is what might be expected in a person aged 60 years. By courtesy of R.A. Cawson, MD, Guy's Hospital, London, UK.

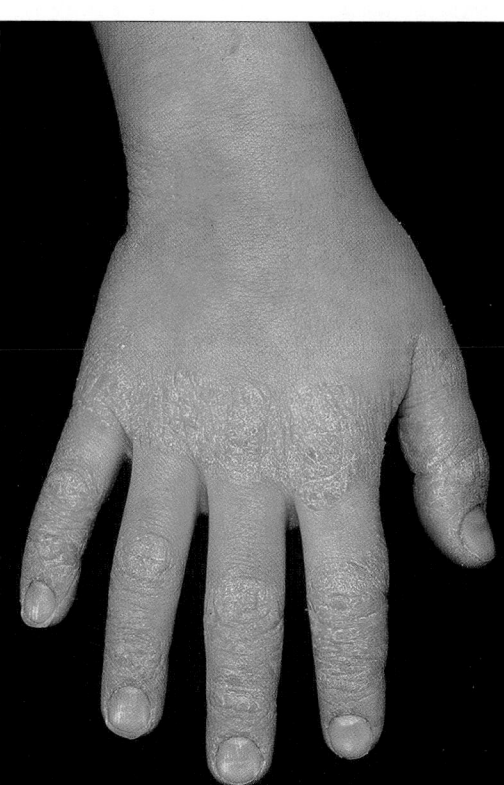

Fig. 2.90
Papillon–Lefèvre syndrome: in this patient, the dorsal aspects of the hands, particularly the knuckles are also affected. By courtesy of W.A.D. Griffiths, MD, Institute of Dermatology, London, UK.

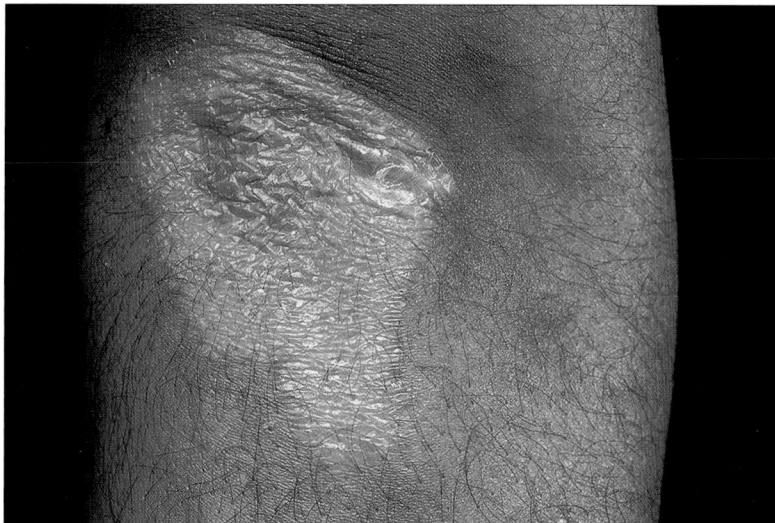

Fig. 2.92
Papillon–Lefèvre syndrome: a scaly psoriasiform plaque is present over the elbow. By courtesy of W.A.D. Griffiths, MD, Institute of Dermatology, London, UK.

Pathogenesis and histological features

Papillon–Lefèvre syndrome has been mapped to 11q14–21.[8] The disease is associated with missense and nonsense mutations, deletions and insertions in the gene for the lysosomal cysteine protease cathepsin C (dipeptidyl aminopeptidase I).[9–12] In homozygous patients, loss of cathepsin C activity results in impaired activation of bone marrow myeloid and macrophage granule serine proteases with resultant defective bacterial phagocytosis.[11,12] The cathepsin C gene is also expressed in squamous epithelium of the palms, soles, knees and the oral keratinized gingiva.[9] At this site, its function is unknown.

The histopathological features of the palmoplantar lesions show marked hyperkeratosis with acanthosis and a thickened granular cell layer (*Fig. 2.93*).[3] Parakeratosis and epidermal psoriasiform hyperplasia have also been described.[7] The elbow and knee lesions show epidermal psoriasiform hyperplasia with parakeratosis, elongation of the dermal papillae and dilatation of the superficial dermal vasculature.[3]

References

1. Haneke, E. (1979) The Papillon–Lefèvre syndrome: keratosis palmoplantaris with periodontopathy. *Hum Genet*, **51**, 1–35.
2. Gorlin, R.J., Sedano, H., Anderson, V.E. (1964) The syndrome of palmar–plantar hyperkeratosis and premature periodontal destruction of the teeth. *J Pediatr*, **65**, 895–908.
3. El Darouti, M.A., Al Raubaie, S.M., Eiada, M.A. (1988) Papillon–Lefèvre syndrome; successful treatment with oral retinoids in three patients. *Int J Dermatol*, **27**, 63–66.
4. Hathway, R. (1982) Papillon–Lefèvre syndrome. *Br Dent J*, **153**, 370–371.
5. Sloan, P., Soames, J.V., Murray, J.J. et al (1984) Histopathological and ultrastructural findings in a case of Papillon–Lefèvre syndrome. *J Periodontol*, **55**, 482–485.
6. Angel, T.A., Hsu, S., Kornbleuth, S.I. et al (2002) Papillon–Lefèvre syndrome: a case report of four affected siblings. *J Am Acad Dermatol*, **46**, S8–10.
7. Nguyen, T.Q., Greer, K.E., Fisher, G.B. et al (1986) Papillon–Lefèvre syndrome: report of two patients treated successfully with isotretinoin. *J Am Acad Dermatol*, **15**, 46–49.
8. Fischer, J., Blanchet-Bardon, C., Prud'homme, J.F. et al (1997) Mapping of Papillon–Lefèvre syndrome to the chromosome 11q14 region. *Eur J Hum Genet*, **51**, 56–60.
9. Hart, T.C., Hart, S., Bowden, D.W. et al (1999) Mutations of the cathepsin C gene are responsible for Papillon–Lefèvre syndrome. *J Med Genet*, **36**, 881–887.
10. Toomes, C., James, J., Wood, A.J. et al (1999) Loss-of-function mutations in the cathepsin C gene result in periodontal disease and palmoplantar keratosis. *Nat Genet*, **23**, 421–424.
11. Hart, P.S., Zhang, Y., Firanti, E. et al (2000) Identification of cathepsin C mutations in ethnically diverse Papillon–Lefèvre syndrome patients. *J Med Genet*, **37**, 927–932.
12. Zhang, Y., Lundgren, T., Renvert, S. et al (2001) Evidence of a founder effect for four cathepsin C gene mutations in Papillon–Lefèvre syndrome patients. *J Med Genet*, **38**, 96–101.

Vohwinkel's syndrome

Clinical features

Vohwinkel's syndrome (keratoderma hereditarium mutilans, palmoplantar ectodermal dysplasia type VII) is a rare keratoderma which is usually inherited as an autosomal dominant although a recessive variant has also been described.[1–3] Onset is in infancy or early childhood.[2] Caucasians are predominantly affected and there is a predilection for females.[3] The clinical features include palmoplantar keratoderma with a papular and honeycomb-like appearance and starfish-like keratoses affecting the dorsal surfaces of the hands, feet, wrists, forearms, elbows and knees (*Figs 2.94–2.96*).[3] Flexion contractures and circumferential hyperkeratotic constriction bands (pseudoainhum) affecting the interphalangeal joints associated with autoamputation are also present.[2,3] In the classical variant, sensorineural deafness is an integral feature.[1,4,5] An ichthyosis-associated variant has also been described.[6–10]

Additional features include alopecia, nail dystrophy and onychogryphosis.[2]

Pathogenesis and histological features

Classical, deafness-associated Vohwinkel's syndrome is due to mutations in the connexin 26 gene.[8] In the ichthyosis-associated variant, a loricrin gene mutation has been described.[9–11]

Histologically, the keratoderma is characterized by hyperkeratosis, hypergranulosis and acanthosis.[3]

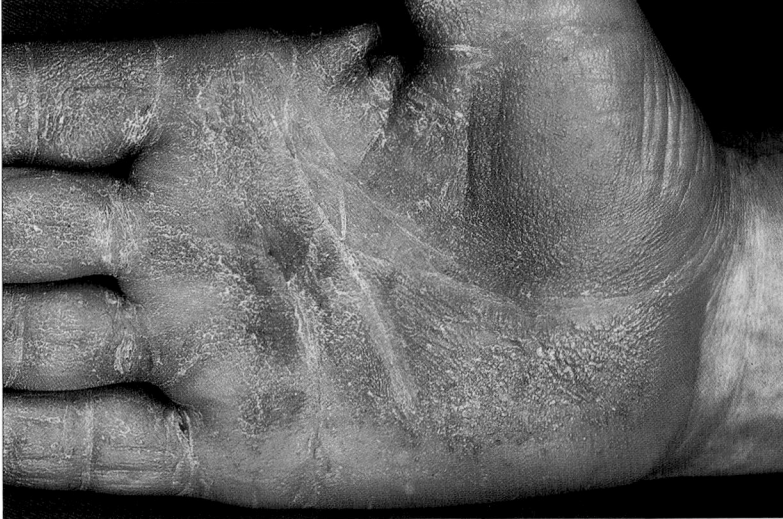

Fig. 2.94
Vohwinkel's syndrome: there is marked palmoplantar keratoderma. By courtesy of W.A.D. Griffiths, MD, Institute of Dermatology, London, UK.

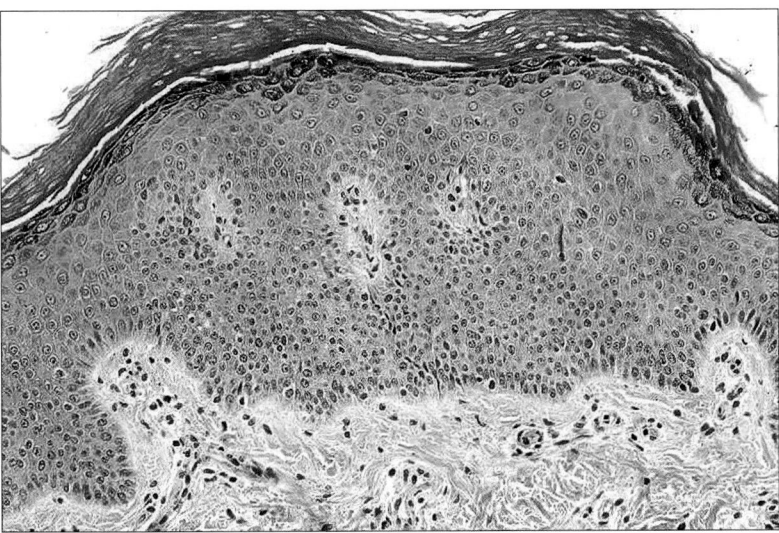

Fig. 2.93
Papillon–Lefèvre syndrome: there is hyperkeratosis, hypergranulosis and psoriasiform hyperplasia.

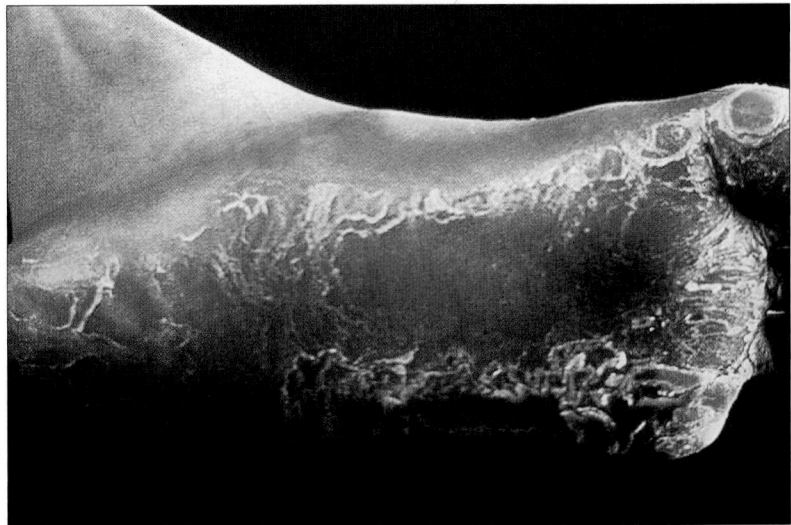

Fig. 2.95
Vohwinkel's syndrome: the sole of the foot is also affected. By courtesy of W.A.D. Griffiths, MD, Institute of Dermatology, London, UK.

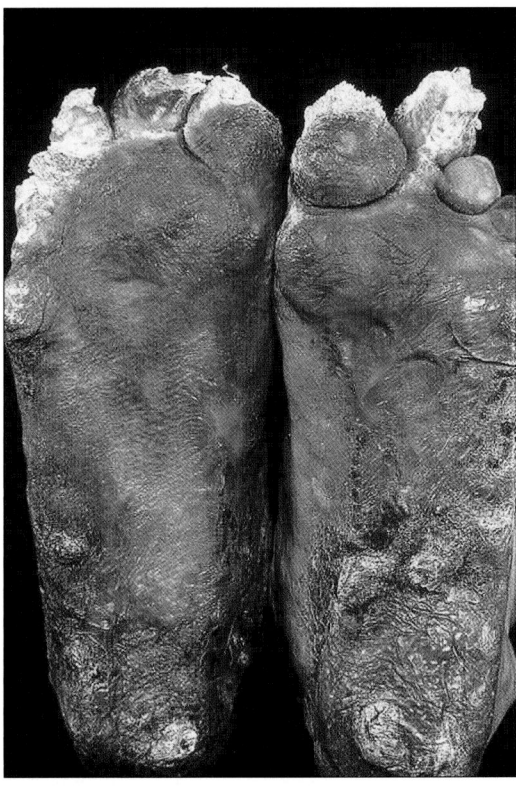

Fig. 2.96
Vohwinkel's syndrome: in this example there is very disfiguring keratoderma, hence the alternative title, keratoderma hereditarium mutilans. By courtesy of W.A.D. Griffiths, MD, Institute of Dermatology, London, UK.

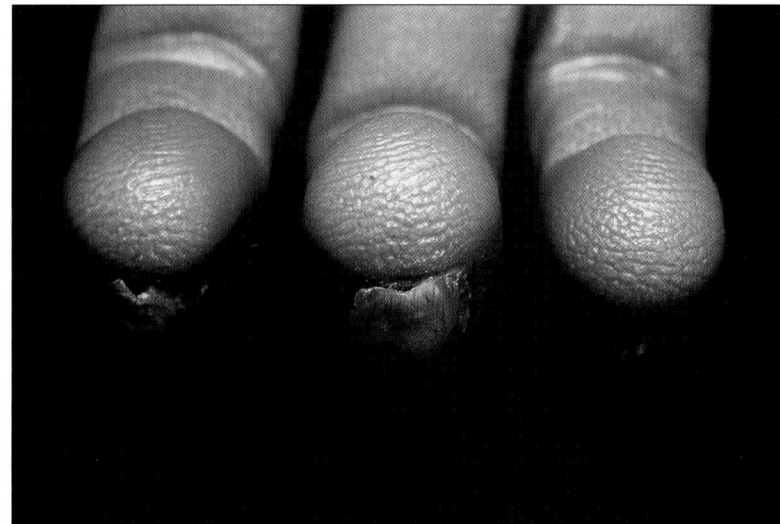

Fig. 2.97
Hidrotic ectodermal dysplasia: there is nail dystrophy accompanied by hyperkeratosis of the fingertips, thereby accentuating the epidermal surface ridges. By courtesy of D. Atherton, MD, the Children's Hospital at Great Ormond Street, London, UK.

References

1. McGrath, J.A., Eady, R.A.J. (2001) Recent advances in the molecular basis of inherited skin diseases. *Adv Genet*, **43**, 1–32.
2. Stevens, H.P., Kelsell, D.P., Bryant, S.P. et al (1996) Linkage of an American pedigree with palmoplantar keratoderma and malignancy (palmoplantar ectodermal dysplasia type III) to 17q24. Literature survey and proposed updated classification of the keratodermas. *Arch Dermatol*, **132**, 640–651.
3. Peris, K., Salvati, E.F., Torlone, G. et al (1995) Keratoderma hereditarium mutilans (Vohwinkel's syndrome) associated with congenital deaf mutism. *Br J Dermatol*, **132**, 617–620.
4. McGibbon, D.H., Watson, R.T. (1977) Vohwinkel's syndrome and deafness. *J Laryngol Otol*, **91**, 853–857.
5. Wereide, K. (1984) Mutilating palmoplantar keratoderma successfully treated with etretinate. *Acta Dermatovenereol Scand*, **64**, 564–569.
6. Camisa, C., Hessel, A., Rossana, C. et al (1975) Autosomal dominant keratoderma, ichthyosiform dermatosis and elevated serum beta-glucuronidase. *Dermatologica*, **177**, 341–347.
7. Camisa, C., Rossana, C. (1984) Variant of keratoderma hereditaria mutilans (Vohwinkel's syndrome). *Arch Dermatol*, **120**, 1323–1328.
8. Maestrini, E., Korge, B.P., Ocana-Sierra, J. et al (1999) A missense mutation in connexin 26, D66H, causes mutilating keratoderma with sensorineural deafness (Vohwinkel's syndrome) in three unrelated families. *Hum Mol Genet*, **8**, 1237–1243.
9. Maestrini, E., Monaco, A.P., McGrath, J.A. et al (1996) A molecular defect in loricrin, the major component of the cornified cell envelope, underlies Vohwinkel's syndrome. *Nat Genet*, **13**, 70–77.
10. Korge, B.P., Ishida-Yamamoto, A., Punter, C. et al (1997) Loricrin mutation in Vohwinkel's keratoderma is unique to the variant with ichthyosis. *J Invest Dermatol*, **109**, 604–610.
11. Armstrong, D.K.B., McKenna, K.B., Hughes, A.E. (1998) A novel insertional mutation in loricrin in Vohwinkel's keratoderma. *J Invest Dermatol*, **111**, 702–704.

Hidrotic ectodermal dysplasia

Clinical features

Hidrotic ectodermal dysplasia (Clouston's syndrome, palmoplantar ectodermal dysplasia type X) is an uncommon disorder with an autosomal dominant mode of inheritance. Nail dystrophy is often predominant, but hair defects and palmoplantar keratoderma are also found (*Fig. 2.97*).[1–7] Rare manifestations include sensorineural deafness, ocular abnormalities, skin hyperpigmentation, polydactyly, syndactyly, mental retardation, epilepsy and dwarfism.[5,6] Changes in the nails are variable, but usually they are short and thickened with longitudinal striations, often with discoloration, and may have grooves, pits and ridges.[5,6] The development of paronychia is a frequent complication.

Scalp alopecia (from hair thinning to complete baldness) is the rule, and facial, axillary and pubic hair is usually sparse or totally absent.[6] The patients have a normal facies and no involvement of the dentition or abnormal sweating.

Although hidrotic ectodermal dysplasia has been documented predominantly in French Canadian families, kindreds have been described in French, Scottish–Irish and Indians.[4,7–10]

Pathogenesis and histological features

The gene responsible for this condition has been mapped to 13q11–12.1.[11–14] Hidrotic ectodermal dysplasia results from a connexin 30 mutation.[15–18]

The palmoplantar keratoderma is typified by hyperkeratosis, thickening of the granular cell layer and acanthosis.[5,7] Elsewhere, eccrine sweat glands are normal, but hair and sebaceous glands are greatly reduced in number and apocrine glands completely absent.[8]

References

1. Priolo, M., Lagana, C. (2001) Ectodermal dysplasias: a new clinical–genetic classification. *J Med Genet*, **38**, 579–585.
2. Pierard, G.E., Van Neste, D., Letot, B. (1979) Hidrotic ectodermal dysplasia. *Dermatologica*, **158**, 168–174.
3. Solomon, L.M., Keuer, E.J. (1980) The ectodermal dysplasias. *Arch Dermatol*, **116**, 1295–1299.
4. Rajagopalan, K., Chong, H.T. (1977) Hidrotic ectodermal dysplasia: study of a large Chinese pedigree. *Arch Dermatol*, **113**, 481–485.
5. Witkop, C.J., Brearley, L.J., Gentry, W.C. Jr (1975) Hypoplastic enamel, onycholysis and hypohidrosis inherited as an autosomal dominant trait. A review of ectodermal dysplasia syndromes. *Oral Surgery*, **39**, 71–86.
6. Freire-Maia, N., Pinheiro, M. (1984) Fischer–Jacobsen–Clouston's syndrome. In: Freire-Maia, N., Pinheiro, M. (eds) Ectodermal dysplasia: a clinical and genetic study. New York: Liss, pp 68–70.
7. Ando, Y., Tanaka, T., Horiguchi, Y. et al (1988) Hidrotic ectodermal dysplasia: a clinical and ultrastructural observation. *Dermatologica*, **176**, 205–211.
8. Escobar, V., Goldblatt, L.I., Bixler, D. et al (1983) Clouston syndrome: an ultrastructural study. *Clin Genet*, **24**, 140–146.
9. Patel, R.A., Bixler, D., Norins, A.L. (1991) Clouston syndrome: a rare autosomal dominant trait with palmoplantar hyperkeratosis and alopecia. *J Craniofac Genet Dev Biol*, **11**, 176–179.
10. Mcnaughton, P.Z., Pierson, L., Rodman, G. (1976) Hidrotic ectodermal dysplasia in a black mother and daughter. *Arch Dermatol*, **112**, 1448–1450.
11. Kibar, Z., Der Kaloustian, V.M., Brais, B. et al (1996) The gene responsible for Clouston hidrotic ectodermal dysplasia maps to the pericentromeric region of chromosome 13q. *Hum Mol Genet*, **5**, 543–547.
12. Radhakrishna, U., Blouin, J.L., Mehenni, H. et al (1997) The gene for autosomal dominant hidrotic ectodermal dysplasia (Clouston syndrome) in a large Indian family maps to the 13q11–q12.1 pericentromeric region. *Am J Hum Genet*, **71**, 80–86.
13. Kibar, Z., Dube, M.P., Powell, J. et al (2000) Clouston hidrotic ectodermal dysplasia (HED): genetic homogeneity, presence of a founder effect in the French Canadian population and fine genetic mapping. *Eur J Hum Genet*, **8**, 372–380.
14. Lamartine, J., Laoudj, D., Blanchet-Bardon, C. et al (2000) Refined localization of the gene for Clouston syndrome (hidrotic ectodermal dysplasia) in a large French family. *Br J Dermatol*, **142**, 248–252.
15. Lamartine, J., Munhoz Essenfelder, G., Kibar, Z. et al (2000) Mutations in GJB6 cause hidrotic ectodermal dysplasia. *Nat Genet*, **26**, 142–144.
16. Taylor, T.D., Hayflick, S.J., McKinnon, W. et al (1998) Confirmation of linkage of Clouston syndrome (hidrotic ectodermal dysplasia) to 13q11–q12.1 with evidence for single independent mutations. *J Invest Dermatol*, **111**, 83–85.
17. Richard, G. (2001) Connexin disorders of the skin. *Adv Dermatol*, **17**, 243–277.
18. Smith, F.J., Morley, S.M., McLean, W.H. (2002) A novel connexin 30 mutation in Clouston syndrome. *J Invest Dermatol*, **118**, 530–532.

Keratitis–ichthyosis–deafness syndrome

Clinical features

Keratitis–ichthyosis–deafness syndrome (KID syndrome, palmoplantar ectodermal dysplasia type XVI) is a very rare genodermatosis. Spontaneous mutations, autosomal dominant and autosomal recessive modes of inheritance have all been documented.[1–4] There is an equal sex incidence.[5] It may present at birth as a 'vernix-like' covering, which soon progresses to a dry, scaling erythema, particularly affecting the face (especially the cheeks) and peripheries, including the palms and soles.[1,3,4,6,7] The skin may be thickened and leathery.[7,8] Later the lesions become verrucous and hyperkeratotic, brownish-yellow plaques (*Fig. 2.98*).[1] Circumoral furrows may lead to a progeria-like effect.[9] Follicular keratoses sometimes develop on the head and extremities and a 'prickly' spiculated appearance on the backs of the hands is occasionally evident.[3,4,8] Palmar and plantar involvement with accentuation of the skin markings has been likened to heavily grained leather.[10] There does, however, appear to be some variation in presentation.[1] Some patients have therefore been described as being normal at birth, developing dry, scaly skin in later childhood, while others have been reported as 'red and wizened at birth'.[11,12]

Inflammation of the cornea with photophobia is usual and a vascularizing keratitis leads to severe visual impairment.[8] The end result is destruction of the cornea by a pannus of vascular or fibrotic tissue (keratoconus).[1]

Deafness is of the congenital neurosensory type, but is occasionally due to recurrent otitis media; conduction defects may also be present.[1,7,8] It is often total and frequently present at birth although not usually recognized until sometime later in early childhood.[8]

Ectodermal dysplasia is variably present and features include alopecia (either partial or complete, including eyebrows and eyelashes), small malformed teeth with increased caries, scrotal tongue, leukokeratosis and a variety of dystrophic nail changes including fragility, hyperkeratosis, dysplasia, leukonychia and aplasia.[1,4,8]

Additional features that may be detected include increased susceptibility to superficial and systemic chronic infections (bacterial and fungal), neuromuscular disease, retraction of the Achilles tendon, hypohidrosis, heat intolerance and growth deficiency.[1,3,8,13–15] The reason for the increased risk of cutaneous infection is unknown. While an abnormality of immunity has been proposed, it is felt more likely that colonization of greatly increased and degenerate keratin is the more important etiological factor.[16] No consistent abnormality of immune function has so far been reported.[3,11,14] Mental retardation is a rare feature, which may be seen in patients with the autosomal recessive variant.[1] Liver disease including cirrhosis has been present in autosomal recessive patients.[1,2] Squamous carcinoma of the tongue and skin (sometimes multiple) are important complications (*Fig. 2.99*).[3,13,17–19]

Pathogenesis and histological features

Recently KID syndrome, at least in some families, has been shown to be associated with mutations in the connexin 26 gene.[20,21]

The histological appearances of the skin lesions are non-specific and include basket-weave hyperkeratosis with occasional foci of parakeratosis, acanthosis and papillomatosis.[8] Follicular plugging is commonly present and occasionally the orifices of the eccrine ducts are similarly affected.[5,11] A superficial perivascular lymphohistiocytic infiltrate is sometimes evident.[8] Eccrine sweat glands may be diminished in number and atrophic, with thickened, hyalinized basement membranes and absent or atrophic hair follicles are seen in the areas of alopecia.[3,8,22] Electron microscopic studies of the epidermis have revealed no significant abnormalities.[7,15]

A recently reported autopsied case has described both ocular and aural changes:[16]

- *Ocular changes* were limited to the cornea and conjunctiva. Dyskeratosis and atrophy of the corneal surface epithelium accompanied by neovascularization and mild chronic inflammation of the substantia propria were evident. The bulbar conjunctiva showed epithelial atrophy, dyskeratosis and mild chronic inflammation. Late changes are characterized by the development of an inflammatory and vascular pannus.[8]

- *Aural changes* related not only to epithelial maturation abnormalities of the external auditory meatus and tympanic membrane, but also to cochlear maldevelopment.[16] The essential features of the former included parakeratosis of the squamous epithelium overlying the tympanic membrane. Immaturity and parakeratosis of the epithelial ridge pattern of the epithelium covering the bony aspect of the external auditory meatus may also

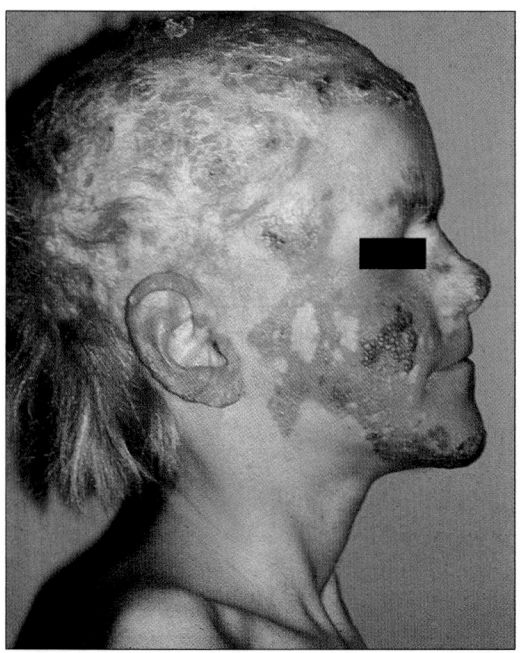

Fig. 2.98
KID syndrome: there is marked scaling of the scalp with alopecia. Note the facial erythema and dark plaques on the cheeks. By courtesy of R.J.G. Rycroft, MD, St John's Dermatology Centre, London, UK.

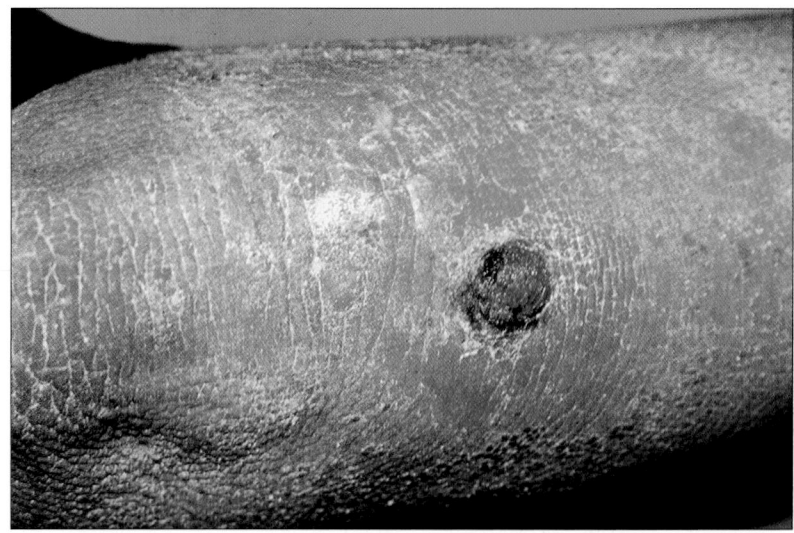

Fig. 2.99
KID syndrome: squamous carcinoma on the knee. Tumors may be multiple. By courtesy of M. Judge, MD, Institute of Dermatology, London, UK.

be present. Changes of the internal ear included maldevelopment of the cochlea and absence of the tectorial membrane and organ of Corti, accompanied by reduction in the number of nerve fibers and spiral ganglion nerve cells.[16] These features are very much in keeping with sensorineural deafness of cochlear origin.

The liver changes include micronodular cirrhosis, cholestasis, Kupffer cell hyperplasia, abundant Mallory's hyaline and marked copper storage.[1]

References

1. Wilson, G.N., Squires, R.H., Weinberg, A.G. (1991) Keratitis, hepatitis, ichthyosis, and deafness: report and review of KID syndrome. *Am J Med Genet*, **40**, 255–259.
2. Desmons, F., Bar, J., Chevillard, Y. (1971) Erythrodermie ichthyosiforme congenitale seche, surdi-mutite, hepatomegalie, de transmission recessive autosomique. *Bull Soc Franc Dermatol Syphiligr*, **78**, 585–588.
3. Grob, J.J., Breton, A., Bonafe, J.L. et al (1987) Keratitis, ichthyosis, and deafness (KID) syndrome. Vertical transmission and death from multiple squamous cell carcinomas. *Arch Dermatol*, **123**, 777–782.
4. Nazzaro, V., Blanchet-Bardon, C., Lorette, G. et al (1990) Familial occurrence of KID (keratitis, ichthyosis, deafness) syndrome. Case reports of a mother and a daughter. *J Am Acad Dermatol*, **23**, 385–388.
5. Caceres-Rios, H., Tamayo-Sanchez, L., Duran-McKinster, C. et al (1996) Keratitis, ichthyosis, and deafness (KID) syndrome: review of the literature and proposal of a new terminology. *Pediatr Dermatol*, **13**, 105–113.
6. Skinner, B.A., Greist, M.C., Norins, A.L. (1981) The keratitis, ichthyosis, and deafness (KID) syndrome. *Arch Dermatol*, **117**, 285–289.
7. Szymko-Bennett, Y.M., Russell, L.J., Bale, S.J., Griffith, A.J. (2002) Auditory manifestations of keratitis–ichthyosis–deafness (KID) syndrome. *Laryngoscope*, **112**, 272–280.
8. McGrae, J.D. (1990) Keratitis, ichthyosis and deafness (KID) syndrome. *Int J Dermatol*, **29**, 89–93.
9. Morris, M.R., Namon, A., Shaw, G.Y. et al (1991) The keratitis, ichthyosis and deafness syndrome. *Otolaryngol Head Neck Surg*, **104**, 526–528.
10. Hazen, P.G., Carney, J.M., Langston, R.H.S. et al (1986) Corneal effects of isotretinoin: possible exacerbation of corneal neovascularization in a patient with the keratitis, ichthyosis, deafness (KID) syndrome. *J Am Acad Dermatol*, **14**, 141–142.
11. Rycroft, R.J.G., Moynahan, E.J., Wells, R.S. (1976) Atypical ichthyosiform erythroderma, deafness and keratitis. *Br J Dermatol*, **94**, 211–217.
12. Senter, T.P., Jones, K.L., Sakati, N. et al (1978) Atypical ichthyosiform erythroderma and congenital neurosensory deafness – a distinct syndrome. *J Pediatr*, **92**, 68–72.
13. Hazen, P.G., Carney, P., Lynch, W.S. (1989) Keratitis, ichthyosis and deafness syndrome with development of multiple cutaneous neoplasms. *Int J Dermatol*, **28**, 190–191.
14. Reynolds, N. J., Kennedy, C.T.C. (1990) Keratitis ichthyosis deafness (KID) syndrome. *Br J Dermatol*, **123** (Suppl.), 77–80.
15. Harms, M., Gilardi, S., Levy, P.M. et al (1984) Kid syndrome (keratitis, ichthyosis, and deafness) and chronic mucocutaneous candidiasis: case report and review of the literature. *Pediatr Dermatol*, **2**, 1–7.
16. de Berker, D., Branford, W.A., Soucek, S. et al (1993) Fatal keratitis, ichthyosis and deafness syndrome (KIDS). Aural, ocular, and cutaneous histopathology. *Am J Dermatopathol*, **15**, 64–69.
17. Madariaga, J., Fromowitz, F., Phillips, M. et al (1986) Squamous cell carcinoma in congenital ichthyosis with deafness and keratitis. *Cancer*, **57**, 2026–2029.
18. Baden, H.P., Alper, J.C. (1977) Ichthyosiform dermatosis, keratitis and deafness. *Arch Dermatol*, **113**, 1701–1704.
19. Lancaster, L., Fournet, L.F. (1969) Carcinoma of the tongue in a child: report of a case. *J Oral Surg*, **27**, 269–270.
20. van Steensel, M.A., van Geel, M., Nahuys, M. et al (2002) A novel connexin 26 mutation in a patient diagnosed with keratitis–ichthyosis–deafness syndrome. *J Invest Dermatol*, **118**, 724–727.
21. Richard, G., Rouan, F., Willoughby, C.E. et al (2002) Missense mutations in GJB2 encoding connexin 26 causes the ectodermal dysplasia keratitis–ichthyosis–deafness syndrome. *Am J Hum Genet*, **70**, 1341–1348.
22. Alli, N., Gungor, E. (1997) Keratitis, ichthyosis and deafness (KID) syndrome. *Int J Dermatol*, **36**, 37–40.

Olmsted syndrome

Clinical features

Olmsted syndrome is exceedingly rare and combines the features of mutilating palmoplantar keratoderma with periorificial plaques. Approximately 20 cases have been documented.[1–5] It is usually associated with sporadic occurrence although X-linked dominant transmission has been suggested at least in one family.[6] There are no racial predilections. There is a striking predominance in males (5:1).

The keratoderma is present at birth or begins in early infancy and when fully developed presents as bilateral and symmetrical massively thickened, yellow, macerated, keratotic plaques covering the whole of the sole and palm and often extending to the lateral and even the dorsal surface of the hands and feet (*Fig. 2.100*).[3,4] The heels and forearms may also be affected. The border of the plaque is sharply defined and surrounded by a pruritic erythematous border. Lesions are often fissured and extremely painful, making walking exceedingly difficult or impossible.[3,4] Blistering has occasionally been described.[5] Flexion contractures, ainhum-like constriction bands and autoamputation are common complications. Superinfection with bacteria and fungi, particularly *Candida albicans*, contributes to the problems and as a result lesions are frequently very malodorous. Squamous carcinoma is an occasional complication.[7,8]

Affected children also develop erythematous keratotic papules and plaques around the body orifices including the mouth, nares, ears and anus.[3,4] The eyelids, umbilical region, inguinal region and gluteal cleft can also be involved.

Additional features include scarring alopecia, keratosis pilaris and nail dystrophy including ridging, transverse striae, thickening, curvature, subungual keratosis and infection.[3,4] Hyperkeratotic linear streaks may develop in the axillae and cubital fossae. Growth retardation, laxity of the large joints and corneal involvement are occasional manifestations.[3,4]

Histological features

The plaques are characterized by massive hyperkeratosis, often with foci of vertically orientated parakeratosis.[2–5] There is hypergranulosis with large coarse granules under the former whereas the granular cell layer is absent beneath the areas of parakeratosis. The epidermis is acanthotic and shows psoriasiform hyperplasia or papillomatosis and there is edema and increased vascularity of the superficial dermis where a lympho-histiocytic infiltrate is also seen.

The plaques show increased mitotic activity, increased Ki-67 expression and increased argyrophilic nucleolar organizer regions (AgNORS).[4,9] Keratinization is abnormal with aberrant expression of keratins 5, 10 and 14, filaggrin and involucrin.[4,5] It has, however, been proposed that the keratin abnormalities might be a result of isotretinoin and etretinate therapy.[10]

References

1. Olmsted, H.C. (1927) Keratodermia palmaris et plantaris congenitalis: report of a case showing associated lesions of unusual location. *Am J Dis Child*, **33**, 757–764.
2. Atherton, D.J., Sutton, C., Jones, B.M. (1990) Mutilating palmoplantar keratoderma with periorificial keratotic plaques (Olmsted's syndrome). *Br J Dermatol*, **122**, 245–252.
3. Perry, H.O., Su, W.P.D. (1995) Olmsted syndrome. *Semin Dermatol*, **14**, 145–151.
4. Larrègue, M., Callot, V., Kanitakis, J. et al (2000) Olmsted syndrome: report of two new cases and literature review. *J Dermatol*, **27**, 557–568.
5. Kress, D.W., Seraly, M.P., Falo, L. et al (1996) Olmsted syndrome: case report and identification of a keratin abnormality. *Arch Dermatol*, **132**, 797–800.
6. Cambiaghi, S., Tadine, G., Barbareschi, M. et al (1995) Olmsted syndrome in twins. *Arch Dermatol*, **131**, 738–739.
7. Barnett, J.H., Estes, S.A. (1985) Multiple epitheliomata cuniculata occurring in mutilating keratoderma. *Cutis*, **35**, 345–347.
8. Yoshizaki, Y., Kanki, H., Ueda, T. et al (2001) A further case of plantar squamous carcinoma arising in Olmsted syndrome. *Br J Dermatol*, **145**, 685–686.
9. Requena, L., Manzarbeitia, F., Moreno, C. et al (2001) Olmsted syndrome: report of a case with study of the cellular proliferation in keratoderma. *Am J Dermatopathol*, **23**, 514–520.
10. Raskin, C.A., Tu, J.H. (1997) Keratin expression in Olmsted syndrome. *Arch Dermatol*, **133**, 389.

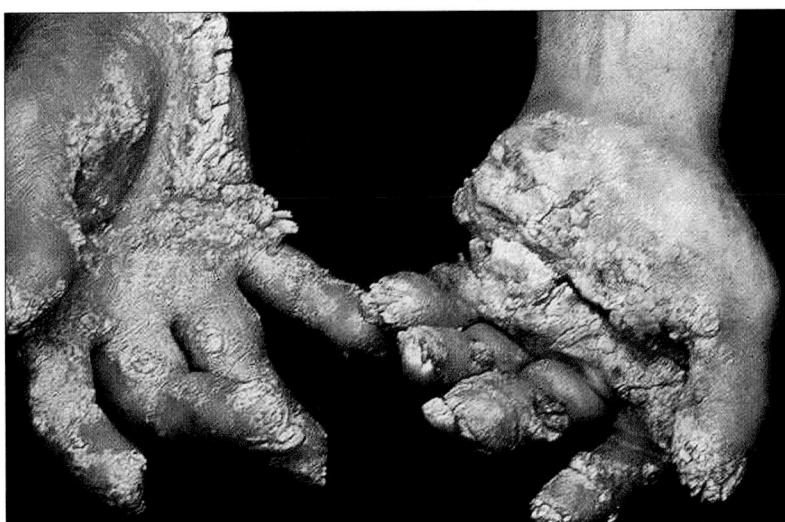

Fig. 2.100
Olmsted syndrome: in this variant, the lesions are very disfiguring. Constriction bands and autoamputation are important complications. By courtesy of W.A.D. Griffiths, MD, Institute of Dermatology, London, UK.

Acrokeratosis verruciformis of Hopf

Clinical features

This is an exceedingly rare dermatosis with an autosomal dominant mode of inheritance.[1–3] The disease presents in infancy or early childhood as dry, rough, brownish or skin-colored verrucoid, keratotic papules, located particularly on the backs of the hands (*Fig. 2.101*) and feet, and on the knees and elbows.[4] Keratotic punctate pits are found on the palms and soles. Lesions, which are clinically and histologically indistinguishable, may occasionally be seen in Darier's disease.[5–7] Exceptionally, a similar association with Hailey–Hailey disease has been documented and there is a report of acrokeratosis verruciformis presenting in a patient with nevoid basal cell carcinoma syndrome.[8,9] Nail involvement, including longitudinal splitting, striations and subungual hyperkeratosis may also be seen.[10]

Histological features

The lesions are acanthotic with a prominent granular cell layer, typically showing a 'church spire' appearance (*Fig. 2.102*). There is usually moderate to marked hyperkeratosis. Parakeratosis is not a feature.

Differential diagnosis

Acrokeratosis verruciformis-like features may occasionally be seen in linear epidermal nevi.[11] There is also considerable histological overlap with stucco keratoses.

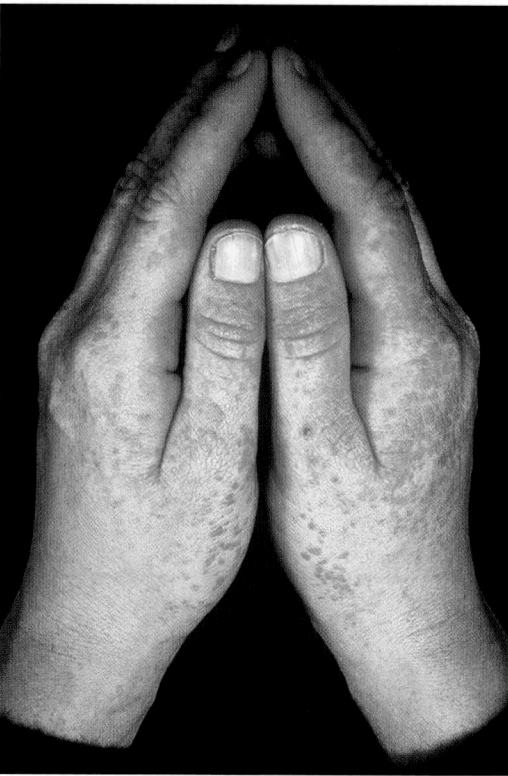

Fig. 2.101 Acrokeratosis verruciformis: numerous brown flat-topped papules are symmetrically distributed over the dorsal aspects of the hands. By courtesy of R.A. Marsden, MD, St George's Hospital, London, UK.

References

1. Hopf, G. (1931) Ueber eine bisher nicht beschriebene disseminierte keratose (akrokeratose verruciformis). *Dermatol Z*, **60**, 227–250.
2. Niedelman, M., McKusick, V. (1962) Acrokeratosis verruciformis (Hopf). *Arch Dermatol*, **86**, 779–782.
3. Panja, R.K. (1977) Acrokeratosis verruciformis (Hopf): a clinical entity? *Br J Dermatol*, **96**, 643–652.
4. Chapman-Rolle, L., DePadova-Elder, S.M., Ryan, E. et al (1994) Persistent flat-topped papules on the extremities. Acrokeratosis verruciformis (AKV) of Hopf. *Arch Dermatol*, **130**, 508–509, 511–512.
5. Burge, S.M., Wilkinson, J.D. (1992) Darier–White disease: a review of the clinical features in 163 patients. *J Am Acad Dermatol*, **27**, 40–50.
6. Niordson, A.M., Sylvest, B. (1965) Bullous dyskeratosis follicularis and acrokeratosis verruciformis. Report of a case. *Arch Dermatol*, **92**, 166–168.
7. Hafner, O., Vakilzadeh, F. (1997) Acrokeratosis verruciformis-like changes in Darier's disease. *Hautarzt*, **48**, 572–576.
8. Yakis, G., Csato, M., Kemeny, L. et al (1996) Hailey–Hailey disease with acrokeratosis verruciformis Hopf. *Acta Derm Venereol*, **76**, 157.
9. Humbert, P., Laurent, R., Faivre, B. et al (1990) Nevoid basal cell carcinoma syndrome and acrokeratosis verruciformis. Occurrence of two rare inherited autosomal dominant conditions in the same patient. *Dermatologica*, **180**, 169–170.
10. Herndon, J., Wilson, J. (1966) Acrokeratosis (Hopf) and Darier's disease. *Arch Dermatol*, **93**, 305–310.
11. Su, W.P. (1982) Histopathologic varieties of epidermal nevus. A study of 160 cases. *Am J Dermatopathol*, **4**, 161–170.

Clavus

Clavi (corns) are extremely common painful keratotic lesions that develop on the dorsal or lateral aspect of the toes often as a consequence of ill-fitting shoes. Histologically, they are characterized by a deep keratin-filled depression often associated with atrophy of the underlying epidermis (*Fig. 2.103*). They are distinguished from plantar warts by the absence of koilocytes and irregular keratohyalin granules.

Callus

In contrast to a clavus, a callus is a non-painful localized focus of hyperkeratosis usually arising on the ball of the foot or heel from pressure or foot deformity. Palmar lesions arise as a consequence of chronic rubbing. Histologically, they are similar to a clavus, consisting of a keratin-filled epidermal dell with hypergranulosis. Parakeratosis is often present.

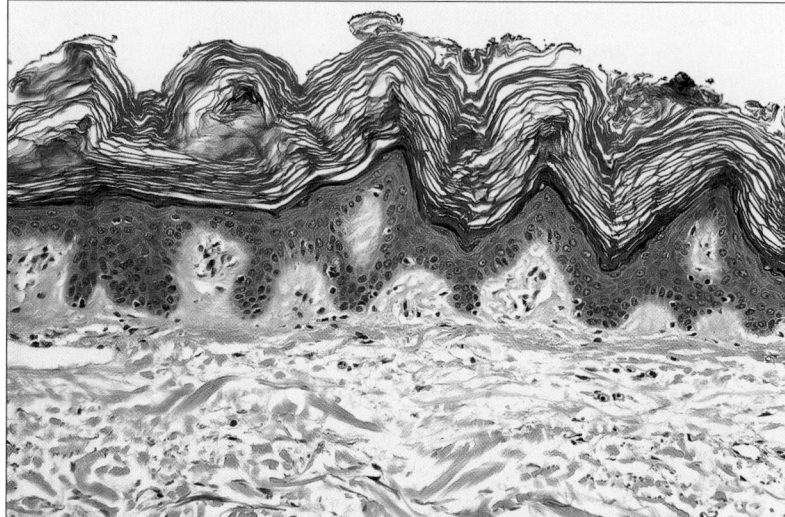

Fig. 2.102 Acrokeratosis verruciformis: there is hyperkeratosis and church-spire papillomatosis.

Porokeratosis

Clinical features

Porokeratosis is a not uncommon pathological process. It consists of an atrophic center bordered by a peripheral grooved keratotic ridge, from the center of which a keratotic core (cornoid lamella) projects at an obtuse angle.[1] There are six major categories: classical, localized, linear, punctate, disseminated superficial porokeratosis (DSP) and disseminated superficial actinic porokeratosis (DSAP), all of which may be inherited as an autosomal dominant.

- In the *classical variant* described by Mibelli, patients develop one or several plaque-like lesions on the extremities (*Figs 2.104, 2.105*). It usually presents in adulthood as persistent lesions that are highly resistant to therapy.
- *Localized porokeratosis* usually consists of a single large lesion.
- *Disseminated superficial actinic porokeratosis*, the most common variant, is characterized by numerous small, dry shallow lesions arising on the sun-damaged skin of adults (*Fig. 2.106*).[2] It may also

complicate PUVA therapy and develop in the immunosuppressed.[3–5] It presents in the third and fourth decades and despite its relationship to sunlight, rarely affects the face. The legs, forearms, back, upper arms and thighs are most commonly affected in decreasing order of frequency.[6]

- *Disseminated superficial (non-actinic) porokeratosis* (porokeratosis palmoplantaris et disseminata) is characterized by asymptomatic lesions with a tendency to involve the trunk, genitalia, palms and soles. An intensely itchy eruptive variant of this has recently been described.[7]
- In *linear porokeratosis*, the lesion is clinically reminiscent of an epidermal nevus affecting the extremities and usually presents in infancy or early childhood (*Fig. 2.107*).[8]
- *Punctate porokeratosis*, which involves the peripheries (particularly the palms and soles), usually presents in the second or third decade.[6] A zosteriform variant most often affects children and shows a predilection for the lower limbs, upper limbs and trunk.[9]

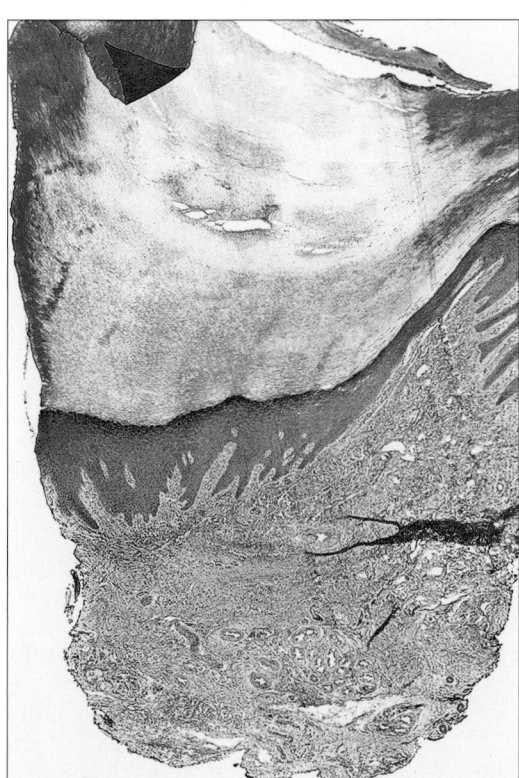

Fig. 2.103
Clavus: massive hyperkeratosis overlies an epidermal depression.

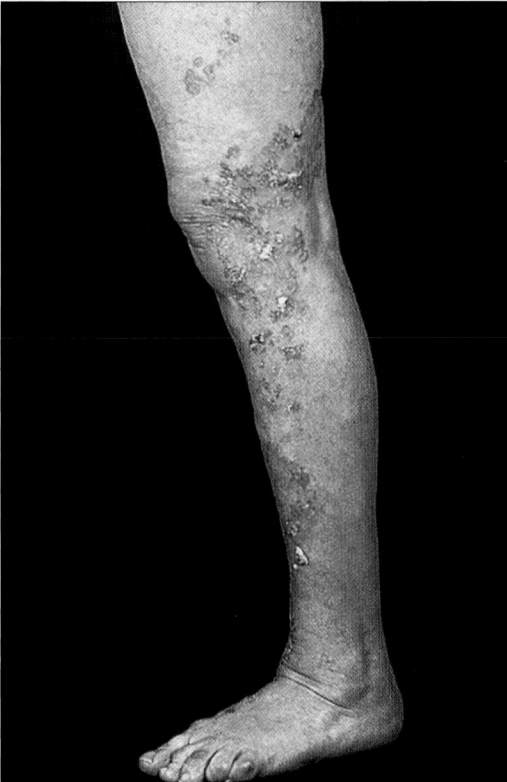

Fig. 2.104
Porokeratosis of Mibelli: these lesions have an extensive and linear distribution. By courtesy of M.M. Black, MD, Institute of Dermatology, London, UK.

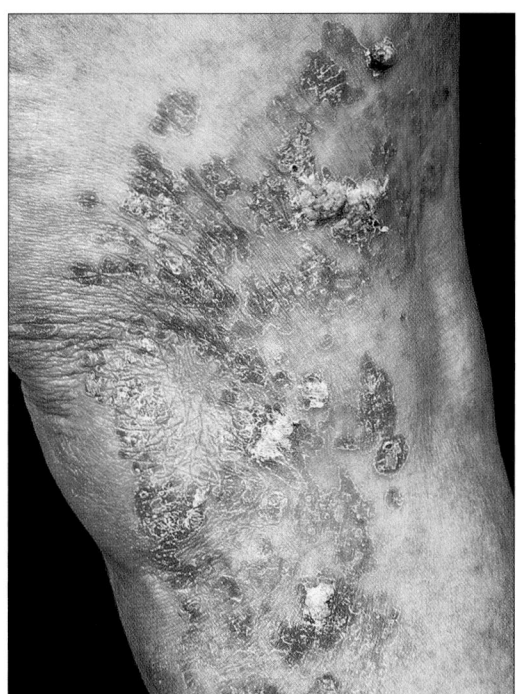

Fig. 2.105
Porokeratosis of Mibelli: the lesions are erythematous, atrophic and scaly, with sharply defined and slightly raised margins. By courtesy of M.M. Black, MD, Institute of Dermatology, London, UK.

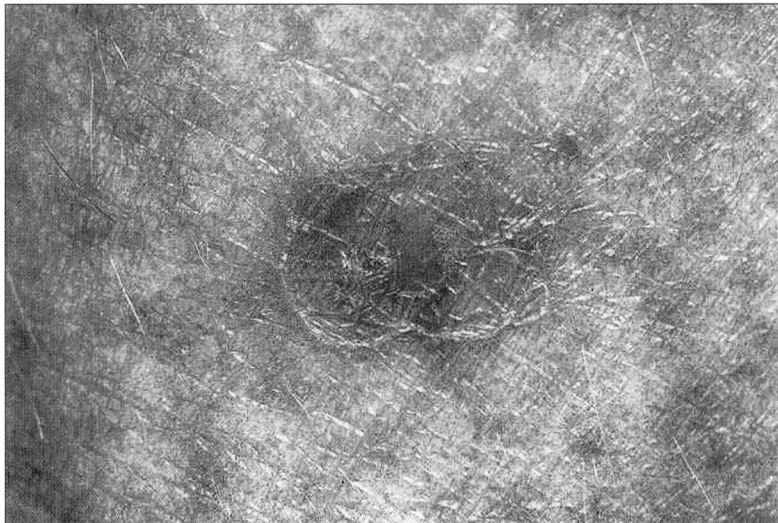

Fig. 2.106
Disseminated superficial actinic porokeratosis: in this variant, the lesions are small and discrete. Note the characteristic raised edge. By courtesy of the Institute of Dermatology, London, UK.

Porokeratosis may involve the mucous membranes, cause nail dystrophy and result in patchy alopecia. It is associated with a slightly increased risk of cutaneous neoplasia. Lesions of porokeratosis may therefore be complicated by the development of Bowen's disease, basal cell and squamous cell carcinomas.[1,8,10–15] The reported incidence has varied from 6.8 to 11.6%.[10,13,14] In some instances there is a probable causal relationship with previous treatment with radiotherapy.[10] Tumors usually develop many years after the onset of the disease, are frequently multiple and arise most often on large or coalescing lesions.[8,10,16] They are most often found on the trunk and extremities.[8]

Pathogenesis and histological features

The pathogenesis of porokeratosis is unknown. The presence of localized dysplastic features was suggested by Reed and Leone to indicate that the disease represented a focal, expanding clone of abnormal keratinocytes associated with the development of a cornoid lamella.[17] The more recent literature appears to support this claim.

Porokeratotic lesions have been shown to be associated with abnormal epidermal DNA ploidies in association with increased DNA indices, midway between normal skin and Bowen's disease.[18,19] Uninvolved skin, however, is usually diploid.[8] Chromosomal abnormalities have been identified within cultured keratinocytes and fibroblasts derived from patients suffering from both the localized and Mibelli variants.[8,10,20,21] These findings have since been confirmed in both cultured fibroblasts from normal untreated skin and lymphocytes, and it has been shown that chromosome 3 is preferentially affected (p12–14).[22] Mutations in the proximal segment of the short arm of chromosome 3 have been associated with a wide variety of malignancies.[22] Ionizing radiation, ultraviolet light including sun tanning beds, and PUVA may be associated with the development of new skin lesions in porokeratosis.[23] The first may be of particular relevance to the development of malignancy in these lesions.[14,24]

Cultured fibroblasts from porokeratosis patients have been shown to be hypersensitive to the lethal effects of X-radiation, but not ultraviolet radiation.[21,22] This has been shown to be associated with chromosomal instability in approximately 50% of patients.[20] While it has been proposed that this may result from abnormal DNA repair mechanisms (see xeroderma pigmentosa) the evidence necessary to support such a hypothesis is not yet available.[21]

Porokeratosis of Mibelli, disseminated superficial porokeratosis and disseminated superficial actinic porokeratosis may also develop against a background of solid organ transplantation or blood transfusion, possibly causally related to hepatitis C infection.[25–29]

p53 and pRb proteins are overexpressed within keratinocytes immediately beneath and adjacent to the cornoid lamellae; mdm-2 and p21^{waf-1} are reduced.[30–33] This imbalance in cell cycle control mechanisms offers a potential explanation for the development of malignancy in porokeratosis although to date p53 mutation has not been identified.[32,34]

Recently, a gene for disseminated superficial actinic porokeratosis has been mapped to chromosome 12q23.2–24.1 in a large Chinese family.[35]

Despite its name, the lesions of porokeratosis are rarely related to the 'pore' of the eccrine duct. While they may involve the follicle, their most common origin is from non-adnexal epithelium. If the biopsy is taken through the peripheral grooved ridge, the typical features can be seen. These consist of a keratin-filled epidermal invagination with an angulated parakeratotic tier, the cornoid lamella (*Figs 2.108, 2.109*).

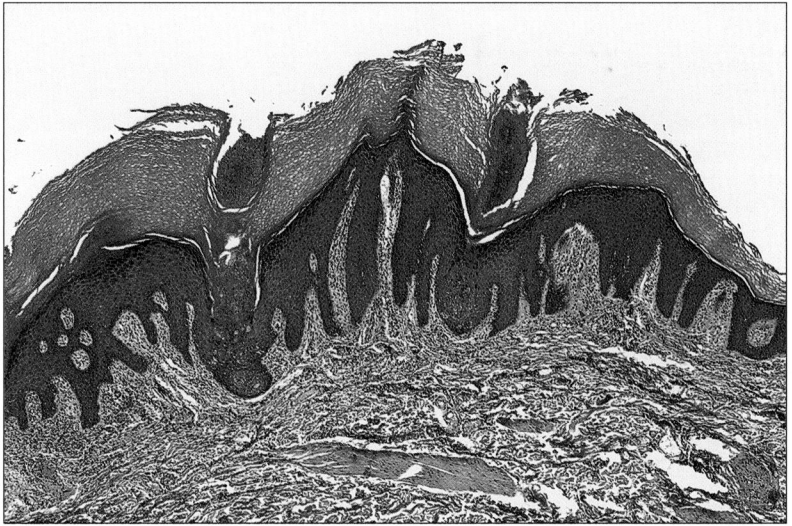

Fig. 2.108
Porokeratosis of Mibelli: there is hyperkeratosis with two well-developed cornoid lamellae projecting at an obtuse angle. Note the epidermal depression at their bases.

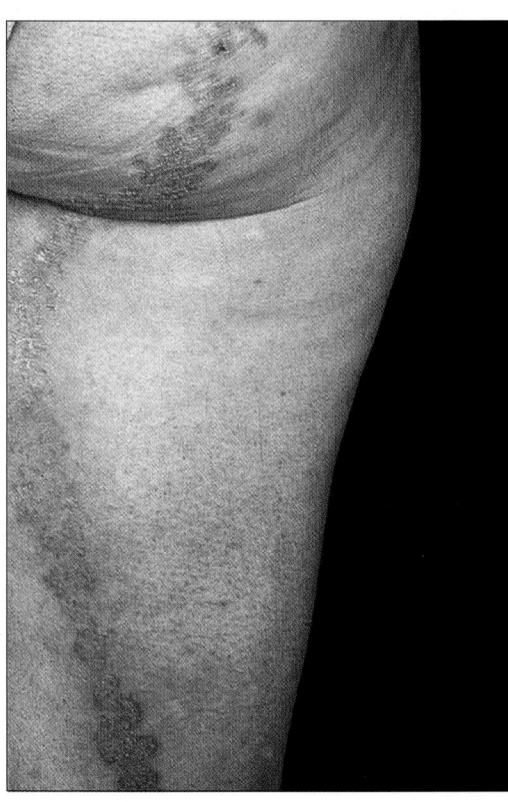

Fig. 2.107
Linear porokeratosis: in this variant, the lesion has a linear, nevoid distribution.

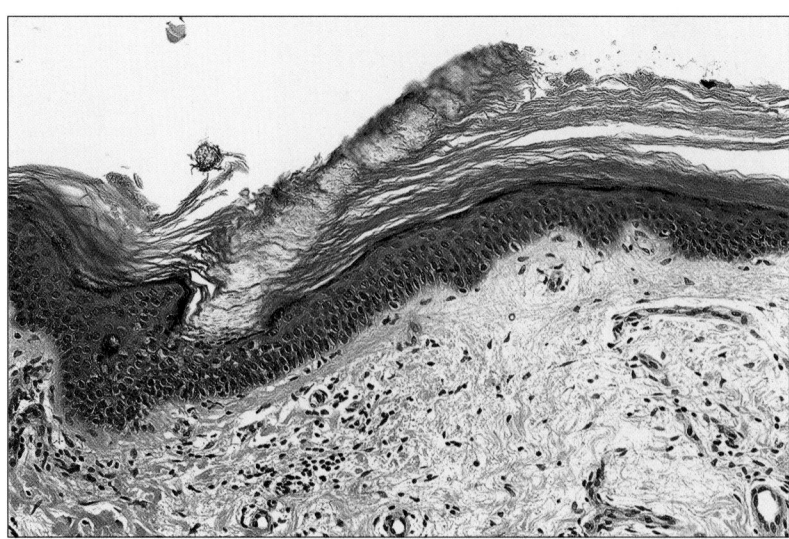

Fig. 2.109
Porokeratosis of Mibelli: in this view, the cornoid lamella can be seen to be composed of an angulated tier of parakeratosis.

The epithelium deep to the tier is vacuolated and devoid of a granular cell layer (*Fig. 2.110*). The adjacent epithelium towards the center is often atrophic, but may be of normal thickness or even acanthotic. Dyskeratotic cells may be present and epithelial dysplasia, ranging from mild changes through to carcinoma in situ, is occasionally a feature. Liquefactive degeneration of the basal cell layer of the epithelium is sometimes present and occasionally there are conspicuous cytoid bodies. In the dermis, a non-specific chronic inflammatory cell infiltrate and telangiectatic vessels are sometimes seen. The typical features are best seen in the Mibelli variant. The changes tend to be less pronounced in the other subtypes (*Fig. 2.111*). In the actinic variant there is often solar elastosis and atrophy of the adjacent epidermis.[6]

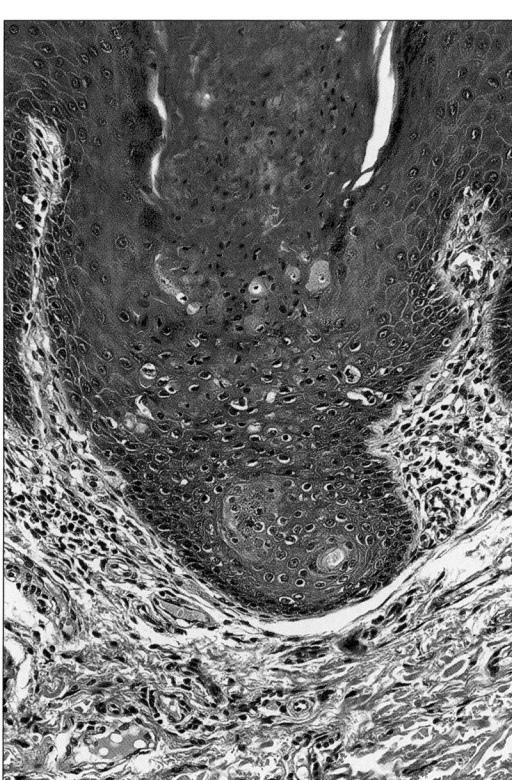

Fig. 2.110
Porokeratosis of Mibelli: the epidermis at the base of the cornoid lamella is vacuolated and the granular cell layer absent.

Differential diagnosis

With the appropriate clinical information the histopathological changes of porokeratosis are diagnostic. Cornoid lamella formation, however, does occur as a non-specific finding in a variety of conditions including seborrheic warts, solar keratoses, verrucae vulgaris, and squamous cell and basal cell carcinomas.[36] Cornoid lamellae are also features of porokeratotic eccrine nevi (see p. 1615).[37,38] They are also not uncommon in normal, particularly actinically damaged skin.

References

1. O'Neill, A., Commens, C.A., Kossard, S. et al (1989) Squamous cell carcinoma in porokeratosis in two patients. *Australas J Dermatol*, **30**, 77–80.
2. Neumann, R.A., Knobler, R.M., Jurecka, W. et al (1989) Disseminated superficial actinic porokeratosis: experimental induction and exacerbation of skin lesions. *J Am Acad Dermatol*, **21**, 1182–1188.
3. MacMillan, A.L., Roberts, S.O.B. (1974) Porokeratosis of Mibelli after renal transplantation. *Br J Dermatol*, **90**, 45–51.
4. Lederman, J.S., Sober, A.J., Lederman, G.S. (1985) Immunosuppression: a cause of porokeratosis. *J Am Acad Dermatol*, **13**, 75–79.
5. Komorowski, R.A., Clowry, L.J. (1989) Porokeratosis of Mibelli in transplant recipients. *Am J Clin Pathol*, **91**, 71–74.
6. Shumack, S.P., Commens, C.A. (1989) Disseminated superficial actinic porokeratosis: a clinical study. *J Am Acad Dermatol*, **20**, 1015–1022.
7. Kanzaki, T., Miwa, N., Kobayashi, T. et al (1992) Eruptive pruritic papular porokeratosis. *J Dermatol*, **19**, 109–112.
8. Otsuka, F., Iwata, M., Watanabe, R. et al (1992) Porokeratosis: clinical and cellular characterization of its cancer-prone nature. *J Dermatol*, **19**, 702–706.
9. Veraldi, S., Bocor, M., Gasparini, G. (1989) Zosteriform porokeratosis: a report of two cases. *Cutis*, **44**, 216–219.
10. Otsuka, F., Someya, T., Ishibashi, Y. (1991) Porokeratosis and malignant skin tumors. *J Cancer Res Clin Oncol*, **117**, 55–60.
11. Coskey, R.J., Mehregan, A.H. (1975) Bowen's disease associated with porokeratosis Mibelli. *Arch Dermatol*, **111**, 1480–1481.
12. Otsuka, F., Huang, J., Sawara, K. et al (1990) Disseminated porokeratosis accompanying multicentric Bowen's disease – characterization of porokeratosis skin lesions progressive to Bowen's disease. *J Am Acad Dermatol*, **23**, 355–359.
13. Cort, D.F., Abdel-Aziz, A.M. (1972) Epithelioma arising in porokeratosis of Mibelli. *Br J Plast Surg*, **25**, 318–328.
14. Goerttler, E.A., Jung, E.G. (1975) Porokeratosis Mibelli and skin carcinoma. *Humangenetik*, **26**, 291–296.
15. Komatsu, T., Tamura, S., Kimura, S. et al (1983) Porokeratosis of Mibelli associated with squamous carcinoma. *Jpn J Clin Dermatol*, **37**, 447–452.
16. Otsuka, F., Umebayashi, Y., Watanabe, S.I. et al (1993) Porokeratosis large skin lesions are susceptible to skin cancer development: histological and cytological explanation for the susceptibility. *J Can Res Clin Oncol*, **119**, 395–400.
17. Reed, R.J., Leone, P. (1970) Porokeratosis: a mutant clonal keratosis of the epidermis. I. Histogenesis. *Arch Dermatol*, **101**, 340–347.
18. Otsuka, F., Shima, A., Ishibashi, Y. (1989) Porokeratosis as a premalignant skin condition. Cytologic demonstration of abnormal DNA ploidy in cells of the epidermis. *Cancer*, **63**, 891–896.
19. Imakado, S., Otsuka, F., Ishibashi, Y. et al (1988) Abnormal DNA ploidy in cells of the epidermis in a case of porokeratosis. *Arch Dermatol*, **124**, 331–332.
20. Taylor, A.M.R., Harnden, D.G., Fairburn, E.A. (1973) Chromosomal instability associated with susceptibility to malignant disease in patients with porokeratosis of Mibelli. *J Natl Cancer Inst*, **51**, 371–378.
21. Watanabe, R., Ishibashi, Y., Otsuka, F. (1990) Chromosomal instability and cellular hypersensitivity to X-radiation of cultured fibroblasts derived from patients with porokeratosis patient's skin. *Mutation Res*, **230**, 273–278.
22. Scappaticci, S., Limbiase, S., Orecchia, G. et al (1989) Clonal chromosomal abnormalities with preferential involvement of chromosome 3 in patients with porokeratosis of Mibelli. *Cancer Genet Cytogenet*, **43**, 89–94.
23. Allen, A.L., Glaser, D.A. (2000) Disseminated superficial actinic porokeratosis associated with topical PUVA. *J Am Acad Dermatol*, **43**, 720–722.
24. Otsuka, F., Watanabe, R., Moro, A. et al (1989) Cultured skin fibroblasts from patients with porokeratosis are hypersensitive to the lethal effects of X-radiation. *Jpn J Cancer Res*, **80**, 41–44.
25. Raychaudhuri, S., Smoller, B. (1992) Porokeratosis in immunosuppressed and non-immunosuppressed patients. *Int J Dermatol*, **31**, 781–782.
26. Kanitakis, J., Euvrard, S., Faure, M. et al (1998) Porokeratosis and immunosuppression. *Eur J Dermatol*, **8**, 459–465.
27. Mizukawa, Y., Shiohara, T. (1999) Porokeratosis in patients with hepatitis C infection: does HCV infection provide a link between porokeratosis and immunosuppression? *Br J Dermatol*, **141**, 163–164.
28. Mizukawa, Y., Shiohara, T. (2001) Onset of porokeratosis of Mibelli in organ transplant recipients: lack of a search for transmissible agents in these patients. *J Am Acad Dermatol*, **44**, 143–144.
29. Kanitakis, J., Euvrard, S., Claudy, A. (2001) Porokeratosis in organ transplant recipients. *J Am Acad Dermatol*, **44**, 144–146.
30. Magee, J.W., McCalmont, T.H., LeBoit, P.E. (1994) Overexpression of p53 tumor suppressor protein in porokeratosis. *Arch Dermatol*, **130**, 187–190.
31. Puig, L., Alegre, M., Costa, I. et al (1995) Overexpression of p53 in disseminated superficial actinic porokeratosis with and without malignant degeneration. *Arch Dermatol*, **131**, 353–354.
32. Nelson, C., Cowper, S., Morgan, M. (1999) p53, mdm-2, and p21^{waf-1} in the porokeratoses. *Am J Dermatopathol*, **21**, 420–425.
33. Chang, S-E., Lim, Y-S., Lee, H-J. et al (1999) Expression of p53, pRb, p16 and proliferating cell nuclear antigen in squamous cell carcinomas arising on a giant porokeratosis. *Br J Dermatol*, **141**, 575–576.
34. Ozkan, S., Fetil, E., Aydogan, T. et al (2000) Lack of TP53 mutations in a case of porokeratosis palmaris, plantaris et disseminata. *Dermatology*, **201**, 158–161.
35. Xia, J-H., Yang, Y-F., Deng, H. et al (2000) Identification of a locus for disseminated superficial actinic porokeratosis at chromosome 12q23.2–24.1. *J Invest Dermatol*, **114**, 1071–1074.
36. Wade, R.T., Ackerman, A.B. (1980) Cornoid lamellation: a histologic reaction pattern. *Am J Dermatopathol*, **2**, 5–14.
37. Kroumpouzos, G., Stefanato, C.M., Wilkel, C.S. et al (1999) Systematized porokeratotic eccrine and hair follicle nevus: report of a case and review of the literature. *Br J Dermatol*, **141**, 1092–1096.
38. Sassmannshausen, J., Bogomilsky, J., Chaffins, M. (2000) Porokeratotic eccrine ostial and dermal duct nevus: a case report and review of the literature. *J Am Acad Dermatol*, **43**, 364–367.

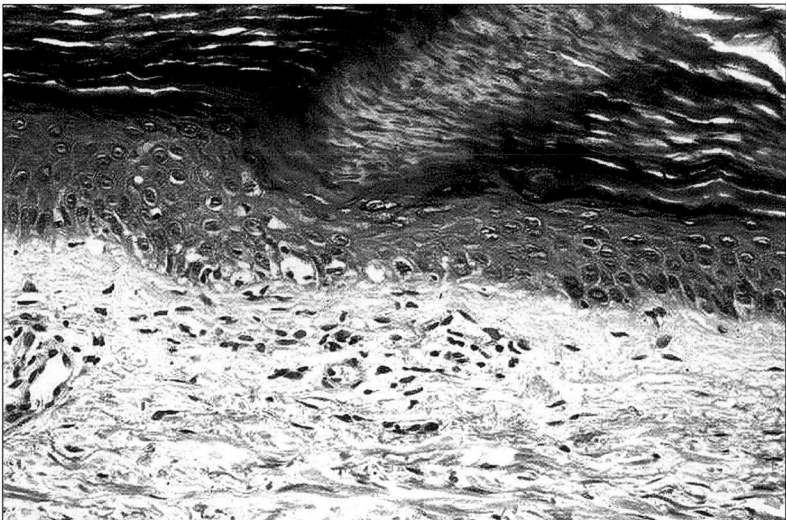

Fig. 2.111
Disseminated superficial actinic porokeratosis: in this example, the cornoid lamella is well formed and vacuolated keratinocytes are conspicuous.

Hyperkeratosis lenticularis perstans

Clinical features

Hyperkeratosis lenticularis perstans (Flegel's disease) is a not uncommon dermatosis that is sometimes mistaken for Kyrle's disease.[1–4] It has an equal sex incidence and patients present most often in their fourth or fifth decade. It is characterized by a very protracted course, many patients having lesions for decades. Patients present with large numbers of 1–5 mm discrete, gray, gray–brown or red–brown, circular scaly papules (*Figs 2.112, 2.113*). Initial lesions often arise on the dorsum of the foot. Other sites of predilection include the lower legs, upper arms and pinnae. The buttocks, trunk and dorsal aspects of the hands may also be affected, and punctate keratoses have been described on the palms and soles. The lesions are either asymptomatic or mildly pruritic. Characteristically removal of the scale is associated with pinpoint bleeding, a feature that distinguishes this disorder from stuccokeratoses. Other than an isolated report of an increased incidence of both basal cell and squamous carcinomas, there is no particular associated disease process (compare with Kyrle's disease).[5] Although most cases appear to be sporadic, there is some evidence to support an autosomal dominant mode of inheritance in a proportion of cases.

Pathogenesis and histological features

Flegel's disease is of unknown etiology and pathogenesis and is characterized by focal areas of abnormal hyperkeratinization.[6–8] Early lesions are not diagnostic, showing merely lamellar hyperkeratosis, focal parakeratosis and an essentially normal epidermis. In an established lesion, in addition to hyperkeratosis and parakeratosis, there is epidermal atrophy with an inconspicuous or absent granular cell layer (*Figs 2.114, 2.115*). The lower layers of the epithelium may show

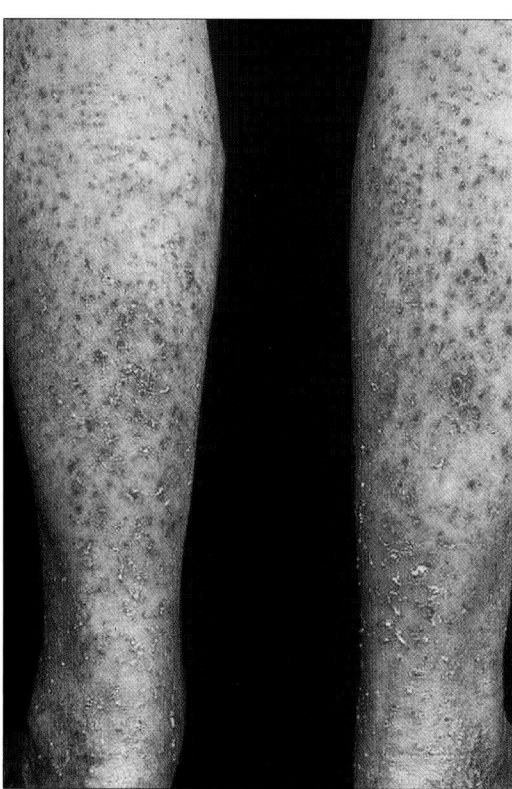

Fig. 2.112
Flegel's disease: there are characteristic disseminated erythematous scaly lesions. By courtesy of M. Price, MD, Institute of Dermatology, London, UK.

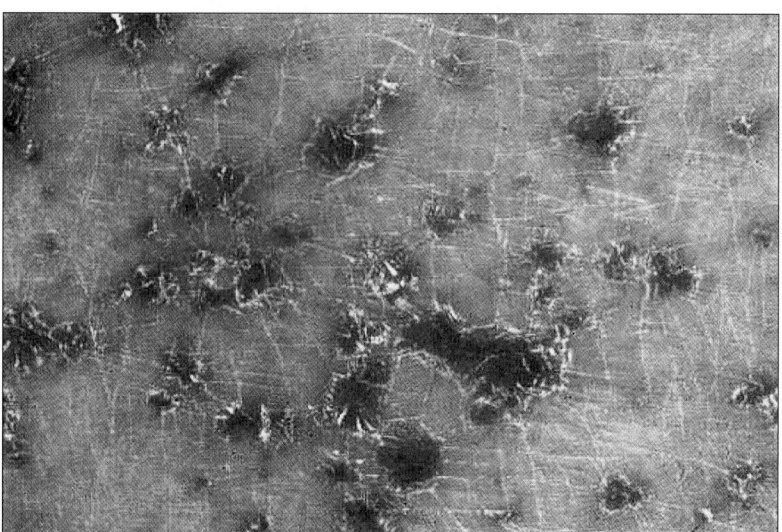

Fig. 2.113
Flegel's disease: the lower legs are commonly affected. Lesions are small, multiple and covered by a well-developed scale. By courtesy of M. Price, MD, Institute of Dermatology, London, UK.

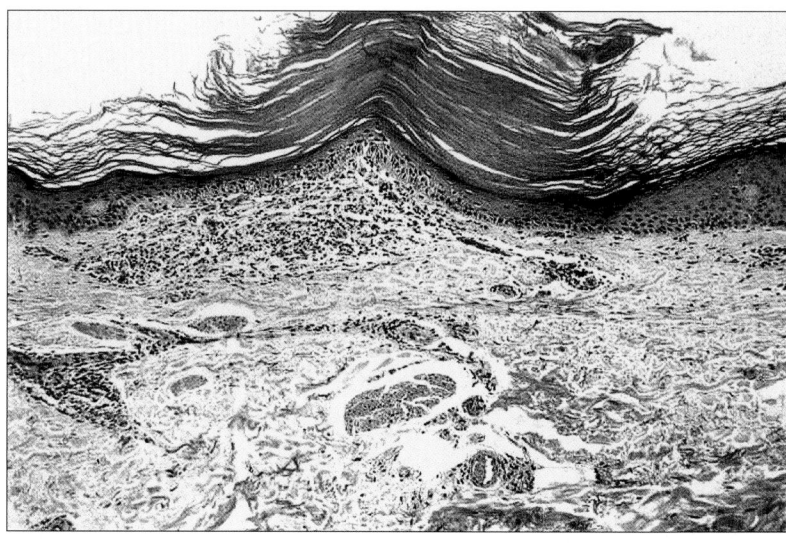

Fig. 2.114
Flegel's disease: there is an angulated tier of hyperkeratosis and parakeratosis with epidermal atrophy and a lichenoid chronic inflammatory cell infiltrate.

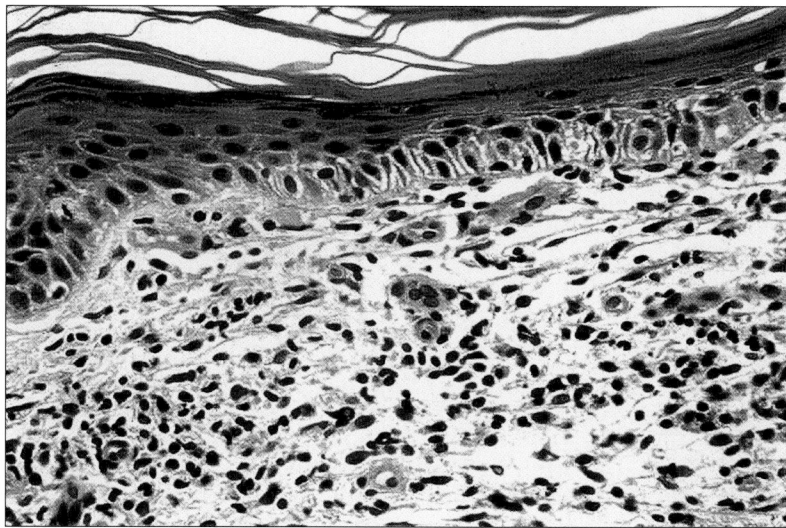

Fig. 2.115
Flegel's disease: there is epidermal atrophy and spongiosis is present.

intercellular edema and occasional foci of basal cell degeneration. Cytoid bodies are sometimes evident. Typically the papillary dermis is edematous and a chronic inflammatory cell infiltrate is often present, adopting a perivascular or lichenoid distribution. Pigmentary incontinence is not usually a feature.

The lymphocytes are an admixture of CD4+ T-helper cells and CD8+ T-suppressor cells.[7] Sézary-like forms have been described.

Ultrastructurally, the most commonly documented changes have been absence, vacuolation or abnormally lamellated membrane coating (Odland) bodies.[7]

Differential diagnosis

Clinically Flegel's disease differs from Kyrle's disease by the absence of keratin-filled penetrating plugs and the frequent presence of palmar and plantar lesions, which are not seen in Kyrle's disease. Flegel's disease is sometimes confused with stuccokeratoses, but these do not affect the trunk, palms and soles and the lesions may be readily removed without bleeding. Histologically, stuccokeratoses are characterized by ortho-hyperkeratosis and 'church spire' papillomatosis (see p. 1165). Although there may be histological overlap with other conditions showing lichenoid features, the striking keratotic tier with parakeratosis and absent granular cell layer are useful diagnostic pointers.

References

1. Flegel, H. (1958) Hyperkeratosis lenticularis perstans. *Hautarzt*, 9, 362–364.
2. Bean, S.F. (1969) Hyperkeratosis lenticularis perstans. *Arch Dermatol*, 99, 705–709.
3. Price, M.L., Wilson Jones, E., Macdonald, D.M. (1987) A clinicopathological study of Flegel's disease (hyperkeratosis lenticularis perstans). *Br J Dermatol*, 116, 681–691.
4. Raffle, E.J., Rogers, J. (1969) Hyperkeratosis lenticularis perstans. *Arch Dermatol*, 100, 423–428.
5. Beveridge, G.W., Langlands, A.D. (1973) Familial hyperkeratosis lenticularis perstans associated with tumours of the skin. *Br J Dermatol*, 88, 453–458.
6. Langer, K., Zonzits, E., Konrad, K. (1992) Hyperkeratosis lenticularis perstans (Flegel's disease). Ultrastructural study of lesional and perilesional skin and therapeutic trial of topical tretinoin versus 5-fluorouracil. *J Am Acad Dermatol*, 27, 812–816.
7. Jang, K-A., Choi, J-H., Sung, K-J. et al (1999) Hyperkeratosis lenticularis perstans (Flegel's disease): histologic, immunohistochemical, and ultrastructural features in a case. *Am J Dermatol*, 21, 395–402.
8. Blaheta, H-J., Metzler, G., Rassner, G. et al (2001) Hyperkeratosis lenticularis perstans (Flegel's disease) – lack of response to treatment with tacalcitol and calcipotriol. *Dermatology*, 202, 255–258.

Granular parakeratosis

Clinical features

Granular parakeratosis is a distinctive acquired disorder of keratinization originally reported in 1991.[1-4] The condition most often affects the axillae but it has also been described involving other intertriginous areas including submammary and intermammary skin, groins, vulva, perianal region and, less commonly, in non-intertriginous skin including the lower back, buttocks and flanks.[5-8] Women are affected more commonly than males. The disease mainly affects the middle aged to elderly; children are rarely involved.[8-10] It presents as pruritic or burning erythematous, hyperpigmented and hyperkeratotic patches. Fissures and a 'cobblestone' appearance may be seen. The condition has been documented to respond to retinoids and to calcipotriene and ammonium lactate.[11,12]

Pathogenesis and histological features

The etiology is unknown. It has been suggested that the condition develops as a result of a contact reaction to an antiperspirant or as a result of excessive use of other topical products including creams, shampoos and soaps.[1-6,8] However, this does not explain the involvement of areas distant from the axilla. The molecular mechanism proposed to explain the disease consists of a failure to transform profilaggrin to filaggrin with the resultant failure in degradation of keratohyalin granules.[1,7]

The histological appearances typically consist of hyperkeratosis with parakeratosis and retention of keratohyalin granules in the stratum corneum (*Figs 2.116, 2.117*). The underlying epidermis may show mild acanthosis or even some degree of thinning.

References

1. Northcutt, A.D., Nelson, D.M., Tschen, J.A. (1991) Axillary granular parakeratosis. *J Am Acad Dermatol*, 24, 541–544.
2. Mehregan, D.A., Vandersteen, P., Sikorski, L. et al (1995) Axillary granular parakeratosis. *J Am Acad Dermatol*, 33, 373–375.
3. Kossard, S., White, A. (1998) Axillary granular parakeratosis. *Australas J Dermatol*, 39, 186–187.
4. Barnes, C.J., Lesher, J.L. Jr, Sangueza, O.P. (2001) Axillary granular parakeratosis. *Int J Dermatol*, 40, 439–441.

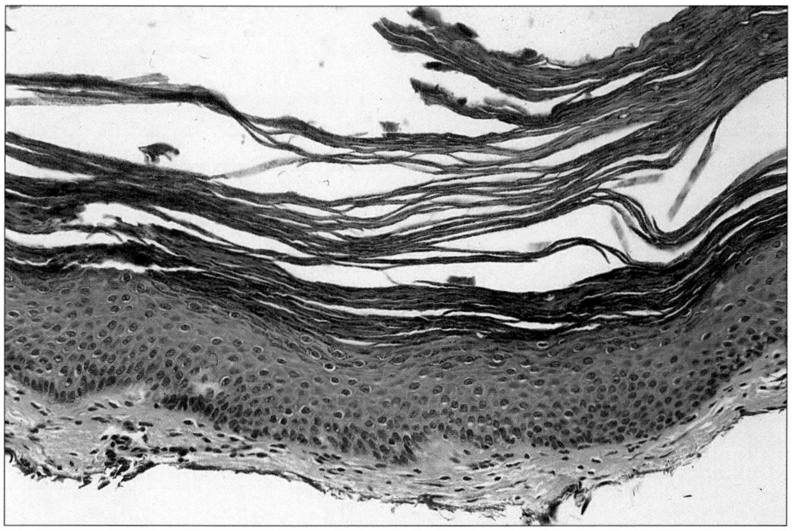

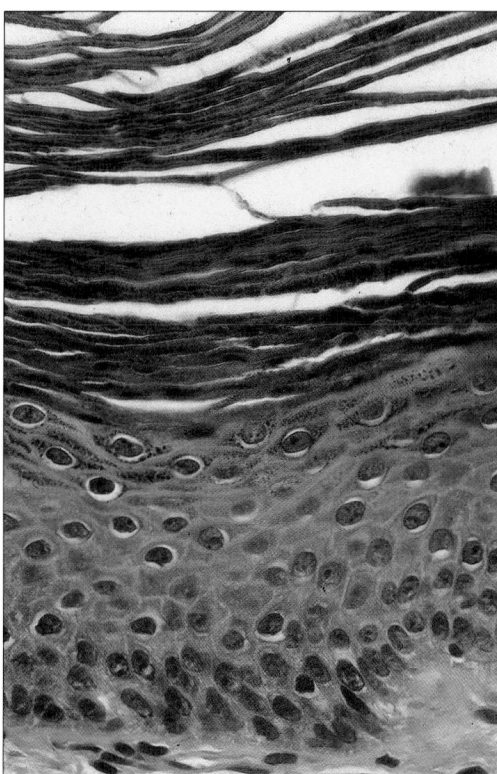

Fig. 2.117
Granular parakeratosis: high power view showing retention of the keratohyalin granules.

Fig. 2.116
Granular parakeratosis: there is marked parakeratosis.

5. Mehregan, D.A., Thomas, J.E., Mehregan, D.R. (1998) Intertriginous granular parakeratosis. *J Am Acad Dermatol*, **39**, 495–496.
6. Wohlrab, J., Luftl, M., Wolter, M. et al (1999) Submammary granular parakeratosis: an acquired punctate hyperkeratosis of exogenic origin. *J Am Acad Dermatol*, **40**, 813–814.
7. Metze, D., Rutten, A. (1999) Granular parakeratosis – a unique acquired disorder of keratinisation. *J Cutan Pathol*, **26**, 339–352.
8. Patrizi, A., Neri, I., Misciali, C. et al (2002) Granular parakeratosis: four paediatric cases. *Br J Dermatol*, **147**, 1003–1006.

9. Pimentel, D.R., Michalany, N., Morgado de Abreu, M.A. et al (2003) Granular parakeratosis in children: case report and review of the literature. *Pediatr Dermatol*, **20**, 215–220.
10. Trowers, A.B., Assaf, R., Jaworsky, C. (2002) Granular parakeratosis in a child. *Pediatr Dermatol*, **19**, 146–147.
11. Contreras, M.E., Gottfried, L.C., Bang, R.H. et al (2003) Axillary intertriginous granular parakeratosis responsive to topical calcipotriene and ammonium lactate. *Int J Dermatol*, **42**, 382–383.
12. Webster, C.G., Resnik, K.S., Webster, G.F. (1997) Axillary granular parakeratosis. *J Am Acad Dermatol*, **37**, 789–790.

Inherited and autoimmune subepidermal blistering diseases

3

Split skin immunofluorescence   81

Immunoperoxidase antigen mapping   83

Epidermolysis bullosa   84

Bullous pemphigoid   98

Pemphigoid gestationis   111

Lichen planus pemphigoides   115

Mucous membrane pemphigoid (Cicatricial pemphigoid)   117

Epidermolysis bullosa acquisita   123

Bullous systemic lupus erythematosus   128

Dermatitis herpetiformis   131

Linear IgA disease   134

Blisters, which are clinically subdivided into vesicles (L. *vesicula*, dim. of vesica, bladder) and bullae (L. bubble), are defined as accumulations of fluid either within or below the epidermis and mucous membranes. Although somewhat arbitrary, the term 'vesicle' is applied to lesions less than 0.5 cm in diameter and 'bulla' to those greater than 0.5 cm. Subepidermal blisters, i.e. those that develop at the epidermal or mucosal basement membrane region, include inherited variants and acquired (often autoimmune mediated) conditions. The former are usually classified as non-inflammatory (cell-poor) blisters whereas the latter are commonly inflammatory (cell-rich) in nature (*Fig. 3.1*).

Subepidermal blisters may develop within the lamina lucida (e.g. bullous pemphigoid) or deep to the lamina densa (e.g. epidermolysis bullosa acquisita) (*Fig. 3.2*). In addition to clinical observations, the precise diagnosis of a blistering disorder requires careful histological and immunofluorescence correlation. When possible the last should include indirect studies and in particular NaCl-split skin should be used as substrate as a mechanism of localizing the site of epidermodermal separation.[1] Alternatively, if a sample has not been taken for indirect immunofluorescence, immunoperoxidase antigen mapping on paraffin-embedded material in many instances may prove to be a satisfactory substitute. Although the results of electron microscopic investigations and in particular molecular studies have formed the basis of the current classification of subepidermal bullous dermatoses, such techniques are not always essential to the everyday investigation of a patient with an acquired blistering disorder.

The mechanisms involved in the development of a subepidermal blister are variable. They include inherited mutational defects of basement membrane proteins, i.e. epidermolysis bullosa, acquired autoimmune bullous diseases such as bullous pemphigoid, cellular immunity-mediated disorders (e.g. erythema multiforme and toxic epidermal necrolysis), metabolic diseases including porphyria cutanea tarda and profound subepidermal edema such as may be seen in bullous arthropod bite reactions and dermal acute inflammatory processes (e.g. Sweet's disease).

In this chapter, only those conditions in which subepidermal blister formation represents an inherited or autoimmune primary event are considered. Other conditions, which may be associated with subepidermal blistering, are dealt with in their more appropriate chapters.

Split skin immunofluorescence

This technique represents a modification of indirect immunofluorescence (IMF) in which normal skin is split through the lamina lucida of the basement membrane region to produce an artificial blister cavity (with the lamina densa lining the floor) for use as substrate. Artificial separation can be achieved by the suction technique (in vivo) or by

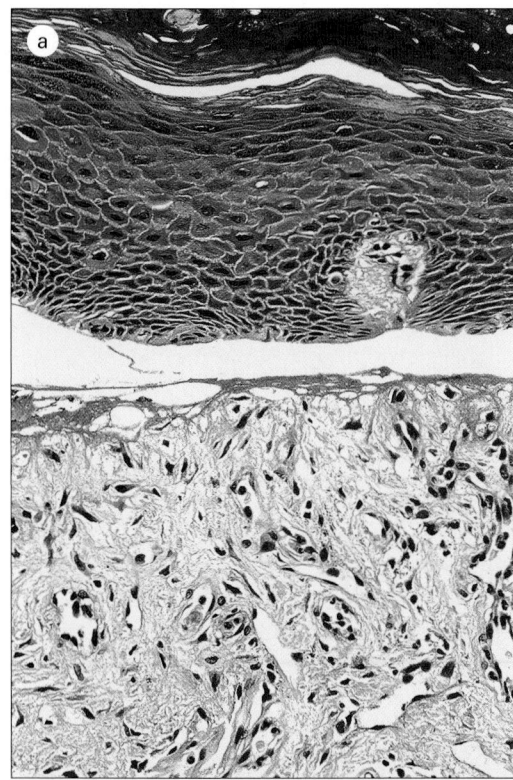

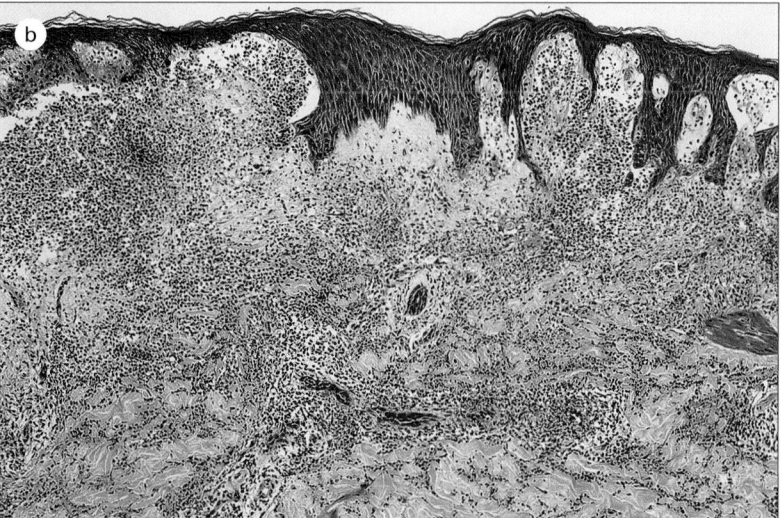

Fig. 3.1
Classification of subepidermal blisters: lesions may be subdivided into (**a**) cell-free and (**b**) cell-rich variants.

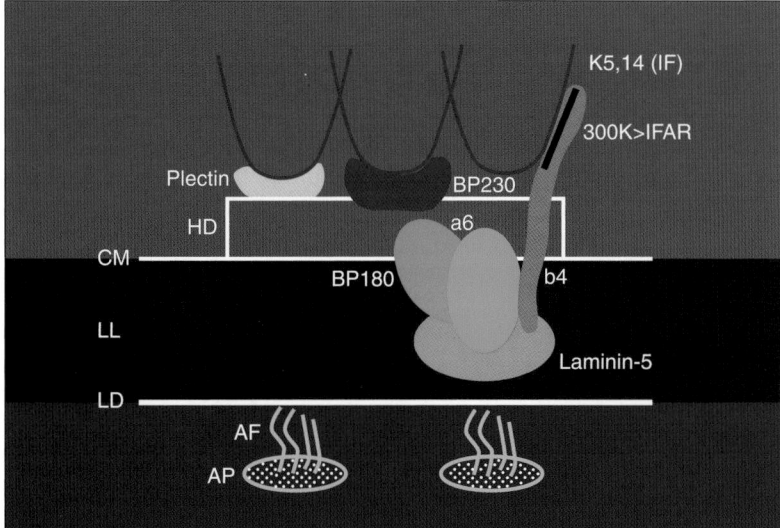

Fig. 3.2
Basement membrane constituents: blisters can be classified into those that develop within the lamina lucida (LL) and those that arise below the lamina densa (LD). (AF, anchoring fibrils; AP, anchoring plaque; CM, cell membrane.)

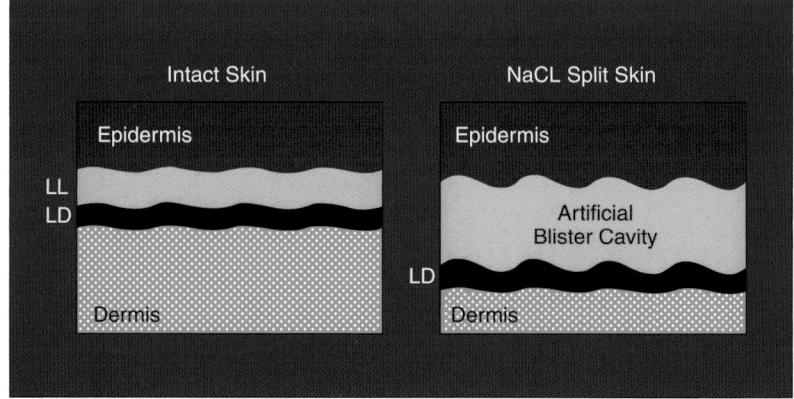

Fig. 3.3
Split skin immunofluorescence.

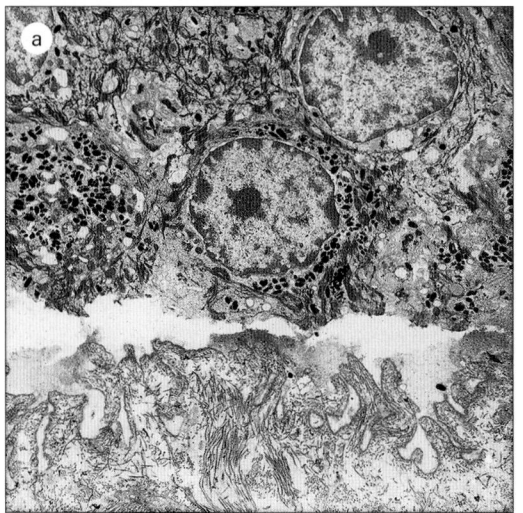

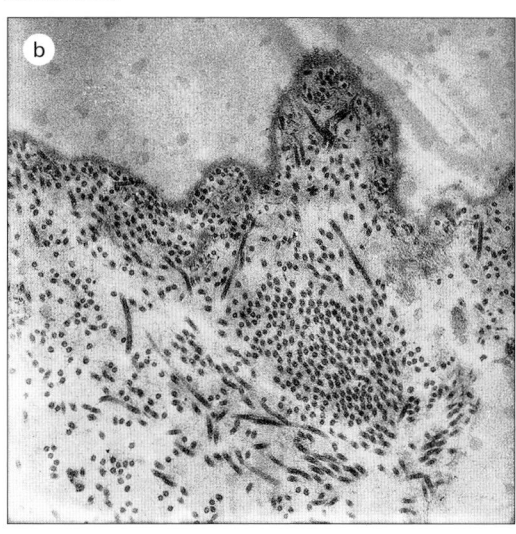

Fig. 3.4
(**a, b**) Split skin immunofluorescence: the split is through the lamina lucida, the lamina densa lining the floor of the artificial blister cavity.

immersion of normal skin in 1 M NaCl for 48 hours at 4°C (*Fig. 3.3*). In general the latter technique is preferred.[2] Such a split is invariably through the lamina lucida region (confirmed by electron microscopy or immunofluorescence) (*Figs 3.4, 3.5*) and therefore the technique enables precise localization of a circulating basement membrane zone antibody to either the floor or the roof of the artificial blister cavity. In bullous pemphigoid, pemphigoid gestationis and the majority of cases of cicatricial pemphigoid, linear immunofluorescence is found along the roof of the artificial blister whereas in diseases characterized by a sublamina densa split (e.g. epidermolysis bullosa acquisita, anti-laminin cicatricial pemphigoid, anti-p105 pemphigoid, anti-p200 pemphigoid and bullous dermatosis of bullous lupus erythematosus), the immuno-fluorescence is found along the floor of the blister (see reference 3 for a review) (*Fig. 3.6*). In some diseases, positive immunofluorescence may be found on either the roof or the floor or even at both sites simultaneously (e.g. linear IgA disease and some variants of cicatricial pemphigoid). Such variable labeling reflects the antigen heterogeneity in a number of these bullous dermatoses.

Immunoperoxidase antigen mapping

As an alternative to split skin immunofluorescence, paraffin embedded sections of lesional skin are used in a direct immunoperoxidase antigen mapping technique to identify the site of the epidermodermal separation.[4–7] This procedure localizes known basement membrane region constituents such as keratins 5/14, laminin and type IV collagen to the roof or floor of the blister cavity. The site of blister formation can therefore be characterized as intrabasal, within the lamina lucida or deep to the lamina densa. For example, in epidermolysis bullosa simplex variants, all of these immunoreactants are present along the floor of the blister cavity. In bullous pemphigoid, keratin is present along the roof of the blister while laminin and type IV collagen are found along the floor (*Fig. 3.7*). In dystrophic epidermolysis bullosa, epidermolysis bullosa acquisita and bullous systemic lupus erythematosus, all three immuno-reactants are present in the roof of the blister (*Fig. 3.8*).

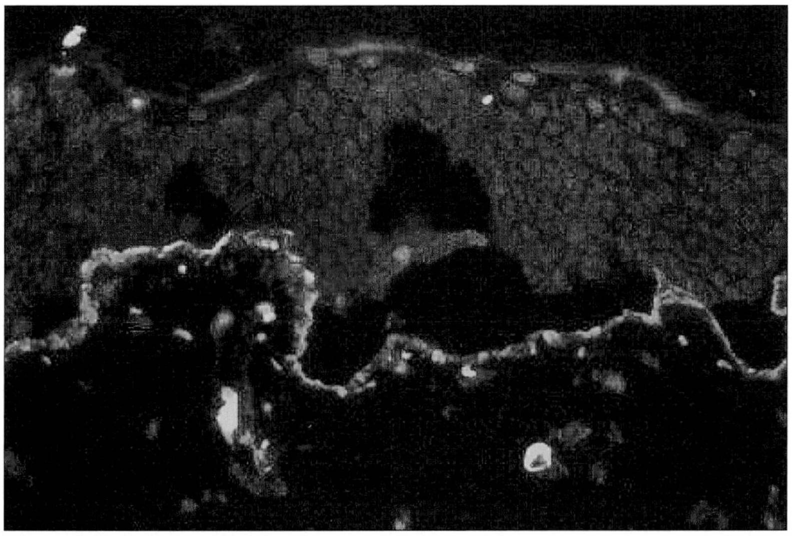

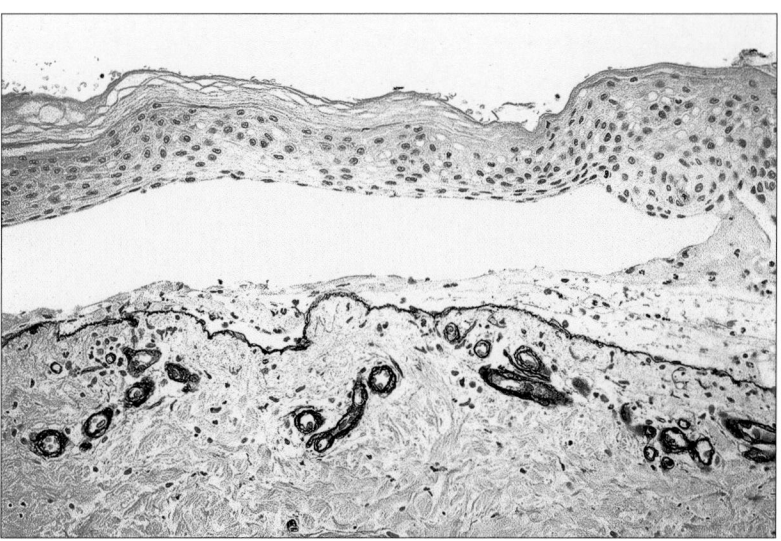

Fig. 3.5
Split skin immunofluorescence: type IV collagen lines the floor of the split skin artificial blister which there forms within the lamina lucida. By courtesy of B. Bhogal, FIMLS, Institute of Dermatology, London, UK.

Fig. 3.7
Paraffin-embedded immunoperoxidase antigen mapping: in bullous pemphigoid, type IV collagen is present along the floor of the blister.

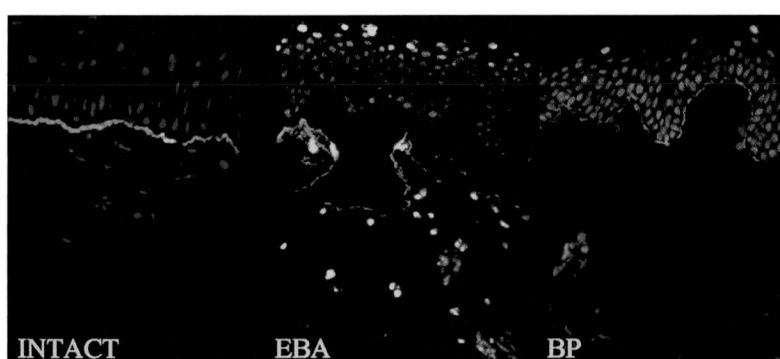

INTACT   EBA   BP

Fig. 3.6
Split skin immunofluorescence: (**left**) linear IgG at the basement membrane; (**middle**) in epidermolysis bullosa acquisita (EBA), the antibody binds to the floor of the blister cavity; (**right**) in bullous pemphigoid (BP), the antibody binds to the roof of the blister. By courtesy of B. Bhogal, FIMLS, Institute of Dermatology, London, UK.

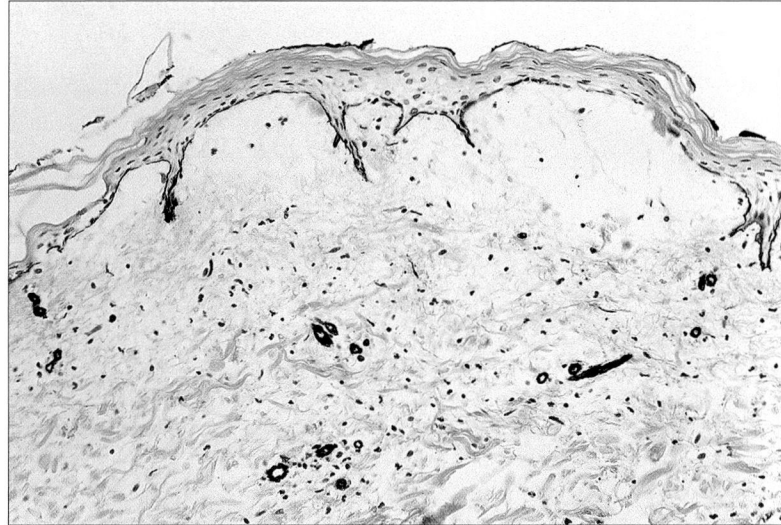

Fig. 3.8
Paraffin-embedded immunoperoxidase antigen mapping: in epidermolysis bullosa acquisita, type IV collagen is present along the roof of the blister cavity.

References

1. Gammon, W.R., Briggaman, R.A., Inman, A.O. et al (1984) Differentiating anti-lamina lucida and anti-sublamina densa anti-BMZ antibodies by indirect immunofluorescence on 1.0 M sodium chloride-separated skin. *J Invest Dermatol*, **82**, 139–144.
2. Willsteed, E., Bhogal, B.S., Black, M.M. et al (1990) The use of IM NaCl split skin in the indirect immunofluorescence of the linear IgA bullous dermatoses. *J Cutan Pathol*, **17**, 144–148.
3. Ghohestani, R.F., Nicolas, J.F., Rousselle, P. et al (1997) Diagnostic value of indirect immunofluorescence on sodium chloride-split skin in differential diagnosis of subepidermal autoimmune bullous dermatoses. *Arch Dermatol*, **133**, 1102–1107.
4. Hallel-Halevy, D., Nadelman, C., Chen, M. et al (2001) Epidermolysis bullosa acquisita: update and review. *Clin Dermatol*, **19**, 712–718.
5. Prieto, V.G., McNutt, N.S. (1994) Immunohistochemical detection of keratin with the monoclonal antibody MNF-116 is useful in the diagnosis of epidermolysis bullosa simplex. *J Cutan Pathol*, **21**, 118–122.
6. Bowszyc-Dmonchowska, M., Hashimoto, T., Dmochowski, M. et al (1997) Evaluation of an avidin-biotin-peroxidase method with a monoclonal antibody to type IV collagen in the differential diagnosis of bullous pemphigoid and epidermolysis bullosa acquisita. *J Dermatol*, **24**, 217–222.
7. Bolte, C., Gonzalez, S. (1995) Rapid diagnosis of major variants of congenital epidermolysis bullosa using a monoclonal antibody against type IV collagen. *Am J Dermatopathol*, **17**, 580–583.

Epidermolysis bullosa

Epidermolysis bullosa (EB) refers to a heterogeneous group of diseases in which the skin and sometimes the mucous membranes blister easily in response to mild trauma, hence the alternative title 'mechanobullous dermatosis', which has sometimes been applied.[1] All are rare conditions; the estimated incidence for the group as a whole is in the order of 1:20,000. Apart from the acquired autoimmune variant (epidermolysis bullosa acquisita), they are all autosomal inherited disorders.

In the second edition of this book (1996), the classification and sub-typing of the major variants was based upon the first (1989) consensus meeting of the Steering Committee of the National EB Registry held in conjunction with the American Academy of Dermatology.[2,3] At that time 23 clinically distinct variants were recognized (*Table 3.1*).[3] In the succeeding decade, a second consensus conference was held.[4] As a result of the considerably increased number of cases available for study, a much greater degree of clinical overlap between the various subtypes has been recognized. For this reason and because of a much better understanding of the molecular basis for many of the variants of EB, a considerably simplified classification system was recommended by this steering committee (*Table 3.2*).[5,6] Research over the past two decades has generated a wealth of literature specifically addressing the molecular basis of the various subtypes of EB. As a result, it is now possible to subgroup EB on the basis of the level of separation within the basement membrane region and on its molecular basis.

Traditionally, EB has been classified into three major groups:

- *simplex* (in which the level of split is within the basal keratinocyte)
- *junctional* (where the level of split is within the lamina lucida)
- *dystrophic* (where the level of split is deep to the lamina densa)

Table 3.2

Second consensus conference (2000): classification of epidermolysis bullosa

Major EB type	Major EB subtype	Protein/gene systems involved
EBS ('epidermolytic EB')	EBS-WC	K5, K14
	EBS-K	K5, K14
	EBS-DM	K5, K14
	EBS-MD	Plectin
Junctional EB	JEB-H	Laminin-5*
	HEB-nH	Laminin-5; type XVII collagen
	JEB-PA†	$\alpha_6\beta_4$ integrin‡
DEB ('dermolytic EB')	DDEB	Type VII collagen
	RDEB-HS	Type VII collagen
	RDEB-nHS	Type VII collagen

Reproduced from Fine et al (2000) *J Am Acad Dermatol*, **42**, 1051–1066 from American Academy of Dermatology.
DDEB, dominant dystrophic EB; EBS-DM, EBS Dowling–Meara; EBS-K, EBS, Koebner; EBS-MD, EBS with muscular dystrophy; EBS-WC, EBS, Weber–Cockayne; JEB-H, junctional EB, Herlitz; JEB-nH, junctional EB, non-Herlitz; JEB-PA, junctional EB with pyloric atresia; RDEB-HS, recessive dystrophic EB, Hallopeau–Siemens; RDEB-nHS, recessive dystrophic EB, non-Hallopeau–Siemens.
* Laminim-5 is a macromolecule composed of three distinct (α_3, β_3, γ_2) laminin chains; mutations in any of the encoding genes result in a junctional EB phenotype.
† Some cases of EB associated with pyloric atresia may have intraepidermal cleavage or both intralamina lucida and intraepidermal clefts.
‡ $\alpha_6\beta_4$ integrin is a heterodimeric protein; mutations in either gene have been associated with the JEB-PA syndrome.

Table 3.1

First consensus conference (1989): classification of subepidermal blisters

EB simplex	Junctional EB	Dystrophic EB
Localized	***Localized***	***Localized***
EB simplex of hands and feet (Weber–Cockayne variant)	Junctional EB, inversa	RDEB, inversa
EB simplex with anodontia/hypodontia (Kallin syndrome)	Junctional EB, acral/minimus	DDEB, minimus
	Junctional EB, progressiva variant	DDEB, pretibial
		RDEB, centripetalis
Generalized	***Generalized***	***Generalized***
EB simplex, Koebner variant	Junctional EB, gravis variant (Herlitz variant)	Autosomal dominant forms of DEB DDEB, Pasini variant DDEB, Cockayne–Touraine variant transient bullous dermolysis of the newborn
EB simplex herpetiformis (Dowling–Meara variant)		
EB simplex with mottled or reticulate hyperpigmentation with or without punctate keratoderma	Junctional EB, mitis variant (non-Herlitz variant; EB atrophicans generalisata mitis; generalized atrophic benign EB)	
EB simplex superficialis	Cicatricial junctional EB	Autosomal recessive forms of DEB RDEB, gravis (Hallopeau–Siemens variant) RDEB, mitis
EB simplex, Ogna variant		
Autosomal recessive EB simplex (letalis) with or without neuromuscular disease		
EB simplex, Mendes da Costa variant		

Reproduced with permission from Fine, J.D. et al (1991) *Pediatrician*, **18**, 175–187.
DDEB, dominant dystrophic EB; DEB, dystrophic EB; RDEB, recessive dystrophic EB.

Table 3.3

Simplified classification of epidermolysis bullosa

Subtype	Mutation
Simplex	Keratin 5 or 14
Hemidesmosomal	BP180, $\alpha_6\beta_4$ integrin, plectin
Junctional	Laminin-5
Dystrophic	Type VII collagen

based on clinical differences, antigen mapping and electron microscopic observations. Recently, a fourth category – *hemidesmosomal* EB (where the level of split is within the hemidesmosome) – has been added (*Table 3.3*).[7] The last classification, which takes into account the most recent, precise molecular data, is particularly valuable when considering the pathological basis of EB and forms the basis for this account.

Mutations of genes encoding keratins 5 and 14, plectin, BP180, α_6 and β_4 integrin subunits, laminin-5 and type VII collagen account for the different subtypes of EB (a full discussion of these basement membrane proteins is given in Chapter 1).[7–9]

Molecular studies including western blot and immunoprecipitation however are not always available for every case of EB, particularly at presentation and therefore initially at least the patient may well be provisionally subclassified on the basis of:

- clinical variation
- presence or absence of extracutaneous manifestations
- mode of inheritance
- immunoepitope mapping and/or electron microscopy.

Clinical evaluation of a patient with suspected EB should include the age of onset and nature and distribution of the cutaneous lesions and whether or not scarring and contractures are present. In addition, the family pedigree should be studied and the patient investigated for the presence or absence of extracutaneous involvement (eyes, oropharynx, larynx, gastrointestinal and genitourinary tracts and musculoskeletal system) and other specific lesions (including enamel hypoplasia, anodontia or hypodontia, pyloric atresia and muscular dystrophy) that might point towards a particular variant.[2,3]

Four major subtypes of EB are now recognized: simplex, hemidesmosomal, junctional and dystrophic:[4–7]

EB simplex (previously known as the epidermolytic variant) is characterized by the level of separation within the epidermis, usually as a consequence of cytolysis. All variants are associated with keratin 5 or 14 gene mutations.[8] Epidermolysis bullosa with late-onset muscular dystrophy, which had traditionally been included in the simplex category, is now known to result from a mutation in the plectin gene and is therefore more appropriately included in the hemidesmosomal group of EB as delineated by Pulkkinen and Uitto.[7,10]

Hemidesmosomal EB is distinguished by the split through the hemidesmosome. The group includes EB with late-onset muscular dystrophy (previously included in the simplex group), some examples of generalized atrophic benign EB (others associated with laminin-5 mutations are included within the junctional group) and EB with pyloric atresia (previously included in the junctional group).[7,11–13] These three variants of EB develop as a consequence of mutations of genes encoding the hemidesmosomal proteins plectin, BP180 and the α_6 and β_4 integrin subunits respectively.[7]

Junctional EB is characterized by the development of cleavage within the lamina lucida. It results from laminin-5 gene mutations.[14] Since cases which have in the past been included in the junctional category are associated with hemidesmosomal protein gene mutations (e.g. BP180 with generalized atrophic benign EB; α_6 or β_4 integrin subunits with EB with pyloric atresia), both of these variants are therefore now included within the hemidesmosomal group of EB.[7]

Dystrophic EB (also known as the dermolytic variant) is defined by a split developing immediately below the lamina densa in the region of the anchoring fibrils. This subtype is invariably due to type VII collagen gene mutations.[15]

Clinical features

EB simplex (EBS)

Five subtypes are currently recognized. Localized EBS with hypodontia (Kallin syndrome) and EB simplex (Ogna), which were discussed in the second edition, are no longer recognized as separate variants of EB following the second consensus conference and are therefore no longer included.[16–18] EB with late-onset muscular dystrophy is more appropriately included in the hemidesmosomal group of EB. Recently, a severe recessive variant of EB simplex has been documented.[19]

EB simplex, Weber–Cockayne (localized EB simplex of the hands and feet)

This is the most common form of epidermolysis bullosa and has an autosomal dominant mode of inheritance.[2,3] Lesions are limited to the palms and soles and are usually detected in infancy or the first few years of life (*Fig. 3.9*). Occasionally in patients with mild involvement, blisters

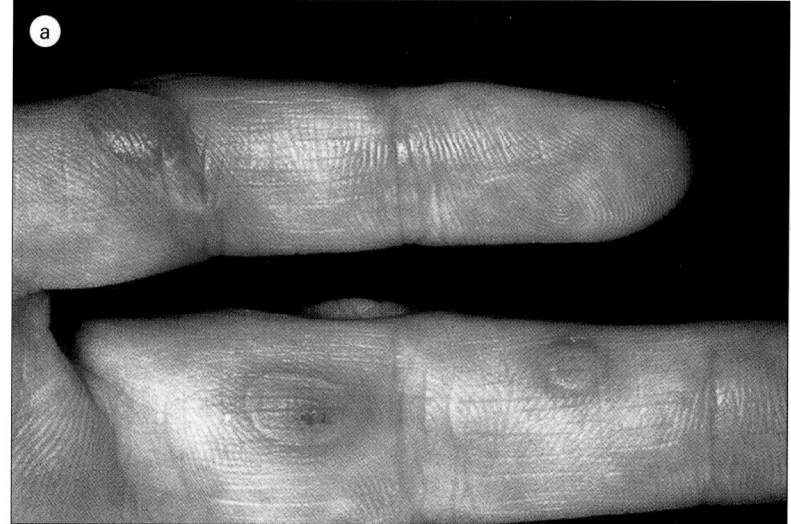

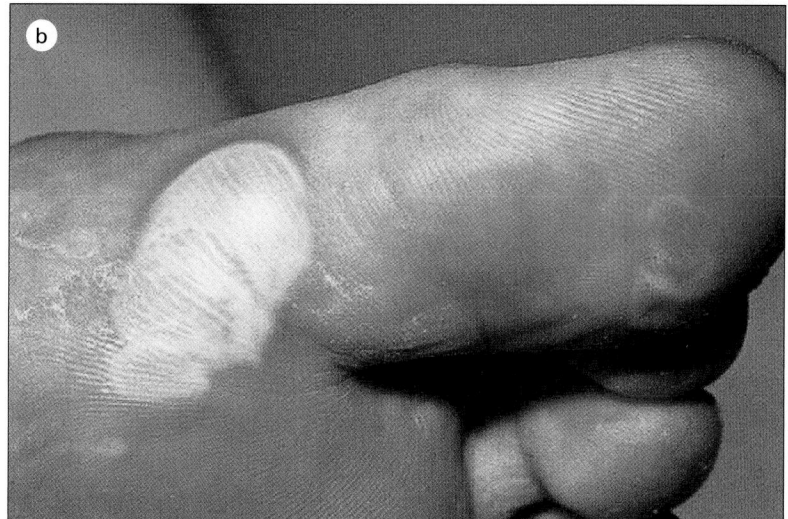

Fig. 3.9

EB simplex (Weber–Cockayne): typical lesions affecting (a) the fingers and (b) the toes. The pale color of the latter is due to the marked thickness of the roof of the blister. By courtesy of the Institute of Dermatology, London, UK.

and erosions may not develop until childhood or even early adulthood in association with strenuous activity. The lesions, which sometimes heal with atrophic scarring, show seasonal variation, often occurring only in the summer months. Hyperhidrosis may sometimes be present. Milia, atrophic scarring and nail dystrophy are uncommon features.[3,6] The teeth are uninvolved and there is no evidence of any systemic involvement, except perhaps for oral erosions, which may affect an appreciable number of patients in infancy.[5] Ocular lesions are not a feature. Repeated episodes of secondary infection may occur in some patients. Postinflammatory hyper- and hypopigmentation may sometimes be a cosmetic problem.[6]

EB simplex (Koebner)

This variant has an autosomal dominant mode of inheritance.[3] Blisters are present at birth or shortly thereafter and although the entire body may be affected, lesions are particularly severe on the extremities, where the dorsal surfaces tend to be involved (*Fig. 3.10*).[3] The blisters usually heal without scarring or atrophy and milia are very uncommon.[3] The eruption often worsens in the summer months. The nails are rarely dystrophic and teeth abnormalities are typically absent. Although oral lesions may be present in infancy, systemic involvement is not a feature of this variant.

EB simplex herpetiformis (Dowling–Meara)

This variant, which is the second commonest form of EB simplex, shows clinical features resembling dermatitis herpetiformis and has an autosomal dominant mode of inheritance (*Fig. 3.11*).[5,20–23] Herpetiform grouping of blisters is characteristic. Lesions are usually present at birth and have a distribution sometimes mimicking severe dystrophic or junctional disease.[5] Some patients die in early infancy due to infection, fluid loss or electrolyte imbalance.[1] Milia formation is common, but atrophy and scarring are rare.[5] Distal flexural contractures are occasionally present.[21] Nail dystrophy is often found and palmar–plantar keratoderma is characteristic. Anodontia and hypodontia have also been described. Normalization during episodes of high fever is a typical finding but seasonal variation is not a feature.[22] Blistering significantly improves with advancing age.[23]

EB simplex herpetiformis with mottled pigmentation and punctate keratoderma

This autosomal dominant variant was originally described in six members of a single kindred.[24] The cutaneous lesions are similar to the Dowling–Meara variant with the addition of mottled or reticulate pigmentation, particularly affecting the neck and trunk. Atrophic scarring, milia and nail dystrophy are uncommon. Punctate keratoderma affecting the palms, and warty hyperkeratotic lesions involving the hands, elbows and knees may be additional features.[24,25] Dental caries is also sometimes present and intraoral lesions are occasionally seen.

EB simplex superficialis

Also inherited as an autosomal dominant, this rare form specifically differs from the other simplex variants by the site of epidermal cleavage: subcorneal rather than intrabasal.[26] Patients present at birth or within the first 2 years of life with erosions and crusts sparing the palms and soles. Atrophic scarring, nail dystrophy and milia are additional common features.[26] As well as the cutaneous manifestations, anemia and gastrointestinal lesions affect a minority of patients.

Hemidesmosomal EB

This group includes three variants:
- some of the patients with generalized atrophic benign EB (GABEB) (others are included in the junctional group; see below)
- EB with late-onset muscular dystrophy (formerly included in the simplex group)
- EB with pyloric atresia (formerly included in the junctional category).

Generalized atrophic benign EB

This category includes patients with either BP180 or laminin-5 mutations which is discussed in full in the junctional EB section (see below).

EB with late-onset muscular dystrophy (pseudojunctional EB)

This is an autosomal recessive variant in which patients concomitantly develop muscular dystrophy or exceptionally myasthenia gravis.[27,28] Blisters and erosions present at birth or soon thereafter and are usually generalized. Patients may also suffer from atrophic scarring, milia, nail dystrophy or anonychia, alopecia and oral lesions.[27,28] The mortality of this variant is high.[4]

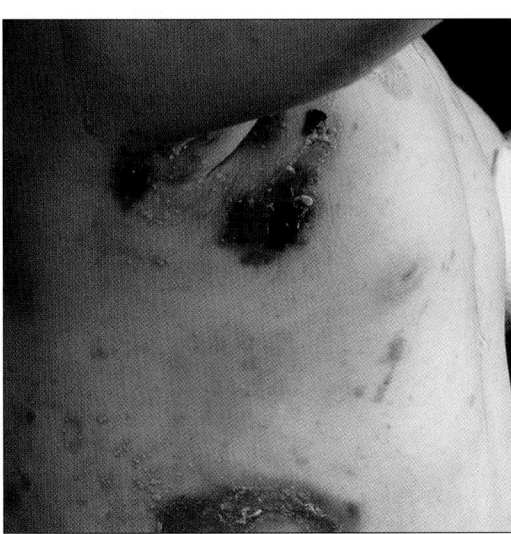

Fig. 3.10
EB simplex (Koebner): intact blisters are present in the axilla and on the chest. By courtesy of M.J. Tidman, MD, Guy's Hospital, London, UK.

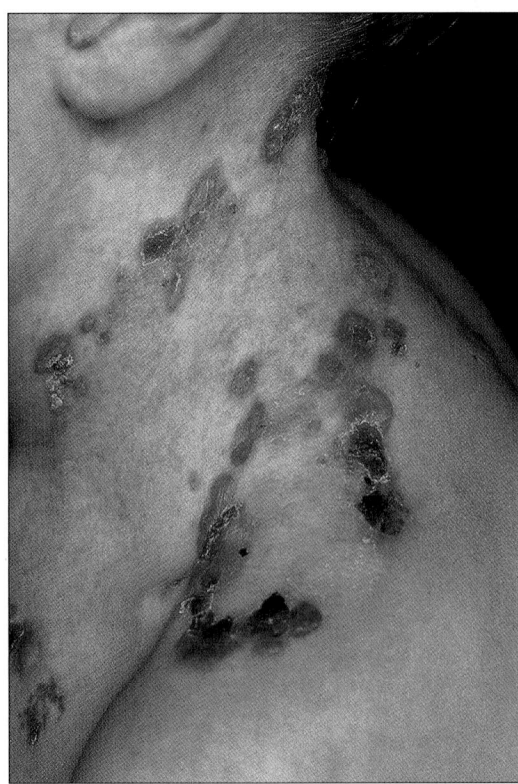

Fig. 3.11
EB bullosa simplex: Dowling–Meara variant showing characteristic grouping of blisters and erosions. By courtesy of R.A.J. Eady, MD, Institute of Dermatology, London, UK.

EB with pyloric atresia (pyloric atresia–junctional EB syndrome)

This is a rare variant of epidermolysis bullosa in which affected infants are at risk of ureterovesical junction obstruction with fibrosis involving the entire urinary tract and aplasia cutis congenita in addition to pyloric atresia (*Figs 3.12, 3.13*).[29–31] The pyloric atresia may be due to a diaphragm or stenosis (*Fig. 3.14*). The mortality of this variant is very high, up to 78% of affected infants succumbing.[31]

Junctional epidermolysis bullosa

Two major subtypes of this variant are recognized: junctional EB-Herlitz and junctional EB-non-Herlitz. Junctional EB with pyloric atresia is now classified in the hemidesmosomal group. Two rare subtypes (junctional EB inversa and junctional EB-late onset) are also still included within the new classification. All have an autosomal recessive mode of inheritance. Cicatricial junctional EB and junctional EB (acral/mimumus) are no longer recognized by the second consensus conference and are therefore not included in the revised classification.

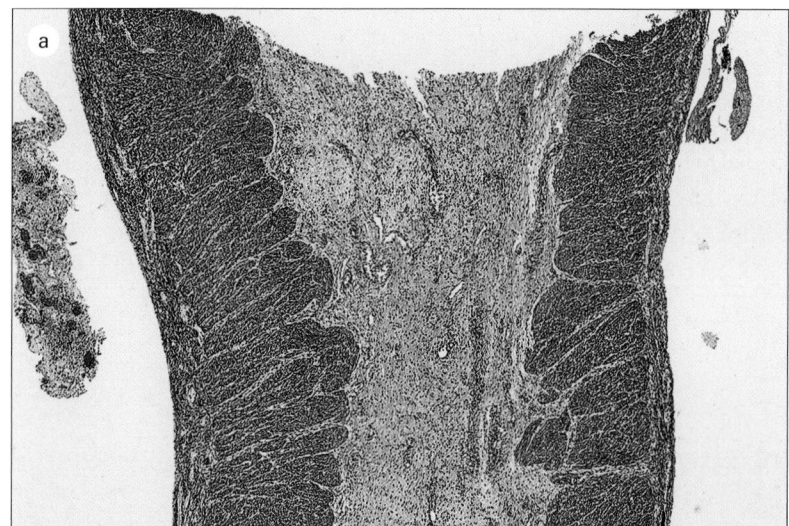

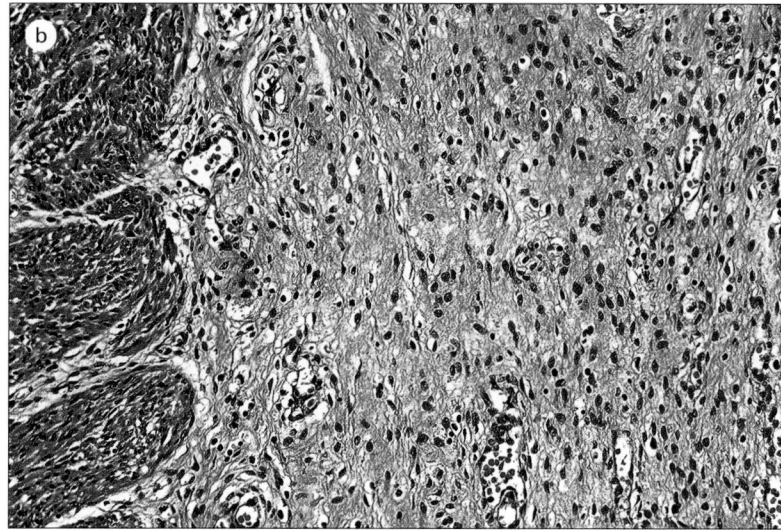

Fig. 3.14
(**a, b**) EB with pyloric atresia: pyloric canal is obliterated by fibrous connective tissue.

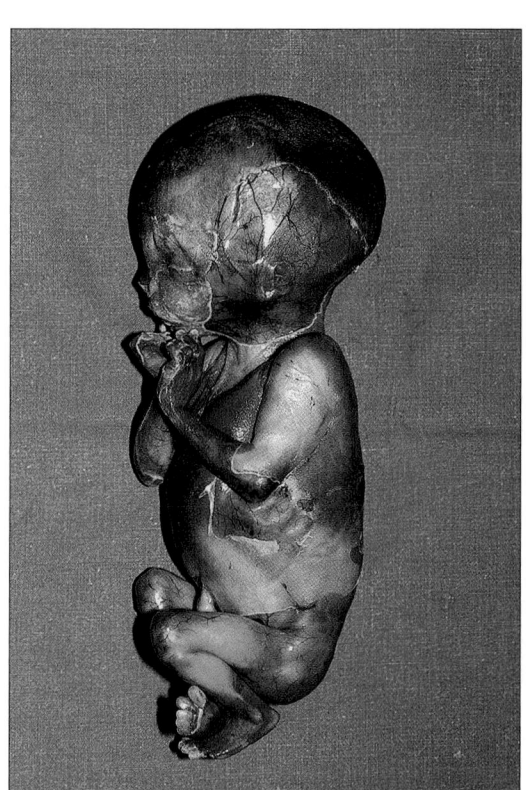

Fig. 3.12
EB with pyloric atresia: stillborn infant with widespread blistering. By courtesy of M.J. Tidman, MD, Institute of Dermatology, London, UK.

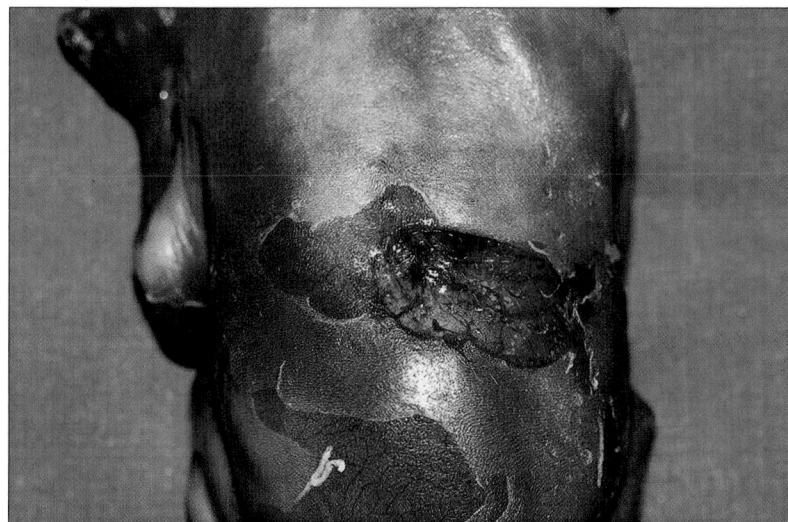

Fig. 3.13
EB with pyloric atresia: in addition to blistering there is also deep ulceration. By courtesy of M.J. Tidman, MD, Institute of Dermatology, London, UK.

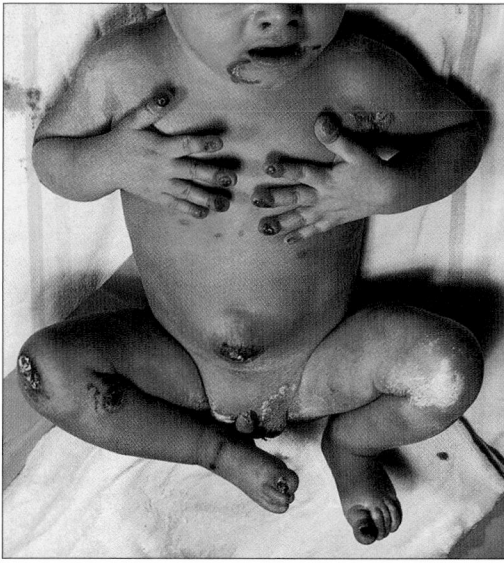

Fig. 3.15
Junctional EB (Herlitz): newly born infant with blistering and nail involvement. By courtesy of J. McGrath, MD, Institute of Dermatology, London, UK.

Junctional EB–Herlitz (Herlitz, gravis variant of junctional EB, EB hereditaria letalis, EB atrophicans generalisata gravis)

In this generalized variant, blisters and erosions are present at birth accompanied by scarring and atrophy (*Fig. 3.15*).[32–34] Milia may be a feature.[5] Healing with the formation of exuberant, vegetative or tumorous granulation tissue is a pathognomonic feature (*Fig. 3.16*).[3] This is found particularly around the mouth, sides of the neck, trunk and about the nails.[2] The nails may be dystrophic or absent and scarring alopecia is sometimes evident.[3] Severe oral involvement (including scarring and microstomia) is usually present and pitted dystrophic enamel is characteristic (*Fig. 3.17*). Dental caries are frequently severe. Other features may include musculoskeletal deformities, gastrointestinal lesions, laryngotracheal stenosis, genitourinary and ocular involvement. Esophageal involvement may result in stenosis. Perforation with resultant infection is an important cause of death. Severe growth retardation and anemia are usually evident. Infantile mortality is high (42.2%).[5]

Junctional EB–non-Herlitz (generalized non-Herlitz junctional EB, EB atrophicans generalisata mitis, generalized atrophic benign EB (GABEB), hemidesmosomal EB, junctional EB mitis)

This somewhat milder form, in which the cutaneous features are similar to the gravis form, includes some patients with laminin-5 gene mutations whereas others with this particular variant are included in the hemidesmosomal group (see above).[35] Systemic involvement is typically mild or absent.[36–39] Patients present at birth with extensive blistering and erosions accompanied by mild scarring and widespread cigarette paper-like atrophy. Variable hyperpigmentation and hypopigmentation is characteristic.[36] Skin lesions may be exacerbated during summer. Milia are variably present. Exuberant granulation tissue is less common than in the Herlitz variant. Other features include dystrophic or absent nails (*Fig. 3.18*), oral erosions with mild scarring, pitted dystrophic enamel and severe dental caries. Ocular lesions include recurrent corneal erosion, blistering and corneal scarring.[37] Follicular atrophy with resultant alopecia involving the scalp, axillary and pubic hair in addition

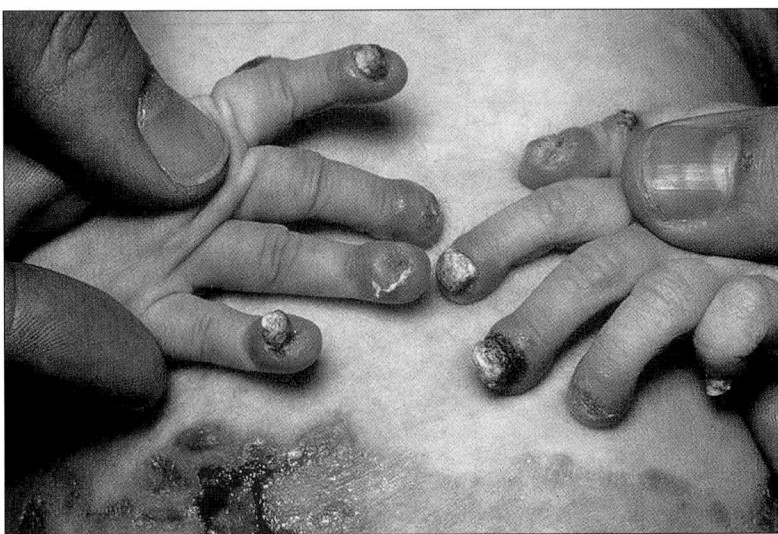

Fig. 3.16
Junctional EB (Herlitz): infant showing granulation tissue at the edge of a healing blister. By courtesy of the Institute of Dermatology, London, UK.

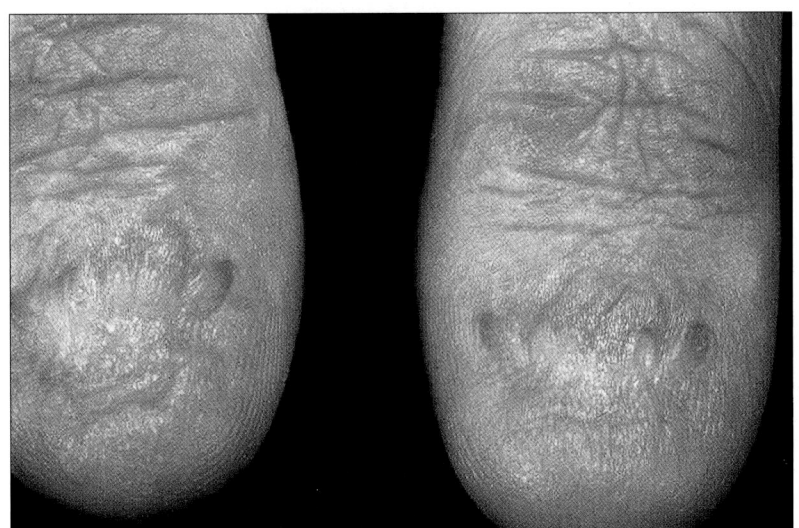

Fig. 3.18
Generalized atrophic benign EB: there is scarring and complete absence of nails. By courtesy of the Institute of Dermatology, London, UK.

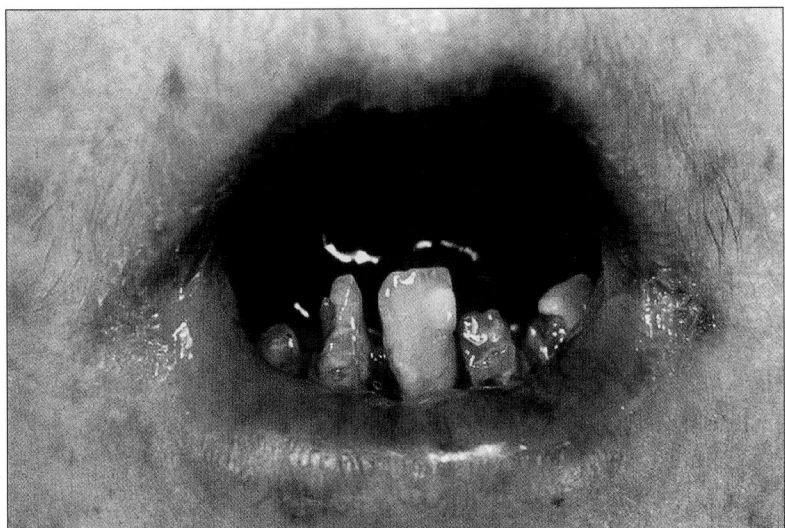

Fig. 3.17
Junctional EB (Herlitz): note the scarring with microstomia and severe dental involvement. By courtesy of J. McGrath, MD, St John's Dermatology Centre, London, UK.

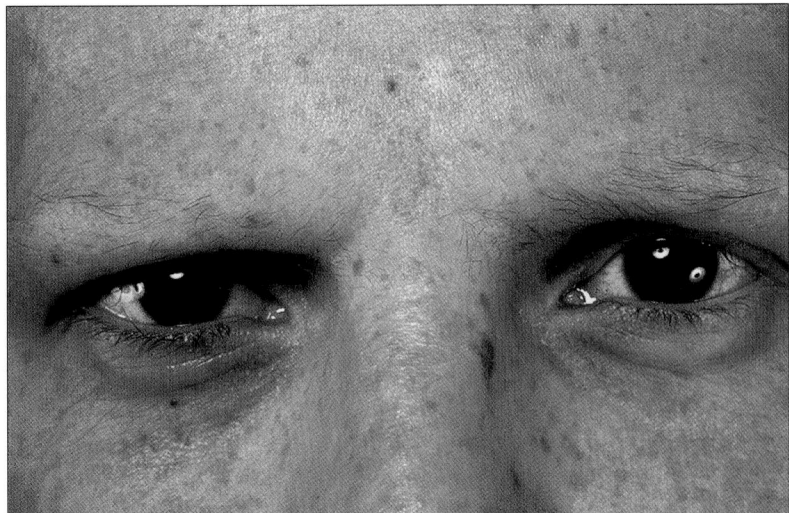

Fig. 3.19
Generalized atrophic benign EB: note the sparsely distributed eyebrows and eye lashes. By courtesy of the Institute of Dermatology, London, UK.

to sparse eyelashes and eyebrows is common (*Fig. 3.19*).[36] Large or multiple melanocytic nevi have also been described as part of the phenotype[34] but this is not currently believed to be a specific feature.[3] Contractures do not develop. Systemic involvement is usually limited to mild laryngeal and/or esophageal lesions.[2] Growth may be retarded and anemia is present in some patients. Infantile mortality is high (38.2%).[5]

Junctional EB inversa

Lesions, which are present at birth or develop in early infancy, are initially generalized, but later are predominantly localized to inverse (flexural) sites including the axillae and groins.[3] Blisters and erosions are accompanied by atrophic scarring and nails may be dystrophic or absent. Other features that can also be evident include mouth erosions, maldeveloped teeth with enamel hypoplasia, and occasional gastrointestinal lesions, particularly affecting the esophagus and anus.

Junctional EB–late onset (progressiva)

In this variant, lesions do not present until late childhood, and consist of blisters and erosions affecting the hands, elbows, knees and feet.[3] Nails may be dystrophic or absent and enamel hypoplasia is characteristic.

Mouth erosions may be evident. Mild finger contractures are sometimes a complication.[3]

Dystrophic EB

Three major subtypes – dominant dystrophic EB, recessive dystrophic EB (Hallopeau–Siemens) and recessive dystrophic EB (non Hallopeau–Siemens) – and six very much rarer variants are recognized.

Dominant dystrophic EB

Autosomal dominant EB includes both the Cockayne–Touraine and Pasini variants. This is because the two conditions are characterized by identical type VII gene mutations and the albopapuloid lesions (white perifollicular papules and plaques) have been found to be an inconsistent finding (*Fig. 3.20*).[4,5] Generalized blisters are seen at birth (*Fig. 3.21a*).[2,6] Alopecia may be present and milia, atrophic scarring and dystrophic or absent nails are typical features (*Fig. 3.21b*). Oral involvement may be mild or absent. Enamel hypoplasia is sometimes present. Gastrointestinal and genitourinary tract involvement is seen in a minority of patients. There is a slightly increased risk of basal cell carcinoma and melanoma.[40]

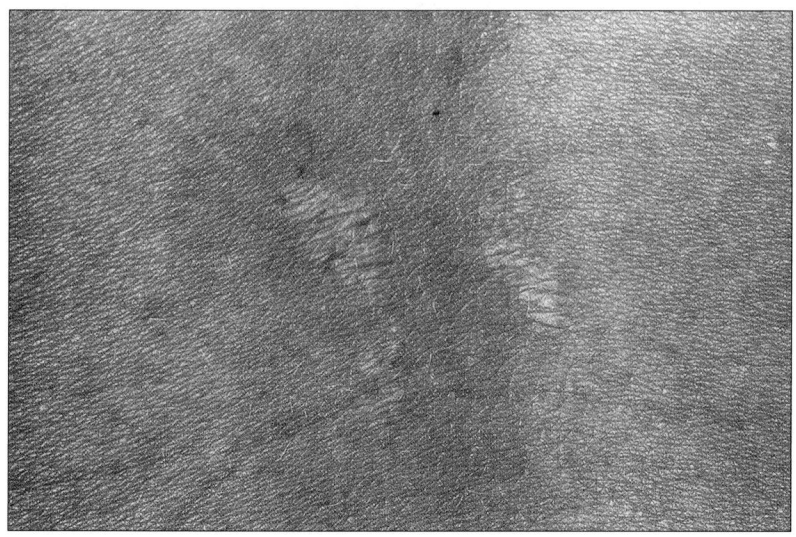

Fig. 3.20
Dystrophic EB: albopapuloid lesions on the lumbosacral area. These are an inconstant finding in junctional EB. The lesions are not preceded by blistering and probably represent connective tissue nevi. By courtesy of M.J. Tidman, MD, Guy's Hospital, London, UK.

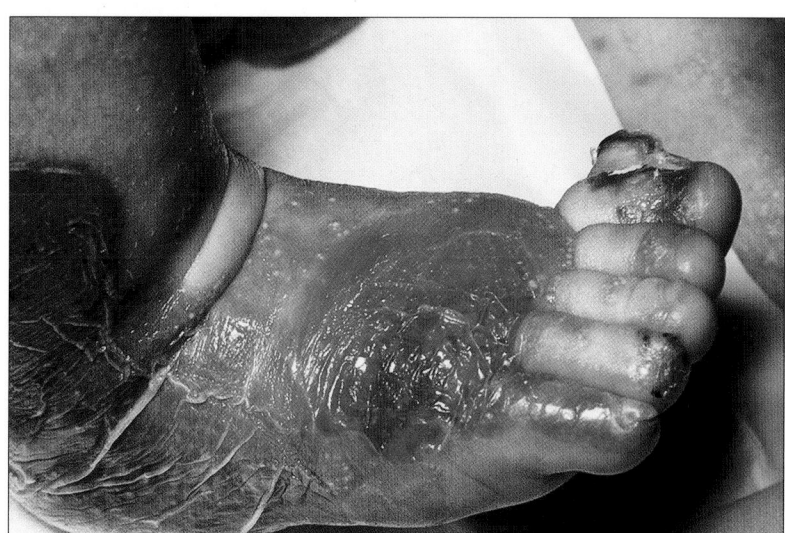

Fig. 3.22
Recessive dystrophic EB (Hallopeau–Siemens): extensive blistering present at birth. The disease process has involved the nails and those of the first two toes are absent. By courtesy of R.A. Marsden, MD, St George's Hospital, London, UK.

Fig. 3.21
Dominant dystrophic EB (Cockayne–Touraine): (a) truncal involvement is present in addition to the more typical limb lesions; (b) hemorrhagic blisters, scarring, milia and nail dystrophy. By courtesy of the Institute of Dermatology, London, UK.

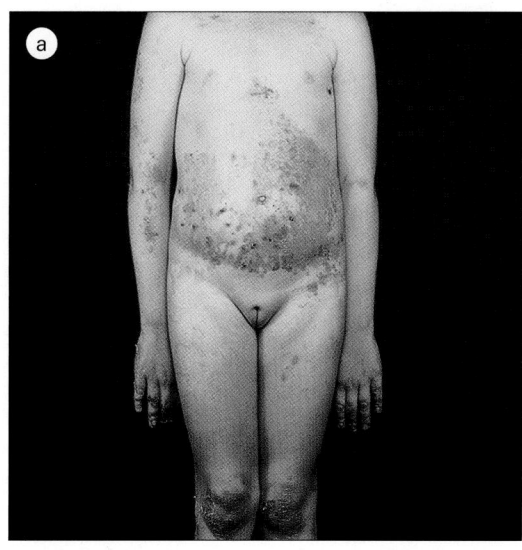

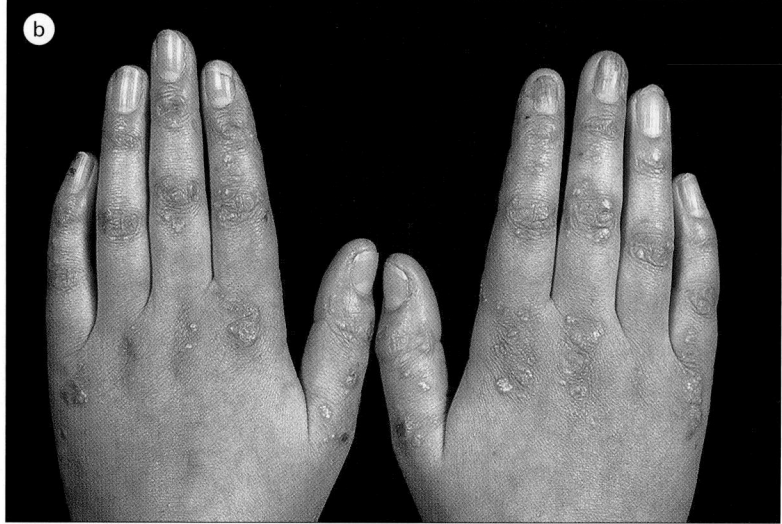

Recessive dystrophic EB–Hallopeau–Siemens (polydysplastic EB, EB gravis)

This autosomal recessive variant is a much more serious form than its autosomal dominant counterpart.[2,6] Blisters and erosions are present at birth and milia, atrophy, scarring, anemia and growth retardation are consistently present (*Figs 3.22, 3.23*). Nikolsky's sign is positive. Destructive involvement of the peripheries results in contractures and severe deformities including the characteristic 'mitten lesions' (pseudosyndactyly) of the hands and feet (*Figs 3.24–3.27*). If the latter is left untreated, there may eventually be resorption of the underlying bones (autoamputation). Nail dystrophy is marked, and scarring alopecia is common. Oral involvement is severe with blisters, erosions and scarring. Excessive caries is usual. There is often conjunctival involvement with keratitis and scarring, and lesions of the mucous membranes result in difficulty in opening the mouth, dysphagia and esophageal stricture formation, with some infants eventually succumbing to terminal respiratory infections (*Fig. 3.28*).[41] Anal and genitourinary involvement may also be present. Squamous cell carcinoma is a common

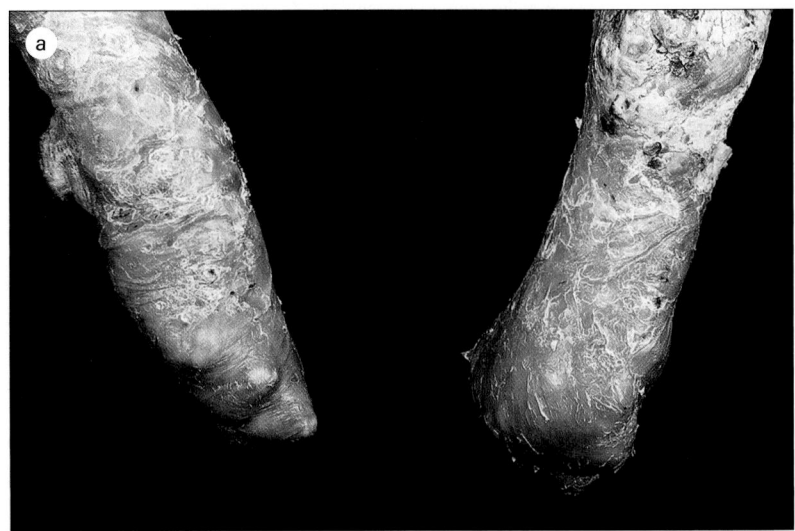

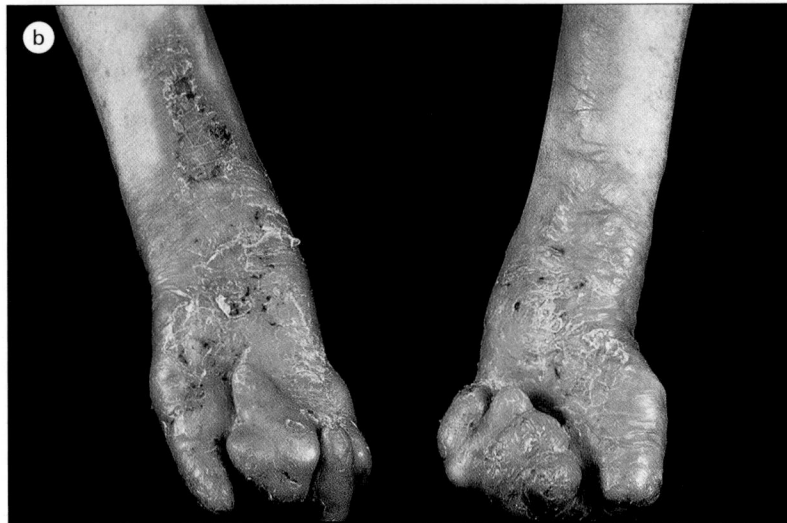

Fig. 3.25
(**a, b**) Recessive dystrophic EB (Hallopeau–Siemens): in addition to the gross mitten deformity, there is very severe scarring and scaling. (**a**) By courtesy of R.A.J. Eady, MD, and B. Mayou, MD, St Thomas' Hospital, London; (**b**) by courtesy of the Institute of Dermatology, London, UK.

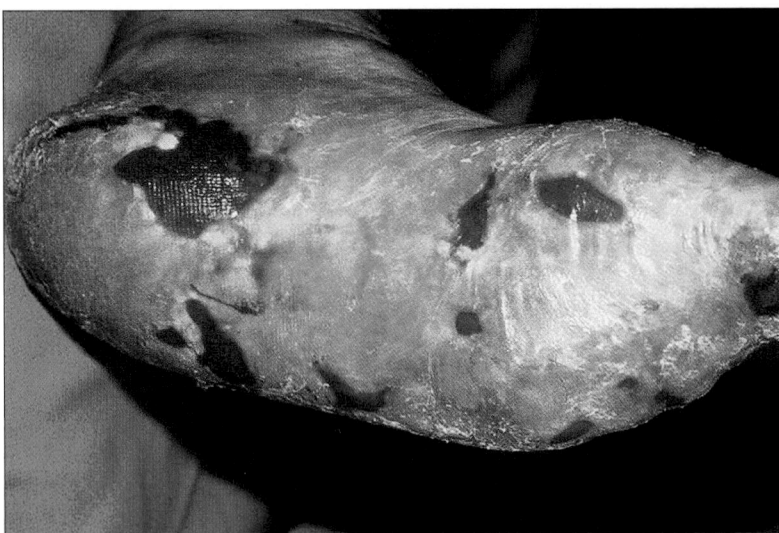

Fig. 3.23
Recessive dystrophic EB (Hallopeau–Siemens): note the scarring and extensive erosions. By courtesy of the Institute of Dermatology, London, UK.

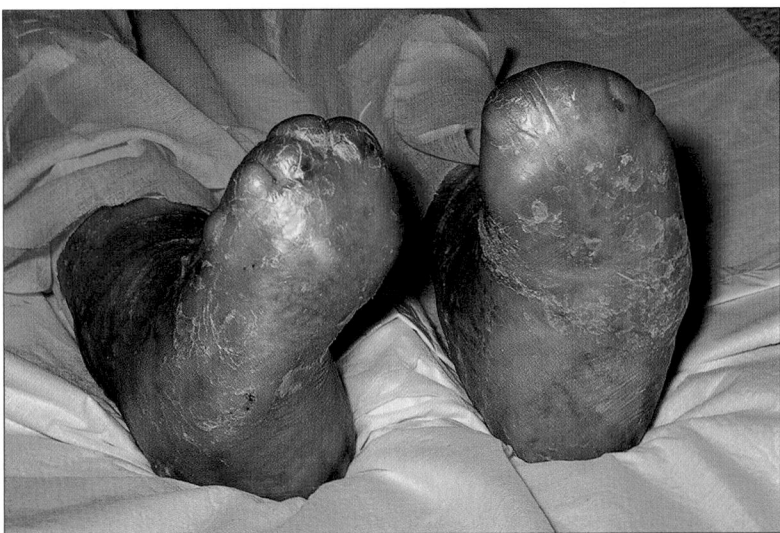

Fig. 3.24
Recessive dystrophic EB (Hallopeau–Siemens): web-like folds enveloping the toes have resulted in a club-like appearance. By courtesy of R.A. Marsden, MD, St George's Hospital, London, UK.

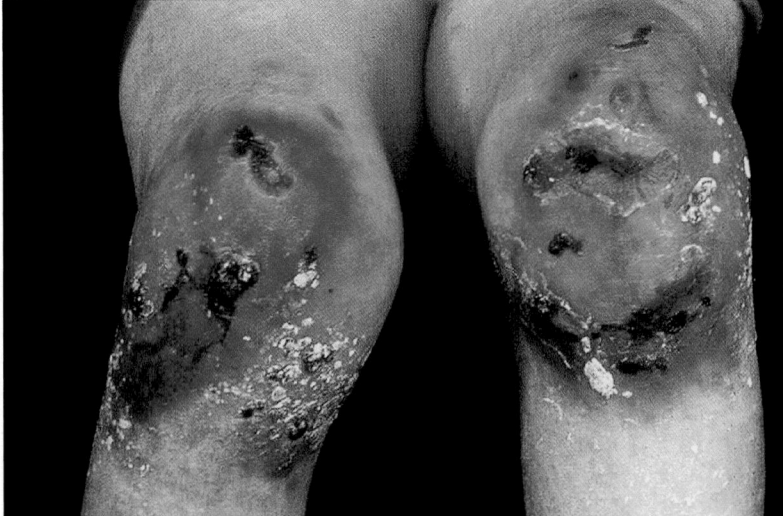

Fig. 3.26
Recessive dystrophic EB (Hallopeau–Siemens): there is gross deformity of the knees. By courtesy of J. McGrath, MD, Institute of Dermatology, London, UK.

complication of the cutaneous scarring (occurring in 39.6% of cases) and is a significant cause of mortality (*Figs 3.29–3.31*).[42,43] Tumors are frequently multiple, have an aggressive behavior and may be associated with extensive metastatic spread. Melanoma much less commonly develops. This variant of EB has a high mortality – 38.7%.[5]

Recessive dystrophic EB–non-Hallopeau–Siemens (EB mitis)

In this variant the features are similar to the Hallopeau–Siemens variant except that the extracutaneous lesions are less severe and the risk of developing cutaneous squamous cell carcinoma is diminished (14.3%).[2,6] The mortality for this variant of EB is 10.0%.

Rare variants of dystrophic EB

Dominant dystrophic EB–pretibial

This is a mild, localized and typically symmetrical autosomal dominant form. An autosomal recessive variant has recently been described.[44] The onset is often delayed, patients usually presenting in early childhood.[45] Blisters and erosions accompanied by atrophic scarring and milia are particularly seen on the pretibial region and dorsal aspects of the feet (*Figs 3.32, 3.33*). The scarring may have a violaceous appearance reminiscent of hypertrophic lichen planus.[44] Lesions may also be evident

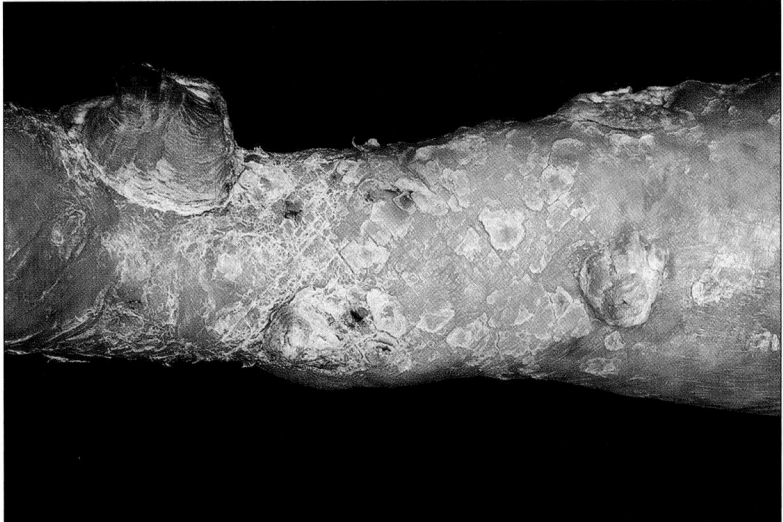

Fig. 3.29
Recessive dystrophic EB (Hallopeau–Siemens): in this patient numerous large keratoses are evident. Many of these progress to squamous cell carcinoma. Courtesy of R.A.J. Eady, MD, and B. Mayou, MD, St Thomas' Hospital, London, UK.

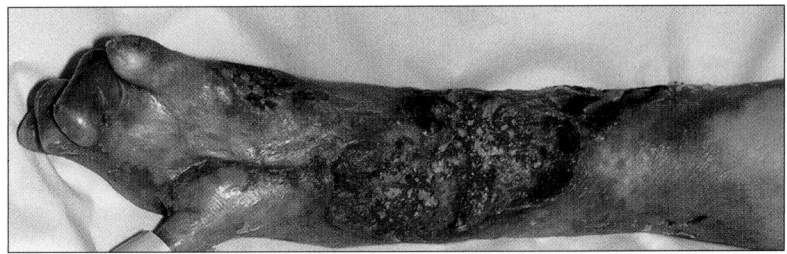

Fig. 3.30
Recessive dystrophic EB (Hallopeau–Siemens): in addition to severe scarring accompanied by autoamputation of the fingertips, there is a large ulcerated squamous cell carcinoma. Courtesy of R.A.J. Eady, MD, and B. Mayou, MD, St Thomas' Hospital, London, UK.

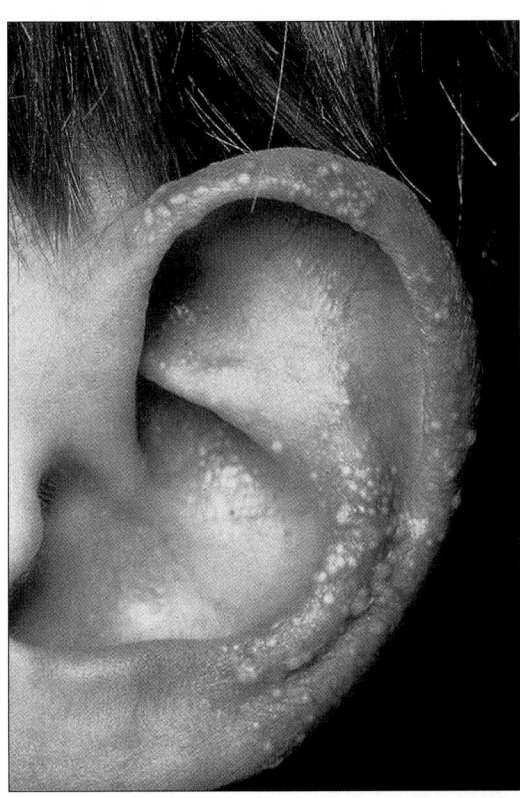

Fig. 3.27
Recessive dystrophic EB (Hallopeau–Siemens): note the conspicuous milia. By courtesy of the Institute of Dermatology, London, UK.

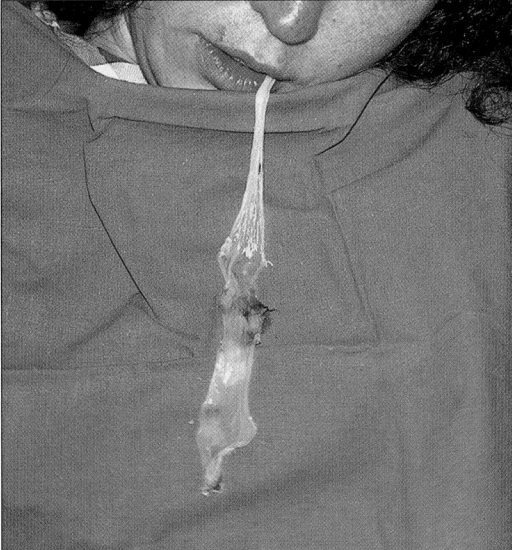

Fig. 3.28
Recessive dystrophic EB: extensive esophageal involvement with complete separation of the mucosa has resulted in this dramatic, but fortunately very rare manifestation. By courtesy of R.A. Marsden, MD, St George's Hospital, London, UK.

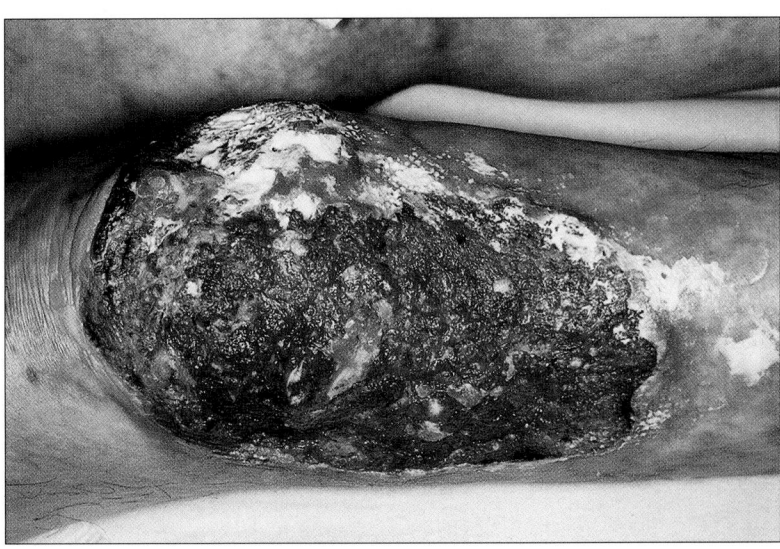

Fig. 3.31
Recessive dystrophic EB (Hallopeau–Siemens): in this patient there is a massive squamous carcinoma, which has destroyed much of the knee. Courtesy of R.A.J. Eady, MD, and B. Mayou, MD, St Thomas' Hospital, London, UK.

on the forearms and trunk.[44] Pruritus and nail dystrophy are common. There are no teeth or hair changes.[45]

Dystrophic EB–pruriginosa

This variant, which presents in childhood, includes dominant and recessive variants.[46] Patients present with highly pruritic, violaceous nodular prurigo-like nodules developing against a background of blisters, milia, nail dystrophy and albopapuloid lesions.

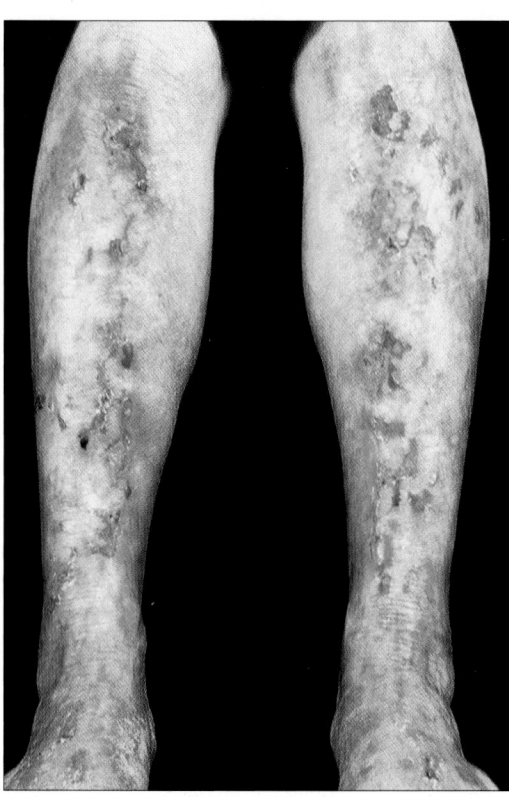

Fig. 3.32
Dystrophic EB–pretibial: extensive erosions with scarring are localized to the front of both shins. By courtesy of the Institute of Dermatology, London, UK.

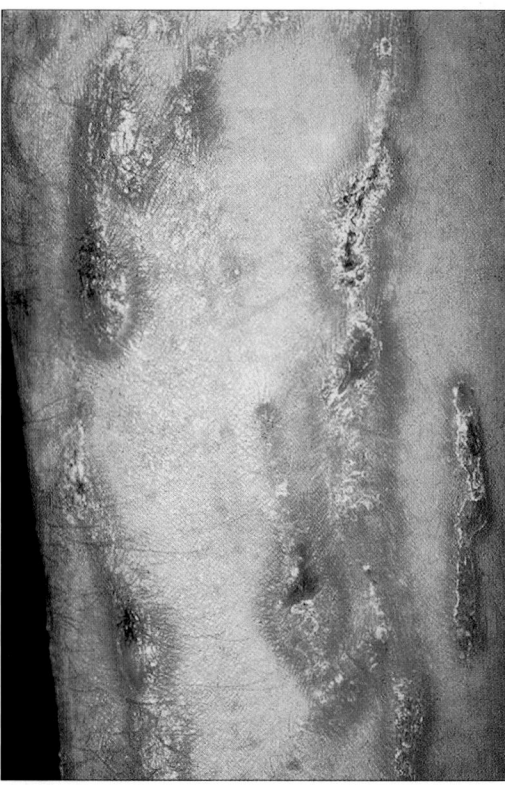

Fig. 3.33
Dystrophic EB–pretibial: close-up view. By courtesy of the Institute of Dermatology, London, UK.

Dystrophic EB–inversa

In this autosomal recessive form, lesions are present at birth and consist of blisters, erosions, milia and atrophic scarring, found particularly about the flexural sites, including the inguinal regions, axillae, neck and the lower back.[47,48] Nail dystrophy is usually evident and sometimes scarring alopecia is seen. Severe oral and esophageal involvement (erosions and scarring) is characteristic.

Dystrophic EB–centripetalis

This autosomal recessive localized form has been described in a single patient. Presentation was at birth with widespread blisters. In adulthood, however, the distribution became acral. The blisters, milia and severe scarring with atrophy then showed a characteristic centripetal spread. Nail dystrophy and/or absence were also present. Despite the severe scarring, contractures and deformities were not features.[49] There were no extracutaneous manifestations.

Dystrophic EB–minimus (acral)

In this mild autosomal dominant localized variant, lesions present at birth or in early childhood, particularly in an acral distribution. Blisters and erosions in the absence of other significant lesions other than atrophic scarring, milia and nail dystrophy may cease altogether after childhood.[1] Extracutaneous manifestations have not been recorded.

Transient bullous dermolysis of the newborn (dominant dystrophic EB–transient bullous dermolysis of the newborn)

This exceptionally rare, self-limiting condition presents in the newborn with blisters that usually resolve within the first 2 years and heal with mild atrophy, milia and scarring.[50,51] Most cases have been inherited as an autosomal dominant although recessive variants have also been documented.[4]

Pathogenesis and histological features

The pathological investigation of a patient with suspected EB should ideally include immunofluorescence antigen mapping, ultrastructural, molecular and gene studies. In general, routine histopathology often contributes little, other to confirm the presence of a subepidermal blister.

Immunofluorescent antigen mapping of basement membrane determinants is a method of identification of the plane of cleavage in the various types of EB that avoids the need for ultrastructural studies.[52,53] Essentially, the location of three antigens – type IV collagen, laminin-1 and bullous pemphigoid antigen-1 – is determined by standard indirect immunofluorescence of lesional (either naturally occurring or mechanically induced) skin:[5]

- in simplex variants, all three antigens are found along the floor of the blister
- in junctional lesions, bullous pemphigoid antigen-1 is identified mainly in the roof of the blister, whereas laminin-5 and type IV collagen are present along the floor
- in dystrophic EB the plane of cleavage is below the lamina densa and therefore all three basement membrane antigens are present in the roof of the blister.

Of late, the immunofluorescent investigation of skin samples for a wide range of more recently recognized basement membrane constituents known to be absent or diminished in the various subtypes of epidermolysis bullosa has proved to be particularly valuable, and has also been shown to be of use in antenatal (16–18 weeks' gestation) diagnosis.[54–56]

The monoclonal antibody KF-1, which localizes to the lamina densa, shows an absence of labeling in non-lesional skin from patients with the severe recessive dystrophic form of EB, whereas in the dominant variant it is reduced.[57,58]

The monoclonal antibodies AF1 and AF2, which recognize antigens in and immediately below the lamina densa (probably constituents of anchoring fibrils), show an absence of immunolabeling in both normal and lesional skin from the recessive dystrophic form, but appear normal in dominant dystrophic EB.[59]

LH7:2 is a monoclonal antibody directed against the NC-1 globular domain of type VII collagen, which binds to the lamina densa and attached anchoring fibrils.[60,61] Labeling is absent or markedly reduced in the severe recessive dystrophic form, patchily reduced in mild or localized recessive dystrophic variants, and normal in the dominant dystrophic variant.[62,63]

Immunolabelling with the monoclonal antibody GB3, which recognizes laminin-5 (nicein/kalinin/epligrin), is reduced or absent in the junctional (Herlitz) form of EB. It may be normal, reduced or absent in the non-Herlitz junctional variants.[64,65] Laminin-5 is a major constituent of the anchoring filaments, which stretch from the hemidesmosomes to the lamina densa.

Two further antibodies, 19-DEJ-1 and AA3, characteristically fail to label the basement membrane zone in all patients with junctional epidermolysis bullosa and are therefore of additional diagnostic value.[66] 19-DEJ-1, which recognizes uncein, has been recommended as the most reliable antibody for evaluation and diagnosis of the major junctional variants.[67,68]

Bullous pemphigoid 180 kD antigen is demonstrably diminished or absent as determined by immunofluorescence in many patients with generalized atrophic benign EB.[69]

EB simplex

In EB simplex variants, blisters develop as a consequence of basal cell cytolysis (*Fig. 3.34*). The plain of cleavage lies deep to the nuclei of the keratinocytes such that wispy remnants of basal cell cytoplasm may be identified along the floor of the blister cavity, which is therefore intraepidermal in location (*Figs 3.35, 3.36*).[70] In older lesions the blister often appears to be subepidermal due to continued lytic changes of the residual keratinocyte cytoplasm (*Fig. 3.37*). By direct immunoperoxidase antigen mapping on paraffin embedded sections, keratin, laminin and type IV collagen staining may be identified along the floor of the blister, confirming its intraepidermal location (*Fig. 3.38*).

Ultrastructural studies have shown that the earliest change is loss of keratin filaments (tonofilaments).[70,71] As a consequence, there is structural

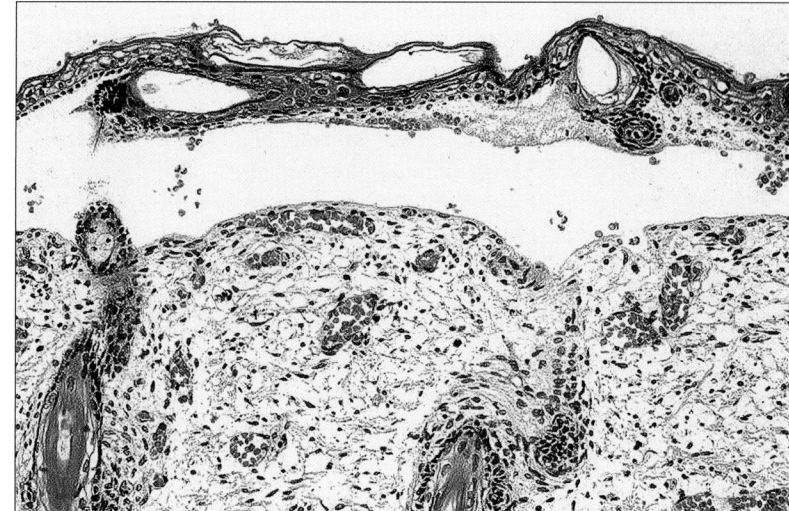

Fig. 3.35
EB simplex: established lesion showing 'subepidermal' vesiculation.

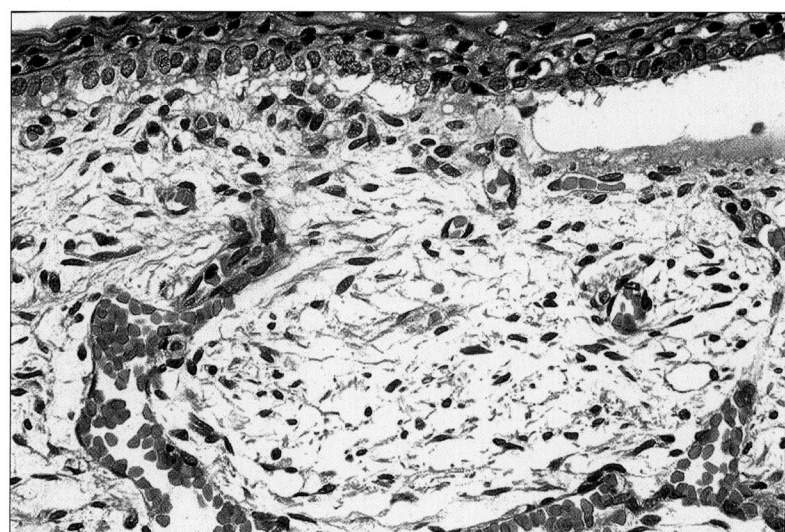

Fig. 3.36
EB simplex: basal keratinocyte cytoplasmic remnants are visible along the floor of the blister cavity.

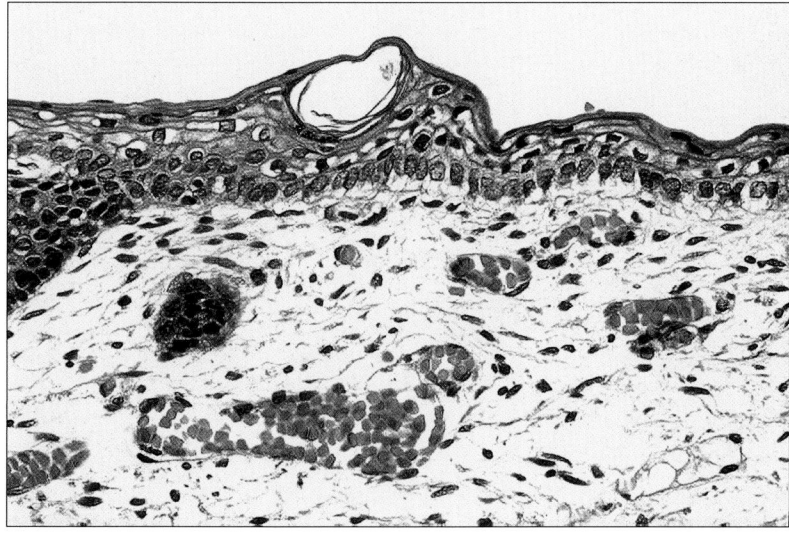

Fig. 3.34
EB simplex: the earliest histological feature in the development of a blister is marked vacuolation of the basal keratinocytes, so-called cytolysis.

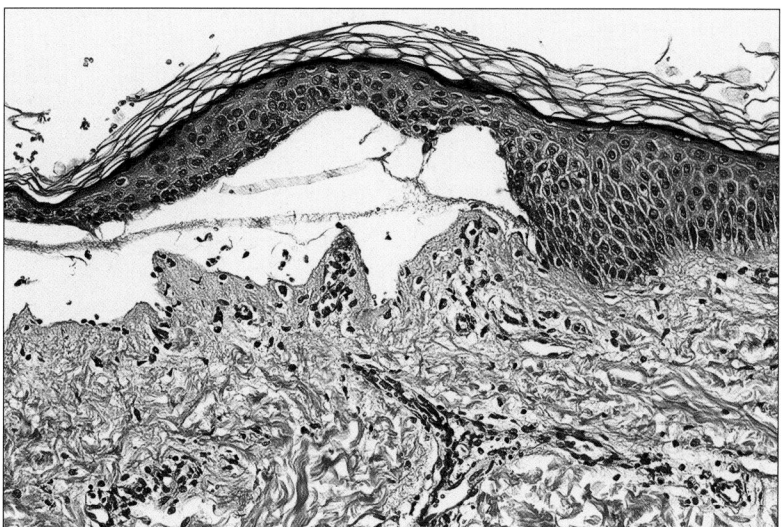

Fig. 3.37
EB simplex: old lesion; the features are those of a cell-free subepidermal blister and are not specific.

instability and fragility of the keratinocytes. Keratin clumps similar to those described in the Dowling–Meara variant (see below) have been a rare finding in EB simplex Koebner.[72] Loss of keratin filaments is subsequently followed by dissolution of the other keratinocyte cytoplasmic constituents. Suprabasal desmosomes appear unaffected. The lamina densa and anchoring fibrils are normal. While the hemidesmosomes have generally appeared normal, reduplication and increased electron density have been described in a recent case report.[73]

The Dowling–Meara variant (including the subset with mottled pigmentation) is characterized by 1–5 μm homogenous intracytoplasmic clumps of keratin filaments in addition to cytolysis (*Fig. 3.39*).[74] These are present in the basal keratinocytes and extend into the overlying prickle cell layer. They may also be identified in the follicular outer root sheaths, dermal eccrine sweat ducts and sebaceous glands. The clumps are composed of keratins 5 (type II) and 14 (type I).[74] In addition to intraepidermal vesiculation, intrakeratinocyte cleavage may also be found in the follicular infundibula. The other skin appendage structures are not affected. The dermis may contain an infiltrate of lymphocytes and eosinophils.

The keratoderma shows hyperkeratosis and acanthosis. Clumps of keratin may also be evident.

Ultrastructurally the level of cleavage is low within the basal keratinocytes, just above the level of the hemidesmosomes (*Figs 3.40, 3.41*). In addition to cytolysis, however, acantholysis may also sometimes be evident. The keratin filament abnormalities include irregular whorled bundles in addition to homogeneous clumps. They are present in normal skin in addition to lesional material (*Fig. 3.42*).[74,75] Desmosomes may appear diminished in number in the keratinocytes showing tonofilament clumps. Basement membrane zone constituents are normal.

In EB simplex superficialis the plane of cleavage is in the upper epidermis just beneath the stratum corneum.[26] Additional clefts may also be evident in the lower third of the epidermis.

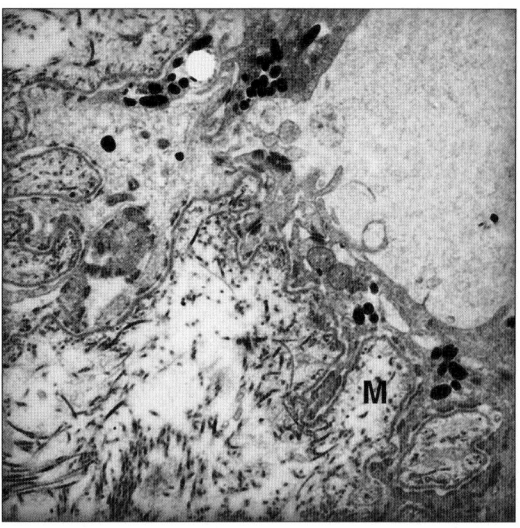

Fig. 3.40
EB simplex (Koebner): the blister cavity forms within the basal keratinocyte. Note the cytoplasmic remnants along the floor of the blister. (M, melanosome.)

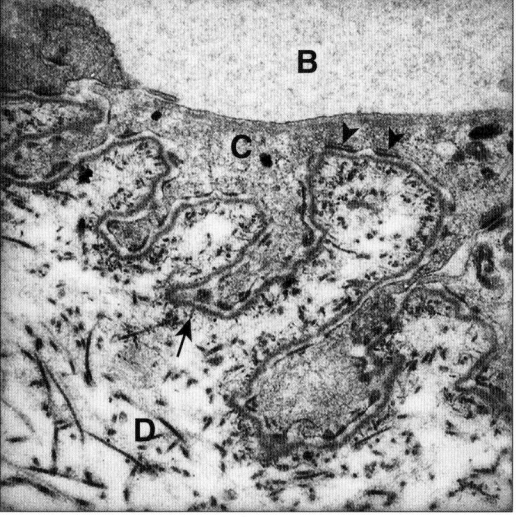

Fig. 3.41
EB simplex (Koebner): this high power view shows the floor of the blister cavity. Note the lamina densa (arrowed), hemidesmosomes (arrowheads) and basal keratinocyte cytoplasm. (B, blister; C, cytoplasm; D, dermis.)

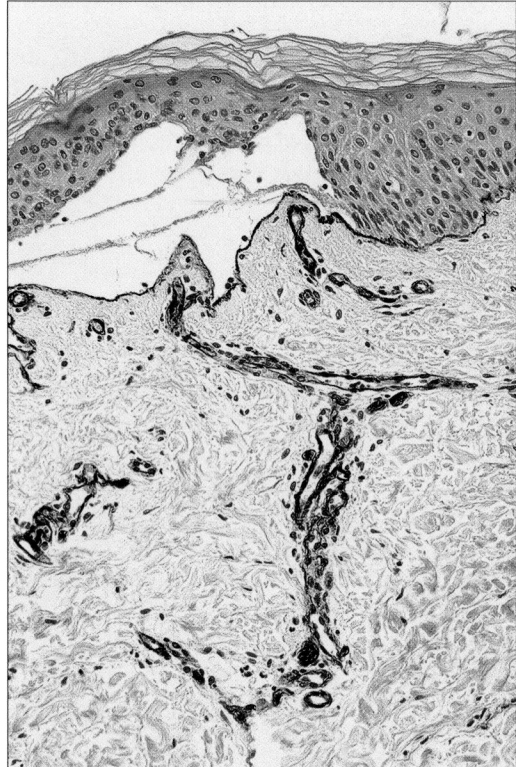

Fig. 3.38
EB simplex: paraffin immunoperoxidase displays type IV collagen along the floor of the blister cavity (same case as *Fig. 3.36*).

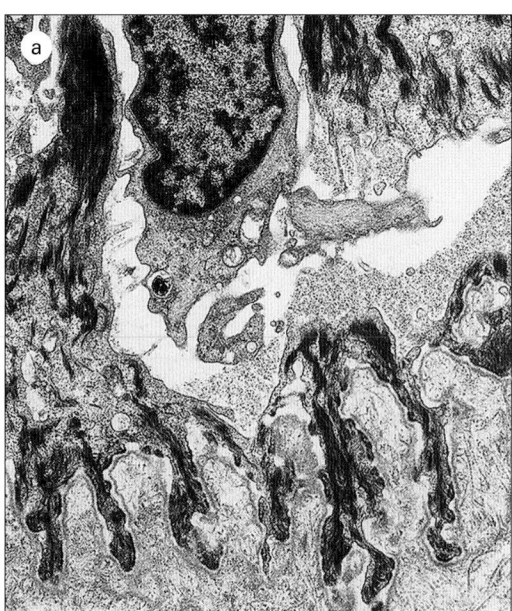
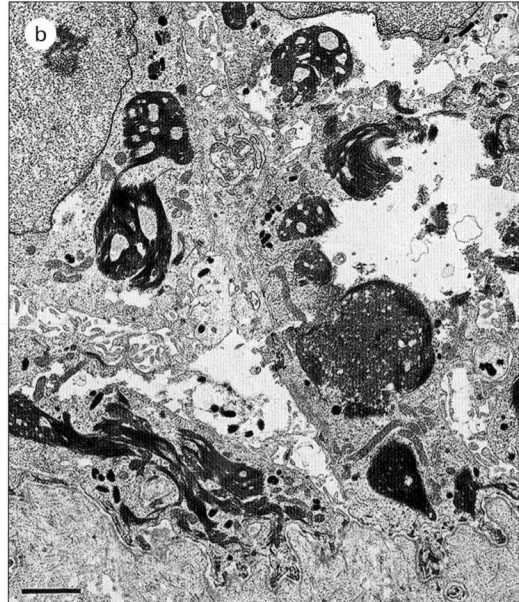

Fig. 3.39
EB simplex (Dowling–Meara): (a) electron micrograph showing intrakeratinocyte splitting; (b) close-up view of tonofilament clumps. By courtesy of J.A. McGrath, MD, and R.A.J. Eady, MD, Institute of Dermatology, London, UK.

It is now apparent that the majority, if not all variants of EB simplex including the severe recessive form, develop as a direct consequence of keratin gene mutation.[76,77] Following the initial discovery of keratin filament clumps in Dowling–Meara EB and their subsequent identification as keratins 5 and 14, it was shown that keratinocyte cultures from patients with this disease exhibited an identical morphological abnormality.[72] Genetic linkage studies showed that EB simplex was associated with keratin gene clusters on chromosomes 12 and 17.[78–82] The gene for keratin 5 is carried on chromosome 12q and that for keratin 14 is located on 17q. Truncated mutant human keratin 14 gene induces the EB phenotype when introduced into transgenic mice and similarly causes an identical keratin abnormality when expressed in transfected human keratinocytes.[83,84] Specific missense mutations or deletions have now been identified in patients with Dowling–Meara, Koebner and Weber–Cockayne variants and EB simplex with mottled pigmentation.[85–90] The highly conserved end domains of the keratin rod are particularly susceptible to significant mutation with resultant instability of the filament assembly and consequent fragility of basal keratinocytes following mild trauma.[76]

Hemidesmosomal (pseudojunctional) EB

The histological features of the three hemidesmosomal variants of EB are not distinctive, showing cell-free subepidermal blisters as with the other variants. They are separated from simplex and junctional variants because the primary defect lies within the constituents of the hemidesmosomes and not in keratin filaments as is typical of simplex variants or in laminin-5 as is characteristic of junctional EB.[7] Mutations of the plectin, BP180 and $\alpha_6\beta_4$ integrin genes account for these variants.

Plectin, which localizes to the inner plaque of the hemidesmosome, is a member of the plakin family and in concert with BP230 is believed to be of importance in keratin filament anchorage.[7,10] Recently, reduced expression of this protein has been described in patients with both the Ogna and muscular dystrophy-associated variants.[91–95]

Generalized atrophic benign EB is most commonly a result of BP180 mutations.[96–98] Nonsense mutations or insertions/deletions with resultant premature termination codons result in absence of BP180 (*BPAG2*/type XVII collagen). This is a transmembrane collagen that is thought via its carboxy-terminal segment to contribute to the anchoring filaments.[7] The amino-terminal globular domain resides within the cytoplasm of the basal keratinocyte localizing to the outer plaque of the hemidesmosome. Less often laminin-5 mutations are responsible for this clinical phenotype (see junctional EB).

EB associated with pyloric atresia results from $\alpha_6\beta_4$ integrin missense mutations resulting in premature termination codons with synthesis of defective or non-functional α_6 or β_4 subunits.[99–101] As a result hemidesmosomes are hypoplastic or reduced in number.[7]

Junctional EB

Junctional EB variants are also characterized by subepidermal blistering, usually unaccompanied by any substantial inflammatory cell infiltrate (*Fig. 3.43*).[102] Ultrastructurally the site of cleavage is through the lamina lucida (*Fig. 3.44*). The hemidesmosomes may appear malformed, be diminished in number or absent.[103–106] Hemidesmosome alterations as detected by electron microscopy, however, are heterogeneous. In a morphometric study of numbers of hemidesmosomes per unit length of basement membrane, one of five patients with the Herlitz variant and two of three patients with non-Herlitz variants had normal results.[107] The same authors recorded an association between junctional EB and a reduction in the numbers of hemidesmosomes with associated sub-basal plates.

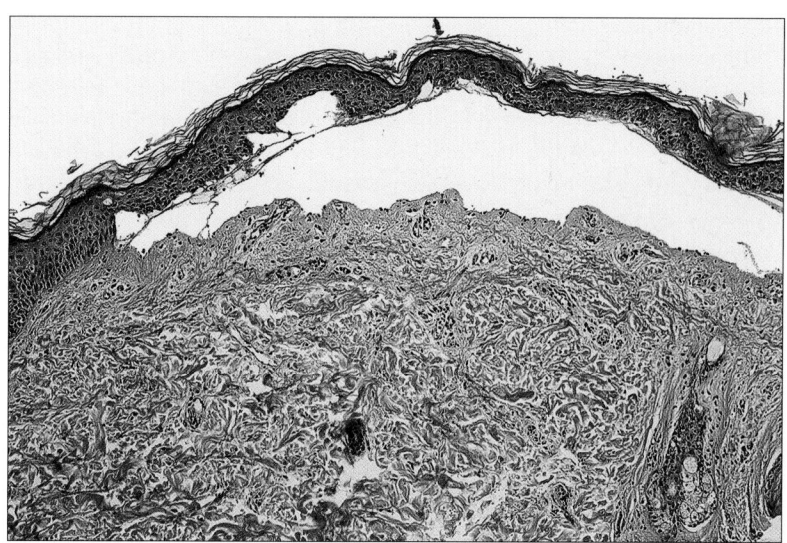

Fig. 3.43
Junctional EB: subepidermal cell-free blister.

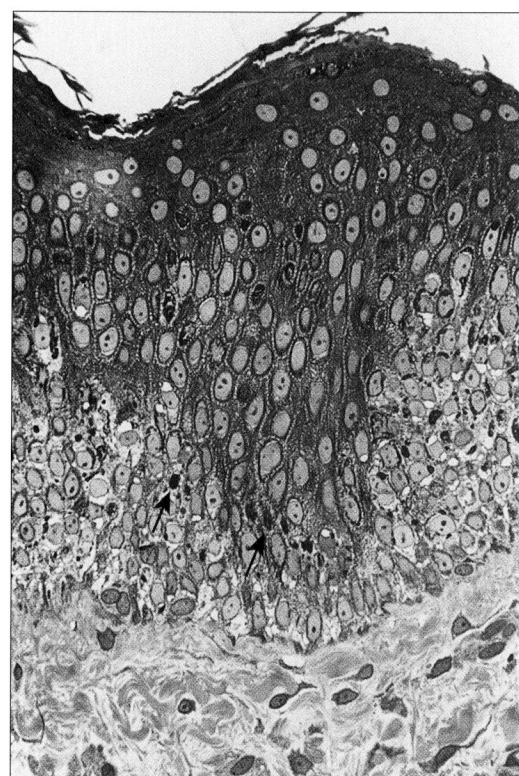

Fig. 3.42
Epidermolysis bullosa simplex (Dowling–Meara): numerous tonofilament clumps are present in the adjacent clinically normal skin (arrowed). By courtesy of J.A. McGrath, MD, Institute of Dermatology, London, UK.

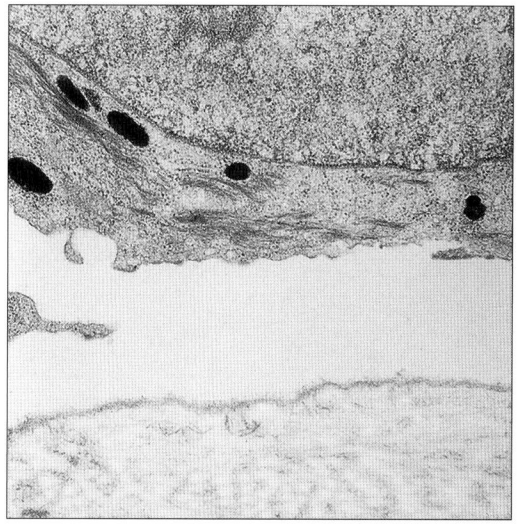

Fig. 3.44
Junctional EB: lesional skin showing separation within the lamina lucida of the dermoepidermal junction. By courtesy of R.A.J. Eady, MD, Institute of Dermatology, and M.J. Tidman, MD, Guy's Hospital, London, UK.

Junctional EB is characterized by mutations in the genes that encode the α_3, β_3 or γ_2 chains of laminin-5.[108–114] Mutations resulting in premature termination codons in the laminin-5 genes are present, for example, in all cases of the Herlitz's lethal variant.[5,7] Nonsense mutations, out-of-frame deletions or insertions and splicing errors affect both alleles, resulting in reduced synthesis and defective assembly of trimeric laminin-5 molecules.[7] The majority of mutations have affected the *LAMB3* gene although *LAMA3* and *LAMC2* gene abnormalities have also been documented. Non-Herlitz junctional EB variants, including some cases of generalized atrophic benign EB, are associated with milder missense mutations or deletions in the laminin-5 gene.[108,115,116] Laminin-5 is located within anchoring filaments and in the lamina densa. The abnormal laminin-5 results in defective anchoring filaments with resultant instability at the basement membrane region.

Dystrophic EB

In the dystrophic variants the histological features are those of subepidermal vesiculation or blister formation in the absence of any significant inflammatory content (*Fig. 3.45*). The clinical subtypes show no particular distinguishing features. The adjacent dermis is often markedly scarred due to previous episodes of blistering.

The squamous carcinomas that develop in association with recessive dystrophic EB are very often well differentiated (*Fig. 3.46*) and occasionally their appearances suggest a verrucous variant. Whether this latter form has the good prognosis usually evident with verrucous carcinoma is uncertain.

Ultrastructurally the site of cleavage is immediately below the lamina densa (*Fig. 3.47*).[117,118] In the autosomal dominant and some localized recessive groups, anchoring fibrils are decreased in number, but may appear morphologically normal, whereas in the generalized recessive variants (and occasionally in severe dominant cases), the fibrils are very sparse or more often absent.[119–121] Frequently, thin wispy filaments immediately adjacent to the lamina densa are all that are visible. In a recent morphometric study of basement membrane in various dystrophic forms, using non-blistered skin, anchoring fibrils were completely absent in generalized recessive dystrophic EB. Reduced numbers of

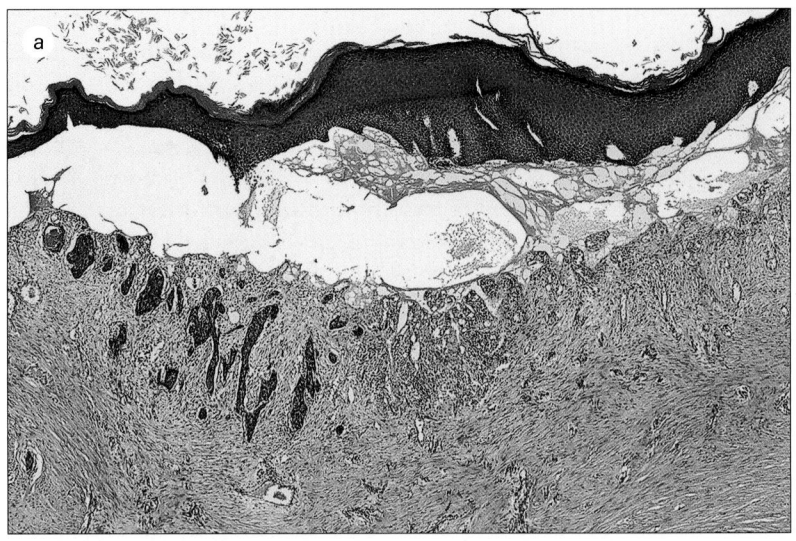

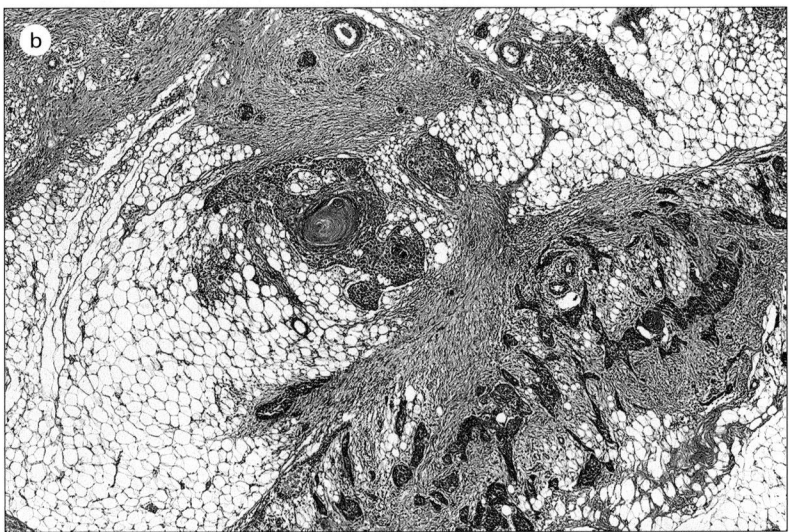

Fig. 3.46
(a, b) Dystrophic EB (Hallopeau–Siemens): biopsy from the forearm of a 30-year-old patient showing a cell-free subepidermal blister. In addition, a well-differentiated squamous cell carcinoma extends into the subcutaneous fat.

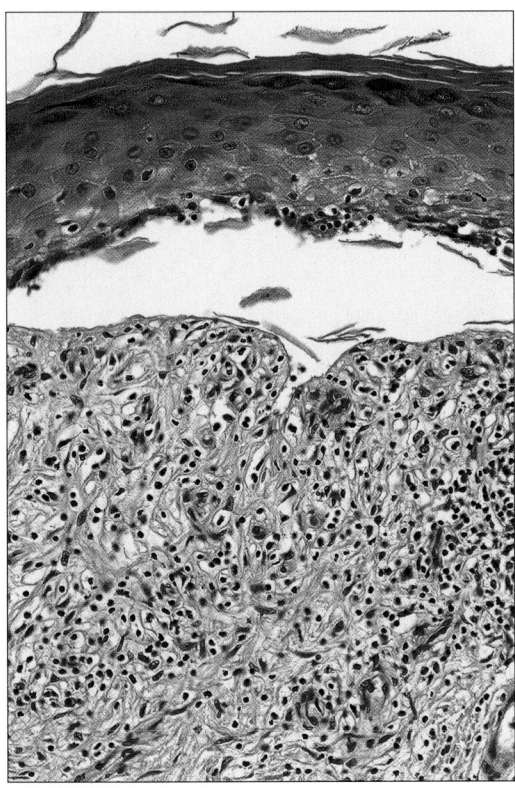

Fig. 3.45
Dystrophic EB (Hallopeau–Siemens): in addition to obvious subepidermal blistering there is dense dermal scarring and chronic inflammation.

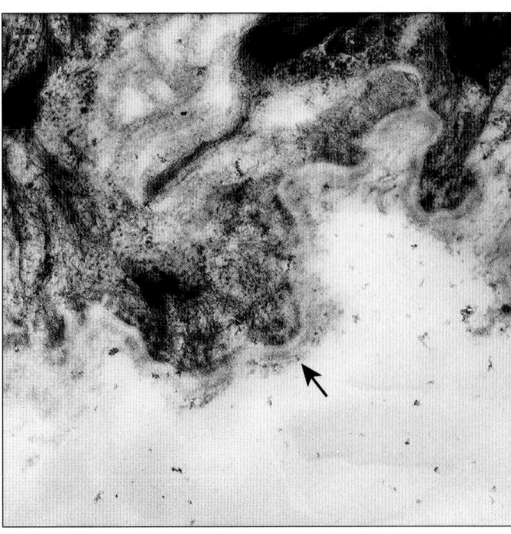

Fig. 3.47
Dystrophic EB (Hallopeau–Siemens): lesional skin demonstrates cleavage immediately beneath the lamina densa of the dermoepidermal junction (arrowed). By courtesy of R.A.J. Eady, MD, Institute of Dermatology, and M.J. Tidman, MD, Guy's Hospital, London, UK.

morphologically normal anchoring fibrils were found in localized recessive and dominant dystrophic variants.[122] Type VII collagen expression in dystrophic EB, however, as determined by LH7:2 immunolabeling is not an all-or-none phenomenon. Even in the recessive variant, some positive staining of thin, ill-formed filamentous structures may be seen immediately below the lamina densa. Collagenolysis in the superficial dermis may also be seen in the more severe variants.

In transient bullous dermolysis of the newborn, in addition to reduced numbers of anchoring fibrils, intracytoplasmic inclusions are seen in the basal keratinocytes. These have a stellate appearance and represent retained type VII and type IV collagen.[123–126]

Dystrophic EB variants are all caused by mutations in the type VII collagen gene *COL7A1*.[127–129] Over 100 distinct mutations have been identified.[7] The Hallopeau–Siemen's severe recessive variant is characterized by nonsense mutations, insertions, deletions or splicing errors, which cause premature termination codons affecting both alleles, resulting in very low levels of mRNA and virtual absence of type VII collagen synthesis.[7,127,128] Premature termination codon, missense, deletion and substitution mutations have been identified in a number of the less severe dystrophic variants.[7] Dominant dystrophic EB is caused by a glycine substitution mutation resulting in a less severe variant in which type VII collagen, although defective, is still produced and anchoring filaments are present albeit in reduced numbers.[130] Transient bullous dermolysis of the newborn also results from a mutation in *COL7A1*.[50,51]

Milia, which are most commonly seen in dystrophic EB, are small cysts within the upper dermis, consisting of a mass of keratinized squames surrounded by a wall of squamous epithelium, thereby representing mini-epidermoid cysts. They are not specific to epidermolysis bullosa, being found in a variety of conditions associated with damage to the cutaneous adnexal structures (e.g. severe burns and porphyria cutanea tarda) and other blistering disorders.

Differential diagnosis

With the appropriate clinical information the histological diagnosis of EB should not pose any particular problems. With the exception, however, of the Dowling–Meara variant, it is not usually possible to predict which subtype the patient suffers from although if specimens from early lesions are provided, it is sometimes possible to identify the simplex variants of the basis of cytolysis. Cell-free subepidermal blisters, however, may be seen in a variety of conditions including autolysis, EB acquisita, cell-free pemphigoid, suction blisters, bullous cutaneous amyloidosis, bullous lichen sclerosus, porphyria cutanea tarda and pseudoporphyria.

References

1. Pearson, R.W. (1988) Clinicopathologic subtypes of epidermolysis bullosa and their non-dermatological complications. *Arch Dermatol*, **124**, 718–725.
2. Fine, J-D., Bauer, E.A., Briggaman, R.A. et al (1991) Revised clinical and laboratory criteria for subtypes of inherited epidermolysis bullosa: a consensus report by the subcommittee on diagnosis and classification of the national epidermolysis bullosa registry. *J Am Acad Dermatol*, **24**, 119–135.
3. Fine, J-D., Johnson, L.B., Wright, J.F. (1991) Inherited blistering diseases of the skin. *Pediatrician*, **18**, 175–187.
4. Fine, J-D., Bauer, E.A., McGuire, J. et al (1999) Epidermolysis bullosa: clinical, epidemiologic, and laboratory advances, and the findings of the National Epidermolysis Bullosa Registry. Baltimore: Johns Hopkins University Press, pp 280–299.
5. Fine, J-D., Eady, R.A.J., Bauer, A.A. et al (2000) Revised classification system for inherited epidermolysis bullosa: report of the second international consensus meeting on diagnosis and classification of epidermolysis bullosa. *J Am Acad Dermatol*, **42**, 1051–1066.
6. Fine, J-D. (1999) The classification of inherited epidermolysis bullosa: current approach, pitfalls, unanswered questions and future directions. In: Fine, J-D., Bauer, E.A., McGuire, J., Moshell, A.N. (eds) Epidermolysis bullosa: clinical, epidemiologic, and laboratory advances, and the findings of the National Epidermolysis Bullosa Registry. Baltimore: Johns Hopkins University Press, pp 20–47.
7. Pulkkinen, L., Uitto, J. (1998) Hemidesmosomal variants of epidermolysis bullosa: mutations in the $\alpha_6\beta_4$ integrin and the 180-kD bullous pemphigoid antigen/type XVII collagen genes. *Exp Dermatol*, **7**, 46–64.
8. McLean, W.H.I., Lane, E.B. (1995) Intermediate filaments in disease. *Curr Opin Cell Biol*, **7**, 118–125.
9. Christiano, A.M., Uitto, J. (1996) Molecular complexity of the cutaneous basement membrane zone. *Exp Dermatol*, **5**, 1–11.
10. Uitto, J., Pulkkinen, L., Smith, F.J.D. et al (1996) Plectin and human genetic disorders of the skin and muscle. The paradigm of epidermolysis bullosa with muscular dystrophy. *Exp Dermatol*, **5**, 237–246.
11. Kunz, M., Rouan, F., Pulkkinen, L. et al (2000) Epidermolysis bullosa simplex associated with severe mucous membrane involvement and novel mutations in the plectin gene. *J Invest Dermatol*, **114**, 376–380.
12. Jonkman, M.F., de Jong, M.C., Heeres, K. et al (1995) 180-kD bullous pemphigoid antigen (BP180) is deficient in generalized atrophic benign epidermolysis bullosa. *J Clin Invest*, **95**, 1345–1352.
13. Gil, S.G., Brown, T.A., Ryan, M.C. et al (1994) Junctional epidermolysis bullosa: defects in the expression of epiligrin/nicein/kalinin and integrin β_4 that inhibit hemidesmosome formation. *J Invest Dermatol*, **103**, 31S–38S.
14. Kivirikko, S., McGrath, J.A., Pulkkinen, L. et al (1996) Mutational hotspots in the LAMB3 gene in the lethal (Herlitz) type of junctional epidermolysis bullosa. *Hum Mol Genet*, **5**, 231–237.
15. Järvikallio, A., Pulkkinen, L., Uitto, J. (1997) Molecular basis of dystrophic epidermolysis bullosa: mutations in the type VII collagen gene (*COL7A1*). *Hum Mutat*, **10**, 338–347.
16. Gamborg Nielsen, P., Sjolund, E. (1985) Epidermolysis bullosa simplex localisata associated with anodontia, hair and nail disorders. A new syndrome. *Acta Derm Venereol*, **65**, 526–530.
17. Olaisen, B., Gedde-Dahl, T. Jr. (1974) GPT–EBS linkage group: general linkage relations. *Hum Hered*, **24**, 178–185.
18. Olaisen, B., Gedde-Dahl, T. (1973) GPT–epidermolysis bullosa simplex (Ogna) linkage in man. *Hum Hered*, **23**, 189–196.
19. Chan, Y., Anton-Lamprecht, I., Yu, Q.C. et al (1994) A human keratin 14 'knockout': the absence of K14 leads to severe epidermolysis bullosa simplex and a function for an intermediate filament protein. *Genes Dev*, **8**, 2574–2587.
20. Dowling, G.B., Meara, R.H. (1954) Epidermolysis bullosa resembling juvenile dermatitis herpetiformis. *Br J Dermatol*, **66**, 139–143.
21. Buchbinder, L.H., Lucky, A., Ballard, E. (1986) Severe infantile epidermolysis bullosa simplex: Dowling–Meara type. *Arch Dermatol*, **122**, 190–195.
22. Anton-Lamprecht, I., Schnyder, U.W. (1982) Epidermolysis bullosa herpetiformis Dowling–Meara, report of a case and pathogenesis. *Dermatologica*, **164**, 221–235.
23. Hacham-Zadeh, S., Rappersberger, K., Livshin, R. et al (1988) Epidermolysis bullosa herpetiformis Dowling–Meara in a large family. *J Am Acad Dermatol*, **27**, 929–934.
24. Medenica-Mojsilovic, L., Fenska, N.A., Espinoza, C.G. (1986) Epidermolysis bullosa herpetiformis with mottled pigmentation and an unusual punctate keratoderma. *Arch Dermatol*, **122**, 900–908.
25. Fisher, T., Gedde-Dahl, T. Jr. (1979) Epidermolysis bullosa simplex and mottled pigmentation: a new dominant syndrome. *Clin Genet*, **15**, 228–238.
26. Fine, J-D., Johnson, L., Wright, T. (1989) Epidermolysis bullosa simplex superficialis. A new variant of epidermolysis bullosa characterized by subcorneal skin cleavage mimicking peeling skin syndrome. *Arch Dermatol*, **125**, 633–638.
27. Niemi, K-M., Sommer, H., Kero, M. et al (1988) Epidermolysis bullosa simplex associated with muscular dystrophy with recessive inheritance. *Arch Dermatol*, **124**, 551–554.
28. Fine, J-D., Stenn, J., Johnson, L. et al (1989) Autosomal recessive epidermolysis bullosa simplex: phenotypic features suggestive of junctional or dystrophic epidermolysis bullosa, and association with neuromuscular diseases. *Arch Dermatol*, **125**, 931–938.
29. Egan, N., Ward, R., Olmstead, M. et al (1985) Junctional epidermolysis bullosa and pyloric atresia in two siblings. *Arch Dermatol*, **121**, 1186–1188.
30. Lacour, J.P., Hoffman, P., Bastiani-Griffet, F. et al (1992) Lethal junctional epidermolysis bullosa with normal expression of BM 600 and antro-pyloric atresia: a new variant of junctional epidermolysis bullosa? *Eur J Pediatr*, **151**, 252–257.
31. Lestringant, G.G., Alkel, S.R., Qayed, K.I. (1992) The pyloric atresia–junctional epidermolysis bullosa syndrome: report of a case and a review of the literature. *Arch Dermatol*, **128**, 1083–1086.
32. Turner, T.W. (1980) Two cases of junctional epidermolysis bullosa (Herlitz–Pearson). *Br J Dermatol*, **102**, 97–107.
33. Pearson, R.W., Potter, B., Strauss, F. (1974) Epidermolysis bullosa hereditaria letalis: clinical and histological manifestations and course of the disease. *Arch Dermatol*, **109**, 349–355.
34. Schachner, L., Lazarus, G.S., Dembritzer, H. (1977) Epidermolysis bullosa hereditaria letalis: pathology, natural history and therapy. *Br J Dermatol*, **96**, 51–58.
35. Jonkman, M.F., De Jong, M.C.J.M., Heeres, K. et al (1996) Generalized atrophic benign epidermolysis bullosa: either 180-kD bullous pemphigoid antigen or laminin-5 deficiency. *Arch Dermatol* **132**, 145–149.
36. Hashimoto, I., Schnyder, U.W., Anton-Lamprecht, I. (1976) Epidermolysis bullosa hereditaria with junctional blistering in an adult. *Dermatologica*, **152**, 72–86.
37. Paller, A.S., Fine, J-D., Kaplan, S. et al (1986) The generalized atrophic form of junctional epidermolysis bullosa: experience with four patients in the United States. *Arch Dermatol*, **122**, 704–710.
38. Foldes, C., Wallach, D., Aubiniere, E. et al (1988) Generalized atrophic benign form of junctional epidermolysis bullosa. *Dermatologica*, **176**, 83–90.
39. Hintner, H., Wolff, K. (1982) Generalized atrophic benign epidermolysis bullosa. *Arch Dermatol*, **118**, 375–384.
40. Briggaman, R.A. (1983) Hereditary epidermolysis bullosa with special emphasis on newly recognized syndromes and complications. *Dermatol Clin*, **1**, 263–280.
41. Orlando, R.C., Bozymski, E.M., Briggaman, R.A. et al (1974) Epidermolysis bullosa: gastrointestinal manifestations. *Ann Intern Med*, **81**, 203–206.
42. Wechsler, H.J., Krugh, F.J., Domonkos, A.N. et al (1970) Polydysplastic epidermolysis bullosa and development of epidermal neoplasms. *Arch Dermatol*, **102**, 374–377.
43. McGrath, J.A., Schofield, O.M.V., Mayou, B.J. et al (1992) Epidermolysis bullosa complicated by squamous cell carcinoma, report of 10 cases. *J Cutan Pathol*, **19**, 116–123.
44. Lichtenwald, D.J., Hanna, W., Sauder, D.N. et al (1990) Pretibial epidermolysis bullosa: report of a case. *J Am Acad Dermatol*, **22**, 346–350.
45. Horiguchi, Y., Leigh, I.M., Oguchi, M. et al (1993) A case of pretibial dystrophic epidermolysis bullosa: decreased expression of the non-helical domain of type VII collagen molecule. *J Dermatol*, **20**, 79–84.
46. McGrath, J.A., Schofield, O.M.V., Eady, R.A.J. (1994) Epidermolysis bullosa pruriginosa: dystrophic epidermolysis bullosa with distinctive clinicopathological features. *Br J Dermatol*, **130**, 617–625.
47. Bruckner-Tuderman, L., Niemi, K-M., Kero, M. et al (1990) Type VII collagen is expressed but anchoring fibrils are defective in dystrophic epidermolysis bullosa inversa. *Br J Dermatol*, **122**, 383–389.
48. Pearson, R.W., Paller, A.S. (1988) Dermolytic (dystrophic) epidermolysis bullosa inversa. *Arch Dermatol*, **124**, 544–547.
49. Fine, J-D., Osment, L.S., Gay, S. (1985) Dystrophic epidermolysis bullosa: a new variant characterized by progressive symmetrical centripetal involvement with scarring. *Arch Dermatol*, **121**, 1014–1017.
50. Christiano, A.M., Fine, J-D., Uitto, J. (1997) Genetic basis of dominantly inherited transient bullous dermolysis of the newborn: a splice site mutation in the type VII collagen gene. *J Invest Dermatol*, **109**, 811–814.
51. Hammami-Hauasli, N., Raghunath, M., Kuster, W. et al (1998) Transient bullous dermolysis of the newborn associated with compound heterozygosity or recessive and dominant *COL7A1* mutations. *J Invest Dermatol*, **111**, 1214–1219.
52. Hintner, H., Stingl, G., Schuler, G. et al (1981) Immunofluorescence mapping of antigenic determinants within the dermal–epidermal junction in mechanobullous diseases. *J Invest Dermatol*, **76**, 113–118.
53. Kero, M., Peltonen, L., Foidart, J.M. et al (1982) Immunohistological localization of three basement membrane components in various forms of epidermolysis bullosa. *J Cutan Pathol*, **9**, 316–328.
54. Eady, R.A.J., Gunner, D.B., Tidman, M.J. et al (1984) Rapid processing of fetal skin for prenatal diagnosis by light and electron microscopy. *J Clin Pathol*, **37**, 633–638.
55. Eady, R.A.J., Tidman, M.J., Heagerty, A.H.M. et al (1987) Approaches to the study of epidermolysis bullosa. *Curr Prob Dermatol*, **17**, 127–141.
56. Uitto, J., Bauer, E.A., Moshell, A.N. (1992) Symposium on epidermolysis bullosa: molecular biology and pathology of the cutaneous basement membrane zone. *J Invest Dermatol*, **98**, 391–395.
57. Breathnach, S., Fox, P.A., Neises, G.R. et al (1983) A unique epithelial basement membrane antigen defined by monoclonal antibody (KF-I). *J Invest Dermatol*, **80**, 392–395.
58. Fine, J-D., Breathnach, S., Hintner, H. et al (1984) KF-1 monoclonal antibody defines a specific basement membrane antigen defect in dystrophic forms of epidermolysis bullosa. *J Invest Dermatol*, **82**, 35–38.
59. Goldsmith, L.A., Briggaman, R.A. (1983) Monoclonal antibodies to anchoring fibrils for the diagnosis of epidermolysis bullosa. *J Invest Dermatol*, **80**, 392–395.
60. Leigh, I.M., Purkis, P.E. (1985) LH7:2 a new monoclonal antibody to lamina densa protein. *J Invest Dermatol*, **84**, 448–449 (A).
61. Heagerty, A.H.M., Kennedy, A.R., Leigh, I.M. et al (1985) LH7:2 monoclonal antibody defines a common dermo-epidermal defect in recessive forms of dystrophic epidermolysis bullosa. *J Invest Dermatol*, **84**, 448 (A).

62. Leigh, I.M., Eady, R.A., Heagerty, A.H. et al (1988) Type VII collagen is a normal component of epidermal basement membrane which shows altered expression in recessive dystrophic epidermolysis bullosa. *J Invest Dermatol*, **90**, 639–642.
63. McGrath, J.A., Ishida-Yamamoto, A., O'Grady, A. et al (1993) Structural variations in anchoring fibrils in dystrophic epidermolysis bullosa: correlation with type VII collagen expression. *J Invest Dermatol*, **100**, 366–372.
64. Verrando, P., Blanchet-Bardon, C., Pisani, A. et al (1991) Monoclonal antibody GB3 defines a widespread defect of several basement membranes and a keratinocyte dysfunction in patients with lethal junctional epidermolysis bullosa. *Lab Invest*, **64**, 85–92.
65. Schofield, O.M.V., Fine, J-D., Verrando, P. et al (1990) GB3 monoclonal antibody for the diagnosis of junctional epidermolysis bullosa: results of a multicenter study. *J Am Acad Dermatol*, **23**, 1078–1083.
66. Heagerty, A.H.M., Kennedy, A.R., Gunner, D.B. et al (1986) Rapid prenatal diagnosis and exclusion of epidermolysis bullosa using novel antibody probes. *J Invest Dermatol*, **86**, 603–605.
67. Fine, J-D. (1990) 19-DEJ-1, a monoclonal antibody to the hemidesmosome–anchoring filament complex, is the only reliable immuno-histochemical probe for all major forms of junctional epidermolysis bullosa. *Arch Dermatol*, **126**, 1187–1190.
68. Fine, J-D., Horiguchi, Y., Couchman, J.R. (1989) 19-DEJ-1, a hemidesmosome–anchoring filament complex-associated monoclonal antibody: definition of a new skin basement membrane antigenic defect in junctional and dystrophic epidermolysis bullosa. *Arch Dermatol*, **125**, 520–523.
69. Jonkman, M.F., de Jong, M.C.J.M., Heeres, K. et al (1995) 180kD bullous pemphigoid antigen (BP180) is deficient in atrophic benign epidermolysis bullosa. *J Clin Invest*, **95**, 1345–1352.
70. Pearson, R.W. (1985) Histopathologic and ultrastructural findings in certain genodermatoses. *Clin Dermatol*, **3**, 143–174.
71. Ito, M., Okuda, C., Shimizu, N. et al (1991) Epidermolysis bullosa simplex (Koebner) is a keratin disorder: ultrastructural and immunohistochemical study. *Arch Dermatol*, **127**, 367–372.
72. Kitajima, Y., Inove, S., Yaoita, H. (1989) Abnormal organization of keratin intermediate filaments in cultured keratinocytes of epidermolysis bullosa simplex. *Arch Dermatol Res*, **281**, 5–10.
73. Kates, S.G., Sueki, H., Honig, P.J. et al (1992) Immunohistochemical and ultrastructural characterization of tonofilament and hemidesmosome abnormalities in a case of epidermolysis bullosa herpetiformis (Dowling–Meara). *J Am Acad Dermatol*, **27**, 929–934.
74. Ishida-Yamamoto, A., McGrath, J.A., Chapman, S.J. et al (1991) Epidermolysis bullosa simplex (Dowling–Meara type) is a genetic disease characterized by an abnormal keratin–filament network involving keratins K5 and K14. *J Invest Dermatol*, **97**, 959–968.
75. Furumura, M., Imayama, S., Hori, Y. (1993) Three neonatal cases of epidermolysis bullosa herpetiformis (Dowling–Meara type) with severe erosive skin lesions. *J Am Acad Dermatol*, **28**, 859–861.
76. Fuchs, E. (1992) Genetic disorders of keratin. *J Invest Dermatol*, **99**, 671–674.
77. Irvine, A.D., McLean, W.H. (1999) Human keratin diseases: the increasing spectrum of disease and subtlety of the phenotype–genotype correlation. *Br J Dermatol*, **140**, 815–828.
78. Coulombe, P.A., Hutton, M.E., Letai, A. et al (1991) Point mutations in human keratin 14 genes of epidermolysis bullosa simplex patients: genetic and functional analyses. *Cell*, **66**, 1301–1311.
79. Coulombe, P., Chan, Y-M., Albers, K. et al (1990) Deletions in epidermal keratins that lead to alterations in filament organization and assembly: *in vivo* and *in vitro* studies. *J Cell Biol*, **111**, 3049–3064.
80. Bonifas, J.M., Rothman, A.L., Epstein, E.H. (1991) Epidermolysis bullosa simplex: evidence in two families for keratin gene abnormalities. *Science*, **254**, 1202–1205.
81. Ryynänen, M., Knowlton, R.G., Uitto, J. (1991) Mapping of epidermolysis bullosa simplex mutation to chromosome 12. *Am J Hum Genet*, **49**, 978–984.
82. McKenna, K.E., Hughes, A.E., Bingham, E.A. et al (1992) Linkage of epidermolysis bullosa simplex to keratin gene loci. *J Med Genet*, **29**, 568–570.
83. Vassar, R., Coulombe, P.A., Degenstein, L. et al (1991) Mutant keratin expression in transgenic mice causes marked abnormalities resembling human genetic skin disease. *Cell*, **64**, 365–380.
84. Coulombe, P.A., Hutton, M.E., Vassar, R. et al (1991) A function for keratins and a common thread among different types of epidermolysis bullosa simplex diseases. *J Cell Biol*, **115**, 1661–1674.
85. Lane, E.B., Rugg, E.L., Navsaria, H. et al (1992) A mutation in the conserved helix termination peptide of keratin 5 in hereditary skin blistering. *Nature*, **356**, 244–246.
86. Rugg, E.L., Morley, S.M., Smith, F.J.D. et al (1993) Missing links: keratin mutations in Weber–Cockayne EBS families implicate the central L12 linker domain in effective cytoskeleton function. *Nat Genet*, **5**, 294–300.
87. Hachisuka, H., Morita, M., Karashima, T. et al (1995) Keratin 14 gene point mutation in the Koebner and Dowling–Meara types of epidermolysis bullosa simplex as detected by the PASA method. *Arch Dermatol Res*, **287**, 142–145.
88. Chen, H., Bonifas, J.M., Matsumura, K. et al (1995) Keratin 14 gene mutations in patients with epidermolysis bullosa simplex. *J Invest Dermatol*, **105**, 629–632.
89. Umoki, K., Nomura, K., Harada, K. et al (1996) Keratin 14 gene mutation in a Japanese patient with the Dowling–Meara type of epidermolysis bullosa simplex. *J Dermatol Sci*, **11**, 64–69.
90. Nomura, K., Shimizu, H., Meng, X.M. et al (1996) A novel K5 gene mutation in Dowling–Meara epidermolysis bullosa simplex. *J Invest Dermatol*, **107**, 253–254.
91. Koss-Harnes, D., Jahnsen, F.L., Wiche, G. et al (1997) Plectin abnormality in epidermolysis bullosa simplex Ogna: non-responsiveness of basal keratinocytes to some anti-rat plectin antibodies. *Exp Dermatol*, **6**, 41–48.
92. Gache, Y., Chavanas, S., Lacour, J.P. et al (1996) Defective expression of plectin/HDI in epidermolysis bullosa simplex with muscular dystrophy. *J Clin Invest*, **97**, 2289–2298.
93. Smith, F.J.D., Eady, R.A.J., Leigh, I.M. et al (1996) Plectin deficiency in muscular dystrophy with epidermolysis bullosa. *Nat Genet*, **13**, 450–457.
94. McLean, W.H.I., Pulkkinen, L., Smith, F.J.D. et al (1996) Loss of plectin causes epidermolysis bullosa with muscular dystrophy: cDNA cloning and genome organization. *Genes Dev*, **10**, 1724–1735.
95. Pulkkinen, L., Smith, F.J.D., Shimizu, H. et al (1996) Homozygous deletion mutations in the plectin gene (PLECI) in patients with epidermolysis bullosa simplex associated with late onset muscular dystrophy. *Hum Mol Genet*, **5**, 1539–1546.
96. McGrath, J.A., Gatalica, B., Christiano, A.M. et al (1995) Mutations in the 180-kD bullous pemphigoid antigen (BPAG2), a hemidesmosomal transmembrane collagen (COL17A1), in atrophic benign epidermolysis. *Nat Genet*, **11**, 83–86.
97. Schumann, H., Hammami-Hauasli, N., Pulkkinen, L. et al (1997) Three novel homozygous point mutations and a new polymorphism in the COL17A1 gene: relation to biological and clinical phenotype of junctional epidermolysis bullosa. *Am J Hum Genet*, **60**, 1344–1353.
98. Darling, T., McGrath, J.A., Yee, C. et al (1997) Premature termination codons are present on both alleles of the bullous pemphigoid antigen 2 (BPAg2) gene in five Austrian families with generalized atrophic benign epidermolysis bullosa. *J Invest Dermatol*, **108**, 463–468.
99. Vidal, F., Aberdam, D., Christiano, A.M. et al (1995) Mutations in the gene for the integrin β4 subunit are associated with junctional epidermolysis bullosa with pyloric atresia. *Nat Genet*, **10**, 229–234.
100. Jonkman, M.F., de Jong, M.C.J.M., Heeres, K. et al (1992) Expression of integrin α6β4 in junctional epidermolysis bullosa. *J Invest Dermatol*, **99**, 489–496.
101. Phillips, R.J., Aplin, J.D., Lake, B.D. (1994) Antigenic expression of integrin α6β4 in junctional epidermolysis bullosa. *Histopathology*, **24**, 571–576.
102. Fine, J-D. (1986) Epidermolysis bullosa: clinical aspects, pathology, and recent advances in research. *Int J Dermatol*, **25**, 143–157.
103. Pearson, R.W., Potter, B., Strauss, F. (1974) Epidermolysis bullosa hereditaria letalis: clinical and histological manifestation and course of the disease. *Arch Dermatol*, **109**, 349–355.
104. Hashimoto, I., Schnyder, U.W., Anton-Lamprecht, I. (1976) Epidermolysis bullosa hereditaria with junctional blistering in an adult. *Dermatologica*, **152**, 72–86.
105. Hashimoto, I., Gedde-Dahl, T. Jr., Schnyder, U.W. et al (1976) Ultrastructural studies in epidermolysis bullosa hereditaria: IV. Recessive dystrophic types with junctional blistering (infantile or Herlitz–Pearson type and adult type). *Arch Dermatol Res*, **257**, 17–32.
106. Schachner, L., Lazarus, G.S., Dembitzer, H. (1977) Epidermolysis bullosa hereditaria letalis: pathology, natural history, and therapy. *Br J Dermatol*, **96**, 51–58.
107. Tidman, M.J., Eady, R.A.J. (1986) Hemidesmosome heterogeneity in junctional epidermolysis bullosa revealed by morphometric analysis. *J Invest Dermatol*, **86**, 51–56.
108. Uitto, J., Christiano, A.M. (1992) Molecular genetics of the cutaneous basement membrane zone: perspectives on epidermolysis bullosa and other blistering skin diseases. *J Clin Invest*, **90**, 687–692.
109. Aberdam, D., Galliano, M-F., Vailly, J. et al (1994) Herlitz's junctional epidermolysis bullosa is linked to mutations in the gene (LAMC2) for the γ2 subunit of nicein/kalinin (laminin-5). *Nat Genet*, **6**, 299–304.
110. Pulkkinen, L., Christiano, A.M., Airenne, T. et al (1994) Mutations in the γ2 chain gene of kalinin/laminin-5 in the junctional forms of epidermolysis bullosa. *Nat Genet*, **6**, 293–298.
111. Uitto, J., Pulkkinen, L., Christiano, A.M. (1994) Molecular basis of the dystrophic and junctional forms of epidermolysis bullosa: mutations in the type VII collagen and kalinin (laminin-5) genes. *J Invest Dermatol*, **103**, 39S–46S.
112. Kivirikko, S., McGrath, J.A., Baudoin, C. et al (1995) A homozygous nonsense mutation in the alpha chain gene of laminin 5 (LAMA3) in lethal (HERLITZ) junctional epidermolysis bullosa. *Hum Mol Genet*, **4**, 959–962.
113. Pulkkinen, L., Christiano, A., Gerecke, D. et al (1994) A homozygous nonsense mutation in the β3 chain gene of laminin-5 (LAMB3) in Herlitz junctional epidermolysis bullosa. *Genomics*, **24**, 357–360.
114. Christiano, A.M., Pulkkinen, L., Eady, R. et al (1996) Compound heterozygosity for nonsense and missense mutations in the LAMB3 gene in nonlethal junctional epidermolysis bullosa. *J Invest Dermatol*, **106**, 775–777.
115. McGrath, J.A., Pulkkinen, L., Christiano, A.M. et al (1995) Altered laminin 5 expression due to mutation in the gene encoding the ß3 chain (LAMB3) in atrophic benign epidermolysis bullosa. *J Invest Dermatol*, **104**, 467–474.
116. Mellerio, J.E., Eady, R.A., Atherton, D.J. et al (1998) E210K mutation in the gene encoding the 3 chain of laminin-5 (LAMB3) is predictive of a phenotype of generalized atrophic benign epidermolysis bullosa. *Br J Dermatol*, **139**, 325–331.
117. Hashimoto, I., Gedde-Dahl, T., Schnyder, U.W. et al (1976) Ultrastructural studies in epidermolysis bullosa: dominant dystrophic type of Cockayne and Touraine. *Arch Dermatol Res*, **255**, 285–295.
118. Hashimoto, I., Schnyder, U.W., Anton-Lamprecht, I. et al (1976) Ultrastructural studies in epidermolysis bullosa hereditaria: III. Recessive dystrophic types with dermolytic blistering (Hallopeau–Siemens types and inverse type). *Arch Dermatol Res*, **256**, 137–150.
119. Tidman, M.J., Eady, R.A.J. (1983) Dystrophic epidermolysis bullosa: ultrastructural morphometry of the dermo-epidermal junction. *J Invest Dermatol*, **80**, 342–346.
120. Briggaman, R.A., Wheeler, C.E. (1975) Epidermolysis bullosa dystrophica recessive: a possible role of anchoring fibrils in the pathogenesis. *J Invest Dermatol*, **65**, 203–211.
121. Briggaman, R.A. (1985) Is there any specificity to defects of anchoring in epidermolysis bullosa dystrophica, and what does this mean in terms of pathogenesis? *J Invest Dermatol*, **84**, 371–373.
122. Tidman, M.J., Eady, R.A.J. (1985) Evaluation of anchoring fibrils and other components of the dermal–epidermal junction in dystrophic epidermolysis by a quantitative ultrastructural technique. *J Invest Dermatol*, **84**, 374–377.
123. Hashimoto, K., Matsumoto, M., Iacobelli, D. (1985) Transient bullous dermolysis of the newborn. *Arch Dermatol*, **121**, 1429–1438.
124. Hashimoto, K., Burk, J.D., Bale, G.F. et al (1989) Transient bullous dermolysis of the newborn: two additional cases. *J Am Acad Dermatol*, **21**, 708–713.
125. Fine, J-D., Horiguchi, Y., Stein, D.H. et al (1990) Intraepidermal type VII collagen. Evidence for abnormal intracytoplasmic processing of a major basement membrane protein in rare patients with dominant and possibly localized recessive forms of dystrophic epidermolysis bullosa. *J Am Acad Dermatol*, **22**, 188–195.
126. Hashimoto, K., Eng, A.M. (1992) Transient bullous dermolysis of the newborn: retention of anchoring fibril- and basal lamina-like structures in keratinocytes and evidence of collagenolysis. *J Cutan Pathol*, **19**, 496–501.
127. Christiano, A.M., Anhalt, G., Gibbons, S. et al (1994) Premature termination codons in the type VII collagen gene (COL7A1) underlie severe, mutilating recessive dystrophic epidermolysis bullosa. *Genomics*, **21**, 160–168.
128. Christiano, A.M., Suga, Y., Greenspan, D. et al (1995) Premature termination codons of the type VII gene (COL7AI) in three brothers with recessive dystrophic epidermolysis bullosa. *J Clin Invest*, **95**, 1328–1334.
129. Christiano, A.M., Greenspan, D.S., Hoffman, G.G. et al (1993) A missense mutation in the human type VII collagen gene in two siblings with recessive dystrophic epidermolysis bullosa. *Nat Genet*, **4**, 62–66.
130. Christiano, A.M., Ryynanen, M., Uitto, J. (1994) Dominant dystrophic epidermolysis bullosa: identification of a glycine to serine substitution in the triple-helical domain of type VII collagen. *Proc Natl Acad Sci USA*, **91**, 3549–3553.

Bullous pemphigoid

Clinical features

Bullous pemphigoid is not a single disease entity. Rather, there are many subtypes, which have been classified into primary cutaneous and mucosal variants and into generalized and localized forms (*Fig. 3.48*).[1–4]

Generalized cutaneous pemphigoid

Bullous pemphigoid (BP) is the most frequently encountered autoimmune bullous dermatosis with an annual incidence of 6.6 new cases per one million of the population.[5,6] Any age group may be affected, but the generalized variant demonstrates a predilection for the later years of life, showing a maximum incidence in the seventh decade and over. Rarely, however, children and even infants may be affected.[7,8] The disease is associated with a worldwide distribution and shows no racial propensity. There are no significant human leukocyte antigen (HLA) associations and the sex incidence is approximately equal.

Prodromal events are numerous and include erythematous, urticarial and, rarely, eczematous phases.[9,10] Erythroderma either preceding the bullous phase or occurring simultaneously is a very rare manifestation (erythrodermic pemphigoid).[11,12] Similarly, patients may present with a history of generalized pruritus in the absence of visible skin lesions (pruritic pemphigoid). In such circumstances, immunofluorescence investigations are essential to establish the correct diagnosis.[13]

The characteristic lesions of established disease are tense and often intact blisters arising on normal or erythematous skin (*Figs 3.49, 3.50*). They may measure up to several centimeters in diameter and are typically dome-shaped (*Fig. 3.51*). Often they contain clear or bloodstained fluid. Any area of the body may be affected, but the blisters are most commonly located about the lower abdomen, the inner aspect of the thighs and on the flexural surfaces of the forearms, the axillae and groins (*Fig. 3.52*).[14] Grouping of lesions as seen in dermatitis herpetiformis is not usually a feature and symmetry is characteristically absent. A 'cluster

of jewels' appearance of new blisters arising at the edge of resolving lesions as seen in linear IgA disease may, however, occasionally be a feature of bullous pemphigoid (*Fig. 3.53*).[15] The lesions are often pruritic and a burning sensation is sometimes a feature. Nikolsky's sign is usually negative. In contrast to cicatricial pemphigoid, generalized bullous pemphigoid is not associated with scarring.

Reported mucosal involvement (frequently as ulcers) is highly variable ranging from 8 to 58%.[16–18] In a recent series of 115 patients, 24% had oral involvement and 7% had genital lesions.[18] Lesions are found most often on the palate, the cheeks, lips and tongue (*Fig. 3.54*). Other sites less commonly involved include mucosae of the nose, pharynx, conjunctiva and rarely the urethra and vulva (see below) (*Fig. 3.55*).[17] In contrast to cicatricial pemphigoid, mucosal involvement in generalized bullous pemphigoid is not associated with scarring.

Although bullous pemphigoid has been reported in association with a variety of internal malignancies, this may just be coincidental, merely reflecting the age incidence of these two diseases.[19] In a series of almost 500 patients from Sweden, no increased incidence of cancer was observed.[20] More recent studies, however, have shown that there may be a positive correlation between internal malignancy and seronegative bullous pemphigoid patients.[21]

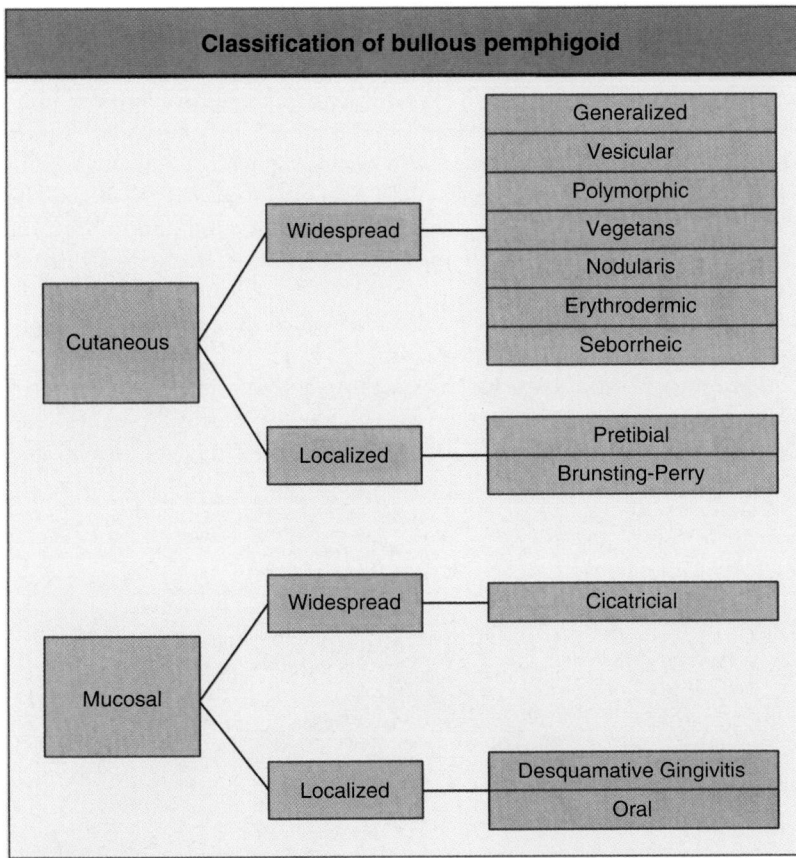

Fig. 3.48
Bullous pemphigoid: clinical subtypes.

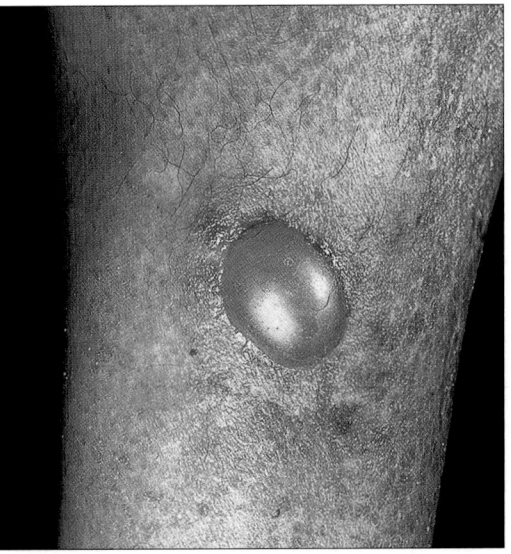

Fig. 3.50
BP: early tense blister arising on an erythematous base. By courtesy of the Institute of Dermatology, London, UK.

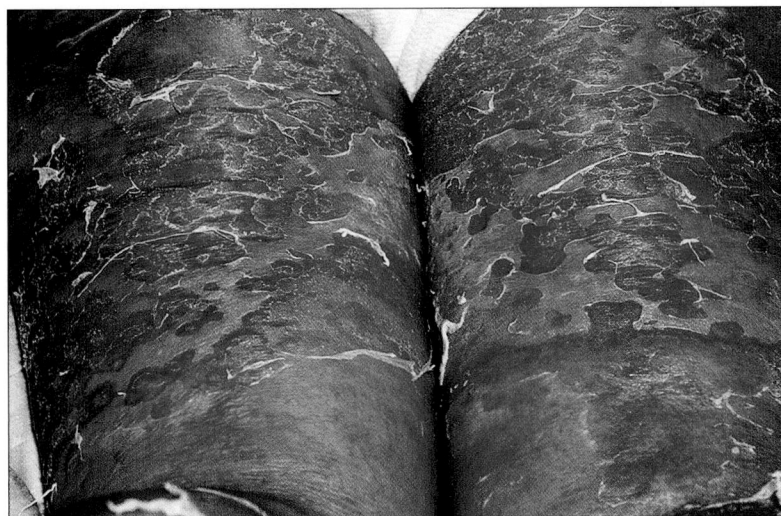

Fig. 3.49
Erythrodermic BP: blistering has developed against a background of generalized erythroderma. By courtesy of the Institute of Dermatology, London, UK.

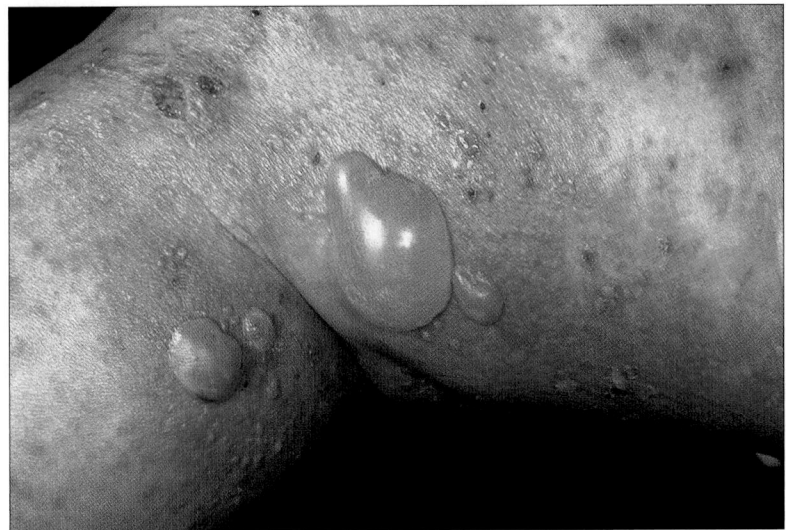

Fig. 3.51
BP: tense, dome-shaped blisters. The flexures are typically affected. By courtesy of the Institute of Dermatology, London, UK.

Generalized bullous pemphigoid is a serious condition with a significant mortality ranging from 10 to 20%.[1] Since the advent of steroid therapy and immunosuppressive agents, patients are more at risk of developing severe iatrogenic disorders than of dying from their disease (*Fig. 3.56*).

Clinical variants of generalized pemphigoid

Urticarial bullous pemphigoid presents with large persistent erythematous plaques, which sometimes adopt an annular or gyrate peripheral component (*Fig. 3.57*).[1] Rarely small vesicles are also to be found.

Vesicular pemphigoid is a rare clinical variant in which the cutaneous manifestations show a striking overlap with dermatitis herpetiformis.[22–24]

Patients present with numerous small tense vesicles that may be symmetrical, intensely pruritic and therefore associated with conspicuous excoriation.

Polymorphic pemphigoid is a somewhat confusing entity, which is similar to vesicular pemphigoid, but probably shows overlap with linear IgA disease.[25–27] Patients present with burning and itching lesions predominantly affecting the extensor aspects of the limbs, back and buttocks. Symmetry, grouping and a polymorphic clinical appearance of papules, vesicles and variably sized bullae emphasize similarity to dermatitis herpetiformis. It has been suggested that polymorphic pemphigoid is not an entity *sui generis*, but represents a *pot-pourri* of conditions including vesicular pemphigoid, linear IgA disease and mixed subepidermal bullous disease in which patients show both linear IgG and linear IgA or dermal papillary granular IgA on direct immunofluorescence.[26]

Pemphigoid vegetans is an exceedingly rare vegetative intertriginous variant that may be associated with chronic inflammatory bowel disease.[28–34] Fewer than 10 cases have been documented. Patients present with vegetative, crusted purulent and sometimes eroded lesions in the groins, axillae, neck, hands, eyelids, inframammary and perioral regions (*Fig. 3.58*). Vesicles and bullae may also be evident. The etiology of the vegetative lesions is unknown.

Seborrheic pemphigoid is a variant in which the clinical features are suggestive of pemphigus erythematosus.[27]

Pemphigoid nodularis represents the extremely rare association of lesions of bullous pemphigoid with intensely pruritic papules and nodules of nodular prurigo predominantly affecting the trunk and extremities[35–37] (*Fig. 3.59*).

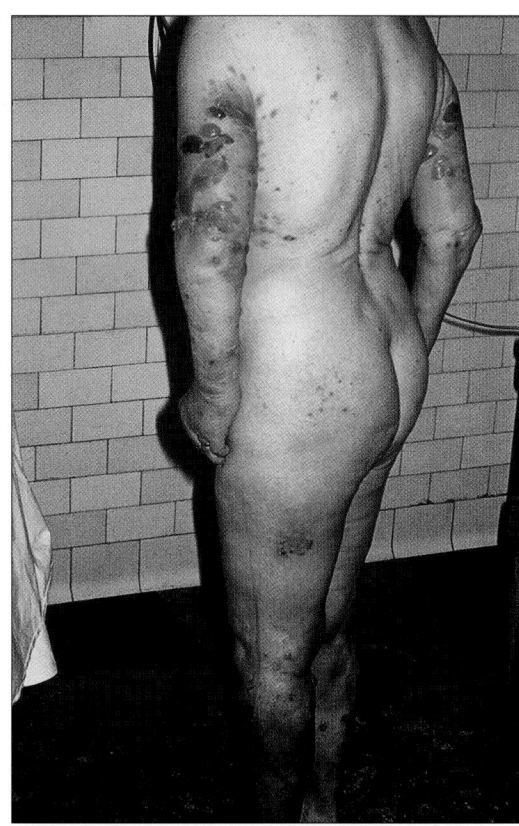

Fig. 3.52
BP: widespread, fluid-filled, hemorrhagic blisters on the arms and legs of an elderly female. By courtesy of the late M. Beare, MD, Royal Victoria Hospital, Belfast, N. Ireland.

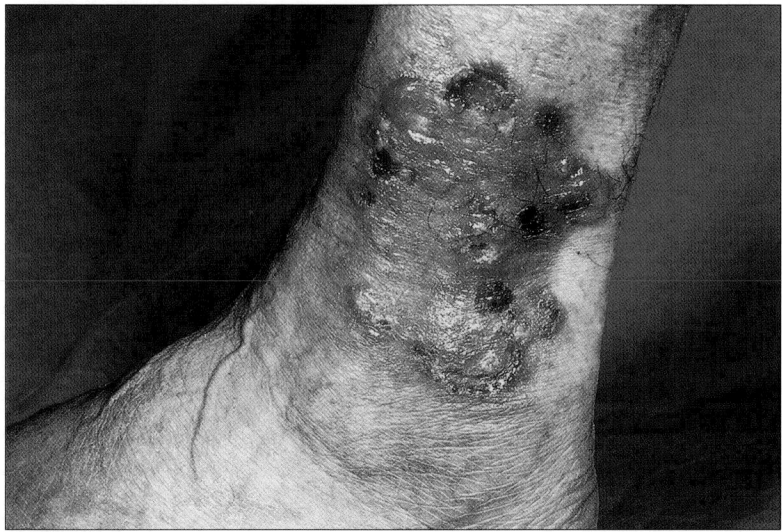

Fig. 3.53
BP: new blisters arising at the edge of a healing lesion (cluster of jewels sign). Although typically seen in childhood linear IgA disease, this is sometimes a feature of bullous pemphigoid. By courtesy of R.A. Marsden, MD, St George's Hospital, London, UK.

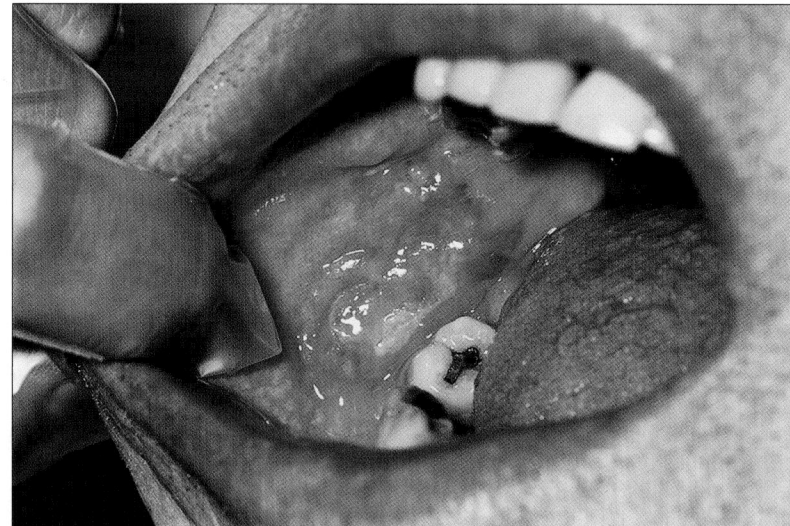

Fig. 3.54
BP: oral erosions are an occasional finding. Intact blisters are rare. By courtesy of R.A. Marsden, MD, St George's Hospital, London, UK.

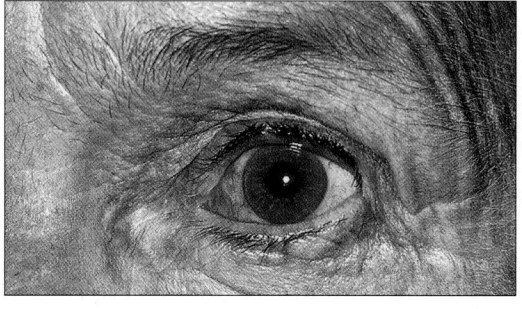

Fig. 3.55
BP: conjunctival injection is present. By courtesy of R.A. Marsden, MD, St George's Hospital, London, UK.

Exceptionally, patients may show immunofluorescent evidence of bullous pemphigoid in the absence of clinical blistering.[37] The cause of this unusual phenomenon is unknown although in some patients at least, chronic scratching probably damages the basement membrane region with exposure of bullous pemphigoid antigens. There is a female predilection (2:1).[37] The age range of this variant extends from 24 to 80 years but, as with classical bullous pemphigoid, the majority of patients are elderly.

Dyshidrosiform pemphigoid is a rare variant of pemphigoid in which patients develop 1–2 mm, tense 'sago-grain-like' vesicles on the palms and soles resembling dyshidrosiform dermatitis (pompholyx).[38–43] Lesions may be localized, or precede or occur simultaneously with generalized disease.

Childhood pemphigoid exhibits lesions that are similar to their adult counterparts, but there is some tendency for lesions to be localized around the face, lower trunk, thighs and genitalia, reminiscent of linear IgA disease in childhood (*Fig. 3.60*).[7,8,44–51] Similarly, a 'cluster of jewels' appearance is sometimes evident.[7] Palmar, plantar and oral lesions are often present and may be the sole site of involvement in infants (*Fig. 3.61*). The mucous membranes may be affected but scarring is absent. A number of children with primary localized vulval lesions have also been described (*Fig. 3.62*).[41,43,51] This latter is of particular clinical importance since it may be mistaken for evidence of sexual abuse. Childhood pemphigoid has a good prognosis and, as in adults, is usually self-limiting. Although generally the etiology is unknown, in some infant cases there appears to be a relationship to prior vaccination or immunization.[51]

Localized cutaneous pemphigoid

Although classical bullous pemphigoid not uncommonly presents initially as localized lesions that after a few months generalize, occasional patients present with localized blisters that do not subsequently disseminate (localized bullous pemphigoid).[52] Traditionally this group has been subdivided into two variants:

- Brunsting–Perry pemphigoid which predominantly affects the head and neck and is associated with scarring[53]
- localized cutaneous non-scarring bullous pemphigoid (Eberhartinger and Niebauer variant),[54] which predominantly affects the lower legs (in particular the pretibial region) of females.

The former variant is considered in the section on cicatricial pemphigoid. Although the latter non-scarring cutaneous form particularly affects the lower legs (*Fig. 3.63*), it may also present at a variety of other sites including forearms and hands, breasts, chest, buttocks and umbilicus. Lesions in localized bullous pemphigoid may be related to

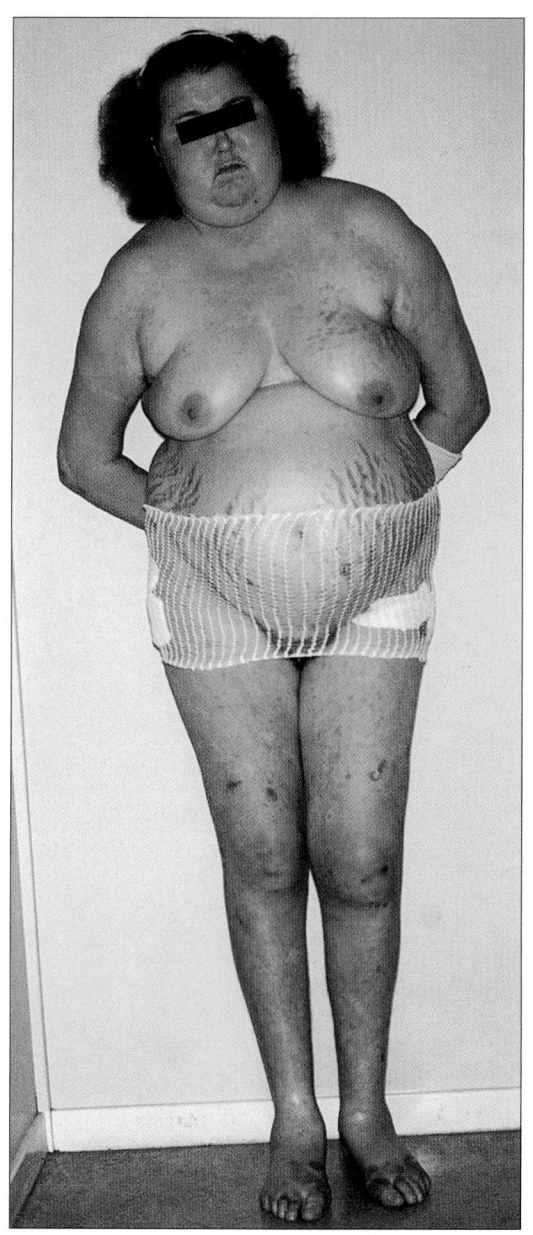

Fig. 3.56
BP: this patient has developed gross Cushing's syndrome as a consequence of steroid therapy. By courtesy of R.A. Marsden, MD, St George's Hospital, London, UK.

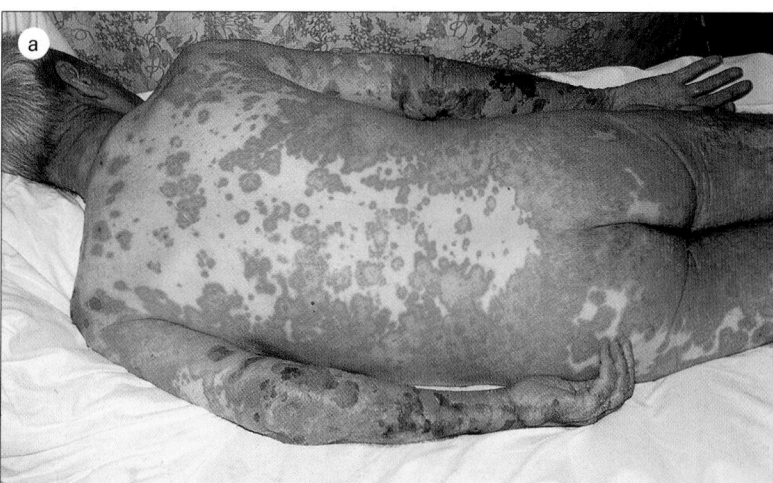

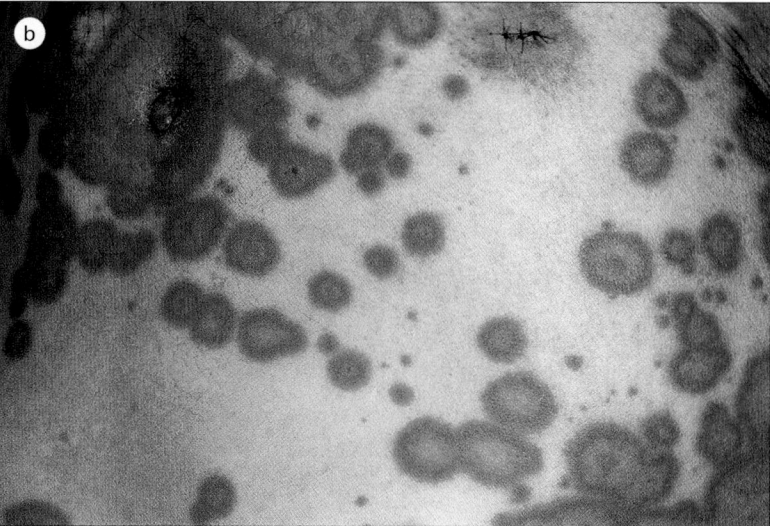

Fig. 3.57
(a, b) Bullous pemphigoid: occasionally erythematous urticarial lesions may be the presenting feature. Blisters may not evolve until several weeks later. By courtesy of R.A. Marsden, MD, St George's Hospital, London, UK.

trauma.[54] This variant shows a peak incidence in the sixth decade. As with generalized bullous pemphigoid, patients present with tense sometimes hemorrhagic bullae that arise on normal or erythematous appearing skin. Localized cutaneous non-scarring bullous pemphigoid is generally associated with a good prognosis.[54]

Mucosal pemphigoid/desquamative gingivitis

Localized oral pemphigoid is a recently described variant of desquamative gingivitis.[55–57] The latter, of multifactorial etiology by definition, affects the marginal and attached gingivae. It shows a female predominance (9:1) and presents most frequently in the middle aged. Desquamative gingivitis may also be a manifestation of lichen planus, cicatricial pemphigoid and pemphigus.[36] The diagnosis of localized oral pemphigoid depends upon the presence of a linear band of immuno-reactants at the epithelial basement membrane region on direct immunofluorescence.[55] Clinical features include erythema, edema, erosions and ulcers. The lesions are non-scarring. Bullous pemphigoid-associated desquamative gingivitis may remain confined to the gingiva (the localized oral pemphigoid type), but approximately equal proportions of patients go on to develop full-blown cicatricial pemphigoid (*Fig. 3.64*).[55]

Pathogenesis and histological features

The histological features of bullous pemphigoid depend to some extent upon the age of the lesion biopsied. Early erythematous and urticarial lesions most often show upper dermal edema associated with a perivascular lymphohistiocytic infiltrate accompanied by usually

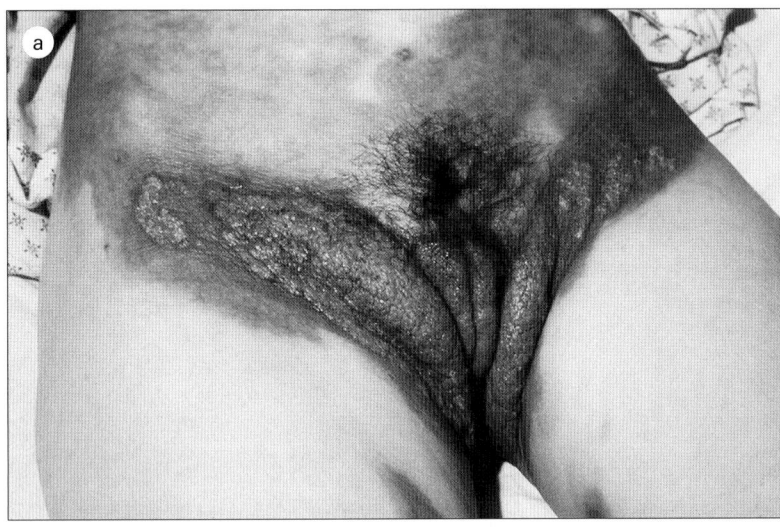

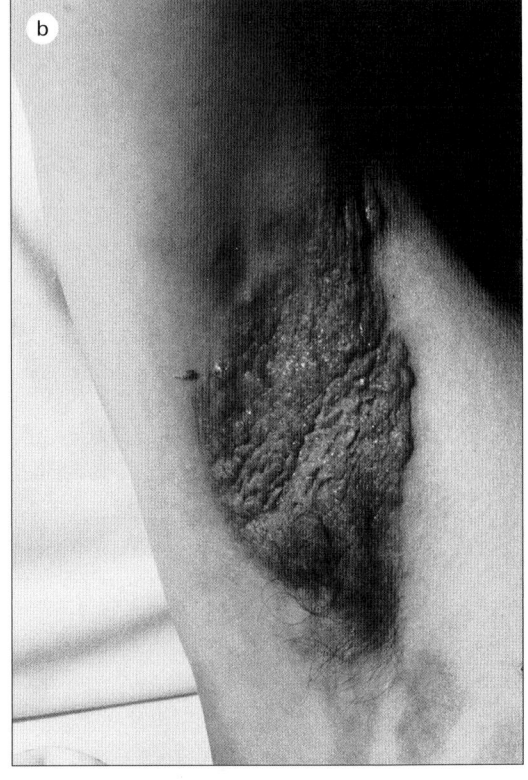

Fig. 3.58
(a, b) Pemphigoid vegetans: presentation as verrucous lesions in the flexures may result in considerable diagnostic difficulties. By courtesy of R.K. Winkelmann, MD, The Mayo Clinic, Scottsdale, Arizona, USA.

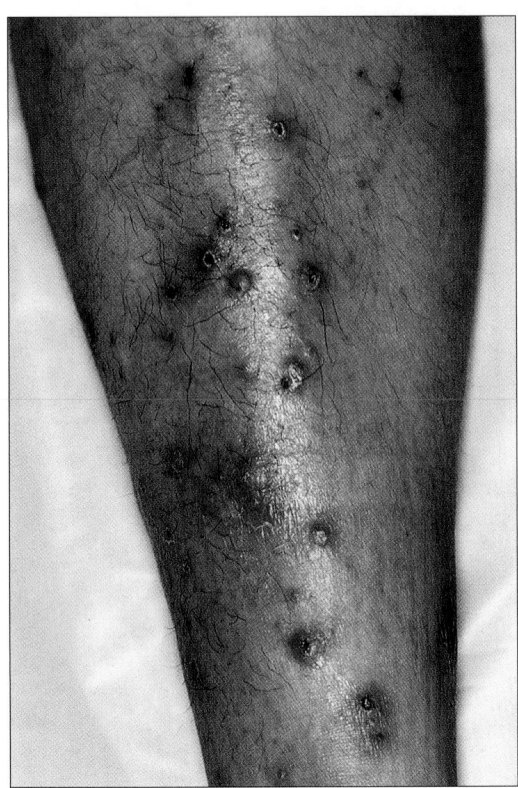

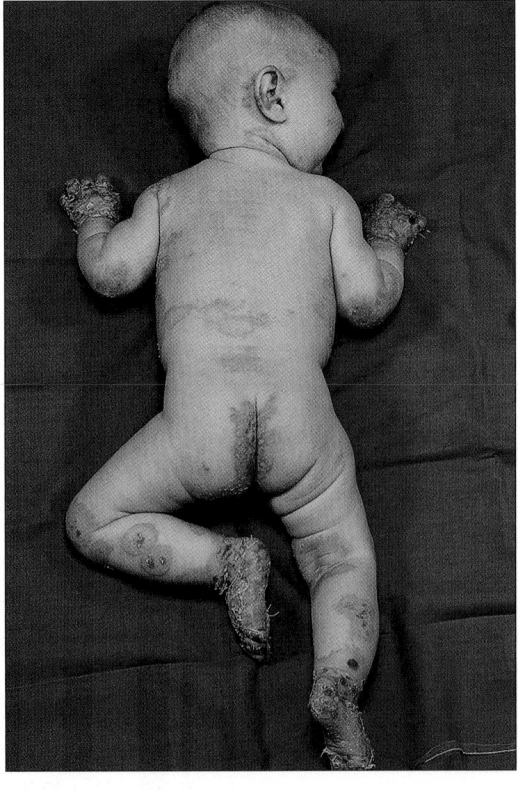

Fig. 3.59
Pemphigoid nodularis: in addition to bullous lesions, this patient also developed these pruritic nodules. By courtesy of H. Shimizu, MD, Keio University School of Medicine, Tokyo, Japan.

Fig. 3.60
Childhood BP: very rarely this disease affects young children and infants. There is a widespread distribution of bullae, which characteristically arise on an erythematous base. By courtesy of R.A. Marsden, MD, St George's Hospital, London, UK.

conspicuous eosinophils (*Figs 3.65, 3.66*). Eosinophilic spongiosis is sometimes evident and occasionally, if eosinophils are present in sufficient numbers, flame figures may be a feature. Mild interface changes characterized by basal cell hydropic degeneration can be seen in early or prodromal lesions.

If the biopsy is taken from an established blister, the changes are most often those of an inflammatory (cell-rich) variant.[58] The blister, which is subepidermal, is typically unilocular and covered by attenuated epithelium (*Fig. 3.67*). In early lesions the roof epidermis may appear unaffected or show occasional to even confluent necrotic basal keratinocytes. The blister contents include coagulated serum, fibrin strands and large numbers of inflammatory cells including conspicuous eosinophils (*Fig. 3.68*). Variable numbers of neutrophils may be present.

A typical finding in bullous pemphigoid is retention of the dermal papillary outline (festooning) which project like sentries into the vesicle cavity (*Fig. 3.69*). The underlying dermis is inflamed and usually shows widespread severe edema. An infiltrate of eosinophils and mononuclears surrounds the blood vessels and extends between the adjacent collagen bundles. Leukocytoclasis is not seen and features of vasculitis are not present. The adjacent papillary dermis is often edematous and, very occasionally, eosinophil microabscesses are a feature (*Fig. 3.70*). Exceptionally rarely, neutrophil microabscesses may be seen (see vesicular pemphigoid), raising diagnostic confusion with dermatitis herpetiformis. Eosinophilic spongiosis is also sometimes evident in the adjacent epidermis (*Fig. 3.71*).[59]

Cell-poor (non-inflammatory) features are occasionally seen if biopsies are taken from lesions arising on non-inflamed skin (*Fig. 3.72*).

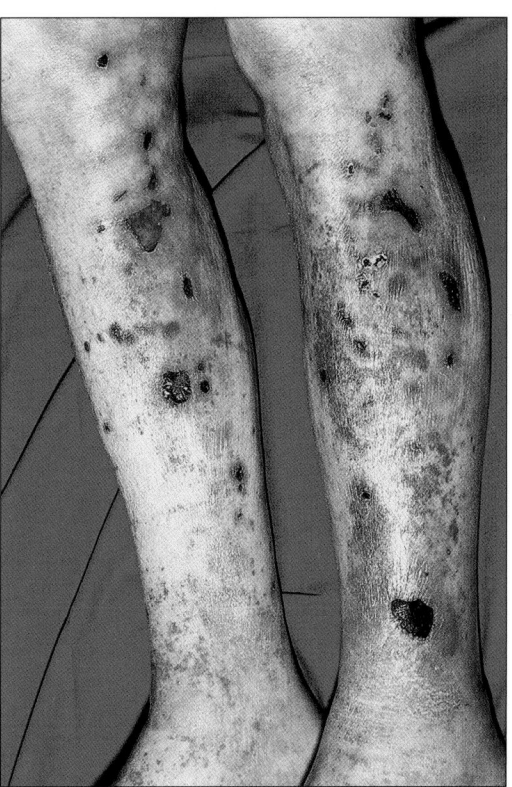

Fig. 3.63
Localized pemphigoid, non-scarring variant: lesions are found particularly on the lower legs of females. The prognosis is usually good, but occasionally the condition can become generalized. By courtesy of R.A. Marsden, MD, St George's Hospital, London, UK.

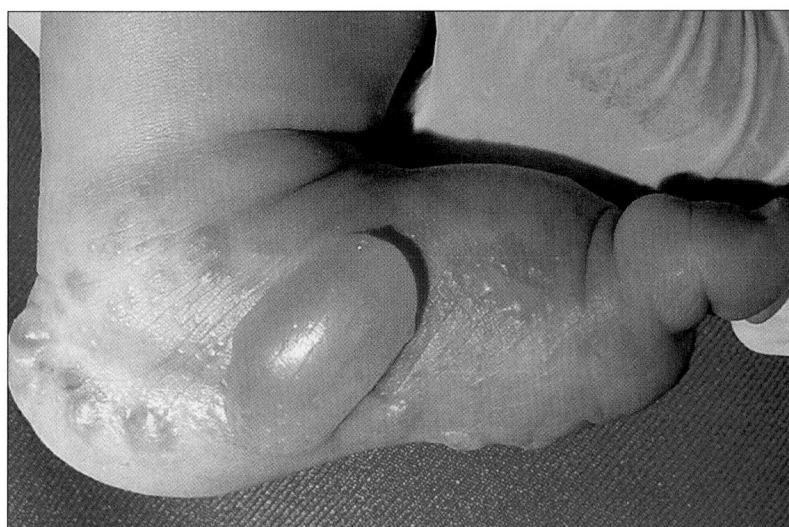

Fig. 3.61
Childhood BP: plantar involvement is sometimes the only site of disease. By courtesy of M. Liang, MD, The Children's Hospital, Boston, USA.

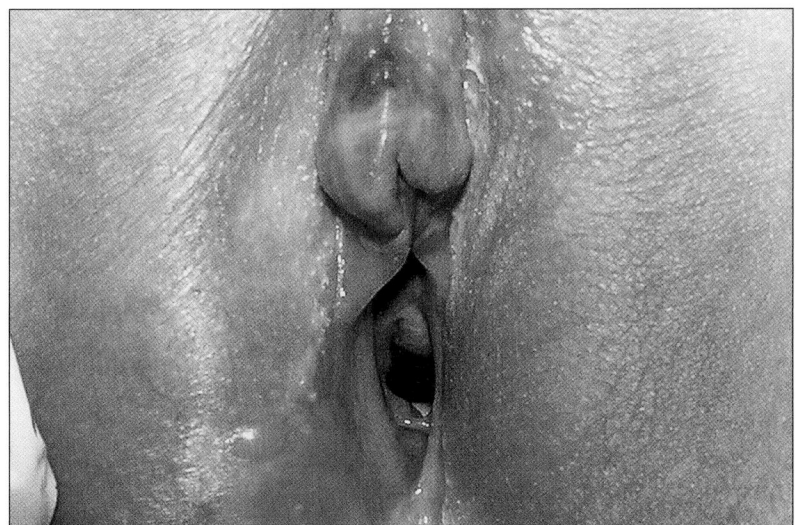

Fig. 3.62
Childhood BP: note the perineal scarring and isolated blister. By courtesy of M. Liang, MD, The Children's Hospital, Boston, USA.

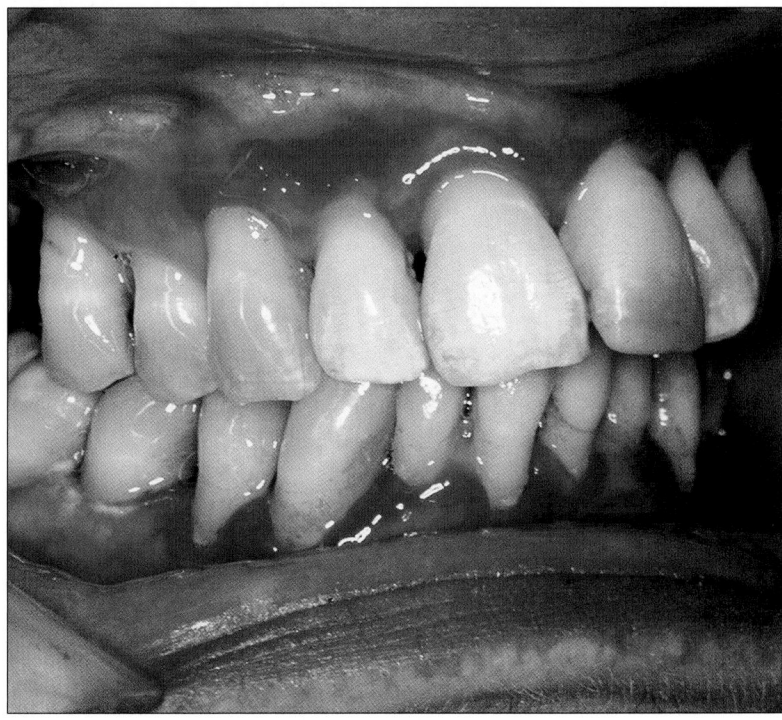

Fig. 3.64
Desquamative gingivitis: note the intense gingival erythema and retraction. Such features may also be seen in cicatricial pemphigoid and pemphigus. By courtesy of P. Morgan, FRCPath, London, UK.

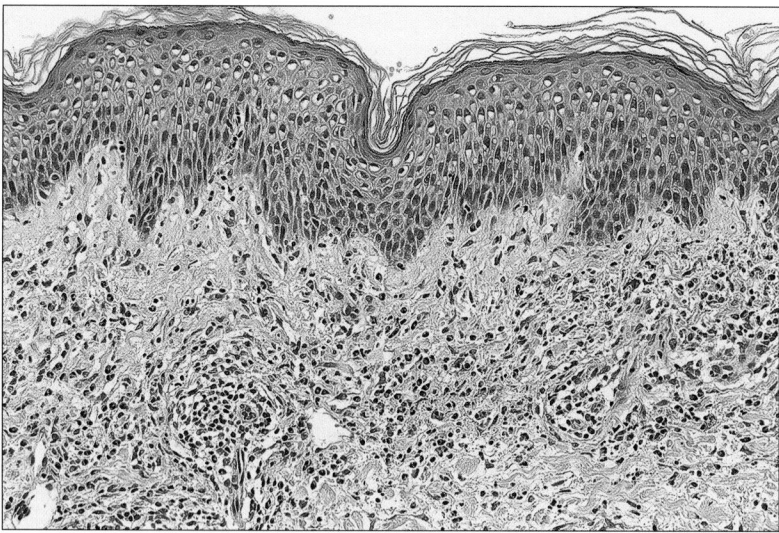

Fig. 3.65
Prebullous pemphigoid: there is upper dermal edema and a perivascular lymphohistiocytic infiltrate with conspicuous eosinophils.

Because inflammatory cells are sparse or, exceptionally, even absent in such cases, problems with the differential diagnosis may be considerable, particularly if adequate clinical information and immunofluorescence findings are not available.

Vesicular/polymorphic pemphigoid is characterized by subepidermal vesicles with features suggesting either bullous pemphigoid or dermatitis herpetiformis or both (*Fig. 3.73*). Neutrophil dermal papillary microabscesses, which are often regarded as pathognomonic of dermatitis herpetiformis, may be seen in this variant (*Fig. 3.74*).

Pemphigoid vegetans is characterized by acanthosis, often with pseudoepitheliomatous hyperplasia, papillary dermal edema with subepidermal clefting or frank vesicle formation and an inflammatory cell infiltrate of eosinophils, mononuclears and occasional neutrophils.

Pemphigoid nodularis exhibits pruriginous lesions which are characterized by hyperkeratosis, acanthosis, and which may amount to pseudoepitheliomatous hyperplasia and dermal fibrosis (*Fig. 3.75*). In the dermis a perivascular infiltrate of lymphocytes and eosinophils is present. The blisters show typical features of bullous pemphigoid (*Fig. 3.76*).

Localized non-scarring (pretibial) bullous pemphigoid usually shows the histology of cell-rich bullous pemphigoid. Localized oral

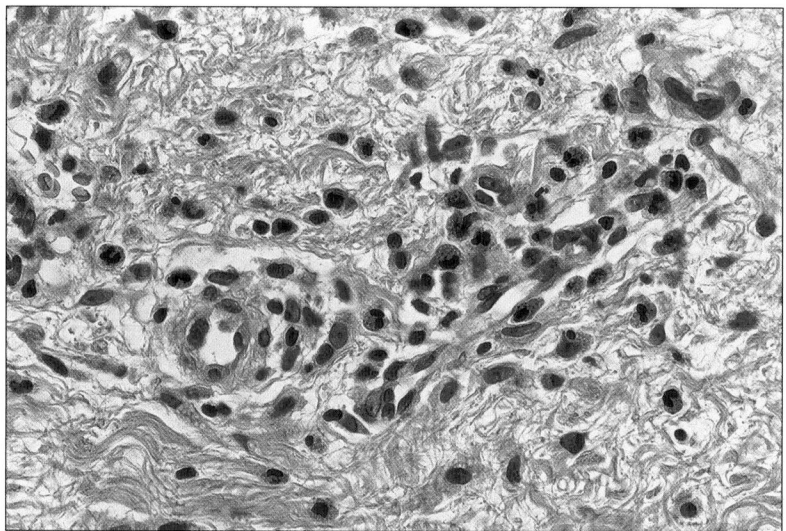

Fig. 3.66
Prebullous pemphigoid: there are numerous eosinophils.

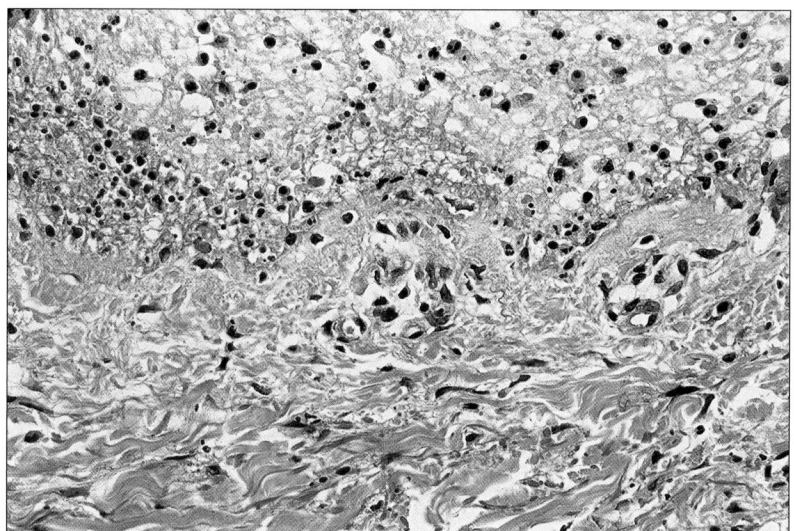

Fig. 3.68
BP: the blister cavity contains large numbers of eosinophils.

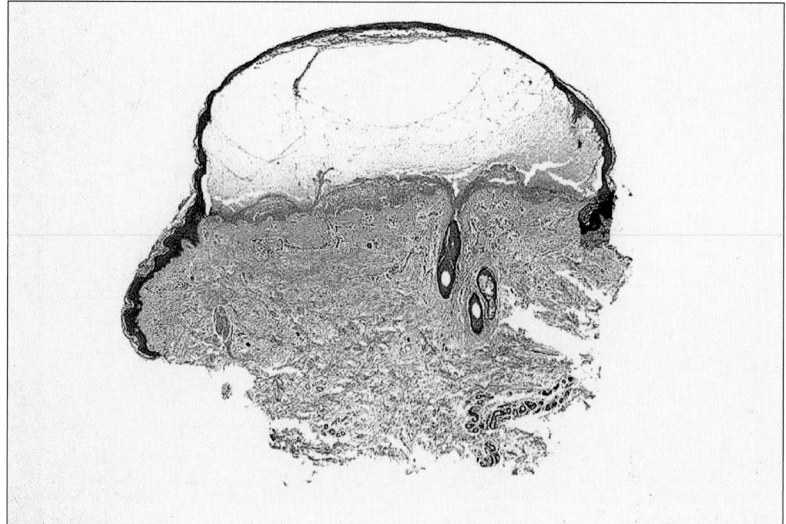

Fig. 3.67
BP: an established lesion showing a subepidermal tense, dome-shaped blister containing edema fluid, fibrin and inflammatory cells.

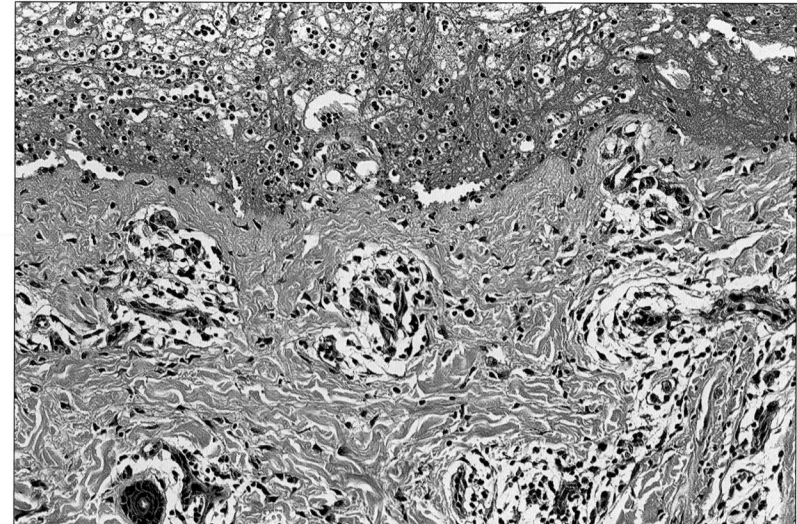

Fig. 3.69
BP: preservation of the dermal papillary outline (festooning) is a characteristic feature.

pemphigoid is typified by a subepithelial vesicle (when present) and cannot be distinguished histologically from oral involvement in cicatricial pemphigoid (see below).

Ultrastructurally, in early lesions of bullous pemphigoid, the dermoepidermal cleavage is seen to have developed between the plasma membrane of the basal keratinocyte and the lamina densa, through the lamina lucida.[60] The lamina densa is therefore located along the floor of the blister (*Figs 3.77, 3.78*). Degenerative changes in the basal cells, including villous process formation, mitochondrial swelling and cytoplasmic vacuolization, are frequently found. Hemidesmosomes may appear reduced in number or may even be absent.[61] Intercellular edema between adjacent basal cells is a common finding.[62] If specimens are examined from established inflammatory lesions the lamina densa may be fragmented or entirely absent.[42]

Bullous pemphigoid is characterized by a linear anti-basement membrane zone antibody using the indirect immunofluorescent technique.[63] Although IgG is invariably present (and most commonly of the IgG4 subclass), other immunoglobulins, including IgE, may be represented.[64]

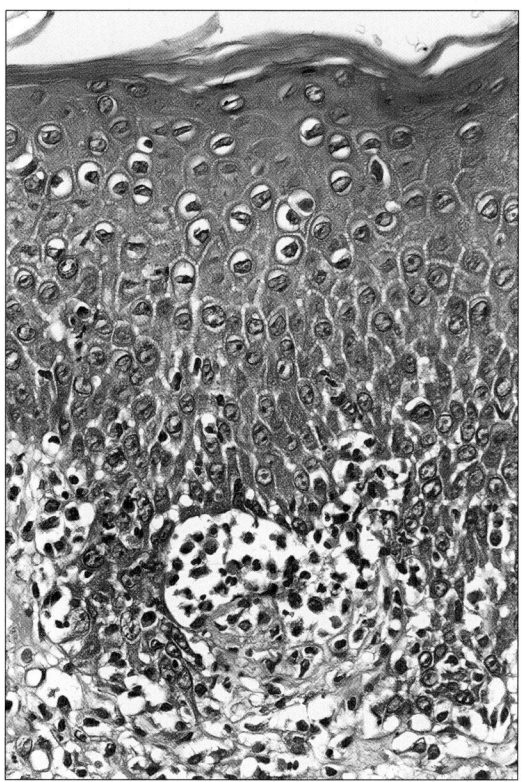

Fig. 3.70
BP: the presence of eosinophil microabscesses in the dermal papillae is a useful although rare diagnostic marker.

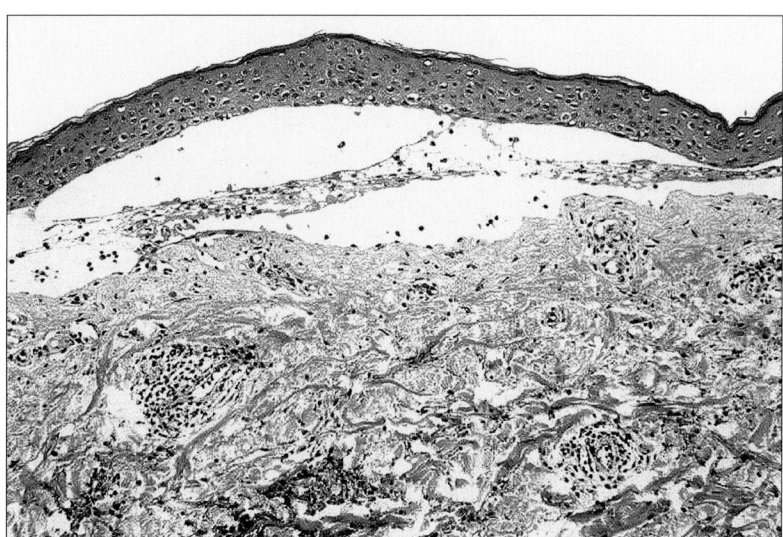

Fig. 3.72
Cell-poor pemphigoid: this is a very uncommon variant and is most often seen if a very early lesion is sampled. The blister contains only a little edema fluid and there is a light chronic inflammatory cell infiltrate in the superficial dermis.

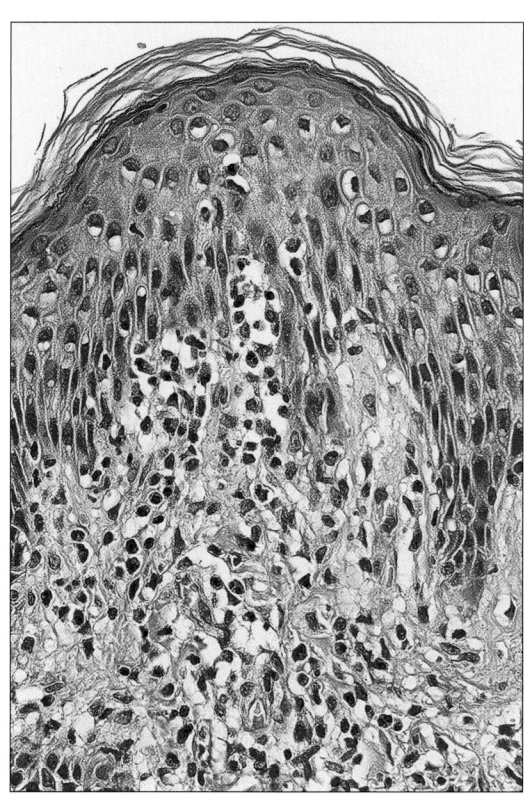

Fig. 3.71
BP: eosinophilic spongiosis is sometimes seen in the epidermis adjacent to the blister.

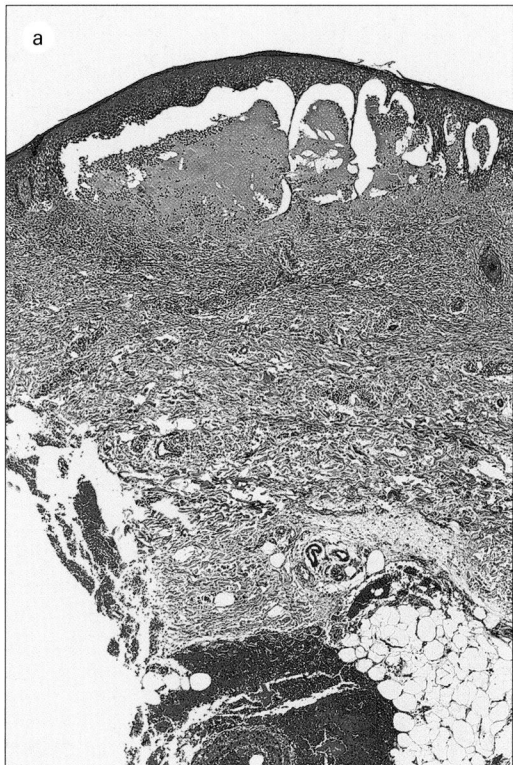
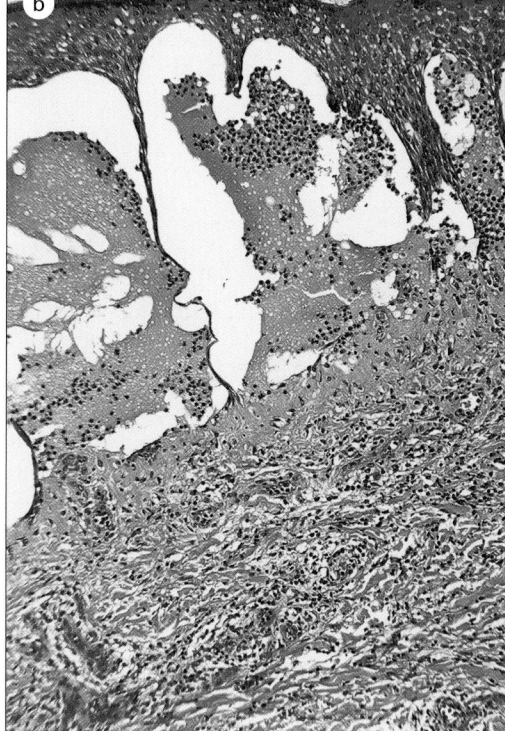

Fig. 3.73
Vesicular pemphigoid: (**a**) low power view showing a multilocular blister; (**b**) the blister contains a neutrophil rich infiltrate.

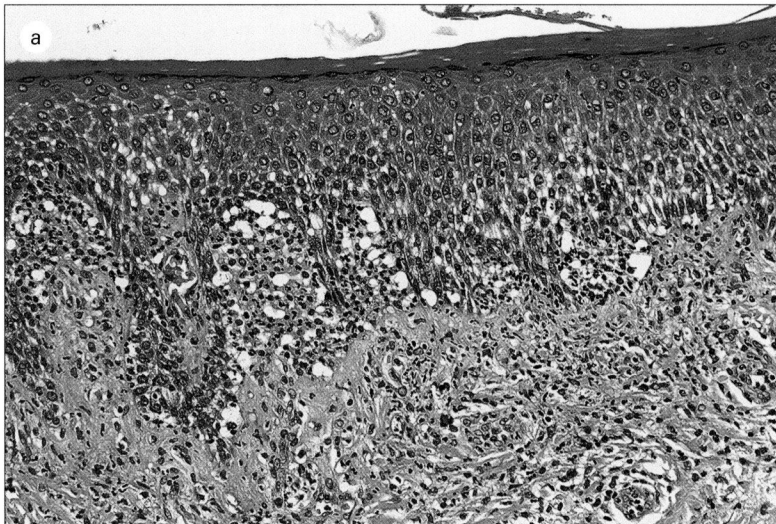

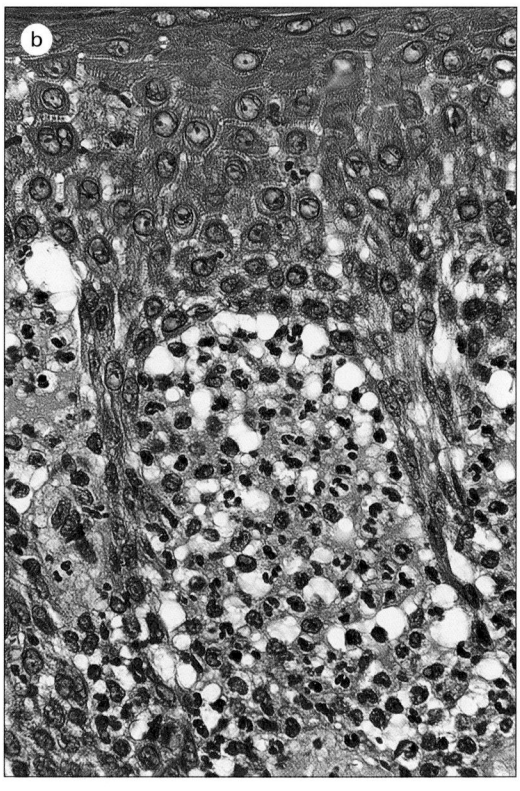

Fig. 3.74
(a, b) Vesicular pemphigoid: neutrophil microabscesses in the adjacent dermal papillae heighten the resemblance to dermatitis herpetiformis. It would be impossible to establish the diagnosis of bullous pemphigoid without appropriate immuno-fluorescent findings.

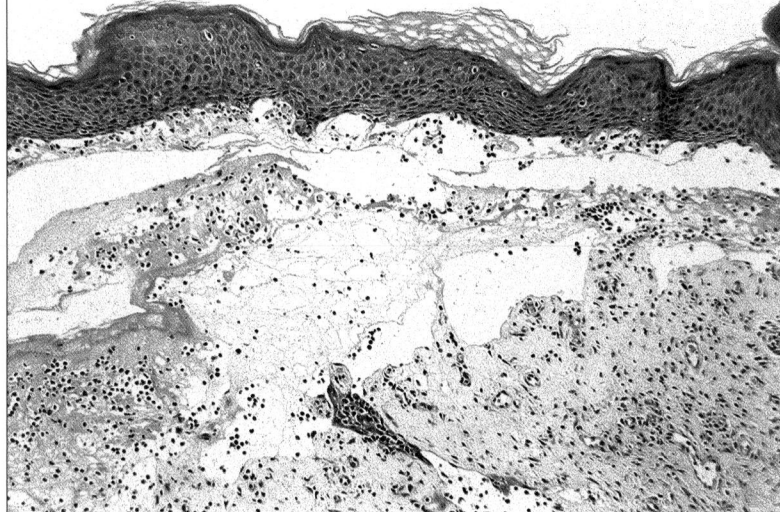

Fig. 3.75
Pemphigoid nodularis: this is a biopsy of a pruritic nodule showing hyperkeratosis, irregular acanthosis, dermal chronic inflammation and scarring.

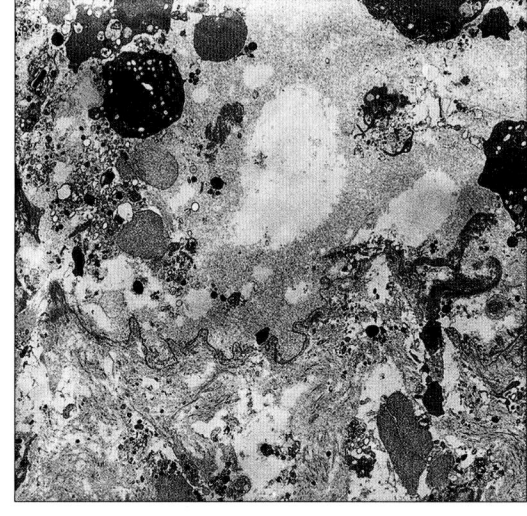

Fig. 3.77
BP: electron micrograph showing the lamina densa lying along the floor of the blister cavity.

Fig. 3.76
Pemphigoid nodularis: this subepidermal blister comes from the same patient as shown in *Fig. 3.75*. Pemphigoid nodularis is of particular importance because the nodular lesions may precede clinical evidence of blistering.

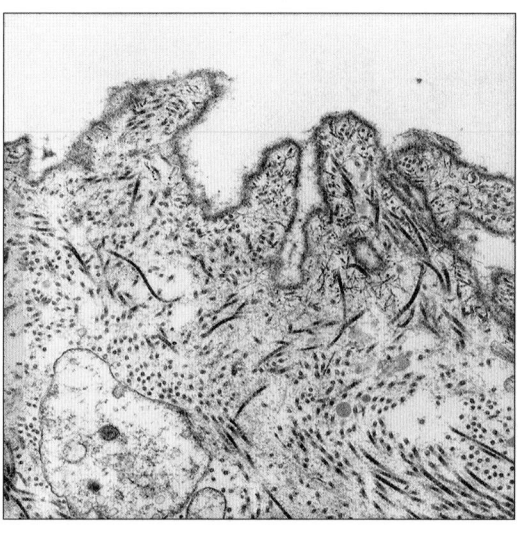

Fig. 3.78
BP: high power view of the lamina densa.

Such antibodies are present in around 75–80% of patients.[65–68] Sensitivity can however be increased to 90% if split skin is used as substrate.[18] Although the antibody titer does not correlate with disease activity, more recently it has been shown that serum antibodies to BP180 NC16A (a subunit of the bullous pemphigoid antigen) do correlate with disease activity (see below).

Split skin indirect studies are essential in the investigation of a patient in whom a linear IgG anti-basement membrane antibody has been detected.[69–71] Such antibodies are also characteristic of cicatricial pemphigoid, herpes (pemphigoid) gestationis, inflammatory epidermolysis bullosa and bullous systemic lupus erythematosus. The antibodies in pemphigoid variants (with the exception of the anti-p105 and anti-p200 variants discussed below) bind to the epidermal side of 1 M NaCl-split skin whereas those of inflammatory epidermolysis bullosa and bullous systemic lupus erythematosus bind to the floor.

In those patients in whom indirect fluorescent studies are not available, similar information may be obtained through the localization of lamina densa constituents such as type IV collagen or laminin-1 using paraffin-embedded direct immunoperoxidase techniques. In pemphigoid, the staining is found along the floor of the blister whereas in inflammatory epidermolysis bullosa and bullous systemic lupus erythematosus, it is located along the roof (see *Figs 3.7, 3.8*).

Bullous pemphigoid antibodies are capable of complement fixation in as many as 75% of patients.[72,73] Most of complement fixation in bullous pemphigoid antibody resides in the IgG4 subclass.[74]

Linear, in vivo-bound immunoglobulin at the epidermodermal interface on direct immunofluorescence is present in 90% or more of patients (*Fig. 3.79*).[18,75] Complement (C3) is also usually present and is sometimes the sole immunoreactants (*Fig. 3.80*).[76] Other immunoglobulin subclasses including IgM, IgA and IgE may be detected occasionally.[68,72] In addition to C3, the other components of the classical complement pathway, in particular C5b–9 (the membrane attack complex) and members of the alternative complement pathway, including properdin, factor B and B-1H-globulin, may also be identified.[68,77] There is therefore evidence that both the classical and alternate complement pathways are involved in the pathogenesis of bullous pemphigoid.[78] The classical complement pathway, however, predominates.

The immunofluorescence findings in erythematous, pruritic, urticarial and eczematous prodromal lesions and childhood, dyshidrosiform, vesicular, nodular and vegetans variants are similar to those seen in the conventional generalized disease.[22–24,28–43] In polymorphic pemphigoid

either linear IgG or IgA deposits may be identified along the basement membrane region.[25–27] The serum may contain either IgG or IgA antibodies.[26]

Immunofluorescence findings in localized cutaneous disease are variable. In some reports, patients show positive direct immunofluorescence for IgG and C3 at the epidermodermal junction and a positive indirect immunofluorescent test for bullous pemphigoid antibody, while others may be positive for in vivo-bound complement, but negative on indirect examination.[53,54,79] A recent series has shown that almost 70% of sera from patients with localized pemphigoid have circulating IgG antibodies.[53]

By direct immunoelectron microscopy, the immunoreactants (IgG and C3) are located within the hemidesmosomal plaque and upper lamina lucida (*Fig. 3.81*).[80–84] Indirect immunoelectron microscopic studies show that the bullous pemphigoid antigen is most often detected intracellularly in the region of the cytoplasmic face of the hemidesmosome (*Fig. 3.82*).[81,85–87]

The immunoelectron microscopic observations in childhood bullous pemphigoid, vesicular pemphigoid, polymorphic pemphigoid, pemphigoid nodularis, pemphigoid vegetans and localized pemphigoid, are identical to those of classical bullous pemphigoid.[88,89]

Two principal bullous pemphigoid antigens are recognized by western blot and immunoprecipitation studies: one is 230 kD (BPAG1) and the

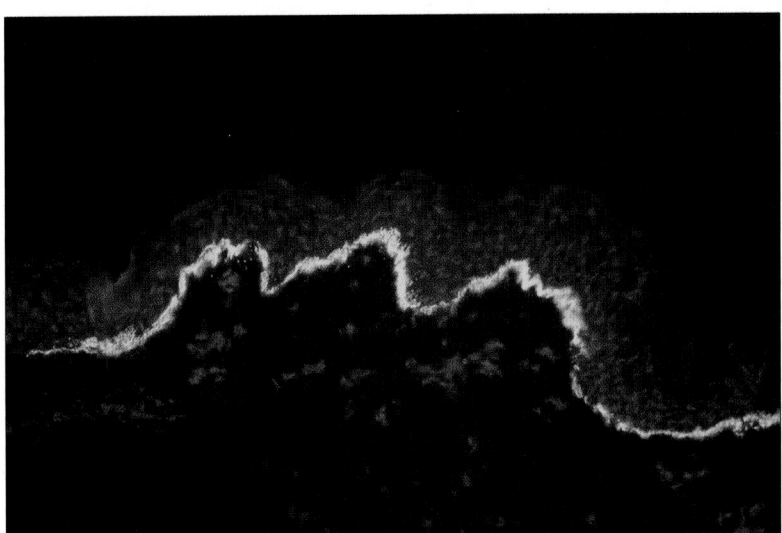

Fig. 3.80
BP: direct immunofluorescence showing C3 deposition. By courtesy of B. Boghal, FIMLS, Institute of Dermatology, London, UK.

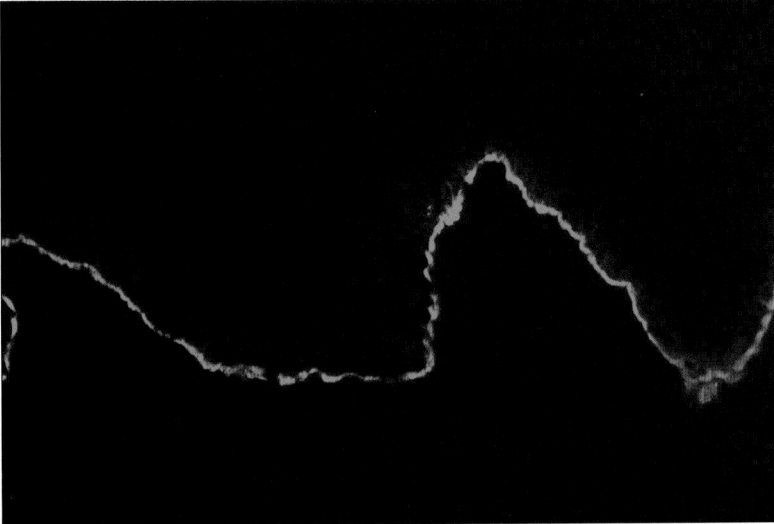

Fig. 3.79
BP: direct immunofluorescence of perilesional skin showing intense linear basement membrane zone staining (IgG).

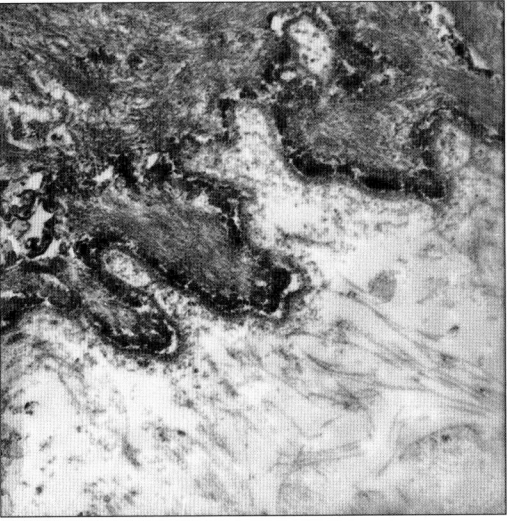

Fig. 3.81
BP: direct immunoperoxidase reaction using frozen tissue substrate showing electron-dense deposits in the lamina lucida.

other is approximately 180 kD (BPAG2) (*Fig. 3.83*).[90–96] These represent distinct gene products.[97–100]

BP230 maps to the short arm of chromosome 6, locus 6p11–12.[98] It belongs to the plakin family and shows homology with plectin and the desmogleins.[100] It is wholly intracellular and localizes to the hemidesmosome. BP230 is not involved in the early stages of the pathogenesis of blistering but is of importance as a secondary event.

BP180 is the major pathogenic antigen in bullous pemphigoid. It maps to the long arm of chromosome 10, locus 10q24.3.[99] It is a transmembrane adhesion molecule comprising an intracytoplasmic N-terminal fragment, a transmembrane region and a collagenous extracellular C-terminal ectodomain.[101] The latter constitutes part of the anchoring filament and distally merges with the lamina densa.

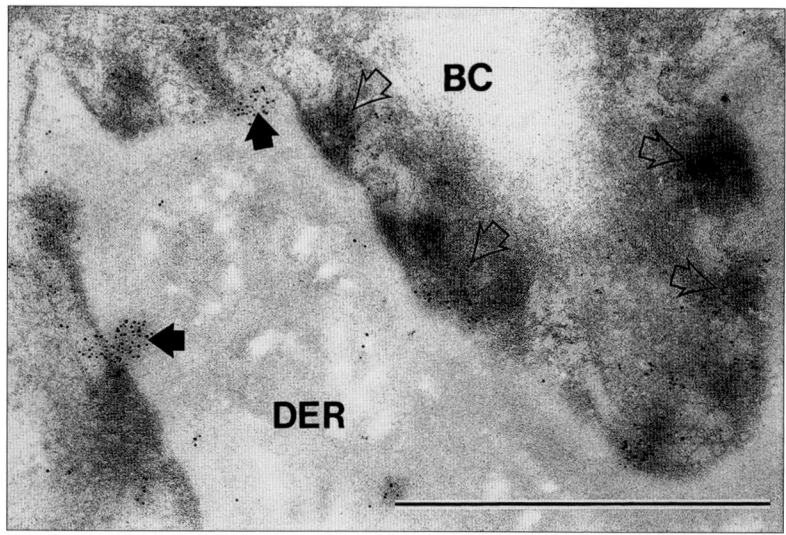

Fig. 3.82
BP: immunogold electron microscopic preparation. Note that the immunoreactant is particularly located on the hemidesmosomes (open arrows). However, deposit is also present within the lamina lucida. (BC, basal cell; DER, dermis.) By courtesy of H. Shimizu, MD, Keio University School of Medicine, Tokyo, Japan.

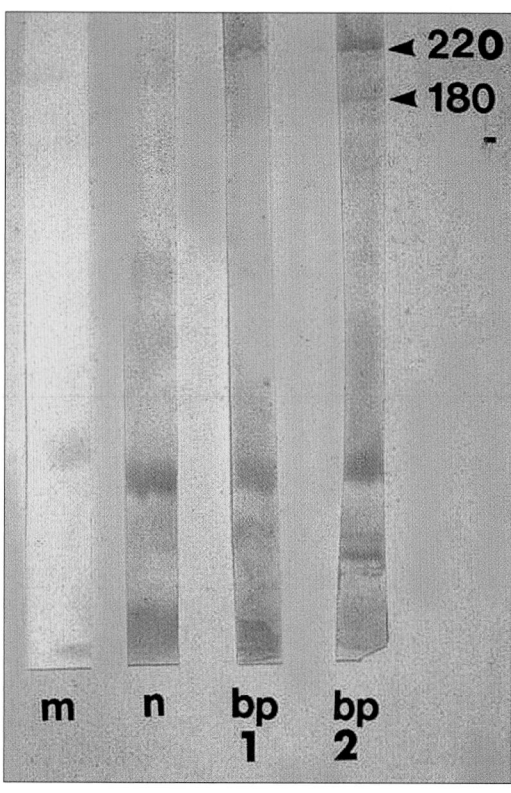

Fig. 3.83
BP: Western blot demonstrating the two quite separate bullous pemphigoid antigens. By courtesy of M.M. Black, MD, Institute of Dermatology, London, UK.

The antibodies directed against BP180 in bullous pemphigoid most commonly react with a short extracellular non-collagenous locus – NC16A (regions MCW0-MCW3) – located within the upper lamina lucida proximal to the collagenous segment (*Fig. 3.84*).[101–104] Antibodies, however, may also target BP180 non-NC16A domains.

Between 50 and 90% of patients with generalized bullous pemphigoid have antibodies that react with BP230 and 35–50% have antibodies that react with BP180.[105] If, however, patients' sera are reacted with a BP180 NC16A domain recombinant protein, the yield for the latter is 100%.[105]

Circulating antibodies against BP180 or BP230 have been also been defined in many of the other variants of bullous pemphigoid, including localized and vesicular forms, pemphigoid vegetans, erythrodermic pemphigoid and pemphigoid nodularis.[105–109]

In childhood pemphigoid, the antibodies also react against these same antigens.[110] In addition, there rarely may also be antibodies reacting with the linear IgA 120 kD antigen.[110] The BP180 antigen is most often targeted and immunoblot analyses have shown that the antibodies react specifically with the NC16A domain as in adult patients. In some children at least, the IgG subclasses differ from adult disease, consisting of all IgG subclasses or IgG2 in isolation.[18] IgE antibodies are not a feature of childhood disease.

More recently, two patients with a non-scarring, bullous pemphigoid-like illness characterized by neutrophil-rich subepidermal blisters resembling dermatitis herpetiformis and antibodies to a unique 105 kD protein – so-called anti-p105 pemphigoid – have been documented.[111–113] This antigen localizes to the dermal side of split skin on indirect immunofluorescence. Its precise nature has not yet been determined.

Anti-p200 pemphigoid is characterized by antibodies to a lower lamina lucida basement membrane antigen.[114,115] Patients generally present with a non-scarring bullous pemphigoid-like illness although linear IgA disease-like and dermatitis herpetiformis-like variants have also been documented.[114] The disease has also been described in association with psoriasis.[115] With split skin indirect IMF, the antibodies bind to the floor of the blister cavity.[114] With indirect immunoelectron microscopy, the antibodies bind to the lower lamina lucida.[116, 117] The identity of the 200 kD antigen has yet to be determined but it is neither laminin nor type VII collagen.[117]

Anti-p450 pemphigoid has been documented in a single patient. The antigen, which has been localized to the basal keratinocyte, belongs to the plectin family.[118] Its precise nature has yet to be determined.

Exceptionally bullous pemphigoid may be associated with antiplectin antibody.[119]

Bullous pemphigoid has been described following PUVA therapy for mycosis fungoides. This observation is discussed on page 1391.

A mechanism for blister development in bullous pemphigoid has been proposed by Jordon et al and is outlined as follows.[78,120] Following antibody–antigen interaction and complement fixation, various chemotactic agents including C3a and C4a are produced.[121] Mast cells degranulate under the influence of the latter or IgE, and release ECF-A, NMW-NCF, ESM, histamine and enzymes.[122] Eosinophils and neutrophils, so recruited, bind (possibly via C3b receptors) to the basement membrane region. By direct cytotoxic action (eosinophils are capable of antibody-dependent cellular cytotoxicity) or via released proteases, particularly elastase, damage at the basement membrane regions results in the development of a vesicle. Lymphocytes elaborate histamine-releasing factor (HRF), which increases mast cell degranulation and perpetuates the process. A broad range of cytokines are involved in this inflammatory reaction including interleukin (IL)-1, IL-4–IL-8, IL-10–IL-13, IL-15 and interferon gamma (IFN-γ).[123] As yet their relative importance and time sequences are unknown.

Bullous pemphigoid is therefore a true autoimmune disease in which antigen–antibody reaction and complement fixation results in a

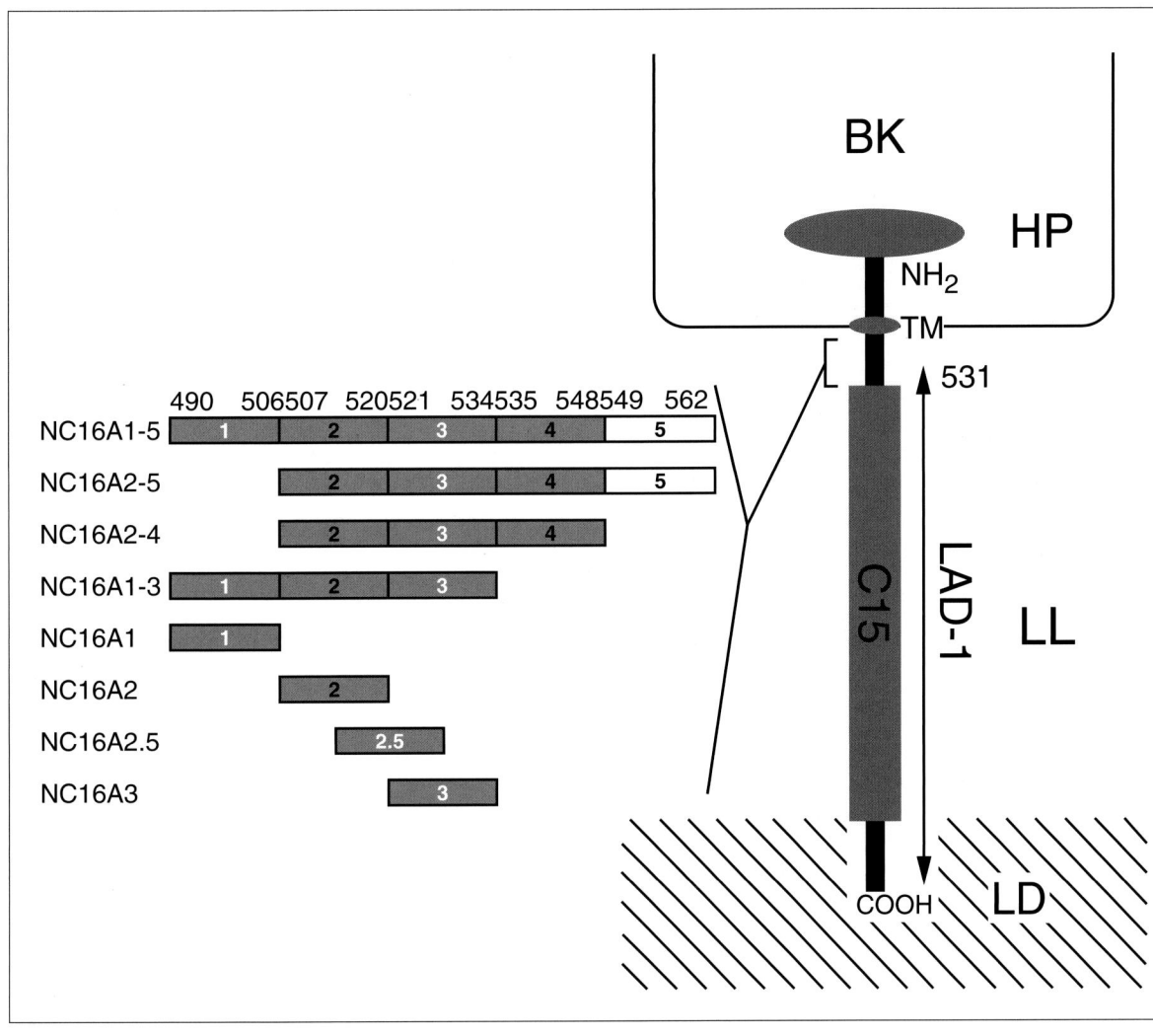

Fig. 3.84
BP: the NC16A domain. (BK, basal keratinocyte; C15, 15th collagenous domain of BP180; COOH, C-terminus; HP, hemidesmosomal plaque; LAD-1, soluble ectodomain of BP180; LD, lamina densa; LL, lamina lucida; NH$_2$, N-terminus; TM, transmembrane region; amino acid residue numbers are shown above the boxes.) By courtesy of D. Zillikens, MD, University of Wuerzburg, Germany. Reproduced with permission from Chimanovitch et al (2000) Archives of Dermatology, **136**, 527–532. Copyright © 2000 American Medical Association. All rights reserved.)

Table 3.4
Differential diagnosis of cell-rich pemphigoid

Parameter	BP	EBA	BSLE	LAD	DH
DIMF	Linear IgG, C3	Linear IgG, C3	Linear IgG, C3	Linear IgA	Granular IgA
IIMF	IgG antibodies 75–80%	IgG antibodies 25–50%	IgG antibodies 60%	IgA antibodies 30%	Antitransglutaminase antibodies
Split skin IMF	Roof	Floor	Floor	Roof or floor or both	N/A
Type IV collagen	Floor	Roof	Roof	Roof or floor	N/A
EM: site of split	LL	Sub-LD	Sub-LD	LL, sub-LD or both	Papillary dermis
Western blot	BP180 kD BP230 kD	290 kD (type VII collagen)	290 kD (type VII collagen)	BP180 kD BP230 kD 200/280 kD 285 kD 250 kD 290 kD	Antigen unknown

BP, bullous pemphigoid; BSLE, bullous systemic lupus erythematosus; DH, dermatitis herpetiformis; DIMF, direct immunofluorescence; EBA, epidermolysis bullosa acquisita; EM, electron microscopy; IIMF, indirect immunofluorescence; IMF, immunofluorescence; LAD, linear IgA disease; LL, lamina lucida; sub-LD, sub-lamina densa.

characteristic and reproducible train of events, which is inevitably accompanied by the development of subepidermal blister formation. The etiology or initiator (other than those associated with drugs or PUVA therapy, the minority) is unknown.

Differential diagnosis

The inflammatory cell-rich variant of bullous pemphigoid must be distinguished from other subepidermal blistering dermatoses in which a heavy inflammatory cell component is a typical finding. These include dermatitis herpetiformis, linear IgA disease, inflammatory epidermolysis bullosa acquisita and bullous systemic lupus erythematosus (*Table 3.4*). Successful differentiation depends upon careful clinicopathological correlation and immunofluorescent studies. Split skin indirect immunofluorescence or lamina densa antigen mapping by type IV collagen or laminin-1 direct immunoperoxidase are essential to determine the level of the split. Although electron microscopy, immunoelectron microscopy and immunoprecipitation or western blotting provide definitive information, in the majority of cases, such techniques are not necessary.

The cell-poor variant of bullous pemphigoid has a very wide range of differential diagnoses including epidermolysis bullosa (congenital and acquired), porphyria cutanea tarda, bullous amyloidosis, bullosa diabeticorum and autolysis.

References

1. Ahmed, A.R., Newcomer, V.D. (1987) Bullous pemphigoid: clinical features. *Clin Dermatol*, **5**, 6–12.
2. Korman, N.J. (1998) Bullous pemphigoid: the latest in diagnosis, prognosis and therapy. *Arch Dermatol*, **134**, 1137–1141.
3. Scott, J.E., Ahmed, A.R. (1998) The blistering diseases. *Med Clin North Am*, **82**, 1239–1283.
4. Cotell, S., Robinson, N.D., Chan, L.S. (2000) Autoimmune blistering skin diseases. *Am J Emerg Med*, **18**, 288–299.
5. Bernard, P., Vaillant, L., Labeille, B. et al (1995) Incidence and distribution of subepidermal autoimmune bullous skin disease in three French regions. *Arch Dermatol*, **31**, 48–52.
6. Zillikens, D., Wever, S., Roth, A. et al (1995) Incidence of autoimmune subepidermal blistering diseases in a region of central Germany. *Arch Dermatol*, **131**, 957–958.
7. Marsden, R.A., McKee, P.H., Bhogal, B. et al (1980) A study of chronic bullous dermatosis of childhood and comparison with dermatitis herpetiformis and bullous pemphigoid. *Clin Exp Dermatol*, **5**, 159–172.
8. Nemeth, A.J., Klein, A.D., Gould, E.W. et al (1991) Childhood bullous pemphigoid. Clinical and immunologic features, treatment and prognosis. *Arch Dermatol*, **127**, 378–386.
9. Asbrink, E., Hovmark, A. (1981) Clinical variations in bullous pemphigoid with respect to early symptoms. *Acta Derm Venereol*, **61**, 417–421.
10. Amato, D.A., Silverstein, J., Zitelli, J. (1988) The prodrome of bullous pemphigoid. *Int J Dermatol*, **27**, 560–563.
11. Korman, N.J., Woods, S.G. (1995) Erythrodermic pemphigoid is a clinical variant of bullous pemphigoid. *Br J Dermatol*, **133**, 967–971.
12. Amato, L., Gallerani, I., Mei, S. et al (2001) Erythrodermic bullous pemphigoid. *Int J Dermatol*, **20**, 343–348.
13. Alonso-Llamazares, J., Rogers, R.S. III, Oursler, J.R. et al (1998) Bullous pemphigoid presenting as generalized pruritus: observations in six patients. *Int J Dermatol*, **37**, 508–514.
14. Liu, H.H., Daniel Su, W.P., Rogers, R.S. (1986) Clinical variants of pemphigoid. *Int J Dermatol*, **25**, 17–27.
15. Trattner, A., Hodak, E., Ingber, A. et al (1989) 'Jewel-like' blisters in bullous pemphigoid. *J Am Acad Dermatol*, **21**, 583–584.
16. Venning, V.A., Frith, P.A., Bron, A.J. et al (1988) Mucosal involvement in bullous pemphigoid. A clinical and immunopathological study. *Br J Dermatol*, **118**, 7–15.
17. Faith, D.A., Venning, V.A., Wojnarowska, F. et al (1989) Conjunctival involvement in cicatricial and bullous pemphigoid: a clinical and immunopathological study. *Br J Ophthalmol*, **73**, 52–56.
18. Kippes, W., Schmidt, E., Roth, A. et al (1999) Immunopathological changes in 115 patients with bullous pemphigoid. *Hautarzt*, **50**, 866–872.
19. Schroeter, A.L. (1987) Pemphigoid and malignancy. *Clin Dermatol*, **5**, 60–63.
20. Lindelöf, B., Islam, N., Eklund, G. et al (1990) Pemphigoid and cancer. *Arch Dermatol*, **126**, 66–68.
21. Hodge, L., Marsden, R., Black, M.M. et al (1982) Bullous pemphigoid: the frequency of mucosal involvement and concurrent malignancy related to indirect immunofluorescence findings. *Br J Dermatol*, **105**, 65–69.
22. Bean, S.F., Michel, B., Furey, N. et al (1976) Vesicular pemphigoid. *Arch Dermatol*, **112**, 1402–1404.
23. Gruber, G.G., Owen, L.G., Callen, J.P. (1980) Vesicular pemphigoid. *J Am Acad Dermatol*, **3**, 619–622.
24. Requena, L., Vázquez, F., Sánchez Yus, E. (1991) Vesicular pemphigoid. *Cutis*, **47**, 333–336.
25. Honeyman, J.F., Honeyman, A.R., de la Parra, M.A. et al (1979) Polymorphic pemphigoid. *Arch Dermatol*, **115**, 423–427.
26. Bernard, P. (1989) Polymorphic pemphigoid: is it still worth using this terminology? *Dermatologica*, **178**, 181–183.
27. Tamaki, K., Furuya, T., Kubota, Y. et al (1991) Seborrheic pemphigoid and polymorphic pemphigoid. *J Am Acad Dermatol*, **25**, 568–570.
28. Winkelmann, R.K., Daniel Su, W.P. (1979) Pemphigoid vegetans. *Arch Dermatol*, **115**, 446–448.
29. Kuokkanen, K., Helin, H. (1981) Pemphigoid vegetans. *Arch Dermatol*, **117**, 56–57.
30. Al-Najjar, A., Reilly, G.D., Bleehen, S.S. (1984) Pemphigoid vegetans: report of a case. *Acta Derm Venereol*, **64**, 450–452.
31. Ueda, J., Otuka, F., Ishibashi, Y. et al (1986) A case of pemphigoid vegetans. *Jpn J Dermatol*, **95**, 527.
32. Chan, L.S., Dorman, M.A., Agha, A. et al (1993) Pemphigoid vegetans represents a bullous pemphigoid variant. Patient's IgG autoantibodies identify the major bullous pemphigoid antigen. *J Am Acad Dermatol*, **28**, 331–335.
33. Ogasawara, M., Matsuda, S., Nishioka, K. et al (1994) Pemphigoid vegetans. *J Am Acad Dermatol*, **30**, 649–650.
34. Delpuget-Bertin, N., Bernard, Ph., Bedane, C. et al (1997) Pemphigoid vegetans: immuno-electron microscopic study. *Ann Dermatol Venereol*, **124**, 467–469.
35. Yung, C.W., Soltani, K., Lorinez, A.L. (1981) Pemphigoid nodularis. *J Am Acad Dermatol*, **5**, 54–50.
36. Ross, J.S., Smith, N.P., Black, M.M. et al (1990) Pemphigoid nodularis: a study of 3 cases. *J Cutan Pathol*, **17**, 315–318.
37. Cliff, S., Holden, C.A. (1997) Pemphigoid nodularis: a report of three cases and review of the literature. *Br J Dermatol*, **136**, 398–401.
38. Levine, N., Freilich, A., Barland, P. (1979) Localized pemphigoid simulating dyshidrosiform dermatitis. *Arch Dermatol*, **115**, 320–321.
39. Rongioletti, F., Parodi, A., Rebora, A. (1985) Dyshidrosiform pemphigoid: report of an additional case. *Dermatologica*, **170**, 84–85.
40. Levine, N., Freilich, A., Barland, P. (1979) Localized pemphigoid simulating dyshidrosiform dermatitis. *Arch Dermatol*, **115**, 320–321.
41. Mohr, C., Duschet, P., Bonsmann, G. et al (1993) Dyshidrosiform bullous pemphigoid. *Hautarzt*, **44**, 785–788.
42. Radloff, P., Vieluf, D., Mensing, H. et al (1994) Initial manifestation of bullous pemphigoid simulating dyshidrosis palmoplantaris. *Hautarzt*, **45**, 97–99.
43. Scola, F., Telang, G.H., Schwartz, C. (1995) Dyshidrosiform pemphigoid. *J Am Acad Dermatol*, **32**, 516–517.
44. Guenther, L.C., Shum, D. (1990) Localized childhood vulvar pemphigoid. *J Am Acad Dermatol*, **22**, 762–764.
45. Nemeth, A.J., Klein, A.D., Gould, E.W. et al (1991) Childhood bullous pemphigoid. *Arch Dermatol*, **127**, 378–386.
46. Saad, R.W., Domloge-Hultsch, N., Yancey, K.B. et al (1992) Childhood localized vulvar pemphigoid is a true variant of bullous pemphigoid. *Arch Dermatol*, **128**, 807–810.
47. Rabinowitz, L.G., Esterly, N.B. (1993) Inflammatory bullous diseases in children. *Dermatol Clin*, **11**, 565–581.
48. Amos, B., Deng, J-S., Flynn, K. et al (1998) Bullous pemphigoid in infancy: case report and literature review. *Pediatr Dermatol*, **15**, 108–111.
49. Trüeb, R.M., Didierjean, L., Fellas, A. et al (1999) Childhood bullous pemphigoid: report of a case with characterization of the targeted antigens. *J Am Acad Dermatol*, **40**, 338–344.
50. Chimanovitch, I., Hamm, H., Georgi, M. et al (2000) Bullous pemphigoid of childhood: autoantibodies target the same epitopes within the NC16A domain of BP180 as autoantibodies in bullous pemphigoid of adulthood. *Arch Dermatol*, **136**, 527–532.
51. Fisler, R.E., Saeb, M., Liang, M.G. et al (2003) Childhood bullous pemphigoid: a clinicopathological study and review of the literature. *Am J Dermatopathol*, **25**, 183–189.
52. Person, J.A., Rogers, R.S., Perry, H.D. (1976) Localized pemphigoid. *Br J Dermatol*, **95**, 531–534.
53. Salomon, R.G., Briggaman, R.A., Wernikoff, S.Y. et al (1987) Localized bullous pemphigoid. *Arch Dermatol*, **123**, 389–392.
54. Kaplan, R.P. (1987) Cutaneous involvement in localized forms of bullous pemphigoid. *Clin Dermatol*, **5**, 43–51.
55. Rogers, R.S., Sheridan, P.J., Nightingale, S.H. (1982) Desquamative gingivitis: clinical, histopathologic, immunopathologic and therapeutic observations. *J Am Acad Dermatol*, **7**, 729–735.
56. McCarthy, P.L., Shklar, G. (1980) Diseases of the oral mucosa, 2nd edn. Philadelphia: Lea & Febiger, pp 306–318.
57. Scully, C., Porter, S.R. (1997) The clinical spectrum of desquamative gingivitis. *Semin Cutan Med Surg*, **16**, 308–313.
58. Lever, W.F. (1951) Pemphigus: a histopathologic study. *Arch Dermatol*, **64**, 727–753.
59. Crotty, C., Pittelkow, M., Muller, S.A. (1983) Eosinophilic spongiosis: a clinicopathological review of seventy-one cases. *J Am Acad Dermatol*, **8**, 337–343.
60. Rodrigo, F.G. (1973) Ultrastructural aspects of pemphigoid. *Br J Dermatol*, **88**, 143–149.
61. Giannotti, B., Fabbri, P., Panconesi, E. (1975) Ultrastructural finding in bullous pemphigoid. *J Cutan Pathol*, **2**,103–108.
62. Schaumburg-Lever, G., Orfanos, C.E., Lever, W.F. (1972) Electron microscopic study of bullous pemphigoid. *Arch Dermatol*, **106**, 662–667.
63. Jordan, R.E., Beutner, E.H., Whitebsky, E. et al (1967) Basement zone antibodies in bullous pemphigoid. *JAMA*, **200**, 91–96.
64. Korman, N. (1987) Bullous pemphigoid. *J Am Acad Dermatol*, **16**, 907–924.
65. Tuffanelli, D.L. (1975) Cutaneous immunopathology: recent observations. *J Invest Dermatol*, **65**, 143–153.
66. Ahmed, A.R., Maize, J.C., Provost, T.T. (1977) Bullous pemphigoid: clinical and immunological follow up after successful therapy. *Arch Dermatol*, **113**, 1043–1046.
67. Anhalt, G.J., Patel, H. (1983) Mechanisms of immunologic injury: pemphigus and bullous pemphigoid. *Arch Dermatol*, **119**, 711–713.
68. Imber, M.J., Murphy, G.F., Jordon, R.E. (1987) The immunopathology of bullous pemphigoid. *Clin Dermatol*, **5**, 81–92.
69. Willsteed, E.M., Bhogal, B.S., Das, A. (1991) An ultrastructural comparison of dermo-epidermal separation techniques. *J Cutan Pathol*, **18**, 8–12.
70. Gammon, W.R., Briggaman, R.A., Inman, A.O. et al (1984) Differentiating anti-lamina lucida and anti-sublamina densa anti-BMZ antibodies by indirect immunofluorescence on 1.0 m sodium chloride-separated skin. *J Invest Dermatol*, **82**, 139–144.
71. Vaillant, L., Bernard, P., Joly, P. et al (1998) Evaluation of clinical criteria for diagnosis of bullous pemphigoid. *Arch Dermatol*, **134**, 1075–1080.
72. Provost, T.T., Tomasi, T.B. (1974) Immunopathology of bullous pemphigoid: basement membrane deposition of IgE, alternative pathway components and fibrin. *Clin Exp Immunol*, **18**, 193–200.
73. Suzuki, M., Watanabe, C., Yaoita, H. (1989) The complement fixing ability of anti-basement membrane zone IgG subclass antibodies of herpes gestationis and bullous pemphigoid. *Acta Derm Venereol*, **69**, 6–11.
74. Bird, P., Friedman, P.S., Ling, N. et al (1986) Subclass distribution of IgG autoantibodies in bullous pemphigoid. *J Invest Dermatol*, **86**, 21–25.
75. Beutner, E.H., Jordon, R.E., Chorzelski, T.P. (1968) The immunopathology of pemphigus and pemphigoid. *J Invest Dermatol*, **51**, 63–80.
76. Lever, W.F. (1979) Pemphigus and pemphigoid. *J Am Acad Dermatol*, **1**, 2–31.
77. Dahl, M.V., Falk, R.J., Carpenter, R. (1984) Deposition of the membrane attack complex of complement in bullous pemphigoid. *J Invest Dermatol*, **82**, 132–135.
78. Jordon, R.E., Kawana, S., Fritz, K.A. (1985) Immunopathologic mechanisms in pemphigus and bullous pemphigoid. *J Invest Dermatol*, **85**, 72S–78S.
79. Sparrow, G.P., Moynahan, E.J. (1976) Localized pemphigoid. *Br J Dermatol*, **95** (Suppl.), 26–28.
80. Schaumburg-Lever, G., Rule, A., Schmidt-Ullrich, B. et al (1975) Ultrastructural localisation of *in vivo* bound immunoglobulins in bullous pemphigoid: a preliminary report. *J Invest Dermatol*, **64**, 47–49.
81. Holubar, K., Wolff, K., Konrad, K. (1975) Ultrastructural localization of immunoglobulins in bullous pemphigoid skin: employment of a new peroxidase anti-peroxidase multi-step method. *J Invest Dermatol*, **64**, 220–227.
82. Schmidt-Ullrich, B., Rule, A., Schaumburg-Lever, G. et al (1975) Ultrastructural localization of *in vivo* bound complement in bullous pemphigoid. *J Invest Dermatol*, **65**, 217–219.
83. Westgate, G.E., Weaver, A.C., Couchman, J.R. (1985) Bullous pemphigoid antigen localisation suggests an intracellular association with hemidesmosomes. *J Invest Dermatol*, **84**, 218–224.
84. Mutasim, D.F., Anhalt, G.J., Diaz, L.A. et al (1987) Linear immunofluorescence staining of the cutaneous basement membrane zone produced by pemphigoid antibodies; the result of hemidesmosome staining. *J Invest Dermatol*, **16**, 75–82.
85. Mutasim, D.F., Takahashi, Y., Labib, R.S. et al (1985) A pool of bullous pemphigoid antigen(s) is intracellular and associated with the basal cell cytoskeleton–hemidesmosome complex. *J Invest Dermatol*, **84**, 47–53.
86. Horiguchi, Y., Imamura, S. (1986) Discrepancy between the localization of *in vivo* bound immunoglobulins in the skin and *in vitro* binding sites of circulating anti-BMZ antibodies in bullous pemphigoid: immunoelectron microscopic studies. *J Invest Dermatol*, **87**, 715–719.
87. Shimizu, H., Hayakawa, K., Nishikawa, T. (1988) A comparative immunoelectron microscopic study of typical and atypical cases of pemphigoid. *Br J Dermatol*, **119**, 717–722.
88. Tani, M., Tani, M., Komura, A. et al (1988) Bullous pemphigoid of childhood: report of a case and immunoelectron microscopic studies. *J Am Acad Dermatol*, **19**, 366–367.
89. Hayakawa, K., Shimizu, H., Amagai, M. et al (1989) Vesicular pemphigoid – ultrastructural and immunoelectron microscopic study. *Dermatologica*, **178**, 213–216.
90. Stanley, J.R., Hawley-Nelson, P., Yuga, S.H. et al (1981) Characterization of bullous pemphigoid antigen: a unique basement membrane protein of stratified squamous epithelia. *Cell*, **24**, 897–903.
91. Stanley, J.R., Woodley, D.T., Katz, S.I. (1984) Identification and partial characterization of pemphigoid antigen extracted from normal human skin. *J Invest Dermatol*, **82**, 108–111.
92. Labib, R.S., Anhalt, G.J., Patel, H.P. et al (1986) Molecular heterogeneity of the bullous pemphigoid antigens as detected by immunoblotting. *J Immunol*, **136**, 1231–1235.
93. Muramatsu, T., IIda, S.T., Yamashina, Y. et al (1988) Antigen specificities of anti-basement membrane zone antibodies: immunofluorescence and Western immunoblotting studies. *Arch Dermatol Res*, **280**, 411–415.
94. Bernard, P., Didierjean, L., Denis, F. et al (1989) Heterogeneous bullous pemphigoid antibodies: detection and characterization by immunoblotting when absent by indirect immunofluorescence. *J Invest Dermatol*, **92**, 171–174.
95. Muellar, S., Klaus-Kovtun, V.S., Stanley, J.R. (1989) A 230-kD basic protein is the major bullous pemphigoid antigen. *J Invest Dermatol*, **92**, 33–38.
96. Cook, A.L., Hanahoe, T.H.P., Mallett, R.B. et al (1990) Recognition of two distinct major antigens by bullous pemphigoid sera. *Br J Dermatol*, **122**, 435–444.
97. Robledo, M.A., Kim, S.C., Korman, N.J. et al (1990) Studies on the relationship of the 230-kD and 180-kD bullous pemphigoid antigens. *J Invest Dermatol*, **94**, 793–797.
98. Sawamura, D., Nomura, K., Sugita, Y. et al (1990) Bullous pemphigoid antigen (BGAG1): cDNA cloning and mapping of the gene to the short arm of human chromosome 6. *Genomics*, **8**, 722–726.
99. Li, K., Sawamura, D., Giudice, G.J. et al (1991) Genomic organization of collagenous domains and chromosomal assignment of human 180-kD bullous pemphigoid antigen-2, a novel collagen of stratified squamous epithelium. *J Biol Chem*, **266**, 24064–24069.
100. Sawamura, D., Li, K.H., Nomura, K. et al (1991) Bullous pemphigoid antigen: cDNA cloning, cellular expression, and evidence for polymorphism of the human gene. *J Invest Dermatol*, **96**, 908–915.
101. Zillikens, D., Giudice, G.J. (1999) BP180/type XVII collagen: its role in acquired and inherited disorders of the dermal–epidermal junction. *Arch Dermatol Res*, **291**, 187–194.
102. Zillikens, D., Rose, P.A., Balding, S.D. et al (1997) Tight clustering of extracellular BP180 epitopes recognized by bullous pemphigoid antibodies. *J Invest Dermatol*, **109**, 573–579.
103. Matsumura, K., Amagai, M., Nishikawa, T. et al (1996) The majority of bullous pemphigoid and herpes gestationis serum samples react with the NC 16A domain of the 180-kDa bullous pemphigoid antigen. *Arch Dermatol Res*, **288**, 507–509.

104. Nakatani, C., Muramatsu, T., Shirai, T. (1998) Immunoreactivity of bullous pemphigoid (BP) autoantibodies against the NC 16A and C-terminal domains of the 180 kDa BP antigen: immunoblot analysis and enzyme-linked immunosorbent assay using BP 180 recombinant proteins. *Br J Dermatol*, **139**, 365–370.

105. Kawahara, Y., Matsumura, K., Hashimoto, T. et al (1997) Immunoblot analysis of autoantigens in localized pemphigoid and pemphigoid nodularis. *Acta Derm Venereol*, **77**, 187–190.

106. Soh, H., Hosokawa, H., Miyauchi, H. et al (1991) Localized pemphigoid shares the same target antigen as bullous pemphigoid. *Br J Dermatol*, **125**, 73–75.

107. Domloge-Hultsch, N., Utecht, L., James, W. et al (1990) Autoantibodies from patients with localized and generalized bullous pemphigoid immunoprecipitate the same 230-kD keratinocyte antigen. *Arch Dermatol*, **126**, 1337–1341.

108. Fujisawa, H., Ishii, Y., Tateishi, T. et al (2000) Pemphigoid nodularis with IgA autoantibodies against the intracellular domain of desmoglein I. *Br J Dermatol*, **142**, 143–147.

109. Schachter, M., Brieva, J.C., Jones, C.R.J. et al (2001) Pemphigoid nodularis associated with autoantibodies to the NC16A domain of BP180 and a hyperproliferative integrin profile. *J Am Acad Dermatol*, **45**, 747–754.

110. Arechalde, A., Braun, R.P., Calza, A.M. et al (1999) Childhood bullous pemphigoid associated with IgA antibodies against BP180 or BP230 antigens. *Br J Dermatol*, **140**, 112–118.

111. Chan, L.S., Fine, J-D., Briggaman, R.A. et al (1993) Identification and partial characterization of a novel 105-kDalton lower lamina lucida autoantigen associated with a novel immune-mediated subepidermal blistering disease. *J Invest Dermatol*, **101**, 262–267.

112. Cotell, S.L., Lapiere, J.C., Chen, J.D. et al (1994) A novel 105-kDa lamina lucida autoantigen: association with bullous pemphigoid. *J Invest Dermatol*, **103**, 78–83.

113. Chan, L.S., Woodley, D.T. (1996) The 105-kDa basement membrane autoantigen p105 is N-terminally homologous to a tumor-associated antigen. *J Invest Dermatol*, **107**, 209–214.

114. Schmidt, E., Zillikens, D. (2000) Autoimmune and inherited subepidermal blistering diseases: advances in the clinic and the laboratory. *Adv Dermatol*, **16**, 113–157.

115. Zillikens, D. (1999) Acquired skin diseases of hemidesmosomes. *J Dermatol Sci*, **20**, 134–154.

116. Zillikens, D., Kawahara, Y., Ishiko, A. et al (1996) A novel subepidermal blistering disease with autoantibodies to a 200-kDa antigen of the basement membrane zone. *J Invest Dermatol*, **106**, 1333–1338.

117. Zillikens, D., Ishiko, A., Jonkman, M.F. et al (2000) Autoantibodies in anti-p200 pemphigoid stain skin lacking laminin 5 and type VII collagen. *Br J Dermatol*, **143**, 1043–1049.

118. Fugiwara, S., Kohno, K., Iwamatsu, A. et al (1996) Identification of a 450-kDa human epidermal autoantigen as a new member of the plectin family. *J Invest Dermatol*, **106**, 1125–1130.

119. Laffitte, E., Favre, B., Fontao, L. et al (2001) Plectin, an unusual target antigen in bullous pemphigoid. *Br J Dermatol*, **144**, 136–138.

120. Liu, Z., Giudice, G.J., Swartz, S.J. et al (1995) The role of complement in experimental bullous pemphigoid. *J Clin Invest*, **95**, 1539–1544.

121. Wintroub, B.U., Mihm, M.C. Jr, Goetzl, E.J. et al (1978) Morphologic and functional evidence for release of mast-cell products in bullous pemphigoid. *N Engl J Med*, **298**, 417–421.

122. Dvorak, A.M., Mihm, M.C. Jr, Osage, J.E. et al (1982) Bullous pemphigoid, an ultrastructural study of the inflammatory response: eosinophil, basophil and mast cell granule changes in multiple biopsies from one patient. *J Invest Dermatol*, **78**, 91–101.

123. D'Auria, L., Fei, P.C., Ameglio, F. (1999) Cytokines and bullous pemphigoid. *Eur Cytokine Netw*, **10**, 123–133.

Pemphigoid gestationis

Pruritus is a very common symptom in pregnancy, occurring in up to 18% of gravid females.[1–4] When it occurs in the absence of significant cutaneous stigmata it is known as pruritus gravidarum. This may occasionally be associated with a cholestatic pathogenesis. The specific pregnancy eruptions have long been a source of considerable confusion and controversy in the literature, largely due to a diverse range of terminologies and classifications. Recently Holmes has attempted to clarify the situation with the introduction of a new and much simplified classification.[2] Therefore the specific dermatoses of pregnancy may be divided into:

- polymorphic eruption of pregnancy, where the predominant lesions are urticarial; in the United States, the term pruritic urticarial papules and plaques of pregnancy (PUPPP) has achieved greater popularity (see p. 114)
- pregnancy prurigo in which the lesions consist of itchy papules (see p. 114)
- pemphigoid (herpes) gestationis, an autoimmune dermatosis belonging to the bullous pemphigoid group of diseases.

Pemphigoid gestationis is a bullous dermatosis of pregnancy and the puerperium. It may be exacerbated by the use of oral contraceptives and rarely complicates hydatidiform mole and gestational (but not non-gestational) choriocarcinoma. The current evidence implicates an autoimmune-mediated pathogenesis in which hormonal influences play a significant role.

Clinical features

The term herpes (gestationis) is neither appropriate nor satisfactory. It is not of viral etiology, nor has it anything to do with creeping (Gr. *herpes*, to creep). It was originally so named because of the tendency of the disease to show 'progressive involvement by peripheral extension'.[3] Because of its intimate relationship to bullous pemphigoid, the designation pemphigoid gestationis is preferred. As the major larger series have consisted of patients derived from a variety of sources, estimates of incidence have been very variable, ranging from 1:3000 to 1:50,000 pregnancies.[4–7] The more recent figures where cases have had immunofluorescent confirmation would suggest that the latter figure is the most accurate.[3]

Pemphigoid gestationis may present in the first or any subsequent pregnancy.[3] It may first also rarely present in the postpartum period. In one series, 30% of patients were primigravidae.[6] In addition to developing in pregnant or postpartum patients, pemphigoid gestationis has rarely been described following a hydatidiform mole and gestational choriocarcinoma.[8,9] It has not, however, been reported in non-gestational variants such as those occurring in the ovary, mediastinum and testis, or complicating malignant teratoma. Pemphigoid gestationis is predominantly a disease of white females, being exceedingly rare in blacks.[10,11] Presentation is usually in the second or third trimester, most often developing in the sixth or seventh month, but the range is variable from 2 months to 4 days postpartum.[7,12] Although the disease may rarely completely remit before delivery, most patients (up to 75%) develop an exacerbation, which is frequently severe, in the immediate puerperium when progesterone levels have fallen.[12,13] Exceptionally, the infant may show transient urticated erythema and blistering.[4]

Pemphigoid gestationis usually complicates subsequent pregnancies, frequently presenting earlier on and with more severe symptomatology.[7] Sometimes, however, it may skip intervening pregnancies.[3] This may be related to a change in paternity, or else due to compatibility at the HLA-D locus.

Pemphigoid gestationis may develop into a very protracted 'post-partum' illness associated with considerable morbidity and lasting up to 12 years.[14,15] In the majority of patients, however, the disease resolves by about 6 months postpartum.[4] The disease may first present following a change in sexual partner.[3] Alternatively, recurrent disease may persist even when there has been a change of sexual partner.[7] This obviously calls into question the role of specific paternal antigens.

Exacerbation following the use of the oral contraceptive is a common complication,[7,16–19] affecting 20–50% of patients.[3] Estrogens in particular have been implicated.[18] The condition may also relapse during menstruation for some weeks or months postpartum and the return of symptoms (pruritus) has also been noted to coincide with ovulation (again suggesting an estrogen influence), although this is rare.[3,7,18]

Evidence has recently been published relating the duration of symptoms postpartum to the practice of breast-feeding. Bullous lesions lasted only 5 weeks in those who breast-fed compared to 24 weeks in those who bottle-fed. Although hormonal factors must be implicated, the precise pathogenetic implications underlying this observation are not fully understood.[18]

Pemphigoid gestationis is associated with intense pruritus, which may be present for days or weeks before the onset of typical cutaneous manifestations.[1] The dermatosis is characteristically polymorphous, consisting of erythematous or urticarial papules and plaques, some with a polycyclic pattern, and later vesicles and bullae develop at the periphery of spreading erythematous plaques (*Fig. 3.85*).[3,7] When fully evolved the blisters are tense and contain clear fluid, but at times this may become hemorrhagic (*Fig. 3.86*). They typically heal without scarring.

The umbilicus is frequently the site of initial involvement; spread to the trunk and extremities then follows (*Figs 3.87, 3.88*).[3] Surprisingly, lesions on the face and mucous membranes are distinctly uncommon. Eventually palmar and plantar manifestations may appear. Other than pruritus, symptoms are usually mild, with stinging, burning and pain being relatively infrequent.[7] Occasionally the presence of target or iris lesions may mimic erythema multiforme.[20] Less commonly features may initially suggest classical bullous pemphigoid.[20] Very occasionally there is clinical overlap with dermatitis herpetiformis.

Pemphigoid gestationis is not associated with pre-eclamptic toxemia and there is no related maternal mortality.

Pemphigoid gestationis is accompanied by a significant increased risk of developing Graves' disease and an increased risk of autoantibodies.[21]

The literature concerning the incidence and nature of fetal morbidity and mortality is a source of some confusion. Kolodney therefore considered that there was no evidence of an increased incidence of stillbirths or abortions; however, this series predates the immunofluorescence era.[5] An investigation by Lawley et al[16] of a large series of cases where immunofluorescent confirmation was available suggested that there was an increased risk of fetal morbidity and mortality. More recently, evidence has been presented that patients with pemphigoid gestationis

are liable to deliver low weight and small-for-dates infants, prematurely.[22] In contrast, however, Shornick et al failed to show any evidence of significant fetal complications.[7] It would seem likely therefore that if there is any degree of fetal risk it is unlikely to be of much significance. The antibody can cross the placenta and, in approximately 5% of cases, this may be associated with a mild and transient vesiculobullous eruption.[23–26]

Pathogenesis and histological features

The histopathological features seen in biopsies from patients with pemphigoid gestationis are variable, depending upon whether early erythematous or urticarial papular lesions are examined or whether fully established vesicles and bullae are studied.[27]

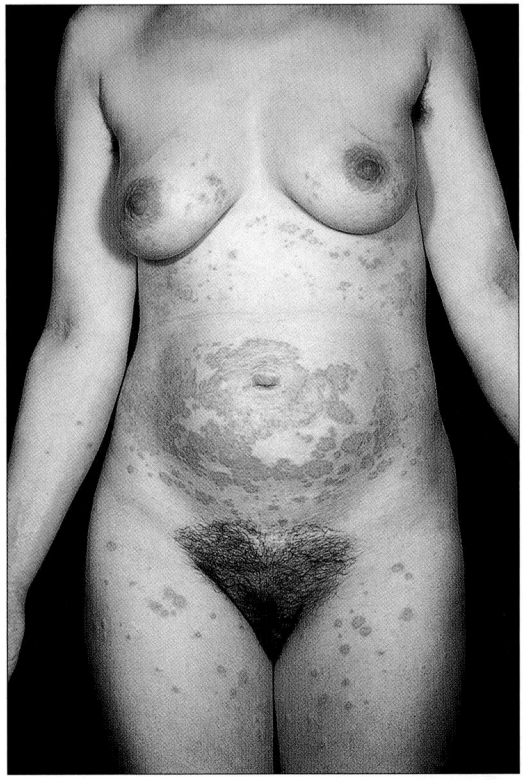

Fig. 3.87
Pemphigoid gestationis: slightly raised erythematous lesions with a propensity to cluster on the abdomen. By courtesy of R.C. Holmes, MD, Warneford Hospital, Oxford, UK.

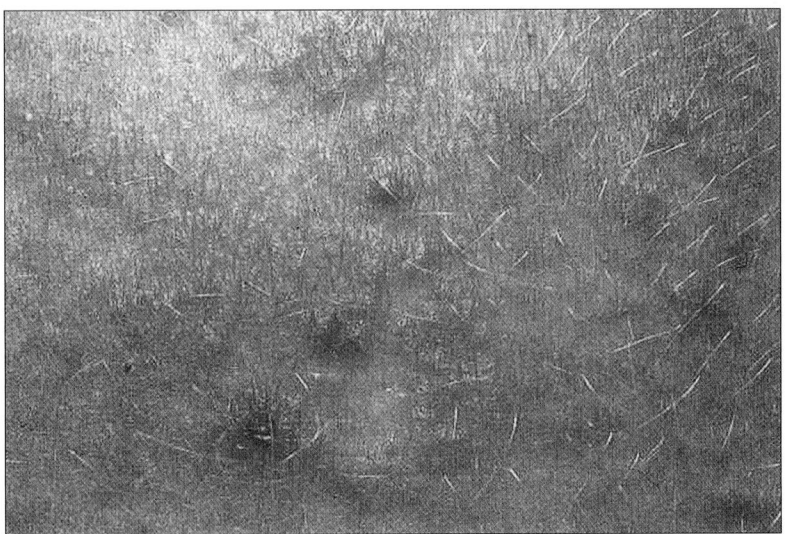

Fig. 3.85
Pemphigoid gestationis: prebullous phase showing erythema and small papules. By courtesy of the Institute of Dermatology, London, UK.

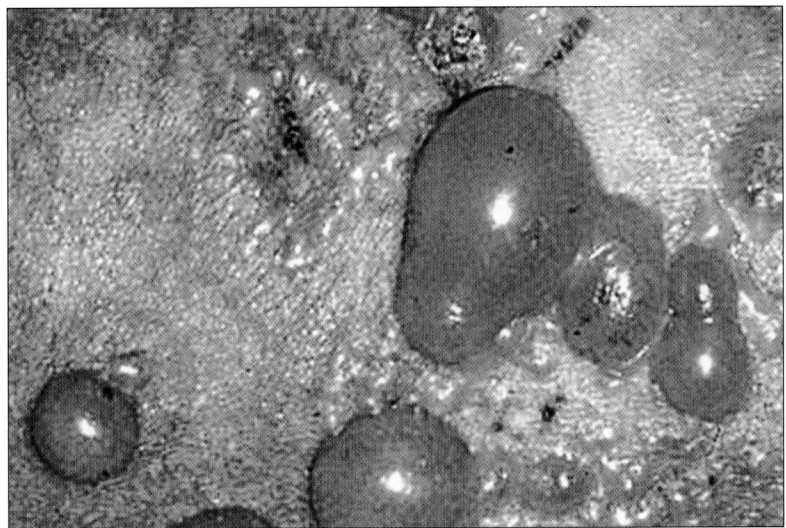

Fig. 3.86
Pemphigoid gestationis: the blisters are tense and dome-shaped. By courtesy of R.C. Holmes, MD, Warneford Hospital, Oxford, UK.

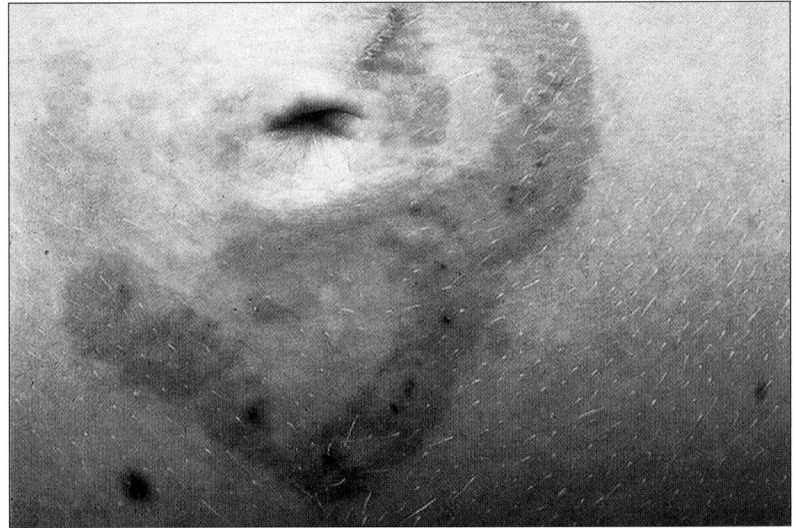

Fig. 3.88
Pemphigoid gestationis: umbilical involvement is a common mode of presentation. By courtesy of the Institute of Dermatology, London, UK.

In early lesions, the major pathological features are seen in the superficial dermis where there is a perivascular inflammatory cell infiltrate consisting of lymphocytes, histiocytes and typically very large numbers of eosinophils. This is associated with edema of the papillary dermis, which when marked may result in a 'tear drop' appearance (*Fig. 3.89*).[27] Sometimes there is accompanying spongiosis and this may be associated with large numbers of eosinophils (eosinophilic spongiosis, *Fig. 3.90*). Occasionally the infiltrate of lymphocytes, histiocytes and eosinophils is present in a linear distribution along the epidermodermal junction.[3]

Vacuolar degeneration of the basal keratinocytes, sometimes accompanied by individual cell necrosis, may be a feature of the early lesions, but is often more evident in the fully established vesicular or bullous stage.[27] In the latter the blister is subepidermal in location and frequently contains large numbers of eosinophils (*Figs 3.91, 3.92*).[28] The underlying and adjacent dermis is edematous and contains a predominantly perivascular lympho/histiocytic infiltrate with large numbers of eosinophils. Leukocytoclasis and eosinophil dermal papillary microabscesses are only rarely identified.[27,28] Ultrastructural studies show that the cleavage plane lies within the lamina lucida.[28,29]

Direct immunofluorescence of perilesional skin in pemphigoid gestationis shows a linear basement membrane zone deposition of C3 in all patients.[3,30–35] About 30–50% of cases also have an IgG band (less frequently IgM or IgA).[30] They are present in non-lesional (perilesional) as well as in lesional skin.[30] Complement pathway components including properdin and properdin factor-B may also be identified.[1] IgG and

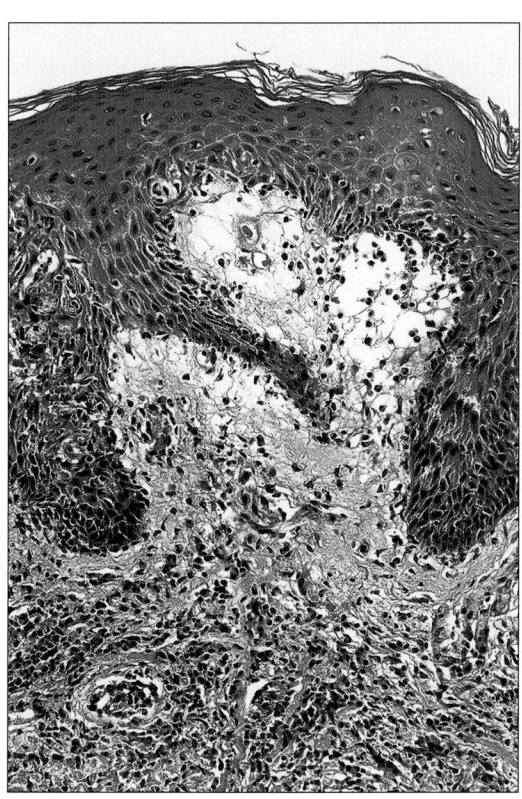

Fig. 3.89
Pemphigoid gestationis: early erythematous lesion showing marked edema of the papillary dermis and conspicuous eosinophils.

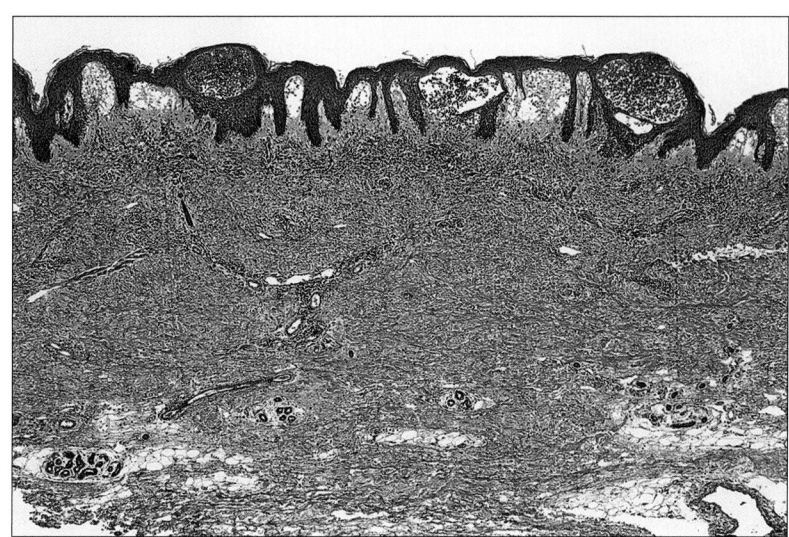

Fig. 3.91
Pemphigoid gestationis: established subepidermal blister.

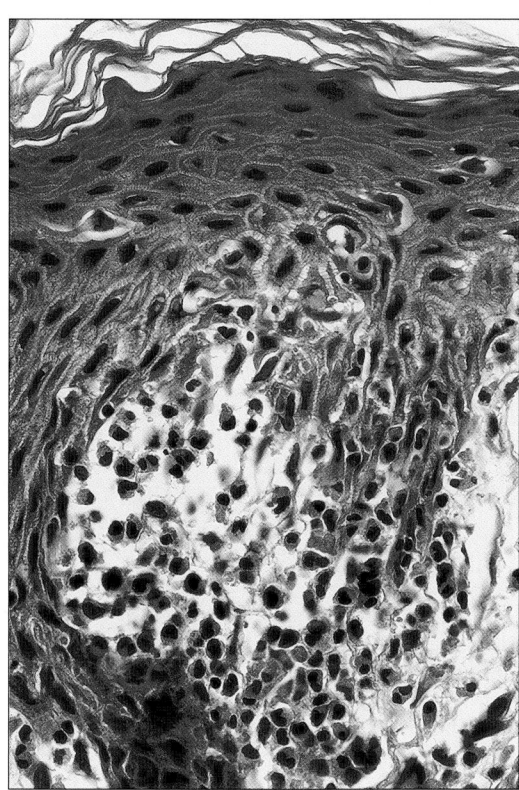

Fig. 3.90
Pemphigoid gestationis: early erythematous lesion showing eosinophilic spongiosis.

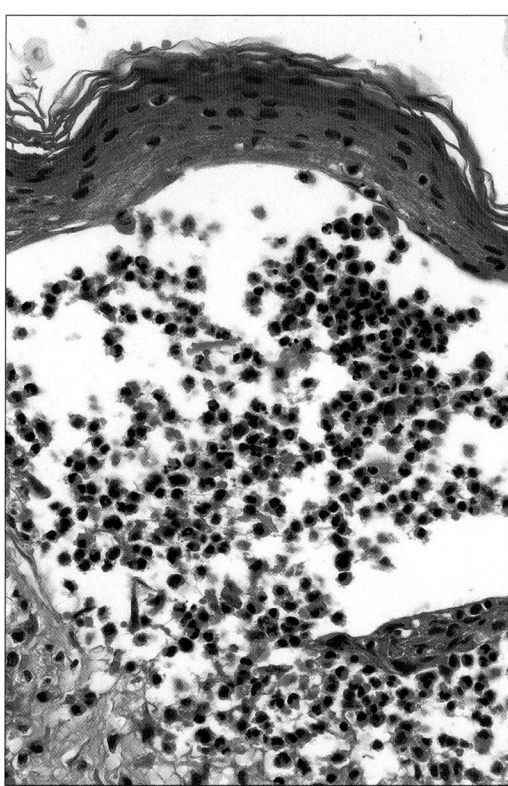

Fig. 3.92
Pemphigoid gestationis: the blister cavity contains a heavy eosinophil infiltrate.

complement may often be detected along the amniotic basement membrane region using direct immunofluorescence.[32,36,37] Pemphigoid gestationis antigen has been detected in the placenta from early in the second trimester onwards.[38] The antibody may also be found in the skin of infants of affected mothers.[24]

Circulating complement-fixing (via the classical pathway) IgG antibodies (pemphigoid (herpes) gestationis (HG) factor) can be detected in 50–75% of cases by indirect complement immunofluorescence (*Fig. 3.93*).[16,30,39–41] The so-called HG factor is nothing more than a low titer IgG complement-fixing anti-basement membrane antibody.[30] The antibody is consistently of the IgG1 subclass.[32] If monoclonal antibodies directed against IgG1 are used, 100% of patients can be shown to possess circulating HG factor.[32] Approximately 25% of patients have anti-basement membrane zone antibodies detectable by conventional techniques.[42] These bind to the roof of 1 M NaCl-split skin.[30] The antibody also reacts with amnion and chorion basement membrane.[36,37]

With immunoelectron microscopy the immunoreactants are deposited within the upper lamina lucida where they are most probably associated with the sub-basal dense plate.[43,44] In pemphigoid gestationis the antibody recognizes the BP 180kD protein on western immunoblot and localizes to the same NC16A domain as described in bullous pemphigoid.[45–48] It may also recognize the 230 kD bullous pemphigoid antigen in 10–26% of cases.[46,47]

Patients with pemphigoid gestationis have an increased incidence of HLA-B8 (43–79%), HLA-DR3 (61–80%) and HLA-DR4 (52–53%). The paired haplotypes HLA-DR3 and -DR4 are present in 54% of patients compared with 3% in the general population.[1,3,18,49,50] The phenotype, however, does not appear to correlate with the clinical features of pemphigoid gestationis.[30] Patients with pemphigoid gestationis also have a high incidence (100%) of anti-HLA cytotoxic antibodies, particularly directed against the paternal antigens.[30,49–52] These are, however, found in 25% of normal multiparous women and therefore their possible role in the pathogenesis of pemphigoid gestationis is uncertain.[21]

The pathogenesis of pemphigoid gestationis relates to antibody-associated complement fixation with the production of leukocyte chemotactic factors, mast cell degranulation and associated dermoepidermal separation.[30]

The presence of pemphigoid gestationis antigen in both skin and amnion raises the possibility that an initial antiplacental antibody cross-reacts with skin giving rise to the clinical features of pemphigoid gestationis.[23] Support for this theory has been the discovery that the HLA antigens -DP and -DR are consistently expressed in the placentas of patients with this condition.[50,53]

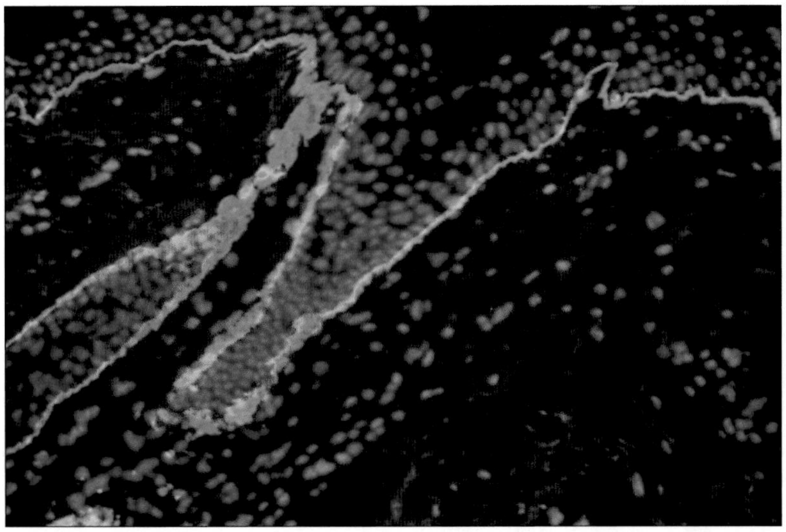

Differential diagnosis

The differential diagnosis includes epidermolysis bullosa acquisita, dermatitis herpetiformis, linear IgA disease and bullous systemic lupus erythematosus (see *Table 3.4*). Pemphigoid gestationis must also be distinguished from pruritic urticarial papules and plaques of pregnancy (PUPPP) and pregnancy prurigo.

PUPPP is predominantly a disorder of first pregnancies. Lesions particularly develop around abdominal striae, and periumbilical sparing is a characteristic feature (*Fig. 3.94*). Eosinophilic spongiosis and subepidermal blistering may be seen in established lesions and therefore in the absence of clinical details and immunofluorescence findings, distinction from pemphigoid gestationis may be impossible.

Pregnancy prurigo, which typically develops in the third trimester, presents with pruritic papules and nodules (*Fig. 3.95*). Blisters are not a feature. Histologically the changes are those of a low-grade, non-specific spongiotic dermatitis.

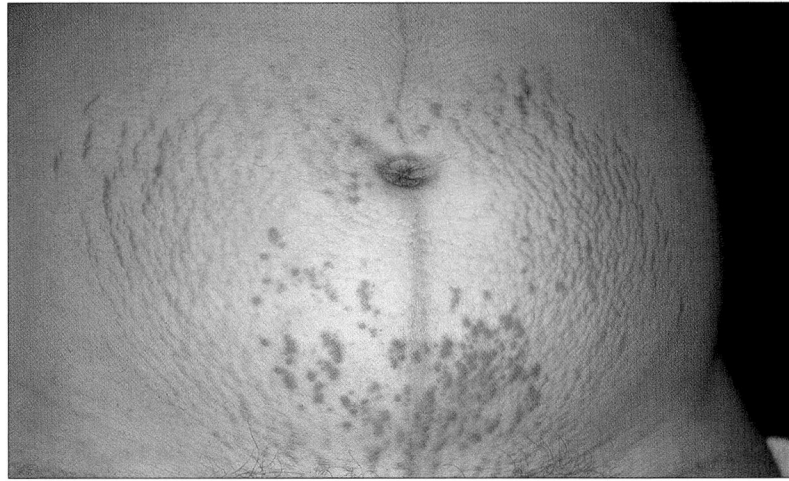

Fig. 3.94
Pruritic papules and plaques of pregnancy: note the erythematous papules particularly related to the abdominal striae, and characteristic umbilical sparing. By courtesy of R.C. Holmes, MD, Warneford Hospital, Oxford, UK.

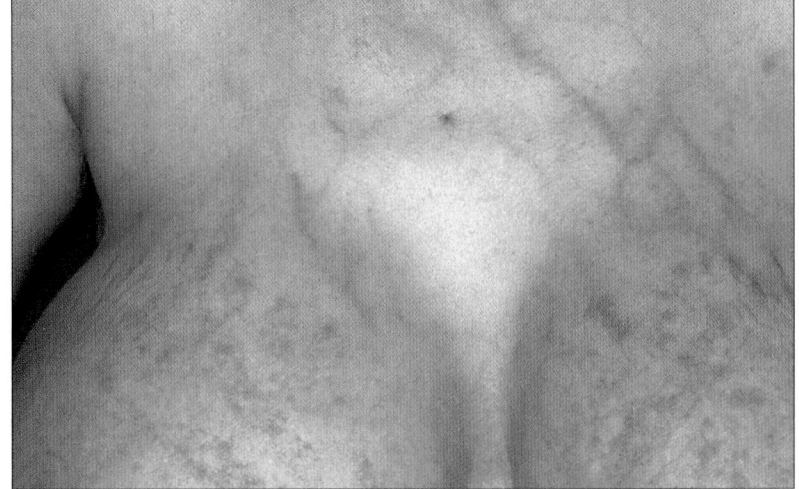

Fig. 3.95
Pregnancy prurigo: there are erythematous papules and excoriations. Blisters are not a feature of this condition. By courtesy of R.A. Marsden, MD, St George's Hospital, London, UK.

Fig. 3.93
Pemphigoid gestationis: indirect complement immunofluorescence showing linear deposition of the IgG.

References

1. Engineer, L., Bhol, K., Ahmed, A.R. (2000) Pemphigoid gestationis: a review. *Am J Obstet Gynecol*, **183**, 483–491.
2. Holmes, R.C., Black, M.M. (1982) The specific dermatoses of pregnancy: a reappraisal with special emphasis on a proposed simplified clinical classification. *Clin Exp Dermatol*, **7**, 65–73.
3. Shornick, J.K. (1987) Herpes gestationis. *J Am Acad Dermatol*, **17**, 539–556.
4. Jenkins, R.E., Hern, S., Black, M.M. (1999) Clinical features and management of 87 patients with pemphigoid gestationis. *Clin Exp Dermatol*, **24**, 255–259.
5. Kolodney, R.C. (1954) Herpes gestationis (dermatitis herpetiformis): report of a case. *Arch Dermatol*, **70**, 331–335.
6. Holmes, R.C., Black, M.M., Dann, J. et al (1982) A comparative study of toxic erythema of pregnancy and herpes gestationis. *Br J Dermatol*, **106**, 449–510.
7. Shornick, J.K., Bangert, J.L., Freeman, R.G. et al (1983) Herpes gestationis: clinical and histologic features of twenty-eight cases. *J Am Acad Dermatol*, **8**, 214–224.
8. Tillman, W.G. (1950) Herpes gestationis with hydatidiform mole and chorion-epithelioma. *BMJ*, **1**, 1471.
9. do Valle Chiossi, M.P., Costa, R.S., Ferreira Roselino, A.M. (2000) Titration of herpes gestationis factor fixing to C3 in pemphigoid herpes gestationis associated with choriocarcinoma. *Arch Dermatol*, **136**, 129–130.
10. Cutler, T.P. (1982) Herpes gestationis. *Clin Exp Dermatol*, **7**, 201–207.
11. Shornick, J.K., Meek, T.J., Nesbitt, L.T. et al (1984) Herpes gestationis in blacks. *Arch Dermatol*, **120**, 511–513.
12. Mayou, S.C., Black, M.M., Holmes, R.C. (1988) Pemphigoid 'herpes' gestationis. *Semin Dermatol*, **7**, 104–110.
13. Baxi, L.V., Kovilam, C.P., Collins, M.H. et al (1991) Recurrent herpes gestationis with postpartum flare: a case report. *Am J Obst Gynecol*, **164**, 778–780.
14. Holmes, R.C., Williamson, D.M., Black, M.M. (1986) Herpes gestationis persisting for 12 years post partum (letter). *Arch Dermatol*, **122**, 375–376.
15. Fine, J-D., Omura, E.F. (1985) Herpes gestationis: persistent disease activity 11 years post partum. *Arch Dermatol*, **121**, 924–926.
16. Lawley, T.J., Stingl, G., Katz, S.I. (1978) Fetal and maternal risk factors in herpes gestationis. *Arch Dermatol*, **114**, 552–555.
17. Winton, G.B., Lewis, C.W. (1982) Dermatoses of pregnancy. *J Am Acad Dermatol*, **6**, 977–998.
18. Holmes, R.C., Black, M.M., Jurecka, W. et al (1983) Clues to the etiology and pathogenesis of herpes gestationis. *Br J Dermatol*, **109**, 131–139.
19. Holmes, R.C., Black, M.M. (1983) The specific dermatoses of pregnancy. *J Am Acad Dermatol*, **8**, 405–412.
20. Holmes, R.C., Black, M.M., Williamson, D.M. et al (1980) Herpes gestationis and bullous pemphigoid: a disease spectrum. *Br J Dermatol*, **103**, 535–541.
21. Shornick, J.K., Black, M.M. (1992) Secondary autoimmune diseases in herpes gestationis (pemphigoid gestationis). *J Am Acad Dermatol*, **26**, 563–566.
22. Holmes, R.C., Black, M.M. (1984) The fetal prognosis in pemphigoid gestationis (herpes gestationis). *Br J Dermatol*, **110**, 67–72.
23. Black, M.M., Stephens, C.J.M. (1991) The specific dermatoses of pregnancy: the British Perspective. *Adv Dermatol*, **7**, 105–127.
24. Chorzelski, T.P., Jablonska, S., Beutner, E.H. et al (1976) Herpes gestationis with identical lesions in the newborn. Passive transfer of the disease? *Arch Dermatol*, **112**, 1129–1131.
25. Bonifazi, E., Meneghini, C.L. (1984) Herpes gestationis with transient bullous lesions in the newborn. *Pediatr Dermatol*, **1**, 215–218.
26. Karna, P., Broecker, A.H. (1991) Neonatal herpes gestationis. *J Pediatr*, **119**, 299–301.
27. Hertz, K.C., Katz, S.I., Maize, J. et al (1976) Herpes gestationis: a clinicopathologic study. *Arch Dermatol*, **112**, 1543–1548.
28. Yaoita, H., Gullino, M., Katz, S.I. (1976) Herpes gestationis. Ultrastructure and ultrastructural localization of *in vivo*-bound complement. *J Invest Dermatol*, **66**, 383–388.
29. Harrington, C.I., Bleehen, S.S. (1979) Herpes gestationis: immunopathological and ultrastructural studies. *Br J Dermatol*, **100**, 389–399.
30. Yancey, K.B. (1990) Herpes gestationis. *Immunodermatol*, **8**, 727–735.
31. Provost, T.T., Tomasi, T.B. (1973) Evidence for complement activation via the alternate pathway in skin disease I. Herpes gestationis, systemic lupus erythematosus and bullous pemphigoid. *J Clin Invest*, **52**, 1779–1787.
32. Kelly, S.E., Cerio, R., Bhogal, B.S. et al (1989) The distribution of IgG subclasses in pemphigoid gestationis: pg factor is an IgG1 autoantibody. *J Invest Dermatol*, **92**, 695–698.
33. Provost, T.T., Tomasi, T.B. (1973) Evidence for complement activation via the alternate pathway in skin diseases: I. Herpes gestationis, systemic lupus erythematosus and bullous pemphigoid. *J Clin Invest*, **52**, 1779–1787.
34. Schaumburg-Lever, G., Saffold, O.E., Orfanos, C.E. et al (1973) Herpes gestationis: histology and ultrastructure. *Arch Dermatol*, **107**, 888–892.
35. Holubar, K., Konrad, K., Stingle, G. (1977) Detection by immunoelectron microscopy of immunoglobulin G deposits in skin of immunofluorescence negative herpes gestationis. *Br J Dermatol*, **96**, 569–571.
36. Ortonne, J.P., Hsi, B-L., Verrando, P. et al (1987) Herpes gestationis factor reacts with the amniotic epithelial basement membrane. *Br J Dermatol*, **117**, 147–154.
37. Kelly, S.E., Bhogal, B.S., Wojnarowska, F. et al (1988) Expression of pemphigoid gestationis related antigen by human placenta. *Br J Dermatol*, **118**, 605–611.
38. Kelly, S.E., Black, M.M. (1989) Pemphigoid gestationis: placental interactions. *Semin Dermatol*, **8**, 12–17.
39. Katz, S.I., Hertz, K.C., Yaoita, H. (1976) Herpes gestationis: immunopathology and characterization of the HG factor. *J Clin Invest*, **57**, 1434–1441.
40. Jordan, R.E., Heine, K.G., Tappeiner, G. et al (1976) The immunopathology of herpes gestationis: immunofluorescence studies and characterization of 'HG factor'. *J Clin Invest*, **57**, 1426–1433.
41. Suzuki, M., Watanabe, C., Yaoita, H. (1989) The complement fixing ability of anti-basement membrane zone IgG subclass antibodies of herpes gestationis and bullous pemphigoid. *Acta Derm Venereol*, **69**, 6–11.
42. Holmes, R.C., Black, M.M. (1983) Herpes gestationis. *Dermatol Clin*, **1**, 195–203.
43. Honigsmann, H., Stringl, G., Holubar, K. et al (1976) Herpes gestationis: fine ultrastructural pattern of immunoglobulin deposits in the skin *in vivo*. *J Invest Dermatol*, **66**, 389–392.
44. Karpati, S., Stolz, W., Meurer, M. et al (1991) Herpes gestationis: ultrastructural identification of the extracellular antigenic sites in diseased skin using immunogold techniques. *Br J Dermatol*, **125**, 317–324.
45. Morrison, L.H., Labib, R.S., Zone, J.J. et al (1988) Herpes gestationis autoantibodies recognise a 180kD human epidermal antigen. *J Clin Invest*, **81**, 2023–2026.
46. Kelly, S.E., Bhogal, B.S., Wojnarowska, F. et al (1990) Western blot analysis of the antigen in pemphigoid gestationis. *Br J Dermatol*, **122**, 445–449.
47. Murakami, H., Amagai, M., Higashiyama, M. et al (1996) Analysis of antigens recognized by autoantibodies in herpes gestationis. Usefulness of immunoblotting using a fusion protein representing an extracellular domain of the 180kD bullous pemphigoid antigen. *J Dermatol Sci*, **13**, 112–117.
48. Matsumura, K., Amagai, M., Nishikawa, T. et al (1996) The majority of bullous pemphigoid and herpes gestationis serum samples react with the NC16A domain of the 180-kDa bullous pemphigoid antigen. *Arch Dermatol Res*, **288**, 507–509.
49. Shornick, J.K., Statsny, P., Gilliam, J.N. (1981) High frequency of histocompatibility antigens DR3 and DR4 in herpes gestationis. *J Clin Invest*, **68**, 553–555.
50. Shornick, J.K., Jenkins, R.E., Briggs, D.C. et al (1993) Anti-HLA antibodies in pemphigoid gestationis (herpes gestationis). *Br J Dermatol*, **129**, 257–259.
51. Reunala, T., Karvonen, J., Tiilikainen, A. et al (1977) Herpes gestationis: a high titer of anti-HLA-B8 antibody in the mother and pemphigoid-like immunohistological findings in the mother and the child. *Br J Dermatol*, **96**, 563–568.
52. Shornick, J.K., Stasyny, P., Gilliam, J.N. (1983) Paternal histocompatibility (HLA) antigens and maternal anti HLA antibodies in herpes gestationis. *J Invest Dermatol*, **81**, 407–409.
53. Kelly, S.E., Black, M.M., Fleming, S. (1989) Pemphigoid gestationis: a unique mechanism of initiation of an autoimmune response by MHC class II molecules. *J Pathol*, **158**, 81–83.

Lichen planus pemphigoides

Clinical features

Lichen planus (lichen ruber) pemphigoides (Kaposi) must be distinguished from the vesicles occasionally seen in lichen planus as a consequence of severe hydropic degeneration (lichen planus vesiculosis).[1,2] Rarely, lichen planus is associated with a generally benign, bullous pemphigoid-like disease: lichen planus pemphigoides. This represents a heterogeneous condition characterized by basement membrane antibodies directed towards a number of antigens.

Clinically, the pemphigoid-like lesions are usually preceded by typical lichen planus although rarely the blisters may develop first (*Fig. 3.96*). The bullae, which are most numerous on the extremities, may arise on normal skin, in areas of erythema or on lichenoid papules (*Figs 3.97, 3.98*). In some patients the blisters are generalized. They are tense, dome-shaped and hemorrhagic or contain clear fluid. Lichen planus pemphigoides more commonly affects males and presents most often in the fourth and fifth decades.[3,4] Exceptionally, however, cases have been documented in childhood.[5,6] All races may be affected.

Pathogenesis and histological features

The lichenoid lesions show the typical histopathological and immunofluorescent changes of lichen planus, but the bullae have features more

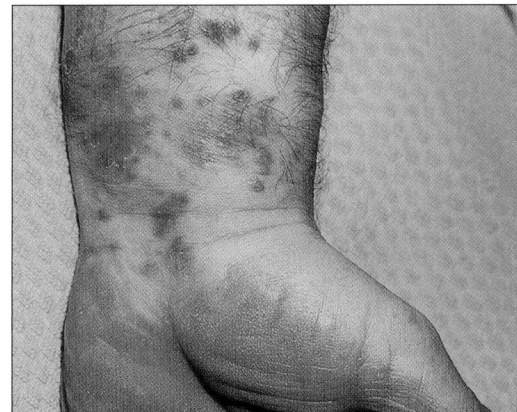

Fig. 3.96
Lichen planus pemphigoides: typical lichenoid papules are present on the anterior aspect of the wrist. By courtesy of M.M. Black, MD, Institute of Dermatology, London, UK.

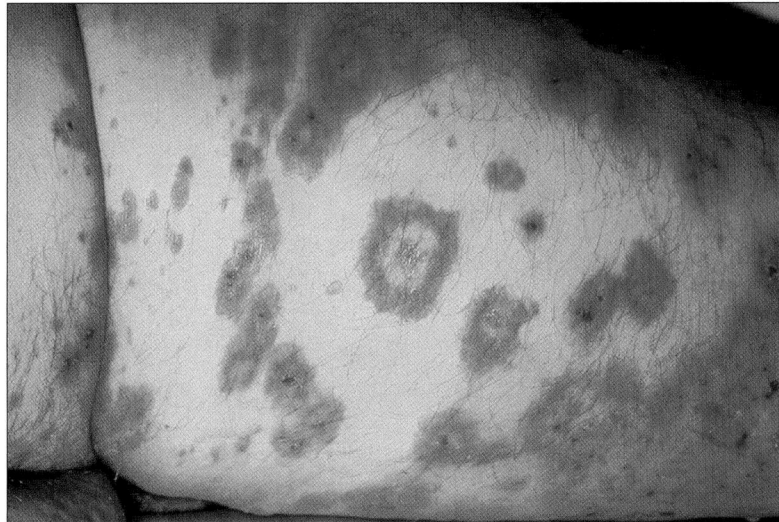

Fig. 3.97
Lichen planus pemphigoides: note the blisters and erosions arising on an erythematous base. Atypical target lesions are present. By courtesy of M.M. Black, MD, Institute of Dermatology, London, UK.

suggestive of bullous pemphigoid (*Fig. 3.99*). A variety of findings have been described. Early erythematous lesions show intense dermal edema with a dense perivascular and interstitial eosinophil infiltrate; eosinophilic spongiosis may also sometimes be evident. Established blisters are subepidermal and both inflammatory (cell-rich) and cell-poor variants have been documented (*Figs 3.100, 3.101*).[3] Eosinophils are variably present but often may be numerous.

Immunofluorescent examination of biopsies from peribullous skin reveals linear deposition of IgG and complement.[7–9] The serum contains an IgG anti-basement membrane antibody in up to 50–60% of patients. With NaCl-split skin, the antibody generally labels the roof of the blister cavity. Ultrastructural investigations have shown that the level of separation is usually through the lamina lucida. By immunoelectron microscopy, the immunoreactants typically localize to the hemidesmosome and lamina lucida.[3,10] Cicatricial pemphigoid and epidermolysis bullosa acquisita (EBA)-like variants have, however, also been documented.[11]

A number of antigens have been recognized in lichen planus including BP180, BP230, and an as yet uncharacterized 200 kD protein of keratinocyte derivation.[1,11–17] The segment of the NC16A domain recognized in lichen planus pemphigoides differs from BP, localizing to MCW-4 as opposed to MCW-0–MCW-3.[18] Type VII collagen has also been implicated in the EBA-like variant although the immunoblot was negative.[11]

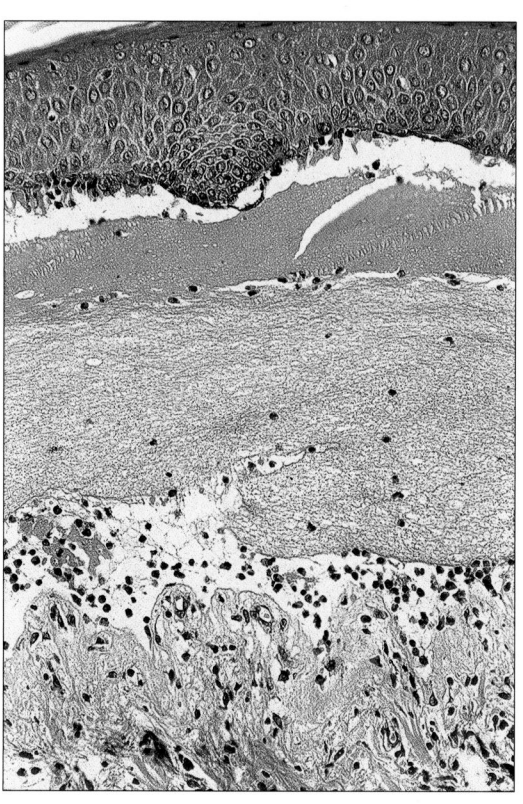

Fig. 3.100
Lichen planus pemphigoides: there is a subepidermal blister.

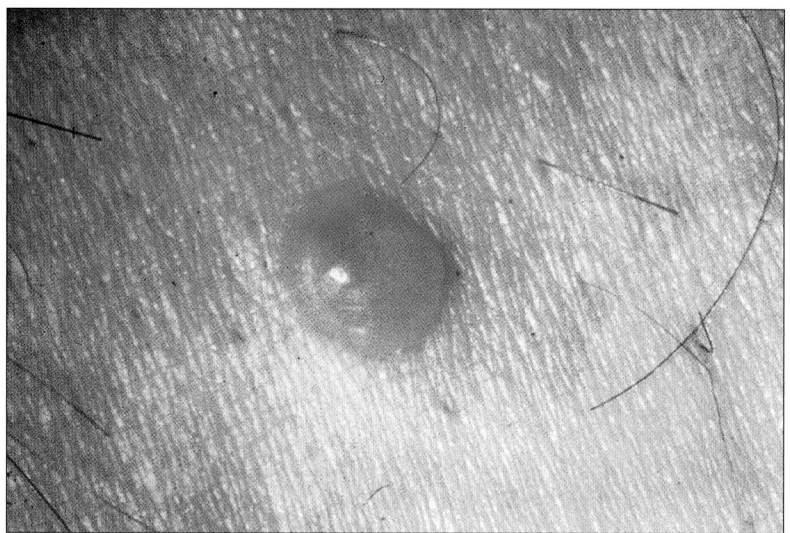

Fig. 3.98
Lichen planus pemphigoides: note the intact dome-shaped tense blister. By courtesy of M.M. Black, MD, Institute of Dermatology, London, UK.

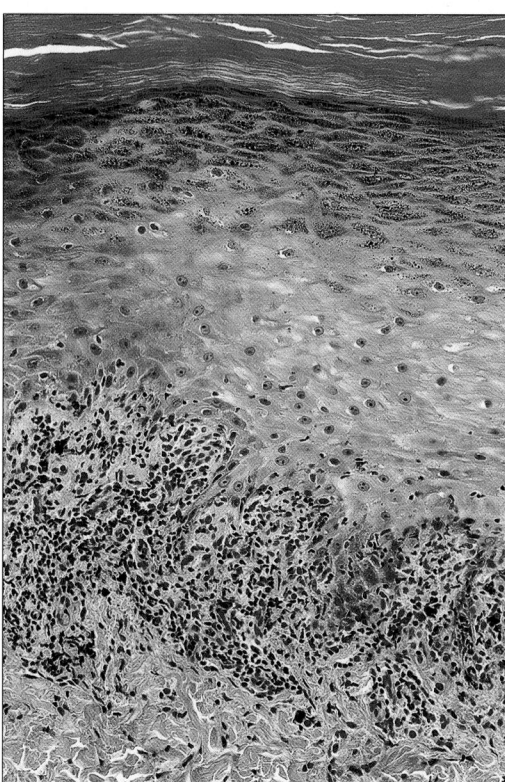

Fig. 3.99
Lichen planus pemphigoides: the lichenoid papules show typical features of lichen planus.

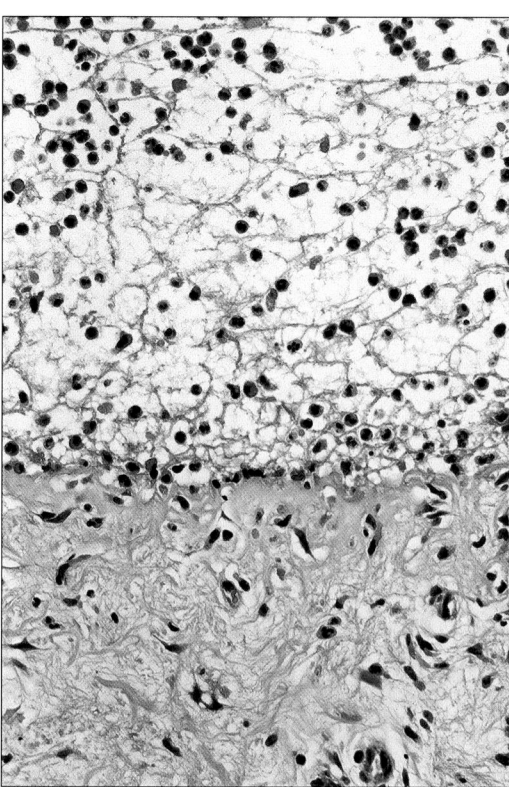

Fig. 3.101
Lichen planus pemphigoides: the blister contains eosinophils.

Although the pathogenesis of lichen planus pemphigoides has not been fully unraveled, it is likely that the basement membrane zone damage associated with lichen planus results in antigen exposure with subsequent autoantibody production and resultant bullous disease. It is so far uncertain why only a small percentage of patients with lichen planus are affected. The pathogenesis in those patients in whom the blisters develop first is unknown although a different antigen may be involved. Exceptionally, cases have been documented as an adverse drug reaction (e.g. to angiotensin-converting enzyme inhibitors or complicating PUVA therapy).[19-23] There has been a suggestion that lichen planus pemphigoides might be associated with internal malignancy but the diagnosis lacked substantiation by immunofluorescence studies.[24]

Differential diagnosis

Lichen planus pemphigoides differs from typical bullous pemphigoid clinically by its earlier age of presentation and predilection for the lower limbs. In those cases associated with antibodies to BP180, epitope mapping may make the distinction.

References

1. Lang, P.G., Maize, J.C. (1983) Coexisting lichen planus and bullous pemphigoid or lichen planus pemphigoides. *J Am Acad Dermatol*, 9, 133–140.
2. Oomen, C.K., Temmerman, L., Kint, A. (1986) Lichen planus pemphigoides. *Clin Exp Dermatol*, 11, 92–96.
3. Willsteed, E., Bhogal, B.S., Das, A.K. et al (1991) Lichen planus pemphigoides: a clinicopathological study of nine cases. *Histopathology*, 19, 147–154.
4. Murphy, A.K., Cronin, E. (1989) Lichen planus pemphigoides. *Clin Exp Dermatol*, 14, 322–324.
5. Flageul, B., Hassan, F., Pinquier, L. et al (1999) Lichen pemphigoid associated with developing hepatitis B in a child. *Ann Dermatol Venereol*, 126, 604–607.
6. Hofman-Wellenhof, R., Salmhofer, W., Kerl, H. (1999) Lichen planus pemphigoides in a 9-year-old child: successful treatment with topical corticosteroids. *Pediatr Dermatol*, 16, 70–71.
7. Mora, R.G., Nesbitt, L.T., Brantley, J.B. (1983) Lichen planus pemphigoides: clinical and immunofluorescent findings in four cases. *J Am Acad Dermatol*, 8, 331–336.
8. Sobel, S., Miller, R., Shatin, H. (1976) Lichen planus pemphigoides: immunofluorescence findings. *Arch Dermatol*, 112, 1280–1283.
9. Stingl, G., Holubar, K. (1975) Coexistence of lichen planus and bullous pemphigoid: an immunopathological study. *Br J Dermatol*, 93, 313–318.
10. Prost, C., Tesserand, F., Laroche, L. et al (1985) Lichen planus pemphigoides: an immuno-electron microscopic study. *Br J Dermatol*, 113, 31–36.
11. Bouloc, A., Vignon-Pennamen, M.D., Caux, F. et al (1998) Lichen planus pemphigoides is a heterogeneous disease: a report of five cases studied by immunoelectron microscopy. *Br J Dermatol*, 138, 972–980.
12. Davis, A., Wojnarowska, F., Bhogal, B. et al (1989) Lichen planus pemphigoides and its relationship to bullous pemphigoid. *Br J Dermatol*, 120, 296.
13. Davis, A.L., Bhogal, B.S., Whitehead, P. et al (1991) Lichen planus pemphigoides: its relationship to bullous pemphigoid. *Br J Dermatol*, 125, 263–271.
14. Tamada, Y., Yokochi, K., Nitta, Y. et al (1995) Lichen planus pemphigoides: identification of 180 kD hemidesmosome antigen. *J Am Acad Dermatol*, 32, 883–887.
15. Hsu, S., Ghohestani, R.F., Uitto, J. (2000) Lichen planus pemphigoides with IgG autoantibodies to the 180kD bullous pemphigoid antigen (type XVII collagen). *J Am Acad Dermatol*, 42, 136–141.
16. Skaria, M., Salomon, D., Jaunin, F. et al (1999) IgG autoantibodies from a lichen planus pemphigoides patient recognize the NC16A domain of the bullous pemphigoid antigen 180. *Dermatology*, 199, 253–255.
17. Swale, V.J., Black, M.M., Bhogal, B.S. (1998) Lichen planus pemphigoides: report of two cases. *Clin Exp Dermatol*, 23, 132–135.
18. Zillikens, D., Caux, F., Mascaro, J.M. et al (1999) Autoantibodies in lichen planus pemphigoides react with a novel epitope within the C-terminal NC16A domain of BP180. *J Invest Dermatol*, 113, 117–121.
19. Miyagawa, S., Ohi, H., Muramatsu, T. et al (1985) Lichen planus pemphigoides-like lesions induced by cinnarazine. *Br J Dermatol*, 112, 607–613.
20. Vollenweider Roten, S., Mainetti, C., Donath, R. et al (1995) Enalapril-induced lichen planus-like eruption. *J Am Acad Dermatol*, 32, 293–295.
21. Ogg, G.S., Bhogal, B.S., Hashimoto, T. et al (1997) Ramipril-associated lichen planus pemphigoides. *Br J Dermatol*, 136, 412–414.
22. Godard, W., Ingargiola, F., Tavernier, B. et al (1983) Lichen plan pemphigoïde et puvathérapie. *Ann Dermatol Venereol*, 110, 69–74.
23. Kuramoto, N., Kishimoto, S., Shibagaki, R. et al (2000) PUVA-induced lichen planus pemphigoides. *Br J Dermatol*, 142, 509–512.
24. Magnusson, B. (1967) Lichen ruber bullosus and tumors in internal organs. *Dermatologica*, 134, 166–172.

Mucous membrane pemphigoid (cicatricial pemphigoid)

Cicatricial pemphigoid represents a spectrum of diseases (e.g. ocular pemphigoid, oral pemphigoid, benign mucous membrane pemphigoid, mucous membrane pemphigoid) which affect the mucosa and skin.[1-3] With the advent of molecular studies identifying the antigens involved, it is becoming clear that there are a number of relatively well-defined clinicopathological variants which arise as a consequence of autoimmune diseases directed against a number of different basement membrane antigens. Although multiple systems are often affected, there is increasing evidence that pure ocular and oral variants may also be encountered.[1,2]

Clinical features

Cicatricial pemphigoid is a rare blistering disorder in which mucosal lesions predominate and in which scarring is a characteristic feature.[1,2] It is often associated with severe morbidity, largely due to the effects of the scarring. As ocular and oral lesions predominate, many patients come to the attention primarily of the dental and oral surgeons or ophthalmologists rather than dermatologists.

The incidence is estimated as being between 1:12,000 and 1:20,000 of the population per year.[2] It is associated with a female preponderance (2:1) and it not uncommonly presents in the seventh decade. Very rare instances of childhood involvement have been reported.[3-7] Cicatricial pemphigoid is a chronic disease and is rarely self-limiting. It shows no racial or geographic predilection.

Oral lesions occur in 85–95% of patients and commonly follow mild trauma.[8] Bullae, erosions and erythema most commonly affect the gingival or buccal mucosa, but the hard and soft palate, tongue and lips are also frequently involved (*Figs 3.102, 3.103*). Desquamative gingivitis is the most common manifestation.[9,10] Patients with this condition present with painful, swollen, erythematous lesions of the gums, which may be associated with bleeding, blistering, erosions and ulceration.[11] Cicatricial pemphigoid limited to the oral cavity is a distinctive subset, usually associated with a good prognosis although characterized by chronicity.[1] Pharyngeal (19% of patients) and esophageal (4% of

patients) lesions may be complicated by scarring, resulting in stenoses. Aspiration pneumonia is sometimes a fatal complication. Nasal lesions, which may occur in up to 15% of patients, lead to obstruction and occasionally cicatricial stenoses and septal perforation.[12] Laryngeal involvement, which occurs in 8% of patients, is sometimes complicated by such severe stricture formation and edema that tracheotomy may be a life-saving necessity.[11]

Ocular lesions, which occur in approximately 64% of patients, are a source of considerable morbidity.[13] The eye (in particular the conjunctiva) may be a sole site of involvement.[11] Early symptoms are those of a non-specific conjunctivitis. In more advanced lesions, subconjunctival fibrosis develops.[14,15] Patients may therefore present with

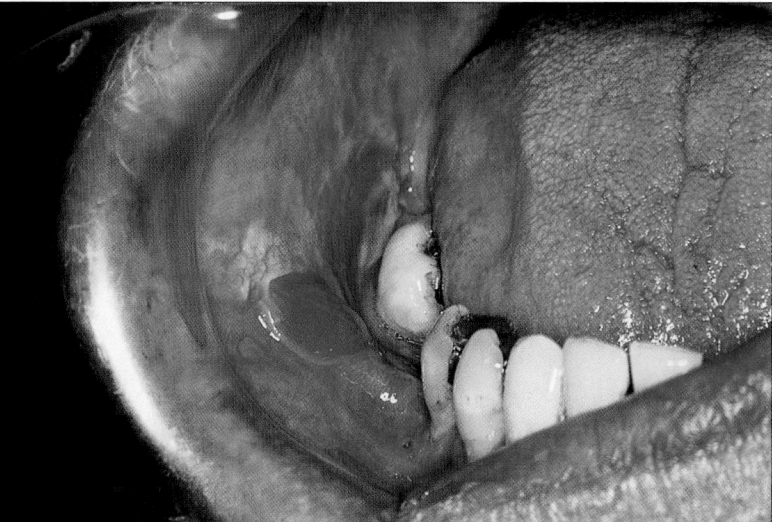

Fig. 3.102
Cicatricial pemphigoid: there is erosion of the buccal mucosa. By courtesy of P. Morgan, FRCPath, London, UK.

fibrous bands (symblephara) stretching between the fornices and the globe (*Fig. 3.104*). Eventually contractures may obliterate the conjunctival sac. An essential feature of ocular cicatricial pemphigoid is the production of an abnormal tear film. This develops because of diminished lacrimal gland secretion (due to ductal stenosis), impaired goblet cell mucus secretion and ocular exposure due to impaired eye closure.[14] The end result is ocular drying and eventual keratinization of the ocular surface epithelium. Other important sequelae include entropion, trichiasis (maldirected eyelashes, which can result in corneal abrasion), erosions and perforation, corneal neovascularization and scarring with opacification (*Figs 3.105, 3.106*). Primary corneal bullae have been described, but are very rare and erosions are more typical.[8] Corneal lesions manifest as foreign body sensations, photophobia and eventual blindness, which may be bilateral, occurring in up to 16% of patients.[7] Ocular involvement may be classified into a number of stages of progression (modified Foster staging system).[16]

Ocular involvement should not be confused with drug-induced pemphigoid (pseudo-ocular cicatricial pemphigoid).[2] This is a self-limiting unilateral scarring disease of the eye, which most commonly develops as a consequence of long-term use of eye-drops containing pilocarpine, echothiophate iodide, idoxuridine, timolol and adrenaline (epinephrine) in the treatment of glaucoma.[17,18]

Lesions of the female genitalia, which occur in 20% of patients, predominantly affect the labia majora and minora.[11] Scarring is common and may occasionally be associated with labial fusion (*Fig. 3.107*). In males, genital lesions most often affect the prepuce and the glans penis and are occasionally complicated by urethral stricture formation. Anal lesions affect up to 4% of patients and sometimes cause stenosis.[11]

Cutaneous lesions are found in approximately 25–33% of patients with cicatricial pemphigoid and most often affect the scalp, face and neck.[2,11,12] In some patients, presentation is similar to bullous pemphigoid and fibrosis is not a feature.[2] Lesions are generally few in number and present as itchy, sometimes burning, tense bullae situated on an erythematous or urticated base (*Fig. 3.108*). They tend to recur on previously affected sites. Rarely patients may suffer from a transient generalized bullous eruption.[11] Nikolsky's sign is negative.[15]

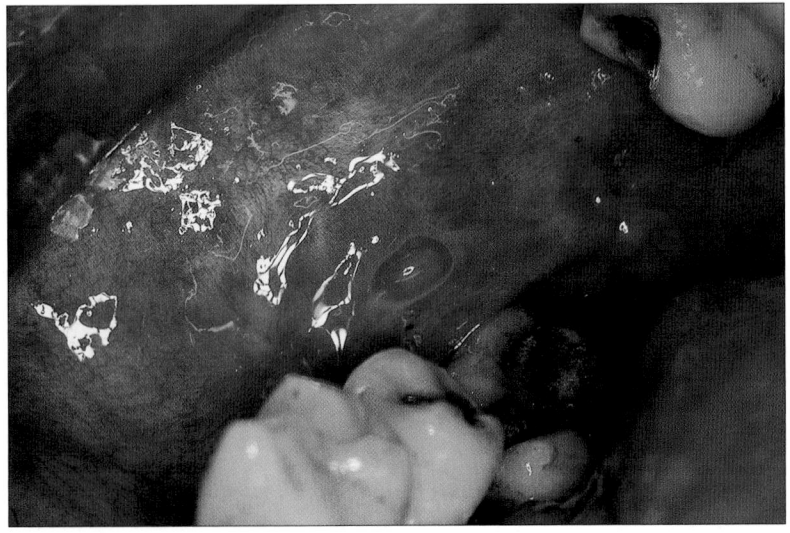

Fig. 3.103
Cicatricial pemphigoid: in addition to erosions, intact blisters are evident. By courtesy of P. Morgan, FRCPath, London, UK.

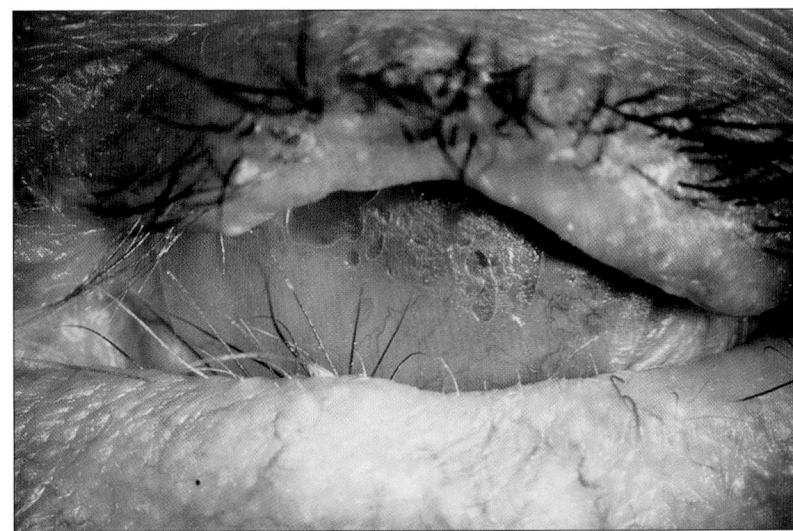

Fig. 3.105
Cicatricial pemphigoid: in this advanced case there is entropion and trichiasis (inwardly directed eyelashes). By courtesy of D. Kerr-Muir, MD, St Thomas' Hospital, London, UK.

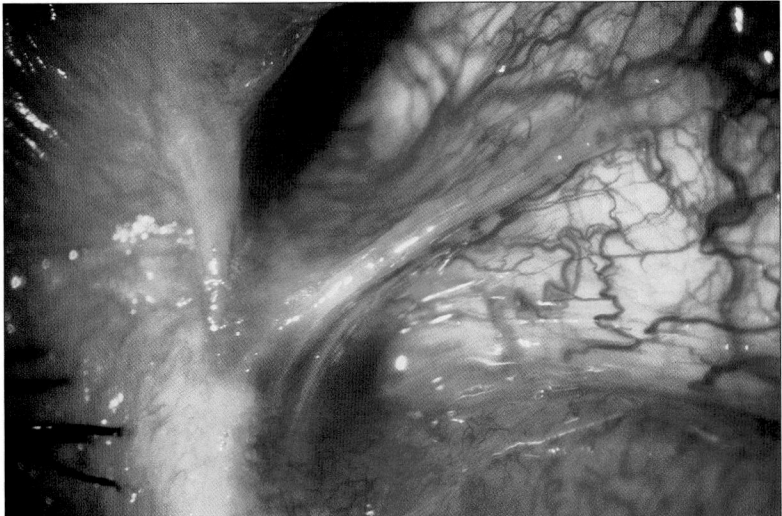

Fig. 3.104
Cicatricial pemphigoid: there is a dense fibrous adhesion (symblepharon) between the conjunctiva lining the eyelid and that covering the globe. By courtesy of D. Kerr-Muir, MD, St Thomas' Hospital, London, UK.

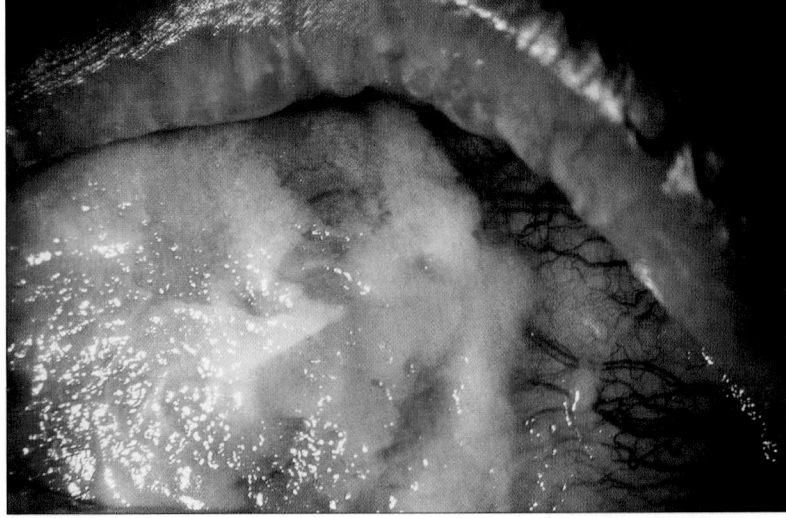

Fig. 3.106
Cicatricial pemphigoid: here there is dense corneal scarring with complete opacification. By courtesy of D. Kerr-Muir, MD, St Thomas' Hospital, London, UK.

In the Brunsting–Perry variant of localized cicatricial pemphigoid, scarring lesions are found predominantly on the head and neck (*Fig. 3.109*).[19,20] This condition shows a male predominance (2:1) and presents most often in the sixth decade. The lesions are slowly enlarging, atrophic or scarred plaques measuring several centimeters or more in diameter and showing vesiculation and/or bullae formation, both centrally and at the enlarging margin.[21] The anterior portion of the scalp, the face (forehead, temporal regions and cheeks) and the anterolateral aspects of the neck are most often affected.[21] In some patients, lesions are few in number and because of crusting, they may be clinically treated as actinic keratosis, thereby delaying the diagnosis. Transient mucous membrane lesions may be a feature, but scarring is not seen.[19]

Pathogenesis and histological features

Cicatricial pemphigoid has been described as a complication of D-penicillamine therapy for rheumatoid arthritis, practolol and clonidine (see adverse drug reactions, p. 648).[11,22] Immunologically characteristic cicatricial pemphigoid has also been described following acute, severe, ocular inflammation in patients with the Stevens–Johnson syndrome.[23] Although the results of HLA associations have been variable, an increased frequency of HLA-DR4 and -DQw3 (DQB1*0301) correlates with a heightened risk of developing ocular disease.[24]

The cutaneous lesions of cicatricial pemphigoid are often indistinguishable from those of cell-rich (inflammatory) bullous pemphigoid, comprising a subepidermal vesicle containing fibrin, edema fluid and variable numbers of inflammatory cells. Although eosinophils are usually evident, they tend to be much less numerous than in generalized bullous pemphigoid. The dermis contains a perivascular lymphohistiocytic infiltrate sometimes with conspicuous plasma cells and accompanied by neutrophils and eosinophils. In older or recurrent lesions, scarring may be a feature (*Fig. 3.110*). Less commonly, a cell-poor subepidermal blister is seen (*Fig. 3.111*).

Oral lesions may rarely be characterized by vesiculation developing between the stratified squamous epithelium (mucosa) and lamina propria (*Figs 3.112, 3.113*). The latter is usually edematous and contains a mixed inflammatory cell infiltrate consisting of lymphocytes, histiocytes, plasma cells and varying numbers of eosinophils and neutrophils (*Fig. 3.114*). More commonly, however, the features seen are those of erosions or ulcers lined by granulation tissue or fibrous tissue and showing non-specific acute or chronic inflammation. The histology is

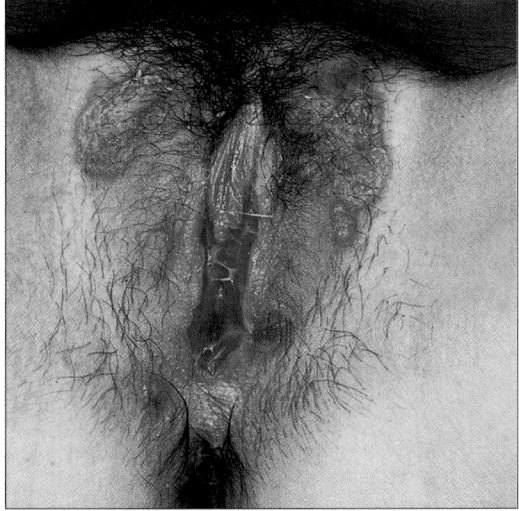

Fig. 3.107
Cicatricial pemphigoid: in addition to erosions, marked scarring of the vulva is present. By courtesy of R.A. Marsden, MD, St George's Hospital, London, UK.

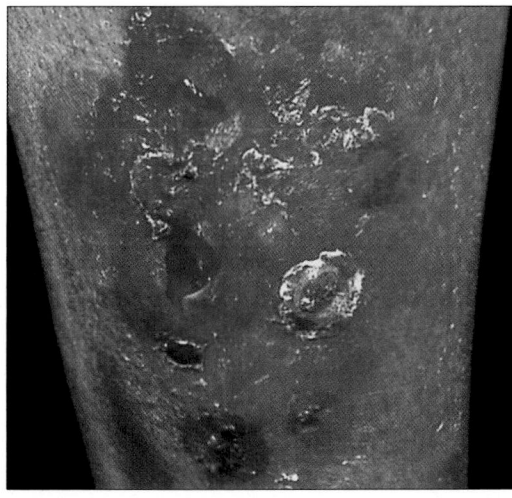

Fig. 3.108
Cicatricial pemphigoid: note the localized blistering and erosion with scarring on the lower leg of an elderly female. By courtesy of R.A. Marsden, MD, St George's Hospital, London, UK.

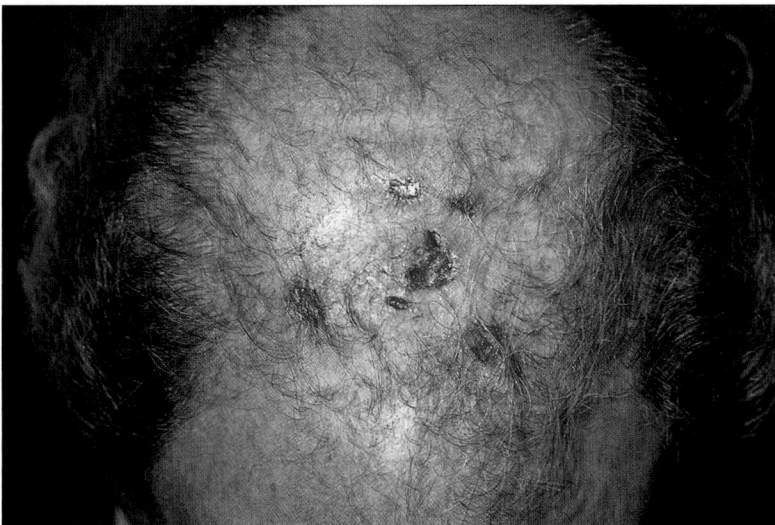

Fig. 3.109
Brunsting–Perry localized pemphigoid: there is extensive alopecia in addition to multiple erosions with scarring. By courtesy of R.A. Marsden, MD, St George's Hospital, London, UK.

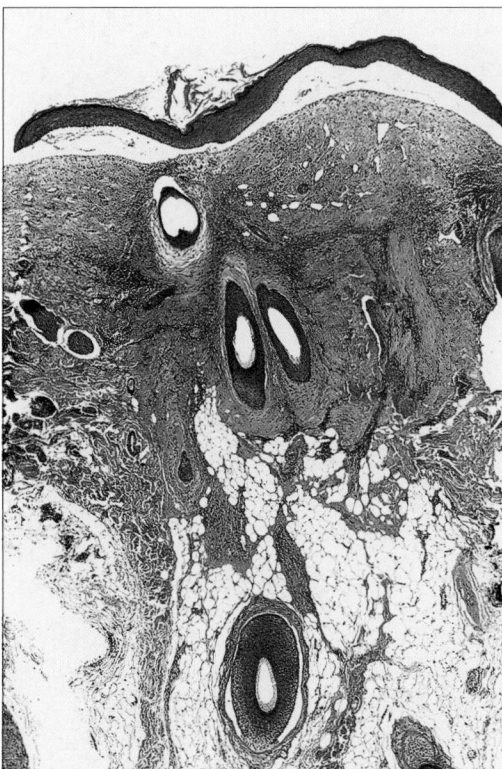

Fig. 3.110
Cicatricial pemphigoid: scalp lesion showing subepidermal vesiculation and dermal scarring.

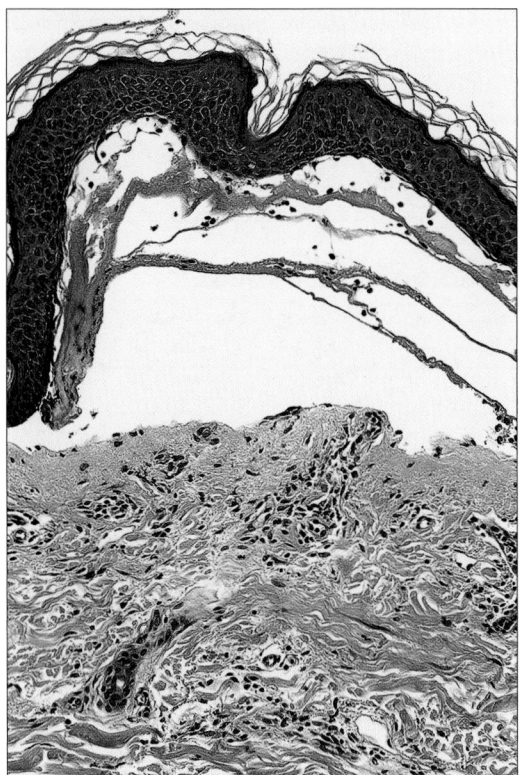

Fig. 3.111
Cicatricial pemphigoid: only very occasional
inflammatory cells are present.

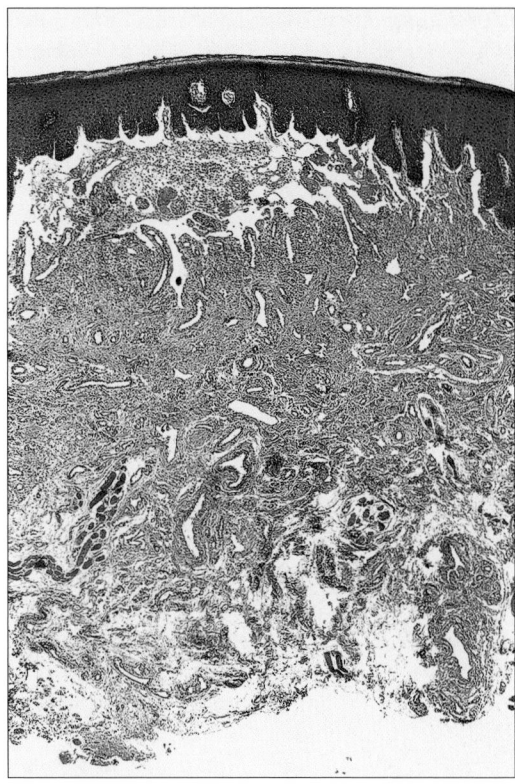

Fig. 3.112
Cicatricial pemphigoid: oral lesion showing an intact
subepithelial blister.

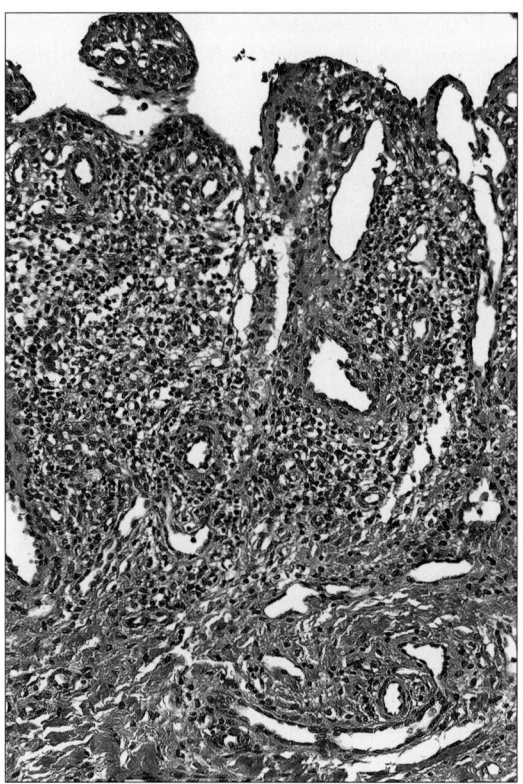

Fig. 3.113
Cicatricial pemphigoid: the lamina propria is intensely
inflamed.

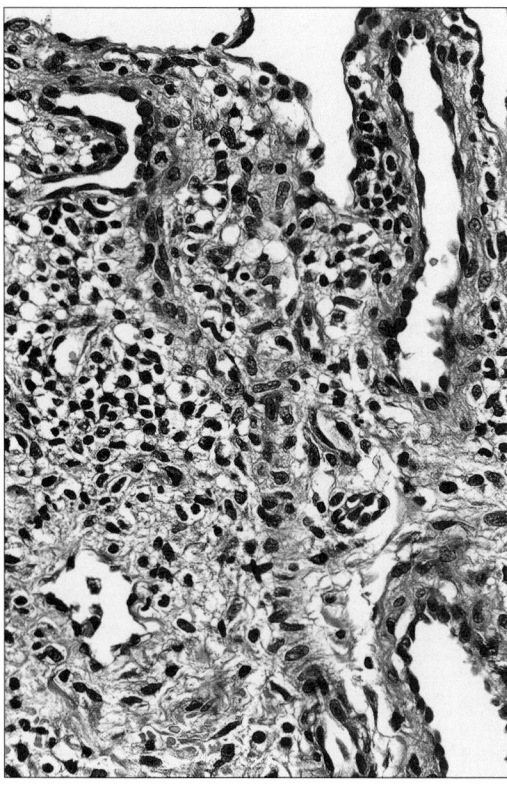

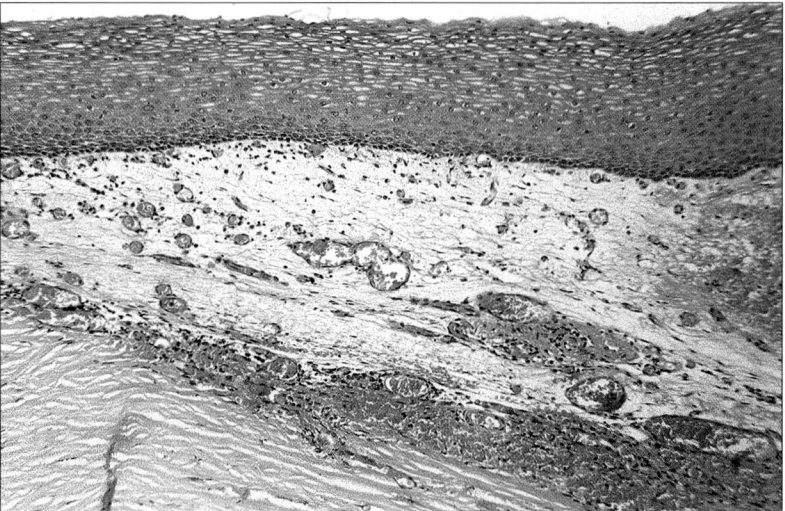

Fig. 3.115
Cicatricial pemphigoid: this specimen of conjunctiva shows complete squamous
metaplasia. Neovascularization of the lamina propria is evident. By courtesy of A.
Garner, MD, Institute of Ophthalmology, London, UK.

Fig. 3.114
Cicatricial pemphigoid:
in this example the
infiltrate consists of
lymphocytes and
histiocytes. Eosinophils
are not a feature.

frequently modified by intense acute inflammatory changes due to
secondary infection.

Conjunctival vesicles or bullae are very rarely seen in ocular cicatricial
pemphigoid. Although erosions may be a feature, more commonly
one may anticipate conjunctival squamous metaplasia with foci of
hyperkeratosis and parakeratosis accompanied by goblet cell depletion
(*Fig. 3.115*).[11] The lamina propria is infiltrated by a mixed inflammatory

cell population consisting of lymphocytes, plasma cells, mast cells and
occasional eosinophils and neutrophils.[15] Granulation tissue may be seen
in early lesions, but dense scarring is a feature of the later stage. In more
severely affected patients, a variety of intraocular manifestations,
including iridocyclitis, rubiosis iridis and the development of synechiae,
may be seen (*Figs 3.116–3.118*).

Laryngeal, pharyngeal and esophageal lesions occasionally show
subepithelial bullae, but erosions, ulcers, inflammatory changes and
fibrosis are more likely to be seen (*Fig. 3.119*). Chronic involvement may
result in serious stenosis.

The histological features of the localized cutaneous scarring (Brunsting–Perry) variant are indistinguishable from those of cicatricial pemphigoid.[21]

Electron microscopic observations are variable. In some patients, the split is in the lamina lucida with the lamina densa lining the floor of the blister cavity whereas in others, lamina densa is found along the roof of the blister and occasionally the lamina densa may be split lining the roof and the floor.[2,25]

Direct immunofluorescent findings in cicatricial pemphigoid are similar to those found in generalized bullous pemphigoid. Therefore a linear deposit of IgG (and sometimes IgA) and C3 is found at the basement membrane region of perilesional mucosa (the site of choice) or perilesional skin in approximately 80–97% of patients.[26–29] The presence of IgA at the basement membrane region accompanied by IgG and C3 is a diagnostic pointer towards cicatricial pemphigoid.[2] Oral mucosa is also of value in the diagnosis of ocular disease.[2] Direct immunoperoxidase of paraffin-embedded tissue can be a satisfactory alternative if a specimen has not been taken for direct immunofluorescence studies.[30]

Circulating anti-basement membrane zone autoantibodies (IgG and/or IgA) are sometimes present (26–36%) and are usually of low titer.[27,31,32] Substitution of normal buccal mucosa as substrate does not increase the yield of circulating antibodies.[31] The antibody consists predominantly of IgG4 and IgG1 subclasses, the presence of the latter conferring complement-fixing ability.[33]

Investigations of cicatricial pemphigoid antibodies using 1 M NaCl-split skin have yielded variable results.[34–36] Circulating antibodies may be detected in from 50 to 100% of cases with active disease.[37,38] Although the majority of sera have reacted with the epidermal side of the split, some have labeled the floor (dermal side, subsequently shown to

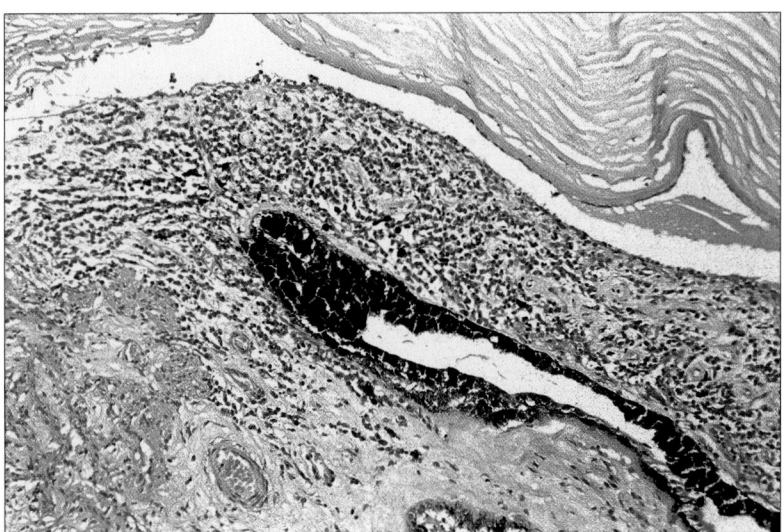

Fig. 3.118
Cicatricial pemphigoid: this field shows anterior uveitis. There is inflammation of the iris and ciliary body. By courtesy of A. Garner, MD, Institute of Ophthalmology, London, UK.

Fig. 3.116
Cicatricial pemphigoid: section of cornea. The overlying pannus shows squamous metaplasia, chronic inflammation and neovascularization. Blood vessels are also present in the cornea. By courtesy of A. Garner, MD, Institute of Ophthalmology, London, UK.

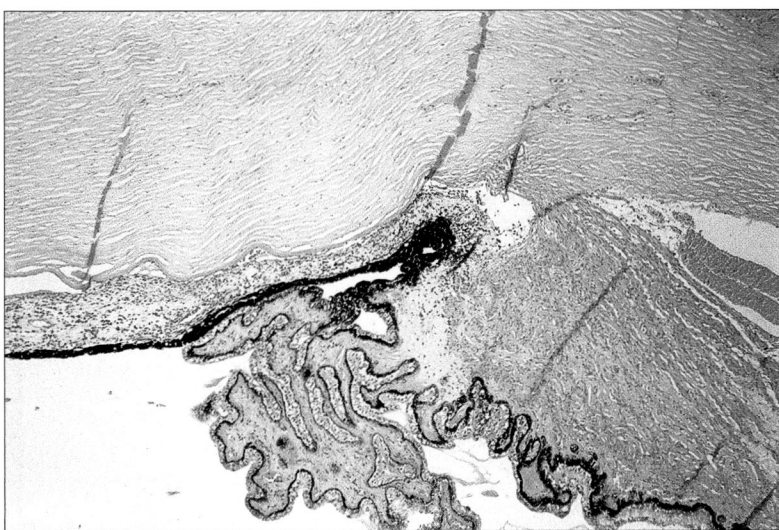

Fig. 3.117
Cicatricial pemphigoid: this section shows iris impaction with anterior synechiae. Iritis and posterior synechiae are also present. By courtesy of A. Garner, MD, Institute of Ophthalmology, London, UK.

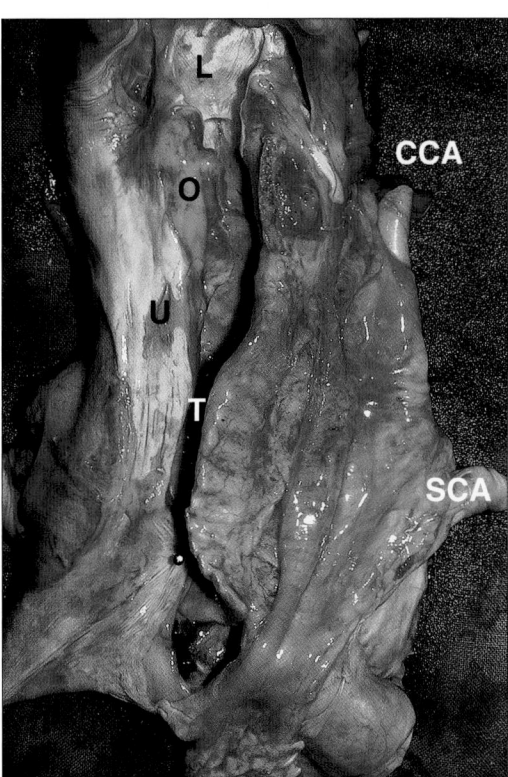

Fig. 3.119
Cicatricial pemphigoid: postmortem specimen showing esophageal erosion and ulceration. (CCA, common carotid artery; L, larynx; O, esophagus; SCA, subclavian artery; T, trachea; U, ulcer.)

be due to anti-laminin-type 5 antibodies – see below), and exceptionally both the roof and the floor have been labeled.[34–38] There is also variation in indirect immunofluorescence findings depending upon the predominant site of involvement. Thus, for example, split skin indirect immunofluorescence may be positive in up to 81% of patients with combined skin and mucosal disease whereas much lower figures have been found in patients with mucosal disease only (18%) or isolated ocular disease (7%).[2,39]

The immunofluorescent findings in the Brunsting–Perry variant are the same as those described for cicatricial pemphigoid.[40–43]

Immunoelectron microscopic observations in cicatricial pemphigoid have revealed two patterns of immune reactant deposition. IgG and C3 may be localized to the lower lamina lucida and lamina densa or else be identified overlying the hemidesmosome.[44–50] There is no involvement of the sublamina densa region. The variation can be explained by the different target antigens involved, i.e. BP180, laminin-5 or β_4 integrin.

In the Brunsting–Perry variant of localized chronic pemphigoid the immunoreactants are localized within the lamina lucida and on the undersurface of basal keratinocytes.[51] Additionally, however, the complement components C3 and C4 may also be detected within the lamina densa and the upper papillary dermis. It is suggested that this latter finding might account for the scarring characteristic of this disease process.[51]

A number of subsets of cicatricial pemphigoid have been delineated by antigen analysis including variants characterized by antibodies to BP180, laminin-5 and β_4 integrin.[33,36,46,52–61] BP180 antibodies react with at least two different sites on the extracellular domain of BP180. One is located on the non-collagenous domain NC16A; the other is located within the carboxy-terminal region.[56] Anti-laminin-5 antibodies to the α_3 subunit (sometimes accompanied by anti-laminin type-6 antibodies) are present in a minority of cases. β_4 integrin implicated in patients with ocular disease and an as yet unidentified 45 kD antigen, which binds to the epidermal side on split skin immunofluorescence, has been implicated in some patients with IgA antibodies.[58,60,61] Autoantibodies to type VII collagen have been documented in some cases of Brunsting–Perry cicatricial pemphigoid (these patients might be better classified within the epidermolysis bullosa acquisita spectrum, see below).[62]

Differential diagnosis

Apart from the presence of scarring in older lesions, cicatricial pemphigoid is indistinguishable from bullous pemphigoid.

References

1. Mobini, N., Nagarwalla, N., Ahmed, A.R. (1998) Oral pemphigoid: subset of cicatricial pemphigoid? *Oral Surg Oral Med Oral Pathol Oral Radiol Endod*, **85**, 37–43.
2. Fleming, T.E., Korman, N.J. (2000) Cicatricial pemphigoid. *J Am Acad Dermatol*, **43**, 571–591.
3. Jolliffe, D.S., Sim-Davis, D. (1977) Cicatricial pemphigoid in a young girl. *Clin Exp Dermatol*, **2**, 281–284.
4. Rogers, M., Painter, D. (1981) Cicatricial pemphigoid in a 4-year-old child. *Aust J Dermatol*, **22**, 21–23.
5. Hauber, I., Fartasch, M., Scheiermacher, E. et al (1987) Disseminated cicatricial pemphigoid in a child and in an adult: ultrastructural diagnostic criteria and differential diagnosis with special reference to acquired epidermolysis bullosa. *Arch Dermatol Res*, **279**, 357–365.
6. Rosenbaum, M.M., Esterly, N.B., Greenwald, M.J. et al (1984) Cicatricial pemphigoid in a six-year-old child: report of a case and review of the literature. *Pediatr Dermatol*, **2**, 13–22.
7. Oranje, A.P., van Joost, T. (1989) Pemphigoid in children. *Pediatr Dermatol*, **6**, 267–274.
8. Hardy, K.M., Perry, H.D., Pingree, G.C. et al (1971) Benign mucous membrane pemphigoid. *Arch Dermatol*, **104**, 467– 475.
9. Williams, D.M. (1990) Vesiculo-bullous mucocutaneous disease: benign mucous membrane and bullous pemphigoid. *J Oral Pathol Med*, **19**, 16–23.
10. Scully, C., Porter, S.R. (1997) The clinical spectrum of desquamative gingivitis. *Semin Cutan Med Surg*, **16**, 308–313.
11. Ahmed, A.R., Kurgis, B.S., Rogers, R.S. III (1991) Cicatricial pemphigoid. *J Am Acad Dermatol*, **24**, 987–1001.
12. Ahmed, A.R., Hombal, S.H. (1986) Cicatricial pemphigoid. *Int J Dermatol*, **25**, 90–96.
13. Mondino, B.J., Linstone, F.A. (1987) Ocular pemphigoid. *Clin Dermatol*, **5**, 28–35.
14. Foster, S. (1986) Cicatricial pemphigoid. *Trans Am Ophthalmol Soc*, **84**, 527–563.
15. Camisa, C., Meisler, D.M. (1992) Immunobullous diseases with ocular involvement. *Dermatol Clin*, **10**, 555–570.
16. Tauber, J., Jabbur, N., Foster, C.S. (1992) Improved detection of disease progression in ocular cicatricial pemphigoid. *Cornea*, **11**, 446–451.
17. Fiore, P.M., Jacobs, I.H., Goldberg, D.B. (1987) Drug-induced pemphigoid: a spectrum of diseases. *Arch Ophthalmol*, **105**, 1660–1663.
18. Fiore, P.M. (1987) Drug-induced ocular cicatrisation. *Int Ophthalmol Clin*, **29**, 147–150.
19. Jacoby, W.D., Bartholome, C.W., Ramchand, S.C. et al (1978) Cicatricial pemphigoid (Brunsting–Perry type). *Arch Dermatol*, **114**, 779–781.
20. Person, J.R., Rogers, R.S., Perry, H.O. (1976) Localized pemphigoid. *Br J Dermatol*, **95**, 531–534.
21. Kaplan, R.P. (1987) Cutaneous involvement in localized forms of bullous pemphigoid. *Clin Dermatol*, **5**, 43–51.
22. Vassileva, S. (1998) Drug-induced pemphigoid: bullous and cicatricial. *Clin Dermatol*, **16**, 379–387.
23. Chan, L.S., Soong, H. K., Foster, C.S. et al (1991) Ocular cicatricial pemphigoid occurring as a sequela of Stevens–Johnson syndrome. *JAMA*, **266**, 1543–1546.
24. Chan, L.S., Hammerberg, C., Cooper, K.D. (1997) Significantly increased occurrence of HLA-DQB1*0301 allele in patients with ocular cicatricial pemphigoid. *J Invest Dermatol*, **108**, 129–132.
25. Person, J.R., Rogers, R.S. (1977) Bullous and cicatricial pemphigoid: clinical, histopathologic, and immunopathologic correlations. *Mayo Clin Proc*, **52**, 54–66.
26. Faith, D.A., Venning, V.A., Wojnarowska, F. et al (1989) Conjunctival involvement in cicatricial and bullous pemphigoid: a clinical and immunopathological study. *Br J Ophthalmol*, **73**, 52–56.
27. Laskaris, G., Angelopoulos, A. (1981) Cicatricial pemphigoid: direct and indirect immunofluorescent studies. *Oral Surg*, **51**, 48–54.
28. Daniels, T.E., Quandra-White, C. (1981) Direct immunofluorescence in oral mucosal disease: a diagnostic analysis of 130 cases. *Oral Surg*, **51**, 38–47.
29. Rogers, R.S., Perry, H.O., Bean, S.F. et al (1977) Immunopathology of cicatricial pemphigoid: studies of complement deposition. *J Invest Dermatol*, **68**, 39–43.
30. Demers, P.E., Robin, H., Prost, C. et al (1998) Immunohistopathologic testing in patients suspected of ocular cicatricial pemphigoid. *Curr Eye Res*, **17**, 823–827.
31. Nisengard, R.J., Jablonska, S., Beutner, E.H. et al (1975) Diagnostic importance of immunofluorescence in oral bullous diseases and lupus erythematosus. *Oral Surg*, **40**, 365–375.
32. Fine, J-D., Neises, G.R., Katz, S.I. (1984) Immunofluorescence and immunoelectron microscopic studies in cicatricial pemphigoid. *J Invest Dermatol*, **82**, 39–43.
33. Bernard, P., Prost, C., Aucouturier, P. et al (1991) The subclass distribution of IgG autoantibodies in cicatricial pemphigoid and epidermolysis bullosa acquisita. *J Invest Dermatol*, **97**, 259–263.
34. Fine, J-D. (1985) Cicatricial pemphigoid, bullous pemphigoid and epidermolysis bullosa acquisita antigens: differences in organ and species specificities and localizations in chemically-separated human skin of three basement membrane regions. *Coll Rel Res*, **5**, 369–377.
35. Kelly, S.E., Wojnarowska, F. (1988) The use of chemically split tissue in the detection of circulating anti-basement membrane zone antibodies in bullous pemphigoid and cicatricial pemphigoid. *Br J Dermatol*, **118**, 31–40.
36. Niimi, Y., Zhu, X-J., Bystryn, J-C. (1992) Identification of cicatricial pemphigoid antigens. *Arch Dermatol*, **128**, 54–57.
37. Kelly, S.E., Wojnarowska, F. (1988) The use of chemically split tissue in the detection of circulating anti-basement membrane zone antibodies in bullous and cicatricial pemphigoid. *Br J Dermatol*, **118**, 31–40.
38. Sarret, Y., Hall, R., Cobo, L.M. et al (1991) Salt-split human skin substrate for the immunofluorescent screening of serum from patients with cicatricial pemphigoid and a new method of immunoprecipitation with IgA antibodies. *J Am Acad Dermatol*, **24**, 952–958.
39. Chan, L.S., Yancey, K.B., Hammerberg, C. et al (1993) Immune-mediated subepithelial blistering diseases of mucous membranes. Pure ocular pemphigoid is a unique clinical and immunopathological entity distinct from bullous pemphigoid and other subsets identified by antigenic specificities of autoantibodies. *Arch Dermatol*, **129**, 448–455.
40. Beno, M., Bean, S.F., Chorzelski, T. et al (1977) Cicatricial pemphigoid of Brunsting–Perry: immunofluorescent studies. *Arch Dermatol*, **113**, 1403–1405.
41. Michel, B., Bean, S.F., Chorzelski, T. et al (1977) Cicatricial pemphigoid of Brunsting–Perry: immunofluorescent studies. *Arch Dermatol*, **113**, 1403–1405.
42. Niebor, C., Roeleveld, C.G., Kalsbeek, G.L. (1978) Localized chronic pemphigoid. *Dermatologica*, **156**, 22–33.
43. Jacoby, W.D., Bartholome, C.W., Ramchand, S.C. et al (1978) Cicatricial pemphigoid (Brunsting–Perry type): case report and immunofluorescence findings. *Arch Dermatol*, **114**, 779–781.
44. Bédane, C., Prost, C., Bernard, P. et al (1991) Cicatricial pemphigoid antigen differs from bullous pemphigoid antigen by its exclusive extracellular localization: a study by indirect immunoelectronmicroscopy. *J Invest Dermatol*, **97**, 3–9.
45. Neiboer, C., Boorsma, D.M., Woerdeman, M.J. (1983) Immunofluorescence and immuno-electron microscopic studies in cicatricial pemphigoid. *J Invest Dermatol*, **106**, 419–422.
46. Horiguchi, Y., Tanaka, T., Akioka, N. et al (1992) Restriction of cicatricial pemphigoid antigens to the lamina densa: confirmation by indirect immunoelectron microscopy. *J Dermatol*, **19**, 449–455.
47. Fine, J-D., Neises, G.R., Katz, S.I. (1984) Immunofluorescence and immunoelectron microscopic studies in cicatricial pemphigoid. *J Invest Dermatol*, **82**, 29–43.
48. Prost, C., Labeille, B., Chaussade, V. et al (1987) Immunoelectron microscopy in subepidermal autoimmune bullous diseases: a prospective study of IgG and C3 bound in vivo in 32 patients. *J Invest Dermatol*, **89**, 567–573.
49. Shimitzu, H., Masunaga, T., Ishiko, A. et al (1995) Autoantibodies from patients with cicatricial pemphigoid target different sites in epidermal basement membrane. *J Invest Dermatol*, **104**, 370–373.
50. Neiboer, C., Boorsma, D.M., Woerdeman, M.J. (1982) Immunoelectron microscopic findings in cicatricial pemphigoid: their significance in relation to epidermolysis bullosa acquisita. *Br J Dermatol*, **106**, 419–421.
51. Murata, Y., Tani, M., Kumano, K. (1983) Localized chronic pemphigoid of Brunsting–Perry. Ultrastructural localization of IgG and complement components. *Arch Dermatol*, **119**, 921–924.
52. Bernard, P., Prost, C., Lecerf, V. et al (1990) Studies of cicatricial pemphigoid autoantibodies using direct immunoelectron microscopy and immunoblot analysis. *J Invest Dermatol*, **94**, 630–635.
53. Domloge-Hultsch, N., Anhalt, G.J., Gammon, W.R. et al (1994) Anti-epiligrin cicatricial pemphigoid. A subepithelial bullous disorder. *Arch Dermatol*, **130**, 1521–1529.
54. Kirtschig, G., Marinkovich, M.P., Burgeson, R.E. et al (1995) Anti-basement membrane zone antibodies in patients with anti-epiligrin cicatricial pemphigoid bind the α3 subunit of laminin-5. *J Invest Dermatol*, **105**, 543–548.
55. Bernard, P., Prost, C., Durepaire, N. et al (1992) The major cicatricial pemphigoid antigen is a 180-kD protein that shows immunologic cross-reactivities with the bullous pemphigoid antigen. *J Invest Dermatol*, **99**, 174–179.
56. Balding, S.D., Prost, C., Diaz, L.A. et al (1996) Cicatricial pemphigoid antibodies react with multiple sites on the BP180 extracellular domain. *J Invest Dermatol*, **106**, 141–146.
57. Zillikens, D., Giudice, G.J. (1999) BP180/type XVII collagen: its role in acquired and inherited disorders of the dermal–epidermal junction. *Arch Dermatol Res*, **291**, 187–194.
58. Chan, L.S., Majmudar, A.A., Tran, H.H. et al (1997) Laminin-6 and laminin-5 are recognized by autoantibodies in a subset of cicatricial pemphigoid. *J Invest Dermatol*, **108**, 848–853.
59. Leverkus, M., Schmidt, E., Lazarova, Z. et al (1999) Antiepiligrin cicatricial pemphigoid: an underdiagnosed entity within the spectrum of scarring autoimmune subepidermal bullous diseases? *Arch Dermatol*, **135**, 1091–1098.
60. Tyagi, S., Bhol, K., Natarajan, K. et al (1996) Ocular cicatricial pemphigoid: partial sequence and biochemical characterization. *Proc Natl Acad Sci USA*, **93**, 14714–14719.
61. Smith, E.P., Taylor, T.B., Meyer, L.J. et al (1993) Identification of a basement membrane zone antigen reactive with circulating IgA antibody in ocular cicatricial pemphigoid. *J Invest Dermatol*, **101**, 619–623.
62. Hallel-Halevy, D., Nadelman, C., Chen, M. et al (2001) Epidermolysis bullosa acquisita: update and review. *Clin Dermatol*, **19**, 712–718.

Epidermolysis bullosa acquisita (dermolytic pemphigoid)

Epidermolysis bullosa acquisita (dermolytic pemphigoid) is a rare, chronic blistering disease, which is characterized by variable clinical presentations and which may therefore be mistaken for a number of other blistering disorders including congenital epidermolysis bullosa and the other acquired autoimmune bullous dermatoses.[1,2] Annual incidence figures from France and Central Germany are 0.17–0.26 per million of the population.[3,4] In contrast to its congenital counterpart, epidermolysis bullosa acquisita (EBA) usually develops in adult life although cases in childhood have been documented.[5] Initially it was characterized as a porphyria cutanea tarda-like mechanobullous dermatosis. More recently, however, patients have been described in whom the disease has presented as a generalized inflammatory bullous dermatosis.[1] For many decades the diagnosis of EBA was one of exclusion. As a result of immunofluorescence and immunoultrastructural techniques combined with immunoblotting and immunoprecipitation, EBA is now recognized as an autoimmune dermatosis, type VII collagen (290 kD) representing the target antigen.[1] A 145 kD antigen is also sometimes identified. This represents a cleavage product of the 290 kD antigen.

Clinical features

EBA was defined in 1971 by Roenigk and colleagues[6] as follows:
- clinical lesions resembling dystrophic epidermolysis bullosa (blisters developing on the hands, feet, elbows and knees following mild trauma and complicated by atrophic scarring, milia formation and nail dystrophy)
- an adult onset
- a negative family history of epidermolysis bullosa
- exclusion of all other recognized bullous dermatoses including porphyria cutanea tarda, bullous pemphigoid, dermatitis herpetiformis, pemphigus, erythema multiforme and bullous drug reactions.[7]

It has a wide age incidence ranging from 11 to 77 years, with a mean age of 47 years. It is associated with a slight female predominance.

In addition to the mechanobullous classical form of EBA, inflammatory variants, including bullous pemphigoid-like, cicatricial pemphigoid-like and linear IgA disease-like variants, may also be encountered.[1,8,9]

Classical variant

The classical variant is the most commonly encountered variant of EBA. Patients present with a porphyria cutanea tarda-like illness showing extreme skin fragility, developing erosions, blistering and crusting in response to mild trauma including shearing forces.[5] Lesions are located on the backs of the fingers and hands in particular and at other sites that are susceptible to trauma, including the knees, elbows and buttocks, but virtually any site may be affected (*Fig. 3.120*).[1,5] The blisters are characteristically non-inflammatory, painless and tense, and may contain clear or bloodstained fluid.

Healing is usually associated with postinflammatory hyperpigmentation, considerable scarring and atrophy. Milia are frequently conspicuous, and nail changes, including distal onycholysis, dystrophy and anonychia with nail bed scarring, are common complications (*Fig. 3.121*). More widespread involvement may resemble dominant or more often recessive dystrophic epidermolysis bullosa. Scarring may then be extreme with resultant contractures and syndactilism. Rarely esophageal involvement has been documented with resultant stricture formation.[8,10,11]

Bullous pemphigoid-like EBA

This is the most commonly encountered inflammatory variant.[12] On the basis of split skin indirect immunofluorescence (see below) it has been suggested that a BP presentation may account for up to 50% of cases of EBA and that 10–15% of patients diagnosed as BP in fact have EBA.[12] Other authors, however, have found that EBA is very rare compared to BP, the relative incidence being approximately 25–50 cases of BP for every one case of EBA diagnosed.[13,14]

Patients present with a generalized eruption of large tense blisters, which are often associated with erythema and show a predilection for the flexural and intertrigenous areas.[15,16] Pruritus is common.[12] Skin fragility is typically absent and scarring and/or milia are not usually features unless the patient concomitantly shows or evolves towards a mechanobullous phase.[1,12] Infrequently, the clinical manifestations may resemble dermatitis herpetiformis (*Fig. 3.122*).

Cicatricial pemphigoid-like variant

Some patients present with a cicatricial pemphigoid-like variant, characterized by mucous membrane involvement. The oral cavity is commonly

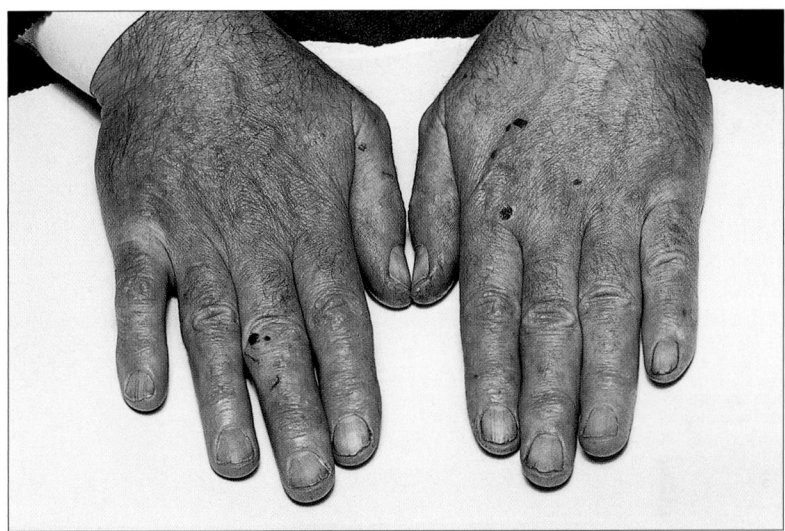

Fig. 3.120
Epidermolysis bullosa acquisita: there are hemorrhagic blisters and scarring on the knuckles similar to those in the autosomal dominant variant of epidermolysis bullosa. By courtesy of M. Shaw, MD, St Thomas' Hospital, London, UK.

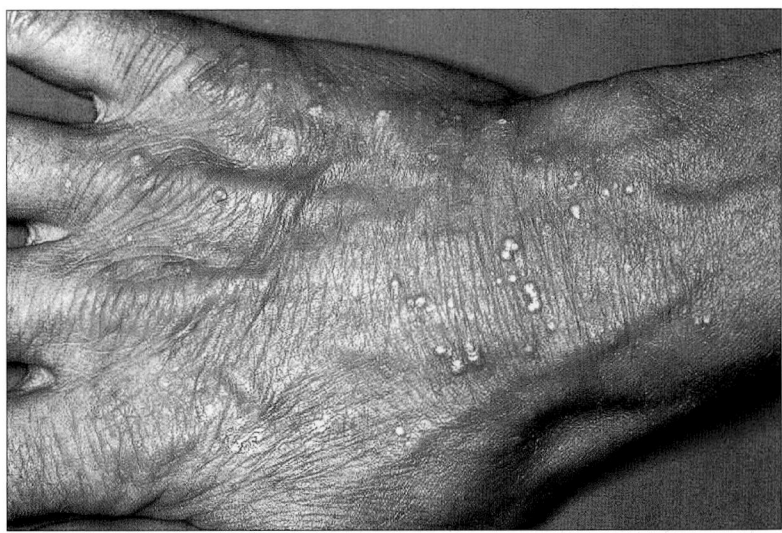

Fig. 3.121
Epidermolysis bullosa acquisita: conspicuous milia are present on the back of the hand. By courtesy of the Institute of Dermatology, London, UK.

affected. Erosions, ulcers and blisters may be seen on the tongue, gums, palate and buccal mucosa.[9] Rarely, the larynx and esophagus are affected with resultant stricture formation.[8] The anus, vulva, vagina and bladder may very occasionally be involved.[17] Conjunctival lesions are an important, but infrequent, cause of morbidity.[8,9] Symblepharon, epiphora and even blindness may occur. Alopecia is sometimes an additional feature.[7,10]

Brunsting–Perry variant

Some patients with the Brunsting–Perry variant of cicatricial pemphigoid (characterized by blistering and scarring confined to the head and neck) have antibodies against type VII collagen and therefore might better be classified within the epidermolysis bullosa acquisita spectrum.[18,19] Facial involvement predominates.[19]

Linear IgA disease-like variant (IgA-EBA)

EBA may also present as a linear IgA disease-like variant in which both adult and childhood patients have IgA autoantibodies directed against type VII collagen (see below).[20–22] In adults, ocular involvement is often severe and blindness is not uncommon.[21]

Childhood EBA

Childhood EBA is extremely rare. Mucosal disease is often severe and clinical manifestations have included classical bullous pemphigoid and linear IgA-like variants.[6]

Systemic disease

EBA has long been known to be associated with a number of systemic illnesses, many with an immunologically mediated pathogenesis. More important are inflammatory bowel disease and diabetes mellitus.[2,8,12,23–34] Approximately 30% of patients with EBA manifest inflammatory bowel

disease, predominantly Crohn's disease.[31] Control of this improves the skin condition in some patients.

Pathogenesis and histological features

The histological features are somewhat variable depending upon whether a mechanobullous or an inflammatory lesion is biopsied.

The mechanobullous lesion is characterized by a bland, 'cell-free' subepidermal vesicle containing only a few erythrocytes and a little fibrin (*Figs 3.123, 3.124*). Usually no significant inflammatory cell infiltrate is present either within the blister cavity or in the adjacent or underlying dermis. Sometimes, however, a small number of neutrophils, histiocytes and eosinophils may be present. The basement membrane lines the roof of the blister. Marked scarring of the adjacent dermis is often a feature and milia are frequently identified.

The inflammatory variant is characterized by a subepidermal vesicle accompanied by a mixed inflammatory cell infiltrate comprising lymphocytes, histiocytes with prominent neutrophils and eosinophils. Neutrophils are usually the predominant cell type and in incipient lesions they may be identified in a linear distribution adjacent to the epider-

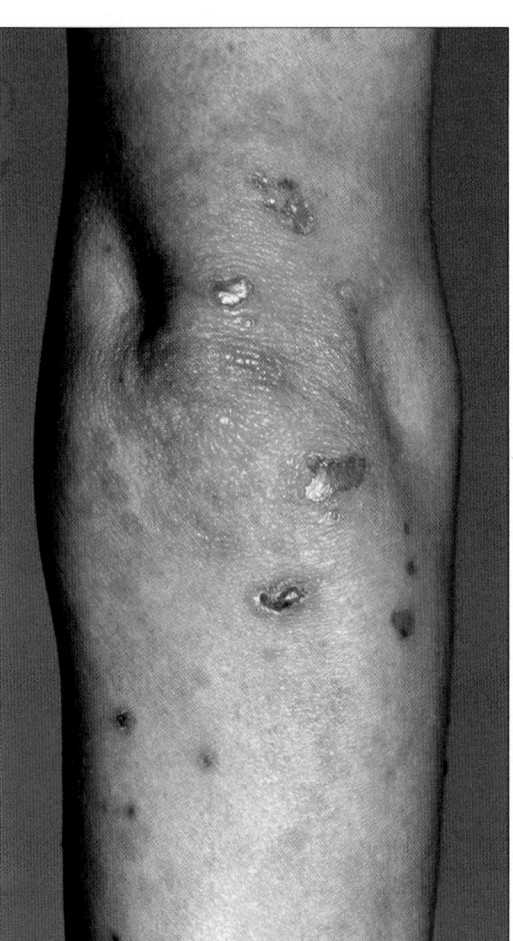

Fig. 3.122
Epidermolysis bullosa acquisita: in this patient with the dermatitis herpetiformis-like inflammatory variant, blisters, erosions and erythematous plaques are evident on the elbow. By courtesy of R.A. Marsden, MD, St George's Hospital, London, UK.

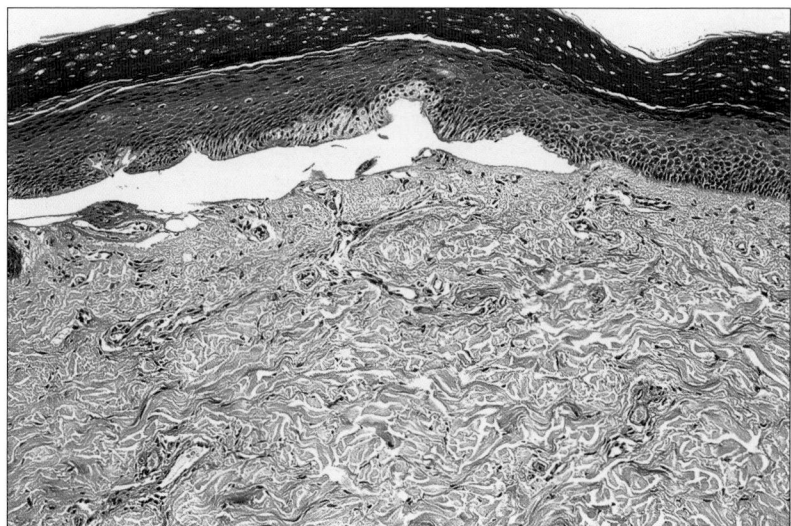

Fig. 3.123
Epidermolysis bullosa acquisita (classical variant): there is a cell-free subepidermal vesicle. Note the dermal scarring.

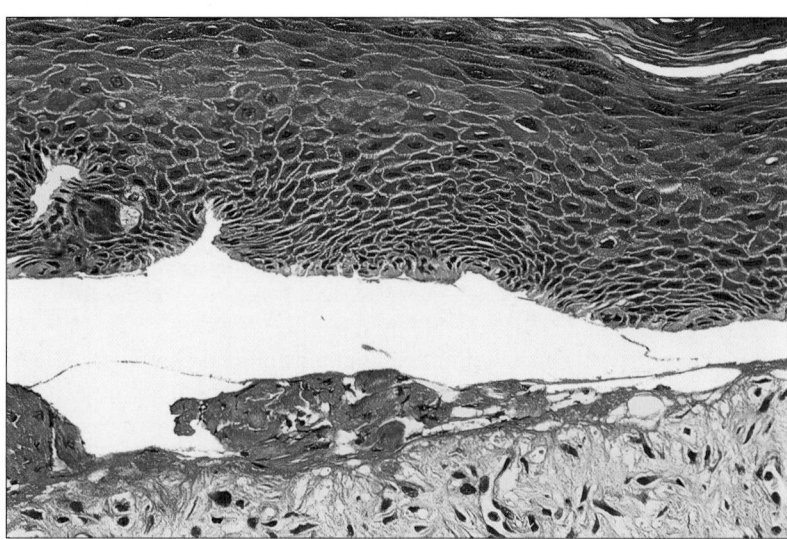

Fig. 3.124
Epidermolysis bullosa acquisita (classical variant): high power view. There is fibrin along the floor of the blister cavity. Note the absence of inflammatory cells.

modermal junction.[12] Occasionally, however, eosinophils predominate.[19] Such inflammatory lesions may resemble BP or dermatitis herpetiformis (*Figs 3.125, 3.126*).[2] Oral lesions show similar features of submucosal vesiculation with an erythrocyte and inflammatory cell content.

By direct immunoperoxidase using paraffin-embedded material, type IV collagen is found in the roof of the blister cavity (see *Fig. 3.8*).

Ultrastructurally, the level of the split in EBA is situated within the superficial dermis immediately below the lamina densa (*Fig. 3.127*).[35–37] The basal keratinocytes appear normal. Anchoring fibrils have been variably reported as reduced in number or absent.[34–37]

An occasional finding is the presence of electron-dense, amorphous granular material within the superficial papillary dermis close to, but separated from, the lamina densa (*Fig. 3.128*).[7,24] When present, the split is usually below the electron-dense amorphous material, which is therefore located within the roof of the blister.

By direct IMF, IgG and C3 are present in a linear distribution along the basement membrane region (identical to BP) in a very high proportion of cases of EBA (*Fig. 3.129*).[7,8,25] Less commonly IgM, IgA, properdin and factor B may also be identified.[1,36,37] In linear IgA disease-like patients, IgA may be present in the absence of IgG.[20–22]

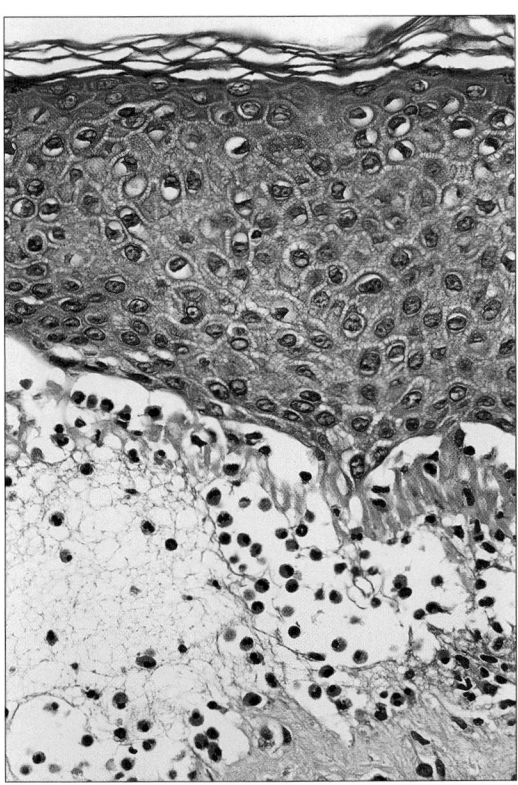

Fig. 3.125
Inflammatory epidermolysis bullosa acquisita: in this bullous pemphigoid-like variant, subepidermal blistering is associated with an eosinophil-rich infiltrate.

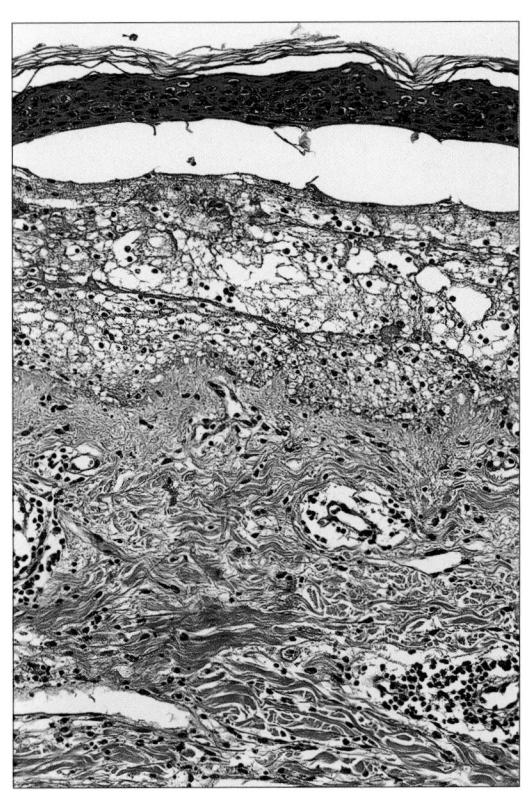

Fig. 3.126
Inflammatory epidermolysis bullosa acquisita: dermatitis herpetiformis-like variant, with a neutrophil-rich infiltrate.

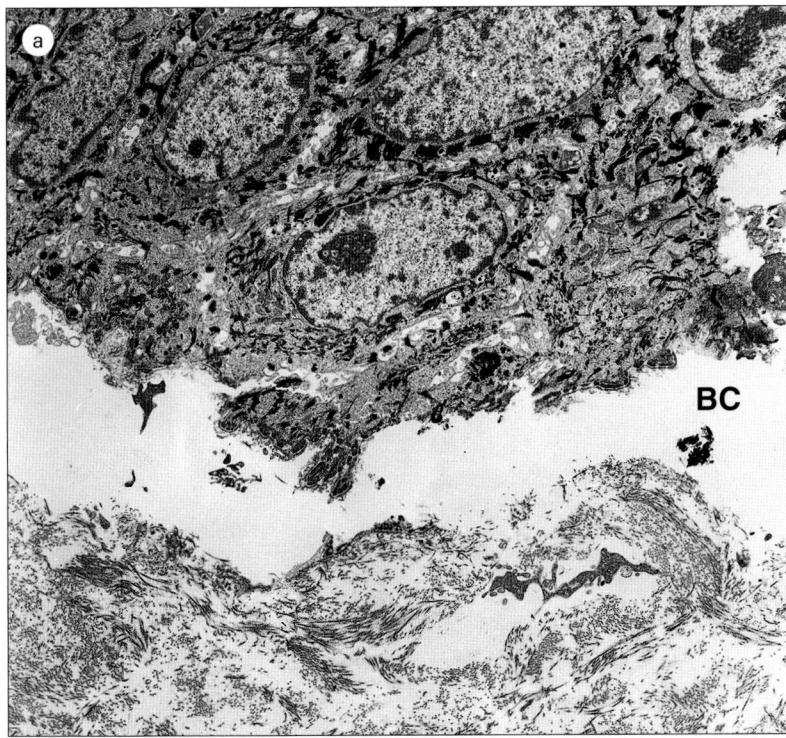

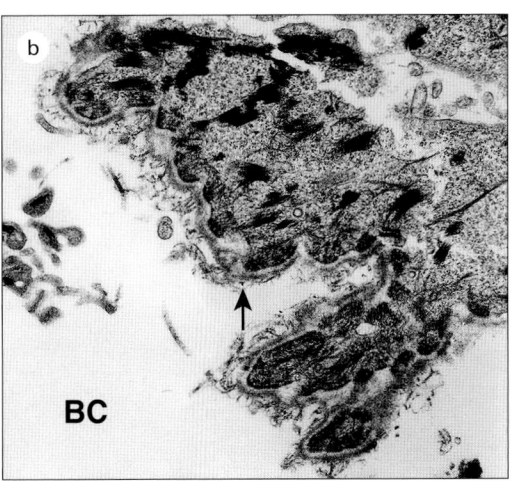

Fig. 3.127
(a, b) Epidermolysis bullosa acquisita: electron micrograph showing the lamina densa (arrowed) in the roof of the blister. (BC, blister cavity.)

Positive direct immunofluorescence has also been reported at a variety of other sites including the oral mucosa, conjunctiva, cornea, esophagus, duodenum and bladder.[17,21,23]

IgG anti-basement membrane antibodies may be identified in 25–50% of patients, thereby increasing the similarity to BP.[2,34,35,38] In many patients the anti-basement membrane antibodies are associated with complement-fixing properties.[39] With split skin indirect IMF, which is more sensitive than conventional indirect IMF, the immunoreactants line the floor of the induced blister cavity.[40–43]

Direct and indirect immunoelectron microscopic studies have determined that the immunoreactants lie on or below the lamina densa, corresponding to the site of the electron-dense amorphous material mentioned above (*Fig. 3.130*).[1,35,37,44] Immunogold labeling confirms that the immunoglobulin deposits are related to the anchoring fibrils (*Fig. 3.131*).[45] As a consequence of these additional observations, a modified set of criteria for the diagnosis of EBA has been recommended:[1,46]

- clinical lesions of trauma-induced bullae occurring over the joints of the hands, feet, elbows and knees, atrophic scars, milia and nail dystrophy, or else, presentation as a clinically inflammatory bullous or cicatricial pemphigoid-like process
- postinfancy onset of the disease
- no family history of EBA
- exclusion of other bullous diseases
- IgG at the basement membrane zone on direct immunofluorescence
- demonstration of blister formation beneath the lamina densa
- demonstration of IgG associated with anchoring fibrils beneath the basal lamina by immunoelectron microscopy
- localization of the immunoreactants to the floor of 1 M NaCl-split skin by direct and or indirect immunofluorescence.

The EBA antigen (290 kD) is the globular (non-collagenous) carboxyl terminus of type VII procollagen (*Fig. 3.132*).[47–51] Type VII collagen is the major constituent of anchoring fibrils which anchor the basement membrane through the lamina densa to the connective tissue constituents of the adjacent dermis. It is synthesized by both human keratinocytes and fibroblasts in culture, and is found within other mammalian skin including dog, cat, guinea pig, rat, mouse and hamster, but not in avian, reptilian, amphibian or fish skin.[52–55] Type VII collagen has also been identified within the esophagus, mouth, anus and vagina. It has a high affinity for fibronectin, which is thought to be responsible (at least in part) for adhesion between cells and matrix within the dermis.[56] The interaction between the EBA antibody and type VII collagen is thought to somehow upset this delicate relationship with consequent epidermodermal separation.[57]

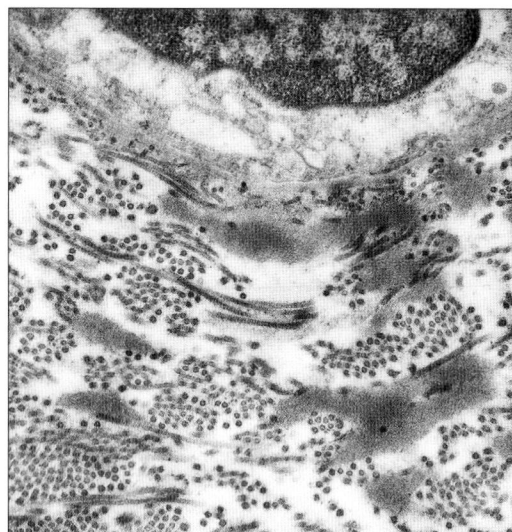

Fig. 3.128
Epidermolysis bullosa acquisita: occasional deposits of finely granular electron-dense material (immunoreactants) as seen in this field may be a useful diagnostic pointer.

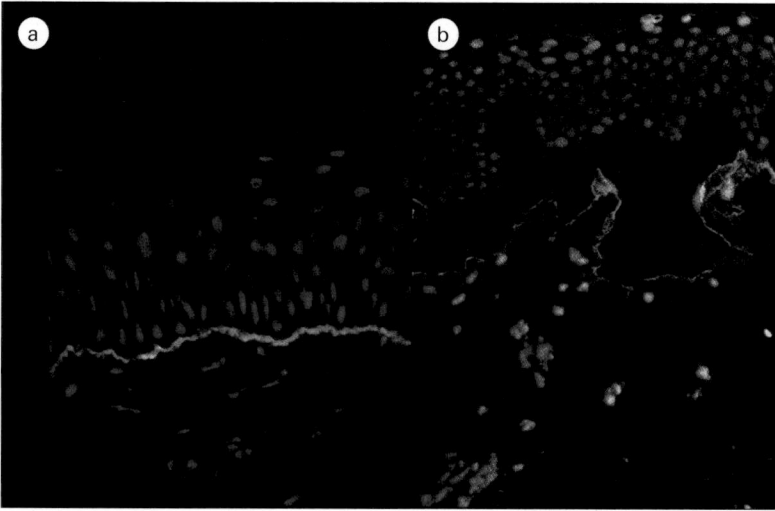

Fig. 3.129
Epidermolysis bullosa acquisita: (a) direct immunofluorescence shows linear IgG deposition along the basement membrane region; (b) with split skin the immunoreactant lines the floor of the induced lesion. By courtesy of Department of Immunofluorescence, Institute of Dermatology, London, UK.

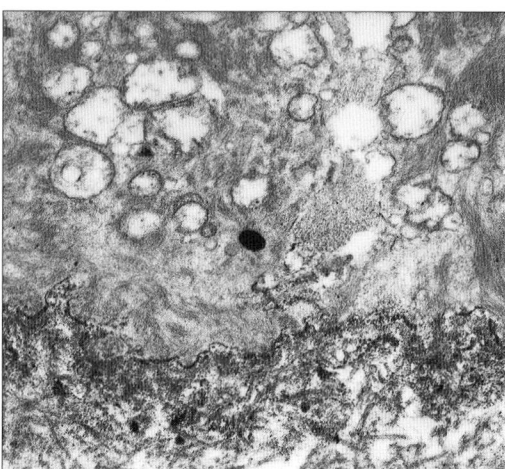

Fig. 3.130
Epidermolysis bullosa acquisita: direct immunoelectron microscopy showing reactant deposition below the lamina densa.

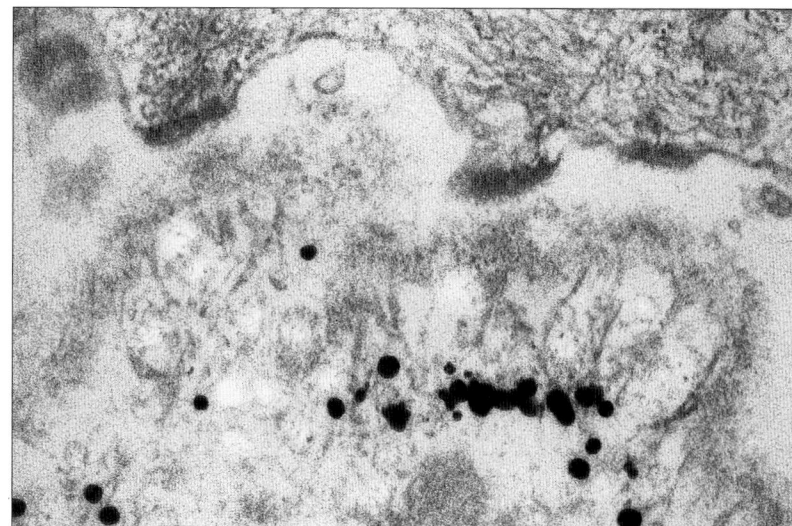

Fig. 3.131
Epidermolysis bullosa acquisita: immunogold preparation showing localization of the immunoglobulin to the anchoring fibrils. By courtesy of H. Shimizu, MD, Keio University School of Medicine, Tokyo, Japan.

The parallel between EBA and BP is obvious and it is tempting to extrapolate a similar pathogenesis. Although the current concept for EBA points to such a similarity, additional confirmatory evidence is required. Recent studies have shown that the pathogenesis is related, at least in part, to neutrophil recruitment mediated by complement activation, and the generation of complement-derived chemotactic activity (C5A) at the epidermal basement membrane region.[57] An experimental model in which immune complexes are produced by treating normal skin in organ culture with EBA complement-fixing antibodies has been shown to result in complement-dependent neutrophil migration to the basement membrane region and eventual dermoepidermal separation.[39] The precise mechanism whereby such blisters evolve is unknown, but it has been suggested that leukocyte-derived proteases and reactive oxygen intermediates may be important.[38]

The pathogenesis of the 'cell-free' mechanobullous variant is poorly understood. It is also associated with anti-basement membrane antibody, but there is little if any evidence for neutrophil chemotactic activity. It has been proposed that separation at the epidermodermal junction may result from an abrogation of affinities between the type VII collagen and laminin-5 in addition to matrix proteins such as fibronectin due to a direct effect of autoantibody deposition at that site.[1,58–60] An additional potential mechanism proposed is a direct effect of the autoantibody on type collagen VII antiparallel dimer assembly leading to diminished anchoring fibril formation.[1,61]

Differential diagnosis

Cell-free EBA must be distinguished from congenital EB, porphyria cutanea tarda, pseudoporphyria and cutaneous bullous amyloidosis. Diagnosis can be achieved easily with the use of immunofluorescence.

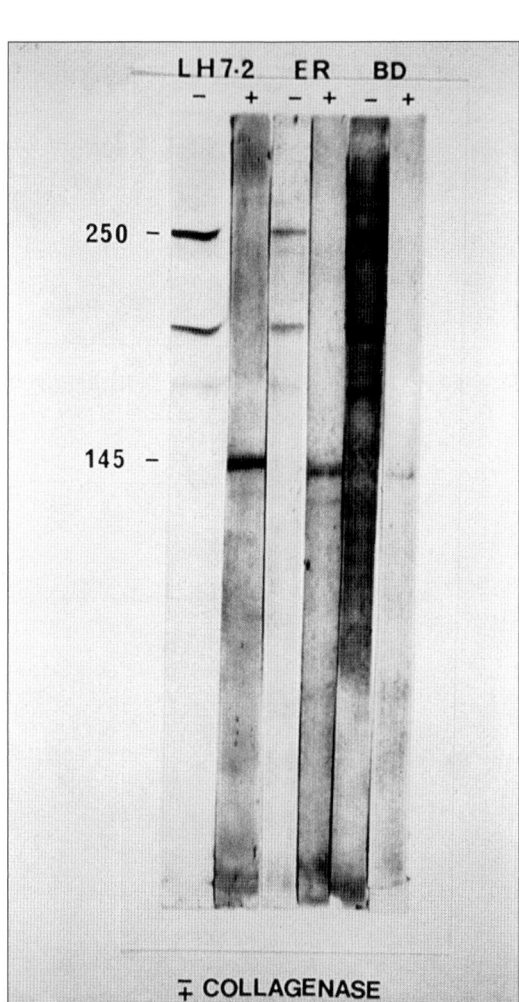

Fig. 3.132
Epidermolysis bullosa acquisita: there are two distinct antigens: one the 290 kD major antigen; the other the 145 kD minor antigen. By courtesy of I. Leigh, MD, Royal London Hospital Trust, London, UK.

Inflammatory EBA can be distinguished from bullous pemphigoid, cicatricial pemphigoid and linear IgA disease by split skin IMF and, when necessary, by western blot (see *Table 3.4*).

It is also important that epidermodermal separation due to autolysis is not confused with in vivo blister formation. In autolysis the epithelium typically shows marked eosinophilia and the nuclei are often lost.

References

1. Hallel-Halevy, D., Nadelman, C., Chen, M. et al (2001) Epidermolysis bullosa acquisita: update and review. *Clin Dermatol*, **19**, 712–718.
2. Briggaman, R.A., Gammon, W.R., Woodley, D.T. (1985) Epidermolysis bullosa acquisita of the immunopathological type (dermolytic pemphigoid). *J Invest Dermatol*, **85**, 795–845.
3. Bernard, P., Valliant, L., Lubeille, B. et al (1995) Incidence and distribution of subepidermal autoimmune bullous skin diseases in three French regions. Bullous Diseases French Study Group. *Arch Dermatol*, **131**, 48–52.
4. Zillikens, D., Wever, S., Hashimoto, T. et al (1995) Incidence of autoimmune subepidermal blistering dermatoses in a region of central Germany. *Arch Dermatol*, **131**, 957–958.
5. Roenigk, H.J., Ryan, J.C., Bergfeld, W.F. (1971) Epidermolysis bullosa acquisita: report of three cases and review of the literature. *Arch Dermatol*, **103**, 1–10.
6. Callot-Mellot, C., Bodemer, C., Caux, F. et al (1997) Epidermolysis bullosa acquisita in childhood. *Arch Dermatol*, **133**, 1122–1126.
7. Gibbs, R.B., Minus, H. R. (1975) Epidermolysis bullosa acquisita with electron microscopical studies. *Arch Dermatol*, **111**, 215–220.
8. Richter, B.J., McNutt, N. S. (1979) The spectrum of epidermolysis bullosa acquisita. *Arch Dermatol*, **115**, 1325–1328.
9. Dahl, M.G.C. (1979) Epidermolysis bullosa acquisita – a sign of cicatricial pemphigoid. *Br J Dermatol*, **101**, 475–484.
10. Stewart, M. I., Woodley, D.T., Briggaman, R.A. (1991) Acquired epidermolysis bullosa and associated symptomatic esophageal webs. *Arch Dermatol*, **127**, 373–377.
11. Harman, K.E., Whittam, L.R., Wakelin, S.H. et al (1998) Severe, refractory epidermolysis bullosa acquisita complicated by esophageal stricture responding to intravenous immune globulin. *Br J Dermatol*, **139**, 1126–1127.
12. Gammon, W.R., Briggaman, R.A., Woodley, B.T. et al (1984) Epidermolysis bullosa acquisita – a pemphigoid-like disease. *J Am Acad Dermatol*, **11**, 820–832.
13. Logan, R.A., Bhogal, B., Das, A.K. (1987) Localization of bullous pemphigoid antibody – an indirect immunofluorescence study of 228 cases using a split skin technique. *Br J Dermatol*, **117**, 471–478.
14. Zhu, X.J., Niimi, Y., Bystryn, J.C. (1990) Incidence of epidermolysis bullosa acquisita in patients with basement membrane zone antibodies. *Arch Dermatol*, **126**, 171–174.
15. Gammon, W.R., Briggaman, R.A., Wheeler, C.E. (1982) Epidermolysis bullosa acquisita presenting as an inflammatory bullous disease. *J Am Acad Dermatol*, **7**, 382–387.
16. Provost, T.T., Maize, J.C., Ahmed, A.R. et al (1979) Unusual subepidermal bullous diseases with immunologic features of bullous pemphigoid. *Arch Dermatol*, **115**, 156–160.
17. Lee, C.W. (1988) Epidermolysis bullosa acquisita associated with vesicular cystitis. *Br J Dermatol*, **119**, 101–105.
18. Joly, P., Ruto, F., Thomine, E. et al (1993) Brunsting–Perry cicatricial bullous pemphigoid: a clinical variant of localized epidermolysis bullosa acquisita? *J Am Acad Dermatol*, **28**, 89–92.
19. Choi, G.S., Lee, E-S., Kim, S-C. et al (1998) Epidermolysis bullosa acquisita localized to the face. *J Dermatol*, **25**, 19–22.
20. Rusenko, K.W., Gammon, W.R., Briggaman, R.A. (1989) Type VII collagen is the antigen recognized by IgA anti-sub lamina densa autoantibodies. *J Invest Dermatol*, **92**, 510.
21. Bauer, J.W., Schaeppi, H., Metze, D. et al (1999) Ocular involvement in IgA-epidermolysis bullosa acquisita. *Br J Dermatol*, **141**, 887–892.
22. Lee, C.W. (2000) Serum IgA autoantibodies in patients with epidermolysis bullosa acquisita: a high frequency of detection. *Dermatology*, **200**, 83–84.
23. Ray, T.L., Levine, J.B., Weiss, W. et al (1982) Epidermolysis bullosa acquisita and inflammatory bowel disease. *J Am Acad Dermatol*, **6**, 242–252.
24. Medenica-Mojsitovic, L., Fenske, H.A., Espinoza, C.G. (1987) Epidermolysis bullosa acquisita: direct immunofluorescence and ultrastructural studies. *Am J Dermatopathol*, **9**, 324–333.
25. Kushniruk, W. (1973) The immunopathology of epidermolysis bullosa acquisita. *Can Med Assoc J*, **108**, 1143–1146.
26. Sherry, F., Dothridge, M.D. (1962) Case for diagnosis: epidermolysis bullosa acquisita. *Proc R Soc Med*, **55**, 409.
27. Duport, A., Bourland, A., Pounce, R. (1969) Epidermolyse bulleuse d'apartition tardive et ileite de Crohn. *Bull Soc Franc Dermatol Syphiligr*, **76**, 311–312.
28. Pegum, J.S., Wright, J.T. (1973) Epidermolysis bullosa acquisita and Crohn's disease. *Proc R Soc Med*, **66**, 234.
29. Livden, J.K., Nilsen, R., Thunold, S. et al (1978) Epidermolysis bullosa acquisita and Crohn's disease. *Acta Derm Venereol*, **58**, 241–244.
30. Hughes, B.R., Horne, J. (1988) Epidermolysis bullosa acquisita and total ulcerative colitis. *J R Soc Med*, **81**, 473–474.
31. Cheesbrough, M.J., Kinmont, P.D.C. (1978) Epidermolysis bullosa acquisita and Crohn's disease. *Br J Dermatol*, **99**, 53–54.
32. Raab, B., Fretzin, D.F., Bronson, D.M. et al (1983) Epidermolysis bullosa acquisita and inflammatory bowel disease. *JAMA*, **250**, 1746–1748.
33. Goodwin, P., Eady, R. (1977) A case of ? epidermolysis bullosa. *Clin Exp Dermatol*, **2**, 409–412.
34. Wilson, B.D., Birnkrant, A.F., Beutner, E.H. et al (1980) Epidermolysis bullosa acquisita – a clinical disorder of varied etiologies. *J Am Acad Dermatol*, **3**, 230–291.
35. Yaoita, H., Briggaman, R.A., Lawley, T.J. et al (1981) Epidermolysis bullosa acquisita: ultrastructural and immunological studies. *J Invest Dermatol*, **76**, 288–292.
36. Benedetto, A.V., Bergfeld, W.F., Taylor, J.S. et al (1976) Epidermolysis bullosa acquisita (diagnosis by electron microscopy). *Cleveland Clin Quart*, **43**, 283–291.
37. Nieboer, C., Boorsma, D.M., Woerdeman, M.J. et al (1980) Epidermolysis bullosa acquisita: immunofluorescence, electron microscopic and immunoelectron microscopic studies in four patients. *Br J Dermatol*, **102**, 383–392.
38. Caughman, S.W. (1986) Epidermolysis bullosa acquisita: the search for identity. *Arch Dermatol*, **122**, 159–161.
39. Gammon, W.R., Inman, A.O., Wheeler, C.E. (1984) Differences in complement-dependent chemotactic activity generated by bullous pemphigoid and epidermolysis bullosa acquisita immune complexes: demonstration by leukocyte attachment and organ culture methods. *J Invest Dermatol*, **83**, 57–61.
40. Gammon, W.R., Kowalewski, C., Chorzelski, T.P. et al (1990) Direct immunofluorescence studies of sodium-chloride separated skin in the differential diagnosis of bullous pemphigoid and epidermolysis bullosa acquisita. *J Am Acad Dermatol*, **22**, 664–670.
41. Woodley, D.T. (1990) Immunofluorescence on salt-split skin for the diagnosis of epidermolysis bullosa acquisita. *Arch Dermatol*, **126**, 229–331.
42. Ghohestani, R.F., Nicolas, J.F., Roussele, P. et al (1997) Diagnostic value of indirect immunofluorescence on sodium chloride-split skin in differential diagnosis of subepidermal autoimmune bullous dermatoses. *Arch Dermatol*, **133**, 1102–1107.
43. Gammon, W.R., Briggaman, R.A., Inman, A.D. et al (1984) Differentiating anti-lamina lucida and anti-sublamina densa anti-BMZ antibodies by direct immunofluorescence on 1.0m sodium chloride separated skin. *J Invest Dermatol*, **82**, 139–144.

44.   Woodley, D.T., Gammon, W.R. (1983) Epidermolysis bullosa acquisita: an autoimmune disease with distinctive immuno-ultrastructural features. *Cutis*, **32**, 521–527.
45.   Kárpáti, S., Stolz, W., Meurer, M. et al (1992) *In situ* localization of IgG in epidermolysis bullosa acquisita by immunogold technique. *J Am Acad Dermatol*, **26**, 726–730.
46.   Roenigk, H.H., Pearson, R.W. (1981) Epidermolysis bullosa acquisita. *J Am Acad Dermatol*, **5**, 43–53.
47.   Woodley, D.T., Briggaman, R.A., O'Keefe, K.J. et al (1984) Identification of the skin basement membrane autoantigen in epidermolysis bullosa acquisita. *New Engl J Med*, **310**, 1007–1013.
48.   Woodley, D.T., Burgeson, R.E., Lunstrun, G.P. et al (1987) The epidermolysis bullosa acquisita antigen is type VII procollagen. *Clin Res*, **35**, 726A.
49.   Woodley, D.T., Burgeson, R.E., Lunstrum, G. et al (1988) Epidermolysis bullosa acquisita antigen is the globular carboxyl terminus of type VII procollagen. *J Clin Invest*, **81**, 683–687.
50.   Whitehead, P., Briggaman, R.A., Wojnarowska, F. et al (1988) Type VII collagen is the target for autoantibody binding in epidermolysis bullosa acquisita. *Br J Dermatol*, **118**, 269.
51.   Tatnall, F.M., Whitehead, P.C., Black, M.M. et al (1989) Identification of the epidermolysis bullosa acquisita antigen by LH7.2 monoclonal antibody: use in diagnosis. *Br J Dermatol*, **120**, 533–539.
52.   Woodley, D.T., Briggaman, R.A., Gammon, W.R. et al (1985) Epidermolysis bullosa acquisita antigen is synthesized by human keratinocytes in serum-free medium. *Biochem Biophys Res Comm*, **130**, 1267–1272.
53.   Woodley, D.T., Briggaman, R.A., Falk, R.J. et al (1986) Epidermolysis bullosa acquisita antigen, a major cutaneous basement membrane component, is synthesized by dermal fibroblasts and other cutaneous tissues. *J Invest Dermatol*, **87**, 227–231.
54.   Stanley, J.R., Rubinstein, N., Klaus-Kovtun, V. (1985) Epidermolysis bullosa acquisita antigen is synthesized by both human keratinocytes and human dermal fibroblasts. *J Invest Dermatol*, **85**, 542–545.
55.   Paller, A.S., Queen, L.L., Woodley, D.T. et al (1986) Organ-specific, phylogenetic and ontogenetic distribution of the epidermolysis bullosa acquisita antigen. *J Invest Dermatol*, **86**, 376–379.
56.   Woodley, D.T., O'Keefe, E.J., McDonald, J.A. et al (1987) Specific affinity between fibronectin and the epidermolysis bullosa acquisita antigen. *J Clin Invest*, **179**, 1826–1830.
57.   Woodley, D.T., Sarret, Y., Briggaman, R.A. (1991) Autoimmunity to type VII collagen. *Semin Dermatol*, **13**, 232–239.
58.   Chen, M., Chan, L.S., Cai, X. et al (1997) Development of an ELISA for rapid detection of anti-type VLL collagen autoantibodies in epidermolysis bullosa acquisita. *J Invest Dermatol*, **108**, 68–72.
59.   Chen, M., Marinkovich, M.P., Jones, J.C. et al (1999) NCI domain of type VII collagen binds to the beta 3 chain of type V laminin via a unique subdomain within the fibronectin-like repeats. *J Invest Dermatol*, **112**, 177–183.
60.   Lapière, J.C., Chen, J.D., Iwasaki, T. et al (1994) Type VII collagen specifically binds fibronectin via a unique subdomain within the collagenous triple helix. *J Invest Dermatol*, **103**, 637–641.
61.   Chen, M., Wang, J., Tahk, S.H. et al (2000) Noncollagenous (NC2) domain of type VII collagen mediates the antiparallel-dimer formation of type VII collagen and constitutes a new antigenic epitope for EBA and BSLE autoantibodies. *J Invest Dermatol*, **114**, 766.

Bullous systemic lupus erythematosus

Blisters may rarely develop as a manifestation of systemic lupus erythematosus (SLE). They can therefore arise in a background of vasculitis or complicate sunburn and photosensitivity.[1] Occasionally vesicles form after extreme basal cell hydropic change and consequent epidermodermal separation.[2]

Patients with SLE manifest a wide range of antibodies and this can result in numerous complications, which have included the development of autoimmune bullous dermatoses such as bullous pemphigoid, dermatitis herpetiformis, pemphigus vulgaris, pemphigus foliaceus, linear IgA disease and epidermolysis bullosa acquisita.[3] More recently, however, an apparently unique dermatosis comprising a widespread vesiculobullous eruption characterized by a dermatitis herpetiformis-like histology, linear basement membrane zone antibody deposition (reacting with type VII collagen) and a striking response to dapsone has been delineated in patients with SLE.[4] This constitutes bullous SLE.

Clinical features

Bullous SLE – also termed bullous eruption of SLE, vesiculobullous SLE, SLE with herpetiform blisters – tends to present in the second and third decades and although young black women are most often affected, all ages, races and both sexes may develop the disease (*Fig. 3.133*).[3–9]

Patients present with a widespread, sometimes pruritic, tense, vesiculobullous eruption that may affect both sun-exposed and non-sun-exposed skin (*Figs 3.134–3.136*). The eruption can precede the onset of SLE or develop subsequently.[6] Lesions develop on flexural and extensor surfaces, and mucosal (mouth and pharynx) lesions have been documented.[3,6,10] A predilection for involvement of the upper trunk and supraclavicular regions has been reported.[3] Lesions may arise against a background of erythema or less commonly urticaria. Unlike EBA with which this disease shares much in common, mechanobullous lesions are not seen, nor is there evidence of scarring.[3] Milia formation, although rare, has been recorded on two occasions and in both instances affected children.[7, 8] Postinflammatory hyperpigmentation is a not uncommon complication. Surprisingly, patients with bullous SLE do not usually develop other cutaneous manifestations of lupus. Bullous SLE has been recorded in a patient whose primary disease developed as a consequence of hydralazine therapy and identical features (including immunological) have been recorded in a patient with mixed connective tissue disease.[11]

Pathogenesis and histological features

Patients with bullous SLE (and EBA) have a significantly higher incidence of HLA-DR2 compared to the normal population.[3] This is thought to be associated with an increased risk of developing autoimmune diseases.[12]

The histological features of bullous SLE (BSLE) are those of a subepidermal vesicle, often indistinguishable from dermatitis herpetiformis. The roof is usually intact and the blister cavity contains fibrin

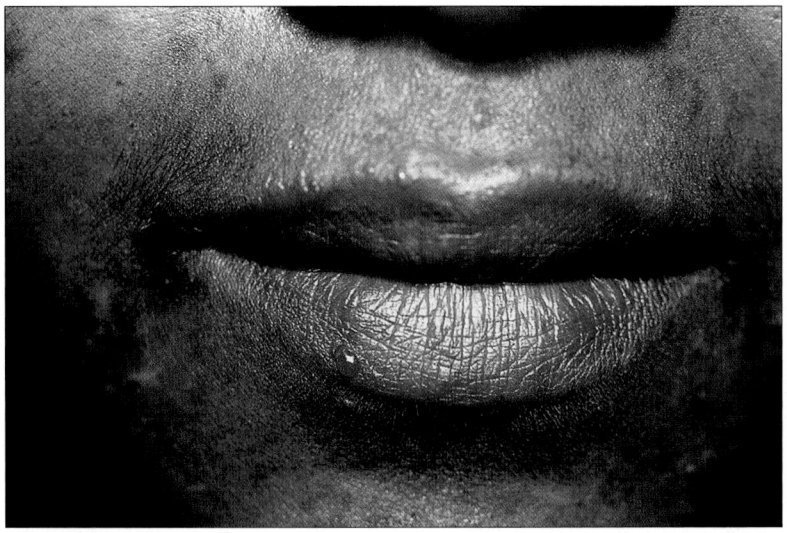

Fig. 3.133
Bullous systemic lupus erythematosus: West Indian female with perioral blistering. By courtesy of R.A. Marsden, MD, St George's Hospital, London, UK.

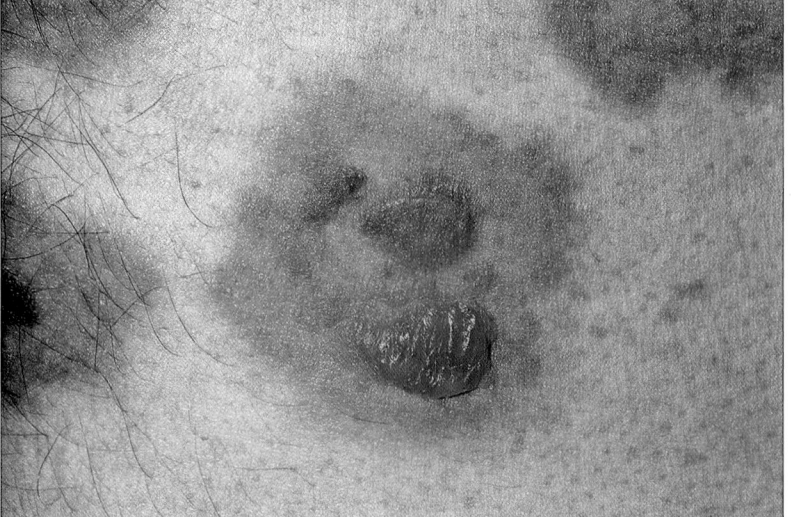

Fig. 3.134
Bullous systemic lupus erythematosus: in this example there is a conspicuous inflammatory background. By courtesy of the Institute of Dermatology, London, UK.

with large numbers of neutrophils and karryorhectic debris (*Fig. 3.137*). Occasionally lymphocytes, histiocytes and eosinophils may also be evident.[3] The adjacent, non-bullous skin characteristically shows subepidermal neutrophil microabscesses (*Fig. 3.138*). The upper dermis contains a perivascular mixed inflammatory cell infiltrate consisting of neutrophils, occasional eosinophils, lymphocytes and histiocytes. Sometimes the features of a leukocytoclastic vasculitis are also present (*Figs 3.139–3.141*).

Electron microscopy shows that the site of the split is below the lamina densa.[3]

Direct immunofluorescence is characterized by the presence of immunoglobulin and complement at the epidermal basement membrane region of both lesional and perilesional skin. Immunoglobulins are frequently multiple: IgG is present in 100% of patients; IgA in 67%; and IgM in 50%.[3,5,6,12,13] Two patterns are recognized: granular in 40% of

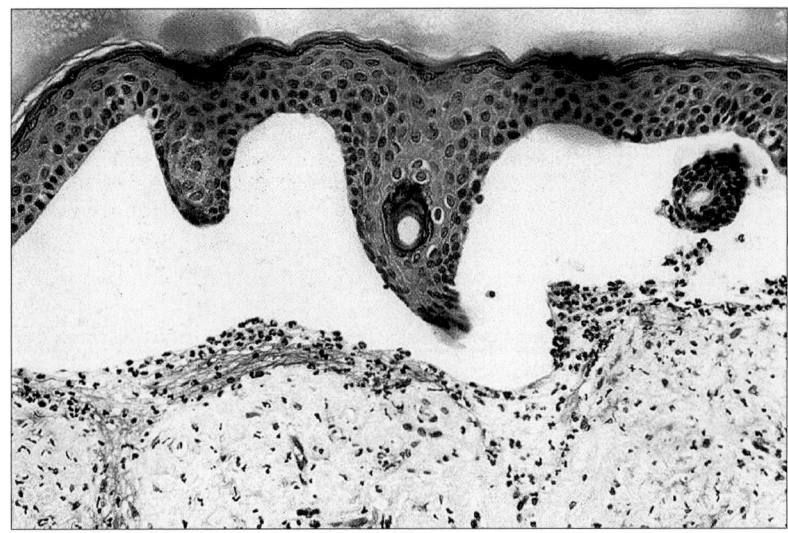

Fig. 3.137
Bullous systemic lupus erythematosus: this shows the typical features of a subepidermal, neutrophil-rich vesicle.

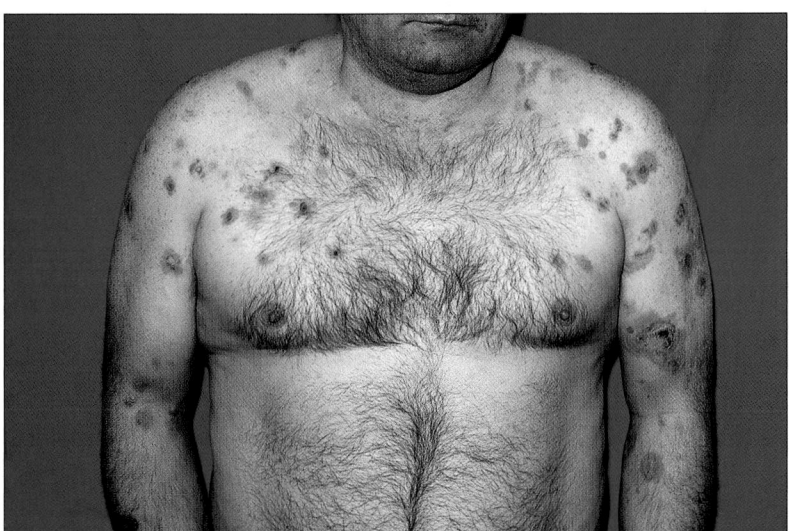

Fig. 3.135
Bullous systemic lupus erythematosus: numerous erosions are present over the chest, shoulders and upper arms. By courtesy of R.A. Marsden, MD, St George's Hospital, London, UK.

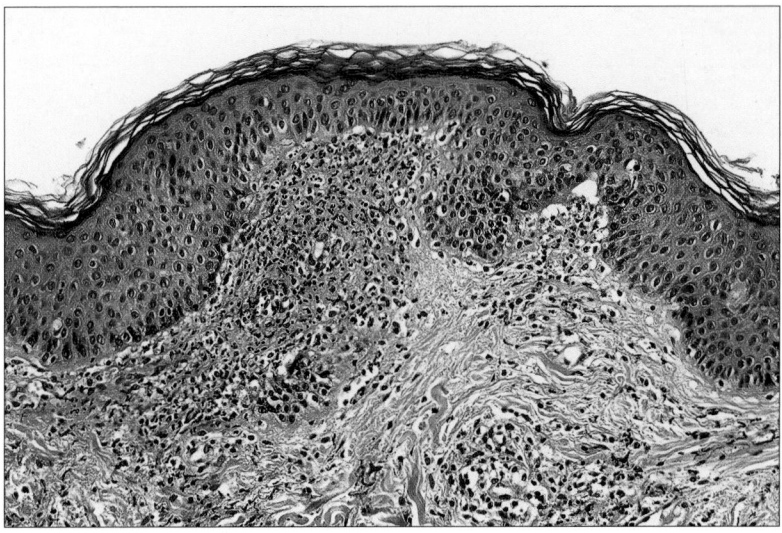

Fig. 3.138
Bullous systemic lupus erythematosus: the presence of a neutrophil abscess in the papillary dermis increases the histological similarity of this condition to dermatitis herpetiformis.

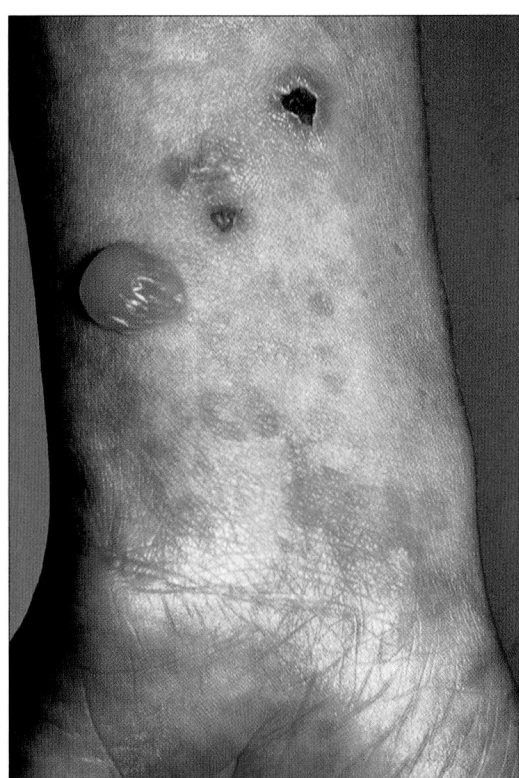

Fig. 3.136
Bullous systemic lupus erythematosus: tense bullous–pemphigoid-like lesions. By courtesy of the Institute of Dermatology, London, UK.

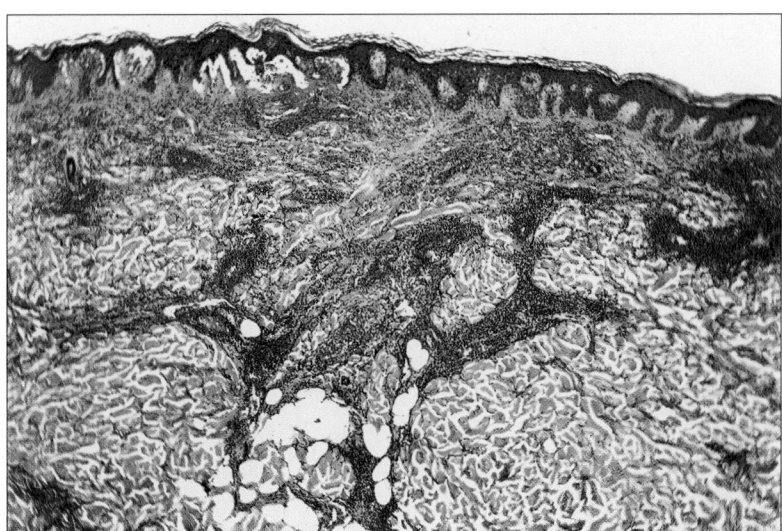

Fig. 3.139
Bullous systemic lupus erythematosus: this scanning view shows a central focus of subepidermal vesiculation. Striking inflammatory changes outline the dermal vasculature.

cases and linear in 60%.[6] Sometimes immunoreactants are also present within the walls of the upper dermal vasculature, particularly venules.[3] Indirect immunofluorescence using 1 M NaCl-split skin as substrate shows the presence of a low titer anti-basement membrane antibody in those patients who demonstrate linear positive direct IMF (type 1 BSLE).[1,3,6,10,11,14–17] The antibodies generally label the floor of the blister cavity although a roof (epidermal) variant has rarely been described.[6] Those that are negative on indirect IMF have been classified as type 2 BSLE.[3] Type 3 BSLE refers to those cases in which the target antigen is an epidermal rather than dermal epitope.[4]

Direct immunoelectron microscopy shows that the immunoreactants are present on and immediately below the lamina densa obscuring the anchoring fibrils and also occasionally somewhat deeper in the papillary

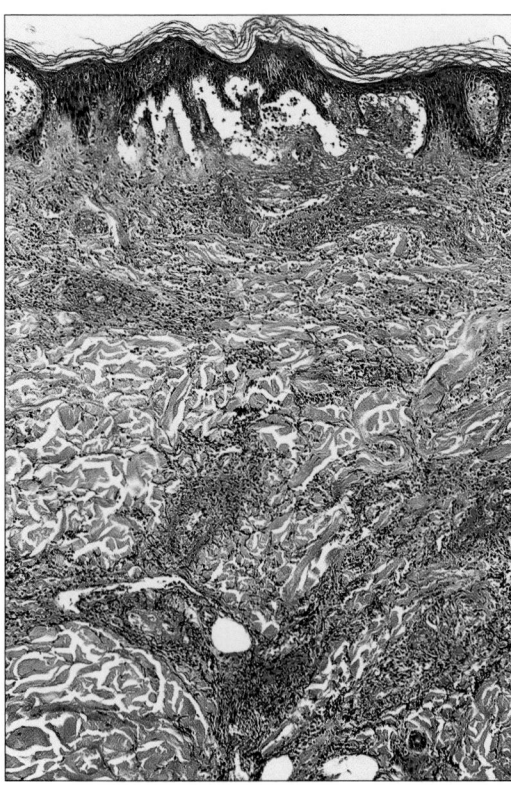

Fig. 3.140
Bullous systemic lupus erythematosus: this view shows florid leukocytoclastic vasculitis.

dermis similar to those seen in non-bullous SLE.[3,18–20] By indirect immunoelectron microscopy, the antibody binds to the lamina densa and sublamina densa in a manner identical to that seen in epidermolysis bullosa acquisita.[3,19]

Western immunoblot has shown that these antibodies bind to antigens of 290 kD and 145 kD as described for EBA (i.e. type VII collagen).[14] Recently, rare patients with SLE have been shown to have circulating antibodies to type VII collagen in the absence of blisters, and occasional patients with bullous SLE have been shown to have antibodies which bind to both the roof and the floor of NaCl-split skin, suggesting that a number of different basement membrane antigens may be involved.[1,3] The target antigen in the epidermal variant of bullous SLE has not yet been identified although bullous pemphigoid antigen 1 was identified in addition to type VII collagen and laminins-5 and -6 in one patient with combined epidermal and dermal staining on NaCl-split skin indirect IMF, most likely representing a manifestation of postinflammatory epitope spreading.[20]

The bullous SLE antibodies are associated with complement activation activity, which results in neutrophil migration and adherence to the basement membrane region.[3] Neutrophil enzyme release is then associated with basement membrane damage and subsequent epidermodermal separation.

Differential diagnosis

Bullous SLE shows obvious overlap with EBA. There are, however, a number of discriminatory features. Bullous SLE is not associated with a mechanobullous pathogenesis and scarring is not a feature. It develops most often in a younger age group than EBA. The dermatitis herpetiformis-like histological features are rarely seen in EBA and probably of greatest importance; bullous SLE responds dramatically to dapsone therapy, but EBA does not.[3]

References

1. Burge, S., Schomberg, K., Wojnarowska, F. (1991) Bullous eruption of SLE – a case report and investigation of the relationship of anti-basement membrane-zone antibodies to blistering. *Clin Exp Dermatol*, **16**, 133–138.
2. Su, W.P., Alegre, V.A. (1991) Bullous lesions in cutaneous lupus erythematosus. *Chang Keng I Hsueh*, **14**, 15–21.
3. Gammon, W.R., Briggaman, R.A. (1993) Bullous SLE: a phenotypically distinctive but immunologically heterogeneous bullous disorder. *J Invest Dermatol*, **100**, 28S–34S.
4. Yell, J.A., Allen, J., Wojnarowska, F., et al (1995) Bullous systemic lupus erythematosus: revised criteria for diagnosis. *Br J Dermatol*, **132**, 921–928.
5. Yell, J.A., Wojnarowska, F. (1997) Bullous skin disease in lupus erythematosus. *Lupus*, **6**, 112–121.
6. Rappersberger, K., Tschachler, M.T., Wolff, K. (1989) Bullous disease in systemic lupus erythematosus. *J Am Acad Dermatol*, **21**, 745–752.
7. Kettler, A.H., Bean, S.F., Duffy, J.O. et al (1988) Systemic lupus erythematosus presenting as a bullous eruption in a child. *Arch Dermatol*, **124**, 1083–1087.
8. Don, P.C. (1992) Vesiculobullous lupus erythematosus with milia formation. *Int J Dermatol*, **31**, 793–795.
9. Janniger, C.K., Kowalewski, C., Mahmood, T. et al (1991) Detection of anti-basement membrane zone antibodies in bullous systemic lupus erythematosus. *J Am Acad Dermatol*, **24**, 643–647.
10. Fleming, M.G., Bergfeld, W.F., Tomecki, K.J. et al (1989) Bullous systemic lupus erythematosus. *Int J Dermatol*, **28**, 321–326.
11. Woodley, D.T., Sarret, Y., Briggaman, R.A. (1991) Autoimmunity to type VII collagen. *Semin Dermatol*, **10**, 232–239.
12. Pedro, S.D., Dahl, M.V. (1973) Direct immunofluorescence of bullous systemic lupus erythematosus. *Arch Dermatol*, **107**, 118–120.
13. Gammon, W.R., Woodley, D.T., Dole, K.C. et al (1985) Evidence that anti-basement membrane zone antibodies in bullous eruption of systemic lupus erythematosus recognize epidermolysis bullosa acquisita antigen. *J Invest Dermatol*, **84**, 472–476.
14. Gammon, W.R., Briggaman, R.A., Iman, A.O. III et al (1983) Evidence supporting a role for immune complex-mediated inflammation in the pathogenesis of bullous lesions of systemic lupus erythematosus. *J Invest Dermatol*, **81**, 320–325.
15. Camisa, C., Grimwood, R.E. (1986) Indirect immunofluorescence in vesiculobullous eruption of systemic lupus erythematosus. *J Invest Dermatol*, **86**, 606.
16. Barton, D.D., Fine, J-D., Gammon, W.R. et al (1986) Bullous systemic lupus erythematosus: an unusual clinical course and detectable circulating autoantibodies to the epidermolysis bullosa acquisita antigen. *J Am Acad Dermatol*, **15**, 369–373.
17. Olansky, A.J., Briggaman, R.A., Gammon, W.R. et al (1982) Bullous systemic lupus erythematosus. *J Am Acad Dermatol*, **7**, 511–520.
18. Burrows, N.P., Bhogal, B.S., Black, M.M. et al (1993) Bullous eruption of systemic lupus erythematosus: a clinicopathological study of four cases. *Br J Dermatol*, **128**, 332–338.
19. Hall, R.P., Lawley, T.J., Katz, S.I. (1983) Bullous eruption of systemic lupus erythematosus. *J Am Acad Dermatol*, **7**, 797–799.
20. Chan, L.S., Lapière, J-C., Chen, M. et al (1999) Bullous systemic lupus erythematosus with autoantibodies recognizing multiple skin basement membrane components, bullous pemphigoid antigen 1, laminin-5, laminin-6, and type VII collagen. *Arch Dermatol*, **135**, 569–573.

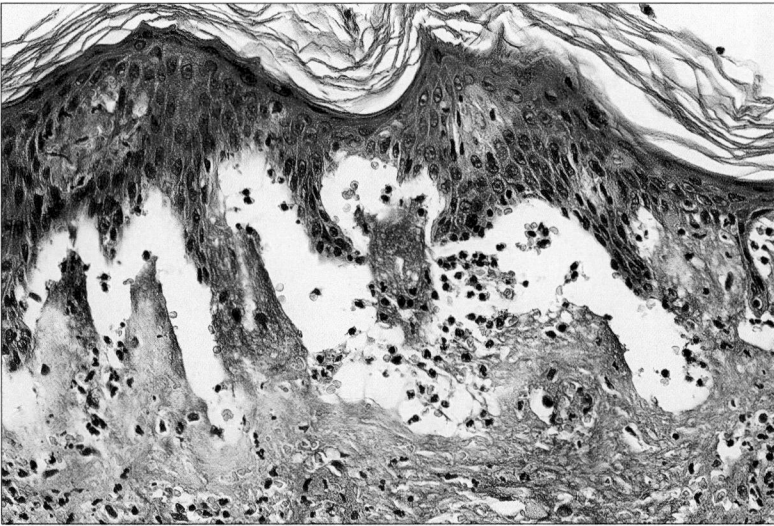

Fig. 3.141
Bullous systemic lupus erythematosus: this is a close-up view of the subepidermal vesicle shown in *Fig. 3.139*.

Dermatitis herpetiformis

Clinical features

Dermatitis herpetiformis and celiac disease are highly interrelated conditions and best regarded as variable expressions of a common inherited tendency to autoimmune disease.

Dermatitis herpetiformis (Duhring–Brocq disease) is a widespread, intensely pruritic, papulovesicular eruption affecting all ages, but particularly people in their second to fourth decade.[1-4] The male to female ratio is 2:1.

The incidence of dermatitis herpetiformis is highest in Northern Europe, Scotland and Ireland.[2,5,6] It is less frequently seen in the United States. Caucasians are mainly affected, the disease being rare in Asians and blacks. Case clustering is common and familial involvement (either dermatitis herpetiformis or celiac disease), possibly autosomal dominantly inherited, has been documented in up to 10.5% of cases.[2,7] Relatives of patients with dermatitis herpetiformis have an increased risk of developing celiac disease.[2]

The lesions, which may be symmetrical, are grouped mainly on the posterior scalp, shoulders, back, buttocks and extensor aspects of the limbs (*Figs 3.142, 3.143*). Often scratching is severe and therefore excoriation and/or lichenification typically predominate with intact vesicles rarely being seen. However, occasionally, larger blisters similar to those found in bullous pemphigoid may be evident. Patients sometimes present with urticarial plaques and crusted erosions.[2] Oral involvement is rare.[3]

The clinical response to dapsone (50–200 mg/day) is dramatic; therefore, the drug is commonly administered for diagnostic as well as therapeutic purposes. Relief from pruritus occurs within a few hours of commencing treatment and is soon followed by clearing of the rash. The eruption returns 2–3 days after dapsone is discontinued. The disease persists for many years and is usually lifelong. A gluten-free diet may result in prolonged remission in some patients or lowering of the daily dapsone requirement in others.

At least 65–75% of patients with dermatitis herpetiformis show histological evidence of celiac disease (gluten-sensitive enteropathy, GSE). However, only about 20% have clinical manifestations of malabsorption, which are usually mild.[8-11] The actual incidence of celiac disease is likely to be higher because the mucosal abnormality in dermatitis herpetiformis is patchy and may be missed unless multiple jejunal biopsies are taken. Interestingly, patients who apparently do not have enteropathy may develop the condition when challenged with large doses of gluten (latent GSE).[11] It is therefore believed that all patients with dermatitis herpetiformis have GSE to a greater or lesser extent.[1-3] Relatives of patients with dermatitis herpetiformis may show no evidence of the skin disease, but can have subclinical or overt symptoms of the enteropathy.

Patients with dermatitis herpetiformis may have antigastric parietal cell antibody (10–25%), gastric hypochlorhydria (50–90%) and gastric atrophy (50–70%).[3] They may also have antithyroid antibodies and show an increased incidence of thyroid disease, insulin-dependent diabetes mellitus and connective tissue diseases including systemic lupus erythematosus and Sjögren's syndrome.[12,13] As with isolated celiac disease, there is an increased risk of intestinal lymphoma.[14]

Pathogenesis and histological features

Patients with dermatitis herpetiformis (and celiac disease) have a high incidence of HLA-B8 (80–90%), HLA-DR3 (90–95%) and HLA-DQ2 (95–100%) compared to a normal control population (21%, 23% and 40%, respectively).[3,15-18] More recent studies, however, have demonstrated that the increased incidences of HLA-B8 and -DR3 are due to positive linkage disequilibrium.[19] The most current data suggest that the significant positive HLA association in dermatitis herpetiformis lies with the class II antigen DQ2.[2,20]

All patients with dermatitis herpetiformis have granular deposits of IgA in the dermal papillae of perilesional skin, and many also show in vivo-bound fibrin (*Fig. 3.144*).[21,22] IgA has also been identified in the oral mucosa.[23] Occasionally, a granular linear pattern may be seen. Other immunoglobulins are not usually found, but C3 is often present.[24] This is associated with formation of the membrane attack complex (C5–C9), which is thought to result in neutrophil chemotaxis and the evolution

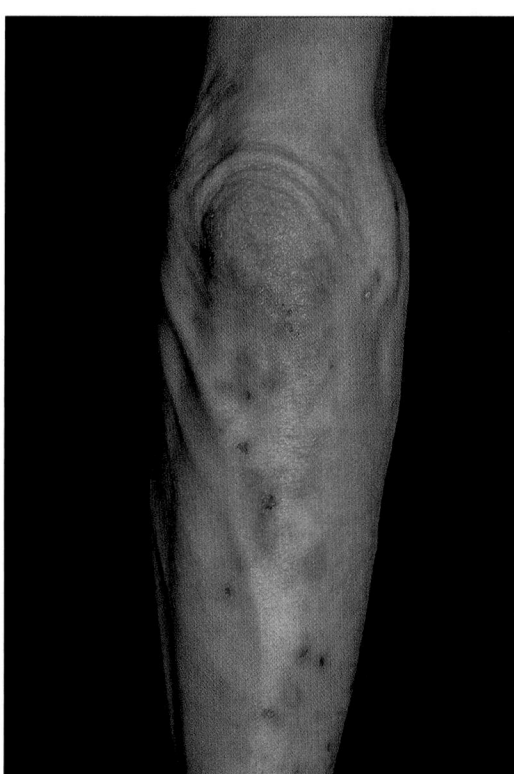

Fig. 3.142
Dermatitis herpetiformis: excoriations are present on the elbow and back of the arm. Intact blisters are uncommon in dermatitis herpetiformis because of the intense pruritus. By courtesy of the Institute of Dermatology, London, UK.

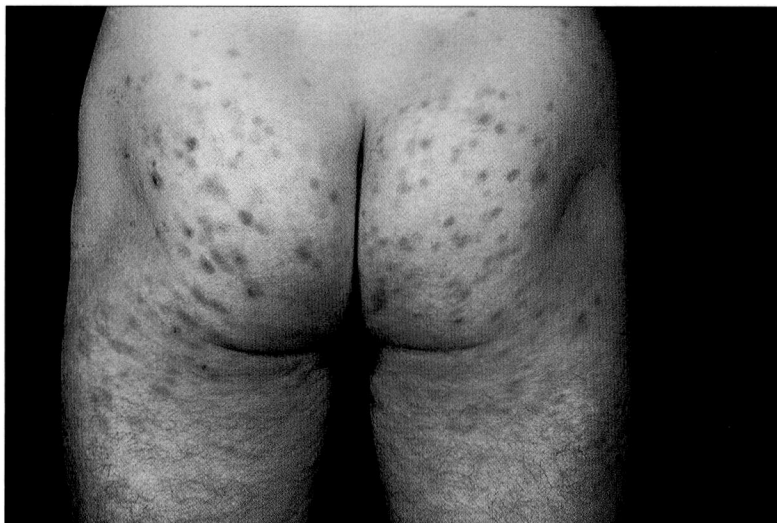

Fig. 3.143
Dermatitis herpetiformis: the buttocks are frequently affected. By courtesy of the Institute of Dermatology, London, UK.

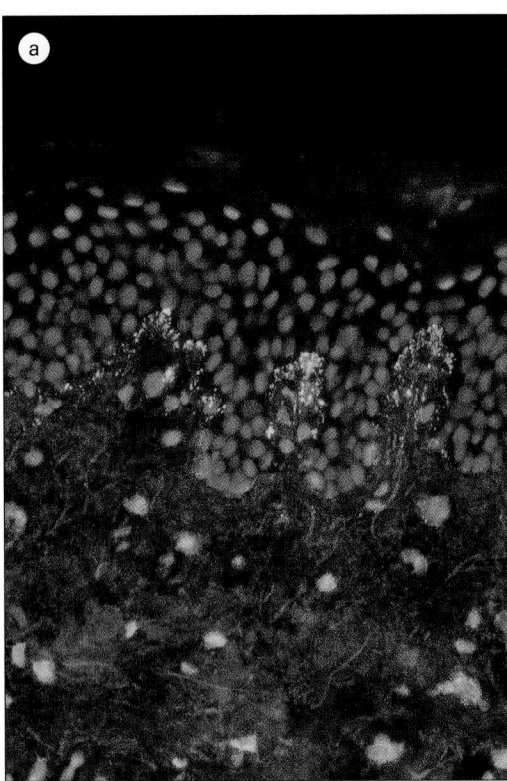
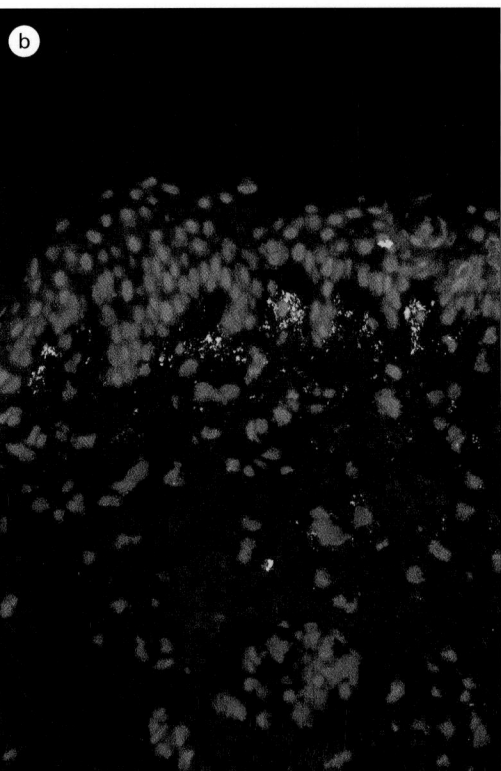

Fig. 3.144
Dermatitis herpetiformis: direct immunofluorescence showing (a) deposits of granular IgA in the dermal papillae; (b) fibrin deposition in the dermal papillae. By courtesy of the Department of Immunofluorescence, Institute of Dermatology, London, UK.

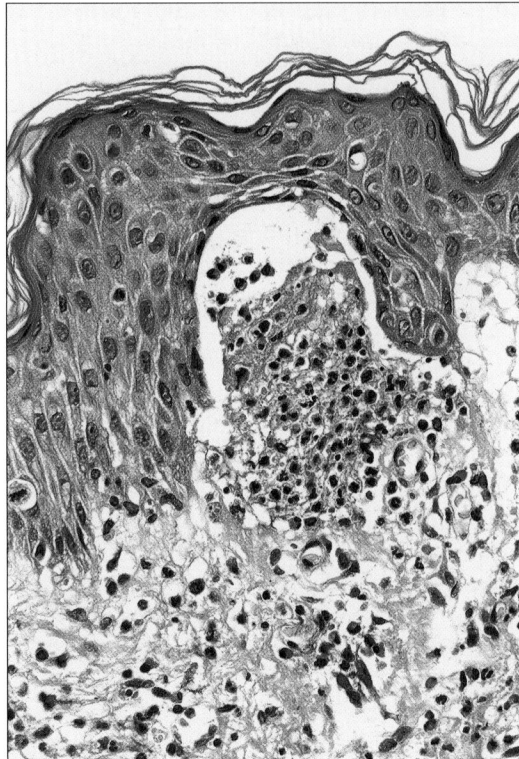

Fig. 3.145
Dermatitis herpetiformis: biopsy from an early lesion showing conspicuous neutrophil microabscesses.

of subepidermal vesiculation.[3,25] Cutaneous IgA deposits may still be detected after dapsone therapy. They do however sometimes disappear after a prolonged gluten-free diet.[2] Cutaneous IgA deposition is not seen in patients with celiac disease.[2]

Electron microscopy reveals electron-dense, amorphous granular deposits in the superficial dermis showing no particular relationship with the basement membrane region or any other specific structure.[26,27]

Immunoelectron microscopic observations initially suggested that the IgA deposits were associated with elastic-containing microfibrillar bundles, but more recently published work using antifibrillin antibodies has discounted this theory.[26,28]

Antigliadin antibodies, which are often used to assess celiac disease status, are of little value in the diagnosis of dermatitis herpetiformis.[11] They have high specificity, but low sensitivity.[11] Anti-smooth muscle endomysial antibody correlates with the gluten-sensitive state and appears before the development of any small intestinal histological abnormality in patients with dermatitis herpetiformis.[11,29,30] Such endomysial antibodies are present in up to 70% of patients and are highly specific; they react with tissue transglutaminase (tTG) (antitransglutaminase antibodies).[31] Gliadin is an important substrate for tissue transglutaminase forming gliadin–gliadin or gliadin–tTG complexes.[32] Circulating IgA antibodies to tTG are pathognomonic of dermatitis herpetiformis and celiac disease.[33] Whether these antibodies react with cutaneous transglutaminases or another cross-reacting dermal antigen, although an attractive hypothesis, is at present unknown. Whatever the underlying mechanism, the IgA in some way 'fixes' in the skin, resulting in complement activation via the alternative pathway.[34–36] Neutrophil chemotaxins are then released and the ensuing inflammatory reaction leads to dermal papillary edema, fibrin deposition and eventual vesiculation.

The histological hallmark of dermatitis herpetiformis is the dermal papillary neutrophilic microabscess, best seen in early erythematous

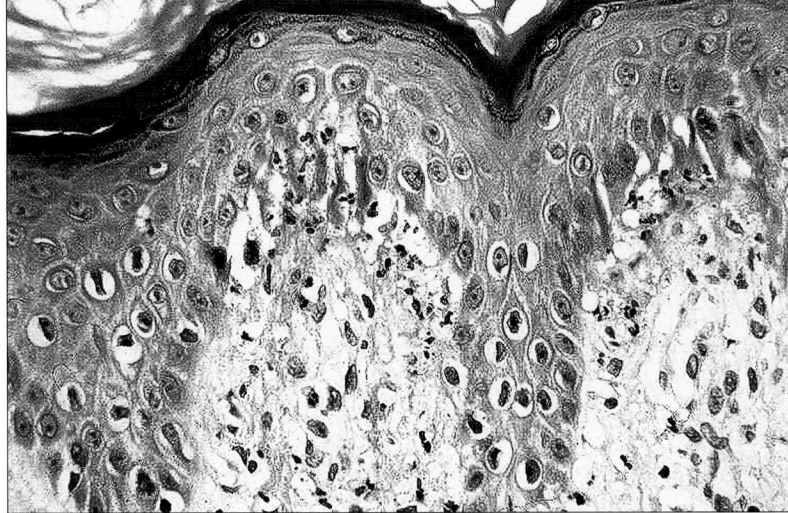

Fig. 3.146
Dermatitis herpetiformis: in this very early lesion, there are thin strands of fibrin and a few neutrophils in the tips of the dermal papillae.

lesions or well away from the blister in an established eruption (*Fig. 3.145*).[37–39] Occasionally, many levels of the biopsy will have to be examined before a microabscess is found.

Abscess evolution depends upon the initial presence of fibrin and polymorphs within the tips of the dermal papillae (*Fig. 3.146*), both of which are associated with degenerative changes of the collagen and the development of edema. Development of small subepidermal microvesicles follows, leading on to the formation of multilocular subepidermal blisters.

Typically the blister cavity contains edema fluid, a reticular network of fibrin and numerous polymorphs (*Figs 3.147, 3.148*). In contrast to bullous pemphigoid, the floor of the blister cavity usually shows effacement of the dermal papillary outline.

Within the dermis is a mixed inflammatory cell infiltrate consisting of lymphocytes, histiocytes and abundant neutrophils. Leukocytoclasis (nuclear dust, *Fig. 3.149*) is characteristic. Although blood vessels frequently show endothelial swelling, there is no evidence of vasculitis. Occasionally, eosinophils are quite numerous in the infiltrate, but usually they are late arrivals, appearing 24–48 hours after the neutrophils. On occasions, biopsies from typical dermatitis herpetiformis may show acantholysis, a cause of considerable confusion (*Fig. 3.150*).

Jejunal biopsy may reveal villous blunting, intestinal crypt elongation, flattening of surface epithelial cells with loss of microvilli and intra-epithelial γ/δ lymphocytic infiltration to a degree ranging from partial to subtotal villous atrophy.[40] If gluten is withheld from the diet, these changes revert to normal.

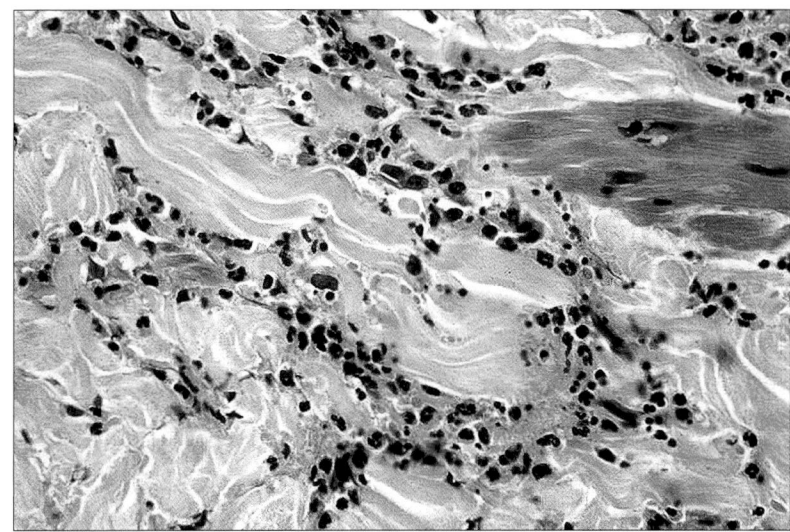

Fig. 3.149
Dermatitis herpetiformis: nuclear debris (karyorrhexis) within the dermis is a characteristic feature.

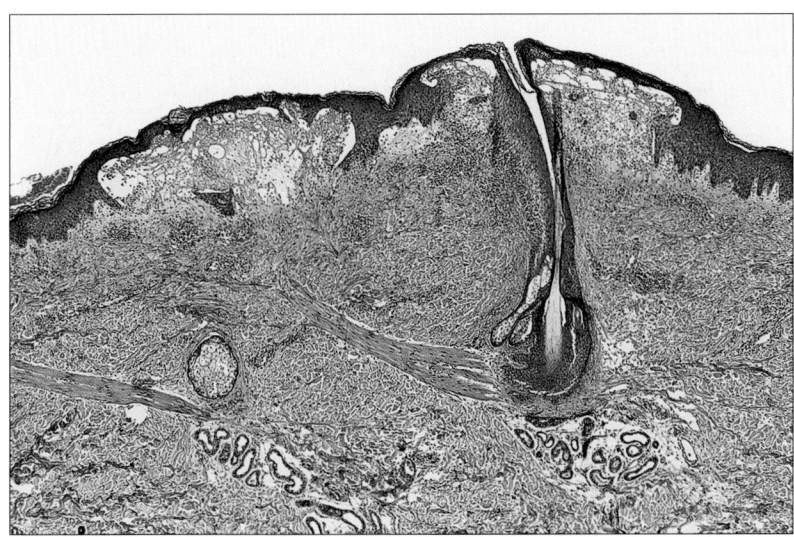

Fig. 3.147
Dermatitis herpetiformis: an established subepidermal blister. Although early lesions are usually multilocular, by 24–48 hours the lesion becomes unilocular.

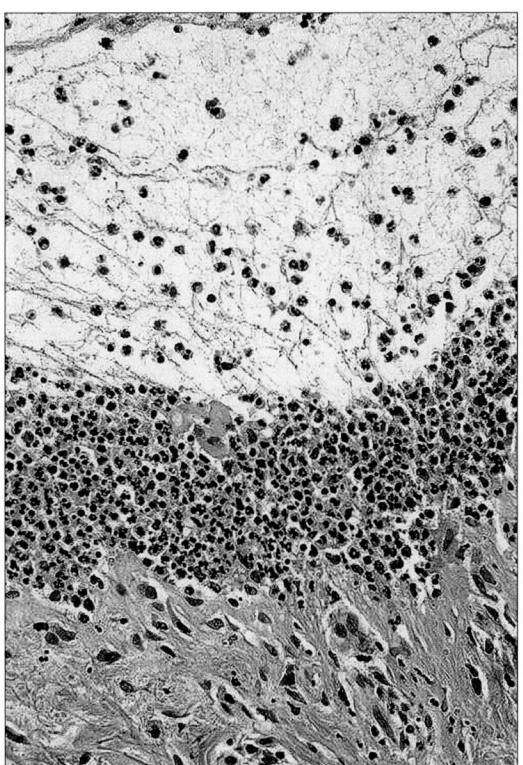

Fig. 3.148
Dermatitis herpetiformis: floor of the blister in *Fig. 3.149* showing an intense neutrophil infiltrate.

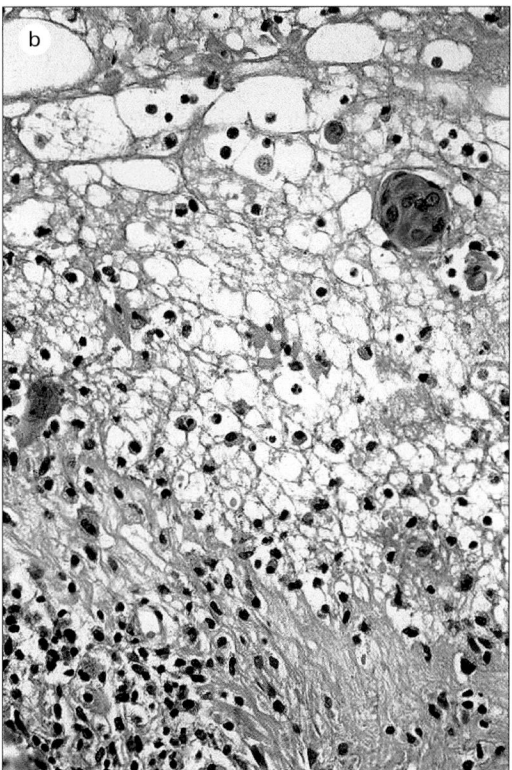

Fig. 3.150
(a, b) Dermatitis herpetiformis: in this example acantholysis may result in diagnostic confusion with pemphigus. Note that the blister is subepidermal.

Differential diagnosis

A neutrophil-predominant subepidermal vesicle accompanied by neutrophil dermal papillary microabscesses in addition to dermatitis herpetiformis may also be seen in vesicular pemphigoid, bullous systemic lupus erythematosus, inflammatory epidermolysis bullosa and linear IgA disease. Distinction depends upon clinical information and the results of immunofluorescent studies (see *Table 3.4*).

References

1. Reunala, T. (1998) Dermatitis herpetiformis: celiac disease of the skin. *Ann Med*, 30, 416–418.
2. Reunala, T.M. (2001) Dermatitis herpetiformis. *Clin Dermatol*, 19, 728–736.
3. Otley, C., Hall, R.P. (1990) Dermatitis herpetiformis. *Derm Clin*, 8, 759–769.
4. Buckley, D.B., English, J., Mollow, W. et al (1983) Dermatitis herpetiformis: a review of 119 cases. *Clin Exp Dermatol*, 8, 477–487.
5. Moi, H. (1984) Incidence and prevalence of dermatitis herpetiformis in a county in central Sweden with comments on the course of the disease and IgA deposits as a diagnostic criterion. *Acta Derm Venereol*, 64, 144–150.
6. Egan, C.A., O'Loughlin, S., Gormally, P. et al (1997) Dermatitis herpetiformis: a review of fifty-four patients. *Ir J Med Sci*, 166, 241–244.
7. Reunala, T. (1996) Incidence of familial dermatitis herpetiformis. *Br J Dermatol*, 134, 394–398.
8. Katz, S.I. (1980) Clinical and histologic overview. In: Dermatitis herpetiformis: the skin and the gut, Katz, S.I. (moderator). *Ann Int Med*, 93, 857–874.
9. Marks, J., Shuster, S., Watson, A.J. (1966) Small bowel changes in dermatitis herpetiformis. *Lancet*, 2, 1280–1282.
10. Marks, J.M. (1977) Dogma and dermatitis herpetiformis. *Clin Exp Dermatol*, 2, 189–207.
11. Beutner, E.H., Chorzelski, T.P., Kumar, V. (1990) Dermatitis herpetiformis – what is it? *Int J Dermatol*, 29, 267–269.
12. Cunningham, M.J., Zone, J.J. (1985) Thyroid abnormalities in dermatitis herpetiformis: prevalence of clinical thyroid disease and thyroid autoantibodies. *Ann Int Med*, 102, 194–196.
13. Reunala, T., Collin, P. (1997) Diseases associated with dermatitis herpetiformis. *Br J Dermatol*, 136, 315–318.
14. Leonard, J.N., Tucker, W.F.G., Fry, J.S. et al (1983) Increased incidence of malignancy in dermatitis herpetiformis. *Brit Med J*, 286, 16–18.
15. Keuning, J.J., Pena, A.S., van Leeuwen, A. et al (1976) HLA-Dw3 associated with celiac disease. *Lancet*, I, 506–508.
16. Hall, R.O. III, Otley, C. (1991) Immunogenetics of dermatitis herpetiformis. *Semin Dermatol*, 10, 240–245.
17. Katz, S.I., Hertz, K.C., Rogentine, G.N. et al (1977) HLA-B8 and dermatitis herpetiformis in patients with IgA deposits in the skin. *Arch Dermatol*, 113, 155–156.
18. Lawley, T.J., Strober, W., Yaoita, H. et al (1980) Small intestinal biopsies and HLA types in dermatitis herpetiformis patients with granular and linear IgA skin deposits. *J Invest Dermatol*, 74, 9–12.
19. Price, P., Witt, C., Allcok, R. et al (1999) The genetic basis of the 8.1 ancestral haplotype (A1, B8, DR3) with multiple immunopathological diseases. *Immunol Rev*, 167, 257–274.
20. Spurkland, A., Ingvarsson, G., Falk, E.S. et al (1997) Dermatitis herpetiformis and celiac disease are both primarily associated with the HLA-DQ (α1*0501, β1*02) or the HLA-DQ (α1*03, β1*0302) heterodimers. *Tissue Antigens*, 49, 29–34.
21. Cormane, R.H. (1967) Immunofluorescent studies of the skin in lupus erythematosus and other diseases. *Pathol Eur*, 2, 170–180.
22. Van der Meer, J.B. (1969) Granular deposits of immunoglobulins in the skin of patients with dermatitis herpetiformis: an immunofluorescent study. *Br J Dermatol*, 81, 493–503.
23. Nisengard, R.J., Chorzelski, T., Maciejawska, E. et al (1982) Dermatitis herpetiformis: IgA deposits in gingiva, buccal mucosa and skin. *Oral Surg*, 54, 22–25.
24. Haffenden, G., Wojnarowska, F., Fry, L. (1979) Comparison of immunoglobulin and complement deposition in multiple biopsies from the uninvolved skin in dermatitis herpetiformis. *Br J Dermatol*, 101, 39–45.
25. Dahl, M.V., Falk, R.J., Carpenter, R., Michael, A.F. (1985) Membrane attack complex of complement in dermatitis herpetiformis. *Arch Dermatol*, 121, 70–72.
26. Lightner, V.A., Sakai, L.Y., Hall, R.P. (1991) IgA binding structures in dermatitis herpetiformis skin are independent of elastic micro-fibrillar bundles. *J Invest Dermatol*, 96, 88–92.
27. Kárpáti, S., Meurer, M., Stolz, W. et al (1990) Dermatitis herpetiformis bodies: ultrastructural study on the skin of patients using direct pre-embedding immunogold labeling. *Arch Dermatol*, 126, 1469–1474.
28. Yaoita, H. (1978) Identification of IgA binding structures in skin of patients with dermatitis herpetiformis. *J Invest Dermatol*, 71, 213–216.
29. Kumar, V., Hemedinger, E., Chorzelski, T. et al (1987) Reticulin and endomysial antibodies in bullous diseases – comparison of specificity and sensitivity. *Arch Dermatol*, 123, 1179–1182.
30. Peters, M.S., McEvoy, M.T. (1989) IgA antiendomysial antibodies in dermatitis herpetiformis. *J Am Acad Dermatol*, 21, 1225–1231.
31. Dieterich, W., Ehnis, T., Bauer, M. et al (1997) Identification of tissue transglutaminase as the autoantigen of celiac disease. *Nat Med*, 3, 797–801.
32. Schmidt, E., Zillikens, D. (2000) Autoimmune and inherited subepidermal blistering diseases: advances in the clinic and the laboratory. *Adv Dermatol*, 16, 113–157.
33. Dieterich, W., Laag, E., Bruckner-Tuderman, L. et al (1999) Antibodies to tissue transglutaminases as serologic markers in patients with dermatitis herpetiformis. *J Invest Dermatol*, 113, 133–136.
34. Hall, R.P. (1987) The pathogenesis of dermatitis herpetiformis: recent advances. *J Am Acad Dermatol*, 16, 1129–1144.
35. Katz, S.I., Strober, W. (1978) The pathogenesis of dermatitis herpetiformis. *J Invest Dermatol*, 70, 63–75.
36. Burne, J. (1980) A possible immunological mechanism for the pathogenesis of dermatitis herpetiformis with reference to coeliac disease. *Clin Exp Dermatol*, 5, 451–463.
37. Blenkinsopp, W.K., Haffenden, G.P., Fry, L. et al (1983) Histology of linear IgA disease, dermatitis herpetiformis and bullous pemphigoid. *Am J Dermatopathol*, 5, 547–554.
38. Connor, B.L., Marks, R., Wilson Jones, E. (1972) Dermatitis herpetiformis: histological discriminants. *Trans St John's Hosp Dermatol Soc*, 58, 191–198.
39. Eng, A.M., Moncada, B. (1974) Bullous pemphigoid and dermatitis herpetiformis: histopathologic differentiation of bullous pemphigoid and dermatitis herpetiformis. *Arch Dermatol*, 110, 51–57.
40. Savilahti, E., Reunala, T., Mäki, M. (1992) Increase of lymphocytes bearing the γ/δ T-cell receptor in the jejunum of patients with dermatitis herpetiformis. *Gut*, 33, 206–211.

Linear IgA disease

Linear IgA disease of adults by definition presents after puberty and is characterized by the development of a sometimes self-remitting dapsone or sulfonamide-responsive dermatosis typified by subepidermal vesicles and blisters in association with in vivo deposition of linear (homogeneous) IgA at the basement membrane region on direct immunofluorescence of normal or perilesional skin.[1–3] Childhood linear IgA disease (chronic bullous dermatosis of childhood) is identical to the adult counterpart; however, there are differences in clinical presentation and therefore these particular aspects are described separately.

Linear IgA disease of adults is a rare disease, which was originally thought to represent a variant of dermatitis herpetiformis[4–6] or bullous pemphigoid.[7,8] Some cases were reported under the rubric polymorphic pemphigoid (see above) or intermediate (mixed) forms of bullous disease.[9,10] More recently, particularly following the application of immunoelectron microscopic and immunoblotting techniques, it has been confirmed as a disease (or at least a disease spectrum) *sui generis*.[11–15]

Its approximate incidence in the South of England is 1:250,000.[16] In France and central Germany, the incidence is 0.5 per million of the population.[17,18] Although data for the United States are limited, the incidence in Utah has been reported as 0.6 per 100,000.[19]

Clinical features

Linear IgA disease of adults affects the sexes equally and while the age distribution is wide, there is a peak in teenagers and young adults and in patients in their sixties.[1] It may present as a somewhat atypical bullous eruption showing features suggestive of dermatitis herpetiformis or more commonly bullous pemphigoid (*Fig. 3.151*). Occasionally it may initially resemble and be mistaken for erythema multiforme clinically.[20] Pruritus and/or a burning sensation are common manifestations and early lesions

may include urticarial, annular, polycyclic and targetoid eruptions.[15,21] The established dermatosis may be vesicular or more often frankly bullous; blisters arising at the edge of erythematous annular lesions ('string of beads' sign) are said to be characteristic.[15]

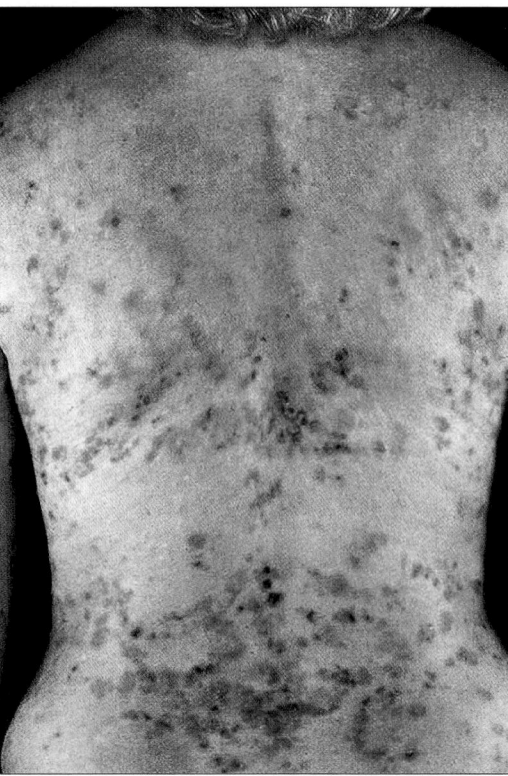

Fig. 3.151
Adult linear IgA disease: in this example the clinical appearances of excoriated lesions are suggestive of dermatitis herpetiformis. By courtesy of the Institute of Dermatology, London, UK.

Sites affected in decreasing order of frequency include the trunk, limbs, hands, scalp, face and perioral region. The perineum and vagina may also be affected with erosions and blisters.[1] Mucous membrane involvement, which is common, is of particular importance because it may be associated with scarring. Important sites that may be affected include the eyes (conjunctivitis, symblepharon, trichiasis, corneal opacification and rarely blindness; *Fig. 3.152*), the mouth (erosions, blisters and chronic ulceration), nasal cavity (crusting and bleeding) and the pharynx (hoarseness).[1,22] When these mucosal symptoms are severe there is clinical overlap and diagnostic confusion with cicatricial pemphigoid.

Childhood linear IgA disease (chronic bullous disease of childhood) not uncommonly develops after an upper respiratory tract illness, often following treatment with penicillin.[23–26] Females are affected more often than males (1.6:1) (*Fig. 3.153*). The average age of onset is 6 years.

Lesions, which can be pruritic or burning in the early stages, may be urticated, annular or polycyclic in appearance and usually arise on normal skin. Vesicles and large bullae (sometimes hemorrhagic) then predominate, and although the perioral regions and genitalia are particularly affected, the face, ears, trunk, limbs, hands and feet are also often involved (*Fig. 3.154*). Usually the new lesions appear around those resolving (the 'cluster of jewels' sign, *Fig. 3.155*). In older and black African children the clinical appearances may suggest bullous pemphigoid. Healing may be associated with postinflammatory hyper- or hypopigmentation. Mucous membrane lesions are common (64%). Ocular symptoms of pain, grittiness, discharge and redness are found in 40% of children; conjunctival scarring is present in approximately 21%; oral lesions are found in up to 57%.

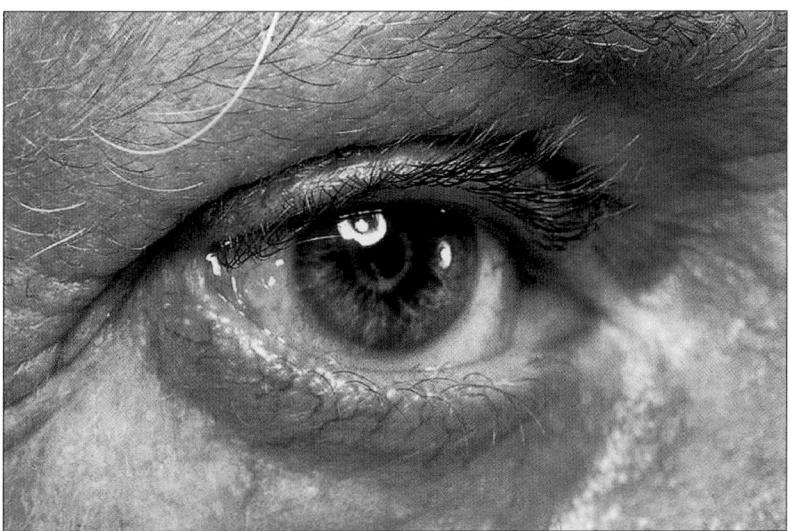

Fig. 3.152
Adult linear IgA disease: there is marked conjunctival injection. By courtesy of the Institute of Dermatology, London, UK.

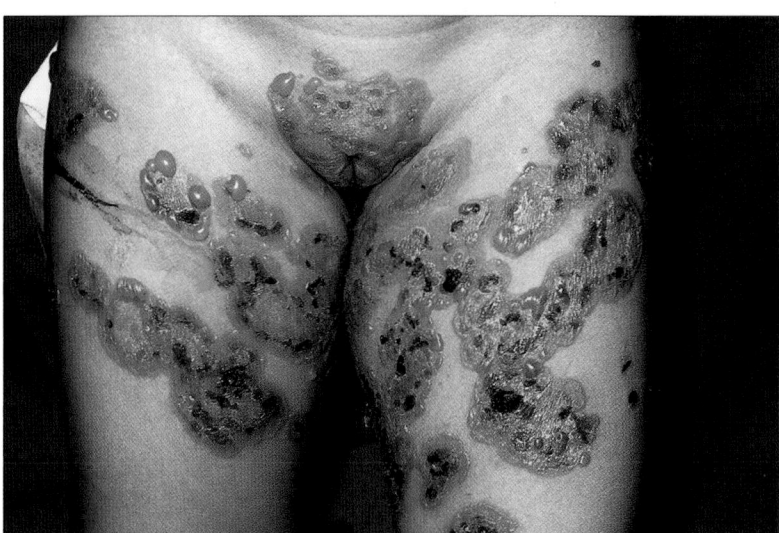

Fig. 3.154
Childhood linear IgA disease: groups of blisters are present on the vulva and inner thighs. By courtesy of R.A. Marsden, MD, St George's Hospital, London, UK.

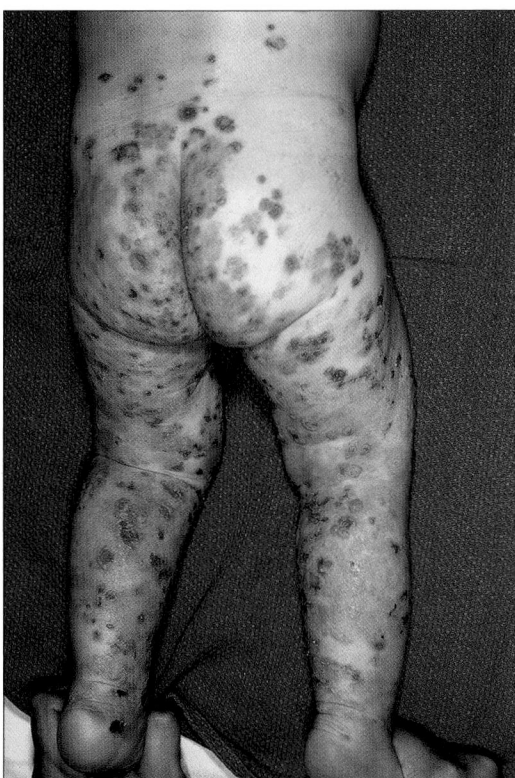

Fig. 3.153
Childhood linear IgA disease: in this case widespread erosions on an erythematous background are present on the buttocks and legs. Occasional intact vesicles are also evident. By courtesy of R.A. Marsden, MD, St George's Hospital, London, UK.

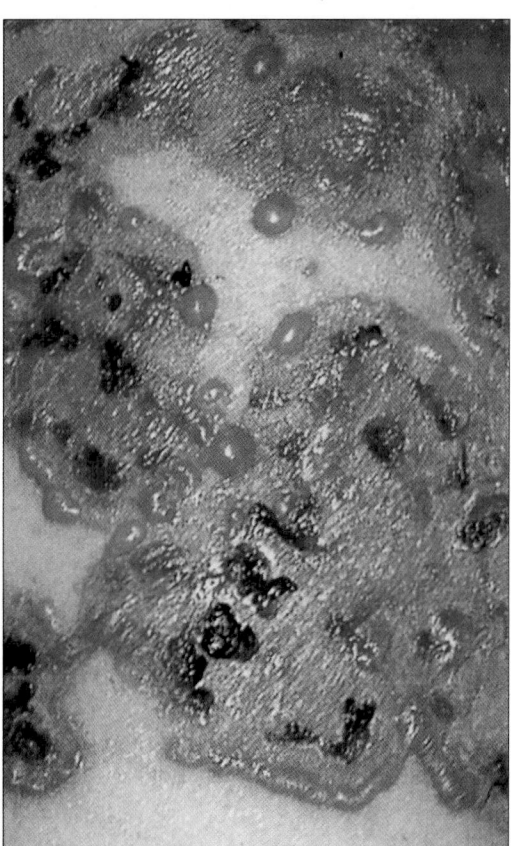

Fig. 3.155
Childhood linear IgA disease: the arrangement of blisters called the 'cluster of jewels'. By courtesy of R.A. Marsden, MD, St George's Hospital, London, UK.

Although linear IgA disease in children was originally thought to be self-limiting, it is now appreciated that symptoms may last over 5 years (25%) and occasionally extend beyond puberty into adult life.

Linear IgA disease is associated with increased expression of HLA-Cw7, -B8, -DR2, -DR3 and -DQ2.[27] The incidence of HLA-B8 association is variable, with reported figures varying from 28 to 56% (normal range 20–25%).[15,21] There is no evidence of an increase in HLA-B12.[15] Linear IgA disease is also associated with HLA-Cw7 and -DR3.[1]

Although in the earlier literature, as many as 24% of patients with linear IgA disease were thought to have associated gluten-sensitive enteropathy, the incidence is almost certainly considerably much lower.[1] There are, however, occasional recent references documenting occasional patients with linear IgA disease with clinical and histological evidence of gluten-sensitive enteropathy in the presence of antiendomysial and antitransglutaminase antibodies.[28,29]

There are a number of reports documenting an association between linear IgA disease and internal malignancy, including lymphoma, although whether this has significance is uncertain.[30,31]

Pathogenesis and histological features

Histologically linear IgA disease is characterized most frequently by dermatitis herpetiformis-like features (*Fig. 3.156*).[23,32,33] Occasionally, however, the histological changes suggest bullous pemphigoid or sometimes a mixture of both (*Fig. 3.157*). Eosinophilic spongiosis may rarely be a feature.[23]

Ultrastructurally the site of cleavage may be through the lamina lucida or below the lamina densa.[20]

A homogeneous linear deposition of IgA along the basement membrane region is found by direct immunofluorescence in 100% of patients (*Fig. 3.158*).[23,34–36] Uninvolved skin (particularly of the back) is suitable.[1] Oral mucosa and conjunctiva may also be positive.[1] The linear IgA antigen is present in all stratified squamous epithelia and amnion but, in contrast to the bullous pemphigoid antigen, is not found in bladder

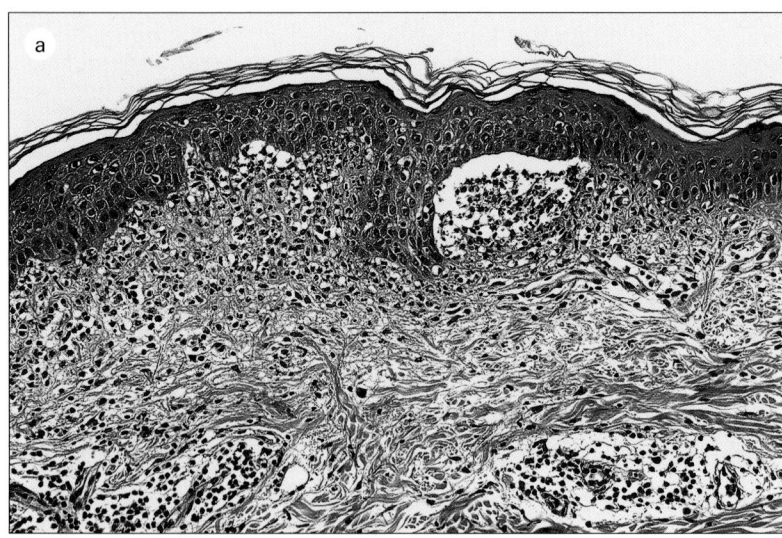

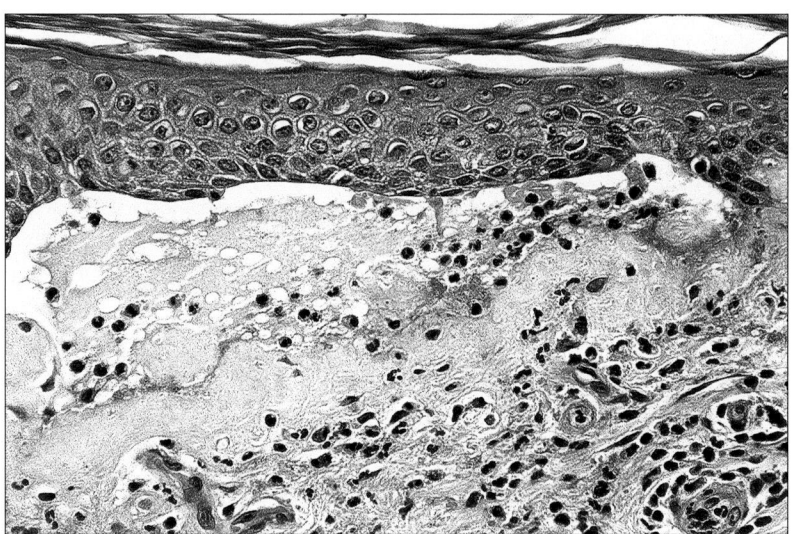

Fig. 3.157
Linear IgA disease: in this field the presence of eosinophils is more suggestive of bullous pemphigoid.

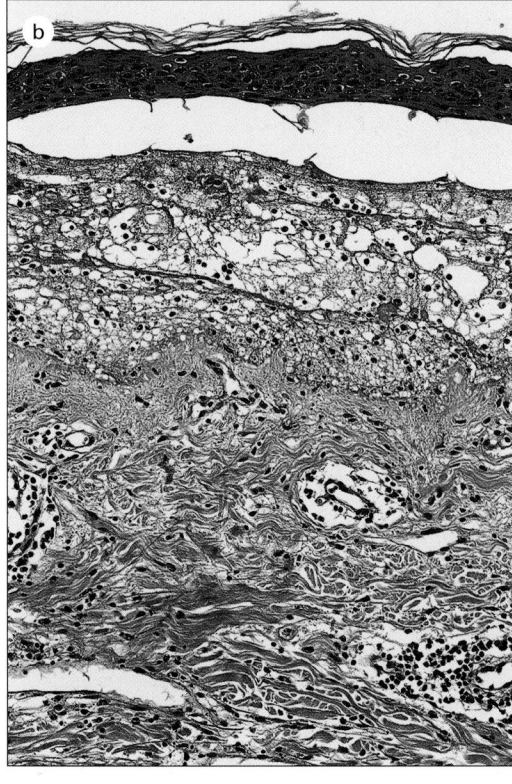

Fig. 3.156
(a, b) Linear IgA disease: in this example the features are those of a neutrophil-rich subepidermal vesicle reminiscent of dermatitis herpetiformis.

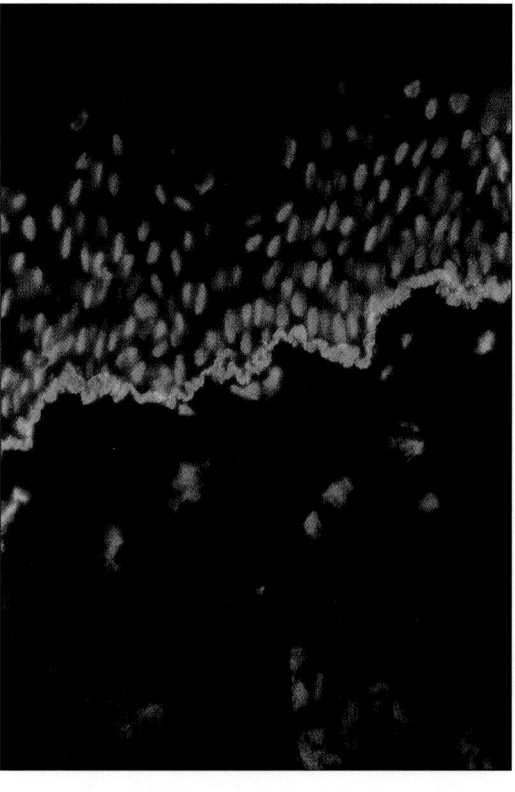

Fig. 3.158
Linear IgA disease: direct immunofluorescence showing linear IgA deposition. By courtesy of the Department of Immunofluorescence, Institute of Dermatology, London, UK.

mucosa.[35] IgG may also be demonstrable in up to 25% of cases.[12,15] IgM and C3 are occasionally present.[36]

A low titer circulating IgA anti-basement membrane zone antibody is present in approximately 30% of patients.[1] Use of conjunctiva as substrate may, however, substantially increase this figure (up to 50%).[22] Circulating IgG or C3-binding anti-basement membrane antibodies are seen only in those patients with overlap syndrome.[37] The IgA antibody is of pathogenetic significance since it causes dermoepidermal separation after incubation with whole skin cultures.[38] Blister fluid is also satisfactory for indirect IMF.[1]

With split skin immunofluorescence, the titer may be higher and sensitivity is increased. The IgA anti-basement membrane zone antibody variably labels the epidermal side, the dermal side or both sides of the artificial blister cavity.[39–41] Immunoelectron microscopy has shown similar results, with IgA being present within the lamina lucida or below the lamina densa in association with anchoring fibrils, and sometimes in both locations (*Fig. 3.159*).[42–47]

Studies by western immunoblotting indicate that linear IgA disease is a heterogeneous condition. Thus, in those cases associated with dermal binding on indirect NaCl-split skin IMF, the dermal antigens include 285 kD and 250 kD proteins and type VII collagen.[14,41,48,49] Epidermal binding antibodies react with BP230, BP180 and 200/280 kD antigens distinct from either of the BP antigens.[50–52] The antigens 120 kD (LAD1) and 97 kD described in earlier reports represent proteolytic cleavage products of BP180.[53–56] Linear IgA disease 180 kD antibodies recognize the NC16A domain.[57–59] LAD1 has been identified as ladinin localizing to the extracellular domain of BP180 kD.[60] Those patients with mixed IgA and IgG antibody-mediated disease also target BP180.[37]

Drug-induced linear IgA disease is considered on p. 646.

Differential diagnosis

The diseases from which linear IgA disease must be differentiated are dermatitis herpetiformis, bullous pemphigoid and inflammatory epidermolysis bullosa. Points of distinction are considered in *Table 3.4*.

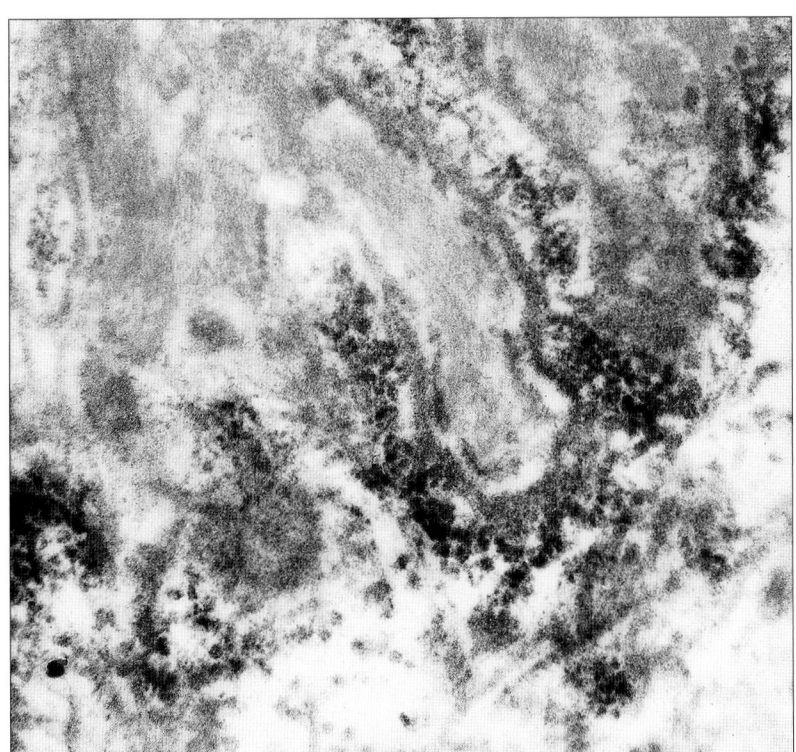

Fig. 3.159
Linear IgA disease: direct immunoperoxidase reaction using frozen tissue substrate. There is an abundance of granular IgA beneath the basal lamina.

References

1. Wojnarowska, F., Frith, P. (1997) Linear IgA disease. *Dev Ophthalmol*, 28, 64–72.
2. Wojnarowska, F. (2000) What's new in linear IgA disease? *JEADV*, 14, 441–443.
3. Schmidt, E., Zillikens, D. (2000) Autoimmune and inherited subepidermal blistering diseases: advances in the clinic and the laboratory. *Adv Dermatol*, 16, 113–157.
4. Pehamberger, H., Konrad, K., Holubar, K. (1977) Circulating IgA anti-basement membrane antibodies in linear dermatitis herpetiformis (Duhring): immunofluorescence and immunoelectron microscopic studies. *J Invest Dermatol*, 69, 490–493.
5. Seah, P.P., Fry, L. (1975) Immunoglobulins in the skin and their relevance in diagnosis. *Br J Dermatol*, 92, 157–166.
6. Chorzelski, T., Jablonska, S. (1988) Evolving concept of IgA linear dermatosis. *Semin Dermatol*, 7, 225–232.
7. Davies, M.G., Eady, R.A. (1980) Bullous pemphigoid with linear basement membrane zone IgA. *Clin Exp Dermatol*, 5, 79–83.
8. Russell-Jones, J.R., Goolamali, S.K. (1980) IgA bullous pemphigoid – a distinct blistering disorder. *Br J Dermatol*, 102, 719–725.
9. Honeyman, J.F., Honeyman, A.R., de la Parra, M.A. et al (1979) Polymorphic pemphigoid. *Arch Dermatol*, 115, 423–427.
10. Jablonska, S., Chorzelski, T.P., Beutner, E.H. et al (1976) Dermatitis herpetiformis and bullous pemphigoid. Intermediate and mixed forms. *Arch Dermatol*, 112, 45–80.
11. Leonard, J.N., Haffenden, G.P., Ring, N.P. et al (1982) Linear IgA disease in adults. *Br J Dermatol*, 107, 301–316.
12. Jablonska, S., Chorzelski, T. (1979) Dermatose á IgA linéaire. *Ann Dermatol Venereol*, 106, 651–655.
13. Aboobaker, J., Bhogal, B., Wojnarowska, F. et al (1987) The localization of the binding site of circulating IgA antibodies in linear IgA disease of adults, chronic bullous disease of childhood and childhood cicatricial pemphigoid. *Br J Dermatol*, 116, 293–302.
14. Wojnarowska, F., Whitehead, P., Leigh, I.M. et al (1991) Identification of the target antigen in chronic bullous disease of childhood and linear IgA disease of adults. *Br J Dermatol*, 124, 157–162.
15. Wojnarowska, F., Marsden, R.A., Bhogal, B. et al (1988) Chronic bullous disease of childhood, childhood cicatricial pemphigoid and linear IgA disease of adults. A comparative study demonstrating clinical and immunopathologic overlap. *J Am Acad Dermatol*, 19, 792–805.
16. Wojnarowska, F. (1990) Linear IgA disease of adults. In: Wojnarowska, F., Briggaman, R.A. (eds) Management of blistering diseases. London: Chapman & Hall Medical, pp 105–118.
17. Bernard, P., Vaillant, L., Labeille, B. et al (1995) Incidence and distribution of subepidermal autoimmune bullous skin disease in three French regions. *Arch Dermatol*, 31, 48–52.
18. Zillikens, D., Wever, S., Roth, A. et al (1995) Incidence of autoimmune subepidermal blistering diseases in a region of central Germany. *Arch Dermatol*, 131, 957–958.
19. Cotell, S., Robinson, N.D., Chan, L.S. (1999) Autoimmune blistering skin diseases. *Am J Emerg Med*, 18, 288–299.
20. Janniger, C.K., Wiltz, H., Schwartz, R.A. et al (1990) Adult linear IgA bullous dermatosis: a polymorphic disorder. *Cutis*, 45, 37–42.
21. Mobacken, H., Kastrop, W., Ljunghall, K. et al (1983) Linear IgA dermatosis: a study of ten adult patients. *Acta Derm Venereol*, 63, 123–128.
22. Kelly, S.E., Frith, P.A., Millard, P.R. et al (1988) A clinicopathological study of mucosal involvement in linear IgA disease. *Br J Dermatol*, 119, 161–170.
23. Marsden, R.A., McKee, P.H., Bhogal, B. et al (1980) A study of benign chronic bullous dermatosis of childhood and comparison with dermatitis herpetiformis and bullous pemphigoid. *Clin Exp Dermatol*, 5, 159–176.
24. Aboobaker, J., Wojnarowska, F., Bhogal, B. et al (1991) Chronic bullous dermatosis of childhood – clinical and immunological features seen in African patients. *Clin Exp Dermatol*, 16, 160–164.
25. Marsden, R.A., Wojnarowska, F., McKee, P.H. et al (1987) Linear IgA dermatosis in childhood. In: Happle, R., Grosshans, E. (eds) Pediatric dermatology. Berlin: Springer-Verlag.
26. Wojnarowska, F., Marsden, R.A., McKee, P.H. et al (1986) A comparative study of benign chronic bullous dermatosis of childhood and linear IgA disease of adults. *Br J Dermatol*, 113 (Suppl. 29), 17.
27. Collier, P.M., Wojnarowska, F., Welsh, K. et al (1999) Adult linear IgA disease and chronic bullous disease of childhood: the association with human lymphocyte antigens Cw7, B8, DR3 and tumor necrosis factor influences disease expression. *Br J Dermatol*, 141, 867–875.
28. Egan, C.A., Smith, E.P., Taylor, T.B. et al (2001) Linear IgA bullous dermatosis responsive to a gluten-free diet. *Am J Gastroenterol*, 96, 1927–1929.
29. Kapur, A., Isaacs, P.E., Kelsey, P.R. (1995) Linear IgA dermatosis, celiac disease, and extraintestinal B cell lymphoma. *Gut*, 37, 731–733.
30. Godfrey, K., Wojnarowska, F., Leonard, J. (1990) Linear IgA disease of adults: association with lymphoproliferative malignancy and possible role of other triggering factors. *Br J Dermatol*, 123, 447–452.
31. McEvoy, M., Connolly, S. (1990) Linear IgA dermatosis: association with malignancy. *J Am Acad Dermatol*, 22, 59–63.
32. Blenkinsopp, W.K., Haffenden, G.P., Fry, L. et al (1983) Histology of linear IgA disease, dermatitis herpetiformis and bullous pemphigoid. *Am J Dermatopathol*, 5, 547–554.
33. Smith, S.B., Harrist, T.J., Murphy, G.F. et al (1984) Linear IgA bullous dermatosis v. dermatitis herpetiformis: quantitative measurements of dermoepidermal alterations. *Arch Dermatol*, 120, 324–328.
34. Chorzelski, T.P., Jablonska, S. (1979) IgA linear dermatosis of childhood (chronic bullous disease of childhood). *Br J Dermatol*, 101, 535–542.
35. Pothupitiya, G.M., Wojnarowska, F., Bhogal, B.S. et al (1988) Distribution of the antigen in adult linear IgA disease and chronic bullous disease of childhood suggests that it is a single and unique antigen. *Br J Dermatol*, 118, 175–182.
36. Wilson, B.D., Beutner, E.H., Kumar, V. et al (1985) Linear IgA bullous dermatosis: an immunologically defined disease. *Int J Dermatol*, 24, 569–574.
37. Hertl, M., Budinger, L., Christophoridis, S. et al (1999) IgG and IgA antibodies in linear IgA/IgG bullous dermatosis target the ectodomain of bullous pemphigoid antigen 2. *Br J Dermatol*, 140, 750–752.
38. Akahoshi, Y., Kanola, G., Anan, S. et al (1987) Dermato-epidermal blister formation by linear IgA dermatosis sera in normal human skin in organ culture. *J Dermatol*, 14, 552–558.
39. Pothupitiya, G.M., Wojnarowska, F., Bhogal, B. (1986) The antigen in linear IgA bullous dermatosis is localized to the lamina lucida and differs from bullous pemphigoid and epidermolysis bullosa antigens. *J Invest Dermatol*, 87, 162A.
40. Willsteed, E., Bhogal, B.S., Black, M.M. et al (1990) The use of 1 M NaCl split skin in the indirect immunofluorescence of the linear IgA bullous dermatoses. *J Cutan Pathol*, 17, 144–148.
41. Dmochowski, M., Hashimoto, T., Bhogal, B.S. et al (1993) Immunoblotting studies of linear IgA disease. *J Dermatol Sci*, 6, 194–200.
42. Yaoita, H., Katz, S.I. (1976) Immunoelectronmicroscopic localisation of IgA in skin of patients with dermatitis herpetiformis. *J Invest Dermatol*, 67, 502–506.
43. Dabrowski, J., Chorzelski, T., Jablonska, S. et al (1979) Immunoelectron microscopic studies on IgA linear dermatosis. *Arch Dermatol Res*, 265, 289–298.
44. Yamasaki, Y., Hashimoto, T., Nishikawa, T. (1982) Dermatitis herpetiformis with linear IgA deposition: ultrastructural localization of in vivo bound IgA. *Acta Derm Venereol*, 62, 401–405.
45. Haffenden, G.P., Ring, N.P., Leonard, J.N. et al (1983) Immuno-electron microscopic studies in patients with linear IgA deposits. *J Invest Dermatol*, 80, 363A.
46. Bhogal, B., Wojnarowska, F., Marsden, R.A. et al (1987) Linear IgA bullous dermatosis of adults and children: an immunoelectron microscopic study. *Br J Dermatol*, 117, 289–296.
47. Prost, C., De Luca, A.C., Combemale, M. et al (1989) Diagnosis of adult linear IgA dermatosis by immunoelectron microscopy in sixteen patients with linear IgA deposits. *J Invest Dermatol*, 92, 39–45.
48. Rusenko, K.W., Gammon, W.R., Briggaman, R.A. (1989) Type VII collagen is the antigen recognized by IgA anti-sub lamina densa autoantibodies. *J Invest Dermatol*, 92, 510A.
49. Zambruno, G., Manca, V., Kanitakis, J. et al (1994) Linear IgA bullous dermatosis with autoantibodies to a 290 kD antigen of anchoring fibrils. *J Am Acad Dermatol*, 31, 884–888.
50. Kanitakis, J., Mauduit, G., Cozzani, E. et al (1994) Linear IgA bullous dermatosis of childhood with autoantibodies to a 230kDa epidermal antigen. *Pediatr Dermatol*, 11, 139–144.
51. Ghohestani, R.F., Nicolas, J.F., Kanitakis, J. et al (1997) Linear IgA bullous dermatosis with IgA antibodies

exclusively directed against the 180- or 230-kD epidermal antigens. *J Invest Dermatol*, **108**, 854–858.

52.   Fujimoto, W., Ohtsu, T., Toi, Y. et al (2000) Linear IgA disease with IgA antibodies directed against 200- and 280-kDa epidermal antigens. *Br J Dermatol*, **142**, 1213–1218.

53.   Hirako, Y., Usukura, J., Uematsu, J. et al (1998) Cleavage of BP180, a 180-kDa bullous pemphigoid antigen, yields a 120-kDa collagenous extracellular polypeptide. *J Biol Chem*, **273**, 9711–9717.

54.   Pas, H.H., Kloosterhuis, G.J., Heeres, K. et al (1997) Bullous pemphigoid and linear IgA dermatosis sera recognize a similar 120-kDa keratinocyte collagenous glycoprotein with antigenic cross-reactivity to BP180. *J Invest Dermatol*, **108**, 423–429.

55.   Marinkovich, M.P., Taylor, T.B., Keene, D.R. et al (1996) LAD-1, the linear IgA bullous dermatosis autoantigen, is a novel 120-kDa anchoring filament protein synthesized by epidermal cells. *J Invest Dermatol*, **106**, 734–738.

56.   Zone, J.J., Taylor, T.B., Meyer, L.J. et al (1998) The 97 kDa linear IgA bullous disease antigen is identical to a portion of the extracellular domain of the 180 kDa bullous pemphigoid antigen, BPAg2. *J Invest Dermatol*, **110**, 207–210.

57.   Herzele, K., Zillikens, D., Schmidt, E. et al (1998) Autoantibodies in a subgroup of patients with linear IgA disease react with the NC16A domain of BP180. *J Invest Dermatol*, **110**, 510A.

58.   Schmidt, E., Herzele, K., Schumann, H. et al (1999) Linear IgA disease with circulating IgA antibodies against the NC16A domain of BP180. *Br J Dermatol*, **140**, 964–966.

59.   Zillikens, D., Herzele, K., Georgi, M. et al (1999) Autoandibodies in a subgroup of patients with linear IgA disease react with the NC16A domain of BP180. *J Invest Dermatol*, **113**, 947–953.

60.   Megahed, M., Motoki, K., McGrath, J. et al (1996) Cloning of the human linear IgA disease gene (LADA) encoding a novel anchoring filament protein, ladinin. *J Invest Dermatol*, **106**, 832(A).

Acantholytic disorders

4

Pemphigus   139
Pemphigus vulgaris   140
Pemphigus vegetans   145
Pemphigus foliaceus   147
Fogo selvagem   149
Pemphigus herpetiformis   151
Pemphigus erythematosus   151
Paraneoplastic pemphigus   152
IgA pemphigus   154
Drug-induced pemphigus   155
Contact pemphigus   155

Acantholytic dermatoses with dyskeratosis   156
Hailey–Hailey disease   156
Relapsing linear acantholytic dermatosis   158
Darier's disease   158
Linear Darier's disease   163
Transient acantholytic dermatosis   164
Acantholytic dermatosis of the genitocrural area   166
Warty dyskeratoma   166
Familial dyskeratotic comedones   168
Acantholytic acanthoma   169
Focal acantholytic dyskeratosis   170

The term acantholysis derives from the Greek *akantha*, a thorn or prickle, and *lysis*, a loosening. In its simplest definition, the term is used to reflect a primary disorder of the skin (and sometimes the mucous membranes) characterized by separation of the keratinocytes at their desmosomal junctions (*Fig. 4.1*). A wide range of conditions are characterized by this feature, from inherited disorders such as Darier's disease and Hailey–Hailey disease in which a calcium pump gene mutation results in desmosomal instability through to the autoimmune pemphigus group of diseases whereby autoantibodies directly damage desmosomes with resultant keratinocyte separation and blister formation (*Table 4.1*). Desmosomes may also be damaged by secondary phenomena, for example following severe edema, either intercellular (spongiosis) or intracellular (e.g. ballooning degeneration as is seen in various viral infections). Such processes, however, are not included in the acantholytic category and are discussed elsewhere. The histological features of the conditions described in this chapter show considerable overlap. The diagnosis is therefore dependent upon adequate clinical information and the results of immunofluorescence investigations.

Pemphigus

Pemphigus (Gr. *pemphix,* blister) refers to a group of chronic blistering diseases which develop as a consequence of autoantibodies directed

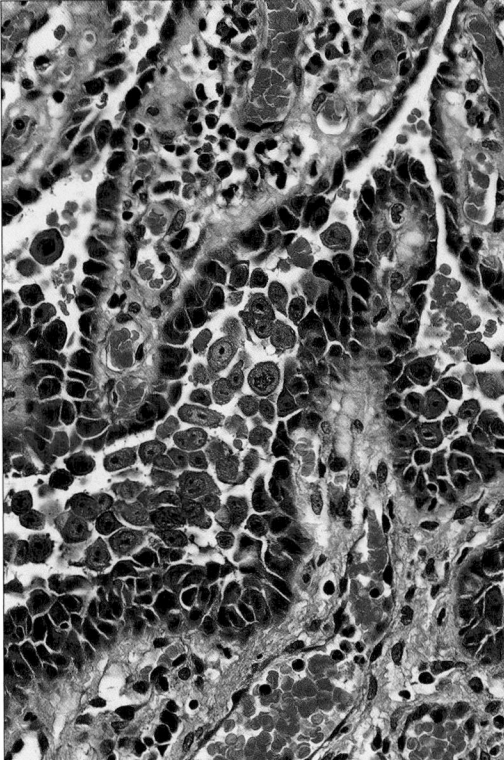

Fig. 4.1
Acantholysis: the keratinocytes are rounded and separated from each other to form an intraepidermal blister. Villi formed from the underlying dermal papillae typically project into suprabasal cavities.

against a variety of desmosomal proteins.[1-4] The condition as a whole is rare, with an annual incidence ranging from 0.1 to 0.5/100,000 of the general population.[2] It is commoner in the Jewish population in which the annual incidence rises to 1.6–3.2/100,000.[5] Ashkenazi Jews are the most frequently affected.[5] There is no sex predilection.

The clinical features and, therefore, classification of these disorders depends upon the level of separation within the epidermis:

- In pemphigus vulgaris (p. vulgaris) and pemphigus vegetans (p. vegetans) the blisters are suprabasal.
- In pemphigus foliaceus (p. foliaceus), pemphigus erythematosus (p. erythematosus) and fogo selvagem, the blisters are situated more superficially.

Pemphigus vulgaris is by far the most common variant, accounting for 80% of cases.[6,7]

In addition to affecting humans, pemphigus has been described in a variety of animals including dogs, cats, goats and horses.[8]

References

1.   Korman, N.J. (1990) Pemphigus. *Dermatol Clin*, **8**, 689–700.
2.   Becker, B.A., Gaspari, A.A. (1993) Pemphigus vulgaris and vegetans. *Dermatol Clin*, **11**, 429–452.
3.   Hertl, M., Veldman, C. (2001) Pemphigus – paradigm of autoantibody-mediated autoimmunity. *Skin Pharmacol Appl Skin Physiol*, **14**, 408–418.
4.   Martel, P., Joly, P. (2001) Pemphigus: autoimmune diseases of keratinocyte's adhesion molecules. *Clin Dermatol*, **19**, 662–674.
5.   Lynch, P., Gallego, R.E., Saied, N.K. (1976) Pemphigus: a review. *Arizona Med*, **33**, 1030–1037.
6.   Krain, I.S. (1974) Pemphigus: epidemiologic and survival characteristics of 59 patients. *Arch Dermatol*, **110**, 862–865.
7.   Rosenberg, F.R., Sanders, S., Nelson, C.T. (1976) Pemphigus: a 20-year review of 107 patients treated with corticosteroids. *Arch Dermatol*, **112**, 962–970.
8.   Holubar, K. (1988) Pemphigus: a disease of man and animal. *Int J Dermatol*, **27**, 516–520.

Pemphigus vulgaris

Clinical features

Pemphigus vulgaris (p. vulgaris) particularly affects the middle aged (onset typically at 40–60 years of age) although occasionally children are affected.[1-6] Self-limiting neonatal disease through transplacental transfer of maternal autoantibodies has also rarely been documented (see pathogenesis).[7] The disease begins in the mouth (*Figs 4.2, 4.3*) in 50–70% of patients with painful erosions or bullae and, after a period of weeks or months, the blisters spread to involve the skin.[8] Oral lesions most commonly affect the buccal, palatine and gingival mucosae.[1]

The typical skin lesion is a fragile, flaccid blister, which develops on normal or erythematous skin, and readily ruptures, leaving a painful crusted, raw, bloody erosion (*Figs 4.4, 4.5*). Lesions are most often seen on the scalp, face, axillae and groins, although in some patients they are

Table 4.1
Antigens targeted in the pemphigus variants

Pemphigus variant	Autoantigen
Pemphigus vulgaris	Dsg3 (mucosal), Dsg1 (cutaneous), desmocollins, pemphaxin, α9-acetylcholine receptor
Pemphigus vegetans	Dsg3, Dsc1 and Dsc2 in some patients
Pemphigus foliaceus	Dsg1
Pemphigus erythematosus	Dsg1
Fogo selvagem	Dsg1, rarely also Dsg3
IgA pemphigus	Dsc1, Dsg1 or Dsg3
Herpetiform pemphigus	Dsg1, rarely also Dsg3
Paraneoplastic pemphigus	Desmoplakins I and II, envoplakin, periplakin, BP230, plectin, Dsg1 and Dsg3
Drug-induced pemphigus	Dsg1 or Dsg3

Dsc, desmocollin; Dsg, desmoglein. Modified from Martel, P., Joly, P. (2001) Pemphigus: autoimmune diseases of keratinocyte's adhesion molecules. *Clinical Dermatology*, **19**, 667.

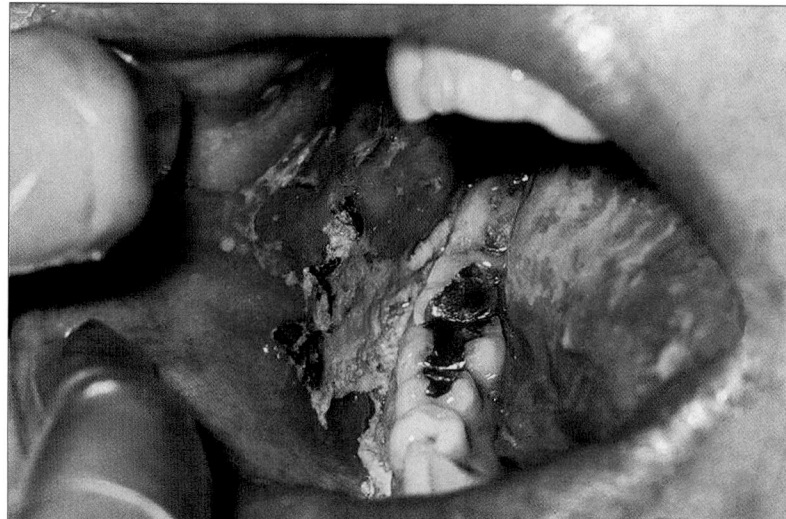

Fig. 4.2
Pemphigus vulgaris: painful erosions are present on the buccal mucosa. By courtesy of R.A. Marsden, MD, St George's Hospital, London, UK.

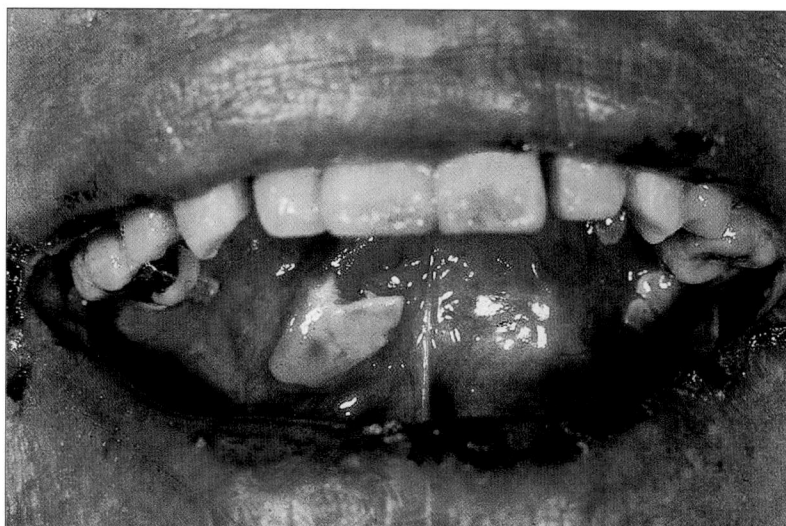

Fig. 4.3
Pemphigus vulgaris: in this patient there is an intact blister on the floor of the mouth. Pemphigus commonly presents in the mouth. By courtesy of the Institute of Dermatology, London, UK.

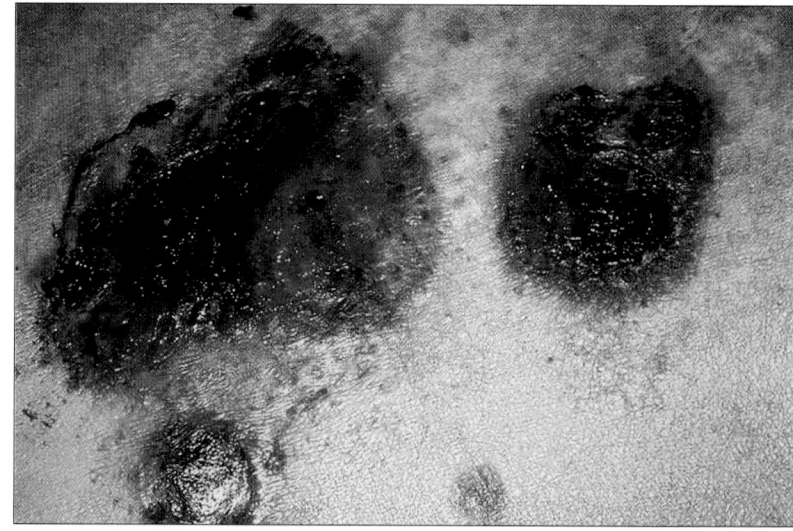

Fig. 4.4
Pemphigus vulgaris: since the blisters are superficial, erosions are more commonly encountered. By courtesy of the Institute of Dermatology, London, UK.

generalized (*Figs 4.6–4.8*).[1–3] Blisters can be induced by rubbing the adjacent, apparently normal skin with a finger – the Nikolsky sign. Direct pressure applied to the center of the blister is also followed by lateral extension – the Asboe–Hansen sign.[2] Healing is often accompanied by postinflammatory hyperpigmentation but scarring is not a feature.[2]

Before the introduction of corticosteroid therapy, the lesions usually became more extensive and in the past often led eventually to death. Treatment with high doses of corticosteroids and immunosuppressants, such as azathioprine, has significantly reduced the mortality to 5–15% and prolonged remissions without treatment are now being reported.[2] A considerable proportion of the deaths that do occur, however, is due to the side-effects of therapy and include staphylococcal infections and, to a lesser extent, pulmonary embolism.[2]

Rarely, nail involvement in the form of hemorrhagic paronychia, chronic paronychia, trachyonychia, onycholysis, or onychomadesis, is encountered in patients with p. vulgaris.[9]

Occasional modes of presentation include linear lesions, postsurgical, postburn and postirradiation pemphigus.[10–16]

In addition to oral and cutaneous involvement, lesions have been described at a wide variety of sites including the pharynx, larynx, esophagus, eye, external genitalia, urethra and anal mucosa.[1] Esophageal lesions, although originally thought to be rare, have more recently been documented in as many as 63–87% of patients.[17,18] Erosions and ulcers are typically found and intact blisters are rare. Exceptionally, the whole mucosa may be affected with subsequent sloughing – esophagitis dissecans superficialis.[19] Ocular lesions are usually restricted to the conjunctiva, presenting as conjunctivitis or small vesicles that rapidly rupture.[2,20,21] Very rarely, scarring may develop and corneal ulceration with perforation has been described.[22] Vulval, vaginal and cervical lesions are well recognized.[23–25] Exceptionally, the vagina may be the sole

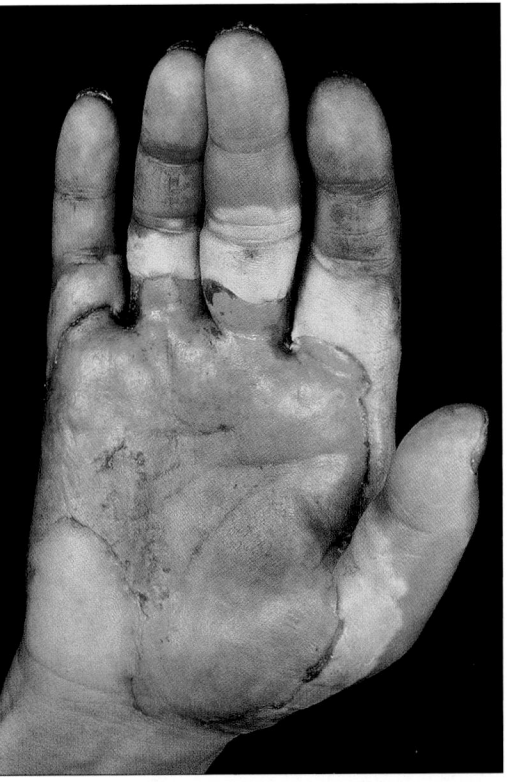

Fig. 4.7
Pemphigus vulgaris: extensive trauma-induced blisters. By courtesy of the Institute of Dermatology, London, UK.

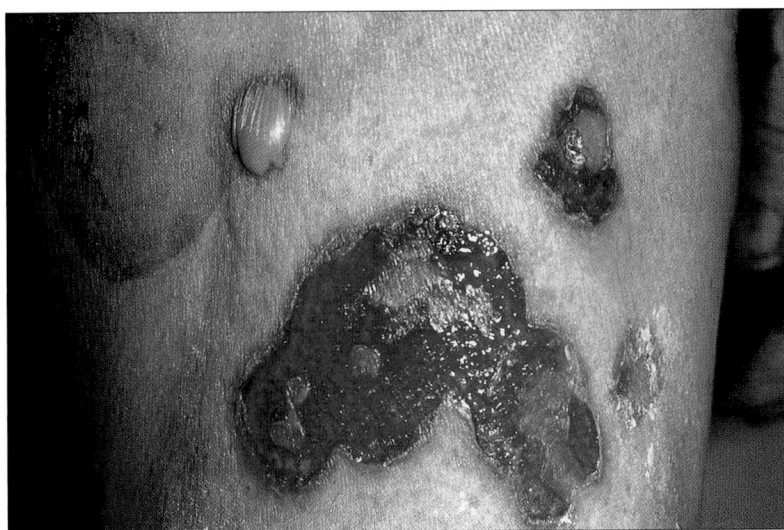

Fig. 4.5
Pemphigus vulgaris: extensive erosions and blisters are present on the shin. By courtesy of R.A. Marsden, MD, St George's Hospital, London, UK.

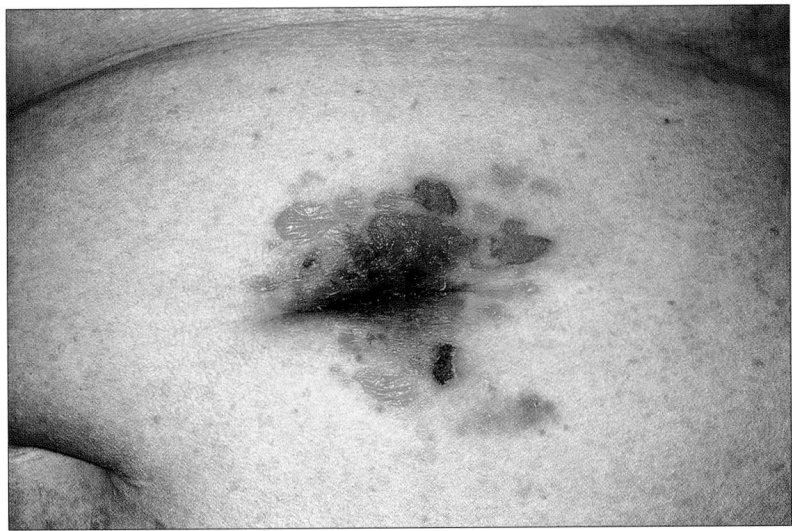

Fig. 4.6
Pemphigus vulgaris: umbilical lesions showing intact blisters as well as raw erosions. By courtesy of R.A. Marsden, MD, St George's Hospital, London, UK.

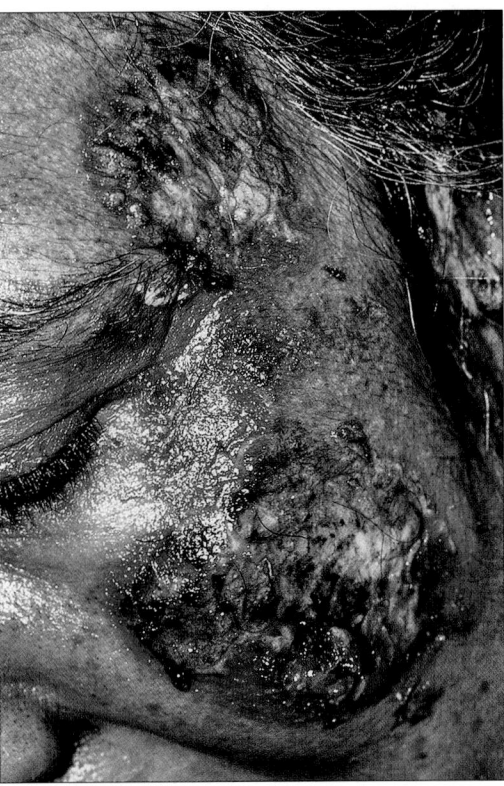

Fig. 4.8
Pemphigus vulgaris: extensive disease can be very disfiguring. By courtesy of the Institute of Dermatology, London, UK.

site of involvement.[26] Penile lesions most commonly affect the glans.[27] They are not usually followed by any significant sequelae.

The development of pemphigus may be associated with a variety of disorders including other autoimmune bullous dermatoses, particularly bullous pemphigoid, lupus erythematosus, thymoma and myasthenia gravis.[28–31] As in the many other diseases with immunological pathogenesis, pemphigus is accompanied by an increased incidence of internal malignancy including thymoma, lymphoma and Kaposi's sarcoma (see paraneoplastic pemphigus).[32]

Pathogenesis and histological features

Pemphigus is an immunologically mediated disease.[33,34] Examination of perilesional skin by direct immunofluorescent techniques reveals in vivo-bound immunoglobulin (usually IgG) and often complement (C3) in the intercellular region of the epidermis (*Fig. 4.9*).[35] Abundant antigen in the follicular outer root sheath and germinal matrix may account for the marked scalp involvement typical of pemphigus.[36] The in vivo-bound IgG is mainly of the IgG1 and IgG4 subclasses.[37]

Indirect immunofluorescent techniques show that the serum of patients with pemphigus contains an IgG antibody that reacts with the intercellular region of normal squamous epithelium – the intercellular substance (pemphigus) antibody.[38] This antibody is, however, not entirely specific as it may be found in a variety of other conditions, such as severe burns, penicillin drug reactions and following radiation therapy.[39–41] Circulating antibodies are predominantly of the IgG1 and IgG4 subclasses; IgG3 is much less often identified.[42]

Circulating IgG is pathogenic.[33,34] The level of the antibody titer closely parallels the clinical state of the disease.[43–46] IgG4 titers diminish during remission whereas circulating IgG1 may continue to be present.[34,44] Relapse is commonly preceded by rising IgG4 antibody titers.[44] P. vulgaris very occasionally may be evident in a neonate born of a mother with active p. vulgaris.[7,47] Such autoantibodies cross the placenta inducing disease in the infant. The disease is, however, short lived, with lesions disappearing as the maternal antibodies are catabolized. Passive transfer of IgG4 into neonatal mice results in the development of blisters.[48] Purified IgG from pemphigus induces acantholysis in human skin explants and keratinocyte cultures.[49,50]

The pemphigus antibody binds to the full thickness of the epidermis. Compared with p. vulgaris, immunofluorescence studies on the sera of p. foliaceus patients tend to show more staining in the superficial

epidermis, correlating with the level of the split.[51,52] Conversely, the sera from patients with p. vulgaris show more affinity for the lower epidermis. Despite these trends, we generally do not base diagnoses on these (often subtle) differences in immunofluorescence staining distribution.

The p. vulgaris antibody is directed at the extracytoplasmic domain of the 130 kD epithelial desmosomal cadherin, desmoglein 3 (Dsg3), which forms a complex with plakoglobin (85 kD).[53–59] The p. vulgaris antibody, however, does not recognize the latter. Many patients also have antibodies that bind to the p. foliaceus antigen, desmoglein 1 (Dsg1), a 160 kD polypeptide.[60,61] Dsg3 is expressed primarily in the oral mucosa and therefore antibodies directed against this antigen result in mucosal pemphigus. In contrast, Dsg1 is a cutaneous antigen and, therefore, antibodies directed against it result in lesions affecting the skin but not the mucosa (cutaneous pemphigus).[51]

Antibodies reactive to a number of other proteins including desmocollins, pemphaxin and acetylcholine receptor have been demonstrated in the sera of p. vulgaris patients.[62–65]

The pathogenesis of the acantholysis is uncertain. It is likely, that direct binding of antibody to the desmosomal cadherins is of major importance.[33] There is also some evidence to suggest that the process may also involve, at least secondarily, the action of local proteolytic enzymes.[33] Pemphigus antibody induces expression of plasminogen activator receptor on the surface of keratinocytes.[66] Binding of plasminogen activator to its keratinocyte cell membrane receptor results in plasminogen activation with resultant production of plasmin.[67,68] This latter has non-specific proteolytic activity, which may be responsible at least in part for the dissolution of the desmosomes.[33] P. vulgaris antibodies stimulate production of keratinocyte phospholipase C, inositol 1,4,5-triphosphate and increase intracellular calcium. Protein kinase C activation results in release of keratinocyte plasminogen activator and increased expression of plasminogen activator receptor.[69–71] Other factors, however, must be of greater importance since p. vulgaris IgG can induce acantholysis in plasminogen activator knockout mice.[72] Complement appears not to be essential for acantholysis and it is thought that any involvement is secondary, perhaps accelerating or extending the process.[33]

T-cells are also critical to the development of the antibody-mediated acantholysis.[34] CD4+ memory T-cells are predominantly involved and both T-helper 1 (Th1) and Th2 Dsg3-specific subtypes are represented.[73,74] Th1 T-cell-derived interferon-γ stimulates production of IgG1, and Th2 cells produce interleukin (IL)-4 and IL-13 which are responsible for secretion of B-cell-derived IgG4. Both populations are therefore of importance in stimulating production of p. vulgaris antibody.[34] In addition, there is evidence that tumor necrosis factor 1 (TNF-1) and IL-1 are also of importance in the development of acantholysis. Knockout mice for both these cytokines show diminished acantholysis in passive antibody transfer experiments.[75]

There is considerable evidence of a genetic background influencing susceptibility to pemphigus as shown by strong associations with human leukocyte antigen (HLA)-DRβ1*0402, HLA-DRβ1*1401 and HLA-DQβ1*0503.[76–79] Perhaps surprisingly, however, there are only occasional documented reports of familial occurrence.[80,81]

Pemphigus blisters rupture easily. It is therefore essential to biopsy an early lesion to establish the correct diagnosis. The characteristic acantholysis develops because of damage to the intercellular bridges. Acantholytic cells are rounded and have intensely eosinophilic cytoplasm, pyknotic nuclei and perinuclear halos. An early lesion of p. vulgaris shows a slit-like suprabasal cleft or vesicle containing occasional acantholytic cells. The established blister contains acantholytic cells in clumps and in isolation (*Figs 4.10, 4.11*). Characteristically, the floor of the cavity is lined by a single layer of intact basal cells, the so-called 'tombstone' pattern (*Fig. 4.12*).[82]

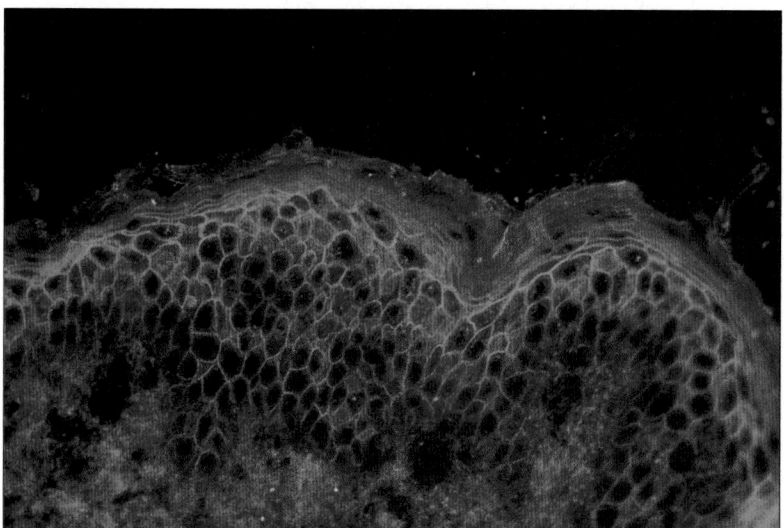

Fig. 4.9
Pemphigus vulgaris: direct immunofluorescence. By courtesy of the Institute of Dermatology, London, UK.

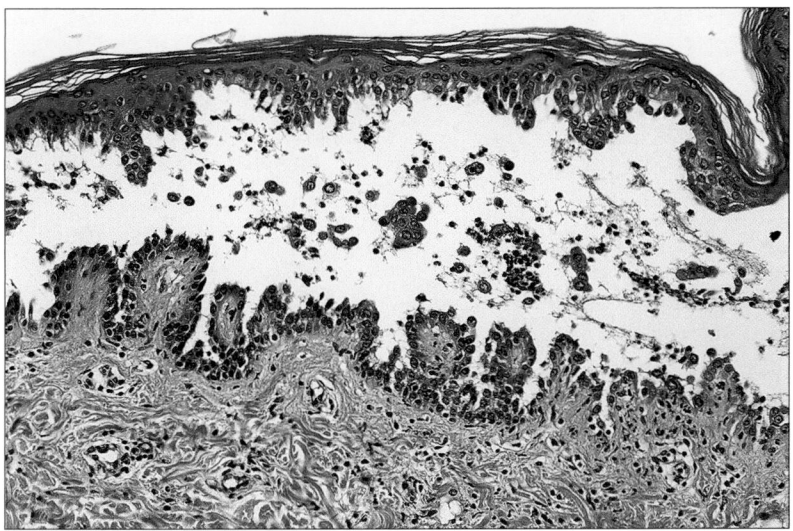

Fig. 4.10
Pemphigus vulgaris: established blister showing marked acantholysis and scattered neutrophils. The dermal papillae project into the cavity as villi.

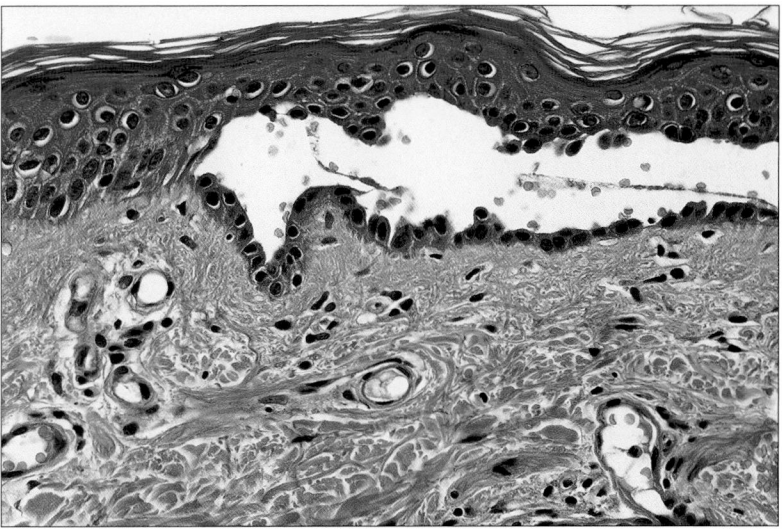

Fig. 4.12
Pemphigus vulgaris: cell-free example showing a linear palisade of intact basal keratinocytes – the so-called 'tombstone' appearance.

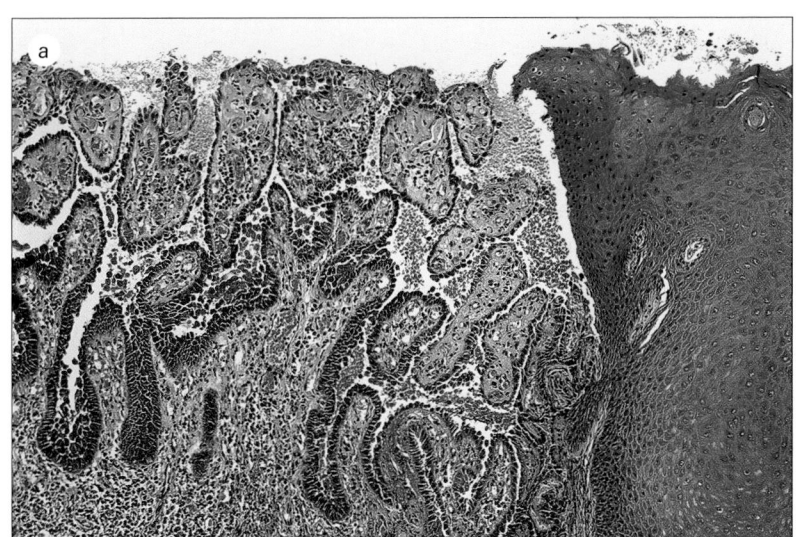

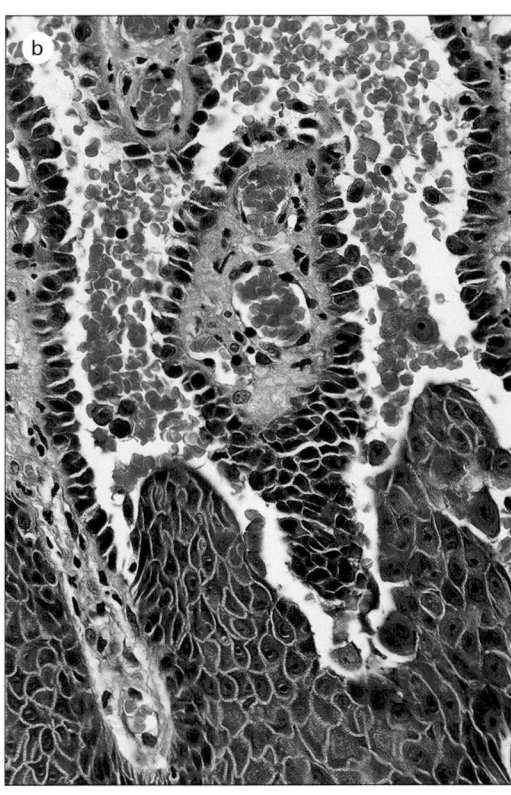

Fig. 4.11
Pemphigus vulgaris: (a) perianal mucosa showing acantholysis and conspicuous villi; (b) high power view.

The acantholytic process frequently involves the epithelium of the adnexae which can be a useful diagnostic clue in those lesions which lack the roof of the blister (*Fig. 4.13*). The dermal papillary outline is usually maintained and, frequently, the papillae protrude into the blister cavity. Sometimes the features of eosinophilic spongiosis are seen on biopsy, particularly in early lesions.[83] The blister cavity often contains a few inflammatory cells (notably eosinophils) and, in the dermis, there is a moderate perivascular chronic inflammatory cell infiltrate with conspicuous eosinophils although sometimes these are scanty or even absent. Mucous membrane lesions show similar histology.

Ultrastructurally, there is dilatation of the intercellular space with consequent stretching of the desmosomal attachment points (*Figs 4.14, 4.15*).[84] With progression these separate and eventually disappear,

residual cell membranes often showing a pseudovillous morphology. Hemidesmosomes are morphologically normal. Immunoelectron microscopy confirms that the immunoreactants are located within the intercellular space.

Differential diagnosis

The differential diagnosis of p. vulgaris includes a variety of conditions such as Darier's disease, Hailey–Hailey disease and transient acantholytic dermatosis (Grover's disease) (*Table 4.2*). In the absence of clinical information or without immunofluorescence studies, it may be impossible to establish a definitive diagnosis. Darier's and Hailey–Hailey diseases are not associated with immunoreactants.

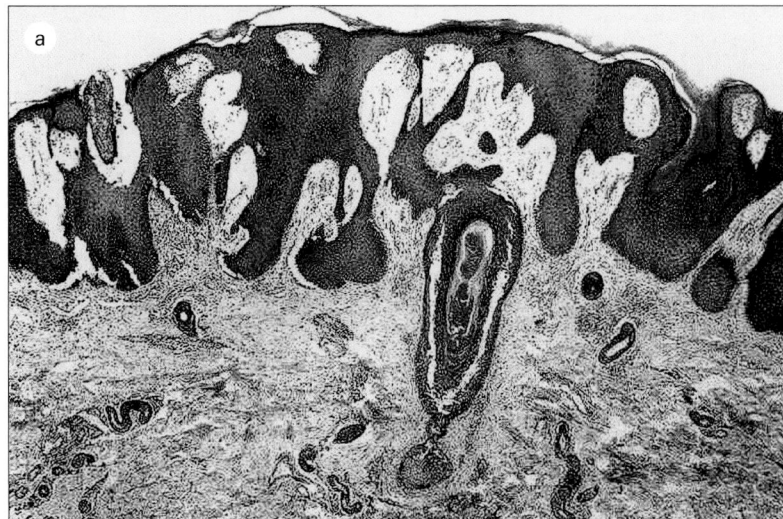

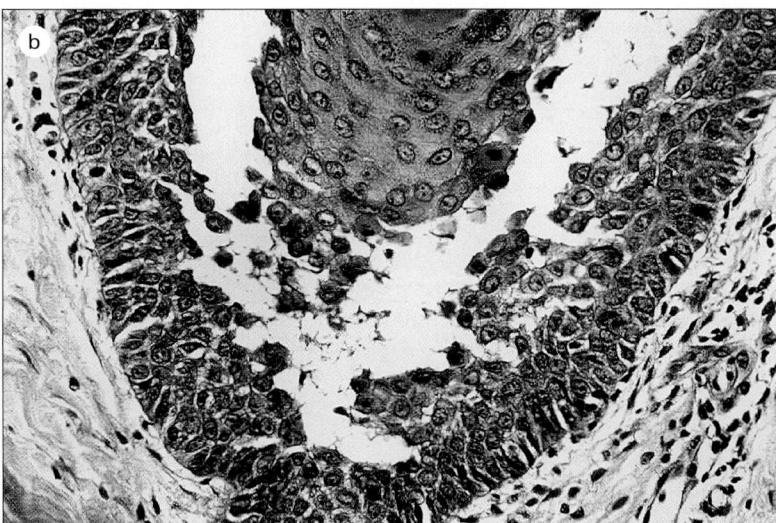

Fig. 4.13
Pemphigus vulgaris: (**a**) follicular involvement distinguishes pemphigus from Hailey–Hailey disease in which it is not a feature; (**b**) high power view.

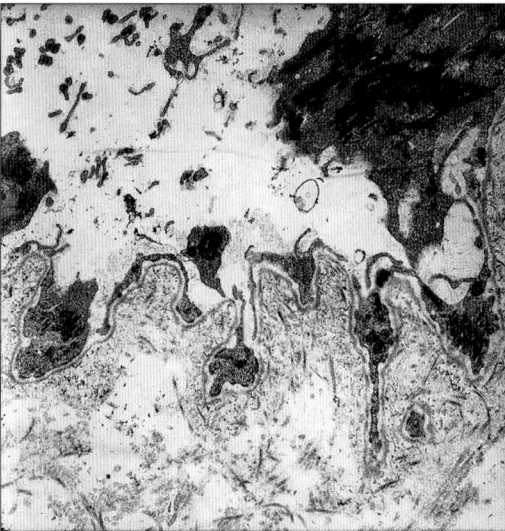

Fig. 4.14
Pemphigus vulgaris: electron photomicrograph of an early lesion showing suprabasal, intraepidermal vesiculation. Residual cytoplasm of basal keratinocytes lines the floor of the blister. The lamina densa is clearly visible.

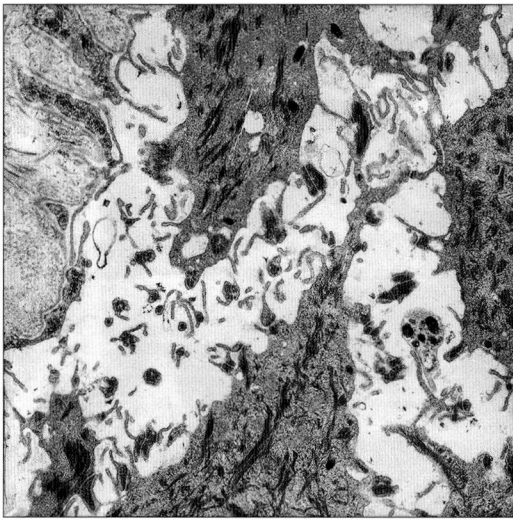

Fig. 4.15
Pemphigus vulgaris: electron photomicrograph of an early lesion showing marked dilatation of the intercellular space. Cytoplasmic 'villus' formation is conspicuous and only occasional desmosomes are apparent.

Table 4.2
Differential diagnosis of suprabasal pemphigus

	Pemphigus vulgaris*	Darier's disease*	Hailey–Hailey disease*
Types of lesion	Intraepithelial bullae	Suprabasal clefts	Intraepithelial bullae
Adjacent epithelium	Intact	Intact	Disintegrating
Involvement of adnexae	Yes	Yes	No
Corps ronds and grains	No	Yes	Rarely
Dermal inflammation	Mononuclears, eosinophils	Mononuclears	Mononuclears
Immunofluorescence	Positive	Negative	Negative

* The lesions of Grover's disease may histologically mimic any of these and can only be distinguished by immunofluorescence.

Dyskeratosis in the form of corps ronds and grains is typical of Darier's disease, but is rarely seen in Hailey–Hailey disease, and is not a feature of pemphigus. In Hailey–Hailey disease, the perivesicular epithelium is likened to a dilapidated brick wall, an effect sometimes seen in p. vulgaris. More frequently, however, the epithelium overlying and adjacent to the blister is essentially intact.

Acantholysis involving the follicular epithelium is often seen in pemphigus, but usually not in Hailey–Hailey disease. The pemphigus-like variant of Grover's disease is histologically indistinguishable from pemphigus, but the clinical history, minute size of the lesions as viewed by the microscope, and negative immunofluorescence findings make distinction relatively easy. Extreme degrees of acantholysis in acantholytic solar keratosis may on rare occasions be confused with the previously mentioned acantholytic disorders. Similarly, it is important not to misinterpret the trivial finding of incidental focal acantholytic dyskeratosis in a skin specimen removed or biopsied for an unrelated finding.

References

1. Korman, N.J. (1990) Pemphigus. *Dermatol Clin*, **8**, 689–700.
2. Becker, B.A., Gaspari, A.A. (1993) Pemphigus vulgaris and vegetans. *Dermatol Clin*, **11**, 429–452.
3. Lynch, P., Gallego, R.E., Saied, N.K. (1976) Pemphigus: a review. *Arizona Med*, **33**, 1030–1037.
4. Simon, D.G., Krutchkoff, D., Kaslow, R.A. et al (1980) Pemphigus in Hartford County, Connecticut from 1972 to 1977. *Arch Dermatol*, **116**, 1035–1037.
5. Kanwar, A.J. (1991) Pemphigus in children. *Int J Dermatol*, **30**, 343–346.
6. Wananukul, S., Pongprasit, P. (1999) Childhood pemphigus. *Int J Dermatol*, **38**, 29–35.
7. Chowdhury, M.M., Natarajan, S. (1998) Neonatal pemphigus vulgaris associated with mild oral pemphigus vulgaris in the mother during pregnancy. *Br J Dermatol*, **139**, 500–503.
8. Meurer, M., Millns, J.L., Rogers, R.S. et al (1977) Oral pemphigus vulgaris. A report of ten cases. *Arch Dermatol*, **113**, 1520–1524.
9. Engineer, L., Norton, L.A., Razzaque Ahmed, A. (2000) Nail involvement in pemphigus vulgaris. *J Am Acad Dermatol*, **43**, 529–535.
10. Ruocco, V., Pisani, M. (1982) Induced pemphigus. *Arch Dermatol Res*, **274**, 123–140.
11. Ruocco, V., Vitale, O., Astarita, C. (1980) Transient pemphigus induced by sunburn. *J Cutan Pathol*, **7**, 429–430.
12. Chorzelski, T., Jablonska, S., Beutner, E.H. et al (1971) Can pemphigus be provoked by a burn? *Br J Dermatol*, **85**, 320–325.
13. Hogan, P. (1992) Pemphigus vulgaris following a cutaneous thermal burn. *Int J Dermatol*, **31**, 46–49.
14. Crovato, F., Desirello, G., Nazzari, G. et al (1989) Linear pemphigus vulgaris after X-ray irradiation. *Dermatologica*, **179**, 135–136.
15. Hasson, A., Requena, L., Arias, D. et al (1991) Linear pemphigus vulgaris along a surgical scar. *Dermatologica*, **182**, 191–192.
16. Mehregan, D.R., Roenigk, R.K., Gibson, L.E. (1992) Postsurgical pemphigus. *Arch Dermatol*, **128**, 414–415.

17. Gomi, H., Akiyama, M., Yakabi, K. et al (1999) Esophageal involvement in pemphigus vulgaris. *Lancet*, **354**, 1794.
18. Mignogna, M.D., Lo Muzio, L., Galloro, G. et al (1997) Oral pemphigus: clinical significance of esophageal involvement: report of eight cases. *Oral Surg Oral Med Oral Pathol Oral Radiol Endod*, **84**, 179–184.
19. Schissel, D.J., David-Bajar, K. (1999) Esophagitis dissecans superficialis associated with pemphigus vulgaris. *Cutis*, **63**, 157–160.
20. Camisa, C., Meisler, D.M. (1992) Immunobullous diseases with ocular involvement. *Dermatol Clin*, **10**, 555–570.
21. Hodok, E., Kremer, I., David, M. et al (1990) Conjunctival involvement in pemphigus: a clinical, histopathological and immunofluorescence study. *Br J Dermatol*, **123**, 615–620.
22. Baykal, H.E., Pleyer, U., Sonnichsen, K. et al (1995) Severe eye involvement in pemphigus vulgaris. *Ophthalmologe*, **92**, 854–857.
23. Wright, C., Pipingas, A., Grayson, W. et al (2000) Pemphigus vulgaris of the uterine cervix revisited: case report and review of the literature. *Diagn Cytopathol*, **22**, 304–307.
24. Chan, E., Thakur, A., Farid, L. et al (1998) Pemphigus vulgaris of the cervix and upper vaginal vault: a cause of atypical Papanicolaou smears. *Arch Dermatol*, **134**, 1485–1486.
25. Lonsdale, R.N., Gibbs, S. (1998) Pemphigus vulgaris with involvement of the cervix. *Br J Dermatol*, **138**, 363–365.
26. Batta, K., Munday, P.E., Tatnall, F.M. (1999) Pemphigus vulgaris localized to the vagina presenting as chronic vaginal discharge. *Br J Dermatol*, **140**, 945–947.
27. Sami, N., Ahmed, A.R. (2001) Penile pemphigus. *Arch Dermatol*, **137**, 756–758.
28. Sami, N., Ahmed, A.R. (2001) Dual diagnosis of pemphigus and pemphigoid. Retrospective review of thirty cases in the literature. *Dermatology*, **202**, 293–301.
29. Sami, N., Bhol, K.C., Beutner, E.H. et al (2002) Diagnostic features of pemphigus vulgaris in patients with bullous pemphigoid. Molecular analysis of autoantibody profile. *Dermatology*, **204**, 108–117.
30. Gibson, L.E., Muller, S.A. (1987) Dermatologic disorders in patients with thymoma. *Acta Derm Venereol*, **67**, 351–356.
31. Oka, D., Shimoda, A., Ueki, H. et al (1986) Coexistence of pemphigus vulgaris, myasthenia gravis and hepatocellular carcinoma. *Dermatologica*, **172**, 177–178.
32. Younus, J., Ahmed, A.R. (1990) The relationship of pemphigus to neoplasia. *J Am Acad Dermatol*, **23**, 498–502.
33. Martel, P., Joly, P. (2001) Pemphigus: autoimmune disease of keratinocyte's adhesion molecules. *Clin Dermatol*, **19**, 662–674.
34. Hertl, M., Veldman, C. (2001) Pemphigus – paradigm of autoantibody-mediated autoimmunity. *Skin Pharmacol Appl Skin Physiol*, **14**, 408–481.
35. Beutner, E.H., Lever, W.F., Witebsky, E. (1965) Autoantibodies in pemphigus vulgaris: response to an intercellular substance of epidermis. *JAMA*, **92**, 682–688.
36. Wilson, C.L., Dean, D., Wojnarowska, F. (1991) Pemphigus and the terminal hair follicle. *J Cutan Pathol*, **18**, 428–431.
37. Tremeau-Martinage, C., Oksman, F., Bazex, J. (1995) Immunoglobulin G subclass distribution of anti-intercellular substance antibodies in pemphigus. *Ann Dermatol Venereol*, **122**, 409–411.
38. Beutner, E.H., Jordon, R.E. (1964) Demonstration of skin antibodies in sera of pemphigus vulgaris patients by indirect immunofluorescent staining. *Proc Soc Exp Biol Med*, **117**, 505–510.
39. Triftshauser, C., Wypych, J., Cloutier, L.C. et al (1971) Fluorescent antibody studies of pemphigus-like antibodies in burn sera. *Ann N Y Acad Sci*, **177**, 227–233.
40. Fellner, M.J., Prutkin, L. (1970) Morbilliform eruptions caused by penicillin. A study by electron microscopy and immunologic tests. *J Invest Dermatol*, **55**, 390–395.
41. Low, G.J., Keeling, J.H. (1990) Ionizing radiation-induced pemphigus. *Arch Dermatol*, **126**, 1319–1323.
42. Jones, C.C., Hamilton, R.G., Jordan, R.E. (1988) Subclass distribution of human IgG autoantibodies in pemphigus. *J Clin Immunol*, **8**, 43–49.
43. Fitzpatrick, R.E., Newcomer, V.D. (1980) The correlation of disease activity and antibody titers in pemphigus. *Arch Dermatol*, **116**, 285–290.
44. Bhol, K., Mohimen, A., Ahmed, A.R. (1994) Correlation of subclass of IgG with disease activity in pemphigus vulgaris. *Dermatology*, **189** (Suppl. 1), 85–89.
45. Bhol, K., Natarajan, K., Nagarwalla, N. et al (1995) Correlation of peptide specificity and IgG subclass with pathogenic and nonpathogenic autoantibodies in pemphigus vulgaris: a model of autoimmunity. *Proc Natl Acad Sci USA*, **29**, 5239–5243.
46. Kricheli, D., David, M., Frusic-Zlotkin, M. (2000) The distribution of pemphigus vulgaris IgG subclasses and reactivity with desmoglein 3 and 1 in pemphigus patients and first-degree relatives. *Br J Dermatol*, **143**, 337–342.
47. Storer, J.S., Galen, W.K., Nesbitt, L.T. et al (1982) Neonatal pemphigus vulgaris. *J Am Acad Dermatol*, **6**, 929–932.
48. Anhalt, G.J., Labib, R.S., Voorhess, J.J. et al (1982) Induction of pemphigus in neonatal mice by passive transfer of IgG from patients with the disease. *N Engl J Med*, **306**, 1189–1196.
49. Hunziker, T., Boillat, C., Gerber, H.A. et al (1989) In vitro pemphigus vulgaris model using organotypic cultures of human epidermal keratinocytes. *J Invest Dermatol*, **93**, 263–267.
50. Barlow, Y., Wray, D. (1991) Ultrastructural alterations associated with in vivo and in vitro bound pemphigus antibodies on cultured oral epithelial cells. *J Oral Pathol Med*, **20**, 241–244.
51. Mahoney, M., Rothenberger, K., Koch, P. et al (1999) Explanation for the clinical and microscopic localization of lesions in pemphigus foliaceus vulgaris. *J Clin Invest*, **103**, 461–468.
52. Kanitakis, J. (2001) Indirect immunofluorescence microscopy for the serological diagnosis of autoimmune blistering skin diseases: a review. *Clin Dermatol*, **19**, 614–621.
53. Stanley, J.R., Yaar, M., Hawley-Nelson, P. et al (1982) Pemphigus antibodies identify a cell surface glycoprotein synthesized by human and mouse keratinocytes. *J Clin Invest*, **70**, 281–288.
54. Eyre, R.W., Stanley, J.R. (1988) Identification of pemphigus vulgaris antigen extracted from normal human epidermis and comparison with pemphigus foliaceus antigen. *J Clin Invest*, **81**, 807–812.
55. Hashimoto, T., Ogawa, M.M., Konohana, A. et al (1990) Detection of pemphigus vulgaris and pemphigus foliaceus antigens by immunoblot analysis using different antigen sources. *J Invest Dermatol*, **94**, 327–331.
56. Amagai, M., Klaus-Kovturn, V., Stanley, J.R. (1991) Autoantibodies against a novel epithelial cadherin in pemphigus vulgaris, a disease of cell adhesion. *Cell*, **67**, 869–877.
57. Amagai, M., Karpati, S., Prussick, R. et al (1992) Autoantibodies against the amino-terminal cadherin-like binding domain of pemphigus vulgaris antigen are pathogenic. *J Clin Invest*, **90**, 919–926.
58. Amagai, M., Hashimoto, T., Shimizu N. et al (1994) Absorption of pathogenic autoantibodies by the extracellular domain of pemphigus vulgaris antigen (Dsg3) produced by baculo-virus. *J Clin Invest*, **94**, 59–67.
59. Korman, N.J., Eyre, R.W., Klaus-Kovtun, V. et al (1989) Demonstration of an adhering junction molecule (plakoglobin) in the autoantigens of pemphigus foliaceus and pemphigus vulgaris. *N Engl J Med*, **321**, 631–635.
60. Emery, D.J., Diaz, L.A., Fairly, J.A. et al (1995) Pemphigus foliaceus and pemphigus vulgaris autoantibodies react with the extracellular domain of desmoglein 1. *J Invest Dermatol*, **104**, 323–328.
61. Ding, X., Diaz, L.A., Fairley, J.A. et al (1999) The anti-desmoglein 1 autoantibodies in pemphigus vulgaris sera are pathogenic. *J Invest Dermatol*, **112**, 739–743.
62. Dmochowski, M., Hashimoto, T., Chidgey, M.A.J. et al (1995) Demonstration of antibodies to bovine desmocollin isoforms in certain pemphigus sera. *Br J Dermatol*, **133**, 519–525.
63. Hashimoto, T., Amagai, M., Watanabe, K. et al (1995) A case of pemphigus vulgaris showing reactivity with pemphigus antigens (Dsg1 and Dsg2) and desmocollins. *J Invest Dermatol*, **104**, 541–544.
64. Nguyen, V.T., Ndoye, A., Grando, S.A. (2000) Pemphigus vulgaris antibody identifies pemphaxin: a novel keratinocyte annexin-like molecule binding acetylcholine. *J Biol Chem*, **275**, 29446–29476.
65. Nguyen, V.T., Ndoye, A., Grando, S.A. (2000) Novel human alpha9 acetylcholine receptor regulating adhesion is targeted by pemphigus vulgaris autoimmunity. *Am J Pathol*, **157**, 1377–1391.
66. Seishima, M., Satoh, S., Nojiri, M. et al (1997) Pemphigus IgG induces expression of urokinase plasminogen activator receptor on the cell surface of cultures keratinocytes. *J Invest Dermatol*, **109**, 650–655.
67. Schaefer, B.M., Jaeger, C.J., Kramer, M.D. (1996) Plasminogen activator system in pemphigus vulgaris. *Br J Dermatol*, **135**, 726–732.
68. Xue, W., Hashimoto, K., Toi, Y. (1998) Functional involvement of urokinase-type plasminogen activator receptor in pemphigus acantholysis. *J Cutan Pathol*, **25**, 469–474.
69. Esaki, C., Seishima, M., Yamada, T. et al (1995) Pharmacologic evidence for involvement of phospholipase C in pemphigus IgG-induced inositol 1,4,5-triphosphate generation, intracellular calcium increase, and plasminogen activator secretion in DJM-1 cells, a squamous cell carcinoma cell line. *J Invest Dermatol*, **105**, 329–333.
70. Osada, K., Seishima, M., Kitajima, Y. (1997) Pemphigus IgG activates and translocates protein kinase C from cytosol to the particulate/cytoskeleton fractions in human keratinocytes. *J Invest Dermatol*, **108**, 482–487.
71. Kitajima, Y., Aoyama, Y., Seishima, M. (1999) Transmembrane signaling for adhesive regulation of desmosomes and hemidesmosomes, and for cell–cell detachment induced by pemphigus IgG in cultured keratinocytes: involvement of protein kinase C. *J Invest Dermatol Symp Proc*, **4**, 137–144.
72. Mahoney, M.G., Wang, Z.H., Stanley, J.R. (1999) Pemphigus vulgaris and pemphigus foliaceus antibodies are pathogenic in plasminogen activator knockout mice. *J Invest Dermatol*, **113**, 22–25.
73. Wucherpfennig, K.W., Yu, W.B., Bhol, K. et al (1995) Structural basis for major histocompatibility complex (MHC)-linked susceptibility to autoimmunity: charged residues of a single MHC binding pocket confer selective presentation of self-peptides in pemphigus vulgaris. *Proc Natl Acad Sci USA*, **92**, 11935–11939.
74. Hertl, M., Amagai, M., Ishii, K. et al (1999) Analysis of the T cells that are potentially involved in autoantibody production in pemphigus vulgaris. *J Dermatol*, **26**, 748–752.
75. Feliciani, C., Toto, P., Amerio, P. et al (2000) In vitro and in vivo expression of interleukin-1alpha and tumor necrosis factor-alpha mRNA in pemphigus vulgaris: interleukin-1alpha and tumor necrosis factor-alpha are involved in acantholysis. *J Invest Dermatol*, **114**, 71–77.
76. Ahmed, A.R., Yunis, E.J., Khatri, K. (1990) Major histocompatibility complex haplotype studies in Ashkenazi Jewish patients with pemphigus vulgaris. *Proc Natl Acad Sci USA*, **87**, 7658–7662.
77. Ahmed, A.R., Wagner, R., Khatri, K. (1991) Major histocompatibility complex haplotypes and class II genes in non-Jewish patients with pemphigus vulgaris. *Proc Natl Acad Sci USA*, **88**, 5056–5061.
78. Sinha, A.A., Brautbar, C., Szafer, F. et al (1988) A newly characterized HLA-DQβ allele associated with pemphigus vulgaris. *Science*, **239**, 1026–1029.
79. Delgado, J.C., Yunis, E.J., Ahmed, A.R. et al (1997) Pemphigus vulgaris autoantibody response is linked to HLA-DQB1*0503 in Pakistani patients. *Hum Immunol*, **57**, 110–119.
80. Revenga-Arranz, F., Martinez-Lasso, J., Vanaclocha-Sebastian, F. (1996) Pemphigus vulgaris in two MHC-haploidentical brothers. *Dermatology*, **193**, 71–72.
81. Brandsen, R., Frusic-Zlotkin, M., Lyubimov, H. et al (1997) Circulating pemphigus IgG in families of patients with pemphigus: comparison of indirect immunofluorescence, direct immunofluorescence, and immunoblotting. *J Am Acad Dermatol*, **36**, 44–52.
82. Lever, W.F. (1951) Pemphigus: a histopathologic study. *Arch Dermatol*, **64**, 727–752.
83. Emmerson, R.W., Wilson-Jones, E. (1968) Eosinophilic spongiosis in pemphigus: a report of an unusual histologic change in pemphigus. *Arch Dermatol*, **97**, 252–257.
84. Ishiko, A., Shimizu, H. (2001) Electron microscopy in diagnosis of bullous disorders. *Clin Dermatol*, **19**, 631–637.

Pemphigus vegetans

Clinical features

Pemphigus vegetans (p. vegetans), a chronic variant of p. vulgaris, has a somewhat better prognosis than p. vulgaris with occasional cases associated with spontaneous remission documented.[1–3] It accounts for 1–2% of all cases of pemphigus.[1] As with the vulgaris variant, p. vegetans typically presents in adults. There have, however, been a small number of cases described in childhood including a dapsone-responsive IgA-mediated variant.[4–6] The lesions, which present as blisters and erosions, are particularly prolific in the flexures, especially the axillae, the groin, the inframammary region, the umbilicus and at the margins of the lips. The scalp is also said to be a site of predilection.[7] Soon thereafter, patients characteristically develop hypertrophic vegetations and pustules at the blistered edges (*Fig. 4.16*).[1]

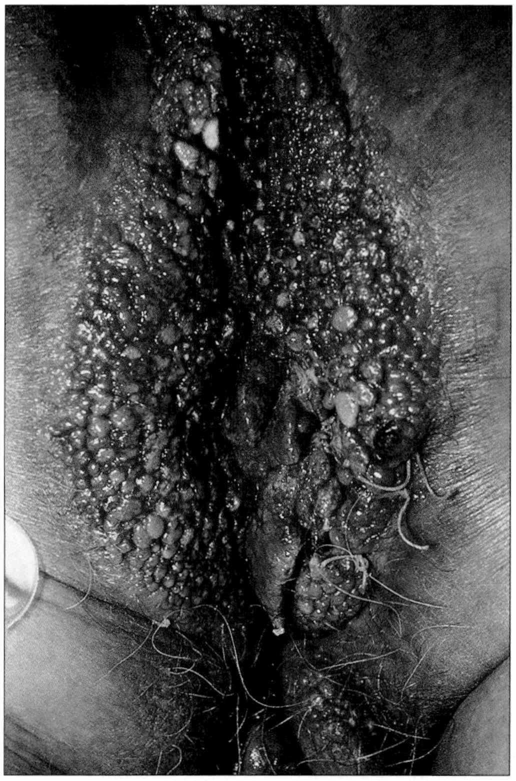

Fig. 4.16
Pemphigus vegetans: perineal view showing characteristic hypertrophic flexural vegetations. Note the numerous intact vesicles. By courtesy of S. Dalziel, MD, University Hospital, Nottingham, UK.

The oral cavity is commonly affected and a cerebriform or "scrotal" tongue is said to be a diagnostic clue in cases of early involvement.[8–10] Esophageal involvement presenting as erosions and white plaques has been described in a number of patients and the nasal mucosa, larynx, vulva, vagina and anus may also be affected.[11–15] Nail involvement including onycholysis and pustules is sometimes seen.[16] Peripheral blood eosinophilia is commonly present.

Two clinical subtypes are recognized:[17,18]

- In the Neumann variant (the more serious form), lesions usually begin as described in p. vulgaris, but the ensuing erosions develop vegetation. The course of this variant is similar to that of p. vulgaris.
- In the Hallopeau variant ('pyodermite vegetante'), the eruption begins as pustular lesions that rapidly evolve into verrucous vegetating plaques.[2] Bullae are usually not seen. This is a milder variant in which spontaneous remission is not uncommon.

Pathogenesis and histological features

Support for the thesis that p. vegetans is a variant of p. vulgaris is based on the finding that both subtypes are associated with IgG and C3 deposition in the epidermal intercellular space on direct immunofluorescence and circulating 'pemphigus' antibody.[18] P. vegetans is characterized by an antibody directed at the desmosomal cadherin, desmoglein 3.[19–21] Antibodies against desmocollins 1 and 2 have also been documented.[22]

Precipitating factors for this variant of pemphigus are largely unknown. Exceptionally, however, p. vegetans has been linked with the angiotensin-converting enzyme (ACE) inhibitors, captopril and enalapril.[23,24] Lesions localized to the nasal mucosa in a patient with longstanding nasal heroin abuse have been reported and an association with human immunodeficiency virus (HIV) infection documented.[15,25,26] There are one or two reports relating p. vegetans with an underlying malignancy and in one patient a p. vegetans-like lesion was a manifestation of paraneoplastic pemphigus.[24,27]

Although a variant of p. vulgaris, p. vegetans shows strikingly different histological features. Suprabasal acantholysis is present but is often subtle, being masked by an exuberant proliferation of squamous

epithelium which may sometimes show pseudoepitheliomatous hyperplasia (*Fig. 4.17*). Characteristically, there is an intense inflammatory cell infiltrate containing numerous eosinophils, and intraepidermal microabscesses are often seen (*Figs 4.18, 4.19*). Eosinophilic spongiosis may sometimes be a feature.[28,29] The inflammatory changes and epithelial proliferation are sometimes so marked that the true nature of the lesions is obscured. Very occasionally, 10–40 μm eosinophilic hexagonal Charcot–Leyden crystals have been described within the eosinophil-rich microabscesses.[23,30] The diagnosis of p. vegetans is easily overlooked and is made by the pathologist with a high index of suspicion.

Differential diagnosis

Since early lesions may be similar, or identical, to p. vulgaris, the same differential diagnosis as discussed for this variant should be considered (see p. 143). In established lesions associated with squamous epithelial hyperplasia, the suprabasal cleft formation is often focal and easily

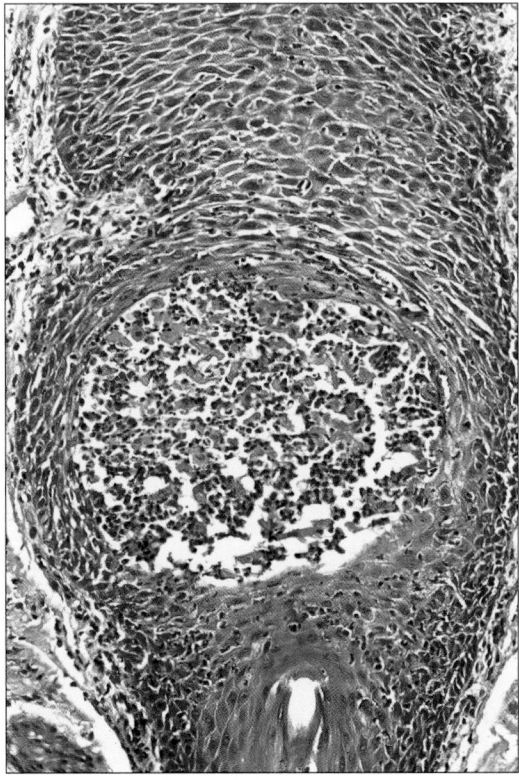

Fig. 4.18
Pemphigus vegetans: higher power view of microabscess.

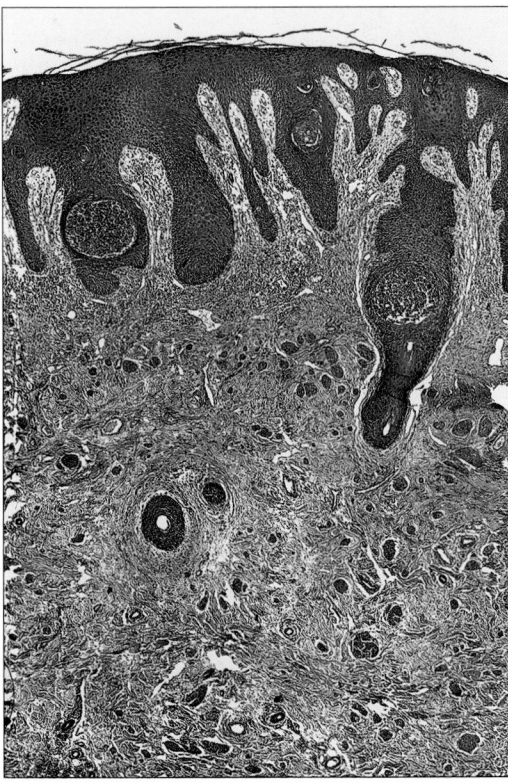

Fig. 4.17
Pemphigus vegetans: the epidermis is hyperplasic and there are scattered abscesses.

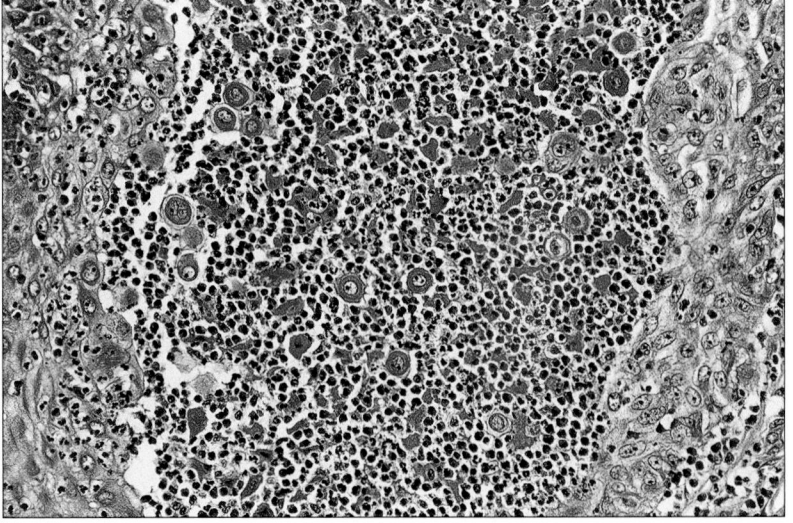

Fig. 4.19
Pemphigus vegetans: there are numerous eosinophils. Note the acantholysis.

overlooked. Infections, particularly fungal and bacterial, that are associated with pseudoepitheliomatous hyperplasia and microabscesses may be confused with p. vegetans. In particular, pyostomatitis vegetans (see p. 405) must be excluded in patients presenting with oral involvement. Halogenoderma may also show similar histological features.

References

1. Korman, N.J. (1990) Pemphigus. *Dermatol Clin*, **8**, 689–700.
2. Pearson, R.W., O'Donoghue, M., Kaplan, S.J. (1980) Pemphigus vegetans: its relationship to eosinophilic spongiosis and favorable response to dapsone. *Arch Dermatol*, **116**, 65–68.
3. Director, W. (1953) Pemphigus vegetans: a clinicopathological correlation. *Arch Dermatol*, **66**, 343–351.
4. Sillevis Smitt, J.H., Mulder, T.J., Albeda, F.W. et al (1992) Pemphigus vegetans in a child. *Br J Dermatol*, **127**, 289–291.
5. Weston, W.L., Friednash, M., Hashimoto, T. et al (1998) A novel childhood pemphigus vegetans variant of intraepidermal neutrophilic IgA dermatosis. *J Am Acad Dermatol*, **38**, 635–638.
6. Wananukul, S., Pongprasit, P. (1999) Childhood pemphigus. *Int J Dermatol*, **38**, 29–35.
7. Rackett, S.C., Rothe, M.J., Hoss, D.M. et al (1995) Treatment-resistant pemphigus vegetans of the scalp. *Int J Dermatol*, **34**, 865–866.
8. Woo, T.Y., Solomon, A.R., Fairley, J.A. (1985) Pemphigus vegetans limited to the lips and oral mucosa. *Arch Dermatol*, **121**, 271–273.
9. Premalatha, S., Jayakumar, S., Yesudion, P. et al (1981) Cerebriform tongue: a clinical sign in pemphigus vegetans. *Br J Dermatol*, **104**, 587–591.
10. Virgili, A., Trombelli, L., Calura, G. (1992) Sudden vegetation of the mouth. Pemphigus vegetans of the mouth (Hallopeau type). *Arch Dermatol*, **128**, 398–399, 401–402.
11. Sawai, T., Kitazawa, K., Danno, K. et al (1995) Pemphigus vegetans with esophageal involvement: successful treatment with minocycline and nicotinamide. *Br J Dermatol*, **132**, 668–670.
12. Akimoto, S., Ishikawa, O., Miyachi, Y. et al (1996) A case of pemphigus vegetans limited to the oral cavity and upper esophagus. *Jpn J Clin Dermatol*, **50**, 434–436.
13. Ichimiya, M., Nakano, J., Muto, M. (1998) Pemphigus vegetans involving the esophagus. *J Dermatol*, **25**, 195–198.
14. Wong, K.T., Wong, K.K. (1994) A case of acantholytic dermatosis of the vulva with features of pemphigus vegetans. *J Cutan Pathol*, **21**, 453–456.
15. Downie, J.B., Dicostanzo, D.P., Cohen, S.R. (1998) Pemphigus vegetans – Neumann variant associated with intra-nasal heroin abuse. *J Am Acad Dermatol*, **39**, 372–375.
16. Leroy, D., Lebrun, J., Maillard, V. et al (1982) Pemphigus vegetans, a clinical type of chronic pustular dermatitis of Hallopeau. *Ann Dermatol Venereol*, **109**, 549–555.
17. Ahmed, A.R., Blose, D.A. (1984) Pemphigus vegetans. Neumann type and Hallopeau type. *Int J Dermatol*, **23**, 135–141.
18. Gerharz, M., Stadler, R. (1987) Pemphigus vegetans of the Hallopeau type. Detection of pemphigus antibodies with direct and indirect immunofluorescence. *Hautarzt*, **38**, 371–374.
19. Parodi, A., Stanley, J.R., Ciaccio, M. et al (1988) Epidermal antigens in pemphigus vegetans: report of a case. *Br J Dermatol*, **199**, 799–802.
20. Hashizume, H., Iwatsuki, K., Takigawa, M. (1993) Epidermal antigens and complement binding anti-intercellular antibodies in pemphigus vegetans, Hallopeau type. *Br J Dermatol*, **129**, 739–743.
21. Ohata, Y., Komiya, H., Kawahara, Y. et al (1996) A case of Neumann type pemphigus vegetans showing reactivity with the 130kD pemphigus vulgaris antigen. *Acta Derm Venereol*, **76**, 169–170.
22. Hashimoto, K., Hashimoto, T., Higashiyama, M. et al (1994) Detection of anti-desmocollins I and II autoantibodies in two cases of Hallopeau type pemphigus vegetans by immunoblot analysis. *J Dermatol Sci*, **7**, 100–106.
23. Pinto, G.M., Lamarão, P., Vale, T. (1992) Captopril-induced pemphigus vegetans with Charcot–Leyden crystals. *J Am Acad Dermatol*, **27**, 281–284.
24. Bastiaens, M.T., Zwan, N.V., Verschueren, G.L.A. et al (1994) Three cases of pemphigus vegetans: induction by enalapril – association with internal malignancy. *Int J Dermatol*, **33**, 168–171.
25. Mahé, A., Flaguel, B., Prost, C. et al (1994) Pemphigus vegetans in an HIV-infected man. *Clin Exp Dermatol*, **19**, 447–450.
26. Lateef, A., Packles, M.R., White, S.M. et al (1999) Pemphigus vegetans in association with human immunodeficiency virus. *Int J Dermatol*, **38**, 778–781.
27. Sapadin, A.N., Anhalt, G.J. (1998) Paraneoplastic pemphigus with a pemphigus vegetans-like plaque as the only cutaneous manifestation. *J Am Acad Dermatol*, **39**, 867–871.
28. Pearson, R.W., O'Donoghue, M., Kaplan, S.J. (1980) Pemphigus vegetans: its relationship to eosinophilic spongiosis and favorable response to dapsone. *Arch Dermatol*, **116**, 65–68.
29. Steiner, A., Diem, E., Rappersberger, K. (1985) Pemphigus vegetans (Hallopeau) with eosinophilic spongiosis – successful retinoid therapy. *Hautarzt*, **36**, 356–359.
30. Kuo, T.T., Wang, C.N. (1986) Charcot–Leyden crystals in pemphigus vegetans. *J Cutan Pathol*, **13**, 242–245.

Pemphigus foliaceus

Clinical features

Pemphigus foliaceus (p. foliaceus) is considerably more rare than p. vulgaris and although it most often affects the middle aged and elderly, it has a very variable age of onset, sometimes affecting younger adults and even, occasionally, children.[1-6] Very exceptionally, maternal antibodies have been known to cross the placenta resulting in neonatal disease.[7,8] In general, non-endemic p. foliaceus in children is relatively benign and of short duration.[6]

The superficial blisters of p. foliaceus are exceedingly fragile and therefore much less obvious; erosions and large leafy scales or crusts are often predominant (*Figs 4.20–4.22*). The lesions may remain localized to the scalp, face and trunk for many months or years, leading to a mistaken diagnosis of seborrheic dermatitis, seborrheic keratosis or even lupus erythematosus. Sometimes the eruption involves the entire surface of the body or produces a clinical resemblance to exfoliative dermatitis (erythroderma) (*Fig. 4.23*).[9,10] Mucous membrane involvement is rare.[1] Exceptionally, patients may present with localized disease, typically

restricted to the face.[11] P. foliaceus often has a much more benign course than p. vulgaris, although patients with severe disease, requiring corticosteroid and immunosuppressant therapy, still have an appreciable mortality.

Very occasionally, patients may develop p. foliaceus during or after a previous episode of p. vulgaris and vice versa.[12,13] This is accompanied by an antigen shift.[13]

In addition to idiopathic p. foliaceus, drug-induced variants, notably due to penicillamine, may also be encountered (*Fig. 4.24*). This is discussed on p. 648.

Pathogenesis and histological features

Like other variants of pemphigus, p. foliaceus is an immunologically mediated disease. Examination of perilesional skin by direct immuno-

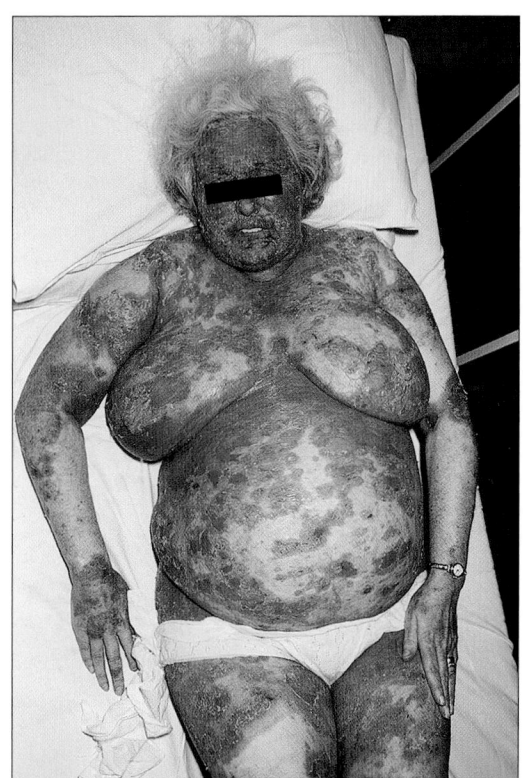

Fig. 4.20
Pemphigus foliaceus: in this patient with severe involvement, there is generalized erosion with crusting. By courtesy of R.A. Marsden, St George's Hospital, London, UK.

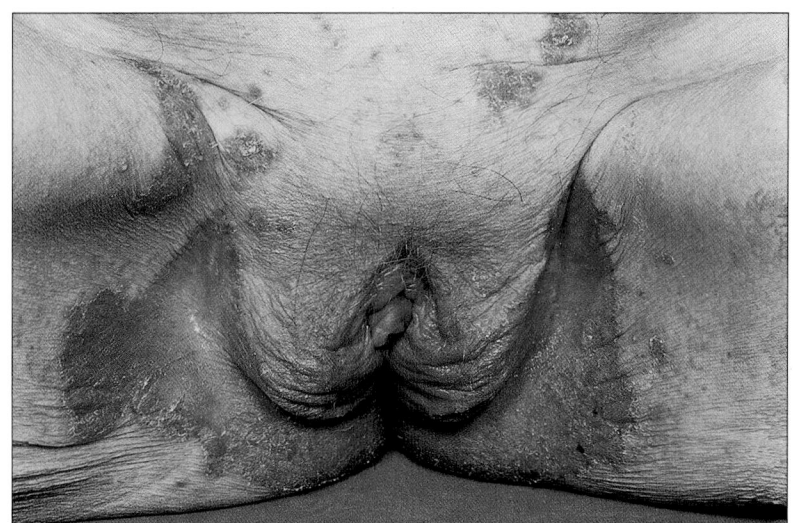

Fig. 4.21
Pemphigus foliaceus: in this patient, there is extensive erosion affecting the groins and the perineum. Small blisters may also be seen. By courtesy of the Institute of Dermatology, London, UK.

fluorescent techniques reveals in vivo-bound immunoglobulin (usually IgG) and often complement (C3) in the intercellular region of the epidermis.[1] Abundant antigen in the follicular outer root sheath and germinal matrix may account for the marked scalp involvement typical of pemphigus.[14]

Indirect immunofluorescent techniques show that the sera of patients with p. foliaceus contain an IgG antibody that reacts with the intercellular region of normal squamous epithelium.[15] IgG4 predominates followed by IgG1.[16] IgG3 is also sometimes present. This may be of importance since IgG3 is the most efficient activator of complement.[16] Some 60–70% of patients are positive with indirect immunofluorescence.[17]

The p. foliaceus antibody binds to a 160 kD desmosomal cadherin, designated desmoglein 1 (Dsg1).[18,19] The sera of p. foliaceus patients bind to the *extracellular* aminoterminal domain of bovine Dsg1 whereas sera from both p. vulgaris and p. vegetans patients react with the *intracellular* domain of Dsg1.[20,21] Compared with p. vulgaris, immunofluorescence studies on the sera of p. foliaceus tend to show more staining in the superficial epidermis, correlating with the level of the split.[22,23]

Conversely, the sera from patients with p. vulgaris show more affinity for the lower epidermis. Anti-Dsg1 antibody is pathogenic.[24] Injection of purified anti-Dsg1 antibodies from sera of patients with p. foliaceus into neonatal mice induces subcorneal acantholysis in a pattern typical of p. foliaceus.[25] The use of D-penicillamine may be associated with the acquisition of a pemphigus-like antibody and the development of p. foliaceus.[26]

Since the blisters of p. foliaceus are superficial, they are therefore fragile and it is often very difficult to obtain an intact lesion for diagnosis. Patients commonly have erosions without blisters, and frequently the clinician does not suspect a bullous disorder. Usually the cleft or blister lies within the granular layer or beneath the stratum corneum (*Fig. 4.25*). The roof of the fragile blister is often not present, having sloughed either before or after biopsy. Acantholysis is frequently difficult to detect, but usually a few acantholytic cells can be found attached to the roof or floor of the blister. In those cases where the blister is missing, a careful inspection of the hair follicles may reveal focal acantholysis. Sometimes the blister contains numerous acute inflammatory cells (*Fig. 4.26*), particularly neutrophils, which can make distinction from subcorneal pustular disorders especially difficult.[27,28] Eosinophilic spongiosis may also be seen.[29]

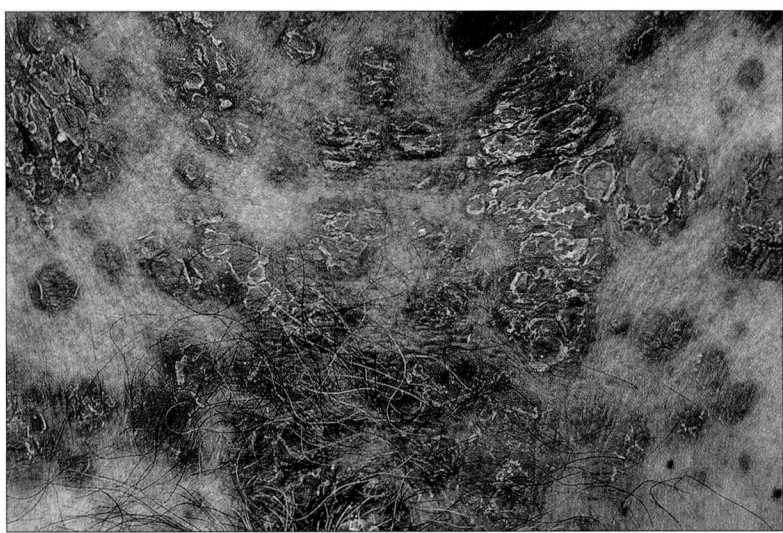

Fig. 4.22
Pemphigus foliaceus: close-up view of crusted erosions. By courtesy of the Institute of Dermatology, London, UK.

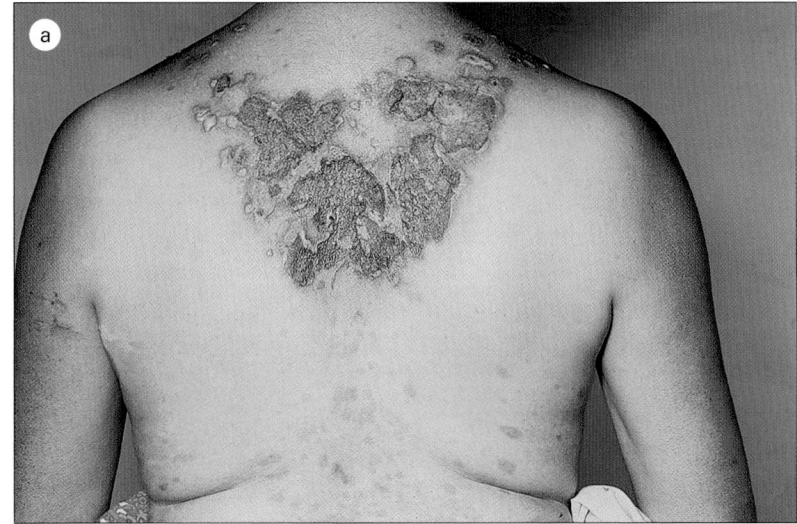

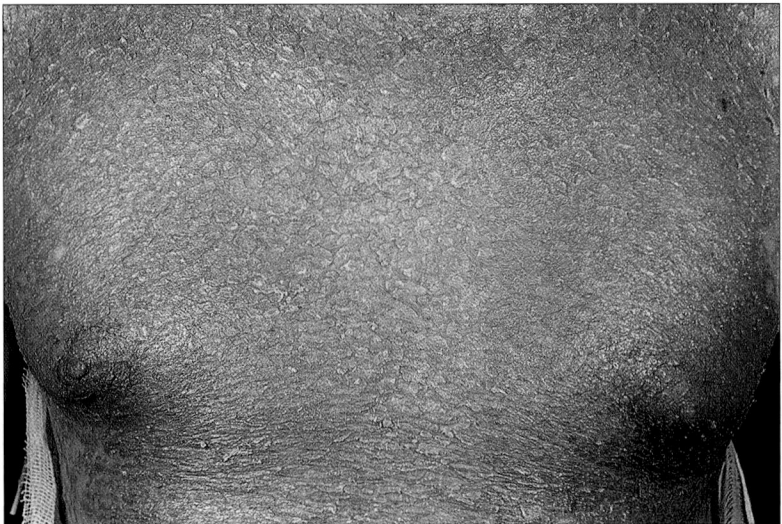

Fig. 4.23
Pemphigus foliaceus: in this patient, there is generalized erosion with scaling and erythroderma. By courtesy of R.A. Marsden, MD, St George's Hospital, London, UK.

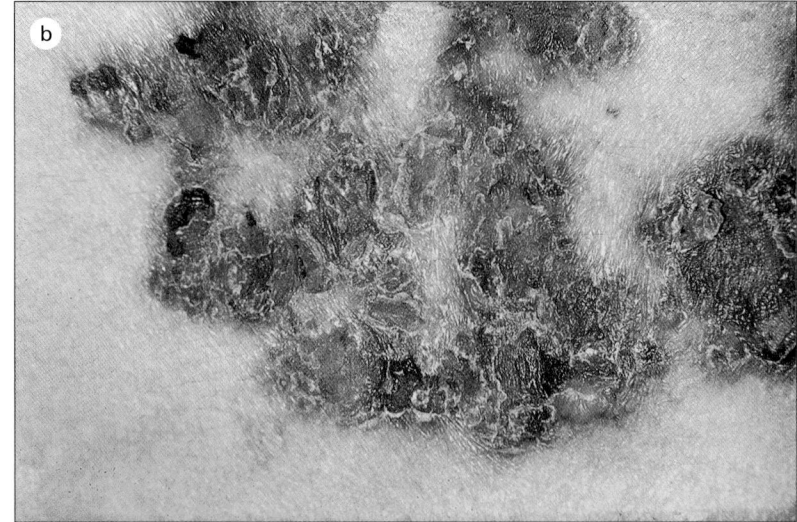

Fig. 4.24
Pemphigus foliaceus: (a) in this patient, the eruption was induced by penicillamine therapy; (b) close-up view of intact blisters, erosions and crusting. By courtesy of R.A. Marsden, MD, St George's Hospital, London, UK.

Differential diagnosis

The histological features in the superficial forms of pemphigus may be easily overlooked and, since bullae are often not appreciated by the clinician, the unwary pathologist may not consider a bullous disorder when evaluating the biopsy. A high index of suspicion is therefore critical. The differential diagnosis of superficial pemphigus includes bullous impetigo, staphylococcal scalded skin syndrome, IgA pemphigus and subcorneal pustular dermatosis (*Table 4.3*). Distinction depends

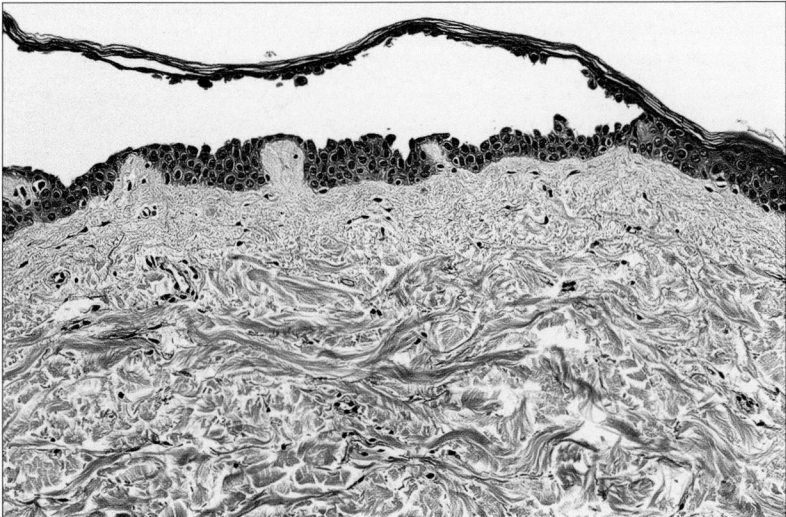

Fig. 4.25
Pemphigus foliaceus: in this example, there is a cell-free, subcorneal blister. Occasional acantholytic cells are present adjacent to the roof.

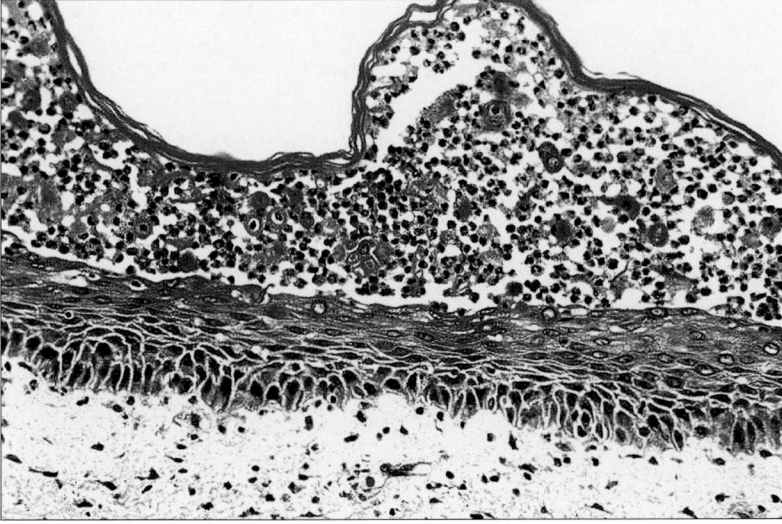

Fig. 4.26
Pemphigus foliaceus: in this example, the blister cavity contains numerous neutrophils. Acantholytic cells are conspicuous.

Table 4.3
Differential diagnosis of superficial pemphigus: conditions characterized by subcorneal pustules

- Superficial pemphigus
- IgA pemphigus
- Subcorneal pustular dermatosis
- Pustular psoriasis
- Reiter's syndrome
- Pustular drug reaction
- Bullous impetigo
- Staphylococcal scalded skin syndrome
- Pustular fungal infection

upon a careful consideration of the clinical information, the results of bacterial culture and immunofluorescent studies.

References

1. Korman, N.J. (1990) Pemphigus. *Dermatol Clin*, 8, 689–700.
2. Rosella, M., Masia, I.M., Satta, R. et al (1996) Pemphigus foliaceus in a child. *Pediatr Dermatol*, 13, 259–260.
3. Galambrun, C., Cambazard, F., Clavel, C. et al (1997) Pemphigus foliaceus. *Arch Dis Child*, 77, 255–257.
4. Mehravaran, M., Morvay, M., Molnar, K. et al (1998) Juvenile pemphigus foliaceus. *Br J Dermatol*, 139, 496–499.
5. Rybojad, M., Ducloy, G., Reymond, J.L. et al (1999) Sporadic superficial pemphigus in the child: 2 cases. *Ann Dermatol Venereol*, 126, 41–43.
6. Metry, D.W., Hebert, A.A., Jordan, R.E. (2002) Nonendemic pemphigus foliaceus in children. *J Am Acad Dermatol*, 46, 419–422.
7. Walker, D.C., Kolar, K.A., Hebert, A.A. et al (1995) Neonatal pemphigus foliaceus. *Arch Dermatol*, 131, 1308–1311.
8. Avalos-Diaz, E., Olague-Marchan, M., Lopez-Swiderski, A. et al (2000) Transplacental passage of maternal pemphigus foliaceus autoantibodies induces neonatal pemphigus. *J Am Acad Dermatol*, 43, 1130–1134.
9. Pal, S., Haroon, T.S. (1998) Erythroderma: a clinico-etiologic study of 90 cases. *Int J Dermatol*, 37, 104–107.
10. Nousari, H.C., Moresi, M., Klapper, M. et al (2001) Nonendemic pemphigus foliaceus presenting as fatal bullous exfoliative erythroderma. *Cutis*, 67, 251–252.
11. Yamamoto, S., Kanekura, T., Gushi, A. et al (1996) A case of localized pemphigus foliaceus. *J Dermatol*, 23, 893–895.
12. Chang, S.N., Kim, S.C., Lee, I.J. et al (1997) Transition from pemphigus vulgaris to pemphigus foliaceus. *Br J Dermatol*, 137, 303–305.
13. Kimoto, M., Ohyama, M., Hata, Y. et al (2001) A case of pemphigus foliaceus which occurred after five years of remission from pemphigus vulgaris. *Dermatology*, 203, 174–176.
14. Wilson, C.L., Dean, D., Wojnarowska, F. (1991) Pemphigus and the terminal hair follicle. *J Cutan Pathol*, 18, 428–431.
15. Beutner, E.H., Jordon, R.E. (1964) Demonstration of skin antibodies in sera of pemphigus vulgaris patients by indirect immunofluorescent staining. *Proc Soc Exp Biol Med*, 117, 505–510.
16. Futei, Y., Amagai, M., Ishii, K. et al (2001) Predominant IgG4 subclass in autoantibodies of pemphigus vulgaris and foliaceus. *J Dermatol Sci*, 26, 55–61.
17. Kanitakis, J. (2001) Indirect immunofluorescence microscopy for the serological diagnosis of autoimmune blistering skin diseases: a review. *Clin Dermatol*, 19, 614–621.
18. Labib, R.S., Rock, B., Robledo, M.A. et al (1991) The calcium-sensitive epitope of pemphigus foliaceus antigen is present on a murine tryptic fragment and constitutes a major antigenic region for human autoantibodies. *J Invest Dermatol*, 96, 144–147.
19. Allen, E.M., Giudice, G.J., Diaz, L.A. (1993) Subclass reactivity of pemphigus foliaceus autoantibodies with recombinant desmoglein. *J Invest Dermatol*, 100, 685–691.
20. Olague Alcala, M., Guidice, M., Diaz, L.A. (1994) Pemphigus foliaceus sera recognize an N-terminal fragment of bovine desmoglein 1. *J Invest Dermatol*, 102, 882–885.
21. Dmochowski, M., Hashimoto, T., Amagai, M. et al (1994) The extracellular aminoterminal domain of bovine desmoglein 1 (Dsg1) is recognized only by certain pemphigus foliaceus sera, whereas its intracellular domain is recognized by both pemphigus vulgaris and pemphigus foliaceus sera. *J Invest Dermatol*, 103, 173–177.
22. Hernandez, C., Amagai, M., Chan, L.S. (1997) Pemphigus foliaceus: preferential binding of IgG1 and C3 at the upper dermis. *Br J Dermatol*, 136, 249–252.
23. Shimizu, H., Masunaga, T., Ishiko, A. et al (1995) Pemphigus vulgaris and pemphigus foliaceus sera show an inversely graded binding pattern to extracellular regions of desmosomes in different layers of the human epidermis. *J Invest Dermatol*, 105, 153–159.
24. Hertl, M., Veldman, C. (2001) Pemphigus – paradigm of autoantibody-mediated autoimmunity. *Skin Pharmacol Appl Skin Physiol*, 14, 408–418.
25. Amagai, M., Nishikawa, T., Shimizu, M. et al (1995) Antigen-specific immunoadsorption of pathogenic autoantibodies in pemphigus foliaceus. *J Invest Dermatol*, 104, 895–901.
26. Kaplan, R.P., Callen, J.P. (1983) Pemphigus associated diseases and induced pemphigus. *Clin Dermatol*, 1, 42–71.
27. Hoss, D.M., Shea, C.R., Grant-Kels, J.M. (1996) Neutrophilic spongiosis in pemphigus. *Arch Dermatol*, 132, 315–318.
28. Matsuo, K., Komai, A., Ishii, K. et al (2001) Pemphigus foliaceus with prominent neutrophilic pustules. *Br J Dermatol*, 145, 132–136.
29. Osteen, F.B., Wheeler, C.E. Jr, Briggaman, R.A. et al (1976) Pemphigus foliaceus. Early clinical appearance as dermatitis herpetiformis with eosinophilic spongiosis. *Arch Dermatol*, 112, 1148–1152.

Fogo selvagem

Clinical features

Fogo selvagem (Brazilian pemphigus foliaceus, 'wild fire', endemic pemphigus foliaceus) is endemic in regions of Brazil and has also been documented in other areas of Central and South America including Colombia, El Salvador, Paraguay and Peru.[1-9] An endemic area has also been described in Tunisia.[10] The condition is associated with poverty and malnutrition and particularly affects children and young adults. There is a striking familial incidence.[4] Most cases are found along major rivers, and people especially at risk include farmers and workers involved in land clearing and road construction.[2] It appears that the majority of patients live at an altitude of between 500 and 800 meters, and that their homes are generally within 10–15 kilometers of running fresh water and in the path of prevailing winds, thus suggesting a likely insect vector.[4] In support of this, a case-controlled epidemiological study has provided evidence that bites by the black fly (family Simuliidae) are a significant risk factor for development of the disease.[11,12] *Simulium nigrimanum*, which is found in the same areas in which Brazilian fogo selvagem occurs, has been identified as being the likely species involved.[12]

The clinical presentation of fogo selvagem has been divided into a number of categories including localized and generalized forms:[2,4]

- *Localized* disease presents in a variety of ways including small blisters and erosions or violaceous papules and plaques distributed mainly in the seborrheic areas. Such lesions may be clinically misdiagnosed as discoid lupus erythematosus.
- *Generalized* presentation includes bullous exfoliative, exfoliative erythrodermic and disseminated plaque and nodular (resembling nodular prurigo) variants (*Fig. 4.27*).[4]

With resolution patients may sometimes develop hyperpigmentation.[13] The antibody does not cross the placenta and therefore neonatal disease is not a feature.[14]

Pathogenesis and histological features

The immunological features of fogo selvagem are similar to p. foliaceus. Indirect immunofluorescent techniques show that the sera of patients with fogo selvagem contain an IgG4 antibody that reacts with the intercellular regions of normal squamous epithelium.[15] Passive transfer of this antibody to BALB/c neonatal mice results in acantholysis and subcorneal blistering clinically indistinguishable from that of human disease.[16–18] Low titer IgG1 and IgG2 antibodies may also be present.[16] Fogo selvagem is histologically and by immunofluorescence indistinguishable from non-endemic foliaceus and, like the latter, the antibody binds to Dsg1.[19] A small subset of patients may also have antibodies to Dsg3.[20] Patients have circulating CD4-positive memory T-cells with a Th2 cytokine profile that proliferate in response to the extracellular domain of Dsg1 and are thought to be of importance in the initiation and progression of the disease by stimulating B-cell production of autoantibodies.[21,22]

Patients often share the HLA phenotype DRB1*0102 and lack DQB1*0201 which is thought to represent a dominant protective gene found in unaffected persons living in endemic regions.[23,24] HLA-DRB1*0404, *1402 and *1406 may also confer susceptibility.[4,19,21]

The histological changes of fogo selvagem are identical to the other forms of superficial pemphigus (p. foliaceus and p. erythematosus).[25] Since the blisters are superficial, often only non-bullous erosions are present for histological examination. It is very difficult to obtain an intact lesion for diagnosis. Typically, the cleft or blister lies within the granular layer or beneath the stratum corneum. Acantholysis is frequently subtle

but usually a few acantholytic cells can be found attached to the floor of the blister. The blister roof is often missing. Blisters may contain numerous inflammatory cells, particularly neutrophils. This feature may cause confusion with infection or other subcorneal pustular disorders. Eosinophilic spongiosis is also sometimes present, particularly if biopsies of early lesions are examined.

The verrucous plaques and nodules seen occasionally in localized or chronic fogo selvagem show acanthosis, hyperkeratosis, parakeratosis and papillomatosis.[26] Acantholysis is invariably present.

The hyperpigmentation characteristic of remission is a direct result of pigmentary incontinence.

Recently criteria have been proposed to establish a diagnosis of fogo selvagem as distinct from non-endemic p. foliaceus:[4]

- clinical evaluation
- presence of subcorneal acantholysis
- positive direct and indirect immunofluorescence and/or immunoprecipitation or ELISA assays
- confirmatory epidemiological data.

Differential diagnosis

As with p. foliaceus, the histological features in fogo selvagem may be easily overlooked and a high index of suspicion is critical to making the diagnosis. The differential diagnosis includes p. foliaceus, p. erythematosus, bullous impetigo, staphylococcal scalded skin syndrome and subcorneal pustular dermatosis. Careful clinical correlation, immunofluorescence studies and sometimes bacterial culture are necessary to establish a definitive diagnosis.

References

1. Castro, R.M., Roscoe, J.T., Sampaio, S.A.P. (1983) Brazilian pemphigus foliaceus. *Clin Dermatol*, 1, 22–41.
2. Diaz, L.A., Sampaio, S.A., Rivitti, E.A. et al (1989) Endemic pemphigus foliaceus (fogo selvagem). I Clinical features and immunopathology. *J Am Acad Dermatol*, 20, 657–669.
3. Crosby, D.L., Diaz, L.A. (1993) Endemic pemphigus foliaceus: fogo selvagem. *Dermatol Clin*, 11, 453–462.
4. Hans-Filho, G., Aoki, V., Rivitti, E. et al (1999) Endemic pemphigus foliaceus (fogo selvagem) – 1998. *Clin Dermatol*, 17, 225–235.
5. Zaitz, C., Campbell, I., Alves, G.F. (2000) Commentary/millennium: endemic pemphigus (fogo selvagem). *Int J Dermatol*, 39, 812–814.
6. Friedman, H., Campbell, I., Rocha-Alvarez, R. et al (1995) Endemic pemphigus foliaceus (fogo selvagem) in native Americans from Brazil. *J Am Acad Dermatol*, 32, 949–956.
7. Hans-Filho, G., dos Santos, V., Katayama, J.H. et al (1996) An active focus of high prevalence of fogo selvagem on an Amerindian reservation in Brazil. Cooperative Group on Fogo Selvagem Research. *J Invest Dermatol*, 107, 68–75.
8. Chiossi, M.P., Roselino, A.M. (2001) Endemic pemphigus foliaceus ('fogo selvagem'): a series from the Northeastern region of the State of Sao Paulo, Brazil, 1973–1998. *Rev Inst Med Trop Sao Paulo*, 43, 59–62.
9. Robledo, M.A., Prada, S.C., Jaramillo, D. et al (1988) South-American pemphigus foliaceus: study of an epidemic in El Bagre and Nechi, Colombia 1982–1986. *Br J Dermatol*, 118, 737–744.
10. Morini, J.P., Jomaa, B., Gorgi, Y. et al (1993) Pemphigus foliaceus in young women: an endemic focus in the Sousse area of Tunisia. *Arch Dermatol*, 129, 69–73.
11. Lombardi, C., Borges, P.C., Chaul, A. et al (1992) Environmental risk factors in endemic pemphigus foliaceus (fogo selvagem). *J Invest Dermatol*, 98, 847–850.
12. Eaton, D.P., Diaz, L.A., Hans-Filho, G. et al (1998) Comparison of black fly species (Diptera: Simuliidae) on an Amerindian reservation with a high prevalence of fogo selvagem to neighboring disease – free sites in the State of Mato Grosso do Sul, Brazil. The Cooperative Group on Fogo Selvagem Research. *J Med Entomol*, 35, 120–131.
13. Vieira, J.P. (1948) Consideracoes sobre o pemfigo foliaceo no Brasil. Empressa Grafica da Sao Paulo, Brazil: Revista dos Tribnais.
14. Rocha-Alvarez, R., Friedman, H., Campbell, I. et al (1992) Pregnant women with endemic pemphigus foliaceus (fogo selvagem) give birth to disease-free babies. *J Invest Dermatol*, 99, 78–82.
15. Beutner, E.H., Prigenzi, L.S., Hale, W. et al (1968) Immunofluorescent studies of autoantibodies to intercellular areas of epithelia in Brazilian pemphigus foliaceus. *Proc Soc Exp Biol Med*, 127, 81–86.
16. Rock, B., Martins, C.R., Theofilopoulos, A.N. (1989) The pathogenic effect of IgG4 autoantibodies in endemic pemphigus foliaceus (fogo selvagem). *N Engl J Med*, 320, 1463–1469.
17. Roscoe, J.T., Diaz, L., Sampaio, S.A. et al (1985) Brazilian pemphigus foliaceus autoantibodies are pathogenic to BALB/c mice by passive transfer. *J Invest Dermatol*, 85, 538–541.
18. Rock, B., Labib, R.S., Diaz, L.A. (1990) Monovalent Fab' immunoglobulin fragments from endemic pemphigus foliaceus autoantibodies reproduce the human disease in neonatal Balb/c mice. *J Clin Invest*, 85, 296–299.
19. Warren, S.J., Lin, M.S., Giudice, G.J. et al (2000) The prevalence of antibodies against desmoglein in endemic pemphigus foliaceus in Brazil. Cooperative group on Fogo Selvagem Research. *N Engl J Med*, 343, 23–30.
20. Arteaga, L.A., Prisayanh, P.S., Warren, S.J. et al (2002) A subset of pemphigus foliaceus patients exhibits pathogenic autoantibodies against both desmoglein-1 and desmoglein-3. *J Invest Dermatol*, 118, 806–811.
21. Lin, M.S., Fu, C.L., Aoki, V. et al (2000) Desmoglein-1-specific T lymphocytes from patients with endemic pemphigus foliaceus (fogo selvagem). *J Clin Invest*, 105, 207–213.
22. Zeoti, D.M., Figueiredo, J.F., Chiossi, M.P. et al (2000) Serum cytokines in patients with Brazilian pemphigus foliaceus (fogo selvagem). *Braz J Med Biol Res*, 33, 1065–1068.
23. Petzl-Erler, M.L., Santamaria, J. (1989) Are HLA class II genes controlling susceptibility and resistance to Brazilian pemphigus foliaceus (fogo selvagem)? *Tissue Antigens*, 33, 408–414.
24. Moraes, J.R., Moraes, M.E., Fernandez-Vina, M. et al (1991) HLA antigens and risk for development of pemphigus foliaceus (fogo selvagem) in endemic areas of Brazil. *Immunogenetics*, 33, 388–391.
25. Furtado, T.A. (1959) Histopathology of pemphigus foliaceus. *Arch Dermatol*, 80, 66–71.
26. Silva dos Reis, V.M. (1989) Anatomopatologia e immunofluorescencia directa e indirecta das lesoes resistentes a corticoterapia do penfigo foliaceo endemico. Thesis. Escola Paulista de Medecina, Sao Paolo, Brazil.

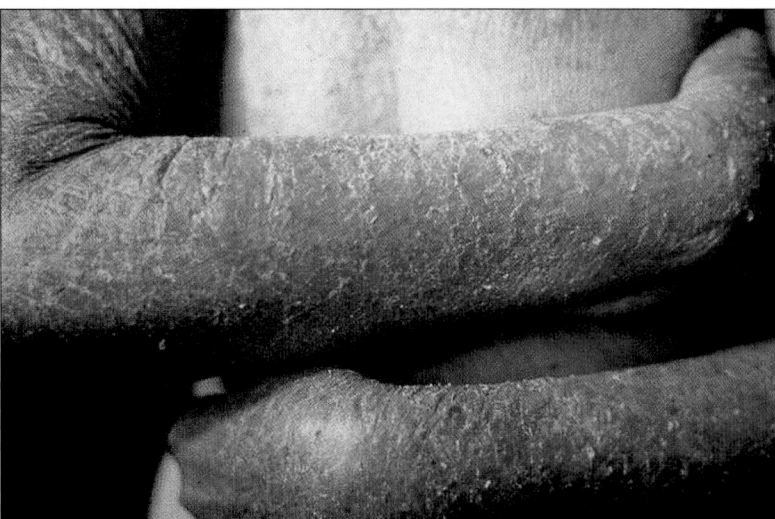

Fig. 4.27
Brazilian pemphigus foliaceus: this woman with chronic disease shows very severe scaling. Blisters are not apparent. By courtesy of S.A. Pecher, MD, Amazonas, Brazil.

Pemphigus herpetiformis

Clinical features

Pemphigus herpetiformis (p. herpetiformis, herpetiform pemphigus, acantholytic dermatitis herpetiformis) is a variant of pemphigus which shows clinical features resembling dermatitis herpetiformis with the histology and immunofluorescent findings of pemphigus.[1–6] It is rare, accounting for only up to 7.3% of cases of pemphigus.[2] The sexes are affected equally and there is a wide age range varying from 31 to 83 years.[3]

Patients typically present with intensely pruritic, grouped, erythematous papules and plaques, vesicles and blisters, sometimes associated with mucous membrane involvement.[2] Urticaria may also be a presenting feature.[7] The Nikolsky sign is variably present. Although lesions are often generalized, there is a tendency for the extensor surfaces of the extremities to be particularly involved. Exceptionally, herpetiform pemphigus may be associated with an underlying malignancy (see paraneoplastic pemphigus).[8] Although in some patients the clinical manifestations remain herpetiform throughout, in others, the features evolve into more typical p. foliaceus, fogo selvagem and, less commonly, p. vulgaris.[2,4–6] Contrariwise, patients with typical p. foliaceus and p. vulgaris may go on to develop a herpetiform eruption.[9] IgA pemphigus may also present with herpetiform lesions.[10] In general, p. herpetiformis has a benign course, most patients responding well to sulfones or steroids.[2,3,11]

Pathogenesis and histological features

Immunofluorescence testing shows IgG in an intercellular pattern characteristic of the pemphigus group of disorders on both direct and indirect techniques.[1,2,4,11] In most patients, Dsg1 (p. foliaceus antigen) is the target autoantigen.[4,6,12,13] However, in some patients, antibodies against Dsg3 (p. vulgaris antigen) have also been documented.[13,14] Why antibodies to Dsg1 in patients with p. herpetiformis often fail to induce appreciable acantholysis compared with p. foliaceus is uncertain. It is postulated that the p. herpetiformis antibody targets a different epitope although this has yet to be confirmed. Recently, two patients with neutrophil-rich histology were shown to co-localize pemphigus antibody and the neutrophil chemoattractant IL-8. In addition, circulating IgG antibody upregulated cultured keratinocyte IL-8 expression, thereby offering an explanation for the neutrophil recruitment.[15]

The biopsy findings are variable and often non-specific. Although eosinophilic spongiosis is most typical, spongiosis associated with either a mixed eosinophilic and neutrophilic, or a neutrophil-predominant infiltrate may also be encountered.[4,16] Intraepidermal vesicles and pustules, also of variable composition, are often present and dermal papillary neutrophil microabscesses have been described.[2,6,11] Acantholytic cells are usually (but not invariably) identified. A requirement for multiple biopsies before a diagnosis can be established is a common theme in the literature.

Differential diagnosis

There is both clinical and histological overlap with IgA pemphigus and dermatitis herpetiformis. Immunofluorescence allows for distinction between these entities. It should also be noted that, exceptionally, dermatitis herpetiformis may histologically show occasional acantholytic cells in the absence of any evidence of pemphigus herpetiformis.

In those cases where eosinophilic spongiosis is the predominant histological feature, the differential diagnosis also includes hypersensitivity reactions and infection (bacterial and fungal). Immunofluorescence studies and special stains for microorganisms will eliminate these possibilities.

References

1. Jablonska, S., Chorzelski, T., Beutner, E.H. et al (1975) Herpetiform pemphigus: a variable pattern of pemphigus. *Int J Dermatol*, **14**, 353–359.
2. Maciejowska, E., Jablonska, S., Chorzelski, T. (1987) Is pemphigus herpetiformis an entity? *Int J Dermatol*, **26**, 571–577.
3. Robinson, N.D., Hashimoto, T., Amagai, M. et al (1999) The new pemphigus variants. *J Am Acad Dermatol*, **40**, 649–671.
4. Santi, C.G., Maruta, C.W., Aoki, V. et al (1996) Pemphigus herpetiformis is a rare clinical expression of nonendemic pemphigus foliaceus, fogo selvagem, and pemphigus vulgaris. *J Am Acad Dermatol*, **34**, 40–46.
5. Dias, M., dos Santos, A.P., Sousa, J. et al (1999) Herpetiform pemphigus. *J Eur Acad Dermatol Venereol*, **12**, 82–85.
6. Cunha, P.R., Jiao, D., Bystryn, J.C. (1997) Simultaneous occurrence of herpetiform pemphigus and endemic pemphigus foliaceus (fogo selvagem). *Int J Dermatol*, **36**, 850–854.
7. Parodi, A., Nunzi, E., Robora, A. (1982) Urticaria as presenting manifestation of pemphigus herpetiformis. *Dermatologica*, **164**, 278–283.
8. Kubota, Y., Yoshino, Y., Mizoguchi, M. (1994) A case of herpetiform pemphigus associated with lung cancer. *J Dermatol*, **21**, 609–611.
9. El Sherif, A.I., Bharija, S.C., Belhaj, M.S. et al (1990) Pemphigus herpetiformis. *Int J Dermatol*, **29**, 737–738.
10. Chorzelski, T.P., Beutner, E.H., Kowalewski, C. et al (1991) IgA pemphigus foliaceus with a clinical presentation of pemphigus herpetiformis. *J Am Acad Dermatol*, **24**, 39–44.
11. Ingber, A., Feuerman, E.J. (1986) Pemphigus with characteristics of dermatitis herpetiformis: a long-term follow-up of five patients. *Int J Dermatol*, **25**, 575–579.
12. Seitz, C.S., Staegemeir, E., Amagi, M. et al (1999) Pemphigus herpetiformis with an autoimmune response to recombinant desmoglein 1. *Br J Dermatol*, **141**, 355–356.
13. Ishii, K., Amagai, K., Komai, A. et al (1999) Desmoglein 1 and desmoglein 3 are the target autoantigens in herpetiform pemphigus. *Arch Dermatol*, **135**, 943–947.
14. Kubo, A., Amagai, M., Hashimoto, T. et al (1997) Herpetiform pemphigus showing reactivity with pemphigus vulgaris antigen (desmoglein 3). *Br J Dermatol*, **137**, 109–113.
15. O'Toole, E.A., Mak, L.L., Guitart, J. et al (1998) Activation of interleukin-8 secretion in pemphigus herpetiformis epidermis by anti-desmoglein 1 IgG autoantibodies. *J Invest Dermatol*, **110**, 509.
16. Huhn, K.M., Tron, V.A., Nguyen, N. et al (1996) Neutrophilic spongiosis in pemphigus herpetiformis. *J Cutan Pathol*, **23**, 264–269.

Pemphigus erythematosus

Clinical features

Pemphigus erythematosus (p. erythematosus, Senear–Usher syndrome) is a mild localized form of superficial pemphigus with the histological and immunofluorescent findings of p. foliaceus combined with features of lupus erythematosus.[1–5] In general, the latter is subclinical, being suggested only by laboratory findings but there are also rare reports of full-blown systemic disease being present.[4] The condition shows a worldwide distribution and a slight female predominance.[5] Exceptionally, it has been described in children although immunological confirmation of the diagnosis is available in only one case.[6–8]

Clinically, it is commonly confined to the head, neck and upper trunk, and typically resembles p. foliaceus. Lesions are erythematous, scaly and crusted, with or without superficial vesicles, blisters or erosions. Facial involvement often shows a butterfly distribution reminiscent of lupus erythematosus or seborrheic dermatitis (*Fig. 4.28*).[1] Mucous membrane involvement is exceedingly rare.[2]

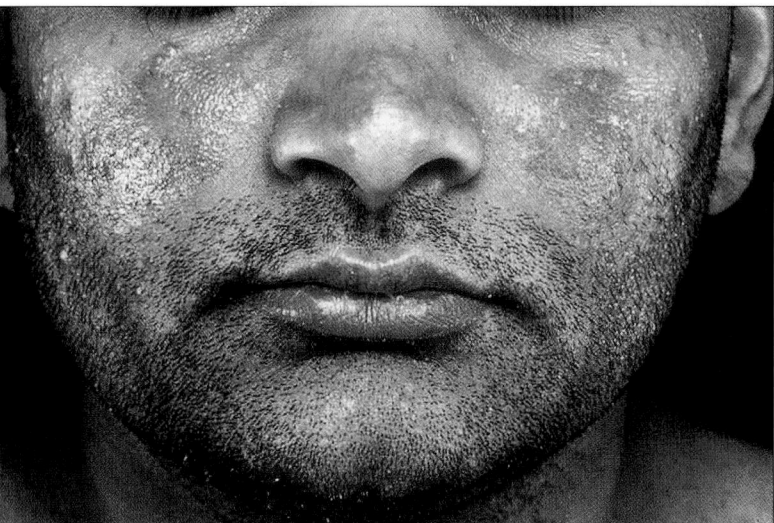

Fig. 4.28
Pemphigus erythematosus: there is scarring and erythema affecting both cheeks. By courtesy of the Institute of Dermatology, London, UK.

There are reports of p. erythematosus developing after treatment with a number of drugs, notably D-penicillamine, and there are also instances attributed to therapy with propranolol, captopril, pyritinol, thiopronine and ceftazidime.[9–12] P. erythematosus has also been described as a complication of heroin abuse.[13]

P. erythematosus may rarely be associated with thymoma.[3,14–16] Typically, the thymoma precedes the onset of cutaneous lesions, which often present following thymectomy.[16] Most tumors have been benign but one malignant variant has been documented.[16] P. erythematosus may also be a manifestation of paraneoplastic pemphigus.[3]

Pathogenesis and histological features

Pemphigus erythematosus, in addition to intercellular staining, also shows granular deposition of IgG and complement along the basement membrane region (positive lupus band test) (*Figs 4.29, 4.30*).[2,17,18] Typically the latter deposits are found within sun-exposed skin but in some patients normal, non-sun-exposed skin may also be positive.[2] Pemphigus antibody is typically present on indirect immunofluorescence and antinuclear factor may also be identified.[17,18] Anti-DNA antibodies and antibodies to extractable nuclear antigens are negative except in those patients with features of systemic lupus erythematosus.[4] In common with p. foliaceus, the antibody reacts with Dsg1.[19]

P. erythematosus has histological changes that are identical to those seen in p. foliaceus and fogo selvagem. As the blisters are superficial, it is often very difficult to obtain an intact lesion for diagnosis. Usually the cleft or blister lies within the granular layer or beneath the stratum corneum. As with the other forms of superficial pemphigus, acantholysis is frequently difficult to detect, but usually a few acantholytic cells can be found attached to the roof or floor of the blister. The blister may contain numerous acute inflammatory cells, particularly neutrophils, which can make distinction from subcorneal pustular disorders especially difficult.

Differential diagnosis

The differential diagnosis includes the other forms of superficial pemphigus (p. foliaceus and fogo selvagem), bullous impetigo and staphylococcal scalded skin syndrome, in addition to subcorneal pustular dermatosis. Distinction depends upon a careful consideration of the clinical information, the results of bacterial culture, and immunofluorescence studies.

References

1. Korman, N.J. (1990) Pemphigus. *Dermatol Clin*, **8**, 689–700.
2. Amerian, M.L., Ahmed, A.R. (1984) Pemphigus erythematosus: presentation of four cases and review of the literature. *J Am Acad Dermatol*, **10**, 215–222.
3. Amerian, M.L., Ahmed, A.R. (1985) Pemphigus erythematosus. Senear–Usher syndrome. *Int J Dermatol*, **24**, 16–25.
4. Weiselthier, J.S., Treloar, V., Koh, H.K. et al (1991) Multiple crusted plaques in a woman with systemic lupus erythematosus. Pemphigus erythematosus (PE). *Arch Dermatol*, **127**, 1572–1573, 1575–1576.
5. Deloach-Banta, L.J., Tenaro, L.J. (1993) Superficial erosions with some oozing and marked crusting. Pemphigus erythematosus. *Arch Dermatol*, **129**, 633, 636–637.
6. Petratos, M.A., Andrade, R. (1967) Pemphigus erythematosus. *Am J Dis Child*, **113**, 394–397.
7. Kowalska, M., Blaszczyk, M., Kupis, B. (1975) Pemphigus erythematosus in an 8-year-old boy. *Przglad Derm*, **62**, 705–708.
8. Lyde, C.B., Cox, S.E., Cruz, P.D. (1994) Pemphigus erythematosus in a five-year-old child. *J Am Acad Dermatol*, **31**, 906–909.
9. Scherak, O., Kolarz, G., Holubar, K. (1977) Pemphigus erythematosus-like rash in a patient on penicillamine. *BMJ*, **1**, 838.
10. Thorvaldsen, J. (1979) Two cases of penicillamine-induced pemphigus erythematosus. *Dermatologica*, **159**, 167–170.
11. Willemsen, M.J., De Coninck, A.L., De Raeve, L.E. et al (1990) Penicillamine-induced pemphigus erythematosus. *Int J Dermatol*, **29**, 193–197.
12. Pellicano, R., Iannantuono, M., Lomuo, M. (1993) Pemphigus erythematosus induced by ceftazidime. *Int J Dermatol*, **32**, 675–676.
13. Fellner, M.J. (1980) Immunology of skin disease. New York: Elsevier Science, pp 146–147.
14. Cruz, P.D. Jr, Coldiron, B.M., Sontheimer, R.D. (1987) Concurrent features of cutaneous lupus erythematosus and pemphigus erythematosus following myasthenia gravis and thymoma. *J Am Acad Dermatol*, **16**, 472–480.
15. Itoh, K., Umehara, F., Iwasaki, H. et al (1997) A case of myasthenia gravis associated with systemic lupus erythematosus and pemphigus erythematosus. *Rinsho Shinkeigaku*, **37**, 111–114.
16. Fuxiang, G., Beutner, E.H. (1999) Pemphigus erythematosus associated with thymoma: a case report. *Cutis*, **64**, 179–182.
17. Chorzelski, T., Jablonska, S., Blaszczyk, M. (1968) Immunopathological investigations in the Senear–Usher syndrome (co-existence of pemphigus and lupus erythematosus). *Br J Dermatol*, **80**, 211–217.
18. Jablonska, S., Chorzelski, T., Blaszczyk, M. et al (1972) Pathogenesis of pemphigus erythematosus. *Arch Dermatol Res*, **258**, 135–140.
19. Gomi, H., Kawada, A., Amagai, M. et al (1999) Pemphigus erythematosus: detection of anti-desmoglein-1 antibodies by ELISA. *Dermatology*, **199**, 188–189.

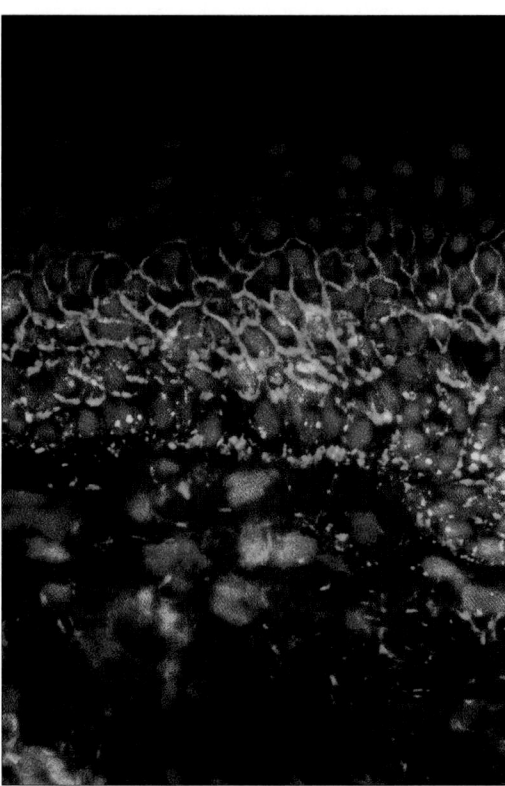

Fig. 4.29
Pemphigus erythematosus: typical intercellular immunofluorescence with granular staining (IgG) at the basement membrane region. By courtesy of B. Bhogal, FIMLS, Institute of Dermatology, London, UK.

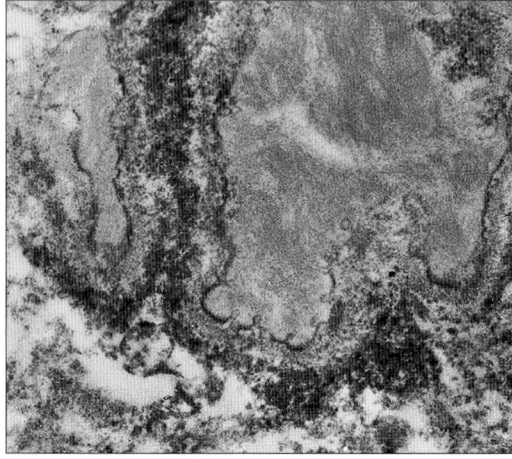

Fig. 4.30
Pemphigus erythematosus: immunoelectron micrograph showing immunoreactant beneath the lamina densa in addition to occupying the intercellular space. By courtesy of B. Bhogal, FIMLS, Institute of Dermatology, London, UK.

Paraneoplastic pemphigus

Clinical features

Paraneoplastic pemphigus is a variant of pemphigus, quite distinct from p. vulgaris and p. foliaceus.[1] Paraneoplastic pemphigus may be associated with a variety of tumors, such as B-cell lymphoproliferative disorders and hematopoietic malignancies, Castleman's disease, Waldenström's macroglobulinemia, thymoma, Hodgkin's lymphoma, carcinomas (e.g. carcinoma of bronchus, pancreas, and breast) and sarcomas.[2–16] Lymphoma is most often the coexistent neoplasm.[1] Paraneoplastic pemphigus has been recently defined by Sapadin and Anhalt[17] as follows:

- painful mucosal erosions and a polymorphous skin eruption in the context of an occult or confirmed neoplasm
- histopathological changes of keratinocyte necrosis, intraepidermal acantholysis, and vacuolar-interface dermatitis
- direct immunofluorescence showing intercellular IgG and complement accompanied by linear or granular complement at the dermal–epidermal junction

- indirect immunofluorescence showing circulating antibodies to simple, columnar and transitional epithelia in addition to a more typical pemphigus pattern of binding to skin and mucosa
- circulating autoantibodies that immunoprecipitate a high molecular weight complex of polypeptides from keratinocyte extracts weighing 250, 230, 210, 190 and 170 kD.

Although the disease may develop in a wide age range (7–83 years), the majority of patients have been in the fifth to eighth decades and there is a male predominance.[5] Exceptionally children may be affected.[4,18] Lesions are seen in both the mucosa and the skin. Patients present with refractory, painful, persistent erosions of the oral mucosa and vermilion border of the lips. In addition, the tongue, gingiva, floor of mouth, palate, oropharynx and nasopharynx can be affected.[5] Exceptionally, oral involvement occurs in the absence of cutaneous lesions.[19] Esophageal disease has been described and the trachea and bronchi may be affected.[20–22] The latter is sometimes accompanied by an invariably fatal bronchiolitis obliterans-like disorder.[21,22] Frequently, patients also have severe pseudomembranous conjunctivitis with symblephara and eventual blindness may occur.[5] The vulva, vagina and penis are sometimes affected.[4]

Cutaneous lesions are typically polymorphic and often present as a pruritic papulosquamous dermatosis with subsequent blistering. The trunk, proximal extremities, palms and soles are characteristically affected.[23] Nail involvement may occur. Although the eruption typically resembles p. vulgaris, it may also mimic bullous pemphigoid, linear IgA disease, lichen planus pemphigoides, erythema multiforme and toxic epidermal necrolysis.[24–26] P. vegetans-like lesions have been described.[17] Paraneoplastic pemphigus is associated with a very high mortality.[5]

Pathogenesis and histological features

In paraneoplastic pemphigus, circulating antibodies bind to desmosomal and hemidesmosomal plakin family members including 250 kD (desmoplakin I), 230 kD (bullous pemphigoid antigen), 210 kD (a doublet originally thought to be desmoplakin II but later determined to represent envoplakin) and a 190 kD antigen (periplakin).[27–30] The presence of antibodies to envoplakin and periplakin (both cornified envelope constituents) is believed to be highly specific for paraneoplastic pemphigus.[31] There are also antibodies to an as yet undetermined 170 kD antigen.[27] Antibodies to Dsg1 and 3 are also usually present and plectin (another plakin family member) antibodies may be found.[32,33] Anti-Dsg antibodies are thought to be of particular importance in the initiation of lesions, disrupting the cell membrane and thereby exposing desmosomal and hemidesmosomal plakin proteins with resultant autoantibody formation.[27,34]

Direct immunofluorescence shows IgG deposition affecting the whole thickness of the epidermis whereas C3 is found only on the lower layers.[27,35–37] Characteristically, the intercellular staining is often focal and faint.[35,36] In addition, complement is present along the basement membrane region. Immunoglobulin deposition in the respiratory epithelium has also been documented.[20–22] Indirect studies confirm the presence of a circulating antibody although the membrane deposition is often masked by strong cytoplasmic labeling.[27] This latter can be reduced or abolished by serum dilution.[27]

In paraneoplastic pemphigus, in addition to binding to stratified squamous epithelium, the antibody labels transitional epithelium, pseudostratified respiratory epithelium, small and large intestinal mucosa and thyroid epithelium.[36] It also reacts with myocardium and skeletal muscle. Rat bladder epithelium is said to be highly specific for paraneoplastic pemphigus.[37] Up to 25% of cases, however, are negative.[38]

Recently, there has been accumulating evidence demonstrating considerable heterogeneity within disorders designated as paraneoplastic pemphigus in addition to overlap with other immunobullous diseases. Immunophenotypic variability among paraneoplastic pemphigus patients has thus been established. The documentation of patients displaying p. vulgaris-like or p. foliaceus-like features has led some authors to suggest that immunobullous disorders arising in association with malignancy would be best viewed as representing a spectrum rather than a distinct entity.[24] Included within this spectrum are other non-pemphigus immunobullous disorders resembling erythema multiforme, graft-versus-host disease and lichen planus. The description of antibodies reactive with desmoplakin I and II in some patients with erythema multiforme raises the possibility that these autoantibodies play a pathogenic role in a subset of patients.[39] However, further study will be necessary to determine the significance of this finding.

The pathological findings in paraneoplastic pemphigus are highly variable but are characterized by an admixture of suprabasal acantholysis, often resembling p. vulgaris, with cleft or vesicle formation (sometimes involving adnexal epithelium), and interface changes with basal cell liquefactive degeneration, dyskeratotic keratinocytes and lymphocytic exocytosis.[28,40] Spongiosis is often present.[3] A perivascular and lichenoid chronic inflammatory cell infiltrate is typically seen in the superficial dermis.[35] Eosinophils, however, are rare. Pigmentary incontinence is frequently evident.[40]

Acantholysis-like change has also been described affecting the bronchial lining epithelium and brochiolitis obliterans-like features may be seen.[20,22]

Differential diagnosis

The biopsy findings of admixed acantholysis and interface change appear to be relatively non-specific. This contention is demonstrated by skin lesions in patients with typical autoimmune pemphigus without evidence of neoplasia that have histological features considered typical of paraneoplastic pemphigus.[37]

The differential diagnosis includes mainly interface dermatitides (e.g. drug eruption, lichen planus, erythema multiforme, graft-versus-host disease) rather than other variants of pemphigus. A very high index of suspicion on the part of the pathologist and clinician alike and confirmatory immunofluorescence studies are prerequisites to achieving a correct diagnosis.

References

1. Anhalt, G.J., Soochan, K., Stanley, J.R. et al (1990) Paraneoplastic pemphigus: an autoimmune mucocutaneous disease associated with neoplasia. *N Engl J Med*, **323**, 1729–1735.
2. Younus, J., Ahmed, A.R. (1990) The relationship of pemphigus to neoplasia. *J Am Acad Dermatol*, **23**, 498–502.
3. Mehregan, D.R., Oursler, J.R., Leiferman, K.M. et al (1993) Paraneoplastic pemphigus: a subset of patients with pemphigus and neoplasia. *J Cutan Pathol*, **20**, 203–210.
4. Anhalt, G.J. (1997) Paraneoplastic pemphigus. *Adv Dermatol*, **12**, 77–96.
5. Kimyai-Asadi, A., Ming, H.J. (2001) Paraneoplastic pemphigus. *Int J Dermatol*, **40**, 367–372.
6. Hertzberg, M.S., Schifter, M., Sullivan, J. et al (2000) Paraneoplastic pemphigus in two patients with B-cell non-Hodgkin's lymphoma: significant response to cyclophosphamide and prednisolone. *Am J Hematol*, **63**, 105–106.
7. Wolff, H., Messer, G. (2002) Paraneoplastic pemphigus triggered by Castleman's disease. *Br J Dermatol*, **146**, 30.
8. Chin, A.C., Stich, D., White, F.V. et al (2001) Paraneoplastic pemphigus and bronchiolitis obliterans associated with a mediastinal mass. A rare case of Castleman's disease with respiratory failure requiring lung transplantation. *J Pediatr Surg*, **36**, E22.
9. van Mook, W.N.K., Fickers, M.M., Theunissen, P.H. et al (2001) Paraneoplastic pemphigus as the initial presentation of chronic lymphocytic leukemia. *Ann Oncol*, **12**, 115–118.
10. Marzano, A.V., Grammatica, A., Cozzani, E. et al (2001) Paraneoplastic pemphigus: a report of two cases associated with chronic B-cell lymphocytic leukemia. *Br J Dermatol*, **145**, 127–131.
11. Leyn, J., Degreef, H. (2001) Paraneoplastic pemphigus in a patient with thymoma. *Dermatology*, **202**, 151–154.
12. Dega, H., Laporte, J.L., Joly, P. et al (1998) Paraneoplastic pemphigus associated with Hodgkin's lymphoma. *Br J Dermatol*, **138**, 196–198.
13. Matz, H., Milner, Y., Frusic-Zlotkin, M. et al (1997) Paraneoplastic pemphigus associated with pancreatic carcinoma. *Acta Derm Venereol*, **77**, 289–291.
14. Krunic, A.L., Kokai, D., Bacetic, B. et al (1997) Retroperitoneal round-cell liposarcoma associated with paraneoplastic pemphigus presenting as lichen planus pemphigoides-like eruption. *Int J Dermatol*, **36**, 526–529.
15. van der Waal, R.I., Pas, H.H., Nousari, H.C. et al (2000) Paraneoplastic pemphigus caused by an epithelioid leiomyosarcoma and associated with fatal respiratory failure. *Oral Oncol*, **36**, 390–393.
16. Kubota, Y., Yoshino, Y., Mizoguchi, M. (1994) A case of herpetiform pemphigus associated with lung cancer. *J Dermatol*, **21**, 609–611.
17. Sapadin, A.N., Anhalt, G.J. (1998) Paraneoplastic pemphigus with a pemphigus vegetans-like plaque as the only cutaneous manifestation. *J Am Acad Dermatol*, **39**, 867–871.
18. Robinson, N.D., Hashimoto, T., Amagai, M. et al (1999) Continuing medical education: the new pemphigus variants. *J Am Acad Dermatol*, **40**, 649–671.

19. Bialy Golan, A., Brenner, S., Anhalt, G.J. (1996) Paraneoplastic pemphigus: oral involvement as the sole manifestation. *Acta Derm Venereol*, 76, 253–254.
20. Fullerton, S.H., Woodley, D.T., Smoller, B.R. (1992) Paraneoplastic pemphigus with autoantibody deposition in bronchial epithelium after autologous bone marrow transplantation. *JAMA*, 267, 1500–1502.
21. Osmanski, J.P. II, Fraire, A.E., Schaefer, O. P. (1997) Necrotizing tracheobronchitis with progressive airflow obstruction associated with paraneoplastic pemphigus. *Chest*, 112, 1704–1707.
22. Nousari, H.C., Deterding, R., Wojtczack, H. et al (1999) The mechanism of respiratory failure in paraneoplastic pemphigus. *N Engl J Med*, 340, 1406–1410.
23. Camisa, C., Helm, T.N., Liu, Y-C. et al (1992) Paraneoplastic pemphigus: a report of three cases including one long-term survivor. *J Am Acad Dermatol*, 27, 547–553.
24. Passerson, T., Bahadoran, P., Lacour, J.P. et al (1999) Paraneoplastic pemphigus presenting as erosive lichen planus. *Br J Dermatol*, 140, 552–553.
25. Stevens, S.R., Griffiths, C.E., Anhalt, G.J. et al (1993) Paraneoplastic pemphigus presenting as a lichen planus pemphigoides-like eruption. *Arch Dermatol*, 129, 866–869.
26. Hsiao, C.J., Hsu, M.M., Lee, J.Y. et al (2001) Paraneoplastic pemphigus in association with a retroperitoneal Castleman's disease presenting with a lichen planus pemphigoides-like eruption. A case report and review of the literature. *Br J Dermatol*, 144, 372–376.
27. Hashimoto, T. (2001) Immunopathology of paraneoplastic pemphigus. *Clin Dermatol*, 19, 675–682.
28. Oursler, J.R., Labib, R.S., Ariss-Abdo, L. et al (1992) Human antibodies against desmoplakins in paraneoplastic pemphigus. *J Clin Invest*, 89, 1775–1782.
29. Kiyokawa, C., Ruhrberg, C., Nie, Z. et al (1998) Envoplakin and periplakin are components of the paraneoplastic pemphigus antigen complex. *J Invest Dermatol*, 111, 1236–1238.
30. Mahoney, M.G., Aho, S., Uitto, J. et al (1998) The members of the plakin family of proteins recognized by paraneoplastic pemphigus antibodies include periplakin. *J Invest Dermatol*, 111, 308–313.
31. Hashimoto, T., Amagai, M., Watanabe, K. et al (1995) Characterization of paraneoplastic pemphigus autoantigens by immunoblot analysis. *J Invest Dermatol*, 104, 819–834.
32. Aho, S., Mahoney, M.G., Uitto, J. (1999) Plectin serves as an autoantigen in paraneoplastic pemphigus. *J Invest Dermatol*, 113, 422–423.
33. Proby, C., Fujii, Y., Owaribe, K. et al (1999) Human autoantibodies against HD 1/plectin in paraneoplastic pemphigus. *J Invest Dermatol*, 112, 153–156.
34. Amagai, M., Nishikawa, T., Nousari, H.C. et al (1998) Antibodies against desmoglein 3 (pemphigus vulgaris antigen) are present in sera from patients with paraneoplastic pemphigus and cause acantholysis in vivo in neonatal mice. *J Clin Invest*, 102, 775–782.
35. Joly, P., Richard, C., Gilbert, D. et al (2000) Sensitivity and specificity of clinical, histologic, and immunologic features in the diagnosis of paraneoplastic pemphigus. *J Am Acad Dermatol*, 43, 619–626.
36. Nguyen, V.T., Ndoye, A., Bassler, K.D. et al (2001) Classification, clinical manifestations, and immunopathological mechanisms of the epithelial variant of paraneoplastic autoimmune multiorgan system. *Arch Dermatol*, 137, 193–206.
37. Kanitakis, J., Wang, Y. Z., Roche, P. et al (1994) Immunohistopathological study of autoimmune pemphigus. *Dermatology*, 188, 282–285.
38. Helou, J., Albritton, L.M., Anhalt, G.J. (1995) Accuracy of indirect immunofluorescence testing in the diagnosis of paraneoplastic pemphigus. *J Am Acad Dermatol*, 32, 441–447.
39. Foedinger, D., Sternickzky, B., Elbe, A. (1996) Autoantibodies against desmoplakin I and II define a subset of patients with erythema multiforme major. *J Invest Dermatol*, 106, 1012–1016.
40. Horn, T.D., Anhalt, G.J. (1992) Histologic features of paraneoplastic pemphigus. *Arch Dermatol*, 128, 1091–1095.

IgA pemphigus

Clinical features

IgA pemphigus is a rare dapsone-responsive variant of pemphigus that, as its name suggests, is characterized by intercellular IgA deposition and presents clinically with pustular rather than bullous or vesicular lesions.[1–4] This disease has been described under a number of different names, such as intraepidermal neutrophilic IgA dermatosis, IgA pemphigus foliaceus, IgA herpetiform pemphigus, intraepidermal IgA pustulosis, intercellular IgA dermatosis, intercellular IgA vesiculo-pustular dermatosis.[5–14] Most patients are middle aged or elderly but children may also be affected.[6,15–18] The sex incidence is equal. There is no racial or geographic predilection.[6,9] Drug-induced variants have occasionally been documented.[19]

IgA pemphigus is divided into two major subtypes: subcorneal pustular dermatosis (SPD) variant (IgA pemphigus foliaceus) and intraepidermal neutrophilic IgA dermatosis (IEN) variant (IgA pemphigus vulgaris).[5] Other less readily classifiable variants may also be encountered.

- Patients with SPD-like IgA pemphigus present with superficial flaccid pustular lesions, often arising on an erythematous base and typically affecting the trunk and proximal limbs although the intertriginous sites are predilected.[9] Occasionally, there is generalized skin involvement. Lesions are crusted and progress with peripheral extension to form ring-like and rosette patterns.[13] The features may be indistinguishable from classical non-IgA-associated SPD.

- Patients with the IEN IgA dermatosis variant present with generalized pustules and crusts and erythematous macules with peripheral vesicles forming the so-called sunflower-like configuration.[5] A dermatitis herpetiformis-like presentation with grouped edematous papules may also be encountered.[9,10,13]

Pruritus is common and is sometimes severe.[6]

The lesions in occasional patients resemble classic p. vulgaris or p. foliaceus. In one childhood case, a p. vegetans-like presentation

associated with α_1-antitrypsin deficiency was documented.[16] Mucous membrane involvement in either variant is exceptional.[15] Nikolsky's sign has been reportedly negative at least in a subset of patients.[2,10,11] IgA pemphigus tends to be a chronic relapsing but relatively benign disorder.[9,10,13]

A significant number of patients (approximately 20%) may have an associated monoclonal gammopathy, usually of the IgA class.[9,20] Two documented cases have been benign and the others have represented B-cell lymphoma or multiple myeloma.[9]

Pathogenesis and histological features

SPD IgA pemphigus is characterized by intercellular IgA deposition in the upper epidermis and circulating IgA antibodies which preferentially bind to the upper epidermis are typically present.[4] In contrast, in the IEN variant, IgA is deposited preferentially in the lower epidermis and circulating antibodies also generally bind to the lower epidermis. In some patients, however, the IgA antibody binds to the entire thickness of the epithelium. A linear subcorneal distribution has also been documented.[9] Complement is not usually present and IgG and IgM are absent.[5] The antibodies are of the IgA 1 subclass and are usually of low titer.[4,15] They have been identified in approximately 50% of patients.[10]

By immunoelectron microscopy performed on a limited number of cases, the immunoglobulin has been identified within the intercellular space, on the keratinocyte cell membrane, in some cases showing desmosomal accentuation.[21–23]

The two subtypes result from autoantibody production to different desmosomal proteins.[24] Patients with the SPD variant show reactivity with desmocollin 1.[25,26] In contrast, anti-Dsg1 or anti-Dsg3 IgA antibodies are present in the IEN variant.[17,27–29] In some patients, neither desmocollins nor desmogleins appear to be involved, suggesting that IgA pemphigus is a heterogeneous group of conditions.[11,16,29]

Histologically, in the SPD variant, vesicles are typically found in a subcorneal location associated with a neutrophil infiltrate (*Figs 4.31, 4.32*). It is thought that the presence of IgA is responsible for the striking neutrophil response of this disorder since IgA is associated with neutrophil chemotaxis and neutrophils bear IgA receptors.[30,31] In the IEN variant, the pustules can be distributed throughout all layers of the epidermis and may also involve the hair follicles.[16] Acantholytic cells are usually (but not always) present. Typically they are sparse and as such, this diagnostic clue may be very easily overlooked.[9,10,11] Significant numbers of eosinophils may also be seen in occasional IEN cases.[18,32]

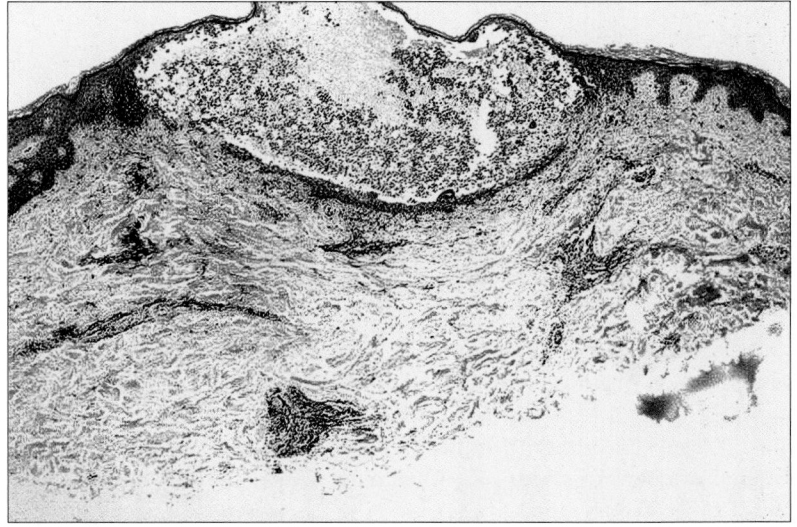

Fig. 4.31
IgA pemphigus: this variant of pemphigus is characterized by a subcorneal vesicle.

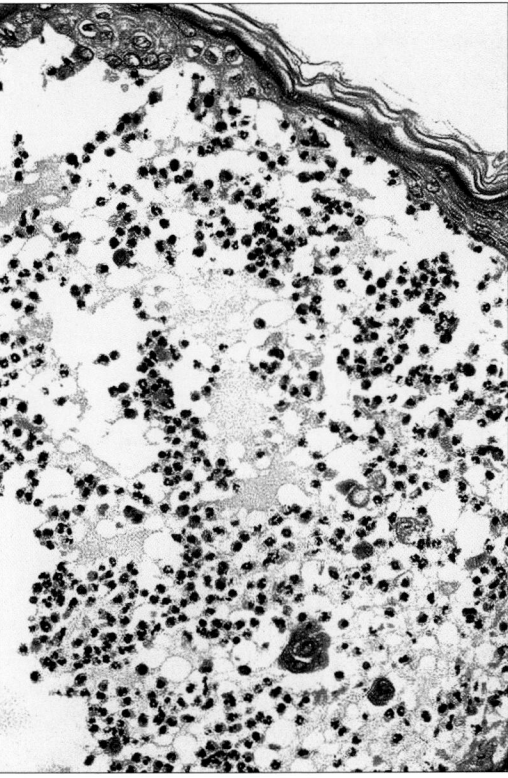

Fig. 4.32
IgA pemphigus: the blister cavity contains neutrophils. Acantholysis is evident.

Neutrophil dermal papillary microabscesses have also been described, sometimes accompanied by neutrophil spongiosis.[10,18] A perivascular infiltrate of neutrophils, lymphocytes and histiocytes surrounds the superficial vascular plexus and eosinophils may also sometimes be present. In addition to the major variants characterized by pustules, some patients with IgA pemphigus show histological features typical of classic p. vulgaris, p. foliaceus or even, exceptionally, p. vegetans.[4,16]

Differential diagnosis

The differential diagnosis includes subcorneal pustular dermatosis, typical p. foliaceus and infections such as bullous impetigo. Although clinically subcorneal pustular dermatosis tends to be more restricted to the flexural sites, absolute distinction from the subcorneal variant of IgA pemphigus depends upon immunofluorescent studies. Gram stain and a periodic acid–Schiff (PAS) should always be included in the histological workup to exclude an infective process.

References

1. Wallach, D., Foldes, C., Cottenot, F. et al (1982) Pustulose sous-cornee acantholyse superficielle et IgA monoclonale. *Ann Dermatol Venereol*, 109, 953–963.
2. Tagami, H., Iwatsuki, K., Iwase, Y. et al (1983) Subcorneal pustular dermatosis with vesiculopustular eruption: demonstration of subcorneal IgA deposits and a leukocyte chemotactic factor. *Br J Dermatol*, 109, 581–587.
3. Huff, J.C., Golitz, L.E., Kunke, S. (1985) Intraepidermal neutrophilic IgA dermatosis. *N Engl J Med*, 313, 1643–1645.
4. Hashimoto, T., Inamoto, N., Nakamura, K. et al (1987) Intercellular IgA dermatosis with clinical features of subcorneal pustular dermatosis. *Arch Dermatol*, 123, 1062–1065.
5. Nishikawa, T., Hashimoto, T. (2000) Dermatoses with intra-epidermal IgA deposits. *Clin Dermatol*, 18, 315–318.
6. Robinson, N.D., Hashimoto, T., Amagai, M. et al (1999) The new pemphigus variants. *J Am Acad Dermatol*, 40, 649–671.
7. Nishikawa, T., Hashimoto, T., Teraki, Y. et al (1991) The clinical and histopathological spectrum of IgA-pemphigus. *Clin Exp Dermatol*, 16, 401–402.
8. Chorzelski, T.P., Beutner, E.H., Kowalewski, C. et al (1991) IgA pemphigus foliaceus with a clinical presentation of pemphigus herpetiformis. *J Am Acad Dermatol*, 24, 39–44.
9. Wallach, D. (1992) Intraepidermal IgA pustulosis. *J Am Acad Dermatol*, 27, 993–1000.
10. Hodak, E., David, M., Ingber, A. et al (1990) The clinical and histopathological spectrum of IgA pemphigus: report of two cases. *Clin Exp Dermatol*, 15, 433–437.
11. Niimi, Y., Kawana, S., Kusunoki, T. (2000) IgA pemphigus: a case report and its characteristic clinical features compared with subcorneal pustular dermatosis. *J Am Acad Dermatol*, 43, 546–549.
12. Yasuda, H., Kobayashi, H., Hashimoto, T. et al (2000) Subcorneal pustular type of IgA pemphigus: demonstration of autoantibodies to desmocollin-1 and clinical review. *Br J Dermatol*, 143, 144–148.
13. Harman, K.E., Holmes, G., Bhogal, B.S. et al (1999) Intercellular IgA dermatosis (IgA pemphigus) – two cases illustrating the clinical heterogeneity of this disorder. *Clin Exp Dermatol*, 23, 464–466.
14. Ongenae, K.C., Temmerman, L.J., Vermander, F. et al (1999) Intercellular IgA dermatosis. *Eur J Dermatol*, 9, 85–94.
15. Teraki, Y., Amagai, N., Hashimoto, T. et al (1991) Intercellular IgA dermatosis of childhood. *Arch Dermatol*, 127, 221–224.
16. Weston, W.L., Friednash, M., Hashimoto, T. et al (1998) A novel childhood pemphigus vegetans variant of intraepidermal neutrophilic IgA dermatosis. *J Am Acad Dermatol*, 38, 635–638.
17. Cordoliani, F., Rybojad, M., Verola, O. et al (1995) Intra-epidermal pustulosis in a child. Demonstration of a target antigen similar to foliaceus pemphigus antigen. *Ann Dermatol Venereol*, 122, 671–674.
18. Saurat, J.-H., Merot, Y., Salomon, D. et al (1987) Pemphigus-like IgA deposits and vesiculo-pustular dermatosis in a 10-year-old girl. *Dermatologica*, 175, 96–100.
19. Kishimoto, K., Iwatsuki, K., Akiba, H. et al (2001) Subcorneal pustular dermatosis-type IgA pemphigus induced by thiol drugs. *Eur J Dermatol*, 11, 41–44.
20. Miyagawa, S., Hashimoto, T., Ohno, H. et al (1995) Atypical pemphigus associated with monoclonal IgA gammopathy. *J Am Acad Dermatol*, 32, 352–357.
21. Iwatsuki, K., Imaizumi, S., Takagi, M. et al (1988) Intercellular IgA deposition in patients with clinical features of subcorneal pustular dermatosis. *Br J Dermatol*, 119, 545–547.
22. Prost, C., Intrator, L., Wechsler, J. et al (1991) IgA autoantibodies bind to pemphigus vulgaris antigen in a case of intraepidermal neutrophilic IgA dermatosis. *J Am Acad Dermatol*, 25, 846–848.
23. Kim, S-C., Won, J.H., Chung, J. et al (1996) IgA pemphigus: report of a case with immunoelectron localization of bound IgA in the skin. *J Am Acad Dermatol*, 34, 852–854.
24. Hashimoto, T. (2001) Immunopathology of IgA pemphigus. *Clin Dermatol*, 19, 683–689.
25. Hashimoto, T., Kiyokawa, C., Mori, O. et al (1997) Human desmocollin 1 (Dsc1) is an autoantigen for the subcorneal pustular dermatosis type of IgA pemphigus. *J Invest Dermatol*, 109, 127–131.
26. Yasuda, H., Kobayashi, H., Hashimoto, T. et al (2000) Subcorneal pustular dermatosis type of IgA pemphigus: demonstration of autoantibodies to desmocollin-1 and clinical review. *Br J Dermatol*, 143, 144–148.
27. Wang, J., Kwon, J., Ding, X. et al (1997) Nonsecretory IgA1 autoantibodies targeting desmosomal component Dsg 3 in intraepidermal neutrophilic IgA dermatosis. *Am J Pathol*, 150, 1901–1907.
28. Kárpáti, S., Amagai, M., Liu, W.L. et al (2000) Identification of desmoglein 1 as autoantigen in a patient with intraepidermal neutrophilic IgA dermatosis type of IgA pemphigus. *Exp Dermatol*, 9, 224–228.
29. Hashimoto, T., Komai, A., Futei, Y. et al (2001) Detection of IgA autoantibodies to desmogleins by an enzyme-linked immunosorbent assay: the presence of new minor subtypes of IgA pemphigus. *Arch Dermatol*, 137, 735–738.
30. Schroder, J.M., Szperalski, B., Koh, C.J. et al (1981) IgA-associated inhibition of polymorphonuclear leukocyte chemotaxis in neutrophilic dermatoses. *J Invest Dermatol*, 77, 464–468.
31. Fanger, M.W., Shen, L., Pugh, H. et al (1980) Subpopulations of human peripheral granulocytes and monocytes express receptors for IgA. *Proc Natl Acad Sci USA*, 77, 3640–3644.
32. Wright, S., Phillips, T., Ryan, J. et al (1989) Intraepidermal neutrophilic IgA dermatosis with colitis. *Br J Dermatol*, 129, 113–119.

Drug-induced pemphigus

Drug-induced pemphigus is discussed in full on p. 648. There are at least 25 drugs that have been shown to be associated with the development of pemphigus.[1] Penicillamine and captopril are the most common offenders; however, enalapril, penicillins, cephalosporins, rifampicin and pyrazolon derivatives, among others, have also been implicated.[1,2] Some drugs such as penicillamine may elicit either p. foliaceus or p. vulgaris, but the former is much more common.

Symptoms disappear in most patients following withdrawal of causative drugs that contain a sulfhydryl group (thiol drugs). Non-thiol drugs are much less likely to be associated with remission following withdrawal.[2]

Histologically, drug-induced pemphigus resembles sporadic counterparts with positive direct immunofluorescence in most, but not all, patients.[3] As expected, given the different variants of pemphigus that drugs may induce, antibodies against both Dsg1 and Dsg3 have been documented.[4]

References

1. Brenner, S., Bialy-Golan, A., Buocco, V. (1998) Drug-induced pemphigus. *Clin Dermatol*, 16, 393–397.
2. Mutasim, D.F., Pelc, N.J., Anhalt, G.J. (1993) Drug-induced pemphigus. *Dermatol Clin*, 11, 463–471.
3. Landau, M., Brenner, S. (1997) Histopathologic findings in drug-induced pemphigus. *Am J Dermatopathol*, 19, 411–414.
4. Brenner, S., Bialy-Golan, A., Anhalt, G.J. (1997) Recognition of pemphigus antigens in drug-induced pemphigus vulgaris and pemphigus foliaceus. *J Am Acad Dermatol*, 36, 919–923.

Contact pemphigus

Clinical features

There is a growing body of literature documenting contact with topical substances preceding the onset of pemphigus. The pathogenesis is not understood, but in some cases the exposure is thought to somehow trigger or induce pemphigus. The term 'contact pemphigus' has been proposed as a designation for this phenomenon, which has been described in the vulgaris, foliaceus and erythematosus variants.[1] Substances that have been implicated include nickel, pesticides, chromium sulfate, tincture of benzoin, phenol, diclofenac, dihydro-diphenyltrichlorethane, ketoprofen and feprazone.[1–10] Clearly, further study is necessary to elucidate the relationship between exposure to topical agents and contact pemphigus.

Pathogenesis and histological features

Whether this phenomenon relates to systemic absorption, contact allergy or a direct 'toxic' effect on epidermal antigens is as yet unknown. It is interesting to note that in the majority of documented cases, the patient has been exposed to the offending agent for a considerable period of time before the onset of the blistering eruption.[5]

Biopsy of contact pemphigus shows histological features similar to those of p. vulgaris. Immunofluorescent studies show intercellular IgG and sometimes C3.

Differential diagnosis

The main differential diagnosis is with classic pemphigus. Only clinical information will allow distinction of contact pemphigus from other members of the pemphigus family of disorders.

References

1. Vozza, A., Ruocco, V., Brenner, S. et al (1996) Contact pemphigus. *Int J Dermatol*, **35**, 199–201.
2. Lynfield, Y.I., Pertshuk, I.P., Zimmerman, A. (1973) Pemphigus erythematosus, provoked by allergic contact dermatitis. Occurrence many years after thymoma removal. *Arch Dermatol*, **108**, 690–693.
3. Dimitrowa, J., Obreschkowa, E., Tsankov, N. et al (1984) Pemphigus vulgaris, induziert durch ultraviolette strahlen und das pestizid Baytan? *Dtsch Deramtologe*, **32**, 971–976.
4. Ruocco, V., Satriano, R.A., Lombardi, M.L. (1993) Drug-induced pemphigus in a predisposed girl. Presented at the 3rd EADV Congress, Copenhagen, September 30.
5. Brenner, S., Wolf, R., Ruocco, V. (1994) Contact pemphigus: a subgroup of induced pemphigus. *Int J Dermatol*, **33**, 843–845.
6. Matz, H., Bialy-Golan, A., Brenner, S. (1997) Diclofenac: a new trigger of pemphigus vulgaris? *Dermatology*, **195**, 48–49.
7. Stransky, L. (1998) Contact pemphigus vulgaris? *Contact Dermatitis*, **38**, 45.
8. Tsankov, N., Kazandjieva, J., Gantcheva, M. (1998) Contact pemphigus induced by dihydrodiphenyl-trichlorethane. *Eur J Dermatol*, **8**, 442–443.
9. Kanitakis, J., Souillet, A-L., Faure, M. et al (2001) Ketoprofen-induced pemphigus-like dermatosis: localized contact pemphigus? *Acta Derm Venereol*, **81**, 304–305.
10. Goldberg, I., Sasson, O., Brenner, S. (2001) A case of phenol-related contact pemphigus. *Dermatology*, **203**, 355–356.

Acantholytic dermatoses with dyskeratosis

Hailey–Hailey disease

Clinical features

Hailey–Hailey disease (benign familial pemphigus) is a rare, episodic, acantholytic disorder with an autosomal dominant mode of inheritance.[1,2] In only about two-thirds of patients, however, is a family history obtained. There is an equal sex incidence.[2,3]

Lesions usually present in the second to fourth decades and appear particularly at sites of minor trauma or friction, especially flexural, around the neck, and in the axillae and groin (*Fig. 4.33*). However, other sites, such as the genitalia, umbilicus, inframammary regions and scalp, may also be affected. Rarely the disease may be generalized.[4] Nikolsky's sign is sometimes positive.[3] Vesicles and bullae, arising on normal or erythematous skin, are soon replaced by erosions, crusting and scaly plaques sometimes resembling impetigo (*Figs 4.34, 4.35*).[2,5] Healing is accompanied by hyperpigmentation, but scarring is not a feature.[3] Lesions are frequently itchy and malodorous. Sometimes pain is a considerable problem, particularly if fissuring is present.[3] Symptoms often improve with advancing age.[1] Superinfection by *Candida albicans*, herpes virus and *Staphylococcus aureus* are frequent complications.[6]

The development of the lesions is related to mechanical trauma, stress and ultraviolet radiation. Symptoms often improve or even disappear during winter, but tend to worsen in summer.[1,7] Mucosal involvement is unusual. Anogenital disease, however, occasionally presents as multiple 3–5 mm diameter warty papules.[8] This occurs most often in females, particularly blacks, and sometimes may be a presenting feature. In such instances there is overlap with papular acantholytic dyskeratosis of the vulva (see p. 166).[9]

Asymptomatic white longitudinal bands may be present on the fingernails in up to 70% of affected patients.[1] The other nail changes of Darier's disease are absent.

Significant associated conditions have not been documented with the possible exception of a bipolar disorder (see Darier's disease).[10]

Exceptionally, squamous carcinoma has been documented as a complication in patients with Hailey–Hailey disease.[11] It is likely, however, that those arising on the vulva have a human papilloma virus-associated basis.[12,13]

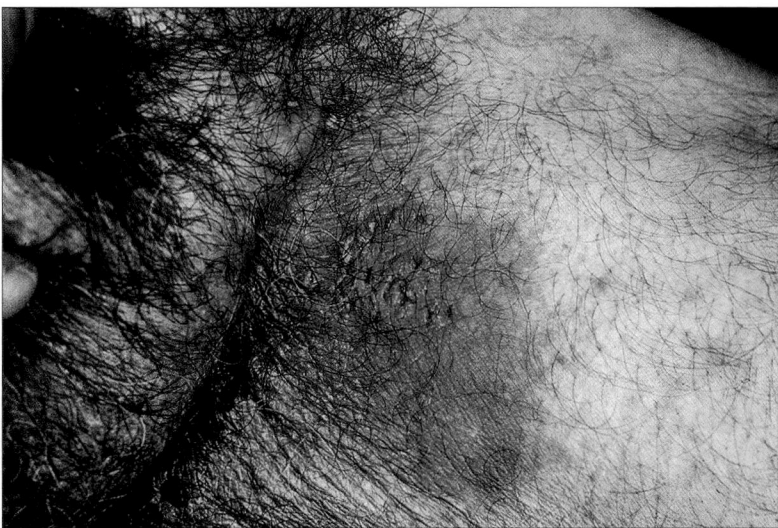

Fig. 4.33
Hailey–Hailey disease: lesions are most often seen in the flexures as a consequence of friction. By courtesy of the Institute of Dermatology, London, UK.

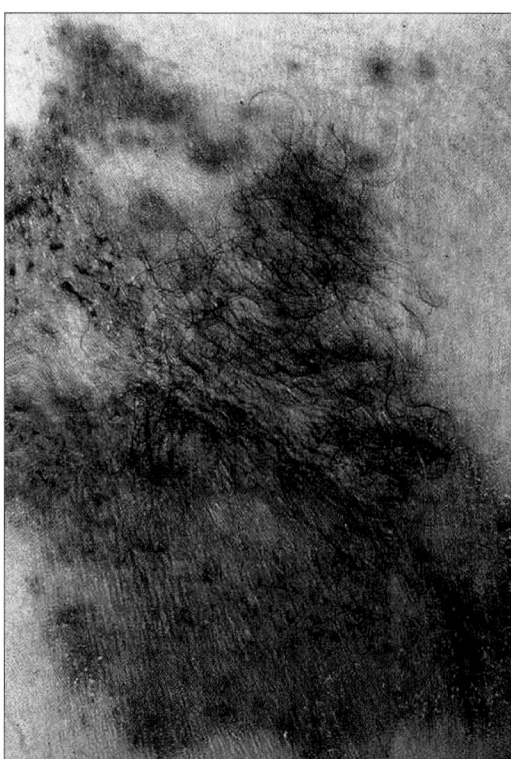

Fig. 4.34
Hailey–Hailey disease: axillary skin showing erythematous eroded and crusted lesions. By courtesy of the Institute of Dermatology, London, UK.

While it has rarely been reported that Darier's disease may coexist with Hailey–Hailey disease, the available evidence supports the contention that these two conditions represent different entities.[14]

Pathogenesis and histological features

Hailey–Hailey disease is primarily an abnormality of cell adhesion. Development of this disease has recently been shown to be caused by multiple mutations in ATP2C1 on chromosome 3q21–24, a gene that encodes for a calcium pump.[15,16] Studies have shown that calcium regulation in cultured keratinocytes is impaired.[15] In addition, there is evidence that integrity of intercellular junctions may be dependent on intracellular calcium stores.[17–20] The precise mechanism by which the abnormality in the calcium pump causes acantholysis is not known. However, the addition of calcium to monolayers of squamous cells in culture elicits stratification.[19] In contrast, cells grown in low calcium medium fail to stratify.[20] It should be noted that Darier's disease, another disorder showing acantholysis, is also associated with a mutation in another calcium pump – ATP2A2. That both of these disorders of acantholysis are associated with mutations in a calcium pump is strong evidence for an important role in maintaining cell–cell cohesion.

Immunocytochemical studies have confirmed that the major desmosomal proteins and glycoproteins are synthesized in Hailey–Hailey disease and distributed along the plasma membranes in uninvolved epidermis.[21] In lesional skin there is marked cytoplasmic labeling for the desmoplakins (DpI, DpII), desmogleins (Dsg2, Dsg3) and the desmocollins.[21–25]

While early lesions show suprabasilar lacunae, established Hailey–Hailey disease is characterized by massive acantholysis associated with suprabasal vesicle or bulla formation.[3] Typically, however, the acantholysis is incomplete, the cell retaining some connections and giving an appearance often likened to a 'dilapidated brick wall' (*Figs 4.36–4.38*). The adnexal epithelium is usually spared. Occasionally, dyskeratotic cells resembling the corps ronds and grains of Darier's disease are seen.

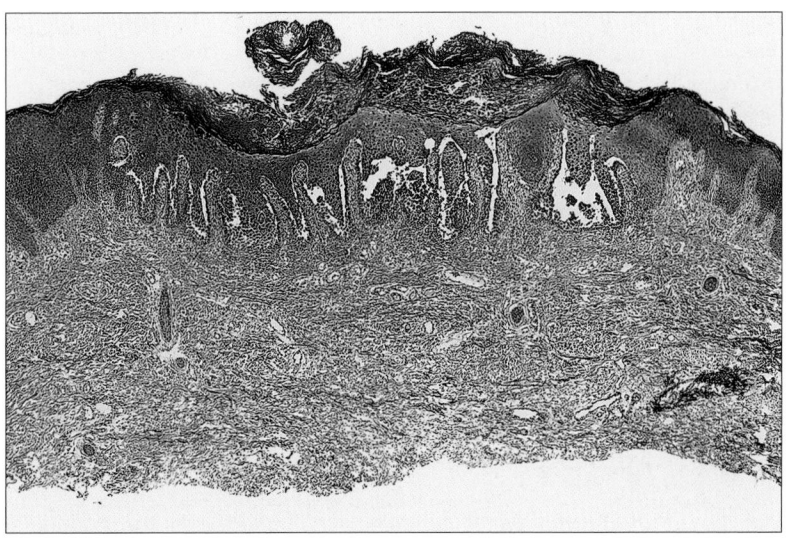

Fig. 4.37
Hailey–Hailey disease: in this example, there is marked hyperkeratosis, parakeratosis and acanthosis. Villi project into the blister cavity.

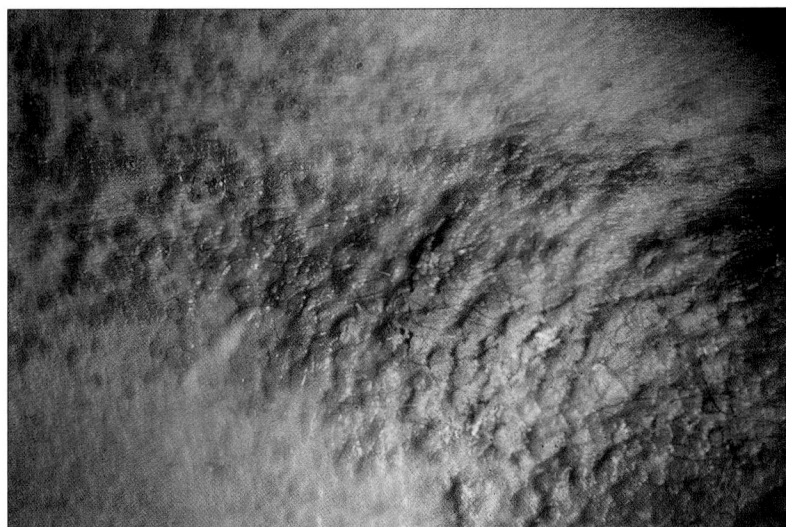

Fig. 4.35
Hailey–Hailey disease: close-up view of keratotic warty lesions. By courtesy of the Institute of Dermatology, London, UK.

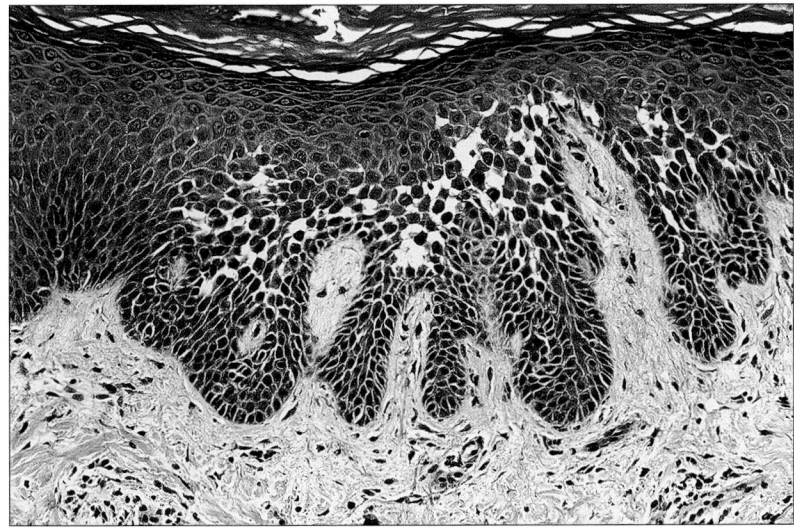

Fig. 4.36
Hailey–Hailey disease: early lesion showing the characteristic 'dilapidated brick wall' appearance.

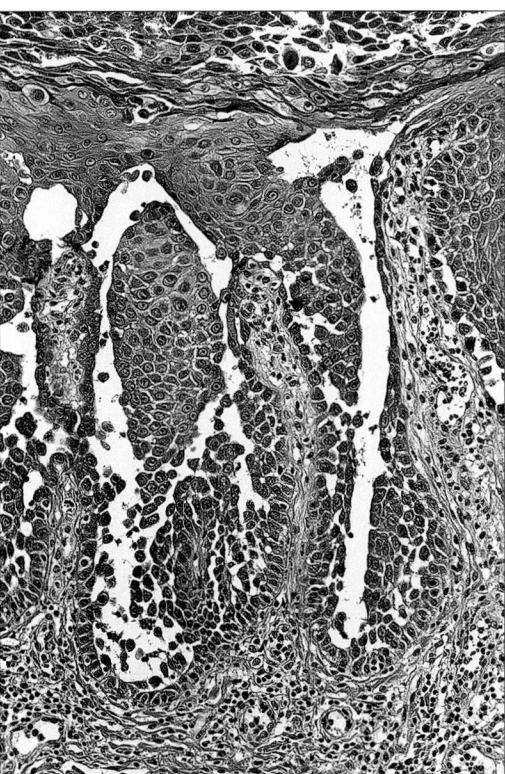

Fig. 4.38
Hailey–Hailey disease: in contrast to Darier's disease, dyskeratosis is usually minimal or even absent.

Ultrastructural studies have primarily disclosed abnormalities of the desmosome–tonofilament units, characterized by diminished numbers of desmosomes and clumped tonofilaments.[26–29] The latter have a linear distribution in the basal keratinocytes, but develop a whorled configuration in the suprabasal layers.[27,29] The cell membranes show microvillus formation.[26] An electron microscopic study of artificially induced early lesions suggests the desmosomal splitting precedes the tonofilament clumping.[28] Dyskeratotic cells are characterized by condensed tonofilaments surrounding pyknotic nuclei.

Differential diagnosis

The histological features of Hailey–Hailey disease must be distinguished from those of Darier's disease, p. vulgaris and Grover's disease. Pemphigus is distinguished from Hailey–Hailey disease by the presence of relatively intact epithelium in the adjacent epidermis (versus disintegrating 'dilapidated brick wall') and involvement of adnexal structures. In difficult cases, positive immunofluorescence staining supports a diagnosis of pemphigus. Darier's disease tends to show prominent suprabasal cleft formation with involvement of adnexae and is associated with numerous corps ronds and grains. These points of distinction are summarized in *Table 4.2*.

Immunofluorescence studies for immunoglobulin and complement are invariably negative, aiding in the distinction from immunobullous disorders. Distinction from acantholytic dermatosis of the genital area can, however, be extremely difficult. In fact, the relationship between these disorders is not well understood. The combination of clinical features of a lesion or lesions localized to the vulvogenital area and a negative family history favors acantholytic dermatosis of the genital area.

References

1. Burge, S.M. (1992) Hailey–Hailey disease: the clinical features, response to treatment and prognosis. *Br J Dermatol*, **126**, 275–282.
2. Palmer, D.D., Perry, H.O. (1962) Benign familial chronic pemphigus. *Arch Dermatol*, **86**, 493–502.
3. Michel, B. (1982) Hailey–Hailey disease. Familial benign chronic pemphigus. *Arch Dermatol*, **118**, 781–783.
4. Marsch, W.C., Stuttgen, G. (1978) Generalized Hailey–Hailey disease. *Br J Dermatol*, **99**, 553–560.
5. Hunt, M.J., Salisbury, E.L., Painter, D.M. et al (1996) Vesiculobullous Hailey–Hailey disease: successful treatment with oral retinoids. *Australas J Dermatol*, **37**, 196–198.
6. Schirren, H., Schirren, C.G., Schlupen, E.M. et al (1995) Exacerbation of Hailey–Hailey disease by infection with herpes simplex virus. Detection with polymerase chain reaction. *Hautarzt*, **46**, 494–497.
7. Saied, N.K., Schwartz, R.A., Hansen, R.C. et al (1981) Atypical familial benign chronic pemphigus. *Cutis*, **27**, 666–669.
8. Denis, J., Ganansia, R., Puy-Montbrun, T. (1994) Rare anorectal pathologic conditions. *Curr Opin Gen Surg*, 103–107.
9. Langenberg, A., Berger, T.G., Cardelli, M. et al (1992) Genital benign chronic pemphigus (Hailey–Hailey disease) presenting as condylomas. *J Am Acad Dermatol*, **26**, 951–955.
10. Wilk, M., Rietschel, M., Korner, J. et al (1994) Pemphigus chronicus benignus familiaris (Hailey–Hailey disease) and bipolar affective disease in 3 members of a family. *Hautarzt*, **45**, 313–317.
11. Holst, V.A., Fair, K.P., Wilson, B.B. et al (2000) Squamous cell carcinoma arising in Hailey–Hailey disease. *J Am Acad Dermatol*, **43**, 368–371.
12. Ochiai, T., Honda, A., Morishima, T. et al (1999) Human papilloma virus types 16 and 39 in a vulval carcinoma occurring in a woman with Hailey–Hailey disease. *Br J Dermatol*, **140**, 509–513.
13. Cockayne, S.E., Rassl, D.M., Thomas, S.E. (2000) Squamous cell carcinoma arising in Hailey–Hailey disease of the vulva. *Br J Dermatol*, **142**, 540–542.
14. Welsh, E.A., Ikeda, S., Peluso, A.M. et al (1994) Hailey–Hailey disease is not allelic to Darier's disease. *J Invest Dermatol*, **102**, 825–826.
15. Sudbrak, R., Brown, J., Dobson-Stone, C. et al (2000) Hailey–Hailey disease is caused by mutations in ATP2C1 encoding a novel Ca2+ pump. *Hum Mol Genet*, **9**, 1131–1140.
16. Hu, K., Bonifas, H.M., Beech, J. et al (2000) Mutations in ATP2C1, encoding a calcium pump, cause Hailey–Hailey disease. *Nat Genet*, **24**, 61–65.
17. Stuart, R.O., Sun, A., Bush, K.T. et al (1996) Dependence of epithelial intercellular junction biogenesis on thapsigargin-sensitive intracellular calcium stores. *J Biol Chem*, **271**, 13636–13641.
18. Hennings, H., Holbrook, K. (1983) Calcium regulation of cell–cell contact and differentiation of epidermal cells in culture. *Exp Cell Res*, **143**, 127–142.
19. Watt, F.M., Mattey, D.L., Garrod, D.R. (1984) Calcium-induced reorganization of desmosomal components in cultured human keratinocytes. *J Cell Biol*, **99**, 2211–2215.
20. de Dobbeleer, G., de Graef, Ch., McPoudi, E. et al (1989) Reproduction of the characteristic morphologic changes of familial benign chronic pemphigus in cultures of lesional keratinocytes onto dead de-epidermized dermis. *J Am Acad Dermatol*, **21**, 961–965.
21. Burge, S.M., Garrod, D.R. (1991) An immunohistological study of desmosomes in Darier's disease and Hailey–Hailey disease. *Br J Dermatol*, **124**, 242–251.
22. Burge, S.M., Cederholm-Williams, S.A., Garrod, D.R. et al (1991) Cell adhesion in Hailey–Hailey disease and Darier's disease: immunocytological and explant-tissue-culture studies. *Br J Dermatol*, **125**, 426–435.
23. Setoyama, M., Hashimoto, K., Tashiro, M. (1991) Immunolocalisation of desmoglein 1 ('band 3' polypeptide) on acantholytic cells in pemphigus vulgaris, Darier's disease and Hailey–Hailey's disease. *J Dermatol*, **18**, 500–505.
24. Setoyama, M., Choi, K.C., Hashimoto, K. et al (1991) Desmoplakin I and II in acantholytic dermatoses: preservation in pemphigus vulgaris and Darier's disease and dissolution in Hailey–Hailey's disease and pemphigus vulgaris. *J Dermatol Sci*, **2**, 9–17.
25. Inohara, S., Tatsumi, Y., Tanaka, Y. et al (1990) Immunohistochemical localization of desmosomal and cytoskeletal proteins in the epidermis of healthy individuals and patients with Hailey–Hailey disease. *Acta Derm Venereol*, **70**, 239–241.
26. Gottlieb, S., Lutzner, M. (1970) Hailey–Hailey disease: an electron microscopic study. *J Invest Dermatol*, **54**, 368–376.
27. Wilgram, G.F., Caulfield, J.B., Lever, W.F. (1962) An electron microscopic study of acantholysis and dyskeratosis in Hailey–Hailey's disease. *J Invest Dermatol*, **39**, 373–381.
28. De Dobbeleer, G., Achten, G. (1979) Disrupted desmosomes in induced lesions of familial benign chronic pemphigus. *J Cutan Pathol*, **6**, 418–424.
29. Piérard, J., Kint, A. (1969) Pemphigus familial bénin chronique (maladie de Hailey–Hailey). *Dermatologica*, **139**, 1–17.

Relapsing linear acantholytic dermatosis

Clinical features

Relapsing linear acantholytic dermatosis (Hailey–Hailey-like epidermal nevus) is an exceptionally rare nevus-like condition, characterized by erythematous plaques with vesicles and erosions arranged in a linear distribution along Blaschko's lines.[1,2] It typically undergoes spontaneous resolution followed by recurrence and has a chronic course. Insufficient cases have been documented to determine its relationship to Hailey–Hailey disease.

Histological features

The features are indistinguishable from Hailey–Hailey disease.

References

1. Vakilzadeh, F., Kolde, G. (1985) Relapsing linear acantholytic dermatosis. *Br J Dermatol*, **112**, 349–355.
2. Duschet, P., Happle, R., Schwartz, T. et al (1995) Relapsing linear acantholytic dermatosis. *J Am Acad Dermatol*, **33**, 920–922.

Darier's disease

Clinical features

Darier's disease (keratosis follicularis, morbus Darier), which is characterized by abnormal keratinocyte adhesion, is a rare hereditary disorder, usually transmitted in an autosomal dominant pattern. In a large series, however, 47% of patients had no clear family history of Darier's disease.[1] Presumably these cases represent new mutations or evidence of incomplete penetrance. Its documented incidence is variable. In Oxfordshire (UK), the incidence is 1:55,000, in the North of England it is 1:36,000, in the west of Scotland it is 1:30,000, whereas in Denmark it is 1:100,000.[2–5] The sex incidence is equal, although males appear to be more severely affected than females. The disease usually presents in the first or second decade (with a peak around puberty) and often follows exposure to ultraviolet light.[1] Exceptionally, patients may not present until their sixth or seventh decade.[6] Darier's disease is a long-term illness. Remissions do not occur although some patients show improvement with increasing age.[6]

The lesions are frequently itchy and less commonly painful.[1,6] They are characterized by greasy, crusted, keratotic yellow–brown papules and plaques found particularly on the 'seborrheic' areas of the body – the scalp, forehead, ears, nasolabial folds, upper chest, back and supraclavicular fossae (*Figs 4.39–4.43*).[1,5] There is mild involvement of the flexures in the majority of patients although sometimes this distribution predominates.[1,6] Lesions may be induced or exacerbated by stress, heat, sweating and maceration.[1,7] In some areas the lesions have a warty appearance, while in the flexures they are often vegetative, malodorous (a particularly distressing problem) and often secondarily infected (*Figs 4.44, 4.45*).[6] Bullous lesions generally following sun exposure can occur, albeit rarely.[8,9] Leukodermic macules in black patients have also been described.[10,11] Additional features including cutaneous horns and hemorrhagic palmar lesions have also been documented.[12–15]

Patients with Darier's disease are susceptible to bacterial (particularly *Staphylococcus aureus*), dermatophyte and viral infections.[1,16,17] There are rare case reports of eczema vaccinatum and eczema herpeticum complicating Darier's disease and a patient who developed localized anogenital cowpox has also been reported.[18–20] Life-threatening Kaposi's varicelliform eruption is a rare but important complication.[21–23] No consistent abnormality of immune function has been found to explain this.[24,25] Recently, however, persistence of intracellular *S. aureus* small-colony variants in a patient with Darier's disease has been shown to be of importance in chronic cutaneous infection and resistance to antibiotic therapy.[26] Whether this mechanism is involved in other patients awaits confirmation.

Other cutaneous manifestations of Darier's disease include unilateral, linear or zosteriform variants, which some regard as acantholytic, dyskeratotic epidermal nevi rather than true Darier's disease (see below).[27] It is more likely that these variants, at least in part, result from genetic mosaicism.[28]

The hands are affected in 96% of patients.[1] Pits and punctate keratoses with focal disruptions of the skin ridges of the palms and soles are characteristic features (*Fig. 4.46*).[1,6,29] Acrokeratosis verruciformis-like lesions are common on the backs of the hands.[1]

Nail changes are a particularly important diagnostic feature.[1,2,6,30] Longitudinal white or red streaks (often both), some of which terminate in a small nick on the free margin, are typical findings (*Figs 4.47, 4.48*).[1] Painful splitting and sublingual hyperkeratoses are additional manifestations.[1] The toenails are affected less often (and less severely) than the fingernails.[1] Subtle hand and nail manifestations may sometimes be a presenting feature.[6]

The mucous membranes of the mouth, pharynx, larynx, esophagus and female genitalia can also be affected.[31] Oral lesions are present in up to 50% of patients and consist of small white papules on the hard palate.[32,33] Large nodular and verrucous plaques are also sometimes

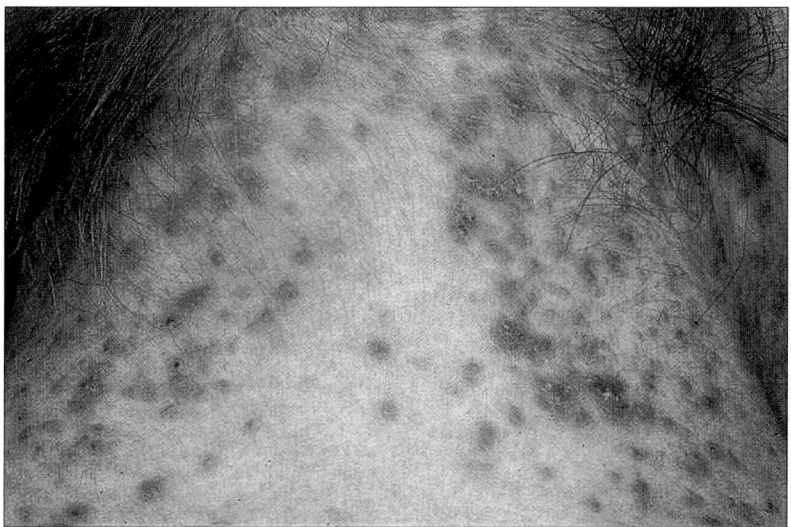

Fig. 4.39
Darier's disease: in this patient keratotic brown papules extend from the back of the neck onto the scalp. By courtesy of the Institute of Dermatology, London, UK.

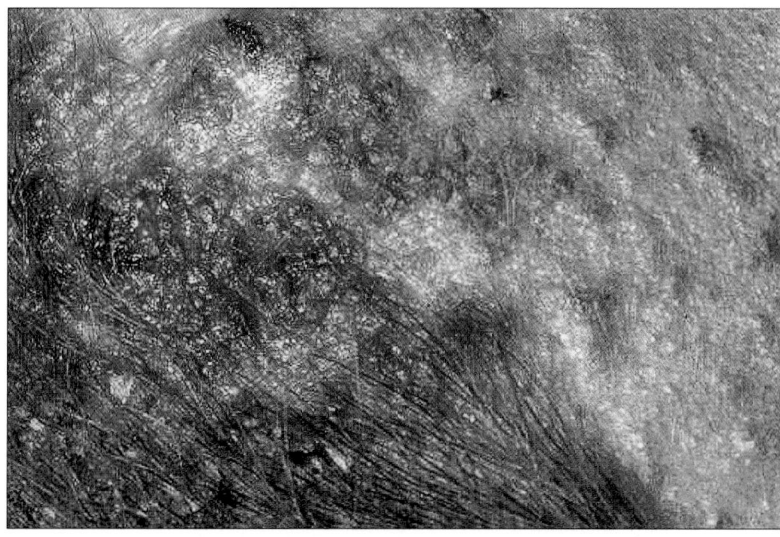

Fig. 4.41
Darier's disease: close-up view showing scaly papules and plaques. By courtesy of the Institute of Dermatology, London, UK.

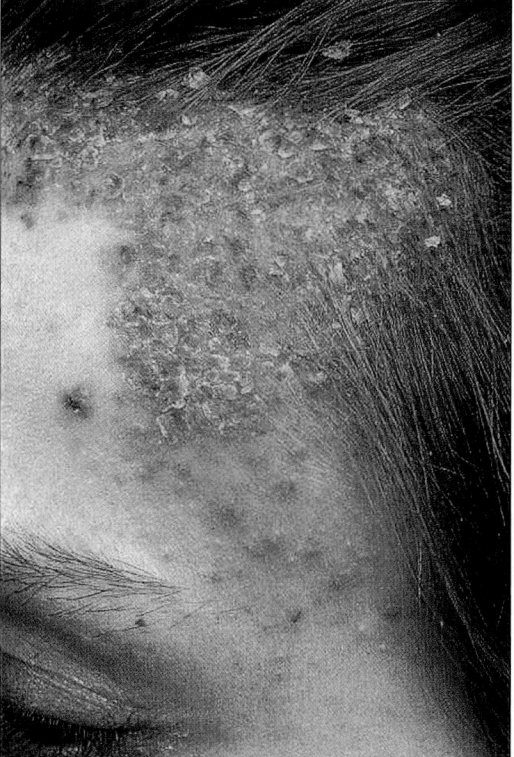

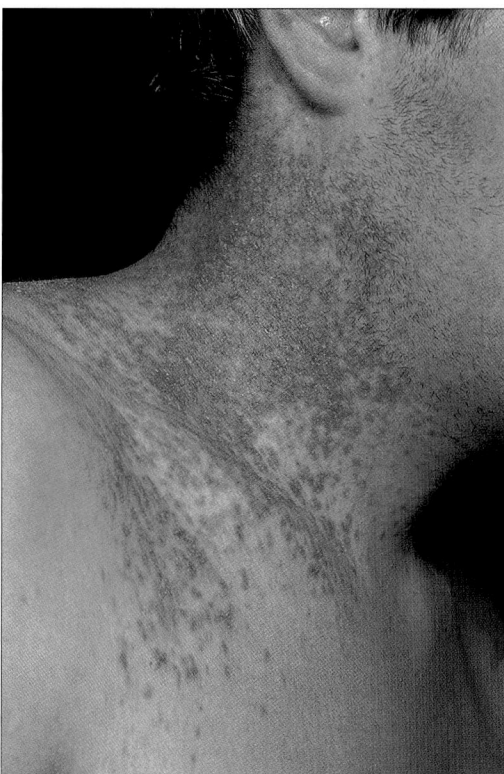

Fig. 4.40
Darier's disease: same patient as *Fig. 4.39* showing typical lesions extending onto the forehead. By courtesy of the Institute of Dermatology, London, UK.

Fig. 4.42
Darier's disease: lesions may be induced by heat, sweating and maceration. By courtesy of the Institute of Dermatology, London, UK.

present and occasionally there are gingival, buccal mucosal and tongue lesions.[12] Involvement of the salivary ducts is said to be uncommon and results in salivary gland swelling with obstruction and sialadenitis.[34,35] Recently, however, one series reported an incidence of 30% involvement of the parotid gland.[32] Anal involvement may present as pruritus ani or less often as vegetating malodorous plaques.[36]

Ocular lesions, particularly affecting the cornea, are seen in up to 76% of patients.[37] Peripheral corneal opacities and central epithelial irregularity are the usual findings. Pannus formation may rarely be present. Lesions are typically asymptomatic.

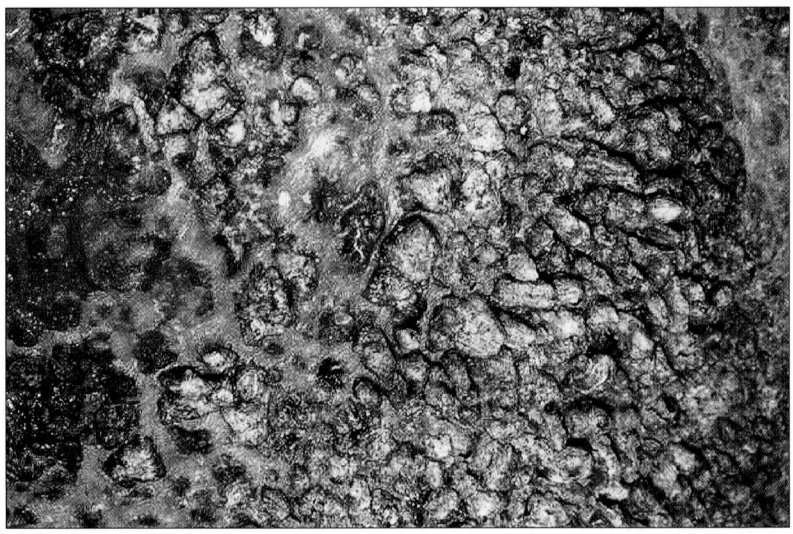

Fig. 4.45
Darier's disease: severe involvement can be very disfiguring and a source of considerable disability and embarrassment. By courtesy of M. Greaves, MD, the Institute of Dermatology, London, UK.

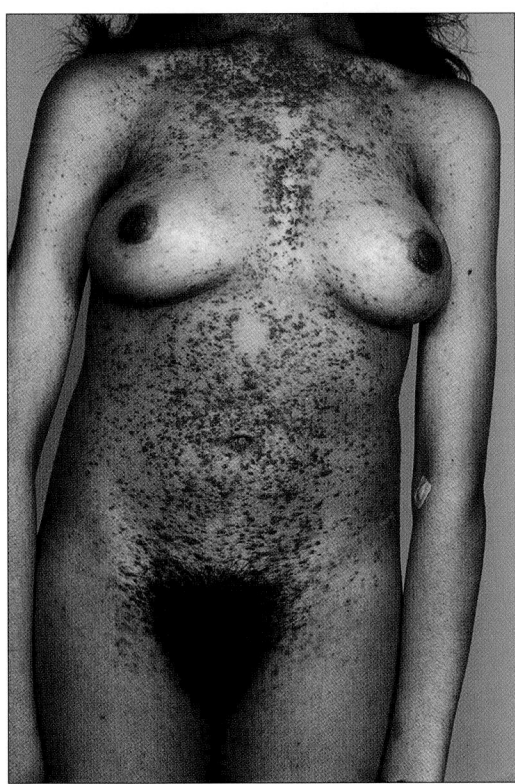

Fig. 4.43
Darier's disease: in this patient, disease is more advanced with lesions involving the chest and abdominal wall with extension into the groins. By courtesy of the Institute of Dermatology, London, UK.

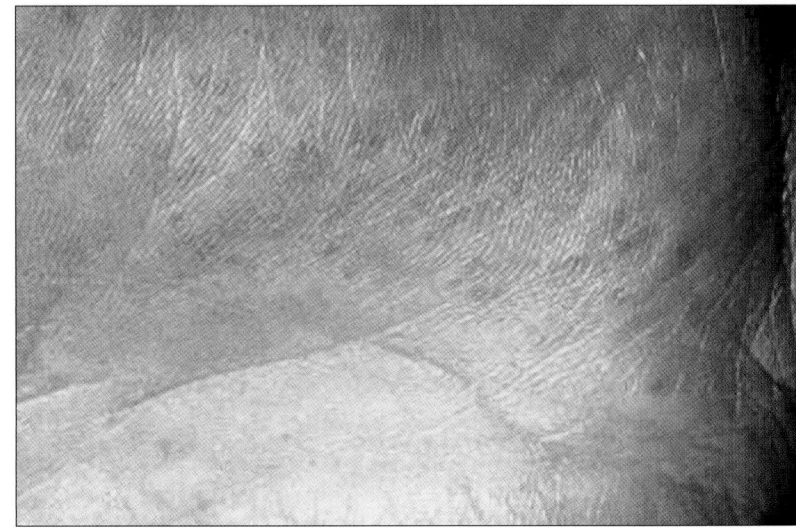

Fig. 4.46
Darier's disease: palmar pits are a helpful diagnostic clue. By courtesy of J. Wilkinson, MD, Wycombe General Hospital, High Wycombe, UK.

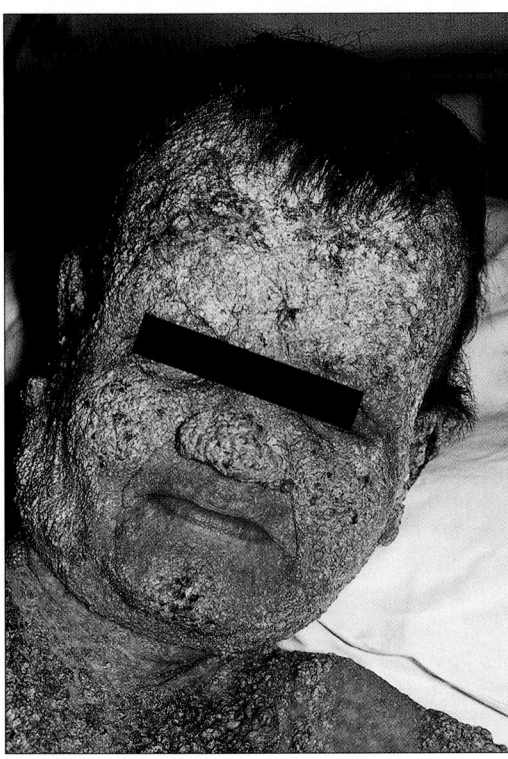

Fig. 4.44
Darier's disease: skin involvement as severe as this is fortunately extremely rare. By courtesy of M. Greaves, MD, the Institute of Dermatology, London, UK.

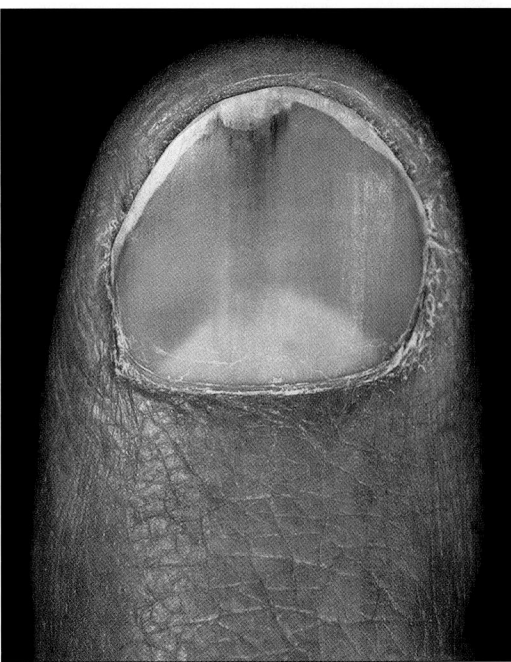

Fig. 4.47
Darier's disease: parallel white and red longitudinal streaks are pathognomonic features. By courtesy of the Institute of Dermatology, London, UK.

Associated systemic abnormalities are unusual, but include epilepsy, pulmonary lesions, bone cysts, low intelligence and small stature.[1] Various neuropsychiatric problems including depression and bipolar disorder have been linked with Darier's disease.[6] There is some evidence to suggest that there is familial cosegregation of bipolar disorder with Darier's disease, at least in a proportion of cases.[38]

Spontaneous remissions in Darier's disease are rare, and in the majority of patients the disease persists throughout life.

Pathogenesis and histological features

Positional cloning studies of different families have all shown the gene of Darier's disease to be located at 12q23–q24.[39,40] Mutations in ATP2A2, a gene that encodes for SERCA2 (a calcium pump of the sarco/endoplasmic reticulum that plays a role in intracellular signaling), cause the disease.[40] Many different mutations within the ATP2A2 gene have been documented to result in the Darier's disease phenotype although the majority is of a missense type.[41,42] It is unclear precisely how such a mutation leads to disease although there is some evidence to suggest that the integrity of intercellular junctions is dependent on the intracellular calcium stores.[43]

No single specific ultrastructural abnormality has been identified in Darier's disease. Changes described have included complete loss of desmosomes in foci of acantholysis with formation of cell membrane microvilli, cytoplasmic vacuolization, cell membrane defects, abnormal tonofilament aggregation, clumping and distribution, premature and abnormal formation of keratohyalin granules and membrane coating (Odland) bodies, and excessive lipid lamellae between the flattened keratinocytes of the stratum corneum.[44–48] Hemidesmosomes and the lamina densa usually appear morphologically normal, although discontinuities of the latter have been described. Ultrastructurally, corps ronds are characterized by large dense keratohyalin masses, numerous membrane coating granules and tonofilament clumps.[44] They are distributed particularly around the nucleus, often surrounding a perinuclear cytoplasmic halo containing distended vesicles. Grains of Darier are composed of nuclear remnants with surrounding dyskeratotic debris.[44]

Acantholysis develops as a consequence of desmosomal breakdown and disassociation of tonofilaments, although which comes first is uncertain.

The histological features of Darier's disease depend upon a variable interplay between acantholysis and abnormal keratinization (dyskeratosis), the acantholysis resulting in suprabasal cleft formation (and rarely vesicles or even blisters), and the dyskeratosis manifesting as corps ronds and grains of Darier.

- Corps ronds are large structures, usually most conspicuous in the granular layer, and consist of an irregular eccentric and sometimes pyknotic nucleus surrounded by a clear halo enclosed within a basophilic or eosinophilic 'shell' (*Fig. 4.49*). Variable amounts of highly irregular keratohyalin granules may also be evident.
- Grains are located within the horny layer and consist of somewhat flattened oval cells with elongated cigar-shaped nuclei and abundant keratohyalin granules (*Fig. 4.50*).

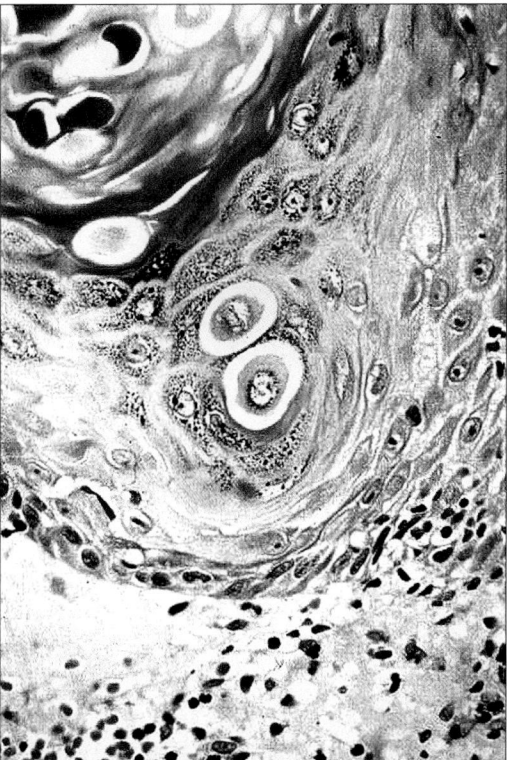

Fig. 4.49
Darier's disease: very early lesion showing two characteristic corps ronds.

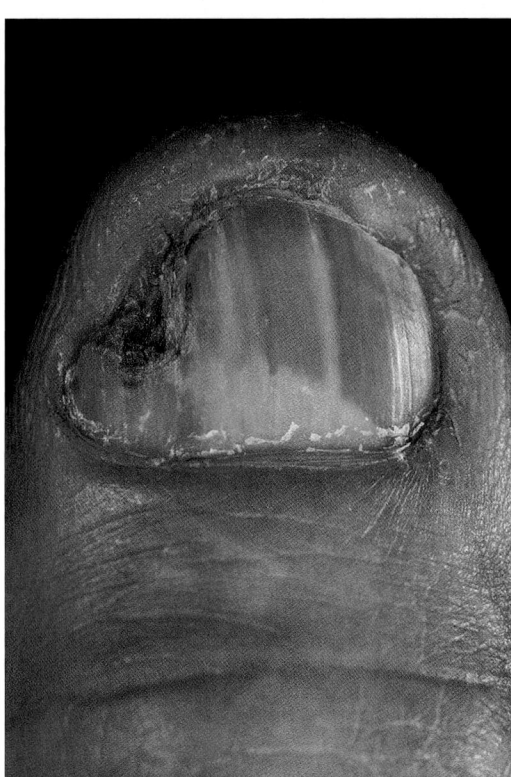

Fig. 4.48
Darier's disease: notches on the free margin of the nail are common findings. By courtesy of the Institute of Dermatology, London, UK.

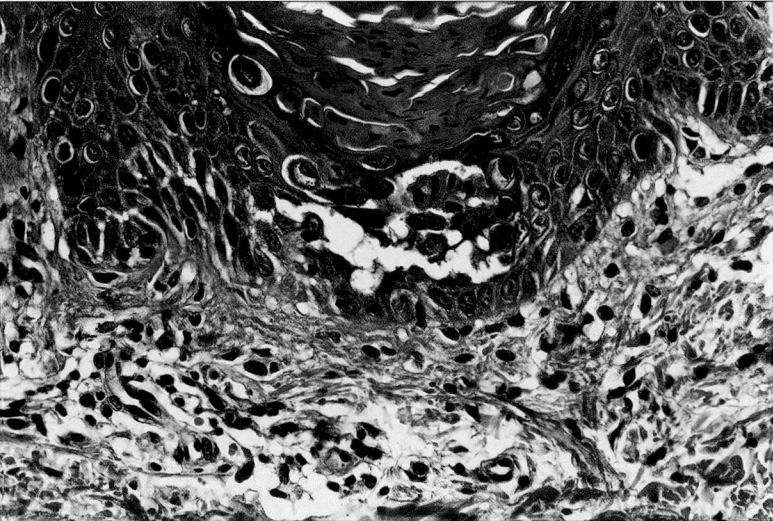

Fig. 4.50
Darier's disease: suprabasal acantholysis with corps ronds and typical grains of Darier in the thickened stratum corneum.

In the fully established lesion there is hyperkeratosis and often parakeratosis, sometimes arranged in a clearly defined tier (*Figs 4.51, 4.52*). The epidermis may appear acanthotic or atrophic and typically shows acantholysis with suprabasal cleft formation in which the underlying dermal papillae, covered by a single layer of epithelium, project into the cavity (villus formation). The roof contains variable numbers of grains and the adjacent epithelium has variable numbers of corps ronds. Occasionally, epithelial proliferation can be marked, resulting in pseudoepitheliomatous hyperplasia. Bullous lesions are illustrated in *Figures 4.53* and *4.54*.

There may be a perivascular chronic inflammatory cell infiltrate in the superficial dermis although this is not a common finding.

The histological features of the oral, pharyngeal, laryngeal and esophageal lesions are similar to those described in the skin although dyskeratosis is said to be less conspicuous.[32] Salivary gland lesions show ductal dilatation and squamous metaplasia of the lining epithelium with acantholysis and dyskeratosis.[34,35]

Corneal lesions are characterized by corneal epithelial edema, subepithelial granular deposits and basement membrane thickening. Acantholysis and dyskeratosis are not seen.[37]

Differential diagnosis

Although warty dyskeratoma, Hailey–Hailey disease and pemphigus are considered in the differential diagnosis with Darier's disease, their distinction is not challenging when clinical information is considered. Warty dyskeratoma is a single umbilicated lesion that typically forms more pronounced papillary structures. Hailey–Hailey disease is characterized by full-thickness epidermal acantholysis and does not show extensive dyskeratosis. Grover's disease may be indistinguishable from Darier's disease in a given biopsy, but the lesions are usually small,

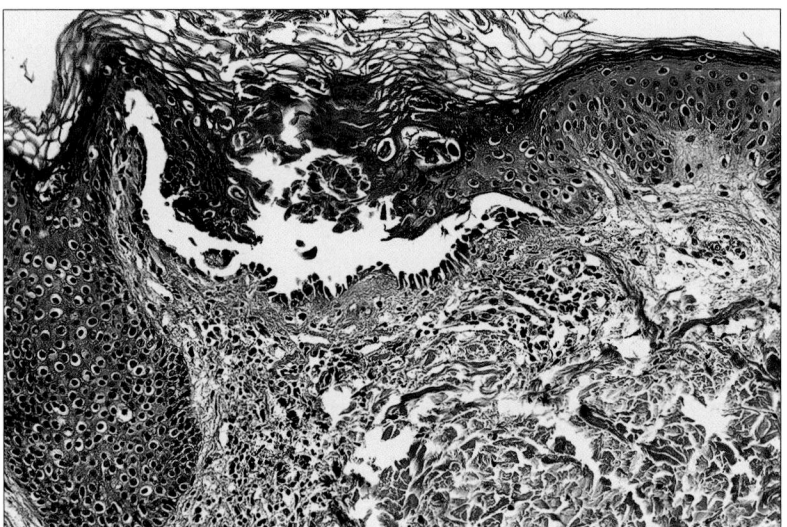

Fig. 4.51
Darier's disease: a well-developed vesicle with suprabasal acantholysis and well-developed corps ronds and grains.

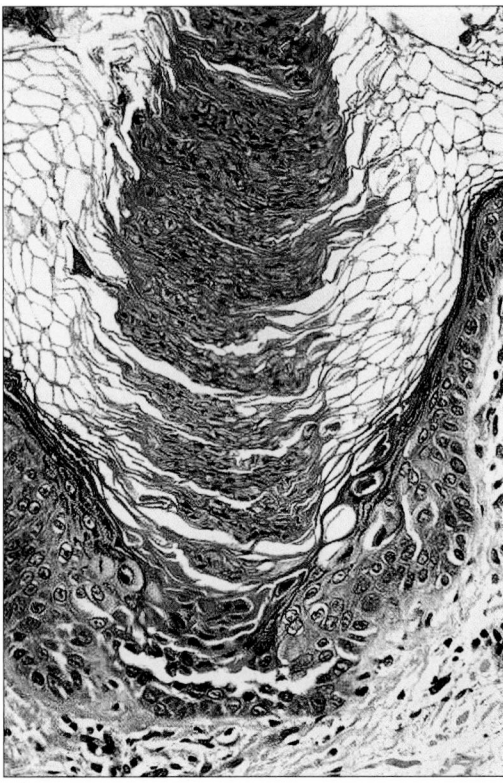

Fig. 4.52
Darier's disease: in this example a vertically orientated parakeratotic tier is present.

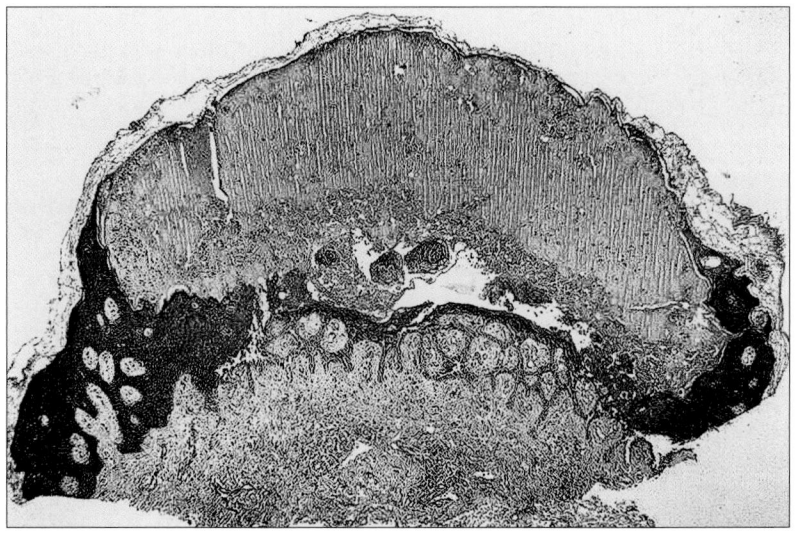

Fig. 4.53
Darier's disease: bullous variant showing suprabasal acantholysis, epidermal regeneration and a subcorneal blister.

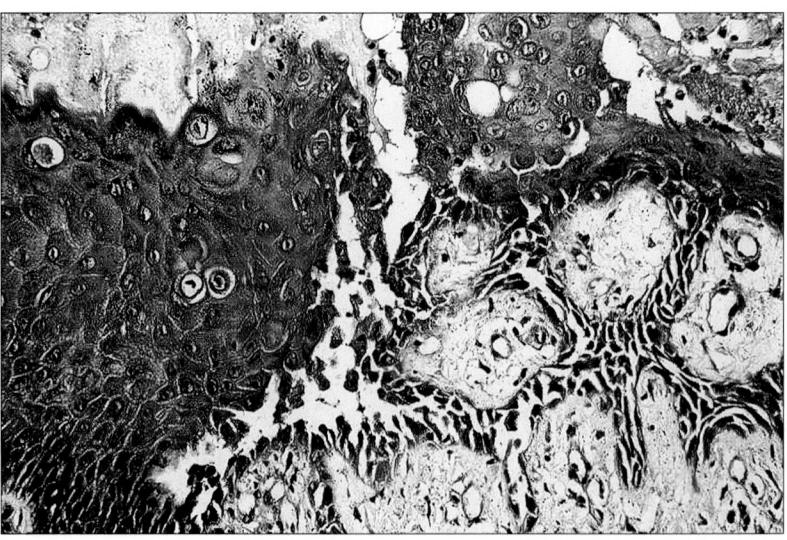

Fig. 4.54
Darier's disease: high power view of *Fig. 4.53* showing multiple corps ronds.

spanning only a few rete. The presence of some combination of spongiosis, and changes mimicking more than one of the acantholytic dermatoses, is characteristic of Grover's disease. In cases that show only Darier-like changes, clinical information should allow for definitive diagnosis.

References

1. Burge, S.M., Wilkinson, J.D. (1992) Darier–White disease: a review of the clinical features in 163 patients. *J Am Acad Dermatol*, 27, 40–50.
2. Wilkinson, J.D., Marsden, R.A., Dawber, R.P.R. (1977) Review of Darier's disease in the Oxford region. *Br J Dermatol*, 15 (Suppl.), 15–16.
3. Munro, C.S. (1992) The phenotype of Darier's disease: penetrance and expressivity in adults and children. *Br J Dermatol*, 127, 126–130.
4. Tavadia, S., Mortimer, E., Munro, C.S. (2002) Genetic epidemiology of Darier's disease: a population study in the west of Scotland. *Br J Dermatol*, 146, 107–109.
5. Svendsen, I.B., Albrectsen, B. (1959) The prevalence of dyskeratosis follicularis (Darier's disease) in Denmark. An investigation of the heredity in 23 families. *Acta Derm Venereol*, 39, 256–259.
6. Burge, S.M. (1994) Darier's disease – the clinical features and pathogenesis. *Clin Exp Dermatol*, 19, 193–205.
7. Burge, S.M., Millard, P.R., Wojnarowska, F. et al (1990) Darier's disease: a focal abnormality of cell adhesion. *J Cutan Pathol*, 17, 160–164.
8. Telfer, N.R., Burge, S.M., Ryan, T.J. (1990) Vesiculo-bullous Darier's disease. *Br J Dermatol*, 122, 831–834.
9. Mei, S., Amato, L., Gallerani, I. et al (2000) A case of vesiculo-bullous Darier's disease associated with bipolar psychiatric disorder. *J Dermatol*, 27, 673–676.
10. Berth-Jones, J., Hutchinson, P.E. (1989) Darier's disease with perifollicular depigmentation. *Br J Dermatol*, 120, 827–830.
11. Rowley, M.J., Nesbitt, L.T., Carrington, P.R. et al (1995) Hypopigmented macules in acantholytic disorders. *Int J Dermatol*, 34, 390–392.
12. Peck, G.L., Kraemer, K.H., Wetzel, B. et al (1976) Cornifying Darier's disease – a unique variant. *Arch Dermatol*, 122, 495–503.
13. Katta, R., Reed, J., Wolf, J.E. (2000) Cornifying Darier's disease. *Int J Dermatol*, 39, 844–845.
14. Peterson, C.M., Lesher, J.L., Sanguenza, O. P. (2001) A unique variant of Darier's disease. *Int J Dermatol*, 40, 278–280.
15. Jorg, B., Erhard, H., Rutten, A. (2000) A hemorrhagic form of dyskeratosis follicularis Darier. *Hautarzt*, 51, 857–861.
16. Tatnall, F.M., Freeman, K., Graham-Brown, R.A.C. et al (1983) Darier's disease: a large family tree with two unusual complications. *Br J Dermatol*, 109 (Suppl. 24), 49.
17. Wheeland, R.G., Donaldson, M.L., Bulmer, G.S. (1985) Localized Darier's disease of the scalp complicated by *Trichophyton tonsurans* infection. *Arch Dermatol*, 121, 905–907.
18. Loeffel, E.D., Meyer, J.S. (1970) Eczema vaccinatum in Darier's disease. *Arch Dermatol*, 102, 451–456.
19. Carney, J.F., Caroline, N.L., Nankervis, G.A. et al (1973) Eczema vaccinatum and eczema herpeticum in Darier disease. *Arch Dermatol*, 107, 613–614.
20. Claudy, A.L., Gaudin, O.G., Granouillet, R. (1982) Pox virus infection in Darier's disease. *Clin Exp Dermatol*, 7, 261–266.
21. Hitselberger, J.F., Burns, R.E. (1961) Darier's disease. Report of a case complicated by Kaposi's varicelliform eruption. *Arch Dermatol*, 83, 425–429.
22. Pantazi, V., Potouridou, I., Katsarou, A. et al (2000) Darier's disease complicated by Kaposi's varicelliform eruption due to herpes simplex virus. *J Eur Acad Dermatol Venereol*, 14, 209–211.
23. Fortuno, Y., Marcoral, J., Kruger, M. et al (2002) Unilateral Darier's disease complicated by Kaposi's varicelliform eruption limited to affected skin. *Br J Dermatol*, 146, 1106.
24. Patrizi, A., Ricci, G., Neri, I. et al (1989) Immunological parameters in Darier's disease. *Dermatologica*, 178, 138–140.
25. Hay, R.J. (1982) Chronic dermatophyte infections: clinical and mycological features. *Br J Dermatol*, 106, 1–7.
26. von Eiff, C., Becker, K., Metze, D. et al (2001) Intracellular persistence of *Staphylococcal aureus* small-colony variants within keratinocytes: a cause for antibiotic treatment failure in a patient with Darier's disease. *Clin Infect Dis*, 32, 1643–1647.
27. Itin, P., Buchner, S., Happle, R. (2000) Segmental manifestation of Darier disease. *Dermatology*, 200, 254–257.
28. Starink, T.H.M., Woerdeman, M.J. (1981). Unilateral systematized keratosis follicularis. A variant of Darier's disease or an epidermal nevus (acantholytic dyskeratotic epidermal nevus)? *Br J Dermatol*, 105, 207–214.
29. Raff, M., Szilvassy, J. (1989) Specific dermatoglyphic patterns: a characteristic manifestation of acantholytic dyskeratotic dermatoses. *J Am Acad Dermatol*, 21, 958–960.
30. Ronchese, F. (1965). The nail in Darier's disease. *Arch Dermatol*, 91, 617–618.
31. Dellon, A.L., Peck, G.L., Chretien, P.B. (1975) Hypopharyngeal and laryngeal involvement with Darier disease. *Arch Dermatol*, 111, 744–746.
32. Weathers, D.R., Driscoll, R.M. (1974) Darier's disease of the oral mucosa: report of five cases. *Oral Surg*, 37, 711–721.
33. MacLeod, R.I., Munro, C.S. (1991) The incidence and distribution of oral lesions in patients with Darier's disease. *Br Dental J*, 171, 133–136.
34. Graham-Brown, R.A.C., Mann, B.S., Downton, D. et al (1983) Darier's disease with salivary gland obstruction. *J R Soc Med*, 76, 609–611.
35. Tegner, E., Jonsson, N. (1990) Darier's disease with involvement of both submandibular glands. *Acta Derm Venereol*, 70, 451–452.
36. Klein, A., Burns, L., Leyden, J.J. (1974) Rectal mucosa involvement in keratosis follicularis. *Arch Dermatol*, 109, 560–561.
37. Blackman, H.J., Rodrigues, M.M., Peck, G.L. (1980) Corneal epithelial lesions in keratosis follicularis (Darier's disease). *J Ophthalmol*, 87, 931–943.
38. Jones, I., Jacobsen, N., Green, E.K. et al (2002) Evidence for familial cosegregation of major affective disorder and genetic markers flanking the gene for Darier's disease. *Mol Psychiatry*, 7, 424–427.
39. Craddock, N., Dawson, E., Burge, S. et al (1993) The gene for Darier's disease map to chromosome 12q23–q24. *Hum Mol Genet*, 2, 1941–1943.
40. Sakuntabhai, A., Ruiz-Perez, V., Carter, S. et al (1999) Mutation in ATP2A2, encoding a Ca2+ pump, cause Darier disease. *Nat Genet*, 21, 271–277.
41. Sakuntabhai, A., Burge, S., Monk, S. et al (1999) Spectrum of novel ATP2A2 mutation in patients with Darier's disease. *Hum Mol Genet*, 8, 1611–1619.
42. Chao, S.C., Yang, M.H., Lee, J.Y. (2002) Mutation analysis of the ATP2A2 gene in Taiwanese patients with Darier's disease. *Br J Dermatol*, 146, 958–963.
43. Stuart, R.O., Sun, A., Bush, K.T. et al (1996) Dependence of epithelial intercellular junction biogenesis on thapsigargin-sensitive intracellular calcium stores. *J Biol Chem*, 271, 13636–13641.
44. Sato, A., Anton-Lamprecht, I., Schnyder, U. (1977) Ultrastructure of dyskeratosis in morbus Darier. *J Cutan Pathol*, 4, 173–184.
45. Lauharanta, J., Niemi, K.M., Lassus, A. (1981). Treatment of Darier's disease with an oral aromatic retinoid (RD–9359). A clinical and light and electron microscopic study. *Acta Derm Venereol*, 61, 535–542.
46. Gottlieb, S., Lutzner, M. (1973) Darier's disease. An electron microscopic study. *Arch Dermatol*, 107, 225–230.
47. Caulfield, J.B., Wilgram, G.F. (1963) An electron microscope study of dyskeratosis and acantholysis in Darier's disease. *J Invest Dermatol*, 41, 57–65.
48. Mann, P.R., Haye, K.R. (1970) An electron microscope study of the acantholytic and dyskeratotic processes in Darier's disease. *Br J Dermatol*, 82, 561–566.

Linear Darier's disease

Clinical features

Linear Darier's disease (acantholytic dyskeratotic epidermal nevus, unilateral Darier's disease, zosteriform Darier's disease, segmental Darier's disease) is a rare acquired condition characterized by the development of grouped, keratotic, sometimes pruritic, yellow–brown papules which affect the trunk, trunk and limbs, limbs, scalp, vulva and face in decreasing order of frequency.[1–7] Their linear distribution corresponds to the lines of Blaschko. Lesions may be aggravated by sunlight, heat and sweating. Although a wide age range may be affected, the majority of patients are in the third or fourth decade. There is an equal sex incidence. There is no family history of Darier's disease. Usually, patients are free from other stigmata of Darier's disease but there are very occasionally reports of patients with linear lesions associated with ipsilateral nail changes and palmar pits typical of Darier's disease.[8,9]

Pathogenesis and histological features

The precise nature of this lesion remains conjectural. Although many authors prefer to regard it as a variant of epidermal nevus with superimposed acantholytic dyskeratosis, there is an alternative school of thought which believes that many, if not all, such lesions represent localized or unilateral Darier's disease, arguing that the condition develops as a consequence of genetic mosaicism. Certainly the late age of onset is unlike a typical epidermal nevus, which usually presents in childhood. The distribution along the lines of Blaschko and the occasional reports of additional Darier-like features on the ipsilateral side of the body offers support to a concept of localized Darier's disease. Recently, ATP2A2 mutations have been identified in lesional tissue but not unaffected skin from two patients with linear acantholytic epidermal nevi, confirming the relationship of these lesions to Darier's disease.[10]

Histologically, these lesions are indistinguishable from Darier's disease.

Differential diagnosis

Very rarely, true epidermal nevus may show histological features of acantholysis and dyskeratosis presenting against a background of a verrucous plaque characterized by marked acanthosis and papillomatosis.[11] Such lesions, which are present at birth, would be best classified as epidermal nevus showing acantholysis and dyskeratosis rather than being included in the spectrum of acantholytic dyskeratotic epidermal nevus.

References

1. O'Malley, M.P., Haake, A., Goldsmith, L. et al (1997) Localized Darier's disease. *Arch Dermatol*, 133, 1134–1138.
2. Starink, T.M., Woerdeman, M.J. (1981) Unilateral systematized keratosis follicularis. A variant of Darier's disease or an epidermal nevus (acantholytic dyskeratotic epidermal nevus)? *Br J Dermatol*, 105, 207–214.
3. van der Wegan-Keijser, M.H., Prevoo, R.L., Bruynzeel, D.P. (1991) Acantholytic dyskeratotic epidermal nevus in a patient with guttate psoriasis on PUVA therapy. *Br J Dermatol*, 124, 603–605.
4. Cottoni, F., Masala, M.V., Cossu, S. (1998) Acantholytic dyskeratotic epidermal nevus localized unilaterally in the cutaneous and genital areas. *Br J Dermatol*, 138, 875–878.
5. Youn, M., Hann, S.K., Moon, T.K. et al (1998) Acantholytic dyskeratotic epidermal nevus induced by ultraviolet B radiation. *J Am Acad Dermatol*, 39, 301–304.
6. Micali, G., Nasca, M.R., de Pasquale, R. (1999) Linear acantholytic dyskeratotic epidermal nevus of the sole. *Pediatr Dermatol*, 16, 166–168.
7. Goldberg, E.I., Lefkovits, A.M., Sapadin, A.N. (2001) Zosteriform Darier's disease versus acantholytic dyskeratotic epidermal nevus. *Mt Sinai J Med*, 68, 339–341.
8. Munro, C.S., Cox, N.H. (1992) An acantholytic dyskeratotic epidermal nevus with other features of Darier's disease on the same side of the body. *Br J Dermatol*, 127, 168–171.
9. Cambiaghi, S., Brusasco, A., Grimalt, R. et al (1995) Acantholytic dyskeratotic epidermal nevus as a mosaic form of Darier's disease. *J Am Acad Dermatol*, 32, 284–286.
10. Sakuntabhai, A., Dhitavat, J., Burge, S. et al (2000) Mosaicism for ATP2A2 causes segmental Darier's disease. *J Invest Dermatol*, 115, 1144–1147.
11. Mazereeuw-Hautier, J., Thibaut, I., Bonafé, J.L. (2002) Acantholytic dyskeratotic epidermal nevus: a rare histopathologic feature. *J Cutan Pathol*, 29, 52–54.

Transient acantholytic dermatosis

Clinical features

Transient acantholytic dermatosis (Grover's disease, persistent acantholytic dermatosis) is a primary acquired, self-limiting, acantholytic disease of unknown etiology, seen predominantly in the middle aged or elderly although there are rare reports of the disorder in children.[1–4] Males are affected more often than females (3:1).[2,3] The white races are predominantly affected. Cases involving blacks are exceptionally rare.[5] Although the disease is usually transient, persistent and recurring variants have also been described (persistent acantholytic dermatosis) in the literature.[6–8]

The skin lesions are usually rather polymorphic, consisting of 1–3 mm erythematous, red–brown or flesh-colored papules, vesicles and eczematous plaques with a predilection for the chest, back and thighs (*Figs 4.55, 4.56*).[2] The palms and soles are unaffected. Superimposed

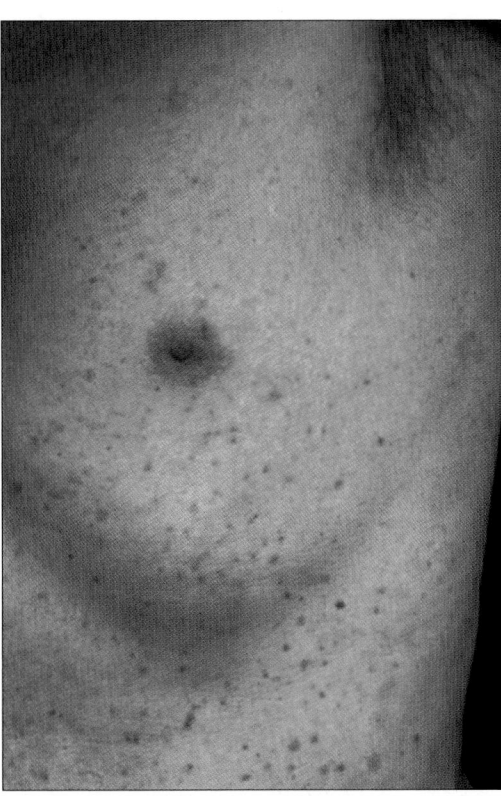

Fig. 4.55
Grover's disease: innumerable erythematous papules are present on the chest wall. By courtesy of the Institute of Dermatology, London, UK.

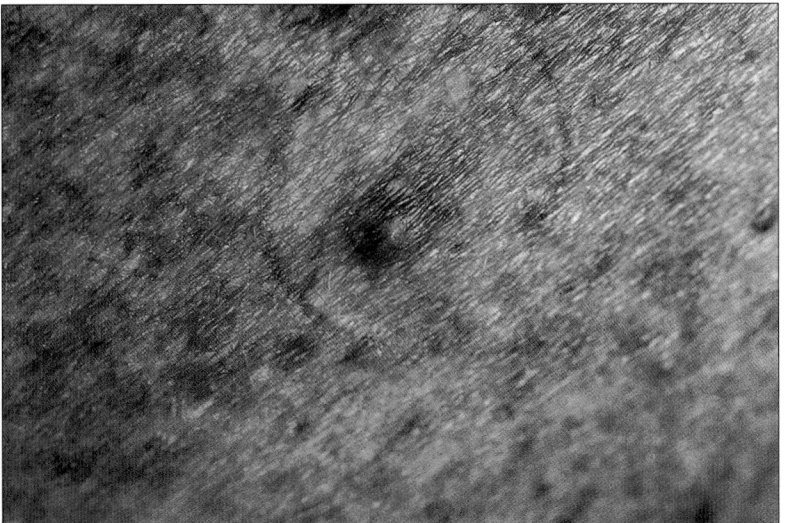

Fig. 4.56
Grover's disease: close-up view. By courtesy of the Institute of Dermatology, London, UK.

excoriations are associated with the intensely pruritic eruption. Pustular, bullous, nummular, follicular herpetiform and zosteriform variants have all been documented.[2,9–12] The mucous membranes, palms and soles are commonly spared although there are rare reports of oral, nasal and laryngeal involvement.[2,13,14] Postinflammatory pigmentary changes following resolution of the acute phase are common. Transient acantholytic dermatosis has been described in association with leukemia and lymphoma in addition to numerous solid tumors including carcinoma of kidney, renal pelvis, bladder and prostate.[2,15–18] In one study, 25% of patients had some form of malignancy.[17] It is likely, however, that the majority of these associations are coincidental. Transient acantholytic dermatosis shows a positive correlation with asteatotic eczema, allergic contact dermatitis and atopic dermatitis.[3,19]

Pathogenesis and histological features

The pathogenesis of Grover's disease is incompletely understood. There are, however, a number of important known etiological factors including:

- sun exposure
- excessive heat and sweating
- ionizing radiation
- adverse reaction to drugs.

Transient acantholytic dermatosis has long been known to be associated with sun exposure.[2,3,20–23] The lesions are photodistributed and the patients commonly give a history of having recently spent time in the sun. There is also a well-established relationship to excessive heat and sweating.[23–26] Bed-ridden, febrile patients are particularly at risk and as a result it has been proposed that the pathogenesis might be analogous to that of miliaria. Occlusion of sweat ducts and increased sweating resulting in acantholysis mediated by high concentrations of sweat urea has been proposed, although this has yet to be proven.[28] More recent immunohistochemistry studies have not generally offered support for this hypothesis although bed-ridden febrile patients may occasionally show prominent involvement of the eccrine duct; this has been termed sudoriferous acrosyringeal acantholytic disease.[17,27,29] Associations with sunlamps, sun parlors, PUVA therapy, steam bath, hot tub, hot water bottle and polyester jogging suits have also been documented.[1,2,17] Despite these well-recognized associations, there must be other important predisposing factors since overexposure to sunlight and excessive sweating are extremely common yet this disease is rare.

Very occasional reports have described transient acantholytic dermatosis developing after radiotherapy for cancer, exceptionally with lesions confined to the area of the port.[2,18,30,31] Only a small number of drugs have been associated (rarely) with the development of transient acantholytic dermatosis.[2] There are reports of lesions following treatment with sulfadoxine-pyrimethamine, 2-chlorodeoxyadenosine, D-penicillamine and recombinant interleukin-4.[32–35] The presence of eosinophils in the dermal inflammatory cell infiltrate raised the possibility of a hypersensitivity reaction.[17] Occasional cases arising in patients with HIV infection have been recorded.[17]

Despite the histological similarity to Darier's and Hailey–Hailey diseases, there is no evidence of a mutation in the ATP2A2 gene.[36]

There have been a variety of both direct and indirect immunofluorescence observations including lupus erythematosus-like, bullous pemphigoid-like and pemphigus-like findings.[17,37] These are reviewed in reference 2. They are the exception rather than the rule and are unlikely to be of any great significance.

Immunohistochemistry observations have included a reduction or absence of desmosomal staining with cytoplasmic redistribution of the proteins, desmoplakins I and II, plakoglobin and desmoglein.[38–40] Redistribution and dissolution of desmosomal attachment plaques have been demonstrated as the first stage in the development of Grover's disease.[40]

Instead of featuring specific histopathological changes, transient acantholytic dermatosis mimics three other diseases: Darier's disease, Hailey–Hailey disease and pemphigus (p. vulgaris and p. foliaceus) (*Figs 4.57–4.60*).[17] The first is by far the most commonly encountered. Thus, in the typical case, there is hyperkeratosis, parakeratosis, acanthosis and acantholysis accompanied by corps ronds formation and grains of Darier. In the Hailey–Hailey pattern, the acantholysis is much more pronounced such that the dilapidated brick wall appearance is seen. Follicular involvement may be present. In the pemphigus-like variant, dyskeratosis is typically absent. Multiple specimens from any one patient may disclose differing histological variants and often superimposed spongiosis is present. Occasional bullae are encountered. A variable dermal mononuclear infiltrate is usual and significant numbers of eosinophils are seen in some cases.[17]

Patients with sudoriferous acrosyringeal acantholytic disease show, in addition to typical features of Grover's disease, acantholysis of the superficial portion of the eccrine duct.

Differential diagnosis

Clinically, transient acantholytic dermatosis is easily differentiated from Darier's disease, Hailey–Hailey disease and pemphigus. However, the biopsy findings often mimic these diseases. A histological clue to the diagnosis is the small size of the lesion. Usually only one or two small discrete lesions that span a few rete ridges are noted. This is in contrast with other acantholytic dermatoses, which tend to involve the entire biopsy. Biopsies from a patient with Grover's disease often show varying features mimicking more than one of the acantholytic dermatoses and occasionally a number of patterns are seen in a single biopsy specimen. Sometimes, a biopsy will show non-specific features of spongiotic dermatitis. The association of both spongiosis and acantholysis may be a useful pointer to the diagnosis of Grover's disease (see also *Table 4.2*).

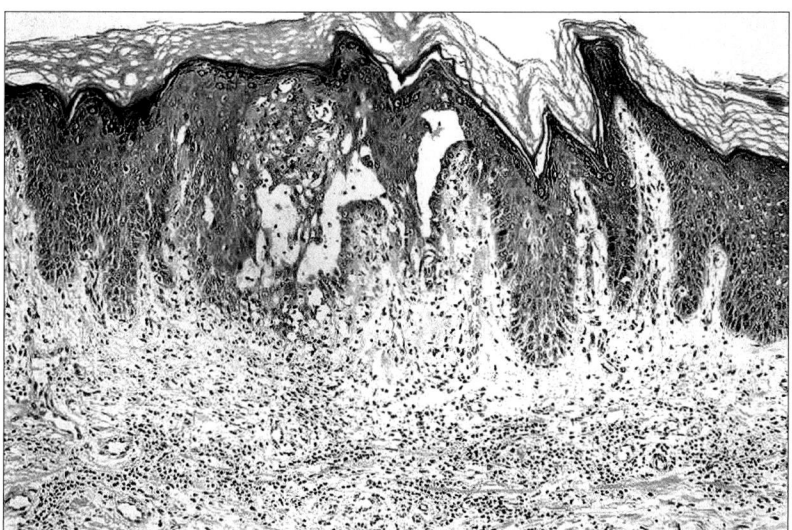

Fig. 4.57
Grover's disease: low power view showing an intact intraepidermal vesicle.

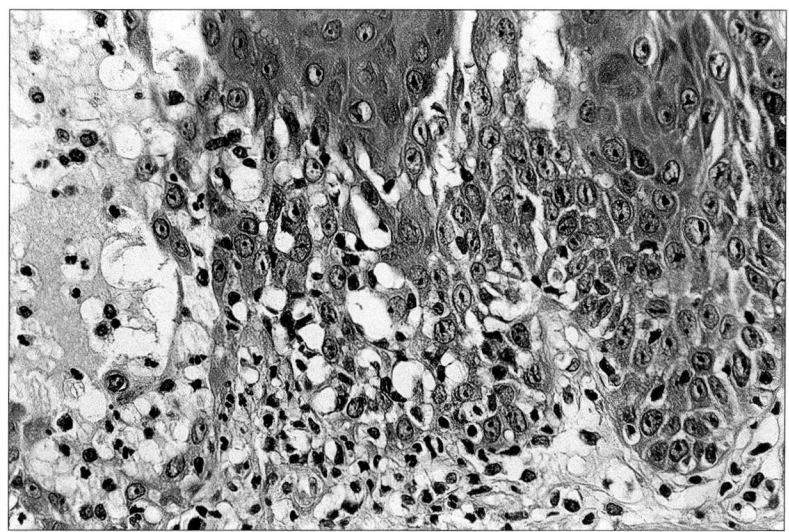

Fig. 4.59
Grover's disease: high power view showing spongiosis and lymphocytic exocytosis.

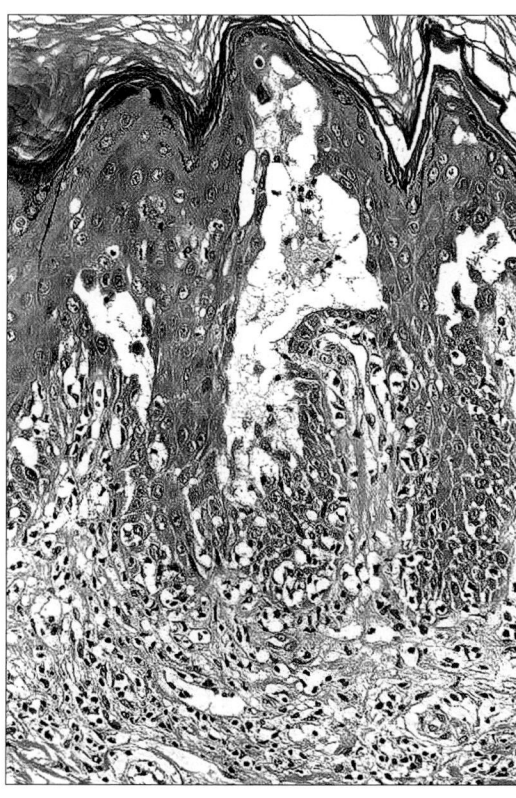

Fig. 4.58
Grover's disease: high power view showing acantholysis.

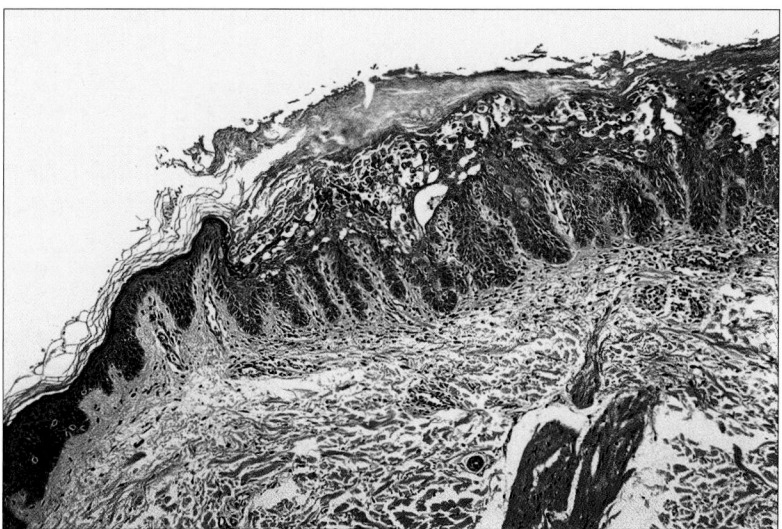

Fig. 4.60
Grover's disease: the features of acantholysis, corps ronds and grains are indistinguishable from Darier's disease.

References

1. Grover, R.W. (1970) Transient acantholytic dermatosis. *Arch Dermatol*, **101**, 426–434.
2. Parsons, J.M. (1996) Transient acantholytic dermatosis (Grover's disease): a global perspective. *J Am Acad Dermatol*, **35**, 653–666.
3. Engst, R. (1980) Transient acantholytic dermatosis and related diseases: a synopsis and case description. *Z Hautkr*, **55**, 748–755.
4. Feinstein, R.P., Einbinder, J.M., Shapiro, L. (1971) Absence of pemphigus-type autoantibodies despite the presence of pemphigus-like histopathology: report of two cases. *Int J Dermatol*, **10**, 115–117.
5. Berger, B.J., Rudolph, R.I., Leyden, J.J. (1974) Transient acantholytic dermatosis. *Arch Dermatol*, **109**, 913.
6. Simon, R., Bloom, D., Ackerman, A.B. (1976) Persistent acantholytic dermatosis: a variant of transient acantholytic dermatosis (Grover's disease). *Arch Dermatol*, **112**, 1429–1431.
7. Fawcett, H.A., Miller, J.A. (1983) Persistent acantholytic dermatosis related to actinic damage. *Br J Dermatol*, **109**, 349–354.
8. Pock, L., Trnka, J., Zlosky, P. (1987) Persistent form of Grover's acantholytic dermatosis. *Cesk Dermatol*, **62**, 259–264.
9. Ujihara, M., Ozaki, M. (1983) Acantholytic dermatosis on both legs. *Dermatologica*, **167**, 145–147.
10. Lisa, W.A., Norins, A.L. (1993) Zosteriform transient acantholytic dermatosis. *J Am Acad Dermatol*, **29**, 797–798.
11. Waisman, M., Stewart, J.J., Walker, A.E. (1976) Bullous transient acantholytic dermatosis. *Arch Dermatol*, **112**, 1440–1441.
12. Lang, I., Lindmaier, A., Honigsmann, H. (1986) The spectrum of transient acantholytic dermatosis. *Hautarzt*, **37**, 485–493.
13. Kanzaki, T., Hashimoto, K. (1978) Transient acantholytic dermatosis with involvement of the oral mucosa. *J Cutan Pathol*, **5**, 23–30.
14. Aloi, F.G., Colonna, S.M., Amasio, M.E. (1985) Grover's disease of the skin and larynx associated with carcinoma of the larynx. *G Ital Dermatol Venereol*, **120**, 407–410.
15. Manteaux, A.M., Rapini, R.P. (1990) Transient acantholytic dermatosis in patients with skin cancer. *Cutis*, **46**, 488–490.
16. Horn, T.D., Groleau, G.E. (1987) Transient acantholytic dermatosis in immunocompromised patients with cancer. *Arch Dermatol*, **123**, 238–240.
17. Davis, M.D.P., Dinneen, A.M., Landa, N. et al (1999) Grover's disease: clinicopathologic review of 72 cases. *Mayo Clin Proc*, **74**, 229–234.
18. Guana, A.L., Cohen, P.R. (1994) Transient acantholytic dermatosis in oncology patients. *J Clin Oncol*, **12**, 1703–1709.
19. Grover, R.W., Rosenblaum, R. (1984) The association of transient acantholytic dermatosis with other skin diseases. *J Am Acad Dermatol*, **11**, 253–256.
20. Chalet, M., Grover, R., Ackerman, A.B. (1977) Transient acantholytic dermatosis: a reevaluation. *Arch Dermatol*, **113**, 431–435.
21. Heenan, P.J., Quirk, C.J. (1980) Transient acantholytic dermatosis. *Br J Dermatol*, **102**, 515–520.
22. Helfman, R.J. (1985) Grover's disease treated with isotretinoin. Report of four cases. *J Am Acad Dermatol*, **12**, 981–984.
23. Heaphy, M.R., Tucker, S.B., Winkelmann, R.K. (1976) Benign papular acantholytic dermatosis. *Arch Dermatol*, **112**, 814–821.
24. Hu, C.H., Michel, B., Farber, E.M. (1985) Transient acantholytic dermatosis (Grover's disease). A skin disorder related to heat and sweating. *Arch Dermatol*, **121**, 1439–1441.
25. Kato, N., Furuya, K. (1991) Two cases of transient acantholytic dermatosis: summary of 20 cases reported in Japan. *Nippon Hifuka Gakkai Zasshi*, **101**, 453–460.
26. French, L.E., Piletta, P-A., Etienne, A. et al (1999) Incidence of transient acantholytic dermatosis (Grover's disease) in a hospital setting. *Dermatology*, **198**, 410–411.
27. Antley, C.M., Carrington, P.R., Mrak, R.E. (1998) Grover's disease (transient acantholytic dermatosis): relationship of acantholysis to acrosyringia. *J Cutan Pathol*, **25**, 545–549.
28. Gretzula, J.C., Penneys, N.S. (1986) Transient acantholytic dermatosis: an immunohistochemical study. *Arch Dermatol*, **122**, 972–973.
29. Hashimoto, K., Moiin, A., Chang, M.W. et al (1996) Sudoriferous acrosyringeal acantholytic disease. A subset of Grover's disease. *J Cutan Pathol*, **23**, 151–164.
30. Held, J.L., Bank, D., Grossman, M.E. (1986) Grover's disease provoked by ionizing radiation. *J Am Acad Dermatol*, **19**, 137–138.
31. Pasolini, G., Lonati, A., Manganoni, A.M. (1992) Grover's like disease associated with radiotherapy. *Eur J Dermatol*, **2**, 91–93.
32. Ott, A. (1987) Persistent acantholytic dermatosis in a patient with increased sensitivity to light. *Z Hautkr*, **62**, 369–378.
33. Mahler, S.J., De Villez, R.L., Pulitzer, D.R. (1993) Transient acantholytic dermatosis induced by recombinant interleukin-4. *J Am Acad Dermatol*, **29**, 206–209.
34. Cohen, P.R., Kurzrock, R. (1998) Transient acantholytic dermatosis after treatment with 2-chlordeoxyadenosine. *Acta Derm Venereol*, **77**, 412–413.
35. Zvulunov, A., Grunwald, M.H., Avinoach, I. et al (1997) Transient acantholytic dermatosis (Grover's disease) in a patient with progressive systemic sclerosis treated with D-penicillamine. *Int J Dermatol*, **36**, 473–478.
36. Powell, J., Sakuntabhai, A., James, S. et al (2000) Grover's disease, despite histological similarity to Darier's disease, does not share an abnormality in the ATP2A2 gene. *Br J Dermatol*, **143**, 658.
37. Bystryn, J.C. (1979) Immunofluorescence studies in transient acantholytic dermatosis. *Am J Dermatopathol*, **1**, 325–327.
38. Machet, M.C., Arbeille, B., Vaillant, L. (1994) Desmosome et maladies acantholytiques. *Ann Dermatol Venereol*, **121**, 581–593.
39. Hashimoto, K., Fujiwara, K., Harada, M. et al (1996) Desmosomal dissolution in Grover's disease, Hailey Hailey's disease and Darier's disease. *J Cutan Pathol*, **22**, 488–501.
40. Hashimoto, K., Fujiwara, K., Harada, M. et al (1995) Junctional proteins of keratinocytes in Grover's disease, Hailey-Hailey's disease, and Darier's disease. *J Dermatol*, **22**, 159–170.

Acantholytic dermatosis of the genitocrural area

Clinical features

In acantholytic dermatosis of the genitocrural area (papular acantholytic dermatosis of the vulvocrural area) focal dyskeratosis and/or acantholysis may present as an isolated phenomenon on the vulvocrural region of young or middle-aged females.[1–6] Lesions sometimes extend on to the thigh and perineum.[5] Patients present with variably pruritic, multiple, 0.1–0.4 mm isolated or groups of white papules, solitary keratotic nodules or less often with erythematous or white plaques measuring up to 1.0 cm in diameter involving the labia majora or inguinal region. More recently, cases with histologically similar findings have been described in males, presenting on the penis, scrotum, thigh, perianal region and in the anal canal.[7,8]

Family history is invariably negative for either Darier's or Hailey–Hailey disease and, by definition, there is no evidence of similar lesions elsewhere on the body.[4] Two cases have developed in the presence of syringomas.[1]

Pathogenesis and histological features

The pathogenesis is unknown although it is likely that the moist environment of the body folds is of importance. Candida infection has accompanied a number of cases although this may have been coincidental.[4,6] Immunofluorescence (when performed) has been negative.[3–5]

The lesions show features of hyperkeratosis, parakeratosis, acanthosis and acantholysis, sometimes with dyskeratosis, resembling Darier's or Hailey–Hailey disease. Warty dyskeratoma-like features associated with follicular involvement may also be encountered.[2,4] Typically, minimal or no inflammation is present.

References

1. King, D.T., Hirose, F.M. (1978) Simultaneous occurrence of familial benign chronic pemphigus (Hailey–Hailey disease) and syringoma on the vulva. *Arch Dermatol*, **114**, 801.
2. Duray, P.H., Merino, M.J., Axiotis, C. (1983) Warty dyskeratoma of the vulva. *Int J Gynecol Pathol*, **2**, 286–293.
3. Chorzelski, T.P., Kudejko, J., Jablonska, S. (1984) Is papular acantholytic dyskeratosis of the vulva a new entity? *Am J Dermatopathol*, **6**, 557–560.
4. Cooper, P.H. (1998) Acantholytic dermatosis localized to the vulvocrural area. *J Cutan Pathol*, **16**, 81–84.
5. Coppola, G., Muscardin, L.M., Piazza, P. (1986) Papular acantholytic dyskeratosis. *Am J Dermatopathol*, **8**, 364.
6. Evron, S., Leviatan, A., Okon, E. (1984) Familial benign chronic pemphigus appearing as leukoplakia of the vulva. *Int J Dermatol*, **23**, 556–557.
7. Wong, T.Y., Mihm, M.C. Jr (1994) Acantholytic dermatosis localized to the genitalia and crural areas of male patients: a report of three cases. *J Cutan Pathol*, **21**, 27–32.
8. Warkel, R.L., Jager, R.M. (1986) Focal acantholytic dyskeratosis of the anal canal. *Am J Dermatopathol*, **8**, 362–363.

Warty dyskeratoma

Clinical features

Warty dyskeratoma is a peculiar hyperkeratotic, umbilicated, persistent nodule that usually presents on the sun-exposed skin of the head and neck of middle-aged adults, although lesions on the trunk and extremities have occasionally been documented (*Fig. 4.61*).[1,2] Most cases

Fig. 4.61
Warty dyskeratoma: scaly nodule on the scalp, a commonly affected site. By courtesy of the Institute of Dermatology, London, UK.

are solitary, but occasional patients with multiple tumors have been reported, particularly in Japanese patients.[3–5] Lesions are commonly asymptomatic but occasionally discharge and bleeding may be encountered.[2] Males are affected more often than females (2.5:1).[2] Although the cutaneous lesions are believed to be of follicular derivation, histologically similar nodules have been described affecting the oral and vulval mucosa.[6–9] The former occur most often on keratinized mucosa of the palate, alveolar ridge and gingiva.[7] Subungual warty dyskeratoma-like lesions have also been documented.[10]

Pathogenesis and histological features

The etiology of warty dyskeratoma is unknown although in the past, authors have suggested an effect of actinic radiation or possibly a viral infection. Neither of these has been substantiated. There is no relationship with Darier's disease. Multiple lesions have been associated with chronic renal disease.[3,4] Warty dyskeratoma is most probably of follicular derivation. Thus, many examples appear in continuity with a dilated hair follicle and, less frequently, a sebaceous gland may be evident.[4] The recent observation of positive staining with antibodies directed towards cortex and inner root sheath provides additional support. Mucosal and subungual variants must have a different derivation.

Histologically, warty dyskeratoma is composed of a widely dilated cystic lesion containing keratinous debris and often associated with a hair follicle (*Fig. 4.62*). Superficially, the keratinous debris contains conspicuous corps ronds and grains of Darier. The adjacent and deeper epithelium shows marked acantholysis and suprabasal villi are a prominent feature (*Figs 4.63, 4.64*). The underlying dermis is often infiltrated by lymphocytes and histiocytes, and sometimes plasma cells are evident.

Oral lesions can be morphologically indistinguishable although a number of cases more likely represent focal acantholytic dyskeratosis arising in a background of a benign trauma-related keratosis. A single case report has documented verruciform xanthoma-like features within a typical oral lesion.[11]

Differential diagnosis

Although there are histological similarities with familial dyskeratotic comedones, Darier's disease, Hailey–Hailey disease and Grover's disease, deeply penetrating crateriform lesions with villus formation are not associated with these entities. In addition, the clinical findings of a solitary umbilicated nodule should not be confused with any of the above disorders with the possible exception of familial dyskeratotic comedones, however; villi are not conspicuous in the latter. There is also considerable overlap with both focal acantholytic dyskeratosis and acantholytic acanthoma; however, in neither of these conditions is there a deeply penetrating crateriform lesion.

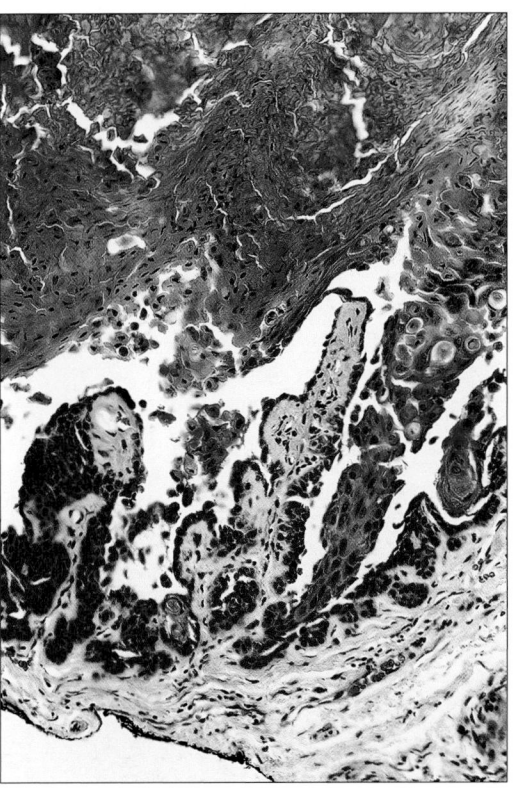

Fig. 4.63
Warty dyskeratoma: note the acantholysis and villi.

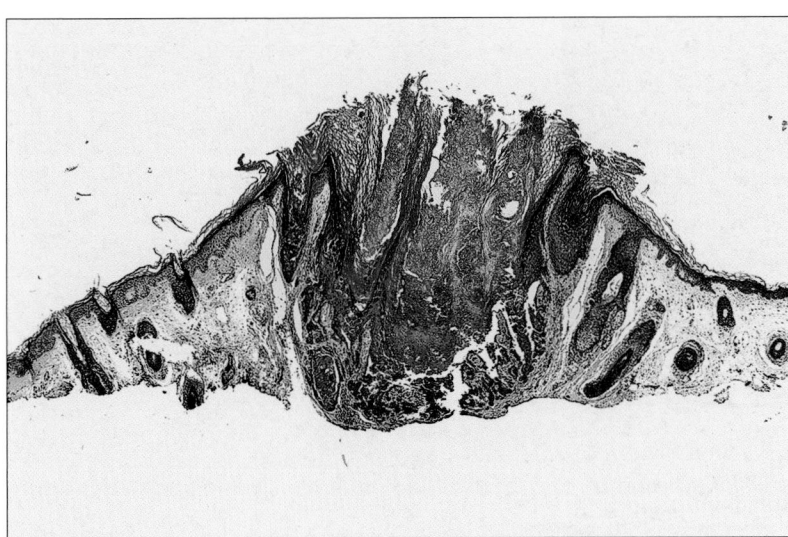

Fig. 4.62
Warty dyskeratoma: typical scanning view of a cystic nodule with acantholysis.

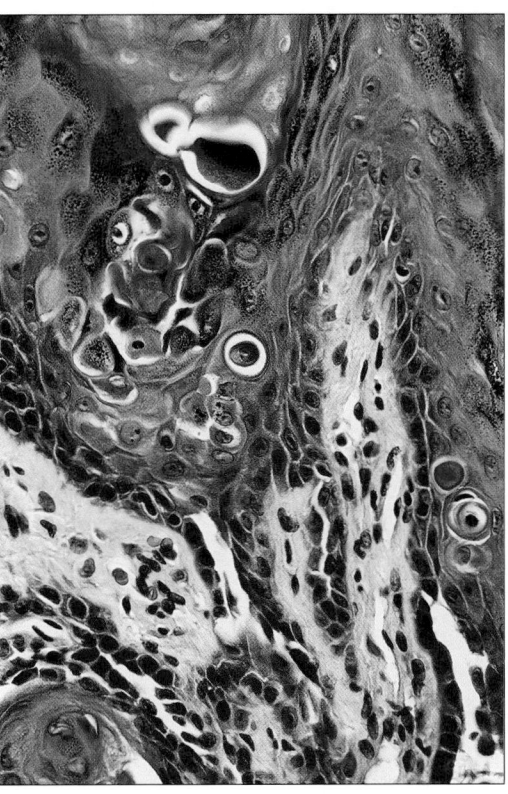

Fig. 4.64
Warty dyskeratoma: corps ronds are conspicuous.

References

1. Szymanski, F.J. (1957) Warty dyskeratoma. *Arch Dermatol*, 75, 567–572.
2. Tanay, A., Mehregan, A.H. (1969) Warty dyskeratoma. *Dermatologica*, 138, 155–164.
3. Shirai, Y., Shirai, K., Oguchui, M. (1987) Multiple warty dyskeratoma. *Rinsho Hifuka*, 41, 615–619.
4. Azuma, Y., Matsukawa, A. (1993) Warty dyskeratoma with multiple lesions. *J Dermatol*, 20, 374–377.
5. Griffiths, T.W., Hashimoto, K., Sharata, H.H. et al (1997) Multiple warty dyskeratomas of the scalp. *Clin Exp Dermatol*, 22, 189–191.
6. Harrist, T.J., Murphy, G.F., Mihm, M.C. (1980) Oral warty dyskeratoma. *Arch Dermatol*, 116, 929–931.
7. Laskaris, G., Sklavounou, A. (1985) Warty dyskeratomas of the oral mucosa. *Br J Oral Maxillofac Surg*, 23, 371–375.
8. Chau, M.N., Radden, B.G. (1984) Oral warty dyskeratomas. *J Oral Pathol*, 13, 546–556.
9. Duray, P.H., Merino, M.J., Axiotis, C. (1983) Warty dyskeratoma of the vulva. *Int J Gynecol Pathol*, 2, 286–293.
10. Baran, R., Perrin, C. (1997) Focal subungual warty dyskeratoma. *Dermatology*, 195, 278–280.
11. Neville, B.W., Coleman, P.J., Richardson, M.S. (1996) Verruciform xanthoma associated with an intraoral warty dyskeratoma. *Oral Surg Oral Med Oral Pathol Oral Radiol Endod*, 81, 3–4.

Familial dyskeratotic comedones

Clinical features

Although thought to be not uncommon, familial dyskeratotic comedones have been extremely rarely documented in the literature. To date only five families have been reported in the English medical literature.[1–5] The condition is characterized by an autosomal dominant mode of inheritance. Lesions develop in childhood or adolescence and are permanent.[5] Patients present with 1–3 mm diameter papules containing small hard keratotic plugs, which on removal leave crateriform lesions resembling comedones (*Fig. 4.65*). Cutaneous horns may also sometimes be apparent (*Fig. 4.66*).[2] Lesions are often generalized but show a predilection for the extremities, particularly the forearms and thighs. The face, scalp, palms, soles and mucous membranes are typically unaffected. Some patients complain of pruritus or inflammation. There is no evidence of ectodermal dysplasia and systemic lesions are absent.

Histological features

The lesions are characterized by a follicle-like crateriform cystic cavity containing laminated hyperkeratotic and parakeratotic debris and lined by squamous epithelium showing dyskeratosis and sometimes acantholysis at the base (*Figs 4.67, 4.68*).[4] Grains of Darier are typically

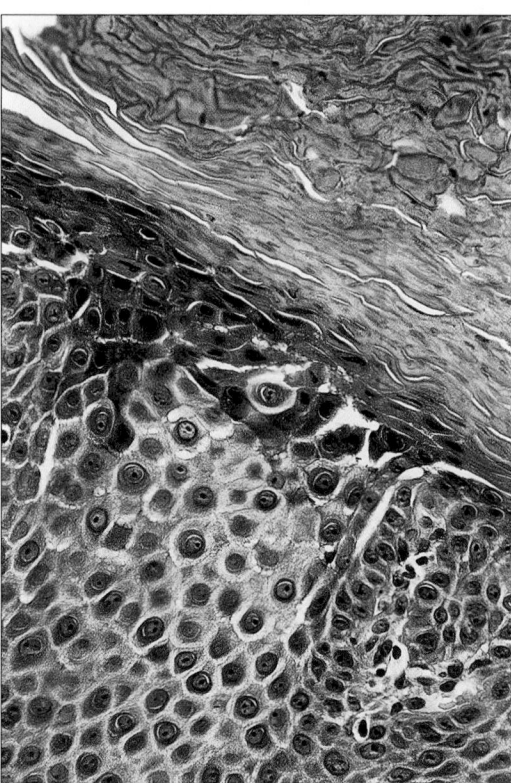

Fig. 4.68
Familial dyskeratotic comedones: note the superficial dyskeratosis. By courtesy of B.J. Leppard, MD, Royal South Hants Hospital, UK.

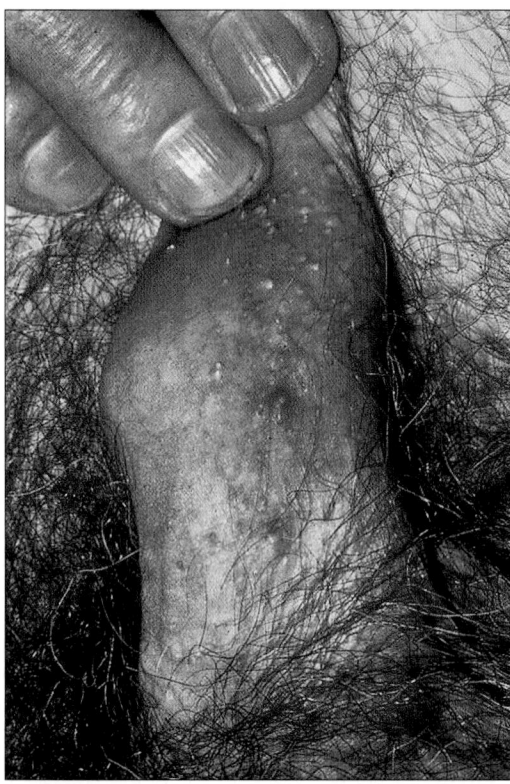

Fig. 4.65
Familial dyskeratotic comedones: numerous comedones are present on the penis and foreskin. By courtesy of B.J. Leppard, MD, Royal South Hants Hospital, UK.

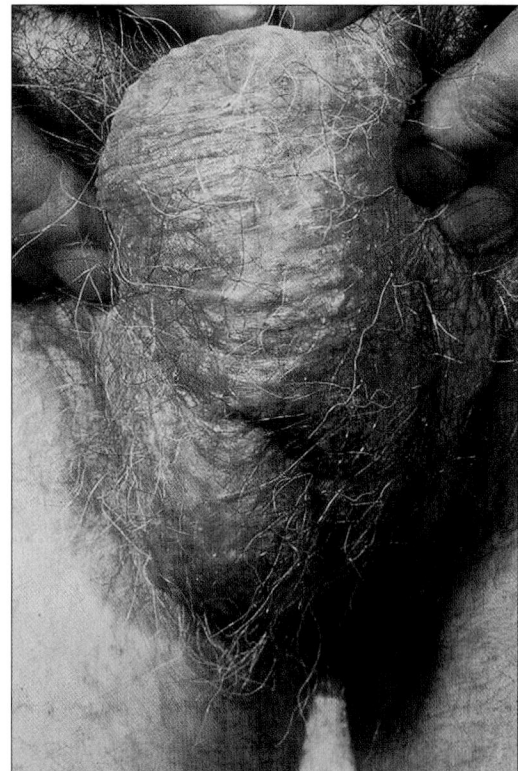

Fig. 4.66
Familial dyskeratotic comedones: a small cutaneous horn is seen arising on the scrotum. By courtesy of B.J. Leppard, MD, Royal South Hants Hospital, UK.

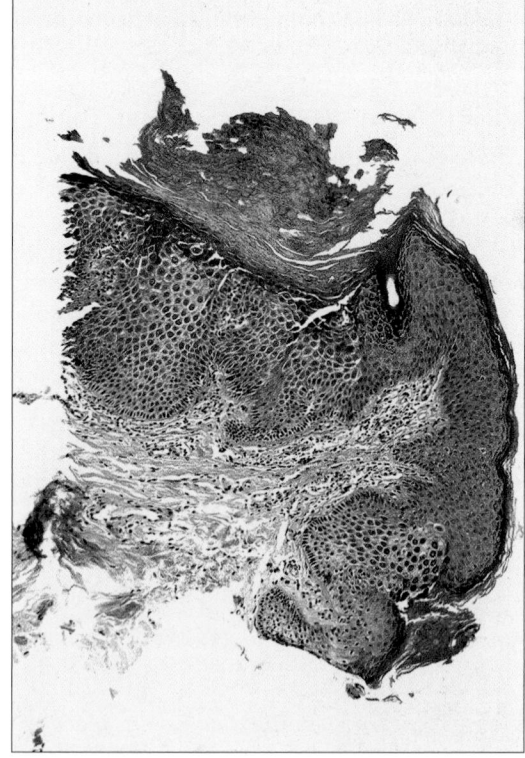

Fig. 4.67
Familial dyskeratotic comedones: this section comes from the edge of a lesion. Note the dell with associated hyperkeratosis and parakeratosis. The acanthosis is in part due to the oblique angle of the cut. By courtesy of B.J. Leppard, MD, Royal South Hants Hospital, UK.

present but corps ronds are sparse and poorly developed. Villi, as seen in Darier's disease, are not a feature. Hair shafts and sebaceous glands are absent.

Differential diagnosis

The consistent folliculocentric nature of the eruption and absence of nail and oral mucosal changes help to distinguish familial dyskeratotic comedones from Darier's disease. Corps ronds, a characteristic finding in Darier's disease, are usually not prominent in familial dyskeratotic comedones. Villus formation and well-developed corps ronds within a solitary lesion distinguish warty dyskeratoma.

Diffuse familial comedones differ by the absence of dyskeratosis.[6,7] Familial dyskeratotic comedones may also be mistaken for Kyrle's and Flegel's diseases:

- *Kyrle's disease* typically presents on the extensor aspect of the lower extremities and presents in adulthood. There is no familial incidence. Histologically, it is characterized by transepidermal elimination of parakeratotic and inflammatory debris. There is no dyskeratosis (see p. 325).
- *Flegel's disease* typically presents in older adults and is characterized by epidermal atrophy, interface change and dyskeratosis. A keratin-filled crateriform lesion is absent (see p. 48).

Perforating folliculitis presents in adults and shows a predilection for the extremities. It is characterized by a crateriform lesion containing a distorted and often curled-up hair shaft (see p. 331).

References

1. Carneiro, S.J.C., Dickson, J.E., Knox, J.M. (1972) Familial dyskeratotic comedones. *Arch Dermatol*, **105**, 249–251.
2. Leppard, B.J. (1982) Familial dyskeratotic comedones. *Clin Exp Dermatol*, **7**, 329–332.
3. Price, M., Russell Jones, R. (1985) Familial dyskeratotic comedones. *Clin Exp Dermatol*, **10**, 147–153.
4. Hall, J.R., Holder, W., Knox, J.M. et al (1987) Familial dyskeratotic comedones. A report of 3 cases and review of the literature. *J Am Acad Dermatol*, **17**, 808–814.
5. Van Geel, N.A.C., Kockaert, M., Neumann, H.A.M. (1999) Familial dyskeratotic comedones. *Br J Dermatol*, **140**, 956–959.
6. Rodin, H.H., Blankenship, M.L., Bernstein, G. (1967) Diffuse familial comedones. *Arch Dermatol*, **96**, 145–146.
7. Cantú, J.M., Gomez-Bustamente, M.O., González-Mendoza, A. et al (1978) Familial comedones. Evidence for autosomal dominant inheritance. *Arch Dermatol*, **114**, 1807–1809.

Acantholytic acanthoma

Clinical features

Acantholytic acanthoma is common entity consisting of a solitary, usually asymptomatic keratotic papule or plaque, 0.5–1.5 cm in diameter, often with overlying scale-crust. It usually presents on the trunk, arm or neck and is clinically thought to be a seborrheic keratosis or actinic keratosis.[1–5] Very occasionally multiple lesions have been described.[6] Some patients report pruritus. Patients are usually elderly (median age 60 years) and there is a predilection for males (2:1).[2,4] Lesions are not seen about the head, palms and soles and the mucous membranes appear to be spared.[2]

Pathogenesis and histological features

The pathogenesis of this lesion is unknown. Although one case has been documented in association with immunosupression, it is likely that this was coincidental.[6]

Diagnosis is one of exclusion and depends upon the solitary nature of the lesion. The histological features are those of hyperkeratosis, acanthosis and papillomatosis accompanied by acantholysis affecting all or any layer of the epidermis (*Figs 4.69, 4.70*).[1] Dyskeratosis may be evident. A perivascular lymphohistiocytic chronic inflammatory cell infiltrate, sometimes with occasional eosinophils, may be present in the superficial dermis.

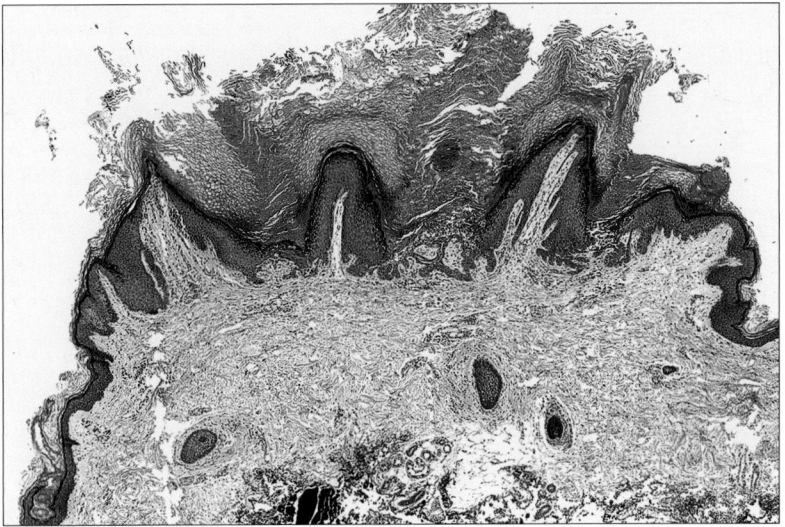

Fig. 4.69
Acantholytic acanthoma: scanning view showing hyperkeratosis, papillomatosis and multiple foci of acantholysis.

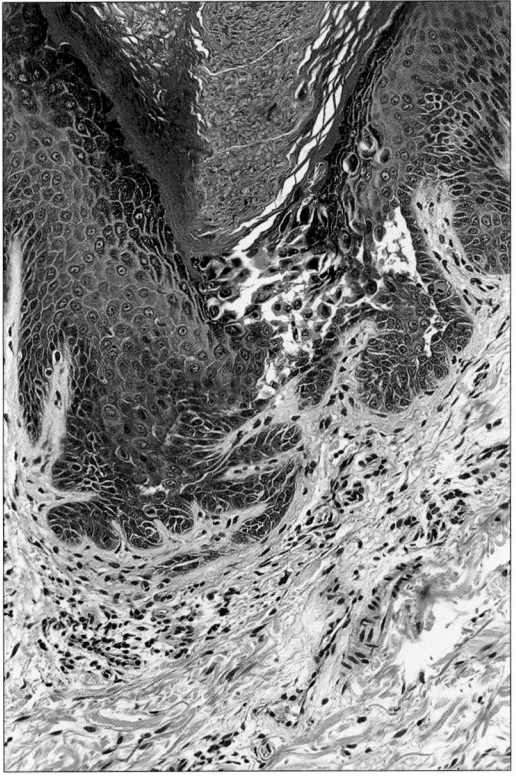

Fig. 4.70
Acantholytic acanthoma: high power view showing acantholysis, corps ronds and grains of Darier.

Differential diagnosis

In acantholytic seborrheic keratosis the acantholysis is typically focal and the lesion elsewhere shows the typical features of horn cysts and squamous eddies (see p. ●●●●).[7] Darier's disease, acantholytic dermatosis of the genitocrural area, warty dyskeratoma and pemphigus, Hailey–Hailey disease and Grover's disease may show similar histological features but are easily distinguished clinically. Acantholytic actinic keratosis also shows dysplasia in addition to acantholysis.

References

1. Brownstein, M.H. (1985) The benign acanthomas. *J Cutan Pathol*, **12**, 172–188.
2. Brownstein, M.H. (1988) Acantholytic acanthoma. *J Am Acad Dermatol*, **19**, 783–786.
3. Megahed, M., Scharffetter-Kochanek, K. (1993) Acantholytic acanthoma. *Am J Dermatopathol*, **15**, 283–285.
4. Barnette, D.J. Jr, Cobb, M. (1995) A solitary, erythematosus, hyperkeratotic papule. Acantholytic acanthomas. *Arch Dermatol*, **131**, 211–212.

5.   Kim, S-H., Choi, J-H., Sung, K-J. et al (2000) Acantholytic acanthoma. *J Dermatol*, **27**, 127–128.
6.   Romos-Caro, F.A., Mack Sexton, F., Browder, J.F. et al (1992) Acantholytic acanthomas in an immunosupressed patient. *J Am Acad Dermatol*, **27**, 452–453.
7.   Tagami, H., Yamada, M. (1978) Seborrheic keratosis: an acantholytic variant. *J Cutan Pathol*, **5**, 145–149.

Focal acantholytic dyskeratosis

Clinical features

By definition, this is an incidental histological feature without a clinical correlate.

Pathogenesis and histological features

Focal acantholytic dyskeratosis is a descriptive histopathological term referring to the finding of Darier-like features within the epidermis overlying or adjacent to an otherwise unrelated pathological lesion.[1] The pathogenesis is not known. The histological features comprise hyperkeratosis, parakeratosis with suprabasal cleft formation, acantholysis and dyskeratosis.[2] These changes may be seen in the overlying or adjacent epithelium in a variety of lesions, such as basal cell carcinoma, melanocytic nevi, chondrodermatitis nodularis helicis, malignant melanoma, dermatofibroma, and as part of an epidermal nevus (*Fig. 4.71*). Focal acantholytic dyskeratosis has recently been described in a patient with pityriasis rubra pilaris.[3] It is important to recognize this as an incidental finding to avoid misdiagnosis as Darier's disease.

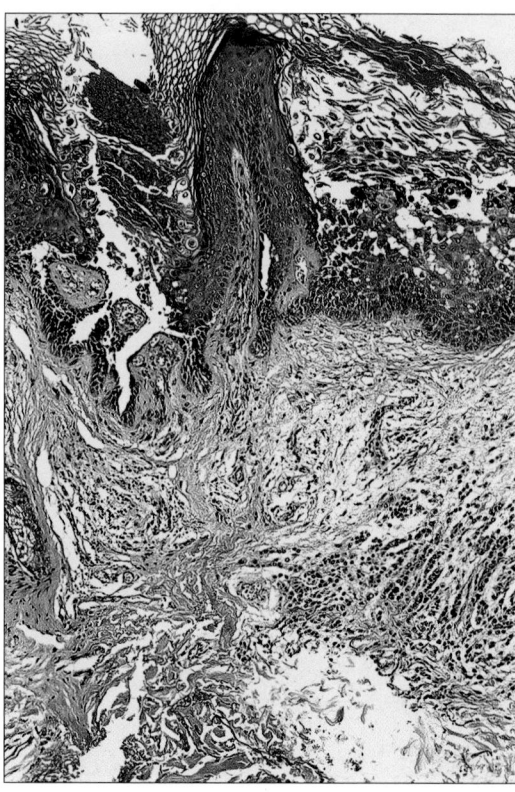

Fig. 4.71
Focal acantholytic dyskeratosis: in this example, the changes of Darier's disease are superimposed upon a dermal melanocytic nevus.

References

1.   Ackerman, A.B. (1972) Focal acantholytic dyskeratosis. *Arch Dermatol*, **106**, 702–706.
2.   DiMaio, D.J.M., Cohen, P.R. (1998) Incidental focal acantholytic dyskeratosis. *J Am Acad Dermatol*, **38**, 243–247.
3.   Kao, G.F., Sulica, V.I. (1989) Focal acantholytic dyskeratosis occurring in pityriasis rubra pilaris. *Am J Dermatopathol*, **11**, 172–176.

Spongiotic, psoriasiform and pustular dermatoses

5

ECZEMATOUS DERMATITIS   171

Eczema – general considerations   171

Endogenous dermatitis   172
Atopic dermatitis   172
Seborrheic dermatitis   173
Discoid dermatitis   174
Hand eczema   174
Autosensitization (Id) reaction   175

Exogenous dermatitis   175
Contact dermatitis   175
Infective dermatitis   177
Asteatotic dermatitis   177
Seborrheic dermatitis-like eruption of AIDS   181
Lichen simplex chronicus   182
Nodular prurigo and prurigo nodule   182
Stasis dermatitis and acroangiodermatitis   185
Pityriasis alba   186
Eosinophilic spongiosis   187
Erythroderma   188
Sulzberger–Garbe syndrome   188
Vein graft site dermatitis   188
Papular acrodermatitis of childhood   188
Pityriasis rosea   190
Juvenile plantar dermatosis   192
Miliaria   193
Fox–Fordyce disease   194
Transient acantholytic dermatosis with prominent eccrine ductal involvement   195

PSORIASIFORM DERMATOSES   195

Psoriasis   195

AIDS-related psoriasis   206

Reiter's syndrome   206

Pityriasis rubra pilaris   206

Inflammatory linear verrucous epidermal nevus   210

Bazex syndrome   211

PUSTULAR DERMATOSES   212

Pustular drug reactions   212

Subcorneal pustular dermatosis   212

Toxic erythema of the neonate   214

Infantile acropustulosis   214

Transient neonatal pustular melanosis   215

Eosinophilic pustular folliculitis of infancy   215

Eczematous dermatitis

This chapter discusses a number of disorders under the rubric eczematous dermatitis, also referred to as eczema and spongiotic dermatitis. The term 'eczema' refers to a group of disorders that share similar clinical and histological features but may have different etiologies. Some object to the term eczema since it does not refer to a specific disease but is a non-specific term that simply refers to any clinical lesion that exhibits spongiosis, which is clinically manifest as moist, often 'bubbly' papules or plaques superimposed on an erythematous base. The pathogenesis of some forms is poorly understood. The histopathologist usually cannot render a more specific diagnosis other than 'spongiotic dermatitis consistent with eczematous dermatitis' and precise classification within the differential diagnosis of spongiotic dermatitis is often not possible. For these reasons, this class of disorders is discussed as a group. Distinguishing clinical, pathogenetic and histological features are presented in the appropriate sections.

Eczema – general considerations

Eczema encompasses a number of disorders with variable etiologies and clinical manifestations and is among the most common complaints of patients visiting dermatology clinics.

The earliest clinical lesions are erythema and aggregates of tiny pruritic vesicles, which rupture readily, exuding clear fluid, and later become encrusted (*Fig. 5.1*). More chronic lesions become scaly and

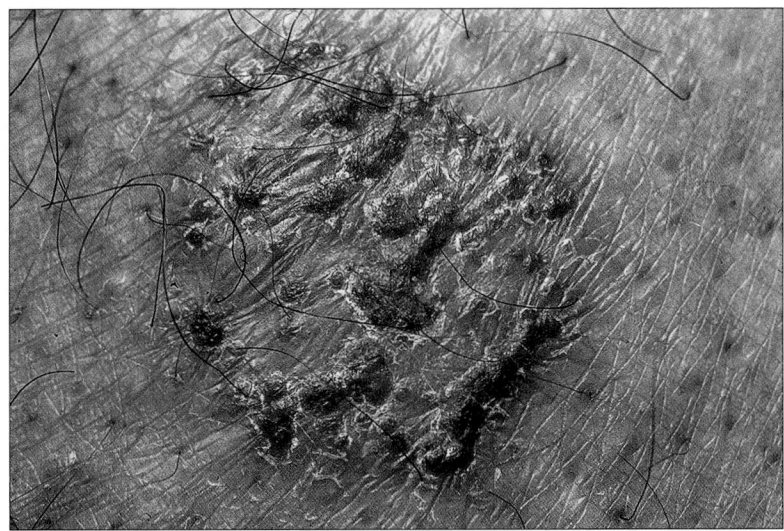

Fig. 5.1
Eczema: this is a plaque of discoid eczema. Small vesicles are present at the edge of the lesion. By courtesy of the Institute of Dermatology, London, UK.

thickened (lichenification), resulting in lichen simplex chronicus (*Fig. 5.2*). Lichenification occurs if the skin is continually scratched or rubbed as, for example, in atopic dermatitis. Therefore, the clinical features of dermatitis depend upon the duration of the lesions, site(s) involved and presence of scratching.

For instance, in pompholyx (acute vesicular dermatitis of the hands and feet), the fluid is trapped beneath the thickened horny layer as small tense white blisters resembling rice grains. In other regions where the skin is loosely attached, as on the eyelids, scrotum and backs of hands, tissue edema is often marked.

Eczematous dermatitis has two major etiological classifications:
- endogenous dermatitis, related to major constitutional or hereditary factors
- exogenous dermatitis, involving environmental factors.

Endogenous dermatitis

Atopic dermatitis

Clinical features

Although atopic (infantile or flexural) dermatitis may begin at any age, it usually commences from about the sixth week onwards. It is characterized by a chronic, relapsing course.[1] In the infantile phase, lesions are present mainly on the head, face, neck, napkin area and extensor aspects of the limbs (*Fig. 5.3*). As the patient grows older and enters childhood, the eruption shifts to the flexural aspects of the limbs. Chronic atopic cheilitis may also be evident.[1] Pruritus is intense, and constant scratching and rubbing leads to lichenification and frequent bouts of secondary bacterial infection (*Fig. 5.4*).[2,3] Atopic eczema is commonly associated with a dry skin (xerosis). Vesiculation is uncommon. There is an increased risk of dermatophyte and viral infections.[1]

The disease improves during childhood and, in over 50% of cases, clears completely by the early teens. Approximately 75% of patients with atopic dermatitis have a family history of atopy and up to 50% have associated asthma or hay fever.[4,5] The disease typically worsens in the

winter months. It is associated with an increased incidence of contact dermatitis, particularly affecting the hand.[6] Other features that may be seen include ichthyosis (50%), nipple eczema, conjunctivitis, keratoconus, bilateral anterior cataracts, sweat-associated itching, wool intolerance,

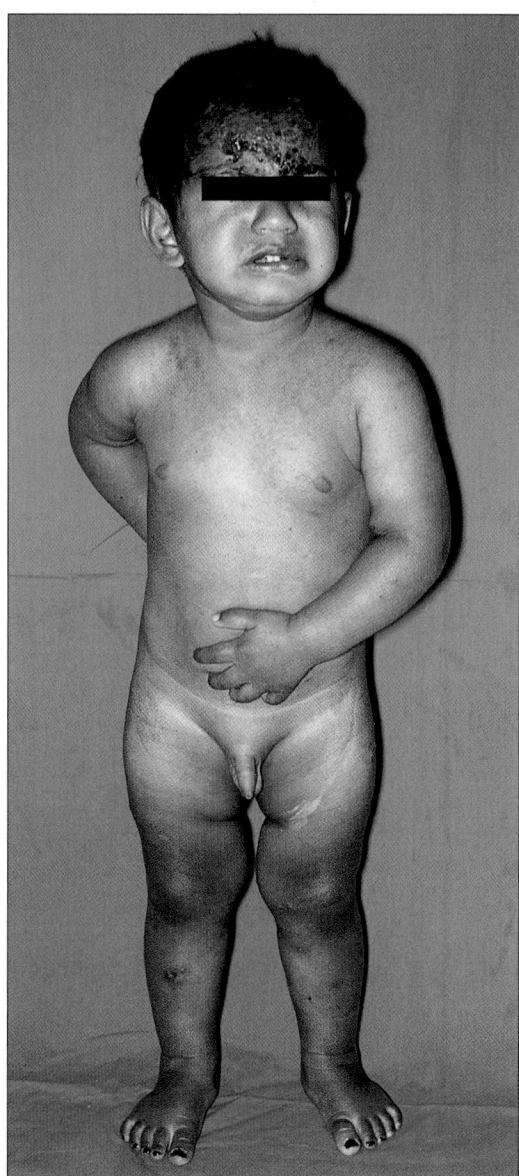

Fig. 5.3
Atopic dermatitis: lesions on the face and trunk are particularly seen in infants and young children. This child has marked blistering and crusting on the forehead. By courtesy of R.A. Marsden, MD, St George's Hospital, London, UK.

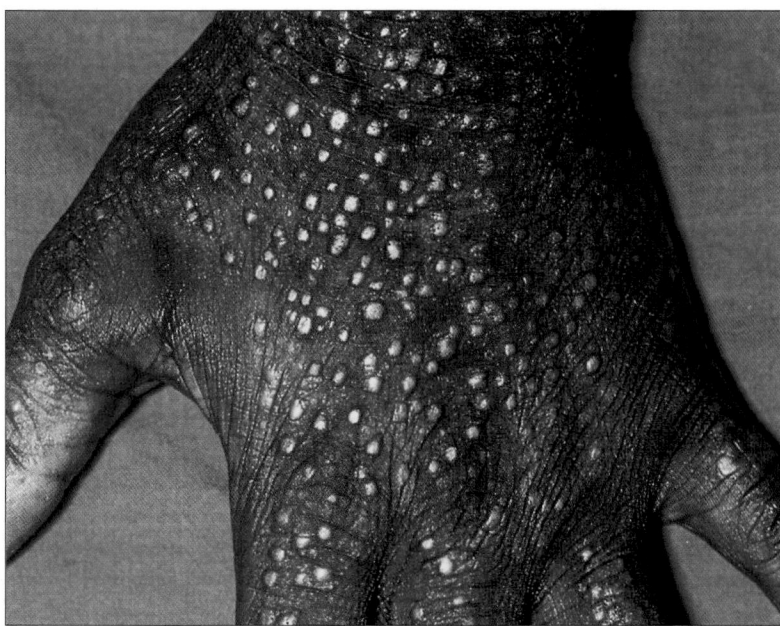

Fig. 5.2
Lichenification: pronounced pebbly lichenification on the dorsum of the hand of a patient with atopic dermatitis. Bizarre forms, as seen here, are not uncommon in black children. By courtesy of R.A. Marsden, MD, St George's Hospital, London, UK.

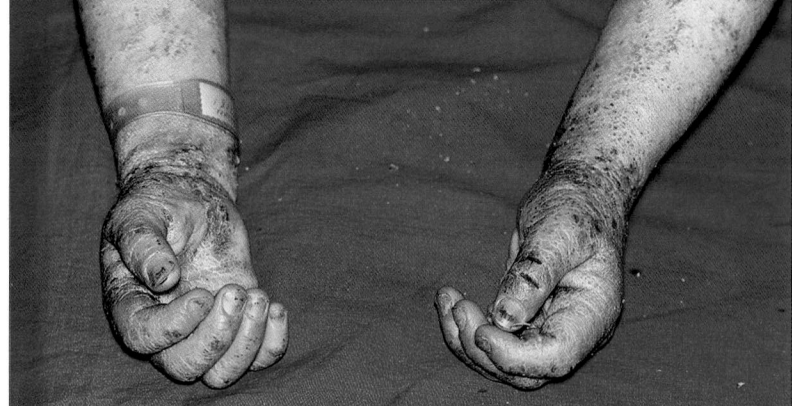

Fig. 5.4
Atopic dermatitis: these crusted, exudative and infected lesions with lichenification are characteristic. By courtesy of R.A. Marsden, MD, St George's Hospital, London, UK.

perifollicular accentuation, food intolerance and white dermatographism.[5] Infraorbital folds (Dennie–Morgan folds) are said to be characteristic of atopic dermatitis, particularly when double.[1]

Pathogenesis

Atopy is defined as a genetically determined disorder encompassing dermatitis, asthma and hay fever. It is associated with excess immunoglobulin E (IgE) antibody formation in response to common environmental antigens. A subset of patients with 'intrinsic atopic dermatitis' represents perhaps 10–30% of patients with atopy; this does not appear to be due to a response to an environmental antigen.[7] The pathogenesis of atopy is not well understood and the mechanism whereby an IgE reaction produces a cell-mediated dermatitis is not clear. Abnormal T-cell, dendritic antigen-presenting cell (Langerhans' cell) and eosinophil activity may play role in the disease.[7–11] An intrinsic epidermal keratinocyte defect and bacterial superantigens may also be important.[7–9] The complex interrelationship between the immune system, the epidermis and various pathogens is currently an area of intense research interest.[7–12]

Many lines of evidence implicate an abnormal immune response as pivotal in the pathogenesis of atopy. It is interesting to note that atopy is cured by bone marrow transplantation in patients with Wiskott–Aldrich syndrome, an immunological disorder characterized by susceptibility to infection and thrombocytopenia, in addition to eczematous dermatitis.[13] Wiskott–Aldrich syndrome shows an X-linked recessive pattern of inheritance and is characterized by depletion of nodal and circulating T-lymphocytes. Contrariwise, patients without a prior history of atopy may develop atopic disease following transplantation of bone marrow from an atopic individual.[14]

Since patients with atopic dermatitis often have a personal or family history of asthma or allergies, a genetic predisposition to the disease is strongly suspected. Currently, an intensive search for genes involved in the pathogenesis of atopy is underway. However, detailed understanding of the genetic basis of atopy has been elusive. Recently, research has focused on the long arm of chromosome 5 in the region of 5q31–33. This area contains the genes for a number of cytokines including interleukin (IL)-3, IL-4, IL-5, IL-13, and granulocyte–macrophage colony stimulating factor (GM-CSF). This region holds particular interest since there is evidence that IL-4 is important in the pathogenesis of asthma and atopic dermatitis, and linkage studies have shown a relationship between IL-4 and total serum IgE concentrations.[15–17] Linkage studies have also suggested a relationship between atopy and polymorphisms of the α-chain of the IL-4 receptor gene located on 16p11.2–12.[18–20]

Patients with atopic dermatitis have an abnormal immune response to a variety of environmental antigens leading to production of IgE antibodies and a T-cell response.[9,21–23] There is evidence that certain subpopulations of T-cells selectively circulate to and perform immune surveillance for the skin and lymph nodes that drain cutaneous sites.[9,23] This subset of lymphocytes is characterized by a unique immunophenotype and is defined by expression of cutaneous lymphocyte antigen (CLA). In patients with atopic dermatitis, antigens such as dust mites and bacteria activate CLA T-cells resulting in the production of cytokines, which stimulate eosinophils to produce IgE, which, in turn, promotes mast cells and basophils to release cytokines and chemotactic factors in what has been termed the intermediate phase response.[8] The so-called late phase reaction is characterized by migration of eosinophils, lymphocytes, histiocytes and neutrophils from the circulation into the dermis and epidermis. The transvascular migration of inflammatory cells is mediated by expression of leukocyte adhesion molecules on endothelial cells.[8,24]

Factors released by the various cells present in the dermis certainly play a role in the generation of the clinical appearance and induction of pruritus, leading to scratching and rubbing. There is evidence that the trauma of scratching and rubbing elicits production of proinflammatory cytokines, growth factors and adhesion molecules that further exacerbate the immune response and symptoms.[25] The demonstration that squamous cells in patients with atopic dermatitis show increased production of GM-CSF, a cytokine thought to play a role in Langerhans'/dendritic cell function, also suggests that a keratinocyte defect may be involved in the pathogenesis of atopy.[26]

Another area of interest has been the role of superantigens in the pathogenesis of atopy as well as other immunologically mediated cutaneous and non-cutaneous disorders.[27–32] Although superantigens have been implicated in the pathogenesis of psoriasis and Kawasaki's disease, in addition to atopic dermatitis, their precise role in these and other diseases is not well understood and is controversial.[28,29] Further research is necessary to clarify the role of superantigens in immunologically mediated diseases.

Superantigens are microbiological (viral, bacterial, fungal) toxins that stimulate CD4+ T-cells. They bind to T-cell receptors and to the class II major histocompatibility complex (MHC), thus stimulating lymphocyte proliferation, activation and release of cytokines, as well as T-cell-mediated tissue damage. They may also stimulate B-cell activation. Superantigens are powerful mediators of the immune system by virtue of their ability to stimulate a large population of T-cells in a *non-specific* manner. Staphylococcal superantigens have, in particular, been an area of research.[31] The skin of most patients with atopic dermatitis is colonized with *Staphylococcus aureus*. In contrast, *S. aureus* is found on the skin of only a minority of control subjects.[32] Disease severity has been shown to correlate with the presence of toxigenic *S. aureus*.[33] It is thought that staphylococcal superantigens SEA and SEB (staphylococcal enterotoxins A and B, respectively) activate T-cells.[33–36] In a study of children with atopic dermatitis, there was a correlation of disease severity and presence of SEA and SEB antibodies.[34] Recently, application of SEB was shown to be associated with T-cell activation in both normal and atopic patients.[37] In summary, there is mounting evidence that staphylococcal superantigens play a role in the symptomatology of atopic dermatitis. Whether superantigens play a key role in the development of disease or simply exacerbate symptoms in atopic patients requires further study.

Seborrheic dermatitis

Clinical features

Seborrheic dermatitis is a common dermatosis which affects up to 1–2% of the population. There is a male predominance. It presents in infants with a second peak affecting adults.[38] There is often a family history of the disease. It particularly affects those areas where sebaceous glands are most numerous, i.e. the scalp, forehead, eyebrows, eyelids, ears, cheeks, presternal and interscapular areas (*Figs 5.5, 5.6*).[39] Occasionally, the flexural regions are affected (intertrigo). Often the lesions of seborrheic dermatitis are sharply marginated, dull red or yellowish and covered by a greasy scale.[39] They are therefore easily confused with psoriasis.

Dandruff and cradle cap are also sometimes included within the spectrum of seborrheic dermatitis.

Seborrheic dermatitis is one of the most common dermatoses seen in patients with acquired immunodeficiency syndrome (AIDS). This topic is discussed separately on page 986. Seborrheic dermatitis has also been associated with stress and neurological disorders including Parkinson's disease, syringomyelia and trigeminal nerve injury.[40]

Pathogenesis

The precise pathogenesis of this condition is unknown. Surprisingly, and in spite of the distribution (and the name) of the disease, sebaceous gland activity and sebum composition appear to be normal.[40]

Seborrheic dermatitis is associated with heavy colonization of the skin by the lipophilic yeast *Malassezia furfur* (*Pityrosporum ovale*).[41–45] Although many workers in the field believe this to be of etiological importance, an almost equal number are unconvinced. The body of evidence favoring a significant relationship relates to the successful treatment of seborrheic dermatitis with antifungal therapy. Whether this implies a causal relationship or merely an exacerbating factor is, however, uncertain.

Discoid dermatitis (Nummular eczema)

Clinical features

The presence of single or multiple pruritic, coin-shaped, erythematous plaques with vesiculation, particularly involving the lower legs, forearms and backs of hands (*Figs 5.7–5.9*)[46] characterize this chronic form of dermatitis. The absence of a raised border clinically distinguishes it from ringworm.[46] There are two peak ages of onset: it affects young women (15–30 years of age) and middle-aged adults of both sexes. The disease tends to chronicity.

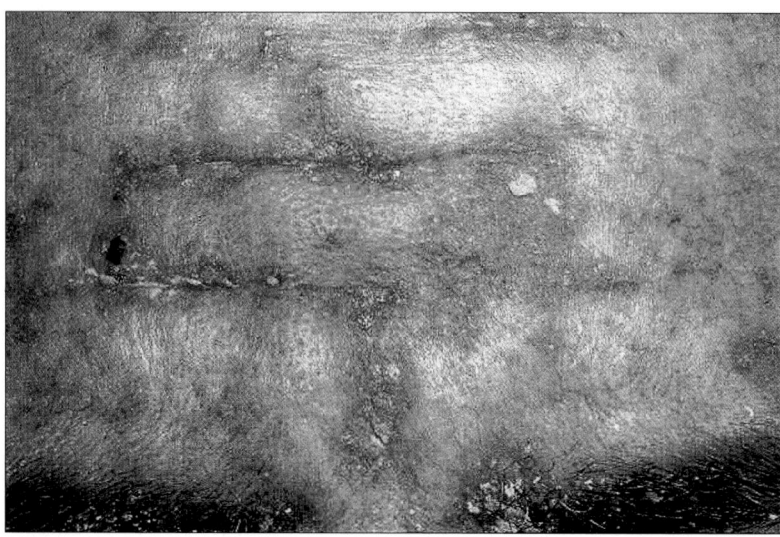

Fig. 5.5
Seborrheic dermatitis: there is diffuse erythema and scaling of the forehead. By courtesy of the Institute of Dermatology, London, UK.

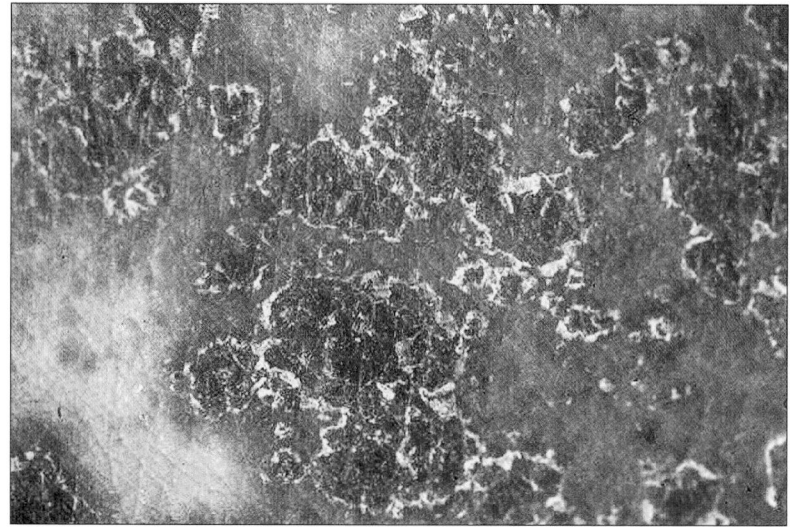

Fig. 5.6
Seborrheic dermatitis: note the marked scaling. By courtesy of the Institute of Dermatology, London, UK.

Pathogenesis

The pathogenesis is poorly understood. A participatory role for organisms in the pathogenesis has been suggested but not been widely accepted.[47] Discoid dermatitis may follow irritants such as soap, acids or alkalis (*Fig. 5.10*).[46] Sometimes it may be a manifestation of atopy and, occasionally, it develops as a consequence of nickel, chromate or cobalt allergy.[48,49]

Hand eczema

Clinical features

Hand eczema (dyshidrotic eczema, palmoplantar eczema, pompholyx) is characterized by a recurrent pruritic vesicular eruption of the palms, soles or digits. Because of the increased thickness of the keratin layer at

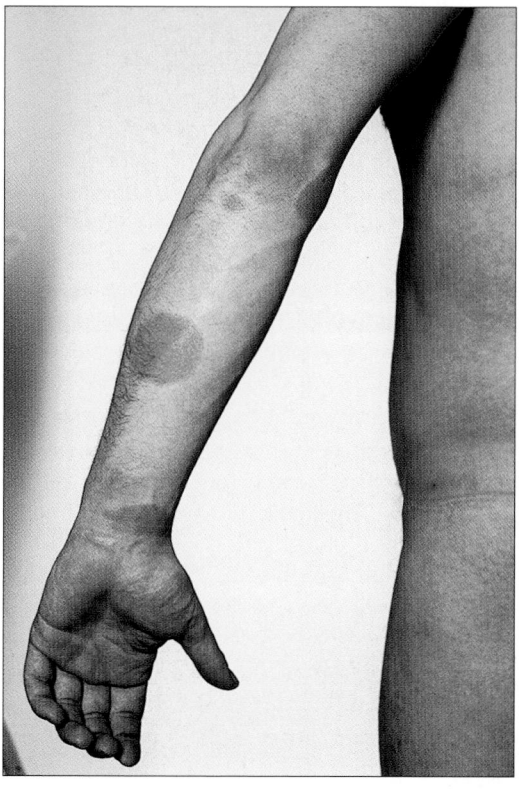

Fig. 5.7
Discoid eczema: circumscribed, erythematous lesions on the forearm, a characteristic site. By courtesy of the Institute of Dermatology, London, UK.

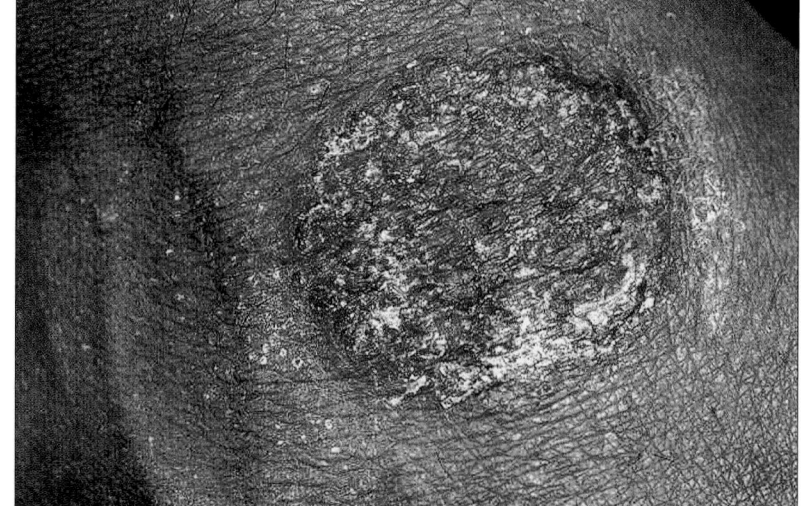

Fig. 5.8
Discoid eczema: the lesion is sharply defined and there is a pronounced scale. By courtesy of the Institute of Dermatology, London, UK.

these sites, the vesicles appear as small pale papules before rupturing (*Fig. 5.11*). Occasionally, frank bullae may form. With the passage of time, the affected parts may show scaling and cracking. The nails sometimes become dystrophic with discoloration and transverse ridging.[50] In the majority of cases the cause is unknown, although heat or psychological stress[50] may precipitate attacks. Occasionally there is a personal or family history of atopy and, sometimes, coexisting tinea pedis. Rubber, latex, chromium, cobalt or nickel sensitivity may trigger it.[51–53]

Pompholyx is often associated with hyperhidrosis.[51] Females are affected slightly more often than males and patients are predominantly in the second to fifth decades.[52]

Pathogenesis

The pathogenesis is obscure. It has been noted that serum IgE levels are often raised.[51]

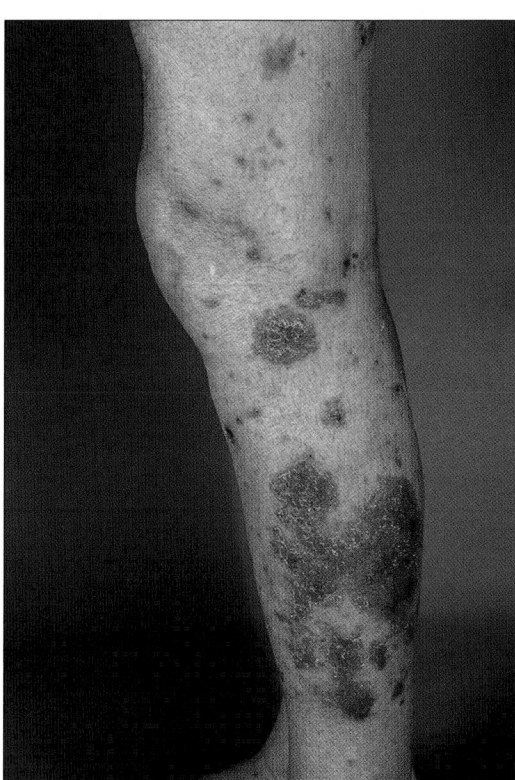

Fig. 5.9
Discoid eczema: there is extensive involvement of the leg. A sharply demarcated erythematous and scaly circular lesion is present just below the knee. By courtesy of R.A. Marsden, St George's Hospital, London, UK.

Autosensitization (Id) reaction

Clinical features

On occasion patients will develop generalized spongiotic dermatitis in response to a dermatosis or infection at a distant site. The eczematous dermatitis resolves if the underlying infection or specific dermatosis is successfully treated. This phenomenon has also been designated an autoeczematization or Id reaction. The lesions that characterize the Id reaction may be a localized pompholyx-like eczematous dermatitis of the hands and feet or scattered papules on the trunk and limbs.[54–58] Disorders that may be associated with the Id reaction include fungal infection (e.g. dermatophyte infection), scabies infestation, molluscum contagiosum, tick bite, pediculosis capitis, and bacterial and mycobacterial infections.[54–58]

Pathogenesis

The pathogenesis of the Id reaction is poorly understood but some data suggest that an abnormal T-cell-mediated immune response directed against skin antigens is responsible for this curious disorder.[59]

Exogenous dermatitis

Contact dermatitis

This form of dermatitis is due to external agents and is divided into two variants: allergic contact and irritant contact.

Allergic contact dermatitis

Allergic contact dermatitis is an idiosyncratic cell-mediated immunological reaction to an environmental allergen, which may be present in very low concentration. Common examples seen in clinical practice include sensitivity to nickel (found in items such as jewelry, buttons, watches and suspenders), constituents of synthetic rubber (e.g. thiuram in rubber gloves), primula, poison ivy, topical medicaments (e.g. neomycin, antihistamines, local anesthetics) and chromates found in cement and leather (*Figs 5.12–5.15*).[60–69]

Dinitrochlorobenzene (DNCB) is a potent contact sensitizer and this is used as a test of cell-mediated immunity.[70,71]

A growing understanding of allergic contact dermatitis has emerged over the last decade with the preponderance of evidence pointing to a

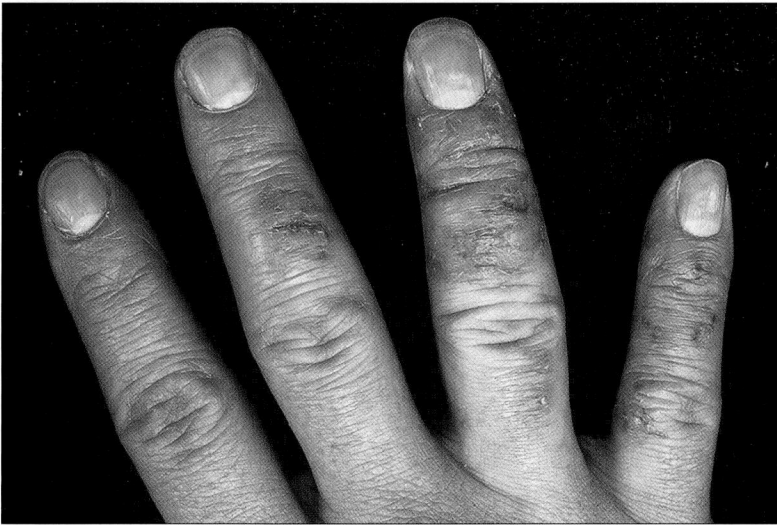

Fig. 5.10
Discoid eczema: lesions localized to the fingers most often represent a contact irritant reaction. By courtesy of R.A. Marsden, St George's Hospital, London, UK.

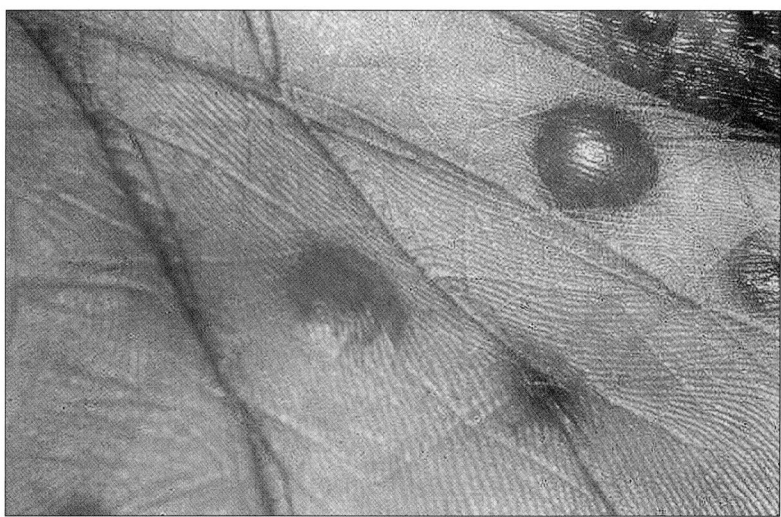

Fig. 5.11
Pompholyx: characteristic tiny tense vesicles on the palm. By courtesy of R.A. Marsden, St George's Hospital, London, UK.

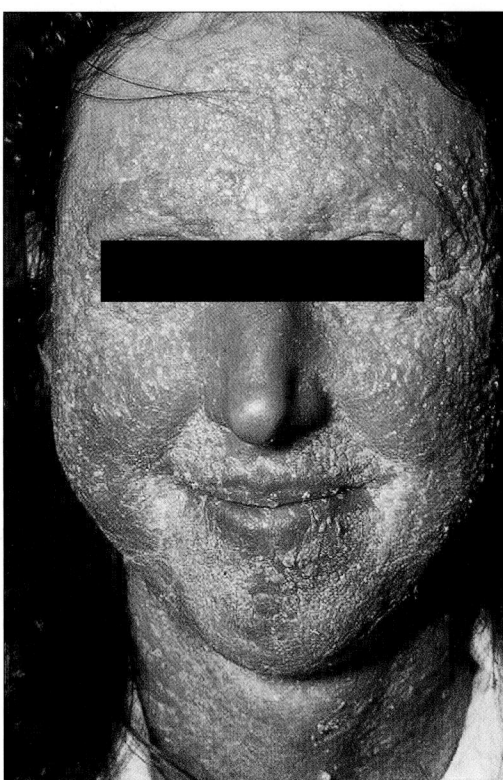

Fig. 5.12
Contact dermatitis: acute vesicular, crusted lesions on the face and neck of a young girl. By courtesy of R.A. Marsden, MD, St George's Hospital, London, UK.

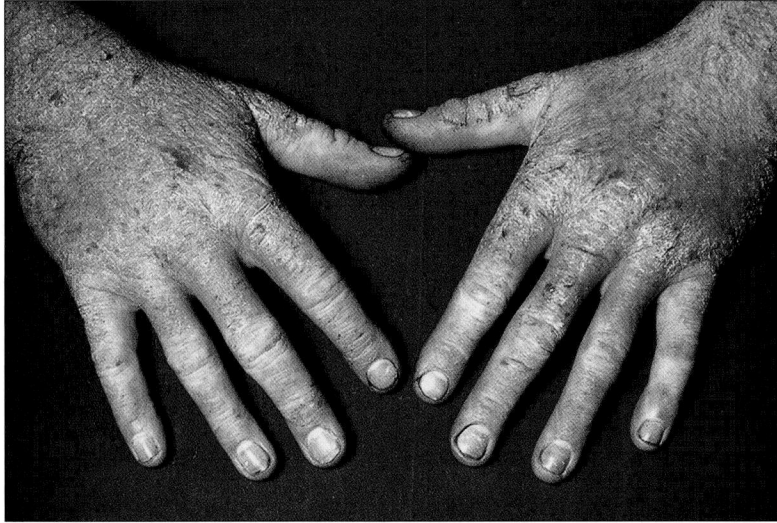

Fig. 5.13
Contact dermatitis: this was due to a reaction to rubber gloves. By courtesy of R.A. Marsden, MD, St George's Hospital, London, UK.

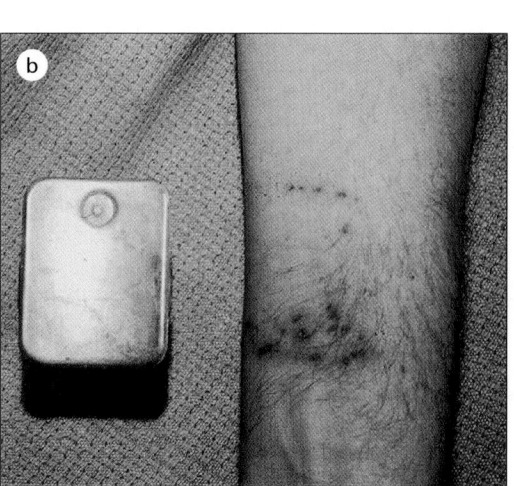

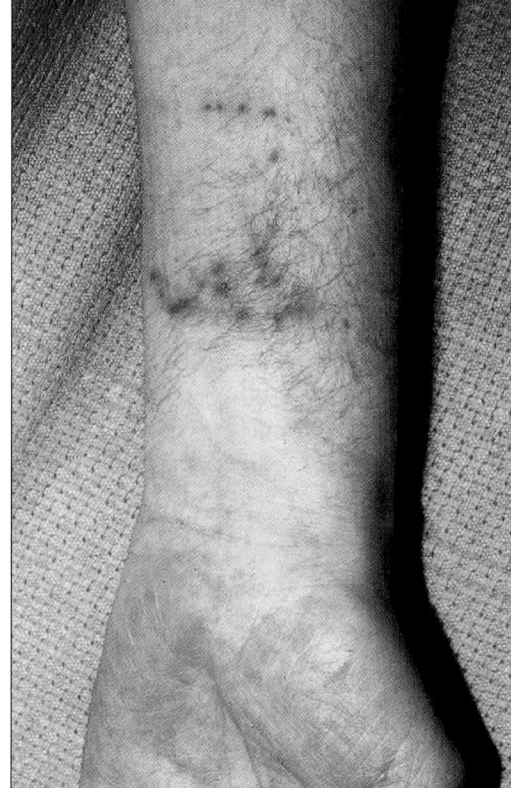

Fig. 5.14
(a, b) Contact dermatitis: nickel dermatitis. By courtesy of the late M. Beare, MD, Royal Victoria Hospital, Belfast, N. Ireland.

T-cell-mediated hypersensitivity reaction.[3,72–75] It is thought that antigens causing allergic contact dermatitis are often unstable and bind to host proteins.[3,72] Langerhans' cells in skin and dendritic cells in lymph nodes process antigen and stimulate appropriate naïve CLA T-cells. CLA-positive T-cells are a subset of T-cells that express a skin selective homing receptor and perform immune surveillance for the skin and lymph nodes that drain cutaneous sites.[76] CLA-positive T-cells proliferate when stimulated by the appropriate antigen or antigen–protein complex. The number of CLA-positive memory T-cells increases with repeated exposures to its antigen.[3,72] When the patient is exposed to the antigen, the CLA-positive T-cells are activated and release cytokines that leads to the immune reaction responsible for the clinical and histological features associated with allergic contact dermatitis.[74] Keratinocytes are also thought to play a role through the release of cytokines after hapten exposure and binding.[75]

Irritant contact dermatitis

Irritant contact dermatitis, which is much more common than allergic contact dermatitis, follows exposure to physical or chemical substances capable of direct damage to the skin. Mechanisms of damage are variable and include keratin denaturation, removal of surface lipids and water-holding substances, damage to cell membranes and/or direct cytotoxic effects.[77] Acute irritant dermatitis usually results from a relatively short single exposure to a potent irritant, such as strong acid or alkali, whereas chronic cumulative insult or 'wear and tear' dermatitis is due to more prolonged contact with one or more weaker irritants, for example, soap and water, detergents or industrial oil.[78–81]

Most forms of occupational dermatitis of the hands, including 'housewives' and wedding ring dermatitis are of the irritant contact type. A diagnosis of contact dermatitis is made from the history and distribution of lesions and, in the case of allergic dermatitis, is confirmed by patch testing to the suspected allergen (*Fig. 5.16*). Although both kinds of contact dermatitis tend to be confined to exposed areas, the reaction may eventually spread to involve non-exposed sites and can persist even when the causative agent is removed from the environment.

Occasionally, an ingested or inhaled allergen in a person who has been previously sensitized by cutaneous absorption may result in a clinical picture similar to allergic contact dermatitis (e.g. ingested nickel, chromium or cobalt may result in the appearances of hand eczema).[82]

Much less commonly, systemic contact dermatitis may be histologically associated with an erythema multiforme-like eruption, vasculitis or urticarial morphology.[82]

Infective dermatitis

Spongiotic dermatitis is commonly associated with infection. For example, it may be triggered by infection with *S. aureus* or an excess of the normal skin flora. It is particularly seen in the flexures, on the ears or feet and sometimes around wounds and ulcers (*Fig. 5.17*). Exudation and crusting is pronounced.

Asteatotic dermatitis

Commonly seen in the elderly, particularly in winter and in those with minor degrees of ichthyosis, asteatotic dermatitis (eczema craquelé) may be precipitated by excessive washing, exposure to detergents, cold winds or low humidity, all of which tend to dry the skin.[83] The affected regions are inflamed and criss-crossed by scaly lines and superficial fissures (*Fig. 5.18*). Asteatotic dermatitis may be associated with internal malignancy, including lymphoproliferative disorders and solid tumors.[84–87]

Pathogenesis and histological features

The histopathological features of spongiotic dermatitis include both dermal and epidermal changes. Their relative proportions vary to some extent with the subtype, but perhaps more importantly, with the stage of evolution of the disease. It is essential not to consider the changes of spongiotic dermatitis as static: different features are seen at different stages.[88–90] Attempting to distinguish the various clinical subtypes based on histological features alone is generally futile. Instead, once the disorder has been recognized as spongiotic in nature, clinical examination is a much more satisfactory method of determining the particular variant.

The histological hallmark of spongiotic dermatitis is the presence of intercellular edema or spongiosis (L., Gr. *spongia*, sponge). Slight degrees of intracellular edema may also be evident but may be easily overlooked. In the early stages of development, spongiosis results in widening of the intercellular spaces, rendering the intercellular bridges conspicuous (*Fig. 5.19*). Further accumulation of fluid leads to the eventual development of an intraepidermal vesicle. A common finding in

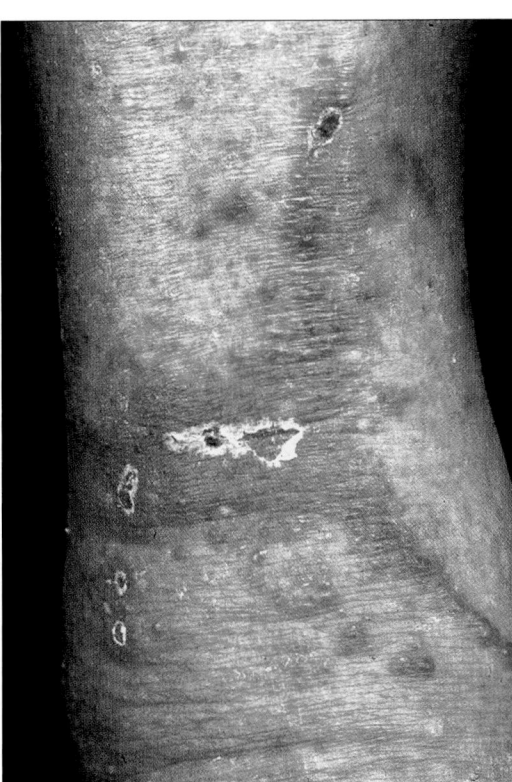

Fig. 5.15
Contact dermatitis: a severe reaction to poison ivy. By courtesy of the Institute of Dermatology, London, UK.

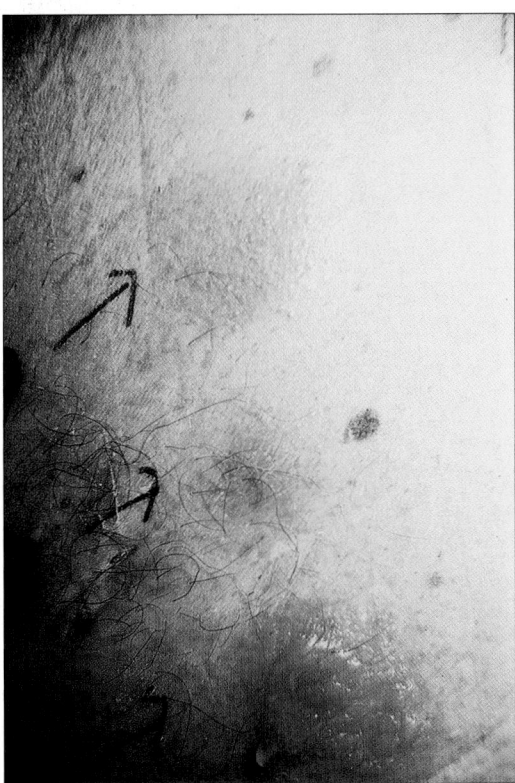

Fig. 5.16
Patch test: three positive reactions seen at 48 hours. By courtesy of R.A. Marsden, MD, St George's Hospital, London, UK.

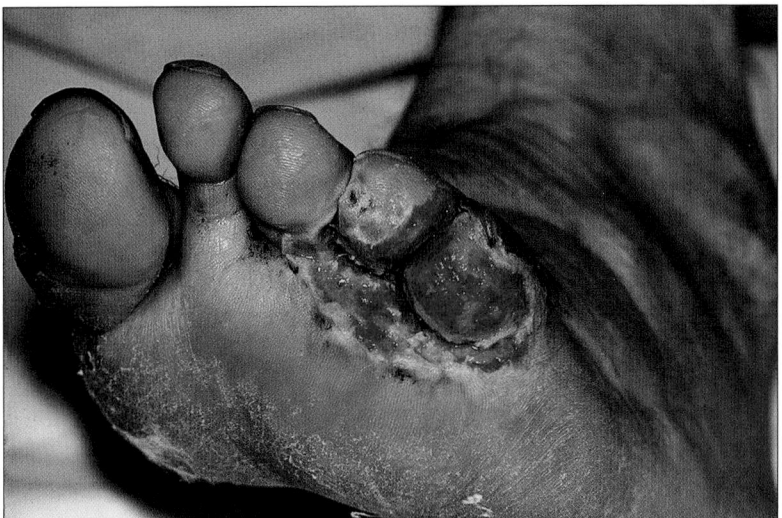

Fig. 5.17
Infective dermatitis: lesions affecting the foot web spaces are often due to staphylococci or streptococci and are associated with excess sweating. By courtesy of R.A. Marsden, MD, St George's Hospital, London, UK.

association with the intercellular edema is lymphocytic infiltration of the epidermis (exocytosis). In severe contact irritant dermatitis, the epidermis may be infiltrated by large numbers of neutrophil polymorphs in association with necrotic keratinocytes.[91] In addition, such reactions may be accompanied by dermoepidermal separation resulting in a vesicle or bulla. The lesions very often become traumatized and may show marked crusting.

Spongiotic dermatitides not uncommonly become infected with bacterial or fungal organisms. Superimposed infection may dramatically alter the histological picture by causing marked acute inflammation with subepidermal, intraepidermal and subcorneal pustules. Such changes may dominate the histological picture and obscure the underlying spongiotic dermatitis. Use of stains for organisms – Gram, periodic acid–Schiff (PAS) – or cultures are necessary to evaluate for infection.

Concomitant with these changes are varying degrees of epithelial proliferation, ranging from mild acanthosis in early acute dermatitis to marked psoriasiform epidermal hyperplasia in chronic variants. Parakeratosis is frequently seen overlying spongiotic foci, while hyperkeratosis is a usual accompaniment of chronic spongiotic dermatitis that has been scratched or rubbed (lichenification).

The dermis is often congested and edema is usually marked in active lesions. The vessels of the superficial vascular plexus are surrounded by a mixed inflammatory cell infiltrate composed of lymphocytes, histiocytes and occasional eosinophils or neutrophils. The degree and composition of dermal inflammation is highly variable. Eosinophils may be numerous in allergic contact dermatitis.[91]

Traditionally, spongiotic dermatitis is subclassified histologically into acute, subacute and chronic variants:

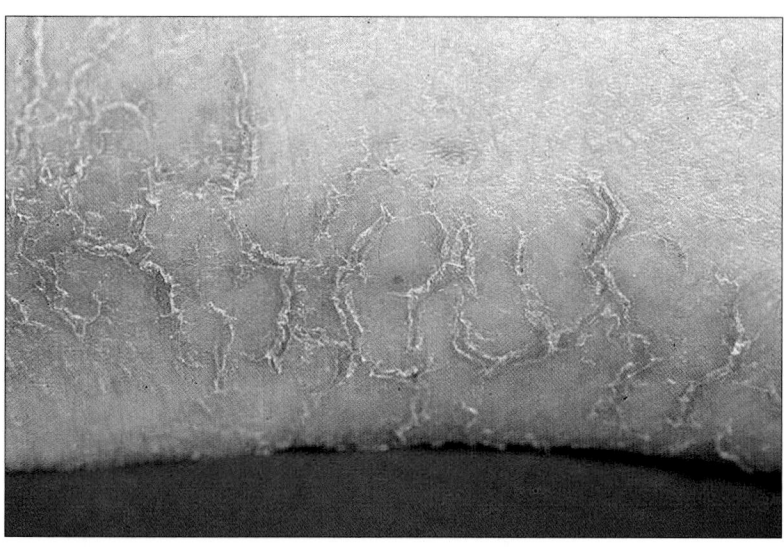

Fig. 5.18
Asteatotic dermatitis: these typical appearances are the result of scaling and fissuring. By courtesy of R.A. Marsden, MD, St George's Hospital, London, UK.

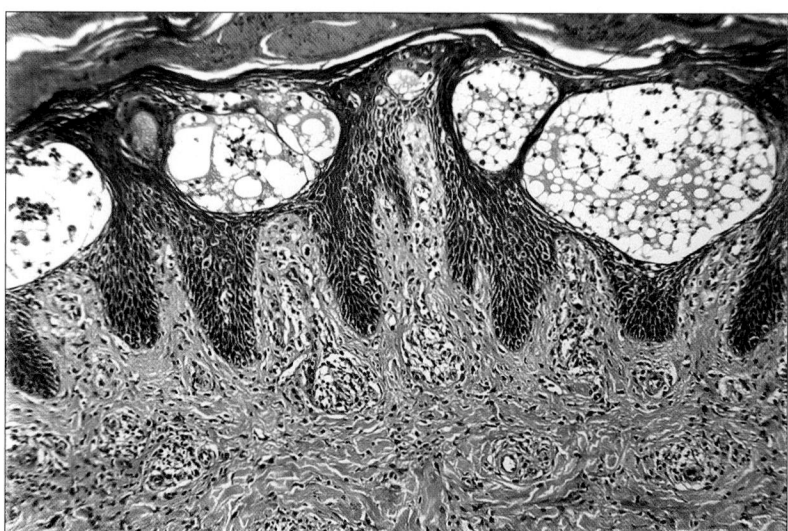

Fig. 5.20
Acute dermatitis: fluid-filled vesicle due to intense spongiosis.

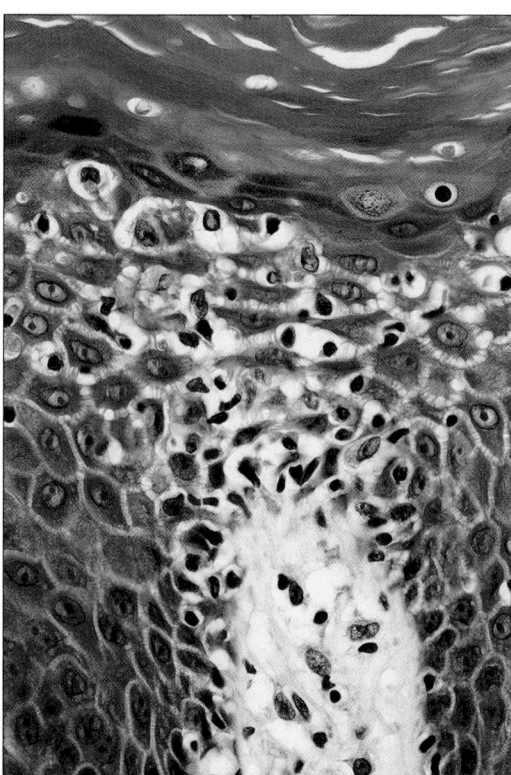

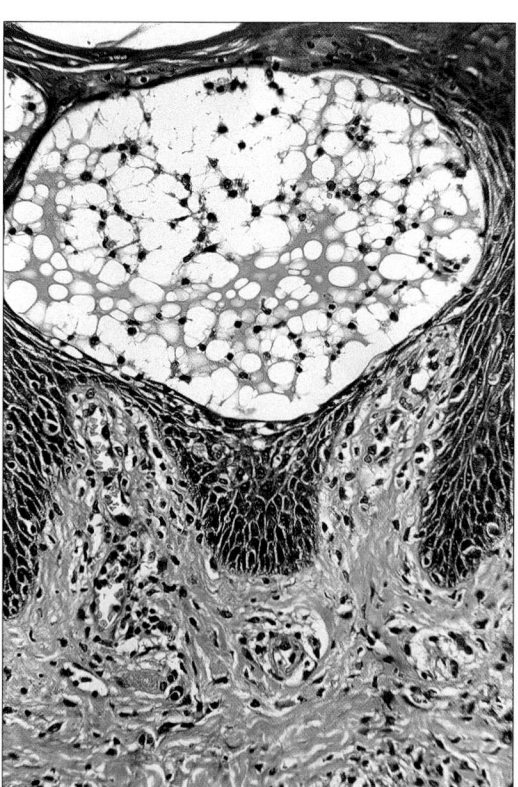

Fig. 5.19
Dermatitis: the earliest visible manifestation of intercellular edema is widening of the intercellular spaces with accentuation of the intercellular bridges.

Fig. 5.21
Acute dermatitis: the vesicle contains lymphocytes and occasional eosinophils. Same case as *Fig. 5.20*, representing an acute contact reaction.

- In *acute* lesions, vesiculation and bullae may be seen (*Figs 5.20–5.22*).
- Acanthosis and spongiosis, often with vesiculation, also characterize *subacute* spongiotic dermatitis (*Fig. 5.23*).
- In *chronic* spongiotic dermatitis, although spongiosis is evident, it may be subtle, and vesicles are uncommon. Epithelial acanthosis is marked and often shows a psoriasiform pattern (*Fig. 5.24*).

Systemic contact dermatitis may be associated with the features of vasculitis or erythema multiforme.[92] As with other forms of spongiotic dermatitis the histological features can be divided into acute, subacute and chronic forms. Spongiosis is more conspicuous in the acute phase although it is never marked. In contrast, the epidermal hyperplasia becomes more conspicuous and psoriasiform towards the chronic end of the spectrum.

The features of seborrheic dermatitis are often non-specific and subtle. It is characterized by hyperkeratosis and parakeratosis, the latter particularly related to hair follicles and typically associated with neutrophil exocytosis (*Figs 5.25, 5.26*). Yeasts may sometimes be found in the stratum corneum particularly if PAS stained sections are examined. Epidermal acanthosis with thickened rete ridges is present and often marked in chronic lesions. It is, however, somewhat irregular in contrast to the uniform hyperplasia characteristic of psoriasis. Variable spongiosis with lymphocyte exocytosis is common. The dermis may be edematous and mild vascular dilatation is usually seen. A mixed inflammatory cell infiltrate consisting of lymphocytes, histiocytes and small numbers of eosinophils surrounds the superficial vascular plexus.

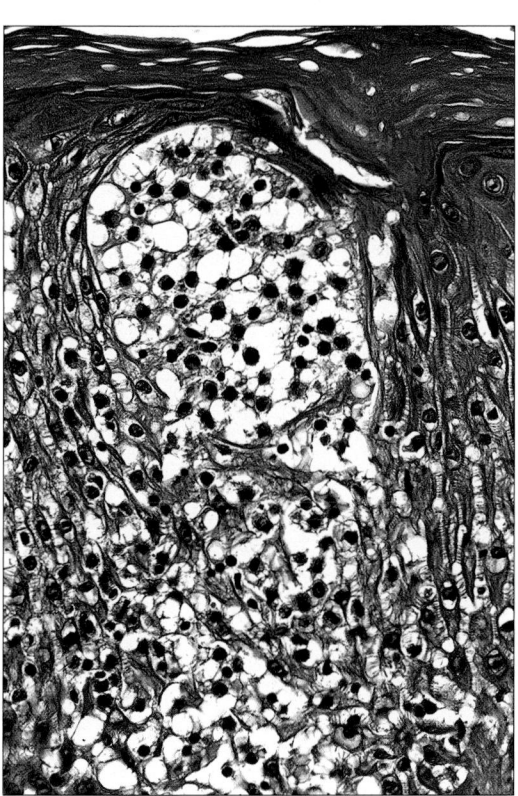

Fig. 5.22
Acute dermatitis: in contact reactions, Langerhans' cell-rich vesicles are often present as shown in this picture. These should not be mistaken for the Pautier micro-abscesses of mycosis fungoides.

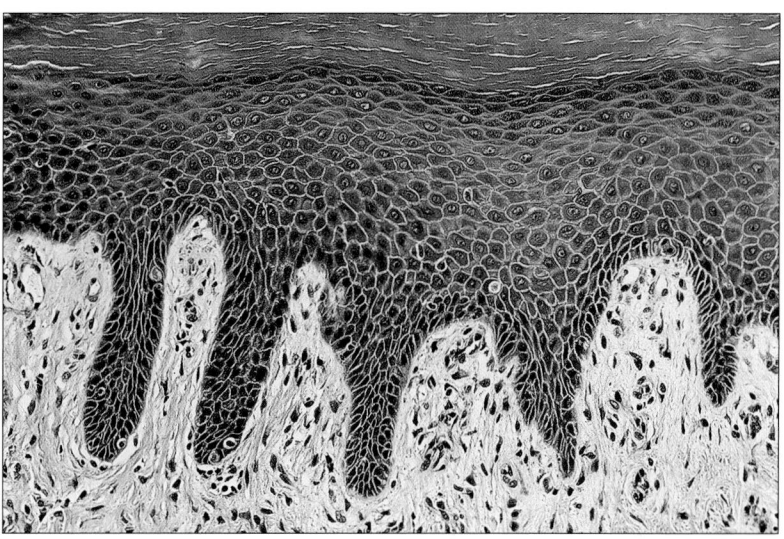

Fig. 5.24
Chronic dermatitis (lichenification): there is hyperkeratosis with hypergranulosis and psoriasiform hyperplasia. The papillary dermis is fibrosed and there is a patchy chronic inflammatory cell infiltrate.

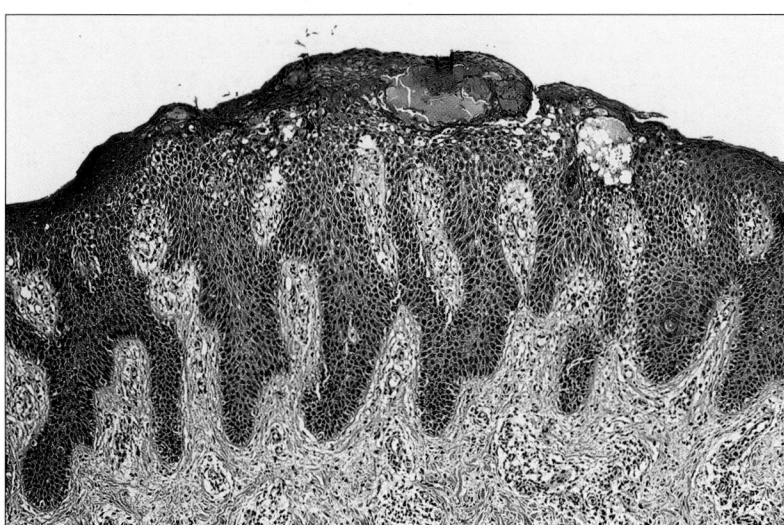

Fig. 5.23
Subacute dermatitis showing patchy parakeratosis, crusting, marked acanthosis with considerable elongation (and fusion) of the epidermal ridges, and focal spongiotic vesiculation. The dermis contains an intense lymphocytic infiltrate.

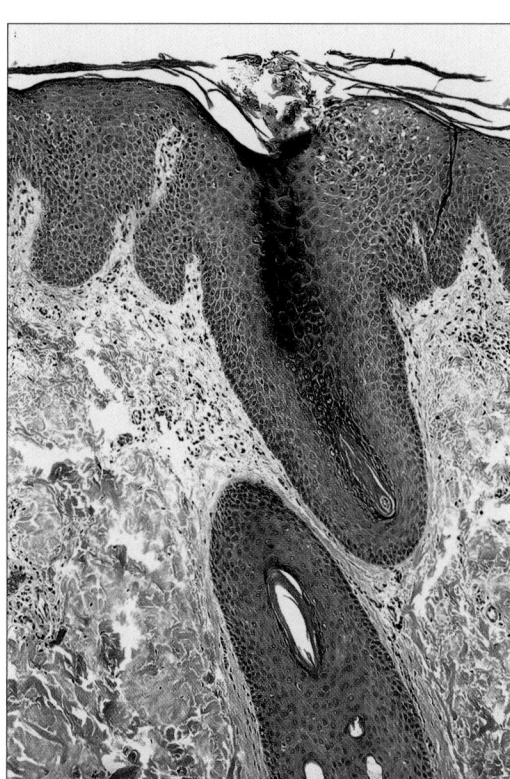

Fig. 5.25
Seborrheic dermatitis: in this field, there is perifollicular psoriasiform hyperplasia. Parakeratosis is present on either side of the follicular ostium.

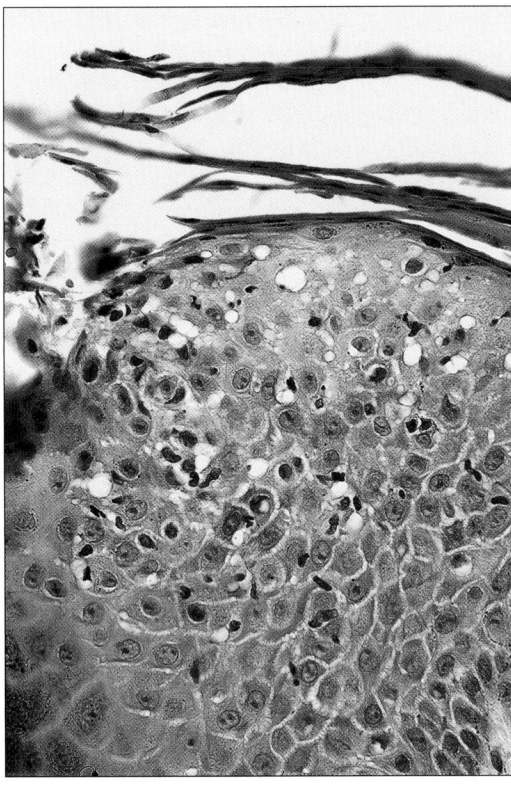

Fig. 5.26
Seborrheic dermatitis: there is parakeratosis and occasional neutrophils are present.

Table 5.1
Conditions featuring spongiosis

- Pityriasis rosea
- Superficial fungal infections
- Herpes gestationis (early lesions)
- Polymorphic eruption of pregnancy
- Erythema multiforme
- Miliaria rubra
- Erythema annulare centrifugum
- Guttate parapsoriasis
- Acral papular eruption of childhood
- Eczema
- Lichen striatus
- Insect-bite reaction
- Prurigo nodularis

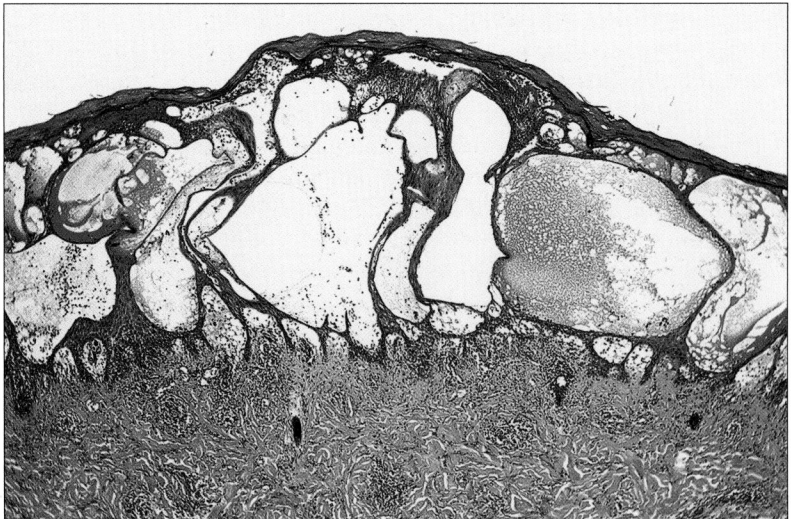

Fig. 5.27
Spongiotic superficial dermatophyte infection: there is marked vesiculation. Subepidermal edema is also present.

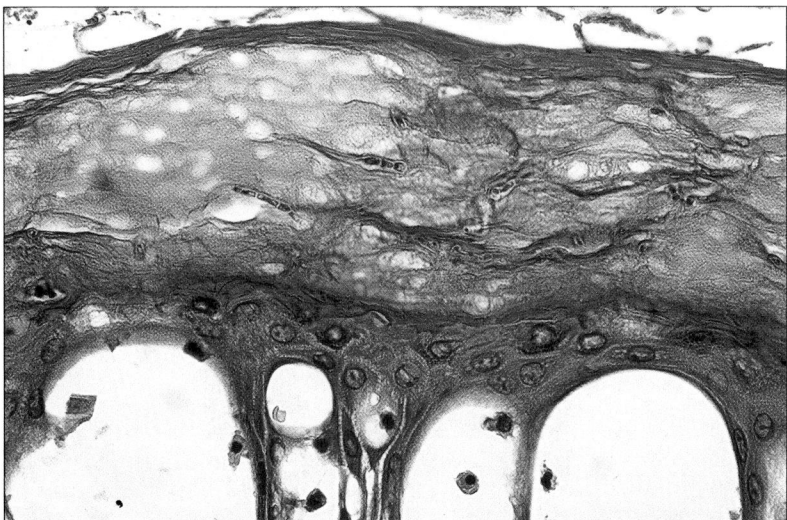

Fig. 5.28
Spongiotic superficial dermatophyte infection: fungi are visible in the stratum corneum in the hematoxylin and eosin stained section

Differential diagnosis

Although spongiosis is a characteristic feature of spongiotic dermatitis, it is also encountered in many other inflammatory dermatoses (*Table 5.1*), particularly superficial dermatophytoses. A diagnosis of spongiotic dermatitis should *never* be rendered until a stain for fungus (e.g. PAS reaction) has been performed to exclude this possibility. This is especially important since the common treatment of spongiotic dermatitides – topical corticosteroids – would exacerbate a fungal infection (tinea incognito) (*Figs 5.27–5.29*).

References

1. Heskel, N., Lobitz, W.C. Jr (1983) Atopic dermatitis in children: clinical features and management. *Semin Dermatol*, 2, 39–44.
2. White, M.I., Noble, W.C. (1986) Consequences of colonization and infection by *Staphylococcus aureus* in atopic dermatitis. *Clin Exp Dermatol*, 11, 34–40.
3. Graham-Brown, R.A.C. (1988) Atopic dermatitis. *Semin Dermatol*, 7, 37–42.
4. Schultz-Larsen, F., Holm, N.V., Henningson, K. (1986) Atopic dermatitis. A genetic–epidemiological study in a population based twin sample. *J Am Acad Dermatol*, 15, 487–493.
5. Hanifin, J., Rajka, G. (1980) Diagnostic features of atopic dermatitis. *Acta Derm Venereol*, 92 (Suppl.), 44–47.
6. Shmunes, E. (1984) Contact dermatitis in atopic individuals. *Dermatol Clin*, 2, 561–566.
7. Wollenberg, A., Kraft, S., Oppel, T. et al (2000) Atopic dermatitis: pathogenic mechanisms. *Clin Dermatol*, 25, 530–534.
8. Leung, D.Y.M., Soter, N.A. (2001) Cellular and immunologic mechanisms in atopic dermatitis. *J Am Acad Dermatol*, 44, S1–S12.

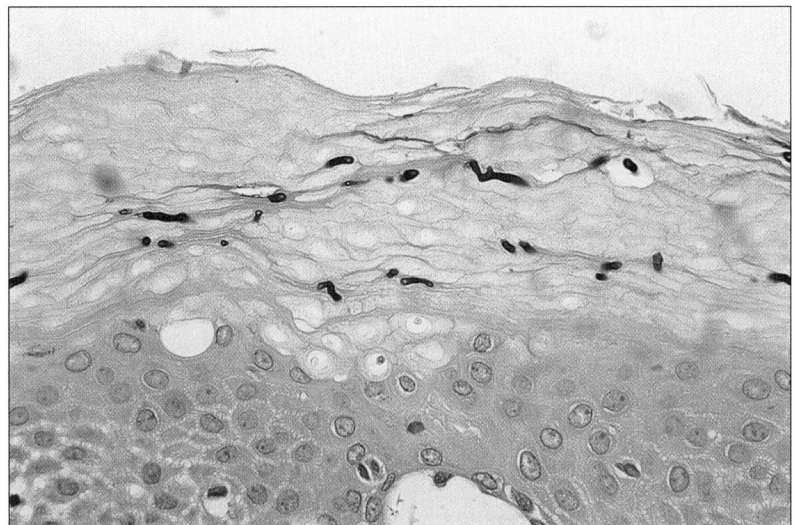

Fig. 5.29
Spongiotic superficial dermatophyte infection: numerous fungi are seen in the PAS stained section.

9. Robert, C., Kupper, T.S. (1999) Inflammatory skin diseases, T cells, and immune surveillance. *N Engl J Med*, **341**, 1817–1828.
10. Hanifin, J.M., Chan, S. (1999) Biochemical and immunologic mechanisms in atopic dermatitis: new targets for emerging therapies. *J Am Acad Dermatol*, **41**, 72–77.
11. Leung, D.Y.M. (1999) Pathogenesis of atopic dermatitis. *J Allergy Clin Immunol*, **104**, S99–S108.
12. Akdis, C.A., Akdis, M., Trautmann, A. et al (2000) Immune regulation in atopic dermatitis. *Curr Opin Immunol*, **12**, 641–646.
13. Surat, J-H. (1985) Eczema in primary immune deficiencies: clues to the pathogenesis of atopic dermatitis with special reference to Wiskott–Aldrich syndrome. *Acta Derm Venereol*, **114**, 125–128.
14. Agosti, J.M., Sprenger, J.D., Lum, L.G. et al (1988) Transfer of allergen-specific IgE-mediated hypersensitivity with allogenic bone marrow transplantation. *N Engl J Med*, **319**, 1623–1628.
15. Marsh, D.G., Neely, J.D., Breazeale, D.R. et al (1994) Linkage analysis of IL4 and other chromosome 5q31.1 and total serum IgE concentrations. *Science*, **264**, 1152–1156.
16. Forrest, S., Dunn, K., Elliott, K. et al (1999) Identifying gene predisposing to atopic eczema. *J Allergy Clin Immunol*, **104**, 1066–1070.
17. Rosenwasser, L.J., Klemm, D.J., Dresback, J.K. et al (1995) Promoter polymorphisms in the chromosome 5 gene cluster in asthma and atopy. *Clin Exp Allergy*, **25**, 74–78.
18. Hershey, G.K., Friedrich, M.F., Esswein, L.A. et al (1997) The association of atopy with a gain-of-function mutation in the alpha subunit of the interleukin-4 receptor. *N Engl J Med*, **337**, 1720–1725.
19. Deichmann, K.A., Heinzmann, A., Forster, J. et al (1998) Linkage and allelic association of atopy and markers flanking the IL4-receptor gene. *Clin Exp Allergy*, **28**, 151–155.
20. Kruse, S., Japha, T., Tedner, M. et al (1999) The polymorphisms S503P and Q576R in the interleukin-4 receptor alpha gene are associated with atopy and influence the signal transduction. *Immunology*, **96**, 365–371.
21. Leung, D.Y. (1993) The immunologic basis of atopic dermatitis. *Clin Rev Allergy*, **11**, 447–469.
22. Cooper, K.D. (1994) Atopic dermatitis: recent trends in pathogenesis and therapy. *J Invest Dermatol*, **102**, 128–137.
23. Picker, L.J., Michie, S.A., Rott, L.S. et al (1990) A unique phenotype of skin-associated lymphocytes in humans: preferential expression of the HECA-452 epitope by benign and malignant T-cells at cutaneous sites. *Am J Pathol*, **136**, 1053–1068.
24. Leung, D.Y.M., Pober, J.S., Cotran, R.S. (1991) Expression of an endothelial leukocyte adhesion molecule (ELAM-1) in elicited late phase allergic skin reactions. *J Clin Invest*, **87**, 1805–1810.
25. Nickoloff, B.J., Naidu, Y. (1994) Perturbation of epidermal barrier function correlates with initiation of cytokine cascade in human skin. *J Am Acad Dermatol*, **30**, 535–546.
26. Pastore, S., Fanales-Belasio, E., Albanesi, C. et al (1997) Granulocyte macrophage colony-stimulating factor is overproduced by keratinocytes in atopic dermatitis. Implications for sustained dendritic cell activation in the skin. *J Clin Invest*, **99**, 3009–3017.
27. Torres, B.A., Kominsky, S., Perrin, G.O. et al (2001) Superantigens: the good, the bad and the ugly. *Exp Biol Med*, **226**, 164–176.
28. Jappe, U. (2000) Superantigens and their association with dermatological inflammatory diseases: facts and hypotheses. *Acta Derm Vernereol*, **80**, 321–328.
29. Yarwood, J.M., Leung, D.Y.M., Schlievert, P.M. (2000) Evidence for bacterial superantigens in psoriasis, atopic dermatitis, and Kawasaki syndrome. *FEMS Microbiol Lett*, **192**, 1–7.
30. Fraser, J., Arcus, V., Kong, P. et al (2000) Superantigens – powerful modifiers of the immune system. *Mol Med Today*, **6**, 125–132.
31. Taskapan, M.O., Kumar, P. (2000) Role of staphylococcal superantigens in atopic dermatitis: from colonization to inflammation. *Ann Allergy Asthma Immunol*, **84**, 3–10.
32. Ulrich, R.G. (2000) Evolving superantigens of Staphylococcus aureus. *FEMS Immunol Med Microbiol*, **27**, 1–7.
33. Leyden, J.E., Marples, R.R., Kligman, A.M. (1974) Staphylococcus aureus in the lesions of atopic dermatitis. *Br J Dermatol*, **170**, 35–39.
34. Bunikowski, R., Mielke, M.E., Skarabis, H. et al (2000) Evidence for a disease-promoting effect of Staphylococcus aureus-derived exotoxins in atopic dermatitis. *J Allergy Clin Immunol*, **105**, 814–819.
35. Bunikowski, R., Mielke, M., Skarabis, H. et al (1999) Prevalence and role of serum IgE antibodies to the Staphylococcus aureus-derived superantigens SEA and SEB in children with atopic dermatitis. *J Allergy Clin Immunol*, **103**, 119–124.
36. Nomura, I., Tanaka, K., Katsunuma, T. et al (1999) Evaluation of the staphylococcal exotoxins and their specific IgE in childhood atopic dermatitis. *J Allergy Clin Immunol*, **104**, 441–446.
37. Skov, L., Olsen, J.V., Giorno, R. et al (2000) Application of staphylococcal enterotoxin B on normal and atopic skin induces up-regulation of T cells by a superantigen-mediated mechanism. *J Allergy Clin Immunol*, **105**, 820–826.
38. Fox, B.J., Odom, R.B. (1985) Papulosquamous diseases: a review. *J Am Acad Dermatol*, **12**, 597–624.
39. Kligman, A.M., Leyden, J.J. (1983) Seborrheic dermatitis. *Semin Dermatol*, **2**, 57–59.
40. Webster, G. (1991) Seborrheic dermatitis. *Int J Dermatol*, **30**, 843–844.
41. Faergemann, J., Bergbrandt, I.M., Dohse, M. et al (2001) Seborrheic dermatitis and Pityrosporum (Malassezia) folliculitis: characterization of inflammatory cells and mediators in the skin by immunohistochemistry. *Br J Dermatol*, **144**, 549–556.
42. Bergbrant, I.M., Andersson, B., Faergemann, J. (1999) Cell-mediated immunity to Malassezia furfur in patients with seborrheic dermatitis and pityriasis versicolor. *Clin Exp Dermatol*, **24**, 402–406.
43. Pechere, M., Krischer, J., Remondat, C. et al (1999) Malassezia spp carriage in patients with seborrheic dermatitis. *J Dermatol*, **26**, 558–561.
44. Parry, M.E., Sharpe, G.R. (1998) Seborrheic dermatitis is not caused by an altered immune response to Malassezia yeast. *Br J Dermatol*, **139**, 254–263.
45. Faergemann, J. (1997) Pityrosporum yeasts – what's new? *Mycoses*, **40** (Suppl. 1), 29–32.
46. Sirot, G. (1983) Nummular eczema. *Semin Dermatol*, **2**, 68–74.
47. Krogh, H.K. (1960) Nummular eczema: its relationship to internal foci of infection. A survey of 84 case records. *Acta Derm Venereol*, **40**,114–126.
48. Veien, N.K., Hattel, T., Justesen, O. et al (1987) Diagnostic procedures for eczema patients. *Contact Derm*, **17**, 35–40.
49. Veien, N.K., Hattel, T., Justesen, O. et al (1983) Oral challenge with metal salts. (II). Various types of eczema. *Contact Derm*, **9**, 407–410.
50. Hansen, O., Kuchler, T., Lotz, G.R. et al (1981) My fingers itch, but my hands are bound. An exploratory psychosomatic study of patients with dyshidrosis of the hands (cheiropompholyx). *Z Psychosom Med Psychoanal*, **27**, 275–290.
51. Lodi, A., Betti, R., Chiarelli, G. et al (1992) Epidemiological, clinical and allergological observations on pompholyx. *Contact Derm*, **26**, 17–21.
52. Christensen, O.B., Moller, H. (1975) Nickel allergy and hand eczema. *Contact Derm*, **1**, 129–135.
53. Veien, N.K., Kaaber, K. (1979) Nickel, cobalt and chromium sensitivity in patients with pompholyx (dyshidrotic eczema). *Contact Derm*, **5**, 371–374.
54. Gianni, C., Betti, R., Crosti, C. (1996) Psoriasiform id reaction in tinea corporis. *Mycoses*, **39**, 307–308.
55. Brenner, S., Wolf, R., Landau, M. (1993) Scabid: an unusual Id reaction to scabies. *Int J Dermatol*, **32**, 128–129.
56. Sander-Jensen, K. (1987) Id reaction associated with chronic Trichophyton rubrum infection: flare-up induced by cimetidine. *Dermatologica*, **174**, 103–104.
57. Rocamora, V., Romani, J., Puig, L. et al (1996) ID reaction to molluscum contagiosum. *Pediatr Dermatol*, **13**, 349–350.
58. Shasky, D.R. (1972) Tick bite granuloma with autoeczematization. *Arch Dermatol*, **106**, 916.
59. Gonzalez-Amaro, R., Baranda, L., Abud-Mendoza, C. et al (1993) Autoeczematization is associated with abnormal immune recognition of autologous skin antigens. *J Am Acad Dermatol*, **28**, 56–60.
60. Lilden, C., Menne, T., Burrows, D. (1996) Nickel containing alloys and platings and their ability to cause dermatitis. *Br J Dermatol*, **134**, 193–198.
61. Emmett, E.A., Risby, T.H., Jiang, L. et al (1988) Allergic contact dermatitis to nickel: bioavailability from consumer products and provocation threshold. *J Am Acad Dermatol*, **19**, 314–322.
62. Zachariae, C.O.C., Agner, T., Menne, T. (1996) Chromium allergy in consecutive patients in a country where ferrous sulfate has been added to cement since 1981. *Contact Derm*, **35**, 83–86.
63. Fregert, S., Gruvberger, B. (1979) Chromium in industrial leather gloves. *Contact Derm*, **5**, 189.
64. Dooms-Goosens, A., Ceuterick, A., Vanmaele, N. et al (1980) Follow-up study of patients with contact dermatitis caused by chromates, nickel, and cobalt. *Dermatologica*, **160**, 249–260.
65. Flowers, M.W. (1978) Burn hazard with cement. *BMJ*, **1**, 108–113.
66. Knudsen, B.B., Larsen, E., Egsgaard, H. et al (1993) Release of thiurams and carbamates from rubber gloves. *Contact Derm*, **28**, 63–69.
67. Angelini, G., Vena, G.A., Meneghini, C.L. (1985) Allergic contact dermatitis to some medicaments. *Contact Derm*, **12**, 263–269.
68. Bandmann, H.J., Calnan, C.D., Cronin, E. et al (1972) Dermatitis from applied medicaments. *Arch Dermatol*, **106**, 335–337.
69. Blondeel, A., Oleffe, J., Achten, G. (1978) Contact allergy in 330 dermatological patients. *Contact Derm*, **4**, 270–276.
70. Adams, R.M., Zimmerman, M.C., Bartlett, J.B. et al (1971) 1-chloro-2,4-dinitrobenzene as an algaecide. Report of four cases of contact dermatitis. *Arch Dermatol*, **103**, 191–193.
71. English, J. (2001) Current concepts in contact dermatitis. *Br J Dermatol*, **145**, 527–529.
72. Girolomoni, G., Sebastiani, S., Albanesi, C. et al (2001) T-cell subpopulations in the development of atopic and contact allergy. *Curr Opin Immunol*, **13**, 733–737.
73. Elias, P.M., Wood, L.C., Feingold, K.R. (1999) Epidermal pathogenesis of inflammatory dermatoses. *Am J Contact Derm*, **10**, 119–126.
74. Belsito, D.V. (1997) The rise and fall of allergic contact dermatitis. *Am J Contact Derm*, **8**, 193–201.
75. Grabbe, S., Schwartz, T. (1998) Immunoregulatory mechanisms involved in elicitation of allergic contact hypersensitivity. *Immunol Today*, **19**, 37–44.
76. Santamaria Babi, L.F., Picker, L.J., Perez Soler, M.T. et al (1995) Circulating allergen-reactive T-cells from patients with atopic dermatitis and allergic contact dermatitis express skin-selective homing receptor, the cutaneous lymphocyte-associated antigen. *J Exp Med*, **181**, 1935–1940.
77. Willis, C.M., Stephens, C.J.M., Wilkinson, J.D. (1989) Epidermal damage induced by irritants in man: a light and electron microscopic study. *J Invest Dermatol*, **93**, 695–699.
78. Malten, K.E. (1981) Thoughts on irritant contact dermatitis. *Contact Derm*, **7**, 238–247.
79. MacKinnon, M.A. (1988) Hydrofluoric acid burns. *Dermatol Clin*, **6**, 67–74.
80. Wood, D.C., Bettley, F.R. (1971) The effect of various detergents on human epidermis. *Br J Dermatol*, **84**, 320–325.
81. Hurkmans, J.F., Bodde, H.E., Van Driel, L.M. (1985) Skin irritation caused by transdermal drug delivery systems during long-term (5 days) application. *Br J Dermatol*, **112**, 461–467.
82. White, C.R. (1990) Histopathology of exogenous and systemic contact eczema. *Semin Dermatol*, **9**, 226–229.
83. Horii, I., Nakayama, Y., Obata, M. et al (1989) Stratum corneum hydration and amino acid content in xerotic skin. *Br J Dermatol*, **121**, 587–592.
84. Guillet, M.H., Schollhammer, M., Sassolas, B. et al (1996) Eczema craquele as a pointer of internal malignancy – a case report. *Clin Exp Dermatol*, **21**, 431–433.
85. Higgins, E.M. (1997) Eczema craquele and internal malignancy. *Clin Exp Dermatol*, **22**, 206.
86. Greenwood, R. (1983) Generalized eczema craquele as a presenting feature of adenocarcinoma. *Br J Dermatol*, **109**, 277–278.
87. Barker, D.J., Cotterill, J.A. (1977) Generalized eczema craquele as a presenting feature of lymphoma. *Br J Dermatol*, **97**, 323–326.
88. White, C.R. Jr (1983) Histopathology of atopic dermatitis. *Semin Dermatol*, **2**, 234–238.
89. Ackerman, A.B. (1986) Histologic findings in different types of contact dermatitis. In: Fisher, A. (ed.) Contact dermatitis. Philadelphia: Lea & Feabiger, pp 46–48.
90. Menne, T., Hjorth, N. (1983) Pompholyx: dyshidrotic eczema. *Semin Dermatol*, **2**, 75–80.
91. Taylor, R.M. (1986) Histopathology of contact dermatitis. *Clin Dermatol*, **4**, 18–22.
92. Andersen, K.E., Benezra, C., Burrows, D. et al (1987) Contact dermatitis: a review. *Contact Derm*, **16**, 55–78.

Seborrheic dermatitis-like eruption of AIDS

Clinical features

Seborrheic dermatitis affects 40–83% of patients with the acquired immunodeficiency syndrome (AIDS).[1–14] A 26–46% incidence has been documented in patients with the AIDS-related complex.[4,6] It may present up to 2 years before the clinical onset of AIDS or it can be a presenting manifestation.[9] Although the distribution of lesions is often similar to the disease in the general population, particularly severe involvement of the scalp with thick, greasy scales is not uncommon and in some patients the eruption involves the trunk and extremities, presenting as generalized erythroderma.[7,8] The disease is more severe in those patients who have central nervous system involvement.[5] Lesions tend to be inflammatory and hyperkeratotic and areas of hyper- or hypopigmentation sometimes develop within the inflammatory plaques.[3] As with seborrheic dermatitis in the immunocompetent population, in many patients there is clinical overlap with psoriasis.

Histological features

Although in some patients the histological features are typical of seborrheic dermatitis, the features are more commonly atypical. Changes suggestive of AIDS-related disease include marked hyperkeratosis with confluent parakeratosis, follicular plugging, acanthosis with slight spongiosis, lymphocyte and neutrophil exocytosis accompanied by keratinocyte necrosis and dyskeratosis with focal interface change.[5,10] A mixed upper dermal inflammatory cell infiltrate consisting of lymphocytes, plasma cells and neutrophils surrounds thick-walled vessels.[10]

References

1. Eisenstat, B.A., Wormser, G.P. (1984) Seborrheic dermatitis and butterfly rash in AIDS. *N Engl J Med*, **311**, 189.
2. Farthing, C.F., Staughton, R.C.D., Roland-Payne, C.M.E. (1985) Skin disease in homosexual patients with acquired immunodeficiency syndrome (AIDS) and lesser forms of human T-cell leukemia virus (HTLV-VIII) disease. *Clin Exp Dermatol*, **10**, 3–12.
3. Sadick, N.S., McNutt, N.S., Kaplan, M.H. (1990) Papulosquamous dermatoses of AIDS. *J Am Acad Dermatol*, **22**, 1270–1277.
4. Mathes, B.M., Douglas, M.C. (1985) Seborrheic dermatitis in patients with acquired immunodeficiency syndrome. *J Am Acad Dermatol*, **13**, 947–951.
5. Smith, K.J., Skelton, H.G., Angritt, P. (1991) Histopathologic features of HIV-associated skin disease. *Dermatol Clin*, **9**, 551–578.
6. Goodman, D.S., Teplitz, E.D., Wishner, A. et al (1987) Prevalence of cutaneous disease in patients with acquired immunodeficiency syndrome (AIDS) or AIDS-related complex. *J Am Acad Dermatol*, **17**, 210–220.
7. Herbst, J.S., Resnick, L. (1989) Mucocutaneous manifestations of HIV infection. *Clin Dermatol*, **7**, 56–64.
8. Kaplan, M.H., Sadick, N.S., McNutt, N.S. et al (1987) Dermatologic findings and manifestation of acquired immunodeficiency syndrome (AIDS). *J Am Acad Dermatol*, **16**, 485–506.
9. Warner, L.C., Fisher, B.K. (1986) Cutaneous manifestations of acquired immunodeficiency syndrome. *Int J Dermatol*, **25**, 337–350.
10. Soeprono, F.F., Scinella, R.A., Cockerall, C.J. et al (1986) Seborrheic-like dermatitis of acquired immunodeficiency syndrome. *J Am Acad Dermatol*, **14**, 242–248.
11. Gelfand, J.M., Rudikoff, D. (2001) Evaluation and treatment of itching in HIV-infected patients. *Mt Sinai J Med*, **68**, 298–308.
12. Jing, W., Ismail, R. (1999) Mucocutaneous manifestations of HIV infection: a retrospective analysis of 145 cases in a Chinese population in Malaysia. *Int J Dermatol*, **38**, 457–463.
13. Barton, J.C., Buchness, M.R. (1999) Nongenital dermatologic disease in HIV-infected women. *J Am Acad Dermatol*, **40**, 938–948.
14. Rosatelli, J.B., Machado, A.A., Roselino, A.M. (1997) Dermatoses among Brazilian HIV-positive patients: correlation with evolutionary phases of AIDS. *Int J Dermatol*, **36**, 729–734.

Lichen simplex chronicus

Clinical features

The term lichen simplex chronicus refers to the development of localized areas of thickened scaly skin complicating prolonged and severe scratching in a patient with no underlying dermatological condition (*Fig. 5.30*).[1] Lichenification is an identical process in which an underlying intensely pruritic dermatosis such as atopic eczema is present.[2] Dermatophyte infections, stasis dermatitis and chronic allergic contact dermatitis may also predispose to lichenification. Picker's nodules and nodular prurigo are related conditions (see below).[3]

Patients present with profound pruritus and localized scaly plaques with accentuated skin markings said to resemble tree bark. There is a predilection for females and young to middle-aged adults are predominantly affected. Accessible skin is particularly affected and the nape and sides of the neck, the thighs, the lower legs and ankles, vulva, and scrotum are sites of predilection.[2]

Pebbly lichenification refers to a distinct variant in which lichenoid papules follow intense scratching in patients with inflammatory dermatoses such as atopic eczema.[2]

Histological features

Lichen simplex chronicus (also known as circumscribed neurodermatitis) is characterized by marked hyperkeratosis, sometimes with small foci of parakeratosis, and a usually prominent granular cell layer (*Fig. 5.31*).[4] The epidermal ridges are elongated and irregularly thickened. Mild spongiosis is variably present depending upon the cause. A perivascular and sometimes interstitial inflammatory cell infiltrate consisting of lymphocytes, histiocytes and small numbers of eosinophils is present in the superficial dermis. Enlarged, angulated myofibroblasts are sometimes evident. Papillary dermal fibrosis is a characteristic feature and in some cases nerve hyperplasia is seen (*Fig. 5.32*).[3]

References

1. Schaffer, B., Beerman, H. (1951) Lichen simplex chronica and its variants. A discussion of certain psychodynamic mechanisms and clinical and histopathologic correlation. *Arch Dermatol Syphilol*, **64**, 340–351.
2. Burton, J.L. (1992) Lichenification and lichen simplex. In: Champion, R.H., Burton, J.L., Ebling, F.J.G. (eds) Rook/Wilkinson/Ebling textbook of dermatology. Oxford: Blackwell Scientific.
3. Rowland-Payne, C.M.E., Wilkinson, J.D., McKee, P.H. et al (1985) Nodular prurigo – a clinicopathologic study of 46 patients. *Br J Dermatol*, **113**, 431–439.
4. Barr, R.J., Young, E.M. (1985) Psoriasiform and related papulosquamous disorders. *J Cutan Pathol*, **12**, 412–425.

Nodular prurigo and prurigo nodule

Clinical features

Nodular prurigo (prurigo nodularis) is characterized by the development of chronic, intensely pruritic, lichenified and excoriated nodules.[1,2] It occurs over a wide age range, from 5 to 75 years, with a mean of 40 years. Rarely children may be affected.[3] Disease duration ranges from 6 months to 33 years, with a mean of 9 years. Nodular prurigo occurs equally in men and women. It shows significant overlap with lichen simplex chronicus, although this is not uniformly accepted.[1,2]

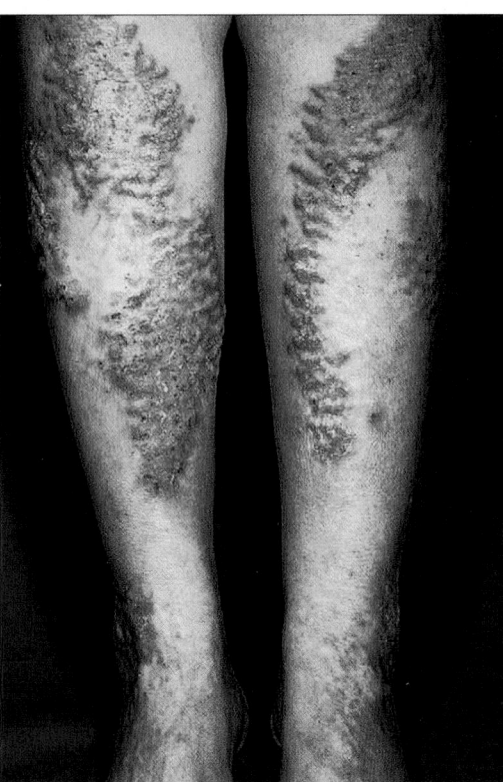

Fig. 5.30
Lichen simplex chronicus: thick, scaly erythematous plaques are present on the shins, a commonly affected site. By courtesy of R.A. Marsden, MD, St George's Hospital, London, UK.

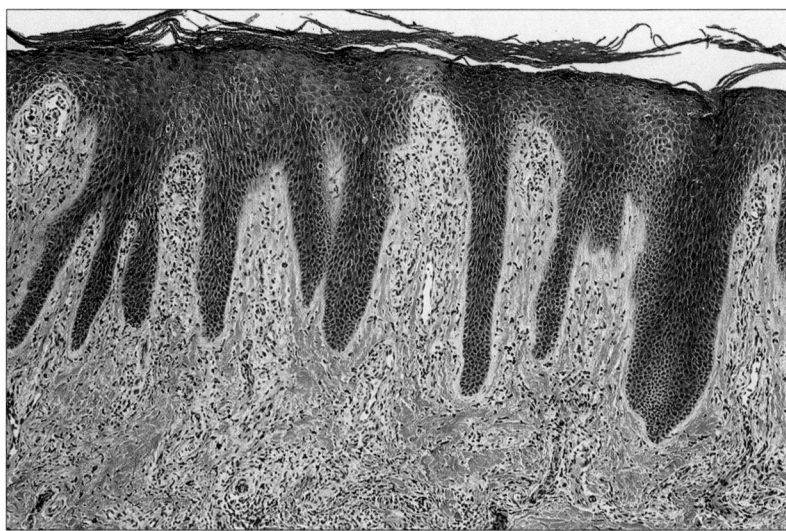

Fig. 5.31
Lichen simplex chronicus: there is hyperkeratosis, patchy parakeratosis and elongation of the rete ridges.

Individual lesions are often described as globular with a warty and excoriated surface and may measure up to 2 cm in diameter (*Fig. 5.33*).[2] They are often grouped, symmetrical and occur predominantly on extensor aspects of the (distal) limbs (*Figs 5.34, 5.35*).[1] The trunk may also be affected.[2] Occasional disseminated cases have been described.[2] The palms and soles are typically uninvolved.[2] The intervening skin usually appears normal. Similar-looking lesions are sometimes seen in patients with eczema (see below). The majority of patients with nodular prurigo are perfectly well and investigations are unhelpful; however, occasionally nodular prurigo is found in patients with gluten enteropathy.[4] Psychosocial disorders have been reported in a high proportion of patients.[5] In some cases the eruption occurs after an insect bite, but subsequent lesions develop spontaneously.[5]

The pruritus is episodic and may be precipitated or aggravated by heat and anxiety.[5] Significant laboratory abnormalities may include anemia, eosinophilia and raised serum IgE levels.[5]

Nodular prurigo (eczema) is defined as lesions of nodular prurigo arising on a background of overt eczema.[5] While this distinction is of academic interest it has no clinical or prognostic importance.

A prurigo nodule (also known as picker's nodule) is a solitary variant that develops as a consequence of localized scratching and picking.

On occasions, nodular prurigo is accompanied by the features of bullous pemphigoid (pemphigoid nodularis, see p. 100).[6]

Pathogenesis and histological features

Classical nodular prurigo, which is focal and characterized by hyperplasia, has recently been related particularly to follicular epithelium.[2,7]

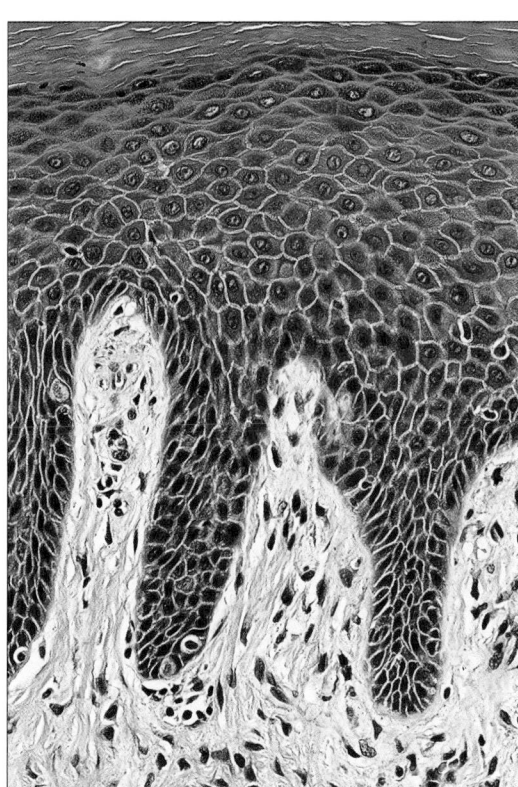

Fig. 5.32
Lichen simplex chronicus: there is hypergranulosis. Note the vertically oriented collagen fibers, a characteristic feature. This is a close up of Fig. 5.24.

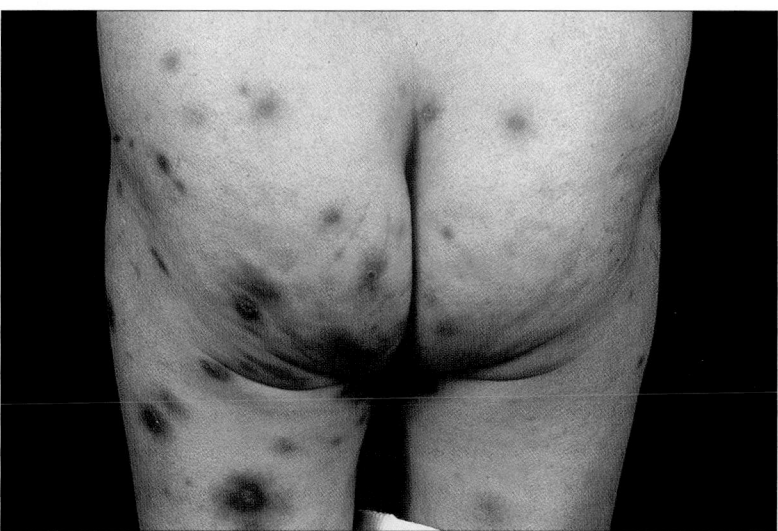

Fig. 5.34
Nodular prurigo: there are scattered, excoriated discrete nodules on the buttocks and thighs. Note the postinflammatory hyperpigmentation. By courtesy of R.A. Marsden, MD, St George's Hospital, London, UK.

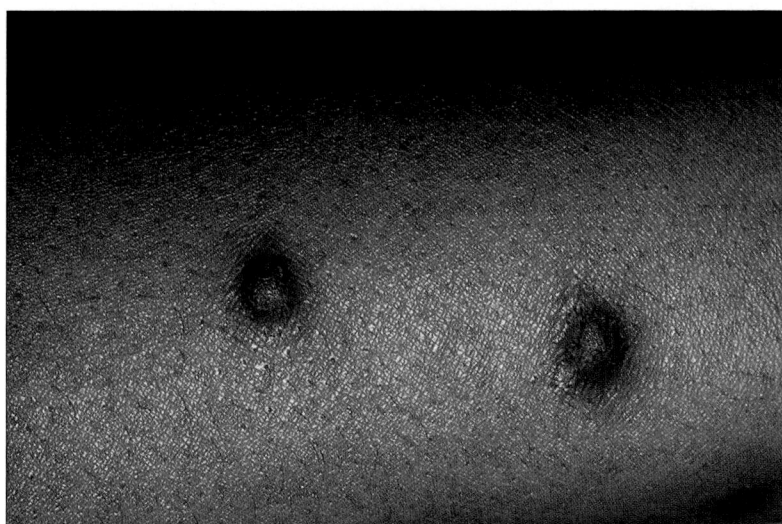

Fig. 5.33
Nodular prurigo: typical globular nodules; the intervening skin appears normal. By courtesy of R.A. Marsden, MD, St George's Hospital, London, UK.

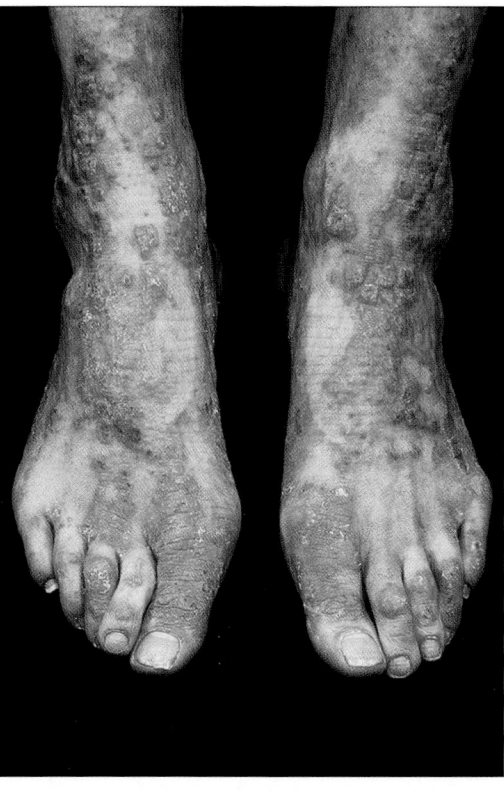

Fig. 5.35
Nodular prurigo: in this patient there is very severe involvement of the shins and dorsal surface of the feet. By courtesy of the Institute of Dermatology, London, UK.

In the epidermis this is manifested as hyperkeratosis and acanthosis, sometimes to the degree of pseudoepitheliomatous hyperplasia (*Figs 5.36, 5.37*). Superficial mild spongiosis is occasionally present and the features may resemble chronic eczema.[5] Subepidermal fibrin deposition is sometimes a feature.[8]

In the dermis there is vascular hyperplasia, with dilated vessels in both the papillary and reticular dermis. New vessel formation is apparent and there is a surrounding perivascular mild inflammatory infiltrate, consisting mainly of lymphocytes and some histiocytes, plasma cells and occasional eosinophils. Mast cells are present in normal numbers.[1] The infiltrate has been described as having an inverted triangular configuration extending from the superficial dermis.[2] This has not been the present authors' experience. Occasionally the dermal features include lymphoid follicles with germinal center formation, thereby resembling persistent insect bite reactions.[5]

With light microscopy the nerves may appear normal, increased in number or occasionally hyperplastic (*Fig. 5.38*).[1,5] Special neural stains or S-100 immunocytochemistry may accentuate mild proliferative changes. Nerve changes, however, do not appear to be essential for the diagnosis.[1] Studies have shown no evidence of true neuroma formation and it is thought by some authors that the neural changes are secondary to chronic trauma and scratching of the intensely pruritic nodules.[1,5,7] This intense pruritus may have been partly responsible for the large amount of attention given to neural changes in nodular prurigo in the past. Very rarely, however, hyperplastic nerve trunks are associated with Schwann cell proliferation, giving rise to small 'neuromata'.[9]

Electron microscopy has shown vacuolation of Schwann cell cytoplasm, together with loss of definition of internal structure of the mitochondria (*Fig. 5.39*).[5,9,10]

References

1. Lindley, R.P., Payne, C.M.E.R. (1989) Neural hyperplasia is not a diagnostic prerequisite in nodular prurigo. A controlled morphometric microscopic study of 26 biopsy specimens. *J Cutan Pathol*, 16, 14–18.
2. Miyauchi, H., Uehara, M. (1988) Follicular occurrence of prurigo nodularis. *J Cutan Pathol*, 15, 208–211.
3. Kanwar, A.J., Dhar, S., Ghosh, S. (1993) Nodular prurigo in a child. *J Pediatr Dermatol*, 10, 200–201.
4. McKenzie, A.W., Stubbing, D.G., Elvy, B.L. (1976) Prurigo nodularis and gluten enteropathy. *Br J Dermatol*, 95, 89–92.
5. Rowland-Payne, C.M.E., Wilkinson, J.D., McKee, P.H. et al (1985) Nodular prurigo – a clinicopathologic study of 46 patients. *Br J Dermatol*, 113, 431–439.
6. Ross, J.S., McKee, P.H., Smith, N.P. et al (1992) Unusual variants of pemphigoid: from pruritus to pemphigoid nodularis. *J Cutan Pathol*, 19, 212–216.
7. Doyle, J.A., Connolly, S.M., Hunziker, N. et al (1979) Prurigo nodularis: a reappraisal of the clinical and histological features. *J Cutan Pathol*, 6, 392–403.
8. Wong, E., MacDonald, D.M. (1982) Localised subepidermal fibrin deposition – a histological feature of friction induced cutaneous lesions. *Clin Exp Dermatol*, 7, 499–503.
9. Feuerman, E.J., Sandbank, M. (1975) Prurigo nodularis. Histological and electron microscopical study. *Arch Dermatol*, 111, 1472–1477.
10. Sandbank, M. (1976) Cutaneous nerve lesions in prurigo nodularis. *J Cutan Pathol*, 3, 125–132.

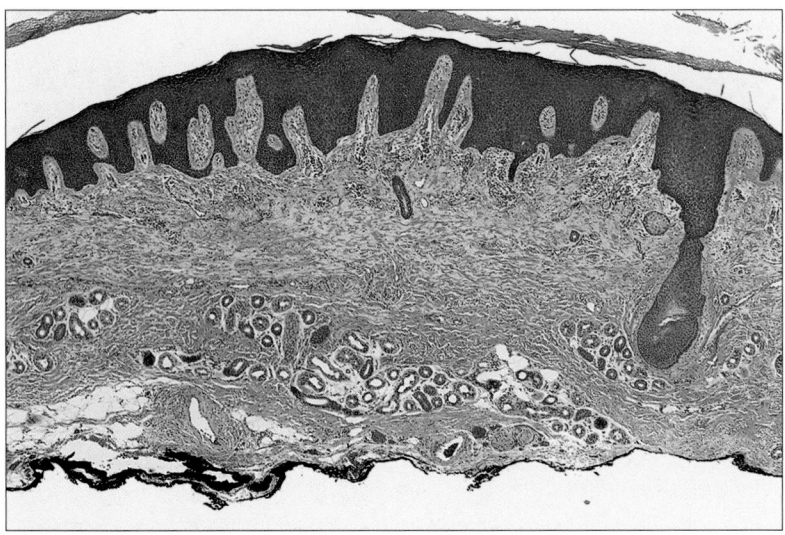

Fig. 5.36
Nodular prurigo: there is hyperkeratosis, hypergranulosis and psoriasiform hyperplasia. The dermis is scarred and there is a light superficial perivascular chronic inflammatory cell infiltrate.

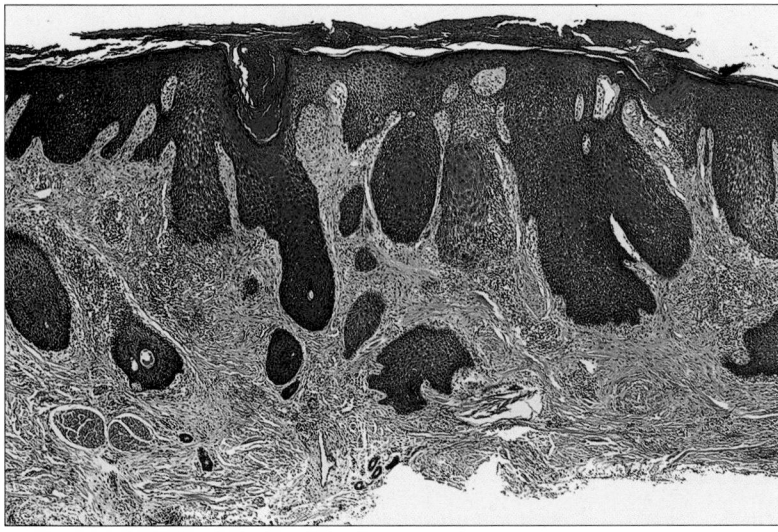

Fig. 5.37
Nodular prurigo: in this example there is pseudoepitheliomatous hyperplasia.

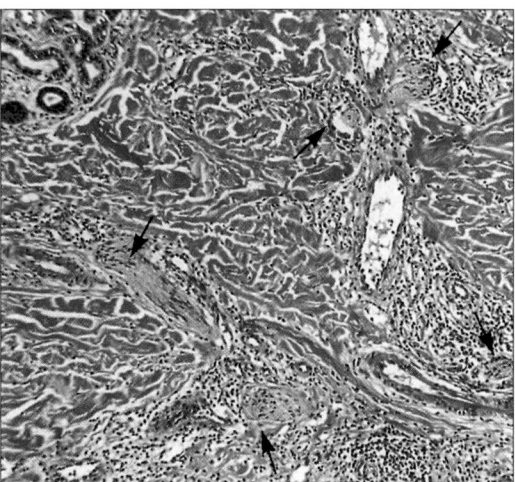

Fig. 5.38
Nodular prurigo: in addition to a perivascular lymphohistiocytic infiltrate, note the excessive numbers of nerves (arrowed).

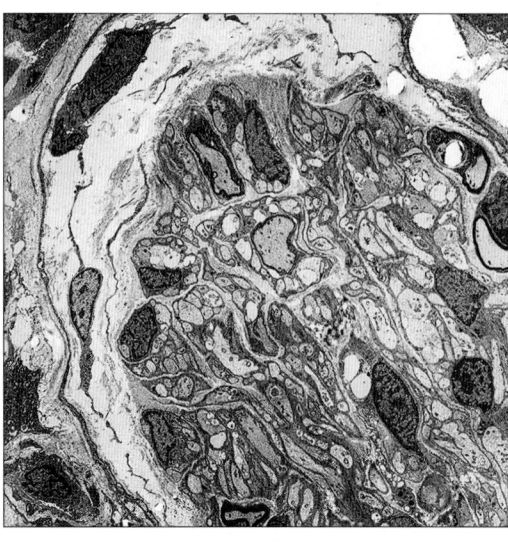

Fig. 5.39
Nodular prurigo: there is marked edema of both axons and Schwann cell cytoplasm.

Stasis dermatitis and acroangiodermatitis

Clinical features

Stasis (varicose) dermatitis usually involves the medial aspect of the lower leg or ankle, but may be more widespread, and develops as a complication of impaired venous return from the lower limbs.[1] Superficial varicose veins are a frequent predisposing factor. The lesion appears as an itchy, scaly, often swollen and hyperpigmented area. Such changes are often seen around chronic stasis ulcers (*Fig. 5.40*). Malignant tumors (both squamous and basal cell carcinomas) may occasionally develop at the edge of these ulcers.[2–5]

Acroangiodermatitis (pseudo-Kaposi's sarcoma, congenital dysplastic angiopathy, arteriovenous malformation with angiodermatitis) refers to the clinical manifestation of purple macules, nodules and sometimes verrucous plaques typically developing on the dorsal aspects of the feet and toes in patients with severe and longstanding venous insufficiency.[6] Varicose veins are often present. The condition is of particular importance in that it may be clinically mistaken for Kaposi's sarcoma.[7] Identical lesions have been described complicating Klippel–Trénaunay, Stewart–Bluefarb and Prader–Willi syndromes, surgical arteriovenous fistulae as seen for example in hemodialysis patients, complicating poorly fitting suction socket prostheses on amputation stumps and on paralysed limbs.[8–18]

Pathogenesis and histological features

The pathogenesis of stasis dermatitis and acroangiodermatitis is unknown although it may be related to the tissue anoxia that typically results from increased venous pressure or circulatory disturbance.[12]

Stasis dermatitis shows, in addition to the epithelial changes of spongiotic dermatitis, marked hemosiderin deposition in the dermis accompanied by fibrosis and a characteristic lobular pattern of superficial and/or deep dermal neovascularization (*Figs 5.41–5.45*). Inflammatory cells – including lymphocytes, histiocytes and variable numbers of plasma cells – are often numerous and erythrocyte extravasation is usually prominent.

In acroangiodermatitis, the vascular proliferation is often so exuberant that it may mimic a vascular neoplasm, most often Kaposi's sarcoma (*Fig. 5.46*).[19]

Differential diagnosis

Acroangiodermatitis differs from Kaposi's sarcoma by the absence of an atypical spindle cell population or irregular vascular channels dissecting the dermal collagen. In addition, the promontory sign (tumor vessels partially surrounding normal vessels and the adnexae) is absent. In acroangiodermatitis, the hallmark is the presence of lobular capillary proliferation.

In cases where the diagnosis is in doubt, CD34 immunocytochemistry may be of value. The spindle cells in Kaposi's sarcoma express this

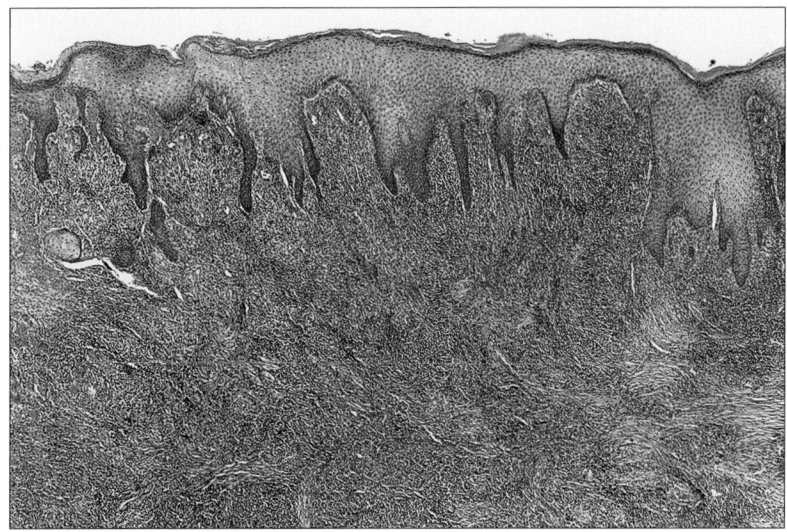

Fig. 5.41
Stasis dermatitis: there is hyperkeratosis, focal parakeratosis and marked epidermal hyperplasia. The dermis is chronically inflamed and scarred.

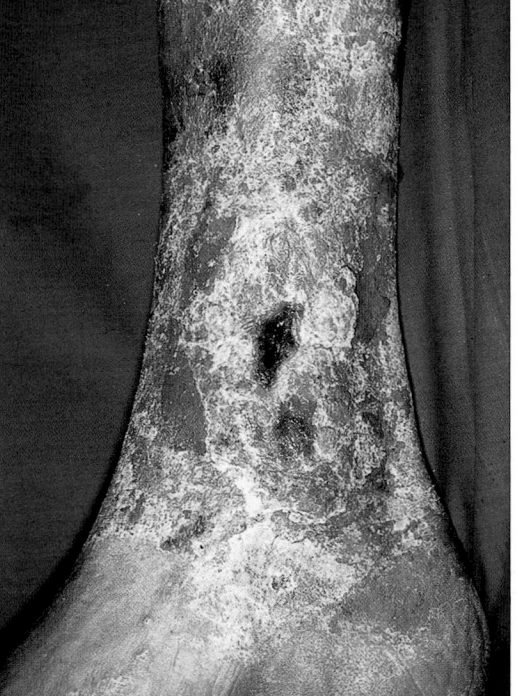

Fig. 5.40
Stasis dermatitis: there is vesiculation, exudation and crusting on the lower leg around a stasis ulcer, which was precipitated by allergy to the antibiotic dressing. By courtesy of R.A. Marsden, MD, St George's Hospital, London, UK.

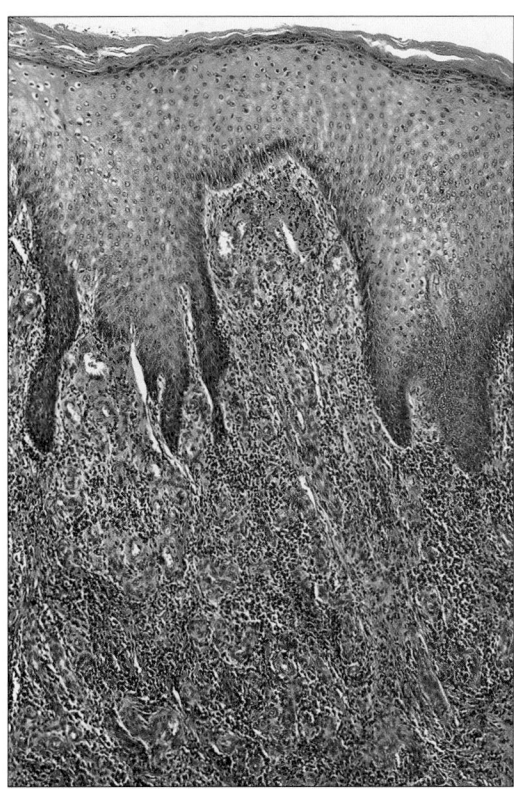

Fig. 5.42
Stasis dermatitis: note the increased vascularity.

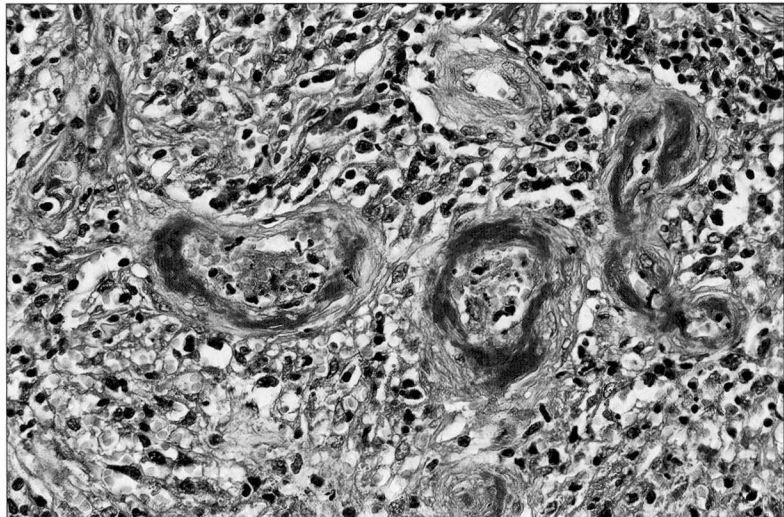

Fig. 5.43
Stasis dermatitis: there is marked mural fibrin deposition. The features often overlap with atrophie blanche.

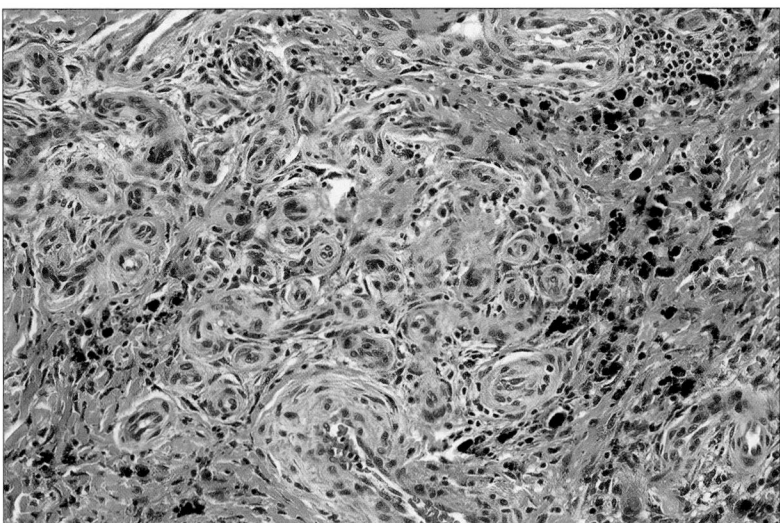

Fig. 5.44
Stasis dermatitis: in this view, there is marked new blood vessel formation and abundant hemosiderin is present.

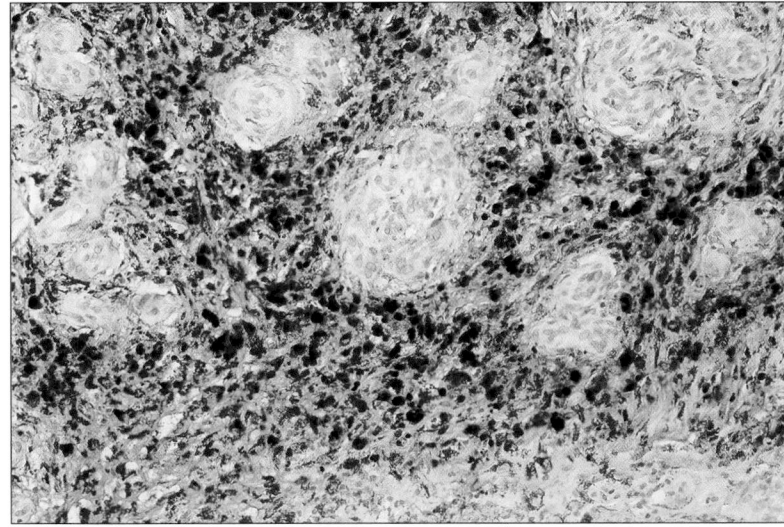

Fig. 5.45
Stasis dermatitis: the hemosiderin can be highlighted with a Prussian blue reaction for iron.

antigen whereas those in acroangiodermatitis do not.[20] Smooth muscle actin emphasizes the pericytes in acroangiodermatitis and a reticulin stain can be used to highlight the lobularity.

References

1. Rietschel, R.L., Ray, M.C. (1988) Nonatopic eczemas. *J Am Acad Dermatol*, **18**, 569–573.
2. Lutz, M.E., Davis, M.D., Otley, C.C. (2000) Infiltrating basal cell carcinoma in the setting of a venous ulcer. *Int J Dermatol*, **39**, 519–520.
3. Ryan, J.F. (1989) Basal cell carcinoma and chronic venous stasis. *Histopathology*, **14**, 657–659.
4. Gosain, A., Sanger, J.R., Yousif, N.J. et al (1991) Basal cell carcinoma of the lower leg occurring in association with chronic venous stasis. *Ann Plast Surg*, **26**, 279–283.
5. Olewiler, S.D. (1995) Marjolin's ulcer due to venous stasis. *Cutis*, **56**, 168–170.
6. Mali, J.W.H., Kuiper, J.P., Hammers, A.A. (1965) Acro-angiodermatitis of the foot. *Arch Dermatol*, **92**, 515–518.
7. Earhart, R.N., Aeling, J.A., Nuss, D.D. et al (1974) Pseudo-Kaposi sarcoma. *Arch Dermatol*, **110**, 907–910.
8. Lund Kofoed, M., Klemp, P., Thestrup-Pedersen, K. (1985) The Klippel–Trénaunay syndrome with acro-angiodermatitis (pseudo-Kaposi's sarcoma). *Acta Derm Venereol*, **65**, 75–77.
9. Lyle, W.G., Given, K.S. (1996) Acroangiodermatitis (pseudo-Kaposi's sarcoma) associated with Klippel–Trénaunay syndrome. *Ann Plast Surg*, **37**, 654–656.
10. Konig, A., Brungger, A., Schnyder, U.W. (1990) Kaposiform acroangiodermatitis with arteriovenous malformation (Stewart–Bluefarb syndrome). *Dermatologica*, **181**, 254–257.
11. Donhauser, G., Eckert, F., Landthaler, M. et al (1991) Pseudo-Kaposi-sarkom bei Prader–Labhart–Willi syndrom. *Hautarzt*, **42**, 467–470.
12. Headley, J.L., Cole, G.W. (1980) The development of pseudo-Kaposi's sarcoma after placement of a vascular access graft. *Br J Dermatol*, **102**, 327–331.
13. Kim, T-H., Kim, K-H., Kim, J-H. et al (1997) Pseudo-Kaposi's sarcoma associated with acquired arteriovenous fistula. *J Dermatol*, **24**, 28–33.
14. Kolde, G., Wordeheide, J., Baumgartner, R. et al (1980) Kaposi-like acroangiodermatitis in an above knee amputation stump. *Br J Dermatol*, **102**, 575–580.
15. Güçlüer, H., Gübrüz, O., Kotiloglü, E. (1999) Kaposi-like acroangiodermatitis in an amputee. *Br J Dermatol*, **141**, 380–381.
16. Santucci, B., Donati, P., Cristaudo, A. et al (1992) Kaposi-like acroangiodermatitis caused by suction socket prosthesis. *Contact Derm*, **27**, 131–132.
17. Baldell, A., Marcoval, J., Graells, J. et al (1994) Kaposi-like acroangiodermatitis induced by a suction-socket prosthesis. *Br J Dermatol*, **131**, 915–917.
18. Meynadier, J., Malbos, S., Guilhou, J.J. et al (1980) Acroangiodermatitis developing on paralytic limbs. *Dermatologica*, **160**, 190–197.
19. Rao, B., Unis, M., Poulos, E. (1994) Acroangiodermatitis: a study of ten cases. *Int J Dermatol*, **33**, 179–181.
20. Kanitakis, J., Narvaez, D., Claudy, A. (1996) Expression of the CD34 antigen distinguishes Kaposi's sarcoma from pseudo-Kaposi's sarcoma (acroangiodermatitis). *Br J Dermatol*, **134**, 44–46.

Pityriasis alba

Clinical features

Pityriasis alba is a very common form of chronic dermatitis usually affecting preadolescent children of either sex.[1] In the United States, the prevalence is 1.9% in a healthy population.[2] The lesions are seen on the face in particular, but the shoulders, upper extremities and legs may also be involved (*Figs 5.47–5.49*).[1,3] Early lesions present as slightly scaly, mildly pruritic, round to oval pink plaques measuring from 0.5 to 5.0 cm or more in diameter, which later appear as scaly hypopigmented lesions.[1] The races are equally affected although lesions are more prominent in dark-skinned persons.[1] The condition usually resolves spontaneously after months or years.

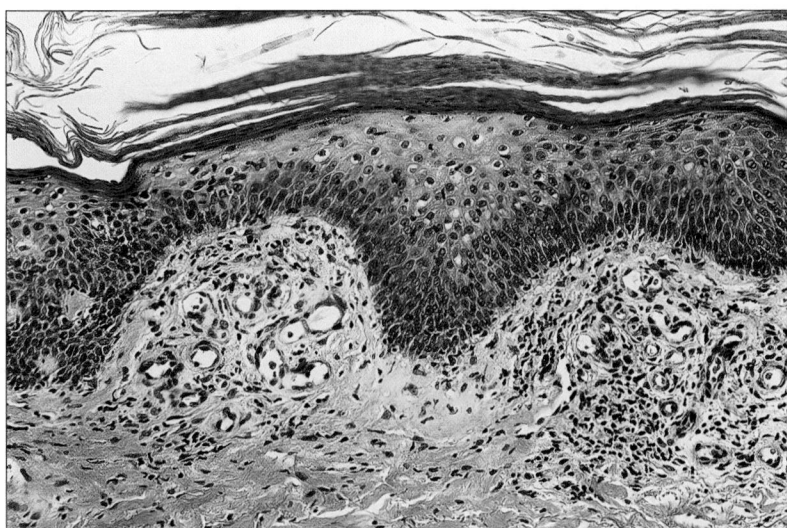

Fig. 5.46
Acroangiodermatitis showing lobular capillary proliferation, red cell extravasation and a chronic inflammatory cell infiltrate.

Pathogenesis and histological features

The etiology is unknown although some authors believe it may be a form of atopic dermatitis since many patients also have features of classic atopic dermatitis or a family history of atopy.[4] However, some patients with pityriasis alba lack typical features of atopy. An association with xerosis has also been postulated and the condition has also been linked to copper deficiency.[5,6]

The histological features of the early stage include follicular dilatation and plugging with infundibular spongiosis, parafollicular parakeratosis and sebaceous gland atrophy accompanied by a superficial perivascular lymphocytic infiltrate and edema.[7] In the later stages, the changes are those of chronic non-specific dermatitis including hyperkeratosis, parakeratosis sometimes accompanied by mild acanthosis and slight spongiosis.[7–9] There is variable hypo- and hyperpigmentation of the basal keratinocytes with reduced numbers of melanocytes and pigmentary incontinence.[7]

References

1. Galan, E.B., Janniger, C.K. (1998) Pityriasis alba. *Cutis*, **61**, 11–13.
2. Vanderhooft, S.L., Francis, J.S., Pagon, R.A. et al (1996) Prevalence of hypopigmented macules in a healthy population. *J Pediatr*, **129**, 355–361.
3. O'Farrell, N.M. (1956) Pityriasis alba. *Arch Dermatol*, **73**, 376–377.
4. Pinto, F.J., Bolognia, J.L. (1991) Disorders of hypopigmentation in children. *Pediatr Clin North Am*, **38**, 991–1017.
5. Urano-Seuhisa, S., Tagami, H. (1985) Functional and morphological analysis of the horny layer of pityriasis alba. *Acta Derm Venereol*, **65**, 164–167.
6. Galdari, E., Helmy, M., Ahmed, M. (1992) Trace elements in serum of pityriasis alba patients. *Int J Dermatol*, **31**, 525–526.
7. Vargas-Ocampo, F. (1993) Pityriasis alba: a histologic study. *Int J Dermatol*, **32**, 870–873.
8. Zaynoun, S.T., Aftimos, B.G., Tenekjian, K.K. et al (1983) Extensive pityriasis alba: a histological, histochemical and ultrastructural study. *Br J Dermatol*, **108**, 83–90.
9. Martin, R.F., Lugo-Somolinos, A., Sánchez, J.L. (1991) Clinicopathologic study on pityriasis alba. *Bol Assoc Med P R*, **82**, 463–465.

Eosinophilic spongiosis

Eosinophilic spongiosis is the histopathological term used to describe spongiosis in which eosinophils are the predominant cell type.[1–5] Eosinophilic spongiosis is a non-specific finding with which a considerable number of dermatoses may be associated. *Table 5.2* lists dermatoses in which eosinophilic spongiosis is commonly encountered. Detailed discussion of each of these disorders is found in the appropriate chapters.

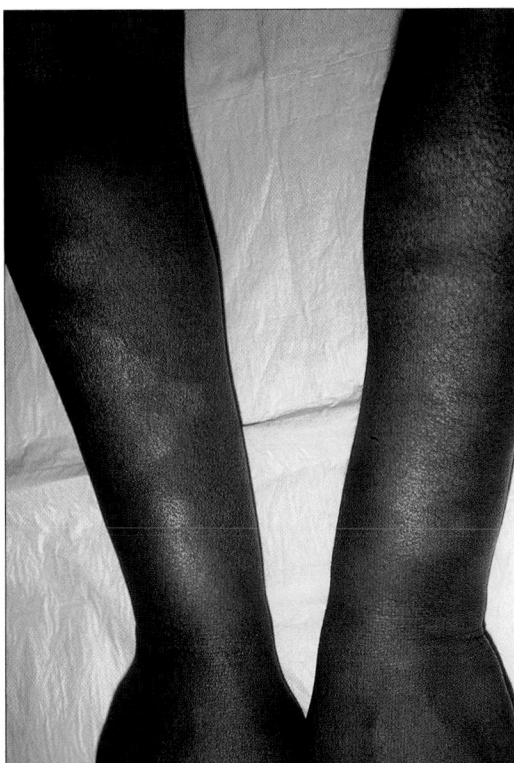

Fig. 5.47
Pityriasis alba: there are multiple hypopigmented, scaly patches on the arms. Lesions are more obvious in the colored races. By courtesy of C. Furlonge, MD, Port of Spain, Trinidad.

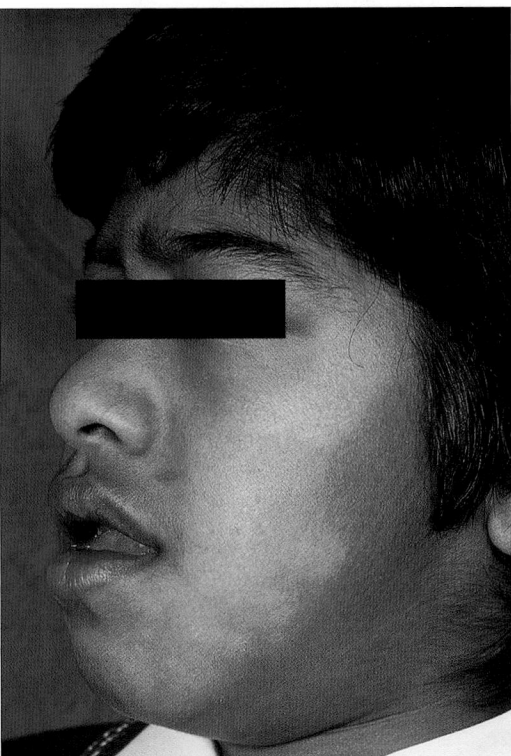

Fig. 5.48
Pityriasis alba: there is striking leukoderma on the cheek and chin, which are commonly affected sites. By courtesy of R.A. Marsden, MD, St George's Hospital, London, UK.

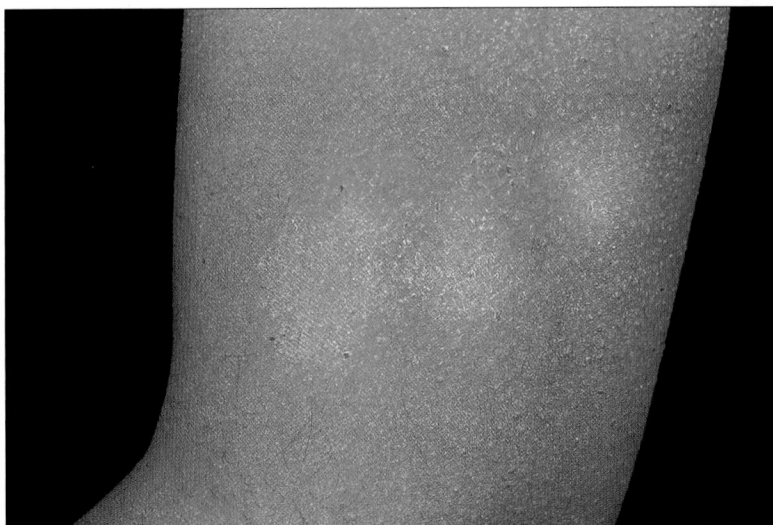

Fig. 5.49
Pityriasis alba: lesions in white-skinned patients are much more subtle. By courtesy of the Institute of Dermatology, London, UK.

Table 5.2
Diseases featuring eosinophilic spongiosis

- Incontinentia pigmenti
- Pemphigus
- Bullous pemphigoid
- Linear IgA disease
- Pemphigoid (herpes) gestationis and polymorphic eruption of pregnancy
- Insect-bite reactions
- Atopic eczema
- Contact dermatitis
- Grover's disease
- Drug reactions

References

1. Crotty, C., Pittelkow, M., Muller, S.A. (1983) Eosinophilic spongiosis: a clinicopathologic review of seventy-one cases. *J Am Acad Dermatol*, **8**, 337–343.
2. Emmerson, P.W., Wilson Jones, E. (1968) Eosinophilic spongiosis in pemphigus: a report of an unusual histological change in pemphigus. *Arch Dermatol*, **97**, 252–258.
3. Knight, A.G., Black, M.M., Delaney, T.J. (1976) Eosinophilic spongiosis: a clinical, histological and immunofluorescent correlation. *Clin Exp Dermatol*, **1**, 141–152.
4. Pearson, R.W., O'Donoghue, M., Kaplan, S.J. (1980) Pemphigus vegetans: its relationship to eosinophilic spongiosis and favorable response to dapsone. *Arch Dermatol*, **116**, 65–68.
5. Ruiz, E., Deng, J.S., Abell, E.A. (1994) Eosinophilic spongiosis: a clinical, histologic, and immunopathologic study. *J Am Acad Dermatol*, **30**, 973–976.

Erythroderma

Spongiotic dermatitis is one of the causes of erythroderma. Sometimes incorrectly called exfoliative dermatitis, erythroderma applies only when the entire skin surface is inflamed, erythematous and scaly (*Fig. 5.50*).[1–5] The clinical features are remarkably consistent irrespective of the underlying disease and therefore often pose a diagnostic challenge. Pruritus is variable, being particularly severe in the Sézary syndrome and in mycosis fungoides. Lymphadenopathy is usually present (dermatopathic lymphadenopathy). Prolonged erythroderma, particularly in the elderly, may be complicated by cardiac failure, peripheral circulatory collapse, hypothermia and infection. Patients with erythroderma are frequently biopsied since the clinical examination findings are often non-specific. Diagnosis without clinical information is often not possible.[1] *Table 5.3* lists the various causes of erythroderma. The specific diseases that cause erythroderma are discussed in detail in the appropriate chapters.

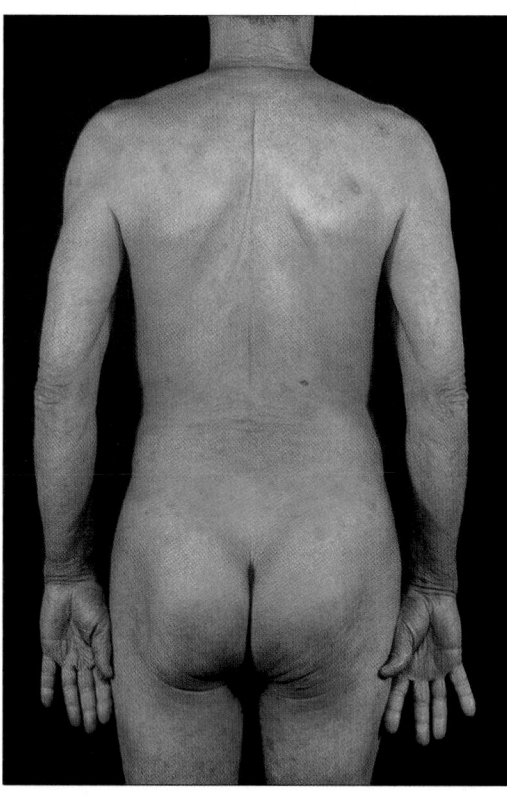

Fig. 5.50
Erythroderma: the entire skin surface is erythematous and slightly scaly. The appearances are relatively non-specific and give no indication of the cause. By courtesy of the Institute of Dermatology, London, UK.

Table 5.3
Causes of erythroderma

- Dermatitis
- Lymphoma (mycosis fungoides, T-cell leukemia, Hodgkin's lymphoma)
- Drugs (gold, penicillin, etc.)
- Psoriasis
- Pityriasis rubra pilaris
- Ichthyosiform erythroderma
- Scabies
- Lichen planus

References

1. Rothe, M.J., Bialy, T.L., Grant-Kiels, H.M. (2000) Erythroderma. *Dermatol Clin*, **18**, 405–415.
2. Botella-Estrada, R., Sanmartin, O., Oliver, V. et al (1994) Erythroderma: a clinicopathological study of 56 cases. *Arch Dermatol*, **130**, 1503–1507.
3. Hasen, T., Jansen, C.T. (1983) Erythroderma: a follow-up of 50 cases. *J Am Acad Dermatol*, **8**, 836–840.
4. Abrahams, I., McCarthy, J.T., Sanders, S.L. (1963) 101 cases of exfoliative dermatitis. *Arch Dermatol*, **87**, 96–101.
5. Walsh, N.M., Prokopetz, R., Tron, V.A. et al (1994) Histopathology in erythroderma: review of a series of cases by multiple observers. *J Cutan Pathol*, **21**, 419–423.

Sulzberger–Garbe syndrome

Clinical features

Sulzberger–Garbe syndrome (distinctive exudative discoid and lichenoid chronic dermatosis) was originally described as a widespread pruritic eruption associated with discoid lesions in middle-aged Jewish males.[1–3] Involvement of the penis was said to be characteristic. Transformation from eczematous to lichenoid lesions and vice versa is also thought to be a characteristic feature. The lesions are chronic, lasting from months to years, but eventuating in resolution.

Pathogenesis and histological features

Biopsy of exudative lesions shows a non-specific spongiotic dermatitis. Biopsy of lichenoid lesions is characterized by a band-like lymphocytic infiltrate. Variable numbers of eosinophils may present.

The existence of Sulzberger–Garbe syndrome as a distinctive entity is controversial. Some authors consider patients classified under this designation as having nummular dermatitis.[3]

References

1. Sulzberger, M.B. (1979) Distinctive exudative discoid and lichenoid chronic dermatosis (Sulzberger and Garbe) re-examined – 1978. *Br J Dermatol*, **99**, 13–20.
2. Stevens, D.M., Ackerman, A.B. (1984) On the concept of distinctive exudative discoid and lichenoid dermatosis (Sulzberger–Garbe). *Am J Dermatopathol*, **6**, 387–395.
3. Rongioletti, F., Corbella, L., Rebora, A. (1989) Exudative discoid and lichenoid chronic dermatosis (Sulzberger–Garbe). *Int J Dermatol*, **28**, 40–43.

Vein graft site dermatitis

Occasionally, patients undergoing coronary artery bypass develop an eczematous dermatitis in the region of the scar from the saphenous vein donor site.[1,2] The pathogenesis is unclear. Since patients often have objective evidence of neuropathy, some authors believe that the neuralgia may play a pathogenic role.[1] It is also possible that stasis changes may play a role in this disorder. Biopsy shows non-specific spongiotic dermatitis.

References

1. Hruza, L.L., Hruza, G.J. (1993) Saphenous vein graft donor site dermatitis. *Arch Dermatol*, **129**, 609–612.
2. Kato, N., Ueno, H. (1995) Saphenous vein graft donor site dermatitis in Japan. *J Dermatol*, **22**, 681–685.

Papular acrodermatitis of childhood

Clinical features

Papular acrodermatitis of childhood (Gianotti–Crosti syndrome, infantile papular acrodermatitis) is a rare disease representing a cutaneous response to a number of viral infections. It is characterized by the acute onset of monomorphic, symmetrical flat-topped papules or papulovesicles, 1–10 mm across, which range in color from pink to red or brown and are located primarily on the face (particularly the cheeks), buttocks and extensor surfaces of the forearms and legs, with the trunk typically being spared (*Figs 5.51–5.53*).[1–4] Lesions are usually blanchable although petechial and hemorrhagic variants may be rarely encountered.[4] A positive Koebner phenomenon is sometimes elicited.[4] The lesions are occasionally pruritic and are self-limiting, lasting up to 3 weeks. Mucous

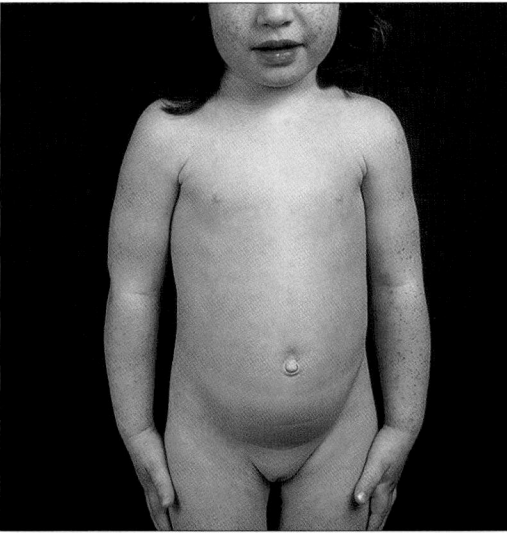

Fig. 5.51
Gianotti–Crosti syndrome: the eruption is present on the face and arms, there is sparing of the trunk. By courtesy of C. Gelmetti, MD, Milan University, Italy.

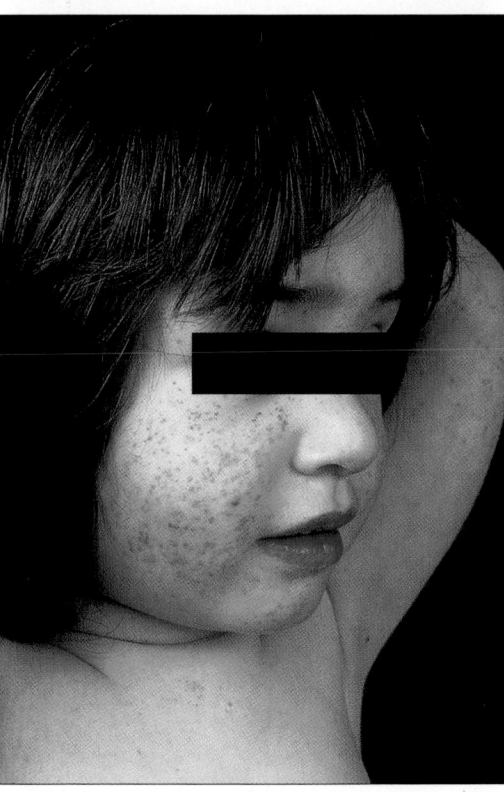

Fig. 5.52
Gianotti–Crosti syndrome: note the widespread erythematous papules on the cheeks of this young girl. By courtesy of C. Gelmetti, MD, Milan University, Italy.

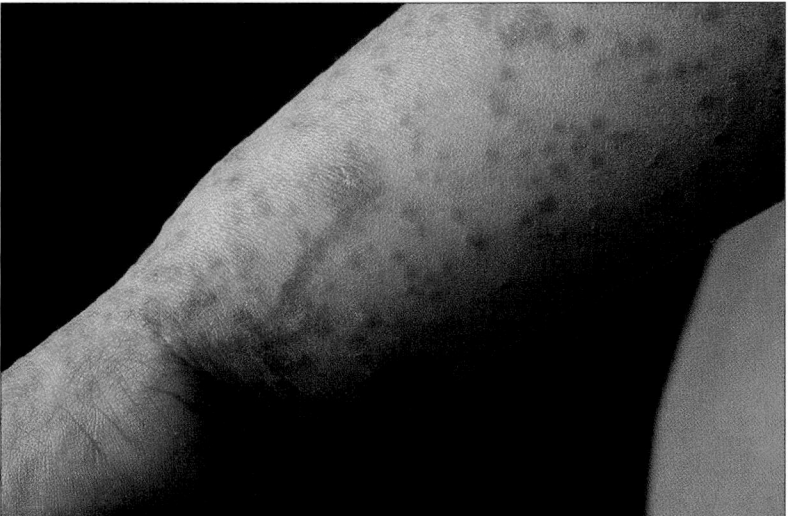

Fig. 5.53
Gianotti–Crosti syndrome: the papules are very uniform. A viral etiology is often identified. By courtesy of C. Gelmetti, MD, Milan University, Italy.

membranes are not affected. Infants and children are predominantly affected although there are occasional reports of the condition developing in adults.[4–8]

Systemic signs include hepatosplenomegaly and axillary and inguinal lymphadenopathy. Sometimes a fever is evident. There may be an anicteric acute hepatitis and occasionally patients progress to chronic liver disease.

Pathogenesis and histological features

In the original and early reports, Gianotti–Crosti syndrome was documented following infection with hepatitis B virus.[9–11] More recently cases have been reported in association with hepatitis A virus, Coxsackie virus, influenza virus, Epstein–Barr virus, cytomegalovirus, parainfluenza virus, human herpesvirus-6 (HHV-6), poxvirus, parvovirus and rotavirus.[12–22] In addition, the disease had been associated with HIV infection.[23] Gianotti–Crosti syndrome has also been reported following *Mycoplasma* infection, Lyme borreliosis and immunization although this last may be coincidental.[24–28] The pathogenesis is unknown although viral antigenemia and immune complex-mediated mechanisms have been proposed.[29]

Biopsies of skin lesions show entirely non-specific histological features. The epidermis often appears normal or it may be mildly acanthotic with parakeratosis. Lymphocytic exocytosis is usually present.[3] The upper dermis contains a lymphohistiocytic infiltrate in a perivascular distribution and there is also swelling of endothelial cells sometimes accompanied by marked papillary dermal edema.[28] Scattered eosinophils may be present.[29] Occasionally, a more lichenoid pattern of inflammation is encountered. There is no evidence of vasculitis.

Direct immunofluorescence is negative.[3]

By immunohistochemistry, the infiltrate consists of an admixture of CD4+ helper T-cells and CD8+ cytotoxic T-cells.[18,29,30]

In cases with hepatitis, the appearances are those of an acute viral hepatitis, which usually resolves over a period of up to 6 months. Rarely, chronic disease ensues.

References

1. Gianotti, F. (1979) Papular acrodermatitis of childhood and other papulovesicular acrolocated syndromes. *Br J Dermatol*, **100**, 49–59.
2. Taieb, A., Plantin, P., Du Pasquier, P. et al (1986) Gianotti–Crosti syndrome: a study of 26 cases. *Br J Dermatol*, **115**, 49–59.
3. Caputo, R., Gelmetti, C., Ermacora, E. et al. (1992) Gianotti–Crosti syndrome: a retrospective analysis of 308 cases. *J Am Acad Dermatol*, **26**, 207–210.
4. Chuh, A.A.T. (2001) Diagnostic criteria for Gianotti–Crosti syndrome: a prospective case-control study for validity assessment. *Cutis*, **68**, 207–231.
5. Claudy, A.L., Ortonne, J.P., Trepo, C. et al (1977) Adult papular acrodermatitis (Gianotti's disease): report of 3 cases. *Ann Dermatol Venereol*, **104**, 190–194.
6. Niitsuma, H., Ishii, M., Ojima, T. et al (1999) A case of acute hepatitis infected with hepatitis B virus during pregnancy and complicated by Gianotti–Crosti syndrome. *Nippon Shokakibyo Gakkai Zasshi*, **96**, 423–426.
7. Mempel, M., Abeck, D., Bye-Hansen, T. et al (1996) Gianotti–Crosti syndrome in an adult patient following a recently acquired Epstein–Barr virus infection. *Acta Derm Venereol*, **76**, 502–503.
8. Gibbs, S., Burrows, N.P. (2000) Gianotti–Crosti syndrome in two unrelated adults. *Clin Exp Dermatol*, **25**, 594–596.
9. Gianotti, F. (1973) Papular acrodermatitis of childhood: an Australian antigen disease. *Arch Dis Child*, **48**, 794–799.
10. Schneider, J.A., Poley, J.R., Millunchick, E.W. et al (1982) Papular acrodermatitis (Gianotti–Crosti syndrome) in a child with anicteric hepatitis B, virus subtype adw. *J Pediatr*, **101**, 219–222.
11. Lee, S., Kim, K.Y., Hahn, C.S. et al (1985) Gianotti–Crosti syndrome associated with hepatitis B surface antigen (subtype add). *J Am Acad Dermatol*, **12**, 629–633.
12. Sagi, E.F., Linder, N., Shouval, D. (1985) Papular acrodermatitis of childhood associated with hepatitis A virus infection. *Pediatr Dermatol*, **3**, 31–33.
13. James, W.D., Odom, R.B., Hatch, M.H. (1982) Gianotti–Crosti like eruption associated with Coxsackie virus A-16 infection. *J Am Acad Dermatol*, **6**, 862–866.
14. Cambiaghi, S., Scarabelli, G., Pistritto, G. et al (1994) Gianotti–Crosti syndrome in an adult after influenza virus vaccination. *Arch Dermatol*, **191**, 340–341.
15. Hofmann, B., Schuppe, H.C., Adams, O. et al (1997) Gianotti–Crosti syndrome associated with Epstein–Barr virus infection. *Pediatr Dermatol*, **14**, 273–277.
16. Maeda, S., Tsuda, H., Haruki, S. et al (1999) Atypical Epstein–Barr virus infection associated with Gianotti–Crosti syndrome and Bell's palsy. *Pediatr Int*, **41**, 315–317.
17. Berant, M., Naveh, Y., Weismann, I. (1983) Papular acrodermatitis with cytomegalovirus hepatitis. *Arch Dis Child*, **58**, 1024–1025.
18. Haki, M., Tsuchida, M., Kotsuji, M. et al (1997) Gianotti–Crosti syndrome associated with cytomegalovirus antigenemia after bone marrow transplantation. *Bone Marrow Transplant*, **20**, 691–693.
19. Balevičiené, G., Maciulvičiené, R., Schwartz, R.A. (2001) Papular acrodermatitis of childhood: the Gianotti–Crosti syndrome. *Cutis*, **67**, 291–294.
20. Yasumoto, S., Tsujita, J., Imayama, S. et al (1996) Case report: Gianotti–Crosti syndrome associated with human herpes-6 virus infection. *J Dermatol*, **23**, 499–501.
21. Carrascosa, J.M., Just, M., Ribera, M. et al (1998) Papular acrodermatitis related to poxvirus and parvovirus B19 infection. *Cutis*, **61**, 265–267.
22. Di Lernia, V. (1998) Gianotti–Crosti syndrome related to rotavirus infection. *Pediatr Dermatol*, **15**, 485–486.

23. Blauvelt, A., Turner, M.L. (1994) Gianotti–Crosti syndrome and human immunodeficiency virus infection. *Arch Dermatol*, **130**, 481–483.
24. Angoulvant, N., Grezard, P., Wolf, F. et al (2000) Acute *Mycoplasma pneumoniae* infection: new cause of Gianotti–Crosti syndrome. *Presse Med*, **29**, 1287.
25. Baldari, U., Cattonar, P., Nobile, C. et al (1996) Infantile acrodermatitis of Gianotti–Crosti and Lyme borreliosis. *Acta Derm Venereol*, **76**, 242–243.
26. Velangi, S.S., Tidman, M.J. (1998) Gianotti–Crosti syndrome after measles, mumps and rubella vaccination. *Br J Dermatol*, **139**, 1122–1123.
27. Murphy, L-A., Buckley, C. (2000) Gianotti–Crosti syndrome in an infant following immunization. *Pediatr Dermatol*, **17**, 225–226.
28. Erkek, E., Senturk, G.B., Özkaya, Ö. et al (2001) Gianotti–Crosti syndrome preceded by oral polio vaccine and followed by varicella infection. *Pediatr Dermatol*, **18**, 516–518.
29. Smith, K.J., Skelton, H. (2000) Histopathologic features seen in Gianotti–Crosti syndrome secondary to Epstein–Barr virus. *J Am Acad Dermatol*, **43**, 1076–1079.
30. Magyarlaki, M., Drobnitsch, I., Schneider, I. (1991) Papular acrodermatitis of childhood (Gianotti–Crosti syndrome). *Pediatr Dermatol*, **8**, 224–227.

Pityriasis rosea

Clinical features

Pityriasis rosea ('rose-colored scale') presents as an acute inflammatory dermatosis characterized by self-limiting oval papulosquamous lesions on the trunk and extremities.[1–3] The disease appears to be more common in females, and 75% of cases occur between the ages of 10 and 35 years.[4] It is characterized by seasonal variation, being most common in the months of December to February.[5] Although pityriasis rosea typically presents as a solitary episode, recurrent disease may occur in up to 2% of patients.[6]

In the majority of cases the disease first manifests itself with the appearance of a 'herald patch', a single red scaly lesion that increases in size over 48 hours up to 2–10 cm in diameter (*Fig. 5.54*).[7] A significant proportion of patients report symptoms, including pyrexia, headache, malaise, arthralgia, chills, vomiting, diarrhea and lymphadenopathy, up to 2–3 weeks before the onset of the eruption.[8]

After the appearance of the herald patch there is a 'secondary incubation period' of 7–14 days before the generalized eruption of pink to salmon-colored elliptical scaly lesions (*Fig. 5.55*).[9] The latter are approximately 1 cm in length and their longest axes occur along the Blaschko skin tension lines, producing the characteristic 'fir' or 'Christmas tree' effect. There is usually an erythematous center, the periphery of the macule being slightly brown and scaly. In dark-skinned patients the macules tend to be darker than the surrounding skin (*Fig. 5.56*). The lesions spread from the chest to the abdomen, thighs, arms and back, generally taking up to 2 weeks to appear, persisting for 2–4 weeks, and fading over a further period of 2 weeks. Pityriasis rosea may be pruritic.

Oral lesions have been described in up to 16% of patients.[4] They may take the form of a single large erythematous plaque, bullae, multiple hemorrhagic puncta, round erythematous macules and plaques or erythematous annular lesions.[4,10–12]

Several morphological variants may occur: a papular variant is seen in young children, pregnant women and Afro-Caribbeans; a vesicular or bullous variant may occur in infants and children; and an urticarial form has also been noted.[5,13] Occasionally pityriasis rosea may have a purpuric, hemorrhagic component.[5,14] Localized and unilateral forms, and an 'inverse' form presenting on the face and extremities, have also been documented.[15]

Pathogenesis and histological features

The exact etiology of pityriasis rosea is unknown; however, most of the evidence points to an infectious, probably viral, cause. It sometimes complicates an upper respiratory tract infection.[16] The herald patch may develop at the site of insect bites, particularly of fleas, but patches have also occurred at the sites of old trauma and scars, suggesting an isomorphic (Koebner's) response.[15] Atypical pityriasis rosea has also been described in bone marrow transplant recipients and following treatment with interferon-alpha (IFN-α).[17,18] Case clustering in establishments with communal living supports an infectious etiology. Recently, HHV-7 has been identified in peripheral blood mononuclear cells in addition to plasma and skin of patients with pityriasis rosea.[19,20] Other workers have failed to confirm this observation.[21] Rarely a pityriasis rosea-like eruption may be a manifestation of AIDS.[22]

The histopathological features are those of a non-specific subacute or chronic dermatitis and comprise focal hyperkeratosis and angulated parakeratosis with slight acanthosis (*Figs 5.57–5.60*).[23] The granular cell layer may be absent beneath the foci of parakeratosis. Intraepidermal cytoid bodies are present in as many as 50% of cases.[24,25] Focal

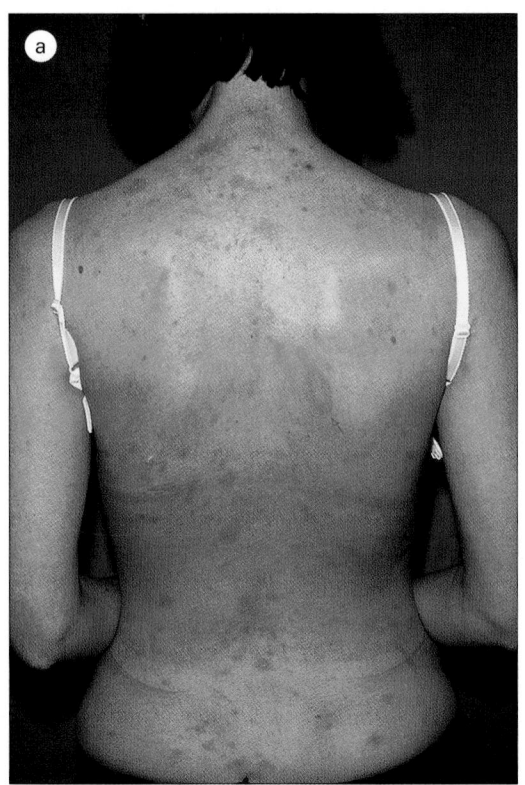

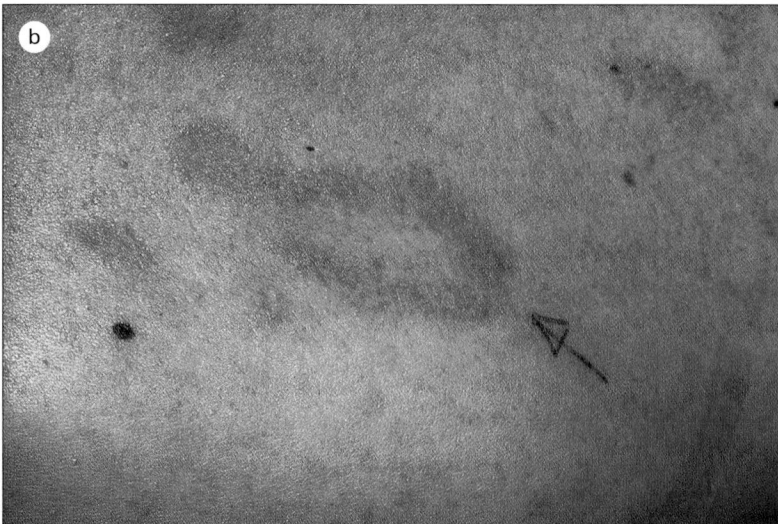

Fig. 5.54
Pityriasis rosea: (a) the 'herald patch' which marks the onset of this dermatosis, is marked by an arrow; (b) close-up view. By courtesy of R.A. Marsden, MD, St George's Hospital, London, UK.

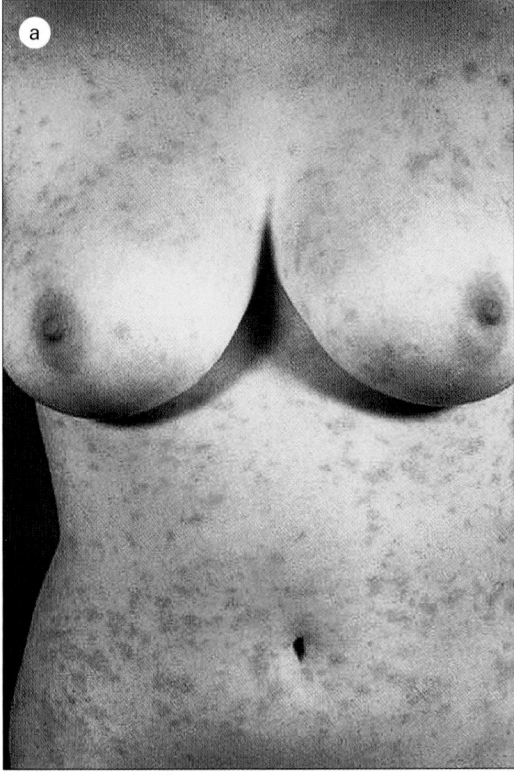
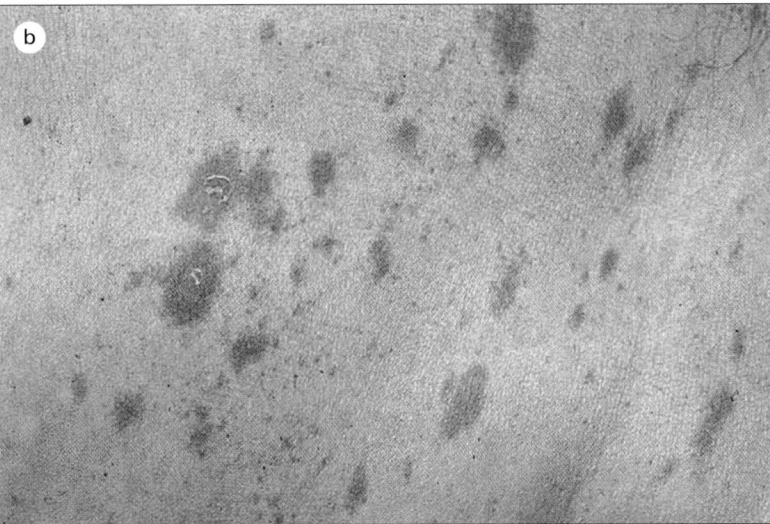

Fig. 5.55
Pityriasis rosea: (a) the secondary rash presents as small pink slightly scaly macules; (b) close-up view. (a) By courtesy of R.A. Marsden, MD, St George's Hospital, London, UK; (b) by courtesy of the Institute of Dermatology, London, UK.

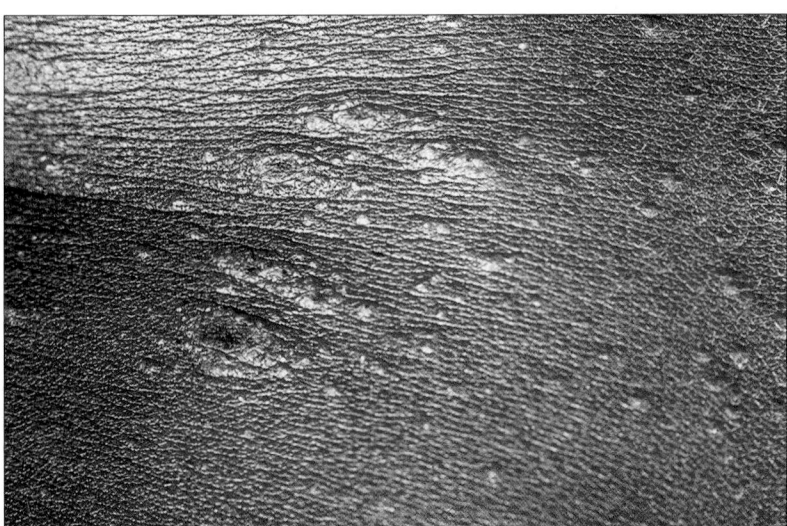

Fig. 5.56
Pityriasis rosea: in pigmented skin, there is often postinflammatory hyperpigmentation and the erythematous nature of the eruption is not apparent. By courtesy of R.A. Marsden, MD, St George's Hospital, London, UK.

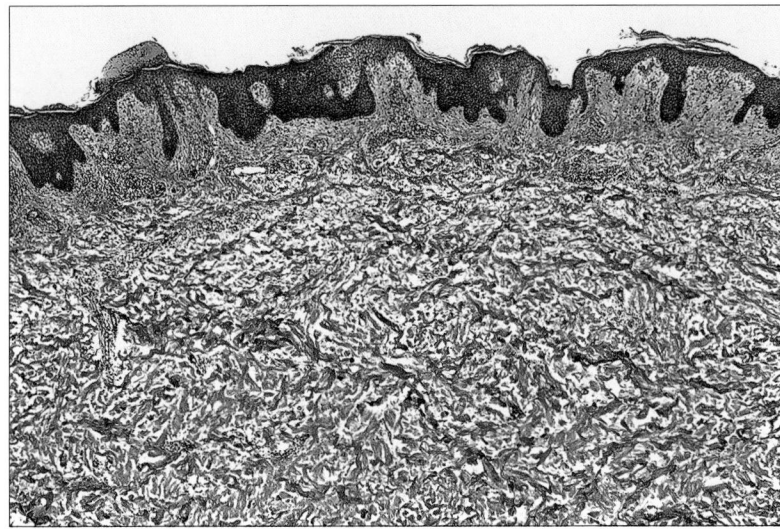

Fig. 5.57
Pityriasis rosea: low power view showing multiple foci of scale with psoriasiform hyperplasia.

acantholytic dyskeratosis has occasionally been documented.[26] A lymphohistiocytic infiltrate surrounds the vessels of the superficial vascular plexus and there is slight spongiosis. Rarely spongiotic vesiculation may be evident.[5] Occasionally scattered eosinophils are present. Purpura is a not infrequent feature and occasional erythrocytes may be seen within the epidermis.

Immunocytochemical staining has demonstrated that the dermal infiltrate consists mainly of T-cells, including helper and suppressor cells, together with large numbers of Langerhans' cells. Human leukocyte antigen DR (HLA-DR, Ia-like antigen) has been demonstrated on the surface of keratinocytes, and this has been interpreted as showing that they are taking an active role in cellular immunity.[27–29] HLA-DR antigen may also be expressed on the surface of the T-helper cells.[28]

Differential diagnosis

Guttate psoriasis shows considerable overlap with pityriasis rosea. The presence of neutrophils within the parakeratotic mounds favors a diagnosis of psoriasis.

A wide range of drugs has been associated with a pityriasis rosea-like eruption including barbiturates, ketotifen, clonidine, captopril, isotretinoin, gold, bismuth, arsenic, organic mercurials, methoxypromazine, D-penicillamine, tripelennamine hydrochloride, metronidazole and salvarsan (see p. 651).[15,17] In such cases, the distinction depends upon clinicopathological correlation. The presence of large numbers of eosinophils is a clue to a hypersensitivity reaction.

Acute and subacute eczematous dermatitis may also be confused with pityriasis rosea. The presence of lens-shaped parakeratosis and limited

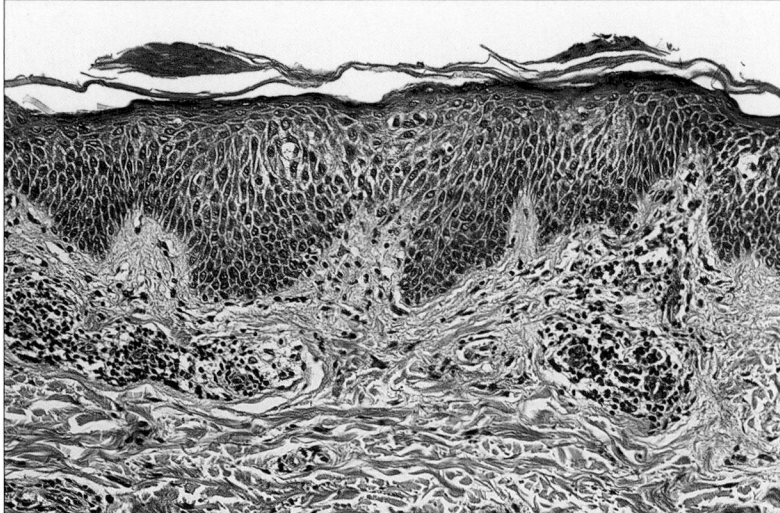

Fig. 5.58
Pityriasis rosea: small foci of parakeratotic scale are a characteristic finding.
The epidermis shows mild spongiosis.

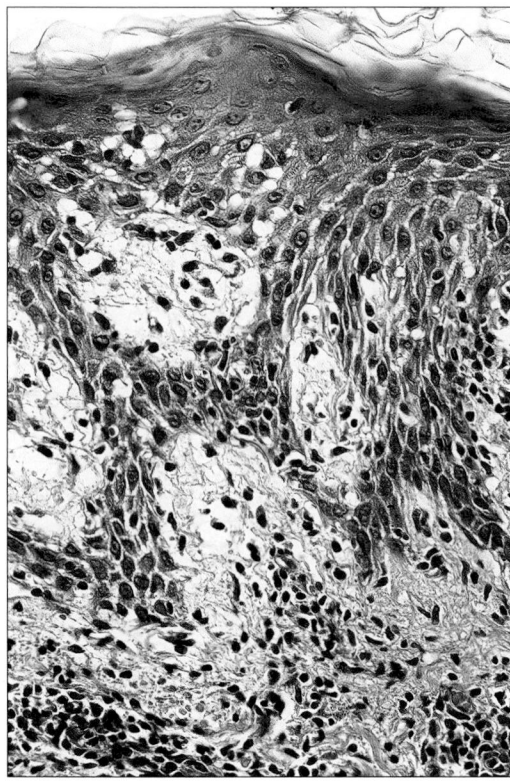

Fig. 5.59
Pityriasis rosea: there is spongiosis and a perivascular lymphocytic infiltrate. One or two plasma cells are also present.

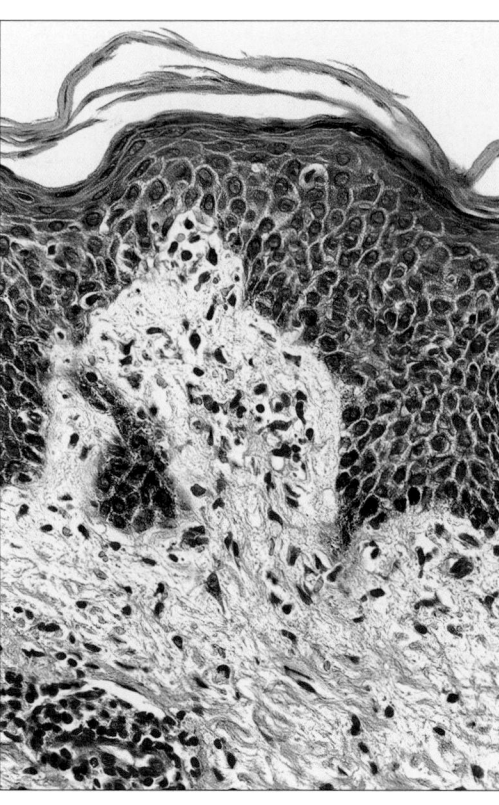

Fig. 5.60
Pityriasis rosea: in this field, there is red cell extravasation.

spongiosis favors pityriasis rosea. Again, clinical findings should help make this distinction.

Pityriasis lichenoides chronica is characterized by interface change and vacuolar degeneration of the basal layer of the epidermis, features not seen in pityriasis lichenoides.

A PAS stain is mandatory in all cases to exclude a dermatophyte infection.

References

1. Percival, G.H. (1932) Pityriasis rosea. *Br J Dermatol*, **44**, 241–253.
2. Parson, J.M. (1986) Pityriasis rosea update. *J Am Acad Dermatol*, **15**, 159–165.
3. Allen, R.A., Janniger, C.K., Schwartz, R.A. (1995) Pityriasis rosea. *Cutis*, **56**, 198–202.
4. Vidimos, A.T., Camisa, C. (1992) Tongue and cheek: oral lesions in pityriasis rosea. *Cutis*, **50**, 276–280.
5. Bari, M., Cohen, B.A. (1991) Purpuric vesicular eruption in a 7 year old girl. Vesicular pityriasis rosea. *Arch Dermatol*, **126**, 1500–1501.
6. Halkier-Søresen, L. (1990) Recurrent pityriasis rosea. *Acta Derm Venereol*, **70**, 179–180.
7. Bjombery, A., Hellgren, I. (1962) Pityriasis rosea: a statistical, clinical and laboratory investigation of 826 patients and matched healthy controls. *Acta Derm Venereol*, **42** (Suppl. 50), 1–68.
8. Graham, R. (1989) What is pityriasis rosea? *Practitioner*, **233**, 555.
9. Chuang, T., Ilstrup, D.M., Perry, H.O. et al (1982) Pityriasis rosea in Rochester, Minnesota, 1969–78. A 10 year epidemiological study. *J Am Acad Dermatol*, **7**, 80–89.
10. Vollum, D.T. (1973) Pityriasis rosea in the African. *Trans St John's Hosp Dermatol Soc*, **59**, 269–273.
11. Jacyk, W.K. (1980) Pityriasis rosea in Nigerians. *Int J Dermatol*, **19**, 397–399.
12. Kay, M.H., Rapini, R.P., Fritz, K.A. (1985) Oral lesions in pityriasis rosea. *Arch Dermatol*, **121**, 1449–1451.
13. Crosby, D.L., Feldman, S.D. (1990) A pruritic vesicular eruption. *Arch Dermatol*, **126**, 1497–1502.
14. Ginsburg, C.M. (1991) Pityriasis rosea. *Pediatr Infect Dis J*, **10**, 858–859.
15. Gibney, M.D., Leonardi, C.L. (1997) Acute papulosquamous eruption of the extremities demonstrating an isomorphic response. *Arch Dermatol*, **133**, 651, 654.
16. Chuang, T., Perry, H.O., Ilstrup, D.M. et al (1983) Recent upper respiratory tract infection and pityriasis rosea: a case-control study of 249 matched pairs. *Br J Dermatol*, **108**, 587–591.
17. Spelman, L.J., Robertson, I.M., Strutton, G.M. et al (1994) Pityriasis rosea-like eruption after bone marrow transplantation. *J Am Acad Dermatol*, **31**, 348–351.
18. Durusoy, Ç., Alpsoy, E., Yilmaz, E. (1999) Pityriasis rosea in a patient with Behçet's disease treated with interferon alpha 2A. *J Dermatol*, **26**, 225–228.
19. Drago, F., Ranieri, E., Malaguti, F. et al (1997) Human herpesvirus in 7 patients with pityriasis rosea: electron microscopy investigations and polymerase chain reaction in mononuclear cells, plasma and skin. *Dermatology*, **195**, 374–378.
20. Black, J.B., Pellett, P.E. (1999) Human herpesvirus 7. *Rev Med Virol*, **9**, 245–262.
21. Aractingi, S., Morinet, F., Mokni, M. et al (1996) Absence of picornavirus genome in pityriasis rosea. *Arch Dermatol Res*, **289**, 60–61.
22. Sadick, N.S., McNutt, N.S., Kaplan, M.H. (1990) Papulosquamous dermatoses of AIDS. *J Am Acad Dermatol*, **22**, 1270–1277.
23. García de Sila, L., Gardner, P.S. (1968) Pityriasis rosea; a histologic and serologic study. *Br J Dermatol*, **80**, 514–515.
24. Okamoto, H., Imamura, S., Aoshima, T. et al (1982) Dyskeratotic degeneration of epidermal cells in pityriasis rosea: light and electron microscopic studies. *Br J Dermatol*, **107**, 189–194.
25. Imamura, S., Ozaki, M., Oguchi, M. et al (1985) Atypical pityriasis rosea. *Dermatologica*, **171**, 474–477.
26. Stern, J.K., Wolf, J.E., Rosen, T. (1979) Focal acantholytic dyskeratosis in pityriasis rosea. *Arch Dermatol*, **115**, 497–500.
27. Aiba, S., Tagami, H. (1984) HLA DR antigen expression on the keratinocyte surface in dermatoses characterized by lymphocytic exocytosis (e.g. pityriasis rosea). *Br J Dermatol*, **111**, 285–294.
28. Aikawa, K., Yoshiike, T., Ogawa, H. (1989) HLA-DR antigen expression on peripheral T cell subsets in pityriasis rosea Gilbert, herpes zoster, and psoriasis. *Jpn J Dermatol*, **99**, 443–447.
29. Aiba, S., Tagami, H. (1985) Immunohistologic studies in pityriasis rosea: evidence for cellular immune reaction in the lesional epidermis. *Arch Dermatol*, **121**, 761–765.

Juvenile plantar dermatosis

Clinical features

Scaly palms and soles with loss of a normal epidermal rete pattern characterize juvenile plantar dermatosis. The affected area often has a shiny red appearance with fissures (*Figs 5.61, 5.62*).[1–4] As its name suggests, the disease is seen in prepubertal children with a mean age of 9.6 years.[1] The most common sites affected are the volar aspect of the great toe and the ball of the foot.[1] The hand is only rarely affected. Patients often have a personal or family history of atopy.[2,4] The disorder usually lasts for 6 months to several years before resolving.[1,3] However, many patients develop features of classic eczema of the hands later in life.[2]

Pathogenesis and histological features

The pathogenesis of this disorder is not understood; however, it has been suggested that synthetic footwear may play a role in its development.[3]

Biopsy shows epidermal acanthosis and subacute to chronic spongiosis.[1] Variable parakeratosis and hypogranulosis may be seen. A lymphocytic infiltrate centered on the eccrine duct is said to be characteristic.[1]

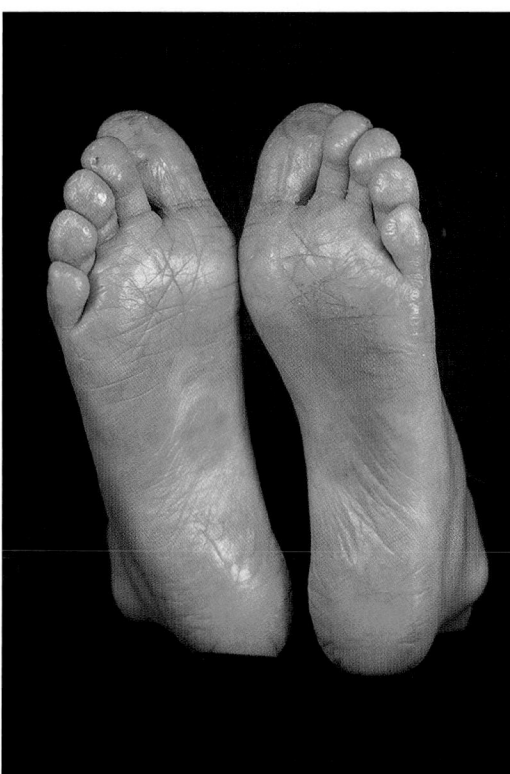

Fig. 5.61
Juvenile plantar dermatosis: multiple erythematous lesions are present on the soles of the feet. By courtesy of the Institute of Dermatology, London, UK.

Fig. 5.62
Juvenile plantar dermatosis: close-up view showing scaling and fissuring. By courtesy of the Institute of Dermatology, London, UK.

Differential diagnosis

The histological changes are probably non-specific but the presence of chronic inflammation centered on the sweat duct should suggest juvenile plantar dermatosis in the appropriate clinical setting and allow distinction from other spongiotic dermatitidies, which typically spare the acrosyringium. One group could not identify PAS-positive material occluding sweat ducts in multiple histological sections of juvenile plantar dermatosis (c.f. miliaria).[1] A PAS stain with diastase digestion should also be performed to evaluate for fungal infection.

References

1. Ashton, R.E., Jones, R.R., Griffiths, A. (1985) Juvenile plantar dermatosis. A clinicopathologic study. *Arch Dermatol*, **121**, 225–228.
2. Svenson, A. (1988) Prognosis and atopic background of juvenile plantar dermatosis and gluteo-femoral eczema. *Acta Derm Vernereol*, **68**, 336–340.
3. Mackie, R.M., Husain, S.L. (1976) Juvenile plantar dermatosis: a new entity? *Clin Exp Dermatol*, **1**, 253–260.
4. Graham, R.M., Verbov, J.L., Vickers, C.F.H. (1987) Juvenile plantar dermatosis. *Clin Exp Dermatol*, **12**, 468–469.

Miliaria

Clinical features

This common disorder, although most often seen in children, may affect any age group. It develops as a consequence of obstruction to the outflow tract of the intraepidermal component of the eccrine sweat duct and is associated with excessive sweating and exposure to high humidity. Traditionally the condition is subdivided into three subtypes: miliaria crystallina, miliaria rubra and miliaria profunda.[1,2]

- In *miliaria crystallina* the level of obstruction is within the stratum corneum, and results in the formation of small, clear vesicles, located particularly on the trunk (*Fig. 5.63*). There are accompanying symptoms of a high fever and pronounced sweating.
- *Miliaria rubra* (prickly heat) is particularly common in hot humid climates and is due to obstruction within the prickle cell layer, resulting in erythematous papules and vesicles, usually located about the trunk and intertriginous regions (*Fig. 5.64*). This form of miliaria is particularly common in infants. The term *miliaria pustulosa* has been applied to the above subtypes when pustules develop.

Fig. 5.63
Miliaria crystallina: tiny vesicles resembling water droplets are scattered over the abdomen of this young male. By courtesy of R.A. Marsden, MD, St George's Hospital, London, UK.

- In *miliaria profunda*, also typically seen in tropical climates, the obstruction is at level of the sweat duct. Small papules are seen on the trunk and occasionally the extremities.

Pathogenesis and histological features

The pathogenesis of miliaria is poorly understood. It has been suggested that bacteria play a role in the development of the disease. There is evidence that extracellular polysaccharide substance (EPS), a PAS-positive material made by some strains of *Staphylococcus epidermidis*, obstructs the sweat duct and causes the disease.[3] Normal controls who had *S. epidermidis* swabbed on to their volar forearms followed by occlusion and heat developed miliaria. These results could not be replicated with other bacteria.[3] Biopsy revealed EPS in lesions from several patients.

A subcorneal vesicle containing a few neutrophils characterizes miliaria crystallina, while rubra involves an intraepidermal spongiotic vesicle. In both variants the lesions can be seen to be centered upon an intraepidermal eccrine sweat duct. Miliaria pustulosa is characterized by features of miliaria in addition to an intraepidermal or subcorneal pustule. Miliaria profunda is characterized by spongiosis of the dermal portion of the eccrine duct, often associated with dermal chronic inflammation adjacent to the affected duct.

References

1. Schachner, L., Press, S. (1983) Vesicular, bullous and pustular disorders in infancy and childhood. *Pediatr Clin North Am*, 30, 609–629.
2. Feng, E., Janninger, C. (1995) Miliaria. *Cutis*, 55, 213–216.
3. Mowad, C.M., McGinley, K.J., Foglia, A. et al (1995) The role of extracellular polysaccharide substance produced by Staphylococcus epidermidis in miliaria. *J Am Acad Dermatol*, 33, 729–733.

Fox–Fordyce disease

Clinical features

Fox–Fordyce disease (apocrine miliaria, chronic itching papular eruption of the axillae and pubic region) presents as a chronic papular eruption, associated with pruritus, and located in areas containing apocrine sweat glands (i.e. the axillae, the pubic area, the vulval labia, the perineum and areola) (*Fig. 5.65*).[1,2] The papules are discrete, firm and flesh-colored or pigmented. Associated hair loss is often present.

The disease is uncommon and over 90% of reported cases have occurred in women, usually aged 13–35 years. Rarely, prepubescent and postmenopausal patients have been described.[3,4]

Patients with Fox–Fordyce disease have apocrine anhidrosis. Although eccrine sweating is normal, apocrine sweating does not occur due to the keratotic plugging of the apocrine duct orifice. The continued secretion of sweat, however, causes the duct to rupture and an apocrine sweat retention cyst forms in the epithelium. The exact cause of the follicular plugging is unknown, but a hormonal link has been postulated.

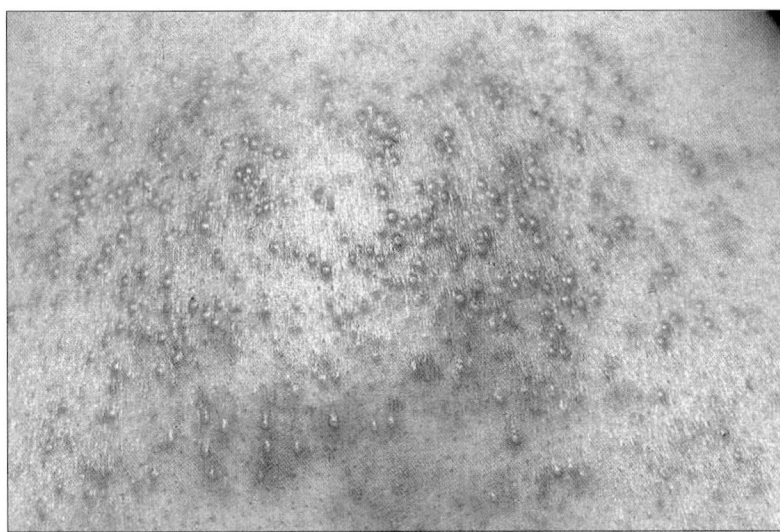

Fig. 5.64
Miliaria rubra: the characteristic appearance is of large numbers of minute papules and vesicles. By courtesy of M.M. Black, MD, Institute of Dermatology, London, UK.

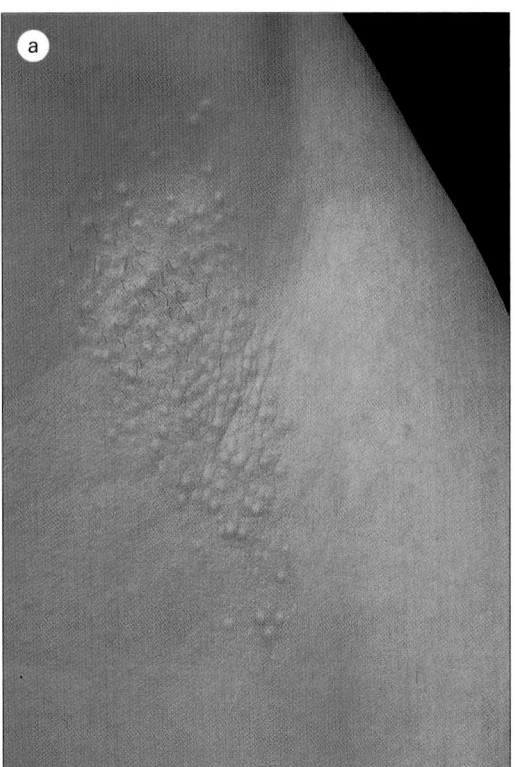
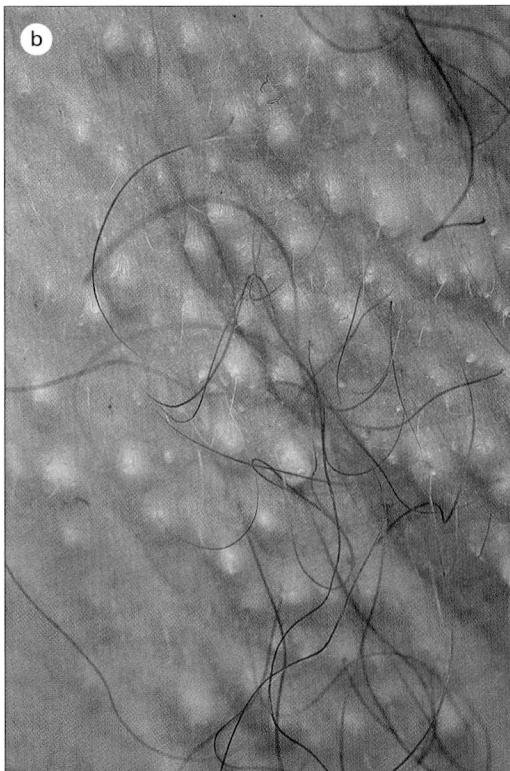

Fig. 5.65
Fox–Fordyce disease: (a) there are numerous white papules. The axilla is a characteristic site; (b) close-up view. By courtesy of the Institute of Dermatology, London, UK.

Occasional instances of coexistent hidradenitis suppurativa have been recorded.[5]

Pathogenesis and histological features

The pathogenesis of Fox–Fordyce disease is not understood. Follicular infundibular plugging is present in association with acanthosis, parakeratosis, spongiosis and an underlying non-specific chronic inflammatory cell infiltrate. The keratinous obstruction prevents the outflow of apocrine secretion and leads to the diagnostic feature of an intrafollicular sweat retention vesicle; serial sections may be needed to demonstrate this lesion.[6]

References

1. MacMillan, D.C., Vickers, H.R. (1971) Fox–Fordyce disease. *Br J Dermatol*, **84**, 181.
2. Feldmann, R., Masouyé, I., Chavaz, P. et al (1992) Fox–Fordyce disease: successful treatment with tropical clindamycin in alcoholic propylene glycol solution. *Dermatology*, **184**, 310–313.
3. Mevorah, B., Duboff, G.S., Wass, R.W. (1968) Fox–Fordyce disease in prepubescent girls. *Dermatologica*, **136**, 43–56.
4. Montes, L.F., Cortés, A., Baker, B.L. et al (1959) Fox–Fordyce disease. A report with endocrinological and histopathological studies of a case, which developed after surgical menopause. *Arch Dermatol*, **80**, 549–553.
5. Spiller, R.F., Knox, J.M. (1958) Fox–Fordyce disease with hidradenitis suppurativa. *J Invest Dermatol*, **31**, 127–135.
6. Winkelmann, R.K., Montgomery, H. (1956) Fox–Fordyce disease. A histopathologic and histochemical investigation. *Arch Dermatol*, **74**, 63–68.

Transient acantholytic dermatosis with prominent eccrine ductal involvement

Grover's disease (transient acantholytic dermatoses) is discussed more comprehensively on page 164; however, since it is commonly associated with spongiosis (often in the absence of acantholysis), it deserves mention in this chapter. Recent studies of Grover's disease have shown a strong correlation with high temperature and sweating and it has been suggested that its pathogenesis may be analogous to that of miliaria.[1–3] Supporting these concepts is the description of Grover's disease in bed-ridden and febrile patients. The lesions are usually present on the back. These patients often have prominent involvement of the eccrine duct and the lesions have been termed sudoriferous acrosyringeal acantholytic disease (sudoriferous Grover's disease).[4] Biopsies taken from patients with sudoriferous acrosyringeal acantholytic disease often show, in addition to typical features of Grover's disease, acantholysis of the superficial portion of the eccrine duct. When acantholysis is present and a clinical history is provided, the diagnosis is usually straightforward. However, not uncommonly, biopsies taken from patients with Grover's disease show spongiosis only (often eosinophilic spongiosis). In these patients, a diagnosis of Grover's disease may still be made in the appropriate clinical setting.

References

1. Hu, C.H., Michel, B., Farber, E.M. (1985) Transient acantholytic dermatosis (Grover's disease). A skin disorder related to heat and sweating. *Arch Dermatol*, **121**, 1439–1441.
2. Heaphy, M.R., Tucker, S.B., Winkelmann, R.K. (1976) Benign papular acantholytic dermatosis. *Arch Dermatol*, **112**, 814–821.
3. Manteaux, A.M., Rapini, R.P. (1990) Transient acantholytic dermatosis in patients with skin cancer. *Cutis*, **46**, 488–490.
4. Hashimoto, K., Moiin, A., Chang, M.W. et al (1996) Sudoriferous acrosyringeal acantholytic disease. A subset of Grover's disease. *J Cutan Pathol*, **23**, 151–164.

It is important to note that myriad cutaneous disorders may show some degree of spongiosis. For example, such disparate conditions as mycosis fungoides and psoriasis are not uncommonly associated with a degree of spongiosis. In this chapter, we have focused our discussion on entities for which spongiosis is a dominant and fairly consistent histological finding. Other entities that may occasionally be associated with some degree of spongiosis are discussed in the appropriate chapters.

Psoriasiform dermatoses

Definition

The psoriasiform reaction pattern is defined by the presence of epidermal hyperplasia with fairly uniform and marked enlargement of the rete ridges. Although confluent parakeratosis with neutrophil exocytosis is characteristic of psoriasis (the prototype of this group of conditions), this feature is not included within the definition, which would otherwise become too restrictive. Diseases in addition to psoriasis which may manifest a psoriasiform pattern include Reiter's syndrome, pityriasis rubra pilaris, lichen simplex chronicus, psoriasiform drug reactions, subacute and chronic spongiotic dermatitis, parapsoriasis and pityriasis rosea (herald patch). Other conditions in which psoriasiform hyperplasia may sometimes be feature include dermatophyte infections and candidiasis, secondary syphilis, scabies infestation, inflammatory linear verrucous epidermal nevus, necrolytic migratory erythema, acrodermatitis enteropathica and pellagra. Neoplastic conditions such as Bowen's disease and mycosis fungoides, which often show marked epidermal hyperplasia, are not included in this definition.

Psoriasis

Clinical features

Psoriasis is a chronic relapsing and remitting disease of the skin that may affect any site.[1] It is one of the commonest of all skin diseases, with a reported incidence of 1–2% in Caucasians.[2] It is rare among blacks, Japanese and native North and South American populations.[3] Males and females are affected equally. Although psoriasis may occur at any age, it most frequently presents in the teens and early adult life (type I psoriasis).[4] A second peak in which the disease is often milder appears around the sixth decade (type II psoriasis).[4]

The classic cutaneous lesion of psoriasis vulgaris (plaque psoriasis) is raised, sharply demarcated, with a silvery scaly surface (*Figs 5.66–5.68*). The underlying skin has a glossy, erythematous appearance. If the parakeratotic scales are removed with the fingernail, small droplets of blood may appear on the surface (Auspitz's sign); this is diagnostic. Plaques, when multiple, are often symmetrical and annular lesions due to central clearing are a common finding (*Fig. 5.69*). The scalp, the extensor surfaces (mainly the knees and elbows), the lower back and around the umbilicus are particularly affected. The clinical features, however, show regional variation: scalp involvement often shows very marked plaque formation whereas on the penis, scaling is commonly minimal and the features may be mistaken for Bowen's disease (*Figs 5.70–5.72*). Linear lesions (linear psoriasis) follow previous trauma (koebnerization) (*Fig. 5.73*).

Psoriasis may manifest in a variety of other ways.

- *Guttate (eruptive) psoriasis* presents as small (0.5–1.5 cm diameter) papules over the upper trunk and proximal extremities, typically in younger patients (*Figs 5.74–5.76*).
- *Psoriasis inversa* is characterized by the development of plaques in the flexures (*Fig. 5.77*).
- *Generalized pustular psoriasis* (von Zumbusch) is an acute variant,

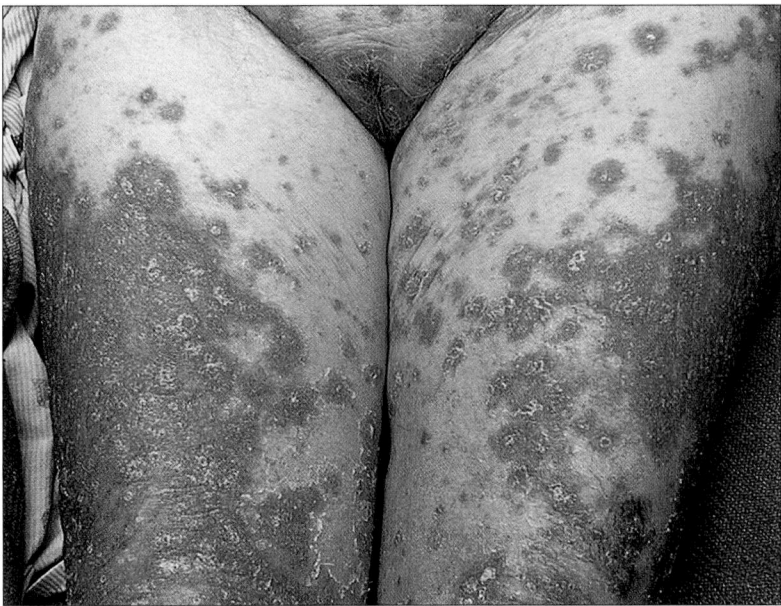

Fig. 5.66
Psoriasis: typical plaque disease showing bilateral and fairly symmetrical distribution. In this example, the silvery scale is well demonstrated. By courtesy of J. Kerner, MD, Harvard Medical School, Boston, USA.

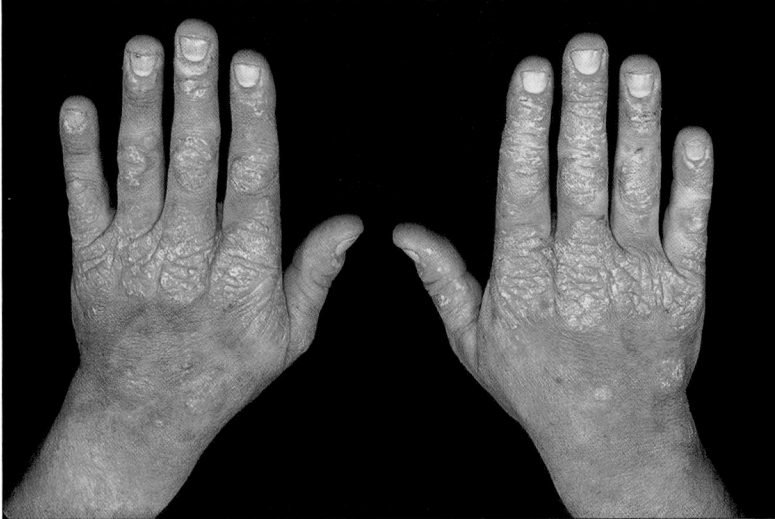

Fig. 5.67
Plaque psoriasis: note the symmetry of these lesions. By courtesy of R.A. Marsden, MD, St George's Hospital, London, UK.

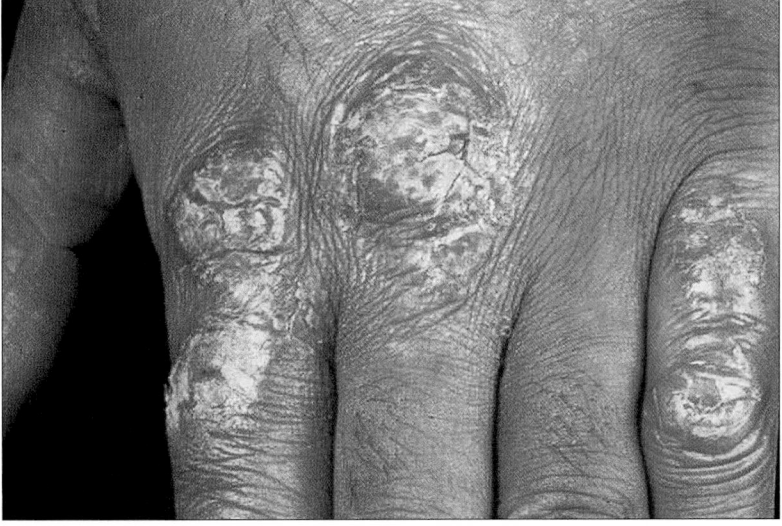

Fig. 5.68
Plaque psoriasis: close-up view showing the thick scale. By courtesy of the Institute of Dermatology, London, UK.

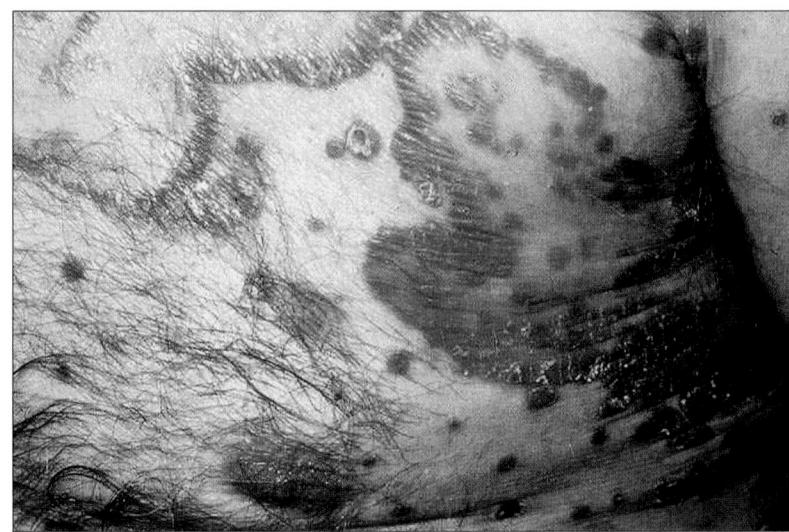

Fig. 5.69
Annular psoriasis: central clearing of plaques results in annular lesions. By courtesy of R.A. Marsden, MD, St George's Hospital, London, UK.

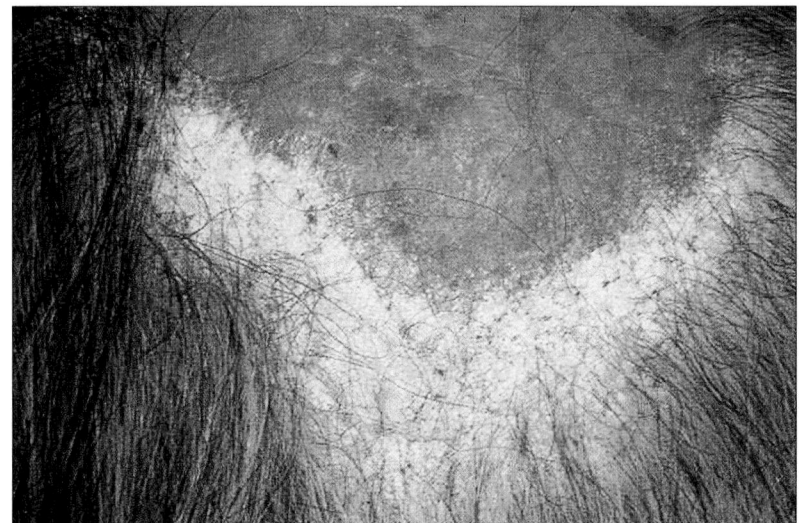

Fig. 5.70
Plaque psoriasis: the scalp is a commonly affected site. By courtesy of the Institute of Dermatology, London, UK.

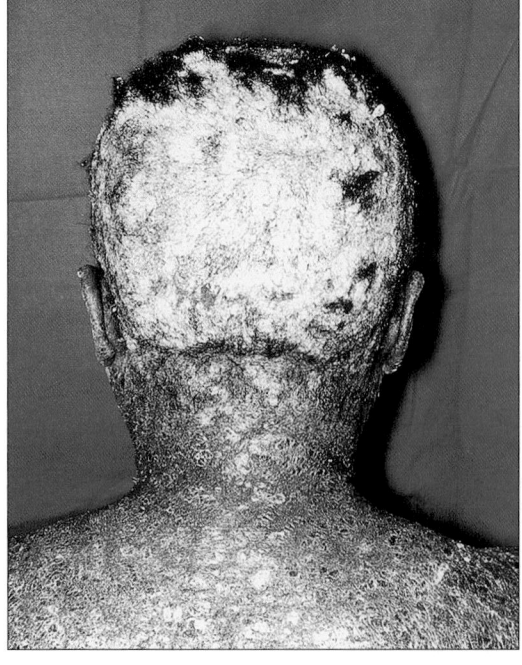

Fig. 5.71
Plaque psoriasis: in this extreme case, the initial diagnosis was Norwegian scabies. Surprisingly alopecia is an uncommon complication. By courtesy of R.A. Marsden, MD, St George's Hospital, London, UK.

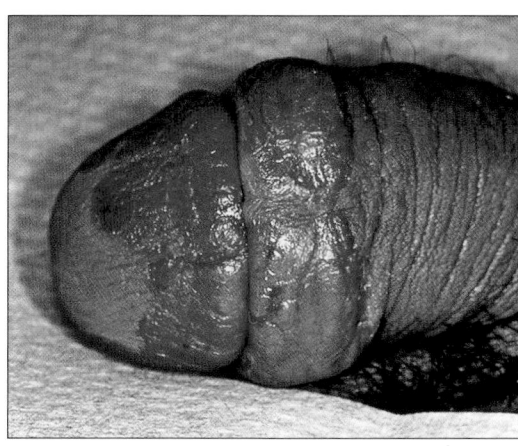

Fig. 5.72
Psoriasis: penile lesion showing a sharply demarcated, erythematous, eroded, slightly scaly plaque. By courtesy of C. Furlonge, MD, Port of Spain, Trinidad.

characterized by fever of several days' duration, together with the sudden appearance of sterile pustules, 2–3 mm across, over the trunk and extremities (*Fig. 5.78*).[5] The surrounding skin is erythematous and confluence may result in a generalized erythroderma (*Fig. 5.79*). Usually recurrent episodes of fever occur, followed by fresh outbreaks of pustules (*Fig. 5.80*). Systemic signs include weight loss, weakness and hypocalcemia, with a raised white cell count and high erythrocyte sedimentation rate (ESR). Although the precipitating factor is often unknown, pustular psoriasis may follow a streptococcal or viral infection. Withdrawal of systemic steroid therapy is also a known predisposing cause.[6] Treatment with systemic steroids or intensive topical regimens has also been incriminated.[7] Other risk factors for developing a pustular episode include drugs, pregnancy, hypocalcemia and sunlight or phototherapy.[8] Uncommon variants of pustular psoriasis include an

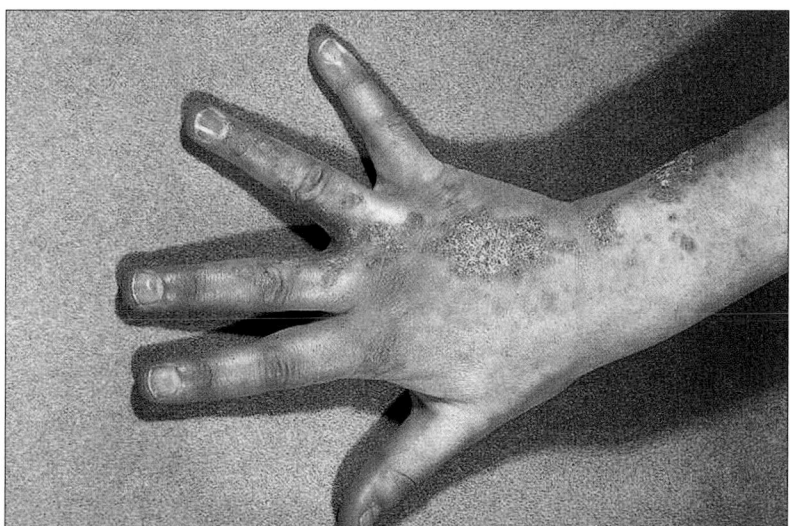

Fig. 5.73
Plaque psoriasis: linear involvement is a manifestation of koebnerization following trauma. By courtesy of the Institute of Dermatology, London, UK.

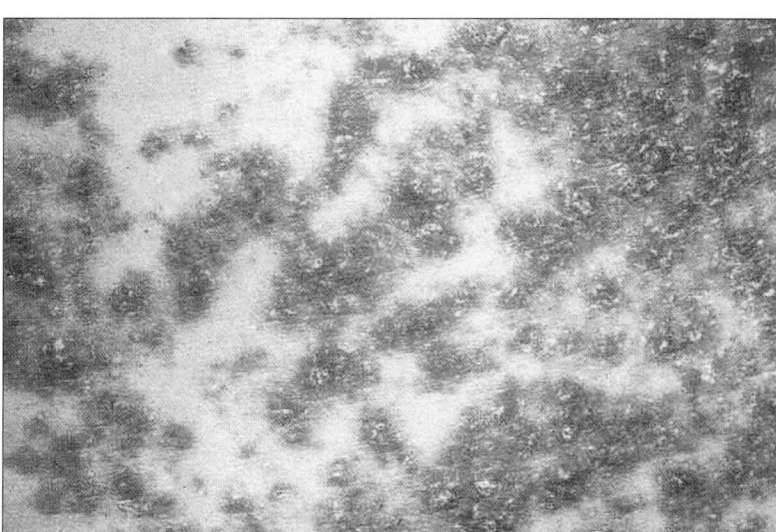

Fig. 5.75
Guttate psoriasis: this close-up view shows the erythema and scaling. By courtesy of the Institute of Dermatology, London, UK.

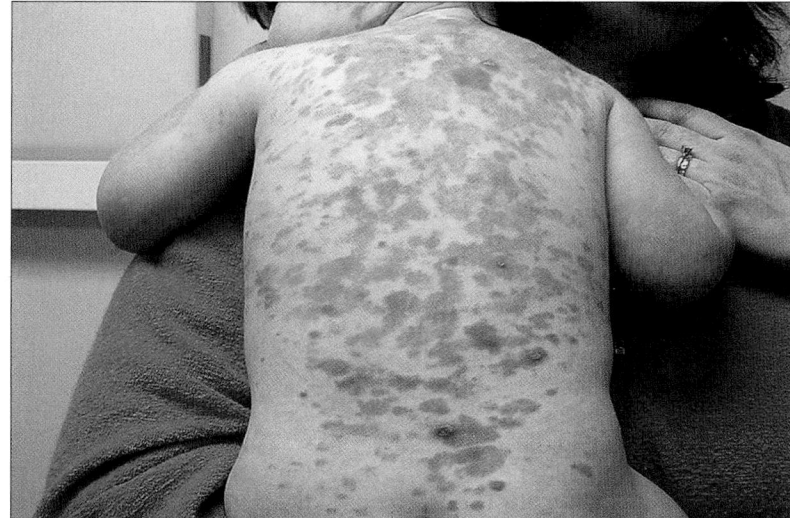

Fig. 5.74
Guttate psoriasis: this infant shows a characteristic distribution over the trunk. By courtesy of M. Liang, MD, Children's Hospital, Boston, USA.

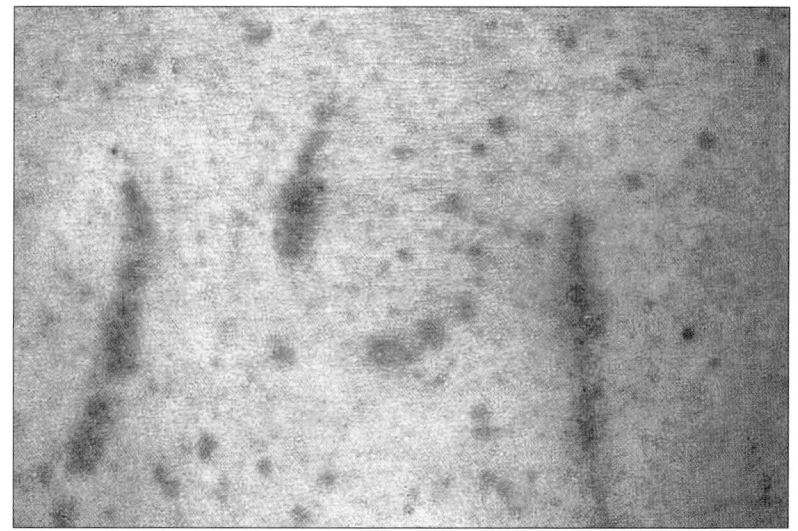

Fig. 5.76
Guttate psoriasis: as with plaque disease, guttate psoriasis is associated with a Koebner phenomenon. By courtesy of the Institute of Dermatology, London, UK.

annular form, exanthematous pustular psoriasis, juvenile and infantile pustular psoriasis.[9,10] The annular variant is a somewhat less serious variant in which, due to central clearing, lesions develop an annular or gyrate morphology.[8] Often the systemic manifestations are less severe. The exanthematous variant, which tends to develop de novo, may sometimes follow an infection or represent a pustular drug reaction.[8] Impetigo herpetiformis most probably represents pustular psoriasis of pregnancy although some authors classify it as a separate entity.[11]

- In *psoriatic erythroderma*, there is an intense generalized erythema affecting the entire skin surface, associated with desquamation (*Fig. 5.81*). Ectropion may be present and scalp involvement is sometimes followed by hair loss. Erythroderma may be precipitated

in patients with psoriasis vulgaris by infection with *Staphylococcus aureus*, abrupt curtailment of steroid or methotrexate therapy, and sunburn.[8] Systemic symptoms including fever, chills, shortness of breath, fatigue and myalgia are commonly present.[8] Biochemical abnormalities include hypoalbuminemia, anemia and dehydration.[12] High output cardiac failure is an important complication.

- *Localized (mixed) pustular psoriasis* represents the development of pustules on pre-existent plaques.[6] This variant most often develops in acute flares of psoriasis or following treatment.[8] It sometimes represents a harbinger of a more generalized process.

- *Palmoplantar pustular psoriasis of Barber* (pustulosis palmaris et plantaris) refers to a chronic recurrent pustular dermatosis localized to the palms and soles (*Figs 5.82, 5.83*).

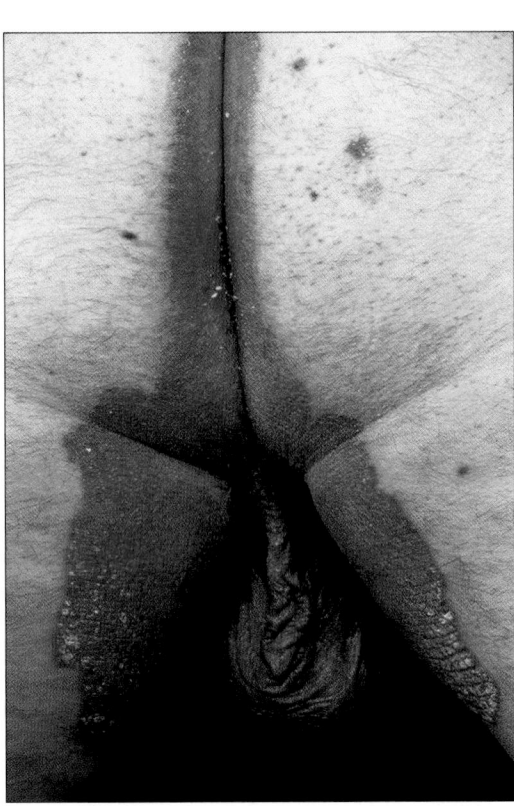

Fig. 5.77
Flexural (inverse) psoriasis: this is a rare variant in which the lesions develop on flexural skin.

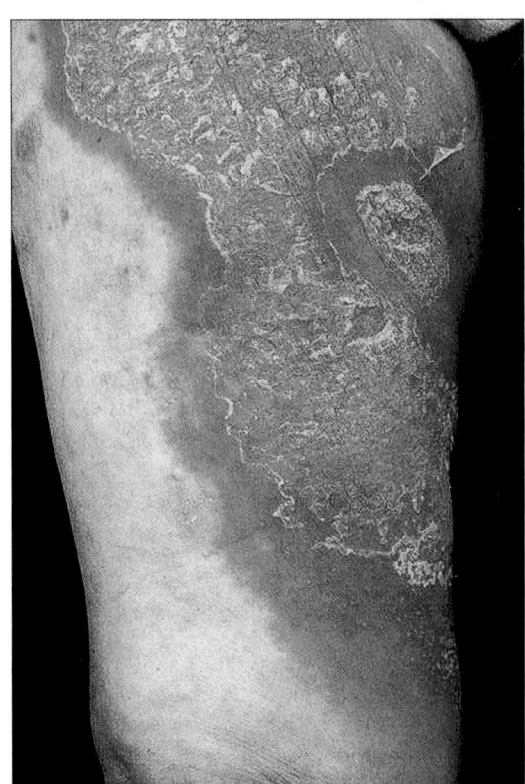

Fig. 5.79
Pustular psoriasis: early stage showing intense erythema. By courtesy of the Institute of Dermatology, London, UK.

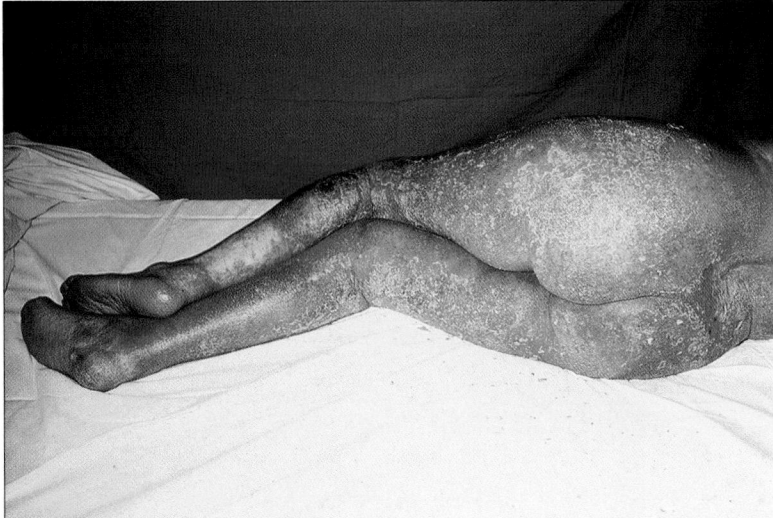

Fig. 5.78
Pustular psoriasis (von Zumbusch): note the extreme generalized erythema and pustulation. This variant is rare and may sometimes prove fatal. By courtesy of R.A. Marsden, St George's Hospital, London, UK.

Fig. 5.80
Pustular psoriasis: close-up view showing typical pustules arising on a background of intense erythema. By courtesy of the Institute of Dermatology, London, UK.

- *Acrodermatitis continua (acropustulosis) of Hallopeau* is a rare sterile pustular eruption of the fingers or toes, involving the nails and slowly extending proximally (*Figs 5.84, 5.85*).

The nail is frequently affected in psoriasis; lesions may include pitting, discoloration, onycholysis, subungual hyperkeratosis, nail grooving, splinter hemorrhages and complete loss in pustular psoriasis.[13] This topic is discussed in greater depth on page 1131.

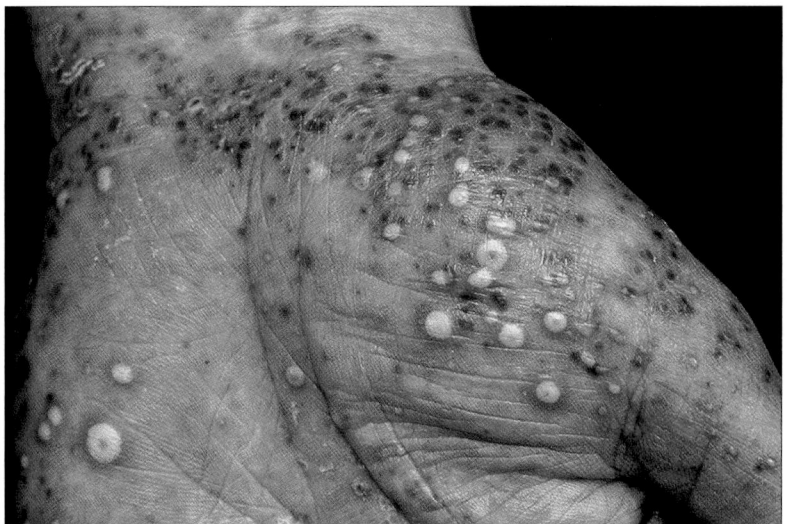

Fig. 5.83
Palmoplantar pustular psoriasis: close-up view of palmar pustules. By courtesy of the Institute of Dermatology, London, UK.

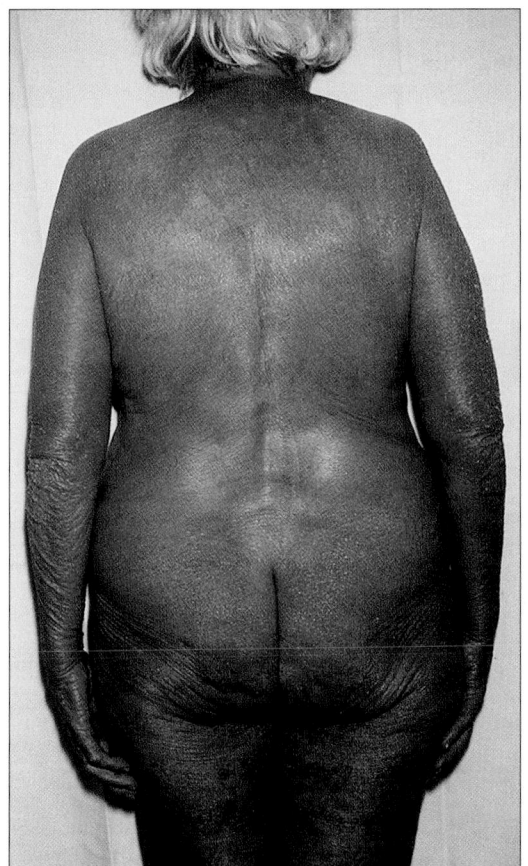

Fig. 5.81
Psoriatic erythroderma: there is generalized erythema. Patients are at risk of dehydration, hypoalbuminemia and anemia. By courtesy of R.A. Marsden, St George's Hospital, London, UK.

Fig. 5.84
Acropustulosis continua: there is pustulation with erythema and scaling, the nail has been shed and there is damage to the nail plate. By courtesy of R.A. Marsden, St George's Hospital, London, UK.

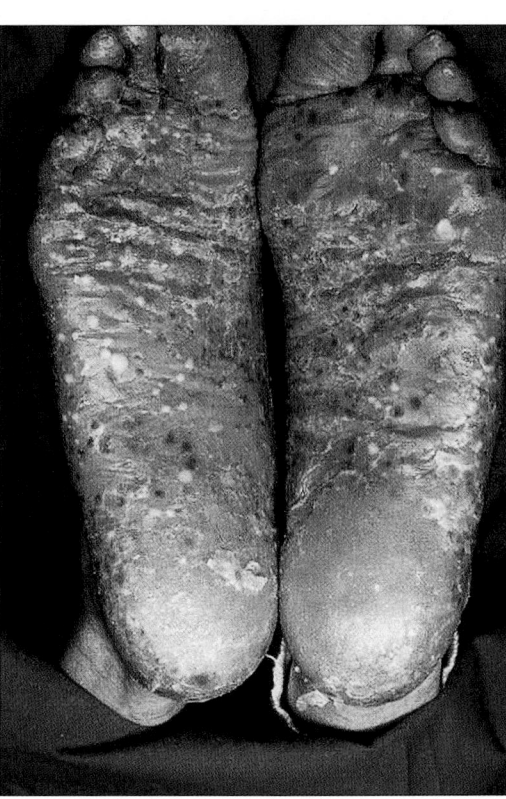

Fig. 5.82
Palmoplantar pustular psoriasis: there is intense erythema, scaling and numerous pustules. By courtesy of the Institute of Dermatology, London, UK.

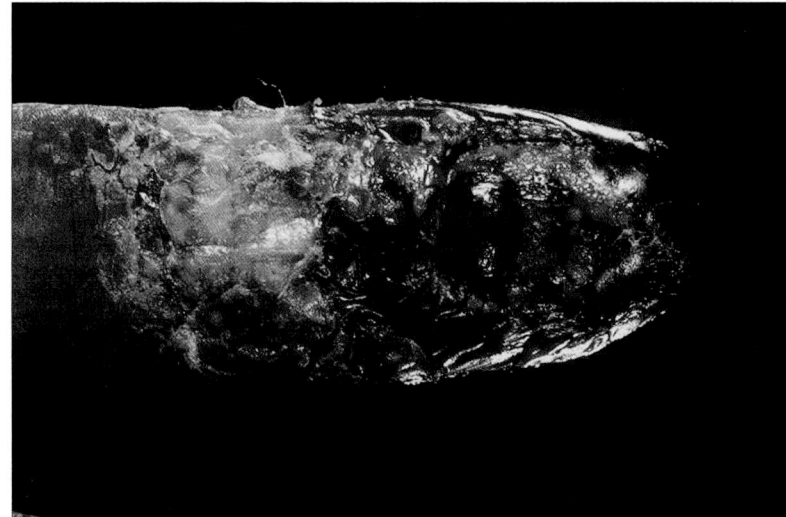

Fig. 5.85
Acropustulosis continua: a particularly severe example. By courtesy of S. Dalziel, MD, University Hospital, Nottingham, UK.

Psoriatic arthritis

Psoriatic arthritis has a prevalence of 0.02–0.1%. It may take a number of different forms (*Fig. 5.86*):[14]

- The most common is an asymmetrical involvement of a few joints of the fingers or toes; this accounts for over 70% of cases.
- In 15% of cases a symmetrical polyarthritis, clinically indistinguishable from rheumatoid arthritis, but seronegative, is seen.
- In approximately 5% of cases the distal interphalangeal joints are involved, the classical picture of psoriatic arthropathy (*Fig. 5.87*).
- A further 5% have a destructive and severely deforming arthritis, arthritis mutilans.
- The remaining cases have ankylosing spondylitis, with or without peripheral joint involvement (*Fig. 5.88*).

Psoriatic arthritis is associated with a high incidence of mitral valve prolapse with resultant incompetence.[15] The peak age of onset is 36–45 years of age, although the destructive form may occur earlier. A high incidence of immunoglobulin gene polymorphism has been identified in patients with psoriatic arthritis, suggesting an inherited predisposition.[16]

Psoriatic arthritis in children, although uncommon, is of importance because frequently the arthritis precedes the onset of the skin lesions. A careful study for nail changes or a family history may be of value in establishing the diagnosis.

Pathogenesis and histological features

Although the etiology of psoriasis remains incompletely understood, considerable advances have been made in the past two decades to unravel the complex mechanisms involved in the pathogenesis of this common dermatosis. For many years psoriasis was considered to represent a primary epidermal hyperproliferative disorder. More recent studies, however, have shown that a T-lymphocyte-driven immune process is central to the development of the psoriatic plaque and in fact may represent the earliest stage in its evolution. Other important factors include genetic influences, the environment and the contribution of keratinocyte-derived mediators of the inflammatory process.

The inherited predisposition to develop psoriasis has long been known. A positive family history is common. Documented prevalence rates in first-degree relatives have ranged from 7.8 to 17.6%.[17,18] Monozygotic twins have a concordance of 64–70% while that of dizygotic twins is in the order of 14–23%.[19]

Psoriasis has been classified into two types:[4]

- Type I disease which affects young adults is characterized by a familial segregation and an association with a number of human leukocyte antigens including Cw6, HLA-B13, HLA-B17 and HLA-DR7.[3] Cw6 is the most powerful, increasing the risk of developing psoriasis by four- to 15-fold.[4]
- Type II disease presents at an older age, shows no familial segregation and is much less significantly associated with specific HLA phenotypes.[3] Patients with pustular psoriasis have a higher incidence of HLA-B27, as do those with psoriasis and peripheral arthritis, and this is most marked if spondylitis is present.[20]

Although the genetic basis of psoriasis has yet to be fully clarified, familial susceptibility has been mapped to loci at 17q and 4q in addition to the MHC on chromosome 6p.[21–23]

Certain factors are known to induce psoriasis in a person who is genetically predisposed. There is a tendency for lesions to develop at sites of previous skin trauma (e.g. mechanical friction, sunburn or childhood illnesses such as varicella); this is termed the isomorphic or Koebner's phenomenon.[24–26]

Infections are well known as predisposing factors in the onset of psoriasis. In children in particular, upper respiratory tract infections frequently trigger psoriasis, while infections with *Streptococcus pyogenes*

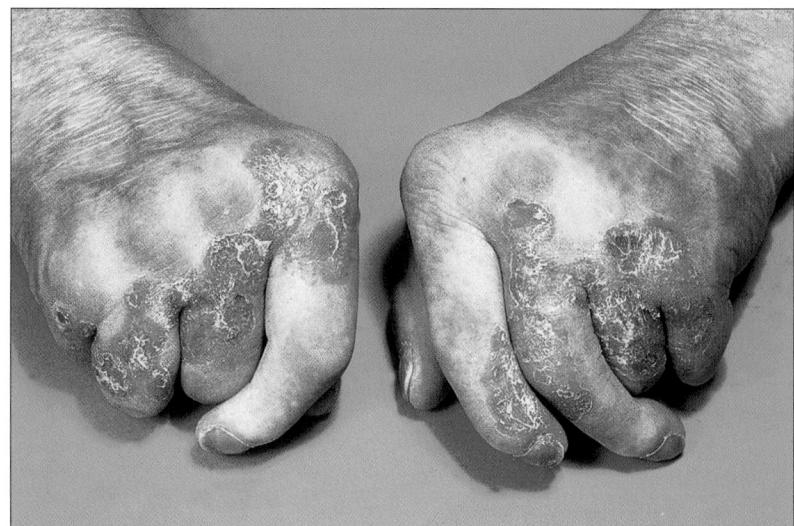

Fig. 5.86
Psoriatic arthropathy: joint involvement is a rare manifestation. Lesions of the interphalangeal joints, while said to be characteristic, are an uncommon finding. In this patient there is gross deformity. By courtesy of R.A. Marsden, St George's Hospital, London, UK.

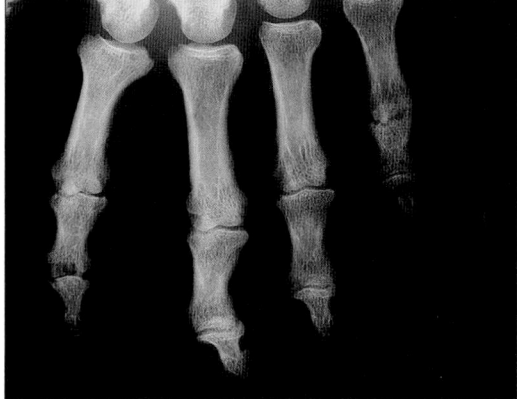

Fig. 5.87
Psoriatic arthropathy: classical type. Note the destruction of the distal interphalangeal joint of the first finger. By courtesy of the Institute of Dermatology, London, UK.

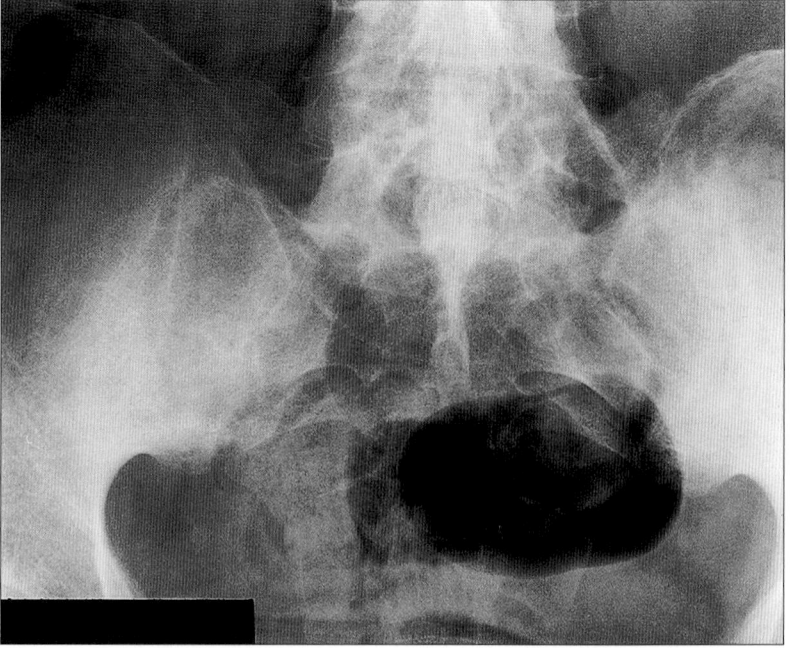

Fig. 5.88
Psoriatic arthropathy: sacroiliitis. Note the virtual obliteration of the sacroiliac joints. By courtesy of R.A. Marsden, St George's Hospital, London, UK.

are implicated in the development of acute guttate psoriasis, together with an exacerbation of other forms of psoriasis.[27] Specific streptococcal serotypes, however, do not appear to be implicated.

Other factors known to exacerbate psoriasis include stress, bereavement, withdrawal of corticosteroids after prolonged use and treatment with a number of drugs including lithium, antimalarials and beta-blocking agents.[28]

The development of the psoriatic plaque results from a complex interplay between keratinocyte hyperproliferation with loss of differentiation, changes in the superficial dermal vasculature and a T-lymphocyte-mediated inflammatory component.[29] The relative roles of keratinocyte hyperplasia, vascular changes and immunological reactions have been the subject of much discussion in the recent literature.[30] Most recently the focus has been particularly directed towards the importance of immune mechanisms.

In the skin there is an increased epidermal proliferation rate: the transit time of keratinocytes through the epidermis in normal skin is 56 days; in psoriatic skin it is shortened to 7 days.[31,32] The epidermal cell cycle is probably shortened, and there is a large increase in the number of proliferating generative cells in the basal layers, where up to three layers of proliferating cells may be seen compared with only one in normal resting epidermis.

Vascular proliferation predominantly affecting the postcapillary venules of the dermal papillae appears to be one of the earliest manifestations of psoriasis.[33] This is mediated by upregulation of $\alpha V \beta 3$ integrin and vascular endothelial growth factor (VEGF).[34–36]

The current weight of evidence suggests that a T-cell-mediated immune reaction is central to the pathogenesis of psoriasis.[29,37] Clinical studies supporting this hypothesis include the response to anti-lymphocyte therapies such as cyclosporin.[38] More recently, remission in patients with severe psoriasis has resulted from treatment with an activated T-lymphocyte selective toxin DAB389 IL-2 that interacts with the receptor-binding domain of IL-2.[39] Successful responses to therapy with monoclonal anti-CD3 and anti-CD4 antibodies adds further support.[40,41] Additional evidence has come from bone marrow transplantation studies. Unaffected patients develop psoriasis following a transplant from an affected donor whereas patients are cured of their disease following transplantation from an unaffected donor.[42] In vitro studies in which intradermal injection of T-helper lymphocytes from an affected patient into severe combined immunodeficient mice results in the development of typical psoriasis further supports a T-lymphocyte-driven pathogenesis.[43]

Although CD4 T-helper (Th) lymphocytes are probably of importance in the earliest stages of plaque development, the major population is characterized by CD8 expression. The immunophenotype of the T-cells includes CD45RO+, HLADR+, CD25+ and CLA+, indicating activated skin-specific memory cells.[44] The lymphocyte cytokine profile, which includes IL-2, interferon-gamma (IFN-γ), and absence of IL-4, IL-10 and tumor necrosis factor alpha (TNF-α), reflects a predominantly Th1-mediated inflammatory reaction.[45,46] IFN-γ is central to the development of the plaque. In vitro studies have shown that the keratinocyte proliferation is IFN-γ dependent.[47] Also, IFN-γ injection in normal human skin results in epidermal proliferation.[48]

In addition to the lymphocyte-derived cytokines discussed above, the keratinocytes themselves are a rich source of inflammatory mediators, which are likely to be of importance in initiating the inflammatory reaction and the development and maintenance of the psoriasiform plaque.[49] In particular, keratinocytes secrete IL-1α, IL-1β and TNF-α. These cytokines play a major role in angiogenesis, in recruitment of circulating lymphocytes and inducing expression of a number of endothelial cell adhesion molecules including E-selectin, intercellular adhesion molecule-1 (ICAM-1) and vascular cell adhesion molecule-1

(VCAM-1).[49–51] These last are of particular importance in facilitating the extravasation of lymphocytes through the endothelium.[37] Keratinocytes are also a valuable source of chemokines including IL-8, melanoma growth stimulatory activity alpha (MGS/GRO-α), gamma inducible protein 10 (IP-10) and molecule chemoattractant protein 1 (MCP-1).[49] IL-8 is of importance in both neutrophil and T-lymphocyte chemotaxis.[52] It also promotes keratinocyte proliferation and induces angiogenesis.[53,54] IL-8 is predominantly derived from superficial keratinocytes and the associated neutrophils within the psoriatic plaque. MGS/GRO-α is an additional powerful neutrophil chemoattractant.[49]

The pathogenesis of psoriasis therefore involves interaction between injured keratinocytes and activated lymphocytes through the release of various cytokines developing in a background of genetic predisposition.[51] The relationship between the T-cell-driven immune reaction and epidermal hyperplasia, however, remains unclear. Similarly, the initiator(s) of this process are uncertain. Although autoantigens and bacterial superantigens are currently favored, the possibility of a direct consequence of lymphocyte–keratinocyte interaction has not yet been disproved.[54]

In biopsies of the early lesions, the histological features consist primarily of dermal changes.[55–59] The evolution of the psoriatic plaque consists initially of the development of tortuous, dilated and frequently congested capillaries in the superficial papillary dermis accompanied by edema and a perivascular mononuclear cell infiltrate (*Fig. 5.89*).[55] This vascular change is common to all forms of psoriasis and may even be seen in biopsies from clinically resolved lesions following treatment.[58] Lymphocytes then migrate into the lower epidermis, which becomes spongiotic. Subsequently the upper epidermis shows focal vacuolation and eventual loss of the granular cell layer with the resultant formation of parakeratotic mounds. Migration of neutrophils from capillaries in the dermal papillae through gaps in the epidermal basement membrane and hence to the stratum corneum completes the process. Psoriasiform hyperplasia of the affected epidermis then follows.

Classical plaque psoriatic lesions show marked and characteristic acanthosis of the epidermal ridges, which are evenly elongated and club-shaped at their bases, alternating with long edematous papillae, which are club-shaped at their tips (*Figs 5.90–5.93*). Fusion of adjacent ridges is commonly present in established lesions. The suprapapillary plate is typically thinned and the epidermal surface is covered by confluent parakeratosis associated with diminution or loss of the granular cell layer. The lower suprabasal layers of the epidermis can

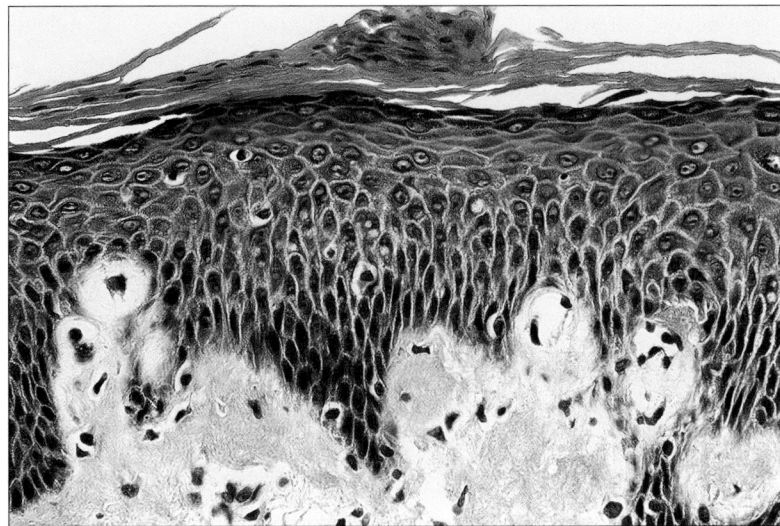

Fig. 5.89
Evolving psoriasis: in the early stages, there is capillary dilatation, with spongiosis as shown in this field. A small parakeratotic mound is also demonstrated.

frequently be seen to be actively dividing. Large tortuous capillaries are present in the papillary dermis and there is a slight perivascular lymphocytic infiltrate in the subpapillary dermis. Palmar and plantar lesions may sometimes cause diagnostic difficulty as spongiosis can be marked and occasionally vesiculation is evident.[58]

The diagnostic features of active lesions include the 'Munro microabscess' and 'spongiform pustule of Kogoj'. Munro microabscesses represent an accumulation of polymorphs within the parakeratotic stratum corneum. Spongiform pustules are seen beneath the keratin layer and consist of small accumulations of neutrophils and occasional lymphocytes intermingled with the epidermal cells in foci of spongiosis.

In guttate psoriasis, the histological features overlap with those of evolving disease.[58] Parakeratosis associated with loss or diminution of the granular cell layer is limited to small foci contrasting with a background of orthokeratosis *(Figs 5.94, 5.95)*. Neutrophils are seen surmounting the parakeratotic tiers. Acanthosis is much less marked than in fully established plaque disease. Neutrophils and lymphocytes are commonly present in the superficial papillary dermis and mild spongiosis is often a feature, particularly if biopsies of early lesions are examined.[60]

In generalized pustular psoriasis and its three variants the histological picture is slightly different in that the spongiform pustule occurs as a macropustule and is the characteristic lesion *(Figs 5.96, 5.97)*.[59] As the spongiform pustule increases in size, the epidermal cells die, with resulting central cavitation. At the edges a shell of thinned epidermal cells remains. Eventually there is migration of neutrophils into the horny layer and the picture resembles that of a large Munro abscess. Although the epidermal and dermal features may be similar to those of psoriasis vulgaris, particularly if the pustule has developed against a background

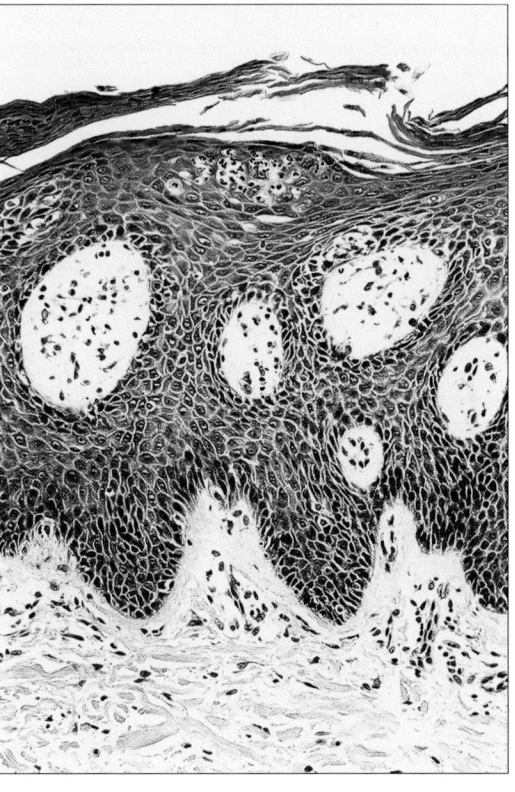

Fig. 5.92
Plaque psoriasis: spongiform degeneration and parakeratosis.

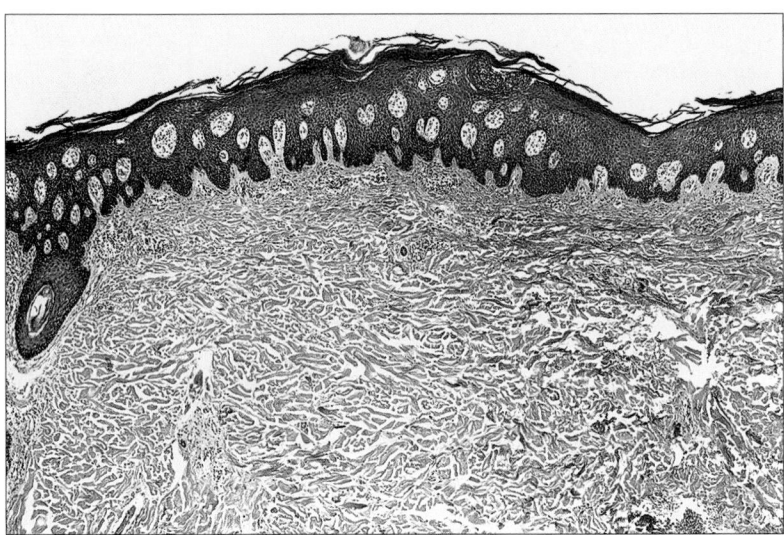

Fig. 5.90
Plaque psoriasis: scanning view showing extensive parakeratosis, regular acanthosis, club-shaped epidermal ridges and ridge fusion.

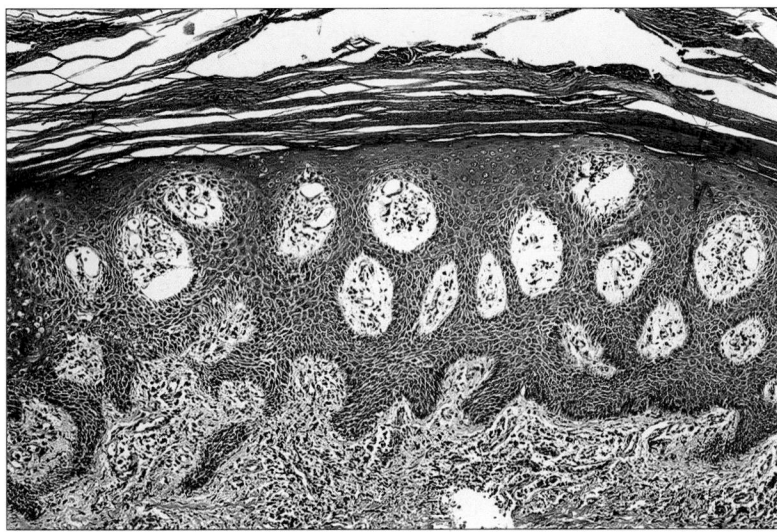

Fig. 5.91
Plaque psoriasis: close-up view showing parakeratosis with neutrophil aggregates (Munro microabscess). There is marked dilatation and tortuosity of the capillaries within the dermal papillae. Mild spongiosis is also present.

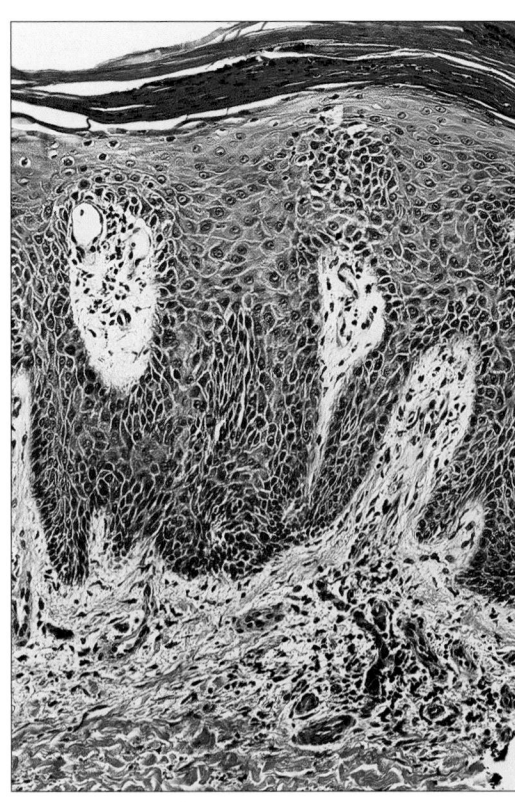

Fig. 5.93
Plaque psoriasis: tortuous and dilated capillaries.

of plaque-type disease, more often the features are much less well developed (*Fig. 5.98*). Frequently, therefore, there is no or only minimal epidermal hyperplasia although tortuous and dilated capillaries accompanied by a lymphocytic or mixed lymphocytic and neutrophil infiltrate are usually seen.[8]

In palmar/plantar pustular lesions, the initial changes are those of spongiosis with lymphocytic exocytosis in the lower epidermis.[60] As the lesion progresses, neutrophils infiltrate the epidermis and a macropustule develops.

In psoriatic erythroderma the histological features are variable but in the majority of cases a positive diagnosis can be established.[61] Most commonly the features are those of evolving psoriasis similar to guttate psoriasis, i.e. slight epidermal hyperplasia, focal diminution or loss of the granular cell layer and mild spongiosis (*Fig. 5.99*). Parakeratosis is often limited to slight change overlying the hyperplastic epithelium and neutrophils are variably present (*Fig. 5.100*). A lymphohistiocytic infiltrate is present in an edematous papillary dermis and dilated, tortuous, spiraling vessels are regularly evident. Extravasated red blood vessels are a constant finding. Less commonly the features are those of psoriasis vulgaris and sometimes the changes overlap regressing psoriasis.

In resolving lesions, foci of hyperkeratosis overlying hypergranulosis are scattered through the parakeratotic scale and the epidermal hyperplasia is less marked (*Fig. 5.101*).

Current treatment for severe widespread plaque psoriasis may include the use of PUVA therapy. Over the recent years it has been shown that this is associated with an increased risk (albeit low) of cutaneous squamous cell carcinoma and dysplastic keratoses.[62–65] Patients at most risk include those who have had more than 200 PUVA treatments and/or

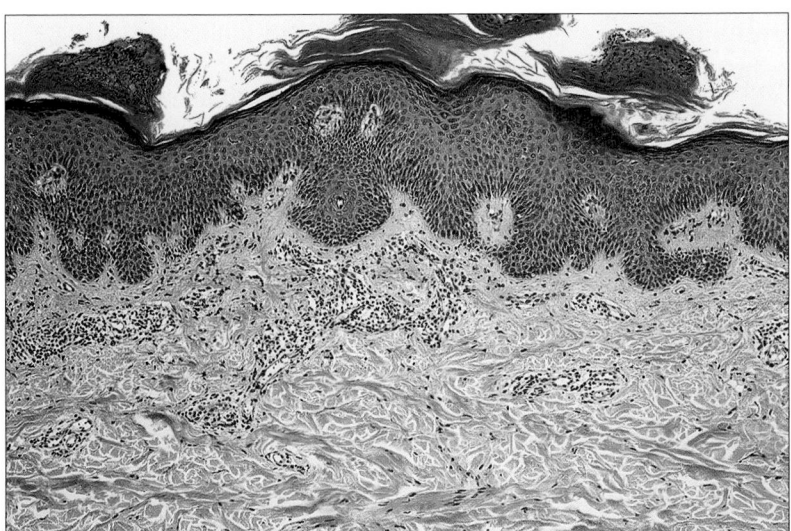

Fig. 5.94
Guttate psoriasis: the multiple discrete, parakeratotic mounds are characteristic. Hyperplasia is not as well developed as in plaque disease.

Fig. 5.96
Pustular psoriasis: a macropustule is present. Typical psoriasiform hyperplasia with parakeratosis is seen in the adjacent epidermis.

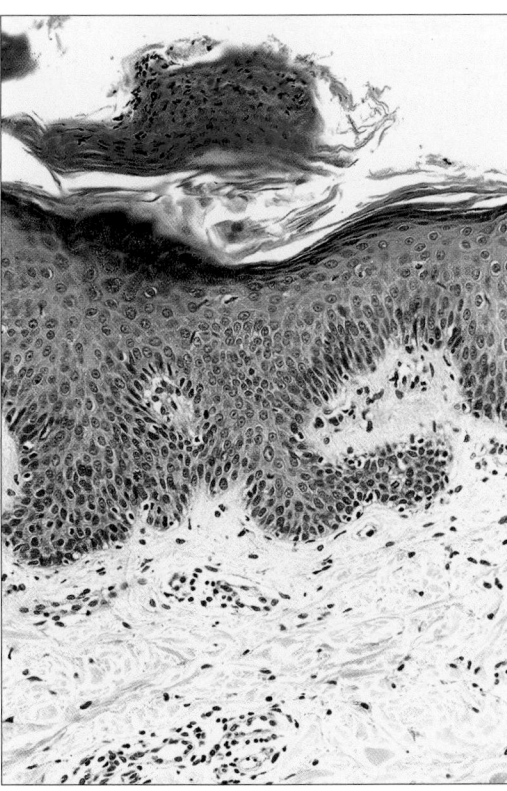

Fig. 5.95
Guttate psoriasis: close-up view.

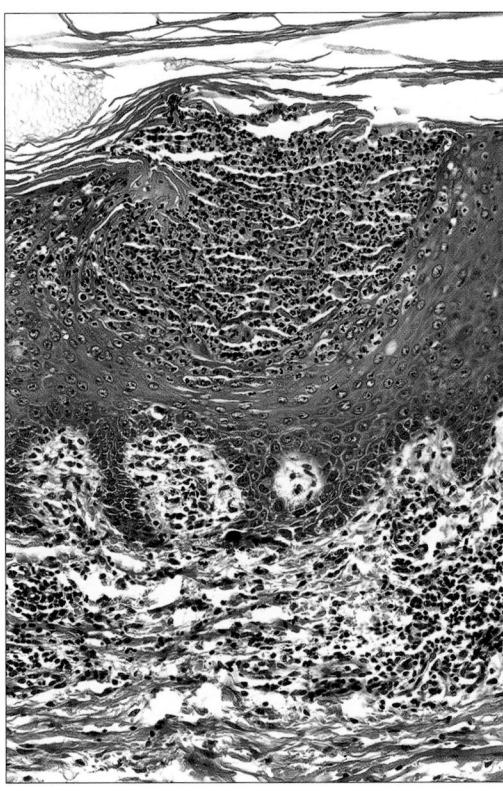

Fig. 5.97
Pustular psoriasis: close-up view.

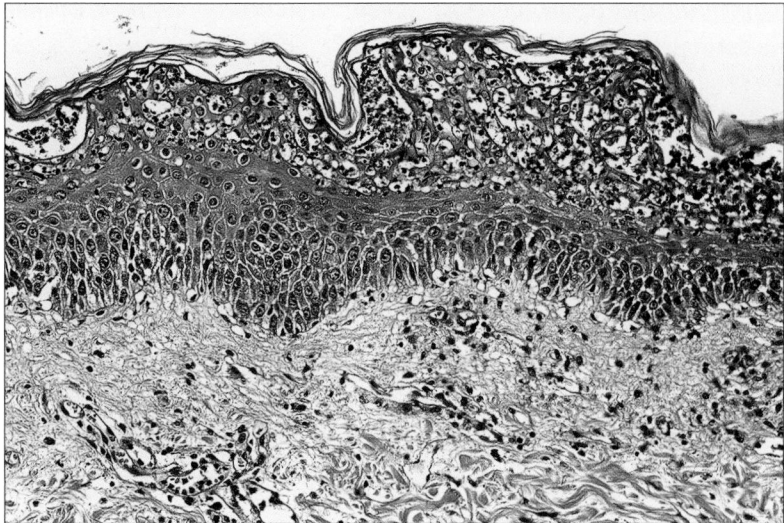

Fig. 5.98
Pustular psoriasis: in this patient, the lesions developed dramatically in the absence of significant plaque disease. There is only mild hyperplasia of the underlying epidermis.

a cumulative dose in excess of 1000 J/cm². There is some evidence to suggest that these tumors behave in a low-grade fashion with little risk of metastatic spread.[65]

Psoriasis may rarely coexist with a number of autoimmune bullous dermatoses including bullous pemphigoid, pemphigus vulgaris, linear IgA disease and epidermolysis bullosa acquisita.[66–72] Although not in all cases, there is often a relationship to treatment, particularly with PUVA therapy. In some instances, the histology may show features of both conditions (*Figs 5.102–5.104*).

Differential diagnosis

The differential diagnosis of psoriatic lesions includes a number of conditions:

- *Pityriasis rubra pilaris* differs from psoriasis by the presence of alternating parakeratosis and hyperkeratosis in both vertical and horizontal directions (spotty parakeratosis). Neutrophil infiltration of the stratum corneum is not a feature of pityriasis rubra pilaris unless there is secondary infection.

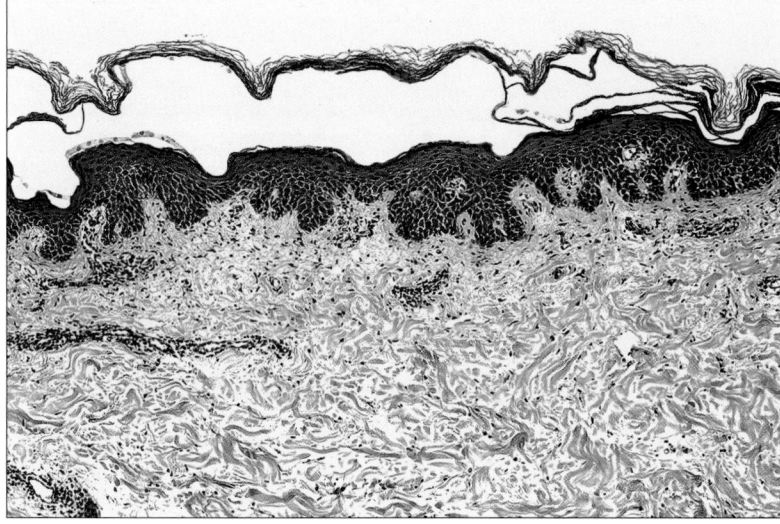

Fig. 5.99
Psoriatic erythroderma: there is only very focal parakeratosis with scattered neutrophils. The epidermal hyperplasia is only slight.

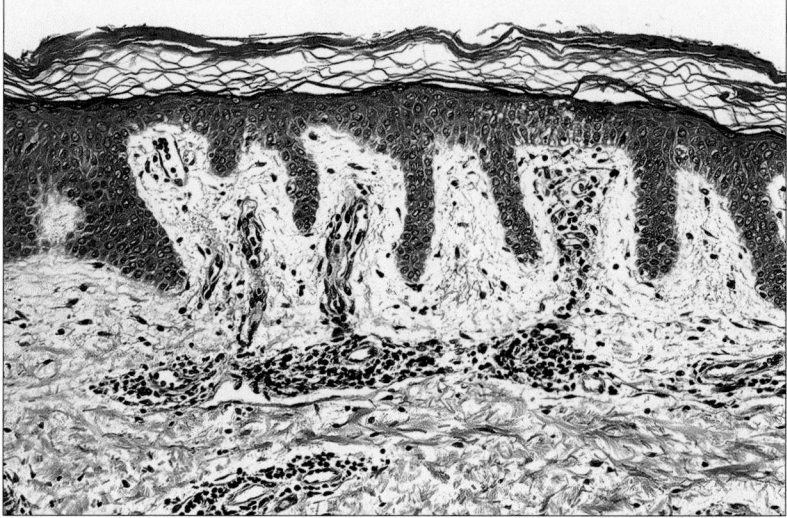

Fig. 5.101
Resolving psoriasis: newly formed basket-weave orthokeratin is seen underlying focal residual parakeratosis.

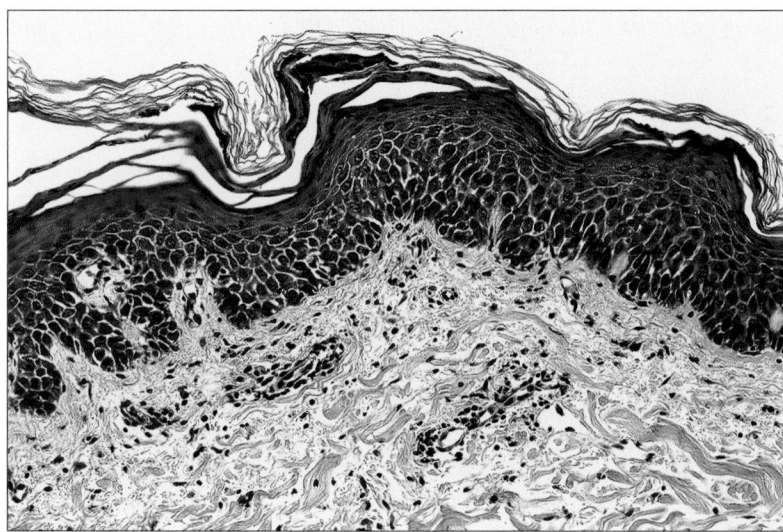

Fig. 5.100
Psoriatic erythroderma: close-up view of parakeratosis and neutrophil karyorrhectic debris.

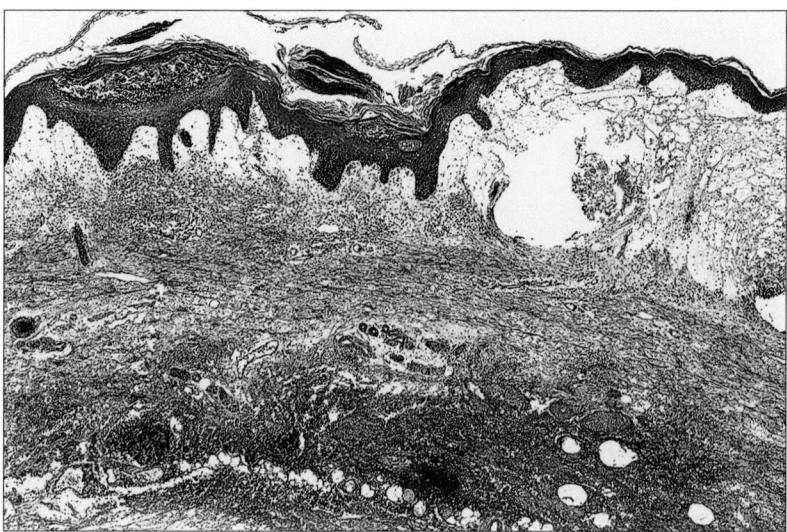

Fig. 5.102
Bullous pemphigoid and pustular psoriasis: on the left is a subcorneal pustule while on the right is a subepidermal blister.

- *Lichen simplex chronicus* typically shows scarring of the dermal papillae due to persistent rubbing, and there is no thinning of the suprapapillary plate. Hyperkeratosis and hypergranulosis are often marked and there is minimal parakeratosis unless there is a background of spongiosis.
- *Papulosquamous drug eruptions* (e.g. due to lithium or propranolol) may appear similar to psoriasis, but a moderate to high number of eosinophils is usually present in the infiltrate.
- *Seborrheic dermatitis* typically shows psoriasiform hyperplasia and corneal neutrophil infiltration may sometimes be a feature. It differs from psoriasis by the presence of a more conspicuous spongiotic component, which in psoriasis only occurs in early lesions and is usually not marked. In those cases where the distinction is not possible, the term 'sebo-psoriasis' is sometimes used.
- *Pustular psoriasis* and its variants are all similar; they must be distinguished from other pustular eruptions, including conditions such as pustular dermatophytoses, bacterial impetigo and pustular drug eruptions. Pustular psoriasis may be differentiated from subcorneal pustular dermatosis by the absence of spongiform change or degeneration in the latter condition (see p. 212). Gram and PAS stains and culture will exclude infective conditions. Superficial pemphigus can be distinguished by the presence of acantholysis and the usual absence of psoriasiform hyperplasia. In IgA pemphigus, acantholytic cells are usually, but not always, present and this diagnostic clue may be very easily overlooked, but should allow distinction from psoriasis. In addition, some lesions may show histological features typical of classic pemphigus vulgaris or pemphigus foliaceus. In lesions of IgA pemphigus that lack acantholytic cells, immunofluorescence studies may be necessary to make the distinction from pustular psoriasis.

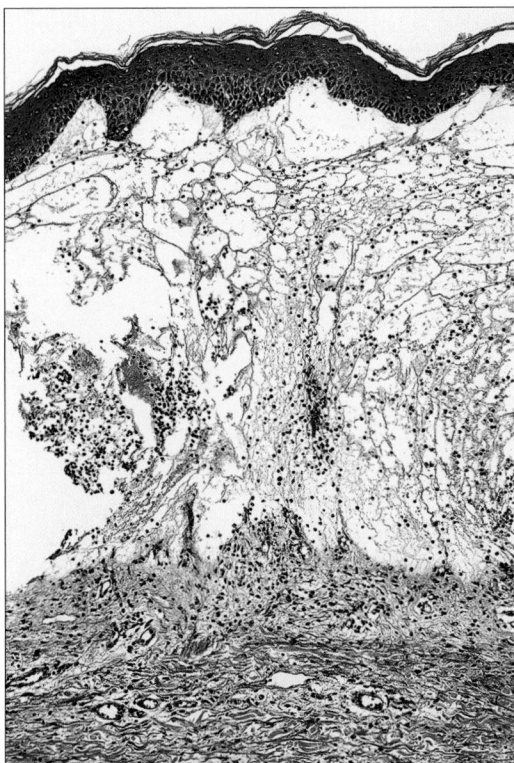

Fig. 5.103
Bullous pemphigoid and pustular psoriasis: higher power view of the blister.

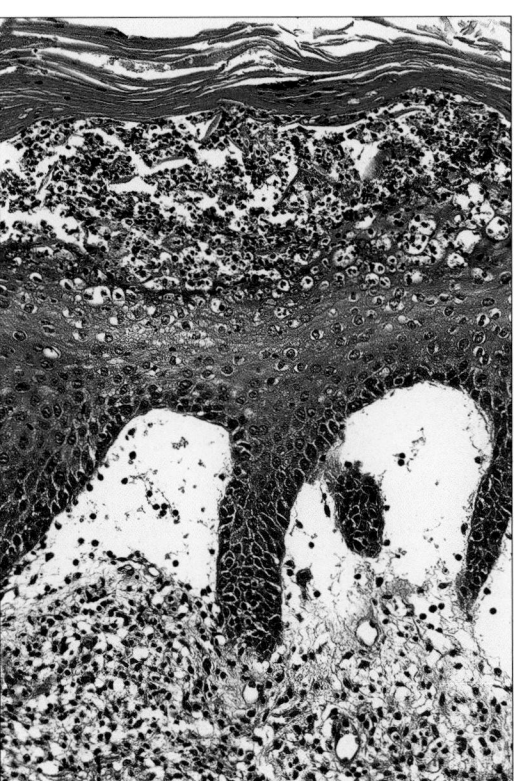

Fig. 5.104
Bullous pemphigoid and pustular psoriasis: higher power view of the pustule.

References

1. Farber, E.M., Nall, M.L. (1974) The natural history of psoriasis in 5600 patients. *Dermatologica*, **148**, 1–18.
2. Rook, A.J., Wilkinson, D.S. (1979) The prevalence, incidence and ecology of diseases of the skin. In: Rook, A. (ed.) Textbook of dermatology. Oxford: Blackwell Scientific, p 31.
3. Henseler, T. (1997) The genetics of psoriasis. *J Am Acad Dermatol*, 37, S1–S11.
4. Henseler, T., Christophers, E. (1985) Psoriasis of early and late onset: characterization of two types of psoriasis vulgaris. *J Am Acad Dermatol*, **13**, 450–456.
5. Zelickson, B.D., Muller, S.A. (1991) Generalized pustular psoriasis: a review of 63 cases. *Arch Dermatol*, **127**, 1339–1345.
6. Baker, H., Ryan, T.J. (1968) Generalized pustular psoriasis. A clinical and epidemiological study of 104 cases. *Br J Dermatol*, **80**, 771–776.
7. Abrahams, I., McCarthy, J.T., Sanders, S.L. (1963) 101 cases of exfoliative dermatitis. *Arch Dermatol*, **87**, 96–101.
8. Prystowsky, J.H., Cohen, P.R. (1995) Pustular and erythrodermic psoriasis. *Dermatol Clin*, **13**, 757–770.
9. Baker, H. (1985) Generalized pustular psoriasis. In: Roenigk, H.H. Jr, Maibach, H.I. (eds) Psoriasis. New York: Marcel Dekker, pp 15–33.
10. Barlow, R.J., Schulz, E.J. (1991) Chronic subcorneal pustulosis with vasculitis: a variant of generalized pustular psoriasis in black South Africans. *Br J Dermatol*, **124**, 470–474.
11. Pierard, G.E., Pierard-Franchimont, C., de la Brassinne, M. (1983) Impetigo herpetiformis and pustular psoriasis during pregnancy. *Am J Dermatopathol*, **5**, 215–220.
12. Boyd, A.S., Menter, A. (1989) Erythrodermic psoriasis. *J Am Acad Dermatol*, **21**, 985–991.
13. Farber, E.M., Nall, L. (1992) Nail psoriasis. *Cutis*, **50**, 174–178.
14. Rose, J.H., Belsky, M.R. (1989) Psoriatic arthritis in the hand. *Hand Clin*, **5**, 137–144.
15. Sakkas, L.I., Demaine, A.G., Panayi, G.S. et al (1988) Arthritis in psoriasis is associated with an immunoglobulin gene polymorphism. *Arthritis Rheum*, **31**, 276–278.
16. Truckenbrodt, H., Hafner, R. (1990) Psoriatic arthritis in childhood. A comparison with subgroups of chronic juvenile arthritis. *Z Rheumatol*, **49**, 88–94.
17. Hellgren, L. (1967) Psoriasis: the prevalence in sex, age and occupational groups in total populations in Sweden. Morphology, inheritance and association with other skin and rheumatic diseases. Stockholm: Almqvist & Wiksell.
18. Farber, E.M., Nall, M.L. (1971) Genetics of psoriasis: twin studies. In: Farber, E.M., Cox, A.J. (eds) Psoriasis. Proceedings of the International Symposium, Stanford, CA: Stanford University Press, pp 7–13.
19. Brandrup, F., Hauge, M., Henningsen, K. et al (1978) Psoriasis in an unselected series of twins. *Arch Dermatol*, **114**, 874–876.
20. Brewerton, D.A., Hart, F.D., Nicholls, A. (1973) Ankylosing spondylitis and HLA 27. *Lancet*, **1**, 904–907.
21. Tomfohrde, J., Silverman, A., Barnes, R. et al (1994) Gene for familial psoriasis susceptibility mapped to the distal end of human chromosome 17q. *Science*, **264**, 1141–1145.
22. Matthews, D., Fry, L., Powles, A. et al (1996) Evidence that a locus for familial psoriasis maps to chromosome 4q. *Nat Genet*, **14**, 231–233.
23. Trembath, R.C., Clough, R.L., Rosbothom, J.L. et al (1997) Identification of a major susceptibility gene locus on chromosome 6p and evidence for further disease loci revealed by a two stage genome wide search in psoriasis. *Hum Mol Genet*, **6**, 813–820.
24. Eyre, R.W., Krueger, G.G. (1982) Response to injury of skin involved and uninvolved with psoriasis and its relation to disease activity: Koebner and 'reverse' Koebner reactions. *Br J Dermatol*, **106**, 153–159.
25. Melski, J.W., Bernhard, J.D., Stern, R.S. (1983) The Koebner (isomorphic) response in psoriasis: associations with early age at onset and multiple previous therapies. *Arch Dermatol*, **110**, 655–659.
26. Rosenberg, E.W., Noah, P.W. (1988) The Koebner phenomenon and the microbial basis of psoriasis. *J Am Acad Dermatol*, **18**, 151–158.
27. Telfer, N.R., Chalmers, R.J., Whale, K. et al (1992) The role of streptococcal infection in the initiation of guttate psoriasis. *Arch Dermatol*, **128**, 39–42.
28. Skoven, I., Thormann, J. (1979) Lithium compound treatment and psoriasis. *Arch Dermatol*, **115**, 1185–1187.
29. Barker, J.N.W.N. (1998) Pathogenesis of psoriasis. *J Dermatol*, **25**, 778–781.
30. Barker, J.N.W.N. (1991) The pathophysiology of psoriasis. *Lancet*, **338**, 227–230.
31. Weinstein, G.D., McCullough, J., Ross, P. (1985) Cell kinetic basis for pathophysiology of psoriasis. *J Invest Dermatol*, **65**, 579–583.
32. Weinstein, G.D., Ross, P., McCullough, J.H., Cotton, A. (1983) Proliferative defects in psoriasis. In: Wright, N.A., Camplejohn, R.S. (eds) Psoriasis: cell proliferation. Edinburgh: Churchill Livingstone, pp 189–207.
33. Creamer, D., Allen, M.H., Sousa, A. et al (1997) Localization of endothelial proliferation and microvascular expansion in active plaque psoriasis. *Br J Dermatol*, **136**, 859–865.
34. Braverman, I.M., Sibley, J. (1982) Role of the microcirculation in the treatment and the pathogenesis of psoriasis. *J Invest Dermatol*, **78**, 12–17.
35. Klemp, P., Staberg, B. (1986) Cutaneous and subcutaneous blood flow in nonlesional skin of patients with minimal psoriatic skin manifestations. *J Invest Dermatol*, **56**, 582–584.
36. Van de Kerkhoff, P. (1986) Dermal microvasculature in psoriasis (letter). *J Invest Dermatol*, **87**, 381.
37. Robert, C., Kupper, T.S. (1999) Inflammatory skin diseases, T cells, and immune surveillance. *N Engl J Med*, **341**, 1817–1828.
38. Ellis, C.N., Fradin, M.S., Messana, J.M. et al (1991) Cyclosporin for plaque-type psoriasis: results of a multidose, double blind trial. *N Engl J Med*, **324**, 227–284.

39. Gottlieb, S.L., Gilleaudeau, P., Johnson, R. et al (1995) Response of psoriasis to a lymphocyte-selective toxin (DAB389IL-2) suggests a primary immune but not keratinocyte, pathogenic basis. *Nat Med*, 1, 442–447.
40. Weinshenker, B.G., Bass, B.H., Ebers, G.C. et al (1989) Remission of psoriatic lesions with muromonab-CD3 (orthoclone OKT3) treatment. *J Am Acad Dermatol*, 20, 1132–1133.
41. Prinz, J.C., Braun-Falco, O., Meurer, M. et al (1991) Chimeric CD4 monoclonal antibody in the treatment of generalized pustular psoriasis. *Lancet*, 338, 320–321.
42. Wrone-Smith, T., Nickoloff, B.J. (1996) Dermal injection of immunocytes induces psoriasis. *J Clin Invest*, 98, 1878–1887.
43. Pitzalis, C., Cauli, A., Piptone, N. et al (1996) Cutaneous lymphocyte antigen-positive T lymphocytes preferentially migrate to the skin but not to the joint in psoriatic arthritis. *Arthritis Rheum*, 39, 137–145.
44. Bos, J.D., Hulsebosch, H.J., Krieg, S.R. et al (1983) Immunocompetent cells in psoriasis: in situ immunophenotyping by monoclonal antibodies. *Arch Dermatol*, 275, 181–189.
45. Schlack, J.F., Buslau, M., Jochum, W. et al (1994) T cells involved in psoriasis vulgaris belong to the Th1 subtype. *J Invest Dermatol*, 102, 145–149.
46. Bonifati, C., Ameglio, F. (1999) Cytokines in psoriasis. *Int J Dermatol*, 38, 241–251.
47. Nickoloff, B.J. (1991) The cytokine network in psoriasis. *Arch Dermatol*, 127, 871–884.
48. Barker, J.N., Goodlad, J.R., Ross, E.L. et al (1993) Increased epidermal cell proliferation in normal human skin *in vivo* following local administration of interferon gamma. *Am J Pathol*, 142, 1091–1097.
49. Barker, J.N.W.N., Mitra, R.S., Griffiths, C.E.M. et al (1991) Keratinocytes as initiators of inflammation. *Lancet*, 337, 211–214.
50. Barker, J.N.W.N., Jones, M.L., Mitra, R.S. et al (1991) Modulation of keratinocyte-derived interleukin-8 which is chemotactic for neutrophils and T lymphocytes. *Am J Pathol*, 141, 869–876.
51. Tuschil, A., Lam, C., Halsberger, A. et al (1992) Interleukin-8 stimulates calcium transients and promotes epidermal cell proliferation. *J Invest Dermatol*, 99, 294–298.
52. Nickoloff, B.J., Mitra, R.S., Varani, J. et al (1994) Aberrant production of interleukin-8 and thrombospondin-1 by psoriatic keratinocytes mediates angiogenesis. *Am J Pathol*, 144, 820–828.
53. Gillitzer, R., Berger, R., Mielke, V. et al (1991) Upper keratinocytes of psoriatic skin lesions express high levels of NAP-I/IL-8 mRNA in situ. *J Invest Dermatol*, 97, 73–79.
54. Valdimarrson, H., Baker, B.S., Jónsdóttir, I. et al (1995) Psoriasis: a T-cell mediated autoimmune disease induced by streptococcal superantigens? *Immunol Today*, 16, 145–149.
55. Ragaz, A., Ackerman, A.B. (1979). Evolution, maturation and regression of lesions of psoriasis. *Am J Dermatopathol*, 3, 199–214.
56. Altman, E.M., Kamino, H. (1999) Diagnosis; psoriasis or not? What are the clues? *Semin Cutan Med Surg*, 18, 25–35.
57. Barr, R.J., Young, E.M. (1985) Psoriasiform and related papulosquamous disorders. *J Cutan Pathol*, 12, 412–425.
58. Brody, I. (1984) Dermal and epidermal involvement in the evolution of acute eruptive guttate psoriasis vulgaris. *J Invest Dermatol*, 82, 465–470.
59. Zelickson, B.D., Muller, S.A. (1991) Generalized pustular psoriasis. *Arch Dermatol*, 127, 1339–1344.
60. Uehara, M., Ofuji, S. (1974) The morphogenesis of pustulosis palmaris et plantaris. *Arch Dermatol*, 109, 518–520.
61. Tomasini, C., Aloi, F., Solaroli, C. et al (1997) Psoriatic erythroderma: a histopathologic study of forty-five patients. *Dermatology*, 194, 102–106.
62. Stern, R.S., Lange, R. (1988) Non-melanoma skin cancer occurs in patients treated with PUVA five to ten years after first treatment. *J Invest Dermatol*, 91, 120–124.
63. Forman, A.B., Roenigk, H.H. Jr, Caro, W.A. et al (1989) Long term follow up of skin cancer in the PUVA-48 co-operative study. *Arch Dermatol*, 125, 515–519.
64. Chuang, T-Y., Heinrich, L.A., Schultz, M.D. et al (1992) PUVA and skin cancer, a historical cohort of 492 patients. *J Am Acad Dermatol*, 26, 173–177.
65. Proby, C.M., Menagé, H. du P., McGregor, J.M. et al (1993) p53 immunoreactivity in cutaneous PUVA tumors is similar to that in other non-melanoma skin neoplasms. *J Cutan Pathol*, 20, 435–441.
66. Koerber, W.A., Price, N.B., Watson, W. (1978) Coexistent psoriasis and bullous pemphigoid: a report of six cases. *Arch Dermatol*, 114, 1643–1646.
67. Gratten, C.E.H. (1985) Evidence of an association between bullous pemphigoid and psoriasis. *Br J Dermatol*, 113, 281–283.
68. Perl, S., Rappersberger, K., Födinger, D. et al (1996) Bullous pemphigoid induced by PUVA therapy. *Dermatology*, 193, 245–247.
69. Kirtschig, G., Chow, E.T.T., Venning, V.A. et al (1996) Acquired subepidermal bullous diseases associated with psoriasis: a clinical, immunopathological and immunogenetic study. *Br J Dermatol*, 135, 738–745.
70. Primka, E.J., Camisa, C. (1998) Psoriasis and bullous pemphigoid treated with azathioprine. *J Am Acad Dermatol*, 39, 121–123.
71. Endo, Y., Tamura, A., Ishikawa, O. et al (1997) Psoriasis vulgaris coexistent with epidermolysis bullosa acquisita. *Br J Dermatol*, 137, 783–786.
72. Takagi, Y., Sawada, S., Yamauchi, M. et al (2000) Coexistence of psoriasis and linear IgA bullous dermatosis. *Br J Dermatol*, 142, 513–516.

AIDS-related psoriasis

Clinical features

The incidence of psoriasis is minimally increased in patients with AIDS, 1.3–2% compared with the normal population (1%).[1–4] Psoriasis may, however, show exacerbation with the development of AIDS, signal the onset of AIDS, or parallel a worsening of the HIV-associated disease.[4] Patients may present with guttate lesions or typical plaques but in some patients there is more generalized involvement accompanied by palmoplantar keratoderma.[2]

Histological features

The histological features are sometimes indistinguishable from typical psoriasis but frequently the changes are atypical. Thus Munro microabscesses are less frequent, the acanthosis is more irregular and the thinning of the suprabasal plate is less conspicuous.[2] Slight spongiosis may be present and there is typically a perivascular infiltrate consisting of lymphocytes, plasma cells, histiocytes, dermal dendrocytes with sometimes conspicuous multinucleate giant cells.[5] The histological features not uncommonly overlap with seborrheic dermatitis.

References

1. Kaplan, M.H., Sadick, N.S., Weider, J. et al (1988) Antipsoriatic effects of zidovudine in human immunodeficiency virus-associated psoriasis. *J Am Acad Dermatol*, 20, 76–82.
2. Sadick, N.S., McNutt, S., Kaplan, M.H. (1990) Papulosquamous dermatoses of AIDS. *J Am Acad Dermatol*, 22, 1270–1277.
3. Duvic, M., Johnson, T.M., Rapini, R.P. (1987) Acquired immunodeficiency syndrome associated psoriasis and Reiter's syndrome. *Arch Dermatol*, 123, 1622–1632.
4. Kaplan, M.H., Sadick, N., McNutt, S. et al (1987) Dermatologic findings and manifestations of AIDS. *J Am Acad Dermatol*, 16, 485–506.
5. Smith, K.J., Skelton, H.G., Angritt, P. (1991) Histopathologic features of HIV-associated skin disease. *Dermatol Clin*, 9, 551–578.

Reiter's syndrome

The skin lesions of Reiter's syndrome typically show psoriasiform hyperplasia with parakeratosis. The epidermis is markedly acanthotic with elongation and hypertrophy of the epidermal ridges. The suprapapillary plates are thinned and there is infiltration of the epidermis by neutrophils, associated with the formation of spongiform pustules, microabscesses and ultimately macropustules indistinguishable from pustular psoriasis. A perivascular lymphohistiocytic infiltrate with neutrophils is seen in the upper dermis. This topic is discussed in depth on page 478.

Pityriasis rubra pilaris

Clinical features

Pityriasis rubra pilaris is an erythematous papulosquamous disorder characterized by follicular plugging (often best seen on the dorsal aspects of the hands and feet), perifollicular erythema that becomes confluent, palmoplantar hyperkeratosis and pityriasis capitis.[1–3] It is an uncommon disease, accounting for approximately one of every 5000 new dermato-logical referrals in the United Kingdom.[3] Males and females are affected equally and the age distribution tends to peak in the first and fifth decades.[3] Although the majority of cases documented have affected Caucasian patients, occasional reports describing pityriasis rubra pilaris in black African patients have recently been published.[4]

Pityriasis rubra pilaris has been classified clinically into five types:[3]

- *Type I, classical adult pityriasis rubra pilaris*, is seen in over 50% of patients. Initially, a single erythematous patch appears on the upper half of the body (typically the face and scalp) and gradually spreads as large areas of sometimes pruritic or burning follicular hyperkeratosis with erythematous perifollicular halos (*Fig. 5.105*).[4] The erythematous areas coalesce and many patients develop generalized erythroderma (*Fig. 5.106*). Characteristically, occasional islands of unaffected skin are present (*Fig. 5.107*). Follicular papules on the dorsal aspects of the fingers and extensor surfaces of the wrists, arms and thighs are said to be characteristic.[5] Fine and powdery scaling occurs on the face and scalp, with coarser scaling on the lower body (*Fig. 5.108*). The erythema has an orange–yellow tint, which is more noticeable on the palms and soles, together with marked hyperkeratosis (*Fig. 5.109*). The nails are also affected, showing distal yellow–brown discoloration, subungual hyperkeratosis, nail thickening and splinter hemorrhages.[6] Ectropion is often present,[7] and there may be diffuse alopecia.[8] Oral lesions are uncommon and include diffuse hyperkeratosis and macular erythema with white streaks reminiscent of lichen planus.[5] Prognosis for patients in this group is good with up to 80% resolving within 3 years.

- *Type II*, *atypical adult pityriasis rubra pilaris*, occurs in approximately 5% of patients and is manifested by atypical morphological features and a lengthy duration, often up to 20 years. The scaling is more ichthyosiform and there are often areas of eczematous change. The prognosis in this group is poor with only 20% resolving within 3 years.

Fig. 5.107
Pityriasis rubra pilaris: characteristic, scattered islands of unaffected skin are evident. By courtesy of the Institute of Dermatology, London, UK.

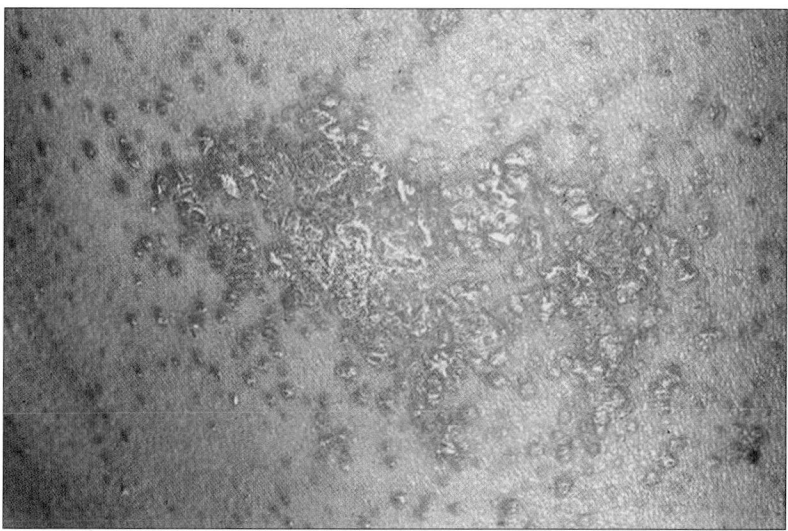

Fig. 5.105
Pityriasis rubra pilaris: there is characteristic hyperkeratosis and surrounding erythema. At the edges individual follicular lesions are evident. By courtesy of M.M. Black, MD, Institute of Dermatology, London, UK.

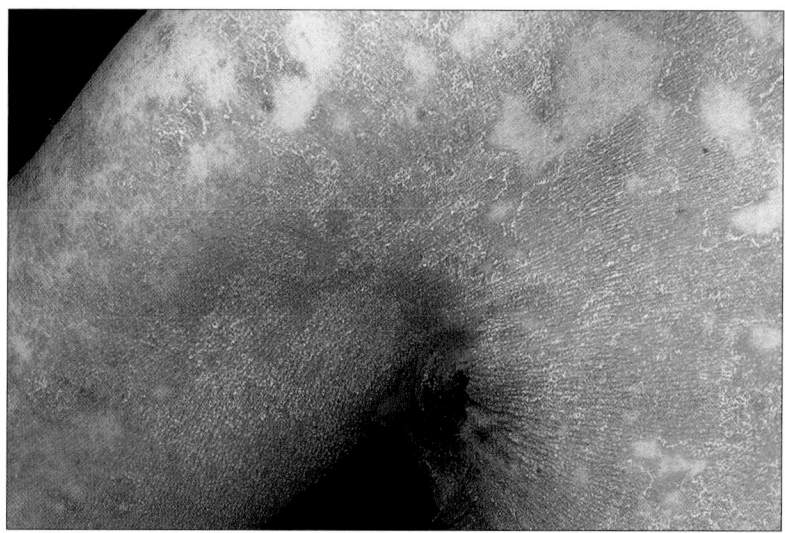

Fig. 5.108
Pityriasis rubra pilaris: in this patient, the scale is conspicuous. By courtesy of the Institute of Dermatology, London, UK.

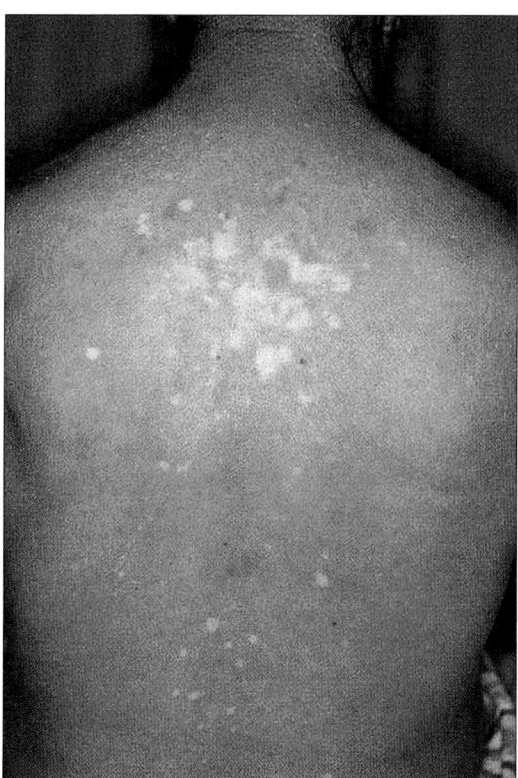

Fig. 5.106
Pityriasis rubra pilaris: confluence of lesions leads to extensive erythroderma. By courtesy of the Institute of Dermatology, London, UK.

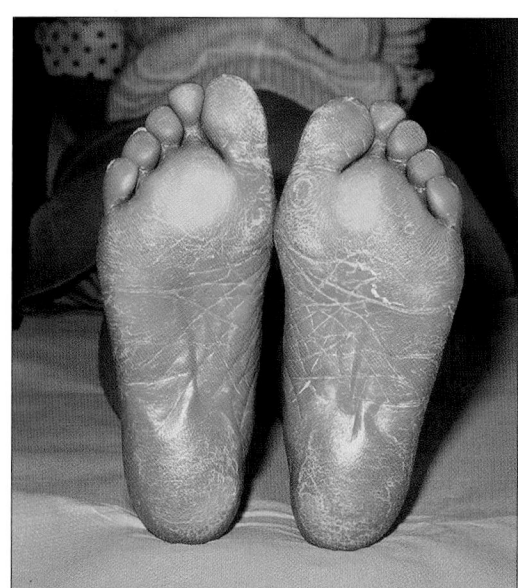

Fig. 5.109
Pityriasis rubra pilaris: palmar and plantar erythema with hyperkeratosis are frequent manifestations. Sometimes, there is an orange–yellow tint, as seen in this patient. By courtesy of the Institute of Dermatology, London, UK.

- *Type III, classical juvenile pityriasis rubra pilaris*, resembles the classical adult form except for its age distribution; it affects children up to 2 years of age, accounting for approximately 10% of patients (*Fig. 5.110*). More often, however, the eruption commences on the lower half of the body. The prognosis in this group is good, most patients clearing within 1 year.
- *Type IV, circumscribed pityriasis rubra pilaris*, affects 25% of patients and is seen in prepubertal children. Sharply defined areas of follicular hyperkeratosis and erythema are seen on the knees and elbows, together with occasional scaly erythematous patches on the rest of the body.
- *Type V, atypical juvenile pityriasis rubra pilaris*, accounts for approximately 5% of patients; presentation occurs early in life and this type has a lengthy duration. Characteristic follicular hyperkeratosis is present, together with a mild erythema. Ichthyosiform features are sometimes seen.[5] The skin of the feet and hands may become thickened and scleroderma-like.

Familial variants which account for 0–6.5% of cases mostly present with atypical features as described in type V pityriasis rubra pilaris.[5] In most families, inheritance has been via an autosomal dominant mechanism with variable expression and reduced penetrance although a recessive form has also been postulated.[9]

Pityriasis rubra pilaris has been reported in association with HIV infection.[10,11] Nodulocystic acneiform or furuncle-like lesions and lichen spinulosus may also be present. This is a particularly severe variant, which responds poorly to therapy.[11]

Pathogenesis and histological features

The etiology of pityriasis rubra pilaris is largely unknown. It has been associated with abnormal vitamin A metabolism but there is little evidence in support for this other than a frequent response to vitamin A or retinoid therapy.[5] Linkage to autoimmune disease, immune dysfunction, internal malignancy, infections and, particularly in recent years, to human immunodeficiency virus, has also been described.[5,11–13] In the majority of cases however, there is no preceding or associated condition. Pityriasis rubra pilaris is associated with an increased rate of epidermopoiesis.[14–18]

Fully developed follicular papules show characteristic features comprising conical follicular plugging, with marked uniform acanthosis of the epidermis and broad epidermal ridges and dermal papillae (*Fig. 5.111*).[14,15,19] There is hyperkeratosis, with foci of parafollicular parakeratosis. In the dermis there is a mild-to-moderate inflammatory cell infiltrate and sebaceous atrophy.

Although the histological features may be non-specific, biopsies from established, non-follicular lesions comprise alternating orthokeratosis and parakeratosis in both vertical and horizontal directions, focal or confluent hypergranulosis, thick suprapapillary plates, broad epidermal ridges, narrow dermal papillae and a perivascular lymphocytic infiltrate in the superficial dermis (*Figs 5.112–5.114*).[20] Small numbers of plasma cells and eosinophils may occasionally be present.[12] Superficial blood

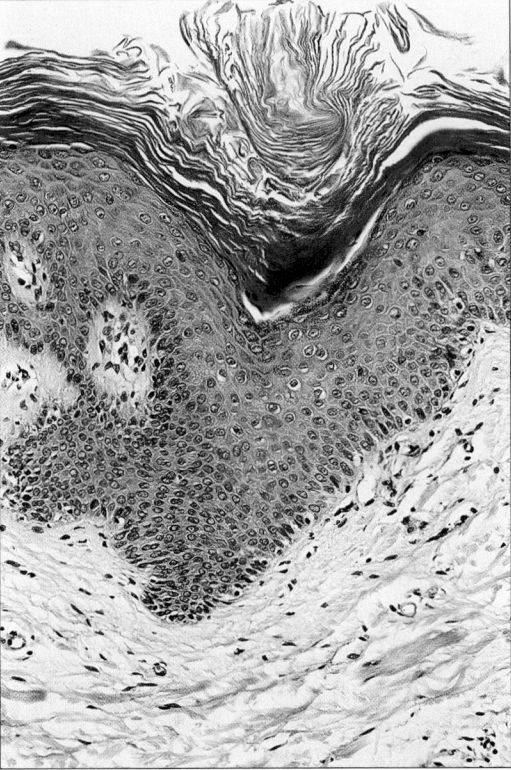

Fig. 5.111
Pityriasis rubra pilaris: follicular lesion showing the conical keratin plug. Parakeratosis is present above the adjacent epithelium.

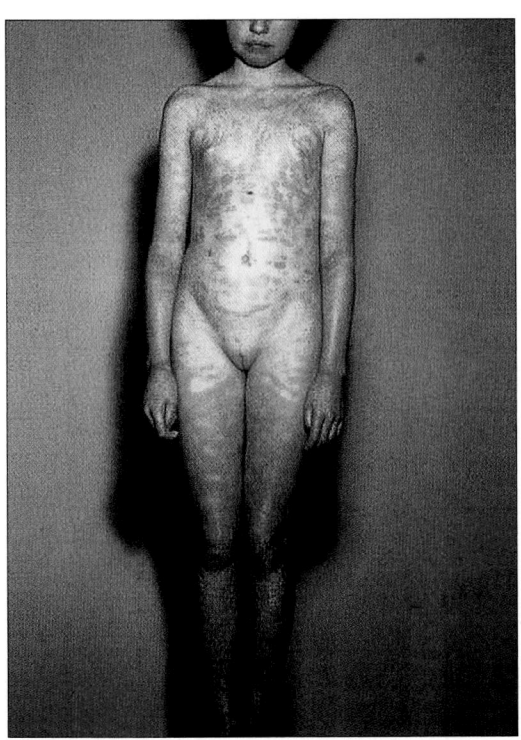

Fig. 5.110
Pityriasis rubra pilaris: classical juvenile type. Note the very extensive distribution of the lesions. By courtesy of M.M. Black, MD, Institute of Dermatology, London, UK.

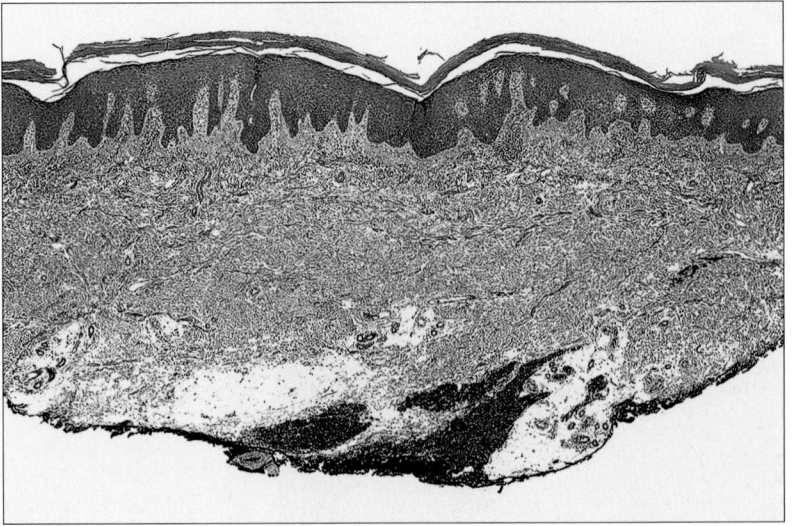

Fig. 5.112
Pityriasis rubra pilaris: there is hyperkeratosis with focal parakeratosis and psoriasiform hyperplasia.

vessels may appear slightly dilated. Occasionally there is also mild spongiosis with scattered intraepidermal lymphocytes.[13] Neutrophil infiltration as seen in psoriasis is not usually a feature of pityriasis rubra pilaris and its presence may indicate a bacterial or fungal superinfection. Acantholysis with or without dyskeratosis involving follicular and interfollicular epithelium has recently been emphasized and exceptionally a lichenoid infiltrate has been documented.[12,21–23]

In early lesions, the diagnosis is often problematical. Parakeratosis is usually poorly developed and lamellar orthohyperkeratosis predominates.[20] Hypergranulosis is present and the rete ridges are broadened and slightly elongated. The suprapapillary plates may be mildly thickened.

In erythrodermic lesions, the keratin layer may be thinned or lost and the granular cell layer diminished.[20]

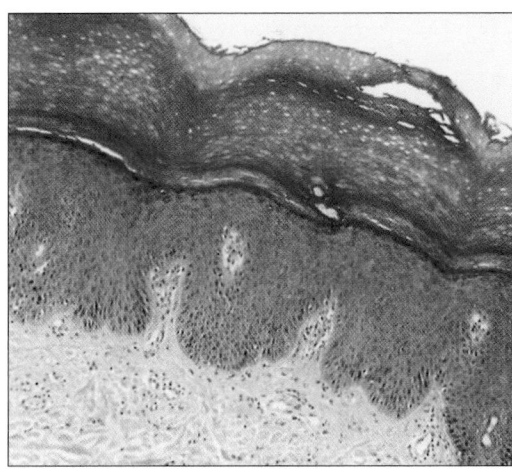

Fig. 5.115
Pityriasis rubra pilaris: plantar lesion showing hyperkeratosis, focal parakeratosis and regular acanthosis with a rounded lower border.

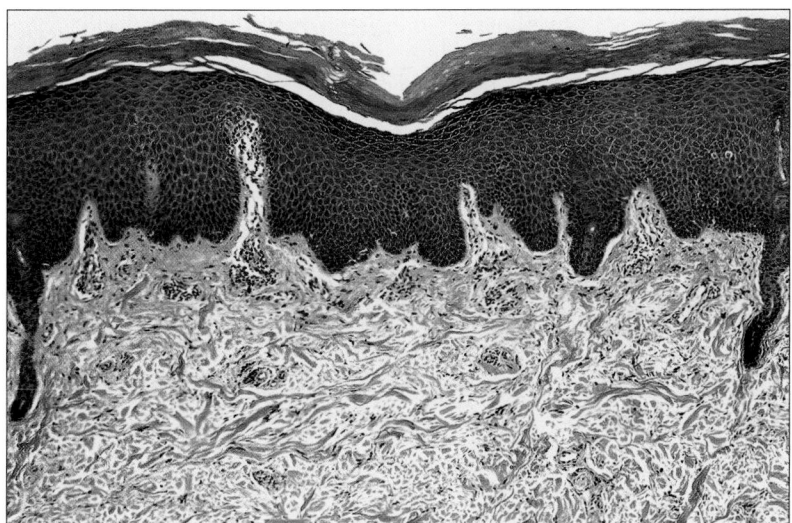

Fig. 5.113
Pityriasis rubra pilaris: alternating hyperkeratosis and parakeratosis.

Palmar and plantar lesions show hyperkeratosis, focal parakeratosis and mild acanthosis (*Fig. 5.115*).

Differential diagnosis

Pityriasis rubra pilaris may be confused both clinically and histologically with psoriasis. Features in favor of pityriasis rubra pilaris include follicular plugging with parakeratosis of the adjacent epithelium, focal parakeratosis, broad rete ridges, thickened suprapapillary plates, increased granular cell layer and an absence of tortuous dilated capillaries immediately adjacent to the epidermis. In psoriasis the acanthosis is typically more marked and often strikingly regular, the rete ridges are thin and often fused, the suprapapillary plate is thinned, parakeratosis is usually confluent and characteristic collections of neutrophils are seen in the overlying parakeratotic stratum corneum in association with spongiform degeneration of the underlying superficial epidermis.

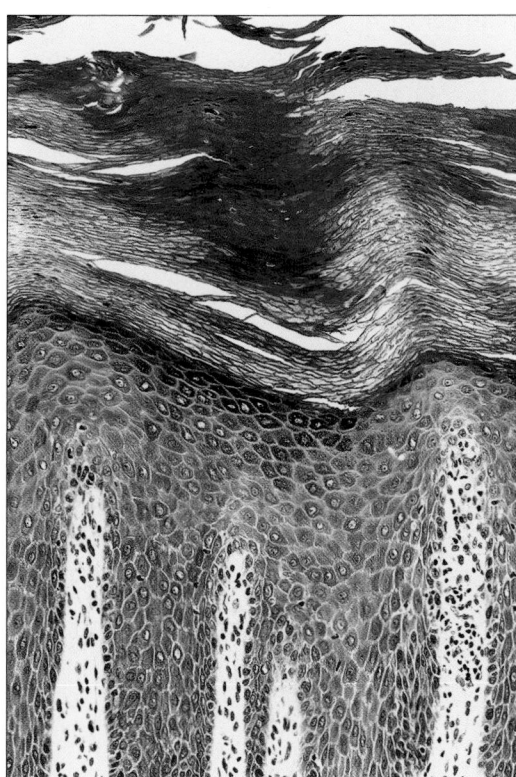

Fig. 5.114
Pityriasis rubra pilaris: in this view, alternating parakeratosis and hyperkeratosis are seen in a vertical plane.

References

1. Griffiths, W.A.D. (1975) Pityriasis rubra pilaris – an historical approach. I. Taxonomy and etiology. *Trans St John's Hosp Dermatol Soc*, **61**, 58–69.
2. Griffiths, W.A.D. (1976) Pityriasis rubra pilaris – an historical approach II. Clinical features. *Clin Exp Dermatol*, **1**, 37–50.
3. Griffiths, W.A.D. (1980) Pityriasis rubra pilaris. *Clin Exp Dermatol*, **5**, 105–112.
4. Jacyk, W.K. (1999) Pityriasis rubra pilaris in black South Africans. *Clin Exp Dermatol*, **24**, 160–163.
5. Albert, M.R., Mackool, B.T. (1999) Pityriasis rubra pilaris. *Int J Dermatol*, **38**, 1–11.
6. Sonnex, T.S., Dawber, R.P.R., Zachary, C.B. et al (1986) The nails in adults type I pityriasis rubra pilaris. A comparison with Sézary syndrome and psoriasis. *J Am Acad Dermatol*, **15**, 956–960.
7. Cohen, P.R., Prystowsky, J.H. (1989) Pityriasis rubra pilaris: a review of diagnosis and treatment. *J Am Acad Dermatol*, **20**, 801–807.
8. Barr, R.J., Young, E.M. (1985) Psoriasiform and related papulo-squamous disorders. *J Cutan Pathol*, **12**, 412–415.
9. Vanderhooft, S.L., Francis, J.S., Holbrook, K.A. et al (1995) Familial pityriasis rubra pilaris. *Arch Dermatol*, **131**, 448–453.
10. Blauvelt, A., Nahass, G.T., Pardo, R.J. et al (1991) Pityriasis rubra pilaris and HIV infection. *J Am Acad Dermatol*, **24**, 703–705.
11. Miralles, E.S., Núñez, M., De Las Heras, M.E. et al (1995) Pityriasis rubra pilaris and human immunodeficiency virus. *Br J Dermatol*, **133**, 990–993.
12. Magro, C.M., Crowson, A.N. (1997) The clinical and histomorphological features of pityriasis rubra pilaris: a comparative analysis with psoriasis. *J Cutan Pathol*, **24**, 416–424.
13. Sánchez-Regaña, M., López-Gil, F., Salleras, M. et al (1995). Pityriasis rubra pilaris as the initial manifestation of internal neoplasia. *Clin Exp Dermatol*, **20**, 436–438.
14. Niemi, K-M., Kousa, M., Storgards, K. et al (1979) Pityriasis rubra pilaris: a clinicopathological study with a special reference to autoradiography and histocompatibility antigens. *Dermatologica*, **152**, 109–118.
15. Braun-Falco, O., Ryckmanns, F., Schmoeckel, C. et al (1983) Pityriasis rubra pilaris: a clinico-pathological and therapeutic study with special reference to histochemistry, autoradiography, and electron microscopy. *Arch Dermatol Res*, **275**, 287–295.
16. Griffiths, A. (1984) Pityriasis rubra pilaris. Etiologic considerations. *J Am Acad Dermatol*, **10**, 1086–1088.
17. Griffiths, W.A.D., Pieris, S. (1982) Pityriasis rubra pilaris – an autoradiographic study. *Br J Dermatol*, **107**, 665–667.
18. Harper, R.A., Rispler, J. (1977) Pityriasis rubra pilaris cells *in vitro*. *Arch Dermatol Res*, **260**, 253–255.
19. Koehn, G.G. (1990) Dramatic follicular plugging in pityriasis rubra pilaris. *J Am Acad Dermatol*, **23**, 526–527.
20. Soeprono, F.F. (1986) Histologic criteria for the diagnosis of pityriasis rubra pilaris. *Am J Dermatopathol*, **8**, 277–283.
21. Kao, G.F., Sulica, V.I. (1989) Focal acantholytic dyskeratosis occurring in pityriasis rubra pilaris. *Am J Dermatopathol*, **11**, 172–176.
22. Howe, K., Foresman, P., Griffin, T. et al (1996) Pityriasis rubra pilaris with acantholysis. *J Cutan Pathol*, **23**, 270–274.
23. Hashimoto, K., Fedoronko, L. (1999) Pityriasis rubra pilaris with acantholysis and lichenoid histology. *Am J Dermatopathol*, **21**, 491–493.

Inflammatory linear verrucous epidermal nevus

Clinical features

Inflammatory linear verrucous epidermal nevus (ILVEN) is an uncommon condition which usually presents in infants or young children as an intensely pruritic, persistent, scaly, unilateral, linear erythematous lesion following the lines of Blaschko. Individual lesions are discrete, scaly papules, which coalesce to form plaques.[1] Superimposed lichenification and excoriations are commonly present. Although lesions may be widely distributed, the leg and thigh are sites of predilection (*Fig. 5.116*). Females are more often affected than males (4:1).[1] The left side of the body is most often involved.[1-3] Much less commonly, the disorder is bilateral and exceptionally, the condition is generalized.[4-6] Familial cases have been documented and adults may sometimes be affected.[5-9] Occasionally inflammatory linear verrucous epidermal nevus coexists with psoriasis and rarely it may present as part of the epidermal nevus syndrome.[10,11] Exceptionally, the condition may coexist with arthritis.[12]

Histological features

Histologically the nevus is characterized by sharply demarcated, alternating parakeratosis and orthohyperkeratosis (*Figs 5.117–5.119*).[1,3,13] The epidermis shows papillomatosis with psoriasiform hyperplasia and absence of the granular layer below the foci of parakeratosis contrasting with a thickened granular cell layer underneath the orthohyperkeratosis. Occasionally, Munro microabscesses are a feature. The rete ridges are elongated and thickened. Focal slight spongiosis is present accompanied by lymphocytic exocytosis. A mild perivascular lymphocytic infiltrate is seen in the superficial dermis.

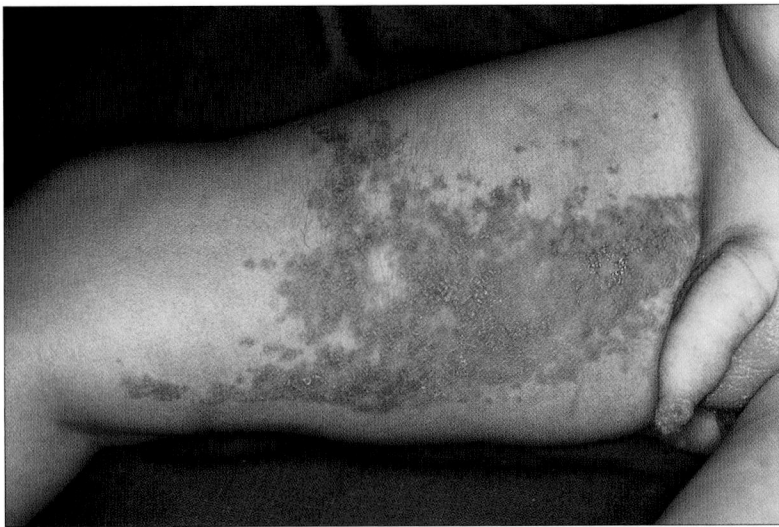

Fig. 5.116
Inflammatory linear verrucous epidermal nevus (ILVEN): patients present with scaly, erythematous, itchy papules and plaques in a linear distribution, showing a predilection for the legs. By courtesy of the Institute of Dermatology, London, UK.

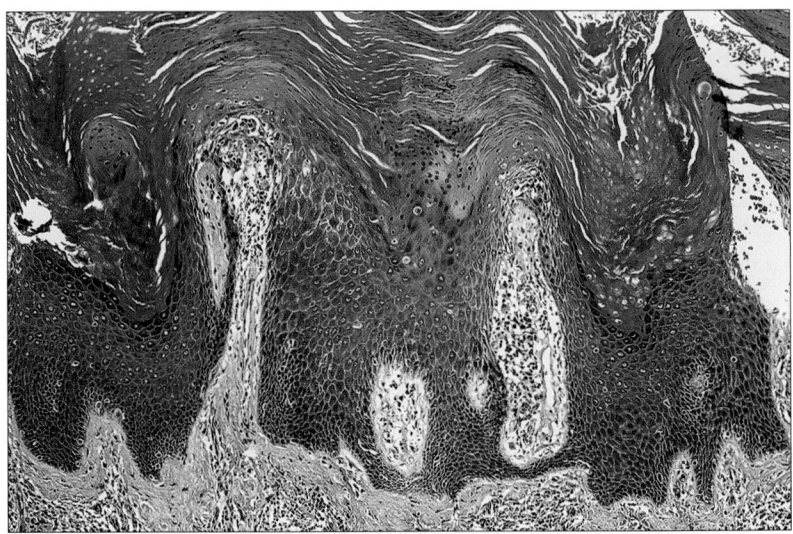

Fig. 5.118
Inflammatory linear verrucous epidermal nevus (ILVEN): alternating hyperkeratosis and parakeratosis is characteristic.

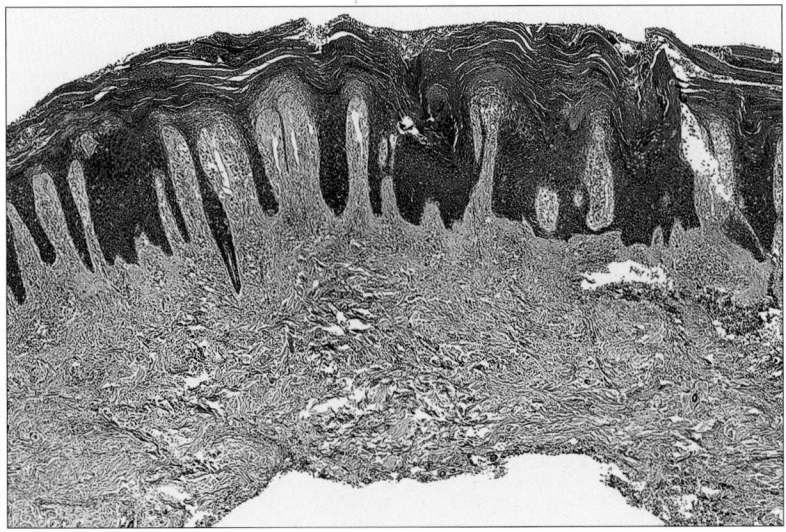

Fig. 5.117
Inflammatory linear verrucous epidermal nevus (ILVEN): in this view there is marked psoriasiform epidermal hyperplasia with massive hyperkeratosis. Mild chronic inflammation is seen in the superficial dermis.

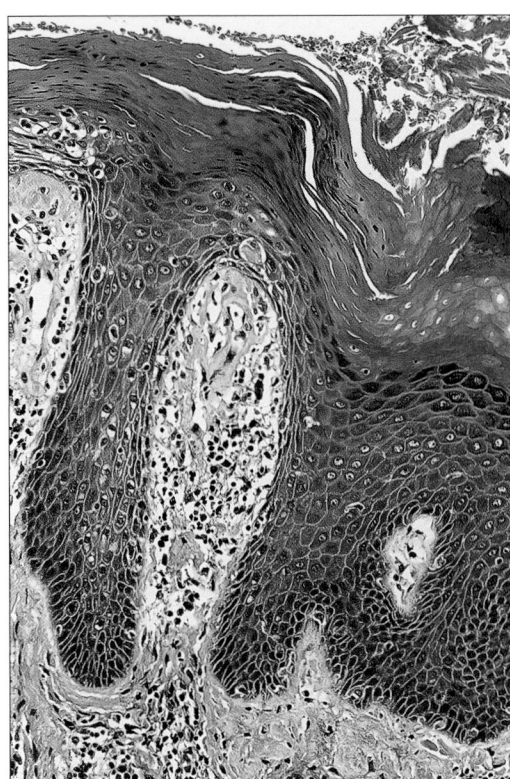

Fig. 5.119
Inflammatory linear verrucous epidermal nevus (ILVEN): close-up view.

Differential diagnosis

ILVEN must be distinguished from linear psoriasis.[14] In ILVEN, parakeratosis alternates with orthohyperkeratosis in contrast with psoriasis where the parakeratosis is confluent. Similarly, the thickened rete ridges of ILVEN contrast with the thinned ones of psoriasis. By immunocytochemistry, in ILVEN, involucrin expression is markedly diminished in the epithelium deep to the parakeratosis, while it is increased in the epithelium underlying the hyperkeratosis.[15] In psoriasis, there is a general increase in involucrin expression throughout the entire lesion.

Rare cases of ILVEN showing histiocyte infiltration of the underlying dermis reminiscent of verruciform xanthoma have been documented.[16–19]

References

1. Altman, J., Mehregan, A.H. (1971) Inflammatory linear verrucose epidermal nevus. *Arch Dermatol*, **104**, 385–389.
2. Hodge, S.J., Barr, J.M., Owen, L.G. (1978) Inflammatory linear verrucose epidermal nevus. *Arch Dermatol*, **114**, 436–438.
3. Morag, C., Metzker, A. (1985) Inflammatory linear verrucous epidermal nevus: report of seven new cases and review of the literature. *Pediatr Dermatol*, **3**, 15–18.
4. Landwehr, A.J., Starink, T.M. (1983) Inflammatory linear verrucous epidermal nevus: report of a case with bilateral distribution and nail involvement. *Dermatologica*, **166**, 107–109.
5. Goldman, K., Don, P.C. (1994) Adult onset of inflammatory linear verrucous epidermal nevus in a mother and her daughter. *Dermatology*, **189**, 170–172.
6. Hamm, H., Happle, R. (1986) Inflammatory linear verrucous epidermal nevus (ILVEN) in a mother and her daughter. *Am J Med Genet*, **24**, 685–690.
7. Kawaguchi, H., Takeuchi, M., Ono, T. et al (1999) Adult onset of inflammatory linear verrucous epidermal nevus. *J Dermatol*, **26**, 599–602.
8. Ito, M., Shimizu, N., Fujiwara, H. et al (1991) Histopathogenesis of inflammatory linear verrucous epidermal nevus: histochemistry, immunohistochemistry and ultrastructure. *Arch Dermatol Res*, **283**, 491–499.
9. Alsaleh, Q.A., Nanda, A., Hassab-El-Naby, N.M.M. et al (1994) Familial inflammatory linear verrucous epidermal nevus. *Int J Dermatol*, **33**, 52–54.
10. Oram, Y., Arisoy, A.E., Hazneci, E. et al (1996) Bilateral inflammatory linear verrucous epidermal nevus associated with psoriasis. *Cutis*, **57**, 275–278.
11. Golitz, L.E., Weston, W.L. (1979) Inflammatory linear verrucous epidermal nevus: association with epidermal nevus syndrome. *Arch Dermatol*, **115**, 1208–1209.
12. Al-Enezi, S., Huber, A.M., Krafchik, B.R. et al (2001) Inflammatory linear verrucous epidermal nevus and arthritis: a new association. *J Pediatr*, **138**, 602–604.
13. Dupre, A., Christol, B. (1977) Inflammatory linear verrucose epidermal nevus: a pathologic study. *Arch Dermatol*, **113**, 767–769.
14. De Jong, E.M.G.J., Rulo, H.F.C., Van de Kerkhof, P.C.M. (1991) Inflammatory linear verrucous epidermal nevus (ILVEN) versus linear psoriasis. A clinical, histological and immunohistochemical study. *Acta Derm Venereol*, **71**, 343–346.
15. Atherton, D.J., Kahana, M., Russell-Jones, R. (1989) Naevoid psoriasis. *Br J Dermatol*, **120**, 837–841.
16. Barr, R.J., Plank, C.J. (1980) Verruciform xanthoma of the skin. *J Cutan Pathol*, **7**, 422–428.
17. Haustein, U.F. (1984) Xanthomatous cells in inflammatory linear verrucous epidermal nevus or nevoid verruciform xanthoma. *Dermatol Monatsschr*, **170**, 475–478.
18. Groshans, E., Laplanche, G. (1981) Verruciform xanthoma or xanthomatous transformation of inflammatory linear verrucous epidermal nevus. *J Cutan Pathol*, **8**, 382–384.
19. Palestine, R.F., Winkelmann, R.K. (1982) Verruciform xanthoma in an epidermal nevus. *Arch Dermatol*, **118**, 686–691.

Bazex syndrome

Clinical features

Bazex syndrome (acrokeratosis paraneoplastica) denotes the presence of an acral psoriasiform dermatosis in association with internal malignancy.[1–3] Elderly patients, usually males, present with a symmetric erythematous or violaceous, scaly eruption affecting the ears, nose, fingers and toes (*Fig. 5.120*).[1] The knees and elbows may sometimes be involved. Vesicles and bullae are less common manifestations.[4] In patients with black or dark-brown skin, the lesions may present with hyperpigmentation.[2] Palmoplantar lesions are keratodermatous and nail involvement ranges from paronychia, horizontal or vertical ridging, yellow discoloration and thickening to onycholysis and subungual keratotic debris (*Fig. 5.121*).[1]

Patients with Bazex syndrome invariably have an associated systemic malignancy, most often affecting the oropharynx, larynx, esophagus and lung in descending order of frequency.[1] Cervical lymph node metastases are commonly present. The cutaneous lesions commonly regress following successful treatment of the underlying malignancy.[2]

Histological features

Histologically, there is considerable overlap with psoriasis and chronic spongiotic dermatitis, the epidermis showing hyperkeratosis, parakeratosis and acanthosis. In addition however, dyskeratosis and interface changes reminiscent of lichen planus are also commonly present.[1] A perivascular or less commonly lichenoid chronic inflammatory infiltrate is present in the superficial dermis.

Bullous lesions may be subepidermal or less often intraepidermal.[1,5]

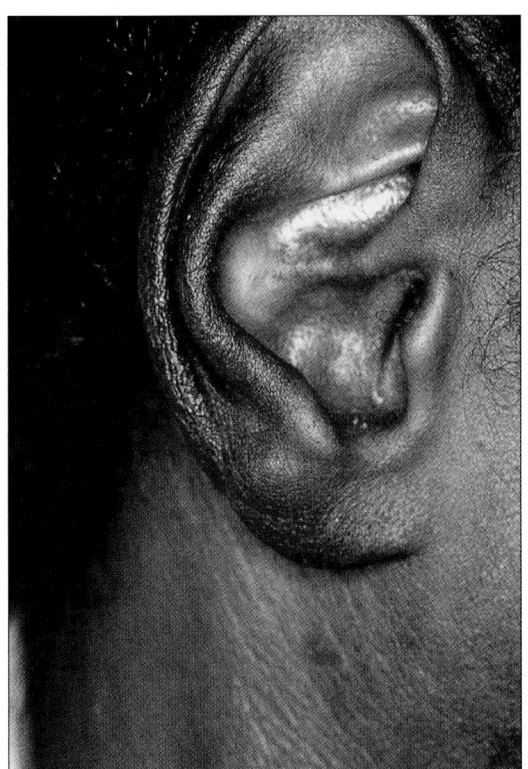

Fig. 5.120
Bazex syndrome: note the violaceous discoloration of the ear. By courtesy of J.L. Bolognia, MD, Yale Medical School, CT, USA.

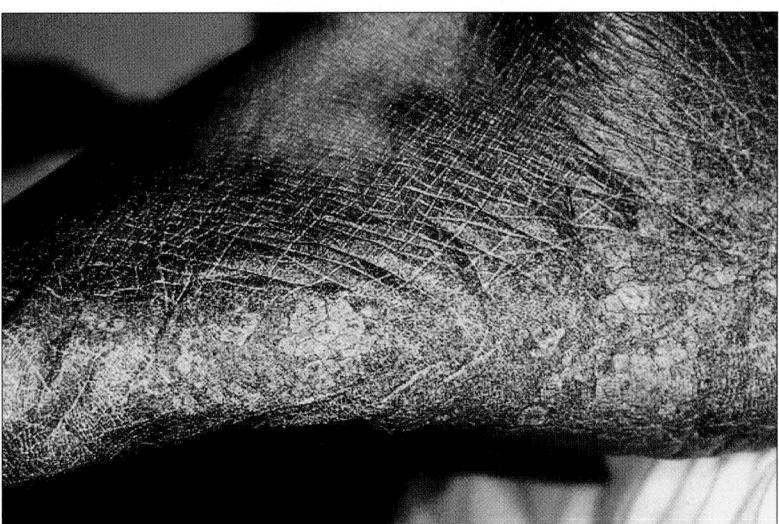

Fig. 5.121
Bazex syndrome: keratoderma. By courtesy of J.L. Bolognia, MD, Yale Medical School, CT, USA.

References

1. Bolognia, J.L., Brewer, Y.P., Cooper, D.L. (1991) Bazex syndrome (acrokeratosis paraneoplastica): an analytic review. *Medicine*, **70**, 269–280.
2. Bolognia, J.L. (1995) Bazex syndrome: acrokeratosis paraneoplastica. *Semin Dermatol*, **14**, 84–89.
3. Bazex, A., Griffiths, A. (1980) Acrokeratosis paraneoplastica: a new cutaneous marker of malignancy. *Br J Dermatol*, **102**, 301–306.
4. Richard, M., Giroux, J.M. (1987) Acrokeratosis paraneoplastica (Bazex syndrome). *J Am Acad Dermatol*, **16**, 178–183.
5. Handfield-Jones, S.E., Matthews, C.N.A., Ellis, J.P. et al (1992) Acrokeratosis paraneoplastica of Bazex. *J R Soc Med*, **85**, 548–550.

Pustular dermatoses

Pustular drug reactions

This topic is discussed on page 651.

Subcorneal pustular dermatosis

Clinical features

Subcorneal pustular dermatosis (Sneddon–Wilkinson disease) is a rare chronic, relapsing and apparently non-infective eruption of unknown etiology.[1,2] It predominantly affects females (4:1) and is usually diagnosed during the middle years of life. Pediatric cases have, however, occasionally been described.[3] It may be associated with a benign or malignant IgA paraproteinemia (up to 40% of cases) or multiple myeloma and sometimes pyoderma gangrenosum may be present.[4–12] Other associations, which have also been documented, include rheumatoid arthritis, systemic lupus erythematosus, hyperthyroidism, Crohn's disease, multiple sclerosis, IgG cryoglobulinemia, bullous pemphigoid, morphea, squamous carcinoma of the bronchus and metastatic gastrinoma, although whether these are of any great significance is doubtful.[13–20]

Clinically, patients present with waves of superficial flaccid pustules in circinate or serpiginous groups and sheets, particularly in the folds of the body, such as the axillae (*Figs 5.122, 5.123*) and groins, beneath the breasts and on the abdomen. Fluid levels are sometimes evident. Typically the mucous membranes, face, scalp and peripheries are spared.

Healing is rapid, usually within a few days or weeks, and the condition responds to dapsone, although not as dramatically as dermatitis herpetiformis. Postinflammatory hyperpigmentation is common.

Canine subcorneal pustular dermatosis, particularly affecting Miniature Schnauzers, has been reported.[21]

Pathogenesis and histological features

The etiology of subcorneal pustular dermatosis is unknown. Intercellular IgA deposits have been identified in a significant number of cases by direct immunofluorescence and many patients have a circulating IgA pemphigus antibody. These cases have been documented in the literature as IgA pemphigus (see p. 154).[22–26] Subcorneal pustular dermatosis should be restricted to the immunofluorescence negative group.

The characteristic lesion is a subcorneal pustule, which appears to sit on the skin surface (*Fig. 5.124*). The contents of the pustules are predominantly neutrophils, although an occasional eosinophil may be identified. The epidermis beneath the pustule shows surprisingly little change except for polymorphs in transit and perhaps slight intercellular edema (*Fig. 5.125*).

Older lesions may contain acantholytic cells (*Fig. 5.126*). In the dermis, superficial blood vessels are surrounded by a non-specific mixed inflammatory cell infiltrate consisting of neutrophil polymorphs and mononuclear cells.

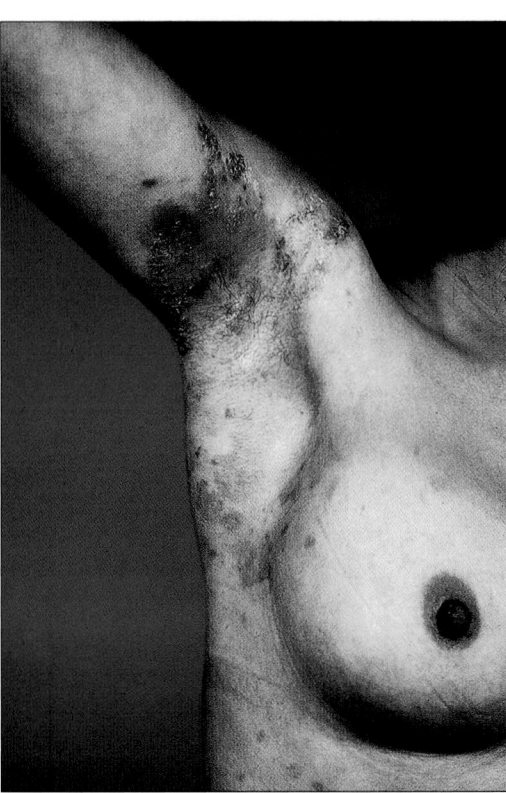

Fig. 5.122
Subcorneal pustular dermatosis: typical example showing a succession of pustules spreading outwards from the axilla. At the periphery the lesions are healing with crust formation. By courtesy of R.A. Marsden, MD, St George's Hospital, London, UK.

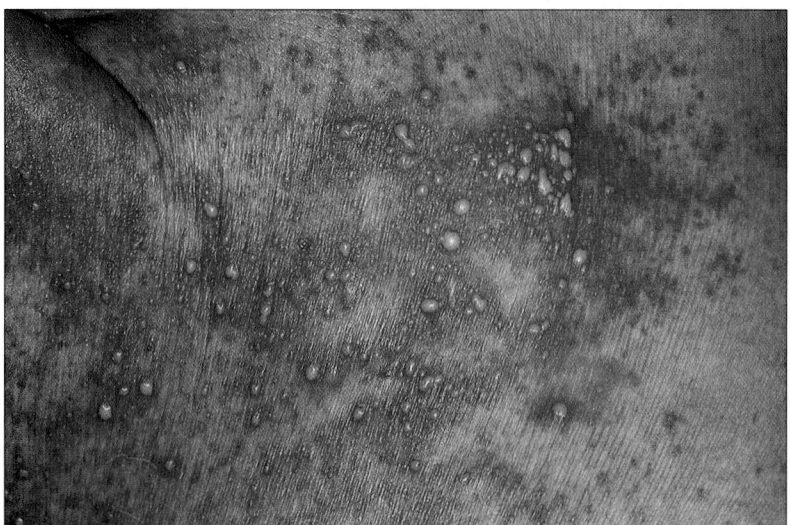

Fig. 5.123
Subcorneal pustular dermatosis: close-up view of early lesions characterized by numerous pustules arising on an erythematous background. By courtesy of R.A. Marsden, MD, St George's Hospital, London, UK.

Differential diagnosis

The histological features of subcorneal pustular dermatosis cannot be reliably distinguished from those of bullous impetigo, staphylococcal scalded skin syndrome, pemphigus foliaceus and IgA pemphigus. Impetigo is, however, a disease of young children and, although a Gram stain is often negative, cultures should grow staphylococci or streptococci.

The staphylococcal scalded skin syndrome (Ritter's disease) is predominantly a disease of infants, but rarely it may present in adults. Clinically it is different from subcorneal pustular dermatosis, being characterized by the development of large flaccid blisters, which rupture, leaving extensive areas of denuded skin.

Although acantholysis is typical of the pemphigus group of diseases, it may occasionally be seen in impetigo, staphylococcal scalded skin syndrome, subcorneal pustular dermatosis and pustular psoriasis. In difficult cases the demonstration of positive immunofluorescence will establish the diagnosis of pemphigus (however, see IgA pemphigus, p. 154).

There has been considerable controversy in the earlier literature concerning the relationship between subcorneal pustular dermatosis and pustular psoriasis, with some authors claiming them to be one and the same condition with others equally determined that they are quite different. In our view, these are two distinct diseases. Thus, in subcorneal pustular dermatosis, there is no family history and there is no evidence of more typical psoriasiform lesions elsewhere. Subcorneal pustular dermatosis responds to dapsone in the vast majority of cases and histologically spongiform change deep to the pustule (typical of psoriasis) is characteristically absent. Psoriasis is not associated with monoclonal gammopathy or multiple myeloma.

References

1. Sneddon, I., Wilkinson, D.S. (1979) Subcorneal pustular dermatosis. *Br J Dermatol*, **100**, 61–68.
2. Lutz, M.E., Daoud, M.S., McEvoy, M.T. et al (1998) Subcorneal pustular dermatosis: a clinical study of ten patients. *Cutis*, **61**, 203–208.
3. Johnson, S.A.M., Cripps, D.J. (1974) Subcorneal pustular dermatosis in children. *Arch Dermatol*, **109**, 73–77.
4. Ryatt, T.J. (1981) Subcorneal pustular dermatosis and IgA gammapathy. *Acta Derm Venereol*, **61**, 560–562.
5. Wallach, D., Cottenot, F., Pelbois, G. et al (1982) Subcorneal pustular dermatosis and monoclonal IgA. *Br J Dermatol*, **107**, 229–234.
6. Burrows, D., Bingham, E.A. (1984) Subcorneal pustular dermatosis and IgA gammapathy. *Br J Dermatol*, **111** (Suppl. 26), 91–93.
7. Dal Tio, R., Di Vito, F., Salvi, F. (1985) Subcorneal pustular dermatosis and IgA myeloma. *Dermatologica*, **170**, 240–243.
8. Kasha, E.E. Jr, Epinette, W.W. (1988) Subcorneal pustular dermatosis (Sneddon–Wilkinson disease) in association with monoclonal IgA gammapathy: a report and review of the literature. *J Am Acad Dermatol*, **19**, 854–858.
9. Todd, D.J., Bingham, E.A., Walsh, M. et al (1991) Subcorneal pustular dermatosis and IgA paraproteinemia: response to both etretinate and PUVA. *Br J Dermatol*, **125**, 387–389.
10. Marsden, J.R., Millard, L.G. (1986) Pyoderma gangrenosum, subcorneal pustular dermatosis and IgA paraproteinemia. *Br J Dermatol*, **114**, 125–129.
11. Kohl, P.K., Hartschuh, W., Tilgen, W. et al (1991) Pyoderma gangrenosum followed by subcorneal pustular dermatosis in a patient with IgA paraproteinemia. *J Am Acad Dermatol*, **24**, 325–328.
12. Venning, V.A., Ryan, T.J. (1986) Subcorneal pustular dermatosis followed by pyoderma gangrenosum. *Br J Dermatol*, **115**, 117–118.
13. Butt, A., Burge, S.M. (1995) Sneddon–Wilkinson disease in association with rheumatoid arthritis. *Br J Dermatol*, **132**, 313–315.
14. Saulsbury, F.T., Kesler, R.W. (1984) Subcorneal pustular dermatosis and systemic lupus erythematosus. *Int J Dermatol*, **23**, 63–64.
15. Taniguchi, S., Tsurata, D., Kutsuna, H. et al (1995) Subcorneal pustular dermatosis in a patient with hyperthyroidism. *Dermatology*, **190**, 64–66.
16. Lin, R.Y., Schwartz, R.A., Lambert, W.C. (1986) Subcorneal pustular dermatosis with polyarthritis. *Cutis*, **37**, 123–126.
17. Bernstein, J.E., Medenica, M., Soltani, K. (1981) Coexistence of localized bullous pemphigoid, morphea, and subcorneal pustulosis. *Arch Dermatol*, **117**, 725–727.
18. Delaporte, E., Colombel, J.F., Nguyen-Mailer, C. et al (1992) Subcorneal pustular dermatosis in a patient with Crohn's disease. *Acta Derm Venereol*, **72**, 301–302.
19. Köhler, L.D., Möhrenschlager, M., Worret, W.I. et al (1999) Subcorneal pustular dermatosis (Sneddon–Wilkinson disease) in a patient with multiple sclerosis. *Dermatology*, **199**, 69–70.

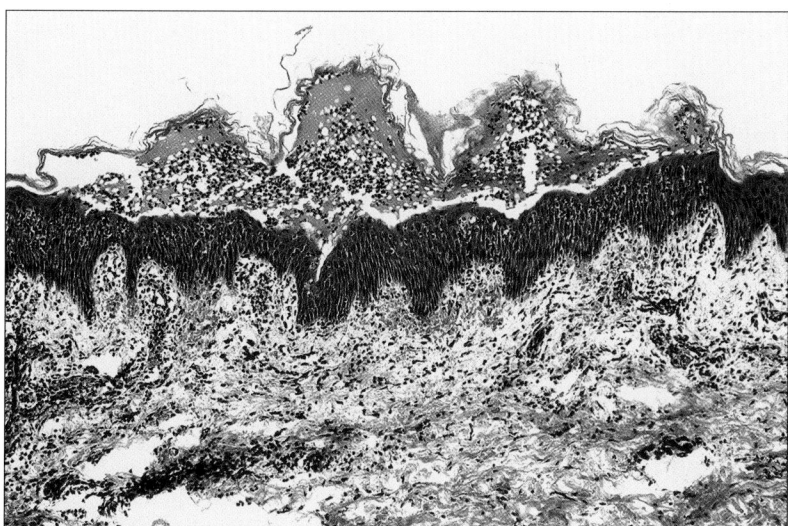

Fig. 5.124
Subcorneal pustular dermatosis: situated immediately below the stratum corneum is a blister cavity containing edema fluid and numerous neutrophils. The epidermis shows neutrophils in transit. Within the papillary dermis is a neutrophil and lymphocytic infiltrate.

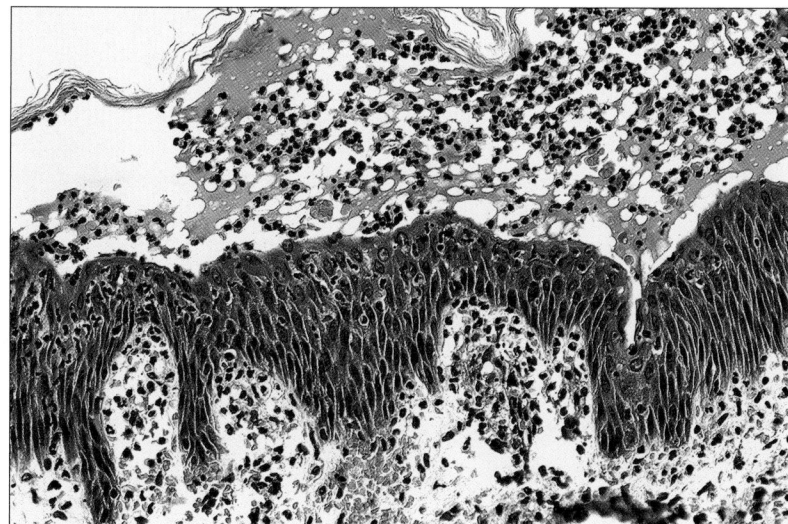

Fig. 5.125
Subcorneal pustular dermatosis: close-up view.

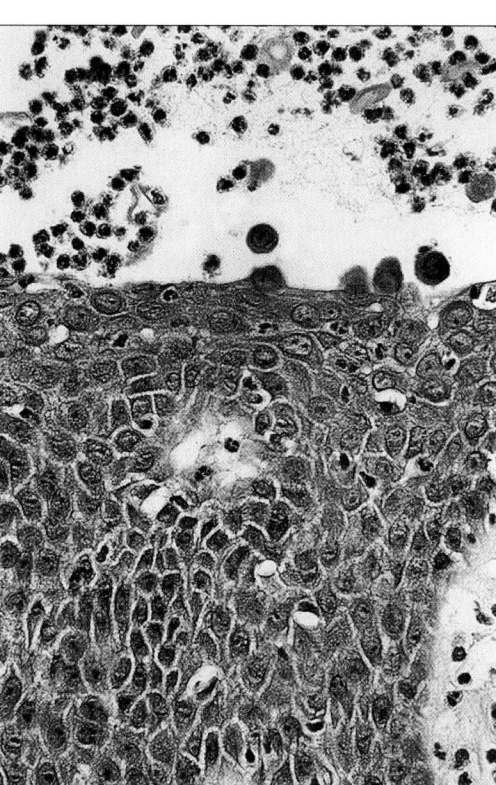

Fig. 5.126
Subcorneal pustular dermatosis: in addition to neutrophils there are scattered acantholytic keratinocytes. These features are indistinguishable from those of pemphigus foliaceus.

20. Buchet, S., Humbert, P., Blane, D. et al (1991) Pustulose sous-cornée associée à un carcinome épidermöide du poumon. *Ann Dermatol Vénéréol*, **118**, 125–128.
21. Kalaher, K.M., Scott, D.W. (1990) Subcorneal pustular dermatosis in dogs and in human beings: comparative aspects. *J Am Acad Dermatol*, **22**, 1023–1028.
22. Beutner, E.H., Chorzelski, T.P., Wilson, R.M. et al (1989) IgA pemphigus foliaceus. Report of two cases and a review of the literature. *J Am Acad Dermatol*, **20**, 89–97.
23. Piette, W., Burken, R.R., Ray, T.L. (1987) Intraepidermal neutrophilic IgA dermatosis: presence of circulating pemphigus-like IgA antibody specific for monkey epithelium. *J Invest Dermatol*, **88**, 512.
24. Huff, J.C., Golitz, L.E., Kunke, K.S. (1985) Intraepidermal neutrophilic IgA dermatosis. *N Engl J Med*, **313**, 1643–1645.
25. Tagami, H., Iwatsuki, K., Iwase, Y. et al (1983) Subcorneal pustular dermatosis with vesiculo-bullous eruption. Demonstration of subcorneal IgA deposits and a leukocyte chemotactic factor. *Br J Dermatol*, **109**, 581–587.
26. Hashimoto, T., Inamoto, N., Nakamura, K. et al (1987) Intercellular IgA dermatosis with clinical features of subcorneal pustular dermatosis. *Arch Dermatol*, **123**, 1062–1065.

Toxic erythema of the neonate

Clinical features

Toxic erythema of the neonate (erythema toxicum neonatorum, erythema neonatorum) is a very common self-limiting disorder affecting from 48 to 72% of all newborn infants.[1-7] There is no racial or sex predilection.[2] It presents as an asymptomatic erythematous macular rash usually in the first 3 days of life.[1] Occasionally, it may be evident at birth and, exceptionally, the onset is delayed until the second week after birth.[5,6,8] Sometimes there are papules and vesicles and, in some patients, pustule formation is evident. The condition most often affects the forehead, face, chest, trunk and extremities.[1] The palms and soles are typically uninvolved. The eruption is asymptomatic and very typically transient with lesions often lasting only a number of hours or days.[1] Full resolution is usually achieved by 1–5 days although recurrences may occur in up to 11% of neonates.[2] Toxic erythema of the neonate is frequently associated with a peripheral blood eosinophilia.

Pathogenesis and histological features

The etiology of this condition is completely unknown.[2] The most intriguing hypothesis to date has been that the condition might represent an acute graft-versus-host type of reaction resulting from transfer of maternal lymphocytes during delivery.[9]

Early erythematous lesions show a somewhat nondescript perivascular inflammatory cell infiltrate with conspicuous eosinophils, which may be seen penetrating the epidermis in close proximity to hair follicles. In an established lesion, the pustules are follicular, lie subcorneally and contain large numbers of eosinophils and occasional neutrophils.[10] The external root sheath of the infundibulum may also be affected.

Differential diagnosis

Toxic erythema of the neonate must be distinguished from incontinentia pigmenti (see Ch. 2). The latter, however, is characterized by eosinophilic spongiosis, a feature not seen in toxic erythema. In miliaria rubra the vesicles are related to sweat ducts rather than hair follicles and typically contain mononuclear cells rather than eosinophils. Toxic erythema of the neonate must also be distinguished from infantile acropustulosis, transient neonatal pustular melanosis and infantile eosinophilic pustular folliculitis.

References

1. Van Praag, M.C.G., Van Rooij, R.W.G., Folkers, E. et al (1997) Diagnosis and treatment of pustular disorders in the neonate. *Pediatr Dermatol*, **14**, 131–145.
2. Schwartz, R.A., Janniger, C.K. (1996) Erythema toxicum neonatorum. *Cutis*, **58**, 153–155.
3. Harris, J.R., Schick, B. (1956) Erythema neonatorum. *Am J Dis Child*, **92**, 27–33.
4. Carr, J.A., Hodgman, J.E., Freeman, R.L. et al (1966) Relationship between toxic erythema and infant maturity. *Am J Dis Child*, **112**, 129–134.
5. Marino, L.J. (1965) Toxic erythema present at birth. *Am J Dis Child*, **92**, 402–403.
6. Leung, A.K.C., Wheeler, B.H., Robson, W.L. et al (1992) Erythema toxicum present at birth. *Pediatr Dermatol*, **9**, 162–163.
7. Schachner, L., Press, S. (1983) Vesicular, bullous and pustular disorders in infancy and childhood. *Pediatr Clin North Am*, **30**, 609–629.
8. Chang, M.W., Jiang, S.B., Orlow, S.J. (1999) Atypical erythema toxicum neonatorum of delayed onset in a term infant. *Pediatr Dermatol*, **16**, 137–141.
9. Bassukas, I.D. (1992) Is erythema toxicum neonatorum a mild self-limited acute cutaneous graft-versus-host-reaction from maternal-to-fetal lymphocyte transfer? *Med Hypotheses*, **38**, 334–338.
10. Freeman, R.G., Spiller, R., Knox, J.M. (1960) Histopathology of erythema toxicum neonatorum. *Arch Dermatol*, **82**, 586–589.

Infantile acropustulosis

Clinical features

This uncommon condition usually presents in the first year of life and is sometimes evident at birth.[1-4] There is a marked male predilection. Although it is most often seen in black children, there are occasional reports of its occurrence in Asians and whites.[5-8]

The disorder presents as crops of intensely itchy, erythematous, 1–5 mm diameter papules, vesicles and pustules, which are found most often on the palms and soles, but the volar surfaces of the wrists, the ankles, the face and scalp may occasionally be affected (*Fig. 5.127*).[6] The mucous membranes are spared.[1] Lesions are often present for 1–2 weeks and tend to recur every 2–4 weeks. With progression, the duration of the eruption diminishes and the remission lasts for gradually increasing periods of time. Spontaneous resolution has usually occurred by 2–3 years of age.

Pathogenesis and histological features

The etiology and pathogenesis of this condition are unknown. However, infantile acropustulosis may be associated with atopy and hypereosinophilia.[6,9-11] Sometimes, a history of prior or concurrent scabies infection is present but whether this is causal is uncertain.[4]

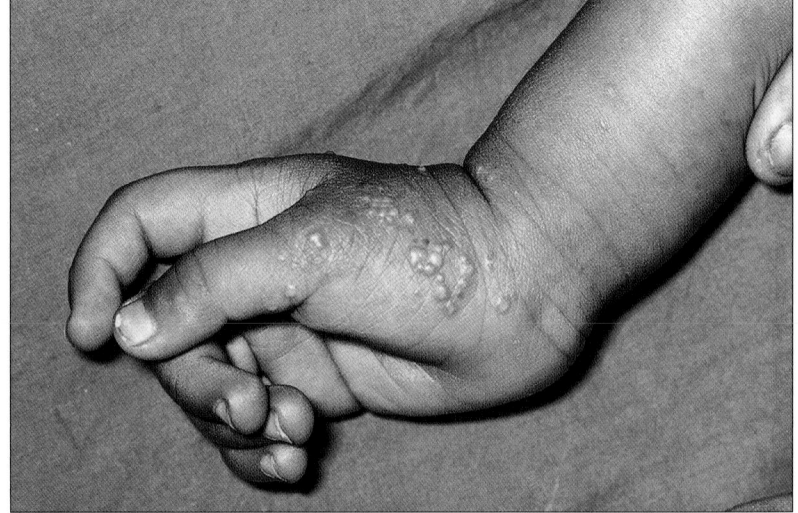

Fig. 5.127
Infantile acropustulosis: typical small pustules centered about the base of the thumb. By courtesy of R.A. Marsden, MD, St George's Hospital, London, UK.

Histology reveals a subcorneal pustule containing predominantly neutrophils, although occasionally small numbers of mononuclears and eosinophils are evident. Eosinophil-rich pustules have also been described but with hindsight most such cases probably represent eosinophilic pustular folliculitis.[11] Slight acantholysis of the adjacent epidermis has been described.[12] The underlying dermis often contains a perivascular chronic inflammatory cell infiltrate, sometimes with scattered neutrophils and eosinophils. Direct and indirect immunofluorescence tests are negative.

Differential diagnosis

The diagnosis of infantile acropustulosis depends upon careful clinicopathological correlation. Conditions that may enter the differential diagnosis include scabies, pompholyx, *Candida* and dermatophytosis, herpes simplex, juvenile dermatitis herpetiformis, toxic erythema of the neonate, bullous impetigo, eosinophilic pustular folliculitis occurring in infancy and transient neonatal pustular melanosis.

References

1. Van Praag, M.C.G., Van Rooij, R.W.G., Folkers, E. et al (1997) Diagnosis and treatment of pustular disorders in the neonate. *Pediatr Dermatol*, **14**, 131–145.
2. Jarrett, M., Ramsdell, W. (1979) Infantile acropustulosis. *Arch Dermatol*, **115**, 834–836.
3. Kahn, G., Rywlin, A.M. (1979) Acropustulosis of infancy. *Arch Dermatol*, **115**, 831–833.
4. Mancini, A.J., Frieda, I.J., Paller, A.S. (1998) Infantile acropustulosis revisited: history of scabies and response to topical steroids. *Pediatr Dermatol*, **15**, 337–341.
5. Bjornberg, A., Friis, B. (1978) Persistent pustulosis in children adopted from Asia: a sequala of scabies. *Int J Dermatol*, **5**, 69–73.
6. Palungwachira, P. (1989) Infantile acropustulosis. *Austr J Dermatol*, **30**, 97–100.
7. Vignon-Pennamen, M.D., Wallach, D. (1986) Infantile acropustulosis: a clinicopathologic study of six cases. *Arch Dermatol*, **122**, 1155–1160.
8. Dromy, R., Raz, A., Metzner, D. (1991) Infantile acropustulosis. *Pediatr Dermatol*, **8**, 184–187.
9. McFadden, N., Falk, E.S. (1985) Infantile acropustulosis. *Cutis*, **36**, 49–51.
10. Bundino, S., Zina, A.M., Ubertalli, A. (1982) Infantile acropustulosis. *Dermatologica*, **165**, 615–619.
11. Falanga, V. (1985) Infantile acropustulosis with eosinophilia. *J Am Acad Dermatol*, **13**, 826–828.
12. Jennings, J.L., Burrows, W.M. (1983) Infantile acropustulosis. *J Am Acad Dermatol*, **9**, 733–738.

Transient neonatal pustular melanosis

Clinical features

Transient neonatal pustular melanosis is an uncommon condition which presents with vesicles and pustules on the forehead, under the chin, on the nape of the neck, chest, back and buttocks.[1–4] In contrast to eosinophilic pustular folliculitis of infancy, the scalp is rarely involved. It affects 4–5% of black infants and 0.1–0.3% of white infants.[2] There is no sex predilection.[3] Lesions, which present at birth or during the first day of life, heal rapidly to leave small brown macules with a peripheral scale, and have usually disappeared by 3 months of age.[3]

Histological features

Histologically, the features are identical to those of infantile acropustulosis; i.e. a subcorneal neutrophil-rich pustule sometimes accompanied by small numbers of eosinophils.[1]

References

1. Ramamurthy, R.S., Reveri, M., Esterly, N.B. et al (1976) Transient neonatal pustular melanosis. *J Pediatr*, **88**, 831–835.
2. Wyre, H.W., Murphy, M.O. (1979) Transient neonatal pustular melanosis. *Arch Dermatol*, **115**, 458.
3. Van Praag, M.C.G., Van Rooij, R.W.G., Folkers, E. et al (1997) Diagnosis and treatment of pustular disorders in the neonate. *Pediatr Dermatol*, **14**, 131–145.
4. Schachner, L., Press, S. (1983) Vesicular, bullous and pustular disorders in infancy and childhood. *Pediatr Clin N Am*, **30**, 609–629.

Eosinophilic pustular folliculitis of infancy

Clinical features

Eosinophilic pustular folliculitis (Ofuji's disease), which is largely a condition of adults and presents as recurrent episodes of itchy follicular papules and pustules on the face, trunk and extremities, may rarely develop in infants.[1–6] There is a predilection for males.[1] In the infantile form, lesions, which may be present at birth or develop during the first 24 hours, are found particularly on the scalp, hands and feet.[1,7] The trunk and limbs may also be affected.[2] Patients present with 1–3 mm white to yellow crusted pustules arising on an erythematous base.[1,2] A blood eosinophilia is often present.[7,8] The condition persists from 3 months to up to 5 years.[2]

Pathogenesis and histological features

The etiology is unknown, although in a small number of cases an association with atopy has been documented.[9] In contrast to the adult disease, HIV infection is very rarely present.[10]

The histological features are those of an eosinophil-rich 'spongiotic' pustule related to the outer root sheath of the hair follicle from the stratum corneum to the level of insertion of the sebaceous duct.[11–15] A heavy inflammatory cell infiltrate consisting of eosinophils, lymphocytes and histiocytes is present in the adjacent dermis.

References

1. Van Praag, M.C.G., Van Rooij, R.W.G., Folkers, E. et al (1997) Diagnosis and treatment of pustular disorders in the neonate. *Pediatr Dermatol*, **14**, 131–145.
2. Buckley, D.A., Munn, S.E., Higgins, E.M. (2001) Neonatal eosinophilic pustular folliculitis. *Clin Dermatol*, **26**, 251–255.
3. Falanga, V. (1985) Infantile acropustulosis with eosinophilia. *J Am Acad Dermatol*, **13**, 826–828.
4. Ofugi, S., Ogini, A., Horio, T. et al (1970) Eosinophilic pustular folliculitis. *Acta Derm Venereol*, **50**, 195–203.
5. Larralde, M., Morales, S., Munoz, S. et al (1999) Eosinophilic pustular folliculitis in infancy: report of two new cases. *Pediatr Dermatol*, **16**, 118–120.
6. Luelmo, A.J., Saez, A.A. (2001) Eosinophilic pustular folliculitis in childhood. *An Esp Pediatr*, **55**, 154–158.
7. Lucky, A.W., Esterly, N.B., Heskel, N. et al (1984) Eosinophilic pustular folliculitis in infancy. *Pediatr Dermatol*, **1**, 202–206.
8. Cutler, T.P. (1981) Eosinophilic pustular folliculitis. *Clin Exp Dermatol*, **6**, 327–332.
9. Ramdial, P.K., Morar, N., Dlova, N.C. et al (1999) HIV-associated eosinophilic folliculitis in an infant. *Am J Dermatopathol*, **21**, 241–246.
10. Boone, M., Dangoisse, C., Andre, J. et al (1995) Eosinophilic pustular folliculitis in three atopic children with hypersensitivity to Dermatophagoides pteronyssinus. *Dermatology*, **190**, 164–168.
11. Duarte, A.M., Kramer, J., Yusk, J.W. et al (1993) Eosinophilic pustular folliculitis in infancy and childhood. *Am J Dis Child*, **147**, 197–200.
12. Giard, F., Marcoux, D., McCuaig, C. et al (1991) Eosinophilic pustular folliculitis (Ofuji disease) in childhood: a review of four cases. *Pediatr Dermatol*, **8**, 189–193.
13. Taieb, A., Bassan-Andrieu, L., Maleville, J. (1992) Eosinophilic pustulosis of the scalp in childhood. *J Am Acad Dermatol*, **27**, 55–60.
14. Darmstadt, G.L. (1992) Eosinophilic pustular folliculitis. *Pediatrics*, **89**, 1095–1098.
15. García-Patos, V., Pujol, R.M., de Moragas, J.M. (1994) Infantile eosinophilic pustular folliculitis. *Dermatology*, **189**, 133–138.

Numerous other pustular dermatoses may be encountered including superficial pemphigus, particularly IgA pemphigus, pustular drug reactions, bullous impetigo and staphylococcal scalded skin syndrome, pustular dermatophyte infections, pustular lesions in pyoderma gangrenosum and necrolytic migratory erythema. These are discussed elsewhere in this book.

Lichenoid and interface dermatoses

6

Lichenoid dermatoses   217
Lichen planus   217
Lichen planus pemphigoides   227
Lupus erythematosus–lichen planus overlap syndrome   227
Lichen nitidus   227
Lichenoid keratosis   229
Lichenoid drug reactions   231
Fixed drug reaction   231
Lichen striatus   231
Adult Blaschkitis   233
Lichen aureus   233
Keratosis lichenoides chronica   233
Twenty-nail dystrophy of childhood   234
Erythema dyschromicum perstans   234

Interface dermatoses   236
Erythema multiforme   237
Toxic epidermal necrolysis and Stevens–Johnson syndrome   240
Paraneoplastic pemphigus   244
Interface dermatitis of HIV infection   244
Poikiloderma   244
Lupus erythematosus and dermatomyositis   245
Large plaque parapsoriasis   245
Poikiloderma of Civatte   245
Mitochondrial DNA syndrome-associated poikiloderma   245
Rothmund–Thomson syndrome   246
Blooms' syndrome   247
Cockayne's syndrome   248
Dyskeratosis congenita   249
Lichen sclerosus et atrophicus   250
Graft-versus-host disease   250
Pityriasis lichenoides   255

In a histological context, the term 'lichenoid' refers to inflammatory dermatoses characterized by the presence of a band-like lymphohistiocytic infiltrate in the upper dermis, hugging and often obscuring the epidermodermal interface. Lichen planus is the prototype (*Table 6.1*). Interface dermatitis refers to the presence of basal cell vacuolization (hydropic degeneration), often accompanied by single cell keratinocyte apoptosis (*Table 6.2*). These two terms are by no means mutually exclusive; in fact most lichenoid infiltrates are accompanied by interface change. By way of contrast, however, many dermatoses characterized primarily by interface change such as lupus erythematosus and poikiloderma, do not show a lichenoid infiltrate.

Lichenoid dermatoses

Lichen planus

Clinical features

Lichen planus (Gr. *leichen*, tree moss) is a common, usually intensely pruritic, symmetrical, papulosquamous dermatosis.[1,2] Its prevalence in the general population is approximately 1%. It presents most often in the fourth to sixth decades and has a slight female predominance.[3,4] It is uncommon in childhood.[5,6] Occasional familial cases have been reported.[7]

The disease is characterized by small, smooth, shiny, flat-topped polygonal papules measuring several millimeters to 1 cm in diameter and

Table 6.1
Causes of lichenoid dermatitis

- Lichen planus
- Lichenoid graft-versus-host disease
- Lichen nitidus
- Lichenoid keratosis
- Lichenoid drug reaction
- Fixed drug reaction
- Lichen planopilaris
- Lichen striatus
- Adult Blaschkitis
- Lichen aureus
- Lichenoid mycosis fungoides
- Ashy dermatoses

Table 6.2
Causes of interface dermatitis

- Lichenoid dermatoses
- Erythema multiforme
- Stevens–Johnson syndrome/toxic epidermal necrolysis
- Lupus erythematosus
- Acute graft-versus-host disease
- Poikiloderma
- Interface drug reactions

often having a violaceous color (*Fig. 6.1*). Delicate white lines known as Wickham's striae typically cross the slightly scaly surface (*Fig. 6.2*). The lesions are found most commonly on the flexor aspect of the wrists, the forearms, the extensor aspect of the hands and ankles, the lumbar area and the glans penis. Lichen planus is associated with a positive Koebner's phenomenon. It is a usually self-limiting although sometimes protracted disorder, patients clearing of lesions within weeks to 1 or 2 years.

Oral involvement, which is very common (affecting up to 60% of patients with cutaneous disease), shows a marked female preponderance and presents most often in the seventh decade. It may sometimes be the sole manifestation (an estimated 15–35% of patients with oral lichen planus never develop skin lesions).[8–12] The buccal mucosa, vestibule, tongue and gingivae are most often affected in decreasing order of frequency.[11] Patients frequently present with a white lace-like pattern, but papules, plaques and erosions, and ulcerated, atrophic and bullous variants may also be found (*Figs 6.3–6.5*).[1,13] Lesions are usually asymptomatic, although erosions and bullae are sometimes tender and painful. Chronic ulcerated oral lichen planus is of particular importance because it has been related to an increased risk, albeit low, of developing squamous cell carcinoma (*Figs 6.6–6.8*). The current literature suggests that 0.2–10% of affected patients will develop an oral malignancy.[11,14–16] The lower estimate is probably closer to the truth.[17] Oral involvement in lichen planus and its relationship to cutaneous squamous cell carcinoma is discussed in greater depth on page 433. Involvement of the gums may present as desquamative gingivitis (see p. 445).[1] Other mucous membranes that may be involved include those of the pharynx, larynx, esophagus, nose, anus and genitalia.[18]

Ocular involvement is rare and may include eyelid lesions, blepharitis, conjunctivitis, keratitis, punctate corneal opacities, iridocyclitis and chorioretinitis.[19,20]

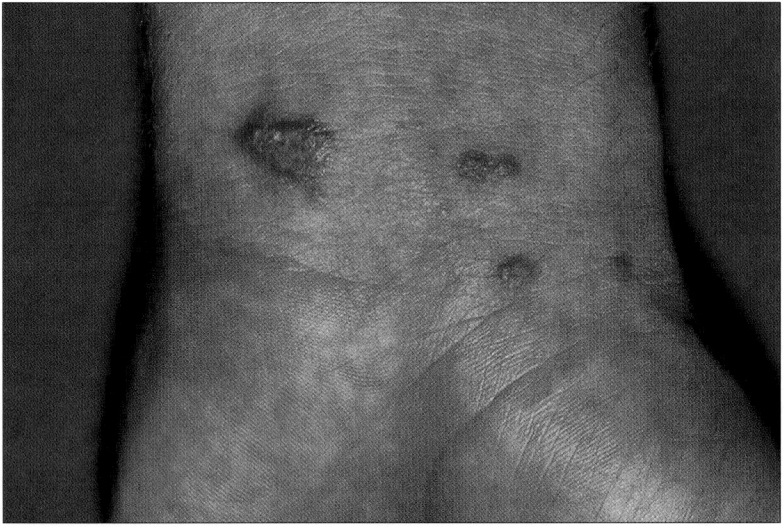

Fig. 6.1
Lichen planus: there are typical flat-topped polygonal papules on the anterior aspect of the wrist. By courtesy of R.A. Marsden, MD, St George's Hospital, London, UK.

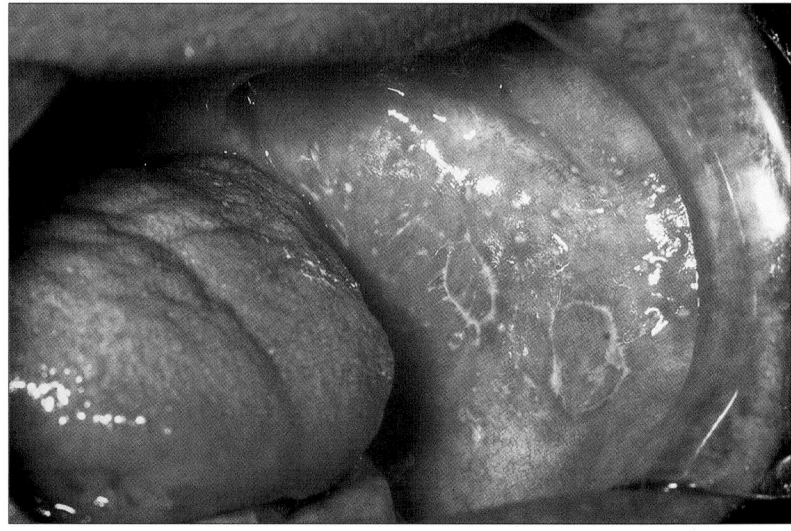

Fig. 6.3
Lichen planus: note the characteristic lacy oral lesions. By courtesy of R.A. Marsden, MD, St George's Hospital, London, UK.

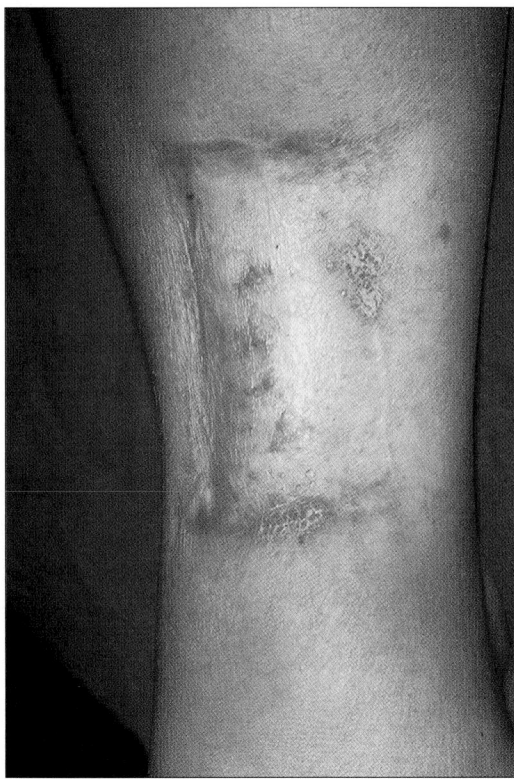

Fig. 6.2
Lichen planus: characteristic Wickham's striae are evident on these lesions, which have arisen on a skin graft for previous malignant melanoma. By courtesy of R.A. Marsden, MD, St George's Hospital, London, UK.

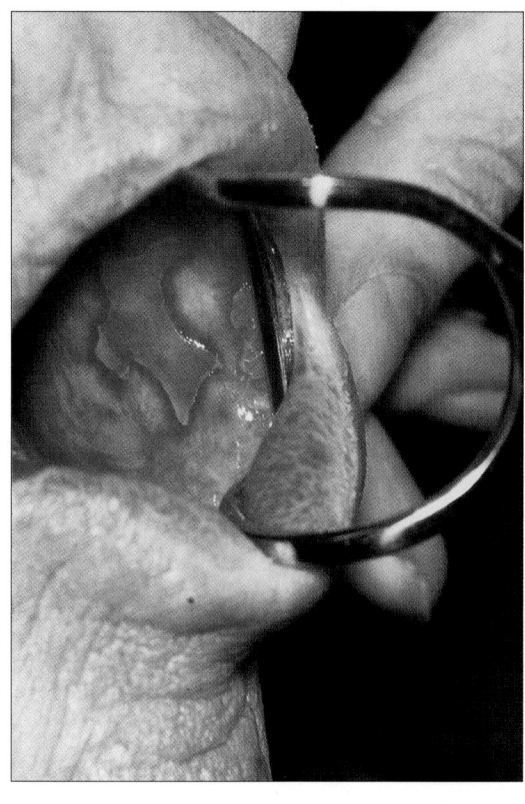

Fig. 6.4
Lichen planus: there is extensive ulceration of the buccal mucosa. By courtesy of R.A. Marsden, MD, St George's Hospital, London, UK.

Esophageal involvement, although rare, is an important potential cause of morbidity. Concomitant oral lesions are invariably present. To date, middle-aged females are affected.[21] Complications include chronic dysphagia and stricture formation affecting the mid or upper esophagus.[21–24] The risk of developing squamous carcinoma in a background of chronic esophageal lichen planus is insignificant.[21]

Genital lesions in lichen planus are common (particularly in males), being present in up to 25% of patients, and sometimes adopting an annular configuration (*Fig. 6.9*).[1] Similar annular lichen planus may be found elsewhere on the body. Occasionally, penile lesions are the sole expression of the disease.[25] Vulval lesions may be found in up to 51% of females with cutaneous involvement.[26] Sometimes gingival and female genital lesions may coexist as a variant of erosive lichen planus, the so-called vulvovaginal–gingival syndrome (see also p. 480).[27,28] Patients present with dyspareunia and intense burning vulval pain. The vulva appears congested and there may be erosions, which are often surrounded by a white reticulate border (*Fig. 6.10*). Vaginal involvement similarly presents as dyspareunia and often postcoital bleeding due to inflammatory, desquamative and erosive changes. More typical features of lichen planus may be encountered elsewhere on the body. Squamous

carcinoma is an important complication of chronic vulval lichen planus.[29] The development of penile cancer is rare.[30] Genital involvement in lichen planus is discussed in greater depth on page 480.

The nails are affected in about 10% of patients with lichen planus; manifestations include thinning of the nail plate, longitudinal ridging, striations, pterygium formation, subungual hyperkeratosis and, very rarely, complete destruction of the nail (*Figs 6.11, 6.12*).[1] Although nail involvement in children is said to be rare some authors regard twenty-nail dystrophy of childhood as a variant of localized lichen planus, although not all accept this hypothesis (see p. 1132).[31–35]

Most lesions of lichen planus heal within 6–18 months of onset, although oral and hypertrophic variants and lichen planopilaris tend to chronicity. Lichen planus is typified by postinflammatory hyperpigmentation, which may be very disfiguring, particularly in colored races (*Fig. 6.13*).

A number of variants of lichen planus merit specific mention:
- *Lichen planopilaris* (follicular lichen planus), which includes a spectrum of clinical lesions ranging from a follicular predominance

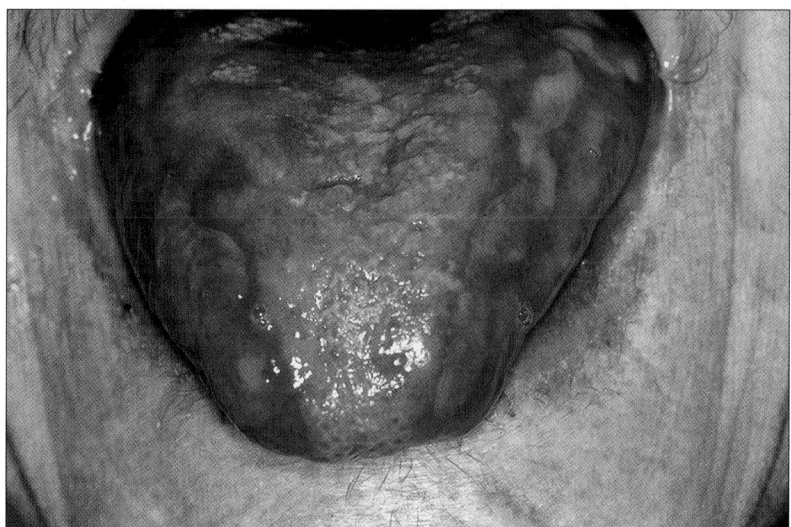

Fig. 6.5
Lichen planus: this patient suffers from severe atrophic and ulcerative lichen planus. By courtesy of S.B. Woo, MD, Harvard Medical School, Boston, USA.

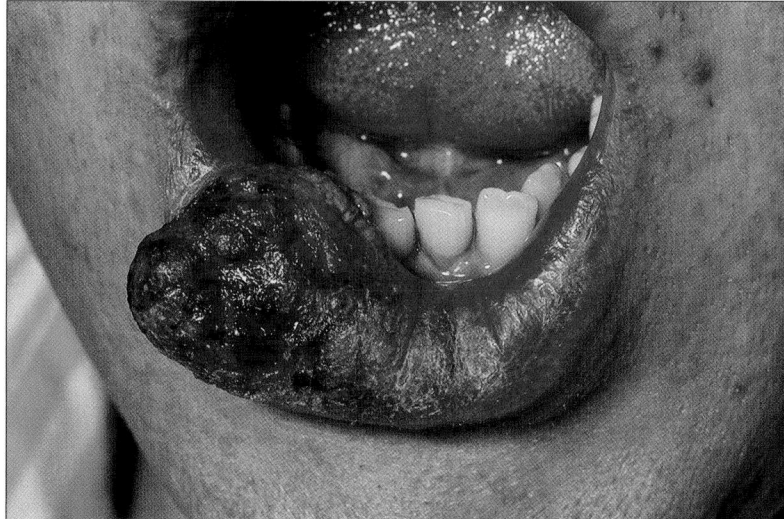

Fig. 6.6
Lichen planus: there is an ulcerated squamous carcinoma on the lower lip. By courtesy of R.A. Marsden, MD, St George's Hospital, London, UK.

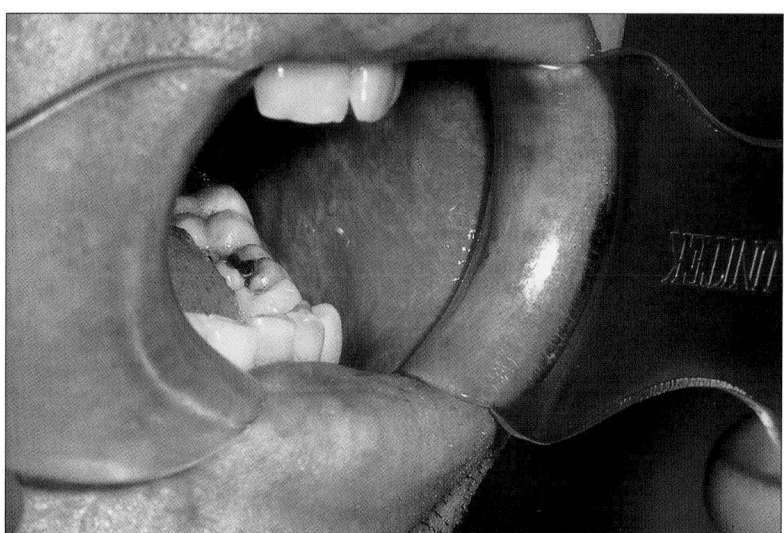

Fig. 6.7
Lichen planus: typical lesions were present on the buccal mucosa. Same patient as shown in *Fig. 6.6*. By courtesy of R.A. Marsden, MD, St George's Hospital, London, UK.

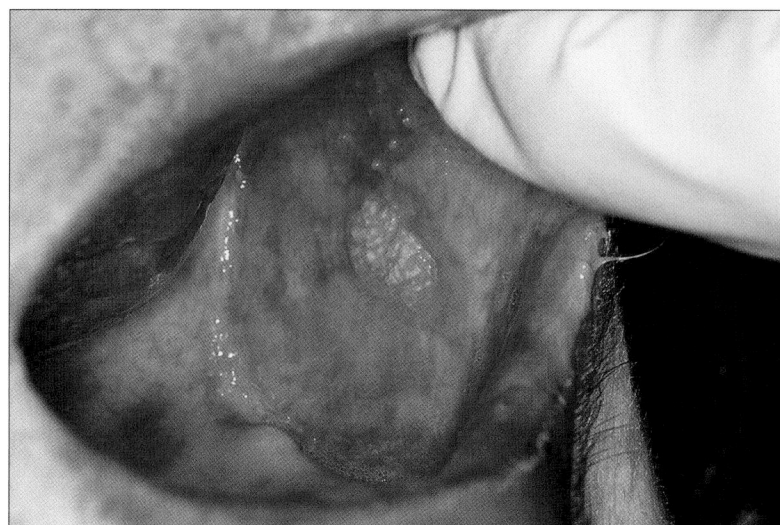

Fig. 6.8
Lichen planus: there is an ulcerated squamous carcinoma of the buccal mucosa. The adjacent epithelium is eroded. By courtesy of S.B. Woo, MD, Harvard Medical School, Boston, USA.

of brown or violaceous keratotic papules particularly affecting the trunk and extremities through to single or multiple plaques of scarring alopecia associated with typical lichenoid papules involving the scalp (*Figs 6.14–6.16*).[36] Non-scarring plaques with prominent follicular papules may also be present. Linear lesions have rarely been described.[37] Some authors believe that scalp lichen planus represents pseudopélade of Brocq (discussed on p. 1093).[38, 39]

- *Atrophic lichen planus*, the clinical features of which merely reflect resolution of the more typical active phase.

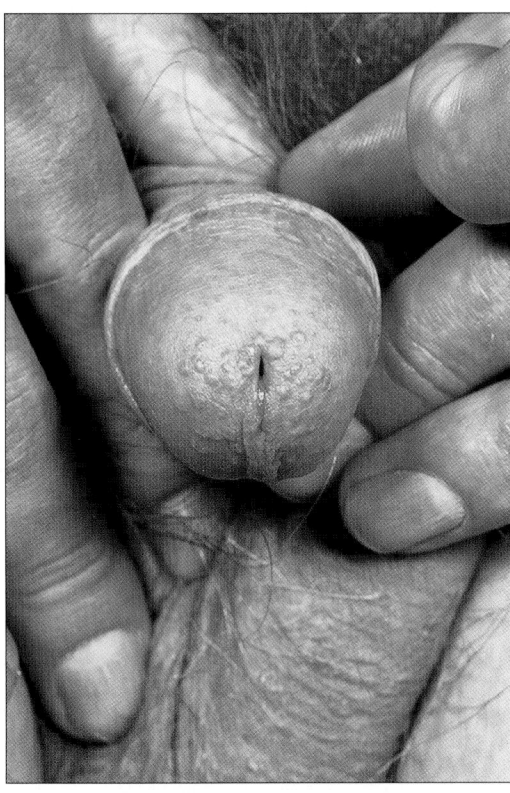

Fig. 6.9
Lichen planus: typical papules are present on the glans penis. By courtesy of R.A. Marsden, MD, St George's Hospital, London, UK.

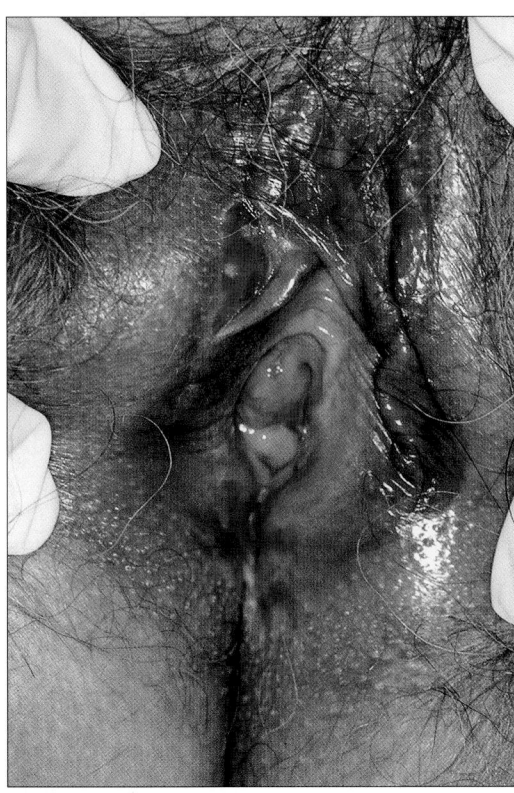

Fig. 6.10
Lichen planus: note the erythematous erosions around the vulval introitus and labia minora. By courtesy of S. Neill, MD, Institute of Dermatology, London, UK.

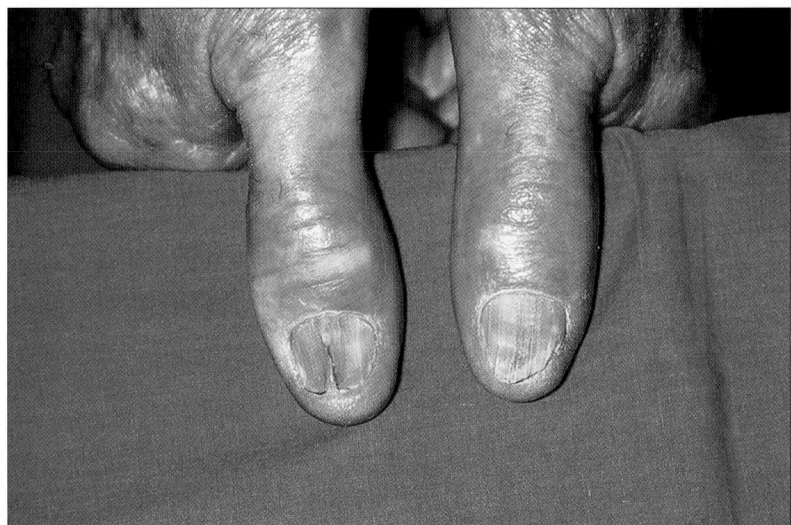

Fig. 6.11
Lichen planus: there is longitudinal ridging and striation affecting the thumbnails, with inflammatory changes in the nail folds. By courtesy of R.A. Marsden, MD, St George's Hospital, London, UK.

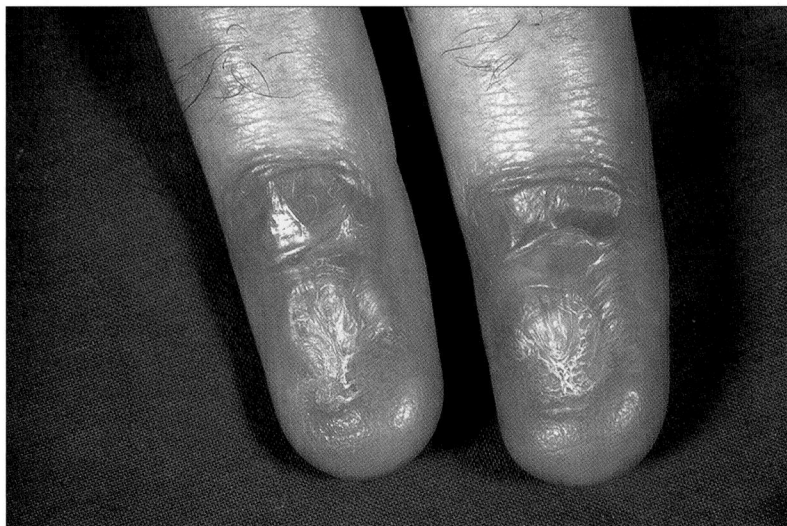

Fig. 6.12
Lichen planus: in this patient, there is complete destruction of the nails and nail folds. The surrounding skin is extremely atrophic. By courtesy of R.A. Marsden, MD, St George's Hospital, London, UK.

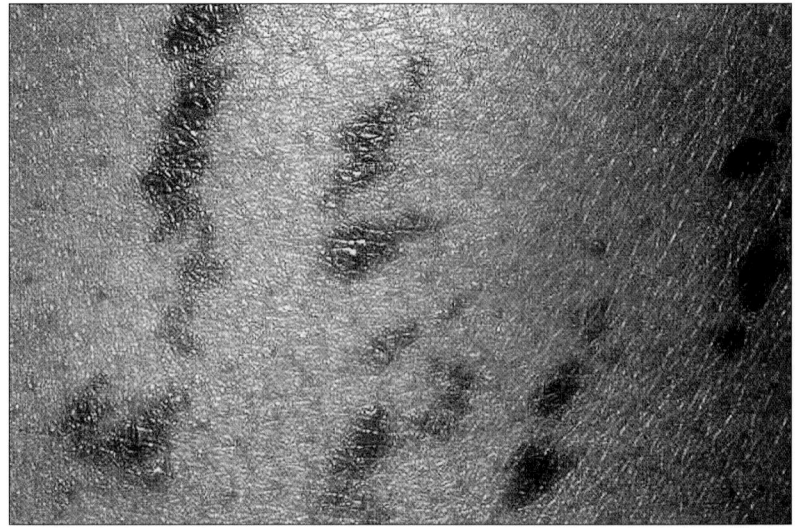

Fig. 6.13
Lichen planus: postinflammatory hyperpigmentation is a common manifestation. By courtesy of R.A. Marsden, MD, St George's Hospital, London, UK.

- *Lichen planus actinicus* (lichen planus subtropicus, summertime actinic lichenoid eruption, SALE), which develops in those who experience prolonged exposure to sunlight and, therefore, usually manifests in spring or summer.[40–44] Improvement or remission may take place in autumn or winter. It occurs particularly in the Middle East (especially Egypt) and Far East and affects younger people, with a maximum incidence in the second and third decades and with a slight female predominance. Affected sites include the lateral aspects of the forehead, the dorsum of the hands, the forearms, face and neck. The eruption includes lichen planus-like and lichen nitidus-like lesions. In some patients these are admixed whereas in others, lesions appear as purely lichen planus or lichen nitidus (see actinic lichen nitidus below). Typically the lichen planus lesions have an annular configuration with a bluish-brown, rather atrophic center and slightly raised border. Lesions may sometimes coalesce to form circinate plaques. Occasionally a melasma-like appearance has been documented.[44] There is usually little pruritus and Koebner's phenomenon is commonly absent. The nails are often unaffected.

- *Lichen planus pigmentosus* (invisible pigmented lichen planus), which is encountered in the tropics in dark-skinned patients, is characterized by the development of variably pruritic pigmented dark-brown macules predominantly affecting exposed skin and the flexures.[45–49] There is no sex predilection. The disorder is characterized by periods of exacerbation and remission.[4] Exceptionally, involvement of the oral mucosa has been documented.[5]

- *Hypertrophic lichen planus*, which represents superimposed lichen simplex chronicus, commonly affects the lower limbs, particularly the shins, and manifests as highly pigmented warty plaques (*Fig. 6.17*).[50] Familial lichen planus shows an increased incidence of this variant.[51] The lesions are intensely itchy and very persistent. There may be an attendant (albeit very slight) risk of neoplastic

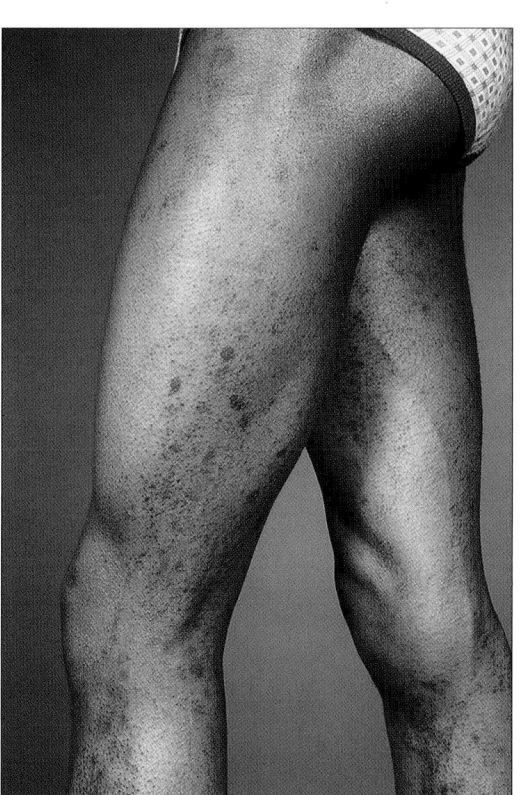

Fig. 6.14
Lichen planopilaris: there are characteristic hyperpigmented follicular papules, which are confluent in some areas. The limbs are commonly affected. By courtesy of R.A. Marsden, MD, St George's Hospital, London, UK.

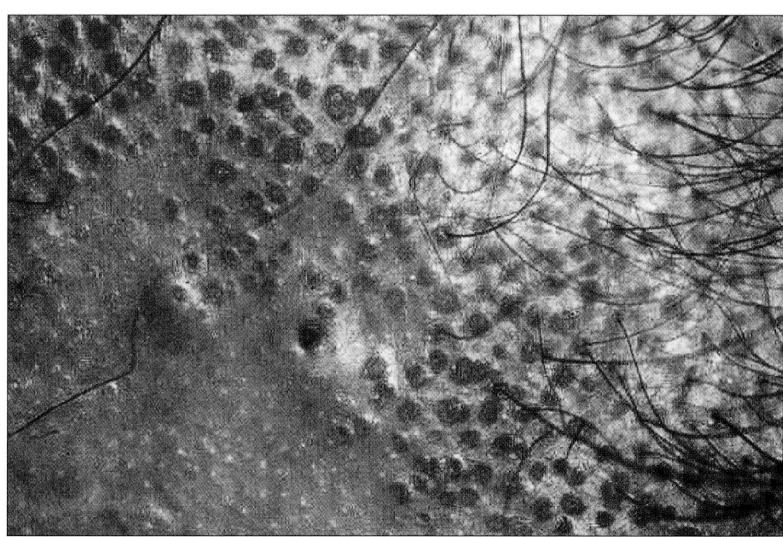

Fig. 6.16
Lichen planopilaris: follicular lichenoid papules are clearly seen in this patient. By courtesy of the Institute of Dermatology, London, UK.

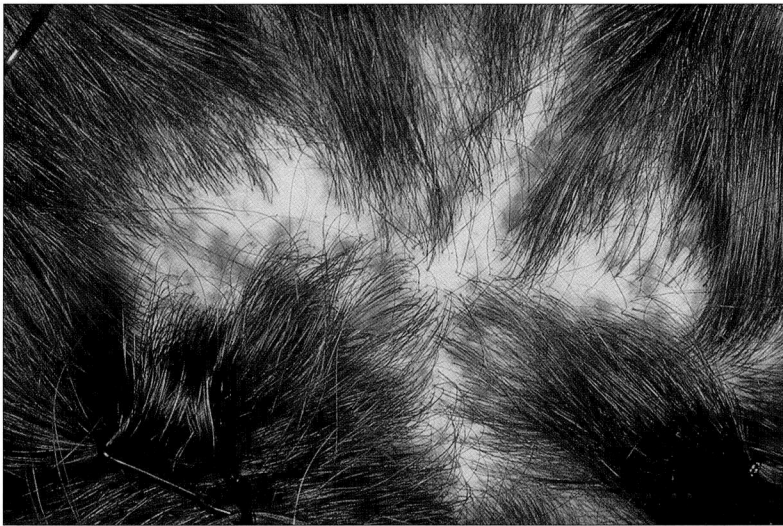

Fig. 6.15
Lichen planopilaris: marked inflammatory changes with scarring and secondary hair loss. These changes are difficult to distinguish from those of pseudopélade and chronic discoid lupus erythematosus. By courtesy of R.A. Marsden, MD, St George's Hospital, London, UK.

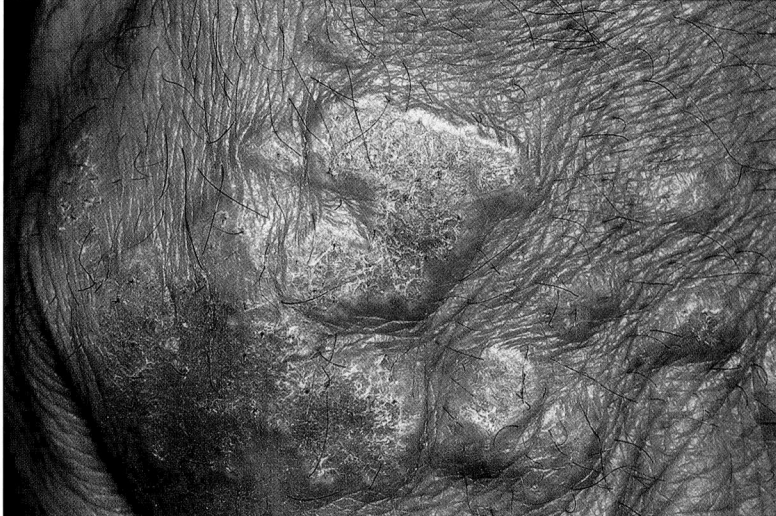

Fig. 6.17
Hypertrophic lichen planus: raised, warty, violaceous plaques on the shin of an elderly man. These lesions had been present for 30 years. By courtesy of R.A. Marsden, MD, St George's Hospital, London, UK.

transformation although the evidence is weak and based largely on case reports.[52]

- *Ulcerative lichen planus*, which is a chronic variant affecting the fingers, hands, soles and toes, is often associated with permanent loss of the nails (*Figs 6.18, 6.19*). Squamous cell carcinoma may exceptionally complicate this variant of lichen planus.[53]

Other variants include lichen planus linearis, which occurs predominantly in children, and the rare vesicular or bullous variants, which must be distinguished from lichen planus pemphigoides. Bullous lichen planus implies the development of vesicles or bullae on pre-existent lichenoid lesions as a consequence of severe basal cell hydropic degeneration. It is more often a histological finding than a clinical observation. Lichen planus pemphigoides on the other hand is characterized by the development of large tense bullae arising on normal or erythematous skin in a patient with typical lichen planus elsewhere. It represents the combined expression of lichen planus and bullous pemphigoid (see p. 115).[54]

Childhood lichen planus shows a male predominance (2:1).[5,6] Although mucosal involvement is said to be rare, the largest series published to date gave a frequency of 30%.[6] Hypertrophic lesions may be seen in up to 26% of cases.[6]

Pathogenesis and histological features

The etiology of lichen planus is unknown. Theories of infectious (bacterial and viral), autoimmune, metabolic, psychosomatic and genetic causes

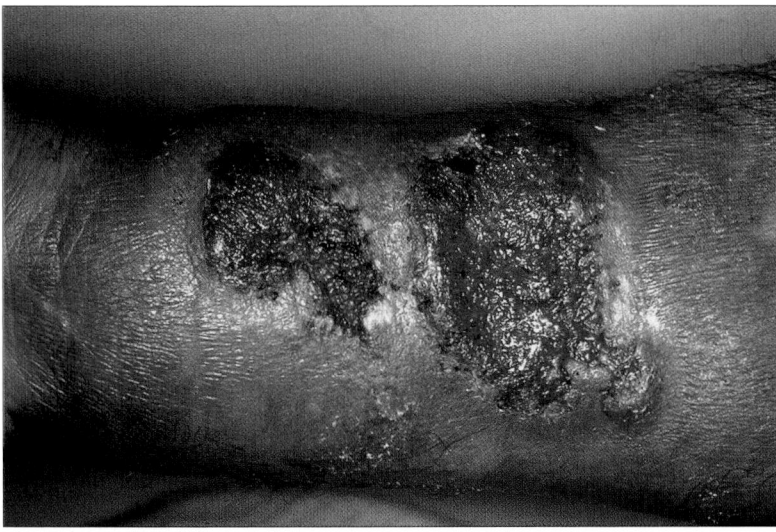

Fig. 6.18
Ulcerative lichen planus: there is marked atrophy of the skin around this crusted ulcer. By courtesy of the Institute of Dermatology, London, UK.

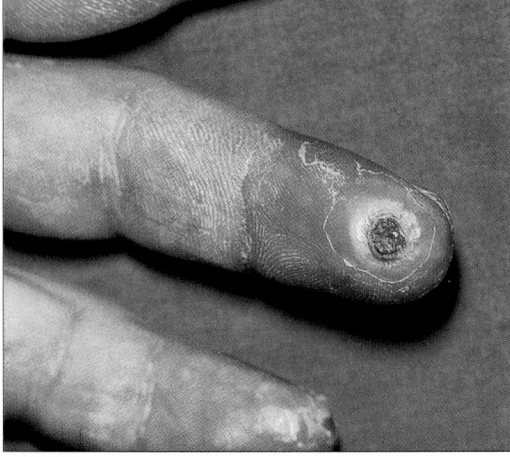

Fig. 6.19
Ulcerative lichen planus: the digits are often affected. This variant is associated with a slightly increased risk of squamous cell carcinoma. By courtesy of R.A. Marsden, MD, St George's Hospital, London, UK.

have all had their proponents. Currently, however, it is thought that lichen planus represents an abnormal delayed hypersensitivity reaction to an as yet undetermined epidermal neoantigen.[55,56] The association of lichen planus with a number of viral infections including hepatitis B and C and human immunodeficiency virus (HIV), combined with the well-recognized relationship to numerous drugs (see lichenoid drug reactions, p. 635), adds support to this hypothesis.

Lichen planus is associated with a variety of liver cell abnormalities including aberrant liver function tests and serology.[57] An increased incidence of chronic active hepatitis, primary sclerosing cholangitis and primary biliary cirrhosis has also been recorded.[58-63] Not all documented series, however, have confirmed these observations, suggesting rather that such positive correlation depends upon the background level of hepatitis B virus infection.[61] Lichen planus has also followed hepatitis B vaccination.[64-67] More recently, lichen planus (particularly oral disease) has been linked to hepatitis C virus and chronic liver disease. The incidence of hepatitis C virus in patients with lichen planus is, however, very variable, ranging from zero in the United Kingdom to 62% in Northern Japan.[68-71]

Evidence of impaired carbohydrate metabolism including overt diabetes mellitus has also documented in lichen planus, particularly the oral variant.[72-76] Whether this is of etiological importance is uncertain.

A significant association between lichen planus and human leukocyte antigen (HLA)-DR1 and HLA-DQ1 has been noted by a number of authors.[77-81] This association pertains to patients with or without mucosal lesions but does not extend to patients with the drug-induced variant. It is suggested that this association relates to antigen presentation by HLA-DR1+ cells to T-helper cells with the resultant development of an autoimmune response.[77]

Although it is generally accepted that the pathogenesis of the basal cell damage in lichen planus primarily involves the cellular immune response, the precise mechanism(s) are as yet unknown. It is unlikely that autoantibody and immune complex-mediated damage have a significant role in the lichenoid tissue reaction.[55,56]

The initial event in the evolution of the lichen planus papule is destruction of the basal epidermal layer (keratinocytes and melanocytes).[82,83] In the earliest stage of development, increased numbers of Langerhans' cells are present within the epidermis and it is believed that these cells process modified epidermal antigens for presentation to T-lymphocytes.[84] Keratinocytes express HLA-DR and this is likely to be of pathogenetic importance. Subsequent migration with resultant CD8+ T-cell activation results in basal keratinocyte death due to the combined effects of interferon-gamma (IFN-γ), interleukin (IL)-6, granulocyte–macrophage colony stimulating factor (GM-CSF) and tumor necrosis factor alpha (TNF-α).[85] The expression of FasR/FasL by the basal keratinocytes suggests that apoptosis is an important mode of cell death in lichen planus.[86] The dermal infiltrate consists predominantly of Ia+, CD4+ lymphocytes.[84,87] CD8+ lymphocytes are also present in close apposition to the dermoepidermal junction adjacent to foci of basal keratinocyte necrosis and are said to predominate in early lesions.[85,87-89] B-lymphocytes are scarce and plasma cells are characteristically absent in cutaneous lesions.

Development of the typical papule appears to be due to a combination of continued keratinocyte destruction and regenerative activity, the latter depending upon migration of epithelium from the edge of the lesion and from adjacent eccrine ducts, rather than from increased mitotic activity. There is little uptake of tritiated thymidine at the site of basal cell damage, but conspicuous uptake at the edges of the lesion and as a reflection of regeneration, keratin 17 expression is upregulated in the suprabasal epithelium.[90] The typical features of lichen planus therefore depend upon a variable interplay between basal cell liquefactive degeneration and irregular epidermal regeneration.

The earliest identifiable change in lichen planus is the presence of cytoid bodies and associated pigmentary incontinence. Cytoid bodies (colloid or Civatte bodies) are round or oval, homogeneous, eosinophilic bodies identifiable within the basal epithelium and the papillary dermis (*Fig. 6.20*). They display diastase-resistant periodic acid–Schiff (PAS) positivity, and may be identified within papules, perilesional skin and even apparently normal skin. Although they may be seen in a variety of dermatoses (including lupus erythematosus, graft-versus-host disease and poikiloderma) and also in normal skin, their presence, either in large numbers or in cluster, suggests lichen planus.

Ultrastructurally, cytoid bodies are composed of tightly arranged aggregates of filaments 6–8 nm in diameter; immunocytochemically they are composed of keratin.

Characteristic histological features of an established papule can usually be recognized at scanning magnification (*Fig. 6.21*). They comprise hyperkeratosis, typically wedge-shaped hypergranulosis (clinically presenting as Wickham's striae) related to the intraepidermal components of sweat ducts and hair follicles, and irregular acanthosis (*Figs 6.22, 6.23*). The acanthosis often has a saw-toothed appearance (*Figs 6.24, 6.25*). The presence of parakeratosis argues strongly against a diagnosis of lichen planus (however, see lichenoid reactions). Lymphocytes and histiocytes may sometimes be seen in the epidermis and very occasionally satellite cell necrosis is a feature. Liquefactive degeneration of the basal layer of the epithelium is characteristic and often subepidermal clefts are present (Max Joseph spaces). Pigmentary incontinence is common (*Fig. 6.26*). A lymphohistiocytic band-like infiltrate occupies the upper dermis and obscures the epidermodermal junction. Hyperkeratosis persists in resolving lichen planus, but the acanthosis regresses, leaving a flattened epidermis (*Fig. 6.27*); there may be focal scarring and the dermal infiltrate is less conspicuous (*Fig. 6.28*).

Lichen planopilaris in its early stages shows an infiltrate surrounding the lower hair follicle and papilla, follicular dilatation and keratin plugging (*Fig. 6.29*).[24] The adjacent interfollicular epithelium may or may not show a typical lichenoid infiltrate (*Fig. 6.30*). Basal cell hydropic degeneration, cytoid body formation and pigmentary incontinence are

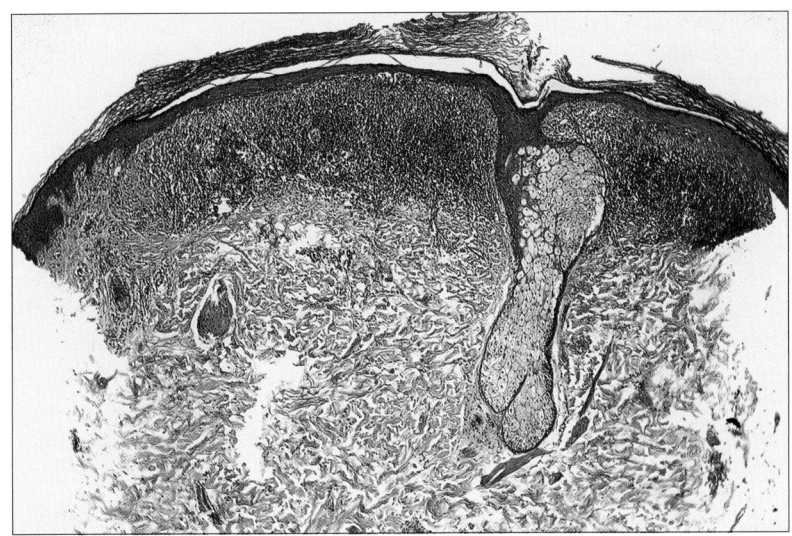

Fig. 6.21
Lichen planus: this scanning view is characteristic and highlights the typical band-like inflammatory cell infiltrate.

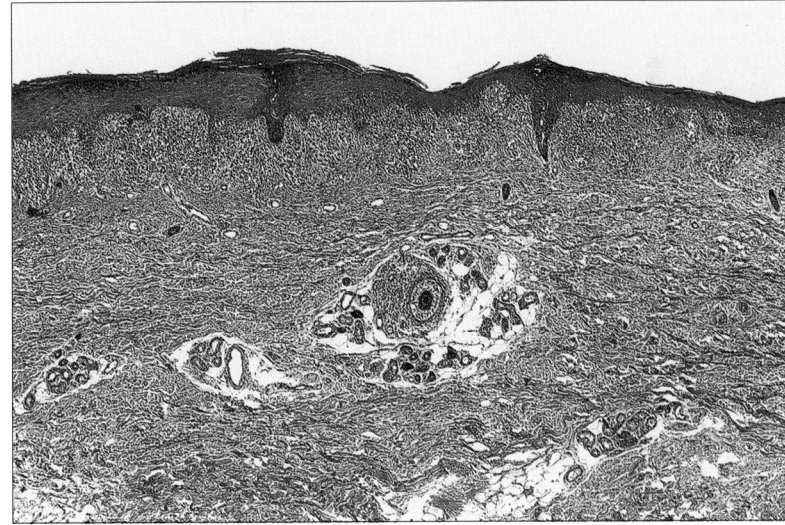

Fig. 6.22
Lichen planus: note the hyperkeratosis, hypergranulosis and irregular acanthosis.

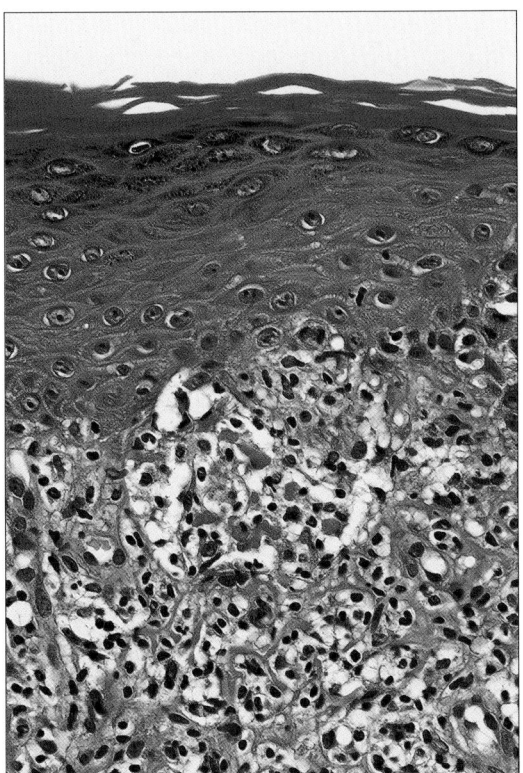

Fig. 6.20
Lichen planus: this view shows characteristic eosinophilic cytoid bodies associated with basal cell liquefactive degeneration and a lymphohistiocytic infiltrate. There is overlying hypergranulosis.

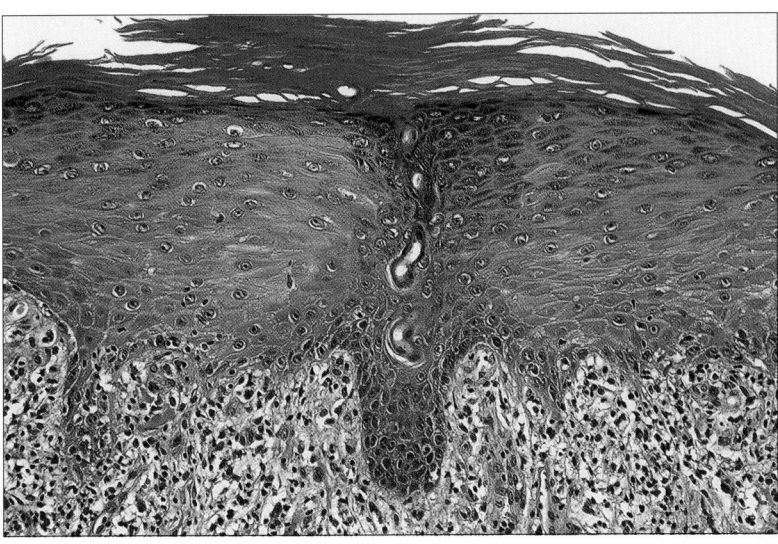

Fig. 6.23
Lichen planus: the hypergranulosis is clearly related to the acrosyringium.

also sometimes evident. In advanced scalp lesions the hair follicles are destroyed and replaced by vertically orientated fibrous scars reminiscent of the fibrous streamers seen in pseudopélade of Brocq.

Lichen planoporitis represents a recently described variant in which lichenoid/interface changes are centered on the acrosyringium and eccrine sweat duct as it enters the epidermis. Squamous metaplasia of the ductal lining epithelium may be a feature.[91]

In lichen planus actinicus the annular borders of the macules show typical features of lichen planus. In the center of the lesions, however, the epithelium is atrophic, thin and flattened, although the lymphohistiocytic infiltrate remains. Foci of parakeratosis and eczematization within the follicular epithelium have also been described. Lichen nitidus-like lesions may sometimes be seen (see below).

Lichen planus pigmentosus is characterized by epidermal thinning accompanied by basal cell vacuolization, pigmentary incontinence and a superficial dermal lichenoid lymphohistiocytic infiltrate.[4]

Hypertrophic lichen planus is characterized by more marked hyperkeratosis and acanthosis, with the epithelium sometimes showing pseudoepitheliomatous hyperplasia such that misdiagnosis as squamous cell carcinoma is a distinct possibility, particularly if clinical information is not available (*Figs 6.31–6.33*).[50] The infiltrate is often associated with dermal scarring and may partially spare the papillary dermis.

The oral lesions of lichen planus, although often displaying the classical features, may show parakeratosis; occasionally alternate foci of both are evident. In contrast to the cutaneous lesions, the epithelium is sometimes rather thin and the saw-toothed pattern indistinct. There

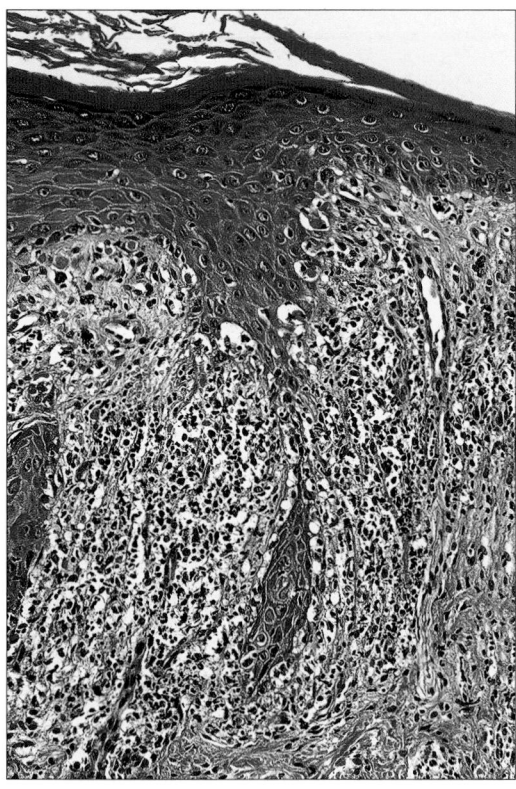

Fig. 6.24
Lichen planus: the acanthosis is irregular and often has a saw-toothed appearance.

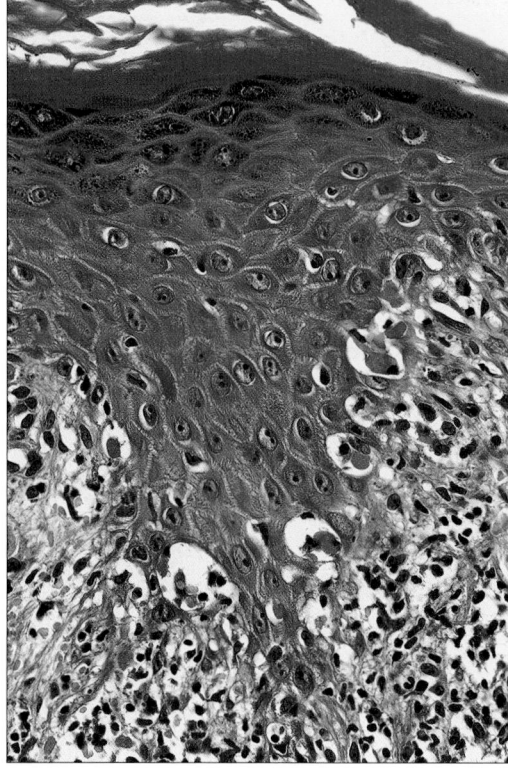

Fig. 6.25
Lichen planus: close-up view of *Fig. 6.24* showing basal cell liquefactive degeneration and cytoid bodies.

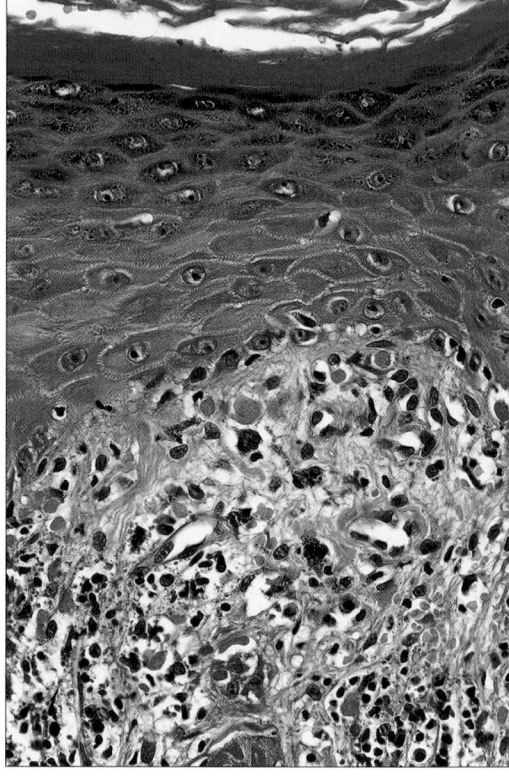

Fig. 6.26
Lichen planus: melanin pigment is present within macrophages (pigmentary incontinence).

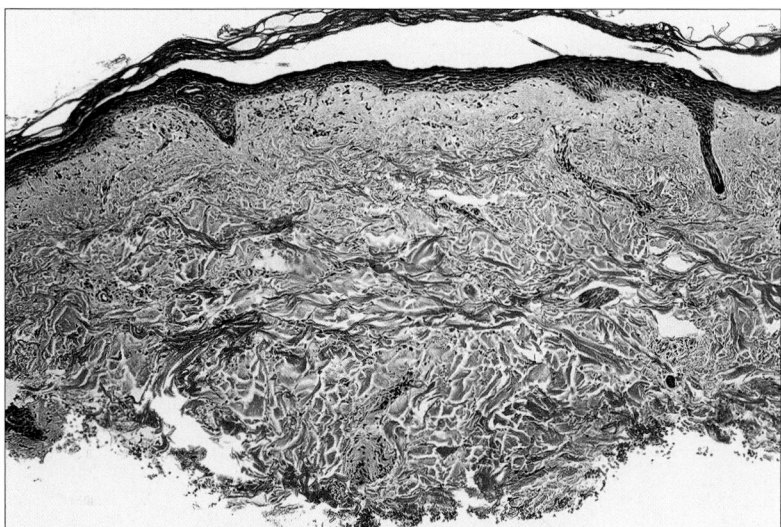

Fig. 6.27
Atrophic (resolving) lichen planus: there is hyperkeratosis, epidermal flattening and a slight residual lymphohistiocytic infiltrate.

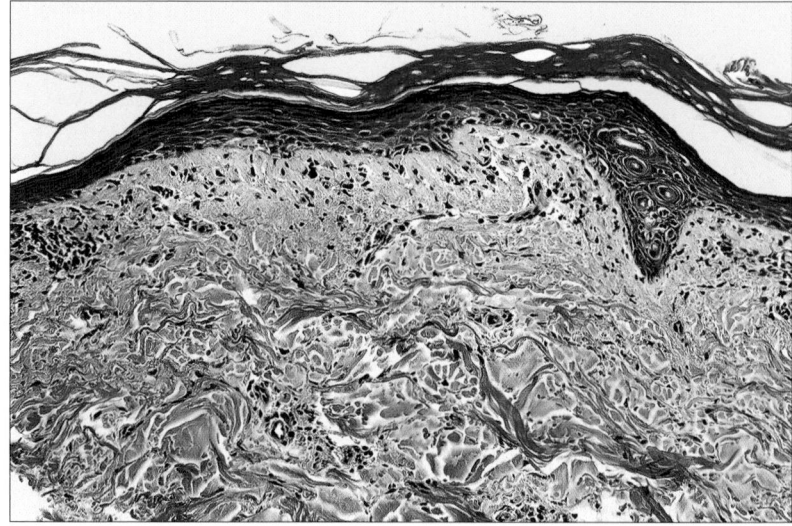

Fig. 6.28
Atrophic (resolving) lichen planus: in addition to the lymphohistiocytic infiltrate, there are excessive numbers of fibroblasts and increased papillary dermal collagen.

is typically basal cell hydropic degeneration. Basement membrane thickening due to the deposition of fibrin-rich eosinophilic amorphous material is commonly present. The cellular infiltrate, in addition to lymphocytes and histiocytes, frequently contains plasma cells. Dysplasia may be seen.

Esophageal lesions show parakeratosis and the granular cell layer is often absent. Variable epithelial atrophy and/or mild thickening are usually seen and the saw-tooth pattern of acanthosis is not a feature.[21–24] As with oral lesions, plasma cells often accompany the lymphocytic infiltrate.

Vesicular or bullous lesions are subepidermal and occur due to excessive edema developing in association with the basement membrane zone damage complicating basal cell hydropic degeneration (*Fig. 6.34*).

Direct immunofluorescence studies on skin biopsies from patients with lichen planus usually show a linear fibrillar band of fibrin at the epidermodermal junction (*Fig. 6.35*). The cytoid bodies may be highlighted non-specifically by the use of antisera, mainly to IgM, but also to IgG, IgA and C3 (*Fig. 6.36*). Recently a lichen planus 'specific antigen', which is present in the prickle cell and granular cell layers, has been demonstrated by indirect immunofluorescence of patients' serum

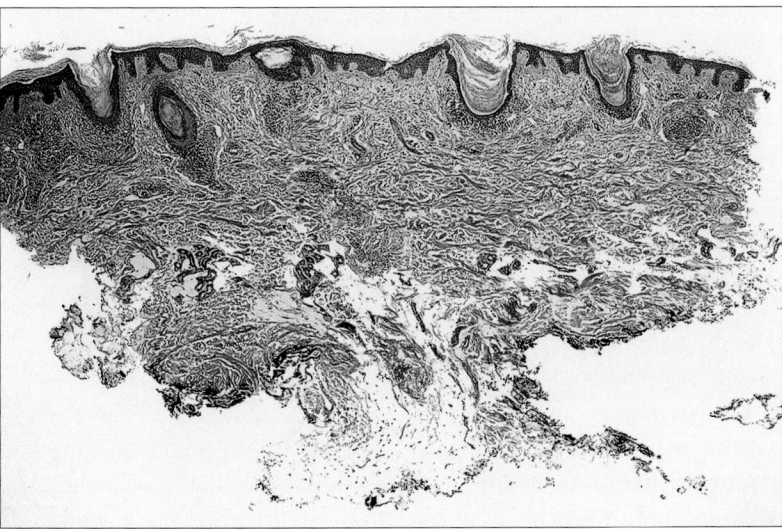

Fig. 6.29
Lichen planopilaris: there is marked follicular dilatation and plugging accompanied by a band-like folliculocentric infiltrate. This patient presented with scarring alopecia and typical lichen planus lesions elsewhere.

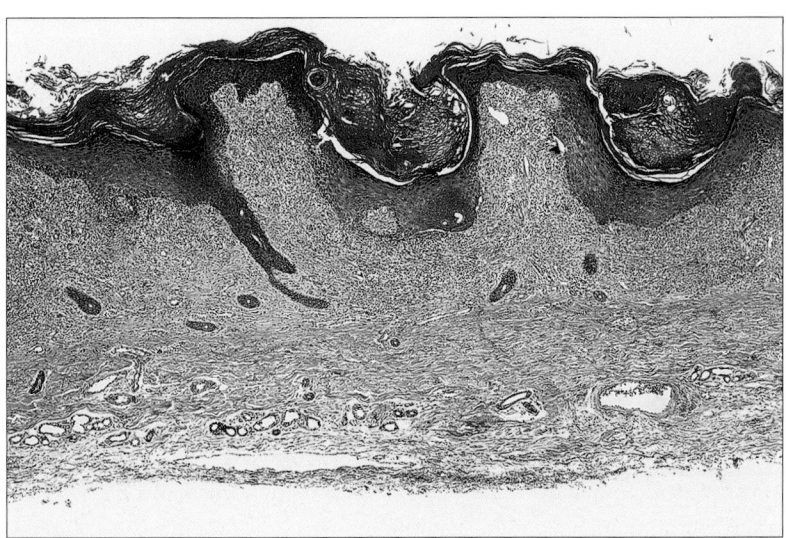

Fig. 6.31
Hypertrophic lichen planus: note the hyperkeratosis, focal wedge-shaped hypergranulosis, very marked irregular acanthosis and superficial band-like infiltrate.

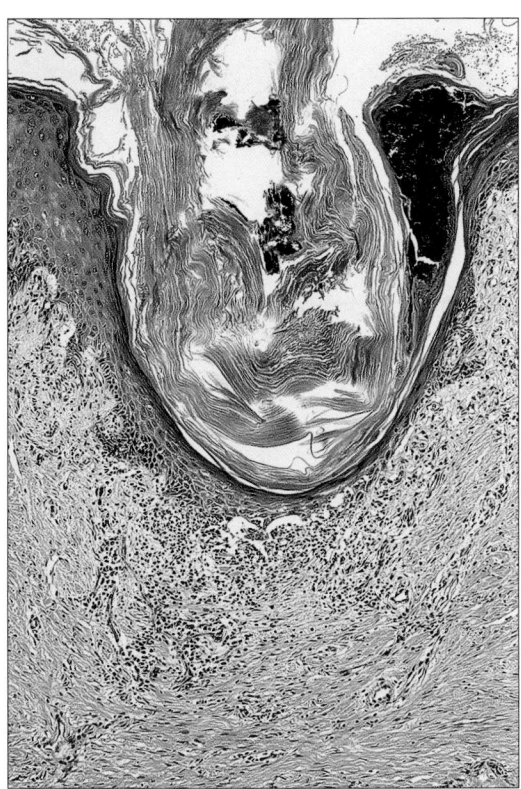

Fig. 6.30
Lichen planopilaris: close-up view of *Fig. 6.29*. Note the basal cell liquefactive degeneration and band-like infiltrate.

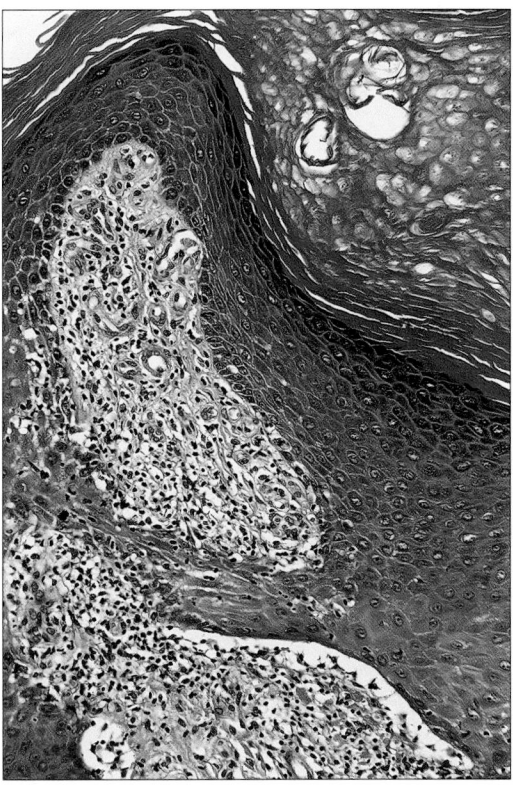

Fig. 6.32
Hypertrophic lichen planus: there is hyperkeratosis and wedge-shaped hypergranulosis. Epidermodermal separation is evident (Max Joseph space).

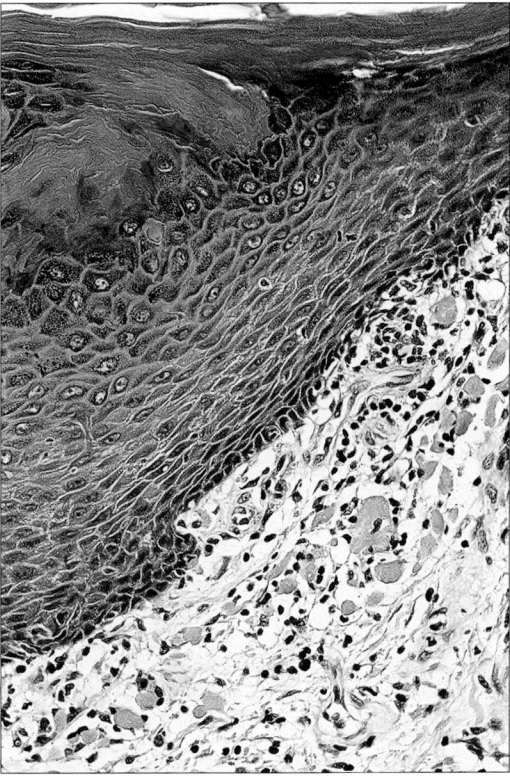

Fig. 6.33
Hypertrophic lichen planus: cytoid bodies are conspicuous.

using fetal skin.[92] Whether this is of pathogenetic significance is unknown. Direct immunofluorescence of lichen planopilaris reveals follicular, linear basement membrane zone labeling with immunoglobulin (primarily IgG or IgA).[93] Fibrin may also be present. The nosological implications of this observation are uncertain. Indirect immunofluorescence for circulating anti-basement membrane zone antibodies is negative.

Differential diagnosis

Lichen planus should be differentiated from other diseases showing a lichenoid infiltrate and hydropic degeneration of the basal layer of the epithelium.[94] Thus lichen planus may be indistinguishable from lichenoid keratosis and their distinction be entirely dependent on clinicopathological correlation. Atrophic lesions may be confused with poikiloderma and chronic discoid lupus erythematosus. A lichen planus-like morphology is typical of the early stages of chronic graft-versus-host disease (GVHD).

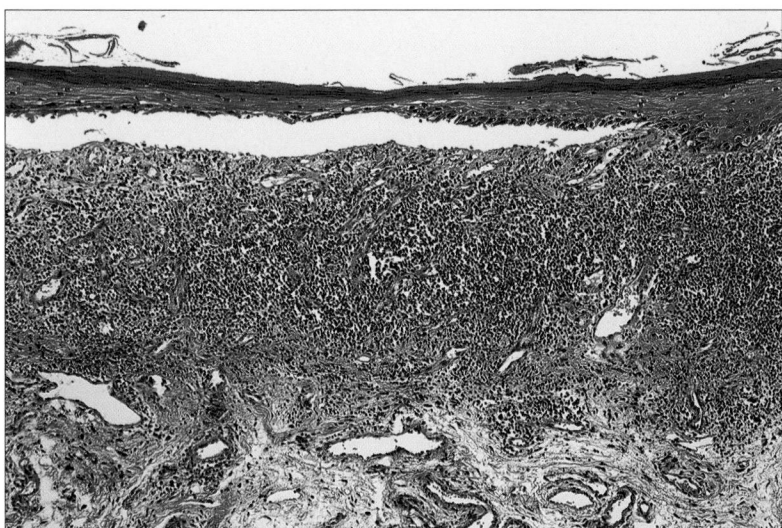

Fig. 6.34
Bullous lichen planus: oral lesion showing separation of the squamous epithelium from the lamina propria. Note the band-like infiltrate.

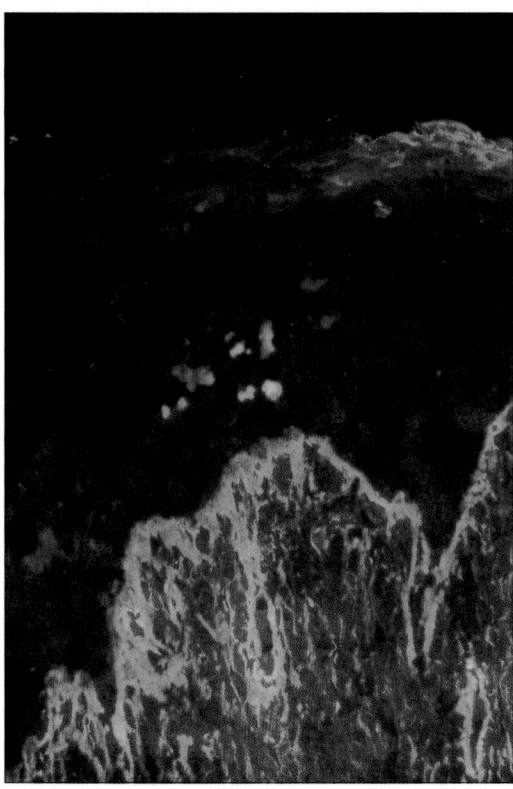

Fig. 6.35
Lichen planus: brilliant green fluorescence indicates the presence of fibrin. By courtesy of the Department of Immunofluorescence, Institute of Dermatology, London, UK.

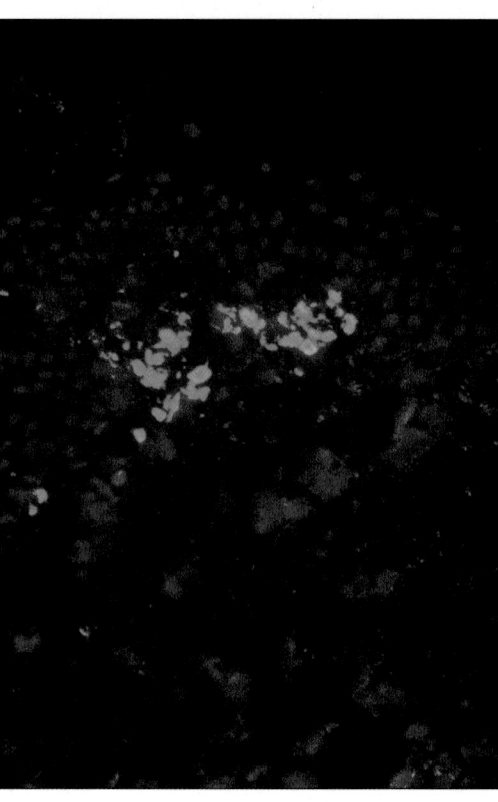

Fig. 6.36
Lichen planus: cytoid bodies labeled positively for IgM. By courtesy of the Department of Immunofluorescence, Institute of Dermatology, London, UK.

Poikiloderma shows epidermal atrophy, with loss of the ridge pattern and no tendency to a saw-tooth appearance. In those examples associated with mycosis fungoides, the lichenoid infiltrate contains variable numbers of atypical lymphocytes and mycosis fungoides cells.

Chronic discoid lupus erythematosus is associated with epidermal atrophy and follicular plugging. The inflammatory cell infiltrate is patchy with a tendency to periappendageal location. A positive lupus band test is a helpful discriminator.

Lichen planus may easily be mistaken for a lichenoid drug reaction, particularly in the absence of clinical information. Histological pointers towards the latter include high level cytoid bodies and eosinophils within the dermal infiltrate.

References

1. Boyd, A.S., Nelder, K.H. (1991) Lichen planus. *J Am Acad Dermatol*, **25**, 593–619.
2. Marshman, G. (1998) Lichen planus. *Australas J Dermatol*, **39**, 1–13.
3. Silverman, S., Gorsky, M., Lozada-Nur, F. (1985) A prospective follow-up study of 570 patients with oral lichen planus: persistence, remission and malignant association. *Oral Surg Oral Med Oral Pathol*, **60**, 30–34.
4. Kaplan, B., Barnes, L. (1985) Oral lichen planus and squamous carcinoma. *Arch Otolaryngol*, **111**, 543–547.
5. Kanwar, A.J., Handa, S., Ghosh, T. et al (1991) Lichen planus in childhood: a report of 17 patients. *Pediatr Dermatol*, **8**, 288–291.
6. Sharma, R., Maheshwari, V. (1999) Childhood lichen planus: a report of fifty cases. *Pediatr Dermatol*, **16**, 345–348.
7. Kofoed, M.L., Wantzin, G.L. (1985) Familial lichen planus. *J Am Acad Dermatol*, **13**, 50–54.
8. Bagan-Sebastian, J.V., Milian-Masanet, M.A., Penarrocha-Diago, M. et al (1992) A clinical study of 205 patients with oral lichen planus. *J Oral Maxillofac Surg*, **50**, 116–118.
9. Silverman, S.Jr, Gorsky, M., Lozada-Nur, F. et al (1991) A prospective study of findings and management in 214 patients with oral lichen planus. *Oral Surg Oral Med Oral Pathol*, **72**, 665–670.
10. Jungell, P. (1991) Oral lichen planus. A review. *Int J Oral Maxillofac Surg*, **20**, 129–135.
11. Altman, J., Perry, H.O. (1961) The variations and course of lichen planus. *Arch Dermatol*, **84**, 179–191.
12. Woo, T.Y. (1984) Systemic isotretinoin treatment of oral and cutaneous lichen planus. *Cutis*, **35**, 385, 390–391, 393.
13. Andreasen, J.O. (1968) Oral lichen planus. 1. A clinical evaluation of 115 cases. *Oral Surg Oral Med Oral Pathol*, **25**, 31–42.
14. Sigurgeirsson, B., Lindelof, B. (1991) Lichen planus and malignancy. An epidemiologic study of 2071 patients and a review of the literature. *Arch Dermatol*, **127**, 1684–1688.
15. Fulling, H.J. (1973) Cancer development in oral lichen planus. A follow-up study of 327 patients. *Arch Dermatol*, **109**, 667–669.
16. Holmstrup, P., Thorn, J.J., Rindum, J. et al (1988) Malignant development of lichen planus-affected oral mucosa. *J Oral Pathol*, **17**, 219–225.
17. Voute, A.B., De Jong, W.F., Schulten, E.A. et al (1992) Possible premalignant character of oral lichen planus. The Amsterdam experience. *J Oral Pathol Med*, **21**, 326–329.
18. Scully, G., El-Kom, M. (1985) Lichen planus: review and update on pathogenesis. *J Oral Pathol*, **14**, 431–458.
19. Vogel, P.S., James, W.D. (1992) Lichen planus of the eyelid: an unusual clinical presentation. *J Am Acad Dermatol*, **27**, 638–639.

20. Itin, P.H., Buechner, S.A., Rufli, T. (1995) Lichen planus of the eyelid. *Dermatology*, **191**, 350–351.
21. Abraham, S.C., Ravich, W.J., Anhalt, G.J. et al (2000) Esophageal lichen planus: case report and review of the literature. *Am J Surg Pathol*, **24**, 1678–1682.
22. Leyva-Leon, F., Wright, A.L., Wright, R.G. et al (1990) Esophageal lichen planus presenting with dysphagia. *Int J Dermatol*, **29**, 354–355.
23. Kirsch, M. (1995) Esophageal lichen planus: a forgotten diagnosis. *J Clin Gastroenterol*, **20**, 145–146.
24. Ukleja, A., Devault, K.R., Stark, M.E. et al (2001) Lichen planus involving the esophagus. *Dig Dis Sci*, **46**, 2292–2297.
25. Barnette, D.J. Jr, Curtin, T.J., Yeager, J.K. et al (1993) Asymptomatic penile lesions. *Cutis*, **51**, 116–118.
26. Lewis, F.M., Shah, M., Harrington, C.I. (1995) Vulval involvement in lichen planus: a study of 37 women. *Br J Dermatol*, **135**, 89–91.
27. Pelisse, M. (1989) The vulvo-vaginal-gingival syndrome. A new form of erosive lichen planus. *Int J Dermatol*, **28**, 381–384.
28. Eisen, D. (1994) The vulvovaginal–gingival syndrome of lichen planus. *Arch Dermatol*, **130**, 1379–1382.
29. Derrick, E.K., Ridley, C.M., Kobza-Black, A. et al (2000) A clinical study of 23 cases of female anogenital carcinoma. *Br J Dermatol*, **143**, 1217–1223.
30. Worheide, J., Bonsmann, G., Kolde, G. et al (1991) Plattenepithelial-karzinom auf dem Boden eines lichen ruber hypertrophicus an der glans penis. *Hautarzt*, **42**, 112–115.
31. Zaias, N. (1970) The nail in lichen planus. *Arch Dermatol*, **101**, 264–271.
32. Scher, R.K., Fischbein, R., Ackerman, A.B. (1978). Twenty-nail dystrophy: a variant of lichen planus. *Arch Dermatol*, **114**, 612–613.
33. Silverman, R.A., Rhodes, A.R. (1984) Twenty-nail dystrophy of childhood: a sign of localised lichen planus. *Pediatr Dermatol*, **1**, 207–210.
34. Wilkinson, J.D., Dawber, R.P.R., Bowers, R.P. et al (1979) Twenty-nail dystrophy of childhood. *Br J Dermatol*, **100**, 217–221.
35. Jerasutus, S., Suvanprakorn, P., Kitchawengkul, O. (1990) Twenty-nail dystrophy. *Arch Dermatol*, **126**, 1068–1070.
36. Matta, M., Kibbi, A-G., Khattar, J. et al (1990) Lichen planopilaris: a clinicopathologic study. *J Am Acad Dermatol*, **22**, 594–598.
37. Gerritsen, M.J.P., de Jong, E.M.G.J., van de Kerkhof, P.C.M. (1998) Linear lichen planopilaris of the face. *J Am Acad Dermatol*, **38**, 633–635.
38. Anderton, R.L., Cullen, S.I. (1976) Pseudopélade of Brocq secondary to lichen planus. *Cutis*, **17**, 916–918.
39. Silvers, D.N., Katz, B.E., Young, A.W. (1993) Pseudopélade of Brocq is lichen plano-pilaris: a report of four that support this nosologie. *Cutis*, **51**, 99–105.
40. Dilnimy, M. (1976) Lichen planus subtropicus. *Arch Dermatol*, **112**, 1251–1253.
41. Salman, S.M., Kibbi, A.G., Zaynoun, S. (1989) Actinic lichen planus. A clinicopathologic study of 16 patients. *J Am Acad Dermatol*, **20**, 226–231.
42. Isaacson, D., Turner, M.L., Elgart, M.L. (1981) Summertime actinic lichenoid eruption (lichen planus actinicus). *J Am Acad Dermatol*, **4**, 404–411.
43. El Zawahry, M. (1965) Lichen planus tropicus. *Int J Dermatol*, **4**, 251–254.
44. Salman, S.M., Khallouf, R., Zaynoun, S. (1988) Actinic lichen planus mimicking melasma. *J Am Acad Dermatol*, **18**, 275–278.
45. Laskaris, G.C., Papavasiliou, S.S., Bovopoulou, O.D. et al (1981) Lichen planus pigmentosus of the oral mucosa: a rare clinical variety. *Dermatologica*, **162**, 61–63.
46. Bhutani, L.K., Bedi, T.R. (1974) Lichen planus pigmentosus. *Dermatologica*, **149**, 43–50.
47. Vega, M.E., Waxtein, L., Arenas, R.A. et al (1992) Ashy dermatosis and lichen planus pigmentosus: a clinicopathologic study of 31 cases. *Int J Dermatol*, **31**, 90–94.
48. Dominguez-Soto, L., Hojvo-Tomoka, T., Vega-memije, E. et al (1994) Pigmentary problems in the tropics. *Dermatol Clin*, **12**, 777–784.
49. Sassolas, B., Zagnoli, A., Leroy, J-P. et al (1994) Lichen planus pigmentosus with acrokeratosis of Bazex. *Clin Exp Dermatol*, **19**, 70–73.
50. Tan, E., Malik, R., Quirk, C.J. (1998) Hypertrophic lichen planus mimicking squamous cell carcinoma. *Australas J Dermatol*, **39**, 45–47.
51. Mahood, J.M. (1983) Familial lichen planus. *Arch Dermatol*, **119**, 292–294.
52. Carsuzaa, F., Pierre, C., Morand, J.J. et al (1996) A case for diagnosis: epidermoid carcinoma complicating hypertrophic lichen planus of the leg. *Ann Dermatol Venereol*, **123**, 583–584.
53. Mayron, R., Grimwood, R.E., Siegle, R.J. et al (1988) Verrucous carcinoma arising in ulcerative lichen planus of the soles. *J Dermatol Surg Oncol*, **14**, 547–551.
54. Willsteed, E., Bhogal, B.S., Das, A.K. et al (1991) Lichen planus pemphigoides: a clinicopathological study of nine cases. *Histopathology*, **19**, 147–154.
55. Shai, A., Halevy, S. (1992) Lichen planus and lichen planus-like eruptions: pathogenesis and associated diseases. *Int J Dermatol*, **31**, 379–383.
56. Lacy, M.F., Reade, P.C., Hay, K.D. (1983) Lichen planus: a theory of pathogenesis. *Oral Surg Oral Med Oral Pathol*, **56**, 521–526.
57. Korkij, W., Chuang, T.Y., Soltani, K. (1984) Liver abnormalities in patients with lichen planus. *J Am Acad Dermatol*, **11**, 609–615.
58. Rebora, A., Rongioletti, F. (1984) Lichen planus and chronic active hepatitis. A retrospective survey. *Acta Derm Venereol*, **64**, 52–56.
59. del Olmo, J.A., Bagan, J.V., Rodrigo, J.M. (1989) Oral lichen planus and hepatic cirrhosis. *Ann Int Med*, **110**, 666.
60. Graham-Brown, R.A.C., Sarkany, I., Sherlock, S. (1982) Lichen planus and primary biliary cirrhosis. *Br J Dermatol*, **106**, 699–703.
61. Gruppo Italiano Studi Epidemiologici in Dermatologia (GISED) (1990) Lichen planus and liver diseases: a multicenter case-control study. *BMJ*, **300**, 227–230.
62. Powell, F.C., Rogers, R.S., Dickson, E.R. (1983) Primary biliary cirrhosis and lichen planus. *J Am Acad Dermatol*, **9**, 540–545.
63. Monk, B. (1985) Lichen planus and the liver. *J Am Acad Dermatol*, **12**, 122–123.
64. Saywell, C.A., Wittal, R.A., Kossard, S. (1997) Lichenoid reaction to hepatitis B vaccination. *Australas J Dermatol*, **38**, 152–154.
65. Rebora, A., Rongioletti, F., Drago, F. et al (1999) Lichen planus as a side effect of HBV vaccination. *Dermatology*, **198**, 1–2.
66. Usman, A., Kimyai-Asadi, A., Stiller, M.J. et al (2001) Lichenoid eruption following hepatitis B vaccination: first North American case report. *Pediatr Dermatol*, **18**, 123–126.
67. Al-Khenaizan, S. (2001) Lichen planus occurring after hepatitis B vaccination: a new case. *J Am Acad Dermatol*, **45**, 614–615.
68. Mignogna, M.D., Muzio, L.L., Favia, G. et al (1998) Oral lichen planus and HCV infection: a clinical evaluation of 263 cases. *Int J Dermatol*, **37**, 575–578.
69. Jubert, C., Pawlotsky, J.M., Pouget, F. et al (1994) Lichen planus and hepatitis C-related chronic active hepatitis. *Arch Dermatol*, **130**, 73–76.
70. Nagao, Y., Sata, M., Tanikawa, K. et al (1995) Lichen planus and hepatitis C virus in the northern region of Japan. *Eur J Clin Invest*, **25**, 910–914.
71. Bonkovsky, H.L., Mehta, S. (2001) Hepatitis C: a review and update. *J Am Acad Dermatol*, **44**, 159–179.
72. Jolly, M. (1972) Lichen planus and its association with diabetes mellitus. *Med J Aust*, **1**, 990–992.
73. Halevy, S., Feuerman, E.J. (1979) Abnormal glucose tolerance associated with lichen planus. *Acta Derm Venereol*, **59**, 167–170.
74. Lundström, I.M.C. (1983) Incidence of diabetes mellitus in patients with oral lichen planus. *Int J Oral Surg*, **12**, 147–152.
75. Hornstein, O.P., Stuhler, C., Schirner, E. et al (1984) Lichen ruber and diabetes mellitus – pathogenetic relations? *Hautarzt*, **35**, 287–291.
76. Nigam, P.K., Sharma, L., Agrawal, J.K. et al (1987) Glucose tolerance studies in lichen planus. *Dermatologica*, **175**, 284–289.
77. Nasa, G. La, Cottoni, F., Mulargia, M. et al (1995) HLA antigen distribution in different clinical subgroups demonstrates genetic heterogeneity in lichen planus. *Br J Dermatol*, **132**, 897–900.
78. Powell, F.C., Rogers, R.S., Dickson, E.R., Moore, S.B. (1986) An association between HLA DR1 and lichen planus. *Br J Dermatol*, **114**, 473–478.
79. Contu, L., Carcassi, C., La Nasa, G. et al (1988) HLA and lichen planus. *Ital Gen Rev Dermatol*, **25**, 95–107.
80. Valsecchi, R., Bontempelli, M., Rossi, A. et al (1988) HLA DR and DQ antigens in lichen planus. *Acta Derm Venereol*, **68**, 77–80.
81. Simon, M., Djawari, D., Schönberger, A. (1984) HLA antigens associated with lichen planus. *Clin Exp Dermatol*, **9**, 435.
82. Smoller, B.R., Glusac, E.J. (1994) Immunofluorescent analysis of the basement membrane in lichen planus suggests destruction of the lamina lucida in bullous lesions. *J Cutan Pathol*, **21**, 123–128.
83. Haapalainen, T., Oksala, O., Kallioinen, M. et al (1995) Destruction of the epithelial anchoring system in lichen planus. *J Invest Dermatol*, **105**, 100–103.
84. Bhan, A.K., Harrist, T.J., Murphy, G.F. et al (1981) T-cell subsets and Langerhans' cells in lichen planus: *in situ* characterization using monoclonal antibodies. *Br J Dermatol*, **105**, 617–622.
85. Yamamoto, T., Osaki, T., Yoneda, K. et al (1994) Cytokine production by keratinocytes and mononuclear infiltrates in oral lichen planus. *J Oral Pathol Med*, **23**, 309–315.
86. Neppelberg, E., Johannessen, A.C., Jonsson, R. (2001) Apoptosis in oral lichen planus. *Eur J Oral Sci*, **109**, 361–364.
87. De Panfilis, G., Manara, G., Sansoni, P. et al (1983) T-cell infiltrate in lichen planus. Demonstration of activated lymphocytes using monoclonal antibodies. *J Cutan Pathol*, **10**, 52–58.
88. Akasu, R., From, L., Kahn, H.J. (1995) Lymphocyte and macrophage subsets in active and inactive lesions of lichen planus. *Am J Dermatopathol*, **15**, 217–223.
89. Al-Fouzan, A.W., Habib, M., Sallam, T.H. et al (1996) Detection of T lymphocytes and T lymphocyte subsets in lichen planus: in situ and in peripheral blood. *Int J Dermatol*, **35**, 426–429.
90. Schofield, J.K., De Berker, D., Milligan, A. et al (1995) Keratin expression in cutaneous lichen planus. *Histopathology*, **26**, 153–158.
91. Kossard, S., Lee, S. (1998) Lichen planoporitis: keratosis lichenoides chronica revisited. *J Cutan Pathol*, **25**, 222–227.
92. Olsen, R.G., Du Plessis, D.P., Schultz, E.J. et al (1984) Indirect immunofluorescence microscopy of lichen planus. *Br J Dermatol*, **110**, 9–15.
93. Ioannides, D., Bystryn, J.C. (1992) Immunofluorescence abnormalities in lichen planopilaris. *Arch Dermatol*, **128**, 214–216.
94. Oliver, G.F., Winkelmann, R.K., Muller, S.A. (1989) Lichenoid dermatitis: a clinicopathologic and immunopathologic review of sixty-two cases. *J Am Acad Dermatol*, **21**, 284–292.

Lichen planus pemphigoides

This dermatosis represents the coexistence of lichen planus and a bullous pemphigoid-like illness. The condition is discussed in full on page 115.

Lupus erythematosus–lichen planus overlap syndrome

The lupus erythematosus–lichen planus overlap syndrome is a rare condition in which patients show features of both conditions. It is discussed on page 777.

Lichen nitidus

Clinical features

Lichen nitidus is a rare but distinctive dermatosis, which shows an equal sex incidence.[1] Children and young adults are predominantly affected. It presents clinically as an eruption of pinhead-sized, flesh-colored, shiny, flat-topped or dome-shaped papules and shows a predilection for the arms, chest, abdomen and genitalia (*Figs 6.37, 6.38*).[1–5] A positive Koebner's phenomenon is typically present.[5] The condition is usually localized and asymptomatic, although occasionally there may be mild or even intense pruritus.[2] Rarely, generalized lesions have been described.[2] Occasionally papules may be encountered on the palms and soles.[3] Exceptionally, familial cases have been documented.[6,7] Lichen nitidus may spontaneously resolve within a few months although occasionally it persists indefinitely.[2]

Mucous membrane involvement presenting as grayish-yellow papules has also been described.[4] Nail involvement, which is extremely rare, presents as thickening with ridges, rippling, terminal splitting, striations and pits.[2,4]

Keratodermic, vesicular, hemorrhagic, purpuric and perforating variants may rarely be encountered.[2,8–11] Perforating lichen nitidus shows a predilection for the forearms and fingers and may be trauma related.[10]

Actinic lichen nitidus refers to the development of lichen nitidus on sun-exposed sites, usually during the summer months. It shows considerable overlap with actinic lichen planus (see above).[12,13]

Histological features

In many cases lichen nitidus is characterized by unmistakable histology. The classical papule is sharply circumscribed and occupies the space of only four or five dermal papillae. It is often depressed in the center and composed of atrophic epidermis, frequently covered by a parakeratotic tier and overlying a cellular infiltrate (*Figs 6.39–6.42*). Claw-like extensions of epidermal ridges mark the lateral boundaries of the lesion. The epithelium shows basal cell hydropic degeneration and cytoid bodies may be a feature. The inflammatory component consists of lymphocytes, histiocytes and variable numbers of epithelioid cells. Giant cells are sometimes a feature and true granulomata may occasionally be found, although caseation is never present. In addition to red cell extravasation, purpuric variants may show increased vascularity and vessel wall thickening with hyalinization.[11]

Palmar lesions may be identical to those seen elsewhere or show a more diffuse band-like upper dermal lymphohistiocytic infiltrate with associated giant cells and focal parakeratosis.[3,14]

Fibrin can be detected at the basement membrane zone by immunofluorescent techniques, but immunoglobulin deposition is not a feature.[15,16]

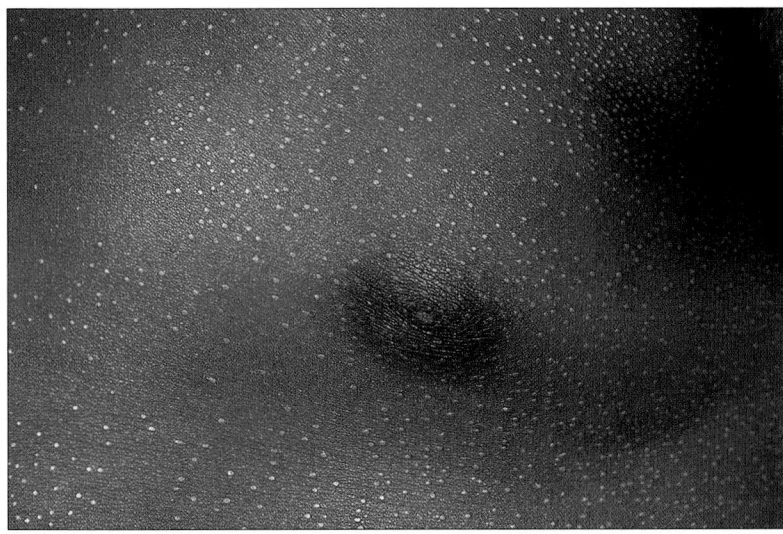

Fig. 6.37
Lichen nitidus: numerous tiny papules are present on the chest of a young child. By courtesy of R.A. Marsden, MD, St George's Hospital, London, UK.

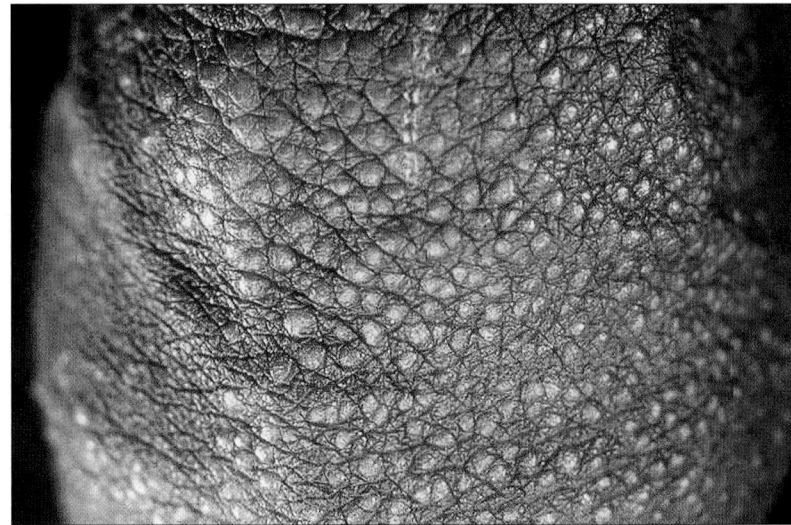

Fig. 6.38
Lichen nitidus: numerous papules are present on the scrotum. The genitalia are commonly affected. By courtesy of the Institute of Dermatology, London, UK.

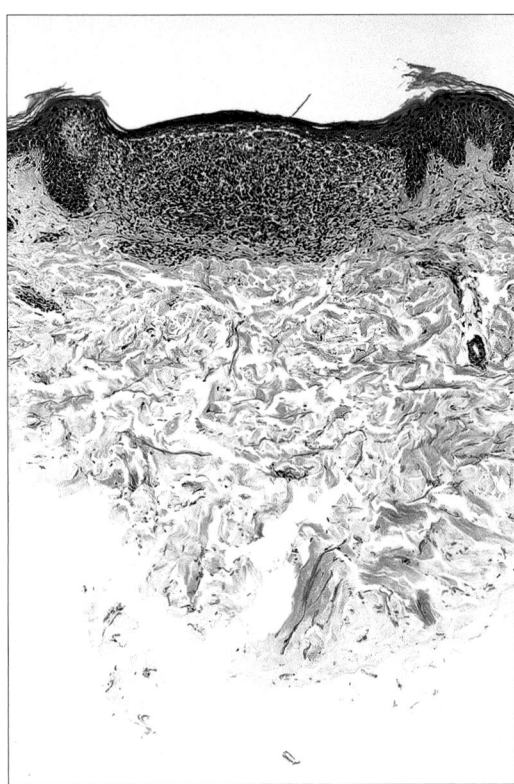

Fig. 6.39
Lichen nitidus: scanning view showing a typical small, circumscribed lesion occupying only a couple of dermal papillae. Note the claw-like epidermal lateral borders.

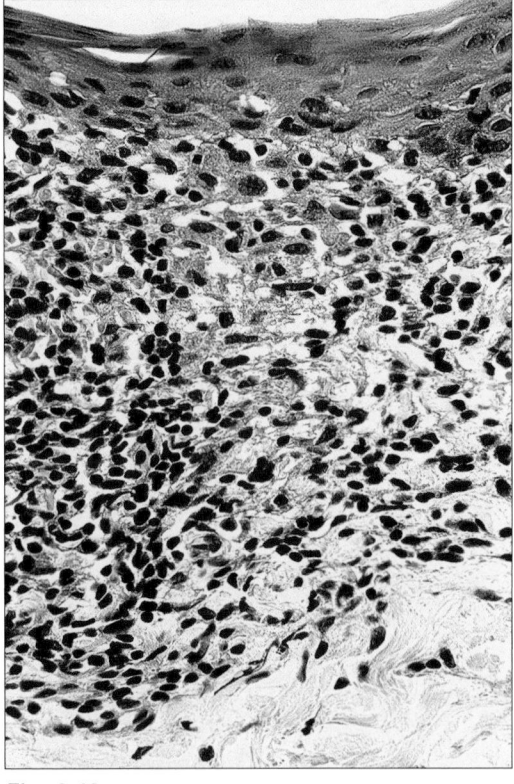

Fig. 6.40
Lichen nitidus: note the parakeratosis and band-like infiltrate.

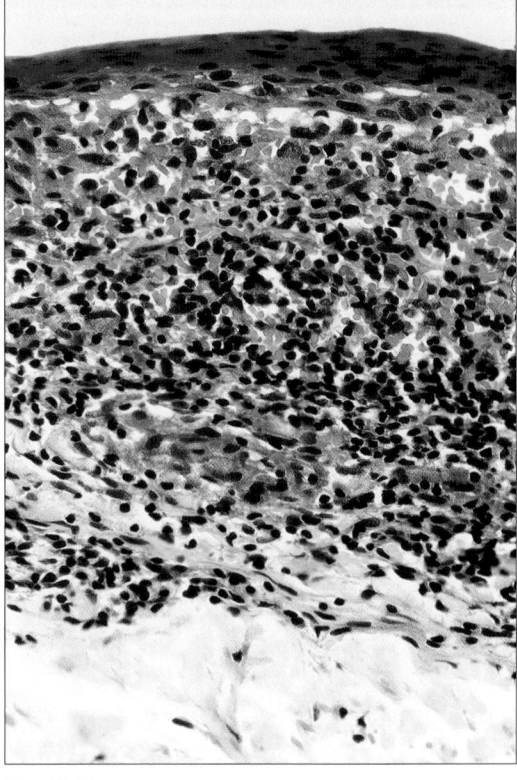

Fig. 6.41
Lichen nitidus: the infiltrate consists of lymphocytes, histiocytes and epithelioid cells. Ill-defined non-caseating granulomata are not uncommon.

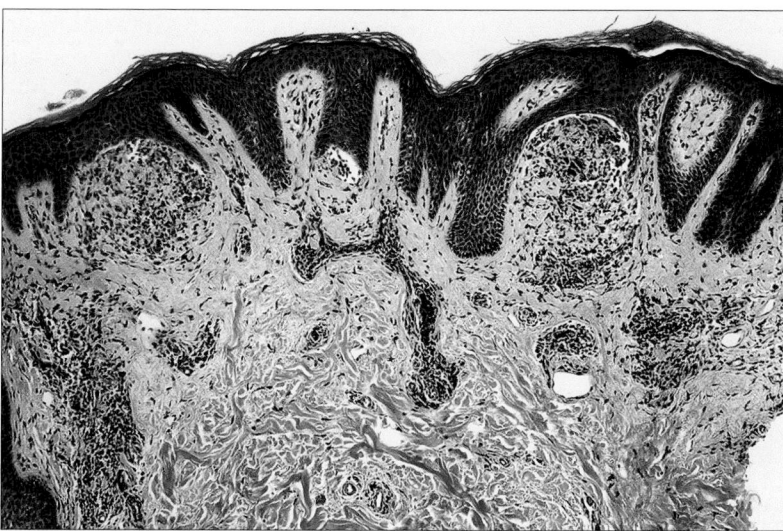

Fig. 6.42
Lichen nitidus: there are multiple lesions of lichen nitidus. The patient also had typical lichen planus lesions. By courtesy of R. Margolis, MD, St Elizabeth's Hospital, Boston, USA.

Immunophenotypic studies show that there is a marked excess of CD4+ cells (helper/inducer T-cells) over CD8+ cells (cytotoxic/suppressor T-cells).[17] Langerhans' cells are conspicuous.[17] These findings are similar to those described for lichen planus.

Ultrastructural examination has revealed rather non-specific findings including epidermal intercellular edema, subepidermal edema, colloid bodies, decreased numbers of desmosomes and disruption or reduplication of the lamina densa.[18–20] Perivascular electron-dense deposits (the nature of which is unknown) have been described in purpuric variants.[11]

Comment

Lichen nitidus may coexist with lichen planus, and lichen nitidus-like lesions may be found in patients with typical lichen planus, but it is unlikely that the conditions are related.[21] Wickham's striae are not a feature of lichen nitidus and mucosal involvement is exceptional.[2,4] Lichen nitidus is associated with parakeratosis and epidermal atrophy, in contrast to the orthohyperkeratosis and acanthosis seen in lichen planus. The saw-toothed appearance of the lower border of the epidermis seen in lichen planus is not a feature of lichen nitidus and immunofluorescence for immunoglobins is negative. Epithelioid cells and giant cells are characteristic of lichen nitidus and are not typically a feature of lichen planus.

References

1. Lapins, N.A., Willoughby, C., Helwig, E.B. (1978) Lichen nitidus: a study of forty-three cases. *Cutis*, **21**, 534–537.
2. Soroush, V., Gurevitch, A.W., Peng, S-K. (1999) Generalized lichen nitidus: case report and literature review. *Cutis*, **64**, 135–136.
3. Weiss, R.M., Cohen, A.D. (1971) Lichen nitidus of the palms and soles. *Arch Dermatol*, **104**, 538–540.
4. Bettoli, V., De Padova, M.P., Corazza, M. et al (1997) Generalized lichen nitidus with oral and nail involvement in a child. *Dermatology*, **194**, 367–369.
5. Maeda, M. (1994) A case of generalized lichen nitidus with Koebner's phenomenon. *J Dermatol*, **21**, 273–277.
6. Marks, R., Wilson Jones, E. (1970) Familial lichen nitidus. The simultaneous occurrence of lichen nitidus in brothers. *Trans St Johns Hosp Dermatol Soc*, **56**, 165–167.
7. Kato, N. (1995) Familial lichen nitidus. *Clin Exp Dermatol*, **20**, 336–338.
8. Jetton, R.L., Eby, C.S., Lejeune, C. et al (1972) Vesicular and hemorrhagic lichen nitidus. *Arch Dermatol*, **105**, 430–431.
9. Bardach, H. (1981) Perforating lichen nitidus. *J Cutan Pathol*, **8**, 111–116.
10. Itami, A., Ando, I., Kukita, A. (1994) Perforating lichen nitidus. *Int J Dermatol*, **33**, 382–384.
11. Endo, M., Baba, S., Suzuki, H. (1998) Purpuric lichen nitidus. *Eur J Dermatol*, **1**, 54–55.
12. Kanwar, A.J., Kaur, S. (1991) Lichen nitidus actinicus. *Pediatr Dermatol*, **8**, 94–95.
13. Hussain, K. (1998) Summer time actinic lichenoid eruption, a distinct entity, should be termed actinic lichen nitidus. *Arch Dermatol*, **134**, 1302–1303.
14. De Eusebio Murillo, E., Sánchez Yus, E., Novo Lens, R. (1999) Lichen nitidus of the palms: a case with peculiar histopathologic features. *Am J Dermatopathol*, **21**, 161–164.
15. Waisman, M., Dundon, B.C., Michel, B (1973) Immunofluorescent studies in lichen nitidus. *Arch Dermatol*, **107**, 200–203.
16. Sysa-Jedrzejowska, A., Wozniacka, A., Robak, E. et al (1996) Generalized lichen nitidus: a case report. *Cutis*, **58**, 170–172.
17. Wright, A.L., McVittie, E., Hunter, J.A.A. (1990) An immunophenotypic study of lichen nitidus. *Clin Exp Dermatol*, **15**, 273–276.
18. Fimiani, M., Alessandrini, C., Castelli, A. et al (1986) Ultrastructural observations in lichen nitidus. *Arch Dermatol Res*, **279**, 77–82.
19. Clausen, J., Jacobsen, P.K., Brandrup, F. (1982) Lichen nitidus: electron microscopic and immunofluorescence studies. *Acta Derm Venereol*, **62**, 15–19.
20. Mihara, M., Nakayama, H., Shimao, S. (1991) Lichen nitidus: a histologic and electron microscopic study. *J Dermatol*, **18**, 475–480.
21. Kawakami, T., Soma, Y. (1995) Generalized lichen nitidus appearing subsequent to lichen planus. *J Dermatol*, **22**, 434–437.

Lichenoid keratosis

Clinical features

Lichenoid keratosis (lichen planus-like keratosis, solitary lichen planus) is not uncommon and usually presents as a solitary, 0.5–2 cm diameter, sharply demarcated, erythematous, violaceous, tan or brown papule or plaque (*Fig. 6.43*).[1] Occasionally, multiple lesions may be present.[2] It is usually of short duration and shows a predilection for the face (particularly the cheeks and nose), forearm and dorsum of the hand, the upper trunk (especially the presternal area), the hand and neck.[3–7] The surface is often scaly. Lesions are commonly asymptomatic, but mild pruritus has sometimes been documented.[7] Patients are frequently Caucasian, but occasionally blacks are affected.[6,7] Females develop these lesions more commonly than males and patients are usually in their fourth to seventh decades.[4]

Lichenoid keratosis is often clinically misdiagnosed as a seborrheic wart, superficial basal cell carcinoma, squamous cell carcinoma, actinic keratosis or Bowen's disease.[4]

Pathogenesis and histological features

The precise nature of lichenoid keratosis is uncertain. In the past it has been regarded as a solitary lesion of lichen planus or it was thought to have an actinic pathogenesis.[8–10] Although neither of these hypotheses has been disproven, more recently it has been proposed that a lichenoid keratosis represents an immunological or regressive response to a pre-existent epidermal lesion in a manner reminiscent of a 'halo' nevus.[2] The frequent association of solar lentigines or, less commonly, seborrheic warts in the adjacent epithelium has been cited as evidence in favor of this hypothesis.[3–5,7] It seems highly likely that lichenoid keratosis represents a heterogeneous condition.

Histologically, as its name suggests, the features are similar to those of lichen planus. Thus there is hyperkeratosis, hypergranulosis, variable

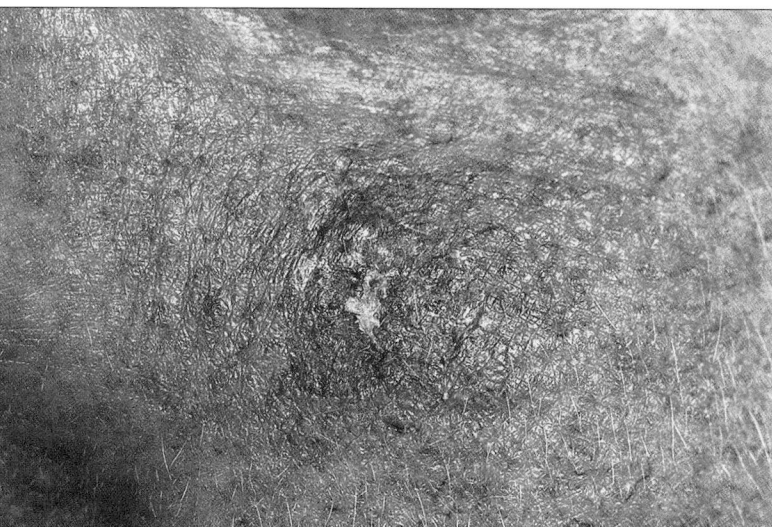

Fig. 6.43
Lichenoid keratosis: there is scaling overlying a slightly raised erythematous plaque. By courtesy of the Institute of Dermatology, London.

acanthosis and basal cell liquefactive degeneration sometimes accompanied by lymphocytic exocytosis (*Fig. 6.44*).[3,5] Foci of parakeratosis are also frequently seen (*Fig. 6.45*).[1] Although the saw-tooth acanthosis of lichen planus is sometimes evident, more often the epithelium merely shows broadened, widened and irregular epidermal ridges.[3] The basal epidermal layers may sometimes show very minor degrees of cytological atypia, including cellular and nuclear enlargement with conspicuous nucleoli, but these changes represent regenerative phenomena.[3] Dysplasia as seen in lichenoid actinic keratosis is not a feature of a lichenoid keratosis. Colloid bodies are usually conspicuous in both the epidermis and dermis and pigmentary incontinence is often marked (*Figs 6.46–6.48*).[1,6]

A dense chronic inflammatory cell infiltrate is typically present in the superficial dermis. Although this characteristically has a lichenoid distribution, on some occasions it may be more discrete and predominantly perivascular in location.[3,6] The infiltrate consists largely of lymphocytes and histiocytes, but small numbers of plasma cells and eosinophils are occasionally present. The adjacent dermis sometimes shows solar elastosis. If present, it is usually mild.

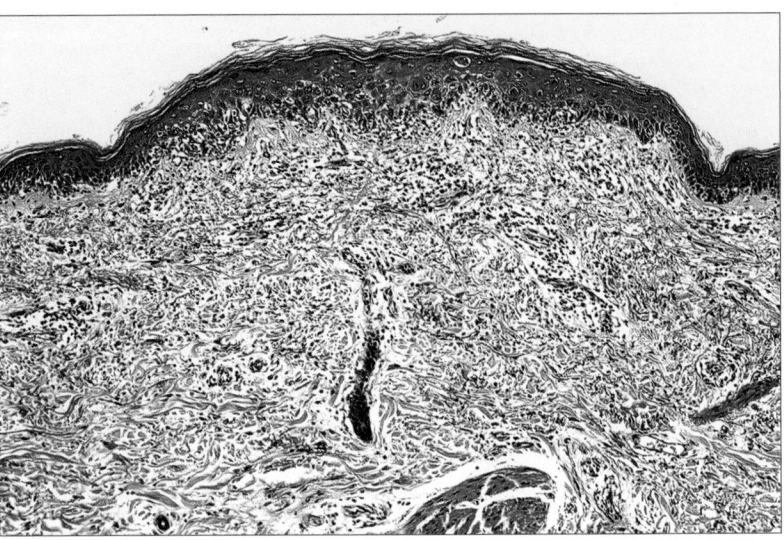

Fig. 6.46
Lichenoid keratosis: in this early lesion, there is more uniform acanthosis.

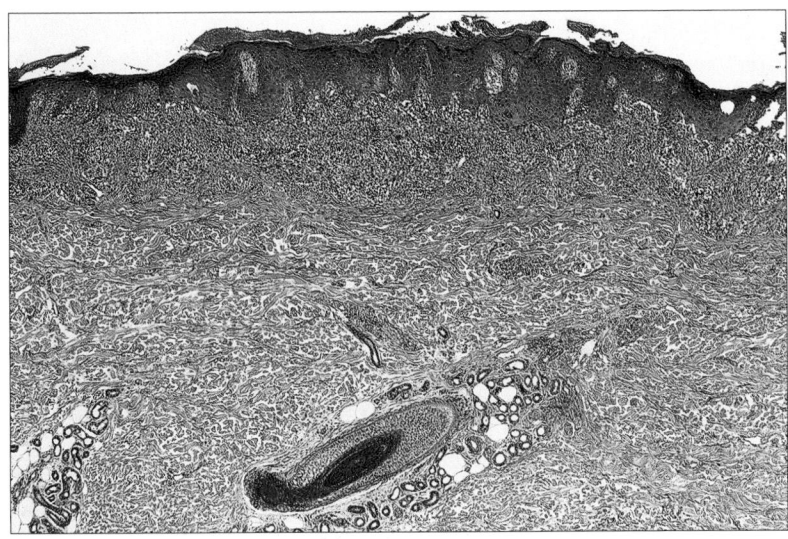

Fig. 6.44
Lichenoid keratosis: scanning view showing hyperkeratosis, hypergranulosis, irregular acanthosis and a band-like chronic inflammatory infiltrate.

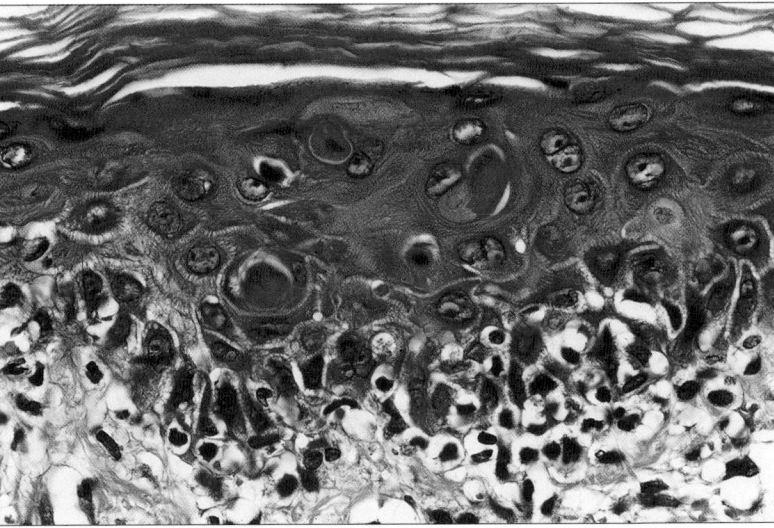

Fig. 6.47
Lichenoid keratosis: high power view showing cytoid bodies.

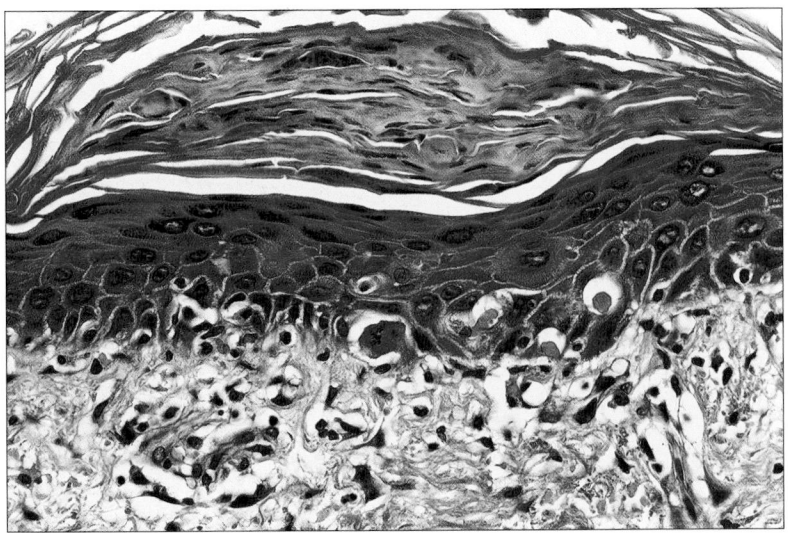

Fig. 6.45
Lichenoid keratosis: in this field there is marked parakeratosis. Cytoid bodies are present.

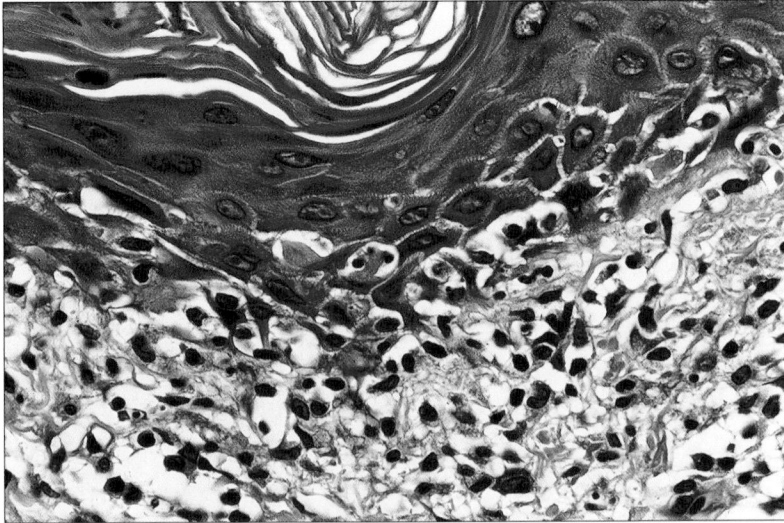

Fig. 6.48
Lichenoid keratosis: basal cell liquefactive degeneration is evident in addition to cytoid bodies. Lymphocytic exocytosis is present.

Immunofluorescence findings, which are similar to those of lichen planus, comprise deposits of IgM and, less commonly, IgG outlining cytoid bodies.[4]

Differential diagnosis

Many conditions show lichenoid histology and therefore come into the differential diagnosis. These include lichen planus and lichenoid drug reactions.

If clinical information is available, differentiation from lichen planus should present little difficulty. Lichen planus is characterized by large numbers of lesions in contradistinction to the single papule or plaque of lichenoid keratosis. In addition, lichen planus is usually itchy. Parakeratosis and dermal plasma cells with eosinophils are not a feature of lichen planus, but are typical of lichenoid keratosis.[6]

Both actinic keratoses and squamous cell carcinoma in situ may sometimes show a lichenoid inflammatory cell reaction. Dysplasia by definition is not a feature of lichenoid keratosis.[1]

References

1. Goette, D.K. (1980) Benign lichenoid keratoses. *Arch Dermatol*, **116**, 780–782.
2. Barranco, V.P. (1985) Multiple benign lichenoid keratoses simulating photodermatoses: evolution from senile lentigines and their spontaneous regression. *J Am Acad Dermatol*, **13**, 201–206.
3. Frigy, A.F., Cooper, P.H. (1985) Benign lichenoid keratosis. *Am J Clin Pathol*, **83**, 439–443.
4. Berger, T.G., Graham, J.H., Goette, D.K. (1984) Lichenoid benign keratosis. *J Am Acad Dermatol*, **11**, 635–638.
5. Prieto, V.G., Casal, M., McNutt, N.S. (1993) Lichen planus-like keratosis. A clinical and histological re-examination. *Am J Surg Pathol*, **17**, 259–263.
6. Scott, M.A., Johnson, W.C. (1976) Lichenoid benign keratosis. *J Cutan Pathol*, **3**, 217–221.
7. Laur, W.E., Posey, R.E., Waller, J.D. (1981) Lichen planus-like keratosis: a clinicohistopathologic correlation. *J Am Acad Dermatol*, **4**, 239–263.
8. Lumpkin, L.R., Helwig, E.B. (1966) Solitary lichen planus. *Arch Dermatol*, **93**, 54–55.
9. Hirsch, P., Marmelzat, W.L. (1967) Lichenoid actinic keratosis. *Dermatol Int*, **6**, 101–103.
10. Shapiro, L., Ackerman, A.B. (1966) Solitary lichen planus-like keratosis. *Dermatologica*, **132**, 386–392.

Lichenoid drug reactions

This topic is discussed on page 635.

Fixed drug reaction

This topic is discussed on page 636.

Lichen striatus

Clinical features

Lichen striatus (Blaschko linear acquired inflammatory skin eruption, BLAISE) is an uncommon, usually asymptomatic, dermatosis of unknown etiology, affecting the limbs or neck in which lesions typically follow Blaschko's lines.[1–6] Infrequently, the condition is pruritic.[6,7] It is self-limiting, normally disappearing within months to a year of onset, shows a female predominance (2:1) and, although it may occur at any age, presents most often in children aged 5–15 years.[2,5] Rarely lichen striatus has been described in adults (adult Blaschkitis, see below).[4,8,9] Exceptionally, a family history is encountered.[2,6] It is associated with seasonal variation, the majority of patients presenting in spring and summer.[2] Case clustering has been documented.[2]

Lesions, usually solitary and unilateral, present as erythematous or flesh-colored lichenoid or sometimes psoriasiform scaly papules, which coalesce into a continuous or interrupted linear or curved band, 1–3 cm wide and often covering the whole length of a limb, most often the lower (*Figs 6.49, 6.50*).[2] Occasional instances of multiple lesions have been recorded, as has bilaterality.[10,11] Nail changes, which may affect a single nail, include onycholysis, longitudinal ridging, splitting and nail loss.[12,13] Lichen striatus is not associated with a positive Koebner's phenomenon.

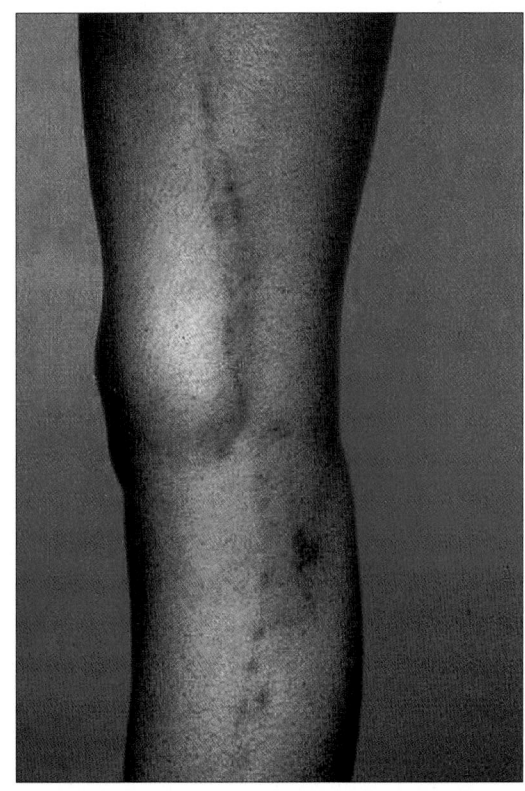

Fig. 6.49
Lichen striatus: a linear band of scaly hyperpigmented papules is present on the inner aspect of the leg, a commonly affected site. By courtesy of R.A. Marsden, MD, St George's Hospital, London, UK.

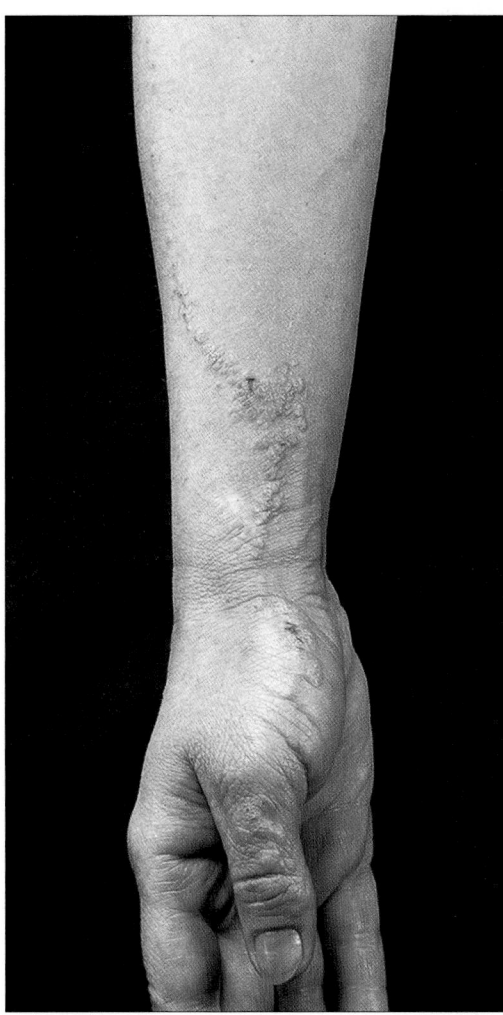

Fig. 6.50
Lichen striatus: the arms are sometimes affected. The condition most often presents in children. By courtesy of the Institute of Dermatology, London, UK.

Hypo- or hyperpigmentation sometimes follows resolution, which may be marked in people of colored races. Lichen striatus is associated with atopy in up to 50% of patients.[1,6]

Pathogensis and histological features

The etiology of this condition is unknown although case clustering and spring/summer preponderance raises the possibility of an environmental or infective basis.[2,14] The development of lesions along Blaschko's lines raises the possibility of a cell-mediated autoimmune reaction to an abnormal clone of cells. Blaschko's lines are believed to represent the direction along which epidermal growth centers expand during early skin development.[1] It has been suggested that the distribution of lesions in lichen striatus may reflect a postzygotic abnormality such as somatic mutation affecting localized stem cells.[1]

The histological changes of lichen striatus may be non-specific and show changes of mild chronic non-specific dermatitis.[15] In an established lesion, however, the changes often consist of an admixture of spongiotic dermatitis with lichenoid and interface features (*Fig. 6.51*).[16] Thus, there is often parakeratosis with a normal or slightly acanthotic epidermis accompanied by intercellular edema, lymphocytic exocytosis and keratinocyte necrosis (*Figs 6.52–6.54*). Satellite cell necrosis may sometimes be a feature and transepidermal elimination of keratinocyte debris (perforating lichen striatus) has occasionally been documented.[4,17] Intraepidermal Langerhans' cell vesicles have occasionally been described.[16] A heavy lymphohistiocytic infiltrate is present in the superficial dermis and also surrounds the vessels of the superficial and deep vascular plexuses and sometimes also the cutaneous adnexae.[4,16] Eosinophils and plasma cells are uncommon.[16]

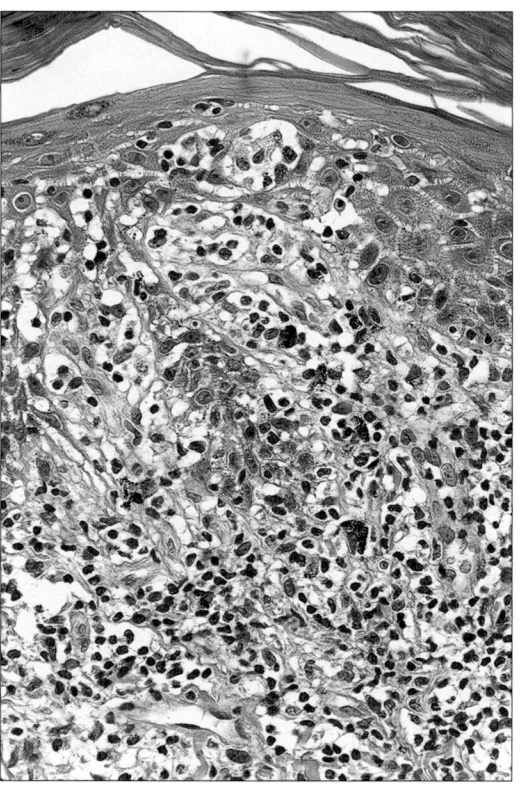

Fig. 6.53
Lichen striatus: there is spongiosis and marked lymphocytic exocytosis. Case courtesy of S. Lyle, MD, Beth Israel Deaconess Medical Center, Boston, USA.

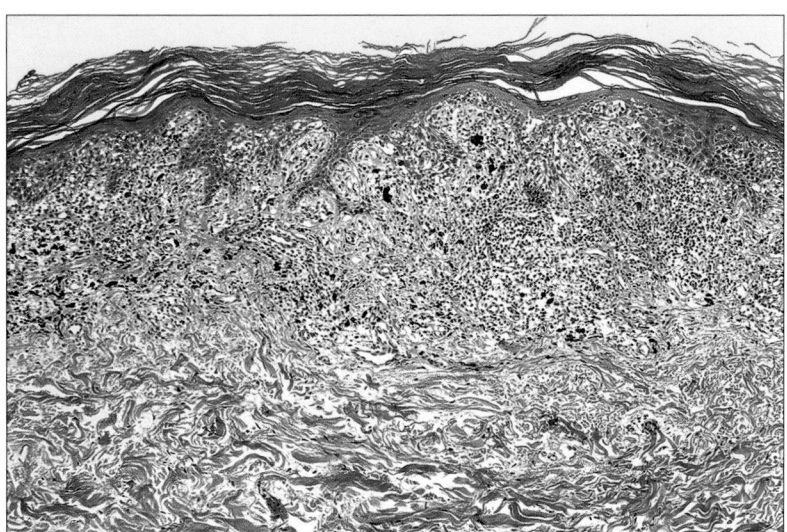

Fig. 6.51
Lichen striatus: scanning view showing hyperkeratosis, focal parakeratosis and acanthosis. A heavy inflammatory cell infiltrate is present in the upper dermis.

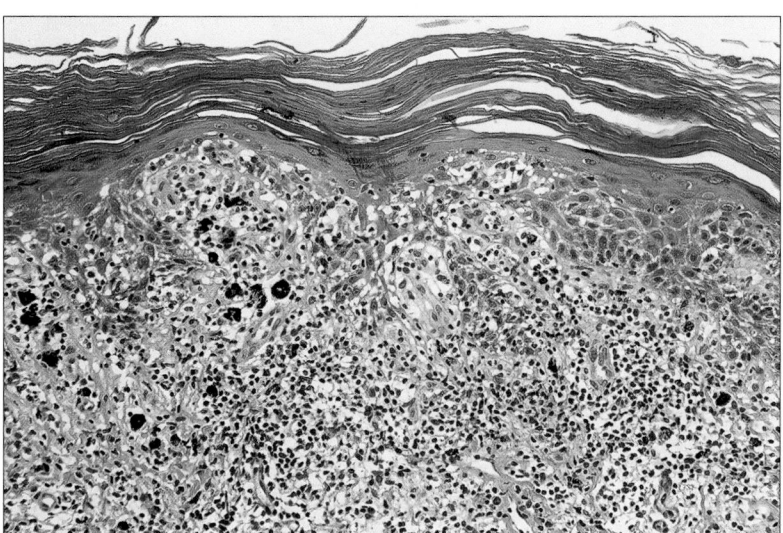

Fig. 6.52
Lichen striatus: in this field, there is parakeratosis and hyperkeratosis. Note the pigment incontinence and intense chronic inflammatory cell infiltrate. Case courtesy of S. Lyle, MD, Beth Israel Deaconess Medical Center, Boston, USA.

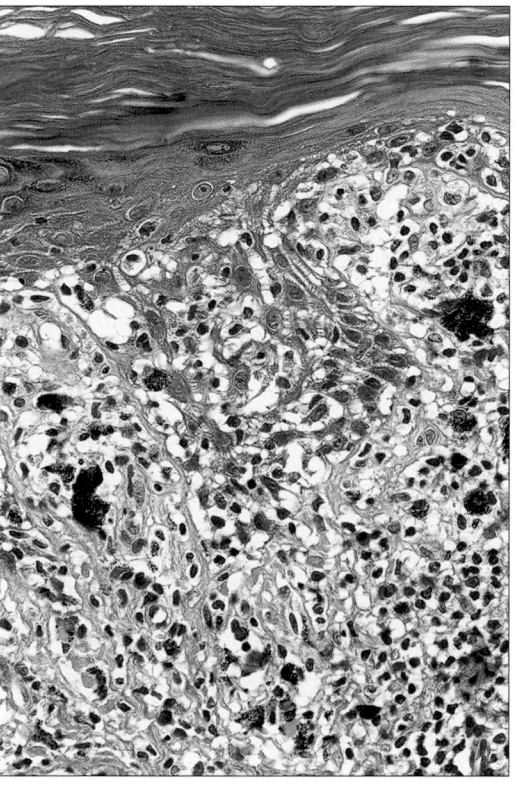

Fig. 6.54
Lichen striatus: note the basal cell liquefactive degeneration, pigmentary incontinence and satellite cell necrosis. Case courtesy of S. Lyle, MD, Beth Israel Deaconess Medical Center, Boston, USA.

Some biopsies, however, may be indistinguishable from lichen planus. In those cases where there is follicular involvement, the features can resemble those of lichen planopilaris, and old lesions sometimes simulate lichen nitidus.

By immunohistochemistry, the majority of the intraepidermal lymphocytes are of a CD8+ cytotoxic phenotype.[4,16] The dermal lymphocytes consist of an admixture of CD4+ and CD8+ subtypes. CD7 is typically conserved.[16] Intraepidermal Langerhans' cells may be normal, increased or decreased.[16]

Nail changes include slight spongiosis with exocytosis, focal hypergranulosis, dyskeratosis and a band-like lymphohistiocytic infiltrate affecting the proximal nail fold, nail bed and nail matrix dermis (see p. 1133).[12]

References

1. Taieb, A., El Youbi, A., Grosshans, E. et al (1991) Lichen striatus: a Blaschko linear acquired inflammatory skin eruption. *J Am Acad Dermatol*, **25**, 637–642.
2. Kennedy, D., Rogers, M. (1996) Lichen striatus. *Clin Lab Invest*, **13**, 95–99.
3. Grosshans, E.M. (1999) Acquired Blaschkolinear dermatoses. *Am J Med Genet*, **85**, 334–337.
4. Gianotti, R., Restano, L., Grimalt, R. et al (1995) Lichen striatus – a chameleon: an histopathological and immunohistological study of forty-one cases. *J Cutan Pathol*, **22**, 18–22.
5. Charles, T.A. (1974) Lichen striatus: a clinical, histologic and electron microscopic study of an unusual case. *J Cutan Pathol*, **1**, 265–274.
6. Hauber, K., Rose, C., Bröcker, E-B. et al (2000) Lichen striatus: clinical features and follow-up in 12 patients. *Eur J Dermatol*, **10**, 536–539.
7. Reed, R.J., Meek, T., Ichinose, H. (1975) Lichen striatus: a model for the histologic spectrum of lichenoid reactions. *J Cutan Pathol*, **2**, 1–18.
8. Mitsuhashi, Y., Kondo, S. (1996) Lichen striatus in an adult. *J Dermatol*, **23**, 710–712.
9. Ro, Y.S., Shin, Y.I. (2001) A case of lichen striatus following Blaschko's lines. *Cutis*, **67**, 31–33.
10. Johnson, H.M. (1946) Lichen striatus. *Arch Dermatol*, **53**, 51–52.
11. Mopper, C., Horwitz, D.C. (1971) Bilateral lichen striatus. *Cutis*, **8**, 140–141.
12. Karp, D.L., Cohen, B.A. (1993) Onychodystrophy in lichen planus. *Pediatr Dermatol*, **10**, 359–361.
13. Tosti, A., Peluso, A.M., Misciali, C. et al (1997) Nail lichen striatus: clinical features and long-term follow-up of five patients. *J Am Acad Dermatol*, **36**, 908–913.
14. Sittart, J.A., Pegas, J.R., Sant Ana, L.A. et al (1989) Lichen striatus: epidemiologic study. *Med Cutan Iber Lat Am*, **17**, 19–21.
15. Muller, S.A., Winkelmann, R.K. (1963) Lichen striatus. Clinical and histologic study with emphasis on vesicular aspects. *JAMA*, **183**, 206–208.
16. Zhang, Y., McNutt, N.S. (2001) Lichen striatus: histological, immunohistochemical, and ultrastructural study of 37 cases. *J Cutan Pathol*, **28**, 65–71.
17. Pujol, R.M., Tuneu, A., Moreno, A. et al (1988) Perforating lichen striatus. *Acta Derm Venereol*, **68**, 171–173.

Adult Blaschkitis

Clinical features

Adult Blaschkitis (acquired relapsing self-healing Blaschko dermatitis) is a rare, relapsing linear eruption with a mean age of onset of 40 years predominantly affecting males.[1–8] Lesions, which are pruritic papules and vesicles, affect multiple sites, particularly the trunk, following Blaschko's lines and typically resolve in days or weeks.[1] The condition, which may be unilateral or more commonly bilateral, recurs over the ensuing months or years. It resembles lichen striatus but differs clinically by the presence of vesicles and by its typically relapsing nature. Pruritus is rare in lichen striatus.

Histological features

Histologically, adult Blaschkitis is characterized by spongiotic changes; lichenoid features are absent.[6,8]

References

1. Grosshans, E.M. (1999) Acquired Blaschkolinear dermatoses. *Am J Med Genet*, **85**, 334–337.
2. Bolognia, J.L., Orlow, S.J., Glick, S.A. (1994) Lines of Blaschko. *J Am Acad Dermatol*, **31**, 157–190.
3. Rongioletti, F., Rebora, A. (1992) Blaschkite de l'adulte. *Ann Dermatol Venereol*, **119**, 45–48.
4. Betti, R., Lodi, A., Crosti, C. (1992) Un autre cas de blaschkite chez l'adulte. *Ann Dermatol Venereol*, **119**, 577.
5. Zaun, H. (1992) Blaschko-Dermatitis. Eine neue Krankheit. *Akt Dermatol*, **18**, 351–353.
6. Megahed, M., Reinauer, S., Scharffeter-Kochanek, K. et al (1994) Acquired relapsing self-healing Blaschko dermatitis. *J Am Acad Dermatol*, **31**, 849–852.
7. Canzona, F., Mazzanti, C., Gobello, T. et al (1995) Lichen striatus e blaschkite dell' adulto: inusuale localizzazione. *Chron Dermatol*, **5**, 139–142.
8. Lee, H.J., King, W.H., Hann, S.K. (1996) Acquired Blaschko dermatitis: acquired relapsing self-healing Blaschko dermatitis. *J Dermatol*, **23**, 639–642.

Lichen aureus

This topic is discussed on page 279.

Keratosis lichenoides chronica

Clinical features

Keratosis lichenoides chronica (Nekam's disease, lichen ruber verrucosus et reticularis) is a very rare, chronic inflammatory dermatosis that combines the features of a seborrheic dermatitis-like eruption of the scalp and face with a progressive lichenoid papulonodular dermatosis affecting the trunk, buttocks and limbs.[1–5] Patients usually present in the third to fifth decades although exceptionally reports of pediatric involvement have been documented.[6,7] It is usually persistent and typically does not respond to treatment although improvement in summer may sometimes be seen.[4]

Facial and scalp lesions are erythematous, greasy and scaly and bear no resemblance to those found on the trunk and extremities, which are erythematous or violaceous lichenoid scaly papules present in a confluent, reticulate or linear distribution, the last perhaps suggesting a Koebner's phenomenon (*Figs 6.55, 6.56*). Papulonodular and infiltrated plaques are sometimes also present. Lesions are typically bilateral, symmetrical and usually asymptomatic although rarely pruritus may be intense. Scarring is not a feature. Associated features include oral papules and ulceration, ocular lesions (blepharitis, conjunctivitis, anterior uveitis and iridocyclitis), laryngeal nodules, palmoplantar keratoderma and nail changes including yellow discoloration and dystrophy (longitudinal ridging, nail plate thickening, onycholysis and paronychia) (*Fig. 6.57*).[8,9–12] Genital involvement including penile and scrotal papules, chronic balanitis and phimosis has been documented.[5,8,9]

Keratosis lichenoides chronica has been described in association with a number of systemic diseases including chronic infections (toxoplasmosis, tuberculosis and viral hepatitis), kidney disease and lymphoma.[2,13–15]

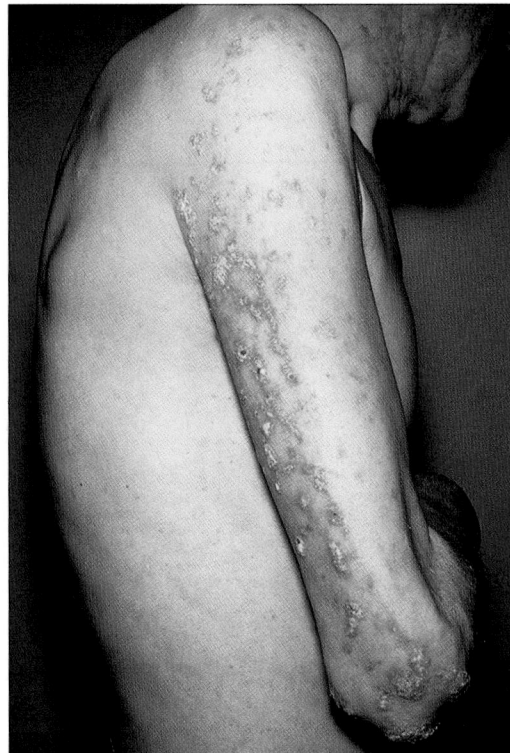

Fig. 6.55
Keratosis lichenoides chronica: there are erythematous hyperkeratotic lichenoid lesions in a linear and reticular distribution. By courtesy of R.A. Marsden, MD, St George's Hospital, London, UK.

Pathogenesis and histological features

Although the precise nature of keratosis lichenoides chronica is uncertain, some authors regard it as a variant of hypertrophic lichen planus.[8,16]

Histologically the lichenoid eruption is characterized by hyperkeratosis and occasionally parakeratosis, variable acanthosis and epidermal atrophy associated with a band-like lymphohistiocytic infiltrate in the superficial dermis, often with conspicuous melanophages.[9] Perifollicular and perivascular chronic inflammation may also be evident. Epidermal basal keratinocytes show hydropic degeneration and cytoid body formation has been described.[9,16] Exceptionally, amyloid deposition has been documented.[17]

The dermal infiltrate consists of lymphocytes, histiocytes and variable plasma cells and eosinophils.[9]

Direct immunofluorescence highlights the cytoid bodies.[16]

The scalp and facial lesions show the features of a chronic dermatitis, namely spongiosis with exocytosis and patchy parakeratosis. A perivascular chronic inflammatory cell infiltrate of lymphocytes, histiocytes and plasma cells may be present in the upper dermis.[4]

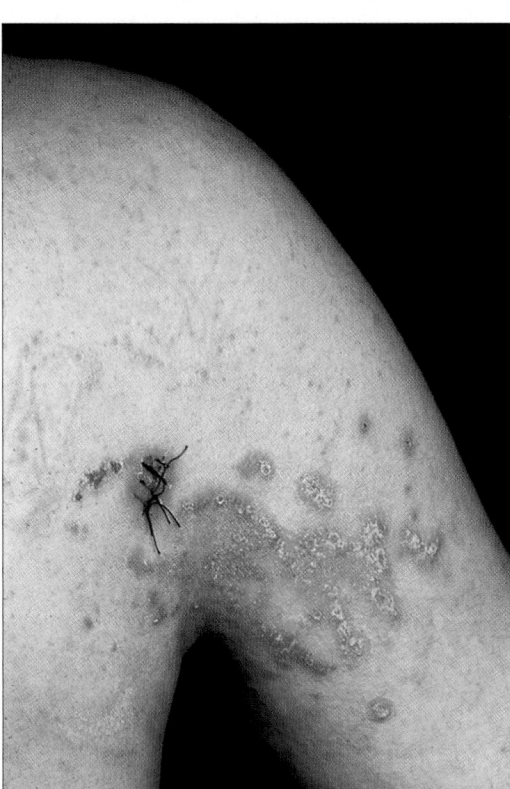

Fig. 6.56
Keratosis lichenoides chronica: close-up view of solitary lichenoid papules and a confluent plaque. By courtesy of R.A. Marsden, MD, St George's Hospital, London, UK.

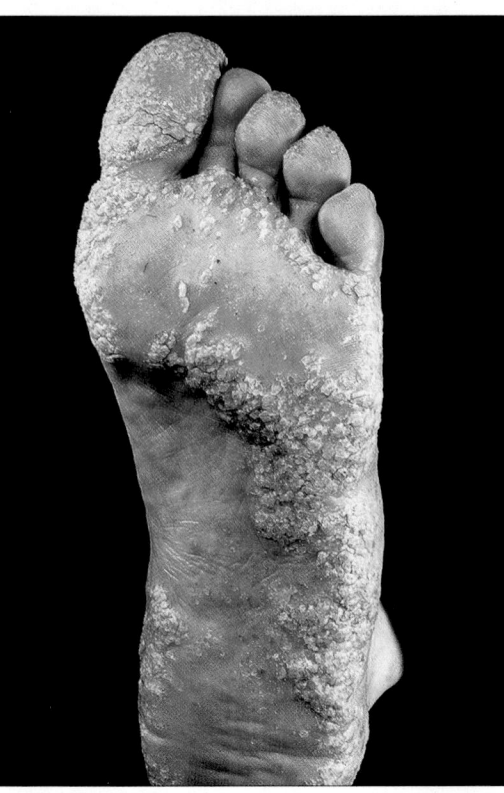

Fig. 6.57
Keratosis lichenoides chronica: plantar involvement showing disfiguring exophytic, hyperkeratotic verrucous plaques. By courtesy of R.A. Marsden, MD, St George's Hospital, London, UK.

References

1. Nekam, L. (1938) Sur la question du lichen moniliforme. *Presse Med*, **46**, 1000–1003.
2. Masouye, I., Saurat, J-H. (1995) Keratosis lichenoides chronica: the centenary of another Kaposi's disease. *Dermatology*, **191**, 188–192.
3. Petrozzi, J.W. (1976) Keratosis lichenoides chronica. *Arch Dermatol*, **112**, 709–711.
4. Nabai, H., Mehregan, A.H. (1980) Keratosis lichenoides chronica: report of a case. *J Am Acad Dermatol*, **2**, 217–220.
5. Margolis, M.H., Cooper, G.A., Johnson, S.A.M. (1972) Keratosis lichenoides chronica. *Arch Dermatol*, **105**, 739–743.
6. Torredo, A., Mediero, I., Zambrano, A. (1994) Keratosis lichenoides chronica in a child. *Pediatr Dermatol*, **11**, 46–48.
7. Patrizi, A., Neri, I., Passarini, B. et al (1995) Keratosis lichenoides chronica: a pediatric case. *Dermatology*, **191**, 264–267.
8. Kersey, P., Ive, F.E. (1982) Keratosis lichenoides chronica is synonymous with lichen planus. *Clin Exp Dermatol*, **7**, 49–54.
9. Konstantinov, K.N., Sondergaard, J., Izuno, G. et al (1998) Keratosis lichenoides chronica. *J Am Acad Dermatol*, **38**, 306–309.
10. Mehregan, A.H., Heath, L.E., Pinkus, H. (1984) Lichen ruber moniliformis and lichen ruber verrucosus et reticularis of Kaposi. *J Cutan Pathol*, **11**, 2–11.
11. Baran, R., Pannizon, R., Goldberg, L. (1984) The nails in keratosis lichenoides chronica: characteristics and response to treatment. *Arch Dermatol*, **120**, 1471–1474.
12. Avermaete, A., Kreuter, J.A., Stücker, M. et al (2001) Keratosis lichenoides chronica: characteristics and response to acitretin. *Br J Dermatol*, **144**, 422–424.
13. Masouyé, I., Salomon, D., Saurat, J-H. (1993) B-cell lymphoma after cyclosporine for keratosis lichenoides chronica. *Arch Dermatol*, **129**, 914–915.
14. Lombardo, G.A., Annessi, G., Baliva, G. et al (2001) Keratosis lichenoides chronica: report of a case associated with panniculitis and B-cell lymphoma. *Dermatology*, **201**, 261–264.
15. Marschalko, M., Papp, I., Szalay, L. et al (1996) Keratosis lichenoides chronica with chronic hepatitis: a coincidence? *Acta Derm Venereol*, **76**, 401–402.
16. Grumwald, M.H., Amichai, B., Finkelstein, E. et al (1997) Keratosis lichenoides chronica: a variant of lichen planus. *J Dermatol*, **24**, 630–634.
17. Stefenato, C.M., Youseff, E.A., Cerio, R. et al (1993) Atypical Nekam's disease – keratosis lichenoides chronica associated with porokeratotic histology and amyloidosis. *Clin Exp Dermatol*, **18**, 274–276.

Twenty-nail dystrophy of childhood

This topic is considered on page 1134.

Erythema dyschromicum perstans

Clinical features

Erythema dyschromicum perstans (dermatosis cenicienta, ashy dermatosis) is an acquired, usually asymptomatic, disfiguring dermatosis which occurs particularly in Latin American (especially Mexican) populations and in Asians.[1-7] It was originally named dermatosis cenicienta after the clinical appearance of affected patients – los cenicientos (the ash-colored ones).[1] White-skinned races may however rarely be affected.[8] It is of unknown etiology, shows a female predilection and can develop at any age although the majority of patients are in their first three decades.[2] Presentation in infancy has, however, been documented.[9]

Patients develop oval, irregular or polycyclic, gray macules with erythematous, indurated, inflammatory borders of 1–2 mm. The lesions extend peripherally, show a tendency to coalesce and often affect large areas of the integument (*Figs 6.58–6.60*). With progression, the eruption develops a gray–blue color and loses the erythematous border, which is sometimes replaced by a hypopigmented periphery. The dermatosis, which is usually symmetrical, particularly affects the trunk and proximal extremities and – to a lesser extent – the face and neck.[2] The palms and soles, scalp, nails and mucous membranes do not appear to be involved.[6]

Pathogenesis and histological features

The etiology is unknown. Cases have followed HIV infection and there is a report of simultaneous development of vitiligo and erythema dyschromicum perstans although the significance of these observations is doubtful.[10,11]

Sections from the inflammatory border show hyperkeratosis and an epidermis of normal thickness or somewhat atrophic accompanied by basal cell hydropic degeneration and cytoid body formation (*Fig. 6.61*). Pigmentary incontinence is marked and a mild perivascular or lichenoid inflammatory cell infiltrate is present in the superficial dermis (*Fig. 6.62*). Sections from the central gray area show epidermal atrophy, follicular hyperkeratosis and pigmentary incontinence.

Direct immunofluorescence reveals non-specific staining of the cytoid bodies with IgG, IgM and C3.[12–14] Fibrinogen may be present at the epidermodermal junction.[13] The immunocytochemical studies are

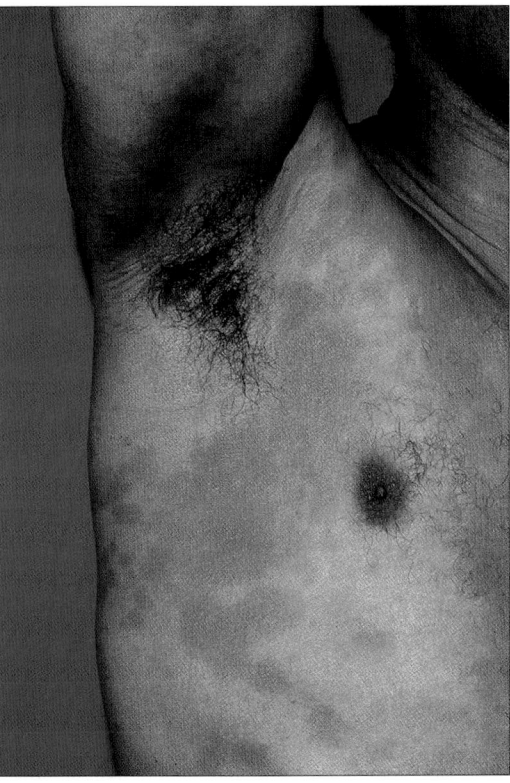

Fig. 6.58
Erythema dyschromicum perstans: this patient shows irregularly distributed gray macules. By courtesy of R.A. Marsden, MD, St George's Hospital, London, UK.

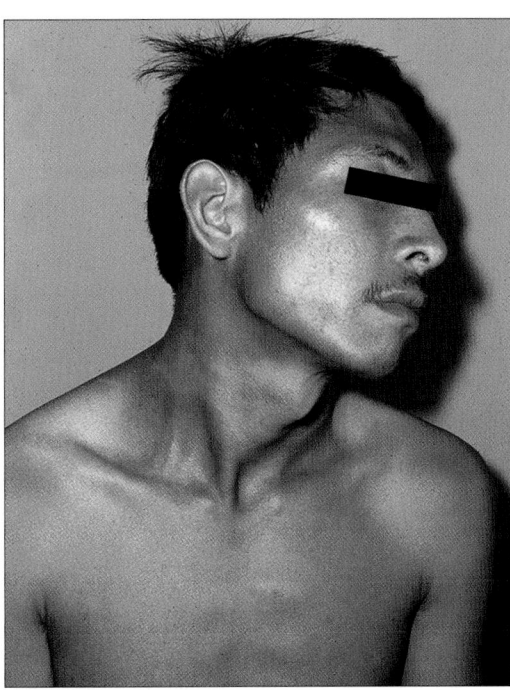

Fig. 6.59
Erythema dyschromicum perstans: in this patient there is extensive involvement of the face, neck and trunk. By courtesy of J. Tschen MD, Baylor College of Medicine, Houston, USA.

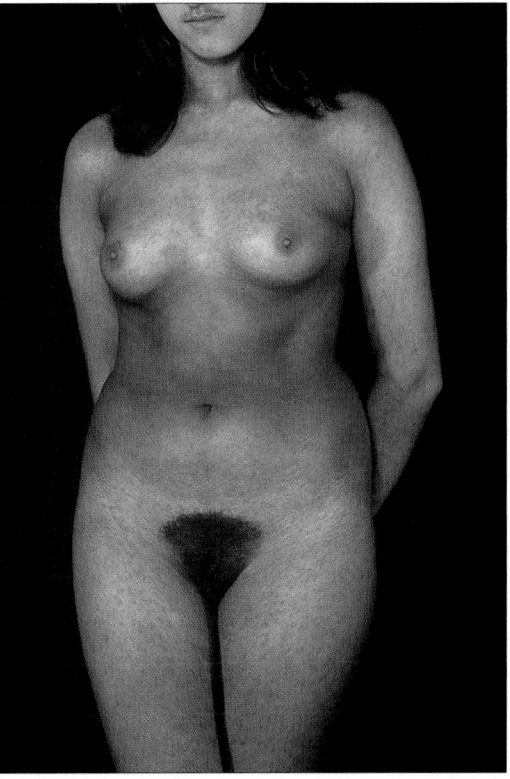

Fig. 6.60
Erythema dyschromicum perstans: in this patient with more advanced disease, there is a generalized bluish discoloration. By courtesy of the Institute of Dermatology, London, UK.

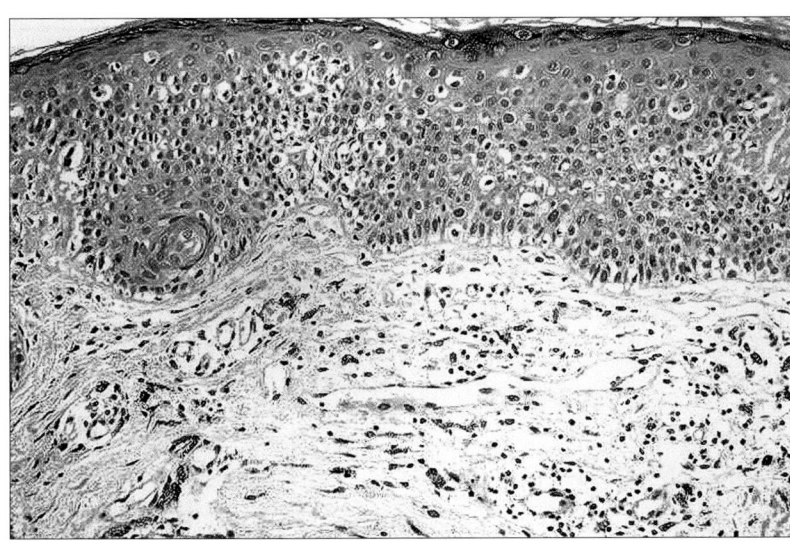

Fig. 6.61
Erythema dyschromicum perstans: there is hyperkeratosis, and marked pigmentary incontinence.

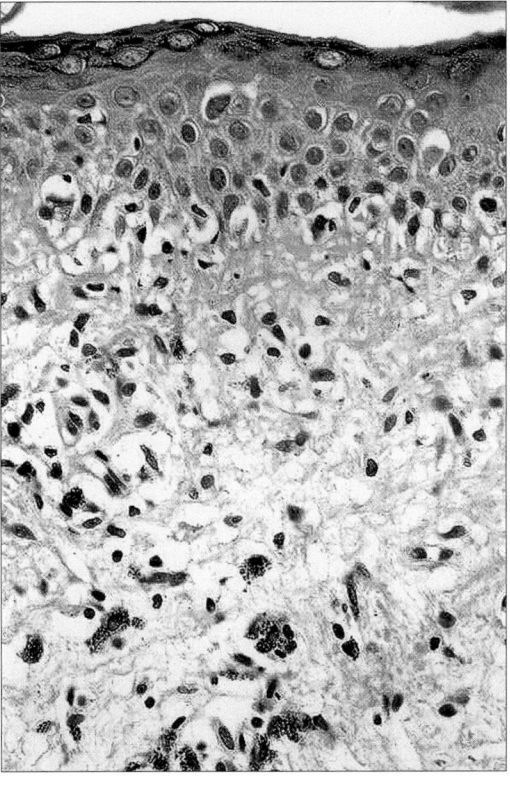

Fig. 6.62
Erythema dyschromicum perstans: note the hydropic degeneration.

therefore similar to lichen planus. The epidermal keratinocytes express Ia antigen and the lymphocytic population comprises both helper/inducer and suppressor/cytotoxic phenotypes similar to lichen planus.[14,15]

Ultrastructural findings are non-specific comprising intra- and interepidermal edema with cytoplasmic vacuolation, separation of keratinocytes and retraction of desmosomes, cytoid body formation, focal gaps in the keratinocyte basal lamina and pigment-laden histiocytes in the papillary dermis.[13,16,17]

Differential diagnosis

The precise relationship of erythema dyschromicum perstans to lichen planus is uncertain. The histological, immunological and ultrastructural findings certainly suggest that they are closely related.[12,13] Typical lichen planus may precede the development of erythema dyschromicum perstans and sometimes the two conditions have presented simultaneously although some of the documented cases may have represented lichen planus pigmentosus.[18,19]

References

1. Ramírez, C.O. (1957) Los cenicientos: problema clinico. *Memoria del Primer Congreso Centroamericano de Dermatologia, San Salvador*, **122**, 122–130.
2. Osswald, S.S., Proffer, L.H., Sartori, C.R. (2001) Erythema dyschromicum perstans: a case report and review. *Cutis*, **68**, 25–28.
3. Domínguez-Soto, L., Hojyo-Tomoka, T., Vega-memije, E. et al (1994) Pigmentary problems in the tropics. *Dermatol Clin*, **12**, 777–784.
4. Ramírez, C.O.L. (1967) The ashy dermatosis (erythema dyschromicum perstans): epidemiological study and report of 139 cases. *Cutis*, **11**, 244–247.
5. Vega, M.E., Waxtein, L., Arenas, R. et al (1992) Ashy dermatosis and lichen planus pigmentosus: a clinicopathologic study of 31 cases. *Int J Dermatol*, **31**, 90–94.
6. Novick, N.L., Phelps, R. (1985) Erythema dyschromicum perstans. *Int J Dermatol*, **24**, 630–633.
7. Knox, J.M., Dodge, B.G., Freeman, R.G. (1968) Erythema dyschromicum perstans. *Arch Dermatol*, **97**, 262–270.
8. Nelson, B.T.R., Ramsey, M.L., Bruce, S .et al (1988) Asymptomatic progressive hyperpigmentation in a 16 year old girl. *Arch Dermatol*, **124**, 769, 772.
9. Lee, S-J., Chung, K-Y. (1999) Erythema dyschromicum perstans in early childhood. *J Dermatol*, **26**, 119–121.
10. Nelson, M.R., Lawrence, A.G., Staughton, R.C.D. et al (1992) Erythema dyschromicum perstans in an HIV antibody-positive man. *Br J Dermatol*, **127**, 127–128.
11. Henderson, C.D., Tschen, J.A., Schaefer, D.G. (1988) Simultaneously active lesions of vitiligo and erythema dyschromicum perstans. *Arch Dermatol*, **124**, 1258–1260.
12. Kark, E.C., Litt, J.Z. (1980) Ashy dermatosis: a variant of lichen planus? *Cutis*, **25**, 631–633.
13. Tschen, J.A., Tschen, E.A., McGavran, M.H. (1980) Erythema dyschromicum perstans. *J Am Acad Dermatol*, **2**, 295–302.
14. Miyagawa, S., Komatsu, M., Okuchi, T. et al (1989) Erythema dyschromicum perstans, immunopathologic studies. *J Am Acad Dermatol*, **20**, 882–886.
15. Gross, A., Tapia, F.J., Mosca, W. et al (1987) Mononuclear cell subpopulations and infiltrating lymphocytes in erythema dyschromicum perstans and vitiligo. *Histol Histopathol*, **2**, 277–283.
16. Soter, N.A., Wand, C.H., Freeman, R.G. (1969) Ultrastructural pathology of erythema dyschromicum perstans. *J Invest Dermatol*, **52**, 155–162.
17. Sánchez, N.P., Pathak, M.A. (1985) Circumscribed dermal melanosis: classification, light histochemical and electron microscopic studies on three patients with erythema dyschromicum perstans. *Int J Dermatol*, **24**, 630–633.
18. Berger, R.S., Hayes, T.J., Dixon, S.L. (1989) Erythema dyschromicum perstans and lichen planus: are they related? *J Am Acad Dermatol*, **21**, 438–442.
19. Naidorf, K.F., Cohen, S.R. (1982) Erythema dyschromicum perstans and lichen planus. *Arch Dermatol*, **118**, 683–685.

interface dermatoses

Definitions

There is such considerable variation in the literature as to the exact definitions and interrelationships between erythema multiforme (particularly the 'major' variant), Stevens–Johnson syndrome and toxic epidermal necrolysis that it is often difficult or impossible to be certain to which disease the authors are actually referring![1–4] In this third edition, the consensus paper published in 1993 by Bastuji-Garin is used as a basis for classification since the authorship included most of the major players in this difficult subject.[1]

Classification of an individual patient depends upon the precise morphology and pattern of individual lesions and the extent of skin involvement (detached and detachable epidermis) as a percentage of total body surface area at the worst stage of the illness.

- *Target lesions* are defined as sharply demarcated and round, less than 3.0 cm in diameter and comprising three distinct zones, namely a central erythematous or purpuric disc with or without a blister, surrounded by a raised edematous ring, in turn bordered by an erythematous rim (*Fig. 6.63*).[1] Target lesions are typically distributed in an acral location, are often seen following a herpetic infection and are characteristic of erythema multiforme. Typical target lesions are not seen in patients with widespread epidermal detachment.

- *Raised atypical target lesions* are ill-defined, round palpable lesions with only two zones including a central raised edematous area with an erythematous border.

- *Flat atypical target lesions* are ill-defined, round lesions with only two non-palpable zones. The center may be blistered (*Fig. 6.64*).

- *Macules with or without blisters* are defined as non-palpable, erythematous or purpuric macules with irregular shape and size and often confluent. Blisters often occur on all or part of the macule. This lesion is characteristically seen in patients with widespread epidermal detachment who have a history of drug ingestion. Working on this basis, the following definitions have been proposed:[1]

- Bullous erythema multiforme is characterized by < 10% detachment, typical target lesions and sometimes raised atypical target lesions.

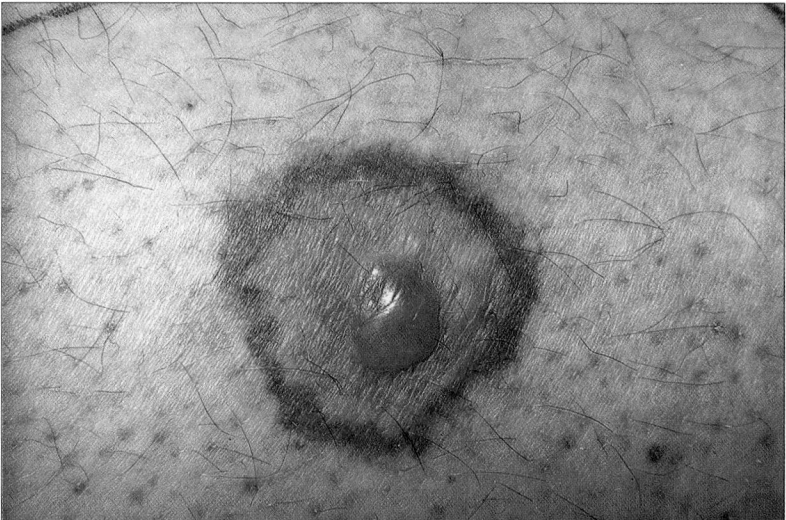

Fig. 6.63
Target lesion: characterized by a central blister surrounded by an edematous ring and an outer erythematous border. By courtesy of R.A. Marsden, MD, St George's Hospital, London, UK.

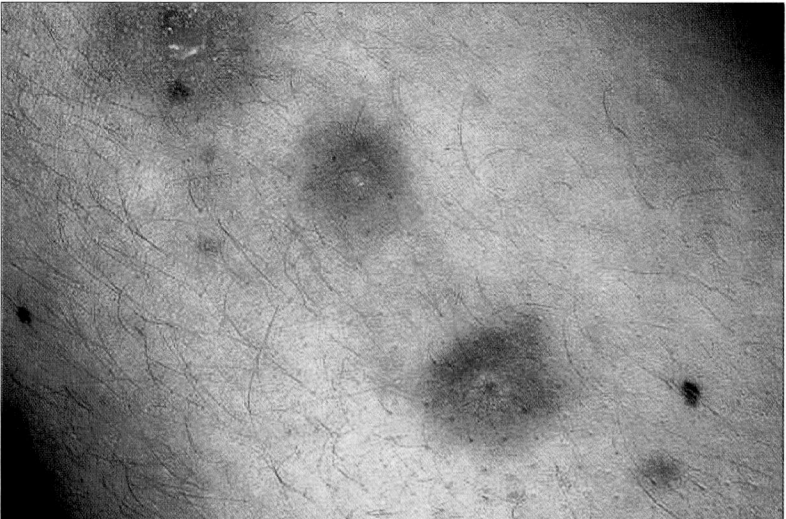

Fig. 6.64
Flat atypical target lesion: characterized by only two components, a central edematous area or blister surrounded by a zone of erythema, these lesions may be seen in erythema multiforme, Stevens–Johnson syndrome and toxic epidermal necrolysis. By courtesy of the Institute of Dermatology, London.

- Stevens–Johnson syndrome is characterized by < 10% detachment, flat atypical target lesions and erythematous macules in addition to blisters and erosions affecting one or more mucous membranes.
- Overlap Stevens–Johnson syndrome/toxic epidermal necrolysis is characterized by 10–30% detachment, atypical target lesions and flat erythematous macules.
- Toxic epidermal necrolysis is characterized by > 30% detachment with flat atypical target lesions and/or erythematous macules. Rarely, toxic epidermal necrolysis may develop as large epidermal sheets in the absence of erythematous macules.

References

1. Bastuji-Garin, S., Rzany, B., Stern, R.S. et al (1993) Clinical classification of cases of toxic epidermal necrolysis, Stevens-Johnson syndrome, and erythema multiforme. *Arch Dermatol*, **129**, 92–96.
2. Goldstein, S.M., Wintroub, B.W., Elias, P.E. et al (1987) Toxic epidermal necrolysis: unmuddying the waters. *Arch Dermatol*, **123**, 1153–1156.
3. Chan, H.L., Stern, R.S., Arndt, K.A. et al (1990) The incidence of erythema multiforme, Stevens–Johnson syndrome, and toxic epidermolysis necrolysis: a population-based study with particular reference to reactions caused by drugs among outpatients. *Arch Dermatol*, **126**, 43–47.
4. Roujeau, J.C., Chosidow, O., Saing, P. et al (1990) Toxic epidermal necrolysis (Lyell syndrome). *J Am Acad Dermatol*, **23**, 1039–1058.

Erythema multiforme

Clinical features

Erythema multiforme is a relatively common condition, which predominantly affects younger individuals (particularly in their second to fourth decades), including children, and shows a slight male predilection.[1-8] All races may be affected. It is self-limiting and commonly recurrent (recurrent erythema multiforme), although rarely continuous episodes of erythema multiforme have been described (persistent erythema multiforme).[9-12] Very occasionally epidemics are seen, as for example in military camps.[4] The eruption shows seasonal variation with many patients presenting in spring and summer.

It presents as symmetrically distributed, fixed, discrete erythematous round maculopapules 1–2 cm in diameter which appear in crops on the acral regions, particularly the elbows, the knees and extensor aspects of the extremities (*Figs 6.65–6.67*). Sometimes, the face, palms and soles, flexural extremities and perineum (*Fig. 6.68*) are affected.[2] The scalp is rarely involved.[13] Typically, the center of the lesions becomes ischemic to produce a bluish discoloration (the classical iris or target lesion) which may eventually blister. Although lesions are often present for up to 7 days, the entire episode is usually over by 6 weeks or less.[13] Lesions often

number a hundred or more. Resolution may be associated with post-inflammatory hyperpigmentation.

Oral lesions are common and are usually mild, typically presenting as multiple ulcers, which may involve the entire oral cavity, or predominantly affect the buccal mucosa and tongue (*Figs 6.69, 6.70*).[14] Target lesion on the lips may also be encountered.

In many patients, episodes of erythema multiforme are recurrent, developing as often as five times each year. Such cases are almost invariably due to herpes simplex infection. Particular clinical features of this variant include a positive Koebner phenomenon, photodistribution,

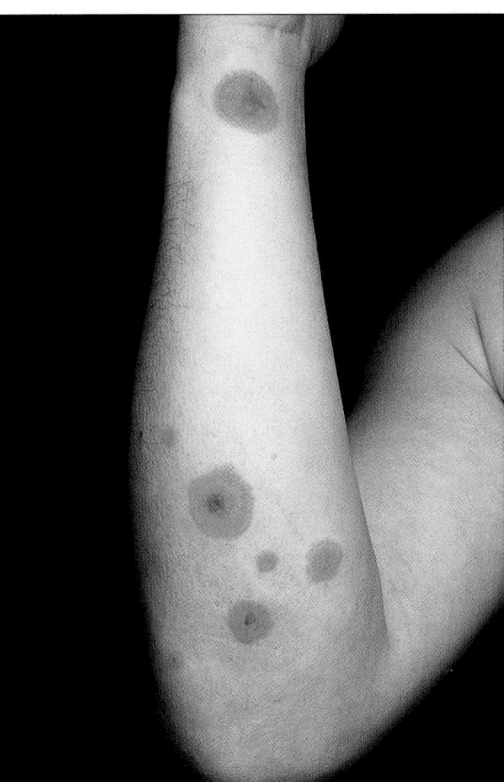

Fig. 6.66
Erythema multiforme: multiple target lesions on the arm. By courtesy of the Institute of Dermatology, London.

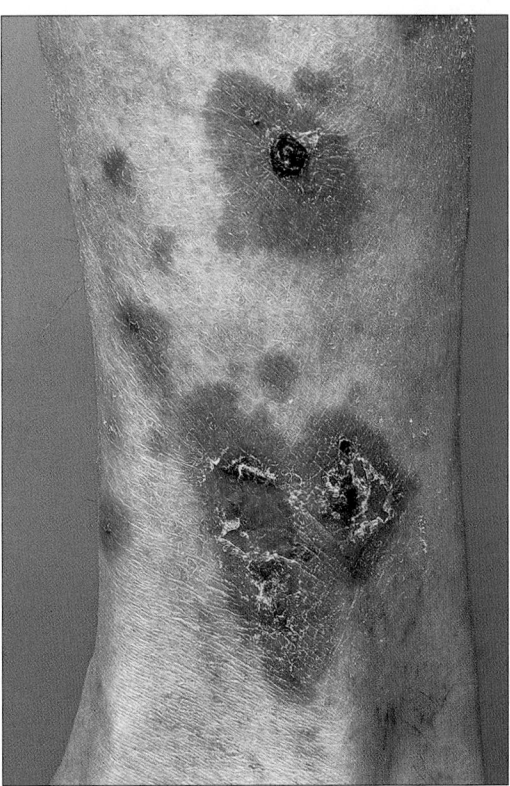

Fig. 6.67
Erythema multiforme: more extensive involvement in an adult with large erythematous lesions. The blisters have ruptured. By courtesy of the Institute of Dermatology, London.

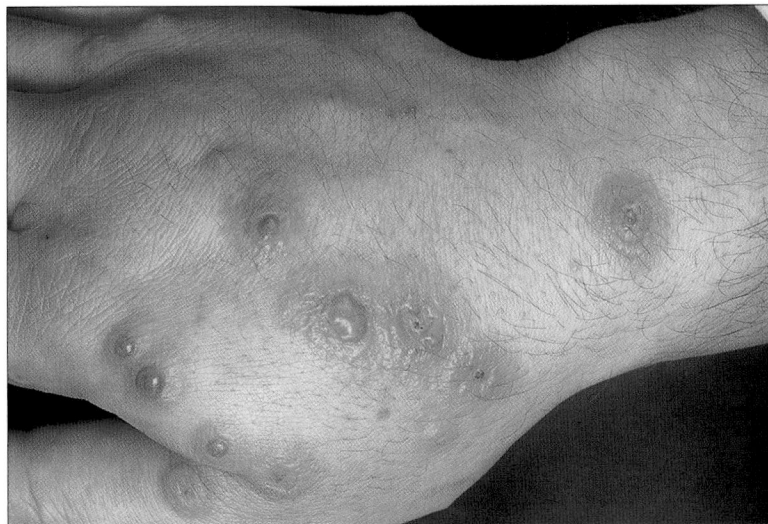

Fig. 6.65
Erythema multiforme: multiple target lesions on a child's hand, a typical site of presentation. By courtesy of the Institute of Dermatology, London.

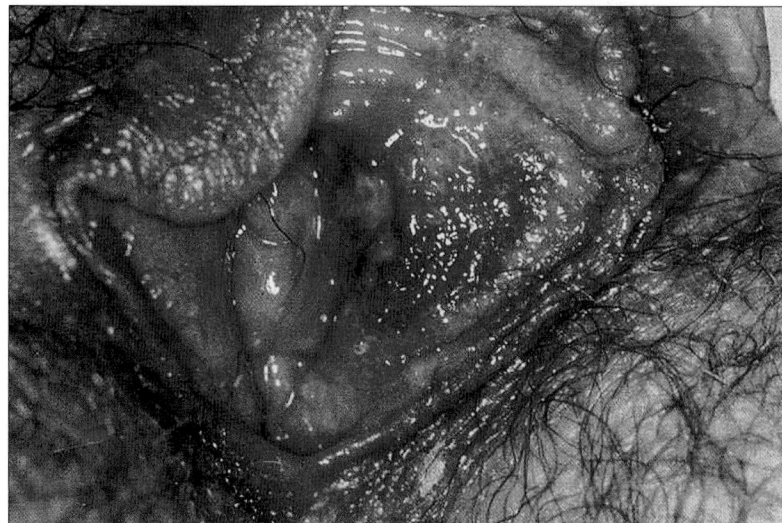

Fig. 6.68
Erythema multiforme: note the presence of erythema and erosion on the labium minus. By courtesy of P. Morgan, MD, London, UK.

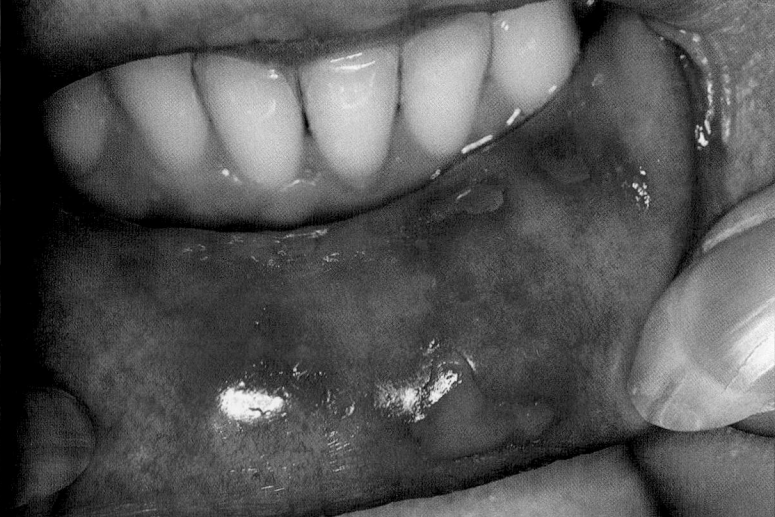

Fig. 6.69
Erythema multiforme: multiple erosions are present on the labial mucosa. By courtesy of P. Morgan, MD, London, UK.

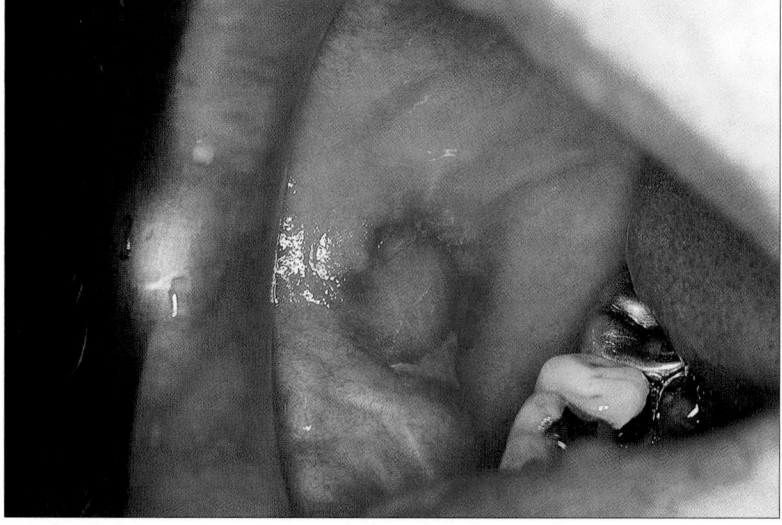

Fig. 6.70
Erythema multiforme: there is a large ulcer on the buccal mucosa. By courtesy of P. Morgan, MD, London, UK.

grouping of lesions over the elbows and knees, and nail fold involvement.[8]

In the older literature, a variant of erythema multiforme was recognized (erythema multiforme major) in which patients developed severe mucosal disease including oral, ocular and anogenital lesions. In keeping with the current thinking on this complex topic, such cases are now included in the spectrum of Stevens–Johnson syndrome.[1,2]

Rarely, patients (usually females) may develop erythema multiforme in association with discoid or systemic lupus erythematosus – Rowell syndrome. This is discussed in depth on page 780.

Pathogenesis and histological features

The etiology in the overwhelming majority of cases is past or present infection with herpes simplex virus (HSV) types I and II. In many patients, disease is subclinical. The relationship is strongest in patients with recurrent disease. Occasionally *Mycoplasma* infection is of etiological importance. Although many other viral and bacterial infections have also been implicated including orf, cowpox, Epstein–Barr virus, streptococcus, meningococcus, histoplasma and various childhood illness immunizations, it is uncertain whether these truly represent erythema multiforme or whether they might be better classified as some other dermatosis including Stevens–Johnson syndrome.[4,13] Erythema multiforme has also been described as a side-effect of a number of drugs including sulfonamides, trimethoprim–sulfamethoxazole combinations, penicillin, barbiturates and the contraceptive pill.[4,13] The same caveat applies. Erythema multiforme has also been associated with internal malignancy, including lymphoma, and may follow radiotherapy.[15,16]

Although cultures of skin lesions in erythema multiforme are negative for herpes simplex, viral DNA has been identified within the epidermis of skin lesions by polymerase chain reaction (PCR); in situ hybridization and immunohistochemistry are commonly positive.[17–24] Viral DNA is absent from healed lesions.[20] Viral gene expression correlates with lesion development.[21] Since there is no evidence of a viremia, it is thought that viral DNA is transported to the skin within circulating lymphocytes rather than directly through the bloodstream or via centrifugal neuronal spread.[20,23] Why it localizes to specific sites in the skin is unknown but this may be related to ultraviolet (UV) exposure. It is likely that an episode of erythema multiforme develops as a delayed hypersensitivity (and/or cytotoxic) reaction to herpes viral antigens including DNA polymerase expressed on the surface of keratinocytes. The identification of IFN-γ in active skin lesions suggests a delayed hypersensitivity reaction with involvement of variable cytokines recruiting additional lymphocytes and macrophages to amplify the inflammatory reaction.[24,25] It has been postulated that HSV DNA polymerase might also be associated with increased expression of transforming growth factor beta (TGF-β) and p21^{waf}, thereby accounting for cell growth arrest and apoptosis.[26] Viral antigens do not persist in lesional skin after resolution of the eruption and therefore in patients with recurrent disease, repeat transportation of viral DNA to the skin must occur.

Erythema multiforme is associated with an increased incidence of HLA-B15 (B62), HLA-B35 and HLA-DR53, particularly in recurrent disease.[27–30] Patients with limited mucosal involvement show an increased frequency of HLA-DQB1*0302 compared with patients in whom mucosal lesions predominate, when HLA-DQB1*0402 is more commonly identified.[30]

Erythema multiforme is characterized by a combination of basal cell hydropic degeneration and keratinocyte apoptosis accompanied by a heavy superficial dermal lymphohistiocytic infiltrate associated with lymphocytic exocytosis and satellite cell necrosis.[31–35] Apoptotic keratinocytes are rounded, intensely eosinophilic and often anucleate, although residual pyknotic forms may be present (*Figs 6.71, 6.72*). Their distribution may be focal, involving only an occasional and often basally located keratinocyte, or it may affect the entire epidermis, thereby resembling toxic epidermal necrolysis (Lyell's syndrome) (*Fig. 6.73*). Marked basal cell hydropic degeneration may result in subepidermal clefting or vesiculation (*Fig. 6.74*). Intra- and intercellular intraepidermal edema is evident and may result in spongiotic vesiculation (*Fig. 6.75*).

In biopsies from early lesions, the changes may be predominantly dermal with marked edema of the papillary dermis accompanied by a chronic inflammatory cell infiltrate and red cell extravasation (*Fig. 6.76*), thereby accounting for the clinical appearance of purpura.

The inflammatory cell infiltrate in erythema multiforme usually comprises lymphocytes and histiocytes; neutrophils are sparse to absent. Eosinophils may sometimes also be present.[36] Leukocytoclasis is not seen.

Histological features similar to those of the skin lesions typify involvement of the mucous membranes; spongiosis and intracellular edema, however, are more obvious and, therefore, intraepithelial blisters may be conspicuous.

By immunohistochemistry, the infiltrate consists predominantly of helper (CD4+ Vβ2+) lymphocytes with a lesser number of cytotoxic lymphocytes and admixed macrophages.[20,37,38] Keratinocytes express intracellular adhesion molecule-1 (ICAM-1) and HLA-DR, the latter thought to be induced by IFN-γ of activated CD4+ T-helper 1 (Th1) cell derivation.[20,39] TNF-α is not expressed in HSV-associated lesions.[26]

Differential diagnosis

Erythema multiforme may show considerable overlap with Steven–Johnson syndrome and toxic epidermal necrolysis. In erythema multiforme, however, there are commonly more marked inflammatory changes than seen in Stevens–Johnson syndrome and toxic epidermal necrolysis in which the epidermal changes of widespread apoptosis are to be expected.

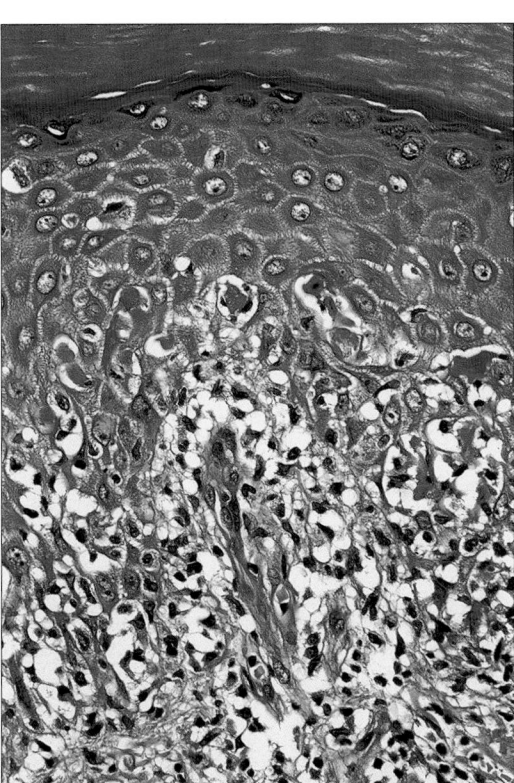

Fig. 6.71 Erythema multiforme: early lesion showing basal cell hydropic degeneration and cytoid bodies.

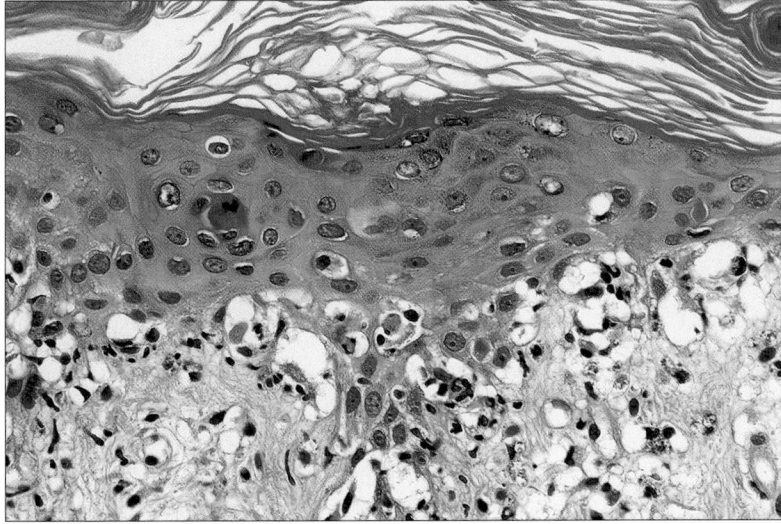

Fig. 6.72 Erythema multiforme: close-up view of basal cell hydropic degeneration, cytoid bodies and satellite cell necrosis.

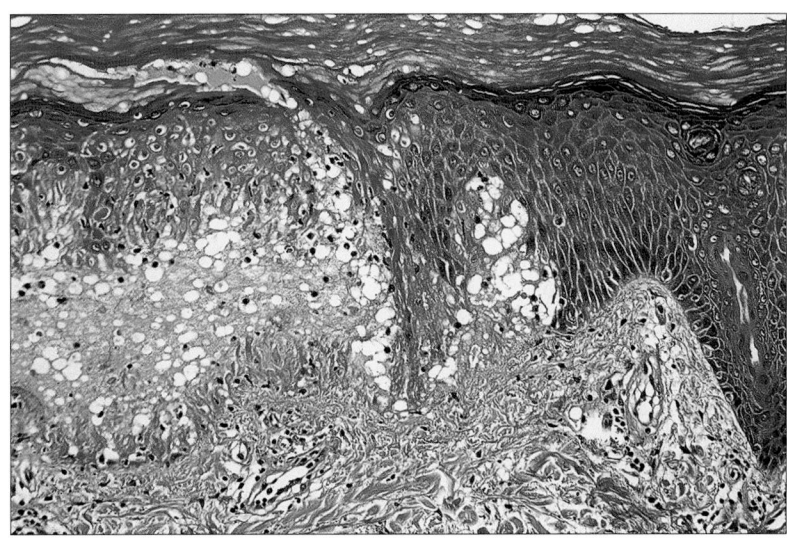

Fig. 6.73 Erythema multiforme: marked apoptosis has resulted in intra-epidermal vesiculation.

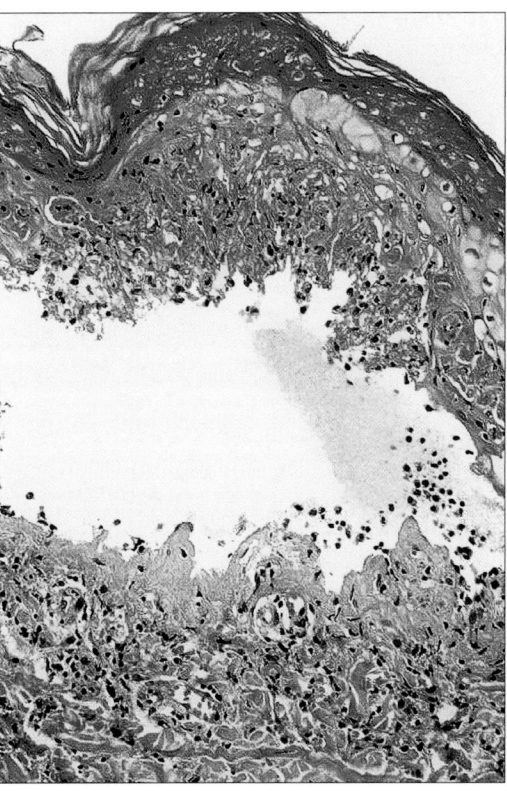

Fig. 6.74 Erythema multiforme: in this example, subepidermal vesiculation is present.

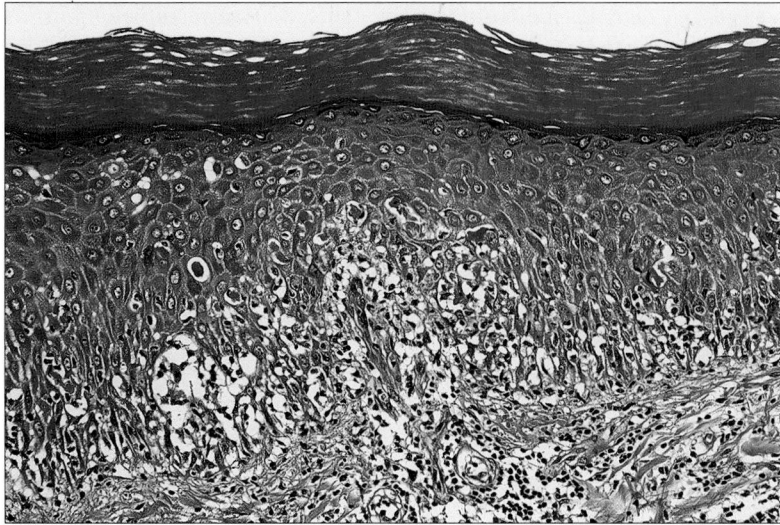

Fig. 6.75
Erythema multiforme: early lesion showing spongiosis, lymphocytic exocytosis and cytoid bodies.

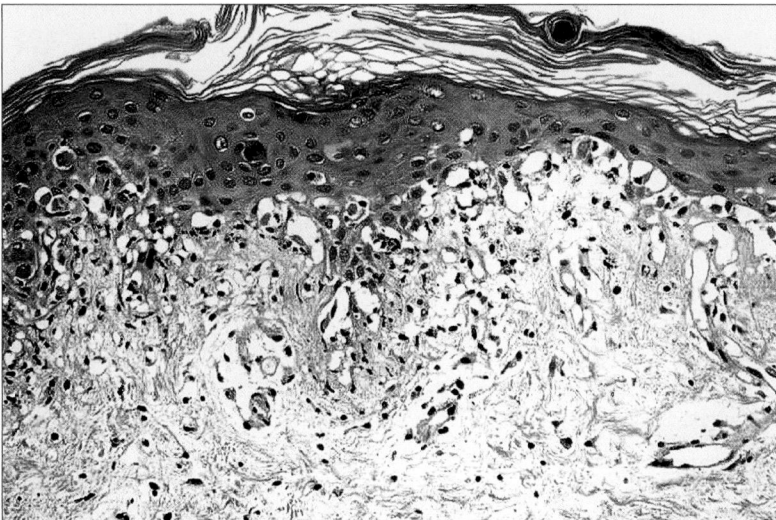

Fig. 6.76
Erythema multiforme: early lesion showing interface change and marked upper dermal edema.

Erythema multiforme may also on occasion be confused with fixed eruption, acute GVHD and subacute cutaneous lupus erythematosus. Clinicopathological correlation will ensure their distinction with ease.

References

1. Côté, B., Weischler, J., Bastuji-Garin, S. et al (1995) Clinicopathologic correlation in erythema multiforme and Stevens Johnson syndrome. *Arch Dermatol*, **131**, 1268–1272.
2. Assier, H., Bastuji-Garin, S., Revuz, J. et al (1995) Erythema multiforme with mucous membrane involvement and Stevens–Johnson syndrome are clinically different disorders with distinct causes. *Arch Dermatol*, **131**, 539–543.
3. Weston, W.L. (1996) What is erythema multiforme? *Pediatr Ann*, **25**, 106–109.
4. Weston, W.L., Brice, S.L., Jester, J.D. et al (1992) Herpes simplex virus in childhood erythema multiforme. *Pediatrics*, **89**, 32–35.
5. Sakurai, M. (1989) Erythema multiforme in children: unusual clinical features with seasonal occurrence. *J Dermatol*, **16**, 361–368.
6. Léauté-Labrèze, C., Lamireau, T., Chawki, D. et al (2000) Diagnosis, classification, and management of erythema multiforme and Stevens–Johnson syndrome. *Arch Dis Child*, **83**, 347–352.
7. Chan, H.L., Stern, R.S., Arndt, K.A. et al (1990) The incidence of erythema multiforme, Stevens–Johnson syndrome, and toxic epidermal necrolysis. *Arch Dermatol*, **126**, 43–47.
8. Huff, J.C., Weston, W.L., Tonnesen, M.G. (1983) Erythema multiforme: a critical review of characteristics, diagnostic criteria and causes. *J Am Acad Dermatol*, **8**, 763–775.
9. Leigh, I.M., Mowbray, J.F., Levene, G.M. et al (1985) Recurrent and continuous erythema multiforme – a clinical and immunological study. *Clin Exp Dermatol*, **10**, 58–67.
10. Huff, J.C., Weston, W.L. (1989) Recurrent erythema multiforme. *Medicine*, **68**, 133–140.
11. Schofield, J.K., Tatnall, F.M., Leigh, I.M. (1993) Recurrent erythema multiforme: clinical features and treatment in a large series of patients. *Br J Dermatol*, **128**, 542–545.
12. Drago, F., Parodi, A., Rebora, A. (1995) Persistent erythema multiforme: report of two new cases and review of literature. *J Am Acad Dermatol*, **33**, 366–369.
13. Ledesma, G.N., McCormack, P.C. (1986) Erythema multiforme. *Clin Dermatol*, **4**, 70–80.
14. Farthing, P.M., Maragou, P., Coates, M. et al (1995) Characteristics of the oral lesions in patients with cutaneous recurrent erythema multiforme. *J Oral Pathol Med*, **24**, 9–13.
15. Delattre, J.Y., Safai, B., Posner, J.B. (1988) Erythema multiforme and Stevens–Johnson syndrome in patients receiving cranial irradiation and phenytoin. *Neurology*, **38**, 194–198.
16. Fleischer, A.B., Rosenthal, D.I., Bernard, S.A. et al (1992) Skin reactions to radiotherapy – a spectrum resembling erythema multiforme: case report and review of the literature. *Cutis*, **49**, 35–39.
17. Orton, P.W., Huff, J.C., Tonnesen, M.G. et al (1984) Detection of a herpes simplex viral antigen in skin lesions of erythema multiforme. *Ann Int Med*, **101**, 48–50.
18. Brice, S.L., Krzemien, D., Weston, W.L. et al (1989) Detection of herpes simplex virus DNA in cutaneous lesions of erythema multiforme. *J Invest Dermatol*, **193**, 183–187.
19. Kokuba, H., Imafuku, S., Huang, S. et al (1998) Erythema multiforme lesions are associated with expression of a herpes simplex virus (HSV) gene and qualitative alterations in the HSV-specific T-cell response. *Br J Dermatol*, **138**, 952–964.
20. Aurelian, L., Kokuba, H., Burnett, J.W. (1998) Understanding the pathogenesis of HSV-associated erythema multiforme. *Dermatology*, **197**, 219–222.
21. Imafuku, S., Kokuba, H., Aurelian, L. et al (1997) Expression of herpes simplex virus DNA fragments located in epidermal keratinocytes and germinative cells is associated with the development of erythema multiforme lesions. *J Invest Dermatol*, **109**, 550–556.
22. Weston, W.L., Morelli, J.G. (1997) Herpes simplex virus-associated erythema multiforme in prepubertal children. *Arch Pediatr Adolesc Med*, **151**, 1014–1016.
23. Brice, S.L., Leahy, M.A., Ong, L. et al (1994) Examination of non-involved skin, previously involved skin and peripheral blood for herpes simplex virus DNA in patients with recurrent herpes-associated erythema multiforme. *J Cutan Pathol*, **21**, 408–412.
24. Kokuba, H., Imafuku, S., Burnett, J.W. et al (1999) Longitudinal study of a patient with herpes-simplex-virus-associated erythema multiforme: viral gene expression and T-cell repertoire usage. *Dermatology*, **198**, 233–242.
25. Colditz, I.G., Watson, D.L. (1992) The effect of cytokines and chemotactic agonists on the migration of T lymphocytes into skin. *Immunology*, **76**, 272–278.
26. Kokuba, H., Aurelian, L., Burnett, J. (1999) Herpes simplex virus associated erythema multiforme (HAEM) is mechanistically distinct from drug-induced erythema multiforme: interferon-gamma is expressed in HAEM lesions and tumor necrosis factor-alpha in drug-induced erythema multiforme lesions. *J Invest Dermatol*, **113**, 808–815.
27. Lepage, V., Douay, C., Mallet, C. et al (1988) Erythema multiforme is associated to HLA-Aw33 and DRw53. *Tissue Antigens*, **32**, 170–175.
28. Khalil, I., Lepage, V., Douay, C. et al (1991) HLA DQB*0301 allele is involved in the susceptibility to erythema multiforme. *J Invest Dermatol*, **97**, 697–700.
29. Schofield, J.K., Tatnall, F.M., Brown, J. et al (1996) Recurrent erythema multiforme: tissue typing in a large series of patients. *Br J Dermatol*, **131**, 532–535.
30. Malo, A., Kampgen, E., Wank, R. (1998) Recurrent herpes simplex virus-induced erythema multiforme: different HLA-DQB1 alleles associate with severe mucous membrane versus skin attacks. *Scand J Immunol*, **47**, 408–411.
31. Ackerman, A.B., Penneys, N.S., Clark, W.H. (1971) Erythema multiforme exudativum: distinctive pathological process. *Br J Dermatol*, **84**, 554–566.
32. Bedi, T.R., Pinkus, H. (1976) Histopathological spectrum of erythema multiforme. *Br J Dermatol*, **95**, 243–250.
33. Orfanos, C.E., Schaumberg-Lever, G., Lever, W.F. (1974) Dermal and epidermal types of erythema multiforme. *Arch Dermatol*, **109**, 682–688.
34. Pierard, J., Whimster, I. (1961) The histological diagnosis of dermatitis herpetiformis, bullous pemphigoid and erythema multiforme. *Br J Dermatol*, **73**, 253–266.
35. Howland, W.W., Golitz, L.E., Weston, W.L. et al (1984) Erythema multiforme: clinical, histopathologic, and immunologic study. *J Am Acad Dermatol*, **10**, 438–446.
36. Rzany, B., Hering, O., Mockenhaupt, M. et al (1996) Histopathological and epidemiological characteristics of patients with erythema exudativum multiforme majus (EEMM), Stevens–Johnson syndrome (SJS) and toxic epidermal necrolysis (TEN). *Br J Dermatol*, **135**, 6–11.
37. Margolis, R.J., Tonnesen, M.G., Harrist, T.J. et al (1983) Lymphocyte subsets and Langerhans' cells/indeterminate cells in erythema multiforme. *J Invest Dermatol*, **81**, 403–406.
38. Zaim, M.T., Giorno, R.C., Golitz, L.E. et al (1987) An immunopathological study of herpes-associated erythema multiforme. *J Cutan Pathol*, **14**, 257–262.
39. Bennion, S.D., Middleton, M.H., David-Bajar, K.M. et al (1995) In three types of interface dermatitis, different patterns of expression of intercellular adhesion molecule-1 (ICAM-1) indicate different triggers of disease. *J Invest Dermatol*, **105**, 71S–79S.

Toxic epidermal necrolysis and Stevens–Johnson syndrome

The original description of toxic epidermal necrolysis included two unrelated conditions:[1]

- the scalded skin syndrome (see p. 872) seen in infants and young children and due to staphylococcal infection with toxin production
- a drug hypersensitivity reaction, predominantly affecting adults, now regarded as the sole representative of this entity.

Clinical features

Classification of a blistering disorder as toxic epidermal necrolysis (Lyell's syndrome) or Stevens–Johnson syndrome is based upon the extent of detached or detachable skin at the worst stage of the illness.[2] In the former condition, 30% or more skin is involved whereas in the latter less than 10% is affected (*Figs 6.77, 6.78*). An intermediate category where 10–30% of the skin is involved has also been recognized.

Toxic epidermal necrolysis and Stevens–Johnson syndrome are very rare conditions, reported incidences ranging from 0.93 to 1.3 cases/million population in Europe and 0.5 in the United States.[3-6] They represent severe drug hypersensitivity reactions except for those instances in which GVHD develops a toxic epidermal necrolysis-like appearance.[4,7] There is no racial predilection and although the elderly are predominantly affected, the conditions may present at any age including children, infants and the newborn.[8–10] In the last group, mucosal lesions may sometimes be the sole manifestation of the disease.[11] Females are affected more often than males (2:1).[10] In children the sex ratio is equal.

Patients typically present with a short prodromal illness of pyrexia, sore throat, muscle ache, headache, anorexia, nausea, vomiting and burning eyes, soon followed by the development of a painful rash most often starting on the face, neck and shoulders before becoming more generalized with trunk and proximal limb accentuation.[10,12,13] The eruption consists of irregular, erythematous and sometimes purpuric or necrotic, flat, atypical target lesions although in some patients an exanthematous, morbilliform eruption is initially seen.[14] Occasionally, typical target lesions overlapping with erythema multiforme may be a feature.[6] In any event, this early stage is soon followed by the development of flaccid, fluid-filled bullae (*Fig. 6.79*). These rapidly ulcerate, leaving painful raw erosions similar to scalding (*Figs 6.80–6.83*). Nikolsky's sign is positive. Eventually, the whole body, with the exception of the hair-bearing scalp, may become affected.

Toxic epidermal necrolysis/Stevens–Johnson syndrome is a multisystem disease. The mucous membranes are affected in all patients and sometimes represent the presenting manifestation.[12] The oropharynx, eyes, genitalia and anus show particular involvement in descending order of frequency.[14] Ocular lesions are especially important, as they are a cause of long-term morbidity in 40–50% of survivors. Patients may manifest conjunctivitis, synechiae, the sicca syndrome, trichiasis and keratitis.[14] Gastrointestinal lesions, esophageal stricture, hepatitis and pancreatitis are occasional manifestations.[15–17] Tracheobronchial involvement is fairly common and adult respiratory distress syndrome is an important and potentially life-threatening complication.[12] Anemia and leukopenia are typically seen.

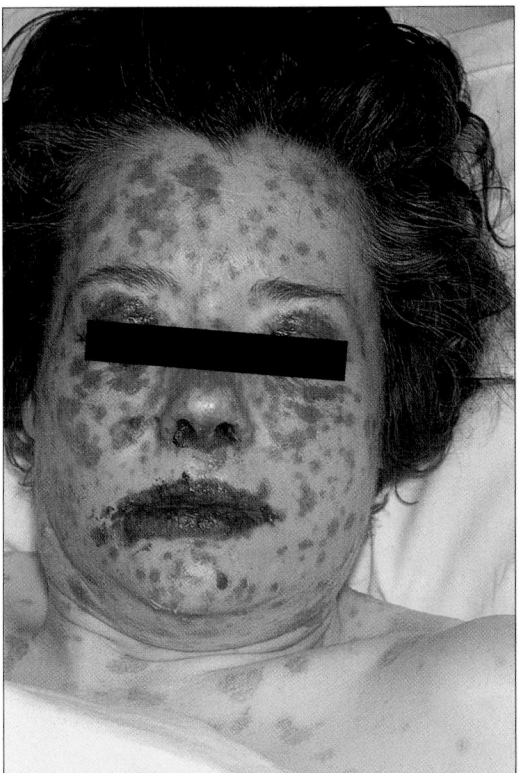

Fig. 6.77
Stevens–Johnson syndrome: this patient developed Stevens–Johnson syndrome following sulfonamide therapy. By courtesy of R.A. Marsden, MD, St George's Hospital, London, UK.

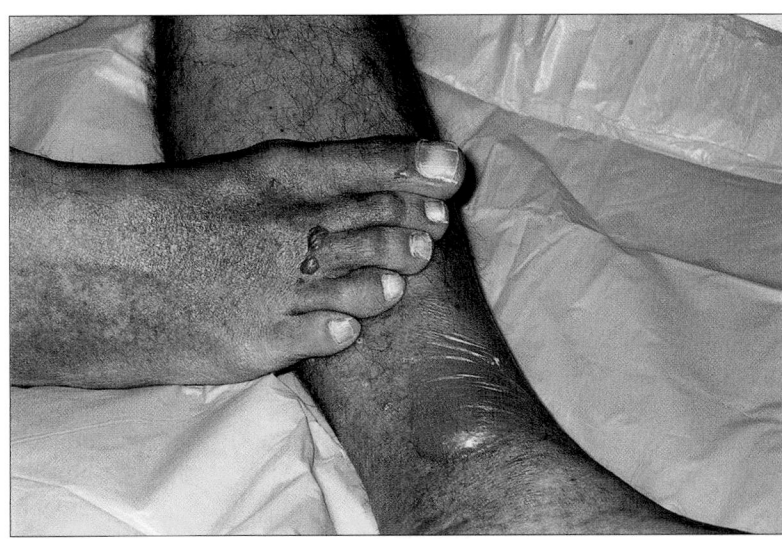

Fig. 6.79
Toxic epidermal necrolysis: early stage showing a large fluid-filled blister. By courtesy of R. Reynolds, MD, Harvard Medial School, Boston, USA.

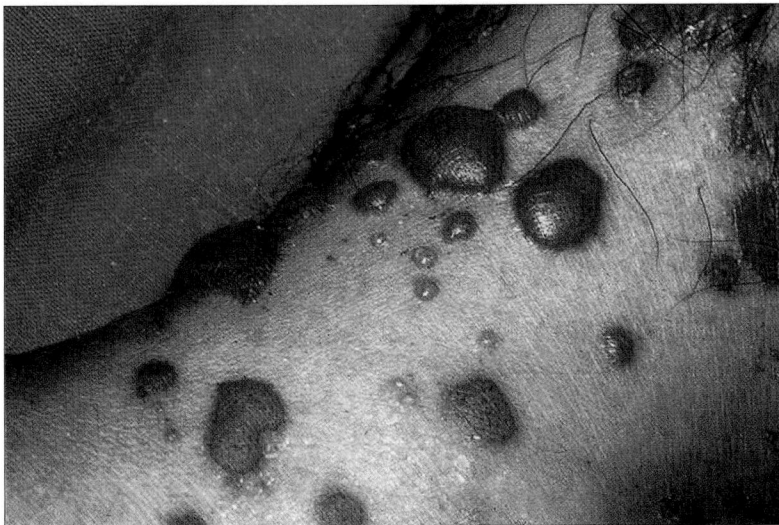

Fig. 6.78
Stevens–Johnson syndrome: this condition is distinguished from toxic epidermal necrolysis by there being less than 10% of the skin involved. Note the tense blisters. By courtesy of the Institute of Dermatology, London, UK.

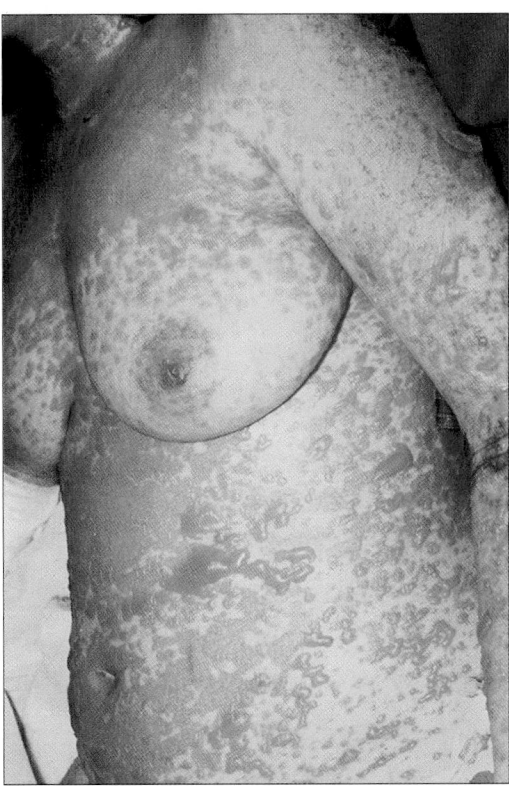

Fig. 6.80
Toxic epidermal necrolysis: there is widespread erythema and numerous blisters are evident. By courtesy of I. Zaki, MD, and S. Dalziel, MD, University Hospital, Queen's Medical Centre, Nottingham, UK.

The mortality of Stevens–Johnson syndrome is approximately 5%, whereas the more extensive skin involvement in toxic epidermal necrolysis is reflected in a higher mortality of up to 40%.[12,16,18,19] Causes of death include sepsis (particularly due to *Staphylococcus aureus* and *Pseudomonas aeruginosa*), heart failure, pulmonary embolism, septic shock, disseminated intravascular coagulation and gastrointestinal bleeding.[14] Increased age, a high proportion of skin loss and deteriorating renal function are all associated with a poor prognosis.[16]

Pathogenesis and histological features

Toxic epidermal necrolysis/Stevens–Johnson syndrome almost always represents an adverse drug reaction[8,12,20] although this is not always reflected in children in whom an infection with *Mycoplasma pneumoniae* has sometimes been implicated.[11] Etiological agents include sulfonamides, anticonvulsants (phenytoin, barbiturates and carbamazepine), antibiotics (aminopenicillins, quinolones and cephalosporins), non-steroidal anti-inflammatory agents (phenylbutazone, oxyphenbutazone, isoxicam and piroxicam) and allopurinol.[12,14] Patients with such adverse reactions may show a positive patch test to the offending drug and lymphocyte transformation may be demonstrable.[20,21]

Toxic epidermal necrolysis may also be a feature of acute GVHD. Although some of these cases are undoubtedly due to an adverse drug reaction, a proportion represents a specific and severe manifestation of acute GVHD. This is associated with a very poor outlook and high mortality.[7]

Toxic epidermal necrolysis/Stevens–Johnson syndrome is an important complication of HIV infection and is seen in up to 1 in 1000 acquired immunodeficiency syndrome (AIDS) patients per year.[22] The high incidence relates in part to the frequent use of sulfonamides in these patients.[23] Patients with systemic lupus erythematosus are also particularly at risk.[10]

Exceptionally, toxic epidermal necrolysis has been documented in adults following an infection including hepatitis A and *M. pneumoniae*.[4,24,25]

The precise mechanisms involved in the pathogenesis of toxic epidermal necrolysis are unclear. Affected patients in sulfonamide-related cases are commonly slow acetylators and detoxification of resultant reactive drug metabolites is impaired.[12,26,27] Although the condition may result from a direct action in some cases, it is thought to be more likely that drug metabolites function as haptens and induce a cellular immune reaction to keratinocytes indirectly. Patients with AIDS are deficient in glutathione and as a result, persistence of such reactive metabolites may explain the increased incidence of this disease in these patients.[27]

Toxic epidermal necrolysis is associated with an increased incidence of HLA-B12: 50% compared with 26% in the normal population.[28]

The histological features are those of variable epidermal apoptosis associated with basal cell hydropic degeneration or subepidermal vesiculation (*Figs 6.84–6.87*).[29,30] Lymphocytic exocytosis may be present and satellite cell necrosis is sometimes apparent.[31,32] Sweat duct epithelium is also involved, and hair follicles may also be affected although much less often (*Fig. 6.88*).[8] A light, predominantly perivascular infiltrate of lymphocytes and macrophages is present in the superficial dermis, which also is commonly edematous (*Figs 6.89, 6.90*). Small numbers of eosinophils may be present.

By immunohistochemistry, the dermal infiltrate consists predominantly of CD4+ T-helper cells whereas in the epidermis CD8+ cells are most numerous.[31,33,34] Histiocytes may be numerous.[35] Langerhans' cells are depleted. Keratinocytes express HLA-DR. Keratinocyte cell death is thought to result from the combined effects of cytolytic enzymes including perforin and cytokines such as soluble TNF-α and IL-6.[13,29,35–37] Fas ligand-mediated apoptosis is believed to be of major importance in the final development of necrolysis.[13,29,35–37]

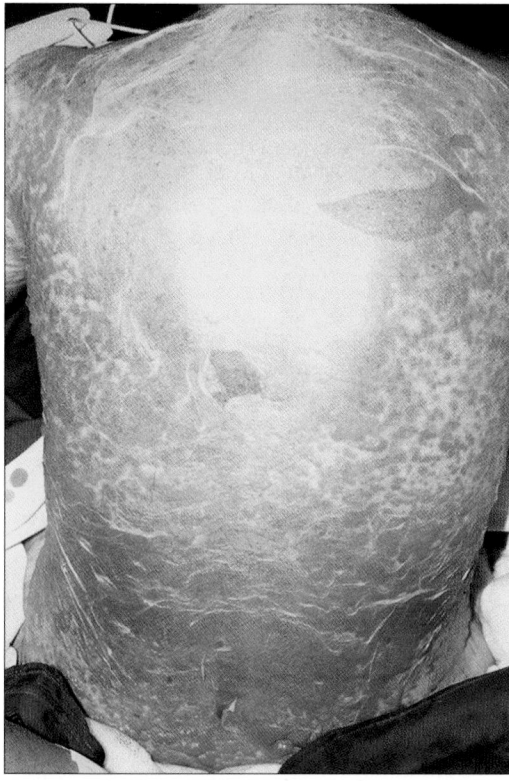

Fig. 6.81
Toxic epidermal necrolysis: note the generalized blistering resembling scalding. By courtesy of I. Zaki, MD, and S. Dalziel, MD, University Hospital, Queen's Medical Centre, Nottingham, UK.

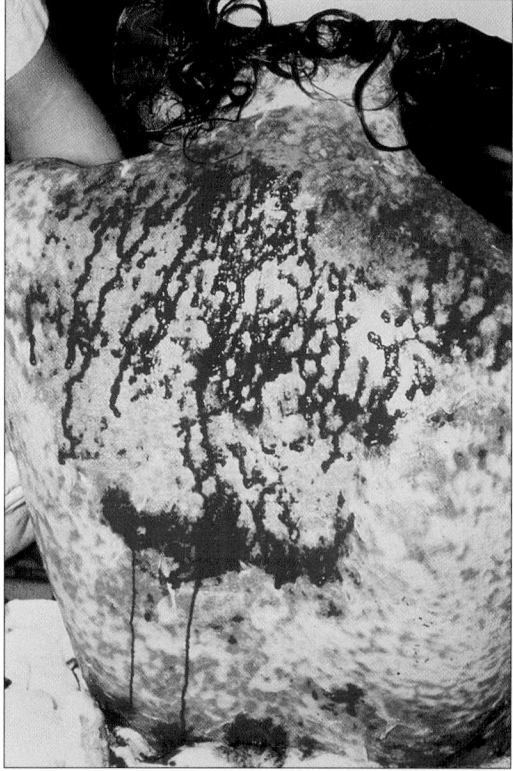

Fig. 6.82
Toxic epidermal necrolysis: this is a serious potentially life-threatening condition. This is a particularly severe example. By courtesy of I. Zaki, MD, and S. Dalziel, MD, University Hospital, Queen's Medical Centre, Nottingham, UK.

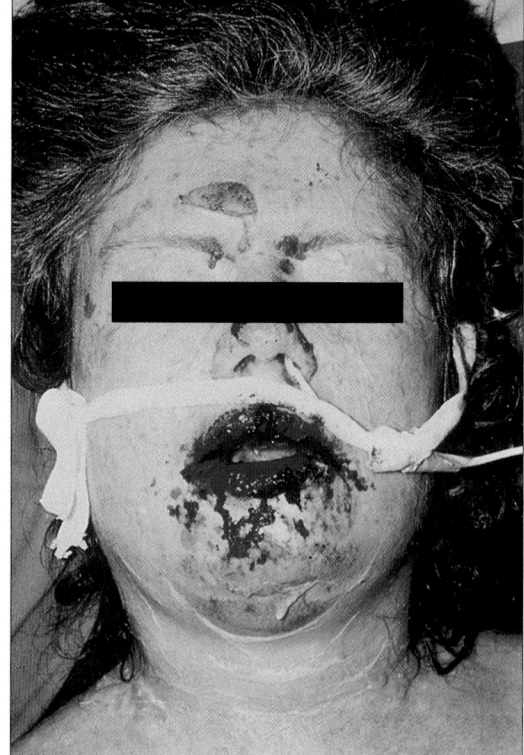

Fig. 6.83
Toxic epidermal necrolysis: mucous membrane involvement is commonly present. By courtesy of I. Zaki, MD, and S. Dalziel, MD, University Hospital, Queen's Medical Centre, Nottingham, UK.

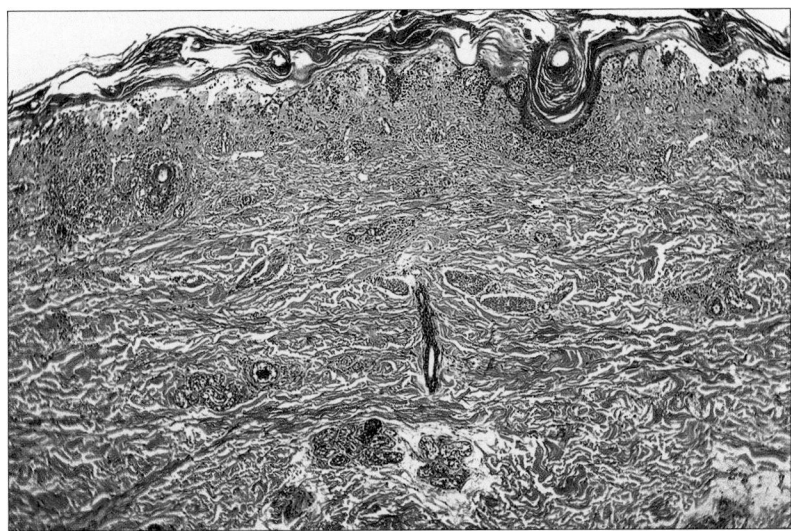

Fig. 6.84
Toxic epidermal necrolysis: scanning view showing subepidermal blistering.

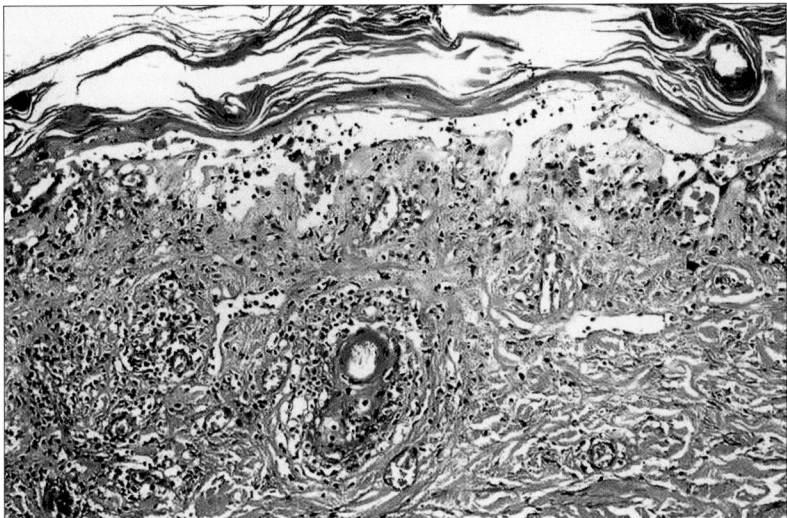

Fig. 6.85
Toxic epidermal necrolysis: the roof of the blister is necrotic. Note the preservation of the dermal papillae.

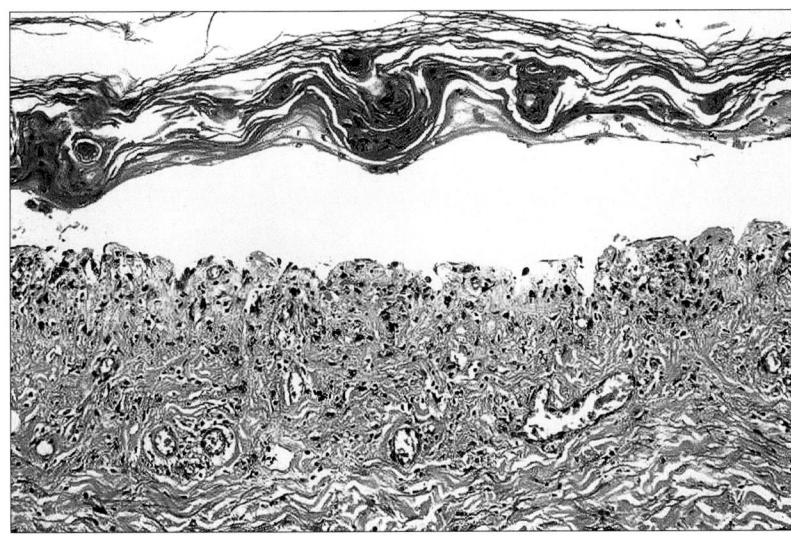

Fig. 6.86
Toxic epidermal necrolysis: in this example there is a cell-free subepidermal blister.

Differential diagnosis

Staphylococcal scalded skin syndrome is an important differential diagnosis. The typical histological finding of a subcorneal pustule in this condition makes the distinction easy.

Toxic epidermal necrolysis/Stevens–Johnson syndrome may sometimes be indistinguishable from severe erythema multiforme. Marked lymphocytic exocytosis, apoptosis predominantly affecting the lower epidermis, intense, lichenoid dermal chronic inflammation with

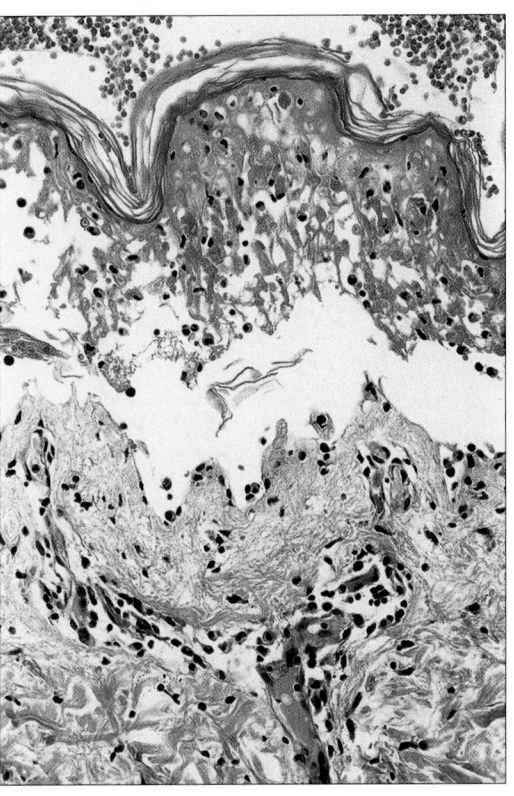

Fig. 6.87
Toxic epidermal necrolysis: high power view showing necrosis of the full thickness of the roof of the blister.

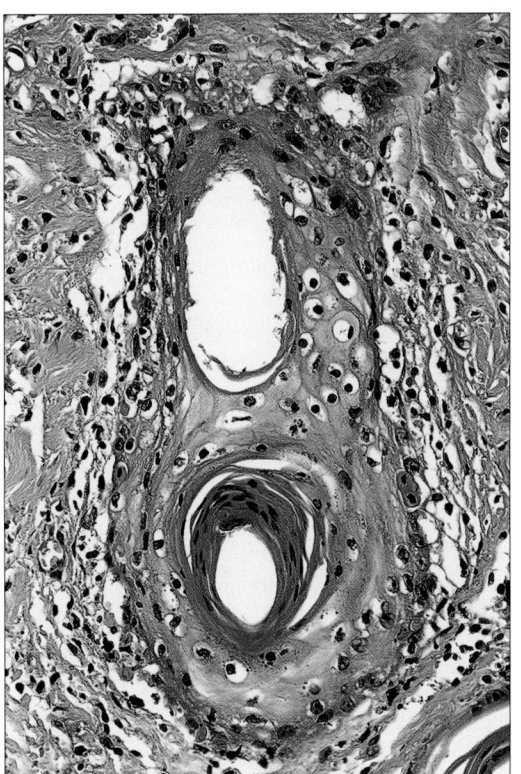

Fig. 6.88
Toxic epidermal necrolysis: follicular involvement showing basal cell hydropic degeneration and apoptosis.

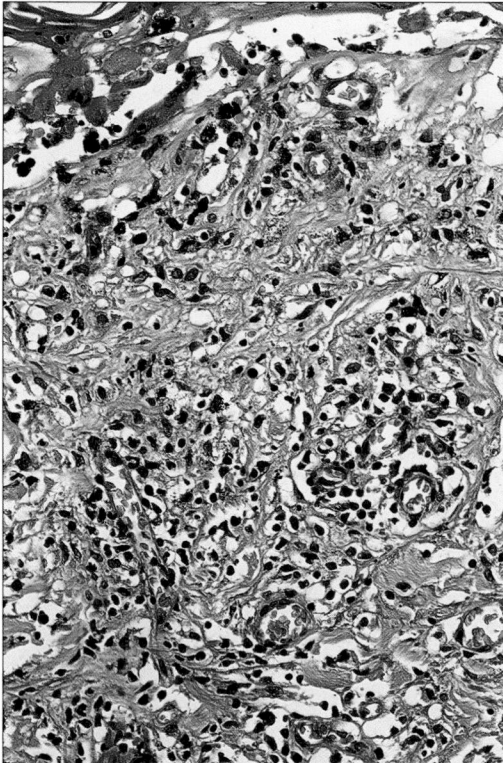

Fig. 6.89
Toxic epidermal
necrolysis: there
is a perivascular
lymphohistiocytic
infiltrate.

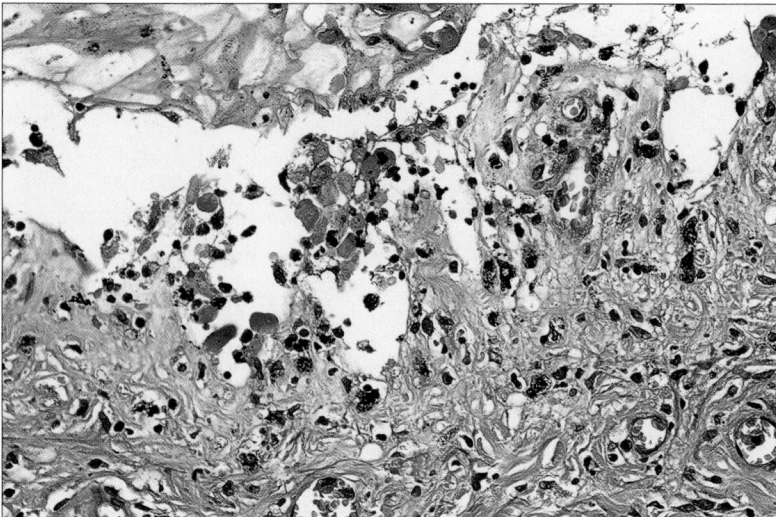

Fig. 6.90
Toxic epidermal necrolysis: note the apoptosis and pigment incontinence.

extension along the superficial and deep vascular plexuses and prominent erythrocyte extravasation are more in favor of erythema multiforme.[30,38] This histological distinction is also mirrored to some extent by the etiology. Thus those cases that result from an infection tend to be more inflammatory than those that represent an adverse drug reaction in which the changes are predominantly epidermal.[38] The presence of eosinophils does not seem to distinguish between drug- and infection-related causes within this histological spectrum.[30]

Toxic epidermal necrolysis resulting from an adverse drug effect and that presenting in a background of severe GVHD are indistinguishable.

References

1. Lyell, A. (1956) Toxic epidermal necrolysis: an eruption resembling scalding of the skin. *Br J Dermatol*, **68**, 355–361.
2. Bastuji-Garin, S., Rzany, B., Stern, R.S. et al (1993) Clinical classification of cases of toxic epidermal necrolysis, Stevens–Johnson syndrome, and erythema multiforme. *Arch Dermatol*, **129**, 92–96.
3. Böttiger, L.E., Strandberg, I., Westerholm, B. (1975) Drug-induced febrile mucocutaneous syndrome. *Acta Med Scand*, **198**, 229–233.
4. Roujeau, J.-C., Guillaume, J.-C., Fabre, J-P. et al (1990) Toxic epidermal necrolysis (Lyell syndrome): incidence and drug etiology in France, 1981–1985. *Arch Dermatol*, **126**, 37–42.
5. Schöpf, E., Stühmer, A., Rzany, B. et al (1991) Toxic epidermal necrolysis and Stevens–Johnson syndrome. An epidemiologic study from West Germany. *Arch Dermatol*, **127**, 839–842.
6. Chan, H.L., Stern, R.S., Arndt, K.A. et al (1990) The incidence of erythema multiforme, Stevens–Johnson syndrome, and toxic epidermal necrolysis. *Arch Dermatol*, **126**, 43–47.
7. Villada, G., Roujeau, J.C., Cordonnier, C. et al (1990) Toxic epidermal necrolysis after bone marrow transplantation: study of nine cases. *J Am Acad Dermatol*, **23**, 870–875.
8. Roujeau, J-C., Chosidow, O., Saiag, P. et al (1990) Toxic epidermal necrolysis (Lyell syndrome). *J Am Acad Dermatol*, **23**, 1039–1058.
9. Ringheanu, M., Laude, T.A. (2000) Toxic epidermal necrolysis in children – an update. *Clin Pediatr*, **39**, 687–694.
10. Wolkenstein, P., Revuz, J. (2000) Toxic epidermal necrolysis. *Dermatol Clin*, **18**, 485–495.
11. Léauté-Labrèze, C., Lamireau, T., Chawki, D. et al (2000) Diagnosis, classification, and management of erythema multiforme and Stevens–Johnson syndrome. *Arch Dis Child*, **83**, 347–352.
12. Revuz, J.E., Roujeau, J.C. (1996) Advances in toxic epidermal necrolysis. *Semin Cutan Med Surg*, **15**, 258–266.
13. Weightman, W. (1996) Toxic epidermal necrolysis. *Australas J Dermatol*, **37**, 167–177.
14. Lyell, A. (1967) A review of toxic epidermal necrolysis in Britain. *Br J Dermatol*, **79**, 662–671.
15. Herman, T.E., Kushner, D.C., Cleveland, R.H. (1984) Esophageal stricture secondary to drug-induced toxic epidermal necrolysis. *Pediatr Radiol*, **14**, 439–440.
16. Revuz, J., Penso, D., Roujeau, J-C. et al (1987) Toxic epidermal necrolysis: clinical findings and prognostic factors in 87 patients. *Arch Dermatol*, **213**, 1160–1165.
17. Tagami, H., Iwatsuki, K. (1986) Elevated serum amylase in toxic epidermal necrolysis. *Br J Dermatol*, **115**, 250–251.
18. Snyder, R., Elias, P.M. (1983) Toxic epidermal necrolysis and staphylococcal skin syndrome. *Dermatol Clin*, **1**, 235–248.
19. Roujeau, J-C. (1997) Severe drug-induced blistering disorders. *Rev Rheum*, **64**, 5–9.
20. Guillaume, J.-C., Roujeau, J.-C., Revuz, J. et al (1987) The culprit drugs in 87 cases of toxic epidermal necrolysis (Lyell's syndrome). *Arch Dermatol*, **123**, 1166–1170.
21. Houwerzijl, J., De Gast, G.C., Nater, J.P. et al (1997) Lymphocyte stimulation tests and patch tests in carbamazepine hypersensitivity. *Clin Exp Immunol*, **29**, 272–277.
22. Mockenhaupt, M., Schöpf, E. (1996) Epidemiology of drug-induced severe skin reactions. *Semin Cutan Med Surg*, **15**, 236–243.
23. Porteous, D.M., Berger, T.G. (1991) Severe cutaneous drug reactions: Stevens–Johnson syndrome and toxic epidermal necrolysis in human immunodeficiency virus infection. *Arch Dermatol*, **197**, 740–741.
24. Werblowsky-Constantini, N., Livshin, R., Burstein, M. (1989) Toxic epidermal necrolysis associated with acute cholestatic viral hepatitis A. *J Clin Gastroenterol*, **11**, 691–693.
25. Fournier, S., Bastuji-Garin, S., Mentec, H. et al (1995) Toxic epidermal necrolysis associated with Mycoplasma pneumoniae infection. *Eur J Clin Microbiol Infect Dis*, **14**, 558–559.
26. Wolkenstein, P., Carrière, V., Charue, D. et al (1995) A slow acylator genotype is a risk factor for sulphonamide-induced toxic epidermal necrolysis and Stevens–Johnson syndrome. *Pharmacogenetics*, **5**, 255–258.
27. Wolkenstein, P., Charue, D., Laurent, P. et al (1995) Metabolic predisposition to cutaneous adverse drug reactions: role in toxic epidermal necrolysis caused by sulfonamides and anticonvulsants. *Arch Dermatol*, **131**, 544–551.
28. Roujeau, J-C., Huynh, T.N., Bracq, C. et al (1987) Genetic susceptibility to toxic epidermal necrolysis. *Arch Dermatol*, **123**, 1171–1173.
29. Paul, C., Wolkenstein, P., Adle, H. et al (1996) Apoptosis as a mechanism of keratinocyte death in toxic epidermal necrolysis. *Br J Dermatol*, **134**, 710–714.
30. Rzany, B., Hering, O., Mockenhaupt, M. et al (1996) Histopathological and epidemiological characteristics of patients with erythema exsudativum multiforme majus (EEMM), Stevens–Johnson syndrome (SJS) and toxic epidermal necrolysis (TEN). *Br J Dermatol*, **135**, 6–11.
31. Villada, G., Roujeau, J-C., Clérici, T. et al (1992) Immunopathology of toxic epidermal necrolysis. Keratinocytes, HLA-DR expression, Langerhans' cells and mononuclear cells: an immunopathologic study of five cases. *Arch Dermatol*, **128**, 50–53.
32. Breathnach, S.M., McGibbon, D.H., Ive, F.E. et al (1982) Carbamazepine (Tegretol) and toxic epidermal necrolysis: report of three cases with histopathological observations. *Clin Exp Dermatol*, 7, 585–591.
33. Miyauchi, H., Hosokawa, H., Akaeda, T. et al (1991) T-cell subsets in drug-induced toxic epidermal necrolysis. *Arch Dermatol*, **127**, 851–855.
34. Correia, O., Delgado, L., Ramos, J.P. et al (1993) Cutaneous T-cell recruitment in toxic epidermal necrolysis. Further evidence of CD8+ recruitment. *Arch Dermatol*, **129**, 466–468.
35. Paquet, P., Nikkels, A., Arrese, J.E. et al (1994) Macrophages and tumor necrosis factor α in toxic epidermal necrolysis. *Arch Dermatol*, **130**, 605–608.
36. Paquet, P., Pierard, G.E. (1998) Soluble fractions of tumor necrosis factor-alpha, interleukin-6 and of their receptors in toxic epidermal necrolysis: a comparison with second degree burns. *Int J Mol Med*, **1**, 459–462.
37. French, L.E., Tschopp, J. (2000) Fas-mediated cell death in toxic epidermal necrolysis and graft-versus-host disease: potential for therapeutic inhibition. *Schweiz Med Wochenschr*, **130**, 1656–1661.
38. Côté, B., Weischler, J., Bastuji-Garin, S. et al (1995) Clinicopathologic correlation in erythema multiforme and Stevens Johnson syndrome. *Arch Dermatol*, **131**, 1268–1272.

Paraneoplastic pemphigus

Erythema multiforme-like histological features are an integral feature of paraneoplastic pemphigus. This topic is considered on page 152.

Interface dermatitis of HIV infection

Interface dermatitis has been described as a reaction pattern in patients with HIV infection. This may represent a drug reaction. It is considered on page 244.

Poikiloderma

Poikiloderma (Gr. *poikilos*, spotted, mottled, varied) is a clinical descriptive term applied to skin showing slight scaling, atrophy, variable pigmentation and telangiectasia. It is a feature of a number of conditions including lupus erythematosus, dermatomyositis, large plaque parapsoriasis, poikiloderma of Civatte, poikiloderma congenitale,

Bloom's syndrome, Cockayne's syndrome, dyskeratosis congenita and DNA mitochondrial syndrome-associated poikiloderma. Histologically, poikiloderma is characterized by hyperkeratosis, epidermal atrophy with basal cell liquefactive degeneration, pigmentary incontinence, telangiectasia and a variable superficial dermal lymphohistiocytic infiltrate (*Figs 6.91, 6.92*).

Lupus erythematosus and dermatomyositis

Interface dermatitis is characteristic of both of these conditions. They are discussed in full on pages 775 and 825, respectively.

Large plaque parapsoriasis

Large plaque parapsoriasis is an old term synonymous with plaque stage mycosis fungoides and is discussed in full on page 1360.

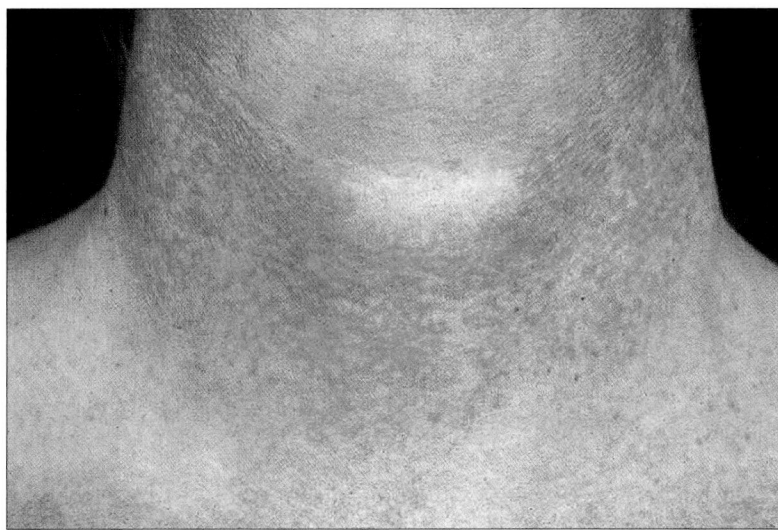

Fig. 6.93
Poikiloderma of Civatte: note the mottled hyperpigmentation in a characteristic distribution. By courtesy of the Institute of Dermatology, London, UK.

Poikiloderma of Civatte

Poikiloderma of Civatte (poikiloderma of head and neck, Derbyshire neck) refers to a fairly common progressive and irreversible disorder in which typical poikiloderma presents in a photodistribution, predominantly affecting the sides of the face and neck and the 'V' of the chest (*Fig. 6.93*).[1-4] Middle-aged and elderly women are predominantly affected, raising the possibility of diminished estrogen as being of etiological importance.[4] Recently familial cases have been documented.[4]

Histological features

In addition to the typical features of poikiloderma, solar elastosis is often very marked.[3] In some biopsies, however, the appearances can be very non-specific.

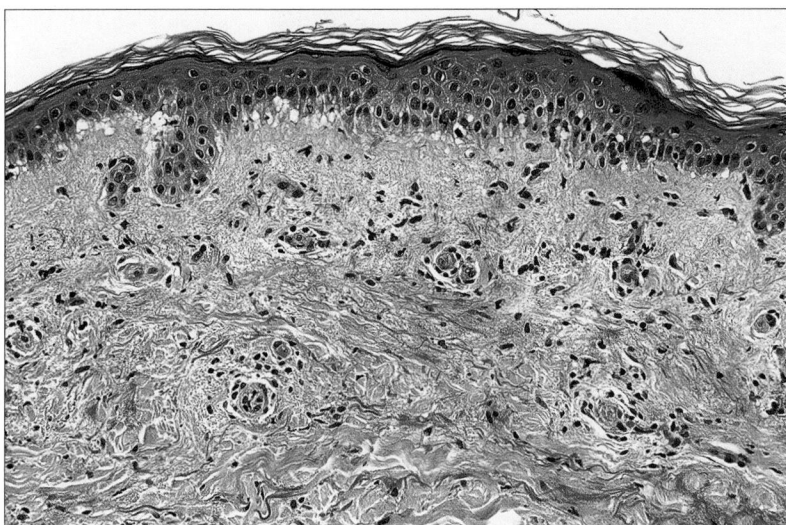

Fig. 6.91
Poikiloderma: there is basal cell hydropic degeneration and a very light perivascular lymphohistiocytic infiltrate.

References

1. Graham, R. (1989) What is poikiloderma of Civatte? *Practitioner*, **233**, 1210.
2. Katoulis, A.C., Sboukis, D., Stavrianeas, N.G. (1995) Poikiloderma of Civatte. *Hellen Dermatol Venereol Rev*, **6**, 165–173.
3. Stavrianeas, N.G., Katoulis, A.C., Koumantaki-Mathioudaki, E. et al (1997) A histopathological approach to the pathogenesis of Civatte's poikiloderma. *Les Nuovelles Dermatologiques*, **16** (Suppl. 4), S13.
4. Katoulis, A.C., Stavrianeas, N.G., Georgala, S. et al (1999) Familial cases of poikiloderma of Civatte: genetic implications in pathogenesis? *Clin Exp Dermatol*, **24**, 385–387.

Mitochondrial DNA syndrome-associated poikiloderma

Photodistributed poikiloderma has been documented in a number of mitochondrial DNA syndromes, particularly Pearson's syndrome, which also includes failure to thrive, exocrine pancreas insufficiency, severe renal tubule dysfunction and bone marrow suppression.[1] Other dermatological manifestations of mitochondrial DNA syndromes include acrocyanosis, dry brittle hair, vitiligo, hyperpigmentation and anhidrosis.[2-7]

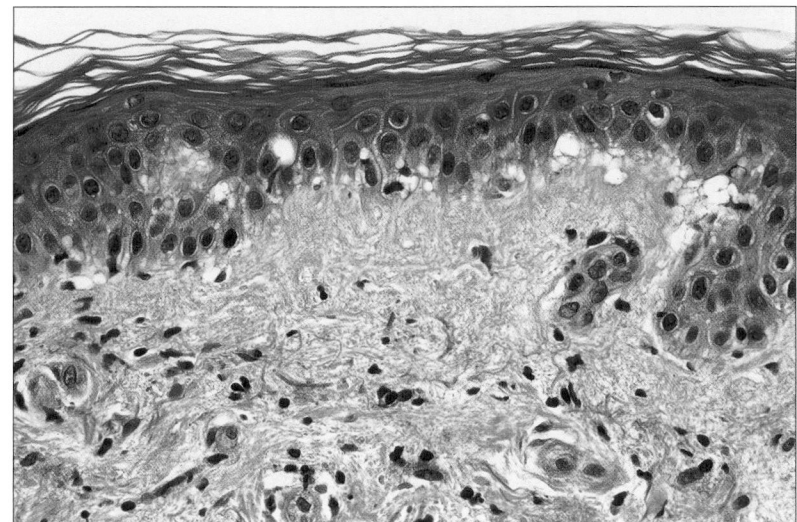

Fig. 6.92
Poikiloderma: close-up view.

References

1. Rötig, A., Cormier, V., Blanche, S. et al (1990) Pearson's marrow-pancreas syndrome: a multisystem mitochondrial disorder in infancy. *J Clin Invest*, **86**, 1601–1608.
2. Simonsz, H., Barlocher, K., Rotig, A. (1992) Kearn's-Sayre's syndrome developing in a boy who survived Pearson's syndrome caused by mitochondrial DNA deletion. *Doc Ophthalmol*, **82**, 73–79.
3. Rötig, A., Blessis, J-L., Romero, N. et al (1992) Maternally inherited duplication of the mitochondrial genome in a syndrome of proximal tubulopathy, diabetes mellitus, and cerebellar ataxia. *Am J Hum Genet*, **50**, 364–370.
4. Niaudet, P., Heidet, L., Munnich, A. et al (1994) Deletion of the mitochondrial DNA in a case of de Toni-Debré-Fanconi syndrome and Pearson syndrome. *Pediatr Nephrol*, **8**, 164–168.

5.   Haferkamp, O., Scheuerle, A., Sclenk, R. et al (1994) Mitochondrial complex I and III mutations and neutral-lipid storage in activated macrophages and neutrophils: a case presenting with necrotizing myopathy, poikiloderma atrophicans vasculare, and xanthogranulomatous bursitis. *Hum Pathol*, 25, 419–423.
6.   Rötig, A., Lehnert, A., Rustin, P. et al (1995) Kidney involvement in mitochondrial disorders. *Adv Nephrol*, 24, 367–378.
7.   Flynn, M.K., Wee, S.A., Lane, A.T. (1998) Skin manifestations of mitochondrial DNA syndromes: case report and review. *J Am Acad Dermatol*, 39, 819–823.

Rothmund–Thomson syndrome

Clinical features

This syndrome, which has been described in Asians and blacks as well as Caucasians, has an autosomal recessive mode of inheritance. In contrast to the earlier finding of an equal sex incidence, the more recent literature suggests a predilection for males (2:1).[1,2] It usually presents between the third and sixth months of life (hence the term 'poikiloderma congenitale') as a reticulated, erythematous rash – sometimes described as marmoreal (L. *marmor*, marble) – on the face, which eventually spreads to involve the extremities and the buttocks (*Figs 6.94–6.96*).[2] The trunk and flexural aspects are usually spared.[1] Affected infants are photosensitive and therefore there is often a history of sun exposure before the development of skin lesions.[3,4] This is later replaced by reticular, linear or punctate foci of atrophy.[4] Telangiectasia is present and areas of hypo- and hyperpigmentation may be noted. The poikilodermatous change is seen most frequently at sun-exposed sites.[1]

A variety of other manifestations may be observed, including variable alopecia particularly involving the scalp, eyebrows and eyelashes, and seen most often in females. This is present in up to 80% of patients.[1] Gastrointestinal problems including chronic emesis and diarrhea may be seen in infancy.[2] Juvenile, subcapsular (unilateral or bilateral) cataracts are common and skeletal abnormalities include short stature, osteopenia, pathological fractures, dislocations, irregular metaphyses, abnormal trabeculation and stippled ossification of the patellae.[2] Small hands with shortened digits are frequently seen.[5] Frontal bossing, saddle nose and prognathism are characteristic.[1] Absent or malformed radii are seen in 10–20% of patients and bifid or absent thumb may also be present.[1,2,6]

Nail dystrophy, dental abnormalities (particularly conical-shaped teeth with caries) and hypogonadism may also be detected. Hyperkeratotic warty or verrucous lesions sometimes develop on the extensor surfaces, particularly overlying joints and especially the feet and hands.[6] While occasionally reported, mental retardation is not usually a feature of this syndrome.[1] The disease is associated with the development of cutaneous squamous cell carcinoma and more rarely basal cell carcinoma.[2,4] Bowen's disease has also been described.[7]

There is also an increased risk of internal malignancies, particularly tibial osteosarcoma and multicentric osteosarcoma (7–32%).[1,2,8–10] An association with duodenal stenosis and annular pancreas has been described in one patient.[11] The life span of the patient, however, is generally normal.

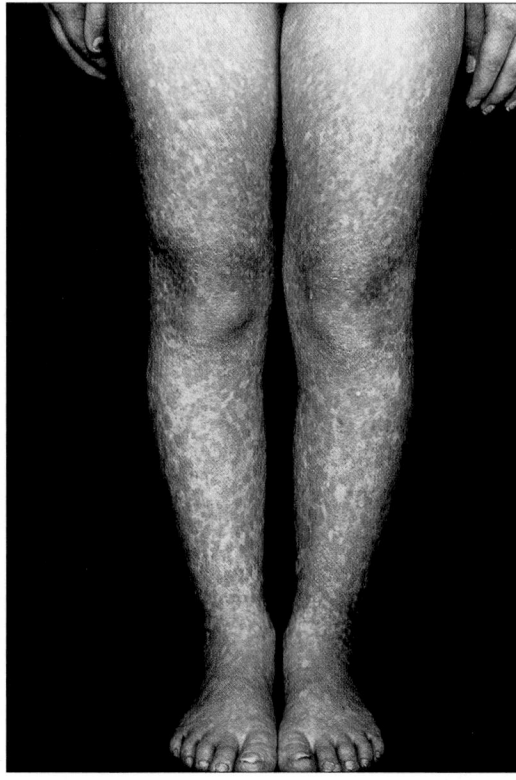

Fig. 6.95
Rothmund–Thomson syndrome: there is symmetrical involvement of the legs. By courtesy of the Institute of Dermatology, London, UK.

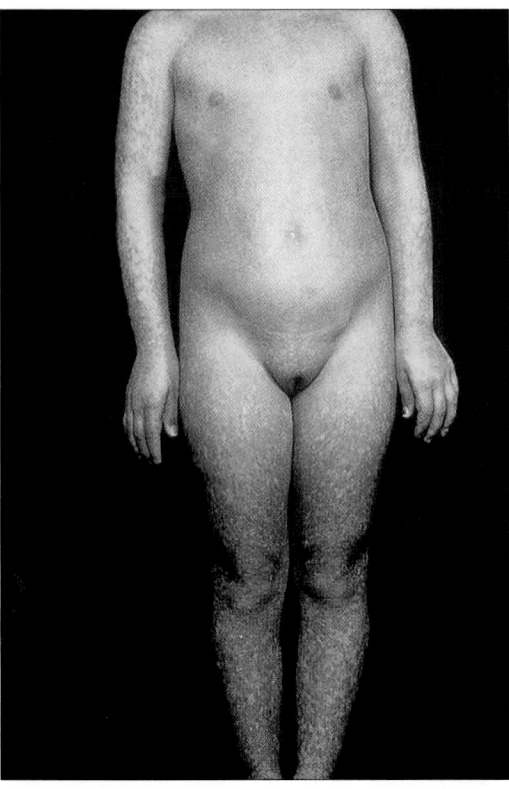

Fig. 6.94
Rothmund–Thomson syndrome: there is a marked mottled hyperpigmentation predominantly affecting the peripheries. By courtesy of the Institute of Dermatology, London, UK.

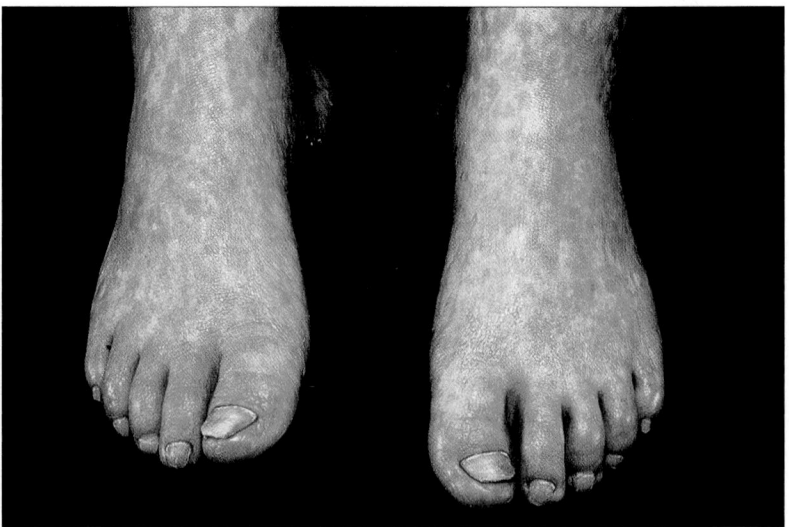

Fig. 6.96
Rothmund–Thomson syndrome: there is atrophy in addition to hyperpigmentation. By courtesy of the Institute of Dermatology, London, UK.

Pathogenesis and histological features

Rothmund–Thomson syndrome in some patients at least has been shown to be associated with a mutation in the *RECQ4* gene, a member of the DNA helicase family (see Bloom's syndrome).[9,12,13] Cytogenetic analysis has revealed mosaicism in a subpopulation including trisomy 8.[2] The underlying defect in Rothmund–Thomson syndrome is unknown. While most investigations have failed to demonstrate abnormal sensitivity to UVA or UVB, there have been occasional recent reports of reduced unscheduled DNA synthesis following irradiation of cultured fibroblasts with UVB and UVC.[3,14]

The histological features of poikiloderma include hyperkeratosis, epidermal atrophy, liquefactive degeneration of the basal epidermal cells and telangiectasia. Pigmentary incontinence may be present and a perivascular chronic inflammatory cell infiltrate is sometimes evident in the superficial dermis. The latter may also show elastic tissue fragmentation and depletion or absence of cutaneous appendages.[1] The squamous cell carcinomas show typical features.

An examination of scalp has revealed hypopigmented vellus hairs without cortices.[6]

References

1. Vennos, E.E.M., Collins, M., James, W.D. (1992) Rothmund–Thomson syndrome: review of the world literature. *J Am Acad Dermatol*, 27, 750–762.
2. Wang, L.L., Levy, M.L., Lewis, R.A. et al (2001) Clinical manifestations in a cohort of 41 Rothmund–Thomson syndrome patients. *Am J Med Genet*, 102, 11–17.
3. Shinya, A., Nishigori, C., Moriwaki, S.I. et al (1993) A case of Rothmund–Thomson syndrome with reduced DNA repair capacity. *Arch Dermatol*, 129, 332–336.
4. Berg, E., Chuang, T.Y., Cripps, D. (1987) Rothmund–Thomson syndrome. *J Am Acad Dermatol*, 17, 332–338.
5. Tailor, W.B. (1957) Rothmund's syndrome, Thomson's syndrome. *Arch Dermatol*, 75, 236–244.
6. Roth, D.N., Campisano, L.C., Callen, J.P.C. et al (1989) Rothmund–Thomson syndrome: a case report. *Pediatr Dermatol*, 6, 321–324.
7. Haneke, E., Gutschmidt, E. (1979) Premature multiple Bowen's disease in poikiloderma congenitale with warty hyperkeratoses. *Dermatologica*, 158, 384–388.
8. Judge, M.R., Kilby, A., Harper, J.I. (1993) Rothmund–Thomson syndrome and osteosarcoma. *Br J Dermatol*, 129, 723–725.
9. Lindor, N.M., Furuichi, Y., Kitao, S. et al (2000) Rothmund–Thomson syndrome due to *RECQ4* helicase mutations: report and clinical and molecular comparisons with Bloom syndrome and Werner syndrome. *Am J Med Genet*, 90, 223–228.
10. el-Khoury, J.M., Haddad, S.N., Atallah, N.G. (1997) Osteosarcomatosis with Rothmund–Thomson syndrome. *Br J Radiol*, 70, 215–218.
11. Blaustein, H.S., Stevens, A.W., Stevens, P.D. et al (1993) Rothmund–Thomson syndrome associated with annular pancreas and duodenal stenosis. *Pediatr Dermatol*, 10, 159–163.
12. Kitao, S., Shimamoto, A., Goto, M. et al (1999) Mutations in *RECQL4* cause a subset of cases of Rothmund–Thomson syndrome. *Nat Genet*, 22, 82–84.
13. Wang, L.L., Levy, M.L., Lewis, R.A. et al (2000) Evidence for genetic heterogeneity in Rothmund–Thomson syndrome. *Am J Hum Genet*, 67 (Suppl. 2), A2107.
14. Cleaver, J.E. (1970) DNA damage and repair in light sensitive human skin disease. *J Invest Dermatol*, 54, 181–195.

Bloom's syndrome

This rare chromosomal instability syndrome (also known as congenital telangiectatic erythema with dwarfism) has an autosomal recessive mode of inheritance and is particularly seen in East European (Ashkenazi) Jews. When found in non-Jews, there is a high incidence of parental consanguinity. It represents a genetically homogenous single locus disease unassociated with any apparent heterogeneity.[1]

Clinical features

There is a characteristic appearance with microcephaly, dolichocephaly and small, narrow 'pinched' facies and stunted growth leading to severe dwarfism.[2,3] An erythematous rash with telangiectasia develops predominantly on the face (in particular the 'butterfly' area) and is exacerbated by sunlight (*Fig. 6.97*). The rash may also affect the backs of the hands and forearms and typically develops in infancy. Café-au-lait spots are a common manifestation and discrete areas of hypopigmentation are usual.[3] A peculiar high-pitched, squeaky (so-called 'Mickey Mouse') voice is sometimes a feature.[4] Male infertility is common.[3] Patients may suffer impaired concentration, short-term memory and general mental organizational disability.[4]

Bloom's syndrome is typified by an inherent propensity to chromosomal abnormalities, in particular, exchanges between sister chromatids. There is an associated increased incidence of most malignancies, but especially acute leukemia, non-Hodgkin's lymphoma, colon carcinoma, breast carcinoma and cutaneous squamous cell carcinoma. Patients are prone to develop multiple tumors, which often develop at an early age (third decade). They may also suffer immunodeficiency (diminished IgG, IgA, IgM) and are therefore at an increased risk of childhood infections, pulmonary infections and chronic lung disease.[4,5] There is also an increased risk of adult onset-like diabetes mellitus.[6]

Pathogenesis and histological features

The gene for Bloom's syndrome, which has been mapped to 15q21.3, is a member of the RecQ helicase protein family, responsible for unwinding DNA and RNA.[7–13] It has been identified as representing part of the BRCA1-associated genome surveillance complex, which is mutated in families with hereditary breast cancer.[14] The protein functions as a 3´–5´ DNA helicase.[10] DNA helicases have essential roles in genetic recombination, transcription, DNA replication and repair.[13] Mutation of the *BLM* gene results in genomic instability. Bloom's syndrome is associated with increased sensitivity to alkylating agents, increased spontaneous chromosome breakages, increased interchromatid exchange (including sister chromatid exchange, 6–10-fold), increased somatic cell mutation frequency and reduced replication fork elongation rate.[9] Mutations include missense, nonsense, frameshift and genomic deletions, most of which result in premature translation terminations and resultant defective Bloom's syndrome protein with impaired function.[12] Multiple defective nuclear enzymes including DNA ligase I have been identified.[15] Monosomy 7 and deletions of the long arm of chromosome 7 are found in the majority of patients with myeloid leukemia.[16]

The cutaneous lesions are typified by a lupus erythematosus-like histology. There is epidermal atrophy accompanied by liquefactive degeneration of the basal layer with cytoid body formation. A lymphohistiocytic infiltrate is present in the superficial dermis. Telangiectatic blood vessels are evident.

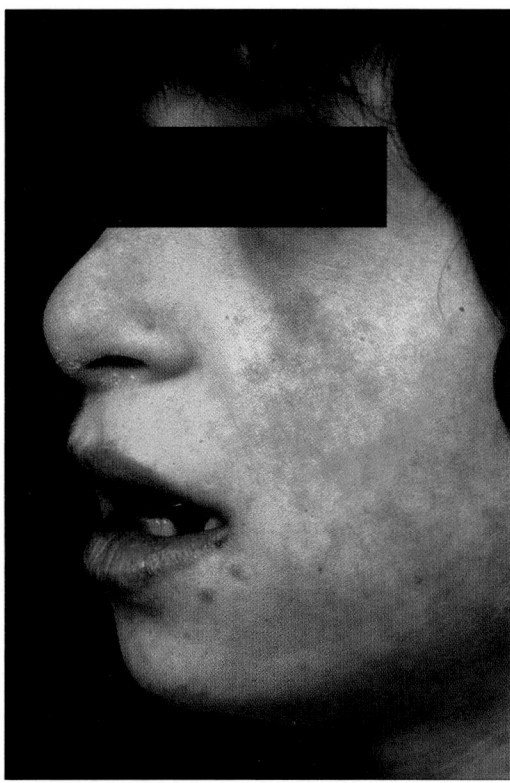

Fig. 6.97
Bloom's syndrome: characteristic facies includes 'pinched' features. Marbled erythema of the cheek and crusted lesions involving the lower lip. By courtesy of D. Atherton, MD, Institute of Dermatology and Children's Hospital at Great Ormond Street, London, UK.

References

1. German, J. (1995) Bloom's syndrome. *Dermatol Clin*, **13**, 7–18.
2. German, J. (1993) Bloom's syndrome: a mendelian prototype of somatic mutational disease. *Medicine*, **72**, 393–406.
3. German, J., Passarge, E. (1989) Bloom's syndrome. XII. Report from the registry for 1987. *Clin Genet*, **35**, 57–69.
4. Passarge, E. (1991) Bloom's syndrome: the German experience. *Ann Genet*, **34**, 179–197.
5. Nicotera, T.M. (1991) Molecular and biochemical aspects of Bloom's syndrome. *Cancer Genet Cytogenet*, **53**, 1–13.
6. German, J., Takebe, H. (1989) Bloom's syndrome. XIV. The disorder in Japan. *Clin Genet*, **35**, 93–110.
7. Ellis, N.A., Groden, J., Ye, T.Z. et al (1995) The Bloom's syndrome gene product is homologous to RecQ helicases. *Cell*, **83**, 655–666.
8. Ellis, N.A. (1996) The molecular genetics of Bloom syndrome. *Hum Mol Genet*, **5**, 1457–1463.
9. Ellis, N.A. (1997) DNA helicases in inherited human disorders. *Curr Opin Genet Dev*, **7**, 354–363.
10. Karow, J.K., Chakraverty, R.K., Hickson, I.D. (1997) The Bloom's syndrome gene product is a 3′–5′ DNA helicase. *J Biol Chem*, **272**, 30611–30614.
11. Woods, C.G. (1998) DNA repair disorders. *Arch Dis Child*, **78**, 178–184.
12. Nakura, J., Ye, L., Morishima, A. et al (2000) Helicases and aging. *Cell Mol Life Sci*, **57**, 716–730.
13. Mohaghegh, P., Hickson, I.D. (2001) DNA helicase deficiencies associated with cancer predisposition and premature aging disorders. *Hum Mol Genet*, **10**, 741–746.
14. Wang, Y., Cortez, D., Yazdi, P. et al (2000) BASC, a super complex of BRCA1-associated proteins involved in the recognition and repair of aberrant DNA structures. *Genes Dev*, **14**, 927–939.
15. Sirover, M.A., Vollberg, T.M., Seal, G. (1990) DNA repair and the molecular mechanisms of Bloom's syndrome. *Crit Rev Oncog*, **2**, 19–33.
16. Poppe, B., Van Limbergen, H., Van Roy, N. et al (2001) Chromosomal aberrations in Bloom syndrome patients with myeloid malignancies. *Cancer Genet Cytogenet*, **128**, 39–42.

Cockayne's syndrome

A very rare disorder with an autosomal recessive mode of inheritance and a male predominance (4:1), the majority of cases reported have had British ancestry. It is a multisystem disease associated with premature aging and particularly affecting the skin, teeth, eyes, skeleton and central nervous system.[1]

Clinical features

Children appear to be normal at birth and have an unremarkable early development. However, usually in the second year of life, they show photosensitivity and acquire a 'butterfly' rash (as in lupus erythematosus) on the malar region, which with time is associated with scarring and hyperpigmentary changes. These features, in association with prognathism, sunken eyes, loss of subcutaneous fat and nasal atrophy ('beaked' nose), give the children a characteristic progeria-like or bird-headed appearance (*Fig. 6.98*).[2–4] Fine hair and anhidrosis may also be evident.[1]

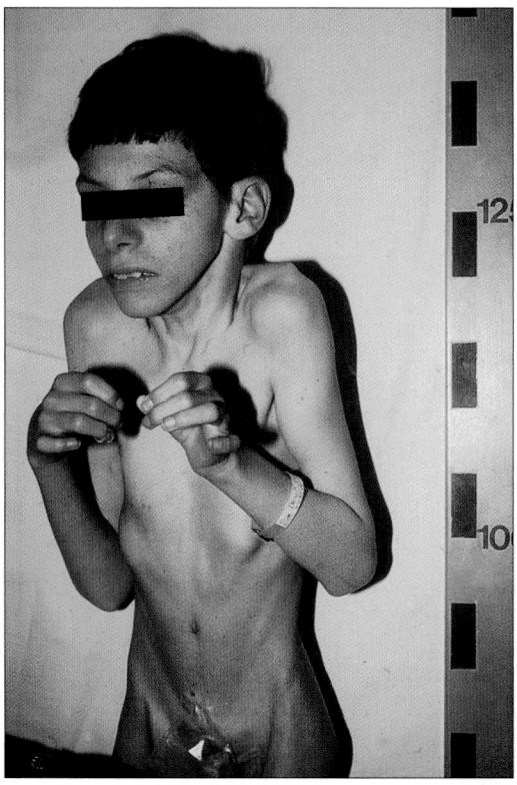

Fig. 6.98
Cockayne's syndrome: the features include prominent ears, prognathism, a 'beaked' nose and flexion contractures. By courtesy of D. Atherton, MD, Institute of Dermatology and Children's Hospital at Great Ormond Street, London, UK.

Ocular lesions include corneal opacity, cataract, retinal degeneration and optic atrophy with resultant blindness.[1] 'Salt and pepper' pigmentation of the fundus is characteristic.[2]

Patients usually suffer from progressive sensorineural deafness.[1] The patients are dwarfs and have disproportionately long limbs with enlarged hands and feet.[2] Microcephaly is common and radiological examination reveals thickening of the skull bones. Kyphosis, ankylosis and flexion contractures are frequent complications, and dental abnormalities include malocclusions and caries. Involvement of the central nervous system presents as microcephaly, normal pressure hydrocephalus, mental subnormality, ataxia, choreoathetosis, spasticity, myoclonus and gait disturbance.[1,2,5] Renal function is usually impaired.[6]

Patients with Cockayne's syndrome have an increased incidence of infections and usually die within the third decade.

An unusually severe form with early onset and quick death associated with abnormal thymidine dimer repair (and hence showing overlap with xeroderma pigmentosum) has recently been described.[5,7]

Prenatal diagnosis of Cockayne's syndrome is now possible.[8]

Pathogenesis and histological features

The two genes responsible for Cockayne's syndrome (CSA and CSB) have been cloned.[9,10] CSA encodes a WD (Trp-Asp) protein, which interacts with a number of proteins including p44 protein, a subunit of transcription/DNA repair factor IIH (TFIIH; see xeroderma pigmentosum, p. 1228).[11] CSB belongs to the yeast SNF2/SW12 protein family, which is of importance in gene transcriptional activation.[11] Unlike CSA, CSB is devoid of helicase activity. CSB protein interacts with CSA and excision repair enzyme XPG.

Patients with Cockayne's syndrome have an impaired DNA excision/repair mechanism and are hypersensitive to the effects of UV radiation with an inability to promote normal levels of DNA and RNA synthesis following UV irradiation.[12–15] The specific defect resides within repair of mutations in transcriptionally active genes rather than in excision/repair mechanisms in general.[16,17] There are five complementation groups identifiable by cell fusion studies: CSA, CSB, XPB, XPD and XPG.[5,11] XPB, XPD and XPG differ from groups CSA and CSB by showing an increased incidence of skin cancer.[11] Cockayne's syndrome may also coexist with trichothiodystrophy.[18]

Biopsy of the malar rash shows epidermal atrophy associated with basal cell hydropic degeneration. A chronic inflammatory cell infiltrate is present in the superficial dermis.

The cerebral lesions are characterized by loss of white matter, cerebellar cortical atrophy, hydrocephalus and widespread calcification.[5] Histologically, there is demyelination and gliosis. Iron-laden neurons, neurofibrillary tangles and giant, bizarre astrocytes have also been reported.[19]

The kidney shows global sclerosis due to marked basement membrane (type IV) collagen deposition associated with tubular atrophy and interstitial fibrosis.[6]

References

1. Boraz, R.A. (1991) Cockayne's syndrome: literature review and case report. *Pediatr Dent*, **13**, 227–230.
2. Lehmann, A.R., Norris, P.G. (1990) DNA repair deficient photodermatoses. *Semin Dermatol*, **9**, 55–62.
3. Lasser, A.E. (1972) Cockayne's syndrome. *Cutis*, **10**, 143–148.
4. Sugarman, G.I., Landing, B.H., Reed, W.B. (1977) Cockayne syndrome: clinical study of two patients and neuropathologic findings in one. *Clin Pediatr*, **16**, 225–232.
5. Patton, M.A., Gianelli, F., Francis, A.J. et al (1989). Early onset Cockayne's syndrome: case reports with neuropathological and fibroblast studies. *J Med Genet*, **26**, 154–159.
6. Sato, H., Saito, T., Kurosawa, K. et al (1988) Renal lesions in Cockayne's syndrome. *Clin Nephrol*, **29**, 206–209.
7. Jaeken, J., Klocker, H., Schwaiger, H. (1989) Clinical and biochemical studies in three patients with severe early infantile Cockayne syndrome. *Hum Genet*, **83**, 339–346.
8. Lehman, A.R., Francis, A.J., Giannelli, F. (1985) Prenatal diagnosis of Cockayne's syndrome. *Lancet*, **I**, 486–488.
9. Henning, K.A., Li, L., Iyer, N. et al (1995) The Cockayne syndrome group A gene encodes a WD repeat protein that interacts with CSB protein and a subunit of RNA polymerase II TFIIH. *Cell*, **82**, 555–564.
10. Troelstra, C., van Gool, A., de Wit, J. et al (1992) ERCC6, a member of a subfamily of putative helicases, is involved in Cockayne's syndrome and preferential repair of active genes. *Cell*, **71**, 939–953.

11. Nakura, J., Ye, L., Morishima, A. et al (2000) Helicases and aging. *Cell Mol Life Sci*, **57**, 716–730.
12. Mayne, L.V., Mullenders, L.H.F., Van Zeeland, A.A. (1988) Cockayne's syndrome: a UV sensitive disorder with defect in the repair of transcribing DNA but with normal excision repair. In: Friedberg E, Hanawalt, P (eds) Mechanisms and consequences of DNA damage processing. New York: Liss, pp 349–353.
13. Venema, J., Mullenders, L.H.F., Natarajan, A.T. et al (1990) The genetic defect in Cockayne syndrome is associated with a defect in repair of UV-induced DNA damage in transcriptionally active DNA. *Proc Natl Acad Sci USA*, **84**, 4707–4711.
14. Wood, R.D. (1991) Human disease associated with defective DNA excision repair. *J R Coll Physicians Lond*, **25**, 300–303.
15. Hansson, J. (1992) Inherited defects in DNA repair and susceptibility to DNA-damaging agents. *Toxicol Lett*, **64/65**, 141–148.
16. Woods, C.G. (1998) DNA repair disorders. *Arch Dis Child*, **78**, 178–184.
17. Goldsmith, L.A. (1997) Genetic skin diseases with altered aging. *Arch Dermatol*, **133**, 1293–1295.
18. Lehmann, A.R. (1987) Cockayne's syndrome and trichothiodystrophy: defective repair without cancer. *Cancer Rev*, **7**, 82–103.
19. Soffer, D., Grotsky, H.W., Rapin, I. et al (1979) Cockayne's syndrome: unusual neuropathological findings and review of the literature. *Ann Neurol*, **6**, 340–348.

Dyskeratosis congenita

Clinical features

This is a rare, but important systemic illness with poor prognosis and high mortality. It has a predominantly X-linked recessive mode of inheritance and occurs mainly in males (6:1), although both autosomal dominant and recessive variants are also recognized.[1–5] The condition consists predominantly of a complex of skin, nail, mucosal and hematological changes associated with an increased incidence of malignancy.[1,2]

The skin acquires a widespread reticular pigmentation with associated poikiloderma, which at first appears most prominently on the face, neck and the 'V' neck region of the upper chest, but later becomes generalized (*Fig. 6.99*).[1,4] During childhood the nails become dystrophic and are often lost (*Fig. 6.100*). There may also be palmoplantar hyperkeratosis associated with hyperhidrosis, development of epiphora, early loss of dentition, caries, poor growth, sparse hair, bullous eruptions, lacrimal duct stenosis and mental subnormality.[1–3,6] A reduced diffusion capacity develops from pulmonary fibrosis.[2]

Premalignant leukoplakia involving particularly the mouth and anus is an important complication, with a significant risk of squamous cell carcinoma developing in these lesions.[2,5] The urethra and vagina may also be affected. Hematological manifestations include thrombocytopenia, aplastic anemia, pancytopenia, myelodysplasia and acute myeloid leukemia.[6–8]

The grave outlook of dyskeratosis congenita relates particularly to the development of infections complicating aplastic anemia, malignancy and pulmonary complications.[2,9]

The clinical features of this disease are most severe in males with the X-linked variant. There is considerable variation in autosomal variants and in some of these patients symptoms may be very mild, allowing a normal life expectancy.[2]

Pathogenesis and histological features

X-linked recessive dyskeratosis congenita is due to mutations of the *DKC1* gene, which has been mapped to Xq28.[10] The mutations, which are predominantly missense, result in single amino acid substitutions in dyskerin, a nucleolar protein believed to be responsible for site-specific pseudouridylation of ribosomal RNA. It is also associated with telomerase RNA (hTR).[11] There is marked chromosomal instability with a striking predisposition to develop rearrangements.[2,12] Dyskeratosis congenita therefore appears to result from defective telomerase activity with resultant impaired stem cell turnover or proliferative activity.[4,13] This is supported by the finding that telomeres are markedly shortened and that this develops at an early age.[14]

The autosomal dominant variant has similarly recently been shown to be associated with a mutation of the RNA component of telomerase.[4]

The histological features of the pigmentary changes are non-specific, showing only pigmentary incontinence.

Biopsies of the mucosal lesions show an acanthotic epithelium with or without dysplastic changes. In the latter case, great care must be taken to exclude the presence of squamous cell carcinoma.

References

1. Sirinavin, C., Trowbridge, A.A. (1975) Dyskeratosis congenita: clinical features and genetic aspects. Report of a family and review of the literature. *J Med Genet*, **12**, 339–354.
2. Dokal, I. (2000) Dyskeratosis congenita in all its forms. *Br J Hematol*, **110**, 768–779.
3. Tchou, R.K., Kohn, K. (1982) Dyskeratosis congenita: an autosomal dominant disorder. *J Am Acad Dermatol*, **6**, 1034–1039.
4. Vulliamy, T., Marrone, A., Goldman, F. (2001) The RNA component of telomerase is mutated in autosomal dominant dyskeratosis congenita. *Nature*, **413**, 432–435.
5. Elliot, A.M., Graham, G.E., Bernstein, M. et al (1999) Dyskeratosis congenita: an autosomal recessive variant. *Am J Med Genet*, **83**, 178–182.
6. Phillips, R.J., Judge, M., Webb, D. et al (1992) Dyskeratosis congenita: delay in diagnosis and successful treatment of pancytopenia by bone marrow transplantation. *Br J Dermatol*, **127**, 278–280.
7. Trowbridge, A.A., Sirinavin, C., Linman, J.W. (1977) Dyskeratosis congenita: hematologic evaluation of a sibship and review of the literature. *Am J Hematol*, **3**, 143–152.
8. Gutman, A., Frumkin, A., Avinoam, A. et al (1978) X-linked dyskeratosis congenital with pancytopenia. *Arch Dermatol*, **114**, 1667–1671.
9. Davidson, H.R., Connor, J.M. (1988) Dyskeratosis congenita. *J Med Genet*, **25**, 843–846.
10. Heiss, N.S., Knight, S.W., Vulliamy, T.J. et al (1998) X-linked dyskeratosis congenita is caused by mutations in a highly conserved gene with putative nucleolar functions. *Nat Genet*, **19**, 32–38.
11. Knight, S.W., Vulliamy, T.J., Morgan, B. et al (2001) Identification of novel DKC1 mutations in patients with dyskeratosis congenita: implications for pathophysiology and diagnosis. *Hum Genet*, **108**, 299–303.
12. Dokal, I., Bungey, J., Williamson, P. et al (1992) Dyskeratosis congenita fibroblasts are abnormal and have unbalanced chromosomal rearrangements. *Blood*, **80**, 3090–3096.
13. Marciniak, R.A., Johnson, F.B., Guarrente, L. (2000) Dyskeratosis congenita, telomeres and human aging. *Trends Genet*, **16**, 193–195.
14. Vulliamy, T.J., Knight, S.W., Mason, P.J. et al (2001) Very short telomeres in the peripheral blood of patients with X-linked and autosomal dyskeratosis congenita. *Blood Cells Mol Dis*, **27**, 353–357.

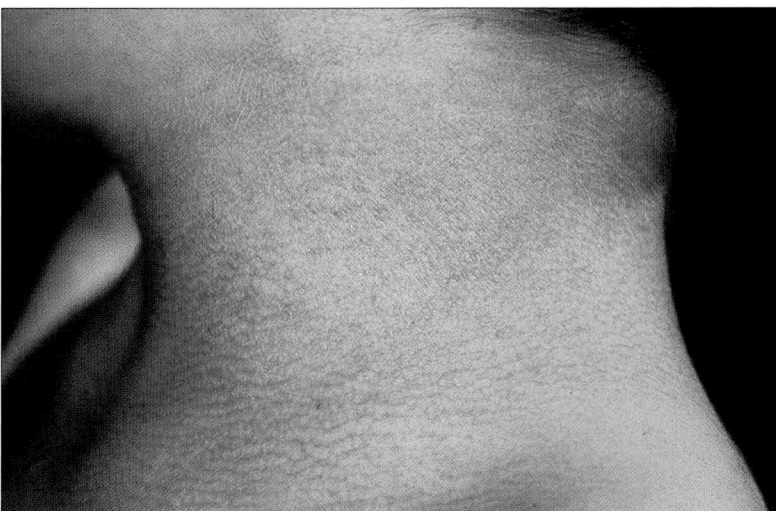

Fig. 6.99
Dyskeratosis congenita: typical poikilodermatous pigmentation on the neck. By courtesy of D. Atherton, MD, Institute of Dermatology and Children's Hospital at Great Ormond Street, London, UK.

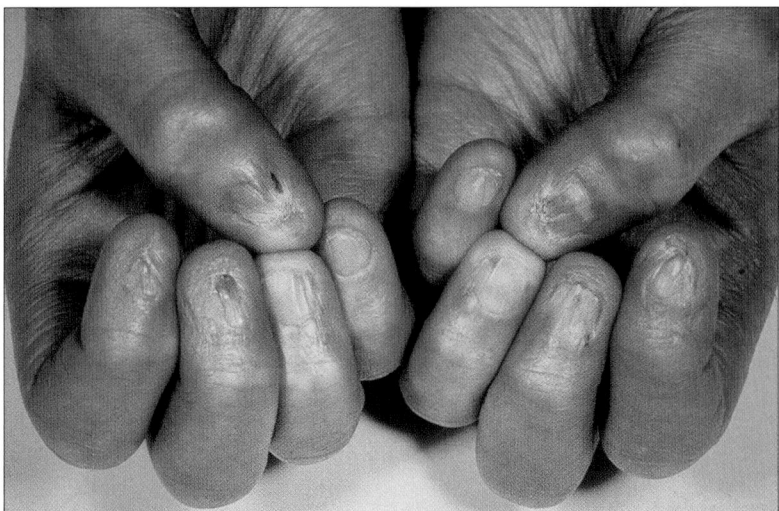

Fig. 6.100
Dyskeratosis congenita: there is dystrophy of the nails with marked atrophy of the surrounding skin. By courtesy of D. Atherton, MD, Institute of Dermatology and Children's Hospital at Great Ormond Street, London, UK.

Lichen sclerosus et atrophicus

Interface change is characteristic of lichen sclerosus (et atrophicus). This disease is discussed in full on page 825.

Graft-versus-host disease

Clinical features

Graft-versus-host disease (GVHD) represents a complex multisystem disorder particularly affecting the skin, intestine and liver that develops when transplanted immunocompetent donor T-lymphocytes are activated, proliferate and respond to foreign host major histocompability complex (MHC)-histoincompatible antigens in a background of recipient immunosuppression.[1-9] In the context of identical class I HLA antigens as may be seen in sibling donors, class II HLA antigens (HLA-DR, -DP and -DQ) and minor histocompatibility antigens are of major pathogenetic significance.[1,2] These latter HLA antigens are expressed on host epithelial cells following pregraft irradiation or chemotherapy, thereby focusing the donor lymphocyte immune response on the skin, liver and intestinal tract.[1,10,11] The condition is a very serious complication of allogeneic bone marrow transplantation and morbidity and mortality is very high. GVHD may also follow solid organ transplantation, develop in severely immunodepressed patients after transfusion of non-irradiated blood or blood products, or complicate transplacental transfer of maternal lymphocytes into an immunodeficient fetus.[12-14]

The clinical features of GVHD therefore develop as a consequence of donor T-lymphocyte-mediated reactions to host tissues. Successful bone marrow transplantation is dependent upon compatibility of the ABO system blood groups and histocompatibility antigens (HLA). The D locus (HLA class II) is of particular importance; successful transplantation has occurred in the presence of identical D loci with dissimilarities at the A and B loci. The development of GVHD is not totally dependent upon HLA incompatibility; it develops in 35% of cases with identical A, B and D loci, suggesting the additional importance of the minor histocompatibility antigens (miH).[2,15]

Development of acute GVHD appears to be a consequence of HLA disparity, sex mismatch, increasing patient age and the presence of infection.[7] While the skin is a major target organ in GVHD, the liver and gastrointestinal tract are also affected.[9] Manifestations include malaise, nausea and vomiting, diarrhea, malabsorption and abnormal liver function. Additionally, patients with GVHD have an increased risk of opportunistic infections, which are an important cause of morbidity and mortality.

GVHD is subdivided into two subgroups:
- *acute GVHD*, occurring within the first 3 months following transplantation (most often presenting between days 7 and 21)[2]
- *chronic GVHD*, presenting after the third month.

Acute GVHD

Acute GVHD develops in between 6 and 90% of patients who undergo bone marrow transplantation.[16] The incidence relates particularly to HLA mismatch, the age of the patient, and the conditioning regimen protocols used.[1,2] Additional risk factors of importance include sex mismatch, i.e. when the donor is a female (particularly if multiparous) and the recipient is male, use of radiation and/or high dosage chemotherapy prior to transplantation, prior blood transfusions, prior splenectomy, viral infections and inadequate immunosuppression.[2]

It presents with the sudden onset of fever and malaise, which are rapidly followed by cutaneous signs including facial erythema and a generalized morbilliform, maculopapular rash characteristically affecting the palms and soles (*Figs 6.101–6.102*). Mucosal lesions may also be a feature (*Fig. 6.103*). The skin lesions particularly affect the upper half of the body and the back of the neck; ears and shoulders are sites of predilection.[1,7] Lichen planus-like features may sometimes supervene. Additional cutaneous lesions include purpura, petechiae, desquamation and a folliculitis-like appearance.[7]

More severe variants include erythroderma or even a toxic epidermal necrolysis-like reaction. The latter has a poor prognosis and may be a manifestation of a drug reaction or represent a true component of acute GVHD. It usually affects a large surface area, shows mucosal involvement and is associated with severe liver and gastrointestinal lesions.[17,18] Mortality is very high (up to 50%), related to the effects of therapy in addition to the lesions themselves.[19] In the event of survival of acute GVHD, the rash may resolve completely or merge into the features of chronic GVHD. It is often difficult on clinical grounds (and histologically) to differentiate between acute GVHD, viral disorders and cytotoxic/adverse drug reactions.

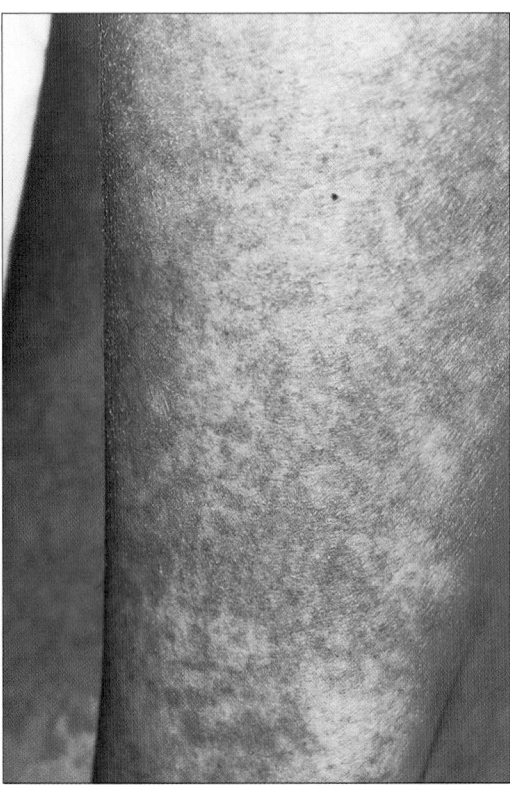

Fig. 6.101
Acute graft-versus-host disease: chest and arm showing widespread macular erythema with fine telangiectasia and mild scaling. By courtesy of R. Touraine, MD, Hôpital Henri Mondor, Paris, France.

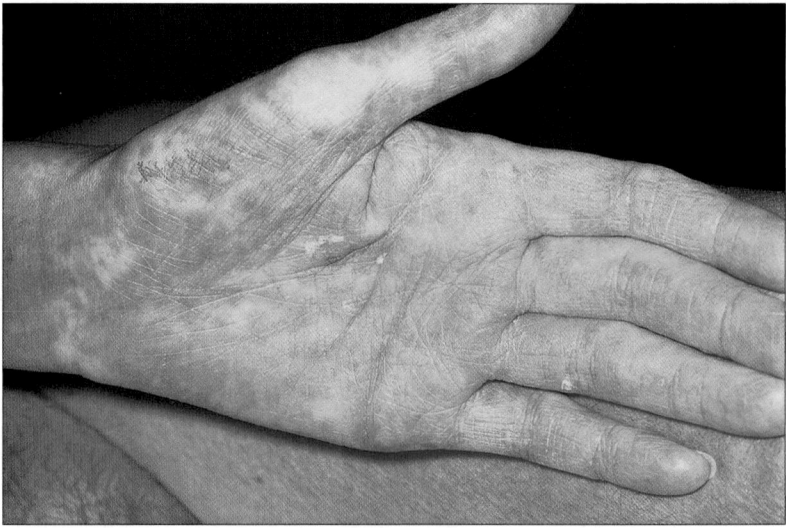

Fig. 6.102
Acute graft-versus-host disease: this vivid palmar erythema is characteristic. By courtesy of R. Touraine, MD, Hôpital Henri Mondor, Paris, France.

The clinical manifestations of acute GVHD are divided into four stages:[1,2]

- *Stage I*: Maculopapular eruption affecting up to 25% of surface area. Bilirubin levels of 2–3 mg/dL and diarrhea in excess of 500 mL/day.
- *Stage II*: Maculopapular erythema affecting 25–50% of surface area. Bilirubin levels of 3–6 mg/dL and diarrhea in excess of 1000 mL/day.
- *Stage III*: Generalized erythroderma. Bilirubin levels of 6–15 mg/dL and diarrhea in excess of 1500 mL/day.
- *Stage IV*: Toxic epidermal necrolysis. Bilirubin levels of 15 mg/dL or more and diarrhea exceeding 1500 mL/day.

Chronic GVHD

Chronic GVHD develops in 10% of all patients undergoing allogeneic bone marrow transplantation and in 30% of all long-term survivors. Systems involved include the skin, eyes, mouth and esophagus, liver, genitalia, muscle, and peripheral and central nervous systems.[7] Virtually all chronic GVHD patients exhibit skin manifestations and 90% develop oral lesions.[2] Some develop chronic GVHD de novo (30%); others show a gradual progression of continuous acute GVHD into the chronic variant (32%).[2] Occasionally, chronic GVHD may follow a period of resolution of acute GVHD, after an interval of quiescence (36%).[2] Chronic GVHD can occur as a lichen planus-like eruption or show features of a poikilodermatous or sclerodermatous reaction. A discoid lupus erythematosus-like reaction is rare. Polymyositis and fasciitis have also been described.[20–22] Risk factors for developing chronic GVHD include prior episode of acute GVHD, increasing age, sex mismatch, i.e. when the donor is a female (particularly if multiparous) and the recipient is male, and use of non-T-cell depleted bone marrow.[2,23]

Although early in chronic GVHD the lesions are typically lichenoid and later in the course of the illness sclerodermatous manifestations develop, in some patients these features may appear simultaneously.[2] UV irradiation, trauma and infection with herpes zoster virus or *Borrelia* precipitate chronic GVHD.[2]

The early chronic GVHD lesion commonly has a classic lichenoid appearance with typical erythematous or violaceous polygonal papules showing Wickham's striae (*Fig. 6.104*). The periorbital region, ears, palms and soles are sites of predilection.[2] Oral mucosal lesions include typical net-like lacy white lesions, and ulcerated areas may also develop (*Figs 6.105–6.107*). The cheeks, tongue, palate and lips are sites of predilection.[2] Sjögren's syndrome is also often present. Onycholysis

and cicatricial alopecia may be features. The rash is sometimes less typical, appearing as a desquamative active dermatitis or as follicular hyperkeratosis.

The late phase of chronic GVHD is typically sclerodermatous and presents 8–18 months after transplantation (*Figs 6.108–6.110*). The development of a poikilodermatous rash is followed by induration, atrophy and sclerosis.[20] The resultant features resemble morphea or systemic sclerosis; chronic ulceration, particularly involving pressure points, can be an unpleasant complication. Blisters may occasionally develop. The development of cutaneous squamous cell carcinoma has occasionally been documented.[21,22]

Chronic GVHD has a mortality of up to 40%. Causes of death include infection, cachexia and liver failure.[2]

Systemic features include chronic hepatitis, diarrhea with malabsorption, bronchiolitis obliterans, peripheral entrapment neuropathy and polymyositis.[2] Opportunistic infections are also of major importance.

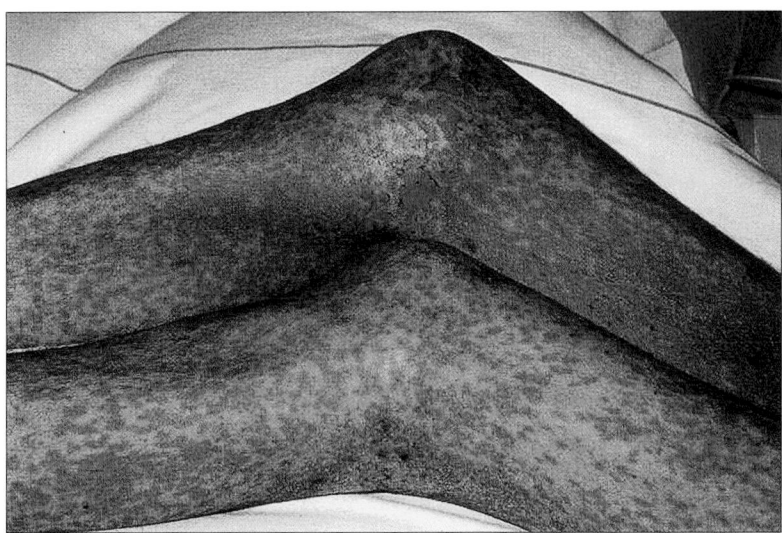

Fig. 6.104
Early chronic graft-versus-host disease: there are widespread, almost confluent hyperpigmented lichenoid papules. Associated erosion of the epidermis gives an appearance similar to toxic epidermal necrolysis (Lyell syndrome). By courtesy of R. Touraine, MD, Hôpital Henri Mondor, Paris, France.

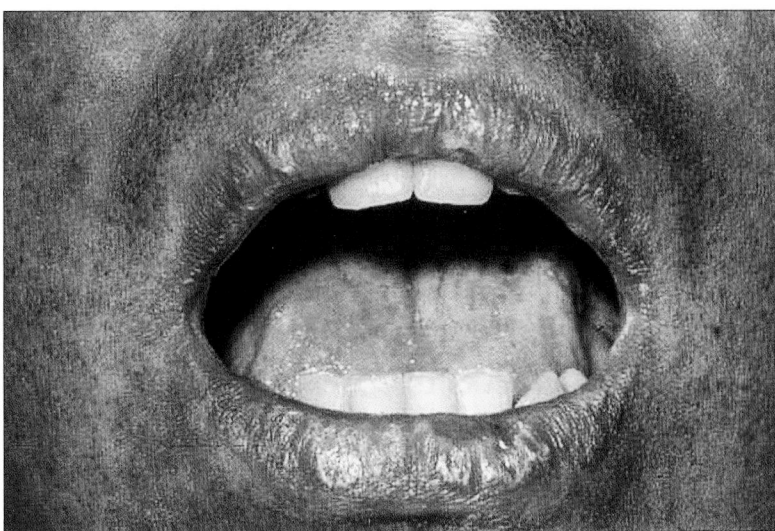

Fig. 6.105
Early chronic graft-versus-host disease: there are diffuse widespread lichenoid changes of the lips. By courtesy of R. Touraine, MD, Hôpital Henri Mondor, Paris, France.

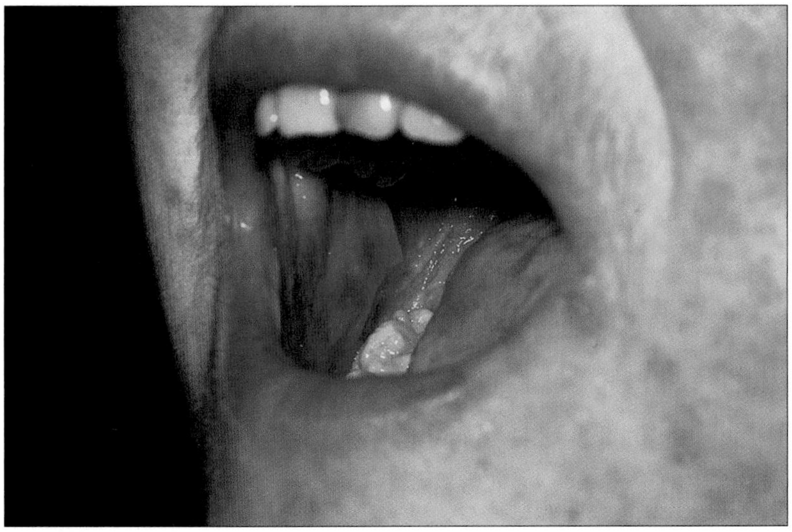

Fig. 6.103
Acute graft-versus-host disease: note the erosions on the buccal mucosa. By courtesy of R. Touraine, MD, Hôpital Henri Mondor, Paris, France.

Pathogenesis and histological features

GVHD is mediated by the combined effects of donor T-lymphocytes (CD4+ cells responding to MHC class II antigens and CD8+ to class I antigens) and cytokines including IL-1, TNF-α, IFN-γ and GM-CSF.[1,2,11,27-35] The development of acute GVHD depends upon a complex interplay between host immunosuppression, tissue damage as a result of pregraft induction therapy and donor lymphocyte proliferation and activation with consequent injury and death of susceptible host tissues.[1]

The lymphocytes may be of CD4+ or CD8+ immunophenotype and commonly there is an admixture. Both Th1 and Th2 CD4+ subtypes are represented. The former produce IL-2 and IFN-γ and are thought to promote GVHD, the latter produce IL-4, IL-6 and IL-10 and are believed to be protective although this has been contested.[36] Natural killer (NK) cells may also be of importance although their presence appears to

be variable.[37] B-cells are absent. Activated keratinocytes following induction chemotherapy or irradiation produce TNF-α and IL-1 and express ICAM-1 and HLA-DR.[38] This may result in increased recognition of histoincompatible MHC antigens by donor T-cells.[1] The superficial dermal endothelial cells express E-selectin, $\alpha_4\beta_1$ integrin, $\alpha_L\beta_2$ integrin, ICAM-1, platelet endothelial cell adhesion molecule-1 (PECAM-1) and vascular cell adhesion molecule-1 (VCAM-1) which mediate lymphocyte adhesion to the endothelium and facilitate recognition, activation and response to MHC molecules.[1,39-41] The mechanisms of cell injury and death result from both cytotoxic T-cell and possibly NK cell-mediated cytotoxic effects and the actions of cytokines. The former includes cytolytic actions mediated by perforin and granzyme B, and apoptosis through the Fas–Fas ligand pathway.[42,43] IL-1, IL-2, IL-6 and TNF-α are thought to be of particular importance in mediating

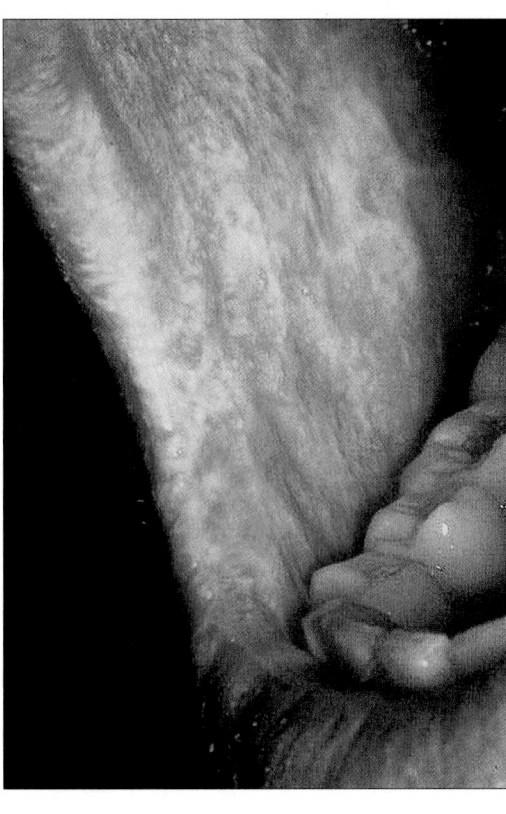

Fig. 6.106
Early chronic graft-versus-host disease: florid reticulate white striae on the buccal mucosa are evident. By courtesy of R. Touraine, MD, Hôpital Henri Mondor, Paris, France.

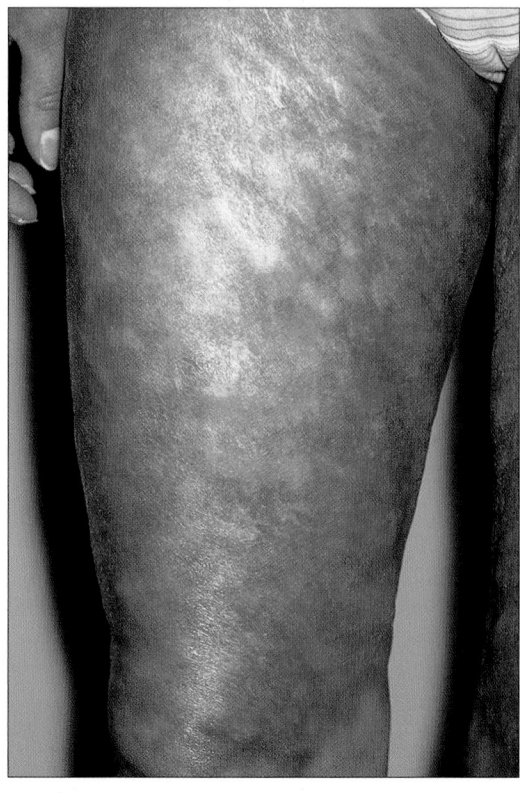

Fig. 6.108
Late chronic graft-versus-host disease: note the grossly hyperpigmented sclerotic limb. By courtesy of R. Touraine, MD, Hôpital Henri Mondor, Paris, France.

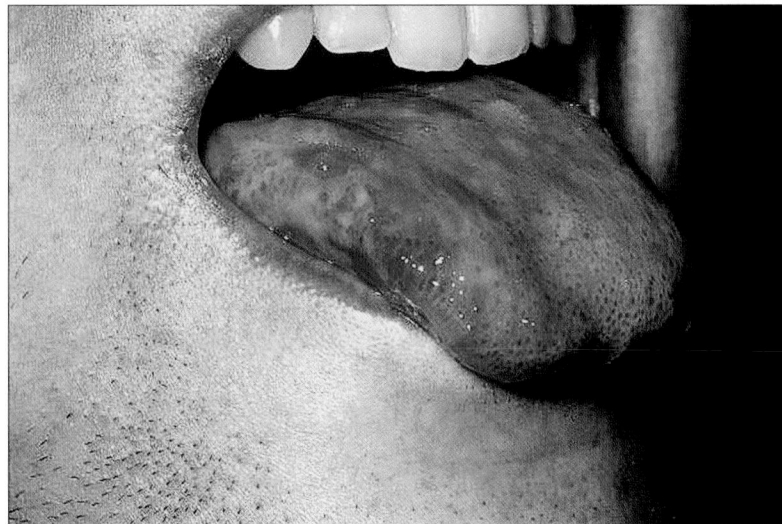

Fig. 6.107
Early chronic graft-versus-host disease: there are erosive changes on the tongue. By courtesy of R. Touraine, MD, Hôpital Henri Mondor, Paris, France.

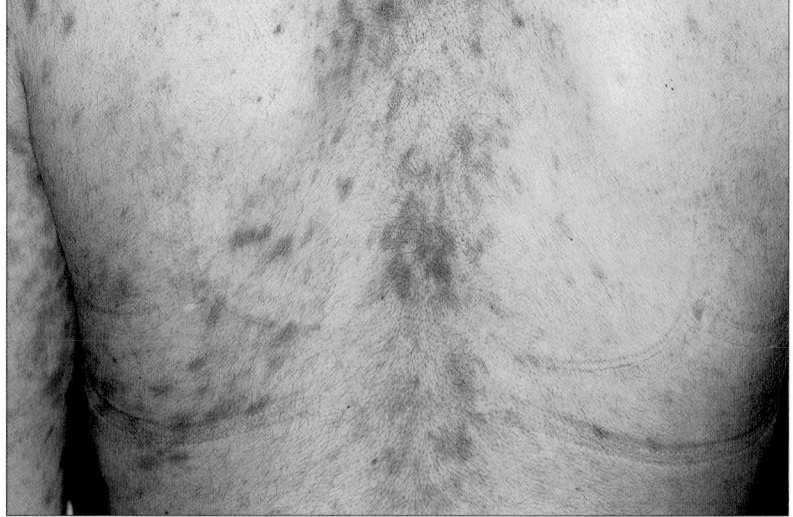

Fig. 6.109
Late chronic graft-versus-host disease: hyperpigmented sclerotic plaques are present on the back. By courtesy of R. Touraine, MD, Hôpital Henri Mondor, Paris, France.

cytotoxicity.[1] Raised serum TNF-α correlates with GVHD and antibodies to TNF-α or its receptor protect against the disease.[1,44–46]

Deposition of IgM and C3 at the epidermodermal junction and around the superficial vasculature in up to 39% of patients with acute GVHD suggests that humoral responses play a significant role in the pathogenesis of GVHD.[47]

The development of chronic GVHD is dependent on a variety of factors including, anti-host tissue activity of donor T-cells and the development of autoimmunity.[2,48] The infiltrate consists predominantly of CD8+ T-cells; NK cells are usually absent.[2] As with acute GVHD, TNF-α and IL-1 are the major cytokines implicated.[2]

The acute lesion of GVHD is characterized by focal or diffuse basal cell hydropic change (*Figs 6.111–6.114*).[49] Apoptotic and dyskeratotic keratinocytes, at all levels of the epidermis and associated with adjacent lymphocytes (satellite cell necrosis), are characteristic.[50] Isolated cytoid bodies are also frequently evident. Lymphocytic exocytosis is invariably present and spongiosis is sometimes a feature. Microvesiculation at the epidermodermal junction occasionally occurs. Follicular involvement is a common feature and the hair bulge is typically affected.[51] Langerhans'

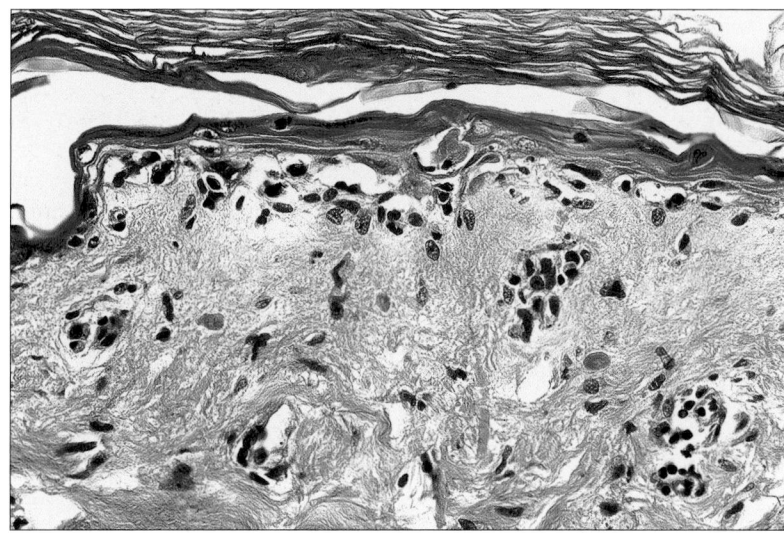

Fig. 6.112
Acute graft-versus-host disease: high power view showing keratinocyte apoptosis. Diagnosis is entirely dependent on the clinical history.

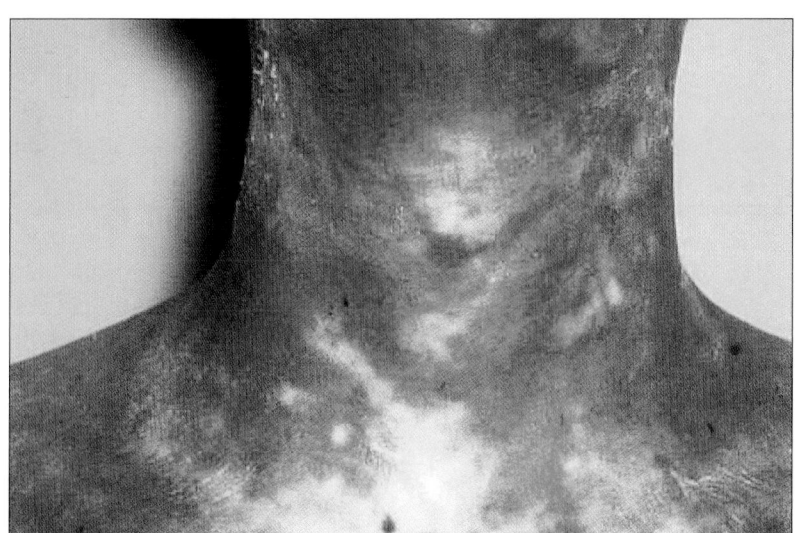

Fig. 6.110
Late chronic graft-versus-host disease: there is mottled hypo- and hyperpigmentation with gross atrophy and scaling. By courtesy of R. Touraine, MD, Hôpital Henri Mondor, Paris, France.

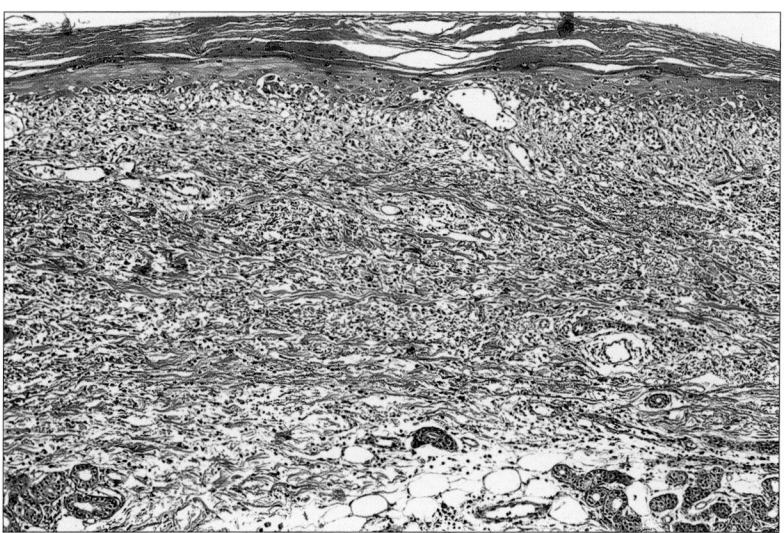

Fig. 6.113
Acute graft-versus-host disease: low power view of an established lesion showing extensive parakeratosis, basal cell hydropic degeneration and apoptosis.

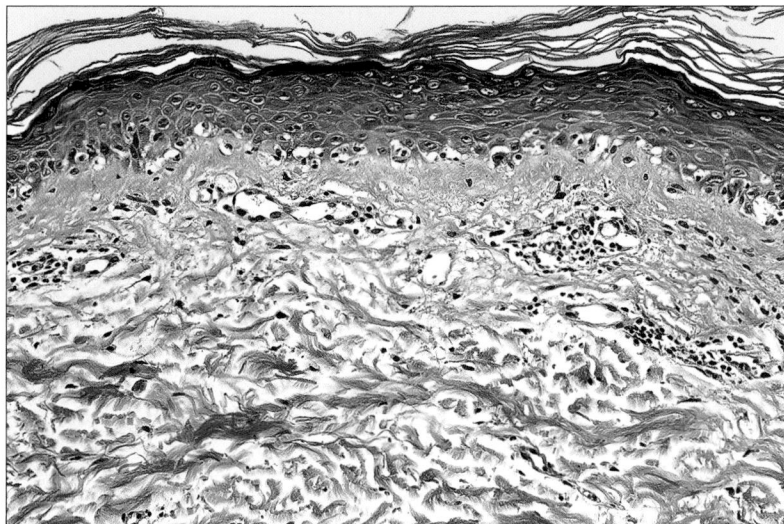

Fig. 6.111
Acute graft-versus-host disease: evolving lesion showing basal cell hydropic degeneration and scattered apoptotic keratinocytes. The dermis contains dilated blood vessels and a light perivascular chronic inflammatory cell infiltrate.

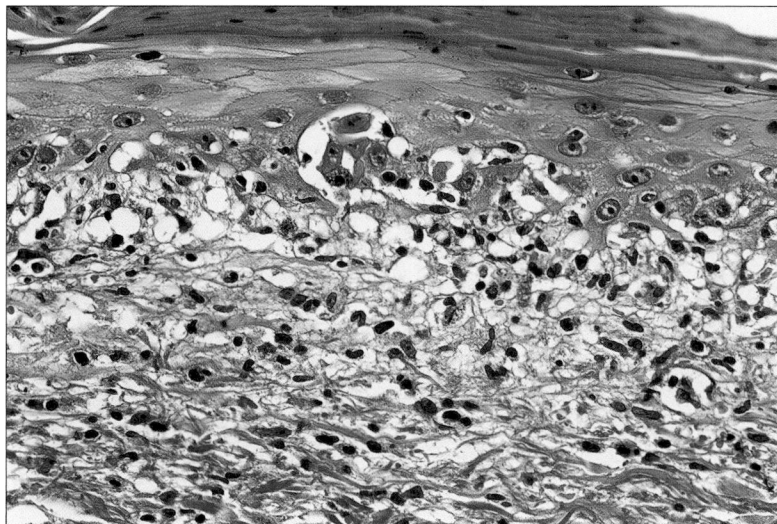

Fig. 6.114
Acute graft-versus-host disease: high power view showing satellite cell necrosis.

cells are often reduced in number. Vascular changes include endothelial cell swelling with sloughing, and intimal and perivascular lymphocytic infiltration. Blood vessel proliferation has also been described. Perivascular edema and nuclear dust may additionally be present and mast cells are also conspicuous.[52,53]

The toxic epidermal necrolysis-like lesions are characterized by severe epidermal necrosis in association with subepidermal vesiculation. Evidence of sweat gland involvement is commonly present.[54,55] Keratinous plugging of the acrosyringium may therefore be seen and the excretory ducts often show cytopathic–degenerative and proliferative changes.[55] The former comprises basal cell hydropic degeneration, lymphocytic infiltration and apoptosis. Follicular involvement is a not uncommon additional manifestation.[56] The histological features of acute GVHD may be subdivided into four stages, which have prognostic significance (*Table 6.3*).[56,57]

The histology of chronic GVHD is typically lichenoid in appearance: indeed, it may be indistinguishable from idiopathic lichen planus (*Fig. 6.115*). The features are hyperkeratosis, hypergranulosis, irregular acanthosis, basal cell hydropic degeneration, cytoid body formation, pigmentary incontinence and a band-like lymphohistiocytic infiltrate obscuring the epidermodermal interface. In contrast to idiopathic lichen planus, satellite cell necrosis is often present in the early phase of chronic GVHD and the infiltrate sometimes contains plasma cells and eosinophils. Squamous metaplasia of the eccrine sweat ducts has been described.[55]

Table 6.3
Grading of acute graft-versus-host disease

Grade	Feature
I	Focal of diffuse vacuolar alteration of basal cells
II	Vacuolar alteration of basal cells; spongiosis and dyskeratosis of epidermal cells
III	Formation of subepidermal cleft in association with dyskeratosis and spongiosis
IV	Complete loss of epidermis

Reproduced with permission from Lerner et al (1974) *Transplantation Proceedings*, **6**, 367–371.

The late stage of chronic GVHD is characterized by epidermal atrophy with abolition of the ridge pattern and scarring of the superficial and deep dermis, with loss of the adnexal structures (*Fig. 6.116*). Features of the early stage of chronic GVHD, i.e. hydropic basal cell degeneration, cytoid body formation and a chronic inflammatory cell infiltrate, may or may not be evident. Dermal mucin deposition has also been documented.[58]

Hepatic changes include bile duct atypia with necrosis, periportal inflammation, focal hepatocyte necrosis and cholestasis.[9] Gastrointestinal lesions show individual crypt cell necrosis accompanied by a mild chronic inflammatory cell infiltrate.[59,60]

Differential diagnosis

The features of acute GVHD can be reproduced by cytotoxic drugs such as cyclophosphamide and by radiotherapy. Viral infections also enter the differential diagnosis, as does an adverse drug reaction as for example to antibiotic therapy. Although the presence of conspicuous eosinophils argues to some extent in favor of an adverse drug reaction, in reality there are no real discriminators between adverse drug reactions and acute GVHD.[61] In short, the regular practice of skin biopsy to differentiate between GVHD, drug reactions, chemotherapy effect and viral infection is of no real practical value.

Acute GVHD may be indistinguishable from erythema multiforme and, in more severely affected patients, toxic epidermal necrolysis. Recently, the intriguing report of bile pigment deposition in the stratum corneum in patients with GVHD offers a possible line of approach to making this important distinction.[62]

The early changes of chronic GVHD may be indistinguishable from lichen planus. However, the dermal infiltrate is usually less conspicuous than that in lichen planus and sometimes contains plasma cells and eosinophils. The presence of satellite cell necrosis may be a diagnostic pointer towards chronic GVHD.

In the absence of clinical information it is usually not possible to distinguish the features of late chronic GVHD from morphea or systemic sclerosis.

The histological features of the eruption of lymphocyte recovery are indistinguishable from acute GVHD (see p. 671).

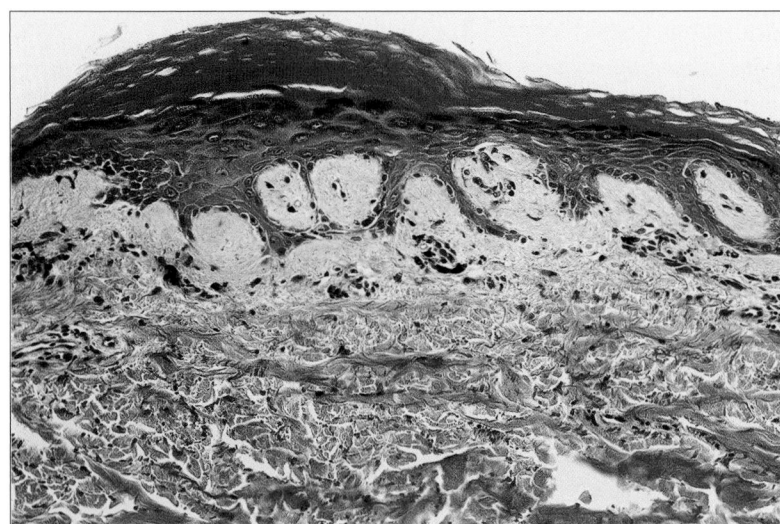

Fig. 6.115
Early chronic graft-versus-host disease: the hyperkeratosis, hypergranulosis, irregular acanthosis and basal cell hydropic degeneration are reminiscent of idiopathic lichen planus.

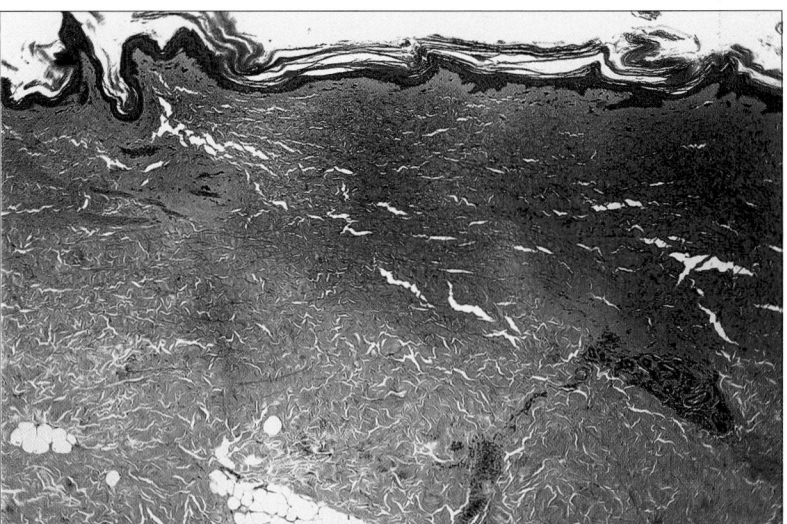

Fig. 6.116
Late chronic graft-versus-host disease: the epidermis appears flattened and there is dense fibrosis of the dermis with tethering of the subcutaneous fat. Epidermal appendages are markedly reduced in number. These appearances are indistinguishable from scleroderma. By courtesy of the late J. Sloan, MD, Royal Marsden Hospital, London, UK.

References

1. Goker, H., Haznedaroglu, I.C., Chao, N.J. (2001) Acute graft-versus-host disease: pathobiology and management. *Exp Hematol*, **29**, 259–277.
2. Aractingi, S., Chosidow, O. (1998) Cutaneous graft-versus-host disease. *Arch Dermatol*, **134**, 602–612.
3. Johnson, M.L., Farmer, E.R. (1998) Graft-vs-host reactions in dermatology. *J Am Acad Dermatol*, **38**, 369–392.
4. Saurat, J.H. (1981) Cutaneous manifestations of graft-versus-host disease. *Int J Dermatol*, **20**, 249–251.
5. Saurat, J.H., Gluckman, E. (1978) Graft versus host reactions. *Arch Dermatol*, **114**, 801–802.
6. Shulman, H.M., Sale, G.E., Lerner, K.G. et al (1978) Chronic cutaneous graft versus host disease in man. *Am J Pathol*, **91**, 545–564.
7. Tanaka, K., Sullivan, K.M., Shulman, H.M. et al. (1991) A clinical review: cutaneous manifestations of acute and chronic graft-versus-host disease following bone marrow transplantation. *J Dermatol*, **18**, 11–17.
8. Parker, C. (1990) Skin lesions in transplant patients. *Dermatol Clin*, **8**, 313–325.
9. Appleton, A.L., Sviland, L. (1993). Current thoughts on the pathogenesis of graft versus host disease. *J Clin Pathol*, **46**, 785–789.
10. Sviland, L., Pearson, A.D.J., Eastham, E.J. et al (1988) Class II antigen expression by keratinocytes and enterocytes: an early feature of graft-vs-host disease. *Transplantation*, **46**, 402–406.
11. Ferrara, J.L.M., Levy, R., Chao, N.J. (1999) Pathophysiologic mechanisms of acute graft-vs-host disease. *Biol Blood Marrow Transplant*, **5**, 347–356.
12. Decoste, S.D., Boudreaux, C., Dover, J.S. (1990) Transfusion-associated graft-vs-host disease in patients with malignancy. *Arch Dermatol*, **26**, 1324–1329.
13. Flidel, O., Barak, Y., Lifschitz-Mercer, B. et al (1992) Graft-versus-host disease in extremely low-birth weight neonates. *Pediatrics*, **89**, 689–690.
14. Jamieson, N.V., Joysey, V., Friend, P.J. et al (1991) Graft-versus-host disease in solid-organ transplantation. *Transpl Int*, **4**, 67–71.
15. Goulmy, E., Schipper, R., Pool, J. et al (1996) Mismatches of minor histocompatibility antigens between HLA identical donors and recipients and the development of graft versus host disease after bone marrow transplantation. *N Engl J Med*, **334**, 281–285.
16. Volc-Platzer, B., Stingl, G. (1991) Cutaneous graft versus host disease. In: Ferrara, J., Deeg, J., Burakoff, S. (eds) Graft versus host disease. New York: Marcel Dekker, pp 245–254.
17. Villada, G., Roujeau, J.C., Cordonnier, C. et al (1990) Toxic epidermal necrolysis after bone marrow transplantation: study of nine cases. *J Am Acad Dermatol*, **23**, 870–875.
18. Peck, G.L., Elias, P.M., Graw, R.G. (1972) Graft-versus-host reaction and toxic epidermal necrolysis. *Lancet*, **2**, 1151–1153.
19. Bortin, M.M., Rimm, A.A. (1981) Treatment of 144 patients with severe aplastic anemia using immunosuppression and allogeneic marrow transplantation. A report from the International Bone Marrow Transplantation Registry. *Transplant Proc*, **13**, 227–229.
20. Prussick, R., Brain, M.C., Walker, I.R. et al (1991) Polymyositis: a manifestation of chronic graft-versus-host disease. *J Am Acad Dermatol*, **25**, 560–562.
21. Pier, N., Dubowitz, V. (1983) Chronic GVHD presenting with polymyositis. *BMJ*, **286**, 2024.
22. Janin-Mercier, A., Socié, G., Devergie, A. et al (1994) Fasciitis in chronic graft versus host disease. *Ann Int Med*, **120**, 993–998.
23. Atkinson, K., Horowitz, M., Gale, R. et al (1990) Risk factors for chronic graft-versus-host disease after HLA-identical sibling bone marrow transplantation. *Blood*, **75**, 2459–2464.
24. Chosidow, O., Bagot, M., Vernant, J.P. et al (1992) Sclerodermatous chronic graft versus host disease: analysis of seven cases. *J Am Acad Dermatol*, **26**, 49–55.
25. Lishner, M., Patterson, B., Kandel, R. et al (1990) Cutaneous and mucosal neoplasms in bone marrow transplant recipients. *Cancer*, **65**, 473–476.
26. Deeg, H.J., Sanders, J., Martin, P. et al (1984) Secondary malignancies after marrow transplantation. *Exp Hematol*, **12**, 660–666.
27. Hill, G.R., Krengler, W., Ferrara, J.M. (1997) The role of cytokines in acute graft-vs-host disease. *Cytokines Cell Mol Ther*, **3**, 257–266.
28. Breathach, S.M. (1986) Current understanding of the etiology and clinical implications of cutaneous graft-versus-host disease. *Br J Dermatol*, **114**, 139–143.
29. Breathnach, S.M., Katz, S.I. (1986) Cell-mediated immunity in cutaneous disease. *Hum Pathol*, **17**, 161–167.
30. Dreno, B., Milpied, N., Harousseau, J.L. et al (1986) Cutaneous immunological studies in diagnosis of acute graft-versus-host disease. *Br J Dermatol*, **114**, 7–15.
31. Woodrouff, J.M., Hansen, J.A., Good, R.A. et al (1976) The pathology of the graft versus host reaction (GVHR) in adults receiving bone marrow transplants. *Transplant Proc*, **8**, 675–684.
32. Lever, R., Turbitt, M., Mackie, R. et al (1986) A prospective study of the histological changes in the skin in patients receiving bone marrow transplants. *Br J Dermatol*, **114**, 161–170.
33. Van Els, C.A., Bakker, A., Zwinderman, A.H. et al (1990) Effector mechanisms in graft-versus-host disease in response to minor histocompatibility antigens. I. Absence of correlation with cytotoxic effector cells. *Transplantation*, **50**, 62–66.
34. Van Els, C.A., Bakker, A., Zwinderman, A.H, et al (1990) Effector mechanisms in graft-versus-host disease in response to minor histocompatibility antigens. II. Evidence of a possible involvement of proliferative T cells. *Transplantation*, **50**, 67–71.
35. Van Els, C.A., Zantvoort, E., Jacobs, N. et al (1990) Graft-versus-host disease associated T helper cell responses specific for minor histocompatibility antigens are mainly restricted by HLA-DR molecules. *Bone Marrow Transplant*, **5**, 365–372.
36. Ju, X., Wang, J., Xu, B. et al (2003) Roles of interleukin-10 in acute graft-versus-host disease and graft rejection. *Chin Med J*, **116**, 534–537.
37. Norton, J., Sloan, J. (1991) ICAM 1 expression on epidermal keratinocytes in cutaneous graft-versus-host disease. *Transplantation*, **51**, 1203–1206.
38. Leskinen, R., Taskinen, E., Volin, L. et al (1992) Immunohistology of skin and rectum biopsies in bone marrow transplant recipients. *APMIS*, **100**, 1115–1122.
39. Shen, N., French, P., Guyotat, D. et al (1994) Expression of adhesion molecules in endothelial cells during allogeneic bone marrow transplantation. *Eur J Hematol*, **52**, 296–301.
40. Behar, E., Chao, N., Hiraki, D. et al (1996) Polymorphism of adhesion molecule CD31 and its role in acute graft-versus-host disease. *N Engl J Med*, **334**, 286–291.
41. Nichols, W.C., Antin, J.H., Lunetta, K.L. et al (1996) Polymorphism of adhesion molecule CD31 is not a significant risk factor for graft-vs-host disease. *Blood*, **88**, 4429–4434.
42. Lowin, B., Hahne, M., Mattmann, C. et al (1994) Cytolytic T-cell cytotoxicity is mediated through perforin and Fas lytic pathways. *Nature*, **370**, 650–652.
43. Via, C.S., Nguyen, P., Shustov, A. et al (1996) A major role for the Fas pathway in acute graft-vs-host disease. *J Immunol*, **157**, 5387–5393.
44. Holler, E., Kolb, H.J., Möller, A. et al (1990) Increased serum levels of tumor necrosis factor-α precede major complications of bone marrow transplantation. *Blood*, **75**, 1011–1016.
45. Herve, P., Flesch, M., Tiberghein, P. et al (1992) Phase I-II trial of a monoclonal anti-tumor necrosis factor α antibody for the treatment of severe refractory acute graft-versus-host disease. *Blood*, **79**, 3362–3368.
46. Piguet, P.F., Grau, G.E., Allet, B. et al (1987) Tumor necrosis factor is an effector of skin and gut lesions of the acute phase of graft-vs-host disease. *J Exp Med*, **166**, 1280–1289.
47. Tsoi, M., Storb, R., Jones, E. et al (1978) Deposition of IgM and complement at the dermoepidermal junction in acute and chronic graft-versus-host disease in man. *J Immunol*, **120**, 1485–1492.
48. Bunjes, D., Theobald, M., Nierle, T. et al (1995) Presence of host-specific interleukin 2-secreting T helper cell precursors correlates closely with active primary and secondary chronic graft-versus-host disease. *Bone Marrow Transplant*, **15**, 727–732.
49. Dickinson, A.M., Sviland, L., Dunn, J. et al (1991) Demonstration of direct involvement of cytokines in graft-versus-host reactions using an *in vitro* human skin explant model. *Bone Marrow Transplant*, **7**, 209–216.
50. Langley, R., Walsch, N., Nevill, T. et al (1996) Apotosis is the mode of keratinocyte death in cutaneous graft versus host disease. *J Am Acad Dermatol*, **35**, 187–190.
51. Sale, G., Beauchamp, M. (1993) The parafollicular hair bulge in human GvHD: a stem cell rich primary target. *Bone Marrow Transplant*, **11**, 223–225.
52. Sale, G.E., Lerner, K.G., Barker, E.A. et al (1977). The skin biopsy in the diagnosis of acute graft-versus-host disease in man. *Am J Pathol*, **89**, 621–635.
53. Dumler, J.S., Beschorner, W.E., Farmer, E.R. et al (1989) Endothelial-cell injury in cutaneous acute graft-versus-host disease. *Am J Pathol*, **135**, 1097–1103.
54. Sloan, J.P., Thomas, J.A., Imrie, S.F. et al (1984) Morphological and immunohistological changes in the skin in allogeneic bone marrow recipient. *J Clin Pathol*, **37**, 919–930.
55. Akosa, A.B., Lampert, I.A. (1990) The sweat gland in graft-versus-host disease. *J Pathol*, **161**, 261–266.
56. Chaudhuri, S.P.R., Smoller, B.R. (1992) Acute cutaneous graft versus host disease: a clinicopathologic and immunophenotypic study. *Int J Dermatol*, **31**, 270–272.
57. Lerner, K.G., Kao, G.F., Storb, R. et al (1974) Histopathology of graft-vs.-host reaction (GvHR) in human recipients of marrow from HL-A-matched sibling donors. *Transplant Proc*, **6**, 367–371.
58. Ameen, M., Russell-Jones, R. (2000) Macroscopic and microscopic mucinosis in chronic sclerodermoid graft-versus-host disease. *Br J Dermatol*, **142**, 529–532.
59. McDonald, G.B., Shulman, H.M., Sullivan, K.M. et al (1986) Intestinal and hepatic complications of human bone marrow transplantation. Part I. *Gastroenterology*, **90**, 460–477.
60. McDonald, G.B., Shulman, H.M., Sullivan, K.M. et al (1986) Intestinal and hepatic complications of human bone marrow transplantation. Part II. *Gastroenterology*, **90**, 770–784.
61. Kohler, S., Hendrickson, M.R., Chao, N.J. et al (1997) Value of skin biopsies in assessing prognosis and progression of acute graft-versus-host disease. *Am J Surg Pathol*, **21**, 988–996.
62. Dilday, B.R., Smoller, B.R. (1998) Intraepidermal bile pigment in skin biopsy specimens from graft-versus-host disease versus erythema multiforme. *Mod Pathol*, **11**, 1005–1009.

Pityriasis lichenoides

Clinical features

Pityriasis lichenoides (Gr. *pityron*, bran+iasis; lichen; Gr. *eidos*, form) is an uncommon dermatosis of unknown etiology, although a hypersensitivity reaction to a number of infectious agents including adenovirus, toxoplasmosis, Epstein–Barr virus and *M. pneumoniae* have been proposed.[1–3] The condition has also been documented in association with a range of autoimmune conditions such as rheumatoid arthritis, hypothyroidism and pernicious anemia.[3] The term includes a spectrum of disease manifestations, ranging from the acute ulceronecrotic lesions of pityriasis lichenoides et varioliformis acuta (PLEVA, also known as Mucha–Haberman disease, acute guttate parapsoriasis) to the more chronic scaly papules of pityriasis lichenoides chronica (chronic guttate parapsoriasis); there is often clinical overlap.[1–7] In addition, a febrile, ulceronecrotic variant (febrile ulceronecrotic Mucha–Habermann disease) is recognized.[3–5]

Pityriasis lichenoides shows a predilection for males (3:1) and tends to occur more commonly in late childhood and early adulthood: patients are therefore often in their second or third decade.

Lesions show a propensity to involve the arms, legs, trunk and buttocks (*Fig. 6.117*). The upper limbs appear to be involved more often than the lower and the flexor more commonly than the extensor surfaces. Lesions are usually asymptomatic, but may be associated with mild itching or a burning sensation. The onset is usually insidious and the

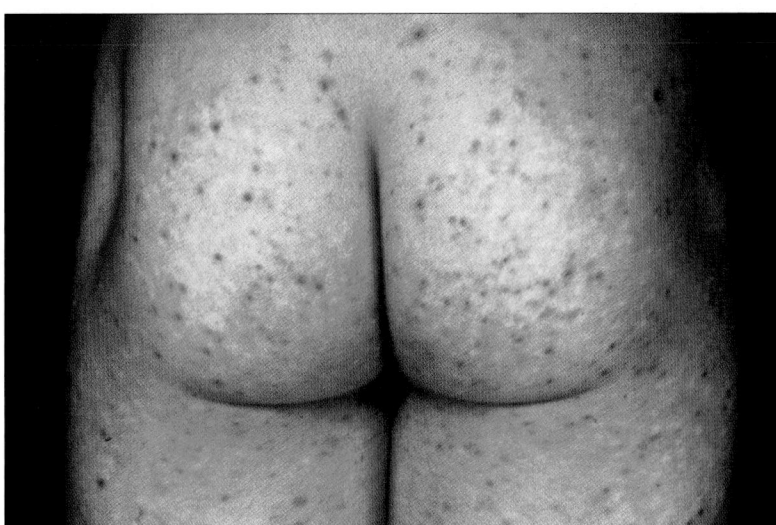

Fig. 6.117

Pityriasis lichenoides acuta: erythematous papules and crusted lesions are present on the buttocks and thighs. In severe cases lesions may be very extensive. By courtesy of the Institute of Dermatology, London, UK.

course fluctuating and episodic, patients experiencing recurrent crops of lesions. Duration of the rash is very variable: although many patients are free of lesions by 3–6 months, others show great persistence of the disease, often for many years. The disease shows some seasonal variation, with lesions worsening in winter and showing improvement in sunlight. Although pityriasis lichenoides is traditionally divided into acute and chronic variants, not uncommonly both sorts of lesion may be seen in the same patient.[6]

In the more acute form of the disease, the initial lesions are crops of pink papules (*Figs 6.118, 6.119*). These may become vesicular or hemorrhagic and ultimately develop necrosis and ulceration (*Fig. 6.120*). Healing is usually associated with the development of superficial varioliform scars. Postinflammatory hyper- or hypopigmentation is not uncommon (*Fig. 6.121*).[6] The rash is often polymorphic, individual patients having lesions at varying stages of evolution. Patients may be pyrexic and sometimes lymphadenopathy is present.[1]

The chronic lesions are typified by numerous, lichenoid, brownish-red, scaly papules, 3–10 mm across, the scale being most noticeable peripherally, sometimes referred to as the mica scale (*Figs 6.122, 6.123*). These lesions usually heal without scarring, but are sometimes associated with hypopigmentation, which may be the most prominent feature in dark-skinned races.

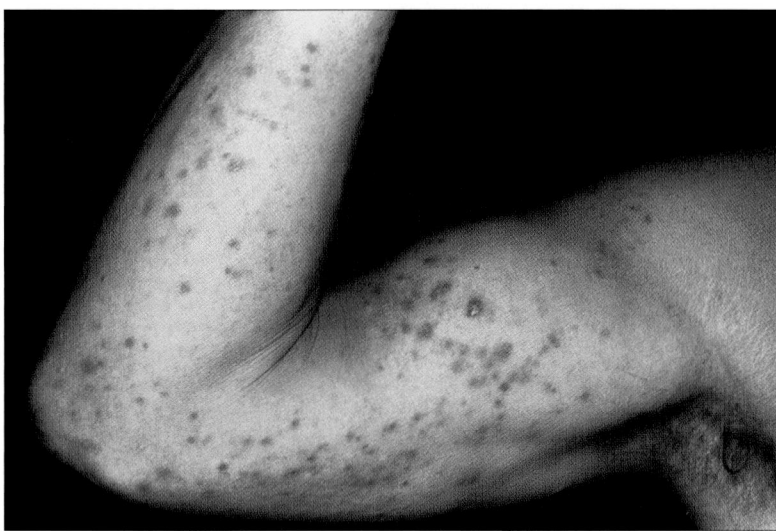

Fig. 6.118
Pityriasis lichenoides acuta: typical lesions with pustulation are present on the arm, a commonly affected site. By courtesy of the Institute of Dermatology, London, UK.

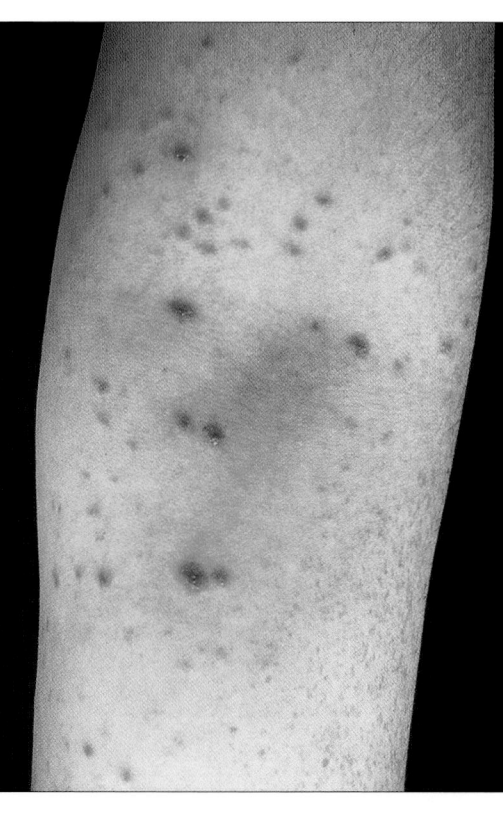

Fig. 6.119
Pityriasis lichenoides acuta: early lesions are erythematous and papular. By courtesy of the Institute of Dermatology, London, UK.

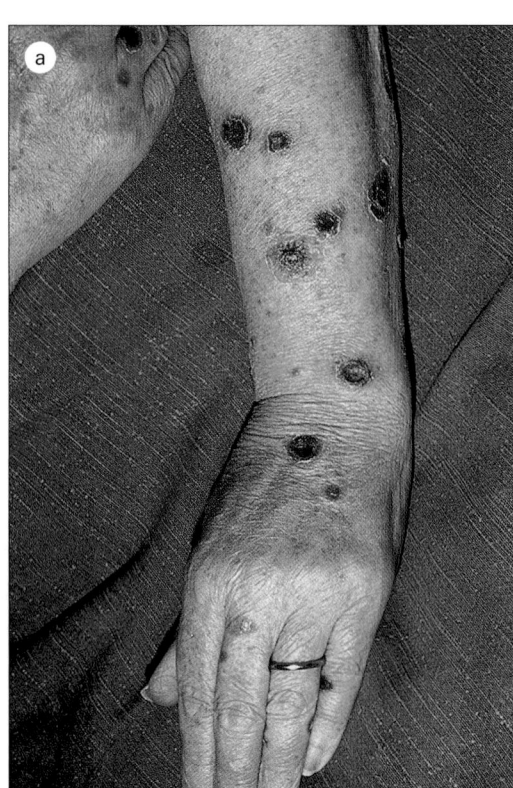

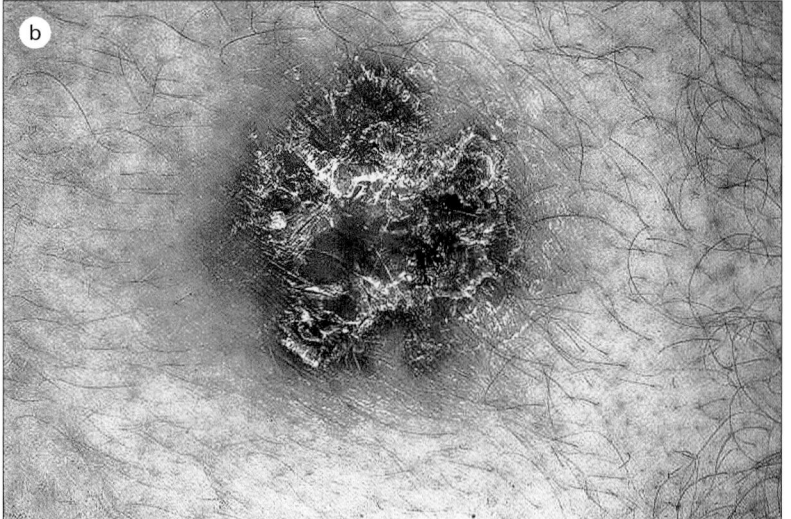

Fig. 6.120
Pityriasis lichenoides acuta: (a) necrotic and ulcerated lesions are present, (b) close-up view. By courtesy of the Institute of Dermatology, London, UK.

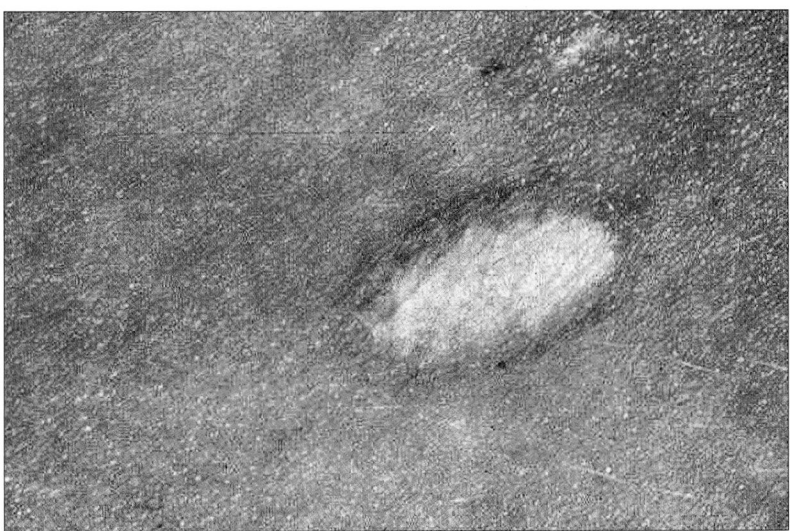

Fig. 6.121
Pityriasis lichenoides acuta: healed lesion showing scarring and hypopigmentation. By courtesy of the Institute of Dermatology, London, UK.

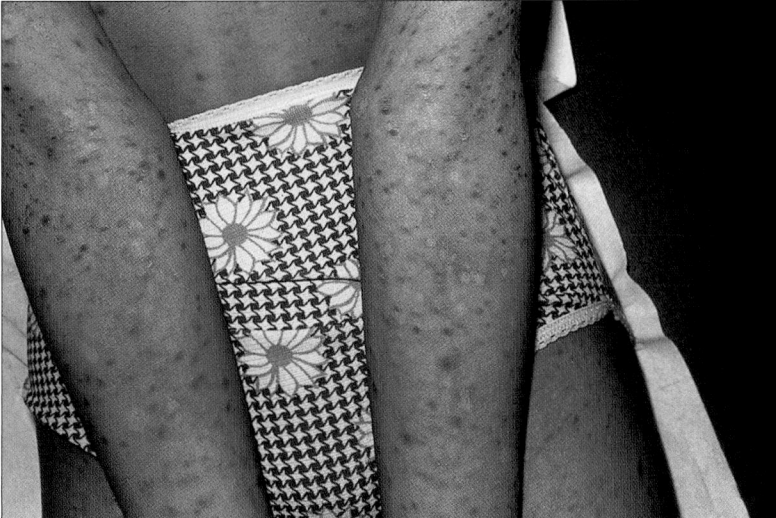

Fig. 6.122
Pityriasis lichenoides acuta: widespread brown scaly papules are present on the arms, a characteristic site. By courtesy of R.A. Marsden, MD, St George's Hospital, London, UK.

Although there are case reports of lymphoma (mycosis fungoides) developing in patients with pityriasis lichenoides, this is a rare event;[8–10] however, see below.[8] Most reported examples would today probably be reclassified as lymphomatoid papulosis.

The rare febrile ulceronecrotic variant is associated systemic features including fever, muscle weakness and pain, malaise, lymphadenopathy, arthritis, myocardial involvement and neuropsychiatric manifestations.[3–5,11,12] Cutaneous manifestations include large 2–6 cm ulceronecrotic lesions, hemorrhagic and necrotic papules and erythema multiforme-like lesions.[3]

Pathogenesis and histological features

Immunofluorescence examination of biopsies from fresh purpuric lesions commonly detects IgM and C3 in the walls of the superficial dermal blood vessels and along the epidermodermal junction in both the acute and chronic forms of the disease.[13–15] A high proportion of patients have elevated circulating immune complexes.[16,17] Cytotoxic suppressor T-cells constitute the majority of the infiltrate in pityriasis lichenoides acuta et varioliformis.[18,19] Lesser numbers are seen in pityriasis lichenoides chronica. These (and the overlying keratinocytes in addition to nearby endothelial cells) have been shown to express HLA-DR.[19] In contrast to lymphomatoid papulosis, the Ki-1 (CD30) activation antigen is not expressed in pityriasis lichenoides acuta except perhaps in overlap cases.[20] Macrophages are also numerous. Langerhans' cells are diminished in number. Clonal T-cell receptor gene rearrangements have been described in small numbers of patients with pityriasis lichenoides acuta raising the possibility of overlap with cutaneous T-cell lymphoma.[21,22] Exceptionally, pityriasis lichenoides acuta may progress to cutaneous T-cell lymphoma.[23]

The histopathological features of pityriasis lichenoides are similar in both variants, although in the acute form the changes are usually more severe. Both are characterized by varying proportions of epidermal and dermal changes.[24–27]

The chronic lesions of pityriasis lichenoides are characterized by parakeratosis in which there are sometimes small collections of lymphocytes reminiscent of the Munro microabscesses of psoriasis (*Figs 6.124, 6.125*). The epidermis may show slight acanthosis and usually small numbers of necrotic keratinocytes are present accompanied

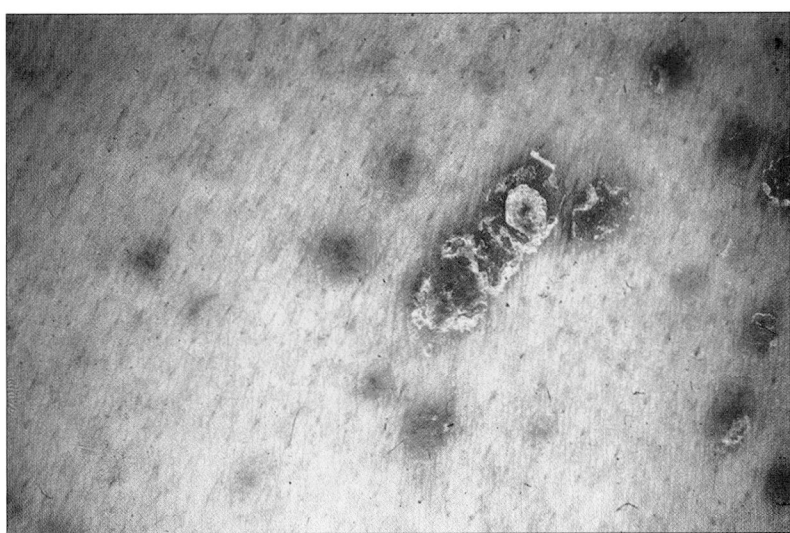

Fig. 6.123
Pityriasis lichenoides chronica: the characteristic mica scale. By courtesy of the Institute of Dermatology, London, UK.

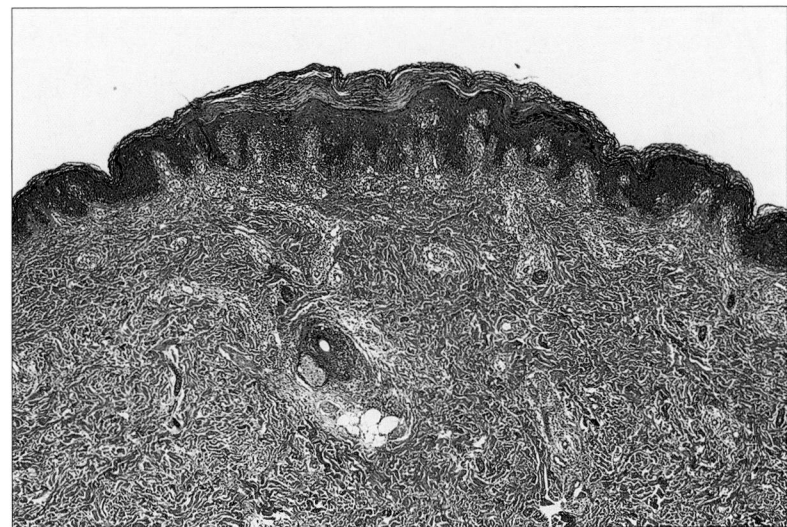

Fig. 6.124
Pityriasis lichenoides chronica: there is hyperkeratosis with parakeratosis and acanthosis.

by a hint of interface change (*Fig. 6.126*). Spongiosis is often a feature. There is a perivascular chronic inflammatory cell infiltrate in the superficial and papillary dermis. Purpura is often present but is usually not marked (*Fig. 6.127*).

The acute lesions of pityriasis lichenoides show similar epidermal features, but on a much exaggerated scale. Marked inter- and intracellular edema accompanied by keratinocyte necrosis and interface change frequently result in vesiculation and ulceration (*Figs 6.128, 6.129*). Exocytosis is usually prominent and intraepidermal red blood cells are characteristic. The upper dermis is edematous and contains chronic inflammatory cell infiltrate (*Fig. 6.130*). This is usually perivascular and varies from sparse to dense; typically is has a wedge-shaped appearance, extending deeply into the reticular dermis although this is only seen in biopsies from established lesions. The infiltrate consists of lymphocytes with an admixture of histiocytes. Red cell extravasation is usually conspicuous (*Fig. 6.131*). The blood vessels of the superficial dermis are dilated and congested. Although the endothelial cells are often blurred or swollen, fibrinoid necrosis indicating necrotizing vasculitis is rarely seen (*Figs 6.132, 6.133*).

In febrile ulceronecrotic Mucha–Habermann disease, the features are those of very severe pityriasis lichenoides acuta often accompanied by the changes of allergic vasculitis.[3,5,28,29]

In the earlier literature, patients having clinical and histological features of both pityriasis lichenoides et varioliformis acuta and lymphomatoid papulosis were documented.[15] In the light of our current understanding of these two conditions, it is now apparent that such patients clearly were suffering from lymphomatoid papulosis. This latter condition is discussed on page 1399.

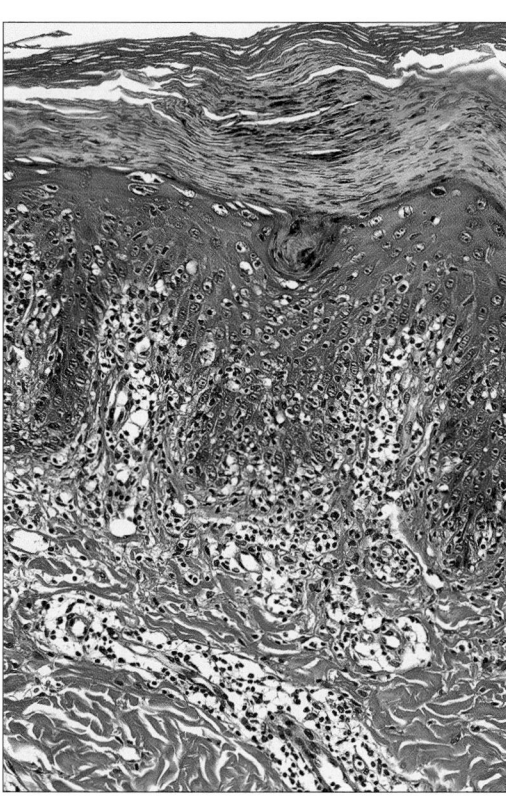

Fig. 6.125
Pityriasis lichenoides chronica: note the parakeratosis, lymphocytic exocytosis, apoptosis and focal interface change.

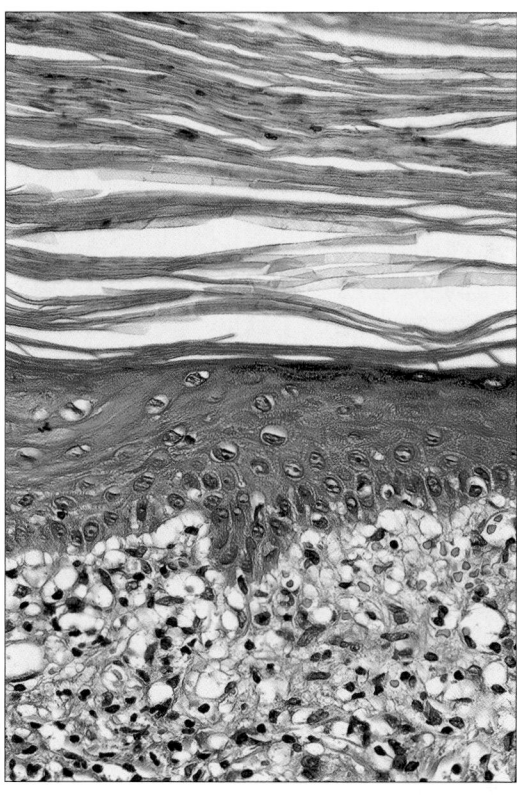

Fig. 6.127
Pityriasis lichenoides chronica: high power view showing red cell extravasation.

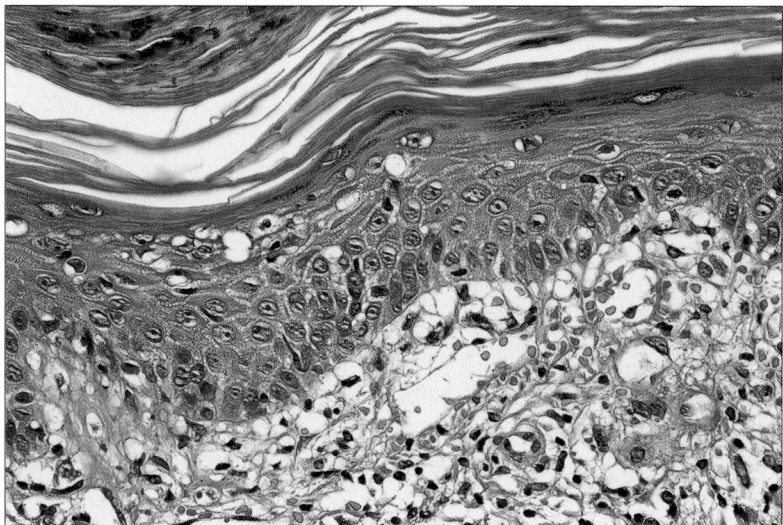

Fig. 6.126
Pityriasis lichenoides chronica: high power view showing basal cell hydropic degeneration.

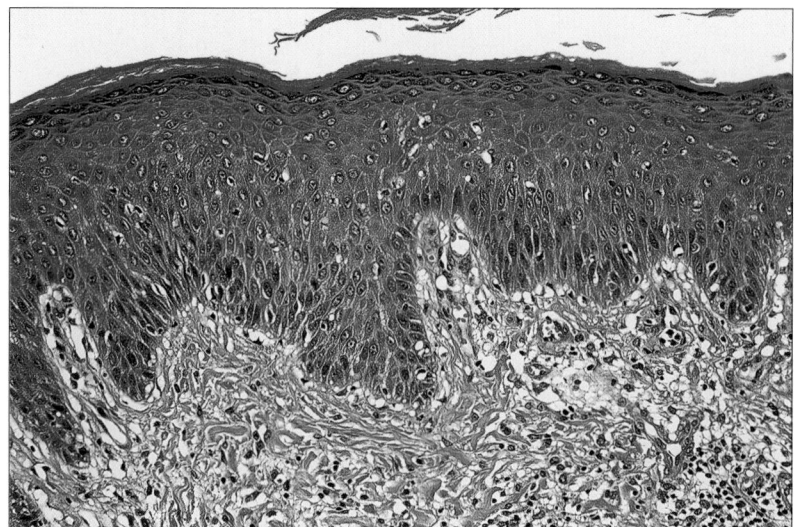

Fig. 6.128
Pityriasis lichenoides acuta: early stage showing extensive basal cell hydropic degeneration.

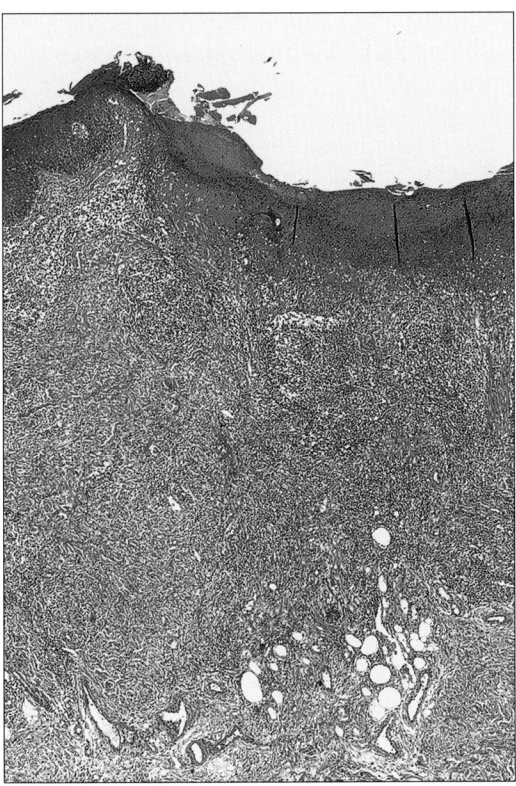

Fig. 6.129
Pityriasis lichenoides acuta: this view shows an ulcerated papule with overlying crust.

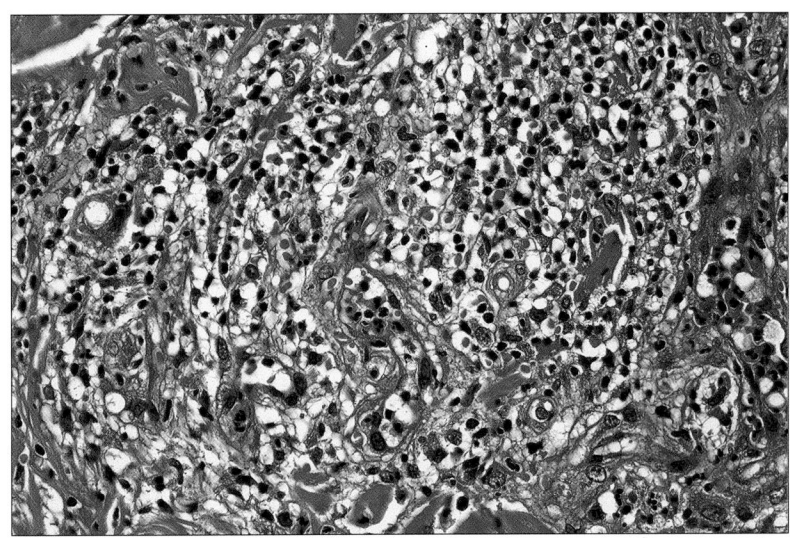

Fig. 6.131
Pityriasis lichenoides acuta: this high power view shows a heavy diffuse lymphohistiocytic infiltrate. Red cell extravasation can also be seen.

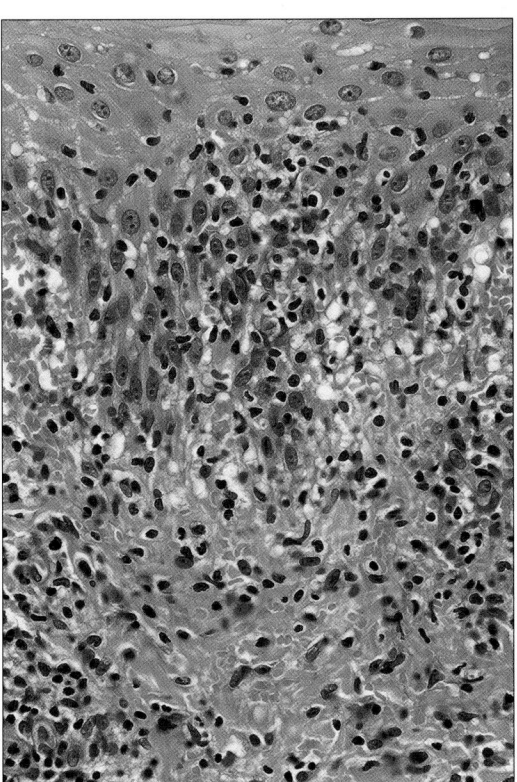

Fig. 6.130
Pityriasis lichenoides acuta: the edge of this established lesion shows basal cell hydropic degeneration and red cell extravasation.

Fig. 6.132
Pityriasis lichenoides acuta: in this example, acute vasculitis can be seen at the interface of the dermis with the subcutaneous fat.

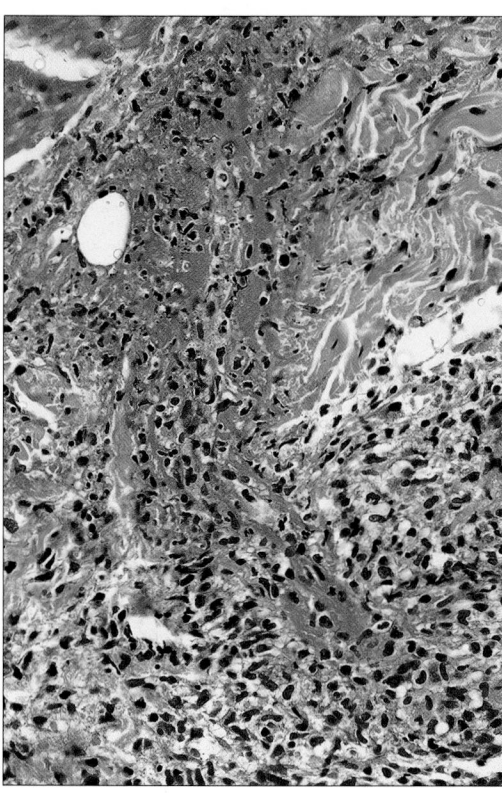

Fig. 6.133
Pityriasis lichenoides acuta: high power view showing fibrinoid necrosis affecting the dermal vasculature.

References

1. Romaní, J., Puig, L., Fernández-Figueras, M. et al (1998) Pityriasis lichenoides in children: clinicopathologic review of 22 patients. *Pediatr Dermatol*, **15**, 1–6.
2. Patel, D.G., Kihiczak, G., Schwartz, R.A. et al (2000) Pityriasis lichenoides. *Cutis*, **65**, 17–23.
3. Tsuji, T., Kasamatsu, M., Yokota, M. et al (1996) Mucha–Habermann disease and its febrile ulceronecrotic variant. *Cutis*, **58**, 123–131.
4. Maekawa, Y., Nakamura, T., Nogami, R. (1994) Febrile ulceronecrotic Mucha–Habermann disease. *J Dermatol*, **21**, 46–49.
5. Suárez, J., López, B., Villalba, R. et al (1996) Febrile ulceronecrotic Mucha–Habermann disease: a case report and review of the literature. *Dermatology*, **192**, 277–279.
6. Rogers, M. (1992) Pityriasis lichenoides and lymphomatoid papulosis. *Semin Dermatol*, **11**, 73–79.
7. Gelmetti, C., Rigoni, C., Alessi, E. et al (1990) Pityriasis lichenoides in children: a long term follow-up of eighty-nine cases. *J Am Acad Dermatol*, **23**, 473–478.
8. Rivers, J.K., Samman, P.D., Spittle, M.F. (1986) Pityriasis lichenoides-like lesions associated with poikiloderma: a precursor of mycosis fungoides. *Brit J Dermatol*, **117** (Suppl. 30), 17.
9. Forston, J.S., Schroeter, A.L., Esterly, N.B. (1990). Cutaneous T-cell lymphoma (parapsoriasis en plaque). An association with pityriasis lichenoides et varioliformis acuta in young children. *Arch Dermatol*, **126**, 1449–1453.
10. Grice, K., Smith, N. (1980) Pityriasis lichenoides with poikiloderma atrophicans vasculare. *Brit J Dermatol*, **103** (Suppl.), 66–67.
11. Hoghton, M.A., Ellis, J.P., Hayes, M.J. (1989) Febrile ulceronecrotic Mucha–Haberman disease: a fatality. *J R Soc Med*, **82**, 500–501.
12. Luberti, A.A., Rabinowitz, L.G., Vernereli, K.O. (1991) Severe febrile Mucha–Habermann's disease in children: case report and review of the literature. *Pediatr Dermatol*, **8**, 51–57.
13. Clayton, R., Haffenden, G., Du Vivier, A. (1978) An immunofluorescence study of pityriasis lichenoides acuta. *Br J Dermatol*, **97**, 491–493.
14. Clayton, R., Haffenden, G. (1978) An immunofluorescence study of pityriasis lichenoides. *Br J Dermatol*, **99**, 491–493.
15. Black, M.M. (1982) Lymphomatoid papulosis and pityriasis lichenoides: are they related? *Br J Dermatol*, **106**, 717–721.
16. Clayton, R., Haffenden, G., Du Vivier, A. et al (1977) Pityriasis lichenoides: an immune complex disease. *Br J Dermatol*, **97**, 629–634.
17. Hayashi, T. (1977) Pityriasis lichenoides et varioliformis acuta: immunohistopathologic study. *J Dermatol*, **4**, 173–178.
18. Muhlbauer, J.E., Bhan, A.K., Harrist, T.J. et al (1984) Immunopathology of pityriasis lichenoides acuta. *J Am Acad Dermatol*, **10**, 783–795.
19. Wood, G.S., Strickler, J.G., Abel, E.A. et al (1987) Immunohistology of pityriasis lichenoides et varioliformis acuta and pityriasis lichenoides chronica: evidence for their interrelationship with lymphomatoid papulosis. *J Am Acad Dermatol*, **16**, 559–570.
20. Varga, F.J., Vonderheid, E.C., Olbricht, S.M. et al (1989) Immunohistochemcial distinction of lymphomatoid papulosis and pityriasis lichenoides et varioliformis acuta. *Am J Pathol*, **136**, 979–987.
21. Weiss, L.M., Wood, G.S., Ellisen, L.W. et al (1987) Clonal T cell populations in pityriasis lichenoides et varioliformis acuta (Mucha–Haberman disease). *Am J Pathol*, **126**, 417–421.
22. Panhans, A., Bodemer, C., Macinthyre, E. et al (1996) Pityriasis lichenoides of childhood with atypical CD30-positive cells and clonal T-cell receptor gene rearrangements. *J Am Acad Dermatol*, **35**, 489–490.
23. Forston, J.S., Schroeter, A.L., Esterly, N.B. (1990) Cutaneous T-cell lymphoma (parapsoriasis en plaque). An association with pityriasis lichenoides et varioliformis acuta in young children. *Arch Dermatol*, **126**, 1449–1453.
24. Hood, A.F., Mark, E.J. (1982) Histopathologic diagnosis of pityriasis lichenoides et varioliformis acuta and its clinical correlation. *Arch Dermatol*, **118**, 478–482.
25. Marks, R., Black, M.M. (1972) The epidermal component of pityriasis lichenoides. *Br J Dermatol*, **87**, 106–113.
26. Marks, R., Black, M., Wilson Jones, E. (1972) Pityriasis lichenoides: a reappraisal. *Br J Dermatol*, **86**, 215–225.
27. Black, M.M., Marks, R. (1972) The inflammatory reaction in pityriasis lichenoides. *Br J Dermatol*, **87**, 533–539.
28. Auster, B.I., Santa Cruz, D.J., Eisen, A.Z. (1979) Febrile ulceronecrotic Mucha–Habermann's disease with interstitial pneumonitis. *J Cutan Pathol*, **6**, 66–76.
29. López-Estebaranz, J.L., Vanaclocha, F., Gil, R. et al (1993) Febrile ulceronecrotic Mucha–Habermann's disease. *J Am Acad Dermatol*, **29**, 903–906.

Superficial and deep perivascular inflammatory dermatoses

7

Chronic superficial dermatitis 261

Toxic erythema 263
Erythema annulare centrifugum 263
Erythema gyratum repens 265

Lymphocytic infiltrate of the skin 267

Reticular erythematous mucinosis 269

Polymorphous light eruption 271

Tumid lupus erythematosus 273

Perniosis 274

Chilblain lupus erythematosus 276

Pigmented purpuric dermatoses 277

Lichen aureus 279

Pruritic urticarial papules and plaques of pregnancy 280

Pregnancy prurigo 281

Urticarial vasculitis 282

Tumor necrosis factor receptor-associated periodic syndrome 285

Eosinophilic, polymorphic and pruritic eruption associated with radiotherapy 285

Viral exanthemata 285

Chronic superficial dermatitis

Clinical features

Chronic superficial dermatitis (digitate dermatosis, superficial scaly dermatitis, small-plaque parapsoriasis, persistent superficial dermatitis) is a not uncommon condition, which presents as erythematous scaly persistent patches, showing a predilection for the limbs and trunk. While the lesions may be round or oval, they often have a finger-like appearance, hence, the alternative designation of digitate dermatosis (*Figs 7.1, 7.2*).[1] The patches are usually a few centimeters in greatest dimension, but may sometimes be much larger. They are associated with a fine 'cigarette-paper' scale that often has a pale white, tan or yellowish color (*Fig. 7.3*). The disorder is most commonly encountered in middle-aged adults and shows a predilection for men. The patient is usually otherwise asymptomatic. Lesions tend to chronicity, often persisting for many years. Chronic superficial dermatitis does not progress to mycosis fungoides.

Histological features

Biopsy shows a superficial perivascular lymphocytic infiltrate (*Figs 7.4, 7.5*). The infiltrate is of variable density but is often very sparse. Cytological atypia is absent. The epidermis often shows foci of spongiosis. A confluent linear band of parakeratosis spanning multiple rete is a characteristic finding.

The infiltrate is largely composed of CD4+ T-lymphocytes with a minor population of CD8+ T-suppressor cells (*Fig. 7.6*).[2] In a small

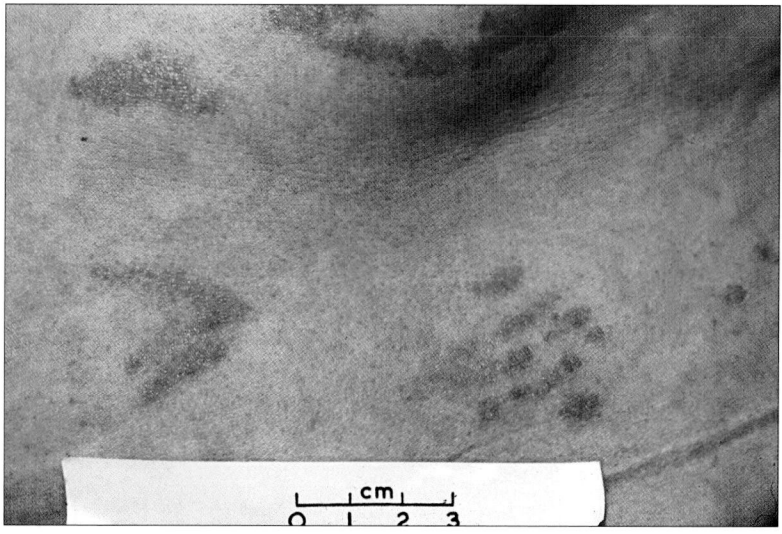

Fig. 7.1
Chronic superficial dermatitis: this patient shows digitate erythematous lesions in a characteristic distribution. By courtesy of the Institute of Dermatology, London, UK.

series, the CD4 to CD8 ratio ranged from 2 to 4.[2] The T-cells are generally reactive for CD2, CD3 and CD5 (*Fig. 7.7*). CD7 expression is variable and may be absent. Scattered CD68 reactive macrophages and CD1+ Langerhans' cells may be seen.

Differential diagnosis

The biopsy findings seen in chronic superficial dermatitis are entirely non-specific. In fact, the constellation of histological findings is among the most often encountered by the dermatopathologist. Certainly, the vast majority of biopsies that shows the histological features described above do not represent chronic superficial dermatitis. Delayed-type hypersensitivity reactions are more commonly associated with these histological features. Many other diseases similarly cause such non-specific biopsy findings including viral exanthems and connective tissue disease. Therefore, clinical correlation is necessary to establish the diagnosis.

The main clinical differential diagnosis is with mycosis fungoides and, accordingly, most biopsies are obtained to exclude this possibility. The patches in chronic superficial dermatitis tend to be uniform in size, shape and color, contrasting vividly with the greater variability of those of mycosis fungoides. The presence of spongiosis favors a diagnosis of chronic superficial dermatitis; however, mycosis fungoides may also be associated with significant spongiosis and this feature does not reliably distinguish these disorders. Diagnostic pointers favoring early mycosis fungoides include the presence of atypical lymphocytes, epidermotropism, and lymphocytes aligned along the basal cell layer of the epidermis ('tagging').

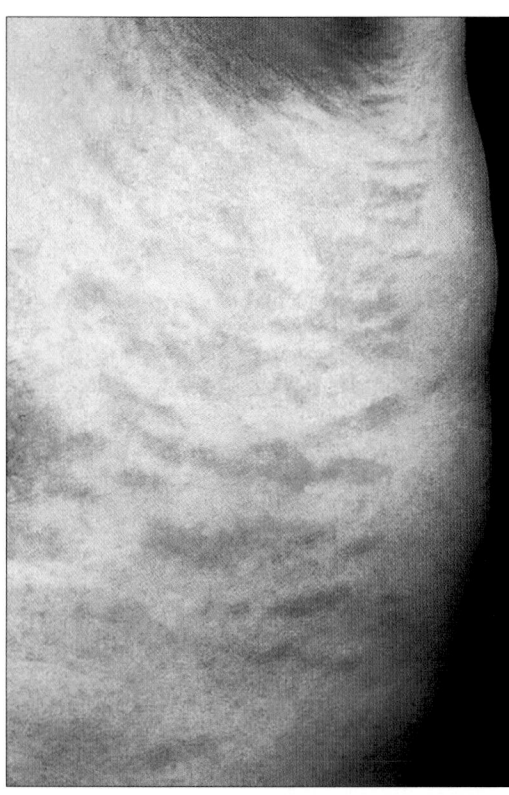

Fig. 7.2
Chronic superficial dermatitis: these uniform, linear lesions had been present for many years. By courtesy of the Institute of Dermatology, London, UK.

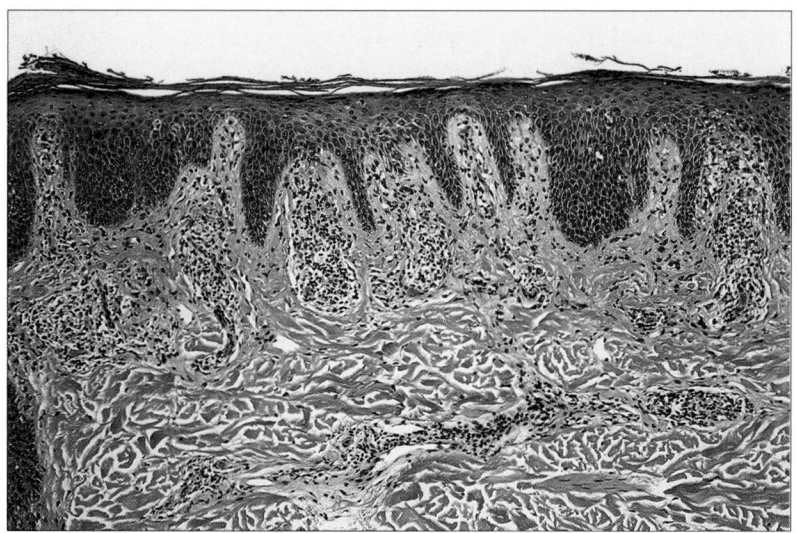

Fig. 7.4
Chronic superficial dermatitis: there is parakeratosis, acanthosis and a superficial perivascular infiltrate.

Fig. 7.3
Chronic superficial dermatitis: closer examination shows that the lesions appear somewhat wrinkled and have a fine scale. By courtesy of R.A. Marsden, MD, St George's Hospital, London, UK.

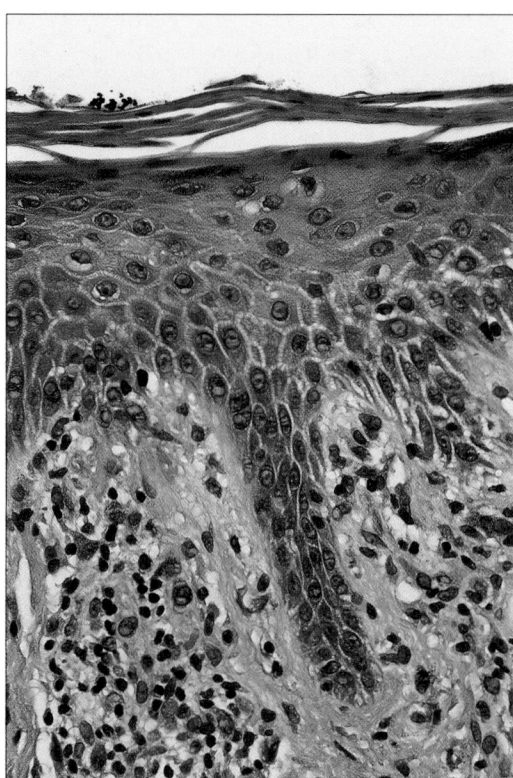

Fig. 7.5
Chronic superficial dermatitis: there is very slight intercellular edema. The infiltrate consists of lymphocytes and histiocytes.

Immunohistochemistry should be viewed with caution. Loss of CD5 and CD7 expression may support a diagnosis of mycosis fungoides provided there are histological features in favor of the diagnosis and if the clinical context is appropriate. Occasionally, only careful review of the clinical information, taken in conjunction with the histological features of previous biopsies (if available) allows for definitive diagnosis. It is important to note that some investigators have demonstrated cases of chronic superficial dermatitis with clonal T-cell gene rearrangements by polymerase chain reaction (PCR).[2] One case with a clonal T-cell popu-lation resolved, underscoring the growing appreciation that clonality and malignancy are not necessarily synonymous.[2] Therefore, it appears that demonstration of a clonal T-cell population may not suffice to reliably distinguish chronic superficial dermatosis from early mycosis fungoides in all cases. In the past, others have concluded that chronic superficial dermatitis *is* mycosis fungoides.[3] The observation that chronic superficial dermatitis rarely, if ever, evolves into (or declares itself as) frank mycosis fungoides has led some authors to cast doubt on this view. More recent publications have asserted that chronic persistent dermatitis does not progress to mycosis fungoides.[4] It is perhaps more likely that some cases of very early mycosis fungoides cannot be reliably distinguished from chronic superficial dermatitis. Recently, clonal T-cell gene rearrange-ments have been demonstrated in circulating lymphocytes in blood but not in skin of patients with digitate dermatitis.[5] Clearly, long-term follow-up studies are necessary to resolve the significance of clonality in putative cases of chronic superficial dermatitis.

Pityriasis lichenoides may also be confused with chronic superficial dermatitis. Spongiosis without interface changes favor the latter. Pityriasis lichenoides is associated with either vacuolar or lichenoid interface changes in the absence of spongiosis.[6]

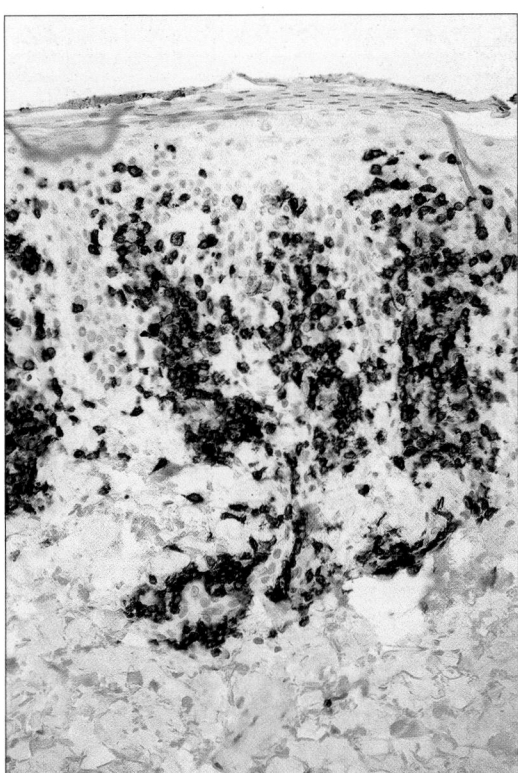

Fig. 7.6
Chronic superficial dermatitis: the infiltrate is composed predominantly of CD4+ T-helper cells.

References

1. Hu, C.H., Winkelman, R.K. (1973) Digitate dermatosis. *Arch Dermatol*, 107, 65–69.
2. Haeffner, A.C., Smoller, B.R., Zepter, K. et al (1995) Differentiation and clonality of lymphocytes in small plaque parapsoriasis. *Arch Dermatol*, 131, 321–328.
3. Ackerman, A.B., Schiff, T.A. (1996) If small plaque parapsoriasis is a cutaneous T-cell lymphoma, even an abortive one, it must be mycosis fungoides. *Arch Dermatol*, 132, 562–566.
4. Liu, V., McKee, P.H. (2002) Cutaneous T-cell lymphoproliferative disorders: recent advances and clarification of confusing issues. *Adv Anat Pathol*, 9, 79–100.
5. Muche, J.M., Lukosky, A., Heim, J. et al (1999) Demonstration of frequent occurrence of clonal T cells in the peripheral blood but not the skin of patients with small plaque parapsoriasis. *Blood*, 15, 3635–3536.
6. Benmaman, O., Sánchez, J.L. (1998) Comparative clinicopathologic study on pityriasis lichenoides chronica and small plaque parapsoriasis. *Am J Dermatopathol*, 10, 189–196.

Toxic erythema

Toxic erythema, annular erythema and gyrate erythema are terms used by dermatologists to describe a number of diseases that share common clinical and histological appearances. Clinically, the terms imply annular erythematous lesions. Pathologists often also use these same terms (particularly gyrate erythema) in a generic manner to describe an inflam-matory lesion with a 'cuffed' perivascular lymphocytic infiltrate. Although such nomenclature may be used as a descriptor (as one might use terms such as 'lichenoid' for example), it should not be taken to imply a specific disease. It is likely that the earlier literature frequently classified different diseases together under these appellations.[1] Therefore, to avoid confusion, it is encouraged that these terms are not used in referring to specific diseases.

Reference

1. Mahood, J.M. (1983) Erythema annulare centrifugum: a review of 24 cases with special reference to its association with underlying disease. *Clin Exp Dermatol*, 8, 383–387.

Erythema annulare centrifugum

Clinical features

Erythema annulare centrifugum has an incidence of 1/100,000 and may be associated with certain underlying factors, including:

*   connective tissue disorders, e.g. Sjögren's syndrome[1,2]
*   drugs, e.g. penicillin, salicylates, amytriptyline, etizolam, gold sodium thiomoalate, hydroxychloroquine sulfate, piroxicam, hydrochlorothiazide and thiacetazone[3–10]
*   bacterial infection, e.g. *Mycobacteria, Streptococcus, Escherichia coli*[11]
*   viral infection, e.g. Epstein–Barr virus, molluscum contagiosum[12]

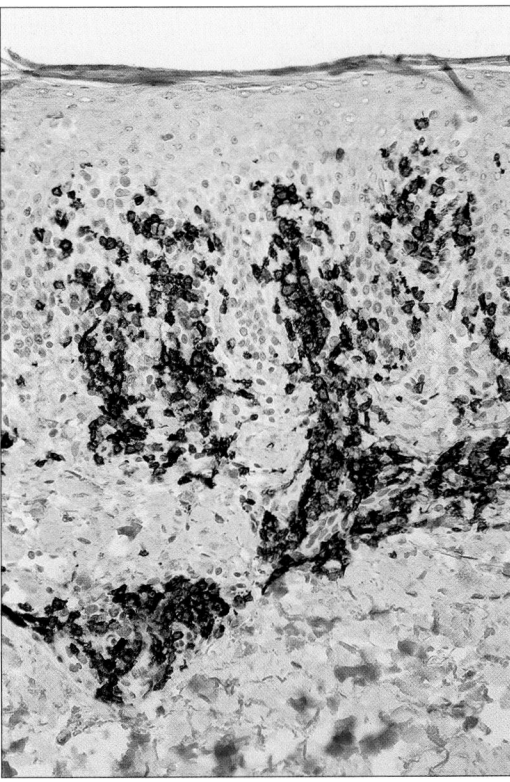

Fig. 7.7
Chronic superficial dermatitis: in this example, there is no significant loss of CD7 expression.

- fungal infection, e.g. dermatophytoses, *Candida*[13–15]
- parasites, e.g. helminths[16]
- sarcoidosis[17]
- hypereosinophilic syndrome[18]
- bullous dermatosis, e.g. linear IgA dermatosis[19,20]
- autoimmune disease, e.g. polyglandular autoimmune disease type 1.[21]

Many of these associations are likely to be coincidental and, in most cases, no underlying etiology is identified.[22–26] It is unclear whether erythema annulare centrifugum is a distinctive entity or simply represents the morphological expression of a number of inflammatory dermatoses such as hypersensitivity reactions sharing common histological features.

Mahood and colleagues emphasized that many earlier reports of neoplasia associated with erythema annulare centrifugum are questionable since different subtypes of annular erythemas were often classified together.[22,27,28] However, more recent cases have recorded erythema annulare centrifugum occurring in patients with underlying malignancy, once again raising the issue of an association with neoplasia. Erythema annulare centrifugum in patients with non-small cell lung carcinoma and Hodgkin's lymphoma have been reported in the last decade.[29–31] In a recent large series, carcinoma was present in 6 of 66 (13%) patients.[32] Of these, two had leukemia (acute myelogenous and acute lymphoblastic); one patient had non-Hodgkin's lymphoma; and three cases were associated with carcinoma (lung, rectal and hepatocellular).[32]

Erythema annulare centrifugum has been reported in all age groups, including infants, but is most commonly seen in young adults.[33] A recent large series found the lower extremities, particularly the thighs, were the most frequent site of involvement.[32] Nearly 50% of patients in this series had lower extremity involvement. The trunk was affected in 28% of patients and the upper extremity in 16%.[32] The hands, feet and face are usually spared. Head and neck involvement was seen in only 8% of patients.[32] Laboratory investigation sometimes reveals a peripheral eosinophilia.[22] Although individual lesions persist for weeks to a few months before resolving, a course of relapses and remissions over months to years is common. Kim et al. found lesions lasted from 3 days to 18 years with a mean duration of 2.8 years.[32]

The lesions take the form of annular erythematous bands, which may spread outwards or remain stationary (*Fig. 7.8*). They are well circumscribed with raised edges, and slight scaling that tends to trail behind the advancing margin.[34] With time, central clearing is seen.

Arcuate and polycyclic variants are therefore occasionally evident.[22] Lesions may be mildly pruritic. Vesiculation is rare.[23]

Some authors have divided the disease into two distinctive subtypes: superficial and deep gyrate erythema.[32]

- The *superficial variant* is associated with pruritus and has a trailing scale.
- The *deep variant* is characterized by erythematous annular lesions with indurated borders but lacking a scale.

Histological features

A spectrum of non-specific histological findings is seen in erythema annulare centrifugum. As noted above, deep and superficial variants are recognized.[32]

In the superficial variant, a well-demarcated perivascular infiltrate of lymphocytes and histiocytes, often described as having a 'coat sleeve' or 'pipe-stem' appearance, is confined to the superficial dermis (*Figs 7.9, 7.10*). The overlying epidermis often may be normal; however, epidermal changes including mild spongiosis, slight and focal basal layer vacuolar degeneration, mounds of parakeratosis or hyperkeratosis are encountered in approximately 50% of patients.[32] In the deep subtype of erythema annulare centrifugum, the perivascular infiltrate involves both the superficial and deep plexuses.[23–25,32]

In the deep variant, epidermal changes are usually absent or minimal.

In both variants, the degree of inflammation is variable; however, the density or inflammation tends to be greater in the deep variant. The vast majority of cells are lymphocytes; however, a minor component of histiocytes and eosinophils may be seen.

Differential diagnosis

Given that the histological features of erythema annulare centrifugum are not distinctive, it is critical to correlate the biopsy and clinical findings. Clinical information is necessary to distinguish this disorder from other gyrate erythemas, pityriasis rosea, hypersensitivity reactions, lupus erythematosus, viral exanthemata and Jessner's lymphocytic infiltrate. In cases with significant epidermal changes, a silver stain to

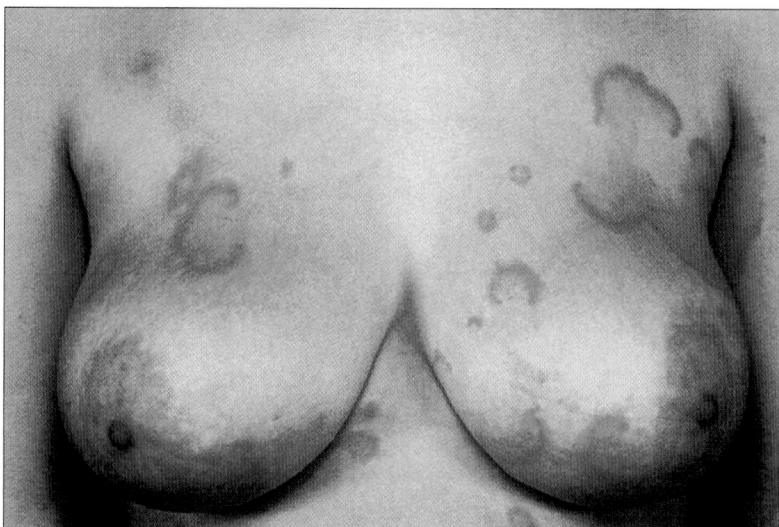

Fig. 7.8
Erythema annulare centrifugum: typical bilateral annular lesions involving the chest, breasts, abdomen and arms. By courtesy of R.A. Marsden, MD, St George's Hospital, London, UK.

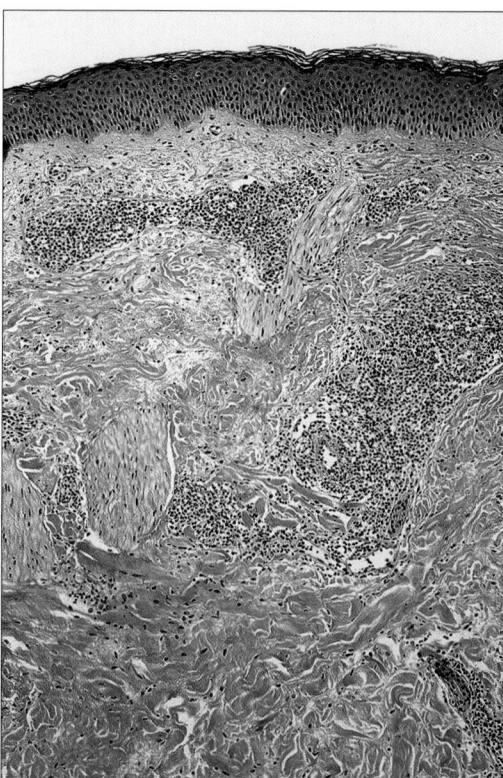

Fig. 7.9
Erythema annulare centrifugum: the superficial vasculature is surrounded by a dense infiltrate.

23. Harrison, P. (1979) The annular erythemas. *Int J Dermatol*, 18, 282–288.
24. Hurley, H.J., Hurley, J.P. (1984) The gyrate erythemas. *Semin Dermatol*, 3, 327–336.
25. White, J.W. Jr (1985) Gyrate erythema. *Dermatol Clin*, 3, 129–139.
26. Bressler, G.S., Jones, R.E. Jr (1981) Erythema annulare centrifugum. *J Am Acad Dermatol*, 4, 597–602.
27. Summerly, R. (1964) The figurate erythemas and neoplasia. *Br J Dermatol*, 76, 370–373.
28. Stillians, A. (1953) Erythema annulare centrifugum. *Arch Dermatol*, 67, 590–593.
29. Monsieur, I., Meysman, M., Noppen, M. et al (1995) Non-small-cell cancer with multiple paraneoplastic syndromes. *Eur Respir J*, 8, 1231–1234.
30. Yaniv, R., Shpielberg, O., Shapiro, D. et al (1993) Erythema annulare centrifugum as the presenting sign of Hodgkin's lymphoma. *Int J Dermatol*, 32, 59–61.
31. Leimert, J.T., Corder, M.P., Skibba, C.A. et al (1979) Erythema annulare centrifugum and Hodgkin's lymphoma: association with disease activity. *Arch Intern Med*, 139, 486–487.
32. Kim, K.J., Chang, S.E., Choi, J.H. et al (2002) Clincopathologic analysis of 66 cases of erythema annulare centrifugum. *J Dermatol*, 29, 61–67.
33. Herbert, T.N., Esterly, N.B. (1986) Annular erythema in infancy. *J Am Acad Dermatol*, 14, 339–343.
34. Tyring, S.K. (1993) Reactive erythemas: erythema annulare centrifugum and erythema gyratum repens. *Clin Dermatol*, 11, 135–139.

Erythema gyratum repens

Clinical features

Erythema gyratum repens (L. *repens*, to crawl or creep) is an extremely rare and clinically distinctive figurate eruption usually associated with an underlying malignancy. The most common associated neoplasm is carcinoma of the lung; other affiliated tumors include carcinoma of the uterus and cervix, esophagus, stomach, kidney and breast.[1–9] Treatment of the cancer may be associated with remission of the cutaneous eruption, while tumor recurrence or metastases can be accompanied by a relapse.[2] Rarely, erythema gyratum repens develops in the absence of an underlying malignancy.[10–15] Erythema gyratum repens may disclose underlying pulmonary tuberculosis. In one patient with no evidence of malignancy, the rash resolved a few days after removal of a cavitary tuberculoid lung lesion.[12]

Ichthyosis may accompany erythema gyratum repens.[16] An example of a patient with transitional cell carcinoma of the kidney who developed erythema gyratum repens and ichthyosis comes as no surprise since both are associated with malignancy. The combination of ichthyosis, palmoplantar keratosis and erythema gyratum repens, in the absence of malignancy, has also been reported.[17]

Erythema gyratum repens-like eruptions have also been described in association with connective tissue diseases. Typical erythema gyratum repens developed in a patient with cutaneous subacute lupus erythematosus following hydroxychloroquine treatment.[18] The authors of this report concluded that the patient's rash represented a peculiar pattern of involvement by subacute lupus which they designated subacute lupus gyratum repens. An erythema gyratum repens-like eruption has been also described in association with Sjögren's syndrome.[19]

Caputo et al. reported a linear IgA dermatosis, erythema and an eruption resembling erythema gyratum repens in a patient without malignancy.[20] Bullous pemphigoid may be associated with erythema gyratum repens.[21,22]

Erythema gyratum repens has been described in patients with hypereosinophilic syndrome and with no evidence of neoplasia.[23]

The eruption, which may precede the malignancy by months, takes the form of concentric bands of erythema in an annular or gyrate arrangement (*Figs 7.11, 7.12*). These bands have been described as having a 'timber grain' or 'zebra-like' pattern and they move (up to about 1 cm) daily.[24] Scaling occurs and there may be pruritus. Lesions often commence on the arms and legs, but frequently become generalized.[1] The hands, feet and face are usually spared.[24] Postinflammatory hyperpigmentation may be a feature.[1] Hyperkeratosis of the palms and soles is also sometimes present.[3,10] Males are affected twice as commonly as females.[3] Patients are usually in their seventh decade.[24]

Pathogenesis and histological features

Erythema gyratum repens may have an immunological pathogenesis, since granular deposits of IgG and C3 have been found at the basement

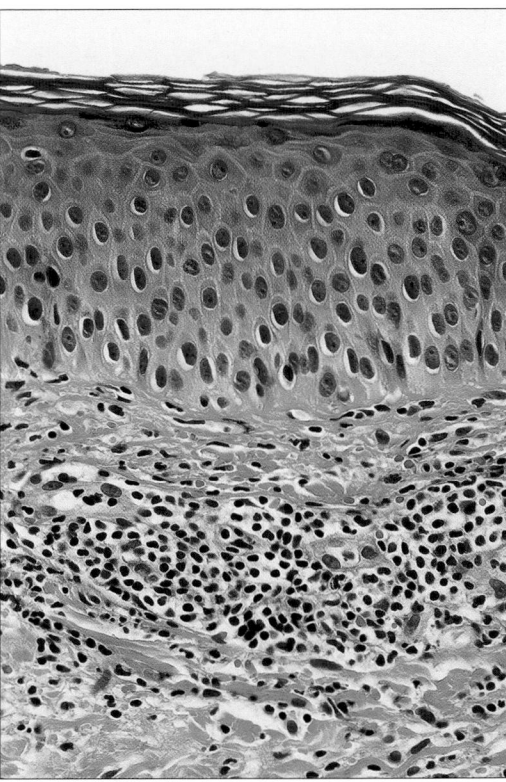

Fig. 7.10
Erythema annulare centrifugum: the infiltrate is composed of mature lymphocytes.

exclude a fungal infection is also advised. Clinically, erythema annulare centrifugum may resemble psoriasis. The presence of parakeratotic mounds associated with neutrophils would favor a diagnosis of psoriasis. In contrast to cutaneous lupus erythematosus, interface changes are not usually well developed and immunofluorescence studies are negative. Erythema chronicum migrans also enters the differential diagnosis. The presence of plasma cells would be in favor of the latter condition. Histochemical stains for spirochetes may be positive.

References

1. Katayama, I., Asai, T., Nishioka, K. et al (1989) Annular erythema associated with primary Sjögren's syndrome: analysis of T-cell subsets in infiltrates. *J Am Acad Dermatol*, 21, 1218–1281.
2. Teramoto, N., Katayama, I., Arai, H. et al (1989) Annular erythema: a possible association with primary Sjögren's syndrome. *J Am Acad Dermatol*, 20, 596–601.
3. García-Doval, I., Peteiro, C., Toiribio, J. (1999) Amitriptyline-induced erythema annular centrifugum. *Cutis*, 63, 35–36.
4. Kuroda, K., Yabunami, H., Hisanaga, Y. (2002) Etizolam-induced superficial erythema annulare centrifugum. *Clin Exp Dermatol*, 27, 34–36.
5. Mahboob, A., Haroon, T.S. (1998) Drugs causing fixed eruptions: a study of 450 cases. *Int J Dermatol*, 37, 833–838.
6. Tsuji, T., Nishimura, M., Kimura, S. (1992) Erythema annulare centrifugum associated with gold sodium thiomalate therapy. *J Am Acad Dermatol*, 27, 282–287.
7. Hudson, L.D. (1985) Erythema annulare centrifugum: an unusual case due to hydroxychloroquine sulfate. *Cutis*, 36, 120–130.
8. Hogan, D.J., Blocka, K.L.N. (1985) Erythema annulare centrifugum associated with piroxicam. *J Am Acad Dermatol*, 13, 840–841.
9. Goette, K.D., Beatrice, E. (1988) Erythema annulare centrifugum caused by hydrochlorthiazide-induced interstitial nephritis. *Int J Dermatol*, 27, 129–130.
10. Ramesh, V. (1987) Eruption resembling erythema annulare centrifugum due to thiacetazone. *Australas J Dermatol*, 28, 44.
11. Borbujo, J., Miguel, C., Lopez, A. et al (1996) Erythema annulare centrifugum and *Escherichia coli* urinary infection. *Lancet*, 347, 897–898.
12. Furue, M., Akasu, R., Ohtake, N. et al (1993) Erythema annulare centrifugum induced by molluscum contagiosum. *Br J Dermatol*, 129, 646–647.
13. Jillson, O.F. (1954) Allergic confirmation that some cases of erythema annulare centrifugum are dermatophytids. *Arch Dermatol Syphilol*, 70, 355–359.
14. Shelly, W.B. (1964) Erythema annulare centrifugum. *Arch Dermatol*, 90, 54–58.
15. Shelly, W.B. (1965) Erythema annulare centrifugum due to *Candida albicans*. *Br J Dermatol*, 77, 383–384.
16. Hendricks, A.A., Lu, C., Elfenbeing, G.J. et al (1981) Erythema annulare centrifugum associated with *Ascaris*. *Arch Dermatol*, 117, 582–585.
17. Altomare, G.F., Capella, G.L., Figero, E. (1995) Sarcoidosis presenting as erythema annular centrifugum. *Clin Exp Dermatol*, 20, 502–503.
18. Shelley, W.B., Shelley, E.D. (1985) Erythema annulare centrifugum as the presenting sign of the hypereosinophilic syndrome: observations on therapy. *Cutis*, 35, 53–55.
19. Dippel, E., Orfanos, C.E., Zouboulis, C. (2000) Linear IgA dermatosis presenting with erythema annulare centrifugum lesions: report of 3 cases in adults. *J Eur Acad Dermatol Venereol*, 15, 167–170.
20. Larregue, M., Bessieux, J.M., Laidet, B. et al (1986) Erythema annulare centrifugum revealing linear IgA dermatitis of childhood. *Ann Dermatol Venereol*, 113, 473–474.
21. Garty, B. (1998) Erythema annulare centrifugum in a patient with polyglandular autoimmune disease type 1. *Cutis*, 62, 231–232.
22. Mahood, J.M. (1983) Erythema annulare centrifugum: a review of 24 cases with special reference to its association with underlying disease. *Clin Exp Dermatol*, 8, 383–387.

membrane zone of both involved and uninvolved skin in a patient with associated bronchial carcinoma and in involved non-sun-exposed skin in another unassociated with neoplasia.[14,25-27] In a separate patient, although basement membrane zone immunofluorescence was negative, epidermal nuclear labeling was identified.[28] Caux et al. reported one patient with squamous cell carcinoma of the lung who had immunoreactants at the basement membrane of involved and normal non-sun-exposed skin. In addition, this patient showed staining of IgG, IgM and C3 along the basement membrane of the bronchus.[26] However, the immunoreactants did not localize to the tumor.

The appearances in erythema gyratum repens are not diagnostic. They include hyperkeratosis, parakeratosis, acanthosis and spongiosis, together with a superficial perivascular lymphohistiocytic infiltrate in the papillary dermis (*Figs 7.13, 7.14*).[2]

Differential diagnosis

As noted above, the histological features are non-specific and vary from patient to patient. Fortunately, the clinical features are so distinctive that confusion with other disorders is unlikely. Obviously, any patient with features of erythema gyratum repens should be very carefully evaluated for an underlying neoplasm. However, accumulating literature has shown that this eruption is also seen in patients without neoplasia and the association between malignancy and erythema gyratum repens is not as invariable as was once believed.

References

1. Hurley, H.J., Hurley, J.P. (1984) The gyrate erythemas. *Semin Dermatol*, 3, 327–355.
2. White, J.W. Jr (1985) Gyrate erythema. *Dermatol Clin*, 3, 129–139.
3. Appell, M.L., Ward, W.Q., Tyring, S.K. (1988) Erythema gyratum repens. A cutaneous marker of malignancy. *Cancer*, 62, 548–550.
4. Eubancks, L.E., McBurney, E., Reed, R. (2001) Erythema gyratum repens. *Am J Med Sci*, 321, 302–305.
5. Lombholt, H., Thestrup-Petersen, K. (2000) Paraneoplastic skin manifestations of lung carcinoma. *Acta Derm Venereol*, 80, 200–202.
6. Kwatra, A., McDonald, R.E., Corriere, J.N. Jr (1998) Erythema gyratum repens in association with renal cell carcinoma. *J Urol*, 159, 2077.
7. Rojo Sánchez, S., Suárez Fernández, R., de Eusebio Murillo, E. et al (1996) Erythema gyratum repens: another case of a rare disorder but no new insight into pathogenesis. *Dermatology*, 193, 336–337.
8. Olsen, T.G., Milroy, S.K., Jones-Olsen, S. (1984) Erythema gyratum repens with associated squamous cell carcinoma of the lung. *Cutis*, 34, 351–353.
9. Larrouy, J.C., Apter, J., Barety, M. et al (1983) Erythema gyratum repens and primary bronchial cancer. Disappearance of the dermatosis under general corticoid therapy. *Ann Dermatol Venereol*, 110, 329–334.

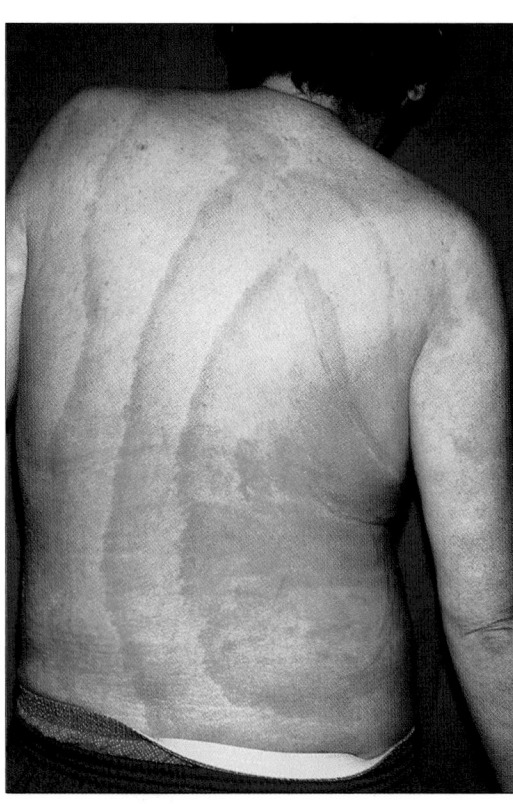

Fig. 7.11
Erythema gyratum repens: the presence of annular erythematous parallel bands with scaling is characteristic. By courtesy of R. Cerio, MD, The London Hospital, London, UK.

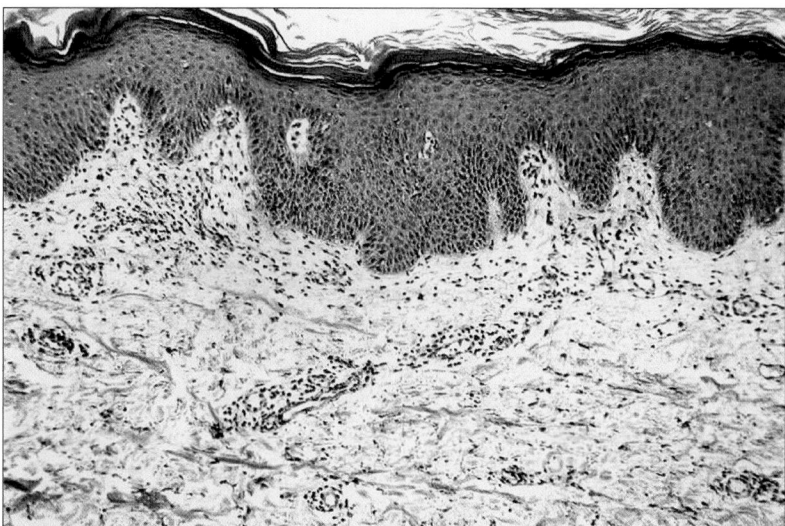

Fig. 7.13
Erythema gyratum repens: there is hyperkeratosis, acanthosis and a mild perivascular chronic inflammatory cell infiltrate.

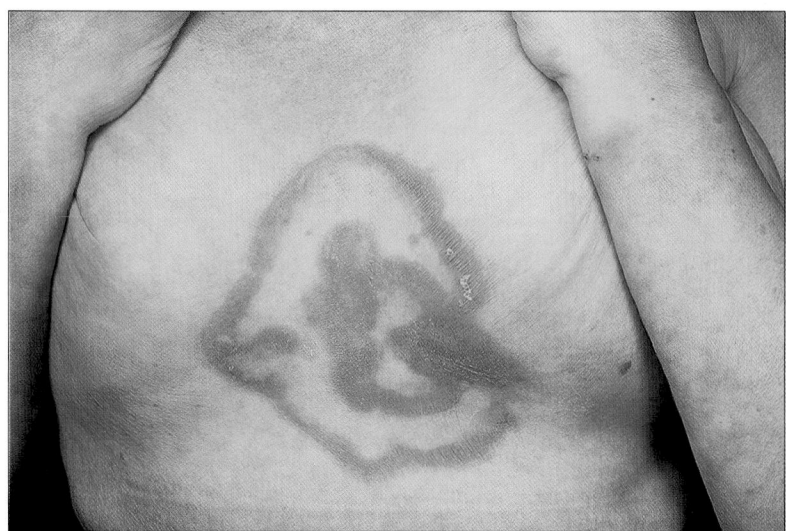

Fig. 7.12
Erythema gyratum repens: the eruption may sometimes have a bizarre appearance. By courtesy of R. Cerio, MD, The London Hospital, London, UK.

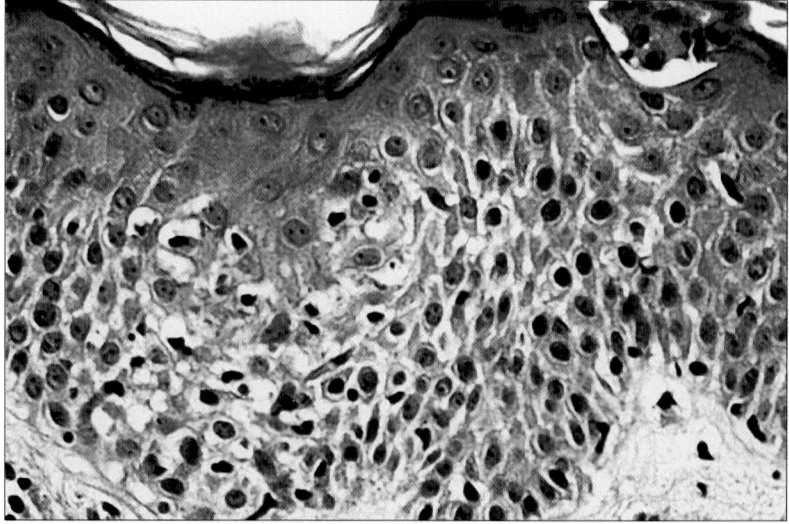

Fig. 7.14
Erythema gyratum repens: spongiosis is present.

10. Langlois, J.C., Shaw, J.M., Odland, G.F. (1985) Erythema gyratum repens unassociated with internal malignancy. *J Am Acad Dermatol*, **12**, 911–913.
11. Shelley, W.B., Hurley, H.J. (1960) Unusual autoimmune syndrome: erythema annulare centrifugum, generalized pigmentation and breast hypertrophy. *Arch Dermatol*, **81**, 889–897.
12. Barber, P.V., Doyle, L., Vichers, D.M. et al (1978) Erythema gyratum repens with pulmonary tuberculosis. *Br J Dermatol*, **98**, 465–468.
13. Cheesbrough, M.J., Williamson, D.M. (1985) Erythema gyratum repens, a stage in the resolution of pityriasis rubra pilaris. *Clin Exp Dermatol*, **10**, 466–471.
14. Garrett, S.J., Roenigk, H.H. (1992) Erythema gyratum repens in a healthy woman. *J Am Acad Dermatol*, **26**, 121–122.
15. Kawakami, T., Saito, R. (1995) Erythema gyratum repens unassociated with underlying malignancy. *J Dermatol*, **22**, 587–589.
16. Ameen, M., Chopra, S., Darvay, A. et al (2001) Erythema gyratum repens and acquired ichthyosis associated with transitional cell carcinoma of the kidney. *Clin Exp Dermatol*, **26**, 510–512.
17. Juhlin, L., Lacour, J.P., Larrouy, J.C. (1989) Episodic erythema gyratum repens with ichthyosis and palmoplantar hyperkeratosis without signs of internal malignancy. *Clin Exp Dermatol*, **14**, 223–226.
18. Hochedez, P., Vasseur, E., Staroz, F. et al (2001) Subacute cutaneous lupus gyratum repens. *Ann Dermatol Venereol*, **128**, 244–246.
19. Matsumura, T., Kumakiri, M., Sato-Matsumura, K.C. et al (1995) Erythema gyratum repens-like eruption in a patient with Sjögren syndrome. *Acta Derm Venereol*, **75**, 327.
20. Caputo, R., Bencini, P.L., Vigo, G.P. et al (1995) Eruption resembling erythema gyratum repens in linear IgA dermatosis. *Dermatology*, **190**, 235–237.
21. Graham-Brown, R.A. (1987) Bullous pemphigoid with figurate erythema associated with carcinoma of the bronchus. *Br J Dermatol*, **117**, 385–388.
22. Breathnach, S.M., Wilkinson, J.D., Black, M.M. (1982) Erythema gyratum repens-like figurate eruption in bullous pemphigoid. *Clin Exp Dermatol*, **7**, 401–406.
23. Morita, A., Sakakibara, N., Tsuji, T. (1994) Erythema gyratum repens associated with hypereosinophilic syndrome. *J Dermatol*, **21**, 612–614.
24. Boyd, A.S., Heldner, K.H., Menter, A. (1992) Erythema gyratum repens: a paraneoplastic eruption. *J Am Acad Dermatol*, **26**, 757–762.
25. Holt, P.J.A., Davies, M.G. (1977) Erythema gyratum repens – an immunologically mediated dermatosis? *Br J Dermatol*, **96**, 343–347.
26. Caux, F., Lebbe, C., Thomine, E. et al (1994) Erythema gyratum repens: a case studied with immunofluorescence, immunoelectron microscopy and immunohistochemistry. *Br J Dermatol*, **131**, 102–107.
27. Bakos, N., Krasznai, G., Begany, A.A. (1997) Erythema gyratum repens: an immunological paraneoplastic dermatosis. *Pathol Oncol Res*, **3**, 59–61.
28. Levine, L.E., Morgan, N.E., Fretzin, D. et al (1985) Erythema gyratum repens. *Arch Dermatol*, **121**, 170–171.

Lymphocytic infiltrate of the skin

Clinical features

Jessner's lymphocytic infiltrate of the skin is an uncommon dermatosis of unknown etiology, although a relationship with sun exposure, at least in the early stages, is occasionally documented.[1] Lesions, which may be single or more often multiple, occur most often on the face, neck, back and upper chest, and present as 1–2 cm diameter, asymptomatic, discoid, erythematous or brownish papules or plaques that often show central clearing to produce circinate lesions (*Figs 7.15, 7.16*).[1,2] Familial cases have occasionally been documented.[3–6]

In contrast to discoid lupus erythematosus, with which it is sometimes confused, there is no hyperkeratosis, telangiectases or follicular plugging, and scarring is not a feature. Rarely, however, the two diseases appear to coexist.[1] The disease tends to affect adults, particularly in the third to fifth decades. Although some have found a predilection for males, 54% of patients in a large series were female.[1] Rarely, the condition presents in children.[7–9] Lesions often resolve within weeks or months, but relapses are not uncommon and, in many patients, the disorder persists for years. The eruption is not characterized by seasonal variation. Lymphocytic infiltrate of the skin is a distinctive dermatosis. It does not evolve into lupus erythematosus, polymorphous light eruption or lymphocytic lymphoma.[1]

Pathogenesis and histological features

The etiology of this curious condition is unknown. Although some patients notice a relationship with sun exposure, many do not, and lesions not uncommonly develop on covered sites.

Braddock and co-authors found that natural killer cell lytic activity and antibody-dependent cell-mediated cytotoxicity was decreased.[8] This same group identified increased levels of circulating immune complexes in patients with lymphocytic infiltrate of skin. In two patients immune complexes decreased to normal levels following treatment but became elevated during recurrence of disease following treatment.[8,9] Based on these observations, these investigators concluded that immune defects might be important in the pathogenesis of Jessner's lymphocytic infiltrate. Of interest, similar findings have been observed in patients with reticular erythematous mucinosis. Clearly, further study is necessary to determine the pathogenesis of this disease.

The epidermis is typically unaffected. Within the superficial and mid-dermis is a perivascular and, much less commonly, a perifollicular infiltrate of mature lymphocytes (*Figs 7.17, 7.18*). Occasional histiocytes and scattered plasma cells may also be present and sometimes there is an increase in dermal ground substance.[10] Lymphoid follicles are not a feature.

The infiltrate consists predominantly of T-cells, most often of the CD4+ helper subtype (*Fig. 7.19*). Occasionally, however, CD8+ suppressor T-cells constitute the majority of cells.[11–14] Leu 8 is commonly expressed but human leukocyte antigen (HLA)-DR is not. B-cells are relatively sparse in number or are absent.

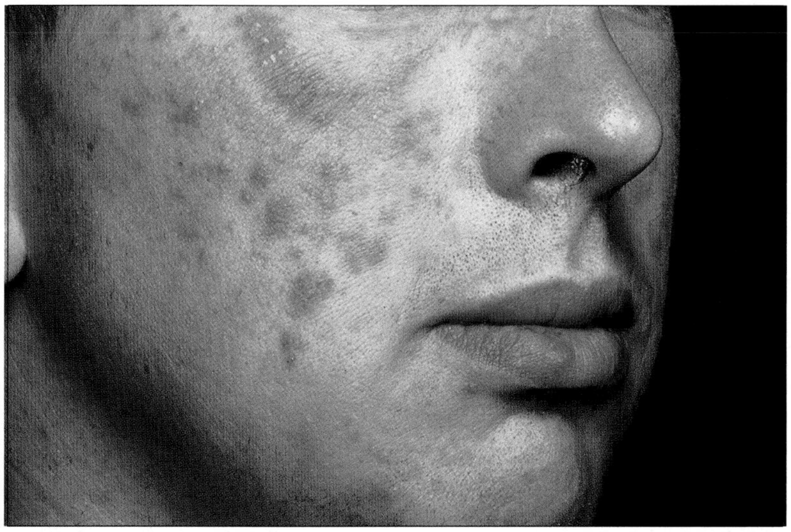

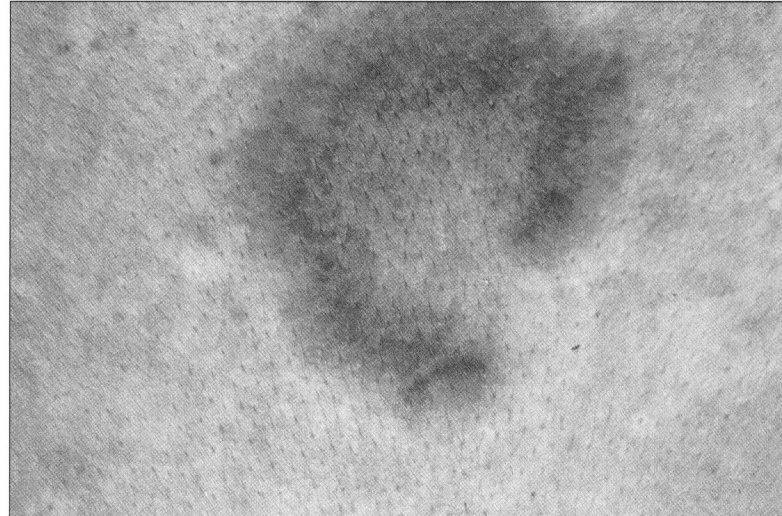

Fig. 7.15
Jessner's lymphocytic infiltrate: there are multiple erythematous plaques on this young man's cheek. By courtesy of the Institute of Dermatology, London, UK.

Fig. 7.16
Jessner's lymphocytic infiltrate: central clearing has resulted in this circinate lesion. By courtesy of the Institute of Dermatology, London, UK.

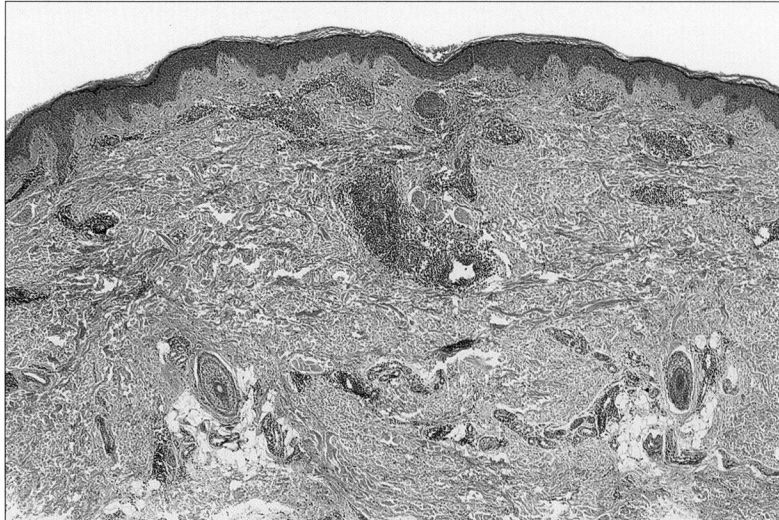

Fig. 7.17
Lymphocytic infiltrate of Jessner: a heavy chronic inflammatory cell infiltrate cuffs the vessels in the superficial and mid-dermis.

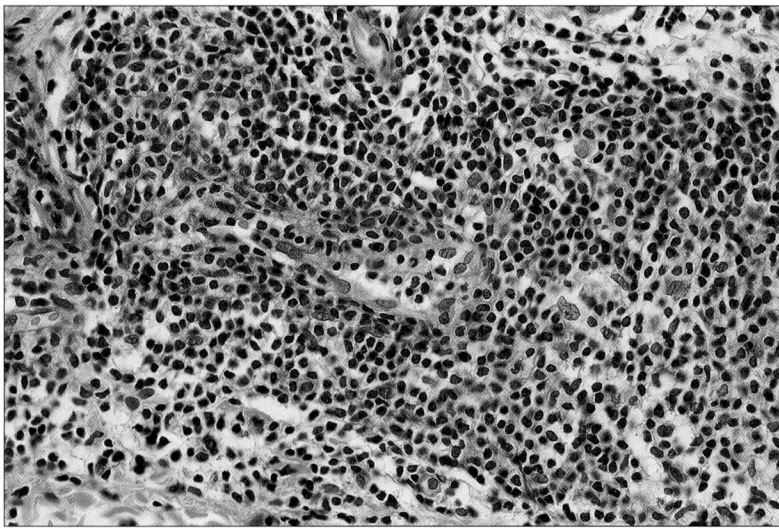

Fig. 7.18
Lymphocytic infiltrate of Jessner: the infiltrate is composed almost entirely of small lymphocytes.

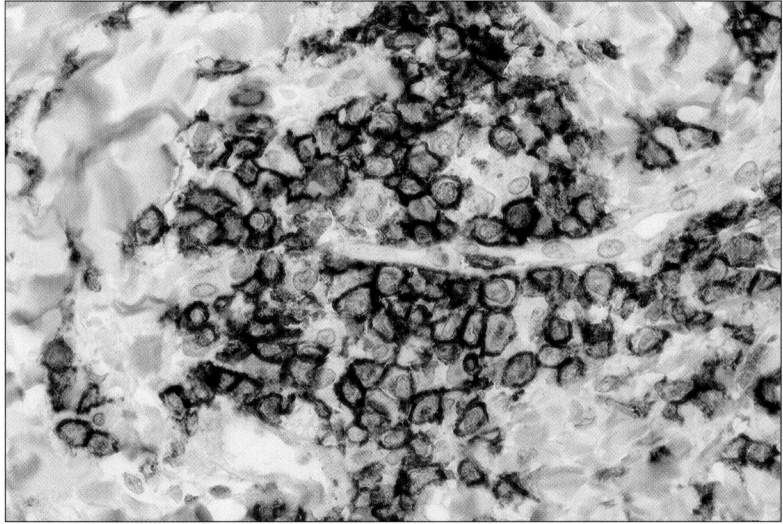

Fig. 7.19
Lymphocytic infiltrate of Jessner: the majority of lymphocytes express CD4 (T-helper cells).

Differential diagnosis

Lymphocytic infiltrate of the skin differs from discoid lupus erythematosus by the absence of epidermal changes, scarring and a negative lupus band test. Immunocytochemistry may sometimes be helpful. The infiltrate in lymphocytic infiltrate is HLA-DR negative in contrast to discoid lupus erythematosus in which the lymphocytes and often the keratinocytes are HLA-DR positive.[15] Leu 8 (immunoregulatory T-cell) expression is also more frequently seen in lymphocytic infiltrate.[11,16] In one study, the average percentage of Leu 8 positive lymphocytes was 65% in lymphocytic infiltrate of skin and only 15% in discoid lupus erythematosus.[16] The presence of CD20+ B-cells favors lupus erythematosus, which tends to be composed of a mixture of B- and T-cells. In contrast, T-cells predominate in lymphocytic infiltrate of skin.[12,17,18] One group of investigators has suggested that the presence of plasmacytoid monocytes favors a diagnosis of lymphocytic infiltrate of skin over lupus erythematosus. They found plasmacytoid monocytes to be present in 58% of patients with lymphocytic infiltrate of skin but only in 7% of patients with discoid lupus erythematosus.[19] Others, however, have not been able to corroborate this finding.[17] The presence of significant dermal mucin would support lupus erythematosus.

Epidermal Langerhans' cells are often increased in lymphocytic infiltrate whereas they are frequently reduced in number in discoid lupus erythematosus.[11]

Lymphocytic infiltrate may often be distinguished from chronic lymphocytic leukemia/lymphocytic lymphoma by careful evaluation of cellular morphology. The benign lymphocytic infiltrate is composed of non-neoplastic lymphocytes with small, regular and hyperchromatic nuclei. In chronic lymphocytic leukemia/lymphocytic lymphoma the nuclei are larger, irregular and paler staining, and a nucleolus may be visible. Regardless of these subtle cytological differences, if the possibility of low-grade lymphoma exists, immunohistochemical studies should be performed. Most often, well-differentiated lymphomas are of B-cell lineage.

Lymphocytic infiltrate is usually histologically indistinguishable from polymorphous light eruption although early lesions of the latter may show edema of the papillary dermis. It should be noted, however, that sometimes the two conditions may coexist. In cases where the diagnosis is in doubt, phototesting may be necessary. One group of investigators has found the presence of plasmacytoid monocytes to favor lymphocytic infiltrate of skin over polymorphous light eruption.[19] However, as noted above, others have not been able to demonstrate this finding.[17]

Histologically, lymphocytic infiltration of Jessner also shows some overlap with reticular erythematous mucinosis. Mucin deposition, however, is not typically a feature of lymphocytic infiltrate of skin. Furthermore, the infiltrate in reticular erythematous mucinosis is usually mild.

References

1. Toonstra, J., Wildschut, A., Boer, J. et al (1989) Jessner's lymphocytic infiltration of the skin. A clinical study of 100 patients. *Arch Dermatol*, **125**, 1525–1530.
2. Helm, K.F., Muller, S.A. (1992) Benign lymphocytic infiltrate of the skin: correlation of clinical and pathologic findings. *Mayo Clin Proc*, **67**, 748–754.
3. Abele, D.C., Anders, K.H. (1990) The many faces and phases of borreliosis II. *J Am Acad Dermatol*, **23**, 401–410.
4. Dippel, E., Poenitz, N., Klemke, C.D. et al (2002) Familial lymphocytic infiltration of the skin: histochemical and molecular analysis in three brothers. *Dermatology*, **204**, 12–16.
5. Toonstra, I., van der Putte, S.C., de la Faille, H.B. et al (1993) Familial Jessner's lymphocytic infiltration of the skin, occurring in a father and a daughter. *Clin Exp Dermatol*, **18**, 142–145.
6. Ashworth, J., Morley, W.N. (1988) Jessner and Kanof's lymphocytic infiltrate of the skin: a familial variant. *Dermatologica*, **177**, 120–122.
7. Mullen, R.H., Jacobs, A.H. (1988) Jessner's lymphocytic infiltrate in two girls. *Arch Dermatol*, **124**, 1091–1093.
8. Braddock, S.W., Kay, H.D., Maennle, D. et al (1993) Clinical and immunologic studies in reticular erythematosus mucinosis and Jessner's lymphocytic infiltrate of the skin. *J Am Acad Dermatol*, **28**, 691–695.
9. Higgins, C.R., Wakeel, R.A., Cerio, R. (1994) Childhood Jessner's lymphocytic infiltrate of the skin. *Br J Dermatol*, **131**, 99–101.
10. Clarke, W.H., Mihm, M.C., Reed, R.J. et al (1974) The lymphocytic infiltrates of the skin. *Hum Pathol*, **5**, 25–42.
11. Rijlaarsdam, J.U., Nieboer, C., De Vries, E. et al (1990) Characterization of the dermal infiltrate in Jessner's lymphocytic infiltrate of the skin, polymorphous light eruption and cutaneous lupus erythematosus: differential diagnostic and pathogenetic aspects. *J Cutan Pathol*, **17**, 2–8.
12. Akasu, R., Kahn, H.J., From, L. (1992) Lymphocytic markers on formalin-fixed tissue in Jessner's lymphocytic infiltrate and lupus erythematosus. *J Cutan Pathol*, **19**, 59–65.

13. Willemze, R., Dijkstra, A., Meijer, C.J.L.M. (1984) Lymphocytic infiltration of the skin (Jessner): a T-cell lymphoproliferative disease. *Br J Dermatol*, **110**, 523–530.
14. David, M., Shohat, B., Hazaz, B. et al (1980) Identification of T and B lymphocytes on skin sections from patients with lymphoproliferative disorders of the skin. *J Invest Dermatol*, **75**, 491–494.
15. Willemze, R., Vermeer, B.J., Meijer, C.J.L.M. (1984) Immuno-histochemical studies in lymphocytic infiltration of the skin (Jessner) and discoid lupus erythematosus. A comparative study. *J Am Acad Dermatol*, **11**, 832–840.
16. Kuo, T.T., Lo, S.K., Chan, H.L. (1994) Immunohistochemical analysis of dermal mononuclear cell infiltrates in cutaneous lupus erythematosus, polymorphous light eruption, lymphocytic infiltration of Jessner, and cutaneous lymphoid hyperplasia: a comparative differential study. *J Cutan Pathol*, **21**, 430–436.
17. Ashworth, J., Turbitt, M., Mackie, R. (1987) A comparison of the dermal lymphoid infiltrates in discoid lupus erythematosus and Jessner's lymphocytic infiltrate of the skin using the monoclonal antibody Leu 8. *J Cutan Pathol*, **14**, 198–201.
18. Kontinnen, Y.T., Bergroth, V., Johansson, E. et al (1987) A long-term clinicopathologic survey of patients with Jessner's lymphocytic infiltrate of the skin. *J Invest Dermatol*, **89**, 205–208.
19. Toonstra, J., van der Putte, S.C. (1991) Plasmacytoid monocytes in Jessner's lymphocytic infiltration of the skin. A valuable clue for the diagnosis. *Am J Dermatopathol*, **13**, 321–328.

Reticular erythematous mucinosis

Clinical features

This rare chronic dermatosis, which shows a female predominance (2:1), has been described worldwide.[1] Although it may affect a wide age range, it most frequently develops in the second to fourth decades.[2] Rarely, it is encountered in children.[2] It usually presents as a persistent, reticulate, urticated, macular, and sometimes papular, erythema with an irregular, but well-defined border. The lesions typically occur on the central chest and upper back (*Figs 7.20, 7.21*).[3–5] Less commonly, they can be found on the face, arms, abdomen and groins, but the peripheries are spared.[1,6,7] Patients frequently notice an exacerbation in the sun, but the relationship between sunlight and the disease (if any) is not well understood.[2,5–9] Although patients are usually asymptomatic, some report pruritus or burning following exposure to sunlight. There is no evidence of systemic involvement.

Occasional patients have more infiltrated papules and plaques; this was originally described as plaque-like cutaneous mucinosis, but is now accepted as a variant of reticular erythematous mucinosis.[10,11] Of particular interest, the plaque-like form of the disease has been documented in association with carcinoma of the breast and colon.[11]

Patients with this condition have an increased risk of thyroid disease, arthritis and diabetes mellitus.[2] In one series of nine patients, one patient had evidence of Hashimoto's disease while another had hyperthyroidism.[11] A patient with reticular erythematous mucinosis and myxedema in the setting of Hashimoto's thyroiditis has been described.[12]

Reticular erythematous mucinosis in patients with human immuno-deficiency virus (HIV) infection has also been documented.[13,14] Of interest, other cutaneous mucinoses that have been described in association with HIV infection include scleredema and lichen myxedematosus (see p. 605).[14] Furthermore, deposition of mucin in the bone marrow of patients with acquired immunodeficiency syndrome (AIDS) is a common finding.[15] The pathogenetic relationship between these various forms of mucin deposition, if any, has not been defined. It is, of course, tempting to postulate that they are related but data to support such a conclusion are not yet established.

Monoclonal IgG (kappa) paraproteinemia has been reported in one patient.[16]

Pathogenesis and histological features

The pathogenesis of reticular erythematous mucinosis is not well understood. Phototoxicity likely plays some role in the disease, either directly or indirectly. Braddock and co-authors found that natural killer cell lytic activity and antibody-dependent cell-mediated cytotoxicity were decreased.[17] This same group found increased levels of circulating immune complexes. Of interest, two patients were observed to have circulating immune complexes that decreased with treatment only to become elevated during recurrence of disease following treatment.[17] Based on these observations, the investigators concluded that immune defects may be of importance in the pathogenesis of reticular erythematous mucinosis. Of interest, similar findings have been observed in patients with Jessner's lymphocytic infiltrate. Clearly, further study is necessary regarding the precise pathogenetic basis of this disease.

The epidermis may be slightly flattened or appear normal. Within the dermis there is moderate vascular dilatation associated with a marked mononuclear perivascular and often perifollicular infiltrate composed mainly of T-helper lymphocytes (*Figs 7.22, 7.23*).[5,11,17–19] Excess mucin (predominantly hyaluronic acid) is usually present in the upper dermis but in more chronic lesions it is sometimes absent (*Fig. 7.24*). The mucin stains positively with alcian blue (pH 2.5) and colloidal iron, but is usually not metachromatic with toluidine blue. The collagen fibers are separated, but appear morphologically normal. Fragmentation of elastic fibers is sometimes a feature.[6] There is no evidence of fibroblastic proliferation.

A few cases with positive direct immunofluorescence have been reported. IgM reactive papillary dermal cytoid bodies were documented

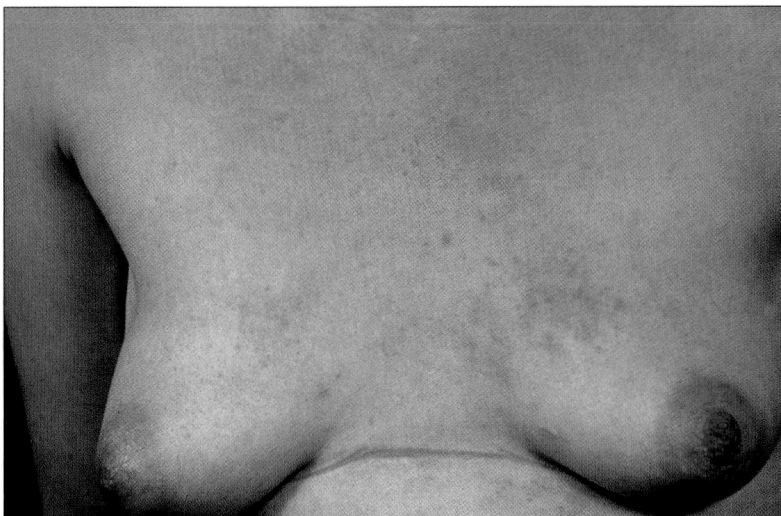

Fig. 7.20
Reticular erythematous mucinosis: erythematous reticular eruption in a characteristic distribution in a young woman. By courtesy of the Institute of Dermatology, London, UK.

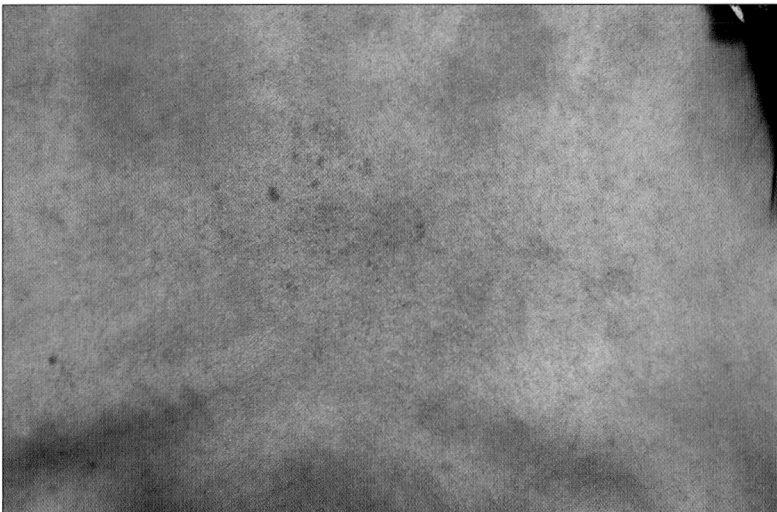

Fig. 7.21
Reticular erythematous mucinosis: in this patient, the lesions are entirely macular. By courtesy of the Institute of Dermatology, London, UK.

in one case.[17] Rare cases show staining for IgM along the dermal–epidermal junction.[2,9,20] The significance of these findings is unclear but may be further evidence of an immunological basis for the pathogenesis of reticular erythematous mucinosis.[20]

Ultrastructural studies are largely unhelpful. Other than demonstrating conspicuous and dilated rough endoplasmic reticulum within dermal fibroblasts, electron microscopy merely serves to confirm the light microscopic observation of widely separated fascicles of collagen fibers.[18] In a number of reports tubuloreticular structures were identified within the cytoplasm of endothelial cells.[6,21,22] Although at one time these were thought to represent paramyxoviruses, more recent studies suggest that they may be derived from infolded endoplasmic reticulum. They have also been identified in pretibial myxedema, lupus erythematosus, dermatomyositis, malignant atrophic papulosis and various lymphomas.[23] An example is shown in *Figure 16.40*.

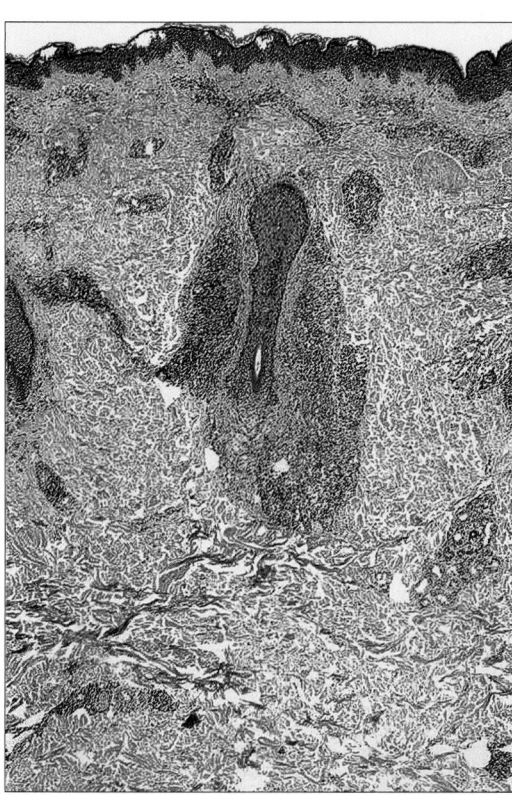

Fig. 7.22
Reticular erythematous mucinosis: there is a perifollicular and perivascular infiltrate in the upper and mid-dermis.

Differential diagnosis

The principal clinical and pathological differential diagnoses include lupus erythematosus and polymorphous light eruption. Distinguishing between lupus erythematosus and reticular erythematous mucinosis may be very difficult, particularly as one condition may evolve into the other.[24] Histologically, reticular erythematous mucinosis lacks the epidermal changes of lupus erythematosus and the immunofluorescent findings are usually, but not always, negative.[6–8] As noted above, there are a few reports in which granular immunoglobulin deposition at the epidermodermal junction was present.[2,9,20] The presence of several immunoreactants favors a diagnosis of lupus erythematosus. Clinical and serological studies are also necessary to establish a diagnosis of lupus erythematosus.

In polymorphous light eruption, mucin deposition is much less striking and is limited to the papillary dermis.[25] Perifollicular inflammation is not a feature of polymorphous light eruption. In addition, epidermal changes of spongiosis – sometimes with vesiculation in papular and eczematous lesions and mild basal cell hydropic change in the plaque variant – serve as further distinguishing features.[26] Polymorphous light eruption resolves once exposure to sunlight has ceased in contrast to reticular erythematous mucinosis where the lesions persist.

Histologically, reticular erythematous mucinosis also shows some overlap with lymphocytic infiltrate of Jessner.[2] Mucin deposition, however, is not generally a feature of the latter condition.

References

1. Braddock, S.W., Davis, C.S., Davis, R.B. (1988) Reticular erythematous mucinosis and thrombocytopenic purpura. *J Am Acad Dermatol*, **19**, 859–868.
2. Cohen, P.R., Rabinowitz, A.D., Ruszkowski, A.M. et al (1990) Reticular erythematous mucinosis syndrome: review of the world literature and report of the syndrome in a prepubertal child. *Pediatr Dermatol*, **7**, 1–10.
3. Funai, T., Aoki, T. (1986) Reticular erythematous mucinosis syndrome: a case report. *J Dermatol (Tokyo)*, **13**, 213–216.
4. Astle, N.J., Rasmussen, J.A. (1987) A reticular eruption on the chest. Reticular erythematous mucinosis (REM). *Arch Dermatol*, **123**, 521–524.
5. Steigleder, G.K., Gartmann, H., Linker, U. (1974) REM syndrome: reticular erythematous mucinosis syndrome (round cell erythematosis), a new entity? *Br J Dermatol*, **91**, 191–199.
6. Bleehen, S.S., Slater, D.N., Mahood, J. et al (1982) Reticular erythematous mucinosis: light and electron microscopy, immunofluorescence and histochemical findings. *Br J Dermatol*, **106**, 9–18.
7. Morison, W.L., Shea, C.R., Parrish, J.A. (1979) Reticular erythematous mucinosis syndrome. Report of two cases. *Arch Dermatol*, **115**, 1340–1342.
8. Dal, B-L., Larsen, T.E. (1977) Reticular erythematous mucinosis syndrome: report of a case. *Acta Derm Venereol*, **57**, 465–467.
9. Dodd, H.J., Sarkany, I., Sadrudin, A. (1987) Reticular erythematous mucinosis syndrome. *Clin Exp Dermatol*, **12**, 36–39.
10. Perry, H.O., Kierland, R.R., Montgomery, H. (1960) Plaque-like form of cutaneous mucinosis. *Arch Dermatol*, **82**, 980–985.
11. Quimby, S.R., Perry, H.O. (1982) Plaque-like cutaneous mucinosis: its relationship to reticular erythematous mucinosis. *J Am Acad Dermatol*, **6**, 856–861.
12. Valasco, J.A., Santos, J.C., Villabona, V. et al (1992) Reticular erythematous mucinosis and acral papulokeratotic lesions associated with myxoedema due to Hashimoto's thyroiditis. *Dermatology*, **184**, 73–77.

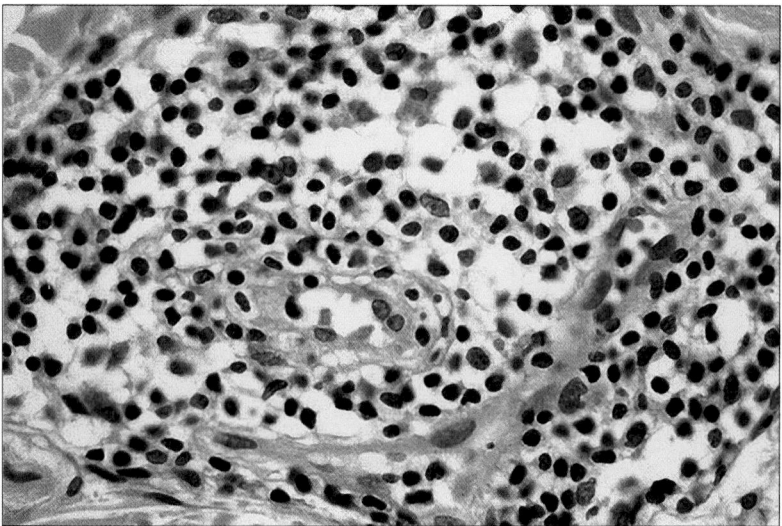

Fig. 7.23
Reticular erythematous mucinosis: the infiltrate consists of mature lymphocytes with a lesser number of histiocytes.

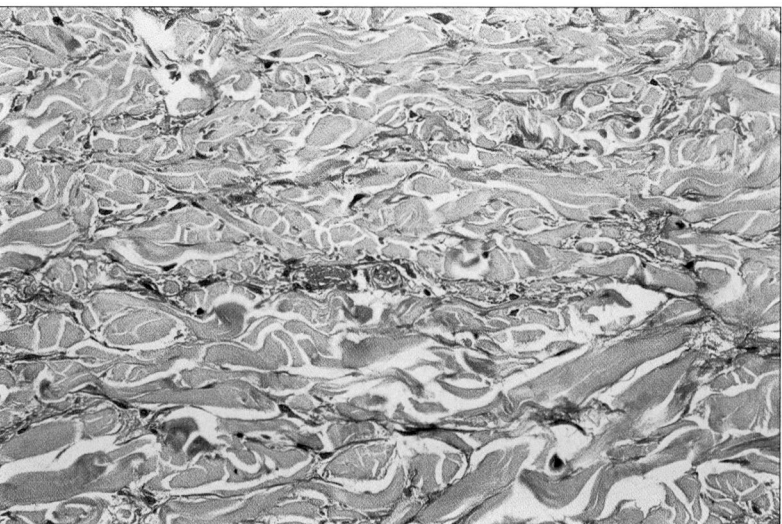

Fig. 7.24
Reticular erythematous mucinosis: increased dermal mucin (hyaluronic acid) separates the collagen fibers (alcian blue stain).

13. Dauden, E., Penas, P.F., Buezo, G.F. et al (1995) Reticular erythematous mucinosis associated with human immunodeficiency virus infection. *Dermatology*, **191**, 157–160.
14. Rongioletti, F., Ghiglioffi, G., Marchi, R. et al (1998) Cutaneous mucinoses and HIV infection. *Br J Dermatol*, **139**, 1077–1080.
15. Mehta, K., Gascon, P., Robboy, S. (1992) The gelatinous bone marrow (serous atrophy) in patients with acquired immune deficiency syndrome. *Arch Pathol Lab Med*, **116**, 504–508.
16. Zaki, I., Shall, L., Millard, L.G. (1993) Reticular erythematous mucinosis syndrome and a monoclonal IgG kappa paraprotein – is there an association? *Br J Dermatol*, **129**, 347–356.
17. Braddock, S.W., Kay, H.D., Maennle, D. et al (1993) Clinical and immunologic studies in reticular erythematous mucinosis and Jessner's lymphocytic infiltrate of the skin. *J Am Acad Dermatol*, **28**, 691–695.
18. Vanuytrecht-Henderickz, D., Dewolf-Peeters, C., Degreef, H. (1984) Morphological study of the reticular erythematous mucinosis syndrome. *Dermatologica*, **168**, 163–169.
19. Truhan, A.P., Roenigk, H.H. Jr (1986) The cutaneous mucinoses. *J Am Acad Dermatol*, **14**, 1–18.
20. Del Pozo, J., Martinez, W., Almagro, M. et al (1997) Reticular mucinosis syndrome. Report of a case with positive immunofluorescence. *Clin Exp Dermatol*, **22**, 234–236.
21. Steigleder, G.K., Kanzow, G. (1980) Muzinablagerungen in der Dermis und REM-syndrom. *Hautarzt*, **31**, 575–583.
22. Chavaz, P., Polla, L., Saurat, J.H. (1982) Paramyxovirus-like inclusions and lymphocyte type in the REM syndrome. *Br J Dermatol*, **106**, 741–742.
23. Eady, R.A.J. (1975) Tubular aggregates: viral or not. *Trans St John's Hosp Dermatol Soc*, **61**, 102–104.
24. Del Pozo, J., Pena, C., Almargo, M. et al (2000) Systemic lupus erythematosus presenting with a reticular erythematous mucinosis-like condition. *Lupus*, **9**, 144–146.
25. Panet-Raymond, G., Johnson, W.C. (1973) Lupus erythematosus and polymorphous light eruption. Differentiation by histochemical procedures. *Arch Dermatol*, **108**, 785–787.
26. Epstein, J.H. (1980) Polymorphous light eruption. *J Am Acad Dermatol*, **3**, 329–343.

Polymorphous light eruption

Clinical features

Polymorphous (polymorphic) light eruption, which is the most common photodermatosis, usually presents in young people as recurrent erythematous papules, vesicles and/or plaques following exposure to ultraviolet (UV) light (*Figs 7.25, 7.26*).[1-5] The face, chest, upper back and extremities are the most common sites of involvement.[5] Most patients have multiple lesions.[5] In one study of 138 patients, the mean age at onset was 26 years.[5] There is a predilection for young women, with 89% of patients being female.[6] The vast majority of lesions are associated with pruritus. Most patients require less than 30 minutes of sun exposure to elicit clinical lesions.[5] Onset of lesions following light exposure typically takes 18–24 hours. Either the UVA or UVB part of the light spectrum may cause lesions.[2,7] Lesions are caused by UVA light in 56% of cases, UVB in 17%, and both UVA and UVB ranges in 26% of cases.[2] However, some authors have not been able to elicit lesions with UVB light.[4] Exposure resulting in sunburn is not necessary for the development of lesions.[4] Some patients report lesions resulting from light exposure through glass.[4]

Polymorphous light eruption most often occurs in patients with fair skin; however, occasionally dark-skinned individuals are affected. The disease is more common in people residing in northern latitudes. One study showed that the prevalence rates for London (UK) and Perth (Australia) were 14.8% and 5.2%, respectively.[8]

It appears that the incidence of polymorphous light eruption is much more common than is demonstrated by contact with health care workers. In one survey, 21% of workers in a Swedish pharmaceutical company had symptoms consistent with polymorphous light eruption; however, only 3% had sought medical attention for their symptoms.[6]

Biopsy of experimentally induced lesions shows similar histological features compared to clinical lesions.[4] Given the role of sun exposure in causing lesions, it comes as no surprise that polymorphous light eruption is most often seen in spring and summer.[4] In addition, it is not uncommon for the first sign of disease to manifest during a vacation to southern latitudes. Lesions, which develop after a latent period of hours to days, commonly subside completely within days and heal without sequelae.[1] However, once the disease is established, persistence for many years is common.[3] Overall, however, there is diminution of light sensitivity over time, but this process often takes years.[3] In a large study, the mean disease duration of the condition was 10.5 years.[5] Patients with a duration of up to 53 years have been studied.[6] The distribution of lesions often changes with time.[5]

One study showed that thyroid disease was present in 14% of patients.[9] This same study found lupus erythematosus in only 2 of 94 patients. The authors concluded that the risk of lupus erythematosus was not increased in patients with polymorphous light eruption. Authors of another study, however, have suggested that a subgroup of patients with polymorphous light eruption may be at an elevated risk for lupus erythematosus.[10]

Juvenile spring eruption appears to be either a form of polymorphous light eruption or a closely related disorder.[11-15] In one study, the prevalence was 6.7% with a male predominance.[11] The lesions are characterized by erythematous papules and vesicles located on sun-exposed portions of the helix of the ear following light exposure. They tend to be pruritic.

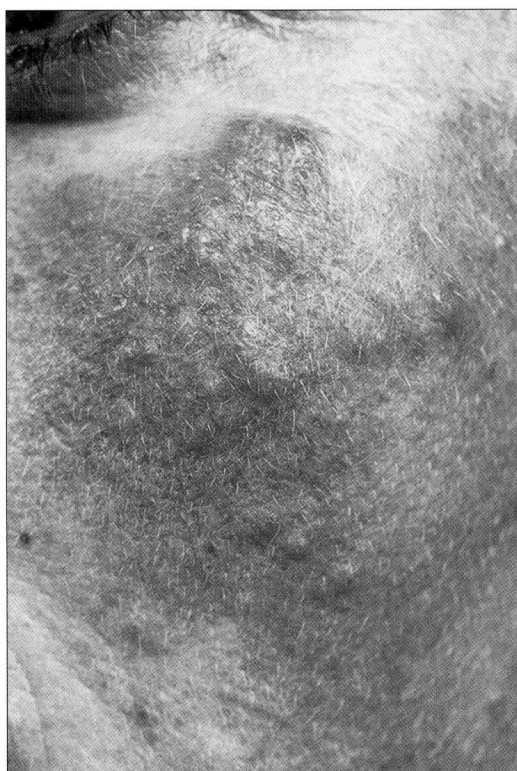

Fig. 7.25
Polymorphous light eruption: patients present with erythematous papules and vesicles on sun-exposed skin. By courtesy of the Institute of Dermatology, London, UK.

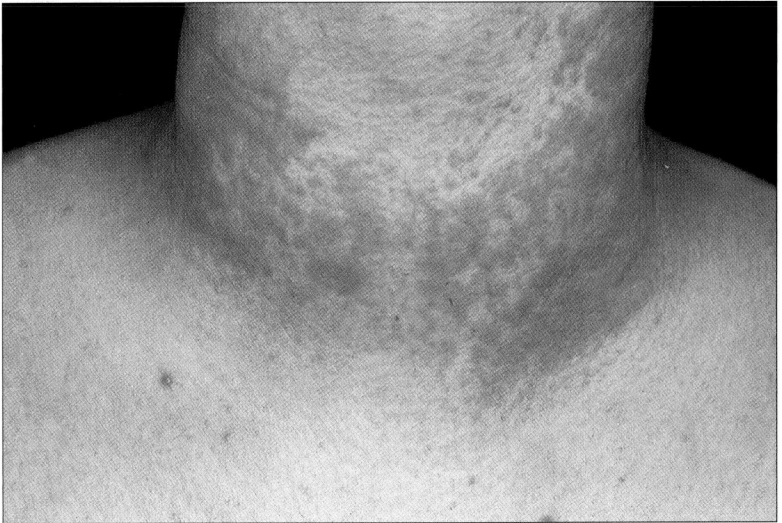

Fig. 7.26
Polymorphous light eruption: the eruption is typically symmetrical and is usually pruritic. By courtesy of the Institute of Dermatology, London, UK.

In one study, 4 of 18 patients also had lesions of typical polymorphous light eruption.[12] As its name implies, the lesions tend to occur in the spring. A positive family history is present in some patients.[14]

Pathogenesis and histological features

The pathogenesis of polymorphous light eruption is poorly understood. Study of adhesion molecule expression has led some authors to propose that polymorphous light eruption is immunologically mediated.[16] Specifically, vascular endothelial expression of endothelial leukocyte adhesion molecule-1 (ELAM-1), vascular cell adhesion molecule-1 (VCAM-1) and keratinocyte and endothelial expression of intercellular adhesion molecule-1 (ICAM-1) in biopsies of induced lesions has been documented.[16] The authors noted that their results were similar to those seen in delayed-type hypersensitivity reactions. However, the triggering antigen(s) are unknown.[16] It appears that polymorphous light eruption may be a heritable disorder. In one study, 46% of patients reported a positive family history.[6]

Histologically, a perivascular lymphohistiocytic infiltrate is present in the superficial and sometimes deep dermis (*Figs 7.27, 7.28*).[17–19] A characteristic, but not uniformly present feature, is papillary dermal edema, which is often marked. The presence of massive papillary dermal edema may be associated with subepidermal or intradermal vesicle formation.

Papular and papulovesicular lesions may show epidermal acanthosis, spongiosis, occasional dyskeratotic cells and lymphocyte exocytosis.[17,19] Spongiosis may sometimes become so severe as to lead to intraepidermal vesicle formation.[17] Other authors, however, have not found spongiosis to be a significant feature.[18] Basal cell vacuolization, usually mild, is found in some cases.[17,19,20] Periadnexal involvement may be present in papular and papulovesicular lesions.[17] Some authors have reported increased eosinophils and neutrophils; however, others have not confirmed this observation.[17,18] Papillary dermal erythrocyte extravasation is commonly present.[17] Finally, features secondary to scratching, such as hyperkeratosis and acanthosis, may be seen.[19]

Immunofluorescence studies have shown that immunoreactants (C3, IgG and IgM) may be seen along the basement membrane zone.[3] However, when staining is present, it is usually weak.[3]

Juvenile spring eruption of the ears is characterized by a perivascular lymphohistiocytic infiltrate often associated with subepidermal vesicle formation.[15]

In early lesions, helper–inducer T-lymphocytes predominate and increased numbers of dermal Langerhans' cells are present.[18] With chronicity, cytotoxic suppressor T-cells become more conspicuous.

Differential diagnosis

It should be noted that there is considerable variability in both the clinical and histological descriptions of polymorphous light eruption. This has led some authors to suggest that polymorphous light eruption likely represents a group of related disorders rather than a single entity.[17,18] Phototesting, therefore, is probably the best 'gold standard' for establishing the diagnosis. Compared with reticular erythematous mucinosis, mucin deposition is absent or much less prominent in polymorphous light eruption. Clinically, polymorphous light eruption resolves once exposure to sunlight has ceased in contrast to the persistent lesions of reticular erythematous mucinosis.

Histologically, polymorphous light eruption also shows some overlap with other causes of gyrate erythema such as lymphocytic infiltration of Jessner. The presence of marked papillary dermal edema, when present, favors polymorphous light eruption. A clinical history of documentation of resolution of lesions with cessation to light exposure may sometimes be the only way to distinguish these entities. In cases where the diagnosis is in doubt, phototesting may often be necessary.

The histological features of lupus erythematosus are sometimes difficult to distinguish from polymorphic light eruption, particularly when the latter is associated with positive immunofluorescence. However, most cases of polymorphous light eruption are negative with immunofluorescence testing. When immunoreactants are present, usually only weak staining is observed. Careful clinical and serological evaluation should resolve any confusion between these conditions.

Actinic reticuloid is another eruption associated with exposure to UV light; this is discussed in detail on page 1427. Compared with polymorphous light eruption, actinic reticuloid is more typically associated with a dense cellular interstitial infiltrate involving the papillary and reticular dermis, and sometimes extending into the subcutaneous fat.

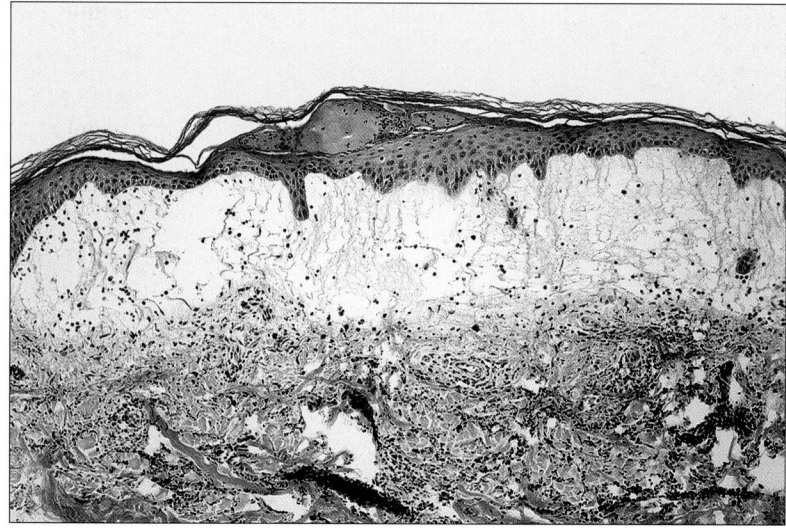

Fig. 7.27
Polymorphous light eruption: note the massive subepidermal edema with incipient vesiculation.

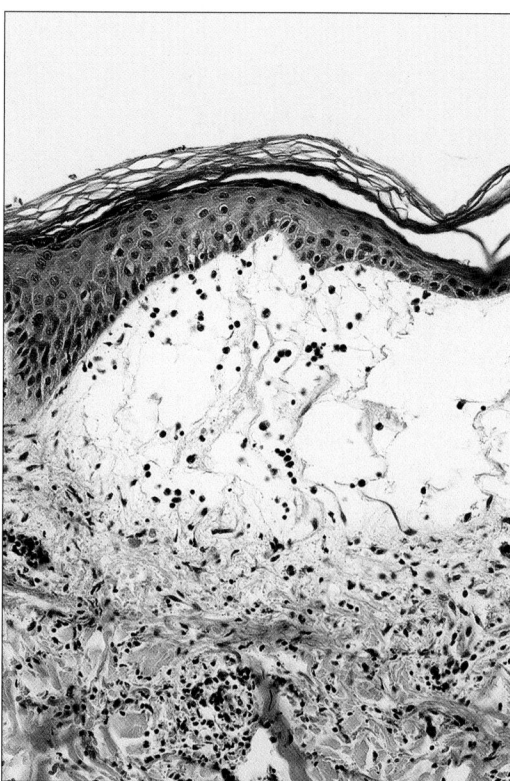

Fig. 7.28
Polymorphous light eruption: there is a predominantly lymphocytic inflammatory cell infiltrate.

It is composed of lymphocytes, histiocytes and variable numbers of eosinophils and plasma cells. The presence of multinucleate stellate myofibroblasts and giant cells is a conspicuous feature that favors actinic reticuloid. Finally, the finding of large atypical, hyperchromatic cerebriform lymphoid cells and blast forms is characteristic of actinic reticuloid.

References

1. Norris, P.G., Hawk, J.L.M. (1990) The acute idiopathic photodermatoses. *Semin Dermatol*, **9**, 32–38.
2. Ortel, B., Tanew, A., Wolff, K. et al (1986) Polymorphous light eruption: action spectrum and photoprotection. *J Am Acad Dermatol*, **14**, 748–753.
3. Jansen, C., Karvonen, J. (1984) Polymorphous light eruption: a seven year follow-up evaluation of 114 patients. *Arch Dermatol*, **120**, 862–865.
4. Holzle, E., Plewig, G., Hofmann, C. et al (1982) Polymorphous light eruption. Experimental reproduction of skin lesions. *J Am Acad Dermatol*, **7**, 111–125.
5. Jansen, C.T. (1979) The natural history of polymorphous light eruption. *Arch Dermatol*, **115**, 165–169.
6. Ros, A.M., Wennersten, G. (1986) Current aspects of polymorphous light eruptions in Sweden. *Photodermatology*, **3**, 298–302.
7. Boonstra, H.E., van Weelden, H., Toonstra, J. et al (2000) Polymorphous light eruption: a clinical, photobiologic, and follow-up study of 110 patients. *J Am Acad Dermatol*, **42**, 199–207.
8. Pao, C., Norris, P.G., Corbett, M. et al (1994) Polymorphic light eruption in Australia and England. *Br J Dermatol*, **130**, 62–64.
9. Hasan, T., Ranki, A., Jansen, C.T. et al (1998) Disease associations in polymorphous light eruption. A long-term follow-up study of 94 patients. *Arch Dermatol*, **134**, 1081–1085.
10. Nyberg, F., Hasan, T., Puska, P. et al (1997) Occurrence of polymorphous light eruption in lupus erythematosus. *Br J Dermatol*, **136**, 217–221.
11. Tan, E., Eberhart-Phillips, J., Sharples, K. (1996) Juvenile spring eruption: a prevalence study. *N Z Med J*, **109**, 293–295.
12. Berth-Norris, J., Norris, P.G., Graham-Brown, R.A. et al (1991) Juvenile spring eruption of the ears: a probable variant of polymorphic light eruption. *Br J Dermatol*, **124**, 375–378.
13. Requena, L., Alegre, V., Hasson, A. (1990) Spring eruption of the ears. *Int J Dermatol*, **29**, 284–286.
14. Berth-Jones, J., Norris, P.G., Graham-Brown, R.A. et al (1989) Juvenile spring eruption of the ears. *Clin Exp Dermatol*, **14**, 462–463.
15. Berth-Jones, J., Hutchinson, P.E., Burns, D.A. et al (1989) Juvenile spring eruption of the ears: a re-examination. *Br J Dermatol*, **121**, 51.
16. Norris, P.G., Barker, J.N.W.N., Allen, M.G. et al (1992) Adhesion molecule expression in polymorphic light eruption. *J Invest Dermatol*, **99**, 504–508.
17. Hood, A.F., Elpern, D.J., Morison, W.L. (1986) Histopathologic findings in papulovesicular light eruption. *J Cutan Pathol*, **13**, 13–21.
18. Norris, P.G., Morris, J., McGibbon, D.M. et al (1989) Polymorphic light eruption: an immunopathological study of evolving lesions. *Br J Dermatol*, **120**, 171–183.
19. Miyamoto, C. (1989) Polymorphous light eruption: successful reproduction of lesions, including papulovesicular light eruption with ultraviolet B. *Photodermatology*, **6**, 69–79.
20. Muhlbauer, J.E., Bhan, A.K., Harrist, T.J. et al (1983) Papular polymorphic light eruption: an immunoperoxidase study using monoclonal antibodies. *Br J Dermatol*, **108**, 153–162.

Tumid lupus erythematosus

Clinical features

Lupus erythematosus is discussed in detail in Chapter 3 and the reader is referred there for a comprehensive discussion of the disease. In this section only the tumid variant of lupus erythematosus is discussed.

Tumid lupus erythematosus (lupus erythematosus tumidus) is a rare manifestation of lupus that some authors believe to be sufficiently characteristic to justify classification as a distinctive subtype of chronic cutaneous lupus.[1] However, the lack of an agreed-upon diagnostic gold standard makes this designation somewhat controversial. Further study and refinement of criteria for inclusion into this subtype of lupus and to allow for reliable distinction from other inflammatory dermatoses is necessary.

Raised erythematous plaques, which have been described as 'succulent', characterize the clinical lesions.[1] Follicular plugging is not a feature. Annular and gyrate lesions are seen in some patients.[1] Lesions are most often present on sun-exposed areas such as the face, chest, arms and shoulders.[1] In the largest series published to date, patients with this clinical appearance accounted for 16% of the total number of patients seen in a large cutaneous lupus clinic.[1] Approximately equal numbers of male and female patients are affected, in contrast to the preponderance of females affected by other subtypes of cutaneous lupus. In this variant, young adults are most often encountered. In most patients, lesions can be reproduced by exposure to UVA or UVB light.[1]

Histological features

Biopsy shows a superficial and perivascular 'cuffed' lymphocytic infiltrate (*Fig. 7.29*). Periadnexal involvement is also seen in many cases. Abundant dermal mucin is commonly present (*Fig. 7.30*).[2] In contrast to other variants of lupus erythematosus, epidermal changes (e.g. follicular plugging, vacuolar interface changes and thickened basement membrane) are generally not apparent.[1]

Direct immunofluorescence staining fails to demonstrate reactivity.[1]

The infiltrate consists of a mixture of CD4+ and CD8+ reactive lymphocytes.[3]

Differential diagnosis

The concept of tumid lupus erythematosus has been expanded in a recent large series of patients.[1] Whether there is justification for classification of the disorder in these patients as a variant of lupus erythematosus or not

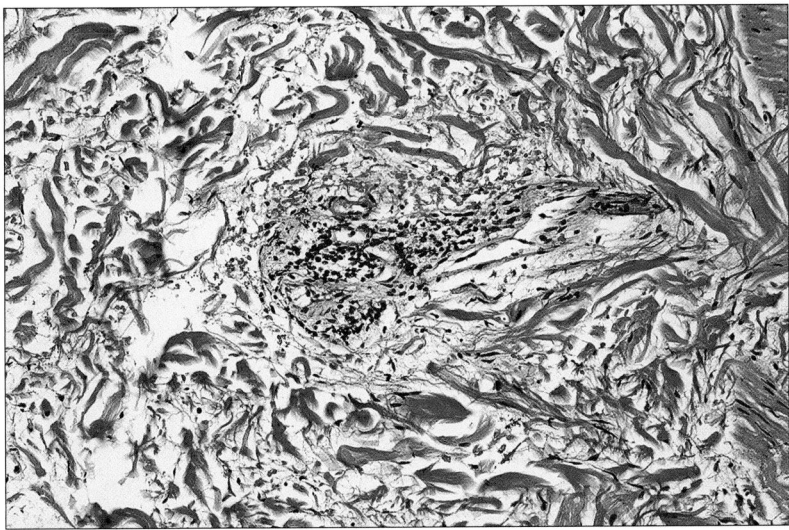

Fig. 7.29
Tumid lupus erythematosus: there is a perivascular lymphocytic infiltrate. The collagen fibers are separated by excess dermal mucin. By courtesy of J. Cohen, MD, Dermatopathology Laboratory, Tucson, Arizona, USA.

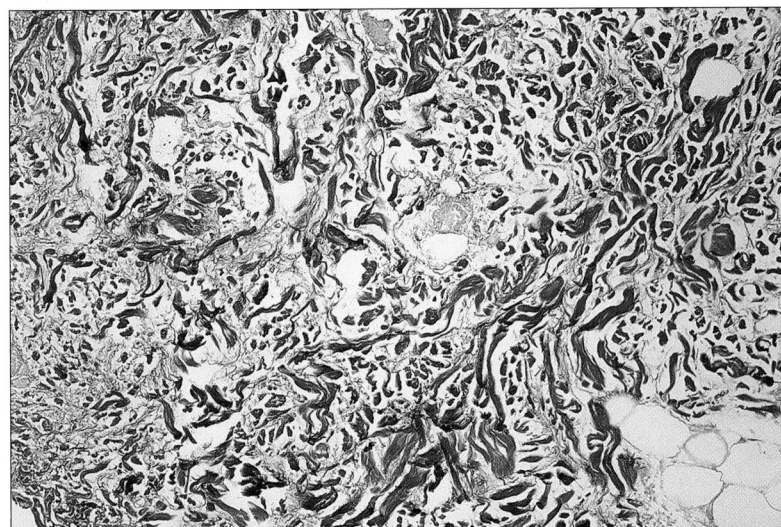

Fig. 7.30
Tumid lupus erythematosus: the mucin is alcian blue positive. By courtesy of J. Cohen, MD, Dermatopathology Laboratory, Tucson, Arizona, USA.

is debatable. None met the criteria for lupus erythematosus and most did not have significantly elevated antinuclear antibodies (ANA). However, occasional patients have been shown to develop skin lesions consistent with discoid lupus erythematosus, including prominent epidermal changes.[2,4]

In addition to patients similar to those described by Kuhn et al.,[1] patients that do fit the criteria for discoid lupus erythematosus (DLE), subacute cutaneous lupus erythematosus (SCLE) or systemic lupus erythematosus (SLE) rarely develop lesions that show a dense superficial and deep perivascular and periappendiceal infiltrate in the absence of significant epidermal changes. Distinction of these subgroups of tumid lupus from lymphocytic infiltrate of Jessner and polymorphous light eruption based on histological examination alone may be difficult if not impossible.[5] Some authors have suggested that some cases reported as lymphocytic infiltrate of Jessner or reticular erythematous mucinosis, in fact, represent tumid lupus.[6]

The histological features of lupus erythematosus tumidus are particularly difficult to distinguish from polymorphic light eruption. The latter, which is the most common photodermatosis, usually presents in young people, particularly females, as recurrent, erythematous papules, vesicles and/or plaques following exposure to UV light. Lesions, which develop after a latent period of hours to days, commonly subside completely within days and heal without sequelae.[7] A dense perivascular lymphohistiocytic infiltrate, often associated with papillary dermal edema, is present in the superficial and sometimes deep dermis.[8] The presence of significant papillary dermal edema favors polymorphic light eruption.

Lymphocytic infiltrate of the skin (Jessner) may be difficult to distinguish from tumid lupus erythematosus. In such cases, immunocytochemistry may sometimes be helpful. The infiltrate in lymphocytic

infiltrate is HLA-DR negative in contrast to lupus erythematosus in which the lymphocytes and often the keratinocytes are HLA-DR positive.[9] Leu 8 (immunoregulatory T-cell) expression is also more frequently seen in lymphocytic infiltrate.[9] Epidermal Langerhans' cells are often increased in number in lymphocytic infiltrate whereas they are frequently reduced in discoid lupus.[10] The presence of significant amounts of dermal mucin favors a diagnosis of tumid lupus.

Erythema annulare centrifugum differs from tumid lupus by the lack of significant dermal mucin.

As can be seen from the above discussion tumid lupus is a controversial entity. To some extent, the problem is a matter of semantics and definitions. Indeed, some authors have taken the position that reticular erythematous mucinosis and Jessner's lymphocytic infiltrate of skin would be more appropriately regarded as tumid lupus.[6] Clearly, further studies are necessary to more clearly define the clinicopathological features of tumid lupus and its distinction from similar entities.

References

1. Kuhn, A., Richter-Hintz, D., Oslislo, C. et al (2000) Lupus erythematosus tumidus – a neglected subset of cutaneous lupus erythematosus: report of 40 cases. *Arch Dermatol*, **136**, 1033–1041.
2. Dekle, C.L., Mannes, K.D., Davis, L.S. et al (1999) Lupus tumidus. *J Am Acad Dermatol*, **41**, 250–253.
3. Kuhn, A., Sonntag, M., Lehmann, P. et al (2002) Characterization of the inflammatory infiltrate and expression of endothelial cell adhesion molecules in lupus erythematosus tumidus. *Arch Dermatol Res*, **294**, 6–13.
4. Ruiz, H., Sanchez, J.L. (1999) Tumid lupus erythematosus. *Am J Dermatopathol*, **21**, 356–360.
5. Hood, A.F., Farmer, E.R. (1985) Histopathology of cutaneous lupus erythematosus. *Clin Dermatol*, **3**, 36–48.
6. Hsu, S., Hwang, L.Y., Ruiz, H. (2002) Tumid lupus erythematosus. *Cutis*, **69**, 227–230.
7. Norris, P.G., Hawk, J.L.M. (1990) The acute idiopathic photodermatoses. *Semin Dermatol*, **9**, 32–38.
8. Norris, P.G., Morris, J., McGibbon, D. et al (1989) Polymorphic light eruption: an immunopathological study of evolving lesions. *Br J Dermatol*, **120**, 173–183.
9. Rijlaarsdam, J.U., Nieboer, C., De Vries, E. et al (1990) Characterization of the dermal infiltrate in Jessner's lymphocytic infiltrate of the skin, polymorphous light eruption and cutaneous lupus erythematosus: differential diagnostic and pathogenetic aspects. *J Cutan Pathol*, **17**, 2–8.
10. Willemze, R., Vermeer, B.J., Meijer, C.J.L.M. (1984) Immunohistochemical studies in lymphocytic infiltration of the skin (Jessner) and discoid lupus erythematosus. A comparative study. *J Am Acad Dermatol*, **11**, 832–840.

Perniosis

Clinical features

Perniosis (chilblains) is characterized by sensitivity to cold damp weather and is therefore seen during cold months of the year. The disease seems to be more common in environments where inadequate heating is problematical for a few months of the year and is less common in localities characterized by harsh frigid winters where adequate home heating is the norm. Exposure to cold water sometimes appears to play a role.[1]

Patients present with painful, erythematous nodules on the distal extremities, especially the fingers and the toes (*Fig. 7.31*).[2] Other exposed sites, such as the nose and ears, may also be affected. Lesions may be complicated by blister formation or ulceration. In most patients, the condition remits during summer but often recurs during winter months. Patients with anorexia nervosa may be at increased risk of developing perniosis.[3,4]

Horse-riding enthusiasts who wear tight clothing during cold weather may develop similar lesions on the thighs (*Fig. 7.32*). This disease is associated with panniculitis and has been termed 'equestrian cold panniculitis'.[5] It is also discussed on page 353.

Patients with lesions that persist into warmer seasons appear to be at a higher risk of developing lupus erythematosus.[6] One group has designated patients with some criteria, but not meeting diagnostic thresholds for connective tissue diseases such as lupus erythematosus, as having 'atypical chilblains'.[6] This subset of patients appears to be at higher risk of developing unequivocal features of connective tissue disease.[6] It is reasonable to evaluate all patients with perniosis for evidence of lupus erythematosus. Occasionally, patients with perniosis

who present without clinical manifestations of connective tissue disease eventually develop SLE.[7]

Pathogenesis and histological features

The pathogenesis of perniosis is not well understood. Clearly, cold is a requirement for development of symptoms. Tight clothing may play a

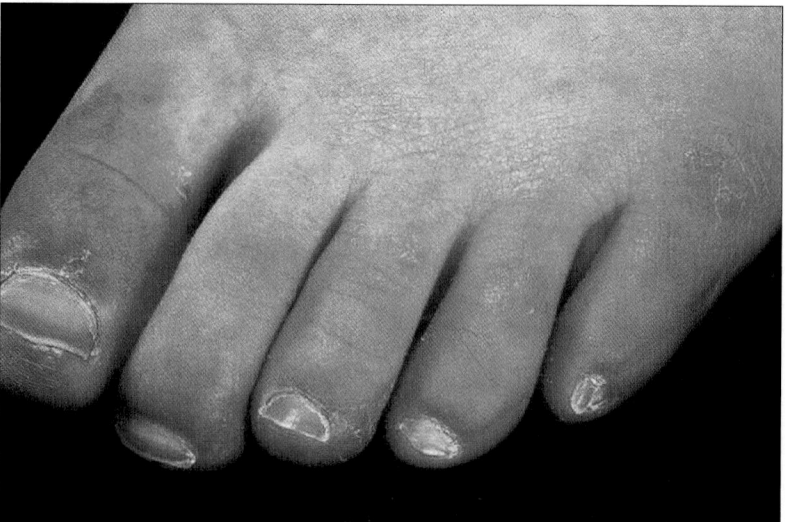

Fig. 7.31
Perniosis: erythematous nodules are present over the toes. By courtesy of the Institute of Dermatology, London, UK.

role in the development of perniosis at non-exposed sites. In some patients, particularly children, the presence of cryoproteins may play a role in the disease.[8]

Biopsy reveals a cuffed perivascular lymphocytic infiltrate with variable vascular fibrinoid change (*Fig. 7.33*). The inflammatory infiltrate may be superficial but often extends into the deep dermis and subcutaneous adipose tissue. In some cases it is difficult to demonstrate strict criteria for lymphocytic vasculitis (*Fig. 7.34*). Occasionally, however, fibrinoid vascular damage with thrombi is extensive. Papillary

dermal edema, which may be marked, is often present.[9] Interface changes, either vacuolar interface or lichenoid dermatitis, may be seen.[10] A perisudoral chronic inflammatory infiltrate is noted in some cases.[6]

Biopsy of cold panniculitis shows a perivascular chronic inflammatory infiltrate that tends to be prominent at the dermal–subcutaneous tissue junction.[5]

The inflammatory infiltrate is mostly composed of CD3+ T-cells with a minor subpopulation of CD20+ B-cells and scattered CD68+ macrophages.[10,11]

Differential diagnosis

The biopsy findings are non-specific and other diseases causing cuffed perivascular lymphocytic reactions and lymphocytic vasculitis enter into the differential diagnosis. The diagnosis is rendered only after careful clinical correlation. Patients often have some features of, but fail to meet criteria for, connective tissue disease.[6] Also, lesions very similar, or identical, to perniosis may be seen in patients with cutaneous or systemic lupus erythematosus.[7,10,12] Frank lymphocytic vasculitis and interface changes seem to be more common in patients with chilblain lupus than idiopathic chilblains; however, the presence or absence of these findings may not be reliable discriminators.[6,10] The presence of a positive lupus band test or antinuclear antibodies favors a diagnosis of chilblain lupus erythematosus.[6]

References

1. Price, R.D., Murdoch, D.R. (2001) Perniosis (chilblains) of the thigh: report of five cases, including four following river crossings. *High Alt Med Biol*, **2**, 535–538.
2. Goette, D.K. (1990) Chilblains (perniosis). *J Am Acad Dermatol*, **23**, 257–262.
3. Rustin, M.H., Foreman, J.C., Dowd, P.M. (1990) Anorexia nervosa associated with acromegaloid features, onset of acrocyanosis and Raynaud's phenomenon and worsening of chilblains. *J R Soc Med*, **83**, 495–496.
4. White, K.P., Rothe, M.J., Milanese, A. et al (1994) Perniosis is association with anorexia nervosa. *Pediatr Dermatol*, **11**, 1–5.
5. Beacham, B.E., Cooper, P.H., Buchanan, C.S. et al (1980) Equestrian cold panniculitis in women. *Arch Dermatol*, **116**, 1025–1027.
6. Viguier, M., Pinquier, L., Cavelier-Balloy, B. et al (2001) Clinical and histopathologic features and immunologic variables in patients with severe chilblains. *Medicine*, **80**, 180–188.
7. Doutre, M.S., Beylot, C., Belot, J. et al (1992) Chilblain lupus erythematosus: report of 15 cases. *Dermatology*, **184**, 26–28.
8. Weston, W.L., Morelli, J.G. (2000) Childhood pernio and cryoproteins. *Pediatr Dermatol*, **17**, 97–99.
9. Wall, L.M., Smith, N.P. (1981) Perniosis: a histopathological review. *Clin Exp Dermatol*, **6**, 263–271.
10. Cribier, B., Djeridi, N, Peltre, B. et al (2001) A histologic and immunohistochemical study of chilblains. *J Am Acad Dermatol*, **45**, 924–929.
11. Crowson, A.N., Magro, C.M. (1997) Perniosis. Idiopathic perniosis and its mimics: a clinical and histological study of 38 patients. *Hum Pathol*, **28**, 478–484.
12. Su, W.P.D., Perniciaro, C., Rogers, R.S. 3rd et al (1994) Chilblain lupus erythematosus (lupus pernio): clinical review to the Mayo experience and proposal of diagnostic criteria. *Cutis*, **54**, 395–399.

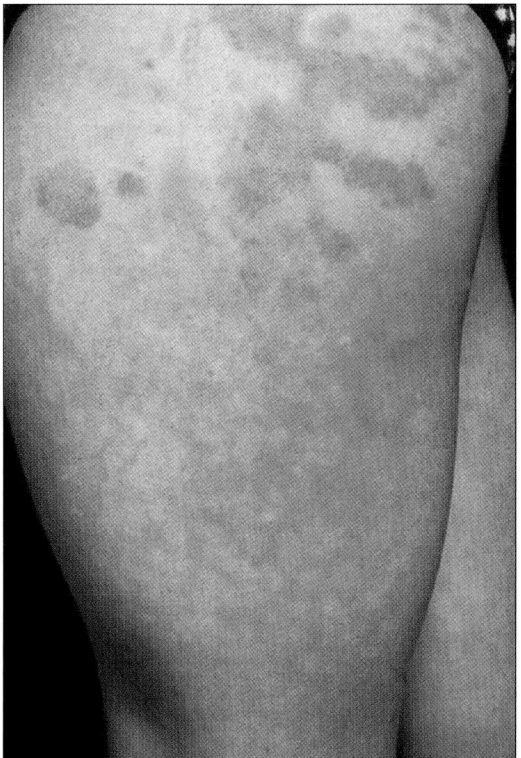

Fig. 7.32
Equestrian cold panniculitis: tender erythematous lesions on buttock and thigh. By courtesy of the Institute of Dermatology, London, UK.

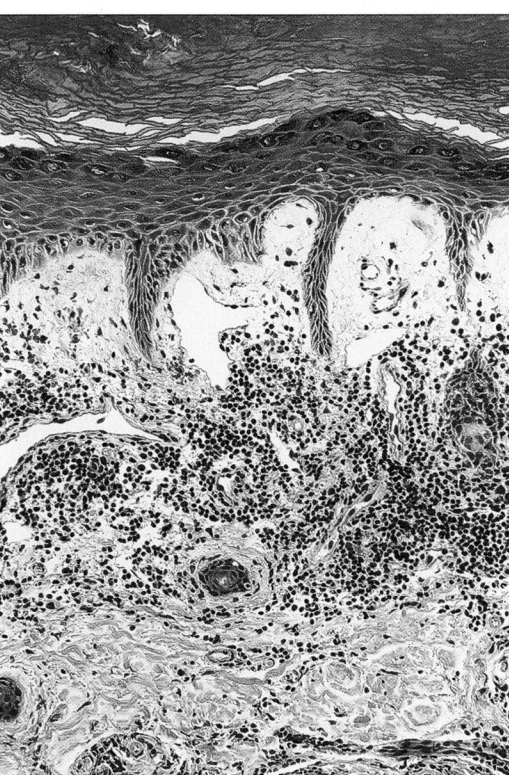

Fig. 7.33
Perniosis: there is hyperkeratosis, acanthosis and a heavy lymphocytic infiltrate. Note the marked subepidermal edema and red cell extravasation.

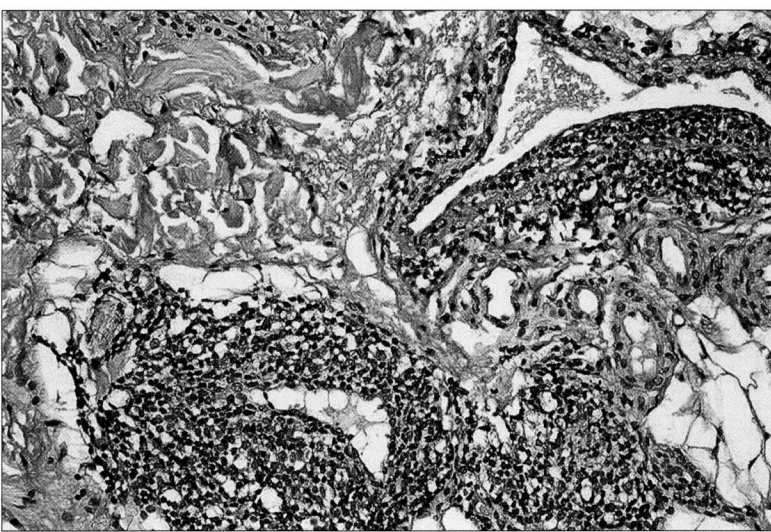

Fig. 7.34
Perniosis: there is a heavy mural lymphocytic infiltrate consistent with lymphocytic vasculitis.

Chilblain lupus erythematosus

Clinical features

Lupus erythematosus is discussed in detail in Chapter 3 and the reader is referred there for a comprehensive discussion of the disease. In this section, only chilblain lupus erythematosus (lupus pernio) will be discussed.

Chilblain lupus erythematosus may be a manifestation of either discoid or systemic lupus and shares many clinical and histological similarities with idiopathic chilblains (*Fig. 7.35*). It develops almost exclusively in females during the winter months.[1] Lesions are characterized by itchy, painful erythematous or blue–purple papules, plaques and nodules on the fingers, heels and soles of the feet; the hands, calves, knees, knuckles, elbows, nose and ears are less often affected.[2] Hyperkeratotic fissured lesions and ulcers are also sometimes present.[3] Patients may develop chilblains many years after the typical discoid rash, or lesions may develop simultaneously. Occasionally, chilblains are the sole manifestation.[3]

Approximately 15% of patients develop SLE, particularly those who develop discoid and perniotic lesions simultaneously and those with DLE–erythema multiforme-like syndrome in addition to perniosis.[1,2] Patients with severe chilblains that persist into warmer seasons appear to be at higher risk of lupus erythematosus compared with the idiopathic form.[5] Patients with some criteria, but not meeting diagnostic thresholds for connective tissue disease, have been designated as having 'atypical chilblains'.[5] Patients with atypical chilblains appear to be at higher risk of eventually developing frank connective tissue disease.[5] Based on the above observations, patients with perniosis should be evaluated for evidence of lupus erythematosus.

Pathogenesis and histological features

Biopsy reveals a cuffed perivascular lymphocytic infiltrate with edema, red cell extravasation and variable vascular fibrinoid change (*Fig. 7.36*).

Some biopsies show frank lymphocytic vasculitis. The inflammatory infiltrate often extends into the deep dermis and subcutaneous adipose tissue. Interface epidermal changes, ranging from focal vacuolar changes to a lichenoid tissue reaction, are often present.[2,7] Perisudoral chronic inflammation is sometimes seen.[5,6]

The infiltrate is mostly composed of T-cells, occasional macrophages and scattered B-cells.

Differential diagnosis

Other diseases associated with a 'cuffed' perivascular lymphocytic infiltrate and lymphocytic vasculitis must be considered in the differential diagnosis. The diagnosis is rendered only after careful clinical and serological correlation. Distinction from idiopathic chilblain perniosis is not possible based on histological features alone. The presence of lymphocytic vasculitis and interface changes seems to be more common in chilblain lupus compared with idiopathic chilblains, but these features may not be reliable discriminators.[5,6] A positive lupus band test and the presence of antinuclear antibodies favor a diagnosis of chilblain lupus erythematosus.

References

1. Millard, L.G., Rowell, N.R. (1978) Chilblain lupus erythematosus (Hutchinson). A clinical and laboratory study of 17 patients. *Br J Dermatol*, **98**, 497–506.
2. Doutre, M.S., Beylot, C., Beylot, J. et al (1992) Chilblain lupus erythematosus: report of 15 cases. *Dermatology*, **184**, 26–28.
3. Rowell, N.R. (1984) The natural history of lupus erythematosus. *Clin Exp Dermatol*, **9**, 217–231.
4. Wechsler, H.L. (1983) Lupus erythematosus. A clinician's coign of vantage. *Arch Dermatol*, **119**, 877–882.
5. Viguier, M., Pinquier, L., Cavelier-Balloy, B. et al (2001) Clinical and histopathologic features and immunologic variables in patients with severe chilblains. *Medicine*, **80**, 180–188.
6. Crowson, A.N., Magro, C.M. (1997) Perniosis. Idiopathic perniosis and its mimics: a clinical and histological study of 38 patients. *Hum Pathol*, **28**, 478–484.
7. Su, W.P.D., Perniciaro, C., Rogers, R.S. 3rd et al (1994) Chilblain lupus erythematosus (lupus pernio): clinical review to the Mayo experience and proposal of diagnostic criteria. *Cutis*, **54**, 395–399.

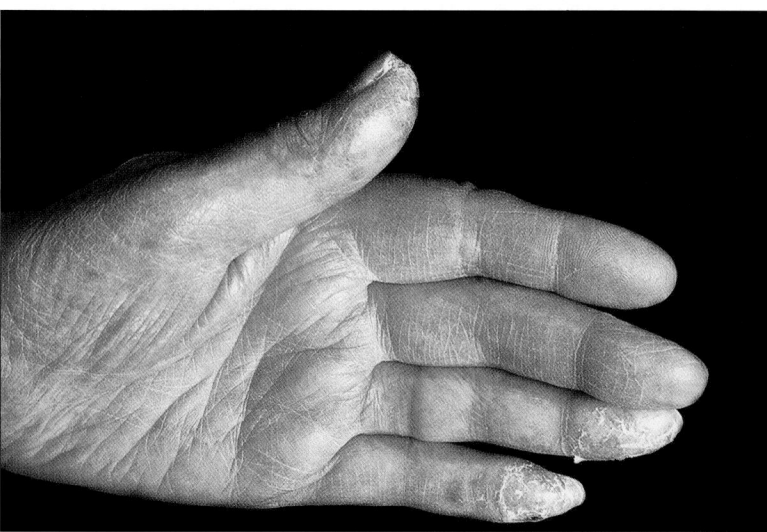

Fig. 7.35
Chilblain lupus erythematosus: resolving perniosis involving the tips of the thumb, ring and little fingers. By courtesy of R.A. Marsden, MD, St George's Hospital, London, UK.

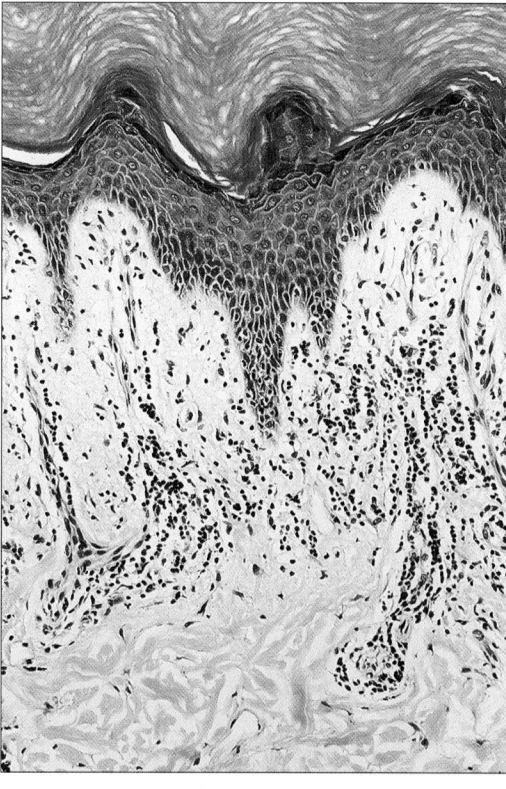

Fig. 7.36
Chilblain lupus erythematosus: there is subepidermal edema with red cell extravasation and a superficial perivascular lymphocytic infiltrate.

Pigmented purpuric dermatoses

Clinical features

The term pigmented purpuric dermatoses (purpura simplex, chronic capillaritis) encompasses a number of clinical syndromes characterized by orange/brown pigmentation (due to hemosiderin deposition likened to cayenne pepper), interspersed with fine pinpoint purpura (due to extravasated red blood cells).[1-4] All are of unknown etiology. These disorders may show overlapping clinical and histological features. Indeed, some authors no longer consider their classification to have nosological value.

- In *Majocchi's disease*, the lesions tend to be discrete and annular, vary from one to several centimeters in diameter, and are associated with telangiectases (*Fig. 7.37*).
- *Schamberg's disease* is characterized by purpura and petechiae with conspicuous pigmentation; there is a marked preponderance of males (*Figs 7.38, 7.39*). Lesions, usually irregular in shape and occurring predominantly on the lower limbs, may remain for 10 years or longer. In some cases, the findings may mimic those of

chronic venous insufficiency. The lesions are asymptomatic in most cases. However, some patients complain of pruritus.

- In *pigmented purpuric lichenoid dermatitis of Gougerot and Blum*, patients, predominantly males, develop lichenoid papules in addition to purpuric lesions, most often on the legs.
- *Itching purpura (pruriginous angiodermatitis)* also shows a male predominance and is associated with an acute onset of widely distributed orange macules (*Figs 7.40, 7.41*). It commonly begins on the dorsal surface of the feet or ankles, but soon spreads to affect the thighs, buttocks, trunk and arms. This variant is associated with a shorter duration than the others, with most patients being free

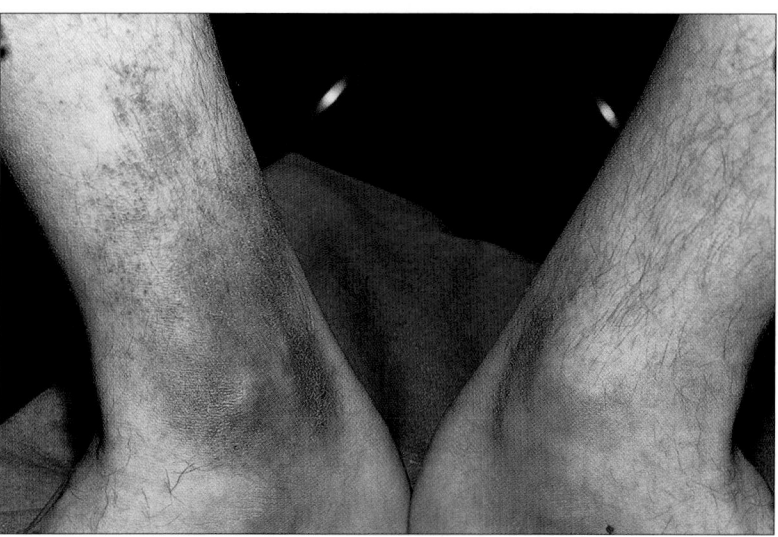

Fig. 7.39
Schamberg's disease: in this patient, the bilateral distribution over the malleoli mimics the effects of venous stasis. By courtesy of R.A. Marsden, MD, St George's Hospital, London, UK.

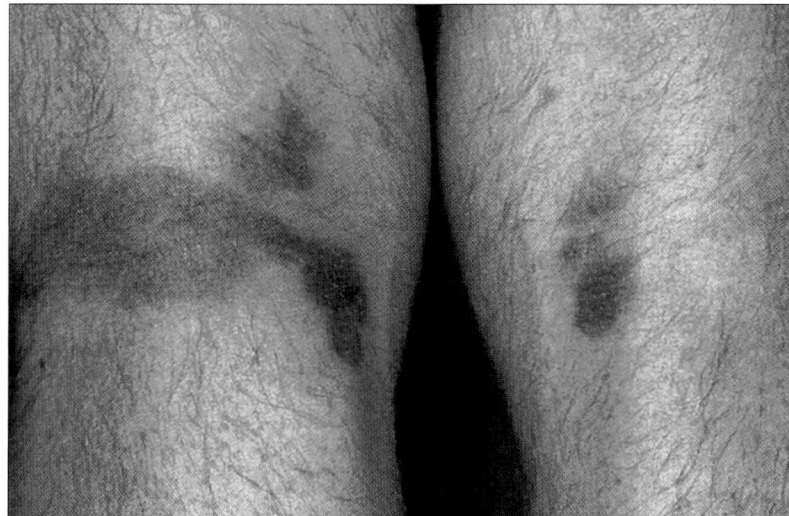

Fig. 7.37
Majocchi's disease: characteristic brown plaques on the backs of the knees in a male. By courtesy of R.A. Marsden, MD, St George's Hospital, London, UK.

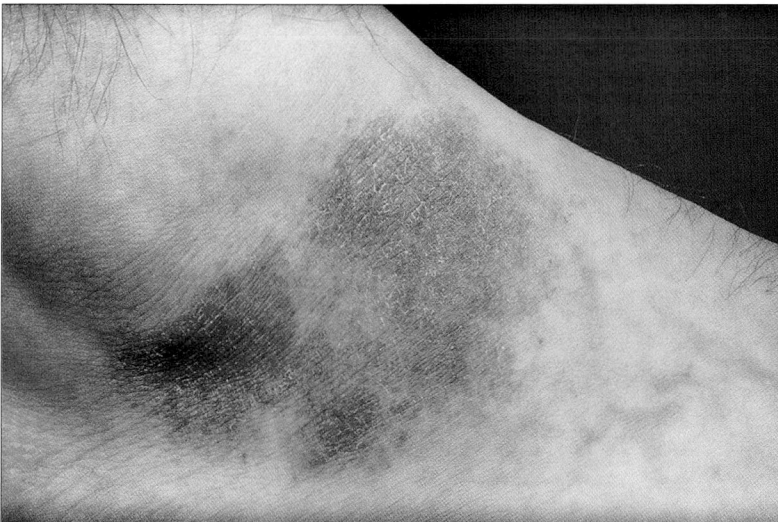

Fig. 7.38
Schamberg's disease: a localized area of capillaritis showing characteristic cayenne pepper speckling over the lateral malleolus of a male. By courtesy of R.A. Marsden, MD, St George's Hospital, London, UK.

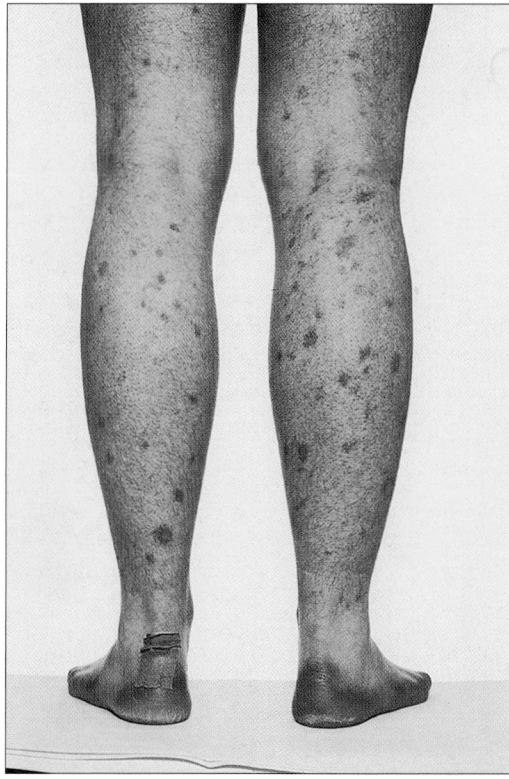

Fig. 7.40
Itching purpura: these small macules are widely distributed over both legs. By courtesy of J. Newton, MD, St Thomas' Hospital, London, UK.

from lesions by 1 month. The itching, which is of unknown etiology, is usually severe. Similar appearances may be caused by drug sensitivity.

Since lichen aureus has more distinctive features, it is discussed separately (see below).

Histological features

All variants show similar histopathological features. A perivascular lymphocytic infiltrate is associated with reactive endothelial changes and extravasated red blood cells (*Figs 7.42, 7.43*).[5] The latter are predominantly of the T-helper subset.[6] The density of the infiltrate is highly variable. The Gougerot–Blum variant is often associated with a dense lichenoid lymphocytic infiltrate. Extravasated red blood cells are usually appreciated in early lesions, while in the later stages they may not be

present but hemosiderin-laden macrophages become conspicuous (*Fig. 7.44*). An iron stain is useful to demonstrate hemosiderin. Recently, cases of pigmented purpuric dermatosis associated with granulomatous inflammation have been described and designated granulomatous pigmented purpuric dermatoses.[7,8]

Differential diagnosis

It should be emphasized that extravasated red blood cells and hemosiderin associated with a lymphocytic capillaritis are non-specific findings. The differential is broad and includes other forms of

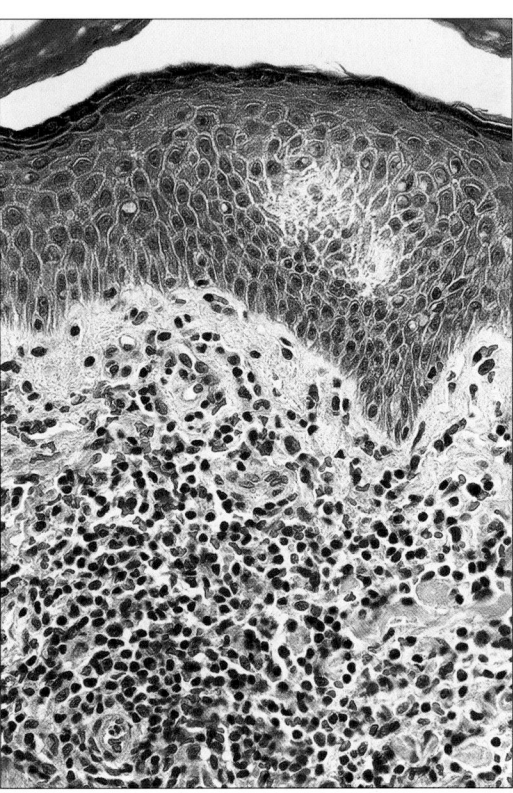

Fig. 7.43
Pigmented purpura: the infiltrate consists of lymphocytes and histiocytes. Note the red cell extravasation.

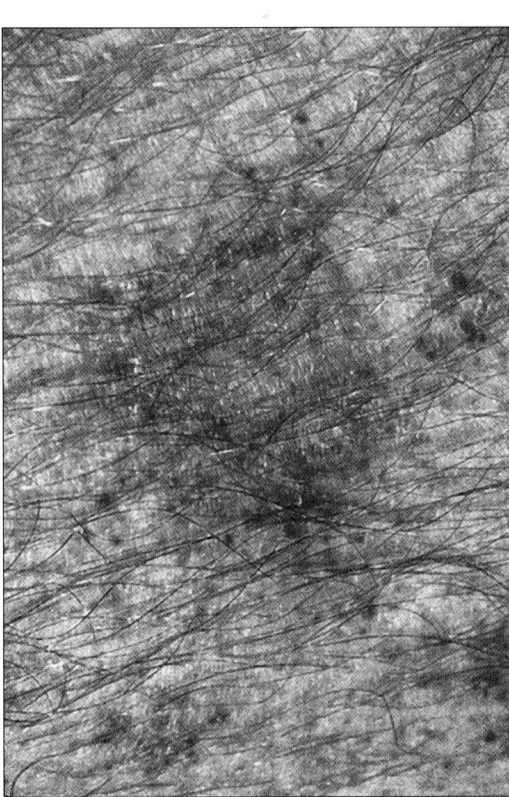

Fig. 7.41
Itching purpura: close-up view of a typical orange macule. By courtesy of J. Newton, MD, St Thomas' Hospital, London, UK.

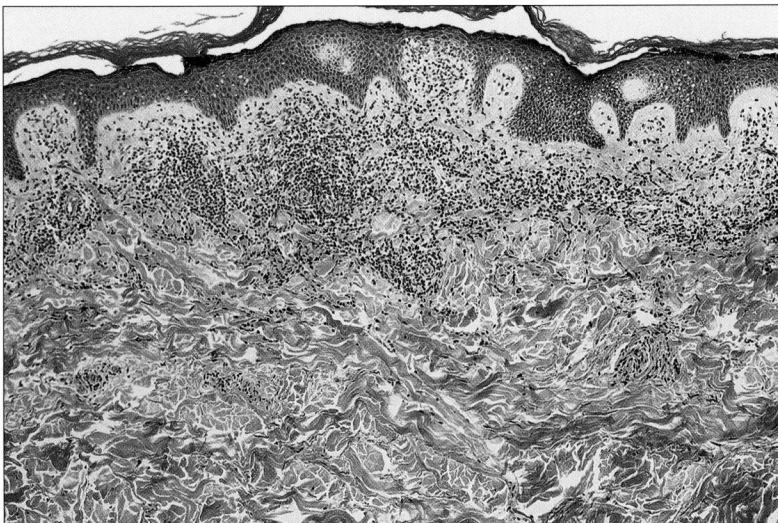

Fig. 7.42
Pigmented purpura: there is an upper dermal heavy perivascular lymphocytic infiltrate.

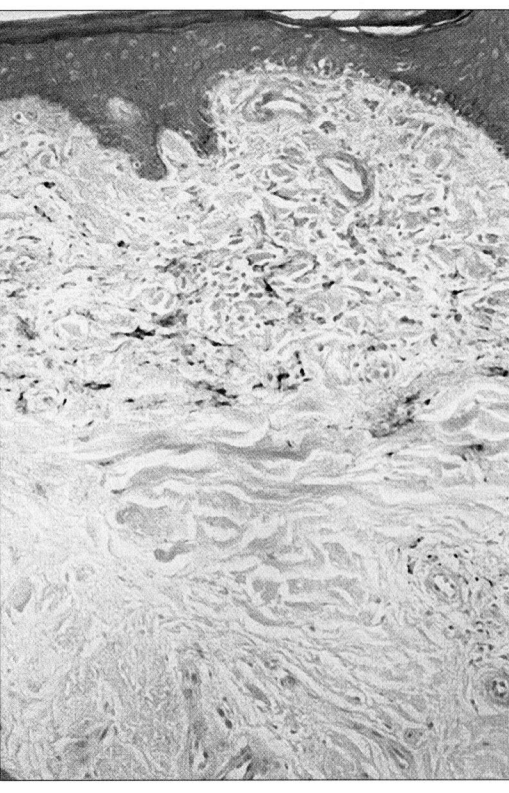

Fig. 7.44
Pigmented purpura: there is abundant hemosiderin deposition as revealed with the Perl Prussian blue stain for iron.

perivascular lymphocytic infiltrates and lymphocytic capillaritis. Careful clinical correlation is necessary to establish a correct diagnosis. Progression of lesions mimicking pigmented purpuric dermatoses to mycosis fungicides has been documented.[9,10] However, this appears to be an uncommon event. The absence of epidermotropism and cytological atypia favors pigmented purpuric dermatitis over a T-cell lympho-proliferative disorder. However, in rare cases, distinction may be difficult or impossible and ancillary investigastions such as immunohistological and T-cell gene rearrangement studies may be indicated. Adding to this occasionally difficult distinction, cases of pigmented purpuric dermatoses with clonal T-cell gene rearrangements have been reported.[7] Therefore, it appears that the results of gene rearrangement studies may not always reliably aid in this differential diagnosis. All information – clinical, histological, immunohistological and genetic – should be evaluated in context.

References

1. Farrokhzad, S., Champion, R.H. (1970) Pigmented purpuric dermatoses. *Dermatologica*, **140**, 45–53.
2. Mosto, S.J., Casala, A.M. (1965) Disseminated pruriginous angiodermatitis (itching purpura). *Arch Dermatol*, **91**, 351–356.
3. Ranall, S.J., Kierland, R.R., Montgomery, H. (1951) Pigmented purpuric eruptions. *Arch Dermatol*, **64**, 177–182.
4. Ratnam, K.V., Su, W.P.D., Peters, M.S. (1991) Purpura simplex (inflammatory purpura without vasculitis): a clinicopathologic study of 174 cases. *J Am Acad Dermatol*, **25**, 642–647.
5. Newton, R.C., Raimer, S.S. (1985) Pigmented purpuric eruptions. *Dermatol Clin*, **3**, 165–169.
6. Simon, M., Heese, A., Gotz, A. (1989) Immunopathological investigations in purpura pigmentosa chronica. *Acta Derm Venereol*, **69**, 101–104.
7. Wong, W.R., Kuo, T.T., Chen, M.J. et al (2001) Granulomatous variant of chronic pigmented purpuric dermatosis: report of two cases. *Br J Dermatol*, **145**, 162–164.
8. Saito, R., Matsuoka, Y. (1996) Granulomatous pigmented purpuric dermatosis. *J Dermatol*, **23**, 551–555.
9. Barnhill, R.L., Braverman, I.M. (1988) Progression of pigmented purpura-like eruptions to mycosis fungoides: report of three cases. *J Am Acad Dermatol*, **19**, 25–31.
10. Toro, J.R., Sander, C.A., Leboit, P.E. (1999) Persistent pigmented purpuric dermatitis and mycosis fungoides: simulant, precursor, or both? A study by light microscopy and molecular methods. *Am J Dermatopathol*, **19**, 108–118.

Lichen aureus

Clinical features

Lichen aureus (lichen purpuricus) is a rare variant of the pigmented purpuric dermatoses. It may be differentiated from the other forms by virtue of its distinctive clinical and histological features.[1–4] It is, therefore, discussed separately.

Lichen aureus shows a male predilection (2:1) and tends to affect the younger age group, with a peak incidence in the fourth decade. Children may occasionally be affected.[3] Lesions are usually asymptomatic, although pruritus is an occasional feature. The disease is characterized by discrete or confluent lichenoid macules and papules, which may be golden yellow, bronze, purple, or dark brown, and may resemble a bruise (*Fig. 7.45*). Sometimes a purpuric element is evident. The lesions of lichen aureus are characteristically very persistent, although occasionally spontaneous resolution is a feature. They occur most often on the lower legs, but may affect quite a wide variety of sites, including the arms, hands, trunk and thighs. Lesions are usually unilateral and limited to only one or two sites; they consist of either solitary ovoid maculopapules 3–5 cm in diameter or irregular plaques up to 20 cm across. Rarely, a zosteriform pattern has been described.[5]

Histological features

The epidermis is structurally normal. A dense lymphohistiocytic infiltrate is present in the upper dermis, usually distributed in a band-like fashion immediately below the epidermis (*Figs 7.46, 7.47*). In contrast to lichen planus, however, there is no evidence of basal cell hydropic degeneration and cytoid bodies are not found. A Grenz zone is sometimes present, although the infiltrate may abut the overlying epidermis. Lymphocytic exocytosis may be present. Scattered within the infiltrate are increased numbers of blood vessels. Hemosiderin-laden macrophages are present in the deeper aspect of the infiltrate or in the adjacent non-infiltrated dermis. Purpura is a variable feature and there is no evidence of frank vasculitis.

Differential diagnosis

There may some histological overlap with the Gougerot–Blum variant of pigmented purpuric lichenoid dermatitis but lichen aureus tends to be more localized.

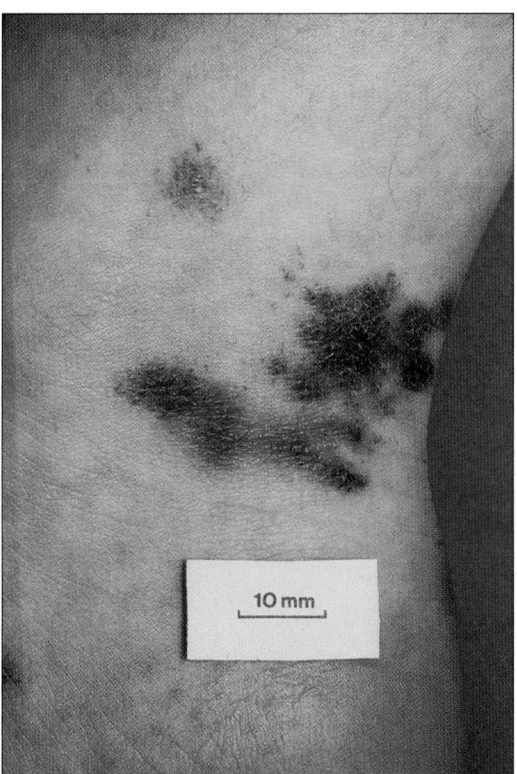

Fig. 7.45
Lichen aureus: golden–red–brown plaques on the ankle. By courtesy of M. Price, MD, St Thomas' Hospital, London, UK.

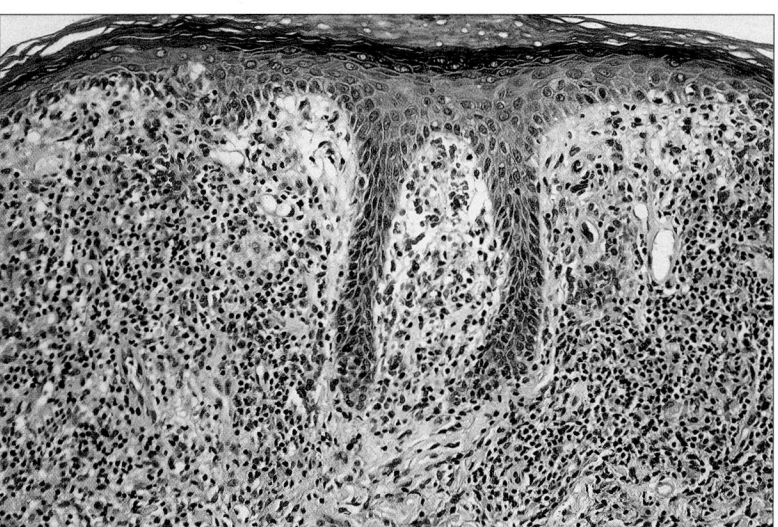

Fig. 7.46
Lichen aureus: there is a dense band-like infiltrate in the upper dermis.

References

1. Gelmetti, C., Cerri, D., Grimalt, R. (1991) Lichen aureus in childhood. *Pediatr Dermatol*, 8, 280–283.
2. Price, M.L., Wilson Jones, E., Calnan, C.D. et al (1985) Lichen aureus: a localised persistent form of pigmented purpuric dermatitis. *Br J Dermatol*, **112**, 307–314.
3. Graham, R.M., English, J.S., Emmerson, R.W. (1984) Lichen aureus: a study of 12 cases. *Clin Exp Dermatol*, 9, 392–401.
4. Kanitakis, C., Tsoitis, G. (1982) Lichen purpurique. *Ann Dermatol Venereol*, **109**, 445–452.
5. Aoki, M., Kawana, S. (2002) Lichen aureus. *Cutis*, **69**, 145–148.

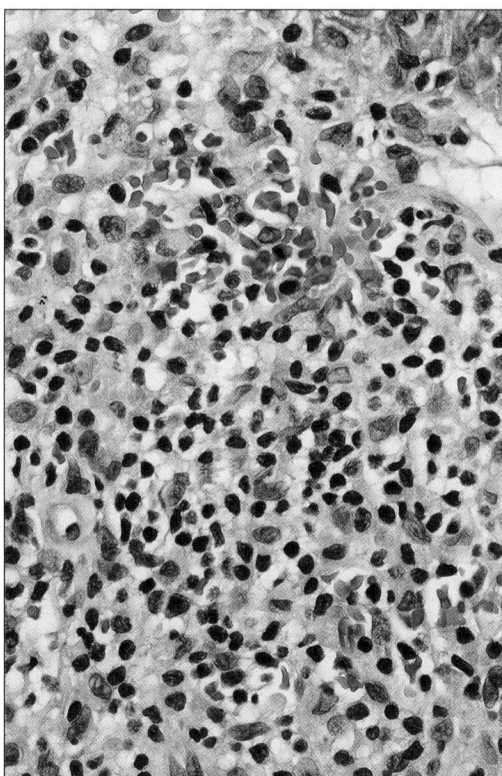

Fig. 7.47
Lichen aureus: the infiltrate consists of lymphocytes and histiocytes. Note the marked red cell extravasation.

Pruritic urticarial papules and plaques of pregnancy

Clinical features

Pruritic and urticarial papules and plaques of pregnancy (PUPPP, also known as polymorphic eruption of pregnancy, toxemic rash of pregnancy, toxic erythema of pregnancy, late onset prurigo of pregnancy) is a common dermatosis of uncertain etiology.[1] The disorder is most frequently seen in primigravidas.[2] Characteristically, it presents late in pregnancy, usually during late third trimester with an average time of onset in the 36th week.[2] Rarely, presentation during the postpartum period has been documented.[2] In a recent study, the female to male infant ratio was 2:1.[3] In one large series, 76% of patients were primigravidas.[2]

As its name indicates, urticarial papules and plaques are associated with vexatious pruritus. Patients frequently complain that pruritus interferes with sleep.[2] At onset, papules are often localized to the abdomen along lines of stria distensae. This pattern is seen in approximately 50% of patients.[1,2] Small vesicles are occasionally present.[2] With time, the papules spread to involve the proximal limbs and torso and coalesce to form plaques. Sparing of the face is a helpful diagnostic clinical clue. Typically, the lesions resolve shortly after delivery. Importantly (see differential diagnosis section below), PUPPP does not usually recur with subsequent pregnancy.

One group found PUPPP was associated with increased maternal weight gain and increased newborn weight compared with a control population.[4,5] Some studies suggest a relationship between PUPPP and twin gestation with two such reports documenting 10% and 16% of cases, respectively, associated with twin gestations.[2,4,5] These data have led some authors to postulate that abdominal distension may play a role in the pathogenesis of PUPPP.[4]

Rarely, congenital abnormalities have been noted in association with PUPPP but this may be due to small statistical sampling. In one report, one child had hypoplastic dental enamel, while the other developed congenital laryngomalacia requiring surgical intervention.[2] In this same series, another child was reported to have a ventriculoseptal defect. Most authors, however, believe that there is no direct association between PUPPP and congenital abnormalities.

Histological features

Early lesions (urticarial papules) of polymorphic eruption of pregnancy show epidermal and upper dermal edema accompanied by a perivascular lymphohistiocytic infiltrate with variable numbers of eosinophils (*Figs 7.48–7.50*). Often the number of eosinophils is modest and in one series only 17% of biopsies had eosinophils in the infiltrate. However, other authors report contrary experience, with most biopsies showing eosinophils. It is our experience that most biopsies show at least rare eosinophils if multiple sections are examined.

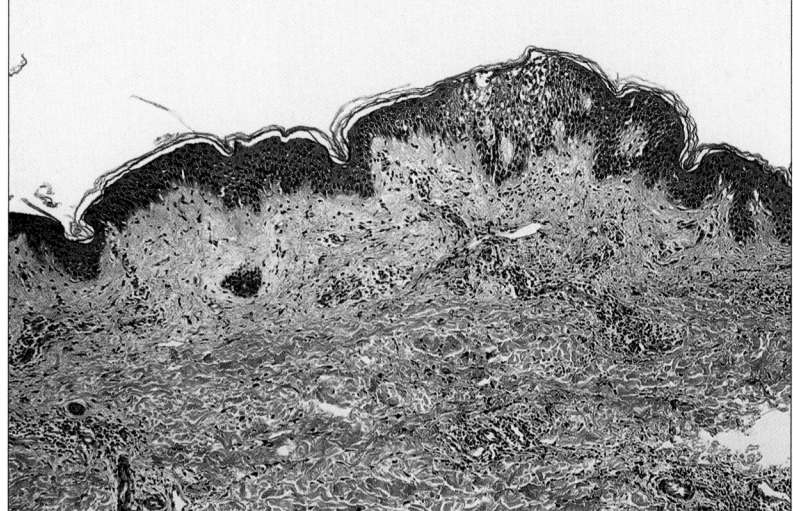

Fig. 7.48
Pruritic urticarial papules and plaques of pregnancy: there is focal spongiosis. Note the perivascular upper dermal infiltrate.

The lymphohistiocytic infiltrate is also variable in density, ranging from modest numbers of cells to a dense infiltrate with a tightly 'cuffed' perivascular distribution.[2] Mild papillary dermal edema is a common finding but marked edema is rarely seen.[2] The additional feature of spongiotic vesiculation characterizes later lesions. Less common manifestations include eosinophilic spongiosis, and rarely eosinophil-rich subepidermal blistering.

Differential diagnosis

As can be deduced from the above histological description, the biopsy findings are non-specific. The main differential diagnosis includes urticaria, hypersensitivity reactions and pemphigoid gestationis. Usually, clinical examination and history will allow distinction from hypersensitivity reactions, which may show identical histological features. Urticaria can be distinguished by the presence of neutrophils. In our experience, distinction between the pre-bullous phase of pemphigoid gestationis and PUPPP is the most common reason for which the clinician performs a biopsy. Distinction is important since pemphigoid gestationis, but not PUPPP, may be associated with significant fetal morbidity. The presence of a subepidermal vesicle or marked papillary dermal edema favors pemphigoid gestationis; however, some early lesions will lack these features. Furthermore, PUPPP is frequently associated with mild papillary dermal edema. Immunofluorescence studies are often necessary for definitive diagnosis. Pemphigoid gestationis is associated with basement membrane staining for C3 and sometimes IgG. Most cases of PUPPP show negative immunofluorescence results.[6] However, it should be noted that there have been a few purported cases of PUPPP in which weak C3 staining in a linear pattern along the basement membrane has been reported.[2] In some laboratories, granular deposits along the basement membrane have also been described in cases of PUPPP.[2,7] However, PUPPP is not associated with positive strong linear immunofluorescence staining along the basement membrane – a result that would strongly favor pemphigoid gestationis.[7] In contrast to pemphigoid gestationis, PUPPP does not tend to recur during subsequent pregnancies.

References

1. Ahmed, A., Kaplan, R. (1981) Pruritic urticarial papules and plaques of pregnancy. *J Am Acad Dermatol*, **4**, 679–681.
2. Yancey, K.B., Hall, R.P., Lawley, T.J. (1984) Pruritic and urticarial papules and plaques of pregnancy (PUPPP): clinical experience in 25 patients. *J Am Acad Dermatol*, **10**, 473–480.
3. Vaughan Jones, S.A., Hern, S., Nelson-Piercy, C. et al (1999) A prospective study of 200 women with dermatoses of pregnancy correlating clinical findings with hormonal and immunopathological profiles. *Br J Dermatol*, **141**, 71–81.
4. Cohen, L.M., Capeless, E.L., Krusinski, P.A. et al (1989) Pruritic urticarial papules and plaques of pregnancy and its relationship to maternal–fetal weight gain and twin pregnancy. *Arch Dermatol*, **125**, 1534–1536.
5. Elling, S.V., McKenna, P., Powell, F.C. (2000) Pruritic urticarial papules and plaques of pregnancy in twin and triplet pregnancies. *J Eur Acad Dermatol Venereol*, **14**, 378–381.
6. Alcalay, J., Ingber, A., Davide, M. et al (1987) Pruritic urticarial papules and plaques of pregnancy. A review of 21 cases. *J Reprod Med*, **32**, 315–316.
7. Aronson, I.K., Bond, S., Fiedler, V.C. et al (1998) Pruritic urticarial papules and plaques of pregnancy: clinical and immunopathologic findings in 57 patients. *Am J Dermatopathol*, **39**, 933–939.

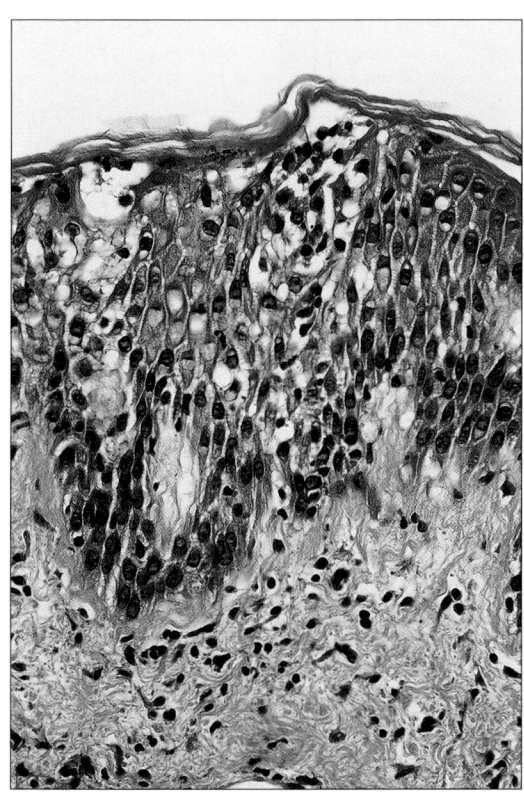

Fig. 7.49
Pruritic urticarial papules and plaques of pregnancy: high power view showing spongiosis.

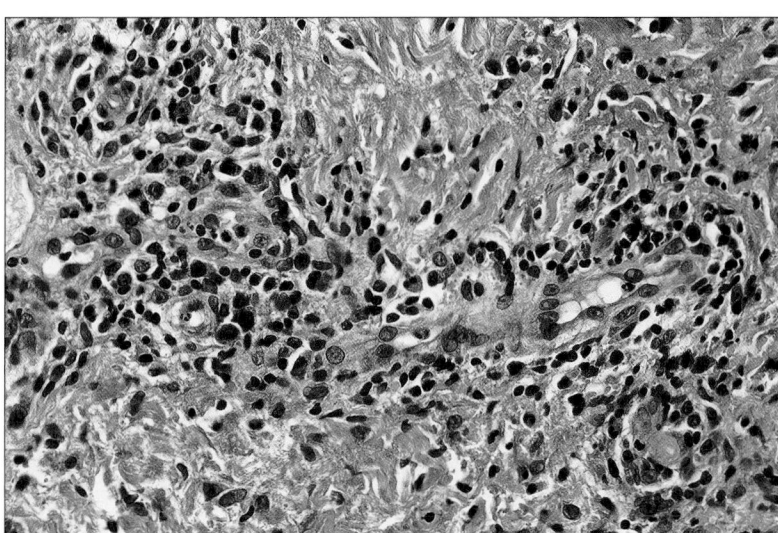

Fig. 7.50
Pruritic urticarial papules and plaques of pregnancy: the infiltrate consists of lymphocytes, histiocytes and eosinophils.

Pregnancy prurigo

Clinical features

Pregnancy prurigo (prurigo gravidarum, prurigo gestationis) affects 1 in 300 pregnancies, presenting as pruritic, erythematous, 0.5–1.0 cm papules and nodules with a predilection for the extensor surfaces of the extremities and the abdomen.[1–5] Superimposed features of excoriation with scale-crust may be seen. Lesions usually present during the third trimester but have been documented to commence in all trimesters of pregnancy. The condition usually disappears following delivery, but in some cases it persists into the puerperium. Blistering is not a feature. Fetal and maternal health does not appear to be adversely affected.[5]

Pathogenesis and histological features

The pathogenesis of pregnancy prurigo is unknown. It has been suggested that the condition represents pruritis gravidarum in a background of atopic dermatitis.[1,5] Patients often have a history of atopy.[5] Serum IgE may be elevated in patients regardless of whether or not there is a positive history of atopy.[5] Of interest, eczematous dermatitis appears to be common in pregnancy.[5] Intrahepatic cholestasis of pregnancy may play a significant role in some patients.[4]

The histological features are not specific, comprising mild spongiosis, lymphocytic exocytosis, and a superficial perivascular lymphohistiocytic infiltrate with occasional eosinophils (*Figs 7.51, 7.52*). Frequently, histological features of excoriation are present. Immunofluorescence studies are negative.

Differential diagnosis

The histological features are non-specific and clinical correlation is necessary to render a firm diagnosis. The diagnosis is perhaps best approached as one of exclusion and underlying etiologies should be sought. The major differential diagnosis includes hypersensitivity reactions (drug eruption, insect bites, etc.) with superimposed prurigo nodularis.

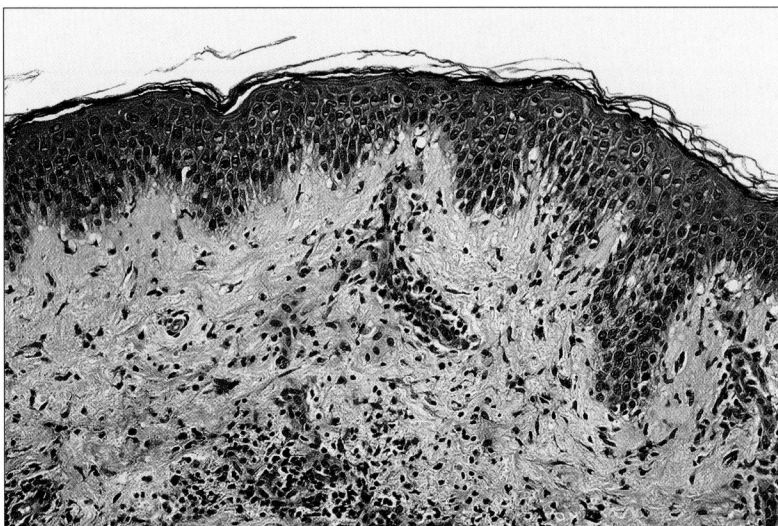

Fig. 7.51
Pregnancy prurigo: there is a superficial perivascular inflammatory cell infiltrate.

References

1. Black, M.M. (1989) Prurigo of pregnancy, papular dermatitis of pregnancy, and pruritic folliculitis of pregnancy. *Semin Dermatol*, **8**, 23–25.
2. Shornick, J.K. (1998) Dermatoses of pregnancy. *Semin Cutan Med Surg*, **17**, 172–181.
3. Vaughan Jones, S.A., Black, M.M. (1999) Pregnancy dermatoses. *J Am Acad Dermatol*, **40**, 233–241.
4. Kroumpouzos, G., Cohen, L. (2001) Dermatoses of pregnancy. *J Am Acad Dermatol*, **45**, 1–19.
5. Vaughan Jones, S.A., Hern, S., Nelson-Piercy, C. et al (1999) A prospective study of 200 women with dermatoses of pregnancy correlating clinical findings with hormonal and immunopathological profiles. *Br J Dermatol*, **141**, 71–81.

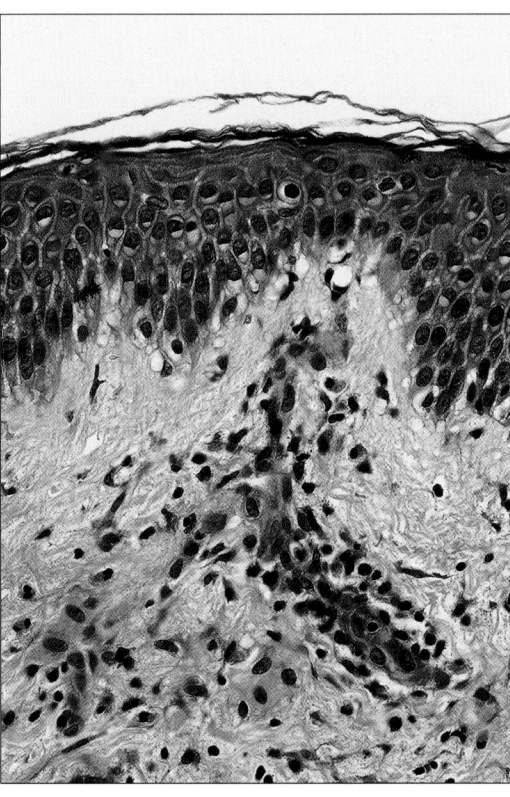

Fig. 7.52
Pregnancy prurigo: the infiltrate consists of lymphocytes with occasional eosinophils.

Urticarial vasculitis

Clinical features

Urticarial vasculitis is an uncommon condition characterized clinically by chronic urticaria and histologically by leukocytoclastic venulitis.[1–3] This disorder is also discussed on page 719. In some patients, urticarial vasculitis is associated with antibody–antigen complexes – a type III hypersensitivity reaction.[4,5] In many patients, however, no underlying cause is discovered.

Patients may have, in addition to urticarial skin lesions, angioedema, arthralgia, gastrointestinal symptoms and evidence of renal involvement. The spectrum of illness ranges from mild symptoms to a serious systemic illness, for which treatment with corticosteroids is sometimes necessary.[6]

The disease shows a female predominance (2:1) and is most often seen in the third, fourth or fifth decades. The cutaneous lesions are urticarial in appearance, but usually last 24–72 hours (*Figs 7.53–7.55*).[7] Pruritus, a burning sensation, or pain, are common complaints. The frequency of attacks varies from daily to monthly. The skin lesions are edematous, raised and erythematous, and are associated with non-blanchable purpura.

Systemic manifestations/associations include joint pain, stiffness and swelling, particularly of the hands, elbows, feet, ankles and knees. Frank arthritis is extremely rare. Proteinuria and hematuria may be seen in some patients. Many patients are hypocomplementemic.[4] Rarely, renal biopsy reveals the features of focal or diffuse proliferative glomerulonephritis. Crescentic glomerulonephritis, mesangial and membranous nephropathy have also been documented.[6,8,9] Abdominal pain associated with nausea, vomiting and diarrhea is a feature in some patients.

The erythrocyte sedimentation rate (ESR) is raised in many cases and in about 50% of patients there is hypocomplementemia. The presence of the latter correlates with systemic involvement.[6,10] There may also be depression of the early classical pathway components C1q, C4 and C2. Patients with hypocomplementemic urticarial vasculitis have a high prevalence of autoantibodies to endothelial cells.[11,12] The term 'Schnitzler's syndrome' has been applied to patients with urticarial vasculitis and monoclonal IgM gammopathy.[13–18] Hepatosplenomegaly, elevated ESR, elevated white blood cell count, fever and joint pain are characteristic features.[14–16] An underlying lymphoproliferative disorder is present in a minor subset of patients.[13]

Importantly, urticarial vasculitis (especially the hypocomplementemic variant) is often associated with, or heralds the onset of, a variety of systemic diseases, including SLE, arthritis, interstitial lung disease, pericarditis, mixed connective tissue disease, hepatitis, inflammatory bowel disease, serum sickness, polyarteritis nodosa and Wegener's granulomatosis, viral infections, Sjögren's syndrome, cryoglobulinemia, polycythemia rubra vera, reaction to drugs, and as a response to sunlight.[6,10,19–25] In one study, more than 50% of patients had uveitis, scleritis, conjunctivitis or episcleritis.[6] It appears that patients with hypocomplementemia have more severe disease.[19] Some authors have postulated that hypocomplementemic urticarial vasculitis represents a form of systemic lupus erythematosus.[26] Others, however, have shown no significant difference in the association with lupus in patients with normocomplementemic compared with hypocomplementemic urticarial vasculitis.[6] A diagnosis of urticarial vasculitis in any patient should initiate an evaluation for underlying disease. Fortunately, urticarial vasculitis usually has a benign outcome.[6]

Urticarial vasculitis has been documented in association with malignancy.[6,27] Given the rarity of this association, it may well be coincidental.

Histological features

In urticarial vasculitis, vascular damage is superimposed on a background of dermal edema and inflammation typical of urticaria. The vasculitis affects the superficial vascular plexus. Extravasation of red blood cells is evidence of vascular damage. The vasculitis shows features of leukocytoclastic vasculitis except that the histological features tend to be subtle and are easily overlooked (*Figs 7.56–7.58*). Mild or focal fibrinoid changes associated with few neutrophils and sparse karyorrhexis are typical. In our experience, the vasculitis is usually low grade in nature. Others have shown that endothelial necrosis is unusual.[28] Nevertheless, more impressive necrotizing vasculitis may sometimes be encountered (*Fig. 7.59*). Urticarial vasculitis appears to represent a spectrum of disease ranging from urticaria with very mild vascular injury to frank necrotizing vasculitis.[29]

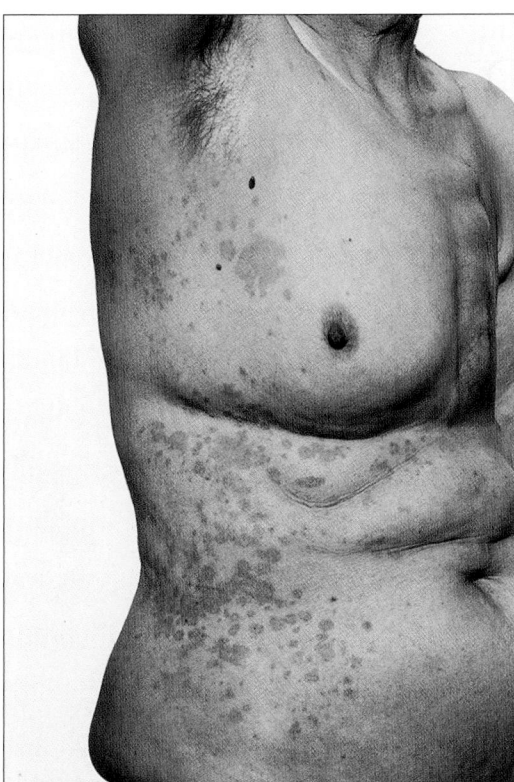

Fig. 7.53
Urticarial vasculitis: note the urticaria with a livid hue. By courtesy of J. Newton, MD, St Thomas' Hospital, London, UK.

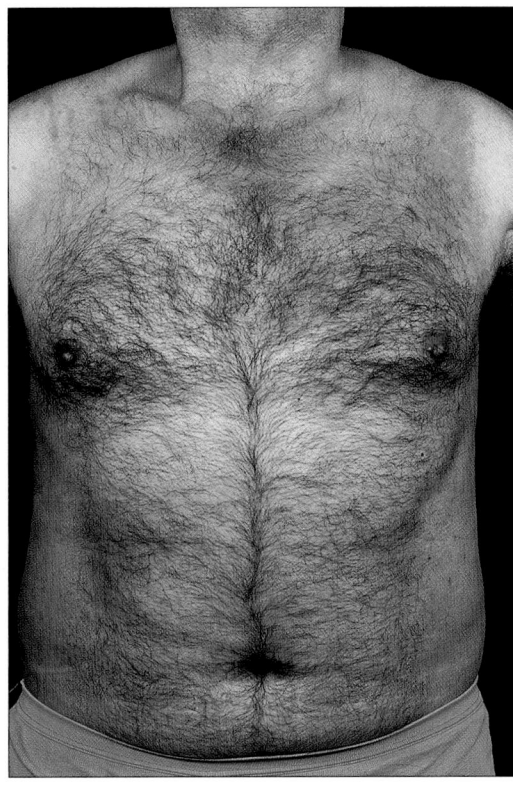

Fig. 7.54
Urticarial vasculitis: in this patient, there is an extensive urticarial plaque. By courtesy of J. Newton, MD, St Thomas' Hospital, London, UK.

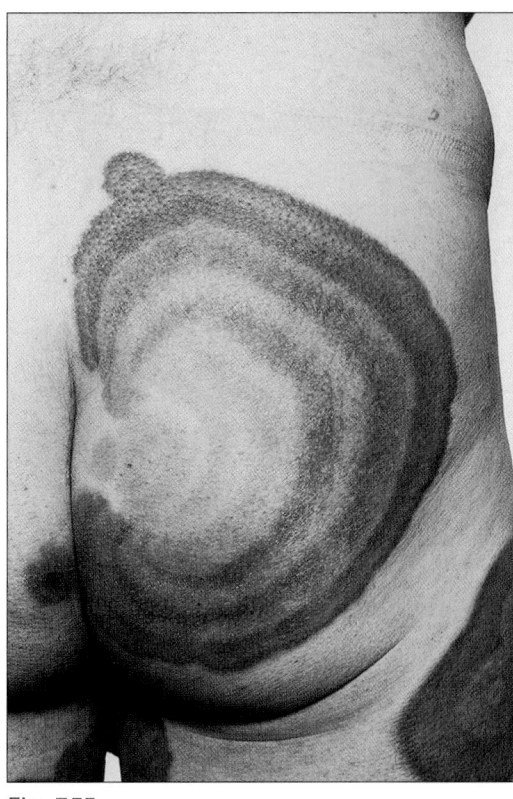

Fig. 7.55
Urticarial vasculitis: note the bizarre annular purpuric urticarial plaque. By courtesy of J. Newton, MD, St Thomas' Hospital, London, UK.

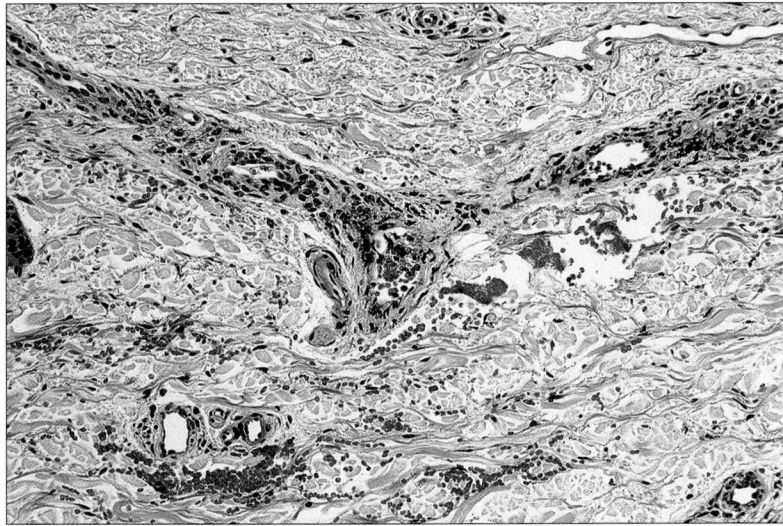

Fig. 7.56
Urticarial vasculitis: in this example of an early lesion, there is a conspicuous perivascular eosinophil infiltrate. There is no evidence of vessel wall damage.

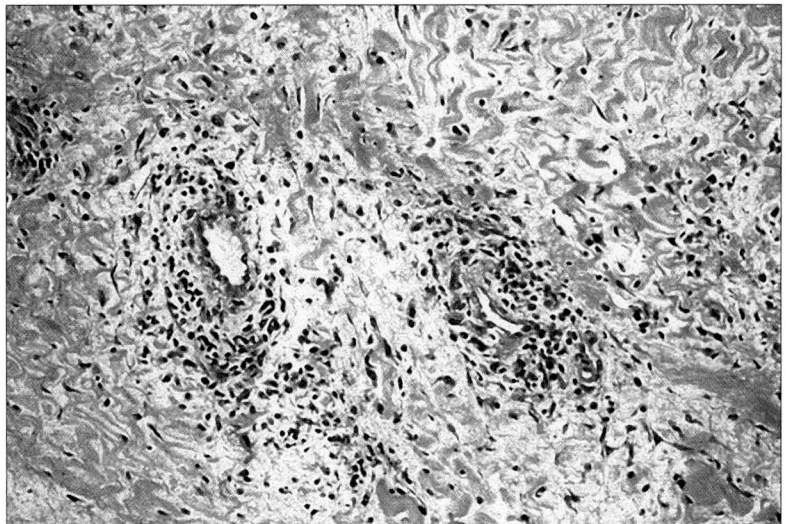

Fig. 7.57
Urticarial vasculitis: in this field, there is marked edema accompanied by a mixed lymphocytic and eosinophil infiltrate.

Differential diagnosis

Clinical correlation is necessary to distinguish urticarial vasculitis from other forms of leukocytoclastic vasculitis. Although urticarial vasculitis is often associated with subtle, low-grade vascular injury, this pattern should not be relied upon in the distinction from other forms of vasculitis. In short, the pathologist's role in diagnosis is to confirm the presence of vasculitis.

References

1. Soter, N.A., Austen, K.F., Gigli, I. (1974) Urticaria and arthralgias as manifestations of necrotizing angiitis (vasculitis). *J Invest Dermatol*, 63, 485–490.
2. Aboobaker, J., Greaves, M.W. (1986) Urticarial vasculitis. *Clin Exp Dermatol*, 11, 436–444.
3. Monroe, E.W. (1981) Urticarial vasculitis: an updated review. *J Am Acad Dermatol*, 5, 88–95.
4. Sanchez, N.P., Winkelman, R.K., Schroeter, A.L. et al (1982) The clinical and histopathologic spectrums of urticarial vasculitis: study of forty cases. *J Am Acad Dermatol*, 7, 599–605.
5. Jones, R.R., Eady, R.A.J. (1984) Endothelial cell pathology as a marker for urticarial vasculitis: a light microscopic study. *Br J Dermatol*, 110, 139–149.
6. Mehregan, D.R., Hall, M.J., Gibson, L.E. (1992) Urticarial vasculitis: a histopathologic and clinical review of 72 cases. *J Am Acad Dermatol*, 26, 441–448.
7. Kobza Black, A., Lawlor, F., Greaves, M.W. (1996) Consensus meeting on the definition of physical urticarias and urticarial vasculitis. *Clin Exp Dermatol*, 21, 424–426.
8. Messiaen, T., Van Damme, B., Kuypers, D. et al (2000) Crescentic glomerulonephritis complicating the course of a hypocomplementemic urticarial vasculitis. *Clin Nephrol*, 54, 409–412.
9. Kobayshi, S., Nagase, M., Hidaki, S. et al (1994) Membranous nephropathy associated with hypocomplementemic urticarial vasculitis: report of 2 cases and a review of the literature. *Nephron*, 66, 1–7.
10. Asherson, R.A., D'Cruz, D., Stephens, C.J. et al (1991) Urticarial vasculitis in a connective tissue disease clinic: patterns, presentations and treatment. *Semin Arthritis Rheum*, 20, 285–296.
11. D'Cruz, D.P., Wisnieski, J.J., Asherson, R. et al (1995) Autoantibodies in systemic lupus erythematosus and urticarial vasculitis. *J Rheumatol*, 22, 1669–1673.
12. Wisnieski, J.J., Baer, A.N., Christensen, J. et al (1995) Hypocomplementemic urticarial vasculitis syndrome. Clinical and serologic findings in 18 patients. *Medicine*, 74, 24–41.
13. Lim, W., Shumak, K.H., Reis, M. et al (2002) Malignant evolution of Schnitzler's syndrome – chronic urticaria and IgM monoclonal gammopathy: report of a new case and review of the literature. *Leuk Lymphoma*, 43, 181–186.
14. Lipsker, D., Veran, Y., Grunenberger, F. et al (2001) The Schnitzler syndrome. Four new cases and review of the literature. *Medicine*, 80, 37–44.
15. Puddu, P., Cianchini, G., Giardelli, C.R. et al (1997) Schnitzler's syndrome: report of a new case and a review of the literature. *Clin Exp Rheumatol*, 15, 91–95.
16. Baty, V., Hoen, B., Hudziak, H. et al (1995) Schnitzler's syndrome: two case reports and review of the literature. *Mayo Clin Proc*, 70, 570–572.
17. Janier, M., Bonvalet, D., Blanc, M.F. et al (1989) Chronic urticaria and macroglobulinemia (Schnitzler's syndrome): report of two cases. *J Am Acad Dermatol*, 20, 206–211.
18. Borradori, L., Rybojad, M., Puissant, A. et al (1990) Urticarial vasculitis associated with a monoclonal IgM gammopathy: Schnitzler's syndrome. *Br J Dermatol*, 123, 113–118.
19. Wisnieski, J.J. (2000) Urticarial vasculitis. *Curr Opin Rheumatol*, 12, 24–31.
20. Hamid, S., Cruz, P.D. Jr, Lee, W.M. (1998) Urticarial vasculitis caused by hepatitis C virus infection: response to interferon alfa therapy. *J Am Acad Dermatol*, 39, 278–280.
21. Chen, H.J., Bloch, K.J. (2001) Hypocomplementemic urticarial vasculitis, Jaccoud's arthropathy, valvular heart disease, and reversible tracheal stenosis. A surfeit of syndromes. *J Rheumatol*, 28, 383–386.
22. Farell, A.M., Sabroe, R.A., Bunker, C.B. (1996) Urticarial vasculitis associated with polycythemia rubra vera. *Clin Exp Dermatol*, 21, 302–304.
23. Kuniyuki, S., Katoh, H. (1996) Urticarial vasculitis with papular lesions in a patient with type C hepatitis and cryoglobulinemia. *J Dermatol*, 23, 279–283.
24. Lin, R.Y., Caren, C.B., Menikoff, H. (1995) Hypocomplementemic urticarial vasculitis, interstitial lung disease and hepatitis C. *Br J Dermatol*, 132, 821–823.
25. Babajanians, A., Chung-Park, M., Wisnieski, J.J. (1991) Recurrent pericarditis and cardiac tamponade in a patient with hypocomplementemic urticarial vasculitis syndrome. *J Rheumatol*, 18, 752–755.
26. Davis, M.D., Daoud, M.S., Kirby, B. et al (1998) Clinicopathologic correlation of hypocomplementemic and normocomplementemic urticarial vasculitis. *J Am Acad Dermatol*, 38, 899–905.
27. Lewis, J.E. (1990) Urticarial vasculitis occurring in association with visceral malignancy. *Acta Derm Venereol*, 70, 345–347.
28. Jones, R.R., Eady, R.A. (1984) Endothelial cell injury as a marker for urticarial vasculitis: a light microscopic study. *Br J Dermatol*, 110, 139–149.
29. Jones, R.R., Bhogal, B., Dash, A. et al (1983) Urticaria and vasculitis: a continuum of histological and immunopathological changes. *Br J Dermatol*, 108, 695–703.

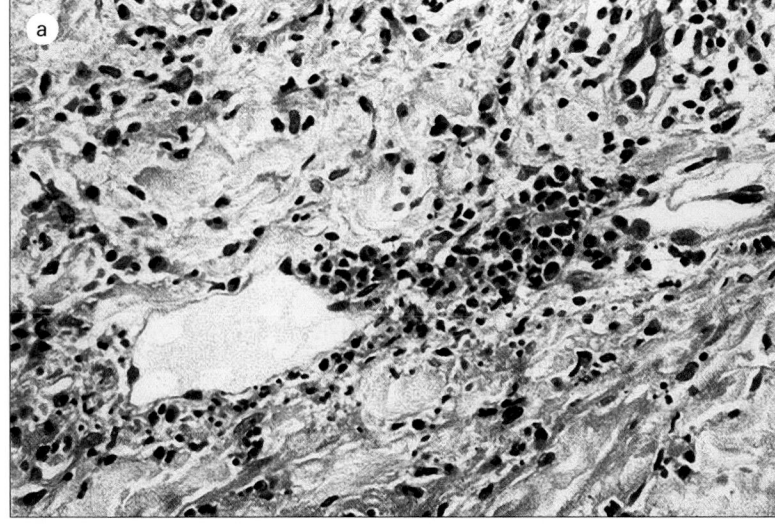

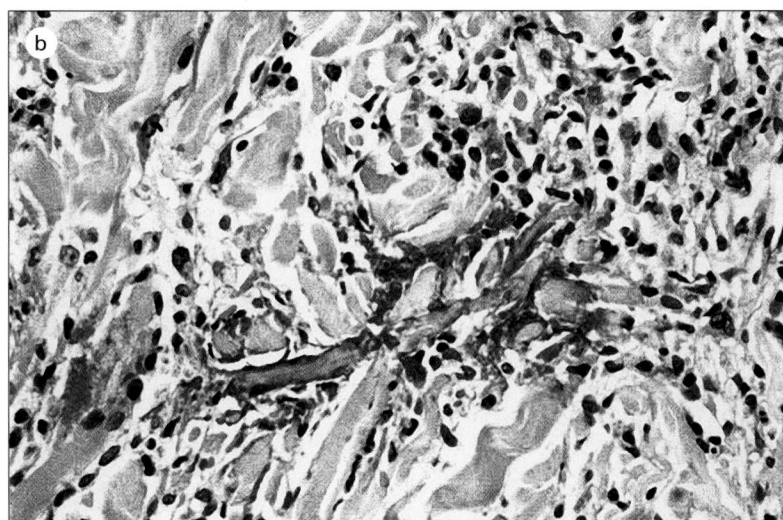

Fig. 7.58
Urticarial vasculitis: (a) there is a heavy lymphocytic and eosinophil infiltrate; (b) in this example, there are conspicuous flame figures.

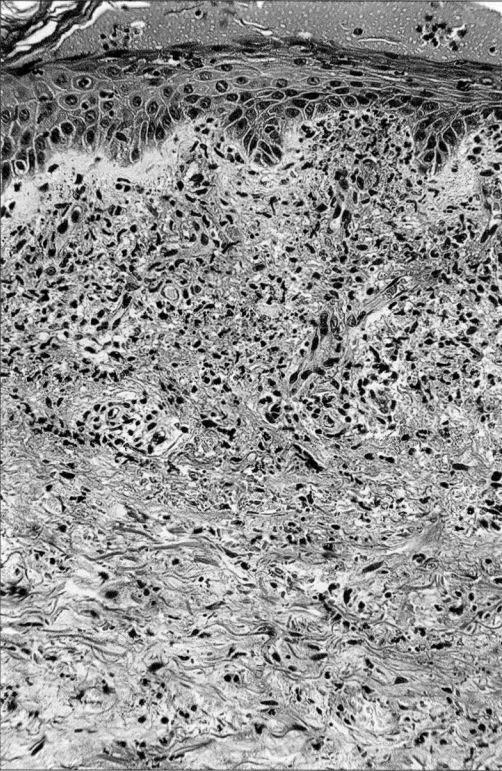

Fig. 7.59
Urticarial vasculitis: this biopsy of a purpuric lesion shows features of florid vasculitis.

Tumor necrosis factor receptor-associated periodic syndrome

Clinical features

Tumor necrosis factor receptor-associated periodic syndrome (TRAPS) is a rare autosomal dominant condition with a predilection for individuals of Irish and Scottish descent.[1–5] Other terms used to describe this disorder include familial Hibernian fever, benign autosomal dominant familial periodic fever and autosomal dominant periodic fever with amyloidosis. Patients usually present in infancy or early childhood with prolonged episodes of fever accompanied by (in descending order of frequency) abdominal pain, cutaneous manifestations, myalgia, headache, athralgia and pleuritic chest pain.[3]

Cutaneous manifestations include migratory asymptomatic, non-scaly erythematous macules and plaques, annular and serpiginous lesions measuring up to 28 cm in diameter.[2,3] The trunk and extremities are predominantly affected with lesions presenting proximally and migrating distally.[3] Patients may also develop conjunctivitis and periorbital edema.[2] Amyloidosis is an occasional complication.[6]

Pathogenesis and histological features

TRAPS is due to a mutation of the TNFRSF1A gene which encodes the tumor necrosis factor receptor.[3] The gene has been localized to chromosome 12p13.[4]

Histologically the skin lesions are characterized by dermal edema and a superficial and deep perivascular and interstitial infiltrate of lymphocytes and a lesser number of macrophages.[1–3] There is no evidence of vasculitis. Small numbers of neutrophils or plasma cells may occasionally be present.[3]

The infiltrate consists of CD3+ T-lymphocytes and CD68+ macrophages. CD4+ T-helper and CD8+ T-suppressor forms are both represented. CD20+ B-lymphocytes are not present.

References

1. Williamson, L.M., Hull, D., Mehta, R. et al (1982) Familial Hibernian fever. *QJM*, **51**, 469–480.
2. McDermott, M.F., Smillie, D.M., Powell, R.J. (1997) Clinical spectrum of familial Hibernian fever: a 14-year follow-up study of the index case and extended family. *Mayo Clin Proc*, **72**, 806–817.
3. Toro, J.R., Aksentijecich, I., Hull, K. et al (2000) Tumor necrosis factor receptor-associated periodic syndrome. *Arch Dermatol*, **136**, 1487–1494.
4. Mulley, J., Saar, K., Hewitt, G. et al (1998) Gene localization for an autosomal dominant familial periodic fever to 12q13. *Am J Hum Genet*, **62**, 884–889.
5. Karenko, L., Petterson, T., Roberts, P. (1992) Autosomal dominant 'Mediterranean fever' in a Finnish family. *J Intern Med*, **232**, 365–369.
6. Gertz, M.A., Petitt, R.M., Perrault, J. et al (1987) Autosomal dominant familial Mediterranean fever-like syndrome with amyloidosis. *Mayo Clin Proc*, **62**, 1095–1100.

Eosinophilic, polymorphic and pruritic eruption associated with radiotherapy

Clinical features

Rueda and co-workers have recently documented a polymorphic cutaneous eruption which develops in females undergoing radiotherapy for cancer (eosinophilic, polymorphic and pruritic eruption associated with radiotherapy, EPPER).[1,2] Although a wide spectrum of tumors may be present, cervical squamous carcinoma is by far the most common. The cutaneous lesions are intensely pruritic and include excoriations, erythematous papules, vesicles, blisters and panniculitis-like lesions. The extremities, particularly the legs, are predominantly affected.

Pathogenesis and histological features

The pathogenesis of this condition is unknown.

Histologically, the eruption is characterized by a superficial and deep lymphohistiocytic infiltrate accompanied by conspicuous eosinophils.

The epidermis is hyperkeratotic and there is mild acanthosis frequently accompanied by spongiosis. Other manifestations include eosinophilic spongiosis, bullous pemphigoid-like subepidermal blistering and eosinophilic panniculitis.

Direct immunofluorescence may disclose perivascular deposits of C3 and IgM. Indirect immunofluorescence studies are negative.

The lymphocytes are of the CD3+ T-cell phenotype with a predominance of CD4+ T-helper cells over CD8+ T-suppressor cells. B-cells are absent.

References

1. Rueda, R.A., Valencia, I.C., Covelli, C. et al (1999) Eosinophilic, polymorphic, and pruritic eruption associated with radiotherapy. *Arch Dermatol*, **135**, 804–810.
2. Gallego, H., Wilke, M.S., Lewis, E.J. (2001) Delayed EPPER syndrome. *Arch Dermatol*, **137**, 821–822.

Viral exanthemata

A variety of viral infections may present with cutaneous eruptions (*Table 7.1*). Although some viruses are associated with an eruption with distinctive clinical features, others are affiliated with a non-specific maculopapular dermatosis. Exceptionally, exanthemata may represent a primary cutaneous infection. More commonly, the clinical features are a manifestation of an immune response, such as an immune complex disease or a cell-mediated hypersensitivity reaction, to an infection at an extracutaneous site.

Biopsy of a viral exanthem often shows a superficial perivascular lymphocytic infiltrate. Some cases may show epidermal pathology such as interface changes with dyskeratotic cells. The histological features are entirely non-specific and distinction from hypersensitivity reactions (e.g. a drug eruption) is impossible without clinical (often including serological investigation) correlation. Viruses that infect cutaneous sites may be visualized by light microscopy including immunohistochemistry,

or demonstrated by viral culture, immunological testing, PCR or DNA hybridization. Skin manifestations of viral infections are described in detail in Chapter 17.

Table 7.1

Viruses associated with cutaneous eruptions

- Cytomegalovirus
- Enterovirus (coxsakievirus, echovirus)
- Epstein–Barr virus
- Hepatitis B virus
- Human immunodeficiency virus
- Paramyxovirus
- Parvovirus
- Roseola (human herpesvirus-6)
- Rubella
- Rubeola (measles)
- Toga virus

Granulomatous, necrobiotic and perforating dermatoses

8

Sarcoidosis 287

Granuloma annulare 297

Necrobiosis lipoidica 305

Rheumatoid nodule 310

Elastolytic granulomata 312
Actinic granuloma (O'Brien) 313
Atypical facial necrobiosis lipoidica 314
Granuloma multiforme 316

Rheumatic fever nodule 317

Necrobiotic xanthogranuloma 318

Palisaded neutrophilic and granulomatous dermatitis 320

'Metastatic' Crohn's disease 321
Granulomatous cheilitis 322

Acne agminata 322

Perioral dermatitis 323

Infective granulomata 324

Foreign body granulomata 324

Granulomata in congenital immunodeficiency syndromes 326

Aluminum granuloma 327

Perforating disorders 328
Reactive perforating collagenosis 328
Perforating folliculitis 331
Elastosis perforans serpiginosa 333
Hyperkeratosis follicularis et parafollicularis in cutem penetrans 335
Perforating pseudoxanthoma elasticum 337

Chondrodermatitis nodularis chronica helicis 338

Sarcoidosis

Clinical features

Sarcoidosis (Gr. *sarkos*, flesh; *eidos*, form), so-named because its histological features were originally thought to resemble a sarcoma (Boeck), is a common systemic disease of unknown etiology. It is characterized and defined by the presence of non-caseating granulomata, usually (but not invariably) affecting multiple organ systems.[1-10] Manifestations are variable. Patients may present with:

* an acute and usually self-limiting variant
* a chronic form exclusively affecting the skin (up to between 20 and 40% of patients with cutaneous sarcoidosis do not have systemic involvement)
* a serious systemic chronic variant with widespread lesions, which affects multiple systems, is associated with high morbidity, and may occasionally be fatal.

Sarcoidosis is more commonly encountered in industrialized countries and shows particularly high incidences in northern Europe (including the UK), the USA and New Zealand, where as many as 20/100,000 of the population may be affected. It presents particularly in people in their third and fourth decades and shows a female predominance.[11] In the USA, sarcoidosis is common among blacks and there is a similar tendency in the UK (*Figs 8.1, 8.2*). An epidemiological study of sarcoidosis in the Detroit, Michigan area found that blacks had a 3.8 times greater risk of developing the disease compared with Caucasians.[12] First- and second-degree relatives of patients with sarcoidosis seem to have a significant risk of developing the disease compared to the normal population.[13] The disease is rare in children and although the

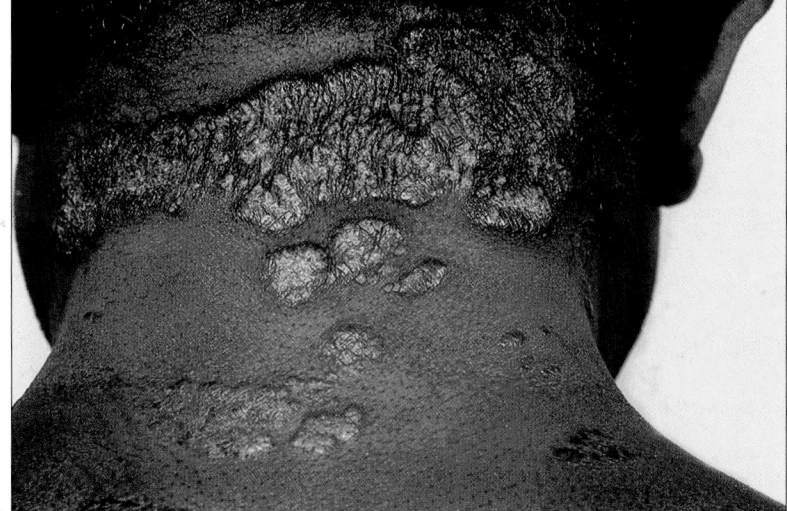

Fig. 8.1
Sarcoidosis: nodules and plaques with a keloidal quality. By courtesy of the Institute of Dermatology, London, UK.

manifestations are usually similar to those seen in adults, infants may present with symptoms simulating juvenile rheumatoid arthritis (*Figs 8.3–8.5*).[14–16] Infantile sarcoidosis should not be confused with Blau's syndrome. This disease is inherited in an autosomal dominant fashion and is characterized by sarcoidal granulomata in the skin, uveal tract and joints but with no pulmonary involvement.[17,18] Despite the similarities between both diseases, no genetic linkage has been identified.

Rarely, sarcoidosis presents in monozygotic twins.[19] Coexistence with common variable immune deficiency is also a rare occurrence.[20]

Cutaneous lesions occur in 20–35% of patients with systemic sarcoidosis and may be classified into non-specific (erythema nodosum) and specific (granulomatous) subtypes.[10] Cutaneous sarcoidal granulomata appear to be associated with a poorer prognosis and an increased incidence of pulmonary fibrosis and uveitis. Erythema nodosum occurs quite commonly in sarcoidosis, reported incidences varying from 11 to 31%.[21] There is a significant female predominance (3:1). Interestingly, erythema nodosum appears to be relatively uncommon in both blacks and Caucasians in the USA. It presents as erythematous, tender, subcutaneous nodules, usually on the anterior tibial regions (see also p. 343). Erythema nodosum may be associated with pyrexia, polyarthralgia (wrists, knees and ankles), a very high erythrocyte sedimentation rate (ESR) and bilateral hilar lymphadenopathy (Lofgren's syndrome) (*Fig. 8.6*). This acute form of sarcoidosis is associated with a good prognosis, with most patients experiencing resolution within 6 months of onset of symptoms.[22–24] In one study, however, 16% of patients who presented with erythema nodosum developed chronic disease.[22]

A not uncommon mode of presentation is the development of a widespread, usually asymptomatic, maculopapular eruption. Individual

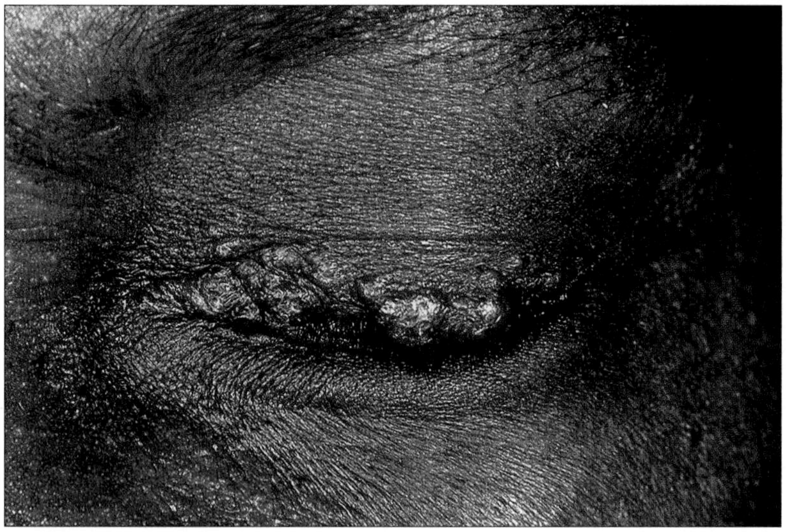

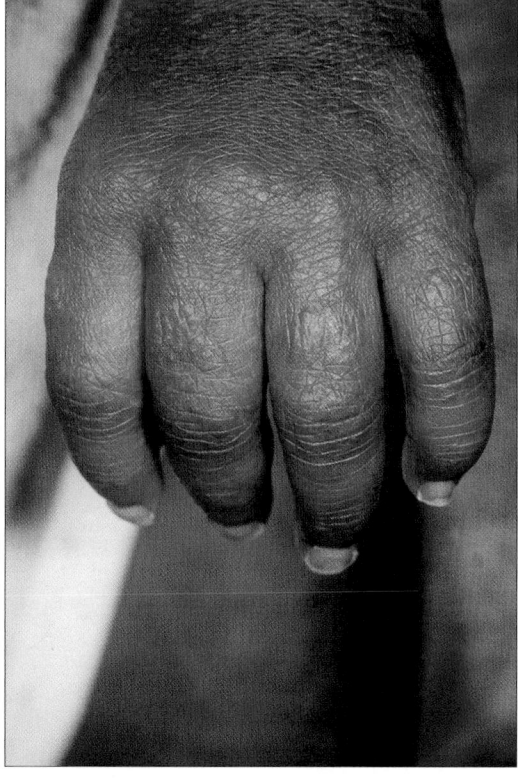

Fig. 8.2
Sarcoidosis: nodular sarcoid producing beaded lesions on the upper eyelids. Sarcoidosis is common in the black population. By courtesy of R.A. Marsden, MD, St George's Hospital, London, UK.

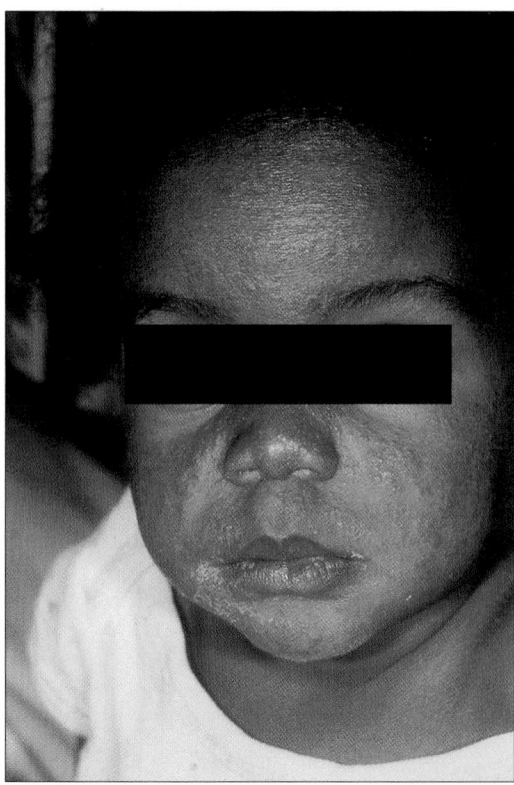

Fig. 8.3
Sarcoidosis: the condition is rare in children. There are widespread micropapules on this child's face. By courtesy of C.T.C. Kennedy, MD, Bristol Royal Infirmary, Bristol, UK.

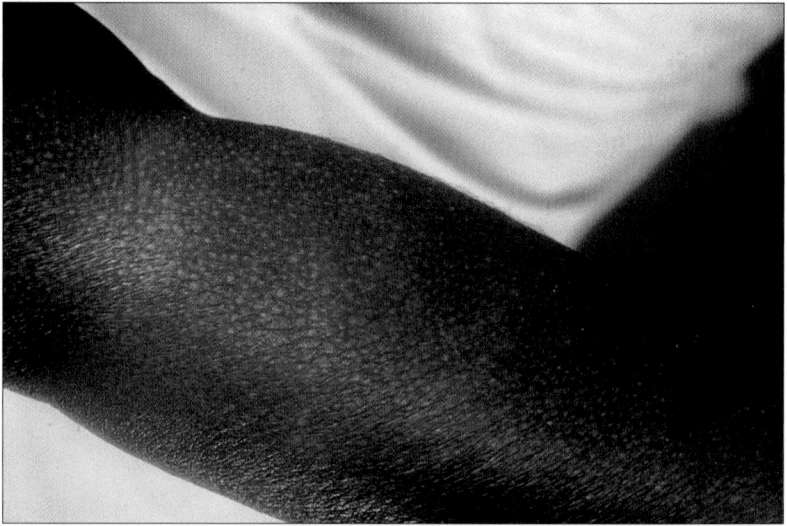

Fig. 8.4
Sarcoidosis: micropapules on the knuckles. By courtesy of C.T.C. Kennedy, MD, Bristol Royal Infirmary, Bristol, UK.

Fig. 8.5
Sarcoidosis: the forearm was also affected. There are hundreds of tiny lesions. By courtesy of C.T.C. Kennedy, MD, Bristol Royal Infirmary, Bristol, UK.

lesions are erythematous or violaceous, 3–6 mm in diameter, and most commonly seen on the face (particularly in a periorbital distribution), the trunk, the extensor aspects of the extremities and the neck (*Figs 8.7, 8.8*). In this variant the patient may also develop acute lymphadenopathy and uveitis, and a chest X-ray examination can reveal features of early respiratory involvement. Spontaneous resolution sometimes occurs. Occasionally, micropapular lesions are seen, particularly on the face and limbs (*Fig. 8.9*). Rarely patients develop sheets of pinhead-sized lichenoid papules on the trunk and limbs. The onset is abrupt and lesions may appear in crops. Some patients develop nodules and plaques, which may occur anywhere on the body, but most often affect the face, extremities, buttocks and shoulders (*Figs 8.10–8.14*). Annular or serpiginous lesions are also encountered and sometimes there is a prominent telangiectatic component (angiolupoid sarcoid) (*Figs 8.15, 8.16*).[10] Rarely, epidermal changes result in a psoriasiform appearance. Chronic skin lesions are associated with pulmonary fibrosis, ocular and bone lesions.

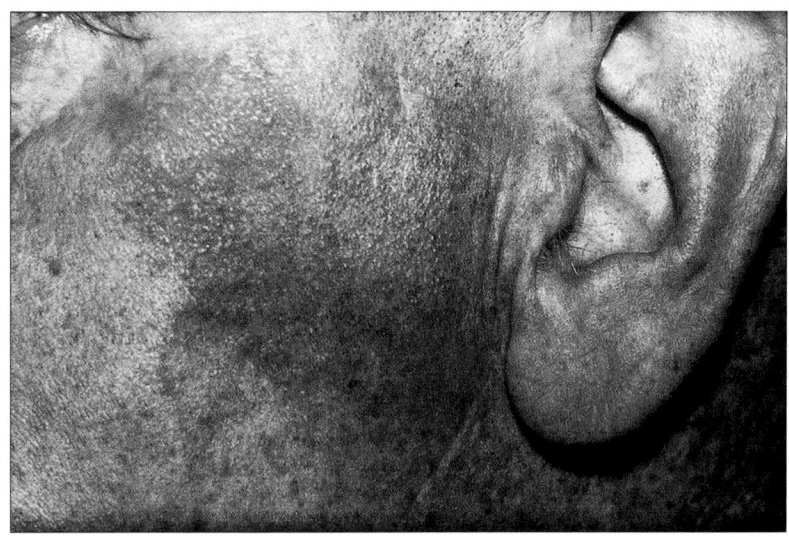

Fig. 8.8
Sarcoidosis: characteristic mauve plaque on the malar area with an infiltrative appearance. By courtesy of R.A. Marsden, MD, St George's Hospital, London, UK.

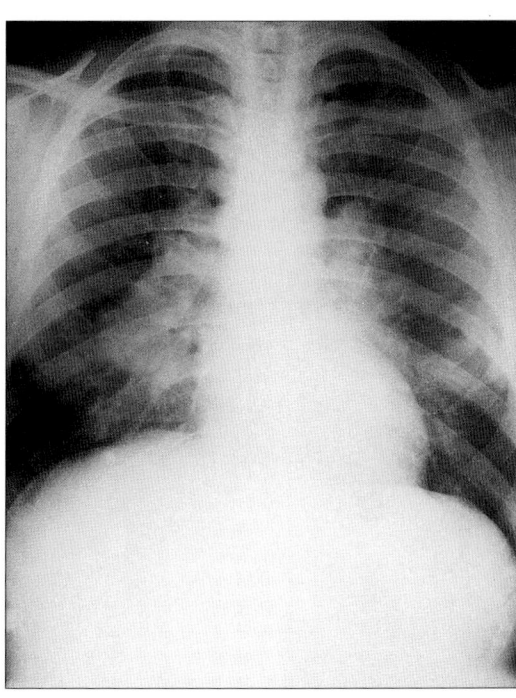

Fig. 8.6
Sarcoidosis: typical bilateral hilar lymphadenopathy. By courtesy of I. Kerr, MD, Brompton Hospital, London, UK.

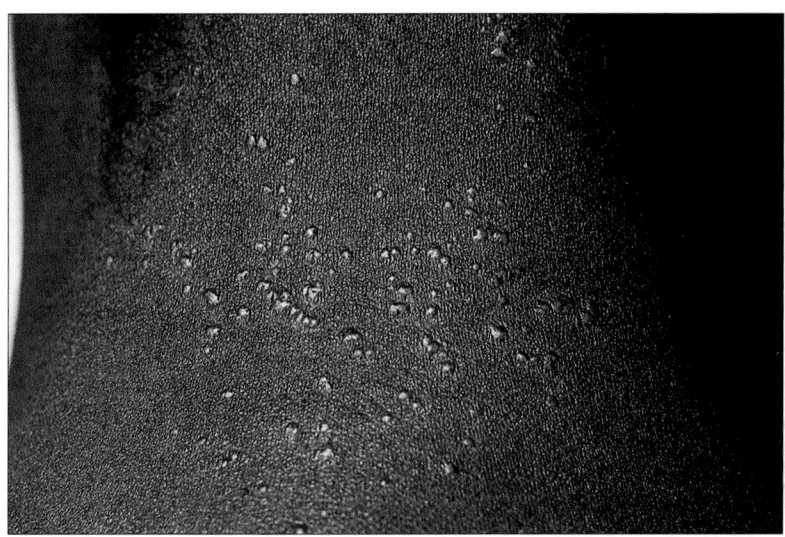

Fig. 8.9
Sarcoidosis: micropapular variant. Note the tiny lichenoid papules. By courtesy of the Institute of Dermatology, London, UK.

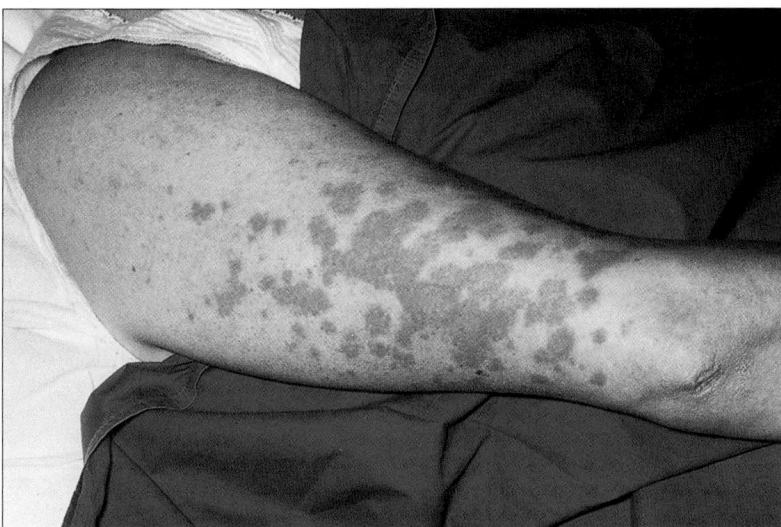

Fig. 8.7
Sarcoidosis: widespread erythematous plaques on the upper arm, some with an annular appearance. By courtesy of R.A. Marsden, MD, St George's Hospital, London, UK.

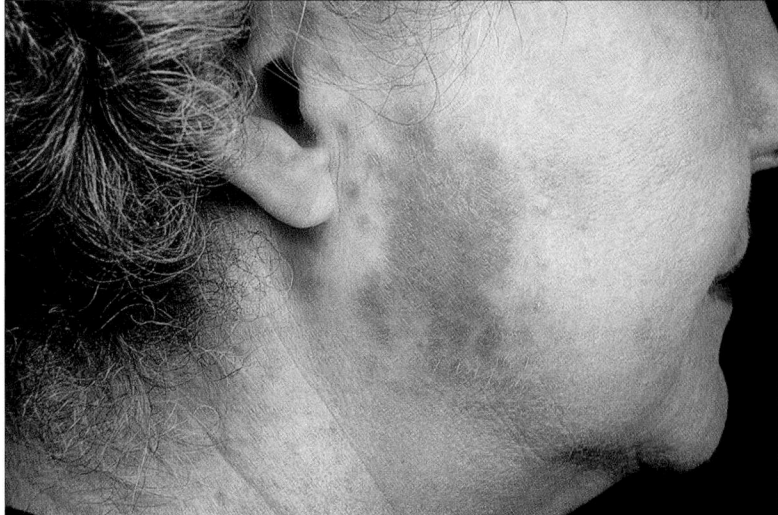

Fig. 8.10
Sarcoidosis: erythematous plaque on the face, a commonly affected site. By courtesy of the Institute of Dermatology, London, UK.

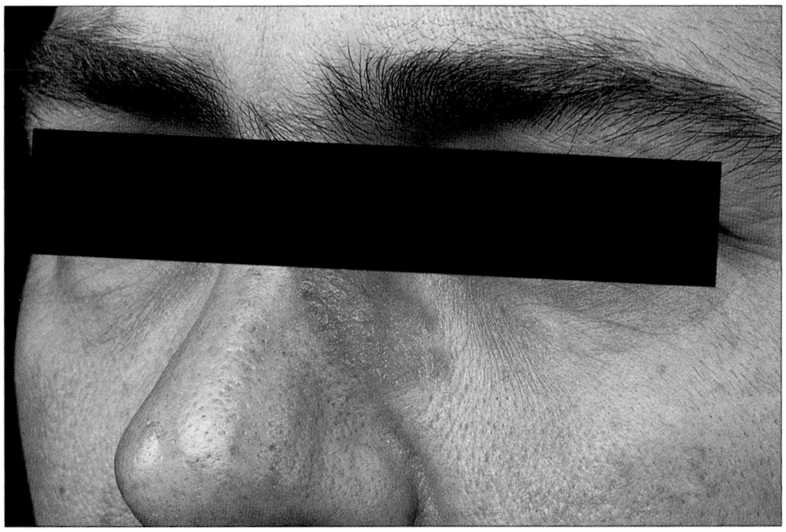

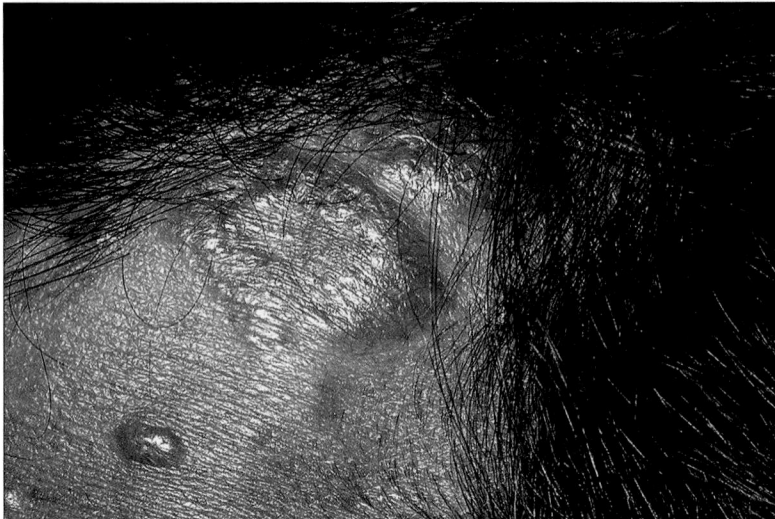

Fig. 8.11
Sarcoidosis: erythematous plaque on the nose. By courtesy of the Institute of Dermatology, London, UK.

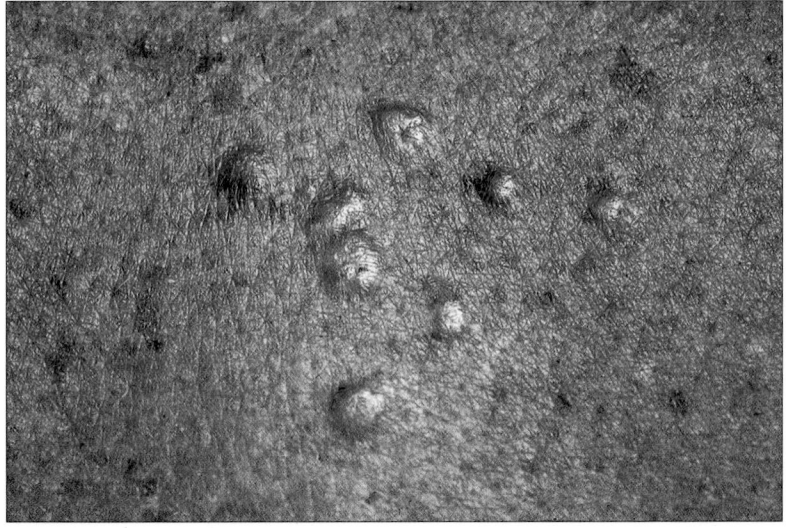

Fig. 8.12
Sarcoidosis: a fixed, erythematous lesion is present on the right side of this woman's forehead. By courtesy of R.A. Marsden, MD, St George's Hospital, London, UK.

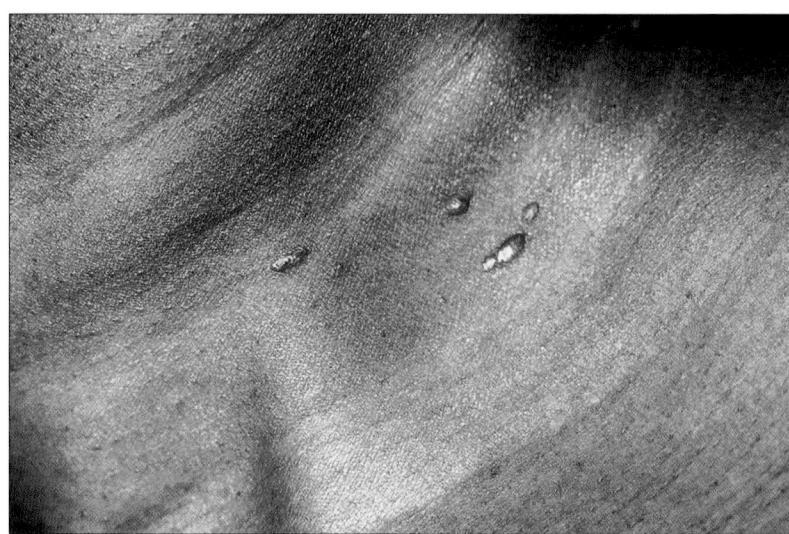

Fig. 8.14
Sarcoidosis: small nodules on the anterior aspect of the neck. By courtesy of R.A. Marsden, MD, St George's Hospital, London, UK.

Most characteristic of sarcoidosis, however, is lupus pernio. This chronic violaceous plaque most often affects the nose, cheek and ears, but lesions also sometimes affect the fingers and knees (*Fig. 8.17*). It is a particularly disfiguring variant and resolution is especially complicated by marked scarring. Lupus pernio is often associated with lesions in the upper respiratory tract and can be followed by nasal obstruction and septal perforation. Patients also have severe pulmonary fibrosis, bone cysts and ocular lesions. This variant has an insidious onset and is associated with a prolonged course and poor prognosis.[14]

Patients with sarcoidosis not uncommonly develop lesions in scar tissue[25] and also in sites of trauma including tattoos, venipuncture and surgery (*Figs 8.18, 8.19*).[26–28] Sarcoidal granulomata in association with foreign bodies do not necessarily imply a diagnosis of sarcoidosis. However, a small number of patients with sarcoidal granulomata in association with silica and tattoo pigment may have systemic sarcoidosis

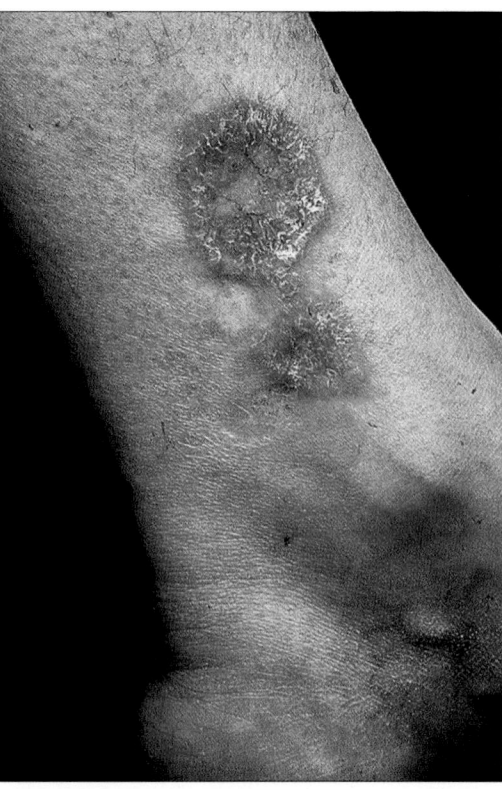

Fig. 8.15
Sarcoidosis: annular lesions on the ankle. By courtesy of the Institute of Dermatology, London, UK.

Fig. 8.13
Sarcoidosis: these grouped nodules are present on sun-damaged skin of the upper chest. By courtesy of the Institute of Dermatology, London, UK.

or the latter may develop subsequently. Awareness of this problem is important, as such cutaneous granulomata may be the first manifestation of the disease. Sarcoidosis has also been documented presenting in a tattoo in association with interferon-alpha (IFN-α) treatment for chronic hepatitis C.[29] Interestingly, sarcoidosis has also been reported in two instances in patients receiving interferon and ribavirin for chronic hepatitis C.[30]

Hypopigmented lesions may be seen in black patients.[31] Unusual cutaneous manifestations include subcutaneous nodules, ichthyosiform lesions, erythroderma, scarring and non-scarring alopecia, lymphedema, nail dystrophy in the absence of underlying bone changes, verrucous lesions, generalized atrophy, leonine facies, palmar erythema and leg ulcers.[32–44] Subcutaneous nodules are rare and present as persistent, freely mobile, often painful lesions measuring 5–15 mm in diameter (see also p. 369). Oral and genital involvement is rare but disease restricted

to the vulva has been documented.[45–47] Sarcoidosis has also been described presenting as a testicular mass.[48]

Ninety per cent of patients with sarcoidosis have pulmonary involvement.[24] Bilateral hilar lymphadenopathy is the commonest intrathoracic manifestation of sarcoidosis and together with pulmonary involvement forms the most frequent lesion. Intrathoracic manifestations in sarcoidosis are classified into five subgroups:[6,10]

- Stage 0, normal chest X-ray
- Stage I, bilateral hilar and/or paratracheal lymphadenopathy with no pulmonary involvement
- Stage II, lymphadenopathy with pulmonary infiltrates
- Stage III, pulmonary infiltrates, but no lymphadenopathy
- Stage IV, irreversible fibrosis and bullae, cysts, emphysema.

Stage I disease is frequently associated with spontaneous resolution; progression to stage II disease is uncommon. Severe pulmonary involve-

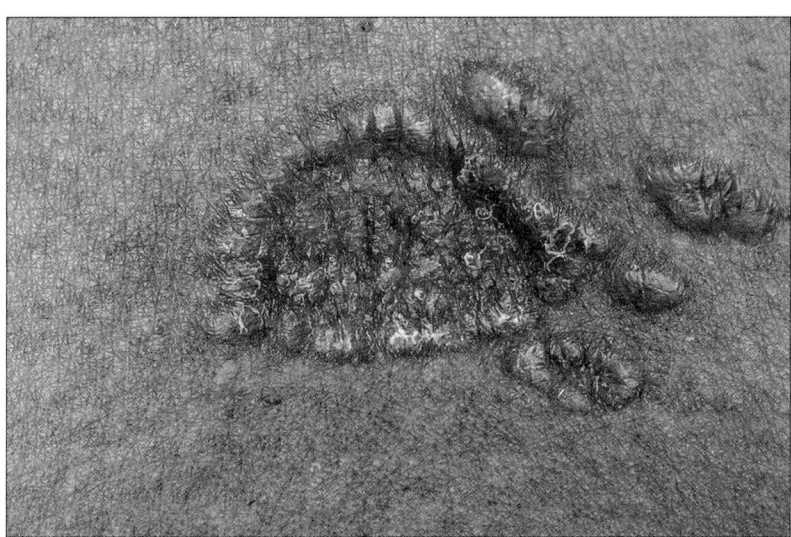

Fig. 8.16
Sarcoidosis: close-up view of an annular lesion. Note the beaded appearance. By courtesy of the Institute of Dermatology, London, UK.

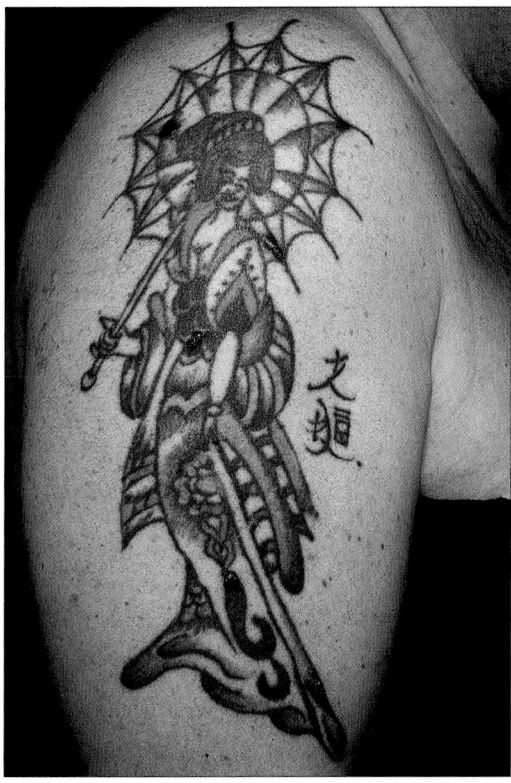

Fig. 8.18
Sarcoidosis: tattoo reaction. There are multiple dome-shaped nodules. By courtesy of the Institute of Dermatology, London, UK.

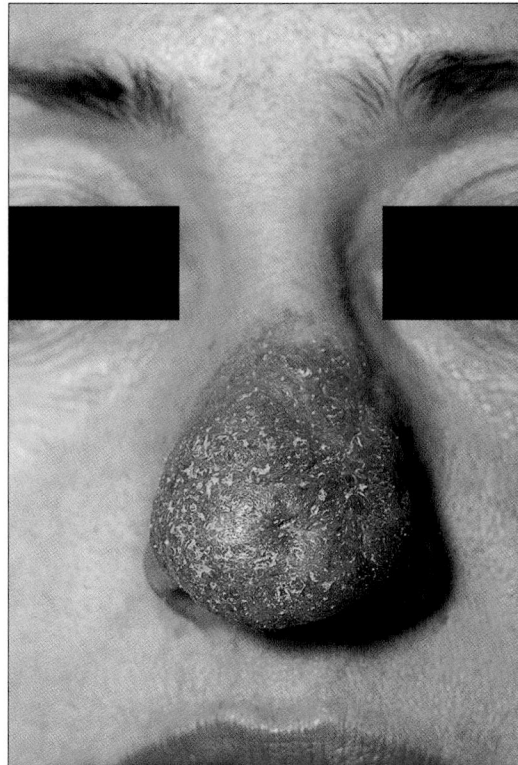

Fig. 8.17
Sarcoidosis: lupus pernio. The nose shows typical scaly violaceous swelling. By courtesy of the Institute of Dermatology, London, UK.

Fig. 8.19
Sarcoidosis: tattoo reaction, close-up view. By courtesy of the Institute of Dermatology, London, UK.

ment as seen in stage III patients correlates with deep chronic plaque lesions and lupus pernio. Patients have interstitial fibrosis and eventual cor pulmonale, which may prove fatal (*Fig. 8.20*).

Systemic vasculitis involving small to large caliber vessels has been found to be present in some adults and children with sarcoidosis.[49] This manifestation tends to be more common in African–American and Asian patients.[49]

Ocular lesions develop in about 20% of patients with sarcoidosis. Acute anterior uveitis is the most common manifestation; it is frequently bilateral and shows a predilection for females. It correlates with a benign outcome and erythema nodosum. Chronic uveitis also affects the anterior chamber and if untreated may progress to glaucoma and blindness. Other lesions include retinal vein perivasculitis, disc edema and neovascularization. Conjunctival granulomata may be present in up to 30% of patients and, therefore, biopsy can be a useful and relatively safe method of establishing the diagnosis. The lacrimal gland is also sometimes affected.

Neurological involvement occurs in 5–15% of patients with systemic sarcoidosis. Clinical manifestations include facial nerve palsy, Guillain–Barré syndrome, optic nerve disease, meningitis, seizure, and encephalopathy.[6,50,51] In one study, neurosarcoidosis was the presenting symptom in 31% of patients.[51] The combination of uveitis, facial nerve palsy, fever and swelling of the parotid gland is known as uveoparotid fever (Heerfordt's syndrome). This condition is often associated with central nervous system involvement. Hypothalamic and pituitary lesions are rare and may manifest as diabetes insipidus or panhypopituitarism.

Peripheral lymphadenopathy develops in about 30% of patients. However, histological examination of peripheral lymph nodes will reveal granulomata in about 75% of patients with sarcoidosis. Although splenomegaly is only present in 10–25% of patients, granulomata are present in about 50% of cases. Splenic disease is usually asymptomatic, but patients may have abdominal pain, hypersplenism and, very rarely, splenic rupture. Splenic disease correlates positively with a high frequency of intrathoracic sarcoidosis. Liver function test abnormalities are quite common and about 20% of patients have hepatomegaly; 60% of patients have hepatic granulomata on histological examination.

Cardiac lesions are uncommon, but are of particular importance due to the associated mortality.[6] In a recent autopsy series, 50% of all deaths were due to cardiac disease.[52] This same study found that the clinician often does not appreciate the presence of cardiac involvement – the antemortem diagnosis of cardiac lesions was made in only 29% of

patients.[52] Granulomata may occur at any site, but appear to show a predilection for the conduction system. Clinical manifestations include ventricular tachycardia, complete heart block, congestive cardiac failure, pericardial effusion and myocardial infarction. Sarcoidal granulomata may affect small and large blood vessels, in particular the pulmonary vasculature.

Muscle involvement is usually asymptomatic. Histological examination of random muscle biopsies reveals granulomata in as many as 50% of patients. Rare features include asymptomatic palpable nodules and a polymyositis-like syndrome.

Radiologically demonstrable bone lesions occur in about 15% of patients. Early lesions consist of osteoporosis, cortical thinning and mottled rarefaction. Established lesions are cystic and are sometimes associated with pathological fractures. The hands and feet are predominantly affected (*Figs 8.21, 8.22*). Destruction of the nasal bones can result from direct infiltration in patients with lupus pernio.

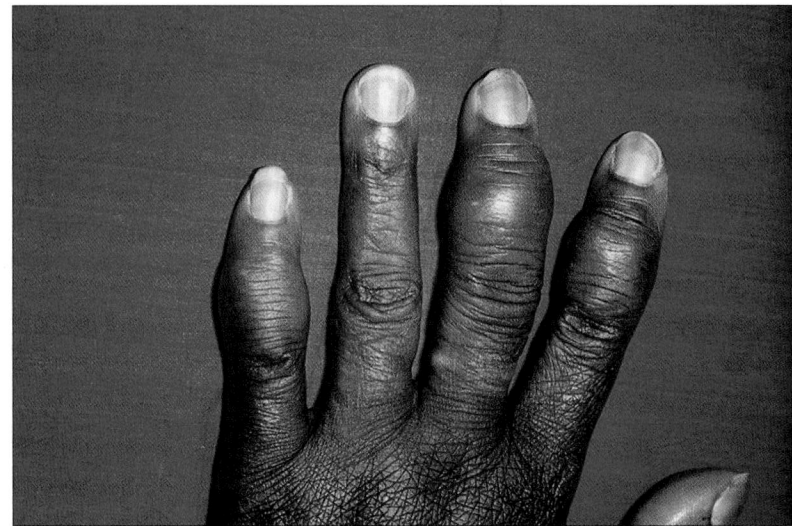

Fig. 8.21
Sarcoidosis: there is marked swelling of the distal interphalangeal joints. By courtesy of R.A. Marsden, MD, St George's Hospital, London, UK.

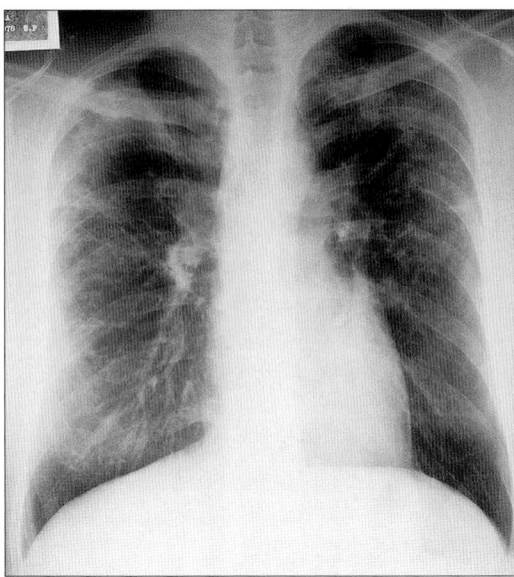

Fig. 8.20
Sarcoidosis: there is extensive fibrotic scarring in both lungs. By courtesy of I. Kerr, MD, Brompton Hospital, London, UK.

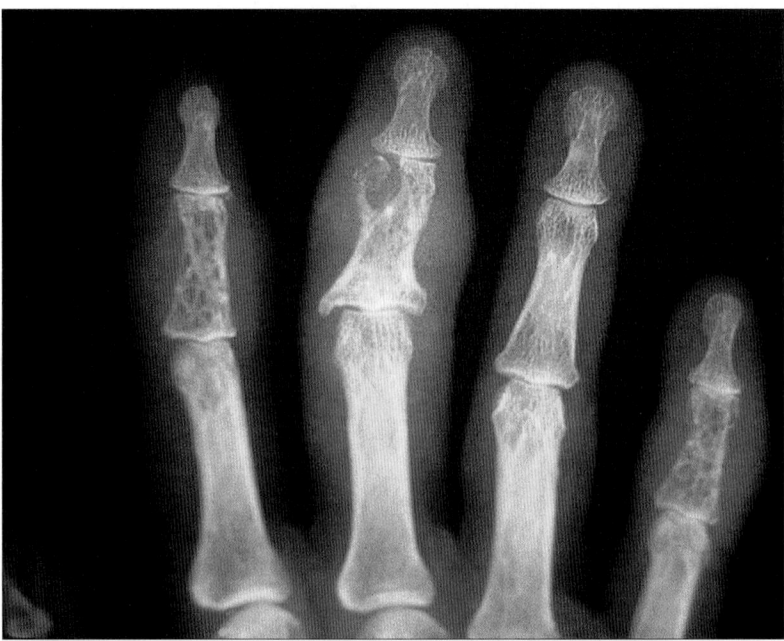

Fig. 8.22
Sarcoidosis: note the erosive changes with cyst formation. By courtesy of R.A. Marsden, MD, St George's Hospital, London, UK.

Hypercalcemia and, particularly, hypercalcuria are important complications of sarcoidosis. This is possibly due to increased intestinal absorption of calcium and abnormal production of 1,25-dihydroxyvitamin D.[53] It is more often transitory, but in a small proportion of patients it is persistent and sometimes complicated by the development of renal failure due to nephrocalcinosis. Granulomata are found on histological examination of the kidney in as many as 40% of patients.

Laboratory investigations reveal a wide variety of abnormalities of the immune system (see below). Patients may demonstrate elevated levels of serum angiotensin-converting enzyme (ACE). Unfortunately, this finding is not specific for sarcoidosis, increased values also being found in patients with diabetes mellitus, alcoholic liver disease and leprosy. It is sometimes of value in monitoring the level of disease activity in patients known to have sarcoidosis. Patients may also display increased levels of serum and urinary lysozyme, serum beta-2-microglobulin and collagenase.

The Kveim test is sometimes (but not widely) used to aid in diagnosis. A homogenate of known sarcoid tissue is injected intradermally at a marked (India ink) site, and 4–6 weeks later the injection site is biopsied. A positive result depends upon the detection of an epithelioid cell granuloma. False positive reactions may occur with other diseases including Crohn's disease, infection (mycobacterial, fungal), berylliosis, silicosis, asbetosis and lymphoma. The stimulatory 'sarcoidal' antigen of the Kveim reagent has not been identified.[54] The Kveim test is rarely used nowadays because of difficulties in obtaining the homogenate of sarcoid tissue.

Although sarcoidosis is associated with a high morbidity, the mortality rate is low, being of the order of 3–6%. Causes of death include cardiac involvement and respiratory or renal failure. The prognosis is better in females and appears to be improved in those with a positive purified protein derivative (PPD) skin test and normal serum immunoglobulin levels. The severity of disease is greater in blacks and Asians compared with Caucasians.[55] Of interest, despite the very marked upset in immunological phenomena, patients do not seem to have an associated greatly increased risk of opportunistic infections except as a consequence of therapy (e.g. corticosteroids).

The association between sarcoidosis and a number of systemic diseases is probably coincidental. Sarcoidosis has been documented in association with vitiligo, pernicious anemia, autoimmune thyroiditis, Graves' disease, chronic hepatitis, Addison's disease, Sjögren's syndrome, diabetes mellitus and ulcerative colitis, lymphoma and human immunodeficiency virus (HIV) infection.[56–66] Interestingly, patients with acquired immunodeficiency syndrome (AIDS) usually develop manifestations of sarcoidosis after antiretroviral therapy is started. This phenomenon has been described as the immune restoration syndrome.[65] Associations with cutaneous autoimmune disease include dermatitis herpetiformis and linear IgA disease.[67,68]

Pathogenesis and histological features

The pathogenesis of sarcoidosis is poorly understood. The demonstration of familial clustering suggests hereditary susceptibility to sarcoidosis in at least a subset of patients.[13,69]

Despite intensive studies, the etiology and pathogenesis of sarcoidosis remains elusive.[70,71] It is likely, however, that sarcoidosis represents a reaction pattern that may develop in a predisposed patient on exposure to one or more infective agents or other antigens.

The role of mycobacteria in the pathogenesis of sarcoidosis is a controversial topic. Attempts at detection of mycobacterial DNA by polymerase chain reaction (PCR) has produced conflicting results. While some authors have failed to detect mycobacterial DNA, others have identified DNA of various strains of tuberculous and non-tuberculous mycobacteria.[72–76] In one study, although amplified mycobacterial DNA

was detected by PCR in 38% of sarcoidosis patients, mycobacterial DNA was also detected in tissue in 44% of control patients.[77] Furthermore, most studies published in the literature fail to report more than 6% positivity for *Mycobacterium tuberculosis* DNA in patients with sarcoidosis.[78] In another interesting study, cell wall deficient acid-fast bacteria (L forms) were cultured from the blood of 19 of 20 patients with sarcoidosis but not from controls.[79] In summary, these mixed results between laboratories have not clarified the role of mycobacteria in the pathogenesis of sarcoidosis. It seems, however, that mycobacteria may be of etiological importance in at least a subset of cases.

Propionibacterium acnes DNA has also been identified in tissues of patients with sarcoidosis including involved lymph nodes.[80,81] The significance of this finding remains uncertain. Human herpesvirus 8 DNA has not been demonstrated in tissues of patients with sarcoidosis.[81]

The occasional association with known autoimmune diseases, such as progressive systemic sclerosis and systemic lupus erythematosus (SLE), has inevitably led to the proposal of an autoimmune pathogenesis. Although many familial cases have been reported in the literature, no consistent pattern of inheritance has emerged. The results of human leukocyte antigen (HLA) typing have shown associations with particular features of the disease; for example, HLA-A1 and HLA-B8 are associated with arthritis, HLA-A1 is also associated with uveitis, and HLA-B13 may be associated with a chronic refractory variant.[10] Patients with HLA-DR17 have a better prognosis.[82] One study has shown that patients with sarcoidosis have an increased frequency of a glutamine residue at position 69 of the B1 chain of the HLA-DPB molecule compared with a control population.[83] This is particularly interesting since a similar polymorphism has been documented in patients with chronic beryllium disease, a disorder also characterized by granulomata and which shares some pathological features in common with sarcoidosis.

The results of immunological investigations in patients with sarcoidosis have produced an immense wealth of data, which reveal that there is clearly an associated state of abnormal immunological hyperactivity. There are alterations of both cell-mediated and humoral immunity. Despite great efforts to clarify the immunobiology of sarcoidosis, particularly with regard to the precise antigens that may facilitate the disease, we still do not have a clear understanding of the disease process. Sarcoidosis, at least in part, appears to be due to a hyperactive T-helper cell proliferation with lymphokine production.[84] Increased T-helper (Th1, Th2) cells are present in the alveolar lung parenchyma. Several studies have demonstrated selective activation of certain oligoclonal T-cell subsets.[85–88] In one study, there was a correlation between the presence of certain oligoclonal T-cell subsets and disease activity.[86] Th1 lymphocytes (T-cells expressing interleukin (IL)-2 and IFN-α) preferentially accumulate in pulmonary parenchyma and the alveolar space compared with Th2 lymphocytes (T-cells expressing IL-4 and IL-5).[89] Compared with T-cells in peripheral blood, T-cells obtained by bronchoalveolar lavage show greater expression of IFN-γ and tumor necrosis factor alpha (TNF-α).[82] Of interest, patients with HLA-DR17 show a muted cytokine response, a finding that is perhaps related to the better prognosis observed in this subset of patients.[82]

T-lymphocytes, in turn, simulate B-cells. Abnormalities of humoral immunity include a non-specific polyclonal hypergammaglobulinemia and circulating immune complexes in acute forms of the disease, particularly in association with erythema nodosum.

The paramount puzzle in unraveling the pathogenesis of sarcoidosis is identifying the initial event(s) that lead to the disease. Despite our increasing knowledge of the immunobiology of sarcoidosis, we seem no closer to answering this key question.

Histologically, sarcoidosis is characterized by a dense, non-caseating granulomatous infiltrate in the dermis (*Fig. 8.23*), which sometimes extends into the subcutaneous fat. The granulomata are discrete and strikingly uniform in size and shape. They are composed of epithelioid histiocytes with abundant eosinophilic cytoplasm and oval or twisted vesicular nuclei often containing a small central nucleolus (*Figs 8.24, 8.25*). Variable numbers of Langhans' giant cells are present and sometimes a scattering of lymphocytes is seen at the peripheral margin of the granuloma. Discrete small central foci of fibrinoid necrosis are sometimes present but caseation necrosis is exceptional (*Fig. 8.26*).[90] Transepidermal elimination is sometimes seen.[91] The epidermis is usually normal although occasional cases display acanthosis and sometimes the granulomata are focally lichenoid.

In some cutaneous lesions, inclusion bodies are present, although much less frequently than in lymph nodes. The Schaumann body, a basophilic, laminated, rounded conchoidal structure composed of calcium carbonate, calcium oxalate, phosphate, iron and dolomite, is not specific for sarcoidosis and is seen in a number of other granulomatous conditions including tuberculosis and berylliosis (*Fig. 8.27*).[92–94] The asteroid body is a small intracytoplasmic eosinophilic star-shaped structure; it is not specific for sarcoidosis, being seen also, for example, in tuberculosis, tuberculoid leprosy, berylliosis and atypical facial necrobiosis (*Fig. 8.28*). It is also commonly found in necrobiotic xanthogranuloma.[95] Initial studies suggested that the asteroid body was composed of collagen but more recent reports, using immunohistochemistry, suggest that it is a product of the microtubular system.[96,97] The presence of foreign material in sarcoidal granulomata does not exclude the diagnosis of sarcoidosis. In fact polarizable material has been found in up to 5% of cases of sarcoidosis.[98,99]

The visceral lesions are characterized by an identical histology of non-caseating granulomata, which may be accompanied by significant

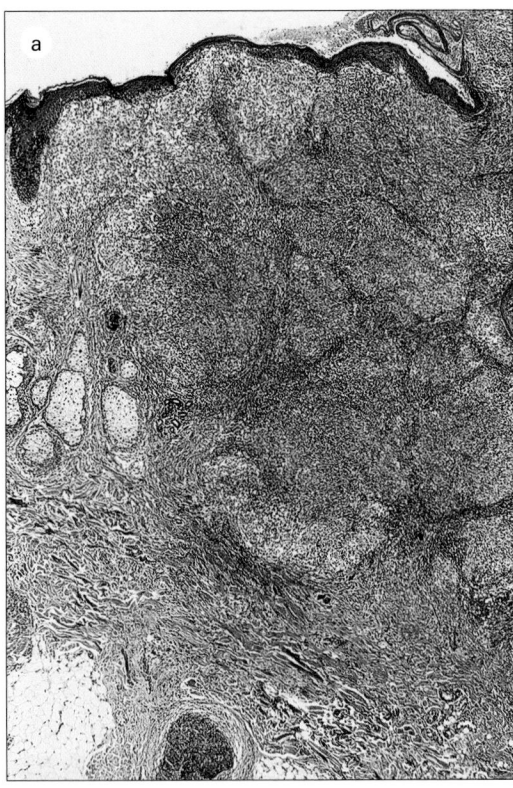
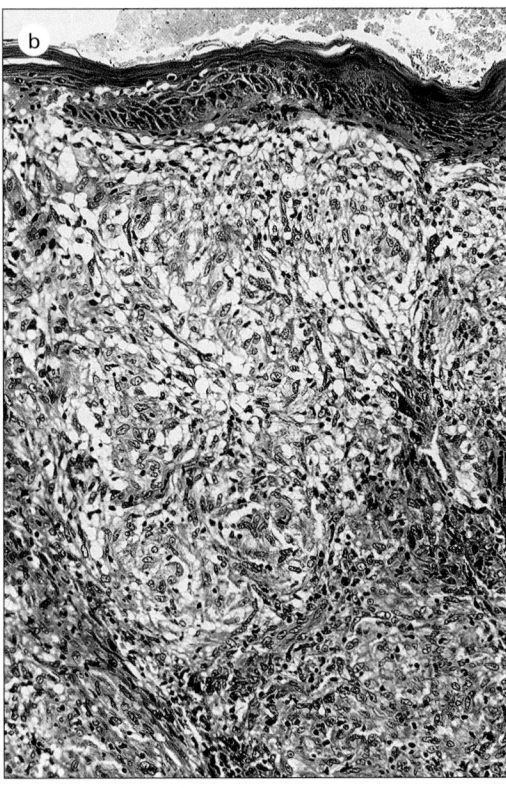

Fig. 8.23
(a, b) Sarcoidosis: the dermis is replaced by uniform circumscribed nests of non-caseating granulomata.

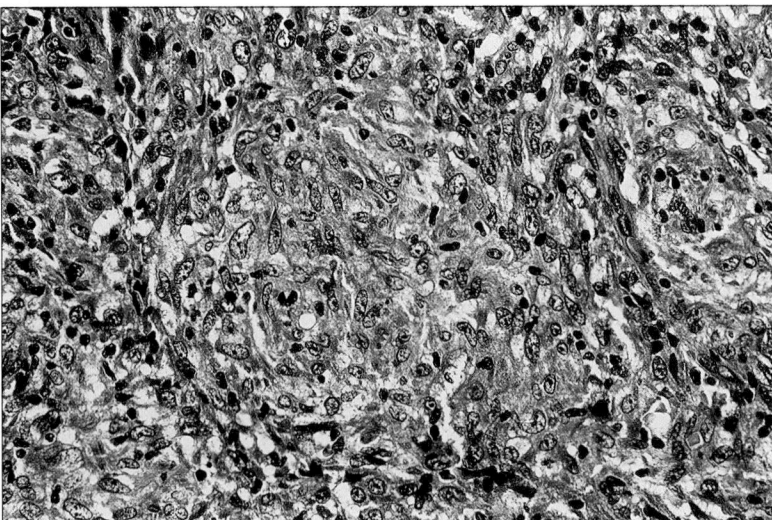

Fig. 8.24
Sarcoidosis: the epithelioid cells are composed of pink cytoplasm with a central oval or sometimes twisted vesicular nucleus containing a small basophilic nucleolus. The granuloma also contains lymphocytes and occasional fibroblasts.

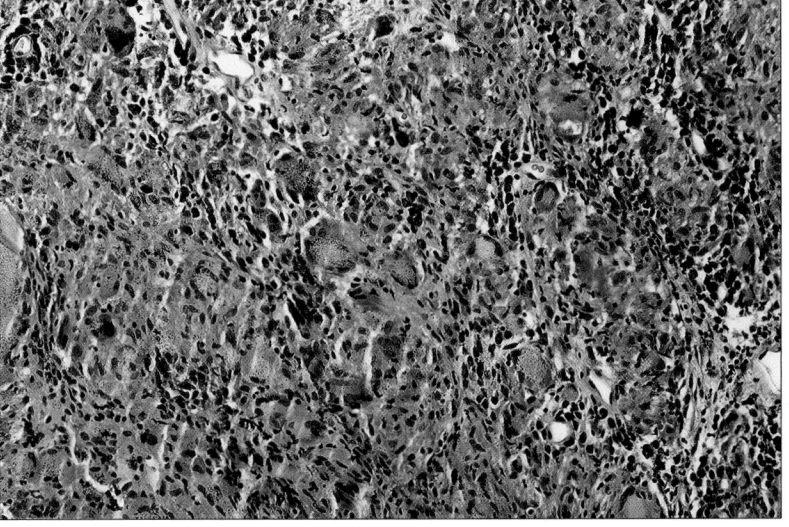

Fig. 8.25
Sarcoidosis: in this example the granulomatous reaction is associated with abundant foreign material.

scarring as, for example, in the lung, where advanced cases are characterized by interstitial fibrosis and sometimes honeycomb lung formation. In the liver, granulomata are most commonly found in the portal tracts or in relation to central veins. Splenic lesions are randomly distributed and are not usually associated with significant fibrosis.

Differential diagnosis

Sarcoidosis must be approached as a diagnosis of exclusion and distinguished from the numerous conditions that may be associated with a non-caseating granulomatous histology, including some forms of tuberculosis, tuberculoid leprosy, berylliosis, fungal infections, Crohn's disease and foreign body granulomatous reactions.[100] Therefore, the use of special stains, including the Ziehl–Neelsen preparation for mycobacteria and the periodic acid–Schiff (PAS) and methenamine silver reactions for fungi, is mandatory before accepting a diagnosis of sarcoidosis. Depending on the clinical context, culture may also be required to evaluate more definitively for an infective etiology. Tuberculoid leprosy is characterized by nerve involvement, a feature that is usually absent in sarcoidosis.

Labial and gingival involvement may be histologically mistaken for Crohn's disease and granulomatous cheilitis (Miescher). It is worth noting that rarely oral involvement in Crohn's disease may precede systemic manifestations by several years.

Granulomatous lesions that have been described in exogenous ochronosis appear to be related to sarcoidosis.[101] However, they have also been described as showing changes mimicking actinic granuloma.[102]

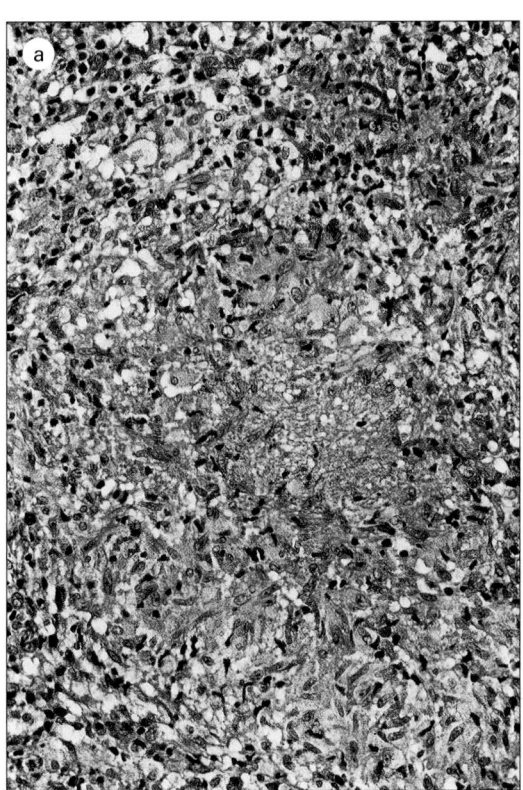
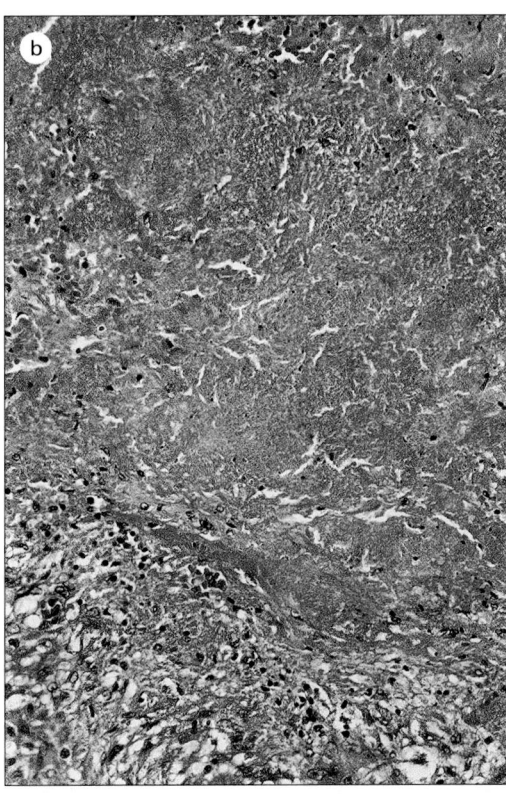

Fig. 8.26
Sarcoidosis: (a) occasionally small foci of 'fibrinoid' necrosis may be seen in the center of the granuloma, but cellular detail is not lost; (b) contrasting structureless caseating necrosis of tuberculosis.

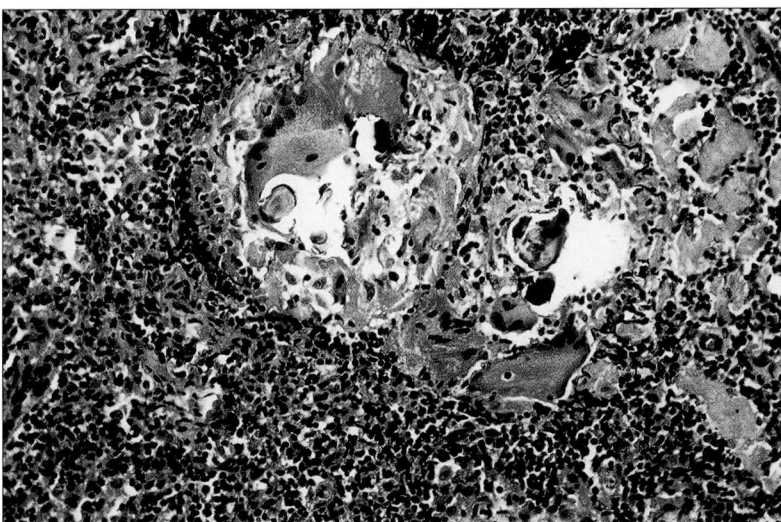

Fig. 8.27
Sarcoidosis: in this lymph node biopsy specimen, fragmented, laminated Schaumann bodies are seen. They are very rarely a feature of cutaneous sarcoidosis.

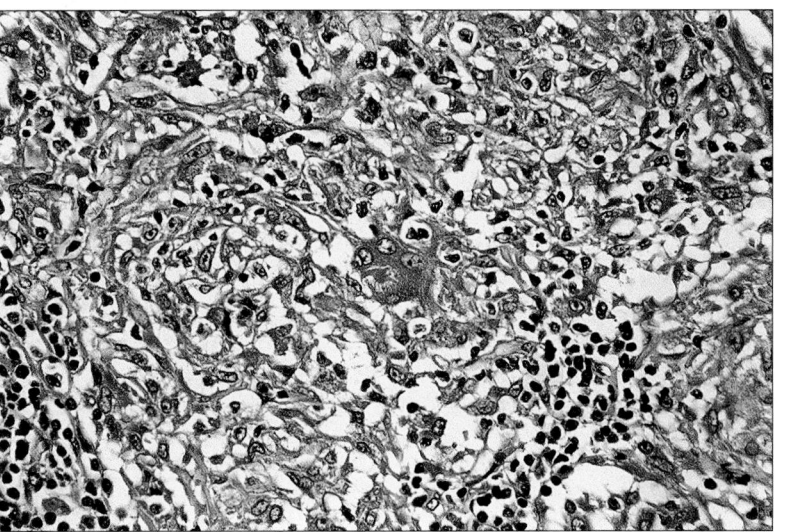

Fig. 8.28
Sarcoidosis: in the center of the field is a typical asteroid inclusion within the cytoplasm of a giant cell.

References

1. English, J.C., Patel, P.J., Greer, K.E. (2001) Sarcoidosis. *J Am Acad Dermatol*, **44**, 725–743.
2. McGrath, D.S., Goh, N., Foley, P.J. et al (2001) Sarcoidosis: genes and microbes – soil or seed? *Sarcoid Vasc Diffuse Lung Dis*, **18**, 149–164.
3. Hart, L.A., Conron, M., du Bois, R.M. (2001) Sarcoidosis. *Int Tuberc Lung Dis*, **5**, 791–806.
4. Geraint James, D. (2001) Sarcoidosis. *Postgrad Med*, **77**, 177–180.
5. Mandel, J., Weinberger, S.E. (2001) Clinical insights and basic science correlates in sarcoidosis. *Am J Med Sci*, **321**, 99–107.
6. Newman, L.S., Rose, C.S., Maier, L.S. (1997) Sarcoidosis. *N Engl J Med*, **336**, 1224–1234.
7. Tozman, E.C.S. (1991) Sarcoidosis: clinical manifestations, epidemiology, therapy and pathophysiology. *Curr Opin Rheumatol*, **3**, 155–159.
8. Hanno, R., Callen, J.P. (1980) Sarcoidosis: a disorder with prominent cutaneous features and their interrelationship with systemic disease. *Med Clin N Am*, **64**, 847–866.
9. Scadding, J.G. (1970) The definition of sarcoidosis etc. Proceedings of a conference held by the Sarcoidosis Unit, Central Middlesex Hospital, London. *Postgrad Med J*, **46**, 465–467.
10. Zax, R.H., Callen, J.P. (1989) Sarcoidosis. *Dermatol Clin*, **7**, 505–515.
11. Rybicki, B.A., Maliarik, M.J., Major, M. et al (1998) Epidemiology, demographics, and genetics of sarcoidosis. *Semin Respir Infect*, **13**, 166–173.
12. Rybicki, B.A., Major, M., Popovich, J. Jr et al (1997) Racial differences in sarcoidosis incidence: a 5-year study in a health maintenance organization. *Am J Epidemiol*, **145**, 234–241.
13. Rybicki, B.A., Ianuzzi, M.C., Frederick, M.M. et al (2001) Familial aggregation of sarcoidosis. A case-control etiologic study of sarcoidosis. *Am J Respir Crit Care Med*, **164**, 2085–2091.
14. Shetty, A.K., Gedalia, A. (2000) Sarcoidosis in children. *Curr Probl Pediatr*, **30**, 149–176.
15. Roy, M., Sharma, O.P., Chan, K. (1999) Sarcoidosis presenting in infancy: a rare occurrence. *Sarcoidosis Vasc Diffuse Lung Dis*, **16**, 224–227.
16. Yotsumoto, S., Takahashi, Y., Takei, S. et al (2000) Early onset sarcoidosis masquerading as juvenile rheumatoid arthritis. *J Am Acad Dermatol*, **43**, 969–971.
17. Scerri, L., Cook, L.J., Jenkins, E.A. et al (1996) Familial juvenile systemic granulomatosis (Blau's syndrome). *Clin Exp Dermatol*, **21**, 445–448.
18. Rybicki, B.A., Maliarik, M.J., Bock, C.H. et al (1999) The Blau syndrome gene is not a major risk for sarcoidosis. *Sarcoidosis Vasc Diffuse Lung Dis*, **16**, 203–208.
19. Swale, V.J., Spector, T.D., Bataille, V.A. (1998) Sarcoidosis in monozygotic twins. *Br J Dermatol*, **139**, 350–352.
20. Ameratunga, R., Becroft, D.M., Hunter, W. (2000) The simultaneous presentation of sarcoidosis and common variable immune deficiency. *Pathology*, **32**, 280–282.
21. Psychos, D.N., Voulgari, P.V., Skopouli, F.N. et al (2000) Erythema nodosum: the underlying conditions. *Clin Rheumatol*, **19**, 212–216.
22. Neville, E., Walker, A.N., James, D.G. (1983) Prognostic factors predicting the outcome of sarcoidosis: an analysis of 818 patients. *QJM*, **52**, 525–533.
23. Mana, J., Marcoval, J., Graells, J. et al (1997) Cutaneous involvement in sarcoidosis. Relationship to systemic disease. *Arch Dermatol*, **133**, 882–888.
24. Statement on sarcoidosis. Joint statement of the American Thoracic Society (ATS), the European Respiratory Society (ERS), and the World Association of Sarcoidosis and Other Granulomatous Disorders (WASOG) adopted by the ATS Board of Directors and by the ERS Executive Committee, February 1999 (1999). *Am J Respir Crit Care Med*, **160**, 736–755.
25. James, D.G. (1959) Dermatologic aspects of sarcoidosis. *QJM*, **28**, 109–124.
26. Burgdorf, W.H.C., Hoxtell, E.O., Bart, B.J. (1979) Sarcoid granulomata in venipuncture sites. *Cutis*, **24**, 52–53.
27. Lewis, F.M., Harington, C.I. (1993) Lupus pernio following facial trauma. *Clin Exp Dermatol*, **18**, 476–477.
28. Girao, L., Bajanca, R., Barata Feio, A. (2000) Systemic sarcoidosis revealed by the coexistence of scar and subcutaneous sarcoidosis. *J Eur Acad Dermatol Venereol*, **14**, 420–430.
29. Nawras, A., Alsolaiman, M.M., Mehboob, S. et al (2002) Systemic sarcoidosis presenting as a granulomatous tattoo reaction secondary to interferon-alpha treatment for chronic hepatitis C and review of the literature. *Dig Dis Sci*, **47**, 1627–1631.
30. Gitlin, N. (2002) Manifestation of sarcoidosis during interferon and ribavirin therapy for chronic hepatitis C: a report of two cases. *Eur J Gastroenterol Hepatol*, **14**, 883–885.
31. Zumla, A., James, G.D. (1989) Sarcoidosis and leprosy – an epidemiological, clinical, pathological and immunological comparison. *Sarcoidosis*, **6**, 88–96.
32. Higgins, E.M., Salisbury, J.R., du Vivier, A.W.P. (1993) Subcutaneous sarcoidosis. *Clin Exp Dermatol*, **18**, 65–66.
33. Shidrawi, R.G., Paradinas, F., Murray-Lyon, I.M. (1994) Sarcoidosis presenting as subcutaneous nodules. *Clin Exp Dermatol*, **19**, 356–358.
34. Feind-Koopmans, A.G., Lucker, G.P., van de Kerkhof, P.C. (1996) Acquired ichthyosiform erythroderma and sarcoidosis. *J Am Acad Dermatol*, **35**, 826–828.
35. Morrison, J.G. (1976) Sarcoidosis in a child, presenting as an erythroderma with keratotic spines and palmar pits. *Br J Dermatol*, **95**, 93–97.
36. Katta, R., Nelson, B., Chen, D. et al (2000) Sarcoidosis of the scalp: a case series and review of the literature. *J Am Acad Dermatol*, **42**, 690–692.
37. Takahashi, H., Mori, M., Muraoka, S. et al (1996) Sarcoidosis presenting as a scarring alopecia: report of a rare cutaneous manifestation of systemic sarcoidosis. *Dermatology*, **193**, 144–146.
38. Nathan, M.P., Pinsker, R., Chase, P.H. et al (1974) Sarcoidosis presenting as lymphedema. *Arch Dermatol*, **109**, 543–544.
39. Wakelin, S.H., James, M.P. (1995) Sarcoidosis: nail dystrophy without underlying bone changes. *Cutis*, **55**, 344–346.
40. Smith, H.R., Black, M.M. (2000) Verrucous cutaneous sarcoidosis. *Clin Exp Dermatol*, **25**, 98–99.
41. Hruza, G.J., Kerdel, F.A. (1986) Generalized atrophic sarcoidosis with ulcerations. *Arch Dermatol*, **122**, 320–322.
42. Ford, P.G., Jorizzo, J.L., Hitchcock, M.G. (2000) Previously undiagnosed sarcoidosis in a patient presenting with leonine facies and complete heart block. *Arch Dermatol*, **136**, 712–714.
43. Cliff, S., Hart, Y., Knowles, G. et al (1998) Sarcoidosis presenting as palmar erythema. *Clin Exp Dermatol*, **23**, 123–124.
44. Saxe, N., Benatar, S.R., Bok, L. et al (1984) Sarcoidosis with leg ulcers and annular facial lesions. *Arch Dermatol*, **120**, 93–96.
45. Gold, R.S., Sager, E. (1976) Oral sarcoidosis: review of the literature. *J Oral Surg*, **34**, 237–244.
46. Klein, P.A., Apeel, J., Callen, J.P. (1998) Sarcoidosis of the vulva: a rare cutaneous manifestation. *J Am Acad Dermatol*, **39**, 281–283.
47. Tatnall, F.M., Barnes, H.M., Sarkany, I. (1985) Sarcoidosis of the vulva. *Clin Exp Dermatol*, **10**, 384–385.
48. Hurd, D.S., Olsen, T. (2000) Cutaneous sarcoidosis presenting as a testicular mass. *Cutis*, **66**, 435–438.
49. Fernandes, S.R., Singsen, B.H., Hoffman, G.S. (2000) Sarcoidosis and systemic vasculitis. *Semin Arthritis Rheum*, **30**, 33–46.
50. Sharma, O.P. (1997) Neurosarcoidosis: a personal perspective based on the study of 38 patients. *Chest*, **112**, 220–228.
51. Chapelon, C., Ziza, J.M., Piette, J.C. et al (1990) Neurosarcoidosis: signs, course and treatment in 35 confirmed cases. *Medicine*, **69**, 261–276.
52. Perry, A., Vuitch, F. (1995) Causes of death in patients with sarcoidosis. A morphologic study of 38 autopsies with clinicopathologic correlations. *Arch Pathol Lab Med*, **119**, 167–172.
53. Sharma, O.P. (1999) Vitamin D, calcium, and sarcoidosis. *Chest*, **109**, 535–539.
54. Conron, M., DuBois, R.M. (2001) Immunological mechanisms of sarcoidosis. *Clin Exp Allergy*, **31**, 543–554.
55. Edmondstone, W.M., Wilson, A.G. (1985) Sarcoidosis in Caucasians, Blacks and Asians in London. *Br J Dis Chest*, **79**, 27–36.
56. Marzano, A.V., Gasparini, L.G., Cavicchini, S. et al (1996) Scar sarcoidosis associated with vitiligo, autoimmune thyroiditis and autoimmune chronic hepatitis. *Clin Exp Dermatol*, **21**, 466–467.
57. Terunuma, A., Watabe, A., Kato, T. et al (2000) Coexistence of vitiligo and sarcoidosis in a patient with circulating autoantibodies. *Int J Dermatol*, **39**, 551–553.
58. Barnadas, M.A., Rodríguez-Arias, J.M., Alomar, A. (2000) Subcutaneous sarcoidosis associated with vitiligo, pernicious anemia and autoimmune thyroiditis. *Clin Exp Dermatol*, **22**, 55–56.
59. Badell, A., Servitje, O., Graells, J. et al. (1998) Hypoparathyroidism and sarcoidosis. *Br J Dermatol*, **138**, 915–917.
60. Papadopoulos, K.I., Hornblat, Y., Lilgeblath, H. et al (1996) High frequency of endocrine autoimmunity in patients with sarcoidosis. *Eur J Endocrinol*, **134**, 331–336.
61. Friedman, J.A., Miller, E.P., Green, L. (2001) Sarcoidosis and Sjögren's syndrome. *Isr Med Assoc J*, **3**, 471.
62. Van de Loosdrecht, A., Kalk, W., Bootsma, H. et al (2001) Simultaneous presentation of sarcoidosis and Sjögren's syndrome. *Rheumatology*, **40**, 113–115.
63. Yoshioko, K., Nishima, S., Kitai, S. et al (1997) Association of sarcoidosis, insulin-dependent diabetes mellitus, and ulcerative colitis. *Arch Intern Med*, **157**, 465.
64. Schmuth, M., Prior, C., Illersperger, B. et al (1999) Systemic sarcoidosis and cutaneous lymphoma: is the association fortuitous? *Br J Dermatol*, **140**, 952–955.
65. Mirmirani, P., Maurer, T.A., Herndier, B. et al (1999) Sarcoidosis in a patient with AIDS: a manifestation of immune restoration syndrome. *J Am Acad Dermatol*, **41**, 285–286.
66. Gómez, V., Smith, P.R., Burack, J. et al (2000) Sarcoidosis after antiretroviral therapy in a patient with acquired immunodeficiency syndrome. *Clin Infect Dis*, **31**, 1278–1280.
67. Reunala, T., Collins. P, (1997) Diseases associated with dermatitis herpetiformis. *Br J Dermatol*, **136**, 315–318.
68. Porter, W.M., Hardman, C.M., Leonard, J.N., Fry, L. (1999) Sarcoidosis in a patient with linear IgA disease. *Clin Exp Dermatol*, **24**, 67–70.
69. Rybicki, B.A., Maliarik, M.J., Major, M. et al (1997) Genetics of sarcoidosis. *Clin Chest Med*, **18**, 707–717.
70. Callen, J.P., Dahl, M.V. (1986) Sarcoidosis. In: Thiers, B.H., Dobson, R.L. (eds) Pathogenesis of skin disease. New York: Churchill Livingstone, pp 331–338.
71. Kerdel, F.A., Moschella, S.L. (1984) Sarcoidosis: an updated review. *J Am Acad Dermatol*, **11**, 1–19.
72. Li, N., Bajoghli, A., Kubba, A. et al (1999) Identification of mycobacterial DNA in cutaneous lesions of sarcoidosis. *J Cutan Pathol*, **26**, 271–278.
73. Popper, H.H., Klemmen, H., Hoefler, G. et al (1997) Presence of mycobacterial DNA in sarcoidosis. *Hum Pathol*, **28**, 796–800.
74. Fidler, H.M., Rook, G.A., Johnson, N.M. et al (1993) Mycobacterium tuberculosis DNA in tissue affected by sarcoidosis. *BMJ*, **27**, 546–549.
75. Vokurka, M., Lecossier, D., du Bois, R.M. et al (1997) Absence of DNA from mycobacteria of the M. tuberculosis complex in sarcoidosis. *Am J Respir Crit Care Med*, **156**, 1000–1003.
76. Richter, E., Geinert, U., Kirsten, D. et al (1996) Assessment of mycobacterial DNA in cells and tissues of mycobacterial and sarcoid lesions. *Am J Respir Crit Care Med*, **153**, 375–380.
77. Bocart, D., Locossier, D., De Lassence, A. et al (1992) A search for mycobacterial DNA in granulomatous tissues from patients with sarcoidosis using the polymerase chain reaction. *Am Rev Respir Dis*, **145**, 1142–1148.
78. Hance, A.J. (1998) The role of mycobacteria in the pathogenesis of sarcoidosis. *Semin Respir Infect*, **13**, 197–205.
79. Almenoff, P.L., Johnson, A., Lesser, M. et al (1996) Growth of acid fast L forms from the blood of patients with sarcoidosis. *Thorax*, **51**, 530–533.
80. Yamada, T., Eishi, Y., Ikeda, S. et al (2002) In situ localization of Propionibacterium acnes DNA in lymph nodes from sarcoidosis patients by signal amplification with catalyzed reporter deposition. *J Pathol*, **198**, 541–547.
81. Gazouli, M., Ikonomopoulos, J., Trigidou, R. et al (2002) Assessment of mycobacterial, propionibacterial, and human herpesvirus 8 DNA in tissues of Greek patients with sarcoidosis. *J Clin Microbiol*, **40**, 3060–3063.
82. Wahlstrom, J., Katchar, K., Wigzell, H. et al (2001) Analysis of intracellular cytotokines in CD4+ and CD8+ lung and blood T cells in sarcoidosis. *Am J Respir Crit Care Med*, **163**, 115–121.
83. Lympany, P.A., Petrek, M., Southcott, A.M. et al (1996) HLA-DPB polymorphisms: Glu 69 positions in sarcoidosis. *Eur J Immunogenet*, **23**, 353–359.
84. Kataria, Y.P., Holter, J.F. (1997) Immunology of sarcoidosis. *Clin Chest Med*, **18**, 719–739.
85. Forman, J.D., Klein, J.T., Silver, R.F. et al (1994) Selective activation and accumulation of oligoclonal V beta-specific T-cells in active pulmonary sarcoidosis. *J Clin Invest*, **94**, 1533–1542.
86. Grunewald, J., Olerup, O., Persson, U. et al (1994) T-cell receptor variable region gene usage by CD4+ and CD8+ T cells in bronchoalveolar lavage fluid and peripheral blood of sarcoidosis patients. *Proc Natl Acad Sci USA*, **91**, 4965–4969.
87. Forrester, J.M., Wang, Y., Ricalton, N. et al (1994) TCR expression of activated T cell clones in the lungs of patients with pulmonary sarcoidosis. *J Immunol*, **153**, 4291–4302.
88. Grunewald, J., Wahlstrom, J., Berlin, M. et al (2002) Lung restricted T cell receptor AV2S3+CD4+ T cell expansions in sarcoidosis patients with a shared HLA-DR beta chain conformation. *Thorax*, **57**, 348–352.
89. Baumer, I., Zissel, G., Schlaak, M. et al (1997) Th-1/Th-2 distribution in pulmonary sarcoidosis. *Am J Respir Cell Mol Biol*, **16**, 171–177.
90. Kuramoto, Y., Shindo, Y., Tagami, H. (1988) Subcutaneous sarcoidosis with extensive caseation necrosis. *J Cutan Pathol*, **15**, 188–190.
91. Batres, E., Klima, M., Tschen, J. (1982) Transepithelial elimination in cutaneous sarcoidosis. *J Cutan Pathol*, **9**, 50–54.
92. Jones Williams, W. (1960) The nature and origin of Schaumann bodies. *J Path Bact*, **79**, 193–201.
93. Reid, J.D., Andersen, M.E. (1988) Calcium oxalate in sarcoid granulomas. With particular reference to the small ovoid body and a note on the finding of dolomite. *Am J Clin Pathol*, **90**, 545–558.
94. Symmons, P.J., Brady, K., Keen, C.E. (1995) Calcium oxalate crystal deposition in epithelioid histiocytes of granulomatous lymphadenitis: analysis by light and electron microscopy. *Histopathology*, **27**, 423–429.
95. Winkelmann, R.K., Dahl, P.R., Peniciaro, C. et al (1998) Asteroid bodies and other cytoplasmic inclusions in necrobiotic xanthogranuloma with paraproteinemia. *J Am Acad Dermatol*, **38**, 967–970.
96. Azar, H.A., Lunardelli, C. (1969) Collagen nature of asteroid bodies of giant cells in sarcoidosis. *Am J Pathol*, **57**, 81–92.
97. Gadde, P.S., Moscovic, E.A. (1994) Asteroid bodies: products of unusual microtubular dynamics in monocyte-derived giant cells. An immunohistochemical study. *Histol Histopathol*, **9**, 633–642.
98. Marcoval, J., Mañá, J., Moreno, A. et al (2001) Foreign bodies in granulomatous cutaneous lesions of patients with systemic sarcoidosis. *Arch Dermatol*, **137**, 427–430.
99. Callen, J.P. (2001) The presence of foreign bodies does not exclude the diagnosis of sarcoidosis. *Arch Dermatol*, **137**, 485–486.
100. Hirsh, B.C., Johnson, W.C. (1984) Pathology of granulomatous diseases: foreign body granulomata. *Int J Dermatol*, **2**, 531–538.
101. Jacyk, W.K. (1995) Annular granulomatous lesions in exogenous ochronosis are manifestations of sarcoidosis. *Am J Dermatopathol*, **33**, 18–22.
102. Jordaan, H.F., Mulligan, R.P. (1990) Actinic granuloma-like change in exogenous ochronosis: case report. *J Cutan Pathol*, **17**, 236–240.

Granuloma annulare

Clinical features

Granuloma annulare is a common, usually asymptomatic, dermatosis of unknown etiology.[1,2] It may be divided into six clinical subsets:

- localized
- generalized
- perforating
- subcutaneous
- papular
- linear.

Unusual clinical variants include pustular follicular lesions and presentation with patches.[3,4] Granuloma annulare (often with widespread disseminated lesions) has been described in patients with HIV infection and sometimes may be the presenting sign.[5–17] Granuloma annulare has also been reported in association with both Hodgkin's and non-Hodgkin's lymphoma.[18–21]

Other documented associations of granuloma annulare include morphea, chronic hepatitis C infection, autoimmune thyroiditis, secondary hyperparathyroidism, sarcoidosis, Plummer disease, myelodysplastic syndrome and metastatic carcinoma.[22–29] Granuloma annulare has also been described after vaccination for tetanus, hepatitis B and tuberculosis.[30–32] Granuloma annulare may also develop in the scars of herpes zoster.[33–35]

Granuloma annulare has developed during treatment with allopurinol and amlodipine.[36,37] It is most likely, however, that granuloma annulare-like eruptions secondary to drug administration represent interstitial granulomatous drug eruptions (see p. 644).

Localized granuloma annulare

The localized variant is the commonest type. It usually presents in the first three decades and is associated with a female preponderance (2.25:1). Lesions consist of one or several papules, which may be skin-colored, red or violaceous, and are typically distributed to form an annular or arcuate lesion 1–5 cm across (*Figs 8.29–8.33*). About 50% of patients have solitary lesions. The acral sites are most commonly affected, in particular the knuckles and dorsum of the fingers. In a small proportion of patients, lesions are present on both the upper and lower limbs, and occasionally the trunk is affected. Lesions on the palms are exceptional.[38] Facial involvement appears to be uncommon.[39,40] Although lesions may be very persistent, approximately 50% of patients can anticipate resolution by about 2 years from onset, although recurrences are, unfortunately, quite common. Interestingly, on occasions lesions regress spontaneously after biopsy.[41] Rarely, granuloma annulare has been reported in families and in monozygotic twins.[42] A case has been documented in which the lesions recurred seasonally with sun-exposed areas.[43] There has only been a single case report of cutaneous granuloma annulare with similar lesions in an intra-abdominal location.[44]

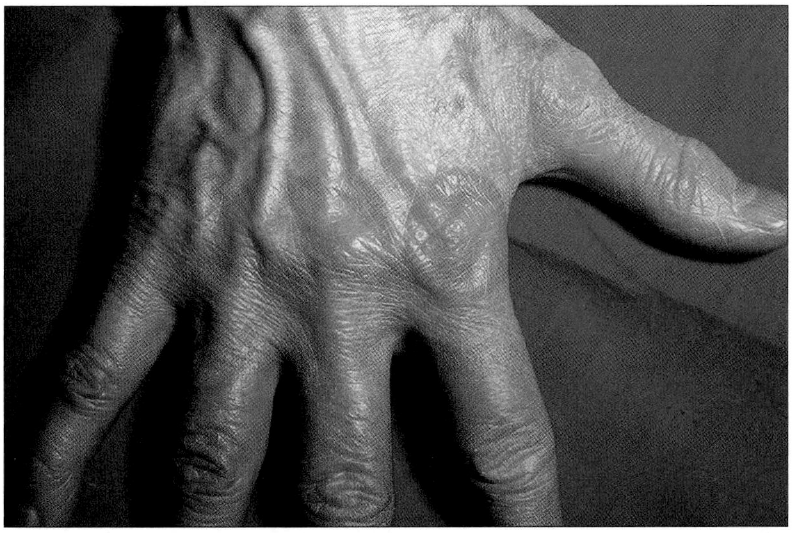

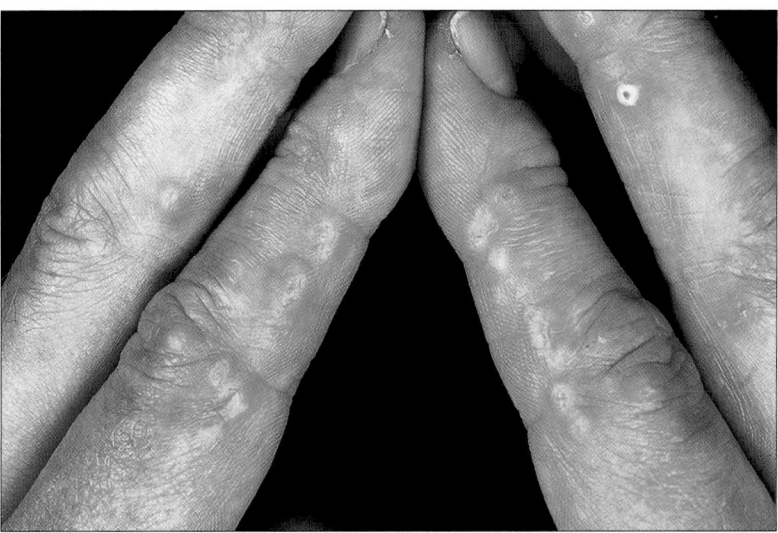

Fig. 8.30
Localized granuloma annulare: in this patient multiple small papules are present on the fingers. By courtesy of the Institute of Dermatology, London, UK.

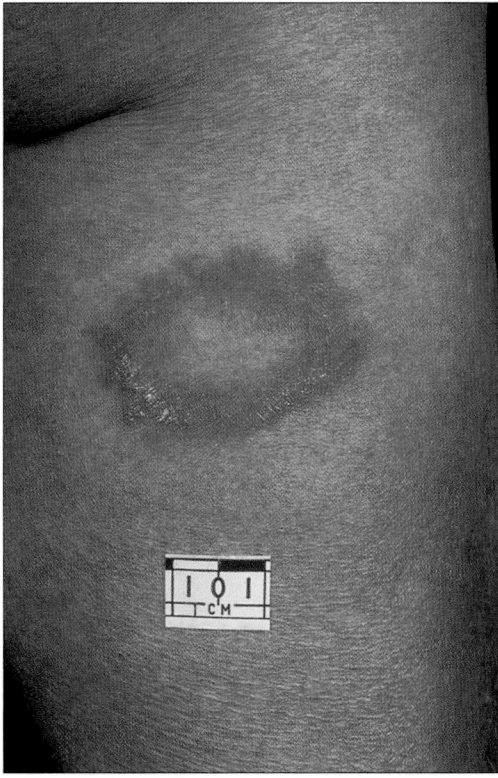

Fig. 8.31
Localized granuloma annulare: this lower leg lesion shows a characteristic beaded margin, but with an unusual overlying scale. By courtesy of R.A. Marsden, MD, St George's Hospital, London, UK.

Fig. 8.29
Localized granuloma annulare: a typical annular lesion over the knuckle. Stretching of the skin reveals a translucent beaded margin. By courtesy of R.A. Marsden, MD, St George's Hospital, London, UK.

Generalized granuloma annulare

Generalized lesions occur in approximately 15% of patients with granuloma annulare.[2,45] As with the localized form, there is an increased incidence in females; however, the median age differs: the majority of cases occur in patients in their fourth to seventh decades, with the rest appearing during the first decade. Patients with generalized granuloma annulare have an increased incidence of HLA-Bw35.[46] Generalized granuloma annulare is defined as lesions occurring on at least the trunk and either upper or lower extremities, or both.[2] Most lesions are papules, which may be distributed in an annular pattern, but maculopapules and nodules also occur. The coloration of the lesions varies from flesh-colored or red, to tan, brown or yellow. Numbers vary from several dozen to hundreds (*Figs 8.34–8.36*). A single patient has been documented with generalized disease accompanied by marked swelling of the hands and another patient developed the disease after erythema multiforme.[47,48] Lesions may be asymptomatic or pruritic.[2] As with the localized form, the disease is very persistent, but some patients experience resolution within 4 years. Anetoderma has been exceptionally reported as a complication of generalized granuloma annulare.[49]

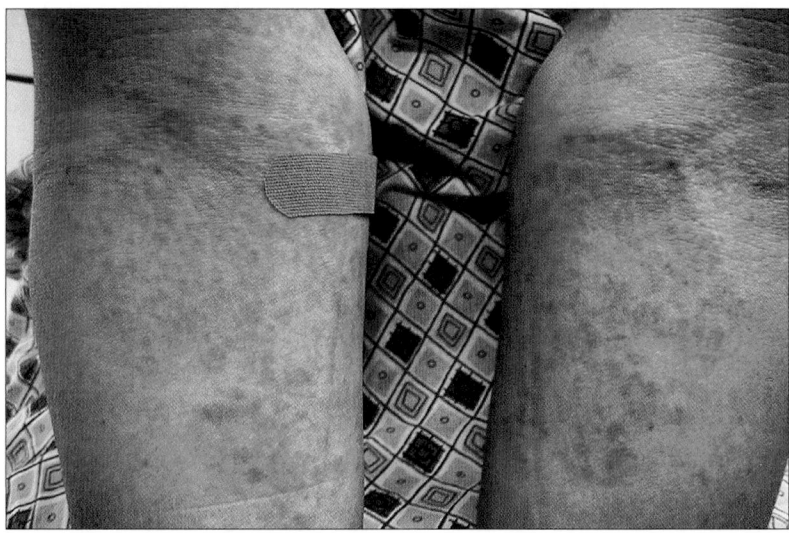

Fig. 8.34
Generalized granuloma annulare: innumerable papules are present on this patient's arms. By courtesy of J. Williams, MD, Brigham and Women's Hospital, Boston, USA.

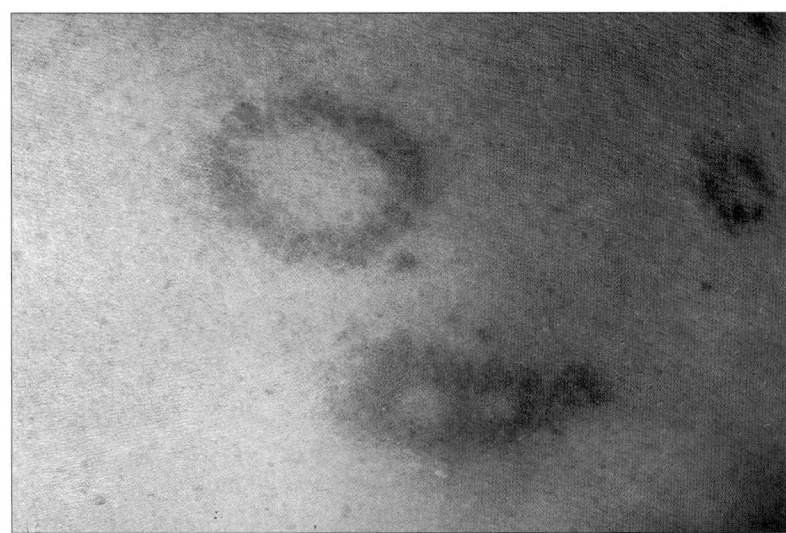

Fig. 8.32
Localized granuloma annulare: close-up view of annular lesions. By courtesy of the Institute of Dermatology, London, UK.

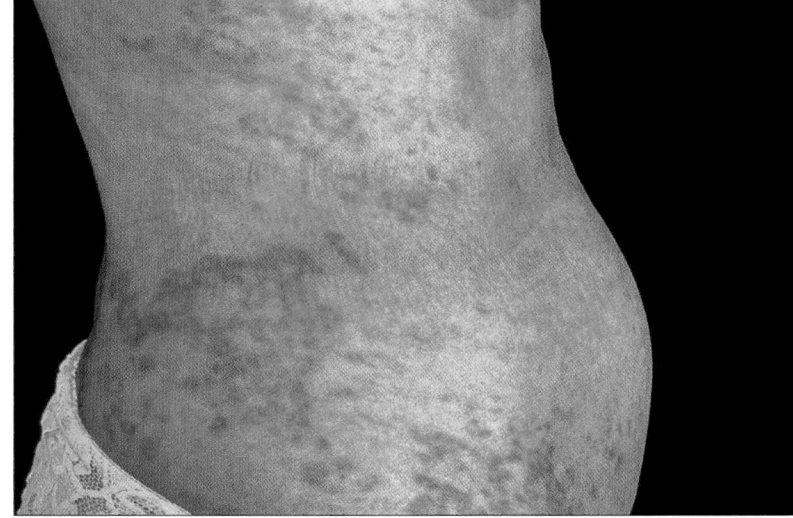

Fig. 8.35
Generalized granuloma annulare: there are widespread papules and plaques. By courtesy of the Institute of Dermatology, London, UK.

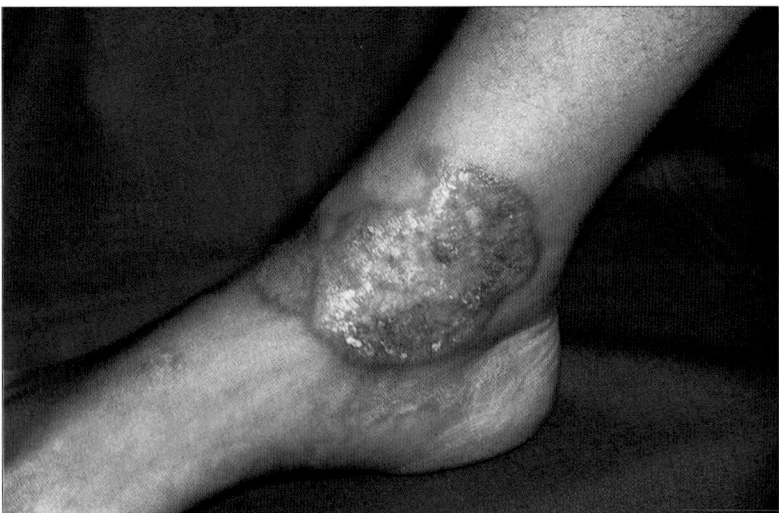

Fig. 8.33
Localized granuloma annulare: in this patient there is a large plaque on the ankle with a hint of central clearing. By courtesy of the Institute of Dermatology, London, UK.

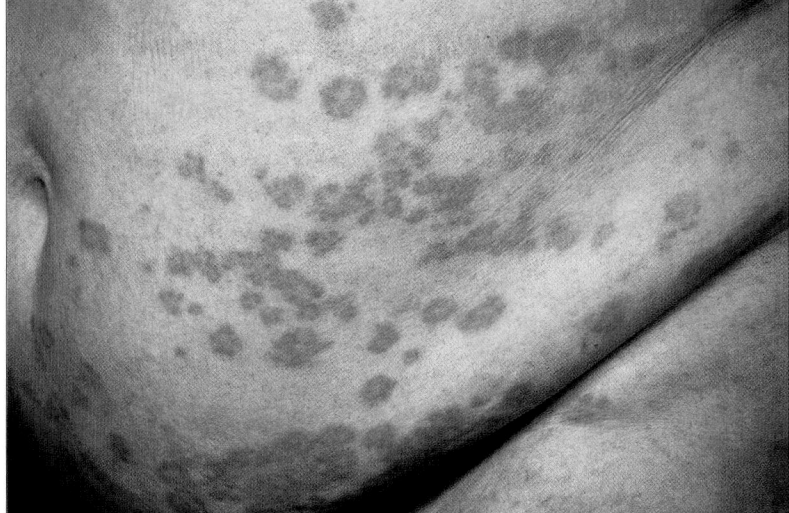

Fig. 8.36
Generalized granuloma annulare: in this patient numerous annular lesions are present on the abdomen. By courtesy of the Institute of Dermatology, London, UK.

Perforating granuloma annulare

Perforating granuloma annulare is distinguished by the presence of transepidermal elimination of necrobiotic collagen.[9,17,50–53] Clinically, the lesion presents as a group of papules with an associated umbilicated crust usually located on the extremities, often the dorsum of the hands (*Fig. 8.37*). Presentation of lesions on the ears has exceptionally been described, as has a generalized variant.[54,55] It may affect both children and adults, and both localized and generalized forms exist. Spontaneous resolution sometimes occurs within months or years of onset. An exceptional case of perforating granuloma annulare which developed following tattooing has been reported.[56]

Subcutaneous granuloma annulare

The subcutaneous variant is synonymous with the pseudorheumatoid nodule of childhood and deep granuloma annulare.[57–60] Lesions may present de novo or may arise in association with typical cutaneous papules. It occurs in childhood, often affecting the underlying periosteum and involving predominantly the lower legs (particularly the tibia), feet, buttocks, hands and head.[60] Lesions may also present on the penis or

eyelid.[62,63] In one study of 47 patients, the mean age was 4.3 years.[61] In some instances, there is a past history of trauma. By definition, such children do not have rheumatoid arthritis or rheumatic fever. The lesion usually regresses after several years. However, recurrences appear in 19% of patients.[61]

Papular granuloma annulare

Papular granuloma annulare presents as flesh-colored or hypopigmented, 1–3 mm diameter papules on the dorsal aspect of the hands, usually in male children. Occasional lesions may be umbilicated or generalized (*Figs 8.38, 8.39*).[64]

Linear granuloma annulare

The linear variant is very rare and may have a bilateral distribution.[66,67] This variant overlaps and may be the same as the condition described as interstitial granulomatous dermatitis (see p. 644).

Pathogenesis and histological features

The cause of granuloma annulare is unknown. The original concept that it represented a tuberculid has long since been discounted. Although it has been reported at the site of previous herpes zoster infection and verruca vulgaris, it is unlikely that an infectious pathogenesis exists. There are a wide variety of currently possible pathogenetic mechanisms, most of which have some merit, but none of which satisfactorily clarifies the precise mechanism by which the lesions of granuloma annulare develop.[67] Particularly popular are an immune complex vasculitic process and a cell-mediated delayed hypersensitivity reaction. Evidence in favor of the former has been the detection, by direct immunofluorescence, of immunoreactants (IgM and complement) in blood vessel walls in some patients.[67] Elevated levels of circulating immune complexes have also been recorded.[68] The histology may reveal features suggestive of a vasculitic process, including endothelial swelling, vessel wall thickening (due to the deposition of PAS-positive material), vascular occlusion and necrosis (*Fig. 8.40*).[69] All of the latter changes may, of course, develop as a consequence of the inflammatory process rather than cause it.

In favor of a cell-mediated delayed hypersensitivity reaction are:
- the finding of activated T-lymphocytes in lesions of granuloma annulare on electron microscopic examination
- the predominance of T-helper–inducer cells in the infiltrate

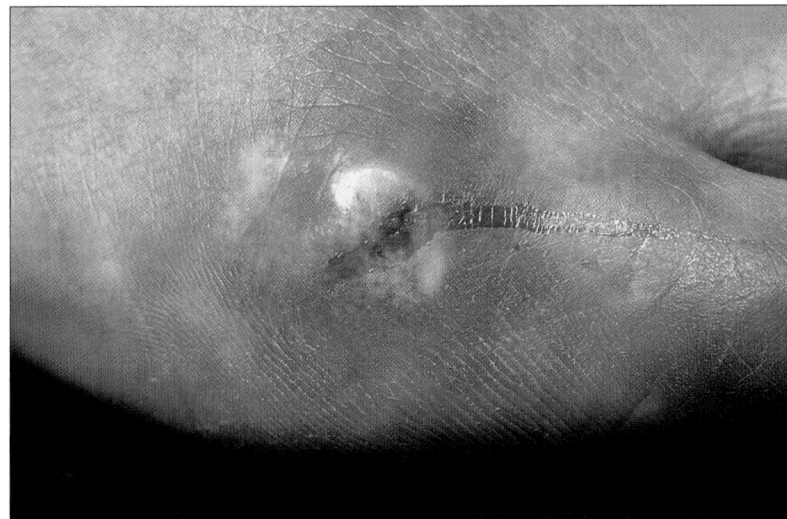

Fig. 8.37
Perforating granuloma annulare: the extremities are most often affected. Necrotic debris can be seen in the center of the lesion. By courtesy of the Institute of Dermatology, London, UK.

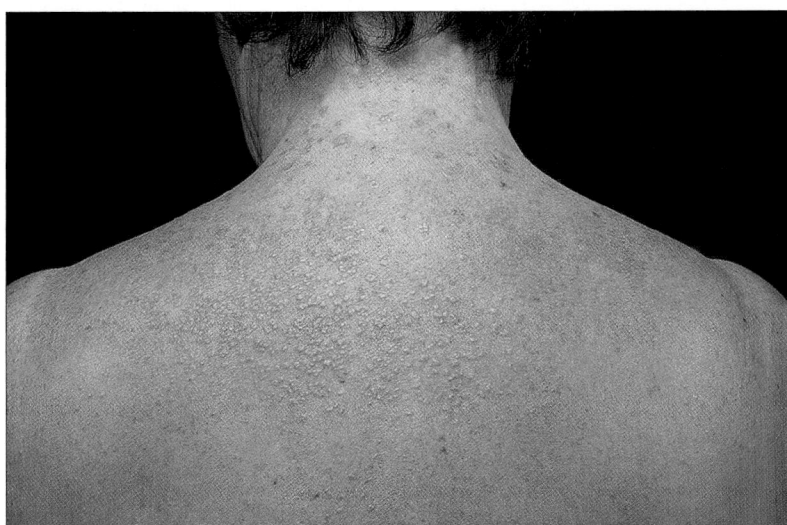

Fig. 8.38
Papular granuloma annulare: widespread papules are present on this patient's back and shoulders. By courtesy of the Institute of Dermatology, London, UK.

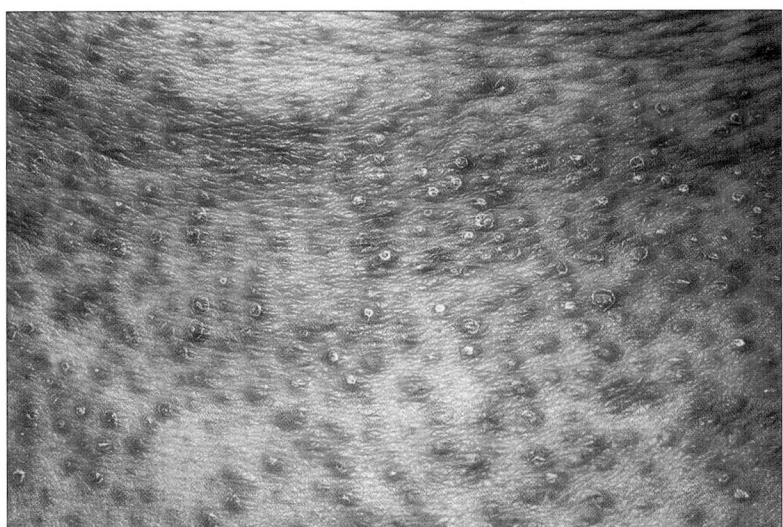

Fig. 8.39
Papular granuloma annulare: numerous small, scaly papules are present. By courtesy of the Institute of Dermatology, London, UK.

• the histopathological resemblance of the infiltrate to that of conditions of known delayed hypersensitivity pathogenesis, including sarcoidosis and tuberculosis.[70]

Patients with granuloma annulare may have raised serum migration inhibition factor activity.[67] Defective neutrophil migration has also been reported.[71,72] Other proposed pathogenetic mechanisms include collagen damage by macrophage lysosomal hydrolytic enzymes as the initial event, or a primary disorder of collagen leading to an allergic or non-allergic tissue reaction. The increased incidences of diabetes mellitus and HLA-B8 may also be of pathogenetic significance (compare with necrobiosis lipoidica).[73] Although there are reports of generalized granuloma being associated with sunlight, this appears to be of doubtful significance.[2]

The most characteristic histological lesion seen in granuloma annulare is the palisading granuloma (*Figs 8.41–8.44*). This consists of a central core of degenerate (necrobiotic) collagen, surrounded by an often radially arranged infiltrate of lymphocytes, histiocytes and fibroblasts. Elastic tissue may be absent within these foci and there may be phagocytosis of elastic fibers by giant cells at the periphery of the granuloma

(*Fig. 8.45*).[74] However, altered elastic fibers are not a constant finding. Solar elastosis is not a feature of granuloma annulare. In some lesions the altered collagen has a somewhat basophilic appearance due to the presence of acid mucopolysaccharides, but more commonly there is eosinophilia, due in part to fibrin deposition (*Fig. 8.46*). Heparin sulfate is an important component of the mucin in granuloma annulare but not of other cutaneous diseases associated with mucin deposition (*Fig. 8.47*).[75]

Occasionally, sparse karryorhectic debris is present in the center of the lesion and sometimes the necrobiotic foci contain lipid droplets. More often, however, the collagenous degeneration is not organized into a nodular pattern, but affects isolated fibers in a random pattern, an appearance often best appreciated on low power examination (*Fig. 8.48*).[76] In this so-called diffuse or interstitial form of granuloma annulare, affected fibers, which are swollen and intensely eosinophilic, alternate with apparently normal fibers to give a rather disorganized

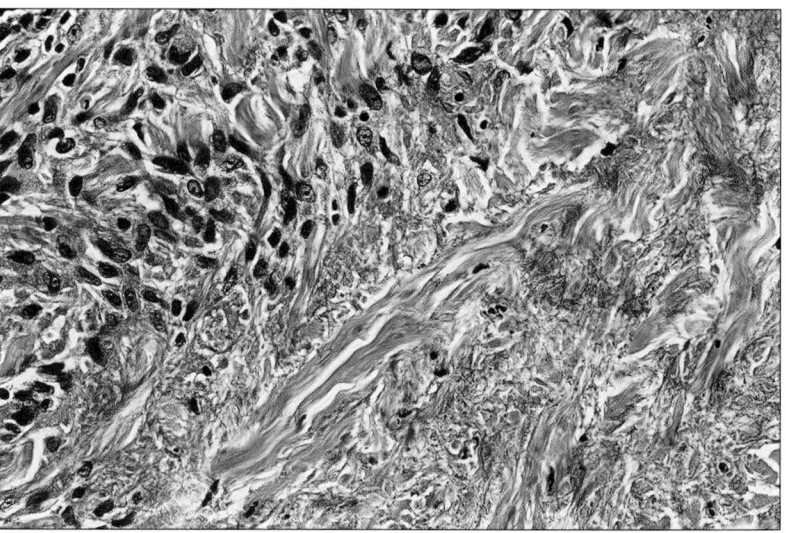

Fig. 8.42
Localized granuloma annulare: the collagen is fragmented and in part granular. Note the peripheral palisade of histiocytes, occasional lymphocytes and fibroblasts.

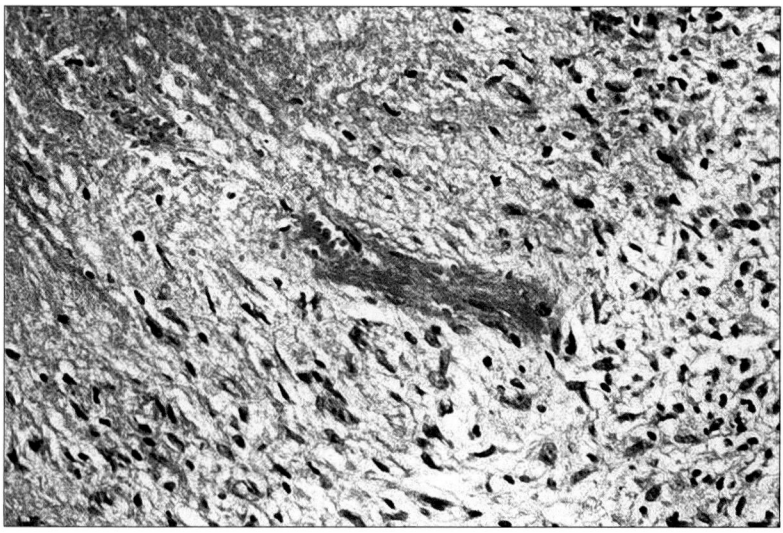

Fig. 8.40
Granuloma annulare: view through the edge of a necrobiotic focus. In the center a small blood vessel shows fibrinoid necrosis with occlusion. This is an uncommon finding.

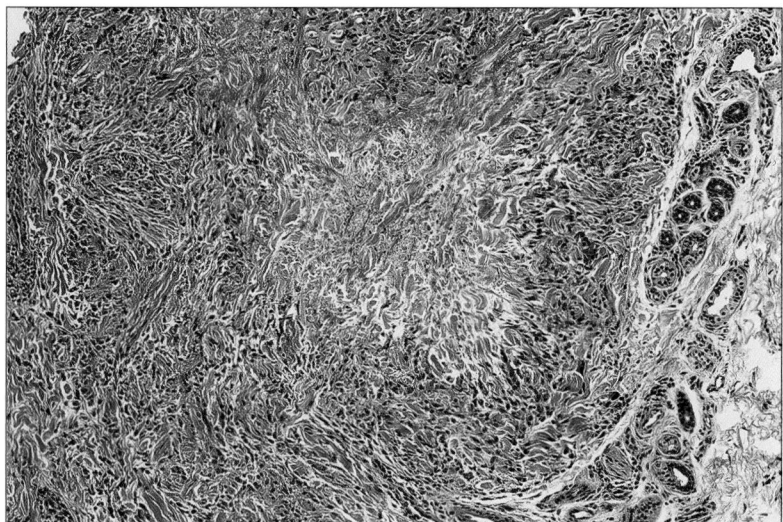

Fig. 8.41
Localized granuloma annulare: the characteristic appearance of a well-circumscribed palisading granuloma consisting of a necrobiotic center surrounded by a cellular infiltrate.

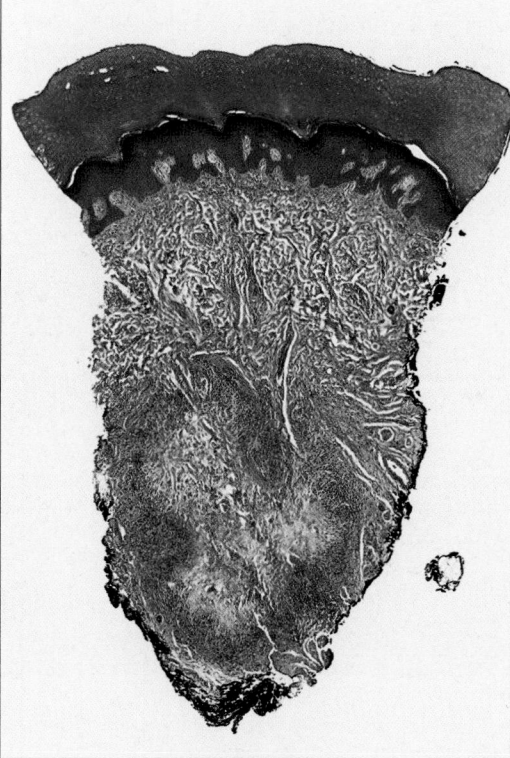

Fig. 8.43
Localized granuloma annulare: this lesion is from the palm of the hand, an uncommonly affected site. There is a sharply delineated focus of necrobiosis in the deep reticular dermis.

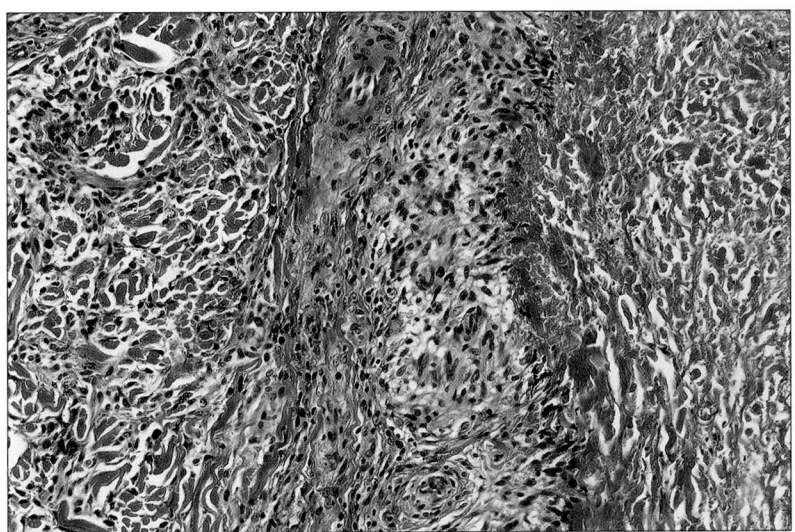

Fig. 8.44
Localized granuloma annulare: the necrobiosis is advanced presenting as eosinophilic granular debris. The histiocytic palisade is well established.

appearance (*Fig. 8.49*). Necrobiosis is minimal or absent. Characteristically, the collagen fibers are separated by mucin, which stains positively with alcian blue at pH 2.5 (*Fig. 8.50*). Histiocytes are often seen infiltrating around and between affected fibers, and this feature may be a helpful clue to the diagnosis in early cases when the collagen changes are inconspicuous and, therefore, promote examination of additional sections to detect more typical features (*Fig. 8.51*).

An almost inevitable feature of granuloma annulare is the presence of a perivascular chronic inflammatory cell infiltrate, both within the lesion and in the adjacent tissue. Well-formed sarcoidal granulomata with associated giant cells are seen in some cases. Significant numbers of eosinophils are often encountered.[77] In one study, eosinophils were present in 66% of biopsies, of which more than 10 eosinophils per high-powered field were seen in 14%.[77] Plasma cells are rare and this is useful in the differential diagnosis with necrobiosis lipoidica (see below). Neutrophils are a rare finding and when present, particularly in association with changes of vasculitis, it is likely that there is an association with systemic disease.[78]

In perforating granuloma annulare the necrobiotic debris is present in close proximity to the epidermis and may be seen to be engulfed by the

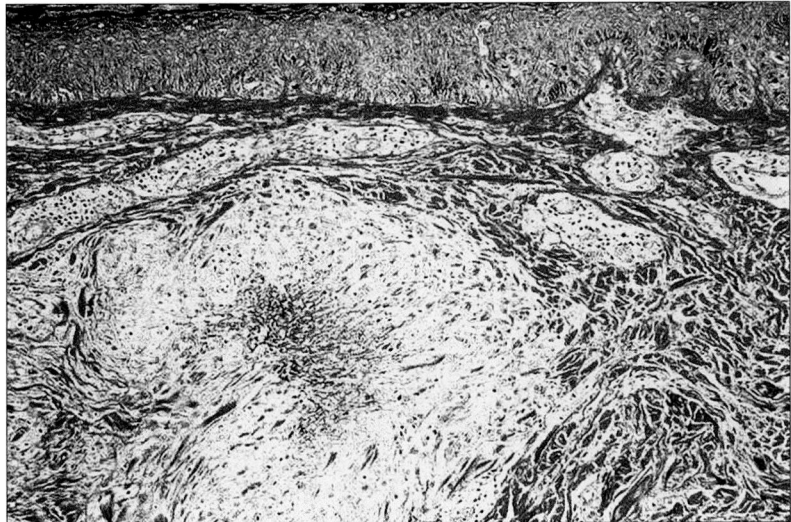

Fig. 8.45
Localized granuloma annulare: there is loss of elastic tissue within the granuloma. The basophilic material in its center is fibrin. Elastic–van Gieson.

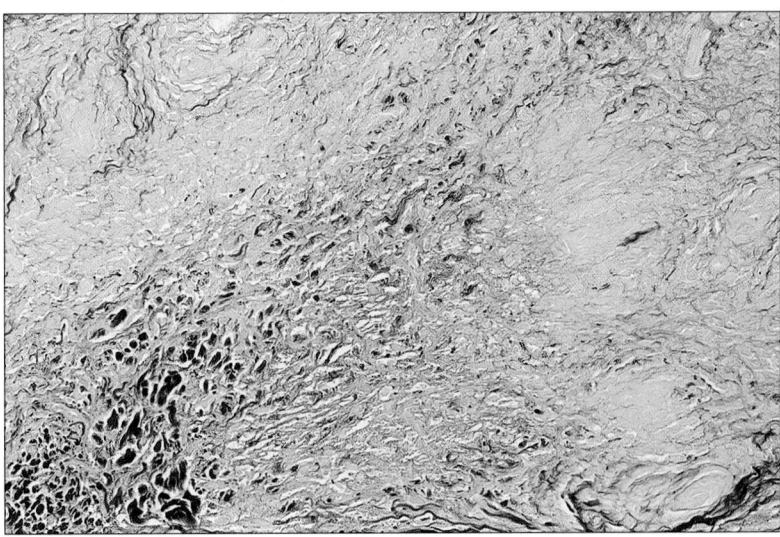

Fig. 8.47
Localized granuloma annulare: in this example there is abundant mucin in the center of the necrobiotic focus. Alcian blue–elastic van Gieson.

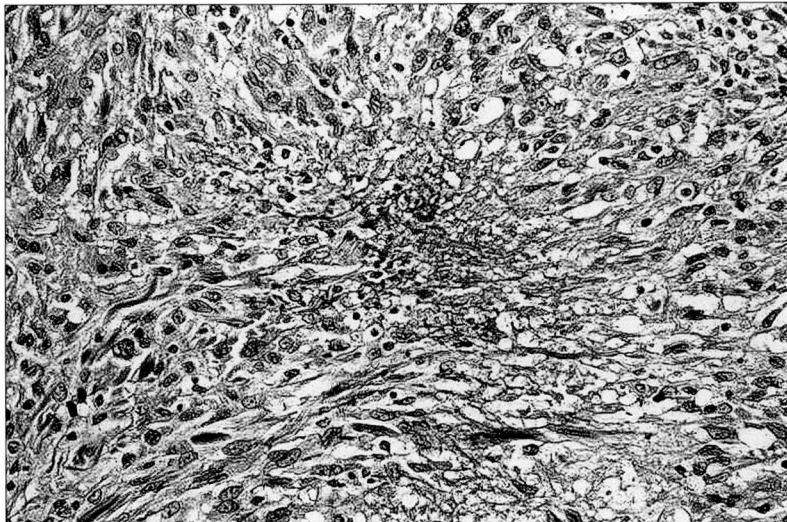

Fig. 8.46
Localized granuloma annulare: the red-staining material in the center of the granuloma is fibrin. Martius scarlet blue.

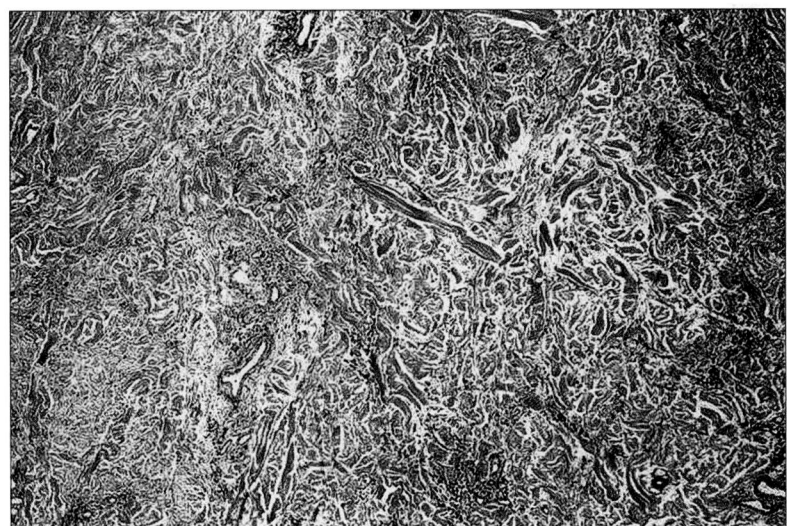

Fig. 8.48
Diffuse granuloma annulare: the collagen bundles are arranged haphazardly. Note the circumferential lymphocytic infiltrate.

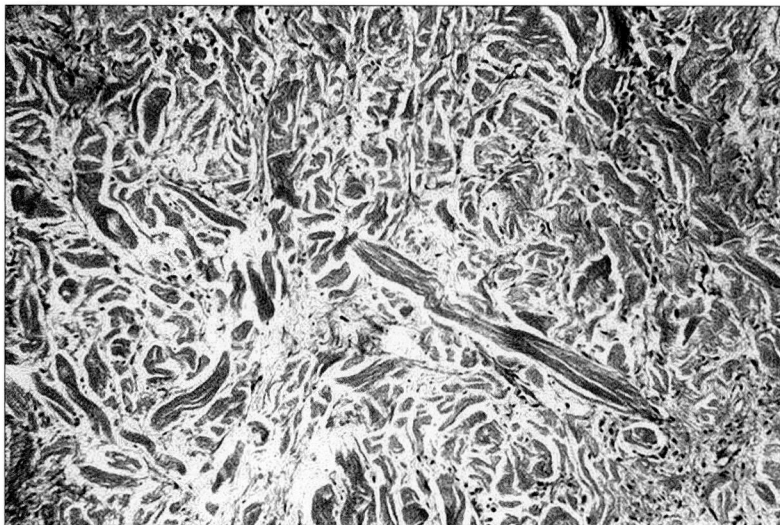

Fig. 8.49
Diffuse granuloma annulare: individual fibers are swollen and intensely eosinophilic. The apparent separation of the fibers is due to increased mucin.

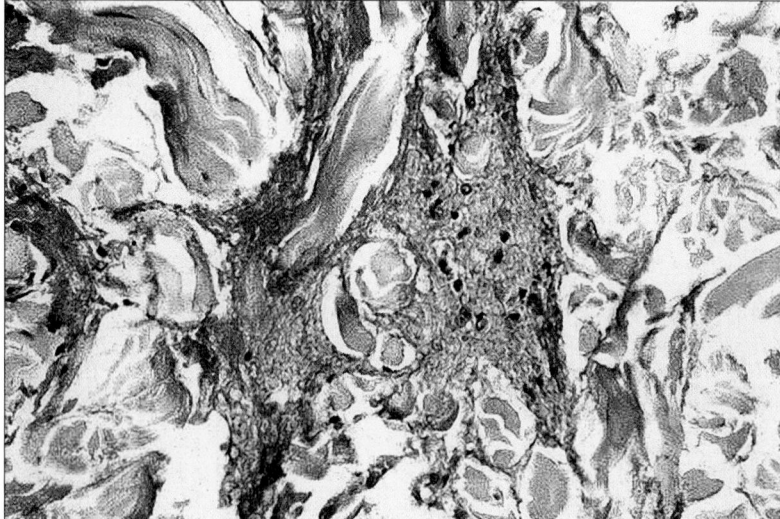

Fig. 8.50
Diffuse granuloma annulare: there is abundant fibrillary mucinous material stained with alcian blue at pH 2.5.

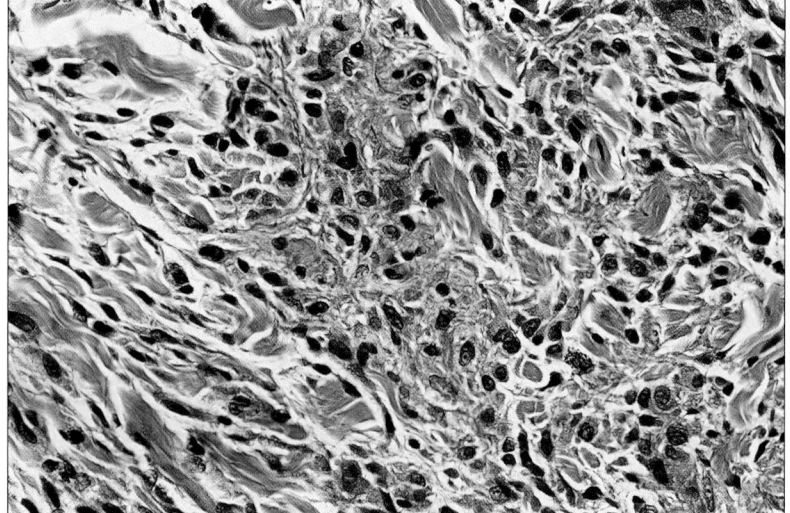

Fig. 8.51
Diffuse granuloma annulare: a heavy histiocytic infiltrate surrounds and separates the collagen fibers.

latter to form a perforating channel by which the necrotic material is extruded to the surface (*Fig. 8.52*). If serial sections are performed, the perforation may often be shown to occur through a hair follicle.

The subcutaneous lesions are much larger than the superficial ones (*Fig. 8.53*) and are frequently composed of multiple nodules. There is usually massive necrobiosis and abundant mucin; on occasions lipid droplets are evident. Mucin, however, may not be apparent and if fibrin deposition is present, distinction from rheumatoid nodule is impossible. A dense rim of lymphocytes, histiocytes and fibroblasts surrounds the necrobiotic center. Multinucleate giant cells are common and eosinophils are often present. Fibrosis of the surrounding tissue may be marked.

Papular and linear variants show histological features similar to those described for typical granuloma annulare.

Differential diagnosis

Granuloma annulare must be distinguished from necrobiosis lipoidica, rheumatoid nodule, actinic granuloma and granuloma multiforme. Points of distinction are summarized in *Table 8.1*.

Granuloma annulare-like lesions with the added features of vasculitis and a significant component of acute inflammatory cells may be encountered in the setting of systemic disease.[78,79] This pattern of disease is discussed in detail in the section on palisaded neutrophilic and granulomatous dermatitis and related disorders (see p. 320).

Granuloma annulare-like drug eruptions have been reported. The presence of associated interface changes favors a drug eruption.[9,80] This topic is discussed in more detail on page 644.

Although epithelioid sarcoma, with its associated geographic necrosis, may bear a superficial resemblance at low power examination to granuloma annulare, the degree of nuclear atypia and pleomorphism in the former condition should afford their distinction in the majority of cases. In addition, epithelioid sarcoma often shows perineural tumor infiltration. It should be noted, however, that mitotic activity may be encountered in granuloma annulare.[81] In difficult cases, keratin and epithelial membrane antigen immunoreactivity in epithelioid sarcoma should assist in this differential diagnosis.

Rare cases of mycosis fungoides may be associated with a tissue reaction resembling granuloma annulare.[82,83] The presence of interstitial lymphocytes with nuclear atypia and epidermotropism, a feature not seen in granuloma annulare, should resolve this differential diagnosis. However, in difficult cases, immunophenotyping and gene rearrangement studies may be required.

References

1. Muhlbauer, J.E. (1980) Granuloma annulare. *J Am Acad Dermatol*, **3**, 217–230.
2. Dabski, K., Winkelmann, R.K. (1989) Generalized granuloma annulare: clinical and laboratory findings in 100 patients. *J Am Acad Dermatol*, **20**, 39–47.
3. Vargas-Díez, E., Feal-Cortizas, C., Fraga, J. et al (1998) Follicular pustulous granuloma annulare. *Br J Dermatol*, **138**, 1075–1078.
4. Mutasim, D.F., Bridges, A.G. (2000) Patch granuloma annulare: clinicopathologic study of 6 patients. *J Am Acad Dermatol*, **42**, 417–421.
5. Ghadially, R., Sibbald, R.G., Walter, J.B. et al (1989) Granuloma annulare in patients with human immunodeficiency virus infections. *J Am Acad Dermatol*, **20**, 232–235.
6. Penneys, N.S., Hicks, B. (1985) Unusual cutaneous lesions associated with acquired immunodeficiency syndrome. *J Am Acad Dermatol*, **13**, 845–852.
7. Warner, L.C., Fisher, B.K. (1986) Cutaneous manifestations of the acquired immunodeficiency syndrome. *Int J Dermatol*, **25**, 337–350.
8. Bakos, L., Hampe, S., da Rocha, J.L. et al (1987) Generalized granuloma annulare in a patient with acquired immunodeficiency syndrome (AIDS). *J Am Acad Dermatol*, **17**, 844–845.
9. Huerter, C.J., Bass, J., Bergfield, W.E. et al (1987) Perforating granuloma annulare in a patient with acquired immunodeficiency syndrome. *Arch Dermatol*, **123**, 1217–1270.
10. Toro, J.R., Chu, P., Yen, T.S. et al (1999) Granuloma annulare and human immunodeficiency virus. *Arch Dermatol*, **135**, 1341–1346.
11. Magro, C.M., Crowson, A.N., Shapiro, B.L. (1998) The interstitial granulomatous drug reaction: a distinctive clinical and pathological entity. *J Cutan Pathol*, **25**, 72–78.
12. McGregor, J.M., McGibbon, D.H. (1992) Disseminated granuloma annulare as a presentation of acquired immunodeficiency syndrome (AIDS). *Clin Exp Dermatol*, **17**, 60–62.
13. Calista, D., Landi, G. (1995) Disseminated granuloma annulare in acquired immune deficiency syndrome: case report and review of the literature. *Cutis*, **55**, 158–160.
14. Cohen, P.R. (1999) Granuloma annulare: a mucocutaneous condition in human immunodeficiency virus-infected patients. *Arch Dermatol*, **135**, 1404–1407.
15. O'Moore, E.J., Nandawni, R., Uthayakumar, S. et al (2000) HIV-associated granuloma annulare (HAGA): a report of six cases. *Br J Dermatol*, **142**, 1054–1056.
16. Morris, S.D., Cerio, R., Page, D.G. (2002) An unusual presentation of diffuse granuloma annulare in an

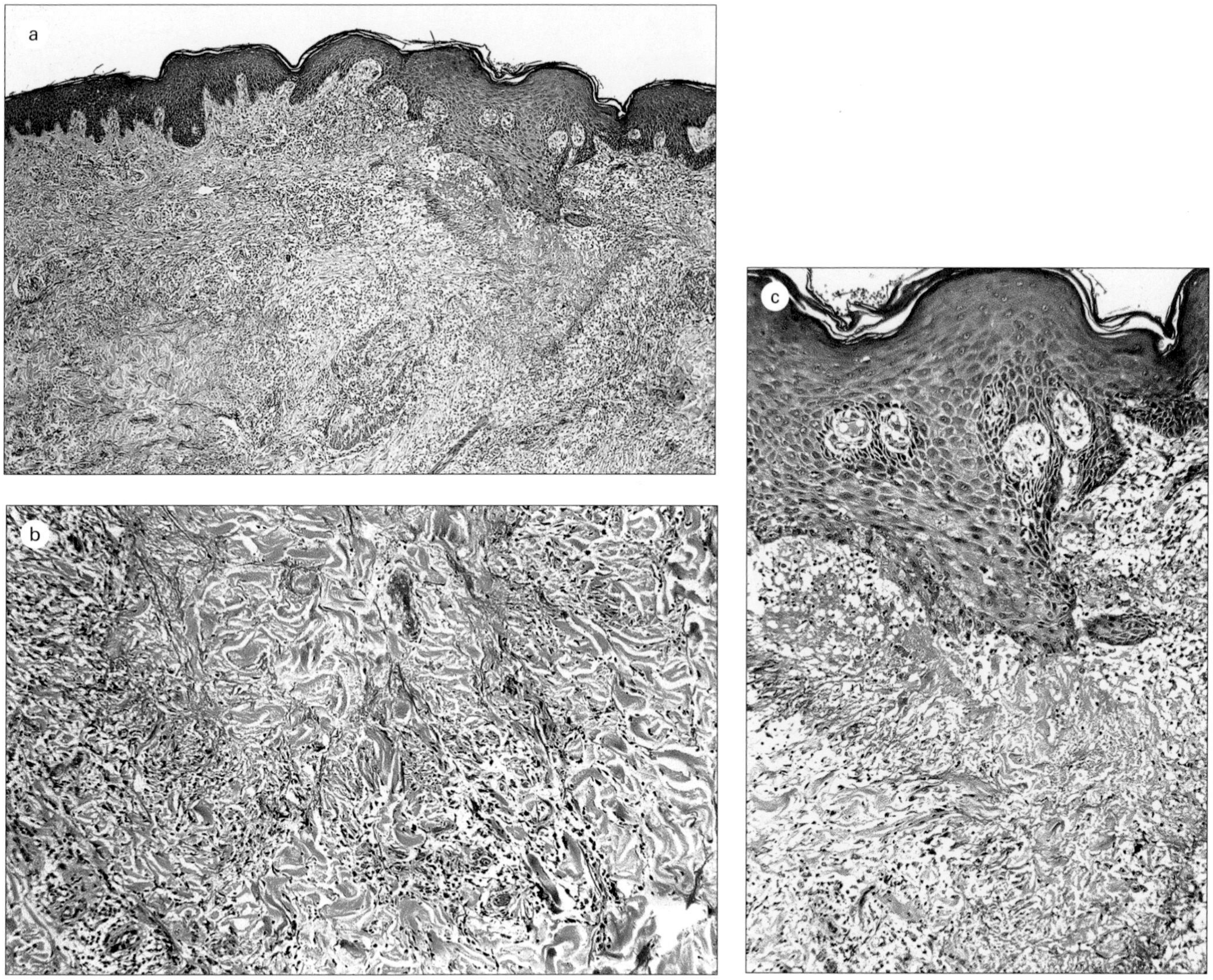

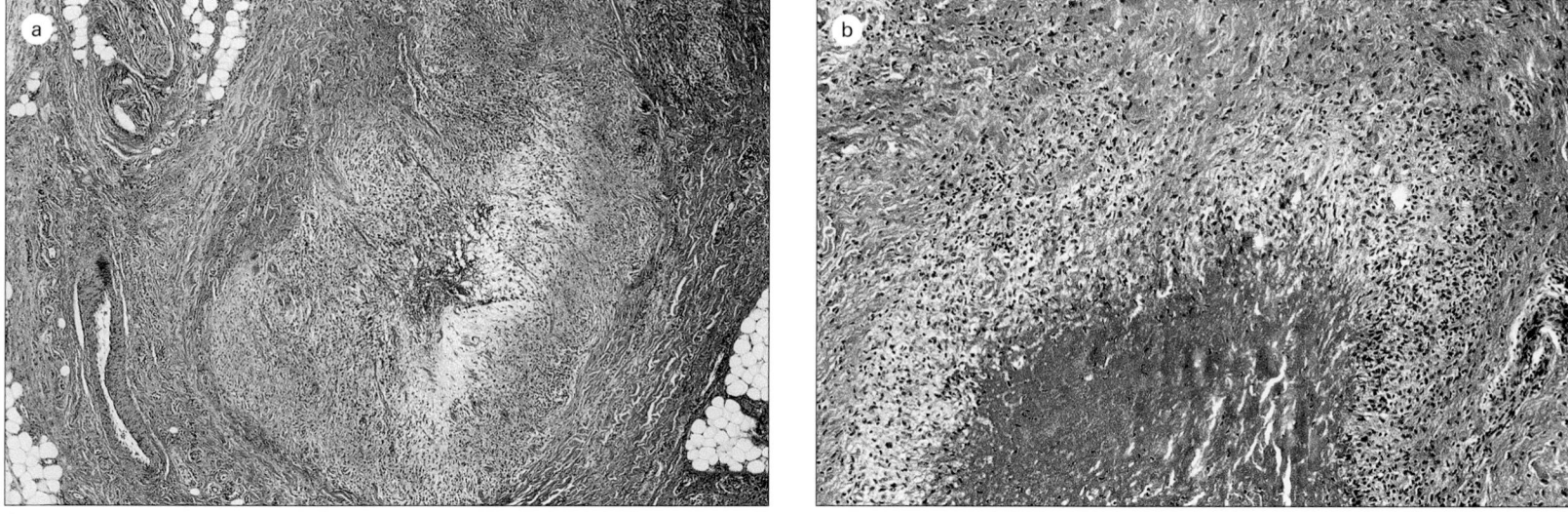

Fig. 8.52
Perforating granuloma annulare: (**a**) scanning view showing widespread typical granuloma annulare (in the upper right quadrant degenerate collagen is impinging upon hyperplastic squamous epithelium); (**b**) high power view of central dermal changes; (**c**) close-up view showing the early features of dermal perforation.

Fig. 8.53
Subcutaneous granuloma annulare: (**a**) within the subcutaneous fat and involving the fascia is a massive necrobiotic nodule; (**b**) Note the intensely eosinophilic necrobiosis and surrounding fibrosis.

Table 8.1

Differential diagnosis of palisading granulomata and variants

	Granuloma annulare (GA)	Subcutaneous GA	Perforating GA	Necrobiosis lipoidica (NL)	Atypical NL	Rheumatoid nodule	Actinic granuloma	Granuloma multiforme
Epidermis	Normal	Normal	Transepidermal elimination	Normal or atrophic or acanthotic	Normal	Normal	Normal or atrophic	Normal
Location of lesion	Superficial dermis	Deep dermis and subcutis	Superficial dermis	Deep dermis and subcutis	Upper and mid dermis	Deep dermis and subcutis	Upper and mid dermis	Upper and mid dermis
Necrobiosis	Circumscribed or ill defined	Massive sharp border	Circumscribed	Diffuse and marked	Rarely present	Massive sharp margin	Absent	Focal
Mucin	Common	Abundant	Common	Variable	Absent	Common	Absent	Present
Lipid	Occasional	Variable	Variable	Common	Absent	Variable	Absent	Absent
Fibrosis	Absent	Marked	Absent	Common; may be marked	Absent	Common	Usually absent	Slight
Loss of elastica	Yes	Yes	Yes	Yes	Yes	Yes	Very marked	Yes
Vasular thickening	Common	Variable	Minimal	Common	Absent	Variable	Absent	Absent
Capillary hyperplasia	Absent	Common	Absent	Variable	Absent	Common	Absent	Absent
Giant cells	Relatively few	Common	Relatively few	Common	Common	Relatively few	Abundant; contain elastica	Common
Asteroid bodies	Absent	Absent	Absent	Absent	Present	Absent	Not uncommon	Absent
Palisading of histiocytes	Common	Common	Common	Variable in degree	Absent	Common	Infrequent	Inconspicuous

HIV-positive patient – immunohistochemical evidence of predominant CD8 lymphocytes. *Clin Exp Dermatol*, **27**, 205–208.

17. Núñez, M., Miralles, E.S., del Olmo, N. et al (1995) Perforating granuloma annulare and HIV. *Acta Derm Venereol*, **75**, 407.
18. Barksdale, S.K., Perniciaro, C., Halling, K.C. et al (1994) Granuloma annulare in patients with malignant lymphoma: clinicopathologic study of thirteen new cases. *J Am Acad Dermatol*, **31**, 42–48.
19. Setoyama, M., Kerdel, F.A., Byrnes, J.J. et al (1997) Granuloma annulare associated with Hodgkin's lymphoma. *Int J Dermatol*, **36**, 445–448.
20. Miyamoto, T., Mihara, M. (1996) Subcutaneous granuloma annulare with Hodgkin's lymphoma. *J Dermatol*, **23**, 405–407.
21. Wong, W.R., Yang, L.J., Kuo, T. et al (2000) Generalized granuloma annulare associated with granulomatous mycosis fungoides. *Dermatology*, **200**, 54–56.
22. Ben-Amital, D., Hodak, E., Lapidoth, M. et al (1999) Coexisting morphoea and granuloma annulare – are the conditions related? *Clin Exp Dermatol*, **24**, 86–89.
23. Granel, B., Serratrice, J., Rey, J. et al Chronic hepatitis C virus infection associated with a generalized granuloma annulare. *J Am Acad Dermatol*, **43**, 918–919.
24. Vázquez-López, F., González-López, M.A., Raya-Aguado, C. et al (2000) Localized granuloma annulare and autoimmune thyroiditis: new case report. *J Am Acad Dermatol*, **43**, 943–945.
25. Mautner, G.H., Knobler, E., Silvers, D.N. (1996) Granuloma annulare-like lesions and secondary hyperparathyroidism. *Cutis*, **57**, 172–174.
26. Ehrich, E.W., McGuire, J.L., Kim, Y.H. (1992) Association of granuloma annulare with sarcoidosis. *Int J Dermatol*, **128**, 855–856.
27. Tursen, U., Pata, C., Kaya, T.I. et al (2002) Generalized granuloma annulare associated with Plummer disease. *J Eur Acad Dermatol Venereol*, **16**, 419–420.
28. Jones, M.A., Laing, V.B., Files, B. et al (1998) Granuloma annulare mimicking septic emboli in a child with myelodysplastic syndrome. *J Am Acad Dermatol*, **38**, 106–108.
29. Lo, J.S., Guitart, J., Bergfeld, W.F. (1991) Granuloma annulare associated with metastatic adenocarcinoma. *Int J Dermatol*, **30**, 281–283.
30. Baykal, C., Ozkaya-Bayazit, E., Kaymaz, R. (2002) Granuloma annulare possibly triggered by antitetanus vaccination. *J Eur Acad Dermatol Venereol*, **16**, 516–518.
31. Wolf, F., Grezard, P., Berard, F. et al (1998) Generalized granuloma annulare and hepatitis B vaccination. *Eur J Dermatol*, **8**, 435–436.
32. Kakurai, M., Kiyosawa, T., Ohtsuki, M. et al (2001) Multiple lesions of granuloma annulare following BCG vaccination: case report and review of the literature. *Int J Dermatol*, **40**, 579–581.
33. Gibney, M.D., Nahass, G.T., Leonardi, C.L. (1996) Cutaneous reactions following herpes zoster infections: report of three cases and a review of the literature. *Br J Dermatol*, **134**, 504–509.
34. Requena, L., Kutzner, H., Escalonilla, P. et al (1998) Cutaneous reactions at sites of herpes zoster scars: an expanded spectrum. *Br J Dermatol*, **138**, 161–168.
35. Ohata, C., Shirabe, H., Takagi, K. et al (2000) Granuloma annulare in herpes zoster scars. *J Dermatol*, **27**, 166–169.
36. Brechtel, B., Kolde, G. (1996) Granuloma annulare disseminatum as a rare side effect of allopurinol. *Hautarzt*, **47**, 143.
37. Lim, A.C., Hart, K., Murrell, D. (2002) A granuloma annulare-like eruption associated with the use of amlodipine. *Australas J Dermatol*, **43**, 24–27.
38. Hsu, S., Lehner, A.C., Chang, J.R. (1999) Granuloma annulare localized to the palms. *J Am Acad Dermatol*, **41**, 287–288.
39. Sandwich, J.T., Davis, L.S. (1999) Granuloma annulare of the eyelid: a case report and review of the literature. *Pediatr Dermatol*, **16**, 373–376.
40. Mills, A., Chetty, R. (1992) Auricular granuloma annulare. A consequence of trauma? *Am J Dermatopathol*, **14**, 431–433.
41. Levin, N.A., Patterson, J.W., Yao, L.L., Wilson, B.B. (2002) Resolution of patch-type granuloma annulare lesions after biopsy. *J Am Acad Dermatol*, **46**, 426–429.

42. Friedman, S.J., Winkelmann, R.K. (1987) Familial granuloma annulare. Report of two cases and review of the literature. *J Am Acad Dermatol*, **16**, 600–605.
43. Uenotsuchi, T., Imayama, S., Furue, M. (1999) Seasonally recurrent granuloma annulare on sun-exposed areas. *Br J Dermatol*, **141**, 367.
44. Thomas, D.J.B., Rademaker, M., Munro, D.D. et al (1986) Visceral and skin granuloma annulare, diabetes, and polyendocrine disease. *BMJ*, **293**, 977–978.
45. Dabski, K., Winkelmann, R.K. (1989) Generalized granuloma annulare: histopathology and immuno-pathology. Systematic review of 100 cases and comparison with localized granuloma annulare. *J Am Acad Dermatol*, **20**, 28–39.
46. Friedman-Birnbaum, R., Haim, S., Gideone, O. et al (1978) Histocompatibility antigens in granuloma annulare: comparative study of the generalised and localised types. *Br J Dermatol*, **98**, 425–428.
47. Kunigvki, S., Kanda, S. (1996) Generalized granuloma annulare showing the unusual clinical feature of marked swelling of the hands. *Acta Derm Venereol*, **76**, 255–256.
48. Abraham, Z., Feuerman, E.J., Schafer, I. et al (2000) Disseminated granuloma annulare following erythema multiforme minor. *Australas J Dermatol*, **41**, 238–241.
49. Ozkan, S., Fetil, E., Izler, F. et al (2000) Anetoderma secondary to generalized granuloma annulare. *J Am Acad Dermatol*, **42**, 335–338.
50. Bardach, H.G. (1977) Granuloma annulare with transfollicular perforation. *J Cutan Pathol*, **4**, 99–104.
51. Abrusci, V., Weiss, E., Planus, G. (1988) Familial generalised perforating granuloma annulare. *Int J Dermatol*, **27**, 126–127.
52. Wright, A.L., Buxton, P.K., McLaren, K.M. (1989) Perforating granuloma annulare. *Int J Dermatol*, **28**, 466–467.
53. Penas, P.F., Jones-Caballer, M., Fraga, J. et al (1998) Perforating granuloma annulare. *Int J Dermatol*, **138**, 522–525.
54. Farrar, C.W., Bell, H.K., Dobson, C.M., Sharpe, G.R. (2002) Perforating granuloma annulare presenting on the ears. *Br J Dermatol*, **147**, 1026–1028.
55. Santos, R., Afonso, A., Cunha, F. et al (1999) Generalized perforating granuloma annulare. *J Eur Acad Dermatol Venereol*, **13**, 62–63.
56. Gradwell, E., Evans, S. (1998) Perforating granuloma annulare complicating tattoos. *Br J Dermatol*, **138**, 360–361.
57. Rubin, M., Lynch, F.W. (1966) Subcutaneous granuloma annulare. *Arch Dermatol*, **98**, 416–420.
58. Burrington, J.D. (1970) Pseudorheumatoid nodules in children: report of ten cases. *Pediatrics*, **45**, 473–478.
59. McDermott, M.B., Lind, A.C., Marley, E.F. et al (1998) Deep granuloma annulare (pseudorheumatoid nodule) in children: clinicopathologic study of 35 cases. *Pediatr Dev Pathol*, **1**, 300–308.
60. Evans, M.J., Blessing, K., Gray, E.S. (1994) Pseudorheumatoid nodule (deep granuloma annulare) of childhood: clinicopathological features of twenty patients. *Pediatr Dermatol*, **11**, 6–9.
61. Felner, E.I., Steinberg, J.B., Weinberg, A.G. (1997) Subcutaneous granuloma annulare: a review of 47 cases. *Pediatrics*, **100**, 965–967.
62. Kossard, S., Collins, A.G., Wegman, A., Hughes, M.R. (1990) Necrobiotic granulomata localized to the penis: a possible variant of subcutaneous granuloma annulare. *J Cutan Pathol*, **17**, 101–104.
63. Cronquist, S.D., Stashower, M.E., Benson, P.M. (1999) Deep dermal granuloma annulare presenting as an eyelid tumor in a child with review of pediatric eyelid lesions. *Pediatr Dermatol*, **16**, 377–380.
64. Lucky, A.W., Prose, N.S., Bove, K. et al (1992) Papular umbilicated granuloma annulare. *Arch Dermatol*, **128**, 1375–1378.
65. Harpster, E.F., Mauro, T., Barr, R.J. (1989) Linear granuloma annulare. *J Am Acad Dermatol*, **21**, 1138–1141.
66. McDow, R.A., Fields, J.P. (1987) Linear granuloma annulare of the finger. *Cutis*, **39**, 43–44.
67. Dahl, M.V., Callen, J.P. (1986) Granuloma annulare. In: Thiers, B.H., Dobson, R.L. (eds) Pathogenesis of skin disease. New York: Churchill Livingstone, pp 319–330.
68. Dahl, M.V., Cherney, K.J., Jordon, R.E. (1979) Circulating immune complexes in granuloma annulare. *Clin Res*, **27**, 312A.
69. Dahl, M.V., Ullman, S., Goltz, R.W. (1977) Vasculitis in granuloma annulare: histopathology and direct immunofluorescence. *Arch Dermatol*, **113**, 463–467.

70. Buechner, S.A., Winkelmann, R.K., Banks, P.M. (1983) Identification of T-cell subpopulations in granuloma annulare. *Arch Dermatol*, **119**, 125–128.
71. Gange, R.W., Black, M.M., Carrington, P. (1979) Defective neutrophil migration in granuloma annulare, necrobiosis lipoidica and sarcoidosis. *Arch Dermatol*, **115**, 32–35.
72. Umbert, P., Belcher, R.W., Winkelmann, R.K. (1976) Lymphokines (MIF) in the serum of patients with sarcoidosis and cutaneous granuloma annulare. *Br J Dermatol*, **95**, 481–485.
73. Andersen, B.L., Verdich, J. (1979) Granuloma annulare and diabetes mellitus. *Clin Exp Dermatol*, **4**, 31–37.
74. Friedman-Birnbaum, R., Weltfriend, S., Kerner, H. et al (1989) Elastic tissue changes in generalized granuloma annulare. *Am J Dermatopathol*, **11**, 429–433.
75. Bandel, C., DePrisco, G., Cockerell, C.J., Ehrig, T. (2002) Abundance of interstitial heparan sulfate in granuloma annulare but not in other mucinous skin diseases. *J Cutan Pathol*, **29**, 524–528.
76. Friedman-Birnbaum, R., Weltfriend, S., Munichor, M. et al (1989) A comparative histopathologic study of generalized and localized granuloma annulare. *Am J Dermatopathol*, **11**, 144–148.
77. Romero, L.S., Kantor, G.R. (1998) Eosinophils are not a clue to the pathogenesis of granuloma annulare. *Am J Dermatopathol*, **20**, 29–34.
78. Magro, C.M., Crowson, A.N., Regauer, S. (1996) Granuloma annulare and necrobiosis lipoidica tissue reactions as a manifestation of systemic disease. *Hum Pathol*, **27**, 50–56.
79. Chu, P., Connolly, K., Leboit, P.E. (1994) The histopathologic spectrum of palisaded neutrophilic and granulomatous dermatitis. *Arch Dermatol*, **130**, 1278–1283.
80. Perrin, C., Lacour, J.P., Castanet, J. et al (2001) Interstitial granulomatous drug eruption with a histological pattern of interstitial granulomatous dermatitis. *Am J Dermatopathol*, **23**, 295–298.
81. Trotter, M.J., Crawford, R.I., O'Connell, J.X. et al (1996) Mitotic activity in granuloma annulare: a clinicopathologic study of 20 cases. *J Cutan Pathol*, **23**, 537–545.
82. Su, L.D., Kim, Y.H., Leboit, P.E. et al (2002) Interstitial mycosis fungoides, a variant of mycosis fungoides resembling granuloma annulare and inflammatory morphea. *J Cutan Pathol*, **29**, 135–141.
83. Shapiro, P.E., Pinto, F.J. (1994) The histologic spectrum of mycosis fungoides/Sézary syndrome (cutaneous T-cell lymphoma). A review of 222 biopsies, including newly described patterns and the earliest pathologic changes. *Am J Surg Pathol*, **18**, 645–667.

Necrobiosis lipoidica

Clinical features

Necrobiosis lipoidica is a disease of unknown etiology, which shows a strong association with diabetes mellitus.[1-6] Although the affiliation is likely to have pathogenic implications, the precise mechanism by which the lesions of necrobiosis lipoidica develop, is nevertheless, unknown and the nature of the relationship between the two diseases is unclear. Therefore, although the diagnosis of diabetes is most often established before the onset of the skin lesions, on occasion, typical plaques may precede the apparent onset of diabetes mellitus by several years. The course of the cutaneous disease does not appear to be related to the hyperglycemia, and treatment of diabetes does not affect the outcome of the cutaneous lesions. In one study, proteinuria, retinopathy and smoking were more common in patients with necrobiosis lipoidica compared with patients with diabetes but no skin disease.[7] Interestingly, however, only a minority of patients with necrobiosis lipoidica have diabetes mellitus. It has been shown recently that 11% of patients with necrobiosis lipoidica have diabetes mellitus and a further 11% develop the disease or altered glucose tolerance on follow-up.[8]

Necrobiosis lipoidica may develop in both juvenile (type I) and maturity-onset (type II) diabetes. Necrobiosis lipoidica has been documented in patients with endocrine disorders other than diabetes such as hypo- and hyperthyroidism, and also in association with inflammatory bowel disease and vasculitis.[9] One non-diabetic patient with necrobiosis lipoidica and ataxia telangiectasia has been reported.[10] Exceptionally, necrobiosis lipoidica and granuloma annulare have presented simultaneously.[11] The disease has also been documented in association with sarcoidosis.[12,13]

Necrobiosis lipoidica shows a marked female preponderance (3.3:1) and, although a wide age range may be affected, patients present most often in their fourth decade (those associated with diabetes mellitus) or fifth decade (those not associated with diabetes mellitus). The condition is rare in childhood and is often associated with diabetes mellitus. It also appears to be related to underlying renal and retinal disease.[14-18] Familial cases may also occur, with, or without, diabetes.[19,20]

The characteristic lesion, sometimes referred to as a sclerodermatous plaque, is round or oval, circumscribed, and often has a slightly elevated rim. It is typically a few millimeters to several centimeters in diameter. Newly acquired lesions are often red–brown in color, but with progression the center of the lesion becomes yellowish and the peripheral border may acquire a violaceous hue. Larger plaques are usually irregular and more variably shaped. Scaling and telangiectasia may become evident. Ulceration appears to be relatively frequent and has been reported in up to 13% of patients.[21-23] Atypical forms may also be found: patients sometimes manifest papules and nodular lesions, and occasionally plaques resembling granuloma annulare are seen (it should be noted, however, that rarely these two conditions appear to coexist).[11,24] Rare clinical presentations with papulonecrotic and nodulo-ulcerative lesions mimicking gummata or erythema induratum have been documented, albeit exceptionally.[20] The lesions may be solitary or multiple, often symmetrical, and show a predilection for the lower extremities, in particular the pretibial area (*Figs 8.54–8.57*). They may also occur on the arms, hands, fingers, abdomen, nipples and back; rarely the face or scalp is affected, in which case diabetes is seldom present.[25]

It is doubtful whether the so-called atypical necrobiosis lipoidica of the face and scalp represents a variant of necrobiosis lipoidica. The name was chosen because of the coexistence of typical lesions of necrobiosis lipoidica on the shins of one of the patients in the original series. However, most patients do not present with classic lesions of necrobiosis lipoidica elsewhere and the microscopic findings do not resemble the latter entity.[26]

Involvement of the penis with lesions resembling chronic balanitis has been described.[27-29] Rarely, lesions are associated with Koebner's phenomenon.[30-32] Necrobiotic and silicotic granulomata developing within phlebectomy scars have also been reported.[33]

The disease tends to chronicity. It is of interest that necrobiosis lipoidica has been reported to be associated with cutaneous hypo- or complete anesthesia in both diabetic and non-diabetic patients.[34,35] One study found loss of nerves within lesions and, based on this finding, the authors postulated that destruction of nerves might explain the sensory loss that is observed in some patients.[35] Hypohidrosis and partial alopecia have also been reported.[36]

Rarely, squamous carcinoma may arise in longstanding lesions.[37-40]

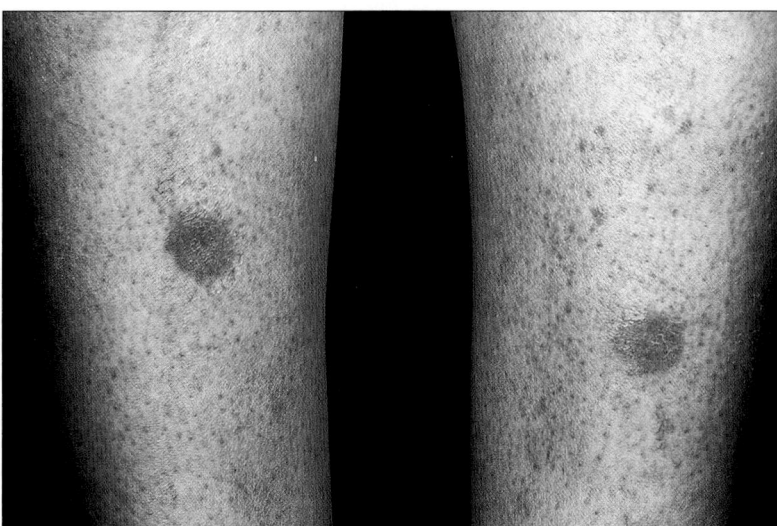

Fig. 8.54
Necrobiosis lipoidica: symmetrical early lesions with erythema. By courtesy of the Institute of Dermatology, London, UK.

Pathogenesis and histological features

The precise pathogenesis of necrobiosis lipoidica is unknown. Of primary importance is the temporal relationship between collagen degeneration and the inflammatory infiltrate.[41] The close association of necrobiosis lipoidica and diabetes mellitus suggests a causal relationship, but the exact mechanism is uncertain. In the past, some 60% of patients with necrobiosis lipoidica were reported as having coexistent diabetes mellitus.[2,4,42,43] However, its reported prevalence in diabetes is only of the order of 3/1000.[41] Furthermore, a recent study has found that only a minority of patients with necrobiosis lipoidica have diabetes.[8]

It has been suggested that the lesions develop as a consequence of diabetic microangiopathy: the vessel walls in lesions of necrobiosis lipoidica are typically thickened by a diastase-resistant PAS-positive material. This does not explain the development of necrobiosis lipoidica in non-diabetic patients or the absence of the disease in patients with established microvascular lesions. Study of microcirculation by Doppler flowmetry and oxygen partial pressure in necrobiosis lipoidica lesions in non-diabetics has demonstrated an altered microcirculation.[44] Low oxygen and high carbon dioxide pressures, presumably reflecting ischemia, characterize necrobiotic plaques.[45] Such vascular changes, although possibly causal, could equally well develop as a consequence of the necrobiotic changes. Aberrant platelet aggregation may also play a role in pathogenesis. Platelet survival times are markedly reduced in patients with necrobiosis lipoidica.[46] Whether this is of pathogenic importance is uncertain.

Autoantibodies against cytoskeleton proteins have been observed in sera from patients with necrobiosis lipoidica. These autoantibodies (IgG antitroponin, antidesmin, antikeratin, anti-insulin, antitrinitrophenol, and IgA and IgM antikeratin) were found to be elevated in patients with necrobiosis lipoidica compared with diabetic patients without evidence of necrobiosis lipoidica.[47] What role, if any, these autoantibodies play in the pathogenesis of necrobiosis lipoidica is unclear. Synthesis of collagen by fibroblasts cultured from lesions is decreased compared with fibroblasts from normal skin.[48]

Also of uncertain significance is the reported detection, by immuno-fluorescence, of immunoreactants (IgM and C3) in blood vessel walls in some cases of necrobiosis lipoidica.[49,50] Epidermal dendritic S-100 positive cells are increased in number.[51] Whether this reflects an immunological aspect to the development of necrobiosis lipoidica has yet to be determined.

Glut-1 (the human erythrocyte glucose transporter) is expressed by the fibroblasts in areas of sclerotic collagen from biopsies of patients with necrobiosis lipoidica.[52] This raises the possibility of an altered transport of glucose in the affected areas contributing to the histopathological features seen in this disease.

The histopathological features are variable, depending to some extent on the presence or absence of coexistent diabetes mellitus.[53,54] The palisading granuloma with necrobiosis is more typical of the diabetes-related variant, whereas a granulomatous sarcoidal type of reaction is more often a feature of non-diabetes-related necrobiosis. Nevertheless, there is very considerable overlap and in the majority of cases one cannot predict, on histological grounds alone which cases are, and which are not, diabetes-related.

The epidermal changes are usually inconspicuous or absent. There may, however, be acanthosis or atrophy and hyperkeratosis is not uncommon.

The hallmark of necrobiosis lipoidica is the palisading necrobiotic granuloma. Large, often confluent areas of necrobiosis are present, usually centered in the lower dermis, although the superficial dermis and subcutaneous fat may also be affected (*Figs 8.58–8.60*). When the

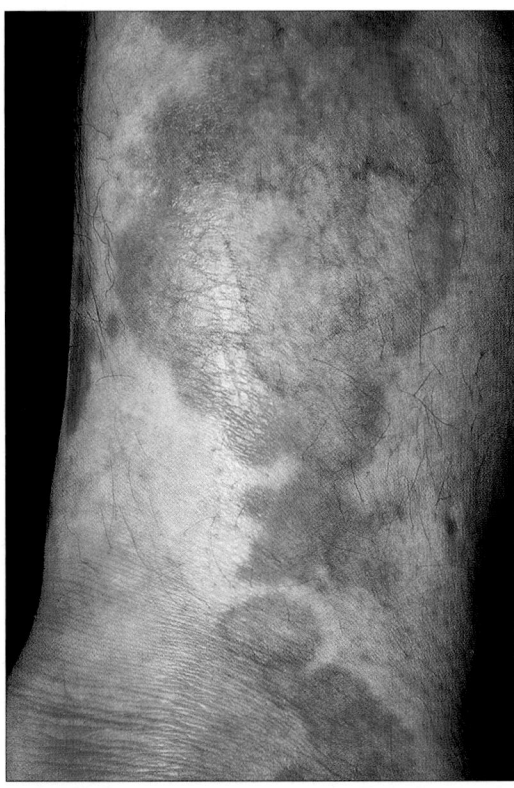

Fig. 8.55
Necrobiosis lipoidica: early lesion with an erythematous border. By courtesy of the Institute of Dermatology, London, UK.

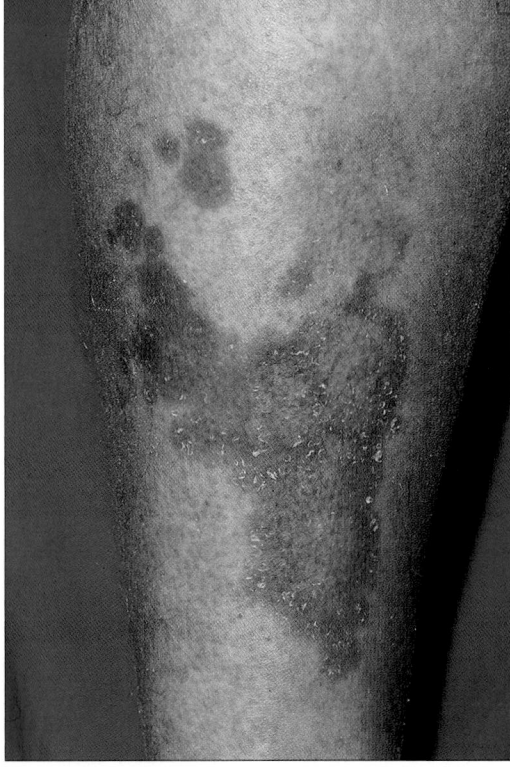

Fig. 8.56
Necrobiosis lipoidica: lesion on shin showing atrophy, telangiectasia and an active inflammatory edge. By courtesy of R.A. Marsden, MD, St George's Hospital, London, UK.

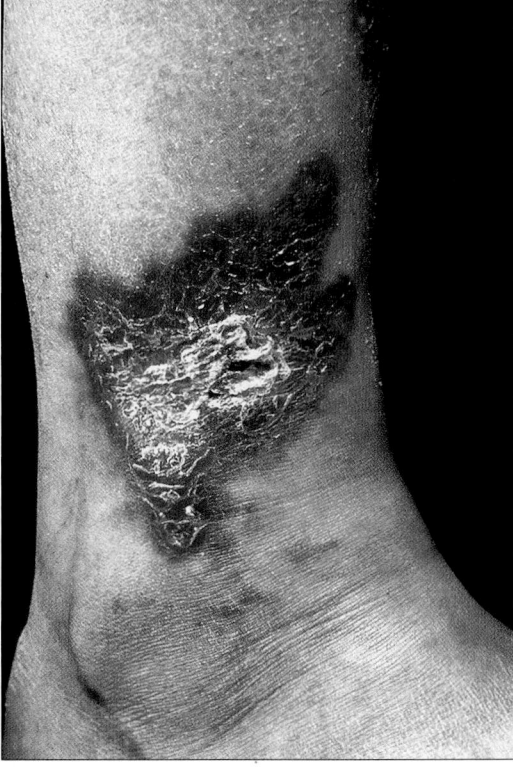

Fig. 8.57
Necrobiosis lipoidica: chronic lesion with ulceration and crusting. By courtesy of the Institute of Dermatology, London, UK.

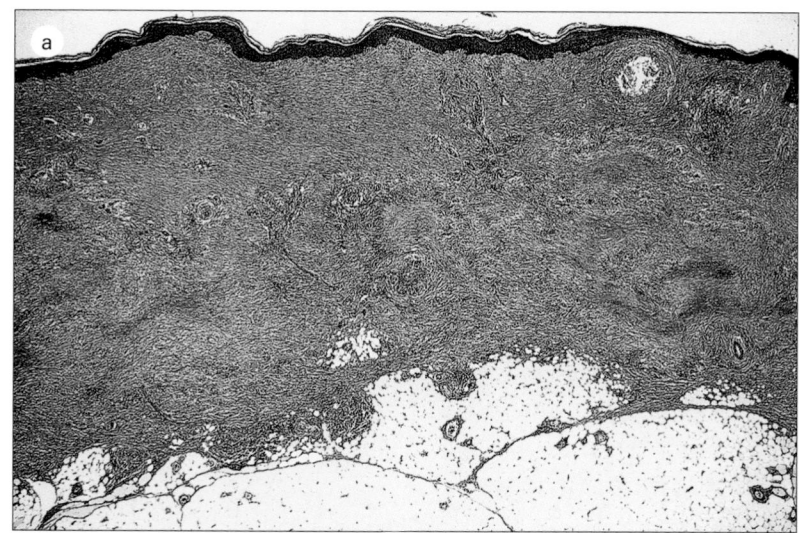

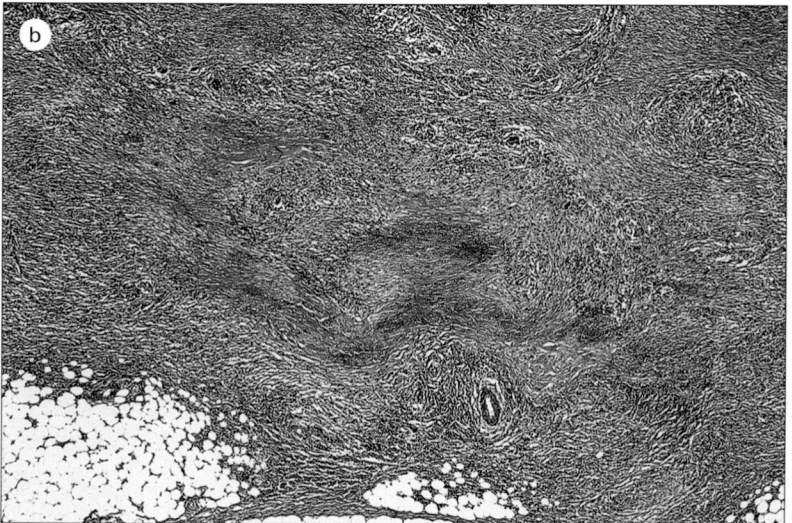

Fig. 8.58
(a, b) Necrobiosis lipoidica: the epidermis is unaffected; there is extensive necrobiosis in the reticular dermis. A heavy chronic inflammatory cell infiltrate is present.

subcutaneous fat is involved, the changes are seen mainly in the septa. The foci of necrobiosis consist of eosinophilic, swollen or degenerate collagen; often appearing hyalinized with a surrounding infiltrate of variable numbers of lymphocytes and histiocytes (*Fig. 8.61*). Aggregates of lymphoid cells, with or without germinal center formation, are frequently found.[55] Plasma cells are almost invariably present. The necrobiotic foci sometimes contain mucin. Palisading is variable, being more conspicuous in those instances associated with a heavy inflammatory cell infiltrate. The areas of necrobiosis are associated with loss of elastic tissue (*Fig. 8.62*). Usually epithelioid histiocytes and giant cells are evident and sometimes there are well-formed granulomata resembling the sarcoidal type of necrobiotic histological reaction (see below) (*Fig. 8.63*). Lipid droplets, best seen with oil red O or Sudan IV staining on frozen tissue, are almost invariably present in the necrobiotic foci. Usually a mild to moderate perivascular lymphocytic infiltrate is seen in the adjacent dermis. Cholesterol clefts are rare and only exceptionally may be prominent.[56,57]

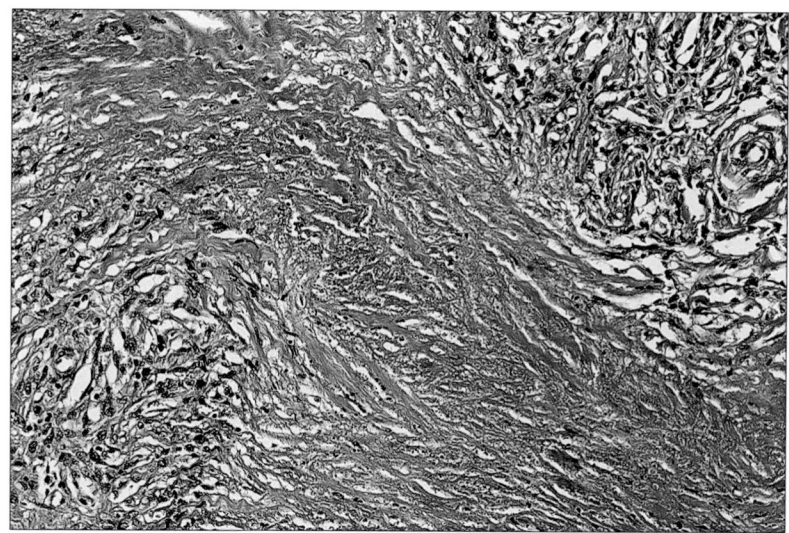

Fig. 8.60
Necrobiosis lipoidica: the degenerate collagen is surrounded by a palisade of histiocytes, lymphocytes and fibroblasts.

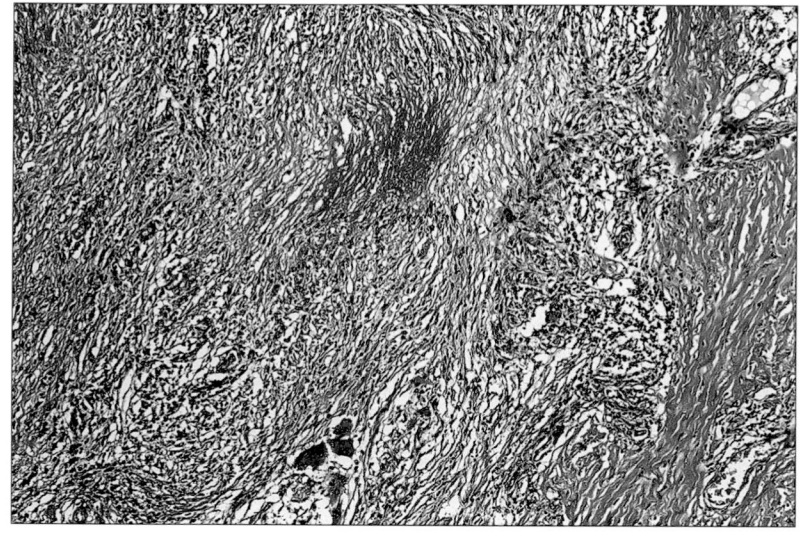

Fig. 8.59
Necrobiosis lipoidica: high power view of *Fig. 8.58*.

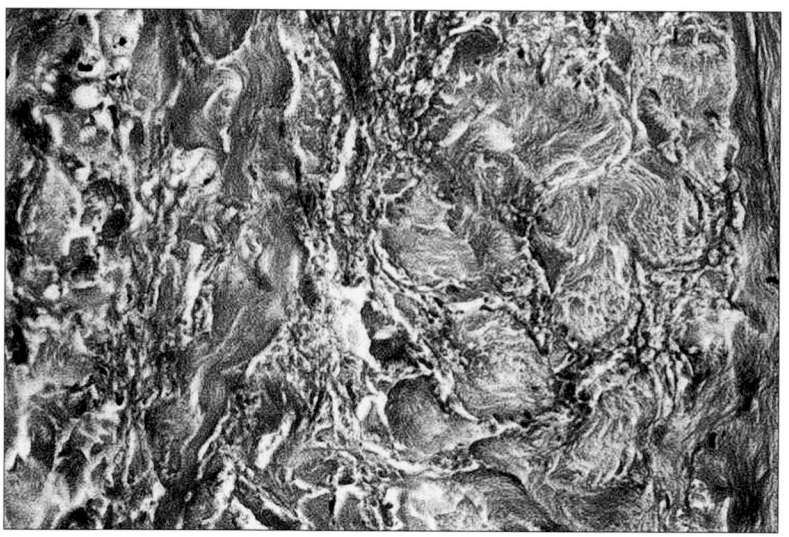

Fig. 8.61
Necrobiosis lipoidica: the necrobiotic collagen is intensely eosinophilic and swollen and, in places, granular.

If one searches carefully, vascular changes are often seen in necrobiosis lipoidica. These consist of blood vessel wall thickening, with intimal proliferation and narrowing of the lumen. Occasionally thrombi are noted. Sometimes increased numbers of vessels are a feature. The vascular changes are more obvious in patients with associated diabetes mellitus or other systemic disease. These changes are particularly severe in those cases where necrobiosis is very marked. One study also showed that neutrophilic and granulomatous vasculopathies correlated with systemic disease.[58] In addition, telangiectatic superficial venules are a common feature. Cases with necrobiosis-like features and significant vasculitis and neutrophilic infiltrates in the setting of systemic disease are discussed in detail in the section on palisaded neutrophilic and granulomatous dermatitis associated with systemic disease (see p. 320).

In the diffuse variant there is very widespread necrobiosis with a minimal inflammatory cell response; such cases are usually associated with diabetes (*Fig. 8.64*). Sometimes linear infiltrates of histiocytes between collagen fibers are a feature, as in granuloma annulare. Lipomembranous fat necrosis is a feature in occasional cases.[59]

In the sarcoidal type of necrobiosis lipoidica, which is more often a feature of the non-diabetes mellitus-associated variant, the appearances are those of naked epithelioid cell granulomata, particularly in the lower dermis (*Fig. 8.65*). Langhans' and foreign body giant cells are usually conspicuous and a lymphocytic and plasma cell infiltrate may be evident (*Fig. 8.66*). Necrobiosis is usually minimal; multiple levels may have to be examined before its presence is confirmed (*Fig. 8.67*). The sarcoidal type of necrobiosis lipoidica in patients without diabetes mellitus has in the past been described as Miescher's granuloma.

Perforating necrobiosis lipoidica is associated with transepidermal elimination of necrobiotic collagen and also degenerated elastotic material (*Figs 8.68–8.70*).[57,60,61] Clinically, this presents as comedo-like plugs localized mainly in the periphery of the lesions.

Differential diagnosis

Necrobiosis lipoidica must be distinguished from granuloma annulare, rheumatoid nodule, actinic granuloma and granuloma multiforme.

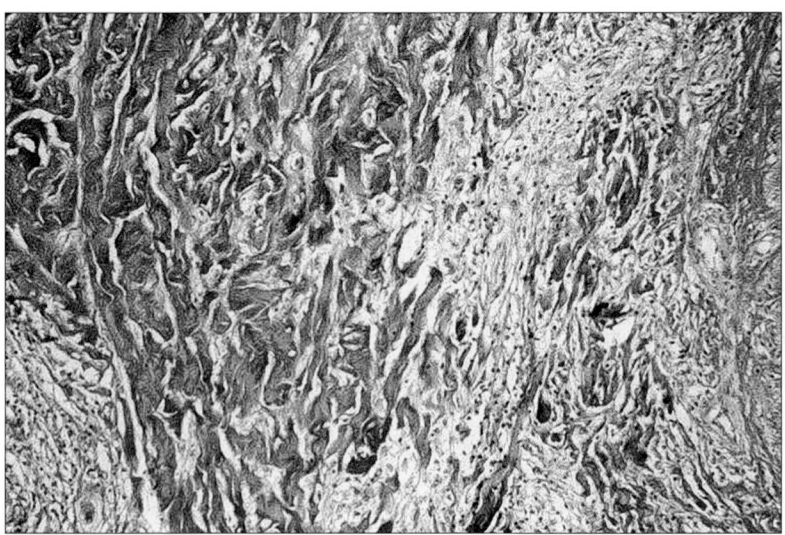

Fig. 8.62
Necrobiosis lipoidica: note the complete absence of elastic tissue. Elastic–van Gieson.

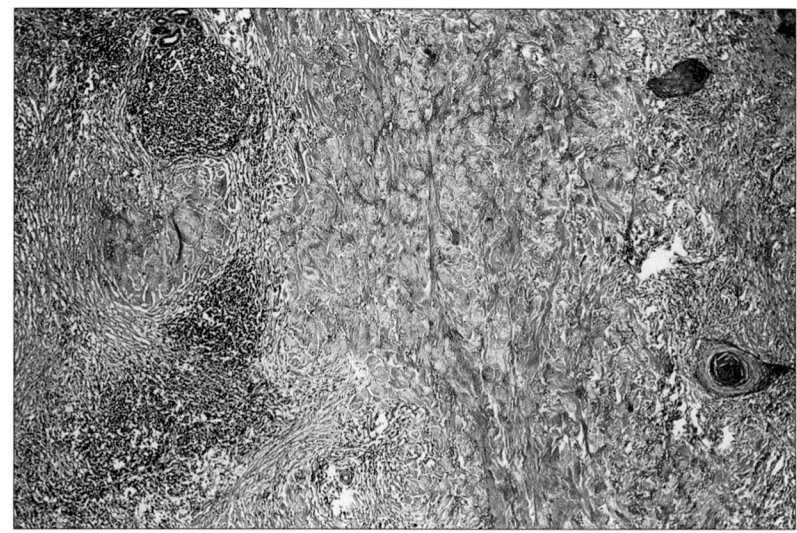

Fig. 8.64
Necrobiosis lipoidica (diffuse variant): a broad band of confluent necrobiosis has destroyed the entire reticular dermis.

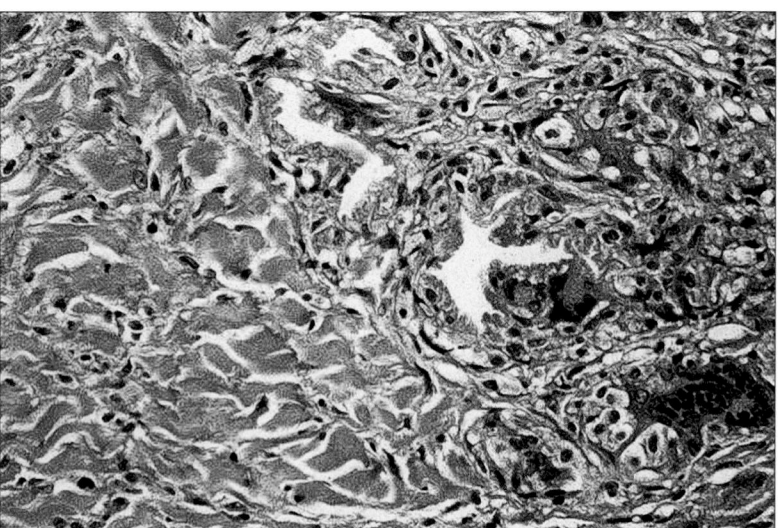

Fig. 8.63
Necrobiosis lipoidica: necrobiosis is present on the left side of the field; on the right there is a granulomatous infiltrate with conspicuous multinucleate giant cells.

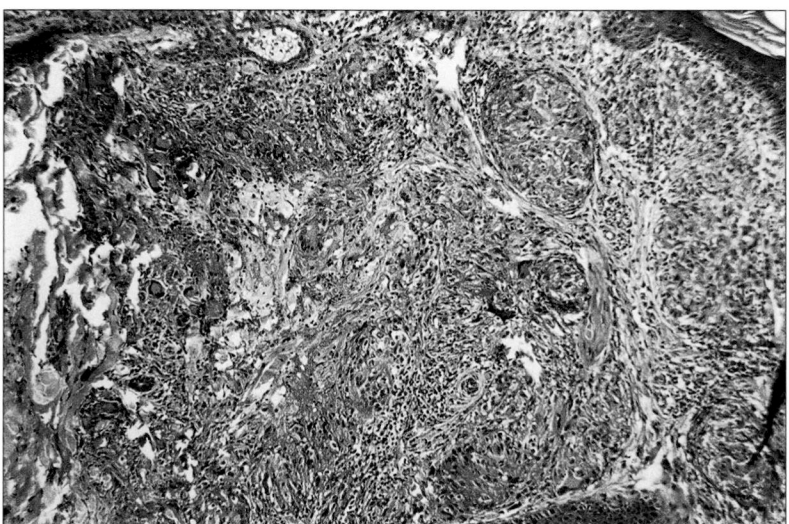

Fig. 8.65
Necrobiosis lipoidica (granulomatous variant): well-defined non-caseating granulomata replace the reticular dermis. Necrobiosis is present to the left of center.

Points of distinction are summarized in *Table 8.1*. The presence of massive necrobiosis associated with numerous cholesterol clefts, bizarre multinucleated giant cells and Touton-type giant cells distinguishes necrobiotic xanthogranuloma from necrobiosis lipoidica. As noted above, prominent cholesterol cleft formation, a feature that usually suggests necrobiotic xanthogranuloma, may rarely be seen in necrobiosis lipoidica.[56,57] Small punch biopsies may not be adequate for definitive evaluation and sampling bias may be misleading. Clinical correlation should be taken into consideration before giving a final diagnosis.

References

1. Hare, P.J. (1955) Necrobiosis lipoidica. *Br J Dermatol*, 67, 365–38.
2. Muller, S.A., Winkelmann, R.K. (1966) Necrobiosis lipoidica diabeticorum. *Arch Dermatol*, 93, 272–281.
3. Wood, M.G., Beerman, H. (1960) Necrobiosis lipoidica, granuloma annulare and rheumatoid nodule. *J Invest Dermatol*, 34, 139–147.
4. Bauer, M., Levan, N.E. (1970) Diabetic dermangiopathy: a spectrum including pigmented pretibial patches and necrobiosis lipoidica diabeticorum. *Br J Dermatol*, 83, 528–535.
5. Jelmek, J.E. (1995) Cutaneous manifestations of diabetes mellitus. *J Am Acad Dermatol*, 32, 143–144.
6. Ferringer, T., Miller, F. 3rd (2002) Cutaneous manifestations of diabetes mellitus. *Dermatol Clin*, 20, 483–492.
7. Kelly, W.F., Nicholas, J., Adams, J. et al (1993) Necrobiosis lipoidica diabeticorum: association with background retinopathy, smoking, and proteinuria. A case controlled study. *Diabet Med*, 10, 725–728.
8. O'Toole, E.A., Kennedy, U., Nolan, J.J. et al (1999) Necrobiosis lipoidica: only a minority of patients have diabetes mellitus. *Br J Dermatol*, 141, 725–727.
9. Murray, C.A., Miller, R.A. (1997) Necrobiosis lipoidica diabeticorum and thyroid disease. *Int J Dermatol*, 36, 799–800.
10. Gotz, A., Eckert, F., Lanthaler, M. (1994) Ataxia-telangiectasia (Loid–Barr syndrome) associated with ulcerating necrobiosis lipoidica. *J Am Acad Dermatol*, 31, 124–126.
11. Schwartz, M.E. (1982) Necrobiosis lipoidica and granuloma annulare. Simultaneous occurrence in a patient. *Arch Dermatol*, 118, 192–193.
12. Monk, B.E., Du Vivier, A.W.P. (1987) Necrobiosis lipoidica and sarcoidosis. *Clin Exp Dermatol*, 12, 294–295.

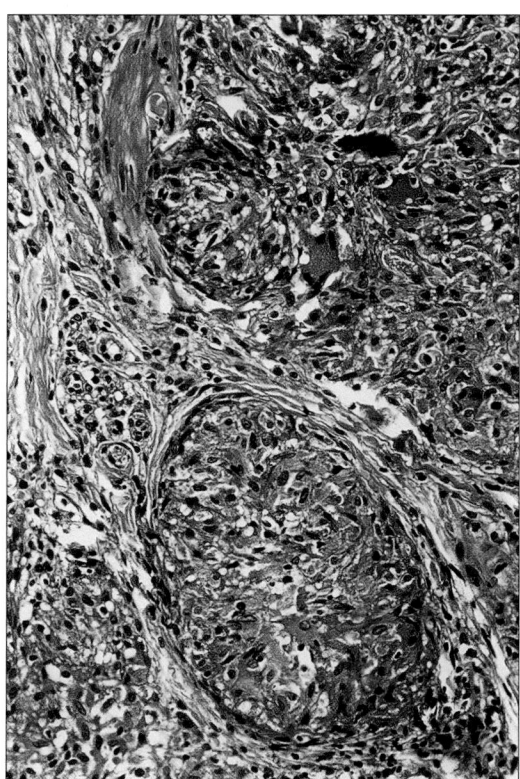

Fig. 8.66
Necrobiosis lipoidica (granulomatous variant): the naked granulomata are very reminiscent of sarcoidosis. Note the multinucleate giant cells.

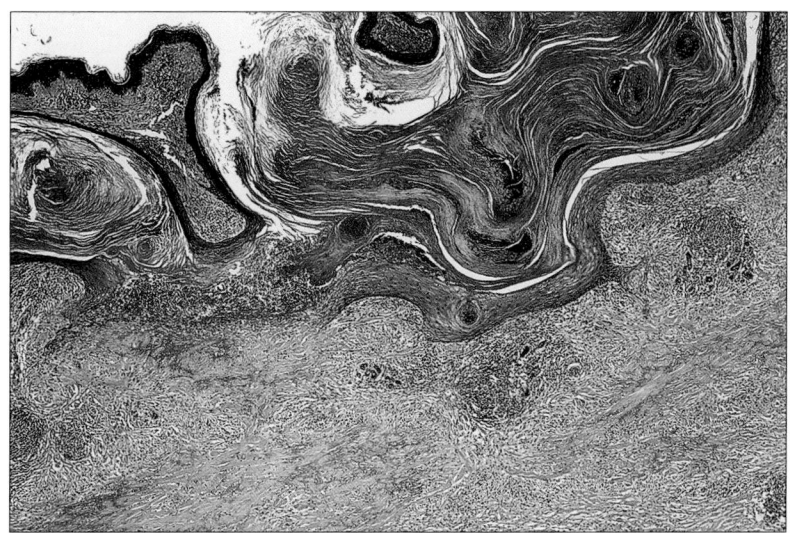

Fig. 8.68
Perforating necrobiosis lipoidica: there is widespread hyperkeratosis and crusting. A perforating channel is seen on the left side of the picture.

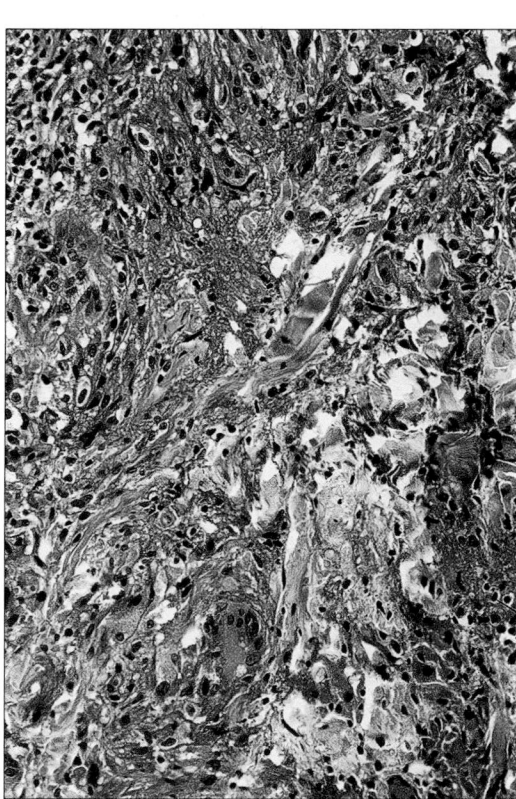

Fig. 8.67
Necrobiosis lipoidica (granulomatous variant): higher power view of the necrobiotic focus seen in *Fig. 8.65*.

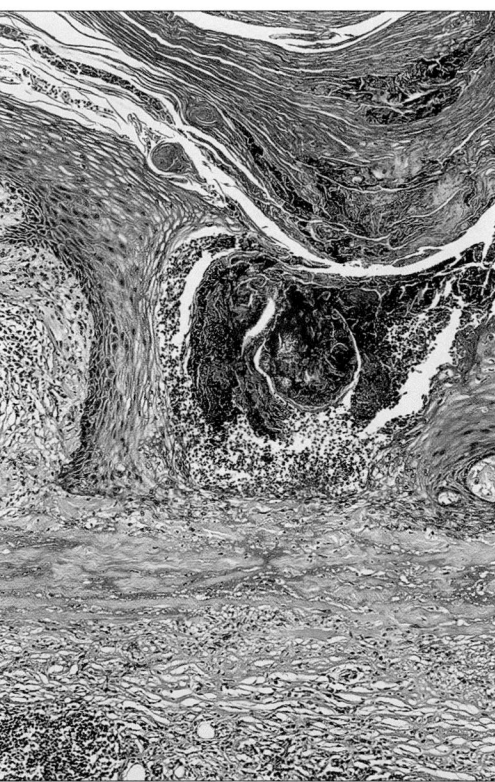

Fig. 8.69
Perforating necrobiosis: close-up view of the perforating channel.

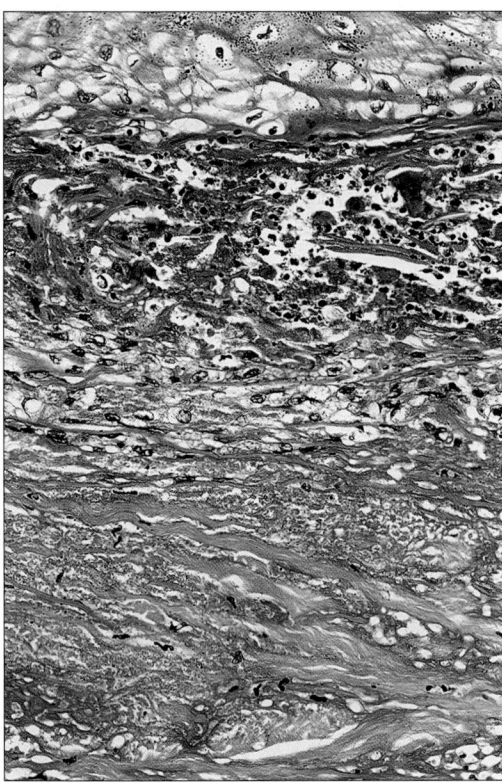

Fig. 8.70
Perforating necrobiosis: the dermis immediately beneath the site of perforation shows severe necrobiotic change.

13. Gudmunsen, K., Smith, O., Dervan, P., Powell, F.C. (1991) Necrobiosis lipoidica and sarcoidosis. *Clin Exp Dermatol*, **16**, 287–291.
14. De Silva, B.D., Schofield, O.M., Walker, J.D. (1999) The prevalence of necrobiosis lipoidica diabeticorum in children with type I diabetes. *Br J Dermatol*, **141**, 593–594.
15. Edidin, D.V. (1985) Cutaneous manifestations of diabetes mellitus in children. *Pediatr Dermatol*, **2**, 161–179.
16. Szabo, R.M., Harris, G.D., Burke, W.A. (2001) Necrobiosis lipoidica in a 9-year-old girl with new-onset type II diabetes mellitus. *Pediatr Dermatol*, **18**, 316–319.
17. Yigit, S., Estrada, E. (2002) Recurrent necrobiosis lipoidica diabeticorum associated with venous insufficiency in an adolescent with poorly controlled type 2 diabetes mellitus. *J Pediatr*, **141**, 280–282.
18. Verrotti, A., Chiarelli, F., Amerio, P. et al (1995) Necrobiosis lipoidica diabeticorum in children and adolescents: a clue for underlying renal and retinal disease. *Pediatr Dermatol*, **12**, 220–223.
19. Seviour, P.W., Elkeles, R.S. (1985) Necrobiosis lipoidica in two diabetic sisters. *Clin Exp Dermatol*, **10**, 155–160.
20. Findlay, G.H., Morrison, J.G., de Beer, H.A. (1981). Non-diabetic necrobiosis lipoidica. Hitherto unrecognized papulonecrotic, nodulo-ulcerative and familial forms of the disease. *S Afr Med J*, **59**, 323–326.
21. Berkson, M.H., Bondi, E.E., Margolis, D.J. (1994) Ulcerated necrobiosis lipoidica diabeticorum in a patient with a history of generalized granuloma annulare. *Cutis*, **53**, 85–86.
22. Evans, A.V., Atherton, D.J. (2002) Recalcitrant ulcers in necrobiosis lipoidica diabeticorum healed by topical granulocyte–macrophage colony-stimulating factor. *Br J Dermatol*, **147**, 1023–1025.
23. Dwyer, C.M., Dick, D. (1993) Ulceration in necrobiosis lipoidica – a case report and study. *Clin Exp Dermatol*, **18**, 366–369.
24. Cohen, I.J.K. (1984) Necrobiosis lipoidica and granuloma annulare. *J Am Acad Dermatol*, **10**, 123–124.
25. Kavanagh, G.M., Novelli, M., Hartog, M. et al (1993) Necrobiosis lipoidica – involvement of atypical sites. *Clin Exp Dermatol*, **18**, 543–544.
26. Wilson Jones, E. (1971) Necrobiosis lipoidica presenting on the face and scalp. *Trans St John's Hosp Dermatol Soc*, **57**, 202–220.
27. España, A., Sánchez-Yus, E., Serna, M.J. et al (1994) Chronic balanitis with palisading granuloma: an atypical genital localization of necrobiosis lipoidica responsive to pentoxifylline. *Dermatology*, **188**, 222–225.
28. el Sayed, F., Elbadir, S., Ferrere, J. et al (1997) Chronic balanitis: an unusual localization of necrobiosis lipoidica. *Genitourin Med*, **73**, 579–580.
29. Velasco-Pastor, A.M., Gil-Mateo, M.P., Martínez-Aparicio, A. et al (1996) Necrobiosis lipoidica of the glans penis. *Br J Dermatol*, **135**, 154–155.
30. Ghate, J.V., Williford, P.M., Sane, D.C. et al (2001) Necrobiosis lipoidica associated with Koebner's phenomenon in a patient with diabetes. *Cutis*, **67**, 158–160.
31. Llajam, M.A. (1990) Koebner's phenomenon and necrobiosis lipoidica. *Br J Clin Pract*, **44**, 715.
32. Patel, G.K., Harding, K.G., Mills, C.M. (2000) Severe disabling Koebnerizing ulcerated necrobiosis lipoidica successfully managed with topical PUVA. *Br J Dermatol*, **143**, 668–669.
33. Vion, B., Burri, G., Ramelet, A.A. (1997) Necrobiotic lipoidica and silicotic granulomata on Muller's phlebectomy scars. *Dermatology*, **194**, 55–58.
34. Mann, R.J., Harmann, R.R.M. (1984) Cutaneous anaesthesia in necrobiosis lipoidica. *Br J Dermatol*, **110**, 323–325.
35. Boulton, A.J., Cutfeld, R.G., Abouganem, D. et al (1988) Necrobiosis lipoidica diabeticorum: a clinicopathologic study. *J Am Acad Dermatol*, **18**, 530–537.
36. Hatzos, J., Varelzidis, A., Tosca, A. et al (1983) Sweat gland disturbances in granuloma annulare and necrobiosis lipoidica. *Br J Dermatol*, **108**, 705–709.
37. Kossard, S., Collins, E., Wargon, O. et al (1987) Squamous cell carcinomas developing in bilateral lesions of necrobiosis lipoidica. *Australas J Dermatol*, **28**, 14–17.
38. Imtiaz, K.E., Khaleeli, A.A. (2001) Squamous cell carcinoma developing in necrobiosis lipoidica. *Diabet Med*, **18**, 325–328.
39. Belijaards, R.C., Groen, J., Starink, T.M. (1990) Bilateral squamous cell carcinoma arising in long-standing necrobiosis lipoidica. *Dermatologica*, **180**, 96–98.
40. Gudi, V.S., Campbell, S., Gould, D.J. et al (2000) Squamous cell carcinoma in an area of necrobiosis lipoidica diabeticorum: a case report. *Clin Exp Dermatol*, **25**, 597–599.
41. Lowitt, M.H., Dover, J.S. (1991) Necrobiosis lipoidica. *J Am Acad Dermatol*, **25**, 735–748.
42. Muller, S.A., Winkelmann, R.K. (1966) Necrobiosis lipoidica diabeticorum. Results of glucose tolerance tests in nondiabetic patients. *JAMA*, **195**, 433–466.
43. Hill, D.M., Rhodes, E.L., Sheldon, J. et al (1966) Necrobiosis lipoidica: serum insulin and prednisone–glycosuria tests in a non-diabetic group. *Br J Dermatol*, **78**, 332–336.
44. Boateng, B., Hiller, D., Albrecht, H.P. et al (1993) Cutaneous microcirculation in pretibial necrobiosis lipoidica. Comparative laser Doppler flowmetry and oxygen partial pressure determinations in patients and healthy controls. *Hautarzt*, **44**, 581–586.
45. Brungger, A. (1989) Transcutaneous measurement of oxygen and carbon dioxide pressure in necrobiosis lipoidica. *Hautarzt*, **40**, 231–232.
46. Quimby, S.R., Muller, S.A., Schroeter, A.L. et al (1989) Necrobiosis lipoidica diabeticorum: platelet survival and response to platelet inhibitors. *Cutis*, **43**, 213–216.
47. Haralambous, S., Blackwell, C., Mappouras, D.G. et al (1995) Increased natural autoantibody activity to cytoskeleton proteins in sera from patients with necrobiosis lipoidica, with or without insulin-dependent diabetes mellitus. *Autoimmunity*, **20**, 267–275.
48. Oikarinen, A., Mortenhumer, M., Kallioinen, M. et al (1987) Necrobiosis lipoidica: ultrastructural and biochemical demonstration of a collagen defect. *J Invest Dermatol*, **88**, 227–232.
49. Quimby, S.R., Muller, S.A., Schroeter, A.L. (1988) The cutaneous immunopathology of necrobiosis lipoidica diabeticorum. *Arch Dermatol*, **124**, 1364–1371.
50. Ullman, S., Dahl, M.V. (1977) Necrobiosis lipoidica: an immunofluorescence study. *Arch Dermatol*, **113**, 1671–1673.
51. Chambers, B., Milligan, A., Fletcher, A. (1990) Epidermal dendritic S-100 positive cells in necrobiosis lipoidica and granuloma annulare. *Br J Dermatol*, **123**, 765–768.
52. Holland, C., Givens, V., Smoller, B.R. (2001) Expression of the human erythrocyte glucose transporter Glut-1 in areas of sclerotic collagen in necrobiosis lipoidica. *J Cutan Pathol*, **28**, 287–290.
53. Muller, S.A., Winkelmann, R.K. (1966) Necrobiosis lipoidica diabeticorum: histopathologic study of 98 cases. *Arch Dermatol*, **94**, 1–10.
54. Gray, H.R., Graham, J.H., Johnson, W.C. (1965) Necrobiosis lipoidica: a histopathological and histochemical study. *J Invest Dermatol*, **44**, 369–380.
55. Alegre, V.A., Winkelmann, R.K. (1988) A new histopathologic feature of necrobiosis lipoidica diabeticorum: lymphoid nodules. *J Cutan Pathol*, **15**, 75–77.
56. Gibson, L.E., Reizner, G.T., Winkelmann, R.K. (1988) Necrobiosis lipoidica diabeticorum with cholesterol clefts in the differential diagnosis of necrobiotic xanthogranuloma. *J Cutan Pathol*, **15**, 18–21.
57. De la Torre, C., Losada, M.J., Cruces, M.J. (1999) Necrobiosis lipoidica: a case with prominent cholesterol clefting and transepithelial elimination. *Am J Dermatopathol*, **21**, 575–577.
58. Magro, C.M., Crowson, A.N., Regauer, S. (1996) Granuloma annulare and necrobiosis lipoidica tissue reactions as a manifestation of systemic disease. *Hum Pathol*, **27**, 50–56.
59. Snow, J.L., Su, W.P. (1996) Lipomembranous (membranocystic) fat necrosis. Clinicopathologic correlation of 38 cases. *Am J Dermatopathol*, **18**, 151–155.
60. Parra, C.A. (1977) Transepithelial elimination in necrobiosis lipoidica. *Br J Dermatol*, **96**, 83–86.
61. McDonald, L., Zanolli, M.D., Boyd, A.S. (1996) Perforating elastosis in necrobiosis lipoidica diabeticorum. *Cutis*, **57**, 336–338.

Rheumatoid nodule

Clinical features

Rheumatoid nodules are subcutaneous lesions that develop at sites of trauma or at pressure points in approximately 30% of adults with rheumatoid arthritis.[1–3] They are most commonly found on the extensor aspect of the forearms and elbows (particularly the olecranon process), the feet, knees, knuckles, buttocks, scalp and back (*Figs 8.71, 8.72*).[4] They have also been described involving a wide variety of other sites, including the abdominal wall, heart (pericardium, myocardium and valves), larynx, lungs, pleura, splenic capsule, peritoneum, eye, bridge of nose, pinna, ischial tuberosity and Achilles tendon. They are often fixed to the underlying periosteum or deep fascia. They present as firm, asymptomatic, dome-shaped masses in the subcutaneous fat or deeper tissues and measure from several millimeters to 5 cm in diameter. Numbers may vary from one to over a hundred. Ulceration sometimes occurs.

Rheumatoid nodules are more commonly found in patients with severe rheumatoid arthritis and are associated with a high titer of rheumatoid factor, joint erosions and an increased incidence of rheumatoid vasculitis.[5] They are not, however, specific for rheumatoid arthritis, being found in approximately 5–7% of patients with SLE (although in this condition they tend to be localized about the hands) and occasionally in seronegative ankylosing spondylitis.[6,7] Clinically similar lesions have also been reported in patients with scleroderma. Presentation of multiple rheumatoid nodules on the fingers in association with little or no arthritis has been described as rheumatoid nodulosis.[8–10] A similar name (cutaneous nodulosis) has been given to the development of multiple small nodules at different sites during methotrexate therapy for rheumatoid arthritis.[11]

Pathogenesis and histological features

Although these lesions develop at sites of pressure and trauma (implying pathogenetic significance), there is some evidence in support of an immune complex-mediated pathogenesis, as both IgG and IgM have been detected by immunofluorescence in the walls of blood vessels adjacent to rheumatoid nodules.[12] Similarly, both rheumatoid factor and complement have been demonstrated within the substance of rheumatoid nodules. Localization of IgM rheumatoid factor and terminal complement complexes C5b–9 has been demonstrated on the luminal surface of endothelial cells in rheumatoid nodules.[13] Proinflammatory cytokines and cell adhesion molecules (TNF-α, IL-1β, IL-Ra RNA, E-selectin) have been demonstrated in rheumatoid nodules and are likely to play a role in mediating injury.[14]

Rheumatoid nodules are typically located in the subcutaneous fat or soft tissues although they may extend into the deeper reticular dermis. This is in contrast to the more superficial location of both granuloma annulare and necrobiosis lipoidica. They are multinodular and associated with very extensive necrobiosis (*Figs 8.73, 8.74*). Fibrin

deposition is often seen in the center of the nodule.[15] Immunoglobulin, lipid, glycosaminoglycans and nucleoproteins may also be present. Old lesions are sometimes associated with cyst formation due to liquefactive degeneration of the contents of the nodules. A well-developed palisade of histiocytes and occasional giant cells characteristically surrounds necrobiotic foci and fibrinoid material (*Fig. 8.75*). Asteroid inclusions are not a feature. The outer layer is composed of vascular granulation tissue and in older lesions marked fibrosis is a frequent accompaniment. An inflammatory cell infiltrate of lymphocytes, plasma cells and eosinophils is often present. Leukocytoclastic vasculitis has occasionally been reported to affect the blood vessels in and around early nodules. A rare case with perforation of the epidermis has been documented.[16]

Differential diagnosis

In some cases of deep granuloma annulare the histological changes are similar to rheumatoid nodule. Deep granuloma annulare ('pseudo-rheumatoid nodule') tends to have more mucin deposition and less fibrin than typical rheumatoid nodule.[17] However, we have noted abundant

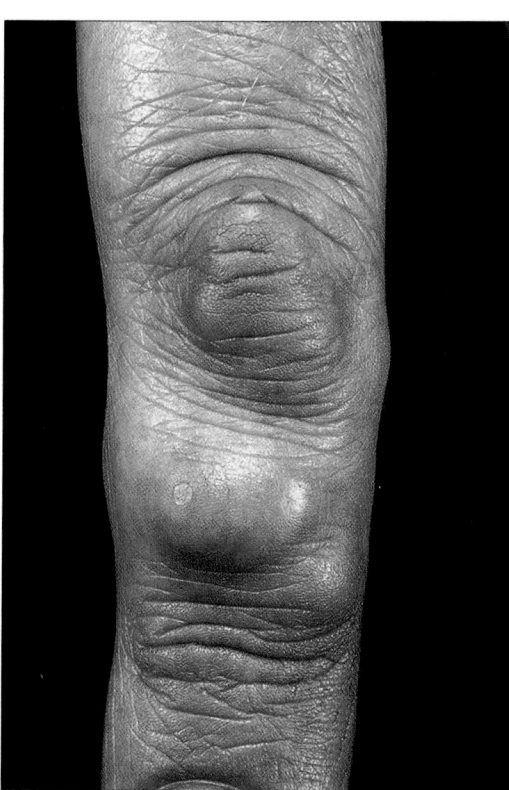

Fig. 8.71
Rheumatoid nodules: lesions on the knuckles are commonly seen in rheumatoid arthritis. By courtesy of the Institute of Dermatology, London, UK.

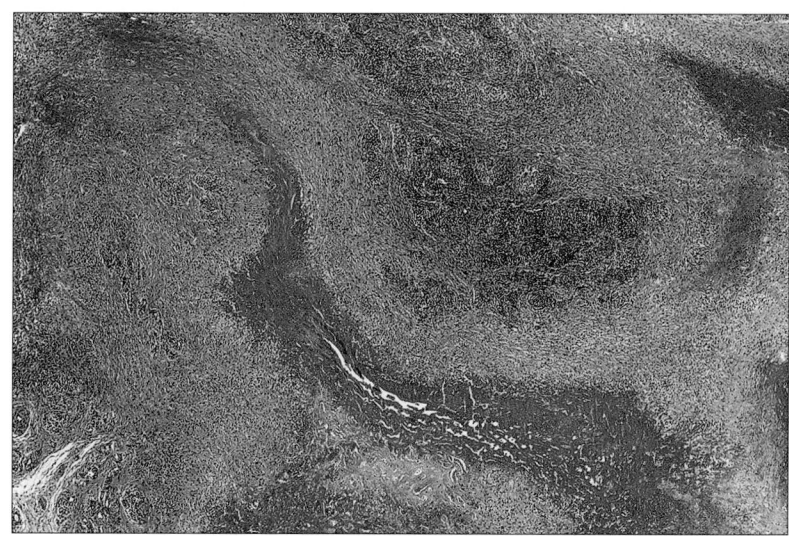

Fig. 8.73
Rheumatoid nodule: there is massive necrobiosis with adjacent scarring and a dense lymphocytic infiltrate. Rheumatoid nodules characteristically occur in the soft tissues.

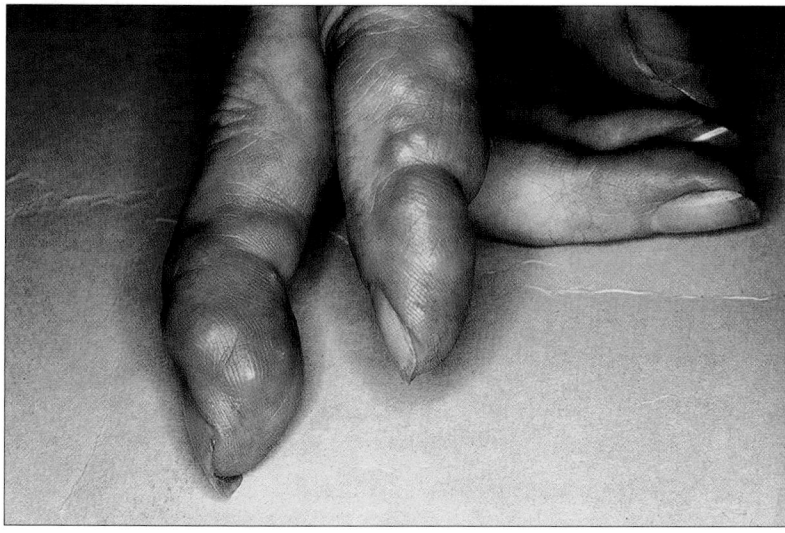

Fig. 8.72
Rheumatoid nodule: in this patient there are multiple small yellowish nodules. By courtesy of the Institute of Dermatology, London, UK.

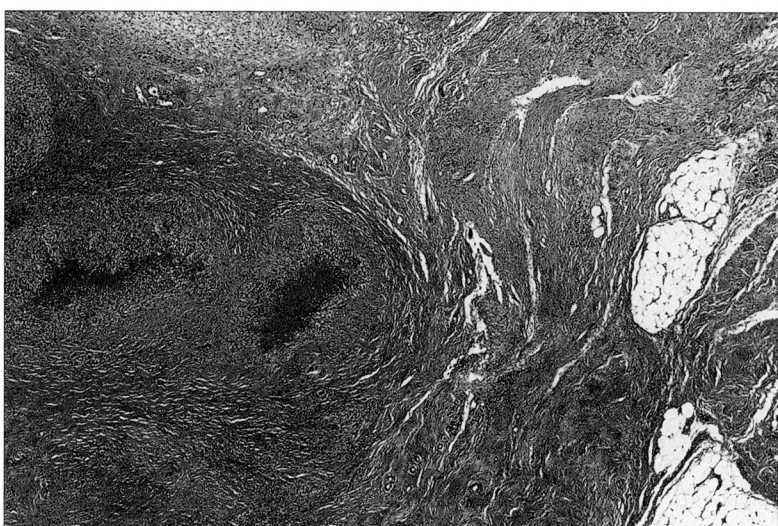

Fig. 8.74
Rheumatoid nodule: in this example, tendon can be seen on the right side of the field.

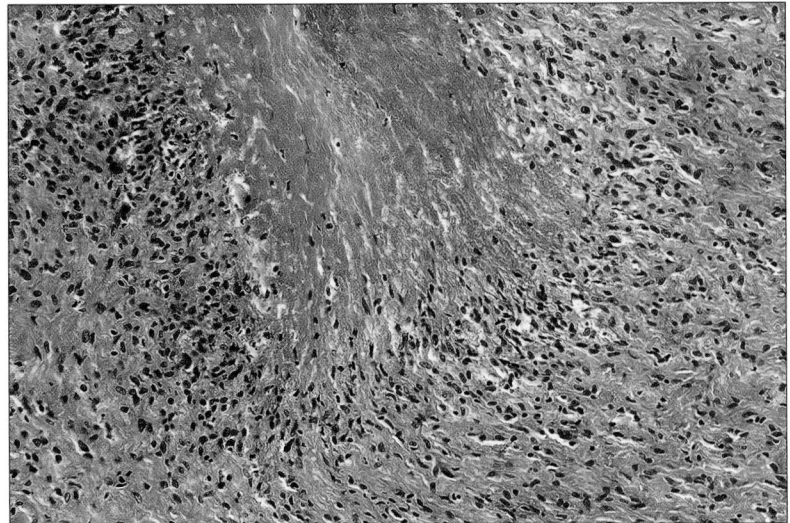

Fig. 8.75
Rheumatoid nodule: the necrobiotic connective tissue is surrounded by a well-developed histiocytic palisade.

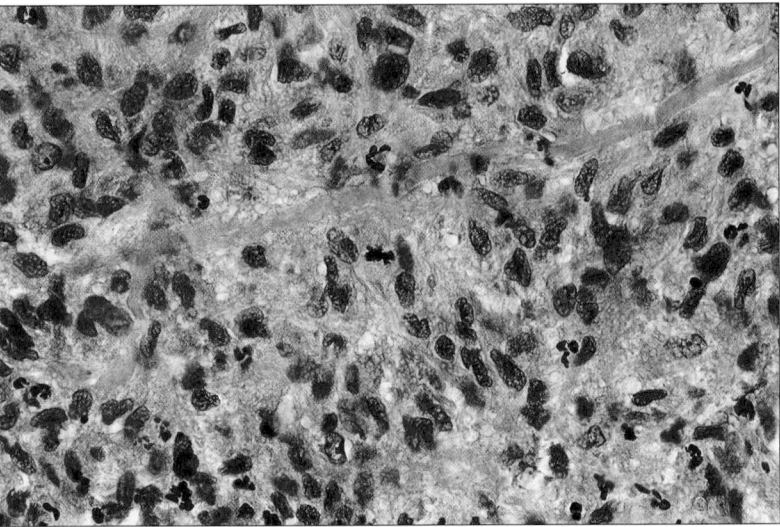

Fig. 8.76
Rheumatoid nodule: the palisading histiocytes may sometimes show mitotic figures which may lead the unwary to consider epithelioid sarcoma.

mucin in rheumatoid nodules. Clinicopathological and serological correlation is advised before establishing a definitive diagnosis.

Compared to rheumatoid fever nodule, rheumatoid arthritis nodules tend to be better circumscribed and surrounded by a well-defined palisade of histiocytes. In addition, the fine fibrinoid strands that form the center of a rheumatic fever nodule contrast with the more dense sheet-like areas of necrobiosis and fibrin deposition in the rheumatoid arthritis nodule.

Patients combining the features of severe rheumatoid arthritis with palisading granulomata accompanied by a neutrophilic infiltrate and leukocytoclastic vasculitis have been described.[5] These lesions are discussed under the rubric of palisaded neutrophilic and granulomatous dermatitis with vasculitis (see p. 320). In short, lesions showing these features may be associated with a number of systemic diseases, including rheumatoid arthritis.

Although epithelioid sarcoma, with its associated geographic necrosis, may bear a superficial resemblance at low power to rheumatoid nodule, the degree of nuclear atypia and pleomorphism in the former should allow easy distinction between these conditions (*Fig. 8.76*). However, in difficult cases, keratin and epithelial membrane antigen immunoreactivity in epithelioid sarcoma should assist in the differential diagnosis.

References

1. Hurd, E.R. (1979) Extraarticular manifestations of rheumatoid arthritis. *Semin Arthritis Rheum*, **8**, 151–176.
2. Jorrizo, J.L., Daniels, J.C. (1983) Dermatologic conditions reported in patients with rheumatoid arthritis. *J Am Acad Dermatol*, **8**, 439–457.
3. Lowney, E.D., Simons, H.M. (1963) 'Rheumatoid' nodules of the skin. *Arch Dermatol*, **88**, 221–226.
4. Veys, E.M., De Keyser, F. (1993) Rheumatoid nodules: differential diagnosis and immunohistochemical findings. *Ann Rheum Dis*, **52**, 625–626.
5. Smith, M.L., Jorizzo, J.L., Semble, E. et al (1989) Rheumatoid papules: lesions showing features of vasculitis and palisading granuloma. *J Am Acad Dermatol*, **20**, 348–352.
6. Schofield, J.K., Cerio, R., Grice, K. (1992) Systemic lupus erythematosus presenting with 'rheumatoid nodules'. *Clin Exp Dermatol*, **17**, 53–55.
7. Hahn, B.H., Yardley, J.H., Stevens, M.B. (1970) 'Rheumatoid' nodules in systemic lupus erythematosus. *Ann Intern Med*, **72**, 49–58.
8. Ginsberg, M.H., Genant, H.K., Yu, T.F. et al (1975) Rheumatoid nodulosis: an unusual variant of rheumatoid disease. *Arthritis Rheum*, **18**, 49–58.
9. Couret, M., Combe, B., van Thoai, C.H. et al (1988) Rheumatoid nodulosis: report of two cases and discussion of diagnostic criteria. *J Rheumatol*, **15**, 1427–1430.
10. Lagier, R., Gerster, J.C. (1995) Palmar rheumatoid nodulosis of the fingers. *Clin Rheumatol*, **14**, 592–593.
11. Williams, F.M., Cohen, P.R., Arnett, F.C. (1998) Accelerated cutaneous nodulosis during methotrexate therapy in a patient with rheumatoid arthritis. *J Am Acad Dermatol*, **39**, 359–362.
12. Moore, C.P., Wilkens, R.F. (1977) The subcutaneous nodule: its significance in the diagnosis of rheumatic disease. *Semin Arthritis Rheum*, **7**, 63–79.
13. Kato, H., Yawakawa, M., Ogino, T. (2000) Complement mediated vascular endothelial injury in rheumatoid nodules: a histopathological and immunohistochemical study. *J Rheumatol*, **27**, 1839–1847.
14. Wikaningrum, R., Highton, J., Parker, A. et al (1998) Pathogenetic mechanisms in the rheumatoid nodule: comparison of proinflammatory cytokine production and cell adhesion molecule expression in rheumatoid nodules and synovial membranes from the same patient. *Arthritis Rheum*, **41**, 1783–1797.
15. Aherne, M.J., Bacon, P.A., Blake, D.R. et al (1985) Immunohistochemical findings in rheumatoid nodules. *Virchows Arch (A)*, **407**, 191–202.
16. Patterson, J.W., Demos, P.T. (1985) Superficial, ulcerating rheumatoid necrobiosis: a perforating rheumatoid nodule. *Cutis*, **36**, 323–328.
17. Patterson, J.W. (1988) Rheumatoid nodule and subcutaneous granuloma annulare. A comparative histologic study. *Am J Dermatopathol*, **10**, 1–8.

Elastolytic granulomata

This is a controversial group of diseases, the prototype of which is the actinic granuloma. Other entities that probably belong to this group include atypical facial necrobiosis lipoidica and granuloma multiforme (see below). It has been suggested that all these conditions represent examples of granuloma annulare occurring in different clinical settings.[1–4] However, the clinicopathological features are distinctive and the pathological process clearly relates to the primary destruction of elastic fibers by a granulomatous infiltrate. In granuloma annulare, as in diseases like sarcoidosis, destruction of elastic fibers does not always occur and when it does, it tends to be only focal and develops as a secondary phenomenon.[5]

The term 'annular elastolytic giant cell granuloma' has been used to describe not only cases of actinic granuloma but also cases in which destruction of elastic fibers occurs in the absence of solar elastosis.[6] In fact, some cases present at sites with little sun exposure and the disease

may also occur in children.[7] Thus, although the terms actinic granuloma and elastolytic giant cell granuloma have been used interchangeably in the literature, the latter term should probably be reserved for elastolytic granulomata occurring in skin without solar elastosis.[8] Elastolytic granulomata have rarely been described in association with adult T-cell leukemia lymphoma.[9] Elastolytic granulomata have also been documented in internal organs.[10] The latter, however, probably represents sarcoidosis with prominent elastolysis.

References

1. Ragaz, A., Ackerman, A.B. (1979) Is actinic granuloma a specific condition? *Am J Dermatopathol*, **1**, 43–50.
2. Weedon, D. (1980) Actinic granuloma: the controversy continues. *Am J Dermatopathol*, **2**, 90–91.
3. Wilson Jones, E. (1980) Actinic granuloma. *Am J Dermatopathol*, **2**, 89–90.
4. Morita, K., Okamoto, H., Miyachi, Y. (1999) Papular elastolytic giant cell granuloma: a clinical variant of annular elastolytic giant cell granulomata or generalized granuloma annulare? *Eur J Dermatol*, **9**, 647–649.
5. Terui, T., Tagami, H. (1998) Annular elastolytic sarcoidosis of the face. *Eur J Dermatol*, **8**, 127–130.
6. Tock, C.L., Cohen, P.R. (1998) Annular elastolytic giant cell granuloma. *Cutis*, **62**, 181–187.

7. Herron, M.D., Coffin, C.M., Vanderhooft, S.L. (2002) Annular elastolytic giant cell granuloma. *Pediatr Dev Pathol*, 5, 305–309.
8. Revenga, F., Rovira, I., Pimentel, J. et al (1996) Annular elastolytic giant cell granuloma – actinic granuloma? *Clin Exp Dermatol*, 21, 51–53.
9. Kuramoto, Y., Watanabe, M., Tagami, H. (1990) Adult T cell leukemia accompanied by annular elastolytic giant cell granuloma. *Acta Derm Venereol*, 70, 164–167.
10. Kurose, N., Nakagawa, H., Iozumi, K. et al (1992) Systemic elastolytic granulomatosis with cutaneous, ocular, lymph nodal, and intestinal involvement. Spectrum of annular elastolytic giant cell granuloma and sarcoidosis. *J Am Acad Dermatol*, 26, 359–363.

Actinic granuloma (O'Brien)

Clinical features

Actinic granuloma develops on the sun-damaged skin of the neck, face, upper chest or arms of middle-aged patients.[1–5] It may also affect the conjunctiva.[6,7] The incidence is equal in men and women, and individuals with blonde hair and freckled skin are predisposed, particularly those living in sunny climes. An association with the longstanding use of sunbeds has also been described.[8]

Lesions present as one or more skin-colored or pink papules, which enlarge to form annular or arcuate plaques up to 1 cm in diameter. The edge of the lesion is somewhat raised, forming a border 0.2–0.5 cm in width. These annular plaques enlarge slowly and the center may gradually clear to appear relatively normal or slightly atrophic with variable depigmentation. Lesions are asymptomatic and there is no evidence of anesthesia. They do not develop on non-sun-damaged skin. Spontaneous resolution may take place after months or years.

Bilateral periocular actinic granuloma has been documented in a patient with renal failure.[9] Other rare associations include relapsing polychondritis, cutaneous amyloidosis and giant molluscum contagiosum.[10–12]

Pathogenesis and histological features

The pathogenesis of actinic granuloma is poorly understood. It has been suggested that the antigenic stimulus for the formation of granulomata in both actinic granuloma and temporal arteritis is the actinically degenerated elastic tissue.[13]

The features are best appreciated by examination of a radial biopsy through the edge of a lesion and including uninvolved skin.[14,15] The epidermis may be normal or atrophic. The peripheral unaffected skin shows gross solar (actinic) elastosis (*Figs 8.77–8.79*). Within the rim of the lesion there is a foreign body giant cell reaction in association with,

and engulfing, fragmented elastotic material (elastoclasis) (*Fig. 8.80*).[15,16] The granulomatous reaction is centered in the zone of solar elastosis and, accordingly, tends to be confined to the superficial dermis.[16] The giant cells may contain asteroid bodies (*Fig. 8.81*). There is an accompanying chronic inflammatory cell infiltrate composed of histiocytes, lymphocytes and plasma cells. Necrobiosis is not a feature of this condition. Palisading of histiocytes is either absent or minimal and, if present, is related to the elastotic debris. Dermal mucin does not appear to be increased.[16] Fibroblasts are scant and fibrosis is minimal. In the actinic granuloma, blood vessels appear normal. Within the central zone the collagen appears relatively normal, although it is more obviously horizontally aligned and may appear more closely packed than normal. Slight scarring is present in the central area where elastic tissue is absent.[16]

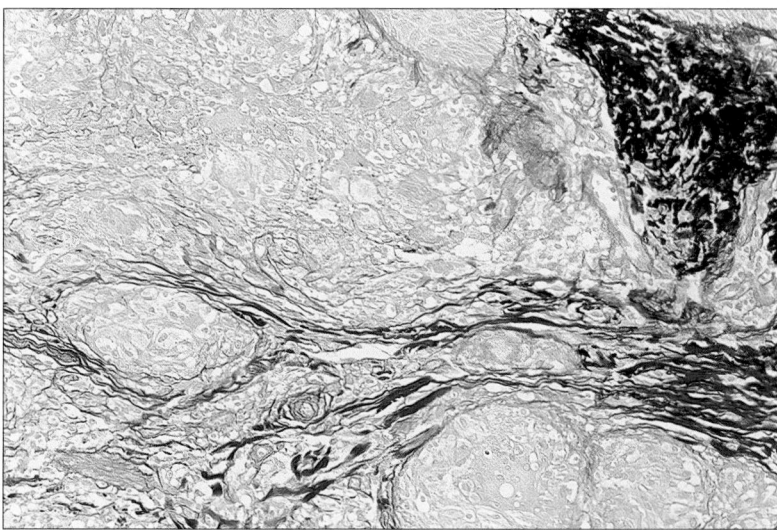

Fig. 8.78
Actinic granuloma: the elastosis is highlighted by use of the elastic–van Gieson stain. Note the absence of elastic tissue within the granulomatous infiltrate.

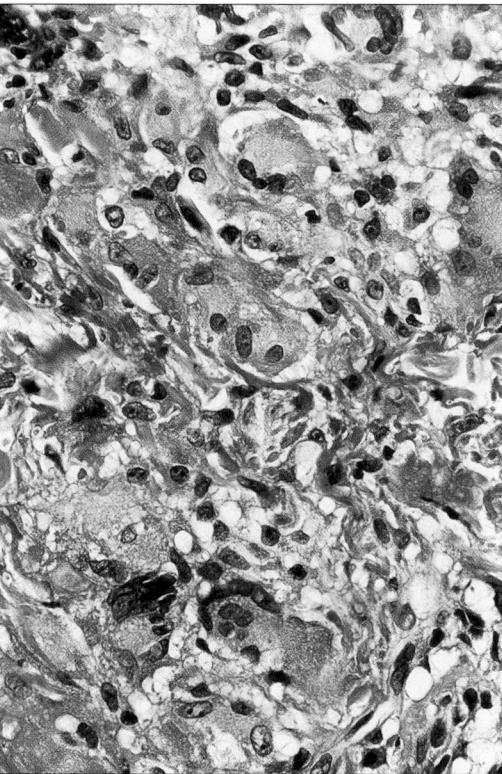

Fig. 8.79
Actinic granuloma: this granulomatous infiltrate surrounds degenerate swollen, eosinophilic elastic fibers.

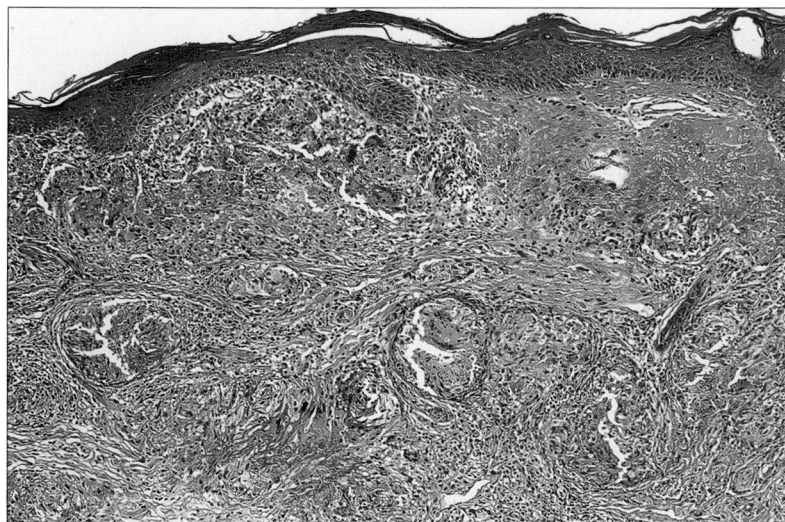

Fig. 8.77
Actinic granuloma: a granulomatous reaction is present in the reticular dermis. Gross solar elastosis is seen as an eosinophilic homogeneous band (top right).

Differential diagnosis

The facial location, presence of elastophagocytosis and absence of necrobiosis aid in distinguishing actinic granuloma from other granulomatous lesions. The absence of dermal mucin and the presence of marked elastoclasis and mild scarring help to distinguish actinic granuloma from granuloma annulare, the disorder that it most resembles.[10]

References

1. Hanke, C.W., Bailin, P.L., Roenigk, H.H. (1979) Annular elastolytic giant cell granuloma. *J Am Acad Dermatol*, **1**, 413–421.
2. McGrae, J.D. (1986) Actinic granuloma: a clinical, histopathologic and immunocytochemical study. *Arch Dermatol*, **122**, 43–47.
3. O'Brien, J.P. (1975) Actinic granuloma. *Arch Dermatol*, **111**, 460–466.
4. Prediville, J., Griffiths, W.A.D., Russell Jones, R. (1985) O'Brien's actinic granuloma. *Br J Dermatol*, **113**, 353–358.
5. Wilson Jones, E. (1980) Actinic granuloma. *Am J Dermatopathol*, **2**, 89–90.
6. Steffen, C. (1992) Actinic granuloma of the conjunctiva. *Am J Dermatopathol*, **14**, 253–254.
7. Ferry, A.P., Kaltreider, S.A., Wyatt, D.B. (1984) Actinic granuloma of the conjunctiva. *Arch Ophthalmol*, **102**, 1200–1202.
8. Davies, M.G., Newman, P. (1997) Actinic granuloma in a young woman following prolonged sunbed usage. *Br J Dermatol*, **136**, 797–798.
9. Spraul, C.W., Wojno, T., Grossniklaus, H.E. (1998) Bilateral periocular actinic granuloma in a patient with renal failure: a clinicopathologic study. *Graefes Arch Clin Exp Ophthalmol*, **236**, 646–651.
10. Pierard, G.E., Henrijean, A., Foidart, J.M. et al (1982) Actinic granuloma and relapsing polychondritis. *Acta Derm Venereol*, **62**, 531–533.
11. Lee, Y.-S., Vijayasingam, S., Chan, H.-L. (1989) Photosensitive annular elastolytic giant cell granuloma with cutaneous amyloidosis. *Am J Dermatopathol*, **11**, 443–450.
12. Agarwal, S., Takwale, A., Bajallan, N. et al (2000) Co-existing actinic granuloma and giant molluscum contagiosum. *Clin Exp Dermatol*, **25**, 401–403.
13. O'Brien, J.P., Regan, W. (1999) Actinically degenerate elastic tissue is the likely antigenic of actinic granuloma of the skin and of temporal arteritis. *J Am Acad Dermatol*, **40**, 214–222.
14. O'Brien, J.P. (1985) Actinic granuloma: the expanding significance – an analysis of its origin in elastotic ('aging') skin and a definition of necrobiotic (vascular), histiocytic, and sarcoid variants. *Int J Dermatol*, **24**, 473–490.
15. Steffen, C. (1988) Actinic granuloma (O'Brien). *J Cutan Pathol*, **15**, 66–74.
16. Al-Hoquail, I.A., Al-Ghamdi, A.M., Martinka, M. et al (2002) Actinic granuloma is a unique and distinct entity. A comparative study with granuloma annulare. *Am J Dermatopathol*, **24**, 209–212.

Atypical facial necrobiosis lipoidica

Clinical features

This variant of necrobiosis lipoidica deserves separate mention because of its unusual clinical features and distinctive histology.[1-5] Atypical facial necrobiosis lipoidica, which predominantly affects females (9:1), usually develops in the absence of diabetes mellitus, and manifests most often in the fourth decade. Patients present with one or more annular, non-scaling plaques on the upper face and scalp, which typically have slightly raised, relatively uniform borders and measure 1–5 cm in diameter (*Figs 8.82–8.84*). Although early lesions are erythematous with a brown

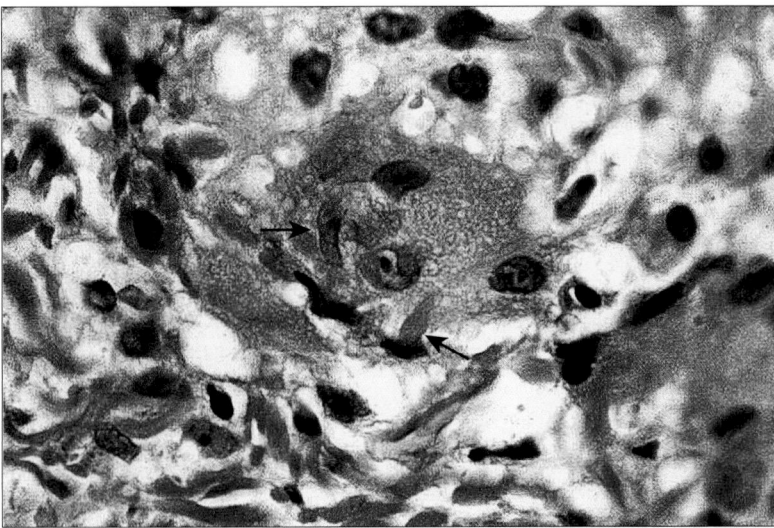

Fig. 8.80
Actinic granuloma: elastotic material is visible (arrowed) within the cytoplasm of a multinucleate giant cell.

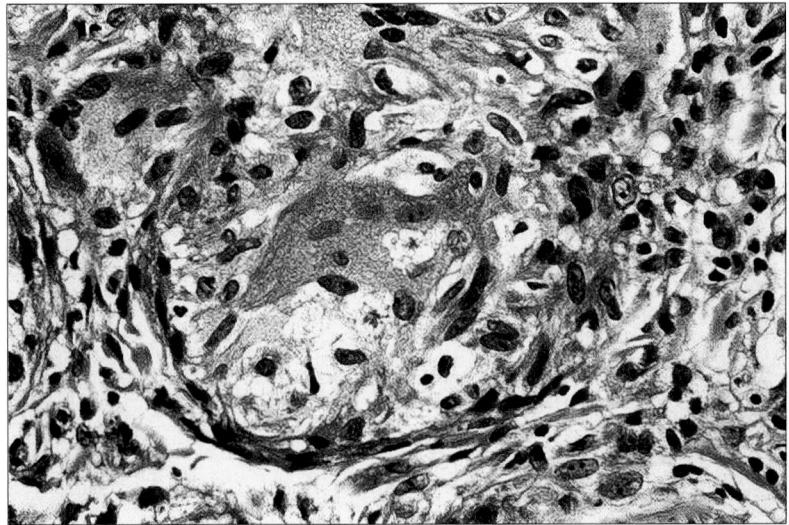

Fig. 8.81
Actinic granuloma: two asteroid inclusions are present in the center of the field.

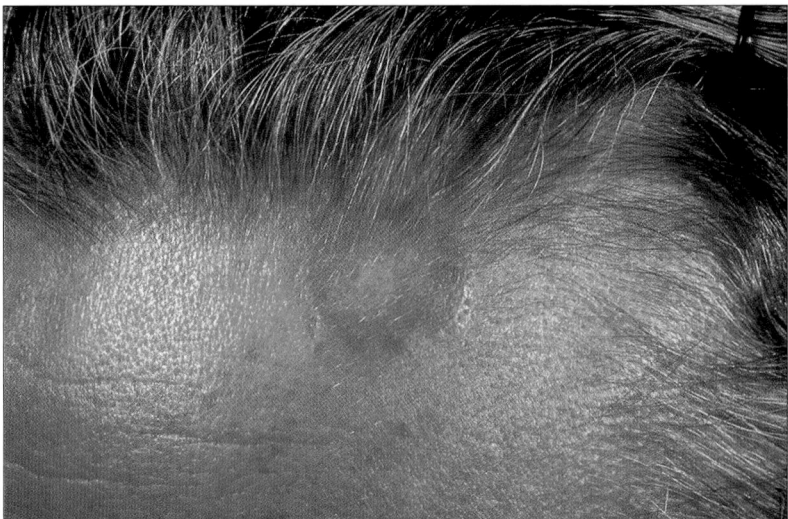

Fig. 8.82
Atypical facial necrobiosis lipoidica: atrophic plaque on the right temple with a well-defined edge. By courtesy of R.A. Marsden, MD, St George's Hospital, London, UK.

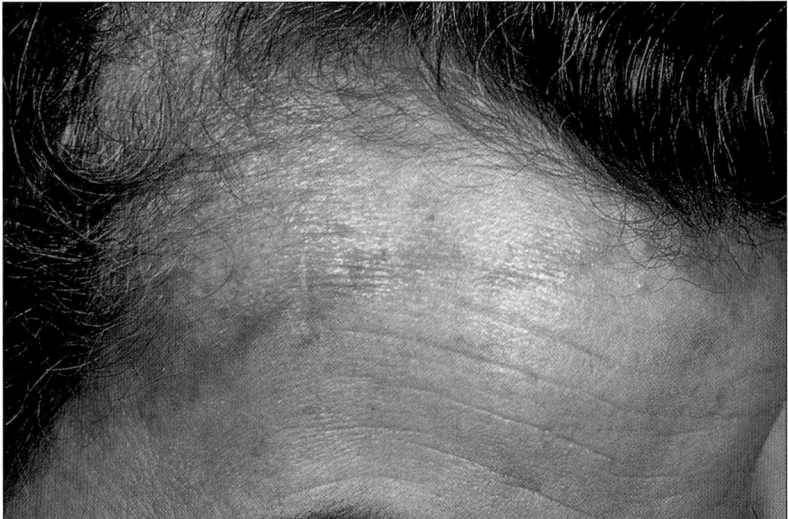

Fig. 8.83
Atypical facial necrobiosis lipoidica: a rather more extensive lesion associated with hair loss. By courtesy of the Institute of Dermatology, London, UK.

border, older lesions are characterized by central depigmentation. Atrophy, however, is minimal or absent. Patients may, in addition, show involvement at other sites, including the arms, hands and trunk. Very rarely, patients have concomitant typical necrobiosis lipoidica on the shins. It is for this reason that the name was originally coined. We now believe, however, that the condition probably has no relationship whatsoever to necrobiosis lipoidica. It is much more likely that it represents a variant of an annular elastolytic granuloma.

Histological features

The condition is characterized by a dense granulomatous infiltrate, with conspicuous giant cells, involving the dermis (*Figs 8.85, 8.86*). The infiltrate has a rather irregular distribution, being dispersed between individual collagen bundles. Occasional circumscribed granulomata may sometimes be a feature. Asteroid bodies are often found in the cytoplasm of giant cells. There is typically loss of elastic tissue in the areas of granulomatous inflammation. Rarely, ill-defined foci of necrobiosis are

a feature (*Fig. 8.87*), but well-defined palisading granulomata are not present. In cases with coexistent necrobiosis lipoidica, the biopsies from the affected areas on the shins show the typical histological features of this condition.

Differential diagnosis

In contrast to the actinic granuloma with which this condition is often confused, the surrounding skin does not show evidence of significant solar elastosis and elastoclasis.

References

1. Dowling, G.B., Wilson Jones, E. (1967) Atypical (annular) necrobiosis of the face and scalp. A report of the clinical and histological features of 7 cases. *Dermatologica*, 135, 11–26.
2. Mehregan, A.H., Altman, J. (1973) Miescher's granuloma of the face. A variant of necrobiosis lipoidica–granuloma annulare spectrum. *Arch Dermatol*, 107, 62–64.
3. Wilson Jones, E. (1971) Necrobiosis lipoidica presenting on the face and scalp. An account of 29 patients and a detailed consideration of recent histochemical findings. *Trans St John's Hosp Dermatol Soc*, 57, 202–220.
4. Vélez, A., Martín-de-Hijas, C., del-Río, E., Ambrojo, P. (1994) Ulcerated plaque of the face. Atypical necrobiosis lipoidica. *Arch Dermatol*, 130, 1433.
5. Helander, I., Niemi, K.M., Tyrkko, J. (1978) Atypical necrobiosis lipoidica of the face. *Acta Derm Venereol*, 58, 276–277.

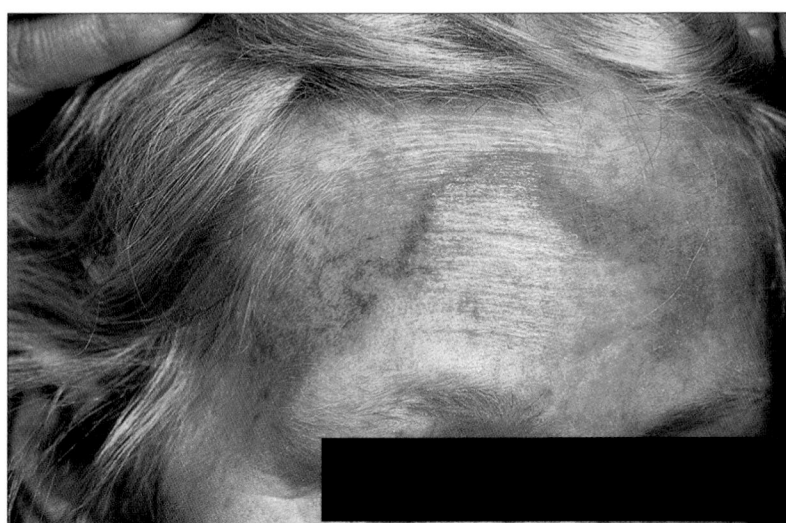

Fig. 8.84
Atypical facial necrobiosis lipoidica: in this patient, the lesion which extends across the forehead is associated with an erythematous border. By courtesy of the Institute of Dermatology, London, UK.

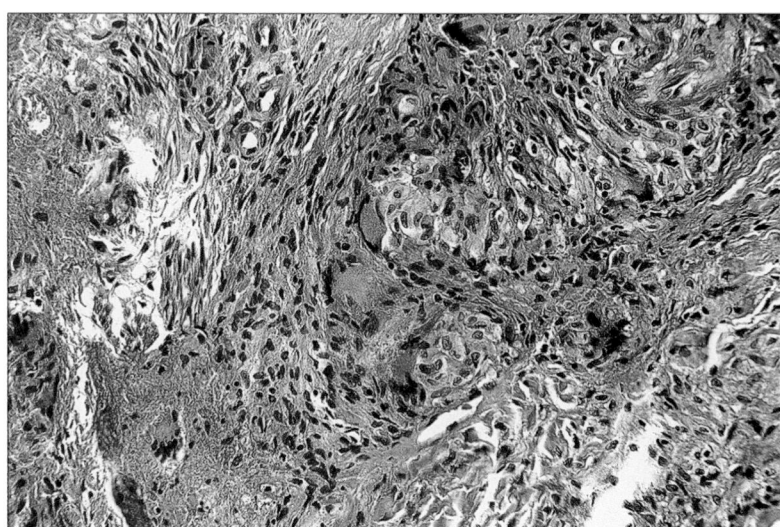

Fig. 8.86
Atypical facial necrobiosis lipoidica: close-up view of the granulomata. Note the conspicuous giant cells.

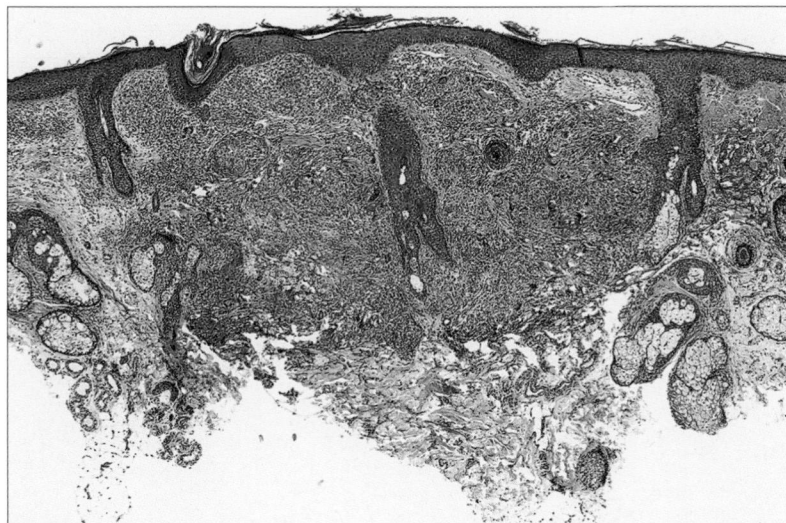

Fig. 8.85
Atypical facial necrobiosis lipoidica: a dense granulomatous infiltrate occupies the dermis.

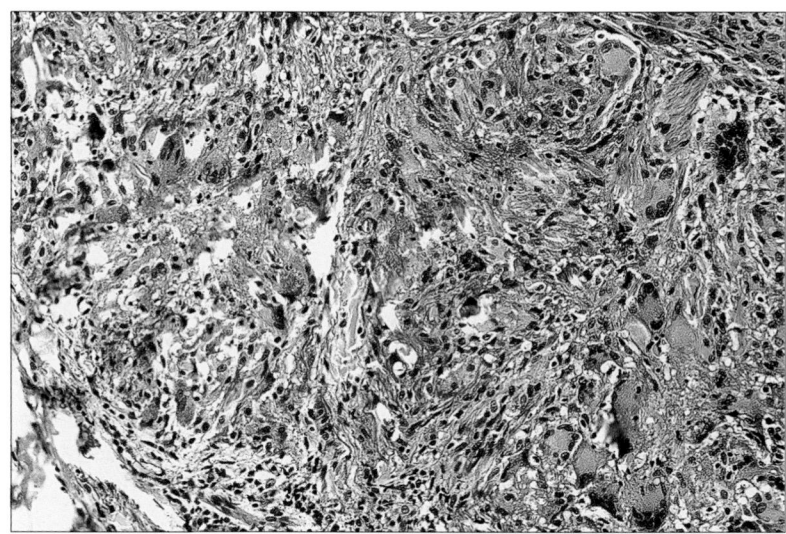

Fig. 8.87
Typical facial necrobiosis lipoidica: an ill-defined focus of necrobiosis is present.

Granuloma multiforme

Clinical features

This dermatosis of unknown etiology is of particular importance because clinically it may be confused with leprosy; however, it is not associated with cutaneous anesthesia.[1,2] Granuloma multiforme, which shows a marked female predominance, is seen most often in Central Africa, especially eastern Nigeria. It has also been documented in the Congo.[3] The disease is very common in some villages. It particularly affects patients over 40 years of age. Lesions, which tend to chronicity, are found on the upper and exposed parts of the body. They commence as small, flesh-colored, indurated, pruritic papulonodules, 1–8 mm in diameter and raised 1–3 mm above the skin surface, which extend peripherally and coalesce to form annular lesions and plaques (Figs 8.88–8.90). Very large lesions become irregular and develop scalloped or gyrate borders. Central healing may be associated with residual hypopigmentation.

Histological features

The epidermis is normal. Situated within the dermis is an ill-defined, irregular, necrobiotic lesion (*Fig. 8.91*).[4] In general, this affects individual collagen fibers, producing a rather haphazard picture of abnormal fibers interspersed with unaffected ones and associated with a histiocytic infiltrate (*Fig. 8.92*). Only rarely is a well-defined palisading granuloma seen. In addition to histiocytes, giant cells are commonly found and the tissues show a perivascular lymphocytic infiltrate with variable numbers of plasma cells and eosinophils (*Fig. 8.93*). The giant cells do not contain

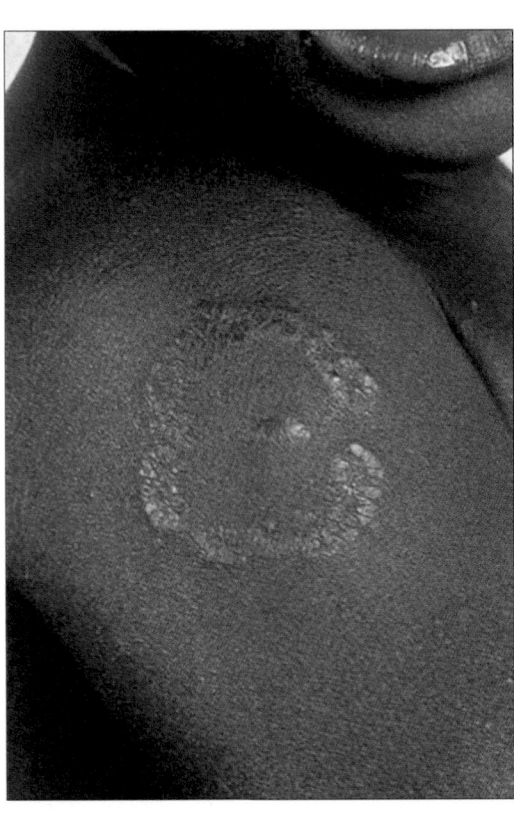

Fig. 8.88
Granuloma multiforme: typical annular lesions with raised borders in a child. By courtesy of R.A. Marsden, St George's Hospital, London, UK.

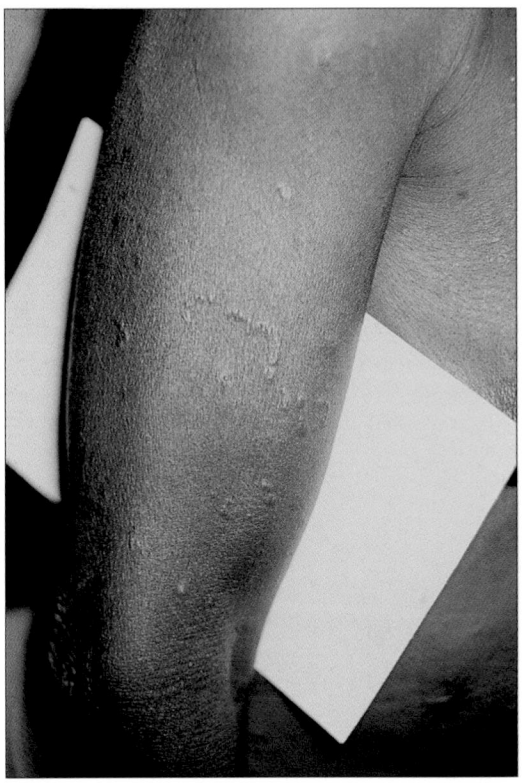

Fig. 8.90
Granuloma multiforme: early lesions on sun-exposed skin. By courtesy of the Institute of Dermatology, London, UK.

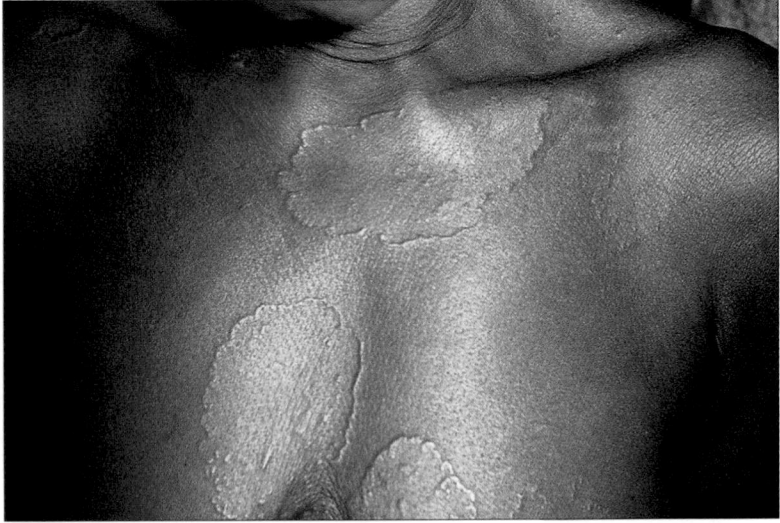

Fig. 8.89
Granuloma multiforme: there are multiple large irregular plaques. By courtesy of the Institute of Dermatology, London, UK.

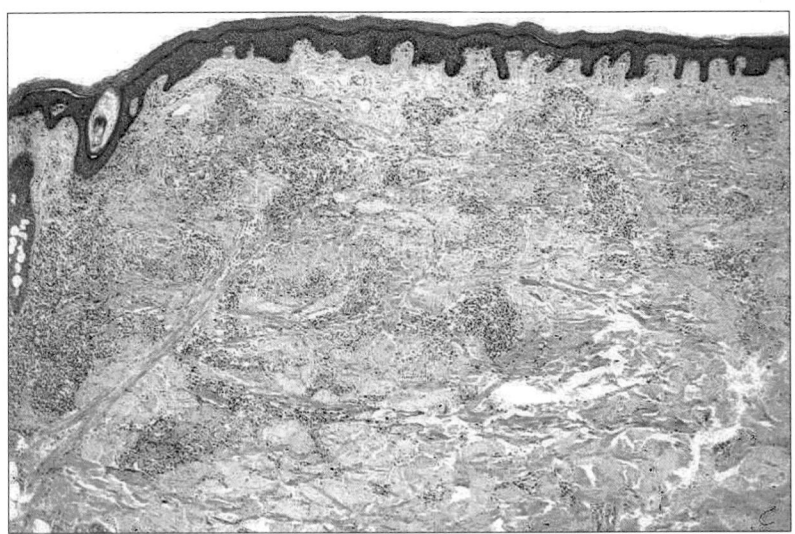

Fig. 8.91
Granuloma multiforme: there is extensive necrobiosis.

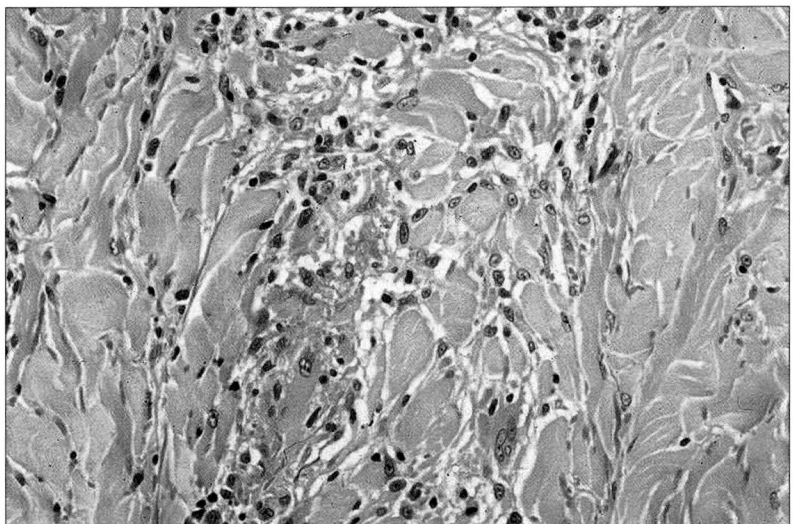

Fig. 8.92
Granuloma multiforme: necrobiosis is seen in the center.

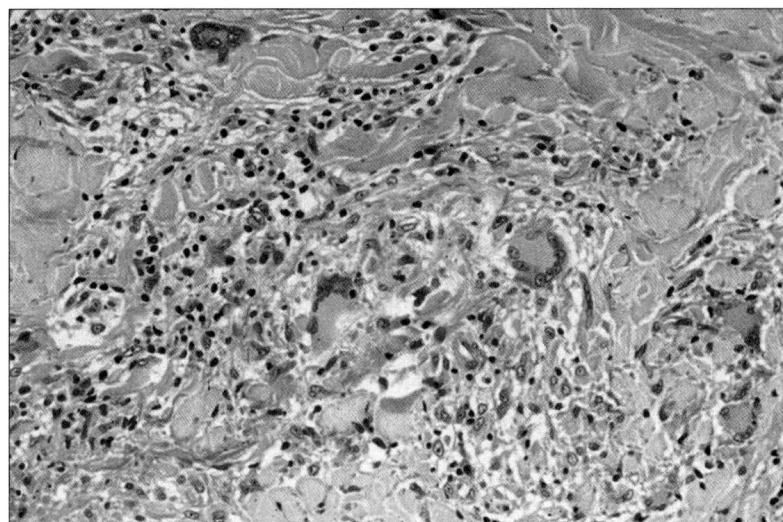

Fig. 8.93
Granuloma multiforme: multinucleate giant cells are present.

asteroid bodies. Perineural involvement is not a feature.[1] The adjacent vasculature is normal. Loss of elastic tissue is typical in relation to the inflammatory infiltrate and healed areas are characterized by absence of elastic tissue and mild superficial scarring.[1]

Differential diagnosis

The exact nosological position of granuloma multiforme is unknown. It is probably a clinicopathological variant of elastolytic granuloma. The granulomata do not show a perineural distribution, helping to distinguish granuloma multiforme from leprosy. Nevertheless, since infection must be excluded before giving a definitive diagnosis, stains for organisms (especially mycobacteria and fungi) must be performed to exclude this possibility. Culture should also be performed when clinically appropriate.

References

1. Allenby, C.F., Wilson Jones, E. (1969) Granuloma multiforme. *Trans St John's Hosp Dermatol Soc*, 55, 88–98.
2. Leiker, D.K., Kok, S.H., Spaas, J.A.J. (1964) Granuloma multiforme. *Int J Leprosy*, 32, 368–376.
3. Chandenier, B., Guillemette, J., Labussiere, J.L. et al (1995) First case of multiforme granuloma in Congo. *Sante*, 5, 245–246.
4. Meyers, W.M., Connor, D.H., Shannon, R. (1970) Histologic characteristics of granuloma multiforme. *Int J Leprosy*, 38, 241–249.

Rheumatic fever nodule

Clinical features

Fortunately, effective antimicrobial therapy has relegated rheumatic fever to a rare pediatric infection. As a consequence, complications of rheumatic fever are only rarely encountered in dermatology practice. Approximately one-third of patients with rheumatic fever develop papules that have a tendency to occur over bony prominence of the knee, elbows, fingers, ankles, spine and scalp.[1–3] However, they may also occur at other sites. Most patients have multiple nodules. In one report, the number of nodules ranged from 1 to 108.[1] Lesions may persist from days to several months.

Histological features

Biopsy shows central gossamer fibrin associated with variable numbers of neutrophils, lymphocytes, plasma cells and karyorrhexis. The lesions are often not well circumscribed and histiocytes surround the lesion forming a poorly defined palisade.

Differential diagnosis

The histological features of the rheumatic fever nodule are not pathognomonic for this disease. Clinical correlation is required to establish a definite diagnosis. The rheumatic fever nodule can be classified under the rubric 'palisaded neutrophilic and granulomatous dermatitis associated with systemic disease'. Rheumatic fever nodule is discussed separately, however, because of its historic interest and its longstanding recognition as distinct clinical entity. The differential diagnosis is therefore that of palisading and necrobiotic granulomatous dermatitis. Other systemic diseases, including connective tissue disease, infection, vasculitis, neoplasia, and inflammatory bowel disease, may be associated with lesions with similar histology. The reader is referred to this section for a more detailed discussion of this group of disorders (see p. 320). In short, a diagnosis of rheumatic fever nodule should only be made in the setting of confirmed rheumatic fever. In the absence of such history, a careful search for other underlying systemic diseases is necessary.

Rheumatoid arthritis nodules tend to be better circumscribed and surrounded by well-defined palisade histiocytes. In addition, the fine fibrinoid strands that form the center of a rheumatic fever nodule contrast with the more dense sheet-like areas of necrobiosis in the rheumatoid arthritis nodule.

References

1. Hayes, R.M., Gibson, S. (1942) An evaluation of rheumatic nodules in children. *JAMA*, 119, 554–555.
2. Bennet, G.A., Zeller, J.W., Bauer, W. (1940) Subcutaneous nodules of rheumatoid arthritis and rheumatic fever. *Arch Pathol*, 30, 70–89.
3. Chopra, P., Narula, J.P., Tandon, R. (1991) Ultrastructure of naturally occurring subcutaneous nodules in acute rheumatic fever. *Int J Cardiol*, 30, 124–127.

Necrobiotic xanthogranuloma

Clinical features

Necrobiotic xanthogranuloma (necrobiotic xanthogranuloma with paraproteinemia) is an extremely rare condition of unknown etiology.[1,2] It occurs equally in men and in women, in the late middle aged and elderly (average age at presentation is 56 years). The disease is characterized by the development of nodules and plaques, which show a predilection for the face, neck, trunk and proximal limbs. The facial lesions are characteristically periorbital (most often infraorbital) in distribution and consist of papules that progress to nodules, and plaques that may form irregular ulcers (*Fig. 8.94*). Although periorbital involvement is fairly constant, in some patients this feature is absent.[3,4] Scarring and telangiectasia are common. Lesions are sharply demarcated and have a distinctive xanthomatous appearance. Ocular complications are common and include episcleritis, keratitis, proptosis, uveitis and iritis.[5] Some patients report pain but this is not a common feature.[2]

The lesions on the trunk and limbs are irregular, well-demarcated, bright yellow, dermal and subcutaneous plaques measuring up to 25 cm across (*Figs 8.95, 8.96*). They may be complicated by ulceration,

hemorrhage, scarring, central atrophy and telangiectases, and typically have a peripheral inflammatory border. Violaceous and flesh-colored nodules may also be present, particularly over the trunk. Unusual presentations include a solitary nodular lesion mimicking a tumor and exceptionally, skin involvement is absent.[6,7]

Involvement of myocardium, lung, larynx and kidneys has been reported.[8–11] Patients may have arthritis, chronic obstructive pulmonary

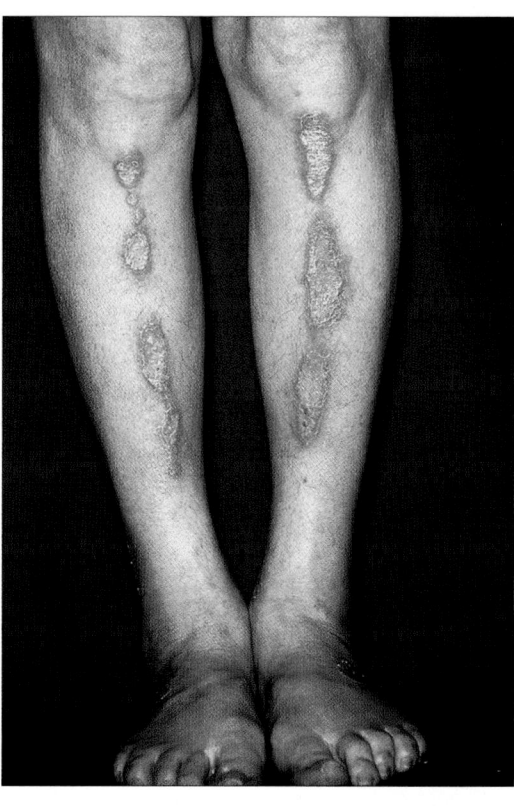

Fig. 8.96
Necrobiotic xanthogranuloma: in this example, there are symmetrical plaques on the shins mimicking necrobiosis lipoidica. By courtesy of the Institute of Dermatology, London, UK.

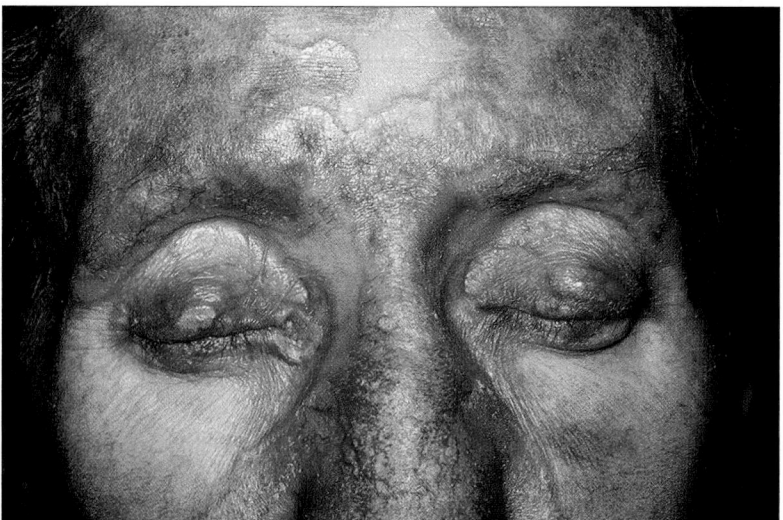

Fig. 8.94
Necrobiotic xanthogranuloma: indurated yellow plaques are present around both eyes and on the eyelids. By courtesy of the Institute of Dermatology, London, UK.

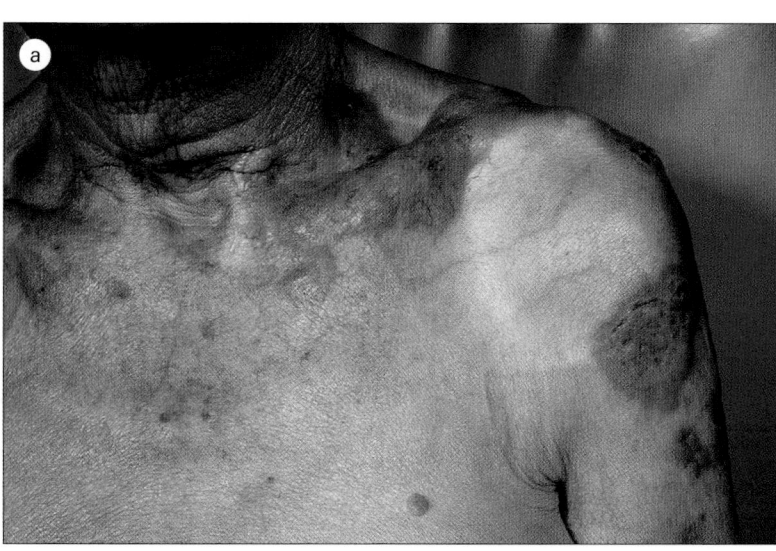

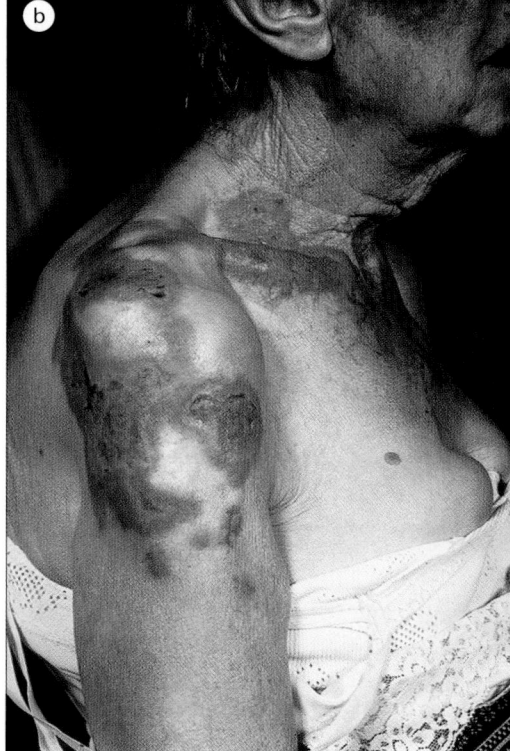

Fig. 8.95
(a, b) Necrobiotic xanthogranuloma: there are multiple yellow plaques around the shoulders and overlying the clavicles. By courtesy of the Institute of Dermatology, London, UK.

disease, neuropathy or hypertension.[2] One case associated with Graves' disease and another associated with linear morphea have been documented.[2,12] Nodular transformation of the liver is an associated feature in some patients.[11,13]

Laboratory investigations reveal anemia, leucopenia and a raised ESR. Most patients with necrobiotic xanthogranuloma have an associated monoclonal paraproteinemia, usually IgG kappa type. Fewer patients present with a lambda paraprotein and an exceptional case has been documented with two monoclonal paraproteins. Some patients have multiple myeloma or B-cell lymphoma.[14–18] A patient with associated Hodgkin's lymphoma has also been reported.[19] Diabetes mellitus is sometimes present and occasional patients have hyperlipidemia. Other associations that may be encountered include low serum complement levels and cryoglobulinemia.

Pathogenesis and histological features

The pathogenesis of necrobiotic xanthogranuloma is unknown. Direct immunofluorescence has shown IgM, C3 and fibrinogen deposition in blood vessel walls.[6] It has more recently been suggested that activation of monocytes is responsible for the intracellular accumulation of lipoprotein-derived lipids and the hypocholesterolemia.[20]

Necrobiotic xanthogranuloma has a very distinctive histological appearance.[6,18] Large areas of marked necrobiosis alternate with foci of xanthogranulomatous infiltration throughout the reticular dermis with extension into the subcutaneous fat (*Fig. 8.97*).[3] Involvement of the subcutaneous fat is predominantly in a septal distribution and may mimic panniculitis.[21] The necrobiotic collagen appears as amorphous eosinophilic debris (*Fig. 8.98*). The granulomatous infiltrate is associated with epithelioid and foamy histiocytes in addition to conspicuous giant cells, many of which are of the Touton type (*Figs 8.99, 8.100*). Foreign body giant cells are also present. Lymphocytes and plasma cells are often prominent and formation of germinal centers is sometimes seen. A characteristic feature is the presence of large and bizarre angulated giant cells with considerable numbers of nuclei irregularly grouped together within copious eosinophilic cytoplasm in the tissue immediately adjacent

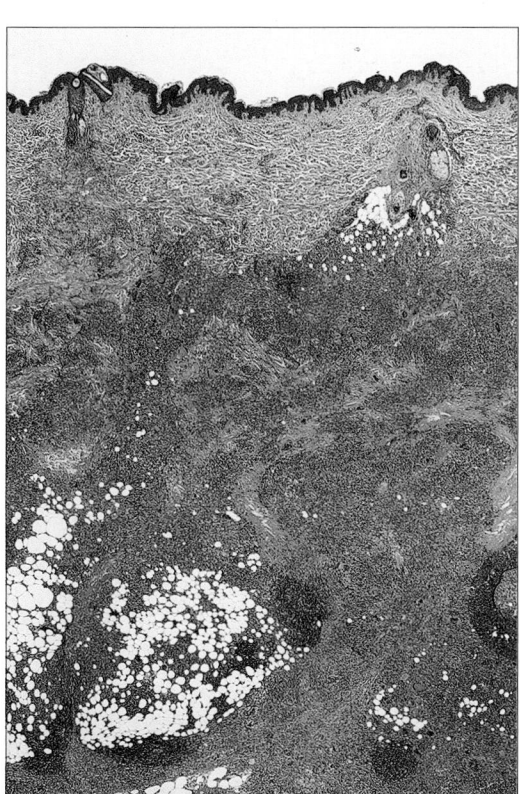

Fig. 8.97
Necrobiotic xanthogranuloma: there is a dense infiltrate extending from the mid-dermis into the subcutaneous fat.

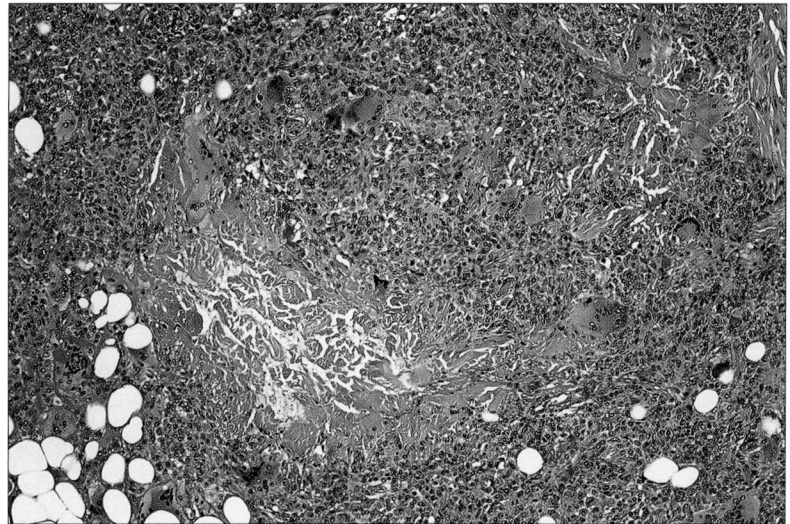

Fig. 8.98
Necrobiotic xanthogranuloma: there is extensive necrobiosis and a dense histiocytic infiltrate with conspicuous giant cells.

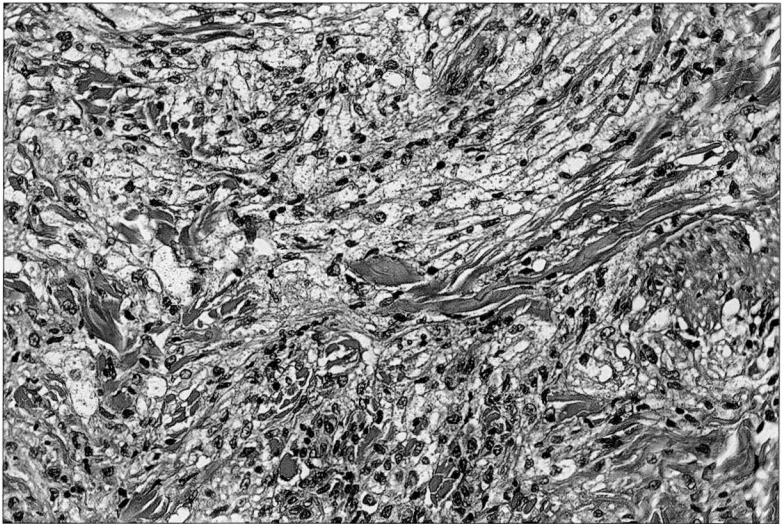

Fig. 8.99
Necrobiotic xanthogranuloma: in this field, there are conspicuous xanthomatized histiocytes.

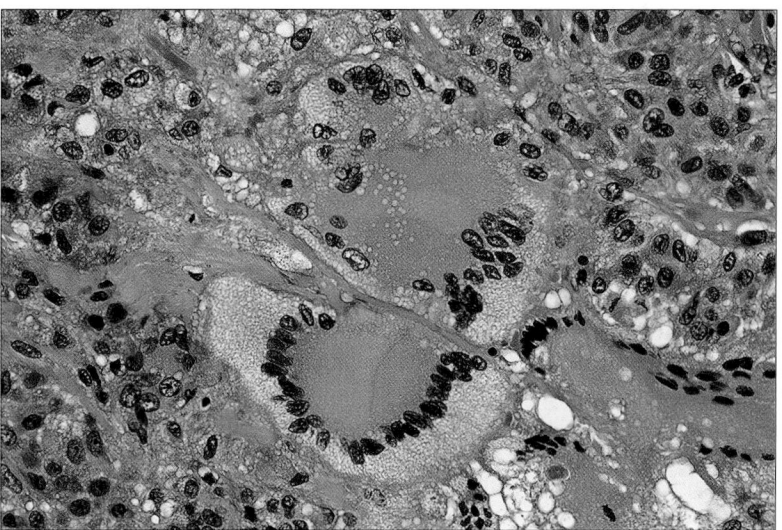

Fig. 8.100
Necrobiotic xanthogranuloma: Touton giant cells are sometimes prominent.

to foci of necrobiosis (*Fig. 8.101*). Asteroid bodies are often found in the cytoplasm of giant cells and have been suggested as a useful diagnostic finding.[22] Frozen sections and oil red O staining for fat may reveal focal lipid droplets. Cholesterol clefts and lipid vacuoles are sometimes seen within the foci of necrobiosis and xanthogranulomatous inflammation (*Fig. 8.102*).[23] In rare cases, however, lipid deposition and giant cells are inconspicuous.[23] The granulomatous and necrobiotic process may affect

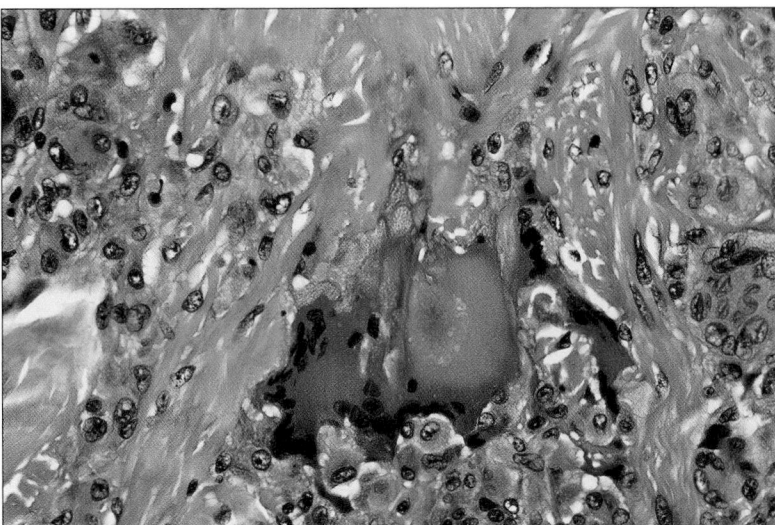

Fig. 8.101
Necrobiotic xanthogranuloma: angulated giant cells with darkly staining nuclei are commonly present.

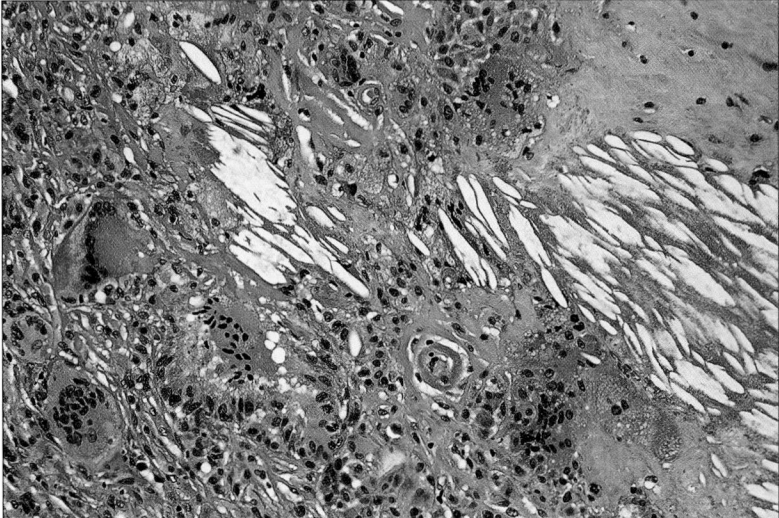

Fig. 8.102
Necrobiotic xanthogranuloma: cholesterol clefts are a characteristic feature.

muscular arteries. Staining for elastic fibers reveals their absence in the necrobiotic areas; alcian blue staining may reveal small amounts of interstitial mucin. As with most necrobiotic disorders, transepidermal elimination of necrobiotic collagen is sometimes a feature.[24]

Lungs and heart may show giant cells, granulomata, necrobiosis or a combination of these features in patients with systemic disease.[9]

Differential diagnosis

The clinical and histological features are distinctive: the presence of massive necrobiosis associated with numerous cholesterol clefts, bizarre multinucleated giant cells and Touton-type giant cells distinguishes necrobiotic xanthogranuloma from necrobiosis lipoidica and other necrobiotic dermatoses. It should, however, be noted that prominent cholesterol cleft formation may rarely be seen in necrobiosis lipoidica.[25] Small punch biopsies may not be adequate for definitive evaluation and sampling bias may be misleading. Clinical correlation should be taken into consideration before making a definitive diagnosis.

References

1. Holden, C.A., Winkelmann, R.K., Wilson Jones, E. (1986) Necrobiotic xanthogranuloma: report of four cases. *Br J Dermatopathol*, **114**, 241–250.
2. Randell, P.L., Heenan, P.J. (1999) Necrobiotic xanthogranuloma with paraproteinemia. *Australas J Dermatol*, **40**, 114–115.
3. Betts, C.M., Pasquinelli, G., Costa, A.M. et al (2001) Necrobiotic xanthogranuloma without periorbital involvement: an ultrastructural study. *Ultrastruct Pathol*, **25**, 437–444.
4. Chave, T.A., Hutchinson, P.E. (2001) Necrobiotic xanthogranuloma with two monoclonal paraproteins and no periorbital involvement at presentation. *Clin Exp Dermatol*, **26**, 493–496.
5. Ugurlu, S., Bartley, G.B., Gibson, L.E. (2000) Necrobiotic xanthogranuloma: long-term outcome of ocular and systemic involvement. *Am J Ophthalmol*, **21**, 575–577.
6. Mehregan, D.A., Winkelmann, R.K. (1992) Necrobiotic xanthogranuloma. *Arch Dermatol*, **123**, 94–100.
7. Stork, J., Kodetova, D., Vosmik, F. et al (2000) Necrobiotic xanthogranuloma presenting as a solitary tumor. *Am J Dermatopathol*, **22**, 453–456.
8. Tucker, N.A., Discepola, M.J., Blanco, G. et al (1997) Necrobiotic xanthogranuloma without dermatologic involvement. *Can J Ophthalmol*, **32**, 369–399.
9. Winkelmann, R.K., Litzow, M.R., Umbert, I.J. et al (1997) Giant cell granulomatous pulmonary and myocardial lesions in necrobiotic xanthogranuloma with paraproteinemia. *Proc Mayo Clin*, **72**, 1028–1033.
10. Umbert, I., Winkelmann, R.K. (1995) Necrobiotic xanthogranuloma with cardiac involvement. *Br J Dermatol*, **133**, 438–443.
11. Novak, P.M., Robbins, T.O., Winkelmann, R.K. (1992) Necrobiotic xanthogranuloma with myocardial lesions and nodular transformation of the liver. *Hum Pathol*, **23**, 195–196.
12. Chandra, S., Finklestein, S., Gill, D. (2002) Necrobiotic xanthogranuloma occurring with linear morphea. *Australas J Dermatol*, **43**, 52–54.
13. Hunter, L., Burry, A.F. (1985) Necrobiotic xanthogranuloma: a systemic disease with paraproteinemia. *Pathology*, **17**, 533–536.
14. Criado, P.R., Vasconcellos, C., Pegas, J.R. (2002) Necrobiotic xanthogranuloma with lambda paraproteinemia: case report of successful treatment with melphalan and prednisone. *J Dermatolog Treat*, **13**, 87–89.
15. Nestle, F.O., Hofbauer, G., Burg, G. (1999) Necrobiotic xanthogranuloma with monoclonal gammopathy of the IgG lambda type. *Dermatology*, **198**, 434–435.
16. Kossard, S., Winkelmann, R.K. (1980) Necrobiotic xanthogranuloma with paraproteinemia. *J Am Acad Dermatol*, **3**, 257–270.
17. Finan, M.C., Winkelmann, R.K. (1986) Necrobiotic xanthogranuloma with paraproteinemia. A review of 22 cases. *Medicine*, **65**, 376–388.
18. Finan, M.C., Winkelmann, R.K. (1987) Histopathology of necrobiotic xanthogranuloma with paraproteinemia. *J Cutan Pathol*, **14**, 92–99.
19. Reeder, C.B., Connolly, S.M., Winkelmann, R.K. (1991) The evolution of Hodgkin's lymphoma and necrobiotic xanthogranuloma syndrome. *Mayo Clin Proc*, **66**, 1222–1224.
20. Matsura, F., Yamashita, S., Hirano, K. et al (1999) Activation of monocytes in vivo causes intracellular accumulation of lipoprotein-derived lipids and marked hypocholesterolemia – a possible pathogenesis of necrobiotic xanthogranuloma. *Atherosclerosis*, **142**, 355–365.
21. Requena, L., Yus, E.S. (2001) Panniculitis. Part I. Mostly septal panniculitis. *J Am Acad Dermatol*, **45**, 458–462.
22. Winkelmann, R.K., Dahl, P.R., Peniciaro, C., Dahl, P.M. (1998) Asteroid bodies and other cytoplasmic inclusions in necrobiotic xanthogranuloma with paraproteinemia. *J Am Acad Dermatol*, **38**, 967–970.
23. Kossard, S., Chow, E., Wilkinson, B. et al (2000) Lipid and giant cell poor necrobiotic xanthogranuloma. *J Cutan Pathol*, **27**, 374–378.
24. Dupre, A., Viraben, R. (1988) Necrobiotic xanthogranuloma: a case without paraproteinemia but with transepidermal elimination. *J Cutan Pathol*, **15**, 116–119.
25. De la Torre, C., Losada, A., Cruces, M.J. (1999) Necrobiosis lipoidica: a case with prominent cholesterol clefting and transepithelial elimination. *Am J Dermatopathol*, **21**, 575–577.

Palisaded neutrophilic and granulomatous dermatitis

Clinical features

Palisaded neutrophilic and granulomatous dermatitis (interstitial granulomatous dermatitis) is a term that has been applied to a reaction pattern of necrobiotic and granulomatous inflammation encountered in the setting of systemic disease.[1] Other terms that have been applied to similar, overlapping and, in some cases, probably identical lesions, include interstitial granulomatous dermatitis with arthritis, rheumatoid

papules, superficial ulcerating rheumatoid necrobiosis, cutaneous extravascular necrotizing granuloma and Churg–Strauss granuloma.[1–6] Myriad underlying systemic diseases have been purported to be associated with these lesions including rheumatoid arthritis, lupus erythematosus, Sjögren's syndrome, thyroiditis, Raynaud's syndrome, hepatitis, inflammatory bowel disease, lymphoproliferative disorders, myelodysplastic syndrome, vasculitis (Wegener's, Churg–Strauss,

Takayasu's arteritis, periarteritis nodosa), hemolytic uremic syndrome, thrombotic thrombocytopenic purpura, mixed cryoglobulinemia, drug reactions (especially sulfonamides), carcinoma, diabetes and infections (streptococcal, HIV, Epstein–Barr virus, parvovirus).[1–4,7–10]

The lesions are usually located on the extremities or trunk in an adult.[1] They are characterized by papules and nodules, and are often arranged in a linear pattern. These linearly arranged lesions may be confluent and have been described as linear bands or cords with a 'rope-like' consistency. Plaques have also been described.[6]

Pathogenesis and histological features

The pathogenesis of palisaded neutrophilic and granulomatous dermatitis most likely depends on the associated/underlying disease. It appears that, in some cases, autoimmune-mediated vasculitis probably plays an important role. Direct immunofluorescence studies have demonstrated fibrin and IgM in the vasculature of some patients.[1]

A variety of histological patterns have been described. A common denominator is the presence of necrobiosis associated with a histiocytic response similar to granuloma annulare or necrobiosis lipoidica. In fact, some would label these lesions as falling within the spectrum of granuloma annulare.[4] In other cases, a well-defined palisade is not present and only a loosely organized zone of histiocytes is seen. Superimposed on this background of granuloma annulare-like features is a neutrophilic infiltrate with karyorrhexis (*Figs 8.103, 8.104*). Variable numbers of eosinophils may be noted and, when present, appear to occur mostly in patients with a peripheral eosinophilia. Frank leukocytoclastic vasculitis is present in some cases. Dermal mucin may be present.

Differential diagnosis

From the above discussion it can be seen that a number of different terms have been proposed to describe lesions resembling granuloma annulare or necrobiosis lipoidica but with the added features of acute and eosinophilic inflammation, karyorrhexis and leukocytoclastic vasculitis. Some have preferred to recognize these changes within the spectrum of granuloma annulare and necrobiosis lipoidica.[4] The precise terminology preferred by the dermatopathologist is probably not important. More significant than any nosological nuances is issuing a report that alerts the clinician to the possibility that the patient may have underlying systemic disease and that when such lesions are encountered appropriate clinical evaluation is necessary.[10]

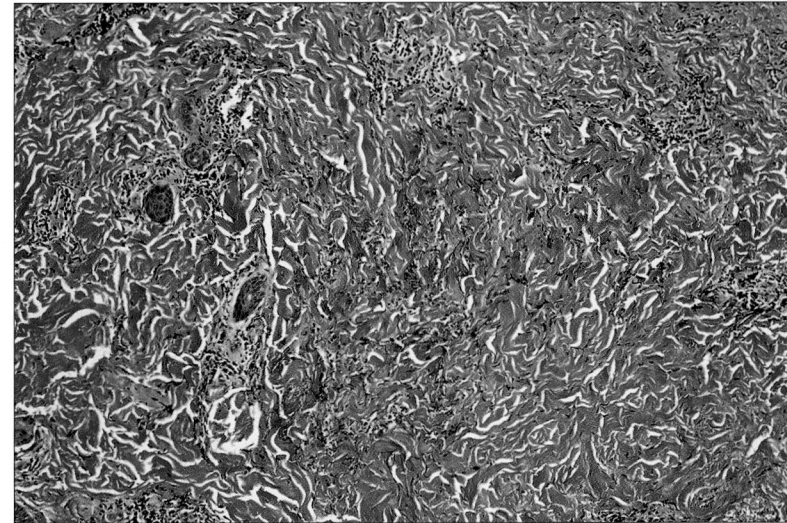

Fig. 8.103
Palisaded neutrophilic and granulomatous dermatitis: an interstitial inflammatory cell infiltrate is present in the center of the field mimicking diffuse granuloma annulare.

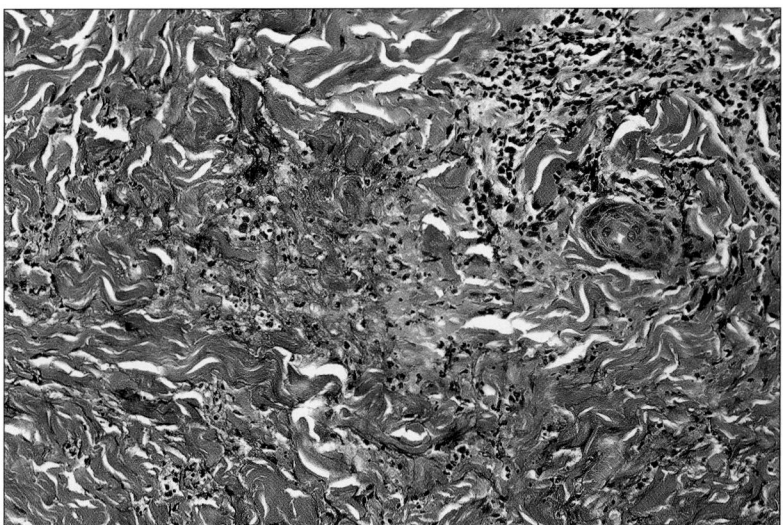

Fig. 8.104
Palisaded neutrophilic and granulomatous dermatitis: close-up view showing necrobiosis, histiocytes and neutrophils associated with karyorrhexis.

References

1. Chu, P., Connolly, K., LeBoit, P.E. (1994) The histopathologic spectrum of palisaded neutrophilic and granulomatous dermatitis. *Arch Dermatol*, **130**, 1278–1283.
2. Finan, M.C., Winkelmann, R.K. (1983) The cutaneous extravascular necrotizing granuloma (Churg–Strauss granuloma) and systemic disease: a review of 27 cases. *Medicine*, **62**, 142–158.
3. Harpster, E.F., Mauro, T., Barr, R.J. (1989) Linear granuloma annulare. *J Am Acad Dermatol*, **21**, 1138–1141.
4. Magro, C.M., Crowson, A.N., Regauer, S. (1996) Granuloma annulare and necrobiosis lipoidica tissue reactions as a manifestation of systemic disease. *Hum Pathol*, **27**, 50–56.
5. Wilmoth, G.J., Perniciaro, C. (1996) Cutaneous extravascular necrotizing granuloma (Winkelmann granuloma): confirmation of the association with systemic disease. *J Am Acad Dermatol*, **34**, 753–759.
6. Aloi, F., Tomasini, C., Pippione, M. (1999) Interstitial granulomatous dermatitis with plaques. *Am J Dermatopathol*, **21**, 320–323.
7. Long, D., Thiboutot, D.M., Majeski, J.T. et al (1996) Interstitial granulomatous dermatitis with arthritis. *J Am Acad Dermatol*, **34**, 957–961.
8. Sangüeza, O.P., Caudell, M.D., Mengesha, Y.M. et al (2002) Palisaded neutrophilic granulomatous dermatitis in rheumatoid arthritis. *J Am Acad Dermatol*, **24**, 209–212.
9. Higaki, Y., Yamashita, H., Sato, K. et al (1993) Rheumatoid papules: a report on four patients with histopathologic analysis. *J Am Acad Dermatol*, **34**, 957–961.
10. Perrin, C., Lacour, J.P., Castanet, J., Michiels, J.F. (2001) Interstitial granulomatous drug reaction with a histological pattern of interstitial granulomatous dermatitis. *Am J Dermatopathol*, **23**, 295–298.

'Metastatic' Crohn's disease

Clinical features

Cutaneous lesions in Crohn's disease predominantly involve the skin of the lower limbs, genitalia, perineum, perianal region and lips. One review of the literature showed that approximately 50% of patients with cutaneous Crohn's disease have involvement of the lower extremities.[1] The lesions present as single or multiple papules, plaques, nodules and ulcers.[1–10] Vulval tumor-like masses and herpes virus-like lesions have occasionally been described.[8,11] Colostomy site involvement has also

been documented. One patient has been reported as presenting with an erysipelas-like eruption involving the lip and nasolabial region.[3] In some patients, mucocutaneous lesions precede evidence of bowel involvement.[5,12,13] Of uncertain significance, cutaneous Crohn's disease seems to be highly associated with involvement of the large bowel.[11] Duration of lesions is variable, typically lasting from months to years. This topic is also discussed on page 489.

Pathogenesis and histological features

The pathogenesis of mucocutaneous Crohn's disease is not understood. Histologically, lesions are usually manifest as ill-defined, non-caseating granulomata present in the superficial (often papillary) dermis; however, granulomata may also involve the deep dermis and even subcutaneous adipose tissue.[14] The granulomata resemble those seen in the bowel. Necrobiotic collagen has been described in a number of cases.[14] Lymphocytes and plasma cells are also commonly present. Recently, the histological features of metastatic Crohn's disease have been expanded to include the findings of significant necrobiosis with leukocytoclasis, and vasculitis (see palisaded neutrophilic and granulomatous dermatitis, above).[14]

Differential diagnosis

Since the histological features of cutaneous Crohn's disease are non-specific, a definitive diagnosis requires clinical confirmation of the presence of associated bowel disease. Therefore, endoscopy, evaluation of gastrointestinal biopsies and review of clinical findings all play a role in confirmation of this diagnosis. Sarcoidosis may be indistinguishable from metastatic Crohn's disease; however, the granulomata of the former tend to be more discrete and compact. Mycobacterial infection is also an important differential diagnosis and, therefore, liberal use of special stains for microorganisms is essential. Culture should be performed as deemed clinically appropriate.

As noted above, cutaneous granulomata may precede evidence of bowel involvement.[5,12,13] Therefore, patients with granulomatous skin disease of uncertain etiology should be followed up carefully for evidence of bowel disease.

Granulomatous cheilitis may also show identical histological features. Studies have documented patients presenting with granulomatous cheilitis (see p. 452) who subsequently developed clinical manifestations of, or pathological evidence (without gastrointestinal symptoms) of, Crohn's disease.[15-20] One group described a patient in whom granulomatous cheilitis antedated development of Crohn's disease by 7 years.[21] It

appears, therefore, that some patients with granulomatous cheilitis are at risk for development of Crohn's disease and require gastrointestinal evaluation and careful clinical follow-up. Similarly, vulval Crohn's disease precedes development of bowel involvement in 25% of cases.[11]

References

1. Shum, D., Guenther, L. (1990) Metastatic Crohn's disease: case report and review of the literature. *Arch Dermatol*, **126**, 645–648.
2. Buckley, C., Bayoumi, A-H.M., Sarkany, I. (1990) Metastatic Crohn's disease. *Clin Exp Dermatol*, **15**, 131–133.
3. Lebwohl, M., Fleischmajer, R., Janowitz, H. et al (1984) Metastatic Crohn's disease. *J Am Acad Dermatol*, **10**, 33–38.
4. Burgdorf, W. (1981) Cutaneous manifestations of Crohn's disease. *J Am Acad Dermatol*, **5**, 689–695.
5. Virgili, A., Corazza, M. (1994) Crohn's disease of the vulva. A case report. *J Reprod Med*, **39**, 115–117.
6. Papiez, J.S., Hassenein, A., Wilkinson, E. et al (2001) Recurrent atypical myxoid fibroepithelial polyp associated with vulvar Crohn's disease. *Int J Gynecol Pathol*, **20**, 271–276.
7. Urbanek, M., Neill, S.M., McKee, P.H. (1996) Vulval Crohn's disease: difficulties in diagnosis. *Clin Exp Dermatol*, **21**, 211–214.
8. Mould, T.A., Rodgers, M.E., Burnham, W.R. et al (1997) Metastatic Crohn's disease causing a vulval mass and involving the cervix. *Int J STD AIDS*, **8**, 461–463.
9. Vettraino, I.M., Merritt, D.F. (1995) Crohn's disease of the vulva. *Am J Dermatopathol*, **17**, 410–413.
10. Tuffnell, D., Buchan, P.C. (1991) Crohn's disease of the vulva in childhood. *Br J Clin Pract*, **45**, 159–160.
11. Greenstein, A.J., Janowitz, H.D., Sachar, D.B. (1976) The extra-intestinal complications of Crohn's disease and ulcerative colitis: a study of 700 patients. *Medicine*, **55**, 401–412.
12. Guerrieri, C., Ohlsson, E., Ryden, G. et al (1995) Vulvitis granulomatosa: a cryptogenic chronic inflammatory hypertrophy of vulvar labia related to cheilitis granulomatosa and Crohn's disease. *Int J Gynecol Pathol*, **14**, 352–359.
13. Acker, S.M., Sahn, E.E., Rogers, H.C. et al (2000) Genital cutaneous Crohn's disease: two cases with unusual clinical and histopathologic features in men. *Am J Dermatopathol*, **22**, 443–446.
14. Hackzell-Bradley, M., Hedbald, M-A., Stephansson, E.A. (1996) Metastatic Crohn's disease: report of 3 cases with special reference to histopathologic findings. *Arch Dermatol*, **132**, 928–932.
15. Kano, Y., Shiohara, T., Yagita, A. et al (1990) Granulomatous cheilitis and Crohn's disease. *Br J Dermatol*, **123**, 409–412.
16. Carr, D. (1974) Granulomatous cheilitis in Crohn's disease. *BMJ*, **4**, 636.
17. Brook, I.M., King, D.H., Miller, I.D. (1983) Chronic granulomatous cheilitis and its relationship to Crohn's disease. *Oral Surg Oral Med Oral Pathol*, **56**, 405–408.
18. Talbot, T., Jewell, L., Schloss, E. et al (1984) Cheilitis antedating Crohn's disease: case report and literature update of oral lesions. *J Clin Gastroenterol*, **6**, 349–354.
19. Wiesenfeld, D., Ferguson, M.M., Mitchell, D.N. (1985) Oro-facial granulomatosis – a clinical and pathological analysis. *QJM*, **54**, 101–113.
20. Williams, A.J., Wray, D., Ferguson, M. (1991) The clinical entity of orofacial Crohn's disease. *QJM*, **79**, 451–458.
21. Rogers, R.S. (1996) Melkersson–Rosenthal syndrome and orofacial granulomatosis. *Dermatol Clin*, **14**, 371–379.

Granulomatous cheilitis

Granulomatous cheilitis (cheilitis granulomatosa, Meischer's cheilitis, orofacial granulomatosis) is discussed on page 452.

Acne agminata

Clinical features

Acne agminata (lupus miliaris disseminatus faciei, acnitis, papular tuberculid) is a rare condition first thought to be a form of tuberculid but an association with tuberculosis has since been excluded.[1-4] Some authors consider this disease to be synonymous with granulomatous rosacea. However, the distinctive clinical presentation, and the absence of typical rosacea in patients affected by the disease, argue against this possibility. Recently, a new name has been suggested for the disease: facial idiopathic granulomata with regressive evolution (F.I.G.U.R.E).[5]

Clinical presentation is characterized by fairly monomorphous yellowish-brown papules typically involving the central face with predilection for periocular areas (*Figs 8.105, 8.106*). Involvement of axillae or upper limbs is exceptionally present.[6] There is no sex predilection and the age range is wide although most cases occur in young to middle-aged adults.[7] An exceptional case has been documented during pregnancy.[8] Response to conventional treatment for rosacea is often ineffective but lesions tend to regress spontaneously over a period of months or even years leaving mild scarring.[9]

Pathogenesis and histological features

As suggested by some synonyms, infection by mycobacteria has been favored by some authors as a potential cause. This theory is no longer

tenable due to the absence of past or present systemic tuberculosis and the constant failure of isolation of bacilli. In one study from Israel, mycobacterial DNA was not detected by PCR.[1] It has been suggested that development of the lesions is due to an unusual granulomatous reaction to ruptured hair follicles.[10]

The histological features vary with the stage of evolution and may be entirely non-specific.[11] A biopsy from a well-established lesion shows a central area of well-defined caseous necrosis surrounded by multinucleate giant cells and epithelioid cells (sometimes indistinguishable from tuberculous infection) (*Figs 8.107, 8.108*). Serial sections often reveal a relationship of the necrosis to a destroyed hair follicle. Special stains may demonstrate a ring of elastic fibers in the center of the necrotic focus, possibly representing the isthmus of the hair follicle. The granulomata are not usually related to *Demodex folliculorum* as is often the case in granulomatous rosacea. Focal vasculitis is only exceptionally seen.

Differential diagnosis

The diagnosis is fairly easy in the presence of granulomata surrounding an area of caseation necrosis since the latter is not usually a feature of either granulomatous rosacea or perioral dermatitis. In biopsies showing only focal granulomatous inflammation, establishing the diagnosis may require very close clinicopathological correlation.

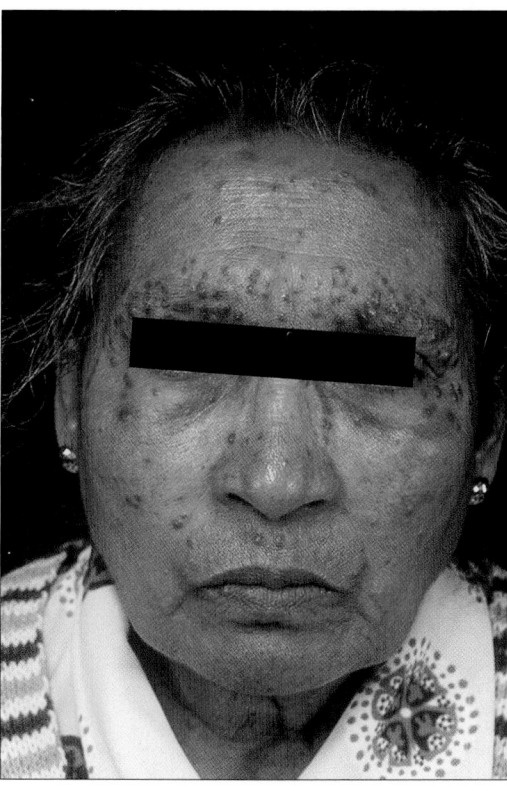

Fig. 8.105
Acne agminata: note the characteristic distribution of symmetrical papules on the forehead, cheeks and around the eyes. By courtesy of R.A. Marsden, MD, St George's Hospital, London, UK.

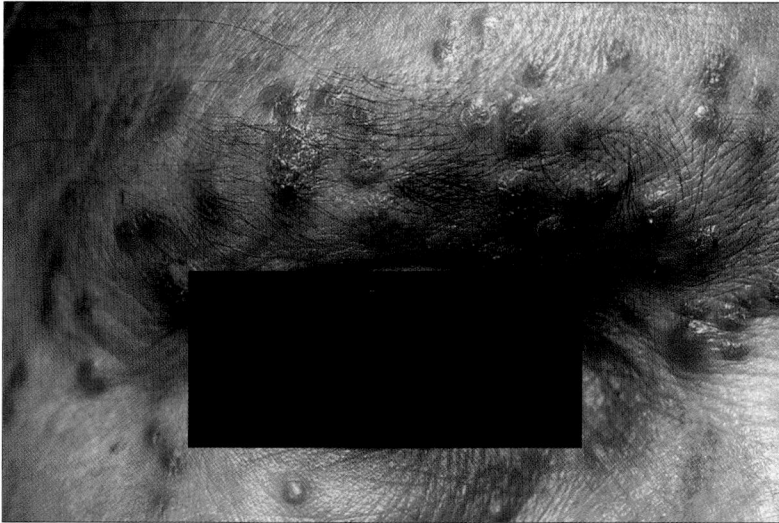

Fig. 8.106
Acne agminata: close-up view. By courtesy of R.A. Marsden, MD, St George's Hospital, London, UK.

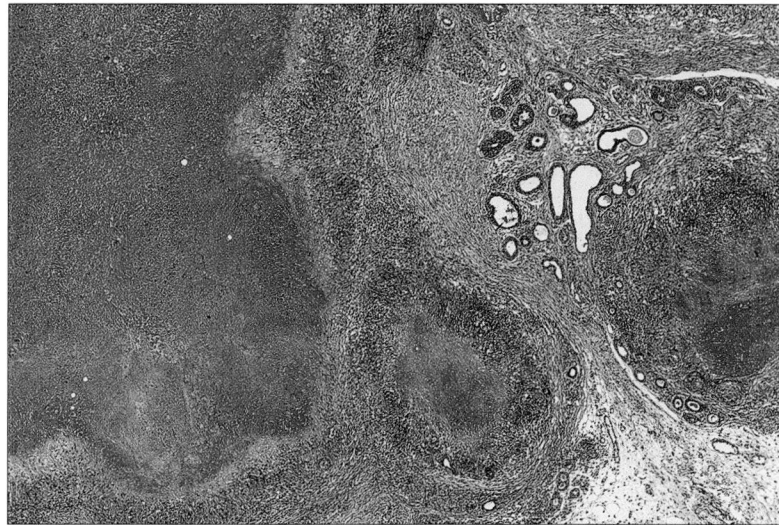

Fig. 8.107
Acne agminata: there are multiple caseating granulomata.

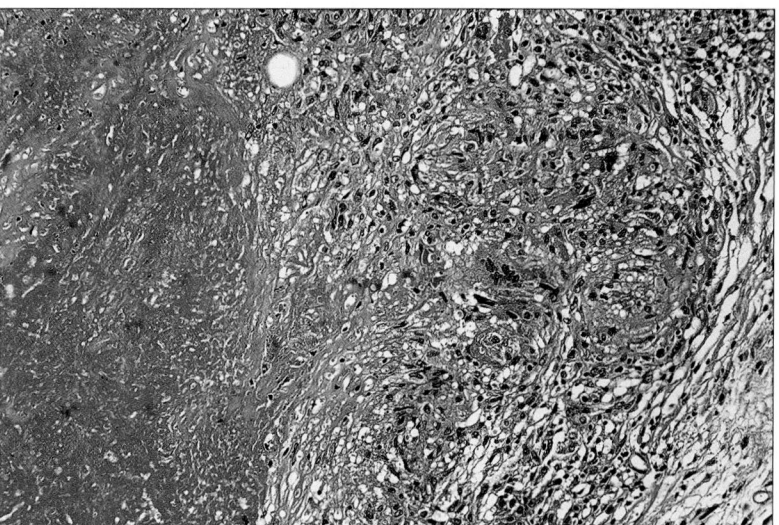

Fig. 8.108
Acne agminata: close-up view. The condition is not a tuberculid. Special stains and culture for tubercle bacilli are invariably negative.

3.   Calnan, C.D. (1966) Acne agminata, lupus miliaris facie and acnitis. *G Ital Dermatol Minerva Dermatol*, **107**, 587–595.
4.   O'Driscoll, T., Morgan, G. (1974) Acne agminata of the eyelid. *Proc R Soc Med*, **67**, 869–870.
5.   Skowron, F., Causeret, A.S., Pabion, C. et al (2001) F.I.G.U.R.E.: facial idiopathic granulomata with regressive evolution. Is 'lupus miliaris disseminatus faciei' still an acceptable diagnosis in the third millennium? *Dermatology*, **201**, 287–289.
6.   Bedlow, A.J., Otter, M., Marsden, R.A. (1998) Axillary acne agminata (lupus miliaris disseminatus faciei). *Clin Exp Dermatol*, **23**, 125–128.
7.   Dekio, S., Jidoi, J., Imaoka, C. (1991) Lupus miliaris disseminatus faciei – report of a case in an elderly woman. *Clin Exp Dermatol*, **16**, 295–296.
8.   Walchner, M., Plewig, G., Messer, G. (1998) Lupus miliaris disseminatus faciei evoked during pregnancy in a patient with cutaneous lupus erythematosus. *Int J Dermatol*, **37**, 864–867.
9.   Uesugi, Y., Aiba, S., Usuba, M. et al (1996) Oral prednisone in the treatment of acne agminata. *Br J Dermatol*, **134**, 1098–1100.
10. Shitara, A. (1984) Lupus miliaris disseminatus faciei. *Int J Dermatol*, **23**, 542–544.
11. el Darouti, M., Zaher, H. (1993) Lupus miliaris disseminatus faciei – pathologic study of early, fully developed, and late lesions. *Int J Dermatol*, **32**, 508–511.

References

1.   Hodak, E., Trattner, A., Feuerman, H. et al (1997) Lupus miliaris disseminatus facei – the DNA of Mycobacterium tuberculosis is not detectable in active lesions by polymerase chain reaction. *Br J Dermatol*, **137**, 614–619.
2.   Scott, K.W., Calnan, C.D. (1967) Acne agminata. *Trans St John's Hosp Dermatol Soc*, **53**, 60–69.

Perioral dermatitis

Clinical features

Perioral dermatitis (perioral granulomatous dermatitis) is a common dermatosis that may represent a variant of rosacea.[1–5] It is discussed in this section since it can, on occasion, be associated with granulomatous histology. Patients are usually young women but the condition may occur in children.[1,6] Presentation in identical twins has exceptionally been documented.[7] A granulomatous variant of perioral dermatitis has been described in children.[8–10] It tends to be more common in Afro-Caribbean children and has been labeled facial Afro-Caribbean childhood eruption (FACE).[8]

Typically, perioral dermatitis consists of erythematous papules and pustules with a characteristic distribution on the chin and nasolabial folds (*Fig. 8.109*). Involvement of the inner cheeks, forehead or periocular area is unusual. Extrafacial and generalized involvement has also been documented.[11] The clinical appearances may mimic acne but comedones are absent.[12]

Pathogenesis and histological features

The pathogenesis of perioral dermatitis is not clearly understood but the condition seems to be etiologically linked in some cases to the use of potent topical steroids, the application of cosmetics, the usage of some toothpastes and the use of epoxy diacrylates in dental composite resins.[13–18] An association has also been reported in renal transplant patients on systemic steroids and azathioprine.[19]

Biopsy shows mild acanthosis, focal spongiosis and hyperkeratosis with parakeratosis and a mild perivascular and periadnexal lymphohistiocytic infiltrate. The appearances are almost indistinguishable from those found in rosacea.[20] Ruptured hair follicles with microabscess formation are occasionally seen. Sometimes granulomata with sarcoidal features are present.[21] Giant cells have also been documented such that distinction from sarcoidosis may be difficult.[1,22] In most cases, clinical correlation resolves any diagnostic difficulties.

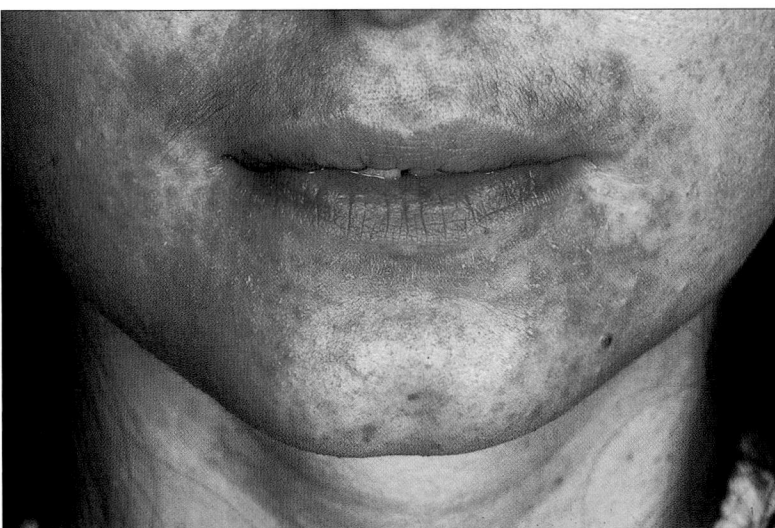

Fig. 8.109
Perioral dermatitis: papules and pustules in a characteristic distribution.
By courtesy of the Institute of Dermatology, London, UK.

References

1. Laude, T.A., Salvemini, J.N. (1999) Perioral dermatitis in children. *Semin Cutan Med Surg*, **18**, 206–209.
2. Smith, K.W. (1990) Perioral dermatitis with histopathologic features of granulomatous rosacea: successful treatment with isotretinoin. *Cutis*, **46**, 413–415.
3. Hjorth, N., Osmundsen, P., Rook, A.J. et al (1968) Perioral dermatitis. *Br J Dermatol*, **80**, 307–313.
4. Sneddon, I. (1972) Perioral dermatitis. *Br J Dermatol*, **87**, 430–434.
5. Hogan, D.J. (1995) Perioral dermatitis. *Curr Probl Dermatol*, **22**, 98–104.
6. Boeck, K., Abeck, D., Werfel, S. et al (1997) Perioral dermatitis in children – clinical presentation, pathogenesis-related factors and response to topical metronidazole. *Dermatology*, **195**, 235–238.
7. Weston, W.L., Morelli, J.G. (1998) Identical twins with perioral dermatitis. *Pediatr Dermatol*, **15**, 144.
8. Sillevis Smitt, J.H., Das, P.K., van Ginkel, C.J.W. (1991) Granulomatous perioral dermatitis (facial Afro-Caribbean childhood eruption [FACE]). *Br J Dermatol*, **125**, 399.
9. Williams, H.C. (1996) Childhood granulomatous periorificial dermatitis. *Pediatr Dermatol*, **13**, 515.
10. Knautz, M.A., Lesher, J.L. Jr (1996) Childhood granulomatous perioral dermatitis. *Pediatr Dermatol*, **13**, 131–134.
11. Urbatsch, A.J., Frieden, I., Williams, M.L. et al (2002) Extrafacial and generalized granulomatous perioral dermatitis. *Arch Dermatol*, **138**, 1354–1358.
12. Kuflik, J.H., Janniger, C.K., Piela, Z. (2001) Perioral dermatitis: an acneiform eruption. *Cutis*, **67**, 21–22.
13. Wells, K., Brodell, R.T. (1993) Topical steroid 'addiction'. A cause of perioral dermatitis. *Postgrad Med*, **93**, 225–230.
14. Velangi, S.S., Humphreys, F., Beveridge, G.W. (1998) Periocular dermatitis associated with prolonged use of a steroid eye ointment. *Clin Exp Dermatol*, **23**, 297–298.
15. Malik, R., Quirk, C.J. (2000) Topical applications and perioral dermatitis. *Australas J Dermatol*, **41**, 34–38.
16. Beacham, B.E., Kurgansky, D., Gould, W.M. (1990) Circumoral dermatitis and cheilitis caused by tartar control dentifrices. *J Am Acad Dermatol*, **22**, 1029–1032.
17. Reilly, K.E., McCarthy, L.H. (2000) Toothpaste allergy with intractable perioral rash in a 10-year old boy. *J Am Board Fam Pract*, **13**, 73–75.
18. Kanerva, I., Alanko, K. (1998) Stomatitis and perioral dermatitis caused by epoxy diacrylates in dental composite resins. *J Am Acad Dermatol*, **38**, 116–120.
19. Adams, S.J., Davidson, A.M., Cunliffe, W.J., Giles, G.R. (1982) Perioral dermatitis in renal transplant recipients maintained on corticosteroids and immunosuppressive therapy. *Br J Dermatol*, **106**, 589–592.
20. Marks, R., Black, M.M. (1971) Perioral dermatitis – a histopathological study of 26 cases. *Br J Dermatol*, **84**, 242–247.
21. Fiedman, I.J., Prose, N.S., Fletcher, V. et al (1989) Granulomatous perioral dermatitis in children. *Arch Dermatol*, **125**, 369–373.
22. Antony, F.C., Buckley, D.A., Russell-Jones, R. (2002) Childhood granulomatous periorificial dermatitis in an Asian girl – a variant of sarcoid? *Clin Exp Dermatol*, **27**, 275–276.

Infective granulomata

Infections, particularly fungal and mycobacterial, are often associated with granulomatous inflammation. Conversely, the vast majority of routine biopsies showing granulomatous inflammation are not due to infection. However, when faced with a specimen showing granulomatous inflammation, the pathologist must maintain a low threshold for performing stains for organisms and for issuing recommendations for microbiology culture. If such an approach is not taken, the vast majority of infectious causes of granulomatous inflammation will be misdiagnosed. In addition, although pathologists tend to associate certain patterns of granulomatous inflammation with infection by specific organisms (e.g. caseating granulomatous inflammation and mycobacterium tuberculosis), it should be remembered that on occasions the same organism may cause several different patterns of granulomatous inflammation (e.g. mycobacterium leprae). Similarly, mixed suppurative and granulomatous inflammation may result from both atypical mycobacteria and deep fungal infections. A practical corollary to this is that the pathologist should order several special stains to evaluate for a variety of organisms rather than relying on a single stain for the most likely culprit.

Specific infectious causes of granulomatous inflammation are discussed in detail in Chapter 17.

Foreign body granulomata

A wide variety of substances when present within the dermis may result in a foreign body giant cell reaction and may mimic primary granulomatous disorders. These are summarized in *Table 8.2* and examples are shown in *Figures 8.110–8.113*. Therefore, when examining specimens with granulomatous inflammation of uncertain etiology, all sections should be examined with polarized light to exclude foreign body reactions. Most foreign body granulomatous reactions occur as a result of external foreign bodies, particularly suture material. Foreign body granulomatous reactions secondary to internal foreign bodies are mainly secondary to hair shafts within the dermis after folliculitis or to fragments of keratin as a result of ruptured epidermoid or trichilemmal cysts. Another source of foreign body granulomatous reaction to internal material is gout (see p. 590).

The pathologist should be particularly aware that beryllium and zirconium may be associated with granulomata that mimic sarcoidosis, the so-called sarcoidal 'naked' granulomata. It is especially important to think of these agents as rare possible causes of granulomata since neither is visible with routine or polarization microscopy. Beryllium was once used in the manufacture of fluorescent light bulbs. Following exposure to beryllium, patients may develop either systemic berylliosis or have cutaneous involvement only. Pulmonary lesions follow inhalation.[1] Skin involvement, in the form of papules, follows direct inoculation.[1] Diagnosis of chronic beryllium disease is based on demonstration of a cell-mediated response to beryllium by patch testing.[1] Diagnosis may also be established by laser microprobe mass spectrometry.[1,2]

Zirconium was once added to antiperspirants.[3] Patients developed papules at sites where the substance was introduced and interstitial lung disease also occurred.[4] More recently, elephantiasis following nodal involvement has been described in patients with beryllium and zirconium exposure from mineral-rich soil (podoconiosis).[5] Diagnosis may be made using spectrographic analysis.[1,2,6]

Foreign body granulomata to esthetic microimplants are relatively uncommon nowadays, as the material used has been greatly improved. Silicone granulomata are sometimes found and occasionally one encounters foreign body granulomata to esthetic microimplants such as Dermalive, artecoll (PMMA-microspheres) and bioplastique (poly-methylsiloxane).[7,8] Histological recognition of granulomatous reactions to artecoll and bioplastique is easy, as the patterns are fairly distinctive. In the former, there are irregularly shaped cystic spaces containing translucent non-birefringent material (*Fig. 8.114*); in the latter, there are small regular round cystic spaces ('Swiss cheese appearance') containing translucent non-birefringent material.

A metastatic silicone granuloma mimicking acne agminata and associated with the sicca complex has been reported in a silicone breast implant patient.[9]

References

1. Jones, W.W. (1988) Beryllium disease. *Postgrad Med*, **64**, 511–516.
2. Bobka, C.A., Stewart, L.A., Engelken, G.J. et al (1997) Comparison of in vivo and in vitro measures of beryllium sensitization. *J Occup Environ Med*, **39**, 540–547.
3. Montemarano, A.D., Sau, P., Johnson, F.B. et al (1997) Cutaneous granulomata caused by an aluminum–zirconium complex: an ingredient of antiperspirants. *J Am Acad Dermatol*, **37**, 496–498.
4. Romeo, L., Cazzadori, A., Bontempini, L. et al (1994) Interstitial lung granulomata as a possible consequence of exposure to zirconium dust. *Med Lav*, **85**, 219–222.
5. Frommel, D., Aynanci, B., Pfeifer, H.R. et al (1993) Podoconiosis in the Ethiopian Rift Valley. Role of beryllium and zirconium. *Trop Geogr Med*, **45**, 165–167.
6. Skelton, H.G. 3rd, Smith, K.J., Johnson, F.B. et al (1993) Zirconium granuloma resulting from an aluminum–zirconium complex: a previously unrecognized agent in the development of hypersensitivity granulomata. *J Am Acad Dermatol*, **28**, 874–876.

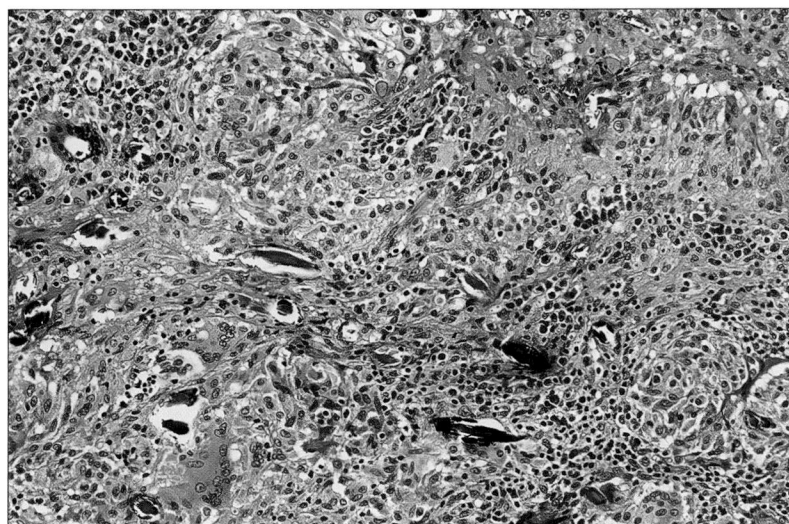

Fig. 8. 110
Foreign body granuloma: there is a florid granulomatous reaction to shrapnel.

Table 8.2
Important causes of foreign body granulomata

Endogenous	Exogenous		
Keratin	Silica	Graphite	Cactus spine
Hair shaft	Beryllium	Paraffin	Vegetable oil
Ruptured cyst	Zirconium	Shrapnel	Mineral oil
contents	Talc	Sutures	Food particles
Released lipids	Silicone	Arthropods	Wood splinters
Urate crystals	Tattoo pigment	Sea urchin spine	

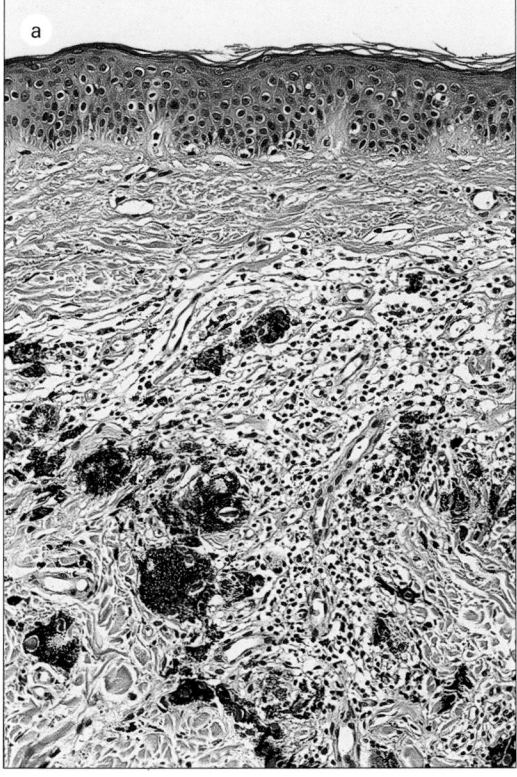

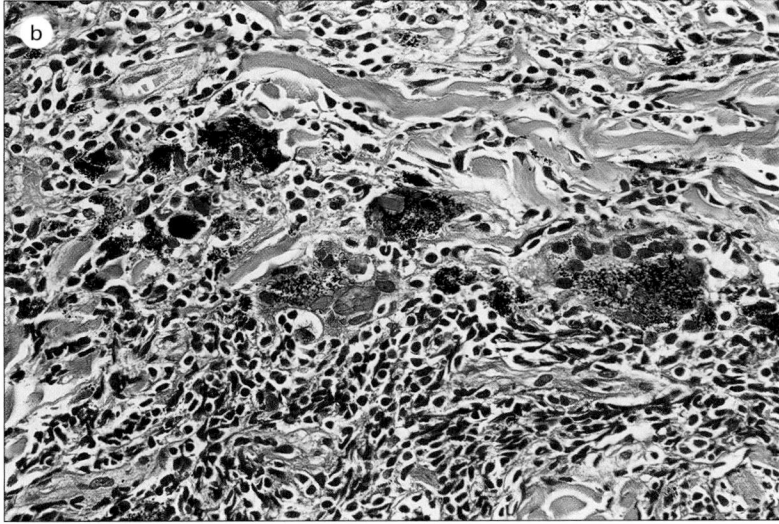

Fig. 8.111
(a, b) Tattoo site: foreign body and sarcoidal responses may occasionally be seen in tattoo reaction.

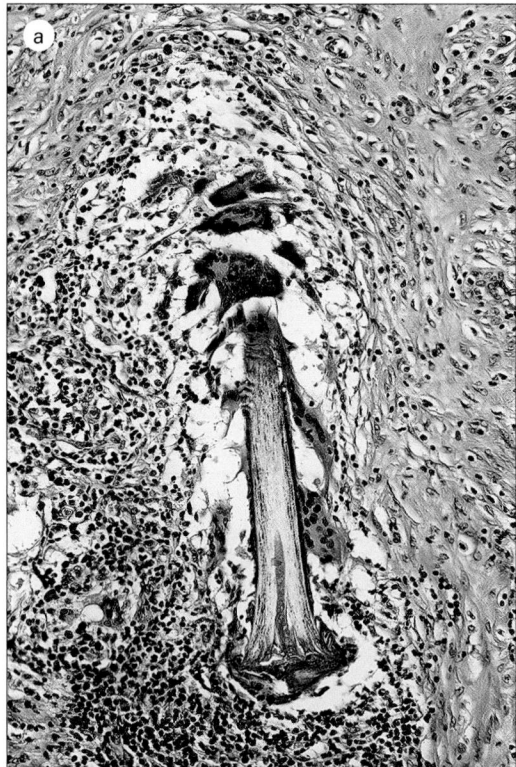

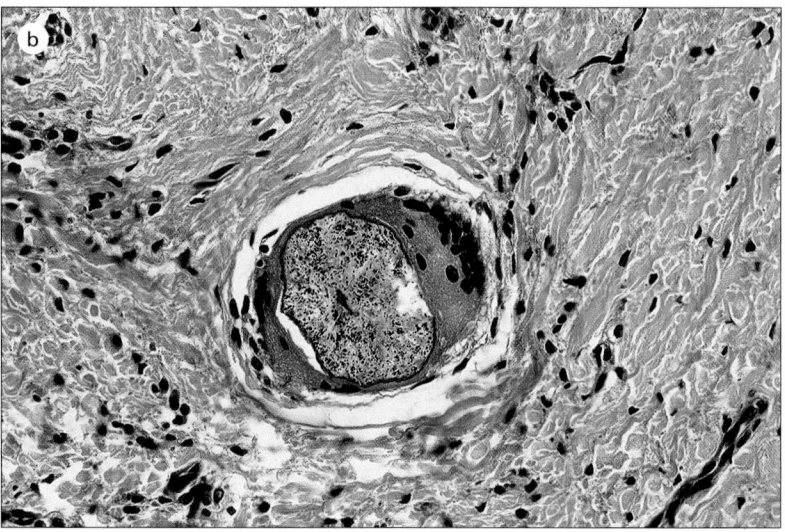

Fig. 8.112
(a, b) Foreign body granuloma: this free hair shaft has been partially engulfed by foreign body giant cells.

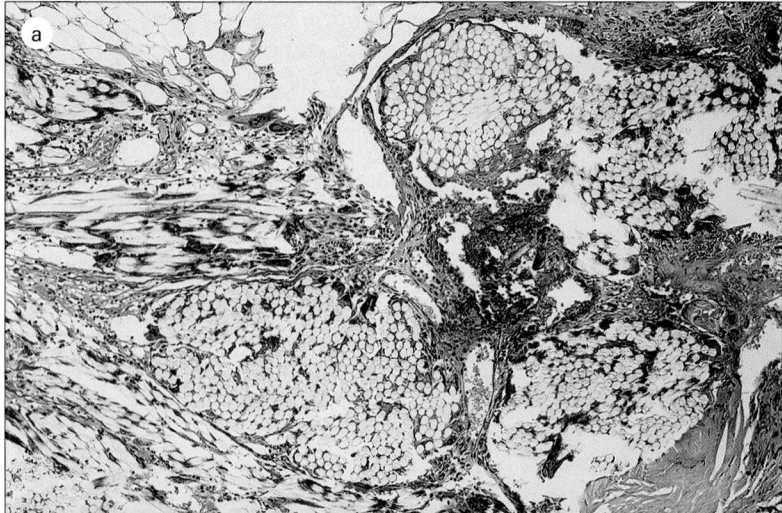

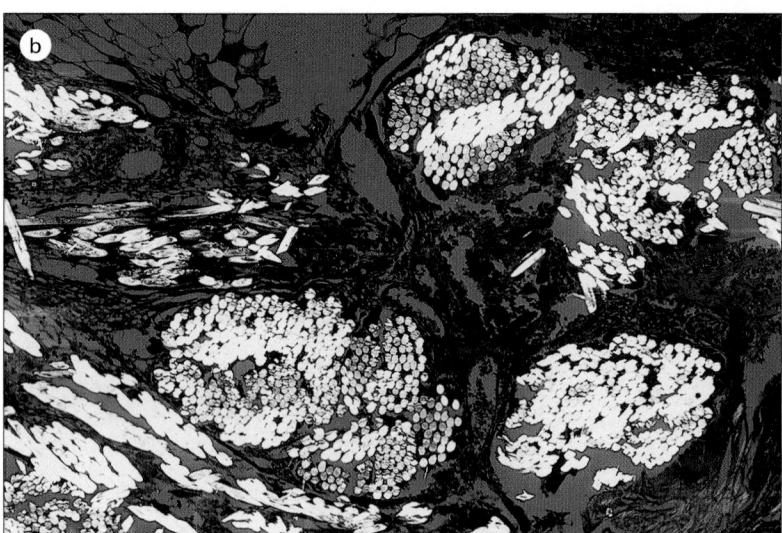

Fig. 8.113
Suture granuloma: (a) suture fragments are present, note the multinucleate giant cells; (b) when viewed with polarized light, suture fragments show birefringence.

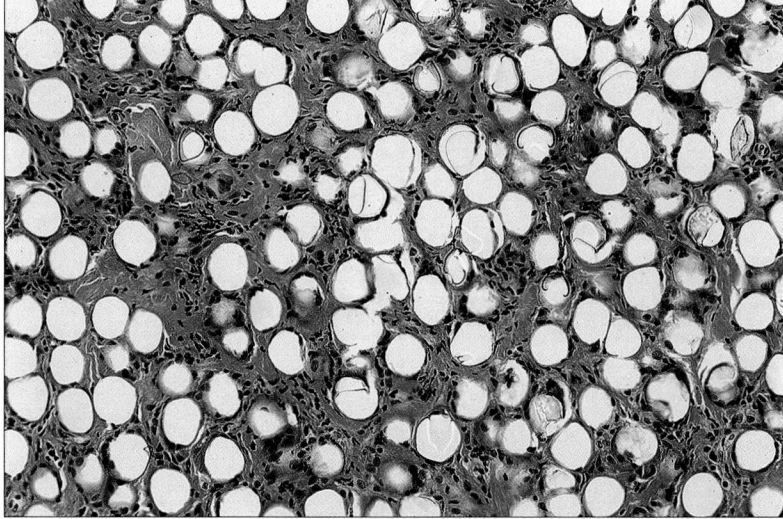

Fig. 8.114
Artecoll granuloma: there are small cystic spaces containing round, slightly refractile foreign bodies.

7. Rudolph, C.M., Soyer, H.P., Schuller-Petrovic, S. et al (1999) Foreign body granulomata to injectable aesthetic microimplants. *Am J Surg Pathol*, **23**, 113–117.
8. Requena, C., Izquierdo, M.J., Navarro, M. et al (2001) Adverse reactions to injectable aesthetic microimplants. *Am J Dermatopathol*, **23**, 197–200.
9. Suzuki, K., Aoki, M., Kawana, S. et al (2002) Metastatic silicone granuloma: lupus miliaris disseminatus faciei-like face nodules and sicca complex in a silicone breast implant patient. *Arch Dermatol*, **138**, 537–538.

Granulomata in congenital immunodeficiency syndromes

A number of inherited immune deficiency diseases may on occasions present with non-infectious granulomata involving different organs including the skin.[1–3] These diseases include combined immune deficiency, chronic granulomatous disease, ataxia telangiectasia, common variable immunodeficiency and X-linked infantile hypogammaglobulinemia.

In combined immune deficiency, cutaneous tuberculoid and necrobiotic granulomata may occur and in a single instance perineural invasion was identified closely mimicking tuberculoid leprosy.[4,5] Cutaneous granulomata in chronic granulomatous disease may show caseation necrosis without a detectable trigger or be associated with foreign bodies.[6,7] In ataxia telangiectasia, patients can present with either necrobiotic or tuberculoid granulomata.[8–10] In common variable immunodeficiency tuberculoid, sarcoidal and caseating granulomata have been documented.[11–13] In X-linked infantile hypogammaglobulinemia, caseating granulomata have been reported.[14]

References

1. Berron-Ruiz, A., Berron-Pérez, R., Ruiz-Maldonado, R. (2000) Cutaneous markers of primary immunodeficiencies in children. *Pediatr Dermatol*, **17**, 91–96.
2. Arbiser, J.L. (1995) Genetic immunodeficiencies: cutaneous manifestations and recent progress. *J Am Acad Dermatol*, **33**, 82–89.
3. Levine, T.S., Price, A.B., Boyle, S. et al (1994) Cutaneous sarcoid-like granulomata in primary immunodeficiency syndromes. *Br J Dermatol*, **130**, 118–120.
4. Siegfried, E.C., Prose, N.S., Friedman, N.J., Paller, A.S. (1991) Cutaneous granulomata in children with combined immunodeficiency. *J Am Acad Dermatol*, **25**, 761–766.
5. Krupnick, A.I., Shim, H., Phelps, R.G. et al (2001) Cutaneous granulomata masquerading as tuberculoid leprosy in a patient with congenital combined immunodeficiency. *Mt Sinai J Med*, **68**, 326–330.
6. Dohil, M., Prendiville, J.S., Crawford, R.I. et al (1997) Cutaneous manifestations of chronic granulomatous disease. A report of four cases and review of the literature. *J Am Acad Dermatol*, **36**, 899–907.
7. Chowdhury, M.M.U., Anstey, A., Matthews, C.N.A. (2000) The dermatosis of chronic granulomatous disease. *Clin Exp Dermatol*, **25**, 190–194.
8. Paller, A.S., Massey, R.B., Curtis, A. et al (1991) Cutaneous granulomatous lesions in patients with ataxia-telangiectasia. *J Pediatr*, **119**, 917–922.
9. Joshi, R.K., Al Asiri, R.H., Haleem, A. et al (1993) Cutaneous granuloma with ataxia-telangiectasia – a case report and review of literature. *Clin Exp Dermatol*, **18**, 458–461.
10. Drolet, B.A., Drolet, B., Zvulunov, A. et al (1997) Cutaneous granulomata as a presenting sign in ataxia-telangiectasia. *Dermatology*, **194**, 273–275.
11. Torrelo, A., Medeiro, I.G., Zambrano, A. (1995) Caseating granulomata in a child with common variable immunodeficiency. *Pediatr Dermatol*, **12**, 170–173.
12. Ziegler, E.M., Seung, L.M., Soltani, K. et al (1997) Cutaneous granulomata with two clinical presentations in a patient with common variable immunodeficiency. *J Am Acad Dermatol*, **37**, 499–500.
13. Cornejo, P., Romero, A., López, S. et al (1999) Cutaneous and hepatic granulomata in a young woman with common variable immunodeficiency. *Br J Dermatol*, **140**, 546–547.
14. Fleming, M.G., Gewurz, A.T., Pearson, R.W. (1991) Caseating cutaneous granulomata in a patient with X-linked infantile hypogammaglobulinemia. *J Am Acad Dermatol*, **24**, 629–633.

Aluminum granuloma

Clinical features

Aluminum granuloma refers to the development of persistent, sometimes painful, subcutaneous nodules that develop at the sites of vaccination or hyposensitization with agents containing aluminum hydroxide as an absorbing agent.[1–5] The lesions develop after a few weeks or years after the injections and are thought to be secondary to a hypersensitivity reaction to aluminum hydroxide. Often, patients have positive patch tests to aluminum hydroxide. The most common vaccine associated with this reaction is tetanus toxoid but any vaccine containing aluminum hydroxide as an absorbent may induce the reaction.

Histological features

Three histological patterns may be found:
- Loose subcutaneous collections of histiocytes with a slightly granular bluish cytoplasm.
- A prominent subcutaneous, predominantly mononuclear, inflammatory cell infiltrate with eosinophils and focal formation of germinal centers (*Figs 8.115–8.117*). This pattern may mimic a lymphoma. Careful examination reveals scattered grouped histiocytes with bluish granular cytoplasm.
- A deep granuloma annulare-like infiltrate with numerous histiocytes surrounding an area of necrobiosis (*Figs 8.118, 8.119*). All the histiocytes show a characteristic bluish granular cytoplasm.

The material within the histiocytes represents aluminum. Confirmation of the presence of aluminum can be done histochemically with the use of azurin stain or by energy dispersive X-ray microanalysis.

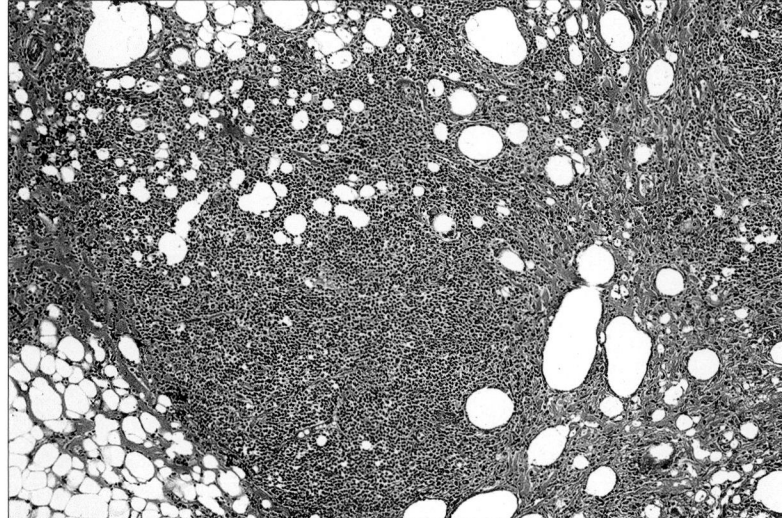

Fig. 8.115
Aluminum granuloma: there is a dense inflammatory cell infiltrate within the subcutaneous fat.

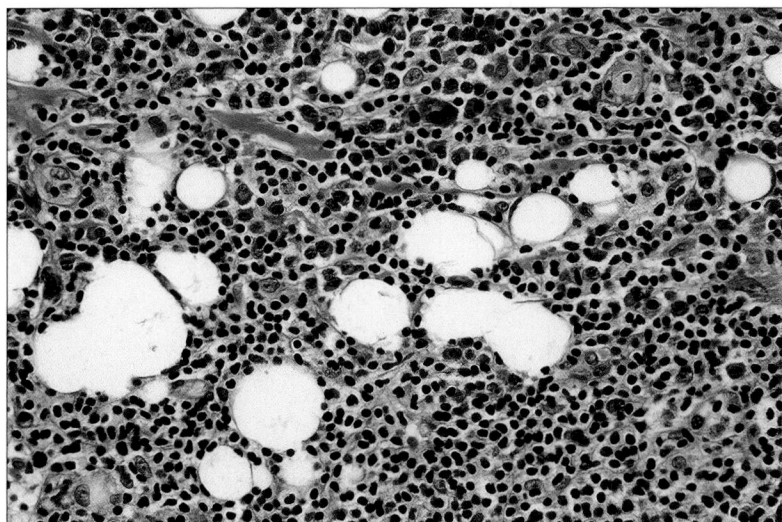

Fig. 8.116
Aluminum granuloma: the infiltrate consists of lymphocytes, histiocytes and plasma cells.

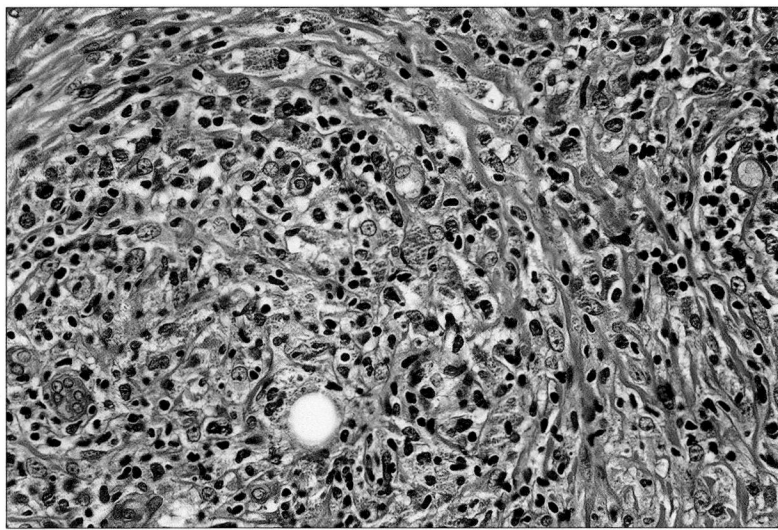

Fig. 8.117
Aluminum granuloma: the histiocytes have markedly granular cytoplasm due to the presence of aluminum.

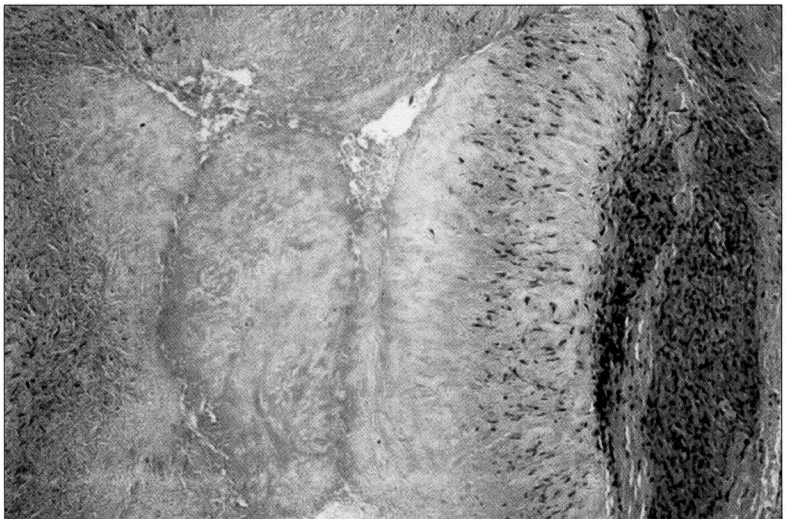

Fig. 8.118
Aluminum granuloma: in this example there is a palisading granuloma surrounding a necrobiotic nodule.

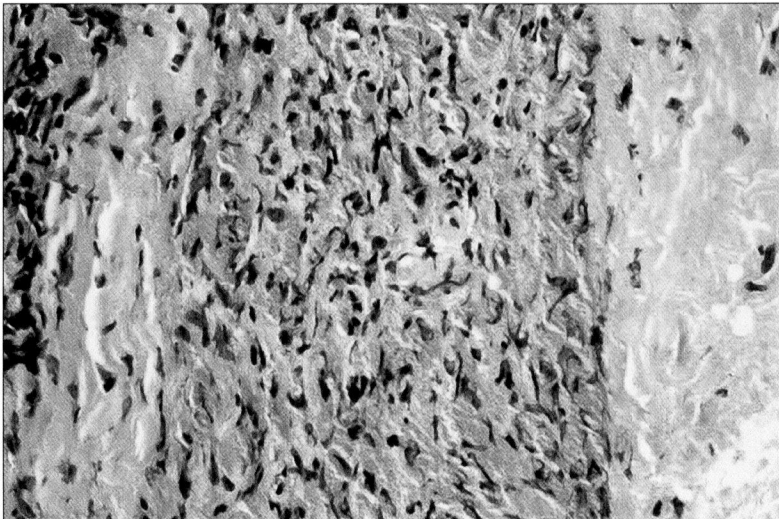

Fig. 8.119
Aluminum granuloma: the histiocytes have finely granular cytoplasm.

References

1. Fawcett, H.A., Smith, N.P. (1984) Injection-site granuloma due to aluminum. *Arch Dermatol*, **120**, 1318–1322.
2. Cominos, D., Strutton, G., Busmains, I. (1993) Granulomata associated with tetanus toxoid immunization. *Am J Dermatopathol*, **15**, 114–117.
3. Morroni, M., Barbatelli, G., Carboni, V. et al (1995) Subcutaneous nodules in a patient hyposensitized with aluminium-containing allergen extracts: a microanalytical study. *Anal Cell Pathol*, **9**, 235–241.
4. García-Patos V., Pujol, R.M., Alomar, A. et al (1995) Persistent subcutaneous nodules in patients hyposensitized with aluminum-containing allergen extracts. *Arch Dermatol*, **131**, 1421–1424.
5. Vogelbruch, M., Nuss, B., Korner, M. et al (2000) Aluminium-induced granulomata after inaccurate intradermal hyposensitization injections of aluminium-adsorbed depot preparations. *Allergy*, **55**, 883–887.

Perforating disorders

Reactive perforating collagenosis

Clinical features

This is a very rare disorder of uncertain etiology in which patients have a predisposition to mount an unusual skin reaction to mild trauma, whereby damaged collagen is extruded through the epidermis.[1–4] Although sporadic cases do occur, in many instances reactive perforating collagenosis appears to be an inherited condition, autosomal recessive and dominant variants having been described.[5–8] Reactive perforating collagenosis has been documented in association with the Treacher Collins syndrome.[9] The disease is characterized by an equal sex incidence; most cases present in childhood although lesions tend to persist into adult life. An acquired variant occurring in adulthood and associated with IgA nephropathy, diabetes mellitus, chronic renal failure, herpes zoster infection, scabies, lymphoma and carcinoma has been described.[10–24] However, the inherited cases are not associated with any systemic disorder. Reactive perforating collagenosis has recently been reported in a patient with AIDS in association with end-stage renal failure.[25] Perforating collagenosis is seen in approximately 10% of patients with renal failure.[1,2] Patients may develop lesions either before or after dialysis treatment.[2] In most cases, underlying diabetes mellitus is also present.[1,2] Patients suffer generalized pruritus and crusting papules. A single case with a zosteriform distribution has also been documented.[26]

Following mild trauma, such as a scratch or insect bite, patients develop flesh-colored papules 1–2 mm in diameter. These enlarge, become umbilicated and, over the course of about 4 weeks, grow to reach a diameter of some 5–10 mm (*Figs 8.120–8.122*). The umbilicated region contains keratinous debris, which is dark brown, hard and leathery. It is very densely adherent and bleeding results if detachment is attempted. This is followed by regression. The papules flatten, and by 6–8 weeks from onset all that remain are residual scars or areas of hypopigmentation. It is of interest that lesions develop only after mild superficial trauma, deep penetrating wounds healing normally. A positive Koebner phenomenon is characteristic and lesions may be induced by gentle needle scratching. Lesions tend to be rather polymorphic: as old lesions are healing, new ones are developing. They are distributed primarily on the upper and lower extremities and face, although the trunk may be affected.[27,28] Rarely, the palms and soles may be involved. A patient showing mucosal involvement has also been described.[29] The severity of this condition seems to be increased in cold weather, whereas there is a reduction in the number of lesions in summer.

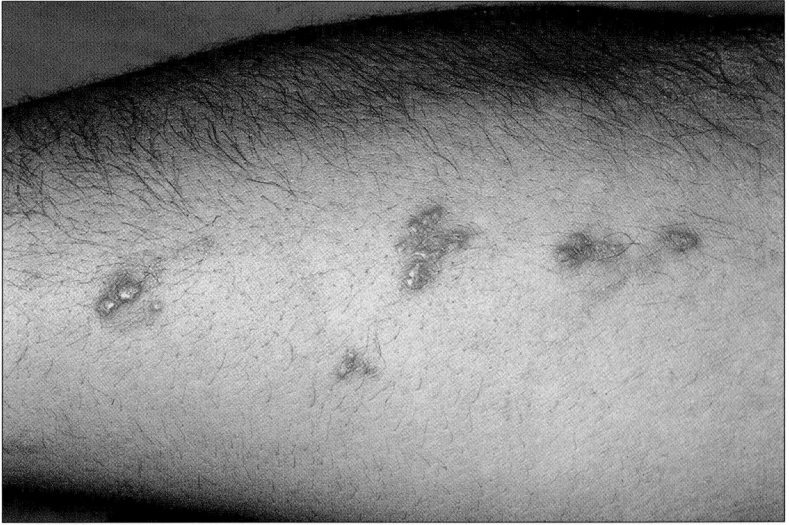

Fig. 8.120
Reactive perforating collagenosis: there are multiple pink papules, some showing central umbilication with crusting. By courtesy of D. McGibbon, MD, St Thomas' Hospital, London, UK.

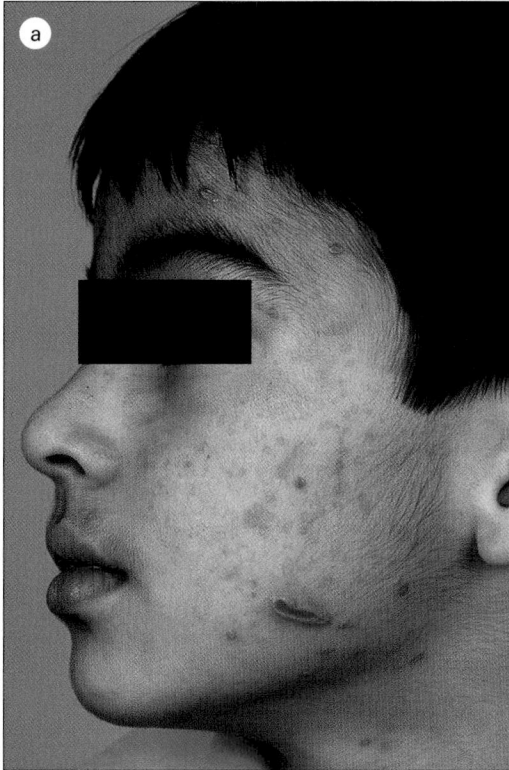

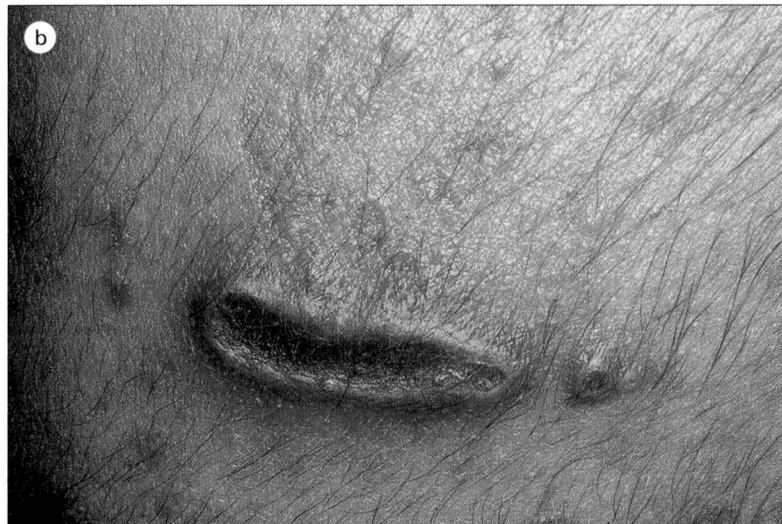

Fig. 8.121
Reactive perforating collagenosis: (a) an example on the cheek of a young boy;
(b) close-up view. By courtesy of E. Young, MD, Wycombe General Hospital, High
Wycombe, UK.

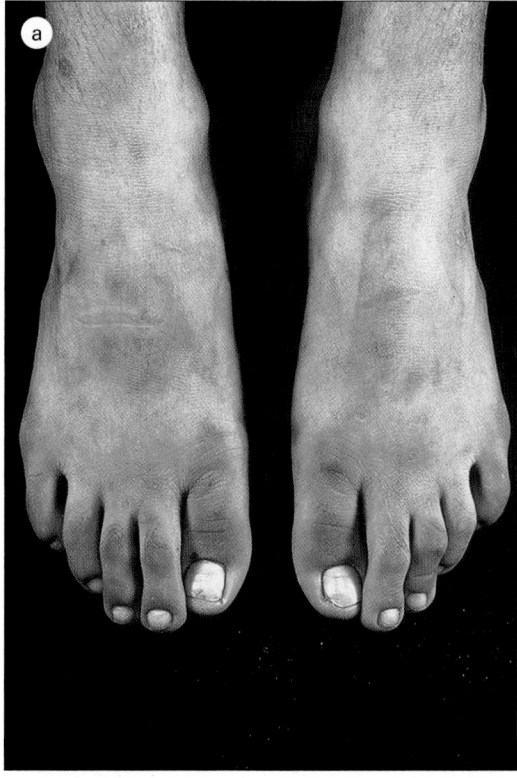

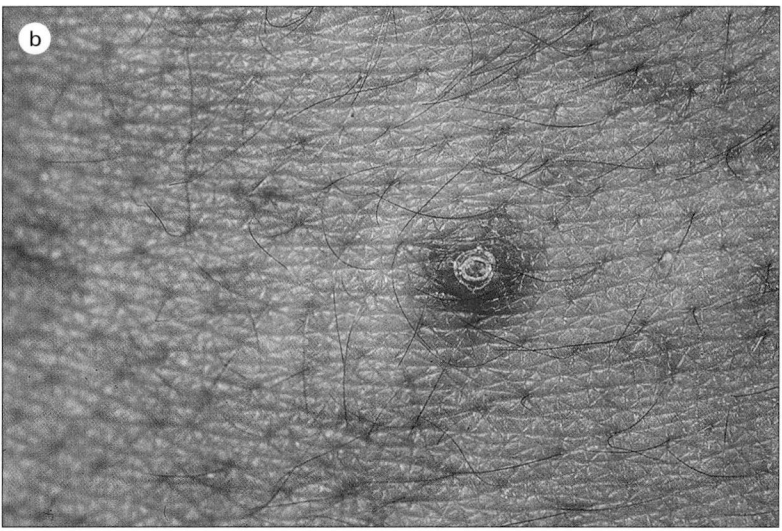

Fig. 8.122
(a, b) Reactive perforating collagenosis: scattered small crusted papules are
present on the dorsa of the feet. By courtesy of the Institute of Dermatology,
London, UK.

Pathogenesis and histological features

The pathogenesis of reactive perforating collagenosis has not been elucidated.[30] Transepidermal elimination of type IV collagen has been demonstrated but the mechanism that triggers its elimination is not clear.[31]

A broadened dermal ridge containing degenerate, basophilic collagen
characterizes early, non-umbilicated lesions. The overlying epithelium is
atrophic and centrally is composed of a thin layer of parakeratotic
material. At the lateral margins there is typically acanthosis. In the
fully established umbilicated lesion the central plug is composed of
parakeratotic debris, degenerate collagen and inflammatory cells
(*Figs 8.123, 8.124*).[32] The epidermis deep to the plug is markedly thinned
and is traversed in foci by vertically orientated collagen fibers
(*Figs 8.125, 8.126*). Elastic fibers are not present within the extruded
connective tissue debris. On either side of the cup-shaped deformity, the
epidermis is acanthotic and hyperkeratotic. A lymphohistiocytic infiltrate
is present in the superficial dermis. The histological appearances in
reactive perforating collagenosis and acquired perforating collagenosis
are identical. Distinction between these disorders requires clinical
correlation (*Fig. 8.127*).

Differential diagnosis

Changes identical to those seen in reactive perforating collagenosis may be seen following trauma in 'normal' patients. Not uncommonly, biopsies of patients with prurigo nodularis/lichen simplex chronicus (but who do not meet clinical criteria for reactive perforating collagenosis) show transepidermal elimination of collagen in a pattern similar to that seen in perforating collagenosis. *Table 8.3* highlights points of distinction among the perforating disorders.

References

1. Mehregan, A.H., Schwartz, O.D., Livingood, C.S. (1967) Reactive perforating collagenosis. *Arch Dermatol*, **96**, 277–282.
2. Patterson, J.W. (1984) The perforating disorders. *J Am Acad Dermatol*, **10**, 561–581.
3. Weiner, A.L. (1970) Reactive perforating collagenosis. *Arch Dermatol*, **102**, 540–544.
4. Faver, I.R., Daoud, M.S., Su, W.P. (1994) Acquired reactive perforating collagenosis. Report of six cases and review of the literature. *J Am Acad Dermatol*, **30**, 575–580.
5. Kanan, M.W. (1974) Familial reactive perforating collagenosis and intolerance to cold. *Br J Dermatol*, **91**, 405–414.
6. Nair, B.K.H., Sarojini, P.A., Basheer, A.M. et al (1974) Reactive perforating collagenosis. *Br J Dermatol*, **91**, 399–403.
7. Kumar, V., Mehndiratta, V., Sharma, R.C. et al (1998) Familial reactive perforating collagenosis: a case report. *J Dermatol*, **25**, 54–56.
8. Kyriaki, A., Ephtichia, Z., Anna, L. et al (1997) Reactive perforating collagenosis and acquired perforating dermatosis: presentation of two cases. *J Dermatol*, **24**, 170–173.
9. Tay, Y.K., Weston, W.I., Aeling, J.L. (1996) Reactive perforating collagenosis in Treacher Collins syndrome. *J Am Acad Dermatol*, **35**, 982–983.
10. Iwamoto, I., Baba, S., Suzuki, H. (1998) Acquired perforating collagenosis with IgA nephropathy. *J Dermatol*, **25**, 597–600.
11. Kawakami, T., Saito, R. (1999) Acquired perforating collagenosis associated with diabetes mellitus: eight cases that meet Faver's criteria. *Br J Dermatol*, **140**, 521–524.
12. Cochrane, R.J., Tucker, S.B., Wilkin, J.K. (1983) Reactive perforating collagenosis of diabetes and renal failure. *Cutis*, **31**, 55–58.
13. Chae, K.S., Park, Y.M., Cho, S.H. et al (1998) Reactive perforating collagenosis associated with periampullary carcinoma. *Br J Dermatol*, **139**, 548–550.
14. Bong, J.L., Fleming, C.J., Kemmett, D. (2000) Reactive perforating collagenosis associated with underlying malignancy. *Br J Dermatol*, **142**, 390–391.
15. Mahanupab, P., Chiewchanvit, S. (2002) Acquired perforating collagenosis: report of a case and review of the literature. *J Med Assoc Thai*, **85**, 1019–1023.
16. Basak, P.Y., Turkmen, C. (2001) Acquired reactive perforating collagenosis. *Eur J Dermatol*, **11**, 466–468.
17. Tang, W.Y., Chong, L.Y., Lam, S.Y. et al (1995) Acquired reactive perforating collagenosis in two Chinese patients. *Int J Dermatol*, **34**, 196–198.
18. Briggs, P.L., Fraga, S. (1995) Reactive perforating collagenosis of diabetes mellitus. *J Am Acad Dermatol*,
19. Satchell, A.C., Crotty, K., Lee, S. (2001) Reactive perforating collagenosis: a condition that may be underdiagnosed. *Australas J Dermatol*, **42**, 284–287.
20. Morton, C.A., Henderson, I.S., Jones, M.C. et al (1997) Acquired perforating collagenosis in British dialysis population. *Br J Dermatol*, **137**, 472–473.

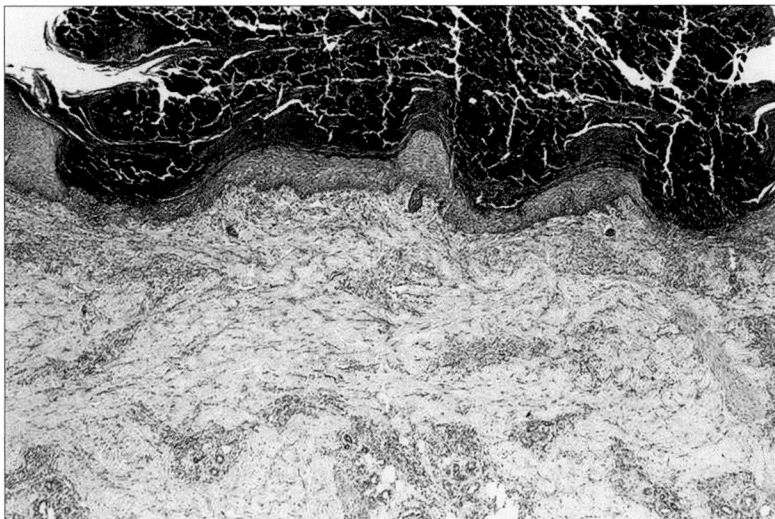

Fig. 8.123
Reactive perforating collagenosis: this is a transverse section through the center of a lesion. Note the crust overlying multiple points of incipient perforation.

Fig. 8.125
Reactive perforating collagenosis: close-up view of collagen fibers within the epidermis.

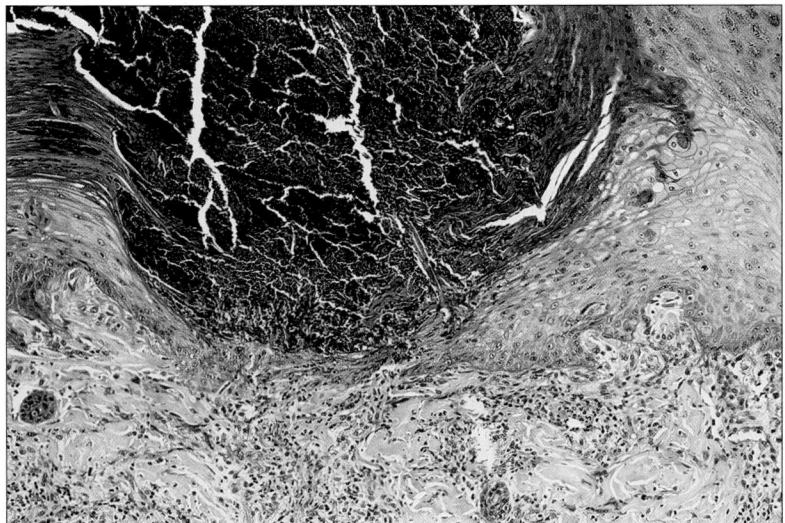

Fig. 8.124
Reactive perforating collagenosis: irregular, swollen collagen fibers have penetrated the epidermis.

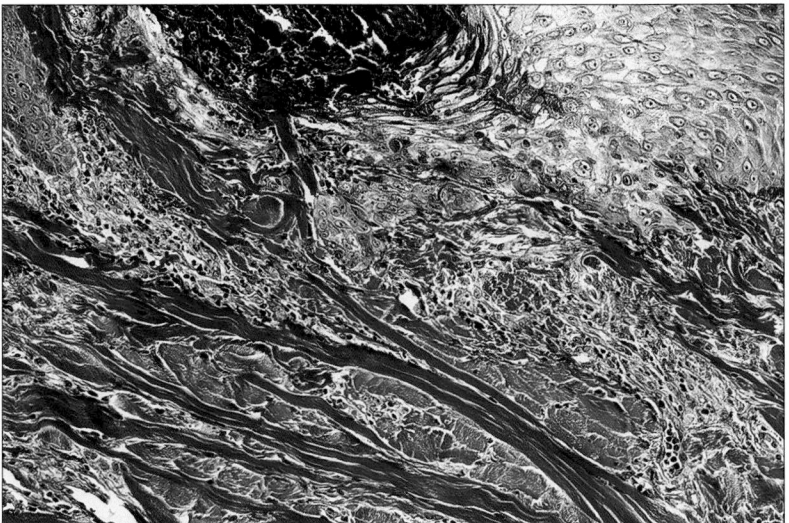

Fig. 8.126
Reactive perforating collagenosis: transepidermal elimination is seen to better advantage with this Masson's trichrome stain.

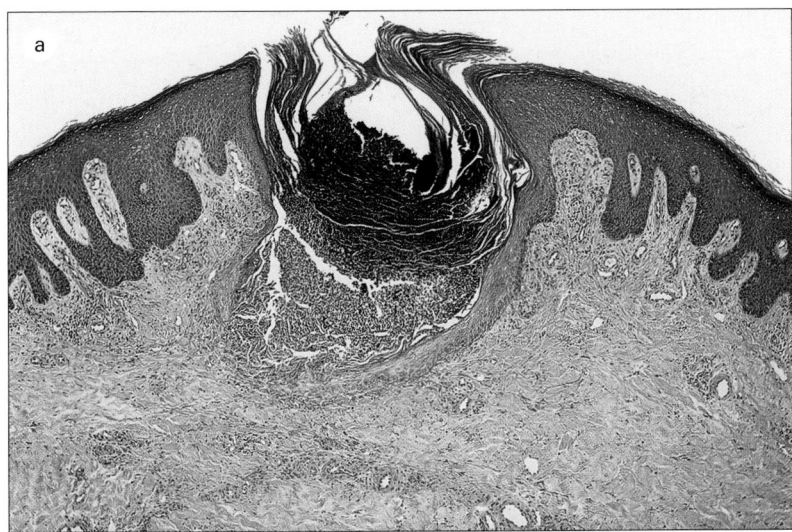

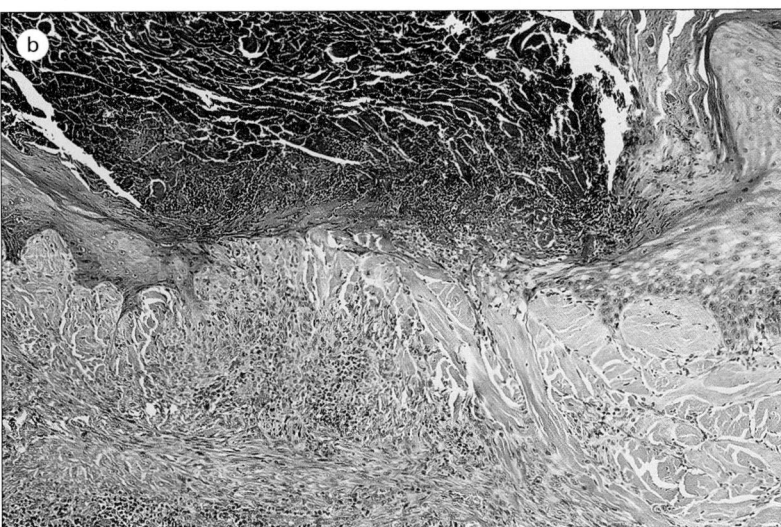

Fig. 8.127
(a, b) Reactive perforating collagenosis: this example developed in a patient with chronic renal failure.

21. Zanardo, L., Stolz, W., Landhaler, M. et al (2001) Reactive perforating collagenosis after disseminated zoster. *Dermatology*, **203**, 273–275.
22. Lee, H.N., Lee, D.W., Lee, J.Y. et al (2001) Two cases of reactive perforating collagenosis arising at the site of healed herpes zoster. *Int J Dermatol*, **40**, 191–192.
23. Bang, S.W., Kim, Y.K., Whank, K.U. (1997) Acquired reactive perforating collagenosis: unilateral umbilicated papules along the lesions of herpes zoster. *J Am Acad Dermatol*, **36**, 778–779.
24. Kurschal, P., Kroger, A., Scharffetter-Kochanek, K. et al (2000) Acquired reactive perforating collagenosis triggered by scabies infection. *Acta Derm Venereol*, **80**, 384–385.
25. Bank, D.E., Cohen, P.R., Kohn, S.R. (1989) Reactive perforating collagenosis in a setting of double disaster: acquired immunodeficiency syndrome and end-stage renal disease. *J Am Acad Dermatol*, **21**, 371–374.
26. Nakanishi, G., Tsunemitsu, R., Akagi, O. (1999) Reactive perforating collagenosis occurring in a zosteriform distribution. *Br J Dermatol*, **141**, 367–369.
27. Cohen, R.W., Auerbach, R. (1989) Acquired reactive perforating collagenosis. *J Am Acad Dermatol*, **20**, 287–289.
28. Oziemski, M.A., Billson, V.R., Crosthwaite, G.L. et al (1991) A new treatment for acquired reactive perforating collagenosis. *Australas J Dermatol*, **32**, 71–74.
29. Trattner, A., Ingber, A., Sandbank, M. (1991) Mucosal involvement in reactive perforating collagenosis. *J Am Acad Dermatol*, **25**, 1079–1082.
30. Yanahigara, M., Fujita, T., Shirasaki, A. et al (1996) The pathogenesis of the transepithelial elimination of the collagen bundles in acquired reactive perforating collagenosis. A light and electron microscopical study. *J Cutan Pathol*, **23**, 398–403.
31. Herzinger, T., Schirren, C.G., Sander, C.A. et al (1996) Reactive perforating collagenosis – transepidermal elimination of type IV collagen. *Clin Exp Dermatol*, **21**, 279–282.
32. Fretzin, D.F., Beal, D.W., Joa, W. (1980) Light and ultrastructural study of reactive perforating collagenosis. *Arch Dermatol*, **116**, 1054–1058.

Perforating folliculitis

Clinical features

Perforating folliculitis is a not uncommon, usually asymptomatic, dermatosis of unknown etiology that superficially resembles Kyrle's disease.[1-3] It shows a female predominance (2:1) and, although a wide range of age groups may be affected, the majority of patients present in the third decade. The disease is characterized by the development of discrete, erythematous follicular papules, 2–8 mm in diameter, each containing a small central white keratotic core. Lesions most often affect the extremities, with a predilection for the hairy portions of the arms, forearms and thighs. The buttocks may also be involved (*Fig. 8.128*). Koebnerization is not usually a feature. Duration of the rash is variable, ranging from several months to years and remissions and exacerbation may punctuate the course.

Perforating folliculitis is associated with renal failure in some patients.[4-6] It has also been reported in the setting of HIV infection[7] and recently it was described in two dialysis patients with markedly elevated serum silicon levels.[8] Primary sclerosing cholangitis may rarely be associated with perforating folliculitis.[9]

Table 8.3
Differential diagnosis of perforating disorders

	Kyrle's disease	Reactive perforating collagenosis	Elastosis perforans serpiginosa	Perforating folliculitis
Age of patient	Average 30 years (20–60)	Childhood	Second decade	Third decade
Sex distribution	♂ = ♀	♂ = ♀	4♂ = ♀	2♀ = ♂
Site	Extensor lower extremities; upper extremities; head, neck and trunk	Upper and lower extremities; face	Side and back of neck; upper extremities; face; lower extremities	Hair-bearing portions of arms, forearms, thighs
Koebner phenomenon	Occasionally positive	Positive	Occasionally positive	Negative
Associated diseases	Diabetes mellitus; renal failure; hepatic insufficiency; congestive cardiac failure	None; (acquired variant renal failure)	Down's syndrome; Ehlers–Danlos syndrome; osteogenesis imperfecta; pseudoxanthoma elasticum	None
Mode of inheritance	—	? autosomal recessive ? autosomal dominant	—	—
Histology	Transepidermal elimination of degenerate parakeratin and inflammatory debris	Transepidermal elimination of collagen	Transepidermal elimination of abnormal elastic tissue	Intrafollicular curled-up hair; transepidermal elimination of degenerate connective tissue

Pathogenesis and histological features

Although the exact etiology is unknown, the frequent finding of a distorted, curled hair within the dilated follicle, often associated with disruption of the epithelium, and the occasional presence of hair fragments within the adjacent dermis suggest that mechanical disruption of follicular epithelium by hair may be the cause of this condition. The lesions of perforating folliculitis occur most commonly on the extensor aspects of the extremities suggesting that trauma may be implicated. It has been proposed that, as with Kyrle's disease, chronic friction leads to abnormal keratinization of the follicular epithelium, which eventually results in follicular perforation. The subsequent exposure of the follicular contents to the underlying dermis results in necrosis of connective tissue and subsequent transepidermal elimination.

The histopathological features of perforating folliculitis are those of a widely dilated hair follicle containing ortho- and parakeratotic keratin, basophilic necrotic debris, connective tissue elements and degenerate inflammatory cells (*Fig. 8.129*).[2] A curled-up hair is sometimes found within the keratinous plug or extruded into the perifollicular dermis. Typically the infundibular follicular epithelium is disrupted at single or multiple foci. The underlying degenerate dermis, including collagen and elastic fibers, may be seen to impinge upon the perforated follicle. The adjacent epidermis often shows pseudoepitheliomatous hyperplasia. A foreign body giant cell reaction is sometimes found within the superficial dermis.

Differential diagnosis

Perforating folliculitis is differentiated from Kyrle's disease by uniform follicular involvement associated with infundibular epithelial perforation (compared with perforation at the base of the lesion in Kyrle's disease) and the presence of tortuous hairs. Although elastic fibers may be found within the dilated follicle, they are neither abnormal in appearance nor increased in quantity as seen in elastosis perforans serpiginosa. *Table 8.3* highlights points of distinction among the perforating disorders. Keratosis pilaris is associated with keratotic plugs that tend to be folliculocentric but perforation and inflammation are not features.

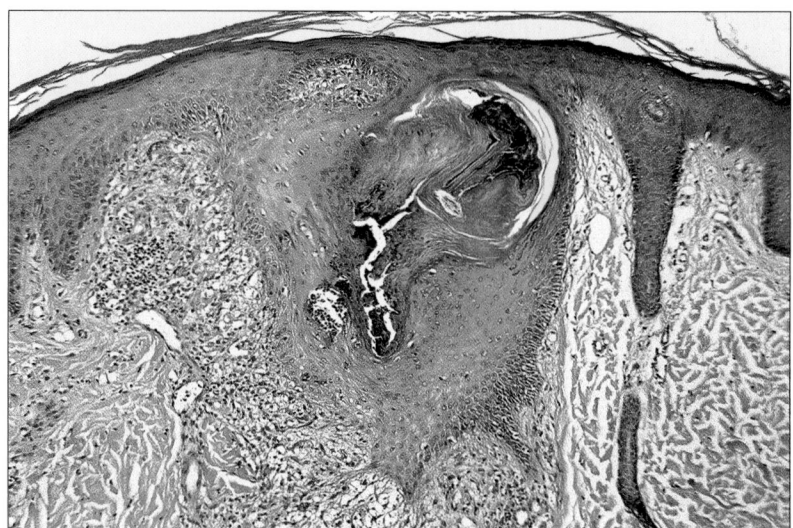

Fig. 8.129
Perforating folliculitis: this field shows a dilated hair follicle containing keratinous and basophilic debris. A hair shaft is visible.

References

1. Mehregan, A.H., Coskey, R.J. (1968) Perforating folliculitis. *Arch Dermatol*, **97**, 394–399.
2. Combermale, P., Courtois, D., Chouvet, B. (1990) Perforating folliculitis. *Ann Dermatol Venereol*, **117**, 515–520.
3. Schgal, V.N., Jain, S., Thappa, D.M. et al (1993) Perforating dermatoses: a review and report of four cases. *J Dermatol*, **20**, 329–340.
4. Hurwitz, R.M. (1985) The evolution of perforating folliculitis in patients with chronic renal failure. *Am J Dermatopathol*, **7**, 231–239.
5. White, R.C. Jr, Heskel, N.S., Pokorny, D.J. (1982) Perforating folliculitis of hemodialysis. *Am J Dermatopathol*, **4**, 109–116.
6. Chang, P., Fernandez, V. (1993) Acquired perforating disease: report of nine cases. *Int J Dermatol*, **32**, 874–876.
7. Rubio, F.A., Herranz, P., Robayna, G. et al (1999) Perforating folliculitis: report of a case in an HIV-infected man. *J Am Acad Dermatol*, **40**, 300–302.
8. Saldanha, L.F., Gonick, H.C., Rodriguez, H.J. et al (1997) Silicon-related syndrome in dialysis patients. *Nephron*, **77**, 48–56.
9. Kahana, M., Trau, H., Dolev, E. et al (1985) Perforating folliculitis in association with primary sclerosing cholangitis. *Am J Dermatopathol*, **7**, 271–276.

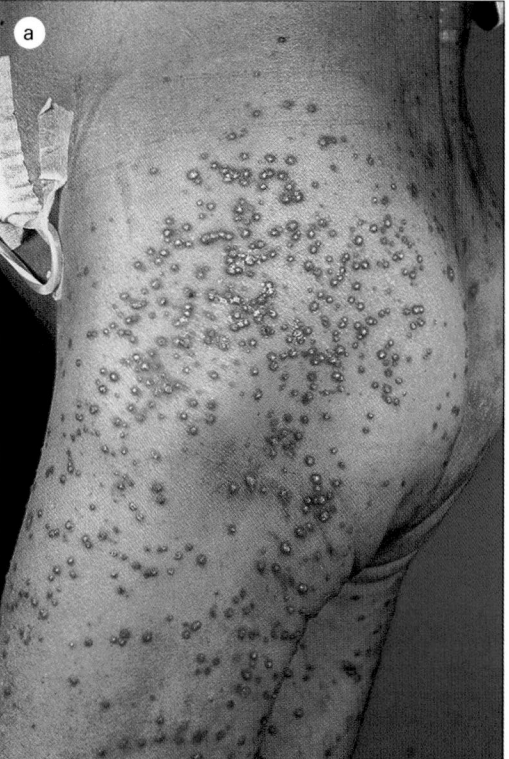
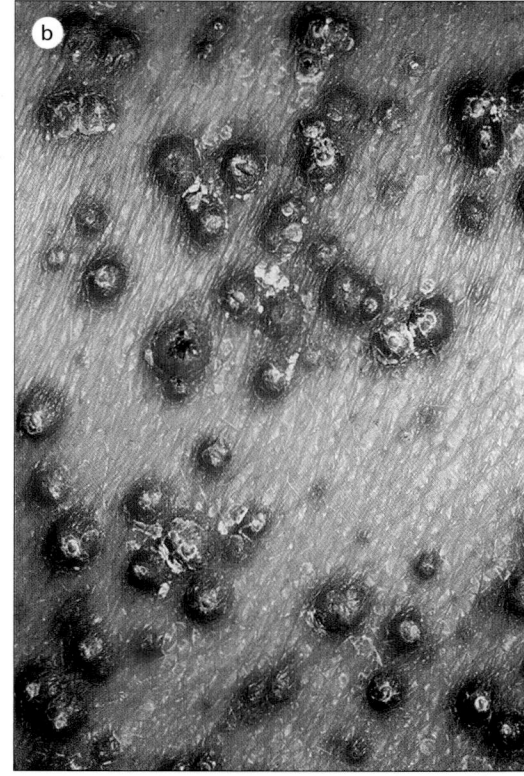

Fig. 8.128
Perforating folliculitis: **(a)** discrete scaly lesions on the buttocks and thighs; **(b)** close-up view. By courtesy of K. Green, MD, Lister Hospital, Stevenage, UK.

Elastosis perforans serpiginosa

Clinical features

Elastosis perforans serpiginosa (L. *serpere*, to creep) is a rare dermatosis associated with transepidermal elimination of abnormal elastic tissue.[1–3] It shows a male predominance (4:1) and presents most often in the second decade. A case with simultaneous onset in two sisters has been reported.[4] Another unusual case has been documented in an individual with a 47 XYY karyotype and unilateral atrophoderma of Pasini and Pierini.[5]

The primary lesion is a 2–5 mm flesh-colored or red keratotic papule containing an adherent plug, removal of which is associated with bleeding. Classically, the papules are arranged in an arcuate or serpiginous pattern, although sometimes they are randomly distributed (*Fig. 8.130*). Most often the lesions are confined to one site, with the back and sides of the neck being most frequently affected. Other sites include the upper extremities, face, lower extremities and abdomen, in decreasing order of frequency. In those cases where multiple sites are involved, symmetrical distribution is characteristic. Rarely, lesions are widely disseminated. The eruption is usually asymptomatic, although mild pruritus is sometimes a feature. Koebnerization is occasionally noted.

Although elastosis perforans serpiginosa may occur as an isolated phenomenon, in quite a high proportion of cases it develops in association with other conditions including Down's syndrome, Ehlers–Danlos syndrome, osteogenesis imperfecta, Marfan's syndrome, pseudoxanthoma elasticum, cutis laxa, acrogeria and the Rothmund–Thomson syndrome.[6–13] Rarely elastosis perforans serpiginosa may develop as a complication of penicillamine therapy for Wilson's disease and cystinuria.[7,14–18] It has been described in a patient with juvenile rheumatoid arthritis.[7]

Pathogenesis and histological features

The pathogenesis of elastosis perforans serpiginosa is not entirely understood. The documentation of familial cases suggests that a genetic component plays a role in a subset of patients.[19] The common association of elastosis perforans serpiginosa with a variety of connective tissue disorders raises the possibility of an elastic tissue defect as being of pathogenetic significance. Histochemical and enzyme studies have confirmed that it is the elastic tissue that is undergoing transepidermal elimination: electron microscopic studies have shown that the elastic fibers are increased in size and have a convoluted and branched pattern.[20] It appears that these abnormal fibers have an irritant effect, resulting in epidermal proliferation and their eventual engulfment by the epidermis. Following epidermal growth with consequent upward migration, the abnormal elastic tissue is expelled via perforating canals. Recently, it has been demonstrated that the 67 kDa elastin receptor is present in the keratinocytes associated with the elimination of elastic material in elastosis perforans serpiginosa.[21,22] This expression varies with the stage of the disease and suggests that the elastin–keratinocyte interaction plays an important role in the transepidermal elimination of elastin.[21,22]

It is of particular interest that this condition has been described following the use of the copper chelating agent penicillamine.[7,14,15] Tissue copper deficiency is known to be associated with damage to the elastica of arteries in experimental animals. The Blotchy mouse, which develops fusiform aortic aneurysms, has a copper metabolism defect that includes a reduced activity of the copper-dependent enzyme lysyl oxidase which is essential for cross-linking the elastin molecules. In Menkes' syndrome, there is an abnormality of copper metabolism associated with reduced numbers of elastic fibers in arterial walls. It may be, therefore, that penicillamine locally depletes the dermis of copper, resulting in abnormally formed elastic tissue and the subsequent development of elastosis perforans serpiginosa.

In the established lesion there is a marked increase in elastic tissue in both the reticular and papillary dermis (*Fig. 8.131*). The vertically orientated fibers of the latter are thicker than normal and can be seen to penetrate the epidermis. A section through the center of the lesion shows characteristic transepithelial perforating canals, which may be transepidermal, parafollicular or transfollicular in location and straight, wavy or screw-like in configuration (*Fig. 8.132*). The canal contents consist of a basophilic mass composed of degenerate epithelial cells, inflammatory debris and numerous elastic fibers (*Fig. 8.133*). Superficially, the plug is composed predominantly of keratinous material and basophilic debris. Sometimes elastic fibers can be identified in the stratum corneum. The epithelium on either side of the perforating canal is acanthotic and may manifest pseudoepitheliomatous hyperplasia.

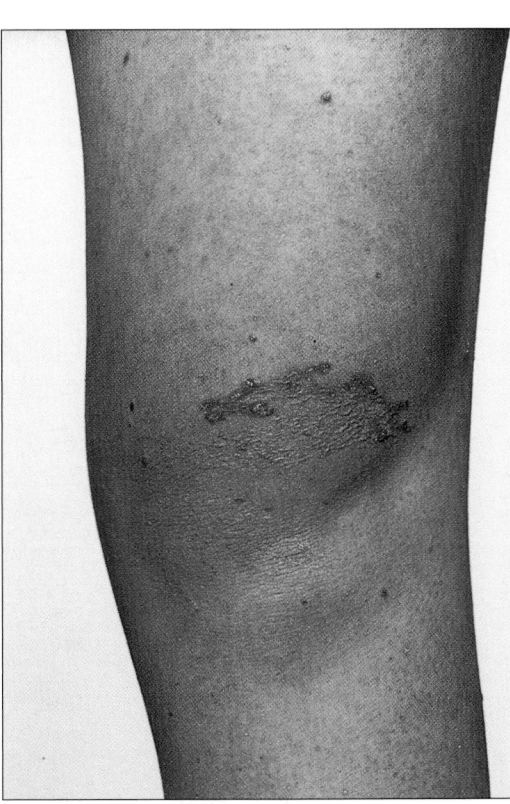

Fig. 8.130
Elastosis perforans serpiginosa: typical scaly serpiginous eruption on the elbow. By courtesy of M.M. Black, MD, St Thomas' Hospital, London, UK.

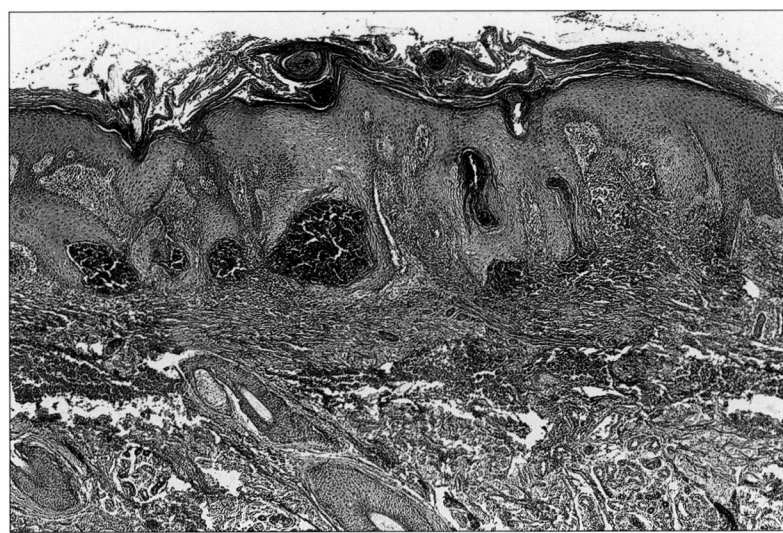

Fig. 8.131
Elastosis perforans serpiginosa: the epidermis is markedly thickened. Multiple perforating channels containing basophilic debris are present.

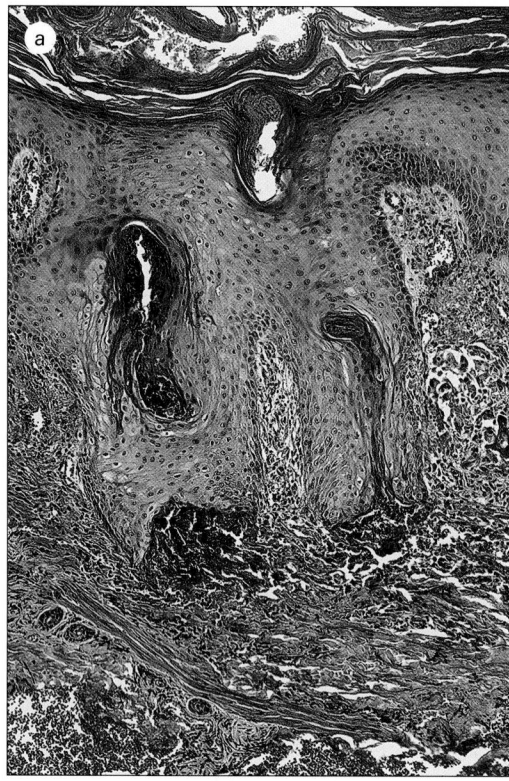
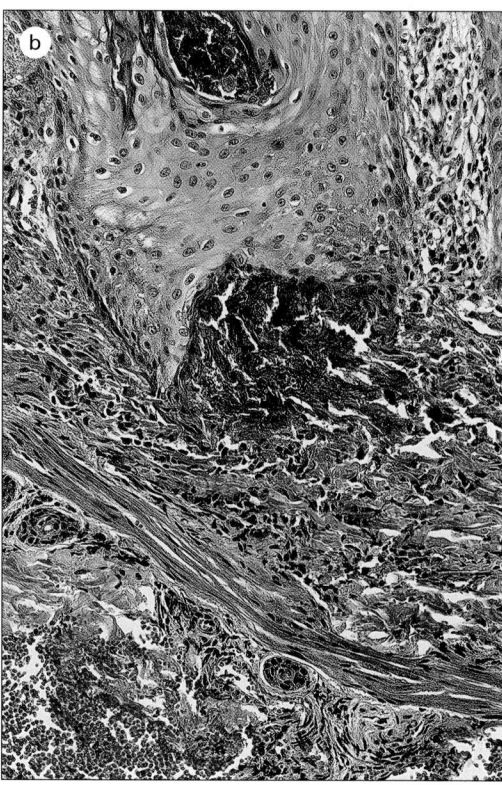

Fig. 8.132
(a, b) Elastosis perforans serpiginosa: this picture is taken through the center of a characteristic tortuous perforating canal. Note the degenerate elastic tissue at the base of the lesion.

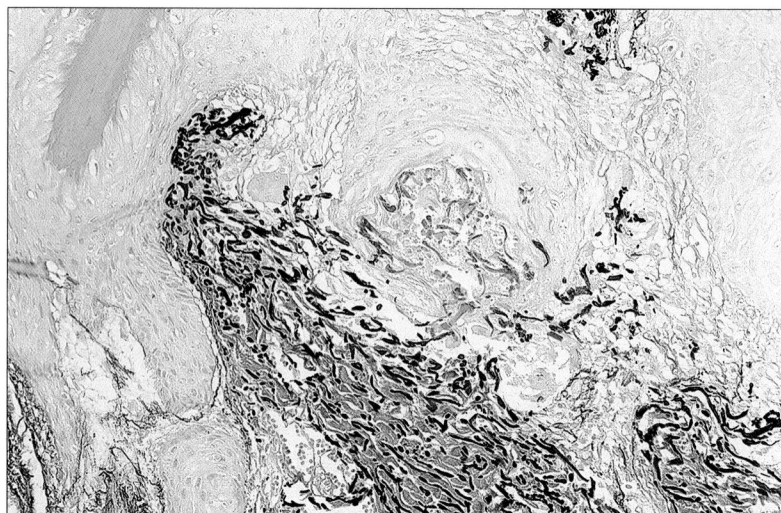

Fig. 8.133
Elastosis perforans serpiginosa: the elastic fibers stain strongly with elastic–van Gieson in the superficial dermis, but less strongly as the fibers undergo transepidermal elimination.

Commonly, a foreign body giant cell reaction is present in the superficial dermis and occasionally elastophagocytosis is evident.

In the penicillamine-induced variant the elastic fibers characteristically have an irregular, serrated, saw-toothed border (see p. 660).[7] Ultrastructurally, this gives the lateral borders of the affected elastic fibers a 'lumpy bumpy' appearance.[5]

Differential diagnosis

Although elastic fibers may be found within the dilated follicle in perforating folliculitis, they are neither abnormal in appearance nor increased in quantity as seen in elastosis perforans serpiginosa. Keratosis pilaris is associated with keratotic plugs that tend to be folliculocentric but perforation and inflammation are not features. Kyrle's disease is differentiated from elastosis perforans serpiginosa by perforation of a keratin plug at the base of the lesion associated with curled hairs in the former. *Table 8.3* summarizes the points of distinction among the perforating disorders.

References

1. Mehregan, A.H. (1968) Elastosis perforans serpiginosa: a review of the literature and report of 11 cases. *Arch Dermatol*, **97**, 381–393.
2. Pedro, S.D., García, R.L. (1974) Disseminate elastosis perforans serpiginosa. *Arch Dermatol*, **109**, 84–85.
3. Catterall, M.D., Padley, N.R. (1979) Elastosis perforans serpiginosa. *Clin Exp Dermatol*, **4**, 119–122.
4. Ríos-Buceta, I., Amigo-Echenagusta, A., Sols-Candelas, M. et al (1993) Elastosis perforans serpiginosa with simultaneous onset in two sisters. *Int J Dermatol*, **32**, 879–881.
5. Armstrong, D.K., Walsh, M.Y., Allen, G.E. (1997) Elastosis perforans serpiginosa associated with unilateral atrophoderma of Pasini and Pierini in an individual with 47 XYY karyotype. *Br J Dermatol*, **137**, 158–160.
6. Whyte, H.J., Winkelmann, R.K. (1960) Elastosis perforans (perforating elastosis). The association of congenital abnormalities, salient facts in the histology, studies of enzyme digestion and a report of a necropsy in a case. *J Invest Dermatol*, **35**, 113–122.
7. Sahn, E.E., Maize, J.C., Garen, P.D. et al (1989) D-penicillamine-induced elastosis perforans serpiginosa in a child with juvenile rheumatoid arthritis. *J Am Acad Dermatol*, **20**, 979–988.
8. O'Donnell, B., Kelly, P., Dervan, P. et al (1992) Generalized elastosis perforans serpiginosa in Down's syndrome. *Clin Exp Dermatol*, **17**, 31–33.
9. Mehta, R.K., Burrows, N.P., Payne, C.M. et al (2001) Elastosis perforans serpiginosa and associated disorders. *Clin Exp Dermatol*, **26**, 521–524.
10. Schepis, C., Barone, C., Siragusa, M. et al (2002) An updated survey on skin conditions in Down syndrome. *Dermatology*, **205**, 234–238.
11. De Pasquale, R., Nasca, M.R., Musumeci, M.I. et al (2002) Elastosis perforans serpiginosa in an adult with Down's syndrome: report of a case with symmetrical localized involvement. *J Eur Acad Dermatol Venereol*, **16**, 387–389.
12. Dourmishev, A., Miteva, I., Mitev, V. et al (2000) Cutaneous aspects of Down syndrome. *Cutis*, **66**, 420–424.
13. Stragusa, M., Romano, C., Cavallari, V. et al (1997) Localized elastosis perforans serpiginosa in a boy with Down syndrome. *Pediatr Dermatol*, **14**, 244–246.
14. Kirsch, N., Hukill, P.B. (1977) Elastosis perforans serpiginosa induced by penicillamine. *Arch Dermatol*, **113**, 630–635.
15. Pass, F., Goldfischer, S., Sternlies, I. et al (1973) Elastosis perforans serpiginosa during penicillamine therapy for Wilson's disease. *Arch Dermatol*, **108**, 713–715.
16. Deguti, M.M., Mucenic, M., Cancado, E.L. et al (2002) Elastosis perforans serpiginosa secondary to D-penicillamine treatment in a Wilson's disease patient. *Am J Gastroenterol*, **97**, 2153–2154.
17. Hill, V.A., Seymour, C.A., Mortimer, P.S. (2000) Penicillamine-induced elastosis perforans serpiginosa and cutis laxa in Wilson's disease. *Br J Dermatol*, **142**, 560–561.
18. Iozumi, K., Nakagawa, H., Tamaki, K. (1997) Penicillamine-induced degenerative dermatoses: report of a case and brief review of such dermatoses. *J Dermatol*, **24**, 458–465.
19. Langeveld-Wildschut, E.G., Toonstra, J., van Vloten, W.A., Beemer, F.A. (1993) Familial elastosis perforans serpiginosa. *Arch Dermatol*, **129**, 205–207.
20. Cohen, A.S., Hashimoto, K. (1960) Electron microscopic observations on the lesion of elastosis perforans serpiginosa. *J Invest Dermatol*, **35**, 15–19.
21. Fujimoto, N., Akagi, A., Tajima, S. et al (2002) Expression of the 67-kDa elastin receptor in perforating skin disorders. *Br J Dermatol*, **146**, 74–79.
22. Fujimoto, N., Tajima, S., Ishibashi, A. (2000) Elastin peptides induce migration and terminal differentiation of cultured keratinocytes via 67 kDa a elastin receptor in vitro: 67 kDa a elastin receptor is expressed.in the keratinocytes eliminating elastic materials in elastosis perforans serpiginosa. *J Invest Dermatol*, **115**, 633–639.

Hyperkeratosis follicularis et parafollicularis in cutem penetrans

Clinical features

Hyperkeratosis follicularis et parafollicularis in cutem penetrans (Kyrle's disease) is a very rare dermatosis of unknown etiology.[1-4] It has an equal incidence in men and women and an age of onset ranging from 20 to 60 years, with an average of 30 years. The disorder is characterized by a widespread, asymptomatic and typically bilateral eruption of 1–8 mm papules, each containing a central cone-shaped keratotic plug. Although lesions are located most often on the extensor aspect of the lower extremities, they may also affect the upper extremities, head, neck and trunk (*Figs 8.134–8.136*). They may or may not be related to hair follicles. The mucous membranes, palms and soles are characteristically spared. Ocular changes have been documented in a single kindred with the disease.[5] Lesions may coalesce into plaques and, occasionally, a Koebner-like appearance is present. There is no evidence to suggest that Kyrle's disease has a genetic etiology. It may be associated with diabetes mellitus, renal failure, hepatic insufficiency and congestive cardiac failure.[6,7] It is unclear whether Kyrle's disease is a distinct entity. Some cases clearly overlap with a perforating folliculitis and reports of examples in patients with diabetes and renal failure may actually represent examples of the latter. An overlap with Flegel's disease may also be seen.[8]

Pathogenesis and histological features

The precise pathogenesis of Kyrle's disease is unknown; however, it has been suggested that the lesions develop as a consequence of rapid and abnormal keratinization, which proceeds at a faster rate than epidermal proliferation, with consequent premature and abnormal differentiation of all the epidermal layers. In most instances, this is complicated by dissolution of the epidermal basement membrane region, with extrusion of keratinous debris into the dermis and subsequent development of a foreign body granulomatous reaction. Following this, the epithelium

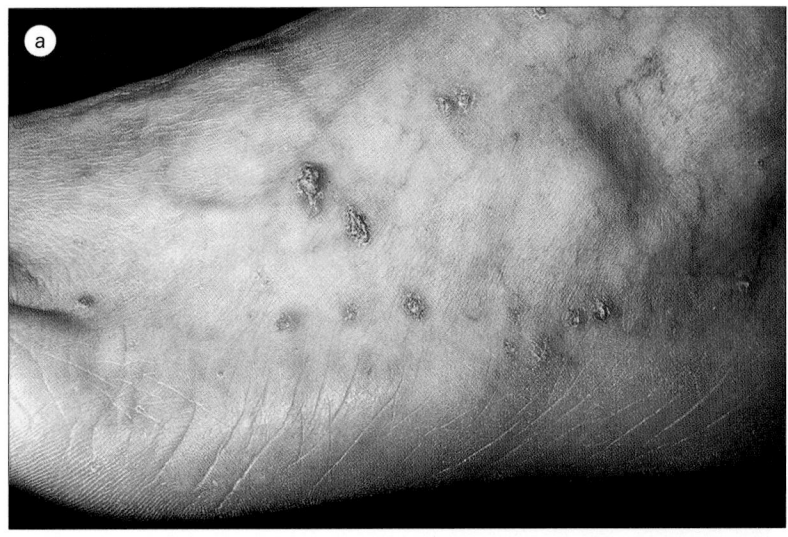

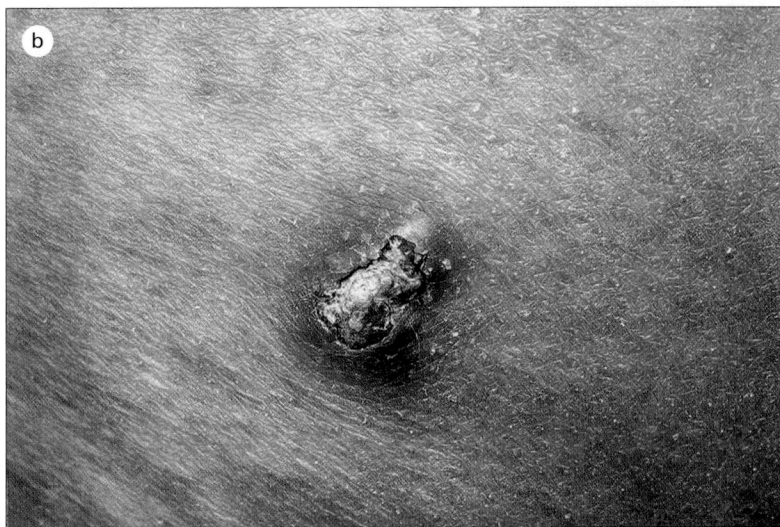

Fig. 8.135
(a, b) Kyrle's disease: multiple keratotic lesions are present on the dorsum of the foot. By courtesy of the Institute of Dermatology, London, UK.

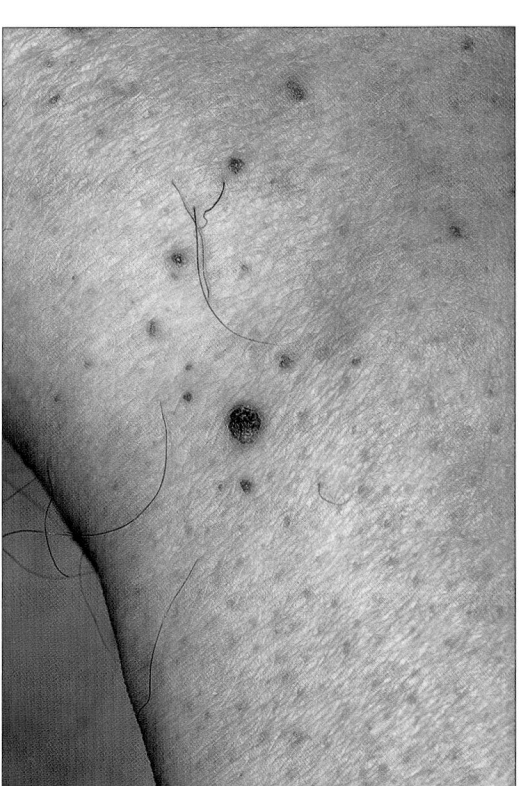

Fig. 8.134
Kyrle's disease: multiple umbilicated lesions are present on the thigh. The largest contains a keratin plug. By courtesy of M.M. Black, MD, St Thomas' Hospital, London, UK.

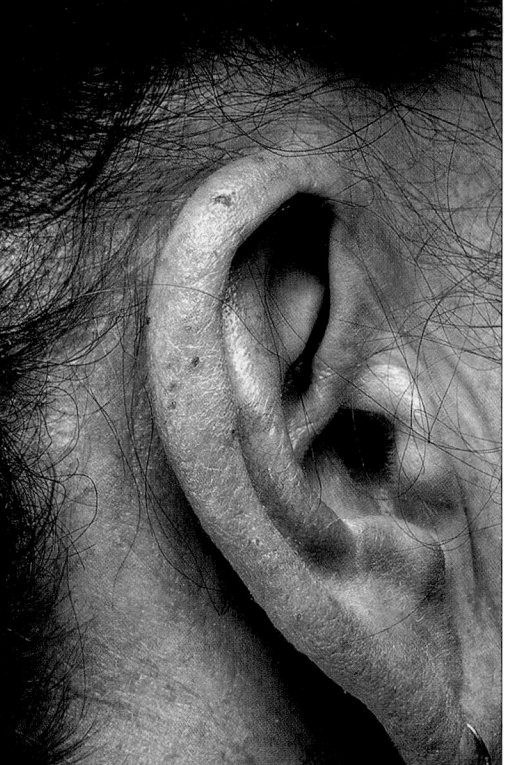

Fig. 8.136
Kyrle's disease: in this patient, there are small lesions on the ear. By courtesy of the Institute of Dermatology, London, UK.

adjacent to the site of the breach proliferates downwards and, by fusion medially, eventually walls off the inflammatory debris. Subsequent epidermal proliferation deep to the debris results in eventual trans-epidermal elimination. Transepidermal elimination or perforation, it seems, is of secondary rather than primary importance in this disorder. From this description, it follows that in early lesions there may be no evidence of an epidermal breach.

The histological features of an established lesion consist of a keratotic plug filling an epidermal invagination.[9–11] The keratinous plug shows parakeratosis and contains basophilic cellular debris (*Figs 8.137, 8.138*). Elastic tissue is absent. The epithelium deep to the plug shows parakeratosis, which extends to the point of epidermal disruption (*Figs 8.139, 8.140*). Where the keratinous debris is in contact with the dermis there is often a granulomatous infiltrate. In more advance cases, downward epidermal proliferation and encirclement results in incorporation of the basophilic keratotic debris into the lower reaches of the epidermis and hence subsequent elimination. A lymphohistiocytic infiltrate is often seen around the epidermal downgrowth and the superficial blood vessels.

Differential diagnosis

Kyrle's disease must be distinguished from reactive perforating collagenosis and elastosis perforans serpiginosa. In the former, collagen bundles may be seen entering the lesion from the dermis; in the latter, the basophilic material is elastic tissue. Kyrle's disease must also be

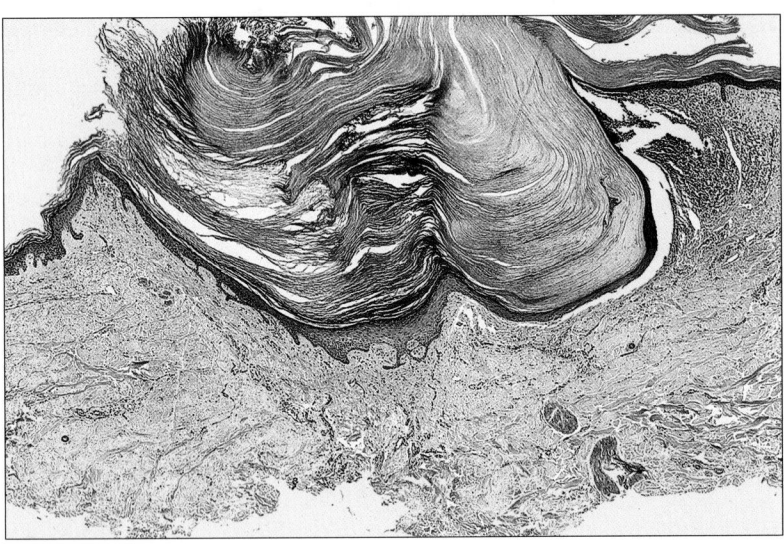

Fig. 8.137
Kyrle's disease: scanning view through the center of an established lesion showing the keratin plug.

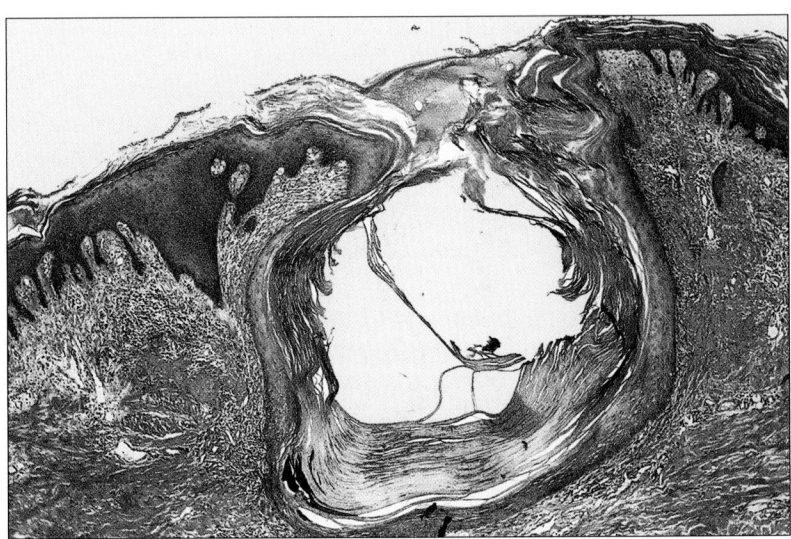

Fig. 8.138
Kyrle's disease: this lesion shows a flask-shaped epidermal invagination containing parakeratotic debris. In the lower left corner of the lesion is a laminated focus of basophilic degenerate material.

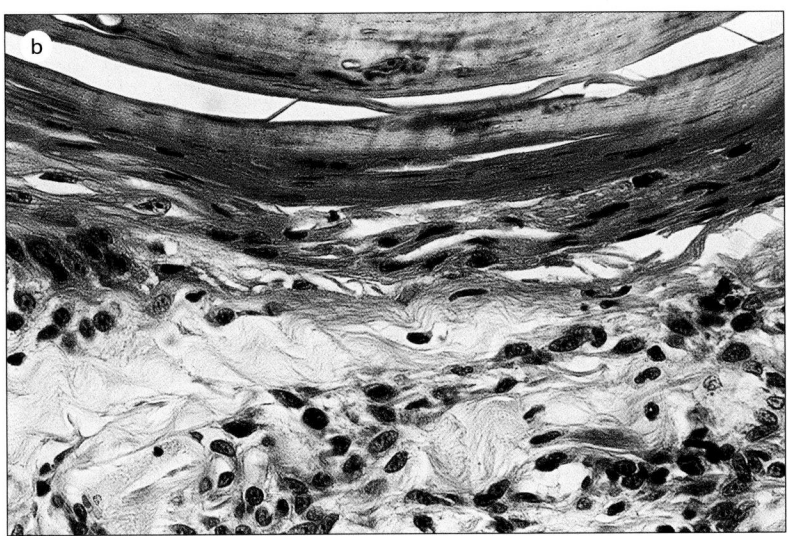

Fig. 8.139
Kyrle's disease: (a) a somewhat earlier lesion in which perforation has not yet occurred. Note the thinning of the epidermis basally. Where parakeratosis is evident there is absence of the granular cell layer; (b) this high power view shows parakeratosis of the residual epithelium.

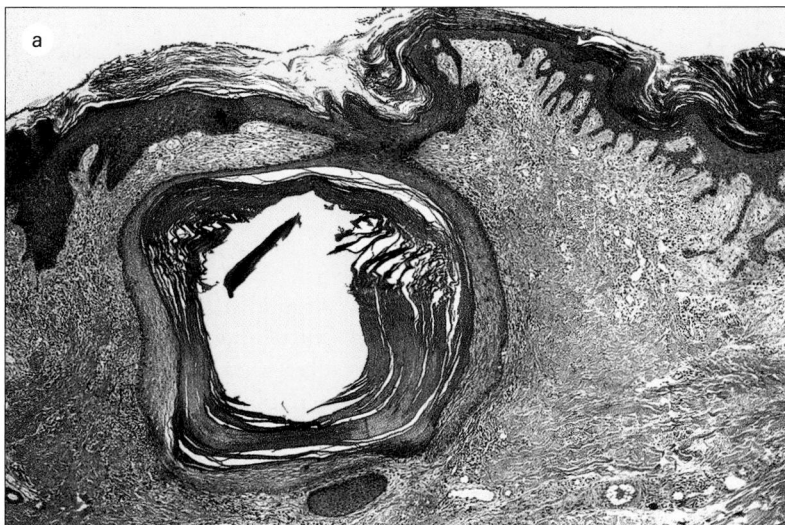

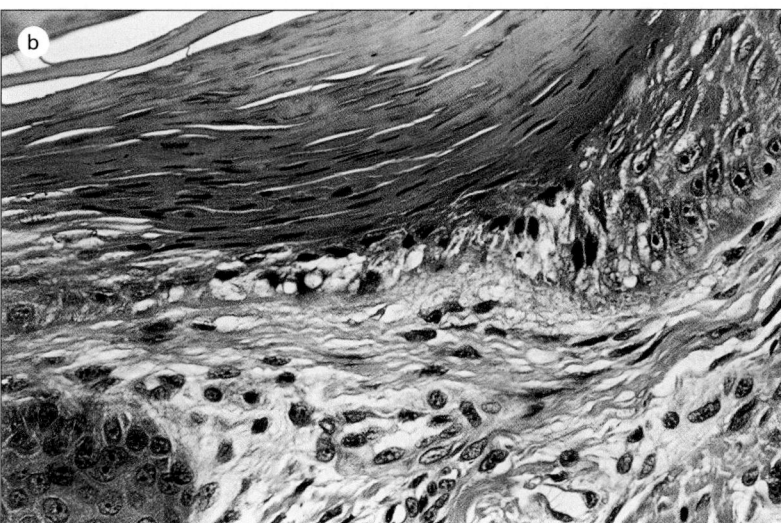

Fig. 8.140
Kyrle's disease: (a) in this example there is incipient perforation; (b) high power view showing liquefactive degeneration of the basal layer.

distinguished from perforating folliculitis (see above). *Table 8.3* highlights points of distinction in the differential diagnosis of perforating disorders.

References

1. Carter, V.H., Constantine, V.S. (1968) Kyrle's disease. I. Clinical findings in five cases and review of the literature. *Arch Dermatol*, **97**, 624–632.
2. Moss, H.V. (1979) Kyrle's disease. *Cutis*, **23**, 463–466.
3. Pajarre, R., Alavaikko, M. (1973) Kyrle's disease. Hyperkeratosis follicularis et parafollicularis in cutem penetrans. *Acta Derm Venereol*, **53**, 505–508.
4. Powell, E.W. (1970) Hyperkeratosis follicularis et parafollicularis in cutem penetrans (? Kyrle's disease). *Br J Dermatol*, **83**, 420–422.
5. Tessler, H.H., Apple, D.J., Goldberg, M.F. (1973) Ocular findings in a kindred with Kyrle disease. Hyperkeratosis follicularis et parafollicularis in cutem penetrans. *Arch Ophthalmol*, **90**, 278–280.
6. Hood, A.F., Hardengen, G.L., Zarate, A.R. et al (1982) Kyrle's disease in patients with chronic renal failure. *Arch Dermatol*, **118**, 85–88.
7. Salomon, R.J., Baden, T.J., Gammon, W.R. (1986) Kyrle's disease and hepatic insufficiency. *Arch Dermatol*, **112**, 18–19.
8. Kossard, E., Palmer, G., Constance, T.J. (1970) Coexistence of hyperkeratosis lenticularis perstans (Flegel) and hyperkeratosis follicularis et parafollicularis in cutem penetrans (Kyrle) in a patient. *Acta Derm Venereol*, **50**, 385–390.
9. Constantine, V.S., Carter, V.H. (1968) Kyrle's disease. II. Histopathologic findings in five cases and review of the literature. *Arch Dermatol*, **97**, 633–639.
10. Ford, T.C., Mirachi, J.A., Castillo, J. (1990) Kyrle's disease. A rare case report and surgical treatment. *J Am Pediatr Med Assoc*, **80**, 151–155.
11. Sorhage, B., Glowania, H.J., Schafer, R. (1990) Kyrle disease – a case report. *Z Hautkr*, **65**, 847–850.

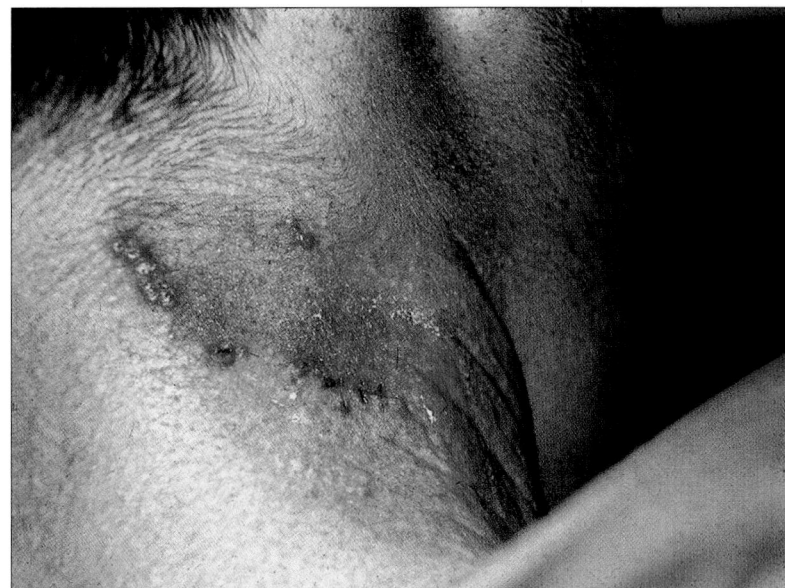

Fig. 8.141
Perforating pseudoxanthoma elasticum: multiple small crusted lesions are seen in a background of typical yellow papules. By courtesy of the Institute of Dermatology, London, UK.

Perforating pseudoxanthoma elasticum

Pseudoxanthoma elasticum (Grönblad–Strandberg syndrome) is an inherited generalized degenerative disease of elastic tissue of which there are autosomal dominant and autosomal recessive variants. The disease is briefly discussed in this section since a perforating variant is recognized. A more detailed description of pseudoxanthoma elasticum can be found on page 1041.

Perforating pseudoxanthoma elasticum is characteristically seen predominantly in multiparous, obese, middle-aged and frequently hypertensive black women who present with isolated abdominal, periumbilical involvement.[1–6] Whether this represents a forme fruste or a distinct entity is not yet known (so-called acquired pseudoxanthoma elasticum). In some cases, however, transepidermal elimination is seen in patients with systemic manifestations (*Fig. 8.141*).[7] The perforating variant may be associated with renal failure.[6]

The perforating subtype is characterized by transepidermal elimination of the degenerate elastic tissue.[7,8]

References

1. Hicks, J., Carpenter, C.L., Reed, R.J. (1979) Periumbilical perforating pseudoxanthoma elasticum. *Arch Dermatol*, **115**, 300–303.
2. Karp, D.L., O'Neill, M.S., Haberman, A.L. et al (1996) A yellow plaque with keratotic papules on the abdomen. Perforating calcific elastosis (periumbilical perforating pseudoxanthoma elasticum [PXE], localized acquired cutaneous PXE). *Arch Dermatol*, **132**, 224–225, 227–228.
3. Pruzan, D., Rabbin, P.E., Heilman, E.R. (1992) Periumbilical perforating pseudoxanthoma elasticum. *J Am Acad Dermatol*, **26**, 642–644.
4. Toporcer, M.B., Kantor, G.R. (1990) Periumbilical hyperpigmented plaque. Periumbilical perforating pseudoxanthoma elasticum (PPPXE). *Arch Dermatol*, **126**, 1639, 1642.
5. Kazakis, A.M., Parish, W.R. (1988) Periumbilical perforating pseudoxanthoma elasticum. *J Am Acad Dermatol*, **19**, 384–388.
6. Nickoloff, B.J., Noodleman, F.R., Abel, E.A. (1985) Perforating pseudoxanthoma elasticum associated with chronic renal failure and hemodialysis. *Arch Dermatol*, **121**, 1321–1322.
7. Kazakis, A.M., Parish, W.R. (1988) Periumbilical perforating pseudoxanthoma elasticum. *J Am Acad Dermatol*, **19**, 384–388.
8. Somasundaram, V., Premalatha, S., Rao, N.A. et al (1987) Periumbilical perforating pseudoxanthoma elasticum. *Int J Dermatol*, **26**, 536–537.

Chondrodermatitis nodularis chronica helicis

Clinical features

Chondrodermatitis nodularis chronica helicis presents as a small, usually solitary, painful dome-shaped nodule on the helix of the ear, most commonly in males over 40 years of age (mean age 60 years) and develops as a consequence of chronic trauma (*Fig. 8.142*).[1–3] The process is less common in women, when it is usually located on the antihelix. The pain is typically severe enough to wake the patient at night if the affected ear touches the pillow. In the majority of patients, symptoms are present for 2–3 years.[3]

On close examination, a firm crust with a small erosion or tiny channel underneath usually covers the nodule. Lesions measure 3–15 mm in diameter.[4] After surgical treatment there is a recurrence rate of 20%. Chondrodermatitis is frequently mistaken for squamous cell or basal cell carcinoma, but the clinical history and auricular location should allow the diagnosis to be made without difficulty. Nevertheless, histological confirmation is advisable. An association with systemic sclerosis has been reported; however, the relationship between these two disorders is unclear.[5]

Pathogenesis and histological features

The etiology is multifactorial, but trauma is likely to be of primary importance. The exposed position of the ear, together with a known history of solar or physical trauma, appears important as many patients have outdoor jobs and evidence of solar damage elsewhere. Of historic interest, in the past there appeared to be a high frequency of cases in telephonists and nuns (wearing a wimple), again supporting the role of physical trauma to the ear. Other factors including cold, anatomical aberrations of the ear (such as a poor vascular supply) and senile degeneration of the cartilage may play a role in development.[3] It is most unlikely, however, that the cartilaginous changes described below are anything other than secondary.

The pathogenetic mechanism of chondrodermatitis nodularis has been interpreted as representing the process of transepidermal elimination.[3] This phenomenon occurs when a disturbance in the dermis initiates an epidermal response. Foreign material in the dermis may elicit one of three responses:

- If the material is inert, there is no response.
- If the material is irritant, either a superficial abscess or necrosis will develop.
- The material (in this case degenerate collagen) may be eliminated by a gradual process of transepidermal elimination (see elastosis perforans serpiginosa, p. 333).

Ulceration, although usual, may not be seen in early lesions.[3,4] The epithelium on either side of the ulcer is hyperplastic and shows features of lichen simplex chronicus (*Figs 8.143, 8.144*). Pseudoepitheliomatous hyperplasia is sometimes evident.[4,6] Lesions have sometimes been shown to be related to the follicular infundibulum.[4] The crateriform ulcer contains keratinous and epidermal debris superimposed on a focus of fibrinoid necrosis of the underlying dermal collagen (*Fig. 8.145*). The base and radial edges of the lesion contain granulation tissue and a variable chronic inflammatory cell infiltrate comprising lymphocytes, histiocytes and occasional plasma cells. Vascular thromboses and hair shaft fragments are sometimes evident.[4]

It is thought that the pathogenetic process at advanced stages of this disease represents the transepidermal or, occasionally, transfollicular elimination of damaged collagen.[3,7] There are often degenerative changes present in the underlying cartilage, including hyalinization, tinctorial changes and perichondritis (*Fig. 8.146*). Occasionally degenerate and fragmented cartilage may also be seen undergoing transepidermal elimination (*Fig. 8.147*). The adjacent dermis often shows marked solar elastosis.[3]

Differential diagnosis

Punch biopsies, which show the characteristic layering of fibrin, granulation tissue and degenerating cartilage, are diagnostic and distinctive. Often, superficial shave biopsies sample only fibrin and granulation

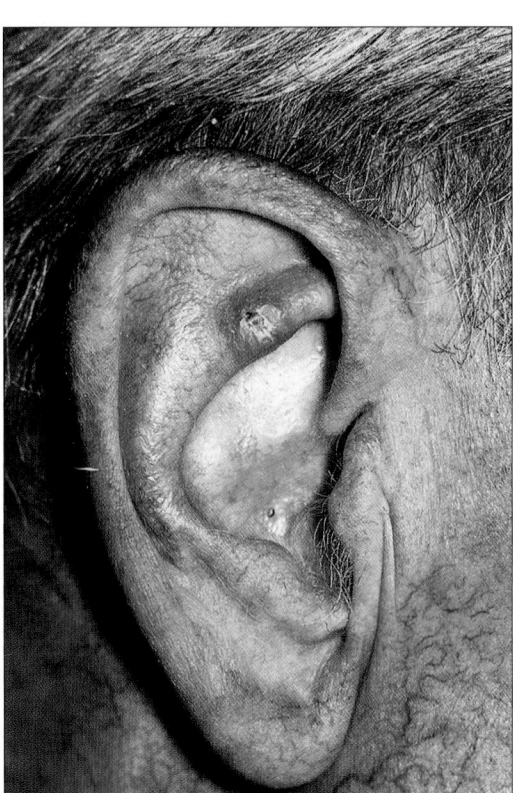

Fig. 8.142
Chondrodermatitis nodularis: this presents as a crusted lesion on the helix and may be clinically misdiagnosed as an epithelial neoplasm. By courtesy of R.A. Marsden, MD, St George's Hospital, London, UK.

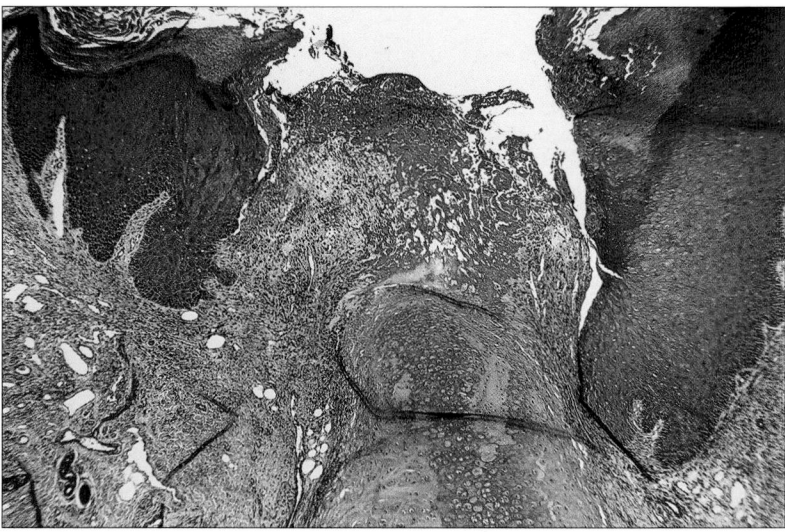

Fig. 8.143
Chondrodermatitis nodularis: this is a section through the center of the lesion showing ulceration. The adjacent epithelium is hyperkeratotic, parakeratotic and acanthotic. There is chronically inflamed granulation tissue at the base of the lesion. Cartilage is evident in the center field.

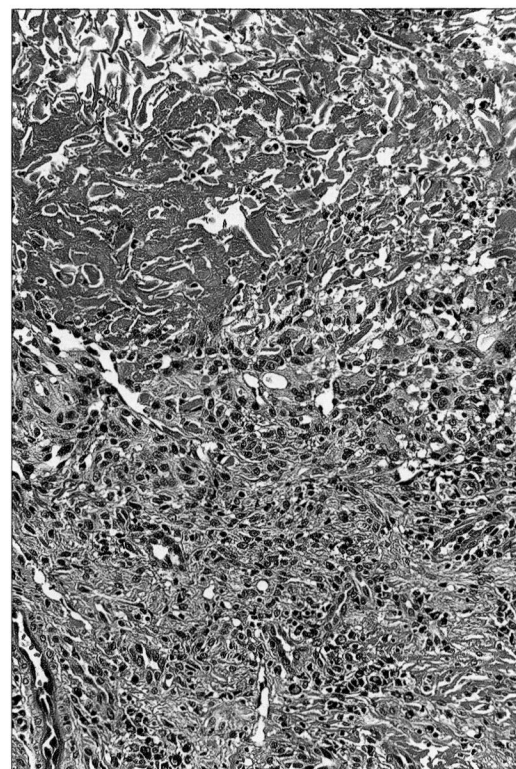

Fig. 8.144
Chondrodermatitis nodularis: there is abundant granulation tissue at the base of the ulcer.

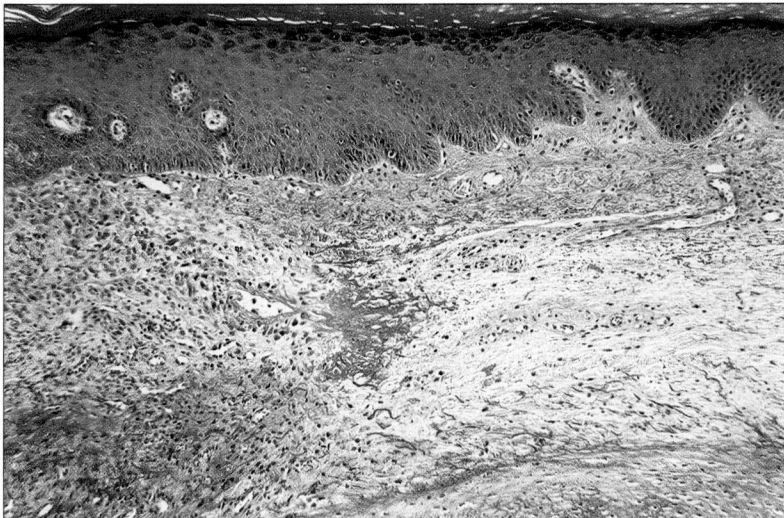

Fig. 8.145
Chondrodermatitis nodularis: in this biopsy from an early recurrence, a focus of fibrinoid degeneration of the dermal connective tissue is present in the center of the field.

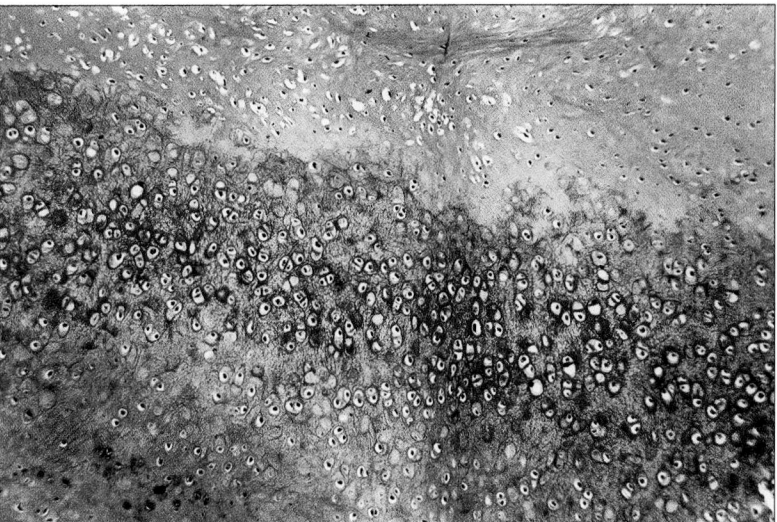

Fig. 8.146
Chondrodermatitis nodularis: in this example the auricular cartilage shows intense eosinophilia and patchy calcification in the lower left quadrant

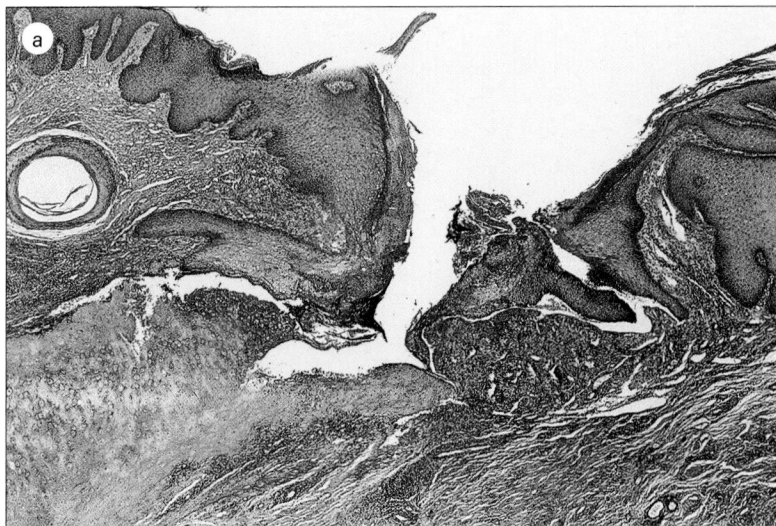

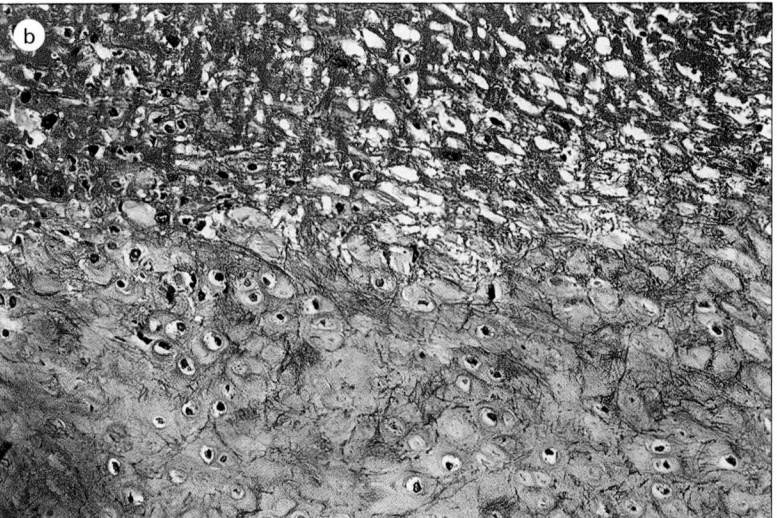

Fig. 8.147
(a, b) Chondrodermatitis nodularis: in this field degenerate cartilage is in direct continuity with abundant fibrinoid material, perhaps in the process of undergoing transepidermal elimination.

tissue without cartilage. Nevertheless, if the clinical setting is appropriate, the diagnosis can still be suggested.

References

1. Bard, J.W. (1981) Chondrodermatitis nodularis chronica helicis. *Dermatologica*, **163**, 376–384.
2. Ackerman, A.B. (1989) Pseudocarcinomatous or infundibular hyperplasia – reply. *Am J Dermatopathol*, **11**, 191–192.
3. Santa Cruz, D.J. (1980) Chondrodermatitis nodularis helicis: a transepidermal perforating disorder. *J Cutan Path*, **7**, 70–76.
4. Hurwitz, R.M. (1987) Painful papule of the ear. A follicular disorder. *J Dermatol Surg Oncol*, **13**, 270–274.
5. Bottomly, W.W., Goofield, M.D.J. (1994) Chondrodermatitis nodularis helicis occurring in systemic sclerosis – an under-reported association? *Clin Exp Dermatol*, **19**, 219–220.
6. Hurwitz, R.M. (1989) Pseudocarcinomatous or infundibular hyperplasia. *Am J Dermatopathol*, **11**, 189–191.
7. Goette, D.M. (1980) Chondrodermatitis nodularis chronica helicis: a perforating necrobiotic granuloma. *J Am Acad Dermatol*, **2**, 148–154.

Inflammatory diseases of the subcutaneous fat

9

Erythema nodosum   343
Erythema nodosum-like lesions in Behçet's disease   348

Weber–Christian disease   348

α₁-Antitrypsin deficiency-associated panniculitis   349

Factitial and traumatic panniculitis   351

Cold panniculitis   353

Cytophagic histiocytic panniculitis   354

Subcutaneous Whipple's disease   357

Pancreatic panniculitis   357

Subcutaneous fat necrosis of the newborn   359

Sclerema neonatorum   361

Cutaneous oxalosis   362

Calciphylaxis   363

Crystal-storing histiocytosis   365
Gouty panniculitis   366

Nodular vasculitis   366

Subcutaneous sarcoidosis   369

Neutrophilic lobular panniculitis associated with rheumatoid arthritis   369

Eosinophilic panniculitis   370

Infective panniculitis   371

Sclerosing panniculitis   372

Membranous fat necrosis   373

LIPODYSTROPHY   375

Familial lipodystrophy   375
Congenital generalized lipodystrophy (Berardinelli–Seip syndrome)   375
Familial partial lipodystrophy (Dunnigan variant)   375
Familial partial lipodystrophy (Köbberling variant)   376
Familial partial lipodystrophy associated with mandibuloacral dysplasia   376

Acquired lipodystrophy   376
Acquired generalized lipodystrophy   376
Acquired partial lipodystrophy   376
Lipodystrophy in HIV positive patients   376

Localized lipoatrophy   377
Lipoatrophic panniculitis   378
Lipophagic panniculitis of childhood   379
Connective tissue panniculitis   379
Lupus erythematosus profundus   379
Scleroderma panniculitis   383
Dermatomyositis panniculitis   383
Postirradiation pseudosclerodermatous panniculitis   383

The inflammatory diseases of the subcutaneous fat are a source of considerable confusion and often cause diagnostic difficulty to clinicians and pathologists alike. This in part stems from the use of classifications and clinical descriptions based upon time-honored but outdated literature.[1–4] Inadequate biopsy specimens are also a source of considerable difficulty, particularly the punch biopsy specimen, which often yields no subcutaneous fat at all. Similarly, the histological subdivision into diseases that affect the lobule and those that affect the septa is to some extent artifactual and sometimes unrewarding since most disorders affect both.[2,3,5] There is also a somewhat monotonous clinical presentation, with most patients complaining of deep-seated, variably tender or painful nodules, often affecting the lower extremities.

The subcutaneous fat has a limited repertoire of responses to noxious stimuli. Fat necrosis is a common manifestation of many forms of panniculitis and as a consequence there is often considerable histological overlap. Although there are many variants of fat necrosis – including enzymatic, crystalline, suppurative, hyalinizing and microcystic – lipophagic fat necrosis is the subtype most commonly encountered and is often a secondary feature in many forms of panniculitis (*Fig. 9.1*). This is characterized by a lobular infiltrate of histiocytes, xanthomatized cells and foreign body giant cells, frequently accompanied by granulomata (*Fig. 9.2*).

It is important to remember that the subcutaneous fat may be involved in a secondary manner, for example, in the vasculitides, the deep cutaneous fungal infections, by metastatic tumor, and following surgery or radiotherapy (*Figs 9.3, 9.4*). In this chapter the panniculitides are classified where possible on an etiological basis (*Table 9.1*).

There is considerable histological overlap in the various types of panniculitis and one must take into account all the clinical information

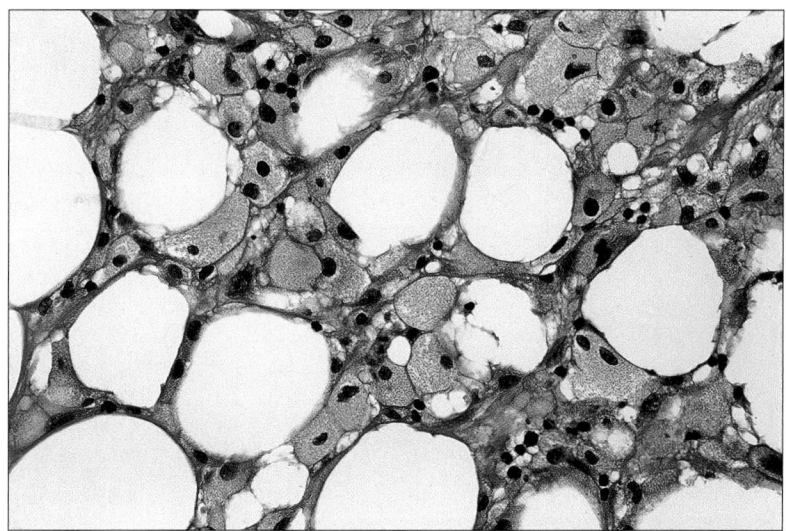

Fig. 9.1
Lipophagic fat necrosis: numerous xanthomatized histiocytes have engulfed free lipid following fat necrosis.

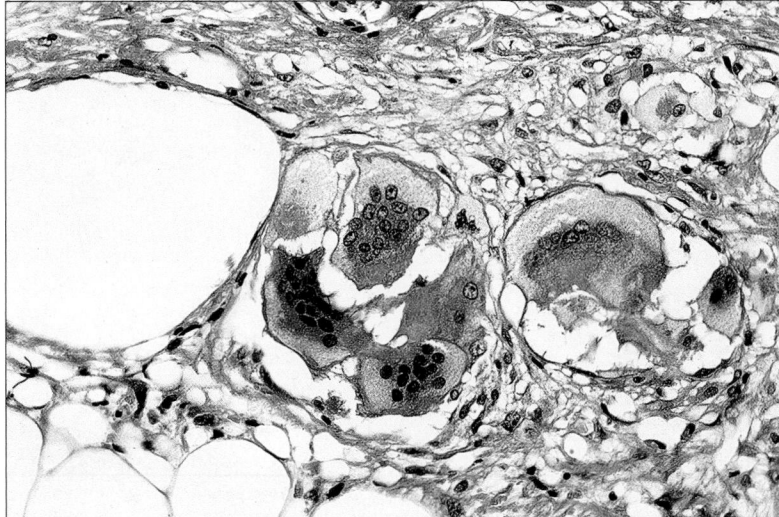

Fig. 9.2
Lipophagic fat necrosis: in this field xanthomatized multinucleated foreign body giant cells are present. Such an infiltrate is a common manifestation of many forms of panniculitis and merely reflects the presence of fat necrosis.

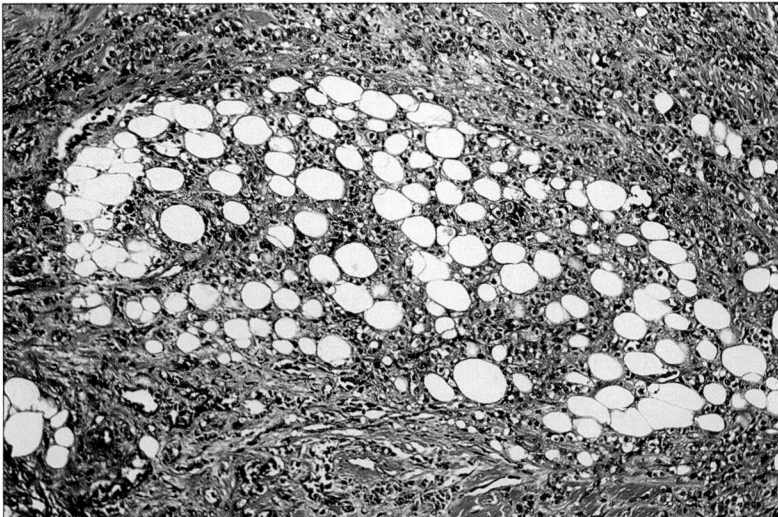

Fig. 9.3
'Malignant' panniculitis: this patient presented with a tumor nodule on the upper chest. Histology revealed a dense cellular infiltrate involving the subcutaneous fat and adjacent fibrous septum.

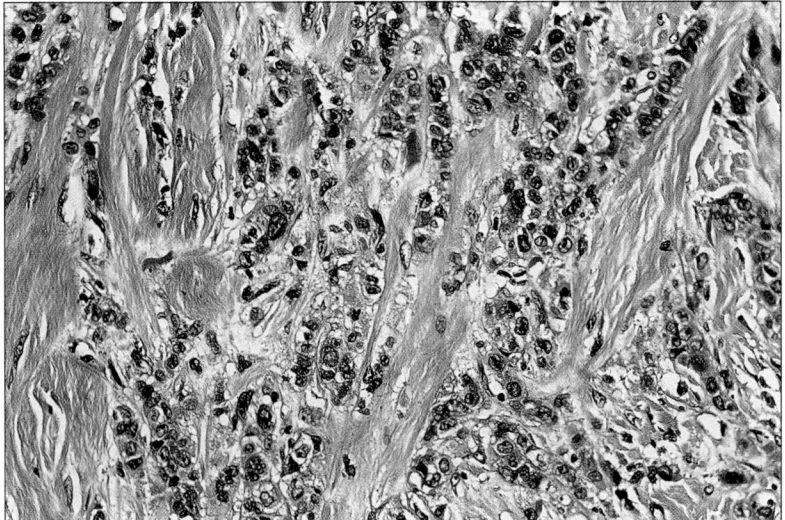

Fig. 9.4
'Malignant' panniculitis: high power view showing large pleomorphic nuclei with prominent nucleoli and mitotic activity. Many cells are arranged in single files. The primary tumor was a pleomorphic lobular carcinoma of breast.

Table 9.1
Classification of panniculitis

- Erythema nodosum
  - subacute nodular migratory panniculitis/erythema nodosum migrans
- Erythema induratum
  - nodular vasculitis
- Panniculitis associated with connective tissue disease
  - lupus panniculitis
  - morphea profunda/scleroderma/eosinophilic fasciitis
  - dermatomyositis
  - connective tissue panniculitis
- Lipoatrophy
  - localized (involutional; inflammatory, e.g. lipophagic panniculitis/granulomatous lipoatrophy)
  - lipodystrophy
- Factitial or traumatic panniculitis
  - injection-induced (steroids, insulin, narcotics, other drugs)
  - sclerosing lipogranuloma
  - blunt trauma
- Cold panniculitis
  - popsicle panniculitis
  - equestrian panniculitis
- Panniculitis of newborn or infants
  - sclerema neonatorum
  - subcutaneous fat necrosis of the newborn
- Drug-induced
  - direct (local) effect, e.g. due to injection
  - systemic effect or reaction
  - poststeroid panniculitis
  - lobular panniculitis secondary to ciprofloxacin
- Panniculitis associated with α_1-antitrypsin deficiency
- Calcifying panniculitis
  - renal failure
  - parathyroid disease
- Pancreatic panniculitis
- Gouty panniculitis
- Panniculitis with cytophagic histiocytes
  - cytophagic histiocytic panniculitis
  - malignant histiocytosis
  - sinus histiocytosis with lymphadenopathy
  - T-cell lymphoma
- Eosinophilic panniculitis
  - parasitic infection
  - Well's syndrome
  - incidental finding of eosinophils in other forms of panniculitis
- Lipomembranous panniculitis
- Non-infectious subcutaneous granulomatous disease
  - granuloma annulare, necrobiotic xanthogranuloma, rheumatoid nodule, sarcoidosis
- Infectious panniculitis
- Subcutaneous Whipple's disease
- Hemorrhagic panniculitis secondary to atheromatous emboli
- Vasculitis involving the panniculus
- Periarteritis nodosa

Reproduced with permission from Peters, M.S. and Daniel Su, W.P. (1992). Panniculitis. *Dermatologic Clinics*, **10**, 37–57.

before attempting to reach a definitive diagnosis. In patients in whom the diagnosis of panniculitis is suspected, a deep surgical incisional biopsy is essential (*Fig. 9.5*). The punch biopsy has no role whatsoever in the diagnosis of panniculitis.

References

1. Cascajo, C.D., Borghi, S., Weyers, W. (2000) Panniculitis: definitions of terms and diagnostic strategy. *Am J Dermatopathol*, **22**, 530–549.
2. Phelps, R.G., Shoji, T. (2001) Update on panniculitis. *Mt Sinai J Med*, **68**, 262–267.
3. Requena, L., Sánchez-Yus, E. (2001) Panniculitis. Part 1. Mostly septal panniculitis. *J Am Acad Dermatol*, **45**, 163–183.
4. Requena, L., Sánchez-Yus, E. (2001) Panniculitis. Part 2. Mostly lobular panniculitis. *J Am Acad Dermatol*, **45**, 325–361.
5. Demirkesen, C., Tüzüner, N., Mat, C. et al (2001) Clinicopathologic evaluation of nodular cutaneous lesions of Behçet's disease. *Am J Clin Pathol*, **116**, 341–346.

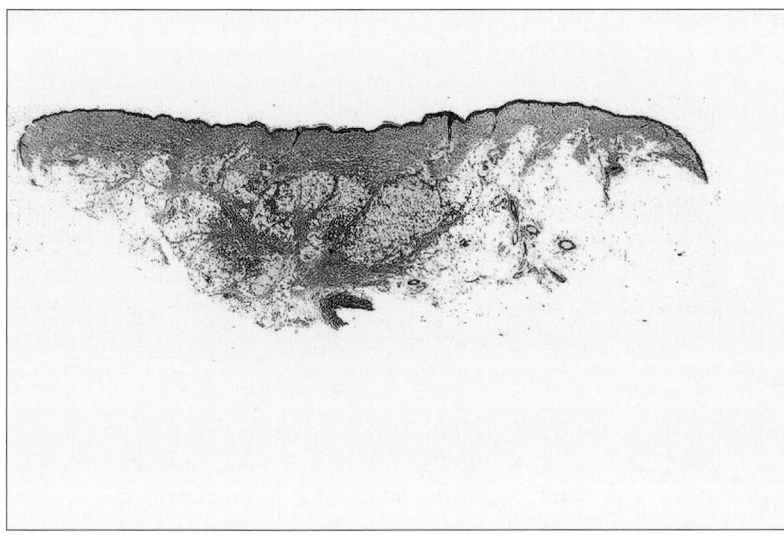

Fig. 9.5
Panniculitis: a deep surgical biopsy is essential in all cases where panniculitis is suspected.

Erythema nodosum

Clinical features

Erythema nodosum represents the commonest form of nodular panniculitis and is the prototype of septal panniculitis.[1,2] It is of course a clinical syndrome rather than a specific disease in its own right, representing a complex of symptoms and signs of multiple and very variable etiologies.[3,4] It typically affects young adults and shows a marked predilection for women (as high as 9:1 in some series). Children are only rarely affected.[5] Patients present with a sudden onset of bright-red, warm tender nodules; these typically affect the anterior and lateral aspects of the lower legs, but the arms, face, calves and trunk are occasionally involved (*Figs 9.6, 9.7*).[6,7] Lesions on the soles of the feet are rare although they appear to be more often encountered in children.[8,9] The lesions are usually multiple, bilateral, symmetrically distributed, elevated above the skin surface, and measure 1–15 cm in diameter.[7] Ulceration and scarring are not features. Subsequently, the erythema fades to a bluish or livid hue and then to a yellow coloration, reminiscent of a bruise (*Fig. 9.8*). The duration of the illness is 3–6 weeks. Patients sometimes also have pyrexia, malaise and vague aches and pains in the joints. Laboratory findings may include a raised erythrocyte sedimentation rate (ESR), leukocytosis and mild anemia.[3]

Two clinical variants have been described.

- *Erythema nodosum migrans* (subacute nodular migratory panniculitis, migratory panniculitis) is similar to classical erythema nodosum, but the lesions appear to migrate due to central clearing of established lesions and the development of new nodules at the periphery.[10–13] Lesions, which may persist for months or years, are usually associated with only mild symptoms.[10] Recurrences are sometimes encountered. Scarring is not a feature. This variant is typically asymmetrical, unilateral and distributed solely on the legs. It also shows a marked female predominance (approximately 9:1), but tends to affect an older age group than classical erythema nodosum (mean age 50 years).[11]

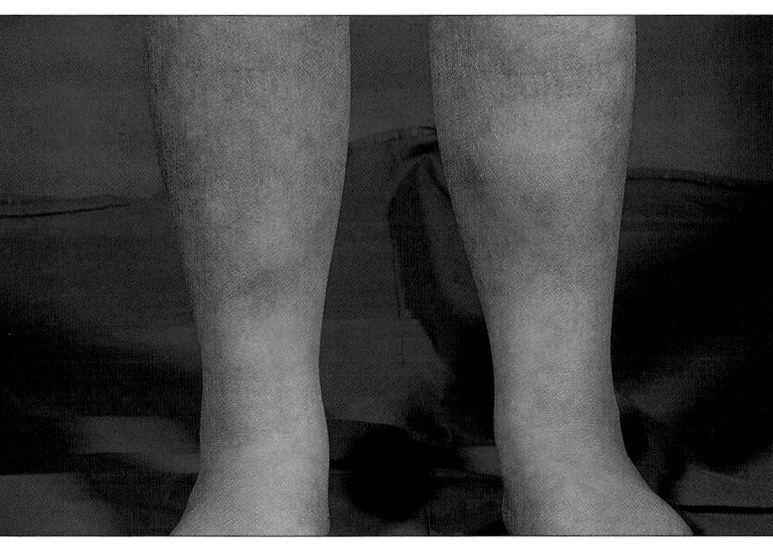

Fig. 9.6
Erythema nodosum: typical erythematous nodule on the shins of a young woman.
By courtesy of the Institute of Dermatology, London, UK.

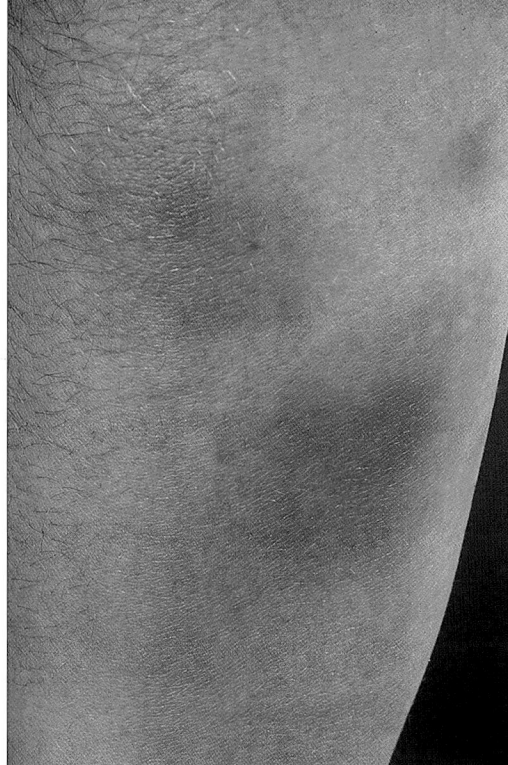

Fig. 9.7
Erythema nodosum: close-up view of *Fig. 9.6*.
By courtesy of the Institute of Dermatology, London, UK.

- *Chronic erythema nodosum*, a somewhat controversial entity, is characterized by the presence of nodules over a time course of months or even years.[14] Otherwise, the clinical features appear indistinguishable from the more typical condition.

Pathogenesis and histological features

The etiology and pathogenesis of erythema nodosum are unknown. Despite the very occasional finding of immunoreactants (IgM or IgG, and C3) in the blood vessel walls, an immune complex-mediated vasculitis is not considered likely.[6] It is probable that erythema nodosum represents a non-specific hypersensitivity reaction that involves delayed hypersensitivity mechanisms in addition to a type 3 component.

There are many known associations. Although some are certainly of significance in the etiology of this dermatosis, many are probably coincidental (*Table 9.2*).[15–27] In the earlier part of the 20th century, tuberculosis was present in up to 90% of adult patients with erythema nodosum, but this is now found in less than 1% of cases. Today, the more frequent associations include streptococcal infections, sarcoidosis, ulcerative colitis and Crohn's disease, Sweet's syndrome, Behçet's disease, menstruation, pregnancy, estrogens and the oral contraceptive, cat scratch disease and various drug treatments (e.g. bromides, antibiotics and sulfonamides). Other infectious conditions that have been described in association with erythema nodosum include cytomegalovirus, *Yersinia*, *Mycoplasma*, *Chlamydia*, hepatitis B, atypical mycobacterial infections (e.g. swimming pool granuloma), *Salmonella*, *Shigella*, meningococcal septicemia, Q fever, *Leptospirosis*, syphilis, human immunodeficiency virus (HIV), kerion, histoplasmosis, blastomycosis, amebiasis and giardiasis.[15,25–37] Additional drugs that have been implicated in the development of erythema nodosum include isotretinoin, interleukin (IL)-2, minocycline, thalidomide, Echinacea, gold salts and hepatitis B vaccine.[16,38–44] Erythema nodosum has also been reported following a variety of malignancies including Hodgkin's lymphoma, hypernephroma, carcinomas of the colon, pancreas and uterine cervix, and after radiotherapy.[45–50] Erythema nodosum leprosum is dealt with in Chapter 17. In 20–30% of patients no obvious cause is identified (idiopathic erythema nodosum).[2]

Erythema nodosum migrans seems to be particularly related to pregnancy, the oral contraceptive, streptococcal infection and thyroid disease.[10–12] Many cases, however, have no obvious associated predisposing factors or condition.

Histologically, erythema nodosum represents the prototype of septal panniculitis. It is characterized by a combination of features, including vascular change, septal inflammation, hemorrhage and a variable degree of acute or chronic panniculitis (*Fig. 9.9*). Although it is often said that

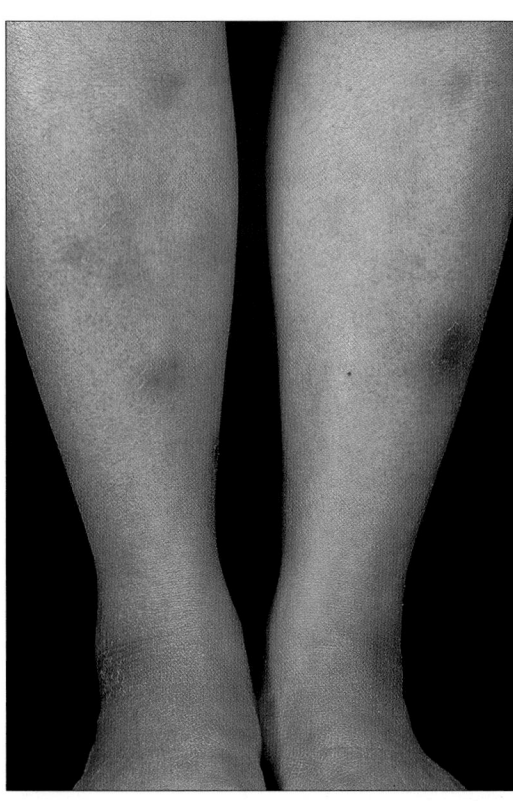

Fig. 9.8
Erythema nodosum: in this patient the lesions are healing and show a characteristic bruise-like appearance. By courtesy of the Institute of Dermatology, London, UK.

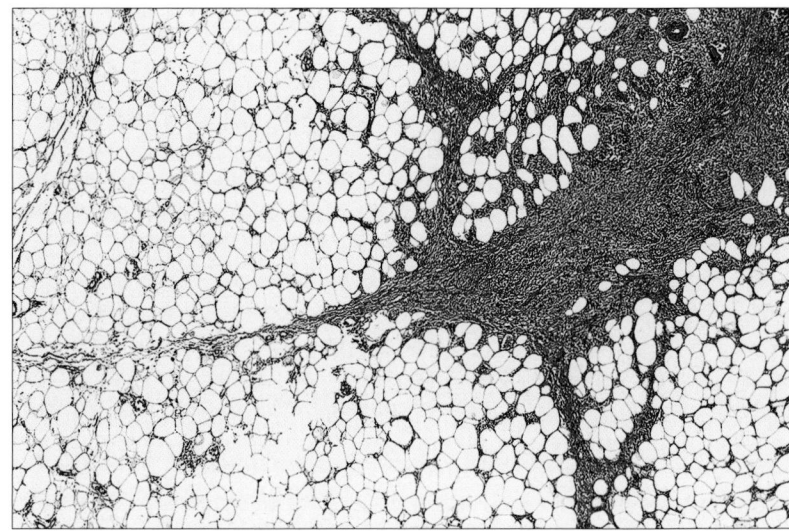

Fig. 9.9
Erythema nodosum: this example shows the classical appearance of septal inflammation with spread into the immediately adjacent lobule, giving rise to a lace-like appearance.

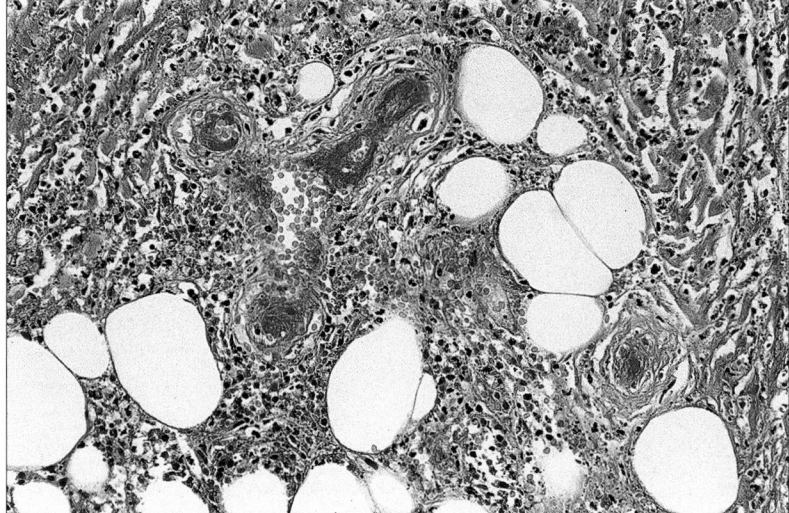

Fig. 9.10
Erythema nodosum: in the acute phase, venulitis is very occasionally present although many sections or levels must be examined before its presence is detected.

Table 9.2
Erythema nodosum: etiology

• *Streptococcus*	• Sarcoidosis
• Tuberculosis	• Sweet's syndrome
• *Chlamydophila psittaci*	• Cat scratch disease
• Crohn's disease	• Yersinia infection
• Drugs	• Ulcerative colitis
• Behçet's disease	• Malignancy

erythema nodosum characteristically affects the septal component of the panniculus, it should be noted that there is not infrequently involvement of the lobule, in part or in whole, particularly if older lesions are biopsied. In the past, cases of the latter might have been diagnosed as Weber–Christian disease.

Frank vasculitis is only very exceptionally encountered. When present it involves the small veins within the connective tissue septa. It may be acute and necrotizing, associated with thrombosis and hemorrhage, or may manifest as chronic venular inflammation associated with endothelial cell swelling (*Figs 9.10, 9.11*). The overlying dermis typically shows a perivascular and periadnexal chronic inflammatory cell infiltrate.

In the early stages, the septal inflammation may be acute and characterized by an infiltrate of neutrophil polymorphs, but this is soon replaced by lymphocytes and histiocytes (*Figs 9.12–9.14*).[51,52]

Eosinophils are sometimes found and rarely they can be conspicuous (see eosinophilic panniculitis, p. 370). Septal collections of histiocytes surrounding a cleft-like space (so-called Miescher's radial granuloma) are said to be a characteristic feature, although they have been reported in Sweet's syndrome, nodular vasculitis and necrobiosis lipoidica (*Figs 9.15–9.17*).[2,53,54] Further progression leads to the development of a frankly granulomatous infiltrate in which giant cells may be conspicuous. Coagulation and caseation-like necrosis is never seen in erythema nodosum (compare with nodular vasculitis below). Sometimes the connective tissue in the fibrous septa shows fibrinoid necrosis, and hemorrhage is almost invariably present (*Figs 9.18–9.20*).

Characteristically, the septal infiltrate (lymphocytes, histiocytes and granulomata) spills over to affect the periphery of the fat lobule to give a delicate lacy appearance, but fat necrosis is not usually present. On occasions, however, otherwise typical erythema nodosum may be associated with fat necrosis and a neutrophil inflammatory cell infiltrate (*Fig. 9.21*).[55]

If an older lesion is biopsied, septal fibrosis can sometimes be quite marked. Residual granulomatous inflammation is usually present.

Erythema nodosum migrans is characterized by densely scarred and thickened interlobular septa accompanied by a conspicuous granulomatous

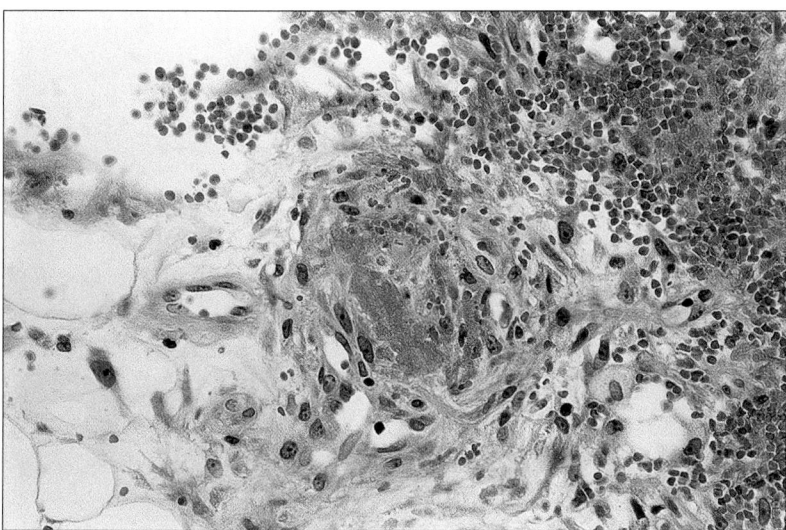

Fig. 9.11
Erythema nodosum: in this field there is a thrombosed venule associated with marked hemorrhage.

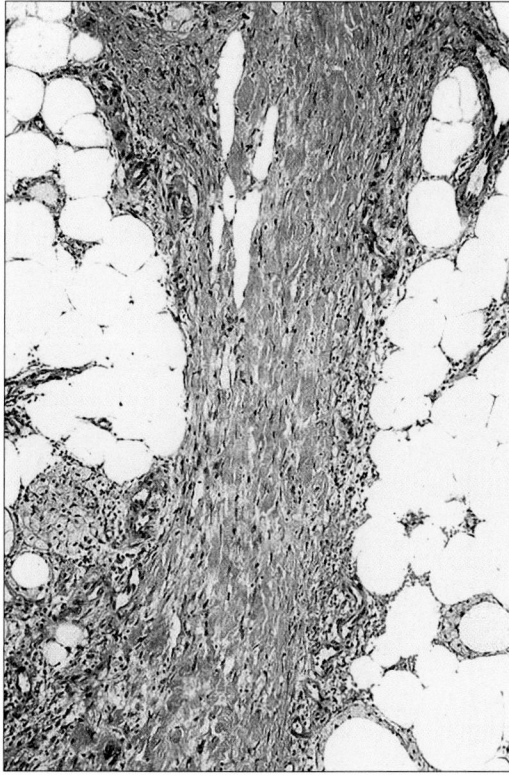

Fig. 9.12
Erythema nodosum: there is septal thickening with a lymphohistiocytic infiltrate.

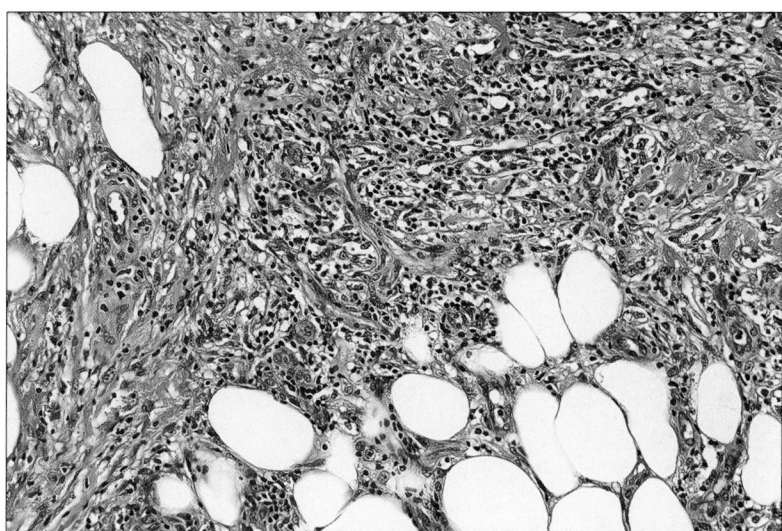

Fig. 9.13
Erythema nodosum: this view shows the interface between the septum and the lobule.

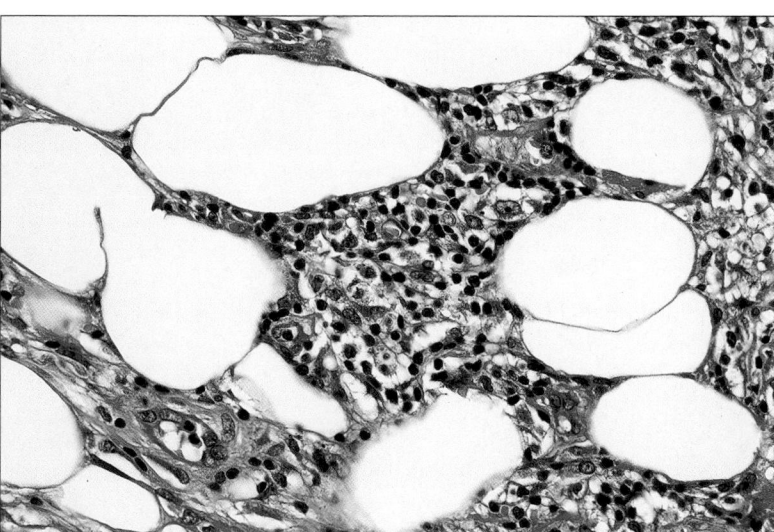

Fig. 9.14
Erythema nodosum: close-up view of cellular infiltrate.

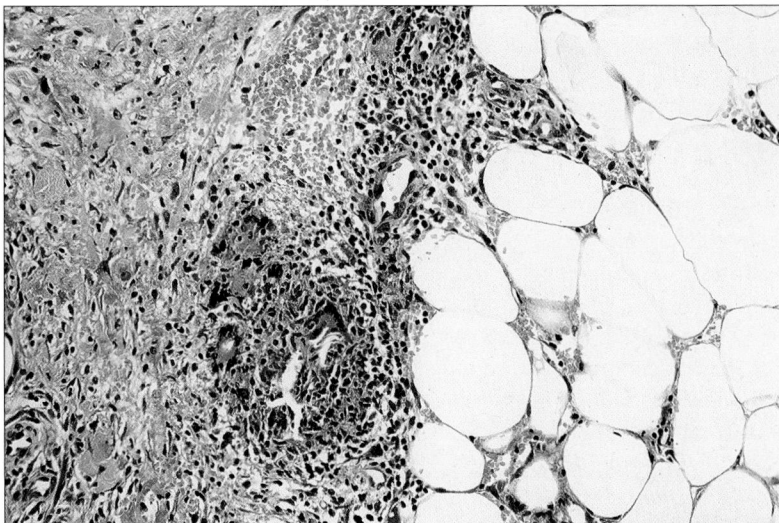

Fig. 9.15
Erythema nodosum: collections of histiocytes known as Miescher's granulomata are a common finding.

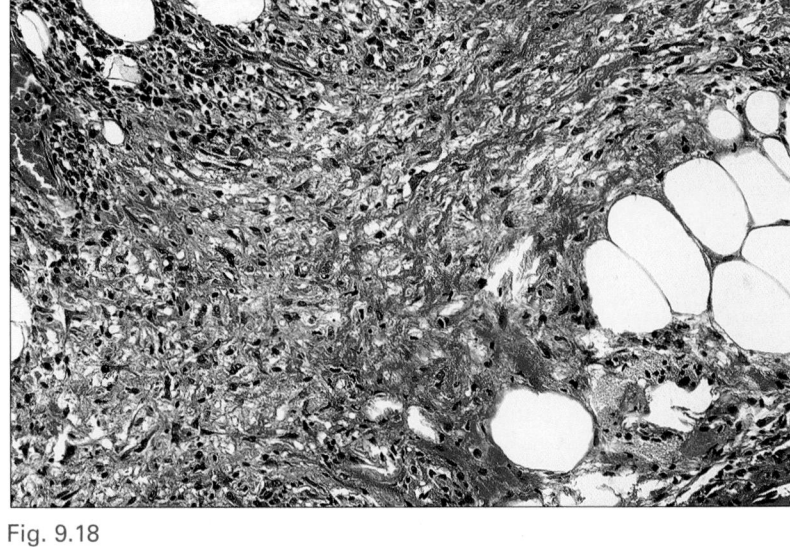

Fig. 9.18
Erythema nodosum: fibrinoid necrosis of the connective tissue septa is an occasional feature.

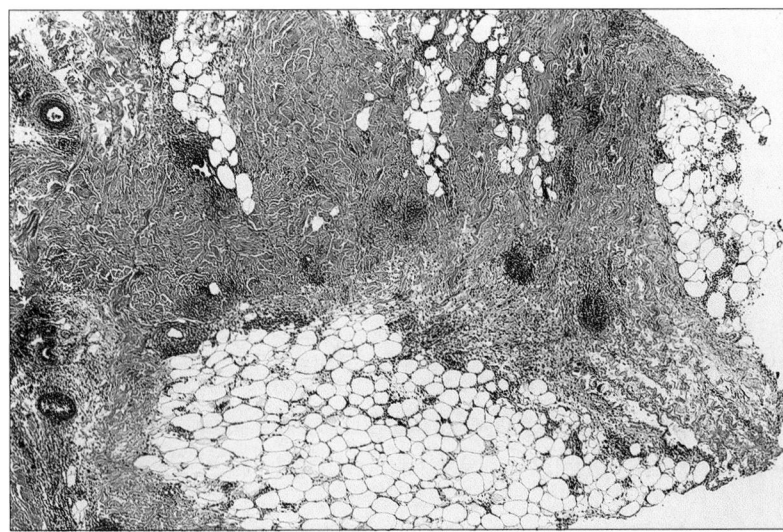

Fig. 9.16
Erythema nodosum: in this example multiple small granulomata are evident in the thickened septa.

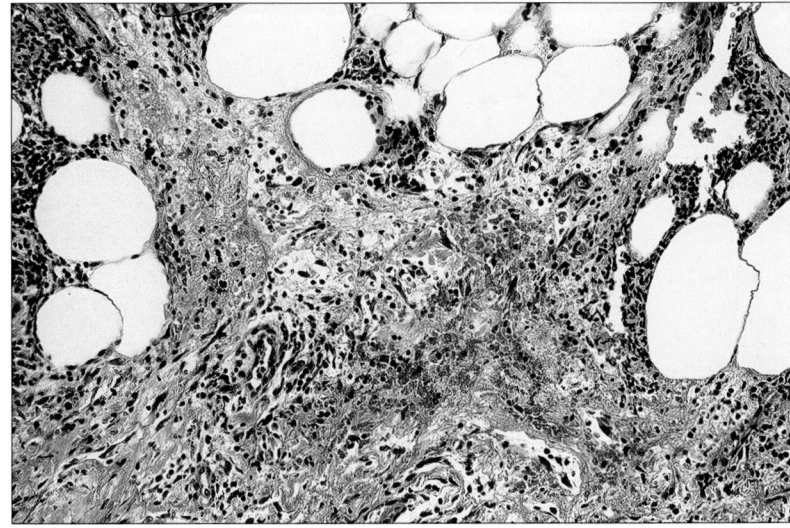

Fig. 9.19
Erythema nodosum: there is marked red cell extravasation.

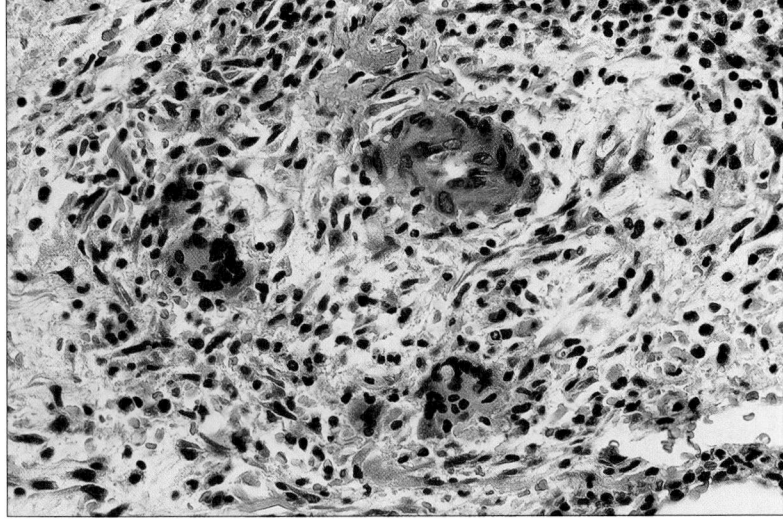

Fig. 9.17
Erythema nodosum: high power view of granulomata.

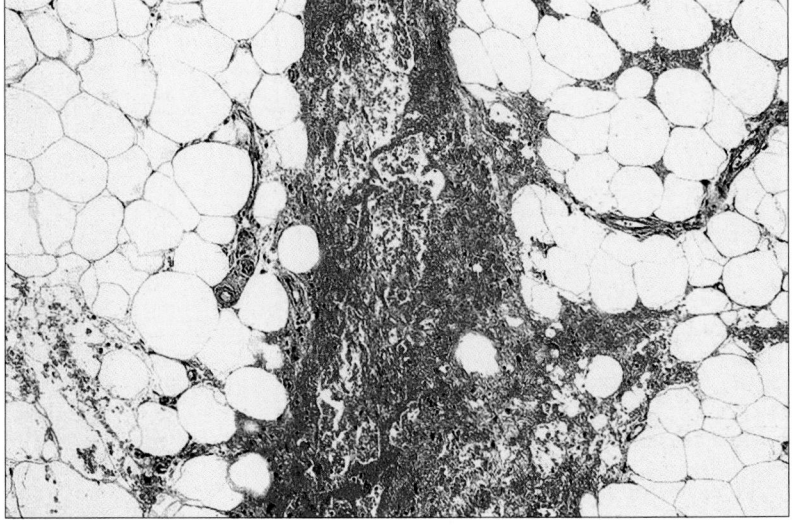

Fig. 9.20
Erythema nodosum: in this example there is massive hemorrhage. Subsequent breakdown with hemosiderin formation accounts for the clinical appearance of bruising.

infiltrate (*Figs 9.22, 9.23*). Numerous giant cells may be seen and often they form a palisade along the septal borders. Granulation tissue-like vascular proliferation is often a conspicuous feature. Vasculitis is absent and hemorrhage is not usually seen.

In chronic erythema nodosum the histological changes are similar to, but usually milder, than those of the acute variant.[11]

Differential diagnosis

At scanning magnification, vasculitic processes affecting the septa of the subcutaneous fat may be mistaken for erythema nodosum. Occasionally, the features of leukocytoclastic vasculitis are seen within the septa of the subcutaneous fat in the absence of the more usual superficial dermal involvement.[56] Such instances present as erythematous nodules usually affecting the lower legs. Similarly, superficial thrombophlebitis presents within the septa of the subcutaneous fat. In this condition, however, the vein is the focus of the inflammatory process with associated thrombosis and there is little or no involvement of the lobule. Cutaneous polyarteritis nodosa affects muscular arteries within the lower dermis and subcutaneous fat septa and, therefore, should not be confused with erythema nodosum.[56]

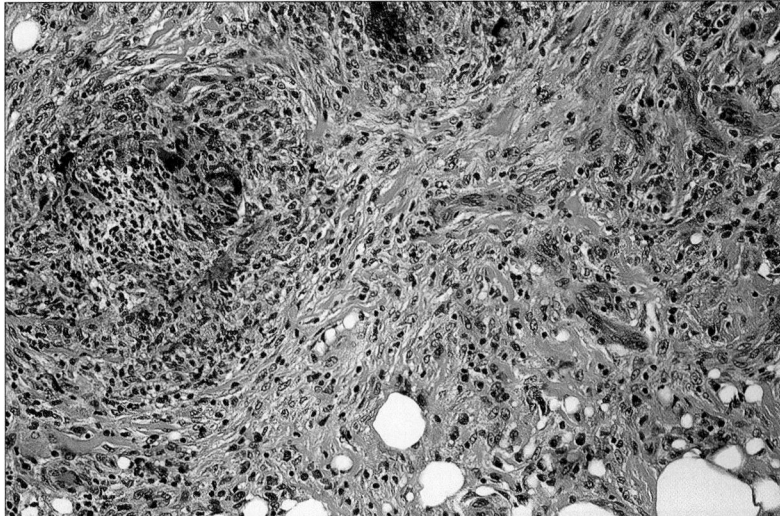

Fig. 9.23
Erythema nodosum migrans: close-up view showing granulomata and newly formed blood vessels.

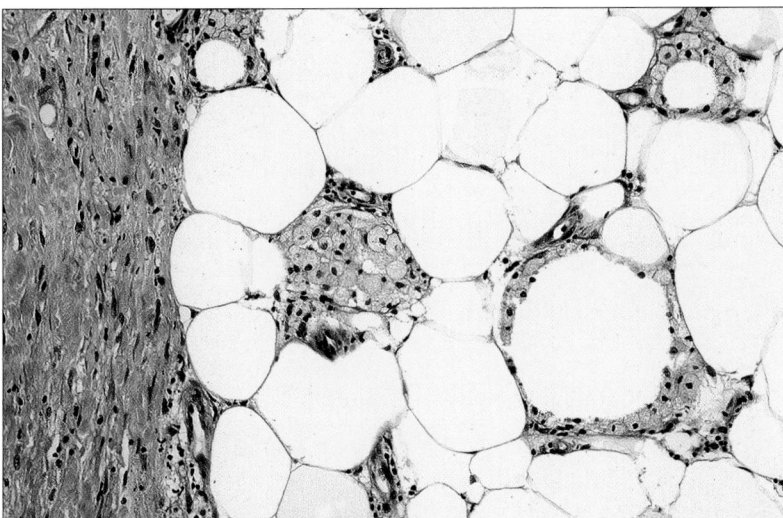

Fig. 9.21
Erythema nodosum: focal fat necrosis associated with lipid-laden histiocytes.

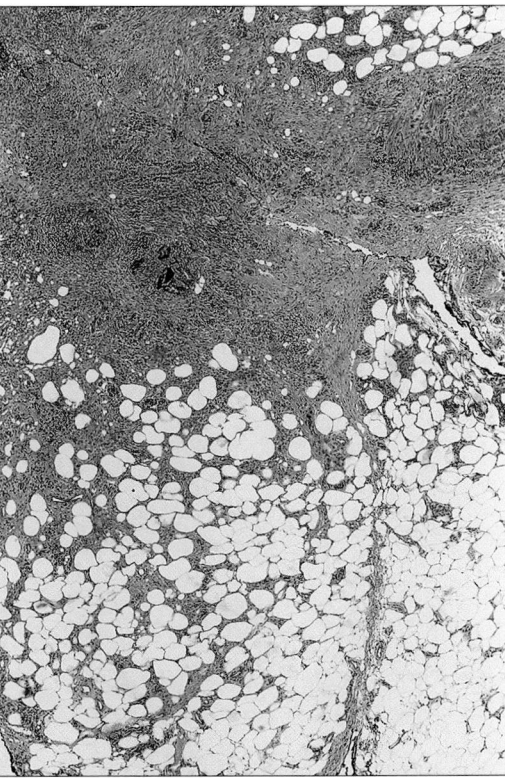

Fig. 9.22
Erythema nodosum migrans: there is marked septal thickening with conspicuous granulomata. Granulation tissue extends into the adjacent lobule.

References

1. Peters, M.S., Daniel Su, W.P. (1992) Panniculitis. *Dermatol Clin*, **10**, 37–57.
2. White, W.L., Wieselthier, J.S., Hitchcock, M.G. (1996) Panniculitis: recent developments and observations. *Semin Cutan Med Surg*, **15**, 278–299.
3. O'Neill, J.H. (1991) The differential diagnosis of erythema nodosum. *Delaware Med J*, **63**, 683–689.
4. Miranda, F.M., Focesca, C.E., Maza, L.P. (1985) Erythema nodosum: a study of 133 cases. *Ann Med Interne*, **2**, 433–437.
5. Kakourou, T., Drosatou, P., Psychou, F. et al (2001) Erythema nodosum in children: a prospective study. *J Am Acad Dermatol*, **44**, 17–21.
6. White, J.W. (1985) Erythema nodosum. *Dermatol Clin*, **3**, 119–127.
7. Hannuksela, M. (1986) Erythema nodosum. *Clin Dermatol*, **4**, 88–95.
8. Suarez, S.M., Paller, A.S. (1993) Plantar erythema nodosum in two children. *Arch Dermatol*, **129**, 1064–1065.
9. Ohtake, N., Kawamura, T., Akiyama, C. et al (1994) Unilateral plantar erythema nodosum. *J Am Acad Dermatol*, **30**, 654–655.
10. Rostas, A., Lowe, D., Smout, M.S. (1980) Erythema nodosum migrans in a young woman. *Arch Dermatol*, **116**, 325–326.
11. de Almeida Prestes, C., Winkelmann, R.K., Daniel Su, W.P. (1990) Septal granulomatous panniculitis: comparison of the pathology of erythema nodosum migrans (migratory panniculitis) and chronic erythema nodosum. *J Am Acad Dermatol*, **22**, 477–483.
12. Hannuksela, M. (1973) Erythema nodosum migrans. *Acta Derm Venerol*, **53**, 313–317.
13. Perry, H.O., Winkelmann, R.K. (1964) Subacute nodular migratory panniculitis. *Arch Dermatol*, **89**, 170–179.
14. Fine, R.M., Meltzer, H.D. (1969) Chronic erythema nodosum. *Arch Dermatol*, **100**, 33–38.
15. Cribier, B., Caille A., Heid, E. et al (1998) Erythema nodosum and associated diseases. A study of 129 cases. *Int J Dermatol*, **37**, 667–672.
16. Bridges, A.J., Graziano, F.M., Calhoun, W. et al (1990) Hyperpigmentation, neutrophilic alveolitis and erythema nodosum resulting from minocycline. *J Am Acad Dermatol*, **22**, 959–962.
17. Macfarlane, J.T. (1981) Recurrent erythema nodosum and pulmonary sarcoidosis. *Postgrad Med J*, **57**, 525.
18. Hannuksela, M. (1977) Human yersiniosis: a common cause of erythematous skin eruptions. *Int J Dermatol*, **16**, 665–666.
19. Schorr-Lesnick, B., Brandt, L.J. (1988) Selected rheumatologic and dermatologic manifestations of inflammatory bowel disease. *Am J Gastroenterol*, **83**, 216–223.
20. Blaustein, A., Moreno, A., Noguera, J. et al (1985) Septal granulomatous panniculitis in Sweet's syndrome: report of two cases. *Arch Dermatol*, **121**, 785–788.
21. Nishie, W., Kimura, T., Kanagawa, M. (2002) Sweet's syndrome evolved from recurrent erythema nodosum in a patient with myelodysplastic syndrome. *J Dermatol*, **29**, 91–95.
22. Chun, S.I., Su, W.P., Lee, S. et al (1989) Erythema nodosum-like lesions in Behçet's syndrome: a histopathologic study of 30 cases. *J Cutan Pathol*, **16**, 259–265.
23. Salvatore, M.A., Lynch, P.J. (1980) Erythema nodosum, estrogens and pregnancy. *Arch Dermatol*, **116**, 557–558.
24. Sundaresh, K.V., Maljar, D.D. Jr, Camisa, C. et al (1986) Cat scratch disease associated with erythema nodosum. *Cutis*, **38**, 317–319.
25. Spear, J.B., Kessler, H.A., Dworin, A. et al (1988) Erythema nodosum associated with acute cytomegalovirus mononucleosis in an adult. *Arch Intern Med*, **148**, 323–324.
26. Garty, B., Tiqva, P. (1991) Swimming pool granuloma associated with erythema nodosum. *Cutis*, **47**, 314–318.
27. Scott, B.B. (1980) Salmonella gastroenteritis: another cause of erythema nodosum. *Br J Dermatol*, **102**, 339–340.
28. Tami, L.F. (1985) Erythema nodosum associated with Shigella colitis. *Arch Dermatol*, **121**, 590.
29. Whitton, T., Smith, A.G. (1999) Erythema nodosum secondary to meningococcal septicaemia. *Clin Exp Dermatol*, **24**, 97–98.
30. Conget, L., Mallolas, J., Mensa, J. et al (1987) Erythema nodosum and Q fever. *Arch Dermatol*, **123**, 867.
31. Derham, R.J.L., Owens, G.G., Wooldridge, M.A.W. (1976) Leptospirosis as a cause of erythema nodosum. *BMJ*, **2**, 403–404.
32. Alinovi, A., Lui, P., Bernoldi, D. (1983) Syphilis: still a cause of erythema nodosum. *Int J Dermatol*, **22**, 310–311.

33. Fegueux, S., Maslo, C., de Truchis, P. et al (1991) Erythema nodosum in HIV-infected patients. *J Am Acad Dermatol*, 25, 113.
34. Martínez Roig, A., Llorens Teral, J., Torres, J.M. (1982) Erythema nodosum and kerion on the scalp. *Am J Dis Child*, 13, 440–442.
35. Ozols, I.I., Wheat, L.J. (1981) Erythema nodosum in an epidemic of histoplasmosis in Indianapolis. *Arch Dermatol*, 117, 709–712.
36. Miller, D.D., Davies, S.F., Sarosi, G.A. (1982) Erythema nodosum and blastomycosis. *Arch Intern Med*, 142, 1839.
37. Harries, A.D., Taylor, J. (1986) Erythema nodosum associated with invasive amoebiasis and giardiasis. *Br J Dermatol*, 114, 394.
38. Kellett, J.K., Beck, M.H., Chalmers, R.J.E. (1985) Erythema nodosum and circulating immunocomplexes in acne fulminans after treatment with isotretinoin. *BMJ*, 290, 820.
39. Tan, B.B., Lear, J.T., Smith, A.G. (1997) Acne fulminans and erythema nodosum during isotretinoin therapy responding to dapsone. *Clin Exp Dermatol*, 22, 26–27.
40. Weinstein, A., Bujak, D., Mittelman, A. et al (1987) Erythema nodosum in a patient with renal cell carcinoma treated with interleukin 2 and lymphokine activated killer cells. *JAMA*, 258, 3120–3121.
41. Viraben, R., Dupre, A. (1988) Erythema nodosum following thalidomide therapy for Behçet disease. *Dermatologica*, 176, 107.
42. Soon, S.L., Crawford, R.I. (2001) Recurrent erythema nodosum associated with echinacea herbal therapy. *J Am Acad Dermatol*, 44, 298–299.
43. Stone, R.L., Claflin, A., Penneys, N.S. (1973) Erythema nodosum following gold sodium thiomalate therapy. *Arch Dermatol*, 107, 602–604.
44. Di Guisto, C.A., Bernhard, J.D. (1986) Erythema nodosum following hepatitis B vaccine. *Lancet*, 2, 1042.
45. Chalmers, R.J.G., Proctor, S.J., Marks, J.M. (1982) Erythema nodosum and Hodgkin's lymphoma. *Br J Dermatol*, 106, 593–595.
46. Lillo, A., Gil, M.J., Jimenez, R. et al (1997) Erythema nodosum and adenocarcinoma of the colon. *Med Clin (Barc)*, 108, 318–320.
47. Durden, F.M., Variyam, E., Chren, M.M. (1996) Fat necrosis with features of erythema nodosum in a patient with metastatic pancreatic carcinoma. *Int J Dermatol*, 35, 39–41.
48. Altomare, G.F., Capella, G.L. (1995) Paraneoplastic erythema nodosum in a patient with carcinoma of the uterine cervix. *Br J Dermatol*, 132, 667–668.
49. Takagawa, S., Nakamura, S., Yokozeki, H. et al (1999) Radiation-induced erythema nodosum. *Br J Dermatol*, 140, 372–373.
50. Fearfield, L.A., Bunker, C.B. (2000) Radiotherapy and erythema nodosum. *Br J Dermatol*, 142, 189.
51. Winkelmann, R.K., Förström, L. (1975) New observations in the histopathology of erythema nodosum. *J Invest Dermatol*, 65, 441–446.
52. White, W.L., Hitchcock, M.G. (1999) Diagnosis: erythema nodosum or not? *Semin Cutan Med Surg*, 18, 47–55.
53. Yus, E.S., Vico, M.D.S., de Diego, V. (1989) Miescher's radial granuloma: a characteristic marker of erythema nodosum. *Am J Dermatopathol*, 11, 434–442.
54. Patterson, J.W. (1991) Differential diagnosis of panniculitis. *Adv Dermatol*, 6, 309–329.
55. Förström, L., Winkelmann, R.K. (1977) Acute panniculitis: a clinical and histopathologic study of 34 cases. *Arch Dermatol*, 113, 909–917.
56. Requena, L., Sánchez-Yus, E. (2001) Panniculitis. Part 1. Mostly septal panniculitis. *J Am Acad Dermatol*, 45, 163–183.

Erythema nodosum-like lesions in Behçet's disease

Recurrent erythematous, tender, nodular lesions on the lower extremities (clinically reminiscent of erythema nodosum) are a common manifestation of Behçet's disease.[1-4] The fronts of the shins are most often affected but lesions may also occur on the arms, face, neck and buttocks.[2] Although histologically they have been described as showing erythema nodosum-like features, more commonly they are characterized by a lobular or mixed septal and lobular panniculitis associated with a neutrophil-rich infiltrate, neutrophilic vasculitis (affecting arterioles and venules) and associated fat necrosis.[2,5] Less often, a lymphocytic vasculitis and, exceptionally, polyarteritis nodosa-like features are encountered. Miescher's granulomata may sometimes be present (see p. 348).[2,6]

References

1. Chun, S.I., Su, W.P.D., Lee, S. et al (1989) Erythema nodosum-like lesions in Behçet's syndrome: a histopathologic study of 30 cases. *J Cutan Pathol*, 16, 259–265.
2. Kim, B.S., LeBoit, P.E. (1998) Erythema nodosum-like lesions in Behçet's disease: is vasculitis the main pathologic feature? *J Cutan Pathol*, 25, 500.
3. Jorizzo, J.L., Abernathy, J.L., White, W.L. et al (1995) Mucocutaneous criteria for the diagnosis of Behçet's disease: an analysis of clinicopathologic data from multiple international centers. *J Am Acad Dermatol*, 32, 968–976.
4. Magro, C.M., Crawson, A.N. (1995) Cutaneous manifestations of Behçet's disease. *Int J Dermatol*, 34, 159–165.
5. Demirkesen, C., Tüzüner, N., Mat, C. et al (2001) Clinicopathologic evaluation of nodular cutaneous lesions of Behçet's syndrome. *Am J Clin Pathol*, 116, 341–346.
6. Liao, Y.H., Hsiao, G.H., Hsiao, C.H. (1999) Behçet's disease with cutaneous changes resembling polyarteritis nodosa. *Br J Dermatol*, 140, 368–369.

Weber–Christian disease

As originally defined by Christian in 1928 (relapsing febrile nodular non-suppurative panniculitis), this disorder was characterized by recurrent attacks of fever associated with the development of subcutaneous tender nodules (particularly over the extremities), which were histologically characterized by the presence of non-suppurative panniculitis and healed to leave a depressed scar.[1-4] Lesions were said to affect mainly young white females, and although the lower extremities were predominantly affected, the upper extremities, buttocks, abdominal wall, breasts and face could also be involved. Arthritis, arthralgias and myalgias were often present.[3] A systemic variant – which was potentially fatal and affected the intestines, mesentery, lungs, heart and kidneys – was also recognized.[3,5]

Since 1928 there have been many case reports in the literature dealing with this so-called 'specific disease'. In general, however, many of the (particularly earlier) studies used imprecise clinical and histological diagnostic criteria. Some were certainly examples of erythema nodosum. In the light of current knowledge of the panniculitides, many cases would now be reclassified. A Weber–Christian-like disease may be seen in erythema nodosum, factitial panniculitis, lupus panniculitis, pancreatic fat necrosis-associated panniculitis, α_1-antitrypsin deficiency-associated panniculitis, connective tissue diseases, cytophagic histiocytic panniculitis and subcutaneous panniculitic T-cell lymphoma.[6-15] The term has also been applied to cases of infective panniculitis, and panniculitis following jejunoileal bypass surgery.[16-19]

It seems unlikely, therefore, that Weber–Christian disease represents a distinct entity in its own right. It is proposed therefore to take this opportunity to bury it once and for all. As suggested by Patterson, 'a clinical diagnosis of Weber–Christian disease should signal the beginning of a search for the true cause of the disorder'.[9] Likewise the term Rothmann–Makai syndrome should be abandoned.[20] More often than not it probably represents erythema nodosum.

References

1. MacDonald, A., Feiwel, M. (1969) A review of the concept of Weber–Christian panniculitis with a report of five cases. *Br J Dermatol*, 80, 355–361.
2. Milner, R.D.G., Mitchinson, M.J. (1965) Systemic Weber–Christian disease. *J Clin Pathol*, 18, 150–156.
3. Panush, R.S., Yonker, R.A., Dlesk, A. et al (1985) Weber–Christian disease: analysis of 15 cases and review of the literature. *Medicine (Baltimore)*, 64, 181–191.
4. Arnot, K.A. (1982) Case records of the Massachusetts General Hospital. *N Engl J Med*, 306, 1035–1043.
5. Aronson, I., West, D.P., Variakojis, D. et al (1985) Fatal panniculitis. *J Am Acad Dermatol*, 12, 535–551.
6. Ackerman, A.B., Moshere, D.T., Schwann, H.A. (1966) Factitial Weber–Christian disease. *JAMA*, 198, 731–736.
7. Förström, L., Winkelmann, R.K. (1974) Factitial panniculitis. *Arch Dermatol*, 110, 747–750.
8. Winkelmann, R.K., Barker, S.M. (1985) Factitial traumatic panniculitis. *J Am Acad Dermatol*, 13, 988–994.
9. Patterson, J.W. (1991) The differential diagnosis of panniculitis. *Adv Dermatol*, 6, 309–329.
10. Förström, L., Winkelmann, R.K. (1977) Acute panniculitis: a clinical and histopathologic study of 34 cases. *Arch Dermatol*, 113, 909–917.
11. Breit, S.N., Clark, P., Robinson, J.P. et al (1983) Familial occurrence of α1-antitrypsin deficiency and Weber–Christian disease. *Arch Dermatol*, 119, 198–202.
12. Bleuminke, E., Klokke, H.A. (1984) Protease-inhibitor deficiencies in a patient with Weber–Christian panniculitis. *Arch Dermatol*, 120, 936–940.
13. Winkelmann, R.K. (1983) Panniculitis in connective tissue disease. *Arch Dermatol*, 119, 336–344.
14. Crotty, C.P., Winkelmann, R.K. (1981) Cytophagic histiocytic panniculitis with fever, cytopenia, liver failure, and terminal hemorrhage diathesis. *J Am Acad Dermatol*, 4, 181–194.
15. Eng, A.M., Aronson, I.K. (1984) Dermatopathology of panniculitis. *Semin Dermatol*, 3, 1–13.
16. Williams, H.J., Samuelson, C.O., Zone, J.J. (1979) Nodular non-suppurative panniculitis associated with jejuno-ileal bypass surgery. *Arch Dermatol*, 115, 1091–1093.
17. Drenick, E.J., Ament, M.E., Finegold, S.M. et al (1976) Bypass enteropathy: intestinal and systemic manifestations following small-bowel bypass. *JAMA*, 236, 269–272.
18. Seff, D.J. (1980) Weber–Christian disease following weight loss after ileal bypass surgery. *Maryland State Med J*, 29, 81–84.
19. White, J.W. Jr, Winkelmann, R.K. (1998) Weber–Christian panniculitis: a review of 30 cases with this diagnosis. *J Am Acad Dermatol*, 391, 56–62.
20. Chan, H.L. (1975) Panniculitis (Rothmann–Makai), with good response to tetracycline. *Br J Dermatol*, 92, 351–354.

α₁–Antitrypsin deficiency-associated panniculitis

Clinical features

Deficiency of α₁-antitrypsin is associated with a severe and particularly intractable form of panniculitis.[1–12] Patients have recurrent episodes of painful or tender nodules, which are particularly resistant to therapy. The disease shows a slight male predominance (3:2), and although a wide age range can be affected (7–73 years), most patients are in their fourth or fifth decade.[5,7] Children, however, may occasionally be affected.[5] The nodules, which are often precipitated by trauma, develop most often on the trunk and proximal extremities, but the buttocks, chest, back and abdomen are sometimes also affected (*Fig. 9.24*). Occasionally, the disease spreads to the genitalia and involvement of the abdominal fat has been described.

The nodules may be erythematous and are frequently associated with ulceration and the spontaneous discharge of clear or serosanguinous fluid.[5] Deeply penetrating sinuses associated with liquefaction of the subcutaneous tissues are an important complication.

Fever is a common accompaniment and patients often have pulmonary problems including effusions and embolic phenomena.[5] Peripheral edema and anasarca are occasional manifestations. This is a particularly severe form of panniculitis, which has recently been successfully treated by the use of infusions of commercial α₁-antitrypsin concentrate or liver transplantation.[5,9,13,14] It is thought that many of the previously reported cases of Weber–Christian disease belong to this group.[15]

Panniculitis in association with α₁-antitrypsin deficiency has been induced by cryosurgery and, in one patient with the enzyme defect, Sweet's syndrome was followed by the development of acquired cutis laxa (Marshall's syndrome).[16,17]

Pathogenesis and histological features

α₁-Antitrypsin (a glycoprotein of hepatic derivation) is a serine protease inhibitor (PI) that greatly modifies the effects of proteolytic enzymes, accounting for at least 90% of serum proteolytic enzyme inhibition. In addition to antitrypsin inhibition, it is also responsible for inhibition of chymotrypsin, collagenase, elastase, factor VIII and kallikrein.[7] Its deficiency has been associated with panacinar emphysema, non-infective (neonatal and adult) hepatitis and cirrhosis. More recently, associations have also been described with cutaneous vasculitis, atopic dermatitis, psoriasis, nodular prurigo and cold urticaria.[18] It has been proposed that absence of the protease inhibitor is associated with unrestrained complement activation with increased inflammatory cell activity, endothelial injury and resultant autolytic tissue damage.[19]

Immunoglobulin (IgM) and complement (C3) have been identified in blood vessel walls in patients with this variant of panniculitis.[6] The significance of this is uncertain.

The gene for α₁-antitrypsin on chromosome 14 has in excess of 75 alleles and is inherited as an autosomal dominant.[7] Deficiency occurs in between 1:3000 to 1:5000 of white North Americans.[20] The MM genotype is most common and individuals with normal activity are coded PiMM. The ZZ genotype is associated with deficient α₁-antitrypsin activity and the panniculitis is usually found in PiZZ individuals.[21] Instances of panniculitis in PiMZ, PiSZ, PiSS and Null patients, however, have also been recorded.[22–24] Panniculitis may also develop as a consequence of dysfunctional α₁-antitrypsin.[25] Recognition of this particular form is of importance as serum α₁-antitrypsin levels are normal and therefore the diagnosis can easily be missed.

The earliest changes consist of necrosis of the connective tissue in the reticular dermis and septa of the subcutaneous fat accompanied by a neutrophil polymorph inflammatory cell infiltrate (*Fig. 9.25*).[26] The histological features of an established lesion are those of a predominantly acute panniculitis (*Fig. 9.26*). The changes, which affect the septa and the paraseptal aspect of the lobule, are characteristically focal in nature. In acutely inflamed areas, large numbers of neutrophil polymorphs infiltrate the lobule. Fat necrosis is common and a characteristic feature is said to be the presence of normal fat adjacent to necrotic and inflamed fat (*Figs 9.27, 9.28*).[6,27] Special stains often show fragmentation and loss of elastic tissue.[6] Foci of hemorrhage associated with vascular thrombosis may be present, but there is no evidence of active vasculitis (*Fig. 9.29*).[6] Elsewhere, a histiocytic infiltrate is conspicuous, involving both the deep vasculature and adjacent panniculus. Lipid-laden foamy macrophages are sometimes evident and multinucleate giant cells are occasionally found. Healing is by fibrous scarring.

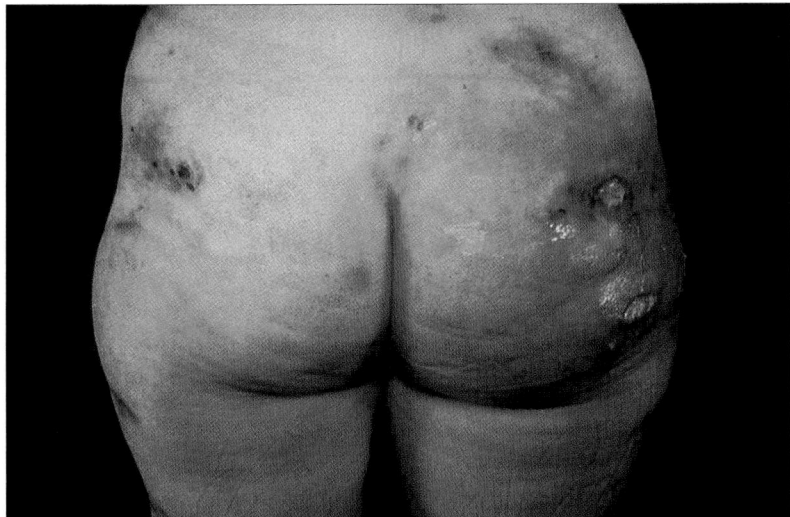

Fig. 9.24
α₁-Antitrypsin deficiency-associated panniculitis: note the extensive involvement of the buttocks in this young female. By courtesy of M.R. Pittelkow, MD, Mayo Clinic, Rochester, New York, USA.

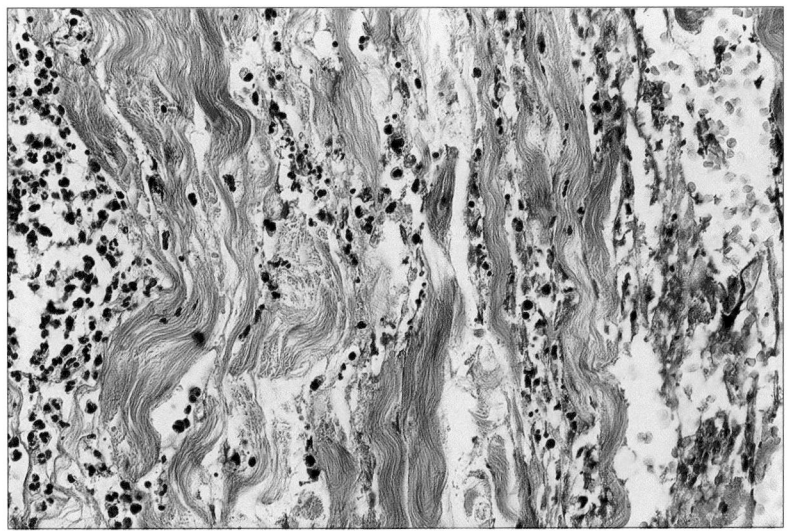

Fig. 9.25
α₁-Antitrypsin deficiency-associated panniculitis: early lesion showing necrosis and acute inflammation of the deep reticular dermis. By courtesy of M.R. Pittelkow, MD, Mayo Clinic, Rochester, USA.

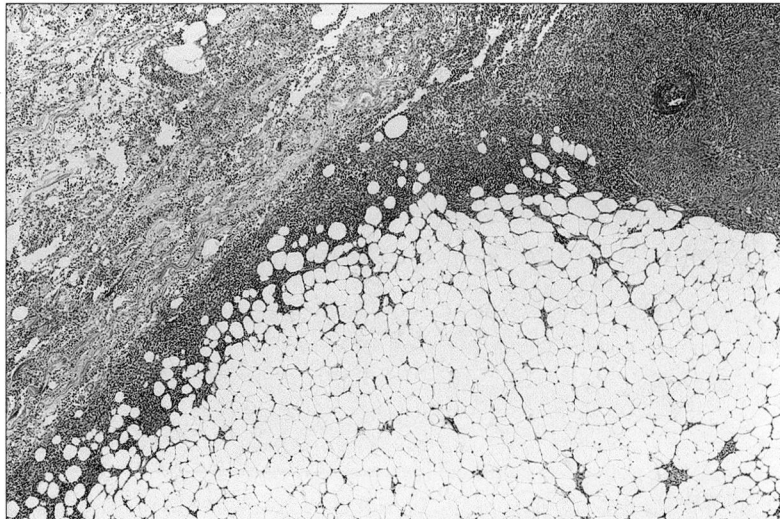

Fig. 9.26
α₁-Antitrypsin deficiency-associated panniculitis: there is intense acute inflammation extending from the septum into the edge of the lobule. Note the necrosis of the overlying dermal connective tissue. By courtesy of M.R. Pittelkow, MD, Mayo Clinic, Rochester, USA.

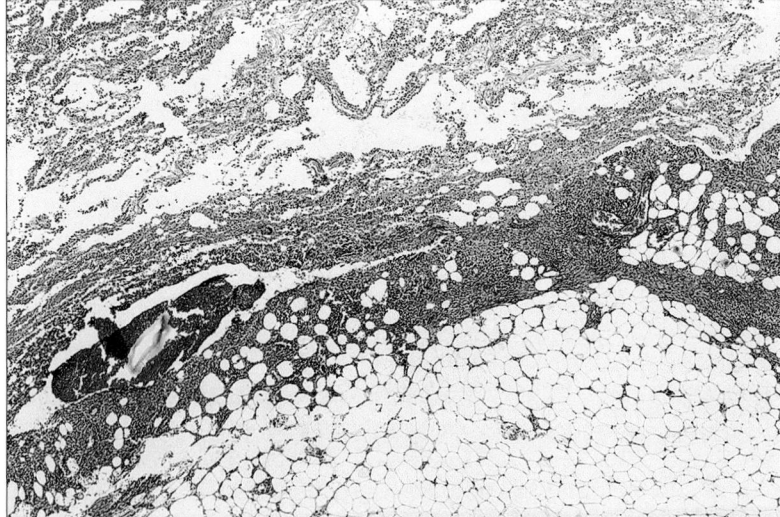

Fig. 9.27
α₁-Antitrypsin deficiency-associated panniculitis: in this field hemorrhage is evident in addition to the inflammatory changes. By courtesy of M.R. Pittelkow, MD, Mayo Clinic, Rochester, USA.

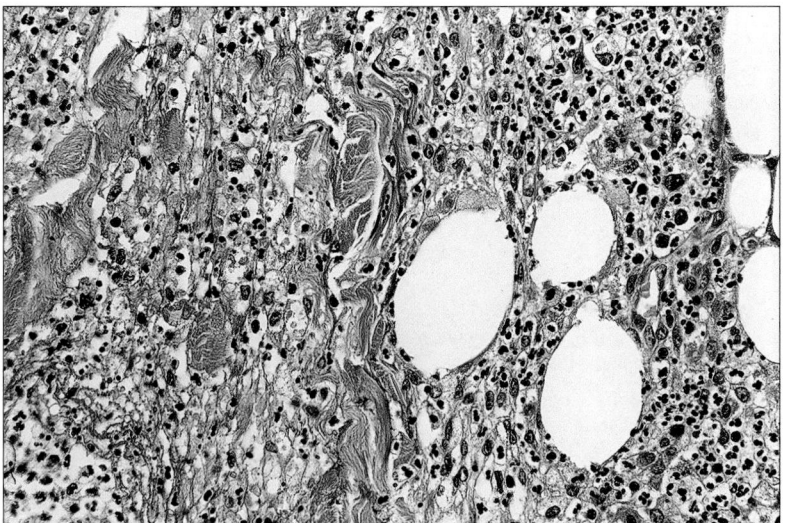

Fig. 9.28
α₁-Antitrypsin deficiency-associated panniculitis: high power view showing an intense neutrophil infiltrate. By courtesy of M.R. Pittelkow, MD, Mayo Clinic, Rochester, USA.

Differential diagnosis

The clinical features may suggest traumatic or factitial panniculitis. The heavy neutrophil infiltrate can cause diagnostic confusion with an infectious etiology.[10] In cases of doubt special stains for microorganisms should be performed.

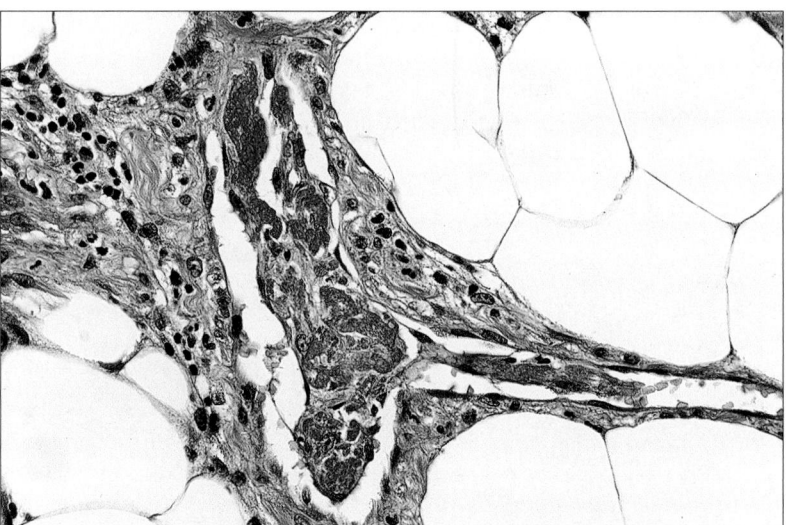

Fig. 9.29
α₁-Antitrypsin deficiency-associated panniculitis: note the organizing thrombus. By courtesy of M.R. Pittelkow, MD, Mayo Clinic, Rochester, USA.

References

1. Warter, J., Storck, D., Grosshans, E. et al (1972) Syndrome de Weber–Christian associe a un deficit en alpha, anti-trypsine. *Ann Med Interne*, **123**, 877–882.
2. Hendrick, S.J., Silverman, A.K., Solomon, A.R. et al (1988) Alpha 1-antitrypsin deficiency associated with panniculitis. *J Am Acad Dermatol*, **18**, 684–692.
3. Su, W.P., Smith, K.C., Pittelkow, M.R. et al (1987) Alpha 1-antitrypsin deficiency panniculitis: a histopathologic and immunopathologic study of four cases. *Am J Dermatopathol*, **9**, 483–490.
4. Bleuminke, E., Klokke, H.A. (1984) Protease inhibitor deficiencies in a patient with Weber–Christian panniculitis. *Arch Dermatol*, **120**, 936–940.
5. Smith, K.C., Pittelkow, M.R., Daniel Su, W.P. (1987) Panniculitis associated with severe α1-antitrypsin deficiency: treatment and review of the literature. *Arch Dermatol*, **123**, 1655–1661.
6. Smith, K.C., Su, W.P.D., Pittelkow, M.R. et al (1989) Clinical and pathologic correlations in 96 patients with panniculitis, including 15 patients with deficient levels of α1-antitrypsin. *J Am Acad Dermatol*, **21**, 1192–1196.
7. Edmonds, B.K., Hodge, J.A., Rietschel, R.L. (1991) Alpha 1-antitrypsin deficiency-associated panniculitis: case report and review of the literature. *Pediatr Dermatol*, **8**, 296–299.
8. Breit, S.N., Clark, P., Robinson, J.P. et al (1983) Familial occurrence of α1-antitrypsin deficiency and Weber–Christian disease. *Arch Dermatol*, **119**, 198–202.
9. Pittelkow, M.R., Smith, K.C., Su, W.P.D. (1988) Alpha-1-antitrypsin deficiency and panniculitis: perspectives on disease relationship and replacement therapy. *Am J Med*, **84** (Suppl. 6A), 80–86.
10. Förström, L., Winkelmann, R.K. (1975) Acute, generalized panniculitis with amylase and lipase in skin. *Arch Dermatol*, **111**, 497–502.
11. Garver, R.I., Mornex, J.F., Nukina, T. (1986) Alpha-1-antitrypsin deficiency and emphysema caused by homozygous inheritance of non-expressing alpha-1-antitrypsin genes. *N Engl J Med*, **314**, 762–766.
12. Hutchinson, D.C. (1990) Epidemiology of alpha-1-protease inhibitor deficiency. *Eur Respir J*, **9** (Suppl.), 29–34.
13. O'Riordan, K.C., Blei, A., Rao, M.S. et al (1997) α1-antitrypsin deficiency-associated panniculitis. *Transplantation*, **63**, 480–482.
14. Furey, N.L., Golden, R.S., Potts, S.R. (1996) Treatment of alpha-1-antitrypsin deficiency, massive edema, and panniculitis with alpha-1 protease inhibitor. *Ann Intern Med*, **125**, 669–674.
15. Patterson, J.W. (1991) Differential diagnosis of panniculitis. *Adv Dermatol*, **6**, 309–329.
16. Linares-Barrios, M., Conejo-Mir, J.S., Artola Igarza, J.L. et al (1998) Panniculitis due to alpha-1-antitrypsin deficiency induced by cryosurgery. *Br J Dermatol*, **138**, 552–553.
17. Hwang, S.T., Williams, M.L., McCalmont, T.H. et al (1995) Sweet's syndrome leading to acquired cutis laxa (Marshall's syndrome) in an infant with alpha 1-antitrypsin deficiency. *Arch Dermatol*, **131**, 1175–1177.
18. Doeglas, H.M.G., Klasen, E.C., Bleumink, E. (1985) Alpha-1-antitrypsin deficiency and PI typing in patients with chronic urticaria. *Br J Dermatol*, **112**, 381–385.
19. Patterson, J.W. (1977) Panniculitis: new findings in the third compartment. *Arch Dermatol*, **123**, 1615–1617.
20. Browne, R.J., Mannino, D.N., Khoury, M.J. (1996) Alpha 1-antitrypsin deficiency deaths in the United States from 1979 to 1991 – an analysis using multiple-cause mortality data. *Chest*, **110**, 78–83.
21. Ginarte, M., Rosón, E., Peteiro, C. et al (2001) Treatment of α-1 antitrypsin-deficiency panniculitis with minocycline. *Cutis*, **68**, 86–88.
22. Gaillard, M.C., Bothwell, J., Dreyer, L. (1997) A case of systemic nodular panniculitis associated with M1 (Val213) Z phenotype of alpha-1-protease inhibitor. *Int J Dermatol*, **36**, 278–280.
23. Pinto, A.R., Maciel, L.S., Carneiro, F. et al (1993) Systemic nodular panniculitis in a patient with alpha-1-antitrypsin deficiency (PiSS phenotype). *Clin Exp Dermatol*, **18**, 154–155.
24. Chng, W.J., Henderson, C.A. (2001) Suppurative panniculitis associated with alpha 1-antitrypsin deficiency (PiSZ phenotype) treated with doxycycline. *Br J Dermatol*, **144**, 1282–1283.
25. Loche, F., Tremeau-Martinage, C., Laplanche, G. et al (1999) Panniculitis revealing qualitative alpha 1 antitrypsin deficiency (MS variant). *Eur J Dermatol*, **9**, 565–567.
26. Peters, M.S., Daniel Su, W.P. (1992) Panniculitis. *Dermatol Clin*, **10**, 37–57.
27. Geller, J.D., Su, W.P.D. (1994) A subtle clue to the histologic diagnosis of early alpha 1-antitrypsin deficiency panniculitis. *J Am Acad Dermatol*, **31**, 241–245.

Factitial and traumatic panniculitis

Clinical features

Factitial panniculitis is by definition self-induced and vigorously denied, and may be caused by mechanical, physical or chemical means. The diagnosis is always worth considering in those patients with bizarre clinical lesions and inflammatory changes in the subcutaneous fat that defy ready classification. It should be particularly sought in those patients with panniculitis in whom there is a known history of psychiatric illness or drug or alcohol abuse. Lesions are most commonly found on the more accessible sites including the buttocks and thighs.

Mechanical causes include local pressure and repeated blunt trauma; the latter may be readily recognized by the presence of obvious bruising. Cold is another possible cause of factitial panniculitis.

By far the most common etiology is the subcutaneous injection of chemical substances including drugs, oily materials and organic matter.[1-4] Panniculitis has been described as a complication of morphine and tetanus antitoxoid injections. Similarly, repeated injections of pentazocine cause a characteristic woody fibrosis of the skin and subcutaneous fat accompanied by deeply penetrating ulcers and hyperpigmented halos.[5-7] Pentazocine abuse has been described, particularly in members of the medical profession.[5] There appears to be a relationship with a personal or family history of diabetes mellitus. It has been suggested that peripheral ischemia may be the pathogenetic link.[7] A similar problem has recently been described following injections of the opioid ketobemidone.[8]

An important cause of factitial panniculitis is the repeated injection of oily materials including paraffin and liquid silicon (paraffinoma, sclerosing lipogranuloma, lipogranulomatous panniculitis) (*Fig. 9.30*).[1,2,4,9-13] Sclerosing lipogranuloma was a condition usually seen in the male genitalia that developed as a consequence of the injection of paraffin oil and related compounds into the penis in the mistaken belief that this would enhance erections. Povidone (polyvinylpyrrolidone), a synthetic dispersing or suspending agent which has been used in both pharmaceutical products and hair sprays, may result in a particular characteristic histological variant of panniculitis.[14,15] Associated features have included pulmonary lesions, lymphadenopathy and hepatosplenomegaly. Organic substances that have been implicated in the etiology of factitial panniculitis include food matter, milk and even feces.

Nodular cystic fat necrosis is a distinct posttraumatic lesion that is seen predominantly in adolescent boys and middle-aged women. Lesions, which are usually found on the legs, are often associated with a history of trauma.[16]

Traumatic fat necrosis is a not uncommon condition and occurs predominantly in middle-aged or elderly females with large pendulous breasts. Its importance is that it may be clinically mistaken for a malignancy. In addition, it may be seen to involve the arms, trunk, buttocks and thighs of the very obese.

A number of therapeutic injections have been associated with the development of panniculitis including interferon-beta (IFN-β) and granulocyte colony stimulating factor.[17,18] Aluminum granuloma may present as a panniculitis. This topic is discussed on page 327. Panniculitis has also been documented following vitamin K1 injections.[19]

Pathogenesis and histological features

The histological features of factitial panniculitis are not usually specific and depend to some extent upon the cause. In some instances, therefore, the changes are those of acute lobular inflammation associated with fat necrosis and a neutrophil polymorph infiltrate. In older lesions, mononuclear cells, lipid-laden histiocytes and foreign body giant cells become predominant and sometimes the response becomes frankly granulomatous. On other occasions the septa may be primarily affected, thereby mimicking erythema nodosum. Calcification is occasionally evident.[2] It is sometimes rewarding to view the sections with polarized light, as birefractile material may be identified and raise the possibility of the factitious nature of the condition.

The paraffinoma is characterized by the presence of round or oval spaces within the dermis and subcutaneous fat ('Swiss cheese' pattern) (*Fig. 9.31*); careful examination may reveal foamy histiocytes or giant cells lining the edges of these cystic cavities (*Fig. 9.32*).[9] There is often associated dense fibrous scarring. Early lesions sometimes show a marked granulomatous component.[9] Similar features have been described following a grease gun injury.[20]

In panniculitis due to pentazocine abuse the histological features include dense dermal fibrosis accompanied by variable scarring of the

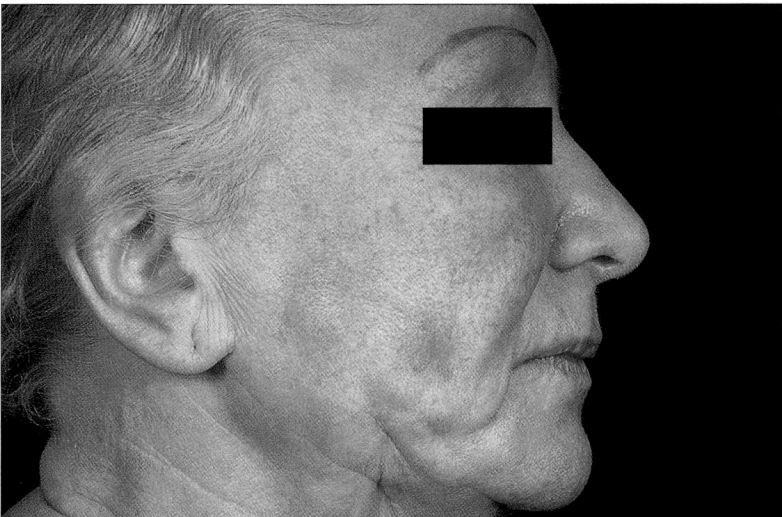

Fig. 9.30
Paraffinoma: note the infiltrated plaque with foci of retraction. By courtesy of the Institute of Dermatology, London, UK.

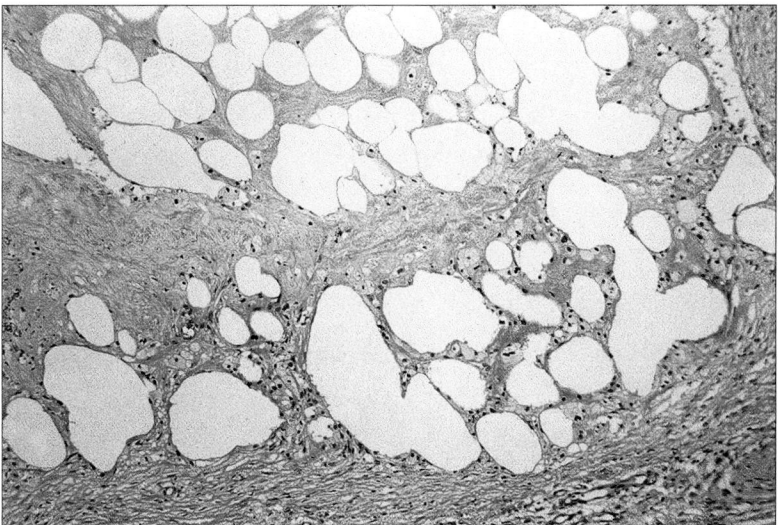

Fig. 9.31
Paraffinoma: empty spaces of variable size (due to the removal of lipid during processing) characterize this lesion. The appearance is often likened to Swiss cheese.

subcutaneous fat.[5] A 'Swiss cheese' appearance may be evident. Small vessel thrombosis is frequently present.[5]

Povidone panniculitis is characterized by histiocytic accumulation of gray–blue, Congo red positive foamy material accompanied by necrosis and hemorrhage.[14]

Lesions caused by blunt trauma show the features of an organizing hematoma. Granulomata and foci of hemosiderin pigment may additionally be present.[21]

Nodular cystic fat necrosis is thought to have an ischemic pathogenesis. Histologically, it is characterized by an encapsulated nodule of necrotic (anucleate) fat cells (*Fig. 9.33*).[22,23] Variable inflammation is present.

Fat necrosis with histiocytes (lipophages) and giant cells is a common histological finding in specimens taken from sites of previous surgery of the subcutaneous fat (or deeper). Zelickson and Winkelmann have described this as lipophagic panniculitis.[22] Hemosiderin deposits are also commonly found and in many instances fragments of suture material may be identified.

The histological features of traumatic fat necrosis are not specific and are characterized by fat necrosis accompanied by a variable inflammatory cell infiltrate (*Figs 9.34, 9.35*). In early lesions this is predominantly composed of neutrophils, later replaced by lymphocytes and monocytes. Aggregates of lipophages are seen frequently and often the reaction becomes frankly granulomatous (*Fig. 9.36*). Fat cysts are a common feature. With resolution fibrosis takes place (*Fig. 9.37*). As evidence of the traumatic nature of the lesion, foci of hemosiderin deposition are not uncommon. Occasionally, the presence of fat necrosis is complicated by focal calcification (*Fig. 9.38*).

References

1. Foucar, E., Downing, D.T., Gerber, W.L. (1983) Sclerosing lipogranuloma of the male genitalia containing vitamin E: a comparison with classical 'paraffinoma'. *J Am Acad Dermatol*, **9**, 103–110.
2. Förström, L., Winkelmann, R.K. (1974) Factitial panniculitis. *Arch Dermatol*, **110**, 747–750.
3. Peters, M.S., Su, W.P.D. (1992) Panniculitis. *Dermatol Clin*, **10**, 37–57.
4. Darsow, U., Bruckbauer, H., Worret, W-I. et al (2000) Subcutaneous oleomas induced by self-injection of sesame seed oil for muscle augmentation. *J Am Acad Dermatol*, **42**, 292–294.
5. Palestine, R.F., Millns, J.L., Spigel, G.T. et al (1980) Skin manifestations of pentazocine abuse. *J Am Acad Dermatol*, **2**, 47–55.
6. Swanson, D.W., Weddige, R.L., Morse, R.M. (1973) Hospitalized pentazocine abusers. *Mayo Clin Proc*, **48**, 85–93.
7. Parks, D.L., Perry, H.O., Muller, S.A. (1971) Subcutaneous complications of pentazocine injections. *Arch Dermatol*, **104**, 231–235.
8. Danielsen, A.G., Huthberg, I.B., Weismann, K. (1994) Skin lesions after injection abuse. Chronic changes caused by ketobemidone (ketogen). *Ugeskr Laeger*, **156**, 162–164.
9. Oertel, Y.C., Johnson, F.B. (1977) Sclerosing lipogranuloma of the male genitalia: review of 23 cases. *Arch Pathol Lab Med*, **101**, 321–326.
10. Hirst, A.E., Heustis, D.G., Rogers-Neufield, B. et al (1984) Sclerosing lipogranuloma of the scalp. A report of two cases. *Am J Clin Pathol*, **82**, 228–231.
11. Klein, J.A., Cole, G., Barr, R.J. et al (1985) Paraffinomas of the scalp. *Arch Dermatol*, **121**, 382–385.

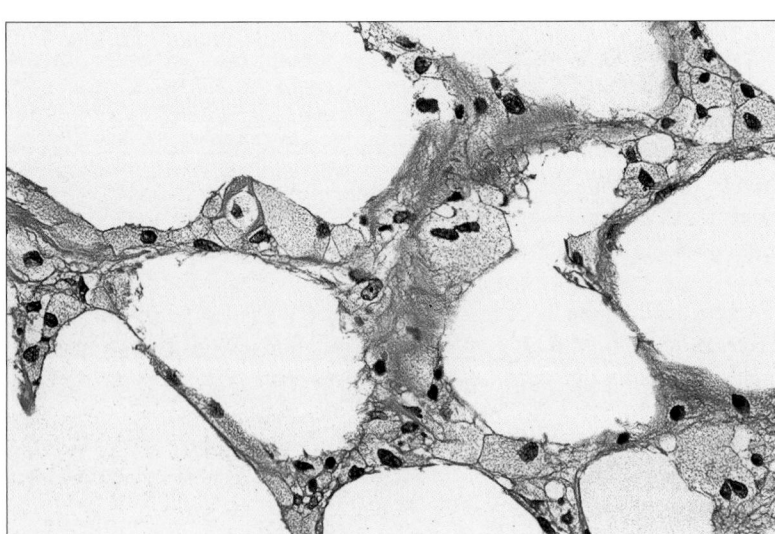

Fig. 9.32
Paraffinoma: on high power examination the cystic spaces can often be seen to be lined by lipophages.

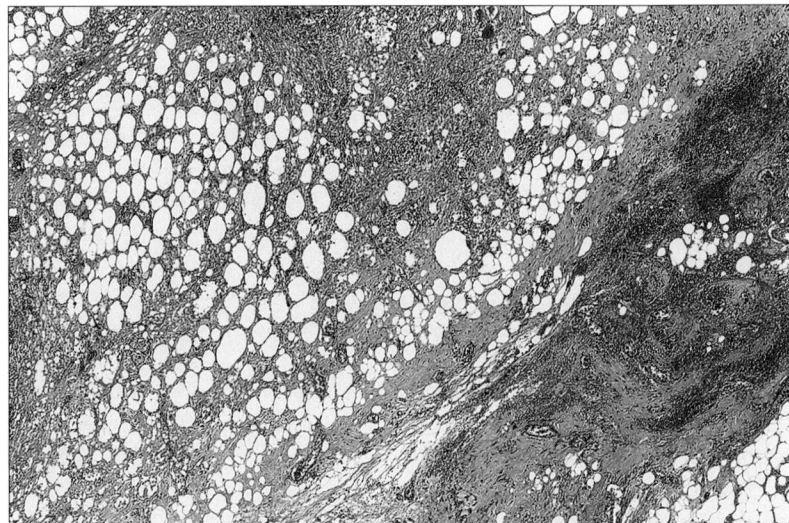

Fig. 9.34
Traumatic fat necrosis: there is intense lobular inflammation with septal fibrosis and hemorrhage.

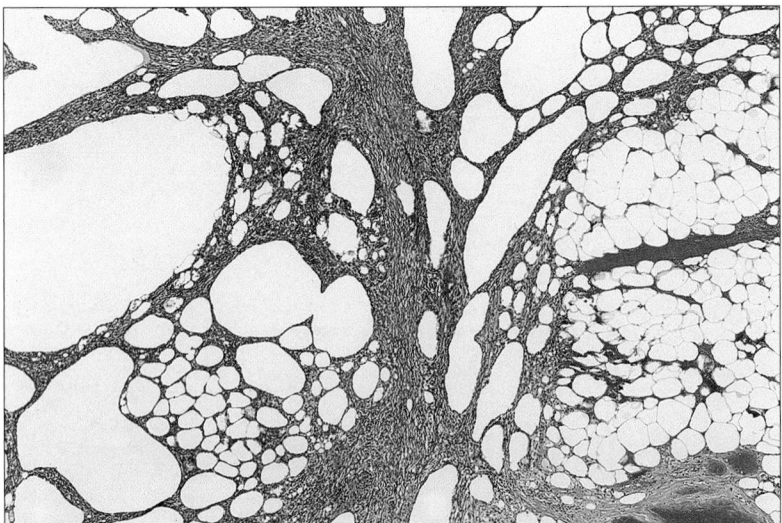

Fig. 9.33
Nodulo-cystic fat necrosis: typical low power appearance; note the variably sized cysts, scarring and chronic inflammation.

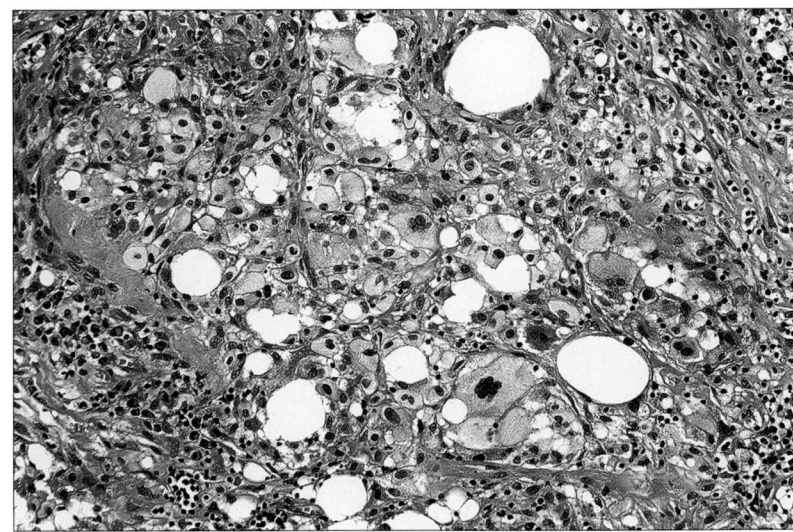

Fig. 9.35
Traumatic fat necrosis: collections of lipophages are characteristic.

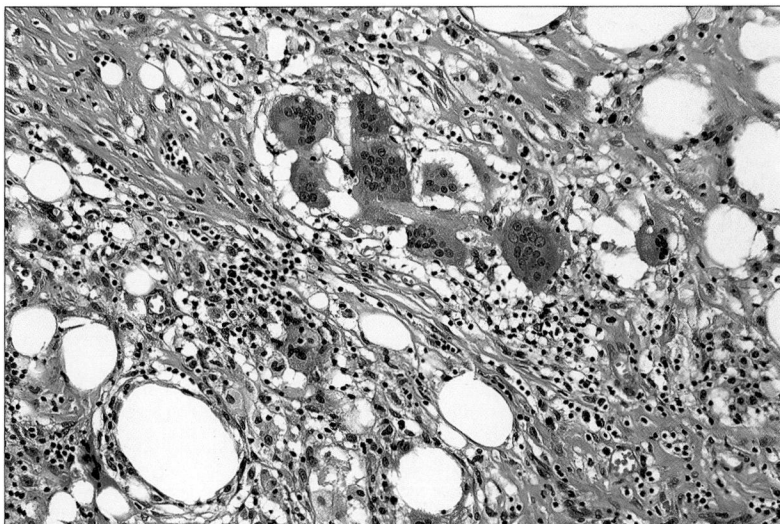

Fig. 9.36
Traumatic fat necrosis: foreign body giant cells are regularly present.

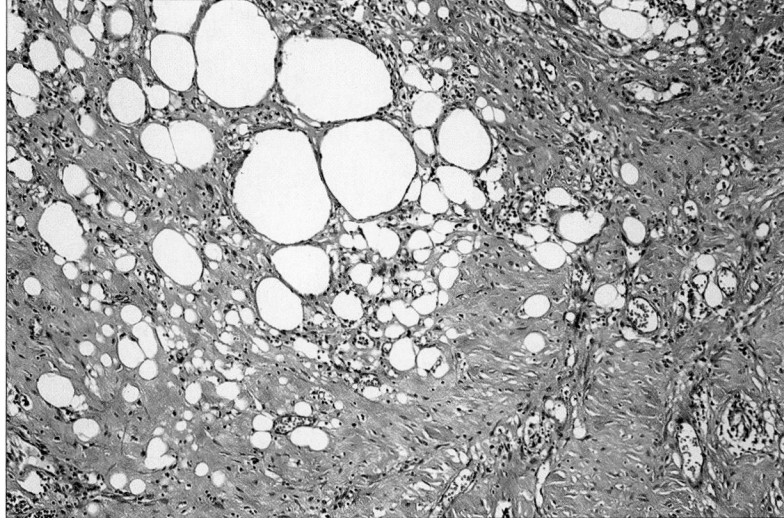

Fig. 9.37
Traumatic fat necrosis: scarring is a feature in more chronic lesions.

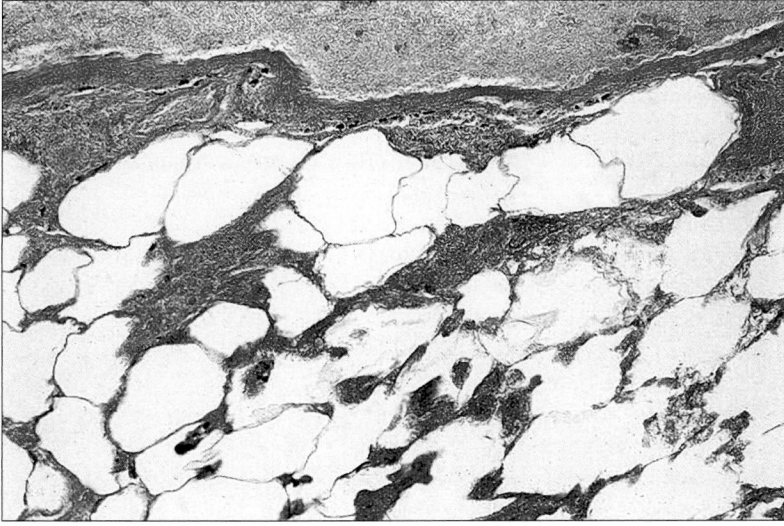

Fig. 9.38
Traumatic fat necrosis: in this example there is marked calcification.

12. Feldmann, R., Harms, M., Chavaz, P. et al (1992) Orbital and palpebral paraffinoma. *J Am Acad Dermatol*, **26**, 833–835.
13. Claudy, A., Garcier, F., Schmitt, D. (1981) Sclerosing granuloma of the male genitalia: ultrastructural study. *Br J Dermatol*, **105**, 451–456.
14. Kossard, S., Ecker, R.I., Dicken, C.H. (1980) Povidone panniculitis. Polyvinylpyrrolidone panniculitis. *Arch Dermatol*, **116**, 704–706.
15. Bergmann, M., Flance, I.J., Cruz, P.T. et al (1962) Thesaurosis due to inhalation of hair spray: report of 12 new cases, including three autopsies. *N Engl J Med*, **266**, 750–755.
16. Hurt, M.A., Santa Cruz, D.J. (1989) Nodular-cystic fat necrosis. A reevaluation of the so-called mobile encapsulated lipoma. *J Am Acad Dermatol*, **21**, 493–498.
17. Heinzerling, L., Dammer, R., Burg, G. et al (2002) Panniculitis after subcutaneous injection of interferon beta in a multiple sclerosis patient. *Eur J Dermatol*, **12**, 194–197.
18. Prendiville, J., Thiessen, P., Mallory, S.R. (2001) Neutrophilic dermatosis in two children with idiopathic neutropenia: association with granulocyte colony stimulating factor (G-CSF). *Pediatr Dermatol*, **18**, 417–421.
19. Janin-Mercier, A., Mosser, C., Souteyrand, P. et al (1985) Subcutaneous sclerosis with fasciitis and eosinophilia after phytonadione injections. *Arch Dermatol*, **121**, 1421–1423.
20. Henrichs, W.D., Helwig, E.B. (1986) Grease gun granulomas. *Military Med*, **151**, 78–82.
21. Winkelmann, R.K., Barker, S.M. (1985) Factitial traumatic panniculitis. *J Am Acad Dermatol*, **13**, 988–994.
22. Zelickson, B.D., Winkelmann, R.K. (1991) Lipophagic panniculitis in re-excision specimens. *Acta Derm Venereol*, **70**, 59–61.
23. Kiryu, H., Rikihisa, W., Furue, M. (2000) Encapsulated fat necrosis – a clinicopathological study of 8 cases and literature review. *J Cutan Pathol*, **27**, 19–23.

Cold panniculitis

Clinical features

This rare condition was originally described in infants and young children who developed tender, warm, erythematous plaques on exposed sites, namely the cheeks and submental region, after experiencing low temperatures.[1–5] These plaques resolved spontaneously after 2–3 weeks, with no residual sequelae. The application of an ice cube to a child's skin may result in the development of similar lesions. Identical changes have also been described in infants following the sucking of ice-lollies ('popsicle panniculitis').[6–8]

A similar phenomenon has recently been described in young women following horse riding in cold weather (equestrian cold panniculitis); these patients develop indurated red–violaceous plaques on the superolateral aspect of the thighs following prolonged riding in freezing conditions (*Fig. 9.39*).[9,10] There is a tendency to ulcerate; healing is associated with postinflammatory hyperpigmentation and the development of depressed scars. It is thought that these lesions occur as a result of extremely cold temperatures combined with the effect of non-insulated, but tight-fitting, clothes which impair the circulation

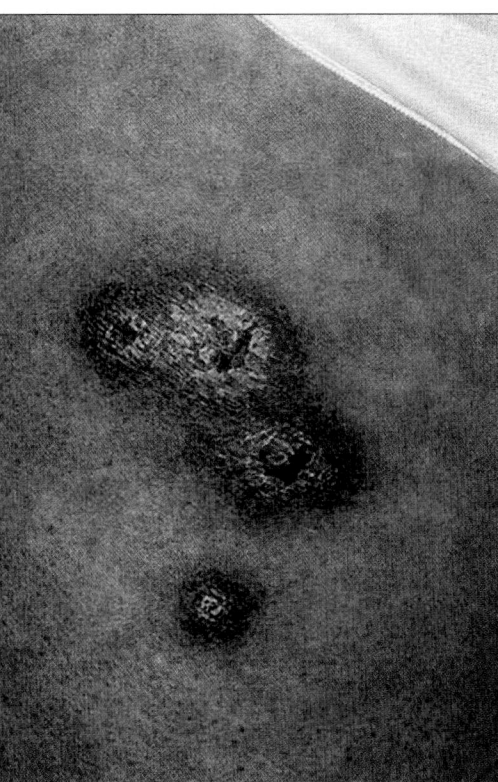

Fig. 9.39
Cold panniculitis: there are ulcerated lesions on this patient's thigh. By courtesy of the Institute of Dermatology, London, UK.

around the thighs. Recently, two patients with cold agglutinins and this condition have been described.[10]

Chilblains (perniosis) also represent localized, abnormal inflammatory responses to the cold.[11] They have an acral distribution (e.g. dorsal surfaces of the fingers and toes) and present as pruritic erythematous lesions, which may blister or ulcerate (see p. 274).

Histological features

The features of cold panniculitis are most noticeable at the interface between the dermis and subcutaneous fat (*Fig. 9.40*).[3,6] The infiltrate, which contains lymphocytes, histiocytes and neutrophils, extends from a perivascular location into the adjacent fat where it is associated with adipocyte necrosis and the development of small cysts (*Fig. 9.41*). Excess hyaluronic acid may sometimes be present. Granulomata are not usually conspicuous.[12] The blood vessels show thickening of their walls and endothelial swelling, but frank vasculitis is not a feature.

The histological features of perniosis include intense papillary dermal edema and a superficial perivascular mononuclear infiltrate. The blood vessel wall characteristically shows very marked edema and often there is fibrin deposition.[11]

References

1. Duncan, W.C., Freeman, R.G., Heaton C.L. (1966) Cold panniculitis. *Arch Dermatol*, **94**, 722–724.
2. Solomon, L.M., Beerman, H. (1963) Cold panniculitis. *Arch Dermatol*, **88**, 897–900.
3. Rotman, H. (1966) Cold panniculitis in children. *Arch Dermatol*, **94**, 720–721.
4. Ter Poorten, J.C., Hebert, A.A., Iikiw, R. (1995) Cold panniculitis. *J Am Acad Dermatol*, **33**, 383–385.
5. Ben-Amitai, D., Metzker, A. (1996) Cold panniculitis in a neonate. *J Am Acad Dermatol*, **35**, 651–652.
6. Epstein, E.H., Oren, M.E. (1970) Popsicle panniculitis. *N Engl J Med*, **23**, 966–967.
7. Rajkumar, S.V., Laude, T.A., Russo, R.M. et al (1976) Popsicle panniculitis of the cheeks. A diagnostic entity caused by sucking on cold objects. *Clin Pediatr*, **15**, 619–621.
8. Day, S., Klein, B.L. (1992) Popsicle panniculitis. *Pediatr Emerg Care*, **8**, 91–93.
9. Beacham, B.E., Cooper, P.H., Buchanan, S. et al (1980) Equestrian cold panniculitis. *Arch Dermatol*, **116**, 1025–1027.
10. De Silva, B.D., McLaren, K., Doherty, V.R. (2000) Equestrian perniosis associated with cold agglutinins: a novel finding. *Clin Exp Dermatol*, **25**, 285–288.
11. Wall, L.M., Smith, N.P. (1981) Perniosis: a histopathological review. *Clin Exp Dermatol*, **6**, 263–271.
12. Patterson, J.W. (1991) Differential diagnosis of panniculitis. *Adv Dermatol*, **6**, 309–329.

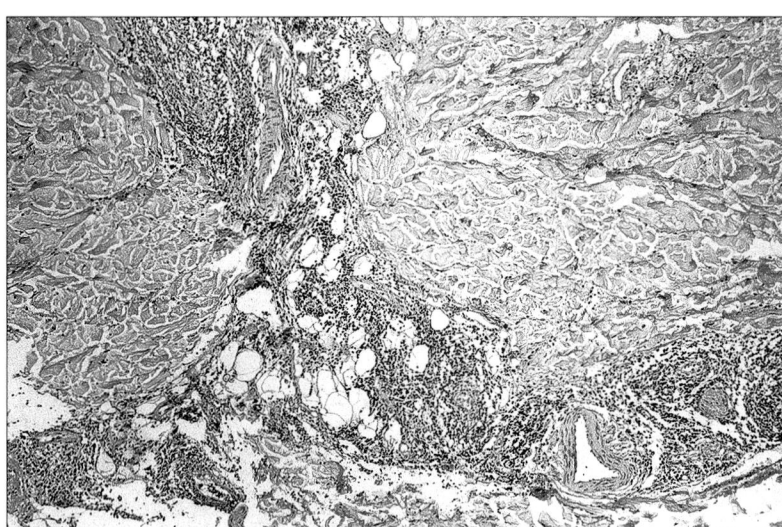

Fig. 9.40
Cold panniculitis: an intense inflammatory cell infiltrate is present at the junction between the dermis and subcutaneous fat. By courtesy of P.H. Cooper, MD, University of Virginia Medical Center, USA.

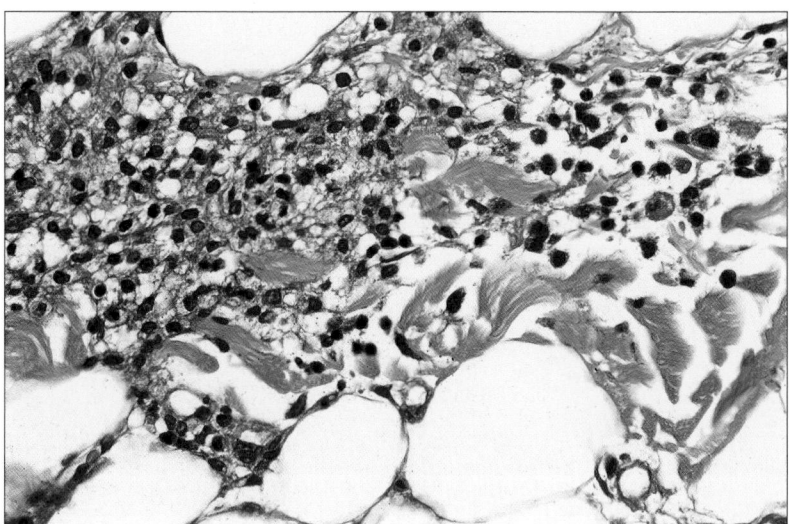

Fig. 9.41
Cold panniculitis: the infiltrate consists of lymphocytes and histiocytes.

Cytophagic histiocytic panniculitis

Clinical features

Cytophagic histiocytic panniculitis (panniculitis associated with hemophagocytic syndrome) represents a serious disorder of immune dysregulation.[1–3] It may develop in association with a number of underlying conditions including viral infections such as cytomegalovirus and Epstein–Barr virus.[4–8] HIV infection has also rarely been incriminated.[7] Bacteria, fungi and parasites are sometimes of etiological significance.[9–11] The condition has been described as a complication of phenytoin therapy, following bone marrow transplantation, in systemic lupus erythematosus (SLE) and as an adverse reaction to interferon-alpha (IFN-α) therapy.[12–15] Some examples in the earlier literature were described as Weber–Christian disease.[16]

Of particular importance, the hemophagocytic syndrome may also be associated with a number of malignancies, most commonly T-cell lymphoma (nodal or cutaneous).[8,16–18] Subcutaneous panniculitic T-cell lymphoma and angiocentric T-cell lymphoma may, therefore, both present with extensive hemophagocytosis. Rarely, an underlying systemic B-cell lymphoma has been incriminated.[19] Most patients are immunosuppressed; however, *very exceptionally*, the cause is unknown (idiopathic histiocytic cytophagic panniculitis).[17,20] It is, therefore, of particular importance that all patients diagnosed with this condition are investigated to exclude an underlying T-cell lymphoma.

Clinically, the cutaneous manifestations of cytophagic histiocytic panniculitis include erythematous to violaceous or hemorrhagic nodules, which particularly affect the lower limbs and trunk (*Figs 9.42, 9.43*). In many patients however, the distribution is much more widespread. Ulceration is sometimes seen. Severe localized or generalized edema may also be a feature.[18] Constitutional symptoms including pyrexia, malaise, weight loss, fatigue and myalgia may be present. Patients commonly develop hepatosplenomegaly, lymphadenopathy, hypertriglyceridemia, anemia, leukopenia, thrombocytopenia and disseminated intravascular coagulopathy.[2-4]

The course of the disease is variable and to some extent depends upon the underlying cause.[21-29] Some patients have a prolonged indolent disease over many years before progressing to clinical evidence of systemic hemophagocytosis. Rarely, patients may present with cutaneous lesions and a relatively benign illness;[20,24,29] others have a rapidly progressive condition with hemophagocytosis and its sequelae from the outset. The mortality rate for these last patients is high. In addition to the direct effects of bone marrow failure and disseminated intravascular coagulation, systemic infections including opportunist bacteria and fungi are important causes of death.[8]

Pathogenesis and histological features

Hemophagocytosis appears to develop as a consequence of excess T-cell cytokine production, either virally induced or as a consequence of neoplastic transformation. Tumor necrosis factor alpha (TNF-α) and IL-2 may be of particular importance.[8]

Histologically, the lesions are characterized by an infiltrate of histiocytes with abundant eosinophilic cytoplasm and uniform, variably hyperchromatic or vesicular nuclei containing small nucleoli. Variable numbers of lymphocytes and neutrophils are also present. Although the distribution is predominantly lobular, septal involvement is usually apparent and the lower dermis is also often involved (*Fig. 9.44*). Red cell extravasation is typically present and frequently the lesions are frankly hemorrhagic. Erythrophagocytosis is invariably a feature and phagocytosis of lymphocytes or nuclear debris is also often evident (*Fig. 9.45*).

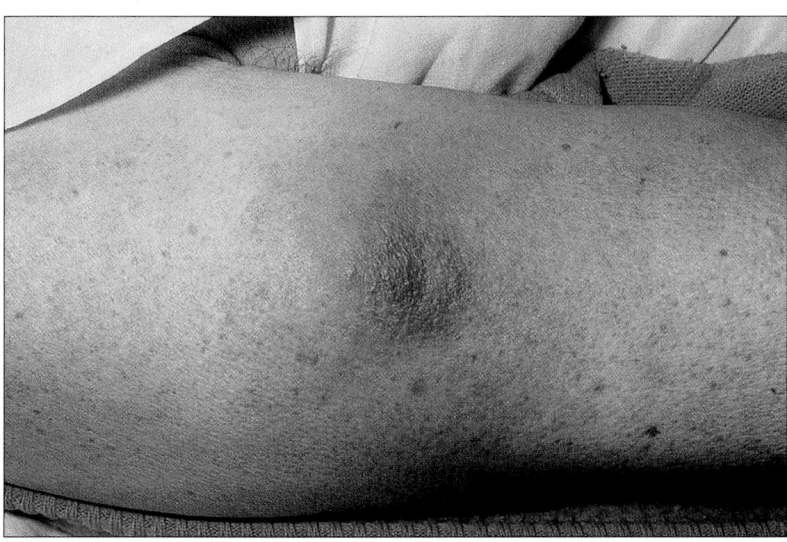

Fig. 9.42
Cytophagic histiocytic panniculitis: an extensive, erythematous, indurated plaque is present on the upper arm. By courtesy of M. Cook, MD, St George's Hospital, London, UK.

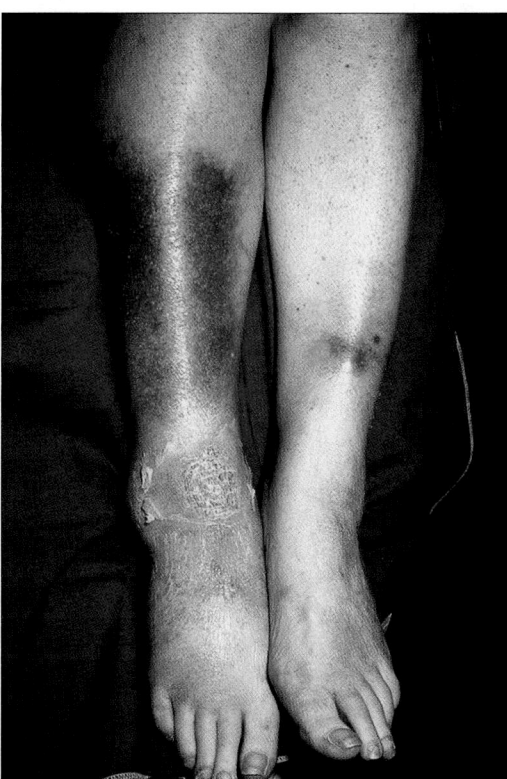

Fig. 9.43
Cytophagic histiocytic panniculitis: in this example the lesions are hemorrhagic and ulcerated. By courtesy of M. Cook, MD, St George's Hospital, London, UK.

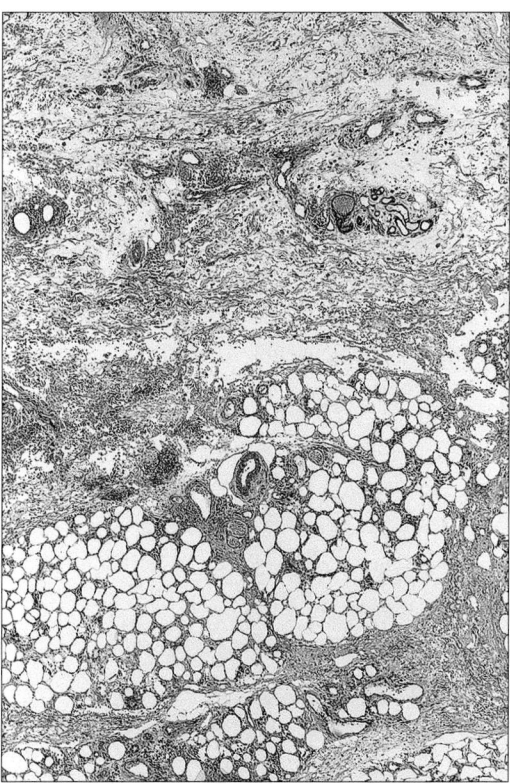

Fig. 9.44
Cytophagic histiocytic panniculitis: there is a lobular cellular infiltrate associated with fat necrosis.

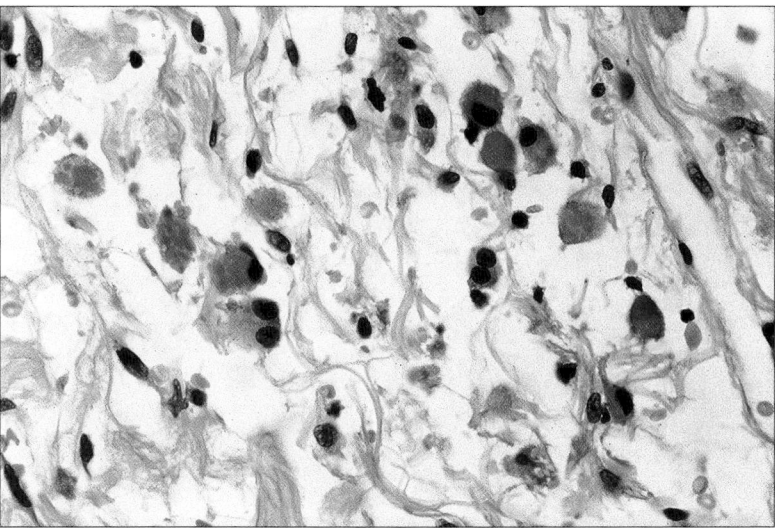

Fig. 9.45
Cytophagic histiocytic panniculitis: note the histiocytes with abundant eosinophilic cytoplasm, many of which show erythrophagocytosis.

The enlarged and distended histiocytes are sometimes described as 'bean-bag' cells (*Fig. 9.46*).[2,3] Giant cells and granulomata are not usually a feature unless there is concomitant fat necrosis. Lymphoid nuclear atypia is evident in those cases in which a T-cell lymphoma is present (see below).

Differential diagnosis

Cytophagic histiocytic panniculitis must be distinguished from other conditions in which erythrophagocytosis or hemophagocytosis may be a feature including subcutaneous T-cell pannaculitic lymphoma, angiocentric lymphoma and cutaneous Rosai Dorfman disease.

In subcutaneous panniculitic T-cell lymphoma, the lymphocytes show cytological atypia with karyorrhexis and mitotic activity (*Fig. 9.47*). Angiocentric T-cell lymphoma is characterized by an angioinvasive and frequently angiodestructive atypical lymphoid infiltrate usually accompanied by widespread coagulative necrosis. In cutaneous Rosai Dorfman disease, the infiltrate is usually centered on the dermis. Lymphophagocytosis is often marked but erythrophagocytosis is not usually present. The histiocytes are characteristically S-100 protein positive.

References

1. Risdall, R.J., McKenna, R.W., Nesbit, M.E. et al (1979) Virus-associated hemophagocytic syndrome: a benign histiocytic proliferation distinct from malignant histiocytosis. *Cancer*, **44**, 993–1002.
2. Winkelmann, R.K., Bowie, E.J. (1980) Hemorrhagic diathesis associated with benign histiocytic, cytophagic panniculitis and systemic histiocytosis. *Arch Intern Med*, **140**, 1460–1463.
3. Alegre, V.A., Winkelmann, R.K. (1989) Histiocytic cytophagic panniculitis. *J Am Acad Dermatol*, **20**, 177–185.
4. Smith, K.J., Skelton, H.G., Yeager, J. et al (1992) Cutaneous histopathologic, immunohistochemical, and clinical manifestations in patients with hemophagocytic syndrome. Military Medical Consortium for Applied Retroviral Research. *Arch Dermatol*, **128**, 193–200.
5. Harada, H., Iwatsuki, K., Kaneko, F. (1994) Detection of Epstein–Barr virus genes in malignant lymphoma with clinical and histologic features of cytophagic histiocytic panniculitis. *J Am Acad Dermatol*, **31**, 379–383.
6. Iwatsuki, K., Ohtsuka, M., Harada, H. et al (1997) Clinicopathologic manifestations of Epstein–Barr virus-associated cutaneous lymphoproliferative disorders. *Arch Dermatol*, **133**, 1081–1086.
7. Iwatsuki, K., Harada, H., Ohtsuka, M. et al (1997) Latent Epstein–Barr virus infection is frequently detected in subcutaneous lymphoma associated with hemophagocytosis but not in non-fatal cytophagic histiocytic panniculitis. *Arch Dermatol*, **133**, 787–788.
8. Smith, K.J., Skelton, H.G., Giblin, W.L. et al (1991) Cutaneous lesions of hemophagocytic syndrome in a patient with T-cell lymphoma and active Epstein–Barr virus infection. *J Am Acad Dermatol*, **25**, 919–924.
9. Smith, K.J., Skelton, H.G., Yeager, J. et al (1992) Cutaneous histopathologic, immunohistochemical, and clinical manifestations in patients with hemophagocytic syndrome. *Arch Dermatol*, **128**, 193–200.
10. Reiner, A.P., Spivak, J.L. (1988) Hematophagic histiocytosis: a report of 23 new patients and a review of the literature. *Medicine (Baltimore)*, **67**, 369–388.
11. Petterson, T., Kariniemi, A.L., Tervonen, S. et al (1992) Cytophagic histiocytic panniculitis: a report of four cases. *Br J Dermatol*, **127**, 635–640.
12. Gutiérrez-Ravé Pecero, V.M., Márquez, R.L. et al (1991) Phenytoin-induced hemocytophagic histiocytosis indistinguishable from malignant histiocytosis. *South Med J*, **84**, 649–650.
13. Galende, J., Vásquez, M.L., Almeida, J. et al (1994) Histiocytic cytophagic panniculitis: a rare late complication of allogeneic bone marrow transplantation. *Bone Marrow Transplant*, **14**, 637–639.
14. Tsukahara, T., Horiuchi, Y., Iidaka, A. (1995) Cytophagic histiocytic panniculitis in systemic lupus erythematosus. *Hiroshima J Med Sci*, **44**, 13–16.
15. Kuno, M., Mimori, A., Fujii, T. et al (1996) Histiocytic cytophagic panniculitis which developed during interferon-alpha therapy. *Intern Med*, **35**, 115–118.
16. Steinger, H., Missmahl, M. (1988) Weber–Christian panniculitis with systemic cytophagic histiocytosis. *Klin Wochenschr*, **66**, 365–372.
17. González, C.L., Medeiros, J., Braziel, R.M. et al (1991) T-cell lymphoma involving subcutaneous tissue: a clinicopathologic entity commonly associated with hemophagocytosis syndrome. *Am J Surg Pathol*, **15**, 17–27.
18. Aronson, I.K., West, D.P., Variakojis, D. et al (1985) Panniculitis associated with cutaneous T-cell lymphoma and cytophagic histiocytosis. *Br J Dermatol*, **112**, 87–96.
19. Huilgol, S.C., Fenton, D., Pambakian, H. et al (1998) Fatal cytophagic panniculitis and haemophagocytic syndrome. *Clin Exp Dermatol*, **23**, 51–55.
20. Marzano, A.V., Berti, E., Paulli, M. et al (2000) Cytophagic histiocytic panniculitis and subcutaneous panniculitis-like T-cell lymphoma. Report of 7 cases. *Arch Dermatol*, **136**, 889–896.
21. Yung, A., Snow, J., Jarrett, P. (2001) Subcutaneous panniculitic T-cell lymphoma and cytophagic histiocytic panniculitis. *Australas J Dermatol*, **42**, 185–187.
22. Peters, M.S., Winkelmann, R.K. (1985) Cytophagic panniculitis and B cell lymphoma. *J Am Acad Dermatol*, **13**, 882–885.
23. Perniciaro, C., Winkelmann, R.K., Ehrhardt, D.R. (1994) Fatal systemic cytophagic histiocytic panniculitis: a histopathologic and immunohistochemical study of multiple organ sites. *J Am Acad Dermatol*, **31**, 901–905.
24. Craig, A.J., Cualing, H., Thomas, G. et al (1998) Cytophagic histiocytic panniculitis – a syndrome associated with benign and malignant panniculitis: case comparison and review of the literature. *J Am Acad Dermatol*, **39**, 721–736.
25. Ito, M., Ohira, I.M., Miyata, M. et al (1999) Cytophagic histiocytic panniculitis improved by combined CHOP and cyclosporin A treatment. *Intern Med*, **38**, 296–301.
26. Guitart, J., Sethi, R., Gordon, K. (1998) Fatal cytophagic histiocytic panniculitis after a short response to cyclosporine. *J Eur Acad Dermatol Venerol*, **10**, 267–268.
27. Okamura, T., Niho, Y. (1999) Cytophagic histiocytic panniculitis – what is the best therapy? *Intern Med*, **38**, 224–225.
28. Koizumi, K., Sawada, K., Nishio, M. et al (1997) Effective high-dose chemotherapy followed by autologous peripheral blood stem cell transplantation in a patient with the aggressive form of cytophagic histiocytic panniculitis. *Bone Marrow Transplant*, **20**, 171–173.
29. White, J.W., Winkelmann, R.K. (1989) Cytophagic histiocytic panniculitis is not always fatal. *J Cutan Pathol*, **16**, 137–144.

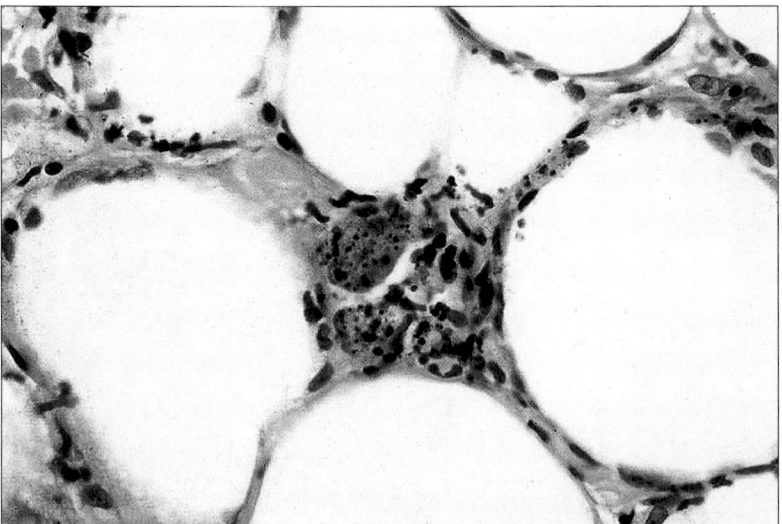

Fig. 9.46
Cytophagic histiocytic panniculitis: in the center of the field are several multinucleated giant cells containing phagocytosed nuclear debris ('bean-bag' cells).

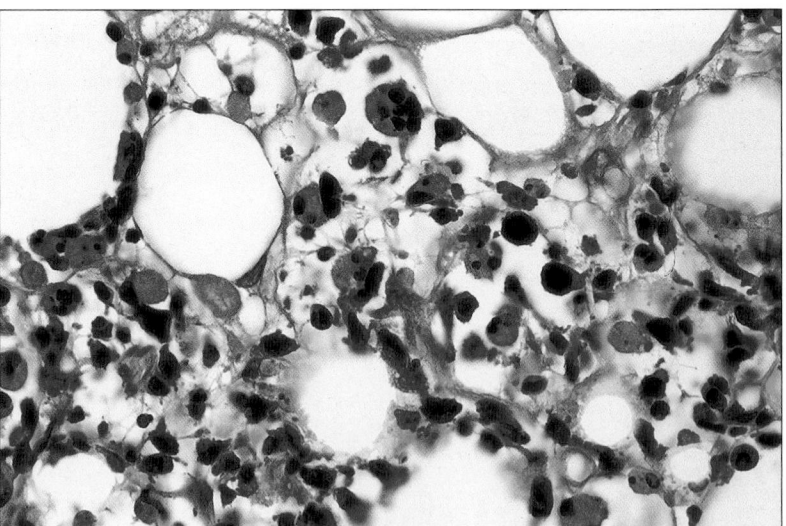

Fig. 9.47
Subcutaneous panniculitic T-cell lymphoma: numerous histiocytes showing hemophagocytosis are present. In addition, however, there are conspicuous hyperchromatic and irregular atypical lymphocytes.

Subcutaneous Whipple's disease

Clinical features

Whipple's disease is a rare condition, which most often affects males and is due to infection with the bacillus Tropheryma whippeli.[1,2] It is characterized by small intestinal involvement leading to malabsorption accompanied by fever and arthritis although virtually any organ system may be involved. Cutaneous lesions include hyperpigmentation, erythroderma, purpura, vasculitis, erythematous and urticarial lesions, eczematous dermatitis and lichenoid granulomatous lesions.[3,4] Exceptionally, subcutaneous nodules have been described.[3,5-7]

Histological features

Involvement of the subcutaneous fat presents as a predominantly septal 'panniculitis' characterized by a mixed inflammatory cell infiltrate consisting of lymphocytes, neutrophils and foamy periodic acid–Schiff (PAS)-positive histiocytes.[4]

Electron microscopy reveals degenerate bacilli within membrane-bound vesicles in the cytoplasm of the histiocytes.[3]

More recently, diagnostic polymerase chain reaction (PCR) and immunohistochemical techniques have become available.[8]

References

1. Relman, D.A., Schmidt, T.M., MacDermott, R.P. et al (1992) Identification of the uncultured bacillus of Whipple's disease. *N Engl J Med*, **327**, 293–296.
2. Dutly, F., Altwegg, M. (2001) Whipple's disease and 'Tropheryma whippelii'. *Clin Microbiol Rev*, **14**, 561–583.
3. Tarroch, X., Vives, P., Salas, A. et al (2001) Subcutaneous nodules in Whipple's disease. *J Cutan Pathol*, **28**, 368–371.
4. Frenk, E., Merot, Y., Pérez, I. et al (1991) Maladie de Whipple à présentation cutanée sarcoidisque. *Ann Dermatol Venereol*, **118**, 115–118.
5. Kwee, D., Fields, J.P., King, L.E. Jr (1987) Subcutaneous Whipple's disease. *J Am Acad Dermatol*, **16**, 188–190.
6. Good, A.E., Beals, T.F., Simmons, J.L. et al (1980) A subcutaneous nodule with Whipple's disease: key to early diagnosis. *Arthritis Rheum*, **23**, 856–859.
7. Balestrieri, G.P., Villanacci, V., Battocchio, S. et al (1996) Cutaneous involvement in Whipple's disease. *Br J Dermatol*, **135**, 666–668.
8. Fenollar, F., Raoult, D. (2001) Molecular techniques in Whipple's disease. *Expert Rev Mol Diagn*, **1**, 299–309.

Pancreatic panniculitis

Clinical features

In pancreatic panniculitis the association of subcutaneous fat necrosis (metastatic fat necrosis) with pancreatic disease is very rare, but is of particular importance because sometimes the underlying pancreatic lesion is clinically silent. The pancreatic diseases include acute pancreatitis, chronic pancreatitis, pancreatic pseudocyst, pancreatic divisum and pancreatic carcinoma (of ductal and more particularly acinic type).[1-11] Pancreatic panniculitis has also been described as a possible adverse drug reaction following renal transplantation for SLE.[12] There are two additional reports of the disease developing in a background of lupus erythematosus.[13,14]

Patients present with multiple, exquisitely tender nodules, which are erythematous or violaceous in appearance (*Figs 9.48, 9.49*). The lower extremities, buttocks and trunk are most often affected, although occasionally the upper arms, thorax and scalp are involved. Occasionally, the nodules ulcerate and release a creamy or oily discharge (*Fig. 9.50*). Joint manifestations (pain and swelling) are an important feature of this syndrome, occurring in approximately 54% (pancreatitis-associated) to 88% (pancreatic carcinoma-associated) of patients.[5,15-18] The ankles are most often affected, but the knees, elbows, wrists, metacarpophalangeal and metatarsophalangeal joints are occasionally involved. Additional features include pleural effusions (in 25%), ascites (in 30%) and, very occasionally, pericardial effusion.[4] Intramedullary fat may also be affected and intestinal involvement has rarely been documented.[1] Peripheral blood eosinophilia is quite a common laboratory finding (19% in pancreatitis-associated; 65% in pancreatic carcinoma-associated). Males are affected more often than females (pancreatitis 2:1; carcinoma 7:1) and patients are most often in the fourth, fifth or sixth decade.

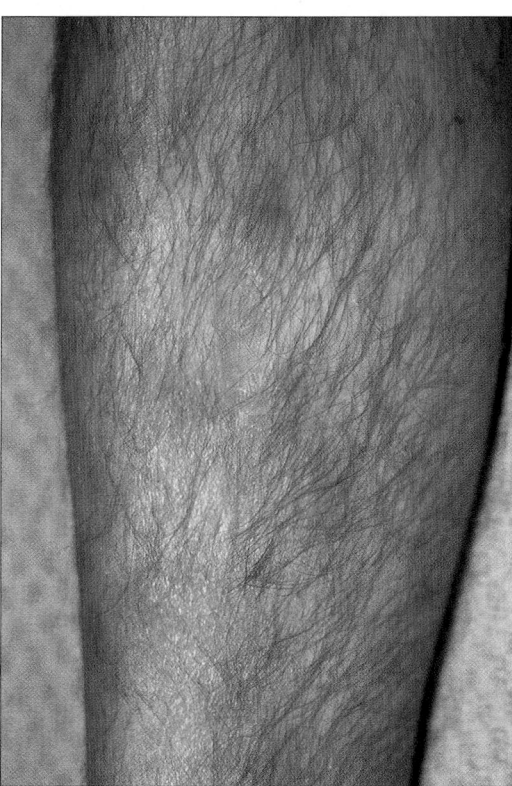

Fig. 9.48
Pancreatic panniculitis: early lesions are often erythematous. By courtesy of D. McGibbon, MD, St Thomas' Hospital, London, UK.

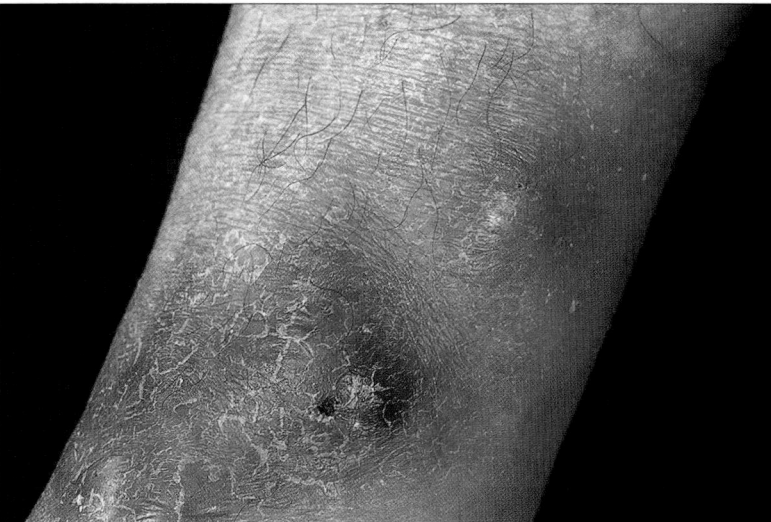

Fig. 9.49
Pancreatic panniculitis: a more advanced lesion. By courtesy of the Institute of Dermatology, London, UK.

This disease is associated with a high mortality, 42% in pancreatitis-associated variants and up to 100% in those cases presenting with an underlying carcinoma.[4]

Pathogenesis and histological features

The development of subcutaneous fat necrosis in association with pancreatic disease is due to the release into the peripheral circulation of trypsin, lipase, phospholipase and amylase.[7,19] It has been postulated that trypsin damages the vasculature, particularly in dependent sites, thereby permitting lipase to enter the surrounding tissues. In vivo evidence suggests that this may be a too simplistic viewpoint.[9] Serum lipase levels do not always correlate with subcutaneous fat necrosis and examples of patients with fat necrosis and normal serum lipase levels have been documented.[10] The reports of Wilson et al. and Simkin et al., however, provide striking in vivo evidence to support a pathogenetic role for released pancreatic enzymes.[15,16]

Histologically, the features are pathognomonic and are identical to those seen in the peripancreatic adipose tissue following an episode of acute hemorrhage pancreatitis (*Fig. 9.51*). The changes are lobular in distribution and are characterized by the presence of ghost cells (*Fig. 9.52*). The latter are anucleate, composed of amorphous granular debris and often show a rim of eosinophilia (*Fig. 9.53*). Stippled baso-philia due to calcification is commonly found (*Fig. 9.54*). A neutrophil polymorph response is usually evident around the foci of fat necrosis and hemorrhage is an almost invariable feature (*Fig. 9.55*). The uninvolved surrounding fat is heavily infiltrated by acute and chronic inflammatory cells including large numbers of macrophages, many of which have foamy cytoplasm due to ingested lipid, and occasional multinucleate giant cells (*Fig. 9.56*). There is no evidence of a vasculitis. Birefringent crystals have been described in the mesenteric fat and within affected joints but not in the subcutaneous fat.[20,21]

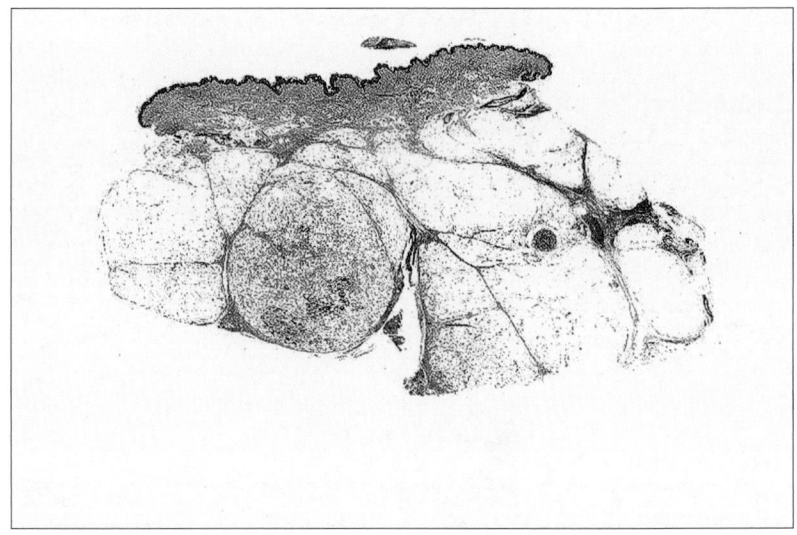

Fig. 9.51
Pancreatic panniculitis: the changes predominantly affect the lobules.

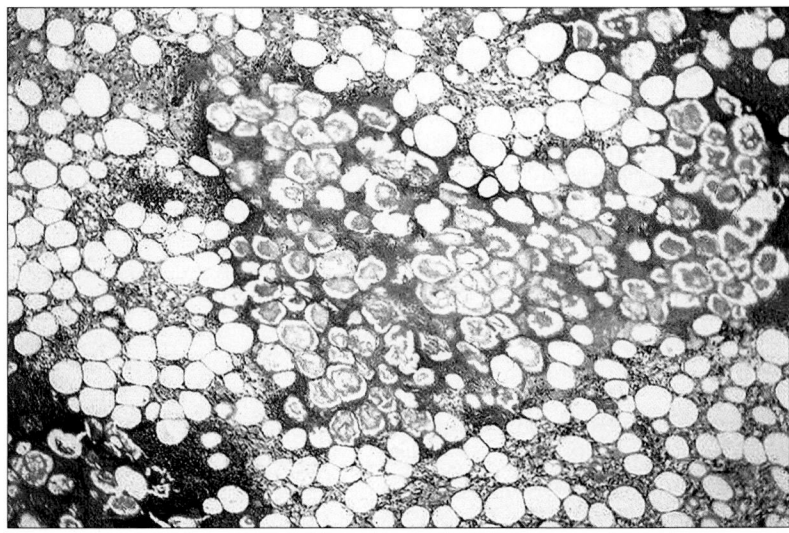

Fig. 9.52
Pancreatic panniculitis: there is extensive enzymatic fat necrosis. Note the characteristic ghost cells.

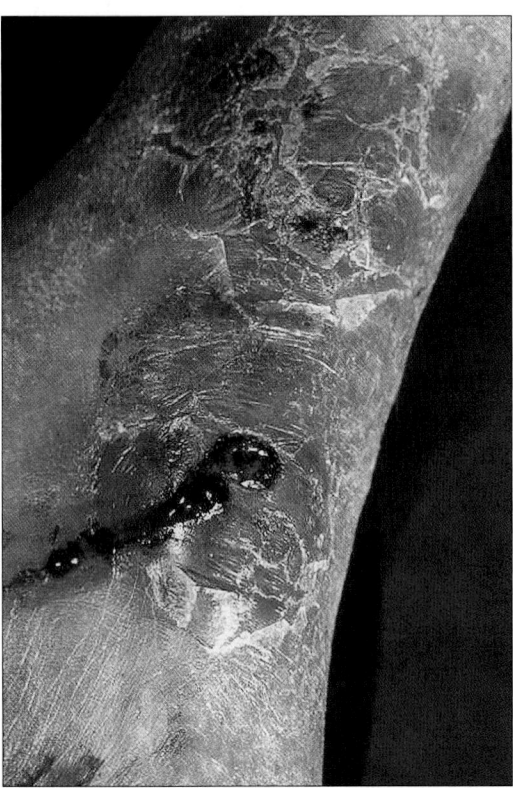

Fig. 9.50
Pancreatic panniculitis: the nodules may ulcerate and release blood-stained fluid. By courtesy of D. McGibbon, MD, St Thomas' Hospital, London, UK.

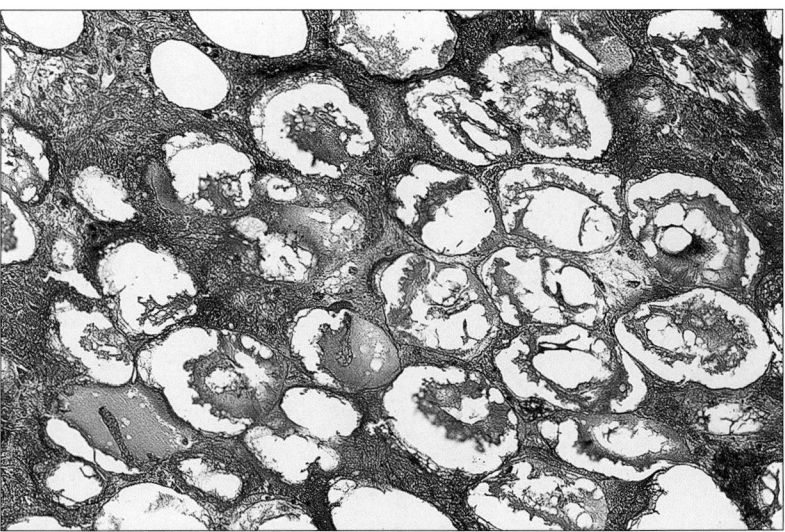

Fig. 9.53
Pancreatic panniculitis: close-up view of ghost cells.

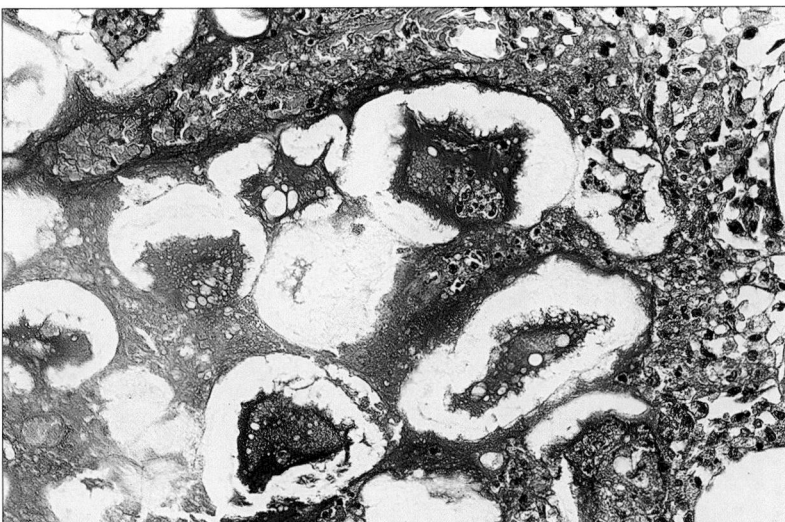

Fig. 9.54
Pancreatic panniculitis: the stippled basophilia represents calcification.

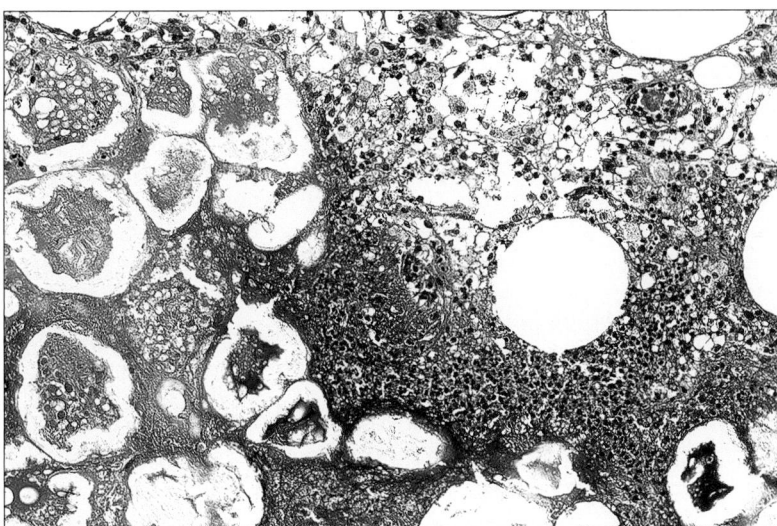

Fig. 9.55
Pancreatic panniculitis: there is a heavy neutrophil infiltrate and lipophages are conspicuous.

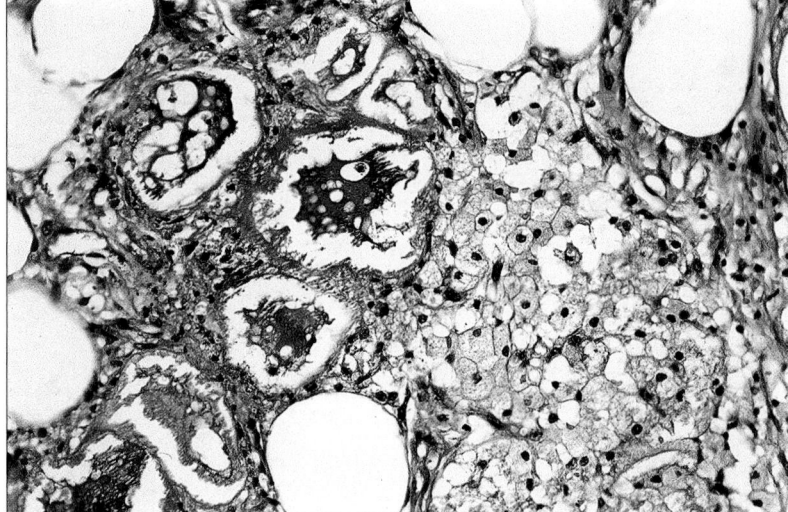

Fig. 9.56
Pancreatic panniculitis: as with other forms of fat necrosis, lipophages are often evident.

References

1. Dahl, P.R., Su, W.P.D., Cullimore, K.C. et al (1995) Pancreatic panniculitis. *J Am Acad Dermatol*, **33**, 413–417.
2. Good, A.E., Schnitzer, B., Kawanishi, H. et al (1976) Acinar pancreatic tumor with metastatic fat necrosis: report of a case and review of rheumatologic manifestations. *Am J Dig Dis*, **21**, 978–987.
3. Hudson-Peacock, M.J., Regnard, C.F.B., Farr, P.M. (1994) Liquefying panniculitis associated with acinous carcinoma of the pancreas responding to octreotide. *J R Soc Med*, **87**, 361–362.
4. Heykarts, B., Anseeuw, M., Degreef, H. (1999) Pancreatitis caused by acinous pancreatic carcinoma. *Dermatology*, **198**, 182–183.
5. Hughes, P.S.H., Apisarnthanarax, P., Mullins, J.F. (1975) Subcutaneous fat necrosis associated with pancreatic disease. *Arch Dermatol*, **111**, 506–510.
6. Fine, R.M. (1983) Subcutaneous fat necrosis, pancreatitis and arthropathy. *Int J Dermatol*, **22**, 575–576.
7. Haber, R.M., Assaad, D.M. (1986) Panniculitis associated with a pancreatic divisum. *J Am Acad Dermatol*, **14**, 331–334.
8. Förström, L., Winkelmann, R.K. (1975) Acute, generalized panniculitis with amylase and lipase in the skin. *Arch Dermatol*, **111**, 497–502.
9. Berman, B., Conteas, C., Smith, B. et al (1987) Fatal panniculitis presenting with subcutaneous fat necrosis. *J Am Acad Dermatol*, **17**, 359–364.
10. Detlefs, R.L. (1985) Drug-induced pancreatitis presenting as subcutaneous fat necrosis. *J Am Acad Dermatol*, **13**, 305–307.
11. Mourad, F.H., Hannoush, H.M., Bahlawan, M. et al (2001) Panniculitis and arthritis as the presenting manifestation of chronic pancreatitis. *J Clin Gastroenterol*, **32**, 259–261.
12. Echeverría, C.M., Fortunato, L.P., Stengel, F.M. et al (2001) Pancreatic panniculitis in a kidney transplant recipient. *Int J Dermatol*, **40**, 751–753.
13. Simons-Ling, N., Schachner, L., Penneys, N. et al (1983) Childhood systemic lupus erythematosus: association with pancreatic subcutaneous fat necrosis, and calcinosis cutis. *Arch Dermatol*, **119**, 491–494.
14. Cutlan, R.T., Wesche, W.A., Jenkins, J.J. III et al (2000) A fatal case of pancreatic panniculitis presenting in a young patient with systemic lupus. *J Cutan Pathol*, **27**, 466–471.
15. Wilson, H.A., Askari, A.D., Neiderhiser, D.H. (1983) Pancreatitis with arthropathy and subcutaneous fat necrosis. *Arthritis Rheum*, **26**, 121–126.
16. Simkin, P.A., Brunzell, J.D., Wisner, D. et al (1983) Free fatty acids in the pancreatic arthritis syndrome. *Arthritis Rheum*, **26**, 127–134.
17. Lopez, A., Garcia-Estan, J., Marras, C. et al (1998) Pancreatitis associated with pleural–mediastinal pseudocyst, panniculitis and polyarthritis. *Clin Rheumatol*, **17**, 335–339.
18. Sang, K.G., Niemann, T.H., Warner, C.A. (1992) Subcutaneous pancreatic fat necrosis associated with acute arthritis. *J Rheumatol*, **19**, 630–632.
19. Phelps, R.G., Shoji, T. (2001) Update on panniculitis. *Mt Sinai J Med*, **68**, 262–267.
20. Keen, C.E., Buk, S.J., Brady, K. et al (1994) Fat necrosis presenting as obscure abdominal mass: birefringent saponified fatty acid crystalloids as a clue to diagnosis. *J Clin Pathol*, **47**, 1028–1031.
21. Saag, K., Niemann, T., Warner, C. et al (1992) Subcutaneous pancreatic fat necrosis associated with acute arthritis. *J Rheumatol*, **19**, 630–632.

Subcutaneous fat necrosis of the newborn

Clinical features

This uncommon disease presents in full-term neonates in the first few weeks of life.[1–3] Affected babies develop painless subcutaneous nodules measuring from a few millimeters to several centimeters in diameter. The overlying skin may appear normal or be erythematous or violaceous. Lesions are symmetrical and distributed over bony prominences, the arms, shoulders, buttocks, thighs and cheeks (*Fig. 9.57*). The nodules frequently soften and become fluctuant, occasionally liquefying. The disease is usually self-limiting and benign, spontaneous resolution occurring within a period of weeks to months in the majority of cases. Occasionally, however, it is associated with hypercalcemia.[4–9] This

may be asymptomatic or associated with failure to thrive, fever, vomiting, irritability and seizures.[1] Exceptionally, this disease can prove fatal. Subcutaneous fat necrosis has also been accompanied by thrombocytopenia.[6]

Pathogenesis and histological features

The pathogenesis of the hypercalcemia is unknown. A number of theories have been proposed including calcium release from resolving plaques, elevated parathormone and prostaglandin E2 levels, increased vitamin D sensitivity and, most recently, lesional histiocytic production of excessive 1,25-dihydroxyvitamin D3 with resultant increased intestinal absorption of calcium.[10–17]

The cause of subcutaneous fat necrosis of the newborn is unknown, but most cases are related to some form of fetal distress, including obstetric or other birth trauma, cord accidents, meconium aspiration, hypothermia, placenta previa, cesarean section and neonatal asphyxia.[2] Pre-eclampsia and maternal diabetes have also been associated.[6] A primary abnormality of subcutaneous fat may be of some importance.[18] Neonatal fat is characterized by elevated levels of saturated fatty acids which have a high melting point and are therefore susceptible to precipitation as a consequence of neonatal hypothermia. Deficiency of brown fat has also been proposed as a potential etiological factor.[19] Although not histologically confirmed, a case of simultaneous development of sclerema neonatorum and subcutaneous fat necrosis of the newborn was described in an infant following cesarean section for fetal distress, hypothermia, neonatal respiratory distress and hypoglycemia.[20]

Subcutaneous fat necrosis has also been described after hypothermic cardiac surgery, as a possible complication of maternal cocaine abuse, following the in partum use of calcium-channel blockers and as a consequence of prolonged exposure in very cold weather.[21–26]

The histological changes are characteristic.[16,27–29] The subcutaneous fat is the scene of intense necrosis. Individual adipocytes are swollen and contain abundant radially arranged eosinophilic crystalline spaces resulting from dissolved lipid (*Figs 9.58, 9.59*). The crystals are largely composed of triglycerides.[28] There is a heavy inflammatory cell infiltrate comprising polymorphs, lymphocytes, histiocytes and numerous foreign body giant cells (*Fig. 9.60*). Large numbers of eosinophils have recently been described in two cases.[16] Older lesions may show fibrosis and foci of calcification. Systemic involvement is sometimes present.[29]

Differential diagnosis

It is of interest to note that identical histological features were seen some years ago in the poststeroid panniculitis syndrome.[30–34] This condition occurred in children who had been treated for rheumatic fever or glomerulonephritis with very large doses of steroids; sudden withdrawal of the steroids resulted in the development of subcutaneous swellings

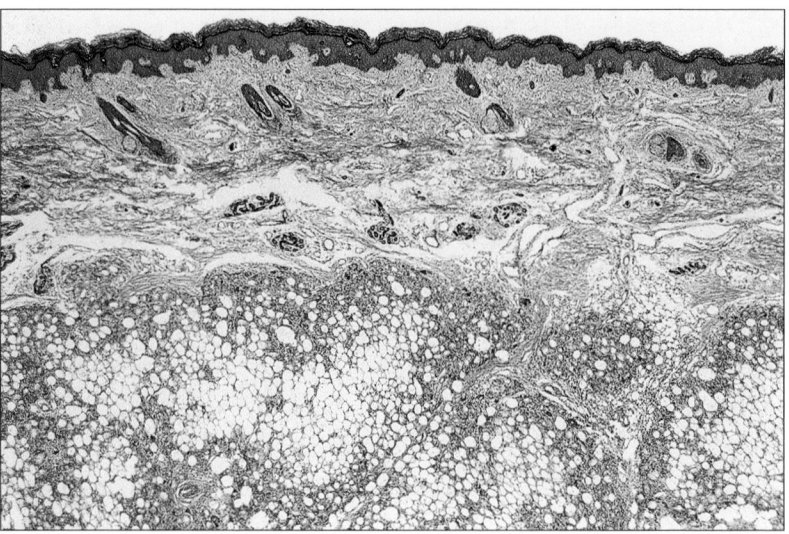

Fig. 9.58
Subcutaneous fat necrosis of the newborn: the changes are lobular in distribution.

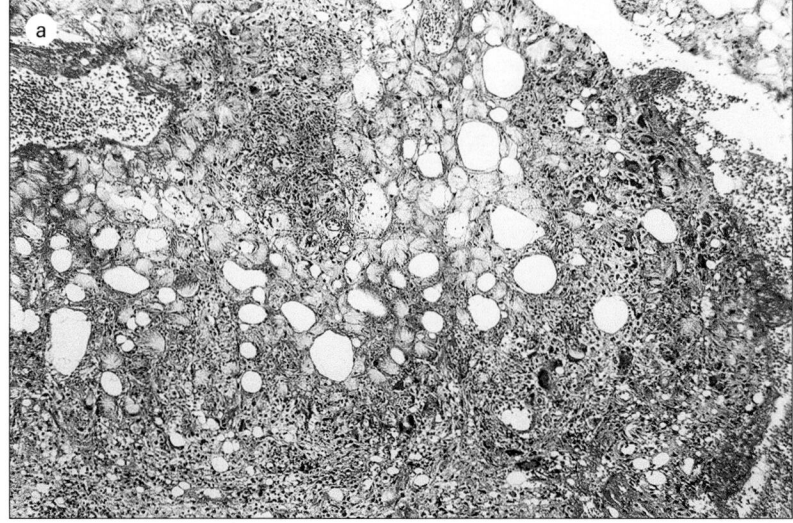

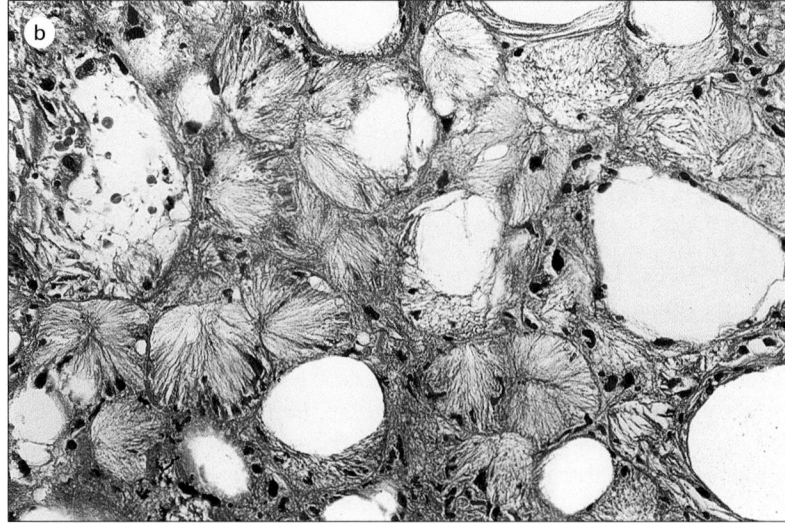

Fig. 9.59
(a, b) Subcutaneous fat necrosis of the newborn: individual adipocytes are swollen and contain characteristic, radial, eosinophilic crystals.

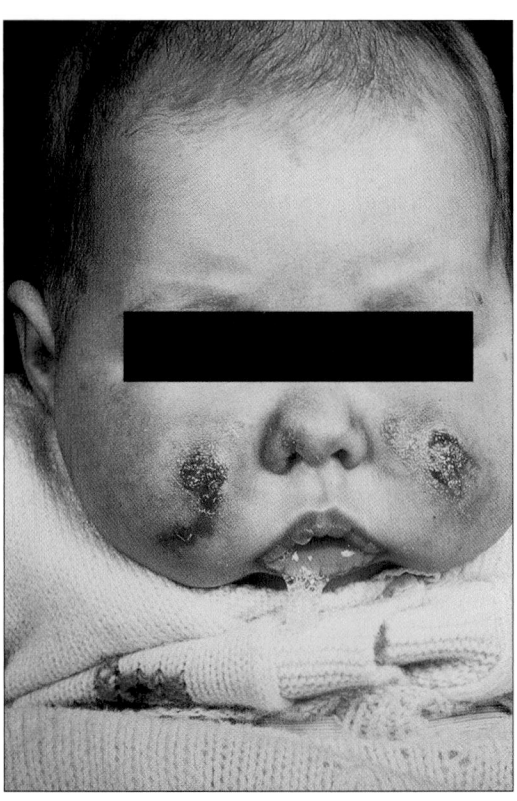

Fig. 9.57
Subcutaneous fat necrosis of the newborn: crusted, ulcerated nodules on both cheeks. By courtesy of the Institute of Dermatology, London, UK.

up to 4 cm across on the cheeks, arms and trunk. The disease is now of historic interest only due to the standard practice of steroid taper when withdrawing the drug. The skin overlying the nodules was erythematous, warm and itchy. In mild cases the panniculitis resolved spontaneously; in more severe examples it subsided following the reintroduction of steroids.

References

1. Hicks, M.J., Levy, M.I., Alexander, J. et al (1993) Subcutaneous fat necrosis of the newborn and hypercalcemia: case report and review of the literature. *Pediatr Dermatol*, 10, 271–276.
2. Mather, M.K., Sperling, L.C., Sau, P. (1997) Subcutaneous fat necrosis of the newborn. *Int J Dermatol*, 36, 450–452.
3. Moreno-Giménez, J.C., Hernández-Aguado, I., Arguisjüela, M.T. et al (1983) Subcutaneous fat necrosis of the newborn. *J Cutan Pathol*, 10, 277–280.
4. Norwood-Galloway, A., Ledwohl, M., Phelps, R.G. et al (1987) Subcutaneous fat necrosis of the newborn with hypercalcemia. *J Am Acad Dermatol*, 16, 435–449.
5. Cook, J.S., Stone, M.S., Hansen, J.R. (1992) Hypercalcemia in association with subcutaneous fat necrosis of the newborn: studies of calcium-regulating hormones. *Pediatrics*, 90, 93–96.
6. Lewis, A., Cowen, P., Rodda, C. et al (1992) Subcutaneous fat necrosis of the newborn complicated by hypercalcemia and thrombocytopenia. *Australas J Dermatol*, 33, 141–144.
7. Thomsen, R. (1980) Subcutaneous fat necrosis of the newborn and idiopathic hypercalcemia. *Arch Dermatol*, 116, 1155–1158.
8. Wiadrowski, T.P., Marshman, G. (2001) Subcutaneous fat necrosis of the newborn following hypothermia and complicated by pain and hypercalcemia. *Australas J Dermatol*, 42, 207–210.
9. Finne, P., Sanderud, J., Aksnes, L. et al (1988) Hypercalcemia with increased and unregulated 1,25-dihydroxyvitamin D production in a neonate with subcutaneous fat necrosis. *J Pediatr*, 112, 792–794.
10. Balfour, E., Antaya, R.J., Lazova, R. (2002) Subcutaneous fat necrosis of the newborn presenting as a large plaque with lobulated cystic areas. *Cutis*, 70, 169–173.
11. Veldhuis, J., Kulin, H., Demers, L. et al (1979) Infantile hypercalcemia with subcutaneous fat necrosis: endocrine studies. *J Pediatr*, 95, 460–462.
12. Repiso-Jiminez, J.B., Marquez, J., Sotillo, I. et al (1999) Subcutaneous fat necrosis of the newborn. *J Eur Acad Dermatol Venereol*, 12, 254–257.
13. Ghirri, P., Bottone, U., Coccoli, L. et al (1999) Symptomatic hypercalcemia in the first months of life: calcium regulating hormones and treatment. *J Endocrinol Invest*, 22, 349–353.
14. Kruse, K., Irle, U., Uhlig, R. (1993) Elevated 1,25-dihydroxyvitamin D serum concentrations in infants with subcutaneous fat necrosis. *J Pediatr*, 122, 460–463.
15. Rice, A.M., Rivkees, S.A. (1999) Etidronate therapy for hypercalcemia in subcutaneous fat necrosis of the newborn. *J Pediatr*, 124, 349–351.
16. So, W.C., Lin, C.H., Lee, J.Y. (1991) Subcutaneous fat necrosis of the newborn: report of two cases. *Acta Pediatr*, 32, 239–243.
17. Burden, A.D., Krafchik, B.R. (1999) Subcutaneous fat necrosis of the newborn: a review of 11 cases. *Pediatr Dermatol*, 16, 384–387.
18. Oswalt, G.C., Montes, L.F., Cassady, G. (1985) Subcutaneous fat necrosis of the newborn. *J Cutan Pathol*, 5, 193–199.
19. Taïeb, A., Douard, D., Maleville, J. (1987) Subcutaneous brown fat necrosis and brown fat deficiency. *J Am Acad Dermatol*, 16, 624–625.
20. Jardine, D., Atherton, D.J., Trompeter, R.S. (1990) Sclerema neonatorum and subcutaneous fat necrosis of the newborn in the same infant. *Eur J Pediatr*, 150, 125–126.
21. Silverman, A.K., Michel, E.H., Rasmussen, J.E. (1986) Subacute fat necrosis in an infant, occurring after hypothermic cardiac surgery. Case report and analysis of etiologic factors. *J Am Acad Dermatol*, 15, 331–336.
22. Glover, M.T., Caterall, M.D., Atherton, D.J. (1991) Subcutaneous fat necrosis in two infants after hypothermic cardiac surgery. *Pediatr Dermatol*, 8, 210–212.
23. Chuang, S.D., Chiu, H.C., Chang, C.C. (1995) Subcutaneous fat necrosis of the newborn complicating hypothermic cardiac surgery. *Br J Dermatol*, 132, 805–810.
24. Carraccio, C., Papadimitriou, J., Feinberg, P. (1994) Subcutaneous fat necrosis of the newborn: link to maternal use of cocaine during pregnancy. *Clin Pediatr*, 33, 317–318.
25. Rosbotham, J.L., Johnson, A., Haque, K.N. et al (1998) Painful subcutaneous fat necrosis of the newborn associated with in partum use of calcium channel blockers. *Clin Exp Dermatol*, 23, 19–21.
26. Lee, S.K., Lee, J.H., Han, C.H. et al (2001) Calcified subcutaneous fat necrosis induced by prolonged exposure to cold weather: a case report. *Pediatr Radiol*, 31, 294–295.
27. Friedman, S.J., Winkelmann, R.K. (1989) Subcutaneous fat necrosis of the newborn: light, ultrastructural and histochemical microscopic studies. *J Cutan Pathol*, 16, 99–105.
28. Fretzin, D.F., Arias, A.M. (1987) Sclerema neonatorum and subacute fat necrosis of the newborn. *Pediatr Dermatol*, 4, 112–122.
29. Fernández-López, E., García-Dorado, J., De Unamino, P. et al (1990) Subcutaneous fat necrosis of the newborn and idiopathic hypercalcemia. *Dermatologica*, 180, 250–254.
30. Roenick, H.H., Haserick, J.R., Arondell, F.D. (1964) Post-steroid panniculitis. *Arch Dermatol*, 90, 387–392.
31. Spagnulo, M., Taranta, A. (1961) Post-steroid panniculitis. *Ann Intern Med*, 54, 1181–1190.
32. Saxena, A.K., Nigam, P.K. (1988) Panniculitis following steroid therapy. *Cutis*, 42, 341–342.
33. Silverman, R.A., Newman, A.J., LeVine, M.J. et al (1988) Poststeroid panniculitis. *Pediatr Dermatol*, 5, 92–93.
34. Reichel, M., Díaz-Cascajo, C. (1995) Bilateral jawline nodules in a child with brain stem glioma: post steroid panniculitis. *Arch Dermatol*, 131, 1448–1449.

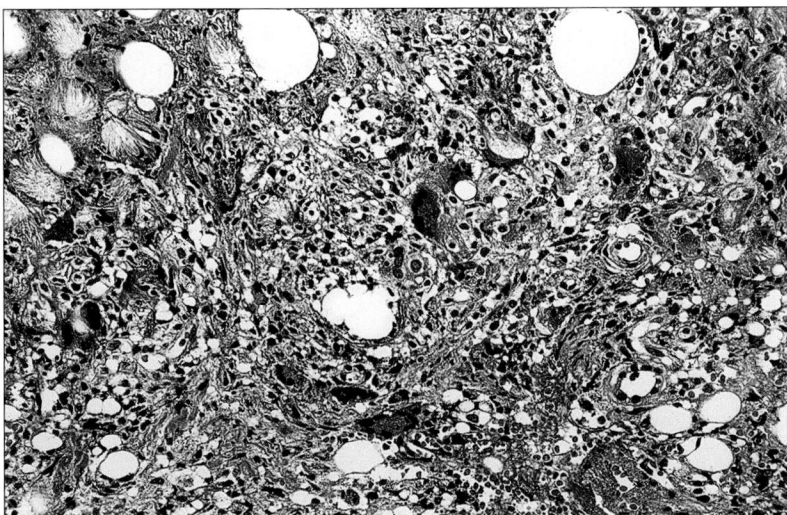

Fig. 9.60
Subcutaneous fat necrosis of the newborn: surrounding the foci of fat necrosis is a chronic inflammatory infiltrate containing numerous foreign body giant cells.

Sclerema neonatorum

Clinical features

Sclerema neonatorum is a very rare condition associated with high morbidity and mortality (75–90%).[1] It is sometimes confused with, and must be distinguished from, subcutaneous fat necrosis of the newborn.[2–4] Infants present in the first week of life (average age of onset, 4 days; range, birth to 70 days) with a diffuse, rapidly spreading, wax-like thickening and induration of the subcutaneous fat, resembling lard. This usually commences about the buttocks, thighs and trunk and often spreads to involve the whole body, excluding the palms, soles and genitalia. The fat is typically tethered to the underlying fascia and the skin cannot be picked up. Pitting edema is not a feature.

Affected infants are usually hypothermic, but body temperature may be normal or, rarely, raised.[5] Some of the infants are premature, but these are a minority. The children commonly have some other associated illness, such as septicemia, pneumonia, diarrhea, dehydration, intestinal obstruction or congenital heart disease. A patient with both sclerema neonatorum and concurrent subacute fat necrosis of the newborn has been described.[6]

Pathogenesis and histological features

The etiology and pathogenesis of this condition are uncertain. It is thought that the structural alterations of the subcutaneous fat probably predate the development of the clinical features. Neonatal subcutaneous fat is characterized by a higher content of saturated fatty acids (palmitic and stearic) and a lower content of unsaturated fatty acids (oleic) than adult subcutaneous fat.[2] It also has higher melting and solidification points. It has been suggested that infants with sclerema neonatorum have an inadequately developed enzyme system for converting saturated to unsaturated fatty acids.[2] It is thought that this, in association with stress, might result in the precipitation of triglycerides and consequent solidification of the subcutaneous fat. Recently, it has been proposed that redistribution of blood flow to the systemic circulation with resultant relative ischemia of the subcutaneous fat may be of pathogenetic importance.[7] Sclerema neonatorum is characterized by increased blood lipid peroxidation and diminished superoxidase dismutase activity which raises the possibility that free radicals may play a role in its pathogenesis.[8] There is no evidence of vasculitis.

The histological features are surprisingly bland. The subcutaneous fat is greatly thickened and the fibrous septa are broader than normal. The adipocytes, which are increased in size, may contain radially orientated fine crystals identical to those described in subcutaneous fat necrosis of the newborn although often they are inconspicuous.[1,9] In contrast to the latter condition, however, there is no necrosis or significant inflammatory cell infiltrate. Calcification is rarely a feature.[1] The dermis may appear sclerotic with hyalinization and the epidermis atrophic with loss of the rete ridges.[9]

References

1. Sadana, S., Mathur, N.B., Thakur, A. (1997) Exchange transfusion in septic neonates with sclerema: effect on immunoglobulin and complement levels. *Indian Pediatr*, **34**, 20–25.
2. Fretzin, D.F., Arias, M. (1987) Sclerema neonatorum and subcutaneous fat necrosis of the newborn. *Pediatr Dermatol*, **4**, 112–122.
3. Horsefield, G.I., Yardley, H.J. (1965) Sclerema neonatorum. *J Invest Dermatol*, **4**, 326–332.
4. Kellum, R.E., Ray, T.L., Brown, G.R. (1968) Sclerema neonatorum. *Arch Dermatol*, **97**, 372–380.
5. Battin, M., Harding, J., Gunn, A. (2002) Sclerema neonatorum following hypothermia. *J Pediatr Child Health*, **38**, 533–534.
6. Jardine, D., Atherton, D.J., Trompeter, R.S. (1990) Sclerema neonatorum and subcutaneous fat necrosis of the newborn in the same infant. *Eur J Dermatol*, **150**, 125–126.
7. Mogilner, B.M., Alkalay, A., Nissim, F. et al (1981) Subcutaneous fat necrosis of the newborn. *Clin Pediatr*, **20**, 748–750.
8. Yao, Y., Gong, F., Xiong, F. et al (1997) Observation on the changes in neonates with sclerema. *Hua Xi Yi Ke Da Xue Xue Bao*, **28**, 440–441.
9. Dasgupta, A., Ghosh, R.N., Pal, R.K. et al (1993) Sclerema neonatorum – histopathologic study. *Ind J Pathol Microbiol*, **36**, 45–47.

Cutaneous oxalosis

Clinical features

Oxalosis, in which there is widespread deposition of calcium oxalate in the tissues, may represent a primary metabolic disease or a secondary phenomenon due to increased intake of oxalate precursors or defective excretion.[1–5] Secondary oxalosis can also result from pyridoxine deficiency, glycerol infusion, methoxyflurane anesthesia, excessive ascorbic acid, extensive hemodialysis, peritoneal dialysis and ethylene glycol poisoning.[2]

Primary oxalosis, which is associated with overproduction of oxalate, is an autosomal recessive condition and includes three subtypes:
- *Type I*, which is most often encountered, develops as a result of deficiency of the hepatic enzyme alanine:glyoxylate aminotransferase with resulting increased urinary excretion of oxalate, glycolate and glyoxylate.[1–3]
- *Type II* (L-glyceric aciduria) results from cytosolic D-glycerate dehydrogenase and glyoxylate reductase deficiencies with associated increased urinary excretion of L-glycerate and oxalate accompanied by normal glycolate and glyoxylate excretion.[4]
- *Type III* develops as a result of primary small intestinal disease associated with excessive oxalate reabsorption.[5]

Calcium oxalate crystal deposition occurs most commonly in the kidneys (calcium oxalate stones and chronic renal failure).[4] With the onset of the latter, hyperoxalemia develops with resultant deposition of oxalate crystals in the blood vessels, retina, myocardium, cardiac conducting system, central nervous system, peripheral nerves, bones and the joints.[6]

Cutaneous manifestations may occur in both primary and secondary forms.[6–22] Lesions most often result from vascular involvement, patients presenting with acrocyanosis, livedo reticularis, Raynaud's phenomenon and distal gangrene (*Fig. 9.61*).[7–12] Ulceronecrotic lesions reminiscent of calciphylaxis have also been documented.[13–15] Less often crystals are deposited in the skin of the face and the fingers as miliary deposits, as dermal/subcutaneous nodules or as painful subungual nodules.[16–21] Exceptionally, generalized cutaneous nodules have been documented.[22] Vascular involvement is said to be more common in patients with primary disease whereas cutaneous extravascular lesions are predominantly seen in patients with secondary disease.[21]

Histological features

Calcium oxalate crystals are yellow to brown, radially arranged, needle-shaped or rectangular crystals (*Figs 9.62, 9.63*). In the skin they may be found in the reticular dermis or within the subcutaneous fat. Vascular involvement may also be seen where the media of arteries is predominantly affected (*Fig. 9.64*). Less commonly, crystals may be seen within the lumina of smaller arteries or arterioles.[1,11,12] The crystals show striking yellow or blue birefringence when examined in polarized light. They are sometimes accompanied by a foreign body giant cell reaction, particularly when present as dermal or subcutaneous deposits.[8,18,22] In those cases associated with gangrene or livedo reticularis, fibrin thrombi may also be detected.[8]

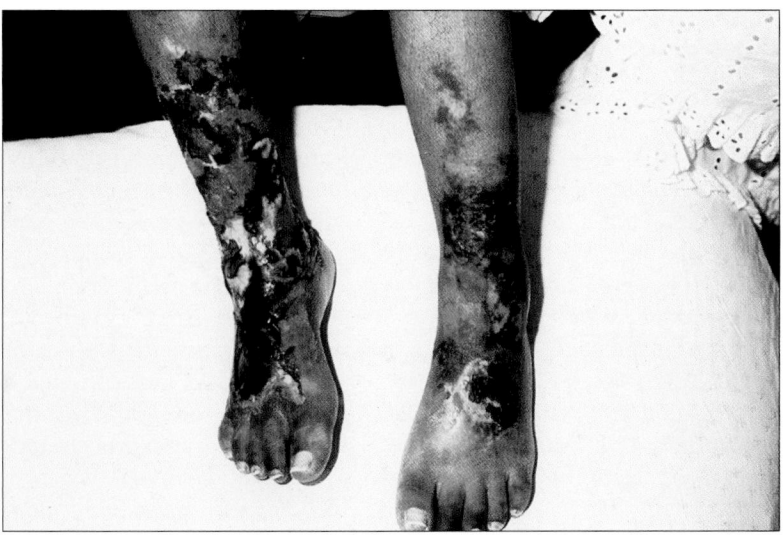

Fig. 9.61
Cutaneous oxalosis: this child shows gangrene with ulceration. By courtesy of N. Saxe, MD, Groote Schuur Hospital, Cape Town, South Africa.

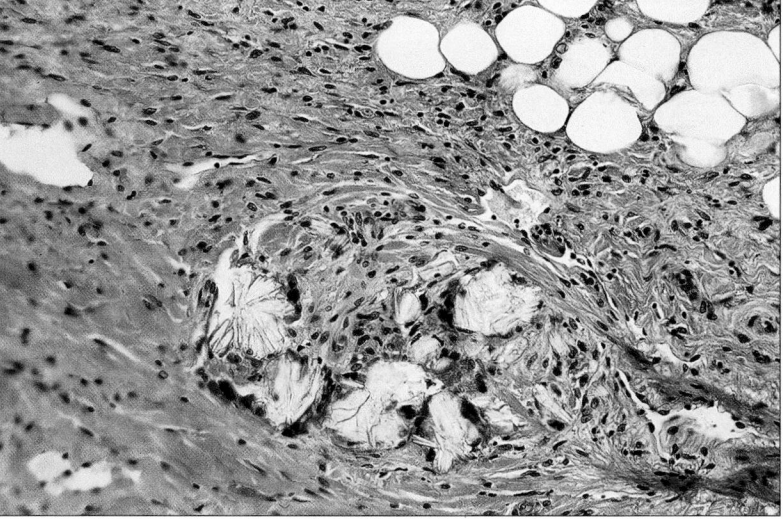

Fig. 9.62
Cutaneous oxalosis: note the radially orientated, needle-shaped crystals.

References

1. Danpure, C.J., Jennings, P.R. (1986) Peroxisomal alanine:glyoxylate aminotransferase deficiency in primary hyperoxaluria type I. *FEBS Lett*, **201**, 20–24.
2. Danpure, C.J., Jennings, P.R., Watts, R.W. (1987) Enzymological diagnosis of primary hyperoxaluria type 1 by measurement of hepatic alanine:glyoxylate aminotransferase activity. *Lancet*, **1**, 289–291.
3. Tolbert, N.E. (1981) Metabolic pathways in peroxisomes and glyoxysomes. *Ann Rev Biochem*, **50**, 133–157.
4. Chelbeck, P.T., Miliner, D.S., Smith, L.H. (1994) Long-term prognosis in primary hyperoxaluria type 2 (L-glyceric aciduria). *Am J Kidney Dis*, **23**, 255–259.
5. Yendt, E.R., Cohanim, M. (1986) Absorptive hyperoxaluria: a new clinical entity – successful treatment with hydrochlorothiazide. *Clin Invest Med*, **9**, 44–50.
6. Spiers, E.M., Sanders, D.Y., Omura, E.F. (1990) Clinical and histologic features of primary oxalosis. *J Am Acad Dermatol*, **22**, 952–956.
7. Arbus, G.S., Sniderman, S. (1974) Oxalosis with peripheral gangrene. *Arch Pathol*, **97**, 107–110.
8. Greer, K.E., Cooper, P.H., Campbell, F. et al (1980) Primary oxalosis with livedo reticularis. *Arch Dermatol*, **116**, 213–214.
9. Winship, I.M., Saxe, N.P., Hugel, H. (1991) Primary oxalosis – an unusual cause of livedo reticularis. *Clin Exp Dermatol*, **16**, 367–370.
10. Farreli, J., Shoemaker, J.D., Otti, T. et al (1997). Primary hyperoxaluria in an adult with renal failure, livedo reticularis, retinopathy, and peripheral neuropathy. *Am J Kidney Dis*, **29**, 947–952.
11. Singh, S., Tai, C., Ganz, G. et al (1999) Steroid-responsive pleuropericarditis and livedo reticularis in an unusual case of adult-onset primary hyperoxaluria. *Am J Kidney Dis*, **33**, e5.
12. Marconi, V., Mofid, M.Z., McCall, C. et al (2002) Primary hyperoxaluria: report of a case with livedo reticularis and digital infarcts. *J Am Acad Dermatol*, **46**, 516–518.
13. Somach, S.C., Davis, B.R., Paras, F.A. et al (1995) Fatal cutaneous necrosis mimicking calciphylaxis in a patient with type 1 primary hyperoxaluria. *Arch Dermatol*, **131**, 821–823.
14. Galimberti, R.L., Parra, I.H., Imperiali, N. et al (1999) Fatal cutaneous necrosis in a hemodialysed patient with oxalosis. *Int J Dermatol*, **38**, 918–920.
15. O'Reilly, M.A., Meadows, K.P., Egan, C.A. (2001) Necrotizing livedo reticularis. Diagnosis: primary hyperoxaluria type 1. *Arch Dermatol*, **137**, 957–962.
16. Jansen, L.H., Groenveld, J.L., van der Meer, J.B. (1974) Deposition of calcium oxalate in the skin in two patients suffering from oxalosis caused by primary hyperoxaluria. *Arch Dermatol Forsch*, **250**, 323–350.
17. Reginato, A.J., Seoane, J.L.F., Alvarez, C.B. et al (1986) Arthropathy and cutaneous calcinosis in hemodialysis oxalosis. *Arthritis Rheum*, **29**, 1387–1396.
18. Sina, B., Lutz, L.L. (1990) Cutaneous oxalate granuloma. *J Am Acad Dermatol*, **22**, 316–318.
19. Abuelo, J.G., Schwartz, S.T., Reginato, A.J. (1992) Cutaneous oxalosis after long-term hemodialysis. *Arch Intern Med*, **152**, 1517–1520.
20. Ohtake, N., Uchiyama, H., Furue, M. et al (1994) Secondary cutaneous oxalosis: cutaneous deposition of calcium oxalate dihydrate after long-term hemodialysis. *J Am Acad Dermatol*, **31**, 368–372.
21. Karakousis, P.C., Tomaszewski, J.E. (2001) Ulcerating subcutaneous nodules and advanced renal failure: is it time for a new liver? *Nephrol Dial Transplant*, **16**, 2095–2096.
22. Isonokami, M., Nishida, K., Okada, N. et al (1993) Cutaneous oxalate granulomas in a hemodyalised patient: report of a case with unique clinical features. *Br J Dermatol*, **128**, 690–692.

Fig. 9.63
Cutaneous oxalosis: note the radial crystals viewed under polarized light.

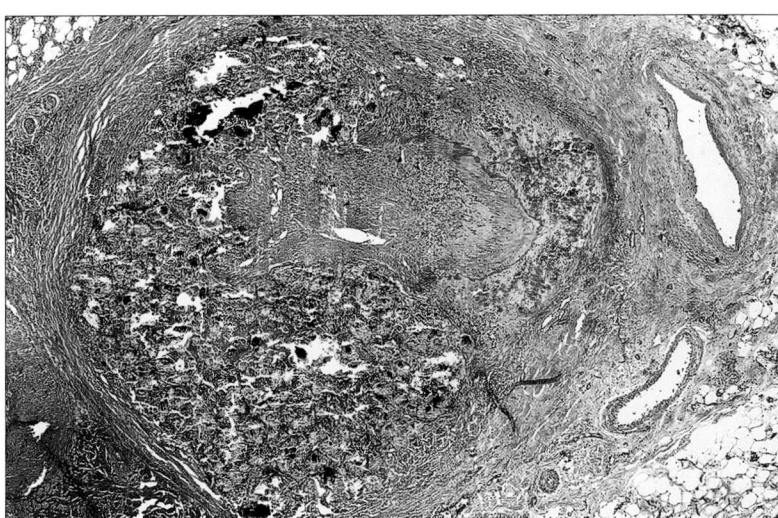

Fig. 9.64
Cutaneous oxalosis: in this field there is dramatic vascular involvement with destruction of the media and massive intimal thickening.

Calciphylaxis

Clinical features

Calciphylaxis was originally defined by an experimental model in rats, in which sensitization with parathormone or dihydrotachysterol followed by the injection of a challenging agent such as a metal salt resulted in localized necrosis and calcification.[1] The term was subsequently adopted to describe a condition in which an abnormality of calcium/phosphate metabolism is followed by calcification of the vasculature of the subcutaneous fat with subsequent thrombosis accompanied by extensive skin necrosis.[2-7]

Calciphylaxis presents clinically as an often bilateral and symmetrical, pruritic and frequently painful/tender eruption most often affecting the lower limbs (*Fig. 9.65*). Less often lesions may affect the breasts, buttocks, abdomen and penis.[8-24] Lesions are often well-delineated, livedoid, violaceous plaques and nodules associated with ischemic necrosis of the underlying tissues sometimes extending down to the fascia. Ulceration is typically present and sometimes bullae are a feature. Gangrene and autoamputation may accompany acral involvement.[6] Intestinal involvement with massive hemorrhage has exceptionally been documented.[16]

Calciphylaxis is associated with considerable morbidity and a high mortality of up to 60%.[4,14] The majority of patients succumb to secondary infection.

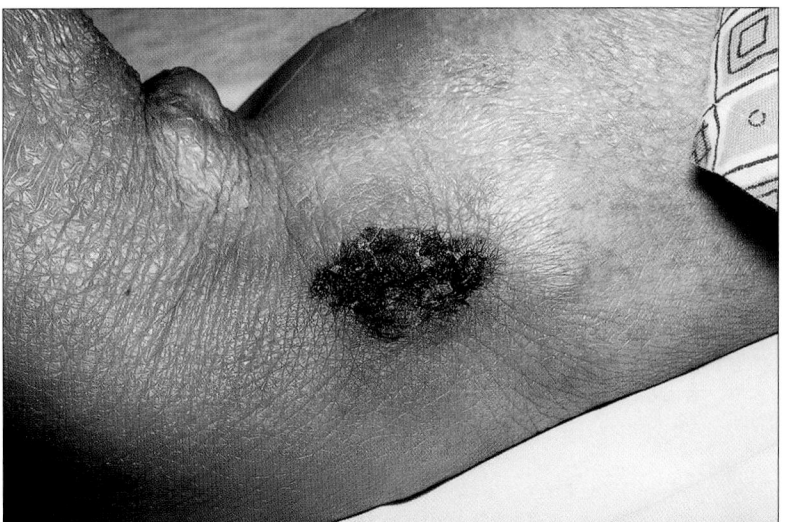

Fig. 9.65
Calciphylaxis: ulcerated gangrenous lesion with surrounding erythema. By courtesy of A. Qureshi, MD, Department of Dermatology, Brigham and Women's Hospital, Boston, USA.

Pathogenesis and histological features

The precise mechanism by which the subcutaneous vasculature undergoes calcification is uncertain but is probably multifactorial. In the majority of patients, however, sensitization occurs as a consequence of abnormal calcium/phosphorus metabolism in a setting of chronic renal failure and secondary or tertiary hyperparathyroidism. Frequently, the patients are undergoing dialysis. Less often, there is a background of primary hyperparathyroidism or hypervitaminosis D.[4,12,14,17] Although in many patients calcium deposition occurs in association with an increased calcium–phosphorus product, in a significant proportion of patients calcium and phosphorus levels are normal.[4] It has been suggested that in such patients the calcification develops as a direct response to excess parathormone or vitamin D. Challenging agents resulting in the vascular precipitation of calcium salts are unknown but a number of substances (including albumin, corticosteroids and immunosuppressives) have been incriminated.[12] Calciphylaxis has also been described in association with decreased functional protein C.[13] Very rarely, the condition has presented in a patient with no evidence of a renal disorder or increase in parathormone level.[17]

Histologically, the characteristic feature is calcification of the small- to medium-sized arteries and arterioles (*Figs 9.66, 9.67*). Calcified debris may sometimes be present within the lumina and occasionally the vessels are thrombosed (*Fig. 9.68*). Intimal fibroblastic proliferation with luminal narrowing has also been described (*Fig. 9.69*).[9] Hemorrhage within the subcutaneous fat may be seen and fat necrosis accompanied by a lobular lymphohistiocytic infiltrate has been documented in a number of cases (*Fig. 9.70*). Interstitial calcification is only rarely a feature.[9] Exceptionally, pseudoxanthoma elasticum-like changes have been documented in calciphylaxis.[25] In a related phenomenon, epidermal and follicular calcification have been described in the absence of vascular lesions in a patient with toxic epidermal necrolysis with a background of hyperparathyroidism.[26]

References

1. Selye, H. (1962) Calciphylaxis. Chicago: University of Chicago Press.
2. Gipstein, R.M., Coburn, J.W., Adams, D.A. et al (1976) Calciphylaxis in man: a syndrome of tissue necrosis and vascular calcification in 11 patients with chronic renal failure. *Arch Intern Med*, **136**, 1273–1280.
3. Lazorik, F.C., Friedman, A.K., Leyden, J.J. (1981) Xeroradiographic observations in four patients with chronic renal disease and cutaneous gangrene. *Arch Dermatol*, **117**, 325–328.
4. Fischer, A.H., Morris, D.J. (1995) Pathogenesis of calciphylaxis: study of three cases with literature review. *Hum Pathol*, **26**, 1055–1064.
5. Coates, T., Kirkland, G.S., Dymock, R.B. et al (1998) Cutaneous necrosis from calcific uremic arteriolopathy. *Am J Kidney Dis*, **32**, 384–391.

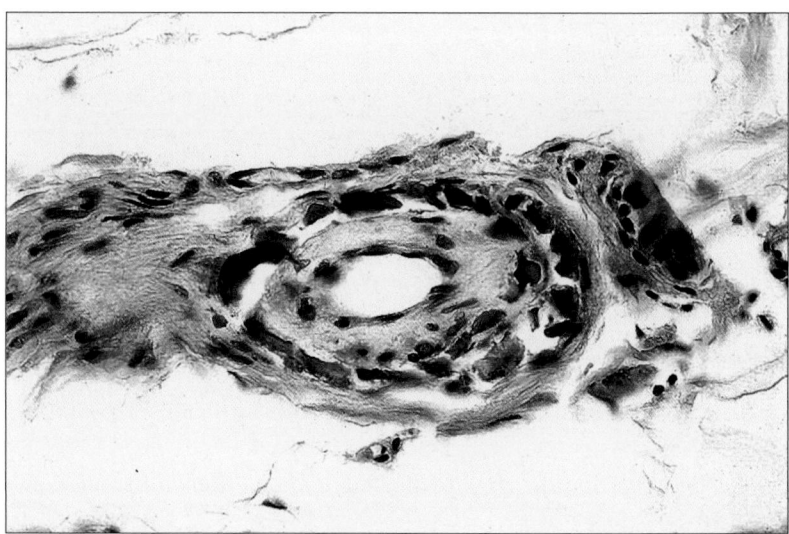

Fig. 9.67
Calciphylaxis: calcification affects both the media and the intima. Involvement of such small vessels is characteristic of this condition.

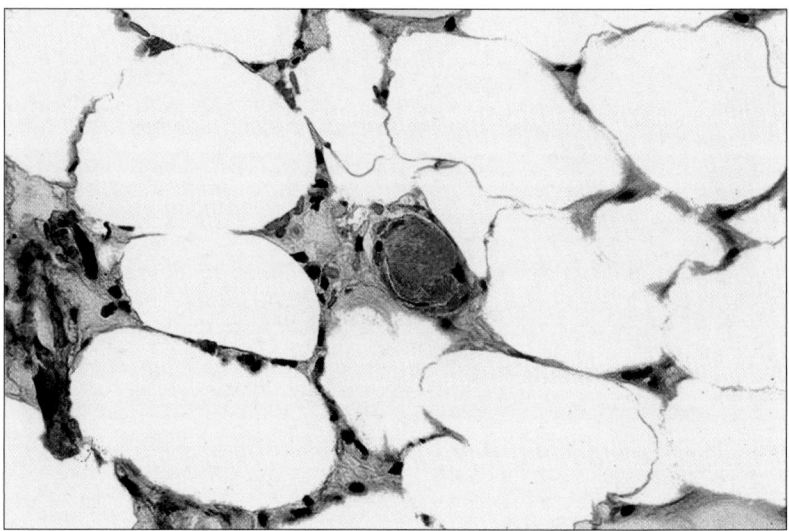

Fig. 9.68
Calciphylaxis: note the thrombosed vessel in the center of the field.

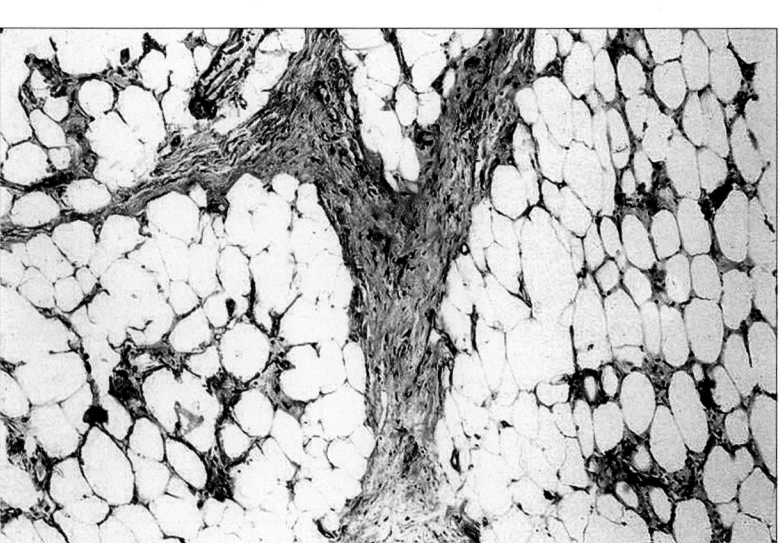

Fig. 9.66
Calciphylaxis: there is focal fat necrosis and widespread calcification affecting the small vessels of the lobule.

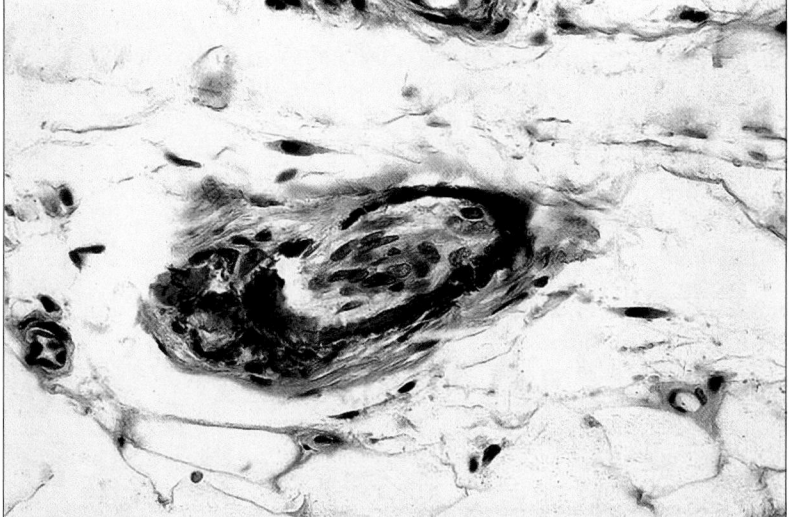

Fig. 9.69
Calciphylaxis: in addition to mural calcification, there is marked intimal fibroblastic proliferation.

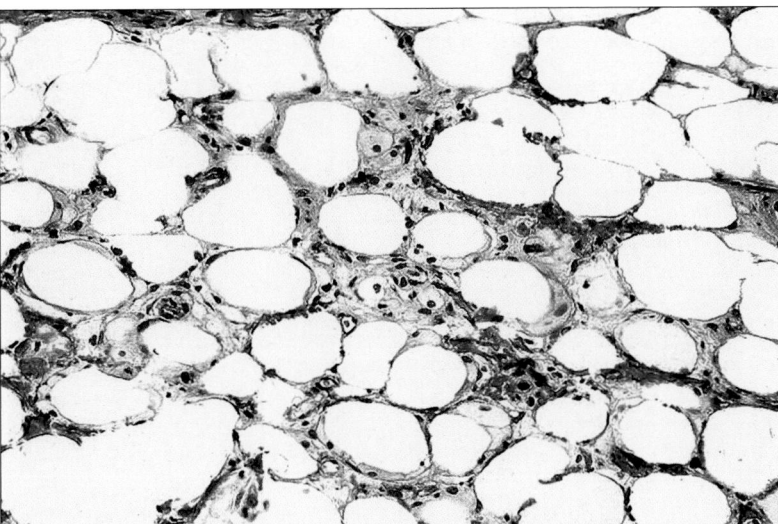

Fig. 9.70
Calciphylaxis: fat necrosis with conspicuous lipophages. In addition there is widespread calcification.

6. Winkelmann, R.K., Keating, F.R. (1970) Cutaneous vascular calcification, gangrene and hyperparathyroidism. *Br J Dermatol*, **83**, 263–268.
7. Kossard, S., Winkelmann, R.K. (1979) Vascular calcification in dermatopathology. *Am J Dermatopathol*, **1**, 177–183.
8. Khafif, R.A., DeLima, C., Silverberg, A. et al (1990) Calciphylaxis and systemic calcinosis. *Arch Intern Med*, **150**, 956–959.
9. Lugo-Somolinos, A., Sanchez, J.L., Mendez-Coll, J. et al (1990) Calcifying panniculitis associated with polycystic kidney disease and chronic renal failure. *J Am Acad Dermatol*, **22**, 743–747.
10. Cockerell, C.J., Dolan, E.T. (1992) Widespread cutaneous and systemic calcification (calciphylaxis) in patients with acquired immunodeficiency syndrome and renal disease. *J Am Acad Dermatol*, **26**, 559–562.
11. Lowry, L.R., Tschen, J.A., Wolf, J.E. et al (1993) Calcifying panniculitis and systemic calciphylaxis in an end-stage renal patient. *Cutis*, **51**, 245–247.
12. Dahl, P.R., Winkelmann, R.K., Connolly, S.M. (1995) The vascular calcification–cutaneous necrosis syndrome. *J Am Acad Dermatol*, **33**, 53–58.
13. Ivker, R.A., Woosley, J., Briggaman, R.A. (1995) Calciphylaxis in three patients with end stage renal disease. *Arch Dermatol*, **131**, 63–68.
14. Walsh, J.S., Fairley, J.A. (1995) Calcifying disorders of the skin. *J Am Acad Dermatol*, **33**, 693–706.
15. Wood, J.C., Monga, M., Hellstrom, W.J. (1997) Penile calciphylaxis. *Urology*, **50**, 622–624.
16. Brown, D.F., Denney, C.F., Burns, D.K. (1998) Systemic calciphylaxis associated with massive gastrointestinal hemorrhage. *Arch Pathol Lab Med*, **122**, 656–659.
17. Oh, D.H., Eulau, D., Tokugawa, D.A. et al (1999) Five cases of calciphylaxis and a review of the literature. *J Am Acad Dermatol*, **40**, 979–987.
18. Essary, L.R., Wick, M.R. (2000) Cutaneous calciphylaxis: an underrecognized clinicopathologic entity. *Am J Clin Pathol*, **113**, 280–287.
19. Goyal, S., Huhn, M.M., Provost, T.T. (2000) Calciphylaxis in a patient without renal failure or elevated parathyroid hormone: possible etiological role of chemotherapy. *Br J Dermatol*, **143**, 1087–1090.
20. Sato, N., Teramura, T., Ishiyama, T. et al (2001) Fulminant and relentless cutaneous necrosis with excruciating pain caused by calciphylaxis developing in a patient undergoing peritoneal dialysis. *J Dermatol*, **28**, 27–31.
21. Kim, Y.J., Chung, B.S., Choi, K.C. (2001) Calciphylaxis in a patient with end-stage renal disease. *J Dermatol*, **28**, 272–275.
22. Pantanowitz, L., Harton, A., Bechwith, B. (2001) Cutaneous gangrene in a renal dialysis patient. *Postgrad Med J*, **77**, 741–742.
23. Filosa, G., Bugatti, L., Nicolini, M. et al (2001) Calciphylaxis in two patients with end-stage renal disease. *J Eur Acad Dermatol Venereol*, **15**, 461–464.
24. Senturk, S., HoSnuter, M., Tosun, Z. et al (2002) Calciphylaxis: cutaneous necrosis in chronic renal failure. *Ann Plast Surg*, **48**, 104–105.
25. Nikko, A.P., Dunningan, M., Cockerell, C.J. (1995) Calciphylaxis with histological changes of pseudoxanthoma elasticum. *Am J Dermatopathol*, **18**, 396–399.
26. Solomon, A.R., Comite, S.L., Headington, J.T. (1988) Epidermal and follicular calciphylaxis. *J Cutan Pathol*, **15**, 282–283.

Crystal-storing histiocytosis

Clinical features

Crystal-storing histiocytosis is an extremely rare condition which has been described in patients with lymphoplasmacytic neoplasms associated with kappa light chain monoclonal gammopathy including lymphoplasmacytic lymphoma (immunocytoma), monoclonal gammopathy of uncertain significance, multiple myeloma, extramedullary plasmacytoma, maltoma and large cell B-cell lymphoma.[1–3] Primary cutaneous involvement is exceptional and the literature on this aspect is limited to only three case reports.[4–6] These patients presented with erythematous asymptomatic subcutaneous nodules and tumors (*Fig. 9.71*).

Histological features

The condition is characterized by the presence of histiocytes containing eosinophilic crystals which have been likened to Gaucher cells (pseudo-Gaucher cells) admixed with lymphoma cells (*Fig. 9.72*).[3] The crystals are variably polygonal to rhomboid or needle-shaped and stain

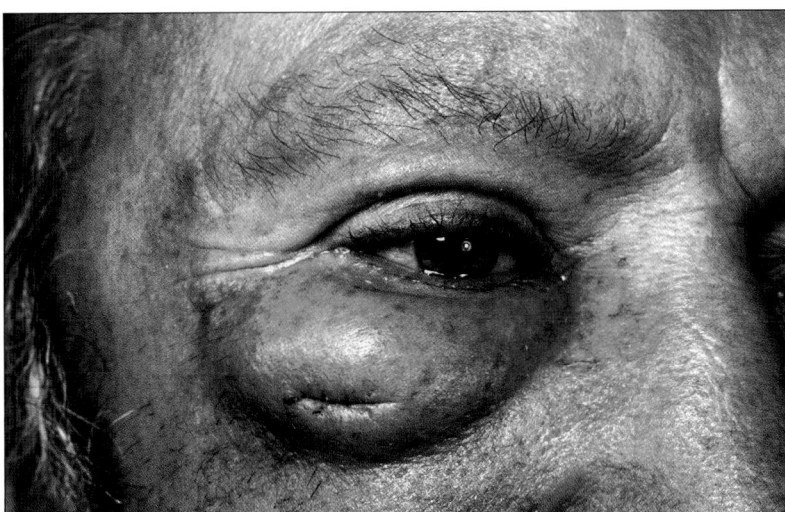

Fig. 9.71
Crystal-storing histiocytosis: this patient presented with marked swelling of the face and the eyelids. From Jenkins, R.E. et al (1994) *Archives of Dermatology*, **130**, 484–488, by courtesy of the editor of *Archives of Dermatology*.

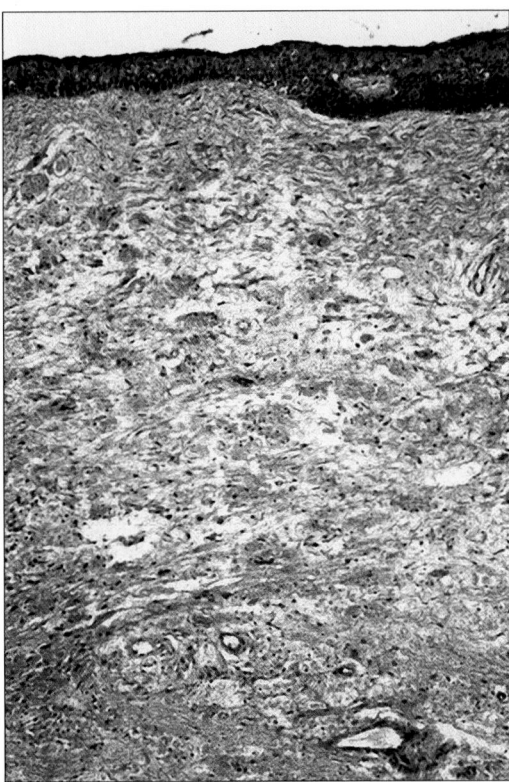

Fig. 9.72
Crystal-storing histiocytosis: within the dermis are large histiocytes with abundant eosinophilic cytoplasm.

positively with PAS and phosphotungstic acid hematoxylin (*Fig. 9.73*).[4,5] Erythrophagocytosis may also be evident.[3]

The histiocytes express CD68, and sometimes immunoglobulin heavy and light chains may be stained weakly.[3]

Ultrastructurally, the crystals are sometimes membrane bound (of lysosomal derivation) and display plate-like, rectangular, trapezoid and rhomboid features with a distinct hexagonal lattice structure.[3–5] The tumor cells may also contain intracytoplasmic crystals.[3]

References

1. Kapadia, S.B., Enzinger, F.M., Heffner, D.K. et al (1993) Crystal-storing histiocytosis associated with lymphoplasmacytic neoplasms. *Am J Surg Pathol*, **17**, 461–467.
2. Yamamoto, T., Hishida, A., Honda, N. et al (1991) Crystal-storing histiocytosis and crystalline tissue deposition in multiple myeloma. *Arch Pathol Lab Med*, **115**, 351–354.
3. Lebeau, A., Zeindl-Eberhart, E., Muller, E.C. et al (2002) Generalized crystal-storing histiocytosis associated with monoclonal gammopathy: molecular analysis of a disorder with rapid clinical course and review of the literature. *Blood*, **100**, 1817–1827.
4. Jenkins, R.E., Calonje, E., Fawcett, H. et al (1994) Cutaneous crystalline deposits in myeloma. *Arch Dermatol*, **130**, 484–488.
5. Kaufmann, O., Hansen, A., Deicke, P. et al (1996) Subcutaneous crystal-storing histiocytosis associated with lymphoplasmacytic lymphoma (immunocytoma). *Pathol Res Pract*, **192**, 1148–1151.
6. Harada, M., Shimada, M., Fukayama, M. et al (1996) Crystal-storing histiocytosis associated with lymphoplasmacytic lymphoma mimicking Weber–Christian disease: immunohistochemical, ultrastructural and gene rearrangement studies. *Hum Pathol*, **27**, 84–87.

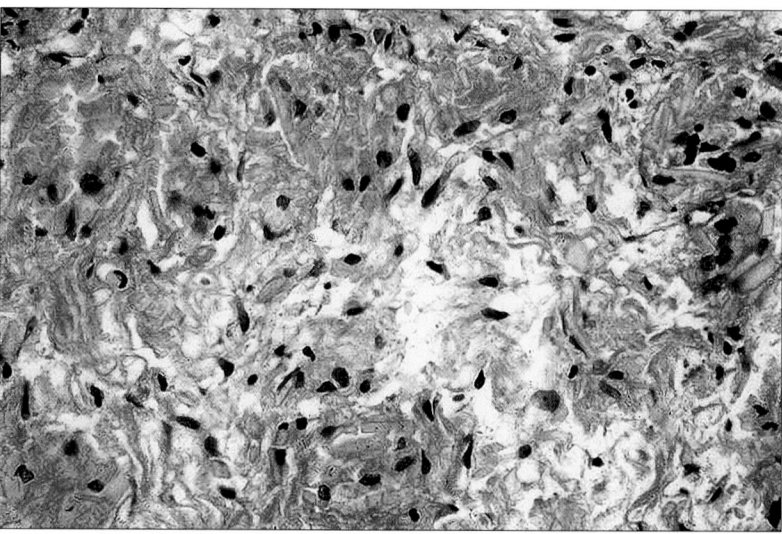

Fig. 9.73
Crystal-storing histiocytosis: the cytoplasm contains large eosinophilic crystals.

Gouty panniculitis

There are very occasional reports of gout presenting as a crystalline lobular panniculitis.[1,2] This topic is discussed in depth on page 590.

References

1. Niemi, K.M. (1977) Panniculitis of the legs with urate crystal deposition. *Arch Dermatol*, **113**, 655–656.
2. LeBoit, P.E., Schneider, S. (1987) Gout presenting as a lobular panniculitis. *Am J Dermatopathol*, **9**, 334–338.

Nodular vasculitis

Clinical features

Nodular vasculitis (erythema induratum) is a rare condition which usually presents in young or middle-aged women, often with an erythrocyanotic circulation.[1] Males are only rarely affected.[2] Patients present with painful, tender, violaceous, indurated nodules particularly affecting the calves although the shins, feet, ankles, thighs and upper limbs may sometimes be involved (*Figs 9.74, 9.75*). Lesions are often bilateral and the overweight with fat calves are most often affected. Seasonal variation has been noted with an increased incidence being recorded in the cold winter months. Skin lesions often recur over many years. Ulceration is common and scarring with hyperpigmentation frequently accompanies healing (*Figs 9.76–9.78*).

In those cases that represent a manifestation of underlying tuberculosis, the term erythema induratum (Bazin's disease) is frequently applied. In this condition, there is invariable hypersensitivity to intradermal injection of purified protein derivative (PPD) at a dilution of 1:10,000 and a complete clearing of all skin lesions following treatment with antituberculous chemotherapy.[3–6]

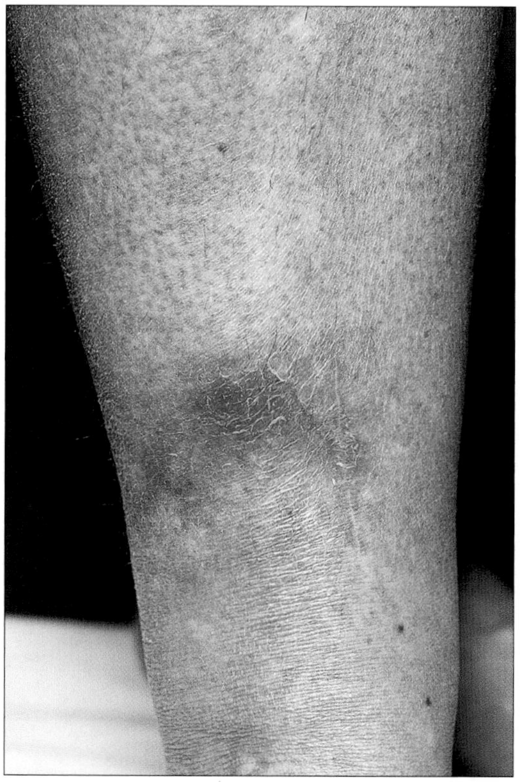

Fig. 9.74
Nodular vasculitis: early lesion presenting as an erythematous nodule on the calf of a middle-aged female. By courtesy of M.M. Black, MD, St Thomas' Hospital, London, UK.

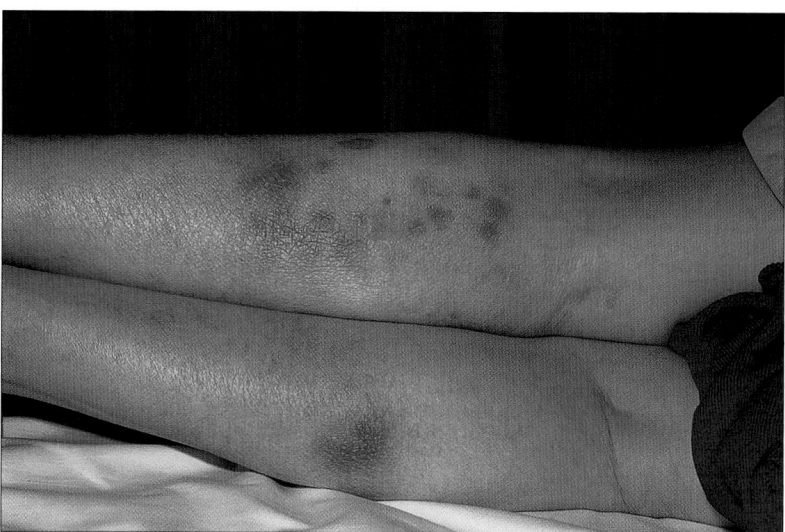

Fig. 9.75
Nodular vasculitis: typical bilateral involvement of the calves. By courtesy of the Institute of Dermatology, London, UK.

Pathogenesis and histological features

The relationship between erythema induratum and nodular vasculitis has for many decades been the subject of controversy. Similarly the association of the former condition with an underlying tuberculous infection has been the subject of prolonged debate.

As outlined above, the more recent literature gives considerable support to the notion that occult tuberculosis is present in many patients with erythema induratum and that the two terms are, therefore, synonymous in a substantial proportion of cases. Thus, erythema induratum may be associated with evidence of active tuberculosis.[7–9] Although cultures of lesions are invariably negative, the more recent demonstration of mycobacterium tuberculosis DNA by PCR in lesional tissue adds strong additional support to the proposal of an underlying tuberculous etiology.[10–16]

Nodular vasculitis can, therefore, be regarded as a hypersensitivity reaction in which mycobacterial antigens are one important cause. Immune complex and delayed hypersensitivity mechanisms have both been proposed.[13] Other predisposing factors for this condition have not yet generally been identified although nodular vasculitis has been described in association with acute myeloid leukemia, chronic hepatitis C infection and as an adverse drug reaction associated with propylthiouracil.[17–20]

The histological features combine septal and lobular changes, with the presence of vasculitis being a diagnostic sine qua non (*Fig. 9.79*).

In a biopsy from an established lesion, the septa are widened and chronically inflamed (*Fig. 9.80*). Acute vasculitis (affecting veins and venules) with a heavy inflammatory cell infiltrate consisting of neutrophils, lymphocytes and histiocytes is typically present, sometimes accompanied by vessel wall necrosis and thrombosis (*Fig. 9.81*).

Occasionally, septal granulomatous inflammation may also be evident.

Lobular inflammation may occasionally be limited to a focal element adjacent to an acutely inflamed vessel.[21] More frequently, however, it

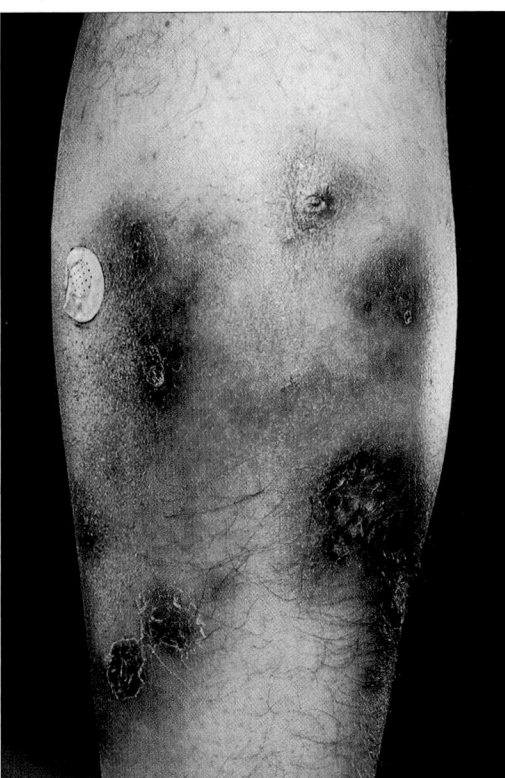

Fig. 9.78
Nodular vasculitis: multiple scarred lesions. Note the marked hyperpigmentation. By courtesy of the Institute of Dermatology, London, UK.

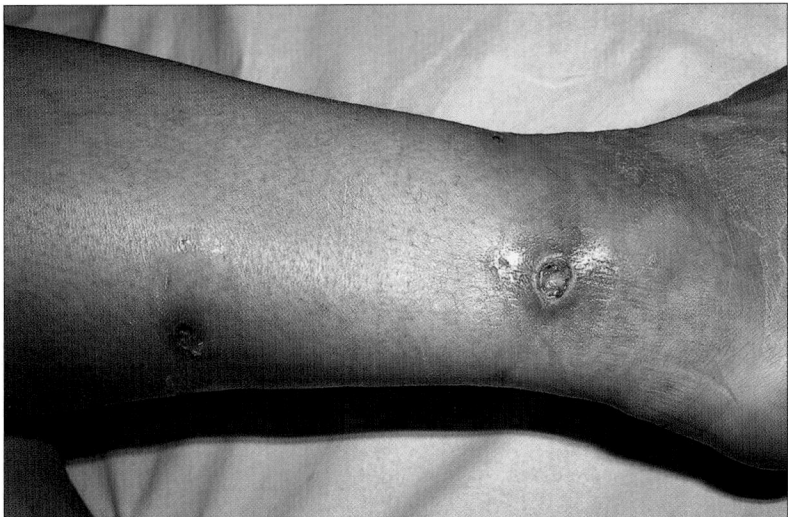

Fig. 9.76
Nodular vasculitis: the nodules frequently ulcerate. By courtesy of R.A. Marsden, MD, St George's Hospital, London, UK.

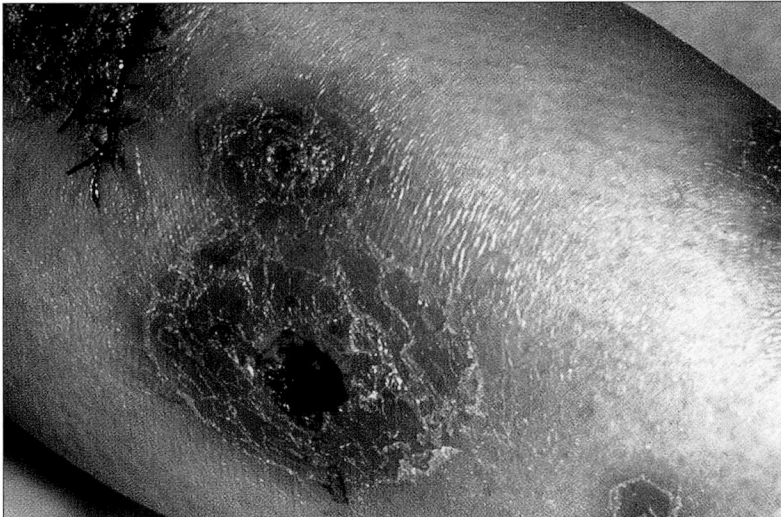

Fig. 9.77
Nodular vasculitis: in this severely affected patient ulcerated lesions are present on the shins in addition to the calves. By courtesy of R.A. Marsden, MD, St George's Hospital, London, UK.

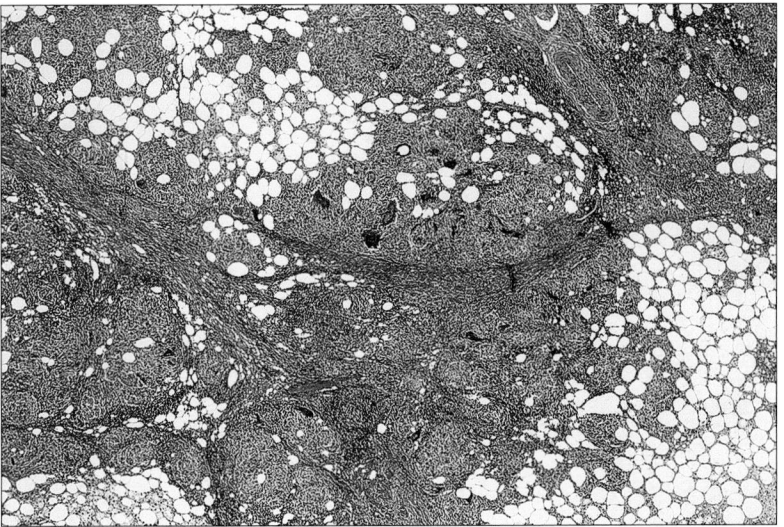

Fig. 9.79
Nodular vasculitis: note the distinct nodules of granulomatous inflammation at the periphery of the lobule.

presents as nodular lesions scattered throughout the whole lobule or affecting multiple lobules. Fat necrosis is invariably present and is often florid. The features are varied and range from typical lipophagic fat necrosis to coagulative or more rarely caseation-like necrosis (*Figs 9.82, 9.83*).[22] Neutrophils, lymphocytes and histiocytes with xanthomatized forms are typically seen. Granulomata are often present and giant cells of both foreign body and Langerhans' type are frequently a feature (*Fig. 9.84*).

In biopsies from chronic or resolving lesions, fibrosis of both the septa and lobules is often present. Giant cells and granulomata may still be present.

Differential diagnosis

Due to the frankly granulomatous nature of the histology, it is mandatory to exclude infective causes of panniculitis, particularly mycobacterial and fungal infections, including cryptococcosis, mycetoma, chromomycosis, sporotrichosis and aspergillosis. Subcutaneous sarcoidosis should also be considered, although in this condition granulomata are also seen in the dermis. Asteroid inclusions and Schaumann bodies, both features of sarcoidosis (see below), are not characteristic of erythema induratum.

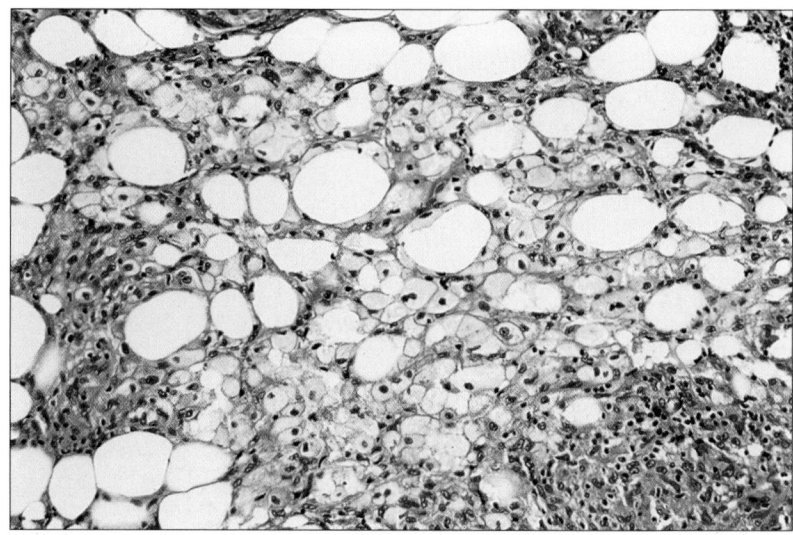

Fig. 9.82
Nodular vasculitis: note the presence of numerous lipophages.

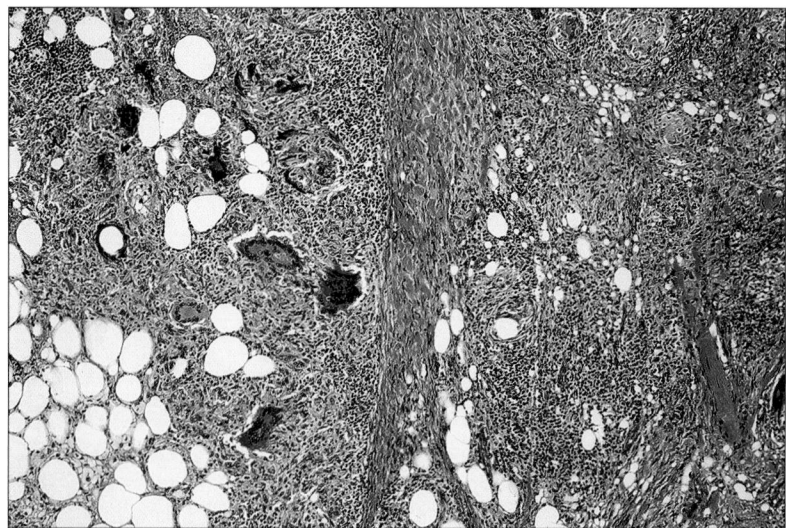

Fig. 9.80
Nodular vasculitis: well-formed epithelioid granulomata and multinucleate giant cells are present.

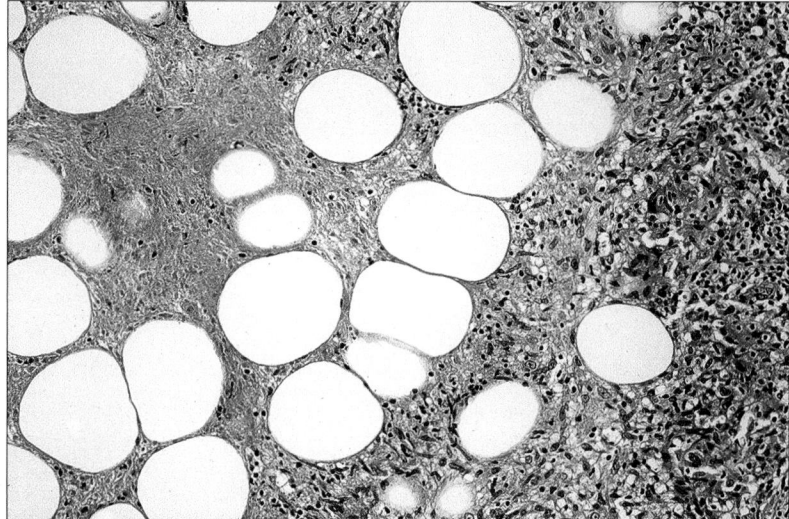

Fig. 9.83
Nodular vasculitis: the eosinophilic necrotic debris reminiscent of caseation is a typical feature.

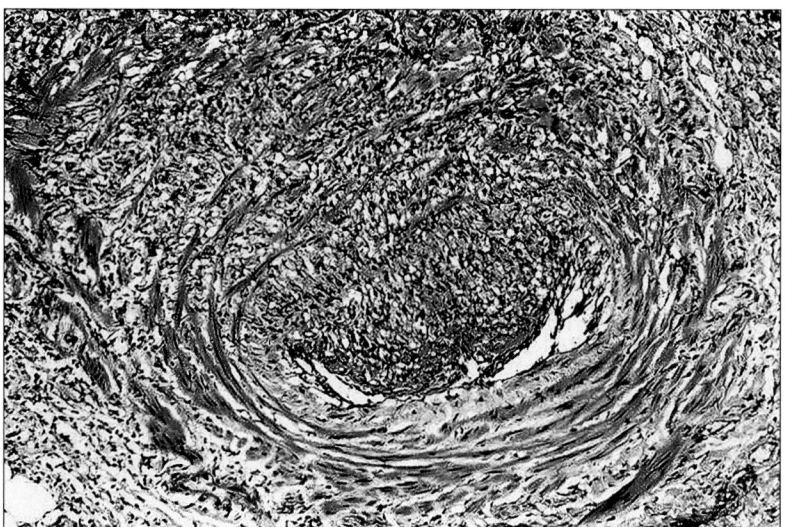

Fig. 9.81
Nodular vasculitis: vascular involvement as seen in this field is a characteristic feature.

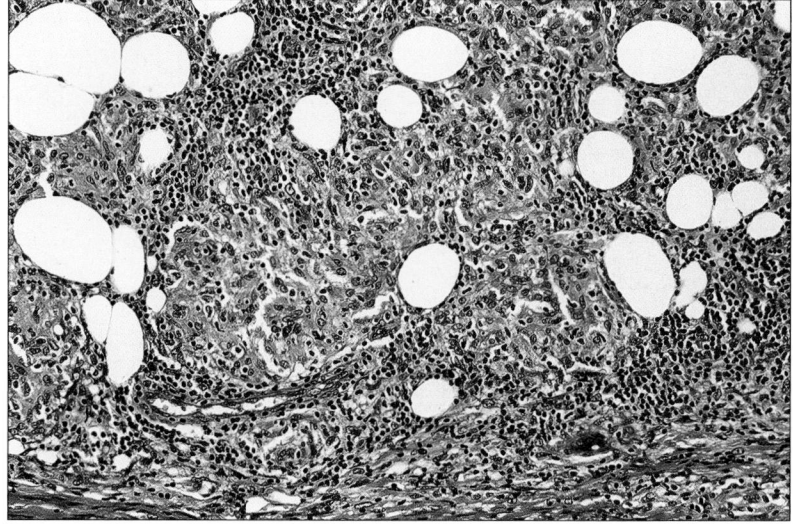

Fig. 9.84
Nodular vasculitis: granulomata may be seen within the lobule and also in the septa.

References

1. Radermaker, M., Lowe, D.G., Munro, D.D. (1989) Erythema induratum (Bazin's disease). *J Am Acad Dermatol*, **21**, 740–745.
2. Montgomery, H., O'Leary, P.A., Barker, N.W. (1945) Nodular vascular diseases of the legs. *JAMA*, **128**, 335–341.
3. Van der Lugt, L. (1965) Some remarks about tuberculosis of the skin and tuberculids. *Dermatologica*, **131**, 266–275.
4. Cho, K.H., Lee, D.Y., Chun, H.S. et al (1995) Erythema induratum with pulmonary tuberculosis: a report of three cases. *J Dermatol*, **22**, 143–148.
5. Kuramoto, Y., Aiba, S., Tagami, H. (1990) Erythema induratum of Bazin as a type of tuberculid. *J Am Acad Dermatol*, **22**, 612–616.
6. Ollert, M.W., Thomas, P., Korting, H.C. et al. (1993) Erythema induratum of Bazin: evidence of T-lymphocyte hyperresponsiveness to purified protein derivative of tuberculin: report of two cases and treatment. *Arch Dermatol*, **129**, 469–473.
7. Fernandez del Moral, R., Ereño, C., Arrinda, J.M. et al (1994) Erythema induratum of Bazin and active renal tuberculosis. *J Am Acad Dermatol*, **31**, 288–290.
8. Boonchai, W., Suthipinittharm, P., Mahaisavariya, P. (1998) Panniculitis in tuberculosis: a clinicopathologic study of nodular panniculitis associated with tuberculosis. *Int J Dermatol*, **37**, 361–363.
9. Del Moral, R.F., Ereño, C., Arrinda, J.M. et al (1994) Erythema induratum of Bazin and active renal tuberculosis. *J Am Acad Dermatol*, **31**, 288–290.
10. Degitz, K., Messer, G., Schirren, H. et al (1993). Successful treatment of erythema induratum of Bazin following rapid detection of mycobacterial DNA by polymerase chain reaction. *Arch Dermatol*, **129**, 1619–1620.
11. Schneider, J.W., Jordaan, H.F., Geiger, D.H. et al (1995) Erythema induratum of Bazin. A clinicopathological study of 20 cases and detection of Mycobacterium tuberculosis DNA in skin lesions by polymerase chain reaction. *Am J Dermatopathol*, **17**, 357–361.
12. Degitz, K. (1996) Detection of mycobacterial DNA in the skin: etiologic insights and diagnostic perspectives. *Arch Dermatol*, **132**, 71–75.
13. Schneider, J.W., Geiger, D.H., Rossouw, D.J. et al (1993) Mycobacterium tuberculosis DNA in erythema induratum of Bazin. *Lancet*, **342**, 747–748.
14. Baselga, E., Margall, N., Barnadas, M.A. et al (1997) Detection of Mycobacterium tuberculosis DNA in lobular granulomatous panniculitis (erythema induratum–nodular vasculitis). *Arch Dermatol*, **133**, 457–462.
15. Wang, T-C., Tzen, C-Y., Su, H-Y. (2000) Erythema induratum associated with tuberculosis lymphadenitis: analysis of a case using polymerase chain reactions with different primer pairs to differentiate Bacille Calmette–Guérin (BCG) from virulent strains of Mycobacterium tuberculosis complex. *J Dermatol*, **27**, 717–723.
16. Lee, Y.S., Lee, S.W., Lee, J.R. et al (2001) Erythema induratum with pulmonary tuberculosis: histopathologic features resembling true vasculitis. *Int J Dermatol*, **40**, 193–196.
17. Yeung, C.K., Au, W.Y., Trendal-Smith, N. et al (2001) Panniculitis heralding blastic transformation of myelofibrosis. *Br J Dermatol*, **144**, 905–906.
18. Cardinali, C., Gerlini, G., Caproni, M. et al (2000) Hepatitis C virus: a common triggering factor in nodular vasculitis and Sjögren's syndrome. *Br J Dermatol*, **142**, 187–189.
19. Ural, I., Erel, A., Ozenirler, S. et al (2002) Nodular vasculitis associated with chronic hepatitis C. *J Eur Acad Dermatol Venereol*, **16**, 298–299.
20. Wolf, D., Ben-Yehuda, A., Oken, E. et al (1992) Nodular vasculitis associated with propylthiouracil therapy. *Cutis*, **49**, 253–255.
21. Schneider, J.W., Jordaan, H.F. (1997) The histopathologic spectrum of erythema induratum of Bazin. *Am J Dermatopathol*, **19**, 323–333.
22. Requena L., Sánchez-Yus, E. (2001) Panniculitis. Part II. Mostly lobular panniculitis. *J Am Acad Dermatol*, **45**, 325–361.

Subcutaneous sarcoidosis

Clinical features

Involvement of subcutaneous fat in patients with sarcoidosis is rarely encountered by histopathologists even though it may occur in as many as 1.4% of all patients with this disease.[1] Most often it presents as asymptomatic or tender, flesh-colored to erythematous, subcutaneous nodules principally affecting the extremities although a more generalized distribution has also been documented.[2–6] Exceptionally, subcutaneous involvement may be the initial or even the only feature of sarcoidosis.[4] More commonly, however, subcutaneous lesions are associated with visceral disease, particularly bilateral hilar lymphadenopathy. Subcutaneous sarcoidosis shows a predilection for females and the majority of patients are in the fifth and sixth decades.[4] Sarcoidosis is discussed in detail on page 287.

Histological features

The changes, which predominantly involve the lobule, consist of well-formed, non-caseating granulomata, sometimes associated with fibrosis, which may extend into the septa. Typically, the granulomata are of the 'naked' type, i.e. devoid of a peripheral rim of lymphocytes, and giant cells of both foreign body and Langerhans' types are usually present. Exceptionally, caseation and calcification have been described.[7,8]

Differential diagnosis

Subcutaneous sarcoidosis is a diagnosis of exclusion; other causes of granulomatous inflammation – including mycobacterial and fungal infections, foreign body reactions and so-called 'metastatic Crohn's disease' – must be considered in the differential diagnosis.[9]

References

1. Scadding, J.G. (1967) Sarcoidosis. London: Eyre & Spottiswoode.
2. Vainsencher, D., Winkelman, R.K. (1984) Subcutaneous sarcoidosis. *Arch Dermatol*, **120**, 1028–1031.
3. Ruiz de Erenchun, F., Vazquez-Doval, F.J., Idoate, M. et al (1992) Subcutaneous nodules as the first clinical manifestation of sarcoidosis. *Clin Exp Dermatol*, **17**, 192–194.
4. Higgins, E.M., Salisbury, J.R., Du Vivier, A.W.P. (1993) Subcutaneous sarcoidosis. *Clin Exp Dermatol*, **18**, 65–66.
5. Shidrawi, R.G., Paradinas, F., Murray-Lyon, I.M. (1994) Sarcoidosis presenting as multiple subcutaneous nodules. *Clin Exp Dermatol*, **19**, 356–358.
6. Curco, N., Pagerols, X., Vives, P. (1995) Subcutaneous sarcoidosis with dactylitis. *Clin Exp Dermatol*, **20**, 434–435.
7. Kuramoto, Y., Shindo, Y., Tagami, H. (1988) Subcutaneous sarcoidosis with extensive caseation necrosis. *J Cutan Pathol*, **15**, 88–90.
8. Kroll, J.J., Shapiro, L., Koplon, B.S. et al (1972) Subcutaneous sarcoidosis with calcification. *Arch Dermatol*, **106**, 84–85.
9. Shum, D.T., Guenther, L. (1990) Metastatic Crohn's disease: case report and review of the literature. *Arch Dermatol*, **126**, 645–648.

Neutrophilic lobular panniculitis associated with rheumatoid arthritis

Clinical features

Also known as pustular panniculitis, this rarely described entity has only been documented in middle-aged females who have presented with painful nodules predominantly affecting the lower legs.[1–5] Blister formation, pustulation, ulceration and discharge of oily, necrotic debris may occur.[3–5]

Pathogenesis and histological features

The pathogenesis may be related to circulating immune complexes since high levels have been identified in patients with this condition.[3,4]

The lobules and septa are infiltrated by neutrophils with central lobular necrosis accompanied by a histiocytic and giant cell response.[2–5] Small numbers of eosinophils are sometimes present.[4] Nuclear dust can be conspicuous and cyst formation with membranous change has been described.[4,5] Leukocytoclastic vasculitis affecting the dermal arterioles and venules may be seen.[4]

Differential diagnosis

Factitial disease and infections must always be excluded in neutrophil-rich panniculitides. Similarly, pancreatic disease-associated panniculitis and α_1-antitrypsin deficiency-associated panniculitis are typically linked with a lobular neutrophil-rich infiltrate. The lobular panniculitis associated with bowel bypass is also typically neutrophil rich.[6,7]

References

1. Yaffee, H.S. (1955) A peculiar nodosity associated with arthritis. *US Armed Forces Med J*, **6**, 1043–1052.
2. Newton, J., Wojnarowska, F.T. (1988) Pustular panniculitis in rheumatoid arthritis. *Br J Dermatol*, **119**, 97–98.
3. Anstey, A., Wilkinson, J.D., Wojnarowska, F. et al (1991) Pustular panniculitis in rheumatoid arthritis. *J R Soc Med*, **84**, 307–308.
4. Kuniyuki, S., Shindow, K., Tanaka, T. (1997) Pustular panniculitis in a patient with rheumatoid arthritis. *Int J Dermatol*, **36**, 292–293.
5. Tran, T-A.N., DuPree, M., Carlson, J.A. (1999) Neutrophilic lobular (pustular) panniculitis associated with rheumatoid arthritis: a case report and review of the literature. *Am J Dermatopathol*, **21**, 247–252.
6. Williams, H.J., Samuelson, C.O., Zone, J.J. (1979) Nodular nonsuppurative panniculitis associated with jejunoileal bypass surgery. *Arch Dermatol*, **115**, 1091–1093.
7. Kennedy, C. (1981) The spectrum of inflammatory skin disease following jejuno-ileal bypass for morbid obesity. *Br J Dermatol*, **105**, 425–435.

Eosinophilic panniculitis

Clinical features

Eosinophilic panniculitis is not a disease in its own right, but represents a reaction pattern that may be found under a variety of circumstances.[1] It is seen more often in females than males (3:1). Although a wide age range is affected, there are two peaks: one in the third decade and one in the sixth decade and above. Patients present predominantly with nodules and plaques, although papules and pustules are sometimes seen.[2–4] Lesions, which may be single or multiple, affect the legs, arms, trunk and face in decreasing order of frequency.

Eosinophilic panniculitis may be found in association with erythema nodosum, immune complex-mediated vasculitis, atopic dermatitis, refractory anemia, chronic recurrent parotitis, artifact, leukocytoclastic vasculitis, drug reactions, eosinophilic cellulitis, insect bites, toxocariasis, gnathostomiasis, Fasciola infection, injection site reactions and in patients with lymphoma.[5–15] Other than in those patients with an associated neoplasm, eosinophilic panniculitis appears to be a self-limiting and benign condition.[6]

Histological features

The histological features affect the lobules and the septa and are characterized by an intense infiltrate of eosinophils, which may be accompanied by variable numbers of other inflammatory cells including neutrophils, lymphocytes and monocytes (*Figs 9.85, 9.86*). Fat necrosis is sometimes present. On occasions typical 'flame figures', as seen in eosinophilic cellulitis, may be noted (*Fig. 9.87*). The changes sometimes extend into the reticular dermis and occasionally the underlying fascia is involved.

References

1. Peters, M.S., Su, W.P.D. (1992) Panniculitis. *Dermatol Clin*, **10**, 37–57.
2. Samlaska, C.P., De Lorimier, A.J., Heldman, L.S. (1995) Eosinophilic panniculitis. *Pediatr Dermatol*, **12**, 35–38.
3. Adame, J., Cohen, P.R. (1996) Eosinophilic panniculitis: diagnostic considerations and evaluation. *J Am Acad Dermatol*, **34**, 229–234.
4. Winkelmann, R.K., Frigas, E. (1986) Eosinophilic panniculitis: a clinicopathologic study. *J Cutan Pathol*, **13**, 1–12.
5. Rook, A., Staughton, R. (1972) The cutaneous manifestations of toxocariasis. *Dermatologica*, **144**, 129–143.
6. Burket, J.M., Burket, B.J. (1985) Eosinophilic cellulitis. *J Am Acad Dermatol*, **12**, 161–164.
7. Ollague, W., Ollague, J., Guevara de Veliz, A. et al (1984) Human gnathostomiasis in Ecuador (nodular migratory eosinophilic panniculitis): first finding of the parasite in South America. *Int J Dermatol*, **23**, 647–651.
8. Ruiz-Maldonado, R., Mosqueda-Cabrera, M.A. (1999) Human gnathostomiasis (nodular migratory eosinophilic panniculitis). *Int J Dermatol*, **38**, 56–57.
9. Rusnak, J.M., Lucey, D.R. (1993) Clinical gnathostomiasis: case report and review of the English language literature. *Clin Infect Dis*, **16**, 33–50.
10. Glass, L.A., Zaghloul, A.B., Solomon, A.R. (1989) Eosinophilic panniculitis is associated with chronic recurrent parotitis. *Am J Dermatopathol*, **11**, 555–559.
11. Marullo, S., Dallot, A., Carelier-Balloy, B. et al (1989) Subcutaneous eosinophilic necrosis with refractory anemia with an excess of myeloblasts. *J Am Acad Dermatol*, **20**, 320–323.
12. Acland, K.M., Churchyard, A., Fletcher, C.L. et al (1998) Panniculitis in association with apomorphine infusion. *Br J Dermatol*, **138**, 480–482.
13. Gómez Rodríguez, N., Ortiz-Rey, J.A., de la Fuente Buceta, A. et al (2001) Auto-induced eosinophilic panniculitis: a diagnostic dilemma. *Ann Med Interne*, **18**, 635–637.
14. Nakayama, F. (1997) Panniculitis with eosinophilic infiltration due to gabexate mesilate (FOY): possibility of allergic reaction. *J Dermatol*, **24**, 235–242.
15. Pérez, C., Vives, R., Montes, M. et al (2000) Recurrent eosinophilic panniculitis associated with Fasciola hepatica infection. *J Am Acad Dermatol*, **42**, 900–902.

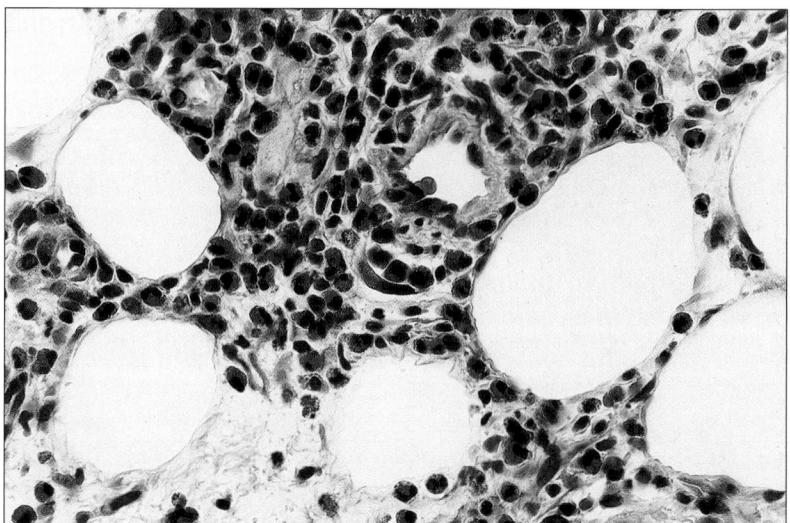

Fig. 9.86
Eosinophilic panniculitis: note the massive eosinophilic infiltrate.

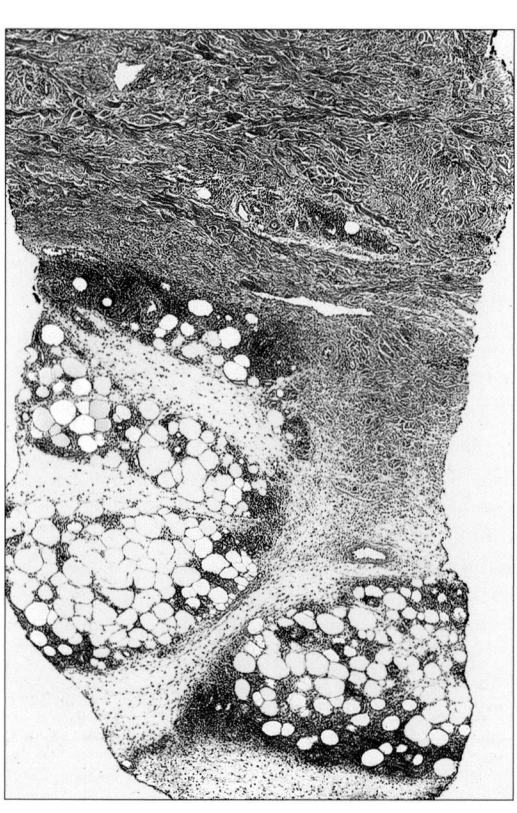

Fig. 9.85
Eosinophilic panniculitis: there is a heavy, predominantly lobular inflammatory cell infiltrate.

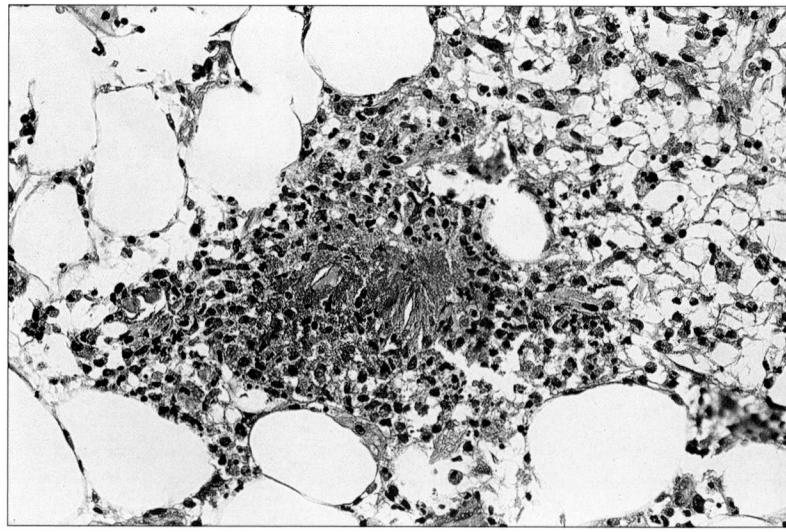

Fig. 9.87
Eosinophilic panniculitis: note the flame figure in the center of the field.

Infective panniculitis

Clinical features

The clinical features in patients with infective panniculitis are not specific and include nodules, ulcerated lesions, abscesses and erythema nodosum-like lesions.[1] Patients are usually, but not invariably, immunosuppressed. The legs and feet are the sites most often affected. Specific infections, which have presented with panniculitis, include *Histoplasma capsulatum*, *Pseudomonas aeruginosa*, *Candida albicans*, *Aspergillus* spp., *Mycobacterium avium intracellulare*, *Mycobacterium ulcerans*, *Mycobacterium marinum* and *Mycobacterium tuberculosis*.[2-12]

Histological features

Epidermal changes may include parakeratosis, acanthosis and spongiosis.[1] The dermis is edematous and often shows a perivascular and interstitial inflammatory cell infiltrate containing many neutrophils. Hemorrhage is sometimes present.

Most commonly, the subcutaneous fat shows features of a mixed septal/lobular panniculitis (*Figs 9.88–9.92*).[1] Erythema nodosum-like features may be evident.[1] Changes suggestive of an infective etiology include a prominent neutrophilic infiltrate, hemorrhage, basophilic necrosis and necrosis of sweat glands, vascular proliferation and discrete abscess formation.[1,13]

Granulomata are sometimes conspicuous in atypical mycobacterial infections. On other occasions acute inflammatory changes with abscess formation are seen (e.g. *Mycobacterium chelonei* infection). In the latter condition, organisms may be identified in microcysts lined by neutrophil polymorphs.[1] Mycobacterial infection may also occasionally manifest as phlebitis.[14] Deep fungal infections commonly involve the subcutaneous fat, presenting as granulomatous or mixed suppurative and granulomatous inflammatory processes.

From the above description, it is obvious that special stains for bacteria and fungi should be performed in all cases of panniculitis where the etiology is uncertain. Culture may also be necessary in some cases.

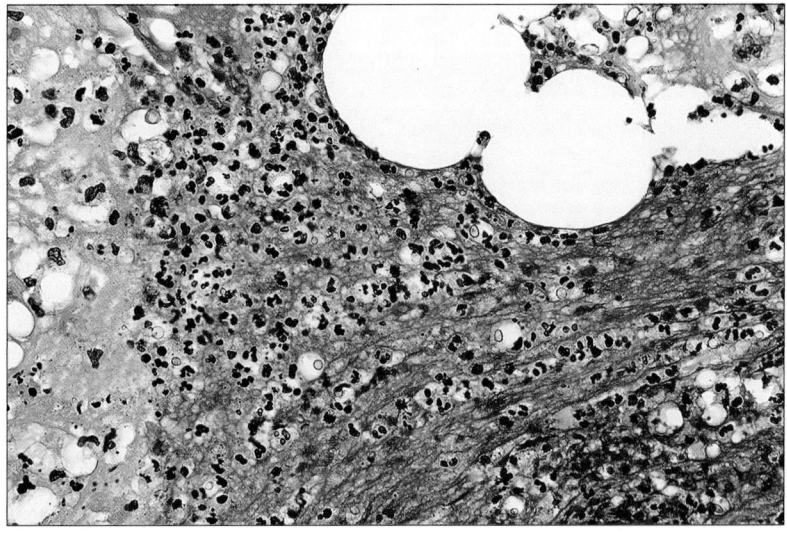

Fig. 9.89
Infective panniculitis: this example is due to cryptococcal infection. Note the typical yeast forms.

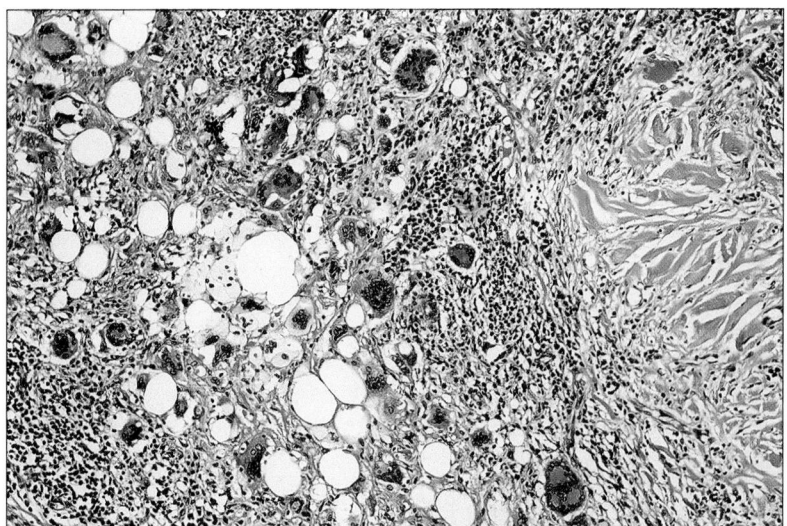

Fig. 9.90
Infective panniculitis: in this example, there is a granulomatous infiltrate.

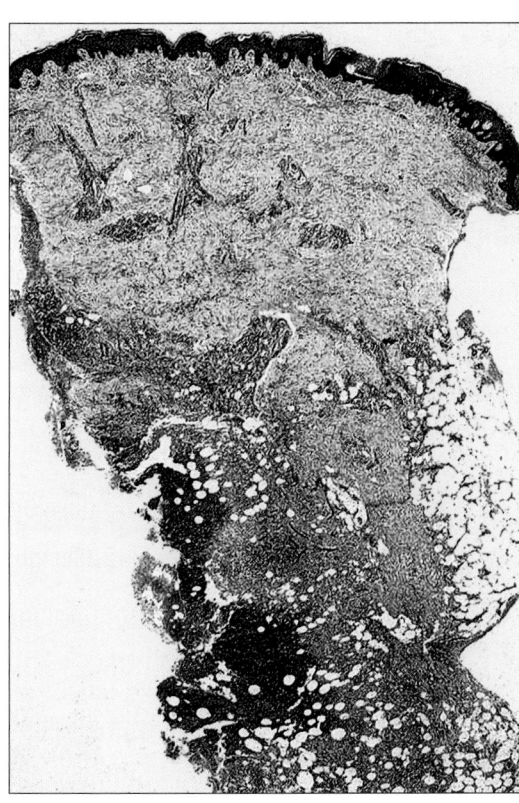

Fig. 9.88
Infective panniculitis: there is widespread fat necrosis with abscess formation.

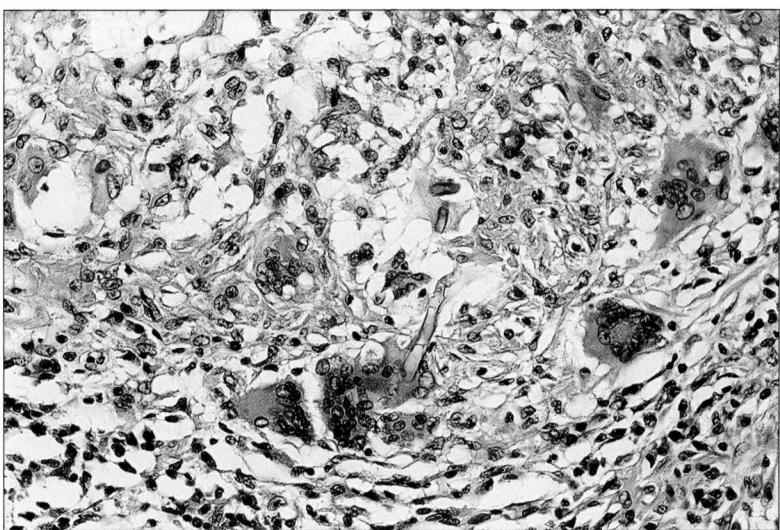

Fig. 9.91
Infective panniculitis: twisted hyphae typical of zygomycosis are present.

References

1. Patterson, J.W., Brown, P.C., Broecker, A.H. (1989) Infection-induced panniculitis. *J Cutan Pathol*, **16**, 183–193.
2. Abildgaard, W.H. Jr, Hargrove, R.H., Kalivas, J. (1985) Histoplasma panniculitis. *Arch Dermatol*, **121**, 914–916.
3. Ginter, G., Rieger, E., Soyer, H.P. et al (1993) Granulomatous panniculitis caused by *Candida albicans*: a case presenting with multiple leg ulcers. *J Am Acad Dermatol*, **28**, 315–317.
4. Murakawa, G.J., Harvell, J.D., Lubitz, P. et al (2000) Cutaneous aspergillosis and acquired immunodeficiency syndrome. *Arch Dermatol*, **136**, 365–369.
5. Bagel, J., Grossman, H.E. (1986) Subcutaneous nodules in Pseudomonas sepsis. *Am J Med*, **80**, 528–529.
6. Smith, R.A., Ross, J.S., Branfoot, C. (1995) Panniculitis with pseudomonas septicemia in AIDS. *J Eur Acad Dermatol Venereol*, **4**, 166–169.
7. Aleman, C.T., Wallace, M.L., Blaylock, W.K. et al (1999) Subcutaneous nodules caused by *P. aeruginosa* without sepsis. *Cutis*, **63**, 161–163.
8. Sanderson, T.L., Moskowitz, L., Henseley, G.T. et al (1982) Disseminated *Mycobacterium avium intracellulare* infection appearing as panniculitis. *Arch Pathol Lab Med*, **106**, 112–114.
9. Weir, E. (2002) Buruli ulcer: the third most common mycobacterial infection. *CMAJ*, **166**, 1691.
10. Zumla, A., Grange, J. (2002) Infection and disease caused by environmental mycobacteria. *Curr Opin Pulm Med*, **8**, 166–172.
11. Larson, K., Glanz, S., Bergfeld, W.F. (1989) Neutrophilic panniculitis caused by *Mycobacterium marinum*. *J Cutan Pathol*, **16**, 315.
12. Langenberg, A., Egbert, B. (1993) Neutrophilic tuberculous panniculitis in a patient with polymyositis. *J Cutan Pathol*, **20**, 177–179.
13. Förström, L., Winkelmann, R.K. (1977) Acute panniculitis: a clinical and histopathologic study of 34 cases. *Arch Dermatol*, **113**, 909–917.
14. Santa Cruz, D.J., Strayer, D.S. (1982) The histologic spectrum of the cutaneous mycobacterioses. *Hum Pathol*, **13**, 485–495.

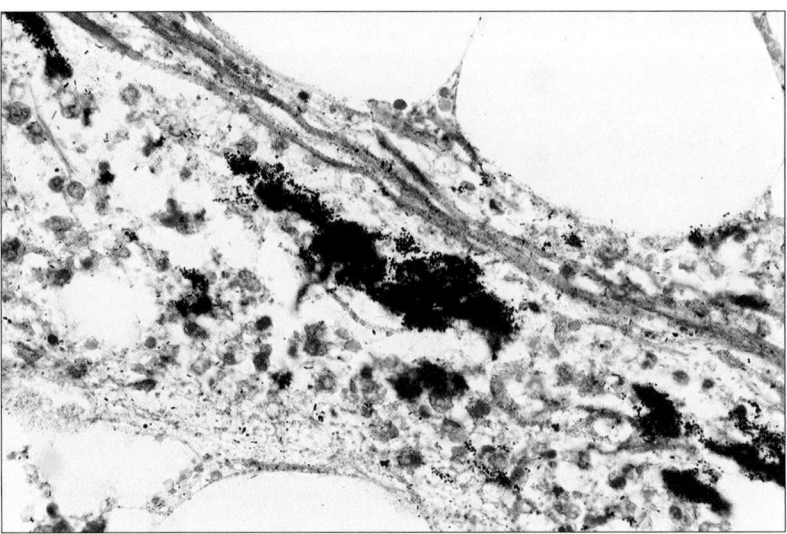

Fig. 9.92
Infective panniculitis: numerous cocci are present in this section from a patient with necrotizing fasciitis.

Sclerosing panniculitis

Clinical features

Sclerosing panniculitis (stasis-associated sclerosing panniculitis, hypodermatitis sclerodermaformis, lipodermatosclerosis, lipomembranous change in chronic panniculitis) is a relatively common condition which most often develops in middle-aged or elderly, overweight females with a history of peripheral venous disease including varicose veins, thrombophlebitis and deep venous thrombosis.[1-7] Less often the condition follows arterial ischemia. Patients present with indurated, wood-like, sclerodermiform plaques affecting the lower legs in a stocking distribution and characteristically resembling an inverted bottle appearance (*Fig. 9.93*).[1,3] Often the changes are bilateral and symmetrical.[2] The overlying skin may show additional changes of venous stasis including atrophy, ulceration, hyperpigmentation and telangiectasia.

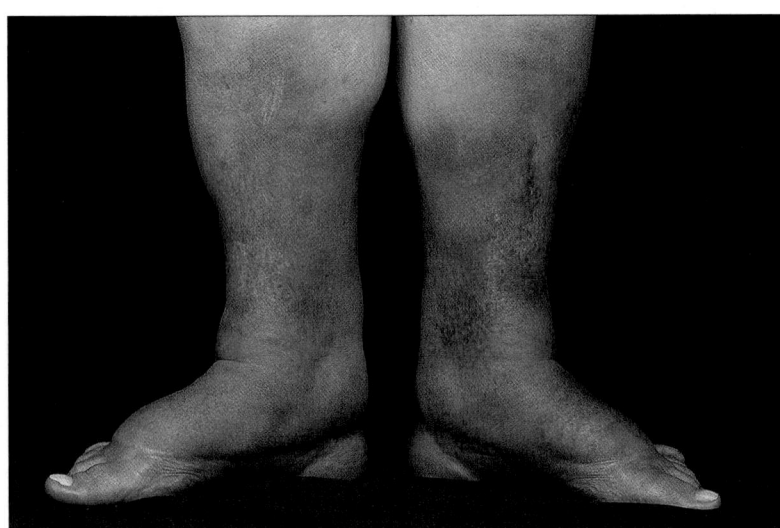

Fig. 9.93
Sclerosing panniculitis: the skin shows features of stasis. Dense fibrosis has resulted in this inverted bottle appearance. Note the characteristic symmetry. By courtesy of the Institute of Dermatology, London, UK.

Pathogenesis and histological features

The pathogenesis of sclerosing panniculitis is venous stasis within the centrilobular capillaries leading to ischemia and eventual infarction of the subcutaneous fat. Increased interstitial fibrinogen as a result of excessive capillary permeability due to venous hypertension is thought to be of importance.[4] Fibrin deposition around the dermal capillaries results in hypoxia. In addition, there is some evidence to suggest that increased matrix metalloproteinases and urokinase-type plasminogen activator may be of importance in the pathogenesis.[8,9]

The histological features are variable depending upon whether the biopsy represents an early stage in the development of this disorder or an established lesion.[5]

Within the subcutaneous fat, early lesions are characterized by centrilobular ischemia with infarction of fat cells and vascular congestion/hemorrhage.[5] Vascular thrombosis may also be seen but there is no evidence of vasculitis. A lymphocytic infiltrate is present in the septa and this may spill over to affect the edge of the lobule. Hemosiderin deposition is commonly present.

In established lesions, ischemic changes may still be evident but more often there is microcystic change with hyalinization with the fat lobule (*Figs 9.94–9.96*). Membranous fat necrosis is often present and lipophagic changes may be evident. Septal scarring is present, which in advanced lesions can be marked with resultant atrophy of the subcutaneous fat.

The dermis typically shows the features of stasis including chronic inflammation, fibrosis, vessel-wall thickening, lobular capillary proliferation and hemosiderin deposition. Acanthosis, spongiosis and lichenification may be evident.

Differential diagnosis

The absence of sclerodermiform dermal changes and the presence of features of venous stasis distinguish end-stage sclerosing panniculitis from morphea profunda, scleroderma and acrodermatitis chronica atrophicans (a late manifestation of Lyme disease).

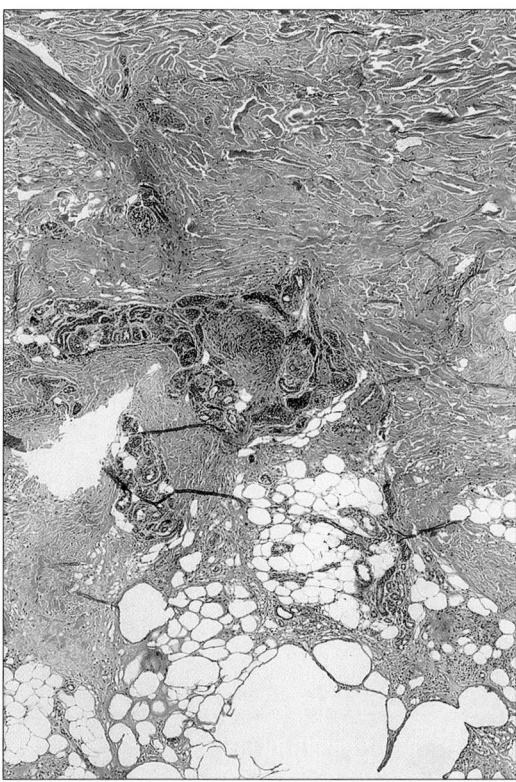

Fig. 9.94
Sclerosing panniculitis: there is typical microcystic change.

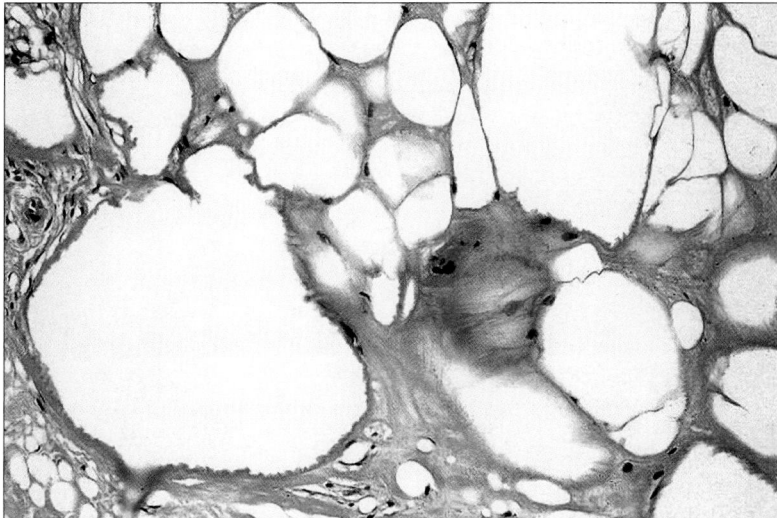

Fig. 9.95
Sclerosing panniculitis: close-up view of microcysts.

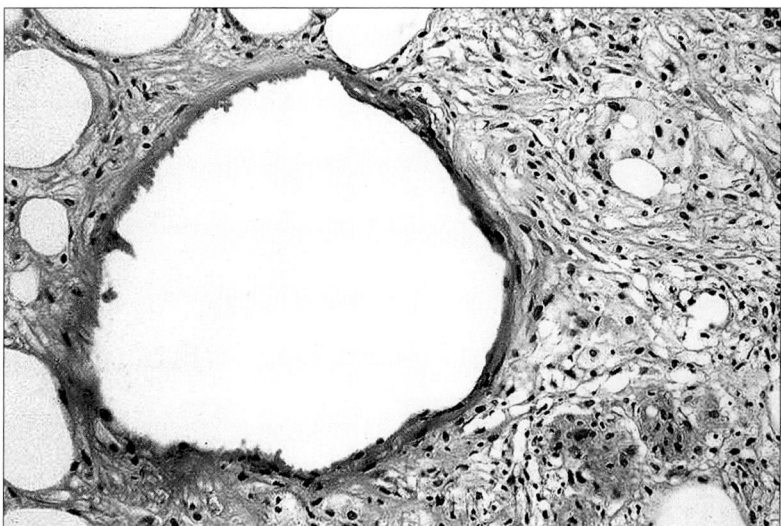

Fig. 9.96
Sclerosing panniculitis: membranous fat necrosis is evident. Lipid laden histiocytes are present in the adjacent septum.

References

1. Alegre, V.A., Winkelmann, R.K., Aliaga, A. (1988) Lipomembranous changes in chronic panniculitis. *J Am Acad Dermatol*, **19**, 39–46.
2. Kirsner, R.S., Pardes, J.B., Eaglstein, W.H. et al (1993) The clinical spectrum of lipodermatosclerosis. *J Am Acad Dermatol*, **28**, 623–627.
3. Browse, N.L., Burnand, K. (1982) The cause of venous ulceration. *Lancet*, **2**, 243–245.
4. Jorizzo, J.L., White, W.L., Zanolli, M.D. et al (1991) Sclerosing panniculitis: a clinicopathologic assessment. *Arch Dermatol*, **127**, 554–558.
5. Machinami, R. (1990) Degenerative change of adipose tissue; the so-called membranous lipodystrophy (editorial). *Virchows Arch A Pathol Anat Histopathol*, **416**, 373–375.
6. Demitsu, T., Okada, O., Yoneda, K. et al. (1999) Lipodermatosclerosis – report of three cases and review of the literature. *Dermatology*, **199**, 271–273.
7. Snow, J.L., Su, W.P.D. (1996) Lipomembranous (membranocystic) fat necrosis: clinicopathologic correlation of 38 cases. *Am J Dermatopathol*, **18**, 151–155.
8. Herouy, Y., May, A.E., Pornschlegel, G. et al (1998) Lipodermatosclerosis is characterized by elevated expression and activation of matrix metalloproteinases: implications for venous ulcer formation. *J Invest Dermatol*, **111**, 822–827.
9. Herouy, Y., Aizpurua, J., Stetter, C. et al (2001) The role of urokinase-type plasminogen activator (UPA) and its receptor (CD87) in lipodermatosclerosis. *J Cutan Pathol*, **28**, 291–297.

Membranous fat necrosis

Clinical features

Membranous fat necrosis is a non-specific change found predominantly in the subcutaneous fat. It was first described, however, in patients with progressive sudanophilic leukoencephalopathy (Nasu-Halola's disease).[1–3] This is a rare condition in which cystic lesions develop in subcutaneous fat and bone marrow associated with pathological fractures and cerebral lesions resulting in seizures and presenile dementia.

Subsequently membranous change has been recognized as a common manifestation of venous stasis-associated disease.[4–7] It has, however, also been observed in association with numerous other conditions including arterial insufficiency, diabetes mellitus, erythema nodosum, nodular vasculitis, infective panniculitis, pancreatic disease-associated panniculitis, subcutaneous sarcoidosis, morphea, morphea profunda, cytophagic histiocytic panniculitis, dermatomyositis, systemic sclerosis, lupus panniculitis, necrobiosis lipoidica and nodular cystic fat necrosis.[6–16] It has also been described in the breast, in appendices epiploicae, within an ovarian cystic teratoma and following subcutaneous elemental mercury injections.[17–21] Membranocystic change accompanied by myospherulosis has also been documented.[22]

Pathogenesis and histological features

Although in the majority of cases an ischemic pathogenesis is likely, its presence following trauma and in a background of infection suggests that other mechanisms are sometimes responsible. The membrane change likely represents altered adipocyte cell membranes although recently a contribution by histiocytes has been postulated.[5–7]

Histologically it presents as amorphous, autofluorescent, eosinophilic, PAS-positive membranes outlining cysts within the lobules of the subcutaneous fat (*Fig. 9.97*). Pseudopapillary and arabesque patterns are commonly present (*Figs 9.98, 9.99*). The membrane also stains for lipid using Sudan black and is luxol fast blue positive.[5] This is thought to represent ceroid, at least in part.[23]

Ultrastructurally, the membrane is composed of perpendicularly orientated microvilli alternating with dilated tubular crypts reminiscent of smooth endoplasmic reticulum with adjacent electron-dense material.[5]

References

1. Hakola, H.P.A., Jaervi, O.H., Sourander, P. (1972) Osteodysplasia polycystica hereditaria combined with sclerosing leukoencephalopathy. *Acta Neurol Scand*, **43** (Suppl.), 1–11.

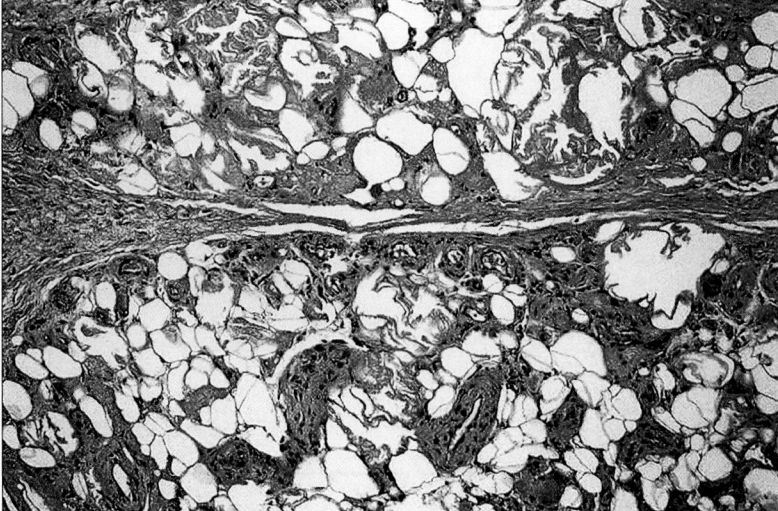

Fig. 9.97
Membranous fat necrosis: note the delicate membranes lying within small cystic spaces.

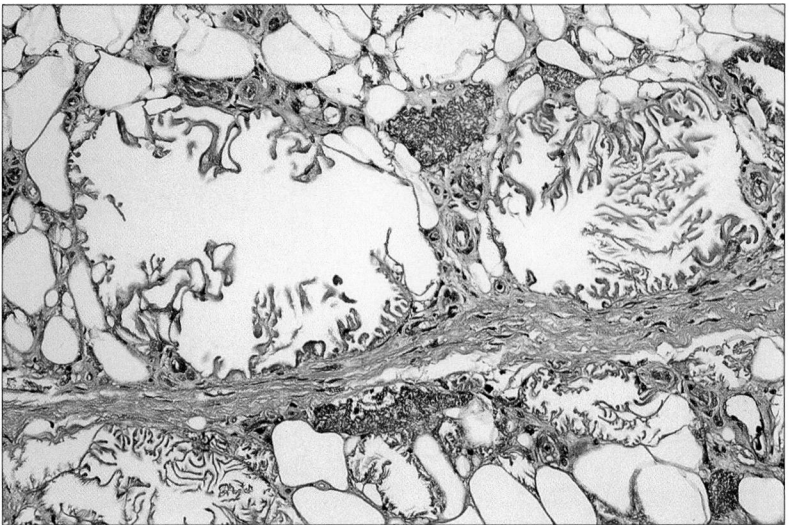

Fig. 9.99
Membranous fat necrosis: the features are highlighted with a Masson's trichrome stain.

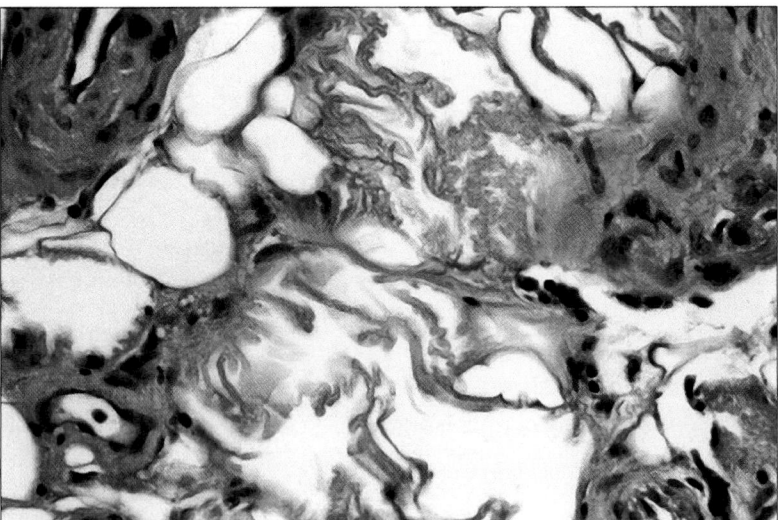

Fig. 9.98
Membranous fat necrosis: close-up view.

2. Nasu, T., Tsukahara, Y., Terayama, K. (1973) A lipid metabolic disease – membranous lipodystrophy – an autopsy case demonstrating numerous peculiar membrane-structures composed of compound lipid in bone and bone marrow and various adipose tissues. *Acta Pathol Jpn*, **23**, 539–543.
3. Tanaka, J. (2000) Nasu-Hakola disease: a review of its leukoencephalopathic and membranolipodystrophic features. *Neuropathology*, **20**, S25–29.
4. White, W.L., Wieselthier, J.S., Hitchcock, M.G. (1992) Panniculitis: recent developments and observations. *Semin Cutan Med Surg*, **15**, 278–299.

5. Machinami, R. (1990) Degenerative change of adipose tissue; the so-called membranous lipodystrophy (editorial). *Virchows Arch A Pathol Anat Histopathol*, **416**, 373–374.
6. Snow, J.L., Su, W.P.D. (1996) Lipomembranous (membranocystic) fat necrosis: clinicopathologic correlation of 38 cases. *Am J Dermatopathol*, **18**, 151–155.
7. Díaz-Cascajo, C., Borghi, S. (2002) Subcutaneous pseudomembranous fat necrosis: new observations. *J Cutan Pathol*, **29**, 5–11.
8. Snow, J.L., Su, W.P.D., Gibson, L.E. (1994) Lipomembranous (membranocystic) changes associated with morphea: a clinicopathologic review of three cases. *J Am Acad Dermatol*, **31**, 246–250.
9. Pujol, R.M., Wang, C-Y., Gibson, L.E. et al (1995) Lipomembranous changes in nodular-cystic fat necrosis. *J Cutan Pathol*, **22**, 551–555.
10. Chun, S.I., Ahn, S.K., Kim, S.C. (1991) Membranous lipodystrophy: primary idiopathic type. *J Am Acad Dermatol*, **24**, 844–847.
11. Chun, S.I.L., Chung, K-Y. (1994) Membranous lipodystrophy: secondary type. *J Am Acad Dermatol*, **31**, 601–605.
12. Ishikawa, O., Tamura, A., Rhuzaki, K. et al (1996) Membranocystic changes in the panniculitis of dermatomyositis. *Br J Dermatol*, **134**, 640–650.
13. Lee, M-W., Lim, Y-S., Choi, J-H. et al (1999) Panniculitis showing membranocystic changes in the dermatomyositis. *J Dermatol*, **26**, 608–610.
14. Toshiyuki, Y., Ohkubo, H., Katayama, I. et al (1994) Dermatomyositis with multiple skin ulcers showing vasculitis and membrano-cystic lesions. *J Dermatol*, **21**, 687–689.
15. Honna, T., Bang, D., Saito, T. et al (1988) Appearance of membranocystic lesion (NASU)-like changes in Behçet syndrome: an electron microscopic study of erythema nodosum-like lesions. *Acta Pathol Jpn*, **38**, 1001–1010.
16. Ohtake, N., Shimada, S., Mizoguchi, S. et al (1998) Membranocystic lesions in a patient with cytophagic histiocytic panniculitis associated with subcutaneous T-cell lymphoma. *Am J Dermatopathol*, **20**, 286–290.
17. Coyne, J.D., Parkinson, D., Baildam, A.D. (1996) Membranous fat necrosis of the breast. *Histopathology*, **28**, 61–64.
18. Ramdial, P.K., Madaree, A., Singh, B. (1997) Membranous fat necrosis in lipomas. *Am J Surg Pathol*, **21**, 841–846.
19. Ramdial, P.K., Singh, B. (1998) Membranous fat necrosis in appendices epiploicae. A clinicopathologic study. *Virchow Arch*, **432**, 223–227.
20. Ramdial, P.K., Bagratee, J.S. (1998) Membranous fat necrosis in mature cystic teratomas of the ovary. *Int J Gynecol Pathol*, **17**, 120–122.
21. Ramdial, P.K., Jogessar, V., Dada, M.A. (1999) Membranous fat necrosis due to subcutaneous elemental mercury injections. *Am J Forensic Med Pathol*, **20**, 369–373.
22. Ono, T., Kageshita, T., Hirai, S. et al (1991) Coexistence of spherulocytic disease (myospherulosis) and membranocystic degeneration. *Arch Dermatol*, **127**, 88–90.
23. Poppiti, R.J., Margulies, M., Cebello, B. et al (1986) Membranous fat necrosis. *Am J Surg Pathol*, **10**, 62–68.

Lipodystrophy

Classification and clinical features

The lipodystrophies are a complex group of disorders characterized by a familial or acquired, complete or partial loss of subcutaneous fat.[1-5] They have recently been classified as follows:[1]

- Familial lipodystrophy including:
  - generalized lipodystrophy (Berardinelli–Seip syndrome)
  - partial lipodystrophy (Dunnigan and Köbberling variants)
- Acquired lipodystrophy including:
  - generalized lipodystrophy (Lawrence syndrome)
  - partial lipodystrophy (Barraquer–Simons syndrome)
  - HIV-associated lipodystrophy
- Localized lipoatrophy (localized lipodystrophy) including:
  - drug-induced lipoatrophy
  - pressure induced lipoatrophy
  - panniculitis-associated lipoatrophy
  - centrifugal variant lipoatrophy
  - idiopathic lipoatrophy.

Familial lipodystrophy

Congenital generalized lipodystrophy (Berardinelli–Seip syndrome)

This exceedingly rare variant of lipodystrophy is inherited in an autosomal recessive mode and is usually recognizable at birth.[1-4] Its prevalence has been estimated as 1:12,000,000.[1] The sex incidence is equal.

It is characterized by a complete absence of metabolically active subcutaneous fat in association with insulin resistance, hyperinsulinemia, hypertriglyceridemia with normal or slightly raised cholesterol and non-ketotic diabetes mellitus.[4] Mechanical fat such as is found in the orbits, on the palms and soles and around the external genitalia is unaffected.[1] Patients also have a voracious appetite associated with a hypermetabolic state and marked hyperhidrosis. Additional features include an anabolic syndrome with increased height velocity, advanced bone age, muscular hypertrophy, masculine body build, acromegaloid stigmata, hepatomegaly, enlarged external genitalia in childhood, abundant curly hair of the scalp, hypertrichosis, umbilical hernia, acanthosis nigricans, mild mental retardation with hydrocephalus and hypothalamic–pituitary dysfunction.[4,5]

Diabetes is thought to develop as a consequence of extensive pancreatic amyloid deposition with loss of β-cells.[6] Postmortem studies have demonstrated fatty liver with cirrhosis.[7]

Recently, the gene for congenital generalized lipodystrophy has been mapped to human chromosome 9q34.[8]

Diagnostic criteria as outlined in *Table 9.3* have recently been recommended.[1]

Familial partial lipodystrophy (Dunnigan variant)

This is another exceedingly rare condition with an estimated prevalence of less than 1 in 15,000,000 of the population.[1] The original cases were all females and therefore a sex-linked dominant mechanism, lethal in hemizygous males, was postulated.[9,10] The more recent publication of families with affected male members suggests, however, that an autosomal dominant mechanism is at play.[11]

Patients are normal at birth but at puberty they lose subcutaneous fat from the extremities and to a lesser extent from the trunk.[12] The face is spared and indeed, in some patients, excessive fat deposition on the face and neck has been documented. Diabetes mellitus, hypertriglyceridemia and low serum high density lipoprotein (HDL) cholesterol levels become manifest in early adulthood.[1,13] Patients may develop chylomicronemia and pancreatitis.[1] Acanthosis nigricans, hirsuitism, menstrual abnormalities and polycystic ovaries are also sometimes evident.[1]

Recently, the gene responsible for familial partial lipodystrophy has been mapped to chromosome region 1q21–22.[14-16] It has been identified as the lamin A/C gene, which codes for a nuclear envelope protein lamin.[17-19]

Diagnostic criteria as outlined in *Table 9.3* have recently been recommended.[1]

Table 9.3
Lipodystrophies: diagnostic criteria

Disorder	Essential criteria	Confirmatory criteria
Congenital generalized lipodystrophy	Generalized lack of body fat Extreme muscularity from birth	Acanthosis nigricans Acromegaloid features Umbilical hernia Clitoromegaly and mild hirsuitism Severe fasting or postprandial hyperinsulinemia Onset of diabetes or impaired glucose tolerance test in teenage years Hypertriglyceridemia with low HDL cholesterol concentration Characteristic body fat distribution on MRI
Familial partial lipodystrophy (Dunnigan variant)	Normal physical appearance at birth Loss of subcutaneous fat of the extremities commencing at puberty Muscular appearing extremities commencing at puberty	Normal or excessive facial adipose tissue Acanthosis nigricans Mild to moderate fasting or postprandial hyperinsulinemia Onset of diabetes or impaired glucose tolerance after age 20 years Hypertriglyceridemia with low serum HDL cholesterol concentrations Characteristic body fat distribution on MRI
Acquired generalized lipodystrophy	Generalized loss of subcutaneous fat developing in childhood or later Extreme muscularity appearing in childhood or later	Loss of fat from palms and soles Severe fasting or postprandial hyperinsulinemia Impaired glucose tolerance or diabetes Hypertriglyceridemia with low serum HDL cholesterol concentrations Nodular panniculitis preceding onset of lipodystrophy Coexistence of autoimmune diseases
Acquired partial lipodystrophy	Gradual loss of subcutaneous fat of the face, neck, trunk and upper extremities developing in childhood or adolescence	Normal or excess fat on hips and lower extremities Proteinuria Biopsy proven mesangiocapillary glomerulonephritis Low serum C3 levels Presence of C3 nephritic factor Absence of insulin resistance Presence of other autoimmune diseases Characteristic body fat on MRI

HDL, high density lipoprotein; MRI, magnetic resonance imaging. Derived from Garg, A. (2000) *American Journal of Medicine*, **108**, 143–152.

Familial partial lipodystrophy (Köbberling variant)

This is an exceedingly rare variant in which only a small number of affected pedigrees have been documented.[1,20,21] Sporadic variants have also been described.[1,22] In these patients, loss of fat is limited to the extremities. There may be increased truncal fat.[1] Hypertriglyceridemia and diabetes mellitus are usually present.[1] To date, documented affected patients have been female.

Familial partial lipodystrophy associated with mandibuloacral dysplasia

This variant of lipodystrophy is characterized by the presence of a variety of bony defects including mandibular and clavicular hypoplasia, acrosteolysis, delayed closure of cranial sutures and joint contractures associated with cutaneous hyperpigmentation.[23,24] Lipodystrophy varies from loss limited to the extremities through to generalized loss. Patients also have insulin-resistant hyperinsulinemia and hypertriglyceridemia and diminished serum HDL cholesterol levels.[24]

Acquired lipodystrophy

Acquired generalized lipodystrophy

Acquired generalized lipodystrophy (Lawrence syndrome, lipoatrophic diabetes, lipoatrophic panniculitis, lipodystrophic diabetes) is similar to the congenital form although there is a predilection for females (3:1).[1,25–27] Patients present in childhood or adolescence with fat loss, which progresses over a period of months or years.[1] The entire body is affected and the muscles of the extremities appear unduly prominent.

Liver involvement may be marked with cirrhosis supervening in a substantial number of cases.[4] Additional features include severe insulin resistance, hyperinsulinemia and hypertriglyceridemia accompanied by low serum HDL cholesterol concentrations.[1]

A preceding viral illness has frequently antedated the development of acquired generalized lipodystrophy although whether this is causal or not is unclear.[1,4]

In some patients, there is an association with autoimmune diseases including Hashimoto's thyroiditis, juvenile rheumatoid arthritis and vitiligo.[1] Features of an inflammatory nodular panniculitis appear to have preceded the onset of lipodystrophy in a number of cases (lipoatrophic panniculitis).[28]

Diagnostic criteria as outlined in *Table 9.3* have recently been recommended.[1]

Acquired partial lipodystrophy

Acquired partial lipodystrophy (Barraquer–Simon syndrome, progressive lipodystrophy, cephalothoracic progressive lipodystrophy) is one of the more common variants of lipodystrophy. Females are affected three times more often than males.[1] Patients present in late childhood or adolescence with gradual loss of the subcutaneous fat of the face followed by the neck, shoulders, arms, thorax and upper abdomen (*Fig. 9.100*).[1,29–31] The distal subcutaneous fat is typically spared and sometimes, in contrast, there is even excessive fat deposition around the pelvis and on the legs.

Mesangiocapillary (membranoproliferative) glomerulonephritis (MCGN II) and hypocomplementemia often accompany this variant.[32–34] C3 levels are usually low in contrast to C1q, C4, C5, C6, factor B and properdin, which are normal.[35,36] The glomerulonephritis and low C3 have been shown to be due to an IgG autoantibody, the C3 nephritic factor (C3NeF).[37] It has been shown that the latter has the capacity to induce adipocyte lysis.[38] An association with a number of other autoimmune diseases including Sjögren's syndrome, dermatomyositis, hypothyroidism and SLE has also been documented.[39–42] Patients may in addition develop hyperlipidemia, non-ketotic diabetes mellitus, acanthosis nigricans and hirsuitism.[1] Hepatomegaly due to fat accumulation is occasionally present.

Diagnostic criteria as outlined in *Table 9.3* have recently been recommended.[1]

Lipodystrophy in HIV positive patients

This acquired variant is characterized by loss of fat from the face, gluteal region and the extremities with deposition around the neck, abdomen

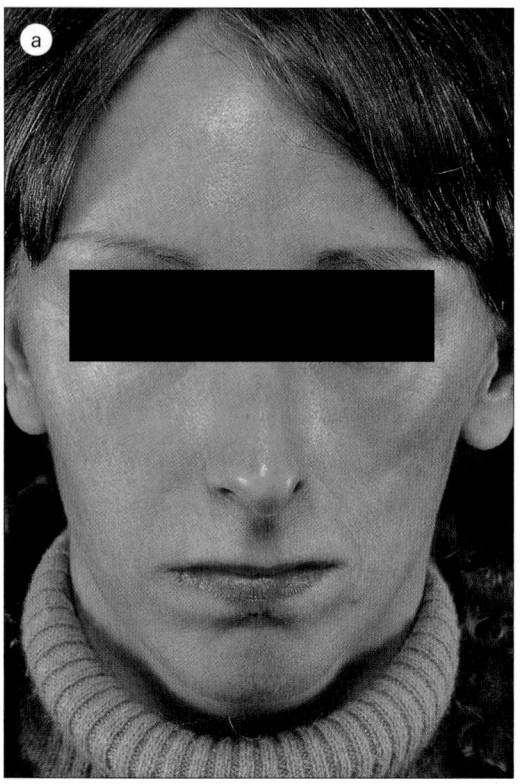
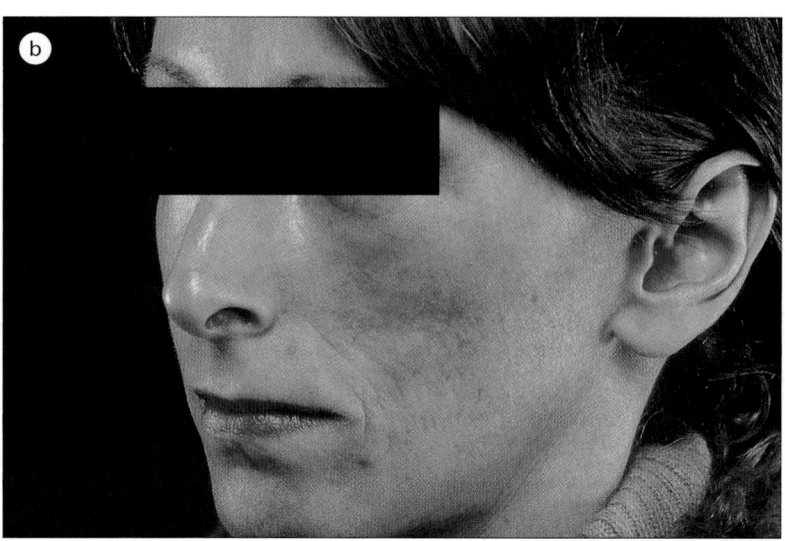

Fig. 9.100
(a, b) Partial lipodystrophy: note the striking loss of symmetry due to diminished fatty tissue of the left side of the face. By courtesy of the Institute of Dermatology, London, UK.

and trunk[1] (*Fig. 9.101*). It has been associated with highly active antiretroviral therapy (HAART), in particular protease inhibitors.[43–50] There is associated insulin resistance with glucose intolerance, diabetes mellitus, hypertriglyceridemia and low serum HDL cholesterol levels.[47]

Localized lipoatrophy

Clinical features

Localized disease (lipoatrophy) is a much more common phenomenon. The subject has, however, been made extremely complicated by virtue of the large number of synonyms that have been used to describe the same disease process over the years (e.g. lipodystrophy, annular lipoatrophy, annular lipodystrophy, semicircular lipoatrophy, postinjection lipoatrophy, involutional lipoatrophy, lipodystrophia centrifugalis abdominalis infantilis, centrifugal lipodystrophy). Essentially, localized lipodystrophy may result from a range of injurious stimuli and present at a wide variety of sites but essentially all of the subtypes listed above are variations of the same disease process which may therefore follow localized panniculitis, connective tissue diseases, injections, trauma, etc.

Lesions affecting the proximal extremities or buttocks should raise the possibility of infection or trauma. Localized lipoatrophy has been described following subcutaneous injections of insulin, triamcinolone acetate and iron dextran, and following vaccinations.[51–54] It has also been described as a complication of idiopathic connective tissue diseases including systemic lupus erythematosus (profundus), dermatomyositis,

polymyositis, linear morphea, facial hemiatrophy, lichen sclerosus et atrophicus and progressive systemic sclerosis.[55–57]

Other types of localized lipodystrophy include annular lipodystrophy and a variant that affects only half the circumference of an extremity (lipoatrophia semicircularis). These distinctive annular lesions are likely to result from a localized pressure effect such as that which may occur with tight clothing or persistent localized trauma.[58,59] Idiopathic variants are also recognized including lipoatrophy associated with Becker's nevus and lipodystrophia centrifugalis abdominalis infantilis.[60–63]

Pathogenesis and histological features

The exact pathogenesis of lipodystrophy is unknown. A variety of theories have been proposed, including hypothalamic–pituitary dysfunction (overproduction of fat-mobilizing peptides and amines), disordered fat metabolism, infection and heredity. A currently favored area of research is directed towards the role of abnormal insulin receptors on fat cells. It has been postulated that abnormal insulin receptors are associated with diminished uptake of lipid by fat cells with resultant lipodystrophy, hyperlipidemia and hyperinsulinemia.

In general, the histopathology of lipodystrophy is non-inflammatory in nature.[64–66] There is a progressive diminution of adipocyte lipid accompanied by a decrease in cell size so that the cells become separated from one another (*Fig. 9.102*). The stroma becomes hyalinized

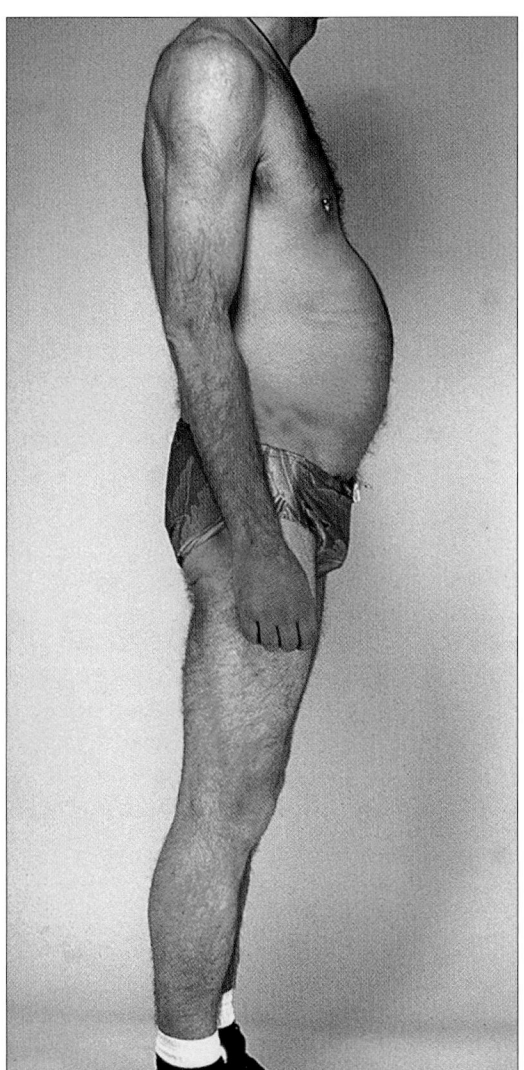

Fig. 9.101
Lipodystrophy associated with HIV infection: there is loss of the fat of the extremities. Note the deposition of fat around the abdomen. By courtesy of D. McGibbon, MD., Institute of Dermatology, London, UK.

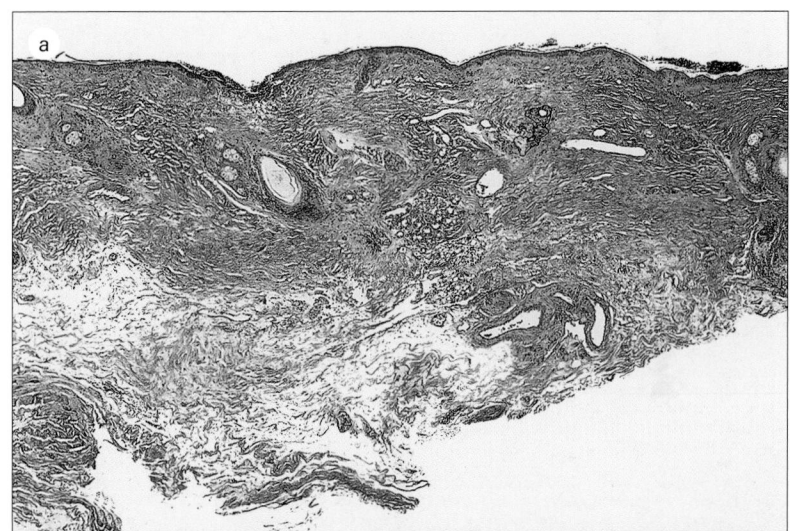

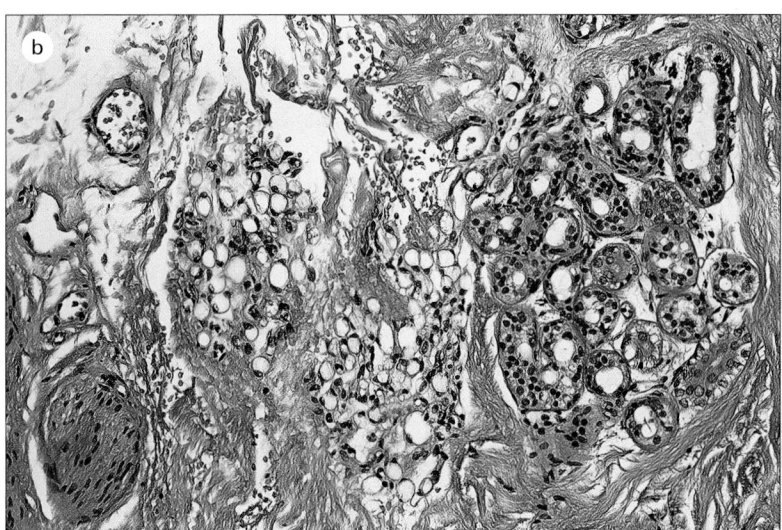

Fig. 9.102
Lipodystrophy: (a) there is only a very small residual amount of subcutaneous fat in the center of the field; (b) these tiny adipocytes are reminiscent of embryonic fat By courtesy of W.P.D. Su, MD, Mayo Clinic, Rochester, USA.

or myxomatous and contains clusters of tortuous capillaries. As the end result resembles embryonic fat, this process of atrophy is sometimes called 'reversal of embryogenesis'.

HIV-associated partial lipodystrophy has been variably characterized by loss of subcutaneous fat without any other recognizable histological abnormality.[49,50]

Patients with multiple areas of localized lipoatrophy may show mild inflammatory changes comprising perivascular and periseptal lymphocytic infiltration accompanied by minor septal fibrosis.

References

1. Garg, A. (2000) Lipodystrophies. *Am J Med*, **108**, 143–152.
2. Berardinelli, W. (1954) An undiagnosed endocrinometabolic syndrome: report of two cases. *J Clin Endocrinol Metab*, **14**, 193–204.
3. Seip, M. (1959) Lipodystrophy and gigantism with associated endocrine manifestations: a new diencephalic syndrome? *Acta Paediatr*, **48**, 555–574.
4. Seip, M., Trygstad, O. (1996) Generalized lipodystrophy, congenital and acquired (lipoatrophy). *Acta Paediatr*, **413** (Suppl.), 2–28.
5. Garg, A., Fleckenstein, J.L., Peshock, R.M. et al (1992) Peculiar distribution of adipose tissue in patients with congenital generalized lipodystrophy. *J Clin Endocrinol Metab*, **75**, 358–361.
6. Garg, A., Chandalia, M., Vuitch, F. (1996) Severe islet amyloidosis in congenital generalized lipodystrophy. *Diabetes Care*, **19**, 28–31.
7. Chandalia, M., Garg, A., Vuitch, F. et al (1995) Postmortem findings in congenital generalized lipodystrophy. *J Clin Endocrinol Metab*, **80**, 3077–3081.
8. Garg, A., Wilson, R., Barnes, R. et al (1999) A gene for congenital generalized lipodystrophy maps to human chromosome 9q34. *J Clin Endocrinol Metab*, **84**, 3390–3394.
9. Dunnigan, M.G., Cochrane, M.A., Kelly, A. et al (1974) Familial lipoatrophic diabetes with dominant transmission: a new syndrome. *QJM*, **49**, 33–48.
10. Köbberling, J., Dunnigan, M.G. (1986) Familial partial lipodystrophy: two types of an X-linked dominant syndrome, lethal in the hemizygous state. *J Med Genet*, **23**, 120–127.
11. Jackson, S.N.J., Howlett, T.A., McNally, P.G. et al (1997) Dunnigan–Köbberling syndrome: an autosomal dominant form of partial lipodystrophy. *QJM*, **90**, 27–36.
12. Garg, A., Peshock, R.M., Fleckenstein, J.L. (1999) Adipose tissue distribution pattern in patients with familial partial lipodystrophy (Dunnigan variety). *J Clin Endocrinol Metab*, **84**, 170–174.
13. Burn, J., Bariatser, M. (1986) Partial lipodystrophy with insulin resistant diabetes and hyperlipidemia (Dunnigan syndrome). *J Med Genet*, **23**, 128–130.
14. Jackson, S.N., Pinkney, J., Bargiotta, A. et al (1998) A defect in the regional deposition of adipose tissue (partial lipodystrophy) is encoded by a gene at chromosome 1q. *Am J Hum Genet*, **63**, 534–540.
15. Peters, J.M., Barnes, R., Bennett, L. et al (1998) Localization of the gene for familial partial lipodystrophy (Dunnigan variety) to chromosome 1q21-22. *Nat Genet*, **18**, 292–295.
16. Anderson, J.L., Khan, M., David, W.S. et al (1999) Confirmation of linkage of hereditary partial lipodystrophy to chromosome 1q21-22. *Am J Med Genet*, **82**, 161–165.
17. Flier, J.S. (2000) Pushing the envelope in lipodystrophy. *Nat Genet*, **24**, 103–104.
18. Vigouroux, C., Magre, J., Vantyghem, M.C. et al (2000) Lamin A/C gene: sex-determined expression of mutations in Dunnigan-type familial partial lipodystrophy and absence of coding mutations in congenital and acquired generalized lipodystrophy. *Diabetes*, **49**, 1958–1962.
19. Garg, A., Vinaitheerthan, M., Weatherall, P.T. et al (2001) Phenotypic heterogeneity in patients with familial partial lipodystrophy (Dunnigan variety) related to the site of missense mutations in lamin a/c gene. *J Clin Endocrinol Metab*, **86**, 59–65.
20. Köbberling, J., Williams, B., Kattermann, R. et al (1975) Lipodystrophy of the extremities. A dominantly inherited syndrome associated with lipoatrophic diabetes. *Humangenetik*, **29**, 111–120.
21. Hook, B., Adam, W. (1983) Partielles lipodystrophie syndrom (Typ Köbberling). *Z Hautkr*, **58**, 1348.
22. Tam, M.M., Berger, P. (1998) Partial face-sparring lipodystrophy (Köbberling–Dunnigan syndrome): a report of a sporadic case. *Australas J Dermatol*, **39**, 100–105.
23. Freidenberg, G.R., Cutler, D.L., Jones, M.C. et al (1992) Severe insulin resistance and diabetes mellitus in mandibuloacral dysplasia. *Am J Dis Child*, **146**, 93–99.
24. Simha, V., Garg, A. (2002) Body fat distribution and metabolic derangements in patients with familial partial lipodystrophy associated with mandibuloacral dysplasia. *J Clin Endocrinol Metab*, **87**, 776–785.
25. Ziegler, L.H. (1928) Lipodystrophies: report of seven cases. *Brain*, **51**, 145–167.
26. Lawrence, R.D. (1946) Lipodystrophy and hepatomegaly with diabetes, lipemia, and other metabolic disturbances. *Lancet*, **i**, 724–731.
27. Senior, B., Gellis, S.S. (1964) The syndromes of total lipodystrophy and partial lipodystrophy. *Pediatrics*, **33**, 593–612.
28. Billings, J.K., Milgraum, S.S., Gupta, A.K. et al (1987) Lipoatrophic panniculitis: a possible autoimmune inflammatory disease of fat. *Arch Dermatol*, **123**, 1662–1666.
29. Barraquer, L. (1907) Histoire clinique d'un cas d'atrophie du tissu cellulodipeux. *Neurolog Zentralblatt*, **26**, 1072.
30. Simons, A. (1911) Eine seltnen Trophoneurose: 'lipodystrophia progressiva'. *Z Ges Neurol Psychiat*, **5**, 29–38.
31. Mitchell, S.W. (1885) Singular absence of adipose matter in the upper half of the body. *Am J Med Sci*, **90**, 105–106.
32. Eisinger, A.J., Shortland, J.R., Moorhead, P.J. (1972) Renal disease in partial lipodystrophy. *QJM*, **41**, 343–354.
33. Houssin, A., Saint-Andre, J.P., Buzelin, F. et al (1981) Partial lipodystrophy (cephalothoracic type) with asymptomatic dense deposit disease. *An Med Intern*, **132**, 44–47.
34. Levy, Y., George, J., Yona, E. et al (1998) Partial lipodystrophy, mesangiocapillary glomerulonephritis, and complement dysregulation: an autoimmune phenomenon. *Immunol Res*, **18**, 55–60.
35. Sissons, J.G.P., West, R.J., Fallows, J. et al (1976) The complement abnormalities of lipodystrophy. *N Engl J Med*, **294**, 461–465.
36. Ipp, M.M., Minta, J.O., Gelfand, E.W. (1977) Disorders of the complement system in lipodystrophy. *Clin Immunol Immunopathol*, **7**, 281–287.
37. McLean, R.H., Hoefnagel, D.H. (1980) Partial lipodystrophy and familial C3 deficiency. *Hum Hered*, **30**, 149–154.
38. Mathieson, P.W., Wurzner, R., Oliviera, D.B.G. et al (1993) Complement-mediated adipocyte lysis by nephritic factor. *J Exp Med*, **177**, 1827–1831.
39. Jasin, H.E. (1979) Systemic lupus erythematosus, partial lipodystrophy and hypocomplementemia. *J Rheumatol*, **6**, 43–50.
40. Cronin, C.C., Higgins, T., Molloy, M. (1995) Lupus, C3 nephritic factor and partial lipodystrophy. *QJM*, **88**, 298–299.
41. Alarcón-Segovia, D., Ramos-Niembro, F. (1976) Association of partial lipodystrophy and Sjögren's syndrome. *Ann Intern Med*, **85**, 474–475.
42. Torrelo, A., España, A., Boixeda, P. et al (1991) Partial lipodystrophy and dermatomyositis. *Arch Dermatol*, **127**, 1846–1847.
43. Lo, J.C., Mulligan, K., Tai, V.W. et al (1998) 'Buffalo hump' in men with HIV-1 infection. *Lancet*, **351**, 867–870.
44. Carr, A., Samaras, K., Thorisdottir, A. et al (1999) Diagnosis, prediction, and natural course of HIV-1 protease-inhibitor-associated lipodystrophy, hyperlipidemia, and diabetes mellitus: a cohort study. *Lancet*, **353**, 2093–2099.
45. Blanch, J., Rousaud, A., Martinez, E. et al (2002) Impact of lipodystrophy on quality of life of HIV-1-infected patients. *J Acquir Immune Defic Syndr*, **31**, 404–407.
46. Manchanda, J., Schedel, D., Fischer, D. et al (2002) Adverse drug reactions to protease inhibitors. *Can J Clin Pharmacol*, **9**, 137–146.
47. Chen, D., Misra, A., Garg, A. (2002) Clinical review 153: lipodystrophy in human immunodeficiency virus-infected patients. *J Clin Endocrinol Metab*, **87**, 4845–4856.
48. Rodwell, G.E.J., Maurer, T.A., Berger, T.G. (2000) Fat redistribution in HIV disease. *J Am Acad Dermatol*, **42**, 727–730.
49. Panse, I., Vasseur, E., Raffin-Sanson, M.L. et al (2000) Lipodystrophy associated with protease inhibitors. *Br J Dermatol*, **142**, 496–500.
50. Pujol, R.M., Domingo, P., Matias-Guiu, X. et al (2000) HIV-1 protease inhibitor-associated partial lipodystrophy: clinicopathologic review of 14 cases. *J Am Acad Dermatol*, **42**, 193–198.
51. Reeves, W., Allan, B., Tattersall, R. (1980) Insulin-induced lipoatrophy: evidence for an immune pathogenesis. *BMJ*, **280**, 1500–1505.
52. Morgan, A.M. (1995) Localized reactions to injected therapeutic material. Part 1, Medical agents. *J Cutan Pathol*, **22**, 193–214.
53. Dahl, P.R., Zalla, M.J., Winkelmann, R.K. (1996) Localized involutional lipoatrophy: a clinicopathologic study of 16 patients. *J Am Acad Dermatol*, **35**, 523–528.
54. Hishamichi, K., Suga, Y., Hashimoto, Y. et al (2002) Two Japanese cases of localized involutional lipoatrophy. *Int J Dermatol*, **41**, 176–177.
55. Winkelmann, R.K., Padilha-Goncalves, A. (1980) Connective tissue panniculitis. *Arch Dermatol*, **116**, 291–294.
56. Winkelmann, R.K. (1983) Panniculitis in connective tissue disease. *Arch Dermatol*, **119**, 336–344.
57. Commens, C., O'Neill, P., Walker, G. (1990) Dermatomyositis associated with multifocal lipoatrophy. *J Am Acad Dermatol*, **22**, 966–999.
58. Rongioletti, F., Rebora, A. (1989) Annular and semi-circular lipoatrophies. Report of three cases and review of the literature. *J Am Acad Dermatol*, **20**, 433–436.
59. Hodak, E., David, M., Sandbank, M. (1990) Semicircular lipoatrophy – a possible pressure-induced lipoatrophy? *Clin Exp Dermatol*, **15**, 464–465.
60. Cox, N.H. (2002) Becker's nevus of the thigh with lipodystrophy: report of two cases. *Clin Exp Dermatol*, **27**, 27-28.
61. Kagoura, M., Toyoda, M., Matsui, C. et al (2001) An ultrastructural study of lipodystrophia centrifugalis abdominalis infantilis with special reference to long-spacing collagen. *Pediatr Dermatol*, **18**, 13–16.
62. Mak, K.H., Ho, H.F., Chan, L.Y. et al (2002) Lipodystrophia centrifugalis abdominalis infantilis: two cases from China. *J Dermatol*, **28**, 320–323.
63. Immamura, S., Taniguchi, S. (2000) Lipodystrophic lesions preceded by pain and erythema – a new clinical entity? *Eur J Dermatol*, **10**, 540–541.
64. Reed, R.J., Clark, W.H., Mihm, M.C. (1973) Disorders of the panniculus adiposus. *Hum Pathol*, **4**, 219–229.
65. Bernstein, R.S., Pierson, R.N., Ryan, S.F. et al (1979) Adipose cell morphology and control of lipolysis in a patient with partial lipodystrophy. *Metabolism*, **28**, 519–526.
66. Patterson, J.W. (1991) The differential diagnosis of panniculitis. *Adv Dermatol*, **6**, 309–329.

Lipoatrophic panniculitis

Clinical features

Lipoatrophic panniculitis (atrophic connective tissue panniculitis) represents a very rarely documented inflammatory form of localized lipoatrophy.[1–6] In the original report, three children developed centrifugally enlarging erythematous nodules and plaques with atrophic centers on the lower extremities. Healing of the lesions resulted in the clinical appearances of localized lipoatrophy. The areas of lipoatrophy coalesced to give an appearance resembling partial or total lipodystrophy.[1] All three patients had elevated ESRs. Two patients had associated diabetes mellitus (one with coexistent Hashimoto's thyroiditis) and one developed juvenile rheumatoid arthritis. Peters and Winkelmann described a similar condition under the rubric 'atrophic connective tissue disease panniculitis'.[2] Nowadays, this entity would probably be best included in the spectrum of acquired total or partial lipodystrophy.

Histological features

In atrophic connective tissue panniculitis the histological features are those of a lobular panniculitis.[1] The deep dermis may manifest a perivascular lymphocytic and histiocytic infiltrate. Lymphocytes and mononuclear phagocytes extensively infiltrate the fatty lobules. Eosinophils and multinucleate giant cells are uncommon. In more advanced lesions, there is fatty atrophy accompanied by an infiltrate composed mainly of foamy macrophages.[3] Vasculitis is not a feature of this disorder.[1]

References

1. Billings, J.K., Milgraum, S.S., Gupta, A.K. et al (1987) Lipoatrophic panniculitis: a possible autoimmune inflammatory disease of fat. *Arch Dermatol*, **123**, 1662–1666.
2. Peters, M.S., Winkelmann, R.K. (1980) Localised lipoatrophy (atrophic connective tissue disease panniculitis). *Arch Dermatol*, **116**, 1363–1368.
3. Peters, M.S., Winkelmann, R.K. (1986) The histopathology of localized lipoatrophy. *Br J Dermatol*, **114**, 27–36.
4. Moragon, M., Jorda, E., Ramon, M.D. et al (1988) Atrophic connective tissue panniculitis. *Int J Dermatol*, **27**, 185–186.

5.   Gupta, A.K., Rasmussen, J.E. (1986) Multiple areas of localized tissue loss in a child. Atrophic connective tissue panniculitis. *Arch Dermatol*, **122**, 1199–1202.
6.   Lutz, B.S., Toussaint, S., Wei, F.C. (1998) Bilateral facial lipoatrophy secondary to connective tissue panniculitis treated with two microsurgically transplanted latissimus dorsi muscles. *Ann Plast Surg*, **40**, 302–307.

Lipophagic panniculitis of childhood

Clinical features

Lipophagic panniculitis of childhood (lipophagic–granulomatous lipoatrophy) is exceedingly rare and presents in children as erythematous asymptomatic or tender plaques and nodules affecting the arms or legs, which are later associated with lipoatrophy.[1] Fever is common and the children usually have a raised ESR, thrombocytosis and microcytic anemia. Antinuclear factor may be present.[1] A similar disorder has rarely been described in adults (adult lipophagic atrophic panniculitis).[2] Winkelmann postulates that many cases of Weber–Christian disease documented in the earlier literature belong to this disorder (literature summarized in reference 1).

Histological features

Histologically, lipophagic panniculitis is characterized by panlobular inflammation with histological features of lipoatrophy.[1] The inflammatory cell infiltrate consists of histiocytes and Touton-like lipophages. Occasional lymphocytes, neutrophils and plasma cells may be evident. Eosinophils are sometimes numerous. There is no evidence of vasculitis.[1]

References

1.   Winkelmann, R.K., McEvoy, M.T., Peters, M.S. (1989) Lipophagic panniculitis of childhood. *J Am Acad Dermatol*, **21**, 971–978.
2.   Umbert, I.J., Winkelmann, R.K. (1991) Adult lipophagic atrophic panniculitis. *Br J Dermatol*, **124**, 291–295.

Connective tissue panniculitis

Clinical features

This extremely rare chronic condition, originally described in two female patients by Winkelmann and Padilha-Goncalves, comprises recurrent tender subcutaneous nodules mainly on the shoulders and upper arms, but the cheek, breast, trunk, neck or leg may also be affected.[1] Healing is sometimes associated with lipoatrophy and hyperpigmentation, which can be particularly disfiguring (*Fig. 9.103*).[2]

Laboratory findings include leukopenia, anemia, a raised ESR, positive antinuclear antibody and an unclassifiable antibody to extractable nuclear antigen.[3]

Histological features

A lymphohistiocytic panniculitis associated with both acute and caseation necrosis characterizes the lesions. Lipophagic histiocytes and giant cells may be present, but granulomata are not a feature and there is no evidence of septal involvement or vasculitis.[1,2]

Comment

At present this variant of chronic panniculitis has defied further classification.

References

1.   Winkelmann, R.K., Padilha-Goncalves, A. (1980) Connective tissue panniculitis. *Arch Dermatol*, **116**, 291–294.
2.   Handfield-Jones, S.E., Stephens, C.J.M., Mayou, B.J. et al (1993) The clinical spectrum of lipoatrophic panniculitis encompasses connective tissue panniculitis. *Br J Dermatol*, **129**, 619–624.
3.   Winkelmann, R.K. (1983) Panniculitis in connective tissue disease. *Arch Dermatol*, **119**, 336–344.

Lupus erythematosus profundus

Clinical features

Lupus erythematosus profundus (lupus panniculitis) is an uncommon variant of panniculitis, which may develop in association with either discoid lupus erythematosus (DLE) or systemic lupus erythematosus (SLE).[1–8] The incidence of lupus panniculitis in SLE ranges from 2 to 10%;[4,9–11] DLE is present in from 33 to 70% of cases.[4,5] Lupus panniculitis may, however, also present in the absence of any other manifestations of lupus erythematosus.[9] In a recent series from the Mayo Clinic, 50% of patients had no evidence of any autoimmune associated disease.[4] Lupus panniculitis shows a predilection for females (4:1) and most patients are middle aged.[4] Rarely, however, children (including infants) may be affected.[7]

Patients develop discrete firm asymptomatic or painful nodules, one to several centimeters across, in the subcutaneous fat; the nodules are often associated with trauma.[9] The overlying skin may appear clinically normal or show discoid lupus plaques, poikiloderma, erythema, atrophy or ulceration (*Fig. 9.104*).[10] The disease is characteristically chronic, patients developing recurrent crops of lesions. Spontaneous resolution may occur and leave depressed atrophic disfiguring scars (lipoatrophy) (*Fig. 9.105*). Sites of predilection include the face, upper and outer parts

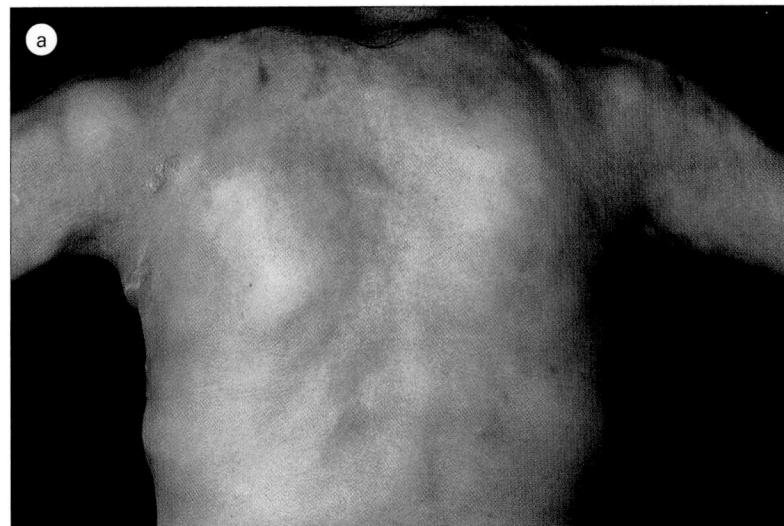

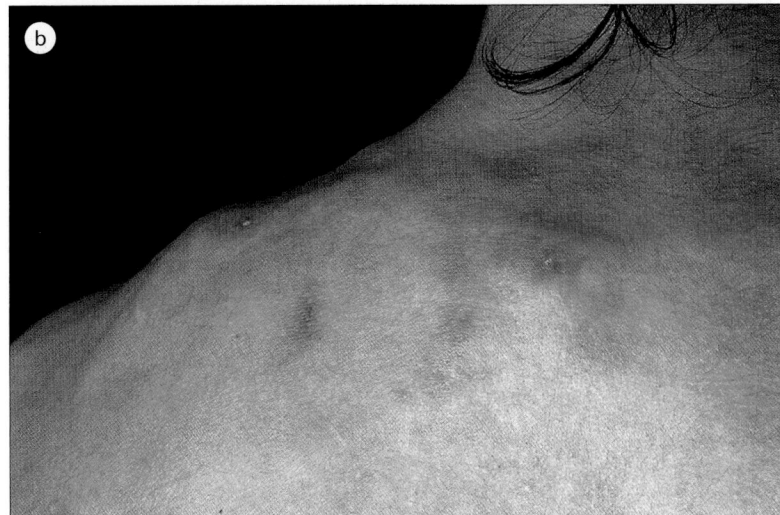

Fig. 9.103

(a, b) Connective tissue panniculitis: this patient shows diffuse hyperpigmentation associated with generalized scarring and deformity. By courtesy of M.M. Black, MD, London, UK.

of the arm, the breasts, back and buttocks. Breast involvement with scarring and calcification may be clinically mistaken for carcinoma (so-called 'lupus mastitis').[12] Salivary gland and primary periorbital lesions have also been documented.[13–17] Rarely, the disease may present with generalized lesions.[8]

In cases with associated SLE, patients frequently manifest arthralgia and Raynaud's phenomenon; there appears to be a relatively low incidence of renal and neurological involvement.[10] Positive serology may include antinuclear antibody, anti-DNA antibody, anti-extractable nuclear antigen (ENA) antibodies and rheumatoid factor.[9] In those patients in whom there is no evidence elsewhere of lupus erythematosus, a raised antinuclear factor may be the only serological abnormality.[4] Although in these latter patients the prognosis is generally thought to be good, in some patients there is considerable mortality and the disfigurement a source of considerable distress.[18,19] Partial C4 deficiency has been described in a patient with lupus erythematosus profundus.[20]

Histological features

In an established lesion the histological features of lupus erythematosus profundus are virtually diagnostic. The overlying epithelium and superficial dermis may show features of DLE, poikiloderma or be unaffected (*Figs 9.106–9.109*).[21,22] Within the deep dermis, and extending into the widened septa of the subcutaneous fat, is a dense chronic inflammatory cell infiltrate consisting predominantly of nodules of lymphocytes with lesser numbers of plasma cells (*Figs 9.110–9.112*).[11,22] Occasionally lymphoid follicles with germinal centers are evident (*Fig. 9.113*). The infiltrate may surround and permeate the walls of blood vessels and sweat glands; involvement of the perineural sheath is occasionally a feature (*Fig. 9.114*).[21,23] Less often, frank lymphocytic vasculitis with mural fibrinoid necrosis and luminal thrombosis is seen (*Fig. 9.115*).

The infiltrate often extends into the periphery of the fat lobules and when associated with fat necrosis there may also be moderate numbers of neutrophil polymorphs. The collagen of the deep dermis and fibrous septa of the subcutaneous fat show striking fibrinoid degenerative changes. Fibers may be markedly swollen and intensely eosinophilic, or fragmented into amorphous granular debris. Similar changes are seen surrounding individual adipocytes. In more advanced examples, glassy eosinophilic necrosis gives a diffusely hyalinized appearance to the subcutaneous fat (*Fig. 9.116*). The foci of collagenous degeneration are sometimes associated with mucin deposition and not infrequently foci of calcification are seen.[10,21,22]

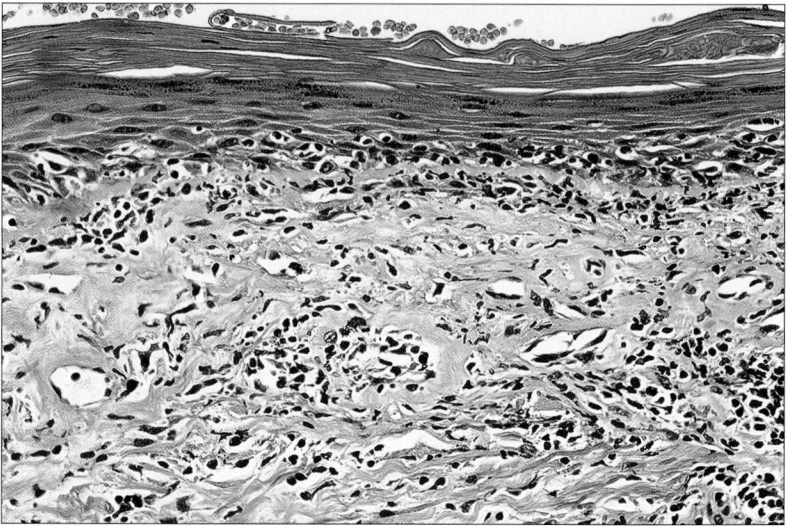

Fig. 9.107
Lupus erythematosus profundus: in this example there are typical features of discoid lupus erythematosus.

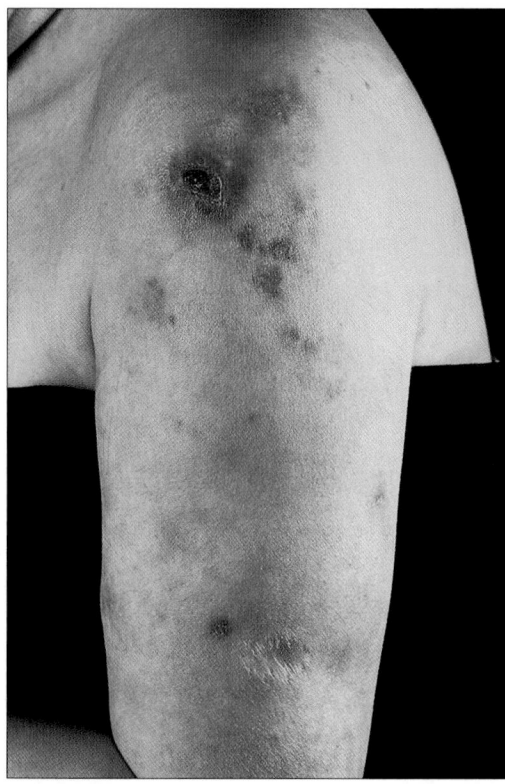

Fig. 9.104
Lupus erythematosus profundus: erythematoviolaceous plaques showing focal ulceration at the characteristic site. By courtesy of the Institute of Dermatology, London, UK.

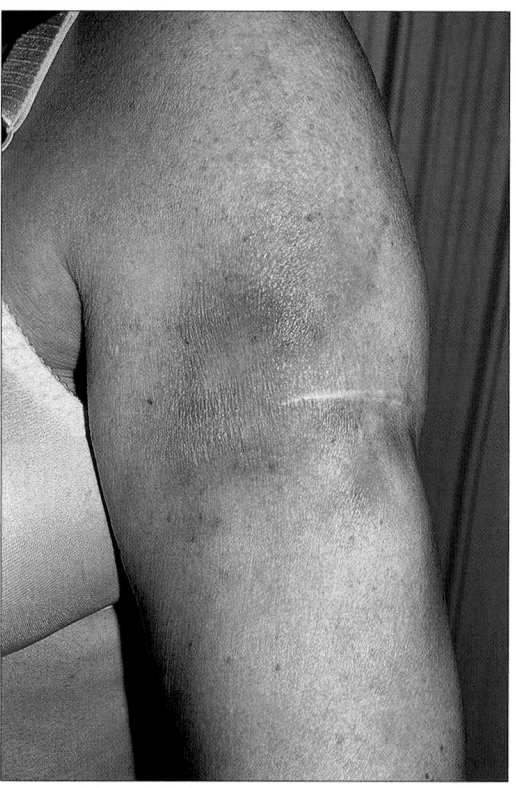

Fig. 9.105
Lupus erythematosus profundus: a depressed scarred area due to end stage lipoatrophy. By courtesy of the Institute of Dermatology, London, UK.

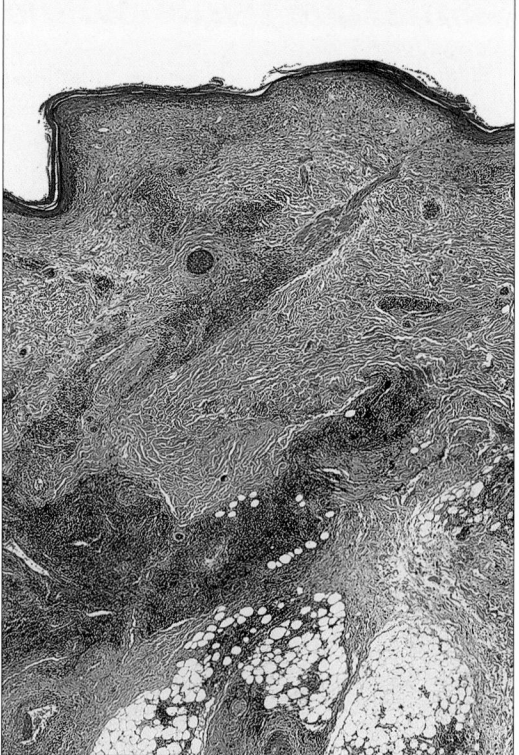

Fig. 9.106
Lupus erythematosus profundus: low power view showing epidermal atrophy with hyperkeratosis and a dense dermal lymphocytic infiltrate with extension into subcutaneous fat.

Immunofluorescence commonly reveals immunoglobulin and complement at the epidermodermal junction and sometimes around the superficial blood vessels.[21]

Differential diagnosis

Similar histological features may be seen in other connective tissue diseases including linear morphea, morphea profunda, systemic sclerosis, dermatomyositis, mixed connective tissue disease and polymyositis.[24–27] Recently, Sjögren's syndrome has been added to the causes of so-called

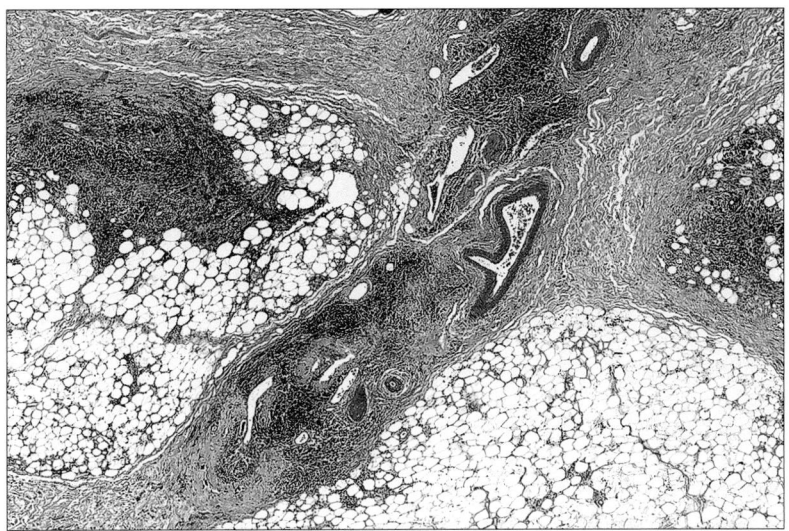

Fig. 9.110
Lupus erythematosus profundus: the septa are thickened and there is a dense infiltrate.

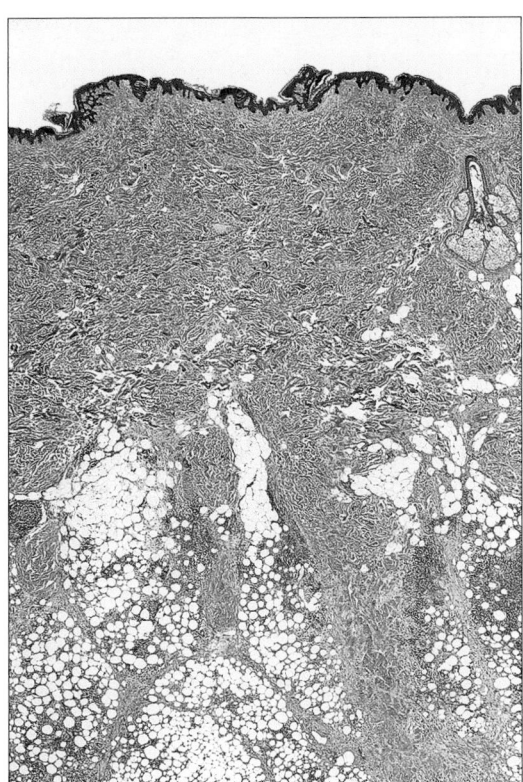

Fig. 9.108
Lupus erythematosus profundus: in contrast, this patient showed disease limited to the subcutaneous fat.

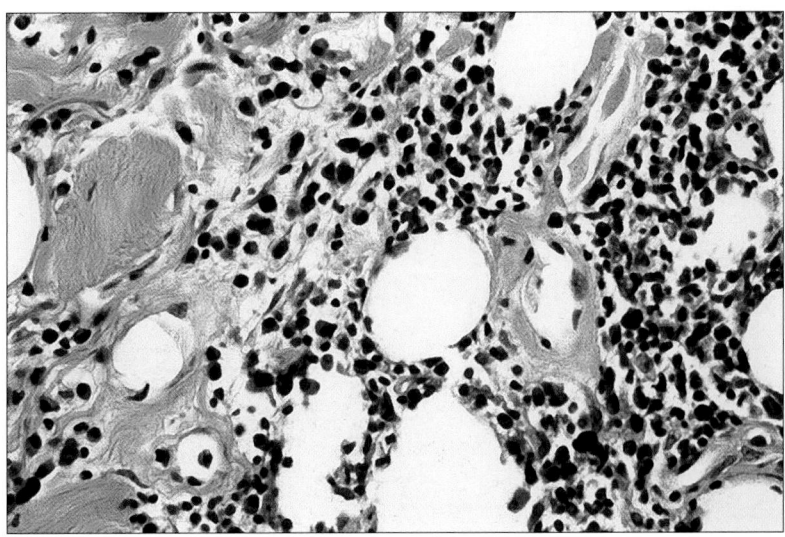

Fig. 9.111
Lupus erythematosus profundus: the infiltrate is largely lymphocytic.

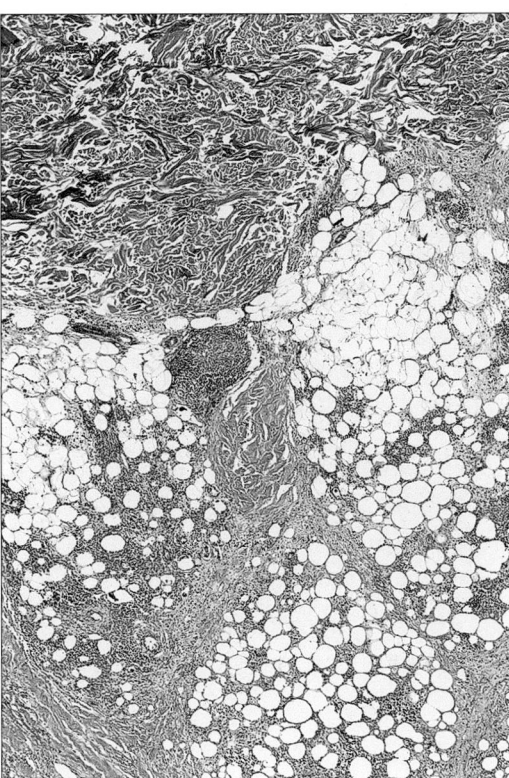

Fig. 9.109
Lupus erythematosus profundus: the subcutaneous fat is infiltrated by large numbers of lymphocytes.

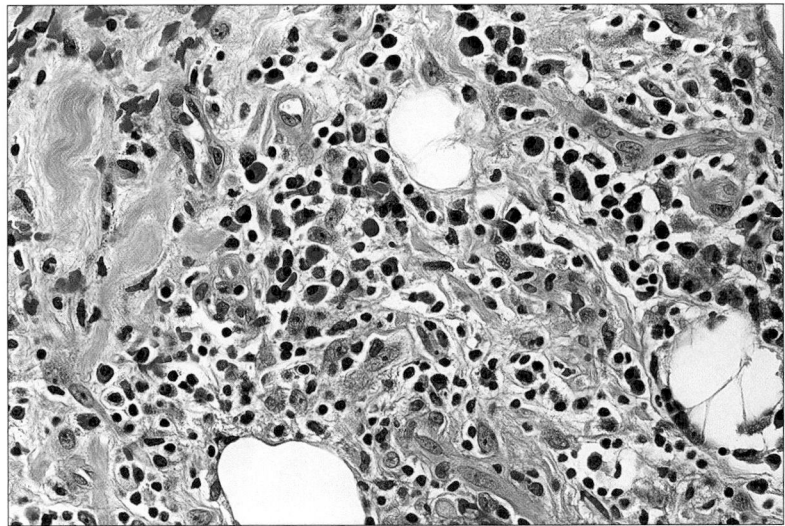

Fig. 9.112
Lupus erythematosus profundus: plasma cells as shown in this field are sometimes conspicuous.

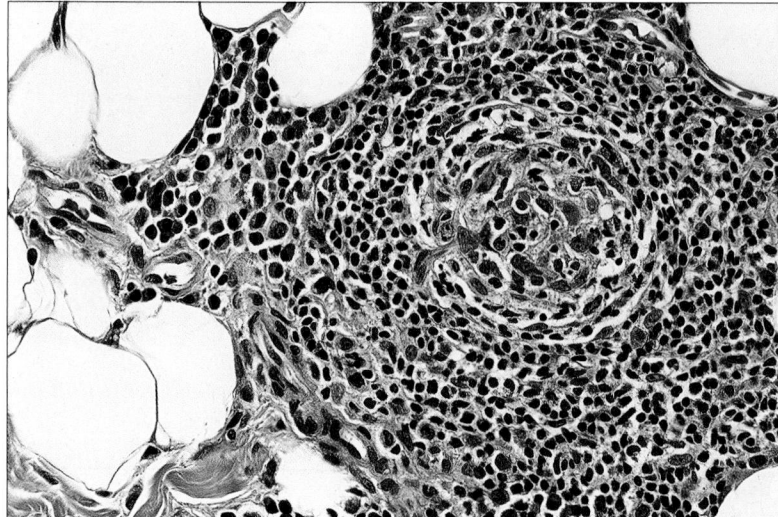

Fig. 9.113
Lupus erythematosus profundus: lymphoid follicles, as shown in this field, may be a prominent feature.

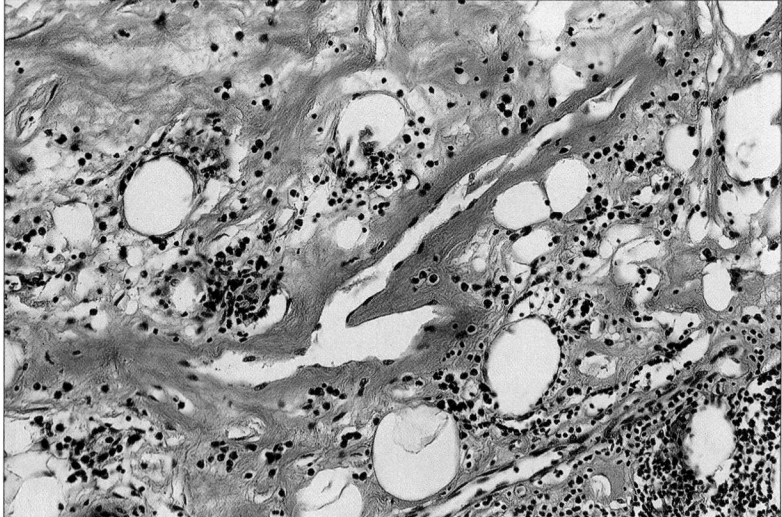

Fig. 9.114
Lupus erythematosus profundus: blood vessel walls are commonly thickened and hyalinized.

plasma cell panniculitis.[28] Lobular panniculitis with sclerosis reminiscent of lupus panniculitis has also been described in a patient with Degos disease (malignant atrophic papulosis).[29]

References

1. Winkelmann, R.K. (1970) Panniculitis and systemic lupus erythematosus. *JAMA*, **211**, 472–475.
2. Tuffanelli, D.L. (1971) Lupus erythematosus panniculitis (profundus). Clinical and immunologic studies. *Arch Dermatol*, **103**, 231–242.
3. Fountain, R.B. (1986) Lupus erythematosus profundus. *Br J Dermatol*, **80**, 571–579.
4. Martens, P.B., Moder, K.G., Ahmed, I. (1999) Lupus panniculitis: clinical perspectives from a case series. *J Rheumatol*, **26**, 68–72.
5. Mascaro, J.M., Herrero, C., Hausmann G. (1997) Uncommon cutaneous manifestations of lupus erythematosus. *Lupus*, **6**, 122–131.
6. Sontheimer, R.D., Provost, T.T. (1996) Lupus erythematosus. In: Sontheimer, R.D., Provost, T.T. (eds) Cutaneous manifestations of rheumatic diseases. Philadelphia: Williams & Wilkins, pp 1–71.
7. Nitta, Y. (1997) Lupus erythematosus profundus associated with neonatal lupus erythematosus. *Br J Dermatol*, **136**, 112–114.
8. Nousari, H.C., Kinyai-Asadi, A., Provost, T.T. (1999) Generalized lupus erythematosus profundus in a patient with genetic partial deficiency of C4. *J Am Acad Dermatol*, **41**, 362–364.
9. Tuffanelli, D.L. (1985) Lupus panniculitis. *Semin Dermatol*, **4**, 79–81.
10. Peters, M.S., Su, W.P.D. (1989) Lupus erythematosus panniculitis. *Med Clin North Am*, **73**, 1113–1127.
11. Peters, M.S., Su, W.P.D. (1992) Panniculitis. *Dermatol Clin*, **10**, 37–57.
12. Harris, R.B., Winkelmann, R.K. (1978) Lupus mastitis. *Arch Dermatol*, **114**, 410–412.
13. White, W.L., Sherertz, E.F., Berg, D. et al (1993) Periparotid lupus erythematosus panniculitis: clinicopathologic correlation of two cases presenting as primary parotid disease. *Arch Pathol Lab Med*, **117**, 535–539.
14. Sheehan-Dare, R.A., Cunliffe, W.J. (1988) Severe periorbital edema in association with lupus erythematosus profundus. *Clin Exp Dermatol*, **13**, 406–407.
15. Magee, K.L., Hymes, S.R., Rapini, R. et al (1991) Lupus erythematosus profundus with periorbital swelling and proptosis. *J Am Acad Dermatol*, **24**, 288–290.
16. Jordan, D.R., McDonald, H., Oldberg, B. et al (1993) Orbital panniculitis as the initial manifestation of systemic lupus erythematosus. *Ophthal Plast Reconstr Surg*, **9**, 71–75.
17. Arthurs, B.P., Khalil, M.R., Chagnon, F. et al (1999) Orbital infarction and melting in a patient with systemic lupus erythematosus. *Ophthalmology*, **106**, 2387–2390.
18. Galindo, E.C., Sánchez de Paz, F., Pérez, I.M. et al (2001) Lupus erythematosus profundus: case reports. *Cutis*, **67**, 465–467.
19. Grossberg, E., Scherschun, L., Fivenson, D.P. (2001) Lupus profundus: not a benign disease. *Lupus*, **10**, 514–516.
20. Burrows, N.P., Russell Jones, R. (1997) Lupus erythematosus profundus with partial C4 deficiency. *Br J Dermatol*, **137**, 651.
21. Sanchez, N.P., Peters, M.S., Winkelmann, R.K. (1981) The histopathology of lupus erythematosus panniculitis. *J Am Acad Dermatol*, **5**, 673–680.
22. Patterson, J.W. (1991) The differential diagnosis of panniculitis. *Adv Dermatol*, **6**, 309–329.
23. Izumi, A.K., Takiguchi, P. (1983) Lupus erythematosus panniculitis. *Arch Dermatol*, **119**, 61–64.
24. Vincent, F., Prokopetz, R., Miller, R.A. (1989) Plasma cell panniculitis: a unique clinical and pathologic presentation of linear scleroderma. *J Am Acad Dermatol*, **21**, 357–360.
25. Su, W.P., Pearson, J.R. (1981) Morphea profunda. A new concept and a histopathologic study of 23 cases. *Am J Dermatopathol*, **3**, 251–260.
26. Janis, J.F., Winkelmann, R.K. (1968) Histopathology of the skin in dermatomyositis: a histopathologic study of 55 cases. *Arch Dermatol*, **97**, 640–650.
27. Nezondot-Chetaille, A.L., Brondino-Riquier, R., Villami, P. et al (2001) Panniculitis in a patient on methotrexate for mixed connective tissue disease. *Joint Bone Spine*, **69**, 324–326.
28. McGovern, T.W., Erickson, A.R., FitzPatrick, J.E. (1996) Sjögren's syndrome, plasma cell panniculitis and hidradenitis. *J Cutan Pathol*, **23**, 170–174.
29. Grilli, R., Soriano, M.L., Izquierdo, M.J. et al (1999) Lupus erythematosus profundus: a new histopathologic finding in malignant atrophic papulosis (Degos disease). *Am J Dermatopathol*, **21**, 365–368.

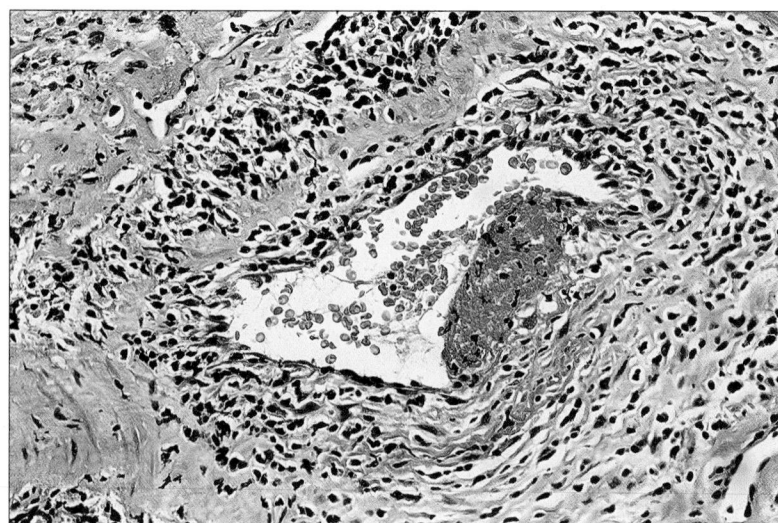

Fig. 9.115
Lupus erythematosus profundus: lymphocytic vasculitis, as noted in this field, is not uncommon.

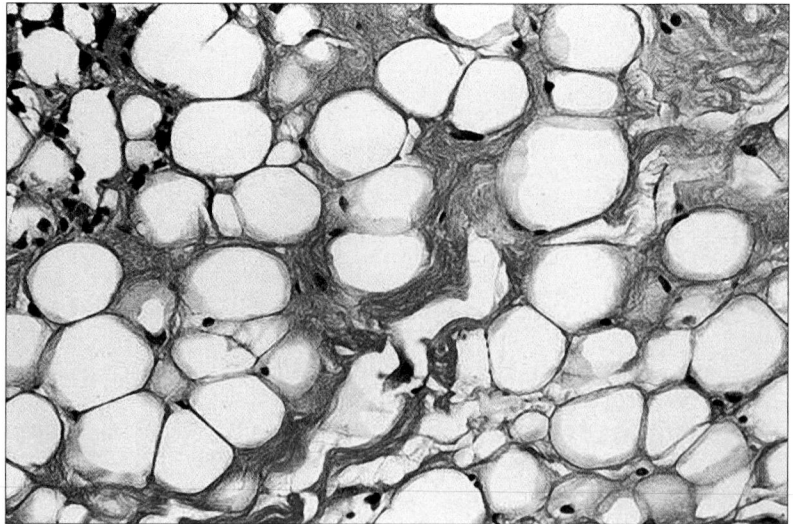

Fig. 9.116
Lupus erythematosus profundus: hyalinization of the fat is a characteristic feature.

Scleroderma panniculitis

Clinical features

Sclerosis and chronic panniculitis have been recorded as main features in both generalized morphea and progressive systemic sclerosis.[1-3] In addition, morphea profunda has been described as a sclerosing variant of morphea, which primarily affects the subcutaneous fat analogous to lupus erythematosus profundus.[4,5] This condition, which shows a female predominance (3:1), affects a wide age range (9–62 years) and presents primarily as subcutaneous sclerosis.[6] The sclerosis may be generalized and extend to the digits, or present as solitary or multiple, localized, inflamed, hyperpigmented or erythematous, asymmetrical and ill-defined plaques with a predilection for the shoulders, upper arms and trunk.[6-8] A variant localized to the paraspinal region in children has also been described.[9,10]

Histological features

The significant features include thickening and hyalinization of the connective tissue of the deep dermis, subcutaneous fat and muscular fascia.[3] A perivascular and focal interstitial lymphocytic and plasma cell infiltrate is present in the subcutaneous fat. Exceptionally, plasma cells may be very numerous – so-called plasma cell panniculitis.[11] Lymphoid nodules (usually without germinal center formation) are evident and mast cells may be increased in number.[6] Scattered eosinophils are occasionally seen. Mucin deposition is sometimes a feature and diminished elastic tissue is a frequent finding, although in some cases it appears increased in quantity.[8] Localized osseous metaplasia with transepidermal elimination has been documented.[12] The changes in the fascia are similar to those described in the subcutaneous fat.

Differential diagnosis

Morphea profunda differs from conventional generalized morphea by the deeper involvement of the sclerotic process and the more intense chronic inflammatory cell infiltrate.[6] Some authors regard eosinophilic fasciitis as part of the spectrum of morphea profunda.[6]

References

1. Fleischmajer, R., Nedwich, A. (1972) Generalized morphea. I. Histology of the dermis and subcutaneous tissue. *Arch Dermatol*, **106**, 509–514.
2. Fleischmajer, R., Damiano, V., Nedwich, A. (1972) Alteration of subcutaneous tissue in systemic scleroderma. *Arch Dermatol*, **105**, 59–66.
3. Winkelmann, R.K. (1983) Panniculitis in connective tissue disease. *Arch Dermatol*, **119**, 336–344.
4. Su, W.P., Pearson, J.R. (1981) Morphea profunda. A new concept and a histopathologic study of 23 cases. *Am J Dermatopathol*, **3**, 251–260.
5. Whittaker, S., Smith, N.P., Russell Jones, R. (1989) Solitary morphea profunda. *Br J Dermatol*, **120**, 431–440.
6. Pearson, J.R., Su, W.P.D. (1979) Subcutaneous morphoea: a clinical study of sixteen cases. *Br J Dermatol*, **100**, 371–380.
7. Requena, L., Sánchez-Yus, E. (2001) Panniculitis. Part 1. Mostly septal panniculitis. *J Am Acad Dermatol*, **45**, 163–183.
8. Balabanova, M., Obreshkova, E. (1999) Scleroderma profunda. Clinicopathological studies. *Adv Exp Med Biol*, **455**, 105–109.
9. Kobayashi, K.A., Lui, H., Prendiville, J.S. (1991) Solitary morphea profunda in a 5-year-old girl: case report and review of the literature. *Pediatr Dermatol*, **8**, 292–295.
10. Kirsner, R.S., Pardes, J.B., Falanga, V. (1993) Solitary fibrosing paraspinal plaques: solitary morphoea profunda. *Br J Dermatol*, **128**, 99–101.
11. Vincent, F., Prokopetz, R., Miller, R.A. (1989) Plasma cell panniculitis: a unique clinical and pathologic presentation of linear scleroderma. *J Am Acad Dermatol*, **21**, 357–360.
12. Ahn, S.K., Won, J.H., Choi, E.H. et al (1996) Perforating plate-like osteoma cutis in a man with solitary morphoea profunda. *Br J Dermatol*, **134**, 949–952.

Dermatomyositis panniculitis

Clinical features

Panniculitis has been described as a non-specific incidental finding in biopsy specimens of skin or muscle from patients with dermatomyositis.[1-3] Rarely, however, it presents as a symptomatic disorder, patients complaining of indurated, erythematous, tender, painful plaques and nodules, located about the arms, thighs, abdomen and buttocks.[3-10]

In some cases, the panniculitis precedes the onset of the myositis.[3] With chronicity patients can develop lipoatrophy.[11] Both children and adults may be affected.

Histological features

Dermatomyositis panniculitis is characterized by a predominantly lobular infiltrate of lymphocytes and plasma cells, sometimes accompanied by lymphoid follicles with germinal centers.[4,5] Focal fat necrosis may be present and lymphocytic vasculitis has occasionally been documented.[6] The septa of the subcutaneous fat become progressively thickened and hyalinized. Membranocystic changes have been described in a number of cases, particularly in the Japanese.[1,10-12] Calcification is a late change.[1]

Mild inflammatory changes may be seen in the subcutaneous fat in patients with dermatomyositis in the absence of panniculitis including focal lymphocytic infiltration, fibrosis and calcification.[5]

The overlying epidermis may show interface change with basal cell vacuolation and lymphocytic exocytosis.[1,7]

Immunofluorescent findings are variable. In the majority of cases it is negative, but C3 was found at the dermoepidermal junction in one case and, in another, C3 and IgM were identified within the blood vessel walls in the superficial dermal vasculature.[6,7]

Differential diagnosis

An association of childhood dermatomyositis with subcutaneous panniculitic T-cell lymphoma has been described in a single case report.[13]

References

1. Solans, R., Cortés, J., Selva, A. et al (2002) Panniculitis: a cutaneous manifestation of dermatomyositis. *J Am Acad Dermatol*, **46** (Suppl.), S148–150.
2. Molnar, K., Kemeny, L., Korom, I. et al (1998) Panniculitis in dermatomyositis: report of two cases. *Br J Dermatol*, **139**, 161–163.
3. Janis, J.F., Winkelmann, R.K. (1968) Histopathology of the skin in dermatomyositis: a histopathologic study of 55 cases. *Arch Dermatol*, **97**, 640–650.
4. Winkelmann, R.K. (1983) Panniculitis in connective tissue disease. *Arch Dermatol*, **119**, 336–344.
5. Raimer, S.S., Solomon, A.R., Daniels, J.C. (1985) Polymositis presenting with panniculitis. *J Am Acad Dermatol*, **13**, 366–369.
6. Winkelmann, W.J., Billick, R.C., Srolovitz, H. (1990) Dermatomyositis presenting as panniculitis. *J Am Acad Dermatol*, **23**, 127–128.
7. Fusade, T., Belanyi, P., Joly, P. et al (1993) Subcutaneous changes in dermatomyositis. *Br J Dermatol*, **128**, 451–453.
8. Neidenbach, P.J., Sahn, E.E., Helton, J. (1995) Panniculitis in juvenile dermatomyositis. *J Am Acad Dermatol*, **33**, 305–307.
9. Ghali, F.E., Reed, A.N., Groben, P.A. et al (1999) Panniculitis in juvenile dermatomyositis. *Pediatr Dermatol*, **16**, 270–272.
10. Tsuchida, T., Tamaki, K., Ando, I. (1987) Panniculitis and interstitial pneumonitis in dermatomyositis. *Jpn J Dermatol*, **97**, 1521–1530.
11. Ishikawa, O., Tamura, A., Rhuzaki, K. et al (1996) Membranocystic changes in the panniculitis of dermatomyositis. *Br J Dermatol*, **134**, 640–650.
12. Lee, M-W., Lim, Y-S., Choi, J-H. et al (1999) Panniculitis showing membranocystic changes in dermatomyositis. *J Dermatol*, **26**, 608–610.
13. Laraki, R., Genestie, C., Wechsler, J. et al (2001) Juvenile dermatomyositis and panniculitis-type subcutaneous T-cell lymphoma. A case report. *Rev Méd Interne*, **22**, 978–983.

Postirradiation pseudosclerodermatous panniculitis

Clinical features

This is a rare complication of high-dose radiotherapy. Thus far, it has only been described in female patients who have received this treatment modality for breast carcinoma following radical mastectomy.[1,2] Patients present with deep-seated and progressive induration of the subcutis in the area of previous irradiation (*Fig. 9.117*).

Histological features

The main histological features are localized to the subcutaneous fat where there is a lobular panniculitis characterized by fat necrosis with foreign body (lipophagic) granulomata and a lymphocyte and plasma cell infiltrate.[1,2] The septa are grossly thickened by hyalinized collagen. Dermal changes may be absent or there can be a perivascular

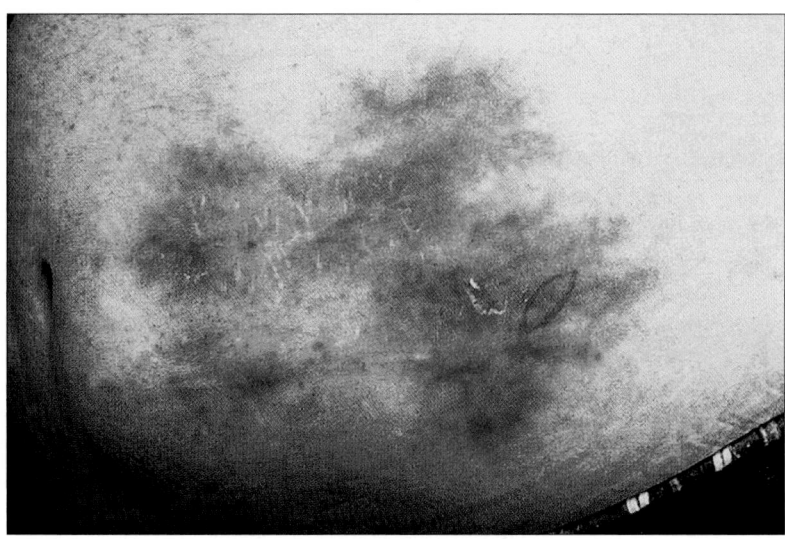

Fig. 9.117
Postirradiation pseudosclerodermatous panniculitis: erythematous irregular plaque.
By courtesy of the Institute of Dermatology, London, UK.

and interstitial lymphocyte and plasma cell infiltrate with atypical myofibroblasts.[1] Epidermal changes of radiotherapy are absent.[2]

Differential diagnosis

In patients with this condition, sections should be very carefully scrutinized for evidence of recurrent/metastatic breast carcinoma. Immunohistochemistry may prove invaluable.

Postirradiation pseudosclerodermatous panniculitis can be histologically confused with both morphea profunda and lupus erythematosus profundus.[2] Clinicopathological correlation should readily establish the correct diagnosis.

References

1.   Winkelmann, R.K., Grado, G.L., Quimby, S. et al (1993) Pseudosclerodermatous panniculitis after irradiation: an unusual complication of megavoltage treatment of breast carcinoma. *Mayo Clin Proc*, **68**, 122–127.
2.   Carrasco, L., Moreno, C., Pastor, M.A. et al (2001) Post irradiation pseudosclerodermatous panniculitis. *Am J Dermatopathol*, **23**, 283–287.

Diseases of the oral mucosa

Sook-Bin Woo

10

HEREDITARY CONDITIONS   387

Macular lesions   387

Tumor-like lesions   390

REACTIVE CONDITIONS   398

Leukoedema   398

Chronic bite injury   399

Benign migratory glossitis   400

Smokeless tobacco keratosis   403

Foreign body gingivitis   405

Pyostomatitis vegetans   405

ULCERATIVE CONDITIONS   406

Recurrent aphthous stomatitis   406

Traumatic ulcerative granuloma   408

PAPILLARY LESIONS   410

Squamous papilloma   410

Verruciform xanthoma   412

TUMOR-LIKE CONDITIONS   413

Fibroma   413

Giant cell fibroma   414

Lipoma   415

Denture-associated fibrous hyperplasia   416

Gingival nodules   417

Gingival fibroma   418

Pyogenic granuloma   419

Peripheral ossifying fibroma   420

Peripheral giant cell granuloma   421

Parulis   422

Peripheral odontogenic fibroma   422

Gingival cyst of the adult   425

Generalized gingival hyperplasia   426

Varix   428

INFECTIONS   430

Hairy leukoplakia   430

Focal epithelial hyperplasia   432

LICHENOID AND HYPERSENSITIVITY REACTIONS   433

Oral lichen planus and lichenoid stomatitis   433

Plasma cell orificial mucositis   438

Orofacial granulomatosis   440

Oral Crohn's disease   441

Wegener's granulomatosis   442

AUTOIMMUNE CONDITIONS   443

Cicatricial pemphigoid   443

Desquamative gingivitis   445

Pemphigus   445

Linear IgA disease   446

Dermatitis herpetiformis   446

Epidermolysis bullosa acquisita   446

Lupus erythematosus   447

REACTIVE SALIVARY GLAND DISEASE   447

Mucocele   447

Sialolithiasis   449

Necrotizing sialometaplasia   449

Nicotinic stomatitis   451

Cheilitis glandularis   452

PREMALIGNANT CONDITIONS   452

Leukoplakia, erythroplakia and epithelial dysplasia   452

Benign alveolar ridge keratosis   457

Submucous fibrosis   458

MALIGNANT LESIONS   459

Squamous cell carcinoma   459

Metaplastic carcinoma   461

Basaloid squamous cell carcinoma   462

Adenoid squamous cell carcinoma   463

Verrucous carcinoma   464

Midline destructive disease   465

PIGMENTED LESIONS   465

Amalgam tattoo   465

Oral melanocytic lesions   467

OTHER TUMORS   470

Granular cell tumor   470

Ectomesenchymal chondromyxoid tumor   471

Oral and maxillofacial pathology is the specialty of dentistry that is involved in the diagnosis and management of diseases of the oral mucosa and supporting bone and soft tissues, teeth, salivary glands, lip vermilion and perioral skin. It would be impossible to discuss diseases affecting all of the above entities in one chapter. As such, this chapter is confined to common and uncommon mucosal lesions that are often seen and biopsied by the oral and maxillofacial surgeon, dermatologist or an otorhinolaryngologist. If a condition presents on the skin in addition to the mouth (such as pemphigus), only a brief mention of the oral manifestations is made since the topic will have been covered in detail elsewhere in the book.

From a histological perspective, the oral mucosa is divided into non-keratinized and keratinized sites. The former include the labial mucosa (wet surface of the lip), buccal mucosa, maxillary and mandibular sulci (sometimes also called the 'vestibule'), ventral tongue, floor of mouth, soft palate, non-attached gingiva and crevicular epithelium (*Fig. 10.1*). The crevicular epithelium is the continuation of attached gingiva where it turns to face the tooth. Any keratin on these surfaces is considered abnormal and should be reported as such. The linea alba ('bite line') which is located on the buccal mucosa where the upper and lower teeth meet may be thinly parakeratinized and this is considered within the realm of normal (*Fig. 10.2*).

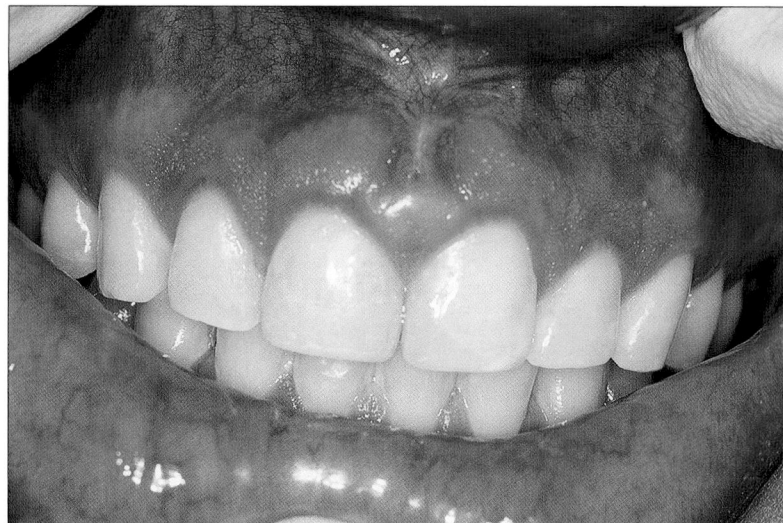

Fig. 10.1
Normal mouth: note the maxillary sulcus, attached and non-attached gingiva and teeth.

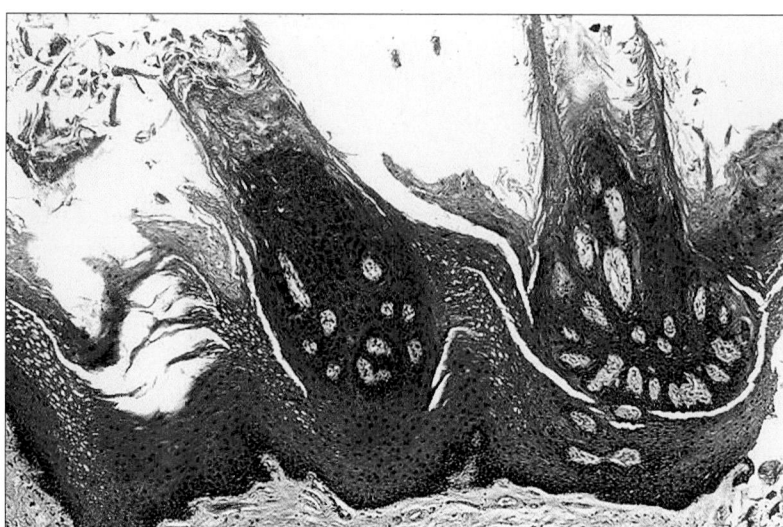

Fig. 10.3
Normal tongue: the filiform papillae are spires of parakeratin usually associated with bacterial colonies.

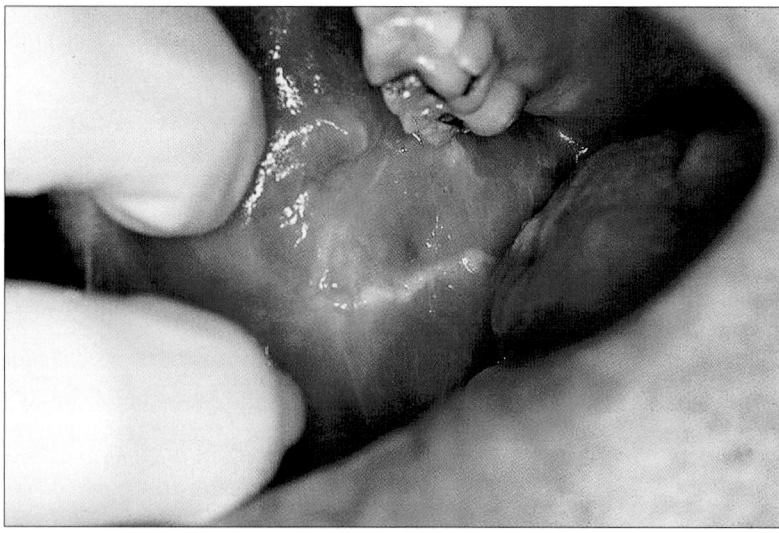

Fig. 10.2
Normal mouth: the linea alba on the buccal mucosa usually exhibits leukoedema and may be thinly parakeratinized.

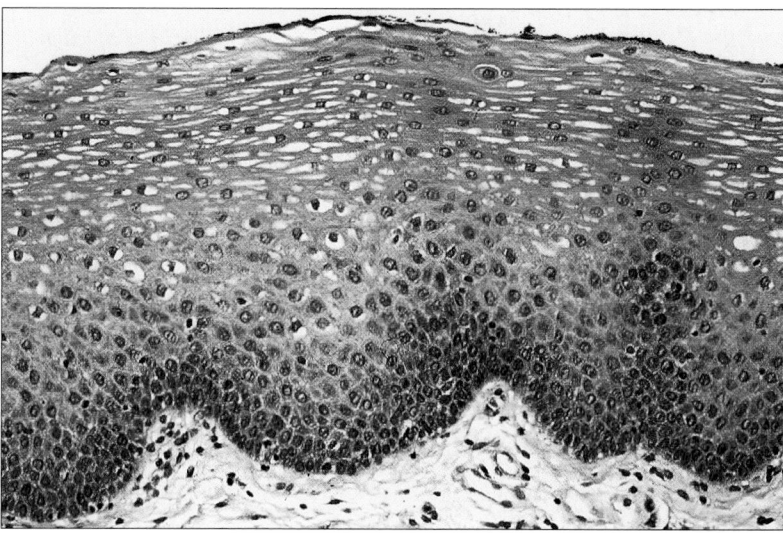

Fig. 10.4
Normal buccal mucosa: the epithelium is non-keratinized and is 12–25 cells thick.

Keratinized sites include the hard palate mucosa, the attached gingiva (extending from the tooth for a band of 3–7 mm) and the tongue dorsum. The tongue is a specialized structure because of its role in taste sensation and has filiform, fungiform and circumvallate papillae, the last two also containing taste buds (*Fig. 10.3*).

The epithelium of the oral mucosa is generally two to four times thicker than the epidermis (*Fig. 10.4*). Pathologists not familiar with this feature tend to diagnose normal mucosa as acanthosis or psoriasiform hyperplasia. The attached gingiva and mucosa of the hard palate abut the periosteum so that the deep lamina propria appears densely fibrotic (*Fig. 10.5*). A diagnosis of 'fibrosis' is therefore inappropriate since this feature is normal for the site.

The tooth is composed of an outer highly calcified thin shell of enamel on the visible crown of the tooth; the non-visible portion within the bone is covered by cementum, which is similar in composition and appearance to bone. The bulk of the tooth consists of dentin and through the tooth runs the pulp containing fibrovascular and neural tissues (the source of

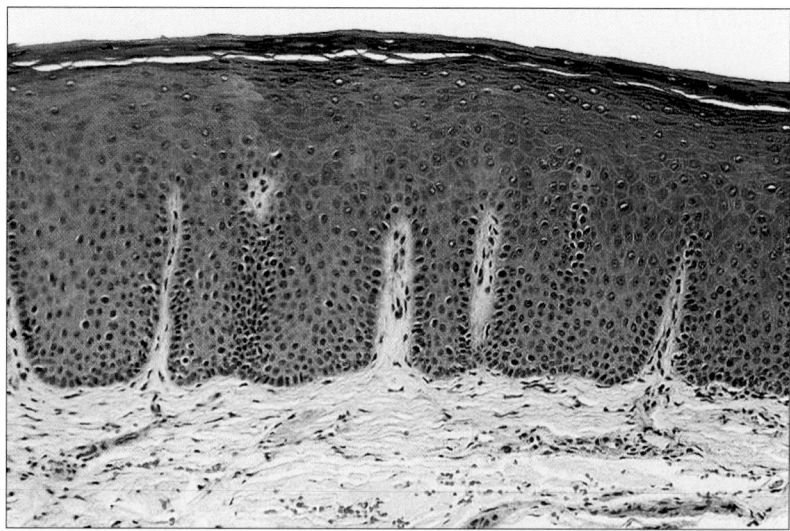

Fig. 10.5
Normal palate: the palate and gingiva both are thinly keratinized. The dense fibrous tissue beneath is normal for these sites.

most toothaches). Odontogenic epithelium is often seen within the gingival tissues and in odontogenic tumors in the gingiva. This consists of clusters of cuboidal epithelium that may have clear cytoplasm and sometimes show palisading of the basal cell nuclei (*Fig. 10.6*).

Finally, the oral mucosa consists of epithelium and underlying lamina propria, which can be arbitrarily divided into superficial and deep portions, and underlying muscle or bone. Since there is no muscularis mucosa, there is no true submucosa.

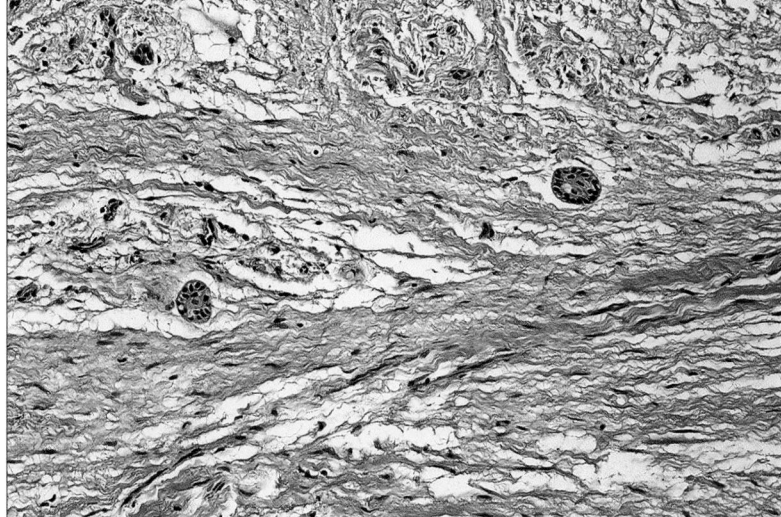

Fig. 10.6
Odontogenic epithelium: note the small rests composed of cuboidal cells, sometimes with subtle palisading of nuclei at the periphery.

Hereditary conditions

Macular lesions

White sponge nevus

Clinical features

White sponge nevus (Canon's white sponge nevus, leukoedema exfoliativum mucosae oris, familial white folded dysplasia of mouth) is an autosomal dominant condition with high penetrance and variable expressivity. Onset is in early childhood with 50% of patients diagnosed before age 20.[1,2] The buccal mucosa is almost invariably affected and other common sites are the labial mucosa, tongue, alveolar mucosa and the floor of mouth. Nasal, esophageal, vaginal, anal and penile mucosae may be affected, but not that of the conjunctiva, although there is one report of associated colobomas.[3] Lesions appear as diffuse, white-to-gray, painless, spongy folded plaques with a tendency to slough off (*Fig. 10.7*).[2,4,5] There may be periods of exacerbation and remission.

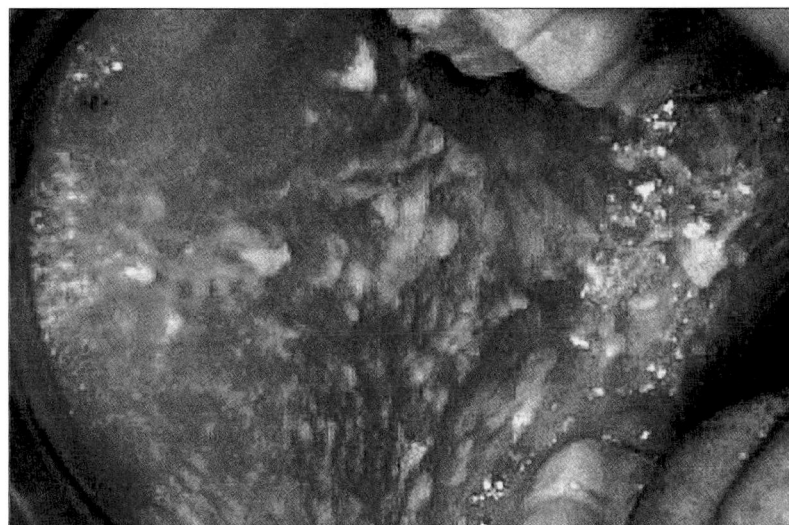

Fig. 10.7
White sponge nevus: typical white, thickened, spongy-appearing mucosa. By courtesy of C. Allen, DDS, Columbus, USA.

Pathogenesis and histological features

White sponge nevus has been traced to a mutation in the helical domain of mucosal-specific keratins K4 (on chromosome 12q) and K13 (on chromosome 17q). The mutations are in the form of amino acid deletions, substitutions and insertions resulting in keratin filament instability and abnormal aggregation of tonofilaments.[6–8] That some cases remit with antibiotic therapy suggests that infections and/or inflamation may play a role in the expression of disease.[9,10]

There is parakeratosis, acanthosis with the formation of large, blunt rete ridges, vacuolation of cells and spongiosis; anucleate keratinocytes are present superficially (*Fig. 10.8*). Dyskeratotic cells exhibit dense peri- and paranuclear eosinophilic condensations and there is insignificant inflammation (*Fig. 10.9*).[4,11,12] Parakeratin plugs and streaks have been noted beneath the superficial keratinocytes. One case that exhibited foci of epidermolytic hyperkeratosis has been documented.[13]

The eosinophilic condensations correspond to tonofilament aggregates in a peri- and paranuclear location.[1,11,12,14] Organelles tend to segregate and are absent in vacuolated cells. Odland bodies are abundant within keratinocytes but few are present in the intercellular spaces, suggesting a lack of acid phosphatase leading to retention, rather than normal shedding of superficial cells.[1]

References

1. Frithiof, L., Banoczy, J. (1976) White sponge nevus (leukoedema exfoliativum mucosae oris): ultrastructural observations. *Oral Surg*, **41**, 607–622.
2. Jorgensen, R.J., Levin, S. (1981) White sponge nevus. *Arch Dermatol*, **117**, 73–76.
3. Wright, S., Levy, I.S. (1991) White sponge naevus and ocular coloboma. *Arch Dis Child*, **66**, 514–516.
4. Nichols, G.E., Cooper, P.H., Underwood, P.B. et al (1990) White sponge nevus. *Obstet Gynecol*, **76**, 545–548.
5. Krajewska, I.A., Moore, L., Brown, J.H. (1992) White sponge nevus presenting in the esophagus – case report and literature review. *Pathology*, **24**, 112–115.
6. Rugg, E.L., McLean, W.H., Allison, W.E. et al (1995) A mutation in the mucosal keratin K4 is associated with oral white sponge nevus. *Nat Genet*, **11**, 450–452.
7. Richard, G., De-Laurenzi, V., Didona, B. et al (1995) Keratin 13 point mutation underlies the hereditary mucosal epithelial disorder white sponge nevus. *Nat Genet*, **11**, 453–455.
8. Terrinoni, A., Candi, E., Oddi, S. et al (2000) A glutamine insertion in the 1A alpha helical domain of the keratin 4 gene in a familial case of white sponge nevus. *J Invest Dermatol*, **114**, 388–391.
9. McDonagh, A.J., Gawkrodger, D.J., Walker, A.E. (1990) White sponge naevus successfully treated with topical tetracycline. *Clin Exp Dermatol*, **15**, 152–153.
10. Lamey, P.J., Bolas, A., Napier, S.S. et al (1998) Oral white sponge naevus: response to antibiotic therapy. *Clin Exp Dermatol*, **23**, 59–63.

11.   McGinnis, J.P. Jr, Turner, J.E. (1975) Ultrastructure of the white sponge nevus. *Oral Surg Oral Med Oral Pathol*, **40**, 644–651.
12.   Morris, R., Gansler, T.S., Rudisil, M.T. et al (1988) White sponge nevus. Diagnosis by light microscopic and ultrastructural cytology. *Acta Cytol*, **32**, 357–361.
13.   Aloi, F.G., Molinero, A. (1988) White sponge nevus with epidermolytic changes. *Dermatologica*, **177**, 323–326.
14.   Whitten, J.B. (1970) The electron microscopic examination of congenital keratoses of the oral mucous membranes. I. White sponge nevus. *Oral Surg Oral Med Oral Pathol*, **29**, 69–84.

Hereditary benign intraepithelial dyskeratosis

Clinical features

This autosomal dominant disorder of the eye and oral cavity was first described in a tri-racial isolate (Caucasian, Native American and African) in North Carolina called the Halowar or Haliwa Indians.[1] Because of migration, cases have been reported in descendants living now in New York, Pennsylvania, Virginia and Washington DC.

The eye lesions, which usually present by the first year of life, are foamy, gelatinous plaques in the bulbar conjunctiva in a perilimbic distribution both nasally and temporally. Patients experience irritation and photophobia and there may be exacerbations in spring. Corneal vascularization sometimes leads to visual loss.[2]

Oral involvement is asymptomatic and is therefore generally not noticed until the second decade. Lesions involve the buccal and labial mucosa, floor of mouth, lateral and ventral tongue and gingiva but not usually the dorsum of tongue or uvula.[3,4] The mucosa is white, opalescent, spongy, macerated, folded and shaggy, often resembling white sponge nevus (*Fig. 10.10*). There is generally no involvement of genital, nasal or rectal mucosa.

Pathogenesis and histological features

Genetic studies have localized the gene for this condition to chromosome 4q35 with a duplication segregating in affected individuals.[5]

There is hyperkeratosis and acanthosis (*Fig. 10.11*). Dyskeratotic cells (also called 'tobacco cells' because of their orange–brown color on Papanicolaou-stained smears) are present in the mid to upper one-third of the epithelium, appearing engulfed by adjacent normal keratinocytes; this 'cell-within-a-cell' appearance is a characteristic feature and is well seen in cytological smears (*Fig. 10.12*).[3,6]

The dyskeratotic cells are packed with tonofilaments and vesicular bodies that may represent Odland bodies.[6] Some keratinocytes also show disappearance of cellular interdigitations and desmosomes.

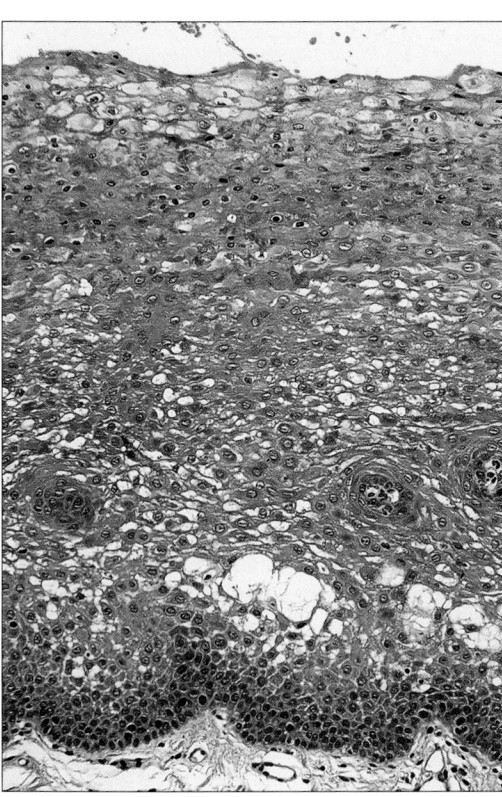

Fig. 10.8
White sponge nevus: the epithelium exhibits spongiosis, acanthosis and dyskeratosis.

References

1.   Von Sallman, L., Paton, D. (1960) Hereditary benign intraepithelial dyskeratosis: I. Ocular manifestations. *Arch Ophthalmol*, **63**, 421–429.
2.   Reed, J.W., Cashwell, F., Klintworth, G.H. (1979) Corneal manifestations of hereditary benign intraepithelial dyskeratosis. *Arch Ophthalmol*, **97**, 297–300.
3.   Witkop, C.J., Shankle, C.H., Graham, J.B. et al (1960) Hereditary benign intraepithelial dyskeratosis. II. Oral manifestations and hereditary transmission. *Arch Pathol*, **70**, 696–711.
4.   McLean, I.W., Riddle, P.J., Schruggs, J.H. et al (1981) Hereditary benign intraepithelial dyskeratosis. A report of two cases from Texas. *Ophthalmology*, **88**, 164–168.
5.   Allingham, R.R., Seo, B., Rampersaud, E. et al (2001) A duplication in chromosome 4q35 is associated with hereditary benign intraepithelial dyskeratosis. *Am J Hum Genet*, **68**, 491–494.
6.   Sadeghi, E.M., Witkop, C.J. (1977) Ultrastructural study of hereditary benign intraepithelial dyskeratosis. *Oral Surg*, **44**, 567–577.

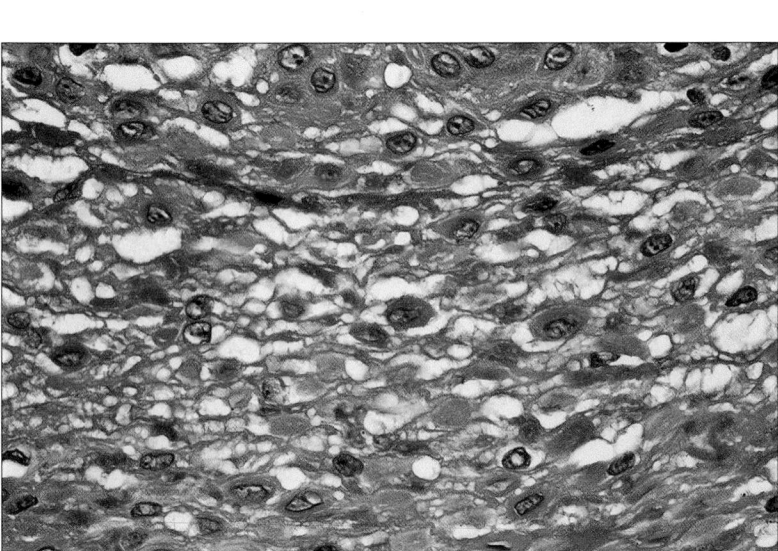

Fig. 10.9
White sponge nevus: there is perinuclear eosinophilic keratin condensations.

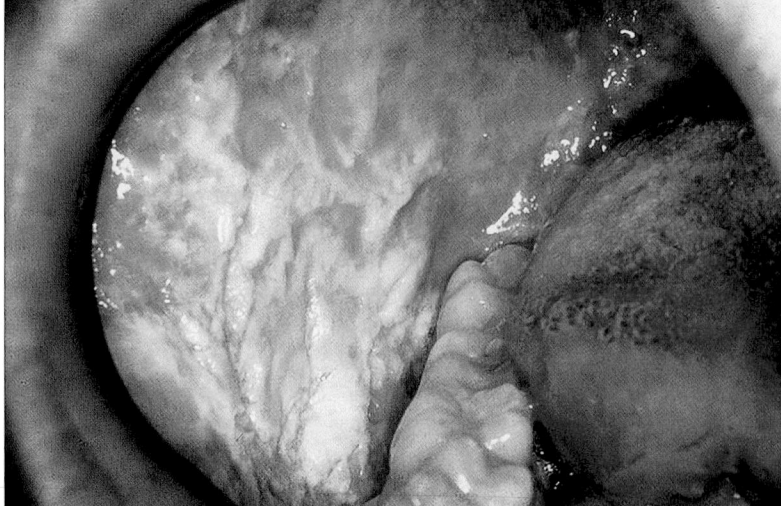

Fig. 10.10
Hereditary benign intraepithelial dyskeratosis: the mucosa appears white and thickened. By courtesy of J. McDonald, DDS, Cincinnati, USA.

Pachyonychia congenita

Clinical features

This genodermatosis is characterized by nail dystrophy, poikiloderma and leukoplakia. The oral findings, usually noted within the first two decades of life, are characterized by focal or generalized white hyperkeratotic plaques on the dorsum and lateral borders of the tongue, gingiva, and on the linea alba.[1–3] Natal teeth (teeth present at birth) are a common finding.[4–6] The mucosa of the larynx, nose and cornea may also be involved.[5,7]

Histological features

There is hyperparakeratosis or hyperorthokeratosis, acanthosis and intracellular vacuolization.[2,8] Because pachyonychia congenita and dyskeratosis congenita are generally diagnosed on clinical findings, there are few detailed reports on the histology of oral lesions.

References

1. Gorlin, R.J., Chaudhry, A.P. (1958) Oral lesions accompanying pachyonychia congenita. *Oral Surg*, **11**, 541–543.
2. Young, L.L., Lenox, J.A. (1973) Pachyonychia congenita. A long-term evaluation of associated oral and dermal lesions. *Oral Surg Oral Med Oral Pathol*, **36**, 663–666.
3. Maser, E.D. (1977) Oral manifestations of pachyonychia congenita. Report of a case. *Oral Surg Oral Med Oral Pathol*, **43**, 373–378.
4. Murray, F.A. (1921) Congenital anomalies of the nails. Four cases of hereditary hypertrophy of the nail-bed associated with a history of erupted teeth at birth. *Br J Dermatol*, **33**, 409–410.
5. Jackson, A.D.M., Fowler, S.D. (1951) Pachyonychia congenita: a report of six cases in one family with a note on linkage data. *Ann Eugenics*, **16**, 142–146.
6. Anneroth, G., Isacsson, G., Lagerholm, B. et al (1975) Pachyonychia congenita. A clinical, histological and microradiographic study with special reference to oral manifestations. *Acta Derm Venereol*, **55**, 387–394.
7. Benjamin, B., Parsons, D.S., Molloy, H.F. (1987) Pachyonychia congenita with laryngeal involvement. *Int J Pediatr Otorhinolaryngol*, **13**, 205–209.
8. Witkop, C.J. Jr, Gorlin, R.J. (1961) Four hereditary mucosal syndromes. *Arch Dermatol*, **84**, 762–771.

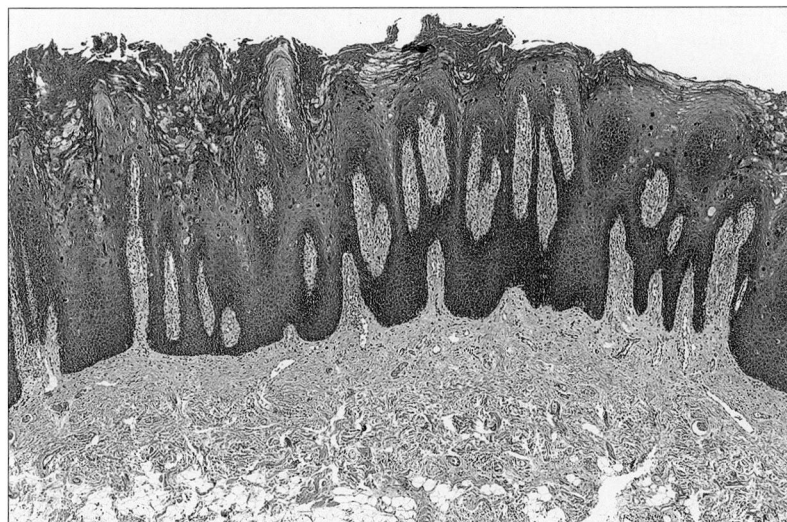

Fig. 10.11
Hereditary benign intraepithelial dyskeratosis: there is hyperkeratosis, dyskeratosis and acanthosis. By courtesy of J. McDonald, DDS, Cincinatti, USA.

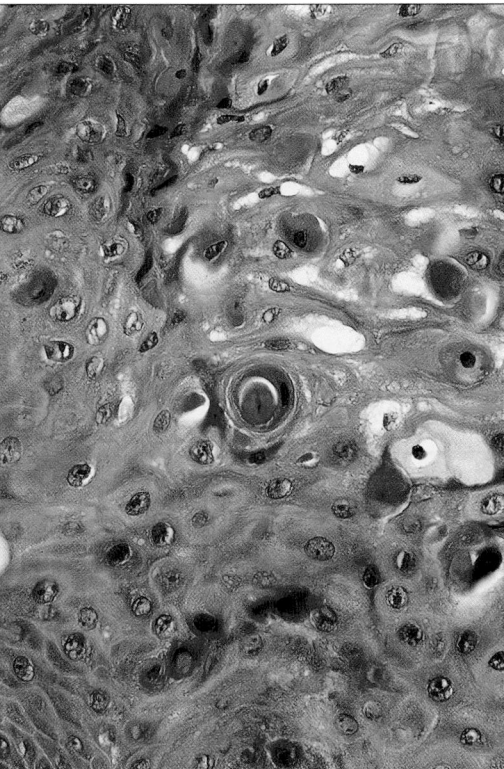

Fig. 10.12
Hereditary benign intraepithelial dyskeratosis: note the dyskeratosis with the typical 'cell-within-a-cell' structures. By courtesy of J. McDonald, DDS, Cincinatti, USA.

Dyskeratosis congenita

Dyskeratosis congenita is another genodermatosis that is associated with nail dystrophy, poikiloderma, oral leukoplakia and development of pancytopenia. The mucosa of the conjunctiva, urethra and genital tract may also be involved.[1,2] Oral leukoplakia, particularly of the tongue, presents in the second decade of life and has a high propensity for developing squamous cell carcinoma at an early age (see p. 249).[3]

References

1. Sirinavin, C., Trowbridge, A.A. (1975) Dyskeratosis congenita: clinical features and genetic aspects. Report of a family and review of the literature. *J Med Genet*, **12**, 339–354.
2. Davidson, H.R., Connor, J.M. (1988) Dyskeratosis congenita. *J Med Genet*, **25**, 843–846.
3. Moretti, S., Spallanzani, A., Chiarugi, A. et al (2000) Oral carcinoma in a young man: a case of dyskeratosis congenita. *J Eur Acad Dermatol Venereol*, **14**, 123–125.

Darier's disease

Clinical features

Oral findings occur in approximately 50% of patients with Darier's disease (Darier–White disease, keratosis follicularis). Mild involvement comprises minute white or pink keratotic papules while in more extensive disease coalescence results in larger plaques or a cobblestone surface. Lesions are generally asymptomatic.[1–4] The palate is the most common site affected, perhaps because of its normally keratinized nature, followed by the gingiva, tongue, buccal mucosa and floor of mouth. The lips are rarely involved.[5] Recurrent parotid or submandibular swelling may be reported in up to approximately one-third of cases and is most likely the result of strictures in the main duct causing obstruction.[4,5] In general, the degree of oral involvement parallels the extent of skin lesions[2,5] (see also p. 158).

Histological features

The typical findings are hyperkeratosis, acanthosis and suprabasal clefting with acantholysis forming vertical villous-like projections protruding into lacunae. Corps ronds and grains may not be as prominent as in skin lesions.[2,5] Papanicolaou-stained smears show an orange–brown staining of the dyskeratotic 'grains' and refractile concentric perinuclear rings and granular bands in corps ronds.[6] The excretory salivary ducts may become metaplastic or involved by the same process leading to stricture formation and obstruction.[1,7,8]

Differential diagnosis

Pemphigus vulgaris and pyostomatitis vegetans both exhibit acantholysis but not generally dyskeratosis; in addition, pemphigus shows intercellular IgG deposits on direct immunofluorescence.

References

1. Spouge, J.D., Trott, J.R., Chesko, G. (1966) Darier–White's disease: a cause of white lesions of the mucosa. Report of four cases. *Oral Surg Oral Med Oral Pathol*, **21**, 441–457.
2. Weathers, D.R., Baker, G., Archard, H.O. et al (1974) Psoriasiform lesions of the oral mucosa (with emphasis on 'ectopic geographic tongue'). *Oral Surg Oral Med Oral Pathol*, **37**, 872–888.
3. Prindiville, D.E., Stern, D. (1976) Oral manifestations of Darier's disease. *J Oral Surg*, **34**, 1001–1006.
4. Ferris, T., Lamey, P.J., Rennie, J.S. (1990) Darier's disease: oral features and genetic aspects. *Br Dent J*, **168**, 71–73.
5. Macleod, R.I., Munro, C.S. (1991) The incidence and distribution of oral lesions in patients with Darier's disease. *Br Dent J*, **171**, 133–136.
6. Burlakow, P., Medak, H., McGrew, E.A. et al (1969) The cytology of vesicular conditions affecting the oral mucosa. 2. Keratosis follicularis. *Acta Cytol*, **13**, 407–415.
7. Green, T.L., Eversole, L.R., Leider, A.S. (1986) Oral and labial verruca vulgaris: clinical, histologic, and immunohistochemical evaluation. *Oral Surg Oral Med Oral Pathol*, **62**, 410–416.
8. Tegner, E., Jonsson, N. (1990) Darier's disease with involvement of both submandibular glands. *Acta Derm Venereol*, **70**, 451–452.

Warty dyskeratoma

Clinical features

This usually solitary lesion resembles Darier's disease and may present as a papule or nodule (warty dyskeratoma, oral focal acantholytic dyskeratosis) in the oral cavity. It generally occurs in the fifth or sixth decade and almost always arises on the keratinized and attached mucosa of the palate or gingiva with a 2:1 female predominance.[1] Most lesions measure less than 1 cm and rare cases develop on the buccal mucosa and tongue.[2-4] Interesting, the majority of cases occur on the left side of the mouth raising the possibility that trauma plays an important role since most individuals are right-handed and tend to brush the left side of the mouth more vigorously. The papular variety appears as a white papule or plaque while the nodular variety has an umbilicated or crateriform appearance. There is an association with tobacco use[3,5] (see also p. 166).

Histological features

Oral warty dyskeratoma is characterized by Darier's disease-like features including suprabasilar clefting with lacunae formation, villous-like projections, corps ronds and grains. The papular lesions show multifocal involvement and sometimes papillary epithelial hyperplasia.[6] There is no association with underlying sebaceous or salivary glands.

Differential diagnosis

Pemphigus vulgaris can be readily distinguished by the clinical history. In addition, intercellular IgG deposition is characteristically present on direct immunofluorescence in pemphigus.

References

1. Laskaris, G., Sklavounou, A. (1985) Warty dyskeratoma of the oral mucosa. *Br J Oral Maxillofac Surg*, **23**, 371–375.
2. Tomich, C.E., Burkes, E.J. (1971) Warty dyskeratoma (isolated dyskeratosis follicularis) of the oral mucosa. *Oral Surg Oral Med Oral Pathol*, **31**, 798–807.
3. Dixter, C.T., Konstat, M.S., Giunta, J.L. et al (1975) Congenital granular-cell tumor of alveolar ridge and tongue. Report of two cases. *Oral Surg Oral Med Oral Pathol*, **40**, 270–277.
4. Leider, A.S., Eversole, L.R. (1984) Focal acantholytic dyskeratosis of the oral mucosa. *Oral Surg Oral Med Oral Pathol*, **58**, 64–70.
5. Kaugars, G.E., Lieb, R.J., Abbey, L.M. (1984) Focal oral warty dyskeratoma. *Int J Dermatol*, **23**, 123–130.
6. Freedman, P.D., Lumerman, H., Kerpel, S.M. (1981) Oral focal acantholytic dyskeratosis. *Oral Surg Oral Med Oral Pathol*, **52**, 66–70.

Tumor-like lesions

Choristomas

Osseous choristoma
Clinical features

The majority of these lesions (93%) occur as sessile or pedunculated masses on the posterior dorsum of the tongue, near the foramen cecum, although other sites such as the buccal mucosa may be involved.[1-4] Most develop in the second and third decades and females are three to five times more likely to be affected.[2,4] There may be dysphagia.

Pathogenesis and histological features

Theories of origin include ossification of branchial arch remnants, metaplastic bone formation secondary to trauma, and osteogenesis of unknown cause from pluripotent mesenchymal cells in the area.

The lesion consists of a well-circumscribed mass of viable lamellar bone with haversian systems surrounded by fibrous connective tissue; osteoblastic rimming, hematopoietic and fatty marrow or even cartilage may be present (*Figs 10.13, 10.14*).[1,5,6]

References

1. Krolls, S.O., Jacoway, J.R., Alexander, W.N. (1971) Osseous choristomas (osteomas) of intraoral soft tissues. *Oral Surg Oral Med Oral Pathol*, **32**, 588–595.
2. Chou, L.S., Hansen, L.S., Daniels, T.E. (1991) Choristomas of the oral cavity: a review. *Oral Surg Oral Med Oral Pathol*, **72**, 584–593.
3. Mesa, M.L., Schneider, L.C., Northington, L. (1982) Osteoma of the buccal mucosa. *J Oral Maxillofac Surg*, **40**, 684–686.
4. Ishikawa, M., Mizukoshi, T., Notani, K. et al (1993) Osseous choristoma of the tongue. Report of two cases. *Oral Surg Oral Med Oral Pathol*, **76**, 561–563.
5. Wesley, R.K., Zielinski, R.J. (1978) Osteocartilaginous choristoma of the tongue: clinical and histopathologic considerations. *J Oral Surg*, **36**, 59–61.
6. Tohill, M.J., Green, J.G., Cohen, D.M. (1987) Intraoral osseous and cartilaginous choristomas: report of three cases and review of the literature. *Oral Surg Oral Med Oral Pathol*, **63**, 506–510.

Cartilaginous choristoma
Clinical features

Cartilaginous choristomas present as discrete nodules, usually along the lateral border of the tongue (85% of cases) and less often on the buccal mucosa and soft palate.[1-3] Most occur in adults.[4]

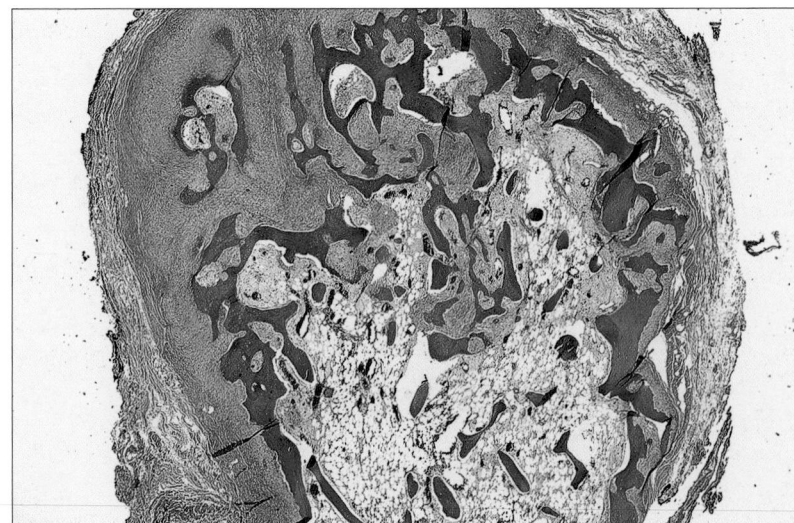

Fig. 10.13
Osseous choristoma from the tongue: there is a discrete nodule of bone and fatty tissue.

Pathogenesis and histological features

They probably represent developmental malformations that arise from pluripotent mesenchymal cells of the tongue. Metaplastic change secondary to trauma is also a possible mechanism.

Cartilaginous choristoma consists of a mass of benign mature hyaline cartilage surrounded by dense perichondrium; loose myxoid tissue akin to primitive mesenchyme or even mature fat may also be present.[2,4,5] Some cases show ossification and association with salivary glands.[2,3] Rare cases of chondrosarcoma have been reported.[6]

Differential diagnosis

Metaplastic cartilaginous nodules are often seen in cases of denture-associated fibrous hyperplasias but these occur in the maxillary and mandibular vestibules associated with denture flanges. Cartilaginous rests are also common in the area of the nasopalatine canal. Some authors believe that cartilaginous rests of the soft palate/tonsillar area are a metaplastic phenomenon, occurring in 20% of tonsils examined.[7]

References

1. Chou, L.S., Hansen, L.S., Daniels, T.E. (1991) Choristomas of the oral cavity: a review. *Oral Surg Oral Med Oral Pathol*, 72, 584–593.
2. Gardner, D.G., Paterson, J.C. (1968) Chondroma or metaplastic chondrosis of soft palate. *Oral Surg Oral Med Oral Pathol*, 26, 601–604.
3. Hankey, G.T., Waterhouse, J.P. (1968) A calcifying chondroma in the cheek. *Br J Oral Surg*, 5, 239–244.
4. Trowbridge, M., McCabe, B., Reznicek, M. (1989) Cartilaginous choristoma of the tongue. A case report and literature review. *Arch Otolaryngol Head Neck Surg*, 115, 627–629.
5. Sultani, F.A., Krolls, S.O., Heckler, F.R. (1983) Cartilaginous choristoma of buccal mucosa: a case report. *Br J Plast Surg*, 36, 395–397.
6. Forman, G. (1967) Chondrosarcoma of the tongue. *Br J Oral Surg*, 4, 218–221.
7. Weller, C.V. (1923) The incidence and histopathology of bone and cartilage in the tonsil. *Ann Otol Rhinol Laryngol*, 32, 687–699.

Sebaceous choristoma and hyperplasia
Clinical features

Sebaceous glands occur as 1–3 mm yellow macules or papules in the buccal and labial mucosa in approximately 80% of the adult population (*Fig. 10.15*).[1] However, these may become hyperplastic, forming painless papules, plaques or nodules, and are termed sebaceous hyperplasia.[2] They occur in the same sites as Fordyce granules.

Rare cases of sebaceous choristomas have been reported in the tongue of adults. They present as dome-shaped masses in the midline of the dorsum in the area of the middle or posterior one-third of the tongue, often associated with a thyroglossal duct.[3–5]

Histological features

Fordyce granules consist of mature lobules of sebaceous glands that communicate with the surface epithelium via a duct. There may be pseudocyst formation with retention of secretions and adenomatous hyperplasia; the rare occurrence of hair follicle within a Fordyce granule has been reported.[6–9]

In sebaceous hyperplasia, at least 15 lobules of mature sebaceous glands empty into ducts that communicate with the surface (*Fig. 10.16*).[2] In the sebaceous choristoma, mature sebaceous units may be associated with eccrine glands, hair follicles and apocrine glands.[3,5] Demodex have been identified in some lesions.[3,10]

References

1. Halperin, V., Kolas, S., Jefferis, K.R. et al (1953) Occurrence of Fordyce glands, benign migratory glossitis, median rhomboid glossitis, and fissured tongue in 2,478 dental students. *Oral Surg*, 6, 1072–1077.
2. Daley, T.D. (1993) Intraoral sebaceous hyperplasia. Diagnostic criteria. *Oral Surg Oral Med Oral Pathol*, 75, 343–347.
3. Trodahl, J.N., Albjerg, L.E., Gorlin, R.J. (1967) Ectopic sebaceous glands of the tongue. *Arch Dermatol*, 95, 387–389.
4. Knapp, M.J. (1971) Lingual sebaceous glands and a possible thyroglossal duct. *Oral Surg Oral Med Oral Pathol*, 31, 70–71 passim.
5. Leider, A.S., Lucas, J.W., Eversole, L.R. (1977) Sebaceous choristoma of the thyroglossal duct. *Oral Surg Oral Med Oral Pathol*, 44, 261–266.
6. Sewerin, I., Praetorius, F. (1974) Keratin-filled pseudocysts of ducts of sebaceous glands in the vermilion border of the lip. *J Oral Pathol*, 3, 279–283.
7. Baughman, R.A., Heidrich, P.D. (1980) The oral hair: an extremely rare phenomenon. *Oral Surg Oral Med Oral Pathol*, 49, 530–531.
8. Lipani, C., Woytash J.J., Greene, G.W. (1983) Sebaceous adenoma of the oral cavity. *J Oral Maxillofac Surg*, 41, 56–60.
9. Ferguson, J.W., Geary, C.P., MacAlister, A.D. (1987) Sebaceous cell adenoma. Rare intra-oral occurrence of a tumor which is a frequent marker of Torre's syndrome. *Pathology*, 19, 204–208.
10. Franklin, C.D., Underwood, J.C. (1986) Demodex infestation of oral mucosal sebaceous glands. *Oral Surg Oral Med Oral Pathol*, 61, 80–82.

Gastrointestinal choristoma
Clinical features

Almost all of these are cystic lesions that present as swellings of the tongue, usually on the ventral surface.[1–3] Sometimes they appear as sinuses.[4] They are most often seen in infancy or early childhood.

Pathogenesis and histological features

Many theories of pathogenesis have been postulated including epithelial entrapment and induction, incomplete coalescence of lacunae and persistence of intestinal epithelial buds.[4,5]

The cystic lesions are lined by epithelium typical for the cardiac, fundic or pyloric regions of the stomach with parietal and Paneth cells.[4] However, some are lined by colonic and/or ciliated epithelium.[5] Smooth

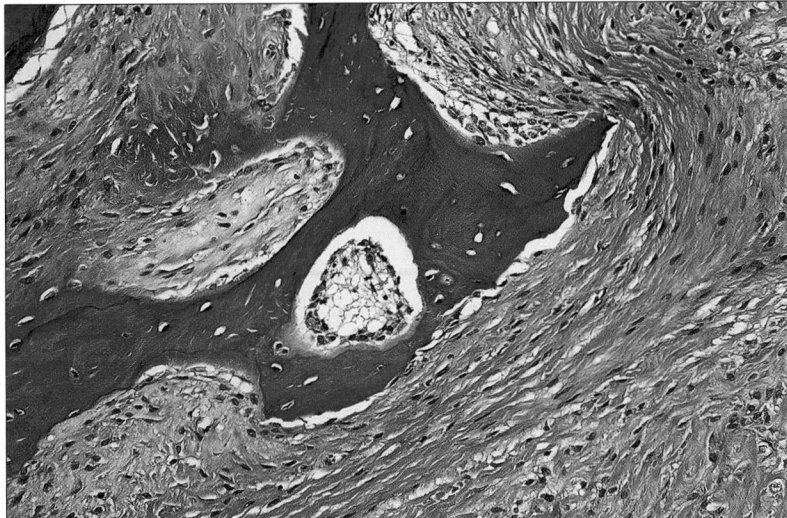

Fig. 10.14
Osseous choristoma from the tongue: the woven bone shows osteoblastic rimming and is laid down by the surrounding mesenchymal cells.

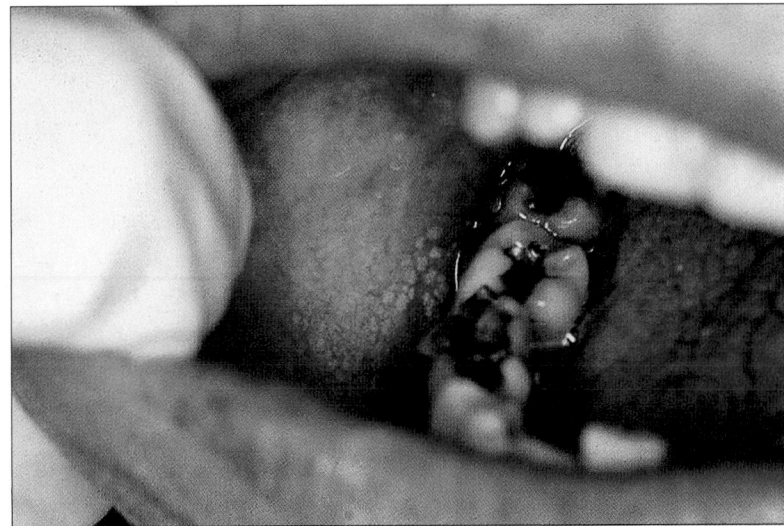

Fig. 10.15
Fordyce granules: typical yellow papules of the buccal mucosa.

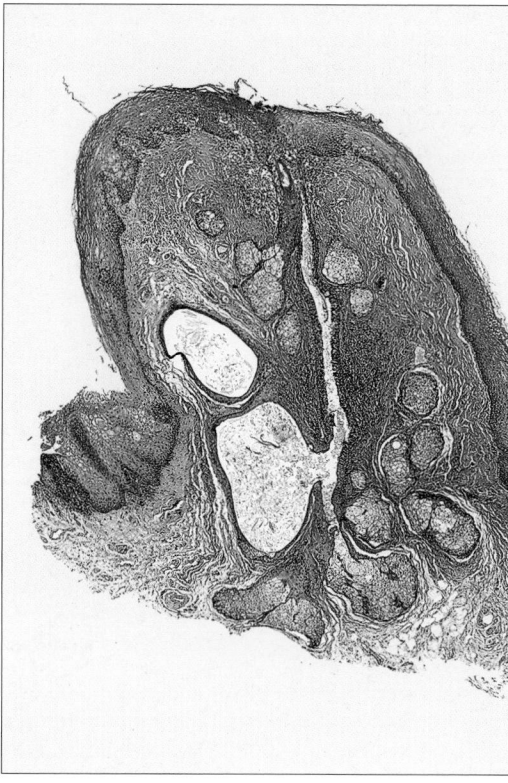

Fig. 10.16
Sebaceous hyperplasia:
numerous lobules of
sebaceous glands empty
into a central duct.

muscle is usually identified. The presence of pancreatic tissue has also been reported.[6]

References

1. Chou, L.S., Hansen, L.S., Daniels, T.E. (1991) Choristomas of the oral cavity: a review. *Oral Surg Oral Med Oral Pathol*, **72**, 584–593.
2. Gruskin, P., Landolfe, F.R. (1972) Heterotopic gastric mucosa of the tongue. *Arch Pathol*, **94**, 184–186.
3. Wurster, C.F., Ossoff, R.H., Rao, M.S. et al (1985) Heterotopic gastric mucosa of the tongue. *Otolaryngol Head Neck Surg*, **93**, 92–95.
4. Daley, T., Gardner, D.G., Smout, M.S. (1984) Canalicular adenoma: not a basal cell adenoma. *Oral Surg Oral Med Oral Pathol*, **57**, 181–188.
5. Lipsett, J., Sparnon, A.L., Byard, R.W. (1993) Embryogenesis of enterocystomas – enteric duplication cysts of the tongue. *Oral Surg Oral Med Oral Pathol*, **75**, 626–630.
6. Khunamornpong, S., Yousukh, A., Tananuvat, R. (1996) Heterotopic gastrointestinal and pancreatic tissue of the tongue: a case report. *Oral Surg Oral Med Oral Pathol Oral Radiol Endod*, **81**, 576–579.

Heterotopic brain tissue

Clinical features

This uncommon condition presents in the first year of life, most often affecting the palate, tongue or oropharynx, as a result of displacement of primitive neural elements in an early stage of development.[1,2] Some patients have associated palatal defects.[3] Respiratory obstruction is a major cause of morbidity and feeding difficulties.[4]

Histological features

Mature elements of the central nervous system including astrocytes, oligodendrocytes, ependymal tissue, choroid plexus-like tissue and, rarely, neuronal tissue may all be identified (*Fig. 10.17*).[1,2,5,6]

References

1. González García, M., Avila, C.G., López Arranz, J.S. et al (1988) Heterotopic brain tissue in the oral cavity. *Oral Surg Oral Med Oral Pathol*, **66**, 218–222.
2. Landini, G., Kitano, M., Urago, A. et al (1990) Heterotopic central neural tissue of the tongue. *Int J Oral Maxillofac Surg*, **19**, 334–336.
3. Chou, L.S., Hansen, L.S., Daniels, T.E. (1991) Choristomas of the oral cavity: a review. *Oral Surg Oral Med Oral Pathol*, **72**, 584–593.
4. Ibekwe, A.O., Ikerionwu, S.E. (1982) Heterotopic brain tissue in the palate. *J Laryngol Otol*, **96**, 1155–1158.
5. Ofodile, F.A., Aghadiuno, P.U., Oyemade, O. et al (1982) Heterotopic brain in the tongue. *Plast Reconstr Surg*, **69**, 120–124.
6. Bychkov, V., Gatti, W.M., Fresco, R. (1988) Tumor of the tongue containing heterotopic brain tissue. *Oral Surg Oral Med Oral Pathol*, **66**, 71–73.

Epidermoid and dermoid cysts

Clinical features

The floor of the mouth is the most common site of presentation and there may be a slight female predilection. Some cases are congenital and more than 80% present before age 25.[1–3] Classification of these lesions is based on anatomical location such as lingual, submental or submandibular and on the histological appearance.[1,2,4]

They present as dome-shaped, yellow masses with a rubbery or doughy consistency. Intraoral lesions cause feeding, swallowing and speech difficulties while extraoral variants below the myohoid muscle lead to a noticeable submental mass. Dumbbell shaped cysts have both intra- and extraoral swellings.[5]

While epidermoid and dermoid cysts are cystic structures that occur in the midline of the floor of mouth in children and young adults, dermoid tumors or hairy polyps are usually large congenital lesions occurring in the nasopharynx and soft palate.

Pathogenesis and histological features

The pathogenesis is uncertain. One theory suggests that they arise from entrapped epithelial rests in the line of fusion of facial processes. Another proposes that the lining develops from displaced embryonic rests or traumatic implantation, possibly occurring even in utero.[3]

Both epidermoid and dermoid cysts are lined by orthokeratinized squamous epithelium and the lumen is filled with keratinaceous material. Epidermoid cysts (also called epithelial inclusion cysts) have no adnexa in the wall, while dermoid cysts always have skin adnexal structures in the wall. Oral dermoid cysts are three times more common than epidermoid cysts.[2]

Some cysts also contain gastrointestinal mucosa.[6,7] If tissues from all three germ layers are represented, the term 'teratoid cyst' may be more appropriate.

Differential diagnosis

Gingival cyst of the adult is generally non-keratinized and is lined by low cuboidal to columnar or stratified squamous epithelium, with occasional epithelial plaques and clear cells.[8] Gingival cysts of the newborn, which are generally not biopsied because they exteriorize on their own, are filled with keratinaceous material.[9] Both can be differentiated from epidermoid cysts by their location on the gingiva.

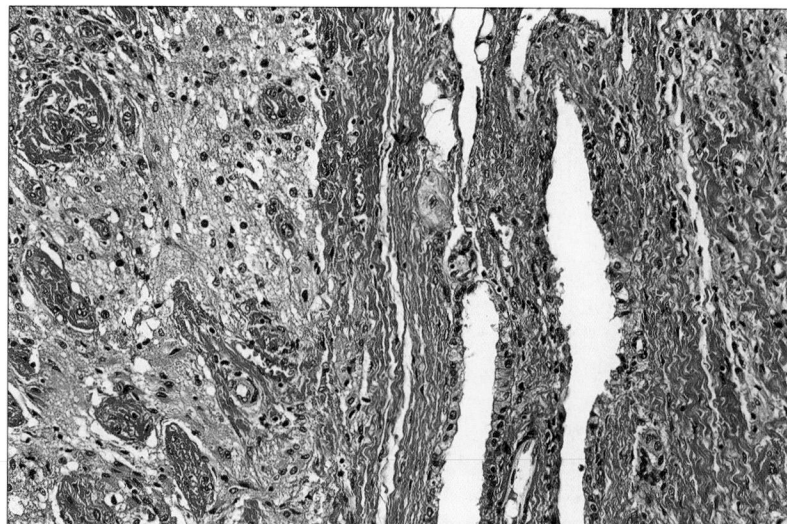

Fig. 10.17
Heterotopic brain tissue: note the presence of glial and ependymal tissue.

References

1. Gibson, W.S. Jr, Fenton, N.A. (1982) Congenital sublingual dermoid cyst. *Arch Otolaryngol*, **108**, 745–748.
2. King, R.C., Smith, B.R., Burk, J.L. (1994) Dermoid cyst in the floor of the mouth. Review of the literature and case reports. *Oral Surg Oral Med Oral Pathol*, **78**, 567–576.
3. Miles, L.P., Naidoo, L.C., Reddy, J. (1997) Congenital dermoid cyst of the tongue. *J Laryngol Otol*, **111**, 1179–1182.
4. Seward, G.R. (1965) Dermoid cysts of the floor of the mouth. *Br J Oral Surg*, **3**, 36–47.
5. Holt, G.R., Holt, J.E., Weaver, R.G. (1979) Dermoids and teratomas of the head and neck. *Ear Nose Throat J*, **58**, 520–531.
6. Arcand, P., Granger, J., Brochu, P. (1988) Congenital dermoid cyst of the oral cavity with gastric choristoma. *J Otolaryngol*, **17**, 219–222.
7. Oygur, T., Dursun, A., Uluoglu, O. et al (1992) Oral congenital dermoid cyst in the floor of the mouth of a newborn. The significance of gastrointestinal-type epithelium. *Oral Surg Oral Med Oral Pathol*, **74**, 627–630.
8. Buchner, A., Hansen, L.S. (1979) The histomorphologic spectrum of the gingival cyst in the adult. *Oral Surg Oral Med Oral Pathol*, **48**, 532–539.
9. Cataldo, E., Berkman, M.D. (1968) Cysts of the oral mucosa in newborns. *Am J Dis Child*, **116**, 44–48.

Dermoid tumor (dermoid), teratoma and epignathus

Clinical features

These rare conditions generally present congenitally or in infancy as masses protruding from the mouth, causing respiratory distress and feeding difficulties. They have been classified as follows:

- *dermoid* where only ecto- and mesodermal structures are present, and therefore the tumor is not strictly a teratoma
- *teratoid* tumor and teratoma with tissue from all three germ layers represented (in general, the tissues in teratoid tumor are not as well organized as in a teratoma)
- *epignathus* where there is recognizable organ and limb formation. Of these, the dermoid is the most common.[1]

Dermoids tend to occur in females (six to seven times more often than in males) as pedunculated masses in the nasopharynx, oropharynx and soft palate.[2,3] The mass is covered by skin, hence its other name, 'hairy polyp'. It may also grossly resemble an accessory auricle.[4]

Teratomas, teratoid tumors and epignathi present as masses that may protrude from the mouth and/or cause airway obstruction; there is no sex predilection and most are present at birth.[5] Unlike dermoids, these tumors are often associated with other findings such as elevated alphafetoprotein and polyhydramnios.[5,6]

Epignathi in particular may be associated with severe congenital malformations and stillbirth is a common occurrence. They most often arise from the hard palate (hence its name), although the posterior nasopharynx and upper lip can be involved, and there may be palatal clefts and cranial extension.[7–9] Grossly, the tumor sometimes contains rudimentary limbs, or even a head resembling an incomplete twin or fetus in fetu.[10]

Lingual teratomas are generally not associated with such developmental defects.[11]

Histological features

Dermoids are covered by skin with its constituent adnexa. In addition, cartilage, bone, muscle, adipose tissue and even salivary glands may be present (*Fig. 10.18*).[3,12] Teratomas contain all of the above. In addition, neural, brain, lung, gastrointestinal and respiratory tissues are sometimes present (*Fig. 10.19*).[6,11]

Epignathi consist of tissues organized to form grossly recognizable specific organ systems such as limbs, a head or eyes.[7,10]

There is no risk for malignant transformation.

References

1. Holt, G.R., Holt, J.E., Weaver, R.G. (1979) Dermoids and teratomas of the head and neck. *Ear Nose Throat J*, **58**, 520–531.
2. Foxwell, P.B., Kelham, B.H. (1958) Teratoid tumours of the nasopharynx. *J Laryngol Otol*, **72**, 647–657.
3. Chaudhry, A.P., Lore, J.M. Jr, Fisher, J.E. et al (1978) So-called hairy polyps or teratoid tumors of the nasopharynx. *Arch Otolaryngol*, **104**, 517–525.
4. Kanzaki, S., Yamada, K., Fujimoto, M. et al (1988) So-called hairy polyp resembling an auricle. *Otolaryngol Head Neck Surg*, **99**, 424–426.

5. Tharrington, C.L., Bossen, E.H. (1992) Nasopharyngeal teratomas. *Arch Pathol Lab Med*, **116**, 165–167.
6. Marras, T., Poenaru, D., Kamal, I. (1995) Perinatal management of nasopharyngeal teratoma. *J Otolaryngol*, **24**, 310–312.
7. Kang, K.W., Hissong, S.L., Langer, A. (1978) Prenatal ultrasonic diagnosis of epignathus. *J Clin Ultrasound*, **6**, 330–331.
8. Zakaria, M.A. (1986) Epignathus (congenital teratoma of the hard palate): a case report. *Br J Oral Maxillofac Surg*, **24**, 272–276.
9. Smith, N.M., Chambers, S.E., Billson, V.R. et al (1993) Oral teratoma (epignathus) with intracranial extension: a report of two cases. *Prenat Diagn*, **13**, 945–952.
10. Hatzihaberis, F., Stamatis, D., Staurinos, D. (1978) Giant epignathus. *J Pediatr Surg*, **13**, 517–518.
11. Lalwani, A.K., Engel, T.L. (1992) Teratoma of the tongue: a case report and review of the literature. *Int J Pediatr Otorhinolaryngol*, **24**, 261–268.
12. Kelly, A., Bough, I.D. Jr, Luft, J.D. et al (1996) Hairy polyp of the oropharynx: case report and literature review. *J Pediatr Surg*, **31**, 704–706.

Oral lymphoepithelial cyst

Clinical features

Oral lymphoepithelial cysts generally occur in the fourth decade of life with an equal sex distribution.[1–3] They present as painless yellowish nodules, usually less than 1 cm in diameter, most commonly affecting the floor of mouth followed by the posterior ventral tongue, soft palate and tonsillar fauces (*Fig. 10.20*).[3–5] They are commonly filled with cheesy, keratinaceous material. Some authors consider lesions which present at sites where tonsillar tissue is normally found to be inflammatory/obstructive tonsillar reactions.[4]

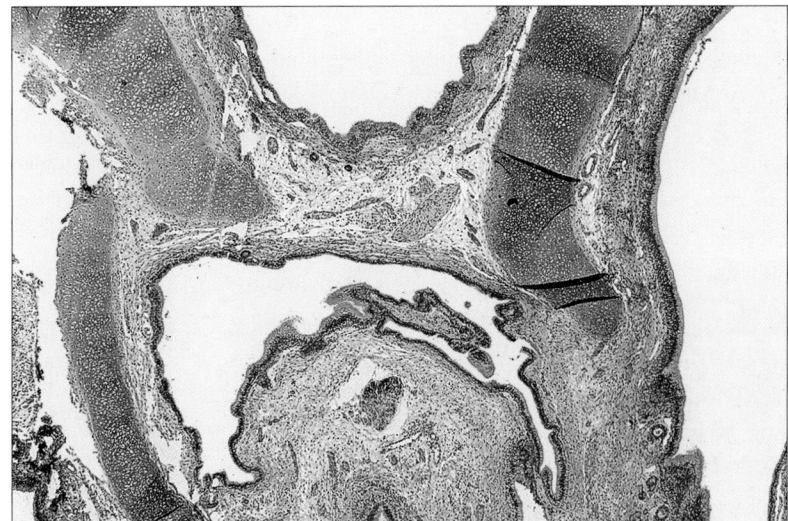

Fig. 10.18
Dermoid tumor: note the presence of cartilage and skin, forming a rudimentary ear. By courtesy of the Registry of Oral Pathology, AFIP, Washington DC, USA.

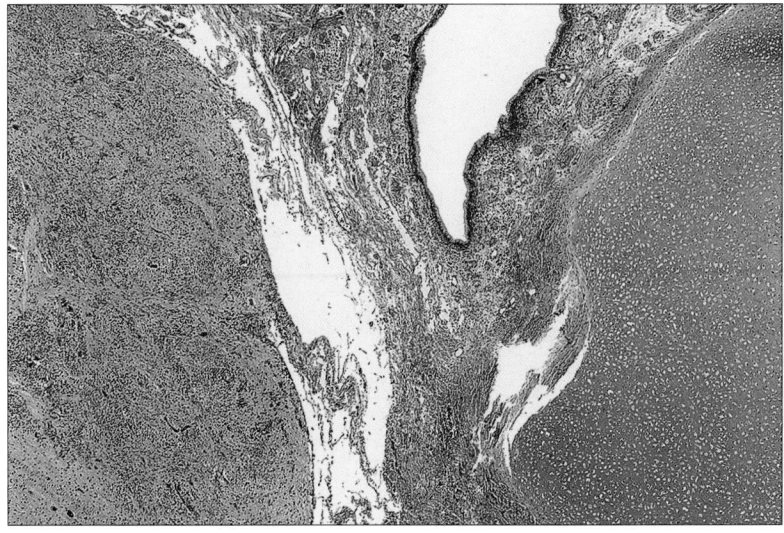

Fig. 10.19
Portion of a teratoma: in addition to ecto- and endoder-mal elements, glial tissue is present. By courtesy of the Registry of Oral Pathology, AFIP, Washington DC, USA.

Pathogenesis and histological features

Three theories of pathogenesis have been proposed:

- There is enclavement of epithelium within oral lymphoid tissue during embryogenesis and subsequent proliferation and cystic degeneration.[1]
- Such lymphoid aggregates are 'ectopic oral tonsils' where the crypt openings have been blocked, resulting in retention of secretions.[5,6]
- The epithelium represents normal excretory salivary ducts and the lymphoid tissue is a reaction to inflammation or immunological stimulation.[3]

The last theory pertains primarily to floor of mouth lesions, a site where tonsillar/lymphoid tissue is not normally found.

The cyst is lined by para- or orthokeratotic stratified squamous epithelium and the lumen is filled with desquamated keratinaceous material (*Fig. 10.21*).[3,4,7] Rare cases may be lined by pseudostratified columnar epithelium with or without mucous cells.[5] The epithelium usually demonstrates lymphocytic exocytosis (*Fig. 10.22*). The surrounding lymphoid tissue may encircle the cyst epithelium completely or partially, and germinal centers are usually well formed although not always present. Some cases demonstrate communication with the overlying surface epithelium, often through a narrow opening.

Salivary glands and ducts may be present in the vicinity, especially floor of mouth lesions.[1,3]

Differential diagnosis

Mucoceles of the retention type are lined by stratified squamous, columnar, oncocytic or respiratory epithelium, sometimes with mucous cell metaplasia. They may show foci of chronic inflammation but not usually the thick mantle of lymphocytes with germinal centers. Dermoid and epidermoid cysts lack the lymphoid mantle, and dermoid cysts contain adnexa in their wall.

Masses and clumps of bacteria may mat together and plug tonsillar crypts, presenting as an opaque yellow mass that is not covered by epithelium and that can readily be scraped off.[8]

References

1. Bhaskar, S.N. (1966) Lymphoepithelial cysts of the oral cavity. Report of twenty-four cases. *Oral Surg Oral Med Oral Pathol*, **21**, 120–128.
2. Sakoda, S., Kodama, Y., Shiba, R. (1983) Lymphoepithelial cyst of oral cavity. Report of a case and review of the literature. *Int J Oral Surg*, **12**, 127–131.
3. Chaudhry, A.P., Yamane, G.M., Scharlock, S.E. et al (1984) A clinico-pathological study of intraoral lymphoepithelial cysts. *J Oral Med*, **39**, 79–84.
4. Giunta, J., Cataldo, E. (1973) Lymphoepithelial cysts of the oral mucosa. *Oral Surg Oral Med Oral Pathol*, **35**, 77–84.
5. Buchner, A., Hansen, L.S. (1980) Lymphoepithelial cysts of the oral cavity. A clinicopathologic study of thirty-eight cases. *Oral Surg Oral Med Oral Pathol*, **50**, 441–449.
6. Knapp, M.J. (1970) Oral tonsils: location, distribution, and histology. *Oral Surg Oral Med Oral Pathol*, **29**, 155–161.
7. Acevedo, A., Nelson, J.F. (1971) Lymphoepithelial cysts of the oral cavity. Report of nine cases. *Oral Surg Oral Med Oral Pathol*, **31**, 632–636.
8. Giunta, J.L. (1987) Bacterial plug versus pseudocyst of the tonsils. *Oral Surg Oral Med Oral Pathol*, **63**, 202–207.

Lingual thyroid

Clinical features

Approximately 10% of cadaveric tongues contain nests of thyroid tissue with no sex predilection.[1,2] However, when thyroid tissue occurs as a mass in the tongue, the term 'lingual thyroid choristoma' or 'ectopic lingual thyroid' is used. Since approximately 86% of such tumors consist of the only thryoid tissue in the body, the terms 'lingual thyroid' or 'ectopic lingual thyroid' are more accurate.[3]

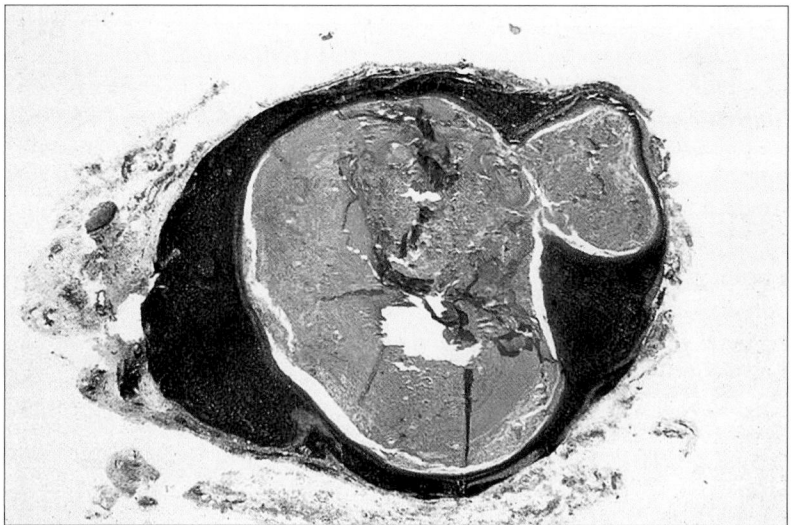

Fig. 10.21
Oral lymphoepithelial cyst: the cyst is completely encircled by lymphoid tissue.

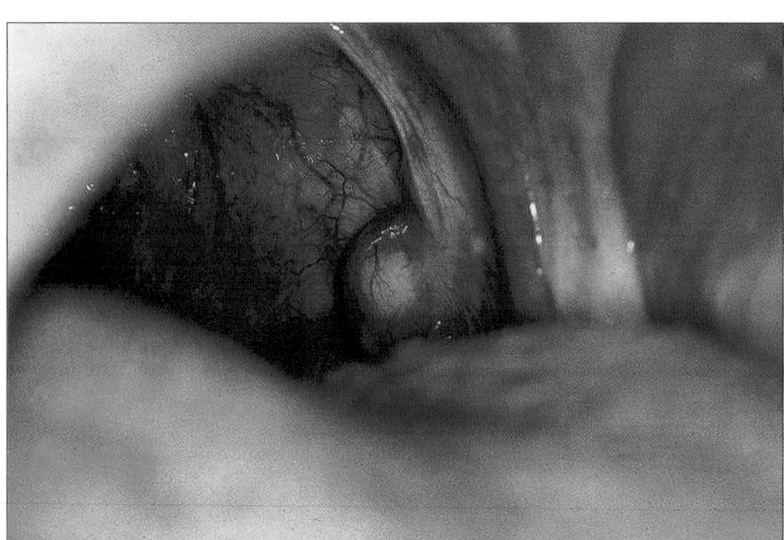

Fig. 10.20
Oral lymphoepithelial cyst: note the yellow nodule located behind the anterior faucial pillar.

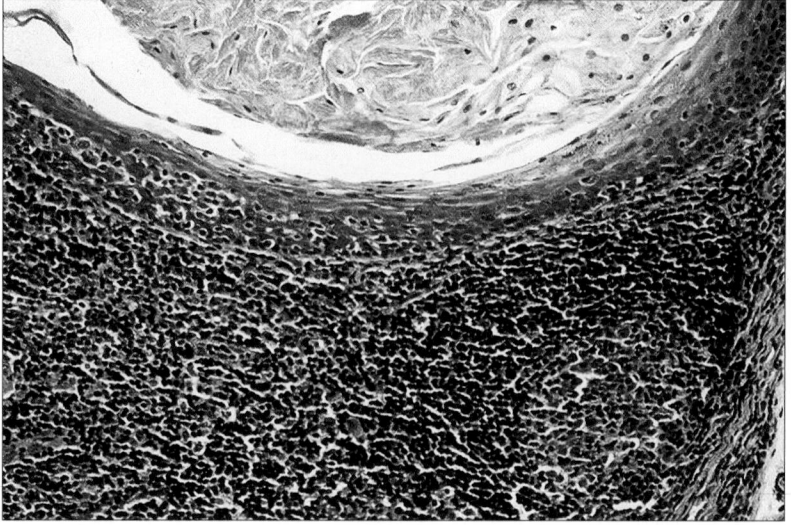

Fig. 10.22
Oral lymphoepithelial cyst: there is lymphocyte exocytosis through the epithelium and a small germinal center is present.

The lesion presents as a rounded, soft-to-firm mass within the base of the tongue between the foramen cecum and the epiglottis. It may cause dysphagia, dyspnea, dysphonia or hemorrhage.[2–4] Females are three to seven times more likely to be affected than males and there are two peaks of presentation, i.e. the first and second decades and the fifth and sixth decades, probably related to hormonal influences.[4–6] One-quarter of patients may be hypothyroid.

Pathogenesis and histological features

Since the thyroid anlage develops in the area of the foramen cecum and descends from there into the neck, failure to descend or persistence of remnants of the anlage which then proliferate, results in a noticeable mass.

In most cases, a biopsy is not indicated if technetium scans are positive for thyroid tissue. Thyroid follicles may contain mature or embryonic thyroid epithelium and exhibit microfollicular, macrofollicular or adenomatous changes.[1,5] There may be an associated thyroglossal duct.[2] Follicular and papillary carcinomas can sometimes occur, in the same frequency as one would expect in the normal thyroid gland.[7,8] As could be anticipated, medullary carcinoma has not been reported.

References

1. Sauk, J.J. Jr (1970) Ectopic lingual thyroid. *J Pathol*, **102**, 239–243.
2. Baughman, R.A. (1972) Lingual thyroid and lingual thyroglossal tract remnants. A clinical and histopathologic study with review of the literature. *Oral Surg Oral Med Oral Pathol*, **34**, 781–799.
3. Chou, L.S., Hansen, L.S., Daniels, T.E. (1991) Choristomas of the oral cavity: a review. *Oral Surg Oral Med Oral Pathol*, **72**, 584–593.
4. Kansal, P., Sakati, N., Rifai, A. et al (1987) Lingual thyroid. Diagnosis and treatment. *Arch Intern Med*, **147**, 2046–2048.
5. Neinas, F.W., Gorman, C.A., Devine, K.D. et al (1973) Lingual thyroid: clinical characteristics of 15 cases. *Ann Intern Med*, **79**, 205–210.
6. Kamat, M.R., Kulkarni, J.N., Desai, P.B. et al (1979) Lingual thyroid: a review of 12 cases. *Br J Surg*, **66**, 537–539.
7. Díaz-Arias, A.A., Bickel, J.T., Loy, T.S. et al (1992) Follicular carcinoma with clear cell change arising in lingual thyroid. *Oral Surg Oral Med Oral Pathol*, **74**, 206–211.
8. Winslow, C.P., Weisberger, E.C. (1997) Lingual thyroid and neoplastic change: a review of the literature and description of a case. *Otolaryngol Head Neck Surg*, **117**, S100–S102.

Congenital granular cell epulis

Clinical features

This benign congenital soft tissue tumor, also known as congenital granular cell tumor, presents as a pink, pedunculated mass usually on the anterior alveolar ridge with an intact surface (*Fig. 10.23*). There is a 10:1 female predilection and it is three times more common in the maxilla.[1] It may cause problems with nursing. Approximately 9% of patients have multiple nodules and some may have concurrent tongue lesions.[2–4]

Pathogenesis and histological features

Theories of histogenesis have included epithelial, pericytic and neural derivation.[5] The current hypothesis is that it represents a mesenchymal tumor of myofibroblastic origin with evidence of degenerative change. The latter is supported by lack of growth after birth of the infant, resolution of some cases over time, histological evidence of degeneration, and lack of recurrence in spite of incomplete removal.[1,6]

Histologically, a Grenz zone may or may not be present and the overlying epithelium is typically atrophic. The cells are round or polygonal with abundant eosinophilic granular cytoplasm, distinct cell borders, eccentric small nuclei and inconspicuous nucleoli; a prominent delicate and arborizing capillary network is usually evident (*Figs 10.24, 10.25*).[3,6] The granules are period acid–Schiff (PAS) positive and diastase resistant; odontogenic rests may also be present.[4,7]

The granular cells do not express S-100 protein but are always vimentin positive; macrophage/histiocytic markers (such as MAC387 and lysozyme) are usually negative although CD68 and Ki-M1P

immunohistochemistry is positive indicating the presence of phagolysosomes.[6,8] Antichymotripsin is sometimes present.[8] Stains for smooth muscle actin, estrogen and progesterone receptors, glial fibrillary acidic protein (GFAP), myelin basic protein (MBP) and neurofilament protein are negative.[1,6] One report identified neuron-specific enolase (NSE) within the granular cells.[9]

Ultrastructural studies reveal the presence of membrane-bound granules with electron-dense contents that most likely represent phagolysosomes.[1,3,8,10] The presence of subplasmalemmal dense bodies, pinocytotic vesicles containing precollagenous material, and intracytoplasmic laminin and fibronectin suggests myofibroblastic differentiation.[3,7,8]

Differential diagnosis

The cells of granular cell tumor are histologically indistinguishable from those of congenital granular cell epulis. However, in congenital granular cell epulis, there is no pseudoepitheliomatous hyperplasia and there is a prominent arborizing delicate vascular network; importantly, the cells are S-100 negative. Angulate bodies, seen ultrastructurally in granular cell tumor, are absent.

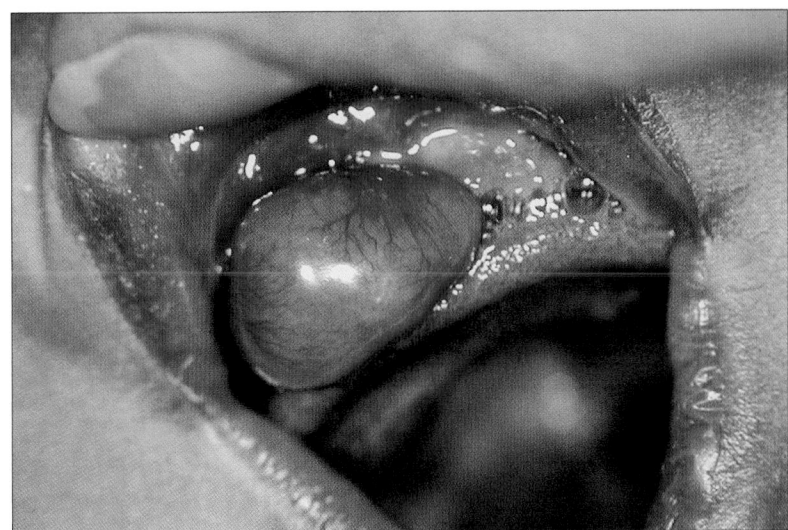

Fig. 10.23
Congenital granular cell epulis: the maxillary alveolus is a typical location for this tumor. By courtesy of B. Padwa, MD DDS, Boston, USA.

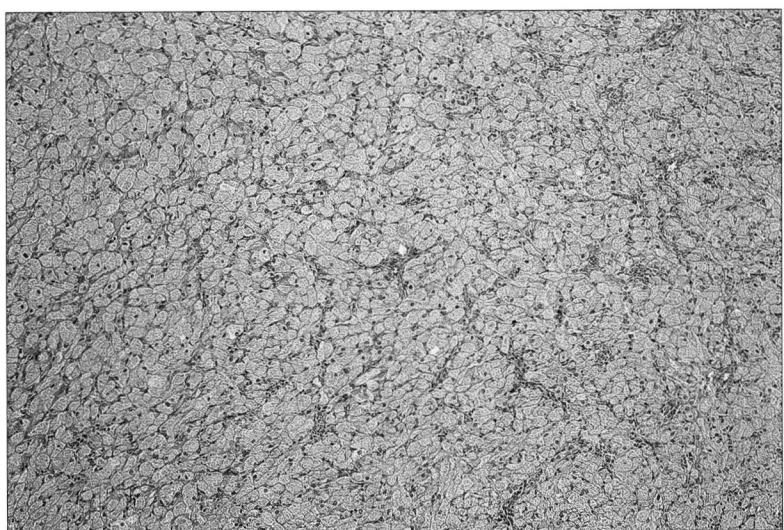

Fig. 10.24
Congenital granular cell epulis: there are sheets of granular cells with a delicate arborizing vasculature.

Congenital gingival leiomyomatous polyp/hamartoma has a similar clinical presentation (usually in the midline of the maxilla) but histologically contains a non-encapsulated proliferation of fusiform and spindle smooth muscle cells that, as expected, express HHF-35, smooth muscle actin and desmin but not S-100 protein.[11–14]

References

1. Lack, E.E., Worsham, G.F., Callihan, M.D. et al (1981) Gingival granular cell tumors of the newborn (congenital 'epulis'): a clinical and pathologic study of 21 patients. *Am J Surg Pathol*, 5, 37–46.
2. Dixter, C.T., Konstat, M.S., Giunta, J.L. et al (1975) Congenital granular-cell tumor of alveolar ridge and tongue. Report of two cases. *Oral Surg Oral Med Oral Pathol*, 40, 270–277.
3. Zarbo, R.J., Lloyd, R.V., Beals, T.F. et al (1983) Congenital gingival granular cell tumor with smooth muscle cytodifferentiation. *Oral Surg Oral Med Oral Pathol*, 56, 512–520.
4. Loyola, A.M., Gatti, A.F., Pinto, D.S. Jr et al (1997) Alveolar and extra-alveolar granular cell lesions of the newborn: report of a case and review of the literature. *Oral Surg Oral Med Oral Pathol Oral Radiol Endod*, 84, 668–671.
5. Fuhr, A.H., Krogh, P.H. (1972) Congenital epulis of the newborn: centennial review of the literature and a report of case. *J Oral Surg*, 30, 30–35.
6. Tucker, M.C., Rusnock, E.J., Azumi, N. et al (1990) Gingival granular cell tumors of the newborn. An ultrastructural and immunohistochemical study. *Arch Pathol Lab Med*, 114, 895–898.
7. Damm, D.D. (1993) Investigation into the histogenesis of congenital epulis of the newborn. *Oral Surg Oral Med Oral Pathol*, 76, 205–212.
8. Kaiserling, E., Ruck, P., Xiao, J.C. (1995) Congenital epulis and granular cell tumor: a histologic and immunohistochemical study. *Oral Surg Oral Med Oral Pathol Oral Radiol Endod*, 80, 687–697.
9. Takahashi, H., Fujita, S., Satoh, H. et al (1990) Immunohistochemical study of congenital gingival granular cell tumor (congenital epulis). *J Oral Pathol Med*, 19, 492–496.
10. Lifshitz, M.S., Flotte, T.J., Greco, M.A. (1984) Congenital granular cell epulis. Immunohistochemical and ultrastructural observations. *Cancer*, 53, 1845–1848.
11. Ng, K.H., Siar, C.G., Latif, H.A. (1992) Leiomyoma of the incisive papilla region: a case report. *Ann Dent*, 51, 29–31.
12. Semba, I., Kitano, M., Mimura, T. (1993) Gingival leiomyomatous hamartoma: immunohistochemical and ultrastructural observations. *J Oral Pathol Med*, 22, 468–470.
13. Takeda, Y., Satoh, M., Nakamura, S. et al (2000) Congenital leiomyomatous epulis: a case report with immunohistochemical study. *Pathol Int*, 50, 999–1002.
14. Correa, L., Lotufo, M., Martins, M.T. et al (2001) Leiomyomatous hamartoma of the incisive papilla. *J Clin Pediatr Dent*, 25, 157–159.

Lymphangioma of the alveolar ridge

Clinical features

Lymphangioma has been identified in approximately 4% of babies, all of African–American descent. They present as dome-shaped, bluish, fluid-filled nodules usually affecting the posterior maxillary and mandibular alveolar ridge and are typically 3–4 mm in diameter. Females are twice as likely to be affected as males and 74% of subjects have more than one lesion.[1,2] Many (if not most) regress by 6 months of age.[1,3,4]

Histological features

Lymphangioma is characterized by slit-like spaces lined by flattened endothelial cells and filled with red blood cells or sparse, fibrillar, eosinophilic material consistent with lymph.[1,2] Rests of odontogenic epithelium may sometimes be present.

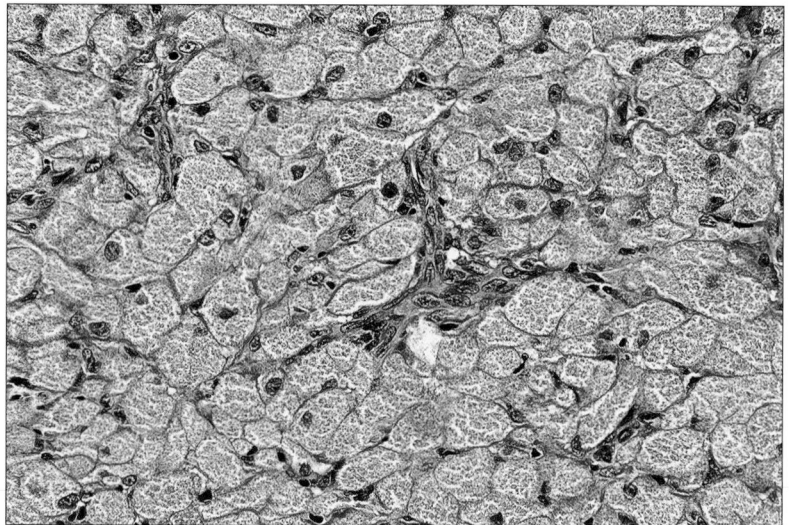

Fig. 10.25
Congenital granular cell epulis: note the large pale cells with granular cytoplasm; they are S-100 negative.

Differential diagnosis

Lymphangioma circumscriptum has an identical histology but is seen in older patients.

References

1. Levin, L.S., Jorgenson, R.J., Bradley, A.J. (1976) Lymphangiomas of the alveolar ridges in neonates. *Pediatrics*, 58, 881–884.
2. Wilson, S., Gould, A.R., Wolff, C. (1986) Multiple lymphangiomas of the alveolar ridge in a neonate: case study. *Pediatr Dent*, 8, 231–234.
3. Jorgenson, R.J., Shapiro, S.D., Salinas, C.F. et al (1982) Intraoral findings and anomalies in neonates. *Pediatrics*, 69, 577–582.
4. Kittle, P.E., Weaver, R.M. (1987) Lymphangiomas of the alveolar ridge in a neonate: report of case. *ASDC J Dent Child*, 54, 277–279.

Gingival fibromatosis

Clinical features

In this condition, there is a benign, diffuse, non-hemorrhagic and fibrotic gingival enlargement, often occurring bilaterally and involving the maxillary and mandibular gingiva, sometimes to the extent that it may reach the occlusal/incisal edges of the teeth.[1,2] Several forms are recognized. The inherited form (usually an autosomal dominant trait, but occasionally an autosomal recessive), which is less common, tends to present congenitally or in the first decade of life coinciding with eruption of teeth and often exhibits generalized gingival involvement (*Fig. 10.26*). There is a strong association with hypertrichosis and mental retardation and/or epilepsy. Gingival fibromatosis may also be a feature of Zimmerman–Laband, Ramon, Rutherford, and Cross syndromes.[3,4] The gene for the non-syndromic form has been localized to chromosome 2p21–22.[5]

An idiopathic form more often occurs later in life with usually limited involvement of the upper or lower jaw or just one quadrant. There is no tendency to regression. The most common presentation is overgrowth of tissue in the area of the maxillary tuberosity and lingual mandible, frequently in a symmetric fashion.[1]

Pathogenesis and histological features

The gingival overgrowth is caused primarily by an increased production and reduced metabolism of connective tissue. Native fibroblasts show elevated rates of proliferation and increased synthesis of fibronectin and type I collagen.[6] Reduced matrix metalloproteinase levels – possibly mediated by increased production of transforming growth factor beta-1 (TGF-β1) – may result in excess accumulation of extracellular matrix.[7]

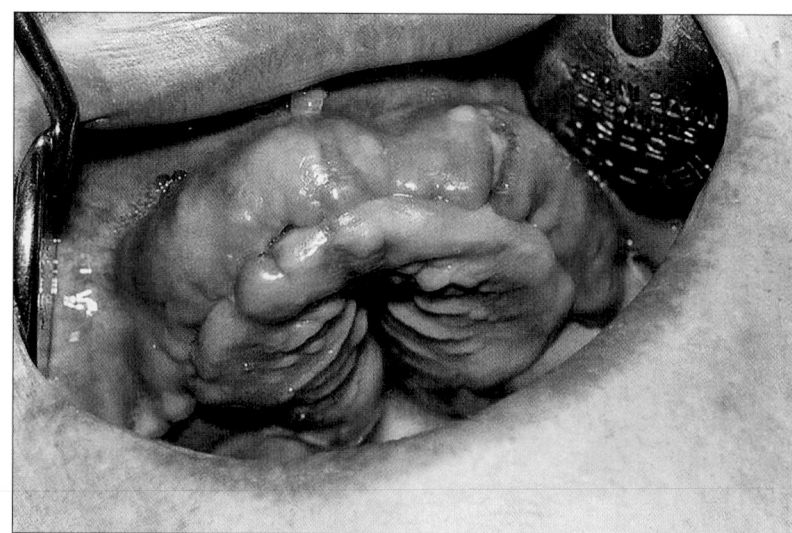

Fig. 10.26
Hereditary gingival fibromatosis: there is extensive involvement of the maxillary soft tissues. By courtesy of G. Gallagher, DMD, Boston, USA.

Histologically, there is a diffuse proliferation of bands and whorls of collagen within a background of excessive ground substance (*Fig. 10.27*). Some lesions contain plump, stellate-shaped fibroblasts (*Fig. 10.28*). Dystrophic calcification may be seen in up to 43% of cases.[2] The overlying epithelium may be slightly acanthotic and there are few inflammatory cells.

Differential diagnosis

Generalized gingival hyperplasia caused by local irritation or systemic influences (such as drugs or hormones) is distinguished from gingival fibromatosis on clinical grounds and by more prominent inflammation.

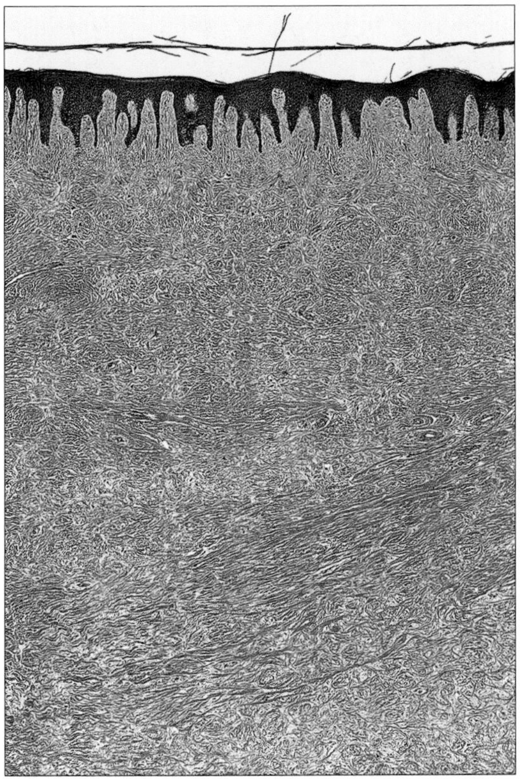

References

1. Witkop, C.J. Jr (1971) Heterogeneity in gingival fibromatosis. *Birth Defects Orig Artic Ser*, 7, 210–221.
2. Takagi, M., Yamamoto, H., Mega, H. et al (1991) Heterogeneity in the gingival fibromatoses. *Cancer*, 68, 2202–2212.
3. Clark, D. (1987) Gingival fibromatosis and its related syndromes. A review. *J Can Dent Assoc*, 53, 137–140.
4. Lacombe, D., Bioulac-Sage, P., Sibout, M. et al (1994) Congenital marked hypertrichosis and Laband syndrome in a child: overlap between the gingival fibromatosis-hypertrichosis and Laband syndromes. *Genet Couns*, 5, 251–256.
5. Hart, T.C., Pallos, D., Bozzo, L. et al (2000) Evidence of genetic heterogeneity for hereditary gingival fibromatosis. *J Dent Res*, 79, 1758–1764.
6. Tipton, D.A., Howell, K.J., Dabbous, M.K. (1997) Increased proliferation, collagen, and fibronectin production by hereditary gingival fibromatosis fibroblasts. *J Periodontol*, 68, 524–530.
7. Coletta, R.D., Almeida, O.P., Reynolds, M.A. et al (1999) Alteration in expression of MMP-1 and MMP-2 but not TIMP-1 and TIMP-2 in hereditary gingival fibromatosis is mediated by TGF-beta 1 autocrine stimulation. *J Periodontal Res*, 34, 457–463.

Juvenile hyalin fibromatosis

Clinical features

Juvenile hyalin fibromatosis is a rare, autosomal recessive disease characterized by pearly papules and larger fibrotic nodules on the skin (around the face, ears, scalp, neck and trunk), gingival overgrowth, flexural contractures of the joints and osteolytic lesions.[1–3] Infantile systemic hyalinosis (another autosomal recessive condition) presents, in addition, with visceral involvement and is fatal within the first 2 years of life[4,5] (see also p. 1722).

Pathogenesis and histological features

Reduced type III collagen production and metabolism, and possibly secondarily elevated type I collagen metabolism, may represent the underlying pathogenesis.[6,7]

The gingival and skin lesions of juvenile hyaline fibromatosis show deposits of PAS-positive, diastase-resistant and Congo red-negative homogenous, eosinophilic, hyalinized material in the connective tissue (*Fig. 10.29*).[1,5] Fibroblasts are sometimes nested, appearing similar to chondrocytes, and, on occasion, present as 'streaks of cells'. The fibroblasts are plump or spindle-shaped with large vesicular nuclei (*Fig. 10.30*).[2,8]

Ultrastructurally, the fibroblasts have distended endoplasmic reticulum and Golgi filled with fibrillogranular material similar to that present in the extracellular space.[2,3,8]

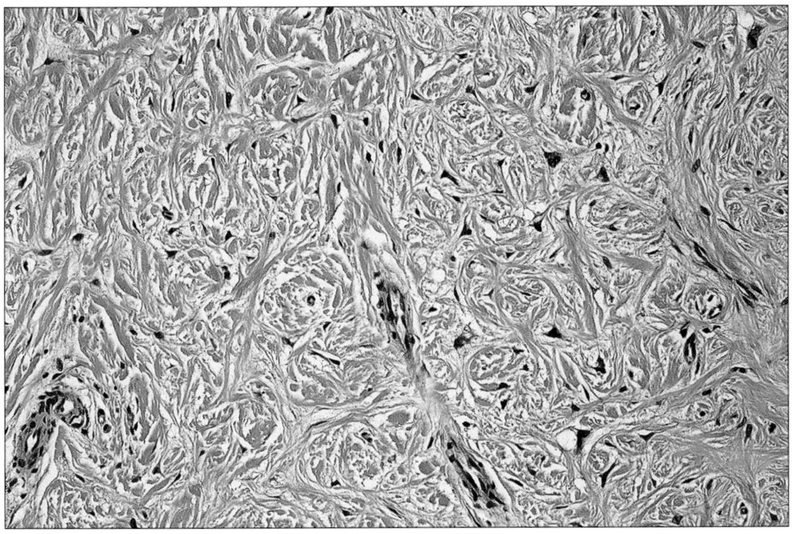

Fig. 10.27
Hereditary gingival fibromatosis: there is massive accumulation of fibrous tissue and ground substance.

Fig. 10.28
Hereditary gingival fibromatosis: plump, stellate-shaped fibroblasts are seen in a densely collagenized stroma.

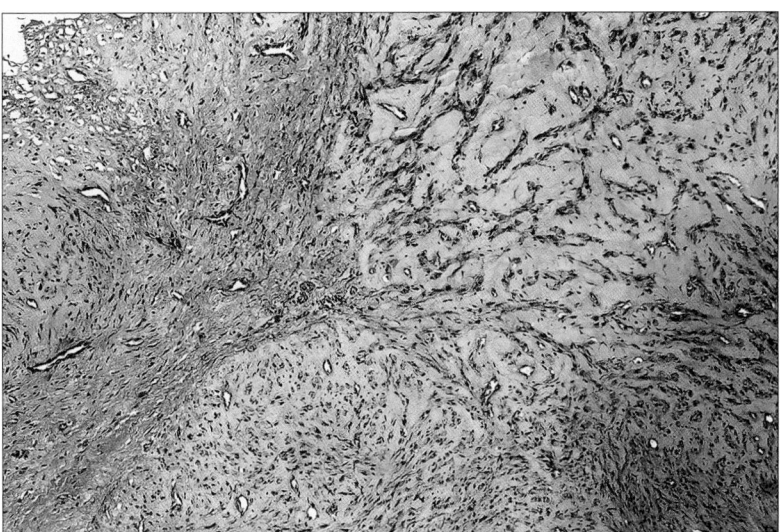

Fig. 10.29
Juvenile hyaline fibromatosis: there are hyper- and hypocellular areas with intervening hyalinized stroma. By courtesy of J. Sciubba, DDS, Baltimore, USA.

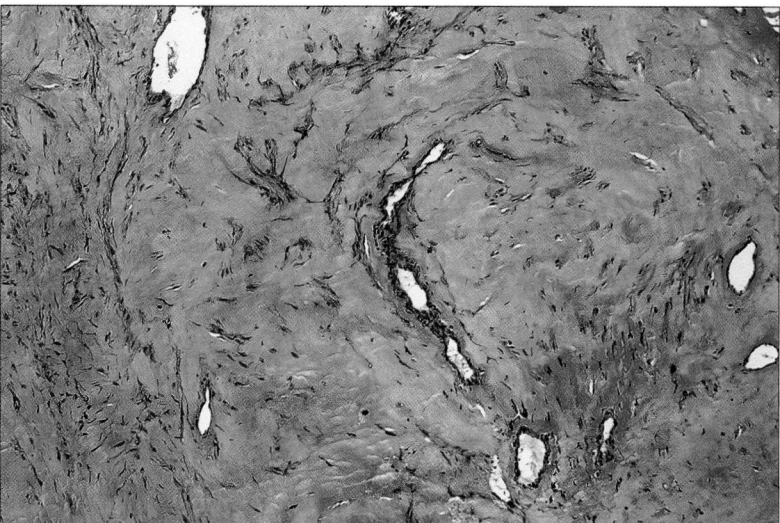

Fig. 10.30
Juvenile hyaline fibromatosis: note the abundant eosinophilic, hyalinized fibrocollagenous material and scattered fibroblasts. By courtesy of J. Sciubba, DDS, Baltimore, USA.

References

1. Kitano, Y., Horiki, M., Aoki, T. et al (1972) Two cases of juvenile hyalin fibromatosis. Some histological, electron microscopic, and tissue culture observations. *Arch Dermatol*, **106**, 877–883.
2. Sciubba, J.J., Niebloom, T. (1986) Juvenile hyaline fibromatosis (Murray–Puretic–Drescher syndrome): oral and systemic findings in siblings. *Oral Surg Oral Med Oral Pathol*, **62**, 397–409.
3. Winik, B.C., Boente, M.C., Asial, R. (1998) Juvenile hyaline fibromatosis: ultrastructural study. *Am J Dermatopathol*, **20**, 373–378.
4. Landing, B.H., Nadorra, R. (1986) Infantile systemic hyalinosis: report of four cases of a disease, fatal in infancy, apparently different from juvenile systemic hyalinosis. *Pediatr Pathol*, **6**, 55–79.
5. Mancini, G.M., Stojanov, L., Willemsen, R. et al (1999) Juvenile hyaline fibromatosis: clinical heterogeneity in three patients. *Dermatology*, **198**, 18–25.
6. Lubec, B., Steinert, I., Breier, F. et al (1995) Skin collagen defects in a patient with juvenile hyaline fibromatosis. *Arch Dis Child*, **73**, 246–248.
7. Breier, F., Fang-Kircher, S., Wolff, K. et al (1997) Juvenile hyaline fibromatosis: impaired collagen metabolism in human skin fibroblasts. *Arch Dis Child*, **77**, 436–440.
8. Woyke, S., Domagala, W., Olszewski, W. (1970) Ultrastructure of a fibromatosis hyalinica multiplex juvenilis. *Cancer*, **26**, 1157–1168.

Reactive conditions

Leukoedema

Clinical features

This is a benign, painless condition usually affecting the buccal mucosa bilaterally. The mucosa has a diffuse gray–white opalescent hue with vertical wrinkles and streaks that usually disappear on stretching except in severe cases (*Fig. 10.31*).[1,2]

The prevalence ranges from 20 to 36% among those who do not use tobacco or chew coca leaves, to 51–68% in those who use tobacco, coca or cannabis.[3–6] Its incidence increases with age.[7] A prevalence of 51% was reported in African–Americans but without mention of tobacco habits.[8] Another study found a prevalence of 93% in a Caucasian population leading the author to question whether this condition is merely a variation of normal.[2] Of all tobacco habits, pipe smoking,

cigarette smoking and snuff are associated with decreasing rates of occurrence.

Pathogenesis and histological features

It is generally believed that a low-grade topical injury, such as occurs with tobacco or coca leaves, gives rise to this condition.

There is acanthosis with little or no parakeratosis. The characteristic feature is the presence of degenerate and swollen cells in the superficial and mid-epithelial layers, respectively, sometimes (but not always) with a layer of compact cells sandwiched between (*Fig. 10.32*).[9] The most superficial cells have pale cytoplasm with many anucleate forms and prominent cell membranes somewhat collapsed upon one another, forming a jigsaw puzzle pattern (*Fig. 10.33*). The ballooned cells in the mid-epithelium are large with pale, watery cytoplasm, sometimes showing reticular cytoplasmic degeneration; pyknotic nuclei are often present. There is no inflammation in the lamina propria.

Ultrastructural studies show abnormal keratohyaline granules and loosely dispersed tonofilaments with fragmented organelles in the superficial degenerate cells. The mid-level swollen cells contain abnormal swollen mitochondria.[9,10] These features support the theory of limited cell damage with swelling, possibly caused by failure of the sodium pump insufficient to cause death and disintegration of the whole cell. Interestingly, a biopsy of the linea alba (the white line on the buccal mucosa bilaterally where the upper and lower teeth meet) essentially reveals identical histological features, supporting the theory of low-grade injury as the primary etiology. Similar features have also been reported in the sucking pads of neonates.[11]

Differential diagnosis

In chronic bite injury, there is papillary and shaggy parakeratosis associated with many bacterial colonies also without inflammation; leukoedema is often present beneath areas of bite injury (see below).

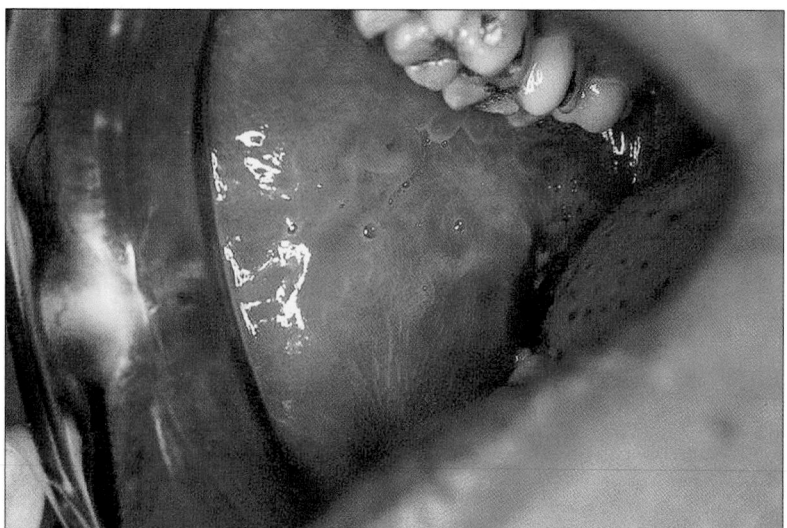

Fig. 10.31
Leukoedema: note the pale, milky film on the buccal mucosa.

Smokeless tobacco keratosis presents with keratin chevrons and shows a band of coagulated and degenerate cells with anucleation similar to leukoedema. The transition zone from normal to degenerate is often abrupt in smokeless tobacco keratosis (see below). Hairy leukoplakia may exhibit leukoedema and concomitant chronic bite injury, but will also exhibit viral cytopathic change (see p. 991).

References

1. Sanstead, H.R., Lowe, J.W. (1953) Leukoedema and keratosis in relation to leukoplakia of the buccal mucosa in man. *J Natl Cancer Inst*, **14**, 423–433.
2. Durocher, R.T., Thalman, R., Fiore-Donno, G. (1972) Leukoedema of the oral mucosa. *J Am Dent Assoc*, **85**, 1105–1109.
3. Borghelli, R.F., Stirparo, M., Andrade, J. et al (1975) Leukoedema in addicts to coca leaves in Humahuaca, Argentina. *Community Dent Oral Epidemiol*, **3**, 40–43.
4. Axell, T. (1981) Leukoedema – an epidemiologic study with special reference to the influence of tobacco habits. *Community Dent Oral Epidemiol*, **9**, 142–146.
5. Van Wyk, C.W. (1985) An investigation into the association between leukoedema and smoking. *J Oral Pathol*, **14**, 491–499.
6. Darling, M.R., Arendorf, T.M. (1993) Effects of cannabis smoking on oral soft tissues. *Community Dent Oral Epidemiol*, **21**, 78–81.
7. Roed-Peterson, B., Pindborg, J.J. (1973) Prevalence of oral leukoedema in Uganda. *Arch Oral Biol*, **18**, 1191–1196.
8. Martin, J.L., Crump, E.P. (1972) Leukoedema of the buccal mucosa in Negro children and youth. *Oral Surg Oral Med Oral Pathol*, **34**, 49–58.
9. Van Wyk, C.W., Ambrosio, S.C. (1983) Leukoedema: ultrastructural and histochemical observations. *J Oral Pathol*, **12**, 319–329.
10. Van Wyk, C.W., Ambrosio, S.C., van der Vyver, P.C. (1984) Abnormal keratohyalin-like forms in leukoedema. *J Oral Pathol*, **13**, 271–281.
11. Heyl, T., Raubenheimer, E.J. (1987) Sucking pads (sucking calluses) of the lips in neonates: a manifestation of transient leukoedema. *Pediatr Dermatol*, **4**, 123–128.

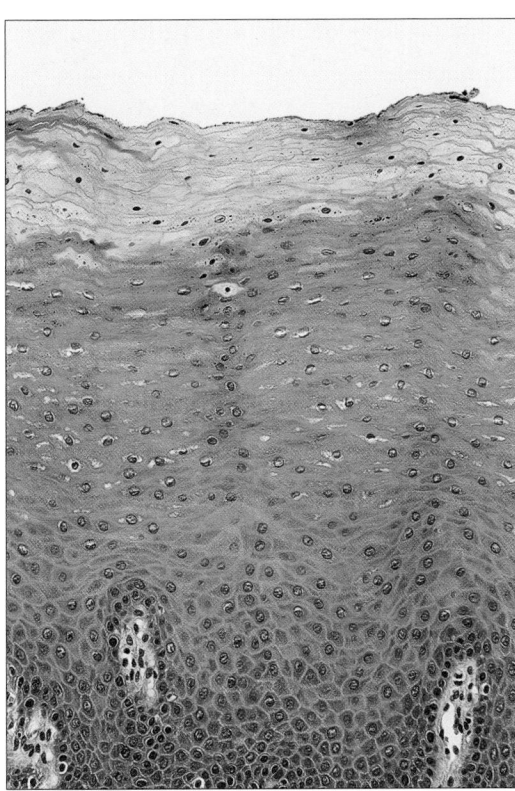

Fig. 10.32
Leukoedema: note the pale superficial cells and acanthosis.

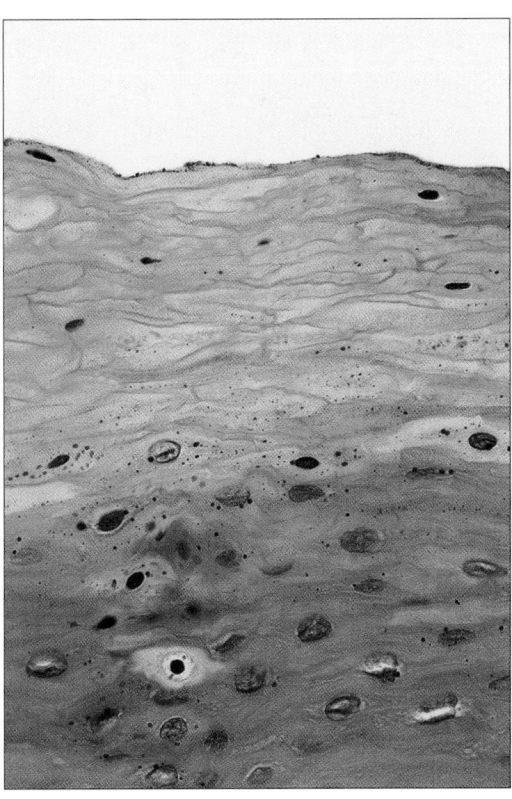

Fig. 10.33
Leukoedema: the superficial cells characteristically are anucleate with a 'jigsaw-like' pattern of cell membranes.

Chronic bite injury

Clinical features

In chronic bite injury (morsicatio buccarum/labiorum/linguorum, pathominia mucosae oris), cheek, lip or tongue biting habits are factitial injuries that occur either subconsciously as part of a neurosis or as a conscious habit or self-mutilating behavior. It is most prevalent in the second and third decade, is usually bilateral and may involve the buccal mucosa (most common), lateral tongue and lower labial mucosa.[1,2] The site of injury exhibits shaggy white plaques that have a peeling, desquamative surface; erosions are often present, and occasionally ulcers are seen (*Figs 10.34, 10.35*). Similar lesions have been noted in areca nut chewers and glass blowers.[3,4]

Histological features

There is hyperparakeratosis, which may be severe. Characteristically, the keratin is thrown into papillations with fissures and clefts, rimmed by bacteria (*Figs 10.36, 10.37*).[1,5,6] There is usually no spongiosis or leukocyte exocytosis. Ballooned and swollen superficial keratinocytes typical for leukoedema are present. There is acanthosis and usually insignificant inflammation in the lamina propria unless there is erosion and ulceration. In betel nut chewers, there is a yellow–brown pigment on the surface of the keratin and within epithelial cells, representing fragments of the betel quid.[4,6]

Differential diagnosis

Chronic bite injury may occur as a primary mucosal disorder such as has been described above, or it may present as a secondary finding related to chronic injury of protruberant plaques and nodules, such as fibromas.

Hairy leukoplakia may show similar shaggy hyperparakeratosis and sometimes there is concurrent bite injury. However, the typical changes of chromatin condensation, eosinophilic inclusions and the presence of Epstein–Barr virus easily afford their distinction. Smokeless tobacco keratosis shows coagulation of the superficial cells, sometimes accompanied by hyalinized, amorphous eosinophilic material in the lamina propria. White sponge nevus exhibits perinuclear eosinophilic keratin condensations.

References

1. Hjorting-Hansen, E., Holst, E. (1970) Morsicatio mucosae oris and suctio mucosae oris. *Scand J Dent Res*, 78, 492–499.
2. Sewerin, I. (1971) A clinical and epidemiologic study of morsicatio buccarum/labiorum. *Scand J Dent Res*, 79, 73–80.
3. Schiodt, M., Larsen, V., Bessermann, M. (1980) Oral findings in glassblowers. *Community Dent Oral Epidemiol*, 8, 195–200.
4. Reichart, P.A., Philipsen, H.P. (1998) Betel chewer's mucosa – a review. *J Oral Path Med*, 27, 239–242.
5. Glass, L.F., Maize, J.C. (1991) Morsicatio buccarum et labiorum (excessive cheek and lip biting). *Am J Dermatopathol*, 13, 271–274.
6. Carmona, I.T., Tejeiro, J., Dios, P.D. et al (2000) Morsicatio linguarum versus oral hairy leukoplakia. *Dermatology*, 201, 281–282.

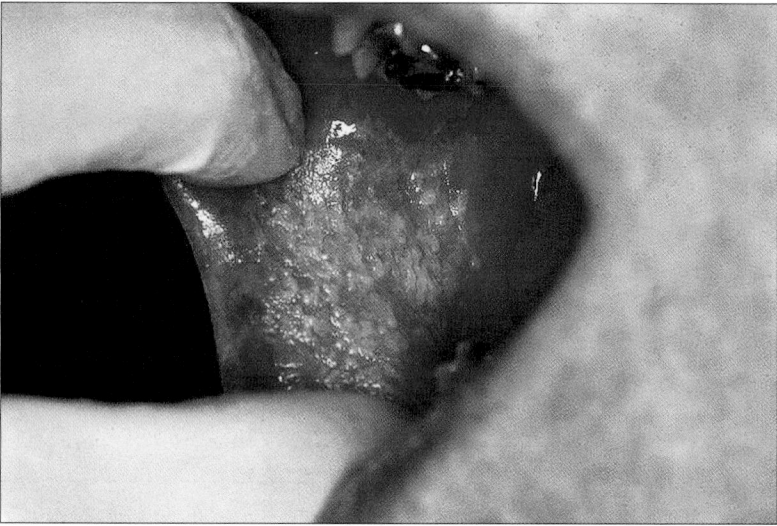

Fig. 10.34
Chronic bite injury: note the rough, shaggy plaques on the buccal mucosa.

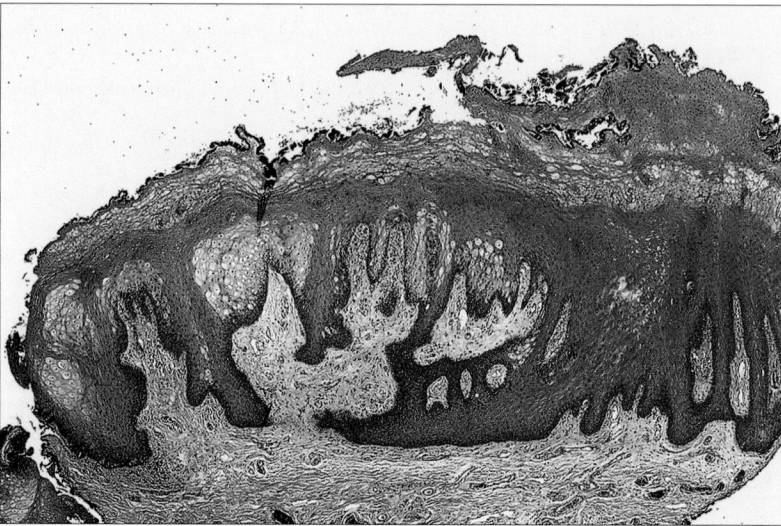

Fig. 10.36
Chronic bite injury: there is marked shaggy hyperparakeratosis with acanthosis and leukoedema but little inflammation.

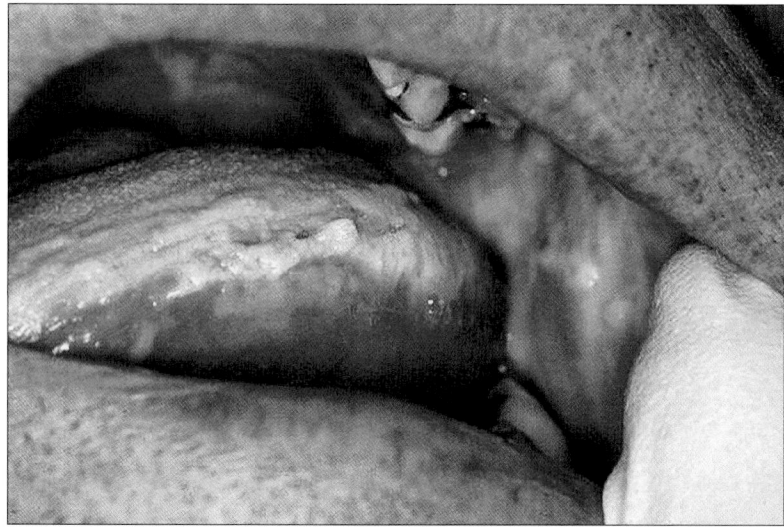

Fig. 10.35
Chronic bite injury: note the macerated, shaggy plaques on the buccal mucosa and lateral border of the tongue.

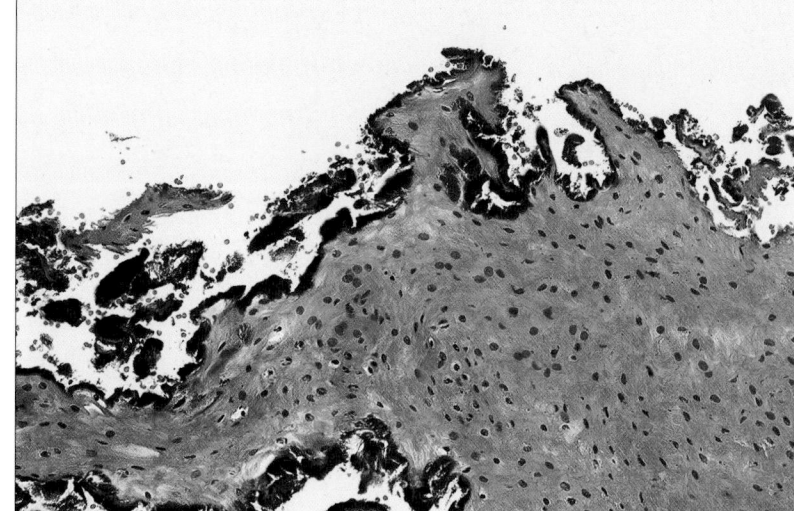

Fig. 10.37
Chronic bite injury: the characteristic fissures and clefts in the parakeratin are rimmed by bacteria with little or no inflammation.

Benign migratory glossitis

Clinical features

Benign migratory glossitis (geographic stomatitis, stomatitis/erythema areata migrans, geographic tongue, annulus migrans, erythema circinata) occurs in 1–2% of the population although this figure may be low because of the evanescent nature of the condition.[1,2] It generally presents in adults with females being twice as often affected.[3] Lesions are recurrent, erythematous and atrophic areas with a serpiginous white, slightly raised border that may appear annular or scalloped (*Figs 10.38, 10.39*). These 'map-like' areas migrate and change in shape over the tongue dorsum as the condition resolves at one edge and involves another. Some lesions, however, are stationary. Pain, in the form of a burning or sensitivity, may or may not be present.[3,4] One-fifth of patients have concurrent fissured tongue.[3]

'Ectopic geographic tongue' or, more appropriately, geographic stomatitis, refers to a similar-appearing lesion at other sites, in particular the buccal and labial mucosae.[5–7]

Approximately 5–19% of patients with psoriasis have benign migratory glossitis.[8–11] This prevalence increases to 17–80% in patients with pustular disease.[12,13] The condition also occurs in 5–19% of patients with Reiter's syndrome.[5,8,10,14] Oral psoriasiform lesions (excluding benign migratory glossitis) have a predilection for the palate. Lithium carbonate (which can exacerbate psoriasis) has also been reported to precipitate migratory glossitis.[15]

Human leukocyte antigen (HLA)-B15 (now Bw62 and Bw63) is seen with higher frequency in affected patients and atopic individuals, as well as in patients with associated type II diabetes mellitus lesions.[16–18] There is also an increased incidence of HLA-Cw6 and HLA-B13 in addition to a reduced incidence of HLA-Cw4.[19] Other authors have shown increased incidences of HLA-DRw6, and -DR5 with reduced incidences of -B51 and -DR2.[20]

Histological features

The tongue dorsum exhibits loss of the filiform papillae (*Fig. 10.40*). There are superficial spongiotic pustules and microabscesses (often involving up to one-third of the thickness of the epithelium) in the absence of candidal infection (*Fig. 10.41*).[3,4] The adjacent epithelium shows variable spongiosis and leukocyte exocytosis. Additional features commonly present are psoriasiform epithelial hyperplasia with broad rete ridges sometimes becoming confluent at their bases, edema of the lamina propria and a variable lymphocytic infiltrate with conspicuous capillary dilatation.

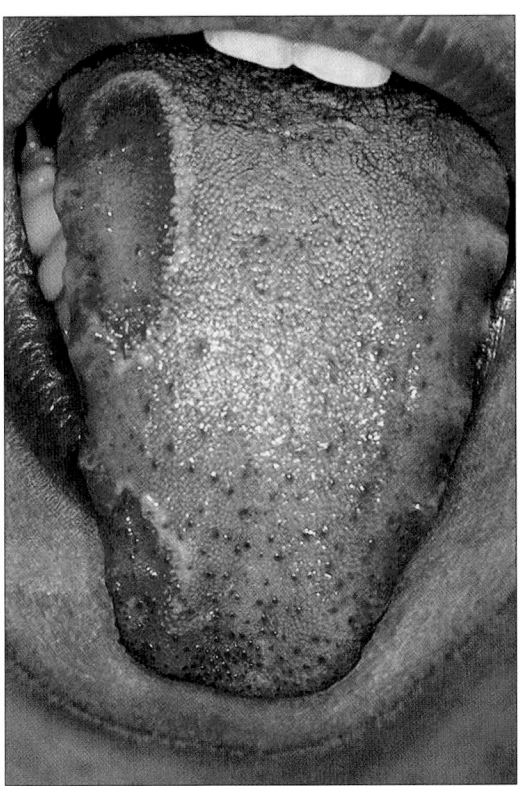

Fig. 10.38
Benign migratory glossitis: note the erythematous depapillated area rimmed by a white margin.

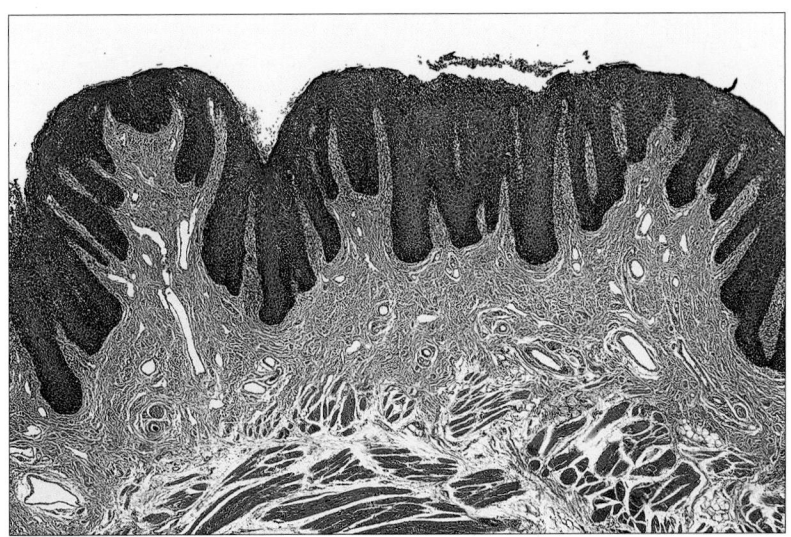

Fig. 10.40
Benign migratory glossitis: note the absence of filiform papillae (filiform papillary atrophy) and psoriasiform epithelial hyperplasia.

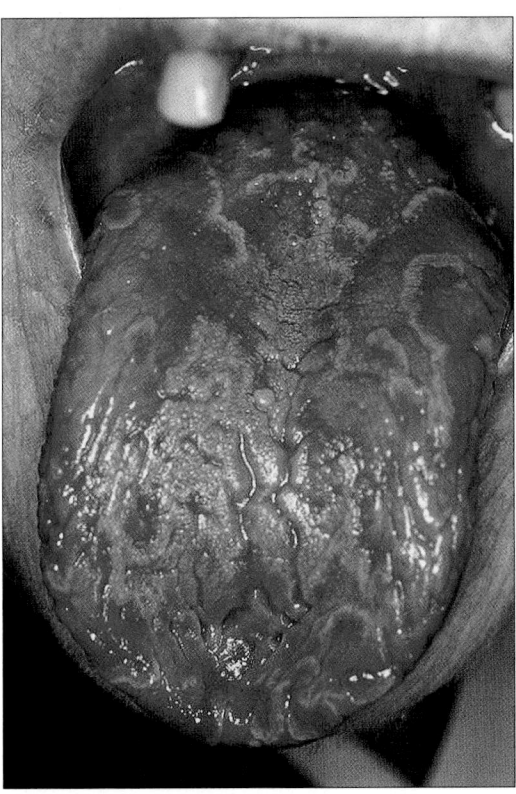

Fig. 10.39
Benign migratory glossitis: more extensive involvement of the tongue.

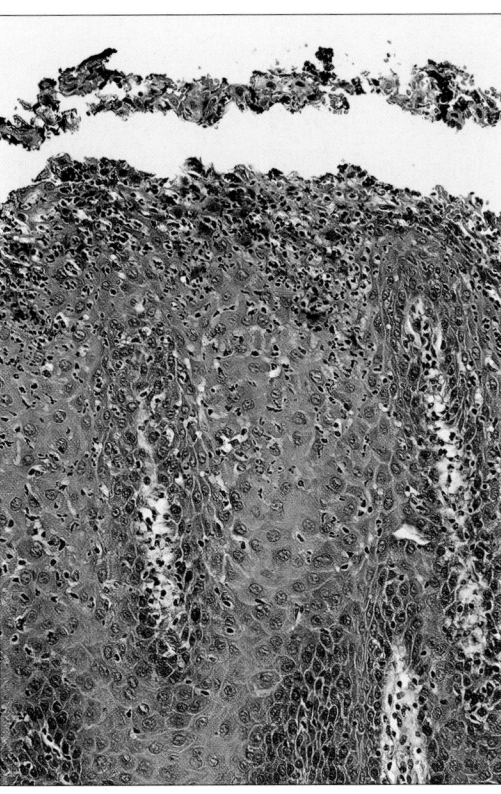

Fig. 10.41
Benign migratory glossitis: note the well-formed spongiotic pustules.

Differential diagnosis

Candidiasis, which must always be excluded, more typically presents with spongiotic pustules affecting only the top two to three layers of keratinocytes. A PAS stain should routinely be performed for all pustular oral lesions. Median rhomboid glossitis also enters the differential diagnosis since it may have a somewhat similar clinical presentation with atrophy of filiform papillae, although the area does not 'migrate' (see below).

The epithelium at the edge of a healing ulcer may show spongiotic pustules devoid of candida and accompanied by neutrophilic exocytosis.

Oral lesions of patients with cutaneous psoriasis are histologically indistinguishable from lesions of benign migratory glossitis.[5,11,21]

References

1. Richardson, E.R. (1968) Incidence of geographic tongue and median rhomboid glossitis in 3,319 Negro college students. *Oral Surg Oral Med Oral Pathol*, **26**, 623–625.
2. Kullaa-Mikkonen, A., Mikkonen, M., Kotilainen, R. (1982) Prevalence of different morphologic forms of the human tongue in young Finns. *Oral Surg Oral Med Oral Pathol*, **53**, 152–156.
3. Banoczy, J., Szabo, L., Csiba, A. (1975) Migratory glossitis. A clinical–histologic review of seventy cases. *Oral Surg Oral Med Oral Pathol*, **39**, 113–121.
4. Marks, R., Radden, B.G. (1981) Geographic tongue: a clinico-pathological review. *Australas J Dermatol*, **22**, 75–79.
5. Weathers, D.R., Baker, G., Archard, H.O. et al (1974) Psoriasiform lesions of the oral mucosa (with emphasis on 'ectopic geographic tongue'). *Oral Surg Oral Med Oral Pathol*, **37**, 872–888.
6. Littner, M.M., Dayan, D., Gorsky, M. et al (1987) Migratory stomatitis. *Oral Surg Oral Med Oral Pathol*, **63**, 555–559.
7. Espelid, M., Bang, G., Johannessen, A.C. et al (1991) Geographic stomatitis: report of 6 cases. *J Oral Pathol Med*, **20**, 425–428.
8. Pogrel, M.A., Cram, D. (1988) Intraoral findings in patients with psoriasis with a special reference to ectopic geographic tongue (erythema circinata). *Oral Surg Oral Med Oral Pathol*, **66**, 184–194.
9. van der Wal, N., van der Kwast, W.A., van Dijk, E. et al (1988) Geographic stomatitis and psoriasis. *Int J Oral Maxillofac Surg*, **17**, 106–109.
10. Morris, L.F., Phillips, C.M., Binnie, W.H. et al (1992) Oral lesions in patients with psoriasis: a controlled study. *Cutis*, **49**, 339–344.
11. Ulmansky, M., Michelle, R., Azaz, B. (1995) Oral psoriasis: report of six new cases. *J Oral Pathol Med*, **24**, 42–45.
12. Dawson, T.A.J. (1974) Tongue lesions in generalized pustular psoriasis. *Br J Dermatol*, **91**, 419–424.
13. Zelickson, B.D., Muller, S.A. (1991) Generalized pustular psoriasis. *Arch Dermatol*, **127**, 1339–1345.
14. O'Keefe, E., Braverman, I.M., Cohen, I. (1973) Annulus migrans. Identical lesions in pustular psoriasis, Reiter's syndrome, and geographic tongue. *Arch Dermatol*, **107**, 240–244.
15. Patki, A.H. (1992) Geographic tongue developing in a patient on lithium carbonate therapy. *Int J Dermatol*, **31**, 368–369.
16. Marks, R., Simons, M.J. (1979) Geographic tongue – a manifestation of atopy. *Br J Dermatol*, **101**, 159–162.
17. Marks, R., Tait, B. (1980) HLA antigens in geographic tongue. *Tissue Antigens*, **15**, 60–62.
18. Wysocki, G.P., Daley, T.D. (1987) Benign migratory glossitis in patients with juvenile diabetes. *Oral Surg Oral Med Oral Pathol*, **63**, 68–70.
19. Gonzaga, H.F. (1996) Both psoriasis and benign migratory glossitis are associated with HLA-Cw6. *Br J Dermatol*, **135**, 368–370.
20. Fenerli, A., Papanicolaou, S., Papanicolaou, M. et al (1993) Histocompatibility antigens and geographic tongue. *Oral Surg Oral Med Oral Pathol*, **76**, 476–479.
21. Hietanen, J., Salo, O.P., Kanerva, L. et al (1984) Study of the oral mucosa in 200 consecutive patients with psoriasis. *Scand J Dent Res*, **92**, 50–54.

Median rhomboid glossitis

Median rhomboid glossitis is a form of oral candidiasis that occurs specifically in the midline of the tongue just anterior to the circumvallate papillae (*Fig. 10.42*).[1,2] Diagnosis depends on the presence of psoriasiform mucositis with spongiotic pustules associated with candidal hyphae (*Figs 10.43, 10.44*). The identification of the median raphe, a densely hyalinized fibrous band within the lamina propria, confirms that the tissue is from the midline of the tongue (*Fig. 10.45*). It is unclear why this particular area of the tongue is predisposed to candidiasis although a developmental etiology had once been in favor.

References

1. Baughman, R.A. (1971) Median rhomboid glossitis: a developmental anomaly? *Oral Surg*, **31**, 56–65.
2. Wright, B.A. (1978) Median rhomboid glossitis: not a misnomer. *Oral Surg*, **46**, 806–814.

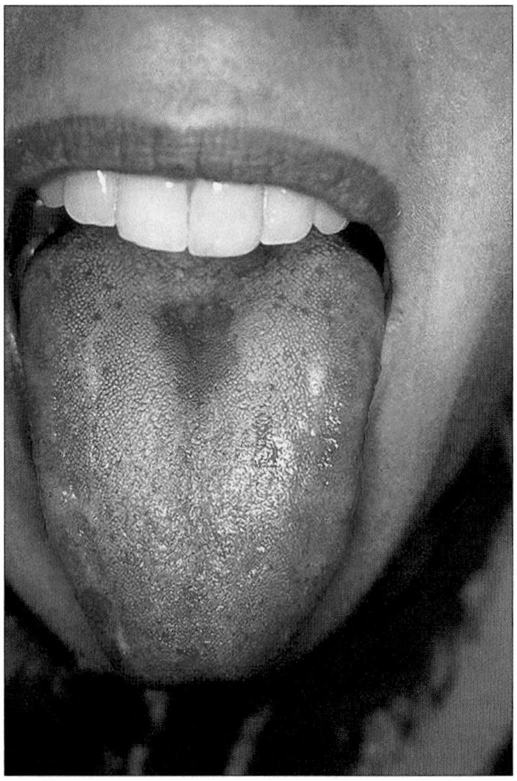

Fig. 10.42
Median rhomboid glossitis: there is a typical rhomboidal-shaped area in the posterior midline of the tongue.

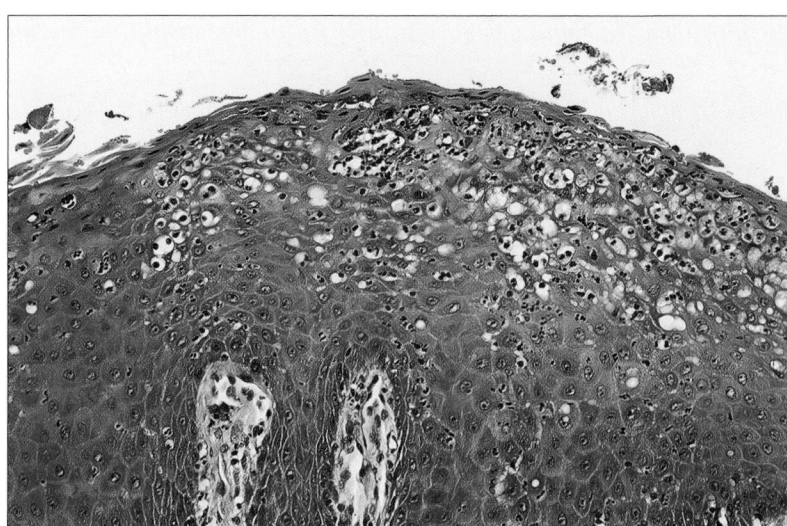

Fig. 10.43
Median rhomboid glossitis: note the presence of spongiotic pustules.

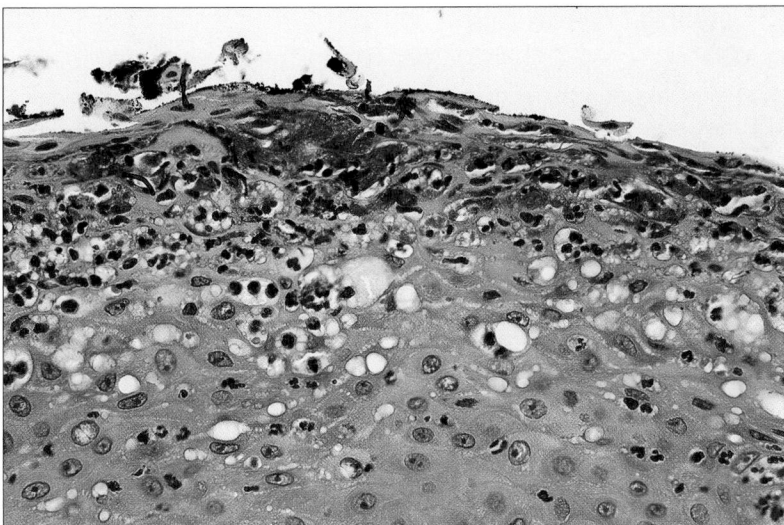

Fig. 10.44
Median rhomboid glossitis: candidal hyphae are present with the PAS stain.

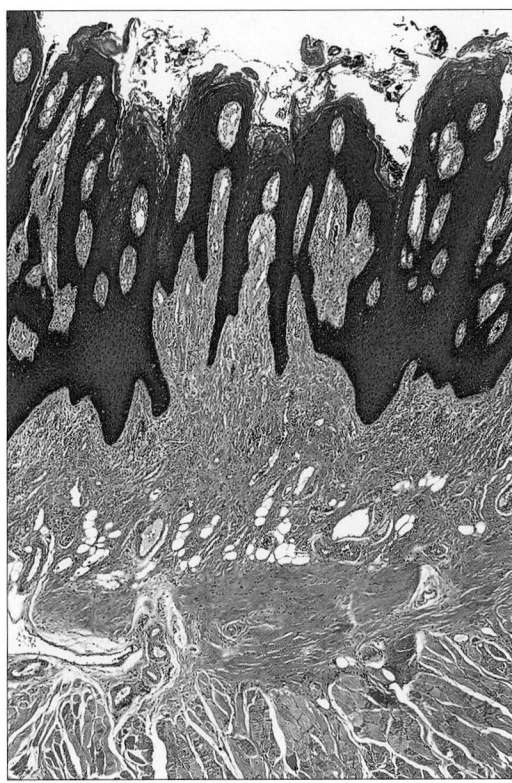

Fig. 10.45
Median rhomboid glossitis: note the psoriasiform epithelial hyperplasia and the dense median raphe just above the muscle fibers.

Smokeless tobacco keratosis

Clinical features

In smokeless tobacco keratosis (snuff dipper's keratosis), smokeless tobacco is usually placed in the mandibular sulcus and its use is associated with the development of white lesions at the site of contact in 13–46% of cases.[1-4] The severity of oral lesions is proportionate to the duration of use and the amount of smokeless tobacco in contact with the mucosa.[2] Discontinuation of use usually results in resolution of oral lesions.[5] Sudanese snuff (toombak) is a mixture of tobacco and sodium bicarbonate and is high in tobacco-specific nitrosamines.[6]

Early and mild lesions show slight wrinkling and pallor of the mucosa while more advanced lesions show deep furrows and thickened white mucosa, more typical of leukoplakia (*Fig. 10.46*).[7]

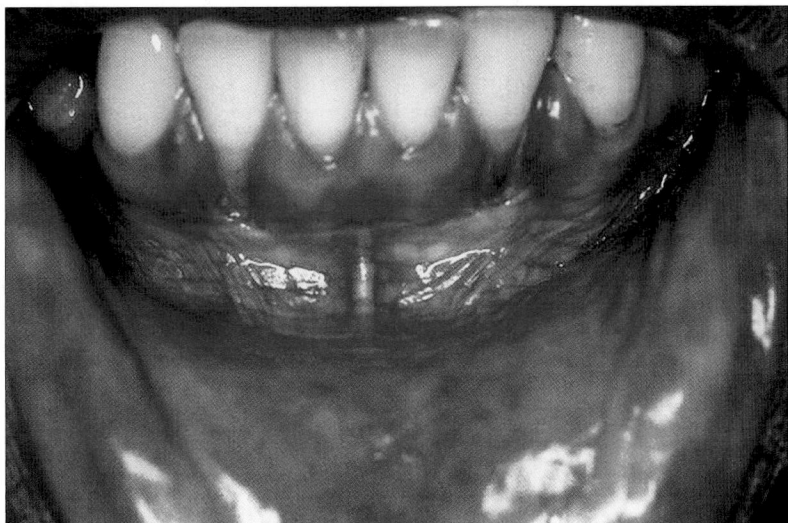

Fig. 10.46
Smokeless tobacco keratosis: note the milky-white, pale, wrinkled mandibular sulcular mucosa.

Pathogenesis and histological features

Smokeless tobacco takes the form of snuff (moist or portion-packed) and chewing tobacco. Scandinavian snuff – and particularly moist snuff which has greater alkalinity (pH 8–9) – has a greater propensity to cause lesions compared with American snuff since it is associated with a greater propensity to induce a contact stomatitis.[1,2] In general, the risk of developing oral cancer is less with smokeless tobacco than with cigarette smoking.[8]

Two histological patterns may be encountered:

- Early lesions show hyperparakeratosis or hyperorthokeratosis with scattered pale vacuolated cells.[7] Such features are difficult to distinguish from other banal leukoplakias.
- More advanced lesions show a characteristic pale-staining surface layer of coagulated and degenerate, often anucleate cells, occasionally covered by a thin layer of para- or orthokeratin (*Fig. 10.47*). This superficial pale layer is sharply demarcated from the underlying viable epithelium, which shows hyperplasia and variable chronic inflammation. In addition, spires of keratin – 'chevrons' – are usually present within this pale surface zone (*Fig. 10.48*).[7,9-11]

Keratin chevrons may also be seen in oral lesions associated with pipe smoking and the use of other tobacco products.[10] Sialadenitis of minor salivary glands has been reported in up to 42% of cases.[12] There is a reduction in the number of intraepithelial Langerhans' cells.[13]

Hyaline deposits may be seen as a continuous, wavy, homogenous, eosinophilic, dense band in the lamina propria in 8–17% of cases, usually between the salivary glands and the surface epithelium but also sometimes involving the glands and surrounding their associated ducts (*Fig. 10.49*).[7,12,14,15] This PAS-positive material does not represent amyloid and is thought to be altered collagen resulting from increased synthesis and/or reduced degradation of collagen.[16]

Epithelial dysplasia (usually mild) is present in up to 8% of cases, usually in areas unassociated with chevrons.[10] Squamous cell carcinoma is an infrequent complication of pure smokeless tobacco usage in the absence of cigarette smoking and/or alcohol consumption.[3,4,7,9,10,15] Some authors believe that these so-called dysplastic changes are merely reactive epithelial atypia since they resolve on discontinuation of the habit.[5,17]

There is disturbed differentiation of keratin as evidenced by increased expression of K13 and K14 in patients using toombak as compared with those using Swedish snuff.[18]

Differential diagnosis

Hyaline deposits may also be seen in lesions of submucous fibrosis. The hyaline material does not stain with Congo red and is not amyloid. Hyalinosis mucosae et cutis has a different clinical presentation.

References

1. Grady, D., Greene, J., Daniels, T.E. et al (1990) Oral mucosal lesions found in smokeless tobacco users. *J Am Dent Assoc*, **121**, 117–123.
2. Kaugars, G.E., Brandt, R.B., Chan, W. et al (1991) Evaluation of risk factors in smokeless tobacco-associated oral lesions. *Oral Surg Oral Med Oral Pathol*, **72**, 326–331.
3. Kaugars, G.E., Riley, W.T., Brandt, R.B. et al (1992) The prevalence of oral lesions on smokeless tobacco users and evaluation of risk factors. *Cancer*, **70**, 2579–2585.
4. Daniels, T.E., Hansen, L.S., Greenspan, J.S. et al (1992) Histopathology of smokeless tobacco lesions in professional baseball players. Associations with different types of tobacco. *Oral Surg Oral Med Oral Pathol*, **73**, 720–725.
5. Larsson, A., Axell, T., Andersson, G. (1991) Reversibility of snuff dippers' lesion in Swedish moist snuff users: a clinical and histologic follow-up study. *J Oral Pathol Med*, **20**, 258–264.
6. Idris, A.M., Nair, J., Oshima, H. et al (1991) Unusually high levels of carcinogenic tobacco-specific nitrosamines in the Sudan snuff (toombak). *Carcinogenesis*, **12**, 1115–1118.
7. Axell, T., Mornstad, H., Sundstrom, B. (1976) The relation of the clinical picture to the histopathology of snuff dipper's lesions in a Swedish population. *J Oral Pathol*, **5**, 229–236.
8. Vigneswaran, N., Tilashalski, K., Rodu, B. et al (1995) Tobacco use and cancer. A reappraisal [see comments]. *Oral Surg Oral Med Oral Pathol Oral Radiol Endod*, **80**, 178–182.
9. Roed-Peterson, B., Pindborg, J.J. (1973) A study of Danish snuff-induced oral leukoplakias. *J Oral Pathol*, **2**, 301–313.
10. Pindborg, J.J., Reibel, J., Roed-Peterson, B. et al (1980) Tobacco-induced changes in oral leukoplakic epithelium. *Cancer*, **45**, 2330–2336.
11. Andersson, G., Axell, T., Larsson, A. (1989) Histologic changes associated with the use of loose and portion-bag packed Swedish moist snuff: a comparative study. *J Oral Pathol Med*, **18**, 491–497.
12. Hirsch, J.M., Heyden, G., Thilander, H. (1982) A clinical, histomorphological and histochemical study on snuff-induced lesions of varying severity. *J Oral Pathol*, **11**, 387–398.
13. Daniels, T.E., Chou, L., Greenspan, J.S. et al (1992) Reduction of Langerhans' cells in smokeless tobacco-associated oral mucosal lesions. *J Oral Pathol Med*, **21**, 100–104.
14. Archard, H.O., Tarpley, T.M. Jr (1972) Clinicopathologic and histochemical characterization of submucosal deposits in snuff dipper's keratosis. *J Oral Pathol*, **1**, 3–11.
15. Idris, A.M., Warnakulasuriya, K.A., Ibrahim, Y.E. et al (1996) Toombak-associated oral mucosal lesions in Sudanese show a low prevalence of epithelial dysplasia. *J Oral Pathol Med*, **25**, 239–244.
16. Idris, A.M., Warnakulasuriya, K.A., Ibrahim, Y.E. et al (1998) Characterization of an amorphous deposit in the lamina propria in oral snuff users in the Sudan as collagen. *J Oral Pathol Med*, **27**, 157–162.
17. Frithiof, L., Anneroth, G., Lasson, U. et al (1983) The snuff-induced lesion. A clinical and morphological study of a Swedish material. *Acta Odontol Scand*, **41**, 53–64.
18. Ibrahim, S.O., Warnakulasuriya, K.A.A.S., Idris, A.M. et al (1998) Expression of keratin 13, 14 and 19 in oral hyperplastic and dysplastic lesions from Sudanese and Swedish snuff-dippers: association with human papillomavirus infection. *Anticancer Res*, **18**, 635–646.

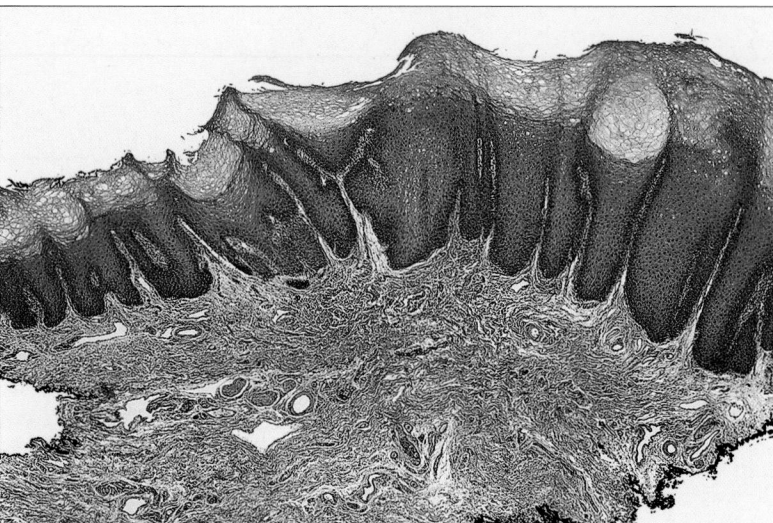

Fig. 10.47
Smokeless tobacco keratosis: the superficial coagulated and degenerate cells are sharply demarcated from the underlying acanthotic epithelium.

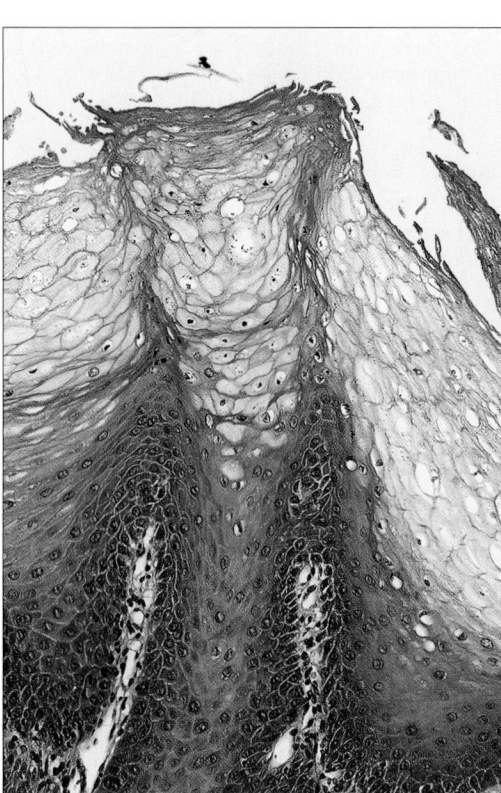

Fig. 10.48
Smokeless tobacco keratosis: note the keratin chevrons and anucleate and degenerate superficial keratinocytes.

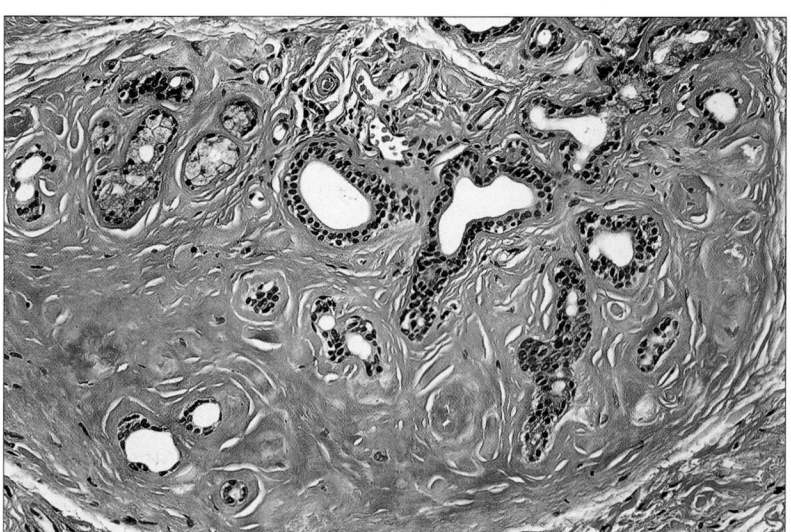

Fig. 10.49
Smokeless tobacco keratosis: the eosinophilic amyloid-like material is often seen within underlying salivary gland parenchyma.

Foreign body gingivitis

Clinical features

This condition occurs more often in females than in males (4:1), most typically in the fifth decade. The gingiva presents with multiple red macules that are sore or painful in the majority of patients. Some lesions are ulcerated and/or inflamed or have white areas. Multifocal areas are occasionally affected.[1,2]

Pathogenesis and histological features

Energy dispersive x-ray microanalyses have revealed Si, Al, Fe and Ti in 23–61% of cases and, in many lesions, the analyses match those of dental abrasives. Some also match those of amalgam.[3]

The epithelium is acanthotic or atrophic and basal cell degeneration is present in up to 50% of cases. The inflammatory infiltrate varies in severity and is lichenoid (band-like and lymphocytic) in half the cases (*Fig. 10.50*). In one-quarter of cases, granulomatous inflammation may be seen, sometimes accompanied by foreign body and/or Langhans' type giant cells.[1,2] Plasma cells are occasionally abundant. Foreign bodies, ranging from 1 to 5 microns in diameter, are present in all cases, and 44% may be refractile (*Fig. 10.51*).

Differential diagnosis

Plasma cell gingivitis exhibits an intense plasmacytic infiltrate, usually in sheets, and foreign material is not identified although there is probably overlap between these two conditions.

References

1. Daley, T.D., Wysocki, G.P. (1990) Foreign body gingivitis: an iatrogenic disease? *Oral Surg Oral Med Oral Pathol*, **69**, 708–712.
2. Gordon, S.C., Daley, T.D. (1997) Foreign body gingivitis: clinical and microscopic features of 61 cases. *Oral Surg Oral Med Oral Pathol Oral Radiol Endod*, **83**, 562–570.
3. Gordon, S.C., Daley, T.D. (1997) Foreign body gingivitis: identification of the foreign material by energy-dispersive x-ray microanalysis. *Oral Surg Oral Med Oral Pathol Oral Radiol Endod*, **83**, 571–576.

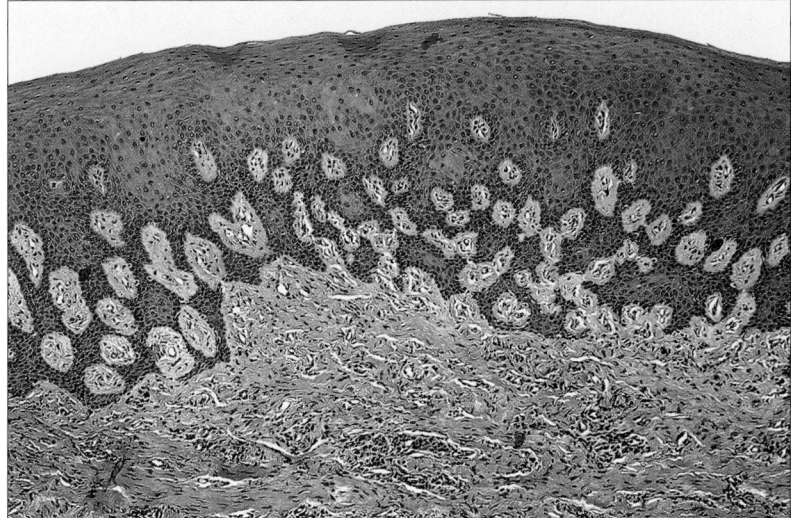

Fig. 10.50
Foreign body gingivitis: there is non-specific mild chronic inflammation in the lamina propria.

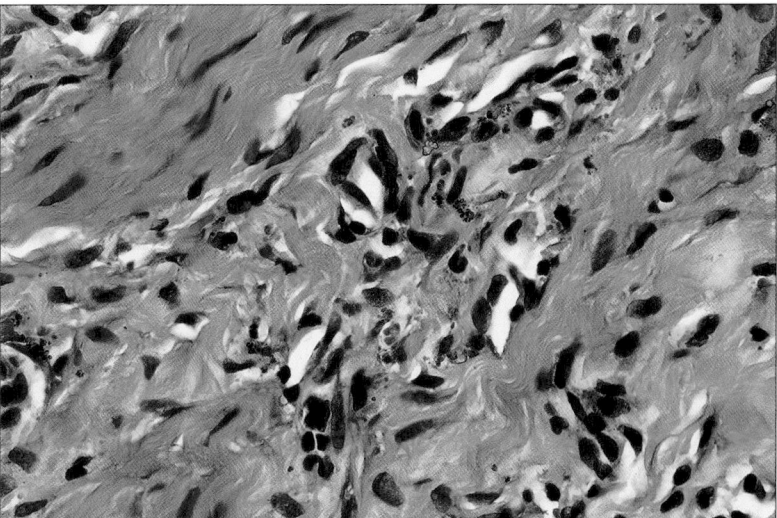

Fig. 10.51
Foreign body gingivitis: small granules of foreign material that are refractile in polarized light are present with some surrounding chronic inflammation.

Pyostomatitis vegetans

Clinical features

This is the oral counterpart of pyoderma vegetans. Men are twice as commonly affected as women.[1] The most common associations are ulcerative colitis (approximately 70%), Crohn's disease (10–15%) and liver disease (21%).[1–4] Patients present with shallow ulcers and erosions, miliary abscesses and pustules that coalesce to form 'snail track' lesions (*Fig. 10.52*). These develop within an erythematous mucosa in which vegetations may be a feature.[5–7] There is sometimes folding and fissuring of the buccal mucosa. The dorsal surface of the tongue is usually spared.[5,8,9] Peripheral blood eosinophilia is present in 90% of cases.[1]

Histological features

There is epithelial hyperplasia, sometimes accompanied by papillomatosis, and spongiosis. Suprabasilar clefting with acantholysis may also be seen (*Fig. 10.53*). Characteristically, neutrophilic and eosinophilic abscesses are present in the connective tissue papillae at the interface, and sometimes within the epithelium itself (*Fig. 10.54*).[1,8–10] Eosinophils and neutrophils may permeate the epithelium and chronic inflammatory cells are abundant in the lamina propria.

Direct immunofluorescence studies for IgG and C3 are generally negative. When positive, the staining is usually weak. It is thought that such weak reactivity and the occasional positive indirect immunofluorescence studies probably represent a secondary reaction to epithelial inflammation and damage rather than represent a primary autoimmune phenomenon.[1,11]

Differential diagnosis

Pemphigus vulgaris may appear similar although typically there is more obvious acantholysis. In addition, neutrophilic and eosinophilic abscesses are absent and papillary epithelial hyperplasia is not usually a feature. Pemphigus vegetans shows considerable histological overlap. Distinction from both of these conditions is readily made by direct immunofluorescence studies which show intercellular IgG deposition.

References

1. Thornhill, M.H., Zakrzewska, J.M., Gilkes, J.J.H. (1992) Pyostomatitis vegetans: report of three cases and review of the literature. *J Oral Pathol Med*, **21**, 128–133.
2. Philpot, H.C., Elewski, B.E., Banwell, J.G. et al (1992) Pyostomatitis vegetans and primary sclerosing cholangitis: markers of inflammatory bowel disease. *Gastroenterology*, **103**, 668–674.
3. Ficarra, G., Cicchi, P., Amorosi, A. et al (1993) Oral Crohn's disease and pyostomatitis vegetans. An unusual association. *Oral Surg Oral Med Oral Pathol*, **75**, 220–224.
4. Soriano, M.L., Martinez, N., Grilli, R. et al (1999) Pyodermatitis–pyostomatitis vegetans: report of a case and review of the literature. *Oral Surg Oral Med Oral Pathol Oral Radiol Endod*, **87**, 322–326.
5. McCarthy, P., Shklar, G. (1963) A syndrome of pyostomatitis vegetans and ulcerative colitis. *Arch Dermatol*, **88**, 913–919.
6. Chan, S.W., Scully, C., Prime, S.S. et al (1991) Pyostomatitis vegetans: oral manifestation of ulcerative colitis. *Oral Surg Oral Med Oral Pathol*, **72**, 689–692.
7. Healy, C.M., Farthing, P.M., Williams, D.M. et al (1994) Pyostomatitis vegetans and associated systemic disease. A review and two case reports. *Oral Surg Oral Med Oral Pathol*, **78**, 323–328.
8. Hansen, L.S., Silverman, S. Jr, Daniels, T.E. (1983) The differential diagnosis of pyostomatitis vegetans and its relation to bowel disease. *Oral Surg Oral Med Oral Pathol*, **55**, 363–373.
9. Neville, B.W., Smith, S.E., Maize, J.C. et al (1985) Pyostomatitis vegetans. *Am J Dermatopathol*, **7**, 69–77.
10. Storwick, G.S., Prihoda, M.B., Fulton, R.J. et al (1994) Pyodermatitis–pyostomatitis vegetans: a specific marker for inflammatory bowel disease. *J Am Acad Dermatol*, **31**, 336–341.
11. Chaudhry, S.I., Philpot, N.S., Odell, E.W. et al (1999) Pyostomatitis vegetans associated with asymptomatic ulcerative colitis: a case report. *Oral Surg Oral Med Oral Pathol Oral Radiol Endod*, **87**, 327–330.

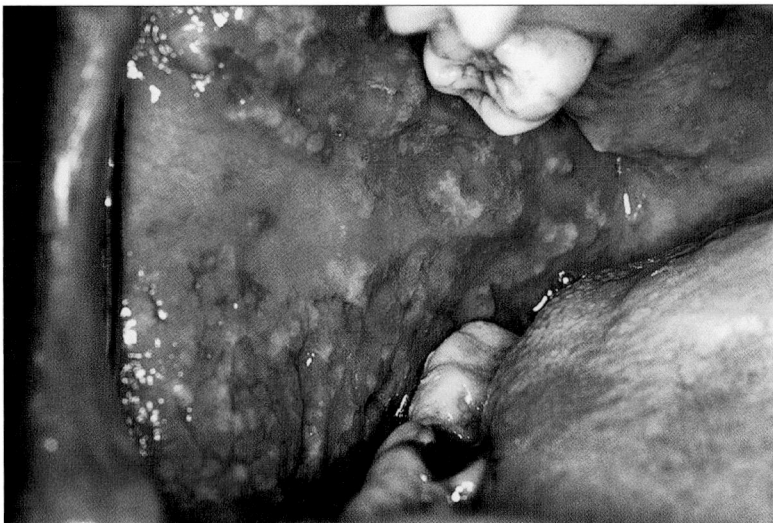

Fig. 10.52
Pyostomatitis vegetans: note the yellow pustular papules and linear lesions on the buccal mucosa. By courtesy of B. Neville, DDS, Charleston, USA.

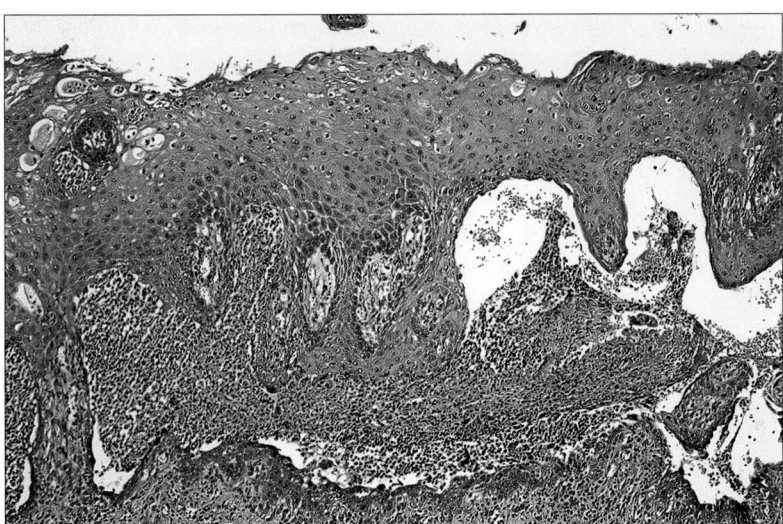

Fig. 10.53
Pyostomatitis vegetans: note the intraepithelial clefting and abscesses.

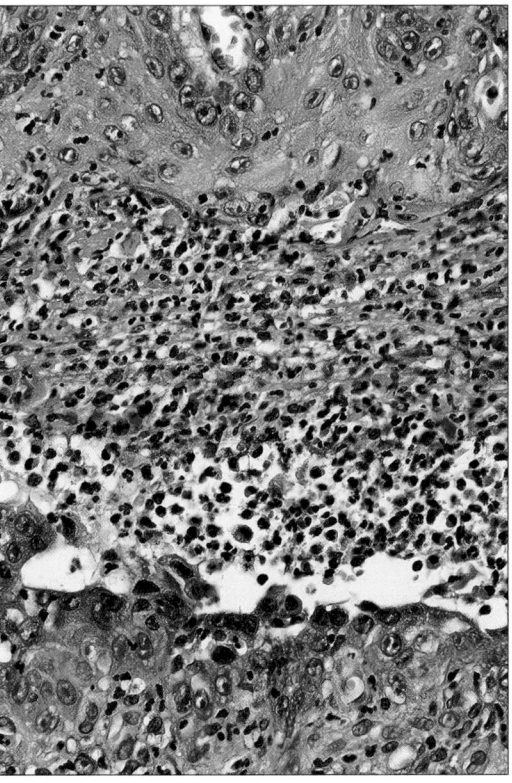

Fig. 10.54
Pyostomatitis vegetans: note the acantholysis and the presence of abscesses present supra-basally

Ulcerative conditions

Recurrent aphthous stomatitis

Clinical features

Recurrent aphthous stomatitis occurs in 15–20% of the adult population, generally below the age of 40.[1,2] It is a chronic, painful, relapsing, ulcerative condition of the non-keratinized mucosa (*Fig. 10.55*). There are three variants: minor, major and herpetiform.

- Ulcers of the minor form (the most common variant) are less than 1 cm, last 7–14 days and heal without scarring.
- Ulcers of the major form are usually greater than 1 cm, last many weeks, and heal with scarring.

- Ulcers of the herpetiform variety occur in small crops of 10–100 ulcers in any one episode.[2,3]

Some conditions frequently associated with the minor variant include Behçet's disease, anemia, inflammatory bowel disease, gluten-sensitive enteropathy, food hypersensitivity and neutropenia.[4,5] Aphthous stomatitis presenting in association with rheumatological or muco-cutaneous disorders is sometimes referred to as complex aphthosis.[6,7] There is also often a family history of aphthous ulcers but there is no evidence at present that the condition is infectious in nature.

Investigations into a possible relationship with *Helicobacter pylori* have proven negative.[8] In children, aphthous stomatitis may be syndromic and associated with fever, lymphadenopathy and pharyngitis (FAPA syndrome, periodic fever syndrome).[9,10]

Pathogenesis and histological features

Cross-reaction of antigens of *Streptococcus mutans* with a mitochondrial heat shock protein may play an important role in the pathogenesis of this condition.[11,12] Expression of HLA class I and class II antigens on epithelial cells may result in targeting for cytotoxic attack.[13] There is no evidence of increased circulating immunoglobins or immune complexes.

The ulcerative process results from T-cell activation. Although the target antigens have yet to be clearly and consistently elucidated, the end result is destruction of the epithelium. Early lesions show a predominance of T-helper cells followed by an increase in T-suppressor cells during the ulcerative phase; T-helper cells re-emerge during the healing phase.[14–17] Increased numbers of peripheral gamma–delta cells have been noted suggesting that antibody-dependent cell-mediated cytotoxicity may play a role in the immunopathogenesis of this disease.[18] Cell lysis may be mediated through tumor necrosis factor alpha (TNF-α).[19]

The histological appearances are non-specific. There is ulceration of the mucosa with a thick fibrin clot enmeshed with neutrophils (*Fig. 10.56*). The adjacent epithelium may exhibit reactive atypia; viral inclusions are not seen. The ulcer bed consists of granulation tissue with acute and chronic inflammatory cells.[20,21] Inflammatory changes and degeneration of superficial skeletal muscle fibers may also be evident.

Differential diagnosis

Traumatic ulcers and the ulcers of Behçet's disease are histologically indistinguishable and their distinction is dependent upon clinicopathological correlation. If there is inflammation of the muscle associated with a histiocytic mononuclear cell infiltrate and a significant number of eosinophils, a diagnosis of traumatic ulcerative granuloma is more appropriate. If the fibrin clot and underlying granulation tissue contain few neutrophils, neutropenia-associated ulceration – such as is seen in human immunodeficiency virus (HIV) disease and cyclic neutropenia – must be considered.

References

1. Ship, I.I., Brightman, V.J., Laster, L.L. (1967) The patient with recurrent aphthous ulcers and the patient with recurrent herpes labialis: a study of two population samples. *J Am Dent Assoc*, 75, 645–654.
2. Axell, T., Henricsson, V. (1985) Association between recurrent aphthous ulcers and tobacco habits. *Scand J Dent Res*, 93, 239–242.
3. Bagan, J.V., Sanchis, J.M., Milian, M.A. et al (1991) Recurrent aphthous stomatitis. A study of the clinical characteristics in 93 cases. *J Oral Pathol Med*, 20, 395–397.
4. Woo, S., Sonis, S.T. (1996) Recurrent aphthous ulcers: a review of diagnosis and treatment. *J Am Dent Assoc*, 127, 1202–1213.
5. Porter, S.R., Scully, C., Pedersen, A. (1998) Recurrent aphthous stomatitis. *Crit Rev Oral Biol Med*, 9, 306–321.
6. Jorizzo, J.L., Taylor, R.S., Schmalstieg, F.C. et al (1985) Complex aphthosis: a forme fruste of Behçet's syndrome? *J Am Acad Dermatol*, 13, 80–84.
7. Ghate, J.V., Jorizzo, J.L.. (1999) Behçet's disease and complex aphthosis. *J Am Acad Dermatol*, 40, 1–18; quiz 19–20.
8. Riggio, M.P., Lennon, A., Wray, D. (2000) Detection of Helicobacter pylori DNA in recurrent aphthous stomatitis tissue by PCR. *J Oral Pathol Med*, 29, 507–513.
9. Marshall, G.S., Edwards, K.M., Butler, J. et al (1987) Syndrome of periodic fever, pharyngitis, and aphthous stomatitis. *J Pediatr*, 110, 43–46.
10. Thomas, K.T., Feder, H.M. Jr, Lawton, A.R. et al (1999) Periodic fever syndrome in children. *J Pediatr*, 135, 15–21.
11. Lehner, T., Lavery, E., Smith, R. et al (1991) Association between 65-kilodalton heat shock protein, Streptococcus sanguis, and the corresponding antibodies in Behçet's syndrome. *Infect Immun*, 59, 1434–1441.
12. Hasan, A., Childerstone, A., Pervin, K. et al (1995) Recognition of a unique peptide epitope of the mycobacterial and human heat shock protein 65-60 antigen by T cells of patients with recurrent oral ulcers. *Clin Exp Immunol*, 99, 392–397.
13. Savage, N.W., Seymour, G.J., Kruger, B.J. (1986) Expression of class I and class II major histocompatibility complex antigens on epithelial cells in recurrent aphthous stomatitis. *J Oral Pathol*, 15, 191–195.
14. Savage, N.W., Seymour, G.J., Kruger, B.J. (1985) T-lymphocyte subset changes in recurrent aphthous stomatitis. *Oral Surg Oral Med Oral Pathol*, 60, 175–181.
15. Hayrinen-Immonen, R., Nordstrom, D., Malmstrom, M. et al (1991) Immune-inflammatory cells in recurrent oral ulcers (ROU). *Scand J Dent Res*, 99, 510–518.
16. Landesberg, R., Fallon, M., Insel, R. (1990) Alterations of T helper/inducer and T suppressor/inducer cells in patients with recurrent aphthous ulcers. *Oral Surg Oral Med Oral Pathol*, 69, 205–208.
17. Savage, N.W., Seymour, G.J. (1994) Specific lymphocytotoxic destruction of autologous epithelial cell targets in recurrent aphthous stomatitis. *Aust Dent J*, 39, 98–104.
18. Pedersen, A., Ryder, L.P. (1994) Gamma delta T-cell fraction of peripheral blood is increased in recurrent aphthous ulceration. *Clin Immunol Immunopathol*, 72, 98–104.
19. Taylor, L.J., Bagg, J., Walker, D.M. et al (1992) Increased production of tumour necrosis factor by peripheral blood leukocytes in patients with recurrent oral aphthous ulceration. *J Oral Pathol Med*, 21, 21–25.
20. Lehner, T. (1969) Pathology of recurrent oral ulceration and oral ulceration in Behçet's syndrome: light, electron and fluorescence microscopy. *J Pathol*, 97, 481–494.
21. Schroeder, H.E., Muller-Glauser, W., Sallay, K. (1984) Pathomorphologic features of the ulcerative stage of oral aphthous ulcerations. *Oral Surg Oral Med Oral Pathol*, 58, 293–305.

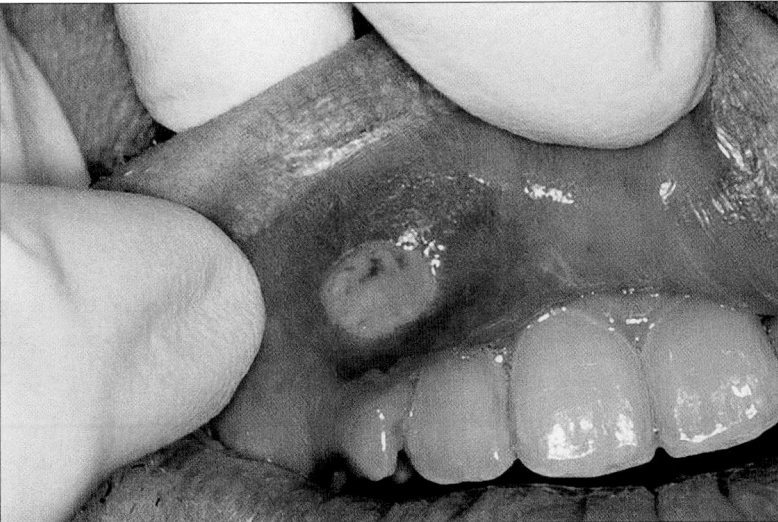

Fig. 10.55
Recurrent aphthous ulcer: a typical aphthous ulcer on the upper labial mucosa.

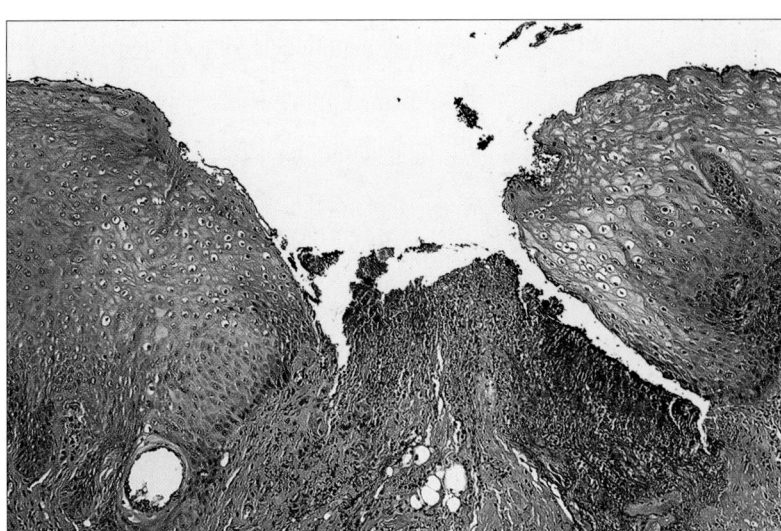

Fig. 10.56
Recurrent aphthous ulcer: the mucosa exhibits non-specific ulceration.

Traumatic ulcerative granuloma

Clinical findings

Traumatic ulcerative granuloma (traumatic ulcerative granuloma with stromal eosinophilia, eosinophilic ulcer/granuloma of the tongue, Riga–Fede disease) may present in two quite different ways. The less common form – and one that is not usually biopsied – occurs in infants in the first year of life. Painful ulcers that may be elevated occur on the sublingual area or ventral tongue as a result of the child rubbing the tongue against the developing lower anterior deciduous teeth (Riga–Fede disease).[1] The second presentation, and the more common, is in the fifth and sixth decades of life. The lateral tongue (up to 64% of cases), followed by the buccal mucosa are most often affected.[2,3] An ulcer or indurated area develops and persists for weeks or months (*Figs 10.57, 10.58*). The lack of pain, often a feature of this condition, raises the clinical suspicion of squamous cell carcinoma.[4] A history of trauma is elicited in only 50% of cases.[2,3] Approximately 7% are multifocal and 12–30% of lesions recur.[4,5]

Pathogenesis and histological features

Lesions similar to but not identical with this condition can be experimentally induced in animals by crush injury.[6] It is thought that the inciting factor is trauma, which leads to acute and chronic inflammation that for unknown reasons becomes deep, penetrating, chronic and exaggerated. It is possible that cytokines released by activated lymphocytes recruit eosinophils. Whether muscle degeneration is primary to the process or merely a secondary phenomenon is unclear.[2,3] Infectious agents and foreign material have not been identified in these lesions.

There is loss of the surface epithelium with abundant granulation tissue at the ulcer base accompanied by a polymorphous inflammatory infiltrate of T-lymphocytes and plasma cells, which penetrates into the deep mucosa and underlying muscle (*Figs 10.59, 10.60*). The presence of many mononuclear histiocyte-like cells accompanied by eosinophils and sometimes mast cells is diagnostic (*Fig. 10.61*).[2,3,7,8] Muscle

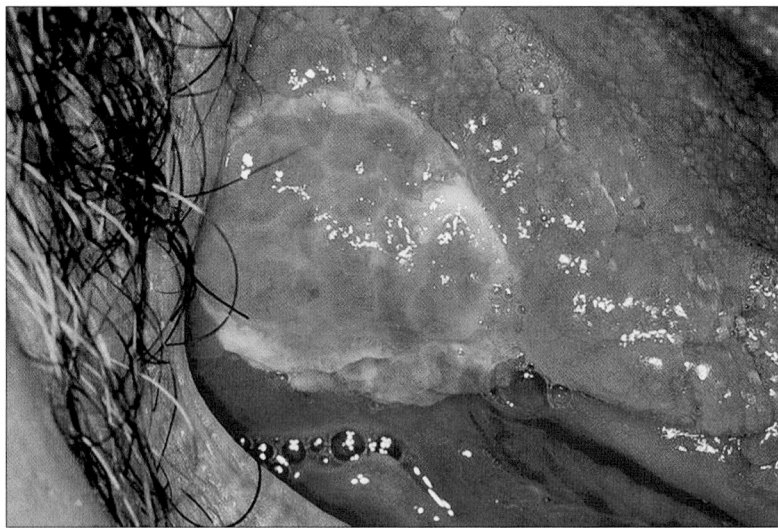

Fig. 10.57
Traumatic ulcerative granuloma: this indurated ulcer had developed after a tongue biopsy at that site.

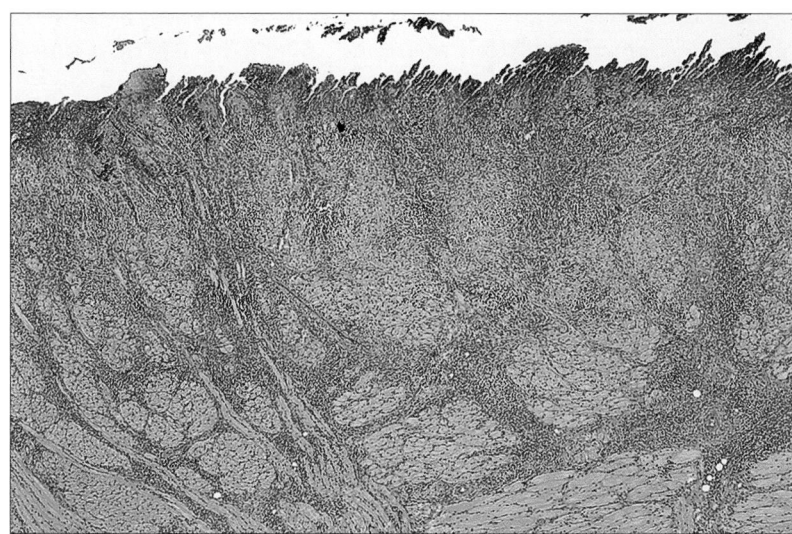

Fig. 10.59
Traumatic ulcerative granuloma: note the ulcerated surface and the penetrating inflammation that separates muscle fascicles.

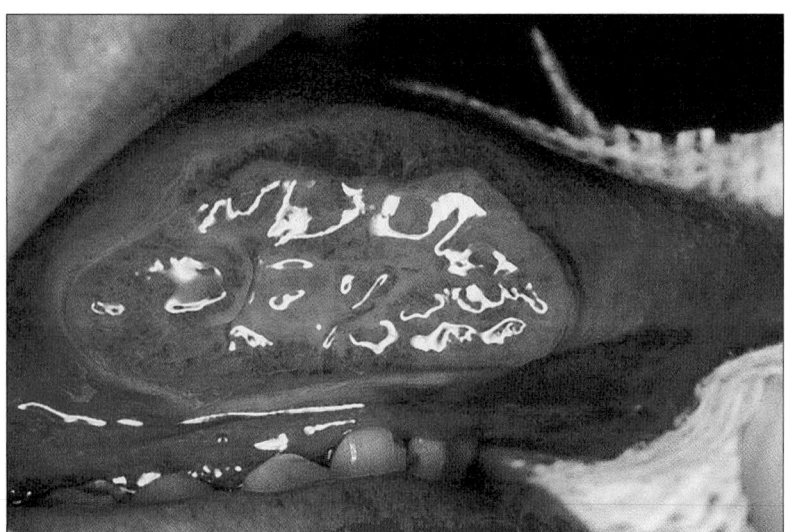

Fig. 10.58
Traumatic ulcerative granuloma: this patient had bitten her tongue during a seizure and the indurated mass developed over a few days.

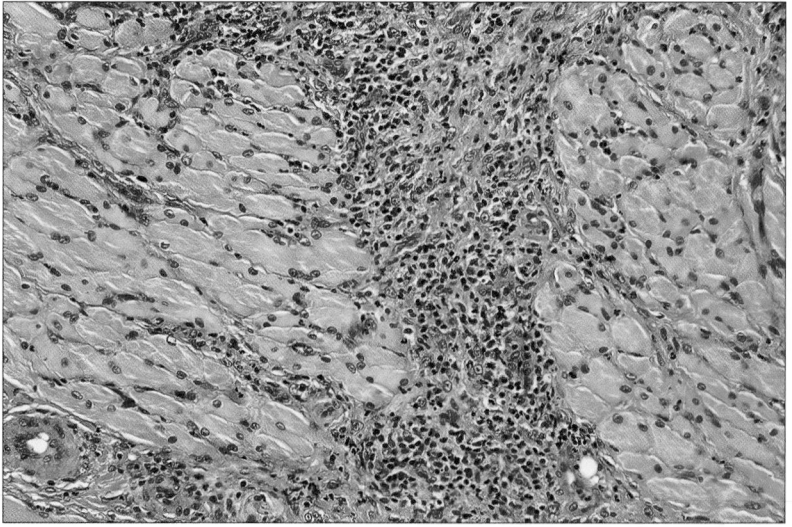

Fig. 10.60
Traumatic ulcerative granuloma: there is prominent interfascicular inflammation and muscle degeneration.

fragmentation, interfascicular inflammation with degeneration and the presence of strap cells are common additional features.[6,9]

The large histiocyte-like cells express either CD68 or factor XIIIa.[7]

Differential diagnosis

In its most florid form, traumatic ulcerative granuloma shares histological features with atypical histiocytic granuloma (pseudolymphoma).[10–14] This condition, which may or may not involve the underlying muscle, is characterized by a dense infiltrate of lymphocytes, including transformed variants and centroblasts, often raising the suspicion of lymphoma including Hodgkin's lymphoma (*Figs 10.62, 10.63*).[12] Clonality and gene rearrangement studies are often necessary to differentiate between these two conditions. Atypical histiocytic granuloma regresses spontaneously in the majority of cases.

Angiolymphoid hyperplasia with eosinophilia may sometimes present in the buccal mucosa or lip.[15,16] Histiocytoid and hobnail endothelial cells stain for Factor VIII antigen. Lymphocytes, plasma cells and eosinophils are commonly seen and occasional lymphoid follicles with germinal centers are present (*Figs 10.64, 10.65*).[16,17]

Histiocyte-like cells and eosinophils are a feature of Langerhans' cell histiocytosis. However, Langerhans' cells have the characteristic grooved nuclei and can be identified with S-100 protein and CD1a immunohistochemistry.

References

1. Eichenfield, L.F., Honig, P.J., Nelson, L. (1990) Traumatic granuloma of the tongue (Riga–Fede disease): association with familial dysautonomia. *J Pediatr*, **116**, 742–744.
2. Elzay, R.P. (1983) Traumatic ulcerative granuloma with stromal eosinophilia (Riga–Fede's disease and traumatic eosinophilic granuloma). *Oral Surg*, **55**, 497–506.
3. El-Mofty, S.K., Wick, M.R., Miller, A.S. (1993) Eosinophilic ulcer of the oral mucosa. *Oral Surg Oral Med Oral Pathol*, **75**, 716–722.
4. Mezei, M.M., Tron, V.A., Stewart, W.D. et al (1995) Eosinophilic ulcer of the oral mucosa. *J Am Acad Dermatol*, **33**, 734–740.
5. Doyle, J.L., Geary, W., Baden, E. (1989) Eosinophilic ulcer. *J Oral Maxillofac Surg*, **47**, 349–352.
6. Bhaskar, S.N., Lilly, G.E. (1964) Traumatic granuloma of the tongue (human and experimental). *Oral Surg*, **18**, 206–218.
7. Regezi, J.A., Zarbo, R.J., Daniels, T.E. et al (1993) Oral traumatic granuloma. Characterization of the cellular infiltrate. *Oral Surg Oral Med Oral Pathol*, **75**, 723–727.

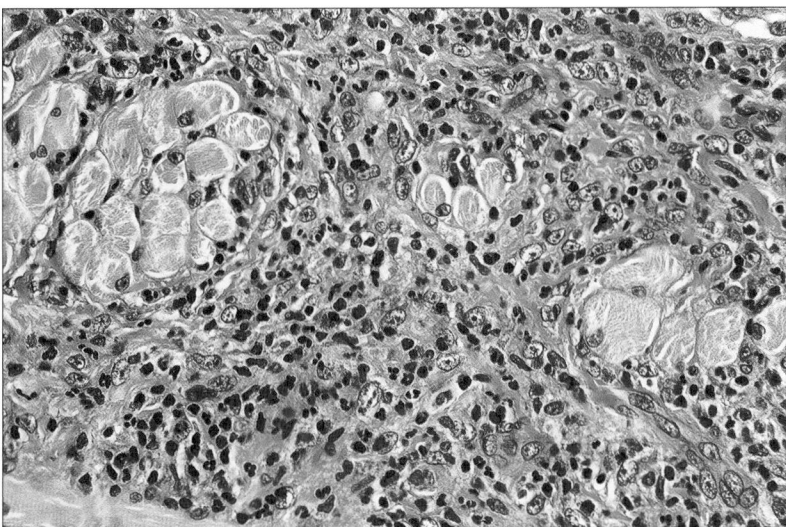

Fig. 10.61
Traumatic ulcerative granuloma: note the presence of histiocyte-like mononuclear cells and many eosinophils.

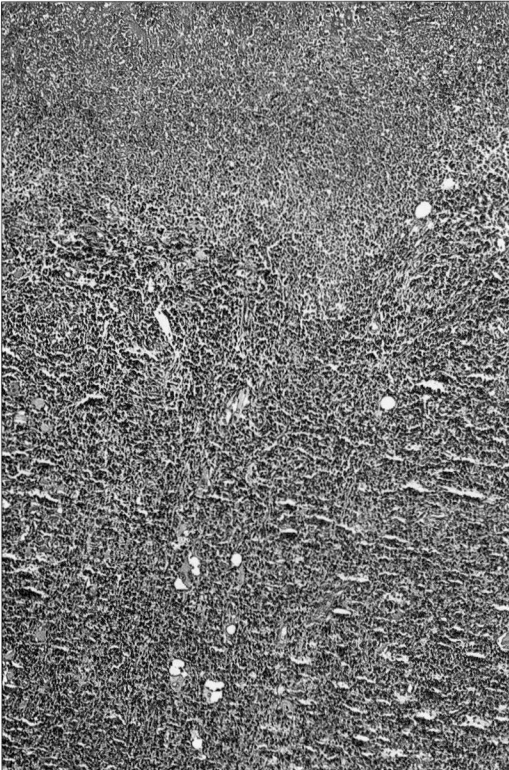

Fig. 10.62
Atypical histiocytic granuloma: there is a diffuse and dense lymphohistiocytic infiltrate.

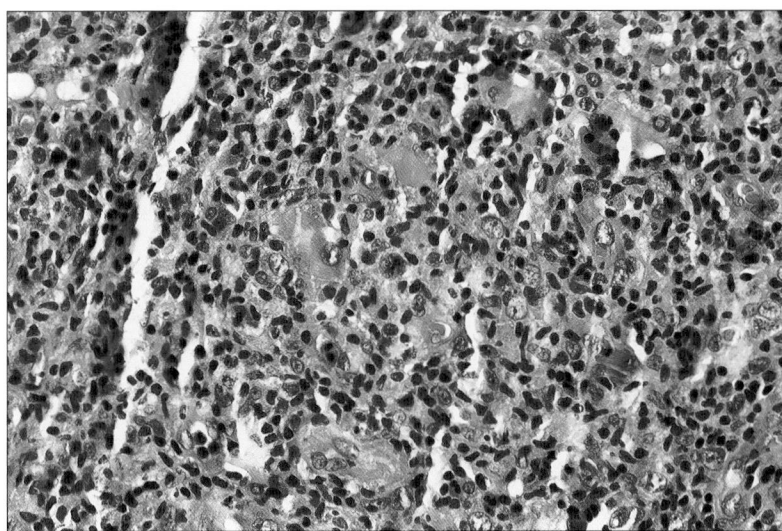

Fig. 10.63
Atypical histiocytic granuloma: many lymphocytes, mononuclear cells and eosinophils are present; there is a mitotic figure.

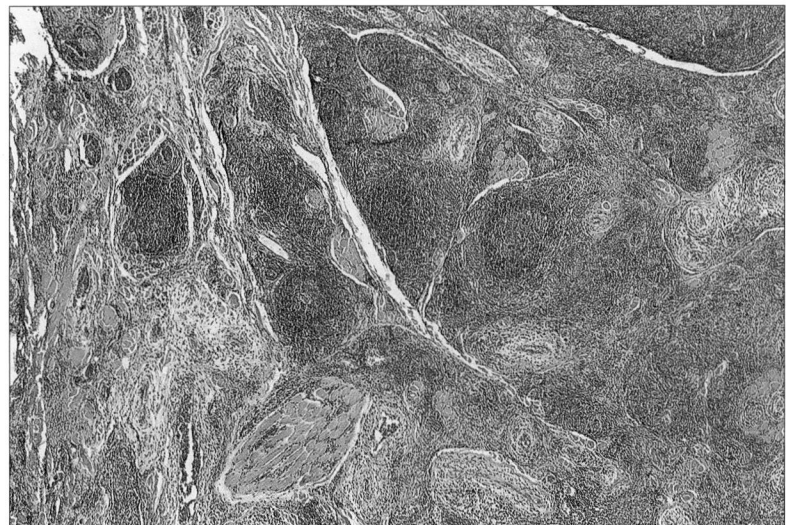

Fig. 10.64
Angiolymphoid hyperplasia with eosinophilia: note the pale lobular areas with central vessels and prominent germinal centers.

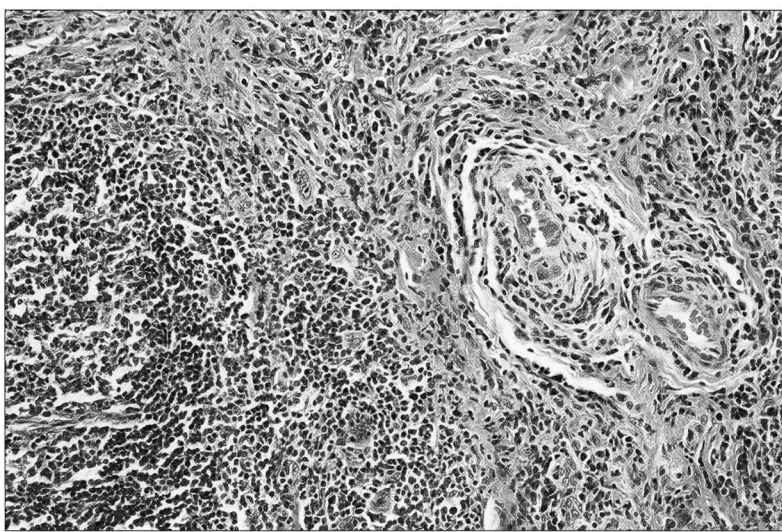

Fig. 10.65
Angiolymphoid hyperplasia with eosinophilia: there are plump epithelioid endothelial cells associated with many lymphocytes and eosinophils.

8. Movassaghi, K., Goodman, K.L., Keith, D. (1996) Ulcerative eosinophilic granuloma: a report of five new cases. *Br J Oral Maxillofac Surg*, **34**, 115–117.
9. McDaniel, R.K., Marano, P.D. (1978) Reparative lesion of the tongue. *Oral Surg Oral Med Oral Pathol*, **45**, 266–272.
10. Ruckley, R.W., Gordon, D., Conroy, B. (1984) Pseudolymphoma of the tongue mimicking Hodgkin's lymphoma (a case report). *J Laryngol Otol*, **98**, 737–741.
11. Eversole, L.R., Leider, A.S., Jacobsen, P.L. et al (1985) Atypical histiocytic granuloma. *Cancer*, **55**, 1722–1729.
12. Kabani, S., Cataldo, E., Folkerth, R. et al (1988) Atypical lymphohistiocytic infiltrate (pseudolymphoma) of the oral cavity. *Oral Surg Oral Med Oral Pathol*, **66**, 587–592.
13. Morrison, J.W., Langston, J.R., Slater, L.J. (1990) Atypical histiocytic granuloma. *J Oral Maxillofac Surg*, **48**, 630–633.
14. Del Rio, E., Sanchez Yus, E., Requena, L. et al (1997) Oral pseudolymphoma: a report of two cases. *J Cutan Pathol*, **24**, 51–55.
15. Ankjaergaard, O., Lawaetz, K.D., Andreassen, U.K. (1988) Atypical histiocytic granuloma with eosinophilia. *J Laryngol Otol*, **102**, 543–545.
16. Tsuboi, H., Fujimura, T., Katsuoka, K. (2001) Angiolymphoid hyperplasia with eosinophilia in the oral mucosa. *Br J Dermatol*, **145**, 365–366.
17. Bartralot, R., Garcia-Patos, V., Hueto, J. et al (1996) Angiolymphoid hyperplasia with eosinophilia affecting the oral mucosa: report of a case and a review of the literature. *Br J Dermatol*, **134**, 744–748.

Papillary Lesions

Squamous papilloma

Clinical features

Squamous papilloma generally presents in adults in the second to fourth decades. Sites of predilection include the soft palate–uvula complex and the tongue, although any region in the oral cavity may be affected. Lesions may be white or erythematous with a warty, finger-like or cauliflower-like appearance (*Figs 10.66, 10.67*).[1,2]

Histological features

The epithelium is thrown into papillary folds and there may be prominent or absent hyperparakeratosis or hyperorthokeratosis. In general, if the papilloma arises from a non-keratinized site (such as the uvula, soft palate, ventral tongue or floor of mouth), it will often be non-keratinized but may exhibit leukoedema (*Figs 10.68, 10.69*).[1] Koilocytes are present in up to 45% of cases.[3] The epithelium may be thickened but rete ridges are not bulbous. The connective tissue cores usually contain congested vessels with perivascular hyaline cuffs. Depending on whether the papilloma has been traumatized or not, there is variable inflammation.[1,2] In situ hybridization and polymerase chain reaction (PCR) studies have identified human papillomavirus (HPV) (usually -6 and -11) in up to 67% of cases; HPV-2 is occasionally present.[3,4]

Differential diagnosis

Verruca vulgaris may occasionally occur in the oral cavity and as in the skin, it is characterized by marked hyperorthokeratosis with prominent

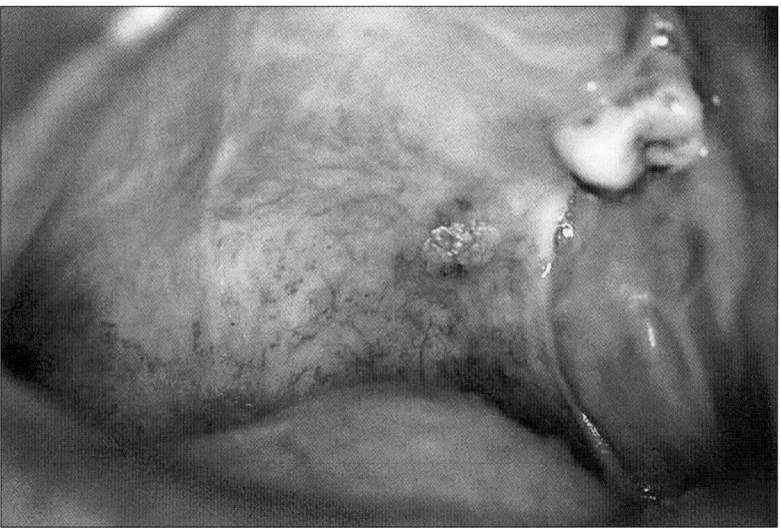

Fig. 10.66
Squamous papilloma: there is a rough, warty lesion of the soft palate.

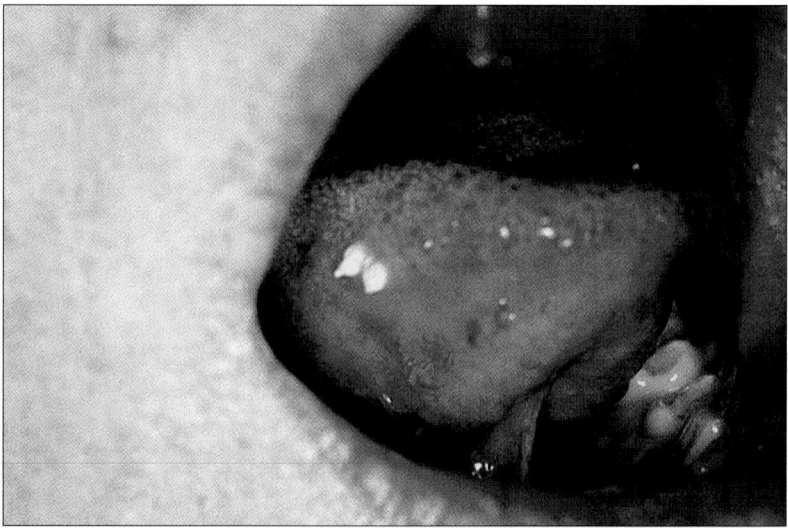

Fig. 10.67
Squamous papilloma: there is a rough, white warty lesion of the lateral tongue.

coarse keratohyaline granules and axial inclination of epithelial papillary projections. HPV-2 is identified in up to 20% of cases of intraoral and up to 100% of lip verruca vulgaris.[5–7]

Oral condyloma acuminatum shows large, bulbous rete ridges and prominent koilocytosis (*Figs 10.70, 10.71*). HPV-6 or -11 is present in up to 85% of cases.[8] This condition occurs most frequently in patients who are on long-term immunosuppression such as organ transplant recipients.

Focal epithelial hyperplasia (Heck's disease), which is associated with infection by HPV-13 and HPV-32, may show papillary epithelial hyperplasia although this is not invariably present. Importantly, 'mitosoid' figures are a characteristic feature (see p. 432).

Rare cases of oral acanthosis nigricans have been reported and these are generally associated with gastrointestinal malignancy.[9–11]

References

1. Greer, R.O., Goldman, H.M. (1974) Oral papillomas. Clinicopathologic evaluation and retrospective examination for dyskeratosis in 110 lesions. *Oral Surg Oral Med Oral Pathol*, **38**, 435–440.
2. Abbey, L.M., Page, D.G., Sawyer, D.R. (1980) The clinical and histopathologic features of a series of 464 oral squamous papillomas. *Oral Surg Oral Med Oral Pathol*, **49**, 419–428.
3. Eversole, L.R., Laipis, P.J. (1988) Oral squamous papillomas: detection of HPV DNA by in situ hybridization. *Oral Surg Oral Med Oral Pathol*, **65**, 545–550.
4. Jiménez, C., Correnti, M., Salma, N. et al (2001) Detection of human papillomavirus DNA in benign oral squamous epithelial lesions in Venezuela. *J Oral Pathol Med*, **30**, 385–388.
5. Adler-Storthz, K., Newland, J.R., Tessin, B.A. et al (1986) Identification of human papillomavirus types in oral verruca vulgaris. *J Oral Pathol*, **15**, 230–233.
6. Eversole, L.R., Laipis, P.J., Green T.L. (1987) Human papillomavirus type 2 DNA in oral and labial verruca vulgaris. *J Cutan Pathol*, **14**, 319–325.
7. Premoli-de-Percoco, G., Galindo, I., Ramirez, J.L. et al (1993) Detection of human papillomavirus-related oral verruca vulgaris among Venezuelans. *J Oral Pathol Med*, **22**, 113–116.
8. Eversole, L.R., Laipis, P.J., Merrell, P. et al (1987) Demonstration of human papillomavirus DNA in oral condyloma acuminatum. *J Oral Pathol*, **16**, 266–272.
9. Mostofi, R.S., Hayden, N.P., Soltani, K. (1983) Oral malignant acanthosis nigricans. *Oral Surg Oral Med Oral Pathol*, **56**, 372–374.
10. Hall, J.M., Moreland, A., Cox, G.J. et al (1988) Oral acanthosis nigricans: report of a case and comparison of oral and cutaneous pathology. *Am J Dermatopathol*, **10**, 68–73.
11. Ramírez-Amador, V., Esquivel-Pedraza, L., Caballero-Mendoza, E. et al (1999) Oral manifestations as a hallmark of malignant acanthosis nigricans. *J Oral Pathol Med*, **28**, 278–281.

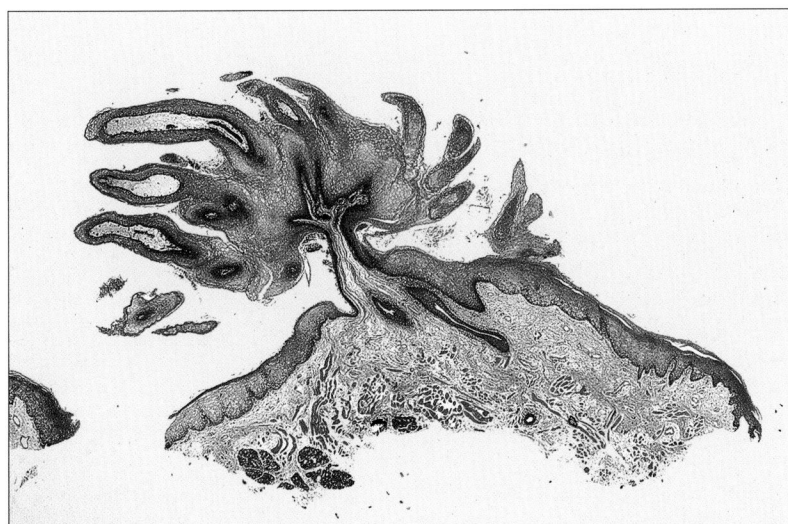

Fig. 10.68
Squamous papilloma: note the finger-like projections of epithelium.

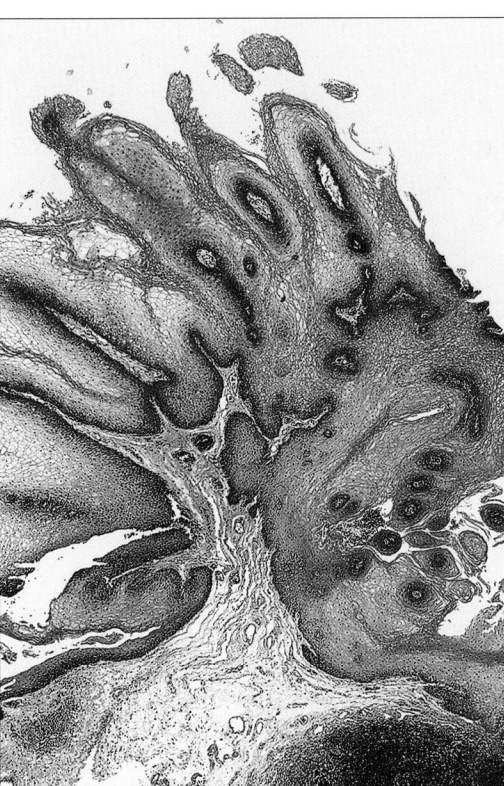

Fig. 10.69
Squamous papilloma: there is no keratosis but there is prominent leukoedema typical for lesions from the soft palate.

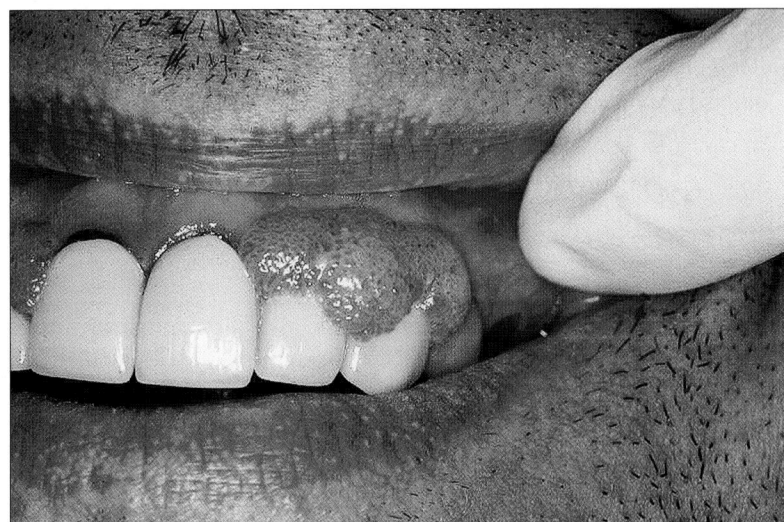

Fig. 10.70
Condyloma acuminatum: this larger warty lesion on the gingiva occurred in a patient on long-term immunosuppression to prevent organ rejection.

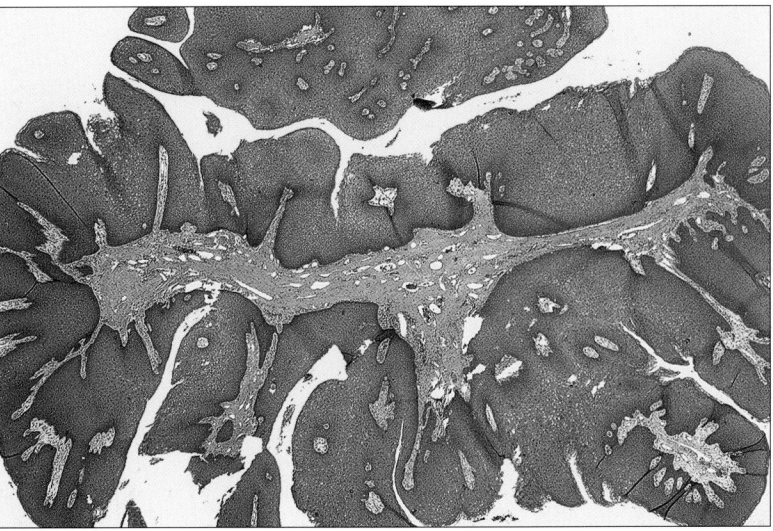

Fig. 10.71
Condyloma acuminatum: unlike squamous papilloma, the rete ridges are large and bulbous and koilocytes are readily identified.

Verruciform xanthoma

Clinical features

Verruciform xanthoma affects adults in the fourth and fifth decades with no significant sex predilection.[1–3] It presents as a well-circumscribed rough, granular or pebbly, raised or depressed, yellowish, reddish or gray plaque (*Fig. 10.72*). Seventy per cent occur primarily on the keratinized attached mucosa of the palate, gingiva or alveolar ridge mucosa. Lesions on the skin (especially of the anogenital area) and other mucosal sites have also been reported (see p. 549).[4] Although there is one report of a patient with multiple lesions and lipid storage disease, most patients do not exhibit hypercholesterolemia or disorders of lipid storage.[5]

Pathogenesis and histological features

It has been postulated that the epithelial cells are damaged and degenerate, releasing lipid that becomes engulfed by macrophages. Neutrophils are also recruited to the area by the degenerating cells.[4,6] The gingiva and palate are constantly traumatized by mastication in support of this hypothesis. Verruciform xanthoma also occurs in association with other conditions where epithelial damage occurs such as lichen planus, pemphigus vulgaris, discoid lupus erythematosus, epidermolysis bullosa, following bone marrow transplantation and possibly graft-versus-host disease (GVHD).[7–13] Such multiple associations suggest that the condition may represent a rather non-specific reaction pattern.

Histologically, there is hyperparakeratosis with the parakeratin exhibiting a bright orange hue. Loose keratin squames are present on the surface or within epithelial crypts. The surface of a verruciform xanthoma generally has a papillary configuration although some lesions are flat.[1] Rete ridges are long and uniform and sometimes coalesce at their bases (*Figs 10.73, 10.74*). Large, foamy, lipid-laden macrophages are found within the connective tissue papillae (*Fig. 10.75*); rarely, such cells extend beyond the deepest portion of the rete ridges or are seen within the epithelium.[15,16] Multinucleate forms are not a feature. Lymphocytes (primarily T-cells) are present at the base.[17,18] Neutrophils may be present superficially and a reduction of Langerhans' cells has been noted in the affected epithelium.[8,17] Rarely, non-mucosal cases may show a cystic and inverted, crateriform configuration.[4,14]

Ultrastructurally, the xanthoma cells contain membrane-bound granules consistent with lysosomes, myelin figures and fragments of desmosomes, the last supporting the theory of phagocytosis of epithelial cell debris.[6,15,19]

The xanthoma cells express CD68 and S-100.[17,18,20] Slight granular staining for cytokeratin within the foam cells also supports the presence of epithelial fragments.[4] HPV immunohistochemistry is negative.[4,18]

Fig. 10.73
Verruciform xanthoma: there is marked hyperparakeratosis and papillomatosis with confluence of rete ridges at the tips; note the unusually brightly stained keratin.

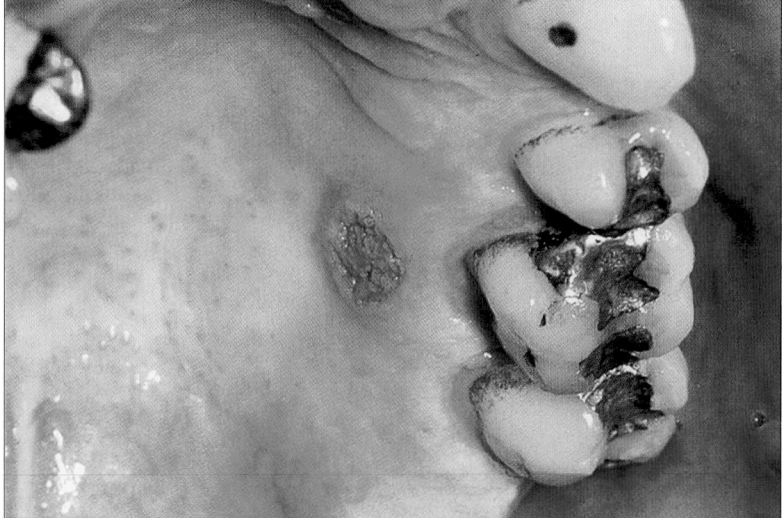

Fig. 10.72
Verruciform xanthoma: note the warty sessile lesion on the left hard palate. By courtesy of C. Allen, DDS, Columbus, USA.

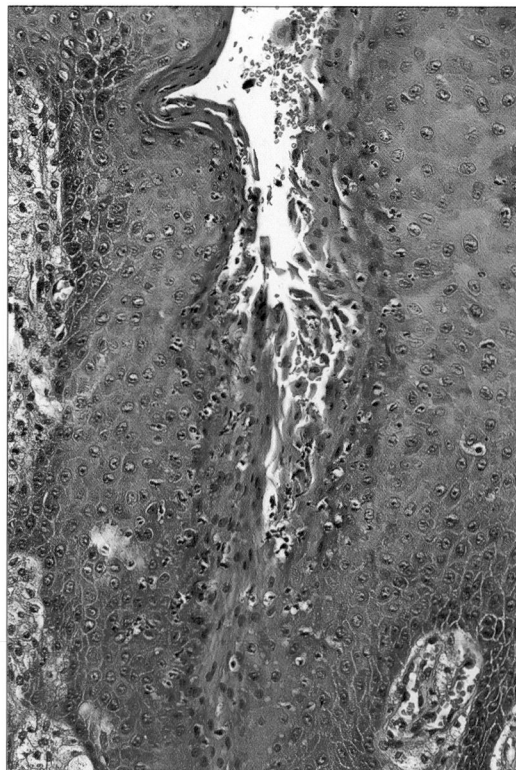

Fig. 10.74
Verruciform xanthoma: parakeratotic squames on the surface of the keratin and in the crypts are a characteristic feature.

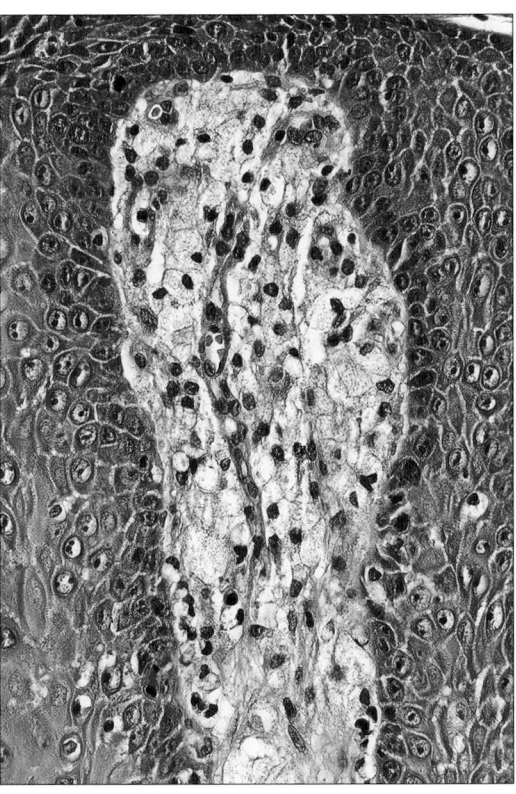

Fig. 10.75
Verruciform xanthoma: the lamina propria contains numerous foamy macrophages.

References

1. Nowparast, B., Howell, F.V., Rick, G.M. (1981) Verruciform xanthoma. *Oral Surg Oral Med Oral Pathol*, **51**, 619–625.
2. Neville, B. (1986) The verruciform xanthoma. A review and report of eight new cases. *Am J Dermatopathol*, **8**, 247–253.
3. Oliveira, P.T., Jaeger, R.G., Cabral, L.A. et al (2001) Verruciform xanthoma of the oral mucosa. Report of four cases and a review of the literature. *Oral Oncol*, **37**, 326–331.
4. Mohsin, S.K., Lee, M.W., Amin, M.B. et al (1998) Cutaneous verruciform xanthoma: a report of five cases investigating the etiology and nature of xanthomatous cells. *Am J Surg Pathol*, **22**, 479–487.
5. Travis, W.D., Davis, G.E., Tsokos, M. et al (1989) Multifocal verruciform xanthoma of the upper aerodigestive tract in a child with a systemic lipid storage disease. *Am J Surg Pathol*, **13**, 309–316.
6. Zegarelli, D.J., Zegarelli-Schmidt, E.C., Zegarelli, E.V. (1975) Verruciform xanthoma. Further light and electron microscopic studies with the addition of a third case. *Oral Surg Oral Med Oral Pathol*, **40**, 246–256.
7. Miyamoto, Y., Nagayama, M., Hayashi, Y. (1996) Verruciform xanthoma occurring within lichen planus. *J Oral Pathol Med*, **25**, 188–191.
8. Polonowita, A.D., Firth, N.A., Rich, A.M. (1999) Verruciform xanthoma and concomitant lichen planus of the oral mucosa. A report of three cases. *Int J Oral Maxillofac Surg*, **28**, 62–66.
9. Gehrig, R.D., Baughman, R.A., Collins, J.F. (1983) Verruciform xanthoma in a young male patient with a past history of pemphigus vulgaris. *Oral Surg Oral Med Oral Pathol*, **55**, 58–61.
10. Meyers, D.C., Woosley, J.T., Reddick, R.L. (1992) Verruciform xanthoma in association with discoid lupus erythematosus. *J Cutan Pathol*, **19**, 156–158.
11. Cooper, T.W., Santa Cruz, D.J., Bauer, E.A. (1983) Verruciform xanthoma. Occurrence in eroded skin in a patient with recessive dystrophic epidermolysis bullosa. *J Am Acad Dermatol*, **8**, 463–467.
12. Allen, C.M., Kapoor, N. (1993) Verruciform xanthoma in a bone marrow transplant recipient. *Oral Surg Oral Med Oral Pathol*, **75**, 591–594.
13. Helm, K.F., Hopfl, R.M., Kreider, J.W. et al (1993) Verruciform xanthoma in an immunocompromised patient: a case report and immunohistochemical study. *J Cutan Pathol*, **20**, 84–86.
14. Poblet, E., McCaden, M.E., Santa Cruz, D.J. (1991) Cystic verruciform xanthoma. *J Am Acad Dermatol*, **25**, 330–331.
15. Cobb, C.M., Holt, R., Denys, F.R. (1976) Ultrastructural features of the verruciform xanthoma. *J Oral Pathol*, **5**, 42–51.
16. Neville, B.W., Weathers, D.R. (1980) Verruciform xanthoma. *Oral Surg Oral Med Oral Pathol*, **49**, 429–434.
17. Mostafa, K.A., Takata, T., Ogawa, I. et al (1993) Verruciform xanthoma of the oral mucosa: a clinicopathological study with immunohistochemical findings relating to pathogenesis. *Virchows Arch Pathol Anat*, **423**, 243–248.
18. Iamaroon, A., Vickers, R.A. (1996) Characterization of verruciform xanthoma by in situ hybridization and immunohistochemistry. *J Oral Pathol Med*, **25**, 395–400.
19. Ronan, S.G., Bolano, J., Manaligod, J.R. (1984) Verruciform xanthoma of penis. Light and electron-microscopic study. *Urology*, **23**, 600–603.
20. Rowden, D., Lovas, G., Shafer, W. et al (1986) Langerhans' cells in verruciform xanthomas: an immunoperoxidase study of 10 oral cases. *J Oral Pathol*, **15**, 48–53.

Tumor-like conditions

Fibroma

Clinical features

Fibroma (fibrovascular polyp, irritation fibroma, bite fibroma) is the most common tumor-like condition in the mouth. It is usually located at sites of trauma, namely the buccal mucosa at or near the linea alba, the lateral borders and tip of the tongue and the lower labial mucosa, as well as on the gingiva.[1,2] It presents as a fleshy, pedunculated or sessile dome-shaped nodule that may be mucosal-colored, ulcerated or hyperkeratotic (*Figs 10.76, 10.77*).

Histological features

The fibroma consists of a proliferation of fibrocollagenous tissue with variable vascularity and usually mild to insignificant inflammation unless there is overlying ulceration (*Figs 10.78, 10.79*). On occasion, the lesion may resemble a keloid. The epithelium may be hyperkeratotic, acanthotic or atrophic. If adipose tissue is present, the term 'fibrolipoma' is sometimes applied.

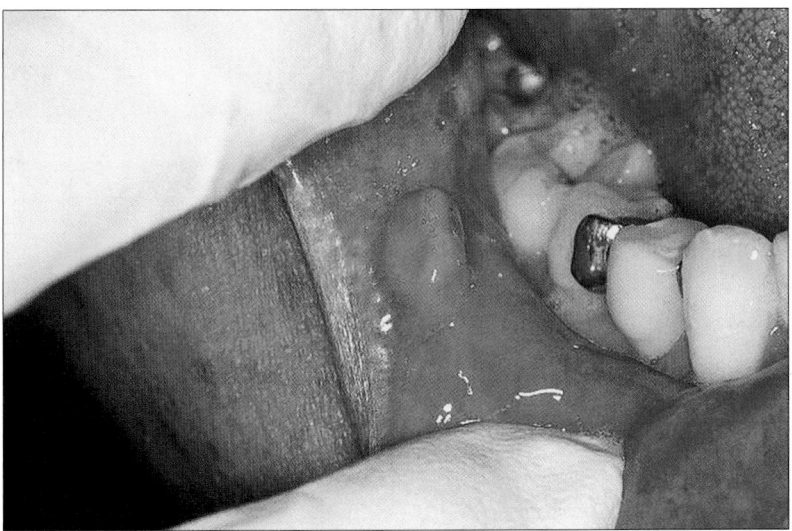

Fig. 10.76
Fibroma: there is a fleshy pink fibroma on the lower labial mucosa.

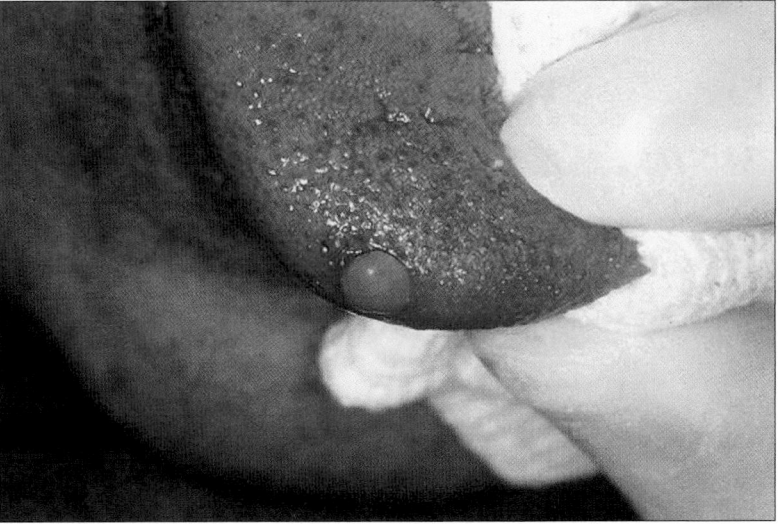

Fig. 10.77
Fibroma: the lateral border of the tongue is a common site for a fibroma.

References

1.   Barker, D.S., Lucas, R.B. (1967) Localised fibrous overgrowths of the oral mucosa. *Br J Oral Surg*, 5, 86–92.
2.   Savage, N.W., Monsour, P.A. (1985) Oral fibrous hyperplasias and the giant cell fibroma. *Austral Dent J*, 30, 582–587.

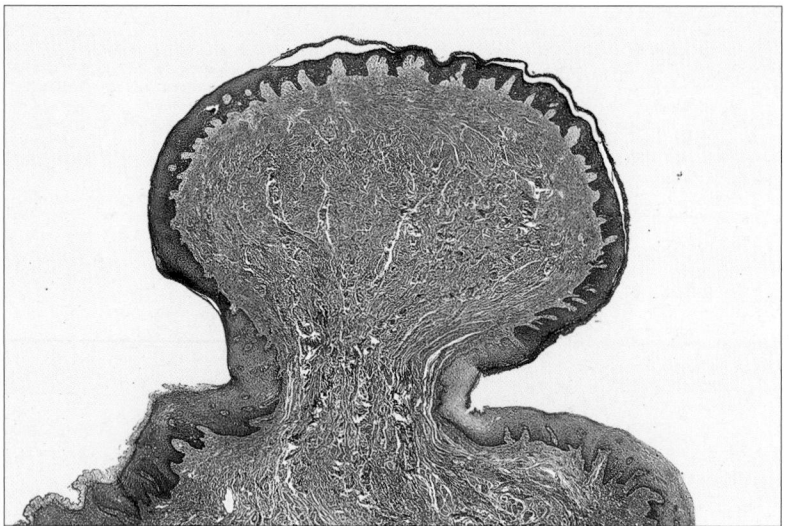

Fig. 10.78
Fibroma: this fibroma from the buccal mucosa exhibits hyperkeratosis as compared to the base which is non-keratinized.

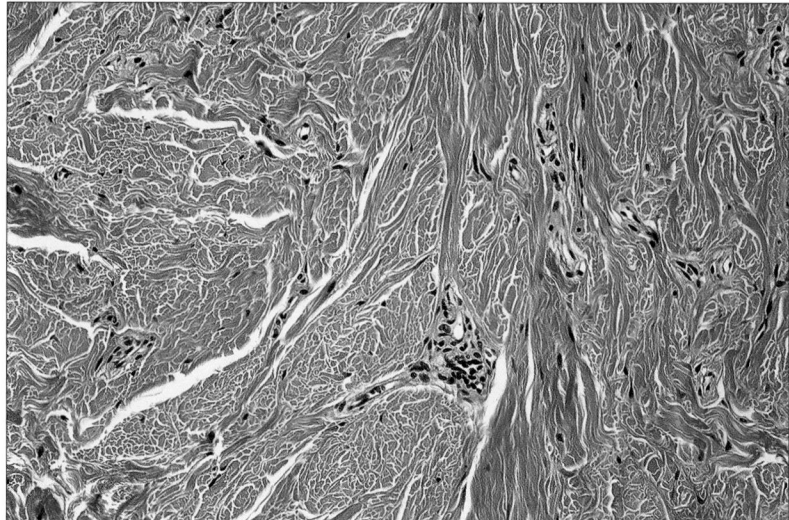

Fig. 10.79
Fibroma: often, the collagen in fibromas may be extremely hyalinized and almost keloidal in appearance.

Giant cell fibroma

Clinical features

Giant cell fibroma occurs in the first three decades of life and the most common sites affected are the gingiva (44–49%), tongue (17–22%) and palate (15–18%).[1,2] It often has a papillary or bosselated surface configuration. It bears some resemblance to the fibrous papule of the nose, angiofibroma and the pearly penile papule. The retrocuspid papilla has a similar histology and is located on the lingual mandibular gingiva in the area of the cuspid.[3,4]

Histological features

The most characteristic feature of the giant cell fibroma is the presence of giant, angulated and stellate-shaped fibroblast-like cells, usually clustered beneath the epithelium (*Figs 10.80, 10.81*).[1,2,5] Multinucleated giant cells ('manta ray cells') are common. The overlying epithelium is usually hyperplastic forming spiky, saw-tooth-shaped rete ridges, and there may be surface papillomatosis.

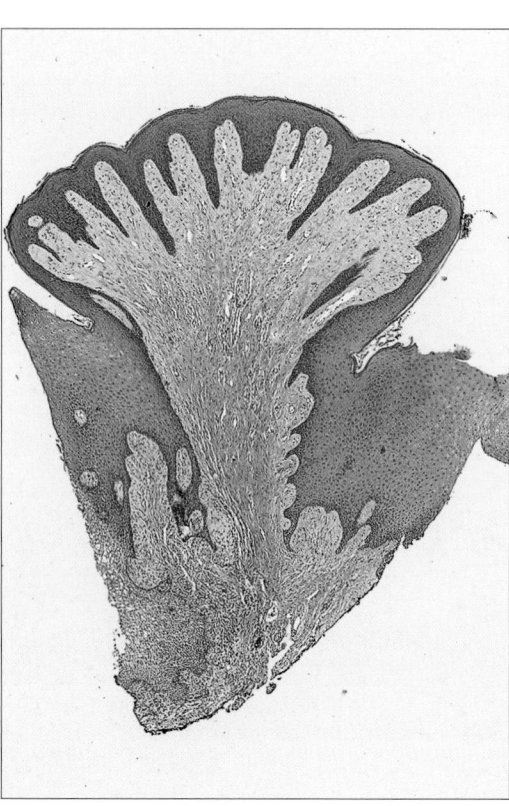

Fig. 10.80
Giant cell fibroma: note the papillary surface and spiky rete ridges.

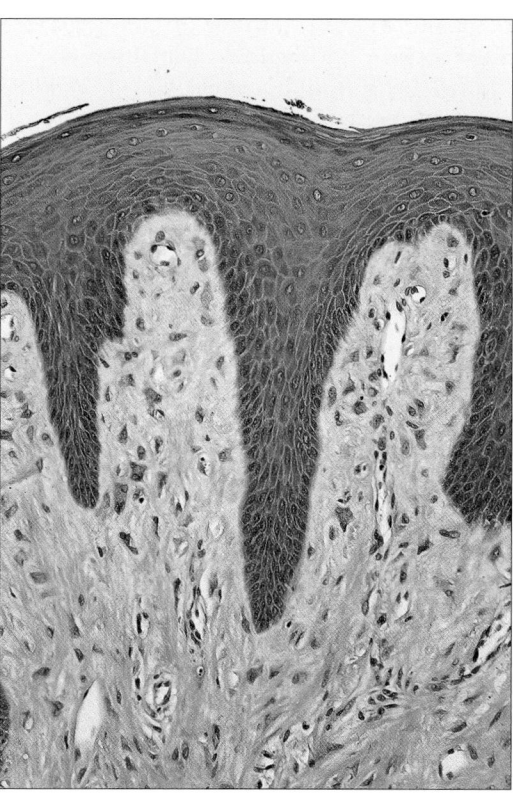

Fig. 10.81
Giant cell fibroma: note the stellate-shaped and multinucleated cells.

The cells express vimentin, occasionally Factor XIIIa, but not S-100 protein or CD68.[5,6]

Differential diagnosis

The multinucleate cell angiohistiocytoma occurs rarely in the oral cavity and contains multinucleated giant cells, branching capillaries and a myxoid stroma.[7,8]

References

1. Weathers, D.R., Callihan, M.D. (1974) Giant-cell fibroma. *Oral Surg Oral Med Oral Pathol*, 37, 374–384.
2. Houston, G.D. (1982) The giant cell fibroma: a review of 464 cases. *Oral Surg Oral Med Oral Pathol*, 53, 582–587.
3. Regezi, J.A., Courtney, R.M., Kerr, D.A. (1975) Fibrous lesions of the skin and mucous membranes which contain stellate and multinucleated cells. *Oral Surg Oral Med Oral Pathol*, 39, 605–614.
4. Berman, F.R., Fay, J.T. (1976) The retrocuspid papilla. A clinical survey. *Oral Surg Oral Med Oral Pathol*, 42, 80–85.
5. Magnusson, B.C., Rasmusson, L.G. (1995) The giant cell fibroma. A review of 103 cases with immunohistochemical findings. *Acta Odontol Scand*, 53, 293–296.
6. Odell, E.W., Lock, C., Lombardi, T.L. (1994) Phenotypic characterisation of stellate and giant cells in giant cell fibroma by immunocytochemistry. *J Oral Pathol Med*, 23, 284–287.
7. Jones, W.E., Cerio, R., Smith, N.P. (1990) Multinucleate cell angiohistiocytoma: an acquired vascular anomaly to be distinguished from Kaposi's sarcoma. *Br J Dermatol*, 122, 651–663.
8. Jones, A.C., Mullins, D., Jimenez, F. (1994) Multinucleate cell angiohistiocytoma of the upper lip. *Oral Surg Oral Med Oral Pathol*, 78, 743–747.

Lipoma

Clinical features

This is a yellowish, soft and doughy, painless, sessile or pedunculated nodule that generally occurs on the buccal mucosa or sulcus (*Fig. 10.82*). It usually presents in adults in the sixth and seventh decades.[1-3] Other sites include the tongue, lips and floor of mouth. Infiltrating or intramuscular lipomas tend to occur two decades earlier and generally involve the tongue.[2,4,5]

Some lipomas of the buccal mucosa are not true tumors but represent herniation of the buccal fat pad.

Histological features

Lipomas represent circumscribed proliferations of mature adipocytes identical to normal adipose tissue.[3] Cartilaginous metaplasia has occasionally been reported.[6] Similar benign adipocytes are present within skeletal muscle fibers in an infiltrating (intramuscular) lipoma.[4] Oral spindle cell lipoma has also been reported and this consists of spindle cells showing slight nuclear pleomorphism within a myxoid stroma.[3]

Differential diagnosis

Distinction must be made between a banal lipoma and atypical lipomatous tumors that generally occur on the tongue of adults, and that represents a superficial form of well-differentiated liposarcoma. These are infiltrative tumors containing lipoblasts (uni-, bi- or multi-vacuolated) with hyperchromatic and atypical nuclei (*Figs 10.83, 10.84*).[7] Foci of spindle cells and dedifferentiation have also been reported.

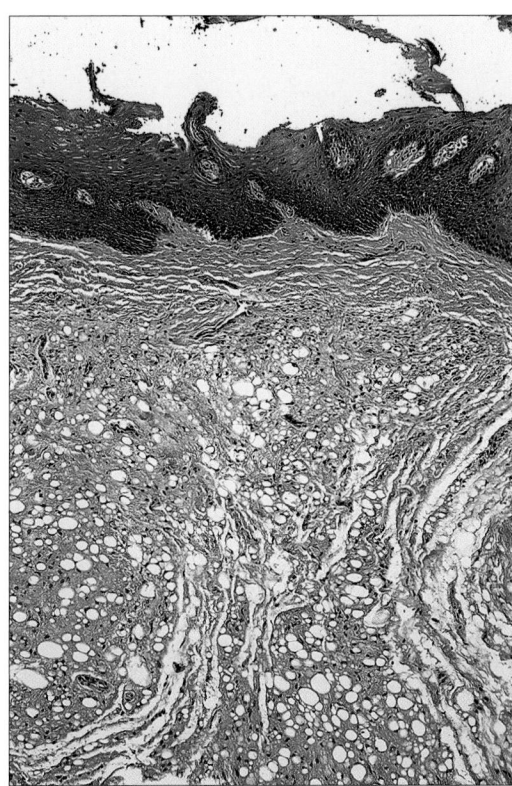

Fig. 10.83
Atypical lipomatous tumor: the tumor has infiltrative margins and cells with variably sized vacuoles.

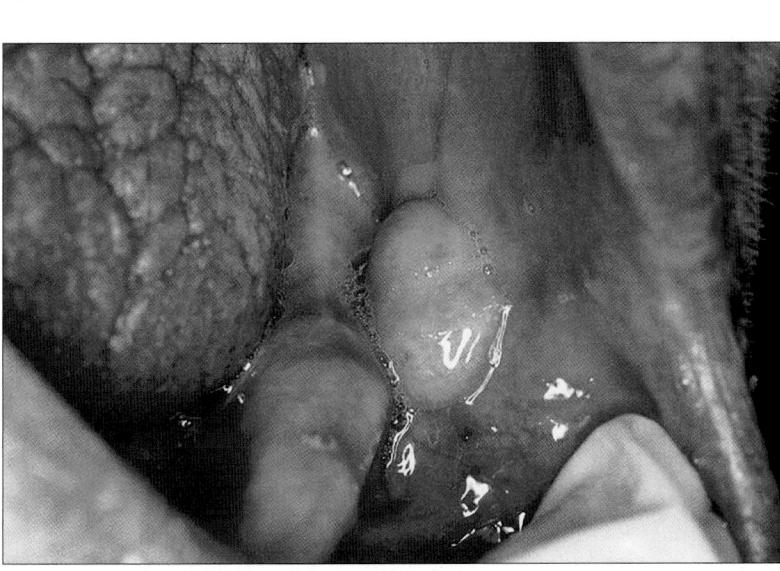

Fig. 10.82
Lipoma: note the yellowish nodule on the buccal mucosa.

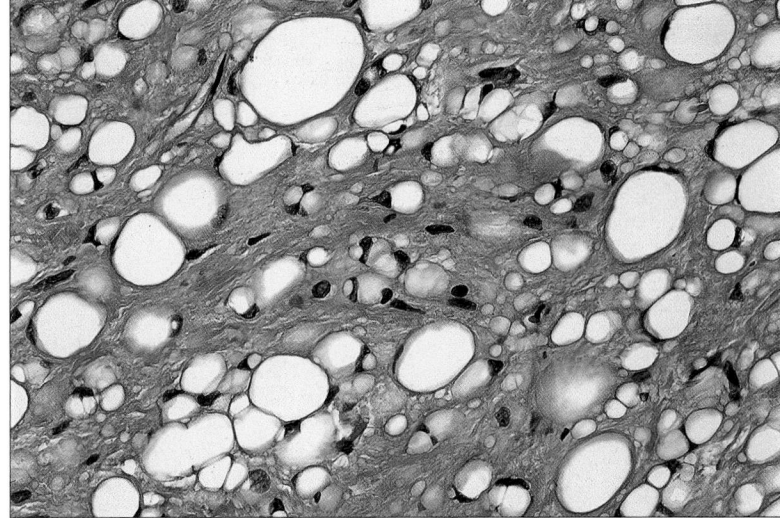

Fig. 10.84
Atypical lipomatous tumor: note the multivacuolated lipoblasts with atypical, hyperchromatic and indented nuclei.

References

1.   de Visscher J.G. (1982) Lipomas and fibrolipomas of the oral cavity. *J Maxillofac Surg*, **10**, 177–181.
2.   Epivatianos, A., Markopoulos, A.K., Papanayotou, P. (2000) Benign tumors of adipose tissue of the oral cavity: a clinicopathologic study of 13 cases. *J Oral Maxillofac Surg*, **58**, 1113–1117; discussion 1118.
3.   Said-Al-Naief, N., Zahurullah, F.R., Sciubba, J.J. (2001) Oral spindle cell lipoma. *Ann Diagn Pathol*, **5**, 207–215.

4.   Garavaglia, J., Gnepp, D.R. (1987) Intramuscular (infiltrating) lipoma of the tongue. *Oral Surg Oral Med Oral Pathol*, **63**, 348–350.
5.   Bataineh, A.B., Mansour, M.J., Abalkhail, A. (1996) Oral infiltrating lipomas. *Br J Oral Maxillofac Surg*, **34**, 520–523.
6.   Fujimura, N., Enomoto, S. (1992) Lipoma of the tongue with cartilaginous change: a case report and review of the literature. *J Oral Maxillofac Surg*, **50**, 1015–1017.
7.   Nascimento, A.F., Mairin, E.M., Fletcher, C.D.M. (2002) Liposarcomas/atypical lipomatous tumors of the oral cavity: a clinicopathologic study of 23 cases. *Ann Diag Pathol*, **6**, 83–93.

Denture-associated fibrous hyperplasia

Clinical features

Denture-associated fibrous hyperplasia (inflammatory fibrous hyperplasia, epulis fissuratum, denture hyperplasia, papillary hyperplasia, inflammatory papillary hyperplasia) presents as a linear mass of tissue arising in the mucobuccal sulcus around the flange of a poorly fitting denture. The redundant tissue cushions the mucosa against ongoing trauma. The anterior maxillary and mandibular sulci are the preferred sites of involvement (*Figs 10.85, 10.86*). There is a 3:1 female predisposition and most occur in the sixth decade.[1–3]

A clinically different form of denture-associated fibrous proliferation is also referred to as papillary hyperplasia or inflammatory papillary hyperplasia of the palate. The movement of a poorly fitting maxillary denture results in the development of an erythematous, edematous and pebbly, multinodular appearance to the mucosa of the hard palate (*Fig. 10.87*).[4,5]

Histological features

Denture-associated fibrous hyperplasia is characterized by a proliferation of dense fibrous tissue with variable vascularity. Lymphocytes are generally diffusely dispersed at the interface of epithelium and fibrous tissue; the epithelium is hyperplastic and thrown into papillary folds (*Figs 10.88, 10.89*). Pooling of plasma on the surface of the mucosa indicates trauma. Osseous and chondroid metaplasia are seen in approximately 5% of cases, particularly in the anterior maxilla.[6] Salivary glands are present in 43% of cases.

In palatal lesions, the histology is that of multiple small nodules of fibrovascular tissue containing chronic inflammatory cells as the lesion is typically removed piecemeal (*Fig. 10.90*).[4] In all cases, if spongiotic pustules are present, Candida superinfection should be excluded.[7]

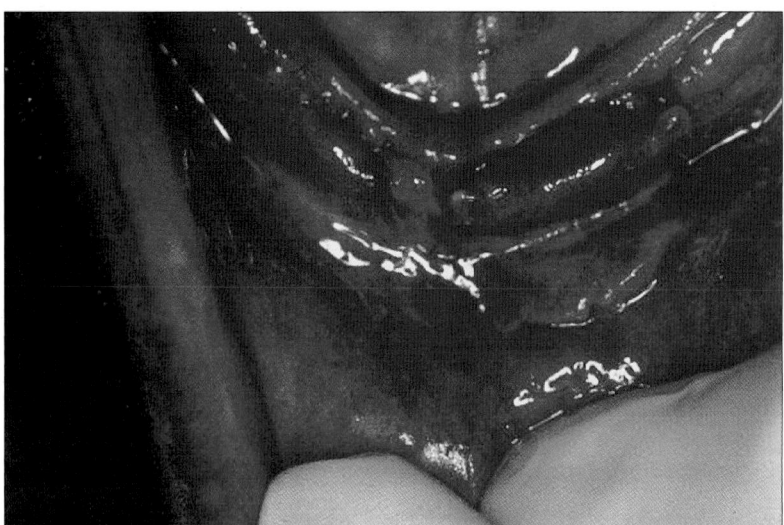

Fig. 10.85
Denture-induced fibrous hyperplasia: there is an elongated mass of soft tissue in the mandibular sulcus with a fissure running through it.

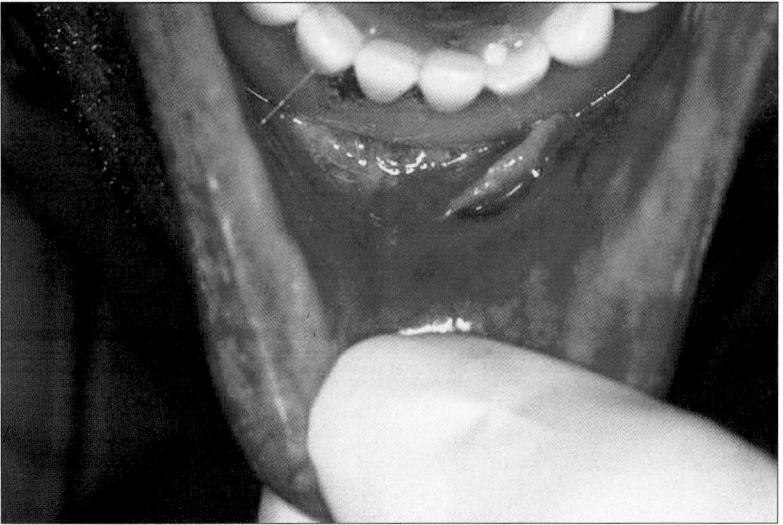

Fig. 10.86
Denture-induced fibrous hyperplasia: the denture flange (edge) fits into the fissure.

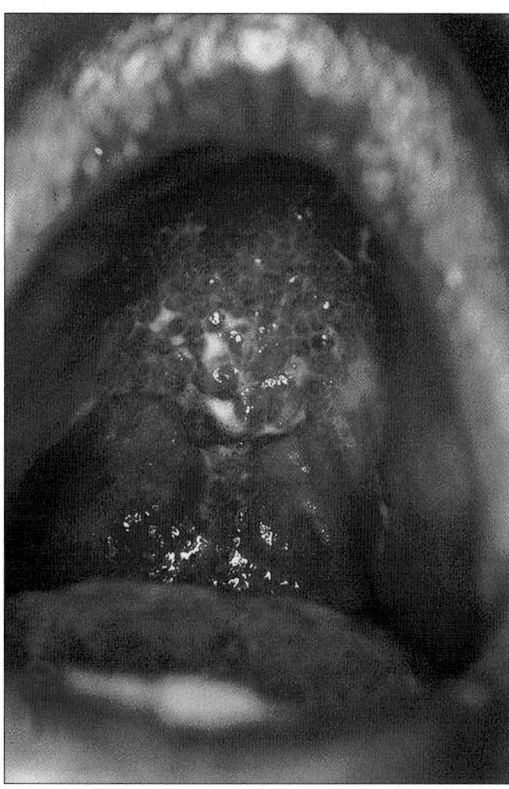

Fig. 10.87
Denture-induced papillary hyperplasia of the palate: note the typical papillary structures on the palate.

References

1. Nordenram, A., Landt, H. (1969) Hyperplasia of the oral tissues in denture cases. *Acta Odontol Scand*, 27, 481–491.
2. Cutright, D.E. (1974) The histopathologic findings in 583 cases of epulis fissuratum. *Oral Surg Oral Med Oral Pathol*, 37, 401–411.
3. Buchner, A., Begleiter, A., Hansen, L.S. (1984) The predominance of epulis fissuratum in females. *Quint Int*, 15, 699–702.
4. Bhaskar, S.N., Beasley, J.D., Cutright, D.E. (1970) Inflammatory papillary hyperplasia of the oral mucosa: report of 341 cases. *J Am Dent Assoc*, 81, 949–952.
5. Cutright, D.E. (1975) Morphogenesis of inflammatory papillary hyperplasia. *J Prosth Dent*, 33, 380–385.
6. Cutright, D.E. (1972) Osseous and chondromatous metaplasia caused by dentures. *Oral Surg Oral Med Oral Pathol*, 34, 625–633.
7. Kaplan, I., Vered, M., Moskona, D. et al (1998) An immunohistochemical study of p53 and PCNA in inflammatory papillary hyperplasia of the palate: a dilemma of interpretation. *Oral Dis*, 4, 194–199.

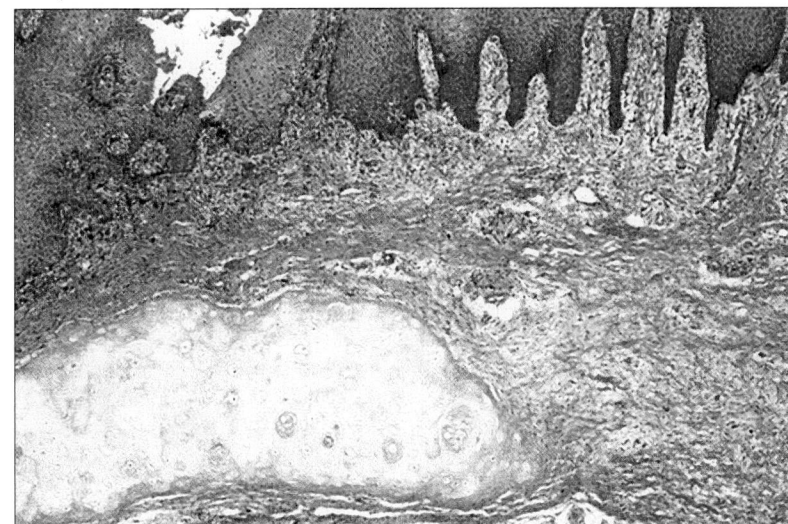

Fig. 10.89
Denture-induced fibrous hyperplasia: a cartilaginous rest is present in this lesion from the anterior maxillary sulcus.

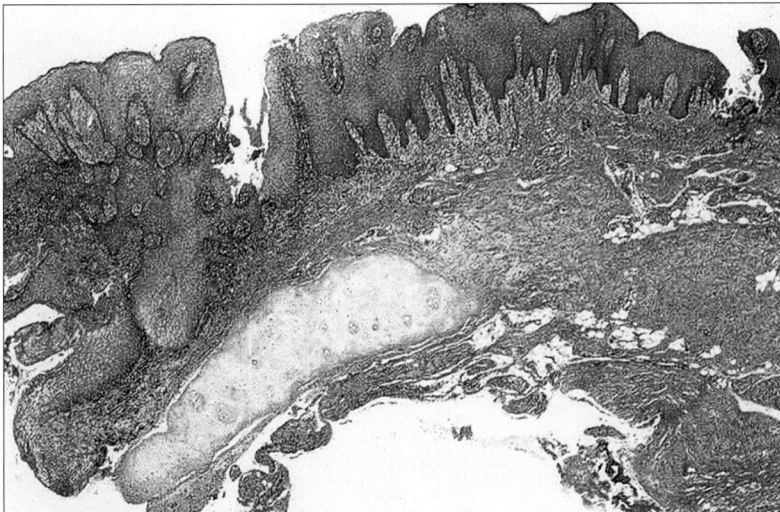

Fig. 10.88
Denture-induced fibrous hyperplasia: there is papillomatosis and hyperplasia of epithelium and fibrous tissue.

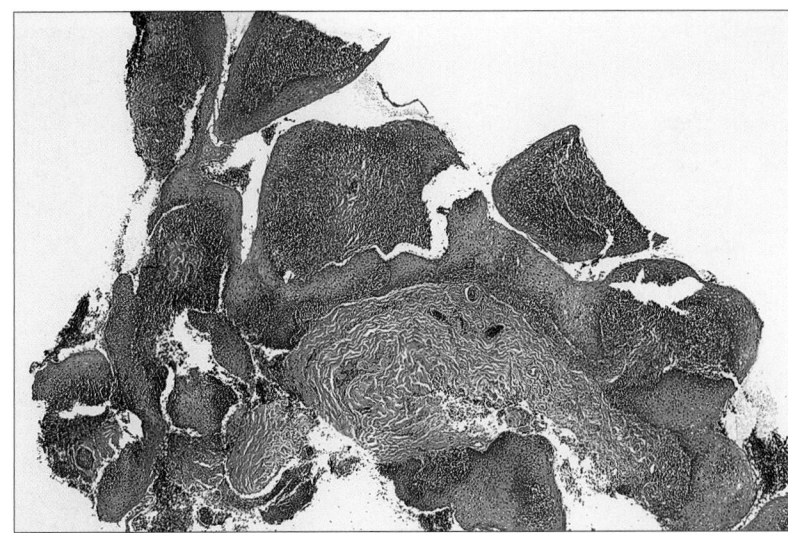

Fig. 10.90
Denture-induced papillary hyperplasia: curettage specimens yield these fibrous nodules with chronic inflammation.

Gingival nodules

Clinical features

The term 'epulis' refers to any mass or nodule on the gingiva or alveolar ridge and should be confined to clinical usage only. The two exceptions are epulis fissuratum and congenital granular cell epulis, referring to two particular clinical and histological entities (see pp. 416 and 395).

Most solitary gingival nodules represent one of the following conditions: reactive tumor-like proliferations, odontogenic cysts, primary odontogenic and non-odontogenic tumors, and metastatic tumors. The first are by far the most common and consist of the following entities:

- fibroma or fibrous hyperplasia with or without inflammation
- giant cell fibroma (see p. 414)
- pyogenic granuloma
- peripheral ossifying fibroma
- peripheral giant cell granuloma.

These lesions are located on the attached or marginal gingiva adjacent to teeth. Depending on the degree of vascularity, inflammation and/or ulceration present, they may be mucosal-colored, erythematous or ulcerated and painful (*Figs 10.91, 10.92*).

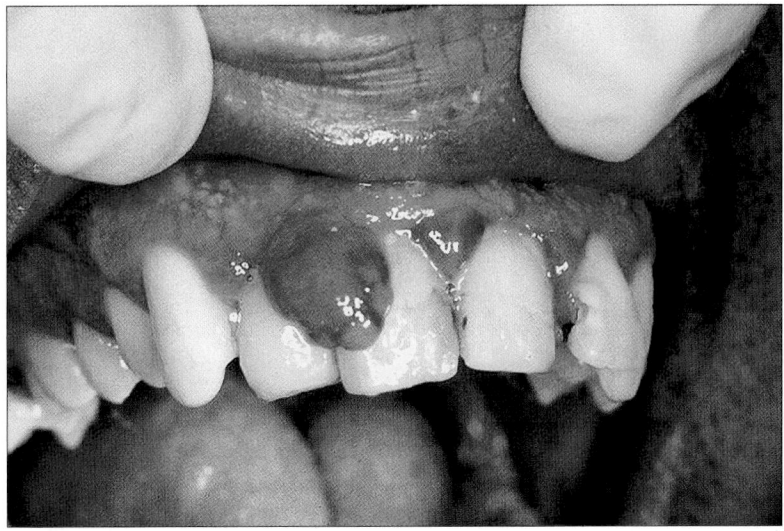

Fig. 10.91
Gingival nodule: note how the nodule arises from the gingival margin and hangs down onto the tooth.

It is thought that these fibrous and vascular reactive nodules develop as a response to irritation from dental plaque and calculus, often exacerbated by the presence of defective restorations or other dental hardware. Undifferentiated mesenchymal cells in the connective tissue proliferate and differentiate into cells that recapitulate tissues in the area such as fibrous tissue (fibroma), endothelial cells (pyogenic granuloma), bone- and cementum-producing cells (peripheral ossifying fibroma), or osteoclasts (peripheral giant cell granuloma). It is therefore not uncommon to see features of all four entities present to varying degrees within any one lesion. Unless the source of irritation is removed completely, it is not unusual for these lesions to recur.

Dental plaque is often present as clumps of Gram-positive filamentous bacteria that morphologically resemble actinomycetic colonies. Unless surrounded by a thick mantle of neutrophils, such colonies are surface colonizers and do not represent *Actinomycosis* infection.

Other gingival nodules and masses include the gingival and periodontal abscess and the parulis.

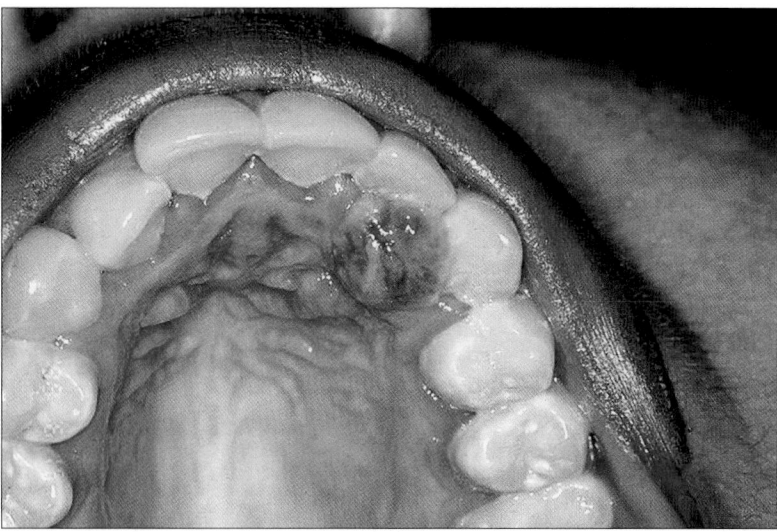

Fig. 10.92
Gingival nodule: such nodules may be located on the palatal aspect of the gingiva.

Gingival fibroma

Clinical features

Some fibromas represent the scarred remnants of pyogenic granulomas. One form of fibroma, the gingival fibrous nodule (also known as fibrous hyperplasia, fibrovascular polyp, inflammatory fibrous hyperplasia, fibrous epulis) occurs not on the free or marginal gingiva but on the attached gingiva and presents as multiple mucosal-colored papules.[1] Another variant is the giant cell fibroma, which often has a papillary surface and may be clinically mistaken for a papilloma (see p. 418).

Histological features

Gingival fibroma is composed of a mass of densely or delicately collagenized tissue with variable vascularity (*Fig. 10.93*).[2] If there is significant chronic inflammation, the stroma may be edematous. The overlying epithelium is sometimes hyperkeratotic and there may be continuity with crevicular epithelium, which generally shows spongiosis, neutrophilic exocytosis and an underlying plasmacytic infiltrate (*Fig. 10.94*).

References

1. Giunta, J.L. (1999) Gingival fibrous nodule. *Oral Surg Oral Med Oral Pathol Oral Radiol Endod*, **88**, 451–454.
2. Zain, R.B., Fei, Y.J. (1990) Fibrous lesions of the gingiva: a histopathologic analysis of 204 cases. *Oral Surg Oral Med Oral Pathol*, **70**, 466–470.

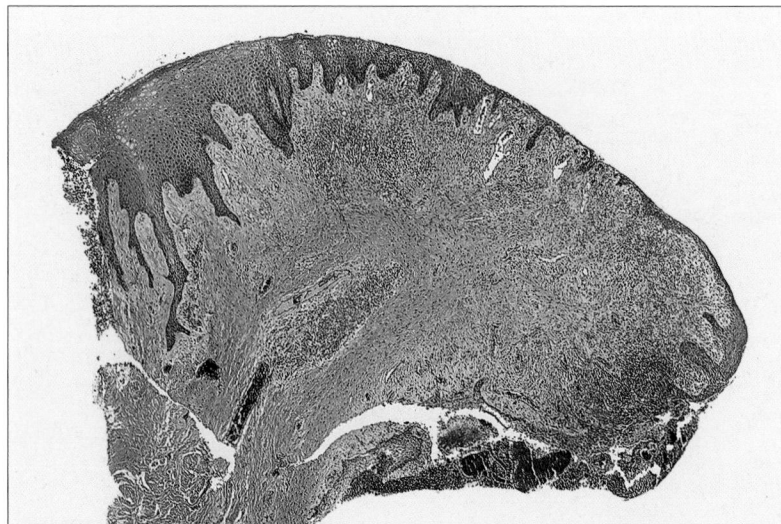

Fig. 10.93
Inflammatory fibrous hyperplasia of the gingiva: the surface keratinized epithelium is in continuity with the non-keratinized crevicular epithelium, where inflammatory cells are present.

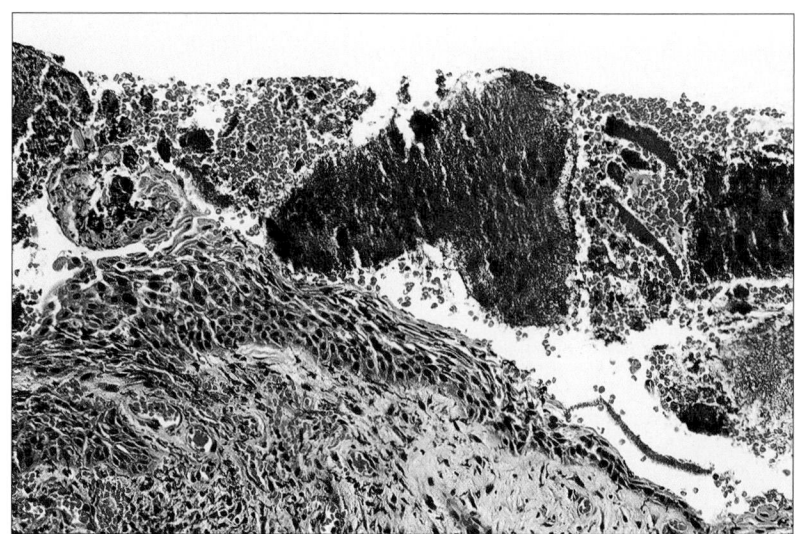

Fig. 10.94
Inflammatory fibrous hyperplasia of the gingiva: note the crevicular epithelium with spongiosis and the piece of dental plaque that morphologically resembles a mass of actinomycotic organisms.

Pyogenic granuloma

Clinical features

These nodules tend to be dark red and bleed readily. One variant of this lesion, the granuloma gravidarum, occurs during pregnancy, usually in the second and third trimesters, probably as a consequence of the neovascularizing effects of estrogen (*Fig. 10.95*). The majority present in the second and third trimesters.[1] They may partially involute and sclerose postpartum and turn into a fibroma or fibrous hyperplasia. The recurrence rate is 16%.[2]

Although the majority of intraoral pyogenic granulomas occur on the gingiva, other sites including the lips, buccal mucosa and tongue may be affected.[3]

Histological features

Gingival pyogenic granuloma is characterized by a lobular (although not as pronounced as in pyogenic granulomas at other sites) or diffuse proliferation of endothelial cells, many of which form canalized and congested capillaries (*Figs 10.96, 10.97*). Dilated, branching vessels are usually present in the center of lobules.[3] The overlying epithelium is ulcerated in 75% of cases and there is a variable neutrophilic, lymphocytic and plasmacytic infiltrate.[2] Some pyogenic granulomas become increasingly sclerotic and may eventuate in gingival fibrous hyperplasias after the bulk of the vasculature is replaced by fibrous tissue (*Figs 10.98, 10.99*).

There is no increase in the number of estrogen receptors on the endothelial cells of such lesions compared with controls although they may express more vascular endothelial growth factor and other angiogenesis enhancing factors and fewer inhibitory factors.[4,5]

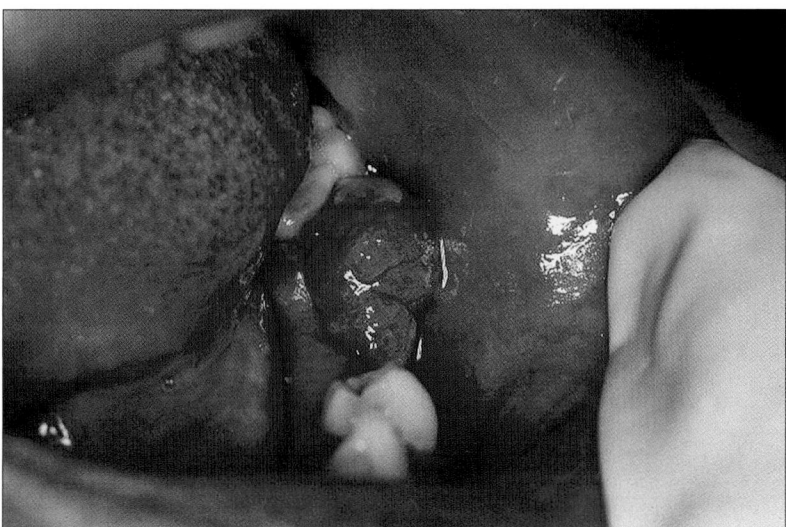

Fig. 10.95
Granuloma gravidarum: this nodule occurred in an edentulous part of the mandible.

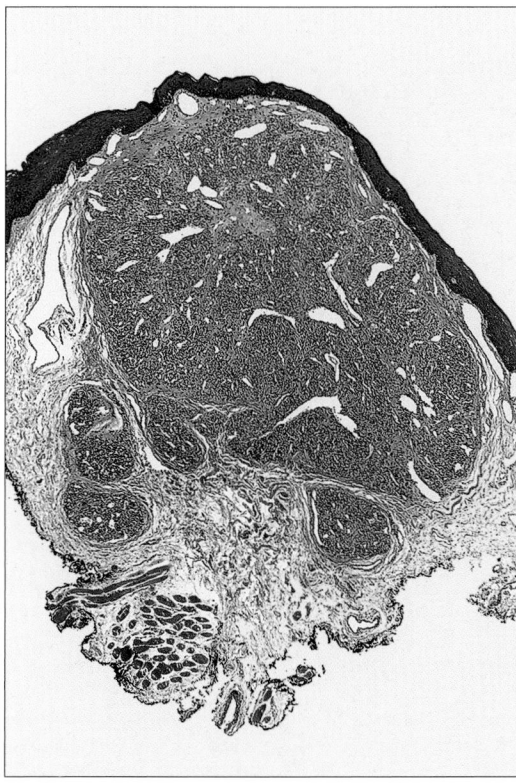

Fig. 10.96
Pyogenic granuloma: there is a typical lobular proliferation of endothelial cells and capillaries.

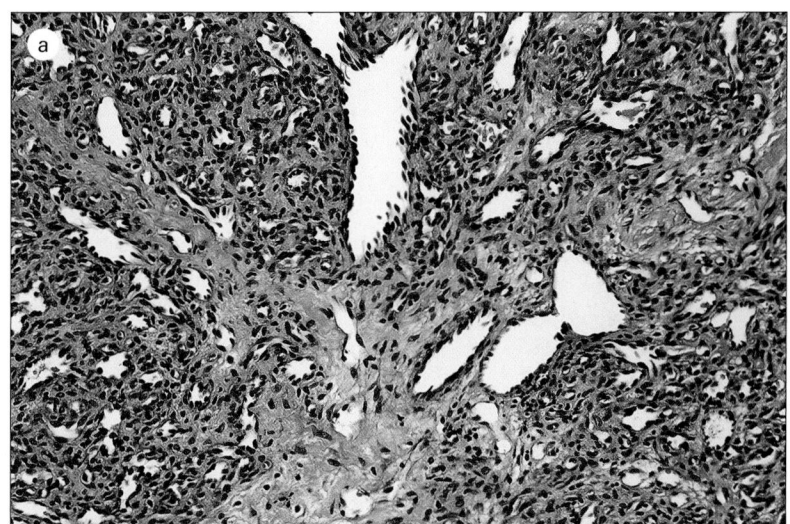

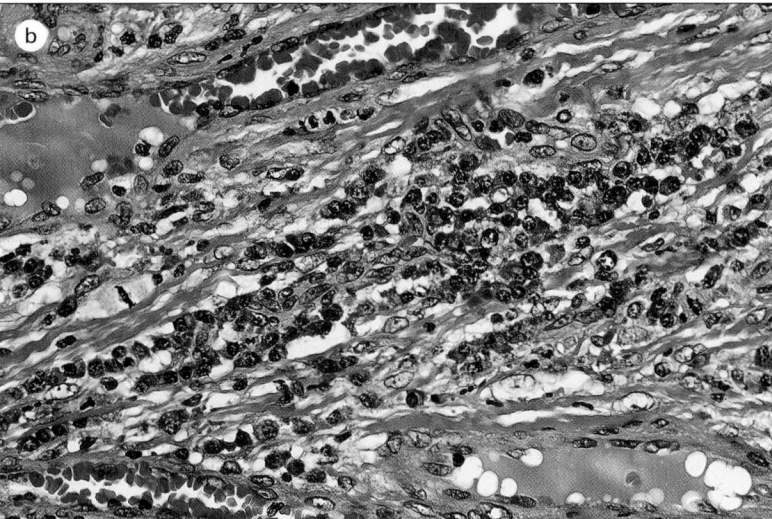

Fig. 10.97
Pyogenic granuloma: (**a**) note benign-appearing endothelial cells and dilated capillaries; (**b**) normal mitoses are not uncommonly seen.

References

1. Daley, T.D., Nartey, N.O., Wysocki, G.P. (1991) Pregnancy tumor: an analysis. *Oral Surg Oral Med Oral Pathol*, 72, 196–199.
2. Bhaskar, S.N., Jacoway, J.R. (1966) Pyogenic granuloma – clinical features, incidence, histology, and result of treatment: report of 242 cases. *J Oral Surg*, 24, 391–398.
3. Mills, S.E., Cooper, P.H., Fechner, R.E. (1980) Lobular capillary hemangioma: the underlying lesion of pyogenic granuloma. A study of 73 cases from the oral and nasal mucous membranes. *Am J Surg Pathol*, 4, 471–479.
4. Whitaker, S.B., Bouquot, J.E., Alimario, A.E. et al (1994) Identification and semiquantification of estrogen and progesterone receptors in pyogenic granulomas of pregnancy. *Oral Surg Oral Med Oral Pathol*, 78, 755–760.
5. Yuan, K., Jin, Y.T., Lin, M.T. (2000) The detection and comparison of angiogenesis-associated factors in pyogenic granuloma by immunohistochemistry. *J Periodontol*, 71, 701–709.

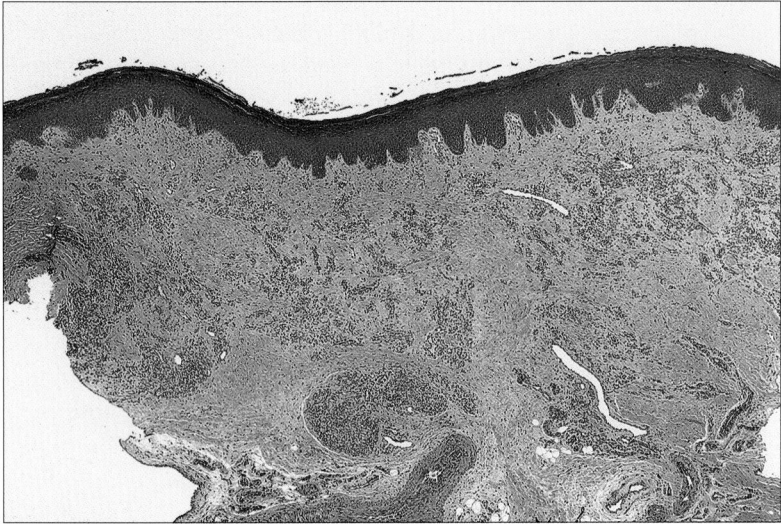

Fig. 10.98
Sclerosing pyogenic granuloma: note the break-up of the lobular architecture by fibrous tissue.

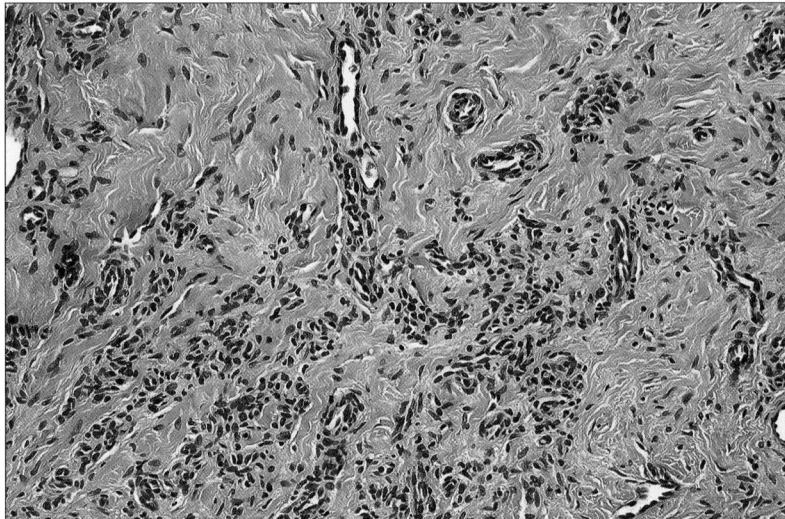

Fig. 10.99
Sclerosing pyogenic granuloma: note marked sclerosis and corresponding reduction in the number of vessels.

Peripheral ossifying fibroma

Clinical features

This tumor, also known as calcifying fibrous epulis or calcifying fibroblastic granuloma, occurs in the second and third decades and women are affected up to two times more often than men (1.5–2:1). Up to two-thirds occur in the maxilla.[1,2] The recurrence rate is 8–16%.[1,2]

Histological features

The lesion presents as a non-encapsulated cellular proliferation of plump, fibroblast-like cells with fusiform-to-ovoid vesicular nuclei and indistinct cell borders (*Figs 10.100, 10.101*). Admixed are varying amounts of osteoid, and woven and lamellar bone (*Fig. 10.102*). The more mature the bone, the less cellular the stroma. The bone may be focally rimmed by osteoblast-like cells. Droplet calcifications and (less commonly) broad anastomosing globular masses of cementum are sometimes seen.[1,3]

Foci of osteoclast-like multinucleated giant cells are occasionally present in addition to areas resembling pyogenic granuloma (*Fig. 10.103*).[1,2]

Even if calcifications are not clearly identified, the cellular proliferation of such fibroblast-like cells should raise the suspicion of this entity and deeper sections will usually reveal the presence of osteoid.

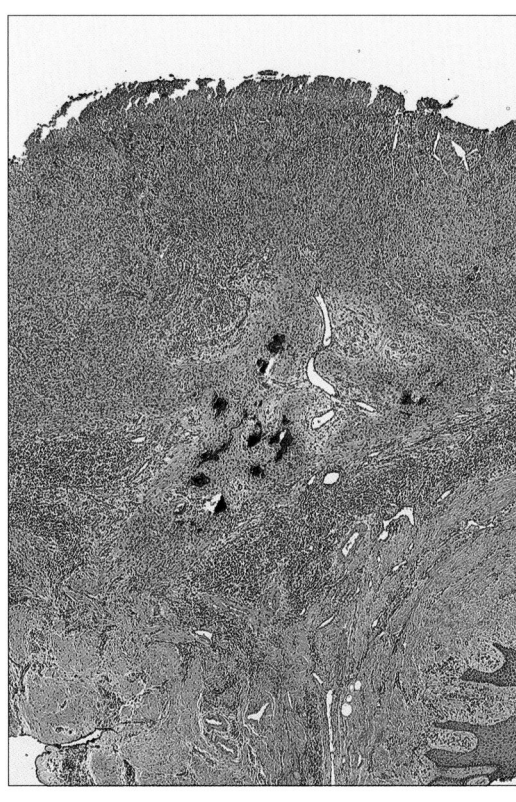

Fig. 10.100
Peripheral ossifying fibroma: there is a mass of cellular fibrous tissue with calcifications and overlying ulceration.

References

1. Zain, R.B., Fei, Y.J. (1990) Fibrous lesions of the gingiva: a histopathologic analysis of 204 cases. *Oral Surg Oral Med Oral Pathol*, **70**, 466–470.
2. Buchner, A., Hansen, L.S. (1987) The histomorphologic spectrum of peripheral ossifying fibroma. *Oral Surg Oral Med Oral Pathol*, **63**, 452–461.
3. Kenney, J.N., Kaugars, G.E., Abbey, L.M. (1989) Comparison between the peripheral ossifying fibroma and peripheral odontogenic fibroma. *J Oral Maxillofac Surg*, **47**, 378–382.

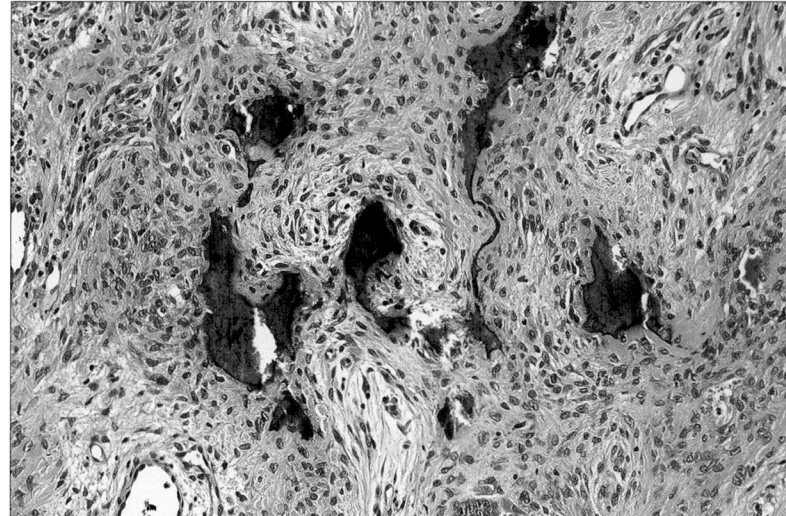

Fig. 10.102
Peripheral ossifying fibroma: the bone may take the form of osteoid, woven and/or lamellar bone, or calcified spherules.

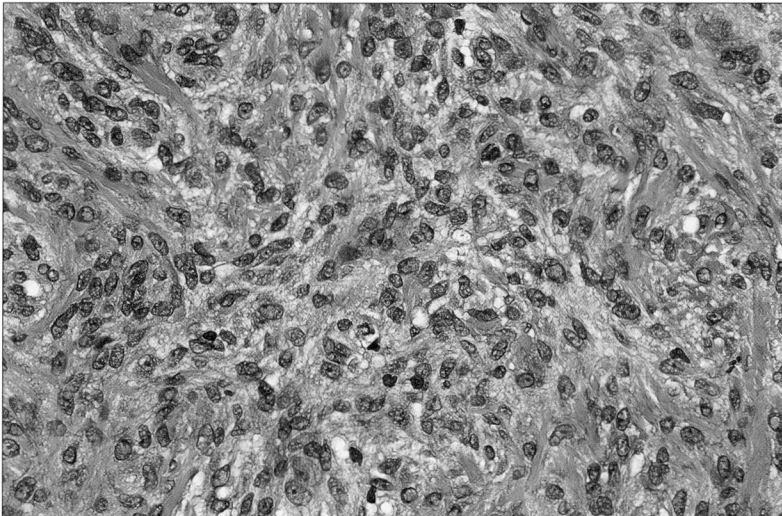

Fig. 10.101
Peripheral ossifying fibroma: note the plump fibroblasts and the marked cellularity.

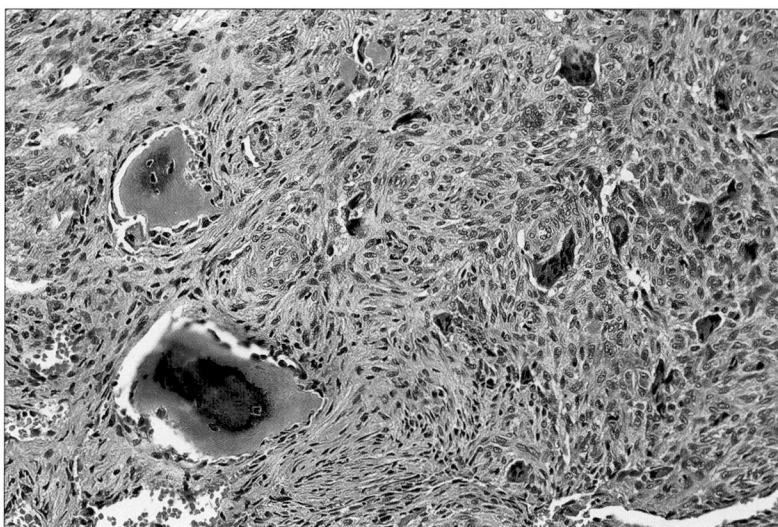

Fig. 10.103
Peripheral ossifying fibroma: it is not uncommon to see clusters of osteoclast-like giant cells in these lesions.

Peripheral giant cell granuloma

Clinical features

This lesion usually occurs in the fourth and fifth decades of life and the mandible may be two to three times more often involved than the maxilla. It often resides in a cup-shaped depression within the underlying bone.[1–3] Some 19–22% occur in edentulous areas.[4] The recurrence rate is up to 22%.[3] Examples of such peripheral lesions associated with hyperparathyroidism most likely represent gingival extension of central giant cell granulomas.[5,6]

Histological features

Peripheral giant cell granuloma is characterized by a discrete but un-encapsulated proliferation of osteocloast-like multinucleate giant cells dispersed in a mononuclear and vascular stroma with abundant fresh hemorrhage and hemosiderin deposition (*Figs 10.104, 10.105*). The giant cells may have vesicular or hyperchromatic nuclei.[7] The mononuclear cells have large vesicular nuclei with prominent nucleoli (*Fig. 10.106*). Mitoses may be numerous.[8] A Grenz zone often separates the infiltrate from an overlying intact or ulcerated epithelium.[1,2] Chronic inflammation may be present. Myofibroblasts have been demonstrated supporting the reactive nature of this lesion.[9] Foci of peripheral ossifying fibroma are present in one-third of cases.[8,10,11]

The giant cells and mononuclear cells express vimentin, muramidase, α_1-antitrypsin, α_1-antichymotrypsin and CD68, suggesting that they are of monocyte–phagocyte lineage.[7,12] Other studies have shown that the multinucleated giant cells stain for MBI, an osteoclast marker.[13] Estrogen but not progesterone receptors have been identified in both mononuclear and giant cells.[14]

References

1. Bhaskar, S.N., Cutright, D.E., Beasley, J.D. 3rd et al (1971) Giant cell reparative granuloma (peripheral): report of 50 cases. *J Oral Surg*, **29**, 110–115.
2. Katsikeris, N., Kakarantza-Angelopoulou, E., Angelopoulos, A.P. (1988) Peripheral giant cell granuloma. Clinicopathologic study of 224 new cases and review of 956 reported cases. *Int J Oral Maxillofac Surg*, **17**, 94–99.
3. Mighell, A.J., Robinson, P.A., Hume, W.J. (1995) Peripheral giant cell granuloma: a clinical study of 77 cases from 62 patients, and literature review. *Oral Dis*, **1**, 12–19.

4. Bodner, L., Peist, M., Gatot, A. et al (1997) Growth potential of peripheral giant cell granuloma. *Oral Surg Oral Med Oral Pathol Oral Radiol Endod*, **83**, 548–551.
5. Smith, B.R., Fowler, C.B., Svane, T.J. (1988) Primary hyperparathyroidism presenting as a 'peripheral' giant cell granuloma. *J Oral Maxillofac Surg*, **46**, 65–69.
6. Burkes, E.J. Jr, White, R.P. Jr (1989) A peripheral-cell granuloma manifestation of primary hyperparathyroidism: report of a case. *J Am Dent Assoc*, **118**, 62–64.
7. Carvalho, Y.R., Loyola, A.M., Gomez, R.S. et al (1995) Peripheral giant cell granuloma. An immunohistochemical and ultrastructural study. *Oral Dis*, **1**, 20–25.
8. Giansanti, J.S., Waldron, C.A. (1969) Peripheral giant cell granuloma: review of 720 cases. *J Oral Surg*, **27**, 787–791.
9. Dayan, D. (1989) Myofibroblasts in peripheral giant cell granuloma. Light and electron microscopic study. *Int J Oral Maxillofac Surg*, **18**, 258–261.
10. Buchner, A., Hansen, L.S. (1987) The histomorphologic spectrum of peripheral ossifying fibroma. *Oral Surg Oral Med Oral Pathol*, **63**, 452–461.
11. Dayan, D., Buchner, A., Spirer, S. (1990) Bone formation in peripheral giant cell granuloma. *J Periodontol*, **61**, 444–446.
12. Regezi, J.A., Zarbo, R.J., Lloyd, R.V. (1987) Muramidase, alpha-1-antitrypsin, alpha-1-antichymotrypsin and S-100 protein immunoreactivity in giant cell lesions. *Cancer*, **59**, 64–68.
13. Bonetti, F., Pelosi, G., Martignoni, G. et al (1990) Peripheral giant cell granuloma: evidence for osteoclastic differentiation. *Oral Surg Oral Med Oral Pathol*, **70**, 471–475.
14. Gunhan, M., Gunhan, O., Celasun, B. et al (1998) Estrogen and progesterone receptors in the peripheral giant cell granulomas of the oral cavity. *J Oral Sci*, **40**, 57–60.

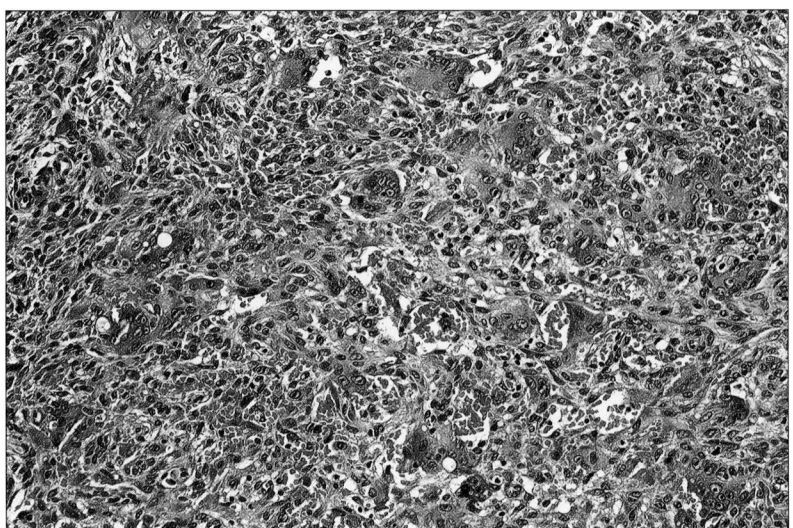

Fig. 10.105
Peripheral giant cell granuloma: note the marked vascularity of the lesion.

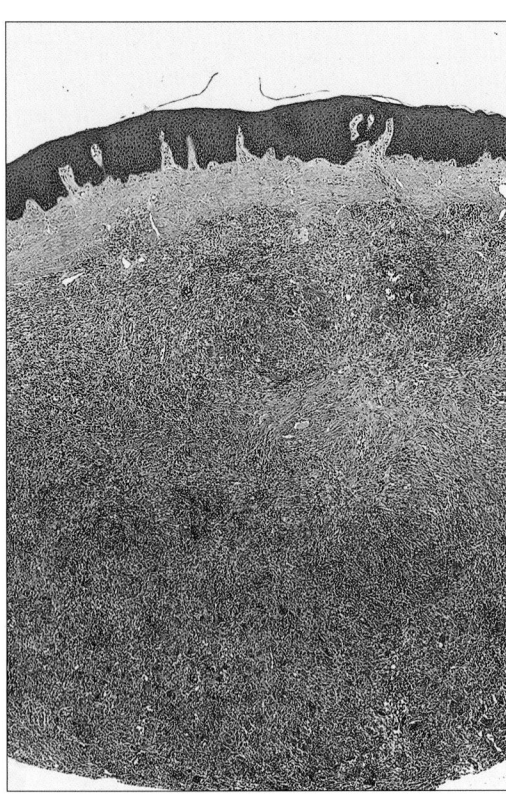

Fig. 10.104
Peripheral giant cell granuloma: there is generally a Grenz zone that separates the giant cells from the epithelium.

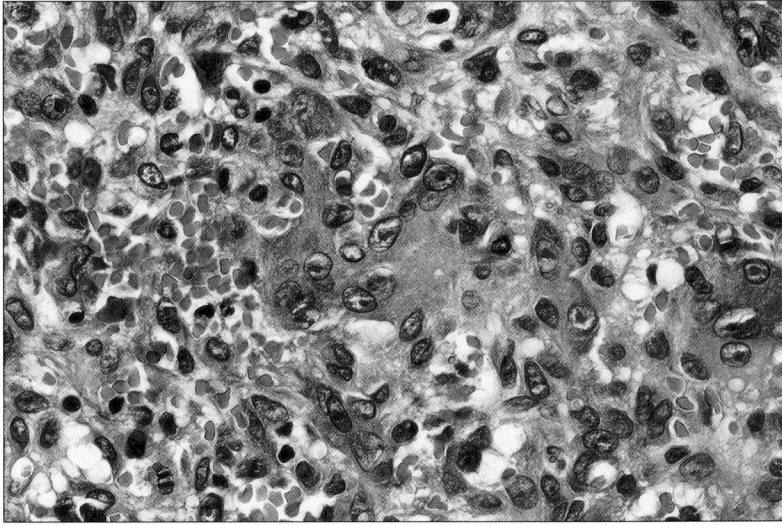

Fig. 10.106
Peripheral giant cell granuloma: giant cells, mononuclear cells and many siderophages are present.

Parulis

Clinical features

The parulis (or gum-boil) is a red or pink, painless papule, sometimes with a central punctum. It is located away from the gingival margin, usually overlying the apex of a tooth, and represents the opening of a draining sinus from an intraosseous odontogenic infection (*Figs 10.107, 10.108*).

Histological features

The nodule consists of a proliferation of edematous granulation tissue containing many acute and chronic inflammatory cells and in particular microabscesses in a linear array – the sinus tract (*Figs 10.109, 10.110*).

Differential diagnosis

Athough this lesion bears a superficial resemblance to a mucocele, no mucin or muciphages are present. Mucoceles almost never occur on the gingiva since salivary gland tissue is absent at this site.

Peripheral odontogenic fibroma

Clinical features

The preferred site for this tumor is the mandibular premolar/cuspid and anterior maxillary region.[1] Also termed 'odontogenic gingival epithelial hamartoma', it mainly occurs in adults in the third decade with an equal sex predilection. Recurrence varies from 3 to 39%.[1,2]

Histological features

The nodule consists of a proliferation of fibrous tissue that may be densely or loosely collagenized and variably hypercellular or hypocellular. More typically, the stroma has a whorled, streaming or fasciculated pattern.[2–4] Islands, strands and nests of odontogenic epithelium are present to a variable extent (*Figs 10.111, 10.112*). Epithelial cells may appear clear or rarely, squamous and hyaline cuffs are sometimes seen around the epithelium (the so-called 'inductive effect'). Calcifications are present in 33–50% of cases and take two forms: as dentinoid, or as dystrophic globular calcifications in the stroma.[1,2,4,5] When epithelium is abundant, the term odontogenic gingival epithelial hamartoma may be applied (*Fig. 10.113*).[6]

One variant contains stromal granular cells that stain for α_1-antitrypsin, suggesting lysosomal content.[1,7] The presence of giant cells has also been reported.[8]

Differential diagnosis

Lack of significant atypia distinguishes this lesion from metastatic carcinoma although it must be borne in mind that many malignant glandular and/or adnexal tumors can sometimes show minimal pleomorphism. Peripheral odontogenic fibroma should also be

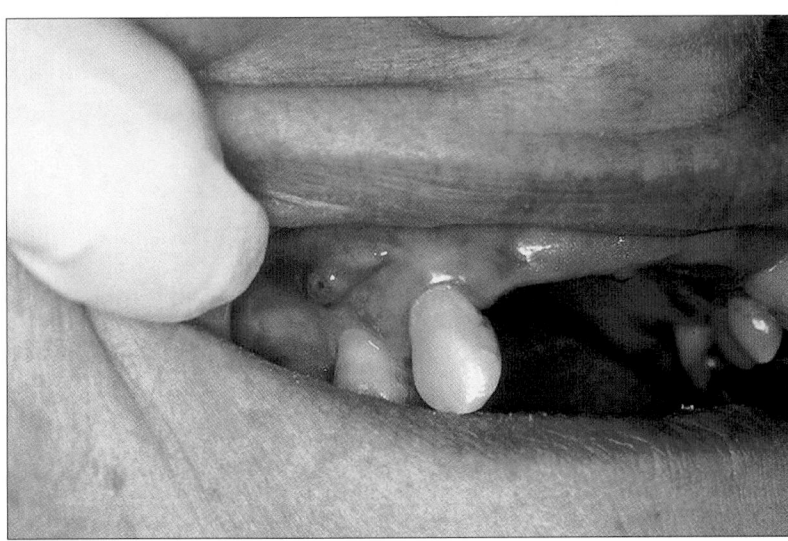

Fig. 10.107
Parulis: note the small papule located on the non-attached gingiva, at some distance from the gingival margin.

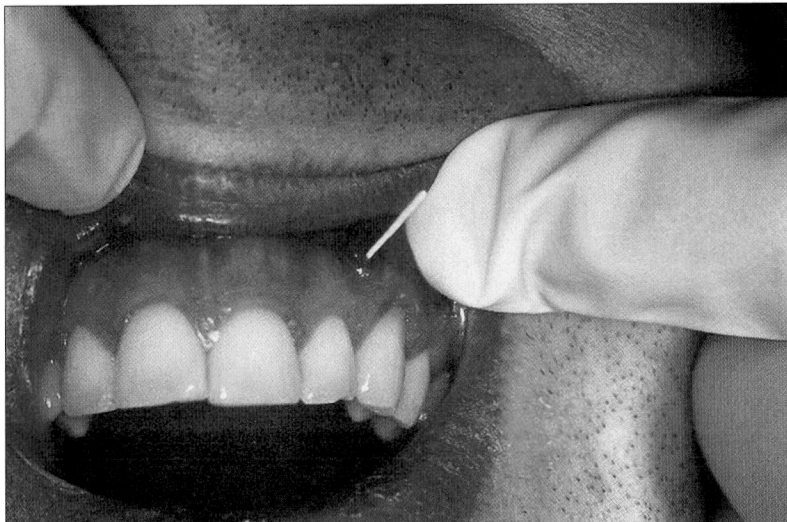

Fig. 10.108
Parulis: this parulis is being traced to its origin in the bone using a pliable probe.

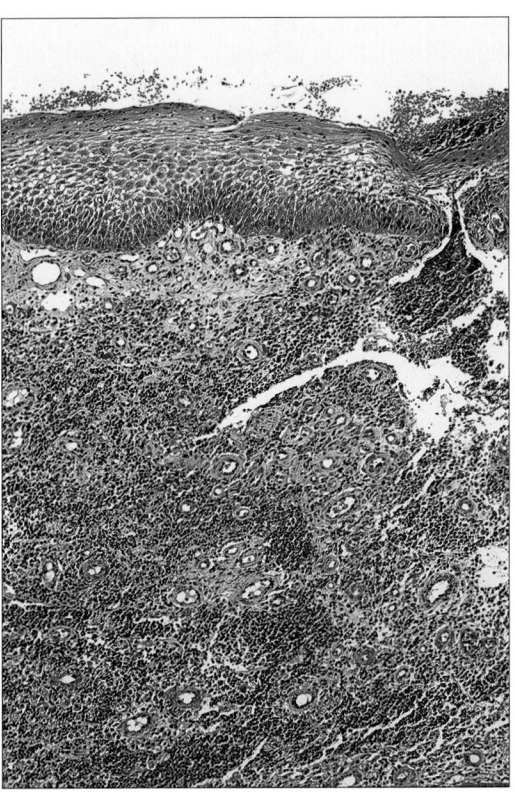

Fig. 10.110
Parulis: note the natural space formed by neutrophils in a linear array.

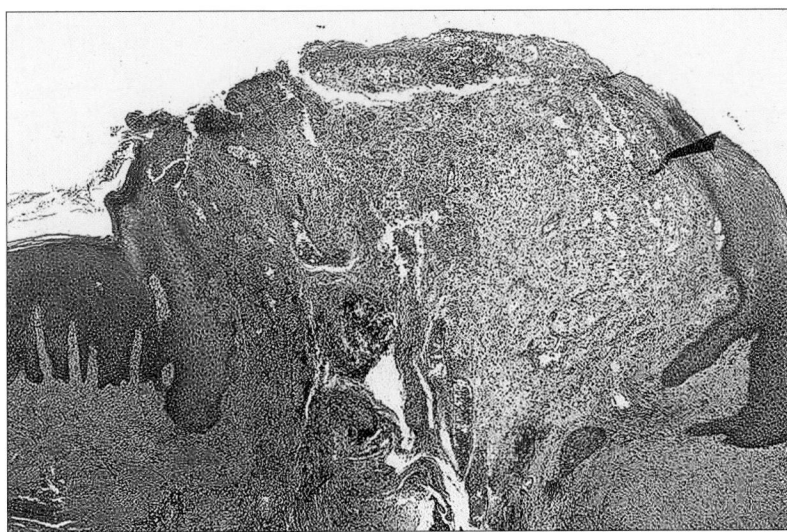

Fig. 10.109
Parulis: the papule is composed of edematous granulation tissue; a tract leads from deep in the tissues to the surface.

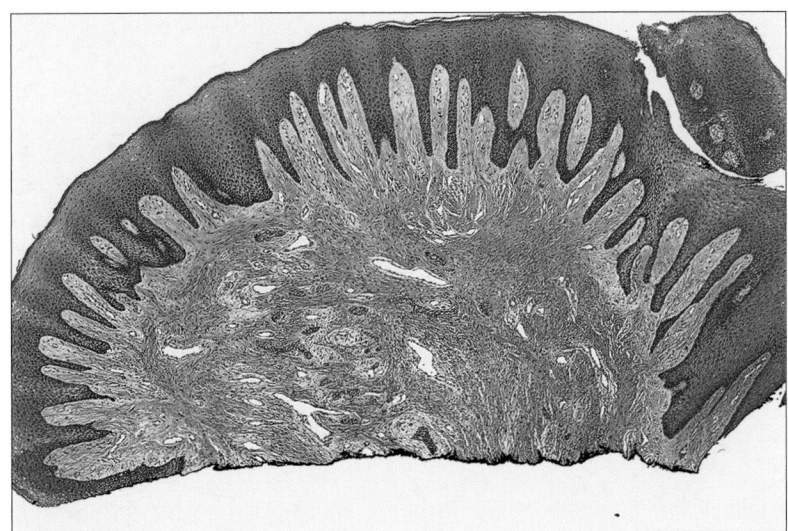

Fig. 10.111
Peripheral odontogenic fibroma: strands of odontogenic epithelium are present in a fibrous stroma.

distinguished from other odontogenic tumors that may present on the gingiva.[9]

The peripheral ameloblastoma contains many large islands of odontogenic epithelium with distinct palisading and reverse polarization of the basal cell nuclei thus resembling a basal cell carcinoma (*Figs 10.114, 10.115*).[10]

Peripheral calcifying odontogenic cyst is lined by basaloid cells containing ghost cells, sometimes with dystrophic calcification (*Figs 10.116, 10.117*).[11] The counterpart of this lesion on the skin is the calcifying epithelioma of Malherbe (pilomatrixoma). A solid variant called the odontogenic ghost cell tumor has a predominance of ghost cells and dentinoid or osteoid.[12]

Peripheral calcifying odontogenic tumor consists of large polyhedral cells with eosinophilic cytoplasm associated with amyloid deposits and ring-like dystrophic calcification (*Fig. 10.118*).[13]

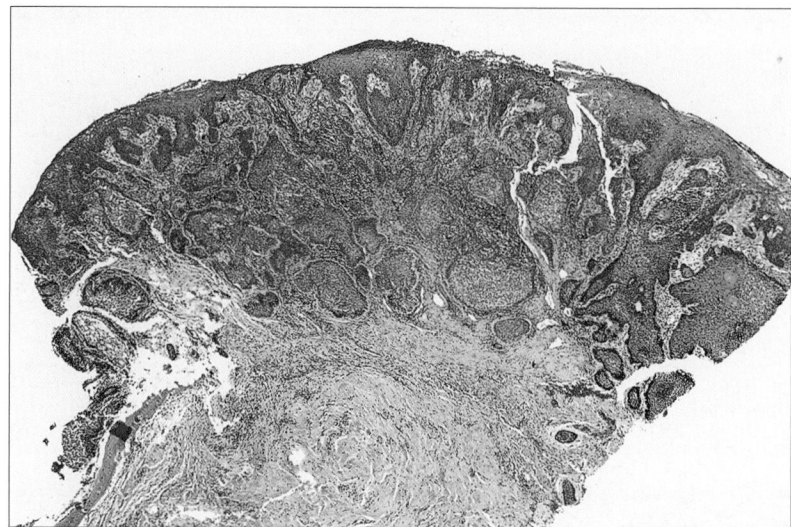

Fig. 10.114
Peripheral ameloblastoma: islands of epithelium grow into the stroma from the surface. By courtesy of C. Allen, DDS, Columbus, USA.

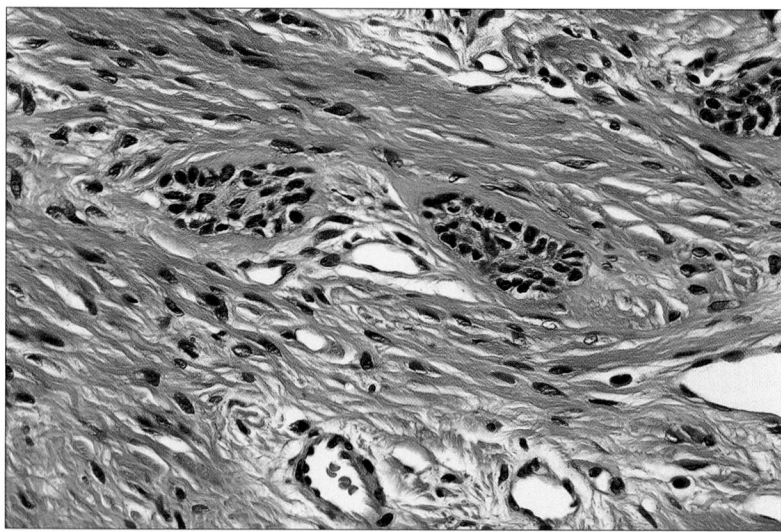

Fig. 10.112
Peripheral odontogenic fibroma: strands of epithelium show a hint of palisading of the peripheral nuclei, typical for odontogenic epithelium.

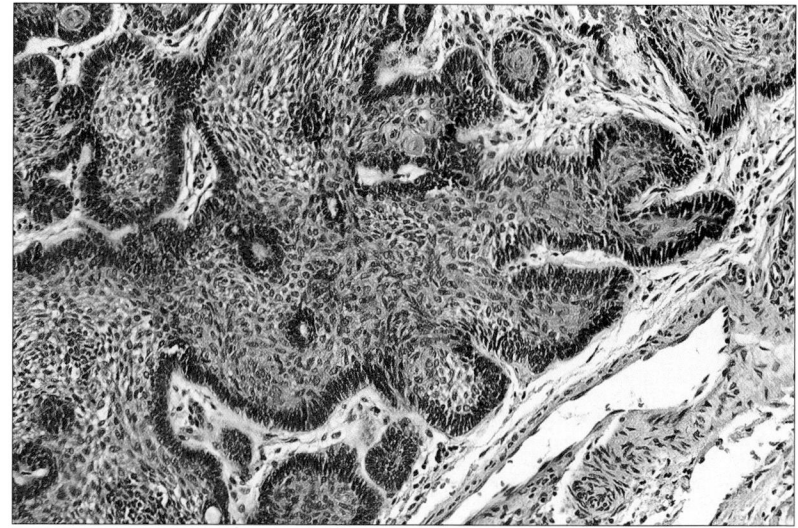

Fig. 10.115
Peripheral ameloblastoma: note the typical palisading of the basal cell nuclei. By courtesy of C. Allen, DDS, Columbus, USA.

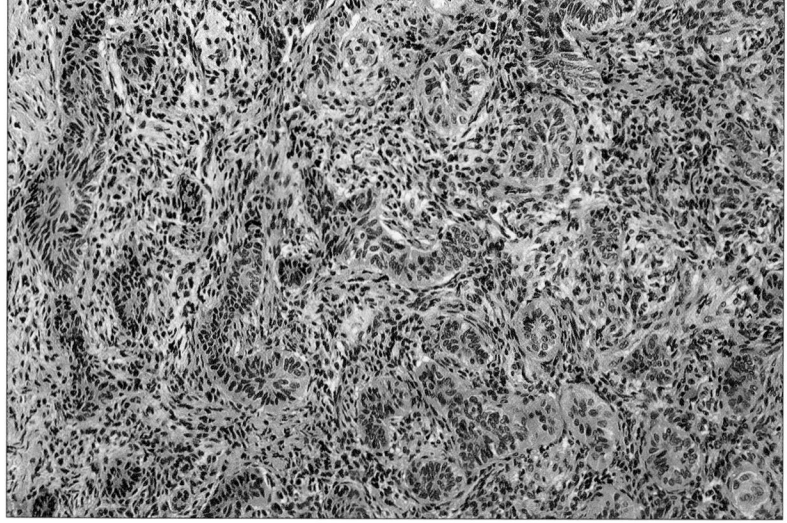

Fig. 10.113
Peripheral odontogenic fibroma: note the abundance of epithelium in this lesion. By courtesy of T. Daley, DDS, Winnipeg, Ontario, Canada.

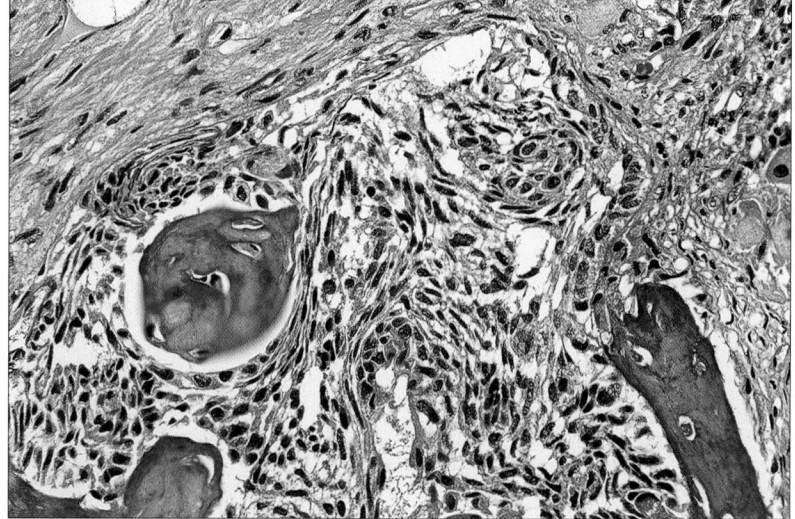

Fig. 10.116
Odontogenic ghost cell tumor: note the basaloid cells and calcified material that abuts the epithelium.

References

1. Daley, T.D., Wysocki, G.P. (1994) Peripheral odontogenic fibroma. *Oral Surg Oral Med Oral Pathol*, 78, 329–336.
2. de Villiers Slabbert, H., Altini, M. (1991) Peripheral odontogenic fibroma: a clinicopathologic study. *Oral Surg Oral Med Oral Pathol*, 72, 86–90.
3. Gardner, D.G. (1982) The peripheral odontogenic fibroma: an attempt at clarification. *Oral Surg Oral Med Oral Pathol*, 54, 40–48.
4. Siar, C.H., Ng, K.H. (2000) Clinicopathological study of peripheral odontogenic fibromas (WHO-type) in Malaysians (1967–95). *Br J Oral Maxillofac Surg*, 38, 19–22.
5. Buchner, A., Ficarra, G., Hansen, L.S. (1987) Peripheral odontogenic fibroma. *Oral Surg Oral Med Oral Pathol*, 64, 432–438.
6. Baden, E., Moskow, B.S., Moskow, R. (1968) Odontogenic gingival epithelial hamartoma. *J Oral Surg*, 26, 702–714.
7. Lownie, J.F., Altini, M., Shear, M. (1976) Granular cell peripheral odontogenic fibroma. *J Oral Pathol*, 5, 295–304.
8. Ficarra, G., Sapp, J.P., Eversole, L.R. (1993) Multiple peripheral odontogenic fibroma, World Health Organization type, and central giant cell granuloma: a case report of an unusual association. *J Oral Maxillofac Surg*, 51, 325–328.
9. Buchner, A., Sciubba, J.J. (1987) Peripheral epithelial odontogenic tumors: a review. *Oral Surg Oral Med Oral Pathol*, 63, 688–697.
10. Gardner, D.G. (1977) Peripheral ameloblastoma: a study of 21 cases, including 5 reported as basal cell carcinoma of the gingiva. *Cancer*, 39, 1625–1633.
11. Buchner, A., Merrell, P.W., Hansen, L.S. et al (1991) Peripheral (extraosseous) calcifying odontogenic cyst. A review of forty-five cases. *Oral Surg Oral Med Oral Pathol*, 72, 65–70.
12. Ellis, G. (1999) Odontogenic ghost cell tumor. *Semin Diagn Pathol*, 16, 288–292.
13. Houston, G.D., Fowler, C.B. (1997) Extraosseous calcifying epithelial odontogenic tumor: report of two cases and review of the literature. *Oral Surg Oral Med Oral Pathol Oral Radiol Endod*, 83, 577–583.

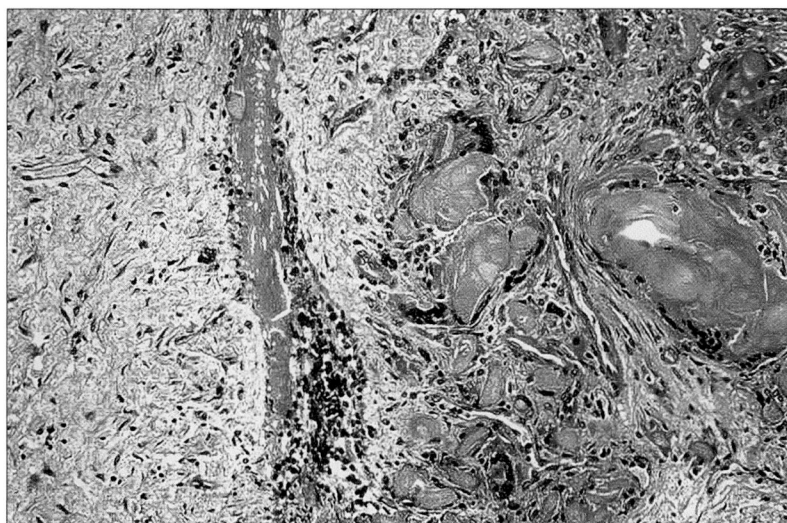

Fig. 10.117
Odontogenic ghost cell tumor: note the ghost cells and the foreign body reaction to them.

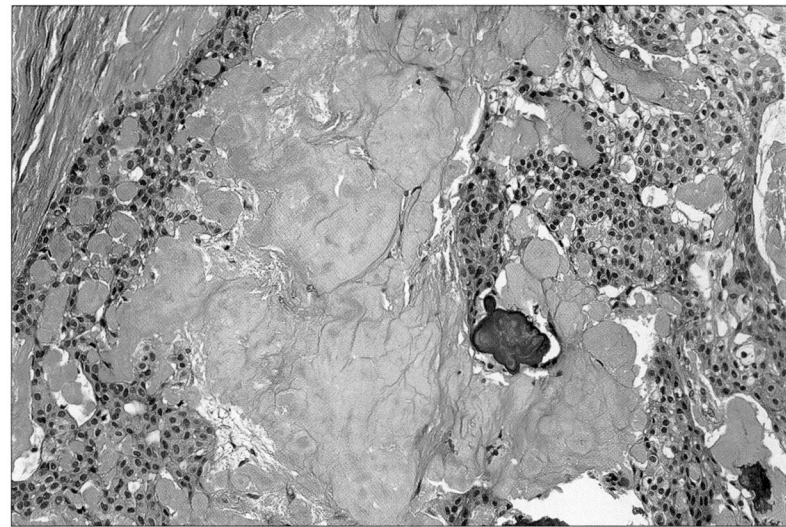

Fig. 10.118
Calcifying epithelial odontogenic tumor: note the presence of epithelial cells and amyloid.

Gingival cyst of the adult

Clinical findings

This lesion occurs in the fifth decade with a roughly equal sex distribution. Three-quarters occur in the mandible, mainly in the cuspid/bicuspid buccal gingiva. It presents as a bluish nodule, usually measuring less than 1 cm in diameter.[1–3]

Pathogenesis and histological features

A variety of origins have been postulated. Gingival cyst may therefore arise from stimulated rests of dental lamina (a residua of odontogenesis) or be derived from epithelium in the gingival crevice.[4,5] A less likely origin is from epithelium in the gingival sulcus.[2]

The cyst is usually lined by non-keratinized epithelium, either low cuboidal or squamous, 1–3 cells thick (*Figs 10.119, 10.120*). Focal epithelial plaques are present in approximately one-third of cases, some of which contain clear cells.[1–3] Occasional lesions resemble intra-osseous odontogenic keratocyst with a thin epithelial lining, corrugated parakeratosis, and palisading of the basal cells.[6] This variant is sometimes referred to as a peripheral odontogenic keratocyst.

Differential diagnosis

In children, dental lamina cysts of the newborn occur on the alveolar ridge (especially maxillary) and are almost always filled with keratin, resembling milia.[7] If the cyst contains oncocytic cells, it is much more likely to be a salivary duct cyst. This does not arise in the gingiva although it may extend onto the gingiva from the maxillary or mandibular sulcus.

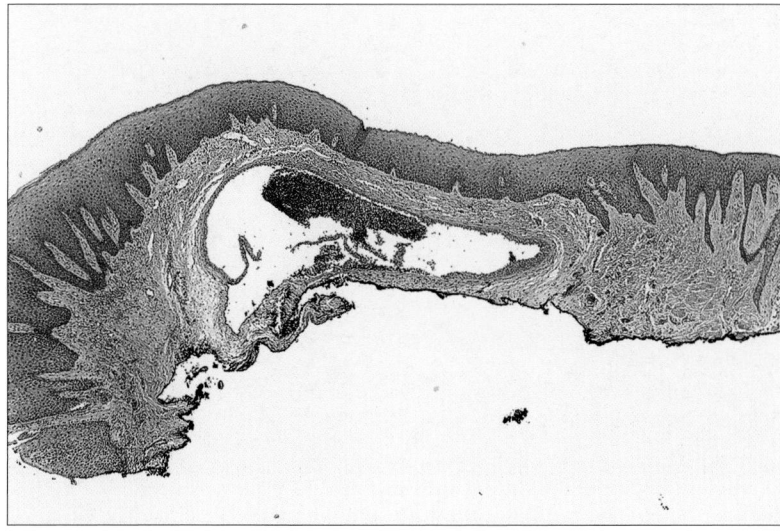

Fig. 10.119
Gingival cyst: note thinly lined cyst in the lamina propria.

References

1. Buchner, A., Hansen, L.S. (1979) The histomorphologic spectrum of the gingival cyst in the adult. *Oral Surg Oral Med Oral Pathol*, **48**, 532–539.
2. Nxumalo, T.N., Shear, M. (1992) Gingival cyst in adults. *J Oral Pathol Med*, **21**, 309–313.
3. Bell, R.C., Chauvin, P.J., Tyler, M.T. (1997) Gingival cyst of the adult: a review and a report of eight cases. *J Can Dent Assoc*, **63**, 533–535.
4. Moskow, B.S., Siegel, K., Zegarelli, E.V. et al (1970) Gingival and lateral periodontal cysts. *J Periodontol*, **41**, 249–260.
5. Wysocki, G.P., Brannon, R.B., Gardner, D.G. et al (1980) Histogenesis of the lateral periodontal cyst and the gingival cyst of the adult. *Oral Surg Oral Med Oral Pathol*, **50**, 327–334.
6. Chehade, A., Daley, T.D., Wysocki, G.P. et al (1994) Peripheral odontogenic keratocyst. *Oral Surg Oral Med Oral Pathol*, **77**, 494–497.
7. Cataldo, E., Berkman, M.D. (1968) Cysts of the mucosa in newborns. *Am J Dis Child*, **116**, 44–48.

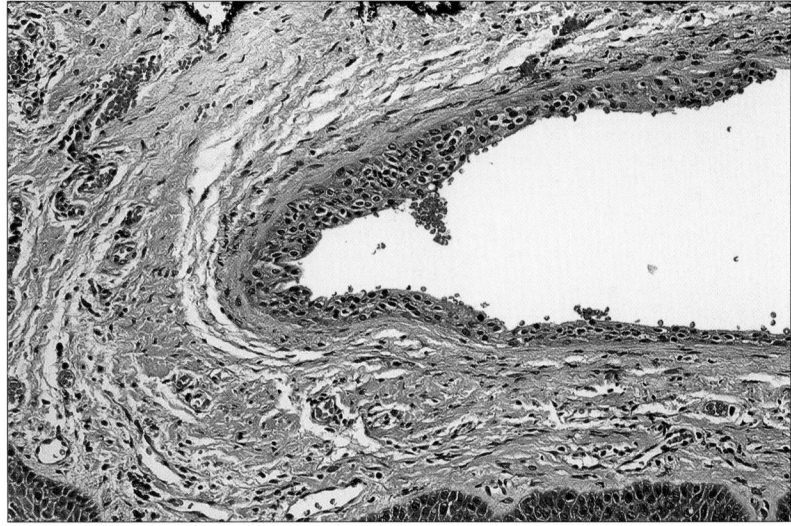

Fig. 10.120
Gingival cyst: the cyst is lined by three to six layers of squamous or low cuboidal cells.

Generalized gingival hyperplasia

Clinical features

In this condition, multiple and usually all quadrants of the upper and lower gingiva are involved, initially by nodular hyperplasia in the interdental areas, which then become coalescent to form diffuse nodular/papillary masses. The gingiva may be edematous and boggy, or it can be firm, fibrotic and so proliferative as to reach the biting surfaces. Provoking factors include:

- poor oral hygiene
- hormonal influences (during puberty and pregnancy)
- ingestion of medications, in particular phenytoin, valproic acid, calcium channel blockers and cyclosporin (*Fig. 10.121*).

Such overgrowths are rare in edentulous patients and if the teeth are extracted, the lesions do not recur, pointing to plaque bacteria as playing an important role in their pathogenesis.[1–3] In general, good oral hygiene measures reduce the severity of disease.

Gingival hyperplasia occurs in approximately 50% of patients taking phenytoin,[4,5] 15–40% of patients taking nifedipine[3,6] and 25–70% of patients on cyclosporin.[7–9] Renal transplant patients taking both cyclosporin and nifedipine show greater gingival overgrowth than those taking cyclosporin alone (*Fig. 10.122*).[10] Of all calcium channel blockers, nifedipine and those of the hydropyridine class are most likely to cause gingival hyperplasia. Verapamil causes hyperplasia in 4% and amlodipine in 3% of cases which is probably not significantly different from patients not taking these medications.[11,12]

Several cases of putative cyclosporin-induced fibrous hyperplasias/pyogenic granulomas of extragingival sites have been reported in patients treated for chronic GVHD (*Fig. 10.123*).[13,14] It is, however, unusual to see significant gingival hyperplasia in patients taking cyclosporin for treatment of chronic GVHD.

One unusual form of gingival hyperplasia is associated with ligneous

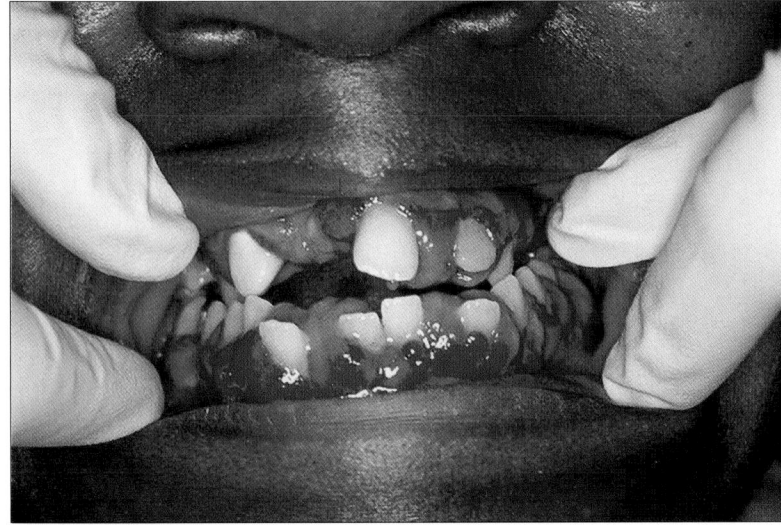

Fig. 10.121
Generalized gingival hyperplasia: this overgrowth of gingiva was caused by poor oral hygiene.

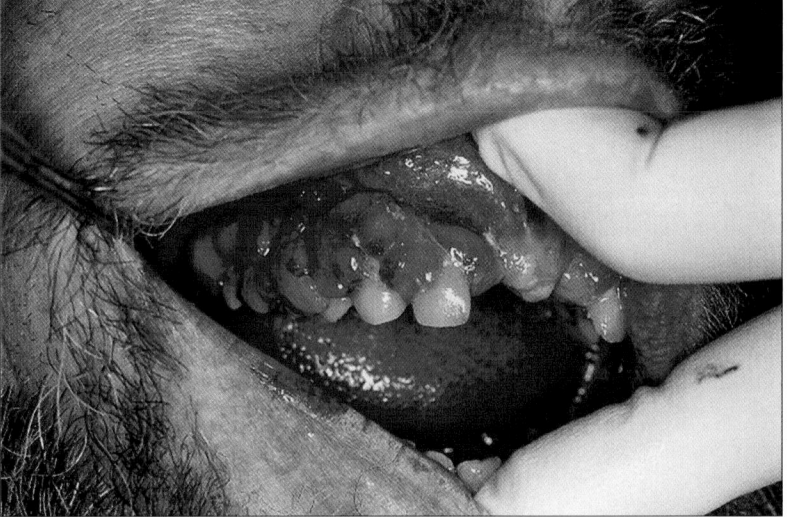

Fig. 10.122
Cyclosporin-induced gingival hyperplasia: this patient was taking cyclosporin to prevent rejection of a renal allograft; he was also taking nifedipine, a calcium-channel blocker.

conjunctivitis, an autosomal recessive disorder leading to functional plasminogen deficiency and characteristic histological features in the conjunctiva and gingiva.[15,16] The gingiva develops painless coalescent waxy nodules similar to those on the conjunctiva.[17,18] Other mucosal surfaces may also be involved.[19] One case occurred after systemic tranexamic acid (an antifibrinolytic agent) therapy.[20]

Pathogenesis and histological features

Gingival hyperplasia caused by cyclosporin (the most widely studied of all the drugs) may result from accumulation of collagen and extracellular matrix as a result of either increased production from susceptible subpopulations of fibroblasts in the gingiva, or else, decreased degradation.[21–23] Cyclosporin may also negate the inhibitory effect of plaque bacteria-associated lipopolysaccharide on fibroblast proliferation.[24] Calcium homeostasis is an important pharmacodynamic feature of these drugs and it has been postulated that impairment of calcium-dependent mechanisms (such as collagenase and metalloproteinase activity) may play an important etiological role. More fibroblasts express TGF-β1 (a stimulator of fibroblast activity) in drug-induced gingival hyperplasia.[25]

Histologically, there is proliferation of fibrous tissue and ground substance with variable hyperplasia of fibroblasts. The epithelium, which is parakeratinized, may also be hyperplastic and there is a variable lymphoplasmacytic infiltrate with variable vascular ectasia (*Fig. 10.124*). Straight-sided 'test tube' rete ridges have been reported in such drug-induced gingival hyperplasias.[6,7,26] There may also be foci that appear myxoid/mucinous.

In cyclosporin-induced non-gingival lesions, the tumors are essentially inflammatory fibrovascular polyps that are extensively ulcerated and composed of edematous granulation tissue with a varying degrees of inflammation (*Figs 10.125, 10.126*).[13,14]

Ultrastructural studies show an increase in cytoplasmic volume of fibroblasts with more extensive rough endoplasmic reticulum and Golgi complexes, reflecting increased synthetic activity and concomitant reduction in phagocytic activity of fibroblasts.[27,28] Increased numbers of fibroblasts exhibiting secretory granules filled with sulfated mucopolysaccharides have been noted.[29] Myofibroblasts are present in increased numbers.[30]

In ligneous gingival hyperplasia, the lamina propria is filled with eosinophilic, PAS-positive amorphous material that stains with MSB phosphotungstic acid–hematoxylin and consists of fibrin (*Fig. 10.127*).[17,18] Stains for amyloid are negative. There may be associated epithelial hyperplasia with acute and chronic inflammation and apoptosis. Early lesions show fibrin deposits around blood vessels.

Differential diagnosis

Accumulations of eosinophilic material in the gingiva may be seen in lipoid proteinosis (hyalinosis cutis et mucosae); these deposits do not stain for fibrinogen or fibrin and there is usually involvement of the skin and other sites.[31,32] Amyloid deposits should also be excluded. Similar amyloid-like material may sometimes be seen in the buccal mucosa but not usually in the gingiva of patients who use snuff.

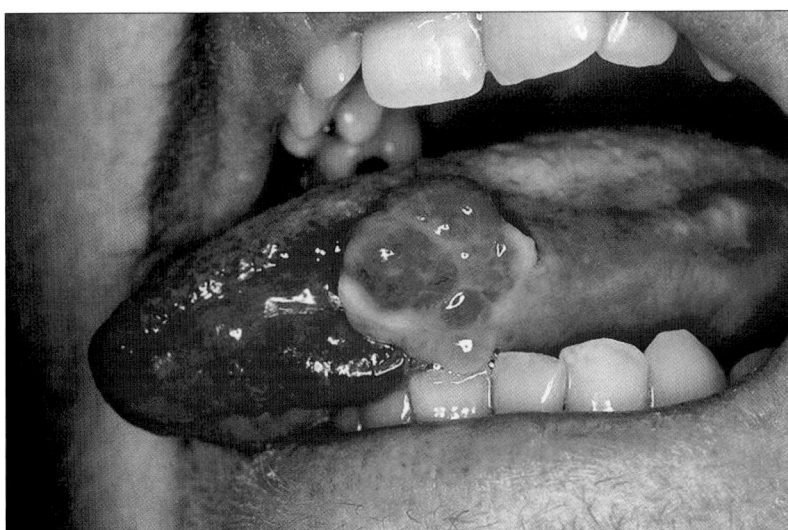

Fig. 10.123
Cyclosporin-induced non-gingival hyperplasia: this patient was taking cyclosporin for treatment of chronic graft-versus-host disease after allogenic bone marrow transplantation.

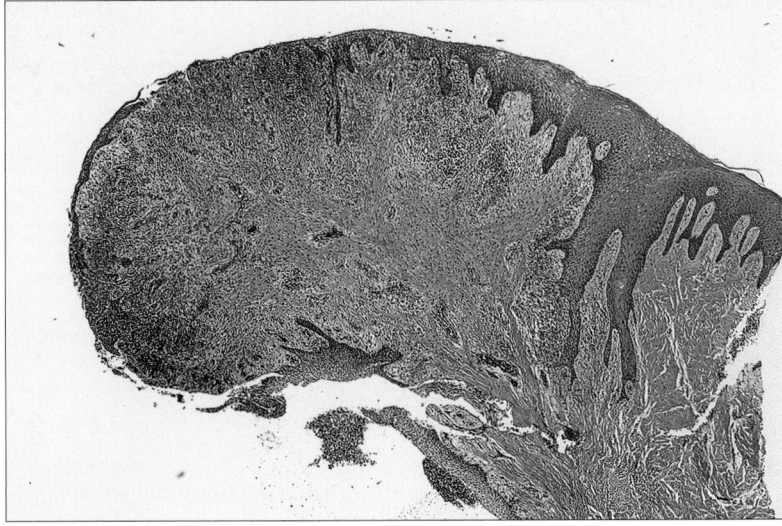

Fig. 10.124
Inflammatory fibrous hyperplasia: the histology is similar to that of the solitary gingival nodules of similar etiology.

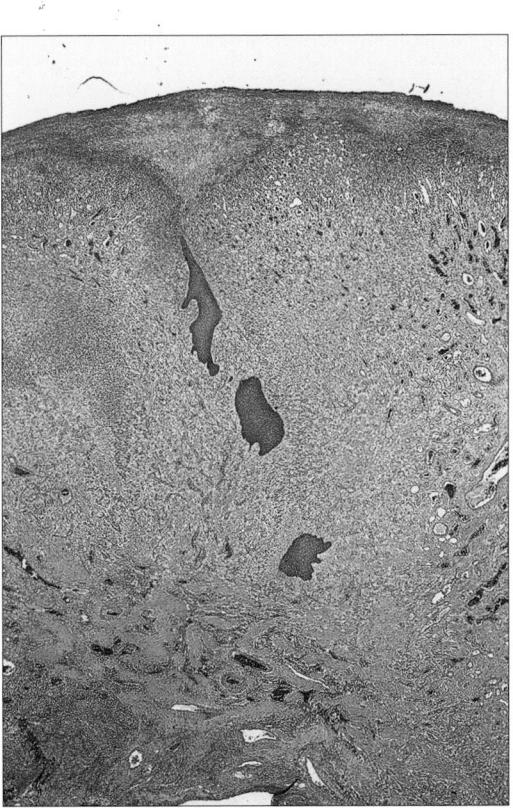

Fig. 10.125
Cyclosporin-induced non-gingival hyperplasia: these are essentially polypoid masses of granulation tissue.

References

1. Rateitschak-Pluss, E.M., Hefti, A., Lortscher, R., Thiel G. (1983) Initial observation that cyclosporin-A induces gingival enlargement in man. *J Clin Periodontol*, **10**, 237–246.
2. Friskopp, J., Klintmalm, G. (1986) Gingival enlargement. A comparison between cyclosporine and azathioprine treated renal allograft recipients. *Swed Dent J*, **10**, 85–92.
3. Nery, E.B., Edson, R.G., Lee, K.K. et al (1995) Prevalence of nifedipine-induced gingival hyperplasia. *J Periodontol*, **66**, 572–578.
4. Angelopoulos, A.P., Goaz, P.W. (1972) Incidence of diphenylhydantoin gingival hyperplasia. *Oral Surg Oral Med Oral Pathol*, **34**, 898–906.
5. Penarrocha-Diago, M., Bagan-Sebastian, J.V., Vera-Sempere, F. (1990) Diphenylhydantoin-induced gingival overgrowth in man: a clinico-pathological study. *J Periodontol*, **61**, 571–574.
6. Barak, S., Engelberg, I.S., Hiss, J. (1987) Gingival hyperplasia caused by nifedipine. Histopathologic findings. *J Periodontol*, **58**, 639–642.
7. Tyldesley, W.R., Rotter, E. (1984) Gingival hyperplasia induced by cyclosporin-A. *Br Dent J*, **157**, 305–309.
8. McGaw, T., Lam, S., Coates, J. (1987) Cyclosporin-induced gingival overgrowth: correlation with dental plaque scores, gingivitis scores, and cyclosporin levels in serum and saliva. *Oral Surg Oral Med Oral Pathol*, **64**, 293–297.
9. Daley, T.D., Wysocki, G.P., Day, C. (1986) Clinical and pharmacologic correlations in cyclosporine-induced gingival hyperplasia. *Oral Surg Oral Med Oral Pathol*, **62**, 417–421.
10. Thomason, J.M., Seymour, R.A., Rice, N. (1993) The prevalence and severity of cyclosporin and nifedipine-induced gingival overgrowth. *J Clin Periodontol*, **20**, 37–40.
11. Miller, C.S., Damm, D.D. (1992) Incidence of verapamil-induced gingival hyperplasia in a dental population. *J Periodontol*, **63**, 453–456.
12. Jorgensen, M.G. (1997) Prevalence of amlodipine-related gingival hyperplasia. *J Periodontol*, **68**, 676–678.
13. Lee, L., Miller, P.A., Maxymiw, W.G. et al (1994) Intraoral pyogenic granuloma after allogeneic bone marrow transplant. Report of three cases. *Oral Surg Oral Med Oral Pathol*, **78**, 607–610.
14. Woo, S.B., Allen, C.M., Orden, A. et al (1996) Non-gingival soft tissue growths after allogeneic marrow transplantation. *Bone Marrow Transplant*, **17**, 1127–1132.
15. Schott, D., Dempfle, C.E., Beck, P. et al (1998) Therapy with a purified plasminogen concentrate in an infant with ligneous conjunctivitis and homozygous plasminogen deficiency. *N Engl J Med*, **339**, 1679–1686.
16. Schuster, V., Seidenspinner, S., Zeitler, P. et al (1999) Compound-heterozygous mutations in the plasminogen gene predispose to the development of ligneous conjunctivitis. *Blood*, **93**, 3457–3466.
17. Gokbuget, A.Y., Mutlu, S., Scully, C. et al (1997) Amyloidaceous ulcerated gingival hyperplasia: a newly described entity related to ligneous conjunctivitis. *J Oral Pathol Med*, **26**, 100–104.
18. Gunhan, O., Gunhan, M., Berker, E. et al (1999) Destructive membranous periodontal disease (ligneous periodontitis). *J Periodontol*, **70**, 919–925.
19. Hidayat, A.A., Riddle, P.J. (1987) Ligneous conjunctivitis. A clinicopathologic study of 17 cases. *Ophthalmology*, **94**, 949–959.
20. Diamond, J.P., Chandna, A., Williams, C. et al (1991) Tranexamic acid-associated ligneous conjunctivitis with gingival and peritoneal lesions. *Br J Ophthalmol*, **75**, 753–754.
21. Hassell, T.M., Romberg, E., Sobhani, S. et al (1988) Lymphocyte-mediated effects of cyclosporine on human fibroblasts. *Transplant Proc*, **20**, 993–1002.
22. Tipton, D.A., Stricklin, G.P., Dabbous, M.K. (1991) Fibroblast heterogeneity in collagenolytic response to cyclosporine. *J Cell Biochem*, **46**, 152–165.
23. Schincaglia, G.P., Forniti, F., Cavallini, R. et al (1992) Cyclosporin-A increases type I procollagen production and mRNA level in human gingival fibroblasts in vitro. *J Oral Pathol Med*, **21**, 181–185.
24. Bartold, P.M. (1989) Regulation of human gingival fibroblast growth and synthetic activity by cyclosporine-A in vitro. *J Periodontal Res*, **24**, 314–321.
25. Wright, H.J., Chapple, I.L., Matthews, J.B. (2001) TGF-beta isoforms and TGF-beta receptors in drug-induced and hereditary gingival overgrowth. *J Oral Pathol Med*, **30**, 281–289.
26. Wysocki, G.P., Gretzinger, H.A., Laupacis, A. et al (1983) Fibrous hyperplasia of the gingiva: a side effect of cyclosporin A therapy. *Oral Surg Oral Med Oral Pathol*, **55**, 274–278.
27. Hall, B.K., Squier, C.A. (1982) Ultrastructural quantitation of connective tissue changes in phenytoin-induced gingival overgrowth in the ferret. *J Dent Res*, **61**, 942–952.
28. McGaw, W.T., Porter, H. (1988) Cyclosporine-induced gingival overgrowth: an ultrastructural stereologic study. *Oral Surg Oral Med Oral Pathol*, **65**, 186–190.
29. Lucas, R.M., Howell, L.P., Wall, B.A. (1985) Nifedipine-induced gingival hyperplasia. A histochemical and ultrastructural study. *J Periodontol*, **56**, 211–215.
30. Yamasaki, A., Rose, G.G., Pinero, G.J., Mahan, C.J. (1987) Ultrastructure of fibroblasts in cyclosporin A-induced gingival hyperplasia. *J Oral Pathol*, **16**, 129–134.
31. Finkelstein, M.W., Hammond, H.L., Jones, R.B. (1982) Hyalinosis cutis et mucosae. *Oral Surg Oral Med Oral Pathol*, **54**, 49–58.
32. Israel, H. (1992) Gingival lesions in lipoid proteinosis. *J Periodontol*, **63**, 561–564.

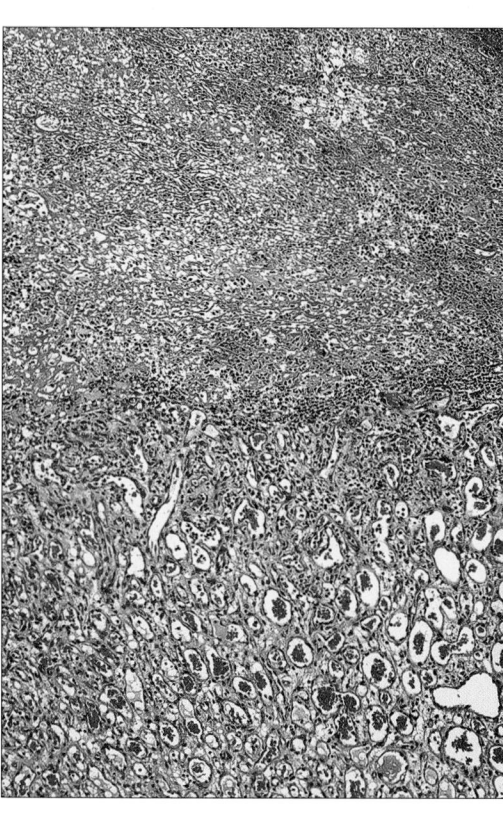

Fig. 10.126
Cyclosporin-induced non-gingival hyperplasia: note the edematous granulation tissue and inflammation.

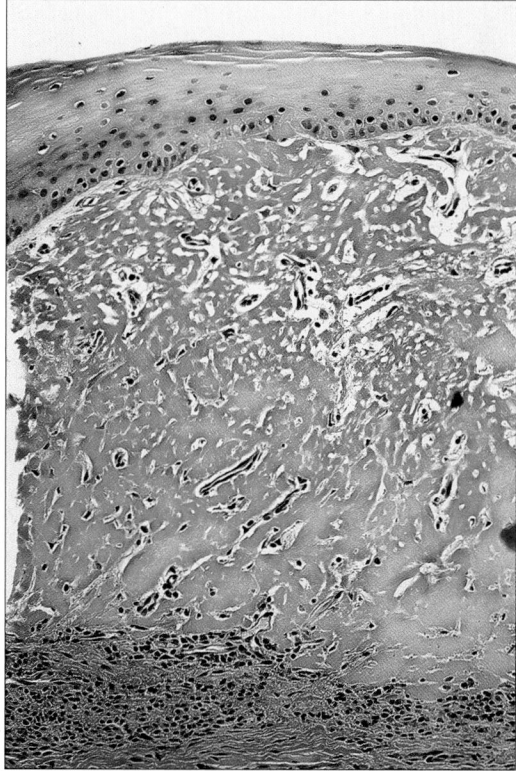

Fig. 10.127
Ligneous gingivitis: there is abundant fibrinous eosinophilic material that fills the lamina propria.

Varix

Clinical features

Varices (or venous lakes) are most common on the ventral surfaces of the tongue (sublingual varicosis) and on the lower lip and buccal mucosa, usually in older individuals (*Figs 10.128, 10.129*).[1,2] They are bluish-purple blebs that become firm if thrombosed.

Histological features

A varix represents a dilatation of an endothelium-lined blood vessel with a very thin muscular wall (*Figs 10.130, 10.131*).[3] Some develop thrombi, which on organization and canalization present as Masson's tumor (intravascular papillary endothelial hyperplasia) (*Fig. 10.132*).

Differential diagnosis

The caliber-persistent labial artery (a pulsatile lesion of the lower lip) consists of an artery that lies close to the surface epithelium with an artery diameter/depth ratio of less than 1.6 (*Fig. 10.133*).[4,5] These putatively represent arterial branches from a main supplying artery that penetrate the superficial mucosa without loss of caliber.[6]

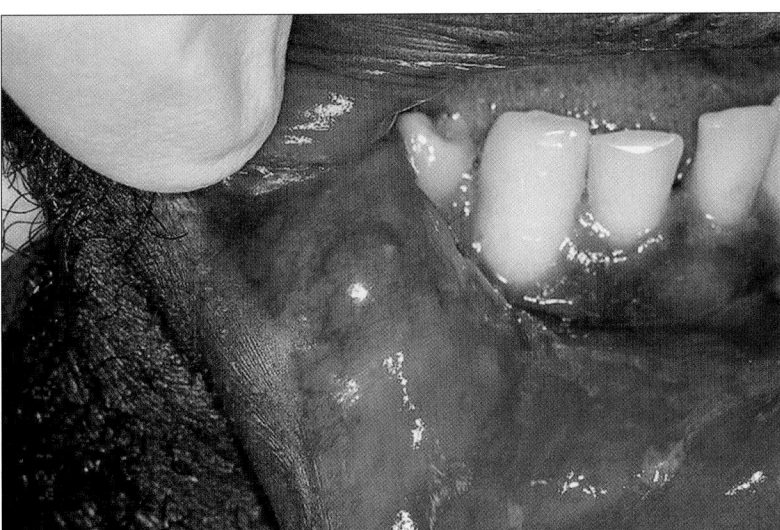

Fig. 10.128
Varix: note the blue bleb on the lower labial mucosa.

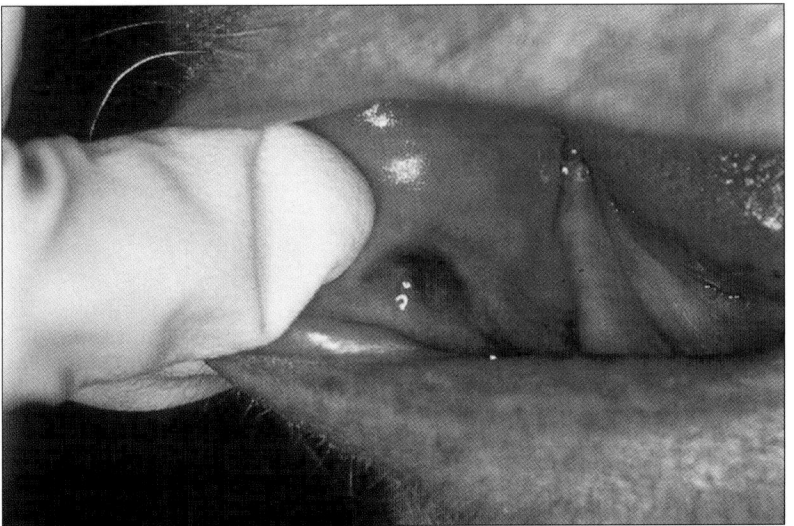

Fig. 10.129
Varix: note the blue bleb on the buccal mucosa.

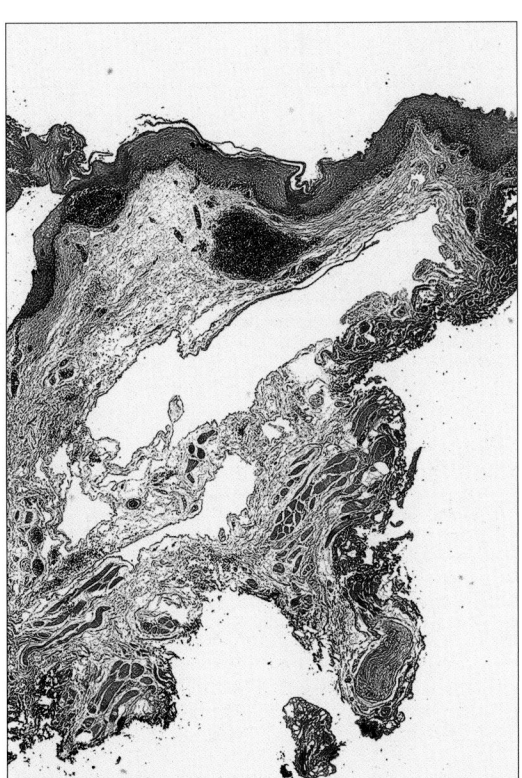

Fig. 10.130
Varix: there are grossly dilated venules in the lamina propria.

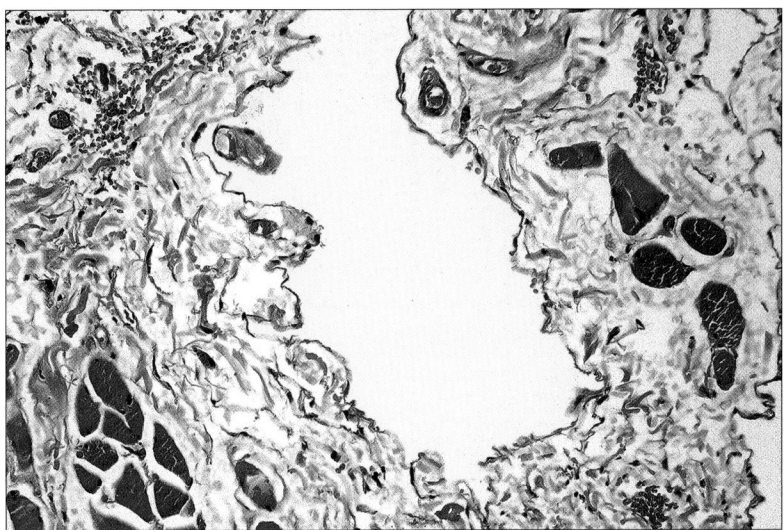

Fig. 10.131
Varix: the grossly dilated venule has a very thin wall.

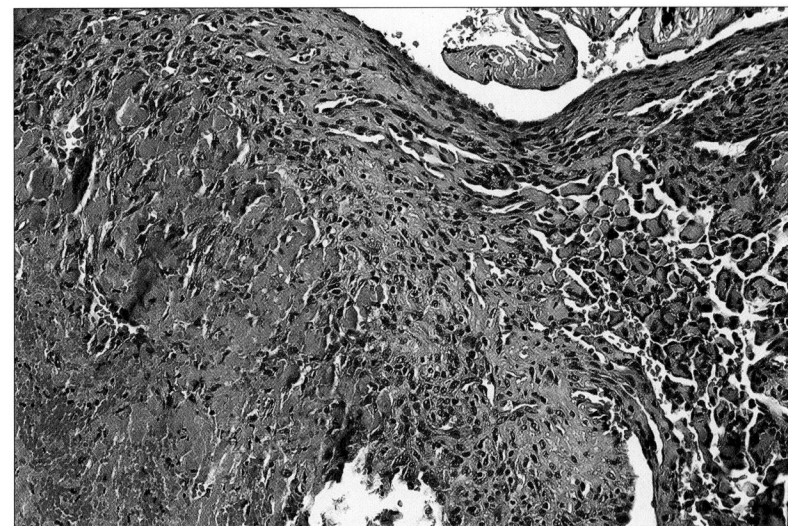

Fig. 10.132
Varix: there is intravascular papillary endothelial hyperplasia within this organizing thrombus.

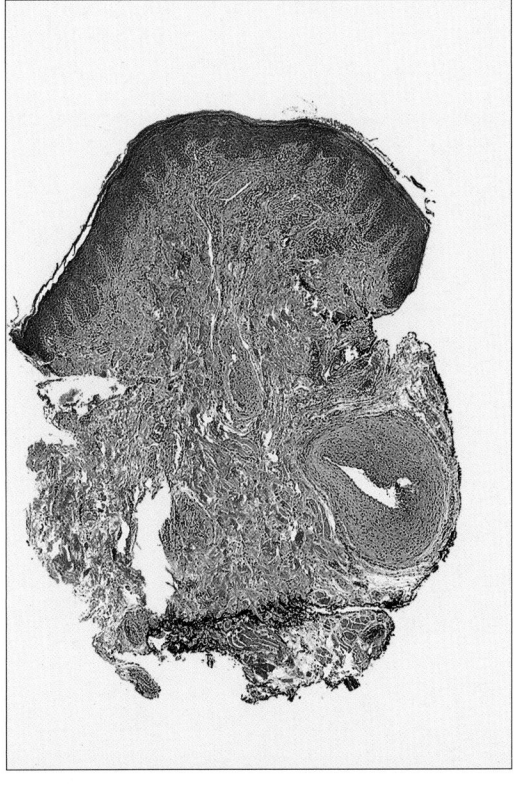

Fig. 10.133
Caliber-persistent artery: this small artery is typically superficially located.

References

1. Bean, W.R., Walsh, J.R. (1956) Venous lakes. *Arch Dermatol*, 74, 459–463.
2. Ettinger, R.L., Manderson, R.D. (1974) A clinical study of sublingual varices. *Oral Surg Oral Med Oral Pathol*, 38, 540–545.
3. Southam, J.C., Ettinger, R.L. (1974) A histologic study of sublingual varices. *Oral Surg Oral Med Oral Pathol*, 38, 879–886.
4. Miko, T., Adler, P., Endes, P. (1980) Simulated cancer of the lower lip attributed to a 'caliber persistent' artery. *J Oral Pathol*, 9, 137–144.
5. Lovas, J.G., Goodday, R.H. (1993) Clinical diagnosis of caliber-persistent labial artery of the lower lip. *Oral Surg Oral Med Oral Pathol*, 76, 480–483.
6. Jaspers, M.T. (1992) Oral caliber-persistent artery. Unusual presentations of unusual lesions. *Oral Surg Oral Med Oral Pathol*, 74, 631–633.

Infections

Hairy leukoplakia

Clinical features

Hairy leukoplakia is an Epstein–Barr virus infection of the oral epithelium that was first described in the HIV-infected population.[1] It may also be seen in patients with other immunodeficiency disorders who are susceptible to opportunistic viral infections or reactivations, such as organ transplant recipients.[2,3] Four cases have been reported in apparently healthy individuals.[3,4] Although the term is now entrenched in the scientific literature, 'hairy leukoplakia' as used in this condition does not ever connote an increased incidence of cytological atypia or propensity for development of squamous cell carcinoma such as is often a feature of 'leukoplakia'.

The majority of cases (> 70%) occur bilaterally on the lateral border of the tongue as a white, corrugated (hence 'hairy') plaque that in early lesions has vertical fissures running perpendicular to the long axis of the tongue (*Figs 10.134, 10.135*).[5,6] Its appearance is associated with the development of acquired immunodeficiency syndrome (AIDS) within 3 years in one-third of patients.[7]

Pathogenesis and histological features

The oropharyngeal epithelia and lymphoid tissue are sites of persistent latent Epstein–Barr virus infection.[8] Reactivation of latent infected tongue mucosa may be the cause of hairy leukoplakia.[9]

Oral hairy leukoplakia is characterized by hyperparakeratosis with a slightly shaggy surface. Candidal hyphae are present in 80% of cases, usually unassociated with spongiotic pustules.[5,6,10,11] Beneath the keratin is a distinct band of vacuolated and ballooned cells (*Fig. 10.136*). Pale cells contain Cowdry Type A eosinophilic inclusions and charac-teristically exhibit peripheral condensation of chromatin ('beaded effect') (*Figs 10.137, 10.138*).[12] This morphology is readily seen even on exfoliative cytology.[13,14] In situ hybridization localizes Epstein–Barr virus within keratinocyte nuclei (*Fig. 10.139*).

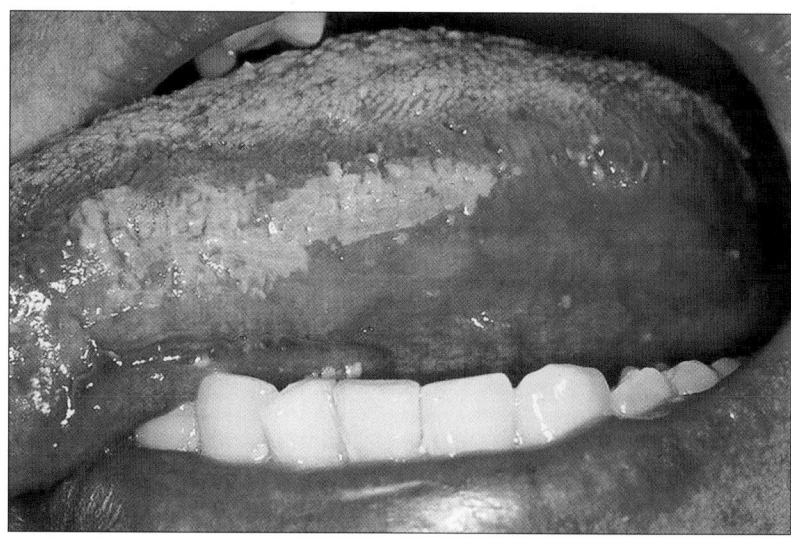

Fig. 10.135
Hairy leukoplakia: this lesion does not have the vertical fissures.

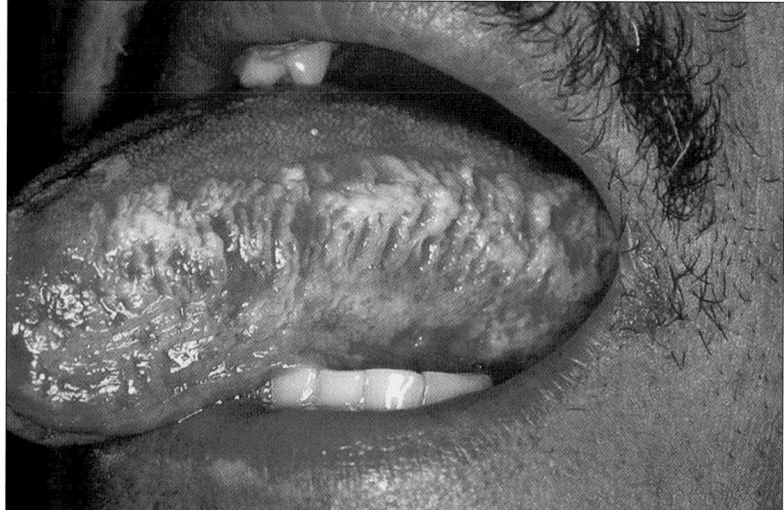

Fig. 10.134
Hairy leukoplakia: the thick white plaque on the lateral border of the tongue has typical vertical fissures.

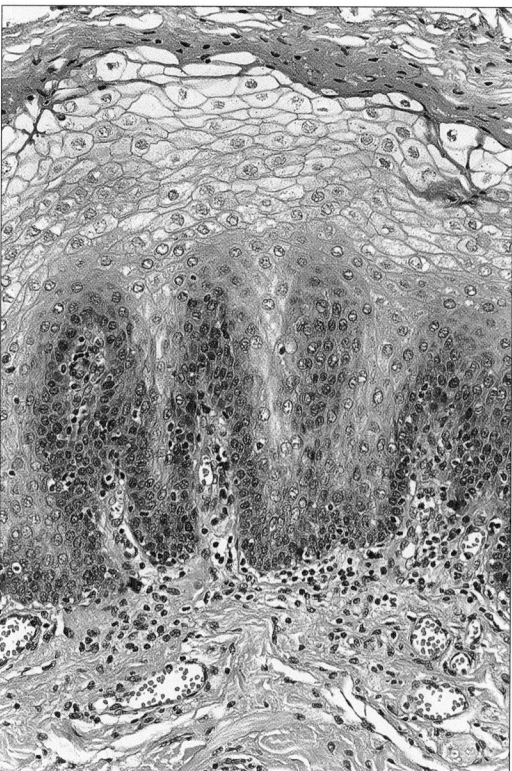

Fig. 10.136
Hairy leukoplakia: note the thick parakeratin and importantly, the vacuolated virally infected cells just beneath.

PCR-in situ hybridization studies demonstrated proteins that disrupt Epstein–Barr virus latency in all layers of the epithelium including basal cells, supporting the concept of reactivation of latent Epstein–Barr virus infection. HIV has also been identified within the keratinocytes.[9]

Although HPV was identified in hairy leukoplakia in earlier studies, more recent studies have disputed this observation.[5,9,15]

Differential diagnosis

Sometimes chronic bite injury is misdiagnosed as hairy leukoplakia. The two conditions share in common shaggy hyperparakeratosis and cytoplasmic vacuolation. However, pure hairy leukoplakia usually does not have the fissures and clefts rimmed by bacteria seen in bite injury unless, of course, there is concomitant secondary bite injury. The vacuolated cells in bite injury represent leukoedema and not viral cytopathic effect. Obviously, identification of Epstein–Barr virus establishes the diagnosis.

References

1. Greenspan, J.S., Greenspan, D., Lennette, E.T. et al (1985) Replication of Epstein–Barr virus within the epithelial cells of oral 'hairy' leukoplakia, an AIDS-associated lesion. *N Engl J Med*, **313**, 1564–1571.
2. Epstein, J.B., Sherlock, C.H., Wolber, R.A. (1993) Hairy leukoplakia after bone marrow transplantation. *Oral Surg Oral Med Oral Pathol*, **75**, 690–695.
3. Lozada-Nur, F., Robinson, J., Regezi, J.A. (1994) Oral hairy leukoplakia in nonimmunosuppressed patients. Report of four cases. *Oral Surg Oral Med Oral Pathol*, **78**, 599–602.
4. Eisenberg, E., Krutchkoff, D. (1992) Incidental oral hairy leukoplakia in immunocompetent persons. *Oral Surg Oral Med Oral Pathol*, **74**, 322–323.
5. Eversole, L.R., Jacobsen, P., Stone, C.E. et al (1986) Oral condyloma planus (hairy leukoplakia) among homosexual men: a clinicopathologic study of thirty-six cases. *Oral Surg Oral Med Oral Pathol*, **61**, 249–255.
6. Schiodt, M., Greenspan, D., Daniels, T.E. et al (1987) Clinical and histologic spectrum of oral hairy leukoplakia. *Oral Surg Oral Med Oral Pathol*, **64**, 716–720.
7. Greenspan, D., Greenspan, J.S., Hearst, N.G. et al (1987) Relation of oral hairy leukoplakia to infection with the human immunodeficiency virus and the risk of developing AIDS. *J Infect Dis*, **155**, 475–481.
8. Yao, Q.Y., Rickinson, A.B., Epstein, M.A. (1985) A re-examination of the Epstein–Barr virus carrier state in healthy seropositive individuals. *Int J Cancer*, **35**, 35–42.
9. Brandwein, M., Nuovo, G., Ramer, M. et al (1996) Epstein–Barr virus reactivation in hairy leukoplakia. *Mod Pathol*, **9**, 298–303.
10. Ficarra, G., Barone, R., Gaglioti, D. et al (1988) Oral hairy leukoplakia among HIV-positive intravenous drug abusers: a clinicopathologic and ultrastructural study. *Oral Surg Oral Med Oral Pathol*, **65**, 421–426.
11. Fernández, J.F., Benito, M.A., Lizaldez, E.B. et al (1990) Oral hairy leukoplakia: a histopathologic study of 32 cases. *Am J Dermatopathol*, **12**, 571–578.
12. Sciubba, J., Brandsma, J., Schwartz, M. et al (1989) Hairy leukoplakia: an AIDS-associated opportunistic infection. *Oral Surg Oral Med Oral Pathol*, **67**, 404–410.
13. Lumerman, H.S., Freedman, P.D., Kerpel, S.M. et al (1990) Screening for oral hairy leukoplakia by cytologic examination. *Diagn Cytopathol*, **6**, 225.
14. Fraga-Fernández, J., Vicandi-Plaza, B. (1992) Diagnosis of hairy leukoplakia by exfoliative cytologic methods. *Am J Clin Pathol*, **97**, 262–266.
15. Greenspan, D., Greenspan, J.S., Conant, M. et al (1984) Oral 'hairy' leucoplakia in male homosexuals: evidence of association with both papillomavirus and a herpes-group virus. *Lancet*, **2**, 831–834.

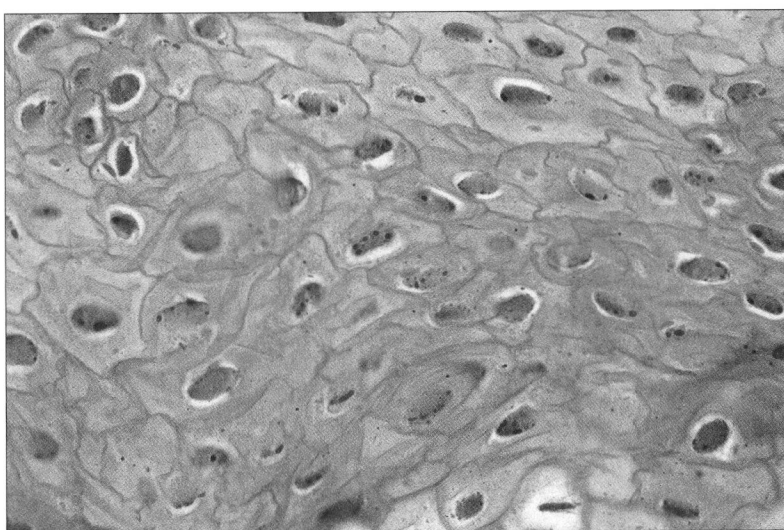

Fig. 10.137
Hairy leukoplakia: note condensation of chromatin in a beaded pattern against the nuclear membrane.

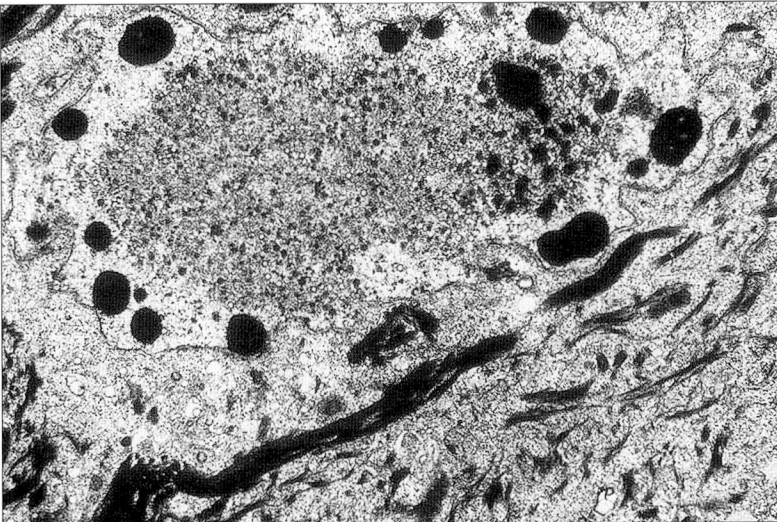

Fig. 10.138
Hairy leukoplakia: ultrastructural confirmation of chromatin condensation; the center of the nucleus is filled with herpesvirus.

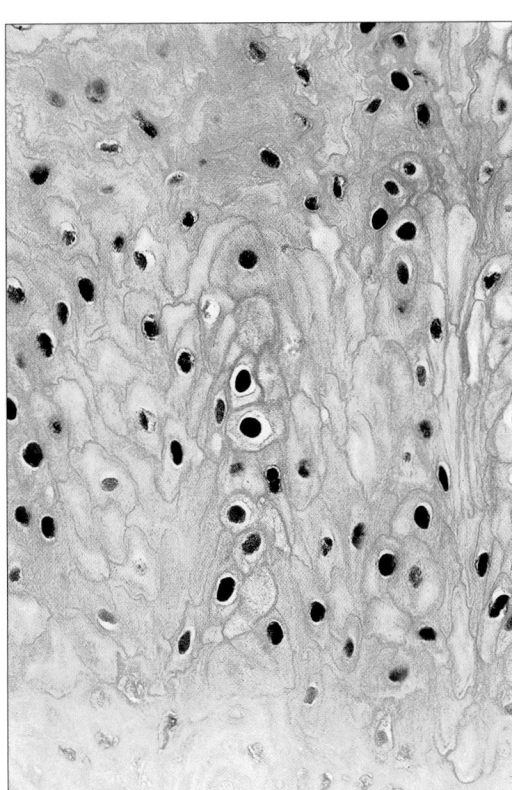

Fig. 10.139
Hairy leukoplakia: in situ hybridization reveals the presence of intranuclear Epstein–Barr virus.

Focal epithelial hyperplasia

Clinical features

Although any racial group may be affected, there is a predilection for focal epithelial hyperplasia (Heck's disease, multifocal papilloma virus epithelial hyperplasia) in Native Americans of Central and South America, Inuits and Africans. Over 90% of cases occur in the first two decades of life and there is a prevalence of 7–13% in predisposed populations with females twice as often affected as males.[1,2] The condition tends to regress over time. Focal epithelial hyperplasia also occurs in patients infected with HIV.[3]

Lesions are almost always multiple and multifocal, favoring the labial mucosa, lips, buccal mucosa and lateral tongue (*Figs 10.140, 10.141*). They are mucosal-colored papules or nodules that sometimes may appear papillary.[2]

Histological features

There is benign epithelial hyperplasia with slight keratinization and broad anastomosing rete ridges (*Fig. 10.142*). Koilocytes are usually present superficially (*Fig. 10.143*). 'Mitosoid' figures are a characteristic finding in the mid and lower third of the epithelium (*Fig. 10.144*). These represent degenerate and karyorrhectic nuclei showing aggregates of coarsely clumped chromatin resembling mitoses. They may be identified in up to 50% of original sections and are almost always present in further levels.[2,4]

HPV-13 and HPV-32 have been identified in 59% and 35% of cases, respectively, in one series, while in another series HPV-32 was found in 60% of cases.[5,6]

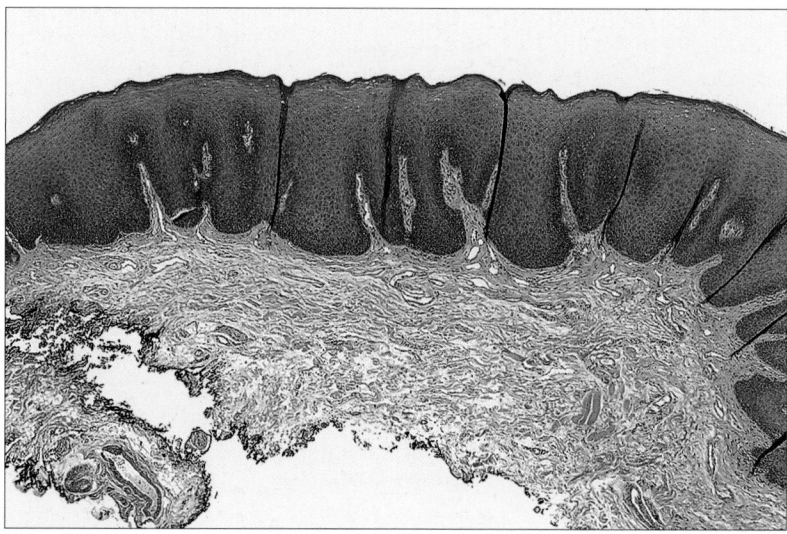

Fig. 10.142
Heck's disease: there is epithelial hyperplasia with the formation of broad rete ridges, somewhat similar to a condyloma.

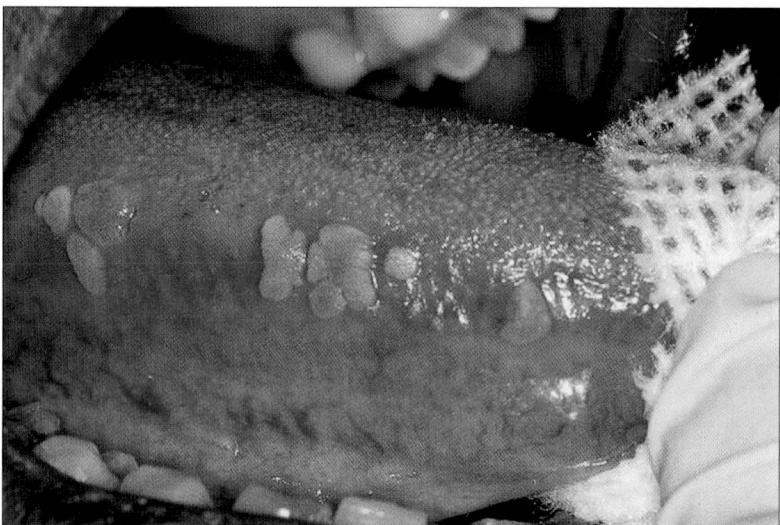

Fig. 10.140
Heck's disease: the lesions are pale, fleshy papules.

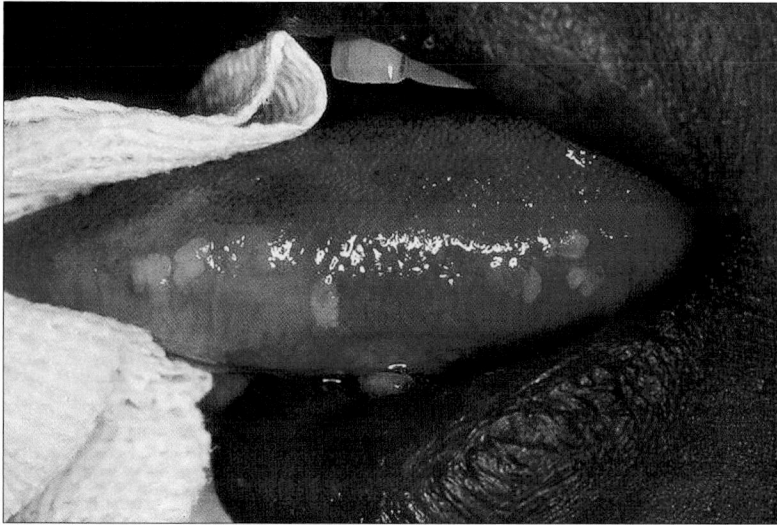

Fig. 10.141
Heck's disease: typical multiple coalescent papules on the lateral tongue.

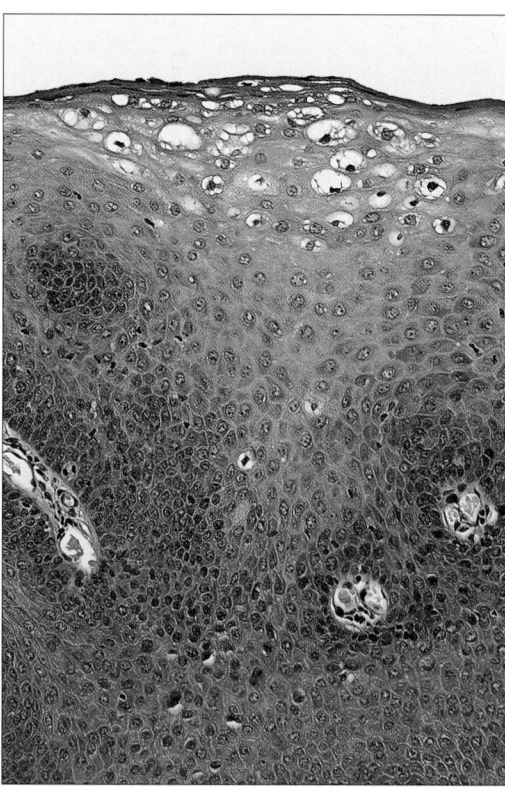

Fig. 10.143
Heck's disease: koilocytes are readily identified.

Differential diagnosis

Condyloma acuminatum may appear similar clinically and histologically but generally this lesion does not contain HPV-13 and HPV-32. Bowenoid papulosis may also exhibit similar 'mitosoid' figures, usually in a more florid fashion and with more epithelial atypia.

References

1. Harris, A.M.P., Van Wyk, C.W. (1993) Heck's disease (focal epithelial hyperplasia): a longitudinal study. *Community Dent Oral Epidemiol*, **21**, 82–85.
2. Carlos, R., Sedano, H.O. (1994) Multifocal papilloma virus epithelial hyperplasia. *Oral Surg Oral Med Oral Pathol*, **77**, 631–635.
3. Vilmer, C., Cavelier-Balloy, B., Pinquier, L. et al (1994) Focal epithelial hyperplasia and multifocal human papillomavirus infection in an HIV-seropositive man. *J Am Acad Dermatol*, **30**, 497–498.
4. Garlick, J.A., Calderon, S., Buchner, A. et al (1989) Detection of human papillomavirus (HPV) DNA in focal epithelial hyperplasia. *J Oral Pathol Med*, **18**, 172–177.
5. Beaudenon, S., Praetorius, F., Kremsdorf, D. et al (1987) A new type of human papillomavirus associated with oral focal epithelial hyperplasia. *J Invest Dermatol*, **88**, 130–135.
6. Henke, R.P., Guerin-Reverchon, I., Milde-Langosch, K. et al (1989) In situ detection of human papillomavirus types 13 and 32 in focal epithelial hyperplasia of the oral mucosa. *J Oral Pathol Med*, **18**, 419–421.

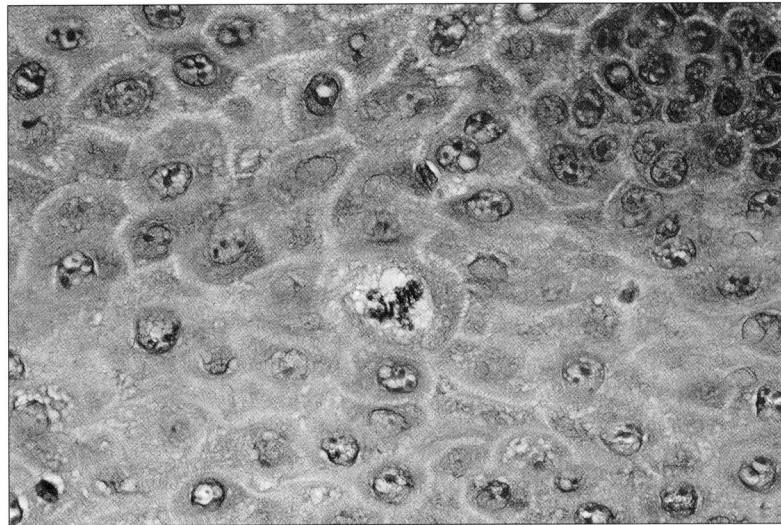

Fig. 10.144
Heck's disease: 'mitosoid' bodies represent human papillomavirus-induced nuclear changes.

Lichenoid and hypersensitivity reactions

Oral lichen planus and lichenoid stomatitis

Clinical features

Oral lichen planus is a chronic inflammatory condition of the mouth that occurs in 1–2% of the population (range 0.08–4.0%).[1–3] There is a 1.5 to 3-fold predilection for women and most patients are in the sixth decade.[1,4,5] The buccal mucosa is affected in 80–90% of cases, followed by the tongue and the gingiva.

While the older literature described between five and six different clinical variants, they can be simply grouped into three main categories:

- *Reticular and/or papular oral lichen planus* in which lesions present with the classic lacy white keratotic striations (Wickham's striae). Annular, papular and linear variants may also be seen. This variant tends to be non- or only mildly symptomatic (*Fig. 10.145*).

- *Erythematous (or erosive) oral lichen planus* in which lesions consist of variably symptomatic reddened mucosa. Because the mouth is a trauma-intense environment, bullae or vesicles of bullous lichen planus are rarely seen. Any blisters that do develop soon rupture, giving rise to erythematous and ulcerative lesions. Another erythematous variant presents clinically as 'desquamative gingivitis' (*Fig. 10.146*) (see p. 445).[6–8]

- *Ulcerative lichen planus*, which presents with a yellow fibrinous exudate on the surface and is almost always painful (*Fig. 10.147*) (see p. 222).

Oral lichen planus often presents with a combination of the above clinical manifestations and may also change from one to another over

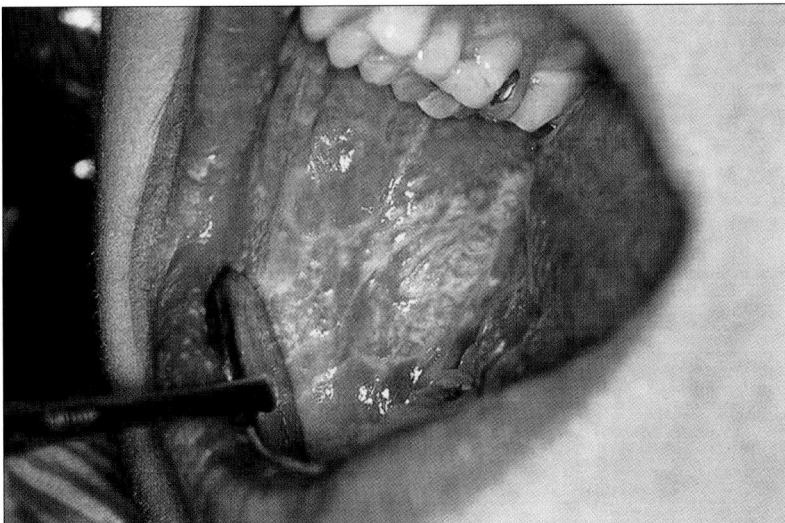

Fig. 10.145
Oral lichen planus: Wikham's striae of reticular lichen planus with mild erythema.

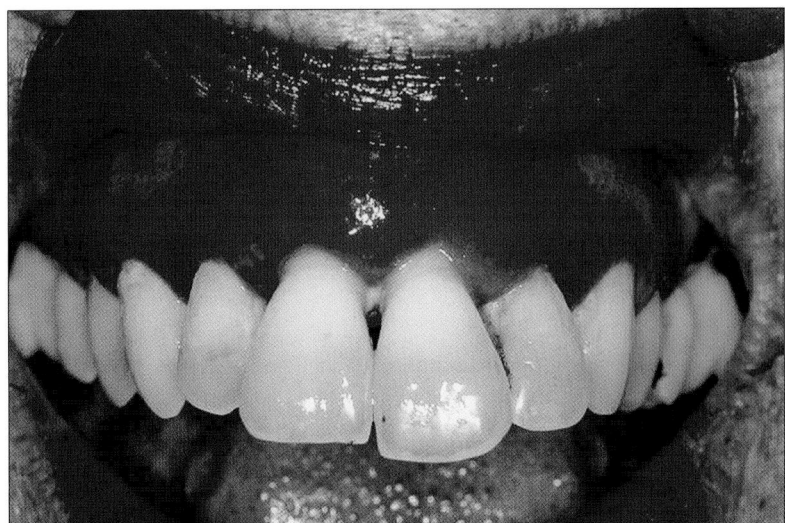

Fig. 10.146
Oral lichen planus: desquamative gingivitis is a form of erythematous lichen planus.

time.[9] From epidemiological studies, reticular lesions are the most common (77%), especially on the buccal mucosa, whereas in studies from referral centers, the erythematous and ulcerative forms predominate because they tend to be symptomatic.[4,10] Similarly, the skin is reportedly involved in approximately 5% of cases in epidemiological studies and 20–44% at referral centers.[1,4,5,11–14] Concurrent involvement of the gingiva with erosive oral lichen planus and lesions affecting the female genitalia is known as the vulvovaginal-gingival syndrome (see p. 480). Other mucosal sites such as the esophagus may also be affected.[15,16] Spontaneous remission occurs in approximately 7% of cases.[4]

Plaque-type lesions resembling leukoplakia should be considered as conventional leukoplakia arising in association with oral lichen planus. Not surprisingly, there is a strong relationship with smoking and malignant transformation.[9,17] The rate for the latter varies from 0 to 12.5% but many reports do not correct for tobacco usage as a confounding factor.[4,5,9,12] The true risk is probably in the order of 0.1–1%. Some authors believe that plaque-type disease has a higher association with malignancy while others believe erosive lesions are particularly susceptible.[12,17]

Pathogenesis and histological features

Local factors that may induce oral lichen planus or oral lichenoid lesions include contact lichenoid reactions to mercury in amalgam restorations. Between 34 and 79% of patients exhibit sensitization to mercury, especially those with lesions in direct contact with the restoration.[18–20] These lesions regress when the restorations are replaced. Similar reactions have been reported to composite restorations, possibly representing a reaction to formaldehyde.[21,22]

Oral lichenoid drug eruptions and oral lichen planus are clinically and histologically indistinguishable. The former occurs much less frequently than cutaneous lichenoid eruptions. The classes of drugs that have been implicated include antihypertensive agents (in particular thiazides), antimalarials, gold, non-steroidal anti-inflammatory drugs (NSAIDs), hypoglycemic agents, penicillamine and allopurinol.[23,24] Patients previously diagnosed with Grinspan's syndrome (oral lichen planus, diabetes mellitus and hypertension) were probably exhibiting a lichenoid mucosal reaction to their medications. Patients with autoimmune conditions such as lupus erythematosus and chronic GVHD may present with oral lesions that are clinically and histologically indistinguishable

from lichen planus (Figs 10.148, 10.149).[25–27] There is also an increased prevalence of oral lichen planus in patients with hepatitis, in particular hepatitis C, and especially in the European and Japanese populations (Fig. 10.150).[28,29]

Patients with oral lichen planus show an increased incidence of HLA-Bw57 in the white British population, HLA-DR9 in the Chinese and Japanese, and HLA-DR3 in the Swedish, with a decrease in incidence of HLA-DQ1 in the white British population.[30–33]

Because so many different conditions can lead to the clinical appearances of oral lichen planus – contact phenomena, hypersensitivity to medications and autoimmune diseases – it is more appropriate to view oral lesions as the final common pathway of expression of the mucosa to local or systemic antigens. It represents a delayed type hypersensitivity reaction characterized by an intense T-cell reaction to altered epithelium and leading ultimately to basal cell lysis.

The pathogenesis of oral disease has been reviewed in several publications and only a summary, albeit somewhat simplistic, is presented here.[24,34,35] The initiating event is alteration of the keratinocyte either from antigen bound or exposed on the cell surface (e.g. drugs, major

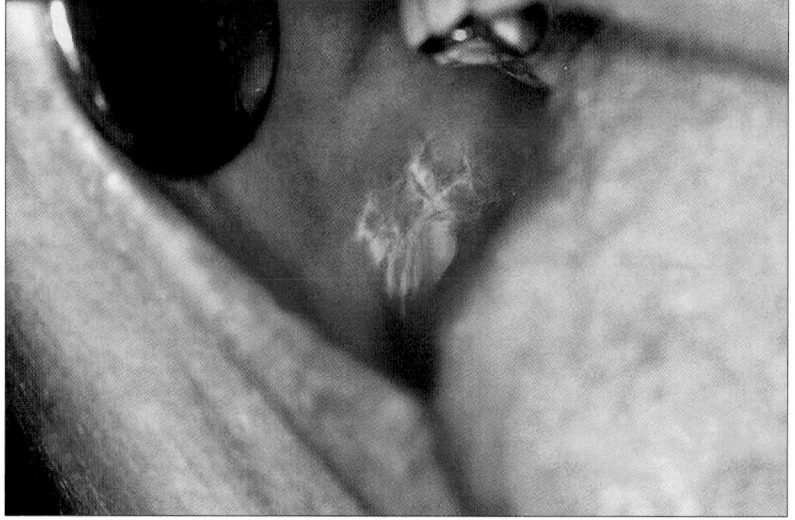

Fig. 10.148
Oral lesions of discoid erythematosus: lichenoid reticulations in a patient with systemic lupus erythematosus.

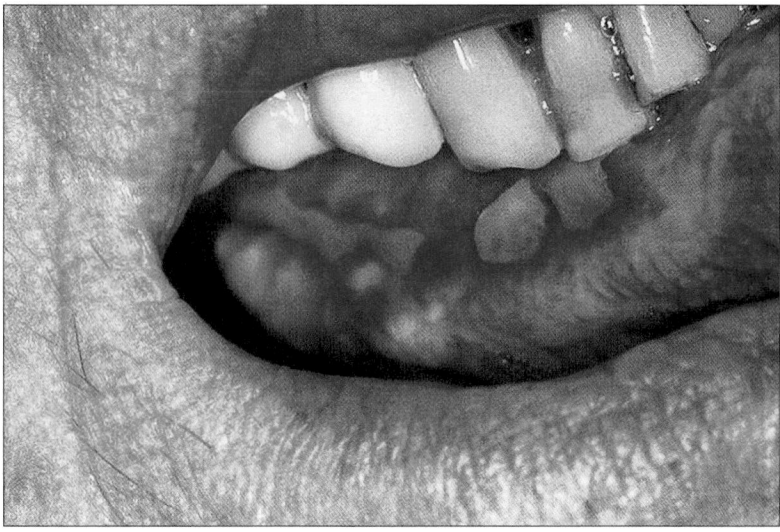

Fig. 10.147
Oral lichen planus: note the presence of some white reticulated areas, erythema and ulcers.

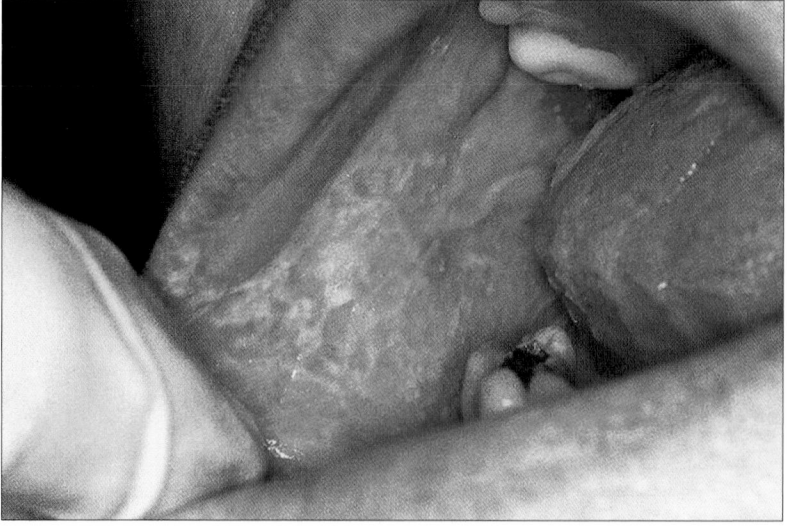

Fig. 10.149
Chronic oral graft-versus-host disease: lichenoid reticulations in a patient with chronic oral graft-versus-host disease.

histocompatibility complex or viral antigens). Langerhans' cells and possibly other antigen-presenting dendritic cells in the epithelium and lamina propria are upregulated or increased in number and ingest antigens and re-present them on the cell membrane.[36–38] Langerhans' cells migrate to lymph nodes where the antigen is recognized by CD4 cells. CD4 cells home to the epithelium where their passage is mediated by adhesion molecules. Extracellular matrix proteins (including type IV and type VII collagen) and laminin are also upregulated, and these facilitate migration of lymphocytes from the vessels to the epithelium.[39]

Meanwhile local mast cells, keratinocytes and lymphocytes are activated and secrete TNF-α which induces endothelial cell adhesion molecule expression, priming the vasculature for lymphocyte adhesion and transmigration.[40,41] Interferon-gamma (INF-γ) additionally plays an important role in lymphocyte trafficking. Keratinocytes release cytokines, which stimulate Langerhans' cell differentiation and which are also growth factors for keratinocytes and lymphocytes, such as interleukin (IL)-1, IL-3, IL-6, IL-8 and granulocyte–macrophage colony stimulating factor (GM-CSF).[42] When T-cells reach the epithelium, adhesion molecules such as major histocompatibility complex (MHC) class I molecules expressed on keratinocytes allow for binding of T-cell receptors, ultimately leading to keratinocyte destruction.

Heat shock proteins (HSP 60 and 70) are also increased in keratinocytes in oral lichen planus but it is unclear whether these are integral to the pathogenesis of oral disease.[43,44]

The reticular/papular type exhibits either hyperparakeratosis or hyperorthokeratosis with hypergranulosis, and variable acanthosis (*Figs 10.151, 10.152*). The erythematous form is non-keratinized and exhibits epithelial atrophy or erosion (*Fig. 10.153*). In both cases, there is lymphocyte exocytosis, mild spongiosis and increased numbers of Langerhans' cells. Common to all variants is destruction of the basal cell layer with blurring of the epithelial–connective tissue interface, and a superficial band-like lymphocytic infiltrate.[35] Early lymphocytic infiltrates contain mainly CD4 cells while older lesions consist predominantly of CD8 cells. Saw-tooth rete ridges and apoptotic cells (cytoid or Civatte bodies) may be present, and the basement membrane zone is sometimes thickly eosinophilic due to fibrinogen deposition. Subepithelial separation is sometimes present but maybe artifactual (*Fig. 10.154*). Although lymphocytes predominate, plasma cells may be seen, particularly in hypersensitivity lichenoid reactions, or if an ulcer or erosion is present. The term 'lichenoid stomatitis/mucositis' is sometimes used when a lesion has only some of the above features, in particular,

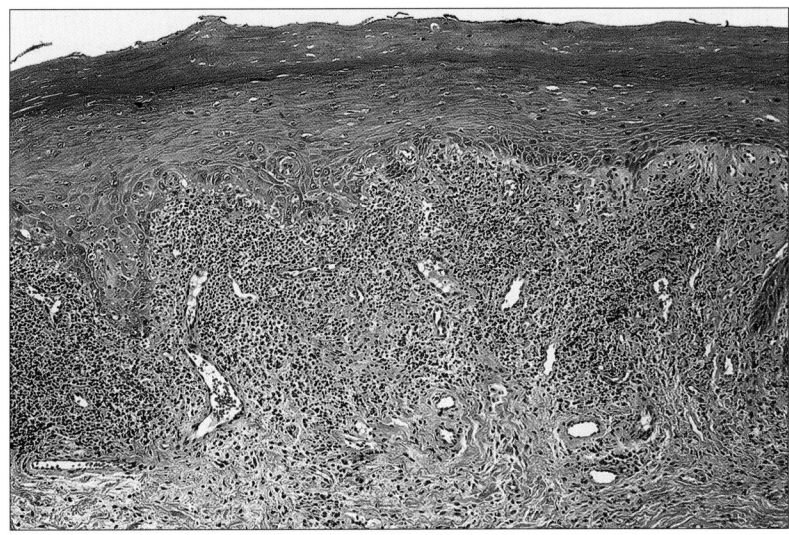

Fig. 10.151
Oral lichen planus: typical features of hyperkeratosis, acanthosis, squamatization of basal cells and a lymphocytic band at the interface.

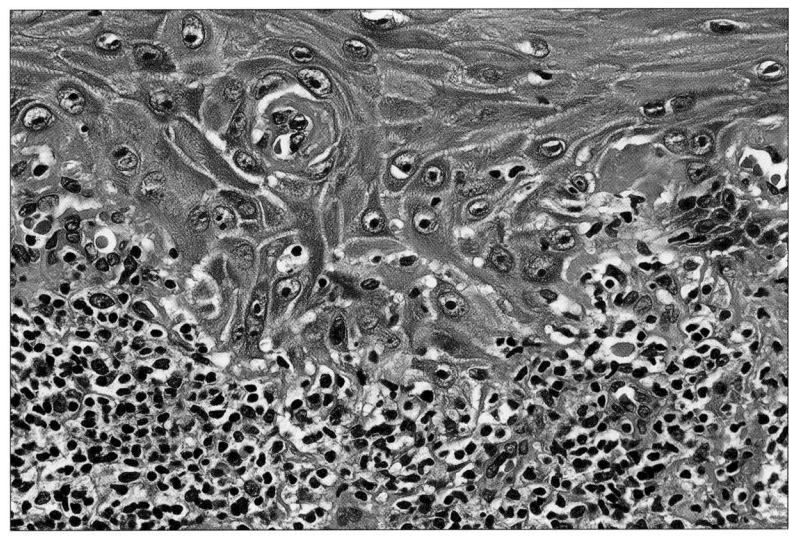

Fig. 10.152
Oral lichen planus: high power view emphasizing the interface stomatitis; note the presence of colloid bodies.

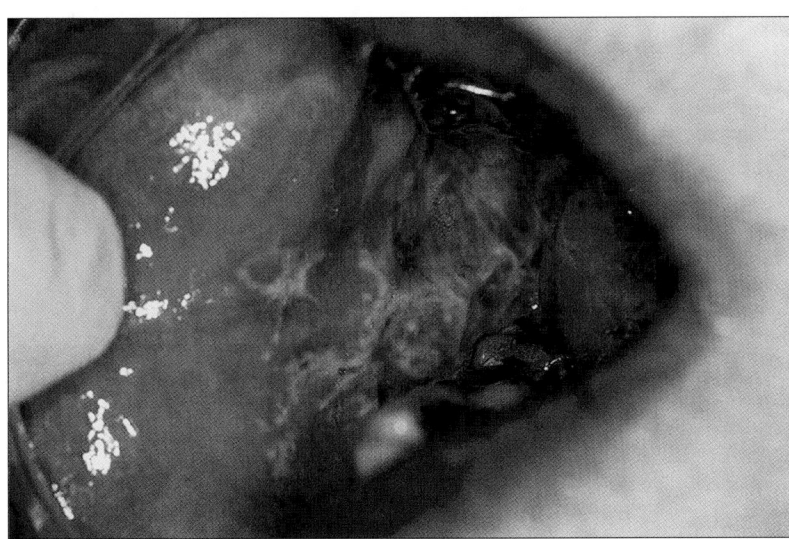

Fig. 10.150
Oral lichen planus: lichenoid reticulations in a patient with hepatitis C.

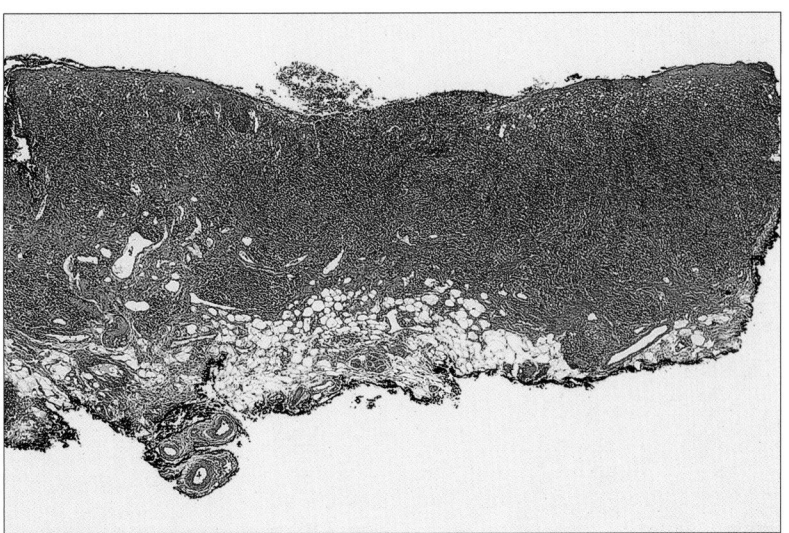

Fig. 10.153
Oral lichen planus: erosive and ulcerative lichen planus without hyperkeratosis.

only focal basal cell degeneration or a sparse lymphocytic band at the interface.

Although reactive epithelial atypia may be present, unequivocal epithelial dysplasia should be reported as such. The term 'lichenoid dysplasia' was originally coined to denote dysplasia arising within lichenoid stomatitis, which subsequently progressed to squamous cell carcinoma.[45,46] These are lesions that exhibit hyperparakeratosis or hyperorthokeratosis, epithelial dysplasia and a band-like lymphocytic infiltrate (*Figs 10.155, 10.156*). They are no different from any other oral epithelial dysplasia and should not be classified separately. Rather, a diagnosis of 'mild/moderate/severe dysplasia with a lichenoid infiltrate' is more appropriate. An important histological feature in true dysplasia is the presence of basal cell hyperplasia and atypia rather than degeneration.

Contact lichenoid hypersensitivity reactions to cinnamon show peri- and paravascular nodular lymphocytic infiltrates (*Figs 10.157, 10.158*).[47,48] It is unclear whether similar features can be seen in oral lichenoid reactions due to ingested medications. The presence of eosinophils is not a reliable marker for oral hypersensitivity reactions.

Direct immunofluorescence demonstrates fibrinogen at the basement membrane zone, often in a fibrillar 'stalactite' pattern with occasional C3 and IgM. Cytoid bodies also stain with IgM or C3.[6,49–51] Indirect immunofluorescence studies have shown that there may be circulating antibodies directed against basal cells.[52,53] Anti-lichen planus-specific antigen antibodies directed against cells in the strata granulosum and spinosum may be present in some cases.[54]

Patients with chronic ulcerative stomatitis (an erosive–ulcerative condition of the mouth that clinically resembles erosive oral lichen planus) have stratified epithelium-specific antinuclear IgG in a speckled pattern primarily affecting the lower epithelium (*Figs 10.159, 10.160*).[55–58] Indirect immunofluorescence using guinea pig esophagus demonstrates nuclear reactivity particularly well (*Fig. 10.161*). The antibody reacts with a 70 kDa epithelial nuclear antigen which is homologous to the p53 tumor suppressor gene.[59] In one case, incubating the

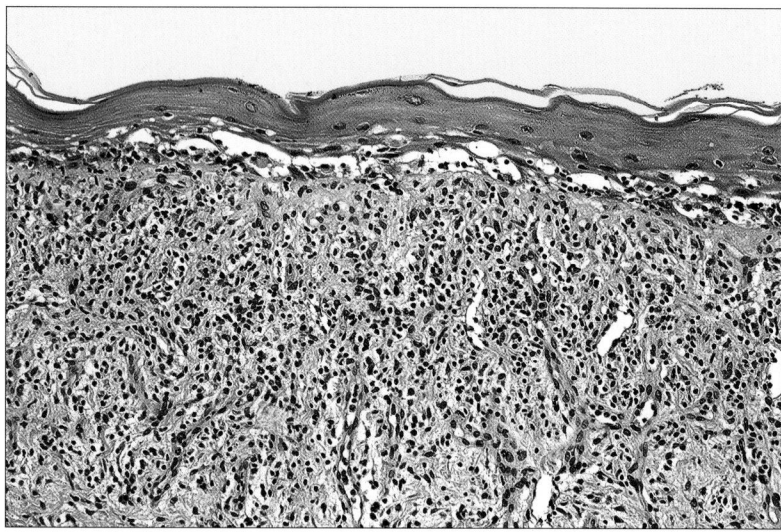

Fig. 10.154
Oral lichen planus: subepithelial separation occurs to varying degrees and is well demonstrated in this case.

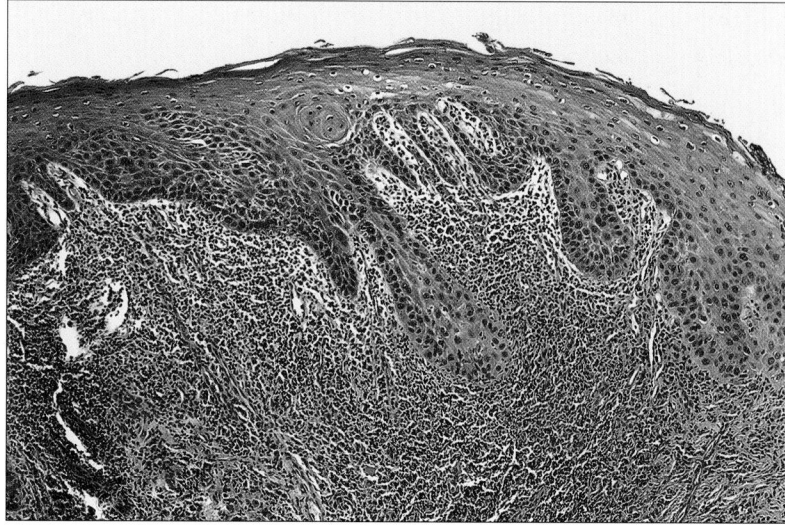

Fig. 10.156
Epithelial dysplasia with lichenoid inflammatory infiltrate: note that there is basal cell prominence and maturation disarray.

Fig. 10.155
Epithelial dysplasia with lichenoid inflammatory infiltrate: note the atypical cells and band-like lymphocytic infiltrate.

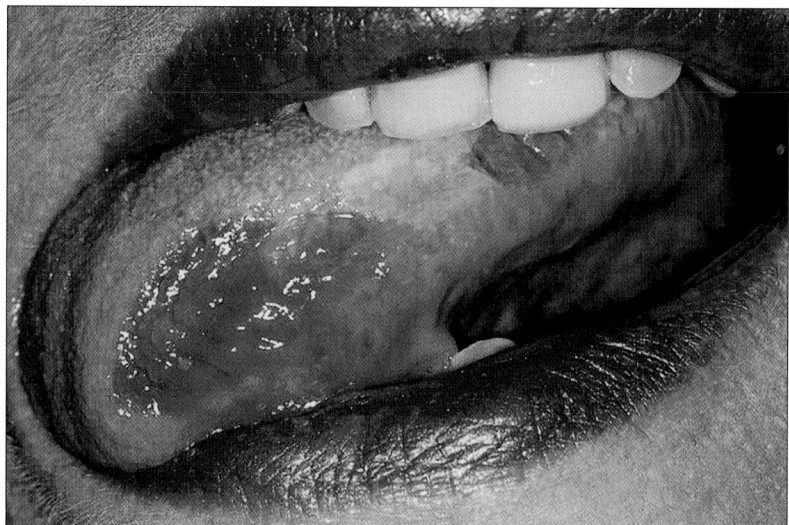

Fig. 10.157
Cinnamaldehyde-associated contact stomatitis: erythematous area on the tongue caused by cinnamon gum contact hypersensitivity reaction.

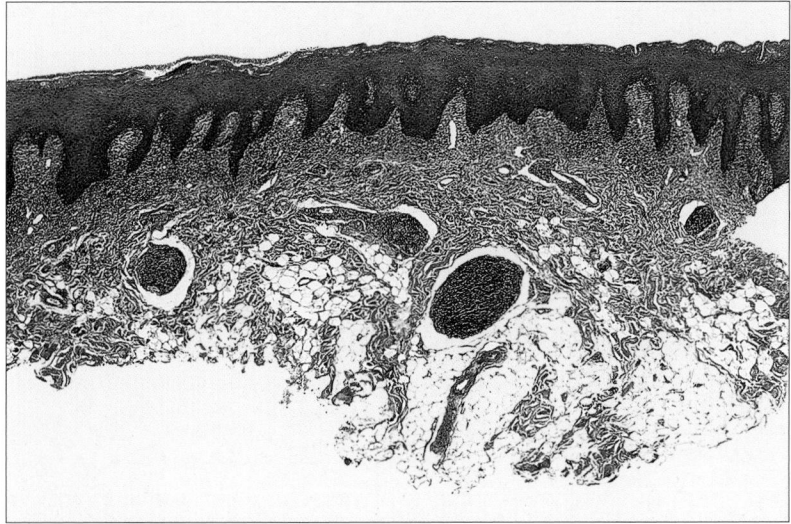

Fig. 10.158
Cinnamaldehyde-associated contact stomatitis: there is a lichenoid inflammatory infiltrate at the interface with peri- and paravascular nodular lymphocytic aggregates; in this case, the basal cells are intact.

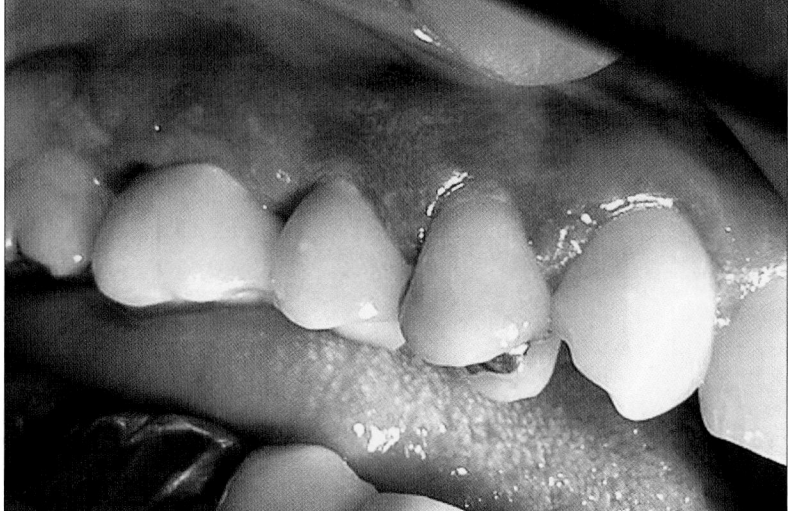

Fig. 10.159
Chronic ulcerative stomatitis: this presents with a vaguely reticulated mucosa. By courtesy of L. Solomon, MD, SUNY, Buffalo, NY, USA.

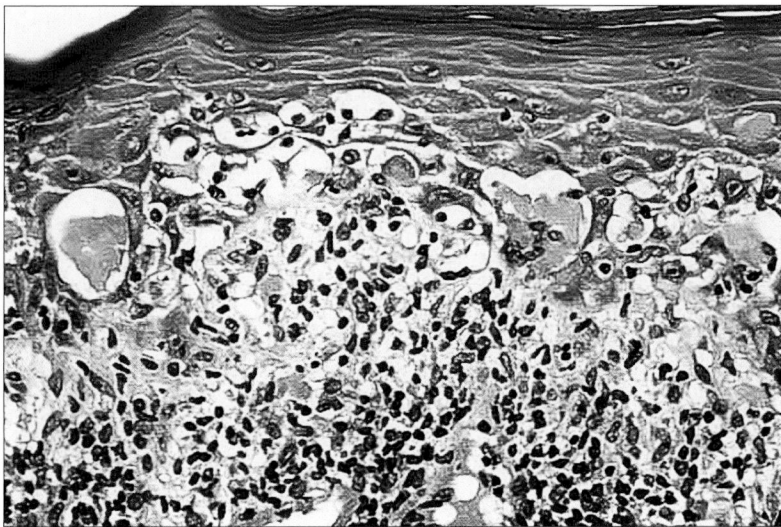

Fig. 10.160
Chronic ulcerative stomatitis: there is epithelial atrophy, many colloid bodies, basal cell degeneration and a lichenoid inflammatory infiltrate. By courtesy of L. Solomon, DDS, Buffalo, NY, USA.

patient's own serum with the patient's own tissue yielded the only positive result.[60]

Loss of heterozygosity on chromosome arms 3p, 9p and 17p is not a feature of oral lichen planus, a finding that supports the hypothesis that this disease is not intrinsically premalignant.[61] However, telomerase activity has been detected in up to 70% of patients.[62] A high rate of TP53 mutations has also been reported in oral lichen planus.[63]

Differential diagnosis

Lesions of discoid lupus erythematosus may also show a lichenoid lymphocytic band at the interface and peri- and paravascular nodular lymphocytic infiltrates (*Fig. 10.162*). Direct immunofluorescence studies are usually positive for the lupus band test in lesional tissue.

An intense chronic inflammatory infiltrate at the interface may also be seen in plasma cell gingivitis although the cells in this condition are, of course, predominantly plasmacytic.

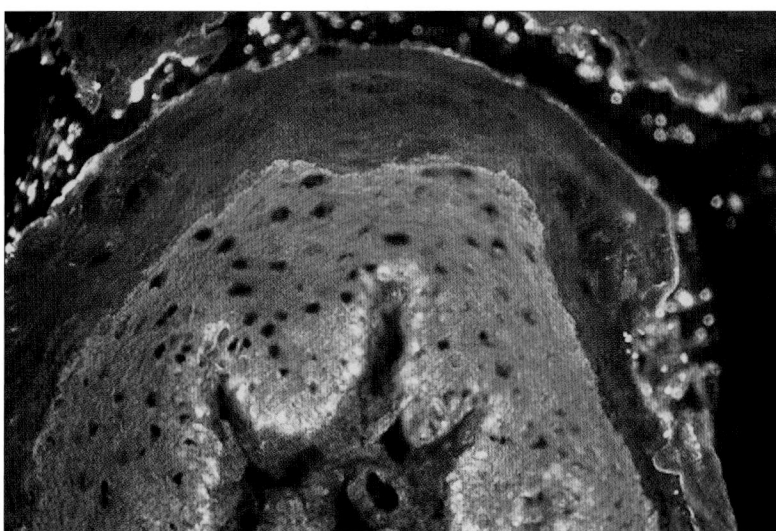

Fig. 10.161
Chronic ulcerative stomatitis: indirect immunofluorescence reveals the presence of nuclear anti-IgG using guinea pig esophagus as a substrate. By courtesy of L. Solomon, DDS, Buffalo, NY, USA.

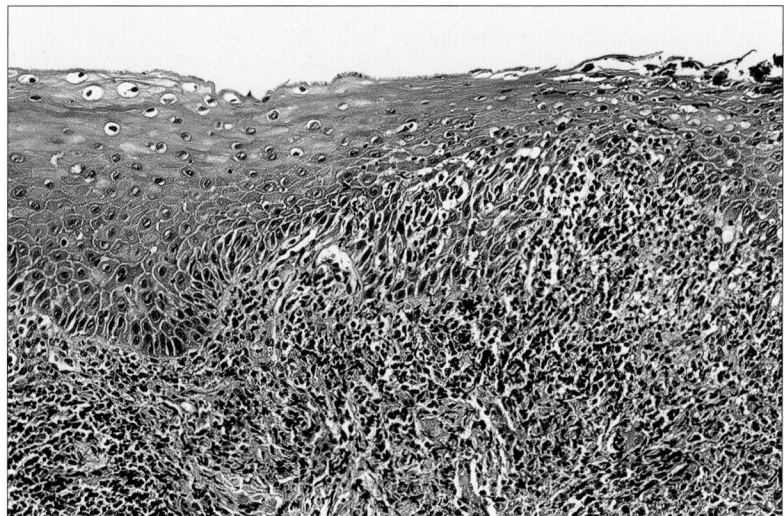

Fig. 10.162
Oral lupus erythematosus: note the lichenoid inflammatory infiltrate.

References

1. Axell, T., Rundquist, L. (1987) Oral lichen planus – a demographic study. *Community Dent Oral Epidemiol*, **15**, 52–56.
2. Banoczy, J., Rigo, O. (1991) Prevalence study of oral precancerous lesions within a complex screening system in Hungary. *Community Dent Oral Epidemiol*, **19**, 265–267.
3. Axell, T., Zain, R.B., Siwamogstham, P. et al (1990) Prevalence of oral soft tissue lesions in out-patients at two Malaysian and Thai dental schools. *Community Dent Oral Epidemiol*, **18**, 95–99.
4. Silverman, S. Jr, Gorsky, M., Lozada-Nur, F. et al (1991) A prospective study of findings and management in 214 patients with oral lichen planus. *Oral Surg Oral Med Oral Pathol*, **72**, 665–670.
5. Gorsky, M., Raviv, M., Moskona, D. et al (1996) Clinical characteristics and treatment of patients with oral lichen planus in Israel. *Oral Surg Oral Med Oral Pathol Oral Radiol Endod*, **82**, 644–649.
6. Daniels, T.E., Quadra-White, C. (1981) Direct immunofluorescence in oral mucosal disease: a diagnostic analysis of 130 cases. *Oral Surg Oral Med Oral Pathol*, **51**, 38–47.
7. Rogers, R.S.I., Sheridan, P.J., Nightingale, S.H. (1982) Desquamative gingivitis: clinical, histopathologic, immunopathologic and therapeutic observations. *J Am Acad Dermatol*, **7**, 729–735.
8. Yih, W.Y., Maier, T., Kratochvil, F.J. et al (1998) Analysis of desquamative gingivitis using direct immunofluorescence in conjunction with histology. *J Periodontol*, **69**, 678–685.
9. Thorn, J.J., Holmstrup, P., Rindum, J. et al (1988) Course of various clinical forms of oral lichen planus. A prospective follow-up study of 611 patients. *J Oral Pathol*, **17**, 213–218.
10. Bagan-Sebastián, J.V., Milian-Masanet, M.A., Penarrocha-Diago, M. et al (1992) A clinical study of 205 patients with oral lichen planus. *J Oral Maxillofac Surg*, **50**, 116–118.
11. Andreasen, J.O. (1968) Oral lichen planus. 1. A clinical evaluation of 115 cases. *Oral Surg Oral Med Oral Pathol*, **25**, 31–42.
12. Barnard, N.A., Scully, C., Eveson, J.W. et al (1993) Oral cancer development in patients with oral lichen planus. *J Oral Pathol Med*, **22**, 421–424.
13. Holmstrup, P., Thorn, J.J., Rindum, J. et al (1988) Malignant development of lichen planus-affected mucosa. *J Oral Pathol*, **17**, 219–225.
14. van der Meij, E.H., Schepman, K.P., Smeele, L.E. et al (1999) A review of the recent literature regarding malignant transformation of oral lichen planus. *Oral Surg Oral Med Oral Pathol Oral Radiol Endod*, **88**, 307–310.
15. Bermejo, A., Bermejo, M.D., Roman, P. et al (1990) Lichen planus with simultaneous involvement of the oral cavity and genitalia. *Oral Surg Oral Med Oral Pathol*, **69**, 209–216.
16. Eisen, D. (1994) The vulvovaginal-gingival syndrome of lichen planus. The clinical characteristics of 22 patients. *Arch Dermatol*, **130**, 1379–1382.
17. Silverman, S. Jr, Griffith, M. (1974) Studies on oral lichen planus. II. Follow-up on 200 patients, clinical characteristics, and associated malignancy. *Oral Surg Oral Med Oral Pathol*, **37**, 705–710.
18. James, J., Ferguson, M.M., Forsyth, A. et al (1987) Oral lichenoid reactions related to mercury sensitivity. *Br J Oral Maxillofac Surg*, **25**, 474–480.
19. Bolewska, J., Hansen, H.J., Holmstrup, P. et al (1990) Oral mucosal lesions related to silver amalgam restorations. *Oral Surg Oral Med Oral Pathol*, **70**, 55–58.
20. Koch, P., Bahmer, F.A. (1999) Oral lesions and symptoms related to metals used in dental restorations: a clinical, allergological, and histologic study. *J Am Acad Dermatol*, **41**, 422–430.
21. Lind, P.O. (1988) Oral lichenoid reactions related to composite restorations. Preliminary report. *Acta Odontol Scand*, **46**, 63–65.
22. Blomgren, J., Axell, T., Sandahl, O. et al (1996) Adverse reactions in the oral mucosa associated with anterior composite restorations. *J Oral Pathol Med*, **25**, 311–313.
23. McCartan, B.E., McCreary, C.E. (1997) Oral lichenoid drug eruptions. *Oral Dis*, **3**, 58–63.
24. Scully, C., Beyli, M., Ferreiro, M.C. et al (1998) Update on oral lichen planus: etiopathogenesis and management. *Crit Rev Oral Biol Med*, **9**, 86–122.
25. Schiodt, M., Halberg, P., Hentzer, B. (1978) A clinical study of 32 patients with oral discoid lupus erythematosus. *Int J Oral Surg*, **7**, 85–94.
26. Schiodt, M. (1984) Oral discoid lupus erythematosus. III. A histopathologic study of sixty-six patients. *Oral Surg Oral Med Oral Pathol*, **57**, 281–293.
27. Schubert, M.M., Sullivan, K.M., Morton, T.H. et al (1984) Oral manifestations of chronic graft-v-host disease. *Arch Intern Med*, **144**, 1591–1595.
28. Nagao, Y., Sata, M., Tanikawa, K. et al (1995) Lichen planus and hepatitis C virus in the northern Kyushu region of Japan. *Eur J Clin Invest*, **25**, 910–914.
29. Carrozzo, M., Gandolfo, S., Carbone, M. et al (1996) Hepatitis C virus infection in Italian patients with oral lichen planus: a prospective case-control study. *J Oral Pathol Med*, **25**, 527–533.
30. Watanabe, T., Ohishi, M., Tanaka, K. et al (1986) Analysis of HLA antigens in Japanese with oral lichen planus. *J Oral Pathol*, **15**, 529–533.
31. Jontell, M., Stahlblad, P.A., Rosdahl, I. et al (1987) HLA-DR3 antigens in erosive oral lichen planus, cutaneous lichen planus, and lichenoid reactions. *Acta Odontol Scand*, **45**, 309–312.
32. Lin, S.C., Sun, A. (1990) HLA-DR and DQ antigens in Chinese patients with oral lichen planus. *J Oral Pathol Med*, **19**, 298–300.
33. Porter, K., Klouda, P., Scully, C. et al (1993) Class I and II HLA antigens in British patients with oral lichen planus. *Oral Surg Oral Med Oral Pathol*, **75**, 176–180.
34. Walsh, L.J., Savage, N.W., Ishii, T. et al (1990) Immunopathogenesis of oral lichen planus. *J Oral Pathol Med*, **19**, 389–396.
35. Eversole, L.R. (1997) Immunopathogenesis of oral lichen planus and recurrent aphthous stomatitis. *Semin Cutan Med Surg*, **16**, 284–294.
36. Rich, A.M., Reade, P.C. (1989) A quantitative assessment of Langerhans' cells in oral mucosal lichen planus and leukoplakia. *Br J Dermatol*, **120**, 223–228.
37. Chou, M.J., Daniels, T.E. (1989) Langerhans' cells expressing HLA-DQ, HLA-DR and T6 antigens in normal oral mucosa and lichen planus. *J Oral Pathol Med*, **18**, 573–576.
38. Farthing, P.M., Matear, P., Cruchley, A.T. (1990) The activation of Langerhans' cells in oral lichen planus. *J Oral Pathol Med*, **19**, 81–85.
39. Eversole, L.R., Dam, J., Ficarra, G. et al (1994) Leukocyte adhesion molecules in oral lichen planus: a T cell-mediated immunopathologic process. *Oral Microbiol Immunol*, **9**, 376–383.
40. Jontell, M., Hansson, H.A., Nygren, H. (1986) Mast cells in oral lichen planus. *J Oral Pathol*, **15**, 273–275.
41. Sugermann, P.B., Savage, N.W., Seymour, G.J. et al (1996) Is there a role for tumor necrosis factor-alpha (TNF-alpha) in oral lichen planus? *J Oral Pathol Med*, **25**, 219–224.
42. Yamamoto, T., Osaki, T., Yoneda, K. et al (1994) Cytokine production by keratinocytes and mononuclear infiltrates in oral lichen planus. *J Oral Pathol Med*, **23**, 309–315.
43. Sugerman, P.B., Savage, N.W., Xu, L.J. et al (1995) Heat shock protein expression in oral epithelial dysplasia and squamous cell carcinoma. *Eur J Cancer B Oral Oncol*, **31B**, 63–67.
44. Chaiyarit, P., Kafrawy, A.H., Miles, D.A. et al (1999) Oral lichen planus: an immunohistochemical study of heat shock proteins (HSPs) and cytokeratins (CKs) and a unifying hypothesis of pathogenesis. *J Oral Pathol Med*, **28**, 210–215.
45. Krutchkoff, D.J., Eisenberg, E. (1985) Lichenoid dysplasia: a distinct histopathologic entity. *Oral Surg Oral Med Oral Pathol*, **60**, 308–315.
46. Eisenberg, E. (1992) Lichen planus and oral cancer: is there a connection between the two? *J Am Dent Assoc*, **123**, 104–108.
47. Allen, C.M., Blozis, G.G. (1988) Oral mucosal reactions to cinnamon-flavored chewing gum. *J Am Dent Assoc*, **116**, 664–667.
48. Miller, R.L., Gould, A.R., Bernstein, M.L. (1992) Cinnamon-induced stomatitis venenata. *Oral Surg Oral Med Oral Pathol*, **73**, 708–716.
49. Schiodt, M., Holmstrup, P., Dabelsteen, E. et al (1981) Deposits of immunoglobulins, complement, and fibrinogen in oral lupus erythematosus, lichen planus, and leukoplakia. *Oral Surg Oral Med Oral Pathol*, **51**, 603–608.
50. Laskaris, G., Sklavounou, A., Angelopoulos, A. (1982) Direct immunofluorescence in oral lichen planus. *Oral Surg Oral Med Oral Pathol*, **53**, 483–487.
51. Firth, N.A., Rich, A.M., Radden, B.G. et al (1990) Assessment of the value of immunofluorescence microscopy in the diagnosis of oral mucosal lichen planus. *J Oral Pathol Med*, **19**, 295–297.
52. Lin, S.C., Sun, A., Wu, Y.C. et al (1992) Presence of anti-basal cell antibodies in oral lichen planus. *J Am Acad Dermatol*, **26**, 943–947.
53. Lamey, P.J., McCartan, B.E., MacDonald, D.G. et al (1995) Basal cell cytoplasmic autoantibodies in oral lichenoid reactions. *Oral Surg Oral Med Oral Pathol Oral Radiol Endod*, **79**, 44–49.
54. Camisa, C., Allen, C.M., Bowen, B. et al (1986) Indirect immunofluorescence of oral lichen planus. *J Oral Pathol*, **15**, 218–220.
55. Parodi, A., Cardo, P.P. (1990) Patients with erosive lichen planus may have antibodies directed to a nuclear antigen of epithelial cells: a study on the antigen nature. *J Invest Dermatol*, **94**, 689–693.
56. Jaremko, W.M., Beutner, E.H., Kumar, V. et al (1990) Chronic ulcerative stomatitis associated with a specific immunologic marker. *J Am Acad Dermatol*, **22**, 215–220.
57. Beutner, E.H., Chorzelski, T.D., Parodi, A. et al (1991) Ten cases of chronic ulcerative stomatitis with stratified epithelium-specific antinuclear antibody. *J Am Acad Dermatol*, **24**, 781–782.
58. Church, L.F. Jr, Schosser, R.H. (1992) Chronic ulcerative stomatitis associated with stratified epithelial specific antinuclear antibodies. A case report of a newly described disease entity. *Oral Surg Oral Med Oral Pathol*, **73**, 579–582.
59. Lee, L.A., Walsh, P., Prater, C.A. et al (1999) Characterization of an autoantigen associated with chronic ulcerative stomatitis: the CUSP autoantigen is a member of the p53 family. *J Invest Dermatol*, **113**, 146–151.
60. Worle, B., Wollenberg, A., Schaller, M. et al (1997) Chronic ulcerative stomatitis. *Br J Dermatol*, **137**, 262–265.
61. Zhang, L., Michelsen, C., Cheng, X. et al (1997) Molecular analysis of oral lichen planus. A premalignant lesion? *Am J Pathol*, **151**, 323–327.
62. Thongprasom, K., Mutirangura, A., Cheerat, S. (1998) Telomerase activity in oral lichen planus. *J Oral Pathol Med*, **27**, 395–398.
63. Ogmundsdottir, H.M., Hilmarsdottir, H., Astvaldsdottir, A. et al (2002) Oral lichen planus has a high rate of TP53 mutations. A study of oral mucosa in Iceland. *Eur J Oral Sci*, **110**, 192–198.

Plasma cell orificial mucositis

Clinical features

In the 1960s and early 1970s, patients presented with symptoms of soreness and burning of the oral mucosa following the use of chewing gum. There was angular cheilitis with fissuring, dry atrophic lips and occasional desquamation. The tongue was often fissured, edematous and crenated (with scalloped borders) and the gingiva (free and attached) was fiery red, often with extension onto the palatal mucosa.[1,2] Some patients had drug allergies while others had atopic states. The gingiva was sometimes the only site of involvement.[3]

Discontinuation of gum chewing led to resolution of lesions in most but not all cases and it was postulated that this condition represented a hypersensitivity reaction to some component of chewing gum or some other unidentified antigen.[1,2] Since that cluster of cases and reformulation of chewing gum, only occasional cases occur now in response to a variety of putative topical irritants.

Subsequent to these reports, patients were identified who not only presented with oral symptoms of pain but also with hoarseness, dysphagia and airway obstruction. On endoscopy, the larynx showed thickened, red, velvety and edematous mucosa; the lips were thickened and fissured with angular cheilitis and fissured tongue.[4–7] The soft palate and gingiva were sometimes concurrently involved. Equivalent lesions have since been noted on the penis (Zoon's balanitis) and the vulva.

It is unclear whether this widespread involvement of the mucosa of the upper respiratory tract indicates a more severe and extensive form of plasma cell gingivostomatitis. No obvious allergen has been identified.

Histological features

Plasma cell orificial mucositis and plasma cell gingivostomatitis have similar histology. There is psoriasiform epithelial hyperplasia with spongiosis, spongiform pustules and leukocyte exocytosis (*Fig. 10.163*). The suprapapillary epithelium is severely thinned.[1,3] Dyskeratosis is often present in more extensive cases of orificial mucositis.[4,6] Characteristically, the lamina propria is filled with sheets of plasma cells with expression of both kappa and lambda light chains (*Fig. 10.164*). Russell bodies maybe present but Dutcher bodies are not seen. Occasional lymphocytes are also present.[1,3]

Differential diagnosis

An intense plasma cell infiltrate is characteristic of banal chronic gingivitis and periodontal disease. However, in these lesions, the plasma cells are not generally present in uninterrupted sheets but have a compartmentalized, slightly lobular character (*Fig. 10.165*). Clinically, even though the gingiva may be hyperplastic and edematous, gingivitis/periodontitis responds well to local therapy.

Plasma cell granuloma, a rare lesion in the oral cavity, is histologically similar to plasma cell orificial mucositis except that the lesions are clinically tumorous masses or nodules.[8–11] Cases of plasma cell granuloma reported from the periodontal space most likely represent chronic periodontitis or banal inflammatory fibrovascular hyperplasias with the usual intense plasma cell infiltrate.[12,13]

Lack of light chain restriction excludes plasmacytoma.

References

1. Kerr, D.A., McClatchey, K.D., Regezi, J.A. (1971) Idiopathic gingivostomatitis. *Oral Surg*, **32**, 402–423.
2. Silverman, S., Lozada, F. (1977) An epilogue to plasma-cell gingivostomatitis (allergic gingivostomatitis). *Oral Surg Oral Med Oral Pathol*, **43**, 211–217.
3. Palmer, R.M., Eveson, J.W. (1981) Plasma-cell gingivitis. *Oral Surg Oral Med Oral Pathol*, **51**, 187–189.
4. White, J.W., Olsen, K.D., Banks, P.M. (1986) Plasma cell orificial mucositis. Report of a case and review of the literature. *Arch Dermatol*, **122**, 1321–1324.
5. Timms, M.S., Sloan, P. (1991) Association of supraglottic and gingival idiopathic plasmacytosis. *Oral Surg Oral Med Oral Pathol*, **71**, 451–453.
6. Ferreiro, J.A., Egorshin, E.V., Olsen, K.D. et al (1994) Mucous membrane plasmacytosis of the upper aerodigestive tract. A clinicopathologic study. *Am J Surg Pathol*, **18**, 1048–1053.
7. Smith, M.E., Crighton, A.J., Chisholm, D.M. et al (1999) Plasma cell mucositis: a review and case report. *J Oral Pathol Med*, **28**, 183–186.
8. Weilbaecher, T.G., Sarma, D.P. (1984) Plasma cell granuloma of the tonsil. *J Surg Oncol*, **27**, 228–231.
9. Soares J., Nunes, J.F., Sacadura, J. (1987) Plasma cell granuloma of the tongue. Report of a case. *Histol Histopathol*, **2**, 199–201.
10. Ballesteros, E., Osborne, B.M., Matsushima, A.Y. (1998) Plasma cell granuloma of the oral cavity: a report of two cases and review of the literature. *Mod Pathol*, **11**, 60–64.
11. Ide, F., Shimoyama, T., Horie, N. (2000) Plasma cell granuloma of the oral mucosa with angiokeratomatous features: a possible analogue of cutaneous angioplasmocellular hyperplasia. *Oral Surg Oral Med Oral Pathol Oral Radiol Endod*, **89**, 204–207.
12. Bhaskar, S.N., Levin, M.P., Frisch, J. (1968) Plasma cell granuloma of periodontal tissues. Report of 45 cases. *Periodontics*, **6**, 272–276.
13. Acevedo, A., Buhler, J.E. (1977) Plasma-cell granuloma of the gingiva. *Oral Surg Oral Med Oral Pathol*, **43**, 196–200.

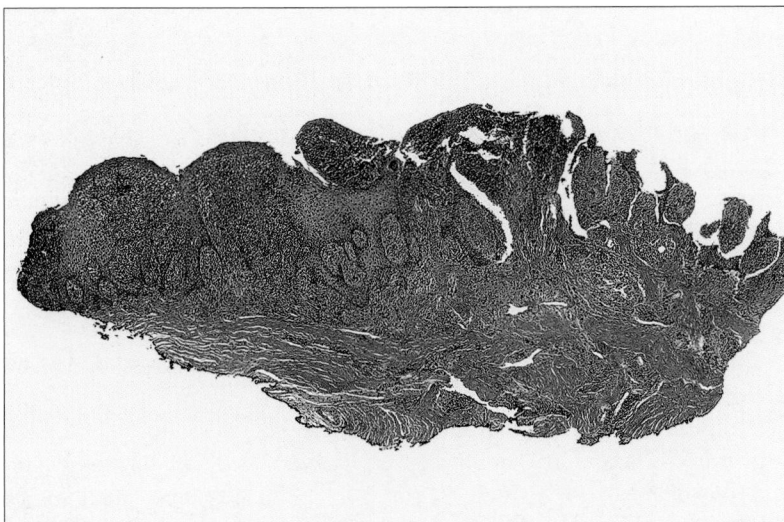

Fig. 10.163
Plasma cell gingivitis: there is a prominent inflammatory infiltrate at the interface with epithelial hyperplasia and atrophy.

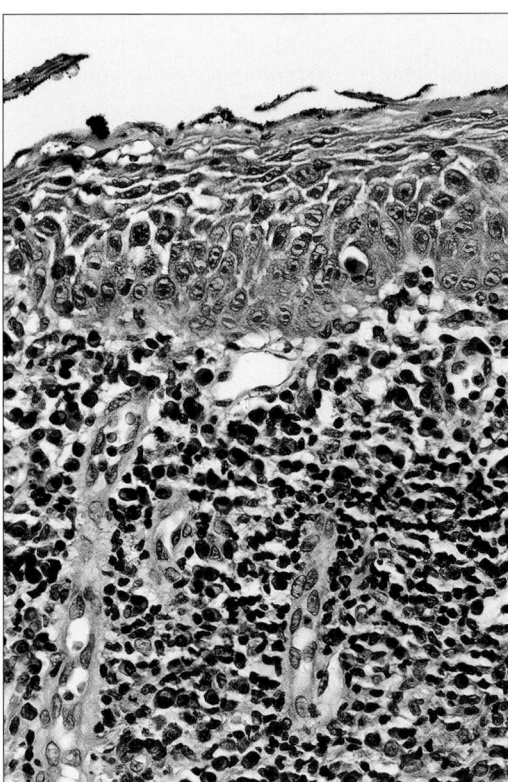

Fig. 10.164
Plasma cell gingivitis: the lamina propria is packed with plasma cells.

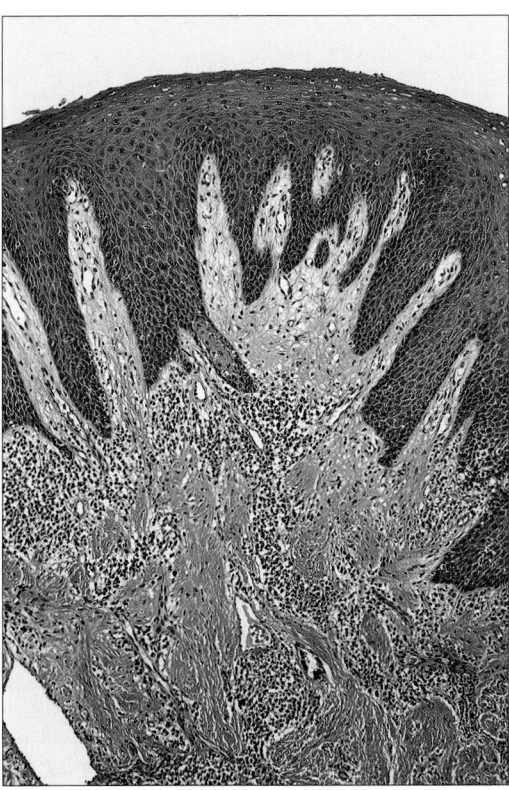

Fig. 10.165
Chronic periodontitis: note the pockets of plasma cells separated by bands of collagen.

Orofacial granulomatosis

Clinical features

Orofacial granulomatosis (cheilitis granulomatosa, granulomatous cheilitis) is a chronic, non-necrotizing, granulomatous and inflammatory condition characterized by non-tender swelling and edema of the lips and/or face, often but not always accompanied by swelling of the gingiva (usually around the anterior teeth), and cobblestoning, folding and erythema of the buccal mucosa. There may be angular cheilitis and prominent vertical fissures in established lesions.[1]

In the Melkersson–Rosenthal syndrome, facial nerve palsy and fissured tongue are additional findings. The triad is present in 18–25% of cases.[2,3]

In general, the swelling of the lips is the most important clinical sign, and is initially soft and relapsing (*Fig. 10.166*). Over the years, it becomes persistent and rubbery. The gingiva is affected in 20–30% of cases.[4,5] Gingival swellings extend onto the alveolar mucosa and become increasingly fibrotic over time (*Fig. 10.167*).[5] Facial nerve palsy is present in 13–47% of cases and may be due to either direct granulomatous involvement of the nerve or edema leading to nerve compression.[3,5,6]

It predates facial/lip swelling in 57–100% of cases.[3,5,6] Migraines and headaches are a feature in 11–20% of patients.[7] Fissured tongue is present in 40–50% of cases although its significance is uncertain since this is a relatively common oral finding.[3,5] Spontaneous improvement or resolution occurs in approximately one-third of patients.[5]

Ten per cent of patients have associated Crohn's disease while only 3% have associated sarcoidosis.[6]

Vulval and eye lesions have been reported in addition to more extensive neurological involvement.

Pathogenesis and histological features

Hypersensitivity to flavorings and antioxidants such as octyl butylated hydroxyanisol, cinnamaldehyde, preservatives (benzoate, metabisulfites), monosodium glutamate and fragrances have been demonstrated in up to 20% of cases.[3,8–12] Patients' symptoms have also been noted to improve when dental sources of infection are eliminated.[5] One report noted the presence of Borrelia within such lesions.[13]

Orofacial granulomatosis is associated with increased HLA-A3, B7 and DR2 expression.[14]

Non-necrotizing granulomata are seen in the lamina propria, sometimes adjacent to lymphatic vessels with associated lymphocytes and plasma cells (*Figs 10.168, 10.169*).[2,4] The granulomata may be subtle and poorly formed and often require serial sectioning to be identified with certainty.[6] They may bulge into and obstruct vessels.[15] Edema and vascular dilatation have also been reported but such features in isolation are insufficient for a diagnosis of orofacial granulomatosis. Foreign material within the granulomata effectively excludes a diagnosis of orofacial granulomatosis. As with any granulomatosis infiltrate, special stains for microorganisms should always be performed.

Mycobacterium tuberculosis and *Borrelia burgdorferi* have been identified by polymerase chain reaction in some cases although this has been disputed.[13,16,17]

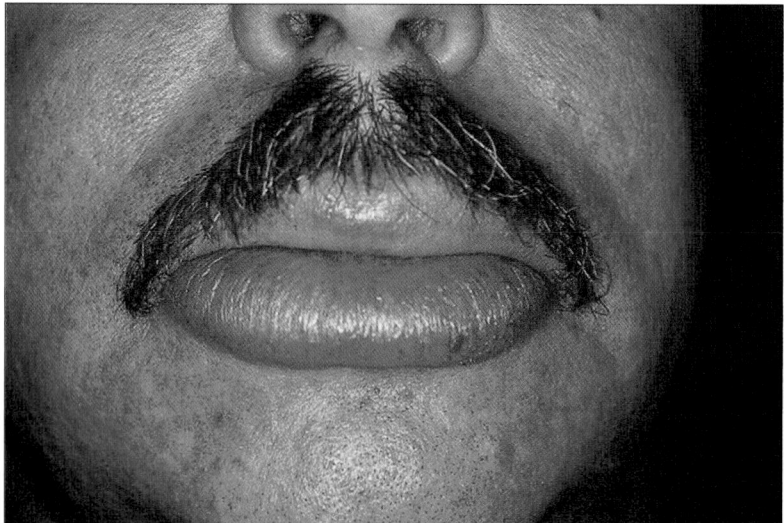

Fig. 10.166
Orofacial granulomatosis: there is diffuse rubbery swelling of the lower lip.

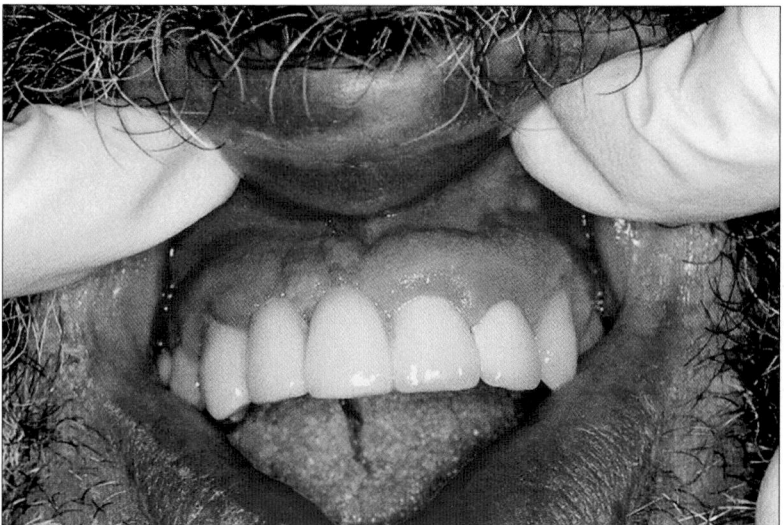

Fig. 10.167
Orofacial granulomatosis: note the thickened anterior maxillary gingiva.

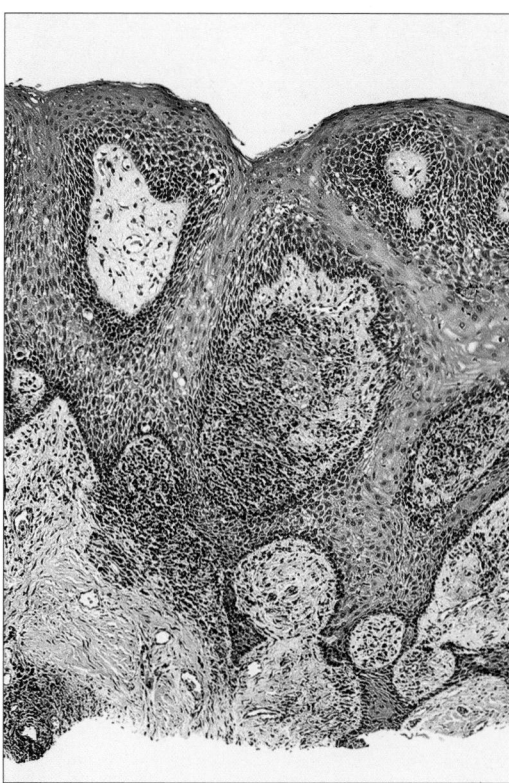

Fig. 10.168
Orofacial granulomatosis: this was the only granuloma present in multiple sections examined.

Differential diagnosis

Granulomata in this clinical setting are histologically indistinguishable from those of extragastrointestinal Crohn's disease; clinical differences help to differentiate between the two. In general, the granulomata of sarcoidosis tend to be more conspicuous. Angioedema and hypersensitivity reactions may present with edema and vascular ectasia in the absense of granulomata. Oral Wegener's granulomatosis is accompanied by pseudoepitheliomatous hyperplasia and a mixed acute and chronic inflammatory infiltrate with abscesses, necrosis and eosinophils.

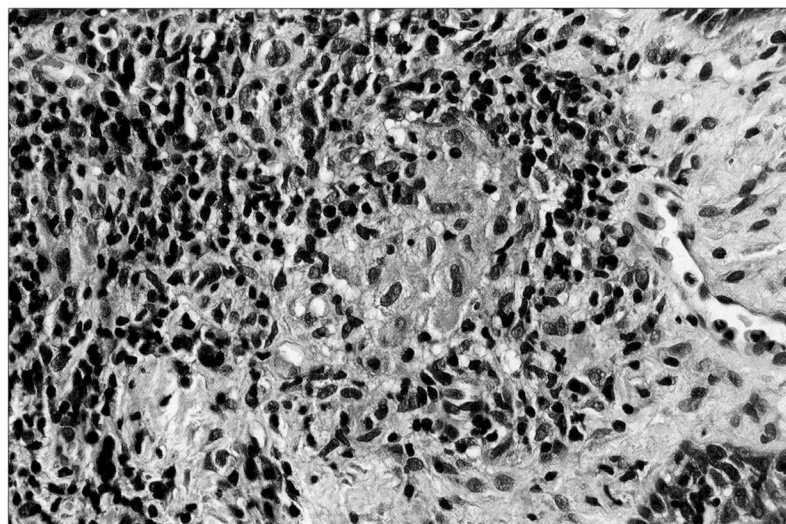

Fig. 10.169
Orofacial granulomatosis: typical subtle non-necrotizing granulomatous inflammation.

References

1. Hornstein, O.P. (1997) Melkersson–Rosenthal syndrome – a challenge for dermatologists to participate in the field of oral medicine. *J Dermatol*, 24, 281–296.
2. Worsaae, N., Christensen, K.C., Schiodt, M. (1982) Melkersson–Rosenthal syndrome and cheilitis granulomatosa. *Oral Surg Oral Med Oral Pathol*, 54, 404–413.
3. Greene, R.M., Rogers, R.S. 3rd (1989) Melkersson–Rosenthal syndrome: a review of 36 patients. *J Am Acad Dermatol*, 21, 1263–1270.
4. Allen, C.M., Camisa, C., Hamzeh, S. et al (1990) Cheilitis granulomatosa: report of six cases and review of the literature. *J Am Acad Dermatol*, 23, 444–450.
5. Worsaae, N., Pindborg, J.J. (1980) Granulomatous gingival manifestations of Melkersson–Rosenthal syndrome. *Oral Surg Oral Med Oral Pathol*, 49, 131–138.
6. Wiesenfeld, D., Ferguson, M.M., Mitchell, D.N. et al (1985) Oro-facial granulomatosis – a clinical and pathological analysis. *QJM*, 54, 101–113.
7. Vistnes, L.M., Kernahan, D.A. (1971) The Melkersson–Rosenthal syndrome. *Plast Reconstr Surg*, 48, 126–132.
8. Patton, D.W., Ferguson, M.M., Forsyth, A. et al (1985) Oro-facial granulomatosis: a possible allergic basis. *Br J Oral Maxillofac Surg*, 23, 235–242.
9. Sweatman, M.C., Tasker, R., Warner, J.O. et al (1986) Oro-facial granulomatosis. Response to elemental diet and provocation by food additives. *Clin Allergy*, 16, 331–338.
10. Lewis, F.M., Shah, M., Gawkrodger, D.J. (1995) Contact sensitivity to food additives can cause oral and perioral symptoms. *Contact Derm*, 33, 429–430.
11. Armstrong, D.K., Biagioni, P., Lamey, P.J. et al (1997) Contact hypersensitivity in patients with orofacial granulomatosis. *Am J Contact Derm*, 8, 35–38.
12. McKenna, K.E., Walsh, M.Y., Burrows, D. (1994) The Melkersson–Rosenthal syndrome and food additive hypersensitivity. *Br J Dermatol*, 131, 921–922.
13. Liu, H.G. (1993) Spirochetes in the cheilitis granulomatosa and sarcoidosis. *Zhonghua Yi Xue Za Zhi*, 73, 142–144, 189–190.
14. Gibson, J., Wray, D. (2000) Human leucocyte antigen typing in orofacial granulomatosis. *Br J Dermatol*, 143, 1119–1121.
15. Nozicka, Z. (1985) Endovasal granulomatous lymphangiitis as a pathogenetic factor in cheilitis granulomatosa. *J Oral Pathol*, 14, 363–365.
16. Apaydin, R., Bilen, N., Bayramgurler, D. et al (2000) Detection of Mycobacterium tuberculosis DNA in a patient with Melkersson–Rosenthal syndrome using polymerase chain reaction. *Br J Dermatol*, 142, 1251–1252.
17. Muellegger, R.R., Weger, W., Zoechling, N. et al (2000) Granulomatous cheilitis and Borrelia burgdorferi: polymerase chain reaction and serologic studies in a retrospective case series of 12 patients. *Arch Dermatol*, 136, 1502–1506.

Oral Crohn's disease

Clinical features

Crohn's disease usually presents in the second decade with a male predominance.[1,2] In one study, 37% of patients had asymptomatic gastrointestinal disease.[3] There is usually swelling of the face or lips; additionally, there may be linear vestibular aphtheiform ulcers, angular cheilitis, papulous and polypoid masses, mucosal tags, lip and gingival swelling, gingival erythema and cobblestoning of the mucosa (*Figs 10.170, 10.171*).[1,3] In 22–60% of cases, oral symptoms precede intestinal symptoms.[1–3] Adhesions may lead to limitation in mouth opening.[2]

Pathogenesis and histological features

Granulomata, which are seen in up to 88% of mucosal lesions, are typically non-caseating, often ill-defined and usually located in the superficial lamina propria, similar to orofacial granulomatosis.[1–4] They are found within the papulous folds, mucosal tags and even ulcers.[4] Salivary glands may also be involved (*Fig. 10.172*). M. paratuberculosis DNA has been identified in the granulomata of some patients with Crohn's disease, suggesting a pathogenic association.[5]

Differential diagnosis

Granulomatous diseases associated with specific infections or foreign material must always be excluded. The histological features of oral Crohn's disease are indistinguishable from those of orofacial granulomatosis of unknown etiology.

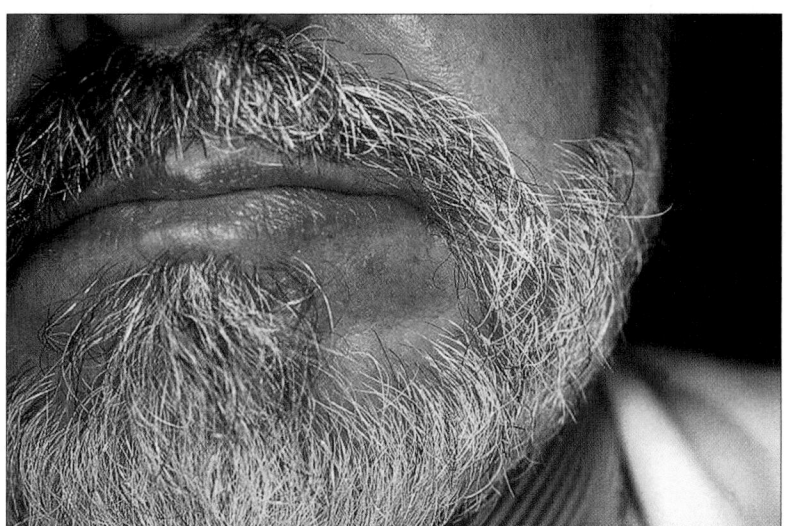

Fig. 10.170
Oral Crohn's disease: there is swelling of the lips and a reddened, indurated area of skin adjacent to the lower vermilion typical for skin involvement by Crohn's disease.

References

1. Plauth, M., Jenss, H., Meyle, J. (1991) Oral manifestations of Crohn's disease. *J Clin Gastroenterol*, **13**, 29–37.
2. Dupuy, A., Cosnes, J., Revuz, J. et al (1999) Oral Crohn's disease: clinical characteristics and long-term follow-up of 9 cases. *Arch Dermatol*, **135**, 439–442.
3. Scully, C., Cochran, K.M., Russell, R.I. et al (1982) Crohn's disease of the mouth: an indicator of intestinal involvement. *Gut*, **23**, 198–201.
4. Pittock, S., Drumm, B., Fleming, P. et al (2001) The oral cavity in Crohn's disease. *J Pediatr*, **138**, 767–771.
5. Fidler, H.M., Thurrell, W., Johnson, N.M. et al (1994) Specific detection of Mycobacterium paratuberculosis DNA associated with granulomatous tissue in Crohn's disease. *Gut*, **35**, 506–510.

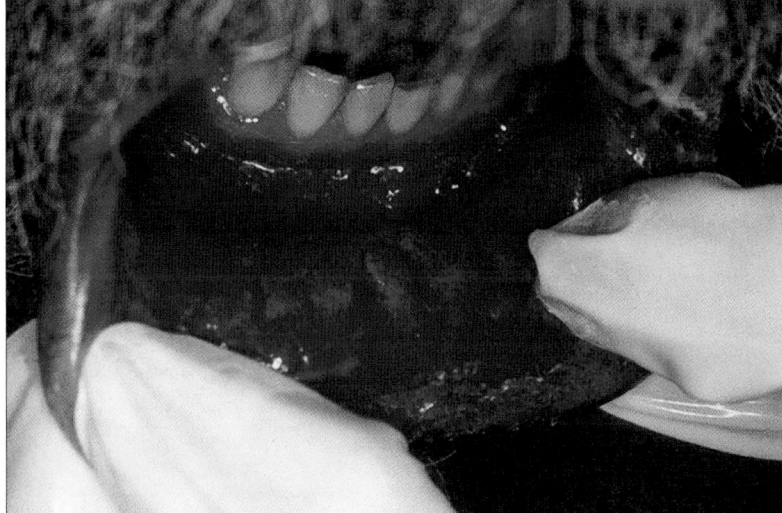

Fig. 10.171
Oral Crohn's disease: note the fissures and cobblestoning of the lower labial mucosa.

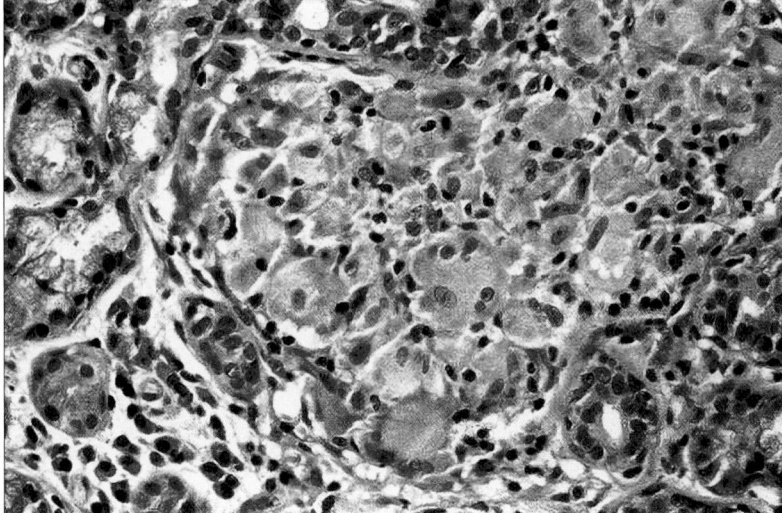

Fig. 10.172
Oral Crohn's disease: there is involvement of the minor salivary glands of the lower labial mucosa by non-necrotizing granulomata.

Wegener's granulomatosis

Clinical features

Wegener's granulomatosis in its complete form is characterized by vasculitis of small- and medium-sized vessels, non-infectious granulomatous inflammation of the upper and lower respiratory tract and glomerulonephritis. Approximately 5% of patients have oral involvement. Although almost all patients show upper and/or lower airway disease, some cases with isolated skin and mucosal disease have been reported. In some patients, the disease runs a protracted course limited to the upper airways before progressing to multiorgan involvement.[1] The gingiva is hyperplastic, often with a friable, granular, erythematous-to-magenta appearance, so-called 'strawberry gingivitis' (*Fig. 10.173*). Ulcerated and necrotic masses may be present.[2,3] The dentition in the affected sites becomes mobile and extraction sockets heal poorly (see also p. 727).

Pathogenesis and histological features

Patients' sera demonstrate the presence of antineutrophil cytoplasmic antibodies (ANCA). There are two main immunofluorescent staining patterns for ANCA:

*   *cytoplasmic* or *c-ANCA staining* (which is more specific for Wegener's granulomatosis) targets proteinase-3, a 29 kD serine protease found in the azurophilic granules of neutrophils
*   *perinuclear* or *p-ANCA staining* targets myeloperoxidase, another constituent of neutrophilic granules.[4,5]

However, disease limited to the upper airway may be negative for such antibodies.[6] Proinflammatory cytokines prime neutrophils causing them to express proteinase-3 and myeloperoxidase on the cell surface. ANCAs are then able to activate such cells, leading to degranulation and the secretion of additional cytokines, thus damaging endothelial cells and recruiting further inflammatory cells to the region.[7]

Oral mucosal biopsies show marked pseudoepitheliomatous hyperplasia with edema, a mixed acute and chronic inflammatory cell infiltrate, hemorrhage and vascular dilatation; many eosinophils may also be present. Granulomata are usually poorly formed or absent although scattered Langhan's-type giant cells are sometimes present.[2] Microabscesses and necrosis may also be seen.[8] Vasculitis with fibrinoid necrosis is sometimes a feature.[3] The typical geographic necrosis with palisaded granulomata is not usually a feature in the oral mucosa, although it is occasionally evident in the major salivary glands.[9]

Direct immunofluorescence studies may show immune deposits of IgG or IgA around blood vessels in skin biopsies.[10]

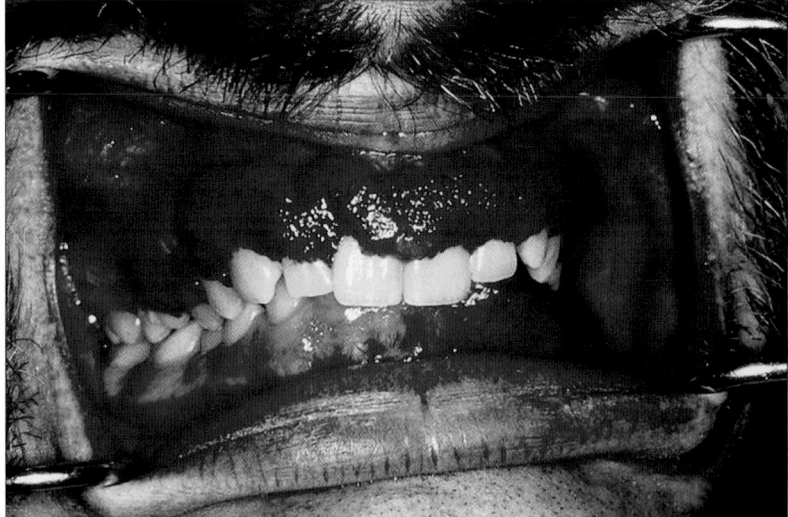

Fig. 10.173
Oral Wegener's granulomatosis: note the typical 'strawberry gingivitis'. By courtesy of S. Zunt, DDS, Indianapolis, USA.

Differential diagnosis

Infectious processes must be excluded in the setting of a mixed inflammatory infiltrate. The presence of pseudoepitheliomatous hyperplasia with eosinophils and scattered giant cells raises the possibility of a fungal infection, such as blastomycosis. Other vasculitides should also be considered although sole presentation in the oral cavity is rare. Microscopic polyarteritis is indistinguishable from lesions of Wegener's granulomatosis but this does not show immune deposition within vessel walls.[11] Pyostomatitis vegetans and pemphigus vegetans do not show vasculitis or granulomata and typically show acantholysis, although both may exhibit pseudoepitheliomatous hyperplasia and eosinophils.

Wegener's granulomatosis is differentiated from natural killer (NK)/T-cell lymphomas of the palate and nasal cavity ('midline destructive disease') by the absence of an atypical lymphocytic infiltrate.

References

1. Fienberg, R. (1981) The protracted superficial phenomenon in pathergic (Wegener's) granulomatosis. *Hum Pathol*, **12**, 458–467.
2. Handlers, J.P., Waterman, J., Abrams, A.M. et al (1985) Oral features of Wegener's granulomatosis. *Arch Otolaryngol*, **111**, 267–270.
3. Allen, C.M., Camisa, C., Salewski, C. et al (1991) Wegener's granulomatosis: report of three cases with oral lesions. *J Oral Maxillofac Surg*, **49**, 294–298.
4. Niles, J.L., McCluskey, R.T., Ahmad, M.F. et al (1989) Wegener's granulomatosis autoantigen is a novel neutrophil serine proteinase. *Blood*, **74**, 1888–1893.
5. Falk, R.J., Jennette, J.C. (1988) Anti-neutrophil cytoplasmic autoantibodies with specificity for myeloperoxidase in patients with systemic vasculitis and idiopathic necrotizing and crescentic glomerulonephritis. *N Engl J Med*, **318**, 1651–1657.
6. Nolle, B., Specks, U., Ludemann, J. et al (1989) Anticytoplasmic autoantibodies: their immunodiagnostic value in Wegener granulomatosis. *Ann Intern Med*, **111**, 28–40.
7. Harper, L., Savage, C.O. (2000) Pathogenesis of ANCA-associated systemic vasculitis. *J Pathol*, **190**, 349–359.
8. Napier, S.S., Allen, J.A., Irwin, C.R. et al (1993) 'Strawberry gums' – a case of Wegener's granulomatosis. *Br Dent J*, **175**, 327–329.
9. Devaney, K.O., Travis, W.D., Hoffman, G. et al (1990) Interpretation of head and neck biopsies in Wegener's granulomatosis. A pathologic study of 126 biopsies in 70 patients. *Am J Surg Pathol*, **14**, 555–564.
10. Brons, R.H., de Jong, M.C., de Boer, N.K. et al (2001) Detection of immune deposits in skin lesions of patients with Wegener's granulomatosis. *Ann Rheum Dis*, **60**, 1097–1102.
11. Jennette, J.C., Thomas, D.B., Falk, R.J. (2001) Microscopic polyangiitis (microscopic polyarteritis). *Semin Diagn Pathol*, **18**, 3–13.

Autoimmune conditions

Cicatricial pemphigoid

Clinical features

Cicatricial pemphigoid is the most common autoimmune subepithelial blistering disease presenting in the mouth. The word 'benign' has been dropped from the synonym because some cases may lead to blindness or severe stenosis of the upper aerodigestive tract. Scarring is not generally a feature of oral disease and although the term mucous membrane pemphigoid might be more appropriate, the designation cicatricial pemphigoid is retained for consistency (see p. 117). It is becoming apparent that several subsets of cicatricial pemphigoid exist, with variable antigenic characteristics and different predilections for the oral cavity or eye, or generalized involvement of the skin and mucosae.[1–3]

Cicatricial pemphigoid usually occurs in the sixth decade and upward with a two-fold female predilection although a three- to five-fold predilection for females has also been reported.[1,4–11] The oral cavity is affected in 84–96% of cases, and the conjunctiva in 52–81%.[4–6,12] Other sites of involvement in order of frequency are the upper airway (40–50%), skin (20–25%) and (less frequently) genitalia (9–17%), anorectal area (3–4%) and esophagus (3–4%).[4–6,12]

The oral cavity is the only site involved in approximately 60% of cases and is the first manifestation of the disease in 48–96% of patients.[4,13,14] The gingiva is the most frequent site of involvement affecting from 64 to 94% of cases; this often takes the form of desquamative gingivitis.[1,6,8,9,14] Desquamative gingivitis may be the sole manifestation of cicatricial pemphigoid in 60% of cases (*Fig. 10.174*).[10] The buccal mucosa, labial mucosa and tongue are less often affected (*Fig. 10.175*). Lesions present as painful areas of erosion, erythema and ulceration. Intact blisters are rarely seen. The collapsed blister roof may take the form of a yellow–white membrane that readily peels off the mucosa. Unlike cases with ocular involvement, cicatrization is an uncommon finding and was noted in only 9% of cases in one series.[4] As such, patients with only oral or oral/skin involvement have been recently classified as 'low risk'.[3]

Paraneoplastic pemphigoid has been reported in association with lymphoma and lung cancer.[15,16]

Oral and ocular cicatricial pemphigoid is associated with increased frequency of HLA-DQB1*0301.[17–19]

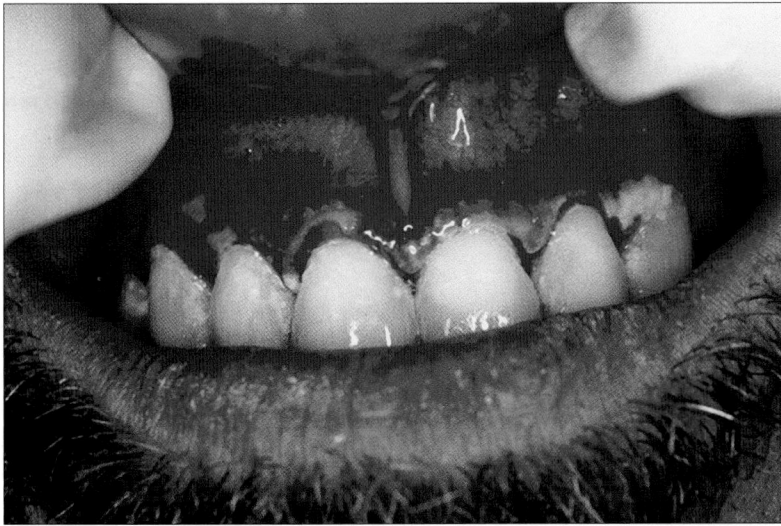

Fig. 10.174
Cicatricial pemphigoid: this typical case presented with erythematous gingiva and white epithelial sloughs.

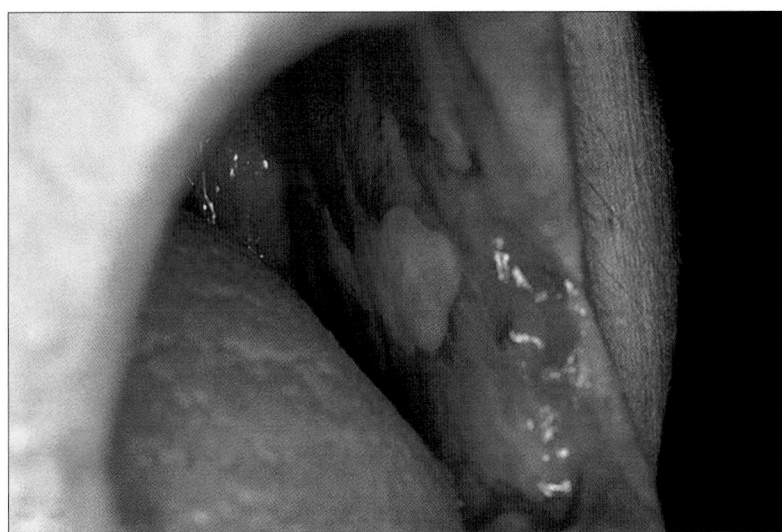

Fig. 10.175
Cicatricial pemphigoid: there are large oral ulcers on the buccal mucosa.

Pathogenesis and histological features

Cicatricial pemphigoid is characterized by separation of the mucosal squamous epithelium from the underlying connective tissue with preservation of the basal keratinocytes (*Figs 10.176, 10.177*).[8–10] A variable lymphoplasmacytic infiltrate is usually present in the lamina propria. Unlike bullous pemphigoid, eosinophils are rarely seen.

Direct immunofluorescence studies reveal basement membrane zone antibodies in a smooth, continuous linear fluorescence pattern in 67–96% of cases.[12,20,21] IgG is present in 39–96% of cases, C3 in 43–97% of cases and IgA in 20–30% of cases.[7,9,20,22]

Indirect immunofluorescence studies for circulating autoantibodies (usually IgG) are present in approximately 20% of cases.[9,12] However, one study using oral mucosa as a substrate elicited a 36% positivity rate.[20] There is no correlation between antibody titer and disease activity.

Indirect immunofluorescence studies in salt-split skin reveal circulating IgG or IgA in 84–100% of cases.[21,23,24] The majority (57–82%) show epidermal binding with 9–22% showing dermal or both epidermal and dermal localization. Those with both circulating IgG and IgA are virtually certain to need systemic immunosuppressive therapy.[21]

Cicatricial pemphigoid is now recognized to be a heterogeneous condition. Thus a number of antigens have been implicated in immunoblotting and immunoprecipitation studies. These include BPAg2 and to a lesser extent BPAg1, laminin-5 and laminin-6, beta-integrin, a 168 kDa antigen and other less well characterized molecules.[12–33]

Differential diagnosis

Oral blisters in cicatricial pemphigoid must be distinguished from subepithelial and autoimmune bullous dermatosis (such as linear IgA disease) and bullous lichen planus. The latter, however, typically shows squamatization of basal cells and apoptosis. In addition, the lymphocytic infiltrate is usually denser.

Direct immunofluorescence studies are essential in helping to differentiate between lichen planus and interface autoimmune stomatitides.

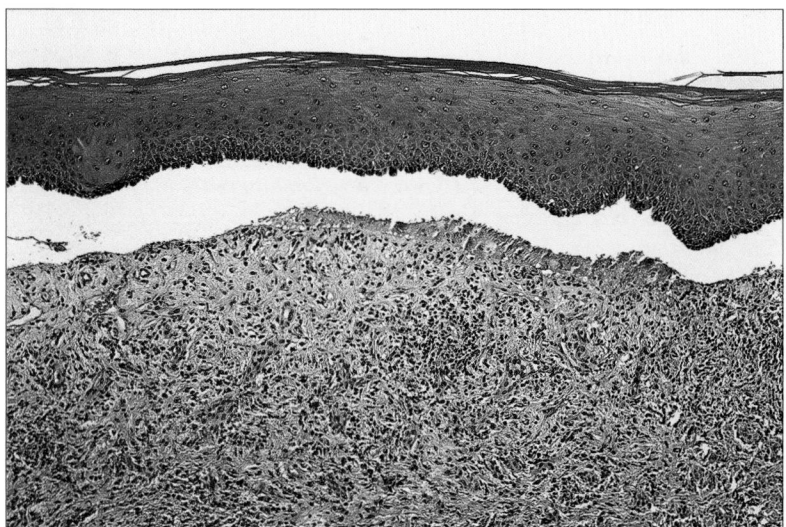

Fig. 10.176
Cicatricial pemphigoid: there is epithelial separation and preservation of the basal cells.

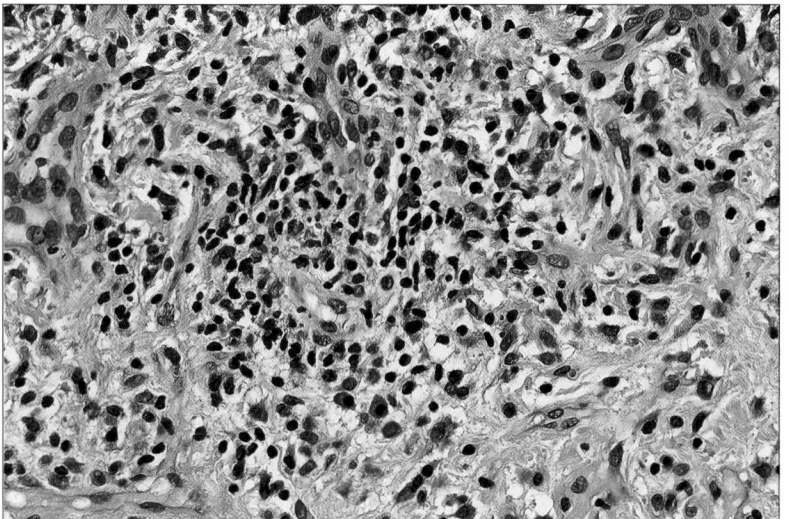

Fig. 10.177
Cicatricial pemphigoid: the lamina propria contains many dilated small capillaries and a variable lymphocytic infiltrate.

References

1. Mobini, N., Nagarwalla, N., Ahmed, A.R. (1998) Oral pemphigoid. Subset of cicatricial pemphigoid? *Oral Surg Oral Med Oral Pathol Oral Radiol Endod*, 85, 37–43.
2. Scully, C., Carrozzo, M., Gandolfo, S. et al (1999) Update on mucous membrane pemphigoid: a heterogeneous immune-mediated subepithelial blistering entity. *Oral Surg Oral Med Oral Pathol Oral Radiol Endod*, 88, 56–68.
3. Chan, L.S., Ahmed, A.R., Anhalt, G.J. et al (2002) The first international consensus on mucous membrane pemphigoid: definition, diagnostic criteria, pathogenic factors, medical treatment, and prognostic indicators. *Arch Dermatol*, 138, 370–379.
4. Hardy, K.M., Perry, H.O., Pingree, G.C. et al (1971) Benign mucous membrane pemphigoid. *Arch Dermatol*, 104, 467–475.
5. Person, J.R., Rogers, R.S. 3rd (1977) Bullous and cicatricial pemphigoid. Clinical, histopathologic, and immunopathologic correlations. *Mayo Clin Proc*, 52, 54–66.
6. Hanson, R.D., Olsen, K.D., Rogers, R.S. 3rd (1988) Upper aerodigestive tract manifestations of cicatricial pemphigoid. *Ann Otol Rhinol Laryngol*, 97, 493–499.
7. Daniels, T.E., Quadra-White, C. (1981) Direct immunofluorescence in oral mucosal disease: a diagnostic analysis of 130 cases. *Oral Surg Oral Med Oral Pathol*, 51, 38–47.
8. Silverman, S. Jr, Gorsky, M., Lozada-Nur, F. et al (1986) Oral mucous membrane pemphigoid. A study of sixty-five patients. *Oral Surg Oral Med Oral Pathol*, 61, 233–237.
9. Manton, S.L., Scully, C. (1988) Mucous membrane pemphigoid: an elusive diagnosis? *Oral Surg Oral Med Oral Pathol*, 66, 37–40.
10. Lamey, P.J., Rees, T.D., Binnie, W.H. et al (1992) Mucous membrane pemphigoid. Treatment experience at two institutions. *Oral Surg Oral Med Oral Pathol*, 74, 50–53.
11. Vincent, S.D., Lilly, G.E., Baker, K.A. (1993) Clinical, historic, and therapeutic features of cicatricial pemphigoid. A literature review and open therapeutic trial with corticosteroids. *Oral Surg Oral Med Oral Pathol*, 76, 453–459.
12. Ahmed, A.R., Hombal, S.M. (1986) Cicatricial pemphigoid. *Int J Dermatol*, 25, 90–96.
13. Shklar, G., McCarthy, P.L. (1971) Oral lesions of mucous membrane pemphigoid. A study of 85 cases. *Arch Otolaryngol*, 93, 354–364.
14. Laskaris, G., Sklavounou, A., Stratigos, J. (1982) Bullous pemphigoid, cicatricial pemphigoid, and pemphigus vulgaris. A comparative clinical survey of 278 cases. *Oral Surg Oral Med Oral Pathol*, 54, 656–662.
15. Bystryn, J.C., Hodak, E., Gao, S.Q. et al (1993) A paraneoplastic mixed bullous skin disease associated with anti-skin antibodies and a B-cell lymphoma. *Arch Dermatol*, 129, 870–875.
16. Setterfield, J., Shirlaw, P.J., Lazarova, Z. et al (1999) Paraneoplastic cicatricial pemphigoid. *Br J Dermatol*, 141, 127–131.
17. Yunis, J.J., Mobini, N., Yunis, E.J. et al (1994) Common major histocompatibility complex class II markers in clinical variants of cicatricial pemphigoid. *Proc Natl Acad Sci USA*, 91, 7747–7751.
18. Delgado, J.C., Turbay, D., Yunis, E.J. et al (1996) A common major histocompatibility complex class II allele HLA-DQB1* 0301 is present in clinical variants of pemphigoid. *Proc Natl Acad Sci USA*, 93, 8569–8571.
19. Carrozzo, M., Fasano, M.E., Broccoletti, R. et al (2001) HLA-DQB1 alleles in Italian patients with mucous membrane pemphigoid predominantly affecting the oral cavity. *Br J Dermatol*, 145, 805–808.
20. Laskaris, G., Angelopoulos, A. (1981) Cicatricial pemphigoid: direct and indirect immunofluorescent studies. *Oral Surg Oral Med Oral Pathol*, 51, 48–54.
21. Setterfield, J., Shirlaw, P.J., Kerr-Muir, M. et al (1998) Mucous membrane pemphigoid: a dual circulating antibody response with IgG and IgA signifies a more severe and persistent disease. *Br J Dermatol*, 138, 602–610.
22. Rogers, R.S. 3rd, Perry, H.O., Bean, S.F. et al (1977) Immunopathology of cicatricial pemphigoid: studies of complement deposition. *J Invest Dermatol*, 68, 39–43.
23. Sarret, Y., Hall, R., Cobo, L.M. et al (1991) Salt-split human skin substrate for the immunofluorescent screening of serum from patients with cicatricial pemphigoid and a new method of immunoprecipitation with IgA antibodies. *J Am Acad Dermatol*, 24, 952–958.
24. Ghohestani, R.F., Nicolas, J.F., Rousselle, P. et al (1997) Diagnostic value of indirect immunofluorescence on sodium chloride-split skin in differential diagnosis of subepidermal autoimmune bullous dermatoses. *Arch Dermatol*, 133, 1102–1107.
25. Domloge-Hultsch, N., Anhalt, G.J., Gammon, W.R. et al (1994) Antiepiligrin cicatricial pemphigoid. A subepithelial bullous disorder. *Arch Dermatol*, 130, 1521–1529.
26. Shimizu, H., Masunaga, T., Ishiko, A. et al (1995) Autoantibodies from patients with cicatricial pemphigoid target different sites in epidermal basement membrane. *J Invest Dermatol*, 104, 370–373.
27. Kirtschig, G., Marinkovich, M.P., Burgeson, R.E. et al (1995) Anti-basement membrane autoantibodies in patients with anti-epiligrin cicatricial pemphigoid bind the alpha subunit of laminin 5. *J Invest Dermatol*, 105, 543–548.
28. Bernard, P., Prost, C., Durepaire, N. et al (1992) The major cicatricial pemphigoid antigen is a 180-kD protein that shows immunologic cross-reactivities with the bullous pemphigoid antigen. *J Invest Dermatol*, 99, 174–179.
29. Balding, S.D., Prost, C., Diaz, L.A. et al (1996) Cicatricial pemphigoid autoantibodies react with multiple sites on the BP180 extracellular domain. *J Invest Dermatol*, 106, 141–146.
30. Bedane, C., McMillan, J.R., Balding, S.D. et al (1997) Bullous pemphigoid and cicatricial pemphigoid autoantibodies react with ultrastructurally separable epitopes on the BP180 ectodomain: evidence that BP180 spans the lamina lucida. *J Invest Dermatol*, 108, 901–907.
31. Yancey, K.B., Kirtschig, G., Yee, C. et al (1995) Studies of patients with anti-epiligrin cicatricial pemphigoid. *J Dermatol*, 22, 829–835.
32. Chan, L.S., Majmudar, A.A., Tran, H.H. et al (1997) Laminin-6 and laminin-5 are recognized by autoantibodies in a subset of cicatricial pemphigoid. *J Invest Dermatol*, 108, 848–853.
33. Bhol, K.C., Goss, L., Kumari, S. et al (2001) Autoantibodies to human alpha6 integrin in patients with oral pemphigoid. *J Dent Res*, 80, 1711–1715.

Desquamative gingivitis

Desquamative gingivitis is a chronic condition of adults, usually women (4:1), affecting either the gingiva diffusely or multifocally. It presents as friable, fiery red, painful, eroded, denuded attached gingiva, primarily on the facial or buccal aspect, with occasional areas of ulceration.[1,2] In approximately half the cases of desquamative gingivitis, the gingiva is the only site affected by disease.

Desquamative gingivitis represents a distinct clinical manifestation of autoimmune blistering diseases, hypersensitivity reactions or oral lichen planus.[2-4] Large studies of desquamative gingivitis have shown that cicatricial pemphigoid accounts for 35-64% of cases of desquamative gingivitis, lichen planus for 25-42% of cases, and pemphigus vulgaris for 3-21% of cases; 10-33% of cases have non-specific findings.[3,5-7]

Occasional cases of linear IgA disease and epidermolysis bullosa acquisita have also been diagnosed in patients with desquamative gingivitis.

References

1. Nisengard, R.J., Alpert, A.M., Krestow, V. (1978) Desquamative gingivitis: immunologic findings. *J Periodontol*, **49**, 27–32.
2. Rogers, R.S.I., Sheridan, P.J., Nightingale, S.H. (1982) Desquamative gingivitis: clinical, histopathologic, immunopathologic and therapeutic observations. *J Am Acad Dermatol*, **7**, 729–735.
3. Nisengard, R.J., Neiders, M. (1981) Desquamative lesions of the gingiva. *J Periodontol*, **52**, 500–510.
4. Scully, C., Porter, S.R. (1997) The clinical spectrum of desquamative gingivitis. *Semin Cutan Med Surg*, **16**, 308–313.
5. Sklavounou, A., Laskaris, G. (1983) Frequency of desquamative gingivitis in skin diseases. *Oral Surg Oral Med Oral Pathol*, **56**, 141–144.
6. Nisengard, R.J., Rogers, R.S. 3rd (1987) The treatment of desquamative gingival lesions. *J Periodontol*, **58**, 167–172.
7. Yih, W.Y., Maier, T., Kratochvil, F.J. et al (1998) Analysis of desquamative gingivitis using direct immunofluorescence in conjunction with histology. *J Periodontol*, **69**, 678–685.

Pemphigus

Clinical features

Oral pemphigus vulgaris typically begins in the sixth decade of life with an equal gender distribution, or perhaps slight female predilection. The mouth is involved in up to 87% of cases.[1-3] Lesions in the oral cavity precede those at other sites in 56-85% of cases.[4,5] The mouth is the only site of involvement in 45% of cases and the buccal mucosa, tongue, palate and floor of mouth are most often affected (*Fig. 10.178*).[3,5] Pemphigus vulgaris presents as desquamative gingivitis in 62% of cases.[6]

In a review of patients with pemphigus vegetans, 92% showed oral involvement.[7] Some of these lesions take the form of a cerebriform tongue that exhibits acantholytic changes on biopsy.[8]

In paraneoplastic pemphigus, the oral mucosa is involved in all cases with persistent, painful, treatment-resistant erosions of the oropharynx and lips; the crusting vermilion lesions are reminiscent of Stevens–Johnson syndrome.[9,10]

Pemphigus variants are considered in greater detail in Chapter 4.

Histological features

Biopsies of lesional tissue of pemphigus vulgaris reveal suprabasilar acantholysis and clefting.[11] Pemphigus vegetans in addition shows papillary epithelial hyperplasia and eosinophilic abscesses.[7]

In paraneoplastic pemphigus there is suprabasilar acantholysis in addition to individual keratinocyte necrosis and vacuolar interface change, suggestive of a lichenoid inflammatory process.[9]

Direct immunofluorescence studies in pemphigus vulgaris and vegetans reveal characteristic staining of the epithelial intercellular space with IgG in all cases with active untreated disease.[11]

In paraneoplastic pemphigus, direct immunofluorescence shows deposition of IgG in the intercellular space, and granular–linear deposition of complement in the intercellular space and along the basement membrane zone.[9]

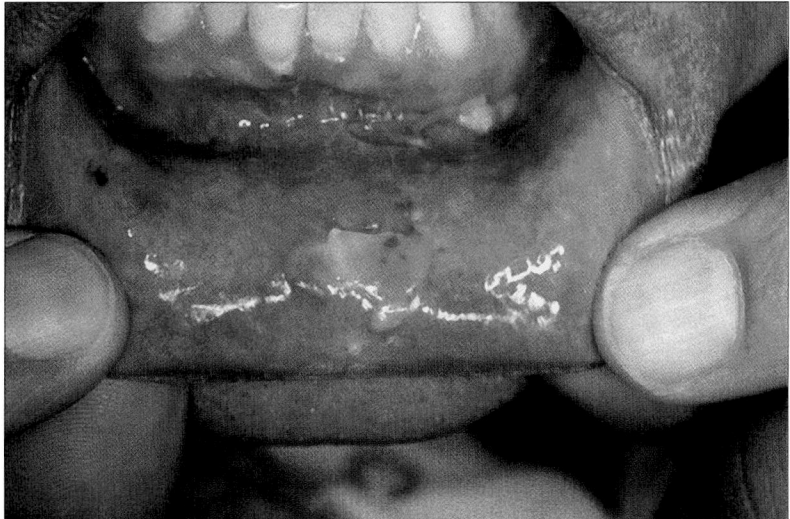

Fig. 10.178
Pemphigus vulgaris: this presented as an ulcer on the lower labial mucosa.

References

1. Laskaris, G., Sklavounou, A., Stratigos, J. (1982) Bullous pemphigoid, cicatricial pemphigoid, and pemphigus vulgaris. A comparative clinical survey of 278 cases. *Oral Surg Oral Med Oral Pathol*, **54**, 656–662.
2. Lamey, P.J., Rees, T.D., Binnie, W.H. et al (1992) Oral presentation of pemphigus vulgaris and its response to systemic steroid therapy. *Oral Surg Oral Med Oral Pathol*, **74**, 54–57.
3. Robinson, J.C., Lozada-Nur, F., Frieden, I. (1997) Oral pemphigus vulgaris: a review of the literature and a report on the management of 12 cases. *Oral Surg Oral Med Oral Pathol Oral Radiol Endod*, **84**, 349–355.
4. Pisanti, S., Sharav, Y., Kaufman E. et al (1974) Pemphigus vulgaris: incidence in Jews of different ethnic groups, according to age, sex, and initial lesion. *Oral Surg Oral Med Oral Pathol*, **38**, 382–387.
5. Laskaris, G., Sklavounou, A., Angelopoulos, A. (1982) Direct immunofluorescence in oral lichen planus. *Oral Surg Oral Med Oral Pathol*, **53**, 483–487.
6. Sklavounou, A., Laskaris, G. (1983) Frequency of desquamative gingivitis in skin diseases. *Oral Surg Oral Med Oral Pathol*, **56**, 141–144.
7. Ahmed, A.R., Blose, D.A. (1984) Pemphigus vegetans. Neumann type and Hallopeau type. *Int J Dermatol*, **23**, 135–141.
8. Premalatha, S., Jayakumar, S., Yesudian, P. et al (1981) Cerebriform tongue – a clinical sign in pemphigus vegetans. *Br J Dermatol*, **104**, 587–591.
9. Anhalt, G.J., Kim, S.C., Stanley, J.R. et al (1990) Paraneoplastic pemphigus. An autoimmune mucocutaneous disease associated with neoplasia. *N Engl J Med*, **323**, 1729–1735.
10. Camisa, C., Helm, T.N., Liu, Y.C. et al (1992) Paraneoplastic pemphigus: a report of three cases including one long-term survivor. *J Am Acad Dermatol*, **27**, 547–553.
11. Daniels, T.E., Quadra-White, C. (1981) Direct immunofluorescence in oral mucosal disease: a diagnostic analysis of 130 cases. *Oral Surg Oral Med Oral Pathol*, **51**, 38–47.

Linear IgA disease

Clinical features

Oral mucosal lesions associated with linear IgA disease occur in 26–100% of cases and present as vesicles, bullae, erosions or ulcerations.[1–3] They may be located on the palate, buccal or labial mucosa, and oropharynx.[3–6] The condition sometimes manifests as desquamative gingivitis and erosive cheilitis (*Fig. 10.179*).[1,7–9]

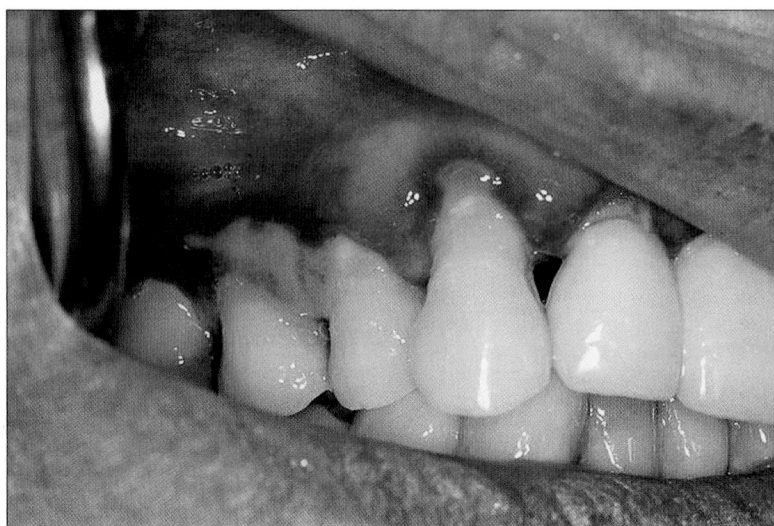

Fig. 10.179
Linear IgA disease: this erythema and ulceration of the gingiva is clinically a desquamative gingivitis.

Histological features

In linear IgA disease, there is a subepithelial vesicle or bulla with neutrophil or eosinophil predominance.[4,5,7,8,10,11] In many lesions, the infiltrate is mixed neutrophilic and eosinophilic. This disease is discussed in detail on page 134. In one report, the infiltrate was lichenoid.[11]

Direct immunofluorescence studies reveal homogeneous smooth linear deposits of IgA along the basement membrane zone.[1,4,5,7,8,10,11] Deposits of C3 may also be present.[7]

References

1. Kelly, S.E., Frith, P.A., Millard, P.R. et al (1988) A clinicopathological study of mucosal involvement in linear IgA disease. *Br J Dermatol*, **119**, 161–170.
2. Leonard, J.N., Wright, P., Williams, D.M. et al (1984) The relationship between linear IgA disease and benign mucous membrane pemphigoid. *Br J Dermatol*, **110**, 307–314.
3. Wojnarowska, F., Marsden, R.A., Bhogal, B. et al (1988) Chronic bullous disease of childhood, childhood cicatricial pemphigoid, and linear IgA disease of adults. A comparative study demonstrating clinical and immunopathologic overlap. *J Am Acad Dermatol*, **19**, 792–805.
4. Wiesenfeld, D., Martin, A., Scully, C. et al (1982) Oral manifestations in linear IgA disease. *Br Dent J*, **153**, 398–399.
5. Hietanen, J., Reunala, T. (1984) IgA deposits in the oral mucosa of patients with dermatitis herpetiformis and linear IgA disease. *Scand J Dent Res*, **92**, 230–234.
6. Chan, L.S., Regezi, J.A., Cooper, K.D. (1990) Oral manifestations of linear IgA disease. *J Am Acad Dermatol*, **22**, 362–365.
7. Porter, S.R., Scully, C., Midda, M. et al (1990) Adult linear immunoglobulin A disease manifesting as desquamative gingivitis. *Oral Surg Oral Med Oral Pathol*, **70**, 450–453.
8. Porter, S.R., Bain, S.E., Scully, C.M. (1992) Linear IgA disease manifesting as recalcitrant desquamative gingivitis. *Oral Surg Oral Med Oral Pathol*, **74**, 179–182.
9. Scully, C., Porter, S.R. (1997) The clinical spectrum of desquamative gingivitis. *Semin Cutan Med Surg*, **16**, 308–313.
10. Cowan, C.G., Lamey, P-J., Walsh, M. et al (1995) Linear IgA disease (LAD): immunoglobulin depositions in oral and colonic lesions. *J Oral Pathol Med*, **24**, 374–378.
11. Cohen, D.M., Bhattacharyya, I., Zunt, S.L. et al (1999) Linear IgA disease histopathologically and clinically masquerading as lichen planus. *Oral Surg Oral Med Oral Pathol Oral Radiol Endod*, **88**, 196–201.

Dermatitis herpetiformis

Clinical features

Oral involvement in dermatitis herpetiformis, a condition associated with gluten-sensitive enteropathy, presents as erythematous, pseudo-vesicular, purpuric or erosive lesions in 70% of patients.[1,2] Aphthous-like ulcers accompanied by mucosal erythema and atrophic glossitis have been described in up to 22% of patients.[3]

Histological features

Mucosal biopsies may sometimes reveal neutrophil microabscesses at the epithelial–connective tissue interface, occasional evidence of subepithelial blistering, and eosinophils and lymphocytes in the lamina propria.[1,2] Extravasated erythrocytes are often conspicuous.

Direct immunofluorescence studies reveal granular deposits of IgA in the basement membrane, particularly at the tips of the papillae.[1,2,4]

References

1. Fraser, N.G., Kerr, N.W., Donald, D. (1973) Oral lesions in dermatitis herpetiformis. *Br J Dermatol*, **89**, 439–450.
2. Economopoulou, P., Laskaris, G. (1986) Dermatitis herpetiformis: oral lesions as an early manifestation. *Oral Surg Oral Med Oral Pathol*, **62**, 77–80.
3. Lahteenoja, H., Irjala, K., Viander, M. et al (1998) Oral mucosa is frequently affected in patients with dermatitis herpetiformis. *Arch Dermatol*, **134**, 756–758.
4. Hietanen, J., Reunala, T. (1984) IgA deposits in the oral mucosa of patients with dermatitis herpetiformis and linear IgA disease. *Scand J Dent Res*, **92**, 230–234.

Epidermolysis bullosa acquisita

Clinical features

The oral mucosa is involved in from 53 to 64% of cases, although in many reports the nature of the lesions is not documented.[1,2] However, all 11 cases of epidermolysis bullosa acquisita in children in one series had involvement of the buccal mucosa, some taking the form of desquamative gingivitis.[3]

Histological features

The histological features are variable. In some lesions, there is a cell-free subepithelial blister (classical variant) whereas in others, a neutrophil-rich or eosinophil-rich lesion is seen.

Direct immunofluorescence studies show linear deposits of IgG and C3 at the basement membrane zone similar to lesions of pemphigoid.[4] Circulating anti-basement membrane antibodies localize exclusively to the floor of the blister in salt-split skin.[5] This disease is discussed in detail on page 123.

References

1. Wojnarowska, F., Marsden, R.A., Bhogal, B. et al (1988) Chronic bullous disease of childhood, childhood cicatricial pemphigoid, and linear IgA disease of adults. A comparative study demonstrating clinical and immunopathologic overlap. *J Am Acad Dermatol*, **19**, 792–805.
2. Matsumura, Y., Hamanaka, H., Horiguchi, Y. et al (1993) Epidermolysis bullosa acquisita (EBA) with nonclassical distribution of eruptions. *J Dermatol*, **20**, 159–163.

3. Callot-Mellot, C., Bodemer, C., Caux, F. et al (1997) Epidermolysis bullosa acquisita in childhood. *Arch Dermatol*, **133**, 1122–1126.
4. Gammon, W.R., Briggaman, R.A., Woodley, D.T. et al (1984) Epidermolysis bullosa acquisita – a pemphigoid-like disease. *J Am Acad Dermatol*, **11**, 820–832.
5. Gammon, W.R., Inman, A.O. 3rd, Wheeler, C.E. Jr (1984) Differences in complement-dependent chemotactic activity generated by bullous pemphigoid and epidermolysis bullosa acquisita immune complexes: demonstration by leukocytic attachment and organ culture methods. *J Invest Dermatol*, **83**, 57–61.

Lupus erythematosus

Clinical features

Oral involvement – mainly in the form of ulcers, erythema with or without white striations, exfoliative areas and discoid plaques – is seen in 26–45% of patients with systemic lupus erythematosus, presenting primarily on the hard palate, buccal mucosa and lips. Some lesions cause burning or soreness while others are asymptomatic.[1–4] Not surprisingly in bullous lupus erythematosus, oral ulcers are occasionally seen.[5,6]

In patients with discoid lupus erythematosus, oral lesions in the form of white plaques, papules and striations associated with erosions and ulcers are seen in 5–50% of cases.[7] These often have a lichen planus-like appearance (see *Fig. 10.148*).

Histological features

Oral lesions of both systemic and discoid lupus erythematosus exhibit hyperparakeratosis or hyperorthokeratosis, epithelial hyperplasia or atrophy, liquefactive degeneration of the basal cells, subepithelial PAS-positive deposits, perivascular inflammatory infiltrates (with some cases showing a band-like lichenoid infiltrate) and collagen degeneration (see *Fig. 10.162*).[2,8,9] This disease is discussed in detail on page 775.

References

1. Urman, J.D., Lowenstein, M.B., Abeles, M. et al (1978) Oral mucosal ulceration in systemic lupus erythematosus. *Arthritis Rheum*, **21**, 58–61.
2. Jonsson, R., Heyden, G., Westberg, N.G. et al (1984) Oral mucosal lesions in systemic lupus erythematosus – a clinical, histopathological and immunopathological study. *J Rheumatol*, **11**, 38–42.
3. Worrall, J.G., Snaith, M.L., Batchelor, J.R. et al (1990) SLE: a rheumatological view. Analysis of the clinical features, serology and immunogenetics of 100 SLE patients during long-term follow-up. *Q J Med*, **74**, 319–330.
4. Callen, J.P. (1997) Oral manifestations of collagen vascular disease. *Semin Cutan Med Surg*, **16**, 323–327.
5. Yell, J.A., Mbuagbaw, J., Burge, S.M. (1996) Cutaneous manifestations of systemic lupus erythematosus. *Br J Dermatol*, **135**, 355–362.
6. Lalova, A., Pramatarov, K., Vassileva, S. (1997) Facial bullous systemic lupus erythematosus. *Int J Dermatol*, **36**, 369–371.
7. Schiodt, M., Halberg, P., Hentzer, B. (1978) A clinical study of 32 patients with oral discoid lupus erythematosus. *Int J Oral Surg*, **7**, 85–94.
8. Shklar, G., McCarthy, P.L. (1978) Histopathology of oral lesions of discoid lupus erythematosus. A review of 25 cases. *Arch Dermatol*, **114**, 1031–1035.
9. Karjalainen, T.K., Tomich, C.E. (1989) A histopathologic study of oral mucosal lupus erythematosus. *Oral Surg Oral Med Oral Pathol*, **67**, 547–554.

Reactive salivary gland disease

Mucocele

Clinical features

In mucocele (mucous extravasation/retention phenomenon, sialocyst, ranula, salivary duct cyst) the most frequent variant is the mucous *extravasation* type, caused by a tear in the excretory duct and spillage of mucin into the connective tissue. This usually arises in children and young adults and the most common locations are the lower labial mucosa (59–73%), buccal mucosa (11–17%), floor of mouth (7–12%) and ventral tongue (4%) (*Fig. 10.180*).[1–3] It presents as a dome-shaped, fluctuant, bluish and sessile lesion, which often increases and decreases in size.

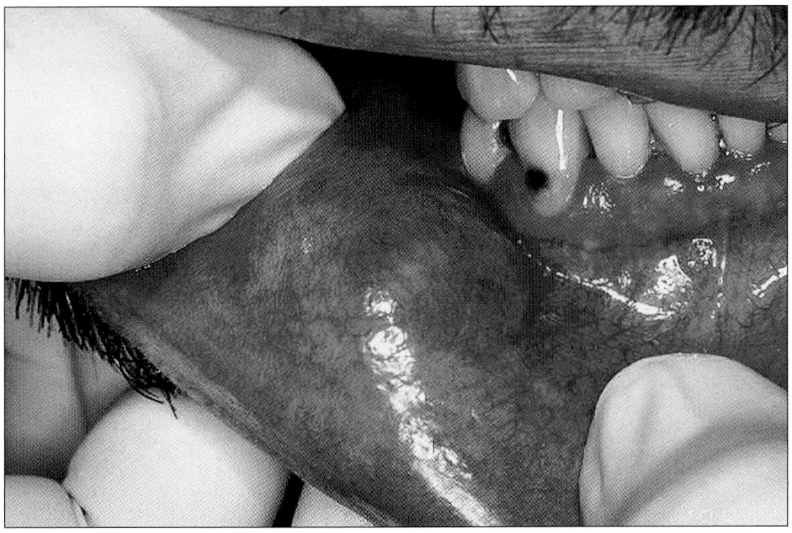

Mucous *retention* cysts result from dilatation of the duct, caused by a distal obstruction. The patients are older and the most common sites are the floor of mouth (50%), buccal mucosa and upper lip.[2]

Superficial mucoceles are distinctly vesicular or dewdrop-like, raising the suspicion of a herpetic infection or autoimmune vesiculobullous disease and occur in older adults, particularly on the palate, retromolar pad and buccal mucosa (*Fig. 10.181*).[4,5]

Floor of mouth mucoceles, when large, are also called ranulas and these may extend below the mylohyoid muscle presenting extraorally as a 'plunging ranula'.[6] There is recurrence in approximately 2% of cases.[1]

Histological features

Extravasation mucoceles consist of pools of mucin containing muciphages and often many neutrophils surrounded by condensed granulation tissue with associated muciphages (*Figs 10.182, 10.183*).[1,2] Some specimens consist only of the collapsed wall of granulation tissue or even a solid mass of granulation tissue containing muciphages (*Fig. 10.184*). Mucin may be dispersed in the inter- and intralobular connective tissue. Portions of a metaplastic duct are seen in 20% of cases.[2] Occasionally, eosinophilic globular masses are present within the mucin pools.[7]

Superficial mucoceles exhibit pools of mucin that are bordered superiorly by surface squamous epithelium only.[5,8]

Retention cysts are lined by cuboidal or columnar epithelium, often with mucous cells or foci of squamous metaplasia; more than half may be lined by oncocytic cells, sometimes with papillary projections (*Figs 10.185, 10.186*).[4] These may also be referred to as oncocytic sialocysts.

Fig. 10.180
Mucocele: note the bluish sessile nodule on the lower labial mucosa, a typical site.

The least common variant is the mucopapillary cyst which is frequently multiloculated and lined by stratified squamous or columnar epithelium with pronounced mucous cell metaplasia and luminal papillary projections.[4] The associated minor salivary glands often exhibit varying degrees of acinar atrophy, ductal dilatation and interstitial chronic inflammation with fibrosis.

Differential diagnosis

Parulides (gum-boils) of the gingiva can sometimes be mistaken for extravasation mucoceles. However, neither pools of mucin nor muciphages are present and microabscesses and sinus tracts are almost always evident.

The mucopapillary retention cyst is distinguished from mucoepidermoid carcinoma by the lack of infiltration of the stroma and absence of discrete, solid islands of neoplastic epidermoid and mucous cells.

Papillary cystadenomas are true tumors consisting of a proliferation of salivary ductal cells in a cystic configuration. In the major salivary glands, papillary cystadenoma lymphomatosum (Warthin's tumor) shows a prominent lymphoid component in addition to oncocytic lining cells.[9]

References

1. Cataldo, E., Mosadomi, A. (1970) Mucoceles of the oral mucous membrane. *Arch Otolaryngol*, **91**, 360–365.
2. Harrison, J.D. (1975) Salivary mucoceles. *Oral Surg Oral Med Oral Pathol*, **39**, 268–278.
3. Sugerman, P.B., Savage, N.W., Young, W.G. (2000) Mucocele of the anterior lingual salivary glands (glands of Blandin and Nuhn): report of 5 cases. *Oral Surg Oral Med Oral Pathol Oral Radiol Endod*, **90**, 478–482.
4. Eversole, L.R. (1987) Oral sialocysts. *Arch Otolaryngol*, **113**, 51–56.
5. Bermejo, A., Aguirre, J.M., López, P. et al (1999) Superficial mucocele: report of 4 cases. *Oral Surg Oral Med Oral Pathol Oral Radiol Endod*, **88**, 469–472.
6. Quick, C.A., Lowell, S.H. (1977) Ranula and the sublingual salivary glands. *Arch Otolaryngol*, **103**, 397–400.
7. Li, T.J., Kitano, M., Yoshida, A. et al (1997) Myxoglobulosis in an extravasation mucocele of the lower lip. *J Oral Pathol Med*, **26**, 342–344.
8. Eveson, J.W. (1988) Superficial mucoceles: pitfall in clinical and microscopic diagnosis. *Oral Surg Oral Med Oral Pathol*, **66**, 318–322.
9. Fantasia, J.E., Miller, A.S. (1981) Papillary cystadenoma lymphomatosum arising in minor salivary glands. *Oral Surg Oral Med Oral Pathol*, **52**, 411–416.

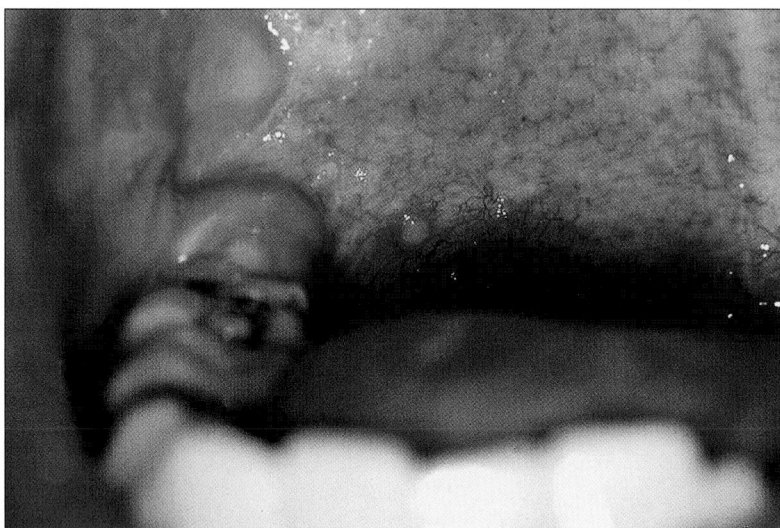

Fig. 10.181
Mucocele: superficial mucoceles on the palate are often clinically mistaken for herpetic infections or autoimmune blistering diseases.

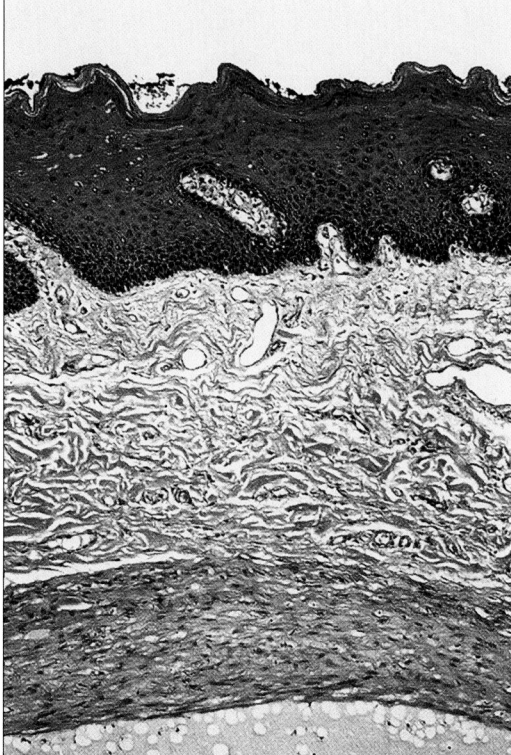

Fig. 10.183
Mucocele: there is no epithelium in the lining, just condensed granulation tissue.

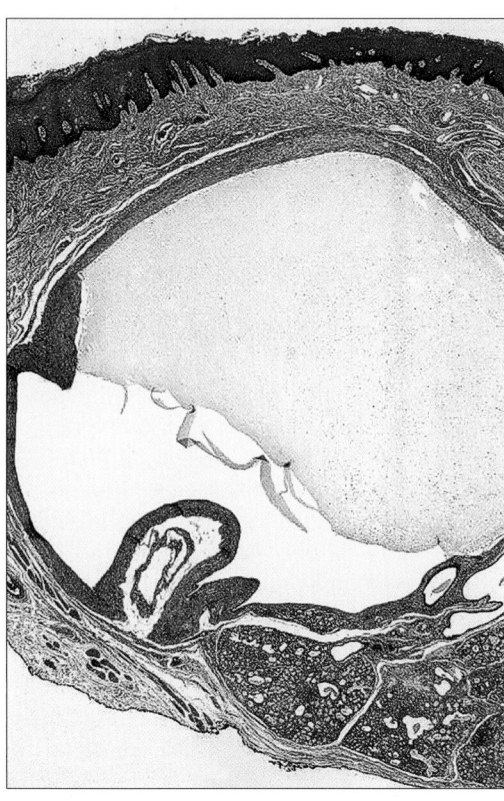

Fig. 10.182
Mucocele: the cyst-like cavity filled with mucin lies in the lamina propria.

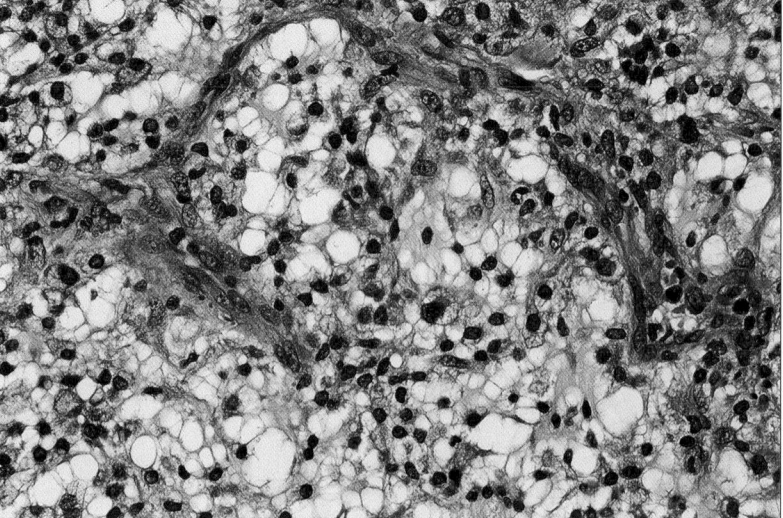

Fig. 10.184
Mucocele: in areas of organization, there are sheets of muciphages with variable amounts of granulation tissue.

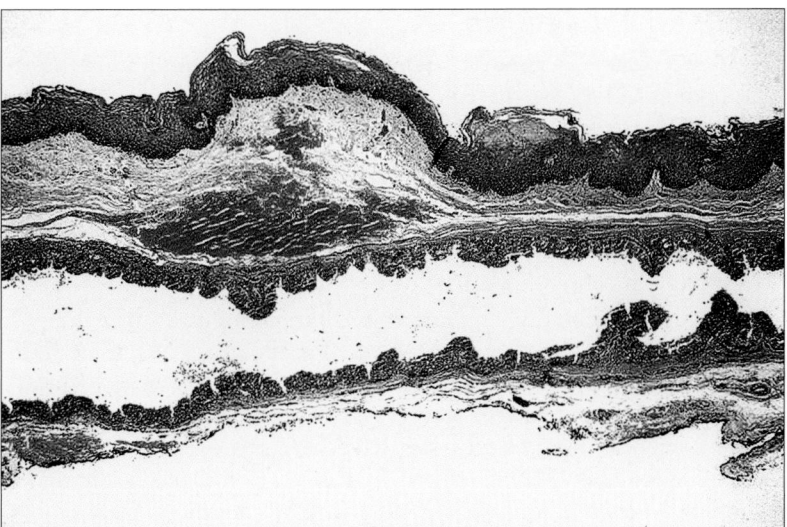

Fig. 10.185
Mucocele: this retention mucocele consists of a grossly ectatic excretory salivary duct; intraluminal papillary projections are evident.

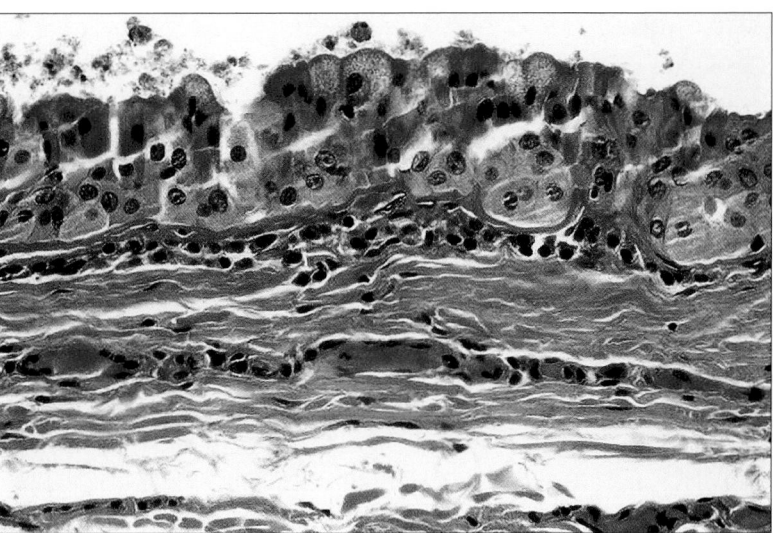

Fig. 10.186
Mucocele: not uncommonly, the lining cells are oncocytic.

Sialolithiasis

Clinical features

In sialolithiasis (salivary gland calculi), affected patients are in their sixth or seventh decade. The most common sites are the upper lip and buccal mucosa which together account for 75–90% of all minor salivary gland lithiasis.[1,2] They present as deep masses, nodules and swellings, sometimes associated with drainage.

Histological features

The calculi have a lamellated appearance with alternating eosinophilic and basophilic bands and a generally homogenous center.[1,2] Globular and granular areas and cellular inclusions may be present. Such calculi generally reside within a cystically dilated excretory duct that exhibits squamous metaplasia and periductal inflammation (*Fig. 10.187*). Bacteria and inflammatory cells may be present between the calculus and the duct lining, or between lamellations. Rupture may lead to acute and chronic inflammation and/or a foreign body reaction. Approximately one-quarter of calculi are unmineralized.[1]

Differential diagnosis

Phleboliths and calcified thrombi are generally not lamellated and occur within vascular lumina lined by endothelial cells.

References

1. Jensen, J.L., Howell, F.V., Rick, G.M. et al (1979) Minor salivary gland calculi. A clinicopathologic study of forty-seven new cases. *Oral Surg Oral Med Oral Pathol*, 47, 44–50.
2. Anneroth, G., Hansen, L.S. (1983) Minor salivary gland calculi. A clinical and histopathological study of 49 cases. *Int J Oral Surg*, 12, 80–89.

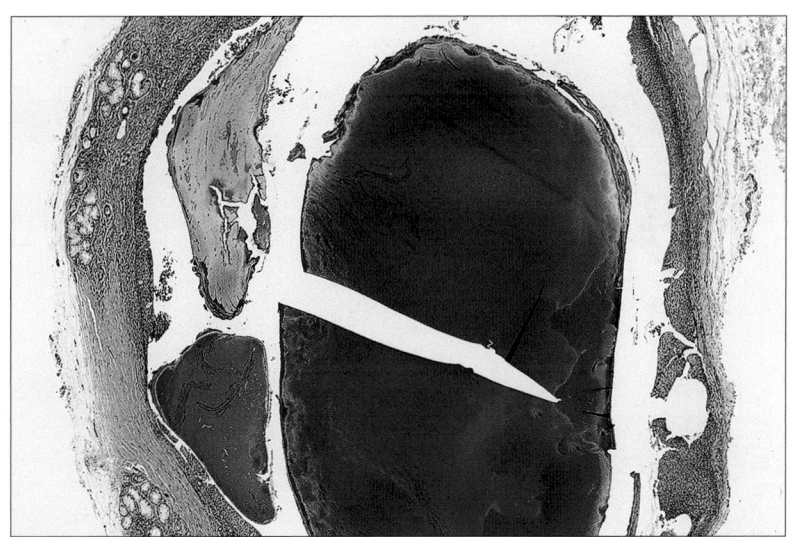

Fig. 10.187
Sialolith: the lith is present within an ectatic salivary duct, the lining of which exhibits squamous metaplasia.

Necrotizing sialometaplasia

Clinical features

This is a self-healing inflammatory condition of salivary glands that may be clinically and histologically mistaken for a malignancy because of its rapidly progressive ulcerative nature and the lack of associated pain in a significant proportion of cases.

Adults (2M:1F) are mainly affected with a mean age of onset in the fifth decade. It usually presents as a painful or painless ulcer or (less often) as a mass, with the majority (approximately 80%) occurring on the hard palate (*Fig. 10.188*). Approximately 10% of cases affect the major glands and (less often) the mucous glands of the nose, maxillary sinus and larynx.[1] One-third of patients give a history of recent surgery at the site. Other predisposing factors include a history of trauma, local anesthetics, alcohol and tobacco use, and there is sometimes an association with tumors.[1] Two cases have been reported in bulimic patients.[2] Generally, healing occurs within 3 weeks of diagnosis.

Pathogenesis and histological features

The putative etiology is vascular compromise leading to infarction of the gland and reactive squamous metaplasia of the ducts and acini. This has been experimentally produced by ligation of salivary ducts and injection with local anesthetics.[3,4] This hypothesis is supported by the development of necrotizing sialometaplasia in a patient with Buerger's disease.[5]

One of the most important features in establishing this diagnosis and distinguishing it from a malignancy, is preservation of the usual lobular architecture of the gland with minimal distortion. Early lesions show infarction of acini resulting in acinar-shaped pools of mucin; more advanced lesions show metaplastic changes with pseudoinvasive islands of benign-appearing squamous epithelium (*Figs 10.189, 10.190*). There is generally a prominent inflammatory infiltrate with granulation tissue formation in later stages.[1,6,7]

Variable features include pseudoepitheliomatous hyperplasia, reactive epithelial atypia and vascular occlusion. Serous and mucoserous glands are less likely to show the necrosis and infarctive changes.[1] Very early lesions may show predominantly mucus spillage.

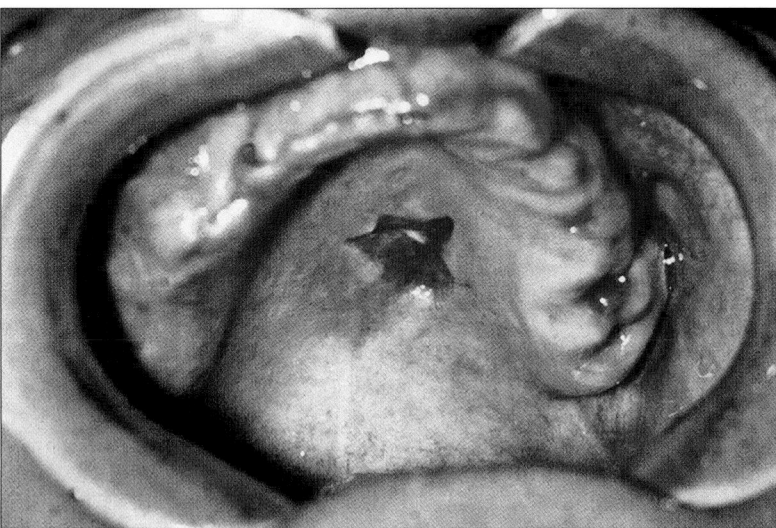

Fig. 10.188
Necrotizing sialometaplasia: there is punched-out ulcer on the hard palate. By courtesy of C. Allen, DDS, Columbus, USA.

Differential diagnosis

The preservation of lobular architecture, lack of infiltration of the surrounding tissues by the epithelial elements, infarction necrosis and generally bland nuclear morphology of the metaplastic islands distinguishes this condition from squamous cell carcinoma and mucoepidermoid carcinoma. Low-grade mucoepidermoid carcinomas exhibit proliferation of mucous cells although this feature is less pronounced in high-grade tumors. The latter, however, will show obvious infiltration of surrounding structures.

Subacute necrotizing sialadenitis characteristically develops in younger patients (third decade), with an almost exclusive location on the palate. Presentation, which is typically acute and over a matter of days, is characterized by a painful, non-ulcerated mass, with rapid resolution within 2 weeks.[8] Since most cases have been reported in the military, there is speculation that this may represent a viral infection that is transmitted between individuals living in close quarters. There is only focal necrosis with little metaplasia. The glands are diffusely infiltrated by a mixed inflammatory infiltrate of neutrophils, lymphocytes, histiocytes and occasionally eosinophils.[9,10] Some contend that subacute necrotizing sialadenitis may fall within the spectrum of necrotizing sialometaplasia but in general, there are sufficient clinical and histological differences to warrant treating them as two distinct entities.

References

1. Brannon, R.B., Fowler, C.B., Hartman, K.S. (1991) Necrotizing sialometaplasia. A clinicopathologic study of sixty-nine cases and review of the literature. *Oral Surg Oral Med Oral Pathol*, **72**, 317–325.
2. Schoning, H., Emshoff, R., Kreczy, A. (1998) Necrotizing sialometaplasia in two patients with bulimia and chronic vomiting. *Int J Oral Maxillofac Surg*, **27**, 463–465.
3. Englander, A., Cataldo, E. (1976) Experimental carcinogenesis in duct–artery ligated rat submandibular gland. *J Dent Res*, **55**, 229–234.
4. Shigematsu, H., Shigematsu, Y., Noguchi, Y. et al (1996) Experimental study on necrotizing sialometaplasia of the palate in rats. Role of local anesthetic injections. *Int J Oral Maxillofac Surg*, **25**, 239–241.
5. Rye, L.A., Calhoun, N.R., Redman, R.S. (1980) Necrotizing sialometaplasia in a patient with Buerger's disease and Raynaud's phenomenon. *Oral Surg Oral Med Oral Pathol*, **49**, 233–236.
6. Abrams, A.M., Melrose, R.J., Howell, F.V. (1973) Necrotizing sialometaplasia. *Cancer*, **32**, 130–135.
7. Anneroth, G., Hansen, L.S. (1982) Necrotizing sialometaplasia. The relationship of its pathogenesis to its clinical characteristics. *Int J Oral Surg*, **11**, 283–291.
8. Fowler, C.B., Brannon, R.B. (2000) Subacute necrotizing sialadenitis: report of 7 cases and a review of the literature. *Oral Surg Oral Med Oral Pathol Oral Radiol Endod*, **89**, 600–609.
9. Werning, J.T., Waterhouse, J.P., Mooney, J.W. (1990) Subacute necrotizing sialadenitis. *Oral Surg Oral Med Oral Pathol*, **70**, 756–759.
10. van der Wal, J.E., Kraaijenhagen, H.A., van der Waal, I. (1995) Subacute necrotising sialadenitis: a new entity? *Br J Oral Maxillofac Surg*, **33**, 302–303.

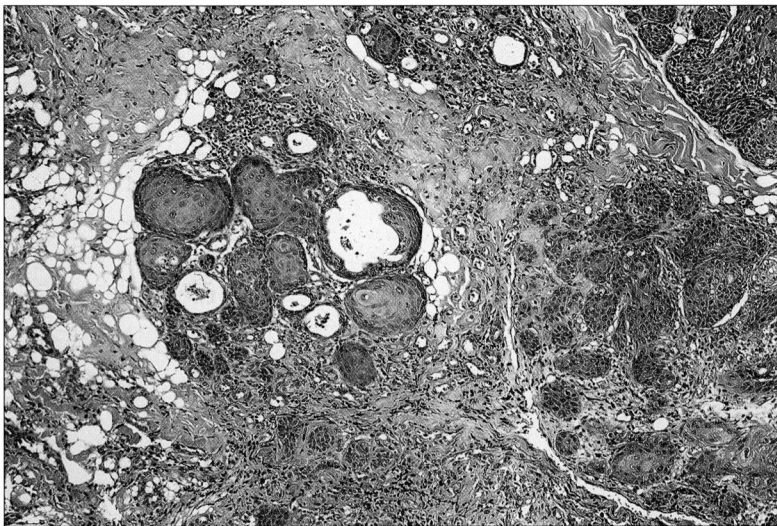

Fig. 10.189
Necrotizing sialometaplasia: there are islands of squamous cells that are organized in the usual salivary gland lobules, with mucous escape and inflammation.

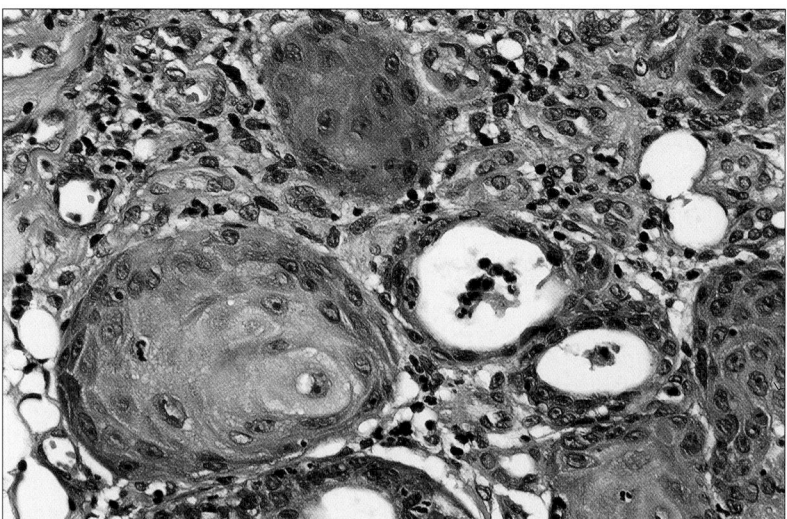

Fig. 10.190
Necrotizing sialometaplasia: the squamous cells are benign and represent metaplastic ducts.

Nicotinic stomatitis

Clinical features

Nicotinic stomatitis (stomatitis nicotina) is associated with pipe smoking and its severity is proportional to the duration of the habit. It is reversible after cessation of pipe smoking.[1–3] It is caused by the heat from the pipe smoke, and not the nicotine itself. The condition has also been noted in a patient who consumed hot beverages.[4]

Early lesions appear as small red punctate areas sometimes associated with whitening of the surrounding mucosa on the posterior half of the palate, a site where many salivary glands are present. Involvement is usually symmetrical. As the lesions progress, the palate may take on a cobblestone appearance with raised white papules having slightly umbilicated central puncta (*Fig. 10.191*).[1,3] The red puncta represent the inflamed ostia of the excretory salivary ducts.

Similar changes have been described in patients who practice reverse smoking (smoking with the lighted end of the cigarette in the mouth as is common in parts of Asia).[5,6]

Histological features

There is hyperparakeratosis or hyperorthokeratosis and acanthosis. The papules represent openings of the excretory salivary ducts that have undergone squamous metaplasia and are usually surrounded by plasma cells and lymphocytes in an edematous stroma (*Figs 10.192, 10.193*).[2,7] Lymphocytes are often seen within the metaplastic ducts. Lobules of minor salivary gland may be present depending on the depth of the biopsy.

Dysplasia or even invasive squamous cell carcinoma may be present in patients who reverse smoke but in general malignant change is not a feature in pipe smokers.[3]

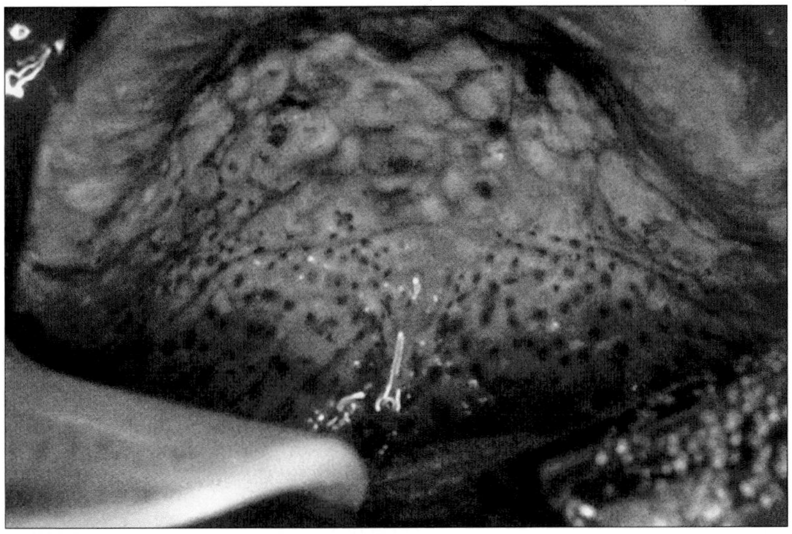

References

1. Forsey, R.R., Sullivan, T.J. (1961) Stomatitis nicotina. *Arch Dermatol*, **83**, 945–950.
2. Schwartz, D.L. (1965) Stomatitis nicotina of the palate. *Oral Surg*, **20**, 306–315.
3. Reddy, C.R., Kameswari, V.R., Ramulu, C. et al (1971) Histopathological study of stomatitis nicotina. *Br J Cancer*, **25**, 403–410.
4. Rossie, K.M., Guggenheimer, J. (1990) Thermally induced 'nicotine' stomatitis. A case report. *Oral Surg Oral Med Oral Pathol*, **70**, 597–599.
5. Gavarasana, S., Susarla, M.D. (1989) Palatal mucosal changes among reverse smokers in an Indian village. *Jpn J Cancer Res*, **80**, 209–211.
6. Ortiz, G.M., Pierce, A.M., Wilson, D.F. (1996) Palatal changes associated with reverse smoking in Filipino women. *Oral Dis*, **2**, 232–237.
7. Reddy, C.R.R.M., Raju, M.V.S., Ramulu, C. et al (1972) Changes in the ducts of the glands of the hard palate in reverse smokers. *Cancer*, **30**, 231–238.

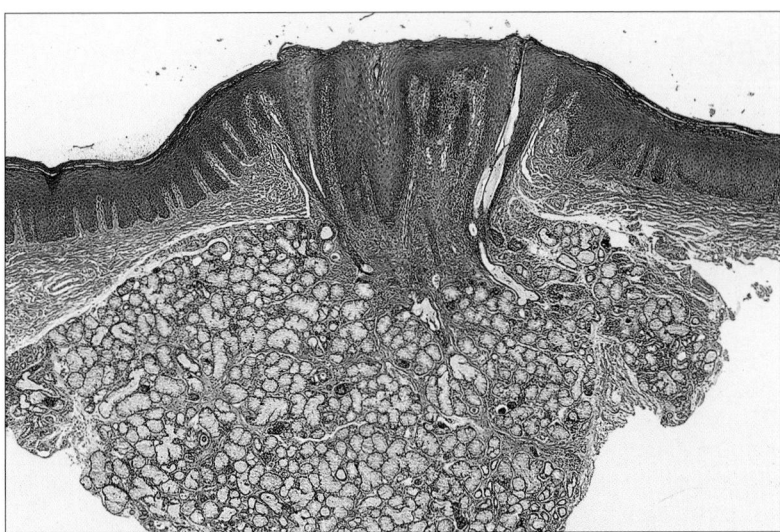

Fig. 10.192
Nicotinic stomatitis: the nodule consists of metaplastic excretory salivary ducts and surrounding chronic inflammation.

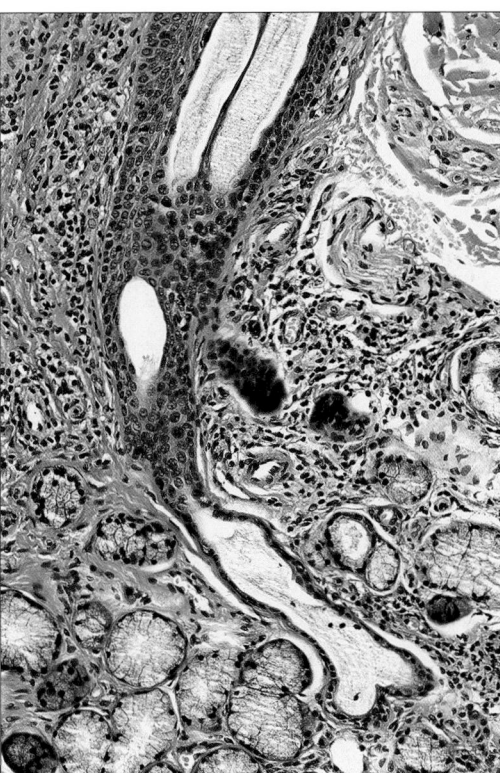

Fig. 10.191
Nicotinic stomatitis: cobblestone appearance of the hard palate in a patient who reverse smokes. By courtesy of L. Lee, DDS, Toronto, Ontario, Canada.

Fig. 10.193
Nicotinic stomatitis: there is chronic inflammation in the surrounding fibrous tissue and lymphocyte exocytosis through the duct epithelium.

Cheilitis glandularis

Clinical features

Cheilitis glandularis (stomatitis glandularis, cheilitis glandularis apostematosa) is a rare chronic, recurrent, inflammatory and, in some cases, suppurative condition of the minor salivary glands, usually of the lower lip. Because salivary glands at other mucosal sites may be affected, the alternative term 'stomatitis glandularis' has been proposed.[1]

Patients present with a painless or painful swelling and eversion of the lip, often with a mucous or mucopurulent discharge through the duct ostia.[1,2] The lip may be dry, scaly and nodular. Simple, deep and deep suppurative forms have been identified.

Pathogenesis and histological features

The etiology is unknown but the condition is likely to represent an inflammatory response to a variety of local irritants. Cases of carcinomatous transformation have occurred in older male patients with outdoor occupations and tobacco smoking; eversion of the lower lip increases its exposure to actinic damage.[3] Factitial injury such as repeated wetting and drying of the lips may also play a role.[4] Familial examples have been reported.[5,6]

There is dilatation and metaplasia (squamous, mucous cell or oncocytic) of the excretory ducts with variable surrounding acute and chronic inflammation. Intraluminal suppuration may be present.[1,2,7,8] The minor salivary glands exhibit non-specific inflammatory changes of acinar atropy, ductal ectasia, interstitial fibrosis and interstitial inflammation (*Fig. 10.194*).[2,8] Hyperplasia or hypertrophy of glands has been refuted in one report.[4]

Differential diagnosis

Similar histological changes are seen in glandular obstruction such as occurs in glands draining into a mucocele and, in particular, in glands that have been plugged by thick mucinous secretions or by small calculi, a common phenomenon in the upper lip. The clinical presentation separates this condition from mucocele or sialolithiasis, both of which are localized and discrete phenomena.

References

1. Lederman, D.A. (1994) Suppurative stomatitis glandularis. *Oral Surg Oral Med Oral Pathol*, **78**, 319–322.
2. Stuller, C.B., Schaberg, S.J., Stokos, J. et al (1982) Cheilitis glandularis. *Oral Surg Oral Med Oral Pathol*, **53**, 602–605.
3. Michalowski, R. (1962) Cheilitis glandularis, heterotopic salivary glands and squamous cell carcinoma of the lip. *Br J Dermatol*, **74**, 445–449.
4. Swerlick, R.A., Cooper, P.H. (1984) Cheilitis glandularis: a re-evaluation. *J Am Acad Dermatol*, **10**, 466–472.
5. Weir, T.W., Johnson, W.C. (1971) Cheilitis glandularis. *Arch Dermatol*, **103**, 433–437.
6. Yacobi, R., Brown, D.A. (1989) Cheilitis glandularis: a pediatric case report. *J Am Dent Assoc*, **118**, 317–318.
7. Rada, D.C., Koranda, F.C., Katz, F.S. (1985) Cheilitis glandularis – a disorder of ductal ectasia. *J Dermatol Surg Oncol*, **11**, 372–375.
8. Winchester, L., Scully, C., Prime, S.S. et al (1986) Cheilitis glandularis: a case affecting the upper lip. *Oral Surg Oral Med Oral Pathol*, **62**, 654–656.

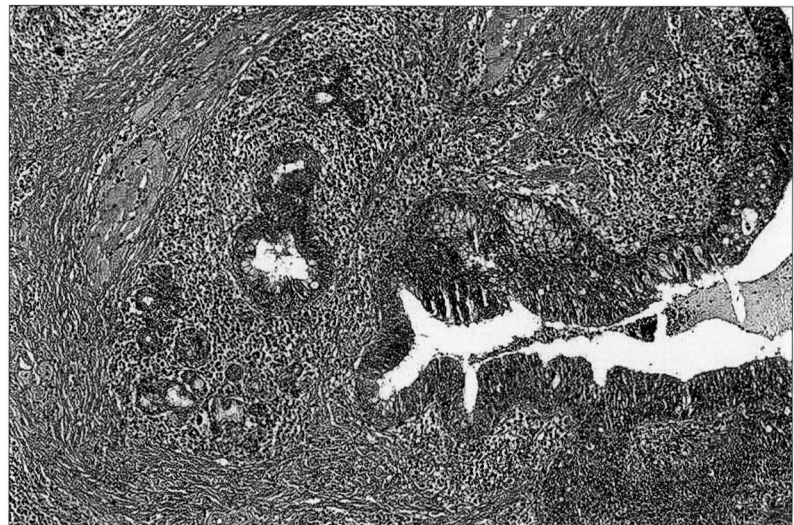

Fig. 10.194
Cheilitis glandularis: there are grossly dilated excretory ducts with mucous cell metaplasia, intraluminal suppuration and surrounding chronic inflammation.

Premalignant conditions

Leukoplakia, erythroplakia and epithelial dysplasia

Clinical features

Leukoplakia, a clinical term, is defined as a white plaque that does not wipe off and cannot be characterized clinically or pathologically as any other disease and is not associated with any physical or chemical agent except tobacco.[1,2] There is a strong association between the appearance of leukoplakia and the use of tobacco products in any form with an incidence rate as high as 15%.[3] Conversely, of all patients who have leukoplakia, 73–90% have a tobacco history.[4–6] Leukoplakia increases in prevalence with age and is present in approximately 3–4% of the general population, usually in the sixth decade in men.[4,7,8]

Clinically, lesions may appear homogenous (in color and texture) or non-homogenous; if the latter they may be referred to as erythroleukoplakia (or speckled leukoplakia), verrucous leukoplakia or nodular leukoplakia (*Figs 10.195–10.197*). The most common sites are the buccal mucosa, gingiva/alveolar mucosa and the palate.[3,9] However, sites associated with dysplasia and carcinoma – so-called 'high risk' sites – are the floor of mouth, tongue and lip (*Fig. 10.198*).[9,10]

Dysplasia, carcinoma-in-situ or invasive squamous cell carcinoma is present in 9–34% of leukoplakias overall.[4,7,9] However, in subcontinental Indians, the rate is generally less than 1%, suggesting alternative factors or that different diagnostic criteria may be at play.[3]

- *Erythroleukoplakia* is associated with an increased risk of dysplasia and malignant transformation.[3,7] The malignant transformation rate of leukoplakia is 5–9%.[11] If epithelial dysplasia is present, the rate increases to 11–36%.[3,6,10] In addition, carcinomatous change occurs more often in patients without a tobacco history.[4,5]

- *Verrucous leukoplakia* most likely represents a precursor lesion of verrucous or papillary squamous carcinoma. Clinically this variant presents as a rough white plaque on the gingiva or alveolar mucosa in patients more than 50 years old with a roughly equal sex distribution.[12]

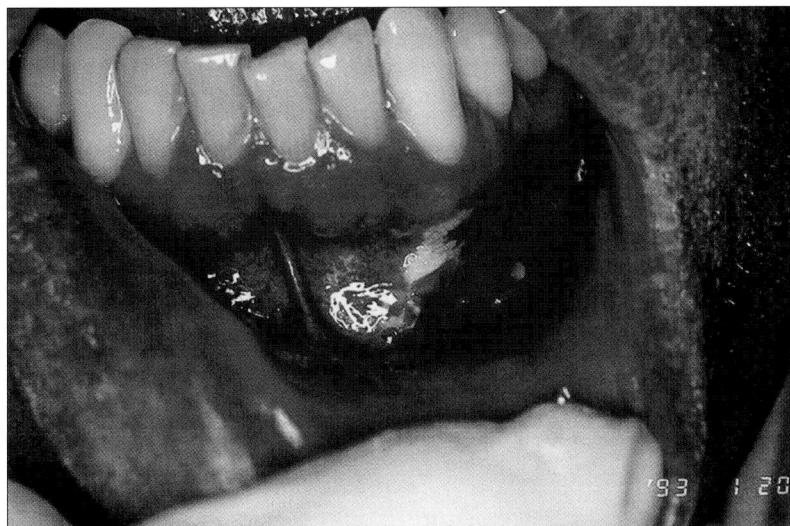

Fig. 10.195
Leukoplakia: there is a small area of homogenous leukoplakia on the mandibular alveolar mucosa. This was histologically benign.

- *Proliferative verrucous leukoplakia* is a persistent and progressive form of leukoplakia that tends to affect women (4:1), with a tobacco habit present in less than 30% of cases.[13,14] It starts as an innocuous leukoplakia that subsequently spreads or develops multifocally, becoming increasingly verrucous over the roughly two decades that it often takes to be recognized (*Figs 10.199, 10.200*). Malignant transformation to squamous cell or verrucous carcinoma occurs in 87–100% of cases.[14,15]
- *Erythroplakia* (similar to erythroplasia) presents as a velvety red papule or plaque that is usually painless. It is much less common than leukoplakia (*Fig. 10.201*). Dysplasia, carcinoma-in-situ or invasive carcinoma is present in 69–91% of cases at the time of biopsy.[16,17]

Pathogenesis and histological features

Leukoplakia is characterized by hyperparakeratosis or hyperorthokeratosis with varying degrees of acanthosis and chronic inflammation. Architectural features of dysplasia include teardrop or bud-shaped rete ridges, often associated with marked papillomatosis such as is seen in verrucous hyperplasia (*Fig. 10.202*). Cytological features are similar to

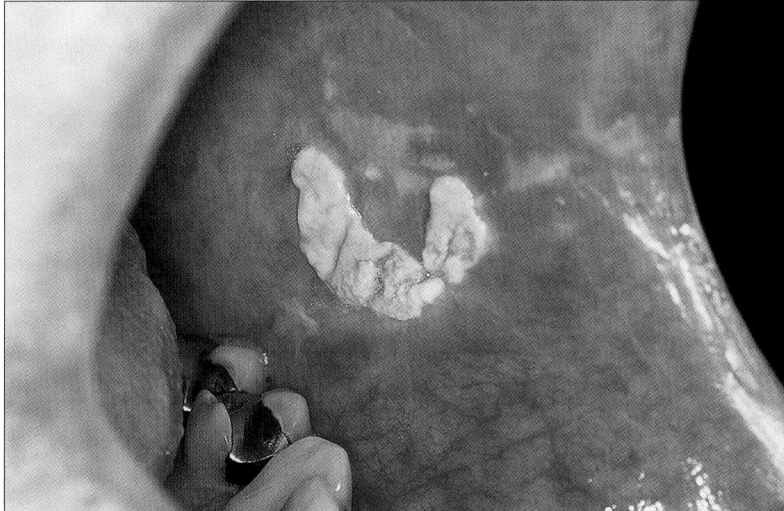

Fig. 10.196
Leukoplakia: there is an area of non-homogenous leukoplakia on the buccal mucosa. This exhibited moderate dysplasia.

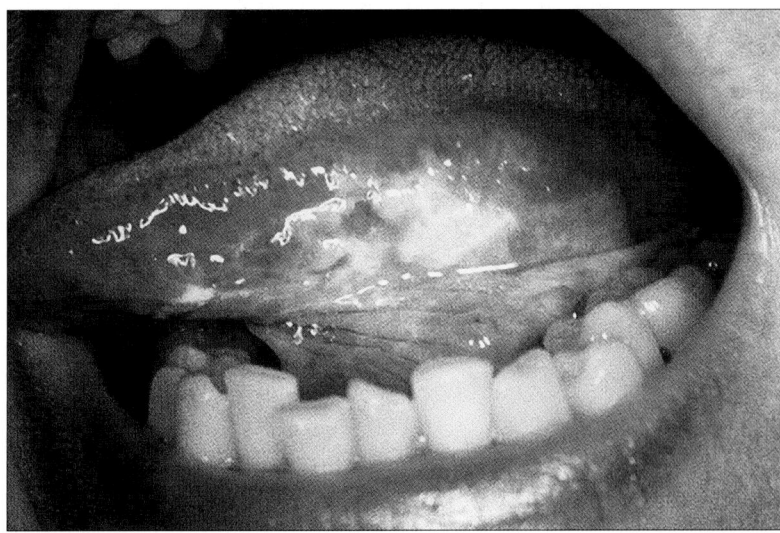

Fig. 10.198
Leukoplakia: this leukoplakia exhibited severe epithelial dysplasia.

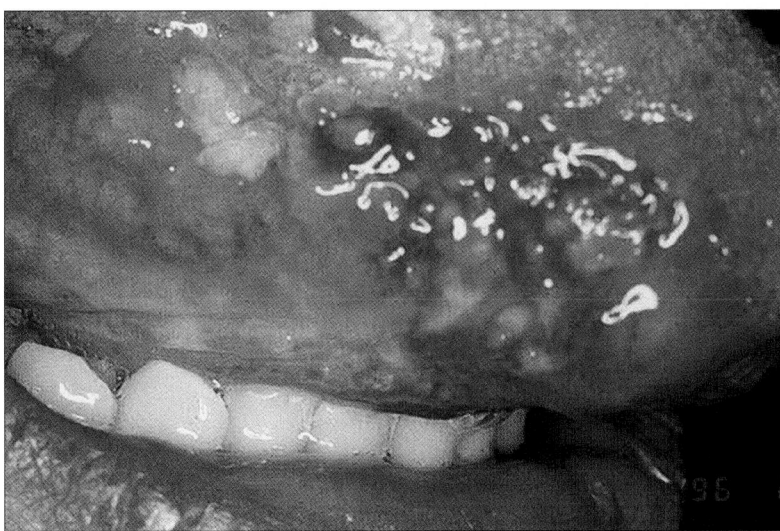

Fig. 10.197
Leukoplakia: erythroleukoplakia on the lateral tongue. This exhibited moderate dysplasia.

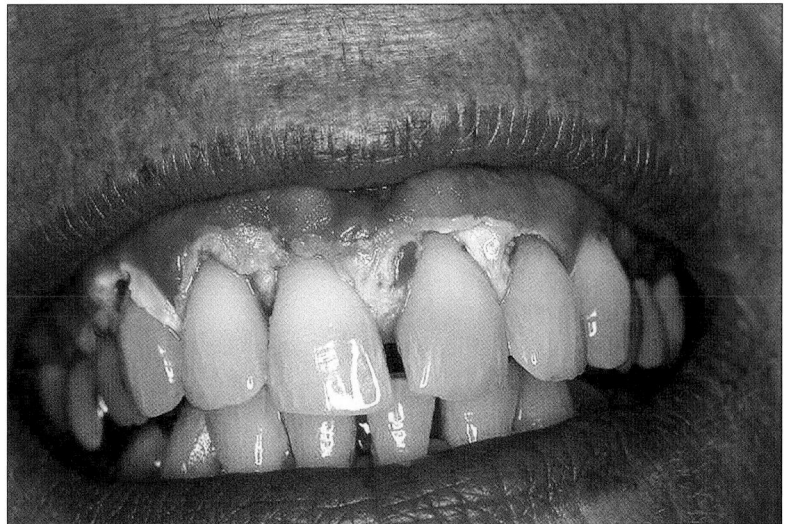

Fig. 10.199
Proliferative verrucous leukoplakia: this patient had been aware of this progressive lesion for approximately 10 years. This was a verrucous carcinoma.

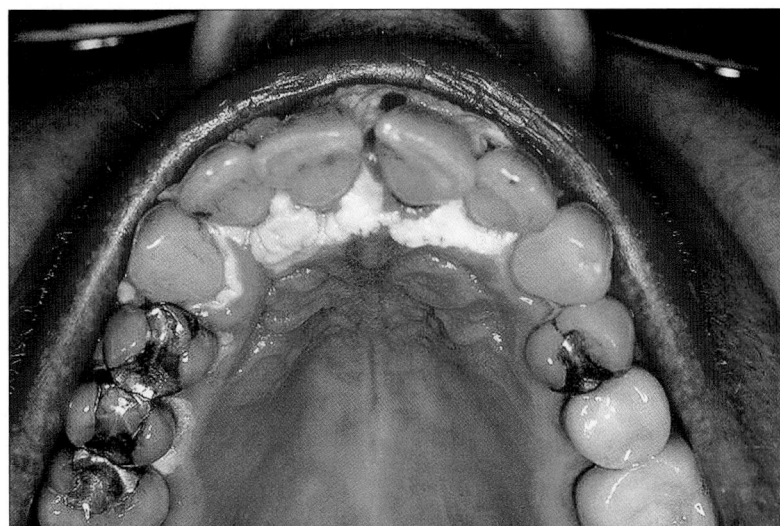

Fig. 10.200
Proliferative verrucous leukoplakia: this is the same patient depicted in *Fig. 10.199*, showing palatal involvement.

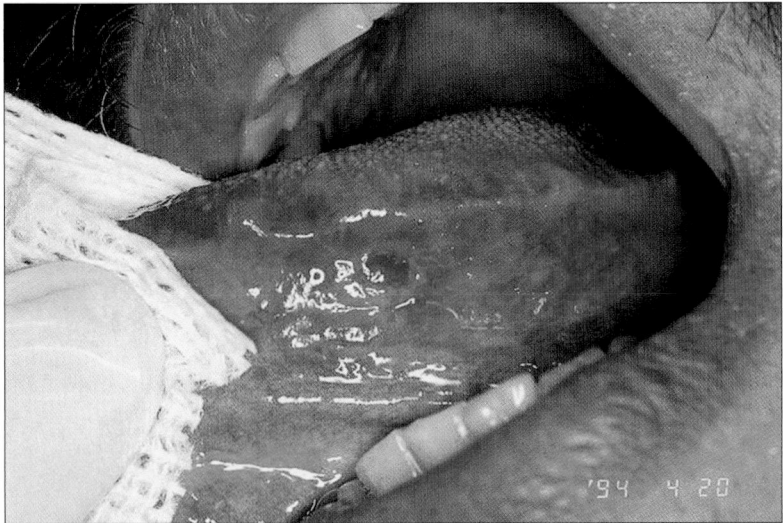

Fig. 10.201
Erythoplakia: this innocuous-appearing red macule on the lateral tongue was an invasive squamous cell carcinoma histologically.

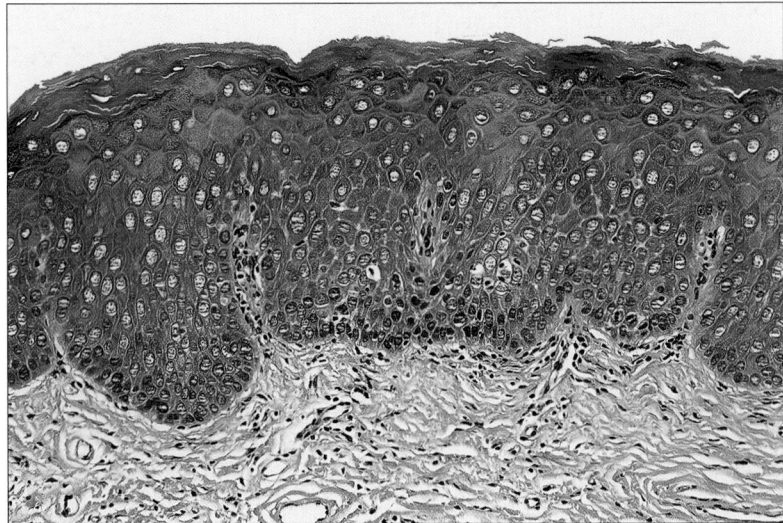

Fig. 10.202
Epithelial dysplasia: there is budding of the rete ridges; dysplastic cells involve less than one-third of the thickness of epithelium.

those used for other epithelia: loss of normal stratification, dyscohesion, dyskeratosis, basal cell hyperplasia, increased nuclear-to-cytoplasmic ratio, mitoses in the mid and upper epithelium, and anaplasia.[2,10,18] By convention, the terms mild, moderate and severe dysplasia are applied if less than one-third, between one- and two-thirds and greater than two-thirds of the epithelium is affected (*Figs 10.203, 10.204*). Full-thickness involvement represents carcinoma-in-situ.

Extension and spread of dysplastic cells from the surface epithelium down excretory salivary ducts (particularly in floor of mouth dysplasias) without evidence of stromal invasion is accompanied by the same

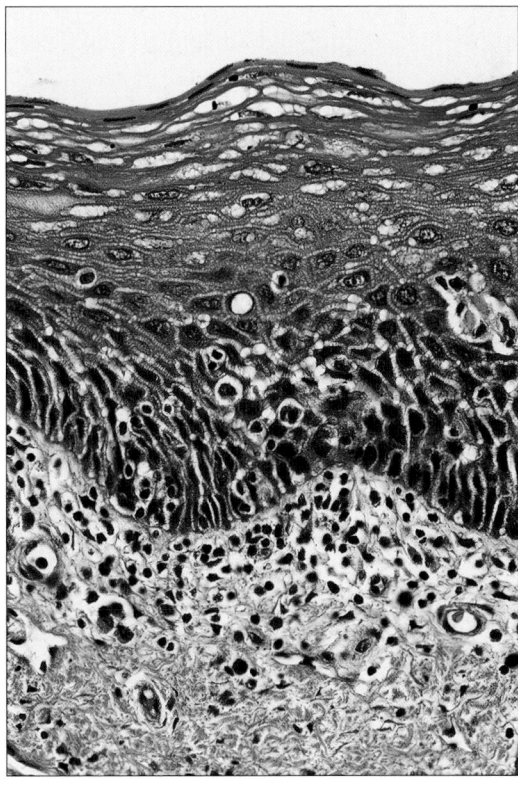

Fig. 10.203
Epithelial dysplasia: dysplastic cells involve greater than one-third but less than two-thirds of the epithelium.

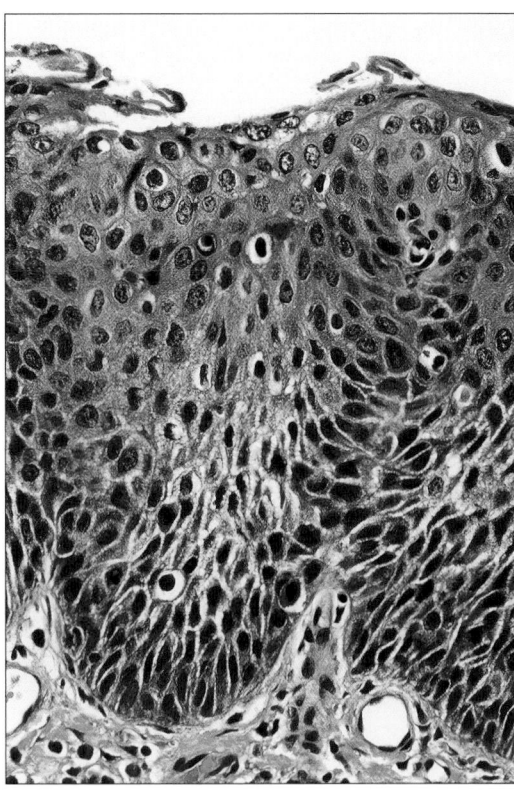

Fig. 10.204
Carcinoma-in-situ: dysplastic cells involve the full thickness of the epithelium.

recurrence rate as for invasive squamous cell carcinoma (*Fig. 10.205*).[19] This may, in part, explain recurrences in the floor of mouth after superficial laser ablation.

Squamous intraepithelial neoplasia is a term used for dysplasia and carcinoma-in-situ of the upper aerodigestive tract, analogous to the concept of cervical intraepithelial neoplasia.[18] Squamous intraepithelial neoplasia connotes not only histomorphological features of malignant change (albeit of a non-invasive lesion) but also molecular and genetic changes of neoplastic transformation.

Allelic imbalance and deletions in chromosome 3 have been reported in dysplastic lesions.[20,21] In particular, there is increased expression of p53 in moderate and severe dysplasia and carcinoma-in-situ.[22–26] p53 has also been demonstrated more frequently in the mucosa of patients who use tobacco.[22,27] The presence of p53 in suprabasal cells correlates with the development of oral squamous cell carcinoma.[28] Inactivation of p16 and changes in cyclin D1 expression have also been reported.[29,30] Telomerase activity is increased in epithelial dysplasia.[31]

A histological diagnosis of verrucous hyperplasia is made for those lesions exhibiting marked hyperorthokeratosis or hyperparakeratosis with the epithelium thrown into slightly endophytic but mostly exophytic papillary projections. This corresponds clinically to verrucous leukoplakia. 'Blunt' and 'sharp' papillary projections are identified with the blunt ones being usually non- to thinly keratinized and the sharp ones being markedly hyperkeratotic (*Figs 10.206, 10.207*).[12] Cytological atypia is minimal. If there is hyperparakeratosis and the papillary fronds of epithelium push endophytically and assume frond-like rete ridges, a diagnosis of verrucous carcinoma should be made (*Figs 10.208, 10.209*).[32,33] Between 20 and 30% of verrucous hyperplasias have been found to harbor human papilloma virus.[34,35]

The histological features of proliferative verrucous leukoplakia are variable. They all show hyperorthokeratosis or hyperparakeratosis and papillomatosis. Epithelial dysplasia may be absent to mild in early lesions. As they spread relentlessly over the mucosa, lesions may show

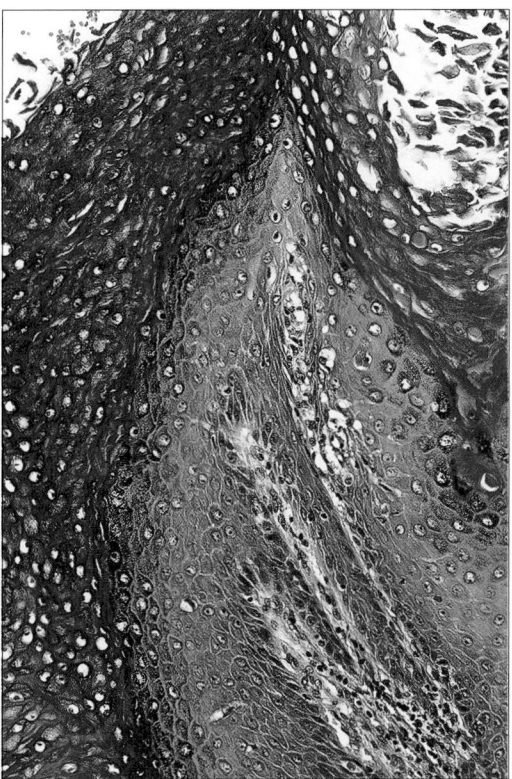

Fig. 10.207
Verrucous hyperplasia: there is hyperorthokeratosis, normal-sized rete ridges and minimal cytological atypia.

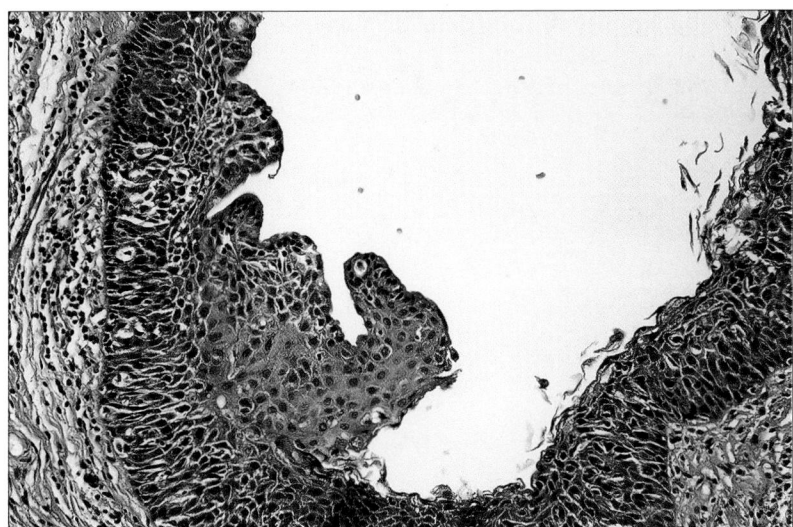

Fig. 10.205
Carcinoma-in-situ: dysplastic cells involve the excretory salivary duct, also in an in-situ pattern; this has important prognostic implications.

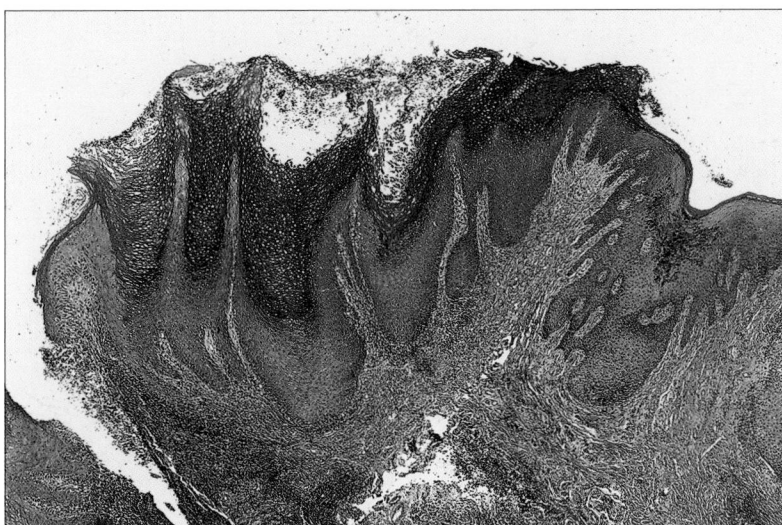

Fig. 10.206
Verrucous hyperplasia: note the exo- and endophytic squamous proliferation with marked hyperkeratosis; normal epithelium is present at one edge.

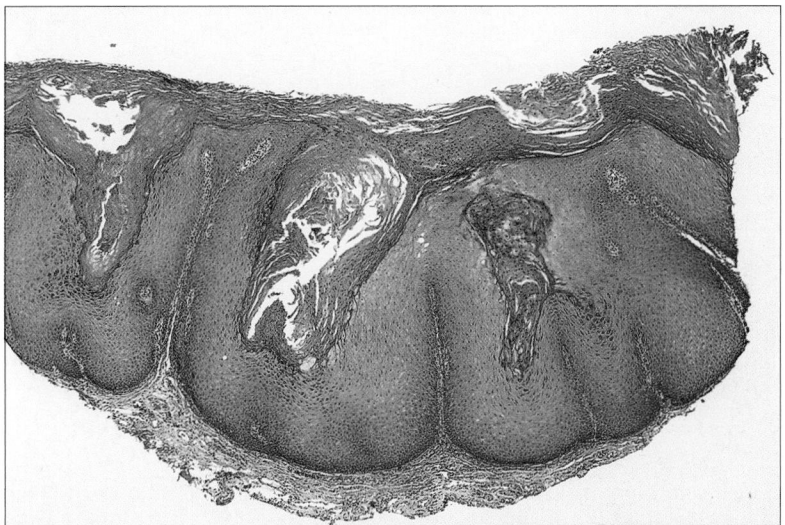

Fig. 10.208
Verrucous hyperplasia/early verrucous carcinoma: note the exo- and endophytic squamous proliferation with bulbous pushing rete ridges.

increasing cytological evidence of dysplasia, more marked exophytic papillomatosis and, finally, an endophytic and/or frankly invasive growth pattern. Conventional squamous cell carcinoma occurs in 70–100% of cases and verrucous carcinoma in up to 30% of cases.[14,15] In one series, 77% of cases were positive for HPV-16.[36] DNA aneuploidy has also been reported.[37]

Differential diagnosis

The use of a sanguinaria-containing dentrifice such as Viadent may lead to a leukoplakia in the maxillary vestibule that exhibits hyperortho-keratosis, atrophy, papillomatosis and usually mild cytological atypia/dysplasia (*Fig. 10.210*).[38,39] No cases have resulted in carcinomatous transformation although discontinuation of the dentrifice has not always led to resolution.

Bowenoid papulosis, a condition of young adults, occurs uncommonly on the lips, tongue and buccal mucosa. In addition to koilocytes, there are atypical, dyskeratotic, apoptotic cells with peculiar fragmented chromatin simulating arrested mitoses involving the full thickness of the epithelium, while the surrounding epithelium exhibits varying degrees of epithelial dysplasia (*Figs 10.211, 10.212*).[40–42] Seventy per cent of cases may be HPV-positive by in situ hybridization and most are positive for high risk HPV-16/18.[42] The authors of another series consider that the term bowenoid papulosis should not be used if dysplasia is present, and recommend that the term 'koilocytic dysplasia' be used instead. In their series, 68% of cases were positive for HPV-16/18.[43]

The term 'lichenoid dysplasia' has been used to denote epithelial dysplasia associated with a band of lymphocytes at the interface, otherwise typical for lichen planus. In such instances, it may be less confusing to use the term 'epithelial dysplasia with lichenoid inflammatory infiltrate'.

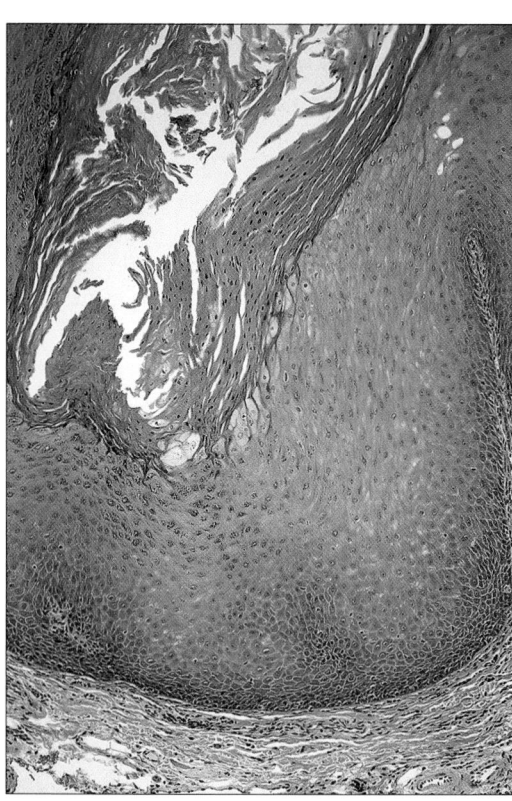

Fig. 10.209
Verrucous hyperplasia/ early verrucous carcinoma: there is hyperparakeratosis, minimal atypia and a broad endophytic front.

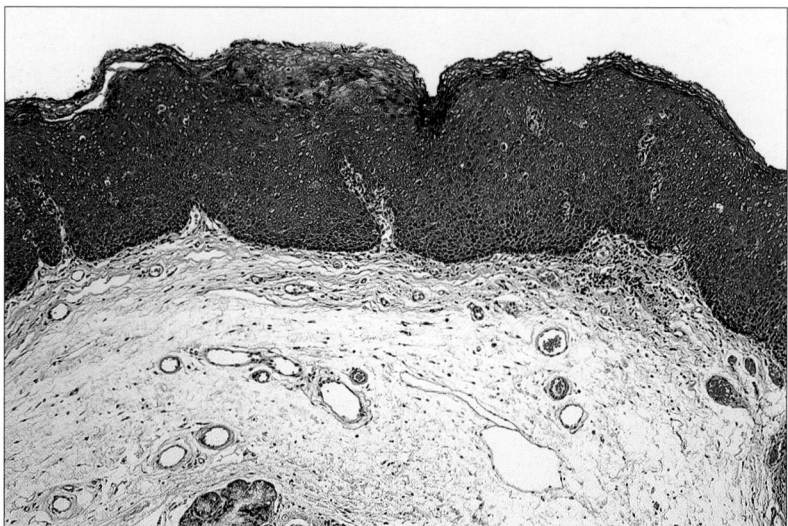

Fig. 10.211
Koilocytic dysplasia: there is carcinoma-in-situ.

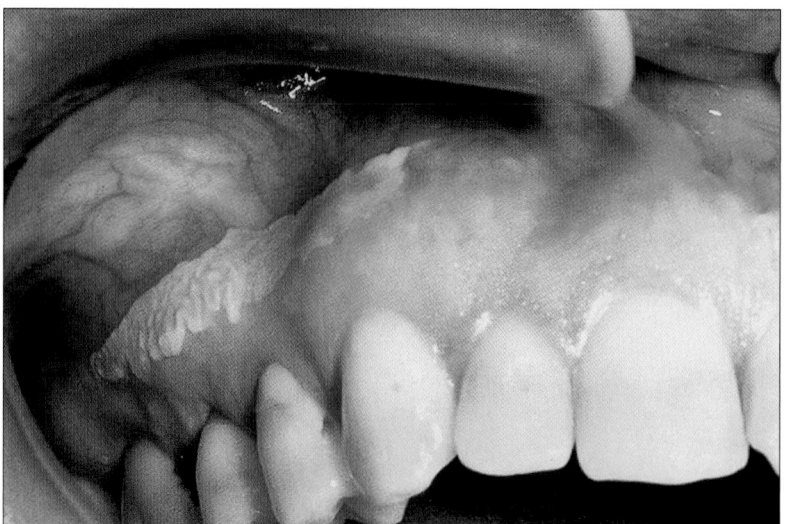

Fig. 10.210
Sanguinaria-induced leukoplakia: the maxillary gingiva and sulcus is a typical location for this condition.

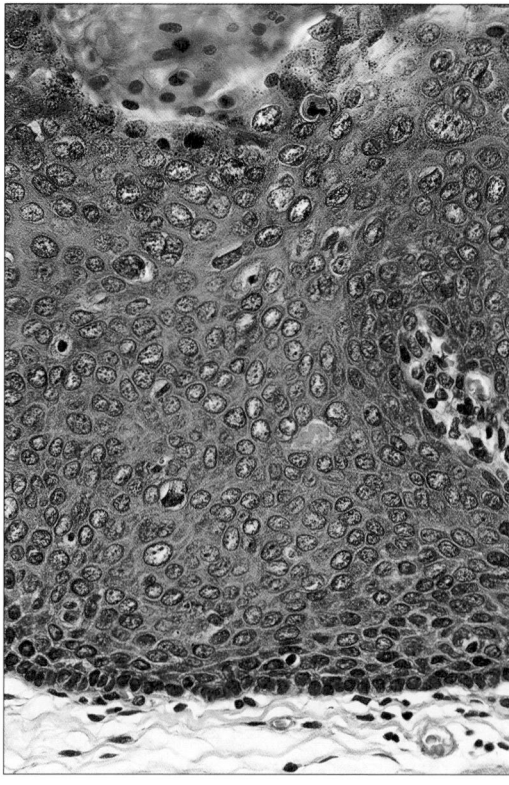

Fig. 10.212
Koilocytic dysplasia: nuclear fragmentation is a characteristic feature of this condition.

References

1. Axell, T., Pindborg, J.J., Smith, C.J. et al (1996) Oral white lesions with special reference to precancerous and tobacco-related lesions: conclusions of an international symposium held in Uppsala, Sweden, May 18–21, 1994. International Collaborative Group on Oral White Lesions. *J Oral Pathol Med*, **25**, 49–54.
2. van der Waal, I., Schepman, K.P., van der Meij, E.H. et al (1997) Oral leukoplakia: a clinicopathological review. *Oral Oncol*, **33**, 291–301.
3. Silverman, S., Bhargava, K., Smith, L.W. et al (1976) Malignant transformation and natural history of oral leukoplakia in 57,518 industrial workers of Gujarat, India. *Cancer*, **38**, 1790–1795.
4. Silverman, S., Gorsky, M., Lozada, F. (1984) Oral leukoplakia and malignant transformation. *Cancer*, **53**, 563–568.
5. Einhorn, J., Wersall, J. (1967) Incidence of oral carcinoma in patients with leukoplakia of the oral mucosa. *Cancer*, **20**, 2189–2193.
6. Mincer, H.H., Coleman, S.A., Hopkins, K.P. (1972) Observations on the clinical characteristics of oral lesions showing histologic epithelial dysplasia. *Oral Surg Oral Med Oral Pathol*, **33**, 389–399.
7. Banoczy, J., Csiba, A. (1976) Occurrence of epithelial dysplasia in oral leukoplakia. Analysis and follow-up study of 12 cases. *Oral Surg Oral Med Oral Pathol*, **42**, 766–774.
8. Axell, T. (1987) Occurrence of leukoplakia and some other oral white lesions among 20 333 adult Swedish people. *Community Dent Oral Epidemiol*, **15**, 46–51.
9. Waldron, C.A., Shafer, W.G. (1975) Leukoplakia revisited: a clinicopathologic study of 3265 oral leukoplakias. *Cancer*, **36**, 1386–1392.
10. Lumerman, H., Freedman, P., Kerpel, S. (1995) Oral epithelial dysplasia and the development of invasive squamous cell carcinoma. *Oral Surg Oral Med Oral Pathol Oral Radiol Endod*, **79**, 321–329.
11. Lind, P.O. (1987) Malignant transformation in oral leukoplakia. *Scand J Dent Res*, **95**, 449–455.
12. Shear, M., Pindborg, J.J. (1980) Verrucous hyperplasia of the oral mucosa. *Cancer*, **46**, 1855–1862.
13. Hansen, L.S., Olson, J.A., Silverman, S. Jr (1985) Proliferative verrucous leukoplakia. A long-term study of thirty patients. *Oral Surg Oral Med Oral Pathol*, **60**, 285–298.
14. Silverman, S. Jr, Gorsky, M. (1997) Proliferative verrucous leukoplakia: a follow-up study of 54 cases. *Oral Surg Oral Med Oral Pathol Oral Radiol Endod*, **84**, 154–157.
15. Zakrzewska, J.M., Lopes, V., Speight, P., Hopper, C. (1996) Proliferative verrucous leukoplakia: a report of ten cases. *Oral Surg Oral Med Oral Pathol Oral Radiol Endod*, **82**, 396–401.
16. Shafer, W.G., Waldron, C.A. (1975) Erythroplakia of the oral cavity. *Cancer*, **36**, 1021–1028.
17. Mashberg, A. (1978) Erythroplasia: the earliest sign of asymptomatic oral cancer. *J Am Dent Assoc*, **96**, 615–620.
18. Crissman, J.D., Visscher, D.W., Sakr, W. (1993) Premalignant lesions of the upper aerodigestive tract: pathologic classification. *J Cell Biochem Suppl*, **17F**, 49–56.
19. Daley, T.D., Lovas, J.G., Peters, E. et al (1996) Salivary gland duct involvement in oral epithelial dysplasia and squamous cell carcinoma. *Oral Surg Oral Med Oral Pathol Oral Radiol Endod*, **81**, 186–192.
20. Emilion, G., Langdon, J.D., Speight, P. et al (1996) Frequent gene deletions in potentially malignant oral lesions. *Br J Cancer*, **73**, 809–813.
21. Roz, L., Wu, C.L., Porter, S. et al (1996) Allelic imbalance on chromosome 3p in oral dysplastic lesions: an early event in oral carcinogenesis. *Cancer Res*, **56**, 1228–1231.
22. Wood, M.W., Medina, J.E., Thompson, G.C. et al (1994) Accumulation of the p53 tumor-suppressor gene product in oral leukoplakia. *Otolaryngol Head Neck Surg*, **111**, 758–763.
23. Sauter, E.R., Cleveland, D., Trock, B. et al (1994) p53 is overexpressed in fifty percent of pre-invasive lesions of head and neck epithelium. *Carcinogenesis*, **15**, 2269–2274.
24. Regezi, J.A., Zarbo, R.J., Regev, E. et al (1995) p53 protein expression in sequential biopsies of oral dysplasias and in situ carcinomas. *J Oral Pathol Med*, **24**, 18–22.
25. Mao, E.J., Schwartz, S.M., Daling, J.R. et al (1996) Human papilloma viruses and p53 mutations in normal pre-malignant and malignant oral epithelia. *Int J Cancer*, **69**, 152–158.
26. Girod, S.C., Pfeiffer, P., Ries, J. et al (1998) Proliferative activity and loss of function of tumour suppressor genes as 'biomarkers' in diagnosis and prognosis of benign and preneoplastic oral lesions and oral squamous cell carcinoma. *Br J Oral Maxillofac Surg*, **36**, 252–260.
27. van Oijen, M.G., van de Craats, J.G., Slootweg, P.J. (1999) p53 overexpression in oral mucosa in relation to smoking. *J Pathol*, **187**, 469–474.
28. Cruz, I.B., Snijders, P.J., Meijer, C.J. et al (1998) p53 expression above the basal cell layer in oral mucosa is an early event of malignant transformation and has predictive value for developing oral squamous cell carcinoma. *J Pathol*, **184**, 360–368.
29. Papadimitrakopoulou, V., Izzo, J., Lippman, S.M. et al (1997) Frequent inactivation of p16INK4a in oral premalignant lesions. *Oncogene*, **14**, 1799–1803.
30. Liu, S.C., Hu, Y., Sauter, E.R. et al (1999) Image analysis of p53 and cyclin D1 expression in premalignant lesions of the oral mucosa. *Anal Quant Cytol Histol*, **21**, 166–173.
31. Mutirangura, A., Supiyaphun, P., Trirekapan, S. et al (1996) Telomerase activity in oral leukoplakia and head and neck squamous cell carcinoma. *Cancer Res*, **56**, 3530–3533.
32. Murrah, V.A., Batsakis, J.G. (1994) Proliferative verrucous leukoplakia and verrucous hyperplasia. *Ann Otol Rhinol Laryngol*, **103**, 660–663.
33. Batsakis, J.G., Suarez, P., el-Naggar, A.K. (1999) Proliferative verrucous leukoplakia and its related lesions. *Oral Oncol*, **35**, 354–359.
34. Greer, R.O. Jr, Eversole, L.R., Crosby, L.K. (1990) Detection of human papillomavirus-genomic DNA in oral epithelial dysplasias, oral smokeless tobacco-associated leukoplakias, and epithelial malignancies. *J Oral Maxillofac Surg*, **48**, 1201–1205.
35. Shroyer, K.R., Greer, R.O. Jr (1991) Detection of human papillomavirus DNA by in situ DNA hybridization and polymerase chain reaction in premalignant and malignant oral lesions. *Oral Surg Oral Med Oral Pathol*, **71**, 708–713.
36. Palefsky, J.M., Silverman, S. Jr, Abdel-Salaam, M. et al (1995) Association between proliferative verrucous leukoplakia and infection with human papillomavirus type 16. *J Oral Pathol Med*, **24**, 193–197.
37. Kahn, M.A., Dockter, M.E., Hermann-Petrin, J.M. (1994) Proliferative verrucous leukoplakia. Four cases with flow cytometric analysis. *Oral Surg Oral Med Oral Pathol*, **78**, 469–475.
38. Damm, D.D., Curran, A., White, D.K. et al (1999) Leukoplakia of the maxillary vestibule – an association with Viadent? *Oral Surg Oral Med Oral Pathol Oral Radiol Endod*, **87**, 61–66.
39. Mascarenhas, A.K., Allen, C.M., Loudon, J. (2001) The association between Viadent use and oral leukoplakia. *Epidemiology*, **12**, 741–743.
40. Lookingbill, D.P., Kreider, J.W., Howett, M.K. et al (1987) Human papillomavirus type 16 in bowenoid papulosis, intraoral papillomas, and squamous cell carcinoma of the tongue. *Arch Dermatol*, **123**, 363–368.
41. Kratochvil, F.J., Cioffi, G.A., Auclair, P.L. et al (1989) Virus-associated dysplasia (bowenoid papulosis?) of the oral cavity. *Oral Surg Oral Med Oral Pathol*, **68**, 312–316.
42. Daley, T., Birek, C., Wysocki, G.P. (2000) Oral bowenoid lesions: differential diagnosis and pathogenetic insights. *Oral Surg Oral Med Oral Pathol Oral Radiol Endod*, **90**, 466–473.
43. Fornatora, M., Jones, A.C., Kerpel, S. et al (1996) Human papillomavirus-associated oral epithelial dysplasia (koilocytic dysplasia): an entity of unknown biologic potential. *Oral Surg Oral Med Oral Pathol Oral Radiol Endod*, **82**, 47–56.

Benign alveolar ridge keratosis

Clinical features

These are white, often rough plaques that occur on the crest of the alveolar ridge, in particular in the area of extracted mandibular third molars and adjacent retromolar pad (*Figs 10.213, 10.214*). They also occur in any other part of the ridge where a previous extraction has occurred. They are most likely caused by frictional trauma to the ridge, not necessarily by direct tooth-to-ridge contact, but by food being crushed between the opposing teeth and the ridge.

This 'white lesion' should be removed from the classification of 'leukoplakia' once the histopathology has been elucidated, because it has distinct histological features and a generally consistent clinical location and putative etiology. It has no malignant potential.

Histological features

These lesions have the typical appearance of skin lesions of lichen simplex chronicus. There is hyperorthokeratosis (often marked) with wedge-shaped hypergranulosis, surface papillomatosis and acanthosis (*Figs 10.215, 10.216*). Rete ridges are tapered and generally uniformly elongated. There is usually minimal to insignificant chronic

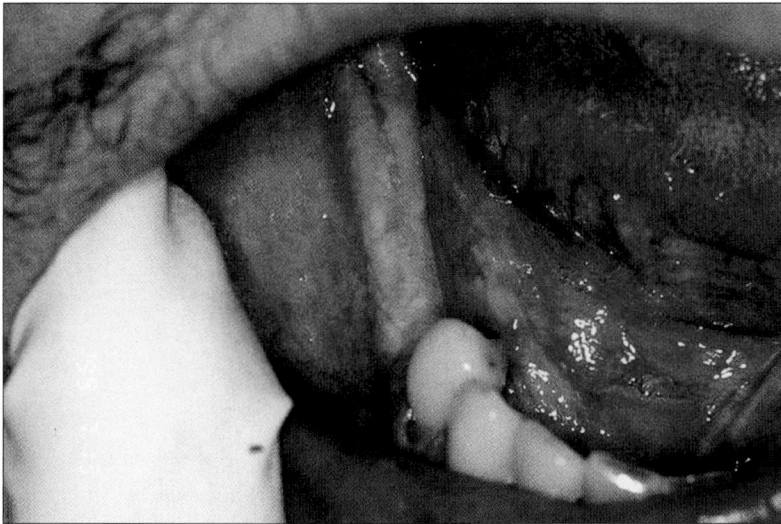

Fig. 10.213
Benign ridge keratosis: the site of a previous mandibular third molar extraction is a typical location for this condition.

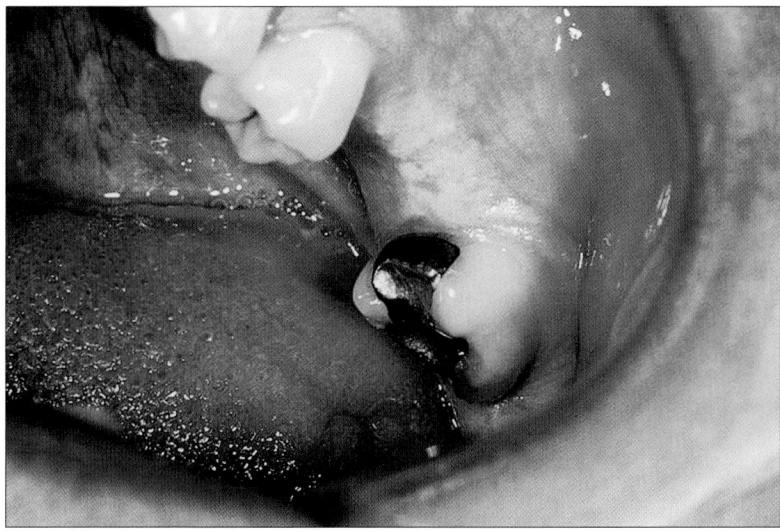

Fig. 10.214
Benign ridge keratosis: the crest of the alveolar ridge, site of a previous tooth extraction, is another typical location for this condition.

inflammation in the lamina propria. Lesions from the retromolar pad often contain stellate-shaped fibroblasts, which are normal for that area.

Submucous fibrosis

Clinical features

This condition affects adults of usually Asian descent (subcontinental Indians in particular) who chew areca (betel) nut.[1] Patients develop progressive pallor, fibrosis and a marble-like rigidity of the tissues usually beginning in the soft palate and fauces, and then involving the buccal mucosa, lips and tongue, not dissimilar to progressive systemic sclerosis. Palpable fibrous bands run vertically down the buccal mucosa in advanced lesions. Ulcers, areas of erythema and symptoms of burning are common.[2] This is a premalignant condition as squamous cell carcinomas develop in 2–8% of cases.[3,4]

Pathogenesis and histological features

Arecoline and arecanoid (areca nut alkaloids) are carcinogenic, stimulate collagen synthesis and also yield nitrosamines.[5,6] Genetic factors and autoimmunity may also play a role in the development of oral squamous cell carcinoma primarily because of increased expression of HLA-DR3, occasional identification of autoantibodies and the condition's similarity to scleroderma.[7–9] HLA-A10 expression is also increased.

The epithelium is hyperkeratotic and atrophic with loss of rete ridges. The subepithelial connective tissue first shows edema, vascular dilatation and chronic inflammation. Progressive thickening of the collagen bundles occurs with increasing degrees of hyalinization (*Fig. 10.217*). In severe cases, hyalinized bands of collagen are devoid of cells.[2,10] Muscle degeneration is also present.[11]

Early ultrastructural studies showed abnormal collagen fibrils that were fragmented, bent/angulated and degenerate.[12] More recent studies have shown the presence of type I and type III collagen in a normal distribution with normal fiber morphology but with increased density.[13] A further study has shown reduced amounts of type III procollagen and type VI collagen in fibrotic areas.[14]

Differential diagnosis

The eosinophilic bands of collagen do not stain for amyloid. Smokeless tobacco keratosis may exhibit similar eosinophilic bands of altered collagen but, in addition, there is surface coagulation and keratin chevrons, as well as epithelial hyperplasia rather than atrophy as is typically seen in submucous fibrosis. Sclerodermatous involvement of the oral mucosa is an important differential diagnosis that can be excluded on clinical grounds and with serological tests.

Lichen sclerosus is a rare oral condition. In addition to the hyalinized eosinophilic subepithelial band, there is basal cell degeneration and a lymphocytic band beneath the area of hyalinization.[15–17]

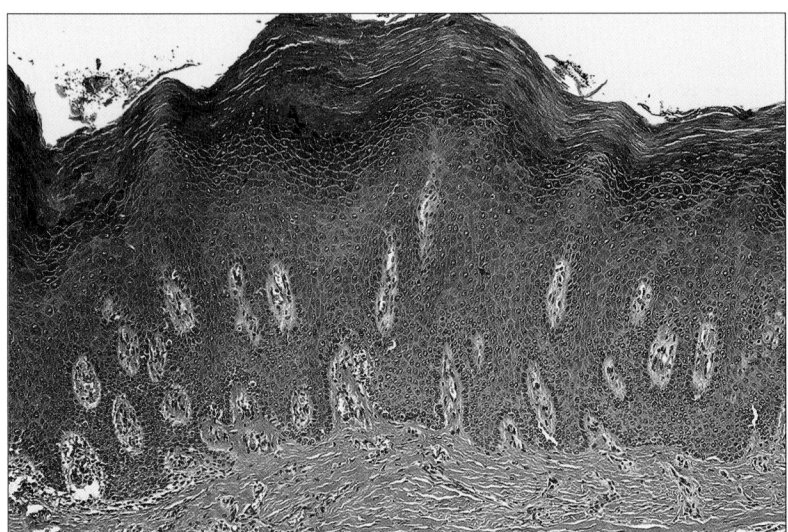

Fig. 10.215
Benign ridge keratosis: there is hyperkeratosis, wedge-shaped hypergranulosis and acanthosis with minimal to no inflammation.

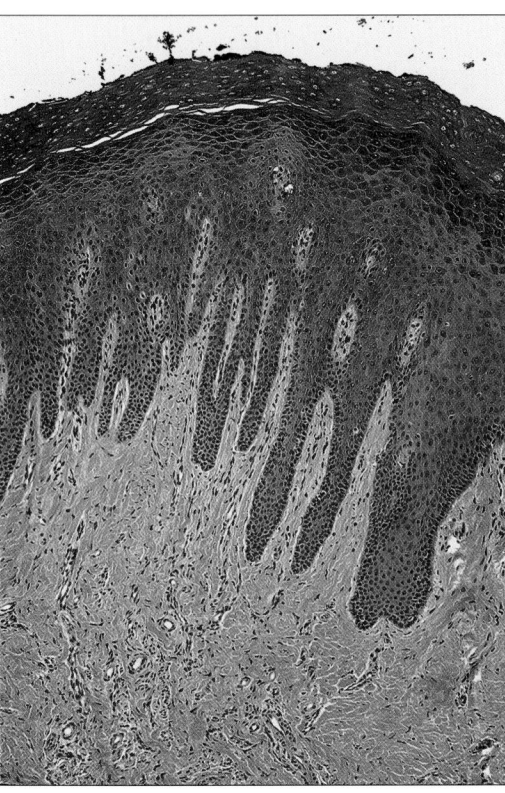

Fig. 10.216
Lichen simplex chronicus: note the marked hyperkeratosis, hypergranulosis and psoriasiform hyperplasia.

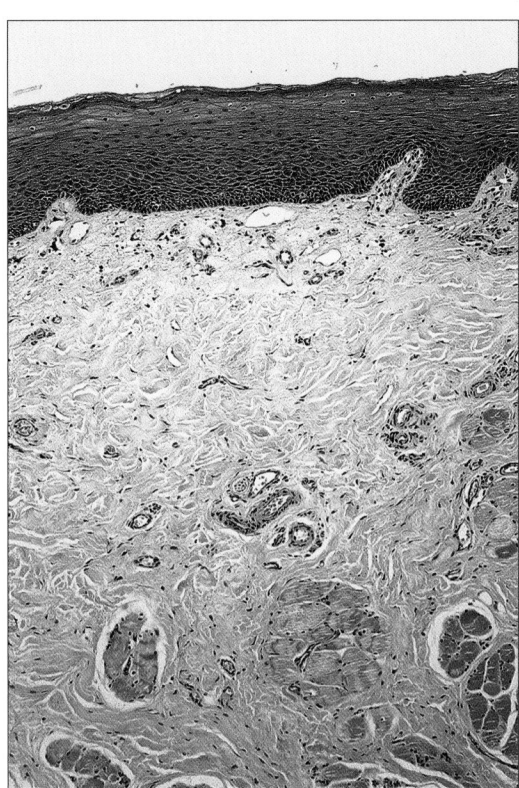

Fig. 10.217
Submucous fibrosis: there is epithelial atrophy and dense fibrosis that surrounds skeletal muscle fibers.

References

1. Rajendran, R. (1994) Oral submucous fibrosis: etiology, pathogenesis, and future research. *Bull World Health Organ*, **72**, 985–996.
2. Pindborg, J.J., Sirsat, S.M. (1966) Oral submucous fibrosis. *Oral Surg Oral Med Oral Pathol*, **22**, 764–779.
3. Pindborg, J.J., Murti, P.R., Bhonsle, R.B. et al (1984) Oral submucous fibrosis as a precancerous condition. *Scand J Dent Res*, **92**, 224–229.
4. Murti, P.R., Bhonsle, R.B., Pindborg, J.J. et al (1985) Malignant transformation rate in oral submucous fibrosis over a 17-year period. *Community Dent Oral Epidemiol*, **13**, 340–341.
5. Canniff, J.P., Harvey, W. (1981) The aetiology of oral submucous fibrosis: the stimulation of collagen synthesis by extracts of areca nut. *Int J Oral Surg*, **10**, 163–167.
6. Harvey, W., Saitt, A., Meghi, S. et al (1986) Stimulation of human buccal fibroblasts in vitro by betel nut alkaloids. *Arch Oral Biol*, **31**, 45–49.
7. Pillai, R., Balaram, P., Reddiar, K.S. (1992) Pathogenesis of oral submucous fibrosis. Relationship to risk factors associated with oral cancer. *Cancer*, **69**, 2011–2020.
8. Murti, P.R., Bhonsle, R.B., Gupta, P.C. et al (1995) Etiology of oral submucous fibrosis with special reference to the role of areca nut chewing. *J Oral Pathol Med*, **24**, 145–152.
9. Canniff, J.P., Batchelor, J.R., Dodi, I.A. et al (1985) HLA-typing in oral submucous fibrosis. *Tissue Antigens*, **26**, 138–142.
10. Sirsat, S.M., Pindborg, J.J. (1967) Subepithelial changes in oral submucous fibrosis. *Acta Pathol Microbiol Scand*, **70**, 161–173.
11. el-Labban, N.G., Canniff, J.P. (1985) Ultrastructural findings of muscle degeneration in oral submucous fibrosis. *J Oral Pathol*, **14**, 709–717.
12. Sirsat, S.M., Khanolkar, V.R. (1957) A histochemical and electron-microscope study of submucous fibrosis of the palate. *J Pathol Bacteriol*, **73**, 439–442.
13. van Wyk, C.W., Seedat, H.A., Phillips, V.M. (1990) Collagen in submucous fibrosis: an electron-microscopic study. *J Oral Pathol Med*, **19**, 182–187.
14. Reichart, P.A., van Wyk, C.W., Becker, J. et al (1994) Distribution of procollagen type III, collagen type VI and tenascin in oral submucous fibrosis (OSF). *J Oral Pathol Med*, **23**, 394–398.
15. Shulten, E.A.J.M., Starink, T.M., van der Waal, I. (1993) Lichen sclerosus et atrophicus of the oral cavity: report of two cases. *J Oral Pathol Med*, **22**, 374–377.
16. Brown, A.R., Dunlap, C.L., Bussard, D.A. et al (1997) Lichen sclerosus et atrophicus of the oral cavity: report of two cases. *Oral Surg Oral Med Oral Pathol Oral Radiol Endod*, **84**, 165–170.
17. Buajeeb, W., Kraivaphan, P., Punyasingh, J. et al (1999) Oral lichen sclerosus et atrophicus: a case report. *Oral Surg Oral Med Oral Pathol Oral Radiol Endod*, **88**, 702–706.

Malignant lesions

Squamous cell carcinoma

Clinical features

Squamous cell carcinoma is the most common malignancy in the oral cavity, accounting for more than 90% of all oral cancers. In the US, it constitutes approximately 3% of all malignancies and accounts for 30,000 cancer cases diagnosed annually.[1] The two most significant risk factors are cigarette smoking (by far the most important) and excessive alcohol consumption.[2,3] In Asian countries, tobacco use and areca nut chewing in its various forms are a major cause of oral cancer. Oral cancer is the most common form of cancer among men in India where such habits are prevalent.[4] These tumors often but not invariably develop within submucous fibrosis. Other risk factors include infection by human papilloma virus, history of a previous oral squamous carcinoma, history of cancer elsewhere in the body, history of immunosuppression and age.[5] Lip carcinoma is generally not included in the discussion on oral lesions because of its different etiology (sunlight) and its better prognosis.

The tumor may present initially as plaque lesions of leukoplakia, erythroplakia and proliferative verrucous leukoplakia, or as non-healing ulcers, masses or nodules (*Figs 10.218–10.220*). Patients are usually in the sixth decade of life or older, although more recent data reveal a rise in these tumors in younger patients, often unassociated with tobacco use.[1] Approximately 14–27% of patients present with synchronous or metachronous tumors of the upper aerodigestive or digestive tract.[6–8]

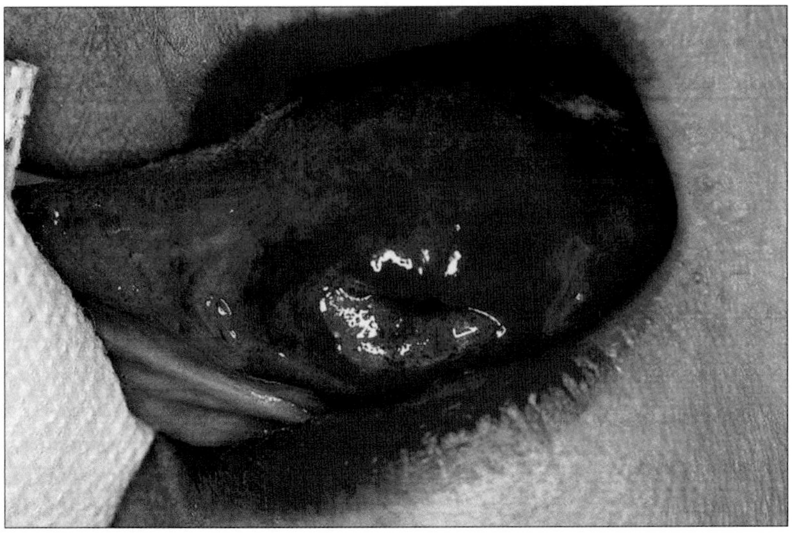

Pathogenesis and histological features

The development of oral squamous cell carcinoma is a multistep process involving allelic imbalance and loss of heterozygosity involving chromosomes 3p, 9p, 11q, 13q and 17p; genetic aberrations involving

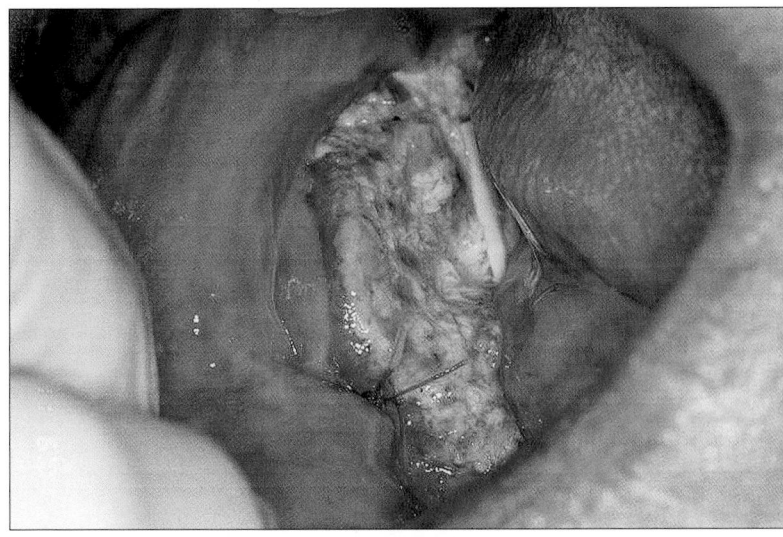

Fig. 10.219
Squamous cell carcinoma: there is a fungating mass on the buccal mucosa.

Fig. 10.218
Squamous cell carcinoma: note the ulcerated nodule on the lateral tongue.

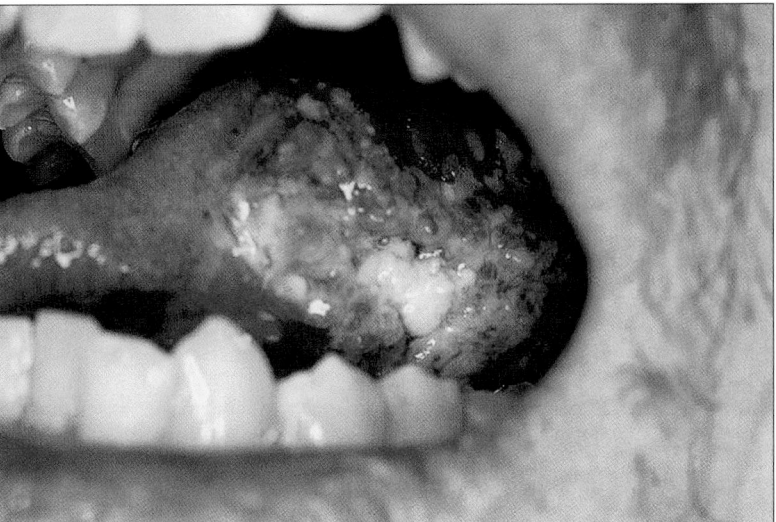

Fig. 10.220
Squamous cell carcinoma: there is an ulcerated mass on the lateral tongue.

practically every gene have recently been reviewed.[9] There may be inactivation and/or mutation of tumor suppressor genes such as p16 (9p) and p53 (17p) and overexpression of such oncogenes as cyclin D1 (11q).[10–12] Genetic aberrations involving deletions on chromosome 3 and those involving chromosome 13 lie close to the Rb gene and often consist of multiple deletions.[13,14] A history of tobacco and alcohol use is associated with a high frequency of p53 mutations.[15]

Histologically, these tumors are similar to squamous cell carcinoma arising at other sites. Pleomorphism varies, as does the degree of differentiation/keratinization. The tumor may invade the stroma as large islands of epithelium on a pushing front (bluntly invasive type) or it may infiltrate the stroma as smaller irregular islands of tumor cells or as single cells. Immunolocalization of type IV collagen and laminin reveals that basement membrane is generally preserved in bluntly invasive patterns of growth and lost in infiltrative tumors.[16] The infiltrative tumor is associated with a significantly higher incidence of lymph node metastasis.[17–20] Tumors thicker than 6–8 mm are more likely to metastasize; however, a figure as low as 1.5–2 mm is quoted for lesions of the tongue and floor of the mouth, both being high risk sites.[19–23] Carcinomas showing perineural or bone involvement have a poorer prognosis.[19–21]

The degree of differentiation/keratinization may or may not correlate with survival or lymph node metastasis.[17,18,20] More recently, sentinel node biopsy in patients without clinical evidence of cervical metastases has disclosed metastatic disease in approximately 50% of cases.[16,24]

A relationship with human papilloma virus (HPV) has been reported in numerous papers. High or intermediate risk HPV variants are present in approximately 20–47%.[25–28] HPV in tonsillar carcinomas is associated with increased survival compared to those who are negative.[29] Diploid tumors are associated with lower incidences of recurrence and lymph node metastasis.[30]

Occult squamous cell carcinoma of the epithelium overlying Waldeyer's ring may present as cystic lesions in cervical nodes. Before making a diagnosis of malignant bronchial cleft cyst/lymphoepithelial cyst, an occult primary in the base of the tongue, tonsil and nasopharynx should be sought.

With molecular techniques, p53 overexpression has been found in histopathologically benign margins. Recurrence has been noted in 38% of patients with such p53 positive margins and metastatic tumor identified in 21% of histologically negative lymph nodes.[31]

An important variant is the papillary squamous cell carcinoma, which predominantly occurs on the alveolar ridge, buccal mucosa, larynx, pharynx, floor of mouth and tongue. The literature regarding this entity is somewhat confusing. There are two variants, both characterized by a papillary growth pattern:

- One occurs in the larynx and upper respiratory tract and consists of an invasive papillary proliferation of minimally to non-keratinizing epithelium with highly atypical epithelial cells and numerous mitoses overlying a fibrovascular core (*Figs 10.221, 10.222*).[32–34] These tumors are HPV positive in approximately one-third of cases and the presence of p53 correlates with poor survival.[34]
- In contrast, oral papillary squamous cell carcinomas are thickly hyperkeratotic and generally well differentiated, although they usually show varying degrees of dysplasia in contrast to the bland histology typical of verrucous carcinoma (*Figs 10.223, 10.224*).[35]

References

1. SEER Cancer Statistics Review 1973–1999. http://seer.cancer.gov/csr/1973_1999/
2. Sankaranarayanan, R. (1990) Oral cancer in India: an epidemiologic and clinical review. *Oral Surg Oral Med Oral Pathol*, 69, 325–330.
3. Johnson, N.W., Warnakulasuriy, S., Tavassoli, M. (1996) Hereditary and environmental risk factors; clinical and laboratory risk markers for head and neck, especially oral, cancer and precancer. *Eur J Cancer Prev*, 5, 5–17.
4. van Wyk, C.W., Stander, I., Padayachee, A. et al (1993) The areca nut chewing habit and oral squamous cell carcinoma in South African Indians. A retrospective study. *S Afr Med J*, 83, 425–429.

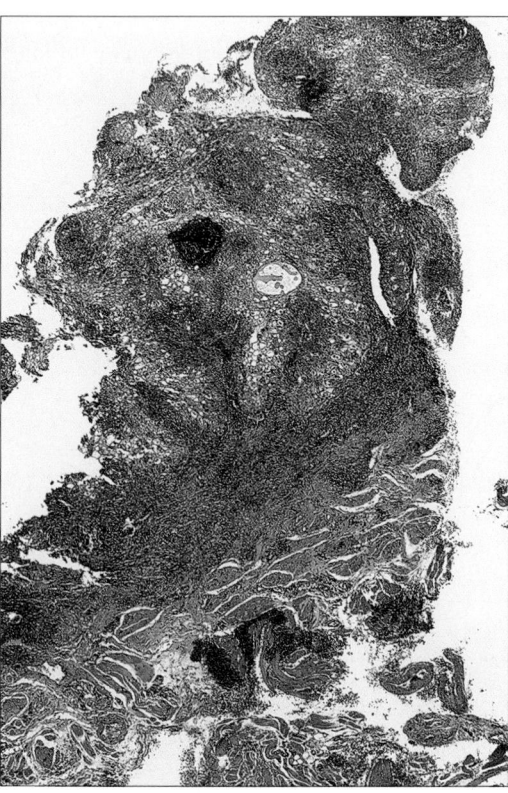

Fig. 10.221
Papillary squamous cell carcinoma: the papillary projections of malignant epithelial cells are non-keratinized and there is stromal invasion.

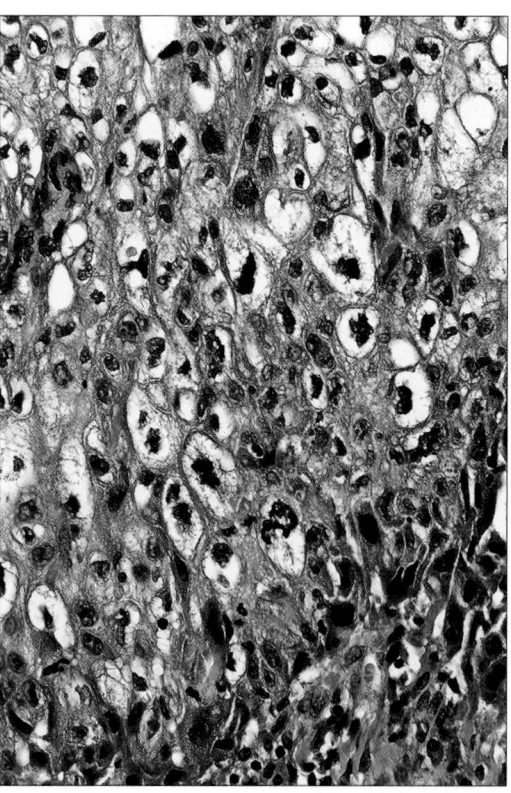

Fig. 10.222
Papillary squamous cell carcinoma: there is marked pleomorphism and koilocyte-like cells.

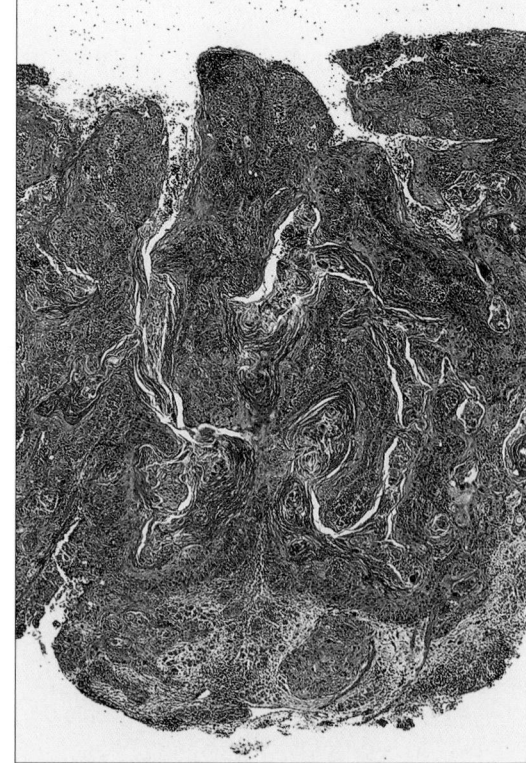

Fig. 10.223
Papillary well-differentiated squamous cell carcinoma: note the abundant keratin formation and papillary and crypt-like formations.

5. Curtis, R.E., Rowlings, P.A., Deeg, J. et al (1997) Solid cancers after bone marrow transplantation. *N Engl J Med*, **336**, 897–904.
6. Tepperman, B.S., Fitzpatrick, P.J. (1981) Second respiratory and upper digestive tract cancers after oral cancer. *Lancet*, **2**, 547–549.
7. Gluckman, J.L., Crissman, J.D. (1983) Survival rates in 548 patients with multiple neoplasms of the upper aerodigestive tract. *Laryngoscope*, **93**, 71–74.
8. Schwartz, L.H., Ozsahin, M., Zhang, G.N. et al (1994) Synchronous and metachronous head and neck carcinomas. *Cancer*, **74**, 1933–1938.
9. Scully, C., Field, J.K., Tanzawa, H. (2000) Genetic aberrations in oral or head and neck squamous cell carcinoma 2: chromosomal aberrations. *Oral Oncol*, **36**, 311–327.
10. van der Riet, P., Nawroz, H., Hruban, R.H. et al (1994) Frequent loss of chromosome 9p21–22 early in head and neck cancer progression. *Cancer Res*, **54**, 1156–1158.
11. Matsumura, T., Yoshihama, Y., Kimura, T. et al (1996) p53 and MDM2 expression in oral squamous cell carcinoma. *Oncology*, **53**, 308–312.
12. Yan, J.J., Tzeng, C.C., Jin, Y.T. (1996) Overexpression of p53 protein in squamous cell carcinoma of buccal mucosa and tongue in Taiwan: an immunohistochemical and clinicopathological study. *J Oral Pathol Med*, **25**, 55–59.
13. Maestro, R., Piccinin, S., Doglioni, C. et al (1996) Chromosome 13q deletion mapping in head and neck squamous cell carcinomas: identification of two distinct regions of preferential loss. *Cancer Res*, **56**, 1146–1150.
14. Gupta, V.K., Schmidt, A.P., Pashia, M.E. et al (1999) Multiple regions of deletion on chromosome arm 13q in head-and-neck squamous-cell carcinoma. *Int J Cancer*, **84**, 453–457.
15. Brennan, J.A., Boyle, J.O., Koch, W.M. et al (1995) Association between cigarette smoking and mutation of the p53 gene in squamous-cell carcinoma of the head and neck. *N Engl J Med*, **332**, 712–717.
16. Taylor, R.J., Wahl, R.L., Sharma, P.K. et al (2001) Sentinel node localization in oral cavity and oropharynx squamous cell cancer. *Arch Otolaryngol Head Neck Surg*, **127**, 970–974.
17. Platz, H., Fries, R., Hudec, M. et al (1983) The prognostic relevance of various factors at the time of the first admission of the patient. *J Maxillofac Surg*, **11**, 3–12.
18. Crissman, J.D., Liu, W.Y., Gluckman, J.L. et al (1984) Prognostic value of histopathologic parameters in squamous cell carcinoma of the oropharynx. *Cancer*, **54**, 2995–3001.
19. Frierson, H.F., Cooper, P.H. (1986) Prognostic factors in squamous cell carcinoma of the lower lip. *Hum Pathol*, **17**, 346–354.
20. Shingaki, S., Suzuki, I., Nakajima, T. et al (1988) Evaluation of histopathologic parameters in predicting cervical lymph node metastasis of oral and oropharyngeal carcinomas. *Oral Surg Oral Med Oral Pathol*, **66**, 683–688.
21. Moore, C., Kuhns, J.G., Greenberg, R.A. (1986) Thickness as prognostic aid in upper aerodigestive tract cancer. *Arch Surg*, **121**, 1410–1414.
22. Mohit-Tabatabai, M., Sobel, H.J., Rush, B.F. et al (1986) Regulation of thickness of floor of mouth stage I and II cancers to regional metastasis. *Am J Surg*, **152**, 351–353.
23. Spiro, R.H., Huvos, A.G., Wong, G.Y. et al (1986) Predictive value of tumor thickness in squamous cell carcinoma confined to the tongue and floor of the mouth. *Am J Surg*, **52**, 345–350.
24. Shoaib, T., Soutar, D.S., MacDonald, D.G. et al (2001) The accuracy of head and neck carcinoma sentinel lymph node biopsy in the clinically N0 neck. *Cancer*, **91**, 2077–2083.
25. Brandwein, M., Zeitlin, J., Nuovo, G.J. et al (1994) HPV detection using 'hot start' polymerase chain reaction in patients with oral cancer: a clinicopathological study of 64 patients. *Mod Pathol*, **7**, 720–727.
26. Snijders, P.J., Scholes, A.G., Hart, C.A. et al (1996) Prevalence of mucosotropic human papillomaviruses in squamous-cell carcinoma of the head and neck. *Int J Cancer*, **66**, 464–469.
27. Badaracco, G., Venuti, A., Morello, R. et al (2000) Human papillomavirus in head and neck carcinomas: prevalence, physical status and relationship with clinical/pathological parameters. *Anticancer Res*, **20**, 1301–1305.
28. Miller, C.S., Johnstone, B.M. (2001) Human papillomavirus as a risk factor for oral squamous cell carcinoma: a meta-analysis, 1982–1997. *Oral Surg Oral Med Oral Pathol Oral Radiol Endod*, **91**, 622–635.
29. Mellin, H., Friesland, S., Lewensohn, R. et al (2000) Human papillomavirus (HPV) DNA in tonsillar cancer: clinical correlates, risk of relapse, and survival. *Int J Cancer*, **89**, 300–304.
30. Hemmer, J., Thein, T., Van Heerden, W.F. (1997) The value of DNA flow cytometry in predicting the development of lymph node metastasis and survival in patients with locally recurrent oral squamous cell carcinoma. *Cancer*, **79**, 2309–2313.
31. Brennan, J.A., Mao, L., Hruban, R.H. et al (1995) Molecular assessment of histopathological staging in squamous-cell carcinoma of the head and neck. *N Engl J Med*, **332**, 429–435.
32. Crissman, J.D., Kessis, T., Shah, K.V. et al (1988) Squamous papillary neoplasia of the adult upper aerodigestive tract. *Hum Pathol*, **19**, 1387–1396.
33. Ferlito, A., Devaney, K.O., Rinaldo, A. et al (1999) Papillary squamous cell carcinoma versus verrucous squamous cell carcinoma of the head and neck. *Ann Otol Rhinol Laryngol*, **108**, 318–322.
34. Suarez, P.A., Adler-Storthz, K., Luna, M.A. et al (2000) Papillary squamous cell carcinomas of the upper aerodigestive tract: a clinicopathologic and molecular study. *Head Neck*, **22**, 360–368.
35. Ishimaya, A., Eversole, L.R., Ross, D.A. et al (1994) Papillary squamous neoplasms of the head and neck. *Laryngoscope*, **104**, 1446–1452.

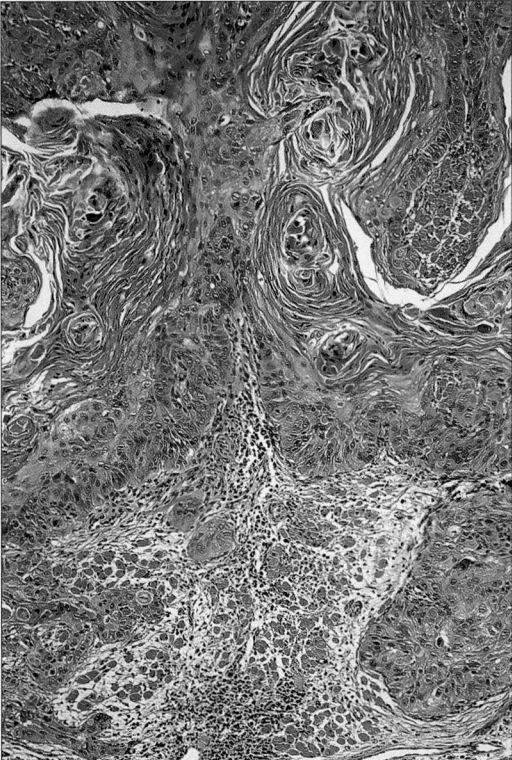

Fig. 10.224
Papillary well-differentiated squamous cell carcinoma: the cells in this tumor are keratinizing.

Metaplastic carcinoma

Clinical features

Metaplastic carcinoma (carcinosarcoma, sarcomatoid squamous carcinoma, spindle cell carcinoma) is a tumor of the sixth to eighth decades with an equal sex distribution.[1] The most common sites to be affected are the lower lip, tongue and alveolar ridge. A polypoid, exophytic configuration is the most common presentation.[1,2] A history of radiation to the site has been noted in 13–67% of cases.[1–3] Oral cavity tumors tend to be deeply invasive and associated with low survival rates; polypoid lesions may have a better prognosis.[2,4]

Histological features

The tumor, which is typically ulcerated, is biphasic with a malignant epithelial component (squamous cell carcinoma) usually present at the base or peduncle of the polypoid lesions, and a malignant spindle cell component in the main body of the tumor.[1] Dysplastic cells can be seen to 'drop off' or stream from the surface epithelium as spindle cells into the underlying stroma. The spindle cells may form streaming fascicles, have a prominent myxoid stroma (reminiscent of granulation tissue) or take on pericytoma and storiform patterns (*Fig. 10.225*).[1,2,5] They sometimes have bipolar processes or appear stellate-shaped and epithelioid; nuclei may be pleomorphic with prominent nucleoli (*Fig. 10.226*). There are usually abundant mitoses, and pleomorphic tumor giant cells as well as osteoclast-like giant cells are sometimes present. Osteoid is present in 7% of cases and malignant cartilage has been reported.[1,4]

Low molecular weight cytokeratins such as AE1/AE3 and CAM 5.2 are present in the spindle cells in 50–62% of cases; spindle cells may also co-express vimentin which is usually diffusely expressed.[4,6] Epithelial membrane antigen (EMA) is seen in less than 10% of cases. S-100 protein and GFAP are typically negative.[3,6]

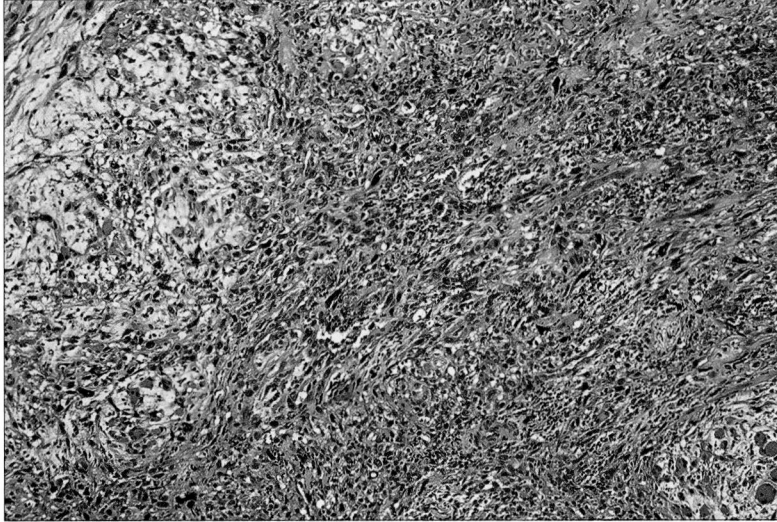

Fig. 10.225
Metaplastic carcinoma: note the streaming, fasciculated pattern.

Ultrastructurally, desmosomes may be well or poorly developed and keratin filaments are variably present. Dilated rough endoplasmic reticulum and the presence of tropocollagen suggest secretory activity.[3–5]

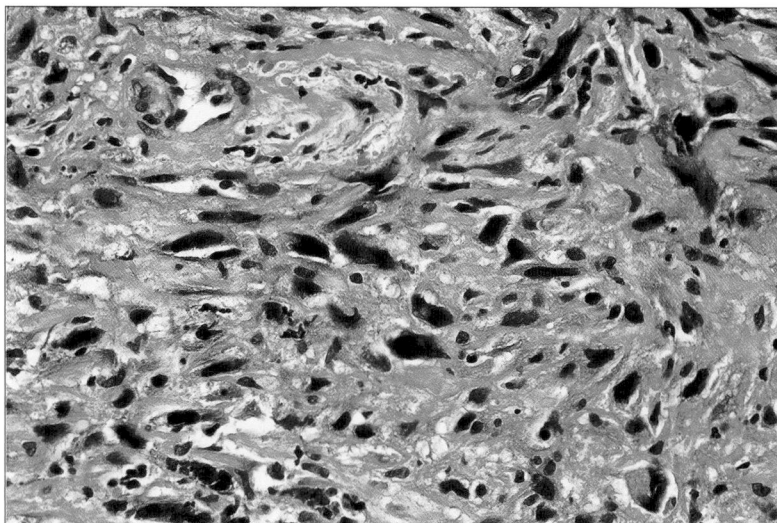

Fig. 10.226
Metaplastic carcinoma: note the large, pleomorphic spindled cells.

Differential diagnosis

The diagnosis is not usually difficult when a spindle cell malignancy is present in association with typical squamous cell carcinoma although the latter may be only evident focally at the base of polypoid lesions. Important differential diagnoses include spindle cell melanoma, sarcomas and malignant myoepithelioma. In difficult cases, immuno-peroxidase studies will usually enable distinction.

References

1. Ellis, G.L., Corio, R.L. (1980) Spindle cell carcinoma of the oral cavity. *Oral Surg Oral Med Oral Pathol*, **50**, 523–534.
2. Leventon, G.S., Evans, H.L. (1981) Sarcomatoid squamous cell carcinoma of the mucous membranes of the head and neck: a clinicopathologic study of 20 cases. *Cancer*, **48**, 994–1003.
3. Takata, T., Ito, H., Ogawa, I. et al (1991) Spindle cell squamous carcinoma of the oral region. An immunohistochemical and ultrastructural study on the histogenesis and differential diagnosis with a clinicopathological analysis of six cases. *Virchows Arch A Pathol Anat Histopathol*, **419**, 177–182.
4. Zarbo, R.J., Crissman, J.D., Venkat, H. et al (1986) Spindle-cell carcinoma of the upper aerodigestive tract mucosa. *Am J Surg Pathol*, **10**, 741–753.
5. Lichtiger, B., Mackay, B., Tessmer, C.F. (1970) Spindle-cell variant of squamous carcinoma. A light and electron microscopic study of 13 cases. *Cancer*, **26**, 1311–1320.
6. Ellis, G.L., Langloss, J.M., Heffner, D.K. et al (1987) Spindle-cell carcinoma of the aerodigestive tract. *Am J Surg Pathol*, **11**, 335–342.

Basaloid squamous cell carcinoma

Clinical features

This is an aggressive variant of squamous cell carcinoma that primarily affects men (M:F = 7:1) in the sixth and seventh decades with a predilection for the tongue and floor of mouth; 60–80% develop local and/or distant metastases.[1–3]

Histological features

This unusual tumor is characterized by well to moderately differentiated squamous cell carcinoma coexisting with a malignant lobular proliferation of basaloid cells. The tumor lobules often exhibit comedo-like necrosis and microcystic spaces filled with PAS-positive material (*Fig. 10.227*). Occasionally, a cribriform pattern is evident and hyalinized material surrounding tumor islands is an occasional feature (*Fig. 10.228*).[1,4] True ductal differentiation or a spindle cell morphology is sometimes seen.[5] The basaloid cells, which are crowded with dark hyperchromatic nuclei and indistinct nucleoli, show palisading at the periphery of the tumor lobules. Mitoses are often abundant and perineural invasion is frequently conspicuous.[3]

Recognizable squamous cell carcinoma must be identified to establish this diagnosis. Dysplasia of overlying epithelium is present in 85% of cases and transition between the squamous and basaloid patterns may be subtle or even absent.[2,4]

The cells express cytokeratin (in particular AE1/AE3, CAM 5.2 and 34betaE12), EMA and NSE (weakly). Carcinoembryonic antigen (CEA) and S-100 protein are present in approximately 50% of cases.[2] Others report vimentin in a perinuclear rim in the basaloid cells, the absence of NSE and S-100 present only within dendritic cells.[3,4,6] Chromogranin and synaptophysin are absent.[2,3]

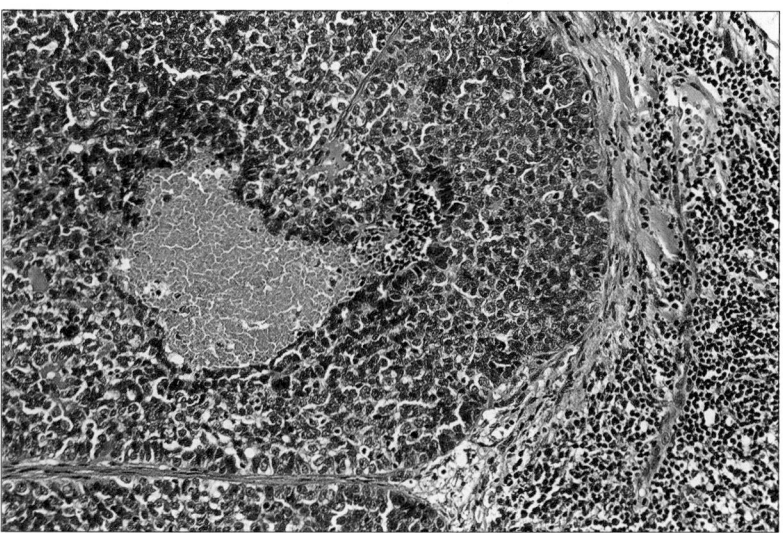

Fig. 10.227
Basaloid squamous cell carcinoma: there is comedonecrosis and lobules of malignant basaloid cells.

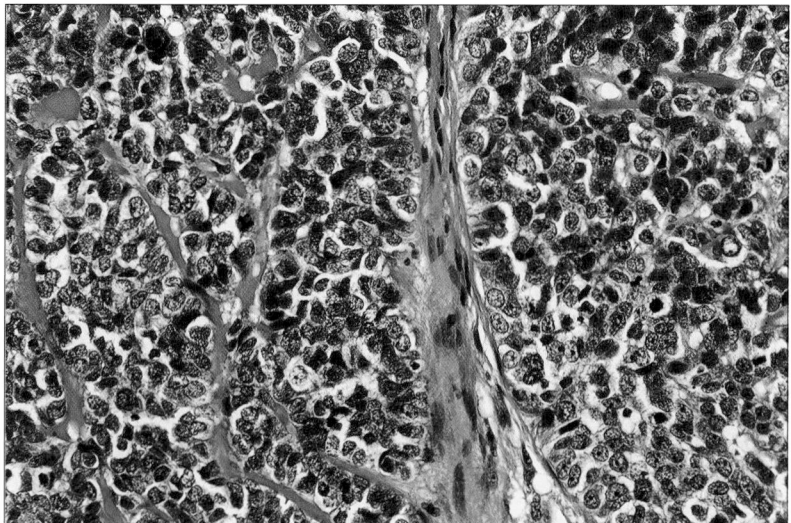

Fig. 10.228
Basaloid squamous cell carcinoma: there are many mitotic figures and trabeculae of hyalinized material.

Approximately 50% of tumors are aneuploid although this may not have prognostic significance.[7,8] These tumors show marked proliferative activity and expression of p53 protein.[9,10]

Differential diagnosis

Salivary gland carcinomas such as adenoid cystic carcinoma and basal cell adenocarcinoma (uncommon in minor salivary glands) contain basaloid cells but do not contain a recognizable conventional squamous cell carcinoma. Adenoid cystic carcinoma also exhibits diffuse cytoplasmic vimentin expression whereas in the basaloid squamous carcinoma it is perinuclear. One study showed that basaloid cell carcinoma almost always stains for 34betaE12 keratin while small cell undifferentiated carcinomas are negative.[11] Merkel cell carcinoma has a trabecular or solid growth pattern and is generally NSE positive. Keratin expression is characterized by paranuclear punctate dots and the tumor cells contain typical neurosecretory granules.[12] Adenosquamous carcinoma has true duct-like structures and produces epithelial mucin.

References

1. Wain, S.L., Kier, R., Vollmen, R.T. et al (1986) Basaloid-squamous carcinoma of the tongue, hypopharynx, and larynx: report of 10 cases. *Hum Pathol*, **17**, 1158–1166.
2. Banks, E.R., Frierson, H.F. Jr, Mills, S.E. et al (1992) Basaloid squamous cell carcinoma of the head and neck. *Am J Surg Pathol*, **16**, 939–946.
3. Coppola, D., Catalano, E., Tang, C. et al (1993) Basaloid squamous cell carcinoma of floor of mouth. *Cancer*, **72**, 2299–2305.
4. Barnes, L., MacMillan, C., Ferlito, A. et al (1996) Basaloid squamous cell carcinoma of the head and neck: clinicopathological features and differential diagnosis. *Ann Otol Rhinol Laryngol*, **105**, 75–82.
5. Muller, S., Barnes, L. (1995) Basaloid squamous cell carcinoma of the head and neck with a spindle cell component. An unusual histologic variant. *Arch Pathol Lab Med*, **119**, 181–182.
6. Klijanienko, J., el-Naggar, A., Ponzio-Prion, A. et al (1993) Basaloid squamous carcinoma of the head and neck: immunohistochemical comparison with adenoid cystic carcinoma and squamous cell carcinoma. *Arch Otolaryngol Head Neck Surg*, **119**, 887–890.
7. Luna, M.A., el-Naggar, A., Parichatikanond, P. et al (1990) Basaloid squamous carcinoma of the upper aerodigestive tract. *Cancer*, **66**, 537–542.
8. Raslan, W.F., Barnes, L., Krause, J.R. et al (1994) Basaloid squamous cell carcinoma of the head and neck: a clinicopathologic and flow cytometric study of 10 new cases with review of the English literature. *Am J Otolaryngol*, **15**, 204–211.
9. Abiko, Y., Muramatsu, T., Tanaka, Y. et al (1998) Basaloid-squamous carcinoma of the oral mucosa: report of two cases and study of the proliferative activity. *Pathol Int*, **48**, 460–466.
10. Coletta, R.D., Cotrim, P., Vargas, P.A. et al (2001) Basaloid squamous carcinoma of the oral cavity: report of 2 cases and study of AgNOR, PCNA, p53, and MMP expression. *Oral Surg Oral Med Oral Pathol Oral Radiol Endod*, **91**, 563–569.
11. Morice, W.G., Ferreiro, J.A. (1998) Distinction of basaloid squamous carcinoma from adenoid cystic and small cell undifferentiated carcinoma by immunohistochemistry. *Hum Pathol*, **29**, 609–612.
12. Vigneswaran, N., Muller, S., Lense, E. et al (1992) Merkel cell carcinoma of the labial mucosa. An immunohistochemical and ultrastructural study with a review of the literature on oral Merkel cell carcinomas. *Oral Surg Oral Med Oral Pathol*, **74**, 193–200.

Adenoid squamous cell carcinoma

Clinical features

In adenoid squamous cell carcinoma (acantholytic squamous cell carcinoma, pseudoglandular squamous cell carcinoma, adenoacanthoma) the majority of tumors present on the lower lip with a five-fold male predilection.[1,2] Approximately 21% occur on the upper lip, an unusual site for the more usual squamous cell carcinoma.[3] While lip lesions generally have a good prognosis, intraoral tumors have a mortality of up to 75%.[2–5]

Histological features

Conventional squamous cell carcinoma must be identified. Pseudoglandular structures with central 'lumina' lined by two to three layers of atypical squamous epithelium are seen within the tumor islands (*Fig. 10.229*). Typically these contain rounded acantholytic tumor cells within the 'lumina' (*Fig. 10.230*).[2,3] In most lesions, the acantholysis appears to begin in the immediate suprabasal cells.[6] In lip lesions, there is typically a background of solar elastosis and sometimes acantholytic solar keratosis is present, supporting the association with sun damage.[7] Clear cell change or a desmoplastic response may also be seen.[8]

The epithelial cells stain for cytokeratins and EMA but not for mucin.[2,3,8]

Differential diagnosis

These lesions must be differentiated from adenosquamous carcinoma in which true glandular differentiation occurs. The latter is mucin positive and runs a more aggressive course (at least compared with lip lesions).

References

1. Tomich, C.E., Hutton, C.E. (1972) Adenoid squamous cell carcinoma of the lip: report of cases. *J Oral Surg*, **30**, 592–598.
2. Jones, A.C., Freedman, P.D., Kerpel, S.M. (1993) Oral adenoid squamous cell carcinoma: a report of three cases and review of the literature. *J Oral Maxillofac Surg*, **51**, 676–681.
3. Jacoway, J.R., Nelson, J.F., Boyers, R.C. (1971) Adenoid squamous-cell carcinoma (adenoacanthoma of the oral labial mucosa). *Oral Surg Oral Med Oral Pathol*, **32**, 444–449.
4. Goldman, R.L., Klein, H.Z., Sung, M. (1977) Adenoid squamous cell carcinoma of the oral cavity: report of the first case arising in the tongue. *Arch Otolaryngol*, **103**, 496–498.
5. Takagi, M., Sakota, Y., Takayama, S. et al (1977) Adenoid squamous cell carcinoma of the oral mucosa: report of two autopsy cases. *Cancer*, **40**, 2250–2255.
6. Batsakis, J.G., Huser, J. (1990) Squamous carcinomas with glandlike (adenoid) features. *Ann Otol Rhinol Laryngol*, **99**, 87–88.
7. Weitzner, S. (1974) Adenoid squamous-cell carcinoma of vermilion mucosa of lower lip. *Oral Surg Oral Med Oral Pathol*, **37**, 589–593.
8. Ferlito, A., Devaney, K.O., Milroy, C.M. et al (1996) Mucosal adenoid squamous cell carcinoma of the head and neck. *Ann Otol Rhinol Laryngol*, **105**, 409–413.

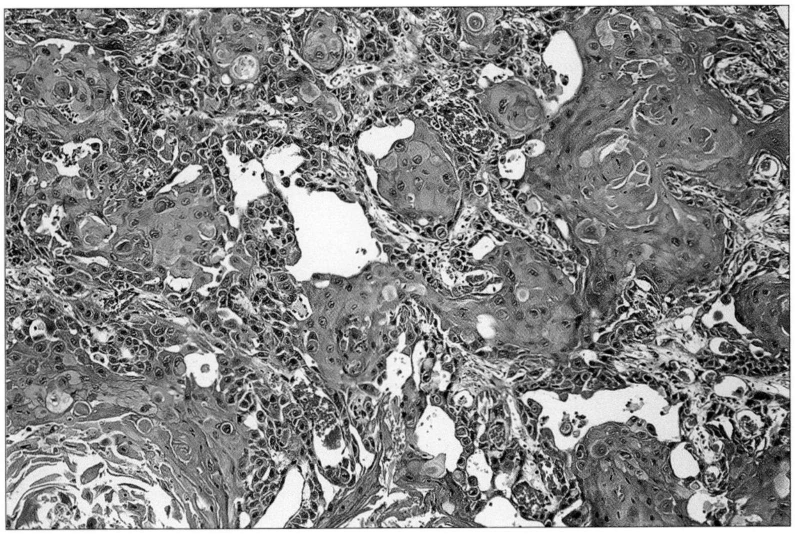

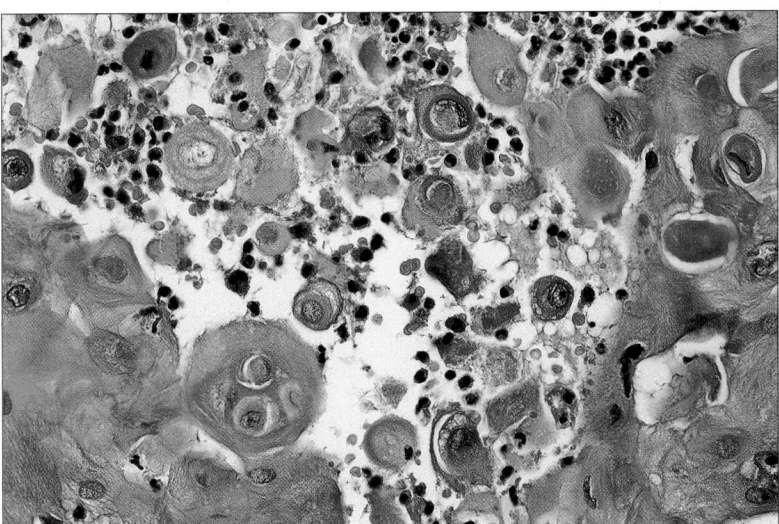

Fig. 10.229
Acantholytic squamous cell carcinoma: note the pseudoglandular structures.

Fig. 10.230
Acantholytic squamous cell carcinoma: note the atypical acantholytic cells.

Verrucous carcinoma

Clinical features

Verrucous carcinoma presents in older individuals (usually seventh decade) with a predilection for the buccal mucosa and gingiva (more than 70% of cases) and is strongly associated with the use of smoke-less tobacco or cigarettes.[1–4] The tumors are white, fungating, cauliflower-like masses, generally several centimeters in size and have usually been present for several years when patients are finally diagnosed (*Fig. 10.231*). There may be destruction of underlying bone and other structures on a broad advancing front. Reactive lymphadenopathy is often present and nodal metastases are distinctly unusual except in irradiated tumors.[1,4] Between 17 and 20% of patients may have associated leukoplakia (most likely verrucous leukoplakia) and up to 38% have a second primary carcinoma.[1,4]

Some controversy exists regarding the use of radiotherapy as primary treatment for oral verrucous carcinoma and the risk of anaplastic transformation and metastasis.[1] A review reports that this modality of treatment controls disease in only 43% of cases and leads to anaplastic transformation in approximately 7% of cases with 100% mortality.[5]

Histological features

Verrucous carcinoma is characterized by marked hyperparakeratosis with keratin plugs between papillary projections of benign-appearing epithelium. The epithelium forms large, bulbous, frond-like rete ridges that push rather than infiltrate, on a broad advancing front (*Fig. 10.232*). Although there may be slight epithelial atypia, pleomorphism or anaplasia is lacking (*Fig. 10.233*). Some of the rete ridges exhibit central

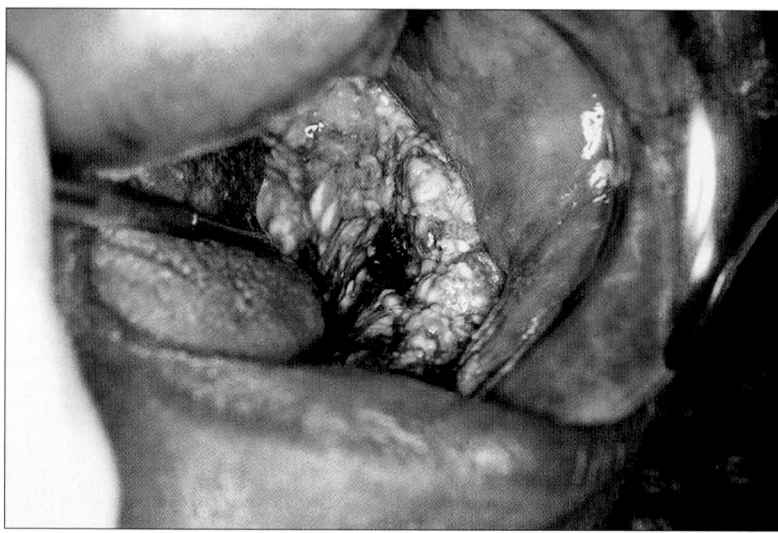

Fig. 10.231
Verrucous carcinoma: there is a warty mass in the mandibular buccal mucosa and sulcus.

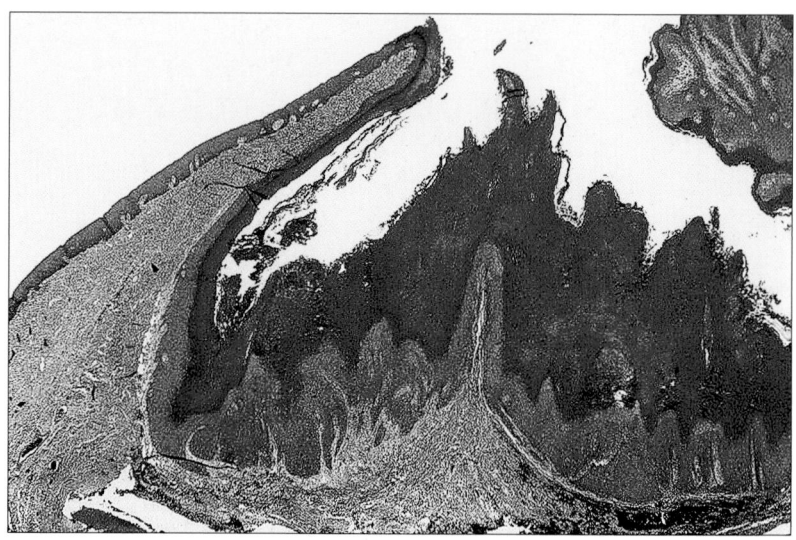

Fig. 10.232
Verrucous carcinoma: there is an endophytic proliferation of squamous epithelium with a broadly invasive front; note the normal gingival epithelium at the periphery.

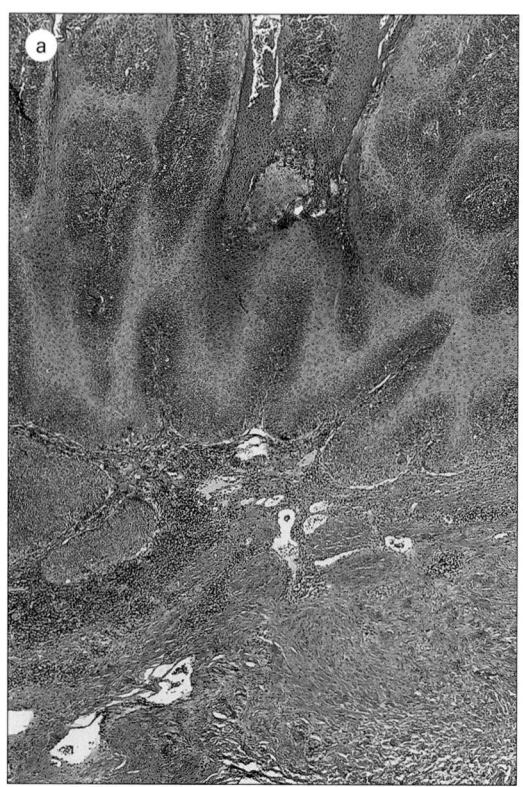
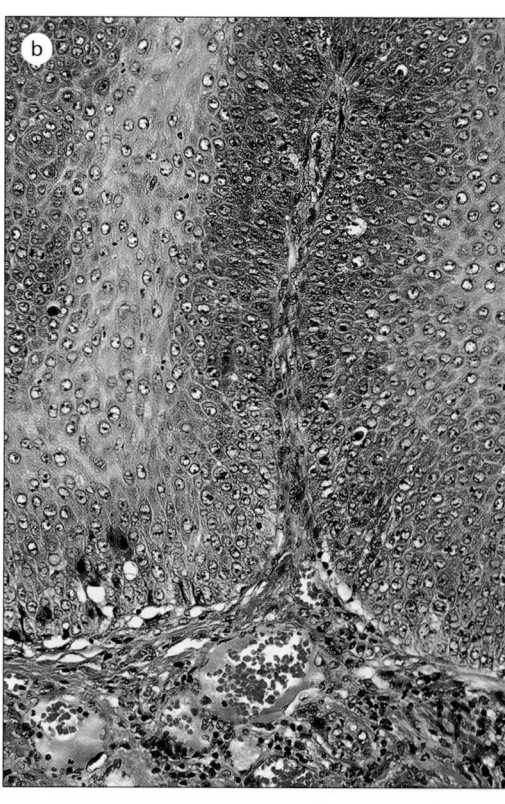

Fig. 10.233
(a, b) Verrucous carcinoma: there is minimal cytological atypia and no single cell infiltration.

degeneration and abscess formation. Foreign body granulomas may develop secondary to keratin spillage.[1,2,4] Lymph node dissections do not usually reveal metastatic disease.

Foci of more typical infiltrative squamous cell carcinoma may be seen in one-fifth of tumors, the so-called 'hybrid tumor'. These foci may be responsible for a higher recurrence rate (approximately 30%) and subsequent anaplastic transformation, independent of radiation treatment.[4]

Differential diagnosis

Strict criteria must be adhered to for the diagnosis of verrucous carcinoma. Papillary squamous cell carcinoma, which is usually minimally if at all keratinized, is composed of convoluted thin ribbons of highly atypical squamous cells, with dysplastic cells involving the full thickness of the epithelium.[6] These are distinct from the papillary well-differentiated squamous cell carcinoma that may also resemble verrucous carcinoma but can be distinguished by the presence of significant atypia, pleomorphism, dyskeratosis, keratin pearl formation and infiltration of the stroma (even if the invasion is of the 'blunt' type). 'Hybrid verrucous carcinoma' in the majority of cases most probably represents papillary well-differentiated squamous cell carcinoma. Cases of verrucous carcinoma exhibiting perineural invasion by 'nests of well-differentiated squamous epithelium' may also actually represent papillary well-differentiated squamous cell carcinoma.[7]

Intraoral so-called keratoacanthomas are rare and may resemble verrucous carcinoma.[8-11] They typically have a crateriform architecture with the cup-shaped depression filled with keratin. Cells have 'glassy' cytoplasm and the underlying stroma is usually infiltrated by cells exhibiting cytological atypia. Keratoacanthomas are best regarded (and treated) as a variant of well-differentiated squamous cell carcinoma.

References

1. Kraus, F.T., Perez-Mesa, C. (1966) Verrucous carcinoma – clinical and pathologic study of 105 cases involving oral cavity, larynx and genitalia. *Cancer*, 19, 26–38.
2. McCoy, J.M., Waldron, C.A. (1981) Verrucous carcinoma of the oral cavity. *Oral Surg Oral Med Oral Pathol*, 52, 623–629.
3. McDonald, J., Crissman, J.D., Gluckman, J.L. (1982) Verrucous carcinoma of the oral cavity. *Head Neck Surg*, 5, 22–28.
4. Medina, J.E., Dichtel, W., Luna, M.A. (1984) Verucous-squamous carcinomas of the oral cavity: a clinicopathologic study of 104 cases. *Arch Otolaryngol*, 110, 437–440.
5. Ferlito, A., Rinaldo, A., Mannara, G.M. (1998) Is primary radiotherapy an appropriate option for the treatment of verrucous carcinoma of the head and neck? *J Laryngol Otol*, 112, 132–139.
6. Crissman, J.D., Kessis, T., Shah, K.V. et al (1988) Squamous papillary neoplasia of the adult upper aerodigestive tract. *Hum Pathol*, 19, 1387–1396.
7. Demian, S.D., Bushkin, F.L., Echevarria, R.A. (1973) Perineural invasion and anaplastic transformation of verrucous carcinoma. *Cancer*, 32, 395–401.
8. Svirsky, J.A., Freedman, P.D., Lumerman, H. (1977) Solitary intraoral keratoacanthoma. *Oral Surg Oral Med Oral Pathol*, 43, 116–122.
9. Freedman, P.D., Kerpel, S.M., Begel, H. et al (1979) Solitary intraoral keratoacanthoma. Report of a case. *Oral Surg Oral Med Oral Pathol*, 47, 74–76.
10. Eversole, L.R., Leider, A.S., Alexander, G. (1982) Intraoral and labial keratoacanthoma. *Oral Surg Oral Med Oral Pathol*, 54, 663–667.
11. Ellis, G.L. (1983) Differentiating keratoacanthoma from squamous cell carcinoma of the lower lip: an analysis of intraepithelial elastic fibers and intracytoplasmic glycogen. *Oral Surg Oral Med Oral Pathol*, 56, 527–532.

Midline destructive disease

Clinical features

Midline destructive disease (also known as midline lethal granuloma, centrofacial malignant granuloma, polymorphic reticulosis) presents with deep ulceration and necrosis of the midline of the face, nasal septum and palate. Although once thought to represent a distinct entity, it is now recognized that the features may be caused by a wide range of conditions, including infections (particularly deep fungal, treponemal and mycobacterial), chronic cocaine use, Wegener's granulomatosis, malignancy and, in particular, NK/T-cell lymphoma of the sinonasal tract.[1-3] T-cell lymphomas constituted 60% of all such midline lesions.[1] These lymphomas (also previously referred to as malignant histiocytosis and angiocentric lymphoma) consist of small and large atypical lymphocytes dispersed in a polymorphic infiltrate of neutrophils, reactive lymphocytes, histiocytes and plasma cells, and showing marked invasion of vessels with consequent necrosis.[4,5] There is a strong association with Epstein–Barr virus and presentation in native South Americans and Asians (see p. 1418).[4,6,7]

References

1. Grange, C., Cabane, J., Dubois, A. et al (1992) Centrofacial malignant granulomas. Clinicopathologic study of 40 cases and review of the literature. *Medicine (Baltimore)*, 71, 179–196.
2. Van Gorp, J., De Bruin, P.C., Sie-Go, D.M. et al (1995) Nasal T-cell lymphoma: a clinicopathological and immunophenotypic analysis of 13 cases. *Histopathology*, 27, 139–148.
3. Trimarchi, M., Gregorini, G., Facchetti, F. et al (2001) Cocaine-induced midline destructive lesions: clinical, radiographic, histopathologic, and serologic features and their differentiation from Wegener granulomatosis. *Medicine (Baltimore)*, 80, 391–404.
4. Chan, J.K., Ng, C.S., Lau, W.H. et al (1987) Most nasal/nasopharyngeal lymphomas are peripheral T-cell neoplasms. *Am J Surg Pathol*, 11, 418–429.
5. Ferry, J.A., Sklar, J., Zukerberg, L.R. et al (1991) Nasal lymphoma. A clinicopathologic study with immunophenotypic and genotypic analysis. *Am J Surg Pathol*, 15, 268–279.
6. Arber, D.A., Weiss, L.M., Albujar, P.F. et al (1993) Nasal lymphomas in Peru. High incidence of T-cell immunophenotype and Epstein–Barr virus infection. *Am J Surg Pathol*, 17, 392–399.
7. Kanavaros, P., Lescs, M.C., Briere, J. et al (1993) Nasal T-cell lymphoma: a clinicopathologic entity associated with peculiar phenotype and with Epstein–Barr virus. *Blood*, 81, 2688–2695.

Pigmented lesions

Amalgam tattoo

Clinical features

These are asymptomatic gray, bluish, black or slate-colored macules that generally occur on the gingiva/alveolar ridge (approximately 50%), the buccal mucosa (approximately 25%) or the floor of mouth (approximately 10%) (*Figs 10.234, 10.235*). However, they can occur anywhere in the oral cavity of adults.[1]

Pathogenesis and histological features

Particles of amalgam restorations may be traumatically implanted into the mucosa by the dentist during placement or removal of a restoration, by the patient from bite injury, from leakage and disintegration of a restoration (or root canal filling material) or from a restoration falling into a tooth socket after extraction.

Amalgam in the tissues takes two main forms: as large dense dark-brown to black fragments that are often macroscopic, and as fine golden- or dark-brown dusty granules (*Fig. 10.236*).[1] The fine granules characteristically are dispersed along connective tissue fibers since the silver deposits on elastin and reticulin. They particularly outline the basement membrane of the epithelium and blood vessels and stain nerve and muscle sheaths (*Fig. 10.237*). The collagen itself may sometimes be stained a golden color. In approximately 50% of cases, a lymphocytic and/or histiocytic and foreign body granulomatous reaction is seen around the larger particles, some of which are present within the cytoplasm of macrophages and giant cells.[1]

Differential diagnosis

Graphite (pencil lead) can present as clumps of black particles. These tend to be coarse and they do not localize to the connective tissue fibers. Aluminum and silicon (hardeners for graphite) may be identified using dispersive x-ray microanalysis.[2]

Silver tattoos of non-amalgam derivation have been reported in patients following silver nitrate cautery.[3]

References

1.   Buchner, A., Hansen, L.S. (1980) Amalgam pigmentation (amalgam tattoo) of the oral mucosa. A clinicopathologic study of 268 cases. *Oral Surg Oral Med Oral Pathol*, **49**, 139–147.
2.   Daley, T.D., Gibson, D. (1990) Practical applications of energy dispersive X-ray microanalysis in diagnostic oral pathology. *Oral Surg Oral Med Oral Pathol*, **69**, 339–344.
3.   Mayall, F., Wild, D. (1996) A silver tattoo of the nasal mucosa after silver nitrate cautery. *J Laryngol Otol*, **110**, 609–610.

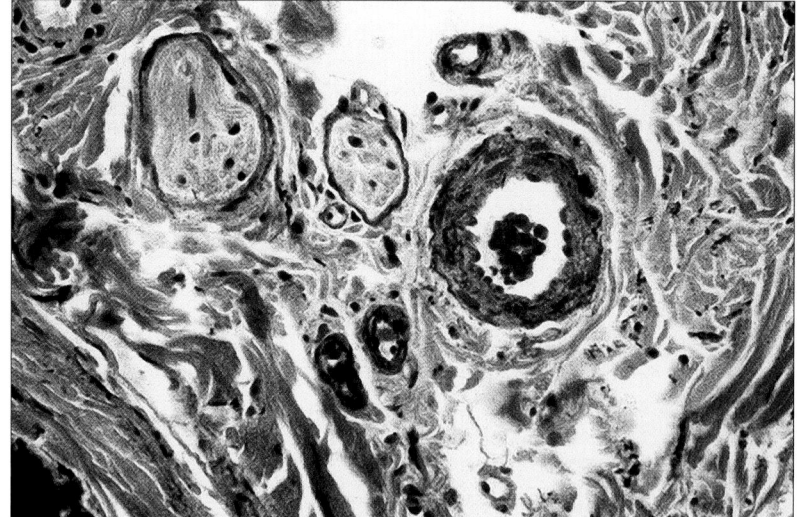

Fig. 10.234
Amalgam tattoo: there are slate-gray macules on the left buccal mucosa corresponding to some large amalgam restorations.

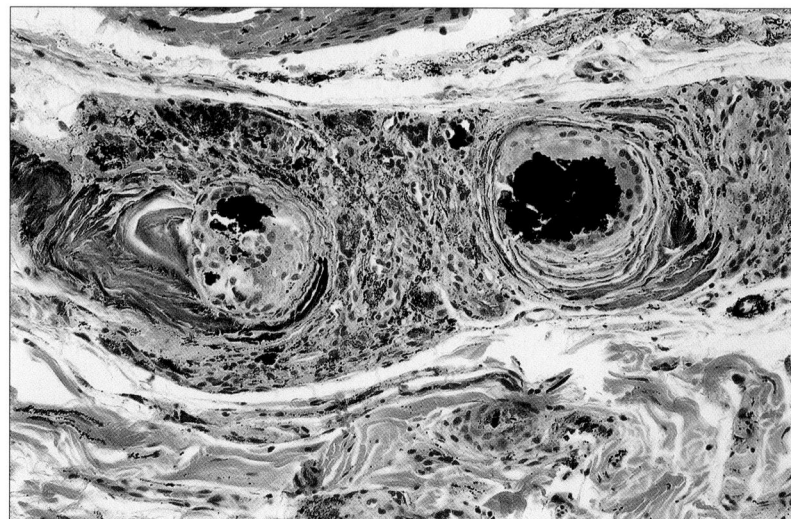

Fig. 10.236
Amalgam tattoo: there are coarse and fine granules of amalgam associated with foreign body granulomas; there is also a golden stain to the collagen fibers.

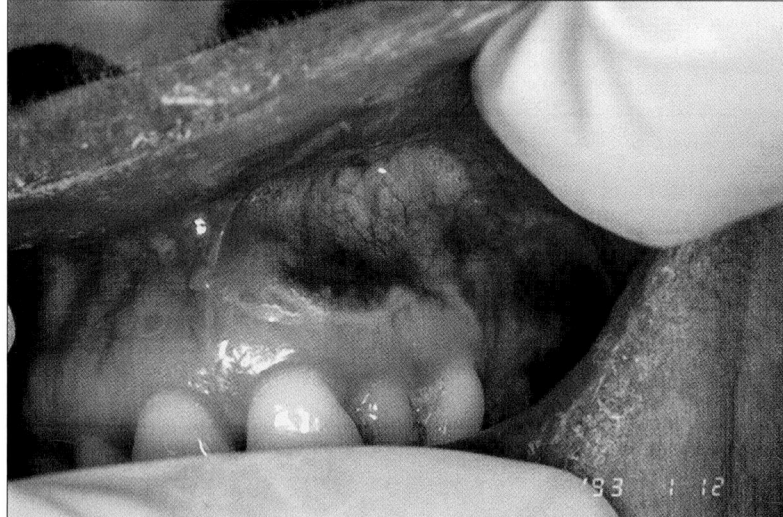

Fig. 10.235
Amalgam tattoo: there is a blue–black macule on the attached gingiva superior to a semi-lunar scar; this tattoo is caused by a root canal-related surgical procedure.

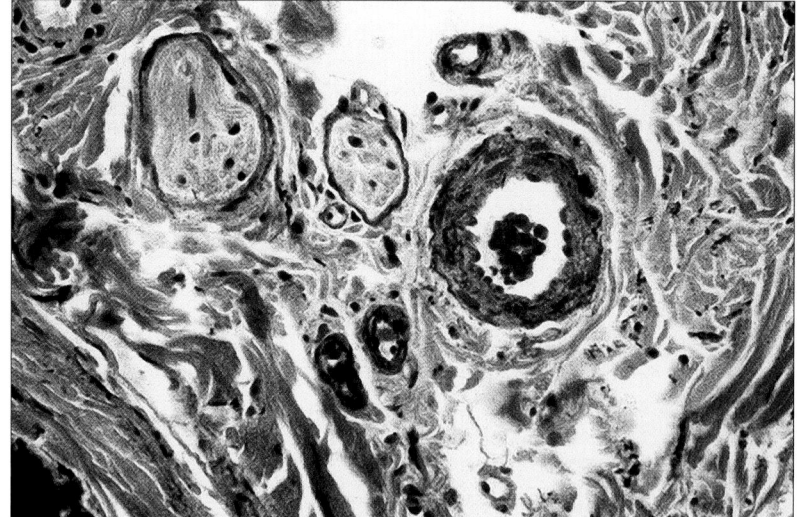

Fig. 10.237
Amalgam tattoo: note the typical staining of the basement membrane and nerve fibers.

Oral melanocytic lesions

Four conditions are of particular importance: melanotic macule, melanoacanthosis, melanocytic nevus and melanoma.

Oral melanotic macule

Clinical features

Originally, these were labeled 'labial melanotic macule' since most of them are found on the lips (*Fig. 10.238*).[1,2] However, subsequent reports identified similar appearing lesions intraorally (especially on the palate) and at other mucosal sites such as on the genitalia (*Fig. 10.239*). The preferred term for such oral lesions is 'oral melanotic macule'.[3]

These are often solitary (two-thirds solitary, one-third multiple), well-defined, brown-to-black macules measuring less than 1.5 cm and occurring on the lips (usually lower), palate, gingiva or buccal mucosa in adults with a female predilection (2:1).[1,4,5] The intensity of pigmentation is usually constant unlike in ephelides, which tend to darken with sun exposure. The lesion has often been present for months to years and 14–25% give a history of increase in size.[1,4] Biopsy is usually performed to exclude a melanoma. Oral melanotic macules tend not to recur except in those associated with HIV infection.[6]

Pathogenesis and histological features

The melanocytes may be functionally hyperactive as suggested by melanin incontinence and the presence of heavily melanized melanosomes seen ultrastructurally although the cause for such activity is unclear.[7] Since 14% of patients with labial melanotic macules give a family history, there may be a genetic predisposition. Some melanotic macules may represent a drug-induced hypermelanosis (such as may occur in HIV-related disease), an unusual distribution of physiologic/racial pigmentation, a manifestation of endocrine disorder, a postinflammatory hypermelanosis, or represent an idiopathic condition. Oral melanotic macules are also associated with longitudinal pigmented bands in the nails (melanonychia striata), pigmentation of the genitalia and other skin and mucosal sites in the Laugier–Hunziker syndrome (see p. 1007).[8–10] Correlation with clinical data is essential in helping to arrive at a definitive diagnosis.

The oral melanotic macule is characterized by increased melanin pigmentation in the basal cell layer of the epithelium, usually localized to the tips of the rete ridges with no or only minimal melanocytic hyperplasia (*Fig. 10.240*).[1,3,7] One study, however, found that melanocytic hyperplasia is a constant feature.[11] There are usually increased numbers of melanophages in the lamina propria that correlate with the degree of chronic inflammation present. There may be associated mild hyperkeratosis and acanthosis.

Ultrastructurally, stage III and stage IV heavily melanized melanosomes are clustered in complexes within melanocytes, keratinocytes and melanophages.[7]

Differential diagnosis

Postinflammatory hypermelanosis exhibits increased melanin in the basal keratinocytes without concentration at the rete ridges. In addition, there is melanin deposition within the lamina propria, with increased numbers

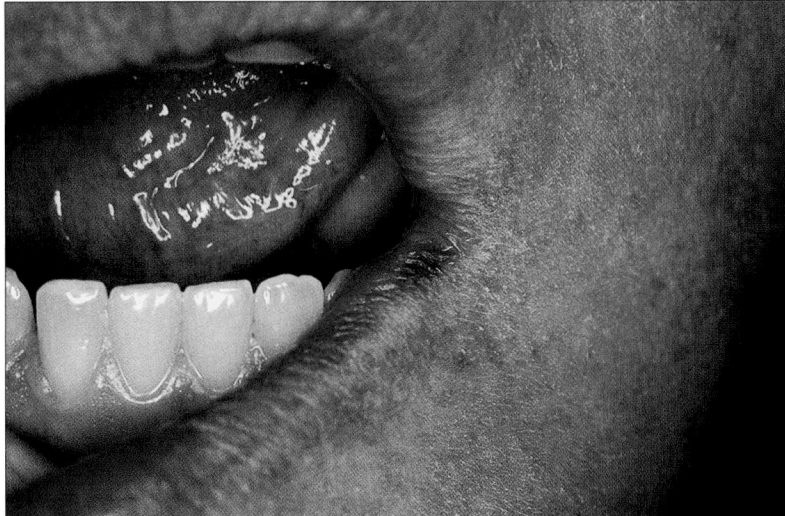

Fig. 10.238
Oral melanotic macule: note the typical dark brown-to-black macule on the vermilion.

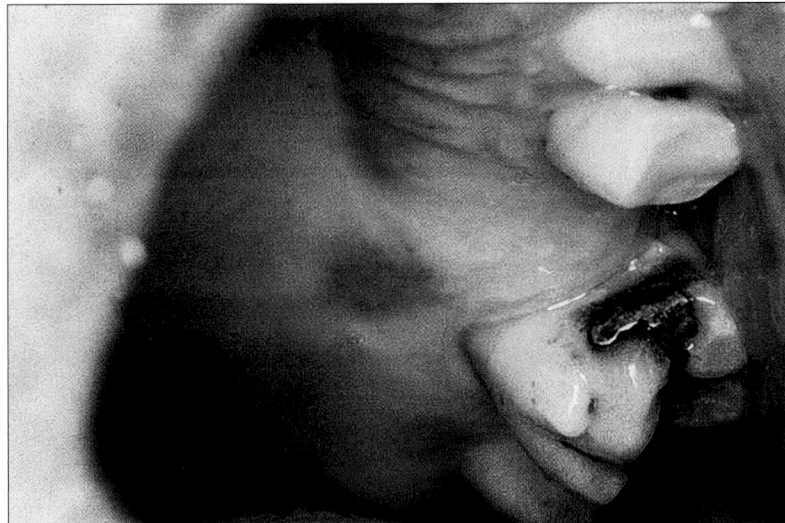

Fig. 10.239
Oral melanotic macule: there is a tan macule on the mucosa of the hard palate.

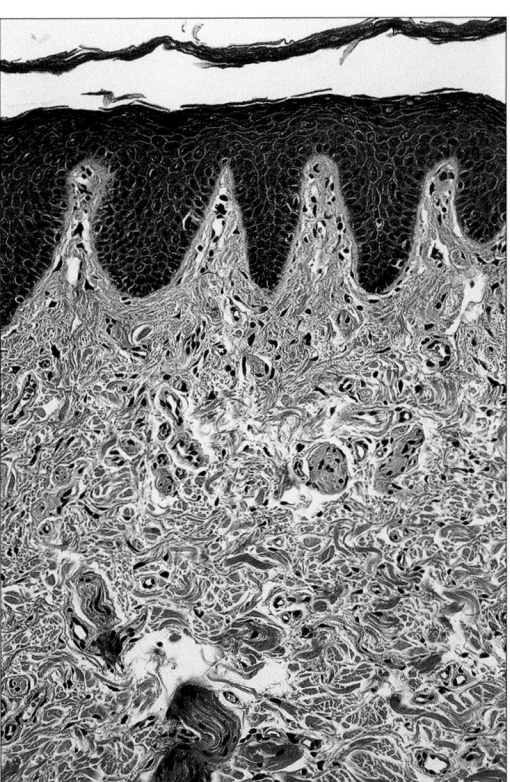

Fig. 10.240
Oral melanotic macule: there is increased melanization of the basal cells in the absence of melanocytic hyperplasia or inflammation.

of melanophages, a more intense lymphoplasmacytic infiltrate and vascular ectasia (*Fig. 10.241*). These features are particularly prominent in resolving lesions, such as may be seen in lichenoid mucositis and oral lichen planus.

Ephelides occur on sun-exposed areas and the darkness of pigmentation increases with sun exposure. Lentigo shows epithelial and melanocytic hyperplasia in addition to increased melanin pigmentation. Rare cases of oral lentigo simplex have been reported where epithelial and melanocytic hyperplasia have been identified.[12]

Syndromes associated with melanotic macules such as Peutz–Jegher's syndrome, Albright's disease, neurofibromatosis and Laugier–Hunziker syndrome are differentiated primarily by clinical features since they are histologically identical. Minocycline-induced pigmentation usually shows a combination of melanin and iron deposits in the lamina propria (see p. 638).

References

1. Weathers, D.R., Corio, R.L., Crawford, B.E. et al (1976) The labial melanotic macule. *Oral Surg Oral Med Oral Pathol*, **42**, 196–205.
2. Spann, C.R., Owen, L.G., Hodge, S.J. (1987) The labial melanotic macule. *Arch Dermatol*, **123**, 1029–1031.
3. Page, L.R., Corio, R.L., Crawford, B.E. et al (1977) The oral melanotic macule. *Oral Surg Oral Med Oral Pathol*, **44**, 219–226.
4. Buchner, A., Hansen, L.S. (1979) Melanotic macule of the oral mucosa. A clinicopathologic study of 105 cases. *Oral Surg Oral Med Oral Pathol*, **48**, 244–249.
5. Kaugars, G.E., Heise, A.P., Riley, W.T. et al (1993) Oral melanotic macules. A review of 353 cases. *Oral Surg Oral Med Oral Pathol*, **76**, 59–61.
6. Ficarra, G., Shillitoe, E.J., Adler-Storthz, K. et al (1990) Oral melanotic macules in patients infected with human immunodeficiency virus. *Oral Surg Oral Med Oral Pathol*, **70**, 748–755.
7. Ho, K.K., Dervan, P., O'Loughlin, S. et al (1993) Labial melanotic macule: a clinical, histopathologic, and ultrastructural study. *J Am Acad Dermatol*, **28**, 33–39.
8. Dupre, A., Viraben, R. (1990) Laugier's disease. *Dermatologica*, **181**, 183–186.
9. Kemmett, D., Ellis, J., Spencer, M.J. et al (1990) The Laugier–Hunziker syndrome – a clinical review of six cases. *Clin Exp Dermatol*, **15**, 111–114.
10. Mignogna, M.D., Lo Muzio, L., Ruoppo, E. et al (1999) Oral manifestations of idiopathic lenticular mucocutaneous pigmentation (Laugier–Hunziker syndrome): a clinical, histopathological and ultrastructural review of 12 cases. *Oral Dis*, **5**, 80–86.
11. Sexton, F.M., Maize, J.C. (1987) Melanotic macules and melanoacanthomas of the lip. *Am J Dermatopathol*, **9**, 438–444.
12. Buchner, A., Merrell, P.W., Hansen, L.S. et al (1991) Melanocytic hyperplasia of the oral mucosa. *Oral Surg Oral Med Oral Pathol*, **71**, 58–62.

Melanoacanthosis

Clinical features

Melanoacanthosis (oral melanoacanthoma, mucosal melanotic macule) should not be confused with cutaneous melanoacanthoma. It occurs in young African–Americans, usually females (greater than 70%), and typically presents in areas that are susceptible to trauma such as the buccal mucosa, lower lip, palate and gingiva.[1,2] The macules have a slightly rough surface and are brown, black or bluish (*Fig. 10.242*). The lesion may be well or poorly demarcated. Most lesions are solitary. A history of trauma is present in only 50% of cases. Lesions may grow rapidly to several centimeters in size. Complete resolution occurs within weeks to months.

Pathogenesis and histological features

It is likely that oral melanoacanthosis is a reactive lesion, most probably precipitated by trauma with subsequent inflammation resulting in stimulation of dendritic melanocytes and transepithelial elimination of melanocytes.[3]

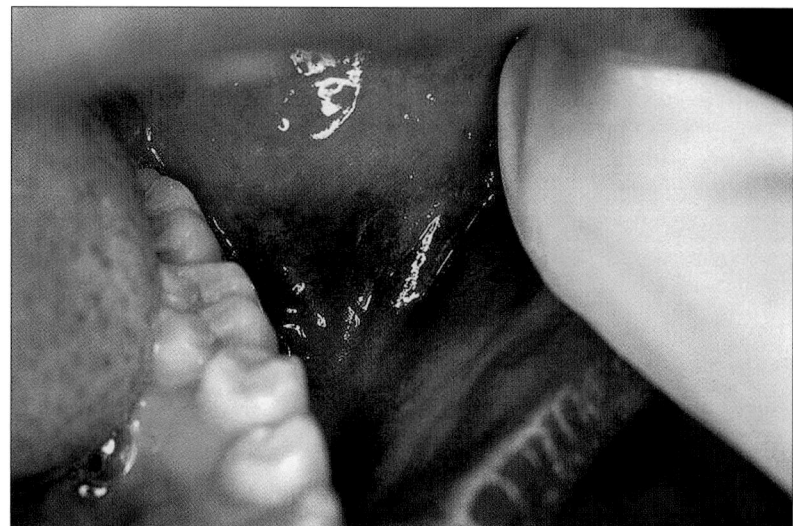

Fig. 10.242
Melanoacanthosis: there is a blue–black macule on the buccal mucosa that enlarged rapidly over a few weeks.

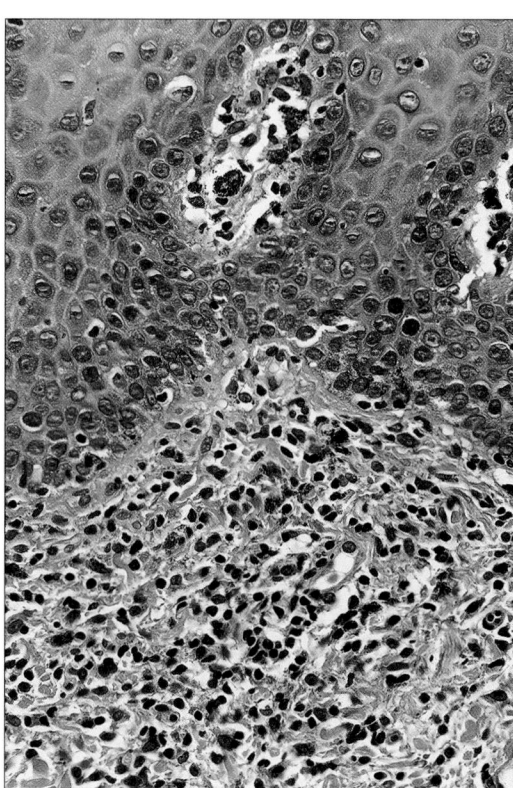

Fig. 10.241
Postinflammatory hypermelaninosis: there is increased melanization of the basal cells, vascular ectasia, chronic inflammation and many melanophages in the lamina propria.

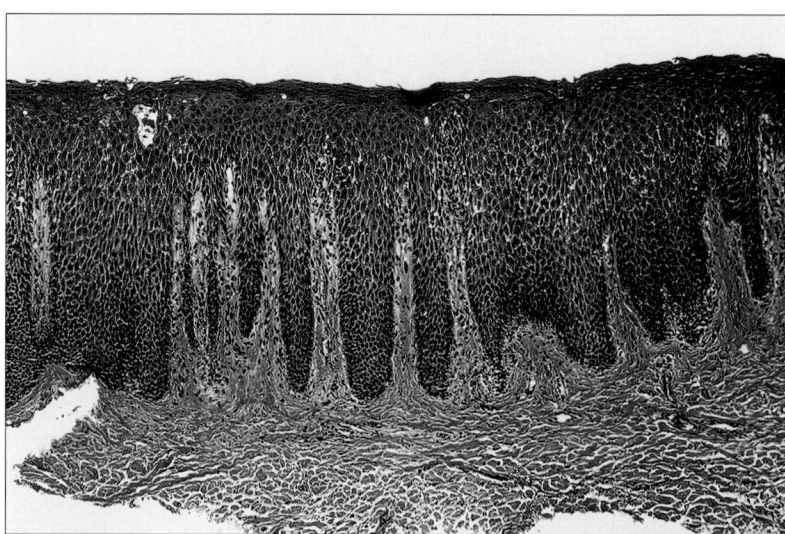

Fig. 10.243
Melanoacanthosis: there is parakeratosis, acanthosis and spongiosis.

There is parakeratosis and acanthosis; spongiosis is also usually evident (*Fig. 10.243*). Numerous dendritic melanocytes and their melanin-laden processes are found insinuating between keratinocytes throughout the full thickness of the epithelium (*Fig. 10.244*).[1,2,4,5] Melanophages, a mild lymphocytic infiltrate and vascular ectasia may all be seen in the lamina propria. Sometimes the spongiosis may be so severe as to form spongiform vesicles.[6]

Differential diagnosis

Melanoacanthosis differs from a nevus by the absence of any junctional activity. The benign cytology readily distinguishes this lesion from oral melanoma.

References

1. Goode, R.K., Crawford, B.E., Callihan, M.D. et al (1983) Oral melanoacanthoma. Review of the literature and report of ten cases. *Oral Surg Oral Med Oral Pathol*, **56**, 622–628.
2. Tomich, C.E., Zunt, S.L. (1990) Melanoacanthosis (melanoacanthoma) of the oral mucosa. *J Dermatol Surg Oncol*, **16**, 231–236.
3. Maize, J.C. (1988) Mucosal melanosis. *Derm Clin*, **6**, 283–293.
4. Sexton, F.M., Maize, J.C. (1987) Melanotic macules and melanoacanthomas of the lip. *Am J Dermatopathol*, **9**, 438–444.
5. Horlick, H.P., Walther, R.R., Zegarelli, D.J. et al (1988) Mucosal melanotic macule, reactive type: a simulation of melanoma. *J Am Acad Dermatol*, **19**, 786–791.
6. Zemtsov, A., Bergfeld, W.F. (1989) Oral melanoacanthoma with prominent spongiotic intraepithelial vesicles. *J Cutan Pathol*, **16**, 365–369.

Oral melanocytic nevus

Clinical features

Oral melanocytic nevi are generally diagnosed and biopsied in the third and fourth decades of life with a female predilection (2:1). Approximately 85% are clinically pigmented (gray, brown, blue or black, or a combination thereof) and almost all are raised, being nodular or papular lesions.[1,2] The hard palate and buccal mucosa are the favored sites, followed by the labial mucosa, gingiva and vermilion. Seventy-five per cent of all intraoral blue nevi occur on the palate followed by the labial mucosa, whereas intramucosal banal nevi occur on the palate and buccal mucosa equally.[3]

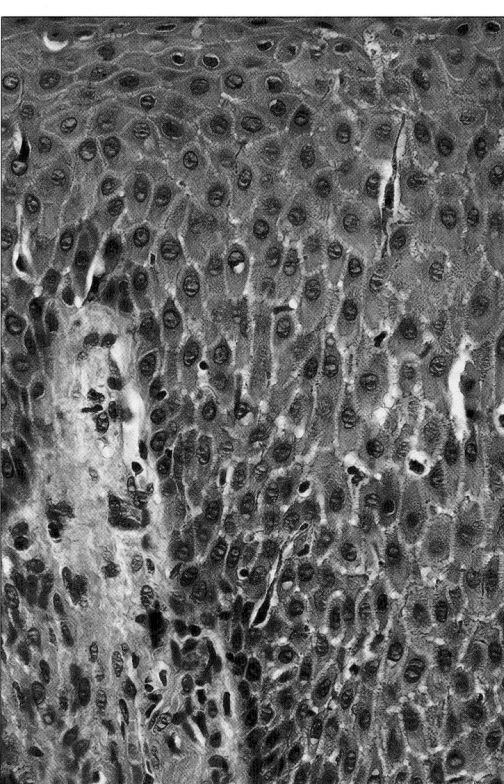

Fig. 10.244
Melanoacanthosis: benign dendritic melanocytes are present throughout the full thickness of the epithelium.

Histological features

Melanocytic nevi in the oral cavity are histologically identical to those found on the skin. The intramucosal nevus (counterpart of the dermal nevus) is the most common (63–66%), followed by the blue nevus (19–25%), compound nevus (6%) and junctional nevus (3–5%).[1,3] Epithelial hyperplasia is seen in association with intramucosal nevi in approximately 50% of cases, sometimes associated with benign lentiginous melanocytic hyperplasia. Approximately 13% may be histologically non-pigmented. Nevus cells are also sometimes seen within the underlying adipose tissue and muscle.[1] The spindle cells of blue nevi are usually separated from the overlying epithelium by a Grenz zone. Intramucosal and oral blue nevi stain for S-100 protein and HMB-45.

Combined nevi (blue and intramucosal) have been reported.[3] Spitz and congenital nevi have also been described, albeit rarely.[4–6]

References

1. Buchner, A., Hansen, L.S. (1979) Pigmented nevi of the oral mucosa: a clinicopathologic study of 32 new cases and review of 75 cases from the literature. Part I. A clinicopathologic study of 32 new cases. *Oral Surg Oral Med Oral Pathol*, **48**, 131–142.
2. Buchner, A., Hansen, L.S. (1980) Pigmented nevi of the oral mucosa: a clinicopathologic study of 32 new cases and review of 75 cases from the literature. Part II. Analysis of 107 cases. *Oral Surg Oral Med Oral Pathol*, **49**, 55–62.
3. Buchner, A., Leider, A.S., Merrell, P.W. et al (1990) Melanocytic nevi of the oral mucosa: a clinicopathologic study of 130 cases from northern California. *J Oral Pathol Med*, **19**, 197–201.
4. Gazit, D., Daniels, T.E. (1994) Oral melanocytic lesions: differences in expression of HMB-45 and S-100 antigens in round and spindle cells of malignant and benign lesions. *J Oral Pathol Med*, **23**, 60–64.
5. Nikai, H., Miyauchi, M., Ogawa, I. et al (1990) Spitz nevus of the palate. Report of a case. *Oral Surg Oral Med Oral Pathol*, **69**, 603–608.
6. Allen, C.M., Pellegrini, A. (1995) Probable congenital melanocytic nevus of the oral mucosa: case report. *Pediatr Dermatol*, **12**, 145–148.

Oral melanoma

Clinical features

Primary oral melanomas comprise up to 37–49% of mucosal head and neck melanomas.[1–3] It is particularly common in the Japanese.[4] Tumors are most often seen in adults with an equal sex distribution. The hard palate mucosa and maxillary gingiva are affected in more than 70% of cases. The lesions are usually pigmented and nodular with surrounding macular melanosis.[4,5] Between 20 and 70% of patients present with lymph node metastases.[1,3,6]

Overall, the prognosis for oral tumors is much worse than for cutaneous melanoma, the 5- and 10-year survival rates being 15% and 6% respectively, although one Japanese study had a 5-year cumulative survival rate of 64%.[7–9] A high rate of nodal metastasis, thick tumor at presentation, extensive tumor spread and the complicated anatomy of the maxillary complex make it difficult to completely excise the majority of these lesions.[5,7]

Histological features

Most tumors consist of malignant epithelioid and spindled melanoma cells, which are only rarely amelanotic. A radial growth phase is commonly seen but pagetoid spread is distinctly uncommon.[5,7] Most tumors present with a thickness of greater than 4 mm regardless of whether they are stage I or stage II tumors.[7] High clinical stage, tumor thickness greater than 5 mm, presence of vascular invasion, absence of melanin in histological sections and the development of nodal and distant metastases predict a worse prognosis.[3] Desmoplastic melanoma has been reported in the oral cavity.[10]

References

1. Berthelsen, A., Andersen, A.P., Jensen, T.S. et al (1984) Melanomas of the mucosa in the oral cavity and the upper respiratory passages. *Cancer*, **54**, 907–912.
2. Conley, J.J. (1989) Melanomas of the mucous membrane of the head and neck. *Laryngoscope*, **99**, 1248–1254.
3. Patel, S.G., Prasad, M.L., Escrig, M. et al (2002) Primary mucosal malignant melanoma of the head and neck. *Head Neck*, **24**, 247–257.

4. Takagi, M., Ishikawa, G., Mori, W. (1974) Primary malignant melanoma of the oral cavity in Japan. With special reference to mucosal melanosis. *Cancer,* **34,** 358–370.
5. Rapini, R.P., Golitz, L.E., Greer, R.O. Jr et al (1985) Primary malignant melanoma of the oral cavity. A review of 177 cases. *Cancer,* **55,** 1543–1551.
6. Doval, D.C., Rao, C.R., Saitha, K.S. et al (1996) Malignant melanoma of the oral cavity: report of 14 cases from a regional cancer centre. *Eur J Surg Oncol,* **22,** 245–249.
7. Umeda, M., Shimada, K. (1994) Primary malignant melanoma of the oral cavity – its histological classification and treatment. *Br J Oral Maxillofac Surg,* **32,** 39–47.

8. Gorsky, M., Epstein, J.B. (1998) Melanoma arising from the mucosal surfaces of the head and neck. *Oral Surg Oral Med Oral Pathol Oral Radiol Endod,* **86,** 715–719.
9. López-Graniel, C.M., Ochoa-Carrillo, F.J., Meneses-Garcia, A. (1999) Malignant melanoma of the oral cavity: diagnosis and treatment experience in a Mexican population. *Oral Oncol,* **35,** 425–430.
10. Kilpatrick, S.E., White, W. L., Browne, J.D. (1996) Desmoplastic malignant melanoma of the oral mucosa. An underrecognized diagnostic pitfall. *Cancer,* **78,** 383–389.

Other tumors

Granular cell tumor

Clinical features

The granular cell tumor (granular cell myoblastoma) presents at a variety of sites, most commonly the skin (38% of cases), the tongue (23–28%), the breast (16%) and the larynx, especially the true cord (8%).[1–3] Females are affected twice as often as males and the mean age at presentation is in the fourth decade.[2,4] In the mouth, the majority of cases (> 80%) occur in the tongue, with the lips, buccal mucosa and floor of mouth being other sites of involvement.[2,4] Approximately 8% of cases are multiple.[1] The lesions are yellowish-white, firm and indurated, painless masses or plaques generally measuring less than 2 cm in greatest dimension (*Fig. 10.245*). There is little tendency to recur even after incomplete excision.[5]

Pathogenesis and histological features

Although many theories of histogenesis have been proposed over the years, including myoblastic, neural, fibroblastic and undifferentiated mesenchymal cells, the consistent staining of the tumor cells with S-100 protein supports schwannian differentiation with degenerative changes.[6] Some investigators (a minority), however, contend that the granular cell tumor may represent either degenerate muscle or Schwann cells.[6,7]

The overlying epithelium exhibits pseudoepitheliomatous hyperplasia in one- to two-thirds of cases, which in some tumors is so marked as to result in a misdiagnosis of invasive squamous cell carcinoma.[3,4,6,7] The tumor is unencapsulated and presents as nests, cords and sheets of granular cells that commonly abut the epithelium, often but not invariably filling the entire lamina propria and infiltrating into the underlying muscle (*Fig. 10.246*).[4] There is usually close association between the tumor cells and skeletal muscle, nerves and blood vessels.[4,7,8]

Cells are large and polygonal with either distinct or indistinct cell borders and a small nucleus (*Fig. 10.247*).[4] The cytoplasm contains granules that are PAS positive and diastase resistant, although this is far from an invariable finding and is of limited diagnostic value. Luxol-fast blue granules have also been identified, suggesting the presence of myelin.[9]

S-100 protein is invariably positive and immunohistochemistry for muscle and histiocytic markers is consistently negative.[7,8,10] Stains for NK1/C3, vimentin, NSE, laminin, CD68 and PGP 9.5 are often positive.[11–16]

Ultrastructurally, the granular cells contain autophagic granules and vesicular bodies.[6,17] Membrane-bound angulate bodies are sometimes present, particularly in undifferentiated or perhaps transitional cells. A basal lamina is sometimes seen around the cells, supporting a schwannian derivation.[4,17] Infoldings of cell membrane similar to the formation of myelin sheaths have been noted.[9]

Malignant granular cell tumors are rare and exhibit pleomorphism, mitoses, necrosis and spindling of cells with a similar staining pattern. They may metastasize.[18,19]

Differential diagnosis

There is a variant of the granular cell tumor that does not stain with S-100 protein – the 'primitive polypoid granular cell tumor'. This lesion is polypoid with an epithelial collarette and the granular cells exhibit

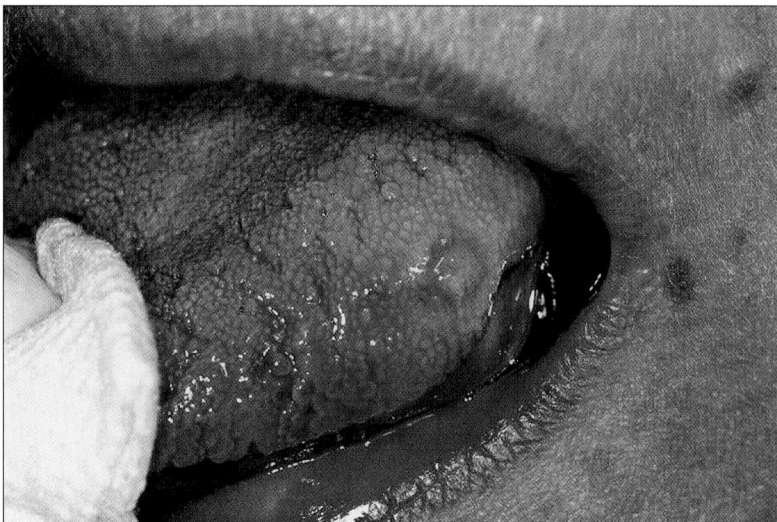

Fig. 10.245
Granular cell tumor: note the yellowish deep mass in the tongue.

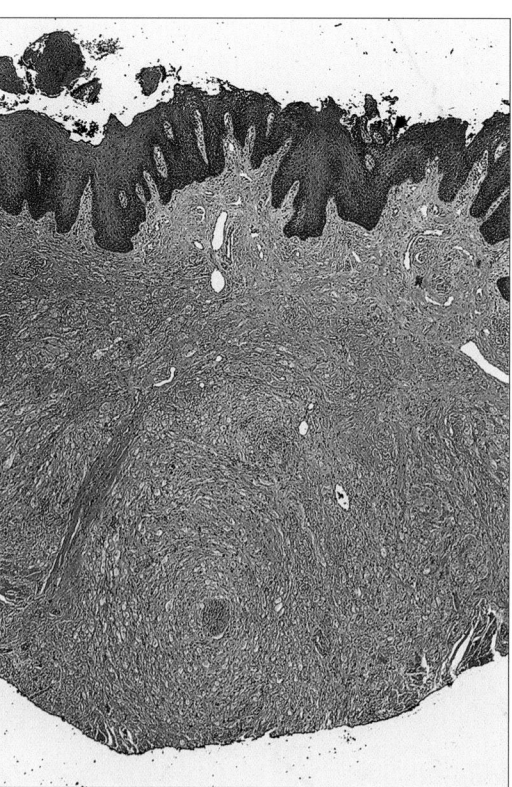

Fig. 10.246
Granular cell tumor: granular cells fill the lamina propria and insinuate between the muscle fibers of the tongue.

slight nuclear atypia.[20] The congenital granular cell tumor is also S-100 negative and has a delicate arborizing vasculature (see p. 1781). Granular cell tumor is further discussed on page 1799.

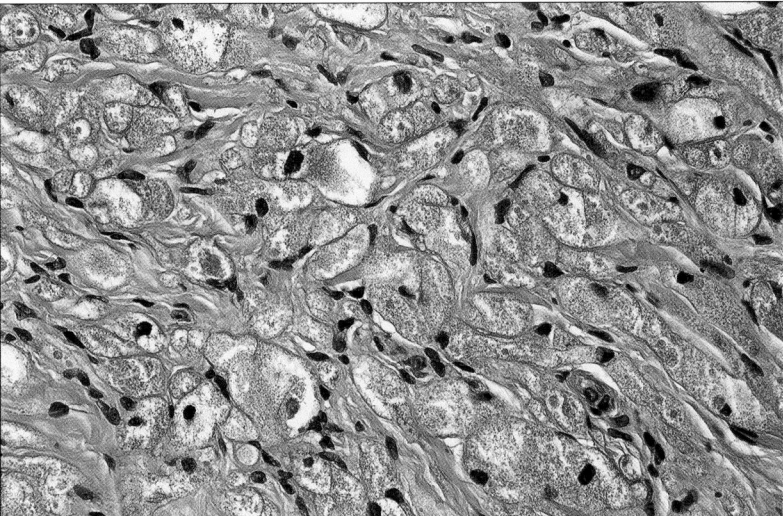

Fig. 10.247
Granular cell tumor: the cells are polyhedral with pale granular cytoplasm and small nuclei.

References

1. Strong, E.W., McDivitt, R.W., Brasfield, R.D. (1970) Granular cell myoblastoma. *Cancer*, 25, 415–422.
2. Peterson, L.J. (1974) Granular-cell tumor. Review of the literature and report of a case. *Oral Surg Oral Med Oral Pathol*, 37, 728–735.
3. Compagno, J., Hyams, V.J., Ste-Marie, P. (1975) Benign granular cell tumors of the larynx: a review of 36 cases with clinicopathologic data. *Ann Otol Rhinol Laryngol*, 84, 308–314.
4. Chaudhry, A.P., Jacobs, M.S., Sunder Raj, M. et al (1984) A clinico-pathologic study of 50 adult oral granular cell tumors. *J Oral Med*, 39, 97–103.
5. Worsaae, N., Schwartz, O., Pindborg, J.J. (1979) Follow-up study of 14 oral granular cell tumors. *Int J Oral Surg*, 8, 133–139.
6. Regezi, J.A., Batsakis, J.G., Courtney, R.M. (1979) Granular cell tumors of the head and neck. *J Oral Surg*, 37, 402–406.
7. Stewart, C.M., Watson, R.E., Eversole, L.R. et al (1988) Oral granular cell tumors: a clinicopathologic and immunocytochemical study. *Oral Surg Oral Med Oral Pathol*, 65, 427–435.
8. Nakazato, Y., Ishizeki, J., Takahashi, K. et al (1982) Immunohistochemical localization of S-100 protein in granular cell myoblastoma. *Cancer*, 49, 1624–1628.
9. Mittal, K.R., True, L.D. (1988) Origin of granules in granular cell tumor. Intracellular myelin formation with autodigestion. *Arch Pathol Lab Med*, 112, 302–303.
10. Stefansson, K., Wollmann, R.L. (1982) S-100 protein in granular cell tumors (granular cell myoblastomas). *Cancer*, 49, 1834–1838.
11. Buley, I.D., Gatter, K.C., Kelly, P.M. et al (1988) Granular cell tumours revisited. An immunohistological and ultrastructural study. *Histopathology*, 12, 263–274.
12. Regezi, J.A., Zarbo, R.J., Courtney, R.M. et al (1989) Immunoreactivity of granular cell lesions of skin, mucosa, and jaw. *Cancer*, 64, 1455–1460.
13. Tsang, W.Y., Chan, J.K. (1992) KP1 (CD68) staining of granular cell neoplasms: is KP1 a marker for lysosomes rather than the histiocytic lineage? *Histopathology*, 21, 84–86.
14. Filie, A.C., Lage, J.M., Azumi, N. (1996) Immunoreactivity of S100 protein, alpha-1-antitrypsin, and CD68 in adult and congenital granular cell tumors. *Mod Pathol*, 9, 888–892.
15. Williams, H.K., Williams, D.M. (1997) Oral granular cell tumours: a histological and immunocytochemical study. *J Oral Pathol Med*, 26, 164–169.
16. Mahalingam, M., LoPiccolo, D., Byers, H.R. (2001) Expression of PGP 9.5 in granular cell nerve sheath tumors: an immunohistochemical study of six cases. *J Cutan Pathol*, 28, 282–286.
17. Sobel, H.J., Schwarz, R., Marquet, E. (1973) Light- and electron-microscope study of the origin of granular-cell myoblastoma. *J Pathol*, 109, 101–111.
18. Klima, M., Peters, J. (1987) Malignant granular cell tumor. *Arch Pathol Lab Med*, 111, 1070–1073.
19. Fanburg-Smith, J.C., Meis-Kindblom, J.M., Fante, R. et al (1998) Malignant granular cell tumor of soft tissue: diagnostic criteria and clinicopathologic correlation. *Am J Surg Pathol*, 22, 779–794.
20. LeBoit, P.E., Barr, R.J., Burall, S. et al (1991) Primitive polypoid granular-cell tumor and other cutaneous granular-cell neoplasms of apparent nonneural origin. *Am J Surg Pathol*, 15, 48–58.

Ectomesenchymal chondromyxoid tumor

Clinical features

This unusual nodular tumor of the anterior tongue dorsum occurs in the fifth decade of life.[1–3]

Histological features

The tumor is a well-circumscribed but unencapsulated, lobular proliferation of tumor cells in the superficial tongue musculature, arranged in sheets, strands and cords in a chondromyxoid stroma with cleft-like spaces (*Fig. 10.248*).[1] Cells are polygonal, round and fusiform with small nuclei and basophilic cytoplasm. There may be focal nuclear hyperchromatism and multinucleation. The myxoid nature of the stroma often gives the tumor a reticular appearance and pseudocyst formation is seen in 50% of cases (*Fig. 10.249*). Muscle fibers are often trapped at the periphery of the tumor.

The tumor cells stain for vimentin, GFAP and S-100 protein and possibly cytokeratin.[1–3] Staining for CD57, smooth muscle actin and Leu-7 is variable. Desmin and EMA are negative.[1]

Ultrastructurally, basal lamina is focally present, but desmosomes and dense bodies are absent.[1]

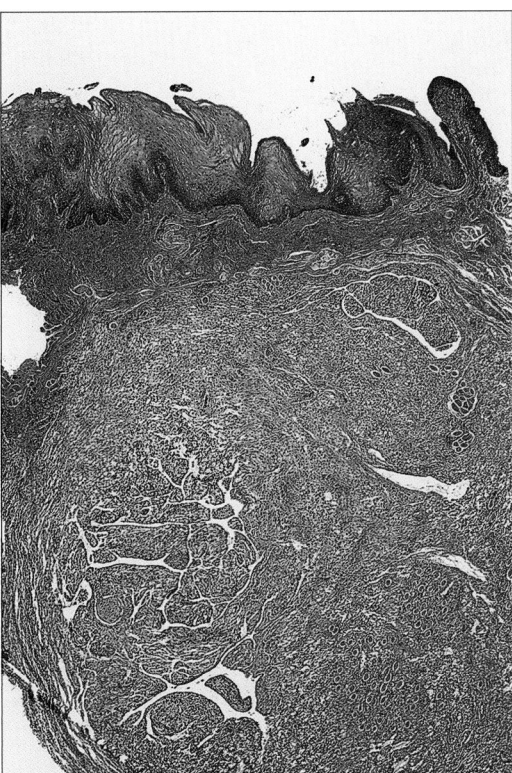

Fig. 10.248
Ectomesenchymal chondromyxoid tumor of the tongue: the tumor is discrete and myxoid, with many cleft-like spaces.

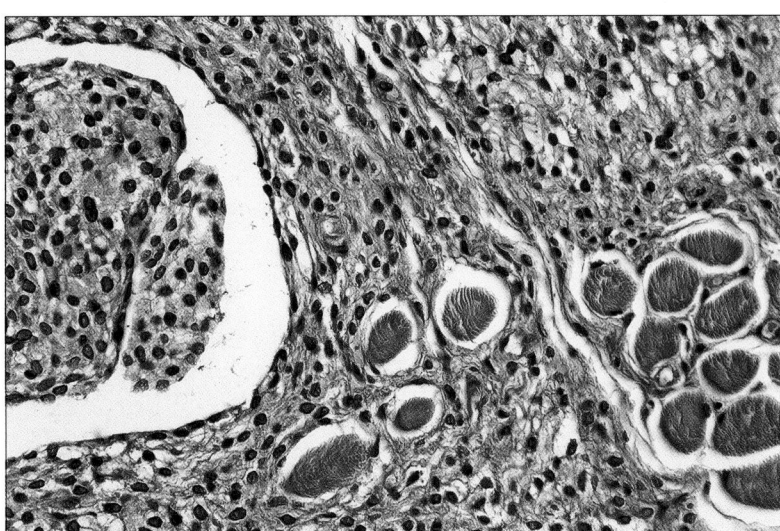

Fig. 10.249
Ectomesenchymal chondromyxoid tumor of the tongue: note the reticular appearance of the tumor and the trapping of muscle fibers.

It is likely that this tumor arises from a pluripotential mesenchymal cell. Osseous and cartilaginous choristomas are, after all, not uncommon on the tongue.

Differential diagnosis

Myoepitheliomas may resemble this tumor because of a similar cytomorphology and immunohistochemistry. The chondromyxoid matrix is also shared by both. The distinction can be readily made, however, by the absence of ductal differentiation and plasmacytoid cells.

In addition, myoepithelioma typically arises in close proximity to a salivary gland and does not extend into or entrap adjacent skeletal muscle.

References

1. Smith, B.C., Ellis, G.L., Meis-Kindblom, J.M., Williams, S.B. (1995) Ectomesenchymal chondromyxoid tumor of the anterior tongue. Nineteen cases of a new clinicopathologic entity. *Am J Surg Pathol*, **19**, 519–530.
2. van der Wal, J.E., van der Waal, I. (1996) Ectomesenchymal chondromyxoid tumor of the anterior tongue. Report of a case. *J Oral Pathol Med*, **25**, 456–458.
3. Kannan, R., Damm, D.D., White, D.K. et al (1996) Ectomesenchymal chondromyxoid tumor of the anterior tongue: a report of three cases. *Oral Surg Oral Med Oral Pathol Oral Radiol Endod*, **82**, 417–422.

Diseases of the genital skin

11

Eduardo Calonje and Sallie Neill

Normal anatomy 473
Labia majora/scrotum/perianal skin 473
Labia minora/penile shaft/prepuce 474
Glans clitoris/glans penis 475
Vestibule 475
Anogenital 'sweat' glands 476

Physiological variants 476
Sebaceous gland hyperplasia 476
Vestibular papillomatosis 476

Inflammatory dermatoses 476
Eczema 476
Infantile gluteal granuloma 477
Lichen simplex chronicus 477
Psoriasis 477
Reiter's syndrome 478
Genital lichen planus 480
Lichen sclerosus 483
Zoon's balanitis/vulvitis 487

Vesiculobullous conditions 488
Genital papular acantholytic dyskeratosis 488
Lipschutz ulcer 488
Sclerosing lymphangitis of the penis 489

Associations with systemic disease 489
Crohn's disease 489
Behçet's disease 490
Necrolytic migratory erythema 490

Infectious diseases 491
Erythrasma 491

Condyloma acuminatum 491
Syphilis 494
Granuloma inguinale 502
Chancroid 504
Lymphogranuloma venereum 505
Schistosomiasis 506
Amebiasis cutis 508
Malakoplakia 508

Miscellaneous conditions 509
Vestibulitis 509
Idiopathic calcinosis 510
Sclerosing lipogranuloma 511
Pilonidal sinus of the penis 511

Pigmented lesions 511
Genital melanosis 511
Genital melanocytic nevi 512
Melanoma 514
Non-Hodgkin's lymphoma 515

Epithelial lesions 515
Benign mucinous metaplasia and mucinous syringometaplasia 515
Endometriosis and endosalpingiosis 516
Median raphe cyst 516
Bartholin duct cyst 517
Mucinous cyst 517
Mesonephric cyst 518
Mesothelial cyst 518
Periurethral cyst 519

Intraepithelial neoplasia 519
Squamous cell carcinoma of the genital epithelia 523
Verrucous carcinoma 526
Pseudoepitheliomatous, keratotic and micaceous balanitis 528
Penile adenosquamous carcinoma 528
Cloacogenic carcinoma 528
Papillary hidradenoma 529
Apocrine carcinoma 530
Extramammary Paget's disease 530
Benign tumors of Bartholin's gland 530
Adenoma of minor vestibular glands 530
Bartholin's gland carcinoma 531
Basal cell carcinoma 531

Metastatic tumors 532
Langerhans' cell histiocytosis 532

Soft tissue tumors 532
Fibroepithelial stromal polyp 532
Angiomyofibroblastoma 533
Aggressive angiomyxoma 534
Cellular angiofibroma 535
Genital leiomyoma 536
Leiomyosarcoma 536
Vulvar leiomyomatosis 537
Myointimoma 537
Postoperative spindle-cell nodule 538
Peyronie's disease 538

Many of the dermatological conditions that present in the skin elsewhere can affect the anogenital area although the clinical and histological features may be modified by the chronicity of the problem and the occlusive effect of this naturally flexural site. Over the years various unsatisfactory classifications have been devised for vulval disorders. The current one is still unsuitable as exemplified by the term 'squamous cell hyperplasia' (SCH).[1] This, at best, is histologically descriptive but clinically meaningless. The Classification Committee of the International Society for the Study of Vulvovaginal Disease (ISSVD) at their meeting in September 2001 in Portugal recommended that no specific classification need be created since the terminology already in existence for dermatology and pathology such as SNOMED ICD-9 and ICD-10 can be employed. The terminology for vulval intraepithelial neoplasia (VIN) is discussed later. Extramammary Paget's disease and in situ melanoma are no longer included in the spectrum of VIN.

The anogenital area is also important as the epithelium covering it includes both skin and mucous membrane, i.e. keratinized and non-keratinized stratified squamous epithelium. The transition from skin to mucosa is characterized by a subtle modification in the properties of the epithelia at their junctions. It is therefore critically important that the site sampled for histological analysis be specified so as to avoid confusion and misinterpretation.

Reference

1. Wilkinson, E.J., Kneale, B., Lynch, P. (1986) Report of the ISSVD Terminology Committee. *J Reprod Med*, 31, 973–974.

Normal anatomy

The vulva comprises the mons pubis, the labia majora and minora, the vestibule of the vagina, the clitoris (including the prepuce and frenulum), the glands of Bartholin and Skene, the hymen, posterior commissure, fossa navicularis, introitus and the external urethral orifice (*Fig. 11.1*).

The male genital organ consists of the glans penis, the balanopreputial sulcus, the prepuce (foreskin), the penile body or shaft and the scrotum.

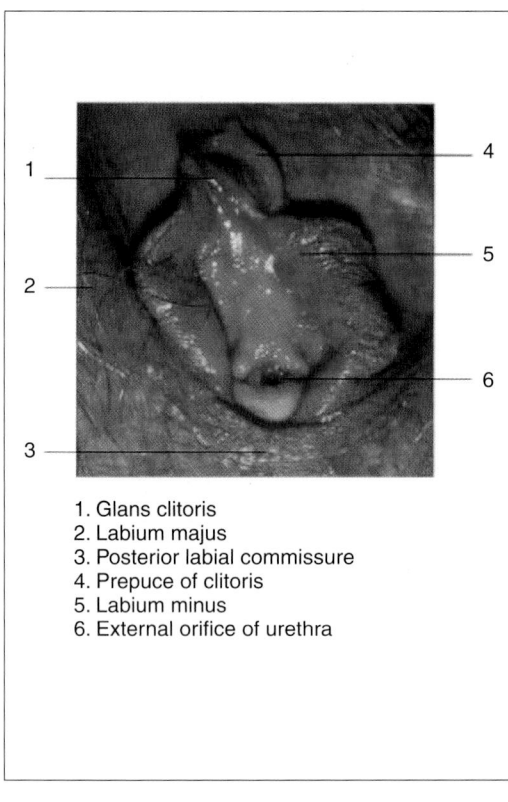

1. Glans clitoris
2. Labium majus
3. Posterior labial commissure
4. Prepuce of clitoris
5. Labium minus
6. External orifice of urethra

Fig. 11.1
Normal vulva showing the major anatomical landmarks.

are represented. The epithelium of the labia majora may normally contain occasional lymphocytes, which can also be found in very small numbers around the superficial dermal vasculature. In the labia majora, sebaceous glands are found in association with hair follicles and both eccrine and apocrine glands are typically present. On the medial aspect of the labia majora there are no hair follicles and the sebaceous glands open directly into the epithelium (*Fig. 11.2*) (Fordyce spots, see below). In the deep dermis a layer of smooth muscle known as the tunica dartos labialis is seen. The subcutaneous tissue of the labia majora tends to be prominent in women of reproductive age but decreases after the menopause. Both the labia majora and the scrotum contain a long smooth muscle called the cremaster. The skin of the scrotum and the perianal area contain numerous terminal hairs with sebaceous glands.

Histological features

The anogenital region, as with other mucocutaneous sites, is characterized by a gradual transition from skin to a mucosal surface.

Labia majora/scrotum/perianal skin

Histological features

These sites most closely resemble skin from other regions of the body since the epithelium is keratinized, stratified and the adnexal structures

Labia minora/penile shaft/ prepuce

Histological features

The labia minora represent the female equivalent of the penile corpus spongiosum. They are located lateral to the vaginal vestibule, medial to the labia majora and are covered by stratified, glycogen-rich, often pigmented, squamous epithelium. In most females, adnexal structures are absent as is subcutaneous tissue. The stroma is richly vascular and contains abundant erectile tissue and elastic fibers.

The penile shaft is covered by stratified squamous epithelium with minimal keratinization. Hair follicles are only present in its proximal portion and they usually lack arrector pili muscle. The pilosebaceous unit is incomplete, as the sebaceous gland is not usually associated with a hair follicle. Sweat glands are sparse. Bundles of smooth muscle known as the penile dartos are present. Subcutaneous fat is not seen.

The prepuce consists of five layers, including epidermis similar to that present in ordinary skin, dermis, a layer of smooth muscle called the dartos, a lamina propria and a mucosal surface. Sweat glands and sebaceous glands are absent.

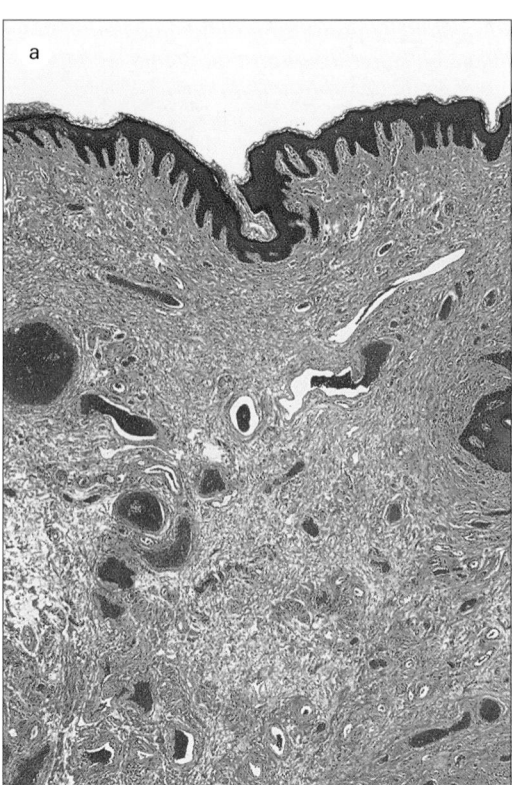

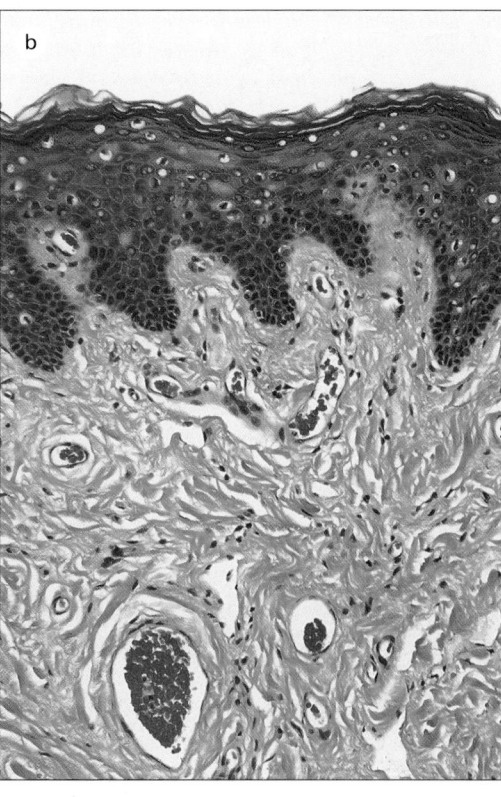

Fig. 11.2
Normal vulva: medial aspect of labium majus. The epidermis is keratinized. The dermis is richly vascular. Hair follicles are absent.

Glans clitoris/glans penis

Histological features

The epithelium is stratified and keratinized. In the uncircumcised male, the epithelium is non-keratinized. No adnexal structures are present. In the glans penis, the lamina propria is composed of loose connective tissue and overlies the main component of the glans, namely the corpus spongiosum. This consists of large venous vascular spaces. The glans clitoris does not contain a corpus spongiosum. The frenulum and the prepuce originate from the labia minora and contain abundant sebaceous and mucous-secreting glands.

Vestibule

Histological features

The epithelium is stratified and non-keratinized, i.e. a mucosa (*Fig. 11.3*). Both the vagina and the urethra open into the vestibule. Bartholin's glands are located deeply in the posterior part of the labia majora. They represent the equivalent of Cowper's glands or the bulbourethral glands in the male. The ducts of Bartholin and Skene's glands and the minor vestibular glands open into the vestibule.

Anogenital 'sweat' glands

These were first described by Van der Putte and are found in anogenital skin, mainly in the interlabial sulci.[1,2] They share morphological and histological features of eccrine, apocrine and mammary glands, making categorization difficult. Superficially, an excretory duct opens directly onto the skin. A deeper coiled or a long straight duct gives rise to several sac-like invaginations forming small glands, which typically extend deeper than the apocrine or eccrine glands. The anogenital sweat glands are lined by simple columnar epithelium surrounded by a layer of myoepithelial cells.

References

1. Van der Putte, S.C.J. (1991) Anogenital sweat glands. Histology and pathology of a gland that may mimic mammary glands. *Am J Dermatopathol*, **13**, 557–567.
2. Van der Putte, S.C.J. (1993) Ultrastructure of the human anogenital 'sweat' gland. *Anat Rec*, **235**, 583–590.

Physiological Variants

Sebaceous gland hyperplasia

The sebaceous glands of the inner labia majora, the labia minora, the prepuce and corona do not usually have an associated hair follicle. The glands open directly onto the surface and may be very prominent and numerous at these sites. The yellow uniform papules (Fordyce spots) are often seen best if the skin is stretched out (*Fig. 11.4*). Sebaceous gland hyperplasia may sometime be associated with pruritus.

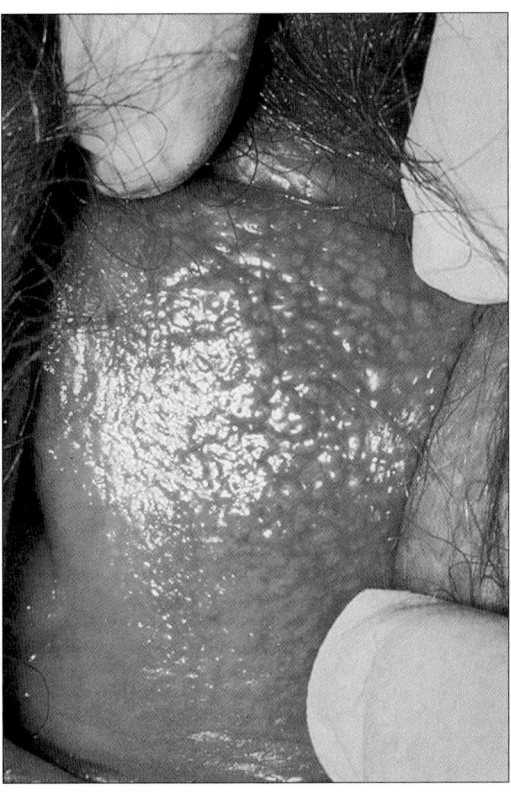

Fig. 11.4
Fordyce spots: hyperplastic sebaceous glands presenting as conspicuous yellow papules. Similar lesions may be seen on the inner lip and oral mucosa. By courtesy of the Institute of Dermatology, London, UK.

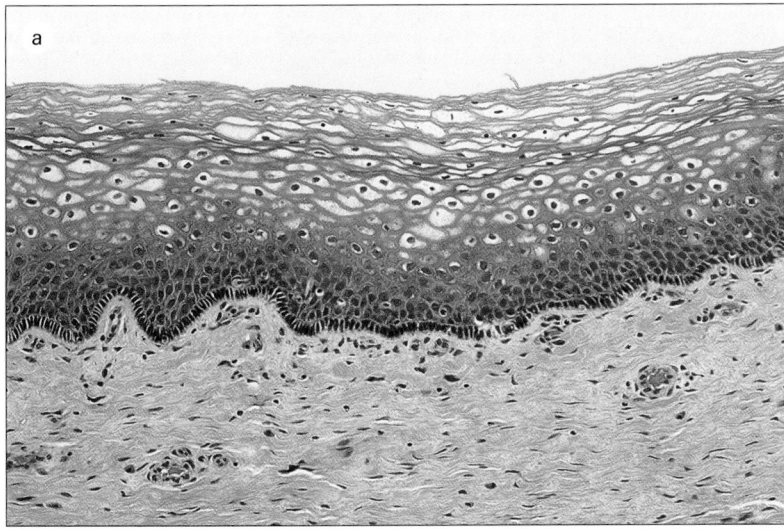

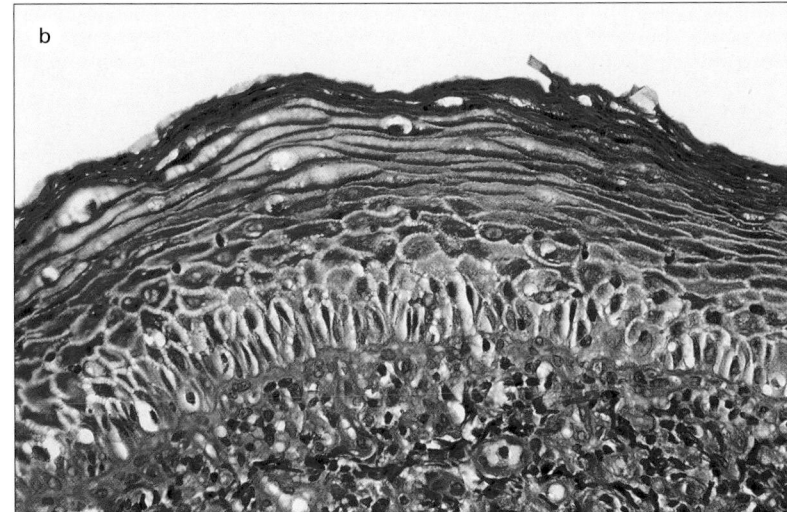

Fig. 11.3
Vestibule: (a) the epithelium is non-keratinizing and rich in glycogen. Cutaneous appendages are absent at this site; (b) the epithelium is strongly PAS positive.

Histological features

One or more enlarged sebaceous glands, each composed of numerous lobules, surround a central duct that opens directly into the epidermis.

Vestibular papillomatosis

Vestibular papillomatosis, also known as penile pearly papules (hirsutoid papillomas), is not due to human papillomavirus infection and is a common finding of no significance. It is asymptomatic. Individual lesions are dome shaped or filiform and arise on a solitary base. They are found on the inner aspect of the labia minora, vestibule and coronal sulcus (*Fig. 11.5*).

Histological features

There is a normal or thickened epidermis overlying a central fibrovascular core.

Inflammatory dermatoses

Eczema

Seborrheic dermatitis is the commonest form of eczema affecting the anogenital skin followed by irritant contact eczema. Allergic contact eczema is rare at genital sites and occurs more typically in a perianal distribution. Involvement of genital skin by atopic eczema is uncommon.

In babies, eczematous reactions are often seen in the napkin area. Most of these represent a primary irritant dermatitis. Seborrheic dermatitis and a psoriasiform napkin rash can also occur. Some but not all of the patients with the latter condition develop psoriasis later in life.[1]

The histological features are identical to those seen in eczema affecting other areas of the skin (see p. 177). The psoriasiform napkin rash shows histological features that overlap with psoriasis.

Reference

1. Neville, E.A., Finn, O.A. (1975) Psoriasiform nappy rash – a follow-up study. *Br J Dermatol*, **92**, 279–285.

Infantile gluteal granuloma

Clinical features

Infantile gluteal granuloma (papuloerosive dermatitis of Jacquet and Sevestre) is a rare condition that has been mainly described in the newborn and infants in the napkin area. It frequently develops against a background of an irritant napkin rash.[1-4] A similar condition has been described in incontinent elderly women with lesions developing on the labia majora (*Fig. 11.6*).[5-7] Oval or round papulonodular lesions present on the convex areas of the perineum, which are in direct contact with the napkin or incontinence pad. They tend to regress spontaneously over a few weeks and occasionally leave scars.

Pathogenesis and histological features

The etiology of the process is unclear but occlusion, *Candida* infection and fluorinated corticosteroids have been implicated. The last, however, does not seem to be of importance in the incontinent, elderly patient.

The histology is fairly non-specific and includes superficial ulceration, focal necrosis and a prominent mixed inflammatory cell infiltrate with granulomata and numerous lymphocytes and plasma cells. Hemorrhage and hemosiderin deposition can sometimes be present.

References

1. Tappeiner, J., Pfleger, L. (1971) Granuloma gluteale infantum. *Hautarzt*, **22**, 383–388.
2. Bonifazi, E., Garofalo, L., Lospalluti, M. et al (1981) Granuloma gluteal infantum with atrophic scars. Clinical and histological observations in 11 cases. *Clin Exp Dermatol*, **6**, 23–29.
3. Uyeda, K., Nakayasu, K., Takaishi, Y. et al (1973) Kaposi sarcoma-like granuloma in diaper dermatitis. *Arch Dermatol*, **107**, 605–607.
4. Lovell, C.R., Atherton, D.J. (1984) Infantile gluteal granulomata: case report. *Clin Exp Dermatol*, **9**, 522–525.
5. Maekawa, Y., Sakazaki, Y., Hayashibara, T. (1978) Diaper area granuloma of the aged. *Arch Dermatol*, **114**, 382–383.
6. Virgili, A., Corazza, M. (1992) Erythema syphiloide de Sevestre et Jacquet. *Ann Dermatol Venereol*, **119**, 744–745.
7. Virgili, A., Corazza, M., Califono, A. (1998) Diaper dermatitis in an adult. A case of erythema papuloerosive of Sevestre and Jacquet. *J Reprod Med*, **43**, 949–951.

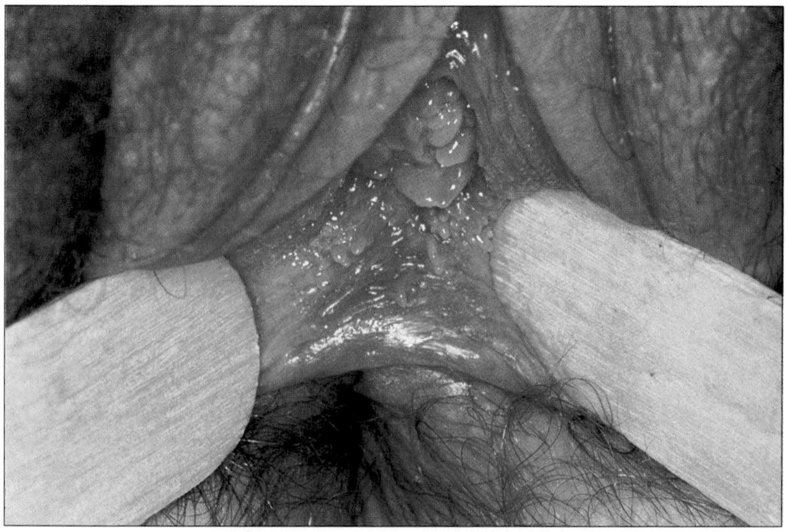

Fig. 11.5
Vulval papillomatosis: numerous pale papillomata are present in the vestibule and on the labia minora. These are a normal finding and are particularly common in pregnancy. By courtesy of the Institute of Dermatology, London, UK.

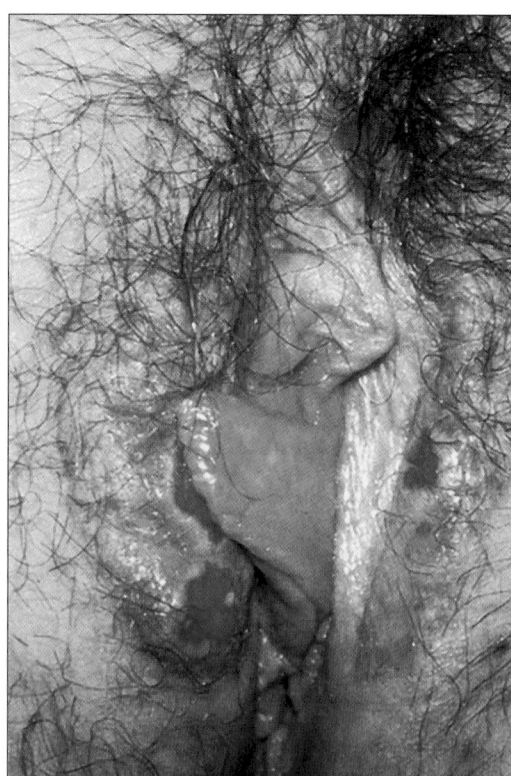

Fig. 11.6
Papuloerosive dermatitis: there are multiple ulcerated papules and nodules predominantly affecting the labia majora. By courtesy of the Institute of Dermatology, London, UK.

Lichen simplex chronicus

The clinical features of lichen simplex chronicus presenting on genital and anal skin are identical to those seen at other sites of the body. The labium majus and scrotum are predominantly affected.

The histological features are discussed in detail elsewhere (see p. 182).

Psoriasis

Flexural psoriasis is the most common pattern seen in the anogenital region with extension into the genitocrural folds and natal cleft (*Figs 11.7–11.10*). There are often difficulties clinically in distinguishing between psoriasis and seborrheic eczema.

Histology is often unhelpful, as the changes can be quite non-specific. The typical features of psoriasis are rarely evident and the presence of secondary spongiosis may be very misleading.

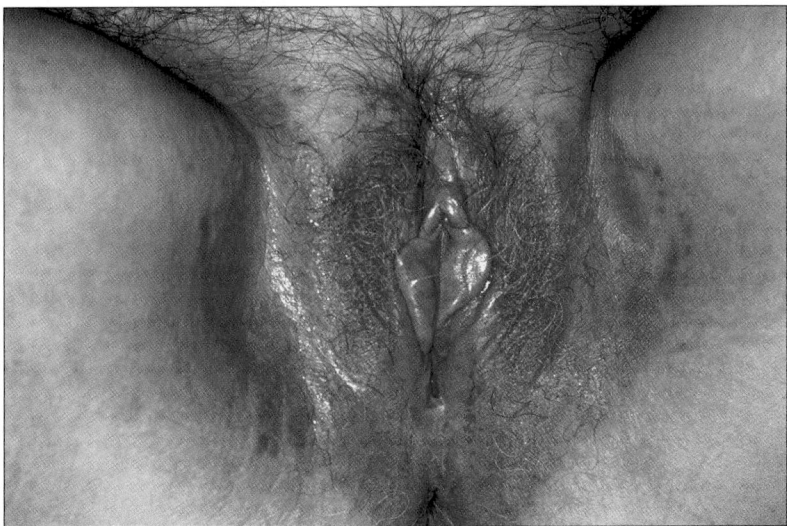

Fig. 11.7
Psoriasis: note the symmetrical, intensely erythematous eruption involving the groins, vulva and perineum. Scaling is typically absent in flexural disease. The sharply demarcated border is characteristic. By courtesy of the Institute of Dermatology, London, UK.

Reiter's syndrome

Clinical features

Reiter's syndrome represents a triad of polyarthritis associated with urethritis and non-gonococcal conjunctivitis.[1–5] A range of other symptoms may also be present and the classical triad may occur together or develop in sequence. It has worldwide distribution. Reiter's syndrome most commonly affects men 20–30 years of age; the male to female sex ratio is approximately 10:1.[1]

Reiter's syndrome is characterized by a relapsing course.[3] The genito-urinary tract is virtually always involved in the form of urethritis, prostatitis, seminal vesiculitis and hemorrhagic cystitis. Urethral strictures also sometimes occur and females may develop cervicitis. Vulvitis has been reported but is rare.[6–8] Vulval lesions often resemble mucocutaneous candidiasis.

Bilateral mucopurulent conjunctivitis is the usual form of eye involvement occurring in up to 35% of patients, but occasionally iritis, iridocyclitis, keratitis or blindness occurs.[9]

Weight-bearing and the larger joints (knees, ankles, feet and wrists) are involved by the arthritis, often together with sacroiliitis. Radiological changes include osteoporosis, erosions and loss of joint space, with multiple joints usually affected.[3,10] Periostitis often affects the metatarsals, the phalanges of the feet and the tarsal bones; occasionally ankylosis develops in the small bones of the hands and feet. Ankylosing spondylitis, which is an important manifestation, correlates with a high erythrocyte sedimentation rate (ESR).[10]

In the initial stages of the arthritis the clinical picture resembles that of an acute joint infection, settling to subacute involvement. Although the arthritis in Reiter's syndrome usually recovers completely, chronic manifestations can sometimes occur; it is important to remember that arthritis may be the only symptom in recurrent episodes.

Cutaneous manifestations include hyperkeratotic lesions on the palms and soles and occasionally affecting the trunk and extremities (*Fig. 11.11*). The lesions initially present as erythematous macules; over the course of several days these become hyperkeratotic waxy papules, with an erythematous halo covered by dry hyperkeratotic material. The papules are numerous and eventually coalesce to form thickened horny plaques. Pustular lesions of the palms and soles may also be evident (keratoderma blenorrhagicum) (*Fig. 11.12*).

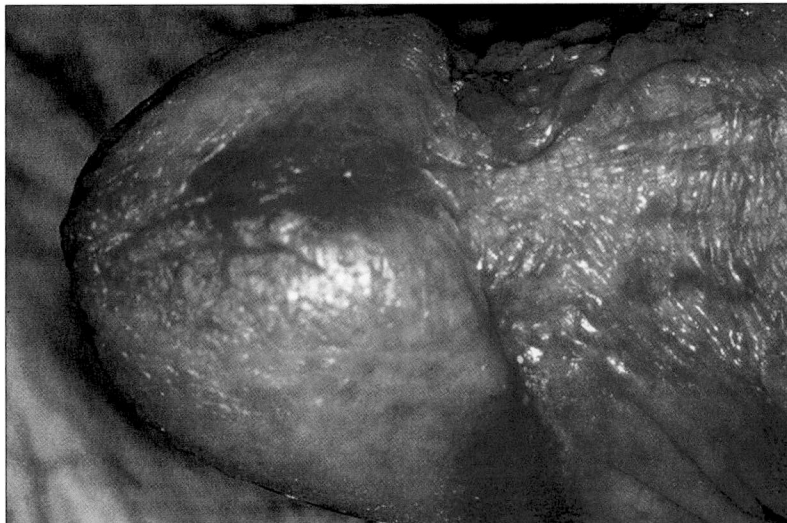

Fig. 11.8
Psoriasis: there are erythematous plaques on the glans penis. By courtesy of the Institute of Dermatology, London, UK.

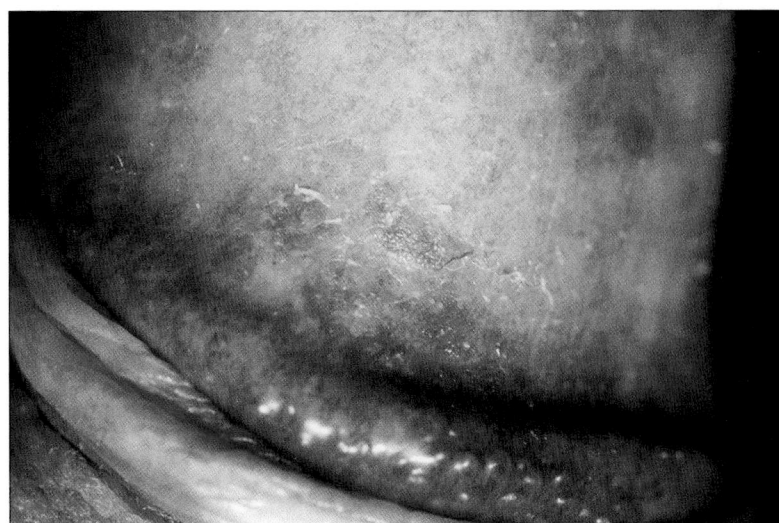

Fig. 11.9
Psoriasis: in this example a slight scale is apparent. By courtesy of the Institute of Dermatology, London, UK.

Circinate balanitis, presenting as a moist superficial erosion, 2–4 mm across, may affect the glans penis and meatus (*Figs 11.13, 11.14*). Superficial ulceration of the oral mucosa may also occur, together with reddening and a granular appearance of the surrounding mucous membrane.[3,4]

Stomatitis and nail dystrophy (indistinguishable from that of psoriasis) may be additional features.[3] Weight loss is common.[11] Aortic incompetence is an important late complication and IgA nephropathy has been described in a number of patients.[3,12]

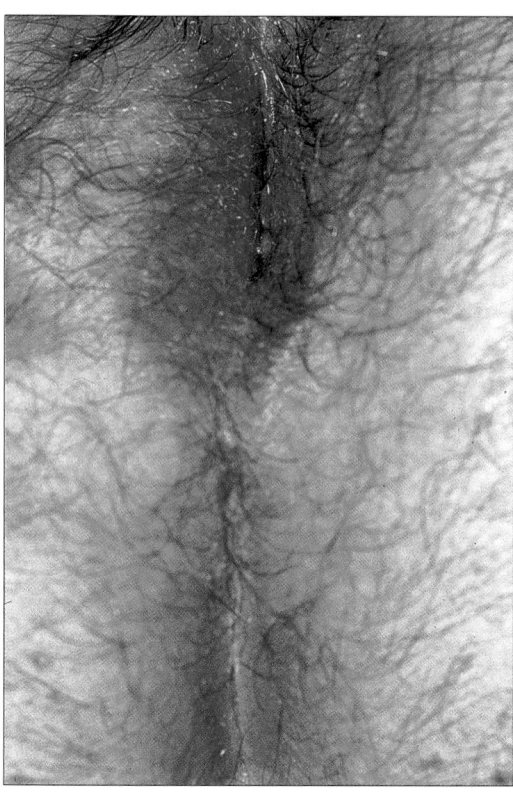

Fig. 11.10
Psoriasis: note the erythematous and slightly scaly plaque affecting the perineum. By courtesy of the Institute of Dermatology, London, UK.

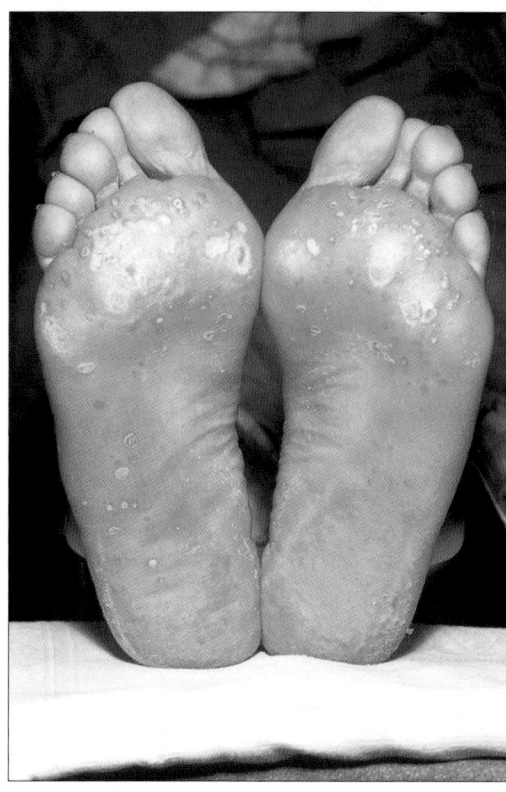

Fig. 11.11
Reiter's syndrome: there are bilateral keratotic papules and plaques affecting the soles of the feet. By courtesy of R.A. Marsden, MD, St George's Hospital, London, UK.

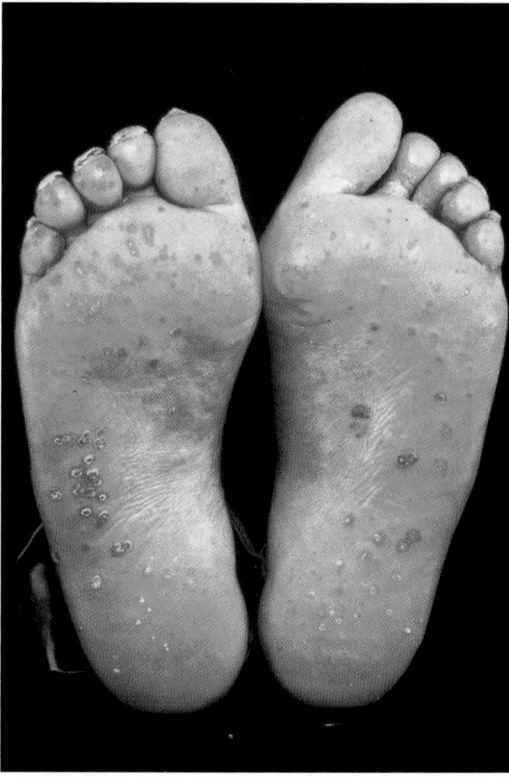

Fig. 11.12
Reiter's syndrome: in addition to keratotic papules there are pustular lesions, many of which have ruptured – keratoderma blenorrhagicum. By courtesy of the Institute of Dermatology, London, UK.

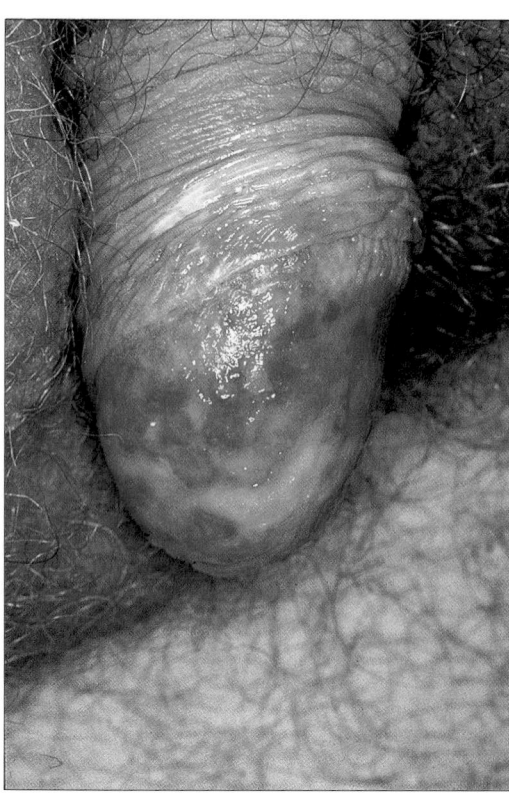

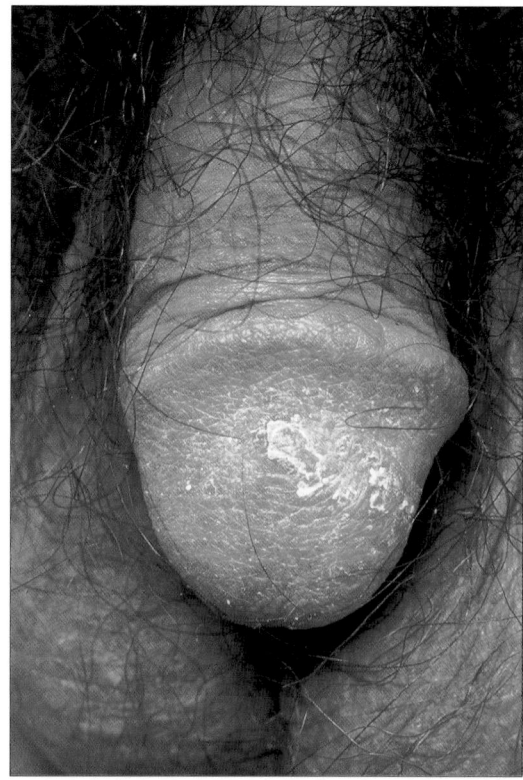

Fig. 11.13
Reiter's syndrome: there are multiple erosions on the glans penis. By courtesy of the Institute of Dermatology, London, UK.

Fig. 11.14
Reiter's syndrome: in this patient there are scaly lesions on the glans penis. By courtesy of the Institute of Dermatology, London, UK.

Reiter's syndrome may resolve spontaneously, but more often it is characterized by chronicity and recurrences.[3] Rarely, it may prove fatal.[3] Causes of death include aortic incompetence, atrioventricular block, terminal cachexia, systemic amyloidosis and iatrogenic effects.[13]

Pathogenesis and histological features

Reiter's syndrome may follow an enteric or a urogenital infection.[14,15] Shigella dysentery was the first associated enteric infection to be recognized when after the two World Wars there were large increases in the incidence of Reiter's syndrome; the causative organisms were either *Shigella flexneri* or *S. dysenteriae*.[16] Recently, *Salmonella*, *Yersinia* and *Campylobacter* have been reported preceding Reiter's syndrome.[17–21]

Sexually transmitted Reiter's syndrome may occur with a non-gonococcal or 'non-specific' urethritis.[14] *Chlamydia trachomatis* is isolated from the genitourinary tract in 40–60% of male cases; isolation is variable, however, and an indirect immunofluorescence test detects chlamydial infection in 90% of patients.[22,23] Mycoplasma infection and *Streptococcus viridans* have also been implicated.[24–26] The condition has also been linked to the acquired immunodeficiency syndrome (AIDS).[11,27,28] Rare associations include *Cyclospora*, *Cryptosporidium*, intravesical bacillus Calmette–Guérin (BCG) immunotherapy, *Gardnerella vaginalis*, hepatitis B immunization and systemic interferon-alpha (IFN-α) treatment.[29–34]

Reiter's syndrome is more likely to occur in predisposed individuals. Human leukocyte antigen (HLA)-B27, which is thought to occur in up to 90% of patients, increases the risk of developing Reiter's syndrome by 25 times; the disease is also more severe in HLA-B27 positive individuals.[3,35] HLA-B27 in patients with Reiter's syndrome correlates with ankylosing spondylitis.[3] Reiter's syndrome develops in 20% of HLA-B27 positive individuals after a specific infective insult.[10] HLA-B27 is found in approximately 10% of the normal population. Recently, an association with HLA-B51 has been reported.[36] Rarely familial instances have been recorded.[10] Therefore, it appears that disease is triggered in genetically predisposed individuals by an unknown mechanism precipitated by infection.

The skin lesions of Reiter's syndrome have a psoriasiform morphology (*Fig. 11.15*). The epidermis is acanthotic with elongation and hypertrophy of the epidermal ridges and parakeratosis. The suprapapillary plates are thinned and there is infiltration of the epidermis by neutrophils, associated with vacuolation of superficial keratinocytes, together with the formation of spongiform pustules and microabscesses (*Fig. 11.16*). The inflammation extends into the adjacent underlying dermis where it is predominantly mononuclear. The histology is essentially identical to that seen in pustular psoriasis.[1] Therefore, close clinicopathological correlation is critical to establish a diagnosis. Occasional biopsies from typical lesions of patients with Reiter's syndrome may disclose an underlying leukocytoclastic vasculitis.[37]

A small number of patients presenting with skin lesions that histologically showed sterile neutrophilic folliculitis with perifollicular vasculopathy have been documented.[38] The authors suggested that this histological pattern may be a marker of systemic disease. Associations may include Reiter's syndrome, inflammatory bowel disease, Behçet's disease, hepatitis B infection, scrofuloderma, connective tissue diseases and hematological dyscrasias. Patients present with systemic symptoms and variable skin lesions including folliculitis, vasculitis, acneiform eruptions, vesiculopustules and erythema nodosum-like features.[38]

Early joint lesions are characterized by a neutrophil polymorph inflammatory cell infiltrate with little if any synovial changes. Older lesions show features suggestive of rheumatoid arthritis, including lymphoid aggregates, a perivascular chronic inflammatory cell infiltrate and synovial hyperplasia.[10]

Differential diagnosis

A periodic acid–Schiff (PAS) stain should always be performed to exclude a fungal infection which may show similar histological features (see also psoriasis, p. 200).

References

1. Lassus, A., Koussa, M. (1981) Reiter's disease. In: Hams, R. (ed.) Recent advances in sexually transmitted diseases No. 2. Edinburgh: Churchill Livingstone, pp 187–199.
2. Weinberger, H.W., Ropes, M.W., Kulka, J.P. et al (1962) Reiter's syndrome, clinical and pathologic observations. A long term study of 16 cases. *Medicine (Baltimore)*, **41**, 35–91.
3. Marks, J.S., Holt, P.J.L. (1986) The natural history of Reiter's disease: 21 years of observation. *QJM*, **60**, 685–697.
4. Callen, J.P. (1979) The spectrum of Reiter's disease. *J Am Acad Dermatol*, **1**, 75–77.
5. Willkens, R.F., Arnett, F.C., Bitter, T. et al (1981) Reiter's syndrome. *Arthritis Rheum*, **24**, 844–849.
6. Thambar, I.V., Dunlop, R., Thin, R.N. et al (1977) Circinate vulvitis in Reiter's disease. *Br J Vener Dis*, **53**, 260–262.
7. Daunt, S.O'N., Kotoeski, K.E., O'Reilly, A.P. et al (1982) Ulcerative vulvitis in Reiter's syndrome: a case report. *Br J Vener Dis*, **58**, 405–407.
8. Edwards, L., Hansen, R. (1992) Reiter's syndrome of the vulva. The psoriasis spectrum. *Arch Dermatol*, **128**, 811–814.

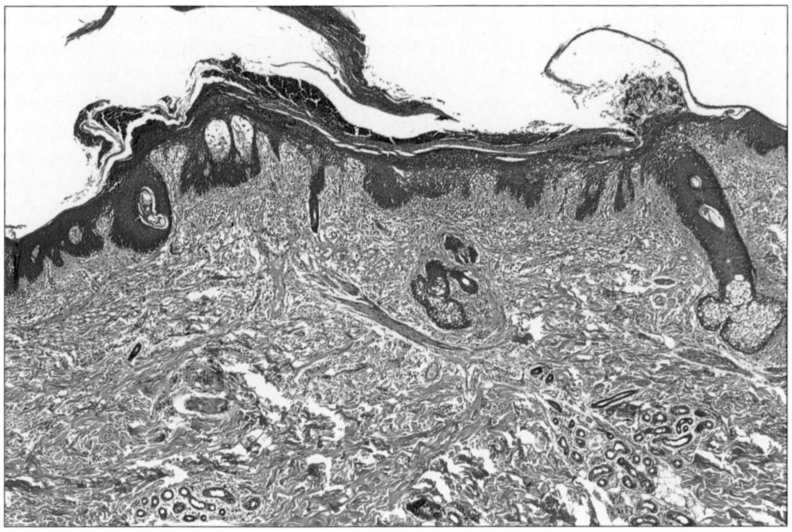

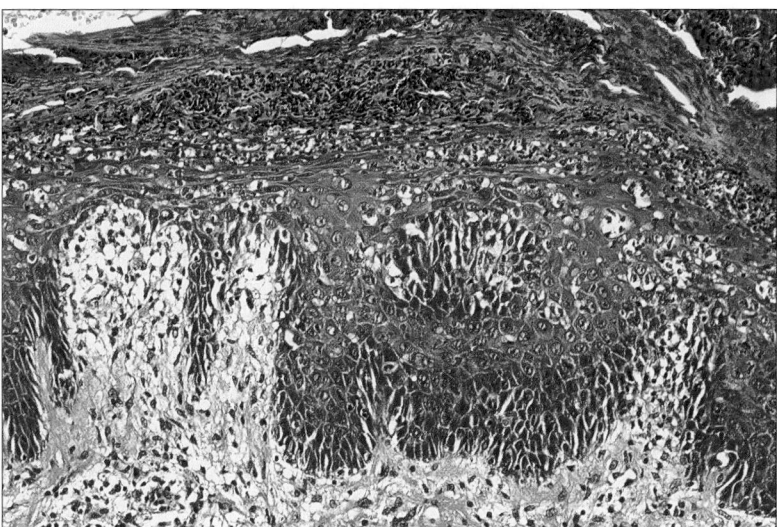

Fig. 11.15
Reiter's syndrome: there is parakeratosis overlying a macropustule. The squamous epithelium shows psoriasiform hyperplasia. These features are indistinguishable from pustular psoriasis.

Fig. 11.16
Reiter's syndrome: high power view showing parakeratosis and a pustule.

9. Callen, J.P., Mahl, C.F. (1992) Oculocutaneous manifestations observed in multisystem disorders. *Dermatol Clin*, **10**, 709–716.
10. Keat, A. (1983) Reiter's syndrome and reactive arthritis in perspective. *N Engl J Med*, **309**, 1606–1615.
11. Winchester, R., Bernstein, D.H., Fischer, H.D. et al (1987) The co-occurrence of Reiter's syndrome and acquired immunodeficiency. *Ann Intern Med*, **106**, 19–26.
12. Satko, S.G., Iskandar, S.S., Appel, R.G. (2000) IgA nephropathy and Reiter's syndrome. Report of two cases and review of the literature. *Nephron*, **84**, 177–182.
13. Wattiaux, M.J., Bourgeois, P., Picard, O. et al (1989) Two familial cases of malignant Reiter's syndrome. *Clin Exp Dermatol*, **7**, 541–545.
14. Catterall, R.D. (1976) The role of microbial infection in Reiter's syndrome. In: Dumonde, D. (ed.) Infection and immunology in the rheumatic diseases. Oxford: Blackwell, pp 147–150.
15. Kousa, M. (1978) Clinical observations on Reiter's disease with special reference to the venereal and non-venereal aetiology. *Acta Dermato-Venereol*, **55** (Suppl. 81), 6–36.
16. Kaslow, R.A., Ryder, R.W., Calin, A. (1979) Search for Reiter's syndrome after an outbreak of Shigella sonnei dysentery. *J Rheumatol*, **6**, 562–566 (F).
17. Warren, C.P.W. (1970) Arthritis associated with salmonella infections. *Ann Rheum Dis*, **29**, 483–487.
18. Winblad, S. (1975) Arthritis associated with Yersinia enterocolitica infections. *Scand J Infect Dis*, **7**, 191–195.
19. Skirrow, M.B. (1977) Campylobacter enteritis: a 'new' disease. *BMJ*, **2**, 9–11.
20. Gumpell, J.M., Martin, C., Sanderson, P.J. (1981) Reactive arthritis associated with Campylobacter enteritis. *Ann Rheum Dis*, **40**, 64–65.
21. Dworkin, M.S., Shoemaker, P.C., Goldoft, M.J. et al (2001) Reactive arthritis and Reiter's syndrome following an outbreak of gastroenteritis caused by Salmonella enteritidis. *Clin Infect Dis*, **33**, 1010–1014.
22. Keat, A.C., Thomas, B.J., Taylor-Robinson, D. et al (1980) Evidence of Chlamydia trachomatis in sexually acquired reactive arthritis. *Ann Rheum Dis*, **39**, 431–437.
23. Koussa, M., Saiku, P., Richmond, S. et al (1978) Frequent association of chlamydial infection with Reiter's syndrome. *Sex Transm Dis*, **5**, 57–61.
24. Ford, D.K. (1967) Relationship between Mycoplasma and the aetiology of nongonococcal urethritis and Reiter's syndrome. *Ann N Y Acad Sci*, **143**, 501–504.
25. Natarajan, U.R., Tan, T.L., Lau, R. (2001) Reiter's disease following Mycoplasma pneumoniae infection. *Int J STD AIDS*, **12**, 349–350.
26. Huang, D.F., Tsai, C.Y., Tsai, Y.Y. et al (2000) Reiter's syndrome caused by Streptococcus viridans in a patient with HLA-B27 antigen. *Clin Exp Rheumatol*, **18**, 394–396.
27. Fuente, C., Vélez, A., Martin, N. et al (1991) Reiter's syndrome and human immunodeficiency virus infection: case report and review of the literature. *Cutis*, **47**, 181–185.
28. Weitzul, S., Duvic, M. (1997) HIV-related psoriasis and Reiter's syndrome. *Semin Cutan Med Surg*, **16**, 213–218.
29. Connor, B.A., Johnson, E.J., Soave, R. (2001) Reiter syndrome following protracted symptoms of Cyclospora infection. *Emerg Infect Dis*, **7**, 453–454.
30. Cron, R.Q., Sherry, D.D. (1995) Reiter's syndrome associated with cryptosporidial gastroenteritis. *J Rheumatol*, **22**, 1962–1963.
31. Hogarth, M.B., Thomas, S., Seifert, M.H. et al (2000) Reiter's syndrome following intravesical BCG immunotherapy. *Postgrad Med J*, **76**, 791–793.
32. Toussirot, E., Plesiat, P., Wendling, D. (1998) Reiter's syndrome induced by Gardnerella vaginalis. *Scand J Rheumatol*, **27**, 316–317.
33. Fraser, P.A., Wilson, J.D. (1994) Reiter's syndrome attributed to hepatitis B immunisation. *BMJ*, **309**, 1513.
34. Cleveland, M.G., Mallory, S.B. (1993) Incomplete Reiter's syndrome induced by systemic interferon alpha treatment. *J Am Acad Dermatol*, **29**, 788–789.
35. Brewerton, D.A., Caffrey, M., Nicholls, A. (1973) Reiter's disease and HLA 27. *Lancet*, **11**, 996–998.
36. Shimamoto, Y., Sugiyama, H., Hirohata, S. (2000) Reiter's syndrome associated with HLA-B51. *Intern Med*, **39**, 182–184.
37. Magro, C.M., Crowson, A.N., Peeling, R. (1995) Vasculitis as the basis of cutaneous lesions in Reiter's disease. *Hum Pathol*, **26**, 633–638.
38. Magro, C.M., Crowson, A.N. (1998) Sterile neutrophilic folliculitis with perifollicular vasculopathy: a distinctive cutaneous reaction pattern reflecting systemic disease. *J Cutan Pathol*, **25**, 215–221.

Genital lichen planus

Clinical features

Anogenital lesions may be found in up to 40% of patients with generalized disease. In some patients, however, the disease is restricted to the genitalia and/or the perianal region and in these instances, the diagnosis may be difficult to establish.[1,2]

The lesions are typical, violaceous, flat-topped shiny papules. Wickham's striae (so frequently seen in oral involvement), although sometimes visible, are less often found on the anogenital skin (*Fig. 11.17*). Erosive disease is commoner at anogenital sites and can lead to scarring and distortion of the architecture (*Figs 11.18–11.20*). The vagina may sometimes be involved and exceptionally is the only site affected. Perianal disease can lead to deep, painful fissuring.

There are several clinical variants of lichen planus (LP) affecting the anogenital skin, notably papular, erosive, hypertrophic and pigmented flexural disease (*Figs 11.21–11.23*). There is also an unusual variant of LP in women that involves the oral gingivae, vulval vestibule and vagina known as the vulvovaginal-gingival syndrome (*Figs 11.24–11.26*).[3–5] This can lead to severe scarring with total sealing of the vagina. Lesions are also sometimes seen on the cervix.[5,6] Patients with genital lesions may have anal, oral, aural, conjunctival and esophageal involvement.[7–12] Those patients with predominantly mucosal disease clinically mimic mucous membrane pemphigoid but immunofluorescence studies are invariably negative.

Lichen planopilaris has also been described on the vulva.[13]

Anogenital lichen planus of either sex carries a small but increased risk of malignancy, usually squamous cell carcinoma (SCC) (*Fig. 11.27*).[14–18]

Pathogenesis and histological features

The histological features of anogenital lichen planus are often more difficult to recognize than those of LP presenting on non-mucosal

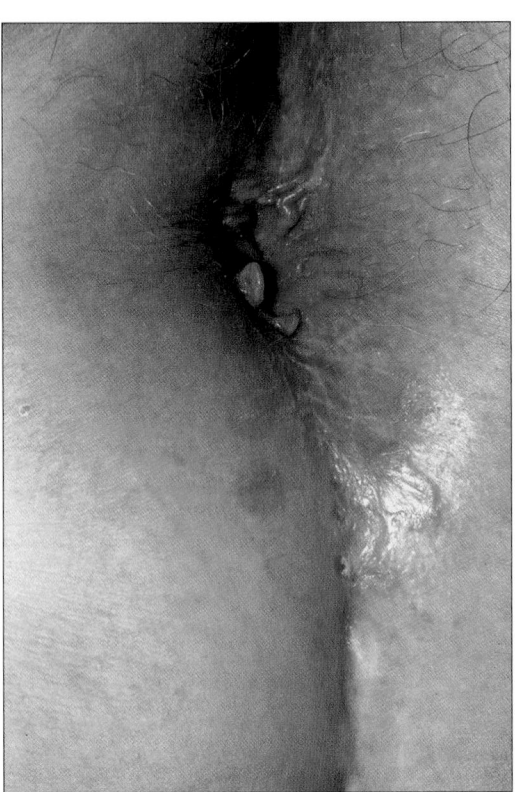

Fig. 11.17
Lichen planus: perineal lesions showing conspicuous striae. By courtesy of the Institute of Dermatology, London, UK.

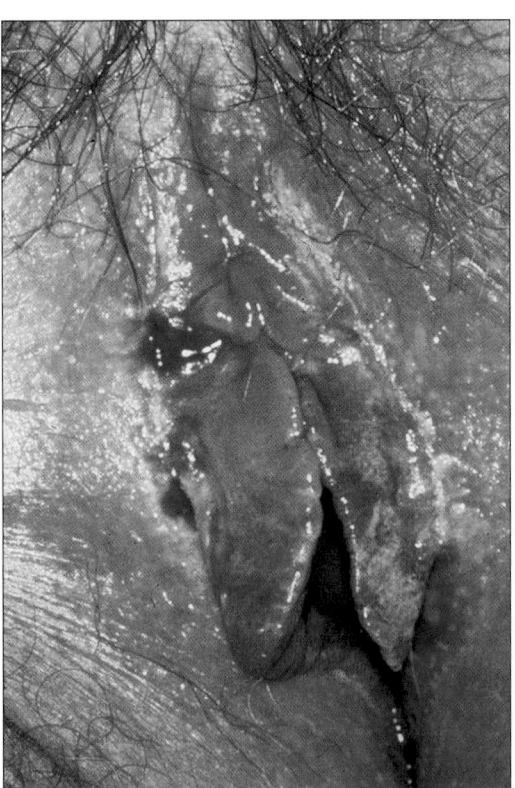

Fig. 11.18
Erosive lichen planus: bilateral erosions are present. By courtesy of the Institute of Dermatology, London, UK.

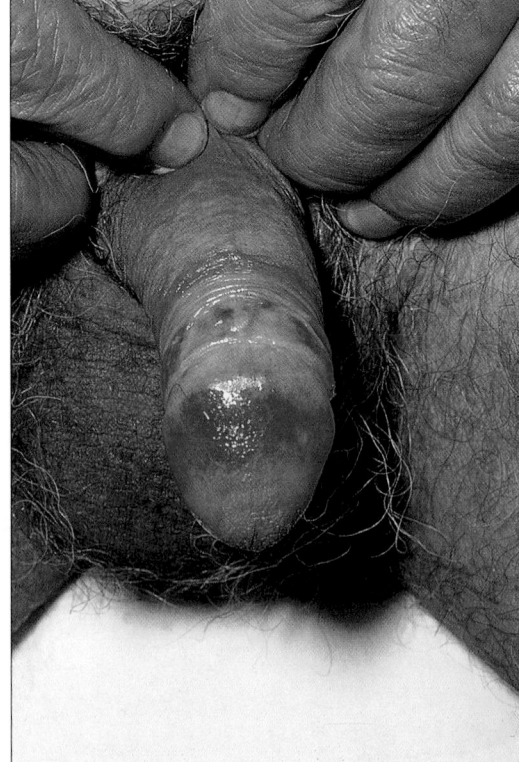

Fig. 11.19
Erosive lichen planus: there is extensive erosion of the glans penis. By courtesy of the Institute of Dermatology, London, UK.

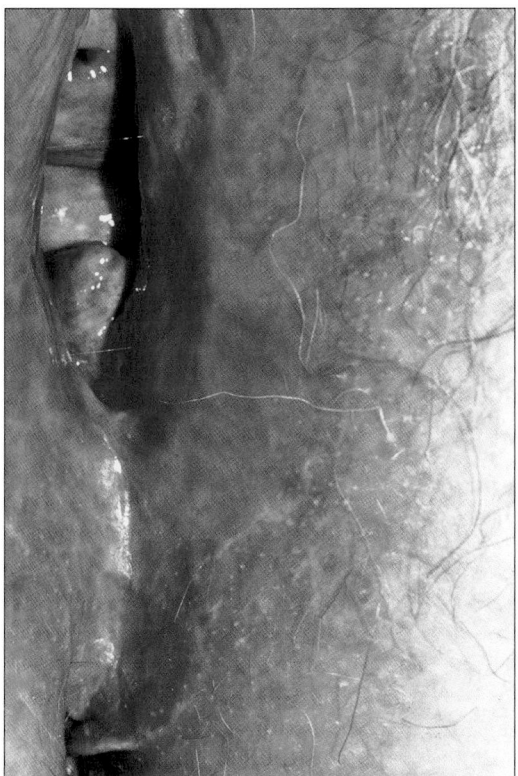

Fig. 11.20
Vulval lichen planus: reticulated lesions of lichen planus extending into the perineum. By courtesy of the Institute of Dermatology, London, UK.

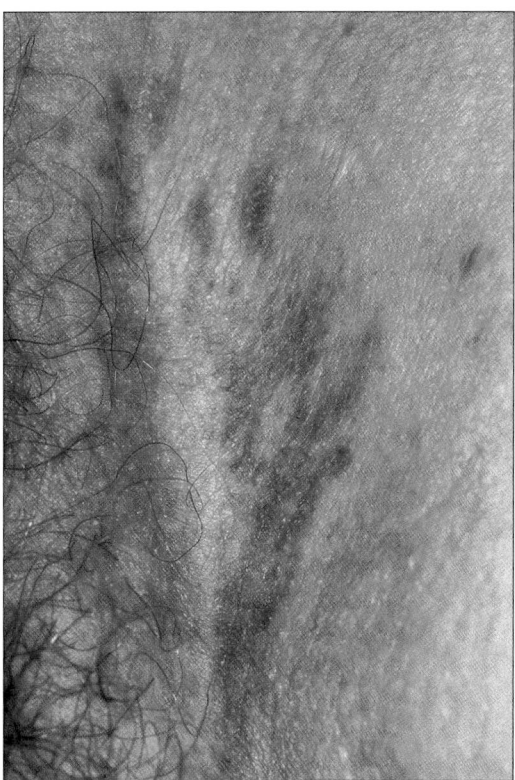

Fig. 11.21
Vulval lichen planus: in this example of resolving disease there are linear hyperpigmented lesions. By courtesy of the Institute of Dermatology, London, UK.

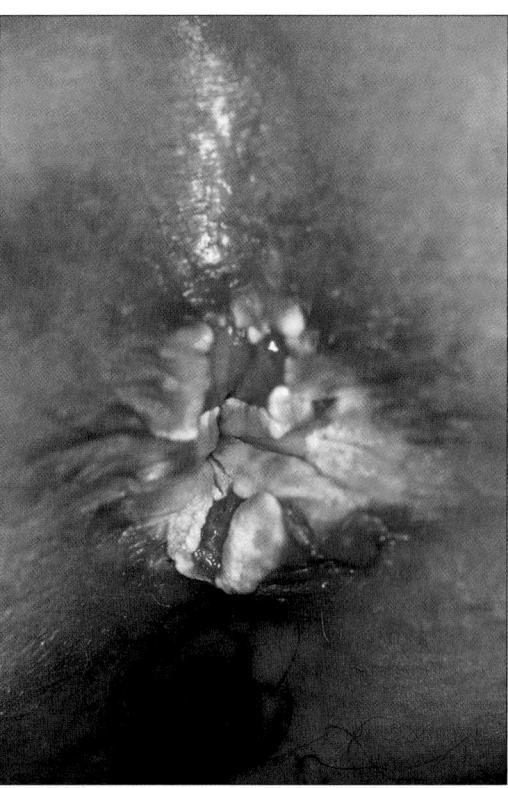

Fig. 11.22
Perineal lichen planus: typical papules with Wickham's striae are present. By courtesy of the Institute of Dermatology, London, UK.

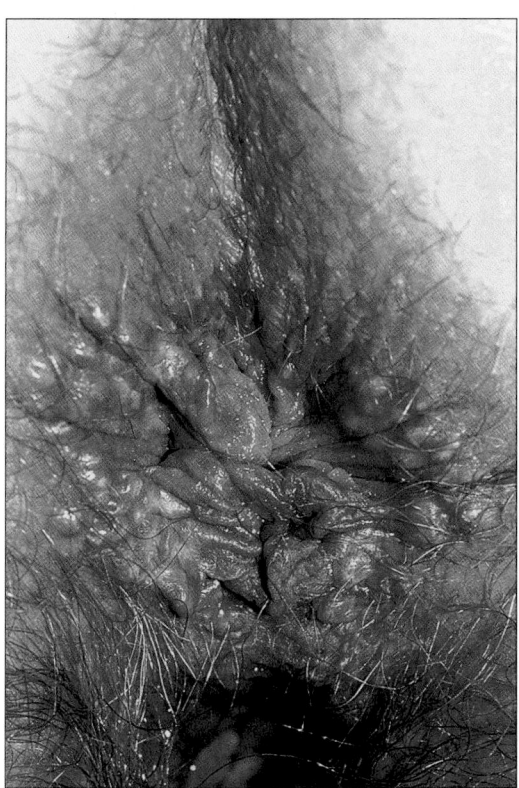

Fig. 11.23
Hypertrophic perianal lichen planus: chronic scratching has resulted in superimposed lichenification. By courtesy of the Institute of Dermatology, London, UK.

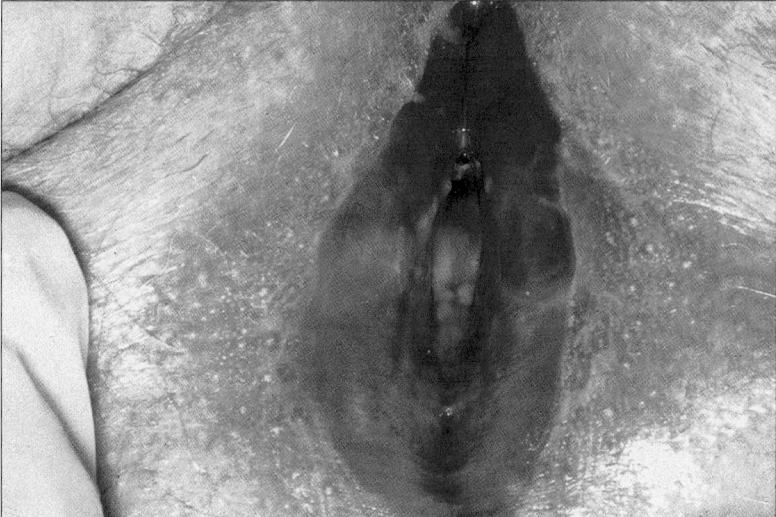

Fig. 11.24
Vulvovaginal-gingival syndrome: there is extensive vestibular erythema and erosion with a surrounding delicate white scale. By courtesy of the Institute of Dermatology, London, UK.

surfaces. The epidermis may be effaced or thickened and there is a dense, band-like infiltrate hugging the dermoepidermal junction (*Fig. 11.28*). Many genital lesions are mucosal and the inflammatory cell infiltrate is often rich in plasma cells, in contrast with lesions of LP elsewhere where lymphocytes and histiocytes predominate (*Fig. 11.29*). The basal layer is often disrupted with some cytological atypia as regeneration takes place.

Cytoid bodies may be seen but tend not to be prominent. Sometimes there is focal accentuation of the granular zone of mucous membrane lesions. This is accompanied by parakeratosis. Focal secondary spongiotic changes are not uncommon, particularly in mucosal surfaces. In longstanding disease the dense, band-like infiltrate may be replaced by a patchy, scant infiltrate with small foci of lichenoid inflammation. Many cases of genital lichen planus are misdiagnosed as Zoon's dermatitis.

Immunofluorescence studies may show fibrinogen and IgM along the basement membrane zone and more rarely IgG or IgA.[19] Cytoid bodies may also be labeled.

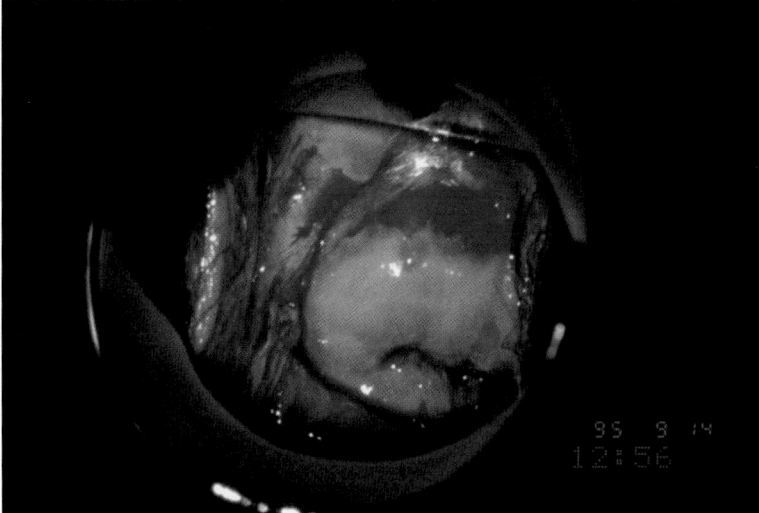

Fig. 11.25
Vulvovaginal-gingival syndrome: there is ulceration of the vagina and cervix. By courtesy of the Institute of Dermatology, London, UK.

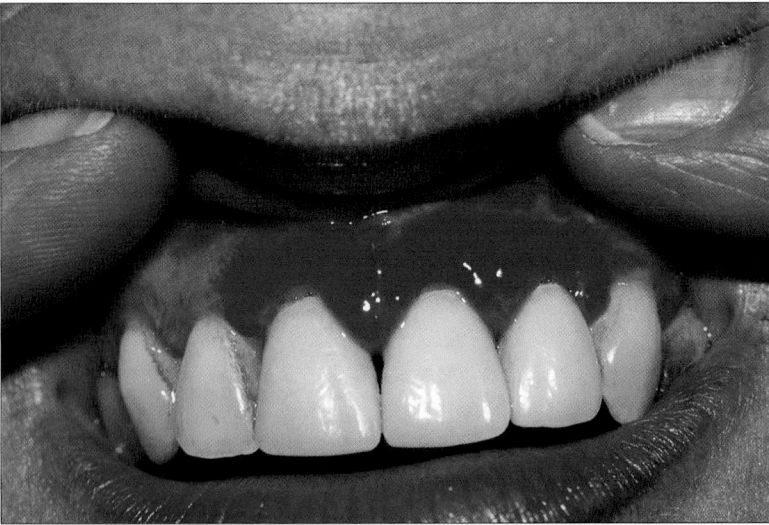

Fig. 11.26
Vulvovaginal-gingival syndrome: note the intense erythema with erosion of the gum. By courtesy of the Institute of Dermatology, London, UK.

Differential diagnosis

Lichen planus often overlaps with the features of lichen sclerosus and, in some patients, the two disorders may coexist. Hyalinization of the papillary dermis or the superficial lamina propria is indicative of the latter condition. In patients suffering from such a chronic overlap syndrome, particular care should be taken to recognize dysplastic areas or SCC.

References

1. Lewis, F., Shah, M., Harrington, C. (1996) Vulval involvement in lichen planus: a study of 37 women. *Br J Dermatol*, **135**, 89–91.
2. Lewis, F.M. (1998) Vulval lichen planus. *Br J Dermatol*, **138**, 569–575.
3. Pelisse, M., Leibowitch, M., Sedel, D. et al (1982) Un nouveau syndrome vulvo-vaginal-gingival. Lichen plan erosif plurimuqueux. *Ann Dermatol Venereol*, **110**, 797–798.
4. Pelisse, M. (1989) The vulvo-vaginal-gingival syndrome: a new form of erosive lichen planus. *Int J Dermatol*, **28**, 381–384.
5. Eisen, D. (1994) The vulvovaginal-gingival syndrome of lichen planus. The clinical characteristics of 22 patients. *Arch Dermatol*, **130**, 1379–1382.
6. Pelisse, M. (1996) Erosive vulvar lichen planus and desquamative vaginitis. *Semin Dermatol*, **15**, 47–50.
7. Ludovic, M., Sylvain, M., Marie-Christine, M. et al (1998) Bilateral conductive deafness related to erosive lichen planus. *J Laryngol Otol*, **112**, 365–366.
8. Moyal-Barracco, M., Lautier-Frau, M., Bechéral, P.A. et al (1993) Lichen plan conjunctival: une observation. *Ann Dermatol Venereol*, **120**, 857–859.
9. Hutnik, C.M., Probst, L.E., Burt, W.L. et al (1999) Progressive refractory keratoconjunctivitis associated with lichen planus. *Can J Ophthalmol*, **30**, 211–214.
10. Sheehan-Dare, R.A., Cotterill, J.A., Simmons, A.V. (1986) Oesophageal lichen planus. *Br J Dermatol*, **115**, 729–730.
11. Dickens, C.M., Hesletine, D., Walton, S. et al (1990) The oesophagus in lichen planus: an endoscopic study. *BMJ*, **300**, 84.
12. Bobadilla, J., van der Hulst, R.W., ten Kate, F.J. et al (1999) Esophageal lichen planus. *Gastrointest Endosc*, **50**, 268–271.
13. Grunwald, M.H., Zvulunov, A., Halevy, S. (1997) Lichen planopilaris of the vulva. *Br J Dermatol*, **136**, 477–478.
14. Worheide, J., Bonsmann, G., Kolde, G. et al (1991) Squamous epithelial carcinoma at the site of lichen ruber hypertrophicus of the glans penis. *Hautarzt*, **42**, 112–115.
15. Leal-Khouri, S., Hruza, G.J. (1994) Squamous cell carcinoma developing within lichen planus of the penis. *J Dermatol Surg Oncol*, **20**, 272–276.
16. Dwyer, C.M., Kerr, R.E., Millan, D.W. (1995) Squamous cell carcinoma following lichen planus of the vulva. *Clin Exp Dermatol*, **20**, 171–172.
17. Lewis, F.M., Harrington, C.I. (1994) Squamous cell carcinoma arising in vulval lichen planus. *Br J Dermatol*, **131**, 703–705.
18. Fundaro, S., Spallanzani, A., Ricchi, E. et al (1998) Squamous cell carcinoma developing within anal lichen planus. *Dis Colon Rectum*, **41**, 111–114.
19. Helander, S.D., Rogers, R.S. (1994) The sensitivity and specificity of direct immunofluorescence testing in disorders of mucous membranes. *J Am Acad Dermatol*, **30**, 65–75.

Lichen sclerosus

Clinical features

Lichen sclerosus (LS) is a dermatosis of unknown etiology.[1–5] It has a predilection for the anogenital skin in women and the genital skin in men. Women are more frequently involved than men (10:1) and it is more common in white than non-white patients.[3]

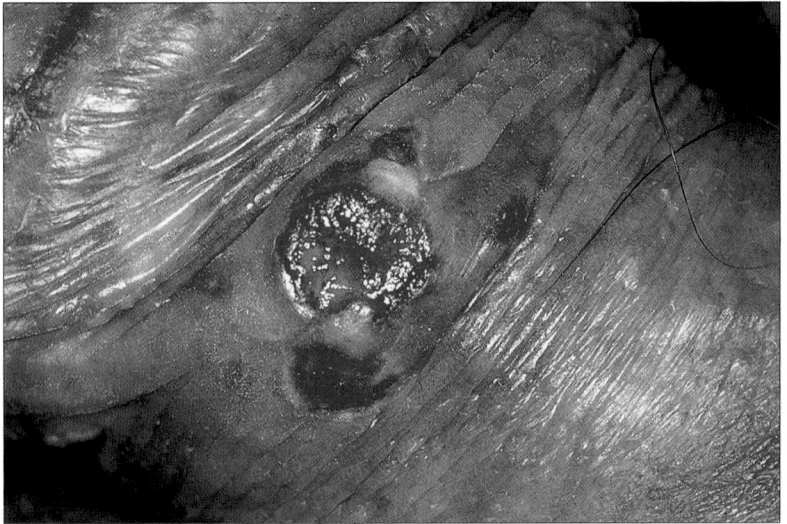

Fig. 11.27
Lichen planus: chronic penile lesion complicated by an ulcerated squamous cell carcinoma. By courtesy of the Institute of Dermatology, London, UK.

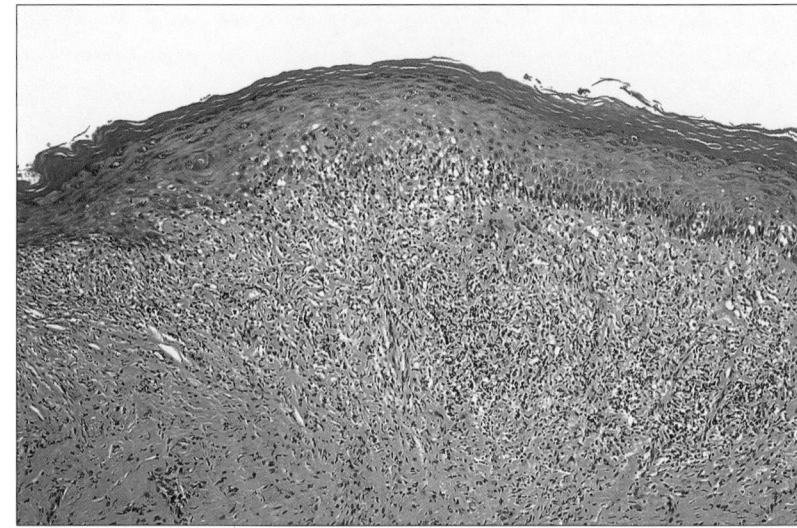

Fig. 11.28
Lichen planus: there is hyperkeratosis, acanthosis and a band-like inflammatory cell infiltrate.

In males, LS predominantly affects the prepuce and glans and thus is sometimes referred to as balanitis xerotica obliterans (*Fig. 11.30*). Perianal disease does not appear to occur. In boys, genital LS is the most common cause of acquired phimosis (*Fig. 11.31*).[6]

In girls, the condition can present at a very early age with hemorrhagic perianal lesions (*Figs 11.32, 11.33*). Constipation can occur as a complication and these signs may lead to the condition being mistaken for sexual abuse.[2] Extragenital lesions occur in 11% of women with genital lichen sclerosus.[7] Such involvement occurs on the upper trunk, groins, upper extremities, neck, lower trunk and lower extremities in decreasing order of frequency (*Figs 11.34, 11.35*). Involvement of the scalp and face is rare.[8] Extragenital lesions may occur in the absence of genital lesions. The Koebner phenomenon is frequent and LS has been described in association with scars and at the sites of radiotherapy.[9–11] Lesions can

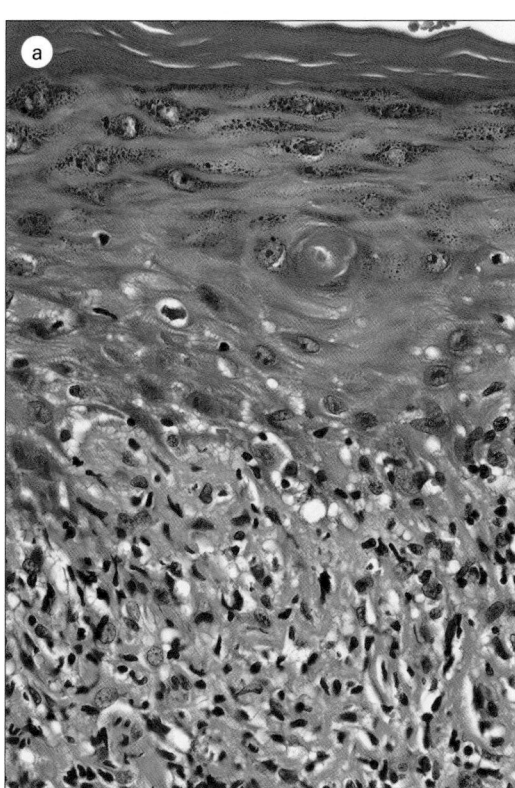

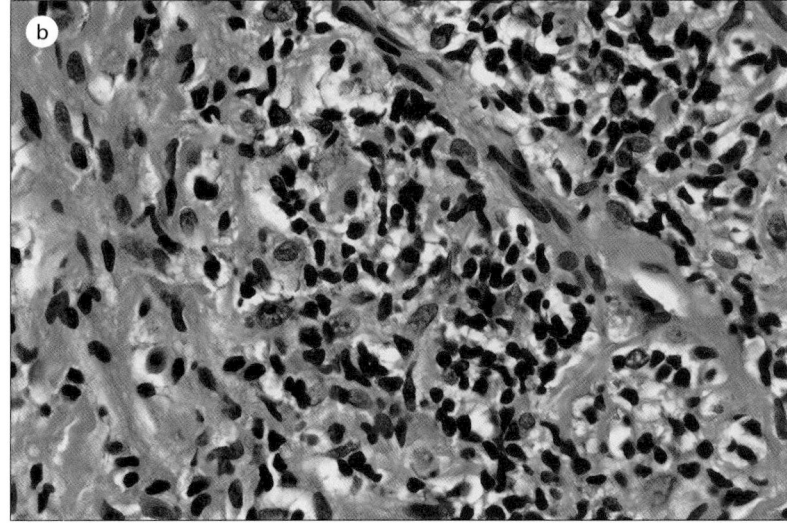

Fig. 11.29
Lichen planus: (a) note the hyperkeratosis, hypergranulosis and basal cell hydropic degeneration; (b) in contrast to cutaneous disease, plasma cells as shown in this field are often present in genital lesions.

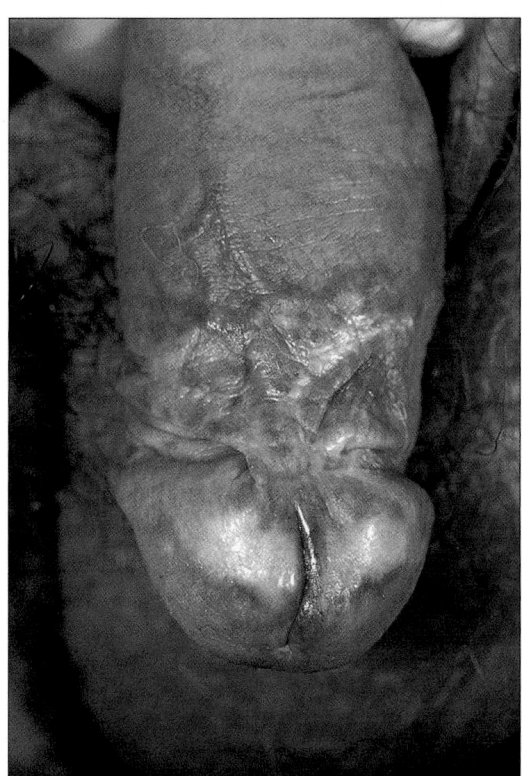

Fig. 11.30
Lichen sclerosus: in males, lesions of the foreskin and glans may be complicated by urethral stricture (so-called balanitis xerotica obliterans). By courtesy of the Institute of Dermatology, London, UK.

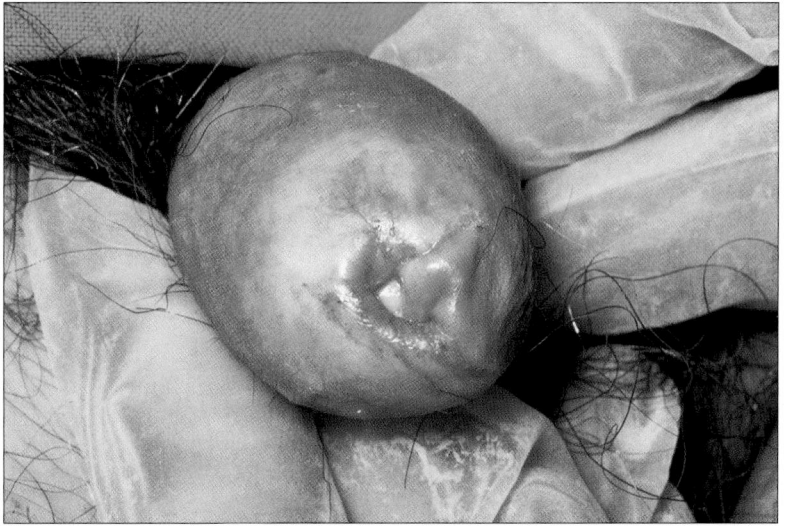

Fig. 11.31
Lichen sclerosus: a more advanced case showing severe phimosis. By courtesy of the Institute of Dermatology, London, UK.

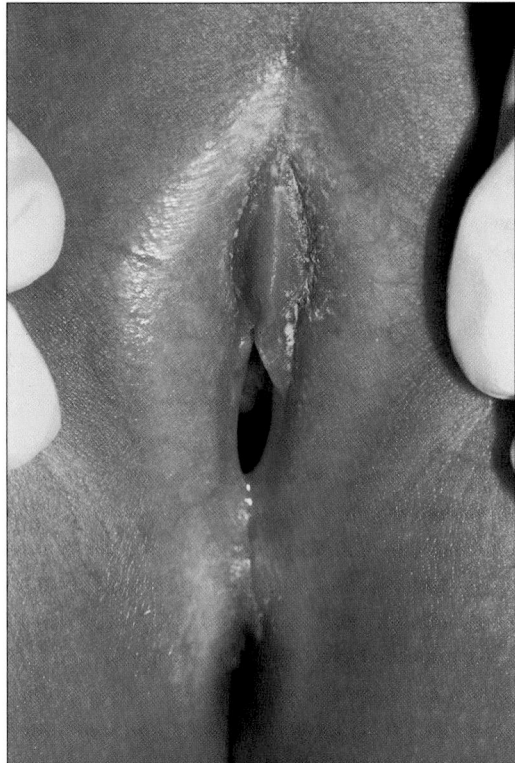

Fig. 11.32
Lichen sclerosus: severe bilateral and symmetrical disease with atrophy and virtual loss of the labia minora. Vulval lesions are intensely pruritic. By courtesy of the Institute of Dermatology, London, UK.

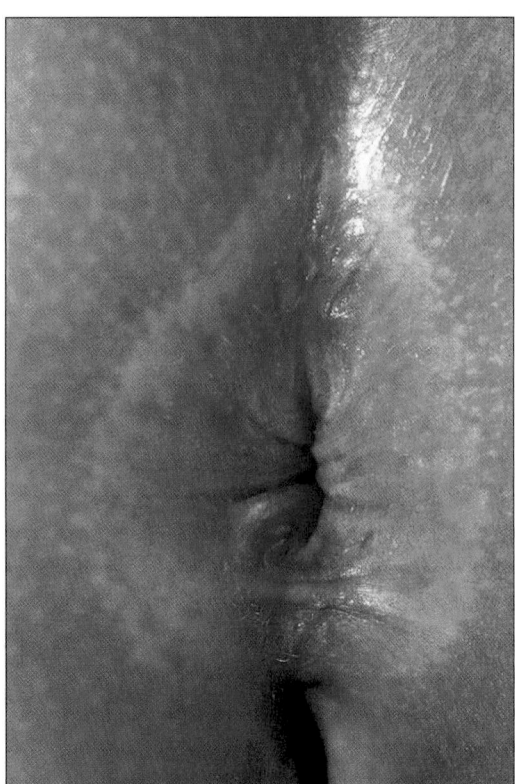

Fig. 11.33
Lichen sclerosus: perianal disease is often present in addition to vulval involvement, giving rise to the so-called hourglass distribution. By courtesy of the Institute of Dermatology, London, UK.

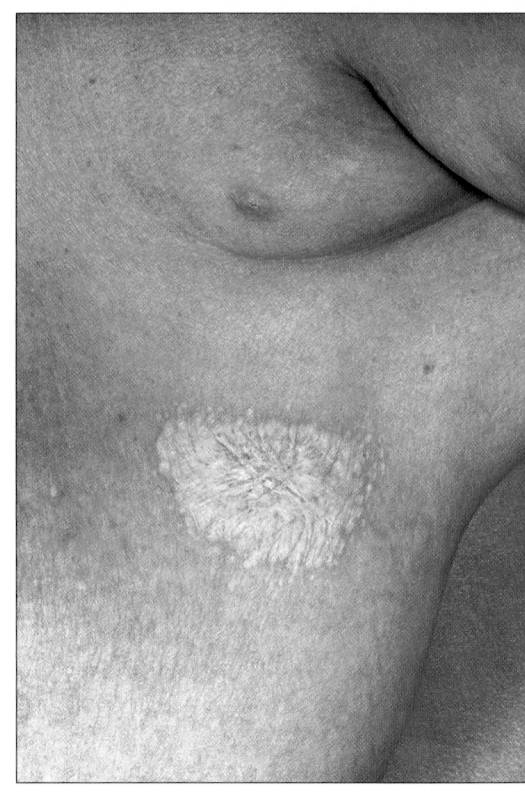

Fig. 11.34
Lichen sclerosus: irregular white plaque. It should be noted that extragenital lesions sometimes occur in the absence of genital lesions. By courtesy of R.A. Marsden, MD, St George's Hospital, London, UK.

also develop or recur in skin grafts.[12] Oral involvement has been described but the exact incidence is unknown, as suspected cases are not often confirmed by histological examination.[13–15] Lichen planus can coexist with LS and this may account for some of the oral lesions.[16] Coexistence of LS with morphea has also been documented.[17]

The typical lesions of LS are porcelain-white papules and plaques with a crinkled surface. They can coalesce to form plaques. There are often associated ecchymoses and areas of hyperkeratosis. The latter occurs in relation to the appendage ostia, which are dilated, giving rise to the physical sign of delling.[16] Bullae only rarely occur. Common symptoms include pruritus, burning and dyspareunia. Although anogenital LS is intensely pruritic, lichenification is often not conspicuous. Female anogenital involvement is typically symmetrical and bilateral, and is described as having a figure-of-eight (hourglass) distribution when it affects the perianal as well as vulval skin.[18] Lesions on the vulva predominantly affect the inner aspect of the labia majora, the labia minora, the prepuce of the clitoris, the fossa navicularis and the posterior commissure (*Figs 11.36, 11.37*). Lichen sclerosus is a scarring disorder and there may be marked anatomical changes with loss of the labia minora, burying of the clitoris, preputial phimosis and urethral perimeatal stenosis. The vagina is unaffected.

An important complication of vulval involvement is the development of dysplasia and SCC (*Figs 11.38, 11.39*).[1] Sites more commonly affected include the clitoral prepuce, the fossa navicularis and the posterior commissure. Dysplastic foci may appear as dry, adherent, gray–white areas. Such changes must be examined histologically. Less than 4% of patients with LS will develop a SCC.[1] SCC has not been described in association with extragenital lesions.[5] Very occasionally, penile tumors complicating lichen sclerosus have been documented.[19]

Pathogenesis and histological features

The etiology of LS is unknown. It has been suggested that genetic, hormonal and autoimmune factors may be of importance. Familial cases are well recognized and have been described in both sexes and in identical and non-identical twins.[20–23] About 21% of patients with LS have an associated autoimmune disease including alopecia areata, vitiligo, hyperthyroidism, hypothyroidism, pernicious anemia and diabetes mellitus.[6,24] Patients and first-degree relatives may have circulating autoantibodies including those to thyroid, gastric parietal cell and smooth muscle in addition to antinuclear factor.[25] A significant association between LS and the presence of class II antigens including HLA-DQ7, -DR7, -DQ8 and -DQ9 (alone or in combination) has been reported.[26] It has also been suggested that HLA-A2 possibly exerts a protective role, as it tends to be absent in patients with extensive extragenital lesions. Also, linkage of HLA-DR4 with -DQ8 is commoner in patients with marked structural damage to the anogenital area.[26]

Additional proposed etiological factors include absence of collagenase, an increase in collagen inhibitor enzyme and decreased elastase activity.[3] Reduced dihydrotestosterone levels have been described in some patients and there is one report documenting the histological presence of variably acid-fast bacilli.[27,28] As with morphea and atrophoderma, a causal relationship with *Borrelia burgdorferi* has been proposed.[29–31] However, findings have been conflicting and a recent study found no evidence of spirochetal organisms.[32]

The histological changes are identical irrespective of the site involved (*Figs 11.40–11.43*).[33–35] Fully developed lesions of LS show a thinned effaced epidermis with interface change and a wide band of hyalinization in the upper dermis and a lymphohistiocytic infiltrate below the hyalinized area.[34] Marked hyperkeratosis, often (on hair bearing) associated

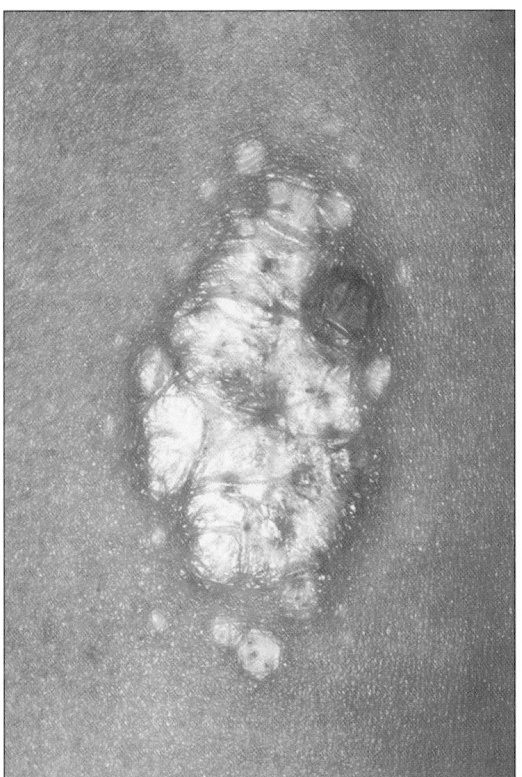

Fig. 11.35
Lichen sclerosus: healing lesion with a typical 'wrinkled tissue paper' appearance. By courtesy of R.A. Marsden, MD, St George's Hospital, London, UK.

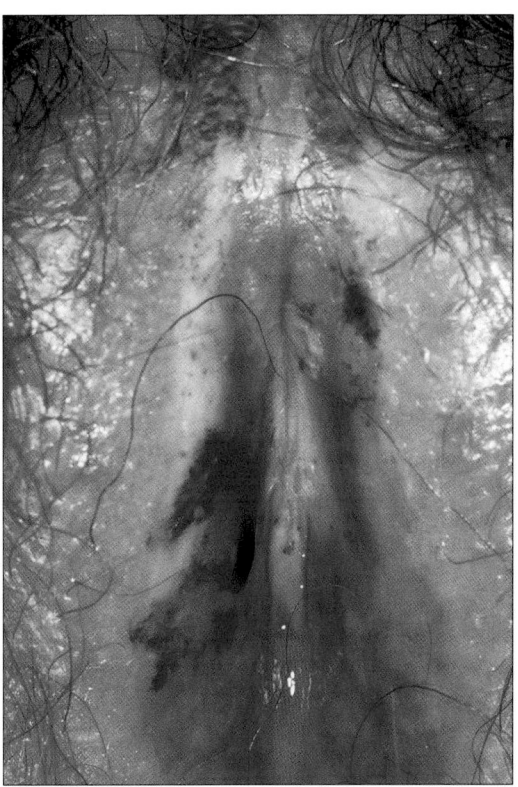

Fig. 11.36
Lichen sclerosus: symmetrical white lesions with gross atrophy and hemorrhage. By courtesy of the Institute of Dermatology, London, UK.

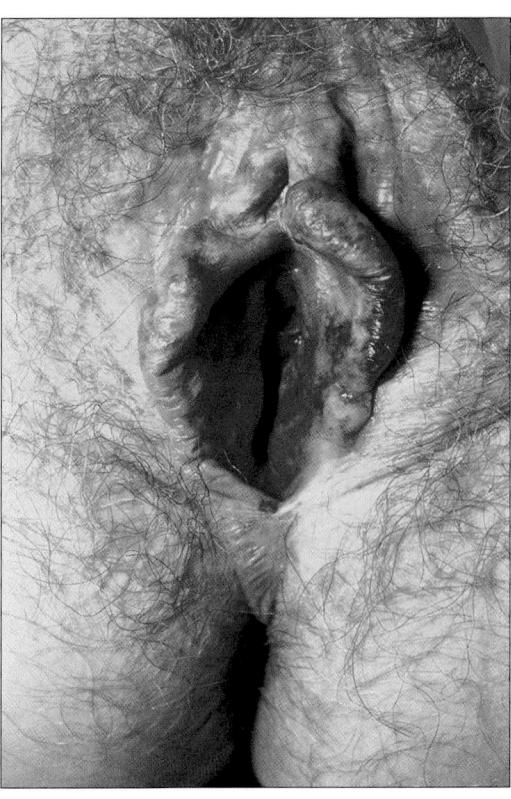

Fig. 11.37
Lichen sclerosus: there is extensive vulval disease with involvement of the perineum and atrophy. By courtesy of the Institute of Dermatology, London, UK.

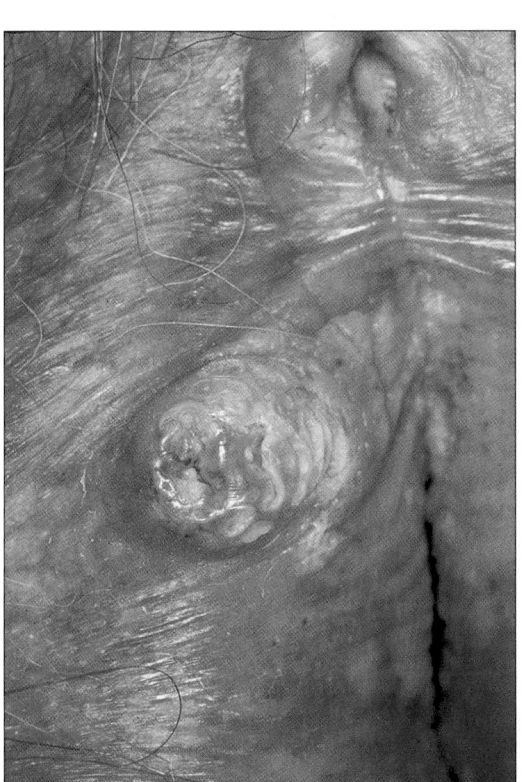

Fig. 11.38
Lichen sclerosus: longstanding disease with complete loss of the vulval architecture complicated by the development of an ulcerated squamous cell carcinoma. By courtesy of the Institute of Dermatology, London, UK.

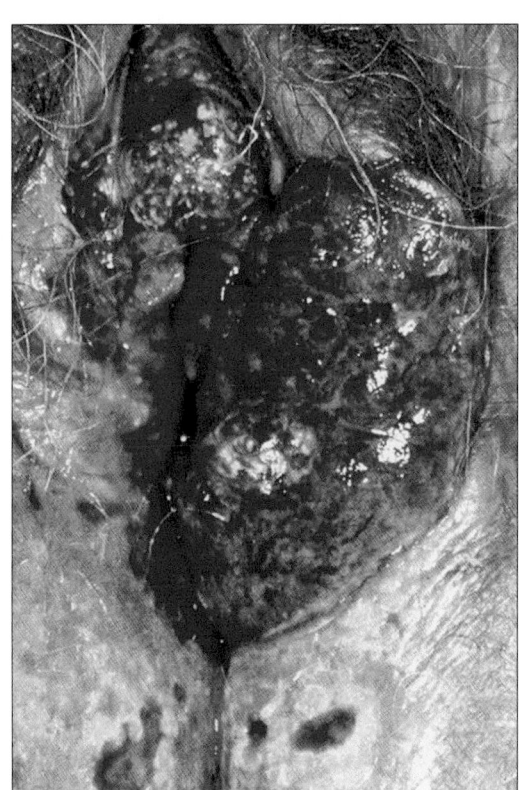

Fig. 11.39
Lichen sclerosus: an ulcerated squamous cell carcinoma has destroyed much of the left side of the vulva. Note the background of ulcerated lichen sclerosus. By courtesy of the Institute of Dermatology, London, UK.

with follicular plugging, is frequently seen. Subepidermal edema is sometimes present and may be sufficient to cause subepithelial vesiculation (*Fig. 11.44*). Telangiectasia is common and purpura may be an additional feature. Early lesions and the periphery of fully developed lesions display lichenoid changes similar to lichen planus (see differential diagnosis).[35] Some cases may be associated with foci of marked and highly irregular acanthosis, often with a very jagged lower border (so-called squamous cell hyperplasia). Such cases should be carefully scrutinized for evidence of epithelial dysplasia or adjacent carcinoma. Currently there is no good evidence to suggest that oncogenic human papillomavirus (HPV) is associated with LS-related SCC.

Ultrastructural studies of LS show fragmentation, reduplication and formation of gaps in the basal lamina.[34,36] Langerhans' cells appear to pass through these gaps.[36] The mononuclear infiltrate in LS is composed of an admixture of T-helper and suppressor lymphocytes. Expression of p53 by epidermal cells has been reported in lichen sclerosus.[37,38]

Differential diagnosis

Anogenital LS, particularly early lesions, may be difficult to distinguish from lichen planus (LP). Changes present in the early stages of LS, and absent in LP, include a psoriasiform lichenoid pattern, epidermotropism affecting the basal cell layer, basement membrane thickening, foci of epidermal atrophy and loss of papillary dermal elastic fibers.[35]

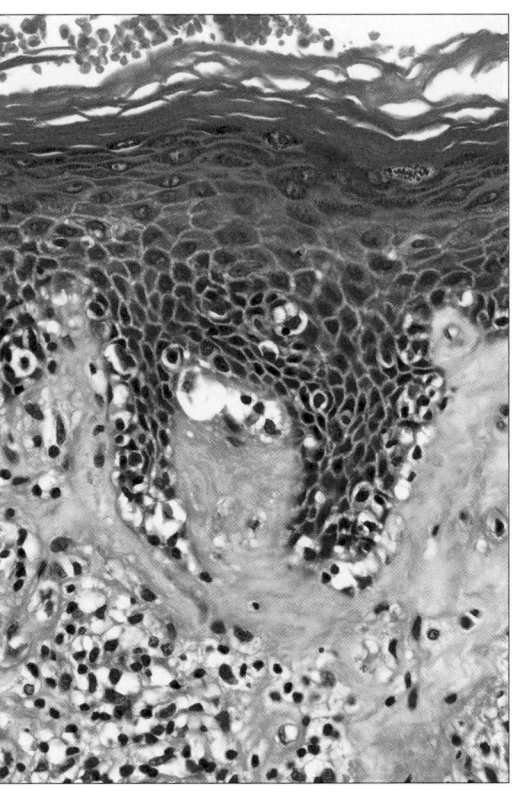

Fig. 11.42
Lichen sclerosus: close-up view of basal cell hydropic degeneration.

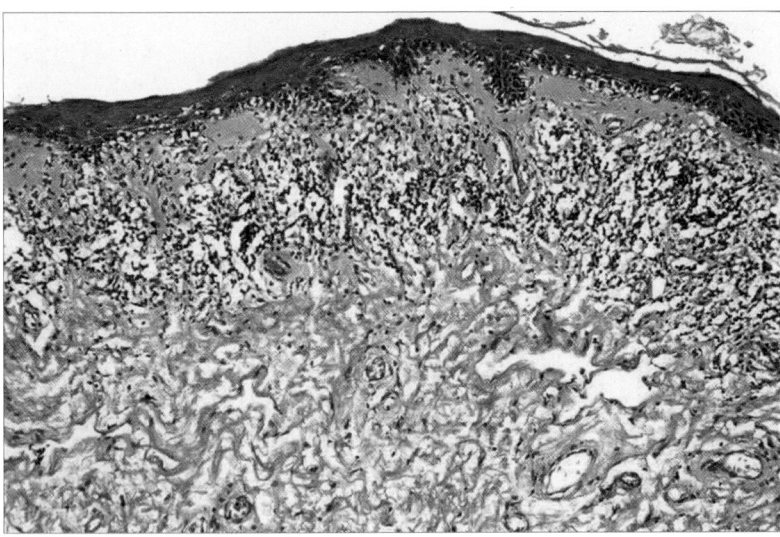

Fig. 11.40
Lichen sclerosus: early lesion showing epidermal atrophy and marked basal cell hydropic degeneration. There is a narrow zone of papillary dermal hyalinization and a band-like infiltrate is present.

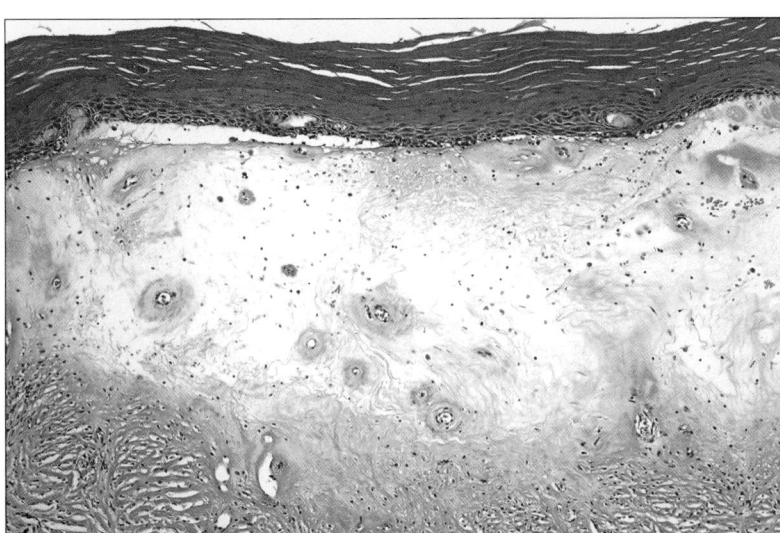

Fig. 11.41
Lichen sclerosus: this example shows the characteristic features of lichen sclerosus. Note the hyperkeratosis, epidermal atrophy and a broad band of dermal hyalinization. Telangiectatic vessels are prominent.

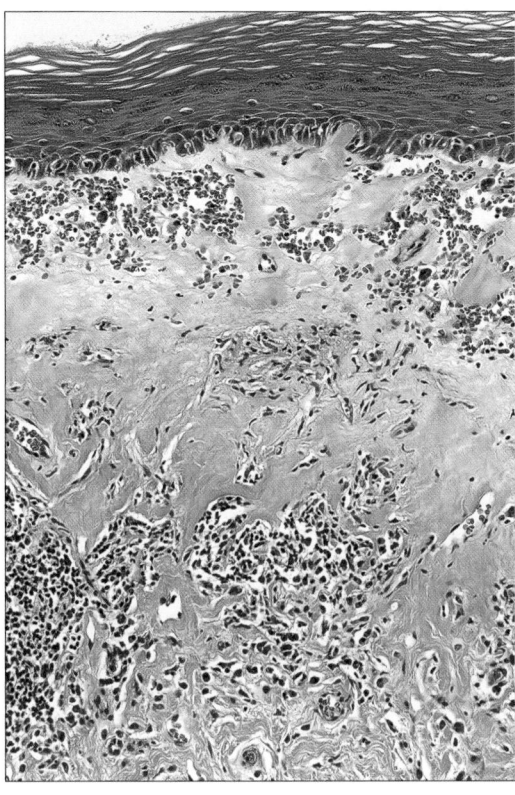

Fig. 11.43
Lichen sclerosus: in this view the lymphohistiocytic infiltrate is present deep to the zone of hyalinization. There is telangiectasia with hemorrhage.

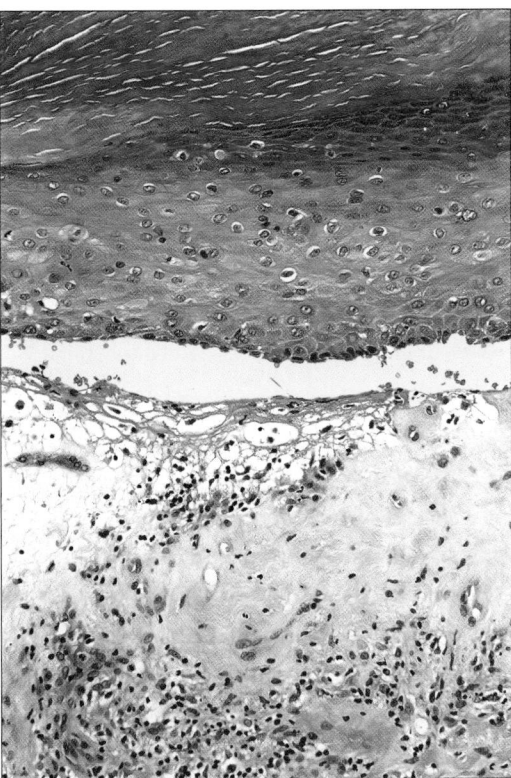

Fig. 11.44
Lichen sclerosus: occasionally, intense edema may result in subepidermal vesiculation.

References

1. Meffert, J.J., Davis, B.M., Grimwood, R.E. (1995) Lichen sclerosus. *J Am Acad Dermatol*, **32**, 393–416.
2. Wallace, H.J. (1971) Lichen sclerosus et atrophicus. *Trans St John's Hosp Dermatol Soc*, **57**, 9–30.
3. Ridley, C.M. (1992) Lichen sclerosus. *Dermatol Clin*, **10**, 309–323.
4. Ridley, C.M. (1989) Lichen sclerosus et atrophicus. *Semin Dermatol*, **8**, 54–63.
5. Tremaine, R.D.I., Miller, R.A.W. (1989) Lichen sclerosus et atrophicus. *Int J Dermatol*, **28**, 10–16.
6. Chalmers, R.J.G., Burton, P.A., Bennett, R.F. et al (1984) Lichen sclerosus et atrophicus. A common and distinctive cause of phimosis in boys. *Arch Dermatol*, **120**, 1025–1027.
7. Meyrick Thomas, R.H., Ridley, C.M., McGibbon, D.H. et al (1996) Anogenital lichen sclerosus in women. *J R Soc Med*, **89**, 694–698.
8. Foulds, I.S. (1980) Lichen sclerosus et atrophicus of the scalp. *Br J Dermatol*, **103**, 197–200.
9. Meffert, J.J., Grimwood, R.E. (1994) Lichen sclerosus appearing in an old burn scar. *J Am Acad Dermatol*, **31**, 671–673.
10. Tegner, E., Vrana, I. (2001) Lichen sclerosus et atrophicus appearing in old scars of burns from welding sparks. *Acta Derm Venereol*, **81**, 211.
11. Yates, V.M., King, C.M., Dave, V.K. (1985) Lichen sclerosus et atrophicus following radiation therapy. *Arch Dermatol*, **121**, 1044–1047.
12. Meyrick Thomas, R.H., Ridley, C.M., McGibbon, D.H. et al (1988) Lichen sclerosus and autoimmunity – a study of 350 women. *Br J Dermatol*, **118**, 41–46.
13. Miller, R.F. (1957) Lichen sclerosus with oral involvement. *Arch Dermatol*, **76**, 43–45.
14. Macleod, R.I., Soames, J.V. (1991) Lichen sclerosus of the oral mucosa. *Br J Oral Maxillofacial Surg*, **29**, 64–65.
15. Brown, A.R., Dunlap, C.L., Bussard, D.A. et al (1997) Lichen sclerosus of the oral cavity: a report of two cases. *Oral Surg Oral Med Oral Pathol Oral Radiol Endod*, **84**,165–170.
16. Marren, P., Millard, P., Chia, Y. et al (1994) Mucosal lichen sclerosus/lichen planus overlap syndromes. *Br J Dermatol*, **131**, 118–123.
17. Uitto, J., Santa Cruz, D.J., Bauer, E.A. et al (1980) Morphea and lichen sclerosus et atrophicus: clinical and histopathologic studies in patients with combined features. *J Am Acad Dermatol*, **3**, 271–279.
18. Ridley, C.M. (1993) Genital lichen sclerosus (lichen sclerosus et atrophicus) in childhood and adolescence. *J R Soc Med*, **86**, 69–75.
19. Campus, G.V., Alia, F., Bosincu, L. (1992) Squamous cell carcinoma and lichen sclerosus et atrophicus of the prepuce. *Plast Reconstr Surg*, **89**, 962–964.
20. Friedrich, E.G., MacLaren, N.K. (1984) Genetic aspects of lichen sclerosus. *Am J Obstet Gynecol*, **150**, 161–166.
21. Murphy, F.R., Lipa, M., Haberman, H.F. (1982) Familial vulvar dystrophy of lichen sclerosus type. *Arch Dermatol*, **118**, 329–331.
22. Meyrick Thomas, R.H., Kennedy, C.T.C. (1986) The development of lichen sclerosus et atrophicus in monozygotic twin girls. *Br J Dermatol*, **114**, 377–379.
23. Cox, N.H., Mitchell, J.N.S., Morley, W.N. (1986) Lichen sclerosus et atrophicus in non-identical female twins. *Br J Dermatol*, **115**, 743.
24. Harrington, C.I., Dunsmore, I.R. (1981) An investigation into the incidence of autoimmune disorders in patients with lichen sclerosus et atrophicus. *Br J Dermatol*, **104**, 563–566.
25. Goolamali, S.K., Barnes, E.W., Irvine, W. et al (1974) Organ specific antibodies in patients with lichen sclerosus. *BMJ*, **IV**, 78–79.
26. Marren, P., Yell, J., Charnock, F.M. et al (1995) The association between lichen sclerosus and antigens of the HLA system. *Br J Dermatol*, **132**, 197–203.
27. Friedrich, E.G., Kaira, P.S. (1984) Serum levels of sex hormones in vulvar lichen sclerosus and the effect of topical testosterone. *N Engl J Med*, **310**, 488–491.
28. Cantwell, A.R. (1984) Histologic observations of pleomorphic, variably acid-fast bacilli in scleroderma, morphea and lichen sclerosus. *Int J Dermatol*, **23**, 42–52.
29. Aberer, E., Stanek, G. (1987) Histological evidence for spirochetal origin of morphea and lichen sclerosus et atrophicans. *Am J Dermatopathol*, **9**, 374–379.
30. Ross, S.A., Sanchez, J.L., Taboas, J.G. (1990) Spirochetal forms in the dermal lesions of morphea and lichen sclerosus et atrophicus. *Am J Dermatopathol*, **12**, 357–362.
31. Schempp, C., Bocklage, H., Lange, R. et al (1993) Further evidence for Borrelia burgdorferi infection in morphea and lichen sclerosus et atrophicus confirmed by DNA amplification. *J Invest Dermatol*, **100**, 717–720.
32. Farrell, A.M., Millard, P.R., Schomberg, K.H. et al (1997) An infective aetiology for lichen sclerosus: myth or reality? *Br J Dermatol*, **137** (Suppl. 50), 25.
33. Hewitt, J. (1986) Histologic criteria for lichen sclerosus of the vulva. *J Reprod Med*, **31**, 781–787.
34. Mihara, Y., Mihara, M., Hagari, Y. et al (1994) Lichen sclerosus et atrophicus. A histological, immunohistochemical, and electron microscopic study. *Arch Dermatol Res*, **286**, 434–442.
35. Fung, M.A., LeBoit, P.E. (1998) Light microscopic criteria for the diagnosis of early vulvar lichen sclerosus. A comparison with lichen planus. *Am J Surg Pathol*, **22**, 473–478.
36. Mann, P.R., Cowan, M.A. (1973) Ultrastructural changes in four cases of lichen sclerosus et atrophicus. *Br J Dermatol*, **89**, 223–231.
37. Tan, S-H., Derrick, E., McKee, P.H. et al (1994) Altered p53 expression and epidermal cell proliferation is seen in vulval lichen sclerosus. *J Cutan Pathol*, **21**, 316–323.
38. Carlson, J.A., Ambros, R., Malfetano, J. et al (1998) Vulvar lichen sclerosus and squamous cell carcinoma: a cohort, case control, and investigational study with historical perspective; implications for chronic inflammation and sclerosis in the development of neoplasia. *Hum Pathol*, **29**, 932–948.

Zoon's balanitis/vulvitis

Clinical features

This variant of balanitis was initially described by Zoon as balanitis circumscripta plasmacellularis.[1–3] Clinically, the condition closely mimics Bowen's disease and is seen almost exclusively in uncircumcised elderly men.[4] Interestingly, although treatment is very difficult, circumcision may result in resolution of the disease.[5] A typical lesions presents as asolitary, glistening, red area, which often appears speckled and hemorrhagic, and measures up to 2 or 3 cm in diameter. Multiple lesions are very rare.

Lesions in females are exceedingly rare and affect the vestibule and the labia minora.[6–11] Few lesions have been described on the clitoris. Many other dermatoses (particularly lichen planus) are mistakenly categorized as Zoon's balanitis and there is some doubt (especially in women) whether an equivalent condition truly exists as a distinct entity.[12] An alternative name proposed for this condition when it presents in females is chronic vulval purpura.[13] Similar lesions have been described in the oral cavity and other mucosal surfaces, including the epiglottis, under such names such as plasma cell orificial mucositis and atypical gingivostomatitis (see p. 438).[14,15]

Pathogenesis and histological features

The etiology and pathogenesis of this condition are unknown.

The histological criteria required for diagnosis have varied in the literature.[4] The essential features, however, include a thinned epidermis, absent granular and horny layers, spongiosis with lozenge- or diamond-shaped keratinocytes and a dense, band-like, plasma cell-rich, dermal inflammatory infiltrate (*Figs 11.45, 11.46*). The infiltrate also contains lymphocytes, histiocytes and, occasionally, neutrophils and eosinophils.

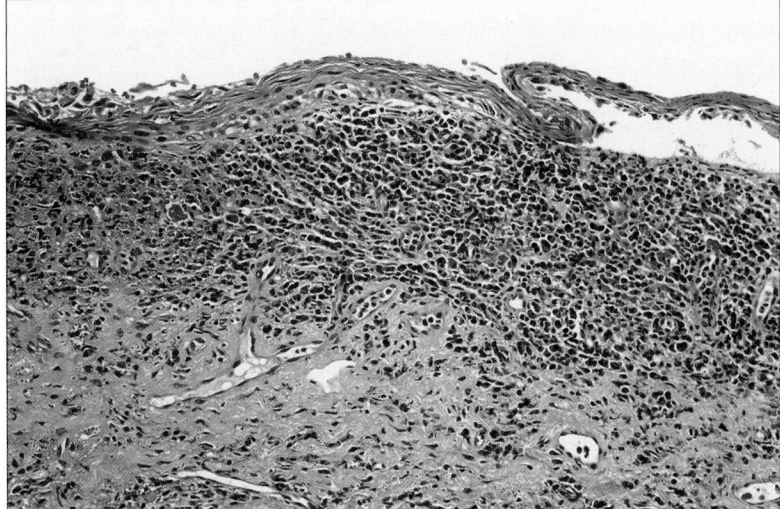

Fig. 11.45
Zoon's balanitis: note the epidermal thinning, spongiosis and a dense superficial inflammatory cell infiltrate.

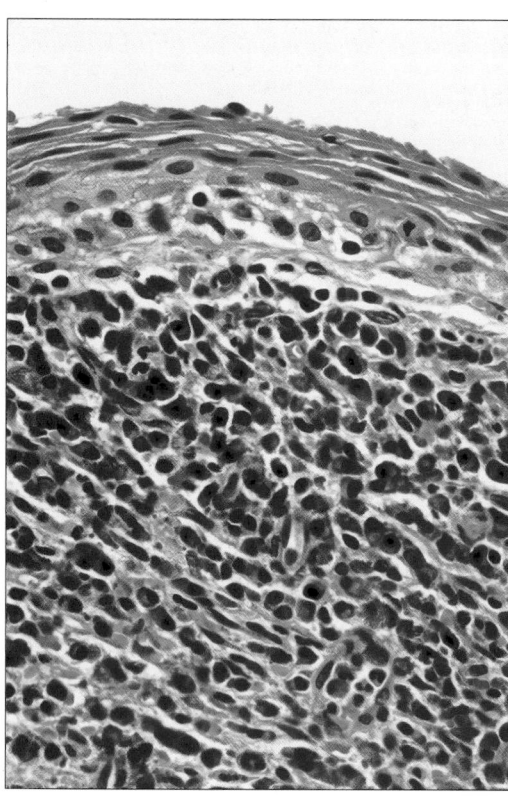

Fig. 11.46
Zoon's balanitis: there is 'lozenge-shaped' spongiosis and an intense plasma cell infiltrate.

Germinal center formation is a rare event. The blood vessels are dilated and increased in number. There is also extravasation of red blood cells and hemosiderin deposition. In rare cases the epidermis may appear partially detached or completely absent. Biopsies of longstanding lesions often show some degree of fibrosis of the lamina propria.

References

1. Zoon, J.J. (1952) Balanoposathite chronique circonscrite benigne a plasmocytes. *Dermatologica*, **105**, 1–7.
2. Brodin, M.B. (1980) Balanitis circumscripta plasmacellularis. *J Am Acad Dermatol*, **2**, 33–35.
3. Stern, J.K., Rosen, T. (1982) Balanitis plasmacellularis circumscripta (Zoon's balanitis plasmacellularis). *Cutis*, **25**, 57–60.
4. Souteyrand, P., Wong, E., MacDonald, D.M. (1981) Zoon's balanitis (balanitis circumscripta plasmacellularis). *Br J Dermatol*, **105**, 195–199.
5. Sonnex, T.S., Dawber, R.P.R., Ryan, T.J. et al (1982) Zoon's (plasma cell) balanitis. *Br J Dermatol*, **106**, 585–588.
6. Garnier, G. (1954) Vulvite erythemateuse circonscrite benigne a type erythroplasique. *Bull Soc Fran Dermatol Syphilol*, **61**, 102–103.
7. Davis, J., Shapiro, L., Baral, J. (1983) Vulvitis circumscripta plasmacellularis. *J Am Acad Dermatol*, **8**, 413–416.
8. Neri, I., Patrizi, A., Marzaduri, S. et al (1995) Vulvitis plasmacellularis: two new cases. *Genitour Med*, **71**, 311–313.
9. Kavanagh, G.M., Burton, P.A., Kennedy, C.T.C. (1993) Vulvitis chronica plasmacellularis (Zoon's vulvitis). *Br J Dermatol*, **129**, 92–93.
10. Woodruff, J.D., Sussman, J., Shakfeh, S. (1989) Vulvitis circumscripta plasmacellularis. A report of 4 cases. *J Reprod Med*, **34**, 369–372.
11. Hautmann, G., Geti, V., Difonzo, E.M. (1994) Vulvitis circumscripta plasma cellularis. *Int J Dermatol*, **33**, 496–497.
12. Scurry, J., Dennerstein, G., Brennan, J. (1993) Vulvitis circumscripta. A clinicopathological entity? *J Reprod Med*, **38**, 14–18.
13. Kato, T., Kuramoto, Y., Tadaki, T. et al (1990) Chronic vulvar purpura. *Dermatologica*, **180**, 174–176.
14. White, J.W. Jr, Olsen, K.D., Banks, P.M. (1986) Plasma cell orificial mucositis. Report of a case and review of the literature. *Arch Dermatol*, **122**, 1321–1324.
15. Perry, H.O., Deffner, N.F., Sheridan, P.J. (1973) Atypical gingivostomatitis. Nineteen cases. *Arch Dermatol*, **107**, 872–878.

Vesiculobullous conditions

Subepidermal autoimmune blistering diseases including bullous pemphigoid and mucous membrane pemphigoid are discussed in Chapter 3. Other blistering disorders including pemphigus, Darier's disease and Hailey–Hailey disease are discussed in Chapter 4.

References

1. Lampert, A., Assier-Bonnet, H., Chevallier, B. et al (1996) Lipschutz's genital ulceration: a manifestation of Epstein–Barr virus primary infection. *Br J Dermatol*, **135**, 663–665.
2. Taylor, S., Drake, S.M., Dedicoat, M. et al (1998) Genital ulcers associated with acute Epstein–Barr virus infection. *Sex Transm Infect*, **34**, 296–297.
3. Sisson, B.A., Glick, L. (1998) Genital ulceration as a presenting manifestation of infectious mononucleosis. *J Pediatr Adolesc Gynecol*, **11**, 185–187.
4. Hudson, L.B., Perlman, S.E. (1998) Necrotizing genital ulcerations in a premenstrual female with mononucleosis. *Obstet Gynecol*, **92**, 642–644.

Genital papular acantholytic dyskeratosis

This rare condition presents as papules, nodules or plaques predominantly affecting the anogenital skin. Histologically, it is characterized by Darier-like or Hailey–Hailey-like features. The condition is discussed in full on page 166.

Lipschutz ulcer

Clinical features

This condition is seen in teenage girls who present with vulval ulceration of sudden onset. Lesions may be solitary or multiple. The ulceration is sometimes accompanied by fever and in many cases it may be a manifestation of Epstein–Barr virus (EBV) infection (infectious mononucleosis).[1–4] The ulcers are painful and show purple margins. Patients usually present with other symptoms of infectious mononucleosis including fever and cervical lymphadenopathy. However, in some cases other signs and symptoms are absent or not prominent and confirmation of the diagnosis requires serological tests.[3]

Histological features

The microscopic appearance has not been described in detail but there is non-specific superficial ulceration with a mixed inflammatory cell infiltrate.

Sclerosing lymphangitis of the penis

Clinical features

Sclerosing lymphangitis of the penis (Mondor's disease) is an exceedingly rare condition which presents as a cord-like thickening of the skin near to the coronal sulcus.[1–4] Rarely, there is involvement of the dorsal aspect of the shaft. There may be some inflammation and local tenderness. The condition is self-limiting and resolves spontaneously after a few weeks. Only occasional cases are persistent.[5] There does not appear to be a female equivalent to this disorder but there has been a report of the disease involving the upper lip and the labium minus.[6]

Pathogenesis and histological features

The etiology is unknown although trauma may be important. Masturbation has occasionally been associated.[7] In general, there does not seem to be any relationship to venereal disease although cases have been reported following genital herpes and Chlamydia infection.[8,9]

The histological features are characterized by a thrombosed vascular channel, thought to be of lymphatic derivation. Focal Masson-like changes may be seen. Later in the course of the disease, the thrombus is replaced by fibrous tissue and a few scattered mononuclear inflammatory cells are also seen. The wall of the affected vessel later becomes thickened and sclerotic.

References

1. Greenberg, R.D., Perry, T.L. (1972) Nonvenereal sclerosing lymphangitis of the penis. *Arch Dermatol*, **105**, 728–729.
2. Fiumara, N.J. (1975) Nonvenereal sclerosing lymphangitis of the penis. *Arch Dermatol*, **111**, 902–903.
3. Tanii, T., Hamada, T., Asai, Y. et al (1983) Mondor's phlebitis of the penis: a study with factor VIII related antigen. *Acta Derm Venereol*, **64**, 337–340.
4. Kandil, E., al-Kashlan, I.M. (1970) Non-venereal sclerosing lymphangitis of the penis. A clinicopathologic treatise. *Acta Derm Venereol*, **50**, 309–312.
5. Broaddus, S.B., Leadbetter, G.W. (1982) Surgical management of persistent, symptomatic nonvenereal sclerosing lymphangitis of the penis. *J Urol*, **127**, 987–988.
6. Stolz, E., van Kampen, W.J., Vuzevski, V. (1974) Sclerosing lymphangitis of the penis, upper lip and labium minus. *Hautarzt*, **25**, 231–237.
7. Sieunarine, K. (1987) Non-venereal sclerosing lymphangitis of the penis associated with masturbation. *Br J Urol*, **59**, 194–195.
8. Van de Staak, W.J. (1977) Non-venereal sclerosing lymphangitis of the penis following herpes progenitalis. *Br J Dermatol*, **96**, 679–680.
9. Kristensen, J.K., Scheibel, J. (1981) Sclerosing lymphangitis of the penis: a possible chlamydia aetiology. *Acta Derm Venereol*, **61**, 455–456.

Associations with systemic disease

Crohn's disease

Clinical features

Anogenital lesions occur in about 30% of patients with intestinal Crohn's disease, either by direct extension of active intestinal disease or as a manifestation of so-called 'metastatic disease' (*Figs 11.47–11.50*).[1–8] Skin involvement is more common in patients with colonic disease (up to 80%).[9] In 'metastatic disease' the affected areas are not contiguous with the involved bowel and may occur in distant cutaneous sites including the face and limbs.[10–14] Anogenital disease may present years before there is evidence of gastrointestinal disease. Vulval edema can be the only manifestation and occasionally it is unilateral.[15] More usually, however, the disease is associated with ulceration, abscesses, skin tags, sinus and fistula formation.[16] Deep fissures ('knife-cut' sign) along the skin creases are a characteristic feature. Exceptionally, the disease presents with unilateral labial hypertrophy.[17] Patients of any age with Crohn's disease may present with anogenital involvement.

Oral involvement includes fissuring and mucosal 'cobblestoning'. In some patients, there is marked edema and the appearances resemble Melkerson–Rosenthal syndrome.[18] One patient presented with 'metastatic' Crohn's disease and oral intraepithelial IgA pustulosis.[19]

Crohn's disease is not uncommonly associated with pyoderma gangrenosum and erythema nodosum. Other associations include leukocytoclastic vasculitis, erythema elevatum diutinum, granulomatous vasculitis, Sweet's syndrome, epidermolysis bullosa acquisita, polyarteritis nodosa, pyostomatitis vegetans, vitiligo, psoriasis, erythema multiforme, lichen nitidus, hidradenitis suppurativa, acne fulminans and a vesiculopustular eruption.[20–35]

The condition runs a chronic course. Development of Bowen's disease in a case of vulvovaginal Crohn's disease has been reported.[36]

Histological features

The histology may show only edema, dilated lymphatics or lymphangiectasia. More commonly, there are dermal or rarely subcutaneous

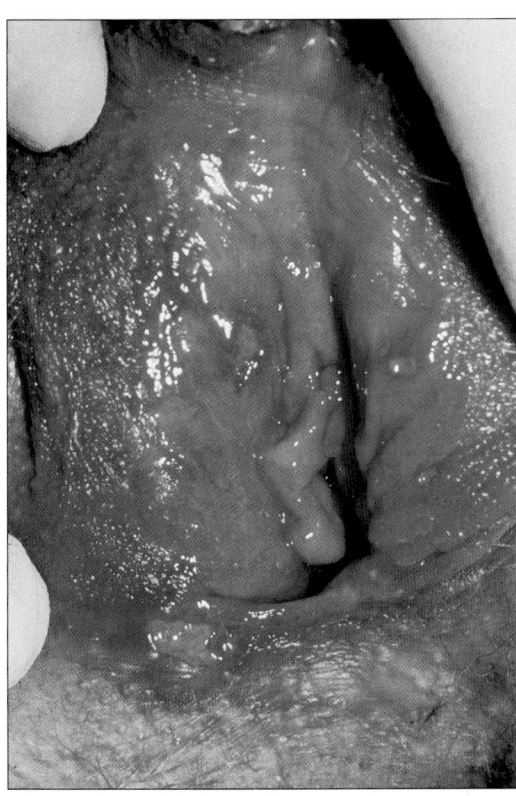

Fig. 11.47
Vulval Crohn's disease: there is intense erythema and multiple vestibular erosions are present. By courtesy of the Institute of Dermatology, London, UK.

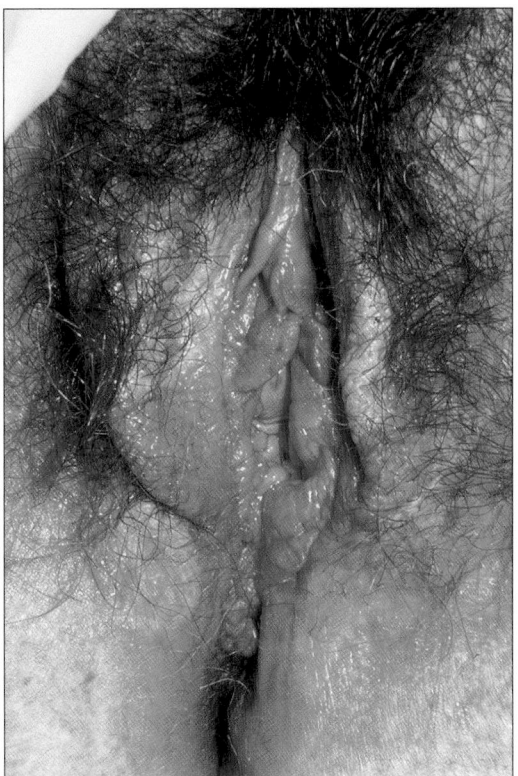

Fig. 11.48
Vulval Crohn's disease: in this patient there is marked edema with erythema and conspicuous granulomatous lesions. By courtesy of the Institute of Dermatology, London, UK.

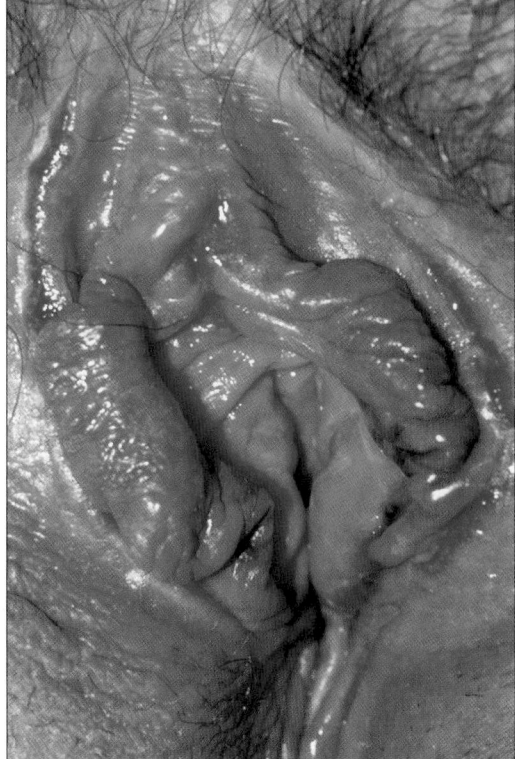

Fig. 11.49
Vulval Crohn's disease: note the erythema, edema and erosions. By courtesy of the Institute of Dermatology, London, UK.

non-caseating granulomata (*Fig. 11.51*). The latter may have a perivascular distribution.[37] The histological diagnosis can only be made after careful clinicopathological correlation.

References

1. McCallum, D.I., Kinmont, P.D. (1968) Dermatological manifestations of Crohn's disease. *Br J Dermatol*, **80**, 1–8.
2. Mountain, J.C. (1970) Cutaneous ulceration in Crohn's disease. *Gut*, **11**, 18–26.
3. Verbov, J.L. (1973) The skin in patients with Crohn's disease and ulcerative colitis. *Trans St John's Hosp Dermatol Soc*, **59**, 30–36.
4. Greenstein, A.J., Jsnowitz, H.D., Sachar, D.B. (1976) The extra-intestinal complications of Crohn's disease and ulcerative colitis: a study of 700 patients. *Medicine (Baltimore)*, **55**, 401–412.
5. Paller, A.S. (1986) Cutaneous changes associated with inflammatory bowel disease. *Pediatr Dermatol*, **3**, 439–445.
6. Apgar, J.T. (1991) Newer aspects of inflammatory bowel disease and its cutaneous manifestations: a selective review. *Semin Dermatol*, **10**, 138–147.
7. Burgdorf, W. (1981) Cutaneous manifestations of Crohn's disease. *J Am Acad Dermatol*, **5**, 689–695.
8. Berkowicz, E.Z., Lebwohl, M. (2000) Cutaneous manifestations of inflammatory bowel disease. *J Eur Acad Dermatol*, **14**, 349–350.
9. Rankin, G.B., Watts, H.D., Melnyk, C.S. et al (1979) National Cooperative Crohn's Disease Study: extraintestinal manifestations and perianal complications. *Gastroenterology*, **77**, 914–920.
10. Witkowski, J.A., Parish, L.C., Lewis, J.E. (1977) Crohn's disease – non-caseating granulomata on the legs. *Acta Derm Venereol*, **57**, 181–183.
11. Lebwohl, M., Fleischmajer, R., Janowitz, H. et al (1984) Metastatic Crohn's disease. *J Am Acad Dermatol*, **10**, 33–38.
12. Shum, D.T., Guenther, L. (1990) Metastatic Crohn's disease. Case report and review of the literature. *Arch Dermatol*, **126**, 645–648.
13. Buckley, C., Bayoumi, A-H.M., Sarkany, I. (1990) Metastatic Crohn's disease. *Clin Exp Dermatol*, **15**, 131–133.
14. Kolansky, G., Kimbrough-Green, C., Dubin, H.V. (1993) Metastatic Crohn's disease of the face: an uncommon presentation. *Arch Dermatol*, **129**, 1348–1349.
15. Martin, J., Holdstock, G. (1997) Isolated vulval oedema as a feature of Crohn's disease. *J Obstet Gynecol*, **17**, 92–93.
16. Urbanek, M., McKee, P.H., Neill, S.M. (1996) Vulval Crohn's: difficulties in diagnosis. *Clin Exp Dermatol*, **21**, 211–214.
17. Werlin, S.L., Esterly, N.B., Oechler, H. (1992) Crohn's disease presenting as unilateral labial hypertrophy. *J Am Acad Dermatol*, **27**, 893–895.
18. Kano, Y., Shiohara, T., Yagita, A. et al (1993) Association between cheilitis granulomatosa and Crohn's disease. *J Am Acad Dermatol*, **28**, 801.
19. Borradori, L., Saada, V., Rybojad, M. et al (1992) Oral intraepidermal IgA pustulosis and Crohn's disease. *Br J Dermatol*, **126**, 383–386.
20. Kay, M.H., Wyllie, R. (1998) Cutaneous vasculitis as the initial manifestation of Crohn's disease in a pediatric patient. *Am J Gastroenterol*, **93**, 1014.
21. Walker, K.D., Badame, A.J. (1990) Erythema elevatum diutinum in a patient with Crohn's disease. *J Am Acad Dermatol*, **22**, 948–952.
22. Chalvardjian, A., Nethercott, J.R. (1982) Cutaneous granulomatous vasculitis associated with Crohn's disease. *Cutis*, **30**, 645–655.
23. Travis, S., Innes, N., Davies, M.G. et al (1997) Sweet's syndrome: an unusual cutaneous feature of Crohn's disease or ulcerative colitis. The South West Gastroenterology Group. *Eur J Gastroenterol Hepatol*, **9**, 715–720.
24. Schattenkirchner, S., Lemann, M., Prost, C. et al (1996) Localized epidermolysis bullosa acquisita of the esophagus in a patient with Crohn's disease. *Am J Gastroenterol*, **91**, 1657–1659.
25. Ray, T.L., Levine, J.B., Weiss, W. et al (1982) Epidermolysis bullosa acquisita and inflammatory bowel disease. *J Am Acad Dermatol*, **6**, 242–252.
26. Goslen, J.B., Graham, W., Lazarus, G.S. (1983) Cutaneous polyarteritis nodosa. Report of a case associated with Crohn's disease. *Arch Dermatol*, **119**, 326–329.
27. Nevile, B.W., Laden, S.A., Smith, S.E. et al (1985) Pyostomatitis vegetans. *Am J Dermatopathol*, **7**, 69–77.
28. Van Hale, H.M., Rogers, R.S. III, Zone, J.J. et al (1985) Pyostomatitis vegetans. A reactive mucosal marker for inflammatory disease of the gut. *Arch Dermatol*, **121**, 94–98.
29. McPoland, P.R., Moos, R.L. (1988) Cutaneous Crohn's disease and progressive vitiligo. *J Am Acad Dermatol*, **19**, 421–425.
30. Yates, V.M., Watkinson, G., Kelman, A. (1982) Further evidence for an association between psoriasis, Crohn's disease and ulcerative colitis. *Br J Dermatol*, **106**, 323–330.
31. Brenner, S.M., Delany, H.M. (1972) Erythema multiforme and Crohn's disease of the large intestine. *Gastroenterology*, **62**, 479–482.
32. Ostlere, L.S., Langtry, J.A., Mortimer, P.S. et al (1991) Hidradenitis suppurativa in Crohn's disease. *Br J Dermatol*, **125**, 384–386.
33. Scheinfeld, N.S., Teplitz, E., McClain, S.A. (2001) Crohn's disease and lichen nitidus: a case report and comparison of common histopathologic features. *Inflamm Bowel Dis*, **7**, 314–318.
34. McAuley, D., Miller, R.A. (1985) Acne fulminans associated with inflammatory bowel disease. Report of a case. *Arch Dermatol*, **121**, 91–93.
35. Matheson, B.K., Gilbertson, E.O., Eichenfield, L.F. (1996) Vesiculopustular eruption of Crohn's disease. *Pediatr Dermatol*, **13**, 127–130.
36. Prezyna, A.P., Kalyanaraman, B. (1977) Bowen's carcinoma in vulvo-vaginal Crohn's disease (regional enterocolitis): report of first case. *Am J Obstet Gynecol*, **128**, 914–915.
37. Acker, S.M., Sahn, E.E., Rogers, H.C. et al (1995) Genital cutaneous Crohn's disease: two cases with unusual clinical and histopathologic features in young men. *Am J Dermatopathol*, **22**, 443–446.

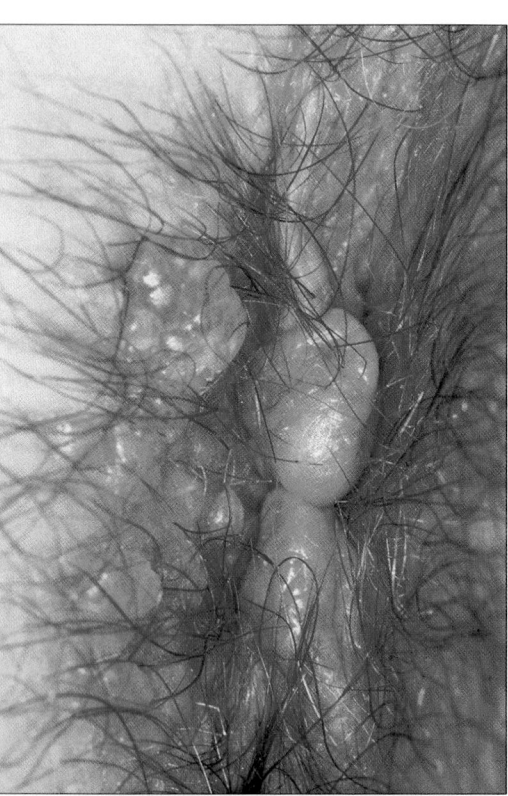

Fig. 11.50
Perianal Crohn's disease: multiple skin tags showing massive edema are present. By courtesy of the Institute of Dermatology, London, UK.

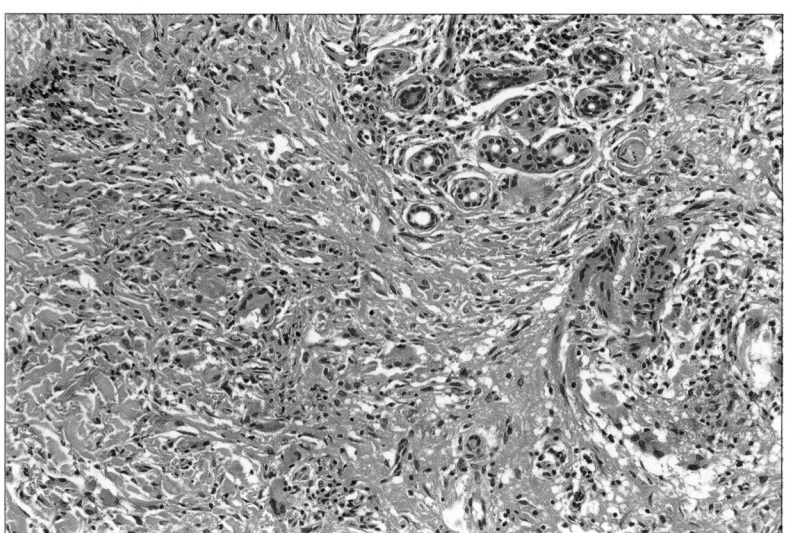

Fig. 11.51
Vulval Crohn's disease: there is an ill-defined granulomatous infiltrate with conspicuous giant cells in the deep reticular dermis.

Behçet's disease

Behçet's disease is discussed on page 685.

Necrolytic migratory erythema

Necrolytic migratory erythema is discussed on page 619.

Infectious diseases

Erythrasma

Clinical features

Erythrasma is a superficial infection of the skin at flexural sites and is common in the inguinal and genitocrural folds (*Fig. 11.52*).[1] The skin between the toes and natal cleft may also be affected. The organism involved is an aerobic, Gram-positive corynebacterium, *C. minutissimum*.[2] The organism normally lives in the skin but causes disease as a result of a warm and humid environment. Obesity, heat, friction and immunosuppression are all contributory factors. Patients with diabetes mellitus are particularly prone to the disease.[3]

The affected areas are covered in red–brown scaly plaques with well-demarcated edges. The rash is usually asymptomatic or mildly itchy. The affected areas fluoresce coral pink under Wood's light. This feature is due to the presence of porphyrin and may be absent in some cases.[4] Very rare cases present with generalized involvement.[5] The disease may appear concomitantly with a dermatophytosis and this often makes the diagnosis difficult.[6]

Histological features

The characteristic clinical picture and the presence of fluorescence under Wood's light obviate the need for biopsies in most cases. A biopsy shows the presence of rods and filamentous organisms in the stratum corneum (*Figs 11.53, 11.54*). Inflammation is minimal.

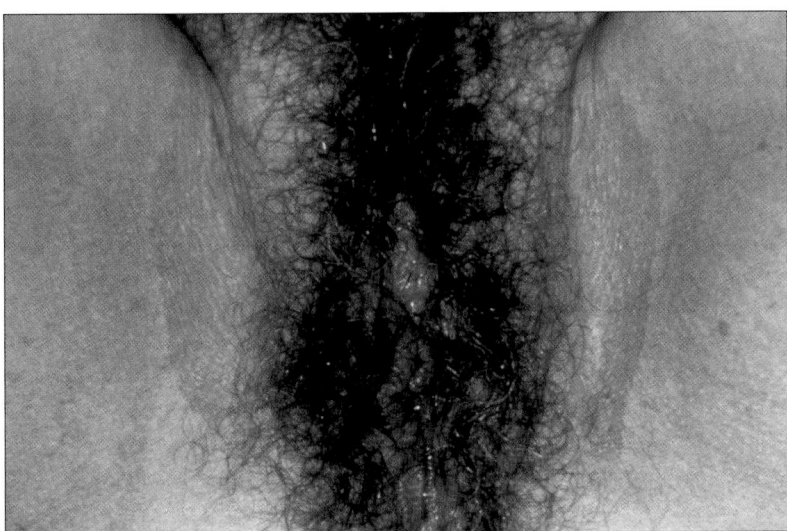

Fig. 11.52
Erythrasma: the flexural distribution and sharply demarcated border are characteristic features. By courtesy of the Institute of Dermatology, London, UK.

References

1. Sarkany, I., Taplin, D., Blank, H. (1961) Erythrasma. *JAMA*, 177, 130–133.
2. Montes, L.F., Black, S.H., McBride, M.E. (1967) Bacterial invasion of the stratum corneum in erythrasma. I. Ultrastructural evidence for a keratolytic action exerted by *Corynebacterium minutissimum*. *J Invest Dermatol*, 49, 474–485.
3. Montes, L.F., Dobson, H., Dodge, B.G. et al (1969) Erythrasma and diabetes mellitus. *Arch Dermatol*, 99, 674–680.
4. Mattox, T.F., Rutgers, J., Yoshimiri, R.N. et al (1993) Nonfluorescent erythrasma of the vulva. *Obstet Gynecol*, 81, 862–864.
5. Engber, P.B., Mandel, E.H. (1979) Generalized disciform erythrasma. *Int J Dermatol*, 18, 633–635.
6. Schlappner, O.L., Rosenblum, G.A., Rowden, G. et al (1979) Concomitant erythrasma and dermatophytosis of the groin. *Br J Dermatol*, 100, 147–151.

Condyloma acuminatum

Clinical features

Condylomata acuminata are particularly caused by HPV types 6, 11, 16, 18, 30–32, 42–44 and 51–55.[1–5] HPV-6 and -11 account for approximately 90% of these lesions.[2] More than one type of HPV can be isolated from a single lesion.[6] They occur on the glans penis and prepuce or shaft as soft, fleshy (sometimes filiform) plaques and may extend into the meatus (*Figs 11.55, 11.56*). On the shaft they are less exophytic. Vulval lesions may be bulky and macerated, and may extend into the introitus (*Figs 11.57–11.59*). Often lesions are difficult to detect on clinical examination.[1,7,8] Vulval condylomata usually involve the labia minora, interlabial sulcus or the area around the introitus. Similar fleshy and filiform soft masses may occur perianally, more often in males (*Fig. 11.60*). Anal and cervical squamous carcinomas have also been shown to contain HPV-6, -16 and -18 in a significant proportion of cases.[4] The lesions are uncommon in children (when they may be a sign of sexual abuse) and are seen most often in young adults (second and third decades), frequently in association with other genital infections.[2,5,9] Lesions in children can also occur by close non-sexual contact.[10] Rarely condyloma acuminatum presents in the oral cavity.[11]

It is important to recognize that a significant proportion of genital HPV infections are asymptomatic.[1,12] The female partners of male patients with condyloma acuminata have been shown to have an increased risk of cervical HPV infection and intraepithelial neoplasia.[13]

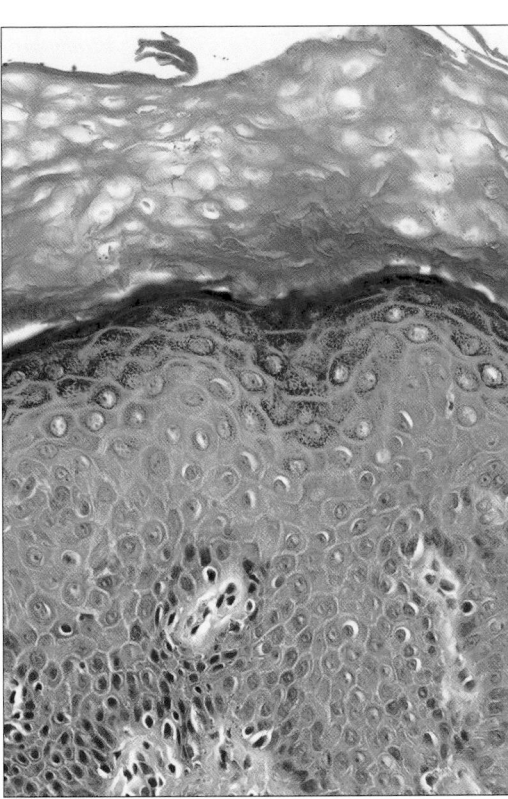

Fig. 11.53
Erythrasma: bacilli are just visible in the upper stratum corneum.

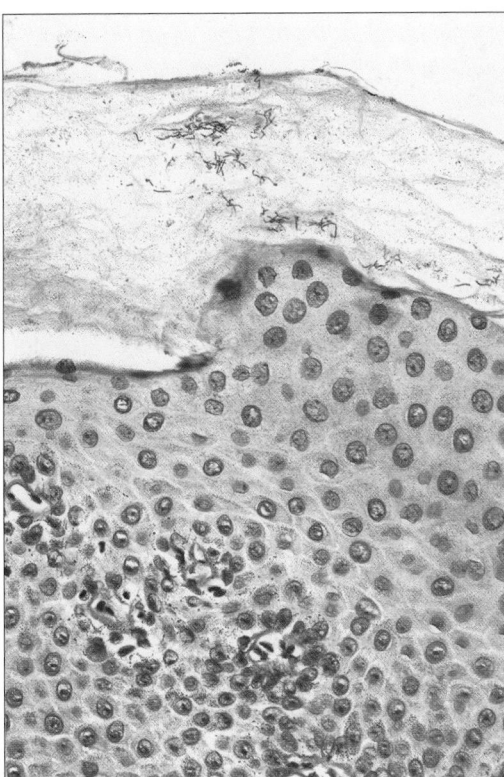

Fig. 11.54
Erythrasma: PAS stain showing elongated bacilli.

Cervical neoplasia associated with pre-existent condylomata acuminata has also been related to immunosuppression, at least in some patients.[14] Up to 80% of invasive cervical squamous carcinomas have been shown to contain HPV DNA.[4] HPV types 16, 18, 31–33, 35, 39, 42, 51–54 are most commonly associated with cancers of the cervix, vulva and penis.[4,5,15] Malignant transformation of condyloma acuminatum is rare.[3,16–18] Condyloma acuminata may occur concomitantly with bowenoid papulosis.[19]

A large, exuberant and locally destructive variant of condyloma (Buschke–Löwenstein tumor) may rarely be encountered.[20,21] This is associated with HPV-6, -11 or -16. It is now considered to be a variant of verrucous carcinoma, a subtype of well-differentiated squamous carcinoma (see below). Juvenile laryngeal papillomata containing HPV-6

and -11 can be seen in children born to mothers with condylomata acuminata.[1] They may show malignant progression if irradiated.

Histological features

Condylomata acuminata are characterized by marked acanthosis with a solid or trabecular pattern and a broad, rounded, exophytic growth (*Figs 11.61, 11.62*). There is a sharp, fairly regular, deep margin. The surface of the lesion is hyperkeratotic and parakeratotic. Superficial

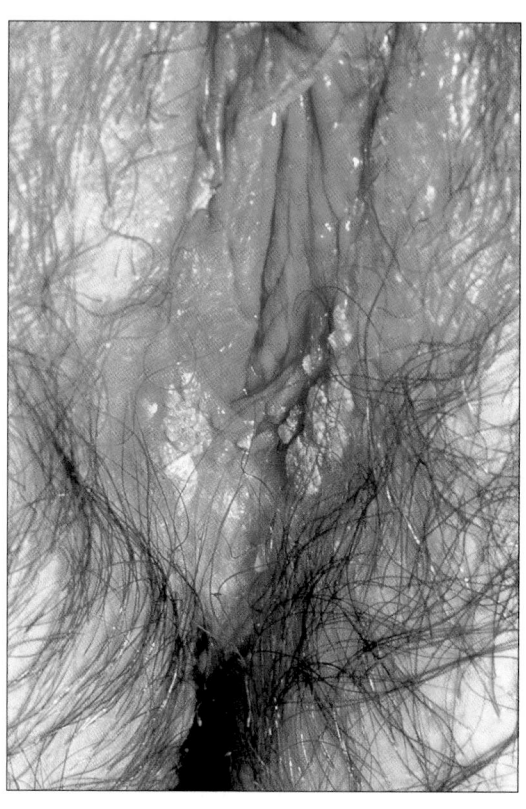

Fig. 11.57
Condyloma acuminatum: multiple gray lesions are evident on the labia minora and around the vestibule. By courtesy of the Institute of Dermatology, London, UK.

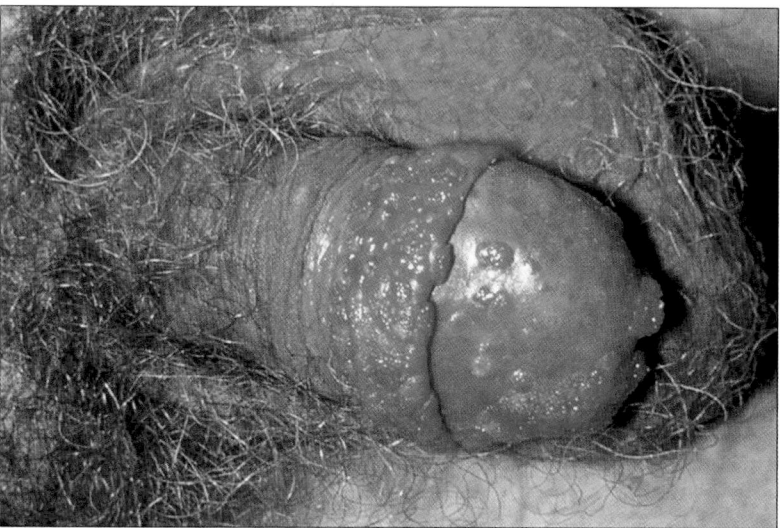

Fig. 11.55
Condyloma acuminatum: multiple erythematous, velvety plaques are present on the glans penis. By courtesy of the Institute of Dermatology, London, UK.

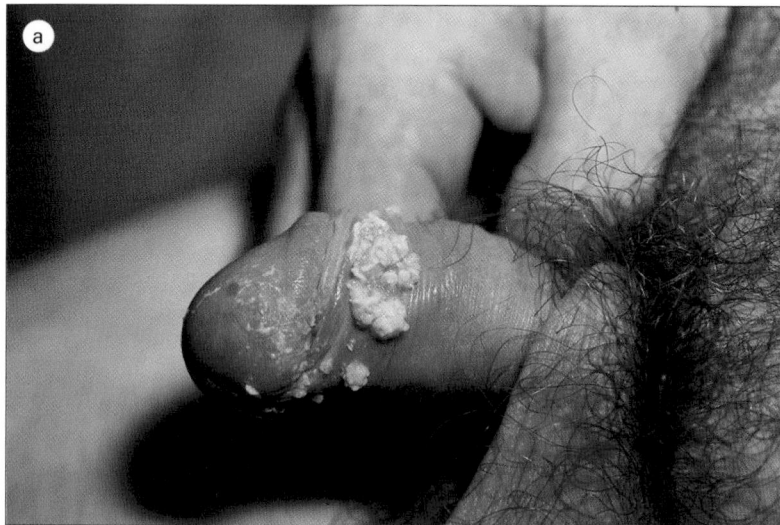

Fig. 11.56
Condyloma acuminatum: (a) in this patient the lesions have a typical filiform appearance; (b) multiple condylomata are present on penis and scrotum. By courtesy of the Department of Genitourinary Medicine, St Thomas' Hospital, London, UK.

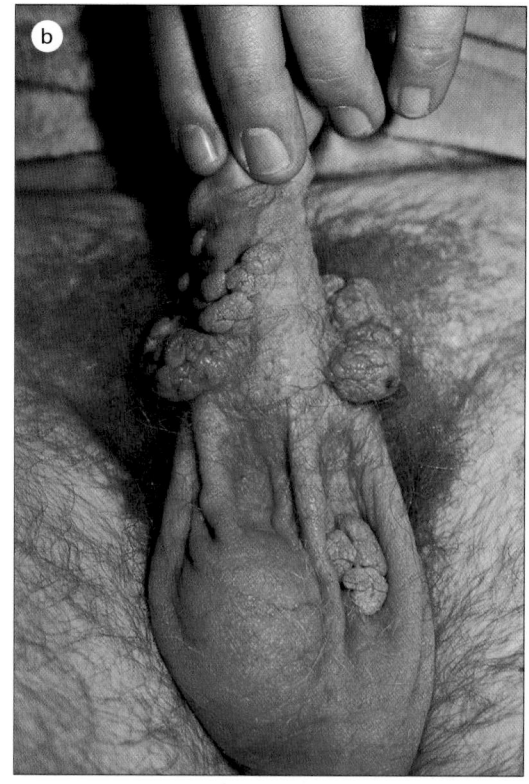

vacuolated keratinocytes (koilocytes) are characteristic (*Fig. 11.63*). The vacuolated epithelium is often most marked in the declivities. Care must be taken not to confuse koilocytes with the vacuolated, glycogenated keratinocytes of mucosal epithelia. Distinction can be made fairly readily as koilocytes have an enlarged, wrinkled, hyperchromatic nucleus.

Care should be taken in the histological interpretation of lesions that have previously been treated with podophyllin.[22,23] These can display prominent degenerative changes with cytoplasmic vacuolation, nuclear enlargement and metaphase arrest. The changes however tend to be more

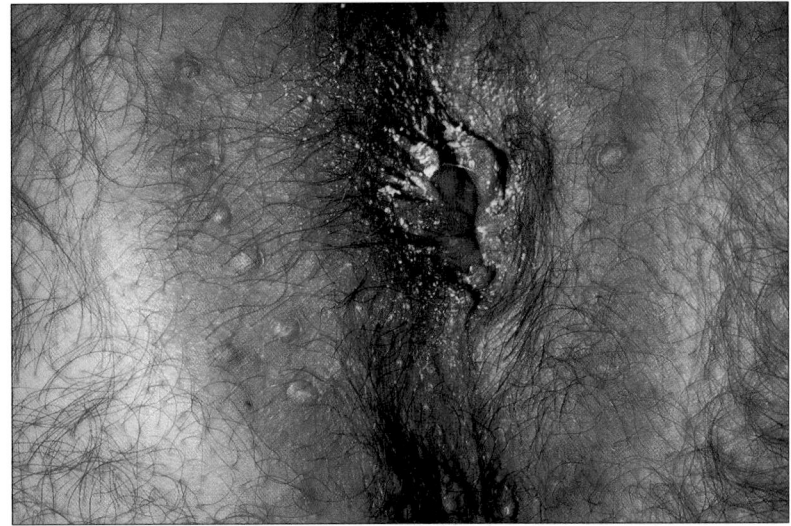

Fig. 11.60
Condyloma accuminatum: perianal involvement is likely to be associated with homosexual activity. By courtesy of R.A. Marsden, MD, St George's Hospital, London, UK.

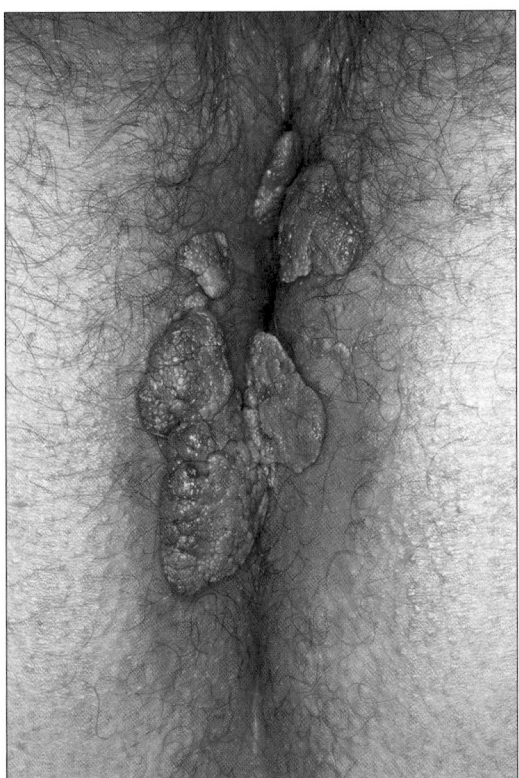

Fig. 11.58
Condyloma accuminatum: in this patient the condylomata are pedunculated and have extended onto the thighs. By courtesy of the Institute of Dermatology, London, UK.

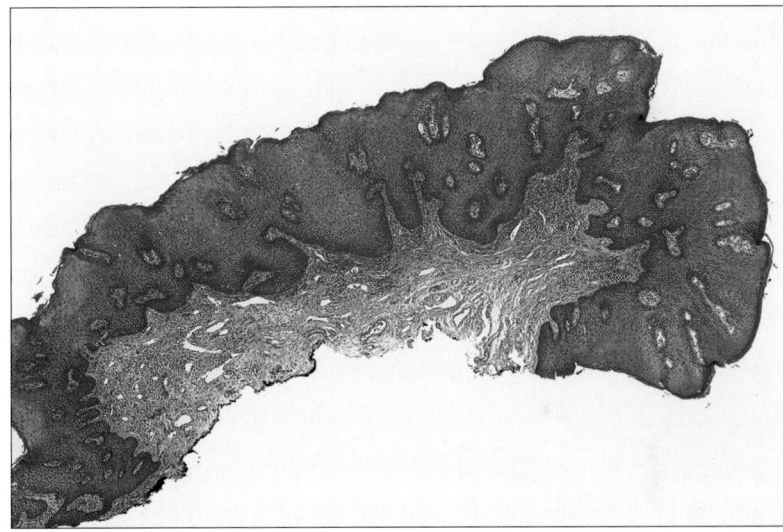

Fig. 11.61
Condyloma accuminatum: there is focal parakeratosis, slight papillomatosis and very marked acanthosis. The lower border is sharply demarcated.

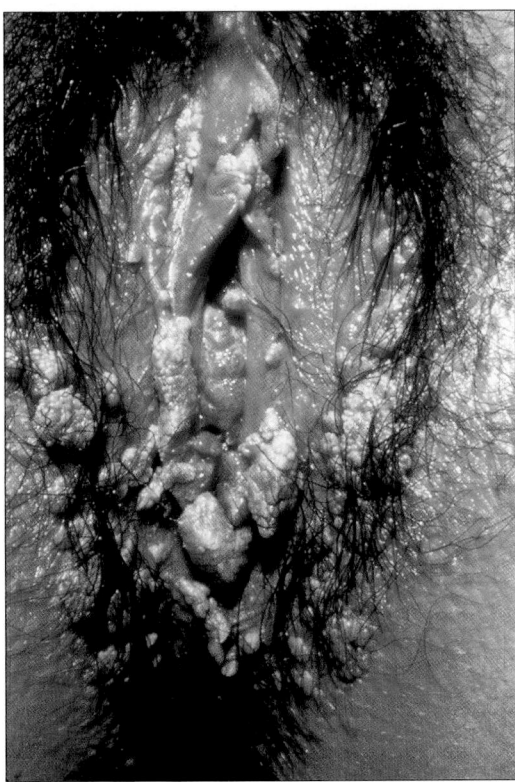

Fig. 11.59
Condyloma accuminatum: there is very extensive disease. The patient is at considerable risk of developing cervical disease. By courtesy of R.A. Marsden, MD, St George's Hospital, London, UK.

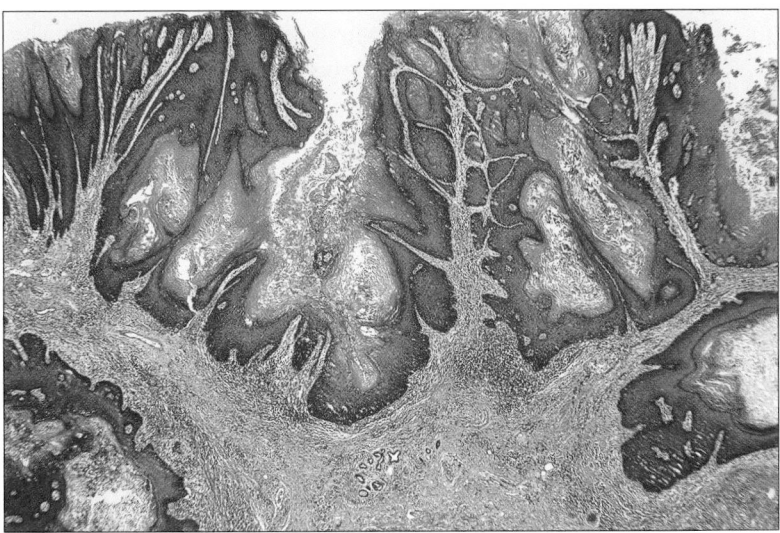

Fig. 11.62
Condyloma accuminatum: this is a much more florid example. Note the gross papillomatosis and very marked acanthosis.

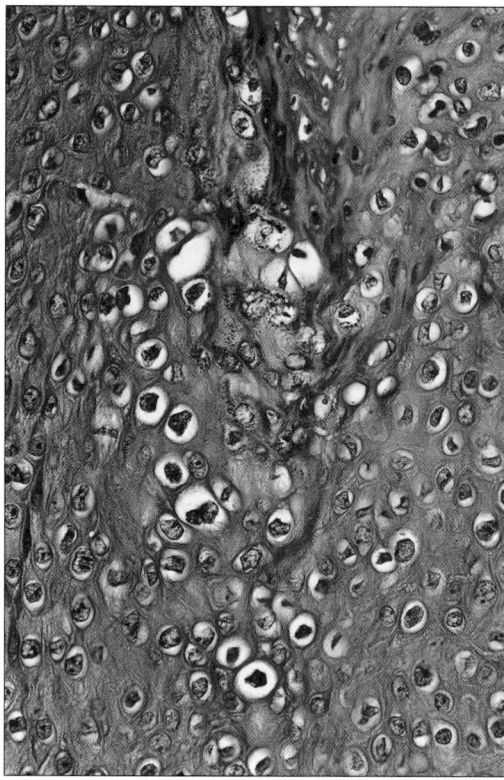

Fig. 11.63
Condyloma acuminatum: there are conspicuous koilocytes with irregular nuclei and vacuolated cytoplasm.

22.   Pope, C., Ingella, H.P., Strecker, H. (1973) Light and electron microscopic observations following repeated podophyllin benzoin therapy of condyloma acuminata. *Arch Ginec*, **215**, 417–425.
23.   Wade, T.R., Ackerman, A.B. (1984) The effects of resin of podophyllin on condyloma acuminata. *Am J Dermatopathol*, **6**, 109–122.
24.   Kimura, S., Masuda, M. (1985) A comparative immunoperoxidase and histopathologic study of condylomata acuminata. *J Cutan Pathol*, **12**, 142–146.
25.   Grasseger, A., Hopfl, R., Hussl, H. et al (1994) Buschke–Loewenstein tumour infiltrating pelvic organs. *Br J Dermatol*, **130**, 221–225.

Syphilis

Clinical features

Following its diminishing incidence after the introduction of penicillin in the 1940s, syphilis is now increasing in frequency, largely due to the increased number of cases among drug abusers and people with high-risk sexual behavior or who tend to bisexuality.[1–3] 'Prostitution for drugs' is particularly important.[2]

In the 16th century syphilis carried a high mortality associated with a chronic disfiguring and disabling disease. In recent times the disease appears less aggressive, even in untreated cases. It is highly infectious, with the risk of transmission from an infected partner ranging from 30 to 51%.[4,5] The chance of acquiring the disease depends upon the number of exposures, type of sexual practice and the location and number of the partner's lesions.[2] There is a close relationship between syphilis and human immunodeficiency virus (HIV) infection and both diseases can be acquired together.[6–8] It is clear that diseases such as syphilis that induce genital ulceration increase the risk of acquiring HIV infection.[8]

The causative organism is *Treponema pallidum*, a spirochete with fastidious growth requirements. Transmission is primarily sexual. An endemic form known as bejel, caused by an identical organism, occurs in children living in conditions of poor hygiene and is transmitted by cutaneous inoculation.[9] Other endemic forms have been associated with shared drinking vessels when some members of the community have oral or labial syphilitic lesions.

The typical initial lesion (or chancre) is seen more often on the glans penis (especially the coronal sulcus), the shaft or prepuce, or on the labia, and usually develops 20–30 days after direct exposure to an infectious lesion (*Figs 11.64–11.68*).[4] At least 5% of primary chancres arise at extragenital locations, most commonly oral or anal sites, but virtually every other part of the skin surface may be affected including the tonsils, fingers, eyelids and nipples (*Figs 11.69, 11.70*).[2,4,10,11] Lesions in the vagina or cervix may go undetected. The chancre appears as an indurated, punched-out, painless ulcer. It is usually accompanied by painless lymphadenopathy. This resolves without scarring after 1–5 weeks.

The secondary cutaneous lesions (syphilids), which are highly infectious, may mimic virtually any skin disorder and present 6–8 weeks after the appearance of the chancre.[12] They develop insidiously (in up to 80% of patients), with a roseolar, macular–erythematous rash, on the head, face and neck followed by a polymorphic papular eruption.[4] The macules measure 5–10 mm in diameter, are not pruritic and particularly occur on the trunk, abdomen and limbs, especially the palms and soles (*Figs 11.71–11.76*).[12] The papular lesions are characteristically coppery red in color and 3–10 mm in diameter. Hypopigmentation of the neck is known as the 'collar of venus'.[12]

Other manifestations described include condylomata (in intertriginous areas), annular, lichenoid, papulosquamous lesions (psoriasiform), arcuate lesions, corymbose brownish-red papules (clustered, Gr. *korymbos*, clusters of ivy flower), bullous, follicular and pustular variants on the skin, with erosive ulcers (mucous patches), often of 'snail track' type, and the (highly infectious) condylomata lata affecting the mucosae (*Figs 11.77–11.80*).[13–18] Large hypertrophic condylomata are known as frambesiform syphilids.[11] Other variants described are acneiform, varioliform and rarely necrotic (*Fig. 11.81*). Lesions tend to be widely disseminated and often symmetrical in distribution.[4] Papular involve-

focal and abnormal mitotic figures are not seen. Immunohistochemical stains for papilloma virus common antigen can be used to confirm the diagnosis but this is only positive in about 60% of cases.[24]

Giant condyloma acuminatum (anogenital verrucous carcinoma, Buschke–Löwenstein tumor), occurs most frequently on the genitalia, and is larger and more cauliflower-like.[19,20,25] It shows some tendency to endophytic growth, but without any suggestion of frank infiltration. It can recur locally, but metastasizes very rarely (see below). Anal condylomata may develop bowenoid features and occasionally invasive tumors supervene.[3,4]

References

1.   Shah, K.V. (1992) Biology of genital tract human papillomaviruses. *Urol Clin N Am*, **19**, 63–69.
2.   Clark, D. (1987) Condyloma acuminatum. *Dermatol Clin*, **5**, 779–788.
3.   Gal, A.A., Meyer, P.R., Taylor, C.R. (1987) Papillomavirus antigens in anorectal condyloma and carcinoma in homosexual men. *JAMA*, **257**, 337–340.
4.   Beckman, A.M., Daling, J.R., Sherman, K.J. et al (1989) Human papilloma virus infection and anal cancer. *Int J Cancer*, **431**, 1042–1049.
5.   Cobb, M.W. (1990) Human papilloma virus infection. *J Am Acad Dermatol*, **22**, 547–566.
6.   Herman-Giddens, M.E., Gutman, L.T., Berson, N.L. (1988) Association of coexisting vaginal infections and multiple abusers in female children with genital warts. *Sex Transm Dis*, **15**, 63–67.
7.   Comite, S.L., Castador, M-J. (1988) Colposcopic evaluation of men with genital warts. *J Am Acad Dermatol*, **18**, 1274–1278.
8.   Oriel, J.D. (1989) Genital papillomavirus infection. *Semin Dermatol*, **8**, 48–53.
9.   Lagenberg, A., Cone, R.W., McDougall, J. et al (1993) Dual infection with human papillomavirus in a population with overt genital condylomas. *J Am Acad Dermatol*, **28**, 434–442.
10.   Stumpf, P.G. (1980) Increasing occurrence of condylomata acuminata in premenarchal children. *Obstet Gynecol*, **56**, 262–264.
11.   Flaitz, C.M. (2001) Condyloma acuminatum of the floor of the mouth. *Am J Dent*, **303**, 718–719.
12.   Siegel, J.F., Mellinger, B.C. (1992) Human papillomavirus in the male patient. *Urol Clin N Am*, **19**, 83–91.
13.   Campion, M.J., Singer, A., Clarkson, P.K. et al (1985) Increased risk of cervical neoplasia in consorts of men with penile condylomata acuminata. *Lancet*, **1**, 943–946.
14.   Krebs, H.B., Schneider, V., Hurt, W.G. et al (1986) Genital condylomas in immunosuppressed women: a therapeutic challenge. *South Med J*, **79**, 183–187.
15.   McCance, D.J., Kalache, A., Ashdown, K. et al (1986) Human papilloma viruses types 16 and 18 in carcinoma of the penis from Brazil. *Int J Cancer*, **37**, 55–59.
16.   Gillatt, D.A., Teasdale, C. (1985) Squamous cell carcinoma of the anus arising within condyloma acuminatum. *Eur J Surg Oncol*, **11**, 369–371.
17.   Woodcock, K. (1991) Condyloma acuminata and the risk of cancer. *BMJ*, **303**, 718–719.
18.   Byars, R.W., Poole, G.V., Barber, W.H. (2001) Anal carcinoma arising from condyloma acuminata. *Am Surg*, **67**, 469–472.
19.   Steffen, C. (1982) Concurrence of condyloma acuminata and bowenoid papulosis. *Am J Dermatopathol*, **4**, 5–8.
20.   Bogomoletz, W.V., Potet, F., Molas, G. (1985) Condylomata acuminata, giant condyloma acuminatum (Buschke–Loewenstein tumour) and verrucous squamous carcinoma of the perianal and anorectal region: a continuous precancerous spectrum? *Histopathology*, **9**, 1155–1169.
21.   Wells, M., Robertson, S., Lewis, F. et al (1988) Squamous carcinoma arising in a giant peri-anal condyloma associated with human papillomavirus types 6 and 11. *Histopathology*, **12**, 319–329.

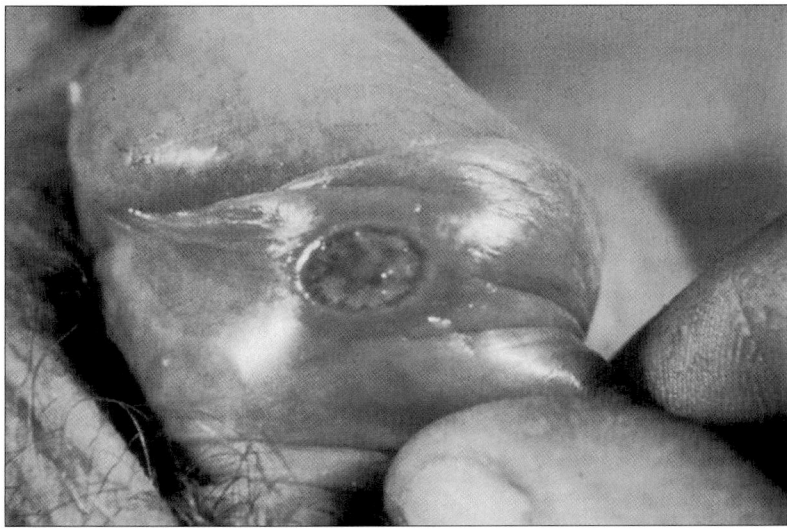

Fig. 11.64
Primary chancre: the chancre is a painless ulcer with an indurated edge. The base is yellow and harbors large numbers of spirochetes. By courtesy of F. Lim, MD, King's College Hospital, London, UK.

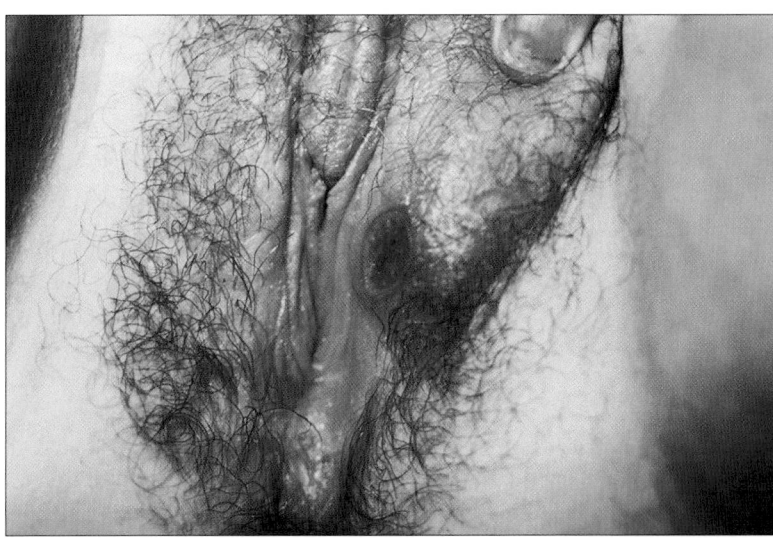

Fig. 11.67
Primary syphilis: a typical chancre is present on the left labium majus. By courtesy of R.N. Thin, MD, St Thomas' Hospital, London, UK.

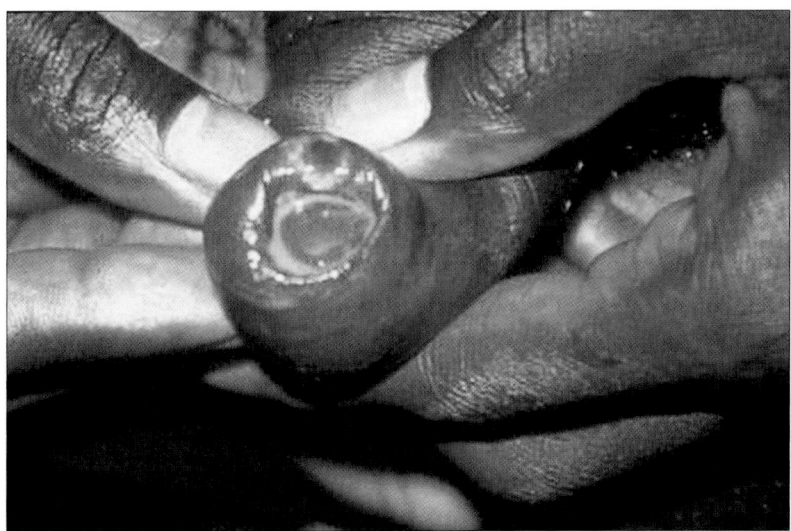

Fig. 11.65
Primary syphilis: painless lymphadenopathy is often present. By courtesy of C. Furlonge, MD, Port of Spain, Trinidad.

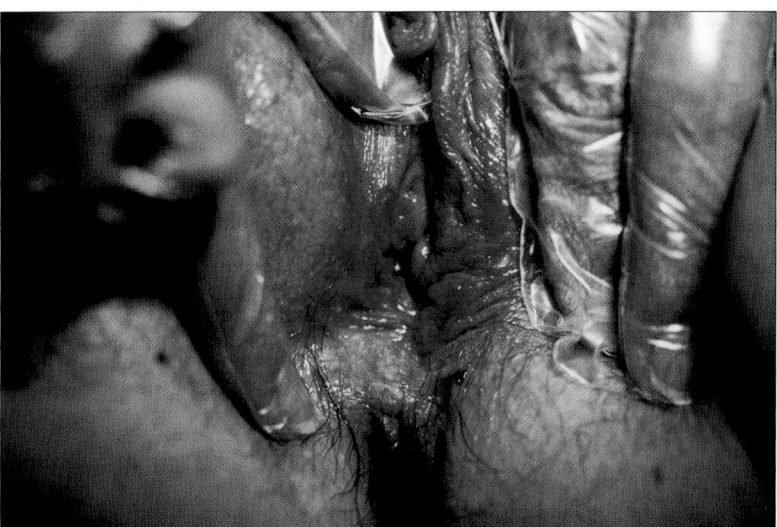

Fig. 11.68
Primary syphilis: typical 'kissing ulcers' are present within the vestibule. By courtesy of D. Barlowe, MD, St Thomas' Hospital, London, UK.

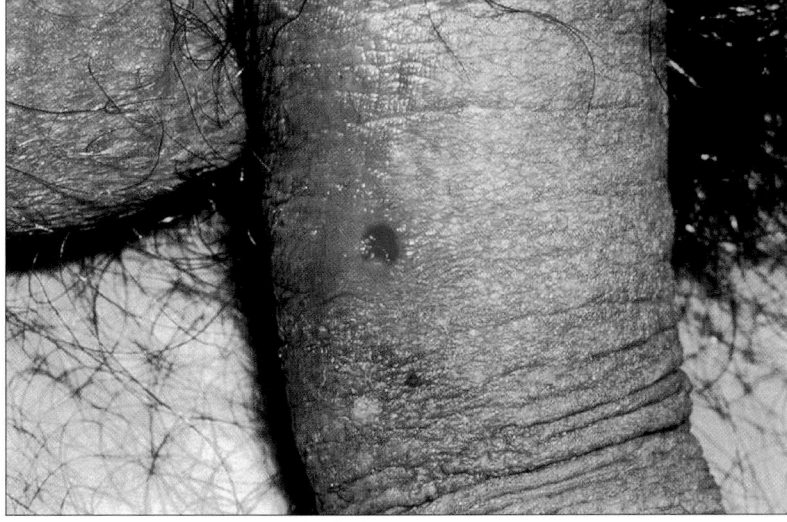

Fig. 11.66
Primary syphilis: in this patient the chancre has a punched-out appearance. By courtesy of the Institute of Dermatology, London, UK.

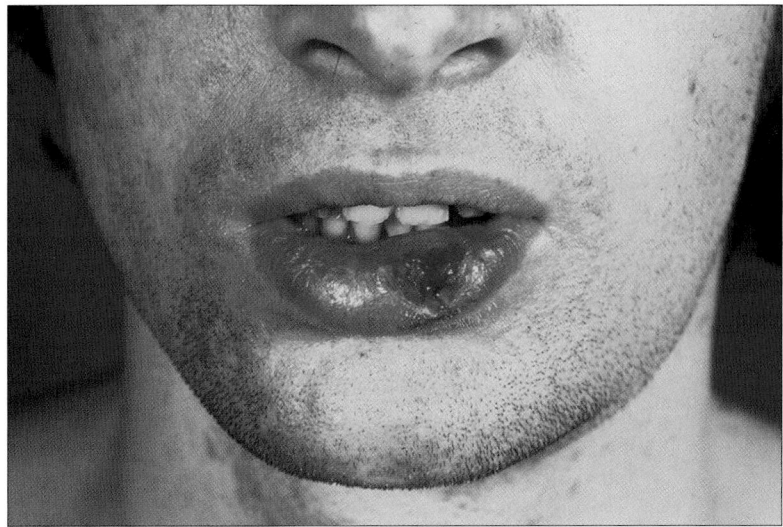

Fig. 11.69
Primary syphilis: oral chancres are most often located on the lip. By courtesy of R.N. Thin, MD, St Thomas' Hospital, London, UK.

ment of the scalp may result in non-scarring, patchy alopecia (*Fig. 11.82*).[19] The alopecia induced by secondary syphilis is known as alopecia syphilitica and has a characteristic, moth-eaten appearance.[20,21] The beard, eyebrows and eyelashes may also be affected.[4] Telogen effluvium has also been described.[12]

Rare 'malignant' forms of syphilis present with rapid progression, much ulceration and rupial lesions (Gr. *rhypos*, filth; necrotic lesions covered by dirty, lamellated encrustation resembling oyster shells).[12,22,23] This form of syphilis has been described in association with HIV infection and is characterized by necrotic and ulcerative lesions.[24,25]

Secondary syphilis manifestations have typically been described as non-pruritic, but recent reports suggest that this is not always the case.[2,4,26] Indeed in the series of 105 patients with secondary syphilis

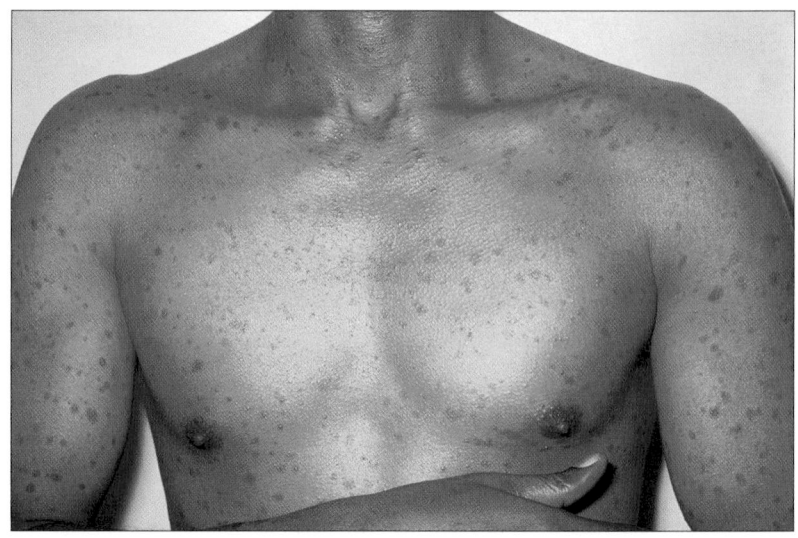

Fig. 11.72
Secondary syphilis: this patient shows a widespread hyperpigmented maculopapular eruption. By courtesy of C. Furlonge, MD, Port of Spain, Trinidad.

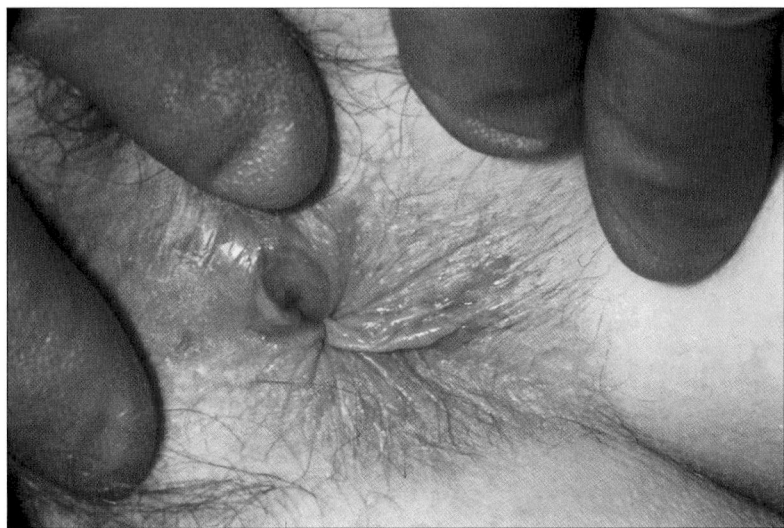

Fig. 11.70
Primary syphilis: a chancre is present at the edge of the anal ostium. By courtesy of R.N. Thin, MD, St Thomas' Hospital, London, UK.

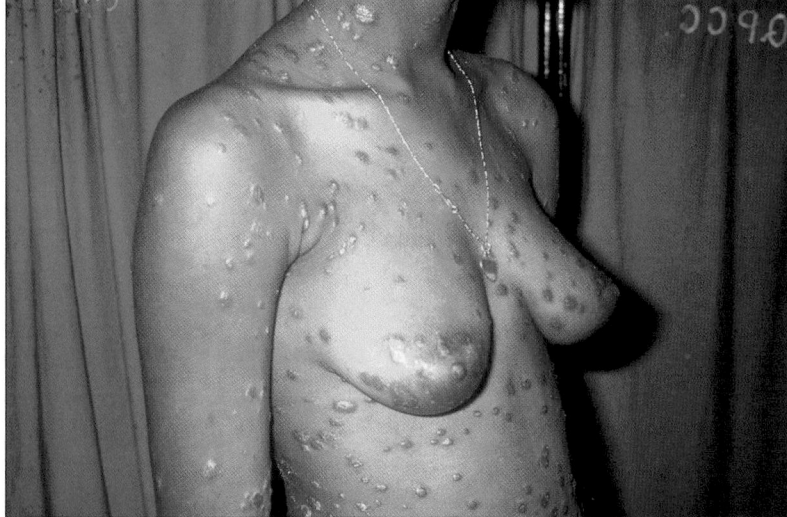

Fig. 11.73
Secondary syphilis: note the widespread papules and nodules many of which have a hypertrophic appearance. By courtesy of C. Furlonge, MD, Port of Spain, Trinidad.

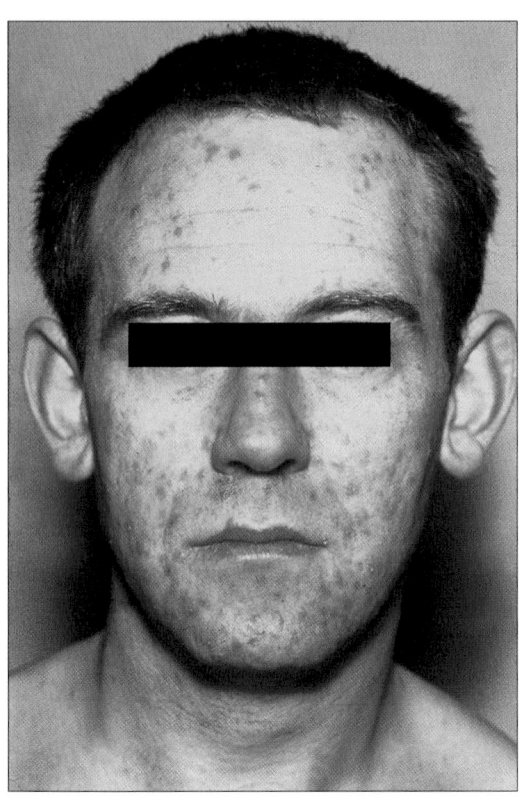

Fig. 11.71
Secondary syphilis: the face is commonly affected. Note the numerous papules. By courtesy of R.N. Thin, MD, St Thomas' Hospital, London, UK.

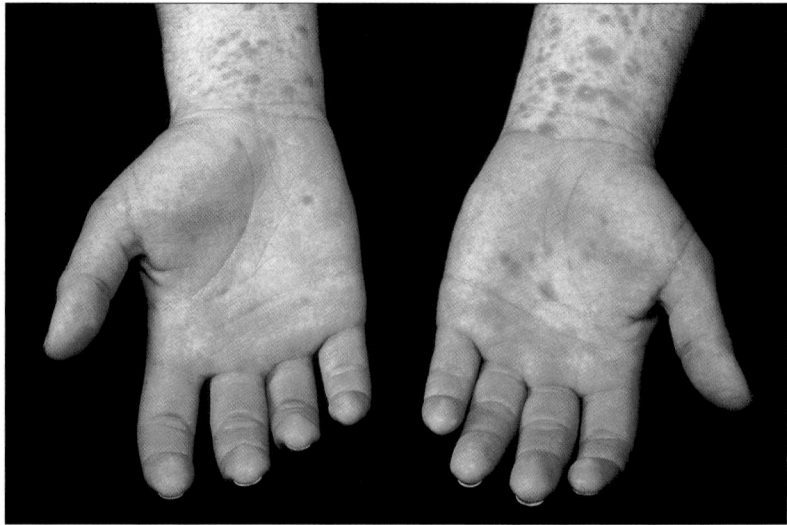

Fig. 11.74
Secondary syphilis: the palms are almost invariably affected. By courtesy of the Institute of Dermatology, London, UK.

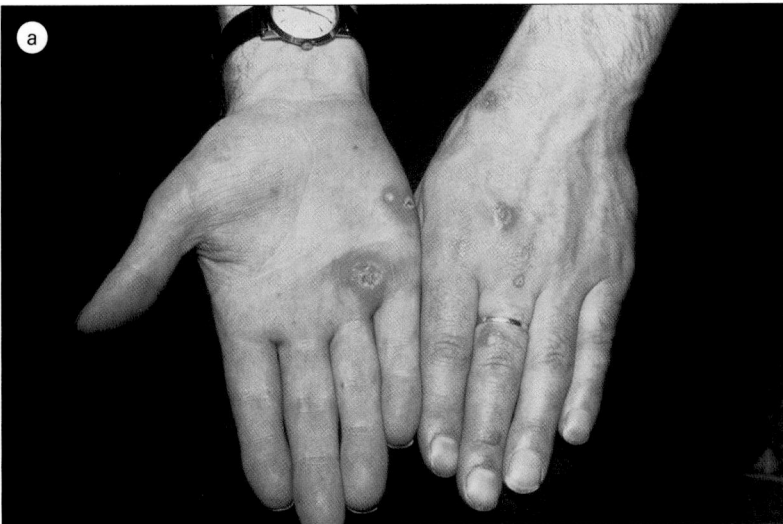

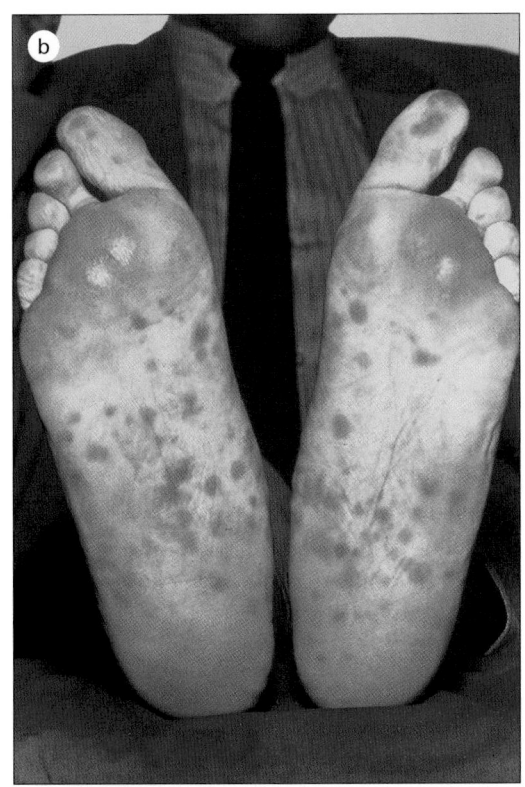

Fig. 11.75
(a, b) Secondary syphilis: erythematous and scaly papules involving the palms and soles are present in this patient with secondary syphilis. (a) By courtesy of R.A. Marsden, MD, St George's Hospital, London, UK; (b) by courtesy of R.N. Thin, MD, St Thomas' Hospital, London, UK.

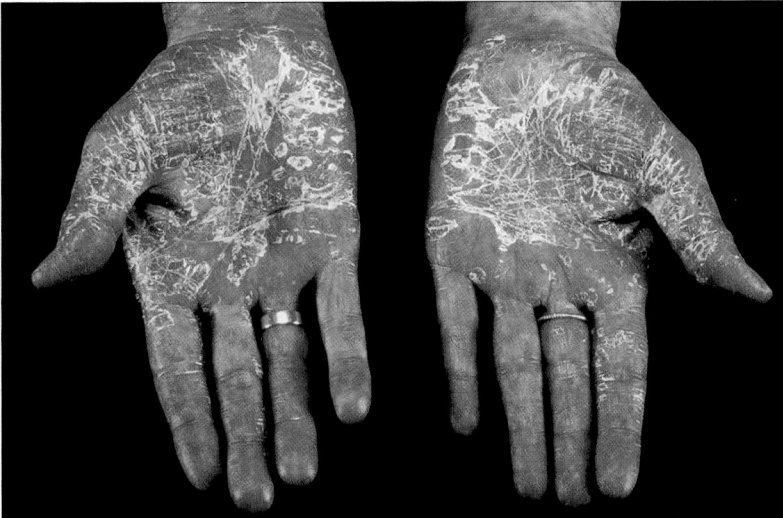

Fig. 11.76
Secondary syphilis: in this patient typical copper penny macules with surrounding annular scale (Biette's collarette) contrast with confluent exfoliation on the palms. By courtesy of the Institute of Dermatology, London, UK.

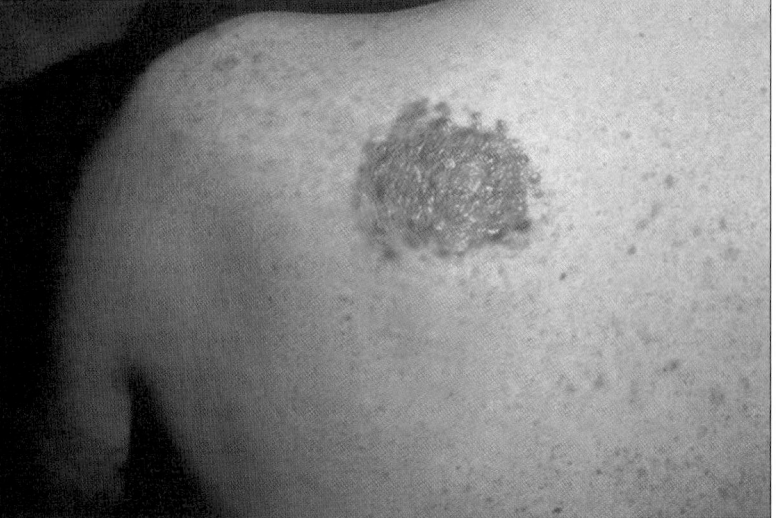

Fig. 11.77
Secondary syphilis: this is a typical corymbose eruption. Note the circumscribed, confluent, erythematous scaly papules. By courtesy of the Institute of Dermatology, London, UK.

published by Chapel, 42% complained of pruritus.[27] Resolution may be accompanied by hypo- or hyperpigmentation.[4] Lymphadenopathy, which may be widespread and is painless and rubbery, occurs in 50–85% of patients.[4] The cutaneous manifestations are often accompanied by pyrexia, headache, weight loss and non-specific muscle and joint aches.[12] Untreated lesions of syphilis resolve in 2–10 weeks.[12] When syphilis is treated with antibiotics, there may be a self-limited febrile reaction known as the Jarisch–Herxheimer reaction associated with systemic symptoms.[28]

Atypical clinical forms of syphilis have been reported in HIV-positive patients.[29,30]

Secondary syphilis is followed by a latent phase, which may precede a change to:

- seronegativity and cure
- persistent seropositivity without further lesions
- development of tertiary lesions.

These late lesions involve mainly the cardiovascular (aortic incompetence) and central nervous system (tabes dorsalis and general paresis of the insane), but cutaneous lesions are seen as noduloulcerative lesions and gummata that tend to break down with central necrosis and suppuration. Gummata may occur up to 15 years after the initial infection. They are painless, frequently ulcerated, firm subcutaneous nodules that show a predilection for the scalp, face, chest and legs (*Fig. 11.83*).[27,31] Noduloulcerative late syphilitic lesions present as superficial nodules that extend peripherally and heal centrally to form ulcerated serpiginous plaques.[32,33]

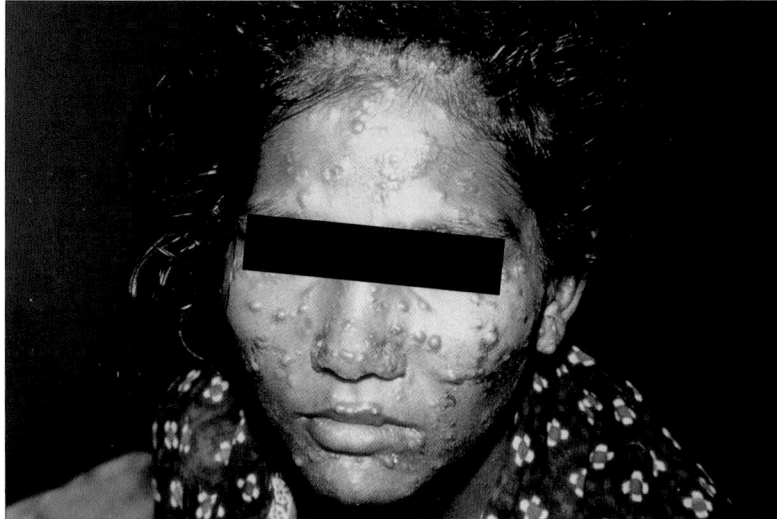

Fig. 11.78
Secondary syphilis: pustular lesions, as seen on this patient's face, are a rare manifestation. By courtesy of R.N. Thin, MD, St Thomas' Hospital, London, UK.

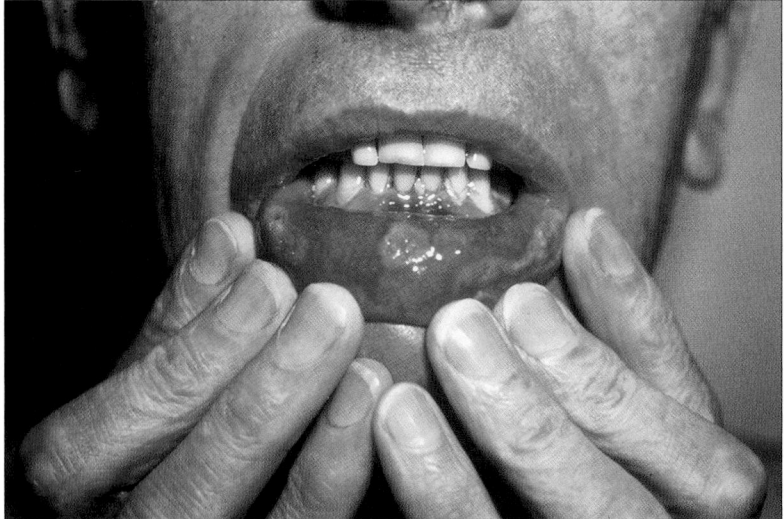

Fig. 11.79
Secondary syphilis: note the symmetrically distributed 'snail track' ulcers. By courtesy of R.N. Thin, MD, St Thomas' Hospital, London, UK.

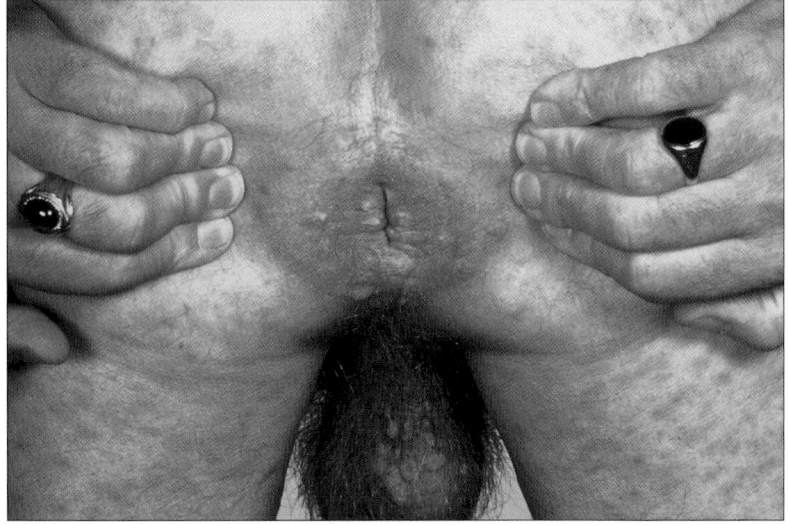

Fig. 11.80
Secondary syphilis: early perianal condylomata lata. By courtesy of R.N. Thin, MD, St Thomas' Hospital, London, UK.

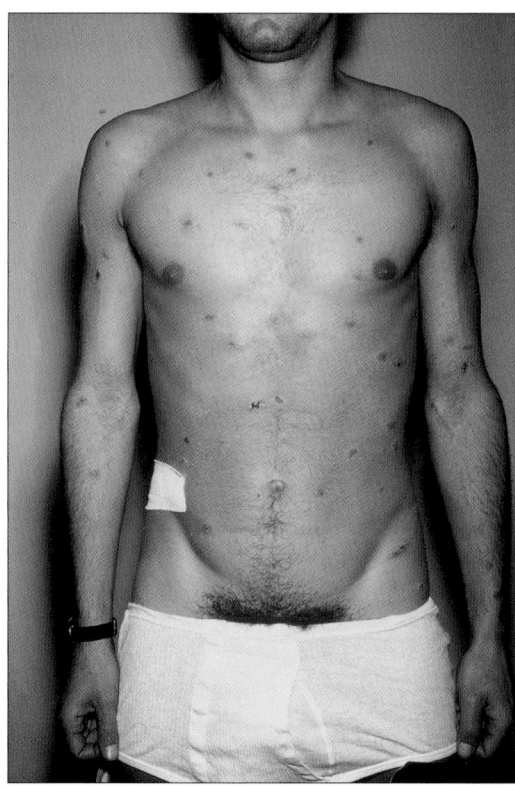

Fig. 11.81
Secondary syphilis: in this patient the lesions greatly resemble pityriasis lichenoides. By courtesy of R.A. Marsden, MD, St George's Hospital, London, UK.

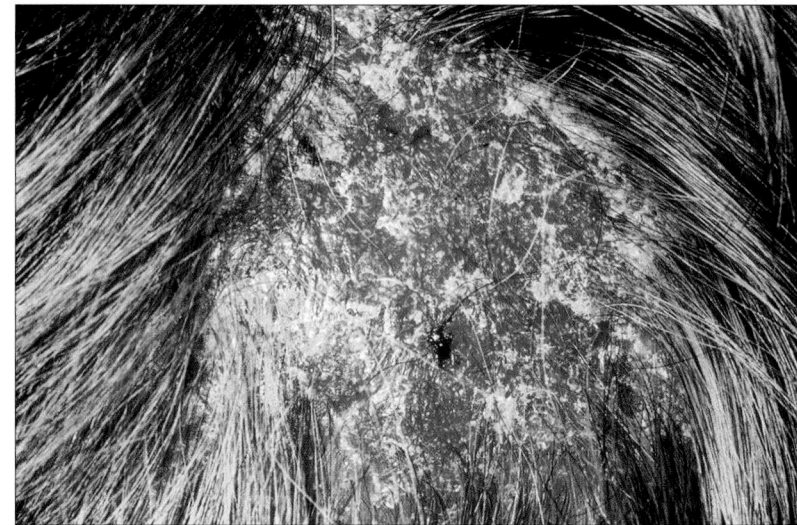

Fig. 11.82
Secondary syphilis: scalp involvement is not uncommon. Note the scaling and hair loss. By courtesy of M.M. Black, MD, Institute of Dermatology, London, UK.

Infants born to infected mothers may have widespread lesions reflecting a systemic infection. These include fibrosis in many organs, with inflammatory changes seen particularly in bones and lung. Vesicular skin lesions and maldevelopment of teeth and bone are also sometimes evident. Later changes of congenital syphilis are classically frontal bossing, a short maxilla, a high arched palate, chronic interstitial keratitis, notched (Hutchinson's) incisors, Mulberry's molars, VIII cranial nerve deafness and saddle nose.[34] Other manifestations include painless hydroarthrosis, perforation of the nasal septum and palate, and cardiovascular and neurological changes, as seen in late stage adult disease.

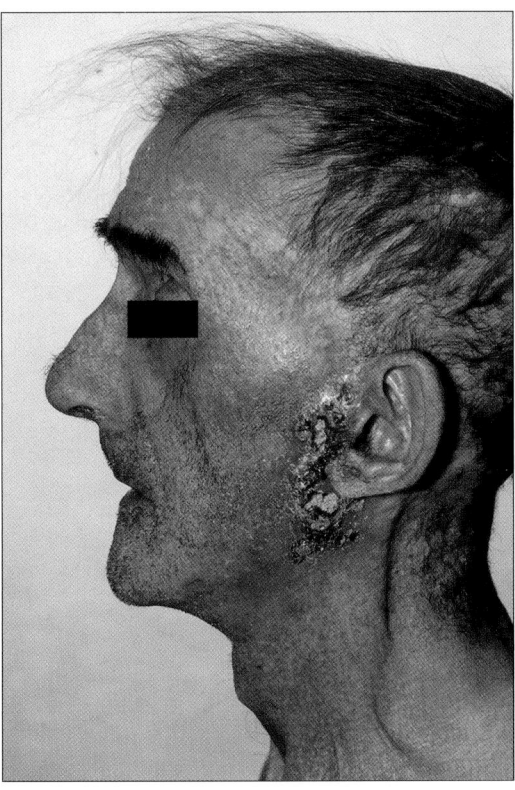

Fig. 11.83
Syphilis: the presence of gummatous cutaneous lesions as seen in this elderly male is now a very rare manifestation. By courtesy of M.M. Black, MD, Institute of Dermatology, London, UK.

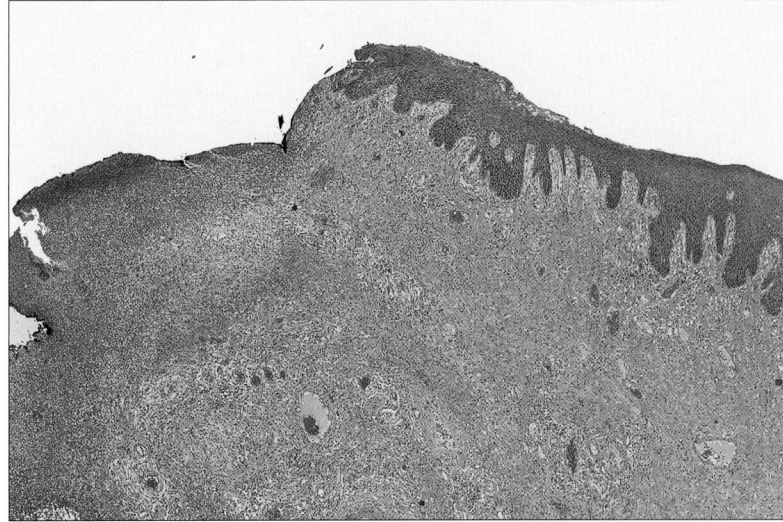

Fig. 11.84
Primary syphilis: biopsy from a chancre on the penis. Note the typical punched-out appearance. By courtesy of W. Grayson, MD, University of Witwatersrand, Johannesburg, South Africa.

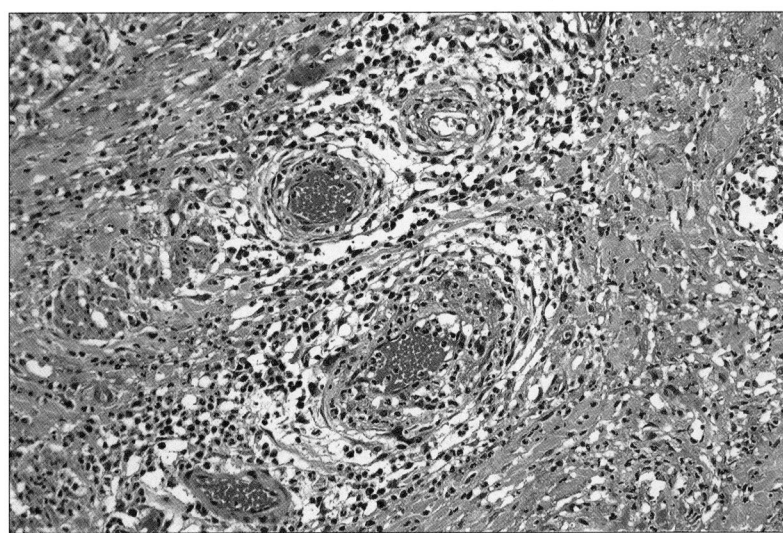

Fig. 11.85
Primary syphilis: note the marked endothelial swelling. By courtesy of W. Grayson, MD, University of Witwatersrand, Johannesburg, South Africa.

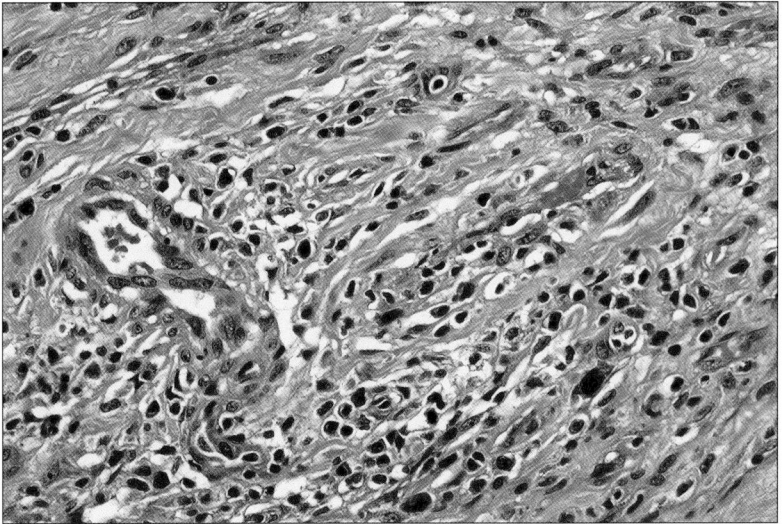

Fig. 11.86
Primary syphilis: the infiltrate consists of lymphocytes, histiocytes and conspicuous plasma cells. By courtesy of W. Grayson, MD, University of Witwatersrand, Johannesburg, South Africa.

Pathogenesis and histological features

T. pallidum is a slender coiled organism, 6–16 μm long, capable of an undulating, corkscrew-like motion. The organisms are readily visualized in material from a primary chancre with dark-field illumination, but have only recently been grown in culture. The usually non-pathogenic spirochetes, which live as commensals around the gingiva, although still termed *Treponema*, are quite different, not least in that they have a right-handed spiral in contrast to the left-handed spiral of *T. pallidum* and other pathogenic spirochetes.

T. pallidum produces a non-antigenic mucin coat, which may be protective in early infections. This mucoid element may be increased by a component produced by host inflammatory cells. A hyaluronidase is associated with the surface of *T. pallidum* and may facilitate dissemination in tissues.[35]

After the first inoculation of the spirochete through mucosa or abraded skin, the organism becomes systemically distributed before the primary chancre develops at the site of inoculation and numerous spirochetes can again be identified.

The chancre is characterized histologically by initial epidermal hyperplasia with an intense lymphohistiocytic and neutrophil infiltrate in the dermis (*Figs 11.84–11.86*). Plasma cells are present, but may be more numerous in papular and papulosquamous secondary lesions (see below). The overlying epithelium becomes ulcerated, and the adjacent epidermis often shows pseudoepitheliomatous hyperplasia and infiltration by neutrophils. The induration of the primary lesion is due to a large amount of mucoid substance. Vascular endothelial cell swelling is often prominent. The organisms can be demonstrated by dark-field examination of a smear taken from the primary lesion. A silver stain such as Warthin–Starry is also useful in demonstrating the organisms in tissue sections. By electron microscopy, the spirochetes are often found in macrophages, endothelial cells, plasma cells and in the intercellular space close to small blood vessels.[36] Resolution of the chancre, while appearing to coincide with immunity to further infection and demonstration of antibodies, nevertheless does not impede the widespread dissemination and proliferation of the treponeme. This leads to its recrudescence in its secondary phase, a paradox that is not understood.

Secondary lesions show variable appearances depending to some extent upon the clinical morphology (*Figs 11.87, 11.88*).[37–40] Purely macular lesions are not distinctive and show a rather sparse perivascular lymphohistiocytic infiltrate with few (if any) plasma cells.[13] The epidermis is normal. As the lesions develop a papular morphology, superficial and deep perivascular infiltrates develop, which may also adopt a band-like distribution. Involvement of the subcutis is rare. Plasma cells become more numerous and parakeratosis, acanthosis, spongiosis and exocytosis may be evident. Thick-walled blood vessels with swollen endothelial cells are characteristic. A prominent infiltrate is often present around hair follicles and sweat glands. Early lesions may show perivascular neutrophils and a heavy neutrophilic infiltrate

mimicking Sweet's syndrome has been reported.[41] Psoriasiform syphilids show parakeratosis and acanthosis with extended (psoriasiform) epidermal ridges. The inflammatory cell infiltrate is both perivascular and superficial, and band-like in distribution. Spongiform pustulation and neutrophil exocytosis may be evident and focal cell hydropic degeneration can sometimes be present.[13,40] Keratinocyte necrosis may occasionally be seen.[40]

Erythrocyte extravasation may be a feature of both papular and papulosquamous variants. A granulomatous element has been described in both papular and papulosquamous eruptions, but this is not a constant feature (*Fig. 11.89*).[40] In addition to a dense dermal infiltrate, large numbers of plasma cells and occasional giant cells are seen in corymbose syphilis. The number of organisms in secondary syphilis is limited and they can be identified by the use of silver stains or immunohistochemistry (*Fig. 11.90*).[42]

The nodular variants of secondary syphilis may be associated with granulomatous or pseudolymphomatous histology (*Figs 11.91, 11.92*).[43–45] These granulomata can mimic sarcoidal granulomata and may rarely have a palisaded distribution.[43,46] The rupial and condylomatous forms are characterized by marked epidermal hyperplasia, spongiosis and a neutrophil infiltrate. The dermis contains a very heavy inflammatory cell infiltrate including numerous plasma cells. Vascular changes are marked.

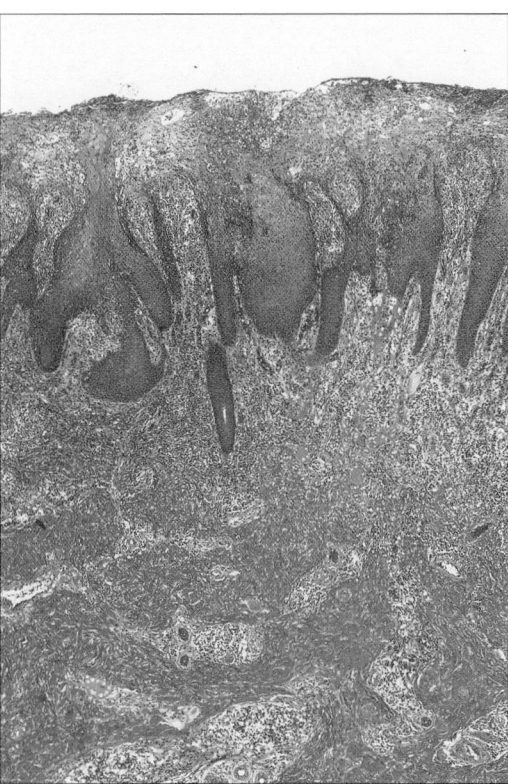

Fig. 11.87
Secondary syphilis: there is very marked hyperkeratosis and parakeratosis. The epidermis shows psoriasiform hyperplasia. A dense inflammatory cell infiltrate is present in the lamina propria. By courtesy of W. Grayson, MD, University of Witwatersand, Johannesburg, South Africa.

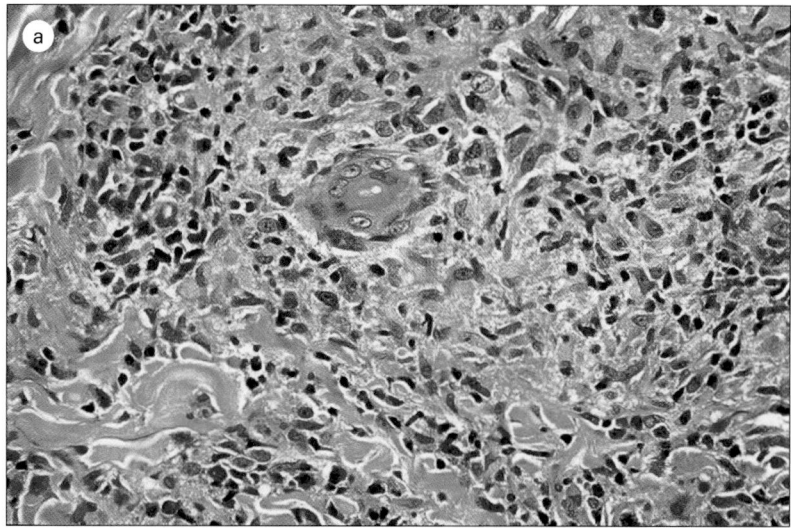

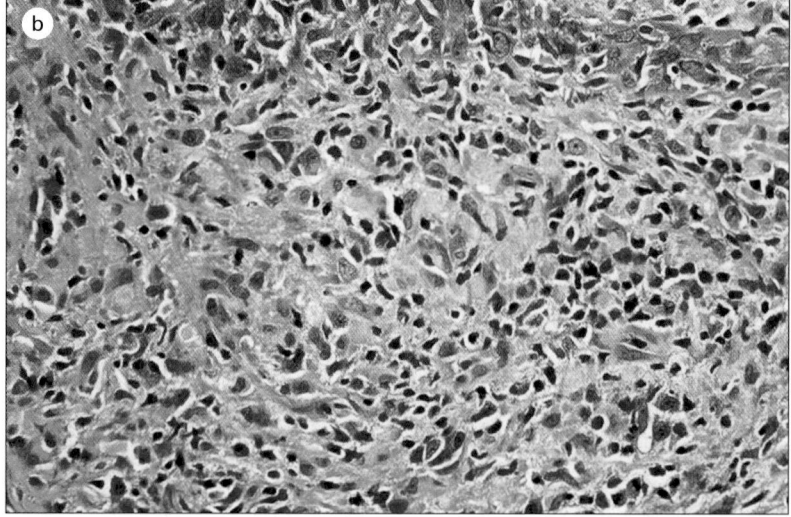

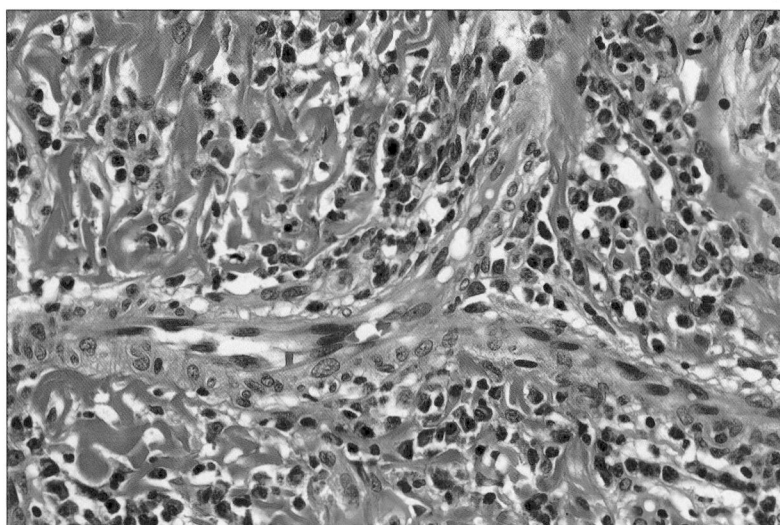

Fig. 11.88
Secondary syphilis: the infiltrate contains large numbers of plasma cells. By courtesy of W. Grayson, MD, University of Witwatersand, Johannesburg, South Africa.

Fig. 11.89
(a, b) Secondary syphilis: sometimes a poorly formed granulomatous component may be evident. By courtesy of W. Grayson, MD, University of Witwatersand, Johannesburg, South Africa.

The late secondary lesions are typified by histiocytic granulomata.[32] These are not well circumscribed and do not usually include multi-nucleated giant cells. They can be distinguished from tuberculosis by the presence of numerous plasma cells peripherally and the swollen endothelia of small blood vessels.

Gummata are characterized by central necrosis similar to caseation, but with a suggestion of residual cell outlines still visible (*Fig. 11.93*). The necrosis is surrounded by a lymphohistiocytic and plasma cell infiltrate with fibrosis. Spirochetes are very scanty and very difficult to find with the use of silver stains. Endarteritis is often evident.

Noduloulcerative lesions are granulomatous and typically there is no significant necrosis. Plasma cells are said to be inconspicuous, which may therefore cause considerable diagnostic difficulty.[33,47]

References

1. Findlay, G.H. (ed.) (1987) Treponemal infections. In: Dermatology of bacterial infections. Oxford: Blackwell, pp 106–130.
2. Buntin, D.M., Rosen, T., Leslier, J.L. et al (1991) Sexually transmitted diseases: bacterial infections. *J Am Acad Dermatol*, **25**, 287–299.
3. Fulford, K.W.M., Catterall, R.D., Hoinville, E. et al (1983) Social and psychological factors in the distribution of STD in male clinic attendees. III. Sexual activity. *Br J Vener Dis*, **59**, 386–393.
4. Minkoff, H.I., McCalla, S., Delke, I. et al (1990) The relationship of cocaine use to syphilis and human immunodeficiency virus infections among inner city parturient women. *Am J Obstet Gynecol*, **163**, 521–526.
5. Chapel, T.A. (1984) Primary and secondary syphilis. *Cutis*, **33**, 47–53.
6. Schober, P.C., Gabriel, G., White, P. et al (1983) How infectious is syphilis? *Br J Vener Dis*, **59**, 217–219.

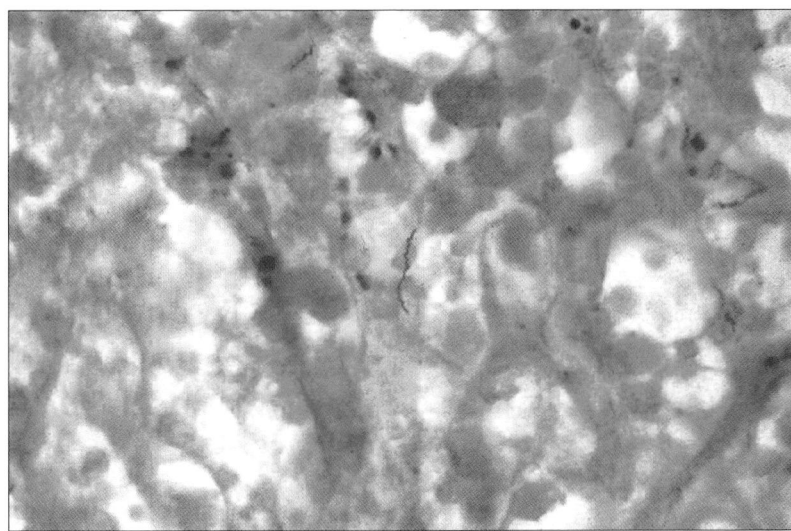

Fig. 11.90
Syphilis: a spirochete is seen in the center of the field. Warthin–Starry stain. By courtesy of R. Cummings, FIMLS, St Thomas' Hospital, London, UK.

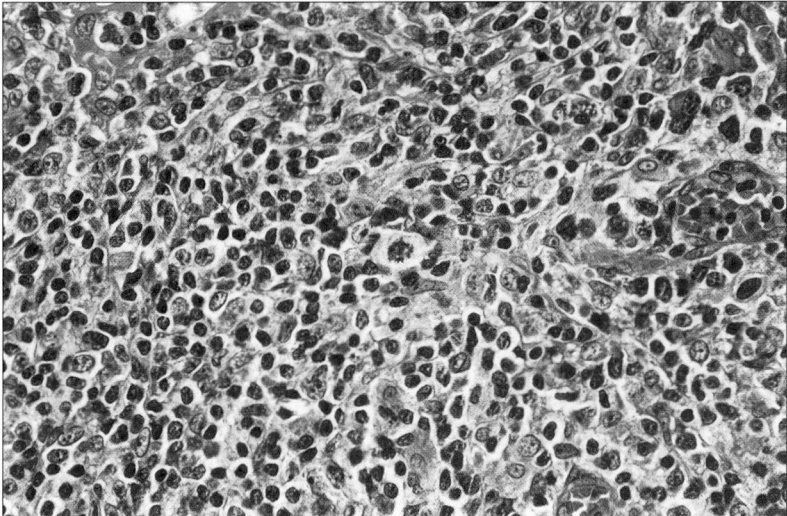

Fig. 11.91
Secondary syphilis: in this nodular variant the infiltrate is very pleomorphic and might suggest a lymphomatous process. The presence of large numbers of mature plasma cells (in the appropriate clinical setting) is a pointer to the correct diagnosis.

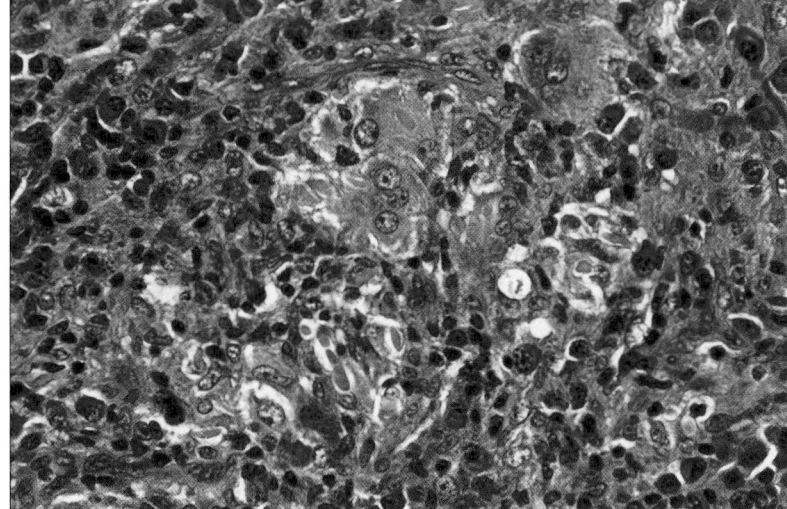

Fig. 11.92
Secondary syphilis: in late lesions granulomata, as seen in this field, are not uncommon.

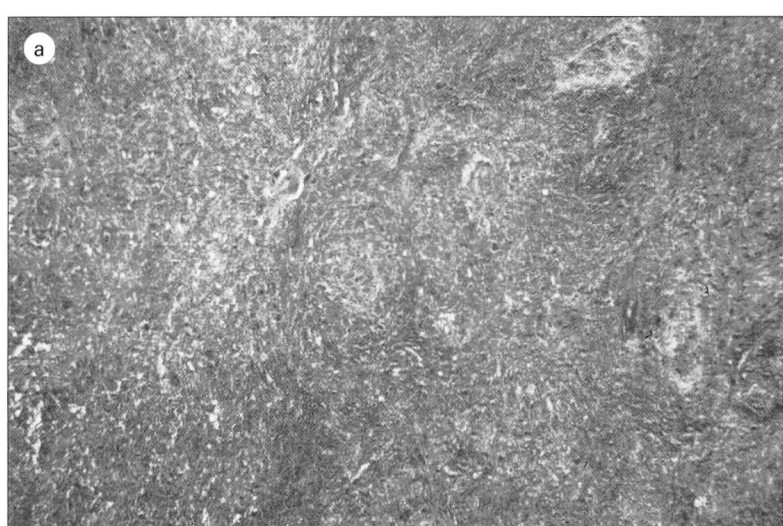

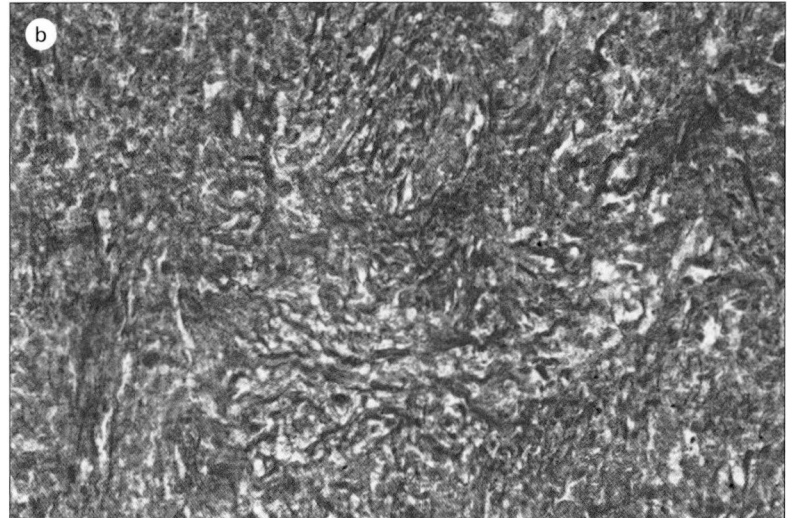

Fig. 11.93
Gumma: (a) superficially gummatous necrosis resembles caseation; (b) closer inspection reveals ghost outlines of cells and connective tissue.

7. Radolf, J.D., Kaplan, R.P. (1988) Unusual manifestations of secondary syphilis and abnormal humoral response to *Treponema pallidum* antigens in a homosexual man with asymptomatic human immunodeficiency virus infection. *J Am Acad Dermatol*, 18, 423–428.
8. Gregory, N., Sanchez, M., Buchness, M.R. (1990) The spectrum of syphilis in patients with human immunodeficiency virus infection. *J Am Acad Dermatol*, 22, 1061–1067.
9. Sehgal, V.N. (1990) Leg ulcers caused by yaws and endemic syphilis. *Clin Dermatol*, 8, 166–174.
10. Chapel, T.A., Prasad, P., Chapel, J. et al (1985) Extragenital syphilitic chancres. *J Am Acad Dermatol*, 13, 582–584.
11. Allison, S.D. (1986) Extragenital syphilitic chancres. *J Am Acad Dermatol*, 14, 1094–1095.
12. Felman, Y.M., Nikitas, J.A. (1982) Secondary syphilis. *Cutis*, 29, 322–334.
13. Jain, H.C., Fisher, B.K. (1988) Annular syphilid mimicking granuloma annulare. *Int J Dermatol*, 27, 340–341.
14. Alessi, S.D., Innocenti, M., Ragusa, G. (1983) Secondary syphilis: clinical, morphology and histopathology. *Am J Dermatopathol*, 5, 11–17.
15. Kennedy, C.T.C., Sanderson, K.V. (1980) Corymbose secondary syphilis. *Arch Dermatol*, 116, 111–112.
16. Lawrence, P., Saxe, N. (1992) Bullous secondary syphilis. *Clin Exp Dermatol*, 17, 44–46.
17. Mikhail, G.R., Chapel, T.A. (1969) Follicular papulopustular syphilid. *Arch Dermatol*, 100, 471–473.
18. Noppakum, N., Dinehart, S.M., Solomon, A.R. (1987) Pustular secondary syphilis. *Int J Dermatol*, 26, 112–114.
19. Lee, J.Y-Y., Hsu, M-L. (1991) Alopecia syphilitica, a simulator of alopecia areata: histopathology and differential diagnosis. *J Cutan Pathol*, 18, 87–92.
20. Jordaan, H.F., Louw, M. (1995) The moth-eaten alopecia of secondary syphilis. A histopathological study of 12 patients. *Am J Dermatopathol*, 17, 158–162.
21. Cuozzo, D.W., Benson, P.M., Sperling, L.C. et al (1995) Essential syphilitic alopecia revisited. *J Am Acad Dermatol*, 32, 840–844.
22. Fisher, D.A., Chang, L.W., Tuffanelli, D.L. (1969) Lues maligna. Report of a case and review of the literature. *Arch Dermatol*, 99, 70–73.
23. Petrozzi, J.W., Lockshin, N.A., Berger, B.J. (1974) Malignant syphilis. Severe variant of secondary syphilis. *Arch Dermatol*, 109, 387–389.
24. Don, P.C., Rubinstein, R., Christie, S. (1995) Malignant syphilis (lues maligna) and concurrent infection with HIV. *Int J Dermatol*, 34, 403–407.
25. Tosca, A., Stavropoulos, P.G., Hatziolou, E. et al (1990) Malignant syphilis in HIV-infected patients. *Int J Dermatol*, 29, 575–578.
26. Cole, G.W., Amon, R.B., Russell, P.S. (1977) Secondary syphilis presenting as a pruritic dermatosis. *Arch Dermatol*, 113, 489–490.
27. Chapel, T.A. (1980) Signs and symptoms of secondary syphilis. *Sex Transm Dis*, 7, 161–164.
28. Rosen, T., Rubin, H., Ellner, K. et al (1989) Vesicular Jarisch–Herxheimer reaction. *Arch Dermatol*, 112, 1451–1454.
29. Glover, R.A., Piaquadio, D.J., Kern, S. et al (1992) An unusual presentation of secondary syphilis in a patient with human immunodeficiency virus infection. *Arch Dermatol*, 128, 530–534.
30. Tikjob, G., Russell, M., Petersen, C.S. et al (1991) Seronegative secondary syphilis in a patient with AIDS: identification of Treponema pallidum in biopsy specimens. *J Am Acad Dermatol*, 24, 506–508.
31. Chung, G., Kantor, G.R., Whipple, S. (1991) Tertiary syphilis of the face. *J Am Acad Dermatol*, 24, 832–835.
32. Tanabe, J.L., Huntley, A.C. (1986) Granulomatous tertiary syphilis. *J Am Acad Dermatol*, 15, 341–344.
33. Pembroke, A.C., Michell, P.A., McKee, P.H. (1980) Nodulosquamous tertiary syphilide. *Clin Exp Dermatol*, 5, 361–364.
34. Fiumara, N.J., Lessell, S. (1970) Manifestations of late congenital syphilis: an analysis of 271 patients. *Arch Dermatol*, 102, 78–83.
35. Fitzgerald, T.J., Repesh, L.A. (1987) The hyaluronidase associated with *Treponema pallidum* facilitates treponemal dissemination. *Infect Immunity*, 55, 1023–1028.
36. Azar, H.A., Pham, T.D., Kurban, A.K. (1970) An electron microscopic study of a syphilitic chancre. *Arch Pathol*, 90, 143–150.
37. Jeerapaet, P., Ackerman, A.B. (1973) Histologic patterns of secondary syphilis. *Arch Dermatol*, 107, 373–377.
38. Abell, E., Marks, R., Wilson Jones, E. (1975) Secondary syphilis: a clinico-pathological review. *Br J Dermatol*, 93, 53–61.
39. Pandhi, R.K., Singh, N., Ramam, M. (1995) Secondary syphilis: a clinicopathologic study. *Int J Dermatol*, 34, 240–243.
40. Jordaan, H.F. (1988) Secondary syphilis. A clinicopathological study. *Am J Dermatopathol*, 10, 399–409.
41. Jordaan, H.F., Cilliers, J. (1986) Secondary syphilis mimicking Sweet's syndrome. *Br J Dermatol*, 115, 495–496.
42. Beckett, J.H., Bigbee, J.W. (1979) Immunoperoxidase localization of Treponema pallidum. *Arch Dermatol*, 103, 135–138.
43. Kahn, L.B., Gordon, W. (1971) Sarcoid-like granulomata in secondary syphilis: a clinical and histopathologic study of five cases. *Arch Pathol*, 92, 334–337.
44. Cochran, R.E.I., Thomson, J., Fleming, K.A. et al (1976) Histology simulating reticulosis in secondary syphilis. *Br J Dermatol*, 95, 251–254.
45. Hodak, E., David, M., Rotham, A. et al (1987) Nodular secondary syphilis mimicking cutaneous lymphoreticular process. *J Am Acad Dermatol*, 17, 914–917.
46. Green, K.M., Heilman, E. (1985) Secondary syphilis presenting as a palisading granuloma. *J Am Acad Dermatol*, 12, 957–960.
47. Tanabe, J.L., Huntley, A.C. (1986) Granulomatous tertiary syphilis. *J Am Acad Dermatol*, 15, 341–344.

Granuloma inguinale

Clinical features

Granuloma inguinale (donovanosis) occurs in people with poor hygiene in tropical regions, mainly in India, Brazil, West Indies, South China and West Africa; it was formerly seen in southern USA, but is now rare.[1-7] The organism is of low infectivity and is presumed to be spread by sexual contact, probably through abraded skin. It occurs most often in the third to fifth decades.[1] The incubation period is uncertain and may range from 2 to 3 weeks to several months.[8]

The initial presentation in females is usually of one or more indurated papules or nodules on the inner aspect of the labia, the fourchette or around the clitoris (*Fig. 11.94*).[9] In males, the glans, prepuce, coronal sulcus or shaft is affected (*Fig. 11.95*). Dorsal perforation of the prepuce can occur as a late complication.[10] The perianal and inguinal regions may also be involved.[11] The papules ulcerate irregularly and extend widely if untreated. The base of the ulcer is 'beefy' and the margins are

undermined and indurated. Spread to contiguous 'kissing' areas may sometimes occur. Variants include verrucous, necrotic and scarring lesions.[1] Primary infection of the lymph nodes does not occur, but painful lymphadenopathy is common due to secondary infection. Rarely primary extragenital lesions may be seen (mainly mouth or lips but also at unusual sites such as the foot).[11-14] Exceptionally, presentation as a psoas abscess has been described.[15]

Very occasionally, there is a systemic infection with involvement of many organs including the liver, and osteolytic lesions in bone.[16] The latter may particularly relate to a primary cervical lesion.[1] Spinal compression has also been reported.[17] Later complications include strictures of the urethra, vagina or anus, destruction of the penile shaft and pseudoelephantiasis.[1,18-20] As with other sexually transmitted

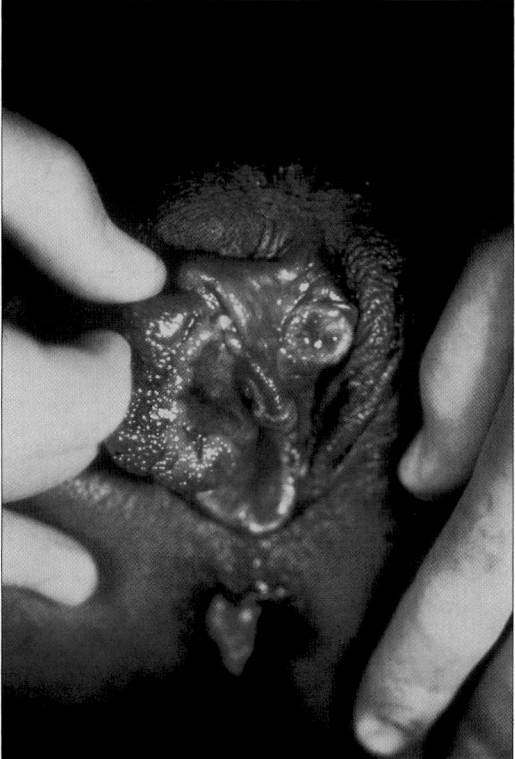

Fig. 11.94
Granuloma inguinale: early lesion showing an ulcerated papule adjacent to the clitoris. By courtesy of J. Lawson, MD, University of Newcastle-upon-Tyne, UK.

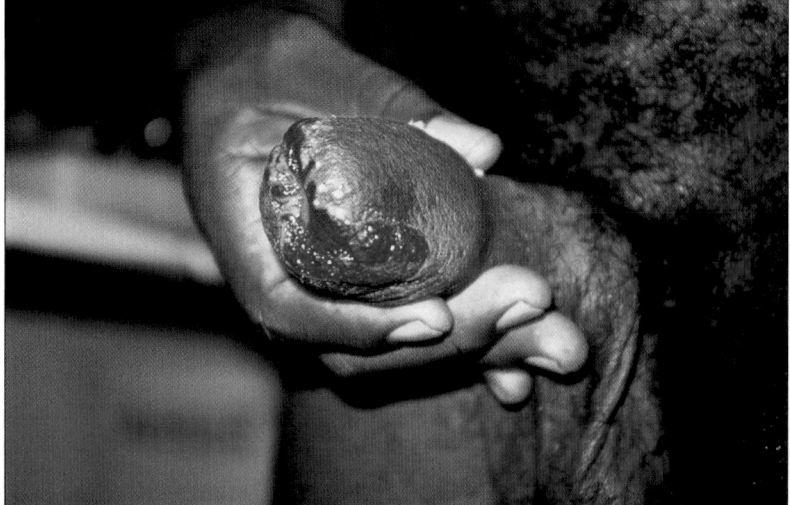

Fig. 11.95
Granuloma inguinale: in this patient there is extensive ulceration of the glans penis. Note the typical 'beefy' appearance. By courtesy of C. Furlonge, MD, Port of Spain, Trinidad.

diseases, patients with granuloma inguinale are often HIV positive[8,21] and may also have syphilis. Genital SCC is an uncommon but important complication.[1,22] Infection in children[23] has rarely been reported and occurs as a result of transmission from an infected mother at birth. Rare manifestations of the disease in children include a mass in the neck, otitis media and mastoiditis.[24,25]

Pathogenesis and histological features

Granuloma inguinale is caused by *Calymmatobacterium granulomatis* (formerly *Donovania granulomatis*), an encapsulated short (1–2 μm) Gram-negative rod with characteristic bipolar staining. It is transmitted by sexual contact, but it is of low infectivity.[1] The organism is found in feces and this may act as a reservoir of infectivity or in occasional cases be the source of genital infection. The higher incidence of infection in homosexuals may support this concept.

The lesion is characterized by a very intense inflammatory infiltrate in which plasma cells are predominant (*Fig. 11.96*). Focal formation of neutrophilic microabscesses is frequent. Pathognomonic macrophages contain cytoplasmic cyst-like vacuoles in which bacteria can be demonstrated by staining with Giemsa or the Warthin–Starry reaction (*Figs 11.97, 11.98*).[26] The bacteria can also be seen extracellularly. In most cases there is associated acanthosis, which sometimes amounts to pseudoepitheliomatous hyperplasia. Ulceration is common. A recent large study has demonstrated frequent transepidermal elimination of organisms.[27] It is likely that this phenomenon may be an important mechanism in the spread of the disease.

Diagnosis is confirmed by the identification of typical organisms (Donovan bodies) on a scraping from an ulcer or on a biopsy stained with Giemsa or Warthin–Starry. More recently, polymerase chain reaction (PCR), has been used successfully to confirm the diagnosis.[28] Dark-field illumination microscopy should be performed to exclude syphilis. By electron microscopy, the encapsulated microorganisms can be demonstrated within the phagosomes of macrophages.[9,29]

References

1. Sehgal, V.N., Shyam Prasad, A.L. (1986) Donovanosis. Current concepts. *Int J Dermatol*, 25, 8–16.
2. Hacker, P., Fisher, B.K., Dekoven, J. et al (1992) Granuloma inguinale: three cases diagnosed in Toronto, Canada. *Int J Dermatol*, 31, 696–699.
3. Niemel, P.L.A., Engelkens, H.J.H., van der Meijden, W.I. et al (1992) Donovanosis (granuloma inguinale) still exists. *Int J Dermatol*, 31, 244–246.
4. Brown, T.J., Yen-Moore, A., Tyring, S.K. (1999) An overview of sexually transmitted diseases. Part I. *J Am Acad Dermatol*, 41, 511–532.
5. O'Farrell, N. (2001) Donovanosis: an update. *Int J STD AIDS*, 12, 423–427.
6. Czelusta, A., Yen-Moore, A., Van der Straten, M. et al (2000) An overview of sexually transmitted diseases. Part III. Sexually transmitted diseases in HIV-infected patients. *J Am Acad Dermatol*, 43, 409–432.
7. Sehgal, V.N., Jain, M.K. (1988) Pattern of epidemics of donovanosis in the 'nonendemic' region. *Int J Dermatol*, 27, 396–399.
8. Ronald, A.R., Plummer, F.A. (1989) Chancroid and granuloma inguinale. *Clin Lab Med*, 9, 535–543.
9. Schwarz, R.H. (1983) Chancroid and granuloma inguinale. *Clin Obstet Gynecol*, 26, 138–142.
10. Gupta, S., Kumar, B. (2000) Dorsal perforation of prepuce: a common end point of severe ulcerative genital disease. *Sex Transm Infect*, 76, 210–212.
11. Hirsch, B.C., Johnson, W.C. (1984) Pathology of granulomatous disease: mixed inflammatory granulomata. *Int J Dermatol*, 23, 585–597.
12. Davis, C.M. (1970) Granuloma inguinale. A clinical, histological and ultrastructural study. *JAMA*, 211, 632–636.
13. Rao, M.V., Thappa, D.M., Jaisankar, T.J. et al (1998) Extragenital donovanosis of the foot. *Sex Transm Infect*, 74, 298–299.
14. Sanders, C.J. (1998) Extragenital donovanosis in a patient with AIDS. *Sex Transm Infect*, 74, 142–143.
15. Mein, J., Russell, C., Knox, J. et al (1999) Intrapelvic donovanosis presenting as a psoas abscess in two patients. *Sex Transm Infect*, 75, 75–76.
16. Buntin, D.M., Rosen, T., Lesher, J.L. et al (1991) Sexually transmitted bacterial infections. *J Am Acad Dermatol*, 25, 287–299.
17. Paterson, D.L. (1998) Disseminated donovanosis (granuloma inguinale) causing spinal cord compression: case report and review of donovanosis involving bone. *Clin Infect Dis*, 26, 379–383.
18. Rosen, T., Tschen, J.A., Ramsdell, W. et al (1984) Granuloma inguinale. *J Am Acad Dermatol*, 11, 433–437.

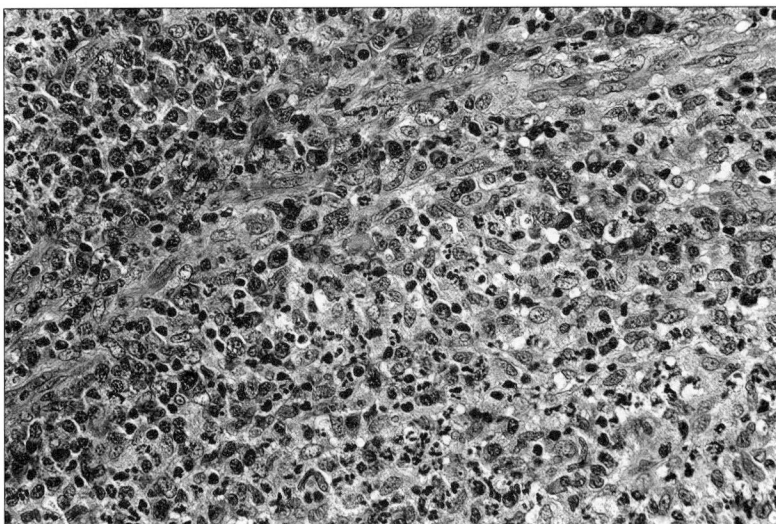

Fig. 11.97
Granuloma inguinale: the infiltrate consists of lymphocytes, neutrophils, plasma cells and conspicuous pale-staining histiocytes.

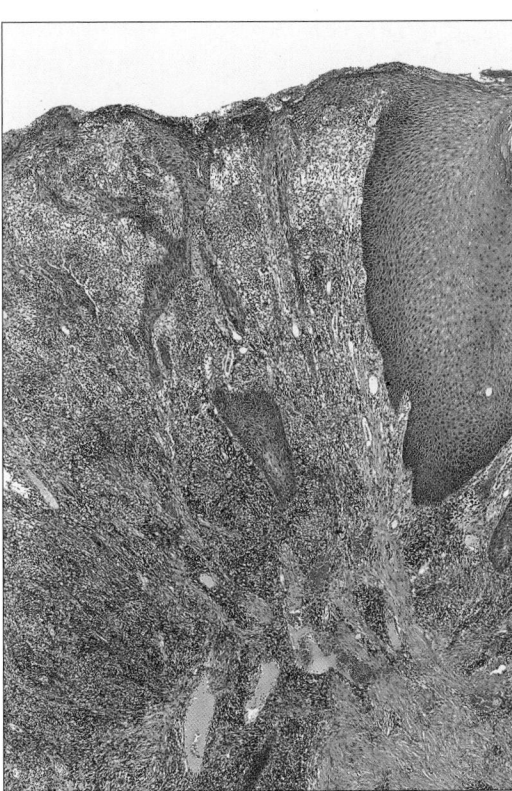

Fig. 11.96
Granuloma inguinale: biopsy from the penis. Note the pseudoepitheliomatous hyperplasia. There are intense inflammatory changes.

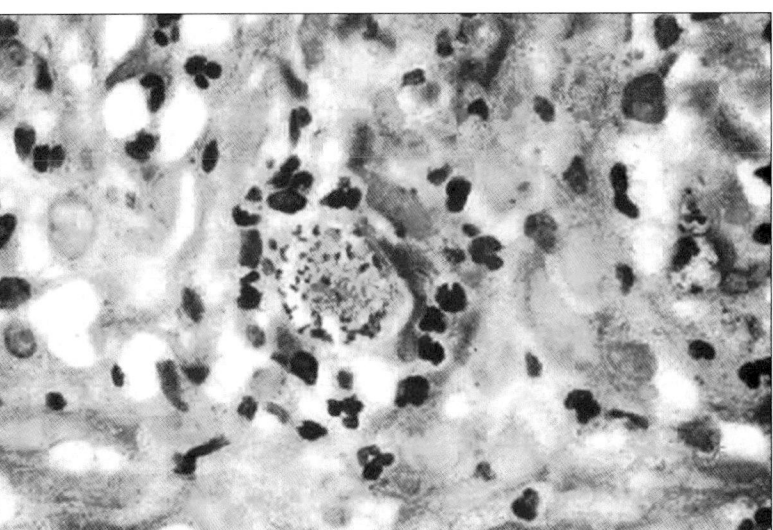

Fig. 11.98
Granuloma inguinale: the histiocytes contain characteristic Donovan bodies (Warthin–Starry stain). By courtesy of W. Grayson, MD, University of Witwatersrand, Johannesburg, South Africa.

19. Fritz, G.S., Hubler, W.R. Jr, Dodson, R.F. et al (1975) Mutilating granuloma inguinale. *Arch Dermatol*, **111**, 1464–1465.
20. Sehgal, V.N., Jain, M.K., Sharma, V.K. (1987) Pseudoelephantiasis induced by donovanosis. *Genitourin Med*, **63**, 54–56.
21. Hoosen, A.A., Mphatsoe, M., Kharsany, A.B.M. et al (1996) Granuloma inguinale in association with pregnancy and HIV infection. *Int J Gynaecol Obstet*, **53**, 133–138.
22. MacKay, C.R., Bunch, W.L. Jr (1952) Carcinoma of the vulva following granuloma inguinale. *Am J Syph Gonorrh Vener Dis*, **36**, 511–514.
23. Bowden, F.J., Bright, A., Rode, J.W. et al (2000) Donovanosis causing cervical lymphadenopathy in a five-month-old boy. *Pediatr Infect Dis J*, **19**, 167–169.
24. Govender, D., Hadley, G.P., Donnellan, R. (1999) Granuloma inguinale (donovanosis) presenting as a neck mass in an infant. *Pediatr Surg Int*, **15**, 129–131.
25. Govender, D., Naidoo, K., Chetty, R. (1997) Granuloma inguinale (donovanosis): an unusual cause of otitis media and mastoiditis in children. *Am J Clin Pathol*, **108**, 510–514.
26. Seghal, V.N., Shyamprasad, A.L., Beohart, P.C. (1984) The histopathological diagnosis of donovanosis. *Br J Vener Dis*, **60**, 45–47.
27. Ramdial, P.K., Kharsany, A.B., Reddy, R. et al (2001) Transepithelial elimination of granuloma inguinale. *J Cutan Pathol*, **27**, 493–499.
28. Carter, J., Bowden, F.J., Sriprakash, K.S. et al (1999) Diagnostic polymerase chain reaction for donovanosis. *Clin Infect Dis*, **28**, 1168–1169.
29. Kuberski, T., Papadimitriou, J.M., Phillips, P. (1980) Ultrastructure of *Calymmatobacterium granulomatis* in lesions of granuloma inguinale. *J Infect Dis*, **142**, 744–749.

Chancroid

Clinical features

Chancroid (soft chancre, genital ulcer disease) is very common in some tropical areas of Africa, Southeast Asia, Central America and the Pacific.[1–4] Poor hygiene is a feature of communities where the disease is endemic.[5] It is associated with an increased risk of transmission or acquisition of HIV.[6,7] It has also been diagnosed more frequently in western Europe and North America in association with increased travel, immigration and prostitution. Chancroid is now endemic in New York City and southern Florida.[6] The disease is acquired solely by sexual contact and has a short incubation period of 3 days to 2 weeks (median 7 days).

The initial lesion is usually a transient vesicular tender papule, which rapidly ulcerates with copious suppuration. The ulcer is sharply circumscribed with an undermined edge and is typically not indurated.[2] These lesions appear much more commonly in the male, usually on the penis (*Fig. 11.99*). The prepuce, coronal sulcus, frenulum and glans are the most favored sites.[6] Lesions in the female are seen on the fourchette, labia or around the clitoris.[2] Cervical and vaginal involvement is uncommon. Variants of primary chancroid ulcers include giant and serpiginous forms, follicular, transient and dwarf lesions; occasionally a condyloma lata-like presentation may occur.[2]

The ulcers are tender and especially painful when in contact with urine. Lymphadenitis occurs in about 50% of cases approximately 1 week after the genital lesion and usually in 50% of these, suppuration

(bubo formation) follows. Sometimes rupture may follow, resulting in inguinal ulceration. In other cases the course is variable, some resolving without treatment in a few days while others go on for several weeks, developing phimosis or even gangrene. Systemic infections do not occur.[2]

Pathogenesis and histological features

Chancroid is caused by *Haemophilus ducreyi*, a Gram-negative coccobacillus, which grows in chains sometimes arranged in parallel. It is transmitted through minor abrasions during sexual intercourse. The subsequent lesion comprises:

- a *superficial* zone of neutrophils, red cells, bacteria and cell debris
- a *middle* zone of edematous granulation tissue
- an *underlying* infiltrate of histiocytes, lymphocytes and plasma cells (*Figs 11.100, 11.101*).

The enlarged lymph nodes show central necrosis with a surrounding mixed inflammatory response of neutrophils and macrophages.

Diagnosis is confirmed by isolation of the organism by culture in a blood-enriched medium containing vancomycin at 33°C. The bacterium may be identified by its chain-like growth in scrapings from the margin of the ulcer, but secondary organisms are often present and it is more helpful to identify the organism in an aspirate from a necrotic lymph node. Recently DNA in situ hybridization for *H. ducreyi* has been developed.[8]

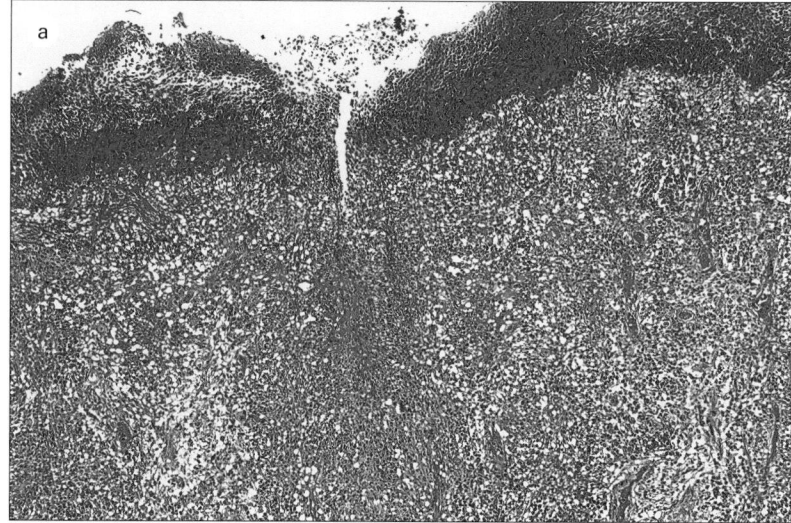
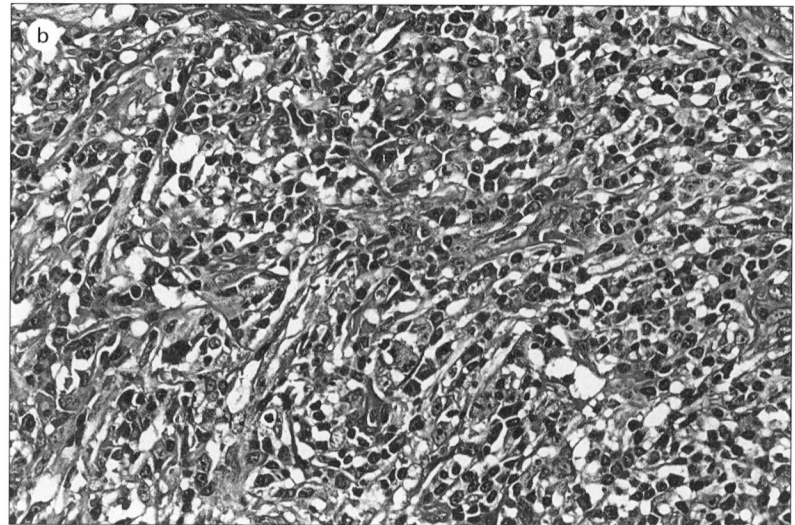

Fig. 11.100
Chancroid: (a) biopsy through an ulcer on the glans penis; (b) note the conspicuous plasma cells. By courtesy of S. Lucas, MD, St Thomas' Hospital, London, UK.

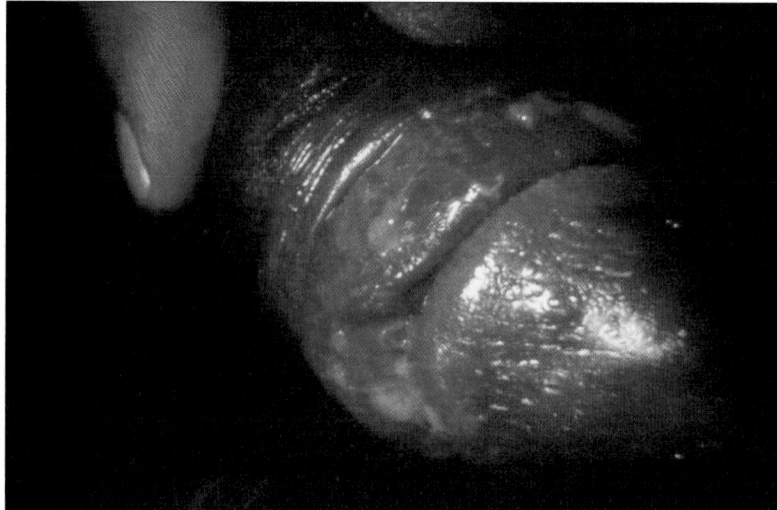

Fig. 11.99
Chancroid: irregular ulcer extending along the coronal sulcus of the penis. By courtesy of R.A. Marsden, MD, St George's Hospital, London, UK.

References

1. Schwarz, R.H. (1983) Chancroid and granuloma inguinale. *Clin Obstet Gynecol*, **26**, 138–142.
2. Morse, S.A. (1989) Chancroid and Haemophilus ducreyi. *Clin Microbiol Rev*, **2**, 137–157.
3. Rosen, T., Brown, T.J. (1996) Cutaneous manifestations of sexually transmitted diseases. *Curr Probl Dermatol*, **24**, 90–96.
4. Brown, T.J., Yen-Moore, A., Tyring, S.K. (1998) An overview of sexually transmitted diseases. Part I. *Med Clin North Am*, **82**, 1081–1104.
5. Buntin, D.M., Rosen, T., Lesher, J.L. et al (1991) Sexually transmitted diseases: bacterial infections. *J Am Acad Dermatol*, **25**, 287–299.
6. Ronald, A.R., Plummer, F.A. (1989) Chancroid and granuloma inguinale. *Clin Lab Med*, **9**, 535–543.
7. Langley, C. (1999) Update on chancroid: an important cause of genital ulcer disease. *J Am Acad Dermatol*, **41**, 511–532.
8. Parsons, L.M., Shayegani, M., Waring, A.L. et al (1989) DNA probe for the identification of Haemophilus ducreyi. *J Clin Microbiol*, **27**, 1441–1445.

Lymphogranuloma venereum

Clinical features

Lymphogranuloma venereum occurs most often in homosexual males in Northern Europe and west America, but is endemic in Asia, Africa and South America.[1–5]

The disease evolves in three stages:

- In *stage 1* disease the primary lesion develops 3–30 days after contact and is a small, transient, frequently asymptomatic papulovesicle or ulcer on the penis, scrotum, rectum, vulva, vagina and/or cervix (*Figs 11.102, 11.103*).[6] The most commonly affected site on the vulva is the fourchette.[6] Primary lesions have been described on the fingers and tongue.[7] Rarely lymphogranuloma venereum has been reported presenting with a psoas abscess.[8] Cat scratch disease may clinically simulate lymphogranuloma venereum.[9]

- *Stage 2* develops within a few weeks of the primary lesion and consists of enlargement of the regional lymph nodes; in the male the inguinal nodes and in the female the inguinal and/or pelvic lymph nodes are involved. The lymphadenopathy is severe and initially painless and hard; later the nodes (buboes) soften and discharge viscous pus. The tissue around the nodes becomes involved in the inflammatory process so that they become matted together. Along with lymphadenopathy, the patient may also experience malaise, joint pains and hepatosplenomegaly. Erythema nodosum, light-sensitive eruptions and erythema multiforme may complicate this phase and are more common in women.

- *Stage 3 disease* consists of complications of the early inflammatory changes. Involvement of the deep iliac and perirectal lymph nodes resulting from drainage from a high vaginal, posterior urethral, cervical or rectal primary lesion may be complicated by a stricture of the rectum 5–10 cm from the anus.[10] This is associated with a periproctitis and proctocolitis, which sometimes fistulates.[11] Rectal carcinoma is an occasional late complication.[12] In both sexes, genital lymphedema and even elephantiasis can develop after the lymphadenopathy. This may remain a continuing problem and be associated with secondary cutaneous erosions and ulceration.

Systemic lesions are rare, and include cardiac and pulmonary involvement, keratoconjunctivitis, episcleritis, uveitis, papilledema and retinal hemorrhages, meningitis, hepatitis and cutaneous manifestations such as erythema nodosum and erythema multiforme.[2,13]

Pathogenesis and histological features

Lymphogranuloma venereum is caused by strains L1, L2 and L3 of the bacterium *Chlamydia trachomatis*.[14,15] *Chlamydiae* are non-mobile,

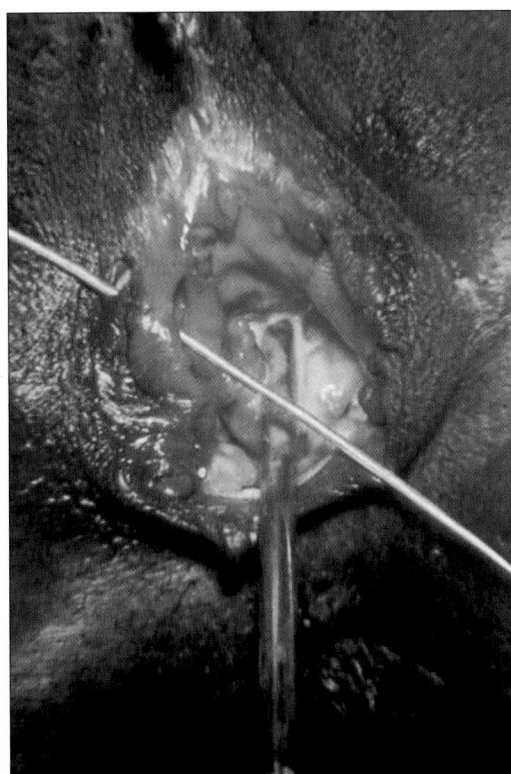

Fig. 11.102
Lymphogranuloma venereum: note the ulcer on the right labium majus. By courtesy of S. Lucas, MD, St. Thomas' Hospital, London, UK.

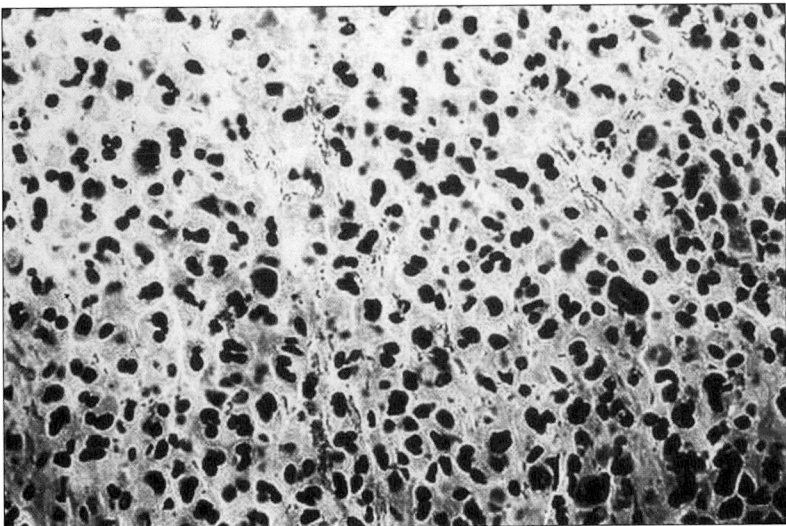

Fig. 11.101
Chancroid: note the coccobacilli growing in chains.

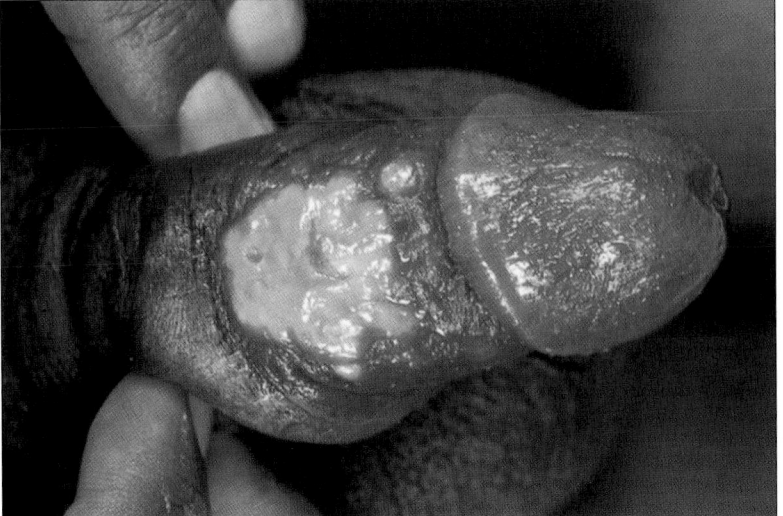

Fig. 11.103
Lymphogranuloma venereum: there is an ulcer on the penile shaft covered with necrotic debris. By courtesy of the Institute of Dermatology, London, UK.

coccoid, obligate intracellular parasites.[16,17] They depend upon their host cells for ATP metabolites and multiply within membrane-bound vacuoles in the host macrophage cytoplasm.[16] They stain faintly blue with hematoxylin and eosin, Gram-negative with the Brown–Hopps tissue Gram stain and black with the Warthin–Starry silver impregnation technique.[18] On the rare occasions that the primary lesion is viewed histologically, the base of the ulcer is lined by intensely inflamed fibrous granulation tissue. Plasma cells and microabscesses are present. The lymphadenitis has a characteristic picture of stellate central necrosis with neutrophils and a surrounding palisaded granulomatous reaction with occasional giant cells.

The central necrosis is slowly absorbed and replaced by fibrosis. As a consequence, lymphedema develops distally. The lymphatics are typically inflamed and granulomata may be seen.

Diagnosis is supported by complement fixation tests (rising titers) or monoclonal antibodies.[17] PCR may also be used to confirm the diagnosis.[17,18] The Frei skin test is no longer performed. Confirmation of the diagnosis is best established by isolation of the organism in tissue culture and by lymph node biopsy.[19]

References

1. Handsfield, H.H. (1981) Lymphogranuloma venereum, chancroid, and granuloma inguinale. In: Braude, A.J. (ed.) Medical microbiology and infectious diseases. Philadelphia: W.B. Saunders, pp 1227–1233.
2. Buus, D.R.E., Pflugfelder, S.C., Schachter, J. et al (1988) Lymphogranuloma venereum conjunctivitis with a marginal corneal perforation. *Ophthalmology*, **95**, 799–802.
3. Penneys, N.S. (1996) Diagnosing sexually transmitted diseases in HIV-positive patients. *Curr Probl Dermatol*, **24**, 77–81.
4. Brown, T.J., Yen-Moore, A., Tyring, S.K. (1999) An overview of sexually tramsmitted diseases. Part I. *J Am Acad Dermatol*, **41**, 511–532.
5. Rosen, T., Brown, T.J. (1998) Cutaneous manifestations of sexually transmitted diseases. *Med Clin North Am*, **82**, 1081–1104.
6. Greenblatt, R.M., Lukehart, S.A., Plummer, F.A. et al (1959) Lymphogranuloma venereum and granuloma inguinale. *Med Clin North Am*, **43**, 1493–1506.
7. Buntin, D.M., Rosen, T., Lesher, J.L. et al (1991) Sexually transmitted diseases: bacterial infections. *J Am Acad Dermatol*, **25**, 287–299.
8. Speers, D. (1999) Lymphogranuloma venereum presenting with a psoas abscess. *Aust N Z J Med*, **29**, 563–564.
9. Philpot, C.R. (1999) A case of cat scratch disease masquerading as lymphogranuloma venereum. *Int J STD AIDS*, **10**, 694–695.
10. Papagrigoriadis, S., Rennie, J.A. (1998) Lymphogranuloma venereum as a cause of rectal strictures. *Postgrad Med J*, **74**, 168–169.
11. Lynch, C.M., Felder, T.L., Scwandt, R.A. et al (1999) Lymphogranuloma venereum presenting as a rectovaginal fistula. *Infect Dis Obstet Gynecol*, **7**, 199–201.
12. Chopda, N.M., Desai, D.C., Sawant, P.D. et al (1994) Rectal lymphogranuloma venereum in association with rectal adenocarcinoma. *Indian J Gastroenterol*, **13**, 103–104.
13. Myhre, E.B., Mardh, P.A. (1982) Unusual manifestations of *Chlamydia trachomatis* infections. *Scand J Infect Dis*, **32** (Suppl.), 122–126.
14. Schachter, J. (1978) Chlamydial infections. *N Engl J Med*, **298**, 428–435 (*first of three parts*).
15. Schachter, J. (1978) Chlamydial infections. *N Engl J Med*, **298**, 494–495.
16. Barnes, R.C. (1989) Laboratory diagnosis of human Chlamydial infections. *Clin Microbiol Rev*, **2**, 119–136.
17. Kellock, D.J., Barlow, R., Suvarna, S.K. et al (1997) Lymphogranuloma venereum: biopsy, serology, and molecular biology. *Genitourin Med*, **73**, 399–401.
18. Hadfield, T.L., Lamy, Y., Wear, D.J. (1995) Demonstration of Chlamydia trachomatis in inguinal lymphadenitis of lymphogranuloma venereum: a light microscopy, electron microscopy and polymerase chain reaction study. *Mod Pathol*, **8**, 924–929.
19. Schachter, J., Caldwell, H.D. (1980) Chlamydiae. *Ann Rev Microbiol*, **34**, 285–309.

Schistosomiasis

Clinical features

Schistosoma haematobium and *Schistosoma mansoni* are both found extensively in Africa. *S. mansoni* also occurs in the West Indies and in parts of South America. *S. japonicum* is present in China, Japan and Southeast Asia. These trematodes (blood flukes) do not often cause major disease of the skin, but skin lesions do occur at various stages of infestation.[1–13]

Invasion of the human host by the aquate cercarial stage may be associated with dermatitis (swimmer's itch).[3,9,11] This rash is erythematous, pruritic and urticarial, but eventually resolves to leave a pigmented spot. It is more often encountered with invasion of avian species.[3]

In schistosomiasis (bilharziasis) the mature worms may be associated non-specifically with erythematous itching macules at the time of release of large numbers of eggs. This probably represents a systemic reaction to antigen liberation. A more severe reaction seen particularly with

S. japonicum is Katayama disease or Yellow River fever. In addition to erythema, macules and pruriginous lesions, patients may also have fever, malaise, chills, sweats, arthralgias, headache, lymphadenopathy, hepatosplenomegaly and peripheral blood eosinophilia.[3]

Specific skin lesions are seen, usually around the genitalia and most often in women mainly before puberty, when ova are deposited there (*Fig. 11.104*). They appear as grouped solid papules, which subsequently become warty and vegetative resembling condyloma acuminatum (*Fig. 11.105*). The labia majora are often involved first. Occasionally progression to squamous cell carcinoma occurs. Periurethral granulomata due to schistosomes may be associated with thrombosis and necrosis, sometimes resulting in fistulation to the perineum ('watering

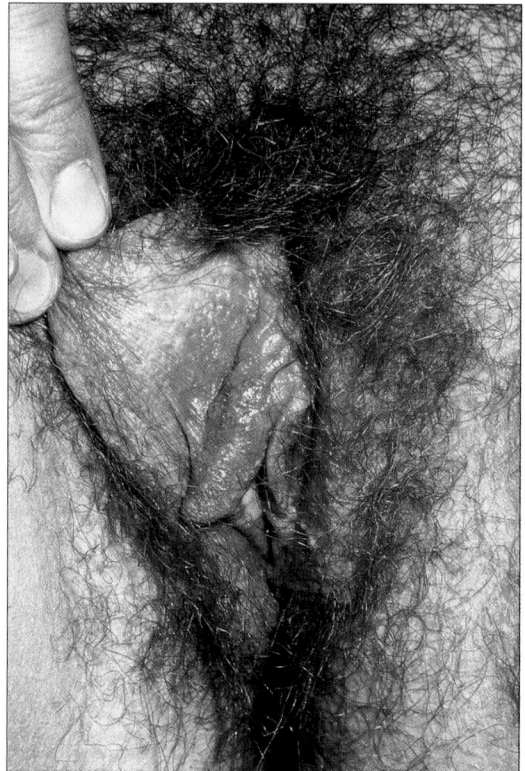

Fig. 11.104
Schistosomiasis: early lesion showing labial erythema and swelling. These features are a response to ova deposition. By courtesy of P. Dowd, MD, Middlesex Hospital, London, UK.

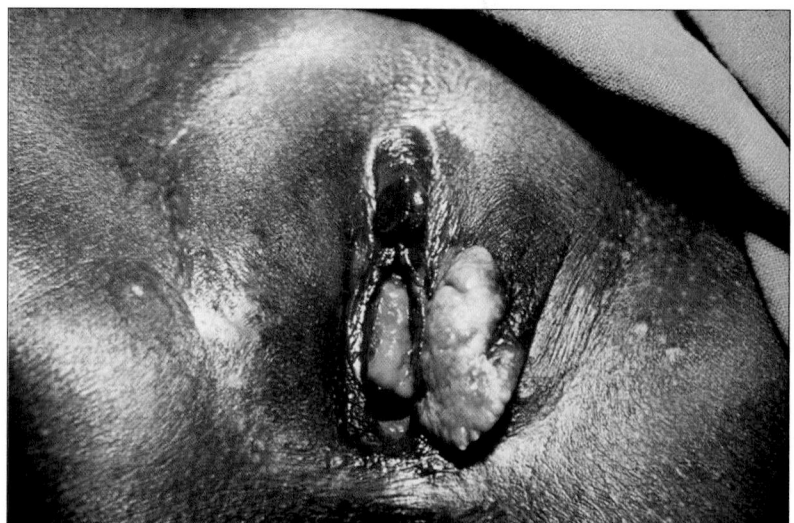

Fig. 11.105
Schistosomiasis: this warty pale nodule has almost completely replaced the left labium majus; other vulval manifestations include schistosomal condylomata, ulcers and rarely, vitiligo. By courtesy of the late M.S.R. Hutt, MD, St Thomas' Hospital, London, UK.

can perineum').[3] In late lesions prominent scarring may occur. More rarely, entrapped ova are seen in other areas of skin, but the means of their migration to those sites is not understood. Extragenital lesions of schistosomiasis have been described in the trunk, face and proximal lower limbs.[4,6,8] Facial lesions may be associated with ocular involvement.[8]

Pathogenesis and histological features

Part of the life cycle of schistosomes takes place in water snails. After their release, the cercariae penetrate the skin and migrate as schistosomes to the portal veins where they mature into adult male and female worms. Adult females then migrate to the mesenteric plexus (*S. mansoni* and *S. japonicum*) or vesical plexus (*S. haematobium*). Ova are deposited in the venules and the clinical and pathological sequelae are a direct consequence of the immunological response to their presence.

Eggs are released into the urine or feces where they hatch, releasing miracidia, which enter the snail host. Involvement of the female genital tract is usually due to *S. haematobium* and occurs as a consequence of worms being transported via anastomoses between the vesical and uterovaginal venous plexuses.

Histologically, adult worms are occasionally seen within the lumina of dilated deep dermal veins and lymphatics (*Fig. 11.106*). Viable ova may be present with a recognizable miracidial structure (*Fig. 11.107*). These

are usually located within abscesses containing numerous neutrophils and variable numbers of eosinophils. Poorly formed granulomata with Langhans' giant cells are also sometimes a feature. *S. haematobium* is recognized by its terminal spine (*Fig. 11.108*). The dead ova typically calcify and provoke a chronic, frequently granulomatous, inflammatory response. The overlying epidermis is usually acanthotic, sometimes to the point of pseudoepitheliomatous hyperplasia, and may occasionally contain intraepidermal ova undergoing transepidermal elimination (*Fig. 11.109*).

References

1. McKee, P.H., Wright, E., Hutt, M.S.R. (1983) Vulval schistosomiasis. *Clin Exp Dermatol*, **8**, 189–194.
2. Grossetete, G., Diabate, I., Pichard, E. et al (1989) Skin manifestations of bilharziasis. Apropos of 24 case reports in Mali. *Bull Soc Pathol Exot Fil*, **82**, 225–232.
3. Amer, M. (1982) Cutaneous schistosomiasis. *Int J Dermatol*, **21**, 44–46.
4. MacDonald, D.M., Morrison, J.G. (1976) Cutaneous ectopic schistosomiasis. *BMJ*, **2**, 619–620.
5. Adeyemi-Doro, F.A., Osboa, A.O., Junaid, T.A. (1979) Perigenital cutaneous schistosomiasis. *Br J Vener Dis*, **55**, 446–449.
6. Jacyk, W.K., Lawande, R.V., Tulpule, S.S. (1980) Unusual presentation of extragenital cutaneous *Schistosomiasis mansoni*. *Br J Dermatol*, **103**, 205–208.
7. Obasi, O.E. (1986) Cutaneous schistosomiasis in Nigeria. An update. *Br J Dermatol*, **114**, 597–602.
8. Milligan, A., Burns, D.A. (1988) Ectopic cutaneous schistosomiasis and schistosoma ocular inflammatory disease. *Br J Dermatol*, **119**, 793–798.
9. Amer, M. (1994) Cutaneous schistosomiasis. *Dermatol Clin*, **12**, 713–717.
10. Farrell, A.M., Woodrow, D., Bryceson, A.D. et al (1996) Ectopic cutaneous schistosomiasis: extragenital involvement with progressive upward spread. *Br J Dermatol*, **135**, 110–112.
11. Davis-Reed, L., Theis, J.H. (2000) Cutaneous schistosomiasis: report of a case and review of the literature. *J Am Acad Dermatol*, **42**, 678–680.
12. Kick, G., Schaller, M., Korting, H.C. (2000) Late cutaneous schistosomiasis representing an isolated skin manifestation of *Schistosoma mansoni* infection. *Dermatology*, **200**, 144–146.
13. Leman, J.A., Small, G., Wilks, D. et al (2001) Localized papular cutaneous schistosomiasis: two cases in travelers. *Clin Exp Dermatol*, **26**, 50–52.

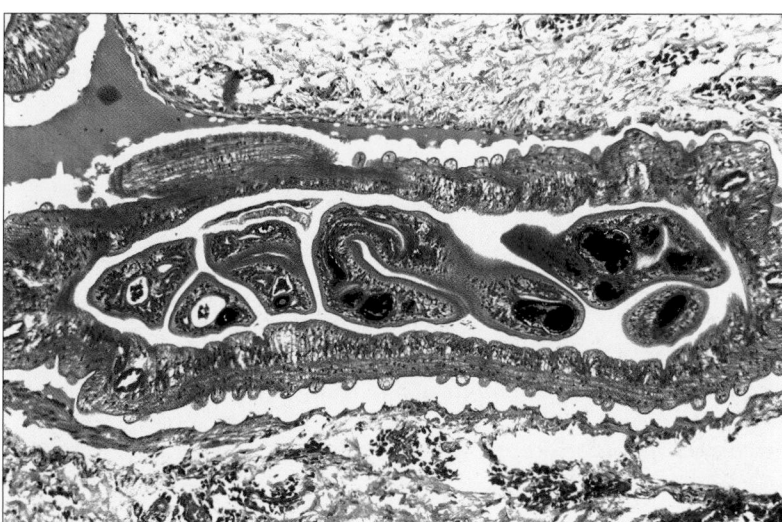

Fig. 11.106
Vulval schistosomiasis: adult worms within a dilated lymphatic; the male characteristically embraces the female in the gynecophoric canal.

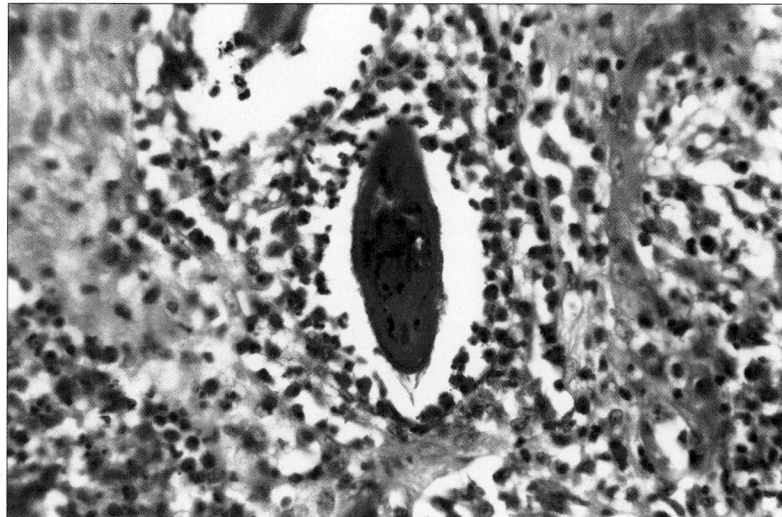

Fig. 11.108
Schistosoma hematobium: the terminal spine is characteristic of this species.

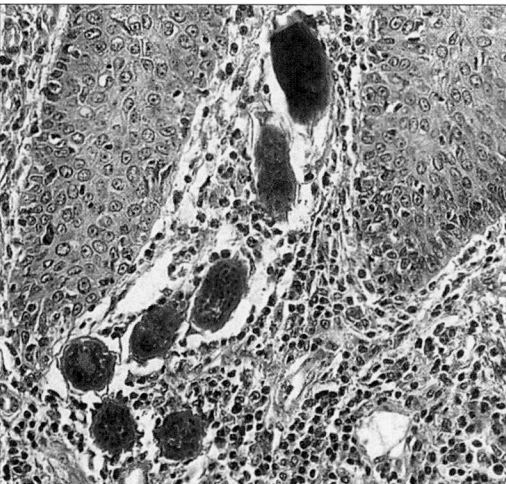

Fig. 11.107
Schistosomiasis: these ova are surrounded by a heavy chronic inflammatory cell infiltrate.

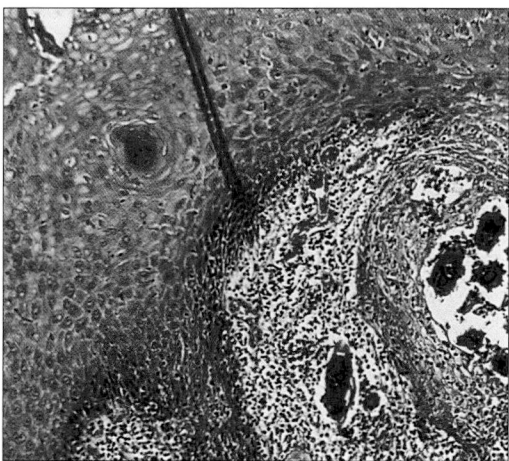

Fig. 11.109
Schistosomiasis: there is marked acanthosis. Intraepidermal ova are present on the right side.

Amebiasis cutis

Clinical features

Cutaneous lesions of *Entamoeba histolytica* are rare and more likely to occur in adults, although cases in children have been described.[1–4] These are most commonly seen after surgical treatment of intestinal or hepatic amebiasis, but may also occur by direct extension, perianally from the bowel or from hepatic involvement, and by direct inoculation of the skin from other infected lesions. Penile amebiasis may follow anal intercourse. Cutaneous lesions have been recorded on the trunk, buttocks, face (including the eyelid and the orbit), genitalia, perineum and on the legs.[3,5–8] The cervix is often affected in genital lesions.[9] Subcutaneous swellings called amebomas have been described.[6]

Lesions present as cutaneous ulcers with a central necrotic zone covered by a purulent exudate, an undermined margin and an erythematous halo. The ulcers are irregular, but sharply defined. They spread and do not heal spontaneously. They are extremely painful and may be destructive. Occasionally they resemble ulcerating tumors and are associated with surrounding verrucous lesions. Sometimes they mimic squamous cell carcinoma.[10]

Histological features

The trophozoites of *E. histolytica* are found within the purulent ulcer exudate and are best identified with PAS staining (*Figs 11.110–11.112*). They are distinguished by their tendency to phagocytose red cells. Trophozoites and cysts are usually found in the patient's feces. The organisms are surrounded by neutrophils, with some lymphocytes and plasma cells. The adjacent epidermis appears acanthotic and this may be marked or pseudoepitheliomatous in verrucous forms.

References

1. Cooke, R. (1986) The colorful people of Papua New Guinea. Some of their habits and some diseases which result from their habits. *Pathol Annual*, **21**, 311–346.
2. Saul, A. (1982) Amebiasis cutis. *Int J Dermatol*, **21**, 472–475.
3. Magana-Garcia, M., Arista-Viveros, A. (1993) Cutaneous amebiasis in children. *Pediatr Dermatol*, **10**, 352–355.
4. Brook, I. (1983) Cutaneous amebiasis. *Pediatrics*, **72**, 746.
5. Fujita, W.H., Barr, R.J., Gottschalk, H.R. (1981) Cutaneous amebiasis. *Arch Dermatol*, **117**, 309–310.
6. El-Zawahry, M., El-Kowy, M. (1973) Amebiasis cutis. *Int J Dermatol*, **12**, 305–307.
7. Baez Mendoza, J., Ramírez Barba, E.J. (1986) Cutaneous amebiasis of the face: a case report. *Am J Trop Med Hyg*, **35**, 69–71.
8. Beaver, P.C., Villegas, A.L., Cuello, C. et al (1978) Cutaneous amebiasis of the eyelid with extension into the orbit. *Am J Trop Med Hyg*, **27**, 1133–1136.

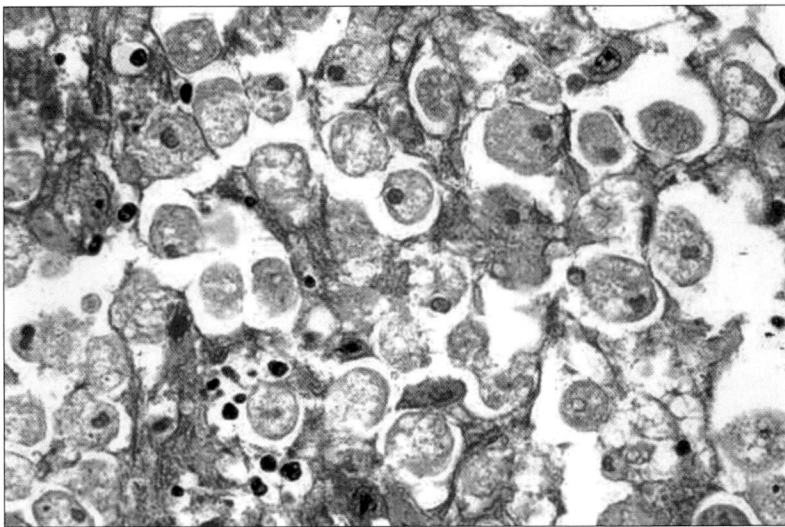

Fig. 11.111
Amebiasis: there are numerous trophozoites present. Note the ingested red blood cells.

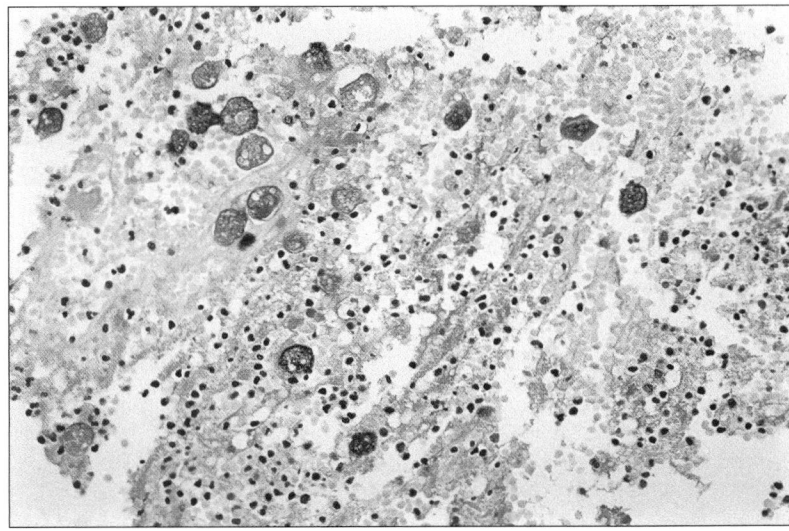

Fig. 11.112
Amebiasis: the trophozoites are strongly PAS positive.

9. Cohen, C. (1973) Three cases of amoebiasis of the cervix uteri. *J Obstet Gynaecol Br Common*, **80**, 476–480.
10. Majmudar, B., Chaiken, M.L., Lee, K.U. (1976) Amebiasis of clitoris mimicking carcinoma. *JAMA*, **236**, 1145–1146.

Malakoplakia

Clinical features

Malakoplakia (soft plaque) most often affects the urinary tract, but it can involve many other organs including the gastrointestinal system, lymph nodes, genitalia, brain, bone, lungs, adrenals and skin.[1–10] Cutaneous lesions may be dermal and/or subcutaneous and are most common around the genitalia (particularly the vulva) or perineum, but are occasionally seen at other sites.[2] Involvement of Bartholin's gland has also rarely been reported.[11] Cutaneous manifestations are variable and include papules, plaques, polyps, ulcers and sinuses. There may be associated malakoplakia at other sites.

Underlying or related conditions, which are usually associated with immunosuppression, include carcinoma, rheumatoid arthritis, systemic lupus erythematosus, leukemia, lymphoma and transplantation.[2,5,12] The skin lesions are non-progressive, but are typically persistent.

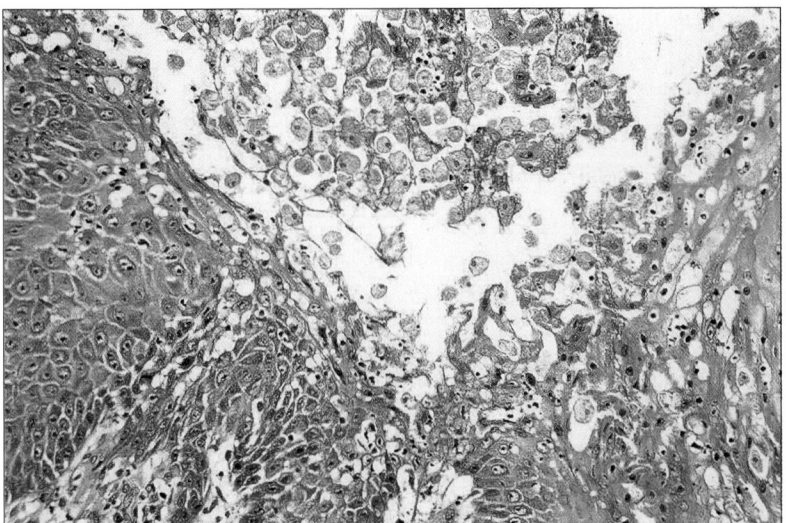

Fig. 11.110
Amebiasis: biopsy from a vulval ulcer, which developed as a result of direct spread from the anus.

Pathogenesis and histological features

Malakoplakia is characterized by confluent sheets of histiocytes with eosinophilic granular cytoplasm and small (usually eccentric) nuclei. There are characteristic cytoplasmic, calcified, von Kossa-positive inclusions known as Michaelis–Gutmann bodies (*Figs 11.113, 11.114*). These are sometimes laminated and this can be accentuated with PAS staining. They may also be positive on staining with Perl's reaction for iron. The Michaelis–Gutmann body is sufficiently distinctive to allow cytological distinction of malakoplakia in a preparation from a skin scraping.[13,14] The histiocytic infiltrate may be mixed with neutrophils, lymphocytes and plasma cells, with associated granulation tissue. Electron microscopy of malakoplakia shows the histiocytes to contain numerous phagolysosomes sometimes with intact and/or partly digested bacteria. It appears that the phagolysosomes accumulate in response to chronic bacterial infections. *Escherichia coli* is most often involved but the disorder may develop with other organisms, including *Staphylococcus aureus*. The cause of this condition is unknown but it most probably reflects impaired macrophage function.[1]

References

1. McClure, J. (1983) Malakoplakia. *J Pathol*, **140**, 275–330.
2. Palazzo, J.P., Ellison, D.J., Garcia, L.E. et al (1990) Cutaneous malakoplakia simulating relapsing malignant lymphoma. *J Cutan Pathol*, **17**, 171–175.
3. Chen, K.T.K., Hendricks, E.J. (1985) Malakoplakia of the female genital tract. *Obstet Gynecol*, **65**, 845–875.
4. Arul, K.J., Emerson, R.W. (1977) Malakoplakia of the skin. *Clin Exp Dermatol*, **2**, 131–135.
5. Nieland, M.L., Borochovitz, D., Silverman, A.R. et al (1981) Cutaneous malakoplakia. *Am J Dermatopathol*, **3**, 287–294.
6. Almagro, U.A., Choi, H., Caya, J.G. et al (1981) Cutaneous malakoplakia: report of a case and review of the literature. *Am J Dermatopathol*, **3**, 295–301.
7. Singh, M., Kaur, S., Vijpayer, B.K. et al (1987) Cutaneous malakoplakia with dermatomyositis. *Int J Dermatol*, **26**, 190–191.
8. Remond, B., Dompmartin, A., Moreau, A. et al (1994) Cutaneous malakoplakia. *Int J Dermatol*, **33**, 538–542.
9. Sarkell, B., Dannenberg, M., Blaylock, W.K. et al (1994) Cutaneous malakoplakia. *J Am Acad Dermatol*, **30**, 834–836.
10. Lowitt, M.H., Kariniemi, A-L., Niemi, K.M. et al (1996) Cutaneous malakoplakia: a report of two cases and review of the literature. *J Am Acad Dermatol*, **34**, 325–332.
11. Paquin, M.L., David, J.R., Weiner, S. (1986) Malakoplakia of Bartholin's gland. *Arch Pathol Lab Med*, **110**, 757–758.
12. Sian, C.S., McCabe, R.E., Lattes, C.G. (1981) Malakoplakia of skin and subcutaneous tissue in a renal transplant recipient. *Arch Dermatol*, **117**, 654–655.
13. Kumar, P.V., Tabbei, S.Z. (1988) Cutaneous malakoplakia diagnosed by scraping cytology. *Acta Cytol*, **32**, 125–127.
14. Sencer, O., Sencer, H., Uluoglu, O. et al (1979) Malakoplakia of the skin. Ultrastructure and quantitative X-ray microanalysis of Michaelis–Gutmann bodies. *Arch Pathol Lab Med*, **103**, 446–450.

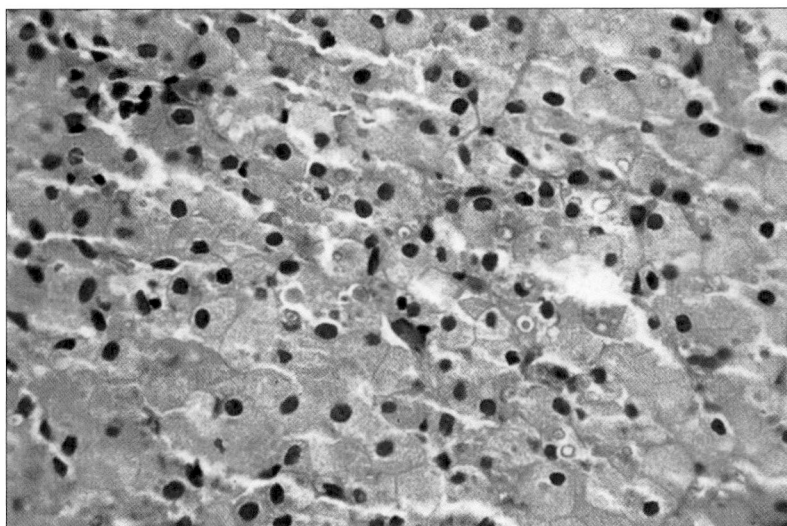

Fig. 11.113
Malakoplakia: the infiltrate consists of histiocytes with eosinophilic cytoplasm. Note the pale blue, laminated Michaelis–Gutmann bodies.

Miscellaneous conditions

Vestibulitis

The term vestibulitis is a misnomer and it is now accepted that it is not an inflammatory dermatosis as was once thought. The inflammatory changes seen on biopsy are non-specific and may also be found in a healthy normal vestibular epithelium.[1-4] Vestibulitis is now recognized as a sensory disorder best categorized as a chronic pain syndrome, and although vestibular dysesthesia is a more accurate description, the term 'vulvodynia' is sometimes used. There is no relationship to HPV infection or chronic candidal infection.[5,6] It is characterized by a constellation of symptoms and signs which include secondary dyspareunia and point tenderness in the vestibule (particularly at 5 and 7 o'clock over the opening to the greater vestibular glands of Bartholin); variable erythema may also be present at these sites (*Fig. 11.115*).[7] In a study to validate these criteria, however, erythema was found to be an unreliable clinical sign.[8]

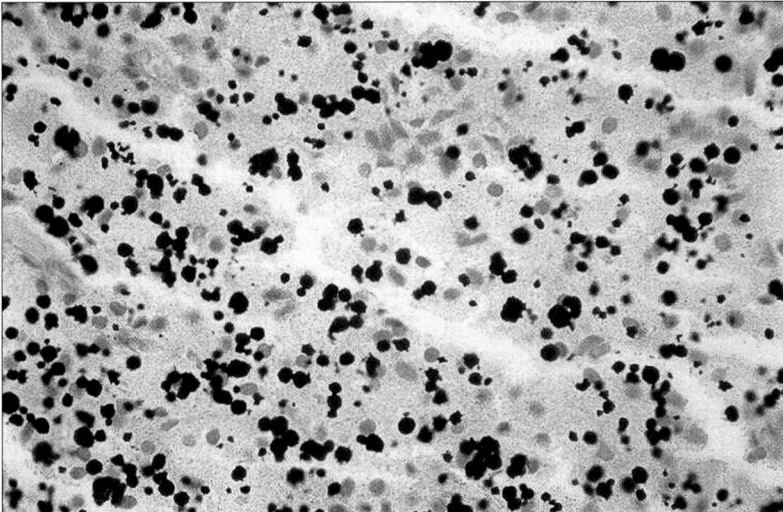

Fig. 11.114
Malakoplakia: the Michaelis–Gutmann bodies can be highlighted with the von Kossa reaction.

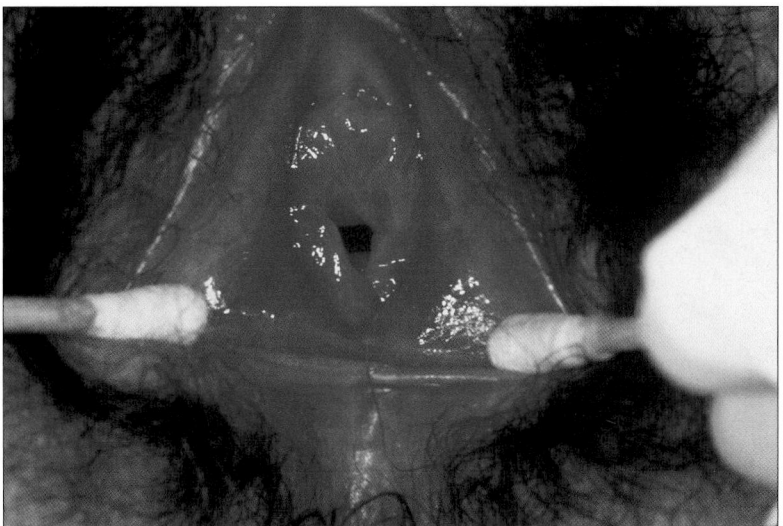

Fig. 11.115
Vestibulitis: there is marked vulval erythema. By courtesy of C. Furlonge, MD, Port of Spain, Trinidad.

References

1. Pyka, R., Wilkinson, E.J., Friedrich, E.G. Jr et al (1988) The histopathology of vulvar vestibulitis syndrome. *Int J Gynecol Pathol*, **7**, 249–257.
2. Furlonge, C.B., Thin, R.N., Evans, B.E. et al (1991) Vulvar vestibulitis syndrome: a clinicopathological study. *Br J Obstet Gynaecol*, **98**, 703–706.
3. O'Keefe, R.J., Scurry, J., Dennerstein, G. et al (1995) Audit of 114 non-neoplastic vulval biopsies. *Br J Obstet Gynaecol*, **102**, 780–786.
4. Nylander Lundqvist, E., Hofer, P-A., Olofsson, J.I. et al (1997) Is vulval vestibulitis an inflammatory condition? A comparison of histological findings in affected and healthy women. *Acta Derm Venereol*, **77**, 319–322.
5. Moyal-Barracco, M., Leibowitch, M., Orth, G. (1990) Vestibular papillae of the vulva. Lack of evidence for human papilloma virus etiology. *Arch Dermatol*, **126**, 1594–1598.
6. Wilkinson, E.J., Guerrero, E., Daniel, R. et al (1993) Vulvar vestibulitis is rarely associated with human papilloma virus infection types 6, 11, 16, or 18. *Int J Gynecol Pathol*, **12**, 344–349.
7. Friedrich, E.G. (1987) Vulvar vestibulitis syndrome. *J Reprod Med*, **32**, 110–114.
8. Bergeron, S., Binik, Y., Khalife, S. et al (2001) Vulvar vestibulitis syndrome: reliability of diagnosis and evaluation of current diagnostic criteria. *Obstet Gynecol*, **98**, 45–51.

Idiopathic calcinosis

Clinical features

Genital calcinosis is uncommon. It occurs much more frequently in the scrotum than in the vulva where it has only seldom been reported.[1–6] Very rarely, idiopathic calcinosis may develop in the penis or areola of the nipple.[7,8] Lesions present as single or multiple hard nodules in children and young adults (*Fig. 11.116*). Occasional nodules break down and discharge a chalky material. Some lesions are polypoid and in this setting the clinical diagnosis is difficult if only a single lesion is present.[9,10] Very young children can exceptionally present with single or multiple calcified scrotal lesions secondary to meconium periorchitis.[11,12]

Pathogenesis and histological features

Although originally thought to represent an idiopathic condition, it is now clear that this disorder develops from dystrophic calcification of epidermoid cysts or the contents of cystically dilated eccrine ducts.[13–18] Scrotal calcinosis is characterized by single or multiple dermal nodules of dystrophic calcification (*Fig. 11.117*). In some cases, there is histological evidence of a pre-existing and partially destroyed cyst.

References

1. Shapiro, L., Platt, N., Torres-Rodriguez, V.M. (1970) Idiopathic calcinosis of the scrotum. *Arch Dermatol*, **102**, 199–204.
2. Moss, R.L., Shewmake, S.W. (1981) Idiopathic calcinosis of the scrotum. *Int J Dermatol*, **20**, 134–136.
3. Song, D.H., Lee, K.H., Kang, W.H. (1988) Idiopathic calcinosis of the scrotum: histopathologic observations of fifty-one nodules. *J Am Acad Dermatol*, **19**, 1095–1101.
4. Gormally, S., Dorman, T., Powell, F.C. (1992) Calcinosis of the scrotum. *Int J Dermatol*, **31**, 75–79.
5. Jamaleddine, F.N., Salman, S.M., Shbaklo, Z. et al (1988) Idiopathic vulvar calcinosis: the counterpart of idiopathic scrotal calcinosis. *Cutis*, **41**, 273–275.
6. Balfour, P.J.T., Vincenti, A.C. (1991) Idiopathic vulvar calcinosis. *Histopathology*, **18**, 183–184.
7. Katoh, N., Okabayashi, K., Wakabayashi, S. et al (1993) Dystrophic calcinosis of the penis. *J Dermatol*, **20**, 114–117.
8. Oh, C.K., Kwon, K.S., Cho, S.H. et al (2000) Idiopathic calcinosis of the areola of the nipple. *J Dermatol*, **27**, 121–122.
9. Dekio, S., Tsukazaki, N., Jidoi, J. (1989) Idiopathic calcinosis of the scrotum presenting as a solitary pedunculated tumour. *Clin Exp Dermatol*, **14**, 60–61.
10. Polk, P., McCutchen, W.T., Phillips, J.G. et al (1996) Polypoid scrotal calcinosis: an uncommon variant of scrotal calcinosis. *South Med J*, **89**, 896–897.
11. Dehner, L.P., Scott, D., Stocker, J.T. (1986) Meconium periorchitis: a clinicopathologic study of four cases with a review of the literature. *Hum Pathol*, **17**, 807–812.
12. Mene, M., Rosenberg, H.K., Ginsberg, P.C. (1994) Meconium periorchitis presenting as scrotal nodules in a five year old boy. *J Ultrasound Med*, **13**, 491–494.
13. Wright, S., Navsaria, H., Leigh, I.M. (1991) Idiopathic scrotal calcinosis is idiopathic. *J Am Acad Dermatol*, **24**, 727–730.
14. Dini, M., Colafranceschi, M. (1998) Should scrotal calcinosis still be termed idiopathic? *Am J Dermatopathol*, **20**, 399–402.
15. Saad, A.G., Zaatari, G.S. (2001) Scrotal calcinosis: is it idiopathic? *Urology*, **57**, 365.
16. Swinehart, J.M., Golitz, L.E. (1982) Scrotal calcinosis. Dystrophic calcification of epidermoid cysts. *Arch Dermatol*, **118**, 985–988.
17. Dare, A.J., Axelsen, R.A. (1988) Scrotal calcinosis: origin from dystrophic calcification of eccrine duct milia. *J Cutan Pathol*, **15**, 142–149.
18. Ito, A., Sakamoto, F., Ito, M. (2001) Dystrophic scrotal calcinosis originating from benign eccrine epithelial cysts. *Br J Dermatol*, **144**, 146–150.

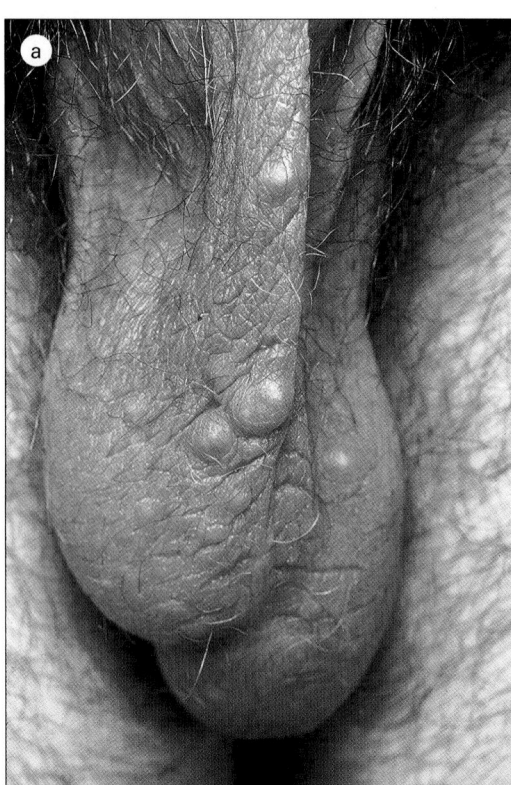

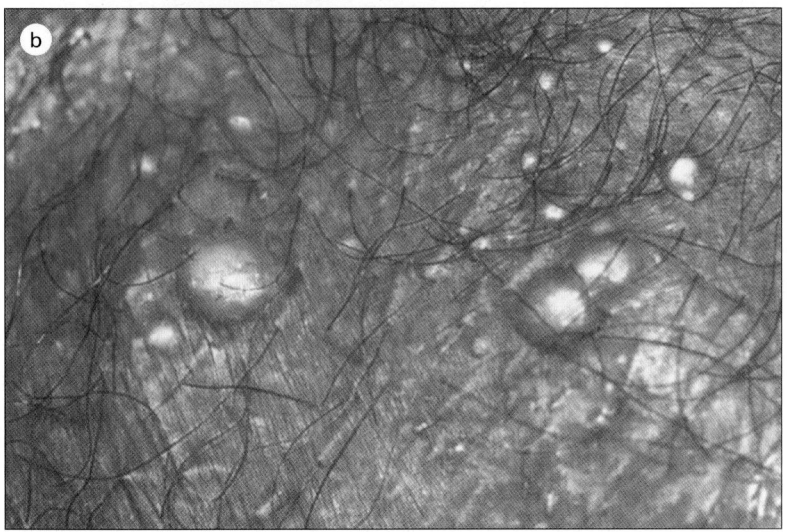

Fig. 11.116
Scrotal calcinosis: (a) characteristic yellow papules and nodules are present; (b) close-up view of the lesions. By courtesy of the Institute of Dermatology, London, UK.

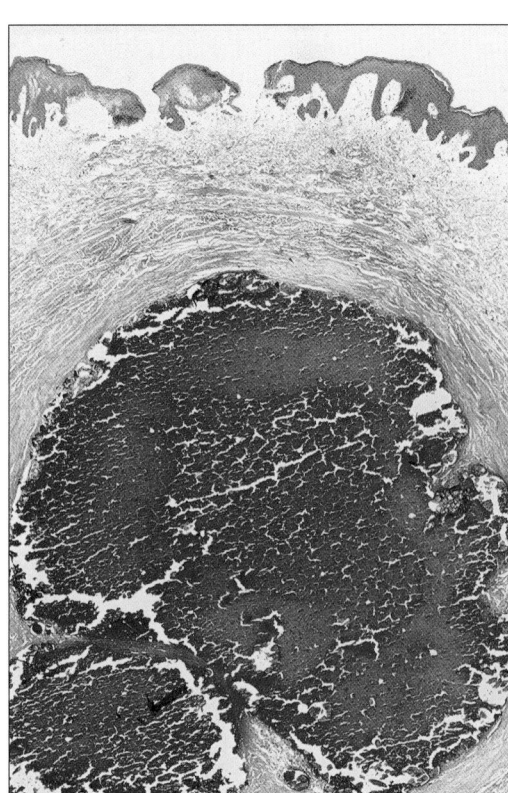

Fig. 11.117
Scrotal calcinosis: the calcium deposits stain purple with hematoxylin and eosin. Sometimes a pre-existent epidermoid cyst can be identified.

Sclerosing lipogranuloma

Clinical features

Sclerosing lipogranuloma (paraffinoma) may involve the scrotum and penis.[1,2] It represents a tissue response to exogenous material (usually paraffin or silicone) and is seen most commonly in the paratesticular area secondary to the injection of size-enhancing materials. Granulomatous penile nodules (Tanko's nodules) have been described due to the insertion of glass spheres under the penile skin.[3] The topic is discussed in greater depth on page 351.

Histological features

There is a foreign body-type granulomatous reaction in the dermis. 'Lipid' vacuoles are surrounded by dense fibrous tissue.

References

1.　Oertel, Y.C., Johnson, F.B. (1977) Sclerosing lipogranuloma of male genitalia. *Arch Pathol*, **101**, 321–326.
2.　Claudy, A., Garcier, F., Schmitt, D. (1981) Sclerosing lipogranulomata of the male genitalia: ultrastructural study. *Br J Dermatol*, **105**, 451–455.
3.　Serour, F. (1993) Artificial nodules of the penis. Report of six cases among Russian immigrants in Israel. *Sex Transm Dis*, **20**, 192–193.

Pilonidal sinus of the penis

This condition mainly occurs in the sacrococcygeal region and has only rarely been reported as occurring in the penis.[1–3] Only 14 cases have been reported in the literature. Lesions present in uncircumcised adults with a predilection for the dorsal aspect of the coronal sulcus. It has been postulated that penile pilonidal sinus develops because the coronal sulcus acts as a cleft where hairs can accumulate and eventually penetrate the shaft and the foreskin as a result of friction between these two surfaces. The symptoms are those of chronic inflammation and abscess formation. Pilonidal sinus has been associated with actinomycosis, squamous cell carcinoma and verrucous carcinoma.[1,4,5]

The histopathology is identical to that of pilonidal sinus occurring elsewhere (see p. 1679).

References

1.　Val-Bernal, J.F., Azcarretazabal, T., Garijo, M.F. (1999) Pilonidal sinus of the penis. A report of two cases, one of them associated with actinomycosis. *J Cutan Pathol*, **26**, 155–158.
2.　Yates-Bell, A.J. (1968) Pilonidal sinus in urology. *Br J Urol*, **40**, 468–471.
3.　Ritchie, J.D. (1975) Pilonidal sinus of the prepuce. *Br J Urol*, **47**, 580.
4.　Kim, Y.A., Thomas, I. (1993) Metastatic squamous cell carcinoma arising in a pilonidal sinus. *J Am Acad Dermatol*, **29**, 272–274.
5.　Norris, C.S. (1983) Giant condyloma acuminatum (Buschke–Löwenstein tumor) involving a pilonidal sinus. A case report and review of the literature. *J Surg Oncol*, **22**, 47–50.

Pigmented lesions

Melanocytic lesions are not the only cause of genital pigmentation. Post-inflammatory hyperpigmentation following inflammatory dermatosis such as lichen planus is much more commonly encountered. However, only melanocytic genital lesions are discussed in this section.

Genital melanosis

Clinical features

This condition of the genital skin is characterized by pigmentation with no evidence of a preceding inflammatory dermatosis.[1–5] The pigmentation may vary in its intensity and is typically irregular. The problem usually affects several sites including cutaneous and mucosal surfaces. The pigmentation develops slowly and can be very extensive.

Unifocal lesions can also sometimes occur. Small discrete single or multiple lesions are usually described as genital melanotic macules.[4] The commonest sites are the glans and shaft of the penis and the inner aspects of the vulva including the vestibule (*Figs 11.118, 11.119*). Lesions may also affect the vagina and cervix.[6,7]

The condition is considered benign but there are rare anecdotal reports of melanoma ensuing in areas of melanosis.[8] This, however, has only been described in penile melanosis. Melanoma only rarely occurs in the context of vulval melanosis and this is likely to be due to the fact that in the latter condition there is no increase in the number of melanocytes but only basal cell layer hyperpigmentation. Penile lesions, on the other hand, often display an increase in the number of basal melanocytes. Single lesions are very difficult to distinguish on clinical grounds from either a lentigo or an early junctional nevus.

Cases of multiple genital lesions associated with oral pigmentation have been described as Laugier–Hunziker disease (idiopathic lenticular mucocutaneous pigmentation).[9,10] It is worth remembering that rare cases of Carney's complex may present with lentigines in genital skin and the correct diagnosis will only be possible if close attention is paid to the presence of other markers of this disease (see p. 1015).[11,12]

Histological features

Genital melanosis is characterized by increased pigmentation of basal keratinocytes and melanocytes (*Fig. 11.120*). By definition, there is no increase in melanocyte number. If, however, melanocytes are present in increased numbers, the term 'genital lentiginosis' may be more appropriate.[13] In real terms, the difference is academic. There is no evidence of junctional activity or cytological atypia. Pigment-laden macrophages may be conspicuous in the underlying dermis.

References

1.　Revuz, J., Clerici, T. (1989) Penile melanosis. *J Am Acad Dermatol*, **20**, 567–570.
2.　Barnhill, R.L., Alber, L.S., Shama, S.K. et al (1990) Genital lentiginosis: a clinical and histopathologic study. *J Am Acad Dermatol*, **22**, 453–460.

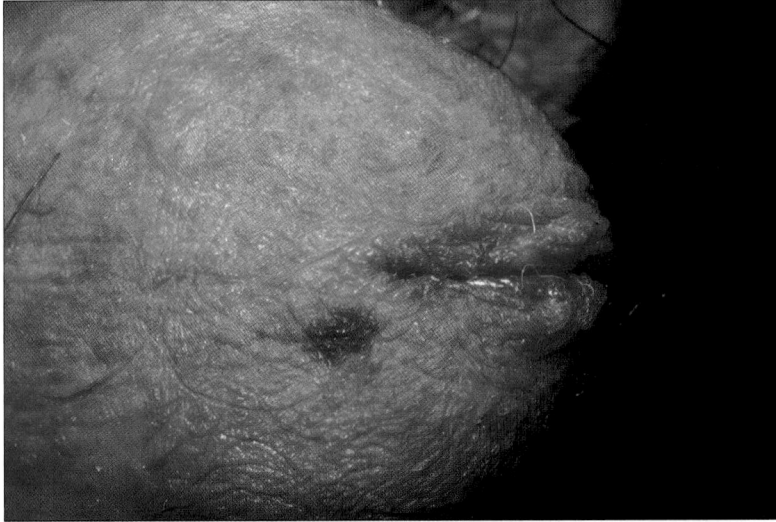

Fig. 11.118
Penile melanotic macule: there is a small irregular pigmented macule on the glans penis. By courtesy of the Institute of Dermatology, London, UK.

3. Estrada, R., Kaufman, R. (1993) Benign vulvar melanosis. *J Reprod Med*, **38**, 5–8.
4. Lenane, P., Keane, C.O., Connell, B.O. et al (2000) Genital melanotic macules: clinical, histologic, immunohistochemical, and ultrastructural features. *J Am Acad Dermatol*, **42**, 640–644.
5. Kanj, L.F., Rubeiz, N.G., Mrouett, A.M. et al (1992) Vulvar melanosis and lentiginosis: a case report. *J Am Acad Dermatol*, **27**, 777–778.
6. Sison-Torre, E.Q., Ackerman, A.B. (1985) Melanosis of the vagina. *Am J Dermatopathol*, **7**, 51–60.
7. Karney, M.Y., Cassidy, M.S., Zahn, C.M. et al (2001) Melanosis of the vagina. A case report. *J Reprod Med*, **46**, 389–391.
8. Testori, A., Mazzarol, G., Viale, G. et al (1999) Medical decision making for melanoma of the glans penis. *J Exp Clin Cancer Res*, **18**, 219–221.
9. Laugier, P., Hunziker, N., Olmos, L. (1977) Pigmentation melanique lenticulare essentialle de la muqueuse jugale et des levres. *Ann Dermatol Venereol*, **104**, 181–184.
10. Gerbig, A.W., Hunziker, T. (1996) Idiopathic lenticular mucocutaneous pigmentation or Laugier–Hunziker syndrome with atypical features. *Arch Dermatol*, **32**, 844–845.
11. Reed, O.M., Mellette, J.R., Fitzpatrick, J.E. (1986) Cutaneous lentiginosis with atrial myxomas. *J Am Acad Dermatol*, **15**, 398–402.
12. Rhodes, A.R., Silverman, R.A., Harrist, T.J. et al (1986) Mucocutaneous lentigines, cardiomuco-cutaneous myxomas and multiple blue nevi: the LAMB syndrome. *J Am Acad Dermatol*, **10**, 72–82.
13. Breathnach, A.S., Balus, L., Amantea, A. (1992) Penile lentiginosis. An ultrastructural study. *Pigment Cell Res*, **5**, 404–413.

Genital melanocytic nevi

Clinical features

Junctional, compound and dermal nevi can all occur on the male and female genitalia and may demonstrate worrisome histological features, often raising the possibility of malignancy.[1–5] Melanocytic lesions presenting in flexural areas (atypical genital nevi, atypical flexural nevi, milk-line nevi, atypical melanocytic nevi of genital type), including the axillae, umbilicus, inguinal creases, pubis, scrotum and perianal area, similarly may show identical disturbing histological features.[5]

The prevalence of vulval nevi is uncertain but has been reported as 2.3% in one series.[1] Most lesions present in young women and vary in size from a few millimeters to up to 1 centimeter (*Figs 11.121, 11.122*). Young girls may also be affected. Lesions are typically located on the labia minora, mucosal surface of the clitoris or labia majora. Atypical genital nevi should not be confused with dysplastic nevi, which may also present on the external genitalia, particularly the labia majora.[3] Melanocytic lesions on male genital organs are much less common than those in females.

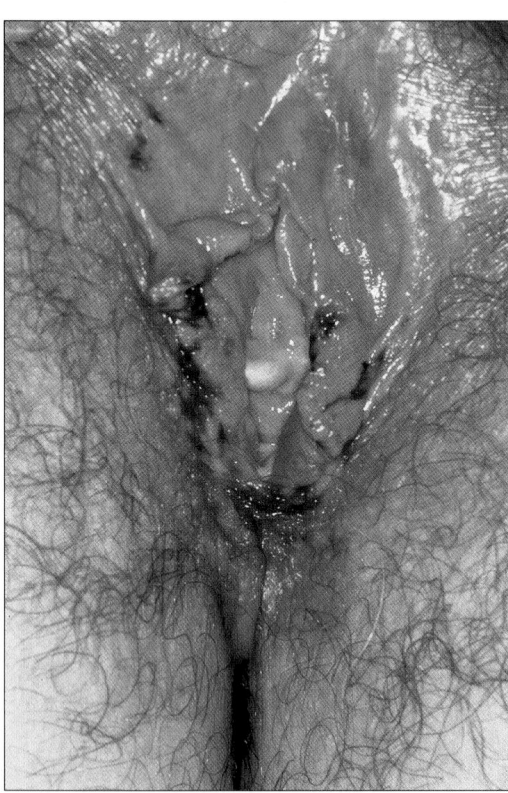

Fig. 11.119
Vulval melanosis: there are multiple irregular pigmented macules on the vulva and adjacent skin. By courtesy of the Institute of Dermatology, London, UK.

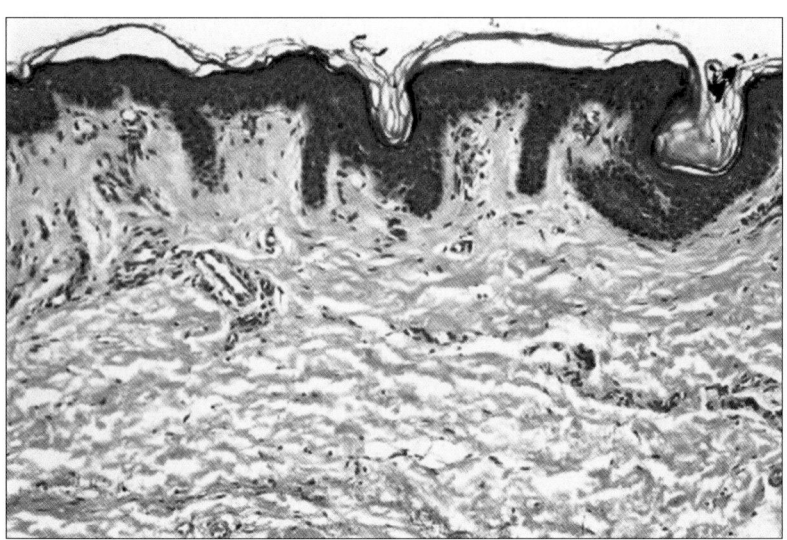

Fig. 11.120
Vulval melanosis: there is marked basal cell pigmentation.

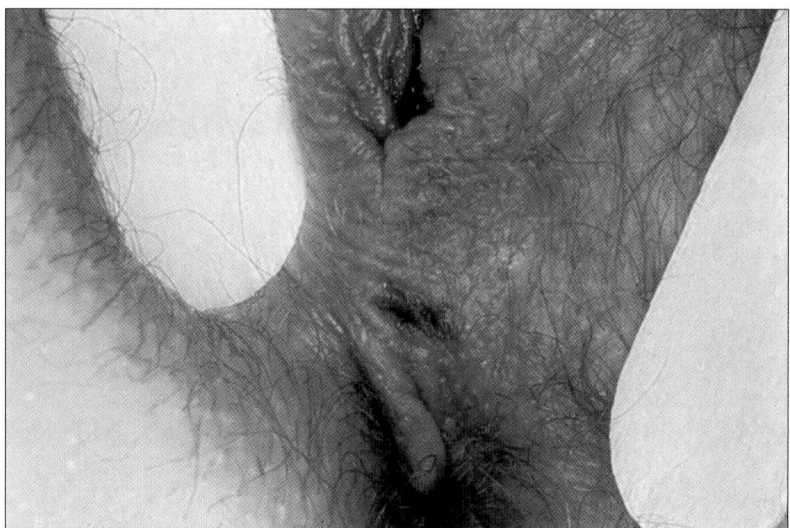

Fig. 11.121
Atypical vulval nevus: there is an irregular darkly pigmented lesion on the perineum. By courtesy of the Institute of Dermatology, London, UK.

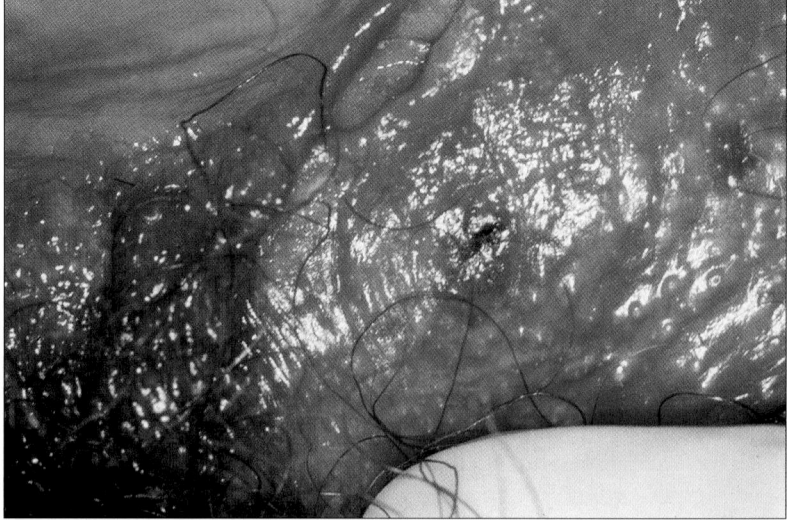

Fig. 11.122
Atypical vulval nevus: there is a small, irregular and variably pigmented melanocytic lesion on the labium minus. By courtesy of the Institute of Dermatology, London, UK.

Histological features

Banal (ordinary type) and dysplastic nevi are identical to their non-genital counterparts and are discussed on pages 1252 and 1286.

Atypical genital nevi can be a source of considerable diagnostic difficulty and sometimes alarm. Flexural nevi at other sites are often similar although the changes are usually less marked. They may be junctional or compound, symmetrical or asymmetrical, and are typically fairly small, measuring only a few millimeters in diameter. The associated epidermis is typically hyperplastic and papillomatosis is often marked (*Fig. 11.123*). The junctional component is usually lentiginous and nested and commonly involves the adnexae in addition to the epidermis. The nests are often large, surrounded by a retraction artifact and, unlike banal nevi, are situated along the sides in addition to the tips of the rete;

they may also be located overlying the dermal papillae (*Fig. 11.124*). Transepidermal elimination of nests is commonly present and some degree of pagetoid spread may be a feature.[6] The nevus cells are epithelioid in type and often atypical (*Figs 11.125–11.127*). The dermal component is composed of morphologically similar nevus cells, which mature with depth. The cytological atypia can affect both junctional and dermal components and in some cases is severe. These features, in addition to dermal mitoses, which are not uncommonly present, may be extreme and raise the possibility of melanoma. Genital melanoma is, however, generally a condition of elderly women. Although the biological potential of these lesions is poorly documented in the literature, they are likely to be benign. Nevertheless, incompletely excised nevi or lesions which extend very close to the radial margin would be best re-excised.

Although there may be some overlap with genital dysplastic nevi, the latter can be distinguished by the presence of elongation of the rete ridges, a more lentiginous distribution of the melanocytes, and the induction of lamellar and eosinophilic fibrosis in the papillary dermis in association with a variable mononuclear inflammatory cell infiltrate and pigmentary incontinence.

Any other type of nevi may occur on genital skin including Spitz nevus, Reed nevus, deep penetrating nevus and blue nevus. Recently, a

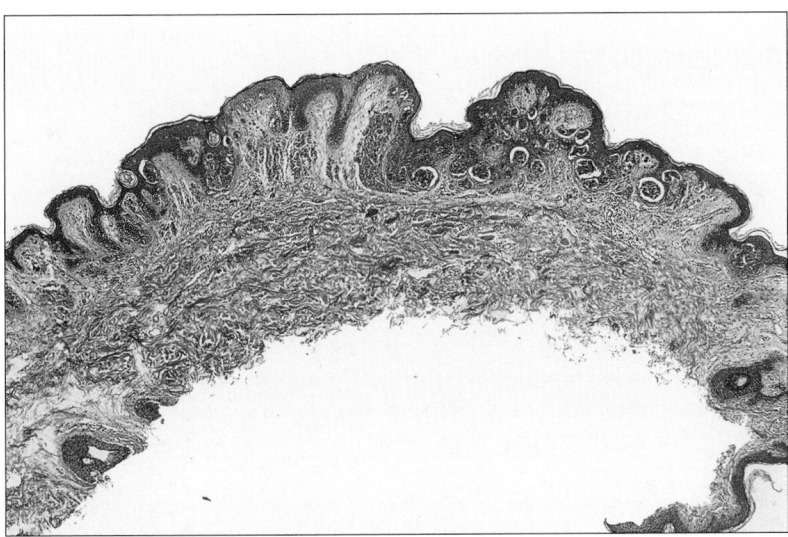

Fig. 11.123
Atypical genital type nevus: this is a shave biopsy from the labium majus showing a compound melanocytic nevus. The papillomatosis and obvious retraction artifact around the junctional nests are typical features.

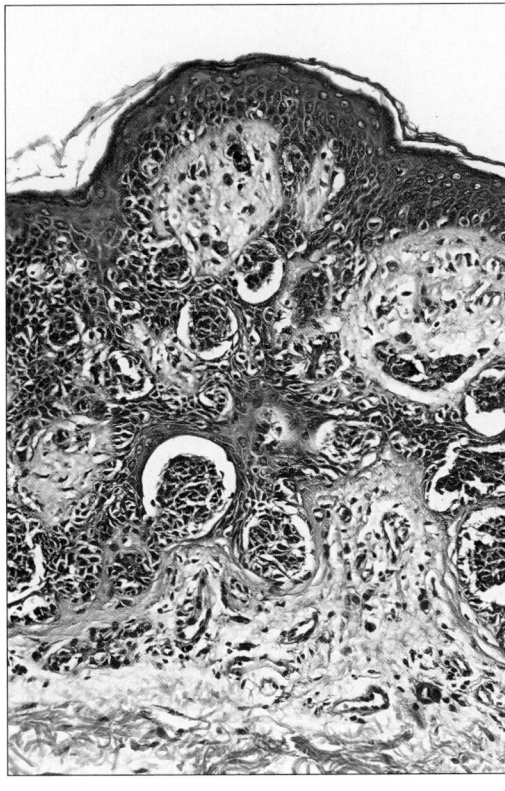

Fig. 11.124
Atypical genital type nevus: high power view highlighting the retraction artifact.

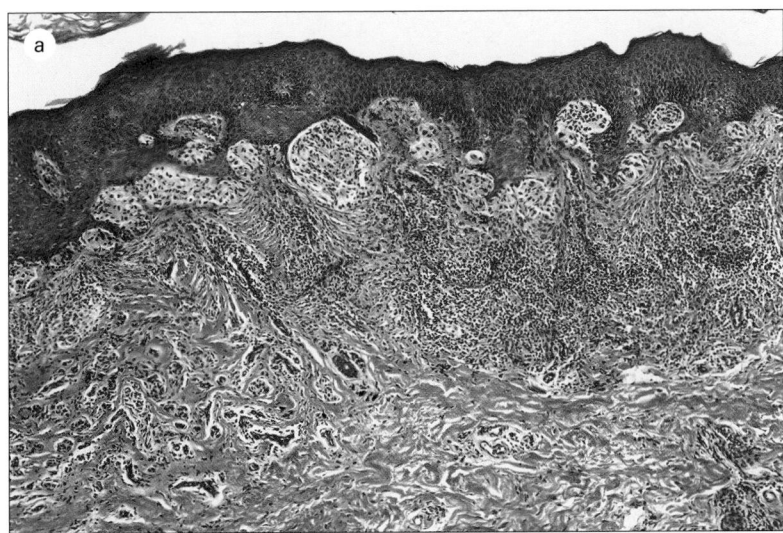

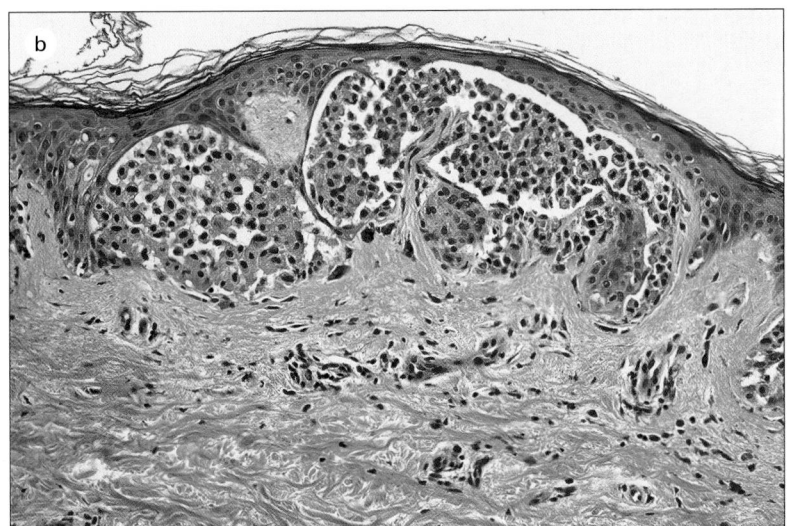

Fig. 11.125
(a, b) Atypical genital type nevus: in this example the junctional nests are large and due to fine melanin pigmentation; the cytoplasm has a grayish hue. Note the nuclear hyperchromatism.

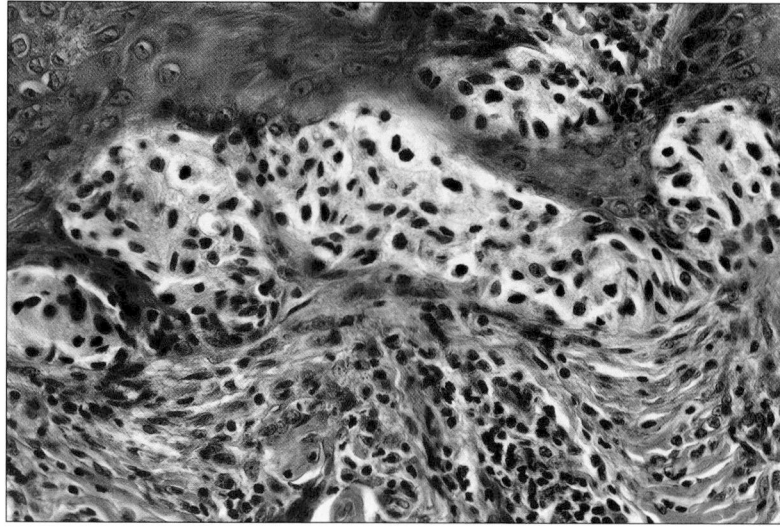

Fig. 11.126
Atypical genital type nevus: in this field, there is nuclear hyperchromatism and mild pleomorphism.

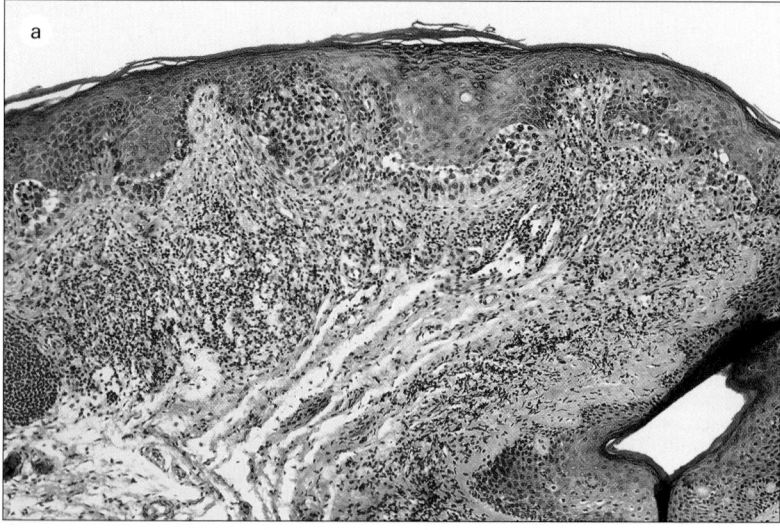

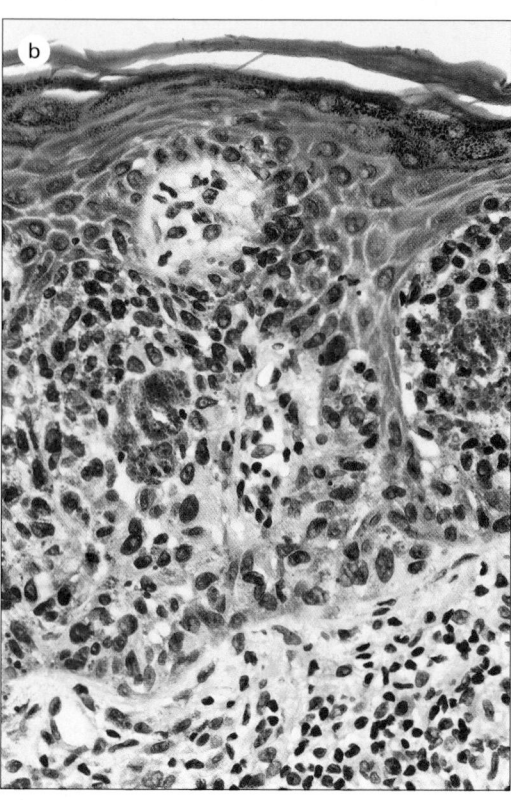

Fig. 11.127
(a, b) Atypical genital type nevus: this example from the vulva of a 20-year-old female shows severe cytological atypia. The biological behavior of this nevus variant is uncertain although the likelihood of malignancy is very low. It should, however, be completely excised.

small series of epithelioid blue nevi of genital skin in patients with no evidence of Carney's complex was reported.[7] These lesions were described on the foreskin and labium minus.

References

1. Rock, B., Hood, A.F., Rock, J.A. (1990) Prospective study of vulvar nevi. *J Am Acad Dermatol*, **22**, 104–106.
2. Christensen, W.N., Friedman, K.J., Woodruff, J.D. et al (1987) Histologic characteristics of vulvar nevocellular nevi. *J Cutan Pathol*, **14**, 87–91.
3. Clark, W.H. Jr, Hood, A.F., Tucker, M.A. et al (1998) Atypical melanocytic nevi of the genital type with a discussion of reciprocal parenchymal–stromal interactions in the biology of neoplasia. *Hum Pathol*, **29** (1 Suppl. 1), S1–S24.
4. Blessing, K. (1999) Benign atypical naevi: diagnostic difficulties and continued controversy. *Histopathology*, **34**, 189–198.
5. Rongioletti, F., Ball, R.A., Marcus, R. et al (2000) Histopathological features of flexural melanocytic nevi: a study of 40 cases. *J Cutan Pathol*, **27**, 215–217.
6. Haupt, H.M., Stern, J.B. (1995) Pagetoid melanocytosis: histologic features in benign and malignant lesions. *Am J Surg Pathol*, **19**, 792–797.
7. Izquierdo, M.J., Pastor, M.A., Carrasco, L. et al (2001) Epithelioid blue naevus of the genital mucosa: report of four cases. *Br J Dermatol*, **145**, 496–501.

Melanoma

Clinical features

Female genital melanoma is rare and accounts for around 3% of all female melanomas and 2–10% of female genital tract malignancies.[1-15] The vulva is the most frequently involved site followed by the vagina and much less often the cervix (*Fig. 11.128*).[5,6,8,10,11,16] The labia majora and the clitoris are the most commonly affected sites.[16] Most patients present in the sixth and seventh decades of life.[17] Less than a third of cases occur in patients younger than 50 years of age. Melanoma of the vulva in children has only been very exceptionally reported.[18]

Clinical presentation varies from flat to raised polypoid brown to black lesions. Ulceration may be present. Less commonly, patients complain of pruritus and/or bleeding. Amelanotic melanomas may clinically mimic squamous cell carcinoma or extramammary Paget's disease. In a recent large Swedish cohort of 219 patients, 27% of vulval melanomas were amelanotic.[16]

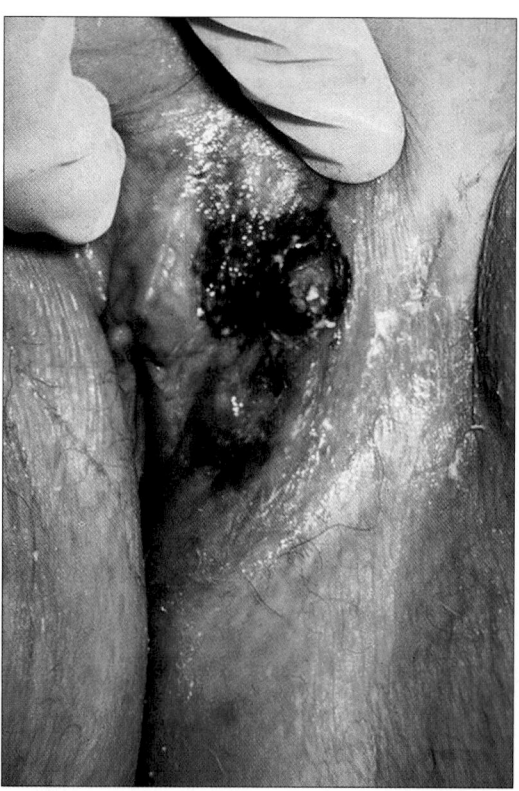

Fig. 11.128
Vulval melanoma: tumors at this site are very rare. They are commonly thick at presentation and therefore generally associated with a poor prognosis. By courtesy of M. Ridley, MD, Institute of Dermatology, London, UK.

Some tumors arise within a pre-existing nevus. A recent study found the latter to occur in around 5% of cases.[16] Most of these are of the superficial spreading type.

The 5-year survival varies enormously, ranging from 15 to 54%.[4-13,19,20] The largest study of vulval melanoma recently published reported a 5-year survival rate of 47%.[21] As with melanomas presenting elsewhere, tumor thickness is the best predictor of survival.[21] Staging has also been found to be an independent predictor of survival.[21] In addition, in stage I disease only, ulceration and the presence of clinical amelanosis were found to be independent predictors of survival.[21] Radical surgery for vulval melanoma does not seem to influence outcome.

Melanomas of the male genital skin are very rare, as are those arising around or on the anus (*Fig. 11.129*).[22-25] The commonest site in men is the glans but rare cases may present elsewhere, including the shaft and the scrotum.[26-28] An exceptional case complicating penile melanosis, and a penile melanoma which developed simultaneously with squamous cell carcinoma have been reported.[29,30] Because of the rarity of the disease, estimation of prognosis is difficult. In the few cases reported, the prognosis appears poor but this seems to be related to late presentation, delay in diagnosis and problems in achieving complete clearance because of the site involved.[25] It is likely that prognosis is related to depth of involvement similar to melanomas occurring elsewhere.

Histological features

Histological features of genital melanoma are identical to melanomas elsewhere and are not discussed further. Until recently, there was no consensus as to the most common type of genital melanoma. Recently, however, a large study found that 57% of vulval melanomas were mucosal lentiginous, 22% nodular, 12% unclassified and 4% superficial spreading.[16] Desmoplastic and neurotropic variants may also be occasionally encountered.

References

1. Giles, G.G., Kneale, B.L. (1995) Vulvar cancer: the Cinderella of gynaecological oncology. *Aust N Z J Obstet Gynaecol*, **35**, 71–75.
2. Pannizon, R.G. (1996) Vulvar melanoma. *Semin Dermatol*, **15**, 67–70.
3. Raber, G., Mempel, V., Jackisch, C. et al (1996) Malignant melanoma of the vulva. Report of 89 patients. *Cancer*, **78**, 2353–2358.
4. Morrow, C.P., Rutledge, F.N. (1972) Melanoma of the vulva. *Obstet Gynecol*, **39**, 745–752.
5. Morrow, C.P., DiSaia, P.J. (1976) Malignant melanoma of the female genitalia: a clinical analysis. *Obstet Gynecol Surv*, **31**, 233–271.
6. Ariel, I.M. (1981) Malignant melanoma of the female genital system: a report of 48 patients and review of the literature. *J Surg Oncol*, **16**, 371–383.
7. Bradgate, M.G., Rollason, T.P., McConkey, C. et al (1990) Malignant melanoma of the vulva: a clinico-pathological study of 30 women. *Br J Obstet Gynaecol*, **97**, 124–133.
8. Ronan, S.G., Eng, A.M., Briele, H.A. et al (1990) Malignant melanoma of the female genitalia. *J Am Acad Dermatol*, **22**, 428–435.
9. Piura, B., Egan, M., Lopes, A. et al (1992) Malignant melanoma of the vulva: a clinicopathologic study of 18 cases. *J Surg Oncol*, **50**, 234–240.
10. Ragnarsson-Olding, B., Johansson, H., Rutqvist, L.E. et al (1993) Malignant melanoma of the vulva and vagina: trends in incidence and distribution, and long term survival among 245 consecutive cases in Sweden 1960–1984. *Cancer*, **71**, 1893–1897.
11. Neven, P., Sheperd, J.H., Masotina, A. et al (1994) Malignant melanoma of the vulva and vagina: a report of 23 cases presenting in a 10-year period. *Int J Gynecol Cancer*, **4**, 379–383.
12. Konstadoulakis, M.M., Ricaniadis, N., Driscoll, D.L. et al (1994) Malignant melanoma of the female genital tract. *Eur J Surg Oncol*, **20**, 141–145.
13. DeMatos, P., Tyler, D., Seigler, H.F. (1998) Mucosal melanoma of the female genitalia: a clinicopathologic study of forty-three cases at Duke University Medical Center. *Surgery*, **124**, 38–48.
14. Kato, T., Takematsu, H., Tomita, Y. et al (1987) Malignant melanoma of mucous membranes. A clinicopathologic study of 13 cases in Japanese patients. *Arch Dermatol*, **123**, 216–220.
15. Khoo, U.S., Collins, R.J., Ngan, H.Y. (1991) Malignant melanoma of the female genital tract. A report of nine cases in the Chinese of Hong Kong. *Pathology*, **23**, 312–317.
16. Ragnarsson-Olding, B.K., Kanter-Lwensohn, L.R., Lagerlöf, B. et al (1999) Malignant melanoma of the vulva in a nationwide, 25 year study of 219 Swedish females: clinical observations and histopathologic features. *Cancer*, **86**, 1273–1284.
17. Heller, D.S., Moomjy, M., Koulos, J. et al (1994) Vulvar and vaginal melanoma. A clinicopathologic study. *J Reprod Med*, **39**, 945–948.
18. Egan, C.A., Bradley, R.R., Logsdon, V.K. et al (1997) Vulvar melanoma in children. *Arch Dermatol*, **133**, 345–348.
19. Blessing, K., Kernohan, N.M., Miller, I.D. et al (1991) Malignant melanoma of the vulva; clinicopathological features. *Int J Gynecol Cancer*, **1**, 81–87.
20. Scheistroen, M., Trope, C., Kaern, J. et al (1995) Malignant melanoma of the vulva: evaluation of prognostic factors with emphasis on DNA ploidy in 75 patients. *Cancer*, **75**, 72–80.
21. Ragnarsson-Olding, B.K., Nilsson, B.R., Kanter-Lwensohn, L.R. et al (1999) Malignant melanoma of the vulva in a nationwide, 25 year study of 219 Swedish females: predictors of survival. *Cancer*, **86**, 1285–1293.
22. Oldbring, J., Mikulowski, P. (1979) Malignant melanoma of the penis and male urethra. Report of nine cases and review of the literature. *Br J Urol*, **51**, 147–150.
23. Manivel, J.C., Fraley, E.E. (1987) Malignant melanoma of the penis and male urethra: 4 case reports and literature review. *J Am Acad Dermatol*, **16** (3 Pt 1), 619–620.
24. Zurrida, S., Bartoli, C., Clemente, C. et al (1990) Malignant melanoma of the penis. A report of four cases. *Tumori*, **76**, 599–602.
25. Larsson, K.B., Shaw, H.M., Thompson, J.F. et al (1997) Primary mucosal and glans penis melanomas: the Sydney Melanoma Unit experience. *Eur J Surg Oncol*, **23**, 277–279.
26. Demitsu, T., Nagato, H., Nishimaki, K. et al (2000) Melanoma in situ of the penis. *J Am Acad Dermatol*, **42** (2 Pt 2), 386–388.
27. Moul, J.W., Ho, C.K., McLeod, D.G. (1992) Primary malignant melanoma of the scrotum. *Int Urol Nephrol*, **24**, 641–643.
28. Konstadoulakis, M.M., Ricaniadis, N., Karakousis, C.P. (1994) Malignant melanoma of the scrotum: report of 2 cases. *J Urol*, **151**, 161–162.
29. Testori, A., Mazzarol, G., Viale, G. et al (1999) Medical decision making for melanoma of the glans penis. *J Exp Clin Cancer Res*, **18**, 219–221.
30. Bundrick, W.S., Culkin, D.J., Mata, J.A. et al (1991) Penile malignant melanoma in association with squamous cell carcinoma of the penis. *J Urol*, **146**, 1364–1365.

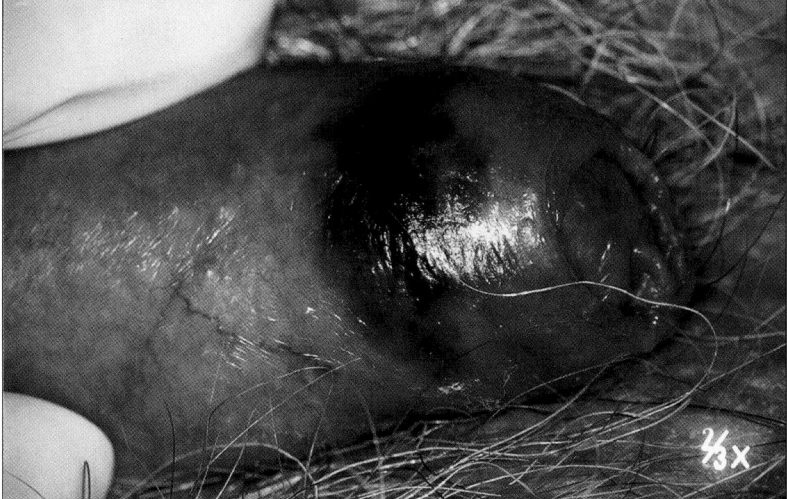

Fig. 11.129
Penile melanoma: note the large size, irregular border and variable pigmentation. By courtesy of the Institute of Dermatology, London, UK.

Non-Hodgkin's lymphoma

Primary and secondary genital involvement by non-Hodgkin's lymphoma is exceptional and only sporadic cases have been reported in the literature.[1,2] Primary anal lymphomas are also extremely rare and the cases described have been anorectal, associated with EBV and AIDS.[3]

The histopathology of genital lymphomas is identical to those occurring elsewhere in the skin (see Ch. 25). The most commonly reported anogenital B-cell lymphoma is of the diffuse large cell type.

References

1. Vang, R., Medeiros, J., Fuller, G.N. et al (2000) Non-Hodgkin's lymphoma involving the gynaecologic tract: a review of 88 cases. *Adv Anat Pathol*, **8**, 200–217.
2. Vang, R., Medeiros, J., Malpica, A. et al (2000) Non Hodgkin's lymphoma involving the vulva. *Int J Gynecol Pathol*, **19**, 236–242.
3. Ioachim, H.L., Antonescu, C., Giancotti, F. et al (1997) EBV associated anorectal lymphomas in patients with acquired immune deficiency syndrome. *Am J Surg Pathol*, **21**, 997–1006.

Epithelial lesions

Benign mucinous metaplasia and mucinous syringometaplasia

Benign mucinous metaplasia of the penis and vulva is exceptionally rare.[1,2] It has been reported on the labia and foreskin. The clinical features are non-distinctive and histologically benign mucus-containing cells are found within the epidermis with a predilection for the upper layers. Distinction from extramammary Paget's disease is difficult but the cells in benign mucinous metaplasia lack cytological atypia and contain nuclei with basal orientation.[1]

Mucinous syringometaplasia is very rare in genital skin and can be distinguished from benign mucinous metaplasia because the cells in the former are not confined to the epidermis but extend into adnexal structures.[3]

References

1. Val-Bernal, J.F., Hernández-Nieto, E. (2000) Benign mucinous metaplasia of the penis. A lesion resembling extramammary Paget's disease. *J Cutan Pathol*, 27, 76–79.
2. Coghill, S.B., Tyler, X., Shaxsted, E.J. (1990) Benign mucinous metaplasia of the vulva. *Histopathology*, 17, 373–375.
3. Kappel, T.J., Abenoza, P. (1993) Mucinous syringometaplasia. A case report with review of the literature. *Am J Dermatopathol*, 15, 62–67.

Endometriosis and endosalpingiosis

Clinical features

Cutaneous endometriosis is uncommon, usually developing in a scar following an abdominal operation on the female internal genitalia, such as a cesarean section.[1–4] On occasions it appears to develop spontaneously in the integument (e.g. in the umbilicus, the inguinal region and the perineum). Endometriosis of the vulva is rare and may occur in an episiotomy scar or after curettage.[5,6] Clinically, it presents as a bluish nodule, which is often painful, and sometimes shows cyclical variation in size and symptoms.[7] Rarely, it may bleed in association with menstruation.

Cutaneous endosalpingiosis is a similar condition in which cysts lined by tubal epithelium develop as a consequence of salpingectomy.[8] It is exceedingly rare in the skin and most cases have presented in an abdominal scar.[9]

Histological features

The diagnosis of cutaneous endometriosis depends upon the detection of both endometrial glands and stroma (*Figs 11.130, 11.131*).[2] Endometrial glands are lined by tall columnar epithelium with basophilic cytoplasm and basally located oval vesicular nuclei. Mitotic activity may sometimes be marked. The stroma is composed of small spindle cells and is usually edematous. Occasionally decidualization is evident. Menstrual bleeding into the deposits often leads to hemosiderin deposition, scarring and chronic inflammation.

Histologically, in endosalpingiosis, the cyst (which is unilocular) is lined by an admixture of ciliated columnar, non-ciliated mucus-secreting columnar and intercalated dark cells.[8] In contrast to endometriosis, there is no associated stroma and foci of hemorrhage and/or hemosiderin are not seen.

References

1. Kurban, R.S., Bhawan, J. (1991) Cutaneous cysts lined by non squamous epithelium. *Am J Dermatopathol*, 13, 509–517.
2. Tidman, M.J., MacDonald, D.M. (1988) Cutaneous endometriosis: a histopathologic study. *J Am Acad Dermatol*, 18, 373–377.
3. Brenner, C., Wohlgemuth, S. (1990) Scar endometriosis. *Surg Gynecol Obstet*, 170, 538–540.
4. Schwayder, T. (1987) Umbilical nodule and abdominal pain. *Arch Dermatol*, 123, 106–107.
5. Catherwood, A.E., Cohen, E.S. (1951) Endometriosis with decidual reaction in episiotomy scar. *Am J Obstet Gynecol*, 62, 1364–1366.
6. Dutta, P. (1987) Vulval endometriosis. *J Ind Med Assoc*, 85, 237–238.
7. Purvis, R.S., Tyring, S.K. (1994) Cutaneous and subcutaneous endometriosis: surgical and hormonal therapy. *J Dermatol Surg Oncol*, 20, 693–695.
8. Dore, N., Landry, M., Cadotte, M. et al (1980) Cutaneous endosalpingiosis. *Arch Dermatol*, 116, 909–912.
9. Sampson, J.A. (1946) The pathogenesis of post salpingectomy endometriosis in laparotomy scars. *Am J Obstet Gynecol*, 50, 597–620.

Median raphe cyst

Clinical features

Median raphe cyst (urethroid cyst) is a rare lesion that usually presents on the ventral aspect of the penis of young adults with a predilection for the glans.[1–4] Perineal and scrotal lesions may occasionally be seen and are rarely polypoid.[5,6] The cyst is usually congenital but tends to become visible only in adult life. Lesions are most commonly solitary, asymptomatic and measure only a few millimeters in diameter. Large lesions are very rare.[7] Exceptional cases present with multiple cysts and spontaneous regression has also been reported.[8] Pigmented cysts are due to the presence of melanocytes in the lining.[7,9] Simple excision is curative.

Pathogenesis and histological features

It is likely that the cyst originates not as a result of defective closure of the median raphe but secondary to anomalous budding and separation of the urethral columnar epithelium from the urethra.[3]

The cyst is lined by pseudostratified columnar epithelium (*Figs 11.132, 11.133*). Rarely, mucin-containing cells are seen. Immunohistochemical stains show that the cells lining the cyst are positive for cytokeratin 7, cytokeratin 13 and CAM 5.2, and negative for cytokeratin 20. It has been suggested that this pattern of keratin expression supports the theory that the cells lining the cyst represent a columnar mucinous epithelium that has undergone immature urothelial metaplasia.[10] Scattered

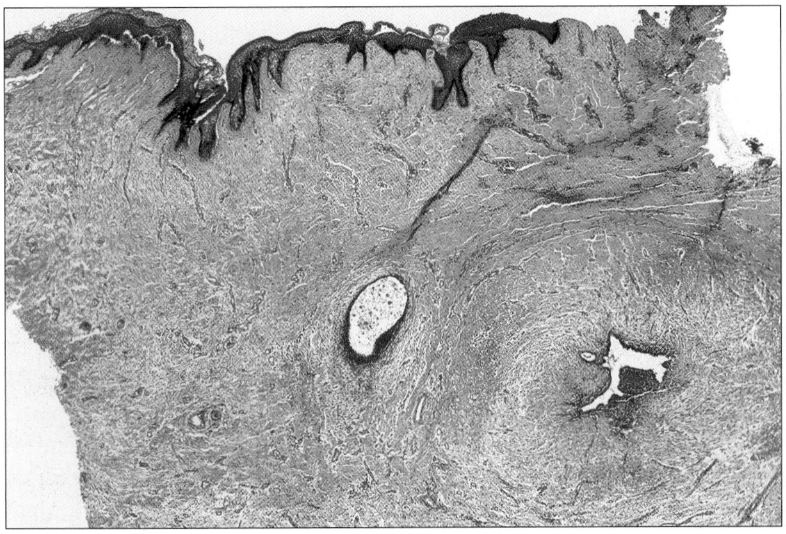

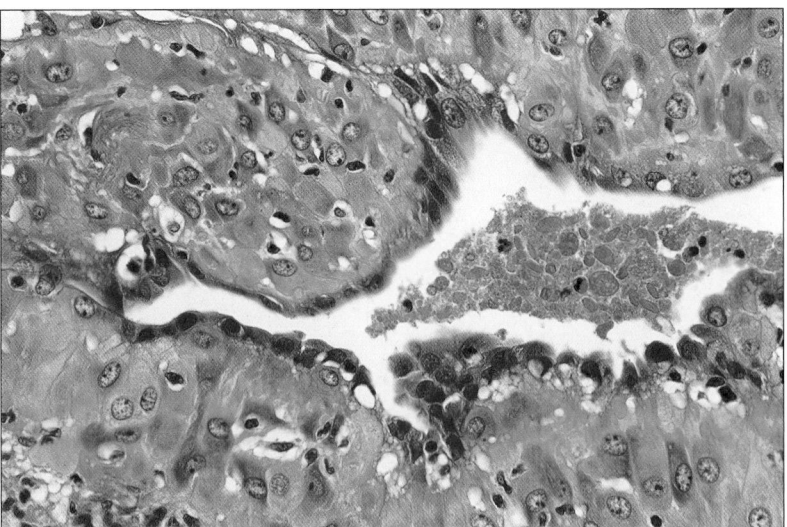

Fig. 11.130
Vulval endometriosis: endometrial glands with edematous stroma are present in the reticular dermis.

Fig. 11.131
Vulval endometriosis: in this example, there is stromal decidualization.

melanocytes and neuroendocrine cells (positive for chromogranin and synaptophysin) may also be identified.[10] Although this lesion may mimic an apocrine cystadenoma, this line of differentiation is unlikely, as the cells in the cyst are negative for human milk fat globulin 1.[11]

References

1. Cole, L.A., Helwig, E.B. (1976) Mucoid cysts of the penile skin. *J Urol*, **115**, 397–400.
2. Asarch, R.G., Golitz, L.E., Sausker, W.F. et al (1979) Median raphe cysts of the penis. *Arch Dermatol*, **115**, 1084–1086.
3. Paslin, D. (1983) Urethroid cyst. *Arch Dermatol*, **119**, 89–90.
4. Nagore, E., Sanchez-Motilla, J.M., Febrer, M.I. et al (1998) Median raphe cysts of the penis: a report of five cases. *Pediatr Dermatol*, **15**, 191–193.
5. Scelwyn, M. (1996) Median raphe cyst of the perineum presenting as a perianal polyp. *Pathology*, **28**, 201–202.
6. LeVasseur, J.G., Perry, V.E. (1997) Perineal median raphe cyst. *Pediatr Dermatol*, **14**, 391–392.
7. Hitti, I.F., Vuletin, J.C., Rapuano, J. (1989) Giant median raphe cyst of the penis with diffuse melanosis of epithelial lining. *Urol Int*, **44**, 121–124.
8. Shibagaki, N., Ohtake, N., Furue, M. (1996) Spontaneous regression of congenital multiple median raphe cysts of the raphe scroti. *Br J Dermatol*, **134**, 376–378.
9. Urahashi, J., Hara, H., Yamaguchi, Z. et al (2000) Pigmented median raphe cysts of the penis. *Acta Derm Venereol*, **80**, 297–298.
10. Dini, M., Baroni, G., Colafranceschi, M. (2001) Median raphe cyst of the penis: a report of two cases with immunohistochemical investigation. *Am J Dermatopathol*, **23**, 320–324.
11. Ohnishi, T., Watanabe, S. (2001) Immunohistochemical analysis of human milk globulin 1 and cytokeratin expression in median raphe cyst of the penis. *Clin Exp Dermatol*, **26**, 88–92.

Bartholin duct cyst

Clinical features

These lesions present in women of reproductive age as a result of obstruction of the main duct of Bartholin's gland.[1] They are relatively uncommon and occur in the posterior aspect of the labium majus. Size varies from 1 cm to several centimeters in diameter. Cysts are usually asymptomatic but the development of a Bartholin's gland abscess is a relatively common complication as the retained glandular secretions become infected.

Histological features

The cyst is lined by transitional epithelium, which frequently undergoes squamous metaplasia (*Figs 11.134, 11.135*).[2] Very rarely, a papilloma has been reported developing within a cyst.[3] The exceptional development of a high-grade squamous cell carcinoma associated with HPV-6 within a cyst has also been described.[4]

References

1. Azzaz, B.D. (1978) Bartholin's gland cyst and abscess: a review of treatment of 53 cases. *Br J Clin Pract*, **32**, 101–105.
2. Rorat, E., Ferenczy, A., Richard, R.M. (1975) Human Bartholin gland, duct and duct cyst. Histochemical and ultrastructural study. *Arch Pathol*, **99**, 367–374.
3. Enghardt, M.H., Valente, P.J., Day, D.H. (1993) Papilloma of Bartholin's gland duct cyst: first report of a case. *Int J Gynecol Pathol*, **12**, 86–92.
4. Sheard, J.D., Vijayanand, R., Herrington, C.S. et al (2000) High-grade squamous intraepithelial neoplasm in a Bartholin's gland cyst associated with HPV 16 infection. *Histopathology*, **37**, 87–88.

Mucinous cyst

Clinical features

This is mainly seen in adult women and presents as a solitary or, less often, multiple lesions in the vestibule.[1–3] Rare cases are found in adolescents. This cyst arises as a result of obstruction of the duct of a minor vestibular gland. Simple excision is curative.

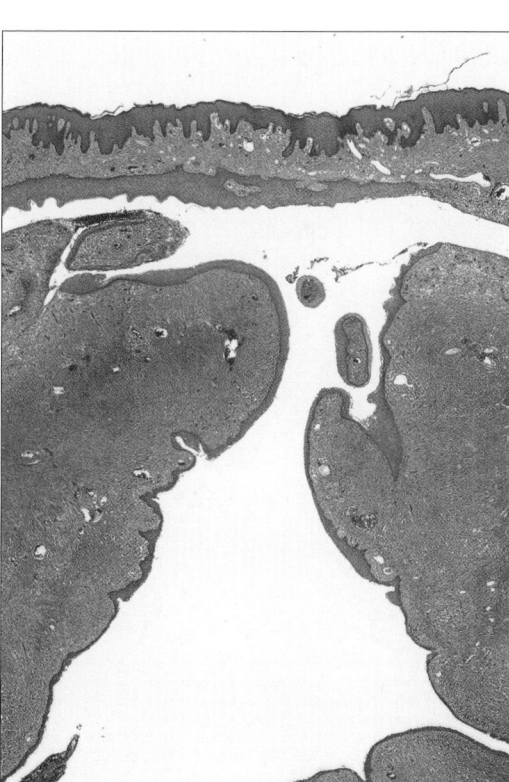

Fig. 11.132
Median raphe cyst: low power view of cyst. By courtesy of C. Gulmann, MD, Beaumont Hospital, Dublin, Eire.

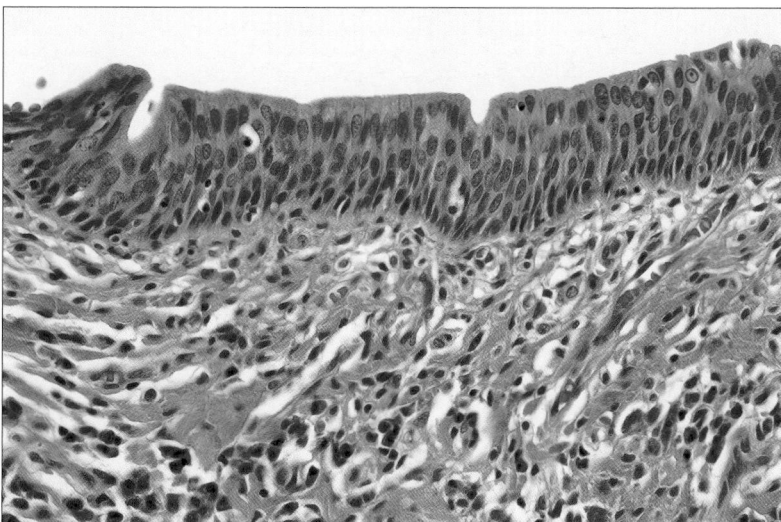

Fig. 11.133
Median raphe cyst: the cyst is lined by pseudostratified epithelium. By courtesy of C. Gulmann, MD, Beaumont Hospital, Dublin, Eire.

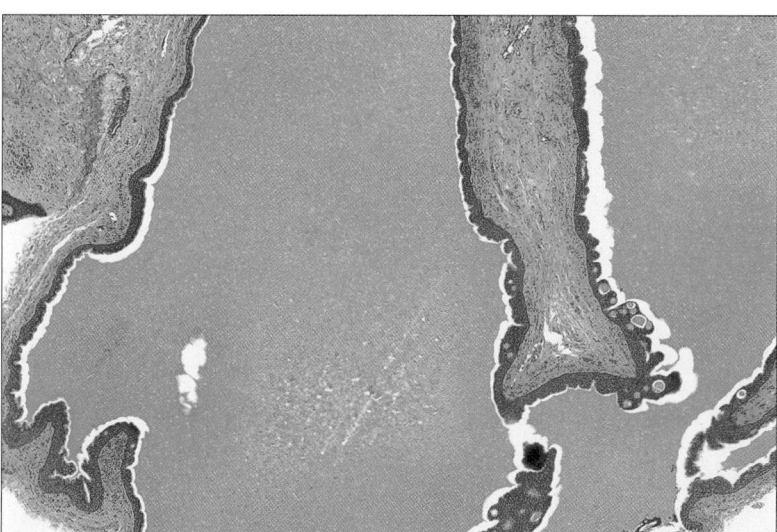

Fig. 11.134
Bartholin duct cyst: low power view of the cyst. By courtesy of C. Crum, MD, Brigham and Women's Hospital and Harvard Medical School, Boston, USA.

Histological features

The cyst is lined by a layer of mucinous epithelium with occasional focal squamous metaplasia (*Figs 11.136–11.138*).[1–3] Myoepithelial cells are not identified. It was originally thought that the cyst originated from Mullerian epithelium but it is more likely that it derives from urogenital sinus epithelium.[2,4,5]

References

1.   Friedrich, E.G. Jr, Wilkinson, E.J. (1973) Mucous cysts of the vulvar vestibule. *Obstet Gynecol*, **42**, 407–414.

2.   Robboy, S.J., Ross, J.S., Prat, J. et al (1978) Urogenital sinus origin of mucinous and ciliated cysts of the vulva. *Obstet Gynecol*, **51**, 347–351.
3.   Friedrich, E.G. Jr (1983) The vulvar vestibule. *J Reprod Med*, **28**, 773–777.
4.   Oi, R.H., Munn, R. (1982) Mucous cysts of the vulvar vestibule. *Hum Pathol*, **13**, 584–586.
5.   Newland, J.R., Fusaro, R.M. (1991) Mucinous cysts of the vulva. *Nebr Med J*, **76**, 307–310.

Mesonephric cyst

Clinical features

This lesion presents in the lateral part of the vulva as a small, asymptomatic, blue–red cystic lesion containing clear fluid. It is thought to be derived from remnants of the mesonephric duct. Simple excision is curative.

Histological features

The cyst is lined by a single layer of cuboidal or columnar non-ciliated cells surrounded by a layer of smooth muscle.[1]

Reference

1.   Deppisch, L.M. (1975) Cysts of the vagina: classification and clinical correlations. *Obstet Gynecol*, **45**, 632–637.

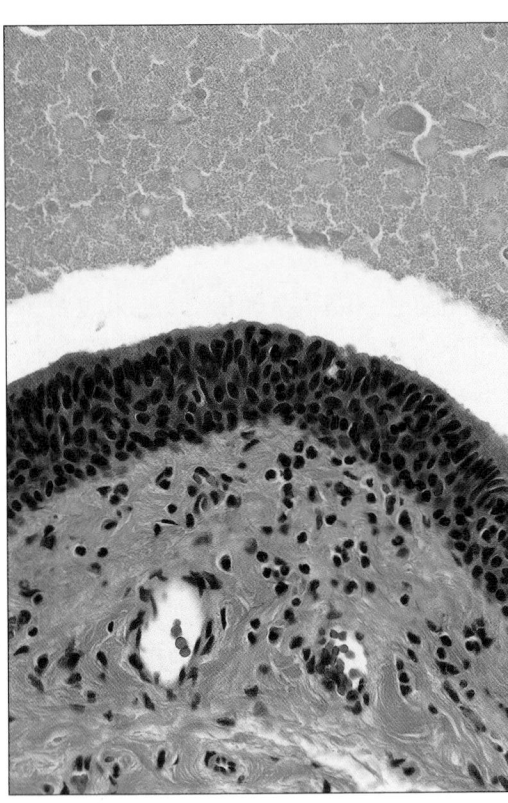

Fig. 11.135
Bartholin duct cyst: the cyst is lined by transitional epithelium. By courtesy of C. Crum, MD, Brigham and Women's Hospital and Harvard Medical School, Boston, USA.

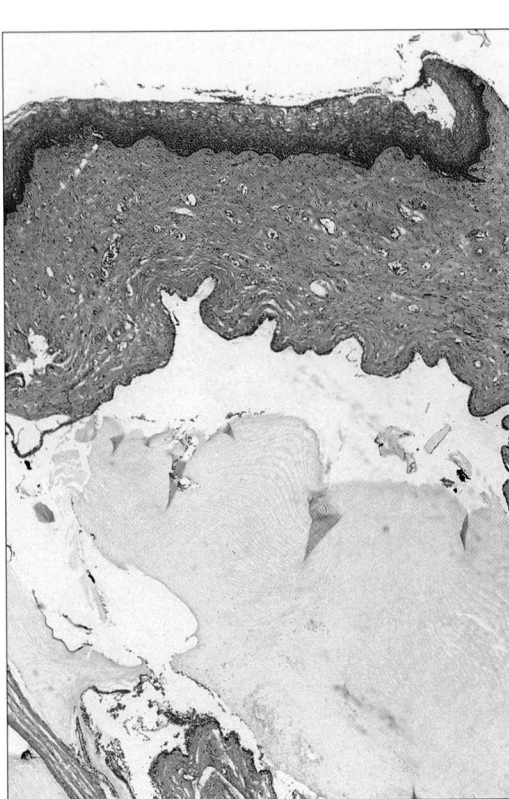

Fig. 11.136
Mucinous cyst: low power view of mucin-containing cyst. Note the non-keratinizing surface epithelium. By courtesy of C. Crum, MD, Brigham and Women's Hospital and Harvard Medical School, Boston, USA.

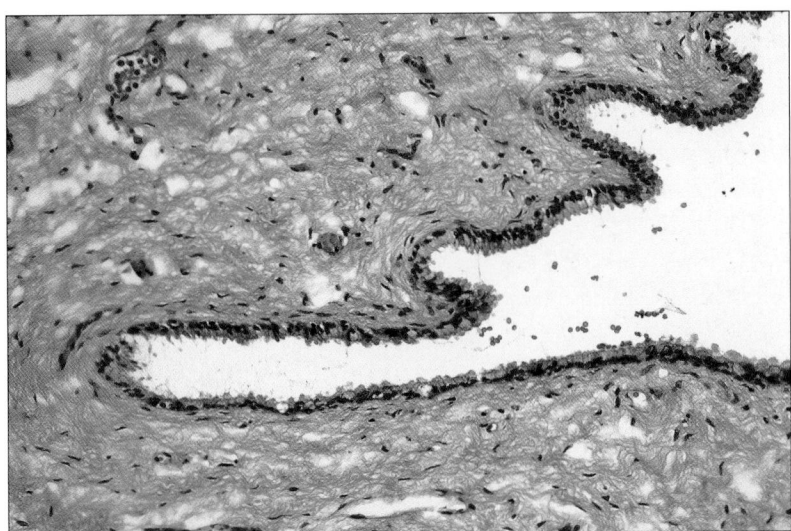

Fig. 11.137
Mucinous cyst: the cyst is lined by mucin-secreting epithelium. By courtesy of C. Crum, MD, Brigham and Women's Hospital and Harvard Medical School, Boston, USA.

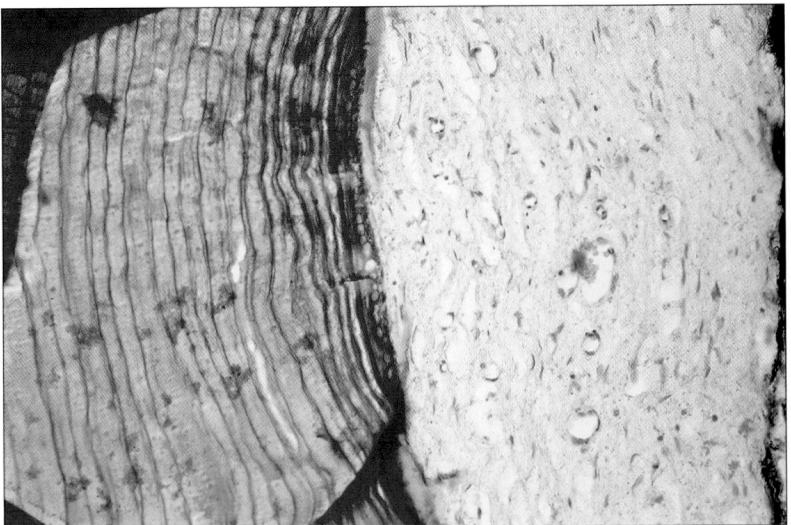

Fig. 11.138
Mucinous cyst: the mucin stains bright red with mucicarmine. By courtesy of C. Crum, MD, Brigham and Women's Hospital and Harvard Medical School, Boston, USA.

Mesothelial cyst

Clinical features

Mesothelial cyst (cyst of the canal of Nuck) presents as a lesion varying in size from less than 1 cm to 5 cm or more. It arises on the upper and lateral aspect of the labium majus at the level of the insertion of the round ligament. Some cases are associated with an inguinal hernia. Simple excision is curative.

Histological features

Microscopic examination reveals a unilocular cavity lined by a single layer of flattened mesothelial cells.[1]

Reference

1. Deppisch, L.M. (1975) Cysts of the vagina: classification and clinical correlations. *Obstet Gynecol*, **45**, 632–637.

Periurethral cyst

Clinical features

This cyst presents as a small swelling lateral to the urethral meatus.

Histological features

Histological examination shows a cavity lined by transitional epithelium[1] (*Figs 11.139, 11.140*).

Reference

1. Deppisch, L.M. (1975) Cysts of the vagina: classification and clinical correlations. *Obstet Gynecol*, **45**, 632–637.

Intraepithelial neoplasia

In this text, the term intraepithelial neoplasia is restricted to squamous intraepithelial neoplasia and does not include extramammary Paget's disease or melanoma in situ. The terminology used for premalignant vulval epithelial lesions has been confusing and unsatisfactory for many years. The most recent revision was 1986.[1] This was devised so that it shared the same terminology as that in use for cervical intraepithelial neoplasia, VIN grades 1, 2 and 3 representing the degree, in thirds, that the epithelium is atypical (*Table 11.1*). Furthermore, 'VIN 3 differentiated' was introduced to describe a variant where the neoplastic cells do not extend throughout the full thickness of the epidermis, which remains well differentiated. However, this terminology does not compare kind-with-kind since the cervix is covered by mucosa and most of the epithelium covering the vulva is skin, the only area that is a mucosa being the vestibule. Older terms such as Bowen's disease, erythroplasia of Queyrat, bowenoid papulosis, multifocal pigmented Bowen's disease, severe dysplasia and carcinoma in situ, which represented full-thickness atypia, were abandoned in this grading system.[2,3] This newer terminology does not take into account the clinical and biological differences between these various entities and also assumes incorrectly that there is a natural progression through grades 1–3 to invasive squamous cell carcinoma (SCC).

Clinical features

Clinically, it is difficult to recognize specific features for VIN 1 and VIN 2. Changes similar to VIN 1 are often found in states where abnormal basal cytology is a result of epithelial reparation (e.g. lichen planus or basal hyperplasia arising from HPV infection). These misinterpretations often arise as a consequence of poor clinicopathological correlation. Furthermore, there is considerable histological overlap between VIN 2 and VIN 3. Recent studies have shown that there is less interobserver variability if VIN 2 and VIN 3 are combined into one category.[4,5]

Atypia throughout the full thickness of the epidermis of the vulva is now known as VIN 3 (undifferentiated VIN) and this terminology has been extended to include other perineal sites, for example perianal intraepithelial neoplasia (PAIN 3). Interestingly, this classification has not been adopted for penile lesions and older terms such as Bowen's disease, bowenoid papulosis and carcinoma in situ are still often used.

Table 11.1
Classification of vulvar intraepithelial neoplasia

• VIN 1 – mild dysplasia
• VIN 2 – moderate dysplasia
• VIN 3 – severe dysplasia or carcinoma in situ (differentiated and undifferentiated VIN)

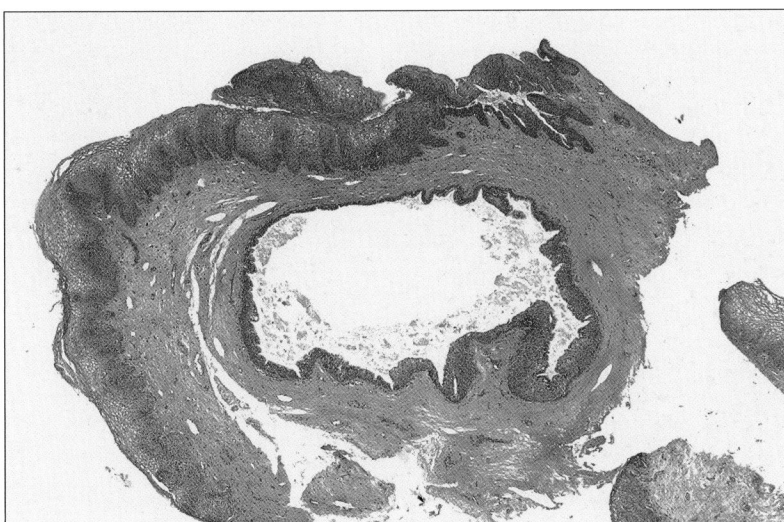

Fig. 11.139
Periurethral cyst: low power view of unilocular cyst. By courtesy of C. Crum, MD, Brigham and Women's Hospital and Harvard Medical School, Boston, USA.

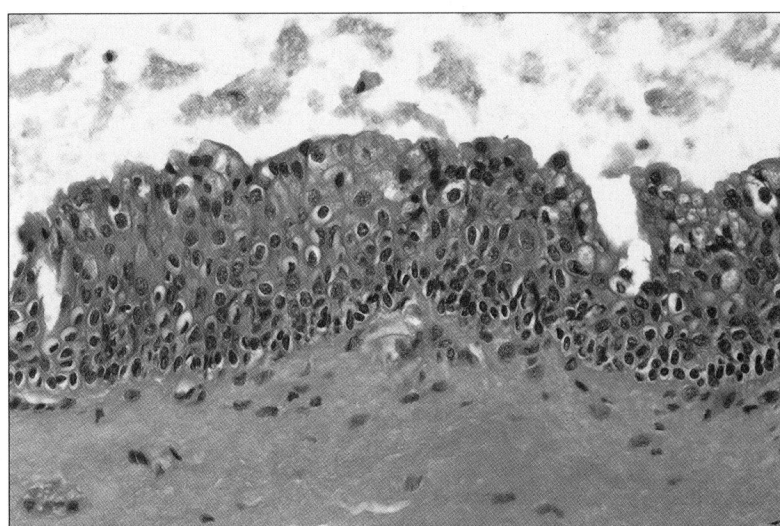

Fig. 11.140
Periurethral cyst: the cyst is lined by transitional epithelium. By courtesy of C. Crum, MD, Brigham and Women's Hospital and Harvard Medical School, Boston, USA.

Clinical lesions of VIN may be unifocal and discrete or multifocal and diffusely distributed about the external genitalia and perineum where the anus may also be affected. Multiple small papules at this site were for many years described as bowenoid papulosis due to the mistaken belief that these lesions could be histologically distinguished from intraepithelial neoplasia and that they were biologically very different. It is now appreciated that histologically the two conditions are indistinguishable and that although in the majority of patients there is only a small risk of progression to invasive disease, the immunocompromised are at a much greater risk, particularly in the setting of perianal disease.[6] Similarly, pigmented multifocal Bowen's disease is now classified within the spectrum of VIN.

The morphology of the lesions ranges from papules to plaques, which may be skin-colored, white, erythematous or pigmented (*Figs 11.141–11.147*). The surface often has a warty texture; less commonly, lesions are papillomatous, particularly around the anus where they may become polypoid (*Fig. 11.148*). The main presenting symptom is pruritus. In male patients, lesions often mimic the appearances of lichen planus, appearing as violaceous papules or as erythematous, velvety plaques (*Fig. 11.149*).

Multifocal vulval, perianal and penile disease is strongly associated with the oncogenic papilloma viruses, particularly HPV-16 and -18, and almost exclusively occurs in smokers.[7,8] It is believed that there is a failure of the host to mount an immune response to HPV and that patients who are immunocompromised are at particular risk. However, many of the patients do not have an identifiable immune deficiency. Anogenital intraepithelial neoplasia, in addition to being multifocal, can be multicentric and there is a history in the majority of female patients of current or past cervical intraepithelial neoplasia.[9]

Vaginal involvement is uncommon. The morphology of the lesions is very variable, some resembling typical warts, others hyperkeratotic papules and plaques which can be white, red or deeply pigmented, akin to seborrheic keratoses.[10,11]

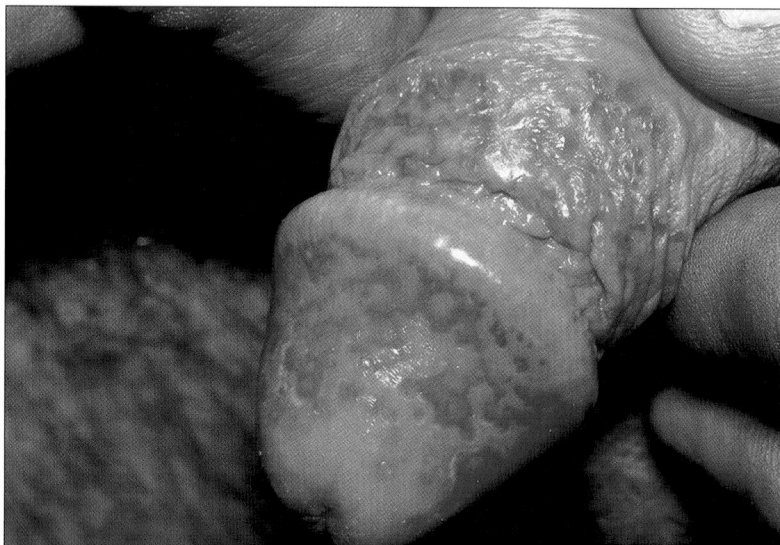

Fig. 11.141
Intraepithelial neoplasia: multiple eroded lesions are present. By courtesy of the Institute of Dermatology, London, UK.

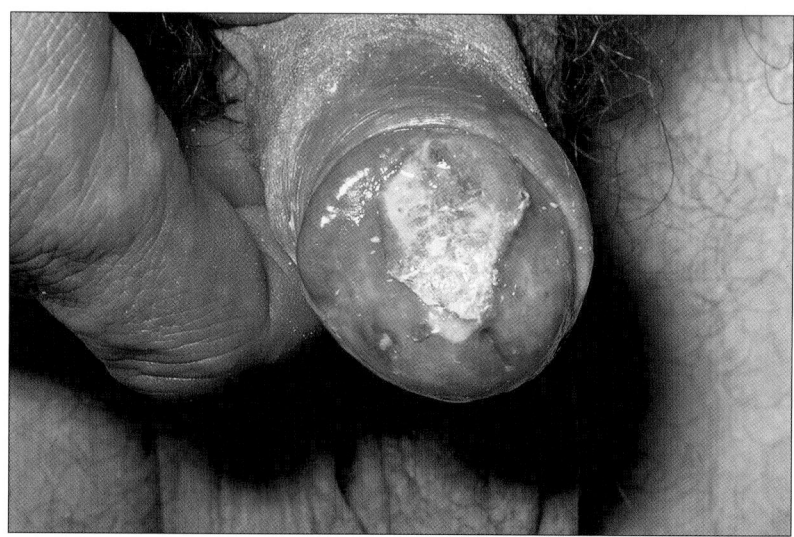

Fig. 11.143
Intraepithelial neoplasia: this patient presented with multiple ulcerated lesions and a thick, scaly plaque. By courtesy of the Institute of Dermatology, London, UK.

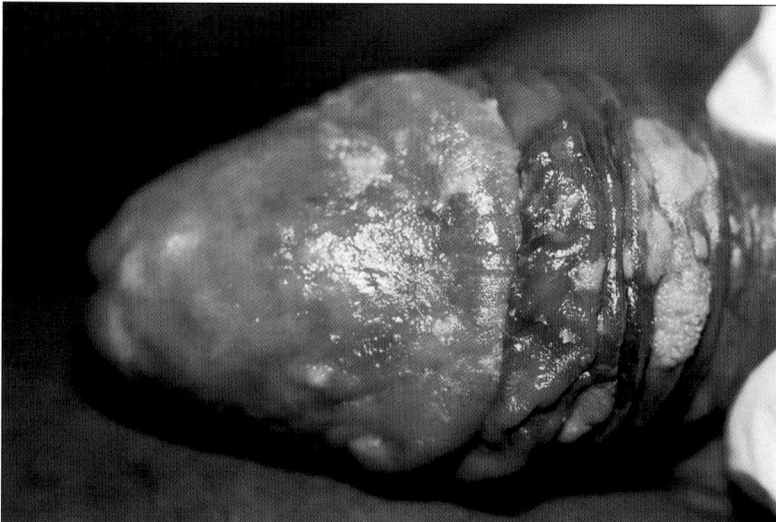

Fig. 11.142
Intraepithelial neoplasia: in this example, viral warts are present in addition to multiple small papules on the glans (Bowenoid papulosis). By courtesy of the Institute of Dermatology, London, UK.

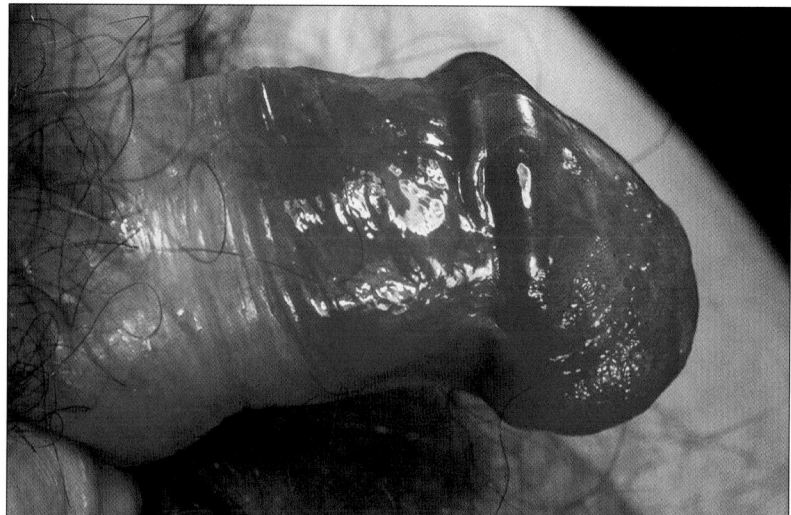

Fig. 11.144
Intraepithelial neoplasia: there is intense erythema of the glans penis and the distal shaft. This lesion is also referred to as Bowen's disease and in the older literature as erythroplasia of Queyrat. By courtesy of the Institute of Dermatology, London, UK.

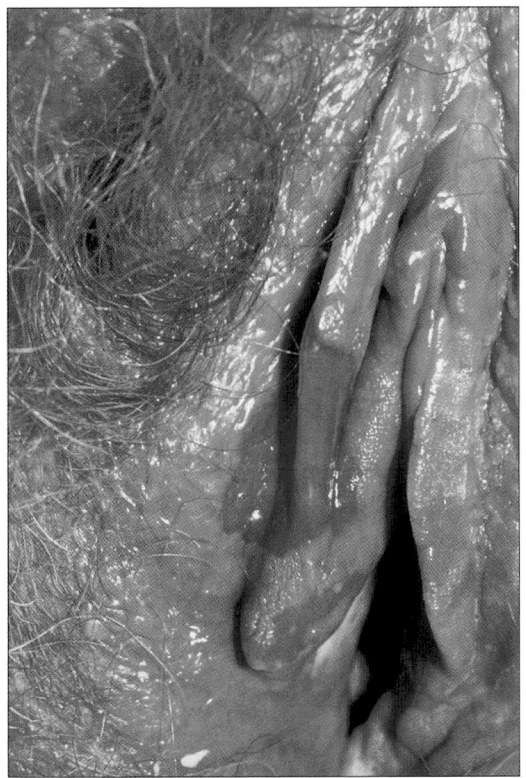

Fig. 11.145
Intraepithelial neoplasia: intensely erythematous ulcerated lesion. By courtesy of the Institute of Dermatology, London, UK.

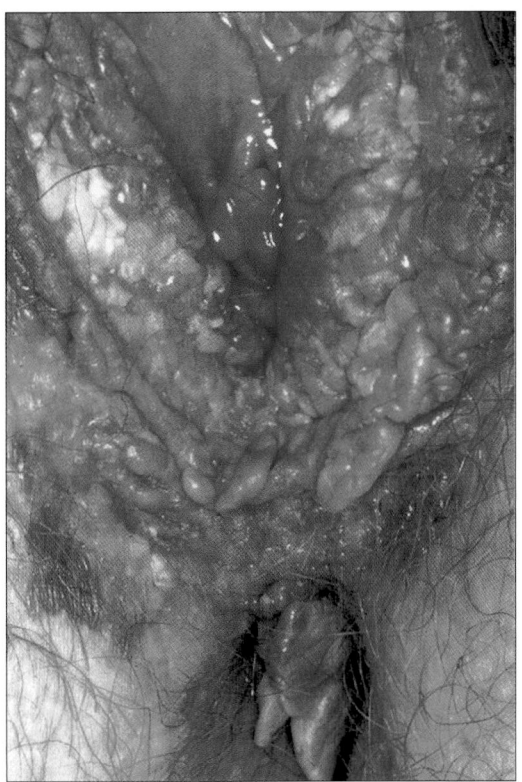

Fig. 11.146
Intraepithelial neoplasia: there are numerous scaly papules accompanied by condylomata. In the older literature, the former was known as bowenoid papulosis. Pigmented lesions are also present. These were once known as multicentric pigmented Bowen's disease. By courtesy of the Institute of Dermatology, London, UK.

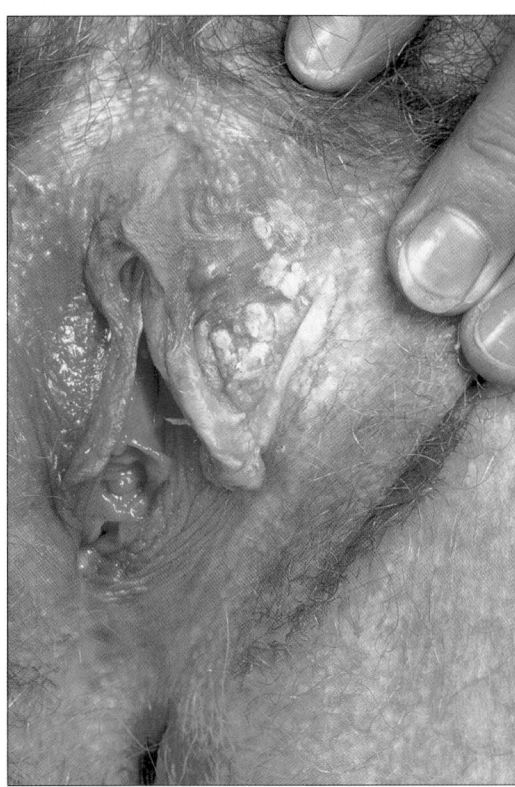

Fig. 11.147
Intraepithelial neoplasia: there is an erythematous plaque with focal scaling. By courtesy of the Institute of Dermatology, London, UK.

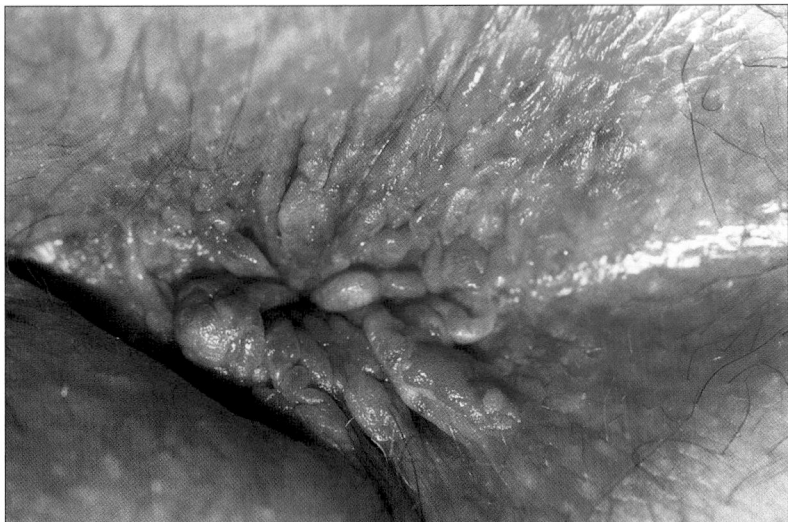

Fig. 11.148
Intraepithelial neoplasia: perianal lesions presenting as multiple small papules (bowenoid papulosis). By courtesy of the Institute of Dermatology, London, UK.

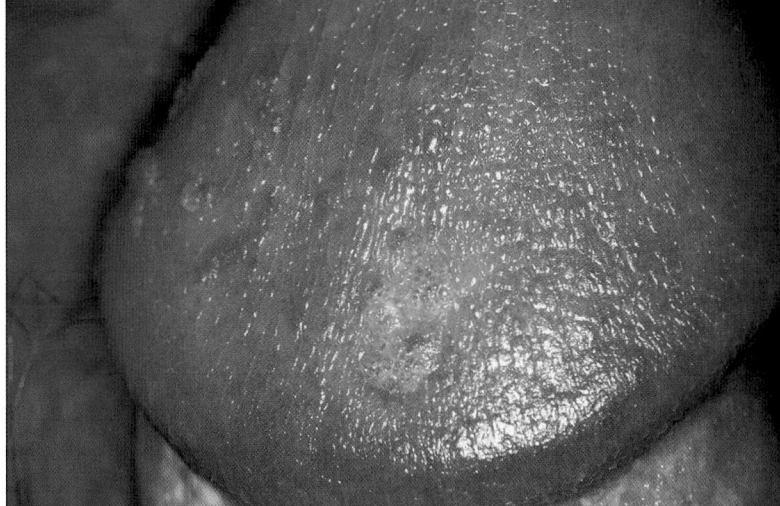

Fig. 11.149
Intraepithelial neoplasia: in this example, small papules are present on the glans penis. By courtesy of the Institute of Dermatology, London, UK.

Traditionally, VIN is classified into three categories depending upon the extent of involvement of the epithelium (*Figs 11.150–11.152*). In order to promote uniform terminology acceptable to both FIGO and the International Society of Gynecological Pathologists, it was proposed at the 2001 ISSVD meeting that VIN 1 be used exclusively for premalignant conditions. A new classification would dispense with numerical grading of VIN and only recognize two subtypes: undifferentiated VIN (i.e. the old VIN 2 and VIN 3) associated with HPV infection, and differentiated VIN. In this latter type, the atypia is confined to the basal region with normal differentiation above. It is very uncommon and not associated with HPV infection. There is a much greater risk of progressing to invasive disease.[12] Most often, it is seen in vulvectomy specimens from women with SCC arising in a background of lichen simplex or lichen planus.

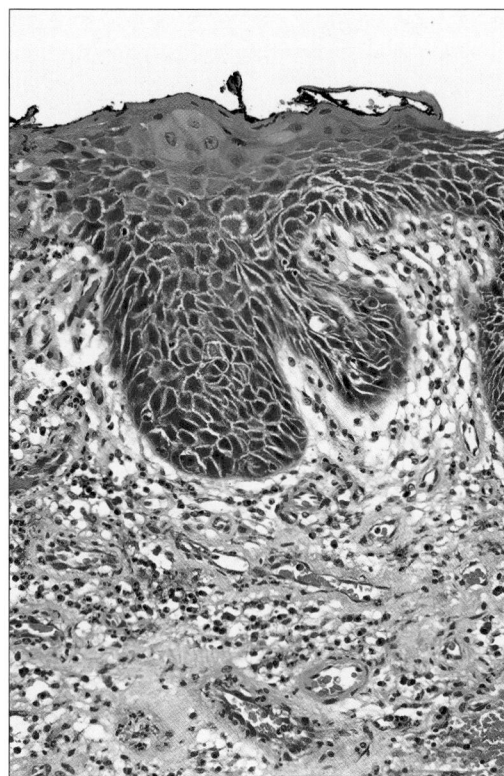

Fig. 11.150
VIN 1: dysplasia is limited to the lower third of the epidermis.

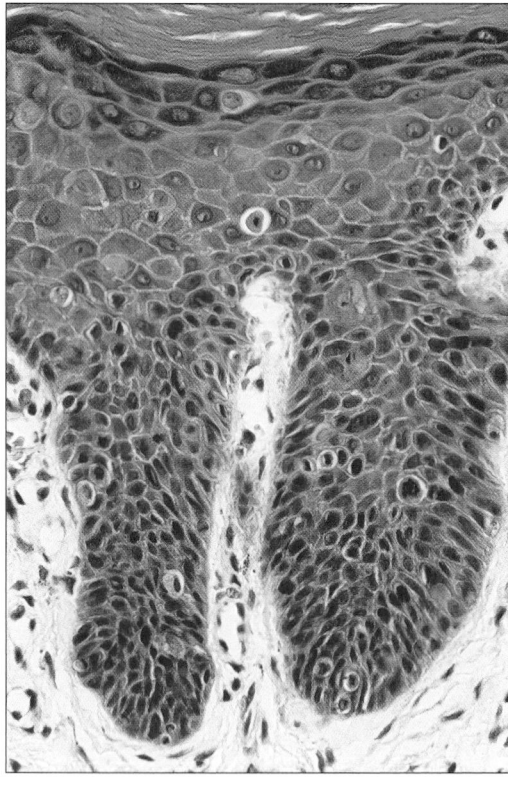

Fig. 11.151
VIN 2: dysplasia affects the lower and middle thirds of the epidermis.

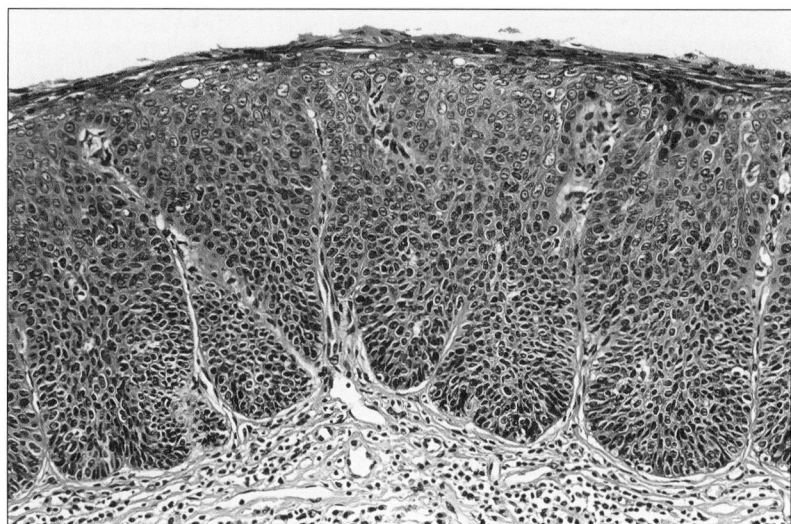

Fig. 11.152
VIN 3: there is full-thickness dysplasia.

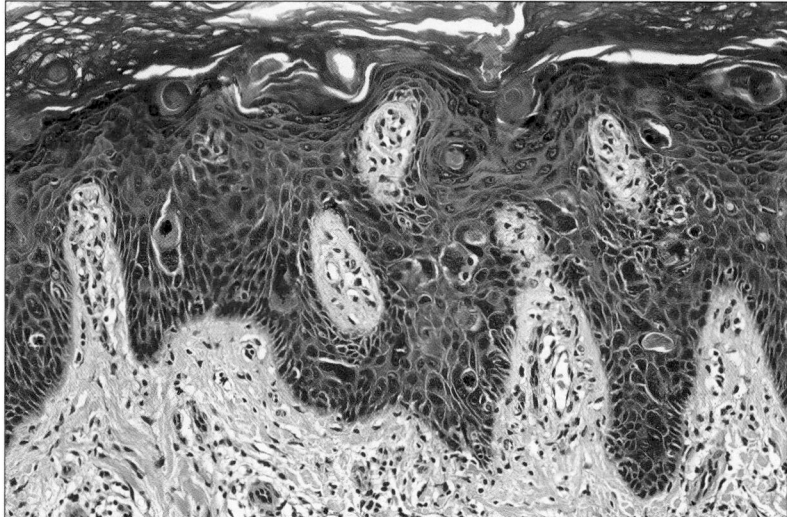

Fig. 11.153
Bowenoid VIN: there is full-thickness dysplasia with very marked nuclear pleomorphism. Note the abnormal mitosis.

This terminology is still far from perfect, particularly as differentiated VIN can be mistakenly thought of as having a better prognosis than undifferentiated VIN. Contrariwise, differentiated VIN developing against a background of lichen sclerosus is much more likely to be associated with progression to invasive tumor and aggressive behavior than HPV-associated undifferentiated lesions.

The newer classification has dispensed with the terms bowenoid and basaloid since they are biologically identical to undifferentiated VIN, and many lesions show an admixture of these histological variants. In this

text, these two variants are retained for descriptive purposes only while fully accepting that both clinically and biologically all variants of undifferentiated VIN are identical.[13,14]

Histological features

Undifferentiated VIN

In this major subtype, there is complete loss of cellular stratification throughout the epidermis with large hyperchromatic cells, dyskeratosis, multinucleated cells and numerous typical and atypical mitoses.[1]

Two distinct types of undifferentiated VIN have been described:
- *bowenoid*, characterized by individual cell keratinization and premature cellular differentiation; pleomorphism may be marked and abnormal mitoses are often conspicuous (*Fig. 11.153*)
- *basaloid*, with atypical parabasal cells extending throughout the full thickness of the epithelium (*Fig. 11.154*).

Differentiated VIN

In some cases of vulval lichen sclerosus there is an associated basal keratinocyte cytological atypia with dyskeratosis and normal differentiation throughout the overlying epithelium (*Fig. 11.155*). The rete ridges

5. van Beurden, M., de Craen, A.J., de Vet, H.C. et al (1999) The contribution of MIB1 in the accurate grading of vulvar intraepithelial neoplasia. *J Clin Pathol*, **52**, 820–824.
6. Rudlinger, R., Buchmann, P. (1986) HPV 16-positive bowenoid papulosis and squamous cell carcinoma of the anus in an HIV positive man. *Dis Colon Rectum*, **32**, 1042–1045.
7. Lookingbill, D.P., Kreider, J.W., Howett, M.K. et al (1987) Human papilloma virus type 16 in Bowenoid papulosis, intraoral papillomas and squamous cell carcinoma of the tongue. *Arch Dermatol*, **123**, 363–368.
8. Buscema, J., Naghashfar, Z., Sawada, E. et al (1988) The predominance of human papilloma virus 16 in vulvar neoplasia. *Obstet Gynecol*, **71**, 601–606.
9. Obalek, S., Jablonska, S., Beaudenon, S. et al (1986) Bowenoid papulosis of the male and female genitalia: risk of cervical neoplasia. *J Am Acad Dermatol*, **14**, 433–444.
10. Wade, T.R., Kopf, A.W., Ackerman, A.B. (1979) Bowenoid papulosis of the genitalia. *Arch Dermatol*, **115**, 306–308.
11. Patterson, J.W., Kao, G.F., Graham, J.H. et al (1986) Bowenoid papulosis. A clinicopathologic study with ultrastructural observations. *Cancer*, **57**, 823–836.
12. Yang, B., Hart, W.R. (2000) Vulvar intraepithelial neoplasia of the simple (differentiated) type. A clinicopathological study including analysis of HPV and P53 expression. *Am J Surg Pathol*, **24**, 429–441.
13. Buckley, C.H., Butler, E.B., Fox, H. (1984) Vulvar intraepithelial neoplasia and microinvasive carcinoma. *J Clin Pathol*, **37**, 1201–1211.
14. Powell, L.C., Dinh, T.V., Rajaraman, S. et al (1986) Carcinoma in situ of the vulva. A clinicopathologic study of 50 cases. *J Reprod Med*, **31**, 808–814.

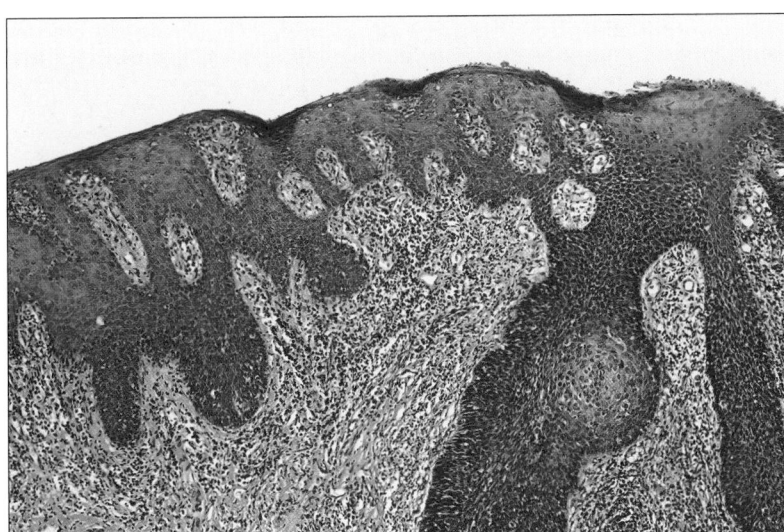

Fig. 11.154
Basaloid VIN: there is full-thickness replacement of the epidermis by a fairly uniform population of small cells with densely basophilic nuclei and imperceptible cytoplasm.

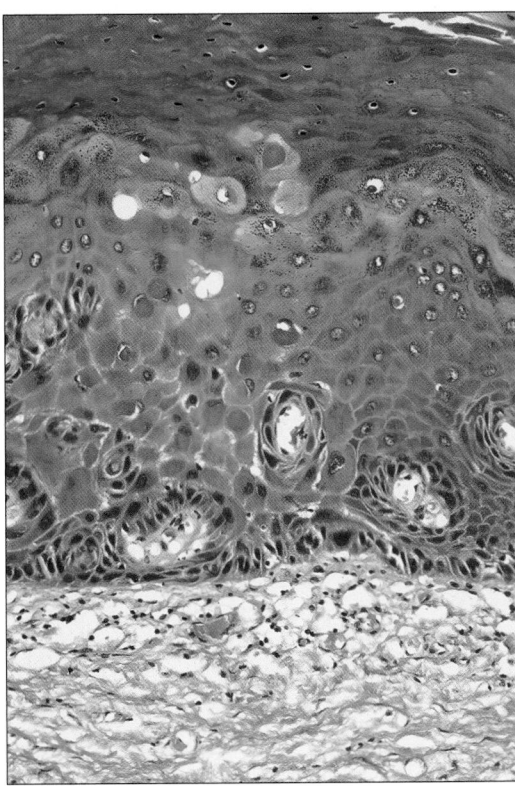

Fig. 11.155
Differentiated VIN: there is basal dysplasia associated with dyskeratosis and normal differentiation. By courtesy of C. Crum, MD, Brigham and Women's Hospital and Harvard Medical School, Boston, USA.

may be long and forked with keratin pearls. This change may reflect invasive disease or herald its imminent onset. To reflect the seriousness of this epithelial change, the term 'VIN 3 differentiated' was coined by the ISSVD. However, this change is poorly recognized by many pathologists and there is a significant risk of a report of VIN 1 being issued with potentially disastrous consequences.

References

1. Wilkinson, E.J., Kneale, B., Lynch, P. (1986) Report of the ISSVD Terminology Committee. *J Reprod Med*, **31**, 973–974.
2. Wilkinson, E.J. (1992) Normal histology and nomenclature of the vulva and malignant neoplasms including VIN. *Dermatol Clin*, **10**, 283–296.
3. Hart, W.R. (2001) Vulvar intraepithelial neoplasia: historical aspects and current status. *Int J Gynecol Pathol*, **20**, 16–30.
4. Preti, M., Mezzetti, M., Robertson, C. et al (2000) Inter-observer variation in histopathological diagnosis and grading of vulvar intraepithelial neoplasia: results of an European collaborative study. *Br J Obstet Gynaecol*, **107**, 594–599.

Squamous cell carcinoma of the genital epithelia

Clinical features

Vulval squamous cell carcinoma

There are two major etiologies for vulval squamous cell carcinoma (SCC):[1–3]

- The majority (75% of cases) arise in elderly women against a background of a chronic scarring dermatosis, usually lichen sclerosus but less often lichen planus. In these patients, the tumors develop directly within the background dermatosis or rarely may be preceded by differentiated VIN. They are not usually associated with HPV.[4–11]

- The second group consists of younger women with a background of undifferentiated VIN associated with HPV-16 and -18, smoking and a previous or current history of squamous intraepithelial lesion (SIL/CIN). In addition, much more rarely, vulval carcinoma has been described in association with chronic granulomatous disease and hidradenitis suppurativa.[12–16]

Patients with the warty and basaloid histological subtypes of vulval SCC tend to be younger than those with conventional keratinizing SCC.[17] There also seems to be a predominance of black patients with the former two histological subtypes.[17] The great majority of vulval SCCs develop on the labia with particular predilection for the labia majora. The second most common site is the clitoris.[18] Patients present with a mass that is sometimes associated with pruritus, ulceration, bleeding, discharge or pain (*Fig. 11.156*). Multifocal tumors are very rare.[19] Vulval SCC usually spreads via lymphatics to inguinal, femoral and pelvic lymph nodes. Up to 30% of patients have inguinal lymph node spread at the time of presentation. Tumors on the clitoris are often associated with bilateral lymph node spread.[20]

The overall 5-year survival for patients with vulval SCC varies according to the presence or absence of lymph node metastasis.[21–27] In the absence of lymph node spread, the 5-year survival is up to 90% but this rate falls to less than 70% in patients with inguinal lymph node metastasis and to less than 25% in those with pelvic lymph node spread.[22] The presence or absence of lymph node metastasis is the single most important factor determining prognosis.[28] Other factors that have been found to be independently associated with prognosis include older age, advanced stage, size of the tumor, positive margins and degree of differentiation. It has been suggested that HPV-positive tumors have a worse prognosis than those that are HPV negative.[29,30] Warty and basaloid SCCs of the vulva are often associated with HPV infection and there is some suggestion (particularly in the penile counterpart) that the prognosis of the basaloid subtype may be worse than that of conventional SCC (see below).[6,17]

Penile squamous cell carcinoma

Penile SCC is commoner than scrotal SCC.[31] Squamous cell carcinoma of the penis is by far the most frequent malignancy affecting this organ. Uncircumcised males, particularly those with associated phimosis, appear to be at increased risk.[32] Phimosis was found in up to 24% of patients with penile carcinoma in one large series.[33] Retention of smegma is thought to be an important factor in the induction of penile carcinoma. Poor hygiene increases the risk of cancer in uncircumcised patients. Circumcision early in life confers more protection than that conferred when the procedure is performed late in life.[34] Other suggested risk factors include HPV infection, lichen sclerosus, psoralen with ultraviolet A light (PUVA) and chemical carcinogens (e.g. 3',4'-benzopyrene).[35]

The role of HPV in penile carcinoma is controversial and appears to be much lower than in cervical carcinoma.[36,37] Furthermore, p53 protein expression is high in cases of penile SCC unrelated to HPV infection.[38] In the past it was believed that penile SCC with classical morphology was only rarely associated with HPV infection and that penile tumors consistently associated with HPV infection were the basaloid and warty variants.[36,37] More recent studies, however, using a novel genotyping line probe assay have demonstrated the presence of HPV in up to a third of verrucous and keratinizing SCCs.[39] These studies have also confirmed the presence of HPV DNA in 80% of warty tumors and in 100% of basaloid lesions.[39-41] The most common HPV type is 16 followed by 18.[36,37,42] Occasionally, HPV-11 and -33 have also been demonstrated.[43,44] Some studies have suggested that there is an increased incidence of cervical cancer in the wives of males with penile carcinoma, offering support to an infectious etiology.[45,46] However, this finding has not been consistently demonstrated in other series.[47] Interestingly, only a third of typical penile SCCs show evidence of HPV in contrast to 90% or more of penile in situ carcinomas and penile squamous intraepithelial lesions.[36,48] This suggests that only a minority of invasive penile tumors originate from HPV-associated squamous intraepithelial lesions. HPV has also been demonstrated in HIV-positive patients with penile SCC.[49,50] There are very occasional reports of penile SCC arising in a background of lichen sclerosus.[51-54] Exceptional cases have been reported in association with Zoon's balanitis and verruciform xanthoma.[55,56]

Penile SCC has a predilection for the glans, followed by the foreskin, coronal sulcus and shaft.[57] It presents mainly in the sixth and seventh decades of life and is very rare in patients less than 40 years of age.[35] The most common presentation is that of an ulcerated mass that may be painful. Multicentricity has been described in up to 8% of cases and tumors develop in squamous intraepithelial lesions in up to 16% of patients.[33,57]

The overall 5-year survival for penile SCC varies according to several parameters that have been found to affect prognosis. The most important prognostic indicators include site, depth of involvement, histological subtype, presence of vascular or lymphatic invasion, lymph node involvement and tumor stage.[33,58-64] Parameters that are independent prognostic indicators include involvement of the corpus cavernosum and the presence of palpable lymph nodes.[33] The histological subtype is also important since basaloid and sarcomatoid carcinomas usually have a poor prognosis; warty and papillary carcinomas have an intermediate prognosis, and verrucous carcinoma has an excellent prognosis. The presence of HPV is not thought to be an important prognostic factor.[65]

Various genetic defects have been described in penile SCC. These include gains in chromosomes 8q24, 16p11–12, 20q11–13, 22q, 19q13 and 5p15, and deletions in chromosomes 13q21–22 and 4q21–32.[66]

Histological features

Squamous carcinoma of the genital skin includes six variants: conventional (typical), warty, papillary, basaloid, sarcomatoid and verrucous.

- *Conventional* (typical) squamous cell carcinoma of the external genitalia is identical to that arising elsewhere on the integument and is described in detail on page 1201.
- *Warty* carcinoma has a cauliflower-like gross appearance and displays prominent papillomatosis with fibrovascular cores, acanthosis and hyperkeratosis.[40] Tumor cells show marked koilocytic change and hyperchromatism. There is a strong association with HPV infection.
- *Papillary* carcinoma has a macroscopic appearance similar to that of warty carcinoma. The growth pattern is endo- and exophytic and mimics that seen in verrucous carcinoma (see below). In contrast to the latter, however, cytological atypia is easily found (*Fig. 11.157*). Changes suggestive of HPV infection are not present.

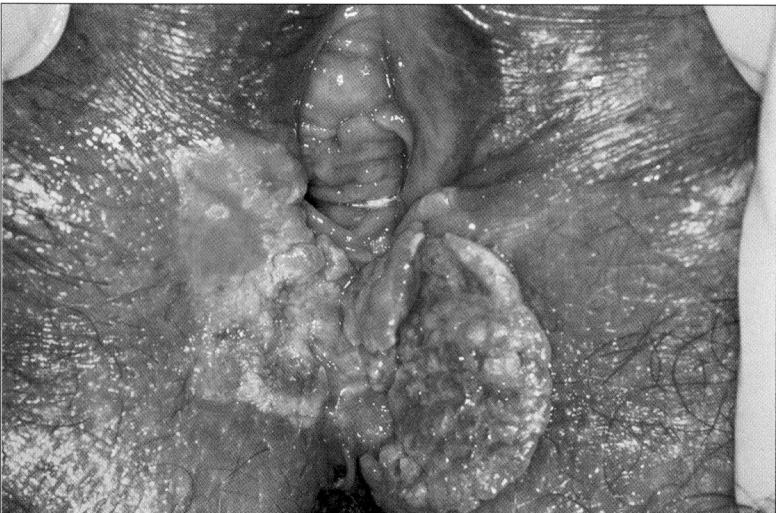

Fig. 11.156
Vulval squamous cell carcinoma: this tumor arose against a background of longstanding carcinoma in situ (Bowen's disease). By courtesy of the Institute of Dermatology, London, UK.

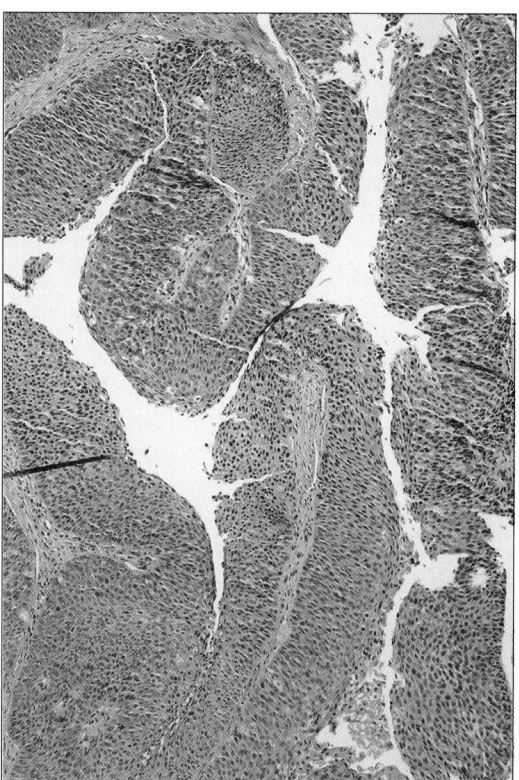

Fig. 11.157
Papillary squamous cell carcinoma: the tumor is characterized by an exophytic and endophytic growth pattern in which the tumor presents as well-formed papillary processes. By courtesy of C. Crum, MD, Brigham and Women's Hospital and Harvard Medical School, Boston, USA.

- *Basaloid* carcinoma is deeply infiltrative and consists of islands and nests of poorly differentiated basaloid cells with cytological atypia, frequent mitotic figures, comedo necrosis and only focal keratinization (*Figs 11.158, 11.159*).[41]
- *Sarcomatoid* carcinoma is the rarest variant of genital SCC.[67] Squamous differentiation is very focal and may not be apparent on hematoxylin and eosin stained sections. An immunohistochemical panel is therefore essential to confirm the diagnosis since it may highlight residual keratin positive cells. Sarcomatoid transformation of a verrucous carcinoma after radiation therapy has also been described.[68]
- *Verrucous* carcinoma is discussed on p. 526.

Rare tumors show a combination of features including conventional SCC with verrucous carcinoma or conventional SCC with basaloid features.[19,69]

Careful evaluation of the gross specimen is very important as this provides important prognostic information, particularly the level and depth of involvement.[70] The pattern of growth of SCC of the penis may be divided into superficial spreading, vertical growth, verrucous and multicentric.[57] Inguinal lymph node metastases are more often found in those tumors with a vertical growth.[57]

References

1. Mabuchi, K., Bross, D.S., Kessler, I.I. (1985) Epidemiology of cancer of the vulva. A case control study. *Cancer*, 55, 1843–1848.
2. Hording, U., Junge, J., Daugaard, S. et al (1994) Vulval squamous cell carcinoma and papilloma viruses; indications for two different etiologies. *Gynecol Oncol*, 52, 241–246.
3. Trimble, C.L., Hildesheim, A., Brinton, L.A. et al (1996) Heterogeneous etiology of squamous cell carcinoma of the vulva. *Obstet Gynecol*, 87, 59–64.
4. Crum, C. (1992) Carcinoma of the vulva: epidemiology and pathogenesis. *Obstet Gynecol*, 79, 448–458.
5. Anderson, W.A., Franquemont, D.W., Williams, J. et al (1991) Vulval squamous cell carcinoma and papillomavirus: two separate entities? *Am J Obstet Gynecol*, 165, 329–336.

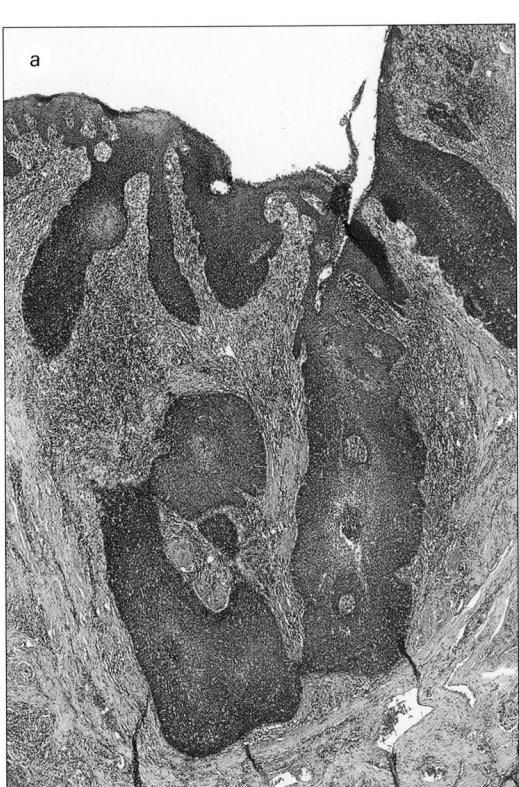
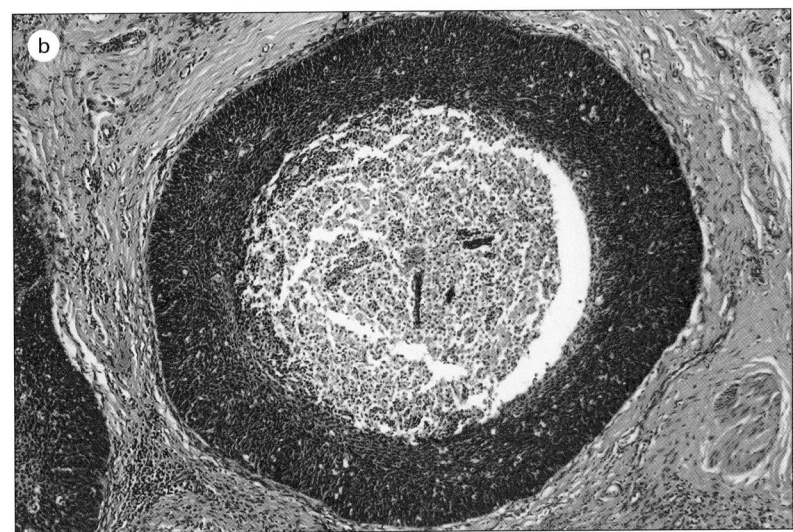

Fig. 11.158
Basaloid carcinoma: (a) the tumor is composed largely of undifferentiated cells. Origin from the surface epithelium is present; (b) there is central (comedo) necrosis.

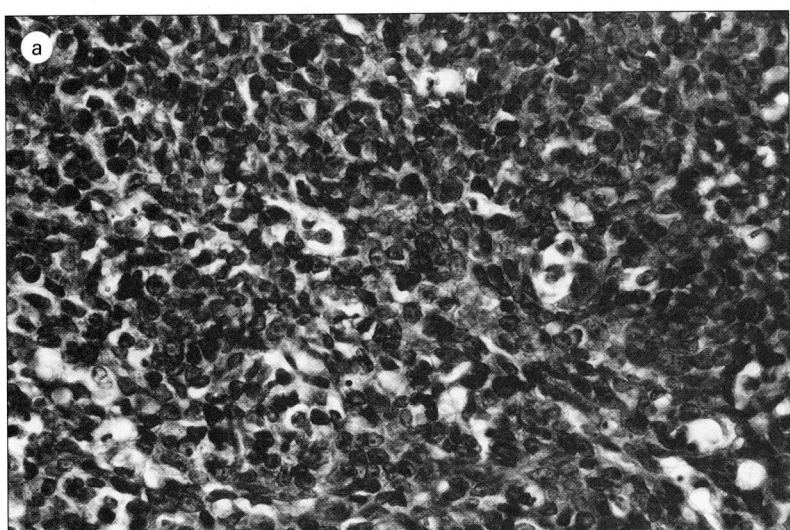
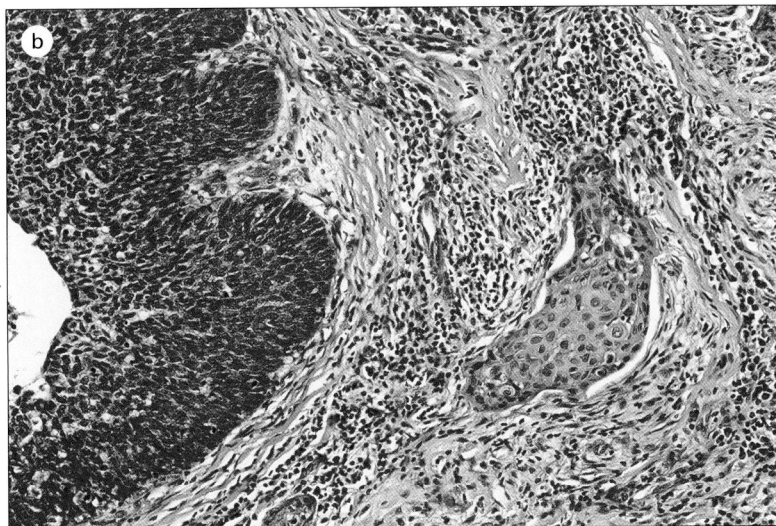

Fig. 11.159
Basaloid carcinoma: (a) the tumor cells have basophilic nuclei showing conspicuous mitotic activity, and cytoplasm is minimal; (b) focal squamous differentiation is evident.

6. Toki, T., Kurma, R.J., Park, J.S. et al (1991) Probable nonpapillomavirus etiology of squamous cell carcinoma of the vulva in older women: a clinicopathologic study using in situ hybridization and polymerase chain reaction. *Int J Gynecol Pathol*, **10**, 107–125.
7. Messing, M.J., Gallup, O.G. (1995) Carcinoma of the vulva in young women. *Obstet Gynecol*, **86**, 51–54.
8. Leibowitch, M., Neill, S., Pelisse, M. et al (1990) The epithelial changes associated with squamous cell carcinoma of the vulva: a review of the clinical, histological and viral findings in 78 women. *Br J Obstet Gynaecol*, **97**, 1135–1139.
9. Walkden, V., Chia, Y., Wojnarowska, F. (1997) The association of squamous cell carcinoma and lichen sclerosus; implications for follow up. *J Obstet Gynecol*, **17**, 551–553.
10. Derrick, E.K., Ridley, C.M., Kobza-Black, A. et al (2000) A clinical study of 23 cases of female anogenital carcinoma. *Br J Dermatol*, **143**,1217–1223.
11. Vilmer, C., Cavelier-Balloy, B., Nogues, C. et al (1998) Analysis of alterations adjacent to invasive vulvar cancer and their relationship with the associated carcinoma: a study of 67 cases. *Eur J Gynaecol Oncol*, **19**, 25–31.
12. Salzstein, S.L., Woodruff, J.D., Novak, E.R. (1956) Postgranulomatous carcinoma of the vulva. *Obstet Gynecol*, **7**, 80–90.
13. Hay, D.M., Cole, F.M. (1970) Postgranulomatous epidermoid carcinoma of the vulva. *Am J Obstet Gynecol*, **108**, 479–484.
14. Black, S.B., Woods, J.E. (1982) Squamous cell carcinoma complicating hidradenitis suppurativa. *J Surg Oncol*, **19**, 25–26.
15. Manolitsas, T., Blankin, S., Jaworski, R. et al (1999) Vulval squamous cell carcinoma arising in chronic hidradenitis suppurativa. *Gynecol Oncol*, **75**, 285–288.
16. Lapins, J., Ye, W., Nyren, O. (2001) Incidence of cancer among patients with hidadenitis suppurativa. *Arch Dermatol*, **137**, 730–734.
17. Kurman, R.J., Toki, T., Schiffman, M.H. (1993) Basaloid and warty carcinoma of the vulva. Distinctive types of squamous cell carcinoma frequently associated with human papillomaviruses. *Am J Surg Pathol*, **17**, 133–145.
18. Benedet, J.L., Turko, M., Fairey, R.N. et al (1979) Squamous carcinoma of the vulva: results of treatment 1938–1976. *Am J Obstet Gynecol*, **134**, 201–207.
19. Kohlberger, P., Kainz, C., Kolbl, H. et al (1995) Basaloid carcinoma and keratinizing squamous cell carcinoma of the vulva: a case of two primary carcinomas. *Anticancer Res*, **15**, 2307–2311.
20. Krupp, P.J. (1992) Invasive tumors of vulva: clinical features, staging and management. In: Coppleson, M. (ed.) Gynecologic oncology, 2nd edn. Edinburgh: Churchill Livingstone, pp 479–491.
21. Rutledge, F.N., Mitchell, M.F., Munsell, M.F. et al (1991) Prognostic indicators for invasive carcinoma of the vulva. *Gynecol Oncol*, **42**, 239–244.
22. Ansink, A. (1996) Vulvar squamous cell carcinoma. *Semin Dermatol*, **15**, 51–59.
23. Drew, P.A., al-Abbadi, M.A., Orlando, C.A. et al (1996) Prognostic factors in carcinoma of the vulva: a clinicopathologic and DNA flow cytometric study. *Int J Gynecol Pathol*, **15**, 235–241.
24. Pinto, A.P., Signorello, L.B., Crum, C.P. et al (1999) Squamous cell carcinoma of the vulva in Brazil: prognostic importance of host and viral variables. *Gynecol Oncol*, **74**, 61–67.
25. Smyczek-Gargya, B., Volz, B., Geppert, M. et al (1997) A multivariate analysis of clinical and morphological prognostic factors in squamous cell carcinoma of the vulva. *Gynecol Obstet Invest*, **43**, 261–267.
26. Wagner, W., Prott, F.J., Weissmann, J. et al (1999) Vulvar carcinoma: a retrospective analysis of 80 patients. *Arch Gynecol Obstet*, **262**, 99–104.
27. Rhodes, C.A., Cummins, C., Shafi, M.I. (1998) The management of squamous cell vulval cancer: a population based retrospective study of 411 cases. *Br J Obstet Gynaecol*, **105**, 200–205.
28. Burger, M.P.M., Hollema, H., Emanuels, A.G. et al (1995) The importance of the groin node status for the survival of T1 and T2 vulval carcinoma patients. *Gynecol Oncol*, **57**, 327–334.
29. Ansink, A.C., Krul, M.R.M., de Weger, R.A. et al (1994) Human papillomavirus, lichen sclerosus and squamous cell carcinoma of the vulva: detection and prognostic significance. *Gynecol Oncol*, **52**, 180–184.
30. Monk, B., Burger, R., Lin, F. et al (1995) Prognostic significance of human papillomavirus DNA in vulvar carcinoma. *Obstet Gynecol*, **85**, 709–715.
31. Micali, G., Innozenci, D., Nasca, M.R. et al (1996) Squamous cell carcinoma of the penis. *J Am Acad Dermatol*, **35**, 432–451.
32. Tsen, H.F., Morgenstern, H., Mack, T. et al (2001) Risk factors for penile cancers: results of a population-based case-control study in Los Angeles County (United States). *Cancer Causes Control*, **12**, 267–277.
33. Soria, J.C., Fizazi, K., Piron, D. et al (1997) Squamous cell carcinoma of the penis: multivariate analysis of prognostic factors and natural history in monocentric study with a conservative policy. *Ann Oncol*, **8**, 1089–1098.
34. Bissada, N.K., Morcos, R.R., El-Senoussi, M. (1986) Post-circumcision carcinoma of the penis. Clinical aspects. *J Urol*, **135**, 283–285.
35. Cubilla, A.L. (1995) Carcinoma of the penis. *Mod Pathol*, **8**, 116–118.
36. Chan, K.W., Lam, K.Y., Chan, A.C.L. et al (1994) Prevalence of human papilloma virus types 16 and 18 in penile carcinoma: a study of 41 cases using PCR. *J Clin Pathol*, **47**, 823–826.
37. Gregoire, L., Cubilla, A.L., Reuter, V.E. et al (1995) Preferential association of human papilloma virus with high-grade histologic variants of penile invasive squamous cell carcinoma. *J Natl Cancer Inst*, **87**, 1705–1709.
38. Zhang, X.H., Sun, G.Q., Yang, Y. et al (2001) Human papillomavirus and p53 protein immunoreactivity in condyloma accuminatum and squamous cell carcinoma of penis. *Asian J Androl*, **3**, 75–77.
39. Rubin, M.A., Kleter, B., Zhou, M. et al (2001) Detection and typing of human papillomavirus DNA in penile carcinoma: evidence for multiple independent pathways of penile carcinogenesis. *Am J Pathol*, **159**, 1211–1218.
40. Cubilla, A.L., Velázques, E.F., Reuter, V.E. et al (2000) Warty (condylomatous) squamous cell carcinoma of the penis. A report of 11 cases and proposed classification of 'verruciform' penile tumors. *Am J Surg Pathol*, **24**, 505–512.
41. Cubilla, A.L., Reuter, V.E., Gregoire, L. et al (1998) Basaloid squamous cell carcinoma: a distinctive human papilloma virus-related penile neoplasm. A report of 20 cases. *Am J Surg Pathol*, **22**, 755–761.
42. McCance, D.J., Kalache, A., Ashdown, K. et al (1986) Human papillomavirus types 16 and 18 in carcinomas of penis from Brazil. *Int J Cancer*, **37**, 55–59.
43. Dianzani, C., Bucci, M., Pierangeli, A. et al (1998) Association of human papillomavirus type 11 with carcinoma of the penis. *Urology*, **51**, 1046–1048.
44. Amerio, P., Offidani, A., Cellini, A. et al (1998) Well-differentiated squamous cell carcinoma of the penis associated with HPV type 33. *Int J Dermatol*, **37**, 128–130.
45. Graham, S., Priore, R., Graham, M. et al (1979) Genital cancer in wives of penile cancer patients. *Cancer*, **44**, 1870–1874.
46. Iversen, T., Tretli, S., Johansen, A. et al (1997) Squamous cell carcinoma of the penis and of the cervix, vulva and vagina in spouses: is there any relationship? An epidemiological study from Norway 1960–92. *Br J Cancer*, **76**, 658–660.
47. Mainche, A.G., Pyrhonen, S. (1990) Risk of cervical cancer among wives of men with carcinoma of the penis. *Acta Oncol*, **29**, 569–571.
48. Cupp, M.R., Malek, R.S., Goellner, J.R. et al (1995) The detection of human papillomavirus deoxyribonucleic acid in intraepithelial, in-situ, verrucous and invasive carcinoma of the penis. *J Urol*, **154**, 1024–1029.
49. Poblet, E., Alfaro, L., Fernander-Segovisno, P. et al (1999) Human papillomavirus-associated penile squamous cell carcinoma in HIV-positive patients. *Am J Surg Pathol*, **23**, 1119–1123.
50. Aboulafia, D.M., Gibbons, R. (2001) Penile cancer and human papillomavirus (HPV) in a human immunodeficiency virus (HIV)-infected patient. *Cancer Invest*, **19**, 266–272.
51. Schnitzler, L., Sayag, J., Sayag, J., Roux, G. (1987) Acute squamous cell carcinoma of the penis and lichen sclerosus et atrophicus. *Ann Dermatol Venereol*, **114**, 979–981.
52. Pride, H.B., Miller, O.F. III, Tyler, W.B. (1993) Penile squamous cell carcinoma arising from balanitis xerotica obliterans. *J Am Acad Dermatol*, **29**, 469–473.
53. Nasca, M.R., Innocenzi, D., Micali, G. (1999) Penile cancer among patients with genital lichen sclerosus. *J Am Acad Dermatol*, **41**, 911–914.
54. Powell, J., Robson, A., Cranston, D. et al (2001) High incidence of lichen sclerosus in patients with squamous cell carcinoma of the penis. *Br J Dermatol*, **145**, 85–89.
55. Porter, W.M., Hawkins, D.A., Dinneen, M. et al (2000) Zoon's balanitis and carcinoma of the penis. *Int J STD AIDS*, **11**, 484–485.
56. Takiwaki, H., Yokota, M., Ahsan, K. et al (1996) Squamous cell carcinoma associated with verruciform xanthoma of the penis. *Am J Dermatopathol*, **18**, 551–554.
57. Cubilla, A.L., Barreto, J.E., Caballero, C. et al (1993) Pathologic features of epidermoid carcinoma of the penis. A prospective study of 66 cases. *Am J Surg Pathol*, **17**, 753–763.
58. Lopes, A., Hidalgo, G.S., Kowalski, L.P. et al (1996) Prognostic factors in carcinoma of the penis: multivariate analysis of 145 patients treated with amputation and lymphadenectomy. *J Urol*, **156**, 1637–1642.
59. Cubillla, A.L., Reuter, V., Velazquez, E. et al (2001) Histologic classification of penile carcinoma and its relation to outcome in 61 patients with primary resection. *Int J Surg Pathol*, **9**, 111–120.
60. Horenblas, S., van Tinteren, H. (1994) Squamous cell carcinoma of the penis. IV. Prognostic factors of survival: analysis of tumor, nodes and metastasis classification system. *J Urol*, **151**, 1239–1243.
61. Heyns, C.F., van Vollenhoven, P., Steenkamp, J.W. et al (1997) Cancer of the penis – a review of 50 patients. *S Afr J Surg*, **35**, 120–124.
62. Lindegaard, J.C., Nielsen, O.S., Lundbeck, F.A. et al (1996) A retrospective analysis of 82 cases of cancer of the penis. *Br J Urol*, **77**, 883–890.
63. Adeyoju, A.B., Thornhill, J., Corr, J. et al (1997) Prognostic factors in squamous cell carcinoma of the penis and implications for management. *Br J Urol*, **80**, 937–939.
64. Soria, J.C., Fizazi, K., Piron, D. et al (1997) Squamous cell carcinoma of the penis: multivariate analysis of prognostic factors and natural history in a monocentric study with a conservative policy. *Ann Oncol*, **8**, 1089–1098.
65. Bezerra, A.L., Lopes, A., Santiago, G.H. et al (2001) Human papillomavirus as a prognostic factor in carcinoma of the penis: analysis of 82 patients treated with amputation and bilateral lymphadenectomy. *Cancer*, **91**, 2315–2321.
66. Alves, G., Heller, A., Fiedler, W. et al (2001) Genetic imbalances in 26 cases of penile squamous cell carcinoma. *Genes Chromosomes Cancer*, **31**, 48–53.
67. Morinaga, S., Nakamura, S., Moro, K. et al (1995) Carcinosarcoma (carcinoma with sarcomatous metaplasia) of the penis. *J Urol Pathol*, **3**, 369–376.
68. Fukunaga, M., Yokoi, K., Miyazawa, Y. et al (1994) Penile verrucous carcinoma with anaplastic transformation following radiotherapy. A case report with human papillomavirus typing and flow cytometric DNA studies. *Am J Surg Pathol*, **18**, 501–505.
69. Kato, N., Onozuka, T., Yasukawa, K. et al (2000) Penile hybrid verrucous–squamous carcinoma associated with a superficial inguinal lymph node metastasis. *Am J Dermatopathol*, **22**, 339–343.
70. Cubilla, A.L., Piris, A., Pfannl, R. et al (2001) Anatomic levels: important landmarks in penectomy specimens: a detailed anatomic and histologic study based on examination of 44 cases. *Am J Surg Pathol*, **25**, 1091–1094.

Verrucous carcinoma

Clinical features

Verrucous carcinoma is a low-grade, slow growing squamous cell carcinoma (SCC) first described in 1948.[1] The precise incidence of verrucous carcinoma is difficult to assess accurately because of the confusing number of different terms that have been applied to this tumor in the past. There has been some debate as to whether verrucous carcinoma, well-differentiated epidermoid SCC, epithelium cuniculatum and giant condyloma of Buschke–Löwenstein are all one and the same or separate entities. It is, however, now generally accepted that they are identical lesions.[2,3]

The tumor presents as a warty exophytic plaque and usually occurs at three anatomical sites: the oropharynx, sole of the foot and the anogenital skin (*Figs 11.160, 11.161*).[2,4–6] Verrucous carcinoma of the penis and vulva may arise on a background of lichen sclerosus or lichen

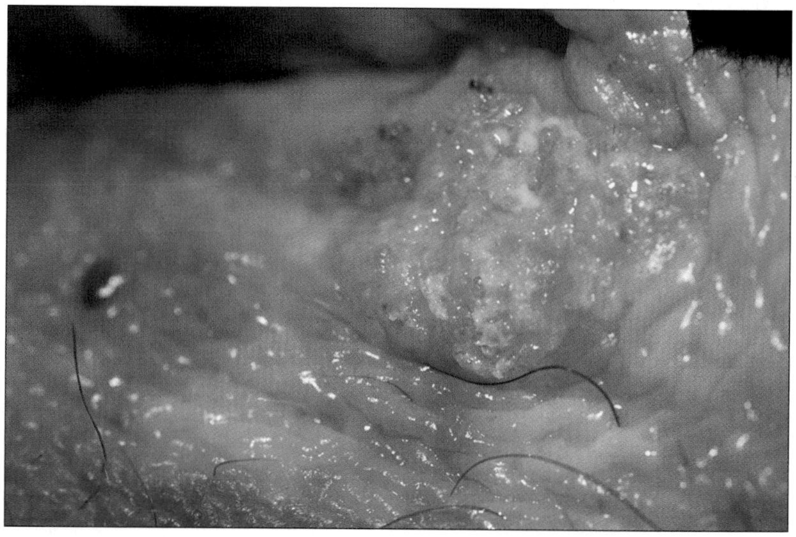

Fig. 11.160
Verrucous carcinoma: note the keratotic warty tumor mass. By courtesy of the Institute of Dermatology, London, UK.

planus.[7,8] Recent advances in the detection of HPV DNA have shown that oral and lower limb neoplasms may be associated with various types of HPV.[9–12] Similarly, genital verrucous carcinoma may be associated with human papillomavirus albeit in a minority of cases.[13,14] The benign histological appearances of verrucous carcinoma often lead to an incorrect histological report of condyloma or squamous papilloma with resultant undertreatment.

Histological features

Verrucous carcinoma is characterized by an exophytic and endophytic growth pattern.[15,16] The latter, which may extend deeply into subcutaneous tissues or beyond, has a bulbous and sharply delineated lower border, lacking the infiltrative characteristics of conventional SCC (*Figs 11.162–11.164*). The epithelium is well differentiated, showing no appreciable cytological atypia; mitoses, which are generally sparse, are confined to the lower layer. Variable keratinization is present, which often is marked. Intraepithelial neutrophil abscesses are commonly present. In some tumors, koilocytes may be seen supporting an HPV-associated etiology.

References

1. Ackerman, L.V. (1948) Verrucous carcinoma of the oral cavity. *Surgery*, 23, 670–678.
2. Gallousis, S. (1972) Verrucous carcinoma: report of three vulval cases and a review of the literature. *Obstet Gynecol*, 40, 503–507.
3. Kraus, F.T., Perez-Mesa, C. (1966) Verrucous carcinoma; clinical and pathologic study of 105 cases including oral cavity, larynx and genitalia. *Cancer*, 19, 26–38.
4. Crowther, M.E., Lowe, D.G., Shepherd, J.H. (1998) Verrucous carcinoma of the female genital tract: a review. *Obstet Gynecol Surv*, 43, 263–280.
5. McKee, P.H., Lowe, D., Haigh, R.J. (1983) Penile verrucous carcinoma. *Histopathology*, 7, 897–906.
6. Seixas, A.L., Ornellas, A.A., Marota, A. et al (1994) Verrucous carcinoma of the penis: retrospective analysis of 32 cases. *J Urol*, 152, 1476–1479.
7. Brisigotti, M., Moreno, A., Murcia, C. et al (1989) Verrucous carcinoma of the vulva: clinicopathologic and immunohistochemical study of five cases. *Int J Gynecol Pathol*, 8, 1–7.
8. Bain, L., Geronemus, R. (1989) The association of lichen planus of the penis with squamous cell carcinoma in situ and with verrucous squamous carcinoma. *J Dermatol Surg Oncol*, 15, 413–417.
9. Schwartz, R.A. (1995) Verrucous carcinoma of the skin and mucosa. *J Am Acad Dermatol*, 32, 1–21.
10. Majewski, S., Jablonska, S. (1997) Human papilloma virus-associated tumors of the skin and mucosa. *J Am Acad Dermatol*, 36, 659–685.
11. Lubbe, J., Kormann, A., Adams, V. et al (1996) HPV-11 and HPV-16 associated oral verrucous carcinoma. *Dermatology*, 192, 217–221.
12. Miyamoto, T., Sasaoka, R., Hagari, Y. et al (1999) Association of cutaneous verrucous carcinoma with human papilloma virus type 16. *Br J Dermatol*, 140, 168–169.
13. Chan, K.W., Lam, K.Y., Chan, A.C. et al (1994) Prevalence of human papillomavirus types 16 and 18 in penile carcinoma: a study of 41 cases using PCR. *J Clin Pathol*, 47, 823–826.
14. Gross, G., Pfister, H. (2003) Role of human papillomavirus in penile cancer, penile intraepithelial squamous cell neoplasia and in genital warts. *Med Microbiol Immunol* (Berl), 28: (in press)
15. Powell, J.L., Franklin, E.W., Nickerson, J.F. et al (1978) Verrucous carcinoma of the female genital tract. *Gynecol Oncol*, 6, 565–573.
16. Lowe, D., McKee, P.H. (1983) Verrucous carcinoma of the penis (Buschke–Löwenstein tumor): a clinicopathological study. *Br J Urol*, 55, 427–429.

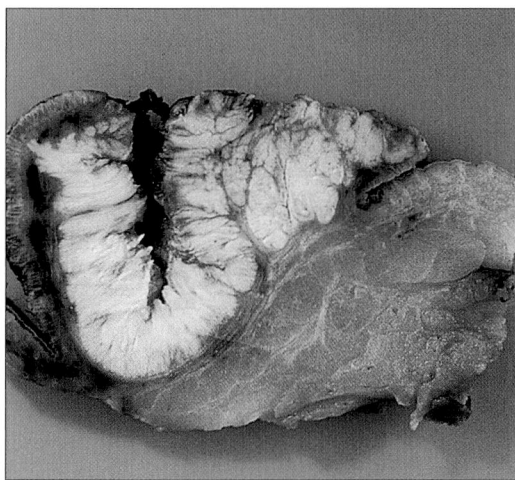

Fig. 11.161
Verrucous carcinoma: this tumor arose in the gluteal cleft of an elderly female. Note the characteristic sharply demarcated lower border.

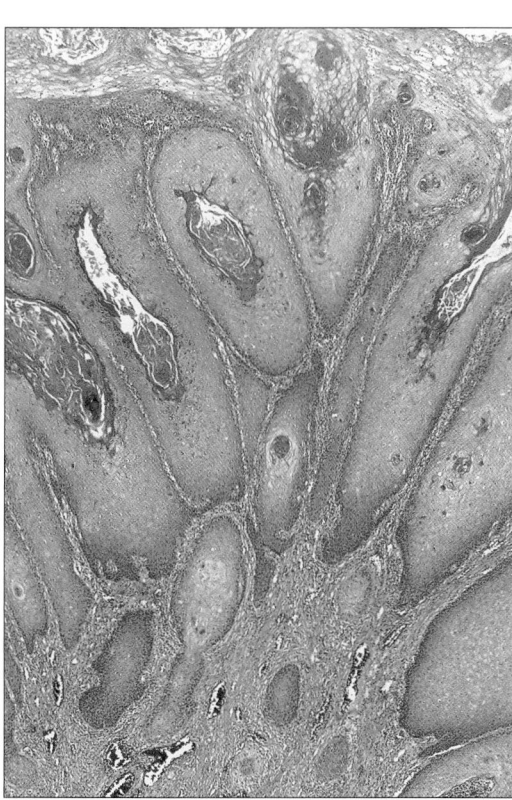

Fig. 11.162
Verrucous carcinoma: low power view showing the characteristic growth pattern comprising deeply penetrating, blunt, finger-like processes.

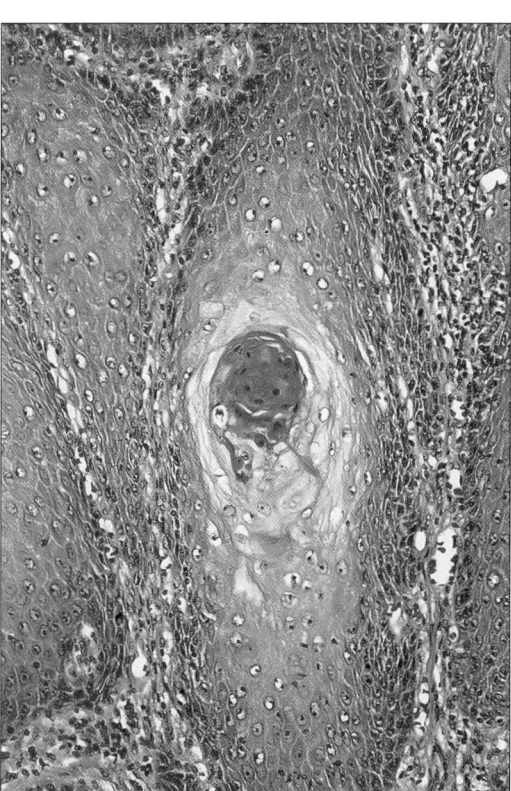

Fig. 11.163
Verrucous carcinoma: the epithelium is uniformly well differentiated and often displays a ground-glass cytoplasmic pallor.

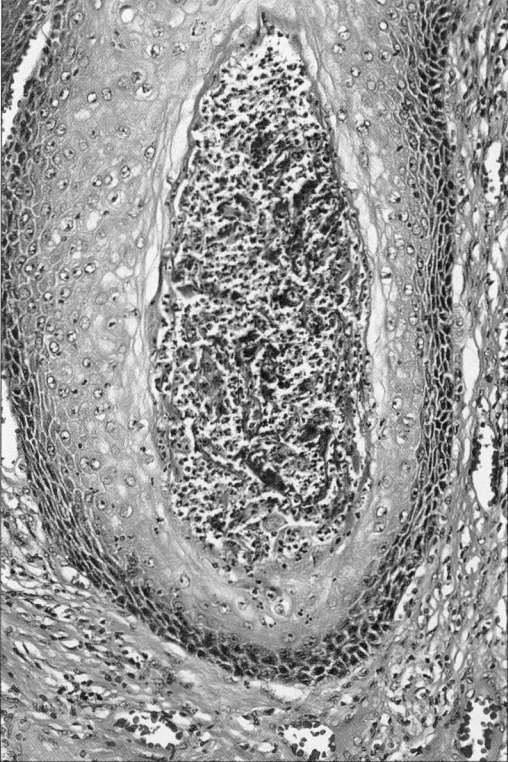

Fig. 11.164
Verrucous carcinoma: intraepithelial neutrophil abscesses are often present.

Pseudoepitheliomatous, keratotic and micaceous balanitis

Clinical features

This rare condition occurs on the glans penis in older men and there is mounting evidence to suggest that it represents a premalignant condition often associated with verrucous carcinoma.[1–7] A case associated with a penile fibrosarcoma has also been described.[8]

Clinically, white, hyperkeratotic and crusted plaques develop on the glans penis. These lesions are resistant to treatment and gradually larger nodular lesions develop.

Histological features

Biopsies from early lesions show mild to moderate epidermal hyperplasia with no cytological atypia and a variable focal lichenoid mononuclear inflammatory cell infiltrate. Larger lesions display pseudoepitheliomatous hyperplasia and often there is transition to verrucous carcinoma. There is no association with human papillomavirus infection.[7]

References

1. Read, S.I., Abell, E. (1981) Pseudoepitheliomatous, keratotic, and micaceous balanitis. *Arch Dermatol*, **117**, 435–437.
2. Beljaards, R.C., van Dijk, E., Hausman, R. (1987) Is pseudoepitheliomatous, micaceous and keratotic balanitis synonymous with verrucous carcinoma? *Br J Dermatol*, **117**, 641–646.
3. Krunic, A.L., Djerdj, K., Stacervic-Bozovic, A. et al (1996) Pseudoepitheliomatous, keratotic and micaceous balanitis. Case report and review of the literature. *Urol Int*, **56**, 125–128.
4. Ridley, C.M. (1988) Pseudoepitheliomatous micaceous and keratotic balanitis. *Br J Dermatol*, **118**, 856–857.
5. Jenkins, D. Jr, Jakubovic, H.R. (1988) Pseudoepitheliomatous, keratotic, micaceous balanitis. A clinical lesion with two histologic subsets: hyperplastic dystrophy and verrucous carcinoma. *J Am Acad Dermatol*, **18**, 419–422.
6. Gray, M.R., Ansell, I.D. (1990) Pseudo-epitheliomatous hyperkeratotic and micaceous balanitis: evidence for regarding it as pre-malignant. *Br J Urol*, **66**, 103–104.
7. Child, F.J., Kim, B.K., Ganesan, R. et al (2000) Verrucous carcinoma arising in pseudoepitheliomatous keratotic and micaceous balanitis without evidence of human papilloma virus. *Br J Dermatol*, **143**, 183–187.
8. Irvine, C., Anderson, J.R., Pye, R.J. (1987) Micaceous and keratotic balanitis and rapidly fatal fibrosarcoma of the penis occurring in the same patient. *Br J Dermatol*, **116**, 719–725.

Penile adenosquamous carcinoma

This very rare tumor presents in adult males on the glans penis.[1] It is not associated with the periurethral glands and is thought to originate from the surface epithelium or from embryologically misplaced mucinous glands located in the perimeatal region of the mucosa of the glans.[1] Of the few reported cases only one tumor has spread to regional lymph nodes.

The tumor combines malignant squamous and glandular elements. The former predominates with the latter presenting as small distinct foci scattered throughout the lesion.

Reference

1. Cubilla, A.L., Ayala, M.T., Barreto, J.E. et al (1996) Surface adenosquamous carcinoma of the penis. A report of three cases. *Am J Surg Pathol*, **20**, 156–160.

Cloacogenic carcinoma

This rare tumor presents in middle-aged women as a superficial ulcerated adenocarcinoma composed of colonic-type glands arising in direct continuity with vulval surface epithelium (*Figs 11.165–11.167*).[1–5] It is independent of the perivulval glands and, by definition, direct extension or metastasis from an underlying large intestinal or visceral adenocarcinoma has been excluded. In a single case, the neoplastic glands also contained Paneth cells.[5] The origin of this tumor is not known but it is thought most probably to arise from an area of gastrointestinal metaplasia or from heterotopic intestinal tissue (*Fig. 11.168*).[6] Vulval

cloacogenic carcinoma should not be confused with the similarly named tumor of the anal canal.

References

1. Zaidi, S.N., Conner, M.G. (2001) Primary vulvar adenocarcinoma of cloacogenic origin. *South Med J*, **94**, 744–746.
2. Willen, R., Bekassy, M., Carlen, B. et al (1999) Cloacogenic adenocarcinoma of the vulva. *Gynecol Oncol*, **74**, 298–301.
3. Ghamande, S.A., Kasznica, J., Griffiths, C.T. et al (1995) Mucinous adenocarcinomas of the vulva. *Gynecol Oncol*, **57**, 117–120.
4. Kennedy, J.C., Majmudar, B. (1993) Primary adenocarcinoma of the vulva, possibly cloacogenic. A report of two cases. *J Reprod Med*, **38**, 113–116.
5. Tiltman, A.J., Knutzen, V.K. (1978) Primary adenocarcinoma of the vulva originating in misplaced cloacal tissue. *Obstet Gynecol*, **51**, 30S–33S.
6. Yeoh, G., Bannatyne, P., Kossard, S. et al (1987) Intestinal heterotopia: an unusual cause of vulval ulceration: a case report. *Br J Obstet Gynaecol*, **94**, 600–602.

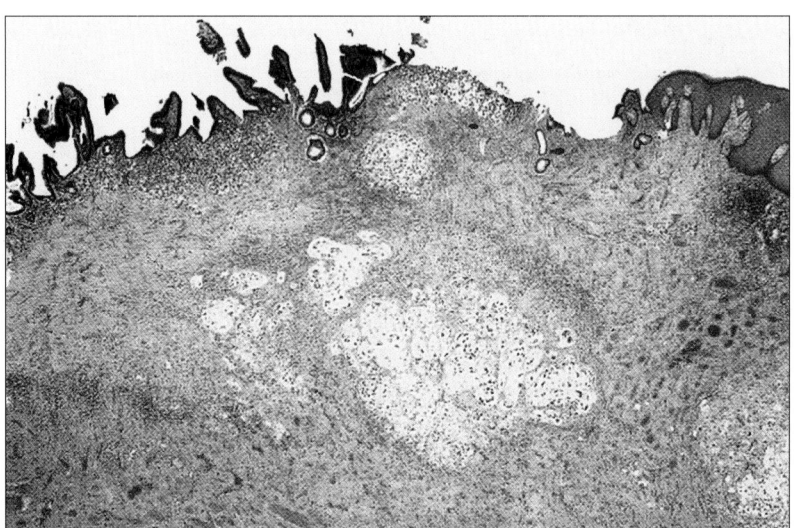

Fig. 11.165
Cloacogenic vulval adenocarcinoma: scanning view showing vulval squamous epithelium on the far right. Colonic epithelium is present on the left. Mucus-secreting carcinoma extends throughout the underlying connective tissue.

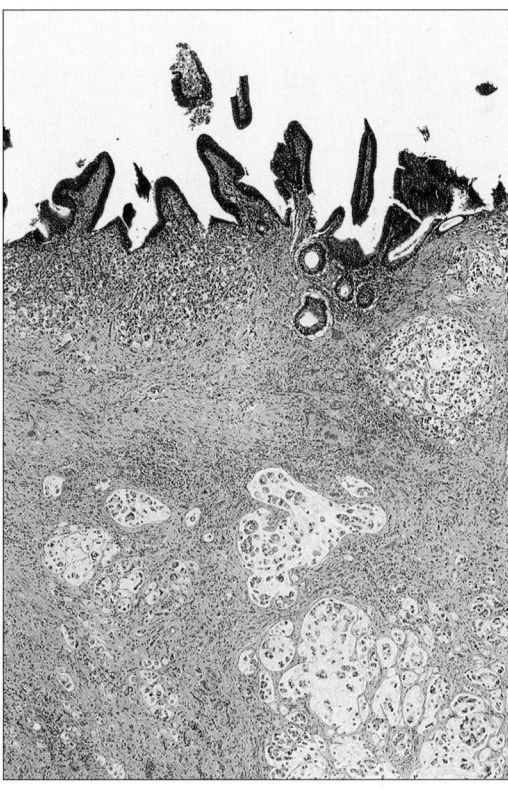

Fig. 11.166
Cloacogenic vulval adenocarcinoma: the tumor is associated with abundant mucin secretion forming large lakes.

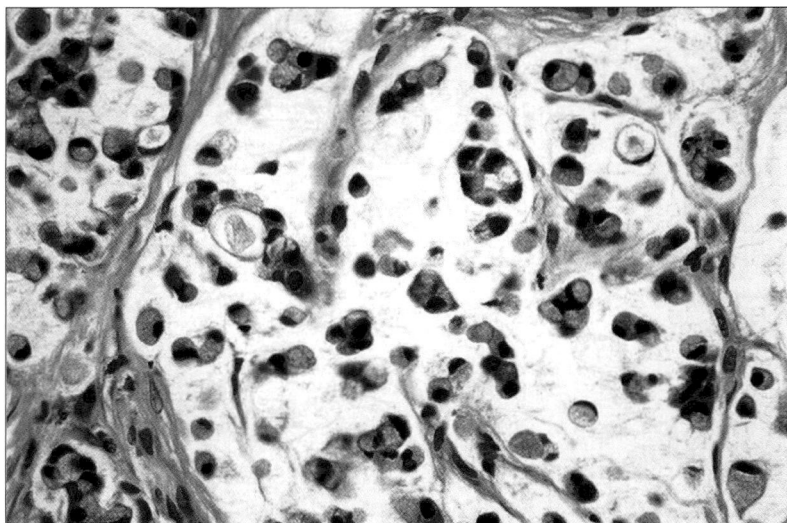

Fig. 11.167
Cloacogenic vulval adenocarcinoma: close-up view showing the tumor cells distended by intracytoplasmic mucin.

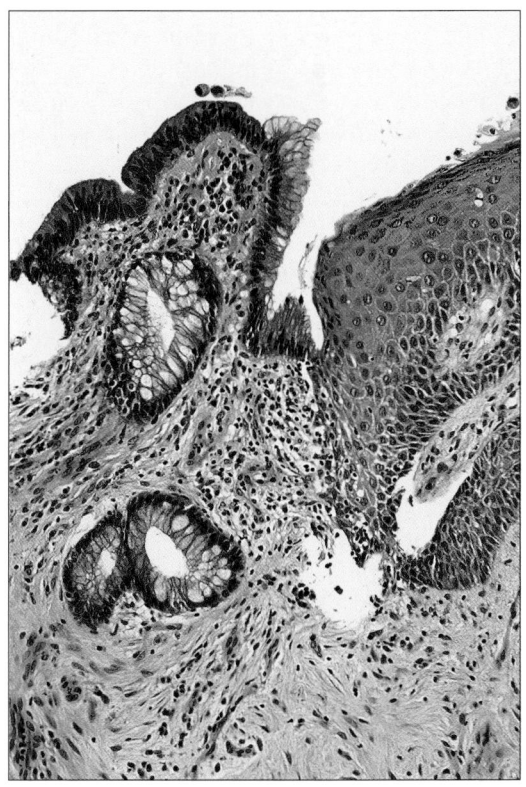

Fig. 11.168
Cloacogenic vulval adenocarcinoma: high power view of the junction between squamous and colonic epithelium.

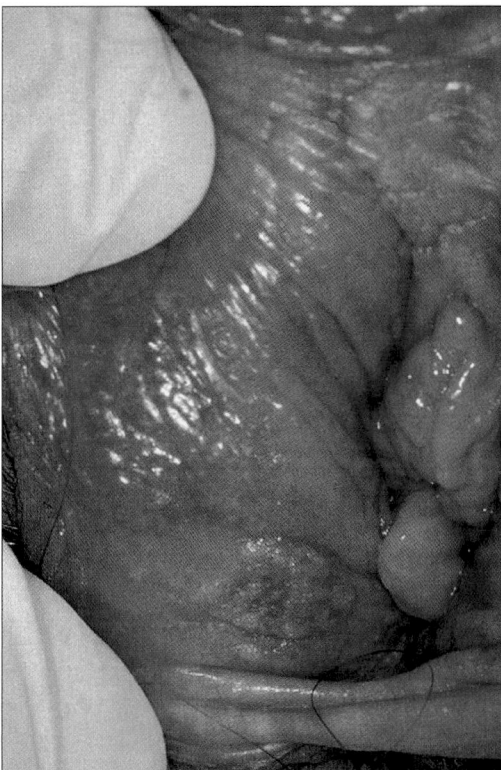

Fig. 11.169
Papillary hidradenoma: the lesion presents as a warty nodule. By courtesy of the Institute of Dermatology, London, UK.

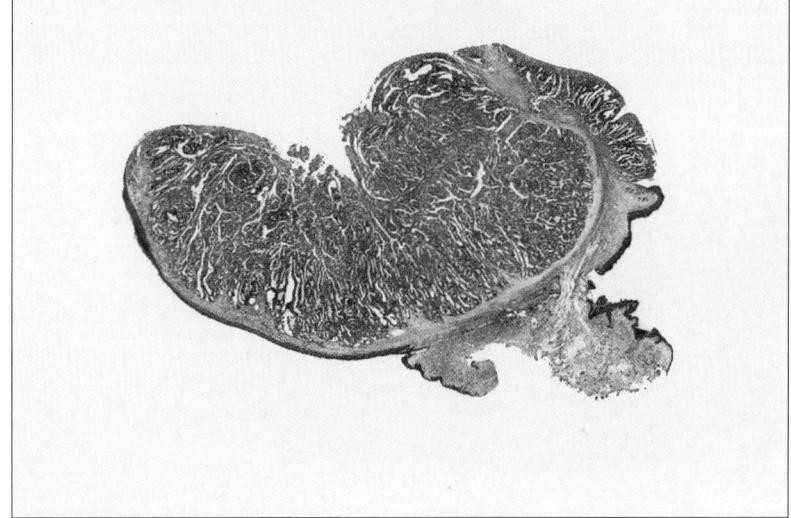

Fig. 11.170
Papillary hidradenoma: whole mount preparation showing sharply circumscribed papillary tumor.

Papillary hidradenoma

Clinical features

Papillary hidradenoma (hidradenoma papilliferum) occurs almost exclusively in females.[1–5] A single example of a perianal variant has been described in a male.[6]

Papillary hidradenoma typically presents in middle-aged women as a small (1–2 cm diameter) solitary asymptomatic nodule in a vulval, perineal or perianal location.[4] Rare lesions attain a large size.[7,8] Ulceration is exceptional. Most often it affects the labium majus, but on occasion it arises on the lateral aspect of the labium minus (*Fig. 11.169*).[9] It is often associated with the anogenital glands.[10] Exceptionally tumors are multiple and such cases tend to be located on the same side of the vulva.[1,2,11] Very rarely lesions may have been described on the nipple, eyelid and external auditory canal.[3,4]

Histological features

The epidermis may be normal, acanthotic or ulcerated. The tumor forms a fairly well demarcated nodule in the dermis or lamina propria and sometimes shows foci of continuity with the overlying epithelium.[5] It is composed of epithelium-covered papillary processes projecting into cystic spaces (*Fig. 11.170*). The epithelium lining is typically double layered, comprising outer small myoepithelial cells with oval hyperchromatic nuclei and inner tall columnar cells with eosinophilic cytoplasm, sometimes manifesting decapitation secretion (*Figs 11.171, 11.172*). Occasionally, the lining is only one cell thick (columnar). Diastase-resistant, PAS-positive intracytoplasmic granules are usually present. Uncommonly, focal sebaceous differentiation may be a feature.[5] The occasional finding of a normal mitotic figure has no sinister implication. The larger villi have a fibrous core in which occasional ductal structures may be identified. Often the fibrous tissue surrounding the tumor is compressed to form a pseudocapsule. An inflammatory cell component is not a significant feature. Exceptionally rarely, a malignant variant may be encountered.[12,13] The malignant component is usually an apocrine carcinoma but an adenosquamous carcinoma has also been documented.[12]

References

1. Meeker, J.H., Neubecker, R.D., Helwig, E.B. (1962) Hidradenoma papilliferum. *Am J Clin Pathol*, **37**, 182–195.
2. Woodworth, H., Dockerty, M.B., Wilson, R.B. et al (1971) Papillary hidradenoma of the vulva: a clinicopathologic study of 69 cases. *Am J Obst Gynecol*, **110**, 501–508.
3. Santa Cruz, D.J., Prioleau, P.G., Smith, M.E. (1981) Hidradenoma papilliferum of the eyelid. *Arch Dermatol*, **117**, 55–56.
4. Nissim, F., Czernobilsky, B., Ostfield, E. (1981) Hidradenoma papilliferum of the external auditory canal. *J Laryngol Otol*, **95**, 843–847.
5. Warkel, R.L. (1984) Selected apocrine neoplasms. *J Cutan Pathol*, **11**, 437–449.
6. Loane, J., Kealy, W.F., Mulcaghy, G. (1998) Perianal hidradenoma papilliferum occurring in a male: a case report. *Ir J Med Sci*, **167**, 26–27.
7. Kaufmann, T., Pawl, N.O., Soifer, I. et al (1987) Cystic papillary hidradenoma of the vulva: case report and review of the literature. *Gynecol Oncol*, **26**, 240–245.
8. Veraldi, S., Schianchi-Veraldi, R., Marini, D. (1990) Hidradenoma papilliferum of the vulva: report of a case characterized by unusual clinical behaviour. *J Dermatol Surg Oncol*, **16**, 674–676.
9. Van der Putte, S.C.J. (1991) Anogenital 'sweat' glands: histology and pathology of a gland that may mimic mammary glands. *Am J Dermatopathol*, **13**, 557–565.
10. Basta, A., Madej, J.G. (1990) Hidradenoma of the vulva: incidence and clinical observations. *Eur J Gynaecol Oncol*, **11**, 185–189.
11. Hobbs, J.E. (1965) Sweat gland tumors. *Clin Obstet Gynecol*, **8**, 946–951.
12. Bannatyne, P., Elliott, P., Russell, P. (1989) Vulvar adenosquamous carcinoma arising in a hidradenoma papilliferum with rapidly fatal outcome: a case report. *Gynecol Oncol*, **35**, 395–398.
13. Pelosi, G., Martignoni, G., Bonetti, F. (1991) Intraductal carcinoma of mammary-type apocrine epithelium arising within a papillary hidradenoma of the vulva: report of a case and review of the literature. *Arch Pathol Lab Med*, **115**, 1249–1254.

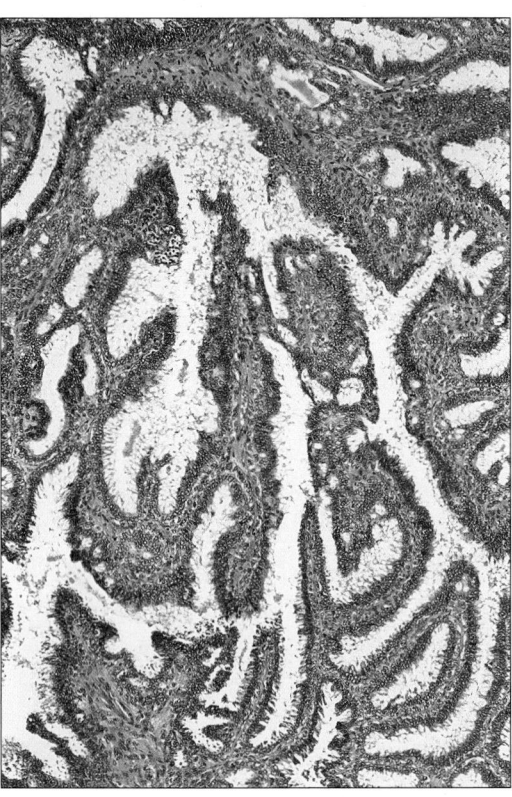

Fig. 11.171
Papillary hidradenoma: the papillae have a fibrovascular core.

Apocrine carcinoma

Apocrine carcinoma is discussed on page 1598.

Extramammary Paget's disease

Extramammary Paget's disease is discussed on page 1514.

Benign tumors of Bartholin's gland

Clinical features

Benign tumors of the Bartholin gland are very rare and the vast majority are nodular hyperplasias.[1] Adenomas are exceptionally rare as are adenomyomas.[1–3] They all present as a small asymptomatic mass on the posterolateral aspect of the vulva and are usually diagnosed clinically as a cyst. Nodular hyperplasia often presents in younger patients.

Histological features

Nodular hyperplasia is well circumscribed and lobular with preservation of the normal duct–acinar relationship.[1] Focal inflammation and squamous metaplasia of the ducts is commonly seen. Adenomas are well circumscribed and composed of small- to medium-sized glands with focal papillary projections and lined by columnar, mucin-producing cells with no cytological atypia and very rare mitotic figures. Tubules and acini proliferate in a haphazard way in contrast to the hyperplasias where the normal architecture is preserved.[1] A single case of a papilloma arising from the duct of a Bartholin's cyst has been reported.[4]

References

1. Koenig, C., Tavassoli, F.A. (1998) Nodular hyperplasia, adenoma, and adenomyoma of Bartholin's gland. *Int J Gynecol Pathol*, **17**, 289–294.
2. Foushee, J.H.S., Reeves, W.J.U., McCool, J.A. (1968) Benign masses of Bartholin's gland: solid adenomas, adenomas with cyst, and Bartholin's gland with varices or thrombosis or cavernous hemangioma. *Obst Gynecol*, **31**, 695–701.
3. Honore, L.H., O'Hara, K.E. (1978) Adenomas of the Bartholin's gland: report of three cases. *Eur J Obstet Gynecol Reprod Biol*, **8**, 335–340.
4. Enghardt, M.H., Valente, P.T., Day, D.H. (1993) Papilloma of Bartholin's gland duct cyst: first report of a case. *Int J Gynecol Pathol*, **12**, 86–92.

Adenoma of minor vestibular glands

Adenoma of minor vestibular glands (paravestibular tumor) is exceedingly rare and occurs in the vulvar vestibule.[1,2] It is likely that it represents a hyperplasia rather than a true neoplasm. It is very small and usually represents an incidental finding in a biopsy taken for another reason.[3]

Histologically it consists of a small nodular aggregate of mucin-secreting glands lined by columnar cells.

References

1. Axe, S., Parmley, T., Woodruff, J.D. et al (1986) Adenomas in minor vestibular glands. *Obstet Gynecol*, **68**, 16–18.
2. Fowler, W.C. Jr, Lawrence, H., Edelman, D.A. (1981) Paravestibular tumor of the female genital tract. *Am J Obstet Gynecol*, **139**, 109–111.
3. Friedrich, E.G. Jr (1987) Vulvar vestibulitis syndrome. *J Reprod Med*, **32**, 110–114.

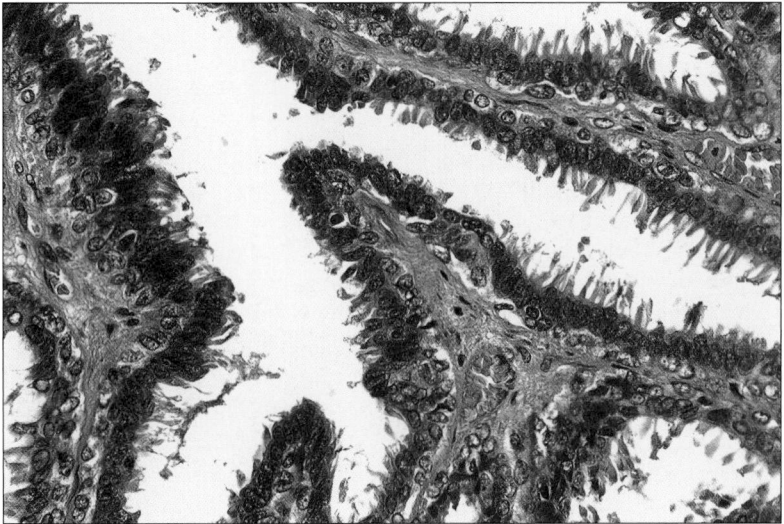

Fig. 11.172
Papillary hidradenoma: the papillae are covered by a double layer of epithelial cells, the inner showing typical decapitation secretion.

Bartholin's gland carcinoma

Clinical features

This rare tumor accounts for only between 2 and 7% of vulvar neoplasms.[1-8] It presents as a painless hard deep subcutaneous nodule, which, as it expands, becomes fixed and painful. The lesion measures from 1 cm to several centimeters and is located in the posterior aspect of the labium majus. It often invades deeply into fat, muscle or bone and may be associated with a Bartholin's gland abscess. The diagnosis is often delayed because of the latter association. Adult and elderly women are usually affected. Exceptional cases have been described during pregnancy.[4]

It is often difficult to decide when a tumor has originated from Bartholin's gland and particular attention should be paid to exclude a metastasis from elsewhere. Distinction from a sweat gland carcinoma can also be a diagnostic problem. Rarely the tumor may be associated with extramammary Paget's disease.[9,10] In recent years, a consistent association has been found between these tumors and HPV-16.[11,12] Recurrence rate varies and has been reported to be as high as 54%.[13] Up to 40% of patients present with inguinofemoral metastases. In the latter patients the 5-year survival is less than 50% but this is decreased to around 18% when two or more lymph nodes are involved.[5,7,8]

Histological features

About 40% of Bartholin's gland carcinomas are adenocarcinomas.[4,7] A further 40% are squamous cell carcinomas and 15% are adenoid cystic carcinomas.[14-16] The remainder are transitional, adenosquamous or anaplastic carcinomas.[5,8]

Exceptional cases of neuroendocrine carcinoma of Bartholin's gland have also been described.[2,17] Malignant mixed tumor very rarely originates from Bartholin's gland.[18] A neoplasm can only be accepted as originating from a Bartholin gland if there is continuity with the gland. Adenocarcinomas may be mucinous or papillary.[5] Cytogenetic analysis of a single case of adenoid cystic carcinoma of Bartholin's gland revealed complex chromosomal abnormalities involving chromosomes 1, 4, 6, 11, 14 and 22.[19]

References

1. Wharton, L.R. Jr, Everett, H.S. (1951) Primary malignant Bartholin's gland tumors. *Obstet Gynecol Surv*, **6**, 1–8.
2. Cardosi, R.J., Speights, A., Fiorica, J.V. et al (2001) Bartholin's gland carcinoma: a 15-year experience. *Gynecol Oncol*, **82**, 247–251.
3. Balat, O., Edwards, C.L., Delclos, L. (2001) Advanced primary carcinoma of the Bartholin gland: report of 18 patients. *Eur J Gynaecol Oncol*, **22**, 46–49.
4. Barclay, D.L., Collins, C.G., Macey, H.B. (1964) Cancer of the Bartholin's gland: a review and report of eight cases. *Obstet Gynecol*, **24**, 329–336.
5. Chamlian, D.L., Taylor, H.B. (1972) Primary carcinoma of Bartholin's gland: a report of 24 patients. *Obstet Gynecol*, **38**, 489–494.
6. Wahlstrom, T., Vesterinen, E., Saksela, E. (1978) Primary carcinoma of Bartholin's glands: a morphological and clinical study of six cases including a transitional cell carcinoma. *Gynecol Oncol*, **6**, 354–362.
7. Leuchter, R.S., Hacker, N.F., Voet, R.L. et al (1982) Primary carcinoma of Bartholin's gland: a report of 14 cases and review of the literature. *Obstet Gynecol*, **60**, 361–368.
8. Wheelock, J.B., Goplerud, D.R., Dunn, L.T. et al (1984) Primary carcinoma of the Bartholin gland: a report of ten cases. *Obstet Gynecol*, **63**, 820–824.
9. Hastrup, N., Andersen, F. (1988) Adenocarcinoma of Bartholin's gland associated with extramammary Paget's disease of the vulva. *Acta Obstet Gynecol Scand*, **67**, 375–377.
10. Tchang, F., Okagaki, T., Richart, R.M. (1973) Adenocarcinoma of Bartholin's gland associated with Paget's disease of vulvar area. *Cancer*, **31**, 221–225.
11. Scinicariello, F., Rady, P., Hannigna, E. et al (1992) Human papillomavirus type 16 found in primary transitional cell carcinoma of the Bartholin's gland and in a lymph node metastasis. *Gynecol Oncol*, **47**, 263–266.
12. Felix, J.C., Cote, R.J., Kramer, E.E. et al (1993) Carcinomas of Bartholin's gland: histogenesis and the etiological role of human papillomavirus. *Am J Pathol*, **142**, 925–933.
13. Jones, M.A., Mann, E.W., Caldwell, C.L. et al (1990) Small cell neuroendocrine carcinoma of Bartholin's gland. *Am J Clin Pathol*, **94**, 439–442.
14. Rosenberg, P., Simonsen, E., Risberg, B. (1989) Adenoid cystic carcinoma of Bartholin's gland: a report of five new cases treated with surgery and radiotherapy. *Gynecol Oncol*, **34**, 145–147.
15. Dunn, S. (1995) Adenoid cystic carcinoma of Bartholin's gland – a review of the literature and report of a patient. *Acta Obstet Gynecol Scand*, **74**, 78–80.
16. DePasquale, S.E., McGuinness, T.B., Mangan, C.E. et al (1996) Adenoid cystic carcinoma of Bartholin's gland: a review of the literature and report of a patient. *Gynecol Oncol*, **61**, 122–125.
17. Obermair, A., Koller, S., Crandon, A.J. et al (2001) Primary Bartholin gland carcinoma: a report of seven cases. *Aust N Z J Obstet Gynaecol*, **41**, 78–81.
18. Ordonez, N.G., Manning, J.T., Luna, M.A. (1981) Mixed tumor of the vulva: a report of two cases probably arising in Bartholin's gland. *Cancer*, **48**, 181–186.
19. Kiechle-Schwarz, M., Kommoss, F., Schmidt, J. et al (1992) Cytogenetic analysis of an adenoid cystic carcinoma of the Bartholin's gland. A rare, semimalignant tumor of the female genitourinary tract. *Cancer Genet Cytogenet*, **61**, 26–30.

Basal cell carcinoma

Exceptionally rarely, basal cell carcinoma arises on anogenital skin (*Figs 11.173, 11.174*). They usually present as an eroded plaque, which may be pigmented. Less commonly the tumor forms a nodule or an ulcer. They occur most frequently on the labia majora, pubis or penis and typically affect the elderly.[1-3]

Histologically the appearances are identical to basal cell carcinomas occurring elsewhere (see p. 1173). Inadequate excision accounts for a

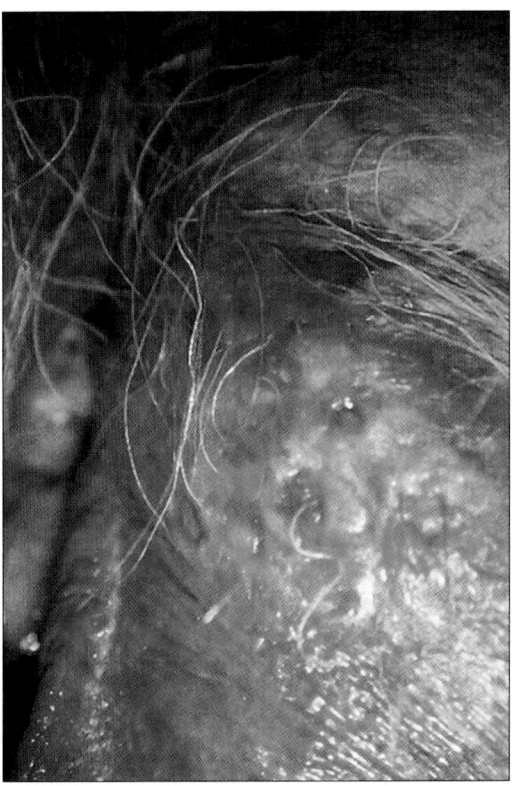

Fig. 11.173
Vulval basal cell carcinoma: erythematous, keratotic plaque on left labium majus. By courtesy of the Institute of Dermatology, London, UK.

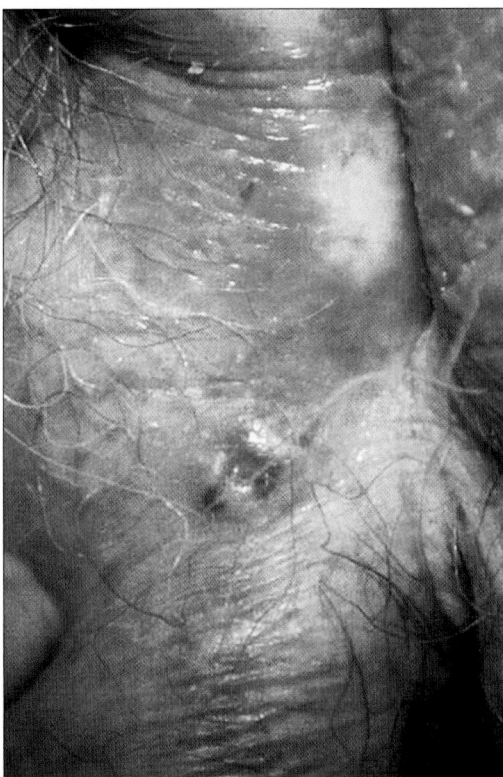

Fig. 11.174
Perianal basal cell carcinoma: ulcerated perianal nodule with a pearly white rolled border. By courtesy of the Institute of Dermatology, London, UK.

high recurrence rate and exceptional metastases to regional lymph nodes. Moh's surgery is often recommended to ensure adequate local excision and acceptable cosmetic results.

References

1.   Kim, E.D.D., Kroft, S., Dalton, D.P. (1994) Basal cell carcinoma of the penis. Case report and review of the literature. *J Urol*, 253, 1557–1559.
2.   Feakins, R.M., Lowe, D.G. (1997) Basal cell carcinoma of the vulva: a clinicopathologic study of 45 cases. *Int J Gynecol Pathol*, 16, 319–324.
3.   Gibson, G.E., Ahmed, I. (2001) Perianal and genital basal cell carcinoma: a clinicopathologic review of 51 cases. *J Am Acad Dermatol*, 45, 68–71.

Metastatic tumors

The anogenital skin is a very rare site for metastatic tumors.[1–3] Those that are described are usually from a nearby primary site, for example vulval metastases may be derived from vaginal, cervical, endometrial, ovarian, renal cell carcinoma and choriocarcinoma; penile metastases most often arise from the prostate, colon, bladder and kidney. The metastases are most commonly sited on the labia majora or periclitorally and in the corpus cavernosum of the penis.[4] Penile metastasis may result in priapism.[4] Metastases can also be found in episiotomy scars.[5] An exceptional metastasis to a Bartholin gland has been reported.[6]

References

1.   Lerner, L.B., Andrews, S.J., Gonzalez, J.L. et al (1999) Vulvar metastases secondary to transitional cell carcinoma of the bladder. A case report. *J Reprod Med*, 44, 729–732.
2.   Kotake, Y., Gohji, K., Suzuki, T. et al (2001) Metastasis to the penis from carcinoma of the prostate. *Int J Urol*, 8, 83–86.
3.   Miyamoto, T., Ikehara, A., Araki, M. et al (2000) Cutaneous metastatic carcinoma of the penis: suspected metastasis implantation from a bladder tumor. *J Urol*, 163, 1519.
4.   Schroeder-Printzen, I., Vosshenrich, R., Weidner, W. et al (1994) Malignant priapism in a patient with metastatic prostate adenocarcinoma. *Urol Int*, 52, 52–54.
5.   Van Dam, P.A., Irvine, L., Lowe, D.G. et al (1992) Carcinoma in episiotomy scars. *Gynecol Oncol*, 44, 96–100.
6.   Patsner, B. (1996) Bartholin's gland metastases from breast cancer: a case report. *Eur J Gynaecol Oncol*, 17, 96–98.

Langerhans' cell histiocytosis

In this condition, exceptionally the anogenital region is the only site affected. More commonly, such involvement represents only one of many sites of disseminated disease.[1–5] Females are affected much more often than males and lesions may present as ulcers, erosions, papules, nodules or plaques. The histological features are described on page 1461.

References

1.   Rivera-Luna, R., Martinez-Guerra, G., Altamirano-Awarez, E. et al (1988) Langerhans' cell histiocytosis: clinical experience with 124 patients. *Pediatr Dermatol*, 5, 145–150.
2.   Stein, S.L., Paller, A.S., Haut, P.R. et al (2001) Langerhans' cell histiocytosis presenting in the neonatal period: a retrospective case series. *Arch Pediatr Adol Med*, 155, 778–783.
3.   Axiotis, C.A., Merino, M.J., Duray, P.H. (1991) Langerhans' cell histiocytosis of the female genital tract. *Cancer*, 67, 1650–1660.
4.   Hoang, M.P., Owen, S.A., Haisley-Royster, C. et al (2001) Papular eruption of the scalp accompanied by axillary and vulvar ulcerations. *Arch Dermatol*, 137, 1241–1246.
5.   Meehan, S.A., Smoller, B.R. (1998) Cutaneous Langerhans' cell histiocytosis of the genitalia in the elderly: a report of three cases. *J Cutan Pathol*, 25, 370–374.

Soft tissue tumors

Fibroepithelial stromal polyp

Clinical features

Fibroepithelial stromal polyp (mesodermal stromal polyp, pseudo-sarcoma botryoides), which presents in women of reproductive age, predominantly affects the vagina and, less commonly, the vulva.[1–9] Involvement of the cervix is rare.[2] In the vagina, the lower third is the most frequent location. Presentation in the very young or the elderly is uncommon. Interestingly, about one-third of patients are pregnant,[5] suggesting that hormonal influences play a significant role in the pathogenesis of these tumors. Lesions can be single or, more rarely, multiple and bilateral,[10] the latter occurrence being most frequently seen in pregnancy. Lesions are usually less than 2 cm in diameter and are often pedunculated. Local recurrence may occur following incomplete excision but the behavior is benign.

Histological features

Low power examination reveals a polypoid and often pedunculated lesion with a fibrovascular stroma and showing variable cellularity. Small- to medium-sized blood vessels with thick walls are conspicuous (*Fig. 11.175*). Hypocellular tumors contain abundant collagen and only scattered spindle-shaped or stellate cells displaying mild focal or no cytological atypia and occasional to frequent multinucleated cells. With increasingly cellular tumors, there is more prominent cytological atypia and mitotic figures may be conspicuous (*Figs 11.176, 11.177*).[8,9,11]

Occasional atypical forms may be seen. Such atypical variants are more frequent in pregnant patients. Multinucleated tumor cells become more prominent with a tendency to concentrate in the stroma adjacent to the epithelium. The cellularity is more prominent towards the center of the lesion.[8] Small collections of mononuclear inflammatory cells are also commonly present.

Tumor cells are positive for desmin, vimentin and estrogen and progesterone receptors.[9,12–15] Positivity for actin is rare and macrophage markers are negative.[12]

Ultrastructural studies show cells with features of fibroblasts and myofibroblasts.[13,14]

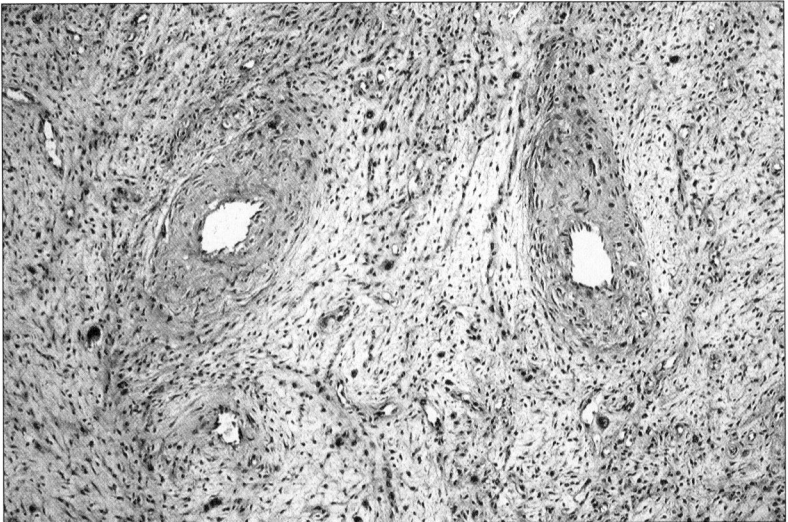

Fig. 11.175
Fibroepithelial stromal polyp: there are thick-walled vessels associated with a variably cellular loose connective tissue stroma. By courtesy of M. Nucci, MD, Brigham and Women's Hospital and Harvard Medical School, Boston, USA.

Differential diagnosis

The main differential diagnosis, particularly for lesions presenting in the vagina, is sarcoma botryoides. The latter lesion, in contrast, tends to occur at a much younger age, lacks a cambium layer, displays invasion of the epithelium by tumor cells, and is composed of small, undifferentiated tumor cells.

References

1. Norris, H.J., Taylor, H.B. (1966) Polyps of the vagina. A benign lesion resembling sarcoma botryoides. *Cancer*, **19**, 227–232.
2. Elliot, G.B., Reynolds, H.A., Fidler, H.K. (1967) Pseudosarcoma botryoides of cervix and vagina in pregnancy. *J Obstet Gynaecol Br Commonw*, **74**, 728–733.
3. Burt, R.L., Prichard, O.W., Kim, B.S. (1976) Fibroepithelial polyp of the vagina. A report of five cases. *Obstet Gynecol*, **47** (Suppl.), 52S–54S.
4. Chirayil, S.J., Tobon, H. (1981) Polyps of the vagina: a clinicopathologic study of 18 cases. *Cancer*, **47**, 2904–2907.
5. O'Quinn, A.G., Edwards, C.L., Gallager, H.S. (1982) Pseudosarcoma botryoides of the vagina in pregnancy. *Gynecol Oncol*, **13**, 237–241.
6. Miettinen, M., Wahlstrom, T., Vesterinen, E. et al (1983) Vaginal polyps with pseudosarcomatous features. A clinicopathologic study of seven cases. *Cancer*, **51**, 1148–1151.
7. Ostor, A.G., Fortune, D.W., Riley, C.B. (1988) Fibroepithelial polyps with atypical stromal cells (pseudosarcoma botryoides) of vulva and vagina. A report of 13 cases. *Int J Gynecol Pathol*, **7**, 351–360.
8. Nucci, M.R., Fletcher, C.D.M. (2000) Vulvovaginal soft tissue tumours: update and review. *Histopathology*, **36**, 97–108.
9. Nucci, M.R., Young, R.H., Fletcher, C.D.M. (2000) Cellular pseudosarcomatous fibroepithelial stromal polyps of the lower female genital tract: an under-recognized lesion often misdiagnosed as sarcoma. *Am J Surg Pathol*, **24**, 231–240.
10. Carter, J., Elliott, P., Russell, P. (1992) Bilateral fibroepithelial polyps of labium minus with atypical stromal cells. *Pathology*, **43**, 604–608.
11. Nucci, M.R., Fletcher, C.D.M. (1998) Fibroepithelial stromal polyps of vulvovaginal tissue. From the banal to the bizarre. *Pathol Case Rev*, **3**, 151–157.
12. Hartmann, C.A., Sperling, M., Stein, H. (1990) So-called fibroepithelial polyps of the vagina exhibiting an unusual but uniform antigen profile characterised by expression of desmin and steroid hormone receptors but no muscle-specific actin or macrophage markers. *Am J Clin Pathol*, **93**, 604–608.
13. Mucitelli, D.R., Charles, E.Z., Kraus, F.T. (1990) Vulvovaginal polyps. Histologic appearance, ultrastructure, immunocytochemical characteristics, and clinicopathologic correlation. *Int J Gynecol Pathol*, **9**, 20–40.
14. Rollason, T.P., Byrne, P., Williams, A. (1990) Immunohistochemical and electron microscopic findings in benign fibroepithelial vaginal polyps. *J Clin Pathol*, **43**, 604–608.
15. Halvorsen, T.B., Johannesen, E. (1992) Fibroepithelial polyps of vagina: are they old granulation tissue polyps? *J Clin Pathol*, **45**, 235–240.

Angiomyofibroblastoma

Clinical features

This recently described benign soft tissue tumor of the external genitalia and perineum must be distinguished from aggressive angiomyxoma (see below).[1–4] It most commonly affects females of reproductive age but has also been described in the elderly.[4] Cases in males are exceptional.[5] A tumor sharing many clinical and histological features with angiomyofibroblastoma has been reported in the male genital tract as angiomyofibroblastoma-like tumor. These are described in the scrotum and groin and histologically show hybrid features between angiomyofibroblastoma and spindle cell lipoma.[6]

Angiomyofibroblastoma presents as a slowly growing, small (usually less than 5 cm diameter), asymptomatic subcutaneous mass in the vulva or, less commonly, in the vagina. They are frequently confused with a Bartholin's gland cyst. In males, tumors occur on the scrotum. Behavior is generally benign with little or no tendency for recurrence although a single malignant case has been reported.[7]

Histological features

Angiomyofibroblastoma is well circumscribed and surrounded by a fibrous pseudocapsule. Scanning magnification reveals a tumor with hypo- and hypercellular areas and a prominent vascular network composed of thin-walled dilated vascular channels (*Figs 11.178, 11.179*). The hypocellular areas display prominent myxoid change. Tumor cells are plump, epithelioid or spindle-shaped with imperceptible to abundant pink cytoplasm, finely dispersed chromatin and inconspicuous nucleoli. They tend to concentrate around the vascular channels. Multinucleated

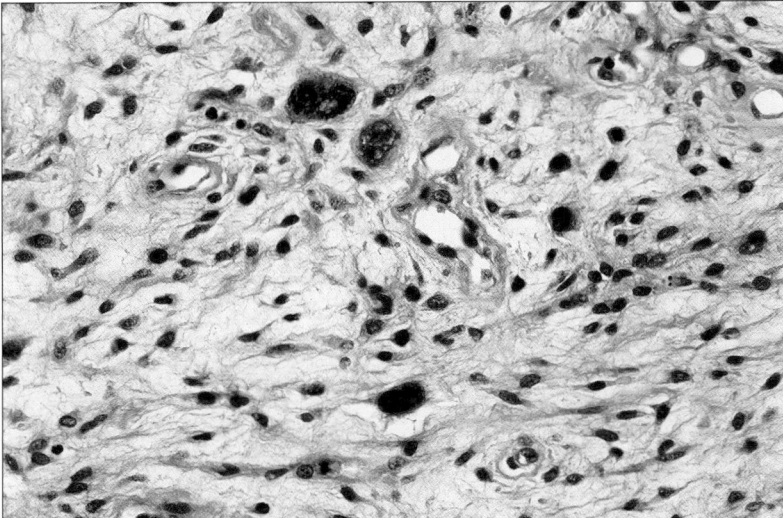

Fig. 11.176
Fibroepithelial stromal polyp: in this field, there is striking nuclear atypia. By courtesy of M. Nucci, MD, Brigham and Women's Hospital and Harvard Medical School, Boston, USA.

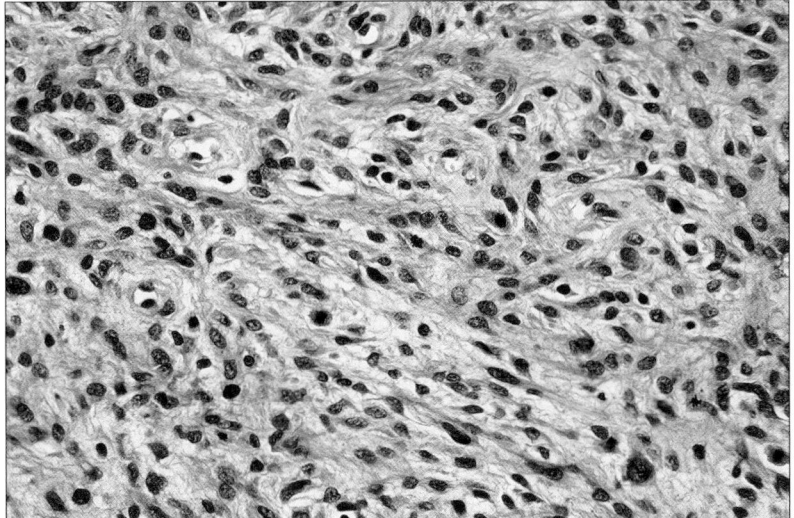

Fig. 11.177
Fibroepithelial stromal polyp: the presence of multiple mitoses as shown in this field can be a source of concern to the unwary. By courtesy of M. Nucci, MD, Brigham and Women's Hospital and Harvard Medical School, Boston, USA.

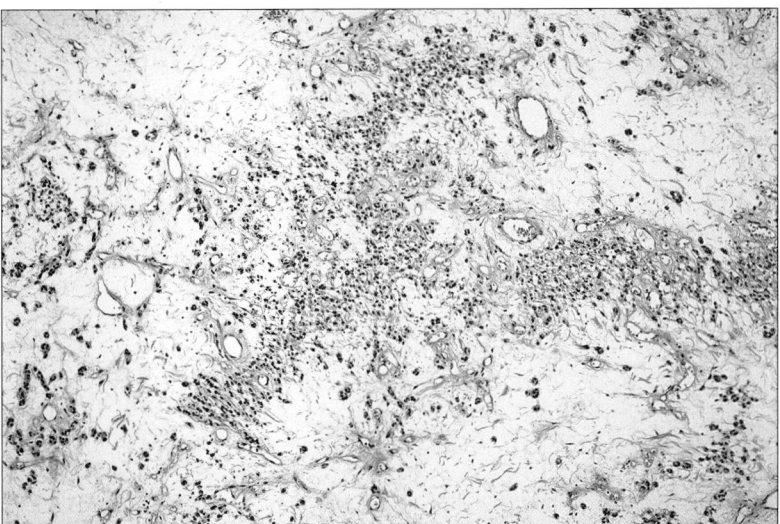

Fig. 11.178
Angiomyofibroblastoma: low power view showing a richly vascular tumor. In this example, there is a strikingly myxoid stroma. By courtesy of M. Nucci, MD, and C.D.M. Fletcher, MD, Brigham and Women's Hospital and Harvard Medical School, Boston, USA.

forms are frequent. Epithelioid cells with hyaline cytoplasm often have a plasmacytoid appearance. Cytological atypia is absent and mitotic figures are very rare. Scattered lymphocytes and mast cells are often present. Intratumoral mature adipocytes are present in a small number of cases although it is uncertain whether they represent normal entrapped fat or an inherent component of the tumor. Degenerative nuclear hyperchromatism may sometimes be present.

The tumor cells are diffusely and strongly positive for desmin but in only occasional cases are they positive for either smooth-muscle actin or pan-muscle actin. Epithelial markers, S-100 and myoglobin are negative.

Ultrastructural studies suggest myofibroblastic differentiation.[1,3,4]

Differential diagnosis

Distinction from aggressive angiomyxoma is not usually difficult as the latter is larger (usually more than 5 cm), infiltrative, less cellular and vascular and contains vessels with thicker walls. However, tumors with hybrid features of angiomyofibroblastoma and aggressive angiomyxoma have been reported.[8] These rare cases are best classified and treated as aggressive angiomyxoma.

References

1. Fletcher, C.D., Tsang, W.Y., Fisher, C. et al (1992) Angiomyofibroblastoma of the vulva. A benign neoplasm distinct from aggressive angiomyxoma. *Am J Surg Pathol*, **16**, 373–382.
2. Katenkamp, D., Kosmehl, H., Mentzel, T. et al (1993) Angiomyofibroblastoma of the vulvar and paravaginal region – a new entity. *Pathologe*, **14**, 131–137.
3. Hisaoka, M., Kouho, H., Aoki, T. et al (1995) Angiomyofibroblastoma of the vulva: a clinicopathologic study of seven cases. *Pathol Int*, **45**, 487–492.
4. Nielsen, G.P., Rosenberg, A.E., Young, R.H. et al (1996) Angiomyofibroblastoma of the vulva and vagina. *Mod Pathol*, **9**, 284–291.
5. Ockner, D.M., Sayadi, H., Swanson, P.E. et al (1997) Genital angiomyofibroblastoma: comparison with aggressive angiomyxoma and other myxoid neoplasms of skin and soft tissue. *Am J Clin Pathol*, **107**, 36–44.
6. Laskin, W.B., Fetsch, J.F., Mostofi, K.F. (1998) Angiomyofibroblastoma-like tumor of the male genital tract: analysis of 11 cases with comparisons to female angiofibroblastoma and spindle cell lipoma. *Am J Surg Pathol*, **22**, 6–16.
7. Nielsen, G.P., Young, R.H., Dickersin, G.R. et al (1997) Angiofibroblastoma of the vulva with sarcomatous transformation ('angiomyofibrosarcoma'). *Am J Surg Pathol*, **28**, 1046–1055.
8. Granter, S.R., Nucci, M.R., Fletcher, C.D. (1997) Aggressive angiomyxoma: reappraisal of its relationship to angiomyofibroblastoma in a series of 16 cases. *Histopathology*, **30**, 3–10.

Aggressive angiomyxoma

Clinical features

This tumor presents as a slowly growing asymptomatic mass involving the pelvis and perineum.[1–6] It mainly affects females in the third or fourth decade of life. Only a single case has been reported in a child.[7] Less than 5% of cases present in males with predilection for the scrotum, perineum or groin.[8–10] Tumors are often 10 cm or more in diameter and can sometimes attain a very large size. Genitourinary and anorectal symptoms usually ensue due to external compression by the tumor. In females, lesions present mainly in the vulva or perineum followed by the vagina and the pelvis. Because of its extensive infiltrative growth, complete surgical excision is often difficult; local recurrences are therefore frequent and occur in up to 30% of cases. Metastasis has not been reported.

Histological features

Macroscopic examination reveals a soft, ill-defined, lobulated tumor with myxoid change. Microscopically, the lesion is infiltrative, with numerous small- and medium-sized blood vessels and a small number of tumor cells in a myxoid stroma (*Figs 11.180–11.182*). The blood vessels have thick walls, which are often hyalinized. Tumor cells are small, spindle-shaped or stellate with ill-defined pale pink cytoplasm and vesicular nuclei. Cytological atypia is absent and mitotic figures are rare.

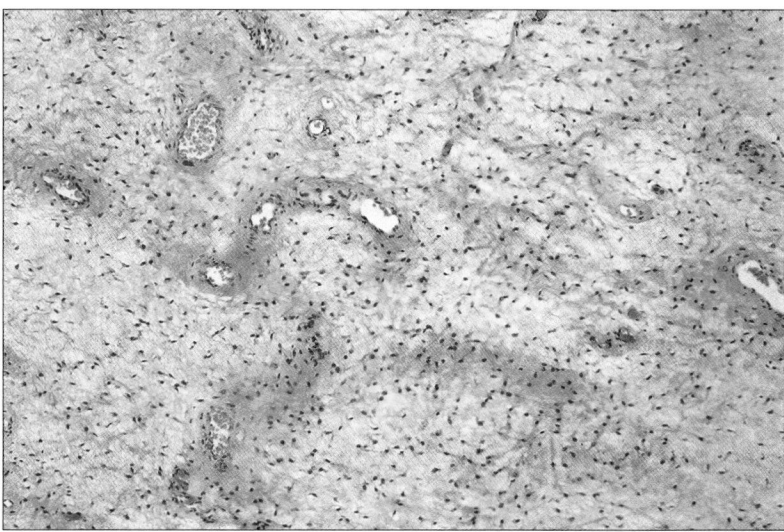

Fig. 11.180
Aggressive angiomyxoma: there are conspicuous blood vessels dispersed in a myxoid stroma. By courtesy of M. Nucci, MD, Brigham and Women's Hospital and Harvard Medical School, Boston, USA.

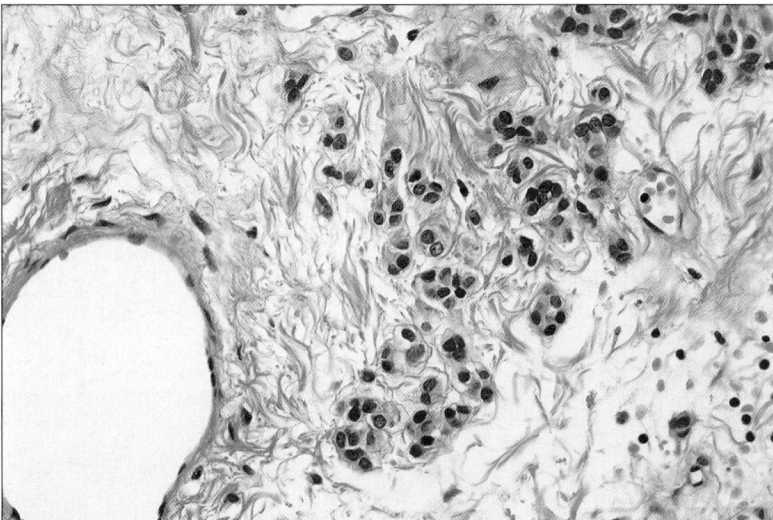

Fig. 11.179
Angiomyofibroblastoma: the tumor cells have eosinophilic cytoplasm and small nuclei. Nucleoli are not apparent. By courtesy of M. Nucci, MD, and C.D.M. Fletcher, MD, Brigham and Women's Hospital and Harvard Medical School, Boston, USA.

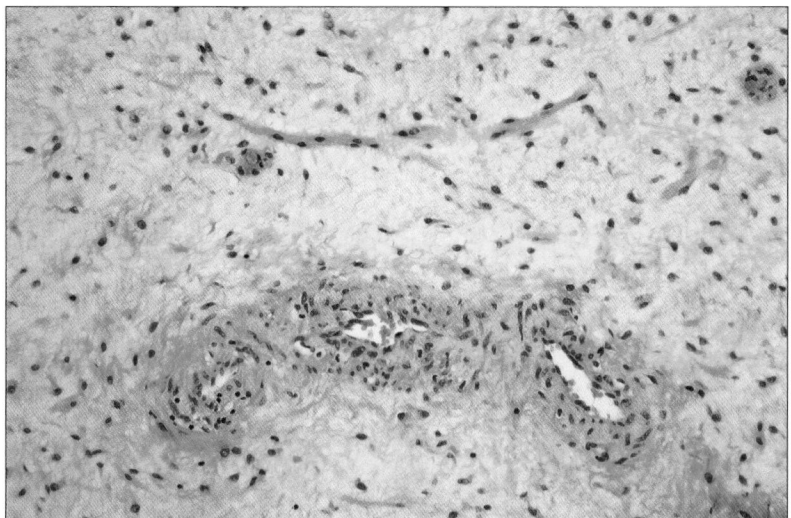

Fig. 11.181
Aggressive angiomyxoma: in this view, a smooth muscle bundle is evident in the upper field. By courtesy of M. Nucci, MD, Brigham and Women's Hospital and Harvard Medical School, Boston, USA.

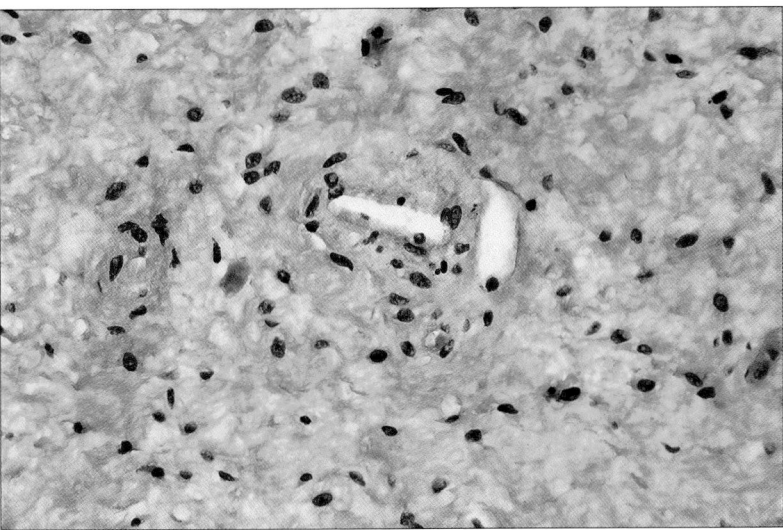

Fig. 11.182
Aggressive angiomyxoma: high power view showing a uniform cellular population. There is no pleomorphism. By courtesy of M. Nucci, MD, Brigham and Women's Hospital and Harvard Medical School, Boston, USA.

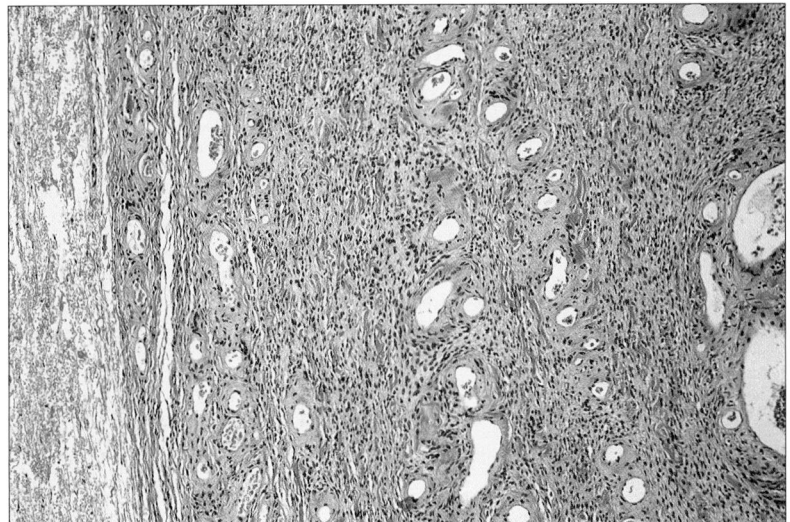

Fig. 11.183
Cellular angiofibroma: the tumor is characterized by thick-walled, hyalinized blood vessels associated with a densely cellular stroma. By courtesy of M. Nucci, MD, Brigham and Women's Hospital and Harvard Medical School, Boston, USA.

Bundles of smooth muscle are frequently seen adjacent to blood vessels, a finding that can be highlighted by a desmin stain.[8] Residual normal structures including glands and smooth muscle are often entrapped by the tumor. Scattered mast cells are often present. Multinucleated giant cells similar to those found in stromal polyps are occasionally found. Some cases overlap histologically with angiomyofibroblastoma (see above).

Immunohistochemically, tumor cells are positive for smooth-muscle actin and desmin. Positivity for estrogen and progesterone receptors has also been documented.[5] A single case has been submitted to cytogenetic analysis and showed a t(5;12). Interestingly, the area involved (12q14–15) is the same as that reported in leiomyoma and lipoma.[11]

Electron microscopy shows cells with features of fibroblasts and myofibroblasts.[5]

Differential diagnosis

See angiomyofibroblastoma.

References

1. Steeper, T., Rosai, J. (1983) Aggressive angiomyxoma of the female pelvis and perineum. *Am J Surg Pathol*, 7, 463–476.
2. Begin, L.R., Clement, P.B., Kirk, M.E. et al (1985) Aggressive angiomyxoma of pelvic soft parts: a clinicopathological study of nine cases. *Hum Pathol*, 16, 621–628.
3. Elchalal, U., Lifshitz-Mercer, B., Dgani, R. et al (1992) Aggressive angiomyxoma of the vulva. *Gynecol Oncol*, 47, 260–262.
4. Simo, M., Zapata, C., Esquius, J. et al (1992) Aggressive angiomyxoma of the female pelvis and perineum: report of two cases and review of the literature. *Br J Obstet Gynaecol*, 99, 925–927.
5. Skalova, A., Michal, M., Husek, K. et al (1993) Aggressive angiomyxoma of the pelviperineal region. Immunohistochemical and ultrastructural study of seven cases. *Am J Dermatopathol*, 15, 446–451.
6. Fetsch, J.F., Laskin, W.B., Lefkowitz, M. et al (1996) Aggressive angiomyxoma. A clinicopathologic study of 29 female patients. *Cancer*, 78, 79–90.
7. White, J., Chan, Y.F. (1994) Aggressive angiomyxoma of the vulva in an 11-year-old girl. *Pediatr Pathol*, 14, 27–37.
8. Tsang, W.Y., Chan, J.K., Lee, K.C. et al (1992) Aggressive angiomyxoma. A report of four cases occurring in men. *Am J Surg Pathol*, 16, 1059–1065.
9. Clatch, R.J., Drake, W.K., Gonzalez, J.G. (1993) Aggressive angiomyxoma in men. A report of two cases associated with inguinal hernias. *Arch Pathol Lab Med*, 117, 911–913.
10. Iezzoni, J.C., Fechner, R.E., Wong, L.S. et al (1995) Aggressive angiomyxoma in males. A report of four cases. *Am J Clin Pathol*, 104, 391–396.
11. Kazmierczak, B., Wanschuwa, S., Meyer-Bolte, K. et al (1995) Cytogenetic and molecular analysis of an aggressive angiomyxoma. *Am J Pathol*, 147, 580–585.

Cellular angiofibroma

Clinical features

Cellular angiofibroma is a recently described tumor that occurs almost exclusively on the vulva of middle-aged women.[1–5] Presentation in males

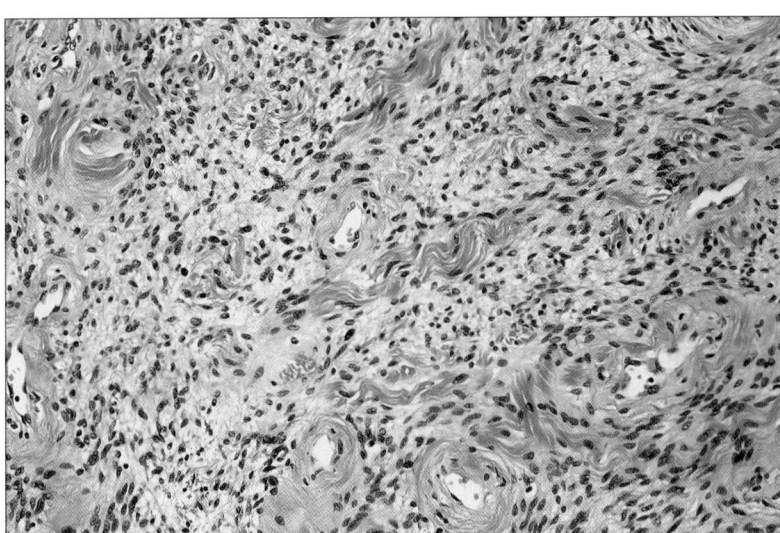

Fig. 11.184
Cellular angiofibroma: note the associated collagen fibers. By courtesy of M. Nucci, MD, Brigham and Women's Hospital and Harvard Medical School, Boston, USA.

is extremely rare and, in this setting, lesions occur in the inguinoscrotal region.[1,2] Exceptional cases have been reported in the retroperitoneum and in the subcutaneous tissue of the chest.[2,6] Tumors tend to be small and behavior is benign with no tendency for local recurrence.[1]

Histological features

Tumors are well circumscribed but unencapsulated with only occasional extension into the surrounding soft tissues (*Figs 11.183–11.185*).[1] Most lesions are fairly cellular and composed of short, bland, spindle-shaped cells with poorly defined pale eosinophilic cytoplasm and vesicular nuclei. The number of mitotic figures varies but sometimes they may be prominent. Thick-walled medium-sized hyalinized blood vessels are frequent in addition to slender collagen bundles and mast cells. Scattered adipocytes are frequently present.

Tumor cells are positive for vimentin and may be positive for CD34. Staining for actin, desmin, S-100 and epithelial markers is negative.[1,2]

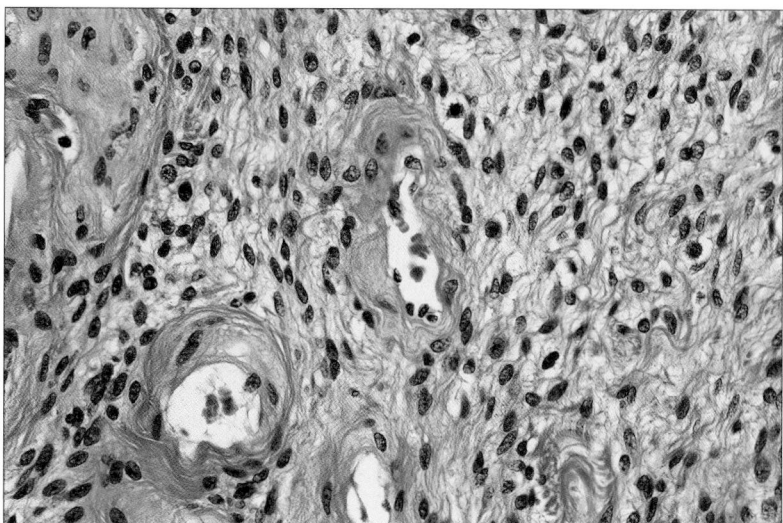

Fig. 11.185
Cellular angiofibroma: the tumor cells are small, uniform and have round to oval vesicular nuclei. By courtesy of M. Nucci, MD, Brigham and Women's Hospital and Harvard Medical School, Boston, USA.

Differential diagnosis

See angiomyofibroblastoma.

References

1. Nucci, M.R., Granter, S.R., Fletcher, C.D. (1997) Cellular angiofibroma: a benign neoplasm distinct from angiomyofibroblastoma and spindle cell lipoma. *Am J Surg Pathol*, **21**, 636–644.
2. Nucci, M.R., Fletcher, C.D.M. (2000) Vulvovaginal soft tissue tumours: update and review. *Histopathology*, **36**, 97–108.
3. Nielsen, G.P., Young, R.H. (2001) Mesenchymal tumors and tumor-like lesions of the female genital tract: a selective review with emphasis on recently described entities. *Int J Gynecol Pathol*, **20**, 105–127.
4. Lane, J.E., Walker, A.N., Mullis, E.N. Jr et al (2001) Cellular angiofibroma of the vulva. *Gynecol Oncol*, **81**, 326–329.
5. Curry, J.L., Olejnik, J.L., Wojcik, E.M. (2001) Cellular angiofibroma of the vulva with DNA ploidy analysis. *Int J Gynecol Pathol*, **20**, 200–203.
6. Garijo, M.F., Val-Bernal, J.F. (1998) Extravulvar subcutaneous cellular angiofibroma. *J Cutan Pathol*, **25**, 327–332.

Genital leiomyoma

Clinical features

Genital leiomyoma describes those lesions arising from the vulva, scrotum and nipple. Tumors arising in the vulva and scrotum are distinctive from other cutaneous leiomyomas including pilar leiomyoma and angioleiomyoma.[1] Leiomyomas arising in the nipple are similar to pilar leiomyoma and are discussed on page 1797.

Vulval leiomyomas are relatively rare and present mainly in women of reproductive age or slightly older as an asymptomatic swelling.[1–5] Clinical features are not distinctive. Tumors are subcutaneous and well circumscribed and are often clinically diagnosed as a cyst. The majority of benign lesions are less than 5 cm in diameter and present in the labia. Rare cases arise in the clitoris.[6] Tumors may increase in size during pregnancy and also in association with estrogen/progesterone replacement therapy.[7] Benign tumors are typically circumscribed and small, but only histological examination allows for distinction between benign, low-grade malignant and malignant tumors.

Scrotal tumors arise from the dartos muscle and are less common and larger than their vulval counterparts.[8,9] They present as an asymptomatic mass thiat may occasionally be polypoid.[9] Rare cases are associated with prominent warty epidermal hyperplasia and resemble condyloma acuminatum.[10] Other benign smooth muscle lesions of the scrotum such as hamartoma of the dartos muscle are exceedingly rare.[11]

Histological features

Tumors are well circumscribed and non-infiltrative with variable cellularity.[1–3] They are composed of admixed spindle-shaped and epithelioid cells, often with a single cell type predominating.[4,12,13] Lesions with a spindle cell component are very similar to those found in the uterus and consist of bundles of cells with well-defined eosinophilic cytoplasm, vesicular cigar-shaped nuclei and an inconspicuous nucleolus. Focal myxoid change and hyalinization are commonly seen and sometimes this results in a plexiform appearance. Epithelioid tumor cells have abundant eosinophilic or pale-staining cytoplasm.

Because of the rarity of vulval smooth muscle tumors, it is often difficult to separate benign lesions from those with potential for local recurrence metastasis (see below). It has been suggested that a tumor with any evidence of mitotic activity, nuclear pleomorphism or an infiltrative margin should be regarded as having at least the potential for local recurrence.[4] In such cases, excision with a margin of at least 1 cm should be recommended.[4]

Because of their rarity, there is even less information relating to histological evaluation of scrotal leiomyoma. Degenerative cytological atypia is accepted in these tumors but these changes occur in non-cellular, well-circumscribed lesions that lack mitotic activity.[14]

References

1. Newman, P.L., Fletcher, C.D.M. (1991) Smooth muscle tumours of the external genitalia: clinicopathological analysis of a series. *Histopathology*, **18**, 523–529.
2. Tavassoli, F.A., Norris, H.J. (1979) Smooth muscle tumors of the vulva. *Obstet Gynecol*, **53**, 213–217.
3. Nielsen, G.P., Rosenberg, A.E., Koerner, F.C. et al (1996) Smooth muscle tumors of the vulva. A clinicopathological study of 25 cases and review of the literature. *Am J Surg Pathol*, **20**, 779–793.
4. Nucci, M.R., Fletcher, C.D.M. (2000) Vulvovaginal soft tissue tumours: update and review. *Histopathology*, **36**, 97–108.
5. Neri, A., Peled, Y., Braslavski, D. (1993) Vulvar leiomyoma. *Acta Obstet Gynecol Scand*, **72**, 221–222.
6. Strenchever, M.A., McDivett, R.W., Fisher, J.A. (1973) Leiomyoma of the clitoris. *J Reprod Med*, **2**, 75–76.
7. Siegle, J.C., Cartmell, L. (1995) Vulvar leiomyoma associated with estrogen/progestin therapy: a case report. *J Reprod Med*, **40**, 58–59.
8. Das, A.K., Bolick, D., Little, N.A. et al (1992) Pedunculated scrotal mass. Leiomyoma of scrotum. *Urology*, **39**, 376–379.
9. Livne, P.M., Nobel, M., Savir, A. et al (1983) Leiomyoma of the scrotum. *Arch Dermatol*, **119**, 358–359.
10. Runne, U., Antz, H., Pullmann, H. (1980) Verrucous leiomyoma of scrotum presenting as condyloma acuminatum. *Z Hautkr*, **55**, 652–660.
11. Quinn, T.R., Young, R.H. (1997) Smooth-muscle hamartoma of the tunica dartos of the scrotum: report of a case. *J Cutan Pathol*, **24**, 322–326.
12. Aneiros, J., Garcia del Moral, B., Beltran, E. et al (1982) Epithelioid leiomyoma of the vulva. *Diagn Gynecol Obstet*, **4**, 351–355.
13. Hopkins-Luna, A.M., Chambers, D.C., Goodman, M.D. (1999) Epithelioid leiomyoma of the vulva. *J Natl Med Assoc*, **91**, 171–173.
14. Slone, S., O'Connor, D. (1998) Scrotal leiomyomas with bizarre nuclei: a report of 3 cases. *Mod Pathol*, **11**, 282–287.

Leiomyosarcoma

Clinical features

Vulval leiomyosarcoma is rare and presents in middle-aged to elderly patients as an asymptomatic mass mainly affecting the labia.[1–5] Malignancy is not usually suspected on clinical examination unless the mass is large and poorly circumscribed.

Scrotal leiomyosarcomas are exceptional and present as an asymptomatic, rapidly growing mass in elderly patients.[6,7]

Wide local excision is the treatment of choice. It is difficult to predict the outcome because of their rarity and the lack of large studies with adequate follow-up information.

Histological features

Accepted criteria for the histological diagnosis of leiomyosarcoma include (*Figs 11.186–11.188*):[1,2,8]

- size larger than 5 cm in diameter
- infiltrative margins
- more than 5 mitoses/10 high power fields (HPF)
- moderate to severe cytological atypia.

More recently, it has been suggested that tumor necrosis should also be regarded as evidence of malignancy.[8]

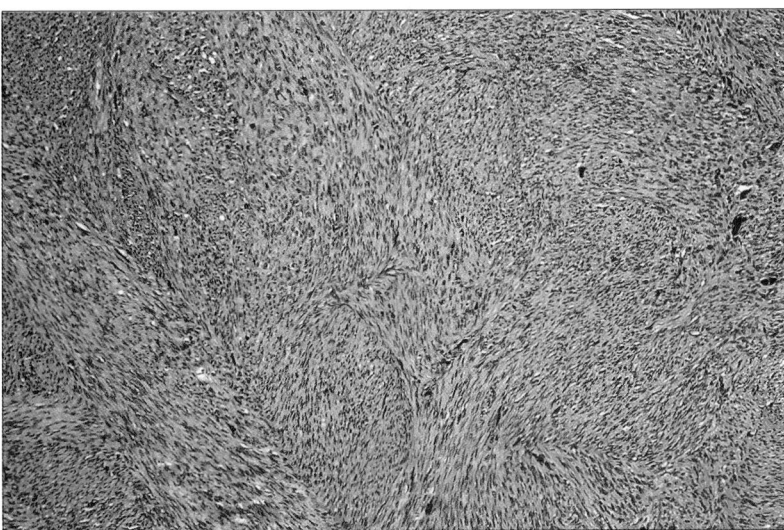

Fig. 11.186
Vulval leiomyosarcoma: this low power view shows fascicles of tumor cells with eosinophilic cytoplasm. By courtesy of C. Crum, MD, Brigham and Women's Hospital and Harvard Medical School, Boston, USA.

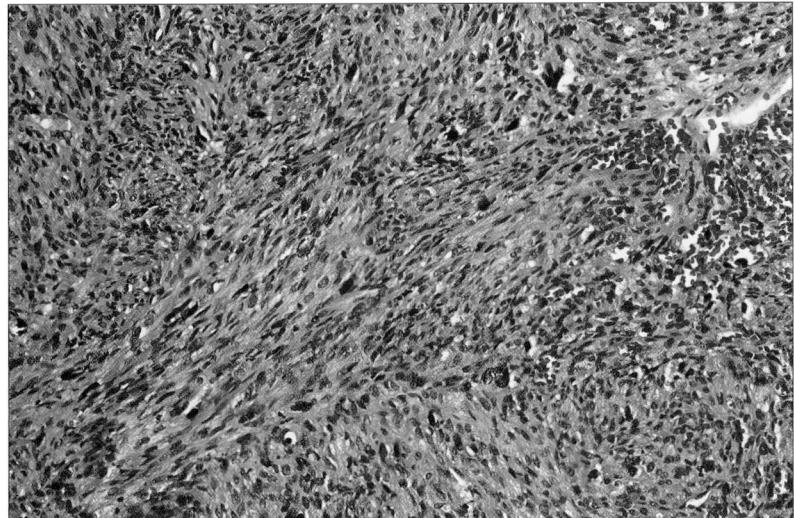

Fig. 11.187
Vulval leiomyosarcoma: note the nuclear pleomorphism. By courtesy of C. Crum, MD, Brigham and Women's Hospital and Harvard Medical School, Boston, USA.

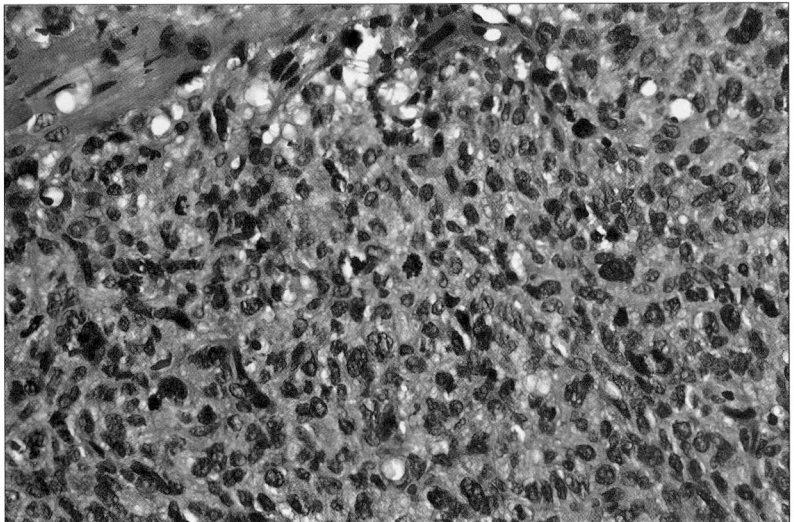

Fig. 11.188
Vulval leiomyosarcoma: high power view showing a mitotic figure in the center of the field. By courtesy of C. Crum, MD, Brigham and Women's Hospital and Harvard Medical School, Boston, USA.

References

1. Tavassoli, F.A., Norris, H.J. (19779) Smooth muscle tumors of the vulva. *Obstet Gynecol*, **53**, 213–217.
2. Nielsen, G.P., Rosenberg, A.E., Koerner, F.C. et al (1996) Smooth muscle tumors of the vulva. A clinicopathological study of 25 cases and review of the literature. *Am J Surg Pathol*, **20**, 779–793.
3. Newman, P.L., Fletcher, C.D.M. (1991) Smooth muscle tumors of the external genitalia: clinicopathological analysis of a series. *Histopathology*, **18**, 523–529.
4. Patel, S., Kapadia, A., Desai, A. et al (1993) Leiomyosarcoma of the vulva. *Eur J Gynaecol Oncol*, **14**, 406–407.
5. Krag-Moller, L.B., Nygaard-Nielsen, M., Trolle, C. (1990) Leiomyosarcoma vulvae. *Acta Obstet Gynecol Scand*, **68**, 187–189.
6. Jeddy, T.A., Vowles, R.H., Southam, J.A. (1994) Leiomyosarcoma of the dartos muscle. *Br J Urol*, **74**, 129–130.
7. Koh, K.B., Joyce, A., Boon, A.P. (1994) Leiomyosarcoma of the scrotum. *Br J Urol*, **73**, 717–718.
8. Nucci, M.R., Fletcher, C.D.M. (2000) Vulvovaginal soft tissue tumours: update and review. *Histopathology*, **36**, 97–108.

Vulvar leiomyomatosis

Clinical features

This rare condition is characterized by multiple leiomyomas in the vulva associated with esophageal leiomyomas.[1-7] The vulval tumors may appear before, concomitantly or after the development of esophageal lesions. Involvement of the clitoris is sometimes present. Patients can also present with Alport's syndrome, characterized by inherited glomerulonephritis, ocular abnormalities and deafness.[5]

Pathogenesis and histological features

The pathogenesis of the disease is unknown but deletions and mutations in the COL4A6 and COL4A5 genes have been described.[5,7] These genetic alterations are associated with defects in type IV collagen in Alport's syndrome.

The vulval and esophageal leiomyomas are identical to those occurring sporadically.

References

1. Whalen, T., Astedt, B. (1965) Familial occurrence of coexisting leiomyoma of the vulva and esophagus. *Acta Obstet Gynecol Scand*, **44**, 197–203.
2. Schapiro, R.L., Sandrock, A.R. (1973) Esophagogastric and vulvar leiomyomatosis: a new radiologic syndrome. *J Can Assoc Radiol*, **24**, 184–187.
3. Fernandez, J.P., Mascarenas, M.J., Costa, J.C. et al (1975) Diffuse leiomyomatosis of the esophagus. A case report and review of the literature. *Dig Dis*, **20**, 684–690.
4. Faber, K., Jones, M.A., Spratt, D. et al (1991) Vulvar leiomyomatosis in a patient with esophagogastric leiomyomatosis: review of the syndrome. *Gynecol Oncol*, **41**, 92–94.
5. Miner, J.H. (1999) Alport syndrome with diffuse leiomyomatosis. When and when not? *Am J Pathol*, **154**, 1633–1635.
6. Compagnoni, G.M., Talamonti, M.S., Joab, A. et al (2000) Esophageal leiomyomatosis in a woman with a history of vulvar leiomyoma and Barrett's esophagus: a case report and review of the literature. *Dig Surg*, **17**, 306–309.
7. Guilliem, P., Delcambre, F., Cohen-Solal, L. et al (2001) Diffuse esophageal leiomyoma with perirectal involvement mimicking Hirschprung disease. *Gastroenterology*, **120**, 216–220.

Myointimoma

Clinical features

This is a rare, recently described tumor involving the corpus spongiosum of the glans penis.[1] The age range is wide and lesions are small (usually less than 1 cm) and asymptomatic. It does not seem to be related to trauma. The behavior is benign with no tendency for local recurrence.

Histological features

Low-power examination reveals a diffuse myointimal proliferation of the blood vessels of the corpus spongiosum of the glans penis in a plexiform growth pattern. The proliferating cells are bland and spindle-shaped with abundant pink cytoplasm and vesicular nuclei. A minority of the cells display features more reminiscent of fibroblasts. The background stroma is sclerotic and myxoid. Focal degenerative changes may be seen and mitotic figures are absent.

The spindle cells are positive for smooth-muscle actin, muscle-specific actin and calponin but negative for desmin.

Differential diagnosis

This tumor must be distinguished from myofibroma, intravascular nodular fasciitis and vascular leiomyoma.

Reference

1. Fetsch, J.F., Brinsko, R.W., Davis, C.J. et al (2000) A distinctive myointimal proliferation ('myointimoma') involving the corpus spongiosum of the glans penis. A clinicopathological and immunohistochemical analysis of 10 cases. *Am J Surg Pathol*, **24**, 1524–1530.

Postoperative spindle-cell nodule

Clinical features

This rare reactive lesion presents as a small nodule at the site of a previous surgical procedure on the vulva and the vagina.[1–3] It grows rapidly and is usually asymptomatic.[1–3] Local recurrence may follow inadequate excision.

Histological features

The nodule is poorly circumscribed and resembles nodular fasciitis.[1–3] It is composed of bundles of plump myofibroblast-like cells dispersed in a myxoid or edematous background. Nuclei may be bland or hyperchromatic. Small blood vessels, foci of hemorrhage, lymphocytes and neutrophils are additional features. Mitotic figures are common.

References

1. Proppe, K.H., Scully, R.E., Rosai, J. (1984) Postoperative spindle cell nodules of the genitourinary tract resembling sarcomas: a report of eight cases. *Am J Surg Pathol*, **8**, 101–108.
2. Manson, C.M., Hirsch, P.J., Coyne, J.D. (1995) Post-operative spindle cell nodule of the vulva. *Histopathology*, **26**, 571–574.
3. Nielsen, G.P., Young, R.H. (2001) Mesenchymal tumors and tumor-like conditions of the female genital tract: a selective review with emphasis on recently described entities. *Int J Gynecol Pathol*, **20**, 105–127.

Peyronie's disease

Peyronie's disease (penile fibromatosis) is discussed on p. 1725.

Degenerative and metabolic diseases

12

The hyperlipidemias 539
Eruptive xanthomata 543
Tendinous xanthomata 544
Tuberous xanthomata 545
Planar xanthomata 547
Verruciform xanthoma 549

Angiokeratoma corporis diffusum 551

The amyloidoses 554
Primary and myeloma-associated systemic
    amyloidoses 555
Secondary amyloidosis 558
Hemodialysis-associated amyloidosis 559
Heredofamilial amyloidoses 559
Amyloid elastosis 559
Primary localized cutaneous amyloidosis, lichen
    and macular types 560
Secondary localized cutaneous amyloidosis 564
Familial primary cutaneous amyloidosis 564
Nodular amyloidosis 565

Colloid milium 567
Juvenile colloid milium 567
Adult colloid milium 568

Hyalinosis cutis et mucosae 571

Cutaneous macroglobulinosis 574

Porphyria 575
Congenital erythropoietic porphyria 576
Erythropoietic protoporphyria 577
Hereditary coproporphyria 579
Porphyria cutanea tarda 579
Hepatoerythropoietic porphyria 582
Variegate porphyria 582

Pseudoporphyria 586

Gout 590

Ochronosis 592
Alkaptonuria 592
Exogenous ochronosis 592

Hartnup disease 594

Pellagra 594

Scurvy 595

Calcinosis cutis 595
Dystrophic calcinosis cutis 596
Metastatic calcinosis cutis 597
Idiopathic calcinosis cutis 597

The mucinoses 600
Generalized myxedema 602
Localized (pretibial) myxedema 603
Lichen myxedematosus 605
Acral persistent papular mucinosis 609
Cutaneous mucinosis of infancy 610
Self-healing juvenile cutaneous mucinosis 610
Reticular erythematous mucinosis 610
Scleredema 610
Papular and nodular cutaneous mucinosis of
    systemic lupus erythematosus 613
Myxoid cyst 613
Cutaneous focal mucinosis 614
Mucinous nevus 614
Neuropathia mucinosa cutanea 614
Self-healing infantile familial cutaneous
    mucinosis 615

Acanthosis nigricans 615

Acrodermatitis enteropathica 617

Necrolytic migratory erythema 619

Bullosis diabeticorum 622

The hyperlipidemias

The hyperlipidemias may present as cutaneous xanthomata which are localized aggregates of histiocytes, containing accumulated lipid (primarily free and esterified cholesterol), and present as five main clinical types:
- eruptive
- tendinous
- tuberous
- planar
- disseminated.[1]

The last, xanthoma disseminatum, in which serum lipid levels are normal, is discussed separately. Xanthoma cells express CD4, CD11c, CD14b and CD68 in addition to human leukocyte antigen (HLA) class II antigens.[2]

Hyperlipidemias may be primary, or secondary to conditions such as diabetes mellitus, obesity, pancreatitis, renal disease (the nephrotic syndrome or chronic renal failure), hypothyroidism, cholestatic liver disease (e.g. primary biliary cirrhosis) and paraproteinemias. Drug-induced hyperlipidemia also occurs as a result of the administration of estrogens, corticosteroids or 13-*cis*-retinoic acid. Hyperlipidemia is often associated with serious, potentially life-threatening disorders such as atherosclerosis (low density lipoproteins) and pancreatitis (hypertriglyceridemia).[3]

The presence of xanthomata commonly represents a cutaneous manifestation of systemic disease and their recognition should therefore be followed by an intensive investigation to exclude the latter (*Table 12.1*).[2] Although not a hard and fast rule, xanthoma morphology and distribution can sometimes point towards specific hyperlipidemia variants.

The plasma lipids are composed of triglycerides and cholesterol; these are highly insoluble and their transport is facilitated by their aggregation into lipoproteins. The latter are macromolecular complexes composed of an outer shell of hydrophilic phospholipids, non-esterified cholesterol and apo(lipo)proteins, which emulsify the associated hydrophobic core of triglycerides and cholesterol ester.[4] There are a large number of apoproteins, with variable structure and function (e.g. ApoB-48, which is required for the secretion of chylomicrons into the thoracic duct).[3] In addition to giving structure to the lipoprotein, apoproteins also represent ligands for specific receptors (e.g. ApoE is a ligand for liver chylomicron receptors). They also act as co-factors for a number of lipid-modifying enzymes (e.g. ApoCII activates lipoprotein lipase).[4] Lipoprotein meta-

Table 12.1
Classification of xanthomatous disorders

Hyperlipidemic xanthomatoses: disorders characterized by elevated plasma triglycerides or cholesterol		Normolipidemic xanthomatoses: disorders characterized by normal plasma triglycerides and cholesterol	

Primary hyperlipo-proteinemias	Elevated plasma triglycerides
	   lipoprotein lipase deficiency
	   familial hyperlipoproteinemia, type V
	   familial hypertriglyceridemia
	Elevated plasma triglycerides and cholesterol
	   familial dysbetalipoproteinemia, typee III
	Elevated plasma cholesterol
	   familial hypercholesterolemia
		Disorders characterized by altered lipoprotein content or structure	Accumulation of unsual sterols in LDL
			   cerebrotendinous xanthomatosis
			     (cholestanol)
			   sitosterolemia (sitosterol, campesterol,
			     stigmasterol, etc.)
			Deficiency of HDL
			   plantar and buccal mucosal xanthomas
			   diffuse plane xanthomas
			Normocholesterolemic dysbetalipoproteinemia
			   tuberous
			   xanthelasmas
			Hyperapobetalipoproteinemia
			   tendon xanthomas
			   xanthelasmas

Secondary hyperlipo-proteinemias	Elevated plasma triglycerides
	   diabetes mellitus
	   drug-induced chylomicronemia
	     alcohol
	     estrogens
	     retinoids
	   hypothyroidism
	   nephrotic syndrome
	   type I glycogen storage disease (von Gierke's
	     disease)
	Elevated plasma cholesterol
	   hepatic cholestasis
	     primary biliary cirrhosis
	     biliary atresia
	   hypothyroidism
	   dysglobulinemias or paraproteinemias
	     multiple myeloma
		Disorders associated with antibodies directed against lipoprotein components	Multiple myeloma
			Other paraproteinemias

		States with no demonstrate lipoprotein abnormalities	Underlying lymphoproliferative disease
			   multiple myeloma
			   cryoglobulinemia
			   Waldenström's macroglobulinemia
			   leukemia
			   lymphoma
			   other
			Xanthomatosis antedated by local tissue
			   alterations
			   normolipemic eruptive xanthomas (after
			     erythema)
			   xanthelasmas and planar xanthomas (after
			     erythroderma)
			   ?verruciform xanthomas (in areas of
			     dystrophic epidermolysis bullosa)
			Other
			   hereditary tendinous and tuberous xanthomas
			   normolipemic tendon and tuberous
			     xanthomas
			   normolipemic subcutaneous xanthomatosis

HDL, high density lipoprotein; LDL, low density lipoprotein. Reprinted from Cruz, P.D., East, C., Bergstresser, P.R. (1988) *Journal of the American Academy of Dermatology*, **19**, 95–111 with permission from the American Academy of Dermatology, Inc.

bolism, which is summarized in *Figure 12.1*, involves both exogenous (dietary) and endogenous pathways.[5] For more detailed information the reader is particularly referred to references 1 and 5.

The classification of hyperlipidemias is based upon the electrophoretic separation, on paper or agarose gel, of abnormal quantities of lipoprotein in the plasma (*Fig. 12.2*). There are seven main classes of lipoprotein, with differing electrophoretic mobilities:

- Chylomicrons, which are composed predominantly of exogenous triglycerides produced by small intestinal mucosal epithelium in response to dietary lipid.
- Very low density (pre-beta) lipoproteins (VLDL) of hepatic derivation, which are particularly involved in the transportation of endogenous triglyceride.
- Intermediate density lipoproteins (IDL), which are thought to be VLDL remnants.
- Low density (beta) lipoproteins (LDL), which are mainly involved in cholesterol transport and derived from IDL or else produced by the liver.
- High density (alpha) lipoproteins (HDL) composed predominantly of lipoprotein and equal quantities of cholesterol and phospholipid.

- High density lipoprotein variant HDL2.[1,4]
- High density lipoprotein variant HDL3.[1,4]

The hyperlipidemias are classified into six types according to the lipoprotein anomaly present (*Table 12.2*). However, it should be noted that each of these six types may result from a variety of pathogeneses, including those of a known or presumed genetic basis and those that complicate a diverse group of disease processes (secondary hyperlipidemia).[6–8] High density lipoproteins are not atherogenic.[3] Indeed their function is to remove cholesterol from the tissues and high levels serve to protect against vascular disease.[4] Conversely HDL deficiency (e.g. Tangier disease) is associated with cholesterol accumulation.[9]

The lipid content of xanthomata is probably mostly derived from the plasma, presumably by lipoprotein (particularly LDL and VLDL) permeation of blood vessel walls with the release of lipid and its subsequent phagocytosis by histiocytes, although localized lipogenesis may also be of importance.[10–13] The subgroups and proportions of lipid deposited within xanthomata are similar to those found in atheromatous plaques, raising the possibility of a shared pathogenesis.[1]

Xanthomata are, however, not always associated with hyper-cholesterolemia or hyperlipoproteinemia.[14] Under such circumstances they may evolve as a consequence of altered lipoprotein content or structure, represent local tissue changes or develop as a consequence of systemic disease including lymphoma, multiple myeloma and Waldenström's macroglobulinemia.[9] Normocholesterolemic xanthomata can therefore arise as a consequence of the accumulation of cholesterol-like substances within histiocytes (e.g. cerebrotendinous xanthomatosis and β-sitosterolemia).

Cerebrotendinous xanthomatosis represents an abnormality of bile acid metabolism inherited as an autosomal recessive.[15,16] As a consequence of hepatic 26-hydroxylase deficiency and resultant impaired oxidation of the cholesterol side chain during the production of cholic acid, cholestanol (and cholesterol) accumulates in the tissues, especially the tendons, lungs and brain. The xanthomata particularly affect the Achilles tendons and the tendons of the knees, elbows and the interphalangeal joints.[17] In addition to tendinous xanthomata, patients develop juvenile cataracts and progressive neurological dysfunction including mental retardation, dementia, pyramidal signs, cerebellar ataxia, spinal cord paresis and sensory changes due to dysmyelination.[17,18] Coronary atherosclerosis and endocrine abnormalities may also be present. In addition to cholestanol accumulation, cerebrotendinous xanthomatosis has been shown to be characterized by abnormal high density lipoproteins, which result in impaired cholesterol (and cholestanol) transport and contribute to the consequent xanthomatization.[15] The mortality is high, patients usually dying in the fourth to sixth decades, most often from progressive neurological dysfunction, pseudobulbar paralysis or myocardial infarction.[18]

Tendinous and tuberous xanthomata may also represent a manifestation of β-sitosterolemia. This is an autosomal recessive condition in which increased intestinal absorption of the plant sterols β-sitosterol, campesterol and stigmasterol results in tissue deposition along with cholesterol and subsequent xanthoma formation.[19,20] Normally these sterols are almost completely unabsorbed from the gastrointestinal tract. β-Sitosterolemia is associated with an increased risk of atherosclerosis.[3]

Xanthomata may occur in extracutaneous locations mimicking tumors in patients with hyperlipidemia. Sites include deep soft tissues and mediastinum.[21]

References

1. Parker, F. (1985) Xanthomas and hyperlipidemias. *J Am Acad Dermatol*, **13**, 1–30.
2. Braun-Falco, O., Eckert, F. (1991) Macroscopic and microscopic structure of xanthomatous eruptions. *Curr Probl Dermatol*, **20**, 54–62.
3. Haber, C., Kwiterovich, P.O. (1984) Dysbetalipoproteinemia and xanthomatosis. *Pediatr Dermatol*, **1**, 261–277.
4. Erkelens, D.W. (1991) Normal and abnormal metabolism of lipoproteins. *Curr Probl Dermatol*, **20**, 45–53.
5. Cruz, P.D., East, C., Bergstresser, P.R. (1988) Dermal, subcutaneous, and tendon xanthomas: diagnostic markers for specific lipoprotein disorders. *J Am Acad Dermatol*, **19**, 95–111.
6. Fredrickson, D.S., Lees, R.S. (1965) A system for phenotyping hyperlipoproteinemia. *Circulation*, **31**, 321–327.
7. Frederickson, D.S., Levy, R.I., Lees, R.S. (1967) Fat transport in lipoproteins – an integrated approach to mechanisms and disorders. *N Engl J Med*, **276**, 32–44, 94–103, 148–156, 215–226, 273–281.
8. Beaumont, J.L., Carlson, L.A., Cooper, G.R. (1970) Classification of the hyperlipidemias and hyperlipoproteinemias. *Bull World Health Organ*, **43**, 891–915.
9. Parker, F. (1986) Normocholesterolemic xanthomatosis. *Arch Dermatol*, **122**, 1253–1256.
10. Scott, P.J., Winterbourn, C.C. (1967) Low density lipoprotein accumulation in actively growing xanthomas. *J Atheroscler Res*, **7**, 207–223.
11. Parker, F., Bagdade, J.D., Odland, G.F. et al (1970) Evidence for the chylomicron origin of lipids accumulating in diabetic eruptive xanthomas: a correlative lipid, biochemical, histochemical and electron microscopic study. *J Clin Invest*, **49**, 2172–2187.
12. Hu, C.H., Ellefson, R.D., Winkelmann, R.K. (1982) Lipid synthesis in cutaneous xanthomas. *J Invest Dermatol*, **79**, 80–85.
13. Parker, F., Odland, G.F. (1973) Ultrastructural and lipid biochemical comparisons of human eruptive, tuberous and planar xanthomas. *Israeli J Med Sci*, **9**, 395–423.
14. Caputo, R., Marcello, M., Berti, E. et al (1986) Normolipemic eruptive cutaneous xanthomatosis. *Arch Dermatol*, **122**, 1294–1297.
15. Oftebro, H., Bjorkhem, I., Skrede, S. et al (1980) Cerebrotendinous xanthomatosis: a defect in mitochondrial 26-hydroxylation required for normal biosynthesis of cholic acid. *J Clin Invest*, **65**, 1418–1430.

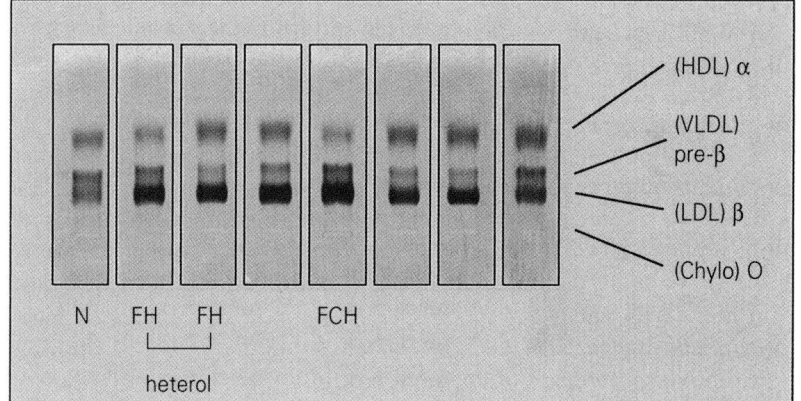

Fig. 12.2
Hyperlipidemia: electrophoretic separation of serum lipids. (Chylo, chylomicron; HDL, high density lipoprotein; LDL, low density lipoprotein; VLDL, very low density lipoprotein.) By courtesy of B. Lewis, MD, St Thomas' Hospital, London, UK.

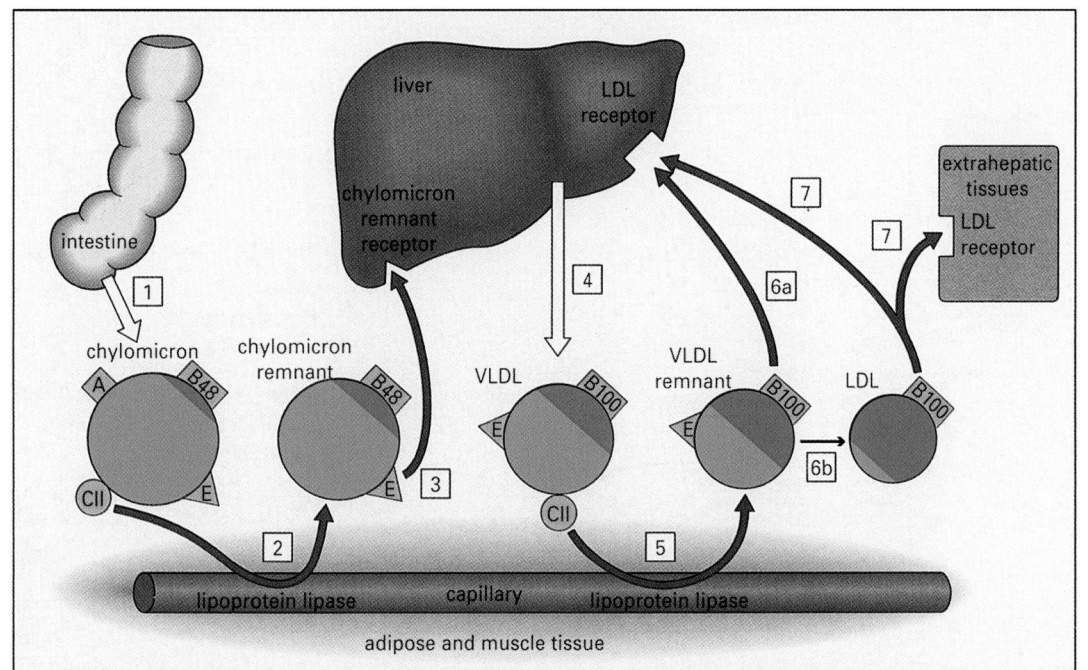

Fig. 12.1
Lipoprotein metabolism. (LDL, low density lipoprotein; VLDL, very low density lipoprotein.) Reproduced with permission from Cruz, P.D., East, C., Bergstresser, P.R. (1988) *Journal of the American Academy of Dermatology*, **19**, 95–111.

Table 12.2
Classification of hyperlipidemias

Type	Anomaly	Primary cause	Secondary cause	Atherogenesis	Xanthoma	Associations
I	Raised chylomicrons	Familial lipoprotein lipase deficiency Apoprotein CII deficiency	–	–	Eruptive	Hepatomegaly Pancreatitis Lipemia retinalis Abdominal pain
IIA	Raised LDL	Familial hypercholesterolemia Familial multiple type hyper-lipoproteinemia Common hypercholesterolemia	Hepatoma Porphyria Myxoedema Anorexia nervosa Nephrotic syndrome Cushing's syndrome	+	Tendinous Xanthelasma Arcus Tuberous (rare)	–
IIB	Raised LDL and VLDL	Familial hypercholesterolemia Familial multiple type hyperlipidemia	Nephrotic syndrome Cushing's syndrome	+	Tendinous Xanthelasma Arcus Tuberous	–
III	Raised IDL	Familial dysbetalipoproteinemia	Paraproteinemia	+	Palmar Tendinous Tuberous	Diabetes Gout Obesity
IV	Raised VLDL	Familial multiple type hyperlipidemia Familial hypertriglyceridemia Sporadic hypertriglyceridemia	Diabetes Uremia Paraproteinemia Alcoholism Lipodystrophy Obesity	+	Eruptive Tendinous Tuberous	–
V	Raised chylomicrons and VLDL	Familial multiple type hyperlipoproteinemia Familial lipoprotein lipase deficiency Apoprotein CII deficiency Familial hypertriglyceridemia Famial type V hyperlipoproteinemia	Diabetes Obesity Pancreatitis	+	Eruptive	Hepatomegaly Pancreatitis Lipemia retinalis

IDL, intermediate density lipoprotein; LDL, low density lipoprotein; VLDL, very low density lipoprotein.

16.　Shore, V., Salen, G., Cheng, T.F. (1981) Abnormal high density lipoproteins in cerebrotendinous xanthomatosis. *J Clin Invest*, **68**, 1295–1304.
17.　Hwang, S.Y., Lee, K.H., Ahn, J.I. (1990) Cerebrotendinous xanthomatosis. *J Dermatol*, **17**, 115–119.
18.　Bouwes Bavinck, J.N., Vermeer, B.J., Gevers Leuven, J.A. et al (1986) Capillary gas chromatography of urine samples in diagnosing cerebrotendinous xanthomatosis. *Arch Dermatol*, **122**, 1269–1272.
19.　Bhattacharyya, A.K., Conner, W.E. (1974) β-sitosterolemia and xanthomatosis. *J Clin Invest*, **53**, 1033–1043.
20.　Matsuo, I., Yoshino, K., Ozawa, A. et al (1981) Phytosterolemia and type IIa hyperlipoproteinemia with tuberous xanthomas. *J Am Acad Dermatol*, **4**, 47–49.
21.　Bhattacharyya, A.K., Preacher, A.B., Connor, W.E. (1980) Ectopic xanthomas in familial (type II) hypercholesterolemia. *Atherosclerosis*, **37**, 319–323.

Eruptive xanthomata

Clinical features

Eruptive xanthomata are small (1–4 mm) yellowish papules with a red halo that have a predilection for the buttocks, shoulders and extensor surfaces of the limbs (*Fig. 12.3*).[1] They may also present in the antecubital and popliteal fossae and the axillae, and on the lips, eyelids and ears.[2] They often appear in crops and may wax and wane with the plasma lipoprotein levels.[3] Lesions usually resolve spontaneously over a period of weeks. Pruritus is frequently present and the papules are sometimes tender.[2] Eruptive xanthomata may rarely display a Koebner phenomenon.[4,5] Healing is occasionally associated with the development of hyperpigmented scars.[2] Cutaneous lesions of Langerhans' cell histiocytosis may mimic eruptive xanthoma.[6]

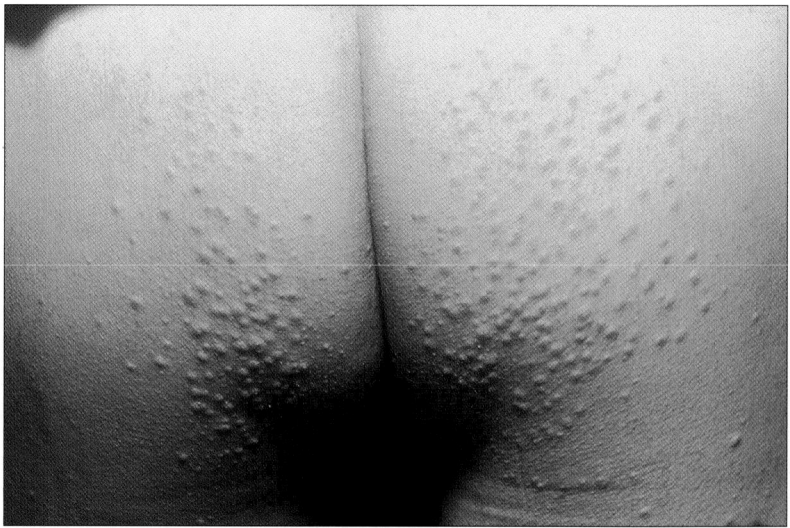

Fig. 12.3
Eruptive xanthoma: numerous small yellow papules are present on the buttocks. By courtesy of R.A. Marsden, MD, St George's Hospital, London, UK.

Eruptive xanthomata are associated with hypertriglyceridemia and most often occur in hyperchylomicronemic states. Sometimes their presence correlates with increased levels of very low density lipoproteins. The most common cause, however, is secondary hyperlipoproteinemia, especially in those cases associated with diabetes mellitus and alcohol ingestion, or in those that are drug-induced (e.g. due to exogenous estrogens, corticosteroids or retinoids).[2,7] They may also develop as a consequence of decreased lipoprotein lipase activity, ApoCII deficiency or increased synthesis of VLDL, which effectively blocks chylomicron access to lipoprotein lipase.[2,8] Eruptive xanthomata are therefore often accompanied by other features of hyperlipidemia, including lipemia retinalis, hepatosplenomegaly, abdominal pain and pancreatitis. They may also rarely develop as a manifestation of primary hyperlipoproteinemia (HPL), particularly autosomal recessive lipoprotein lipase deficiency (HLP type I) in children and familial HPL type V in adults.[9,10] An exceptional association with β-sitosterolemia, a condition usually presenting with tuberous or tendinous xanthomata, has been documented.[11] Much rarer associations include familial hypertriglyceridemia, the nephrotic syndrome, chronic pancreatitis, von Gierke's disease and hypothyroidism.[7,12,13] An association with acanthosis nigricans has also been reported.[14]

Histological features

The histological features are seen predominantly within the superficial reticular dermis. In early lesions histiocytes are numerous and the fully developed 'foam cells', which characterize xanthomata, are sometimes few in number. The infiltrate may also contain an admixture of lymphocytes and neutrophils.[15,16] In an established papule, xanthoma cells with characteristic clear or foamy cytoplasm form the predominant cell type (*Figs 12.4–12.6*).

Eruptive xanthomata often develop rapidly over the course of several days and occasionally are associated with spontaneous resolution. The quantity of intracytoplasmic lipid (predominantly triglyceride in contrast to other xanthomata, which contain mostly cholesterol) is in a state of

flux and may be associated with extracellular deposition, a phenomenon that is rare or absent in the other types of xanthomata. In all xanthomata the lipid within the macrophage stains positively with fat stains such as oil red O, scarlet or Sudan red (*Fig. 12.7*).

References

1. Parker, F. (1985) Xanthomas and hyperlipidemias. *J Am Acad Dermatol*, **13**, 1–30.
2. Cruz, P.D., East, C., Bergstresser, P.R. (1988) Dermal, subcutaneous, and tendon xanthomas: diagnostic markers for specific lipoprotein disorders. *J Am Acad Dermatol*, **19**, 95–111.
3. Parker, F., Odland, G.F. (1973) Ultrastructural and lipid biochemical comparisons of human eruptive, tuberous and planar xanthomas. *Israeli J Med Sci*, **9**, 395–423.
4. Goldstein, G.D. (1984) The Koebner response with eruptive xanthomas. *J Am Acad Dermatol*, **10**, 1064–1065.
5. Miwa, N., Kanzaki, T. (1992) The Koebner phenomenon in eruptive xanthoma. *J Dermatol*, **19**, 48–50.
6. Chi, D.H., Sung, K.J., Koh, J.K. (1996) Eruptive xanthoma-like cutaneous Langerhans' cell histiocytosis in an adult. *J Am Acad Dermatol*, **34**, 688–689.
7. Braun-Falco, O., Eckert, F. (1991) Macroscopic and microscopic structure of xanthomatous eruptions. *Curr Probl Dermatol*, **20**, 54–62.
8. Shore, V., Salen, G., Cheng, T.F. (1981) Abnormal high density lipoproteins in cerebrotendinous xanthomatosis. *J Clin Invest*, **68**, 1295–1304.
9. Nikkila, E.A. (1983) Familial lipoprotein lipase deficiency and related disorders of chylomicron metabolism. In: Standbury, J.B., Wyngaarden, J.B., Frederickson, D.J. (eds) The metabolic basis of inherited disease. New York: McGraw–Hill, pp 622–642.
10. Schreiber, M.M., Shapiro, S.I. (1969) Secondary eruptive xanthoma. Type V hyperlipoproteinemia. *Arch Dermatol*, **100**, 601–603.
11. Hidaka, H., Sugiura, H., Nakamura, T. et al (1997) β-sitosterolemia with generalized eruptive xanthomatosis. *Endocrin J*, **44**, 59–64.
12. Cooper, P.H. (1986) Eruptive xanthoma: a microscopic stimulant of granuloma annulare. *J Cutan Pathol*, **13**, 207–215.

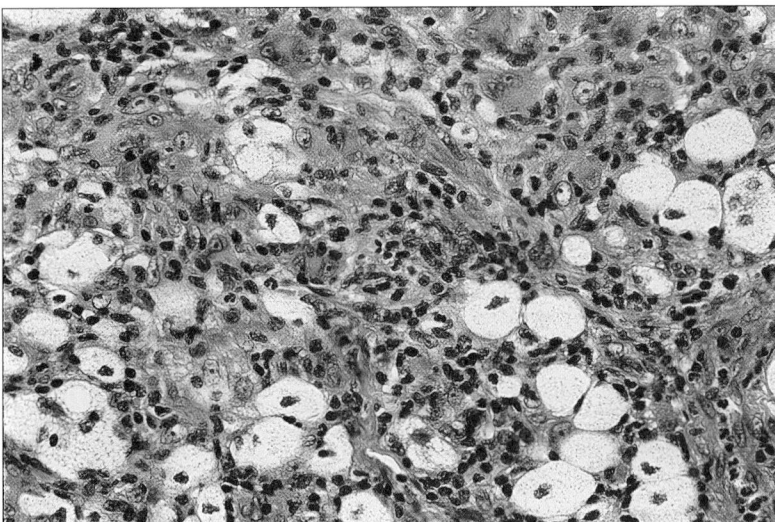

Fig. 12.5
Eruptive xanthoma: high power view showing an admixture of vacuolated xanthoma cells and non-lipidized variants with abundant eosinophilic cytoplasm.

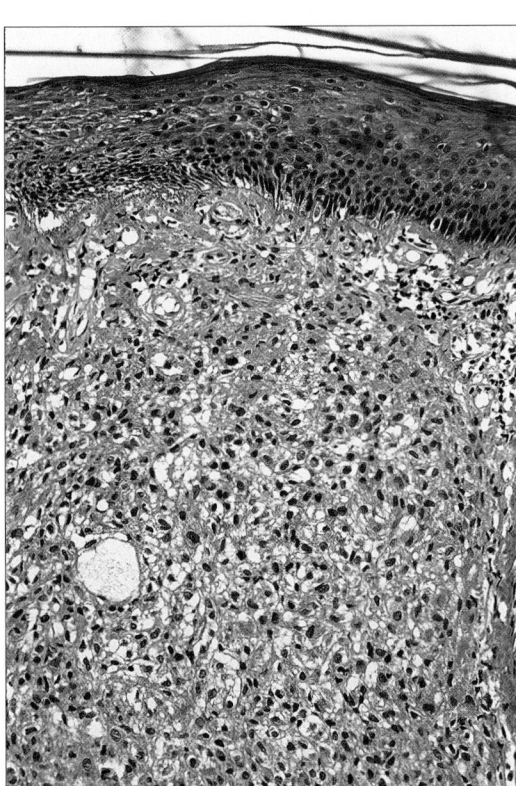

Fig. 12.4
Eruptive xanthoma: biopsy of an established lesion. The histiocytes have abundant vacuolated cytoplasm.

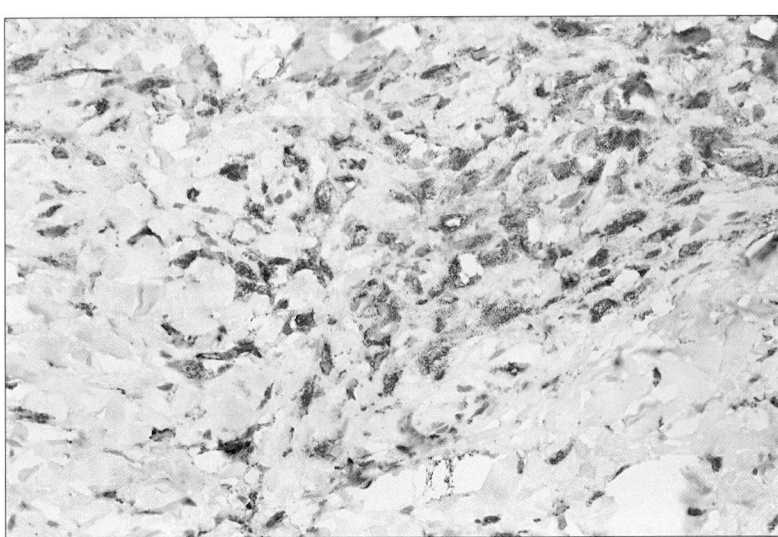

Fig. 12.6
Eruptive xanthoma: the histiocytes express CD68.

13. Dotsch, J., Zepf, K., Schellmoser, S. et al (2001) Unmasking of childhood hypothyroidism by disseminated xanthomas. *Pediatrics*, **108**, E96.
14. Emmerson, R.W. (1976) Acanthosis nigricans and eruptive xanthoma. *Proc R Soc Med*, **13**, 207–215.
15. Teltscher, J., Silverman, R.A., Stork, J. (1989) Eruptive xanthomas in a child with the nephrotic syndrome. *J Am Acad Dermatol*, **21**, 1147–1149.
16. Crowe, M.J., Gross, D.J. (1992) Eruptive xanthoma. *Cutis*, **50**, 31–32.

Tendinous xanthomata

Clinical features

Tendinous xanthomata, which are associated with raised low density lipoprotein levels, are slowly enlarging, subcutaneous tumors that occur in tendons (especially those of the hands, knees, elbows and the Achilles tendon), ligaments, fascia and periosteum (*Figs 12.8, 12.9*).[1] The overlying skin, which appears normal, is freely moveable over the surface and small tendon xanthomata may be difficult to palpate.[1] Tendinous xanthomata characteristically 'move with the tendons' and are thought to be trauma related.[2] The presence of these xanthomata is most frequently a feature of heterozygous familial (LDL receptor deficiency) hypercholesterolemia.[2–4] There is a high risk of associated coronary atherosclerosis. Tendinous xanthomata are also seen in familial combined hyperlipidemia, normocholesterolemic states such as cerebrotendinous xanthomatosis (cholestanolosis) and β-sitosterolemia, and the nephrotic syndrome.[2,5–9]

Clinically, tendinous xanthomata, which may be mistaken for gouty tophi and rheumatoid nodules, are sometimes found in association with tuberous xanthomata and xanthelasmata.

Histological features

Tendinous xanthomata are composed of multiple nodules containing xanthoma cells, accompanied in early lesions by an admixture of inflammatory cells including histiocytes, lymphocytes and neutrophil polymorphs. The deposits in tendinous xanthoma are doubly refractile to polarized light (*Fig. 12.10*). Older lesions are characteristically associated with fibrosis.

References

1. Parker, F. (1985) Xanthomas and hyperlipidemias. *J Am Acad Dermatol*, **13**, 1–30.
2. Cruz, P.D., East, C., Bergstresser, P.R. (1988) Dermal, subcutaneous, and tendon xanthomas: diagnostic markers for specific lipoprotein disorders. *J Am Acad Dermatol*, **19**, 95–111.

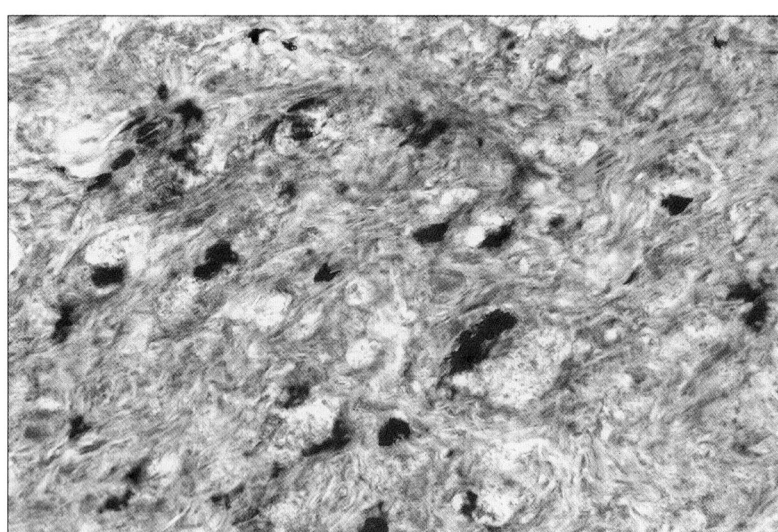

Fig. 12.7
Eruptive xanthoma: the lipid within the macrophages stains positively with oil red O.

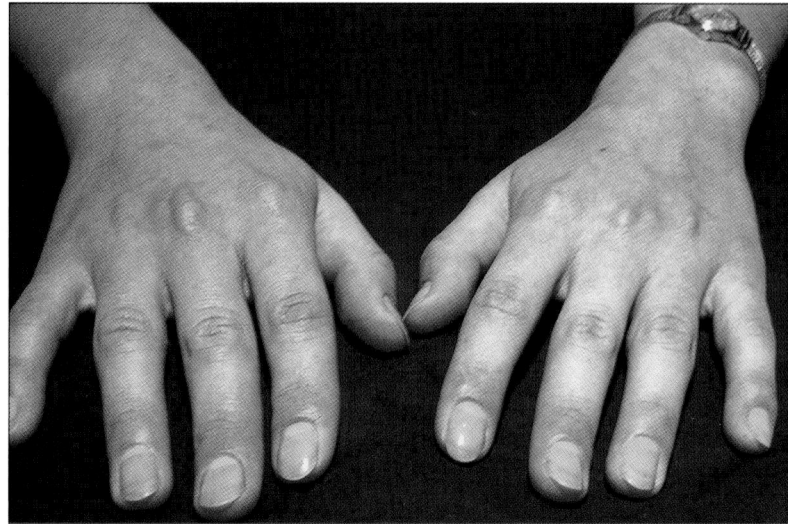

Fig. 12.9
Tendinous xanthoma: xanthomata are present overlying the knuckles. By courtesy of the Institute of Dermatology, London, UK.

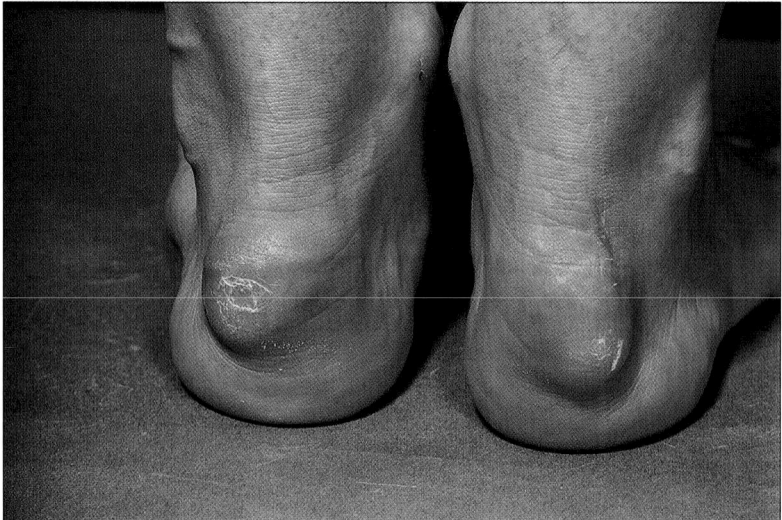

Fig. 12.8
Tendinous xanthoma: typical nodules on the heels. These lesions are often related to trauma; the Achilles tendon is a classical site. By courtesy of A.F. Lant, MD, and J. Dequeker, MD, London, UK.

Fig. 12.10
Tendinous xanthoma: intense birefringence of deposits in polarized light (oil red O).

3. Goldstein, J.L., Brown, M.S. (1975) Familial hypercholesterolemia, a genetic regulatory defect in cholesterol metabolism. *Am J Med*, **58**, 147–150.
4. Tsang, R.C., Glueck, C.J., Fallat, R.W. (1975) Neonatal familial hypercholesterolemia. *Am J Dis Child*, **129**, 83–91.
5. Oftebro, H., Bjorkhem, I., Skrede, S. et al (1980) Cerebrotendinous xanthomatosis: a defect in mitochondrial 26-hydroxylation required for normal biosynthesis of cholic acid. *J Clin Invest*, **65**, 1418–1430.
6. Bhattacharyya, A.K., Conner, W.E. (1974) β-sitosterolemia and xanthomatosis. *J Clin Invest*, **53**, 1033–1043.
7. Matsuo, I., Yoshino, K., Ozawa, A. et al (1981) Phytosterolemia and type IIa hyperlipoproteinemia with tuberous xanthomas. *J Am Acad Dermatol*, **4**, 47–49.
8. Philippart, M., Van Bogaert, L. (1969) Cholestanolosis (cerebrotendinous xanthomatosis). *Arch Neurol*, **21**, 603–610.
9. Lussier-Cacan, S., Cantin, M., Roy, C.C. et al (1986) Tendon xanthomas associated with cholestanolosis and hyperapolipoproteinemia. *Clin Invest Med*, **9**, 94–99.

Tuberous xanthomata

Clinical features

Tuberous xanthomata are firm yellow–red papules and nodules, which are found most frequently on the extensor aspect of the knees, elbows and buttocks (*Figs 12.11–12.13*).[1] Lesions sometimes also occur on the hands and palms.[2] They are most characteristically seen in familial dysbetalipoproteinemia type III, and there is a particular risk of peripheral vascular disease.[3] Four other conditions may also be characterized by tuberous xanthomatosis:

- homozygous familial hypercholesterolemia
- cerebrotendinous xanthomatosis
- β-sitosterolemia[1]
- type IV hyperlipoproteinemia.[4]

Tuberous xanthomata also occur in secondary hyperlipidemia (e.g. due to the nephrotic syndrome or hypothyroidism). Clinically, tuberous xanthomata occasionally resemble the lesions of erythema elevatum diutinum. Tuberous and tendinous normolipemic xanthomata have been described but it seems that with adequate follow-up, patients usually develop some form of hyperlipidemia.[5] Cholesterotic fibrous histiocytomas may be associated with hyperlipidemia and often simulate a tuberous xanthoma clinically and histologically.[6] A rare case of malignant fibrous histiocytoma clinically presenting as a tuberous xanthoma in a patient with type IIA hyperlipoproteinemia has been documented.[7]

Histological features

Tuberous xanthomata consist of multiple nodules in the reticular dermis and sometimes the subcutaneous fat (*Fig. 12.14*). Their appearance varies, depending upon their stage of evolution (*Fig. 12.15*). Xanthoma cells predominate in early lesions, but with maturity fibrosis supervenes (*Fig. 12.16*). On occasions, foreign body giant cell granulomata containing cholesterol clefts are seen and a perivascular chronic inflammatory cell infiltrate is sometimes evident (*Fig. 12.17*).

Differential diagnosis

Heavily lipidized fibrous histiocytomas that tend to occur mainly around the ankle may mimic tuberous xanthoma histologically.[8]

References

1. Cruz, P.D., East, C., Bergstresser, P.R. (1988) Dermal, subcutaneous, and tendon xanthomas: diagnostic markers for specific lipoprotein disorders. *J Am Acad Dermatol*, **19**, 95–111.
2. Braun-Falco, O., Eckert, F. (1991) Macroscopic and microscopic structure of xanthomatous eruptions. *Curr Probl Dermatol*, **20**, 54–62.
3. Havel, R.J. (1982) Familial dysbetalipoproteinemia: new aspects of pathogenesis and diagnosis – symposium on lipid disorders. *Med Clin North Am*, **66**, 441–454.

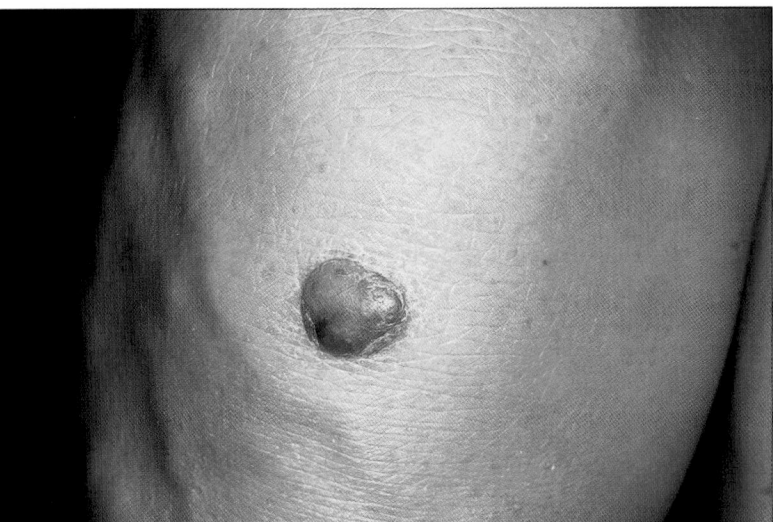

Fig. 12.12
Tuberous xanthoma: erythematous nodule on the back of the arm. By courtesy of the Institute of Dermatology, London, UK.

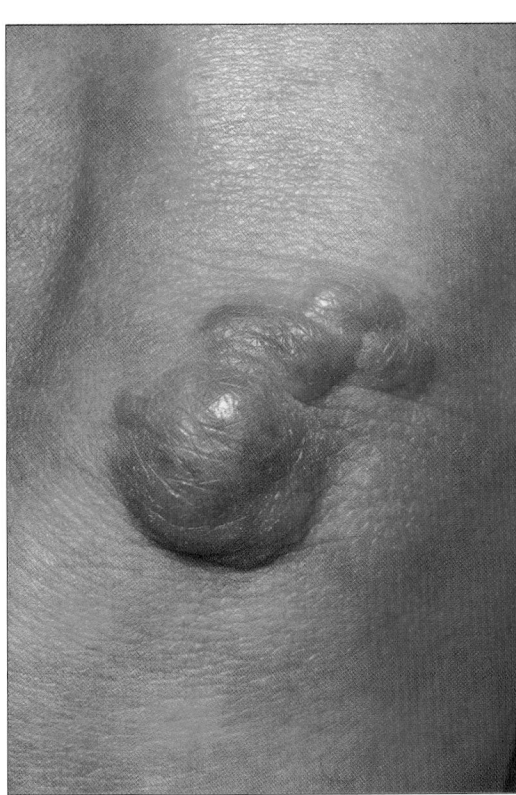

Fig. 12.11
Tuberous xanthoma: firm erythematous nodules over the elbow. By courtesy of R.A. Marsden, MD, St George's Hospital, London, UK.

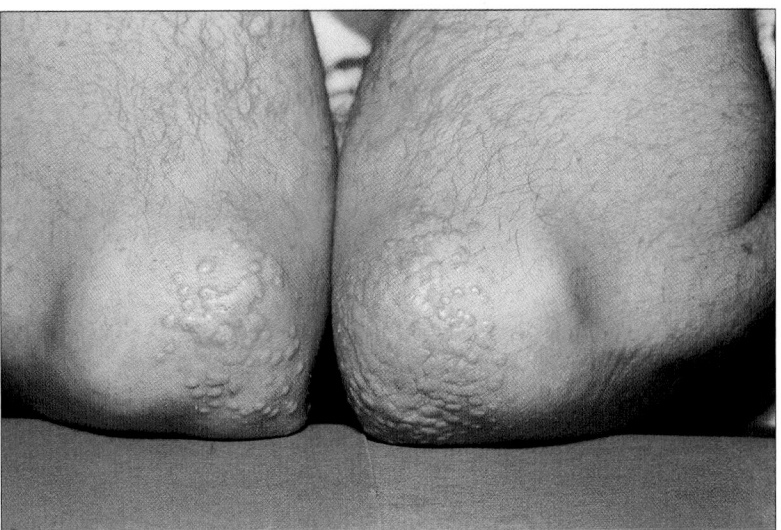

Fig. 12.13
Tuberous xanthoma: in this example, eruptive lesions are present on the elbows. By courtesy of the Institute of Dermatology, London, UK.

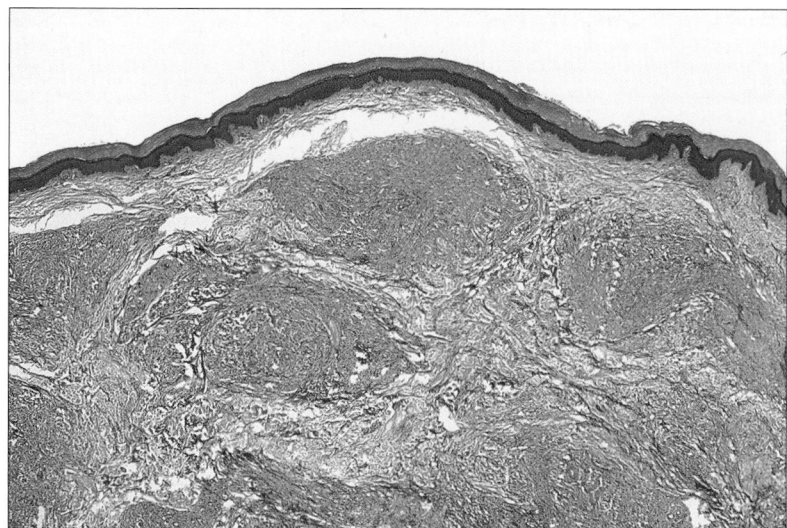

Fig. 12.14
Tuberous xanthoma: several nodules are present in the reticular dermis.

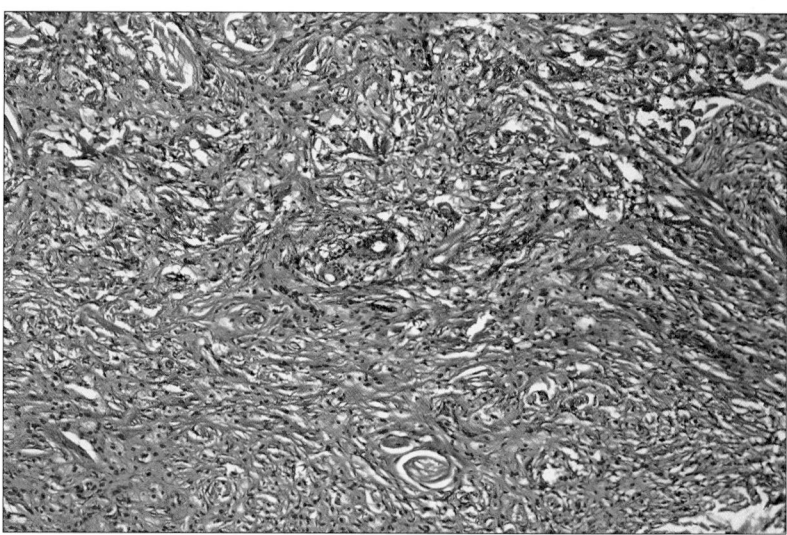

Fig. 12.16
Tuberous xanthoma: there is marked scarring.

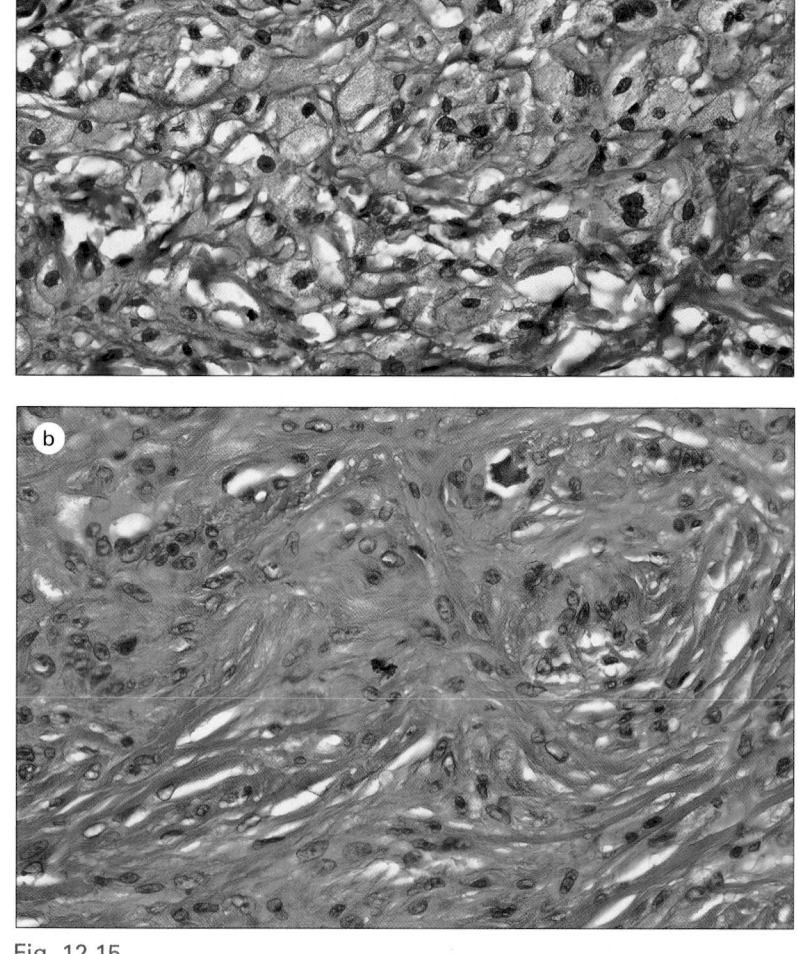

Fig. 12.15
Tuberous xanthoma: (a) the infiltrate is composed of uniform xanthoma cells characterized by pale, foamy cytoplasm and small central vesicular nuclei; (b) occasional normal mitoses are commonly present.

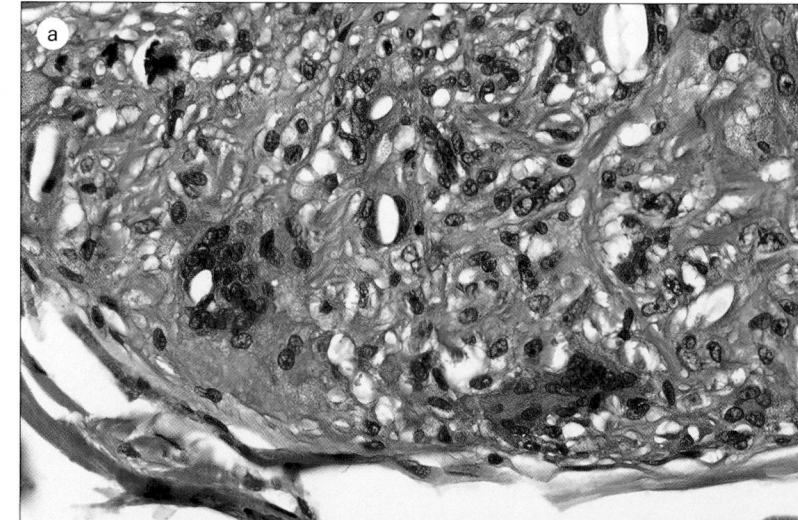

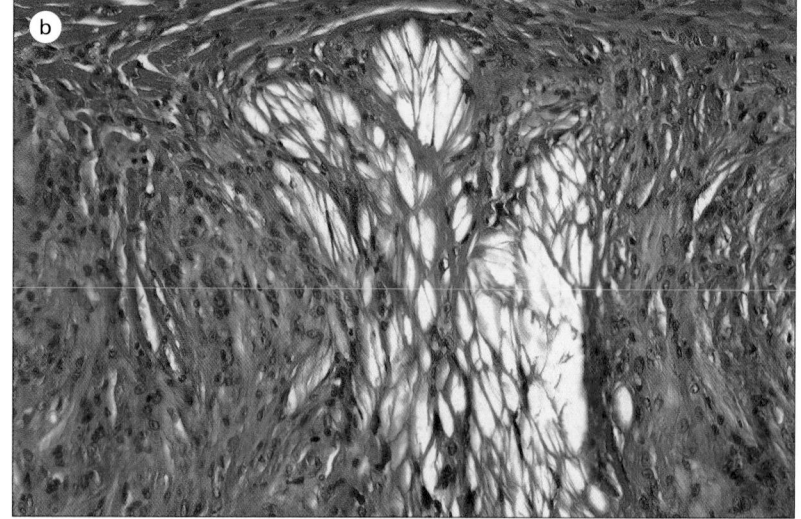

Fig. 12.17
(a, b) Tuberous xanthoma: in addition to xanthoma cells, occasionally there are foreign body giant cells containing cholesterol clefts. The lipid has been dissolved out during processing.

4. Cho, H.R., Lee, M.H., Haw, C.R. (1997) Generalized tuberous xanthoma with type IV hyperlipoproteinemia. *Cutis*, **59**, 315–318.
5. Mancuso, G., La Regina, G., Bagnoli, M. et al (1996) 'Normolipidemic' tendinous and tuberous xanthomatosis. *Dermatology*, **193**, 27–32.
6. Hunt, S.J., Santa Cruz, D.J., Miller, C.W. (1990) Cholesterotic fibrous histiocytoma. Its association with hyperlipoproteinemia. *Arch Dermatol*, **126**, 506–508.
7. Laskin, W.B., Conklin, R.C., Enzinger, F.M. (1988) Malignant fibrous histiocytoma associated with hyperlipoproteinemia. *Am J Surg Pathol*, **12**, 727–732.
8. Iwata, J., Fletcher, C.D. (2000) Lipidized fibrous histiocytoma: clinicopathologic analysis of 22 cases. *Am J Dermatopathol*, **22**, 126–134.

Planar xanthomata

Clinical features

Planar xanthomata are typically soft yellow dermal macules or plaques that occur most frequently around the eyes, where they are known as xanthelasmata (*Fig. 12.18*).[1,2] About 50% of patients with xanthelasmata have associated hyperlipidemia (hypercholesterolemia or hyperlipoproteinemia type III) which is often accompanied by a cholesterol corneal arcus.[3–5] Many of those who appear biochemically normal on routine testing, however, can be shown to have subtle abnormalities of lipid metabolism on more detailed analysis.[6] There is a particularly increased risk of coronary artery atherosclerosis in younger patients.[1] When very extensive (diffuse or generalized plane xanthomatosis) and associated with orange–yellow planar xanthomata around the head and neck, and occasionally the upper trunk and arms, there may be an associated systemic disorder such as multiple myeloma with paraproteinemia, cryoglobulinemia, benign paraproteinemia or, less commonly, leukemia and rheumatoid arthritis (necrobiotic xanthogranuloma, see p. 318) (*Fig. 12.19*).[1,3,7–13] More exceptional associations include idiopathic Bence Jones proteinuria, Sézary's syndrome, Castleman's disease, relapsing polychondritis and acquired palmoplantar keratoderma.[14–18] A patient with monoclonal gammopathy and cutaneous lesions with features of both plane xanthoma and amyloidosis has been documented.[19] The latter case was also associated with myeloma.

In cases of myeloma and plane xanthoma it has been demonstrated that there is formation of complexes between serum lipoproteins and paraprotein suggesting that this interaction may induce a hyperlipidemia and xanthoma formation.[20,21] The serum lipid levels of patients with diffuse plane xanthomata are normal or raised. Plane xanthomata may present in the gingiva and, in this location, are usually associated with hyperlipidemia.[22] An exceptional case has been described in an infant presenting with normolipemic papular and nodular lesions progressing to plane xanthomata and resulting in spontaneous resolution.[23] Diffuse plane normolipemic xanthomata with mucosal and conjunctival involvement and aortic valve xanthomatosis may occur exceptionally.[24] Lesions have been reported that clinically resembled plane xanthoma in a patient with systemic lupus erythematosus but histologically showed degeneration of collagen bundles with secondary fat deposition.[25]

Intertriginous xanthomata seen in patients with raised low density lipoproteins and pathognomonic of homozygous familial hypercholesterolemia present as yellow papules and plaques, often with a cobblestone appearance. These occur in the finger webspaces and to a lesser extent in the axillae and antecubital and popliteal fossae.[2,26] They have a particularly high association with early and severe atherosclerosis. Intertriginous xanthomata may also rarely be seen in heterozygous familial hypercholesterolemia.[27]

Planar xanthomata presenting as yellow–orange macules in the skin creases of the palm and fingers (xanthoma striatum palmare) are diagnostic of familial dysbetalipoproteinemia (HLP type III, broad beta disease) (*Fig. 12.20*), which is due to an abnormality of the apoprotein ApoE (homozygous ApoE2/E2).[1,2,28] This results in impaired uptake of lipoprotein remnant particles by the liver and macrophages with resultant hyperlipoproteinemia and increased atherogenesis.[27]

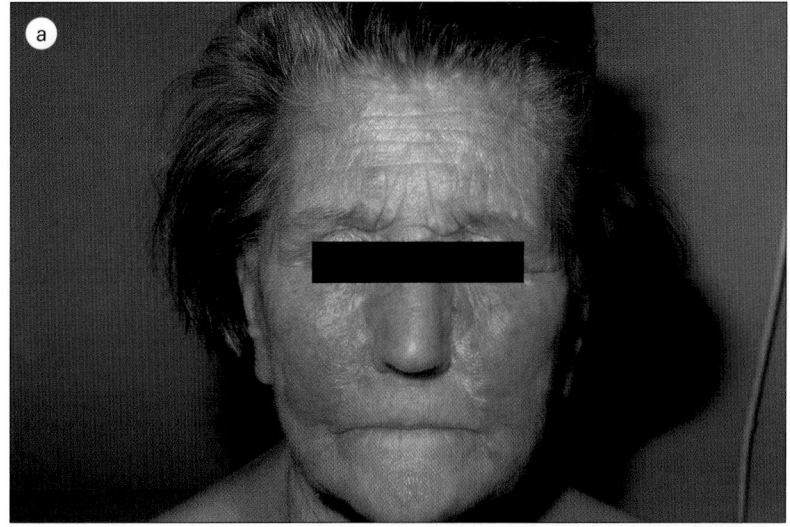

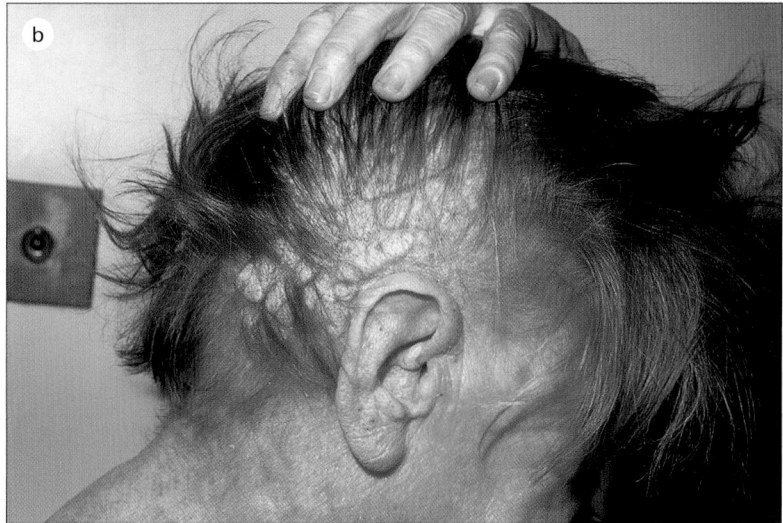

Fig. 12.19
Planar xanthoma: (a) widely distributed lesions over the forehead, eyelids and cheeks; (b) extensive yellow plaques on the scalp. This appearance should prompt a search for an associated paraproteinemia. By courtesy of R.A. Marsden, MD, St George's Hospital, London, UK.

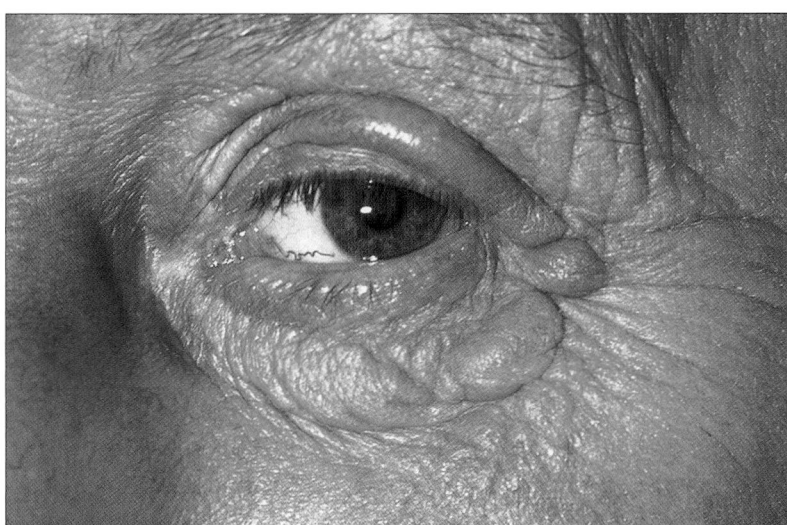

Fig. 12.18
Xanthelasmata: note the yellow, periorbital plaques. These are a common manifestation of hypercholesterolemia. By courtesy of the Institute of Dermatology, London, UK.

Interestingly, the tendency to familial dysbetalipoproteinemia is present in 1% of the population, but a second lipid abnormality appears to be necessary to induce symptoms.[27]

Plane xanthomata of cholestasis, for example due to primary biliary cirrhosis and biliary atresia, present as well-demarcated, beige–orange plaques that are particularly found on the hands and feet, but may occur elsewhere.[2] They can also develop in patients with diabetes mellitus.

Planar xanthomata have also been described as a feature of HDL deficiency.[29]

Histological features

In planar xanthomata the characteristic lipid-laden foam cells are situated within the superficial dermis (*Figs 12.21–12.23*). There is minimal fibrosis. In rare cases the histology may overlap with that of necrobiotic xanthogranuloma.[30]

References

1. Parker, F. (1985) Xanthomas and hyperlipidemias. *J Am Acad Dermatol*, **13**, 1–30.
2. Cruz, P.D., East, C., Bergstresser, P.R. (1988) Dermal, subcutaneous, and tendon xanthomas: diagnostic markers for specific lipoprotein disorders. *J Am Acad Dermatol*, **19**, 95–111.
3. Braun-Falco, O., Eckert, F. (1991) Macroscopic and microscopic structure of xanthomatous eruptions. *Curr Probl Dermatol*, **20**, 54–62.
4. Polano, M.D. (1974) Xanthomatosis and hyperlipoproteinemia. *Dermatologica*, **149**, 1–9.
5. The Lipid Research Clinic's Program Prevalence Study (1986) The association of lipoproteinaemia with corneal arcus and xanthelasma. *Circulation*, **73**, 1108–1118.
6. Douste-Blazy, P., Marcel, Y.L., Cohen, L. et al (1982) Increased frequency of apoE-ND phenotype and hyperapobetalipoproteinaemia in normal lipidemic subjects with xanthelasmas of the eyelids. *Ann Intern Med*, **96**, 164–169.
7. Lynch, P.J., Winkelmann, R.K. (1966) Generalized plane xanthoma and systemic disease. *Arch Dermatol*, **93**, 639–642.
8. Marien, K.J., Smeenk, G. (1975) Plane xanthomata associated with multiple myeloma and hyperlipoproteinaemia. *Br J Dermatol*, **93**, 407–415.
9. Mosschella, S.L. (1970) Plane xanthomatosis associated with myelomatosis. *Arch Dermatol*, **101**, 683–687.
10. Vail, J.T., Adler, K.R., Rothenberg, J. (1985) Cutaneous xanthoma associated with chronic myelomonocytic leukemia. *Arch Dermatol*, **121**, 1318–1320.
11. Taylor, J.S., Lewis, L.A., Battle, J.D. Jr et al (1978) Plane xanthoma and multiple myeloma with lipoprotein–paraprotein complexing. *Arch Dermatol*, **114**, 425–431.
12. Derrick, E.K., Price, M.L. (1993) Plane xanthomatosis with chronic lymphatic leukaemia. *Clin Exp Dermatol*, **18**, 259–260.
13. Marcoval, J., Moreno, A., Bordas, X. et al (1998) Diffuse plane xanthoma: clinicopathologic study of 8 cases. *J Am Acad Dermatol*, **39**, 439–442.
14. Ginarte, M., Peteiro, C., Toribio, J. (1997) Generalized plane xanthoma and idiopathic Bence Jones proteinuria. *Clin Exp Dermatol*, **22**, 192–194.
15. Schloss, E., Brown, J. (1978) Sezary's syndrome and generalized plane xanthoma. *Can Med Assoc J*, **118**, 377–378.
16. Sherman, D., Ramsay, B., Theodorou, N.A. et al (1992) Reversible plane xanthoma, vasculitis, and peliosis hepatis in giant lymph node hyperplasia (Castleman's disease): a case report and review of the cutaneous manifestations of giant lymph node hyperplasia. *J Am Acad Dermatol*, **26**, 105–109.
17. Yoshimura, T., Aiba, S., Tadaki, T. et al (1994) Generalized normolipemic plane xanthomatosis associated with relapsing polychondritis. *Acta Derm Venereol*, **74**, 221–223.
18. Smith, C.H., Barker, J.N., Hay, R.J. (1995) Diffuse plane xanthomatosis and acquired palmoplantar keratoderma in association with myeloma. *Br J Dermatol*, **132**, 286–289.
19. Buezo, G.F., Porras, J.I., Fraga, J. et al (1996) Coexistence of diffuse plane normolipaemic xanthoma and amyloidosis in a patient with monoclonal gammopathy. *Br J Dermatol*, **135**, 460–462.

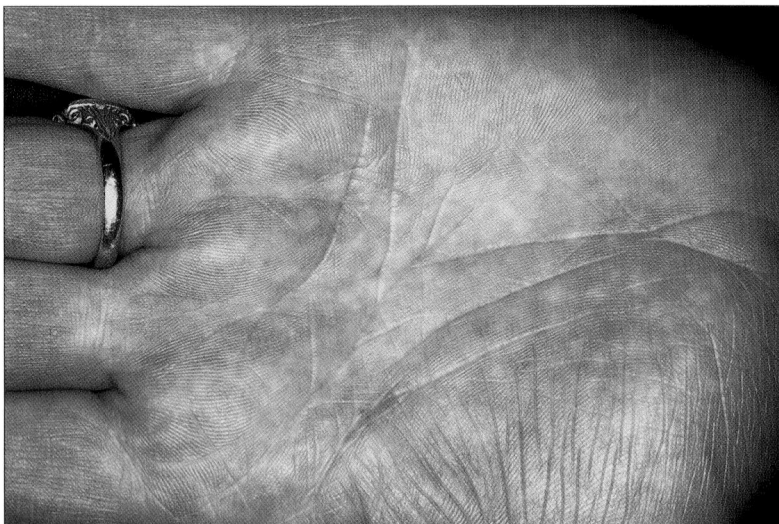

Fig. 12.20
Planar xanthoma: palmar lesions presenting as discrete macules with accentuation in the skin creases. By courtesy of R.A. Marsden, MD, St George's Hospital, London, UK.

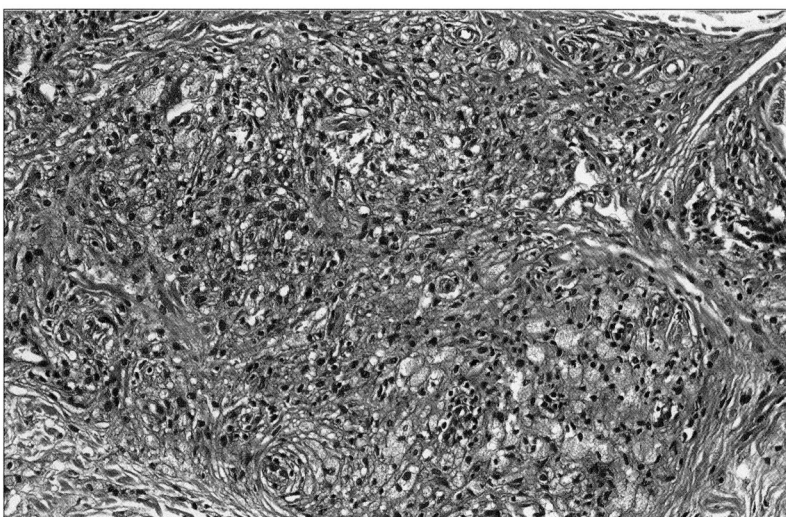

Fig. 12.22
Planar xanthoma: there is an admixture on non-lipidized and lipidized histiocytes.

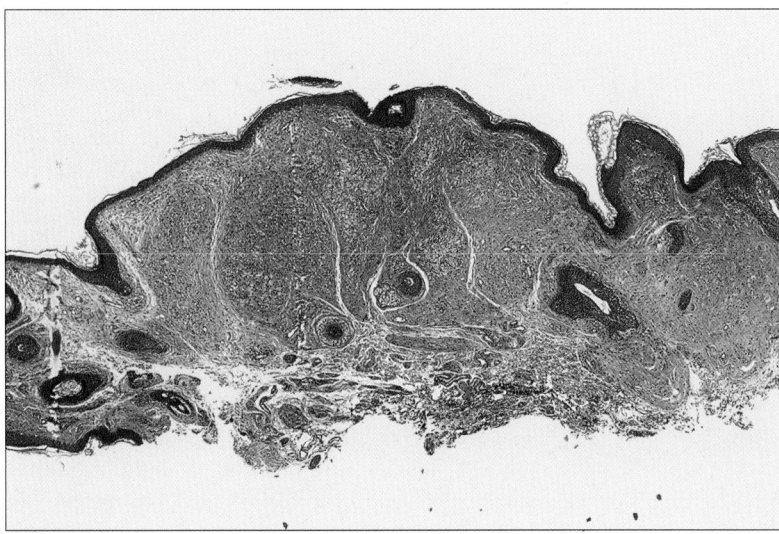

Fig. 12.21
Planar xanthoma: a dense infiltrate is present in the upper dermis.

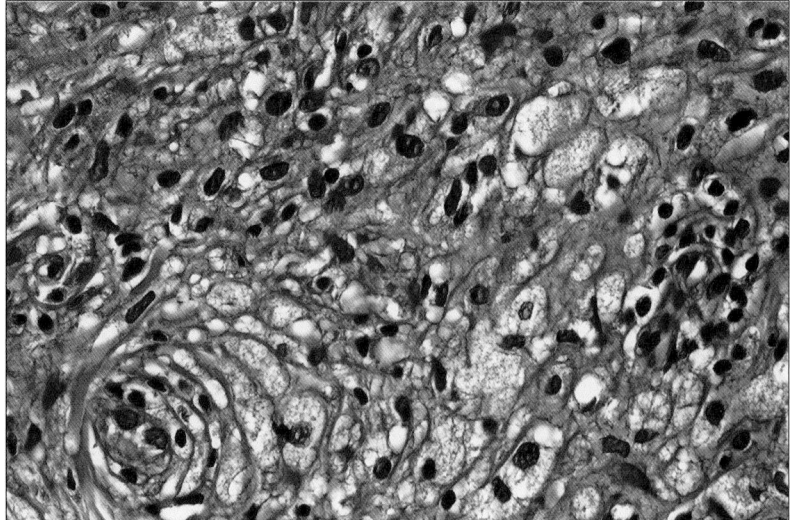

Fig. 12.23
Planar xanthoma: in addition to xanthoma cells, there are scattered lymphocytes.

20. Taylor, J.S., Lewis, L.A., Battle, J.D. Jr et al (1978) Plane xanthoma and multiple myeloma with lipoprotein–paraprotein complexing. *Arch Dermatol*, **114**, 425–431.
21. Berard, M., Antonucci, M., Beaumont, J.L. (1986) Cytotoxic effect of serum on fibroblasts in one case of normolipidemic plane xanthoma and myeloma IgG lambda. *Atherosclerosis*, **62**, 111–115.
22. Warnock, G.R., Correll, R.W., Schorn, V. (1987) Multiple asymptomatic yellowish-white nodules on the free gingiva. *J Am Dent Assoc*, **114**, 367–368.
23. Horiuchi, Y., Ito, A. (1991) Normolipemic papuloeruptive xanthomatosis in an infant. *J Dermatol*, **18**, 235–239.
24. Winkelmann, R.K., McEvoy, M.T. (1991) Diffuse-plane normolipaemic xanthoma with aortic-valve xanthoma. *Clin Exp Dermatol*, **16**, 38–40.
25. Yasaka, N., Otake, N., Furue, M. et al (1997) Pseudoxanthomatous lesions with membranocystic changes of collagen fibers in an SLE patient receiving long-term steroid treatment. *Dermatology*, **194**, 162–165.
26. Elias, P., Goldsmith, L.A. (1973) Intertriginous xanthomata in type II hyperbetalipoproteinemia. *Arch Dermatol*, **107**, 761–762.
27. Vermeer, B.J., Gevers Leuven, J. (1991) New aspects of xanthomatosis and hyperlipoproteinemia. *Curr Probl Dermatol*, **20**, 63–72.
28. Brewer, H.B., Zech, L.A., Gregg, R.E. et al (1983) Type III hyperlipoproteinemia: diagnosis, molecular defects, pathology and treatment. *Ann Intern Med*, **98**, 623–640.
29. Haber, C., Kwiterovich, P.O. (1984) Dysbetalipoproteinemia and xanthomatosis. *Pediatr Dermatol*, **1**, 261–277.
30. Williford, P.M., White, W.L., Jorizzo, J.L. et al (1993) The spectrum of normolipemic plane xanthoma. *Am J Dermatopathol*, **15**, 572–575.

Verruciform xanthoma

Clinical features

The verruciform xanthoma is an uncommon, asymptomatic lesion, which occurs predominantly in the oral cavity of adults in their fifth or sixth decade and shows a male predilection (1.7:1).[1–5] It is most often found on the premolar gingiva of the mandible or maxilla.[1] In this site it usually produces a solitary, well-circumscribed, asymptomatic, erythematous or yellow–tan lesion, 3–20 mm in diameter, which may be papillomatous or ulcerated. The patients are normolipidemic. The clinical differential diagnosis includes viral warts, leukoplakia and squamous cell carcinoma.

Verruciform xanthomata of the skin, which are extremely rare, have been described at a variety of sites including the ear, nose and digits.[6–9] Most cases described, however, have arisen on anogenital skin (*Fig. 12.24*).[10–16] It may also develop as a reactive phenomenon within epidermal nevi (including patients with inflammatory linear verrucous epidermal nevus or with the epidermal nevus syndrome) and has been recorded as a complication of lymphedema.[9,17–19] It has been described in association with longstanding discoid lupus erythematosus, complicating ulceration in epidermolysis bullosa and in association with squamous cell carcinoma of the penis.[20–22] Occasionally verruciform xanthomata are multifocal.[6] Such a case has been described as multiple lesions in the upper aerodigestive tract of a child with a systemic lipid storage disease.[23]

In the skin, verruciform xanthoma usually presents as a gray or pink nodule or as a plaque with a variably warty surface. Untreated, the lesions have a long duration and behave in a benign fashion, recurrence being very uncommon after local excision.

Pathogenesis and histological features

The etiology and pathogenesis of the verruciform xanthoma are unknown. Originally a viral infection was suspected, but there has been no evidence to support this hypothesis either by immunohistochemistry or molecular biology studies including in situ hybridization and polymerase chain reaction (PCR).[24–26] Alternatively it has been suggested that keratinocyte necrosis may lead to the release of intracellular lipids, with resultant macrophage influx and xanthomatization.[3,26,27] The inciting event leading to keratinocyte necrosis has not been identified. Immunohistochemical and electron microscopic studies tend to give support to this latter hypothesis (see below).

Verruciform xanthoma is an exophytic lesion characterized by massive, but regular epidermal proliferation, parakeratosis and hyperkeratosis (*Fig. 12.25*).[28] Neutrophils, neutrophilic debris and bacterial colonies may be evident in the parakeratotic stratum corneum. The acanthosis is associated with uniform, bulbous epidermal ridges, all of which penetrate to the same depth, giving a characteristically level lower border. The expanded ridges are associated with marked central keratinocyte necrosis and a heavy neutrophil polymorph inflammatory cell infiltrate (*Fig. 12.26*). There is no epithelial atypia and viral inclusions are invariably absent. The accentuated papillary dermis between the elongated epidermal ridges contains large numbers of eosinophilic foamy to granular xanthoma cells, which stain positively with lipid stains, but not usually with the diastase–periodic acid–Schiff (PAS) technique (*Fig. 12.27*). No foreign body or Touton giant cells are present. At the base of the lesion the epidermis may show focal basal cell hydropic degeneration associated with patchy loss of basement membrane. The reticular dermis deep to the lesion often contains a moderately dense lymphocyte–plasma cell infiltrate, which at the edge of the lesion sometimes adopts a lichenoid distribution. Typically vascular ectasia is seen beneath the lesion.

By immunohistochemistry, fully formed foamy cells are negative for histiocytic markers including Factor XIIIa, Mac 387, Ham-56 and KP1.[26,29] Cells with incompletely lipidized cytoplasm show diffuse

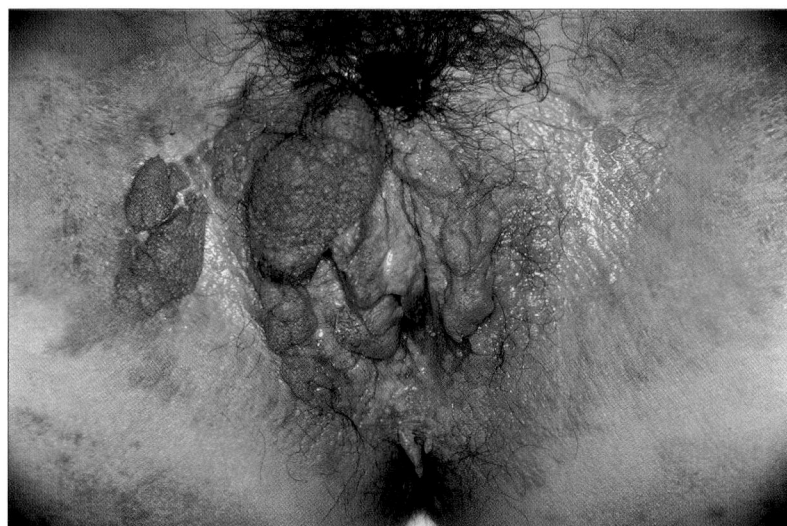

Fig. 12.24
Verruciform xanthoma: in this unusual gross example there are numerous warty and polypoid lesions showing extensive involvement of the vulva, perineum and thighs. A viral etiology was initially suspected clinically.

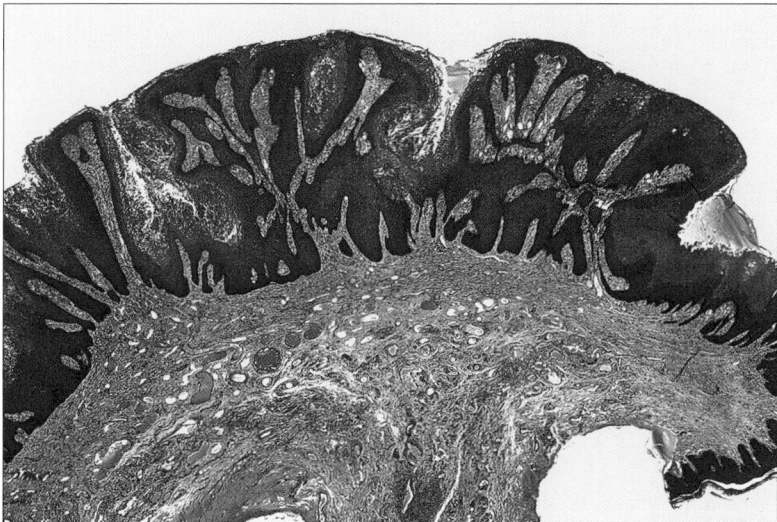

Fig. 12.25
Verruciform xanthoma: there is marked acanthosis, hyperkeratosis and a level lower border.

positivity for KP1 and weak positivity for FXIIIa and keratin. Cells with little cytoplasmic lipid are diffusely positive for FXIIIa and weakly positive for keratin. Non-lipidized cells located in the periphery of the infiltrate are diffusely positive for FXIIIa only. This staining pattern has led to the suggestion that FXIIIa positive dermal dendritic cells play an active role in the formation of the lipid cells seen in this condition.[26] It also tends to give further support to the role of damaged keratinocytes in the pathogenesis of verruciform xanthoma.[26]

Ultrastructural studies have revealed histiocytes containing numerous non-membrane-bound lipid droplets, lysosomes and myelin figures.[11,30]

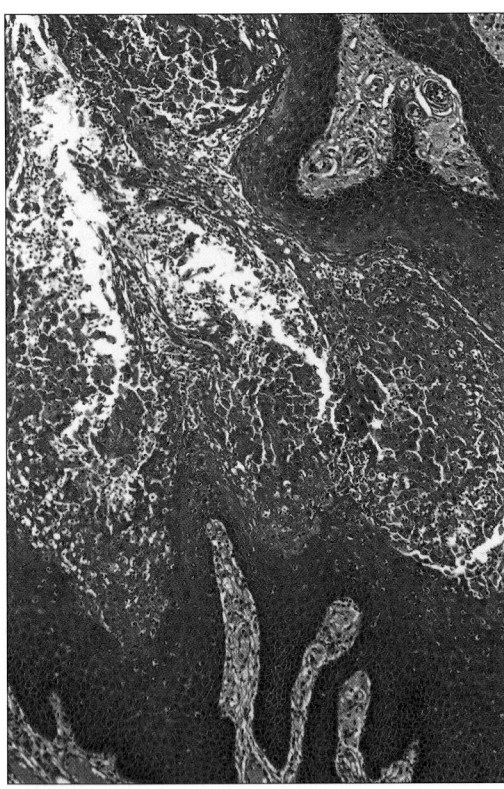

Fig. 12.26
Verruciform xanthoma: there is extensive keratinocyte necrosis associated with a polymorph infiltrate.

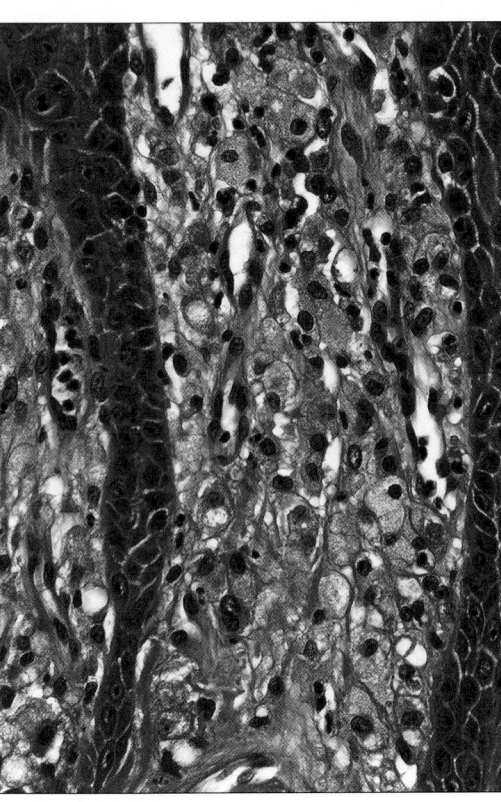

Fig. 12.27
Verruciform xanthoma: in the papillary dermis there is an infiltrate of uniform xanthoma cells.

Smaller numbers of these lipid inclusions may be found in the overlying keratinocytes and in the intercellular space. In one report, basal melanocytes were found to contain conspicuous lipid droplets.[31] This was accompanied by evidence that the latter had been released into the basal intercellular space in association with disruption of the basal lamina, thereby providing a source for the lipid within the dermal macrophages.

Differential diagnosis

Verruciform xanthoma must be distinguished from viral warts, granular cell tumor and verrucous carcinoma:

- *Viral warts:* Verruciform xanthoma lacks the vacuolation, clumped keratohyalin granules and tiers of parakeratosis seen in a viral wart. Inclusions are not a feature.
- In *granular cell tumor* the hyperplastic overlying squamous epithelium often shows an infiltrative growth pattern, in contrast to the exophytic nature of verruciform xanthoma. The granular cells are larger, often have a syncytial appearance and typically stain positively with the PAS reaction.
- *Verrucous carcinoma* has both exophytic and endophytic components, the latter appearing as deeply penetrating bulbous epithelial processes. The epithelium often has a 'watery' appearance and xanthoma cells are not a feature.

References

1. Takehana, S., Kameyama, Y., Fukaya, M. et al (1989) Verruciform xanthoma of the gingiva: report of three cases. *J Oral Maxillofac Surg*, **47**, 1079–1081.
2. Shafer, W.G. (1971) Verruciform xanthoma. *Oral Surg*, **31**, 784–789.
3. Zegarelli, D.J., Zegarelli-Schmidt, E.C., Zegarelli, E.V. (1975) Verruciform xanthoma. Further light microscopic studies, with the addition of a third case. *Oral Surg*, **40**, 246–256.
4. Nowparast, B., Howell, F.V., Rick, G.M. (1981) Verruciform xanthoma. A clinicopathological review and report of fifty-four cases. *Oral Surg*, **51**, 619–625.
5. Buchner, A., Hansen, L.S., Merell, P.W. (1981) Verruciform xanthoma of the oral mucosa. Report of five cases and review of the literature. *Arch Dermatol*, **117**, 563–565.
6. Mouncastle, E.A., Lupton, G.P. (1989) Verruciform xanthomas of the digits. *J Am Acad Dermatol*, **20**, 313–317.
7. Duray, P.H., Johnston, Y.E. (1986) Verruciform xanthoma of the nose in an elderly male. *Am J Dermatopathol*, **8**, 237–240.
8. Jensen, J.L., Liao, S-Y., Jeffes, E.W.B. III (1992) Verruciform xanthoma of the ear with coexisting epidermal dysplasia. *Am J Dermatopathol*, **14**, 426–430.
9. Chyu, J., Medenica, M., Whitney, D.H. (1987) Verruciform xanthoma of the lower extremity – report of a case and review of the literature. *J Am Acad Dermatol*, **17**, 695–697.
10. Santa Cruz, D.J., Martin, S.A. (1979) Verruciform xanthoma of the vulva: report of two cases. *Am J Clin Pathol*, **71**, 224–228.
11. Nakamura, S-I., Kanamori, S., Nakayama, K. et al (1989) Verruciform xanthoma of the scrotum. *J Dermatol*, **16**, 397–401.
12. Ronan, S.G., Bolano, J., Manaligod, J.R. (1984) Verruciform xanthoma of the penis. Light and electron microscopic study. *Urology*, **13**, 600–603.
13. Neville, B. (1986) The verruciform xanthoma: a review and report of eight new cases. *Am J Dermatopathol*, **8**, 247–253.
14. Al-Nafussi, A.I., Azzopardi, J.G., Salm, R. (1985) Verruciform xanthoma of the skin. *Histopathology*, **2**, 245–252.
15. De Rosa, G., Barra, E., Gentile, R. et al (1989) Verruciform xanthoma of the vulva: case report. *Genitourin Med*, **65**, 252–254.
16. Griffel, B., Cordoba, M. (1980) Verruciform xanthoma in the anal region. *Am J Proctol Gastroenterol Colon Rectal Surg*, **31**, 24–25.
17. Palestine, R.F., Winkelmann, R.K. (1982) Verruciform xanthoma in an epithelial nevus. *Arch Dermatol*, **118**, 686–691.
18. Grosshans, E., Laplanche, G. (1981) Verruciform xanthoma or xanthomatous transformation of inflammatory epidermal nevus? *J Cutan Pathol*, **8**, 382–384.
19. Haustein, U.F. (1984) Xanthoma cells in inflammatory verrucous epidermal nevus or nevoid verruciform xanthoma. *Dermatol Monatsschr*, **170**, 475–478.
20. Cooper, T.W., Santa Cruz, D.J., Bauer, E.A. (1983) Verruciform xanthoma. Occurrence in eroded skin in a patient with recessive dystrophic epidermolysis bullosa. *J Am Acad Dermatol*, **8**, 463–467.
21. Meyers, D.C., Woosley, J.T., Reddick, R.L. (1992) Verruciform xanthoma in association with discoid lupus erythematosus. *J Cutan Pathol*, **19**, 156–158.
22. Takiwaki, H., Yokota, M., Ahsan, K. et al (1996) Squamous cell carcinoma associated with verruciform xanthoma of the penis. *Am J Dermatopathol*, **18**, 551–554.
23. Travis, W.D., Davis, G.E., Tsokos, M. et al (1989) Multifocal verruciform xanthoma of the upper aerodigestive tract in a child with a systemic lipid storage disease. *Am J Surg Pathol*, **13**, 309–316.
24. Helm, K.F., Hopfl, R.M., Kreider, J.W. et al (1993) Verruciform xanthoma in an immunocompromised patient: a case report and immunohistochemical study. *J Cutan Pathol*, **20**, 84–86.
25. Orchard, G.E., Wilson Jones, E., Russell Jones, R. (1994) Verruciform xanthoma: an immunocytochemical study. *Br J Biomed Sci*, **51**, 28–34.
26. Mohsin, S.K., Lee, M.W., Amin, M.B. et al (1998) Cutaneous verruciform xanthoma. A report of five cases investigating the etiology and nature of xanthomatous cells. *Am J Dermatopathol*, **22**, 479–487.
27. Zegarelli, D.J., Zegarelli-Schmidt, E.C., Zegarelli, E.V. (1974) Verruciform xanthoma. A clinical, light microscopic and electron microscopic study of two cases. *Oral Surg*, **38**, 725–734.
28. Barr, R.J., Plank, C.J. (1980) Verruciform xanthoma of the skin. *J Cutan Pathol*, **7**, 422–428.
29. Furue, M., Suzuki, H., Kodama, T. et al (1995) Colocalization of scavenger receptor in CD68 positive foam cells in verruciform xanthoma. *J Dermatol Sci*, **10**, 213–219.
30. Cobb, L.M., Holt, R., Denys, R.F. (1976) Ultrastructural features of the verruciform xanthoma. *J Oral Pathol*, **5**, 42–51.
31. Balus, S., Breathnach, A.S., O'Grady, A.J. (1991) Ultrastructural observations on 'foam cells' and the source of their lipid in verruciform xanthoma. *J Am Acad Dermatol*, **24**, 760–764.

Angiokeratoma corporis diffusum

Clinical features

Angiokeratoma corporis diffusum (Anderson–Fabry's disease) is a sex-linked recessive disorder of glycosphingolipid metabolism with a high mortality. It is very rare with an approximate incidence of 1 in 200,000.[1] Deficiency of the lysosomal enzyme α-galactosidase A leads to the widespread accumulation of neutral glycolipids, mainly globotriaosyl-ceramide (GB3, ceramidetrihexoside), and elevated urinary trihexoxylceramide levels.[1–4]

Globotriaosylceramide is normally broken down by α-galactosidase A to produce galactose and lactosylceramide. The full-blown syndrome is normally seen only in men, since female carriers have 15–40% greater enzyme activity than their male siblings or offspring. Heterozygotes, however, usually display abnormal ophthalmological and ultrastructural features.[5] Occasionally heterozygous females may manifest signs and symptoms due to extreme X inactivation (lyonization) of the healthy X chromosome.[5,6] Cutaneous lesions are believed to occur in about 20% of heterozygous females.[7]

In males, the disease normally presents in childhood as episodes of excruciating intermittent pain, frequently in the fingers and toes.[8] The attacks may be accompanied by fever, edema and malaise. Patients may also have hypohidrosis, acroparesthesiae and peripheral vasomotor disturbance affecting the heart, kidney and central nervous system. Heat intolerance and telangiectases of the ears are often present early in the course of the disease.[9]

The characteristic angiokeratomata develop after puberty and present as tiny red–black bilaterally symmetrical papules, 0.5–2 mm in diameter, with slight hyperkeratosis.[8] Lesions are typically seen in the bathing trunk distribution including the thighs, buttocks, lower back, penis and scrotum, although occasional lesions may also be seen on the trunk or buccal mucosa (*Figs 12.28, 12.29*). The number of angiokeratomata is very variable and bears no relationship to the degree of systemic involvement. Atypical cases can present with an oligosymptomatic phenotype which includes only very few cutaneous angiokeratomata and asymptomatic involvement of organs such as the kidney and the heart.[10]

In a patient in whom the diagnosis is suspected, confirmation can usually be obtained by an ophthalmic examination. The conjunctival vessels may be tortuous or aneurysmal, as may the retinal vessels, and slit-lamp examination of the eyes reveals characteristic whorled, corneal linear opacities (verticillate cornea) (*Fig. 12.30*). Enzyme assay of α-galactosidase A can be performed using peripheral leukocytes or cutaneous fibroblasts. Hair root analysis has been recommended for the detection of heterozygotes.[11]

Affected males may develop transient cerebrovascular accidents, but the most common cause of death is renal failure. In the early stages, proteinuria is seen and microscopy of the urinary sediment may reveal characteristic lipid-laden cells even before proteinuria develops (*Fig. 12.31*). Electron microscopy may reveal the typical inclusions (*Fig. 12.32*).

Cardiac involvement is found in approximately 20% of patients.[12] Glycosphingolipid deposits in the conducting system, myocardium, endocardium and valves may give rise to angina, electrocardiographic abnormalities, hypertrophic cardiomyopathy, hypertension, mitral valve incompetence and aortic medial degeneration.[13,14]

Oral and dental abnormalities are more common than previously realized and include the presence of cysts/pseudocysts of the maxillary sinuses and maxillary prognathism.[15]

Pathogenesis and histological features

A variety of genetic defects have been identified including point mutations, gene rearrangements and deletions.[16–19] A symptomatic heterozygous female Fabry's disease patient without detectable mutation in the α-galactosidase gene has recently been described.[20]

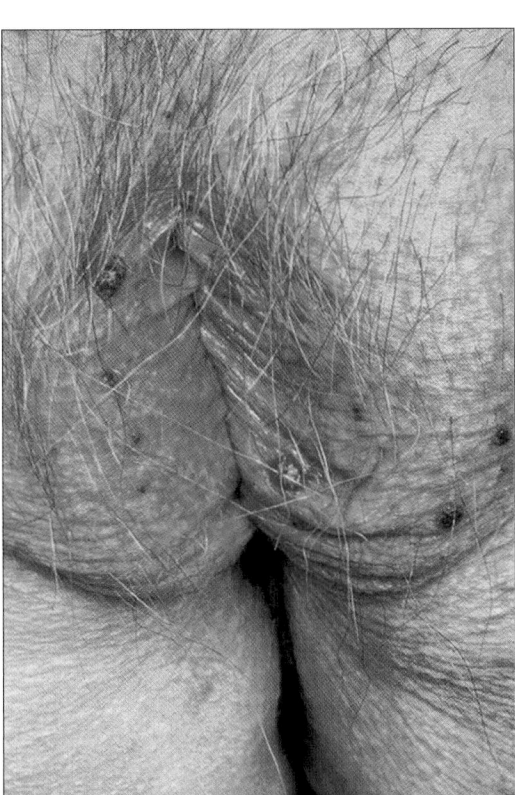

Fig. 12.28
Angiokeratoma corporis diffusum: tiny grouped red papules are present on the buttocks, a characteristic site. By courtesy of the Institute of Dermatology, London, UK.

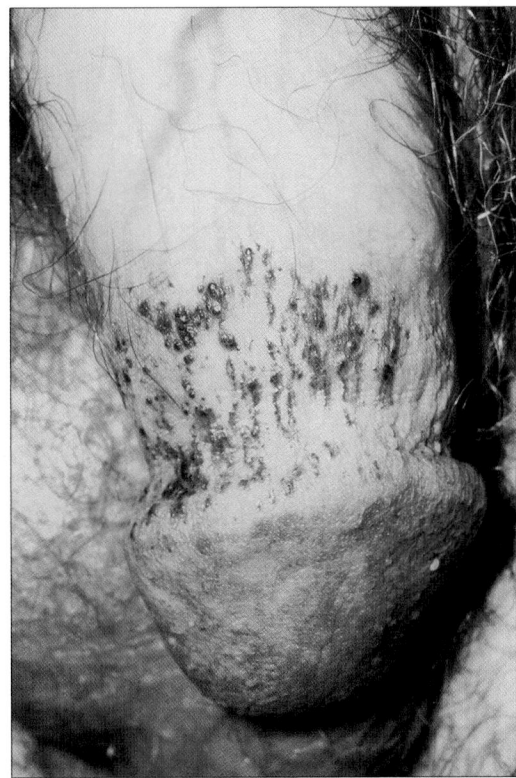

Fig. 12.29
Angiokeratoma corporis diffusum: conspicuous angiokeratomata on the penis, a commonly affected site. By courtesy of R.A. Marsden, MD, St George's Hospital, London, UK.

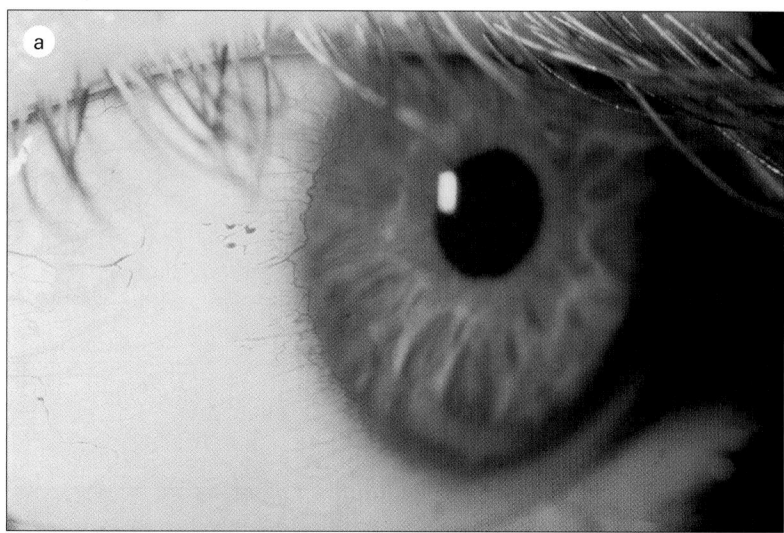

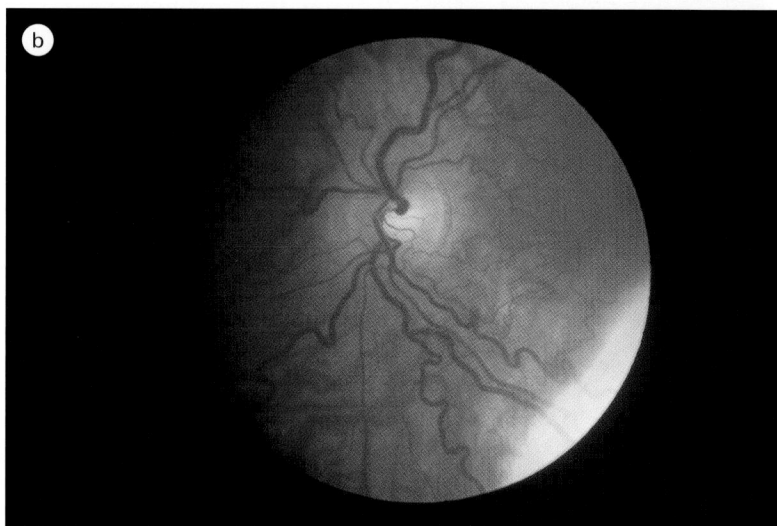

Fig. 12.30
Angiokeratoma corporis diffusum: (**a**) tortuous conjunctival vessels; (**b**) tortuous retinal vessels. By courtesy of S. Parker, MD, St Thomas' Hospital, London, UK.

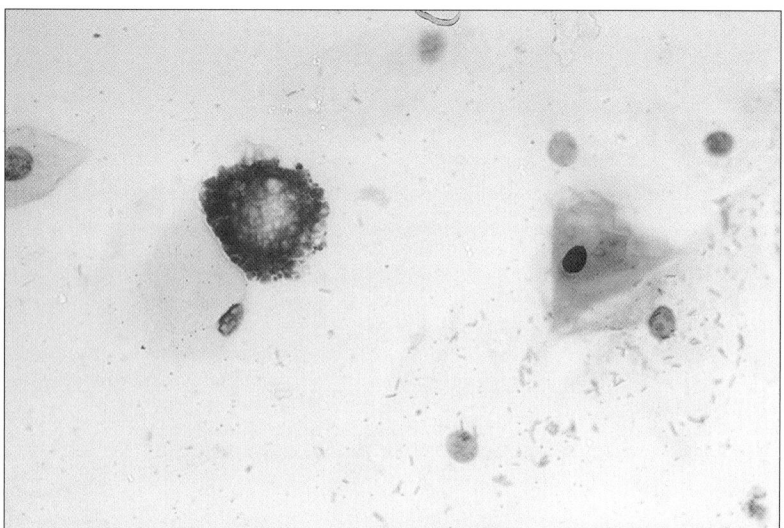

Fig. 12.31
Angiokeratoma corporis diffusum: urinary sediment stained with toluidine blue. The metachromasia (purple coloration) is due to the presence of intracytoplasmic sulfatides.

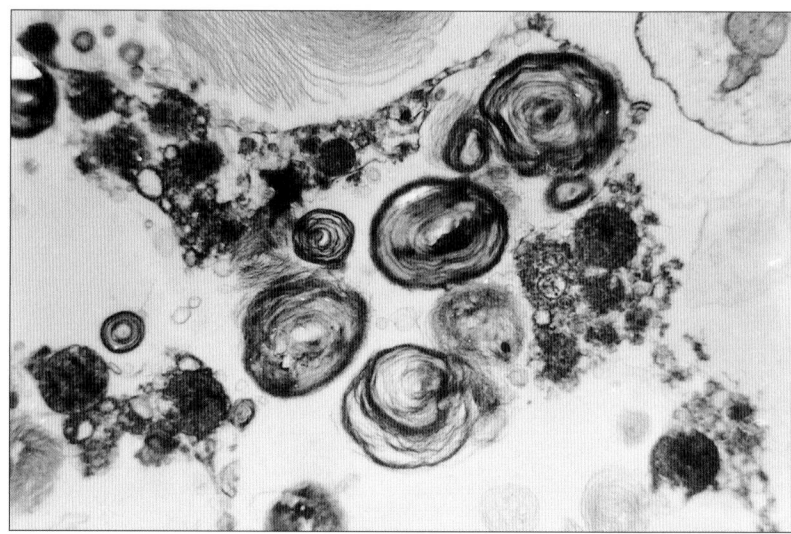

Fig. 12.32
Angiokeratoma corporis diffusum: electron micrograph of urine sediment, showing typical concentrically lamellated inclusions.

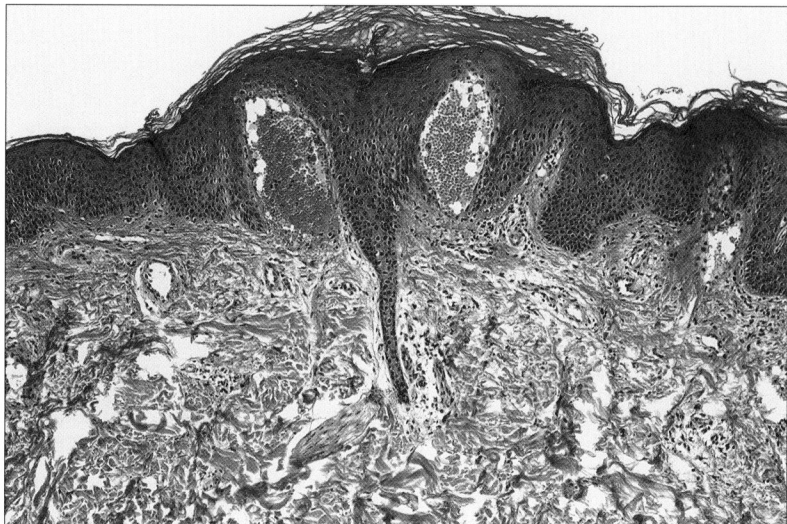

Fig. 12.33
Angiokeratoma corporis diffusum: ectatic blood-filled vascular channels expand the papillary dermis. Note the hyperkeratosis.

The skin lesions are composed of ectatic blood-filled vessels in the papillary dermis, associated with slight hyperkeratosis (*Figs 12.33, 12.34*). A characteristic feature is vacuolation of endothelial cells due to lipid deposits. The latter are doubly refractile and can usually be demonstrated in frozen material tissue sections. They may also be identified in toluidine blue-stained material. On electron microscopy, lamellar electron-dense inclusion bodies can be seen within the endothelial cells, pericytes, smooth muscle cells, fibroblasts, sweat gland epithelium and macrophages. It is thought that these are due to lipid deposition within lysosomes (*Fig. 12.35*).

Differential diagnosis

Other forms of angiokeratomata, for example those of Mibelli or Fordyce, should be clinically distinguishable by their site and distribution although their histopathological appearances are identical. It should be noted, however, that diffuse angiokeratomata may also be seen in fucosidosis, α-galactosidosis, sialidosis, aspartylglycosaminuria, α-N-acetylgalactosaminidase deficiency (Kanzaki disease), adult-onset GM1 gangliosidosis and indeed, diffuse angiokeratomata of a benign type may

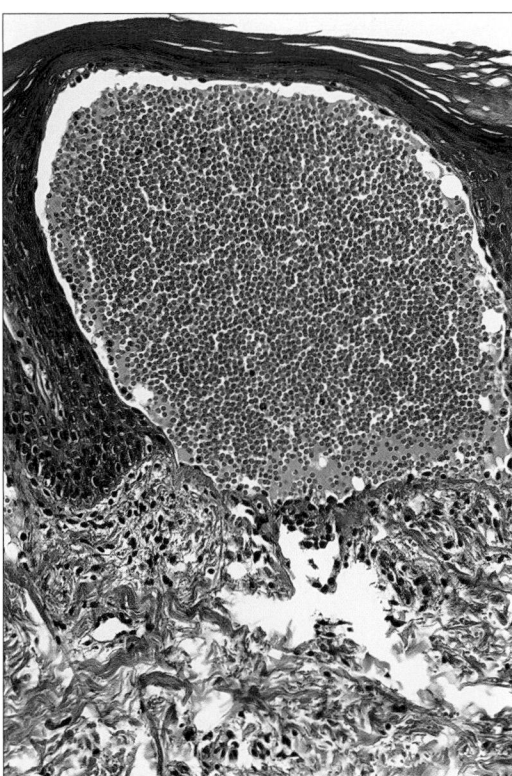

Fig. 12.34
Angiokeratoma corporis diffusum: close-up view.

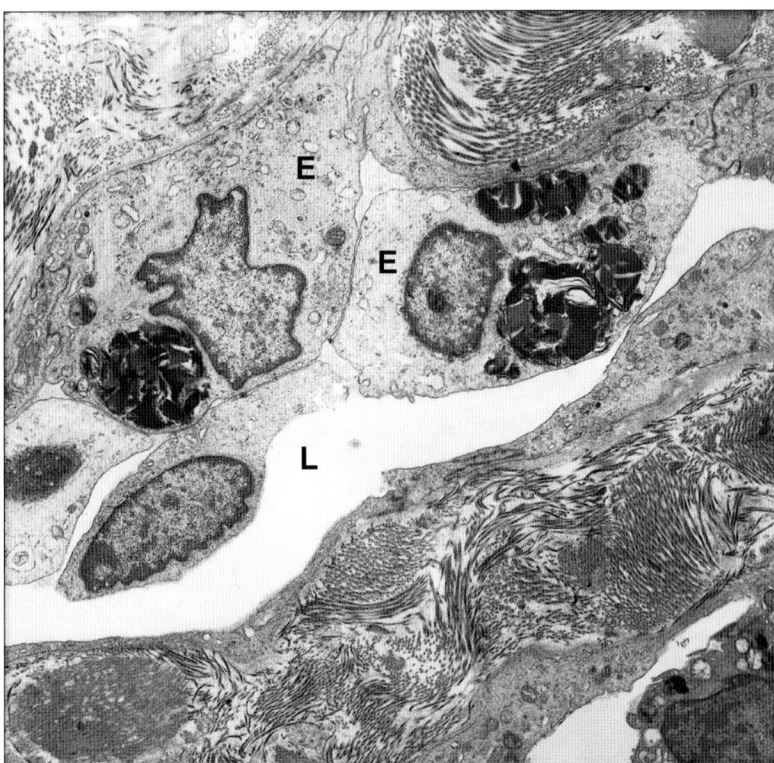

Fig. 12.35
Angiokeratoma corporis diffusum: the endothelial cells of this small blood vessel contain typical inclusions. (L, lumen; E, endothelial cell.)

occur in patients with normal enzyme activities.[21–25] Widespread angiokeratomata have also been described as an exceptional finding in tuberous sclerosis.[26]

References

1. Desnick, R.J., Sweeley, C.C. (1983) Fabry's disease: α-galactosidase A deficiency. In: Stanbury, J.B., Wyngaarden, J.B., Fredrickson, D.S. (eds) The metabolic basis of inherited disease, 5th edn. New York: McGraw-Hill, p 906.
2. Brady, R.O., Schiffmann, R. (2000) Clinical features and recent advances in therapy for Fabry disease. *JAMA*, **284**, 2771–2775.
3. Carsuzaa, F., Rommel, A., Bobin, P. (1985) La maladie de Fabry. *Ann Dermatol Venereol*, **112**, 643–656.
4. Hashimoto, K., Lieberman, P., Lamkin, N., Jr (1976) Angiokeratoma corporis diffusum (Fabry disease): a lysosomal disease. *Arch Dermatol*, **112**, 1416–1423.
5. Marguery, M.C., Giordano, F., Parant, M. et al (1993) Fabry's disease: heterozygous form of different expression in two monozygous twin sisters. *Dermatology*, **187**, 9–15.
6. Pravata, G., Noto, G., Arico, M. (1991) Fabry disease: classic hemizygote and residual alpha-galactosidase A activity. *Int J Dermatol*, **30**, 367–369.
7. Opitz, J.M., Stiles, F.C., Wise, D. et al (1965) The genetics of angiokeratoma corporis diffusum and its linkage with Xg(a) locus. *Am J Hum Gen*, **17**, 325–342.
8. Wallace, H.J. (1973) Anderson–Fabry disease. *Br J Dermatol*, **88**, 1–23.
9. Shelley, E.D., Shelley, W.B., Kurczynski, T.W. (1995) Painful fingers, heat intolerance, and telangiectases of the ear: easily ignored childhood signs of Fabry disease. *Pediatr Dermatol*, **12**, 215–219.
10. Ko, Y.H., Kim, H.J., Roh, Y.S. et al (1996) Atypical Fabry's disease. An oligosymptomatic variant. *Arch Pathol Lab Med*, **120**, 86–89.
11. Hatton, C.E., Cooper, A., Sardharwalla, I.B. (1989) Detection of Fabry's disease carriers by enzyme assay of hair roots. *J Inher Metab Dis*, **12**, 369–371.
12. Desnick, R.J., Blieden, L.C., Sharp, H.L. et al (1976) Cardiac valvular anomalies in Fabry disease: clinical, morphologic and biochemical studies. *Circulation*, **54**, 818–824.
13. Fisher, E.A., Desnick, R.J., Gordon, R.E. et al (1992) Fabry disease: an unusual case of severe coronary disease in a young man. *Ann Intern Med*, **117**, 221–223.
14. Nagao, Y., Nakashima, H., Fukuhara, Y. et al (1991) Hypertrophic cardiomyopathy in late-onset variant of Fabry disease with high residual activity of alpha-galactosidase A. *Clin Genet*, **39**, 233–237.
15. Baccaglini, L., Schiffmann, R., Brennan, M.T. et al (2001) Oral and craniofacial findings in Fabry's disease: a report of 13 patients. *Oral Surg Oral Med Oral Pathol Oral Radiol Endod*, **92**, 415–419.
16. Inaoki, M., Otsuki, N., Ishise, S. et al (1992) Two cases of Fabry's disease: a hemizygote with a point mutation in the α-galactosidase A gene and his relative. *J Dermatol*, **19**, 481–486.
17. Sakuraba, H., Oshima, A., Fukuhara, Y. et al (1990) Identification of point mutations in the alpha-galactosidase A gene in classical and atypical hemizygotes with Fabry disease. *Am J Hum Genet*, **47**, 784–789.
18. Bernstein, H.S., Bishop, D.F., Astrin, K.H. et al (1989) Fabry disease: six gene rearrangements and an exonic point mutation in the alpha-galactosidase gene. *J Clin Invest*, **83**, 1390–1399.
19. Cariolou, M.A., Christodoulides, M., Manoli, P. et al (1996) Novel trinucleotide deletion in Fabry's disease. *Hum Genet*, **97**, 468–470.
20. Handa, Y., Yotsumoto, S., Isobe, E. et al (2000) A case of symptomatic heterozygous female Fabry's disease without detectable mutation in the alpha-galactosidase A gene. *Dermatology*, **200**, 262–265.
21. Kanzaki, T., Yokota, M., Irie, F. et al (1993) Angiokeratoma corporis diffusum with glycopeptiduria due to deficient lysosomal α-N-acetylgalactosaminidase activity. *Arch Dermatol*, **129**, 460–465.
22. Beratis, N.G., Varvarigou-Frimas, A., Beratis, S. et al (1989) Angiokeratoma corporis diffusum in GM1 gangliosidosis, type 1. *Clin Genet*, **36**, 59–64.
23. Pravata, G., Noto, G., Arico, M. (1990) Angiocheratoma corporis diffusum with normal enzyme activiites. *G Ital Dermatol Venereol*, **125**, 401–403.
24. Crovato, F., Rebora, A. (1985) Angiokeratoma corporis diffusum and normal enzyme activities. *J Am Acad Dermatol*, **12**, 885–887.
25. Gasparini, G., Sarchi, G., Cavicchini, S. et al (1992) Angiokeratoma corporis diffusum in a patient with normal enzyme activities and Turner's syndrome. *Clin Exp Dermatol*, **17**, 56–59.
26. Gil-Mateo, M.P., Miquel, F.J., Velasco, A.M. et al (1996) Widespread angiokeratomas and tuberous sclerosis. *Br J Dermatol*, **135**, 280–282.

The amyloidoses

Amyloidosis is characterized by the extracellular deposition of a protein associated with particular tinctorial and ultrastructural properties. The amyloidoses are classified according to whether the amyloid deposition is systemic or localized (*Table 12.3*).

The most characteristic staining patterns of amyloid are seen with Congo red or Dylon (cotton dye pagoda red No. 9), which show apple-green birefringence under polarized light (*Fig. 12.36*). Unfortunately this is not specific, and green birefringence may also be seen with collagen and in colloid milium, porphyria and lipoid proteinosis. Amyloid deposits, which are PAS positive, may also be identified by the cotton dye Sirius red, or metachromatically using methyl or cresyl violet.[1] Further confirmatory evidence can be obtained by staining with thioflavine-T and examination using fluorescence microscopy or by immunocyto-chemistry (see below) (*Fig. 12.37*).

Amyloid shows characteristic and specific electron microscopic features of rigid, straight, non-branching amyloid filaments with a diameter of 6–10 nm showing a hollow core on cross-section (*Fig. 12.38*).[2] They are haphazardly distributed, lack the cross-banding of collagen, and are embedded in an electron-dense amorphous ground substance, which is probably composed of polysaccharides.

X-ray diffraction and infrared spectroscopy reveal a beta-pleated antiparallel configuration.[3,4] Fibrils with a beta-pleated configuration are

Table 12.3
Classification of the amyloidoses

Systemic amyloidosis	Localized amyloidosis
Primary (due to an occult plasma cell dyscrasia)	Organs other than the skin*
Myeloma associated	Primary cutaneous
Secondary	Lichen, macular and biphasic
Hemodialysis associated	Secondary cutaneous
Heredofamilial†	Associated with neoplasms, porokeratosis and PUVA therapy
Amyloid elastosis	Familial cutaneous Nodular

* Not discussed further in this chapter.
† Including familial Mediterranean fever, Muckle–Wells syndrome, familial amyloidotic polyneuropathy.

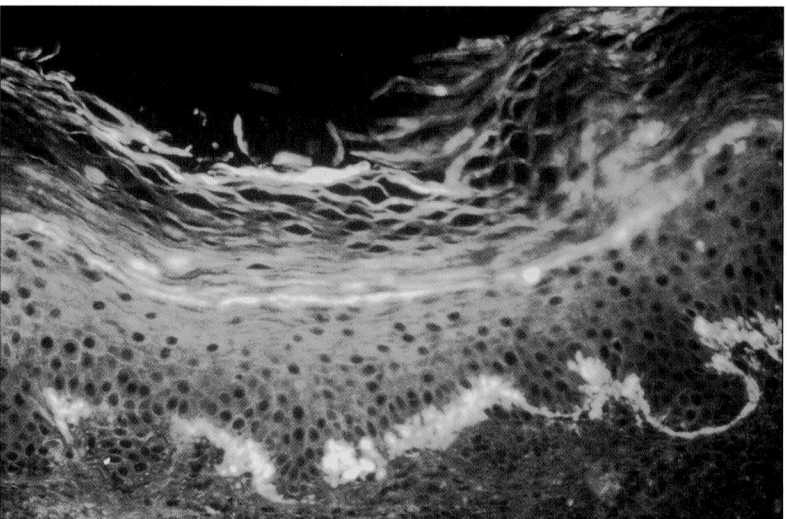

Fig. 12.37
Cutaneous amyloidosis: positive immunofluorescence just beneath the epidermis in a case of macular amyloid (thioflavine-T).

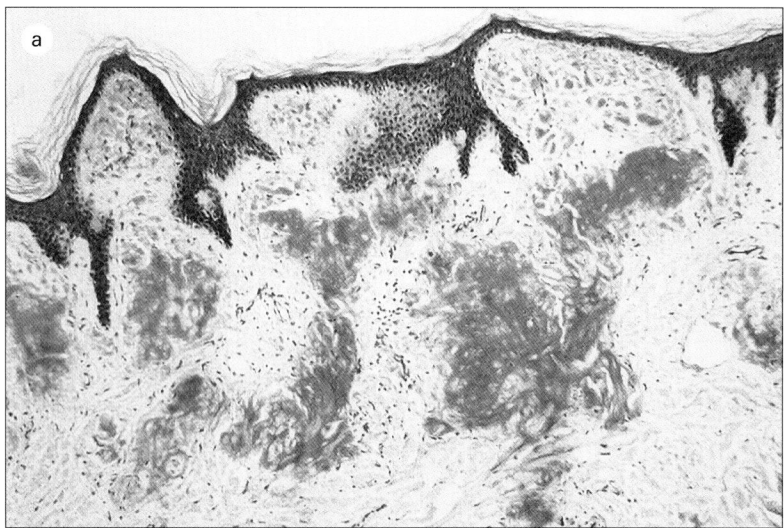

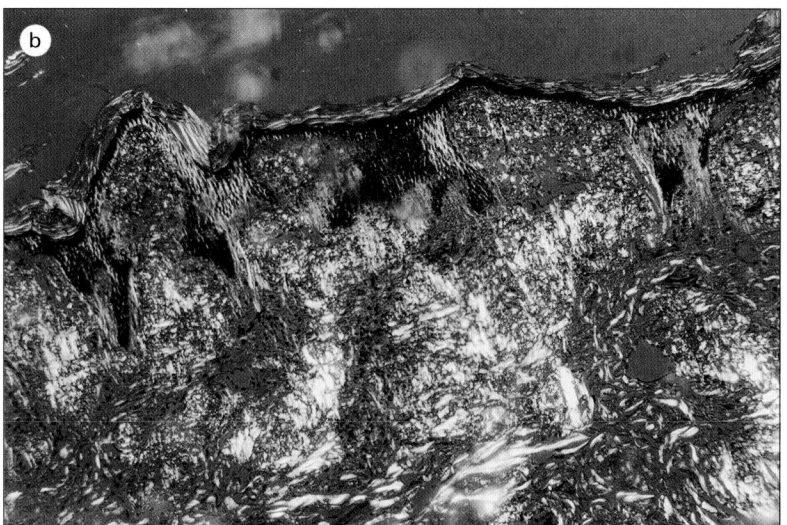

Fig. 12.36
Cutaneous amyloidosis: (a) positive staining with Congo red; (b) there is intense apple-green birefringence when viewed with polarized light.

insoluble and highly resistant to proteolysis. This, combined with a lack of immunogenicity, results in their persistence at the site of deposition and subsequent tissue-damaging effects.

All forms of amyloid contain up to 14% by dry weight of a non-fibrillary protein, the amyloid P component.[1,5] The function of amyloid P component is unknown, but it has been suggested that it may be primarily involved in the deposition and maintenance of the fibrillary components.[1] Its presence, identified immunohistochemically, is a useful adjunct to the diagnosis of amyloidosis.[6] However, it should be appreciated that the antibody also labels degenerate elastic fibers. The fibrillary component, however, may be derived in very different ways in each of the recognized types of amyloidosis:[7]

- In primary and myeloma-associated amyloidoses it consists of immunoglobulin light chains (most often of lambda type, or a part thereof).
- In the secondary form the fibrillary component is composed of amyloid A protein, which is derived from a normal serum constituent known as serum amyloid A protein. This serum protein, which is an HDL3-associated apolipoprotein, is an acute phase reactant.[1,7]
- Primary cutaneous amyloidosis is derived from filamentous degeneration of keratin filaments (amyloid-K) (see below).[8,9]

The capacity to form amyloid in the primary and myeloma-associated variants appears to be dependent upon the inherent ability of a segment of the variable region of the light chain to adopt a beta-pleated configuration.[2] This capability is only evident in a proportion of (so-called amyloidogenic) Bence Jones proteins, which explains why not all patients with multiple myeloma develop amyloidosis. Primary and myeloma-associated amyloidoses can be distinguished histochemically from secondary amyloidosis using the potassium permanganate reaction.[10] The former are potassium permanganate resistant whereas the latter is sensitive and loses its affinity for Congo red following exposure. 'Endocrine' amyloid is also resistant to the effects of potassium permanganate solution as is senile cardiac amyloid. Therefore, although the amyloidoses all include, by definition, amyloid deposition, they in fact represent a very diverse group of conditions.

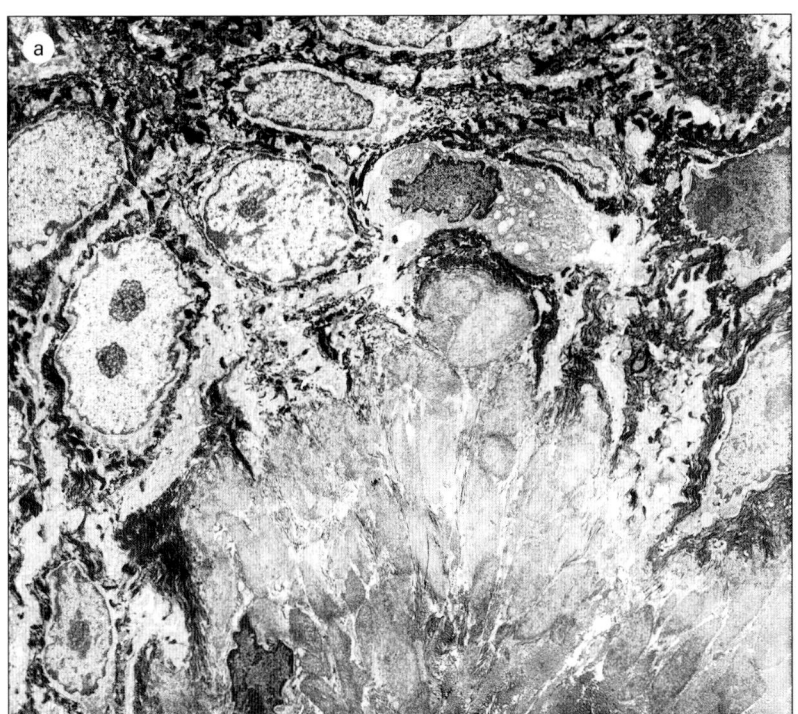
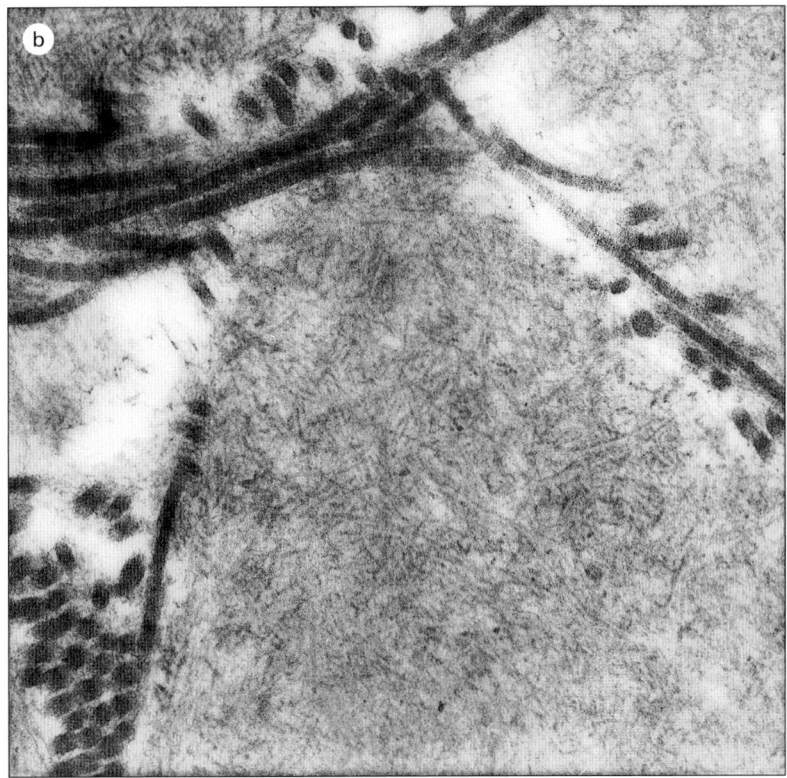

Fig. 12.38
Cutaneous amyloidosis: (a) electron micrograph of macular amyloidosis showing nodular deposits in the superficial dermis; (b) the characteristic randomly orientated, straight, non-branching appearance of amyloid filaments.

References

1. Breathnach, S.M. (1988) Amyloid and amyloidosis. *J Am Acad Dermatol*, **18**, 1–16.
2. Glenner, G.G. (1980) Amyloid deposits and amyloidoses: the beta fibrilloses. *N Engl J Med*, **302**, 1283–1292.
3. Eanes, E.D., Glenner, G.G. (1968) X-ray diffraction studies on amyloid filaments. *J Histochem Cytochem*, **16**, 673–677.
4. Termine, J.D., Eanes, E.D., Ein, D. et al (1972) Infrared spectroscopy of human amyloid fibrils and immunoglobulin proteins. *Biopolymers*, **11**, 1103–1113.
5. Skinner, M., Pepys, M.B., Cohen, A.S. et al (1980) Studies on amyloid protein AP. In: Glenner, G.G., Costa, P., Freitas, A.F. (eds) Amyloid and amyloidosis. Amsterdam: Excerpta Medica, pp 384–391.
6. Breathnach, S.M., Bhogal, B., Dyck, R.F. et al (1981) Immunohistochemical demonstration of amyloid P component in skin of normal subjects and patients with cutaneous amyloidosis. *Br J Dermatol*, **105**, 115–124.
7. Breathnach, S.M. (1985) The cutaneous amyloidoses: pathogenesis and therapy. *Arch Dermatol*, **121**, 470–475.
8. Hashimoto, K. (1984) Progress on cutaneous amyloidoses. *J Invest Dermatol*, **82**, 1–3.
9. Kobayashi, H., Hashimoto, K. (1983) Amyloidogenesis in organ-limited cutaneous amyloidosis: an antigenic identity between epidermal keratin and skin amyloid. *J Invest Dermatol*, **80**, 66–72.
10. Wright, J.R., Calkins, E., Humphrey, R.L. (1977) Potassium permanganate reaction in amyloidosis: a histological method to assist in differentiating forms of this disease. *Lab Invest*, **36**, 274–281.

Primary and myeloma-associated systemic amyloidoses

Cutaneous disease occurs in up to 40% of patients with primary (due to occult plasma cell dyscrasia) and myeloma-associated systemic amyloidosis.[1–4]

Clinical features

Primary and myeloma-associated systemic amyloidoses predominantly affect the elderly (mean onset at 65 years of age) and show a slight predilection for males.[2] Up to 15% of patients with myeloma have coexisting primary amyloidosis. Occasional patients present with primary systemic amyloidosis and only develop multiple myeloma later.[5]

The early clinical changes, which are often mild, non-specific and very difficult to diagnose, include weight loss, hoarseness, dyspnea, fatigue, paresthesia and lightheadedness.[4] Subsequently the most frequent features are development of the carpal tunnel syndrome and edema due to renal and cardiac involvement. Bilateral carpal tunnel syndrome may be the first symptom of the disease.[6]

The commonest cutaneous manifestation is hemorrhage (purpura, petechiae and frank ecchymoses) due to deposition of amyloid within blood vessel walls, with resultant fragility (*Figs 12.39–12.42*). It occurs most typically on the hands (often posttraumatic) and around the eyes, when the purpura may follow proctoscopy or vomiting (*Fig. 12.43*). Lesions are sometimes also evident in the nasolabial folds, the neck, axillae, umbilicus, anogenital region and within the oral cavity.[4,7–9] Prominent hemorrhagic bullae may be present.[9] Rarely, systemic amyloidosis presents with solitary vulval lesions which may mimic a condyloma acuminatum.[10,11]

Blistering may be an additional feature and occurs due to cleavage developing within the amyloid deposits as a consequence of shearing stresses.[12–21] The blisters are often hemorrhagic, and occur most often on the tongue, buccal or labial mucosa although they may be more widespread and therefore mimic those of bullous pemphigoid.[12] Blisters may sometimes arise on the dorsal surfaces of the hands and fingers and the extensor aspect of the forearms and epidermolysis bullosa acquisita may then enter the differential diagnosis (*Fig. 12.44*). Healed lesions are sometimes associated with the development of milia.[17] Bullous amyloidosis most often develops in patients with systemic disease, particularly myeloma associated.[14] Rarely, however, it may complicate primary cutaneous amyloidosis.[12] Rare cases present an elastolytic appearance and the occurrence of cord-like indurations associated with intermittent claudication and due to prominent perivascular deposition of amyloid has been documented.[22,23]

In more advanced cases, waxy, smooth, shiny papules, plaques and even nodules develop. Cystic nodular lesions have also been reported.[24] The papules are skin-colored or yellow and have a dome-shaped appearance.[7,25] They are found predominantly on the face (especially the eyelids), head and neck, axillae, umbilicus, inguinal region and the

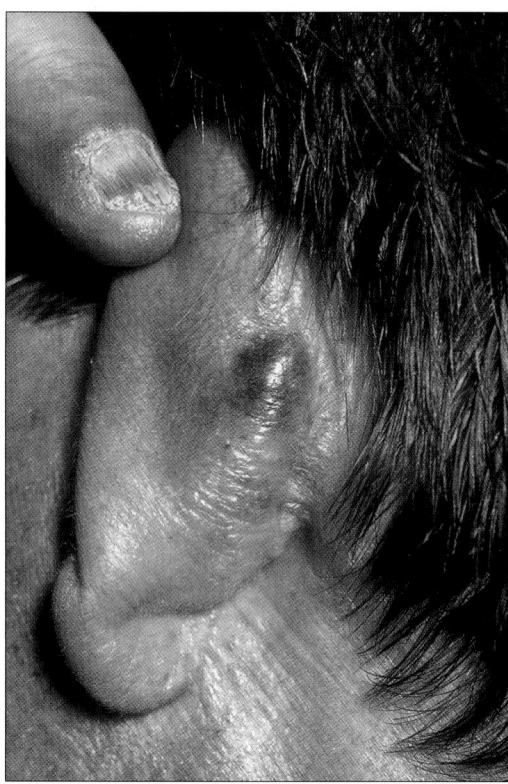

Fig. 12.39
Primary systemic amyloidosis: a waxy nodule is present behind the ear. Note the purpura. By courtesy of R.A. Marsden, MD, St George's Hospital, London, UK.

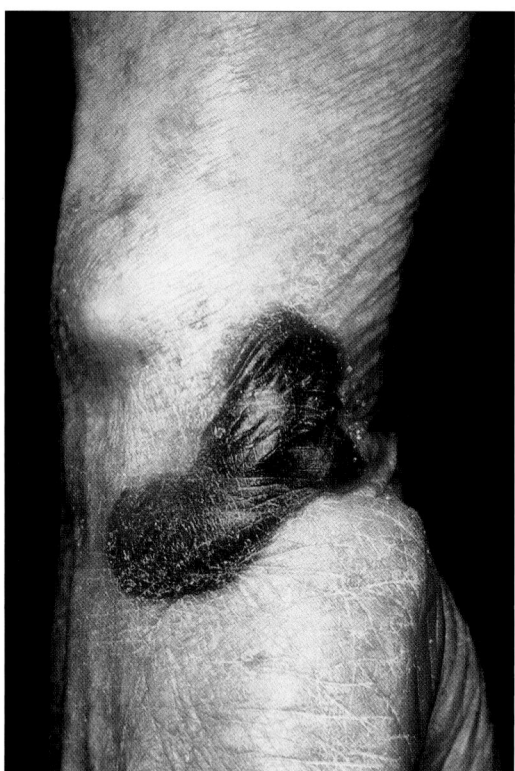

Fig. 12.40
Primary systemic amyloidosis: hemorrhagic bullous lesion on wrist. By courtesy of the Institute of Dermatology, London, UK.

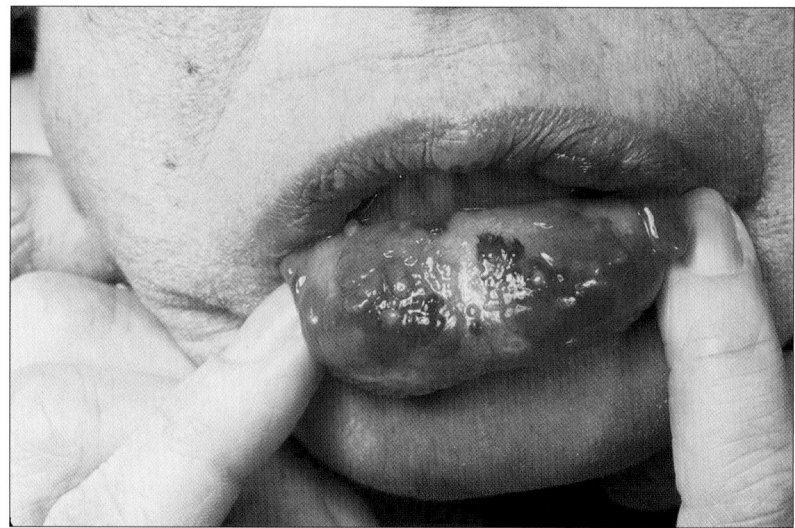

Fig. 12.41
Primary systemic amyloidosis: papular mucosal lesions with hemorrhage on the inner aspect of the lower lip. By courtesy of R.A. Marsden, MD, St George's Hospital, London, UK.

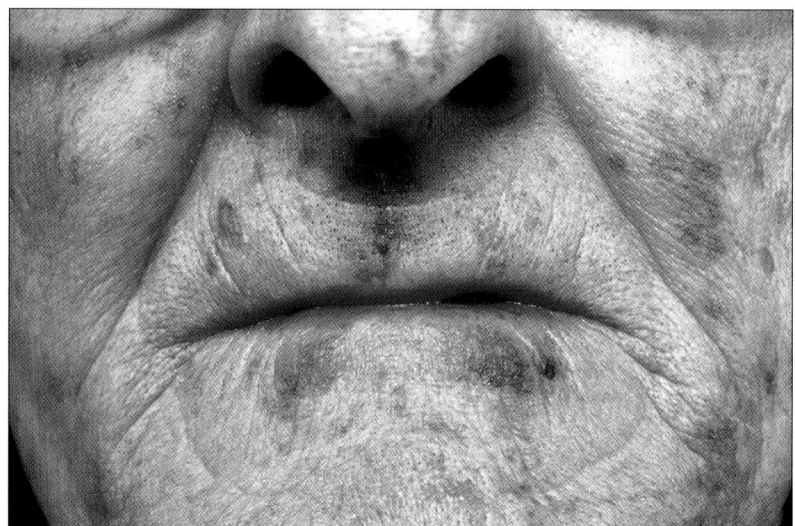

Fig. 12.42
Primary systemic amyloidosis: erythematous and purpuric lesions on the face of an elderly male. By courtesy of the Institute of Dermatology, London, UK.

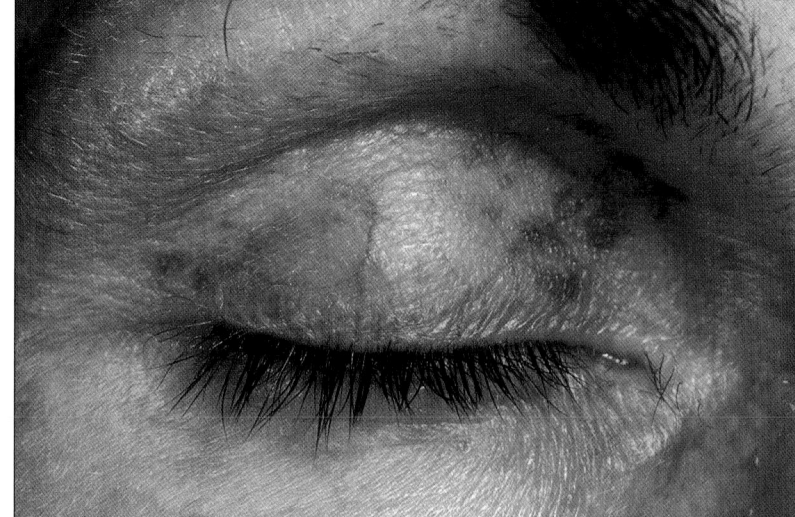

Fig. 12.43
Primary systemic amyloidosis: small macular purpuric lesions at a classical site. By courtesy of R.A. Marsden, MD, St George's Hospital, London, UK.

perineum.[4,7] In severely affected patients the clinical appearances with taut skin, particularly affecting the face, hands and digits, may mimic scleroderma.[7,25] Alopecia and nail dystrophy are sometimes evident (*Fig. 12.45*). Chronic paronychia, palmodigital erythematous swelling and induration of the hands have been described.[26] The presence of these features in conjunction with macroglossia and the carpal tunnel syndrome is highly suggestive of primary or myeloma-associated systemic amyloidosis (*Fig. 12.46*). In addition to macroglossia, the tongue may be covered with waxy papules, nodules and plaques and occasionally it is ulcerated or fissured.[4] As a consequence, speaking and swallowing difficulties are not infrequently encountered. The sicca syndrome may also be a manifestation of primary systemic amyloidosis.[27] Exceptional association with normolipemic xanthoma has also been documented.[28]

Hepatomegaly is found in about 50% of cases and there may also be evidence of cardiomyopathy with arrhythmia or heart failure, peripheral neuropathy and renal failure or the nephrotic syndrome. Splenomegaly is a feature in less than 10% of cases.[3] Intestinal involvement can lead to malabsorption or an ulcerative colitis-like picture, sometimes with hemorrhage.[4] There is no effective treatment for systemic primary amyloidosis and the prognosis is therefore grave. Mortality relates primarily to cardiac and renal involvement.[2,3]

Histological features

Masses of eosinophilic, amorphous, fissured material are present in the dermis and subcutaneous tissues (*Fig. 12.47*).[7,29] The overlying epidermis

is often stretched and flattened, but – in contrast to the macular and lichenoid variants – shows no evidence of amyloid deposition. In mild cases the changes may be limited to the perivascular tissues, but in more extensive disease large aggregates are usually evident. Involvement of blood vessel walls, arrector pili muscles, skin adnexa and subcutaneous fat (amyloid rings) is frequently present (*Fig. 12.48*).[4,7,25] Amyloid deposits around the pilosebaceous units may be accompanied by follicular atrophy with resultant hair loss.[7] There is usually little secondary inflammatory cell infiltration.

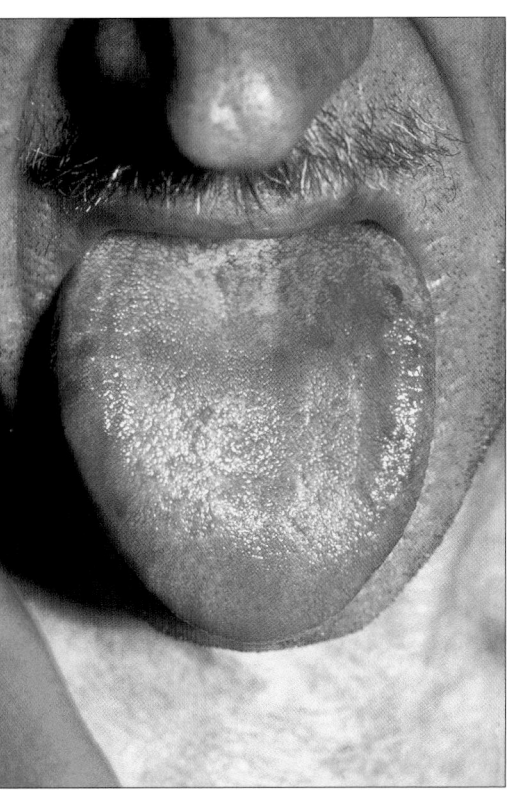

Fig. 12.46
Primary systemic amyloidosis: macroglossia. By courtesy of R.A. Marsden, MD, St George's Hospital, London, UK.

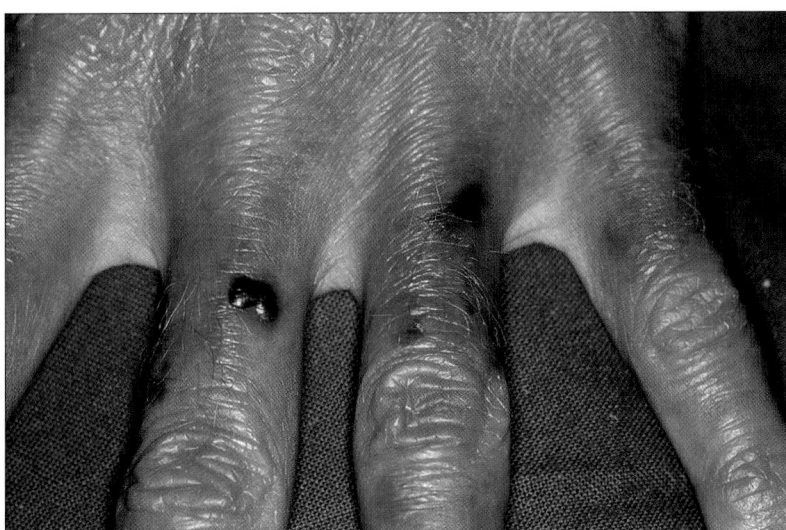

Fig. 12.44
Primary systemic amyloidosis: blood-filled blisters on the dorsal aspect of the fingers. By courtesy of R.A. Marsden, MD, St George's Hospital, London, UK.

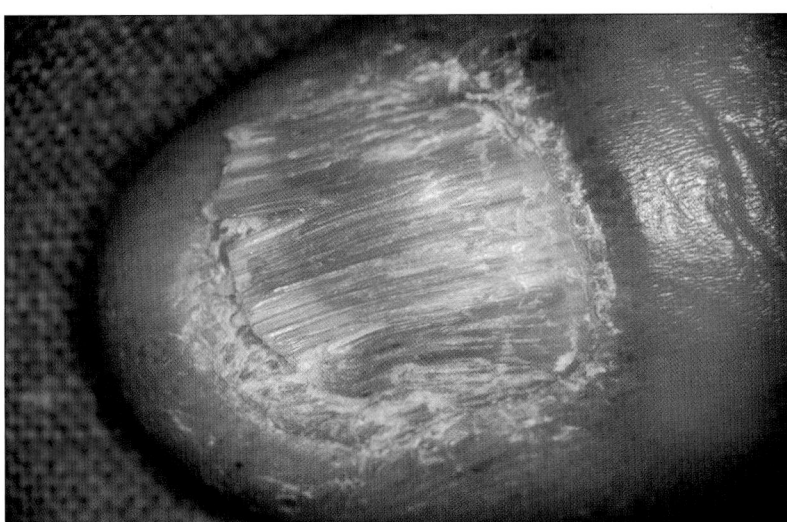

Fig. 12.45
Primary systemic amyloidosis: nail dystrophy as seen in this example is a very rare manifestation. By courtesy of R.A. Marsden, MD, St George's Hospital, London, UK.

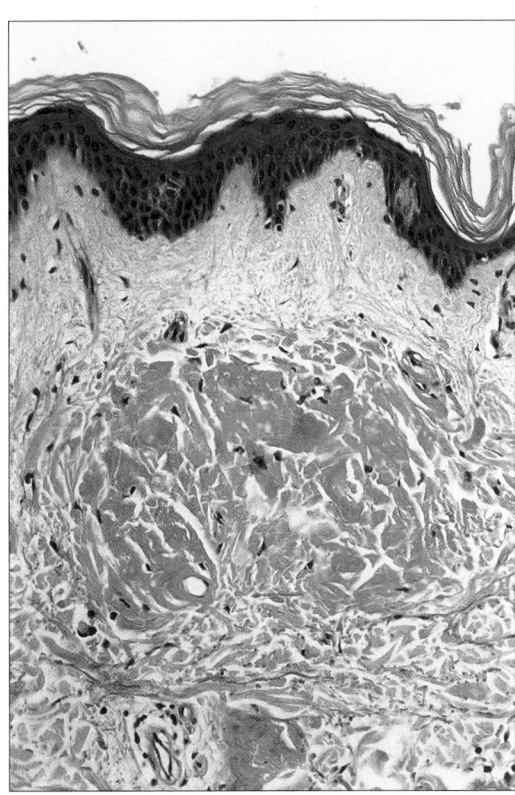

Fig. 12.47
Primary systemic amyloidosis: a circumscribed deposit of amyloid is present in the superficial dermis.

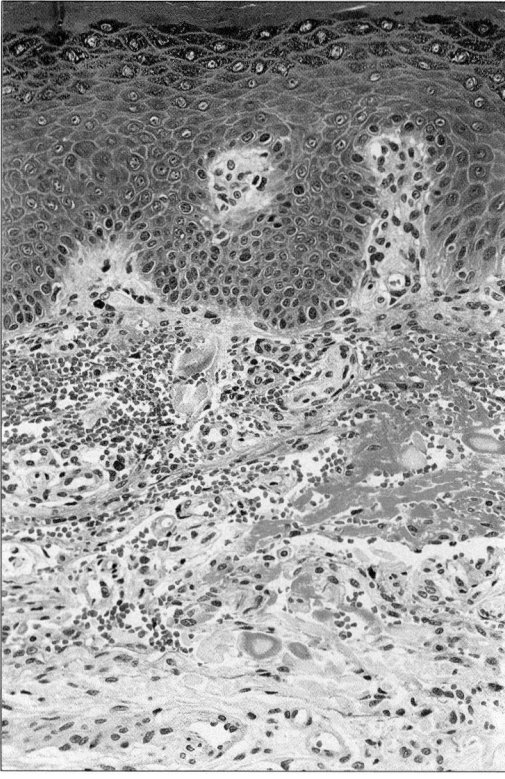

Fig. 12.48
Primary systemic amyloidosis: in this field deposits of amyloid can be seen in intimate association with dilated superficial blood vessels. Note the red cell extravasation.

In those cases associated with blistering, the vesicle appears in an intradermal or less commonly subepidermal location. The dermis, in addition to showing amyloid deposits, often in association with blood vessel walls, also shows a fragmented appearance due to the presence of cleft-like spaces.[11] Purpura is frequently marked.

Clinically normal skin shows histological evidence of amyloid deposition in up to 50% of patients.[25]

References

1. Alexanian, R., Fraschini, G., Smith, L. (1984) Amyloidosis in multiple myeloma or without apparent cause. *Arch Intern Med*, **114**, 2158–2160.
2. Kyle, R.A., Greipp, P.R. (1983) Amyloidosis (AL): clinical and laboratory features in 229 cases. *Mayo Clin Proc*, **58**, 665–683.
3. Kyle, R.A., Bayrd, E.D. (1975) Amyloidosis: review of 236 cases. *Medicine*, **54**, 271–299.
4. Breathnach, S.M. (1988) Amyloid and amyloidosis. *J Am Acad Dermatol*, **18**, 1–16.
5. Rajkumar, S.V., Gertz, M.A., Kyle, R.A. (1998) Primary systemic amyloidosis with delayed progression to multiple myeloma. *Cancer*, **82**, 1501–1505.
6. Nestle, F.O., Burg, G. (2001) Bilateral carpal tunnel syndrome as a clue for the diagnosis of systemic amyloidosis. *Dermatology*, **202**, 353–355.
7. Brownstein, M.H., Helwig, E.B. (1970) The cutaneous amyloidoses. II. Systemic forms. *Arch Dermatol*, **102**, 20–28.
8. Taylor, S.C., Baker, E., Grossman, M.E. (1991) Nodular vulval amyloid as a presentation of systemic amyloidosis. *J Am Acad Dermatol*, **24**, 139.
9. Grundmann, J.U., Bonnekoh, B., Gollnick, H. (2000) Extensive hemorrhagic-bullous skin manifestation of systemic AA-amyloidosis associated with IgG lambda myeloma. *Eur J Dermatol*, **10**, 139–142.
10. Konig, A., Wennemuth, G., Soyer, H.P. et al (1999) Vulvar amyloidosis mimicking giant condylomata acuminata in a patient with multiple myeloma. *Eur J Dermatol*, **9**, 29–31.
11. Persoons, J.H., Sutorius, F.J., Koopman, R.J. et al (1999) Vulvar paraneoplastic amyloidosis with the appearance of a vulvar carcinoma. *Am J Obst Gynecol*, **180**, 1041–1044.
12. Beacham, B.E., Greer, K.A., Andrews, B.S. et al (1980) Bullous amyloidosis. *J Am Acad Dermatol*, **3**, 506–510.
13. Ruzicka, T., Schmoeckel, C., Ring, J. et al (1985) Bullous amyloidosis. *Br J Dermatol*, **113**, 85–95.
14. Johnson, T.M., Rapini, R.P., Hebert, A.A. et al (1989) Bullous amyloidosis. *Cutis*, **43**, 346–352.
15. Hodl, S., Turek, T., Kerl, H. (1982) Plasmozytom-assoziierte bullos-hamorrhagische amyloidose der Haut. *Hautarzt*, **33**, 556–558.
16. Northover, J.M.A., Pickard, J.D., Murray-Lyon, I.M. et al (1972) Bullous lesions of the skin and mucous membranes in primary amyloidosis. *Post Med J*, **48**, 351–353.
17. Bluhm, J.F., Johnson, S.C., Norback, D.H. (1980) Bullous amyloidosis: case report with ultrastructural studies. *Arch Dermatol*, **116**, 1164–1168.
18. Westermark, P., Ohman, S., Domar, M. et al (1981) Bullous amyloidosis. *Arch Dermatol*, **117**, 782–784.
19. Holden, C.A., Weston, M.J., MacDonald, D.M. (1982) Trauma-induced bullae; the presenting feature of systemic amyloidosis associated with plasma cell dyscrasia. *Br J Dermatol*, **107**, 701–706.
20. Isobe, T., Hata, S., Murakami, M. et al (1984) Bullous amyloidosis associated with Bence Jones proteinuria without proteinuria. *Jpn J Med*, **23**, 245–257.
21. Levi, L., Sala, G.P., Crippa, D. et al (1983) Amiloidosi sistemica emorragica e bullosa, rivelatrice di un mieloma non secernente. *G Ital Dermatol Venereol*, **118**, 31–35.
22. Yoneda, K., Kanoh, T., Momura, S. et al (1990) Elastolytic cutaneous lesions in myeloma-associated amyloidosis. *Arch Dermatol*, **126**, 657–660.
23. Breathnach, S.M., Wells, G.C. (1980) Amyloid vascular disease: cord-like thickening of mucocutaneous arteries, intermittent claudication and angina in a case with underlying myelomatosis. *Br J Dermatol*, **102**, 591–595.
24. Akiyama, T., Seishima, M., Nojiri, M. et al (1999) Partial amino acid sequence of an amyloid fibril protein from unusual cutaneous cystic lesions in myeloma-associated amyloidosis. *Eur J Dermatol*, **9**, 624–628.
25. Rubinow, A., Cohen, A.S. (1978) Skin involvement in generalized amyloidosis: a study of clinically involved and uninvolved skin in 50 patients with primary and secondary amyloidosis. *Ann Intern Med*, **83**, 781–785.
26. Ahmed, I., Cronk, J.S., Crutchfield, C.E. 3rd et al (2000) Myeloma-associated systemic amyloidosis presenting as chronic paronychia and palmodigital erythematous swelling and induration of the hands. *J Am Acad Dermatol*, **42**, 339–342.
27. Richey, T.K., Bennion, S.D. (1996) Etiologies of the sicca syndrome: primary systemic amyloidosis and others. *Int J Dermatol*, **35**, 553–557.
28. Buezo, G.F., Porras, J.I., Fraga, J. et al (1996) Coexistence of diffuse plane normolipaemic xanthoma and amyloidosis in a patient with monoclonal gammopathy. *Br J Dermatol*, **135**, 460–462.
29. Westermark, P. (1979) Amyloidosis of the skin: a comparison between localized and systemic amyloidosis. *Acta Derm Venereol*, **59**, 341–345.

Secondary amyloidosis

Cutaneous involvement has not been recognized as a clinical feature of secondary systemic amyloidosis. Yet in one publication it was described in eight out of nine patients with amyloidosis complicating rheumatoid arthritis.[1] It is of interest to note that a considerable number of chronic dermatoses may be associated with the development of secondary amyloidosis including psoriasis, lepromatous leprosy, hidradenitis suppurativa, chronically infected burns and dystrophic epidermolysis bullosa.[2–4] In patients with no cutaneous lesions and symptoms suggestive of systemic amyloidosis, the diagnosis can be confirmed by Congo red staining of abdominal fat aspirates.[5]

Although frank clinical lesions are not commonly a feature of secondary amyloidosis, sometimes small deposits are found in specimens of normal skin.[1,6] Usually these are present in a perivascular location, but may occasionally be present elsewhere in the dermis or even in subcutaneous fat.[7] Deposition of amyloid around sweat glands may also be seen. Deposits are said to be focal and abdominal subcutaneous fat has been recommended as the site that is most likely to be positive.[1,5] Hemodialysis-associated amyloidosis is a distinctive form of secondary amyloidosis and is described below.

References

1. Westermark, P. (1972) Occurence of amyloid deposits in the skin in secondary systemic amyloidosis. *Acta Pathol Microbiol Scand (Section A)*, **80**, 718–720.
2. Breathnach, S.M. (1988) Amyloid and amyloidosis. *J Am Acad Dermatol*, **18**, 1–16.
3. Wlittenberg, G.P., Oursler, J.R., Peters, M.S. (1995) Secondary amyloidosis complicating psoriasis. *J Am Acad Dermatol*, **32**, 465–468.
4. Brownstein, M.H., Helwig, E.B. (1970) Systemic amyloidosis complicating dermatoses. *Arch Dermatol*, **102**, 1–7.
5. Masouye, I. (1997) Diagnostic screening of systemic amyloidosis by abdominal aspiration: an analysis of 100 cases. *Am J Dermatopathol*, **19**, 41–45.
6. Brownstein, M.H., Helwig, E.B. (1970) The cutaneous amyloidoses. II. Systemic forms. *Arch Dermatol*, **102**, 20–28.
7. Rubinow, A., Cohen, A.S. (1978) Skin involvement in generalized amyloidosis: a study of clinically involved and uninvolved skin in 50 patients with primary and secondary amyloidosis. *Ann Intern Med*, **83**, 781–785.

Hemodialysis-associated amyloidosis

Clinical features

This variant of amyloidosis, induced by beta-2-microglobulin, occurs in patients on long-term hemodialysis.[1–3] Exceptional cases present after short-term hemodialysis.[4] The most commonly involved organs are the heart, gastrointestinal tract and lungs.[1] Interestingly, the disease does not seem to involve the spleen.[1] Carpal tunnel syndrome has also been documented.[5] The walls of blood vessels are often involved whereas bone lesions are relatively rare, although pathological fractures may occur.[5,6] Cutaneous involvement, which is very uncommon, has been reported to present as subcutaneous masses in the buttocks, lichenoid papules and a wrinkled appearance of the skin of the palmar aspect of the fingers.[4,5,7,8]

Histological features

In those cases with skin involvement in which biopsies have been performed, the amyloid deposits have been found either in the subcutaneous tissue or in the papillary and reticular dermis, around sweat glands and hair follicles.[4,5,7,8] Occasionally, special stains are unhelpful in demonstrating amyloid and confirmation of the diagnosis by electron microscopy is necessary.

References

1. Gal, R., Korzets, A., Schwartz, A. et al (1994) Systemic distribution of beta-2-microglobulin-derived amyloidosis in patients who undergo long-term hemodialysis. Report of seven cases and review of the literature. *Arch Pathol Lab Med*, 118, 718–721.
2. Drueke, T., Zingraff, J. (1987) Beta-2-microglobulin-related amyloidosis in long-term hemodialysis patients: possible pathogenetic mechanisms. *Contrib Nephrol*, 59, 99–109.
3. Picken, M.M., Shen, S. (1994) Beta-2-microglobulin amyloidosis: illustrative cases. *Ultrastruct Pathol*, 18, 133–136.
4. Albers, S.E., Fenske, N.A., Glass, L.F. et al (1994) Atypical β2-microglobulin amyloidosis following short-term hemodialysis. *Am J Dermatopathol*, 16, 179–184.
5. Tom, Y., Htwe, M., Chandra, R. et al (1994) Bilateral beta 2-microglobulin amyloidomas of the buttocks in a long-term hemodialysis patient. *Arch Pathol Lab Med*, 118, 651–653.
6. Casey, T.T., Stone, W.J., DiRaimondo, C.R. et al (1986) Tumoral amyloidosis of bone of beta 2-microglobulin origin in association with long-term hemodialysis: a new type of amyloid disease. *Hum Pathol*, 17, 731–738.
7. Lipner, H.I., Minkowitz, S., Neiderman, G. et al (1995) Dialysis-related amyloidosis manifested as masses in buttocks. *South Med J*, 88, 876–888.
8. Sato, K.D., Kumakiri, M., Koizumo, H. et al (1993) Lichenoid skin lesions as a sign of β2-microglobulin-induced amyloidosis in a long-term hemodialysis patient. *Br J Dermatol*, 128, 686–689.

Heredofamilial amyloidoses

Familial Mediterranean fever

This is a rare variant of autosomal recessive inherited systemic amyloidosis. It is characterized by episodes of fever associated with pleuritis, peritonitis and synovitis.[1,2] Cutaneous lesions are rare and consist of Henoch–Schönlein purpura and an erythema of the lower limbs mimicking erysipelas.[1,3] Panniculitis and recurrent urticaria may also occur. Nail fold capillary abnormalities consisting of increased tortuosity and enlargement of capillary loops have also been documented.[4–6] Cutaneous amyloid deposition has not been described.

A serum precursor protein forms the amyloid in this condition. This precursor is a high density lipoprotein known as serum amyloid A. The histopathology of the cutaneous lesions has not been reported.

References

1. Sohar, E., Gafni, J., Pras, M. et al (1967) Familial Mediterranean fever: a survey of 470 cases and a review of the literature. *Am J Med*, 43, 227–253.
2. Oizel, A.M., Demirturk, L., Yazgan, Y. et al (2000) Familial Mediterranean fever. A review of the disease and clinical and laboratory findings in 105 patients. *Dig Liver Dis*, 32, 504–509.
3. Barzilai, A., Langevitz, P., Goldberg, I. et al (2000) Erysipelas-like erythema of familial Mediterranean fever: clinicopathologic correlation. *J Am Acad Dermatol*, 42, 791–795.
4. Danar, D.A., Kwan, T.H., Stern, R.S. et al (1987) Panniculitis in familial Mediterranean fever. Case report and histopathologic findings. *Am J Med*, 82, 829–832.
5. Alonso, R., Cistero-Bahima, A., Enrique, E. et al (2002) Recurrent urticaria as a rare manifestation of familial Mediterranean fever. *J Investig Allergol Clin Immunol*, 12, 60–61.
6. Dinc, A., Melikoglu, M., Korkmaz, C. et al (2001) Nailfold capillary abnormalities in patients with familial Mediterranean fever. *Clin Exp Rheumatol*, 19, S42–44.

Muckle–Wells syndrome and familial cold autoinflammatory syndrome

Muckle–Wells syndrome is an autosomal inherited disease with variable penetrance. It is characterized by urticaria, amyloidosis and deafness.[1,2] The disease has been mapped to chromosome 1q44. The gene is called CIAS1 and encodes a pyrin-like protein that appears to play a role in regulation of inflammation and apoptosis.[3,4] Familial cold autoinflammatory syndrome (familial cold urticaria) is very similar to Muckle–Wells syndrome but in the former, there is no deafness and the episodes of urticaria are precipitated by cold. The same serum precursor protein (serum amyloid A) produces the amyloid in both conditions.

Histological evidence of cutaneous amyloid deposition is not usually seen in this disease.

References

1. Muckle, T.J. (1979) The 'Muckle-Wells' syndrome. *Br J Dermatol*, 100, 87–92.
2. Lieberman, A., Grossman, M.E., Silvers, D.N. (1998) Muckle–Wells syndrome: case report and review of cutaneous pathology. *J Am Acad Dermatol*, 39, 290–291.

3. Hoffman, H.M., Mueller, J.L., Broide, D.H. et al (2001) Mutation of a new gene encoding a putative pyrin-like protein causes familial cold autoinflammatory syndrome and Muckle–Wells syndrome. *Nat Genet*, 29, 301–305.
4. Dode, C., Le Du, N., Cuisset, L. et al (2002) New mutations of CIAS1 that are responsible for Muckle–Wells syndrome and familial cold urticaria: a novel mutation underlies both syndromes. *Am J Hum Genet*, 70, 1498–1506.

Familial amyloidotic polyneuropathy

Familial amyloidotic polyneuropathy is an autosomal dominant disease in which the deposition of amyloid occurs predominantly in peripheral nerves. The amyloid deposits in this disease consist in most cases of variant transthyretin with single amino acid substitutions.[1,2] Clinical manifestations include peripheral neuropathy predominantly affecting the limbs and diarrhea with sphincter abnormalities due to involvement of autonomic nerves. The cutaneous manifestations comprise non-healing ulcers, multiple atrophic scars and anhidrosis of the lower limbs.[3,4] In some patients petechiae can be induced by gentle stroking of the skin.

Histologically, biopsies from clinically normal skin reveal the presence of amyloid in blood vessel walls, sweat glands and arrector pili muscles.[3]

References

1. Murakami, T., Uchino, M., Ando, M. (1995) Genetic abnormalities and pathogenesis of familial amyloidotic polyneuropathy. *Pathol Int*, 45, 1–9.
2. Takahashi, K., Sakashita, N., Ando, Y. et al (1997) Late onset type I familial amyloidotic polyneuropathy: presentation of three autopsy cases in comparison with 19 autopsy cases of the ordinary type. *Pathol Int*, 47, 353–359.
3. Ohnishi, A., Yamamoto, T., Murai, Y. (1998) Denervation of eccrine glands in patients with familial amyloidotic polyneuropathy type I. *Neurology*, 51, 714–721.
4. Rubinow, A., Cohen, A.S. (1981) Skin involvement in familial amyloidotic polyneuropathy. *Neurology*, 31, 1341–1345.

Amyloid elastosis

Amyloid elastosis is a very rare disease, characterized by systemic and cutaneous deposits of amyloid. Only two cases have been reported to date and the manifestations of the disease included papular and nodular lesions, a sclerodermatous facial appearance, a pseudoxanthoma-like appearance of the neck, cord-like thickening of superficial blood vessels, livedo reticularis-like changes on trunk, Raynaud's phenomenon, venous and arterial thrombosis and the nephrotic syndrome.[1,2] One of the patients had a lambda light chain paraprotein.

Amyloid is seen in the dermis, around adnexal structures and in blood vessel walls, together with a striking deposition of amyloid in the dermal, subcutaneous and serosal elastic tissue.[1,2]

References

1. Winkelmann, R.K., Peters, M.S., Venencie, P.Y. (1985) Amyloid elastosis. A new cutaneous and systemic pattern of amyloidosis. *Arch Dermatol*, 121, 498–502.
2. Sepp, N., Pichler, E., Breathnach, S.M. et al (1990) Amyloid elastosis: analysis of the role of amyloid P component. *J Am Acad Dermatol*, 22, 27–34.

Primary localized cutaneous amyloidosis, lichen and macular types

Clinical features

Lichen and macular amyloidoses (skin-limited amyloidoses) represent different manifestations of the same process and both entities may coexist (biphasic amyloidosis) or one may transform into the other.[1–4] A recent large study of primary cutaneous amyloidosis found that 67% of cases represented lichen amyloidosis, 8% macular amyloidosis and 25% biphasic variants.[5]

Macular primary cutaneous amyloidosis

This is most commonly seen in patients from the Middle East, Asia and Central and South America.[1,6] It affects females more often than males

(3:1), is seen in younger age groups and is usually a very chronic condition.[7,8] Patients present with a macular, dark brown or grayish, symmetrical pigmentation, which occurs most frequently on the upper chest and back although the extremities and face may also be affected (*Fig. 12.49*).[1,7] The lesions sometimes have a very characteristic reticulated or rippled appearance, which can be quite subtle, and they are usually moderately pruritic (*Fig. 12.50*). More commonly, however, macular amyloid appears as small, 2–3 mm diameter lesions or else as confluent macular foci, which sometimes have superimposed micropapules.[6] Exceptionally, widespread diffuse pigmentation may occur.[9]

Papular or lichen amyloidosis

In papular or lichen amyloidosis, discrete papules and/or plaques occur, which are often scaly, persistent and pigmented. They are usually severely pruritic (*Fig. 12.51*). Excoriations, lichenification and nodular prurigo-like lesions due to chronic scratching are sometimes evident.[8] Lesions are especially common on the front of the shins and extensor aspect of the forearms (*Figs 12.52, 12.53*).[10] The calves, ankles, dorsa of the feet, thighs and trunk may also be affected.[1,11] Presentation is most often in young adults. The sex incidence is equal.[1,11] Lichen amyloidosis shows a predilection for the Chinese race and familial cases have been recorded (see p. 564).[12,13] An association with Epstein–Barr virus infection has been reported in a single case but this was not confirmed in a larger study.[14,15]

Association with systemic disease is probably coincidental but there have been a number of cases described with progressive systemic sclerosis.[16,17]

Other primary cutaneous amyloidoses

These include anosacral and poikilodermatous variants:

- *Anosacral amyloidosis* presents as scaly hyperpigmented macules and lichenoid papules spreading out from the perianal skin.[18,19] It is seen in patients from Japan and China and is very rare. The disease

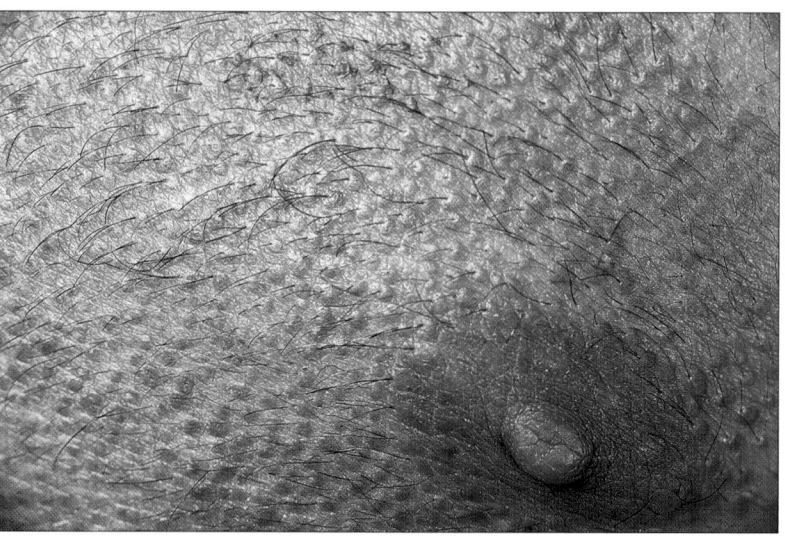

Fig. 12.51
Lichen amyloidosis: pigmented papules on the chest. By courtesy of R.A. Marsden, MD, St George's Hospital, London, UK.

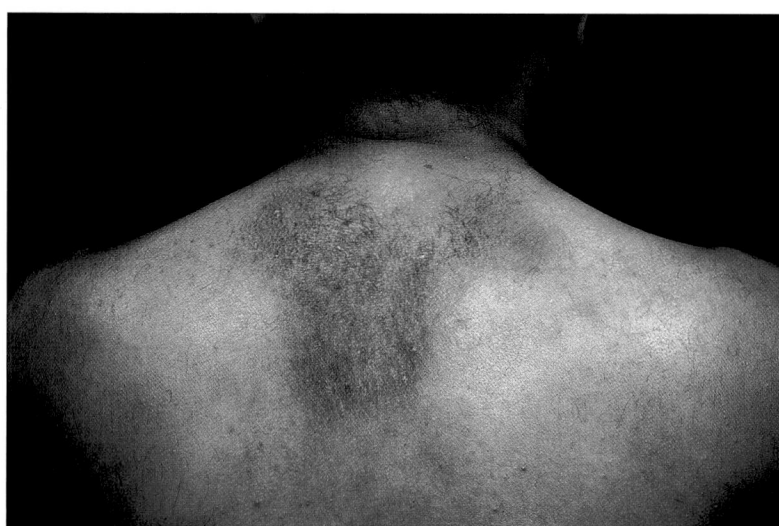

Fig. 12.49
Macular amyloid: hyperpigmented lesion in a characteristic site. By courtesy of R.A. Marsden, MD, St George's Hospital, London, UK.

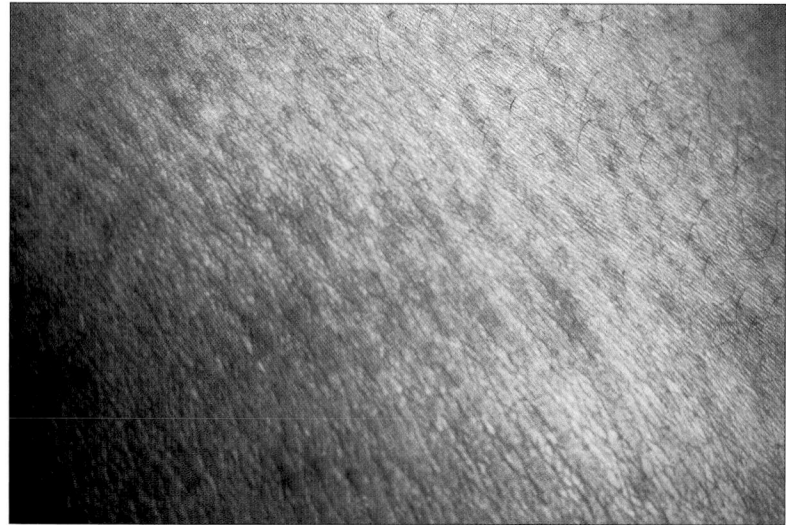

Fig. 12.50
Macular amyloid: close-up view of a lesion showing the typically rippled appearance. By courtesy of R.A. Marsden, MD, St George's Hospital, London, UK.

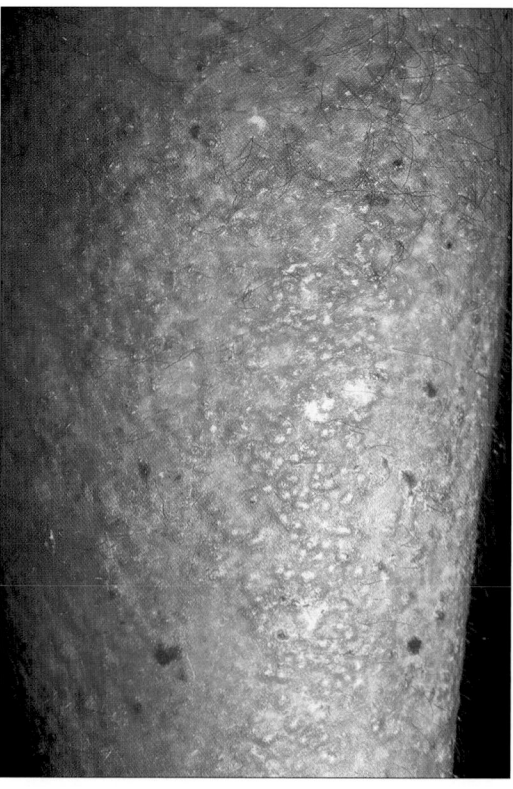

Fig. 12.52
Lichen amyloidosis: scaly lichenoid papules on the shin. By courtesy of R.A. Marsden, MD, St George's Hospital, London, UK.

may present early in life and its cause has not been established although a relationship to keratinocyte apoptosis has been suggested.[19] Clinically, lesions may be confused with lichen simplex chronicus, a dermatophyte infection or even postinflammatory hyperpigmentation.

- *Poikiloderma-like cutaneous amyloidosis* is an extremely rare manifestation of localized cutaneous amyloidosis.[20,21] Patients present with poikilodermatous skin lesions and lichenoid papules. It may be associated with photosensitivity, short stature and palmoplantar keratoderma.[21] Blisters are rarely seen. The condition may present early in life or in young adults. Confusion with other conditions associated with poikiloderma including poikiloderma atrophicans vasculare is possible.

Pathogenesis and histological features

Chronic irritation to the skin has been proposed as a cause of amyloid deposition in the macular and lichenoid variants although this has never been proven.[22,23] The documentation, however, of friction amyloidosis due to nylon brush skin massage and towels does offer some support to this hypothesis.[24–27] It may be that chronic trauma in a susceptible or 'primed' individual may be associated with an increased risk of developing cutaneous amyloidosis. It has been suggested that amyloid deposition in lichen amyloidosis is a consequence of scratching as pruritus tends to be the presenting symptom even before amyloid is detected in skin biopsies.[28] The chronic damage to the epidermis induces apoptosis of keratinocytes and this leads to amyloid deposition in the papillary dermis. A similar mechanism has been proposed in notalgia paresthetica. This is a condition characterized by pruritus, a burning sensation and paresthesia or hyperesthesia in an area of the back between dermatomes D2 and D6.[29,30] The resultant irritation and scratching induces cutaneous hyperpigmentation and amyloid deposition. It has even been suggested that the cutaneous amyloidosis observed in patients with multiple endocrine neoplasia type 2A is secondary to notalgia paresthetica (see below).[31]

In both variants the amyloid is deposited high in the papillary dermis, often immediately adjacent to the epidermis.[6,7,11,32,33]

In the macular type, the amount of amyloid present is often very small and focally distributed. It frequently has a faceted appearance (*Figs 12.54–12.56*).[2,7] Special stains and/or immunocytochemistry are

sometimes necessary as the deposits can easily be missed. Intraepidermal cytoid bodies are present in about 33% of cases.[6] Typically there is associated pigmentary incontinence, but only minor epidermal changes of hyperkeratosis and acanthosis are generally evident. Melanin pigment may be present in the stratum corneum. A slight perivascular chronic inflammatory cell infiltrate is often found in the superficial dermis.[7]

In papular or lichen amyloidosis, the histopathological changes are similar and cannot be reliably distinguished from those of the macular variant, except that the quantities deposited are greater and there is often more marked epidermal acanthosis, hypergranulosis and hyperkeratosis. Basal cell hydropic degeneration may be evident and colloid bodies are usually visible (*Figs 12.57, 12.58*).[1] Satellite cell necrosis is sometimes a feature.[1] A superficial perivascular chronic inflammatory cell infiltrate is typically present.

When special stains fail to demonstrate the presence of amyloid, ultrastructural studies are usually successful in detecting the presence of the protein.[34]

In contrast to skin involvement in systemic disease, blood vessel deposits are not a feature of primary cutaneous localized lesions.

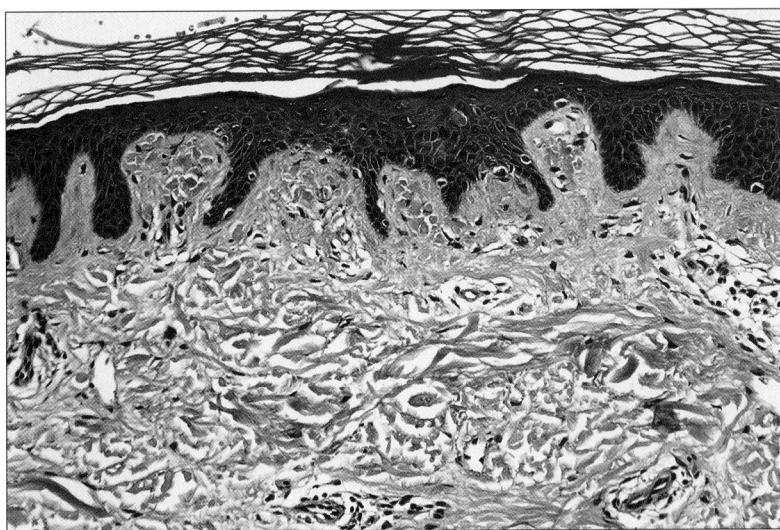

Fig. 12.54
Macular amyloidosis: typical eosinophilic faceted deposits are present in the papillary dermis.

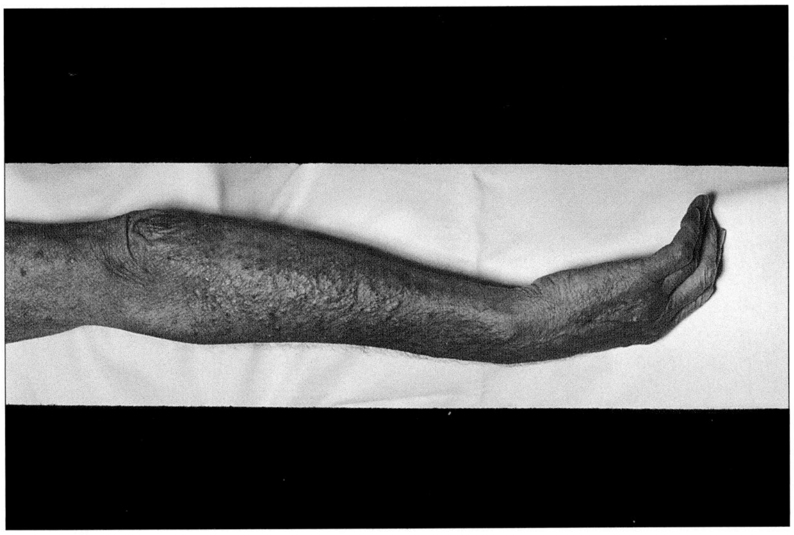

Fig. 12.53
Lichen amyloidosis: grouped, erythematoviolaceous papules, with a lichenoid surface and showing excoriations in some areas. By courtesy of R.A. Marsden, MD, St George's Hospital, London, UK.

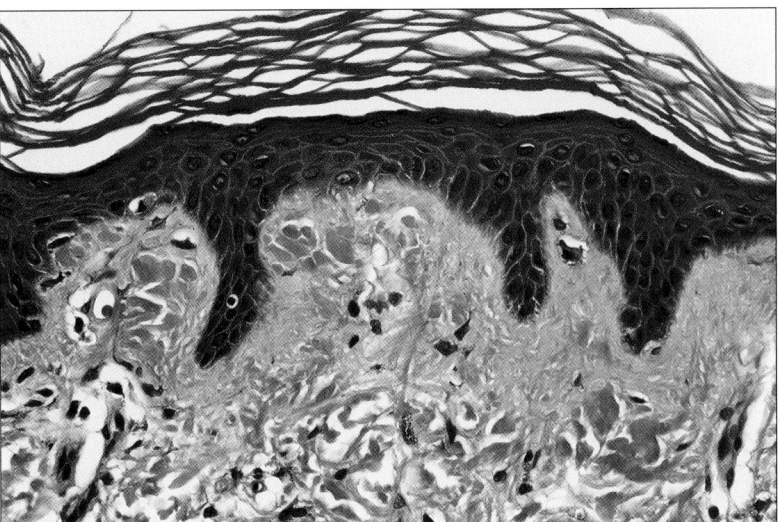

Fig. 12.55
Macular amyloidosis: close-up view of faceted deposits.

In earlier literature it was postulated that the amyloid might have been derived from mast cells or fibroblasts. The application of newer technology, however, has shown that it is indisputably of keratinocyte derivation,[6] and amyloid deposits have been shown to contain disulfide bonds and bullous pemphigoid antigen. Numerous recent publications confirm the presence of epidermal keratin in the deposits in both macular and lichenoid forms using monoclonal immunocytochemistry.[3,35–43] The amyloid of the skin-limited variants, so-called amyloid-K, has been shown to contain 50 and 67 kD keratin filaments.[22,42] Apolipoprotein E, one of the proteins found in the amyloid plaque of Alzheimer's disease and in systemic amyloidosis, has also been demonstrated in the amyloid present in localized cutaneous amyloidosis.[44,45] Electron microscopic studies have provided further evidence that amyloid-K is of keratinocyte

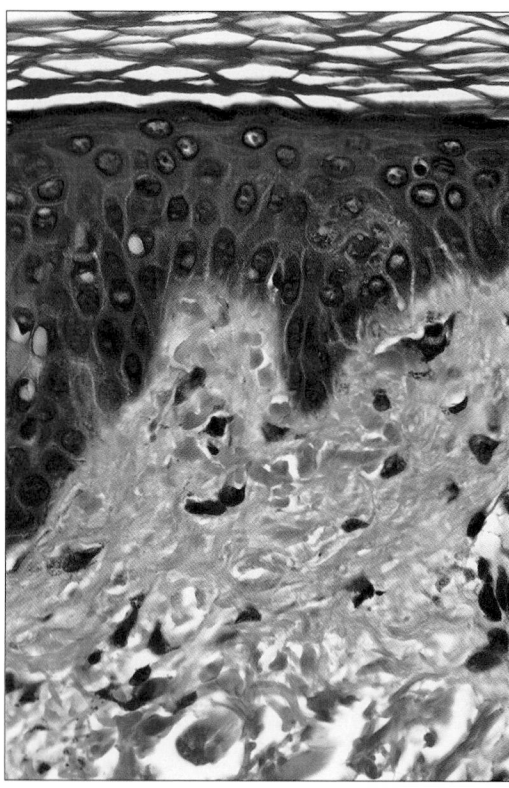

Fig. 12.56
Macular amyloidosis: pigmentary incontinence is typically present.

origin by showing tonofilament filamentous (apoptotic) degeneration into amyloid filaments both within the epidermis and in the immediately adjacent dermis.[46] Under normal circumstances apoptotic keratinocytes (cytoid bodies) are either shed as a consequence of epidermal upward migration or are released into the dermis where they are removed by an inflammatory response as is seen, for example, in lichen planus. In macular and lichenoid cutaneous amyloidosis it appears that the above disposal mechanism is either overwhelmed or non-functioning.

Early ultrastructural changes consist of loss of tonofilament electron density and development of a wavy morphology accompanied by internalization of desmosomes, thickening of the keratinocyte cell membrane and the acquisition of hemidesmosome-like attachments to neighboring cells.[22] Cytoplasmic and nuclear remnants are frequently present in the more superficial deposits. It is thought that on entering the dermis, fibroblasts and macrophages convert the degenerate keratin into amyloid filaments (*Fig. 12.59*).[46] The precise mechanism is unknown, but it must involve the conversion of the normal alpha tertiary structure of tonofilaments into the beta-pleated configuration of amyloid. The filaments of amyloid and cytoid bodies show ultrastructural differences. Amyloid fibrils are irregularly distributed whereas the filaments in cytoid bodies are arranged in bundles or whorls.[47]

It is postulated that the development of localized cutaneous amyloidosis is dependent upon mild chronic trauma resulting in excessive production of cytoid bodies and their subsequent conversion into amyloid deposits. It would seem that despite a normal humoral response as shown by the presence of IgM and IgG in association with complement fixation, the normal cellular response whereby apoptotic keratinocytes are removed is lacking.[22,48–50]

Amyloid deposits are frequently found in intimate association with dermal elastic fibers and the deposits in macular amyloidosis have been shown to contain fibrillin.[51] Whether this is of pathogenetic significance or is merely a secondary phenomenon is uncertain.

The apoptotic theory of amyloidogenesis in the cutaneous variants has, however, been challenged. On the basis of finding amyloid deposits immediately below the basal keratinocyte, separating its cell membrane from the lamina densa in the absence of any evidence of filamentous degeneration, it has been suggested that cutaneous amyloid deposits may also be a direct secretory product of keratinocytes.[52,53] It may be that both mechanisms are in operation.

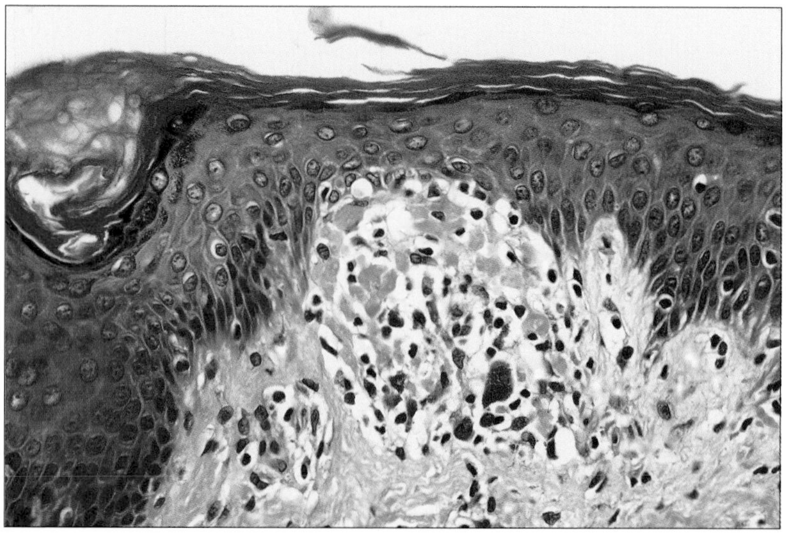

Fig. 12.57
Lichen amyloidosis: there is hyperkeratosis, acanthosis and basal cell hydropic degeneration; small eosinophilic globules are present in the papillary dermis. A mild chronic inflammatory cell infiltrate is present. Note the pigmentary incontinence.

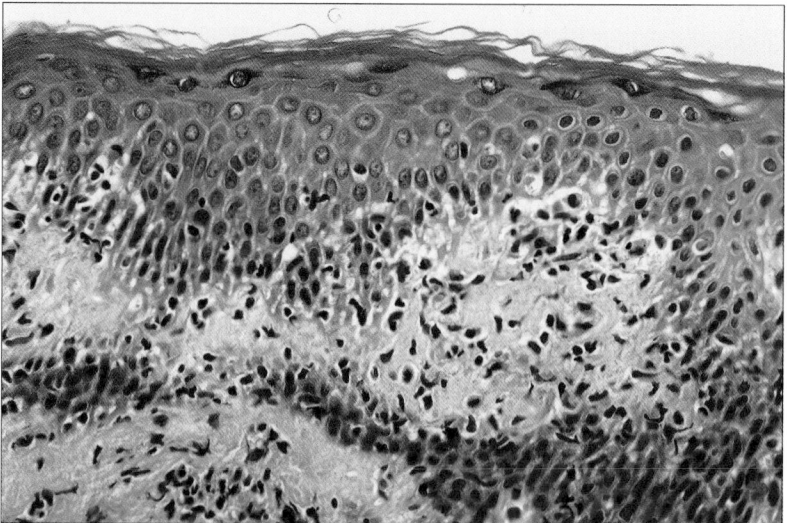

Fig. 12.58
Lichen amyloidosis: in this view, there is interface change and a lymphocytic infiltrate.

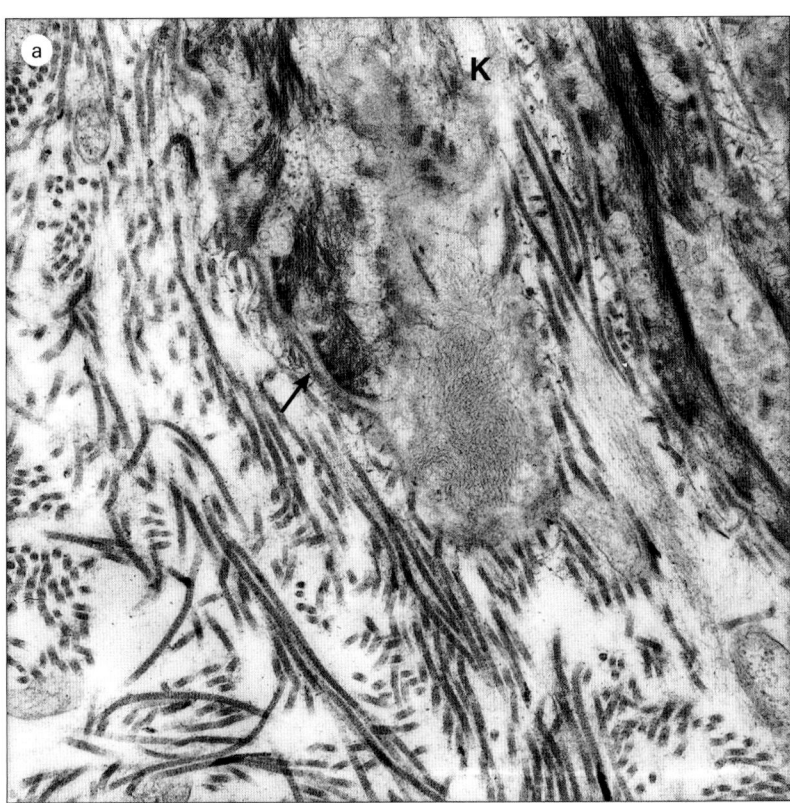 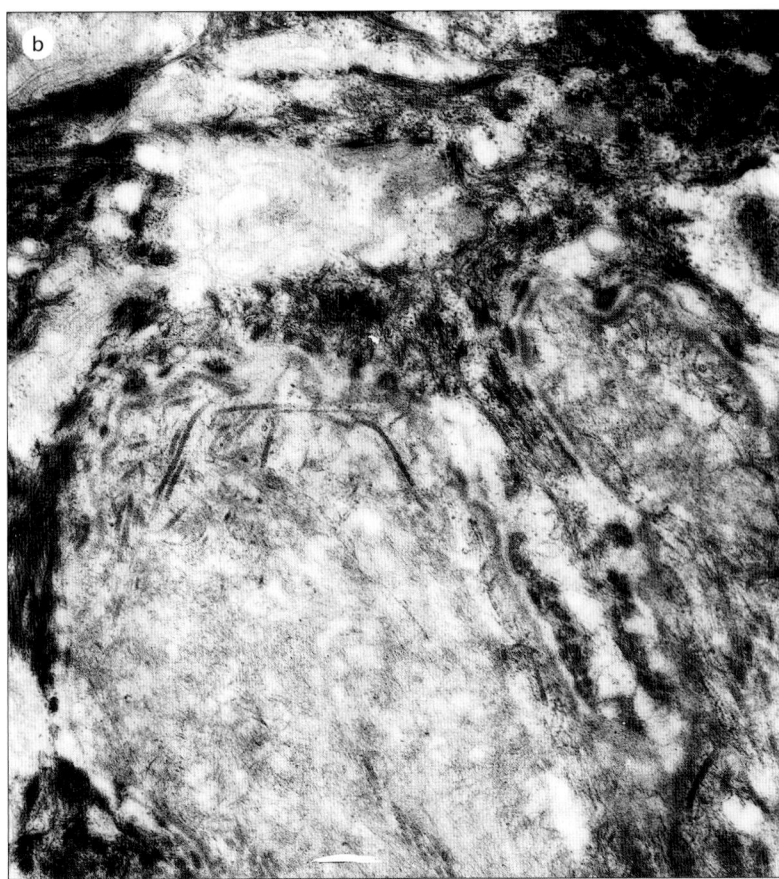

Fig. 12.59
Lichen amyloidosis: (**a**) early filamentous degeneration is seen in this basal keratinocyte (K), lamina densa is arrowed; (**b**) compare the organized appearance of the tonofilaments with the haphazardly orientated amyloid immediately adjacent to the lamina densa.

References

1. Kibbi, A-G., Rubeiz, N.G., Zaynoun, S.T. et al (1992) Primary localized cutaneous amyloidosis. *Int J Dermatol*, **31**, 95–98.
2. Brownstein, M.H., Hashimoto, K., Greenwald, G. (1973) Biphasic amyloidosis: link between macular and lichenoid forms. *Br J Dermatol*, **88**, 25–29.
3. Bourke, J.F., Berth-Jones, J., Burns, D.A. (1992) Diffuse primary cutaneous amyloidosis. *Br J Dermatol*, **127**, 641–644.
4. al-Ratrout, J.T., Satti, M.B. (1997) Primary localized cutaneous amyloidosis: a clinicopathologic study from Saudi Arabia. *Int J Dermatol*, **36**, 428–434.
5. Wang, W.J., Chang, Y.T., Huang, C.Y. et al (2001) Clinical and histopathological characteristics of primary cutaneous amyloidosis in 794 Chinese patients. *Zhonghua Yi Xue Za Zhi (Taipei)*, **64**, 101–107.
6. Black, M.M., Wilson Jones, E. (1971) Macular amyloidosis: a study of 21 cases with special reference to the role of the epidermis in its histogenesis. *Br J Dermatol*, **84**, 199–209.
7. Brownstein, M.H., Hashimoto, K. (1972) Macular amyloidosis. *Arch Dermatol*, **106**, 50–57.
8. Wang, W-J. (1990) Clinical features of cutaneous amyloidoses. *Clin Dermatol*, **2**, 13–19.
9. Wang, C.K., Lee, J.Y. (1996) Macular amyloidosis with widespread diffuse pigmentation. *Br J Dermatol*, **135**, 135–138.
10. Wong, C-K. (1987) Cutaneous amyloidoses. *Int J Dermatol*, **26**, 273–277.
11. Brownstein, M.H., Helwig, E.B. (1970) The cutaneous amyloidoses: I. Localized forms. *Arch Dermatol*, **102**, 8–19.
12. Rajagopalan, K., Tay, C.H. (1972) Familial lichen amyloidosis. Report of 19 cases in 4 generations of a Chinese family in Malaysia. *Br J Dermatol*, **87**, 123–129.
13. Tay, C.H., Dacosta, J.L. (1970) Lichen amyloidosis: clinical study of 40 cases. *Br J Dermatol*, **82**, 129–136.
14. Drago, F., Ranieri, E., Pastorino, A. et al (1996) Epstein–Barr virus-related primary cutaneous amyloidosis. Successful treatment with acyclovir and interferon-alpha. *Br J Dermatol*, **134**, 170–174.
15. Chang, Y.T., Liu, H.N., Wong, C.K. et al (1997) Detection of Epstein–Barr virus in primary cutaneous amyloidosis. *Br J Dermatol*, **136**, 823–826.
16. Chanoki, M., Suzuki, S., Hayashi, Y. et al (1994) Progressive systemic sclerosis associated with cutaneous amyloidosis. *Int J Dermatol*, **33**, 648–649.
17. Ogiyama, Y., Hayashi, Y, Kuo, C. et al (1996) Cutaneous amyloidosis in patients with progressive systemic sclerosis. *Cutis*, **57**, 28–32.
18. Yanagihara, M., Mori, S. (1981) Ano-sacral cutaneous amyloidosis. *J Dermatol (Tokyo)*, **91**, 463–471.
19. Wang, W.J., Huang, C.Y., Chang, Y.T. et al (2000) Anosacral cutaneous amyloidosis: a study of 10 Chinese cases. *Br J Dermatol*, **143**, 1266–1269.
20. Ogino, A., Tanaka, S. (1977) Poikiloderma-like cutaneous amyloidosis: report of a case and review of the literature. *Dermatologica*, **155**, 301–309.
21. Ho, M.H., Chong, L.Y. (1998) Poikiloderma-like cutaneous amyloidosis in an ethnic Chinese girl. *J Dermatol*, **25**, 730–734.
22. Hashimoto, K. (1990) Keratin in cutaneous amyloidoses. *Clin Dermatol*, **8**, 55–65.
23. Esmaramoorthy, V., Kaur, I., Das, A. et al (1999) Macular amyloidosis: etiological factors. *J Dermatol*, **26**, 305–310.
24. Hashimoto, K., Ito, K., Kumakiri, M. et al (1987) Nylon brush macular amyloidosis. *Arch Dermatol*, **123**, 633–637.
25. MacSween, R.M., Saihan, E.M. (1997) Nylon cloth macular amyloidosis. *Clin Exp Dermatol*, **22**, 28–29.
26. Sumitra, S., Yesudian, P. (1993) Friction amyloidosis: a variant or an etiologic factor in amyloidosis cutis? *Int J Dermatol*, **32**, 422–423.
27. Siragusa, M., Ferri, R., Cavallari, V. et al (2001) Friction melanosis, friction amyloidosis, macular amyloidosis, towel melanosis: many names for the same clinical entity. *Eur J Dermatol*, **11**, 545–548.
28. Weyers, W., Weyers, I., Bonczkowitz, M. et al (1999) Lichen amyloidosus: a consequence of scratching. *J Am Acad Dermatol*, **37**, 923–928.
29. Goulden, V., Higher, A.S., Shamy, H.K. (1994) Notalgia paresthetica – report of an association with macular amyloidosis. *Clin Exp Dermatol*, **19**, 346–349.
30. Raison-Peyron, N., Meunier, L., Acevedo, M. et al (1999) Notalgia paresthetica: clinical, physiopathological and therapeutic aspects. A study of 12 cases. *J Eur Acad Dermatol Venereol*, **12**, 215–221.
31. Chabre, O., Labat, F., Pinel, N. et al (1992) Cutaneous lesion associated with multiple endocrine neoplasia type 2A: lichen amyloidosis or notalgia paresthetica? *Henry Ford Hosp Med J*, **40**, 245–248.
32. Kurban, A.K., Malak, J.A., Afifi, A.K. et al (1971) Primary localized macular cutaneous amyloidosis: histochemistry and electron microscopy. *Br J Dermatol*, **85**, 52–60.
33. Westermark, P. (1979) Amyloidosis of the skin: a comparison between localized and systemic amyloidosis. *Acta Derm Venereol*, **59**, 341–345.
34. Schepis, C., Siragusa, M., Gagliardi, M.E. et al (1999) Primary macular amyloidosis: an ultrastructural approach to diagnosis. *Ultrastruct Pathol*, **23**, 279–284.
35. Kobayashi, H., Hashimoto, K. (1983) Amyloidogenesis in organ-limited cutaneous amyloidosis: an antigenic identity between epidermal keratin and skin amyloid. *J Invest Dermatol*, **80**, 66–72.
36. Mukai, H., Kanazaki, T., Nishiyama, S. (1984) Sulfhydryl and disulfide stainings in amyloids of skin-limited and systemic amyloidosis. *J Invest Dermatol*, **82**, 4–8.
37. Kumakiri, M., Hashimoto, K., Tsukinaga, I. et al (1983) Presence of basal lamina-like substance with anchoring fibrils within the amyloid deposits of primary localized cutaneous amyloidosis. *J Invest Dermatol*, **82**, 153–157.
38. Yoneda, K., Watanabe, H., Yanagihara, M. et al (1989) Immunohistochemical staining properties of amyloids with anti-keratin antibodies using formalin-fixed, paraffin-embedded sections. *J Cutan Pathol*, **16**, 133–136.
39. Masu, S., Hosokawa, M., Seiji, M. (1980) Studies on cutaneous amyloidosis with anti-keratin antibody. *Jpn J Dermatol*, **90**, 623–626.
40. Maeda, H., Ohta, S., Saito, Y. et al (1982) Epidermal origin of the amyloid in localized cutaneous amyloidosis. *Br J Dermatol*, **106**, 345–352.
41. Eto, H., Hashimoto, K., Kobayashi, H. et al (1984) Differential staining of cytoid bodies in skin-limited amyloids with monoclonal anti-keratin antibodies. *Am J Pathol*, **116**, 473–481.
42. Hashimoto, K. (1984) Progress on cutaneous amyloidoses. *J Invest Dermatol*, **82**, 1–3.
43. Huilgol, S.C., Ramnarain, N., Carrington, P. et al (1998) Cytokeratins in primary cutaneous amyloidosis. *Australas J Dermatol*, **39**, 81–85.
44. Furumoto, H., Shimizu, T., Asagami, C. et al (1998) Apolipoprotein E is present in primary localized cutaneous amyloidosis. *J Invest Dermatol*, **111**, 417–421.
45. Chang, Y.T., Tsai, S.F., Wang, W.J. et al (2001) A study of apolipoproteins E and A-I in cutaneous amyloids. *Br J Dermatol*, **145**, 422–427.
46. Kumakiri, M., Hashimoto, K. (1979) Histogenesis of primary localized cutaneous amyloidosis: sequential change of epidermal keratinocytes to amyloid via filamentous degeneration. *J Invest Dermatol*, **73**, 150–162.
47. Ebner, H., Gebhart, W. (1975) Light and electron microscopic differentiation of amyloid and colloid or hyaline bodies. *Br J Dermatol*, **92**, 637–645.
48. MacDonald, D.M., Fergin, P.E., Black, M.M. (1980) Localized cutaneous amyloidosis: a clinical review of 100 cases including immunofluorescent studies. In: Glenner, G.G., Pinhoe Costa, P., Falcao de Freitas, A. (eds) Amyloid and amyloidosis. Amsterdam: Excerpta Medica, pp 239–242.
49. MacDonald, D.M., Black, M.M., Ramnarain, N. (1977) Immunofluorescence studies in primary localized cutaneous amyloidosis. *Br J Dermatol*, **96**, 635–641.
50. Habermann, M.C., Montenegro, M.R. (1980) Primary cutaneous amyloidosis: clinical, laboratorial and histopathological study of 25 cases: identification of gamma globulins and C3 in the lesions by immunofluorescence. *Dermatologica*, **160**, 240–248.

51. Dahlbäck, K., Sakai, L. (1990) Immunohistochemical studies on fibrillin in amyloidosis, lichen ruber planus and porphyria. *Acta Derm Venereol*, **70**, 275–280.
52. Lee, Y.-S., Fong, P.-H. (1991) Macular and lichenoid amyloidosis: a possible secretory product of stimulated basal keratinocytes. An ultrastructural study. *Pathology*, **23**, 322–326.
53. Westermark, P., Noren, P. (1986) Two different pathogenetic pathways in lichen amyloidosis and macular amyloidosis. *Arch Dermatol Res*, **278**, 206–213.

Secondary localized cutaneous amyloidosis

Microscopic foci of amyloid may be seen in quite a number of cutaneous neoplasms including basal cell carcinoma, sweat gland tumors, syringocystadenoma papilliferum, pilomatrixoma, trichoepithelioma, trichoblastoma, intradermal nevi, dermatofibroma, seborrheic wart, solar keratosis and Bowen's disease (*Fig. 12.60*).[1–6] The amyloid in most cases appears to be derived from tumor cells. Porokeratosis has also been reported in association with dermal amyloid deposition as a result of apoptosis of keratinocytes.[7] Mycosis fungoides may exceptionally be seen associated with localized cutaneous amyloidosis.[8]

Cutaneous amyloid deposition may also rarely be seen as a consequence of chronic epidermal damage following PUVA therapy.[9,10] So-called concha amyloidosis due to chronic actinic damage to the ear has also been documented.[11]

Repeated insulin injections at the same site have been reported as inducing amyloid in the skin.[12]

References

1. Breathnach, S.M. (1988) Amyloid and amyloidosis. *J Am Acad Dermatol*, **18**, 1–16.
2. Wang, W.J., Huang, J.Y., Wong, C.K. et al (2000) A study of secondary cutaneous amyloidosis in basal cell carcinoma in Chinese patients: lack of correlation with bcl-2 and p53 protein expression. *Arch Dermatol Res*, **292**, 379–383.
3. Jennings, R.C., Ahmed, E. (1970) An amyloid forming nodular syringocystadenoma. *Arch Dermatol*, **101**, 224–226.
4. MacDonald, D.M., Black, M.M. (1980) Secondary localized cutaneous amyloidosis in melanocytic nevi. *Br J Dermatol*, **103**, 553–556.
5. Hashimoto, K., King, L.E. (1973) Secondary localized cutaneous amyloidosis associated with actinic keratosis. *J Invest Dermatol*, **61**, 293–299.
6. Speight, E.L., Milne, D.S., Lawrence, C.M. (1993) Secondary localized cutaneous amyloid in Bowen's disease. *Clin Exp Dermatol*, **18**, 286–288.
7. Amantea, A., Giuliano, M.C., Balus, L. (1998) Disseminated superficial porokeratosis with dermal amyloid deposits: case report and immunohistochemical study of amyloid. *Am J Dermatopathol*, **20**, 86–88.
8. Romero, L.S., Kantor, G.R., Levin, M.W. et al (1997) Localized cutaneous amyloidosis with mycosis fungoides. *J Am Acad Dermatol*, **37**, 124–127.
9. Greene, I., Cox, A.J. (1979) Amyloid deposition after psoriasis therapy with psoralen and long-wave ultraviolet light. *Arch Dermatol*, **115**, 1200–1202.
10. Hashimoto, K., Kumakiri, M. (1979) Colloid-amyloid bodies in PUVA-treated human patients. *J Invest Dermatol*, **72**, 70–80.
11. Hicks, B.C., Weber, P.J., Hashimoto, K. et al (1988) Primary cutaneous amyloidosis of the auricular concha. *J Am Acad Dermatol*, **18**, 19–25.
12. Dische, F.E., Wernstedt, C., Wilander, E. et al (1988) Insulin as an amyloid-fibril protein at sites of repeated insulin injections in a diabetic patient. *Diabetologia*, **31**, 158–161.

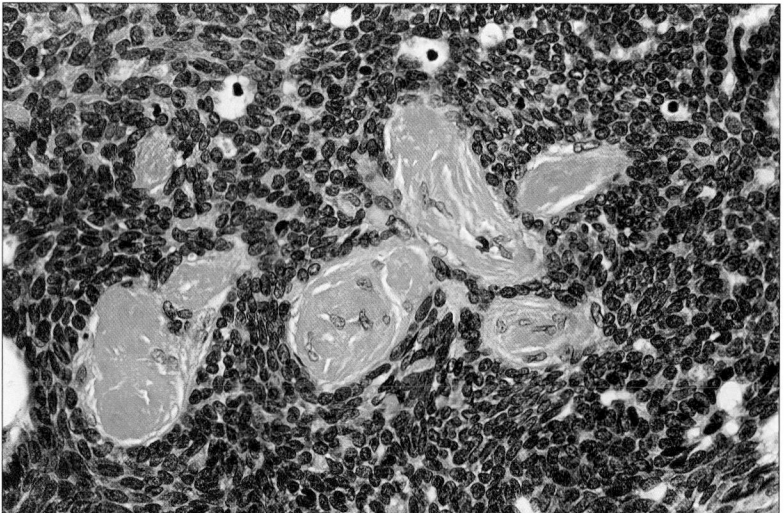

Fig. 12.60
Tumor-associated amyloid: amyloid deposits in a trichoblastoma.

Familial primary cutaneous amyloidosis

Familial primary cutaneous amyloidosis is a very rare autosomal dominant variant of amyloidosis that presents with manifestations of either macular and/or lichenoid amyloidosis.[1–5] Lichen amyloidosis is also seen in patients with multiple endocrine neoplasia type 2A (Sipple syndrome).[6–8] Germline mutations of the RET proto-oncogene on chromosome 10 involving cysteine residues have been consistently described in Sipple syndrome. However, familial primary cutaneous amyloidosis without Sipple syndrome does not show RET mutations, clearly indicating that they are different conditions.[6,9] The histopathological findings are identical to those described in the primary non-familial variants of localized cutaneous amyloidosis.

Amyloidosis cutis dyschromica (vitiliginous) is another familial variant of primary cutaneous amyloidosis characterized by reticulate hyper- and hypopigmentation of the trunk and limbs.[10–13] Papules, atrophy and telangiectasia are usually not present. It has been suggested that the disease is caused by hypersensitivity to ultraviolet B light with possible DNA repair defects.[12] Histologically, the amyloid is present in the papillary dermis. Amyloidosis cutis dyschromica may represent the same disease described as X-linked reticulate pigmentary disorder in which cutaneous amyloidosis occurs as a secondary phenomenon in patients with a disease characterized by failure to thrive, chronic respiratory disease, photophobia with corneal dystrophy and gastrointestinal disease.[14,15]

References

1. Newton, J.A., Jagjivan, A., Bhogal, B. et al (1985) Familial primary cutaneous amyloidosis. *Br J Dermatol*, **112**, 201–208.
2. Vasily, D.B., Bhatia, S.G., Uhlin, S.R. (1978) Familial primary cutaneous amyloidosis. Clinical, genetic, and immunofluorescent studies. *Arch Dermatol*, **114**, 1173–1176.
3. LeBoit, P.E., Greene, I. (1986) Primary cutaneous amyloidosis: identically distributed lesions in identical twins. *Pediatr Dermatol*, **3**, 244–246.
4. Wang, W.J., Chang, Y.T., Huang, C.Y. et al (2001) Clinical and histopathological characteristics of primary cutaneous amyloidosis in 794 Chinese patients. *Zhonghua Yi Xue Za Zhi*, **64**, 101–107.
5. Hartshorne, S.T. (1999) Familial primary cutaneous amyloidosis in a South African family. *Clin Exp Dermatol*, **24**, 438–442.
6. Kousseff, B.G., Espinoza, C., Zamore, G.A. (1991) Sipple syndrome with lichen amyloidosis as a paracrinopathy: pleiotropic, heterogeneity, or a contiguous gene? *J Am Acad Dermatol*, **25**, 651–657.
7. Hofstra, R.M., Sijmons, R.H., Stelwagen, T. et al (1996) RET mutation screening in familial cutaneous lichen amyloidosis and in skin amyloidosis associated with multiple endocrine neoplasia. *J Invest Dermatol*, **107**, 215–218.
8. Seri, M., Celli, I., Betsos, N. et al (1997) A Cys634Gly substitution of the RET proto-oncogene in a family with recurrence of multiple endocrine neoplasia type 2a and cutaneous lichen amyloidosis. *Clin Genet*, **51**, 86–90.
9. Lee, D.D., Huang, J.Y., Wong, C.K. et al (1996) Genetic heterogeneity of familial primary cutaneous amyloidosis: lack of evidence for linkage with the chromosome 10 pericentromeric region in Chinese families. *J Invest Dermatol*, **107**, 30–33.
10. Eng, A.M., Cogan, L., Gunnar, R.M. et al (1976) Familial generalized dyschromic amyloidosis cutis. *J Cutan Pathol*, **3**, 102–108.
11. Vijaikumar, M., Thappa, D.M. (2001) Amyloidosis cutis dyschromica in two siblings. *Clin Exp Dermatol*, **26**, 674–676.
12. Moriwaki, S., Nishigori, C., Horiguchi, Y. et al (1992) Amyloidosis cutis dyschromica. DNA repair reduction in the cellular response to UV light. *Arch Dermatol*, **128**, 966–970.
13. Choohakarn, C., Wittayachanyapong, S. (2002) Familial amyloidosis cutis dyschromica: six cases from three families. *J Dermatol*, **29**, 439–442.
14. Gedeon, A.K., Mulley, J.C., Kozman, H. et al (1994) Localisation of the gene for X-linked reticulate pigmentary disorder with systemic manifestations (PDR), previously known as X-linked cutaneous amyloidosis. *Am J Med Genet*, **52**, 75–78.
15. Ades, L.C., Rogers, M., Sillence, D.O. (1993) An X-linked reticulate pigmentary disorder with systemic manifestations: report of a second family. *Pediatr Dermatol*, **10**, 344–351.

Nodular amyloidosis

Clinical features

In this rare variant, which is more common in females, pink–brown single or multiple nodules develop on the trunk, extremities, genitalia, face or scalp (*Fig. 12.61*).[1–4] Bilateral nodular amyloidosis of the eyelids in the absence of systemic amyloidosis has rarely been documented.[5] The lesions often have a waxy appearance and the surface may be atrophic or ulcerated. Most cases of nodular amyloidosis are limited to skin, and only 7% show progression to systemic amyloidosis.[6] Occasional reports have documented monoclonal paraproteinemia, lymphoplasmacytoid lymphoma, Sjögren's syndrome, proteinuria, bone marrow abnormalities and a positive rectal biopsy.[7–9] Nodular cutaneous amyloidosis has also been documented in association with carpal tunnel syndrome induced by the amyloidogenic transthyretin His 114 variant.[10] An unusual variant of nodular amyloidosis with bilateral plantar involvement is very occasionally encountered.[11]

Histological features

The histological appearances cannot be distinguished from those of systemic amyloidosis and, indeed, as in primary amyloidosis, the amyloid consists of light chain-derived AL protein.[12–15] It is thought likely that this nodular variant results from local production of light chains by a localized group of plasma cells.[1] PCR studies have demonstrated that the infiltrating plasma cells in cases of nodular amyloidosis are usually monoclonal.[16,17] Polyclonality, however, has also been reported.[8] In all patients with nodular amyloidosis, it is important to exclude systemic disease.[2]

The deposits of amyloid are present in both the papillary and reticular dermis and may involve the subcutaneous fat (*Figs 12.62–12.64*). Sometimes the vasculature and nerve sheaths are affected (*Figs 12.65–12.67*).[2] Characteristically, plasma cells are seen around blood vessels and at the margin of the amyloid deposits (*Fig. 12.68*).[4,18] Rarely, an associated foreign body giant cell reaction and/or calcification are evident.[4]

References

1. Breathnach, S.M. (1988) Amyloid and amyloidosis. *J Am Acad Dermatol*, **18**, 1–16.
2. Brownstein, M.H., Helwig, E.B. (1970) The cutaneous amyloidoses: I. Localized forms. *Arch Dermatol*, **102**, 8–19.
3. Vestey, J.P., Tidman, M.J., Mclaren, K.M. (1994) Primary nodular cutaneous amyloidosis – long-term follow-up and treatment. *Clin Exp Dermatol*, **19**, 159–162.
4. Northcutt, A.D., Vanover, M.J. (1985) Nodular cutaneous amyloidosis involving the vulva. *Arch Dermatol*, **121**, 518–521.
5. Pelton, R.W., Desmond, B.P., Mamalis, N. et al (2001) Nodular cutaneous amyloid tumors of the eyelids in the absence of systemic amyloidosis. *Ophthalmic Surg Lasers*, **32**, 422–424.
6. Woollons, A., Black, M.M. (2001) Nodular localized primary cutaneous amyloidosis: a long-term follow-up study. *Br J Dermatol*, **145**, 105–109.
7. Badell, A., Servitje, O., Graells, J. et al (1996) Salivary gland plasmacytoid lymphoma with nodular cutaneous amyloid deposition and lambda chain paraproteinemia. *Br J Dermatol*, **135**, 327–329.
8. Inazumi, T., Hakuno, M., Yamada, H. et al (1994) Characterization of the amyloid fibril from primary localized cutaneous nodular amyloidosis associated with Sjögren's syndrome. *Dermatology*, **189**, 125–128.
9. Hashimoto, K. (1990) Keratin in cutaneous amyloidoses. *Clin Dermatol*, **8**, 55–65.
10. Mochizuki, H., Kamakura, K., Masaki, T. et al (2001) Nodular cutaneous amyloidosis and carpal tunnel syndrome due to the amyloidogenic transthyretin His 114 variant. *Amyloid*, **8**, 105–110.
11. Helm, T.N., Danzinger, J., Helm, K.F. (1997) Bilateral plantar amyloidosis: a unique presentation of localized cutaneous amyloidosis. *Cutis*, **59**, 142–144.
12. Breathnach, S.M. (1985) The cutaneous amyloidoses: pathogenesis and therapy. *Arch Dermatol*, **121**, 470–475.
13. Ito, K., Hashimoto, K., Kambe, N. et al (1987) Role of immunoglobulins in amyloidogenesis in cutaneous nodular amyloidosis. *J Invest Dermatol*, **89**, 415–419.
14. Masuda, C., Mohri, S., Nakajima, H. (1988) Histopathological and immunohistochemical study of amyloidosis cutis nodularis – comparison with systemic amylodiosis. *Br J Dermatol*, **119**, 33–43.

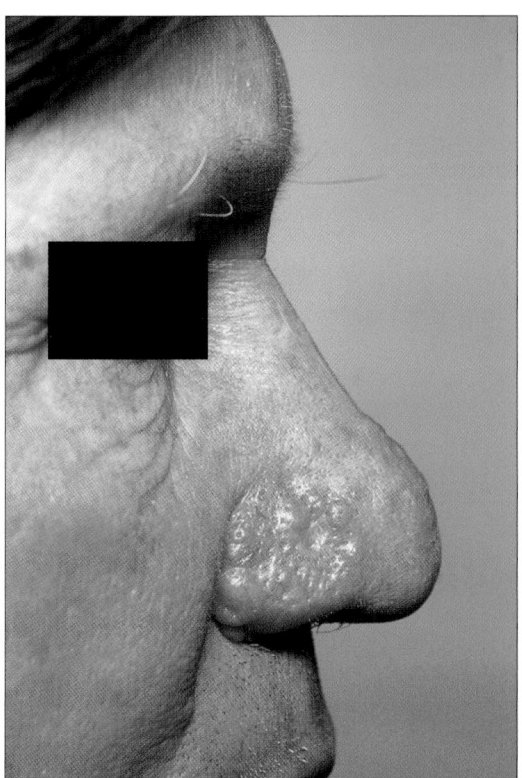

Fig. 12.61
Nodular amyloidosis: an irregular infiltrated plaque limited to the nose.

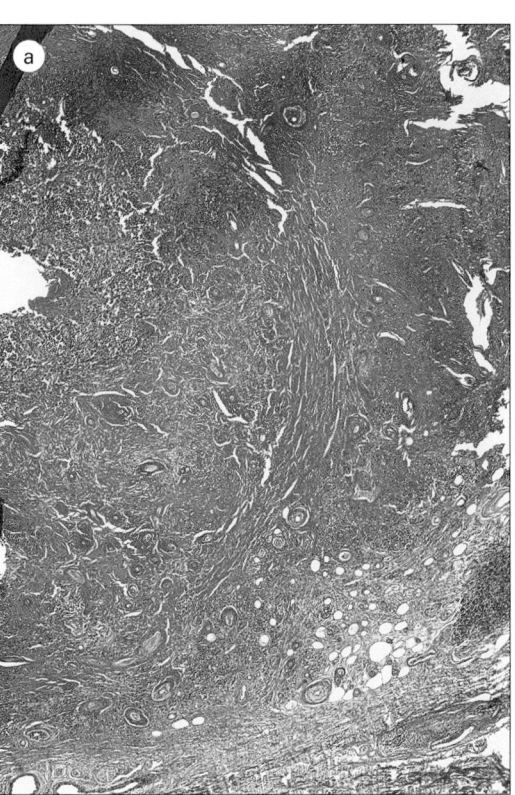

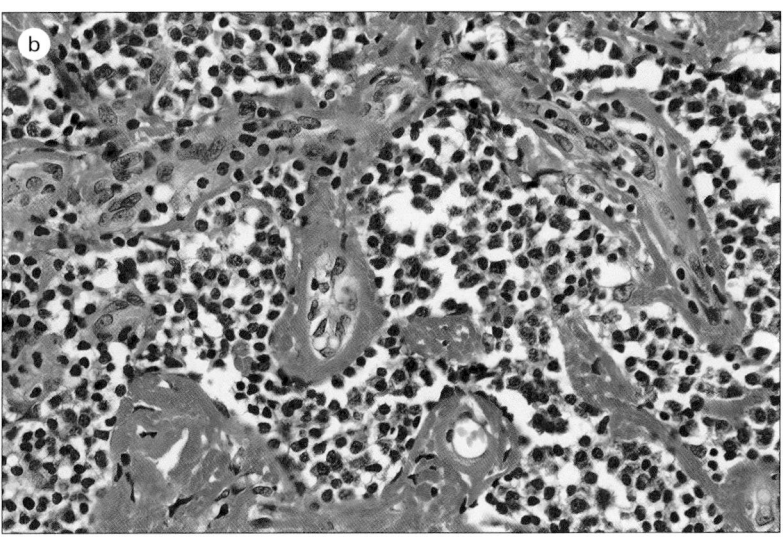

Fig. 12.62
Nodular amyloidosis: (a) massive deposits of amyloid are present in both the papillary and reticular dermis; (b) there is a very heavy associated plasma cell infiltrate.

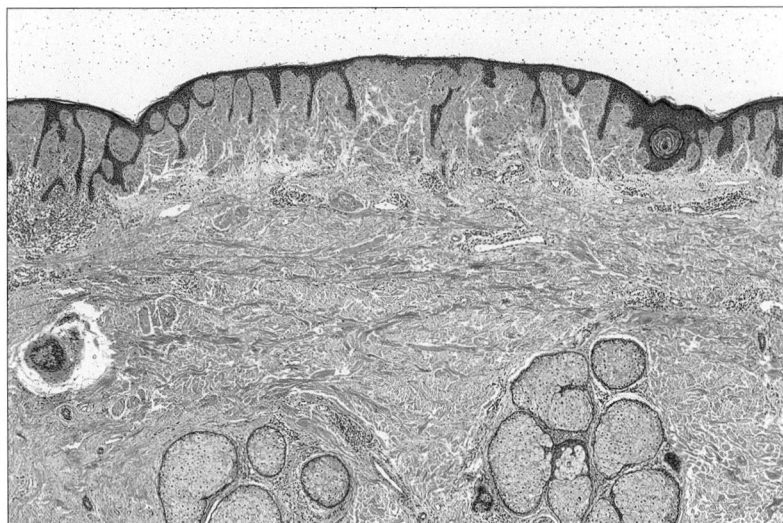

Fig. 12.63
Nodular amyloidosis: in this example there is a broad band-like deposit in the upper dermis.

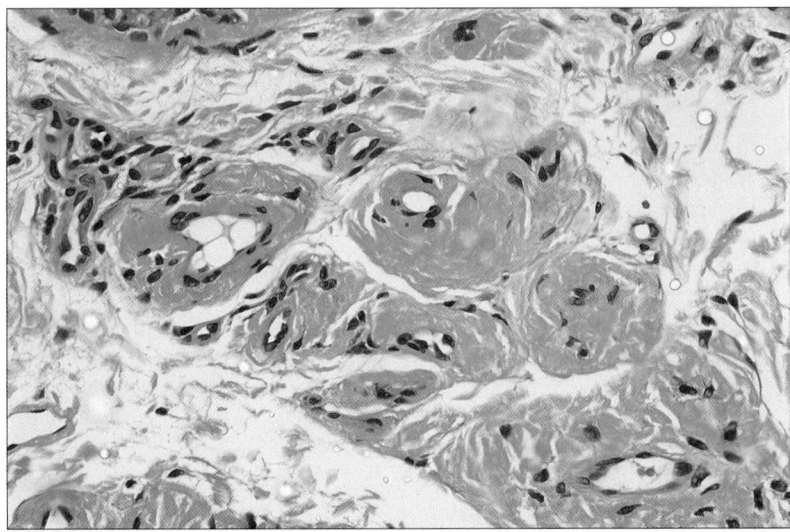

Fig. 12.65
Nodular amyloidosis: amyloid deposits have thickened the blood vessel walls.

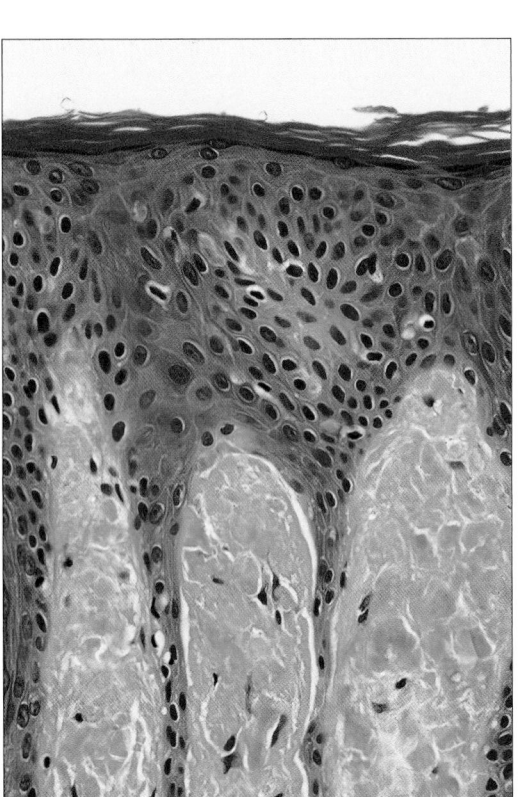

Fig. 12.64
Nodular amyloid: the amyloid deposits fill the papillary dermis.

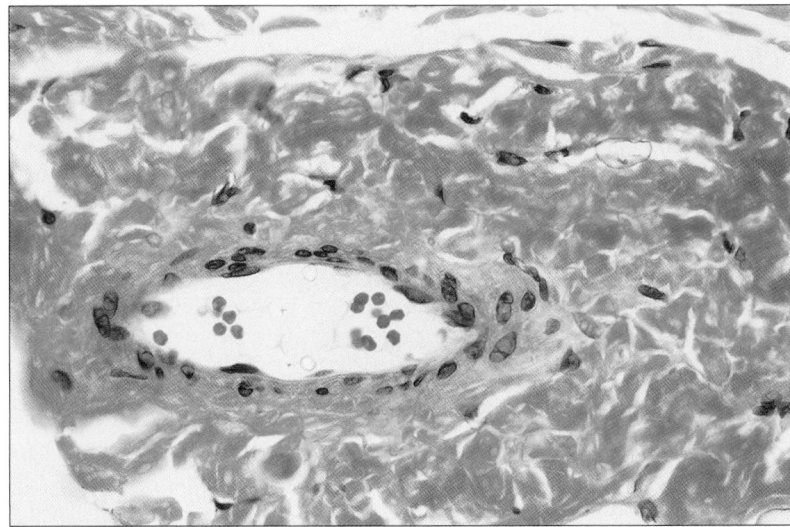

Fig. 12.66
Nodular amyloid: the deposits are strongly Congo red positive.

15.   Kitajima, Y., Seno, J., Aoki, S. et al (1986) Nodular primary cutaneous amyloidosis. *Arch Dermatol*, **122**, 1425–1430.
16.   Hagari, Y., Mihara, M., Hagari, S. (1996) Nodular localized cutaneous amyloidosis: detection of monoclonality of infiltrating plasma cells by polymerase chain reaction. *Br J Dermatol*, **135**, 630–633.
17.   Hagari, Y., Mihara, M., Konohana, I. et al (1998) Nodular localized cutaneous amyloidosis: further demonstration of monoclonality of infiltrating plasma cells in four additional Japanese patients. *Br J Dermatol*, **138**, 652–654.
18.   Horiguchi, Y., Takahashi, C., Imamura, S. (1993) A case of nodular cutaneous amyloidosis. Amyloid production by infiltrating plasma cells. *Am J Dermatopathol*, **15**, 59–63.

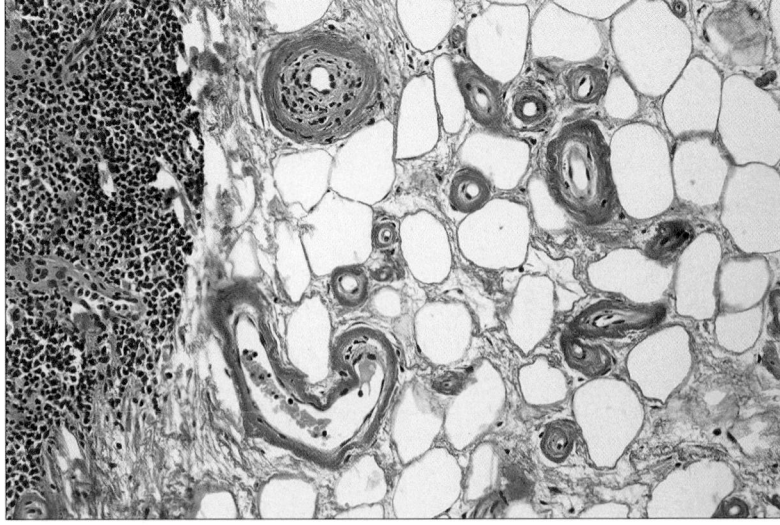

Fig. 12.67
Nodular amyloid: in this example, vessels in the subcutaneous fat showing striking involvement.

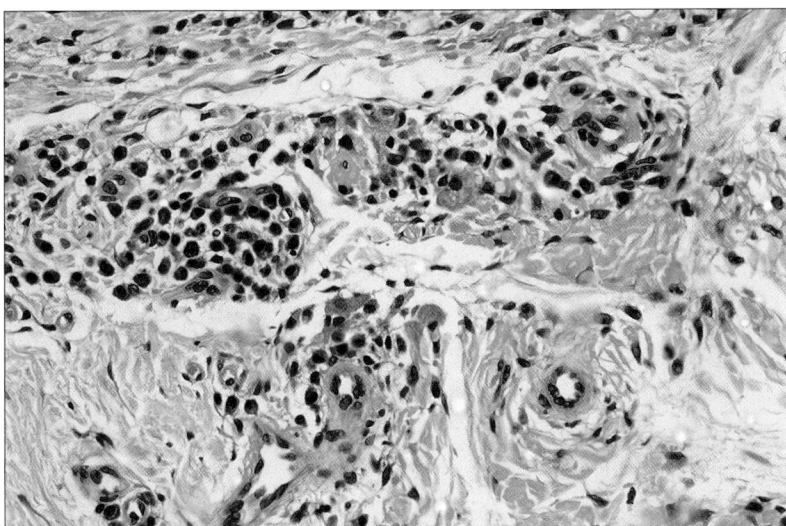

Fig. 12.68
Nodular amyloidosis: there is a conspicuous plasma cell infiltrate.

Colloid milium

Colloid milium, which is characterized by the deposition of amorphous, eosinophilic granular deposits in the superficial dermis, has a number of subtypes including the juvenile and adult variants. It may also develop as a manifestation of ochronosis due to use of the skin bleaching agent hydroquinone.[1] Two other variants – nodular colloid degeneration and paracolloid of the skin – are probably variants of nodular amyloidosis.[2–4] An alternative name proposed for adult colloid milium is that of papular elastosis.[5]

Juvenile colloid milium

Clinical features

The juvenile variant, which is exceedingly rare, develops in children before puberty and sometimes has a familial incidence.[6] Patients present with discrete, or sometimes confluent, papules measuring 0.2–1.5 cm in diameter.[7] Lesions, which are yellow–brown in color, appear translucent and when punctured characteristically express gelatinous material. The underlying tissues often feel indurated. Juvenile colloid milium predominantly affects the face, in particular the cheeks, nose and around the mouth (*Figs 12.69–12.71*). Induction of purpura after stroking has been described in both juvenile and adult colloid milium.[8] This phenomenon has been attributed to vascular fragility due to infiltration of the blood vessel walls by colloid material. Exceptionally juvenile colloid milia may present with gingival deposits and ligneous conjunctivitis as a result of infiltration of these tissues by colloid-like material.[9]

Pathogenesis and histological features

Although the etiology remains unknown, in some cases at least, sunlight plays an important role. The pathogenesis, however, shows considerable overlap with macular and lichenoid amyloidosis. Juvenile colloid milium represents a primary degenerative disorder of epidermal keratinocytes, which through the process of apoptosis are transformed into colloid bodies within the superficial dermis.

The initial change is one of filamentous transformation whereby the relatively straight electron-dense keratin filaments are converted into shortened curved 8–10 nm filaments arranged in weaved or whorled fascicles (*Fig. 12.72*).[7] Occasionally both types of filament may be iden-

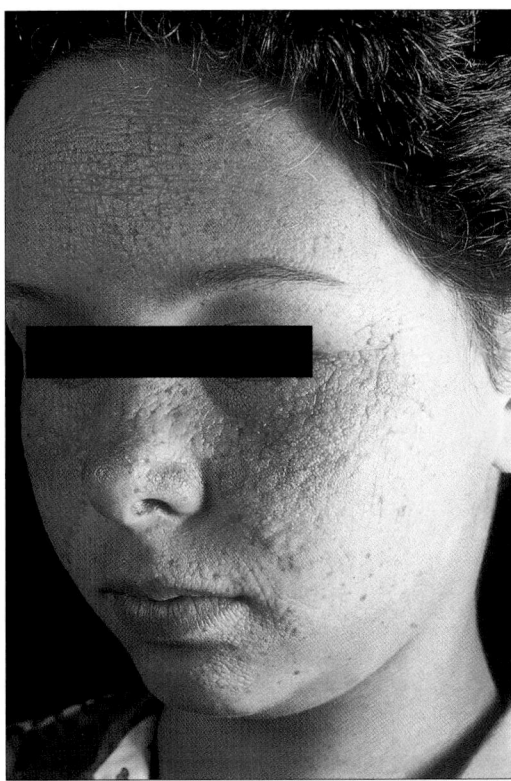

Fig. 12.69
Juvenile colloid milium: there is papular thickening of the skin, particularly involving the cheeks, nose and forehead. By courtesy of S. Hendfield-Jones, MD, Institute of Dermatology, London, UK.

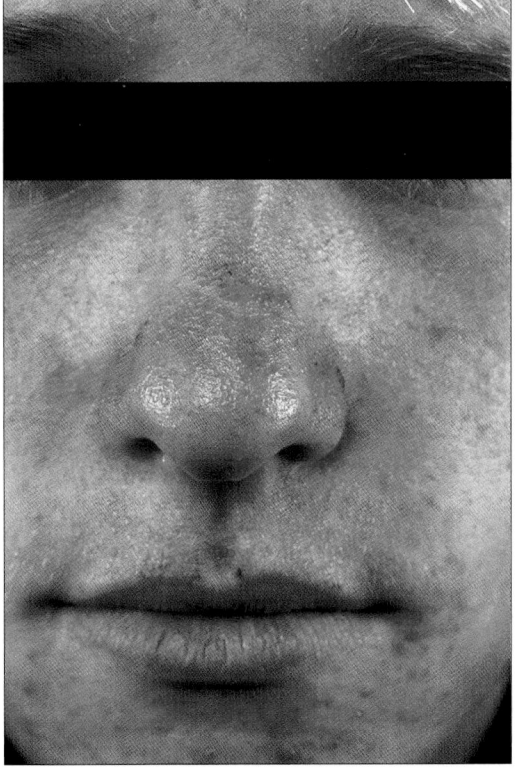

Fig. 12.70
Juvenile colloid milium: this less severely affected child shows typical yellow–brown translucent papules on the nose and upper lip. By courtesy of S. Hendfield-Jones, MD, Institute of Dermatology, London, UK.

tified simultaneously within the cytoplasm of basal keratinocytes. With progression, filamentous transformation comes to affect the entire cell, and nuclear, cytoplasmic and desmosomal remnants may be identified within the filamentous mass (*Fig. 12.73*). Residual desmosomes are sometimes present around the border of the colloid deposit. Finally, the apoptotic cell is extruded into the adjacent dermis. In addition to the transformed filaments characteristic of all cytoid bodies, amyloid filaments have also been identified recently in juvenile colloid milium, thereby prompting the authors to classify this entity along with other

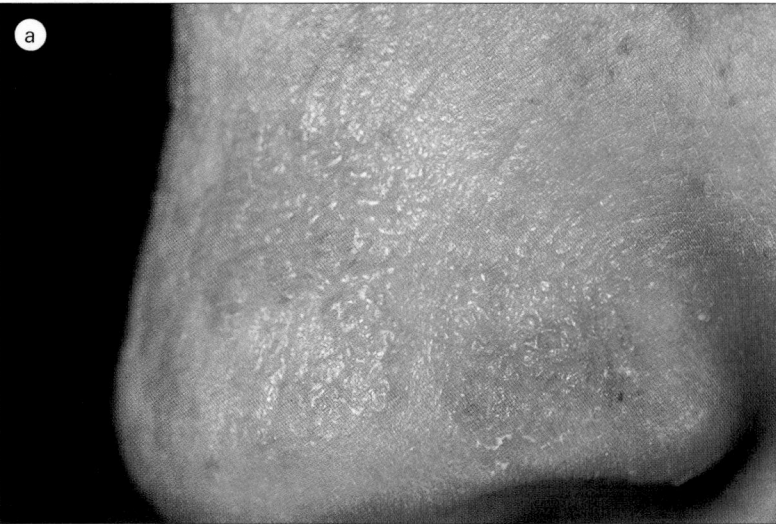

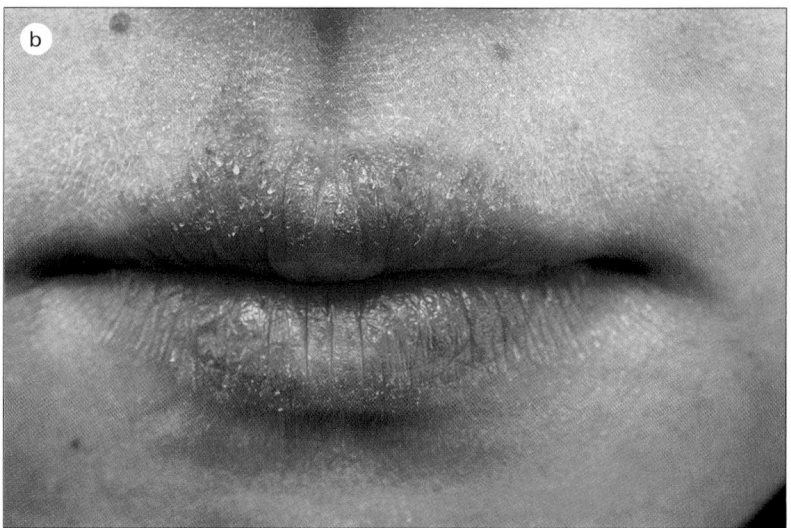

Fig. 12.71
(a, b) Juvenile colloid milium: these close-up views are from the brother of the patient shown in *Fig. 12.70*. By courtesy of S. Hendfield-Jones, MD, Institute of Dermatology, London, UK.

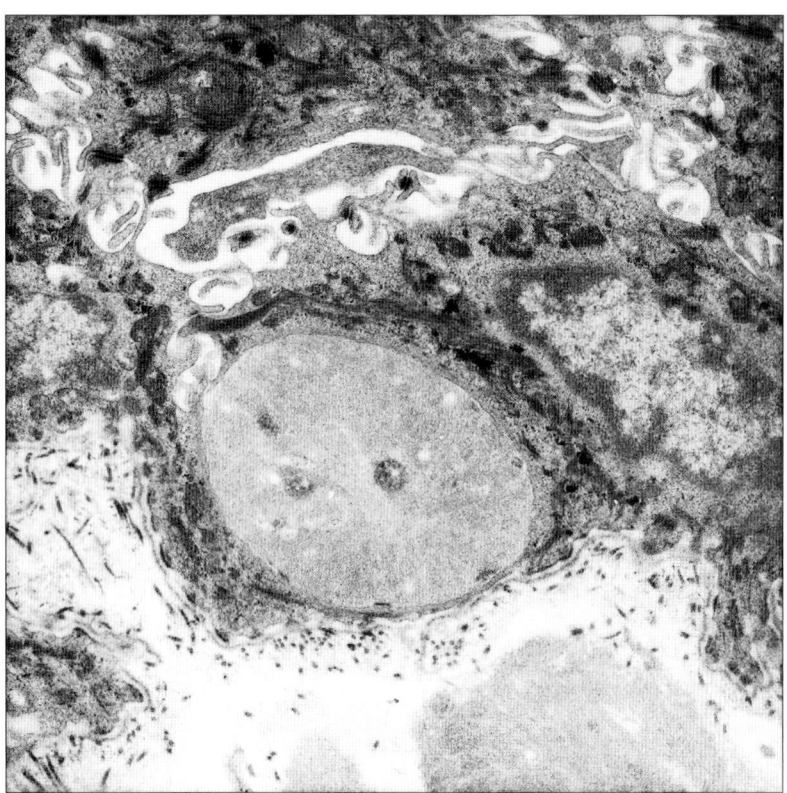

Fig. 12.72
Juvenile colloid milium: this shows an apoptotic keratinocyte, the cytoplasm of which is filled with fascicles of pale-staining filaments that contrast strikingly with adjacent tonofilaments.

amyloid-K dermatoses.[2] Positive labeling of the deposits for epidermal keratin gives support to this hypothesis.[2,10]

Juvenile colloid milium has also been shown by direct immuno-fluorescence to be accompanied by immunoglobulin, complement and fibrin deposits.[7] Whether this represents an autoimmune-mediated reaction as is seen in macular–lichenoid amyloidosis or a secondary non-specific reactive phenomenon has yet to be determined.

Histologically the deposits are present in the superficial dermis where they impinge on the overlying and often somewhat frayed epidermis (*Figs 12.74–12.77*). The colloid consists of eosinophilic amorphous aggregates, often showing a fractured appearance. The overlying epithe-lium shows prominent cytoid bodies, while laterally acanthosis associated with downward and inward growth results in cuffing or even encirclement of the colloid islands by an epidermal collarette.[2] An admixture of fibroblasts and mast cells may be evident and pigmentary incontinence is sometimes present. Juvenile colloid milium is histo-chemically indistinguishable from amyloid: it is diastase-resistant, PAS positive, thioflavine-T positive and shows positive staining with Congo red with apple-green birefringence.

Adult colloid milium

Clinical features

This variant, which is much commoner than the childhood form, affects middle-aged patients and shows a predilection for males. Outdoor workers are most often affected and lesions seen on sun-exposed skin are often accompanied by the features of solar elastosis, giving rise to the synonym of papular elastosis.

Adult colloid milium presents as dome-shaped yellowish translucent papules measuring 0.1–0.5 cm in diameter and, in common with juvenile colloid milium, they contain gelatinous material. Lesions are most often seen on the face, ears, neck and the dorsum of the hands (*Fig. 12.78*).[2] Adult colloid milium affects fair-skinned patients and follows excessive sun exposure. This has been dramatically illustrated in patients whose lesions are limited to sun-exposed areas of the body.[11,12] Adult colloid milium has also been reported following the excessive use of cosmetic ultraviolet A (UVA) sunbed exposure.[13] A rare association with multiple myeloma has been described.[14] A further report described a patient who developed lesions of adult colloid milia in areas exposed to mineral oils.[15]

Pathogenesis and histological features

In contrast to the keratinocyte changes seen in the juvenile variant, adult colloid milium represents an extreme degree of actinic damage centered upon the upper dermal elastic fibers. Although earlier studies suggested that the colloid might have represented abnormal collagen or a fibroblast secretory product, more recent studies suggest that it derives from actinic elastoid.[11,16–18]

Ultrastructural studies have shown that there is direct continuity between actinic elastoid and the colloid deposits and that within the electron-dense colloid, remnants of both normal and elastotic fibers may sometimes be identified.[17,19] Amyloid filaments are not present. Further

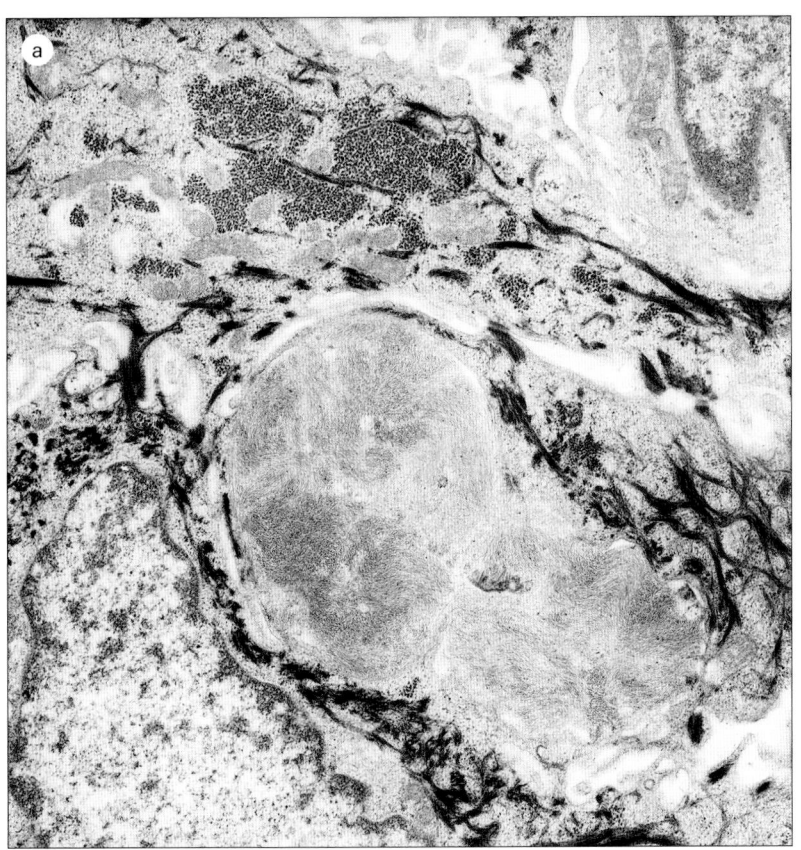

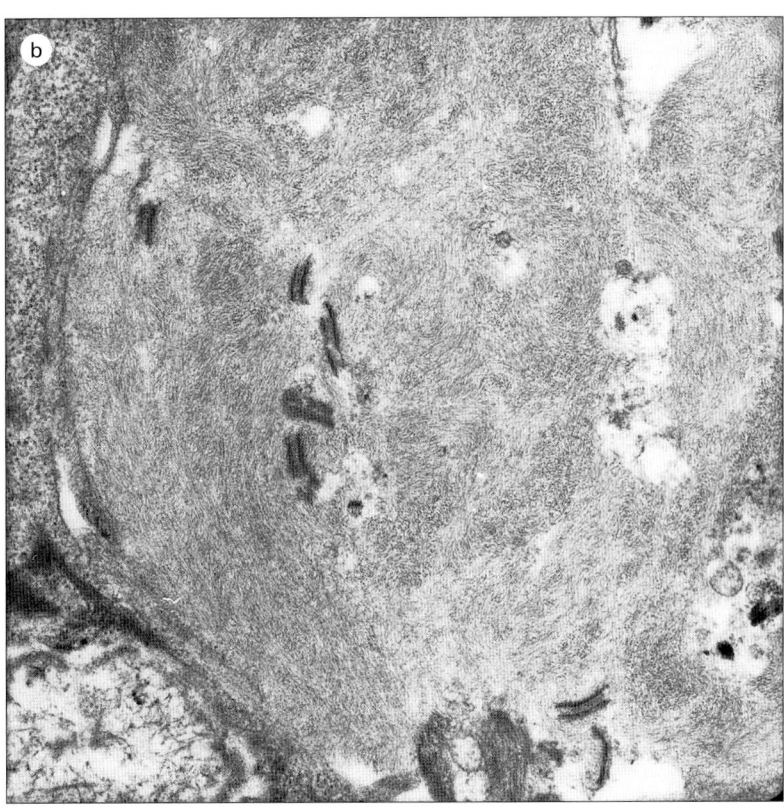

Fig. 12.73
Juvenile colloid milium: (**a**) this high power view shows the whorled arrangement of the filaments. An adjacent keratinocyte shows abundant glycogen particles (G);
(**b**) internalized desmosomes are evident within this degenerate keratinocyte.

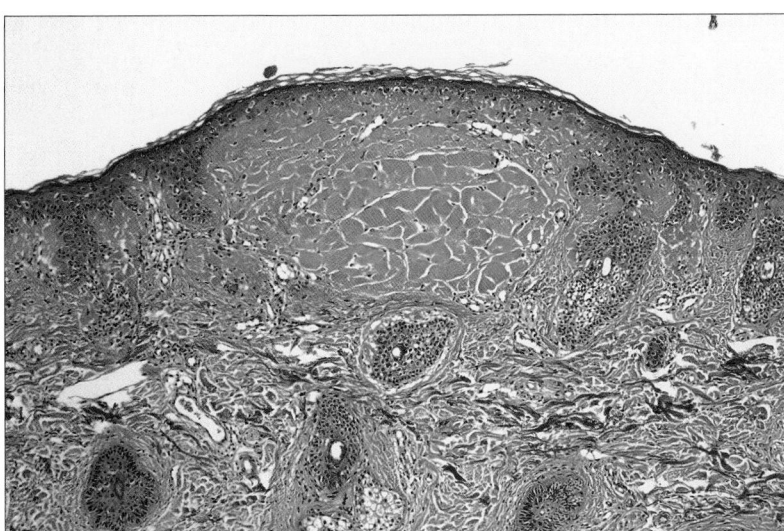

Fig. 12.74
Juvenile colloid milium: the papule consists of an intradermal deposit of eosinophilic material. There is no inflammatory response.

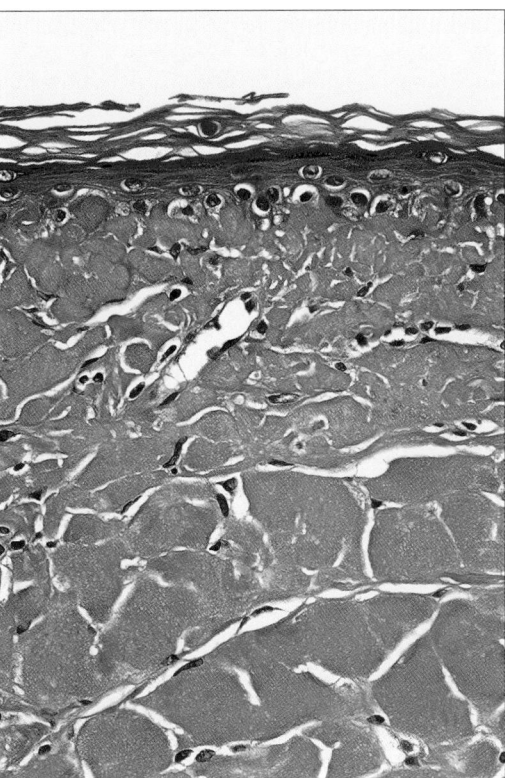

Fig. 12.75
Juvenile colloid milium: this high power view shows the faceted nature of the deposit.

support for this hypothesis is given by the identification of serum amyloid P component within the colloid deposits.[17] Although this protein is characteristically present within amyloid, it is also a constant component of normal elastic tissue and has also been identified in actinic elastoid.[20,21] Adult colloid milium does not label with antikeratin antibodies, and immunoglobulins and complement are absent.

Histologically, in adult colloid milium, the eosinophilic amorphous, autofluorescent clefted deposits are typically separated from the epidermis by a Grenz zone containing normal collagen (*Figs 12.79,*

12.80).[17] Fibroblasts often occupy the fissures between the fragmented deposits.[17]

Histochemically, adult colloid milium is diastase-resistant, PAS positive, thioflavine-T positive and demonstrates apple-green birefringence with Congo red.[11] It is also Dylon positive.[2]

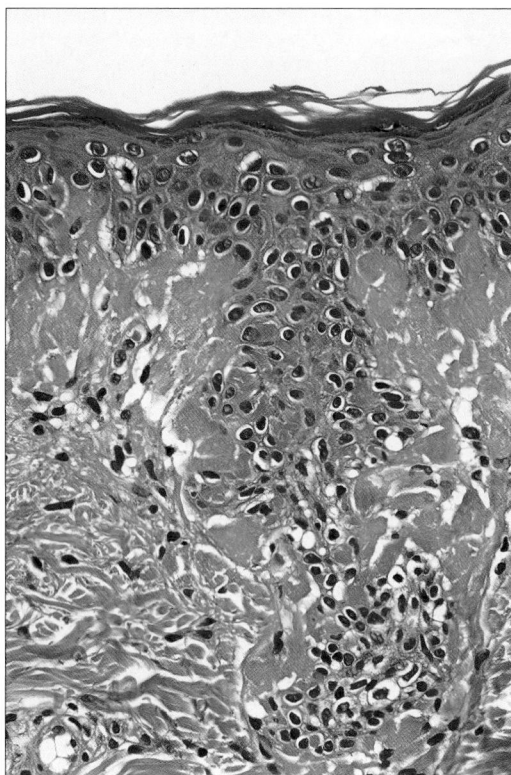

Fig. 12.76
Juvenile colloid milium: the adjacent epidermis shows massive apoptosis.

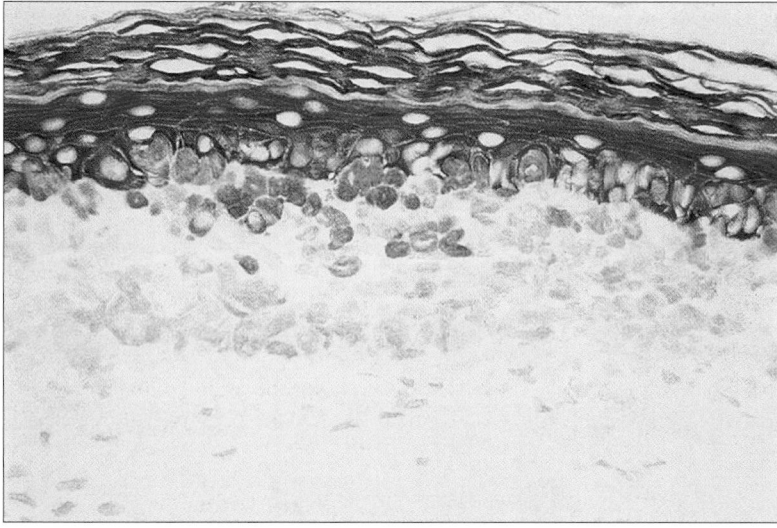

Fig. 12.77
Juvenile colloid milium: the amorphous material that characterizes this condition is of epidermal derivation. Tonofilaments undergo filamentous degeneration (apoptosis). Note the keratin positivity of the colloid aggregates (pankeratin).

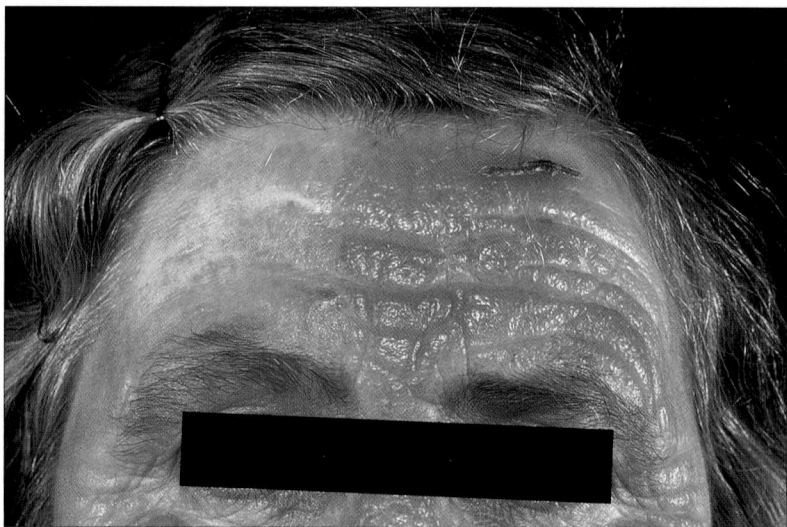

Fig. 12.78
Adult colloid milium: predominantly unilateral, streaked, orange plaque involving the forehead and nose. By courtesy of the Institute of Dermatology, London, UK.

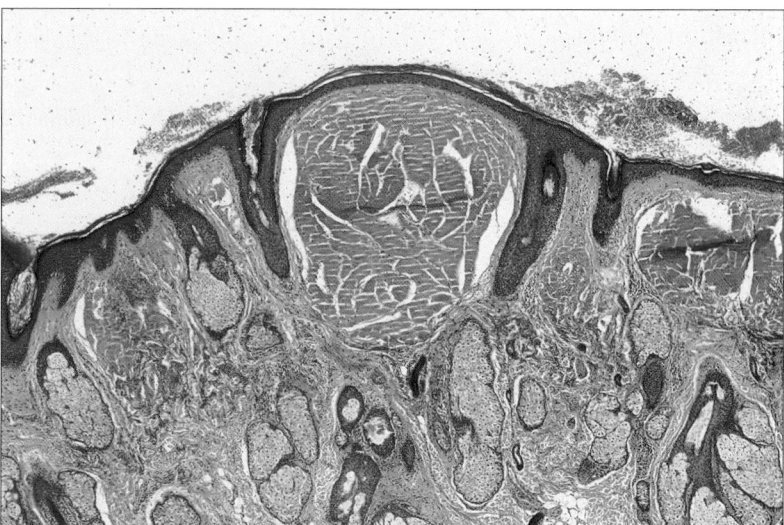

Fig. 12.79
Adult colloid milium: deposits of eosinophilic material are present in the superficial dermis. There is adjacent solar elastosis.

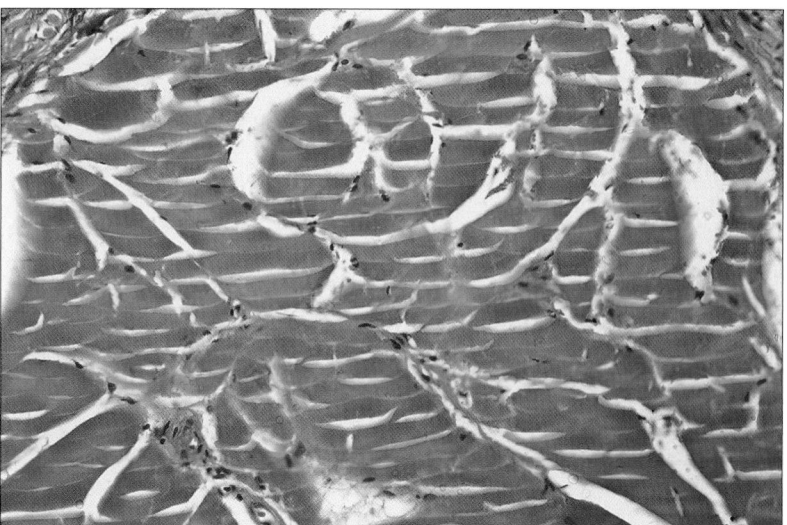

Fig. 12.80
Adult colloid milium: the typical faceted appearance.

References

1. Findlay, G.H., Morrison, J.G.L., Simson, I.W. (1975) Exogenous ochronosis and pigmented colloid milium from hydroquinone bleaching creams. *Br J Dermatol* **93**, 613–622.
2. Hashimoto, K., Nakayama, H., Chimenti, S. et al (1989) Juvenile colloid milium: immunohistochemical and ultrastructural studies. *J Cutan Pathol*, **16**, 164–174.
3. Sullivan, M., Ellis, F.A. (1961) Facial colloid degeneration in plaques. *Arch Dermatol*, **84**, 816–823.
4. Dupre, A., Bonafe, J.F., Pieraggi, M.T. et al (1979) Paracolloid of the skin. *J Cutan Pathol*, **6**, 304–309.
5. Kwittken, J. (2000) Papular elastosis. *Cutis*, **66**, 81–83.
6. Percival, B.H., Duthie, D.A. (1948) Notes on a case of colloid pseudo-milium. *Br J Dermatol*, **60**, 399–404.
7. Ebner, H., Gebhart, W. (1977) Colloid milium: light and electron microscopic investigations. *Clin Exp Dermatol*, **2**, 217–226.
8. Sevigny, G.M., Ford, M.J. (1995) Stroke-induced purpura in lesions of colloid milium. *Cutis*, **56**, 109–113.
9. Chowdhury, M.M., Blackford, S., Williams, S. (2000) Juvenile colloid milium associated with ligneous conjunctivitis: report of a case and review of the literature. *Clin Exp Dermatol*, **25**, 138–140.
10. Handfield-Jones, S.E., Atherton, D., Black, M.M. (1992) Juvenile colloid milium. *J Cutan Pathol*, **19**, 434–438.
11. Hashimoto, K., Miller, F., Bereston, E.S. (1972) Colloid milium: histochemical and electron microscopic studies. *Arch Dermatol*, **105**, 684–694.
12. Mayer, F.E., Milburn, P.B. (1990) Unilateral colloid milium. *J Am Acad Dermatol*, **23**, 1166–1167.
13. Innocenzi, D., Barduagni, F., Cerio, R. et al (1993) UV-induced colloid milium. *Clin Exp Dermatol*, **18**, 347–350.

14. Sanjuan, E.B., Planas, G., Piquero, J. et al (1994) Colloid milium associated with multiple myeloma. *Int J Dermatol*, **33**, 793–795.
15. Muscardin, L.M., Bellocci, M., Balus, L. (2000) Papuloverrucous colloid milium: an occupational variant. *Br J Dermatol*, **143**, 884–887.
16. Hashimoto, K., Katzman, R.L., Kang, A.H. et al (1975) Electron microscopical and biochemical analysis of colloid milium. *Arch Dermatol*, **111**, 49–59.
17. Hashimoto, K., Black, M.M. (1985) Colloid milium: a final degeneration product of actinic elastoid. *J Cutan Pathol*, **12**, 147–156.
18. Matsuta, M., Kunimoto, M., Kosegawa, G. et al (1989) Electron microscopy study of the colloid-like substance in solar elastosis. *Am J Dermatopathol*, **16**, 191–195.
19. Kobayashi, H., Hashimoto, K. (1983) Colloid and elastic fibre: ultrastructural study on the histogenesis of colloid milium. *J Cutan Pathol*, **10**, 111–112.
20. Breathnach, S.M., Melrose, S.M., Bhogal, B. et al (1981) Amyloid P component is located on elastic fibre microfibrils in normal human tissue. *Nature*, **293**, 652–654.
21. Breathnach, S.M., Melrose, S.M., Bhogal, B. et al (1982) Immunohistochemical studies of amyloid P component distribution in normal human skin. *J Invest Dermatol*, **80**, 86–90.

Hyalinosis cutis et mucosae

Clinical features

Hyalinosis cutis et mucosae (Urbach–Wiethe disease), more commonly known as lipoid proteinosis, is a very rare, autosomal recessive condition first described in 1929 in which a hyaline material is deposited in virtually any organ in the body, but particularly the skin, the pharyngeal mucosa and the larynx.[1–6] It has been reported most frequently in South Africa (descendants of German and Dutch immigrants) and Sweden and it has been suggested that up to 35% of documented cases have had South African lineage.[7–10]

The gene for lipoid proteinosis has been mapped to chromosome 1q21 and the disease is caused by mutations in the extracellular matrix protein 1 gene (ECM1).[11] The initial symptom, hoarseness, develops in infancy and results from incomplete closure of the vocal cords, which are thickened and irregular due to the hyaline deposits. Induration of the oral mucosa (including the inner aspect of the lips, the gingivae, uvula, palate and floor of the mouth) begins in childhood and is progressive, so that adults have extensive yellow infiltration (*Fig. 12.81*).[4,12] The lower lip often assumes a cobblestone appearance. The tongue also tends to be thick and immobile. Nail growth is frequently abnormal and the upper incisors, premolars or molars can be hypoplastic or aplastic.[5]

Early inflammatory skin lesions (bullae, pustules and crusts) are followed by acneiform infiltrated scars on the face and limbs (*Fig. 12.82*).[9] Papulonodular lesions develop on the face, fingers and around the eyelashes, where they produce the pathognomonic 'string of beads' appearance (moniliform blepharosis) (*Fig. 12.83*). Thicker

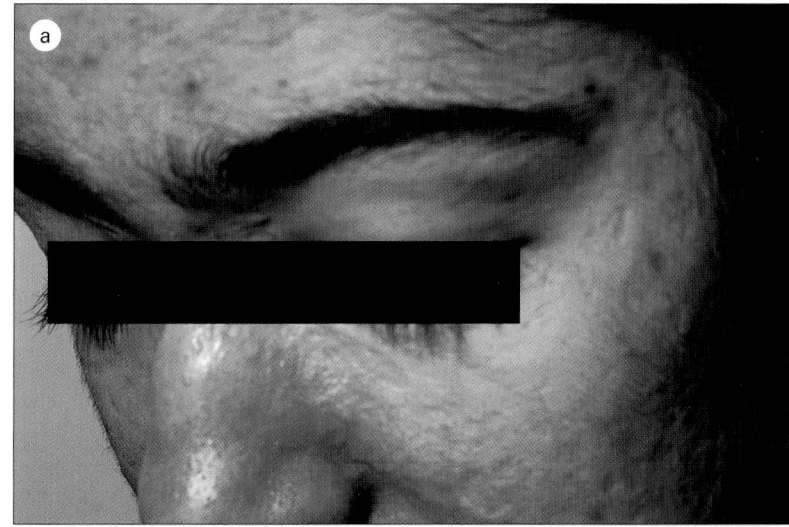

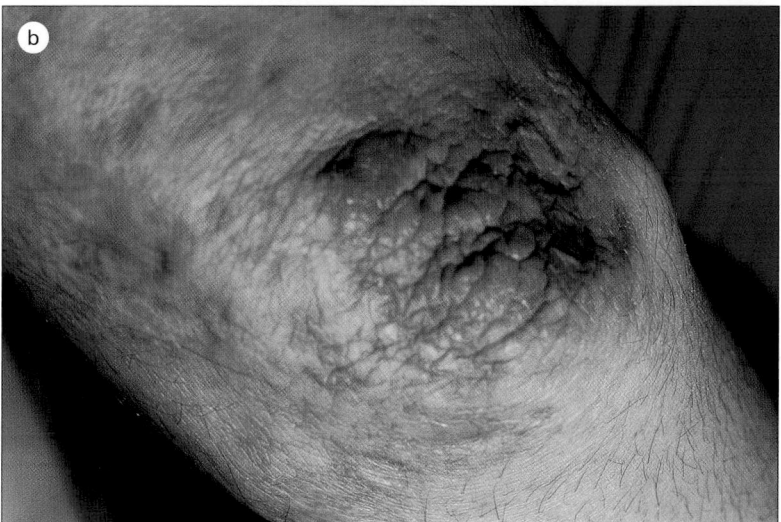

Fig. 12.82
Lipoid proteinosis: (a) there is extensive facial scarring; (b) marked thickening of the skin is present with conspicuous scarring. By courtesy of R.A. Marsden, MD, St George's Hospital, London, UK.

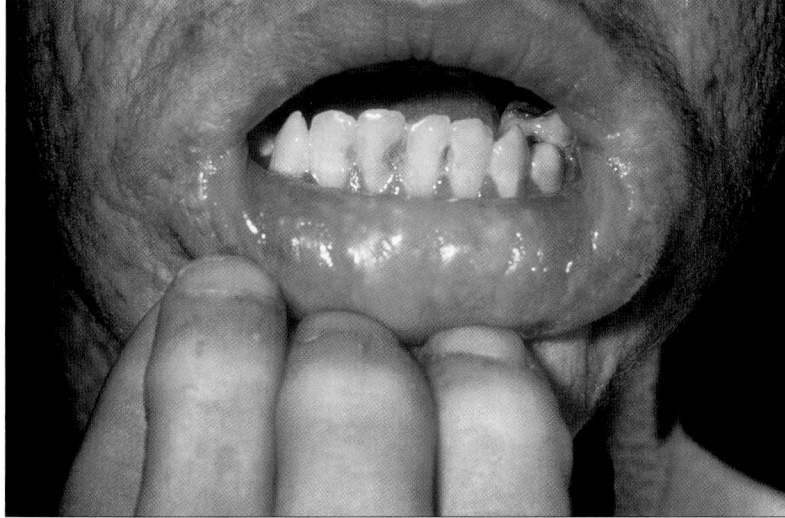

Fig. 12.81
Lipoid proteinosis: small pale papules are present on the mucosal aspect of the lower lip. By courtesy of the Institute of Dermatology, London, UK.

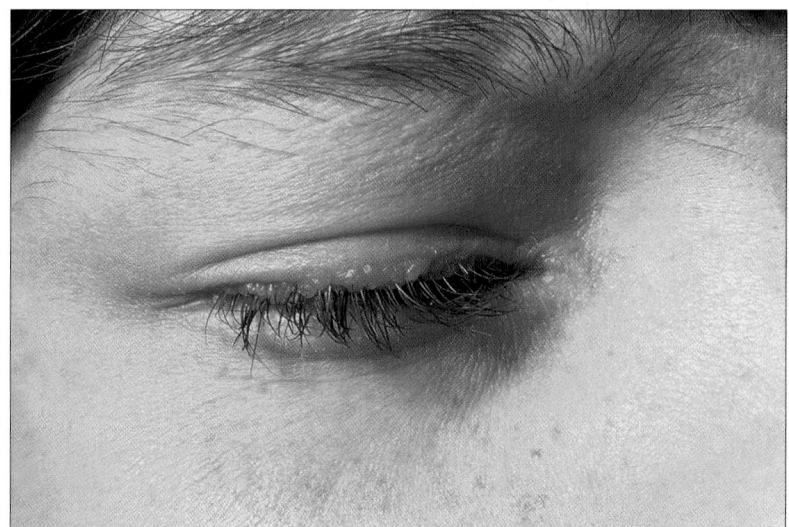

Fig. 12.83
Lipoid proteinosis: note the waxy nodules on the lower eyelid, producing the typical 'string of beads' appearance. By courtesy of the Institute of Dermatology, London, UK.

xanthoma-like plaques, which sometimes become verrucous, later develop on the areas of trauma including the knees, elbows, feet and hands.[13] With chronicity in severely affected patients the entire skin becomes yellow, waxy and thickened, particularly the flexures.[14] Similar lesions in the scalp can produce alopecia which can be patchy or diffuse.[5,7]

Intracranial disease may occur, associated with calcification, which is thought to complicate deposition of hyaline material around cerebral blood vessels and basal ganglia.[4] Epilepsy is a not uncommon result.[13,15,16] Other neurological manifestations include memory loss and rage attacks.[17]

Involvement of the small bowel by the disease may lead to intestinal bleeding.[18]

The disease is usually associated with normal life expectancy although there might be some increase in the mortality rate during childhood due to respiratory insufficiency.[2]

Pathogenesis and histological features

The epidermis is acanthotic and occasionally papillomatous, with overlying hyperkeratosis. Homogeneous eosinophilic material is distributed in a very characteristic pattern in the dermis.[7] Initially it is found around capillaries and concentrically around sweat coils (*Figs 12.84, 12.85*); later, more extensive deposits are seen, which tend to be vertically orientated within the dermis. The hair follicles and arrector pili muscles are often surrounded by a hyaline mantle.[19] In advanced cases, the perineurium of nerves can also be affected.[20] This material stains very strongly with PAS (diastase-resistant) and only very weakly with Congo red and thioflavine-T (*Fig. 12.86*). The name lipoid is used because the hyaline material usually has a lipid component.[21]

Ultrastructurally, the deposit is amorphous, electron dense and may contain ill-defined, anastomosing amyloid-like (5–10 nm) filaments and delicate collagen fibers (*Figs 12.87, 12.88*).[19] Reduplication of basal lamina is evident around blood vessels, hair follicles and sweat glands, and excess type IV collagen has been demonstrated immunohistochemically.[7,13,14,22] The fibroblasts contain abundant rough endoplasmic reticulum and numerous mitochondria. Intracytoplasmic inclusions, probably lysosomal in nature, have also been described.

Despite considerable research, the precise pathogenesis of lipoid proteinosis remains an enigma. Quantitative abnormalities of dermal collagen have been clearly demonstrated, but little is known about the nature of the hyaline deposits other than that they are probably composed of an admixture of glycoproteins, glycosaminoglycans and lipids, as may be determined by special staining techniques.[7]

Numerous mechanisms have been hypothesized, but none has satisfactorily unraveled the nature of the primary disturbance in this disease. The identification of lipid droplets within the hyaline deposits therefore led to the suggestion that lipoid proteinosis might represent a systemic lipoidosis.[7] However, the lipid deposition is very variable and lesional chemical analyses have not demonstrated any consistent

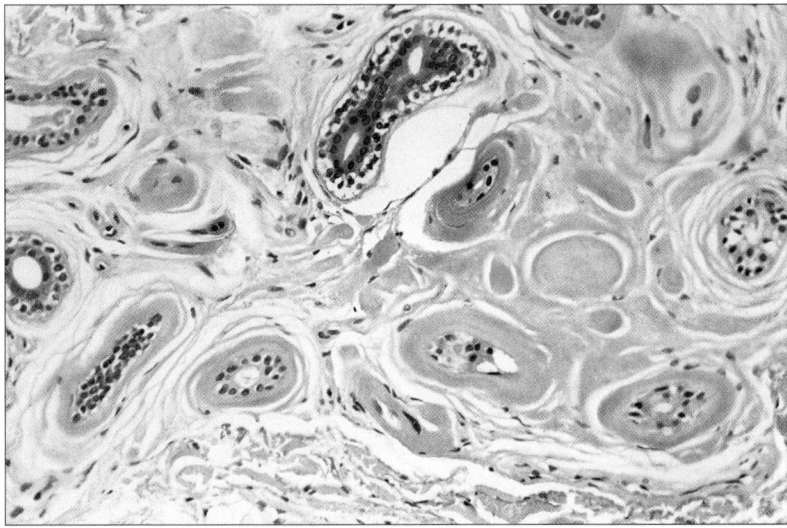

Fig. 12.85
Lipoid proteinosis: in this advanced example, there is considerable involvement of eccrine sweat glands which, as a result, are atrophic.

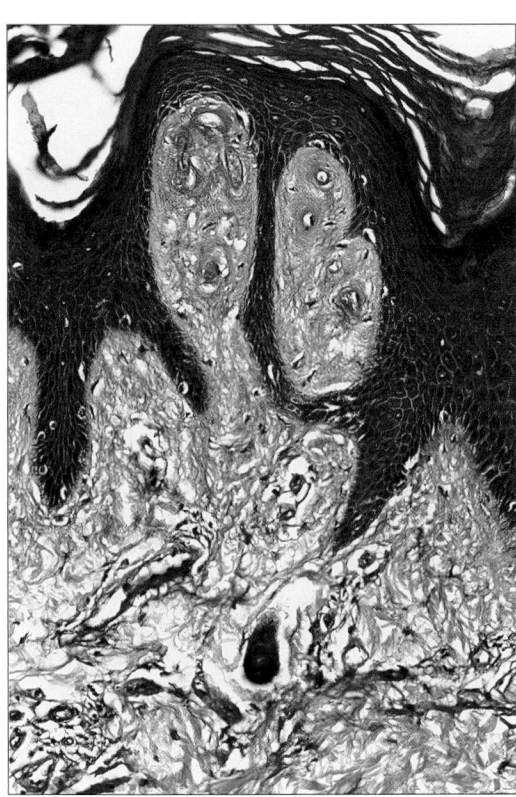

Fig. 12.84
Lipid proteinosis: the blood vessel walls are thickened by pale-staining, eosinophilic homogeneous material.

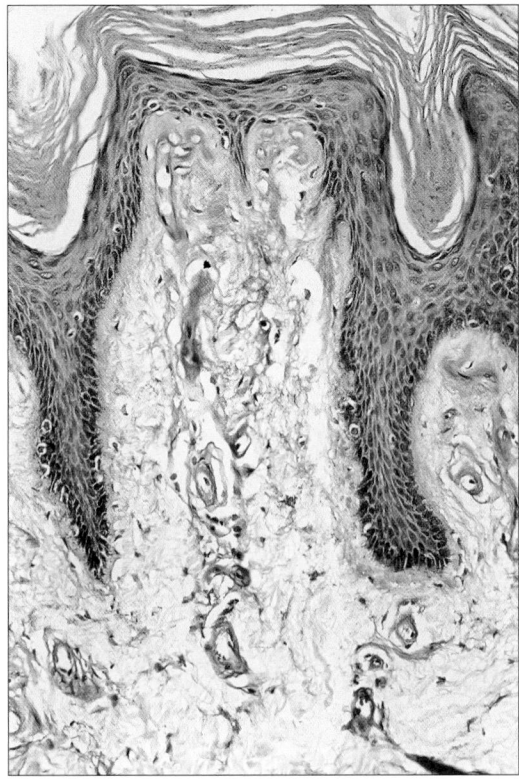

Fig. 12.86
Lipoid proteinosis: the deposit is strongly periodic acid–Schiff positive (diastase-resistant).

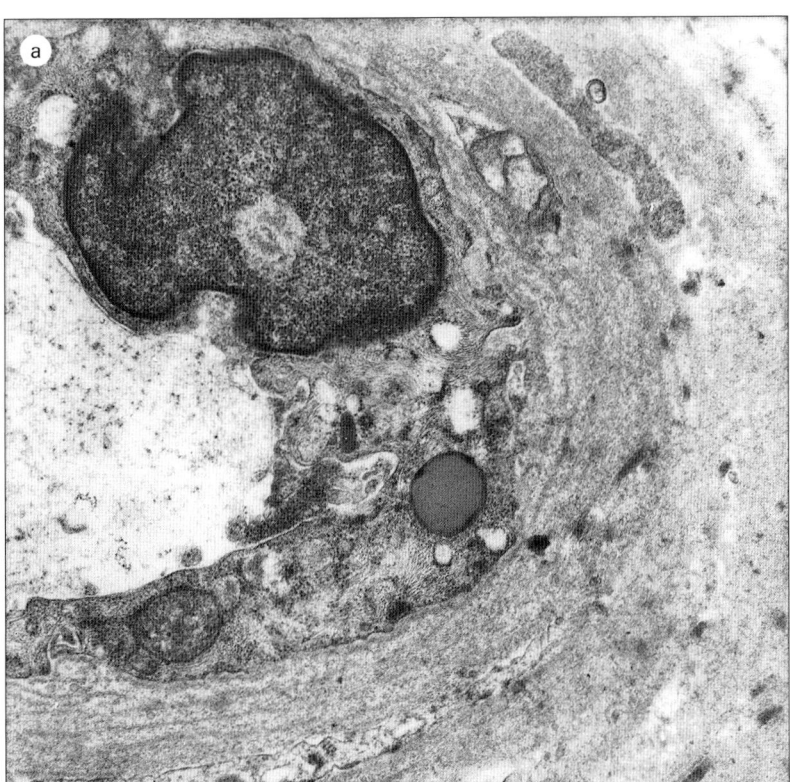 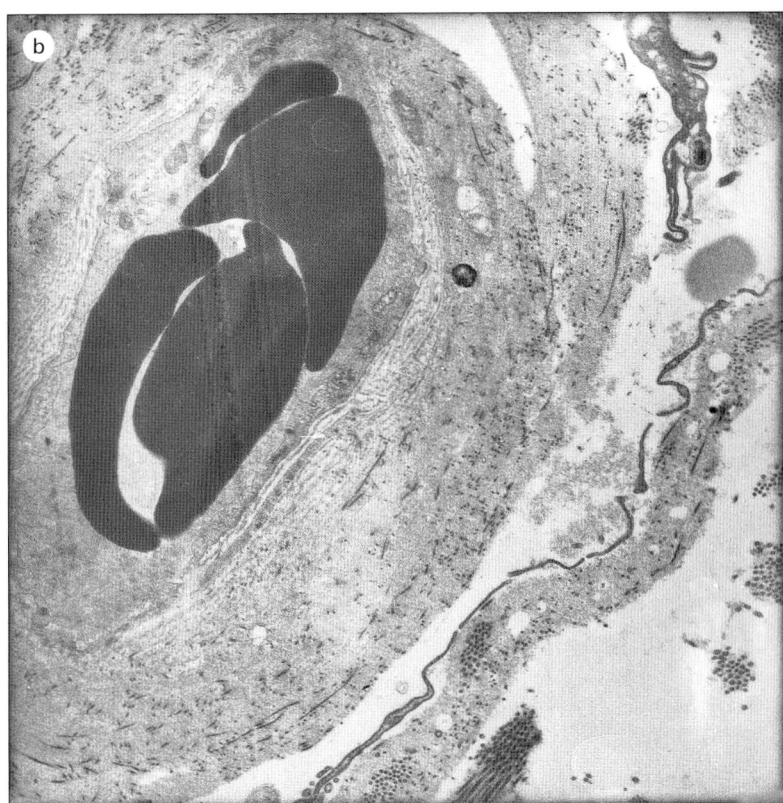

Fig. 12.87
(a, b) Lipoid proteinosis: transverse section through blood vessel showing reduplication of the basement membrane.

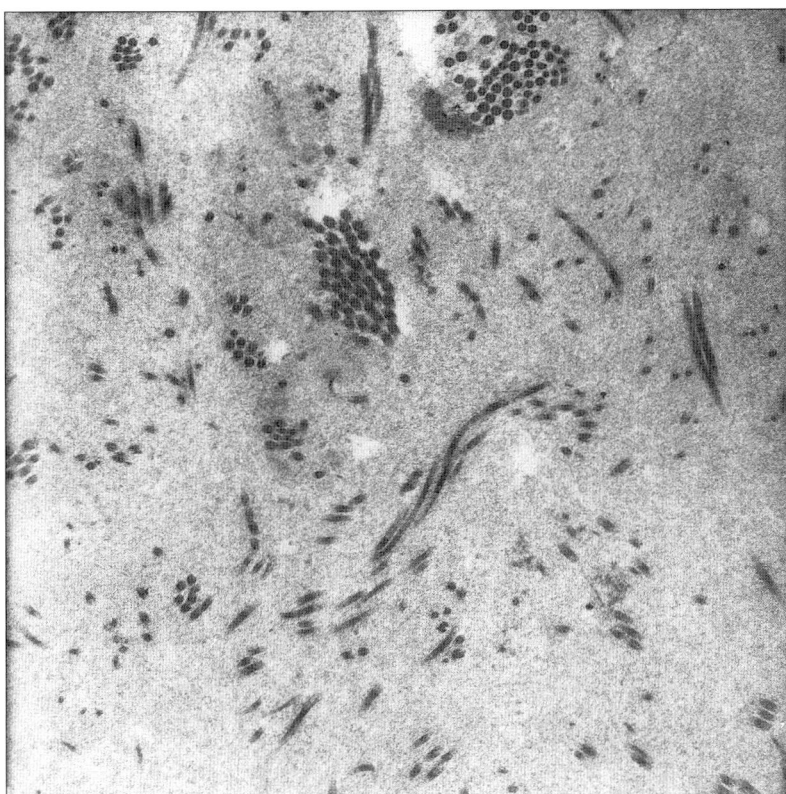

Fig. 12.88
Lipoid proteinosis: high power view of amorphous electron-dense material containing occasional collagen fibers.

abnormalities. Fibroblast tissue culture experiments have not supported this concept.[21] It probably denotes a secondary phenomenon. The ultrastructural finding of intracytoplasmic inclusions – including myelin figures and lysosomes accompanied by an increased fibroblast hexuronic

acid content – has raised the possibility of a lysosomal storage disorder.[23] This has recently been given further support by the demonstration of abnormal lysosomes in eccrine cells and histiocytes in two patients with this disease.[24] These lysosomes were found to contain amorphous granular material, zebra bodies and curved tubular profiles. The curved tubular profiles are similar to those found in Farber disease and it has been suggested that lipoid proteinosis represents not only a disease with impaired production of collagen but also a disease with alterations in ceramide metabolism.

A number of recent publications have described a variety of changes in the dermal collagen content. The reduplicated basement membrane laminae noted ultrastructurally have been shown to be composed of laminin accompanied by collagen types III and IV.[25] This feature, however, is of doubtful significance as similar appearances have been described in a wide variety of conditions including psoriasis, systemic lupus erythematosus and diabetes mellitus.[7] Basement membrane replication most likely represents a non-specific secondary response to a range of stimuli.

Dry weight studies of lipoid proteinosis dermis have shown an apparent decrease in collagen content although there appears to be a relative increase in collagen types III and V compared with collagen type I.[26] Immunofluorescence data, however, suggest that there are reduced absolute levels of both type I and type III collagen.[7] In vitro studies of fibroblast collagen synthesis as determined by radioactive hydroxy-proline synthesis have revealed no significant abnormality.[13] Fibroblasts, however, have reduced replicative capacity. Recent investigations have disclosed reduced fibroblast type I procollagen mRNA and a diminished type I:III procollagen mRNA ratio.[13] Type IV procollagen mRNA levels have been shown to be raised.[27] No DNA abnormalities or chromosomal alternations have yet been identified in lipoid proteinosis.

It is likely that the collagen changes are not directly responsible for the accumulation of the granular hyaline material so characteristic of this disorder. It is, however, likely to be of fibroblast derivation.[28]

References

1. Urbach, E., Wiethe, C. (1929) Lipoidosis cutis et mucosae. *Virchows Arch (Pathol Anat)*, **27**: 286–319.
2. Hoffer, P-A. (1973) Urbach–Wiethe disease (lipoglycoproteinosis; lipoid proteinosis; hyalinosis cutis et mucosae): a review. *Acta Derm Venereol*, **53** (Suppl. 71), 1–52.
3. Caplan, R. (1967) Visceral involvement in lipoid proteinosis. *Arch Dermatol*, **95**, 149–155.
4. Van Rooy, C.H., Swart, J.G., Pietrzak, J.T. (1991) Lipoid proteinosis. A report of four cases. *S Afr Med J*, **79**, 160–162.
5. Touart, D.M., Sau, P. (1998) Cutaneous deposition diseases. Part I. *J Am Acad Dermatol*, **39**, 149–171.
6. Nanda, A., Alsaleh, Q.A., Al-Sabah, H. et al (2001) Lipoid proteinosis: report of four siblings and brief review of the literature. *Pediatr Dermatol*, **18**, 21–26.
7. Newton, J.A., Rasbridge, S., Temple, A. et al (1991) Lipoid proteinosis – new immunopathological observations. *Clin Exp Dermatol*, **16**, 350–354.
8. Heyl, T. (1971) Lipoid proteinosis in South Africa. *Dermatologica*, **142**, 129–132.
9. Rook, A. (1976) Lipoid proteinosis: Urbach–Wiethe disease. *Br J Dermatol*, **94**, 341–342.
10. Findlay, G., Scott, F., Cripps, D. (1966) Porphyria and lipoid proteinosis: a clinical, histological and biochemical comparison of 19 South African cases. *Br J Dermatol*, **78**, 69–80.
11. Hamada, T., McLean, W.H., Ramsay, M. et al (2002) Lipoid proteinosis maps to 1q21 and is caused by mutations in the extracellular matrix protein 1 gene (ECM1). *Hum Mol Genet*, **11**, 833–840.
12. Israel, H. (1992) Gingival lesions in lipoid proteinosis. *J Periodont*, **63**, 561–564.
13. Moy, L.S., Moy, R.L., Matsuoka, L.Y. et al (1987) Lipoid proteinosis: ultrastructural and biochemical studies. *J Am Acad Dermatol*, **16**, 1193–1201.
14. Konstantinov, K., Kabakchiev, P., Karchev, T. et al (1992) Lipoid proteinosis. *J Am Acad Dermatol*, **27**, 293–297.
15. Weidner, W.A., Wenzl, J.E., Swischuk, L.E. (1970) Roentgenographic findings in lipoid proteinosis: a case report. *Am J Roentgenol*, **110**, 457–461.
16. Tranel, D., Hyman, B.T. (1990) Neuropsychological correlates of bilateral amygdala damage. *Arch Neurol*, **47**, 349–355.
17. Newton, F.H., Rosenberg, R.N., Lampert, P.W. et al (1971) Neurologic involvement in Urbach–Wiethe's disease (lipoid proteinosis): a clinical, ultrastructural, and chemical study. *Neurology*, **21**, 1205–1213.
18. Caccano, D., Jaen, A., Telenta, M. et al (1994) Lipoid proteinosis of the small bowel. *Arch Pathol Lab Med*, **118**, 572–574.
19. Hashimoto, K. (1985) Diseases of amyloid, colloid and hyalin. *J Cutan Pathol*, **12**, 322–333.
20. van der Walt, J.J., Heyl, T. (1971) Lipoid proteinosis and erythropoietic protoporphyria. *Arch Dermatol*, **104**, 501–507.
21. Shore, R.N., Howard, B.V., Howard, W.J. et al (1974) Lipoid proteinosis. *Arch Dermatol*, **110**, 591–594.
22. Hausser, I., Biltz, S., Rauterberg, E. et al (1991) Hyalinosis cutis et mucosae (Urbach–Wiethe disease) – ultrastructural and immunological characteristics. *Hautarzt*, **42**, 28–33.
23. Bauer, E.A., Santa-Cruz, D.J., Eisen, A.Z. (1981) Lipoid proteinosis: in vivo and in vitro evidence for a lysosomal storage disease. *J Invest Dermatol*, **76**, 119–125.
24. Navarro, C., Fachal, C., Rodriguez, C. et al (1999) Lipoid proteinosis. A biochemical and ultrastructural investigation of two new cases. *Br J Dermatol*, **141**, 326–331.
25. Fleischmajer, R., Krieg, T., Dziadek, M. et al (1984) Ultrastructure and composition of connective tissue in hyalinosis cutis et mucosae skin. *J Invest Dermatol*, **82**, 252–258.
26. Harper, J.I., Duance, V.C., Sims, T.J. et al (1985) Lipoid proteinosis: an inherited disorder of collagen metabolism. *Br J Dermatol*, **113**, 145–151.
27. Olsen, D.R., Chu, M-L., Uitto, J. (1988) Expression of basement membrane zone genes coding for type IV procollagen and laminin by human skin fibroblasts in vitro: elevated (IV) collagen mRNA levels in lipoid proteinosis. *J Invest Dermatol*, **90**, 734–738.
28. Hashimoto, K., Klingmuller, G., Rodermund, O.E. (1972) Hyalinosis cutis et mucosae. An electron microscopic study. *Acta Derm Venereol*, **52**, 179–195.

Cutaneous macroglobulinosis

Clinical features

Cutaneous macroglobulinosis (IgM storage papules) is a rarely documented manifestation of Waldenström's macroglobulinemia.[1–7] The latter is a chronic lymphoproliferative condition that typically presents in the fifth and sixth decades and shows a slight predilection for males.[5] It is characterized by proliferation of lymphoplasmacytoid cells in the bone marrow, lymph node and spleen and IgM paraproteinemia.[5] Patients present with weakness, fatigue, weight loss, anemia, mucous membrane bleeding, retinal hemorrhages, lymphadenopathy, hepatosplenomegaly, peripheral neuropathy and the hyperviscosity syndrome.[7,8] Skin involvement is very uncommon and includes tumors, plaques and macroglobulinosis cutis. Additional features that may sometimes be encountered are purpura, xanthomata, cryoglobulinemia and Raynaud's phenomenon.[7]

Clinically, macroglobulinosis presents as sometimes pruritic, skin-colored, erythematous or translucent papules measuring up to 1.0 cm in diameter distributed predominantly on extensor sites including knees, elbows, buttocks and the arms and legs.[7] Umbilication, erosion and crusting are commonly seen.[5] Cutaneous tumor deposits present as violaceous nodules and plaques.

Histological features

The papules are characterized by homogeneous eosinophilic material in the papillary and reticular dermis (*Fig. 12.89*).[2] Hair follicles may be encased.[2] The deposits are PAS positive but are Congo red negative (*Fig. 12.90*). A lymphoplasmacytoid infiltrate is variably present.[7] The plasma cells may contain intracytoplasmic IgM-rich vacuoles.[4]

Direct immunofluorescence shows that the deposits stain strongly for IgM.[2,5,7]

Ultrastructurally, the deposits are composed of amorphous or granular and sometimes filamentous material which by immunoelectron microscopy consists of IgM.[1–3,7] The periodicity of amyloid is absent in the filamentous component.[7]

The plaques and tumor nodules are composed of lymphoplasmacytoid infiltrates.

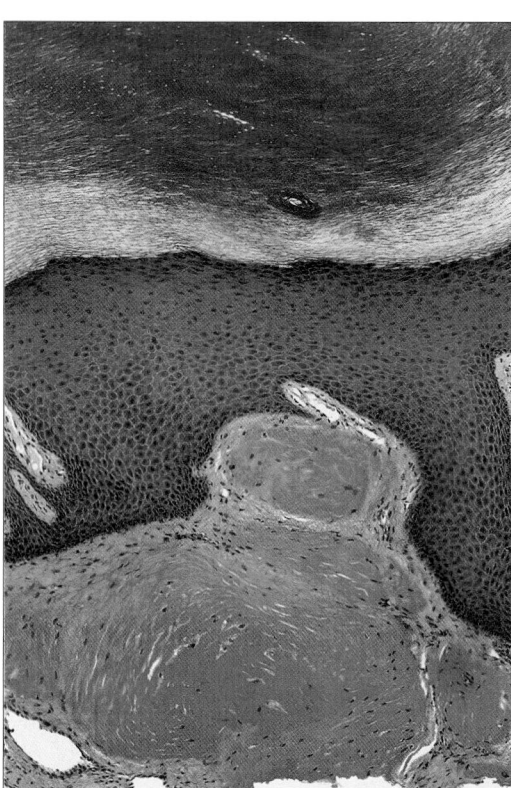

Fig. 12.89
Macroglobulinosis cutis: these are nodular deposits of eosinophilic material in the superficial dermis. By courtesy of A. Wang, MD, Brigham and Women's Hospital, Boston, USA.

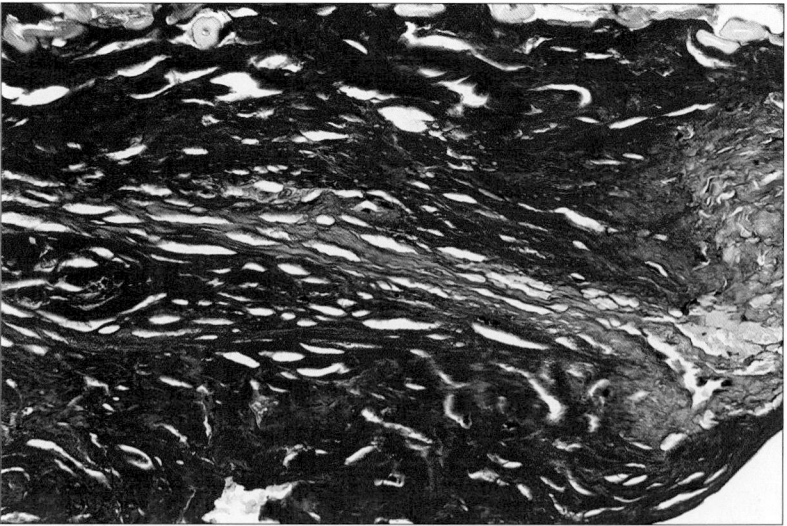

Fig. 12.90
Macroglobulinosis cutis: the material is strongly periodic acid–Schiff positive. By courtesy of A. Wang, MD, Brigham and Women's Hospital, Boston, USA.

References

1. Tichenor, R.E., Rau, J.M., Mantz, F.A. (1978) Macroglobulinemia cutis. *Arch Dermatol*, **114**, 280–281.
2. Hanke, C.W., Steck, W.D., Bergfeld, W.F. et al (1980) Cutaneous macroglobulinosis. *Arch Dermatol*, **116**, 575–577.
3. Mascaro, J.M., Montserrat, E., Estrach, T. et al (1982) Specific cutaneous manifestations of Waldenström's macroglobulinemia. A report of two cases. *Br J Dermatol*, **106**, 217–222.
4. Brookins-Reddix, N., Spivak, J.L., Watson, R.M. (1988) Violaceous plaques on the lower extremities: cutaneous macroglobulinosis. *Arch Dermatol*, **124**, 1851–1856.
5. Lowe, L., Fitzpatrick, J.E., Huff, J.C. et al (1992) Cutaneous macroglobulinosis. A case report with unique ultrastructural findings. *Arch Dermatol*, **128**, 377–380.
6. Ardura, A.E., Porta, J., Gatti, Y.C.F. (1993) Macroglobulinosis cutis. *Arch Argent Dermatol*, **43**, 309–313.
7. Lipsker, D., Cribier, B., Spehner, D. et al (1996) Examination of cutaneous macroglobulinosis by immunoelectron microscopy. *Br J Dermatol*, **135**, 287–291.
8. Mackenzie, R.E., Fudenberg, H.H. (1972) Macroglobulinemia: an analysis of 40 patients. *Blood*, **39**, 874–889.

Porphyria

The porphyrias constitute a heterogeneous group of conditions characterized by the excessive production of porphyrins or their precursors resulting from defects in the activity of the enzymes regulating heme synthesis (*Fig. 12.91*).[1–9] Porphyrin synthesis occurs mainly in the erythropoietic system and the liver. Deficiency of a specific enzyme results in an accumulation of heme precursors due to stimulation of the rate-limiting enzyme aminolevulinic acid synthetase as a consequence of diminished heme concentration.[10]

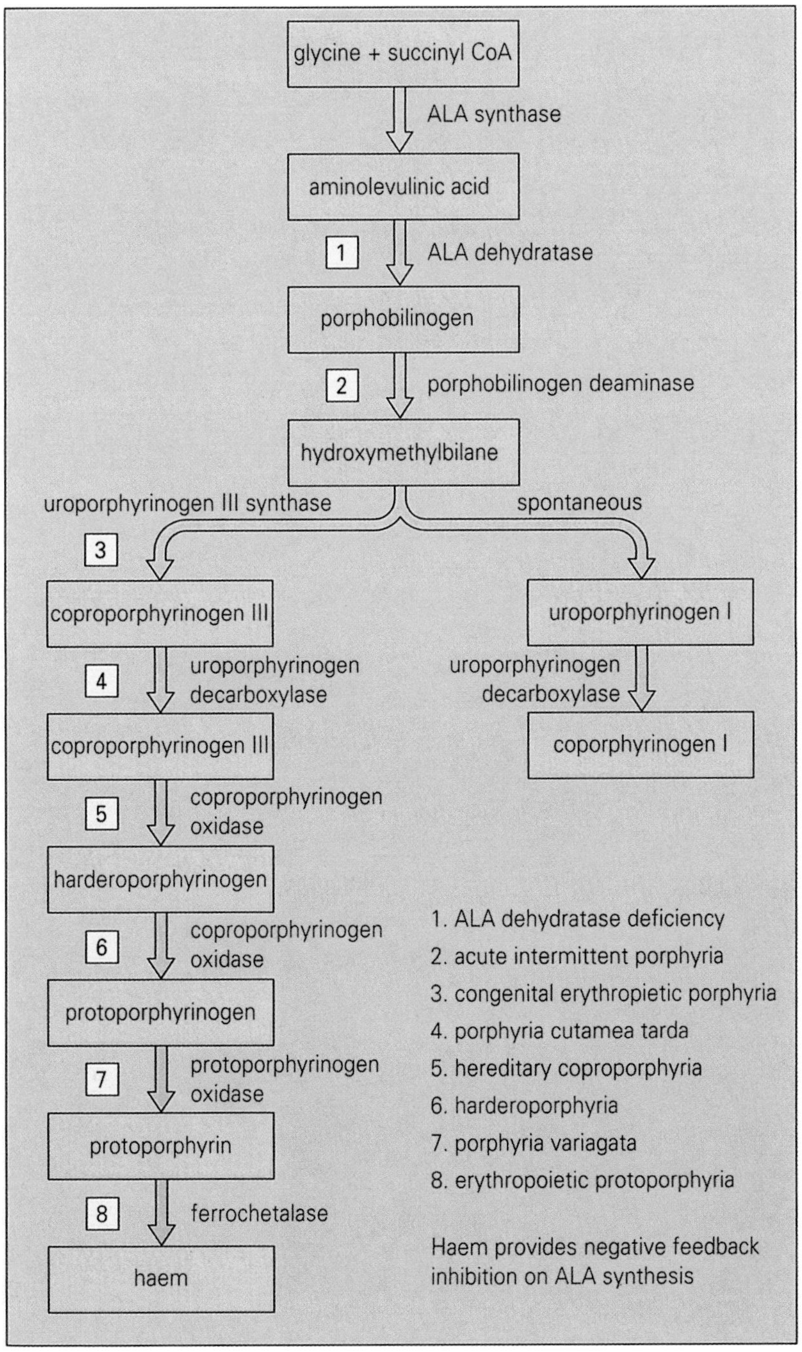

Genetic mutations account for the enzyme deficiencies seen in the various types of porphyria. These mutations have all been delineated at a molecular level, are very heterogeneous and often result in enzyme deficiencies that may remain silent throughout life.[10] If a patient is homozygous for a specific mutation, however, symptoms usually develop even in early life.

Patients may present with acute porphyria (abdominal pain with neurological and/or psychiatric symptoms) often induced by drugs, fasting, alcohol or sex hormones.[11–14] The enzyme defect leads to the accumulation in the skin of a photosensitizing porphyrin, which absorbs light predominantly in the 400–410 nm range. The energy absorbed may then be released to adjacent nucleic acids or proteins, either directly or indirectly by involving acceptor molecules such as oxygen, and toxic changes causing damage to lysosomal and cellular membranes result.[13,14] There is also some evidence to suggest that activation of the complement cascade may be involved in the phototoxic reaction mechanism.[13,14] The cutaneous manifestations in acute attacks consist of prominent erythema in sun-exposed areas with a burning sensation. Subacute or chronic skin involvement consists of skin fragility, blister formation and progressive scarring. Exceptional cases of a photosensitive bullous eruption associated with transient elevation of porphyrin levels have been described in neonates during phototherapy for treatment of hyperbilirubinemia due to hemolytic disease.[15,16]

Porphyria is primarily classified into erythropoietic and hepatic types depending upon which tissue is predominantly affected. The erythropoietic porphyrias (congenital erythropoietic porphyria and erythropoietic protoporphyria) are characterized by altered heme synthesis mainly in the bone marrow. In the hepatic porphyrias the altered synthesis mainly occurs in the liver (porphyria cutanea tarda, hepatoerythropoeitic porphyria, acute intermittent porphyria, aminolevulinic acid (ALA) dehydratase deficiency, variegate porphyria and hereditary coproporphyria). Of the eight major types of porphyria, six are associated with cutaneous disease (*Table 12.4*). The clinical and biochemical findings are very different in these six types of porphyria, although the cutaneous histology is similar in all.[17–20] Type II porphyria cutanea tarda, hereditary coproporphyria, variegate porphyria and erythropoietic protoporphyria are all inherited as autosomal dominants with incomplete penetrance. Less than 20% of affected individuals display symptoms and patients often deny a family history.[2]

Fig. 12.91
Biochemistry of porphyria. Reproduced with permission from Young, J.W., and Conte, E.T. (1991) *International Journal of Dermatology*, **30**, 399–406.

Within the figure:

glycine + succinyl CoA
↓ ALA synthase
aminolevulinic acid
1 ↓ ALA dehydratase
porphobilinogen
2 ↓ porphobilinogen deaminase
hydroxymethylbilane
uroporphyrinogen III synthase / spontaneous
3 ↓ coproporphyrinogen III — uroporphyrinogen I
4 ↓ uroporphyrinogen decarboxylase — uroporphyrinogen decarboxylase
coproporphyrinogen III — coporphyrinogen I
5 ↓ coproporphyrinogen oxidase
harderoporphyrinogen
6 ↓ coproporphyrinogen oxidase
protoporphyrinogen
7 ↓ protoporphyrinogen oxidase
protoporphyrin
8 ↓ ferrochetalase
haem

1. ALA dehydratase deficiency
2. acute intermittent porphyria
3. congenital erythropietic porphyria
4. porphyria cutamea tarda
5. hereditary coproporphyria
6. harderoporphyria
7. porphyria variagata
8. erythropoietic protoporphyria

Haem provides negative feedback inhibition on ALA synthesis

References

1. Young, J.W., Conte, E.T. (1991) Porphyria and porphyrins. *Int J Dermatol*, **30**, 399–406.
2. Elder, G.H. (1990) The cutaneous porphyrias. *Semin Dermatol*, **9**, 63–69.
3. Paslin, D.A. (1992) The porphyrias. *Int J Dermatol*, **31**, 527–539.
4. Meola, T., Lim, H.W. (1993) The porphyrias. *Dermatol Clin*, **11**, 583–596.
5. Murphy, G. (1999) The cutaneous porphyrias: a review. The British Photodermatology Group. *Br J Dermatol*, **140**, 573–581.
6. Bonkovsky, H.L., Barnard, G.F. (2000) The porphyrias. *Curr Treat Options Gastroenterol*, **3**, 487–500.
7. Gross, U., Hoffmann, G.F., Doss, M.O. (2000) Erythropoietic and hepatic porphyrias. *J Inherit Metab Dis*, **23**, 641–661.
8. Harber, L.C., Poh-Fitzpatrick, M., Walther, R.R. et al (1982) Cutaneous aspects of the porphyrias. *Acta Derm Venereol*, **100** (Suppl.), 9–15.
9. Werman, H.A. (1989) The porphyrias. *Emerg Med Clin North Am*, **7**, 927–942.

Table 12.4
Classification of porphyria

Condition	Mode of inheritance	Enzyme defect	Site of metabolic expression	Laboratory abnormality
Non-acute porphyrias producing cutaneous lesions				
Congenital erythropoietic porphyria	Autosomal recessive	URO-S	Erythroid cells	Elevated uroporphyrin Coproporphyrin in urine and feces
Porphyria cutanea tarda				
inherited	Autosomal dominant	URO-D	Hepatocytes	Urinary uroporphyrin:coproporphyrin = 3:1
sporadic	Acquired/sporadic	URO-D		Elevated urinary uroporphyrin
toxic	Acquired			Urinary and stool isocoproporphyrins
Erythropoietic protoporphyria	Autosomal dominant	Ferrochetalase	Erythroid cells and hepatocyte	Normal urine Elevated plasma, RBC and stool protoporphyrin Elevated fecal and RBC coproporphyrin
Hepatoerythropoietic porphyria	Autosomal recessive	URO-D (severe)	Erythroid cells and hepatocyte	Increased urine and stool URO Elevated stool coproporphyrin and isocoproporphyrin Elevated RBC protoporphyrin
Acute porphyrias (porphyrias producing abdominal, neurological and psychiatric symptoms)				
Acute intermittnt porphyria	Autosomal dominant	Porphobilinogen deaminase	Hepatocyte	Stool and blood usually normal Elevated urinary ALA and PBG
ALA dehydratase deficiency	Autosomal recessive	ALA dehydratase (porphobilinogen synthase)	?	ALA alone elevated
Prophyrias producing abdominal, neurological, psychiatric and cutaneous manifestations				
Variegate porphyria	Autosomal dominant	Protoporphyrinogen oxidase	Hepatocyte	Urine normal between attacks Increased stool protoporphyrins and coproporphyrin Increased urinary ALA and PBG during attacks
Hereditary coproporphyria	Autosomal dominant	Coproporphyrinogen oxidase	Hepatocyte	Increased stool and urine coproporphyrins

ALA, aminolevulinic acid; PBG, porphobilinogen; RBC, red blood cell; URO, uroporphyrinogen. Reproduced with permission from Young, J.W., Conte, E.T. (1991) *International Journal of Dermatology*, **30**, 399–406.

10. Sassa, S., Kappas, A. (2000) Molecular aspects of the inherited porphyrias. *J Intern Med*, **247**, 169–178.
11. Targovnik, S.E., Targovnik, J.H. (1986) Cutaneous drug reactions in porphyrias. *Clin Dermatol*, **4**, 110–117.
12. Tefferi, A., Colgan, J.P., Solberg, L.A. Jr (1994) Acute porphyrias: diagnosis and management. *Mayo Clin Proc*, **69**, 991–995.
13. Poh-Fitzpatrick, M.B. (1985) Porphyrin-sensitized cutaneous photosensitivty. Pathogenesis and treatment. *Clin Dermatol*, **3**, 41–82.
14. Poh-Fitzpatrick, M.B. (1982) Pathogenesis and treatment of photocutaneous manifestations of the porphyrias. *Semin Liver Dis*, **2**, 164–176.
15. Mallon, E., Wojnarowska, F., Hope, P. et al (1995) Neonatal bullous eruption as a result of transient porphyrinemia in a premature infant with hemolytic disease of the newborn. *J Am Acad Dermatol*, **33**, 333–336.
16. Crawford, R.I., Lawlor, E.R., Wadsworth, L.D., Prendiville, J.S. (1996) Transient erythroporphyria of infancy. *J Am Acad Dermatol*, **35**, 833–834.
17. Epstein, J.H., Tuffanelli, D.L., Epstein, W.L. (1973) Cutaneous changes in the porphyrias. *Arch Dermatol*, **107**, 689–698.
18. Corey, T.J., DeLeo, V.A., Christianson, H. et al (1980) Variegate porphyria: clinical and laboratory features. *J Am Acad Dermatol*, **2**, 36–43.
19. Wolff, K., Hönigsmann, H., Rauschmeier, W. et al (1982) Microscopic and fine structural aspects of porphyrias. *Acta Derm Venereol*, **100** (Suppl.), 17–28.
20. Maynard, B., Peters, M.S. (1992) Histologic and immunofluorescence study of cutaneous porphyrias. *J Cutan Pathol*, **19**, 40–47.

Congenital erythropoietic porphyria

Clinical features

Congenital erythropoietic porphyria (Gunther's disease) is the most severe and mutilating of the erythropoietic porphyrias. It is inherited as an autosomal recessive and develops as a consequence of deficiency of the fourth enzyme of the heme pathway (uroporphyrinogen III synthase) resulting in excessive production of uroporphyrin I isomers, which give the urine a pink–burgundy color.[1–3] Patients with the more severe form of the disease may present with fetal hydrops.[4] The diapers of affected children usually show a characteristic pink stain. Uroporphyrin I accumulates in the bone marrow, peripheral blood and other organs. It has been demonstrated that there is a clear correlation between the degree of porphyrin excess and disease severity.[5] There is increased

production of uroporphyrins and coproporphyrins in the urine and coproporphyrins in the feces.

Affected patients develop intense photosensitivity to sunlight as well as to fluorescent light, typically in infancy (*Fig. 12.92*). Vesicles and bullae are supervened by a mutilating scarring process on the face and hands, where autoamputation may occur (*Figs 12.93, 12.94*). Sclerodermoid change is sometimes seen.[6] Coarse hair may be found on

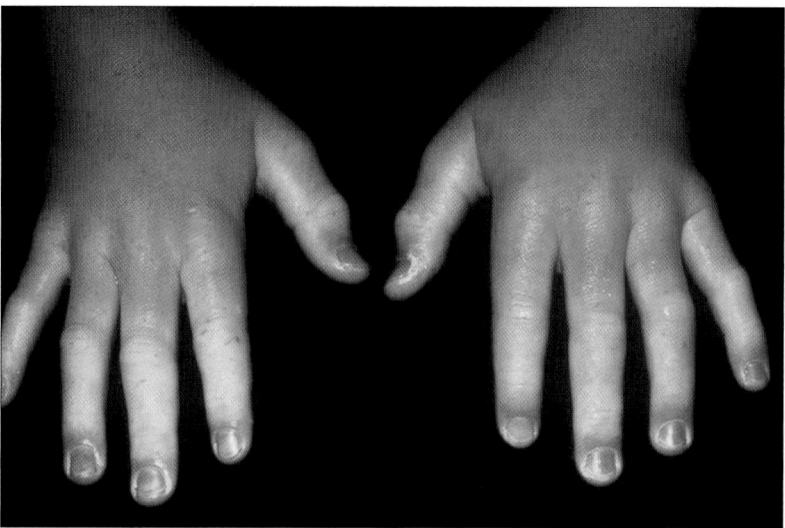

Fig. 12.92
Congenital erythropoietic porphyria (Gunther's disease): this variant is associated with severe photosensitivity. There is marked erythema and edema of the backs of the hands and fingers. Scarring frequently supervenes. By courtesy of G. Murphy, MD, Beaumont Hospital, Dublin, Eire.

the face and lanugo hair develops on the limbs. Pigmentary changes are sometimes evident. In addition, patients may develop cicatricial alopecia of the scalp, nail changes, conjunctivitis, ectropion, keratoconjunctivitis, symblepharon, blepharitis, or brown staining of the teeth.[1,7–9] The teeth characteristically fluoresce intense orange–red with Wood's light (400 nm). The sclera also demonstrates pink fluorescence under Wood's light.[9]

Hemolytic anemia and splenomegaly occur in a large proportion of the patients and hypersplenism is sometimes a feature. Patients with congenital erythropoietic porphyria have an increased risk of bone

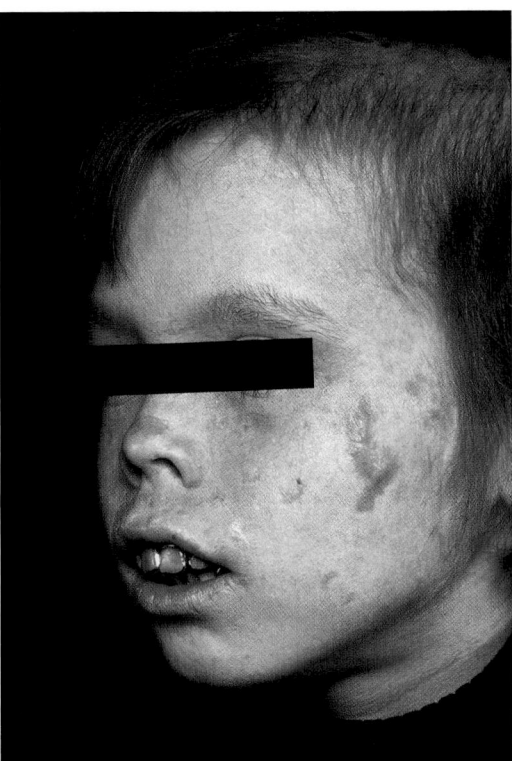

Fig. 12.93
Congenital erythropoietic porphyria (Gunther's disease): in this severely affected patient there is marked hyperpigmented scarring on the cheeks, nose and around the mouth. The brownish discoloration of the teeth is characteristic. By courtesy of G. Murphy, MD, Beaumont Hospital, Dublin, Eire.

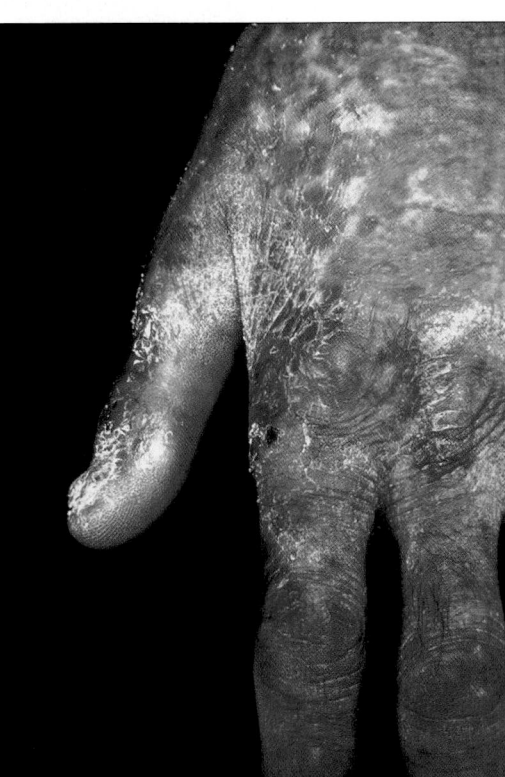

Fig. 12.94
Congenital erythropoietic porphyria (Gunther's disease): adult patient showing very severe photodamage. By courtesy of the Institute of Dermatology, London, UK.

fragility with resultant fractures and developmental defects.[2] Acroosteolysis, soft tissue calcifications and widening of the diploic space have also been documented.[10] Early death may result, often in the third decade. Rare cases are associated with the nephrotic syndrome, probably secondary to renal siderosis.[11] A delayed late-onset variant has rarely been described.[12–14] Some of these patients present with thrombocytopenia and others with myelodysplasia.[13,14]

The URO-synthase gene has been mapped to chromosome 10q25.3–q26.3.[15] The molecular defects in this disease are very heterogeneous and up to 18 mutations in the URO-synthase gene have already been described.[16–19] These include single base substitutions, insertions and deletions and splicing defects. By far the most common mutation is C73R, which has been found in up to 40% of patients with the disease. Two other relatively common mutations include L4F and T228M, seen in 8 and 7% of patients respectively.[17] Prenatal diagnosis of the disease is possible not only by measurement of uroporphyrin I levels in amniotic fluid but also by DNA mutation analysis.[20]

References

1. Young, J.W., Chonte, E.T. (1991) Porphyria and porphyrins. *Int J Dermatol*, **30**, 399–406.
2. Werman, H.A. (1989) The porphyrias. *Emerg Med Clin North Am*, 7, 927–942.
3. Jensen, J.D., Resnick, S.D. (1995) Porphyria in childhood. *Semin Dermatol*, **14**, 33–39.
4. Linhardt, A., Aubard, Y., Laroche, C. et al (1999) A rare cause of fetal ascites: a case report of Gunther's disease. *Fetal Diagn Ther*, 14, 378.
5. Freesemann, A.G., Bhutani, L.K., Jacob, K. et al (1997) Interdependence between degree of porphyrin excess and disease severity in congenital erythropoietic porphyria (Gunther's disease). *Arch Dermatol Res*, **289**, 272–276.
6. Murphy, G.M., Hawk, J.L.M., Nicholson, D.C. et al (1987) Congenital erythropoietic porphyria (Gunther's disease). *Clin Exp Dermatol*, 12, 61–65.
7. Kurihara, K., Takamura, N., Imaizumi, S. et al (2001) Ocular involvement caused by the accumulation of porphyrins in a patient with congenital erythropoietic porphyria. *Br J Ophthalmol*, **85**, 1265–1266.
8. Tanigawa, K., Takamura, N., Nakata, K. et al (1996) Ocular complication in congenital erythropoietic porphyria. *Ophthalmologica*, 21, 183–185.
9. Oguz, F., Sidal, M., Bayram, C. et al (1993) Ocular involvement in two symptomatic congenital erythropoietic porphyria. *Eur J Pediatr*, **152**, 671–673.
10. Laorr, A., Greenspan, A. (1994) Severe osteopenia in congenital erythropoietic porphyria. *Can Assoc Radiol*, **45**, 307–309.
11. Lange, B., Hofweber, K., Waldherr, R., Scharer, K. (1995) Congenital erythropoietic porphyria associated with nephrotic syndrome and renal siderosis. *Acta Paediatr*, **84**, 1325–1328.
12. Horiguchi, Y., Horio, T., Yamamoto, M. et al (1989) Late-onset erythropoietic porphyria. *Br J Dermatol*, **121**, 255–262.
13. Kontos, A., Ozog, D., Lim, H.W. (2002) Late onset congenital erythropoietic porphyria (Gunther's disease). *Photodermatol Photoimmunol Photomed*, **18**, 105.
14. Murphy, A., Gibson, G., Elder, G.H. et al (1995) Adult-onset congenital erythropoietic porphyria (Gunther's disease) presenting with thrombocytopenia. *J R Soc Med*, **88**, 357P–358P.
15. Warner, C.A., Poh-Fitzpatrick, M.B., Zaider, E.F. et al (1992) Congenital erythropoietic porphyria. *Arch Dermatol*, **128**, 1243–1248.
16. Fontanellas, A., Bensidhoum, M., Enriquez de Salamanca, R. et al (1996) A systematic analysis of the mutations of the uroporphyrinogen III synthase gene in congenital erythropoietic porphyria. *Eur J Hum Genet*, **4**, 274–282.
17. Desnick, R.J., Glass, I.A., Xu, W. et al (1998) Molecular genetics of congenital erythropoietic porphyria. *Semin Liver Dis*, **18**, 77–84.
18. Tanigawa, K., Bensidhoum, M., Takamura, N. et al (1996) A novel point mutation in congenital erythropoietic porphyria in two members of Japanese family. *Hum Genet*, **97**, 557–560.
19. Xu, W., Warner, C.A., Desnick, R.J. (1995) Congenital erythropoietic porphyria: identification expression of 10 mutations in the uroporphyrinogen III synthase gene. *J Clin Invest*, **95**, 905–912.
20. Ged, C., Moreau-Gaudry, F., Taine, L. et al (1996) Prenatal diagnosis in congenital erythropoietic porphyria by metabolic measurement and DNA mutation analysis. *Prenat Diagn*, **16**, 83–86.

Erythropoietic protoporphyria

Clinical features

Although this condition was not recognized until 1961, it is now known to be the second commonest type of porphyria. It results from increased production of protoporphyrin due to diminished ferrochelatase (heme synthase) activity.[1,2] Ferrochelatase is the enzyme responsible for the combination between protoporphyrin IX and iron to form heme. Urinary porphyrins are normal because protoporphyrins are insoluble in water. Protoporphyrin is elevated in plasma, erythrocytes and occasionally in the feces.[1] Coproporphyrins may be found in erythrocytes and feces. The mode of inheritance is predominantly autosomal dominant with incomplete penetrance but an autosomal recessive inheritance has also rarely been reported.[3] The gene for ferrochelatase has been mapped to the long arm of chromosome 8.[4]

The variable clinical manifestations of this disease are probably the result of heterogeneity of the ferrochelatase gene defects.[5] Acute photosensitivity usually presents in early childhood.[6] A painful burning erythema with edema occurs immediately after exposure to sunlight.[7] Vesicles are uncommon, but a scaly, erythematous reaction may be seen, leading to circular or linear depressed scars on the face (particularly on the bridge of the nose and around the mouth) and over the knuckles (*Figs 12.95–12.99*).[1] Purpura and urticaria are sometimes seen. There may also be a wax-like thickening of the skin, particularly of the dorsum of the hands and, more rarely, the face (*Fig. 12.100*).[1] Bulla and milia have been documented exceptionally.[2] A further case presented with pseudoainhum.[8] An association with lupus erythematosus is very rare.[9]

In the majority of cases the disease is limited to the skin, but some affected patients develop protoporphyrin-rich gallstones, and 5–10% of patients develop liver disease, which may progress to liver failure in less than 5% of patients and rarely to cirrhosis.[4,10,11] Patients that develop liver failure have a different form of the disease with an autosomal recessive form of transmission.[12] Neurological manifestations are not common. Anemia is rare and if present is very mild.

Recently a late-onset variant has been described.[13] Exacerbation of the disease by blood transfusion and by iron ingestion has been described.[14,15]

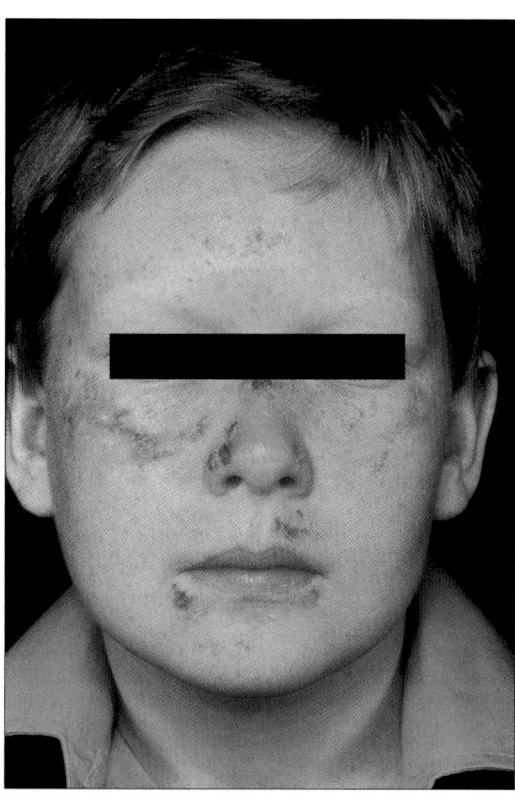

Fig. 12.95
Erythropoietic protoporphyria: crusted lesions are present on the cheeks, nose and around the mouth. By courtesy of G. Murphy, MD, Beaumont Hospital, Dublin, Eire.

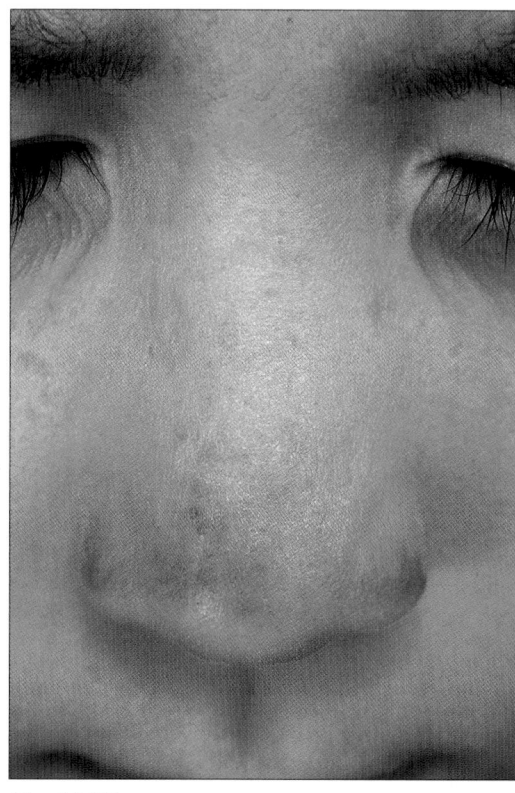

Fig. 12.97
Erythropoietic protoporphyria: there are characteristic, depressed, small linear scars on the bridge and sides of this patient's nose. By courtesy of the Institute of Dermatology, London, UK.

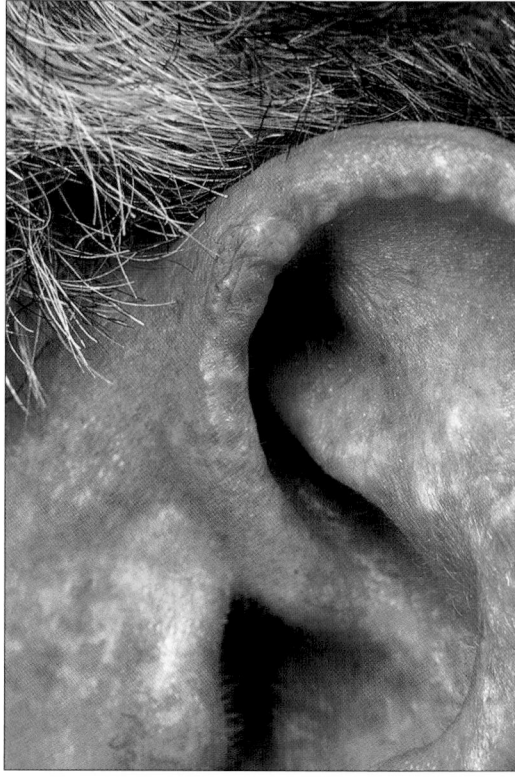

Fig. 12.98
Erythropoietic protoporphyria: there is very severe actinic damage. By courtesy of the Institute of Dermatology, London, UK.

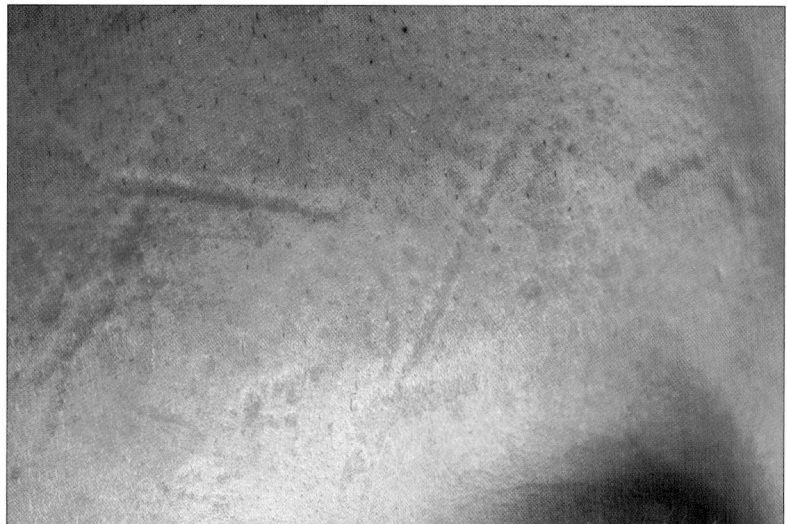

Fig. 12.96
Erythropoietic protoporphyria: there is marked scarring. Note the depressed linear lesions. By courtesy of G. Murphy, MD, Beaumont Hospital, Dublin, Eire.

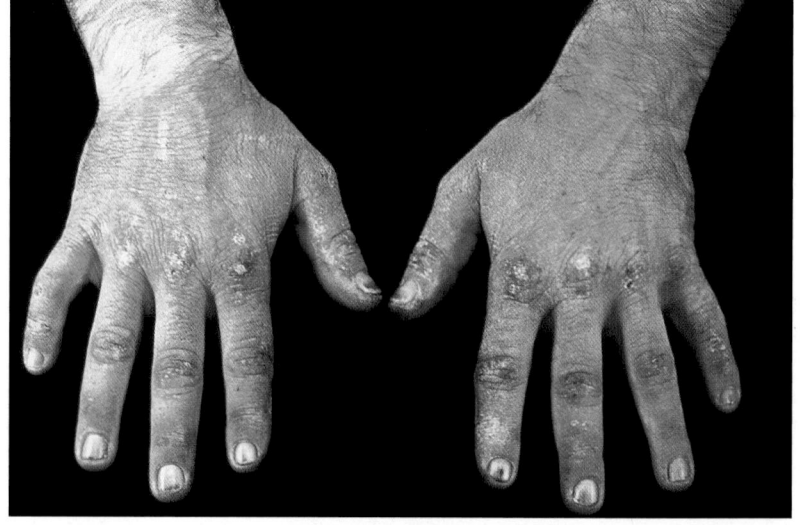

Fig. 12.99
Erythropoietic protoporphyria: note the characteristic scaly scars over the knuckles. By courtesy of the Institute of Dermatology, London, UK.

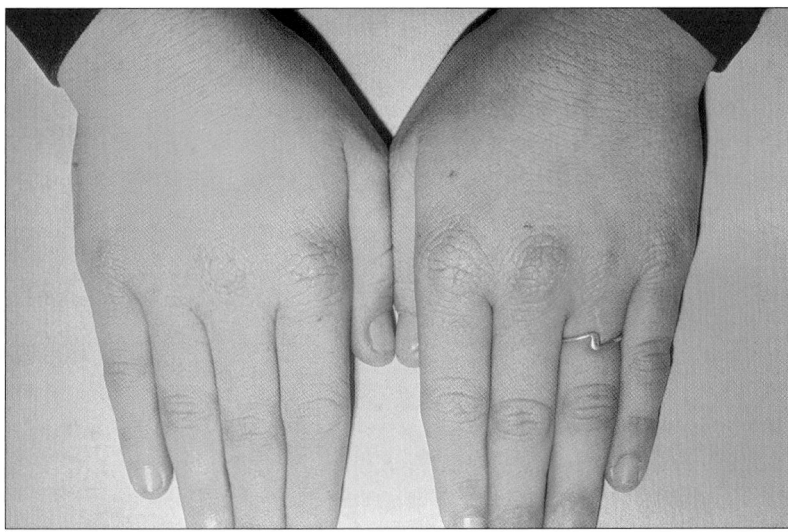

Fig. 12.100
Erythropoietic protoporphyria: there is characteristic waxy thickening of the skin of the hands. By courtesy of G. Murphy, MD, Beaumont Hospital, Dublin, Eire.

References

1. Elder, G.H. (1990) The cutaneous porphyrias. *Semin Dermatol*, **9**, 63–69.
2. Schmidt, H., Snitker, G., Thomsen, K., Lintrup, J. (1974) Erythropoietic protoporphyria. A clinical study based on 29 cases in 14 families. *Arch Dermatol*, **110**, 58–64.
3. Norris, P.G., Nunn, A.V., Hawk, J.L.M. et al (1990) Genetic heterogeneity in erythropoietic protoporphyria: a study of the enzymatic defect in nine affected families. *J Invest Dermatol*, **95**, 260–263.
4. Todd, D.J. (1994) Erythropoietic protoporphyria. *Br J Dermatol*, **131**, 751–766.
5. DeLeo, V.A., Poh-Fitzpatrick, M.B., Matthews-Roth, M.M. et al (1976) Erythropoietic protoporphyria: ten years experience. *Am J Med*, **60**, 8–22.
6. Wang, X., Poh-Fitzpatrick, M.B., Piomelli, S. (1994) A novel splicing mutation in the ferrochelatase gene responsible for erythropoietic protoporphyria. *Biochim Biophys Acta*, **1227**, 25–27.
7. Baart de la Faille, H., Bijlmer-Lest, J.C., Van Hattum, J. et al (1991) Erythropoietic protoporphyria: clinical aspects with emphasis on the skin. *Curr Prob Dermatol*, **20**, 123–134.
8. Christopher, A.P., Grattan, C.E.H., Cowan, M.A. (1988) Pseudoainhum and erythropoietic protoporphyria. *Br J Dermatol*, **118**, 113–116.
9. Mutasin, D.F., Pelc, N.J. (1994) Erythropoietic protoporphyria and lupus erythematosus: case report and review of the literature. *Arch Dermatol*, **130**, 1330–1332.
10. Young, J.W., Conte, E.T. (1991) Porphyria and porphyrins. *Int J Dermatol*, **30**, 399–406.
11. Meerman, L. (2000) Erythropoietic protoporphyria. An overview with emphasis on the liver. *Scan J Gastroenterol*, **232** (Suppl.), 79–85.
12. Sarkany, R.P. (1999) Porphyria. From Sir Walter Raleigh to molecular biology. *Adv Exp Med Biol*, **455**, 235–241.
13. Murphy, G.M., Hawk, J.L.M., Magnus, I.A. (1985) Late-onset erythropoietic protoporphyria with unusual clinical features. *Arch Dermatol*, **121**, 1309–1312.
14. Todd, D.J., Callender, M.E., Mayne, E.E. et al (1990) Erythropoietic protoporphyria, transfusion therapy and liver disease. *Br J Dermatol*, **127**, 534–537.
15. Milligan, A., Graham-Brown, R.A.C., Sarkany, I. et al (1988) Erythropoietic protoporphyria exacerbated by oral iron therapy. *Br J Dermatol*, **119**, 63–66.

Hereditary coproporphyria

Clinical features

This very rare autosomal dominant form of porphyria develops as a result of a deficiency of coproporphyrinogen oxidase.[1,2] This enzyme catalyzes the sixth step in the heme biosynthetic pathway. A number of different mutations have been documented.[3] Heterozygous patients often do not manifest symptoms of the disease.[4] In those in whom symptoms arise, these usually appear after puberty. Affected patients develop intermittent attacks of abdominal pain in association with neurological and psychiatric manifestations. About 30% of cases develop photosensitivity, usually at the time of the acute attacks. The cutaneous changes are similar to those described for porphyria cutanea tarda. The disease may be precipitated by pregnancy, the contraceptive pill and the anabolic steroid methandrostenolone.[5–7] Diagnosis is confirmed by the presence of increased excretion of coproporphyrinogen III in urine and feces. Porphobilinogen and aminolevulinic acid are increased during the episodic attacks.

Harderoporphyria is regarded as a variant form of hereditary coproporphyria in which hematological alterations predominate.[2,8] Patients present with jaundice, severe chronic hemolytic anemia starting in the neonatal period, hepatosplenomegaly and photosensitivity. Neuropsychiatric symptoms or abdominal pain are not seen. These patients usually have a specific mutation (K404E) on one or both alleles of the coproporphyrinogen gene.[9]

References

1. Topi, G.C., D'Alessandro Gandolfo, L., Fazio, M. et al (1977) Coproporphyrie erythropoietique congenitales observée chez un frère et une soeur. *Ann Dermatol Venereol*, **104**, 68–70.
2. Elder, G.H., Evans, G.O., Thomas, N. et al (1976) The primary enzyme defect in hereditary coproporphyria. *Lancet*, **2**, 1217–1219.
3. Wiman, A., Floderus, Y., Harper, P. (2002) Two novel mutations and coexistence of the 991C.T and the 1339C.T mutation on a single allele in the coproporphyrinogen oxidase gene in Swedish patients with hereditary coproporphyria. *Hum Genet*, **47**, 407–412.
4. Gross, U., Puy, H., Kuhnel, A. et al (2002) Molecular, immunological, enzymatic and biochemical studies of coproporphyrinogen oxidase deficiency in a family with hereditary coproporphyria. *Cell Mol Biol (Noisy-le-grand)*, **48**, 49–55.
5. Hunter, J.A.A., Khan, S.A., Hope, E. et al (1971) Hereditary coproporphyria. Photosensitivity, jaundice and neuropsychiatric manifestations associated with pregnancy. *Br J Dermatol*, **84**, 301–310.
6. Roberts, D.T., Brodie, M.J., Moore, M.R. et al (1977) Hereditary coproporphyria presenting with photosensitivity induced by the contraceptive pill. *Br J Dermatol*, **96**, 549–554.
7. Lane, P.R., Massey, K.L., Worobetz, L.J. et al (1994) Acute hereditary coproporphyria induced by the androgenic/anabolic steroid methandrostenolone (Dianabol). *J Am Acad Dermatol*, **30**, 308–312.
8. Lamoril, J., Puy, H., Whatley, S.D. et al (2001) Characterization of mutations in the CPO gene in British patients demonstrates absence of genotype–phenotype correlation and identifies relationship between hereditary coproporphyria and harderoporphyria. *Am J Hum Genet*, **68**, 1130–1138.
9. Lamoril, J., Puy, H., Gouya, L. et al (1998) Neonatal hemolytic anemia due to inherited harderoporphyria: clinical characteristics and molecular basis. *Blood*, **91**, 1453–1457.

Porphyria cutanea tarda

Clinical features

This is the commonest type of porphyria and usually manifests in middle age.[1,2] It shows a marked male predominance.[3] The highest incidence is found in the South African Bantu.[3] Cases are also often seen in Europe and North America.

There are two main forms of porphyria cutanea tarda: familial and sporadic.[1] Both variants have in common a reduced activity of uroporphyrinogen decarboxylase (URO-D), which catalyzes the decarboxylation of uroporphyrinogen to coproporphyrinogen. In the familial variant there is decreased URO-D activity in erythrocytes and most other tissues while in the sporadic form there is decreased URO-D activity restricted to the liver.[4,5] In rare familial cases, normal URO-D activity has been reported in erythrocytes.[6]

The rare familial form exhibits an autosomal dominant inheritance. The onset tends to be earlier than that of the sporadic form and the exceptional cases occurring in childhood are usually familial. The disease is related to many different mutations in the URO-D gene.[7] There is no clear correlation between disease severity and the type of mutation.[8] Porphyria cutanea tarda may be precipitated by many exogenous factors including alcohol abuse, iron overload, childbirth and sun exposure. Pregnancy may exacerbate the symptoms of the disease during the first trimester.[9] Multiple factors often contribute to precipitate the disease in a given patient.[10] Rare cases of familial porphyria cutanea tarda present with constrictive pericarditis.[11]

The second much more common form is sporadic or acquired. Up to 80% of patients with porphyria cutanea tarda have the sporadic form of the disease. It has been demonstrated that sporadic porphyria cutanea tarda is a multifactorial disorder involving a combination of genetic and environmental factors. Recent studies have demonstrated that the hemochromatosis gene mutations C282Y and H63D represent a susceptibility factor in Western European and Australian patients affected by this form of the disease.[12–15] These mutations probably induce the disease through iron overload. It has also been suggested that the IVS4+198 T allele in the human transferrin receptor-1 may play an independent role in the development of the disease.[12] However, this has not been substantiated in other studies.[15] Coinheritance of mutations in the uroporphyrinogen decarboxylase and in the hemochromatosis genes appears to accelerate the onset of porphyria cutanea tarda.[16] Sporadic cases mainly occur in patients exposed to a variety of hepatotoxic chemicals, such as ethanol, estrogens, griseofulvin, vitamin B12, sulphonamides, tamoxifen, pravastatin, barbiturates, hydantoins and chlorinated hydrocarbons; for example, an epidemic form occurred in Turkey due to exposure to the fungicide hexachlorobenzene.[17–21] Rare associations include diabetes mellitus, Wilson's disease, myelofibrosis, the CREST syndrome and hepatocellular carcinoma.[22–25]

Increased hepatic iron stores are a major predisposing factor.[5,26] The mechanism by which this happens is not well understood. Iron catalyzes the formation of reactive oxygen species and this may enhance uroporphyrin formation by increasing the rate at which uroporphyrinogen is oxidized to uroporphyrin leading to the manifestations of the disease. A second possible proposed mechanism considers the indirect inhibition of uroporphyrinogen decarboxylase by iron. Whatever the mechanism, the iron overload has important therapeutic implications as venesection can induce a remission.

Hepatitis C virus infection is often associated with porphyria cutanea tarda.[27,28] A frequent association is also the acquired immunodeficiency syndrome (AIDS).[29–34] AIDS patients with porphyria cutanea tarda are often hepatitis C virus-positive.[35] Patients who have had both acquired and familial variants have developed the typical features of increased skin fragility, blistering, hyperpigmentation and hypertrichosis, but scarring and milia have rarely been evident.[36] Often the development of porphyria has preceded the diagnosis of HIV infection.[36] In many instances this has been related to excessive alcohol consumption and/or infectious hepatitis, particularly hepatitis C.[33,37] The association has been reported too often to be merely fortuitous and liver damage seems to be the common denominator. The causal agent (be it hepatitis C virus or HIV) seems to have a direct effect upon hepatocyte porphyrin metabolism. It has been demonstrated that elevated serum porphyrin levels occur in early stage HIV infection and hepatitis C infection.[38] Porphyria cutanea tarda has also been described in association with non-alcoholic liver disease, chronic hemodialysis, non-insulin dependent diabetes mellitus and systemic lupus erythematosus (SLE).[1,39] A recent autoantibody study in a large series of patients with SLE suggests that the association is fortuitous.[40] The association with hematological malignancies including leukemia and lymphoma is usually related to the treatment, particularly repeated blood transfusions.[41,42]

Typically, blisters occur on light-exposed skin and are traumatic or actinically induced (*Figs 12.101–12.103*).[3] Cutaneous fragility is usually marked. The blisters are slow to heal and leave superficial atrophic scars

with milia. Although they are most often seen on the backs of the hands, they may also be found on the palms, face, scalp, forearms, trunk and under the finger nails.[3] Hypertrichosis and premature aging with chronic actinic damage are usual and sclerodermatous changes may be marked (*Fig. 12.104*). The hypertrichosis is characterized by long dark lanugo hair developing about the cheeks and temples, the eyebrows, ears and arms (*Fig. 12.105*).[3] The sclerodermatous features, which are more common in females, are found on both light-exposed and unexposed skin. Sites that are particularly affected include the face, neck, scalp, chest and backs of hands, and often there is hyper- or hypopigmentation or both.[3,43] Hyperpigmentation, if present, may be diffuse, reticulate or spotty. Preauricular calcification is a common complication. The dermal fibrosis appears to be related particularly to high uroporphyrin levels.[43] Uroporphyrin has been shown to stimulate fibroblast collagen synthesis independent of ultraviolet light.[44]

Uncommon cutaneous manifestations of porphyria cutanea tarda include alopecia affecting the frontoparietal, temporal and occipital regions of the scalp, and centrofacial papular lymphangiectasis.[45,46] Hair

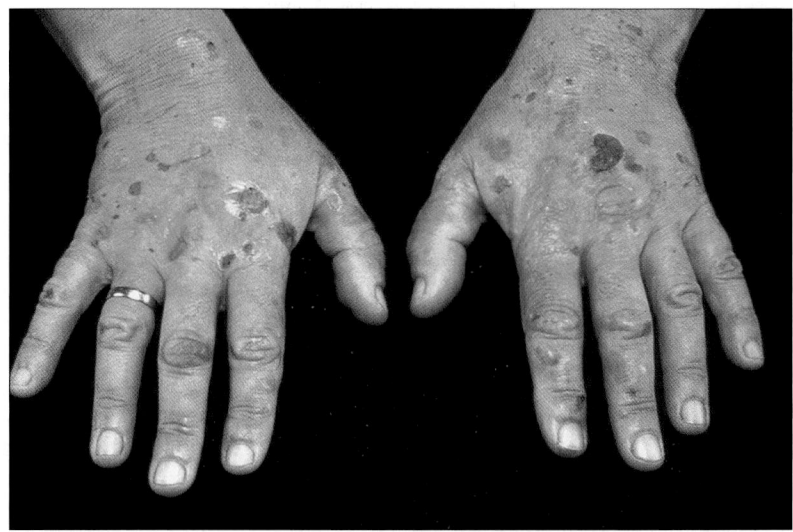

Fig. 12.102
Porphyria cutanea tarda: there are numerous ruptured blisters. Milia are also evident. By courtesy of the Institute of Dermatology, London, UK.

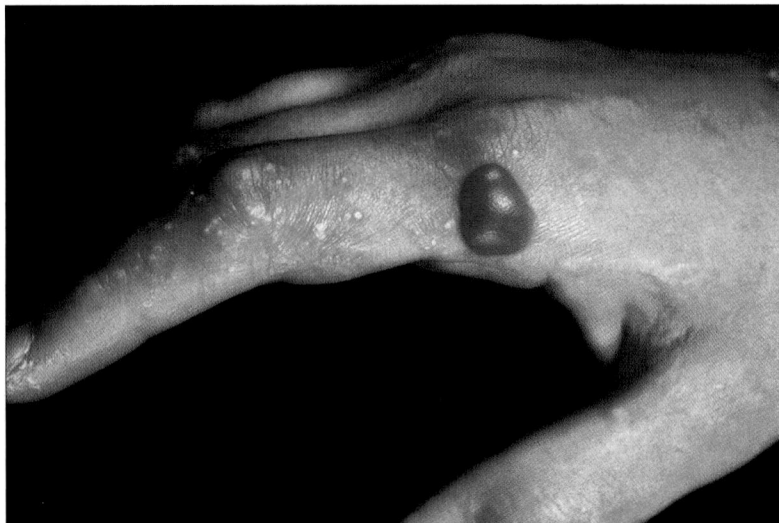

Fig. 12.101
Porphyria cutanea tarda: in addition to a blood-filled vesicle there are numerous milia. By courtesy of G. Murphy, MD, Beaumont Hospital, Dublin, Eire.

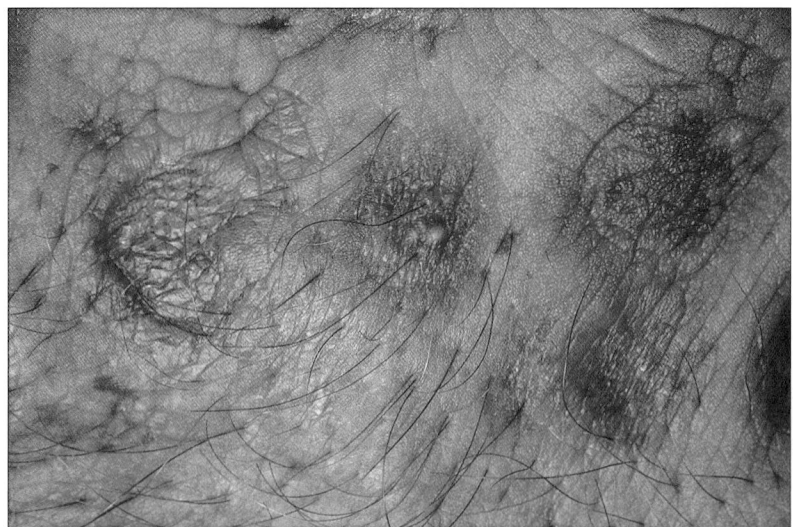

Fig. 12.103
Porphyria cutanea tarda: note the scarring and milia. By courtesy of the Institute of Dermatology, London, UK.

darkening has also been reported.[47] Very rare cases have been documented presenting with plaques or simulating solar urticaria.[48,49]

Acute attacks are not a feature of this variant. Biochemical evidence of liver involvement is common, but clinical manifestations are unusual.[1] Urinary porphyrin levels are increased and result in pink–red fluorescence with a Wood's lamp.[50]

The diagnosis is confirmed by the presence of uroporphyrin and heptacarboxylic porphyrins in urine and plasma and by the presence of isocoproporphyrin in feces.

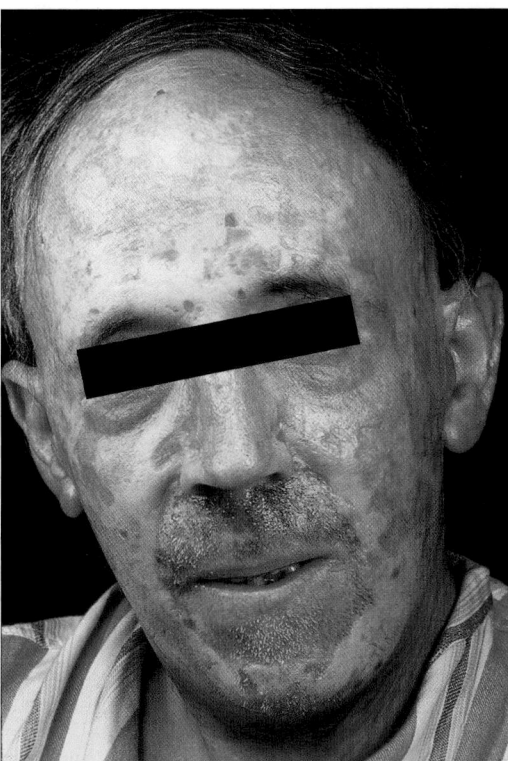

Fig. 12.104
Porphyria cutanea tarda: there is marked facial scarring with sclerodermiform features. By courtesy of G. Murphy, MD, Beaumont Hospital, Dublin, Eire.

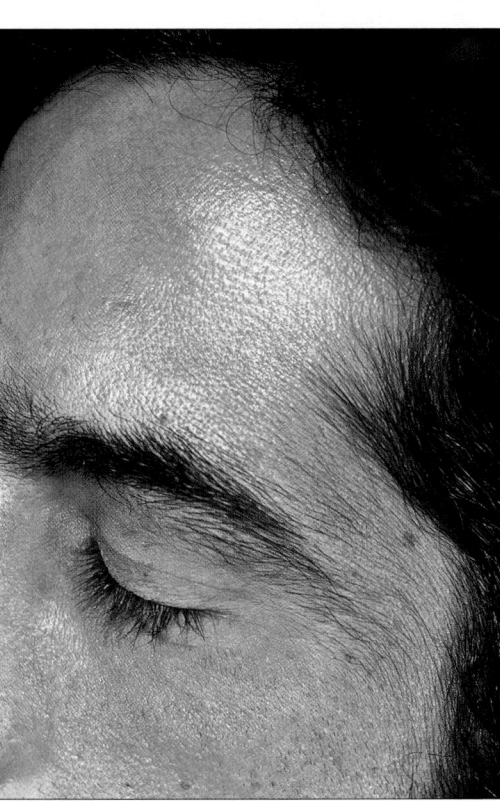

Fig. 12.105
Porphyria cutanea tarda: hypertrichosis as seen in this patient is a very typical feature. By courtesy of the Institute of Dermatology, London, UK.

References

1. Young, J.W., Conte, E.T. (1991) Porphyria and porphyrins. *Int J Dermatol*, **30**, 399–406.
2. Grossman, M.E., Bickers, D.R., Poh-Fitzpatrick, M.B. et al (1979) Porphyria cutanea tarda. Clinical features and laboratory findings in 40 patients. *Am J Med*, **67**, 277–286.
3. Mascaró, J.M. (1991) Porphyria cutanea tarda: clinical manifestations. *Curr Probl Dermatol*, **20**, 79–90.
4. Elder, G.H., Sheppard, D.M., De Salamanca, R.E. et al (1980) Identification of two types of porphyria cutanea tarda by measurement of erythrocyte uroporphyrinogen decarboxylase. *Clin Sci (Lond)*, **58**, 477–484.
5. Elder, G.H. (1991) Porphyria cutanea tarda: pathogenesis in relation to therapy. *Curr Probl Dermatol*, **20**, 91–96.
6. Held, J.L., Sassa, S., Kappas, A. et al (1989) Erythrocyte uroporphyrin decarboxylase activity in porphyria cutanea tarda: a study of 40 consecutive patients. *J Invest Dermatol*, **93**, 332–334.
7. McManus, J.F., Begley, C.G., Sassa, S. et al (1996) Five new mutations in the uroporphyrinogen decarboxylase gene identified in families with cutaneous porphyria. *Blood*, **88**, 3589–3600.
8. Méndez, M., Sorkin, L., Rossetti, M.V. et al (1998) Familial porphyria cutanea tarda: characterization of seven novel uroporphyrinogen decarboxylase mutations and frequency of common hemochromatosis alleles. *Am J Hum Genet*, **63**, 1363–1375.
9. Loret de Mola, J.R., Muise, K.L., Duchon, M.A. (1996) Porphyria cutanea tarda and pregnancy. *Obstet Gynecol Surv*, **51**, 493–497.
10. Egger, N.G., Goeger, D.E., Payne, D.A. et al (2002) Porphyria cutanea tarda: multiplicity of risk factors including HFE mutations, hepatitis C, and inherited uroporphyrinogen decarboxylase deficiency. *Dig Dis Sci*, **47**, 419–426.
11. Adachi, S., Amano, J., Ito, H. et al (1997) Porphyria cutanea tarda with constrictive pericarditis in a family. *Jpn Heart J*, **38**, 749–753.
12. Lamoril, J., Andant, C., Gouya, L. et al (2002) Hemochromatosis (HFE) and transferrin receptor (TFRC1) genes in sporadic porphyria cutanea tarda (sPCT). *Cell Mol Biol (Noisy-le-grand)*, **48**, 33–41.
13. Elder, G.H. (1998) Update on enzyme and molecular defects in porphyria. *Photodermatol Photoimmunol Photomed*, **14**, 66–69.
14. Stuart, K.A., Busfield, F., Jazwinska, E.C. et al (1998) The C282Y mutation in the hemochromatosis gene (HFE) and hepatitis C virus infection are independent cofactors for porphyria cutanea tarda in Australian patients. *J Hepatol*, **28**, 404–409.
15. Dereure, O., Aguilar-Martínez, P., Bessis, D. et al (2001) HFE mutations and transferrin receptor polymorphism analysis in porphyria cutanea tarda: a prospective study of 36 cases from southern France. *Br J Dermatol*, **144**, 533–539.
16. Brady, J.J., Jackson, H.A., Roberts, A.G. et al (2000) Co-inheritance of mutations in the uroporphyrinogen decarboxylase and hemachromatosis genes accelerates the onset of porphyria cutanea tarda. *J Invest Dermatol*, **115**, 868–874.
17. Becker, F.T. (1965) Porphyria cutanea tarda induced by estrogens. *Br J Dermatol*, **92**, 252–255.
18. Agarwal, R., Peters, T.J., Coombes, R.C. et al (2002) Tamoxifen-related porphyria cutanea tarda. *Med Oncol*, **19**, 121–123.
19. Schindl, A., Trautinger, F., Pernerstorfer-Schon, H. et al (1998) Porphyria cutanea tarda induced by the use of pravastatin. *Arch Dermatol*, **134**, 1305–1306.
20. Cam, C., Nigogosyan, G. (1963) Acquired toxic porphyria cutanea tarda due to hexachlorobenzene: report of 348 cases caused by this fungicide. *JAMA*, **183**, 88–91.
21. Crips, D.J., Peters, H.A., Gocmen, A. et al (1984) Porphyria turcica due to hexachlorobenzene: a 20 to 30 year follow-up study on 204 patients. *Br J Dermatol*, **111**, 413–422.
22. Grossman, M.E., Bickers, D.R., Poh-Fitzpatrick, M.B. et al (1979) Porphyria cutanea tarda. Clinical features and laboratory findings in 40 patients. *Am J Med*, **67**, 277–286.
23. Chesney, T.M., Wardlaw, L.L., Kaplan, R.J. et al (1981) Porphyria cutanea tarda complicating Wilson's disease. *J Am Acad Dermatol*, **4**, 64–66.
24. Lee, S.C., Yun, S.J., Lee, J.B. et al (2001) A case of porphyria cutanea tarda in association with idiopathic myelofibrosis and CREST syndrome. *Br J Dermatol*, **144**, 182–185.
25. O'Reilly, K., Snape, J., Moore, M.R. (1988) Porphyria cutanea tarda resulting from primary hepatocellular carcinoma. *Clin Exp Dermatol*, **13**, 44–48.
26. Lambrecht, R.W., Bonkovsky, H.L. (2002) Hemochromatosis and porphyria. *Semin Gastrointest Dis*, **13**, 109–119.
27. Tsukazaki, N., Watanabe, M., Irifune, H. (1998) Porphyria cutanea tarda and hepatitis C virus infection. *Br J Dermatol*, **138**, 1015–1017.
28. Rivanera, D., Lilli, D., Griso, D. et al (1998) Hepatitis C virus in patients with porphyria cutanea tarda: relationship to HCV-genotypes. *New Microbiol*, **21**, 329–334.
29. Wissel, P.S., Sordillo, P., Anderson, K.E. et al (1987) Porphyria cutanea tarda associated with the acquired immunodeficiency syndrome. *Am J Hematol*, **25**, 107–113.
30. Lobato, M.N., Berger, T.C. (1988) Porphyria cutanea tarda associated with the acquired immunodeficiency syndrome. *Arch Dermatol*, **124**, 1009–1010.
31. Conrad, M.E. (1988) AIDS and porphyria cutanea tarda. *Am J Hematol*, **28**, 207–208.
32. Scannell, K.A. (1990) Porphyria cutanea tarda and acquired immunodeficiency syndrome: case reports and literature review. *Arch Dermatol*, **126**, 1658–1659.
33. Boisseau, A-M., Couzigou, P., Forestier, J-F. et al (1991) Porphyria cutanea tarda associated with human immunodeficiency virus infection. A study of four cases and review of the literature. *Dermatologica*, **182**, 155–159.
34. Chuang, T.Y., Brashear, R., Lewis, C. (1999) Porphyria cutanea tarda and hepatitis C virus: a case-control study and meta-analysis of the literature. *J Am Acad Dermatol*, **41**, 31–36.
35. Mansourati, F.F., Stone, V.E., Mayer, K.H. (1999) Porphyria cutanea tarda and HIV/AIDS: a review of pathogenesis, clinical manifestations and management. *Int J STD AIDS*, **10**, 51–56.
36. O'Connor, W.J., Murphy, G.M., Darby, C. et al (1996) Porphyrin abnormalities in acquired immunodeficiency syndrome. *Arch Dermatol*, **132**, 1443–1447.
37. Cohen, P.R. (1991) Porphyria cutanea tarda in human immunodeficiency virus-seropositive men: case report and literature review. *J Acquir Immune Defic Syndr*, **4**, 1112–1117.
38. Lim, H.W., Pereira, A., Sassa, S. et al (1998) Early-stage HIV infection and hepatitis C virus infection are associated with elevated serum porphyrin levels. *J Am Acad Dermatol*, **39**, 956–959.
39. Gibson, G.E., McEvoy, M.T. (1998) Coexistence of lupus erythematosus and porphyria cutanea tarda in fifteen patients. *J Am Acad Dermatol*, **38**, 569–573.
40. Griso, D., Macri, A., Biolati, G. et al (1989) Does an association exist between PCT and SLE? Results of a study on autoantibodies in 158 patients affected with PCT. *Arch Dermatol Res*, **281**, 291–292.
41. Remenyik, E., Ujj, G., Kiss, A. et al (1996) Porphyria cutanea tarda and chronic lymphoid leukemia. *Photodermatol Photoimmunol Photomed*, **12**, 180–182.
42. McKenna, D.B., Browne, M., O'Donnell, R. et al (1997) Porphyria cutanea tarda and hematologic malignancy – a report of 4 cases. *Photodermatol Photoimmunol Photomed*, **13**, 143–146.
43. Friedman, S.J., Doyle, J.A. (1985) Sclerodermoid changes of porphyria cutanea tarda: possible relationship to urinary uroporphyrin levels. *J Am Acad Dermatol*, **13**, 70–74.
44. Varigos, G., Schiltz, J.R., Bickers, D.R. (1982) Uroporphyrin I stimulation of collagen biosynthesis in human skin fibroblasts: a unique dark effect of porphyrin. *J Clin Invest*, **69**, 129–135.
45. Piñol Aguade, J., Mascaro, J.M., Galy-Mascaro, C. (1971) La alopecia porfirica. *Medicina Cutanea Ibero Latino Americana*, Año V, 235–240.
46. Piñol Aguadé, J., Mascaró, J.M., Galy-Mascaró, C. et al (1969) Sur quelques manifestations cutanées et oculaires peu connues des porphyries. Les lymphangiectasies papuleuses centro-faciales de la porphyrie. *Ann Dermatol Syphil (Paris)*, **96**, 265–270.
47. Shaffrali, F.C., McDonagh, A.J., Messenger, A.G. (2002) Hair darkening in porphyria cutanea tarda. *Br J Dermatol*, **146**, 325–329.
48. Creamer, D., McGregor, J.M., McFadden, J. et al (1999) Lichenoid tissue reaction in porphyria cutanea tarda. *Br J Dermatol*, **141**, 123–126.
49. Dawe, R.S., Clark, C., Ferguson, J. (1999) Porphyria cutanea tarda presenting as solar urticaria. *Br J Dermatol*, **141**, 392.
50. Young, J.W., Conte, E.T. (1991) Porphyria and porphyrins. *Int J Dermatol*, **30**, 399–406.

Hepatoerythropoietic porphyria

Clinical features

Hepatoerythropoietic porphyria is very rare and, in fact, represents the homozygous form of familial porphyria cutanea tarda.[1] Both diseases share some of the mutations that have been described.[2] This form of porphyria is also heterogeneous and different mutations in the URO-D gene may occur.[3,4] The activity of uroporphyrinogen decarboxylase is much lower than in porphyria cutanea tarda. Extreme immediate photosensitivity occurs in infancy.[5–7] Erythema, edema and vesicles lead to severe scarring, with hypertrichosis and sclerodermatous changes in exposed areas.[8] Ocular features include photophobia, conjunctivitis and scleromalacia perforans.[9] Hepatitis, cirrhosis and normochromic anemia may also occur.

References

1. Elder, G.H., Smith, S.G., Herrero, C. et al (1981) Hepatoerythropoietic porphyria, a new uroporphyrinogen decarboxylase defect on homozygous porphyria cutanea tarda? *Lancet*, I, 916–919.
2. Mendez, M., Rossetti, M.V., De Siervi, A. et al (2000) Mutations in familial porphyria cutanea tarda: two novel and two previously described for hepatoerythropoietic porphyria. *Hum Mutat*, 16, 269–270.
3. Koszo, F., Elder, G.H., Roberts, A. et al (1990) Uroporphyrinogen decarboxylase deficiency in hepatoerythropoietic porphyria: further evidence for genetic heterogeneity. *Br J Dermatol*, 122, 365–370.
4. Meguro, K., Fujita, H., Ishida, N. et al (1994) Molecular defects of uroporphyrinogen decarboxylase in a patient with mild hepatoerythropoietic porphyria. *J Invest Dermatol*, 102, 681–685.
5. Smith, S.G. (1986) Hepatoerythropoeitic porphyria. *Semin Dermatol*, 5, 125–137.
6. Czarnecki, D.B. (1980) Hepatoerythropoietic porphyria. *Arch Dermatol*, 116, 307–311.
7. Lim, H.W., Poh-Fitzpatrick, M.B. (1984) Hepatoerythropoietic porphyria: a variant of childhood-onset porphyria cutanea tarda. Porphyrin profiles and enzymatic studies of two cases in a family. *J Am Acad Dermatol*, 11, 1103–1111.
8. Young, J.W., Conte, E.T. (1991) Porphyria and porphyrins. *Int J Dermatol*, 30, 399–406.
9. Mascaro, J.M. (1991) Porphyria cutanea tarda: clinical manifestations. *Curr Probl Dermatol*, 20, 79–90.

Variegate porphyria

Clinical features

This familial type of porphyria manifests the cutaneous features of porphyria cutanea tarda and the acute abdominal and neurological attacks of acute intermittent porphyria, both of which usually become apparent in the second or third decade (*Figs 12.106–12.109*).[1,2] It is particularly common in South Africa where it can be traced to the descendants of a single Dutch family.[2,3] It is an autosomal dominantly

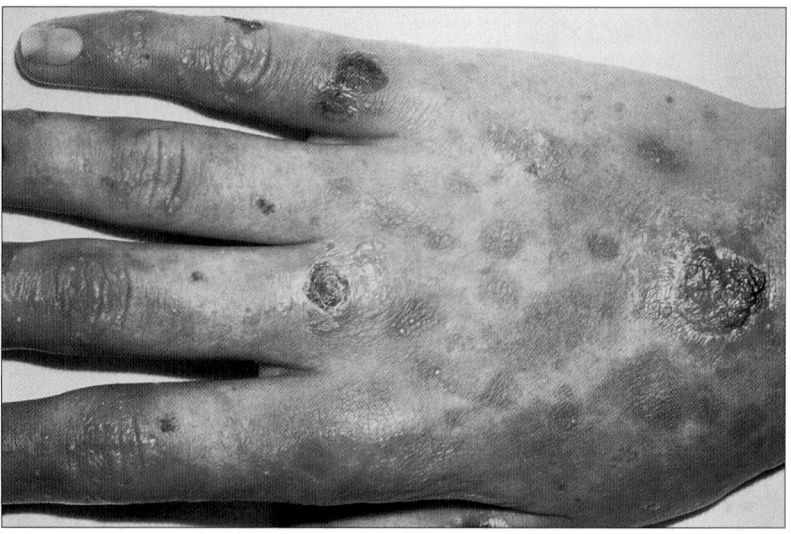

Fig. 12.107
Variegate porphyria: there are ruptured blisters with scarring and milia. By courtesy of the Institute of Dermatology, London, UK.

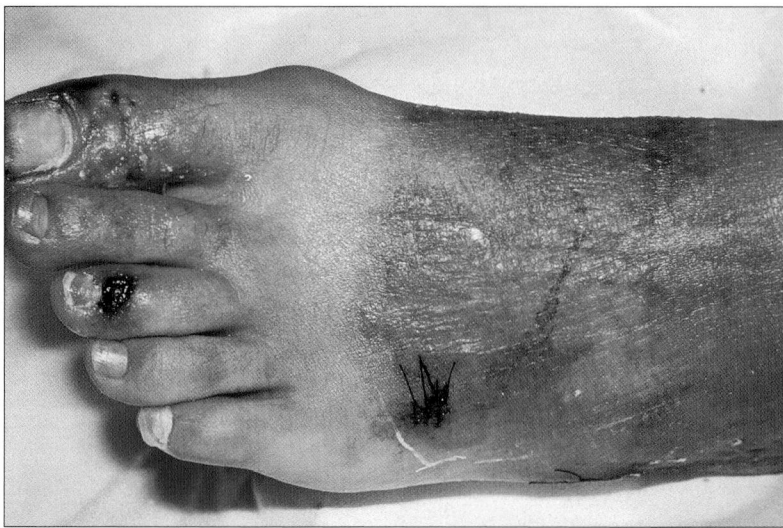

Fig. 12.108
Variegate porphyria: note the blistering over the toes and dorsum of the foot. By courtesy of the Institute of Dermatology, London, UK.

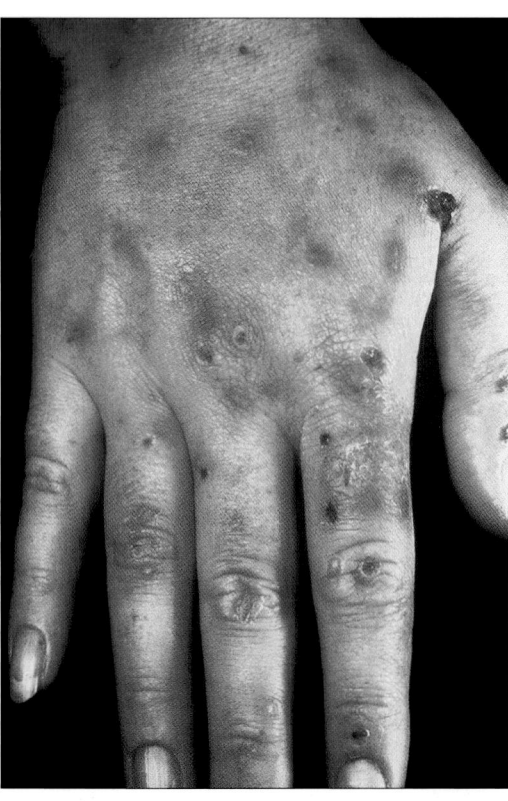

Fig. 12.106
Variegate porphyria: numerous ruptured vesicles are present on the back of the hand and fingers. By courtesy of G. Murphy, MD, Beaumont Hospital, Dublin, Eire.

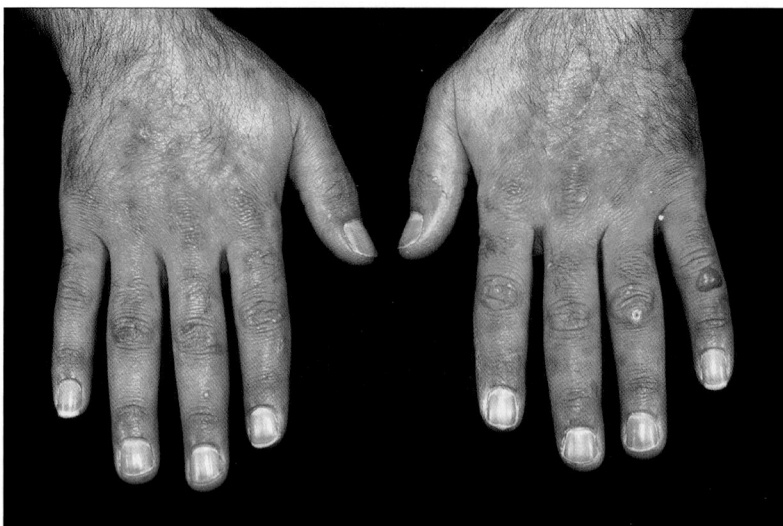

Fig. 12.109
Variegate porphyria: an intact blister is present on the left little finger. Elsewhere there is marked scarring and milia are present. By courtesy of the Institute of Dermatology, London, UK.

inherited condition and more severely affected homozygotes have been recognized (*Figs 12.110, 12.111*). Variegate porphyria is associated with diminished activity of protoporphyrinogen oxidase, the penultimate enzyme in the heme biosynthetic pathway.[4] Several different mutations have been demonstrated in the protoporphyrin oxidase gene on chromosome 1q22–23.[5,6] The genotype is not a significant determinant of the clinical manifestations.[7–9] Usually there is approximately 50% reduction in the activity of the enzyme.[9]

Acute attacks may be precipitated by a wide range of drugs that induce hepatic microsomal activity including barbiturates, alcohol, oral contraceptives, anticonvulsants and sulphonamides.[10–12] Acute variegate porphyria has also presented during an episode of viral hepatitis.[10] The cutaneous manifestations are sometimes mild or absent during the acute attack and the condition may therefore be misdiagnosed as acute intermittent porphyria.[2]

References

1. Elder, G.H. (1990) The cutaneous porphyrias. *Semin Dermatol*, 9, 63–69.
2. Mustajoki, P. (1978) Variegate porphyria. *Ann Intern Med*, 89, 238–244.
3. Young, J.W., Conte, E.T. (1991) Porphyria and porphyrins. *Int J Dermatol*, 30, 399–406.
4. Perrot, H., Thivolet, J., Boucherat, M. et al (1976) La porphyrie variegata (a propos de 4 cas). *Lyon Med*, 235, 905–915.
5. Frank, J., McGrath, J.A., Poh-Fitzpatrick, M.B. et al (1999) Mutations in the translation initiation codon of the protoporphyrinogen oxidase gene underlie variegate porphyria. *Clin Exp Dermatol*, 24, 296–301.
6. Frank, J., Christiano, A.M. (1998) Variegate porphyria: past, present and future. *Skin Pharmacol Appl Skin Physiol*, 11, 310–320.
7. Corrigall, A.V., Hift, R.J., Davids, L.M. et al (2001) Identification of the first variegate porphyria mutation in an indigenous black South African and further evidence for heterogeneity in variegate porphyria. *Mol Genet Metab*, 73, 91–96.
8. Whatley, S.D., Puy, H., Morgan, R.R. et al (1999) Variegate porphyria in Western Europe: identification of the PPOX gene mutations in 104 families, extent of allelic heterogeneity, and absence of correlation between phenotype and type of mutation. *Am J Hum Genet*, 65, 984–994.
9. Mustajoki, P. (1980) Variegate porphyria: twelve years experience in Finland. *QJM*, 49, 191–203.
10. Coburn, P.R., Coleman, J.C., Cream, J.J. et al (1985) Porphyria cutanea tarda and porphyria variegata unmasked by viral hepatitis. *Clin Exp Dermatol*, 10, 169–173.
11. Targovnik, S.E., Targovnik, J.H. (1986) Cutaneous drug reactions in porphyrias. *Clin Dermatol*, 4, 110–117.
12. Quiroz-Kendall, E., Wilson, F.A., King, L.E. Jr (1983) Acute variegate porphyria following a Scarsdale Gourmet diet. *J Am Acad Dermatol*, 8, 46–49.

Histological features of the porphyrias

Direct immunofluorescence reveals immunoglobulin (particularly IgG and to a lesser extent IgM), fibrinogen and C3 outlining characteristic donut-shaped blood vessels in the papillary dermis (*Fig. 12.112*). Although this is particularly evident in erythropoietic protoporphyria, it is also a feature of the other 'cutaneous' variants.[1,2] Immunoreactants are also frequently present at the epidermodermal junction and have been identified within the basement membrane region of eccrine sweat glands and ducts.[1–4] This finding is believed to be due to the non-specific binding of serum components rather than an immunologically mediated reaction.[3] In addition both type IV collagen and laminin are present in increased amounts thereby contributing to the vessel wall thickening.[5] Cytoid bodies are also commonly evident.[3] Indirect immunofluorescence is invariably negative for basement membrane zone autoantibodies.

The dermatopathological changes for all types of porphyria are very similar. The characteristic feature is the presence of a PAS-positive, diastase-resistant, hyaline material around the blood vessels of affected skin (*Figs 12.113, 12.114*). In mild disease the deposits are delicate and are usually limited to the papillary dermal capillaries, but in more severe cases the deposits are widespread, occur more deeply in the dermis and give the vessel walls a characteristic lamellated appearance. These appearances are particularly conspicuous in erythropoietic proto-porphyria.[1,6] Alcian blue positive mucin is sometimes evident around the blood vessels and to a lesser extent at the epidermodermal junction in both porphyria cutanea tarda and erythropoietic protoporphyria.[1] Lipid

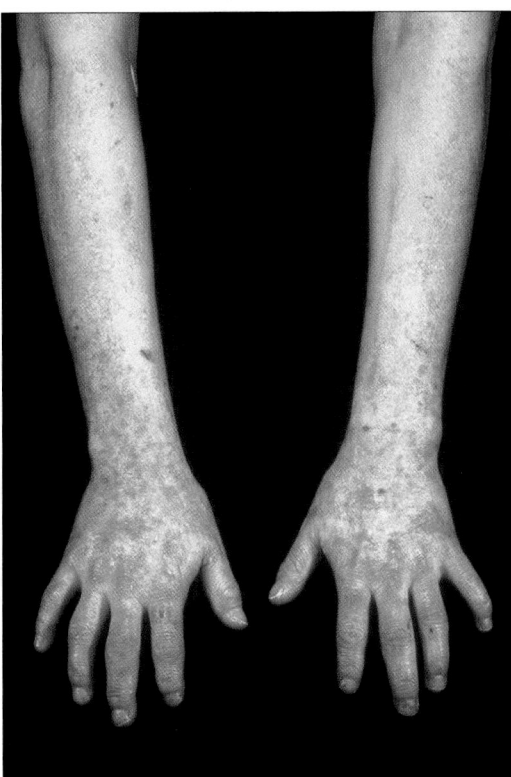

Fig. 12.110
Homozygous variegate porphyria: there is marked scarring of the dorsal surface of the forearms, hands and fingers. By courtesy of G. Murphy, MD, Beaumont Hospital, Dublin, Eire.

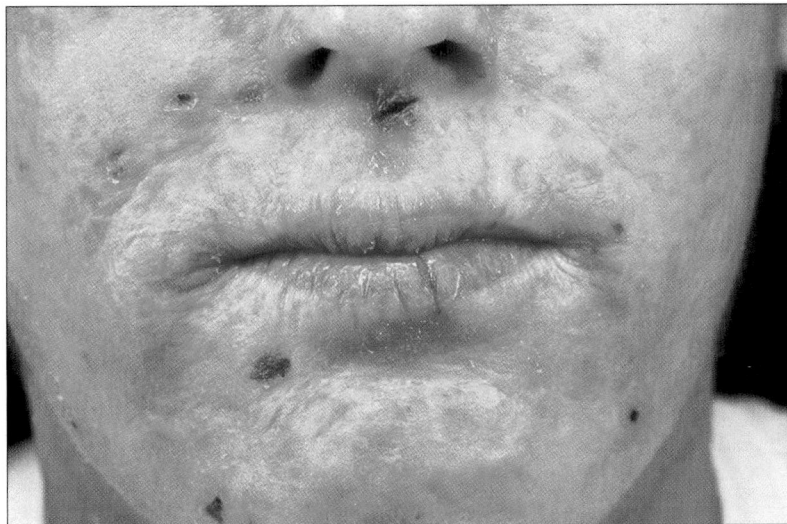

Fig. 12.111
Homozygous variegate porphyria: note the perioral erosions and scarring. By courtesy of the Institute of Dermatology, London, UK.

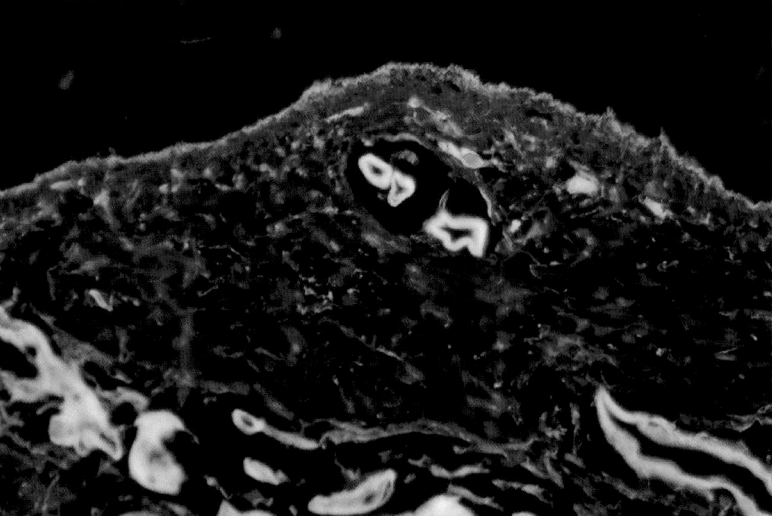

Fig. 12.112
Porphyria cutanea tarda: the superficial blood vessels show striking IgG circumferential deposition.

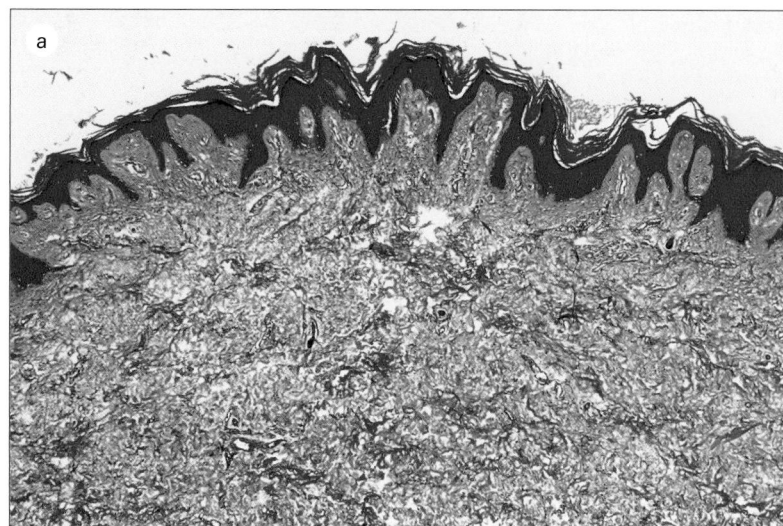

Fig. 12.113
(a, b) Porphyria cutanea tarda: the superficial vessels are thickened and appear hyalinized.

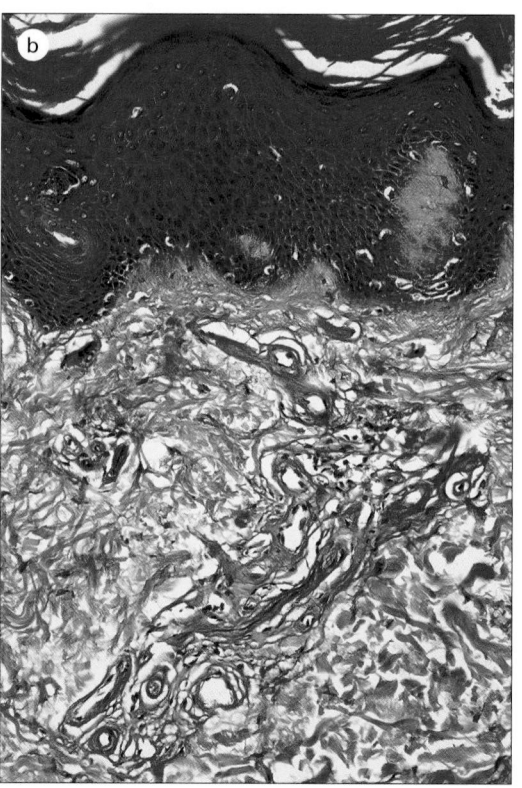

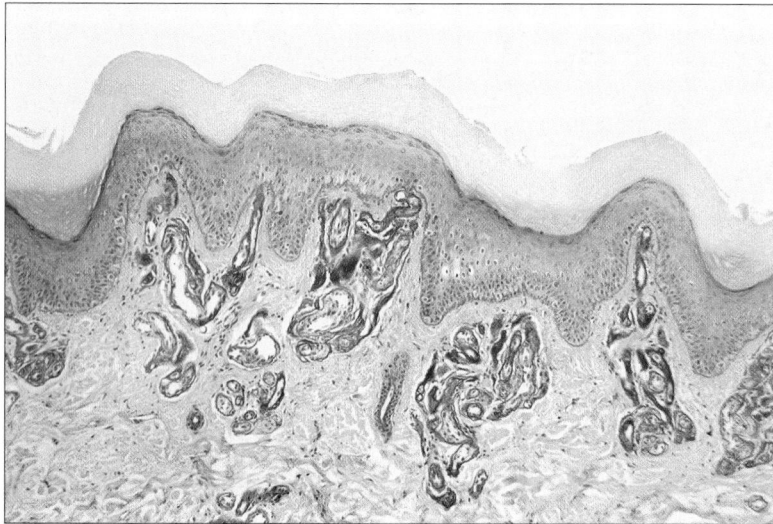

Fig. 12.114
Erythropoietic protoporphyria: the appearances are much more dramatic in this periodic acid–Schiff stained section.

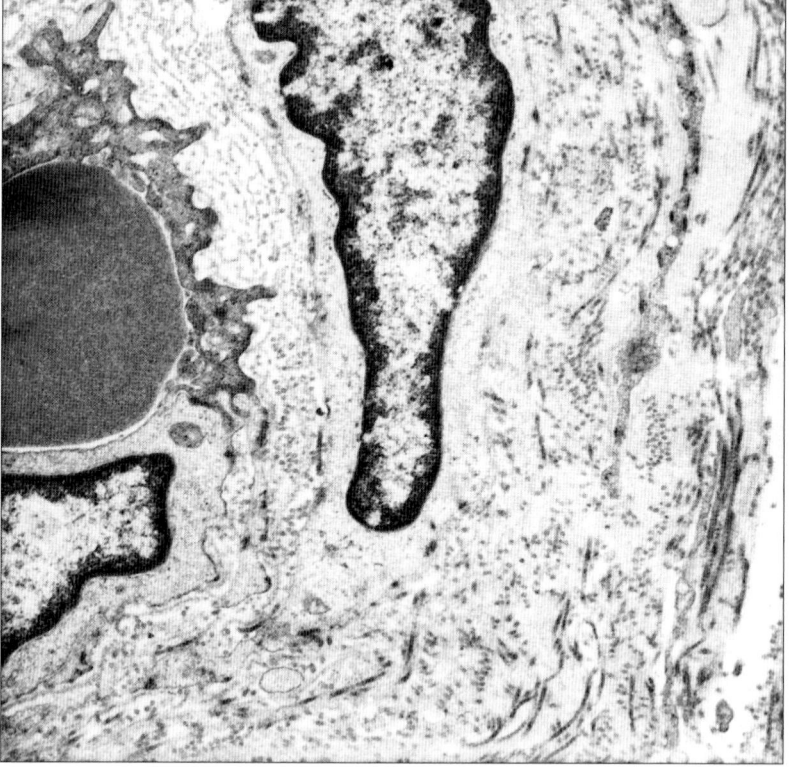

Fig. 12.115
Porphyria cutanea tarda: there is striking basement membrane reduplication surrounding this small dermal vessel. An erythrocyte is present in the lumen.

droplets are sometimes also demonstrable. A false positive Congo red stain for amyloid may be evident in the lower dermis.[1]

Electron microscopic observations include considerable basement membrane reduplication around the dermal vasculature and to a lesser extent at the epidermodermal junction (*Fig. 12.115*).[1,6] This is consistent with the effects of repetitive endothelial cell injury and regeneration with subsequent new basement membrane formation. In addition finely fibrillar material is typically present both around the vessels and at the epidermal basement membrane region. Irregular electron-dense amorphous deposits may also be evident.[1]

There may be subepidermal blisters, characteristically associated with slight mononuclear inflammatory cell infiltration (*Figs 12.116, 12.117*). Neutrophil polymorphs showing leukocytoclasis have been described in acute lesions of erythropoietic protoporphyria and purpura is sometimes evident.[7] Festooning of the dermal papillae is often, but not invariably

present. The plane of cleavage appears to be variable.[8] Some blisters arise beneath the lamina densa in the superficial dermis similar to epidermolysis bullosa acquisita. In others they develop within the reduplicated basement membrane constituents. Most often, however, as shown by antigen mapping experiments, blistering commences in the lamina lucida.[8,9] Type IV collagen and laminin are therefore usually present along the floor of the blister while bullous pemphigoid antigen is evident

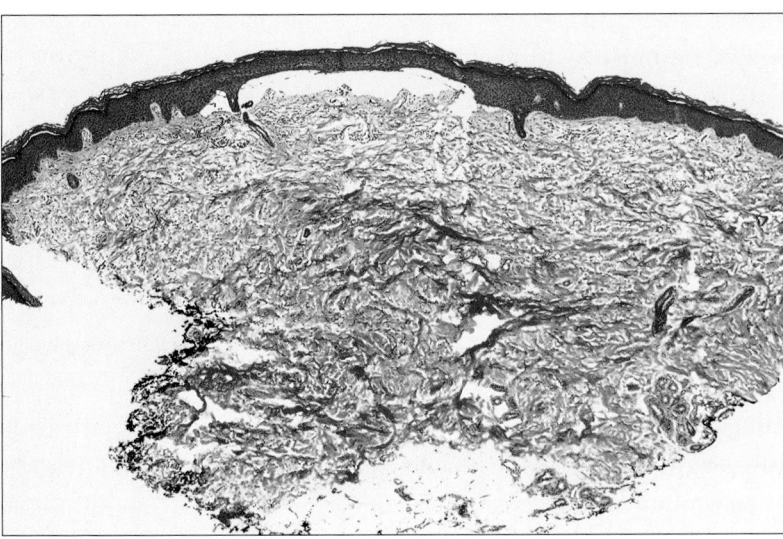

Fig. 12.116
Porphyria cutanea tarda: a bland subepidermal blister is present.

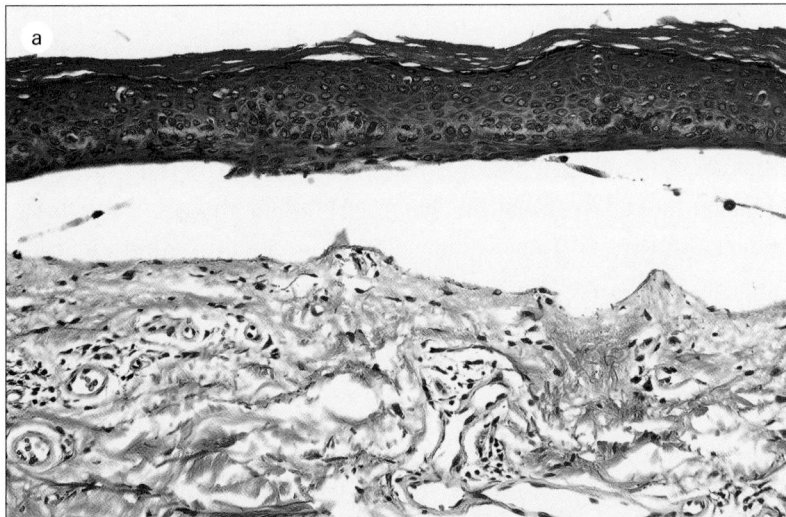

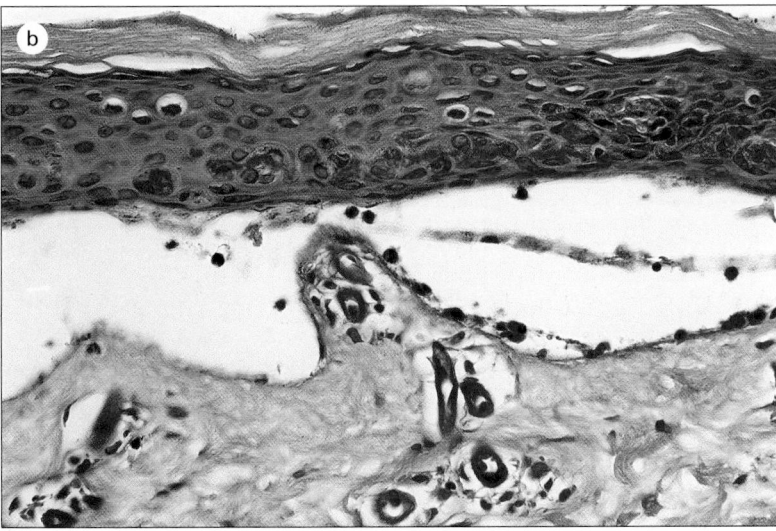

Fig. 12.117
Porphyria cutanea tarda: **(a)** the blister is cell free; **(b)** the superficial vessels are thickened (periodic acid–Schiff). Note the caterpillar bodies in the overlying epidermis.

in the roof. Recently, linear segmented structures composed of type IV collagen and laminin have been identified in the roof of blisters from patients with porphyria cutanea tarda.[10] These so-called caterpillar bodies may also be seen in specimens from patients with erythropoietic protoporphyria and drug-induced pseudoporphyria (*Fig. 12.117*).[11] They are PAS positive and appear as globules arranged in a linear fashion in the epidermis overlying the subepidermal blisters. Ultrastructural studies suggest that these bodies represent a combination of degenerating keratinocytes, colloid bodies and basement membrane fragments formed by repeated blistering and re-epithelialization.[12]

Rarely, a lichenoid tissue reaction has been documented in porphyria cutanea tarda.[13]

The histological features of the blisters seen in variegate porphyria are identical to those described for porphyria cutanea tarda.[14]

A secondary sclerodermatous change is frequently present in more chronic lesions, characterized by thickened collagen bundles and reduced numbers of cutaneous adnexae (*Fig. 12.118*).[3,6,15] Diastase-resistant, PAS-positive material may be identified throughout the involved dermis.[1] This is particularly marked in porphyria cutanea tarda. Its distinction from the dermal changes of scleroderma may be very difficult, but it has been said that the texture of the collagen bundles is somewhat looser in porphyria.[1] Basement membrane thickening due to diastase-resistant, PAS-positive material is usually present particularly in porphyria cutanea tarda.[1,6] Solar elastosis is often evident in the latter condition, but this is probably largely a consequence of the age of the patient and is unlikely to be a fundamental process (*Fig. 12.119*). It is not a feature of erythropoietic protoporphyria.[1,6]

In the alopecia associated with porphyria cutanea tarda, the initial changes are those of swelling and homogenization of the perifollicular connective tissue sheath.[16] Later the features of sclerodermatous transformation of the reticular dermis supervene. Centrofacial papular lymphangiectasis is characterized by the presence of dilated lymphatics in the superficial dermis.[17]

The hepatic changes of porphyria cutanea tarda are variable and include needle-shaped uroporphyrin crystals, hepatitis, liver cell degeneration and regeneration, fatty change, hemosiderosis and scarring, sometimes amounting to cirrhosis (*Fig. 12.120*).[16,18,19] There is an increased risk of hepatocellular carcinoma.[19] Hepatic changes of erythropoietic protoporphyria include birefringent, dark brown, protoporphyrin crystal deposition in the hepatocytes and Kupffer cells, hepatocyte

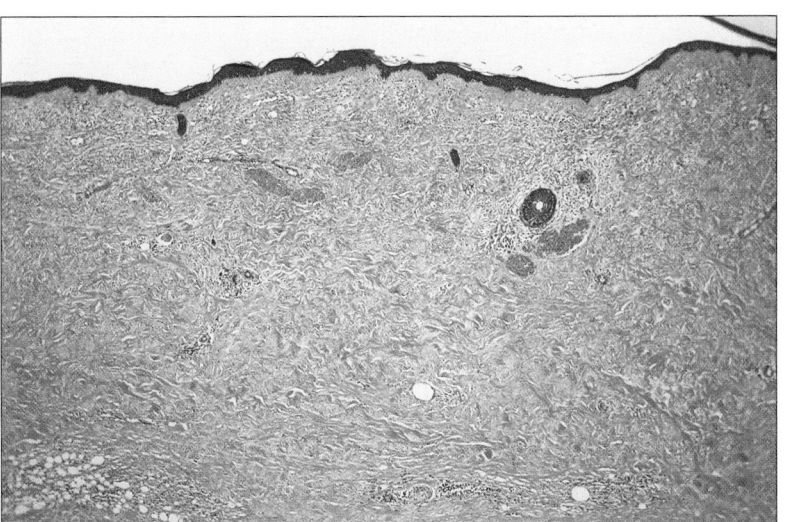

Fig. 12.118
Porphyria cutanea tarda: there is intense scarring of the entire dermis. The fat entrapment is reminiscent of scleroderma.

necrosis, portal and periportal fibrosis, cholestasis and, less commonly, cirrhosis (*Fig. 12.121*).[20]

Differential diagnosis

The major differential diagnosis histologically is between porphyria, pseudoporphyria, epidermolysis bullosa acquisita and congenita, and bullous amyloidosis. All produce cell-poor or cell-free subepidermal blisters. Their distinction is readily made in the majority of cases with clinical information, immunofluorescence studies and Congo red staining.

References

1. Epstein, J.H., Tuffanelli, D.L., Epstein, W.L. (1973) Cutaneous changes in the porphyrias. *Arch Dermatol*, **107**, 689–698.
2. Cormane, R.H., Szabo, E., Hauge, L.S. (1970) Immunofluorescence of the skin, the interpretation of the staining of blood vessels and connective tissue aided by new techniques. *Br J Dermatol*, **82** (Suppl. 5), 26–43.
3. Maynard, B., Peters, M.S. (1992) Histologic and immunofluorescence study of cutaneous porphyrias. *J Cutan Pathol*, **19**, 40–47.
4. Cormane, R.H., Szabò, E., Hoo, T.T. (1971) Histopathology of the skin in acquired and hereditary porphyria cutanea tarda. *Br J Dermatol*, **85**, 531–539.
5. Wick, G., Hönigsmann, H., Timpl, R. (1979) Immunofluorescence demonstration of type IV collagen and a noncollagenous glycoprotein in thickened vascular basal membranes in protoporphyria. *J Invest Dermatol*, **73**, 335–338.
6. Wolff, K., Hönigsmann, H., Rauschmeier, W. et al (1982) Microscopic and fine structural aspects of porphyrias. *Acta Derm Venereol*, **100** (Suppl.), 17–28.
7. Baart de la Faille, H., Bijlmer-Lest, J.C., Van Hattum, J. et al (1991) Erythropoietic protoporphyria: clinical aspects with emphasis on the skin. *Curr Probl Dermatol*, **20**, 123–134.
8. Dabski, C., Beutner, E.H. (1991) Studies of laminin and type IV collagen in blisters of porphyria cutanea tarda and drug-induced pseudoporphyria. *J Am Acad Dermatol*, **25**, 28–32.
9. Pardo, R.J., Penneys, N.S. (1990) Location of basement membrane type IV collagen beneath subepidermal bullous diseases. *J Cutan Pathol*, **17**, 336–341.
10. Austin, C., Egbert, B., Hu, C. et al (1986) A new clue to aid in the histological diagnosis of porphyria cutanea tarda. *J Cutan Pathol*, **13**, 80.
11. Egbert, B.M., LeBoit, P.E., McCalmont, T. et al (1993) Caterpillar bodies: distinctive, basement membrane-containing structures in blisters of porphyria. *Am J Dermatopathol*, **15**, 199–202.
12. Raso, D.S., Greene, W.B., Maize, J.C. et al (1996) Caterpillar bodies of porphyria cutanea tarda ultrastructurally represent a unique arrangement of colloid and basement membrane bodies. *Am J Dermatopathol*, **18**, 24–29.
13. Creamer, D., McGregor, J.M., McFadden, J. et al (1999) Lichenoid tissue reaction in porphyria cutanea tarda. *Br J Dermatol*, **141**, 123–126.
14. Corey, T.J., DeLeo, V.A., Christianson, H. et al (1980) Variegate porphyria: clinical and laboratory features. *J Am Acad Dermatol*, **2**, 36–43.
15. Friedman, S.J., Doyle, J.A. (1985) Sclerodermoid changes of porphyria cutanea tarda: possible relationship to urinary uroporphyrin levels. *J Am Acad Dermatol*, **13**, 70–74.
16. Mascaro, J.M. (1991) Porphyria cutanea tarda: clinical manifestations. *Curr Probl Dermatol*, **20**, 79–90.
17. Piñol Aguade, J., Mascaro, J.M., Galy-Mascaro, C. et al (1969) Sur quelques manifestations cutanées et oculaires peu connues des porphyries. Les lymphangiectasies papuleuses centro-faciales de la porphyrie. *Ann Dermatol Syphil (Paris)*, **96**, 265–270.
18. Elder, G.H. (1990) The cutaneous porphyrias. *Semin Dermatol*, **9**, 63–69.
19. Fakan, F., Chlumska, A. (1987) Demonstration of needle-shaped hepatic inclusions in porphyria cutanea tarda using the ferric ferricyanide reduction test. *Virchows Archives (A)*, **411**, 365–368.
20. Bloomer, J.R. (1988) The liver in protoporphyria. *Hepatology*, **8**, 402–407.

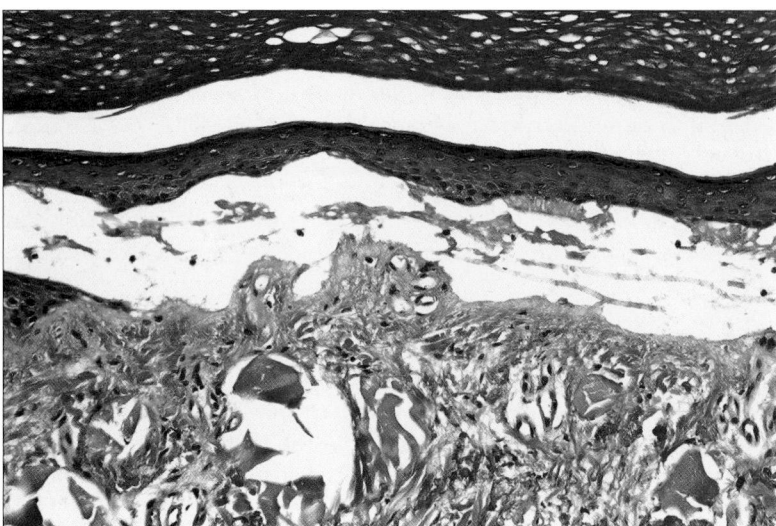

Fig. 12.119
Porphyria cutanea tarda: there is colloid milium-like solar elastosis deep to this blister.

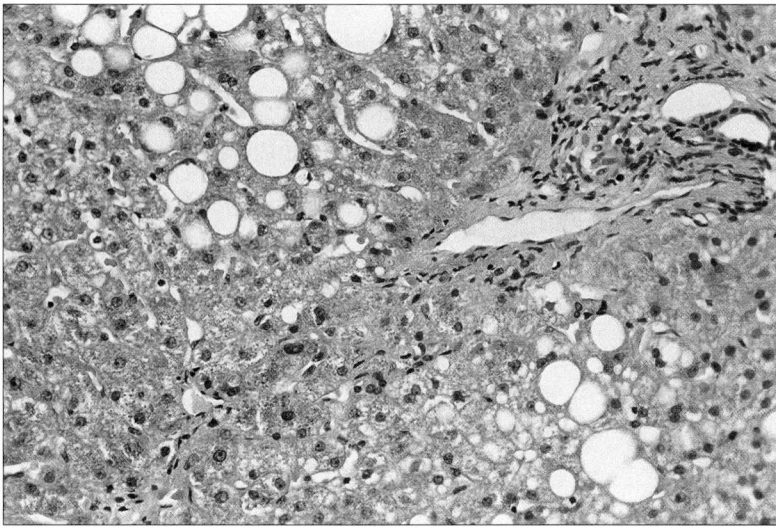

Fig. 12.120
Porphyria cutanea tarda: in addition to fatty change and mild chronic inflammation, brown uroporphyrin crystals are evident.

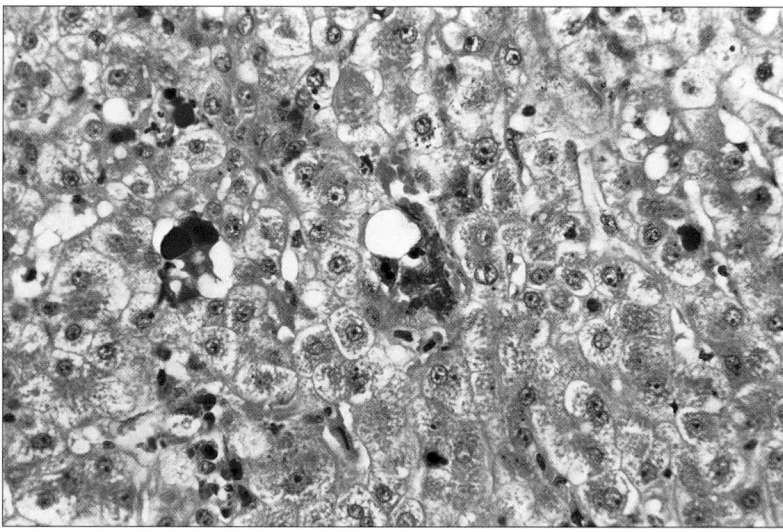

Fig. 12.121
Erythropoietic protoporphyria: the Kupffer cells contain abundant brown pigment. By courtesy of D.R. Davies, MD, St Thomas' Hospital, London, UK.

Pseudoporphyria

Clinical features

Pseudoporphyria (drug-induced pseudoporphyria, drug-induced pseudoporphyria cutanea tarda, pseudoporphyria cutanea tarda, bullous dermatosis in end-stage renal failure, bullous dermatosis of hemodialysis) refers to a photodistributed blistering dermatosis resembling porphyria cutanea tarda but in the absence of any serum, urine or stool porphyrin abnormality (*Figs 12.122–12.125*).[1] It is now recognized as having many causes including drugs, excessive UVA (including the use of sunbeds) and sunlight exposure and may develop in patients undergoing hemodialysis for chronic renal failure.[1–9] Pseudoporphyria occurs in up to 6% of patients receiving hemodialysis therapy.[10]

Small tense blisters develop on the backs of the hands and fingers and, occasionally involve the face, upper chest and legs.[1,2] Milia, skin fragility, photosensitivity and scarring are often present. Hypertrichosis, hyperpigmentation, sclerodermoid changes and dystrophic calcification as seen in porphyria cutanea tarda are not features of pseudoporphyria.[1] In children affected with this condition (usually receiving naproxen for juvenile arthritis), facial scarring reminiscent of erythropoietic protoporphyria has been documented.[5,11] In general, hepatic abnormalities appear to be absent.[1]

Pathogenesis and histological features

Pseudoporphyria is a UVA-related phototoxic dermatosis.[1] It may develop following both hemodialysis and peritoneal dialysis and also in patients with chronic renal failure in the absence of dialysis. Suggested risk factors in such patients include iron overload, aluminum intoxication, PVC-induced photosensitivity, drugs and ethanol.[1,2] The condition has also been documented following use of non-steroidal anti-inflammatory medications including naproxen.[5] A wide variety of other drugs including various antibiotics (e.g. nalidixic acid and tetracyclines) and diuretics (e.g. furosemide (frusemide)) have also been incriminated (for details see references 1 and 2). The use of UVA suntanning beds is also a well-recognized cause of pseudoporphyria.[12] Young females are almost exclusively affected and PUVA therapy has also rarely been incriminated.[1]

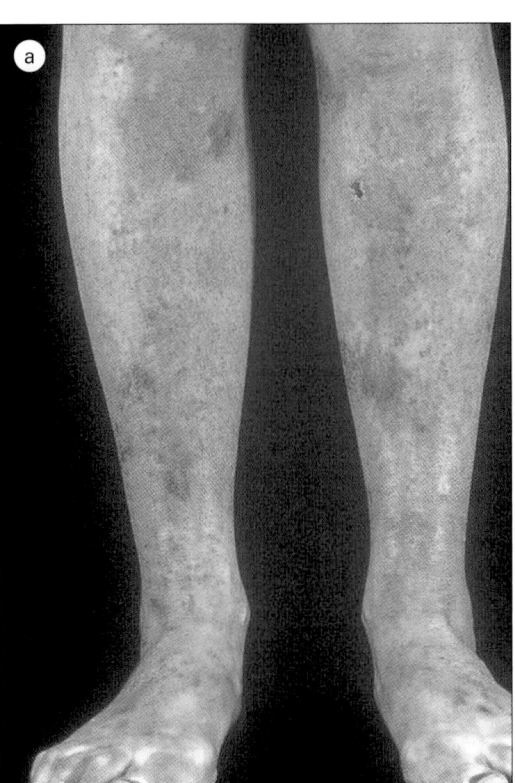
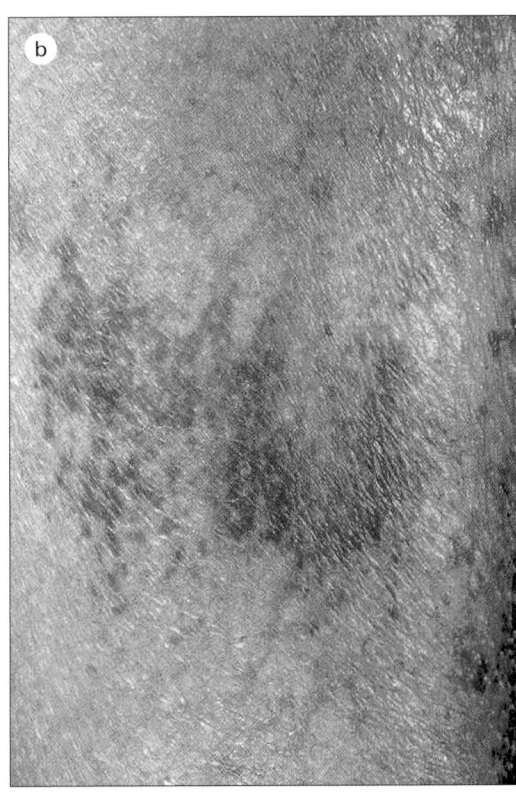

Fig. 12.122
(a, b) Pseudoporphyria: there is extensive purpura with freckling and conspicuous excoriations. The patient had used sunbeds for a number of years. By courtesy of G.M. Murphy, MD, Beaumont Hospital, Dublin, Eire.

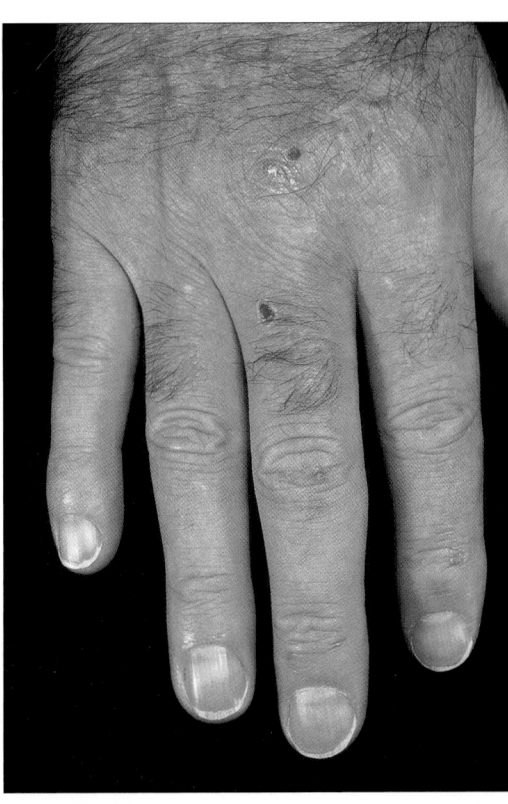

Fig. 12.125
Pseudoporphyria: there are multiple erosions and milia. By courtesy of the Institute of Dermatology, London, UK.

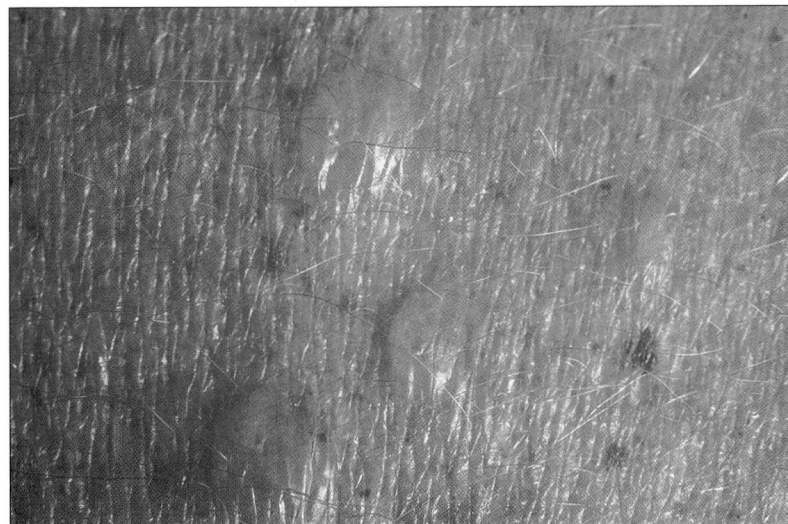

Fig. 12.123
Pseudoporphyria: small tense grouped vesicles are present on the arm. By courtesy of G.M. Murphy, MD, Beaumont Hospital, Dublin, Eire.

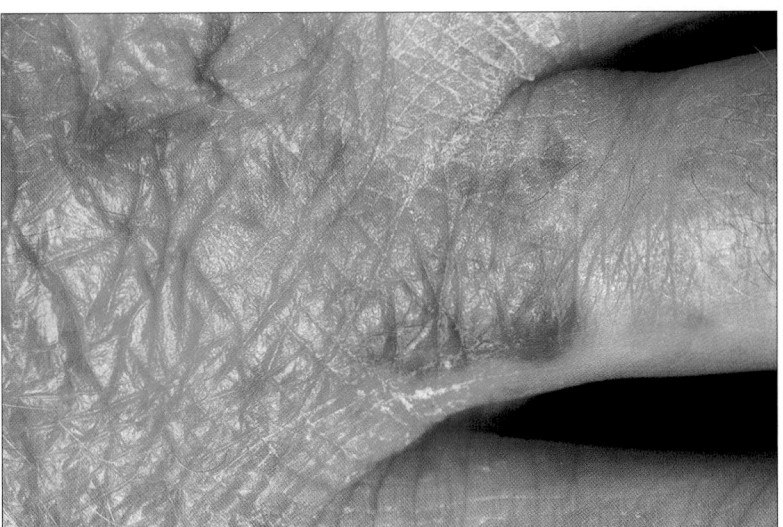

Fig. 12.124
Pseudoporphyria: note the hemorrhagic blister overlying the knuckle. By courtesy of G.M. Murphy, MD, Beaumont Hospital, Dublin, Eire.

The blisters are subepidermal and rather bland, containing perhaps a little fibrin and, occasionally, red blood cells (*Fig. 12.126*).[5,6,13,14] The floor of the blister is typically lined by well-preserved dermal papillae (festooning). There is usually no significant inflammatory component although occasionally, a light perivascular lymphocytic infiltrate may be seen in the superficial dermis. Thickening of the superficial vessels (highlighted by a PAS stain) and dermal sclerosis with elastosis may be apparent.

Direct immunofluorescence reveals Ig (usually IgG, IgM and sometimes IgA) with C3 around the superficial vasculature in a donut distribution and as a fine granular deposit at the epidermal basement membrane region (*Fig. 12.127*).[2,5,11–15] Indirect immunofluorescence is invariably negative.[2]

On electron microscopic examination, the plane of cleavage is variable: in some, it has been shown to be within the lamina lucida whereas in others it has been deep to the lamina densa (*Fig. 12.128*).[5,16,17] As in porphyria cutanea tarda, basement membrane reduplication is typically present both at the epidermodermal junction and also around the superficial vasculature (*Fig. 12.129*).[5]

Differential diagnosis

The invariably negative indirect immunofluorescence and absence of porphyrin abnormalities distinguish this disease from autoimmune bullous dermatoses and porphyria cutanea tarda.[18,19]

References

1. Green, J.J., Manders, S.M. (2001) Pseudoporphyria. *J Am Acad Dermatol*, **44**, 100–108.
2. Schambacher, C.F., Vanness, E.R., Daoud, M.S. et al (2001) Pseudoporphyria: a clinical and biochemical study of 20 patients. *Mayo Clin Proc*, **76**, 488–492.
3. Gupta, A.K., Gupta, M.A., Cardella, C.J. et al (1980) Cutaneous associations of chronic renal failure and dialysis. *Int J Dermatol*, **25**, 498–504.
4. Gilchrest, B., Rowe, J.W., Mihm, M.C. (1975) Bullous dermatosis of hemodialysis. *Ann Intern Med*, **83**, 480–483.
5. De Silva, B., Banney, L., Uttley, W. et al (2000) Pseudoporphyria and nonsteroidal antiinflammatory agents in children with juvenile idiopathic arthritis. *Pediatr Dermatol*, **17**, 480–483.
6. Webster, S.B., Dahlberg, P.J. (1980) Bullous dermatosis of hemodialysis: case report and review of the dermatologic changes in chronic renal failure. *Cutis*, **25**, 322–326.
7. Farr, P.M., Marks, J.M., Diffey, B.L. et al (1988) Skin fragility and blistering due to use of sunbeds. *BMJ*, **296**, 1708–1709.
8. Epstein, J.H., Tuffanelli, D.L., Seibert, J.S. et al (1976) Porphyria-like cutaneous changes induced by tetracycline hydrochloride photosensitization. *Arch Dermatol*, **112**, 661–666.
9. Stenberg, A. (1990) Pseudoporphyria and sunbeds. *Acta Derm Venereol*, **70**, 354–356.
10. Perrot, H., Germain, D., Euvrard, S. et al (1977) Porphyria cutanea tarda-like dermatosis: ultrastructural study of exposed skin. *Arch Dermatol Res*, **259**, 177–185.
11. Wallace, C.A., Farrow, D., Sherry, D.D. (1994) Increased risk of facial scars in children taking non-steroidal antiinflammatory drugs. *J Pediatr*, **125**, 819–822.
12. Murphy, G.M., Wright, J., Nicholls, D.S.H. et al (1989) Sunbed-induced pseudoporphyria. *Br J Dermatol*, **120**, 555–562.
13. Magro, C.M., Crowson, A.N. (1999) Pseudoporphyria associated with relafen therapy. *J Cutan Pathol*, **26**, 42–47.
14. Maynard, B., Peters, M.S. (1992) Histologic and immunofluorescence study of cutaneous porphyrias. *J Cutan Pathol*, **19**, 40–47.
15. Breier, F., Feldmann, R., Pelzl, M. et al (1998) Pseudoporphyria cutanea tarda induced by furosemide in a patient undergoing peritoneal dialysis. *Dermatology*, **197**, 271–273.
16. Judd, L.E., Henderson, D.W., Hill, D.C. (1986) Naproxen-induced pseudoporphyria: a clinical and ultrastructural study. *Arch Dermatol*, **122**, 451–454.
17. Dabski, C., Beutner, E.H. (1991) Studies of laminin and type IV collagen in blisters of porphyria cutanea tarda and drug-induced pseudoporphyria. *J Am Acad Dermatol*, **25**, 28–32.
18. Goldsman, G.I., Taylor, J.S. (1983) Porphyria cutanea tarda and bullous dermatosis associated with chronic renal failure: a review. *Cleve Clin Q*, **50**, 151–161.
19. Harber, L.C., Bickers, D.R. (1984) Porphyria and pseudoporphyria. *J Invest Dermatol*, **82**, 207–209.

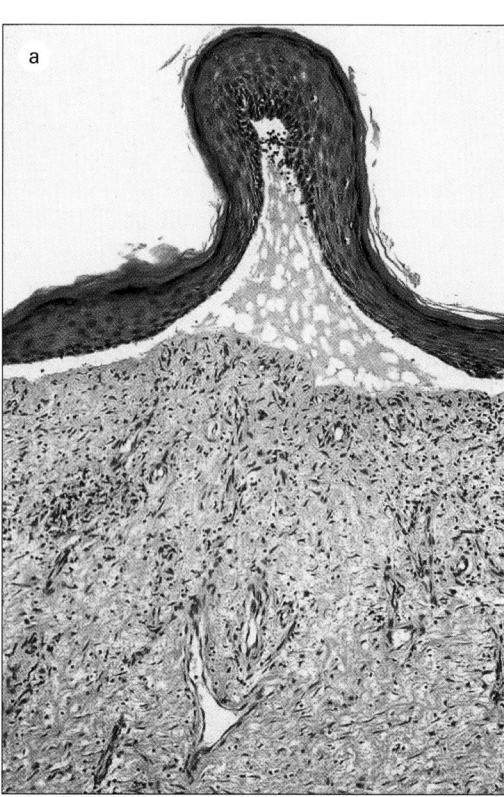

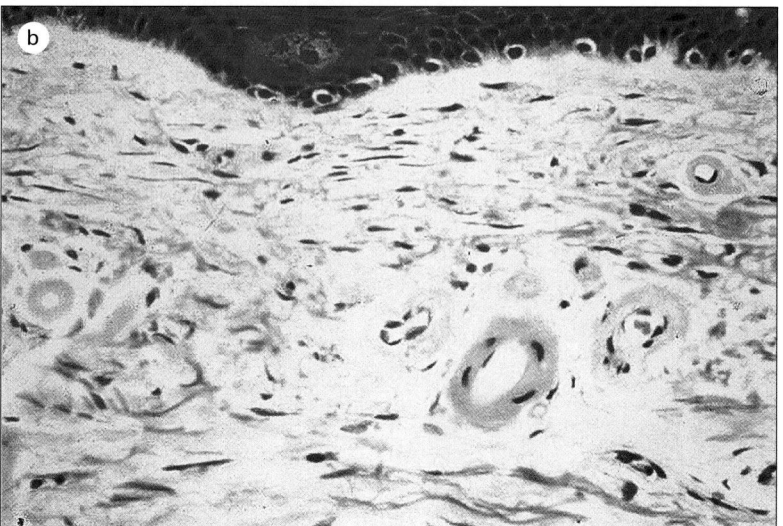

Fig. 12.126 Pseudoporphyria: (a) there is a subepidermal blister; (b) the superficial dermal vessels are thickened with a hyaline deposit. (b) By courtesy of G.M. Murphy, MD, Beaumont Hospital, Dublin, Eire.

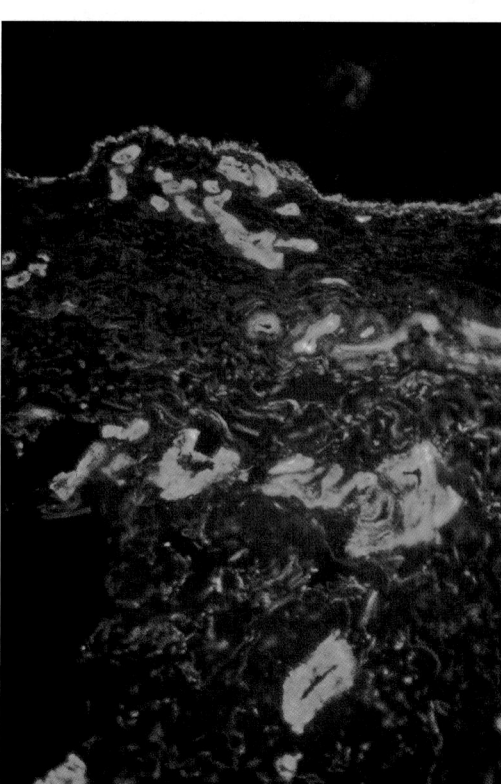

Fig. 12.127 Pseudoporphyria: the vessel wall thickening is in part due to excess type IV collagen, as shown in this field. By courtesy of G.M. Murphy, MD, Beaumont Hospital, Dublin, Eire.

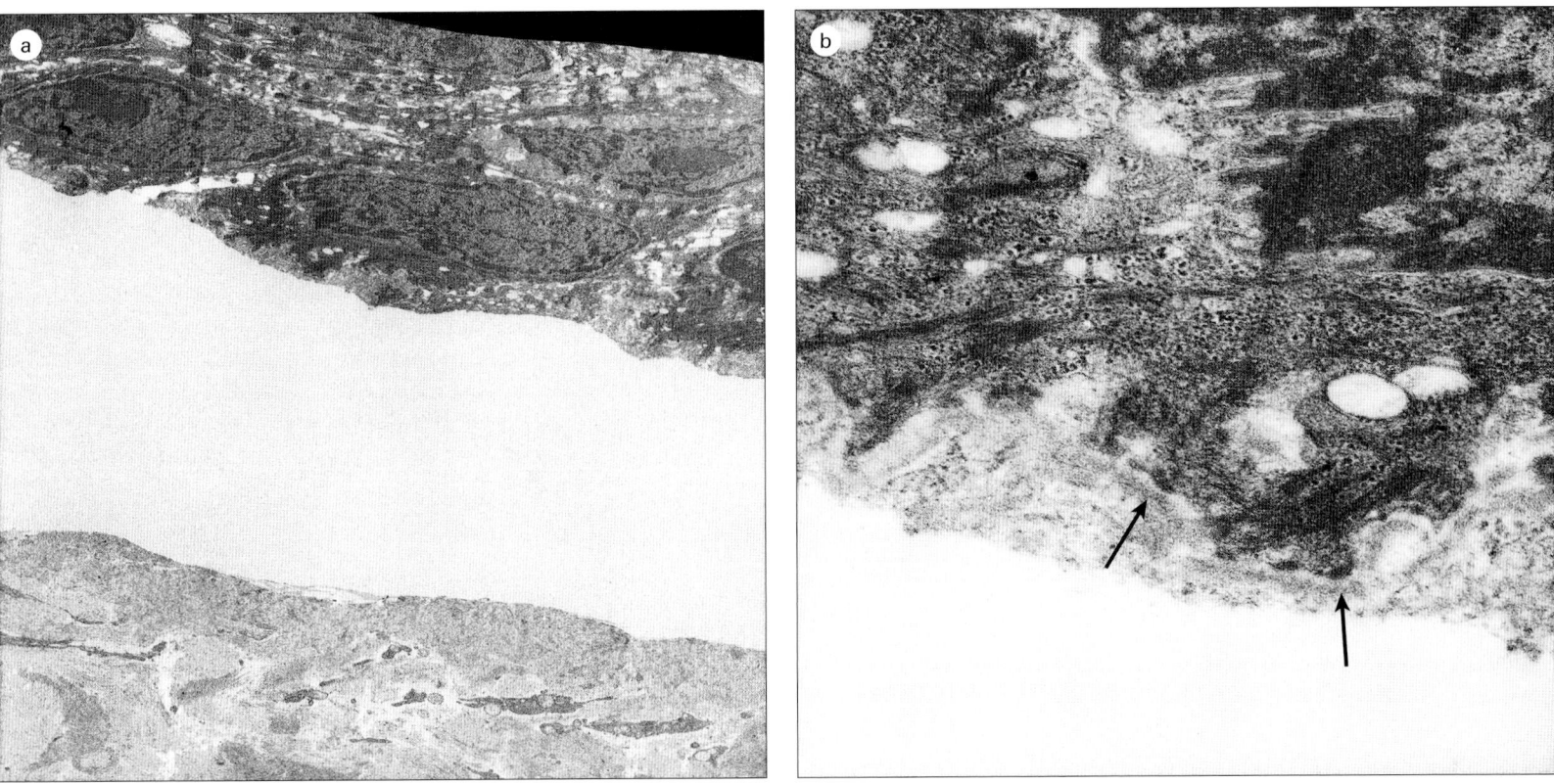

Fig. 12.128
(a, b) Pseudoporphyria: in this example the blister is located in the superficial papillary dermis deep to the lamina densa (arrowed).

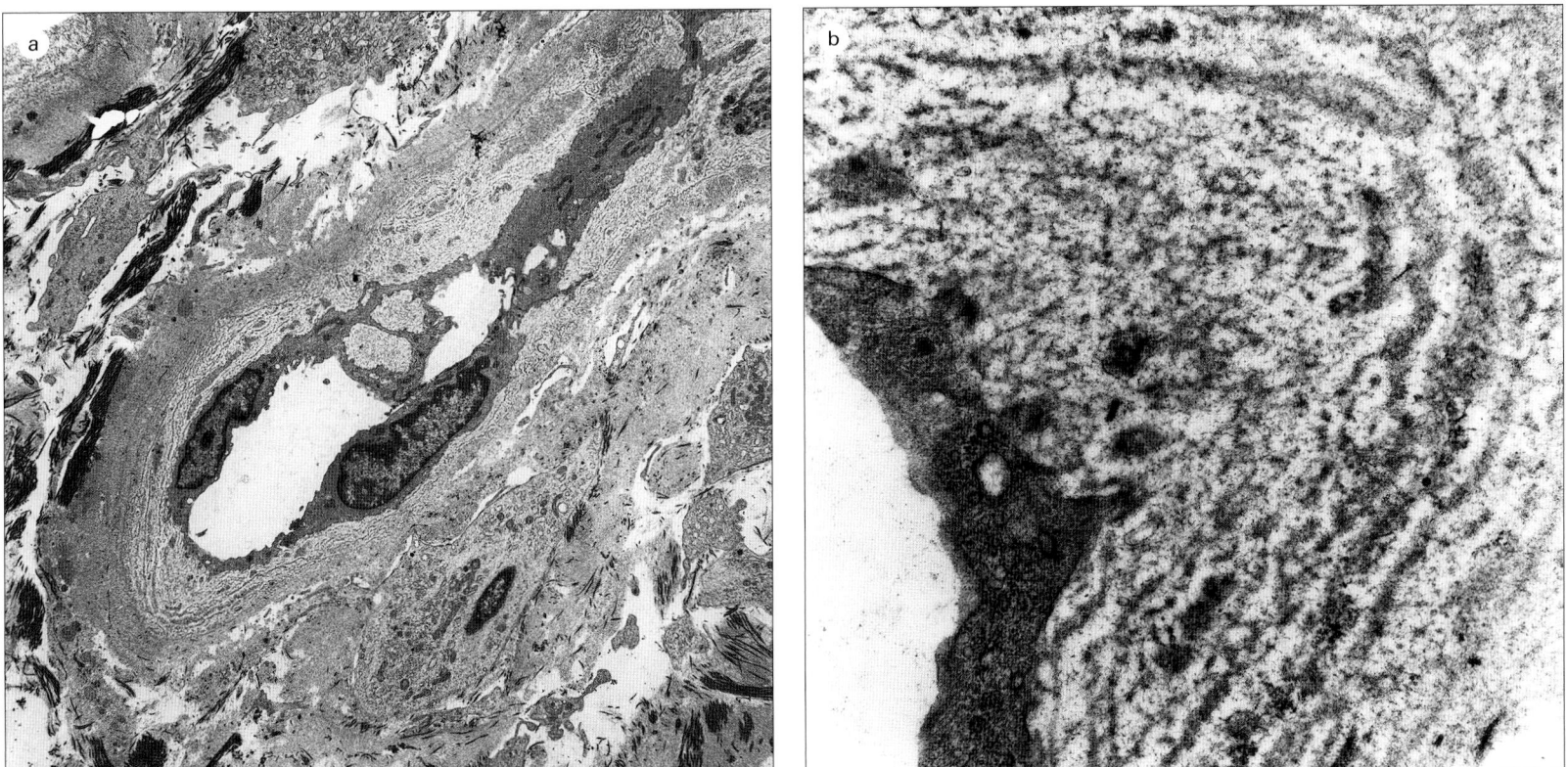

Fig. 12.129
(a, b) Pseudoporphyria: note the striking basement membrane duplication.

Gout

Clinical features

Gout represents a group of disorders of purine metabolism in which elevated levels of uric acid occur.[1-3] The majority of affected patients have reduced excretion of purines which may be caused by diuretic therapy or renal disease. Hyperuricemia may also complicate diabetic ketoacidosis and starvation, and may develop in patients with sarcoidosis and psoriasis.[4,5] Some have increased purine synthesis and this type of disturbance can occur dramatically in the myeloproliferative diseases, particularly following therapy with cytotoxic drugs. Less commonly, gout represents a primary inherited disorder of purine metabolism. A number of enzymatic defects are recognized including hypoxanthine guanine phosphoribosyltransferase activity (X-linked recessive), abnormal phosphoribosylpyrophosphate synthetase variants (X-linked dominant) and glucose-6-phosphatase deficiency.[3]

Males are affected more often than females and presentation is usually in the fourth to sixth decades. However, the incidence in females is rising, particularly in those on diuretics and those with altered renal function.[6] The prevalence of the disease is higher in black patients.[7]

Gout produces recurrent, acute, exceedingly painful monoarticular arthritis, classically of the great toe, but also of the large joints of the legs. Many patients present initially with acute inflammation of the first metatarsophalangeal joint (podagra).[8] The affected joint is characteristically exceedingly tender, hot and erythematous, and cellulitis may therefore enter the differential diagnosis. Precipitating factors include trauma, excessive alcohol consumption, dietary excess, lead exposure, hypertension, renal insufficiency, surgery and infections.[3,8] Alcohol and obesity are associated with increased nucleotide catabolism and decreased urate excretion.[9-11] With chronicity a disabling and often crippling arthritis may develop, particularly affecting the hands and feet.[3] Subsequently, uric acid crystal deposition in skin and soft tissues produces gouty tophi; these nodules are seen most commonly on the external ear, but also over the elbows and on the digits. When large, they often discharge a chalky material (Fig. 12.130). Rare clinical presentations include bullous lesions, a fungating mass and sparing of hemiplegic limbs by the tophi.[12-14] Nowadays, only a minority of patients present with tophi because of improvement in the diagnosis and treatment of the disease.[15] Tophi are rarely the first manifestation of the disease.[16,17] They have exceptionally been described in the mitral valve, breast, nose, cervical spine, sacroiliac joint, larynx and eyes.[18-24] Bone involvement gives rise to characteristic lytic lesions in the distal subchondral region of the digits.[3]

Renal disease, which is an important complication, presents as urate nephropathy and/or uric acid nephrolithiasis.[11,25] In secondary types associated with increased cell turnover, including myeloproliferative disease and multiple myeloma, acute precipitation of uric acid crystals sometimes occurs in the collecting ducts of the kidney during chemotherapy. Uric acid nephropathy may also develop in patients with the inherited variants. Patients present with acute renal failure. More commonly, in primary gout, renal stones are a feature, and chronic urate nephropathy (due to deposition of monosodium urate monohydrate salt crystals in the interstitial tissues of the kidney), presenting as mild proteinuria and hypertension, occasionally develops.[3] Uric acid stones develops in about 40% of patients with gout secondary to myeloproliferative diseases and in 10–25% of patients with the primary variants.[3]

The diagnosis of gout rests primarily on the identification of uric acid crystals within joint fluid or tophi rather than on serum uric acid levels, which can be unreliable. Acute attacks of gout can be associated with normal uric acid levels.[8]

Histological features

The demonstration of uric acid crystals in tophi requires alcohol fixation and anhydrous processing because monosodium urate is water soluble (Fig. 12.131).[26] In formalin-fixed sections, uric acid crystals appear as amorphous material in the dermis or subcutaneous tissues, surrounded by a marked granulomatous response in which many giant cells are usually evident (Figs 12.132, 12.133). Calcification may be a late complication. In secondarily infected lesions, a neutrophil polymorph infiltrate is sometimes present.[27] In alcohol-fixed sections, the deposits are seen to be composed of needle-shaped brown crystals, which lie in bundles and show negative birefringence with polarized light and a first order red compensator filter (Figs 12.134, 12.135).[28]

References

1. Becker, M.A. (1988) Clinical aspects of monosodium urate monohydrate crystal deposition (gout). *Rheum Dis Clin North Am*, **14**, 377–394.
2. Rejinato, A.J., Schumacher, H.R. Jr (1988) Crystal-associated arthropathies. *Clin Geriatric Med*, **4**, 295–322.

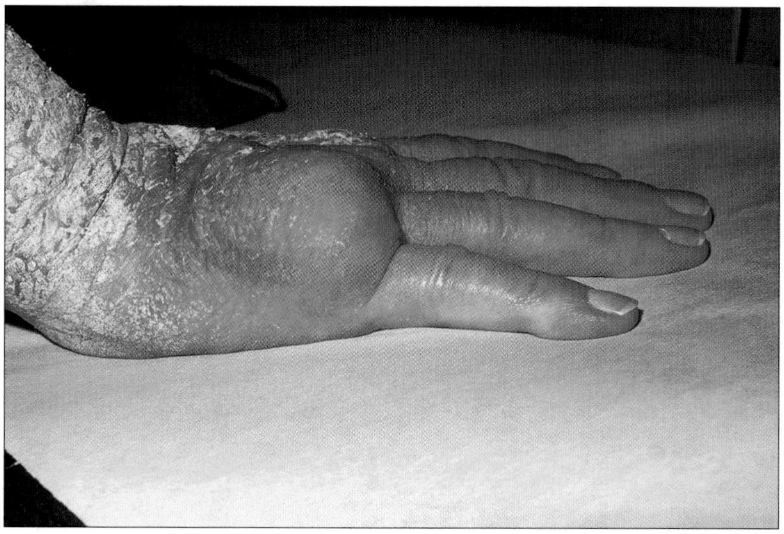

Fig. 12.130
Gout: massive deposit on the dorsal aspect of the hand.

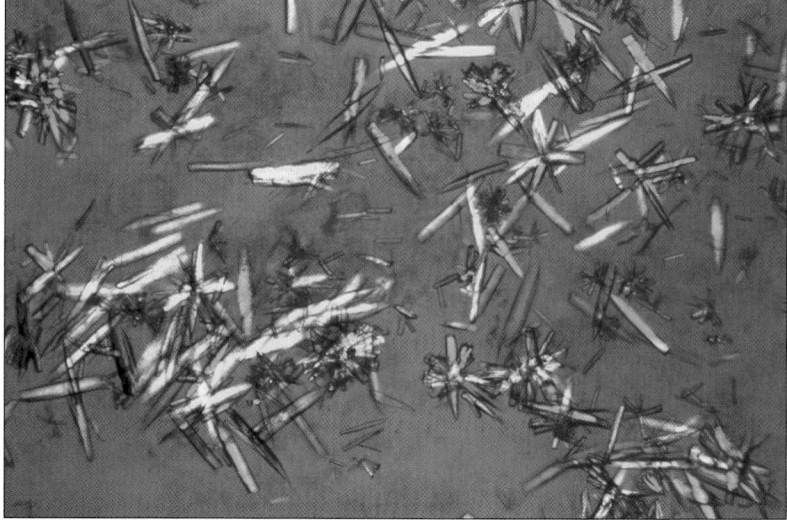

Fig. 12.131
Gout: characteristic needle shaped crystals. By courtesy of G.T. McKee, MD, Massachusetts General Hospital, Boston, USA.

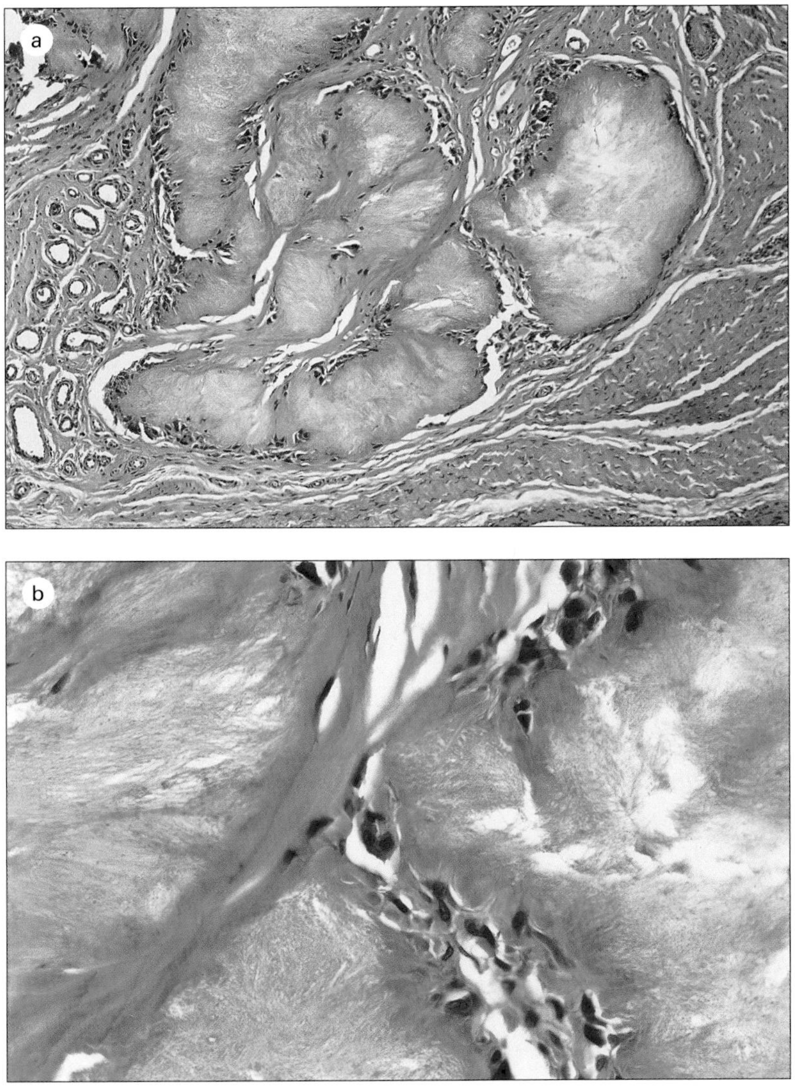

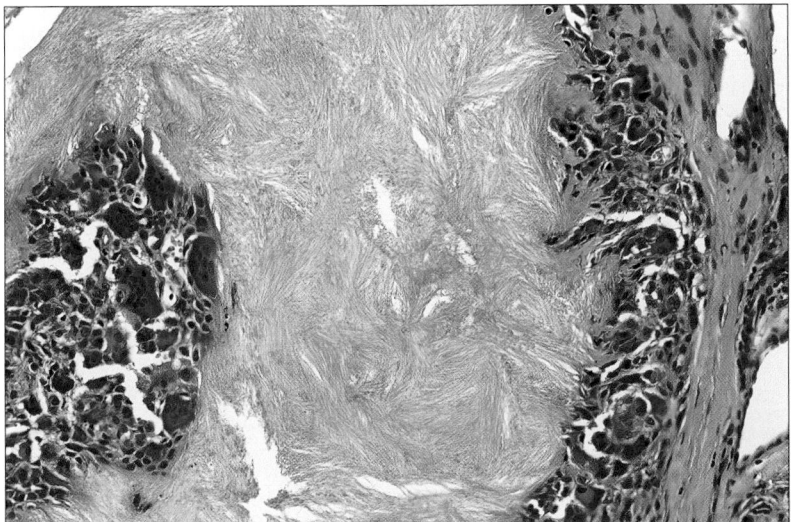

Fig. 12.132
Gout: (a) circumscribed deposits of uric acid are scattered within the dermis, note the accompanying fibrosis; (b) formalin fixation has destroyed the uric acid crystals to leave amorphous eosinophilic material.

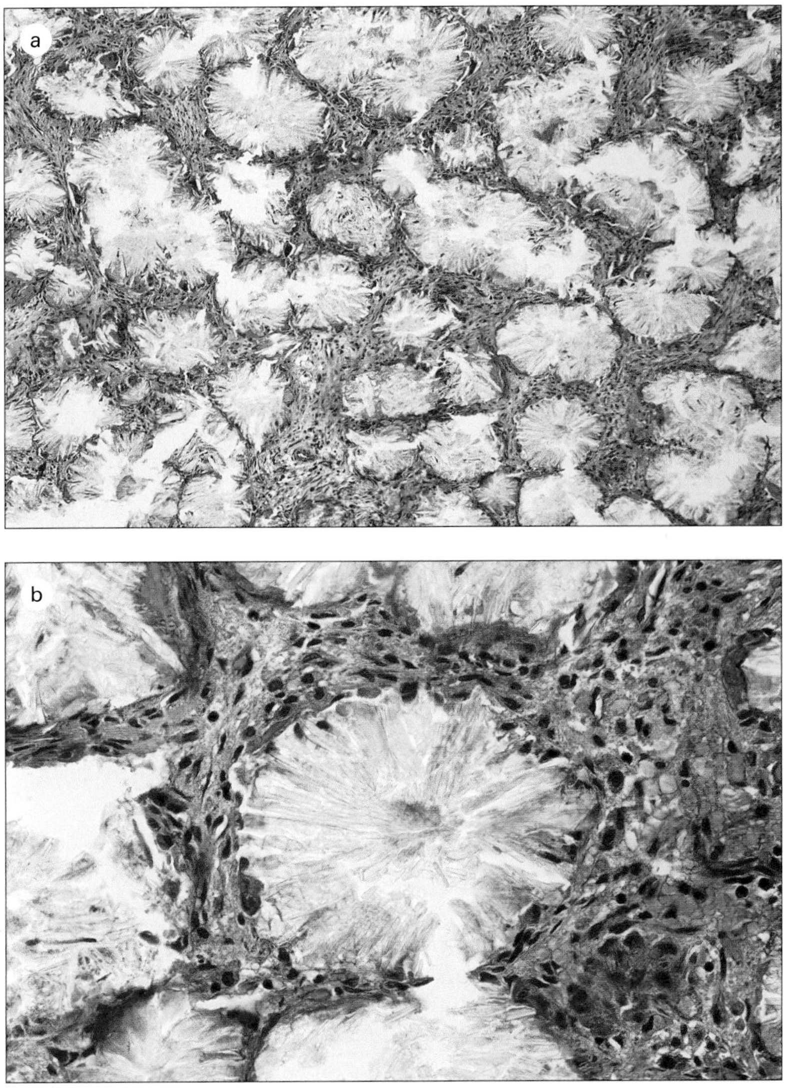

Fig. 12.134
(a, b) Gout: characteristic needle-shaped uric acid crystals are seen in alcohol-fixed and anhydrous processed material.

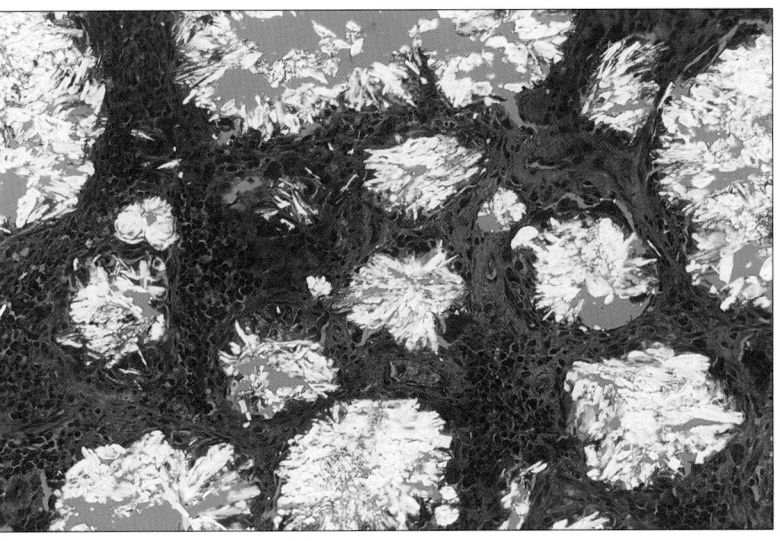

Fig. 12.133
Gout: multinucleate giant cells are present.

Fig. 12.135
Gout: the crystals display striking birefringence when viewed with polarized light.

3. German, D.C., Holmes, E.W. (1986) Hyperuricemia and gout. *Med Clin North Am*, 70, 419–436.
4. Lambert, J.R., Wright, V. (1977) Serum uric acid levels in psoriatic arthritis. *Ann Rheum Dis*, 36, 264–267.
5. Zimmer, J.G., Demis, D.J. (1966) Associations between gout, psoriasis and sarcoidosis: with consideration of their pathologic significance. *Ann Intern Med*, 64, 786–796.
6. Terkeltaub, R.A. (1993) Gout and mechanisms of crystal-induced inflammation. *Curr Opin Rheumatol*, 5, 510–516.
7. Roubenoff, R. (1990) Gout and hyperuricemia. *Rheum Dis Clin North Am*, 16, 539–550.
8. Touart, D.M., Sau, P. (1998) Cutaneous deposition diseases. Part II. *J Am Acad Dermatol*, 39, 527–544.
9. Faller, J., Fox, I.H. (1982) Ethanol-induced hyperuricemia: evidence for increased urate production by activation of adenine nucleotide turnover. *N Engl J Med*, 307, 1598–1602.
10. Lieber, C.S., Jones, D.P., Losowsky, M.S. (1962) Interrelation of uric acid and ethanol metabolism in man. *J Clin Invest*, 41, 1863–1870.
11. Emmerson, B.T. (1973) Alteration of urate metabolism by weight reduction. *Aust N Z J Med*, 3, 410–412.
12. Schumacher, H.R. (1977) Bullous tophi in gout. *Ann Rheum Dis*, 36, 91–93.
13. Low, L.L., Cervantes, A.G., Melcher, W.L. (1992) Tophaceous gout as a fungating mass. *Arthritis Rheum*, 35, 1399–1400.
14. Glynn, J.J., Clayton, M.L. (1976) Sparing effect of hemiplegia on tophaceous gout. *Ann Rheum Dis*, 35, 534–535.
15. O'Duffy, J.D., Hunder, G.G., Kelley, P.J. (1975) Decreasing prevalence of tophaceous gout. *Mayo Clinic Proc*, 50, 227–228.
16. Wernick, R., Winkler, C., Campbell, S. (1992) Tophi as the initial manifestation of gout. *Arch Intern Med*, 152, 873–876.
17. López-Redondo, M.J., Requena, L., Macia, M. et al (1993) Fingertip tophi without gouty arthritis. *Dermatology*, 187, 140–143.
18. Scalapino, J.N., Edwards, W.D., Steckelberg, J.M. et al (1984) Mitral stenosis associated with valvular tophi. *Mayo Clin Proc*, 59, 509–512.
19. Gisser, S.D., Kletter, I. (1982) Gouty mammary tophus. *South Med J*, 75, 773–774.
20. Rask, M.R., Kopf, E.H. (1978) Nasal gouty tophus. *JAMA*, 240, 636.
21. Vaccaro, A.R., An, H.S., Cotler, J.M. et al (1993) Recurrent cervical subluxations in a patient with gout and end-stage renal disease. *Orthopedics*, 16, 1273–1276.
22. Malawista, S.E., Seegmiller, J.E., Hathaway, B.E. et al (1965) Sacroiliac gout. *JAMA*, 194, 954–956.
23. Marion, R.B., Alperin, J.E., Maloney, W.H. (1972) Gouty tophus of the true vocal cord. *Arch Otolaryngol*, 96, 161–162.
24. Martínez-Cordero, E., Barreira-Mercado, E., Katona, G. (1986) Eye tophi deposition in gout. *J Rheumatol*, 13, 471–473.
25. Barlow, K.A., Beilin, L.J. (1968) Renal disease in primary gout. *QJM*, 37, 79–96.
26. King, D.F., King, I.A. (1982) The appropriate processing of tophi for microscopy. *Am J Dermatopathol*, 4, 239.
27. Lichenstein, L., Scott, H.W., Levin, M.H. (1956) Pathologic changes in gout. *Am J Pathol*, 32, 871–895.
28. Cohen, P.R., Schmidt, W.A., Rapini, R.P. (1991) Chronic tophaceous gout with severely deforming arthritis: a case report with emphasis on histopathologic considerations. *Cutis*, 48, 445–451.

Ochronosis

The term 'ochronosis' was first used by Virchow in 1866 to describe a condition in which clinically blue–black cutaneous pigmentation in the skin was associated with the microscopic deposition of an ochre-colored pigment. There are two main types: alkaptonuria and exogenous ochronosis.

Alkaptonuria

Clinical features

This is an autosomal recessively inherited condition (with an approximate incidence of 1:1,000,000) in which deficiency of homogentisate 1,2-dioxygenase in the liver and kidneys (necessary for the catabolism of phenylalanine and tyrosine) leads to the accumulation of homogentisic acid (2,5-hydroquinone acetic acid) in cartilage, tendon, skin and fibrous tissue.[1,2] The condition is particularly seen in patients of Eastern European origin, mainly those from Slovakia where the incidence is as high as 1:19,000.[3] Clinical features relate particularly to joint and cardiovascular involvement, renal and prostatic stones, and ocular and cutaneous lesions. Alkaptonuria, or blackening of the urine after standing due to oxidation of homogentisic acid, usually becomes obvious in childhood. The blue–black discoloration of the tissues involved is due in part to the Tyndall effect.

The cutaneous changes that are seen particularly on sun-exposed skin and areas with maximum numbers of sweat glands develop later, at about 30–40 years of age.[1,2] Deposition of polymerized oxidase pigment in the ear cartilage produces painful thickening and blue–black speckled discoloration. Involvement of the eardrum and ossicles may result in tinnitus and deafness.[2] Subsequently, discoloration of the sclera, tendons and skin of the face, hands and flexures occurs. The skin pigmentation may be more prominent on the palms and soles.[4] Finally, a characteristic arthritis, which is often severe, presents in almost all patients. Low back pain is followed by involvement of the large joints of the limbs. Spinal involvement leads to disc herniation, spondylosis and osteophytosis with resultant limitation of movement and loss of height.[1] Despite widespread morbidity, alkaptonuria is not associated with significant mortality.[1]

Osteoarticular involvement – which is particularly evident in the knees, shoulders, and hips, and in advanced cases the vertebral column – is characterized by pigmentation of the articular cartilage, synovium and capsule-associated with fibrillation, fragmentation and erosion.[5] Osteoarthritis may also be evident and chronic non-specific synovitis is commonly present. Cardiovascular involvement occurs in up to 50% of patients and mainly consists of pigmentation and calcification of the aortic valve, which may lead to stenosis.[6,7] Cardiovascular pigmentation, which is especially seen on the endocardium and valves (aortic and mitral), also affects the intima and media of arteries. Surprisingly, even with heavy pigment deposition and smooth muscle cell degeneration, aneurysm formation is not a feature of vascular involvement.[8]

Kidneys that typically show very marked pigmentation, especially involving the pyramids and calculi, are found in up to 60% of patients.[9] Ochronotic prostatic stones are a nearly invariable feature, but bladder calculi are much less frequent.[2,8]

Asymptomatic ocular involvement is seen in up to 70% of patients.[10] Pigmentation particularly affects the sclera and to a lesser extent the conjunctiva and cornea.[8] The lesions are typically non-inflammatory.

Ochronotic pigmentation is frequently seen in the hyaline cartilage of the larynx, trachea and bronchi.[8] Involvement of endocrine organs, central nervous system and teeth is rarely seen.[11–13]

Exogenous ochronosis

Clinical features

Deposition in the skin of an identical pigment to that seen in alkaptonuria may occur as a result of the application of phenol (carbolic acid) to leg ulcers, therapy with resorcinol and picric acid, the oral and intramuscular administration of antimalarials such as chloroquine, and the application to dark skin of bleaching creams containing hydroquinone, most often in black women.[14–21] Antimalarials result in slate-gray pigmentation affecting the knees, face, palate and subungual regions.[22] In hydroquinone-induced ochronosis, lesions occur particularly over bony prominences such as the forehead, temples, nose and lower jaws and also on the sides of the neck (*Fig. 12.136*).[23] In addition to increased pigmentation, patients develop widespread 'caviar-like' black papules; cutaneous atrophy and colloid milia may also occur.[23–25] Hydroquinone-induced ochronosis is a major problem in the black population of South Africa. In one series the prevalence among users of skin lighteners was almost 70%.[18] Exogenous ochronosis due to hydroquinone is thought to be photoactivated. Exogenous ochronosis tends to chronicity.

Pathogenesis and histological features

In alkaptonuria, as a result of the deficiency of homogentisate 1,2-dioxygenase, homogentisic acid is oxidized and polymerized by polyphenol oxidase, to form benzoquinone acetic acid. This results in a black pigment that binds irreversibly to collagen. Polyphenol oxidase is particularly common in cartilage and skin and this reflects in their preferential involvement. The pigment formed has not been characterized but there are some similarities to melanin.[26] It appears that the pigment deposition occurs both in previously damaged collagen and in normal collagen. The gene responsible for alkaptonuria has been localized to chromosome 3q.[27,28] The human homogentisate 1,2-dioxygenase gene has been cloned and it has been shown that patients with alkaptonuria carry two copies of a loss-of-function homogentisate 1,2-dioxygenase allele.[29] A study of patients with alkaptonuria has demonstrated that they have a significantly higher prevalence of HLA-DR7 than normal patients.[30]

The exact pathogenesis of exogenous ochronosis is not known. Proposed mechanisms include:

- the inhibition in the skin of homogentisate 1,2-dioxygenase by hydroquinone with formation of pigment[31]
- increased tyrosinase activity induced by hydroquinone.[14]

Ochronosis presents as yellow–brown, sharply defined, irregularly shaped and frequently fragmented fibers in the superficial dermis (*Fig. 12.137*).[1,16] The ochronotic pigment is autofluorescent, appears black with methylene blue, but does not stain with van Gieson or Perl's stains or the Masson–Fontana reaction.[1] Pigment granules are often present in the epithelium and basement membrane of sweat glands, in endothelial cells and within dermal macrophages.[8]

In ochronosis due to hydroquinones the skin may, in addition, show melanophages in the upper dermis associated with depigmentation of the epidermal melanocytes.[23]

In early lesions the collagen fibers appear basophilic and swollen before developing the characteristic yellow ochronotic morphology (*Fig. 12.138*). With chronicity, large amorphous eosinophilic granules may develop, resembling colloid milium.[23] Solar elastosis and foreign body granulomata (sometimes indistinguishable from sarcoidosis) are less common features.[16,17,25,32] An actinic granuloma-like variant has been described.[24] Transepidermal and transfollicular elimination of ochronotic fibers has occasionally been documented.[25,33]

Antimalarial pigmentation is due to melanin and hemosiderin deposition in addition to the classical ochronotic fibers.[1]

Electron microscopic studies have shown that initially electron-dense ochronotic pigment is deposited around swollen collagen fibrils that characteristically lose their banding pattern.[23] These fibrils subsequently degenerate until the whole collagen fiber is replaced by amorphous ochronotic pigment. Rupture of the fibrils also occurs, so that the pigment comes to lie scattered free in the dermis. Phagocytosis of the latter by macrophages and giant cells may be seen.[8,16] The colloid milium-like deposits in hydroquinone-associated ochronosis consist of electron-dense granular material lacking a significant fibrillar component.[23]

References

1. Albers, S.E., Brozena, S.J., Glass, L.F. et al (1992) Alkaptonuria and ochronosis: case report and review. *J Am Acad Dermatol*, 27, 609–614.
2. O'Brien, W.M., La Du, B.N., Bunim, J.J. (1963) Biochemical, pathologic and clinical aspects of alkaptonuria, ochronosis and ochronotic arthropathy. Review of the word literature (1584–1962). *Am J Med*, 34, 813–838.
3. Zatkova, A., de Bernabe, D.B., Polakova, H. et al (2000) High frequency of alkaptonuria in Slovakia: evidence for the appearance of multiple mutations in HGO involving different mutational hot spots. *Am J Hum Genet*, 67, 1333–1339.
4. Vijaikumar, M., Thappa, D.M., Srikanth, S. et al (2000) Alkaptonuric ochronosis presenting as palmoplantar pigmentation. *Clin Exp Dermatol*, 25, 305–307.

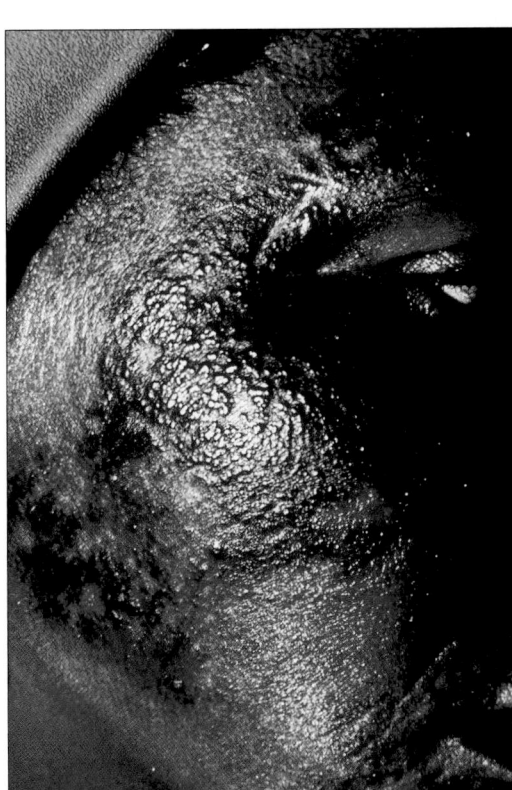

Fig. 12.136
Exogenous ochronosis: hyperpigmented plaque with numerous colloid milia in a Bantu female. The lesions developed as a consequence of the application of hydroquinone bleaching cream.

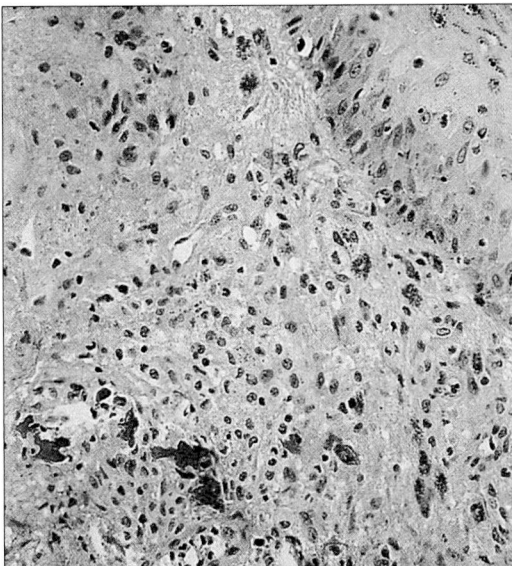

Fig. 12.137
Ochronosis: typical swollen, irregular, golden brown fibers are seen (bottom left).

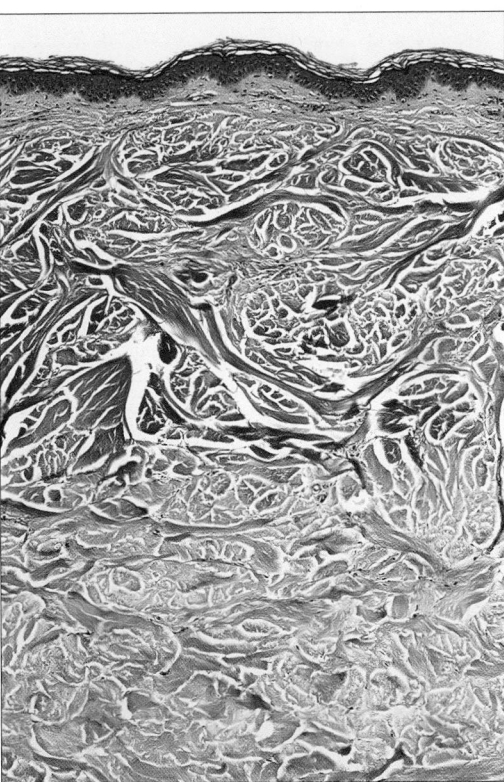

Fig. 12.138
Exogenous ochronosis: early lesion showing markedly swollen collagen fibers.

5. Schumacher, H.R., Holdsworth, D.E. (1977) Ochronotic arthropathy. I. Clinicopathologic studies. *Semin Arthritis Rheum*, 6, 207–246.
6. Levine, H.D., Parisi, A.F., Holdsworth, D.E. et al (1978) Aortic valve replacement for ochronosis of the aortic valve. *Chest*, 74, 466–467.
7. Gaines, J.J., Pai, G.M. (1987) Cardiovascular ochronosis. *Arch Pathol Lab Med*, 111, 991–994.
8. Gaines, J.J. Jr (1989) The pathology of alkaptonuric ochronosis. *Hum Pathol*, 20, 40–46, 500.
9. Koar, J., Krizek, V.L. (1968) Roentgen signs of alkaptonuric ochronosis. *Fortschritte auf dem Gebiete der Rontgenstrahlen und der Nuklearmedizin erganzungsband*, 109, 203.
10. Daicker, B., Riede, U.N. (1974) Histologische und ultrastrukturelle befunde bei alkaptonurischer ochronosis oculi. *Ophthalmologica*, 169, 377–388.
11. Cooper, J.A., Moran, T.J. (1957) Studies on ochronosis: report of a case with death from ochrontic nephrosis. *Arch Pathol Lab Med*, 64, 46–53.
12. Siekert, R.G., Gibilisco, J.A. (1970) Discoloration of teeth in alkaptonuria (ochronosis) and parkinsonism. *Oral Surg*, 29, 197–199.
13. Galdston, M., Steele, J.M., Dobriner, K. (1952) Alcaptonuria and ochronosis with a report of three patients and metabolic studies in two. *Am J Med*, 13, 432–452.
14. Engasser, P.J. (1984) Ochronosis caused by bleaching creams. *J Am Acad Dermatol*, 10, 1072–1073.
15. Bruce, S., Tshen, J.A., Chow, D. (1986) Exogenous ochronosis resulting from quinine injections. *J Am Acad Dermatol*, 15, 357–361.
16. Tidman, M.J., Horton, J.J., MacDonald, D.M. (1985) Hydroquinone induced ochronosis – light and electron microscopic features. *Clin Exp Dermatol*, 11, 224–228.
17. Lawrence, N., Bligard, C.A., Reed, R. et al (1988) Exogenous ochronosis in the United States. *J Am Acad Dermatol*, 18, 1207–1211.
18. Hardwick, N., Van Gelder, L.W., Van der Merwe, C.A. et al (1989) Exogenous ochronosis: an epidemiological study. *Br J Dermatol*, 120, 229–238; 121, 153.
19. Cullison, D., Abele, D.C., O'Quinn, J.L. (1983) Localized exogenous ochronosis: report of a case and review of the literature. *J Am Acad Dermatol*, 8, 882–889.
20. Howard, K.L., Furner, B.B. (1990) Exogenous ochronosis in a Mexican–American woman. *Cutis*, 45, 180–182.
21. Mahler, R., Sissons, W., Watters, K. (1986) Pigmentation due to quinidine therapy. *Arch Dermatol*, 122, 1062–1064.
22. Tuffanelli, D., Abraham, R.K., Dubois, E.J. (1963) Pigmentation from antimalarial therapy. *Arch Dermatol*, 88, 113–120.
23. Phillips, J.I., Isaacson, C., Carman, N. (1986) Ochronosis in black South Africans who used skin lighteners. *Am J Dermatopathol*, 8, 14–21.
24. Jordaan, H.F., Mulligan, R.P. (1990) Actinic granuloma-like change in exogenous ochronosis: case report. *J Cutan Pathol*, 17, 236–240.
25. Findlay, G.H., Morrison, J.G.L., Simson, I.W. (1975) Exogenous ochronosis and pigmented colloid milium from hydroquinone bleaching creams. *Br J Dermatol*, 93, 613–622.
26. Touart, D.M., Sau, P. (1998) Cutaneous deposition diseases. Part II. *J Am Acad Dermatol*, 39, 527–544.
27. Janocha, S., Wolz, W., Srsen, S. et al (1994) The human gene for alkaptonuria (AK) maps to chromosome 3q. *Genomics*, 19, 5–8.
28. Pollak, M.R., Chou, Y.H.W., Cerda, J.J. et al (1993) Homozygosity mapping of the gene for alkaptonuria to chromosome 3q2. *Nat Genet*, 5, 201–204.
29. Granadino, B., Beltran-Valero de Bernabe, D., Fernandez-Canon, J.M. et al (1997) The human homogentisate 1,2-dioxygenase (HGO) gene. *Genomics*, 43, 115–122.
30. Aliberti, G., Proietta, M., Pulignano, I. et al (2001) HLA antigens in alkaptonuric patients. *Panminerva Med*, 43, 145–148.
31. Penneys, N.S. (1985) Ochronosis like pigmentation from hydroxyquinone bleaching creams. *Arch Dermatol*, 121, 1239–1240.
32. Dogliotti, M., Leibowitz, M. (1979) Granulomatous ochronosis – a cosmetic-induced skin disorder in blacks. *S Afr Med J*, 56, 757–760.
33. Jordaan, H.F., Van Niekerk, D.J.T. (1991) Transepidermal elimination in exogenous ochronosis: a report of two cases. *Am J Dermatopathol*, 13, 418–424.

Hartnup disease

Clinical features

Hartnup disease is an autosomal recessive disorder characterized by defective gastrointestinal absorption and renal reabsorption of mono-amine and monocarboxylic amino acids due to a defect in the neutral brush border system.[1] One of the effects is tryptophan deficiency.[2] In addition to a pellagra eruption (see below), patients also have a characteristic aminoaciduria and cerebellar ataxia.[3,4] The skin may appear atrophic. The disease may, however, sometimes be so mild as to remain asymptomatic.[5] Additional symptoms include diarrhea and central nervous system dysfunction ranging from mild apathy to frank dementia.[6] An exceptional case of a patient with identical symptoms and signs of Hartnup disease in the absence of a recognized metabolic abnormality or aminoaciduria has been described.[7] The disease has been mapped to chromosome 11q13.[8] Linkage analysis of two Japanese families, however, has mapped the locus of this disease to 5p15.[8]

Histological features

The cutaneous histology is identical to that of pellagra (see below).

References

1. Miller, S.J. (1989) Nutritional deficiency and the skin. *J Am Acad Dermatol*, 21, 1–30.
2. Milne, J.D., Crawford, M.A., Girao, C.B. (1959) The metabolic abnormality of Hartnup disease. *Biochem J*, 72, 30P.
3. Halvorsen, K., Halvorsen, S. (1963) Hartnup disease. *Pediatrics*, 31, 29–38.
4. Schmidtke, K., Endres, W., Roscher, A. et al (1992) Hartnup syndrome, progressive encephalopathy and allo-albuminemia. A clinicopathological case study. *Eur J Pediatr*, 151, 899–903.
5. [No Authors Listed] (1984) Treatment of Hartnup disease with nicotinic acid. *Nutr Rev*, 42, 251–253.
6. Mahon, B.E., Levy, H.L. (1986) Maternal Hartnup disorder. *Am J Med Genet*, 24, 513–518.
7. Da Gloria, E.R., Assuncao, J.G., Costa, M.A. (1990) Clinical picture of Hartnup disease. Without urine amino acids or any other identified metabolic disorder (a new entity). *Med Cutan Ibero Lat Am*, 18, 227–231.
8. Nozaki, J., Dakeishi, M., Ohura, T. et al (2001) Homozygosity mapping to chromosome 5p15 of a gene responsible for Hartnup disorder. *Biochem Biophys Res Commun*, 284, 255–260.

Pellagra

Clinical features

Pellagra develops as a consequence of deficiency of nicotinic acid (niacin, vitamin B3) or its precursor tryptophan.[1,2] The cause may be dietary: in developed countries it is most frequently observed in alcoholics, in those living in conditions of socioeconomic deprivation and in those with anorexia nervosa or malabsorption due to extensive gastrointestinal disease (e.g. partial gastrectomy, gastroenterostomy and Crohn's disease).[1,3] A severe case of cytomegalovirus colitis in an immunocompetent patient has also been associated with pellagra.[4] It is sometimes also a feature of the carcinoid syndrome because the tumor cells consume available tryptophan to produce serotonin.[5] Pellagra occasionally develops after therapy with a number of drugs including isoniazid, 6-mercaptopurine and 5-fluorouracil.[5–8] Finally, it can occur in Hartnup disease and in association with defects in the metabolism of tryptophan.[9] Pellagra is particularly prominent in parts of Africa and Asia where nutritional deficiencies are prevalent.[1] A rare case of pellagra has been described in association with the intake of alternative medicines.[10] A further case has been described in association with amyloidosis secondary to multiple myeloma.[11]

The skin eruption of pellagra is photosensitive in nature. An initial painful sunburn-like erythema subsides to leave a dusky brownish discoloration with a dry scaly appearance (*Figs 12.139, 12.140*). Blisters may sometimes be evident. The eruption is typically sharply demarcated, symmetrical and occurs on the backs of the hands, the forearms, the knees, central chest, neck and face.[6] The thickened skin around the photoexposed skin of the neck typically resembles a necklace (Casal's necklace). Other features sometimes present include cheilosis, glossitis, angular stomatitis, and oral or perianal sores.[6]

Histological features

The appearances in pellagra are usually non-specific. There is hyperkeratosis, parakeratosis and acanthosis associated with increased melanin pigmentation and in early lesions, keratinocyte vacuolation in the upper reaches of the epidermis.[6] Telangiectasia and a perivascular chronic inflammatory cell infiltrate in the upper dermis may also be evident. Older lesions sometimes show epidermal psoriasiform hyperplasia.[12] In some instances the histology can resemble that of necrolytic migratory erythema and acrodermatitis enteropathica.

Differential diagnosis

The diagnosis is very much dependent upon clinicopathological correlation, particularly in those cases that resemble necrolytic migratory erythema and acrodermatitis enteropathica.

References

1. Stratigos, J.K., Katsambas, A. (1977) Pellagra: a still existing disease. *Br J Dermatol*, **96**, 99–106.
2. Hendricks, W.M. (1991) Pellagra and pellagra-like dermatoses: etiology, differential diagnosis, dermatopathology, and treatment. *Semin Dermatol*, **10**, 282–292.
3. Kertesz, S.G. (2001) Pellagra in 2 homeless men. *Mayo Clin Proc*, **76**, 315–318.
4. Lu, J.Y., Yu, C.L., Wu, M.Z. (2001) Pellagra in an immunocompetent patient with cytomegalovirus colitis. *Am J Gastroenterol*, **96**, 932–934.
5. Castiello, R.J., Lynch, P.J. (1972) Pellagra and the carcinoid syndrome. *Arch Dermatol*, **105**, 574–577.
6. Miller, S.J. (1989) Nutritional deficiencies and the skin. *J Am Acad Dermatol*, **21**, 1–30.
7. Stevens, H.P., Ostlere, L.S., Begent, R.H. et al (1993) Pellagra secondary to 5-fluorouracil. *Br J Dermatol*, **128**, 578–580.
8. Darvay, A., Basarab, T., McGregor, J.M. et al (1999) Isoniazid induced pellagra despite pyridoxine supplementation. *Clin Exp Dermatol*, **24**, 167–169.
9. Clayton, P.T., Bridges, N.A., Atherton, D.J. et al (1991) Pellagra with colitis due to a defect in tryptophan metabolism. *Eur J Pediatr*, **150**, 498–502.
10. Wood, B., Rademaker, M., Oakley, A. et al (1998) Pellagra in a woman using alternative remedies. *Australas J Dermatol*, **39**, 42–44.
11. Itami, A., Ando, I., Kukita, A. et al (1997) Pellagra associated with amyloidosis secondary to multiple myeloma. *Br J Dermatol*, **137**, 829.
12. Moore, R.A., Spies, T.D., Cooper, Z.K. (1942) Histopathology of the skin in pellagra. *Arch Dermatol*, **46**, 100–111.

Scurvy

Clinical features

Scurvy, due to vitamin C deficiency, results from a diet inadequate in fresh fruit and vegetables and is nowadays most often encountered following inappropriate dieting, food fads and in alcoholics and socially isolated individuals.[1]

Cutaneous manifestations include dry skin, follicular hyperkeratoses particularly affecting the forearms, legs and abdomen, perifollicular hemorrhages particularly affecting the legs, petechiae and subungual splinter hemorrhages, leg edema, alopecia, erythematous, swollen and bleeding gums with tooth loss and clinical evidence of poor wound healing.[1,2]

Pathogenesis and histological features

Vitamin C is necessary for hydroxylation of proline and lysine residues during the conversion of procollagen into collagen fibers. As a result of impaired collagen synthesis, basement membrane synthesis is defective with consequent loss of blood vessel wall integrity. This, combined with impaired dermal connective tissue constituents, results in a bleeding tendency.

The cutaneous features include follicular dilatation and keratin plugging, perifollicular hemorrhages with chronic inflammation and hemosiderin deposition.[2–4] The alopecia is characterized by hair shaft fracture and corkscrew hairs within a dilated and plugged follicle (*Fig. 12.141*).[1,2,5]

References

1. Hirschmann, J.V., Raugi, G.J. (1999) Adult scurvy. *J Am Acad Dermatol*, **41**, 895–906.
2. Prendiville, J.S., Manfredi, L.N. (1992) Skin signs of nutritional disorders. *Semin Dermatol*, **11**, 88–97.
3. Onorato, J., Lynfield, Y. (1992) Scurvy. *Cutis*, **49**, 321–322.
4. Yalcin, A., Ural, A.U., Beyan, C. et al (1996) Scurvy presenting with cutaneous and articular signs and decrease in red and white blood cells. *Int J Dermatol*, **35**, 879–881.
5. Walter, J.F. (1979) Scurvy resulting from a self-imposed diet. *West J Med*, **130**, 177–179.

Calcinosis cutis

Calcinosis cutis may occur when connective tissue is abnormal (dystrophic) or where calcium or phosphate levels in the blood are high (metastatic); alternatively, there may be no obvious underlying cause (idiopathic) (*Table 12.5*).[1–3]

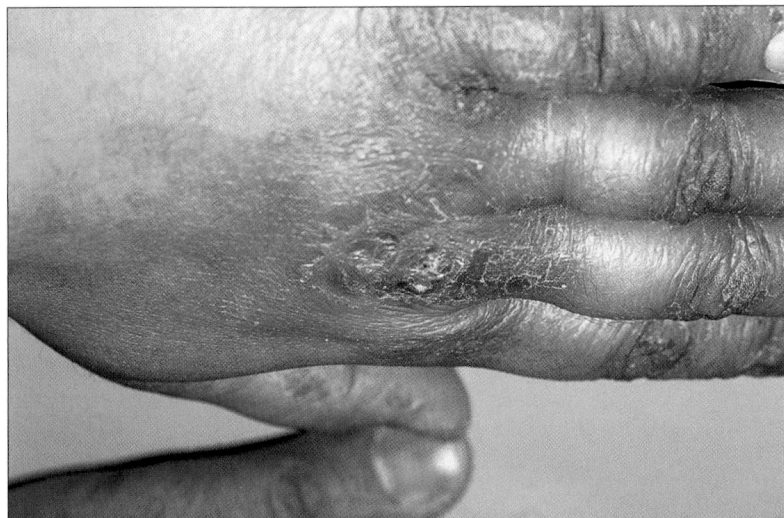

Fig. 12.139
Pellagra: scaling and hyperpigmentation are present on the dorsal aspect of the knuckles and fingers. By courtesy of the Institute of Dermatology, London, UK.

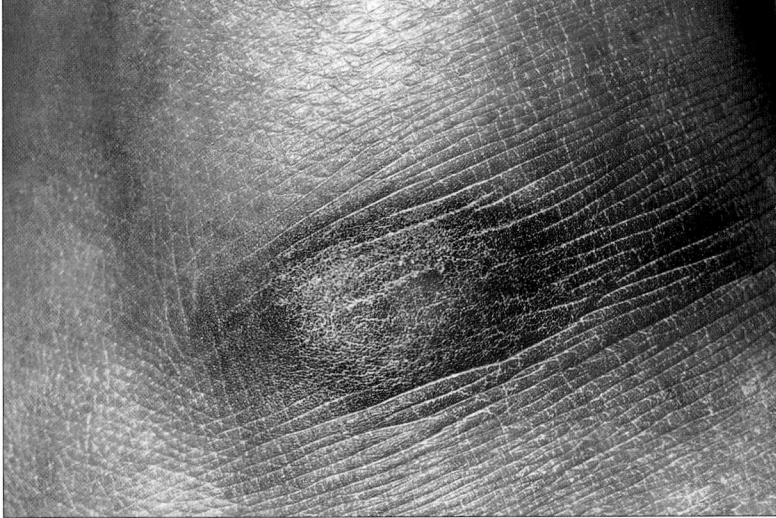

Fig. 12.140
Pellagra: close-up view of hyperpigmentation and scaling. By courtesy of the Institute of Dermatology, London, UK.

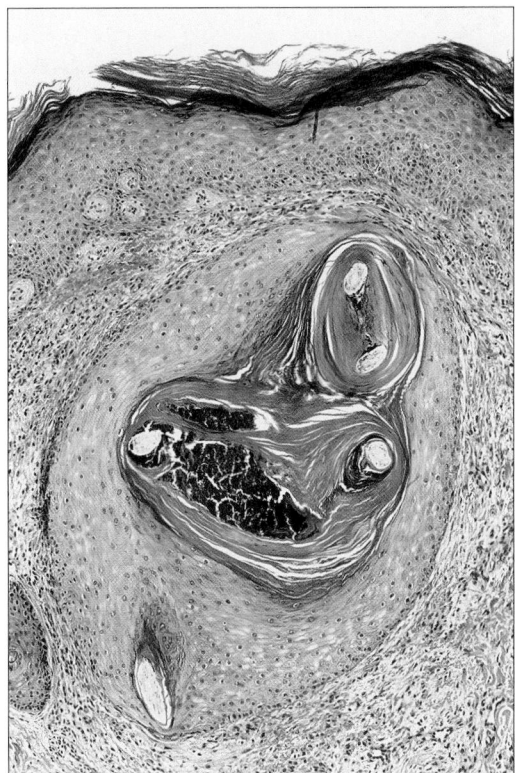

Fig. 12.141
Scurvy: the hair follicle is dilated and there is a typical corkscrew hair cut in multiple planes. Note the surrounding chronic inflammation and red cell extravasation. By courtesy of S. Tahan, MD, Beth Israel and Deaconess Medical Center, Boston, USA.

Table 12.5
Classification of calcinosis cutis

Type	Distribution	Clinical features
Dystrophyic	Localized Widespread	Acne scars; fat cell necrosis; epidermoid cysts; pilomatrixoma; infantile calcinosis of the heel Dermatomyositis; systemic lupus erythematosus; Ehlers–Danlos syndrome; pseudoxanthoma elasticum
Metastatic	Hypercalcemic Normocalcemic	Hyperparathyroidism; sarcoidosis; vitamin D excess; milk alkali syndrome; destructive bone disease Chronic renal failure; pseudohypoparathyroidism
Idiopathic	Generalized Localized	Calcinosis universalis Subepidermal calcified nodule; localized idiopathic dermal calcinosis; tumoral; scrotal

Dystrophic calcinosis cutis

Clinical features

In this, the most common variant of calcinosis, the changes are limited to the dermis and subcutaneous tissues and there is no involvement of internal organs. This form of calcinosis always occurs in tissue that has been previously damaged either by external agents or as the result of a disease. Under this variant, iatrogenic calcinosis cutis induced by local application of chemicals or medications is also included. In the localized form of dystrophic calcinosis cutis, the underlying anomaly may be inflammatory or traumatic in nature, for example acne scars, burns, fat necrosis or subcutaneous and intramuscular injections.[4,5] Calcification and necrosis have been reported following electroencephalography and electromyography.[6,7] Calcification is a characteristic feature of pancreatic disease-associated panniculitis and in older lesions of subcutaneous fat necrosis of the newborn. Auricular calcification may occur as a result of chondritis, trauma or frostbite.[1] A distinct example of this condition is infantile calcinosis cutis of the heel, in which calcific dermal nodules develop approximately 1 year after birth in infants who have had multiple heel punctures for venesection.[8,9]

Localized dystrophic calcinosis may also complicate epithelial cysts or neoplasms (*Fig. 12.142*). It is particularly seen within the keratin of trichilemmal cysts. Calcification may occur in many adnexal tumors, for example pilomatrixoma and trichoepithelioma. It is much more common in basal cell carcinoma than in squamous cell carcinoma.[10,11]

Calcinosis cutis has also been documented following the intravenous administration of calcium chloride, phosphate and gluconate (iatrogenic calcinosis cutis) (*Fig. 12.143*).[12,13] Deep soft tissue calcification has been described in association with pentazocine and pitressin.[14,15]

Widespread dystrophic calcification occurs most commonly as a sequel to connective tissue disease (*Figs 12.144, 12.145*). Localized dystrophic calcification with bone formation has also been described in mixed connective tissue disease.[16] Dermatomyositis, especially in children, may be complicated by extensive deposits of calcium in the skin and subcutaneous tissues, as well as in muscles and tendons. Scleroderma, especially the CREST variant, tends to show localized deposition of calcium, particularly on the digits and over bony prominences (see *Fig. 12.146*). Systemic lupus erythematosus is infrequently associated

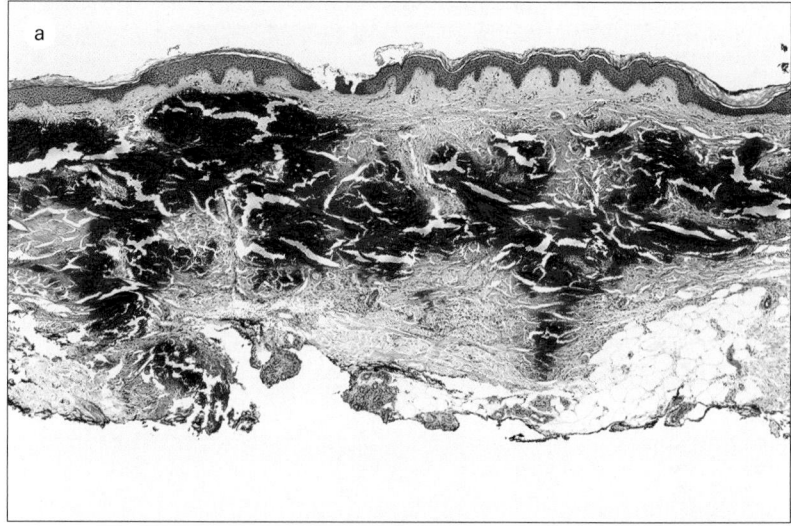

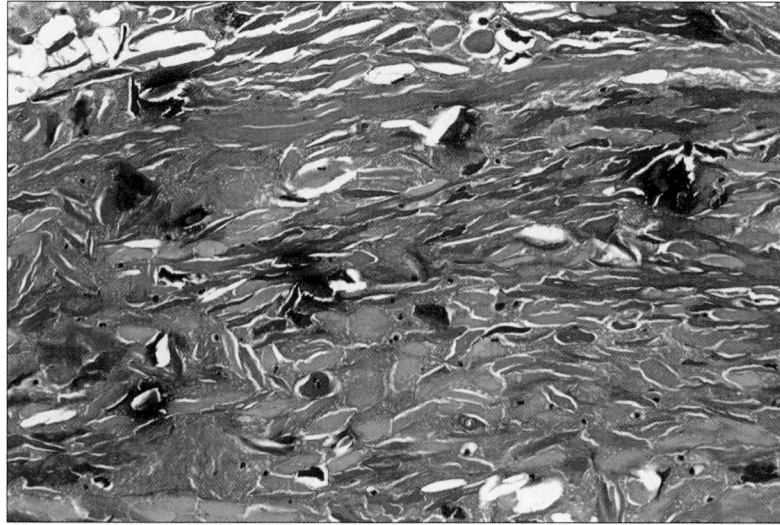

Fig. 12.142
Dystrophic calcinosis cutis: calcification has developed in this ruptured cyst.

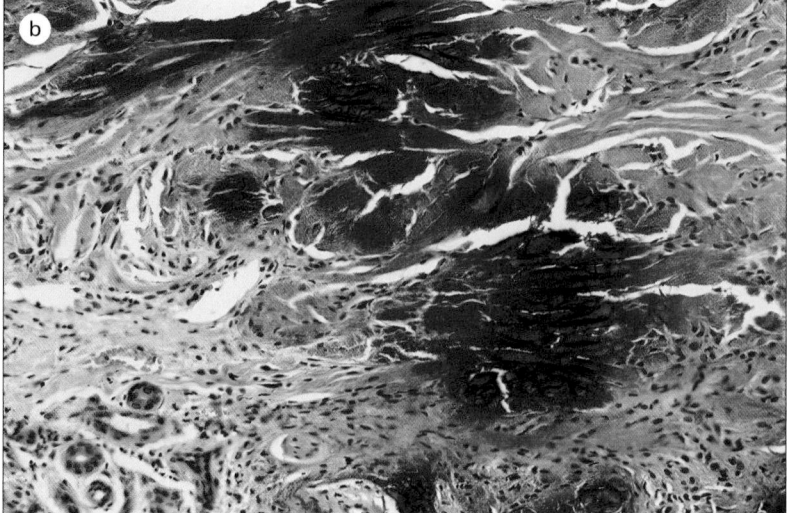

Fig. 12.143
(a, b) Iatrogenic calcinosis cutis: this widespread dermal calcification followed calcium gluconate infusion.

with calcinosis.[17] It is usually an incidental radiological observation, most commonly seen in the buttocks and extremities and unassociated with panniculitis. Mostly it develops in patients with severe acute disease including cardiac, renal or central nervous system (CNS) manifestations.[2] It also appears to correlate with high doses of corticosteroids and myositis.[18,19] Calcification complicating discoid lupus erythematosus and subacute lupus erythematosus is limited to a few case reports.[20–22] Lupus panniculitis and other types of panniculitis (including pancreatic fat necrosis, see p. 357) may also be associated with calcification.[23]

Calcium is also deposited in inherited connective tissue disorders, especially Werner's syndrome, pseudoxanthoma elasticum and Ehlers–Danlos syndrome, in which small calcific nodules typically develop within atrophic scars over bony prominences.

Metastatic calcinosis cutis

Clinical features

Metastatic calcification occurs as a result of hypercalcemia or hyperphosphatemia as may for example be seen in chronic renal failure, hyperparathyroidism and sarcoidosis.[24–26] Calcium deposits occur in the skin, subcutaneous tissues, muscle, tendon and internal organs. In the

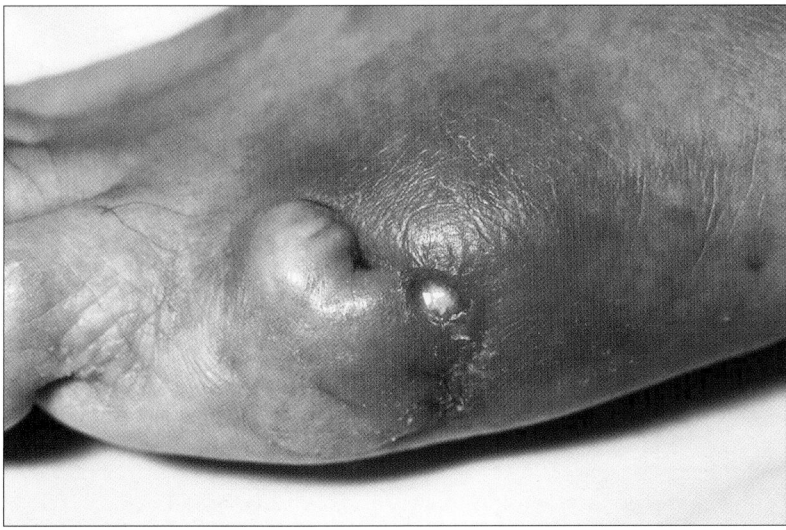

Fig. 12.144
Dystrophic calcinosis cutis: this large deposit is associated with focal ulceration and transepidermal elimination. By courtesy of the Institute of Dermatology, London, UK.

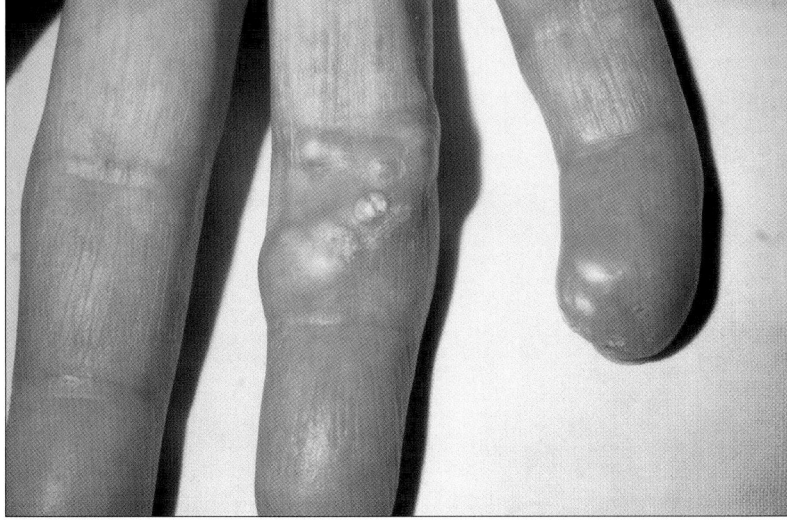

Fig. 12.145
Dystrophic calcinosis cutis: multiple digital deposits are present. By courtesy of the Institute of Dermatology, London, UK.

skin, the clinical appearances are of hard nodules and plaques, which may ulcerate to liberate chalky material and ultimately leave a scar (*Fig. 12.146*). This may be particularly frequently seen over large joints, the iliac crest or in the flexures. Fingertip lesions are usually very painful.

Vascular calcification with thrombosis may lead to livedo reticularis, ulceration and gangrene, particularly affecting the hands, fingers, toes and lower legs (so-called clinical calciphylaxis).[26–28] A frequent complication is sepsis and this often results in death. Patients usually have chronic renal failure in association with hyperphosphatemia and hyperparathyroidism.[29–31] Other conditions associated with calciphylaxis include hypervitaminosis D and A, hypercalcemia, primary or secondary hyperparathyroidism, AIDS and protein C deficiency.[32,33] The exact mechanism of calciphylaxis is not clear but it seems to be related to an imbalance in the calcium and/or phosphorus metabolism.[34] Rarely, the condition may occur in patients with normal levels of calcium and phosphorus.[34]

Idiopathic calcinosis cutis

Clinical features

There are five main clinical types of calcinosis in which there is no known predisposing condition:

- In *calcinosis universalis*, there is progressive deposition of calcium in the skin and subcutaneous tissue, producing discharging hard nodules and plaques very similar clinically to those seen in metastatic calcification. Some cases may represent dermatomyositis in which the acute phase was not diagnosed.
- In contrast, *idiopathic calcinosis* may occur as a solitary nodule on the extremities and face, particularly the eyelids (subepidermal calcified nodule, cutaneous calculus). It usually presents in early childhood and is more common in males; the majority of the nodules are hyperkeratotic and tender on palpation. Rarely it may be present at birth and occasionally multiple lesions are present.[35]
- *Localized idiopathic dermal calcinosis* may also occur as a solitary nodule on the limbs.[36] The fingers and elbows are particularly affected.[1] An equivalent lesion, designated oral mucosal calcified nodule and which affects the gingiva and tongue, has recently been documented.[37]
- In *tumoral calcinosis*, large deposits of calcium are present in the skin and subcutaneous tissues, typically over bony prominences (hip, elbow and scapula) (*Figs 12.147, 12.148*). It is rare in Europe and

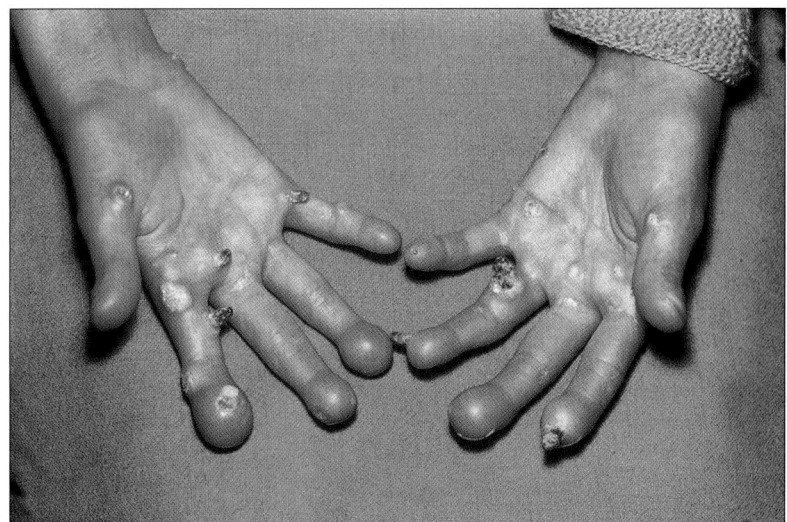

Fig. 12.146
Metastatic calcinosis cutis: there are gross deposits, many ulcerated. By courtesy of R.A. Marsden, MD, St George's Hospital, London, UK.

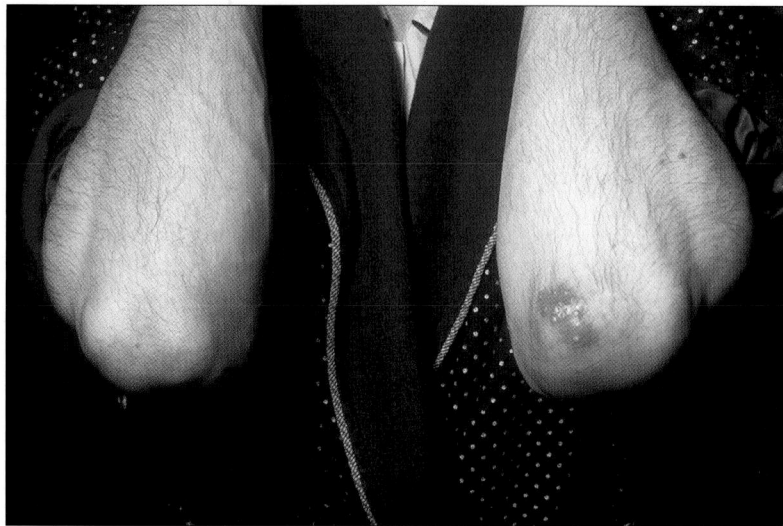

Fig. 12.147
Tumoral calcinosis: bilateral nodules over the elbows, with perforation on the patient's left. By courtesy of R.A. Marsden, MD, St George's Hospital, London, UK.

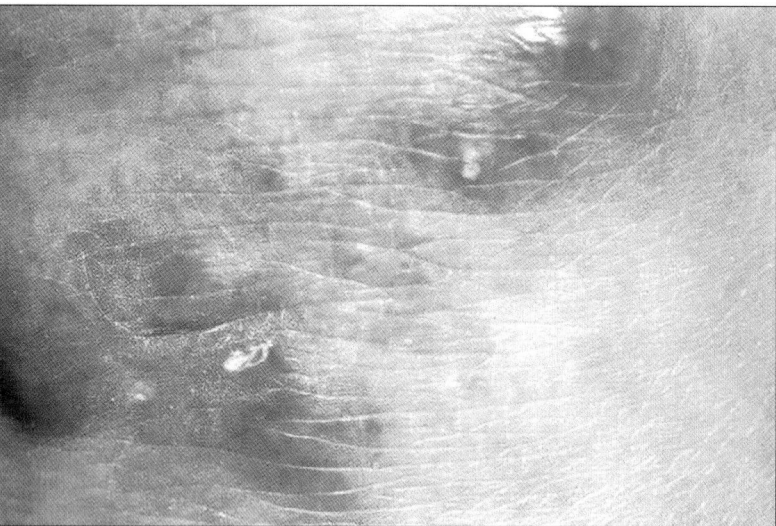

Fig. 12.148
Tumoral calcinosis: these small deposits are undergoing transepidermal elimination. By courtesy of R.A. Marsden, MD, St George's Hospital, London, UK.

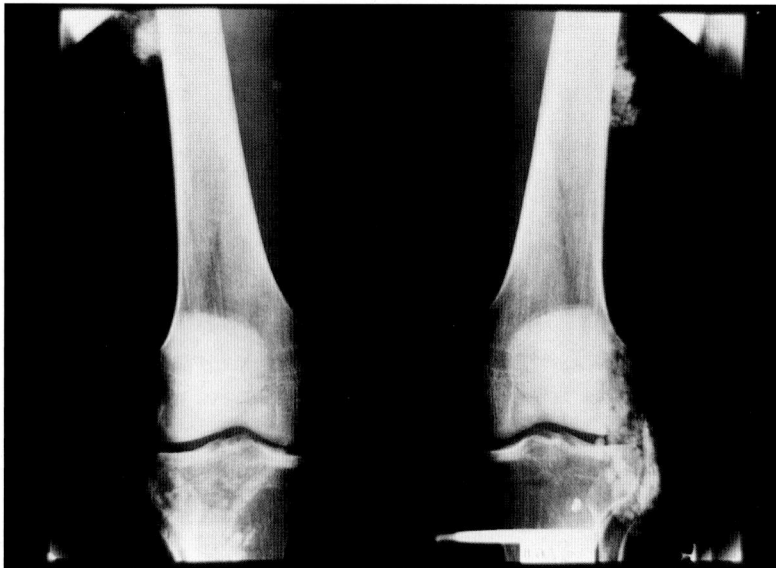

Fig. 12.149
Tumoral calcinosis: subcutaneous deposits are present overlying the thigh and lateral border of the knee. By courtesy of R.A. Marsden, MD, St George's Hospital, London, UK.

North America, but is not uncommon in South, Central and East Africa and Papua New Guinea, where it is known as hip stone. It shows a female preponderance (2:1) and affects the younger age groups. These deep deposits may be visualized radiologically (*Fig. 12.149*).

- Finally, *scrotal calcinosis* may occur spontaneously (see p. 510). Patients present in childhood or early adulthood with multiple, asymptomatic, flesh-colored or yellow nodules of varying sizes, which often release granular chalky material.[38]

Pathogenesis and histological features

Calcium stains blue with hematoxylin and eosin. In calcinosis cutis a rather homogeneous deep blue material is seen, which may present as small superficial deposits or as deeper globular ones (*Fig. 12.150*). Owing to the concomitant presence of phosphate and carbonate, the deposit stains black with the Von Kossa stain (*Fig. 12.151*).

The presence of calcium in the skin variably excites a foreign body reaction so giant cells may sometimes be seen at the edge of the deposit. On other occasions a chronic inflammatory cell infiltrate is present. Transepidermal elimination of calcified debris is sometimes a feature.[4]

In calciphylaxis, there is prominent calcification of walls of dermal and subcutaneous small blood vessels (*Fig. 12.152*).[34] Often the findings also include some degree of intimal proliferation and thrombosis. These changes result in prominent ischemic necrosis. Calcification of the subcutaneous fat accompanied by lipophagic necrosis may also be seen.

A report of an exceptional case of metastatic calcification only showed calcification of sweat ducts.[39]

There may be histological evidence of the underlying disease process. In localized dystrophic calcinosis, for example, there is sometimes evidence of a preceding epidermoid cyst. In widespread dystrophic calcinosis cutis secondary to connective tissue disease, there is occasionally evidence of preceding collagen necrosis.

In subepidermal calcified nodule, there may be pseudoepitheliomatous hyperplasia, associated with transepidermal elimination of calcium.

In tumoral calcinosis the histological features depend upon the stage of evolution of the lesion (*Figs 12.153–12.155*).[40] In early examples multiple cystic spaces lined by epithelioid and giant cells are seen. The cyst lumina contain eosinophilic debris undergoing calcification. In advanced lesions, densely calcified material is seen embedded in hyalinized connective tissue. The occasional finding of necrobiosis and vasculitis may have pathogenetic significance.

The pathogenesis of the scrotal variant is most probably calcification of the contents of pre-existent dermal cysts, mostly epidermoid, but occasionally pilar.[38,41,42] Some authors have failed to detect an epithelial component;[43] however, this may be a reflection of the age of the lesion. In many examples typical epidermoid lining epithelium surrounds the calcified deposit and sometimes residual keratinous contents are visible. A foreign body giant cell reaction is not uncommon.

References

1. Mehregan, A.H. (1984) Calcinosis cutis: a review of the clinical forms and report of 75 cases. *Semin Dermatol*, 3, 53–61.
2. Orlow, S.J., Watsky, K.L., Bolognia, J.L. (1991) Skin and bones II. *J Am Acad Dermatol*, 25, 447–462.
3. Walsh, J.S., Fairley, J.A. (1995) Calcifying disorders of the skin. *J Am Acad Dermatol*, 33, 693–706.
4. Pitt, A.E., Ethington, J.E., Troy, J.L. (1990) Self-healing dystrophic calcinosis following trauma with transepidermal elimination. *Cutis*, 45, 28–30.
5. Kanda, A., Uchimiya, H., Ohtake, N. et al (1999) Two cases of gigantic dystrophic calcinosis cutis caused by subcutaneous and/or intramuscular injections. *Dermatology*, 198, 371–374.
6. Mancuso, G., Tosti, A., Fanti, P.A. et al (1990) Cutaneous necrosis and calcinosis following electroencephalography. *Dermatologica*, 181, 324–326.
7. Johnson, R.C., Fitzpatrick, J.E., Hahn, D.E. (1993) Calcinosis cutis following electromyographic examination. *Cutis*, 52, 161–164.
8. Leung, A. (1985) Calcification following heel sticks. *J Pediatr*, 106, 168.
9. Sell, E.J., Hansen, R.C., Struck-Pierce, S. (1980) Calcified nodules of heel: a complication of neonatal intensive care. *J Pediatr*, 96, 473–475.
10. Walsh, J.S., Perniciaro, C., Randle, H.W. (1999) Calcifying basal cell carcinomas. *Dermatol Surg*, 25, 49–51.
11. Goldminz, D., Barnhill, R., McGuire, J. et al (1988) Calcinosis cutis following extravasation of calcium chloride. *Arch Dermatol*, 124, 922–925.

12. Mills, C.M., Knight, A.G. (1993) Cutaneous calcinosis: an unusual complication of intravenous phosphate administration. *Clin Exp Dermatol*, **18**, 370–372.
13. Hertzman, A., Toone, E., Resnik, C.S. (1986) Pentazocine-induced myocutaneous sclerosis. *J Rheumatol*, **13**, 210–214.
14. Adam, A., Rakhit, G., Beeton, S. et al (1984) Extensive subcutaneous calcification following injections of pitressin tannate. *Br J Radiol*, **57**, 921–922.
15. Nakagawa, S., Tagami, H. (1997) Metaplastic bone formation in the subcutaneous nodule of a patient with mixed connective tissue disease. *Acta Derm Venereol*, **77**, 64–65.
16. Rothe, M.J., Grant-Kels, J.M., Rothfield, N.F. (1990) Extensive calcinosis cutis with systemic lupus erythematosus. *Arch Dermatol*, **126**, 1060–1063.
17. Savin, J.A. (1971) Systemic lupus erythematosus with ectopic calcification. *Br J Dermatol*, **84**, 191–192.
18. Quismorio, F.P., Dubois, E.L., Chandor, S.B. (1975) Soft tissue calcification in systemic lupus erythematosus. *Arch Dermatol*, **111**, 352–356.
19. Kabir, D.J., Malkinson, F.D. (1969) Lupus erythematosus and calcinosis cutis. *Arch Dermatol*, **100**, 17–22.
20. Johansson, E., Kanerva, L., Niemi, K.M. et al (1988) Diffuse soft tissue calcifications (calcinosis cutis) in a patient with discoid lupus erythematosus. *Clin Exp Dermatol*, **13**, 193–196.
21. Marzano, A.V., Kolesnikova, L.V., Gasparini, G. et al (1999) Dystrophic calcinosis cutis in subacute lupus. *Dermatology*, **198**, 90–92.
22. Winkelmann, R.K. (1983) Panniculitis in connective tissue disease. *Arch Dermatol*, **119**, 336–344.
23. Khafif, R.A., Delima, C., Silverberg, A. et al (1989) Acute hyperparathyroidism with systemic calcinosis: report of a case. *Arch Intern Med*, **149**, 681–684.
24. Zouboulis, C.C., Weihe, J., Gollnick, H. et al (1990) Calcinosis cutis: cutaneous manifestations of generalized calcinosis in renal hyperparathyroidism. *Hautarzt*, **41**, 212–217.
25. Scheinman, P.L., Helm, K.F., Fairley, J.A. (1991) Acute necrosis in a patient with chronic renal failure. *Arch Dermatol*, **127**, 247–251.
26. Touart, D.M., Sau, P. (1998) Cutaneous deposition diseases. Part II. *J Am Acad Dermatol*, **39**, 527–546.
27. Khafif, R.A., Delima, C., Silverberg, A. et al (1990) Calciphylaxis and systemic calcinosis: collective review. *Arch Intern Med*, **150**, 956–959.
28. Ledbetter, L.S., Khoshnevis, M.R., Hsu, S. (2000) Calciphylaxis. *Cutis*, **66**, 49–51.
29. Seyle, H., Gabbiani, G., Strebel, R. (1962) Sensitization to calciphylaxis by endogenous parathyroid hormone. *Endocrinology*, **71**, 554–558.
30. Duh, Q-Y., Lim, R.C., Clark, O.H. (1991) Calciphylaxis in secondary hyperparathyroidism. *Arch Surg*, **126**, 1213–1219.
31. Pulitzer, D.R., Martin, P.C., Collins, P.C. et al (1990) Cutaneous vascular calcification with ulceration in hyperparathyroidism. *Arch Pathol Lab Med*, **114**, 482–484.
32. Cockerell, C.J., Dolan, E.T. (1992) Widespread cutaneous and systemic calcification (calciphylaxis) in patients with the acquired immunodeficiency syndrome and renal disease. *J Am Acad Dermatol*, **26**, 559–562.

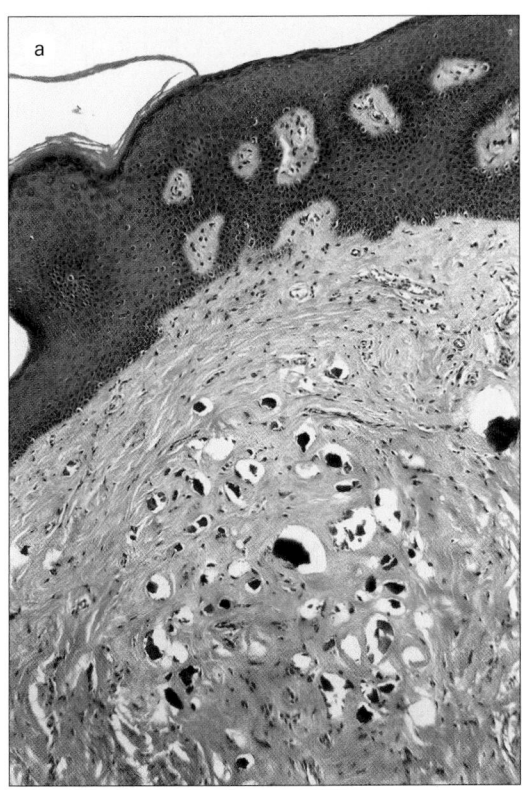 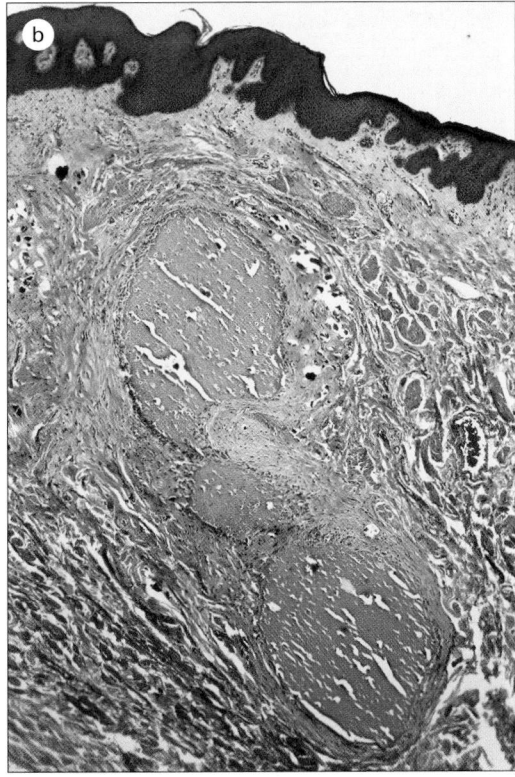

Fig. 12.150
Calcinosis cutis: (a) small deposits of intensely basophilic material are present in the superficial dermis; (b) these calcium deposits are associated with scarring.

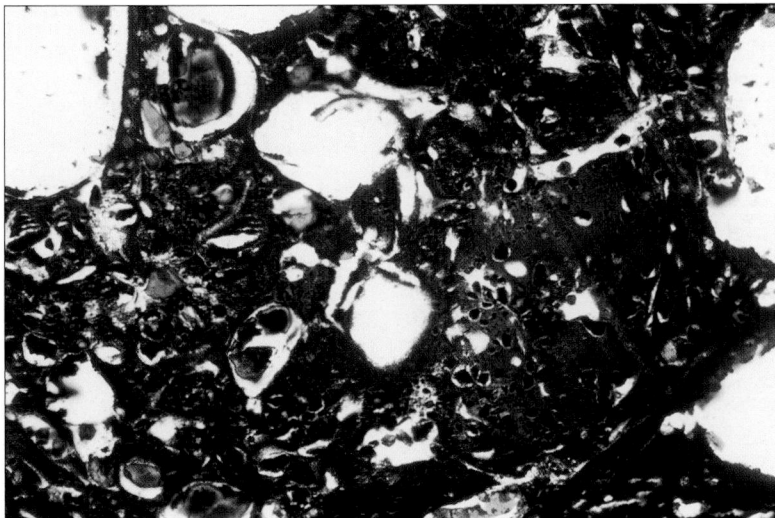

Fig. 12.151
Calcinosis cutis: the calcified deposit stains positively with the Von Kossa reaction.

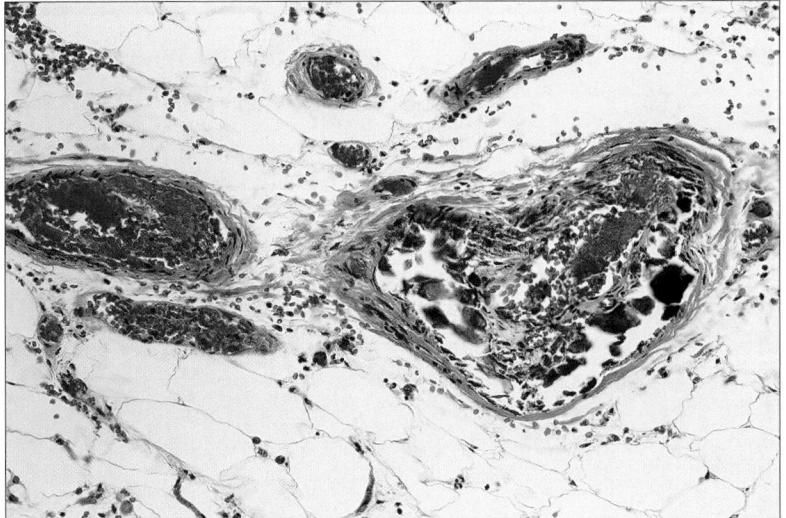

Fig. 12.152
Calciphylaxis: note the mural calcification and thrombosis.

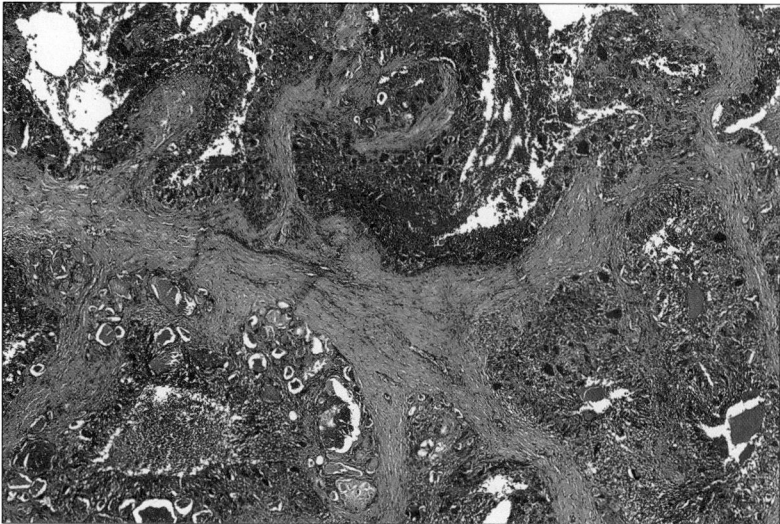

33. Mehta, R.L., Scott, G., Sloand, J.A. et al (1990) Skin necrosis associated with acquired protein C deficiency in patients with renal failure and calciphylaxis. *Am J Med*, **88**, 252–257.
34. Fischer, A.H., Morris, D.H.J. (1995) Pathogenesis of calciphylaxis: study of three cases with literature review. *Hum Pathol*, **26**, 1055–1064.
35. Tezuka, T. (1980) Cutaneous calculus: its pathogenesis. *Dermatologica*, **161**, 191–199.
36. Mendoza, L.E., Lavery, L.A., Adam, R.C. (1990) Calcinosis cutis circumscripta. A literature review and case report. *J Am Pediatr Assoc*, **80**, 97–99.
37. El Mofty, S.K., Santa Cruz, D. (1992) Mucosal calcified nodule. The oral counterpart of the subepidermal calcified nodule. *Oral Surg Oral Med Oral Pathol*, **73**, 472–475.
38. Song, D.H., Lee, K.H., Kang, W.H. (1988) Idiopathic calcinosis of the scrotum: histopathologic observations of fifty one nodules. *J Am Acad Dermatol*, **19**, 1095–1101.
39. Greenbaum, E. (1980) Metastatic calcification in skin: exclusive involvement of eccrine sweat ducts. *Hum Pathol*, **11**, 287–289.
40. McKee, P.H., Liomba, N.G., Hutt, M.S.R. (1982) Tumoral calcinosis: a pathologic study of fifty-six cases. *Br J Dermatol*, **107**, 669–674.
41. Swinehart, J.M., Golitz, L.E. (1982) Scrotal calcinosis: dystrophic calcification of epidermoid cysts. *Arch Dermatol*, **118**, 985–988.
42. Sarma, D.P., Weilbaecher, T.G. (1984) Scrotal calcinosis: calcification of epidermoid cysts. *J Surg Oncol*, **27**, 76–79.
43. Shapiro, L., Platt, N., Torres-Rodriguez, V.M. (1970) Idiopathic calcinosis of the scrotum. *Arch Dermatol*, **102**, 199–204.

Fig. 12.153
Tumoral calcinosis: this low power view shows a dense hyalinized stroma with numerous cystic cavities containing necrotic and calcified debris.

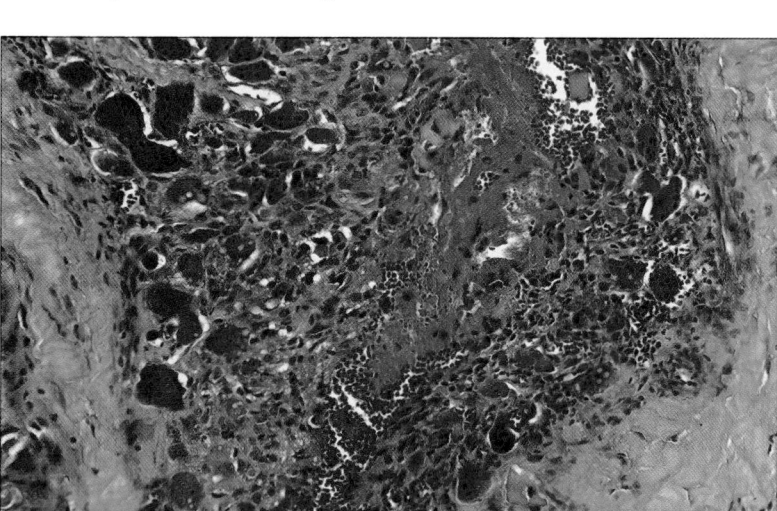

Fig. 12.154
Tumoral calcinosis: early lesions characteristically show a histiocytic and giant cell palisade around eosinophilic, degenerate connective tissue.

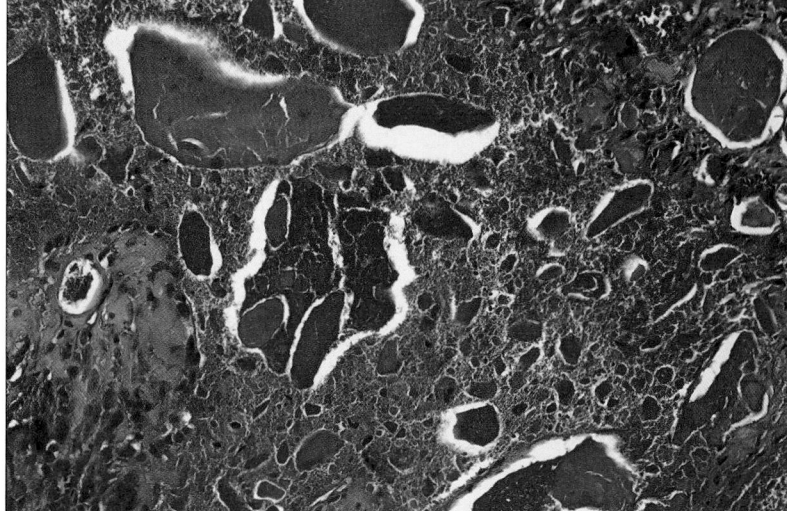

Fig. 12.155
Tumoral calcinosis: in older lesions calcified deposits lie within lacunae.

The mucinoses

The mucinoses are a group of conditions in which accumulation of acid glycosaminoglycans (mucin), particularly hyaluronic acid and to a lesser extent chondroitin (-4 and -6) sulfate and heparin, occurs either diffusely or focally in the dermis (*Table 12.6*).[1–5] Mucinosis also may occur as a secondary phenomenon in dermatoses such as lupus erythematosus, scleroderma, dermatomyositis, Degos disease, granuloma annulare and chronic graft-versus-host disease.[5,6] In this chapter, however, only primary cutaneous mucinoses are discussed.

The glycosaminoglycans, which are secreted by fibroblasts, are constituents of normal cell membranes and connective tissue. This substance is usually secreted in only small amounts by fibroblasts. It is not clear why mucin production is increased in pathological states. Although the cause is probably multifactorial, it has been suggested that cytokines and/or immunoglobulins and unidentified factors in the serum of affected patients can induce the synthesis of glycosaminoglycans.[5,7–9] Cytokines that can play an important role in this process include tumor necrosis factor, interleukin-1 and transforming growth factor beta (TGF-β).[5,10,11]

Table 12.6
Classification of the dermal mucinoses

- Diffuse
  - lichen myxedematosus – generalized form (scleromyxedema)
  - scleredema
  - reticular erythematous mucinosis
  - generalized myxedema
  - pretibial myxedema

- Focal
  - lichen myxedematosus – descrete papular form
  - acral persistent papular mucinosis
  - papular and nodular mucinosis associated with lupus erythematosus
  - self-healing juvenile cutaneous mucinosis
  - cutaneous mucinosis of infancy
  - cutaneous focal mucinosis
  - myxoid cyst

- Follicular
  - follicular mucinosis

Actively secreting fibroblasts have a characteristic stellate shape and contain intracytoplasmic secretory vesicles; their presence in sections should therefore prompt a careful search for mucin deposition (*Figs 12.156–12.158*).

Hyaluronic acid stains with colloidal iron (blue–green), alcian blue at pH 2.5 (blue) (but not at pH 0.4) and mucicarmine (red) but it is negative for PAS. It also stains metachromatically with toluidine blue, methylene blue and thionine.[12] Sulfated acid mucins stain with alcian blue at pH 0.5 and aldehyde–fuschin.[2] Hyaluronic acid absorbs enormous amounts of water, which accounts for the induration and thickening common to this group of conditions.[13]

Routine fixation and processing results in an anhydrous state so that mucin presents as basophilic strands and granules in hematoxylin and eosin stained sections.[3] In normal skin it is found particularly around appendages and the vasculature (*Fig. 12.159*). In the cutaneous

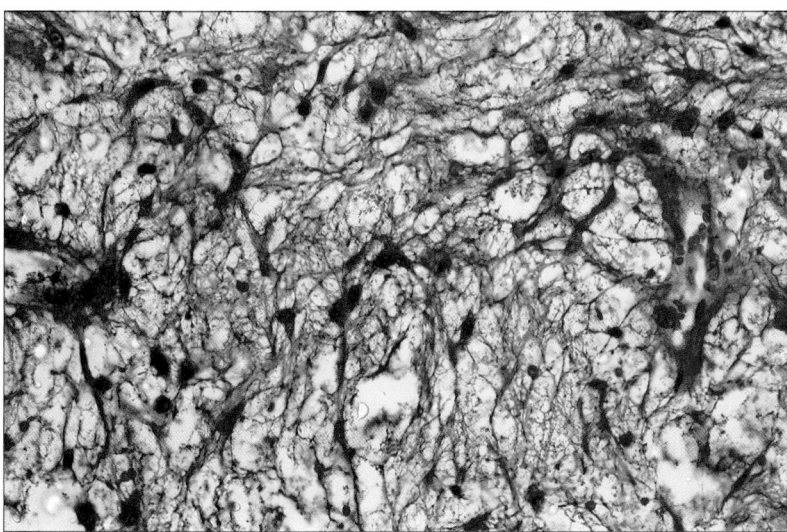

Fig. 12.156
Myxoma: in the center is a stellate fibroblast with multiple cell processes.

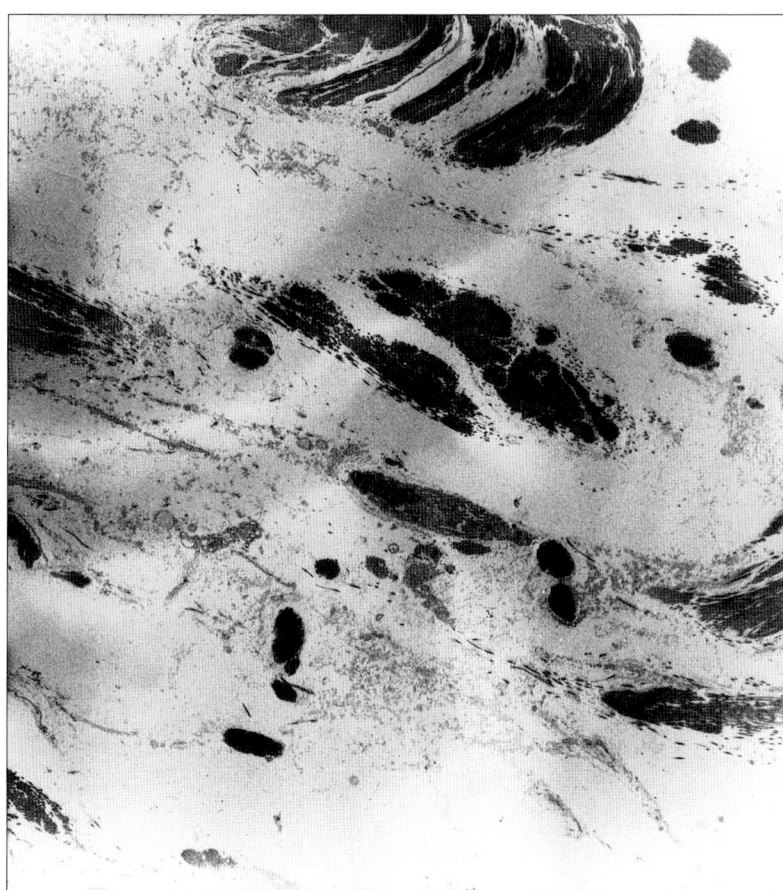

Fig. 12.157
Mucinosis: this electron micrograph from a patient with acral persistent papular mucinosis shows collagen bundles widely separated by a faintly electron-dense granular deposit.

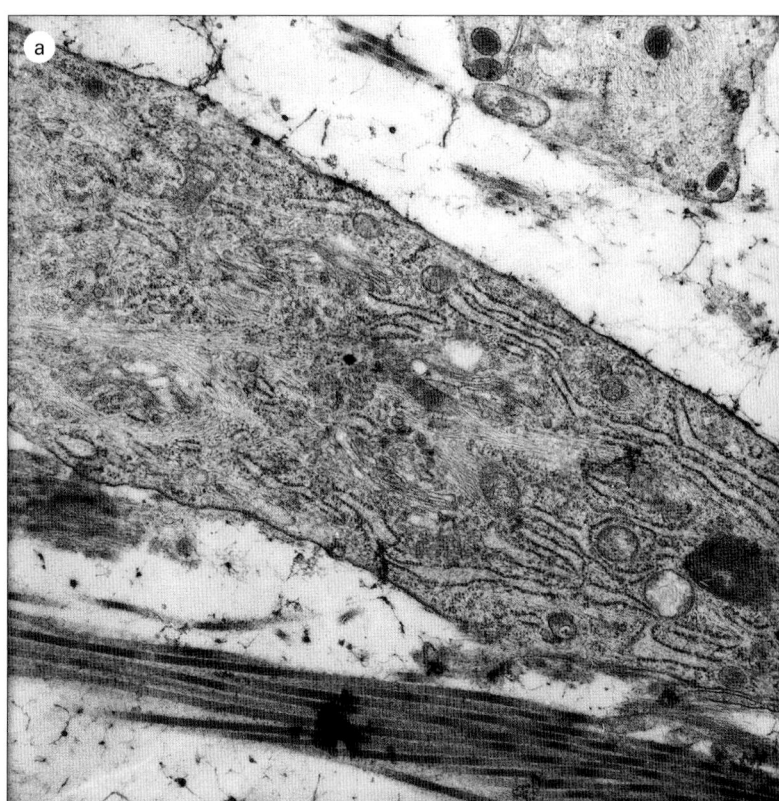

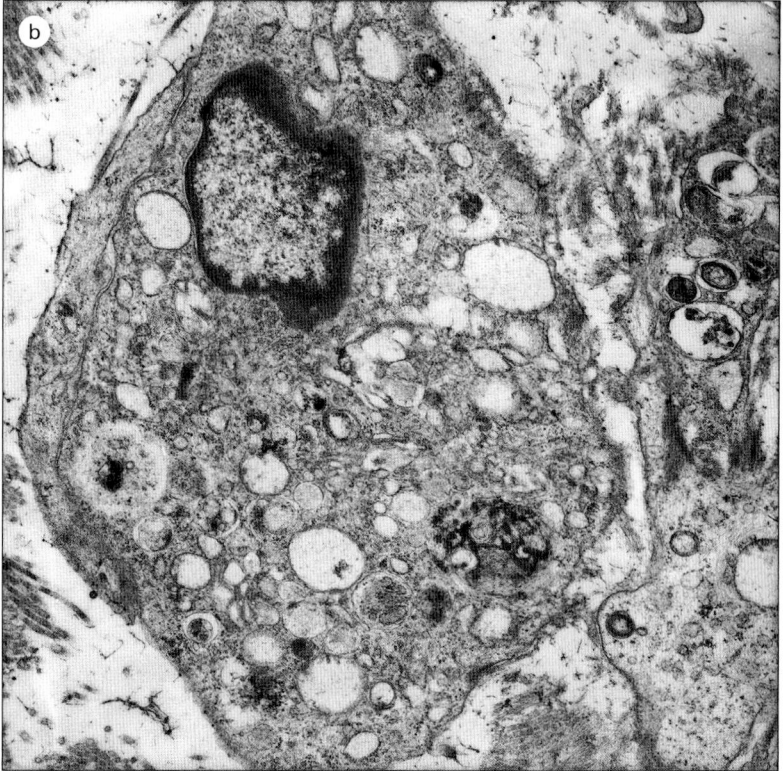

Fig. 12.158
Mucinosis: (a) actively secreting fibroblasts contain abundant rough endoplasmic reticulum; (b) numerous intracytoplasmic vesicles containing amorphous material are commonly present.

mucinoses the deposits are hyaluronidase sensitive because most of the mucin present is hyaluronic acid. The excessive mucin disrupts the collagen fibers giving them a frayed appearance. In general, with the exception of scleromyxedema, there is considerable histological overlap within this group of conditions. Diagnosis depends considerably upon clinical features and the results of biochemical investigations.[13]

There are five major mucinoses:
- generalized myxedema
- pretibial myxedema
- lichen myxedematosus
- reticular erythematous mucinosis (see p. 269)
- scleredema.

Follicular mucinosis is considered on page 1387.

References

1. Schaeffer, D., Bruce, S., Rosen, T. (1983) Cutaneous mucinosis associated with thyroid dysfunction. *Cutis*, 32, 449–456.
2. Stephens, C.J.M., Das, A.K., Black, M.M. et al (1990) The dermal mucinoses: a clinicopathological and ultrastructural study. *J Cutan Pathol*, 17, 319.
3. Truhan, A.P., Roenigk, H.H. (1986) The cutaneous mucinoses. *J Am Acad Dermatol*, 14, 1–18.
4. Rongioletti, F., Rebora, A. (1991) The new cutaneous mucinoses: a review with an up-to-date classification of cutaneous mucinoses. *J Am Acad Dermatol*, 24, 265–270.
5. Rongioletti, F., Rebora, A. (2001) Cutaneous mucinoses. Microscopic criteria for diagnosis. *Am J Dermatopathol*, 23, 257–267.
6. Ameen, M., Russell-Jones, R. (2000) Macroscopic and microscopic mucinosis in graft versus host disease. *Br J Dermatol*, 142, 529–532.
7. Pandya, A.G., Sontheimer, R.D., Cockerell, C.J. et al (1995) Papulonodular mucinosis associated with systemic lupus erythematosus: possible mechanisms of increased glycosaminoglycan accumulation. *J Am Acad Dermatol*, 32, 199–205.
8. Harper, R.A., Rispler, J. (1978) Lichen myxedematous serum stimulates human skin fibroblast proliferation. *Science*, 194, 545–547.
9. Cheung, H.S., Nicoloff, J.T., Kamiel, M.B. et al (1978) Stimulation of fibroblast biosynthetic activity by serum of patients with pretibial myxedema. *J Invest Dermatol*, 71, 12–17.
10. Duncan, M.R., Berman, B. (1989) Differential regulation of collagen, glycosaminoglycan, fibronectin and collagenase activity production in cultured human adult dermal fibroblasts by interleukin 1-alpha and beta and tumor necrosis factor alpha and beta. *J Invest Dermatol*, 92, 699–706.
11. Falanga, V., Tiegs, S.L., Alstadt, S.P. et al (1987) Transforming growth factor-beta: selective increase in glycosaminoglycans synthesis by cultures of fibroblasts from patients with progressive systemic sclerosis. *J Invest Dermatol*, 89, 100–104.
12. Stephens, C.J.M., McKee, P.H., Black, M.M. (1993) The dermal mucinoses. *Adv Dermatol*, 8, 201–227.
13. Matsuoka, L.Y., Wortsman, J., Carlisle, K.S. et al (1980) The acquired cutaneous mucinoses. *Arch Intern Med*, 144, 1974–1980.

Generalized myxedema

Clinical features

Patients with myxedema may appear pale yellow due to the combined effects of edema, anemia and carotenemia.[1,2] The last, which is due to defective conversion of betacarotene to vitamin A in the liver, is seen particularly on the palms, soles and in the nasolabial folds.[3] Rarely the color change may be generalized.[4] The skin is cool, dry, coarse, waxy and puffy, especially around the eyes and cheeks, and the hands and feet may show non-pitting edema (*Fig. 12.160*).[3,5–7] The face is often expressionless. Eccrine and sebaceous gland secretions are reduced and this may result in xerosis, an ichthyotic appearance or asteatotic eczema.[4] Hyperkeratosis over bony prominences resembling avitaminosis A is also sometimes evident.[8] Alopecia is a common finding and the outer third of the eyebrows is typically affected. There is usually thinning of the beard and sexual hair in addition to loss of the scalp hair. Myxedema is associated with a greatly increased percentage of hair follicles in the telogen phase.[9] Residual hair is dry, coarse and brittle.[3] The nails often become thin, brittle and striated.[1] Additional cutaneous manifestations have included pruritic papular lesions, purpura and ecchymoses, impaired healing, generalized follicular mucinosis and multiple focal cutaneous mucinoses.[1,5,9–11] Oropharyngeal and laryngeal involvement is common and many patients are hoarse. Patients with myxedema have an increased risk of developing hyperlipidemia with resultant eruptive and tuberous xanthomata (*Fig. 12.161*).

Histological features

The epidermis may show mild hyperkeratosis with occasional follicular plugging.[3] Most frequently the dermal changes are subtle and non-diagnostic. However, in cases of greater severity there is slight swelling and separation of the collagen bundles with edema, and special stains show that small quantities of mucin are present within the dermis and occasionally in the subcutaneous fat.[12] Fibroblastic proliferation is not a feature of primary myxedema.[13]

References

1. Christianson, H.B. (1976) Cutaneous manifestations of hypothyroidism including purpura and ecchymoses. *Cutis*, 17, 45–51.
2. Niepomniszcze, H., Amad, R.H. (2001) Skin disorders and thyroid diseases. *J Endocrinol Invest*, 24, 628–638.
3. Truhan, A.P., Roenigk, H.H. (1986) The cutaneous mucinoses. *J Am Acad Dermatol*, 14, 1–18.
4. al-Jubouri, M.A., Coombes, E.J., Young, R.M. et al (1994) Xanthoderma: an unusual presentation of hypothyroidism. *J Clin Pathol*, 47, 850–851.
5. Schaeffer, D., Bruce, S., Rosen, T. (1983) Cutaneous mucinosis associated with thyroid dysfunction. *Cutis*, 32, 449–456.
6. Heymann, W.R. (1992) Cutaneous manifestations of thyroid disease. *J Am Acad Dermatol*, 26, 885–886.
7. Heymann, W.R. (1997) Advances in the cutaneous manifestations of thyroid disease. *Int J Dermatol*, 36, 641–645.

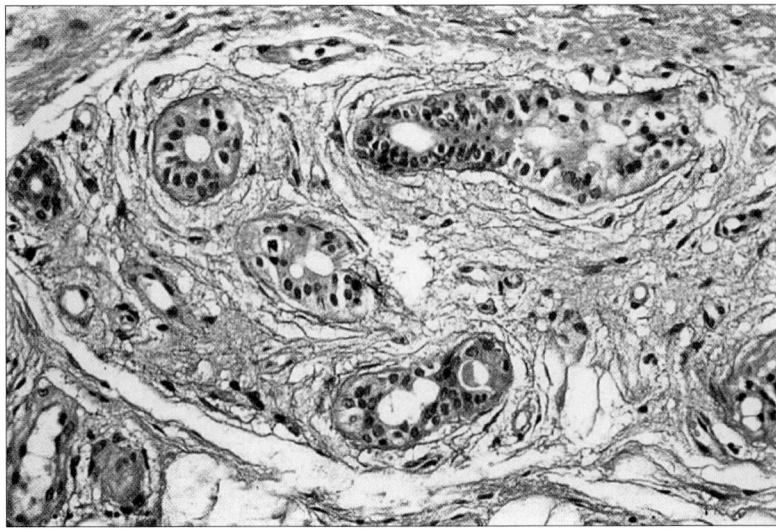

Fig. 12.159
Eccrine sweat gland: this section of normal skin from the sole of the foot shows abundant dermal mucin when stained with Ehrlich's hematoxylin.

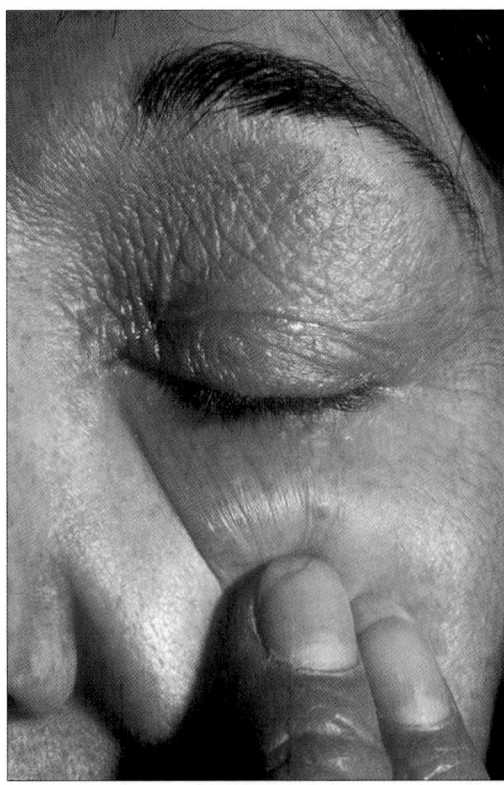

Fig. 12.160
Generalized myxedema: note the waxy infiltrated plaques on the eyelid. By courtesy of R.A. Marsden, MD, St George's Hospital, London, UK.

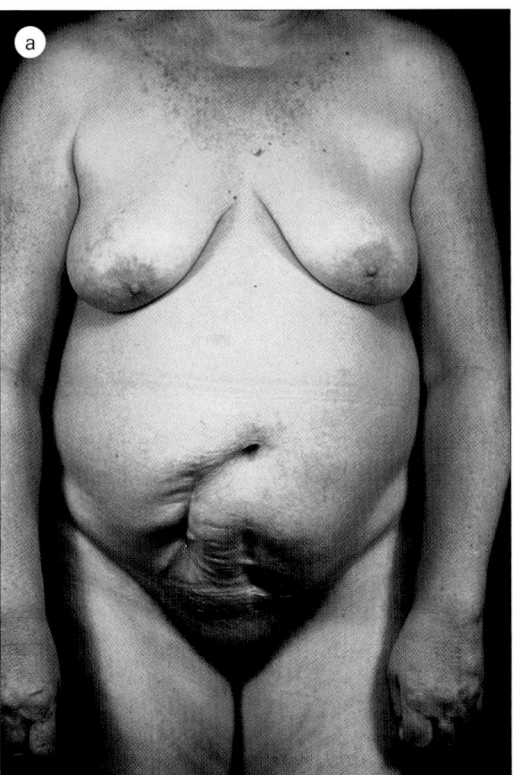

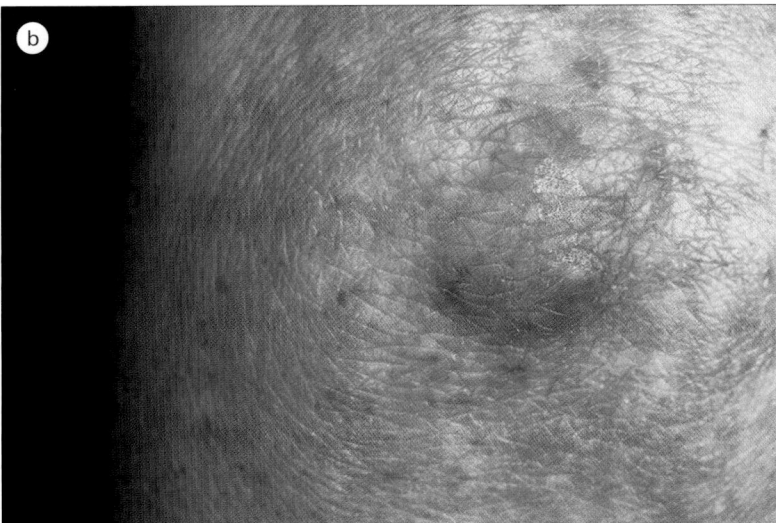

Fig. 12.161
(a, b) Generalized myxedema: this patient has widespread xanthomata. By courtesy of the Institute of Dermatology, London, UK.

8. Warin, A.P. (1973) Eczema craquelé as the presenting feature of myxedema. *Br J Dermatol*, **89**, 289–291.
9. Freinkel, R.K., Freinkel, N. (1972) Hair growth and alopecia in hypothyroidism. *Arch Dermatol*, **106**, 349–352.
10. Jakubovic, H.R., Samith, S.S.S., Rosenthal, D. (1982) Multiple cutaneous focal mucinosis with hypothyroidism. *Ann Intern Med*, **96**, 56–58.
11. Grice, K., Doniach, D., Wilson-Jones, E. et al (1968) Generalized follicular mucinosis with myxedema. *Proc R Soc Med*, **61**, 717–720.
12. Schermer, D.R. (1968) Cutaneous myxedematous (mucoid) states. *Cutis*, **4**, 939–948.
13. Stephens, C.J.M., McKee, P.H., Black, M.M. (1993) The dermal mucinoses. *Adv Dermatol*, **8**, 201–227.

Localized (pretibial) myxedema

Clinical features

Localized (pretibial) myxedema is most often associated with hyperthyroidism.[1] It occurs in 3–5% of cases.[2] It is one of three processes classically seen in autoimmune thyroid (Graves') disease, the other two being exophthalmos and thyroid acropachy (clubbing of the digits associated with subperiosteal new bone formation). Pretibial myxedema is usually a late manifestation of Graves' disease and has only been reported exceptionally preceding the diagnosis of Graves' disease and in the absence of ophthalmopathy.[3] In 10% of cases of Graves' disease, patients are not clinically hyperthyroid.[4] Hyperthyroidism (and also hypothyroidism) may also be associated with glycosaminoglycan deposition around the forearm, so-called preradial myxedema.[5] Pink or yellow waxy plaques, nodules and sometimes 'tumors' develop, most frequently first on the anterolateral aspects of the lower legs (*Fig. 12.162*). In some patients there is induration with prominence of the follicles, giving

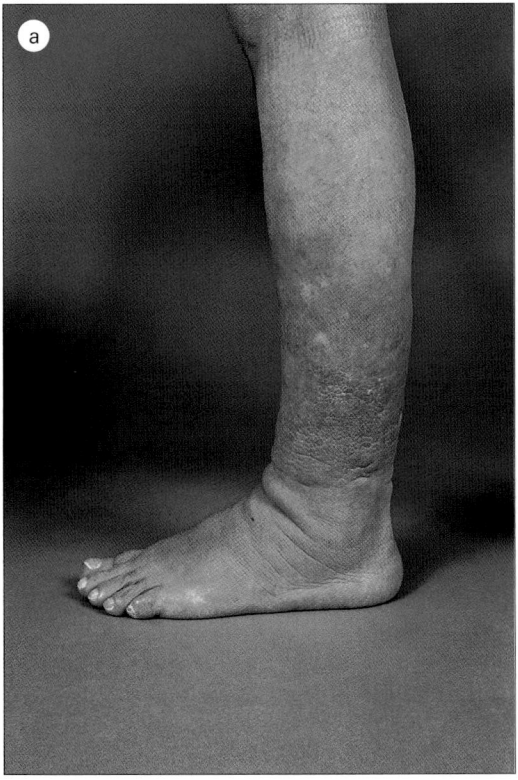

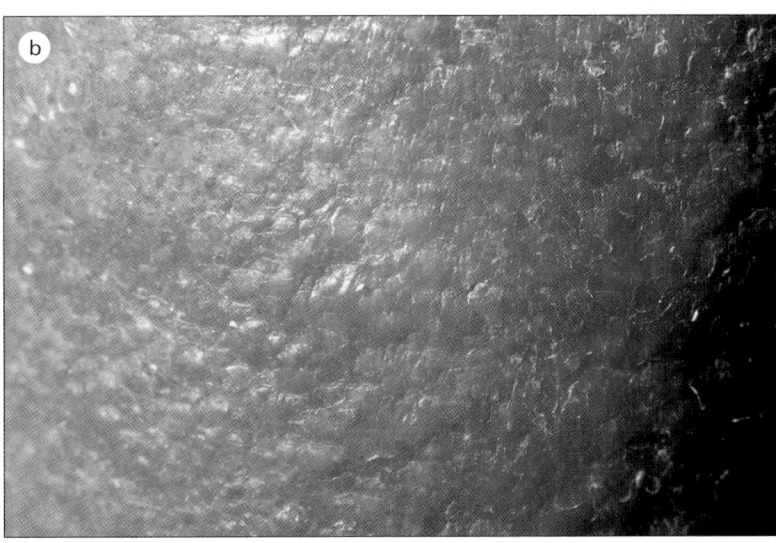

Fig. 12.162
Pretibial myxedema: (a) erythematous, somewhat translucent plaques are present over the shin; (b) close-up view. By courtesy of R.A. Marsden, MD, St George's Hospital, London, UK.

rise to a peau d'orange appearance, and secondary hypertrichosis is occasionally marked. Localized hyperhidrosis at the site of the myxedema may also rarely occur.[6] The disease may progress to involve much of the lower leg, which rarely becomes grossly elephantiasiform (*Fig. 12.163*).[2,7] Small lesions are usually asymptomatic or mildly pruritic, the larger plaques are often painful.[8] Infrequently, localized myxedema occurs on other sites such as the arms, shoulders, abdomen, neck, face, and even the ears (*Fig. 12.164*).[9] Nodular lesions rarely occur on the hands.[10] It has also been described localized to scar tissue.[11–13] The

latter includes the site of a smallpox vaccination scar.[14] Presentation at the site of a thigh donor graft site has also been reported.[15]

Rare patients with pretibial myxedema have no evidence of thyroid disease. Biopsies from these patients tend to show changes associated with stasis and this feature is useful in the histological differential diagnosis.[16]

Pretibial myxedema is sometimes self-limiting, involution occurring after a number of years. Complete remission occurs in up to 26% of cases but this depends on the severity of the disease.[4,17]

An exceptional form of pretibial mucin deposition that may be confused with pretibial myxedema associated with Graves' disease has been documented in association with Sjögren's syndrome under the name acral ichthyosiform mucinosis.[18] In the cases described, the patients had normal thyroid function tests and the mucin deposition was predominantly in the papillary dermis.

Pathogenesis and histological features

The etiology is uncertain; the presence of pretibial myxedema is usually associated with detection of long-acting thyroid stimulator (LATS) in the serum, but LATS is not believed to be causal.[19] It was suggested in 1978 that a fibroblast stimulating factor associated with mucigenic properties isolated from the serum of patients with pretibial myxedema might play a role in the pathogenesis of the disease.[20] More recent studies have shown that fibroblasts in pretibial skin and in the orbit of affected patients contain sequences identical to those of the thyroid stimulating hormone receptor.[21,22] It has also been proposed that the fibroblasts might contain a cross-reacting protein rather than the true receptor, which binds with the autoantibodies against thyroid stimulating factor receptor.[23,24] Based on these observations, it has been proposed that autoantibodies against thyroid-stimulating hormone receptor react with fibroblasts containing these sequences, resulting in production of cytokines and induction of increased glycosaminoglycan secretion.[23,24]

The epidermis is often hyperkeratotic, with follicular plugging; in gross cases it may be papillomatous and acanthotic. The dermis shows separation of collagen bundles by large quantities of mucin (*Figs 12.165,*

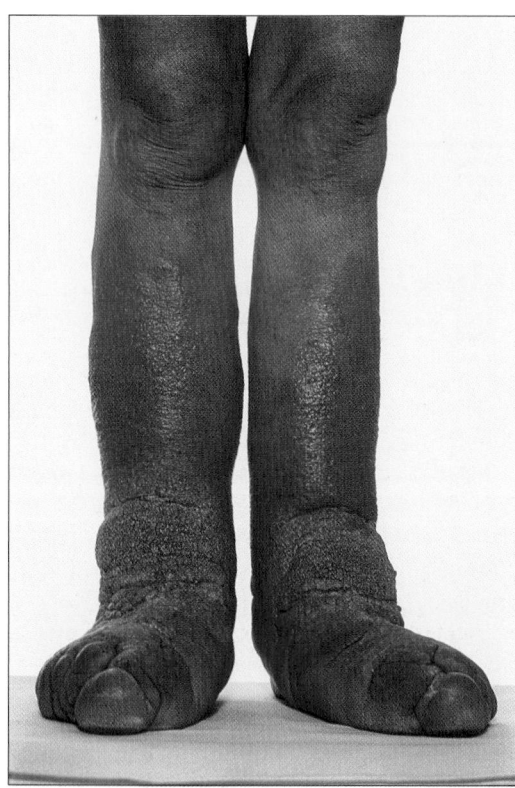

Fig. 12.163
Pretibial myxedema: in this extreme example the features resemble elephantiasis. By courtesy of R.A. Marsden, MD, St George's Hospital, London, UK.

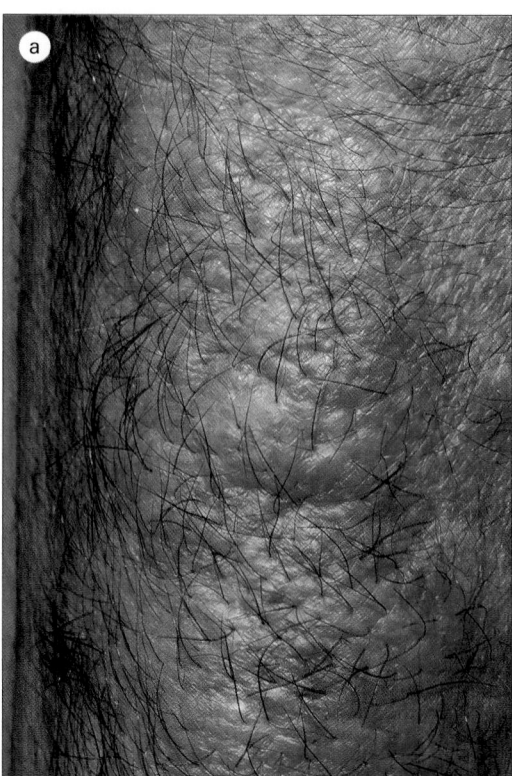

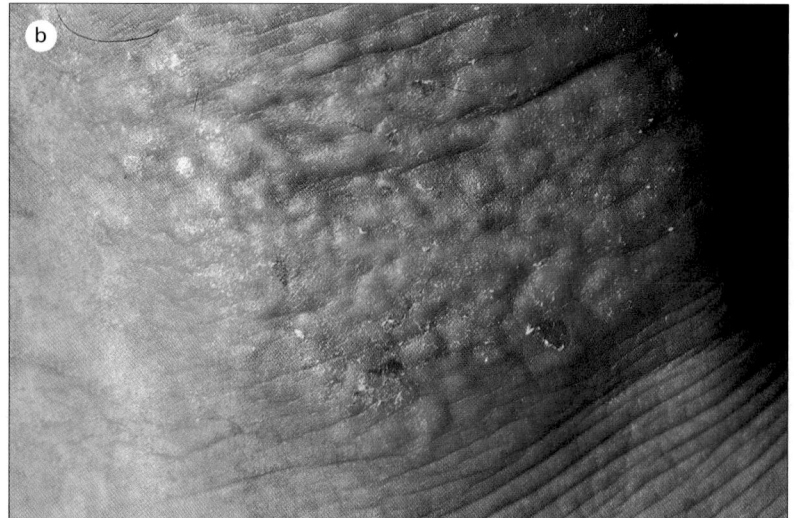

Fig. 12.164
(a, b) Localized myxedema: these pictures came from same patient shown in *Fig. 12.162*. Following a road traffic accident, the patient developed additional mucinous deposits on her arm close to the site of a fracture. By courtesy of P.G. Goodwin, MD, The Royal Bournemouth Hospital, UK.

12.166).[1] Stellate fibroblasts are evident, but there is usually no increase in their number except perhaps for the more elephantiasiform examples.

Immunofluorescent studies are usually negative, although granular deposits of IgM have been identified within the superficial papillary dermis.[8]

Electron microscopic studies show amorphous granular material both within fibroblast endoplasmic reticulum, coating the surface of the fibroblast, and in the interstitium surrounding the widely separated collagen and elastic fibers.[8] Tubuloreticular structures have been identified in the cytoplasm of endothelial cells in one case and in the dermis of another.[8,11]

References

1. Truhan, A.P., Roenigk, H.H. Jr (1986) The cutaneous mucinoses. *J Am Acad Dermatol*, **14**, 14–18.
2. Albers, S.E., Fenske, N.A. (1991) Exuberant tumoral lesions on the dorsum of the foot. Pretibial myxedema. *Arch Dermatol*, **127**, 247–248, 250–251.
3. Omohundro, C., Dijkstra, J.W., Camisa, C. et al (1996) Early onset pretibial myxedema in the absence of ophthalmopathy: a morphologic evolution. *Cutis*, **58**, 211–214.
4. Fatourechi, V., Pajouhi, M., Fransway, A.F. (1994) Dermopathy of Graves disease (pretibial myxedema). Review of 150 cases. *Medicine (Baltimore)*, **73**, 1–7.
5. Wortsman, J., Dietrich, J., Traycoff, R.B. et al (1981) Preradial myxedema in thyroid disease. *Arch Dermatol*, **117**, 635–636.
6. Kato, N., Ueno, H., Matsubara, M. (1991) A case report of EMO syndrome showing localized hyperhidrosis in pretibial myxedema. *J Dermatol*, **18**, 598–604.
7. Stephens, C.J.M., McKee, P.H., Black, M.M. (1993) The dermal mucinoses. *Adv Dermatol*, **8**, 201–227.
8. Konrad, K., Brenner, W., Pehamberger, H. (1980) Ultrastructural and immunological findings in Graves' disease with pretibial myxedema. *J Cutan Pathol*, **7**, 99–108.
9. Noppakun, N., Bancheun, K., Chandraprasert, S. (1986) Unusual locations of localized myxedema in Graves' disease. *Arch Dermatol*, **122**, 85–88.
10. Cho, S., Choi, J.H., Sung, K.J. et al (2001) Graves' disease presenting as elephantiasic pretibial myxedema and nodules of the hands. *Int J Dermatol*, **40**, 276–277.
11. Slater, D.N. (1987) Cervical nodular localized myxedema in a thyroidectomy scar, light and electron microscopy and histochemical findings. *Clin Exp Dermatol*, **12**, 216–219.
12. Wright, A.L., Buxton, P.K., Menzies, D. (1990) Pretibial myxedema localized to scar tissue. *Arch Dermatol*, **29**, 54–55.
13. Tong, D.W., Ho, K.K. (1998) Pretibial myxedema presenting as a scar infiltrate. *Australas J Dermatol*, **39**, 255–257.
14. Pujol, R.M., Monmany, J., Bague, S. et al (2000) Graves' disease presenting as localized myxedematous infiltration in a smallpox vaccination scar. *Clin Exp Dermatol*, **25**, 132–134.
15. Missner, S.C., Ramsay, E.W., Houck, H.E. et al (1998) Graves' disease presenting as localized myxedema in a thigh donor graft site. *J Am Acad Dermatol*, **39**, 846–849.
16. Somach, S.C., Helm, T.N., Lawlor, K.B. et al (1993) Pretibial mucin. Histologic patterns and clinical correlation. *Arch Dermatol*, **129**, 1152–1156.
17. Schwartz, K.M., Fatourechi, V., Ahmed, D.D. et al (2002) Dermopathy of Graves' disease (pretibial myxedema): long-term outcome. *J Clin Endocrinol Metab*, **87**, 438–446.
18. Yamazaki, S., Katayama, I., Satoh, T. et al (1993) Acral ichthyosiform mucinosis in association with Sjögren's syndrome: a peculiar form of pretibial myxedema? *J Dermatol*, **20**, 715–718.
19. Schermer, D.R., Roenigk, H.H., Schmacher, O.P. et al (1970) Relationship of long-acting thyroid stimulator to pretibial myxedema. *Arch Dermatol*, **102**, 62–67.
20. Cheung, H.S., Nicoloff, J.T., Kamiel, M.B. et al (1978) Stimulation of fibroblast biosynthetic activity by serum of patients with pretibial myxedema. *J Invest Dermatol*, **71**, 12–17.
21. Stadlmayr, W., Spitzweg, C., Bichlmair, A.M. et al (1997) TSH receptor transcripts and TSH receptor-like immunoreactivity in orbital and pretibial fibroblasts of patients with Graves' ophthalmopathy and pretibial myxedema. *Thyroid*, **7**, 3–12.
22. Wu, S.L., Chang, T.C., Chang, T.J. et al (1996) Cloning and sequencing of complete thyrotropin receptor transcripts in pretibial fibroblast culture cells. *J Endocrinol Invest*, **19**, 365–370.
23. Chang, T.C., Wu, S.L., Hsiao, Y.L. et al (1994) THS and TSH receptor antibody-binding sites in fibroblasts of pretibial myxedema are related to extracellular domain of entire TSH receptor. *Clin Immunol Immunopathol*, **71**, 113–120.
24. Daumarie, C., Ludgate, M., Costagliola, S. et al (2002) Evidence for thyrotropin receptor immunoreactivity in pretibial connective tissue from patients with thyroid-associated dermopathy. *Eur J Endocrinol*, **146**, 35–38.

Lichen myxedematosus

Clinical features

As originally classified there were four variants of this rare disease of adults.[1] These consisted of:

- a generalized lichenoid papular eruption (*Figs 12.167, 12.168*)
- a discrete papular variant presenting as much smaller numbers of flesh-colored papules on the trunk and extremities (*Fig. 12.169*)
- localized and generalized lichenoid plaques mimicking lichen planus
- urticarial or nodular lesions, which often evolved into the generalized papular form.[2,3]

With the recent delineation of new entities, the validity of this classification has been called into question.[4] Lichen myxedematosus is now therefore divided into two forms:[5,6]

- a localized form, which includes several variants: discrete papular lesions occurring at any site, acral persistent papular mucinosis (see below), self-healing papular mucinosis (see below), papular mucinosis of infancy (see below) and nodular mucinosis.

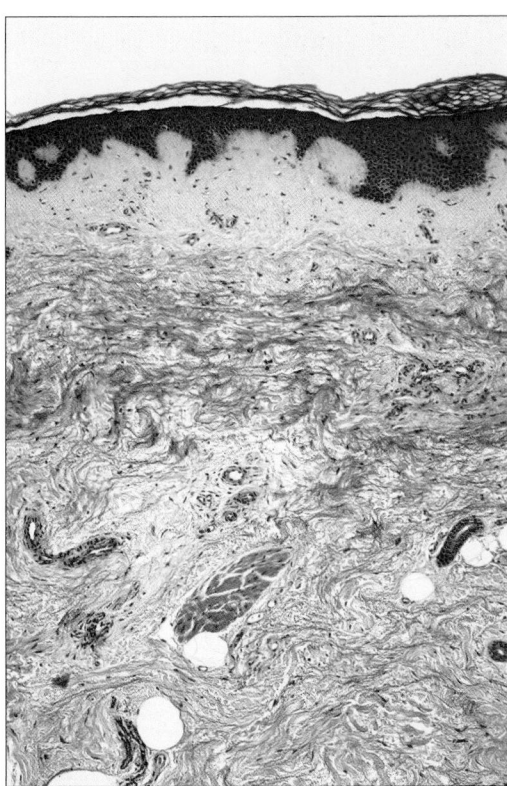

Fig. 12.165
Pretibial myxedema: there is loss of collagen fibers associated with mucin deposition.

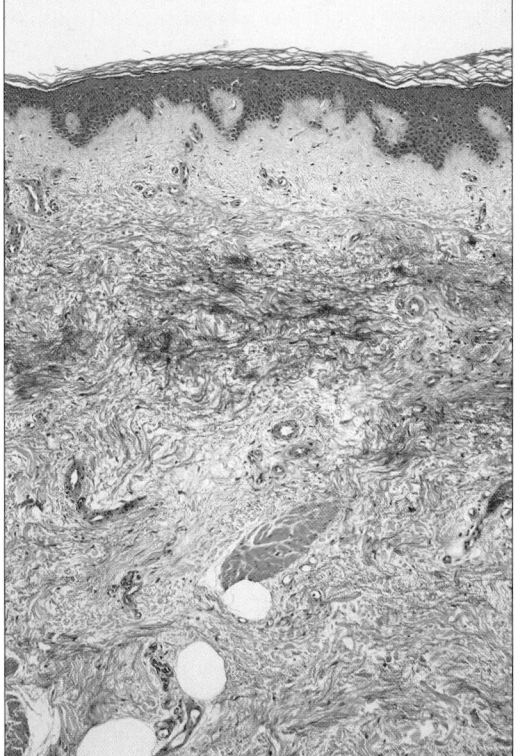

Fig. 12.166
Pretibial myxedema: the mucin (hyaluronic acid) stains positively with alcian blue.

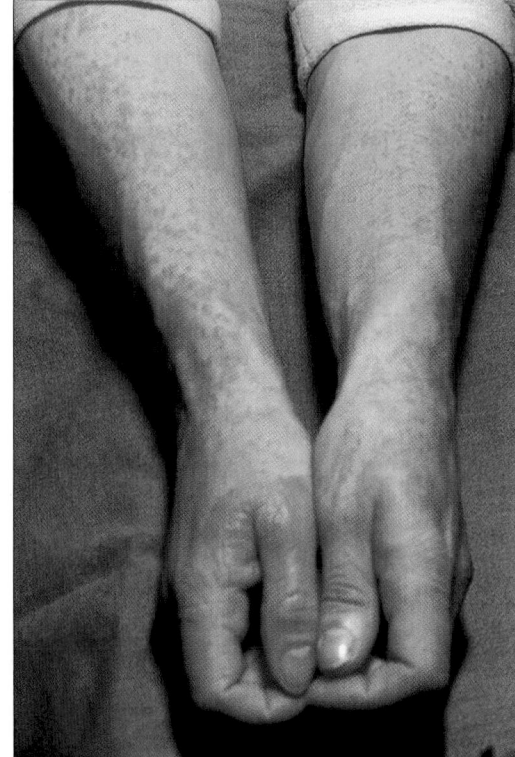

Fig. 12.167
Lichen myxedematosus: erythematous papules are widely distributed over the forearms. A more diffuse plaque is present over the dorsum of the left hand.

- a generalized form (scleromyxedema) characterized by lichenoid papules, indurated and thickened skin and a monoclonal gammopathy. Although most patients who present with scleromyxedema have a coexisting monoclonal gammopathy, very occasional patients may be encountered in whom no evidence of gammopathy can be found. By definition, thyroid function is invariably normal.

A small number of cases are atypical and do not strictly fulfill criteria for either the localized or generalized variants.[6] In such cases, features of both are often present.

The generalized form of lichen myxedematosus (scleromyxedema) occurs equally in males and females and is seen most often in the fourth and fifth decades.[3] It often presents on the hands and wrists, but soon becomes generalized although lesions are particularly seen on the hands,

elbows, neck, face and upper trunk.[7,8] Prominent linear papules may be evident on the forehead, neck, axillae and behind the ears.[9] The papules are small, 2–3 mm in diameter, white or erythematous and often have a waxy consistency. They tend to coalesce to form infiltrated plaques and when associated with hardening and thickening of the underlying skin (scleromyxedema) result in tethering and limitation of movement, so that sclerodactyly, microstomia and a mask-like facies may result (*Fig. 12.170*).[4] Gross involvement of the glabellar skin sometimes causes a leonine appearance.[10] The lack of acral calcification and absence of Raynaud's phenomenon help to distinguish this condition from scleroderma. The mucous membranes are not usually affected.[3]

There are occasional reports of systemic symptoms. Esophageal aperistalsis, peripheral neuropathy, proximal myopathy, and cardiac and cerebrovascular diseases have all been described.[4,11] There has, however, been little postmortem confirmation of visceral involvement and therefore it is likely that many of these associations are no more than coincidental. Neurological manifestations have, however, been reported most often and are probably of significance. They have included acute

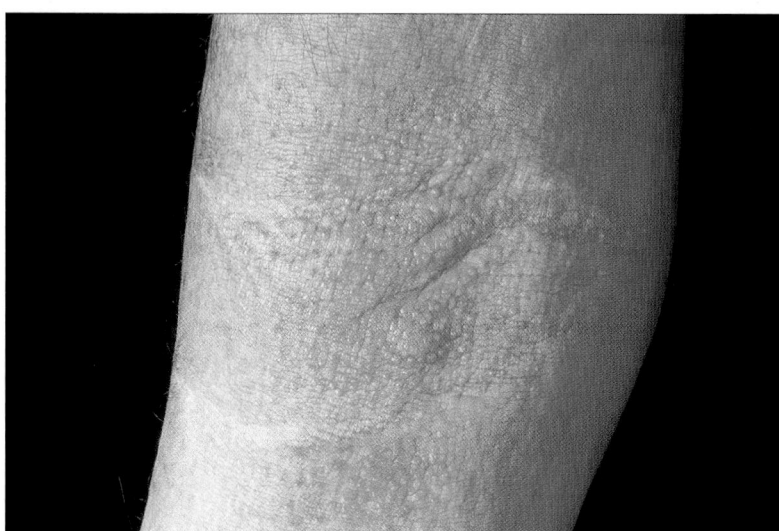

Fig. 12.168
Lichen myxedematosus: numerous papules are present in the antecubital fossa. By courtesy of R.A. Marsden, MD, St George's Hospital, London, UK.

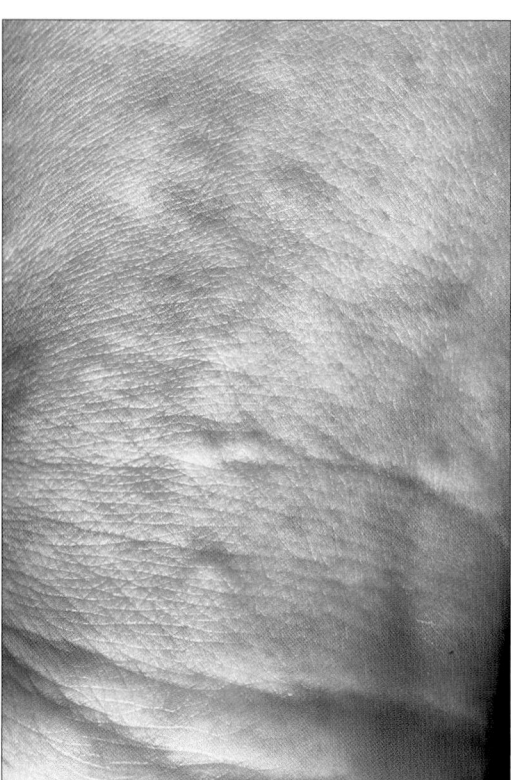

Fig. 12.169
Lichen myxedematosus: this is an example of the discrete papular form showing small numbers of papules on the anterior wrist. By courtesy of R.A. Marsden, MD, St George's Hospital, London, UK.

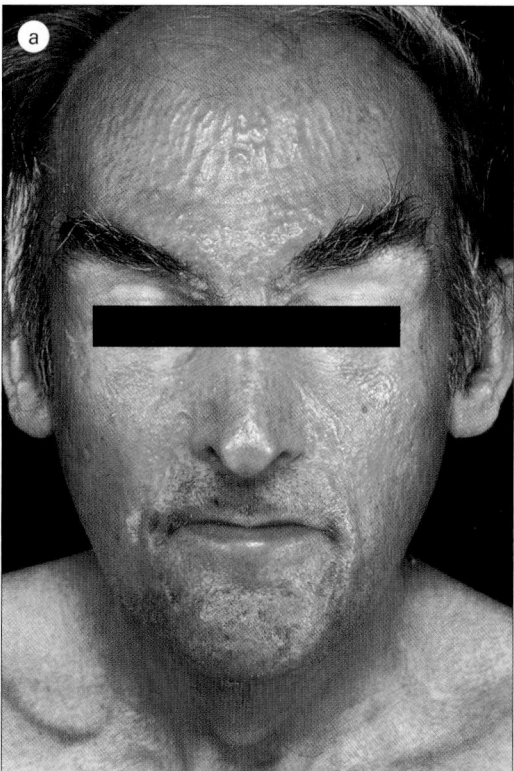

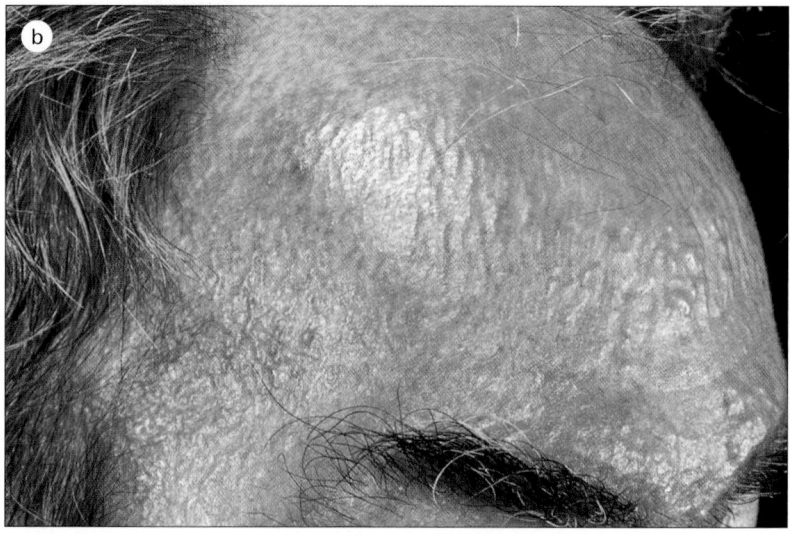

Fig. 12.170
(a, b) Scleromyxedema: this severely affected patient shows sclerosis and linear papules on the forehead. Note the pinched, masked-like facies. By courtesy of R.A. Marsden, MD, St George's Hospital, London, UK.

psychoses, encephalopathy and coma, epileptiform seizures, aphasia, memory loss, depression and motor dysfunction.[7,11–13] Carpal tunnel syndrome has also been reported fairly frequently.[14–16] There is usually no relationship between lichen myxedematosus and neoplasia. An exceptional case of lichen myxedematosus and hepatocellular carcinoma has been reported.[17] Rare cases associated with HIV infection have also been documented.[18,19] Further associations include chronic hepatitis C and dermatomyositis.[20–22] The latter finding is interesting because inflammatory myopathy but not dermatomyositis has been described in the past in association with scleromyxedema.[23] It has been suggested that the development of myopathy is associated with a poor prognosis.[23]

Scleromyxedema is usually (but not invariably) associated with a paraproteinemia; most often this is IgG with lambda light chains.[12,24–27] Occasionally it has been of the IgM or IgA class.[3] An occasional association with multiple myeloma has also been noted.[7]

Pathogenesis and histological features

The pathogenesis of lichen myxedematosus is unknown. There is no evidence to suggest that the paraprotein is responsible for the fibroblastic proliferation. However, serum from scleromyxedema patients has been shown to contain a non-paraprotein-associated fibroblast growth factor. This requires further characterization.[6,28] There is some evidence to suggest that the paraprotein may, however, have mucinogenic properties.[29,30] Fibroblasts grown in tissue culture produce greater quantities of hyaluronic acid and sulfated glycosaminoglycans than normal controls.[31] Collagen synthesis, as determined by H3-hydroxyproline estimations, is diminished.

Immunofluorescent studies have revealed immunoglobulin (IgG and to a lesser extent IgM) in the reticular dermis or just below the epidermis in about 35% cases.[10] Indirect immunofluorescence is invariably negative.

The epidermis may be normal, acanthotic or atrophic and sometimes hyperkeratosis with parakeratosis is evident. In early lesions stellate fibroblasts are seen between disorganized collagen fibers in the reticular dermis (*Figs 12.171, 12.172*).[3,5] The papillary dermis is not affected. Increased numbers of mast cells are sometimes present.[22] Focal deposits of mucin are readily identifiable (*Fig. 12.173*).[2] A slight perivascular chronic inflammatory cell infiltrate is often seen in the superficial dermis.

In the more severe scleromyxedema variant, fibroblasts are numerous and there is consequent fibrosis and thickening of the dermis (*Figs 12.174–12.176*).[4] Mucin deposits may be less evident or even absent.[10] Decreased elastic fibers have occasionally been reported.[3] A

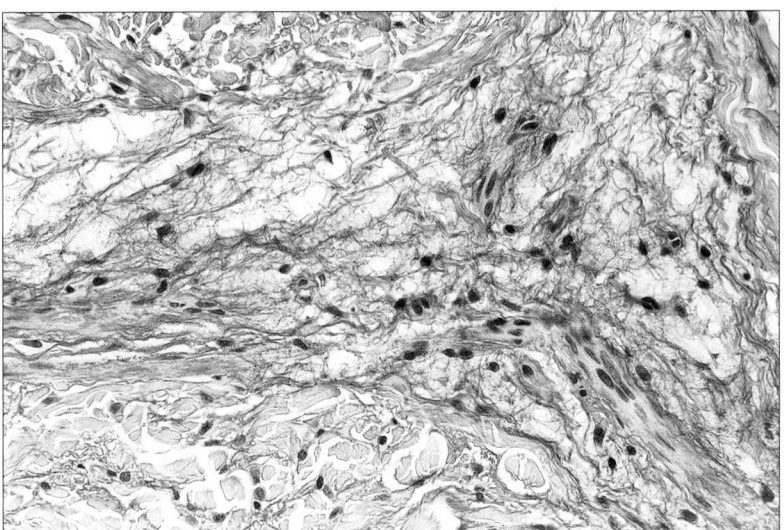

Fig. 12.173
Lichen myxedematosus: staining with colloidal iron emphasizes the mucin deposits.

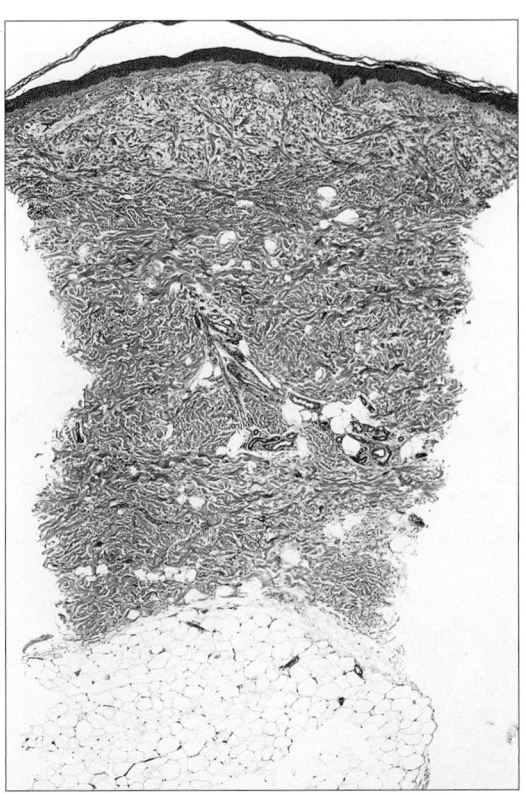

Fig. 12.171
Lichen myxedematosus: increased mucin is evident in the superficial dermis.

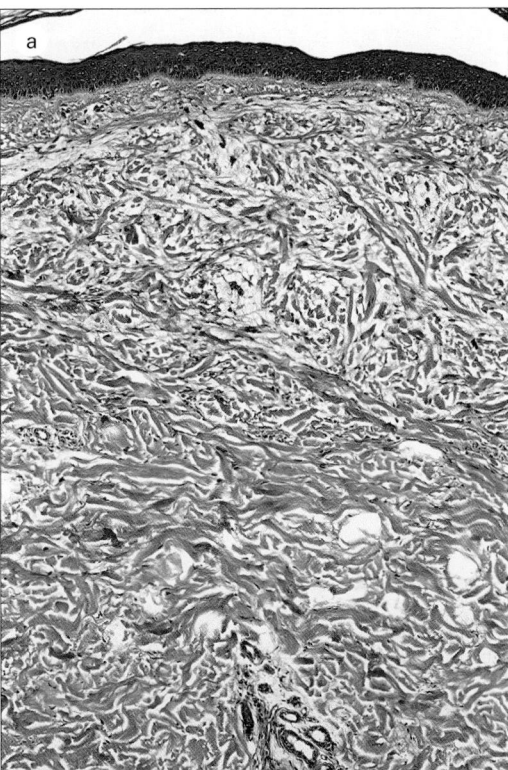

Fig. 12.172
(a, b) Lichen myxedematosus: the collagen fibers are widely separated by mucin deposits. Fibroblasts are increased in number.

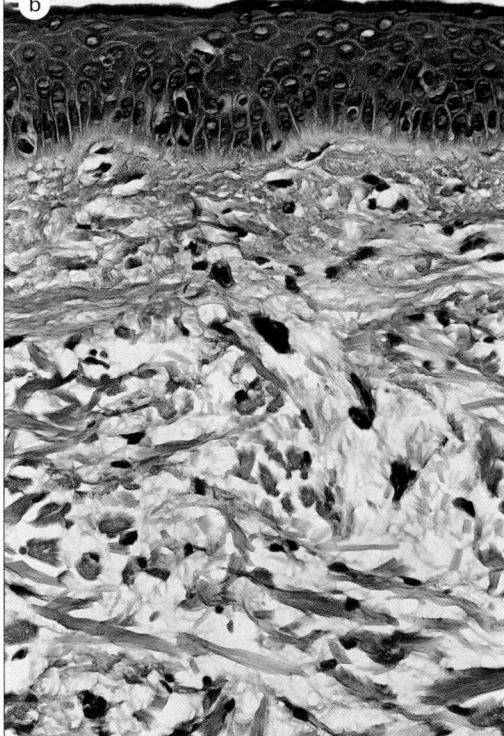

chronic inflammatory cell infiltrate is frequently present surrounding the superficial vasculature.

Ultrastructural studies show active fibroblasts characterized by abundant rough endoplasmic reticulum and Golgi apparatus, increased numbers of mitochondria, and cytoplasmic inclusions accompanied by collagen deposition.[32]

Systemic involvement has only rarely been documented. Mucin deposition has been described in the adventitia of visceral blood vessels and in the renal papillae in single case reports.[7,32] It has also been described within rectal mucosa and in muscle in one patient with scleromyxedema. Whether this represents true primary involvement or a secondary unrelated phenomenon is uncertain. In a particularly unusual case the features of systemic sclerosis were found in the kidney.[7] In the absence of any autopsy evidence of further sclerodermatous lesions, it may be that the renal vascular and glomerular changes reflected unrecognized scleromyxedematous pathology. Demyelination and focal gliosis have also been reported.[10,33] Nevertheless autopsy studies have usually shown no evidence of widespread mucinosis and it is likely that in the great majority of cases the pathological changes are limited to the skin.

References

1. Montgomery, H., Underwood, L.J. (1952) Lichen myxedematosus (differentiation from cutaneous myxedemas or mucoid states). *J Invest Dermatol*, **20**, 213–236.
2. Coskey, R.J., Mehregan, A. (1977) Papular mucinosis. *Arch Dermatol*, **16**, 741–744.
3. Truhan, A.P., Roenigk, H.H. (1986) The cutaneous mucinoses. *J Am Acad Dermatol*, **14**, 1–18.
4. Stephens, C.J.M., McKee, P.H., Black, M.M. (1993) The dermal mucinoses. *Adv Dermatol*, **8**, 201–227.
5. Rongioletti, F., Rebora, A. (2001) Cutaneous mucinosis. Microscopic criteria for diagnosis. *Am J Dermatopathol*, **23**, 257–267.
6. Rongioletti, F., Rebora, A. (2001) Updated classification of papular mucinosis, lichen myxedematosus and scleromyxedema. *J Am Acad Dermatol*, **44**, 273–281.
7. Kantor, G.R., Bergfeld, W.F., Katzin, W.E. et al (1986) Scleromyxedema associated with scleroderma renal disease and acute psychosis. *J Am Acad Dermatol*, **14**, 879–888.
8. Perry, H.O., Montgomery, H., Stickney, J.M. (1960) Further observations on lichen myxedematosus. *Ann Intern Med*, **55**, 955–969.
9. Stephens, C.J.M., Ross, J.S., Black, M.M. (1990) A case of scleromyxedema associated with paraproteinemia and leg ulceration. *J Cutan Pathol*, **17**, 320.
10. Farmer, E.R., Hambrick, G.W. Jr, Shulman, L.E. (1982) Papular mucinosis: a clinicopathologic study of four patients. *Arch Dermatol*, **118**, 9–13.
11. Loggini, B., Pingitore, R., Avvenente, A. et al (2001) Lichen myxedematosus with systemic involvement: clinical and autopsy findings. *J Am Acad Dermatol*, **45**, 606–608.
12. Rudner, E.J., Mehregan, A., Pinkus, H. (1966) Sclermyxedema. *Arch Dermatol*, **93**, 3–12.
13. Ochitill, H.N., Amberson, J. (1978) Acute cerebral symptomatology, a rare presentation of scleromyxedema. *J Clin Psych*, **39**, 471, 473–475.
14. Milam, C.P., Cohen, L.E., Fenske, N.A. et al (1988) Sclermyxedema: therapeutic response to isotretinoin in three patients. *J Am Acad Dermatol*, **19**, 469–477.
15. Harris, R.B., Perry, H.O., Kyle, R.A. et al (1979) Treatment of scleromyxedema with melphalan. *Arch Dermatol*, **115**, 295–299.
16. Howsden, S.M., Herndon, J.H., Freeman, R.G. (1975) Lichen myxedematosus: a dermal infiltrative disorder responsive to cyclophosphamide therapy. *Arch Dermatol*, **111**, 1325–1330.
17. Lo, P.Y., Tzung, T.Y. (2000) Lichen myxedematosus in a patient with hepatocellular carcinoma. *Br J Dermatol*, **143**, 452–453.
18. Rongioletti, F., Ghigliotti, G., de Marchi, R. et al (1998) Cutaneous mucinosis and HIV infection. *Br J Dermatol*, **139**, 1077–1080.
19. Gildersleeve, R.F., Kirk, J.F., Cooper, P.H. et al (1995) Papular mucinosis with acquired immunodeficiency syndrome. *Cutis*, **55**, 174–176.
20. Banno, H., Takama, H., Nitta, Y. et al (2000) Lichen myxedematosus with chronic hepatitis C. *Int J Dermatol*, **39**, 212–214.
21. Montesu, M.A., Cottoni, F., Sanna, R. et al (2001) Lichen myxedematosus with chronic hepatitis C: a case report. *Acta Derm Venereol*, **81**, 67–68.
22. Launay, D., Hatron, P.Y., Delaporte, E. et al (2001) Scleromyxedema (lichen myxedematosus) associated with dermatomyositis. *Br J Dermatol*, **144**, 359–362.
23. Kaufman, D., Truhan, A.P., Roenigk, H.H. (1987) Scleromyxedema: systemic manifestations, cosmetic improvement from dermabrasion. *Cutis*, **39**, 321–324.
24. James, K., Fudenberg, H., Epstein, W.L. et al (1967) Studies on a unique diagnostic serum globulin in papular mucinosis (lichen myxedematosus). *Clin Exp Immunol*, **2**, 153–166.
25. Kitamura, W., Matsuoka, Y., Miyagawa, S. et al (1978) Immunochemical analysis of the monoclonal paraprotein in sclermyxedema. *J Invest Dermatol*, **70**, 305–308.
26. Chanda, J.J. (1979) Scleromyxedema. *Cutis*, **24**, 549–552.
27. Harper, R.A., Rispler, J. (1978) Lichen myxedematosus serum stimulates human skin fibroblast proliferation. *Science*, **199**, 545–547.
28. Muldrow, M.L., Bailin, P.L. (1983) Scleromyxedema associated with IgG lambda multiple myeloma. *Cleve Clin Q*, **50**, 189–195.
29. Harvey, J.M., Zilko, P.J., Cheah, P.S. et al (1986) Scleromyxedema and inflammatory myopathy: a clinicopathologic study of three patients. *Aust N Z J Med*, **16**, 329–335.
30. Yaron, M., Yaron, I., Yust, I. et al (1985) Lichen myxedematosus (scleromyxedema) serum stimulates hyaluronic acid and prostaglandin E production by human fibroblasts. *J Rheumatol*, **12**, 171–175.
31. Turakainen, H., Välimäki, M., Penttinen, R. (1985) Synthesis of glycosaminoglycans and collagen in skin fibroblasts cultured from a patient with lichen myxedematosus. *Arch Dermatol Res*, **277**, 55–59.
32. Matsuoka, L.Y., Wortsman, J., Carlisle, K.S. et al (1984) The acquired cutaneous mucinoses. *Arch Intern Med*, **144**, 1974–1980.
33. McCuistion, C.H., Schoch, E.P. Jr (1956) Autopsy findings in lichen myxedematosus. *Arch Dermatol*, **74**, 259–262.

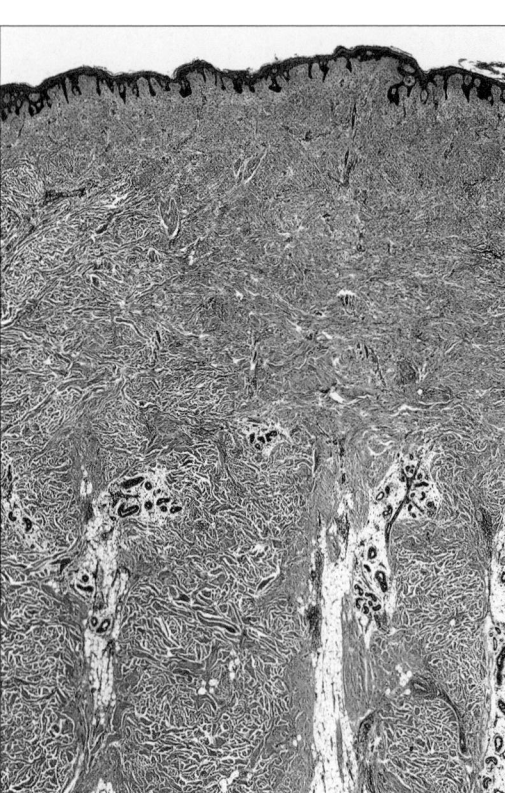

Fig. 12.174
Scleromyxedema: the dermis is markedly thickened. There is fibrosis and increased numbers of fibroblasts are evident.

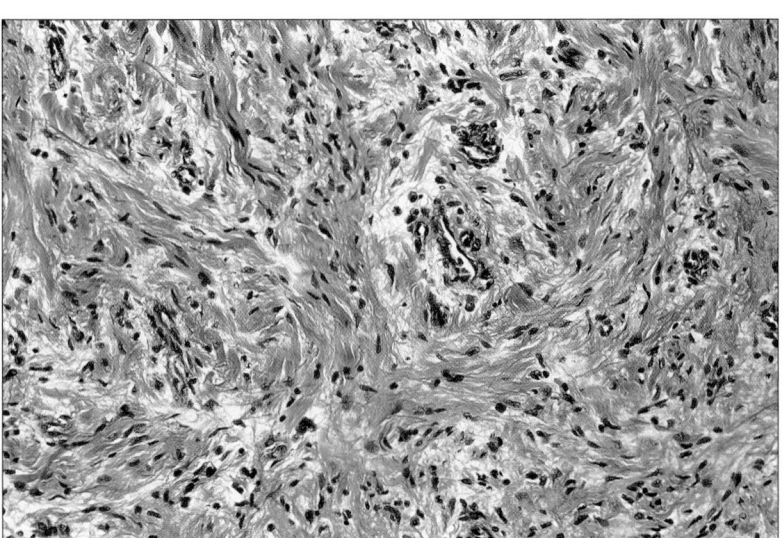

Fig. 12.175
Scleromyxedema: delicate strands of mucin separate the collagen fibers.

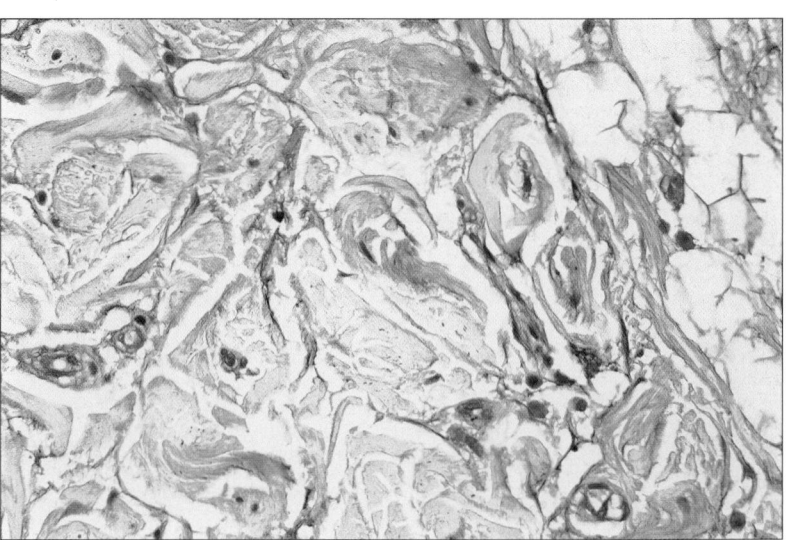

Fig. 12.176
Scleromyxedema: alcian blue.

Acral persistent papular mucinosis

Clinical features

This rare condition, which predominantly affects females, is characterized by the development of persistent multiple discrete and often symmetrical smooth-surfaced small papules (2–7 mm) on the dorsal aspects of the hands and wrists, sometimes extending on to the forearms (*Fig. 12.177*).[1–4] The condition is generally regarded as a localized variant of lichen myxedematosus.[5–8] The papules are ivory or flesh-colored and translucent, and on puncture characteristically contain clear viscous fluid.[2] Lesions do not occur on the face or trunk and there is no thickening or induration of the skin.[9] Pruritus is exceptional.[10] Occurrence in two sisters has been reported raising the possibility of a familial form of the disease.[11] Acral persistent papular mucinosis is not usually known to be associated with any systemic abnormalities such as thyroid disease or paraproteinemia.[12,13] An exceptional case associated with IgA monoclonal gammopathy has been reported.[14]

Histological features

The papules show extensive mucin deposition in the upper reticular dermis separated by a Grenz zone from the overlying epidermis (*Figs 12.178, 12.179*).[9,15] Increased numbers of spindle or stellate-shaped fibroblasts may occasionally be evident.[16] Fibrosis, however, as seen in lichen myxedematosus, is not a feature of this condition. Direct immunofluorescence has revealed granular IgM at the epidermodermal junction and linear IgG around the eccrine glands in one case.[2] Ultrastructural studies reveal active fibroblasts with prominent dilated rough endoplasmic reticulum. The collagen bundles are widely separated and focal deposits of electron-dense amorphous material are evident.[5] Conspicuous lamellated electron-dense lysosomes have been described in one case.[16] This probably represents a non-specific secondary change.

References

1. Rongioletti, F., Rebora, A. (1991) The new cutaneous mucinoses: a review with an up-to-date classification of cutaneous mucinoses. *J Am Acad Dermatol*, **24**, 265–270.
2. Rongioletti, F., Rebora, A., Crovato, F. (1986) Acral persistent papular mucinosis: a new entity. *Arch Dermatol*, **122**, 1237–1239.
3. Flowers, S.L., Cooper, P.H., Landes, H.B. (1989) Acral persistent papular mucinosis. *J Am Acad Dermatol*, **21**, 293–297.
4. Ross, J.S., Stephens, C.J.M., McKee, P.H. et al (1990) An unusual case of localized papular mucinosis. *J Cutan Pathol*, **17**, 315.
5. Naeyaert, J.M., Geerts, M.L., Kudsi, S. et al (1990) Acral persistent papular mucinosis: a peculiar variant of the discrete form of lichen myxedematosus. *J Am Acad Dermatol*, **126**, 1372–1374.
6. Rebora, A., Rongioletti, F. (1992) Acral persistent papular mucinosis and lichen myxedematosus. *Dermatology*, **126**, 283–285.
7. Rongioletti, F., Rebora, A. (2001) Updated classification of papular mucinosis, lichen myxedematosus and scleromyxedema. *J Am Acad Dermatol*, **44**, 273–281.
8. Gartner, S., Schoppelrey, H.P., Agathos, M. et al (1998) Acral papular lichen myxedematosus. *Hautarzt*, **49**, 855–858.
9. Stephens, C.J.M., McKee, P.H., Black, M.M. (1993) The dermal mucinoses. *Adv Dermatol*, **8**, 201–227.
10. Bayerl, C., Nurnberger, M., Moll, I. (1994) Acral persistent papular mucinosis (APPM) with pruritus. A case report and mast cell quantification. *Acta Derm Venereol*, **74**, 410–412.
11. Menni, S., Cavicchini, S., Brezzi, A. et al (1995) Acral persistent papular mucinosis in two sisters. *Clin Exp Dermatol*, **20**, 431–433.
12. Ravella, A., Garcia, P., Moreno, A. et al (1987) Mucinose papuleuse persistante acrale. *Ann Dermatol Venereol*, **114**, 1438–1440.
13. Royer, P., Beylot, C., Garabiol, B. et al (1988) Acromucinose papuleuse persistante. *Ann Dermatol Venereol*, **115**, 827–831.
14. Borradori, L., Aractingi, S., Blanc, F. et al (1992) Acral persistent papular mucinosis and IgA monoclonal gammopathy: report of a case. *Dermatology*, **185**, 134–136.
15. Crovato, F., Nazzari, G., Desirello, G. (1990) Acral persistent papular mucinosis. *J Am Acad Dermatol*, **23**, 121–122.
16. Ahó, H.J., Forsten, Y., Hopsu-Havu, V.K. (1991) Ultrastructural signs of altered intracellular metabolism in acral persistent papular mucinosis. *J Cutan Pathol*, **18**, 347–352.

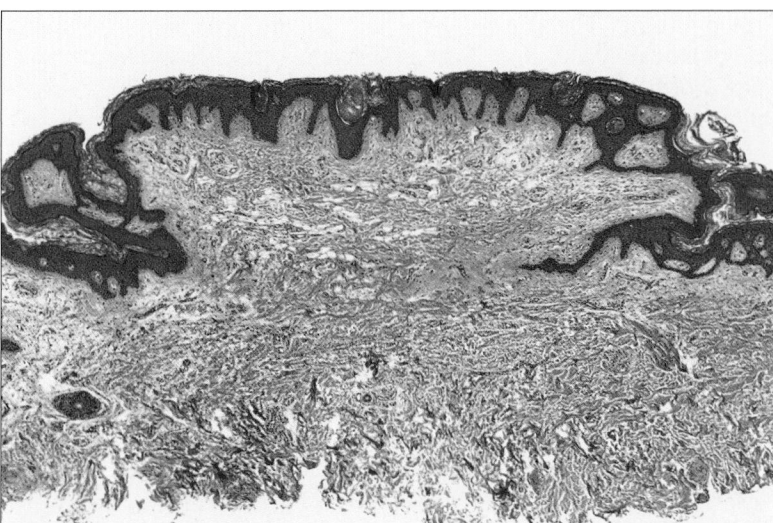

Fig. 12.178
Acral persistent papular mucinosis: note the presence of a discrete superficial papule with a well-developed collarette.

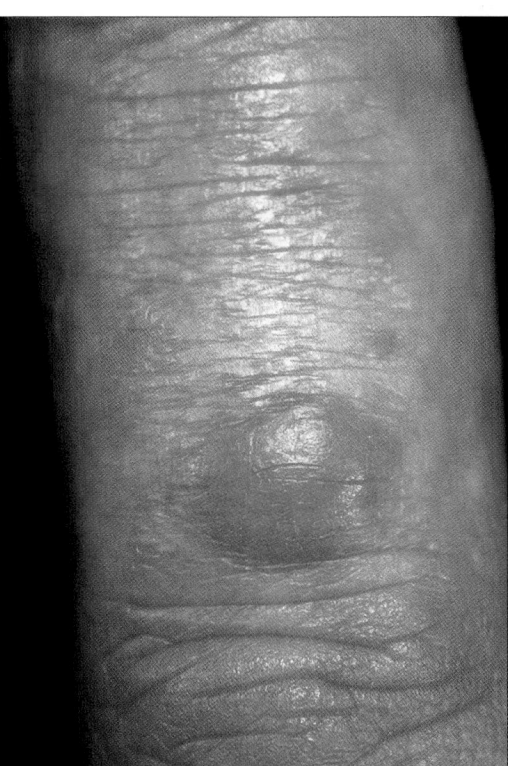

Fig. 12.177
Acral persistent papular mucinosis: discrete papule on the dorsal surface of a forefinger. This patient had similar lesions on the arms. By courtesy of R.A. Marsden, MD, St George's Hospital, London, UK.

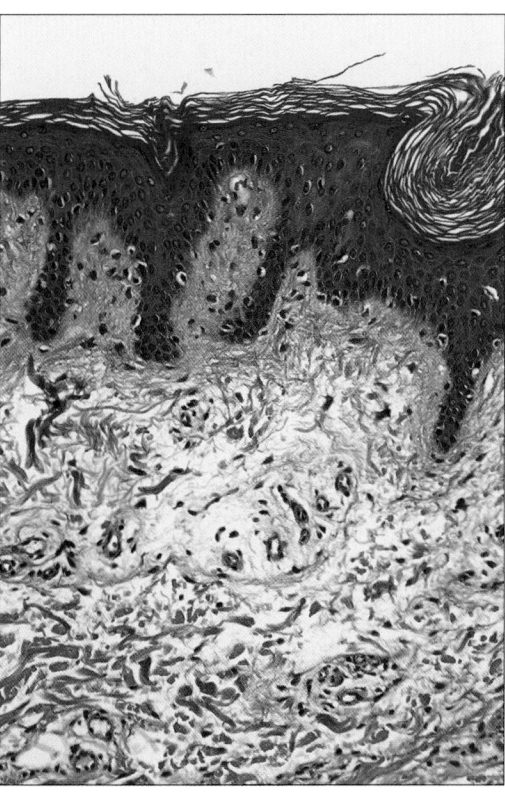

Fig. 12.179
Acral persistent papular mucinosis: close-up view showing mucin deposits.

Cutaneous mucinosis of infancy

Clinical features

This variant of papular mucinosis is very rare.[1–3] It has recently been suggested that this condition might represent a pediatric localized form of lichen myxedematosus.[4] Familial cases have been documented.[4]

The eruption consists of densely grouped, firm, 1–2 mm papules on the elbows and smaller numbers of more dispersed lesions about the forearms and dorsa of the hands.[1] Congenital linear papules on the backs of two fingers have been reported in one infant and another was born with clustered papules on the lower back.[2,3] Owing to the paucity of cases the natural history and prognosis of this condition is unknown.

Histological features

Excessive mucin (hyaluronic acid) is present in the papillary dermis under an acanthotic epidermis. Sectioning artifact may make the deposits appear to have an intraepidermal location. Biopsies from late lesions show features identical to those of lichen myxedematosus with fibrosis and proliferation of dermal fibroblasts.[4] A perivascular chronic inflammatory cell infiltrate is evident in the superficial dermis.

References

1. Lum, D. (1980) Cutaneous mucinosis of infancy. *Arch Dermatol*, **116**, 198–200.
2. McGrae, J.D. (1983) Cutaneous mucinosis of infancy: a congenital and linear variant. *Arch Dermatol*, **119**, 272–273.
3. Carapeto, F.J., Charlez, L., Marron, J. et al (1987) Infantile and progressive papular mucinosis. *Pediatr Dermatol*, **4**, 62.
4. Podda, M., Rongioletti, F., Greiner, D. et al (2001) Cutaneous mucinosis of infancy: is it a real entity or the paediatric form of lichen myxoedematosus (papular mucinosis)? *Br J Dermatol*, **144**, 590–593.

Self-healing juvenile cutaneous mucinosis

Clinical features

This is an extremely rare condition, only a handful of cases having been documented.[1–7] It presents in teenagers with a rapid onset of asymptomatic erythematous papules and plaques, which show a predilection for the face, neck, scalp, abdomen and thighs, accompanied by deep nodules on the face and periarticular regions.[1] The plaques have a characteristic appearance as linear groups of papules, giving the skin a corrugated appearance.[3] The eruption resolves within a period of weeks to months. Mild arthritis involving the elbows, knees and interphalangeal joints has been documented as has possible polychondritis.[1,3] These latter manifestations may be persistent.[1] In one patient bilateral carpal tunnel syndrome was present. Non-specific features of fatigue, weight loss and myalgia may also be evident. Exceptionally, the disease may present in adults, although only a single case has been documented.[8] There is no evidence of thyroid dysfunction or paraproteinemia.

Pathogenesis and histological features

The etiology is unknown although it has been suggested that the fibroblast activity may have been stimulated by a preceding viral infection.[3]

Histologically, the epidermis is normal or may show mild hyperkeratosis. Mucin deposition is seen in the papillary and upper reticular dermis separating and splitting the collagen bundles. In one case the mucin was PAS positive and identified as a sialomucin whereas in another it was found to consist of hyaluronic acid.[1,3] Fibroblasts are slightly increased in number and a mild chronic inflammatory cell infiltrate surrounds the superficial vasculature.

References

1. Pucevich, M.V., Latour, D.L., Bale, G.F. et al (1984) Self-healing juvenile cutaneous mucinosis. *J Am Acad Dermatol*, **11**, 327–332.
2. Colomb, D., Racouchot, J., Vittori, F. (1973) Mucinose d'évolution régressive sans paraprotéine chez une jeune fille. *Lyon Med*, **230**, 474–475.
3. Bonerandi, J-J., Andrac, L., Follana, J. et al (1980) Mucinose cutanée juvénile spontanément résolutive: étude anatomo-clinique et ultrastructurale. *Ann Dermatol Venereol*, **107**, 51–57.
4. Wadee, S., Roode, H., Schulz, E.J. (1994) Self-healing juvenile cutaneous mucinosis in a patient with nephroblastoma. *Clin Exp Dermatol*, **19**, 90–93.
5. Caputo, R., Grimalt, R., Gelmetti, C. (1995) Self-healing juvenile cutaneous mucinosis. *Arch Dermatol*, **131**, 459–460.
6. Kim, Y.J., Kim, Y.T., Kim, J.H. (1994) Self-healing juvenile cutaneous mucinosis. *J Am Acad Dermatol*, **31**, 815–816.
7. Aydingoz, I.E., Candan, I., Dervent, B. (1999) Self-healing juvenile cutaneous mucinosis. *Dermatology*, **199**, 57–59.
8. De las Heras, M.E., Pérez, B., Arrazola, J.M. et al (1996) Self-healing cutaneous mucinosis. *Dermatology*, **192**, 268–270.

Reticular erythematous mucinosis

This condition is described on page 269.

Scleredema

Clinical features

Scleredema (Buschke) is a rare primary mucinosis that presents with non-pitting indurated edema and associated dermal hardening in the absence of any significant clinical abnormality of the overlying skin.[1,2] Three distinct subtypes are recognized:[2–4]

- Most commonly seen is an acute variant predominantly affecting children and characterized by a rapid onset arising a few weeks after an infection, most often of the upper respiratory tract. Streptococcal infections are particularly implicated, but cases have followed a variety of viral illnesses including measles, mumps, influenza, cytomegalovirus infection and chickenpox.[5,6] Although many of these cases resolve spontaneously within a period of months and years, a significant number are persistent and exacerbations are not uncommon.[7] Females are affected more often than males and the disease is more common in the winter months.[8] Sometimes there is a prodromal illness of malaise, myalgia, generalized myasthenia and arthralgias.[7] Some patients develop a variety of cutaneous manifestations including transient erythema, urticarial or annular eruptions and dermographism before the onset of the more typical features.[4] Scleredema in children may exceptionally present overlapping features with eosinophilic fasciitis.[9]
- Secondly, scleredema may have an insidious onset unaccompanied by any previous acute illness.[2]
- Lastly, scleredema sometimes develops in association with late-onset diabetes mellitus. Patients, more often males, are often obese and there are usually other manifestations of diabetes including nephropathy, hypertension, coronary and peripheral vascular insufficiency, retinopathy and peripheral neuropathy.[2,10,11] The diabetes commonly precedes the development of scleredema, which is usually widespread and associated with a chronic course.[1,12] This variant of scleredema does not tend to resolve spontaneously or with treatment.

Scleredema is occasionally associated with a paraproteinemia (usually IgG, but sometimes IgA) and rarely multiple myeloma.[13,14] There is no evidence that the paraprotein results in the skin lesions and is probably a secondary phenomenon.

It should be noted that despite the original nomenclature of scleredema adultorum, many of the patients are in fact children.[7,8,15] Only very rarely are cases in children associated with diabetes.[15] An exceptional case of congenital scleredema has been reported.[16]

Rare cases have been associated with primary and secondary hyperparathyroidism and with rheumatoid arthritis and Sjögren's syndrome.[17–19] Scleredema has also been described in HIV infection, in association with a nuchal fibroma and following exposure to organic solvent, in the setting of a malignant insulinoma, with acanthosis nigricans and with generalized hyperpigmentation.[13,20–23] The cutaneous manifestations are similar for all three subtypes, differences being merely a matter of degree.

Patients present with symmetrical non-pitting edema and dermal hardening, which particularly affects the posterior and lateral aspects of the neck (*Fig. 12.180*).[2] The face, anterior neck, upper trunk and upper limbs are also frequently affected.[1] Rarely the disease may spread to the lower abdomen and legs. Confinement of the changes to the thighs has been described.[24] The palms and soles are rarely affected and genital involvement is uncommon.[7] Lesional skin is shiny and feels hard, and wrinkling is impossible due to involvement of the papillary dermis (*Fig. 12.181*). In severely affected patients reduced mobility is often a problem. The face may be expressionless, the lines of cleavage lost, and smiling and mouth opening may be difficult.[1]

In some patients systemic disease may be evident, including pericardial, pleural and peritoneal effusions, dysarthria and dysphagia due to tongue and pharyngeal lesions, hepatosplenomegaly, cardiac and skeletal muscle manifestations, parotid gland involvement and ocular changes presenting as induration of the eyelids and conjunctivae.[7,8,25] In cases with systemic involvement mucin deposition has been demonstrated in the bone marrow, liver, nerve, salivary gland and heart.[26,27]

Pathogenesis and histological features

The pathogenesis of scleredema is unknown. The serum from one patient with scleredema and a paraprotein markedly stimulated collagen production in normal skin fibroblast cultures, suggesting that a circulating factor(s) probably related to the paraprotein might induce the dermal fibrosis.[28] The involved skin shows increased synthesis of type I collagen, which appears to be responsible, at least in part, for the dermal fibrosis.[29,30] The fibroblasts in involved skin from individuals with scleredema show increased protein production, collagen synthesis and glucosamine incorporation. This correlation is associated with increased levels of type I and type III collagen.[31] Biochemical analysis of involved skin in scleredema has confirmed an increase in glycosaminoglycans, the main component being hyaluronic acid.[32]

The histological features are often subtle and the diagnosis is difficult. The epidermis may be slightly thinned or appear normal. The reticular dermis is greatly thickened, often at the expense of the subcutaneous fat, and the eccrine glands therefore become abnormally situated within the upper third or mid-dermis (*Figs 12.182, 12.183*).[1] The collagen fibers are broadened and, particularly in the earlier stages, are abnormally separated by clear spaces (dermal fenestration).[2] The latter may contain small quantities of mucin, but often special stains (alcian blue, colloidal iron) and multiple biopsies are necessary for their demonstration (*Fig. 12.184*).[12,33] Fibroblasts are present in normal numbers. A mild chronic inflammatory cell infiltrate is sometimes evident in the superficial dermis and mast cells may be increased in number (*Fig. 12.185*).[1] Direct immunofluorescence studies are negative.[2,13]

Differential diagnosis

Scleredema may be distinguished clinically from scleroderma by the absence of Raynaud's phenomenon, acral sclerosis with calcification, pigmentary changes and telangiectasia.[2] Histologically the appendages are atrophic and compressed or absent in scleroderma and there is diffuse dermal sclerosis rather than the fenestrated appearance seen in scleredema.

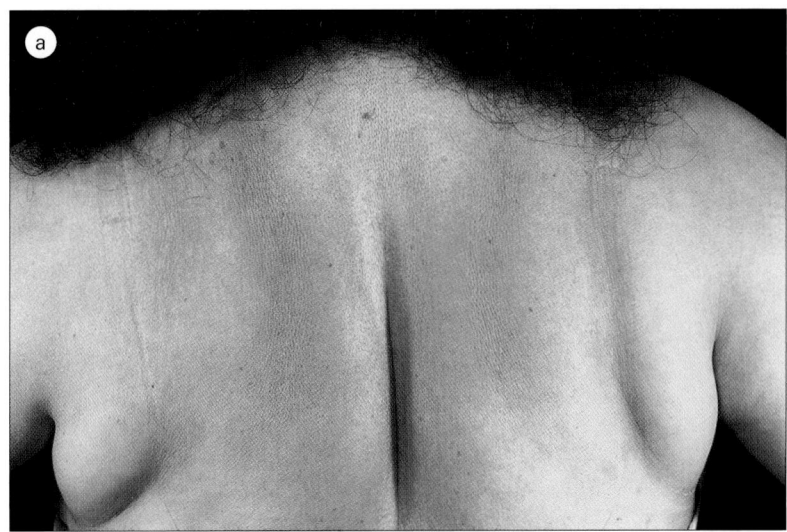

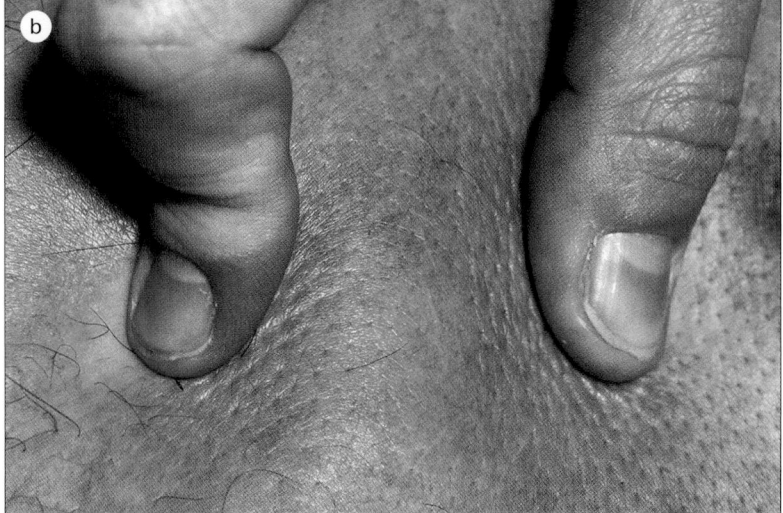

Fig. 12.180
Scleredema: a diffuse, firm thickening of the tissues is present over the neck and shoulders. By courtesy of G. Murphy, MD, Institute of Dermatology, London, UK.

Fig. 12.181
(a, b) Scleredema: there is marked thickening and induration of the skin of the upper back. By courtesy of G. Murphy, MD, Beaumont Hospital, Dublin, Eire.

References

1. Truhan, A.P., Roenigk, H.H. (1986) The cutaneous mucinoses. *J Am Acad Dermatol*, **14**, 1–18.
2. Venencie, P.Y., Powell, F.C., Su, W.P.D. et al (1984) Scleredema: a review of 33 cases. *J Am Acad Dermatol*, **11**, 128–134.
3. Steigleder, G.K., Kuchmeister, B. (1985) The cutaneous mucinous deposits. *J Cutan Pathol*, **12**, 334–347.
4. Carrington, P.R., Sanusi, I.D., Winder, P.R. et al (1984) Scleredema adultorum. *Int J Dermatol*, **23**, 514–522.
5. Cron, R.Q., Swetter, S.M. (1994) Scleredema revisited. A poststreptococcal complication. *Clin Pediatr (Phila)*, **33**, 606–610.
6. Parmar, R.C., Bavdekar, S.B., Bansal, S. et al (2000) Scleredema adultorum. *J Postgrad Med*, **46**, 91–93.
7. Heilbron, B., Saxe, N. (1986) Scleredema in an infant. *Arch Dermatol*, **122**, 1417–1419.
8. Greenberg, L.M., Geppert, C., Worthen, H.G. et al (1963) Scleredema 'adultorum' in children: report of three cases with a histochemical study and review of the world literature. *Pediatrics*, **32**, 1044–1054.
9. Huemer, M., Seeber, A., Huemer, C. (2000) Scleroderma-like syndrome in a child: eosinophilic fasciitis or scleredema adultorum. *Eur J Pediatr*, **159**, 520–522.
10. Krakowski, A., Cavo, J., Berlin, C. (1973) Diabetic scleredema. *Dermatologica*, **146**, 193–198.
11. Tate, B.J., Kelly, J.W., Rotstein, H. (1996) Scleredema of Buschke: a report of seven cases. *Australas J Dermatol*, **37**, 139–142.
12. Fleischmajer, R., Faludi, G., Krol, S. (1970) Scleredema and diabetes mellitus. *Arch Dermatol*, **101**, 21–26.
13. McFadden, N., Lee, K., Soyland, E. et al (1987) Scleredema adultorum associated with a monoclonal gammopathy and generalized hyperpigmentation. *Arch Dermatol*, **123**, 629–632.
14. Kövary, P.M., Vakilzadeh, F., Macher, E. et al (1981) Monoclonal gammopathy in scleredema: observations in three new cases. *Arch Dermatol*, **117**, 536–539.
15. Mitsuhashi, Y., Kondo, S., Shimizu, Y. (1996) Scleroedema in a child. *J Dermatol*, **23**, 495–498.
16. Hwang, J.H., Cho, K.H., Park, K.C. et al (1998) A case of congenital scleredema. *Clin Exp Dermatol*, **23**, 139–140.
17. Berk, M.A., Lorincz, A.L. (1988) Scleredema adultorum of Buschke and primary hyperparathyroidism. *Int J Dermatol*, **27**, 647–649.
18. Jacob, N., Gleichmann, U., Stadler, R. (2002) Scleredema adultorum in secondary hyperparathyroidism. *Hautarzt*, **53**, 121–125.
19. Miyagawa, S., Dohi, K., Tsuruta, S. et al (1989) Scleredema of Buschke associated with rheumatoid arthritis and Sjögren's syndrome. *Br J Dermatol*, **121**, 517–520.
20. Rongioletti, F., Ghigliotti, G., De Marchi, R. et al (1998) Cutaneous mucinoses and HIV infection. *Br J Dermatol*, **139**, 1077–1080.
21. Banney, L.A., Weedon, D., Muir, J.B. (2000) Nuchal fibroma associated with scleredema, diabetes mellitus and organic solvent exposure. *Australas J Dermatol*, **41**, 39–41.
22. Matsugana, J., Hara, M., Tagami, H. (1992) Scleredema of Buschke associated with malignant insulinoma. *Br J Dermatol*, **126**, 527–528.
23. Valente, L., Velho, G.C., Farinha, F. et al (1997) Scleredema, acanthosis nigricans and IgA/Kappa multiple myeloma. *Ann Dermatol Venereol*, **124**, 537–539.
24. Farrell, A.M., Branfoot, A.C., Moss, J. et al (1996) Scleredema diabeticorum of Buschke confined to the thighs. *Br J Dermatol*, **134**, 1113–1115.
25. Stephens, C.J.M., McKee, P.H., Black, M.M. (1993) The dermal mucinoses. *Adv Dermatol*, **8**, 201–227.
26. Basarab, T., Burrows, N.P., Munn, S.E. et al (1997) Systemic involvement in scleredema of Buschke associated with IgG-kappa paraproteinaemia. *Br J Dermatol*, **136**, 939–942.
27. Rimon, D., Lurie, M., Storch, S. et al (1988) Cardiomyopathy and multiple myeloma. Complication of scleredema adultorum. *Arch Intern Med*, **148**, 551–553.
28. Ohtoa, A., Uitto, J., Oikarinen, A.I. et al (1987) Paraprotein in patients with scleredema. Clinical findings and serum effects on skin fibroblasts in vitro. *J Am Acad Dermatol*, **16**, 96–107.

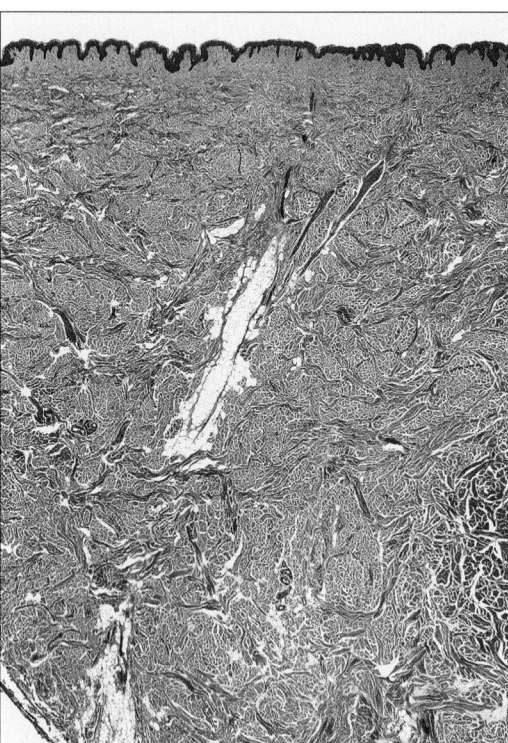

Fig. 12.182
Scleredema: the dermis is thickened.

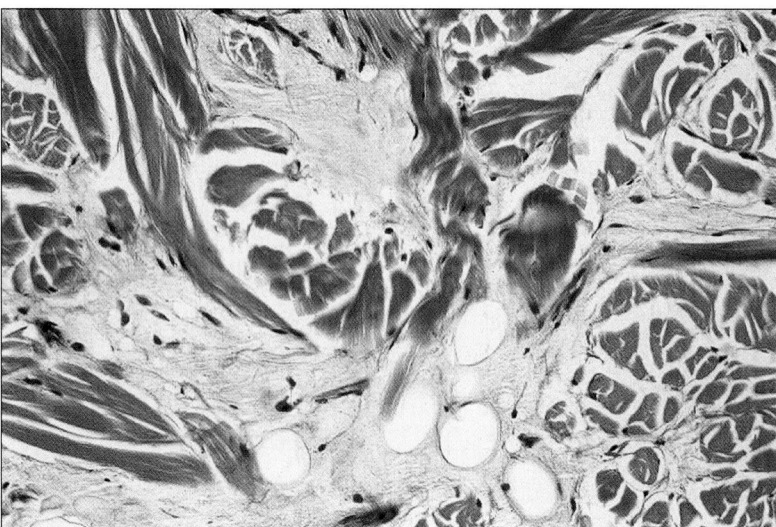

Fig. 12.183
Scleredema: the collagen fibers appear swollen.

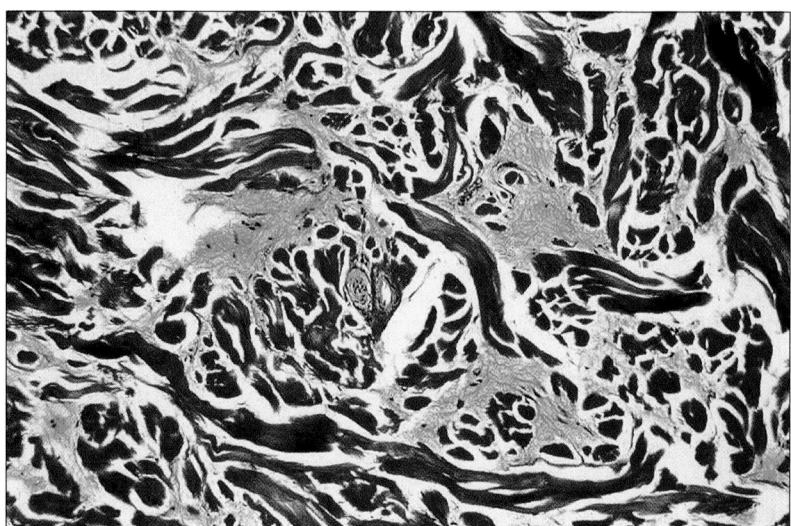

Fig. 12.184
Scleredema: the abundant mucin is highlighted by alcian blue/chromotrophe 2R staining.

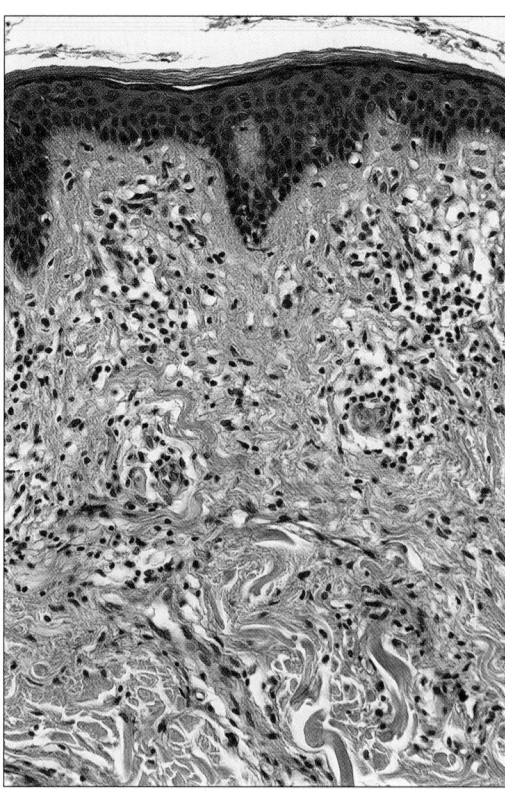

Fig. 12.185
Scleredema: superficial dermal lymphohistiocytic infiltrate.

29. Tasanen, K., Palatsi, R., Oikarinen, A. (1998) Demonstration of increased levels of type I collagen mRNA using quantitative polymerase chain reaction in fibrotic and granulomatous skin diseases. *Br J Dermatol*, **139**, 23–26.
30. Haapasaari, K.M., Kallioinen, M., Tasanen, K. et al (1996) Increased collagen propeptides in the skin of a scleredema patient but no change in re-epithelialization rate. *Acta Derm Venereol*, **76**, 305–309.
31. Varga, J., Gotta, L.L., Sollberg, S. et al (1995) Scleredema adultorum: case report and demonstration of abnormal expression of extracellular matrix genes in skin fibroblasts in vivo and in vitro. *Br J Dermatol*, **132**, 992–999.
32. Kobayashi, T., Yamasaki, Y., Watanabe, T. (1997) Diabetic scleredema: a case report and biochemical analysis of glycosaminoglycans. *J Dermatol*, **24**, 100–103.
33. Cole, H.G., Winkelmann, R.K. (1990) Acid mucopolysaccharide staining in scleredema. *J Cutan Pathol*, **17**, 211–213.

Papular and nodular cutaneous mucinosis of systemic lupus erythematosus

Clinical features

Mucin deposition as a specific clinical manifestation of lupus erythematosus has been recorded only rarely in the literature yet is said to occur in up to 1.5% of dermatological patients with this disease.[1–3] The condition presents as asymptomatic, flesh-colored, occasionally umbilicated papules and nodules on the neck, trunk and upper limbs.[4–8] Presentation with massive cutaneous mucinosis has also rarely been reported.[9] The papules may rarely be hyperpigmented.[10] Lesions are best appreciated using tangential light, which gives the skin a lumpy appearance.[5] Mucin deposition occurs most often in patients with the systemic variant, usually with diffuse antinuclear factor and anti-DNA antibodies and is particularly associated with joint and kidney lesions.[4,11] There are, however, occasional reports of its occurrence in patients with discoid lupus erythematosus.[4,7] An inconstant relationship to sunlight has been recorded.[4,12] Exceptionally, systemic sclerosis may present with similar papular and nodular mucinous lesions.[13]

Histological features

The epidermis shows no significant features; in particular the changes of lupus erythematosus are usually absent. However, an interface change has been described in a single case.[14] The mucin is present in the papillary and upper reticular dermis associated with a slight perivascular chronic inflammatory cell infiltrate.[4,15]

Direct immunofluorescence may show linear or granular immunoglobulin (IgG, IgM) deposits and complement at the epidermodermal junction.

References

1. Rongioletti, F., Rebora, A. (1991) The new cutaneous mucinoses: a review with an up-to-date classification of cutaneous mucinoses. *J Am Acad Dermatol*, **24**, 265–270.
2. Gold, S.C. (1954) An unusual papular eruption associated with lupus erythematosus. *Br J Dermatol*, **66**, 429–433.
3. Gammon, W.R., Caro, I., Long, J.C. et al (1978) Secondary cutaneous mucinosis with systemic lupus erythematosus. *Arch Dermatol*, **114**, 432–435.
4. Rongioletti, F., Parodi, A., Rebora, A. (1990) Papular and nodular mucinosis as a sign of lupus erythematosus. *Dermatologica*, **180**, 221–223.
5. Rongioletti, F., Rebora, A. (1986) Papular and nodular mucinosis associated with systemic lupus erythematosus. *Br J Dermatol*, **115**, 631–636.
6. Revier, J., Kienzler, J.L., Blanc, D. et al (1982) Papular mucinosis associated with lupus erythematosus. A case presentation and review of the literature. *Ann Dermatol Venereol*, **109**, 331–338.
7. Aquilina, C., Sayag, J. (1991) Lupus erythematosus and papules. 4 cases. *Ann Dermatol Venereol*, **118**, 593–605.
8. Storck, R., Schirren, C.G., Meurer, M. et al (1994) Papular mucinosis. A rare cutaneous manifestation of lupus erythematosus. *Hautarzt*, **45**, 642–646.
9. Maruyama, M., Miyauchi, S., Hashimoto, K. (1997) Massive cutaneous mucinosis associated with systemic lupus erythematosus. *Br J Dermatol*, **137**, 450–453.
10. Lacour, J.P., Juhlin, L., el Baze, P. et al (1989) Hyperpigmented acral papular mucinosis, systemic lupus erythematosus and universal alopecia. *Acta Derm Venereol*, **69**, 212–216.
11. Choi, E.H., Hann, S.K., Chung, K.Y. et al (1992) Papulonodular cutaneous mucinosis associated with systemic lupus erythematosus. *Int J Dermatol*, **31**, 649–652.
12. Moulin, G., Bouchet, B., Souteyrand, P. et al (1980) Mucinose papuleuse photodépendante et lupus érythémateux disséminé. *Ann Dermatol Venereol*, **107**, 1193–1198.
13. Van Zander, J., Shaw, J.C. (2002) Papular and nodular mucinosis as a presenting sign of progressive systemic sclerosis. *J Am Acad Dermatol*, **46**, 304–306.
14. Pandya, A.G., Sontheimer, R.D., Cockerell, C.J. et al (1995) Papulonodular mucinosis associated with systemic lupus erythematosus: possible mechanisms of increased glycosaminoglycan accumulation. *J Am Acad Dermatol*, **32**, 199–205.
15. Rongioletti, F., Rebora, A. (2001) Cutaneous mucinoses. Microscopic criteria for diagnosis. *Am J Dermatopathol*, **23**, 257–267.

Myxoid cyst

Clinical features

Cutaneous myxoid cyst, sometimes inappropriately referred to as synovial cyst, presents as a soft or fluctuant cystic nodule on the dorsal aspect of the distal interphalangeal, the metacarpophalangeal and, less frequently, the metatarsophalangeal joints (*Figs 12.186, 12.187*).[1,2] Occasionally lesions are multiple. Cutaneous myxoid cysts may present at any age and are more common in females. The surface is usually smooth, although verrucous variants are occasionally encountered. The cyst contains yellow, clear viscous fluid. Lesions are often painful or tender. Myxoid cyst involving the proximal nail fold may be associated with longitudinal grooving of the nail.[3] Osteoarthrosis is sometimes evident.[1]

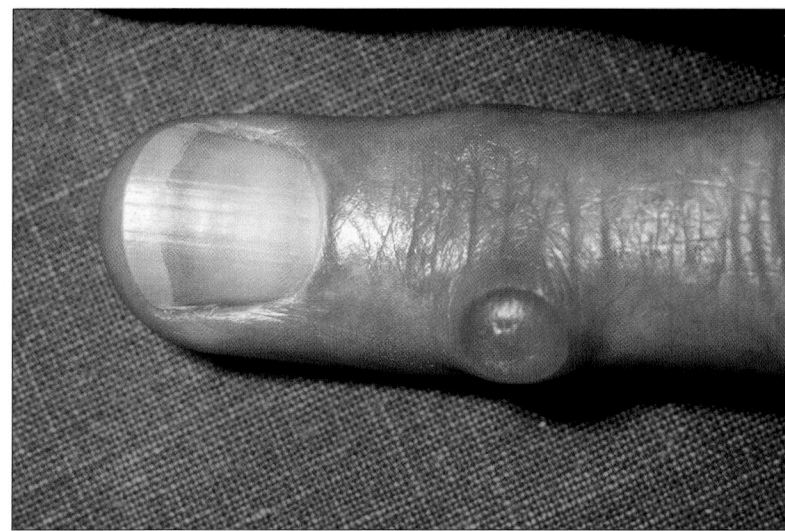

Fig. 12.186
Myxoid cyst: the translucency is typical. By courtesy of R.A. Marsden, MD, St George's Hospital, London, UK.

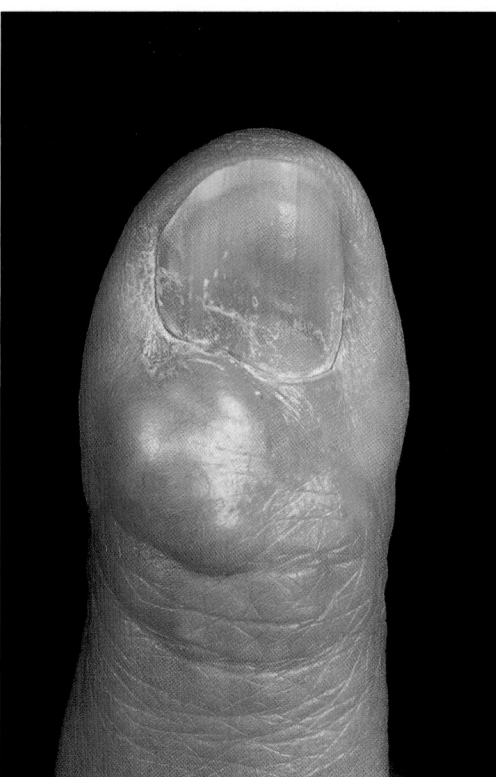

Fig. 12.187
Myxoid cyst: localization over the distal interphalangeal joint is characteristic. By courtesy of the Institute of Dermatology, London, UK.

Histological features

The cyst is devoid of any lining and consists of a large pool of mucin containing spindle/stellate fibroblasts with prominent cytoplasmic processes (*Fig. 12.188*). The overlying epidermis is often atrophic and hyperkeratotic and acanthosis may be seen at the edges. Early lesions are sometimes indistinguishable from cutaneous focal mucinosis. There is no evidence of any connection with an underlying joint.

References

1. Johnson, W.C., Graham, J.H., Helwig, E.B. (1965) Cutaneous myxoid cyst: a clinicopathological and histochemical study. *JAMA*, **191**, 15–20.
2. Armijo, M. (1982) Mucoid cysts of the fingers. *J Dermatol Surg Oncol*, **7**, 317–322.
3. Smith, E.B., Skipworth, G.B., Van der Ploeg, D.E. (1964) Longitudinal grooving of nails due to synovial cysts. *Arch Dermatol*, **89**, 364–366.

Cutaneous focal mucinosis

Clinical features

Cutaneous focal mucinosis presents as an asymptomatic, usually solitary, benign dermal papule or nodule most commonly on the face, neck, trunk or extremities of adults.[1–5] It is not seen in relation to the joints of the hands, feet or wrists. The lesion is usually dome-shaped, white or flesh-colored and sometimes has an erythematous halo.[2] Occasional verrucous variants have been documented.[1] There is usually no evidence of an associated thyroid abnormality. Exceptional cases, however, are associated with reticular erythematous mucinosis or scleromyxedema.[6]

Histological features

The lesion is usually located in the mid and upper dermis, often separated from the epidermis by a Grenz zone of dermal sparing.[2] It consists of a localized, but usually poorly delineated, focus of mucin deposition containing increased numbers of spindle cells and stellate fibroblasts with elongated cytoplasmic processes.[2] Sometimes these contain conspicuous intracytoplasmic vacuoles.[3] Collagen fibers are usually diminished in number.[4] A mild perivascular chronic inflammatory cell infiltrate is often present in the adjacent dermis.

Ultrastructurally the fibroblasts contain prominent rough endoplasmic reticulum and membrane-bound intracytoplasmic vesicles containing abundant granular electron-dense material.[3]

Differential diagnosis

Cutaneous focal mucinosis must be distinguished from superficial angiomyxoma, a benign myxoid cutaneous and subcutaneous lesion with a tendency for local recurrence (see p. 1858).

References

1. Johnson, W.C., Helwig, E.B. (1966) Cutaneous focal mucinosis: a clinicopathological and histochemical study. *Arch Dermatol*, **93**, 13–20.
2. Stephens, C.J.M., McKee, P.H., Black, M.M. (1993) The dermal mucinoses. *Adv Dermatol*, **8**, 201–227.
3. Wilk, M., Schmoeckel, C. (1994) Cutaneous focal mucinosis – a histopathologic and immunohistochemical analysis of 11 cases. *J Cutan Pathol*, **21**, 446–452.
4. Hazelrigg, D.E. (1974) Cutaneous focal mucinosis. *Cutis*, **14**, 241–242.
5. Nishiura, S., Mihara, M., Shimao, S. et al (1989) Cutaneous focal mucinosis. *Br J Dermatol*, **121**, 511–515.
6. Rongioletti, F., Amantea, A., Balus, L., Rebora, A. (1991) Cutaneous focal mucinosis associated with reticular erythematous mucinosis and scleromyxedema. *J Am Acad Dermatol*, **24**, 656–657.

Mucinous nevus

Clinical features

Mucinous nevus (nevus mucinosis) is a rare lesion that may be congenital or acquired.[1–5] The most common site affected is either the trunk or lower limbs. Patients present with papules, nodules and/or plaque-like lesions, usually with a linear or dermatomal distribution.[4]

Histological features

Histologically, the mucin is located in the superficial dermis where it replaces the collagen and elastic fibers.[5] Some cases are associated with epidermal hyperplasia and these cases may represent a combined epidermal and mucinous nevus.[3]

References

1. Redondo Bellon, P., Vázquez-Doval, J., Idoate, M. et al (1993) Mucinous nevus. *J Am Acad Dermatol*, **28**, 797–798.
2. Brakman, M., Starink, T.M., Tafelkruyer, J. et al (1994) Linear connective tissue naevus of the proteoglycan type ('naevus mucinosus'). *Br J Dermatol*, **131**, 368–370.
3. Rongioletti, F., Rebora, A. (1996) Mucinous nevus. *Arch Dermatol*, **132**, 1522–1523.
4. Suhr, K.B., Ro, Y.W., Kim, K.H. et al (1997) Mucinous nevus: report of two cases and review of the literature. *J Am Acad Dermatol*, **37**, 312–313.
5. Rongioletti, F., Rebora, A. (2001) Cutaneous mucinoses. Microscopic criteria for diagnosis. *Am J Dermatopathol*, **23**, 257–267.

Neuropathia mucinosa cutanea

There is only one case report of this condition that presented in a young male with hyperesthesia and livedoid lesions on the lower limbs. A biopsy of these lesions revealed hypertrophic nerves surrounded by mucin.[1]

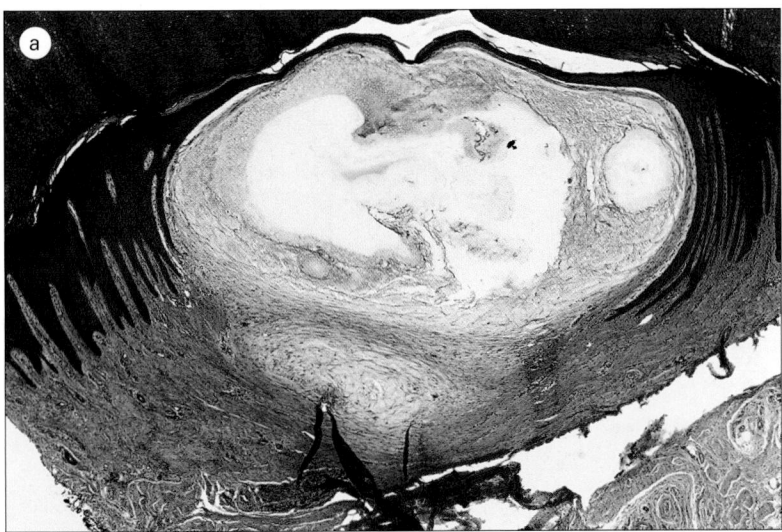
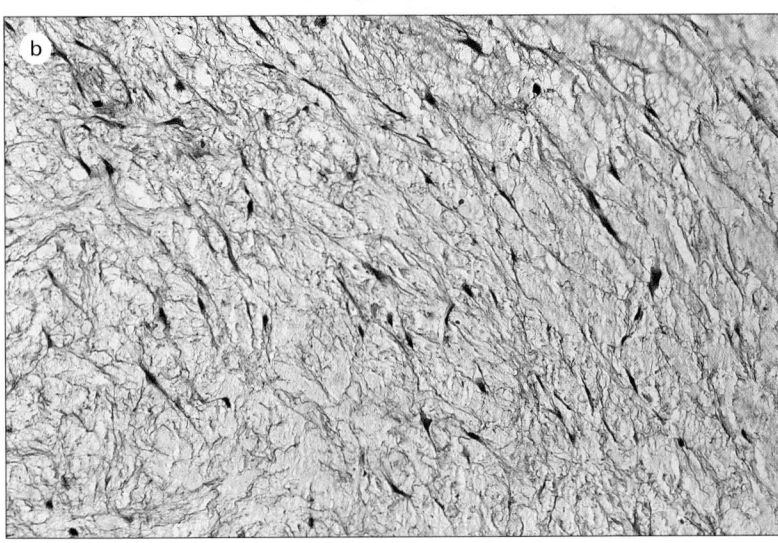

Fig. 12.188

(a, b) Myxoid cyst: excessive mucin deposition has resulted in this fluid-filled cyst. The overlying epithelium may appear attenuated or verrucous and occasionally the cyst is in part intraepidermal in location.

Reference

1. Vakilzadeh, F. (1988) Neuropathia mucinosa cutanea. *Hautartz*, **40**, 167–169.

Self-healing infantile familial cutaneous mucinosis

This very rare entity has been reported only once, in two brothers. Multiple lesions developed during the first few months of life and in one patient regressed spontaneously over a few years.[1]

Reference

1. González-Ensenat, M.A., Vicente, M.A., Castella, N. et al (1997) Self-healing infantile familial cutaneous mucinosis. *Pediatr Dermatol*, **14**, 460–462.

Acanthosis nigricans

Clinical features

Acanthosis nigricans may develop under a variety of circumstances.[1,2] In addition to the well-recognized tumor-associated variant, acanthosis nigricans may present with benign familial forms, endocrinopathy and drug-related variants, and the condition may be seen in association with a range of congenital conditions including lipoatrophy, leprechaunism and the type A and type B syndromes described below. Genetic conditions associated with acanthosis nigricans include:

- Alstrom syndrome (retinopathy, progressive sensorineural hearing loss, truncal obesity)
- Crouzon syndrome (facial palsy, sensorineural hearing loss and skeletal and mental retardation)
- Seip–Lawrence syndrome (congenital lipodystrophic diabetes)
- Costello syndrome (postnatal growth deficiency, coarse facies, redundant skin of the neck, palms, soles and fingers, dark skin and papillomas)
- Bannayan–Riley–Ruvalcaba syndrome (subcutaneous lipomas, vascular malformations, lentigines of the penis and vulva, warty lesions, macrocephaly, mental retardation, intestinal polyposis, skeletal abnormalities, vascular malformations of the central nervous system and thyroid tumors).[3–7]

Recently, acanthosis nigrans has been described in association with a missense mutation of the fibroblast growth factor receptor.[3] This disease is also associated with severe neurological impairment and severe achondroplasia.[8] Additional rare associations include Wilson's disease (hepatolenticular degeneration) and primary biliary cirrhosis.[9,10] In the latter case, the acanthosis nigricans resolved after liver transplantation. An exceptional family with several members affected by acanthosis nigricans, absence of the eyebrows and eyelashes and sparse hair elsewhere has also been reported.[11]

Development of acanthosis nigricans may also antedate or present concomitantly with a variety of connective tissue diseases including systemic lupus erythematosus, systemic sclerosis and dermatomyositis.[12–14]

Acanthosis nigricans is characterized by the presence of symmetrical brown velvety or verrucous plaques with a predilection for intertriginous sites such as the back of the neck, groin and axillae (*Figs 12.189, 12.190*). In more extreme forms the changes may be generalized.[15] Involvement of the eyelids also rarely occurs.[16] In addition there is sometimes brown thickening of the skin over the dorsum of the fingers or, rarely, the palms of the hands (tripe palms) (*Fig. 12.191*). The latter is a distinctive appearance due to broadened epidermal ridges and deep sulci giving the skin a velvety rugose texture.[17] Tripe palms are usually associated with internal malignancy and often (but not invariably) accompany acanthosis nigricans. Tripe palms, however, may also represent a benign reversible phenomenon unassociated with neoplasia. Less frequently there may be similar changes on mucosal surfaces such as the mouth (particularly the tongue and upper lip) or genitalia (*Fig. 12.192*).[18,19] These latter changes are more common in cases related to malignancy.

Oral lesions have been reported in up to 25–50% of all cases of acanthosis nigricans and in at least 35% of patients with associated malignancy.[18,20] The tongue lesions consist of hypertrophied filiform

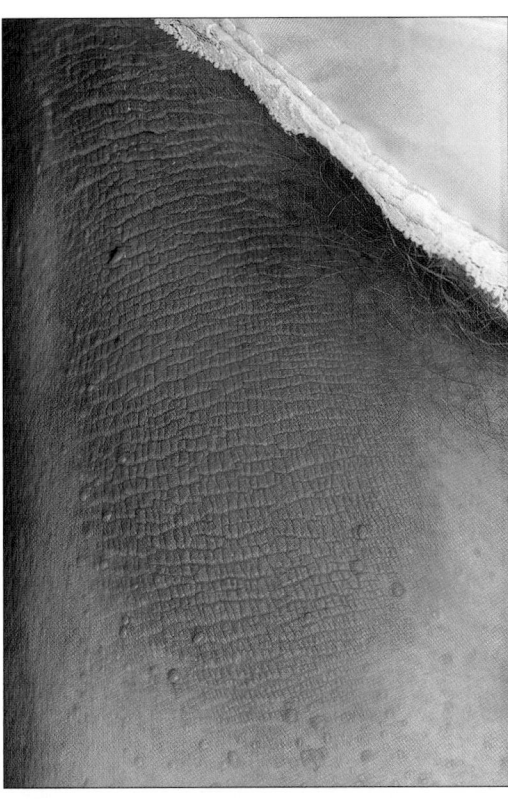

Fig. 12.189
Acanthosis nigricans: thickening of the skin of the groin. By courtesy of R.A. Marsden, MD, St George's Hospital, London, UK.

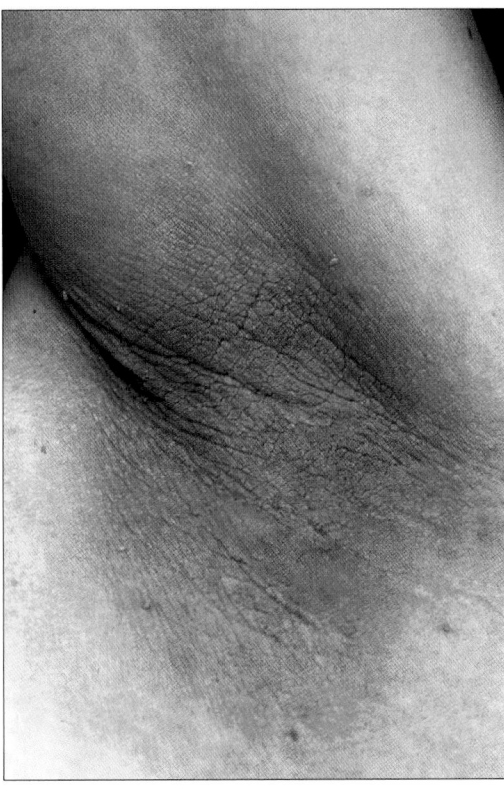

Fig. 12.190
Acanthosis nigricans: there is velvety thickening of the axillary skin. By courtesy of the Institute of Dermatology, London, UK.

papillae producing a deeply fissured papillomatous surface and the lips develop papillary and verrucous lesions.[18] Oral lesions are usually non-pigmented. Involvement of the esophagus is rare and it is almost invariably associated with malignancy, particularly in the gastrointestinal tract.[21]

A drug-induced variant has been documented, and glucocorticoids, nicotinic acid, oral contraceptives and diethylstilbestrol have been implicated.[22] Acanthosis nigricans has also been reported in association with somatotrophin therapy.[23]

Rarely acanthosis nigricans presents as an autosomal dominant nevoid lesion, which may present at birth, in childhood or at puberty.[24] The condition has also been reported in association with Cohen syndrome (truncal obesity, hypotonia, mental retardation, microcephaly and ocular abnormalities).[25]

So-called benign familial acanthosis nigricans occurs more commonly in females. This autosomal dominantly inherited condition usually presents in early childhood with lesions that particularly affect the face, dorsal surfaces of the fingers and the flexures.[26] There are usually no associated endocrinopathies or congenital abnormalities.

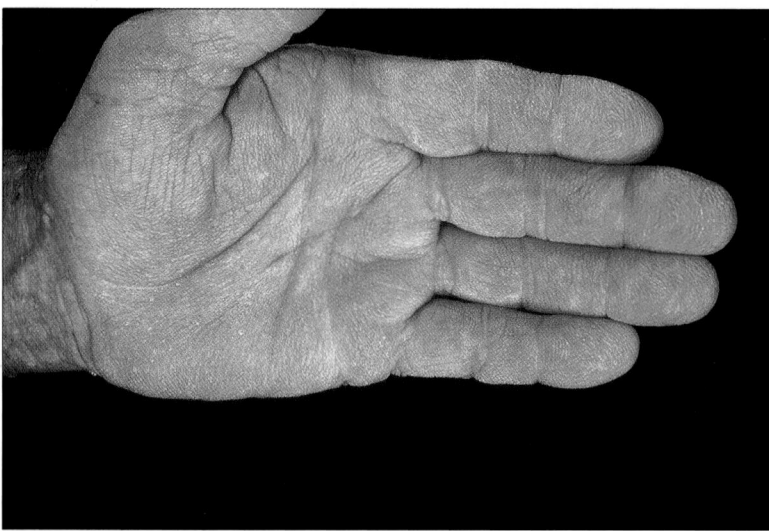

Fig. 12.191
Acanthosis nigricans: tripe palms. The palmar skin is thickened and the creases are accentuated. By courtesy of the Institute of Dermatology, London, UK.

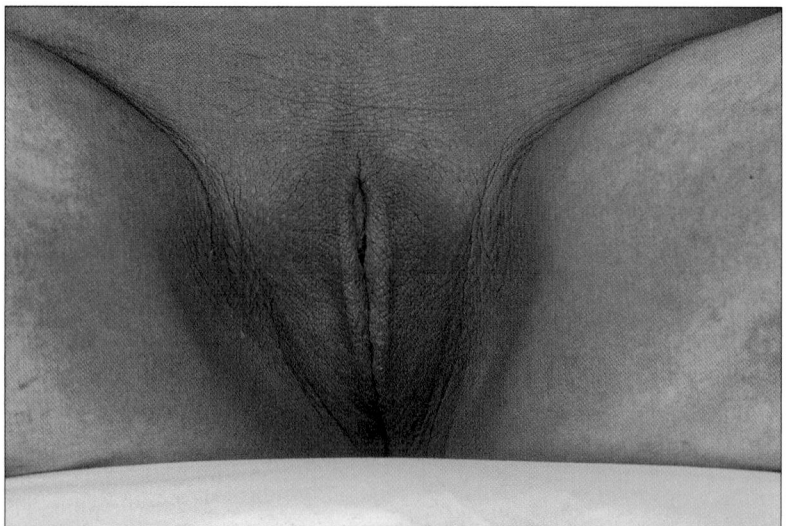

Fig. 12.192
Acanthosis nigricans: the skin of the groins and vulva is thickened and hyperpigmented. By courtesy of R.A. Marsden, MD, St George's Hospital, London, UK.

Acanthosis nigricans presents in up to 51% of patients with Down's syndrome and is probably due to insulin resistance.[27] It has also been described in up to 5% of patients with severe atopic dermatitis but the pathogenesis in this setting is unknown.[27]

Acanthosis nigricans may occur as a sign of occult malignancy and obesity. The sex incidence is equal. Malignant acanthosis nigricans is often widely disseminated and has a rapid course. Tumors that are particularly associated include gastric adenocarcinoma, and, less often, malignancies of the extrahepatic biliary tree, breast, pancreas, bladder and colon.[21,28] Ovarian and uterine tumors, bronchial squamous and adenocarcinoma, and lymphoma have also been implicated.[29]

Acanthosis nigricans as an indicator of insulin resistance has been reported in HIV-positive patients receiving treatment with protease inhibitors.[30]

Malignant acanthosis nigricans sometimes develops in association with other cutaneous markers of internal malignancy including palmoplantar hyperkeratosis, eruptive seborrhoeic warts (Leser–Trélat sign) and florid cutaneous papillomatosis.[31] The last condition presents as numerous viral wart-like itchy papillomas, which show a predilection for the trunk and extremities and invariably accompany an internal malignancy, most often gastric adenocarcinoma. The course of malignant acanthosis nigricans usually parallels that of the underlying neoplasm, which is usually aggressive and associated with a high mortality. Lesions may sometimes abate following surgical removal of the tumor only to return with its recurrence.

Acanthosis nigricans may also be associated with a wide range of endocrine diseases, including Cushing's disease, acromegaly, gigantism, Addison's disease, polycystic ovary syndrome, diabetes mellitus, acromegaly and thyroid disorders. The association between hyperandrogenism (HA), insulin resistance (IR) and acanthosis nigricans (AN) is known as HAIR-AN syndrome. There appears to be an association between acanthosis nigricans, obesity, hypertension, ischemic heart disease and type 2 diabetes, the inheritance of which is autosomal dominant.[32]

Acanthosis nigricans may also occur in non-obese patients in association with diabetes mellitus and insulin resistance due to diminished receptor binding.[33–37] Patients with this sporadic syndrome may be divided into two groups:

- In type A, the patients are young (particularly black) women with acanthosis nigricans, primary amenorrhea with hypertestosteronemia, virilization, increased somatic growth, hyperglycemia and hyperinsulinemia, with insulin resistance due to a congenital defect of insulin receptors.
- In type B, the patients are older and have features suggesting other autoimmune diseases, including raised erythrocyte sedimentation rate (ESR), proteinuria and hypocomplementemia with antinuclear and anti-DNA antibodies. Antibodies directed against the insulin receptor may be detected.
- A third type, type C, has recently been proposed, in which acanthosis nigricans and insulin resistance are associated with a postinsulin receptor defect.

Recent studies have found that the presence of acanthosis nigricans in African–Americans and Native Americans is a cutaneous marker of hyperinsulinemia and insulin resistance.[38,39]

Pseudoacanthosis nigricans develops in the flexures of obese patients and is thought to be related to heat, friction and maceration. By definition there are no underlying disease associations.

Transient acanthosis nigricans-like lesions have been described at the sites of healing lesions of pemphigus vulgaris[40] and pemphigus foliaceous.[40,41]

Acanthosis nigricans-like lesions have been described after local application of fusidic acid.[42]

Pathogenesis and histological features

The pathogenesis is uncertain, although in the diabetes-associated patients hyperinsulinemia is likely to be of importance.[36] In malignancy-related acanthosis nigricans, peptide or hormonal secretion appears to be of significance in at least a proportion of cases.[28] It has been demonstrated that some malignant tumors secrete transforming growth factor alpha (TGF-α) in large quantities and this stimulates proliferation of keratinocytes.[43]

The histopathological findings are subtle, comprising delicate, elongate papillomatosis, hyperkeratosis and slight acanthosis, sometimes alternating with foci of atrophy (*Fig. 12.193*). The occasional presence of keratin-filled cysts may result in a seborrhoeic wart-like appearance.[18] Despite the clinically obvious brown appearance of the lesions, there is normally little increase in the amount of melanin present. A non-specific perivascular chronic inflammatory cell infiltrate is sometimes evident in the superficial dermis. Distinguishing this type of benign acanthosis from other benign acanthoses, such as epidermal nevi, may be difficult.

Oral lesions show hyperkeratosis and patchy parakeratosis associated with marked acanthosis and epithelial papillary hyperplasia.[18]

Tripe palms are characterized by hyperkeratosis, acanthosis and papillary hypertrophy.[17]

Florid cutaneous papillomatosis is also characterized by hyperkeratosis, papillomatosis and acanthosis.[31]

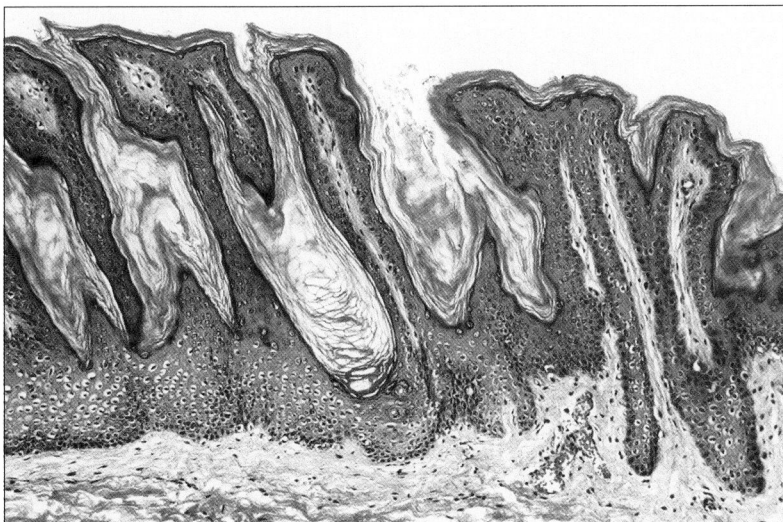

Fig. 12.193
Acanthosis nigricans: there is hyperkeratosis, papillomatosis and slight acanthosis.

References

1. Brown, J., Winkelmann, R.K. (1968) Acanthosis nigricans: a study of 90 cases. *Medicine (Baltimore)*, **47**, 33–51.
2. Curth, H.O. (1976) Classification of acanthosis nigricans. *Int J Dermatol*, **15**, 592–593.
3. Chang, K.W., Hou, J.W., Lin, S.J. et al (2000) Alstrom syndrome with hepatic dysfunction: report of one case. *Acta Paediatr Taiwan*, **41**, 270–272.
4. Nagase, T., Nagase, M., Hirose, S. et al (2000) Crouzon syndrome with acanthosis nigricans: case report and mutational analysis. *Cleft Palate Craniofac J*, **37**, 78–82.
5. Reed, W.B., Dexter, R., Corley, C., Fish, C. (1965) Congenital lipodystrophic diabetes with acanthosis nigricans. The Seip–Lawrence syndrome. *Arch Dermatol*, **91**, 326–334.
6. Philip, N., Sigaudy, S. (1998) Costello syndrome. *J Med Genet*, **35**, 238–240.
7. Fargnoli, M.C., Orlow, S.J., Semel-Concepcion, J. et al (1996) Clinicopathologic findings in the Bannayan–Riley–Ruvalcaba syndrome. *Arch Dermatol*, **132**, 1214–1218.
8. Tavormina, P.L., Bellus, G.A., Webster, M.K. et al (1999) A novel skeletal dysplasia with developmental delay and acanthosis nigricans is caused by a Lys650 Met mutation in the fibroblast growth factor receptor 3 gene. *Am J Hum Genet*, **64**, 722–731.
9. Thaipisuttikul, Y. (1997) Acanthosis nigricans associated with hepatolenticular degeneration. *J Dermatol*, **24**, 395–400.
10. Pham, T.H., Kaushik, S., Lin, B.P. et al (1996) Case report: acanthosis nigricans in association with primary biliary cirrhosis: resolution after liver transplantation. *J Gastroenterol Hepatol*, **11**, 1021–1023.
11. Chuang, S.D., Jee, S.H., Chiu, H.C. et al (1995) Familial acanthosis nigricans with madarosis. *Br J Dermatol*, **133**, 104–108.
12. Baird, J.S., Johnson, J.L., Elliot-Mills, D. et al (1997) Systemic lupus erythematosus with acanthosis nigricans, hyperpigmentation, and insulin receptor antibody. *Lupus*, **6**, 275–278.
13. Sturner, R.A., Denning, S., Marchase, P. (1981) Acanthosis nigricans and autoimmune reactivity. *JAMA*, **246**, 763–765.
14. Tuna Castro, M.A., García Kutzbach, A. (1996) Acanthosis nigricans associated with longstanding dermatomyositis. *J Rheumatol*, **23**, 1487–1488.
15. Andreev, V.C., Boyanov, L., Tsankov, N. (1981) Generalised acanthosis nigricans. *Dermatologica*, **163**, 19–24.
16. Pinto, G.L., Meyer, D.R. (1994) Ophthalmic manifestations of acanthosis nigricans. *Ophthal Plast Reconstr Surg*, **10**, 49–50.
17. Breathnach, S.M., Wells, G.C. (1980) Acanthosis nigricans: tripe palms. *Clin Exp Dermatol*, **5**, 181–189.
18. Hall, J.M., Moreland, A., Cox, G.J. et al (1988) Oral acanthosis nigricans: report of a case and comparison of oral and cutaneous pathology. *Am J Dermatopathol*, **10**, 68–73.
19. Shafer, W.G., Hine, M.K., Levy, B.M. (1983) A textbook of oral pathology, 4th edn. Philadelphia: Saunders.
20. Cairo, F., Rubino, I., Rotundo, R. et al (2001) Oral acanthosis nigricans as a marker of internal malignancy. A case report. *J Periodontol*, **72**, 1271–1275.
21. Kozlowski, L.M., Nigra, T.P. (1992) Esophageal acanthosis nigricans in association with adenocarcinoma from an unknown primary site. *J Am Acad Dermatol*, **26**, 348–351.
22. Stals, H., Vercammen, C., Peeters, C. et al (1994) Acanthosis nigricans caused by nicotinic acid: case report and review of the literature. *Dermatology*, **189**, 203–206.
23. Downs, A.M., Kennedy, C.T. (1999) Somatotrophin-induced acanthosis nigricans. *Br J Dermatol*, **141**, 390–391.
24. Krishnaram, A.S. (1991) Unilateral nevoid acanthosis nigricans. *Int J Dermatol*, **30**, 452–453.
25. Kumandas, S., Gumus, H., Kurtuglu, S. et al (2001) Cohen syndrome with acanthosis nigricans and insulin resistance. *J Pediatr Endocrinol Metab*, **14**, 807–810.
26. Tasjan, D., Jarrat, M. (1984) Familial acanthosis nigricans. *Arch Dermatol*, **120**, 1351–1354.
27. Munoz-Perez, M.A., Camacho, F. (2001) Acanthosis nigricans: a new cutaneous sign in severe atopic dermatitis and Down syndrome. *J Eur Acad Dermatol*, **15**, 325–327.
28. Rigel, D.S., Jacobs, M.I. (1980) Malignant acanthosis nigricans: a review. *J Dermatol Surg Oncol*, **6**, 923–927.
29. Mekhail, T.M., Markman, M. (2002) Acanthosis nigricans with endometrial carcinoma: case report and review of the literature. *Gynecol Oncol*, **84**, 332–334.
30. Mellor-Pita, S., Yebra-Bango, M., Alfaro-Martinez, J. et al (2002) Acanthosis nigricans: a new manifestation of insulin resistance in patients receiving treatment with protease inhibitors. *Clin Infect Dis*, **34**, 716–717.
31. Gheeraert, P., Goens, J., Schwartz, R.A. et al (1991) Florid cutaneous papillomatosis, malignant acanthosis nigricans, and pulmonary squamous cell carcinoma. *Int J Dermatol*, **30**, 193–197.
32. Kerem, N., Guttmann, H., Hochberg, Z. (2001) The autosomal dominant trait of obesity, acanthosis nigricans, hypertension, heart disease and diabetes type 2. *Horm Res*, **55**, 298–304.
33. Garcier, F., Claudy, A.L. (1985) Acanthosis nigricans in monozygotic twins with post receptor defects causing insulin resistance. *Clin Exp Dermatol*, **10**, 358–364.
34. Kahn, C.R., Flier, J.S., Bar, R.S. et al (1976) The syndromes of insulin resistance and acanthosis nigricans: insulin receptor disorders in man. *N Engl J Med*, **294**, 739–745.
35. Editorial (1986) Insulin receptors, acanthosis nigricans and insulin resistance. *Lancet*, **1**, 595–596.
36. Plourde, P.V., Marks, J.G. Jr, Hammond, J.M. (1984) Acanthosis nigricans and insulin resistance *J Am Acad Dermatol*, **10**, 887–891.
37. Rendon, M.I., Cruz, P.D. Jr, Sontheimer, R.D. et al (1989) Acanthosis nigricans: a cutaneous marker of tissue resistance to insulin. *J Am Acad Dermatol*, **21**, 461–469.
38. Stuart, C.A., Gilkison, C.R., Keenan, B.S. et al (1997) Hyperinsulinemia and acanthosis nigricans in African Americans. *J Natl Med Assoc*, **89**, 523–527.
39. Stuart, C.A., Smith, M.M., Gilkison, C.R. et al (1994) Acanthosis nigricans among Native Americans: an indicator of high diabetes risk. *Am J Public Health*, **84**, 1839–1842.
40. Usui, K., Konod, A., Nakagawa, H. (1998) Pemphigus vulgaris associated with transient acanthosis nigricans-like lesion. *J Dermatol*, **25**, 550–552.
41. Bossuyt, L., Morren, M., Degreef, H. (1992) Transient acanthosis nigricans-like dermatosis in re-epithelializing lesions of pemphigus foliaceus. *Dermatology*, **185**, 309–310.
42. Teknetzis, A., Lefaki, I., Joannides, D. et al (1993) Acanthosis nigricans-like lesions after local application of fusidic acid. *J Am Acad Dermatol*, **26**, 501–502.
43. Koyama, S., Ikeda, K., Sato, M. et al (1997) Transforming growth factor-alpha (TGF alpha)-producing gastric carcinoma with acanthosis nigricans: an endocrine effect of TGF alpha in the pathogenesis of cutaneous paraneoplastic syndrome and epithelial hyperplasia of the esophagus. *J Gastroenterol*, **32**, 71–77.

Acrodermatitis enteropathica

Clinical features

Acrodermatitis enteropathica is a rare autosomal recessive inherited disorder of zinc malabsorption, which predominantly affects infants and responds dramatically to dietary zinc supplements.[1–3] It presents with diarrhea, stomatitis, irritability and failure to thrive, accompanied by erythematous, scaly and crusted lesions with vesicles, pustules and erosions predominantly affecting the extremities, perineal and periorificial region (*Figs 12.194, 12.195*). Non-scarring alopecia may also be present. Additional features include nail dystrophy, short stature, psychiatric symptoms and photophobia.[1–5] Corneal lesions and decreased visual acuity have also exceptionally been reported.[6,7] Patients are also prone to developing infections, particularly by bacteria and fungi, illustrating the importance of normal zinc levels in maintaining the integrity of the immune system.[8–10] The disease may persist into adulthood or rarely be diagnosed for the first time in adult life.[11–13] An acquired variant may complicate breast-fed and artificially fed infants either full term or premature.[14–23] This is due to the low concentration of zinc in breast milk. In prematures, the problem is aggravated by the low gastrointestinal absorption of zinc.

Many other conditions with acquired zinc deficiency have been associated with signs and symptoms of acrodermatitis enteropathica including Crohn's disease, alcoholic cirrhosis, alcoholic pancreatitis, intestinal bypass operation, chemotherapy for hematological malignancies, anorexia nervosa, lymphoma, biotin deficiency, dialysis, cystic fibrosis, essential fatty acid deficiency, citrullinemia, deficiency of ornithine transcarbamylase and following total intravenous hyperalimentation.[7,24–37] A picture similar to this condition has also been described in a number of aminoacidopathies and organic acidemias. The latter include methylmalonic acidemia, propionic acidemia, glutaric aciduria type I, and non-ketotic hyperglycinemia.[38–41] The changes are due not only to zinc deficiency, but also to a deficiency in branched chain amino acids including isoleucine. This is induced by the low protein diet that these patients receive. Acrodermatitis enteropathica has also been described in relation to HIV infection.[42]

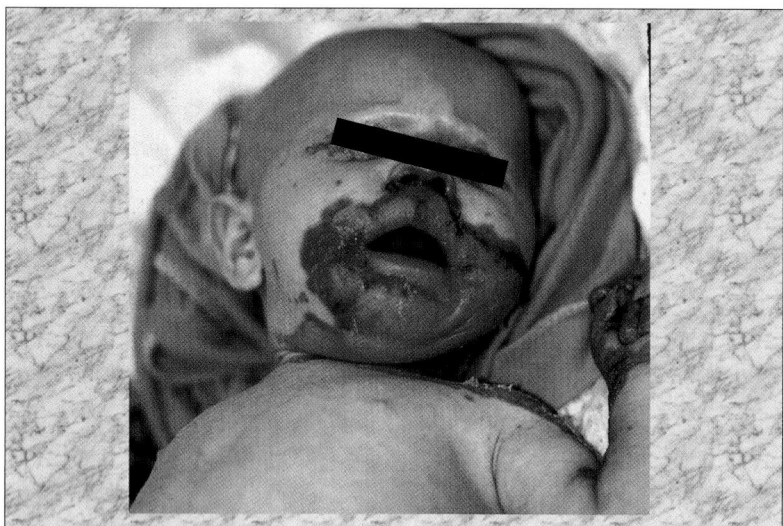

Fig. 12.194
Acrodermatitis enteropathica: extensive crusted erosions in a characteristic distribution. By courtesy of Z.S. Tannous, MD, Harvard Medical School, Boston, USA.

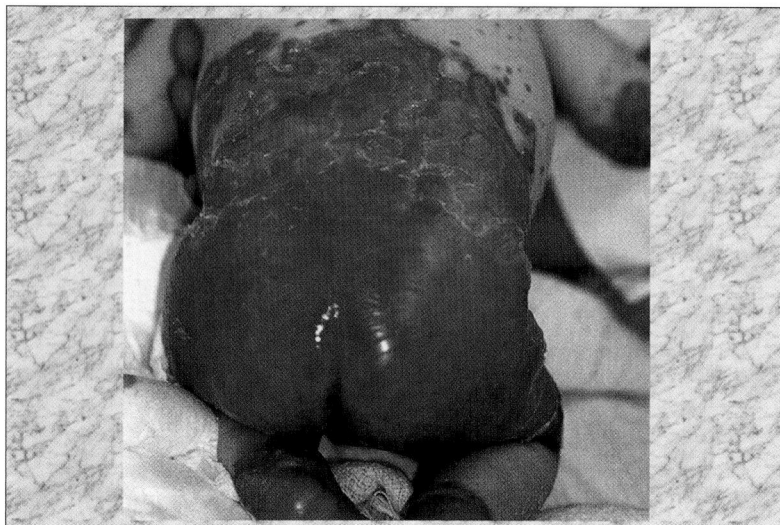

Fig. 12.195
Acrodermatitis enteropathica: in this infant, there is very extensive involvement with widespread erosion. By courtesy of Z.S. Tannous, MD, Harvard Medical School, Boston, USA.

Pathogenesis and histological features

The manifestations of acrodermatitis enteropathica result from insufficient absorption of zinc by the intestine. The exact molecular mechanism of the disease is not known but it is thought that the disease results from a defect in a zinc transporting protein. Initial studies of genes that encode for proteins important in the transport of zinc including SLC30A4 and ZNT4 did not show association with the disease.[43–45] More recently, the gene for acrodermatitis enteropathica has been identified on chromosome 8q24.3.[46] This gene, designated SLC39A4, encodes a histidine-rich transmembrane protein known as hZIP4 which is involved in zinc uptake.[47,48] A defect in this protein is likely to be paramount in the pathogenesis of acrodermatitis enteropathica. The mutation in acrodermatitis enteropathica also affects zinc metabolism in fibroblasts and reduces the activity of 5′-nucleotidase.[49,50]

The mechanism of infections in acrodermatitis enteropathica is related to alterations in the immune system due to zinc deficiency.[10] Lymphopenia and thymic atrophy are frequent findings in this disease and are due to the loss of B- and T-cell precursors in the bone marrow. The zinc deficiency induces apoptosis mediated by glucocorticoids with resultant decrease in lymphopoiesis.

The histopathology varies according to the stage of evolution.[51] Very early lesions show subtle changes consisting of focal parakeratosis alternating with orthokeratosis. As lesions advance, the parakeratosis becomes more prominent and confluent and the stratum granulosum is decreased or absent. The keratinocytes in the upper layers of the epidermis display marked cytoplasmic pallor (*Figs 12.196, 12.197*). In addition there is focal spongiosis. Dyskeratotic cells are rarely seen.

In late stages there is cytoplasmic vacuolation and necrosis which may result in vesicles or occasionally progress to blister formation.[52] Subcorneal pustules may be seen and usually indicate secondary infection.

Differential diagnosis

Histologically, acrodermatitis enteropathica is indistinguishable from necrolytic migratory erythema and pellagra. Very similar histological features are also seen in necrolytic acral erythema, a condition that occurs on the dorsum of the feet of patients with hepatitis C infection.[53] Prominent pallor of keratinocytes in the upper layers of the epidermis is also seen in deficiency of the M subunit of lactate dehydrogenase.[54,55] The cutaneous manifestation of the latter condition has been described as annually recurring acroerythema.[56]

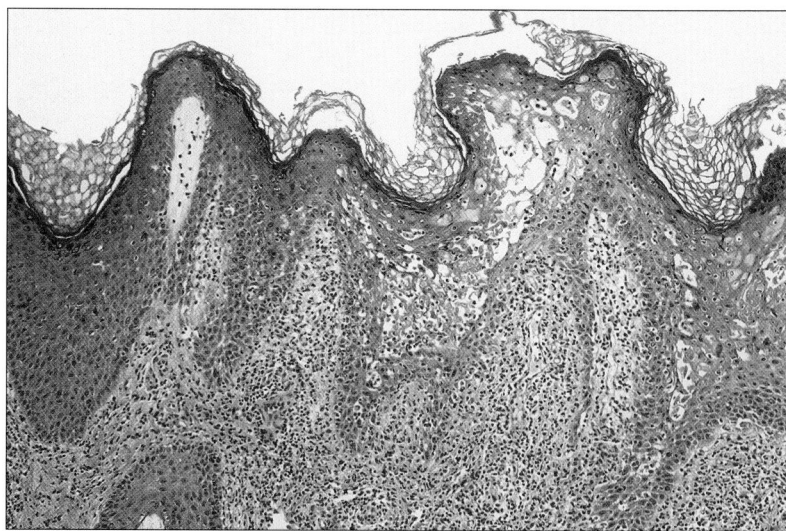

Fig. 12.196
Acrodermatitis enteropathica: there is spongiosis and cytoplasmic pallor. Note the marked secondary inflammation.

References

1. Danbolt, N., Closs, K. (1942) Acrodermatitis enteropathica. *Acta Derm Venereol*, **23**, 127–169.
2. Moynahan, E. (1974) Acrodermatitis enteropathica: a lethal inherited human zinc deficiency disorder. *Lancet*, **2**, 399–400.
3. Sehgal, V.N., Jain, S. (2000) Acrodermatitis enteropathica. *Clin Dermatol*, **18**, 745–748.
4. Deffner, N.F., Perry, H.O. (1973) Acrodermatitis enteropathica and failure to thrive. *Arch Dermatol*, **108**, 658–662.
5. Neldner, K.H., Hagler, L., Wise, W.R. et al (1974) Acrodermatitis enteropathica. A clinical and biochemical survey. *Arch Dermatol*, **110**, 711–721.
6. Prabiputaloong, A., Prakitrittranon, W. (1992) Corneal involvement in acrodermatitis enteropathica: a case report. *J Med Assoc Thai*, **75**, 423–427.
7. Myung, S.J., Yang, S.K., Jung, H.Y. et al (1998) Zinc deficiency manifested by dermatitis and visual dysfunction in a patient with Crohn's disease. *J Gastroenterol*, **33**, 876–879.
8. Sandstrom, B., Cederblad, A., Lindblad, B.S. et al (1994) Acrodermatitis enteropathica, zinc metabolism, copper status and immune function. *Arch Pediatr Adolesc Med*, **148**, 980–985.
9. Ozkan, S., Ozkan, H., Fetil, E. et al (1999) Acrodermatitis enteropathica with Pseudomonas aeruginosa sepsis. *Pediatr Dermatol*, **16**, 444–447.
10. Fraker, P.J., King, L.E., Laakko, T. et al (2000) The dynamic between the integrity of the immune system and zinc status. *J Nutr*, **130**, 1399S–1406S.
11. Tompkins, R.R., Livingood, C.S. (1969) Acrodermatitis enteropathica persisting into adulthood. *Arch Dermatol*, **99**, 190–195.
12. Graves, K., Kestenbaum, T., Kalivas, J. (1980) Hereditary acrodermatitis in an adult. *Arch Dermatol*, **116**, 562–564.
13. Bronson, D.M., Barsky, R., Barsky, S. (1983) Acrodermatitis enteropathica. Recognition at long last during a recurrence in a pregnancy. *J Am Acad Dermatol*, **9**, 140–144.
14. Niemi, K.M., Anttila, P.H., Kanerva, L. et al (1989) Histopathological study of transient acrodermatitis enteropathica due to decreased zinc in breast milk. *J Cutan Pathol*, **16**, 382–387.
15. Kuramoto, Y., Igarashi, Y., Tagami, H. (1991) Acquired zinc deficiency in breast-fed infants. *Semin Dermatol*, **10**, 309–312.
16. Glover, M.T., Atherton, D.J. (1988) Transient zinc deficiency in two full-term breast-fed siblings associated with low maternal breast milk concentration. *Pediatr Dermatol*, **5**, 10–13.
17. Bye, A.M.E., Goodfellow, A., Atherton, D.J. (1985) Transient zinc deficiency in a full-term breast-fed infant of normal birth weight. *Pediatr Dermatol*, **2**, 308–311.
18. Bonifazi, E., Rigillo, N., de Simone, B. et al (1980) Acquired dermatitis to zinc deficiency in a premature infant. *Acta Derm Venereol*, **60**, 449–451.
19. Munro, C.S., Lazaro, C., Lawrence, C.M. (1989) Symptomatic zinc deficiency in a breast-fed, premature infant. *Br J Dermatol*, **121**, 773–778.
20. Bilinski, D.L., Ehrenkranz, R.A., Cooley-Jacobs, J. et al (1987) Symptomatic zinc deficiency in a breast-fed premature infant. *Arch Dermatol*, **123**, 1221–1224.
21. Buehning, L.J., Goltz, R.W. (1993) Acquired zinc deficiency in a premature breast-fed infant. *J Am Acad Dermatol*, **28**, 499–501.
22. Stapleton, K.M., O'Loughlin, E., Relic, J.P. (1995) Transient zinc deficiency in a breast-fed premature infant. *Australas J Dermatol*, **36**, 157–159.
23. Piela, Z., Szuber, M., Mach, B. et al (1998) Zinc deficiency in exclusively breast-fed infants. *Cutis*, **61**, 197–200.
24. Krasovec, M., Frenk, E. (1996) Acrodermatitis enteropathica secondary to Crohn's disease. *Dermatology*, **193**, 361–363.
25. Ecker, R.I., Schroeter, A.L. (1978) Acrodermatitis and acquired zinc deficiency. *Arch Dermatol*, **114**, 937–939.
26. Taniguchi, S., Kaneto, K., Hamada, T. (1995) Acquired zinc deficiency associated with alcoholic liver cirrhosis. *Int J Dermatol*, **34**, 651–652.
27. Weismann, K., Wadskov, S., Mikkelsen, H.I. et al (1978) Acquired zinc deficiency in man. *Arch Dermatol*, **114**, 1509–1511.
28. Sawai, T., Sugigura, H., Danno, K. et al (1996) Acquired acrodermatitis enteropathica during chemotherapy for acute lymphocytic leukaemia in a child with Down syndrome. *Br J Dermatol*, **135**, 659–660.
29. Van Voorhees, A.S., Riba, M. (1992) Acquired zinc deficiency in association with anorexia nervosa: case report and review of the literature. *Pediatr Dermatol*, **9**, 268–271.
30. Mortureux, P., Adamski, H., Perromat, M. et al (1993) Acrodermatite entéropathique acquise associée à un lymphome. *Ann Dermatol Venereol*, **120**, 767–769.
31. Bodokh, I., Lacour, J.P., Nonis, E. et al (1991) Aspect d'acrodermatite entéropathique par défect en vitamines du groupe B. *Ann Dermatol Venereol*, **118**, 806–810.
32. Parra, E., Campistol, J.M., Soy, D. et al (1995). Acrodermatitis enteropathica-like syndrome in a dialysis patient. *Nephron*, **70**, 389–390.
33. Hansen, R.C., Lemen, R., Revsin, B. (1983) Cystic fibrosis manifesting with acrodermatitis enteropathica-like eruption. *Arch Dermatol*, **119**, 51–55.
34. Horrobin, D.F., Cunnane, S.C. (1980) Interactions between zinc, essential fatty acids and prostaglandins. *Med Hypotheses*, **6**, 277–296.
35. Goldblum, O.M., Brusilow, S.W., Maldonado, Y.A. et al (1986) Neonatal citrullinemia associated with cutaneous manifestations and arginine deficiency. *J Am Acad Dermatol*, **14**, 321.
36. Lee, J.Y., Chang, S.E., Suh, C.W. et al (2002) A case of acrodermatitis enteropathica-like dermatosis caused by ornithine transcarbamylase deficiency. *J Am Acad Dermatol*, **46**, 965–967.
37. Van Vloten, W.A., Bos, L.P. (1978) Skin lesions in acquired zinc deficiency due to parenteral nutrition. *Dermatologica*, **156**, 175–183.
38. Howard, R., Frieden, I.J., Crawford, D. et al (1997) Methylmalonic acidemia, cobalamin C type, presenting with cutaneous manifestations. *Arch Dermatol*, **133**, 1563–1566.
39. De Raeve, L., De Meirleir, L., Ramet, J. et al (1994) Acrodermatitis enteropathica-like cutaneous lesions in organic aciduria. *J Pediatr*, **124**, 416–420.
40. Niiyama, S., Koelker, S., Degen, I. et al (2001) Acrodermatitis acidemia secondary to malnutrition in glutaric aciduria type I. *Eur J Dermatol*, **11**, 244–246.
41. Samady, J.A., Schwartz, R.A., Shih, L.Y. et al (2000) Acrodermatitis enteropathica-like eruption in an infant with nonketotic hyperglycinemia. *J Dermatol*, **27**, 604–608.
42. Reichel, M., Mauro, T.M., Ziboh, V.A. et al (1992) Acrodermatitis enteropathica in a patient with the acquired immunodeficiency syndrome. *Arch Dermatol*, **128**, 415–417.
43. Kury, S., Devilder, M.C., Avet-Loiseau, H. et al (2001) Expression pattern, genomic structure and evaluation of the human SLC30A4 gene as candidate for acrodermatitis enteropathica. *Hum Genet*, **110**, 201–202.
44. Bleck, O., Ashton, G.H., Mallipedi, R. et al (2001) Genomic localization, organization and amplification of the human zinc transporter protein gene, ZNT4, and exclusion as a candidate gene in different clinical variants of acrodermatitis enteropathica. *Arch Dermatol Res*, **293**, 392–396.
45. Nakano, A., Nakano, H., Hanada, K. et al (2002) ZNT4 gene is not responsible for acrodermatitis enteropathica in Japanese families. *Hum Genet*, **110**, 201–202.
46. Wang, K., Pugh, E.W., Griffen, S. et al (2001) Homozygosity mapping places the acrodermatitis enteropathica gene on chromosomal region 8q24.3. *Am J Hum Genet*, **68**, 1055–1060.
47. Wang, K., Zhou, B., Kuo, Y.M. et al (2002) A novel member of a zinc transporter family is defective in acrodermatitis enteropathica. *Am J Hum Genet*, **71**, 66–73.
48. Kury, S., Dreno, B., Bezieau, S. et al (2002) Identification of SCLC39A4, a gene involved in acrodermatitis enteropathica. *Nat Genet*, **31**, 239–240.
49. Grider, A., Young, E.M. (1996) The acrodermatitis enteropathica mutation transiently affects metabolism in human fibroblasts. *J Nutr*, **126**, 219–224.
50. Grider, A., Lim, Y.F., Muga, S.J. (1998) Differences in the cellular zinc content and 5'-nucleotidase activity of normal and acrodermatitis enteropathica (AE) fibroblasts. *Biol Trace Elem Res*, **61**, 1–8.
51. González, J.R., Botet, M.V., Sánchez, J.L. (1982) The histopathology of acrodermatitis enteropathica. *Am J Dermatopathol*, **4**, 303–311.
52. Borroni, G., Brazzelli, V., Vignati, G. et al (1992) Bullous lesions in acrodermatitis enteropathica: histopathologic findings regarding two patients. *Am J Dermatopathol*, **14**, 304–309.
53. el Darouti, M., Abu el Ela, M. (1996) Necrolytic acral erythema: a cutaneous marker of viral hepatitis C. *Int J Dermatol*, **35**, 252–256.
54. Yoshikuni, K., Tagami, H., Yamada, M. et al (1986) Erythematosquamous skin lesions in hereditary lactate dehydrogenase M-subunit deficiency. *Arch Dermatol*, **122**, 1420–1424.
55. Takayasu, S., Fujiwara, S., Waki, T. (1991) Hereditary lactate dehydrogensase M-subunit deficiency: lactate dehydrogenase activity in skin lesions and in hair follicles. *J Am Acad Dermatol*, **24**, 339–342.
56. Nazzari, G., Crovato, F. (1992) Annually recurring acroerythema and hereditary lactate dehydrogenase M-subunit deficiency. *J Am Acad Dermatol*, **27**, 262–263.

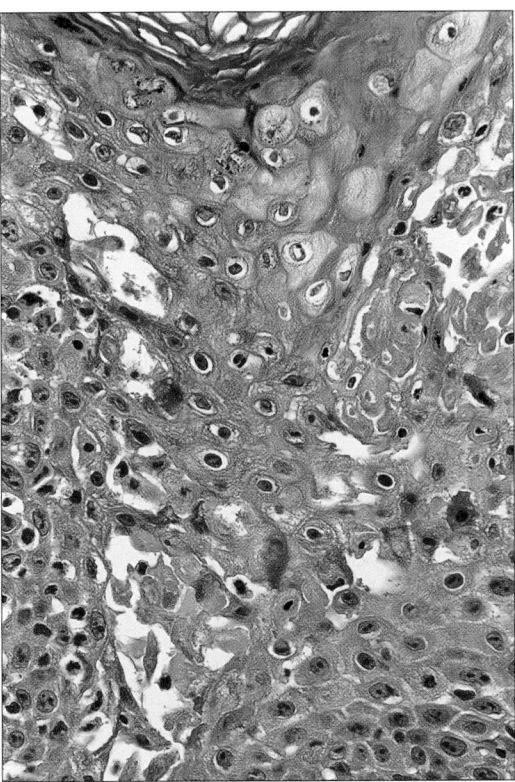

Fig. 12.197
Acrodermatitis enteropathica: close-up view to show cytoplasmic pallor.

Necrolytic migratory erythema

Clinical features

Necrolytic migratory erythema is a distinctive dermatosis that is seen predominantly in patients with the glucagonoma syndrome.[1–6] The latter, due to a slowly progressive malignant cell tumor of the pancreatic islets, consists of hyperglucagonemia, diabetes mellitus, glossitis, normochromic normocytic anemia, nausea, diarrhea, abdominal pain, neurological symptoms (ataxia and fecal and urinary incontinence), thromboembolic pathology (deep vein thrombosis and pulmonary thromboembolism) and weight loss in addition to the cutaneous manifestations.[7] About 57% of patients present with the typical visceral, cutaneous and laboratory abnormalities.[8] Exceptional cases of glucagonoma arise from the duodenum, kidney and lung.[9–11]

Necrolytic migratory erythema, so-called because of its superficial resemblance to toxic epidermal necrolysis and the waxing and waning nature of the eruption, is seen most frequently on the central face, particularly around the mouth, on the perineum and other intertriginous sites, the thighs, buttocks and distal limbs (*Fig. 12.198*).[3] Patients most often present in their sixth decade (median 52 years) with intense erythema, which progresses to flaccid bullae that rupture readily and develop crusting.[8,12] Pressure, friction and trauma have occasionally been noted to precipitate the eruption.[5] Central healing with active borders gives rise to annular and serpiginous lesions.

Postinflammatory hyperpigmentation follows resolution. Individual lesions usually last 1–2 weeks and characteristically lesions in varying stages of evolution are evident at any one time.[5,12]

Additional features may include stomatitis, angular cheilitis, blepharitis, conjunctivitis, hair loss and nail changes.[6–8] Laboratory investigations commonly reveal an abnormal glucose tolerance test, normochromic normocytic anemia, hypoproteinemia, hypoalbuminemia and hypoaminoacidemia.[6,13] Low amino acid levels were detected in 96% of patients in one reported series.[14] However, in larger series the percentage of patients with low amino acid levels has been lower, ranging between 41 and 78%.[7,8]

Glucagonoma syndrome may constitute part of the multiple endocrine neoplasia syndrome.[15]

Rarely necrolytic migratory erythema has been described in the absence of a glucagonoma.[16–21] Abnormal liver function tests have usually been present and it has been suggested that this may have resulted in impaired glucagon catabolism with resultant hyperglucagonemia or raised levels of one of the glucagon immunofractions.[17] Patients have had associated celiac disease, cirrhosis, other malignancies, hepatitis, ulcerative colitis, Crohn's disease and chronic pancreatitis.[20,22,23] A study of 24 patients with non-glucagonoma-associated necrolytic migratory erythema found increased glucagon in 52% of patients and low zinc levels in 37% of patients.[20]

Despite its relatively indolent growth characteristics, a large majority of tumors have metastasized by the time of diagnosis.

Pathogenesis and histological features

The precise etiology of necrolytic migratory erythema is unknown. Although it is certainly related to hyperglucagonemia, this is not necessarily causal. Therefore, although the signs and symptoms rapidly abate following surgery or the use of glucagon secretion inhibitors such as somatostatin, hyperglucagonemia does not readily explain the intermittent nature of the eruption.[17] The topical or intradermal application of glucagon does not produce the dermatoses.[5] Similarly there are alternative causes of hyperglucagonemia including burns and acute trauma, diabetes mellitus, septicemia, cirrhosis, renal failure, Cushing's syndrome and primary hyperglucagonemia, in which necrolytic migratory erythema is not a feature.[13]

Hypoaminoacidemia is an extremely common manifestation and it may have pathogenetic significance for the cutaneous lesions. It has been proposed that the diminished amino acid availability may result in epidermal protein depletion and eventual necrosis.[12] Certainly treatment with intravenous amino acids has been shown to control the eruption, but this of course may have been coincidental considering the characteristic fluctuating course of the dermatoses.[17] Fatty acid and zinc deficiency and abnormal arachidonic acid distribution have also been proposed as pathogenetic mechanisms.[6,24] It has been suggested that diminished tryptophan levels may be the cause of the dermatoses.[6] A further hypothesis tends to point to hepatic dysfunction as having a role in the pathogenesis of the disease.[17,18,20,25] This is mainly based on the fact that patients with necrolytic migratory erythema and absence of glucagonoma often have liver dysfunction.

Histological examination reveals parakeratosis accompanied by vacuolation and pallor of the mid and upper keratinocytes (*Figs 12.199, 12.200*).[26] Dyskeratosis has been described as a clue to early diagnosis.[27] This is accompanied by necrosis and separation of the upper layers of the epidermis to give rise to intraepidermal clefting or vesiculation (*Figs 12.201, 12.202*).[26] A neutrophil polymorph infiltrate may be evident, particularly in well-established lesions.[28] Subcorneal pustulation has also been described.[13] This may develop in a background of epidermal necrosis or less often represent an isolated phenomenon.[28] Suprabasal acantholysis has exceptionally been described.[29] The dermis shows a lymphohistiocytic chronic inflammatory cell infiltrate surrounding dilated blood vessels. In lesions associated with pustulation, neutrophils may also be present. Older lesions may show parakeratosis, marked acanthosis and papillary dermal angiogenesis, and psoriasis may therefore enter the differential diagnosis.[4,26,28] Pustular folliculitis in association with more typical features has also been described.[28]

Immunofluorescence studies are invariably negative.[10,12,24,28,30]

An ultrastructural study revealed widening of the intercellular space with reduced numbers of desmosomes in the absence of acantholysis.[31] Cytoplasmic vacuolation with lysed organelles and dyskeratotic cells was also present. These changes are largely degenerative and non-specific.

Differential diagnosis

Necrolytic migratory erythema shows considerable clinicopathological overlap with acrodermatitis enteropathica, and niacin and zinc deficiencies, suggesting a possible shared pathogenesis.[6] Pellagra can

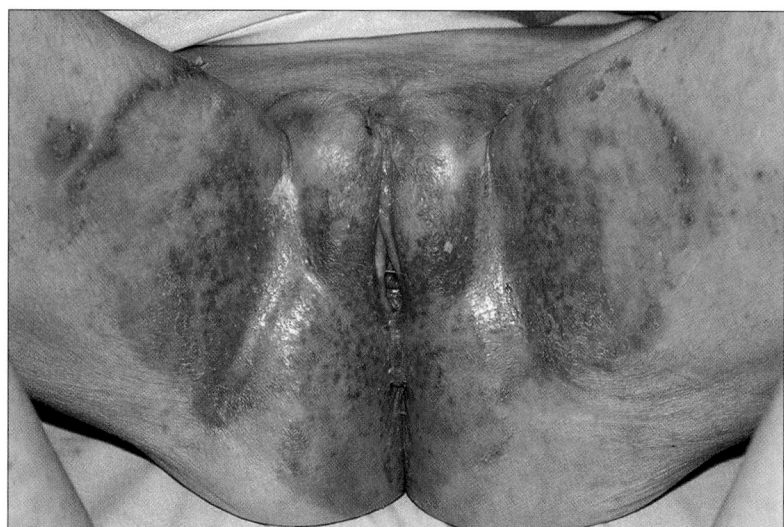

Fig. 12.198
Necrolytic migratory erythema: note the intense erythema in a characteristic distribution. By courtesy of the Institute of Dermatology, London, UK.

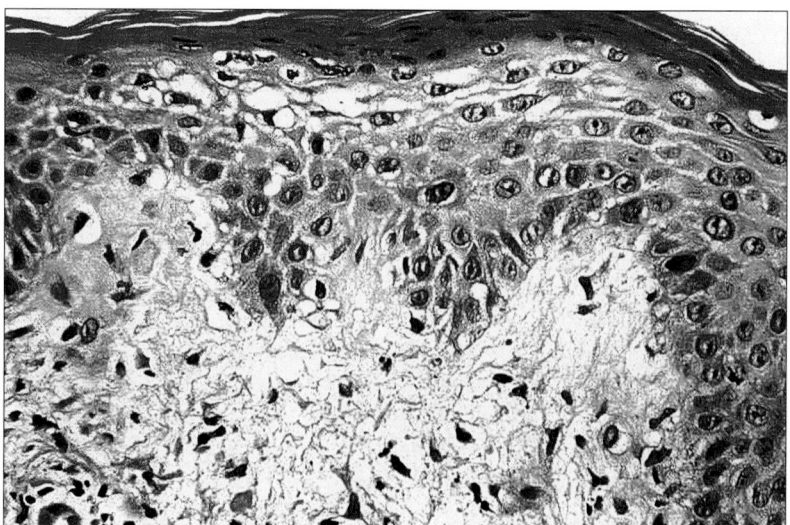

Fig. 12.199
Necrolytic migratory erythema: early lesion showing parakeratosis and vacuolation of the superficial keratinocytes.

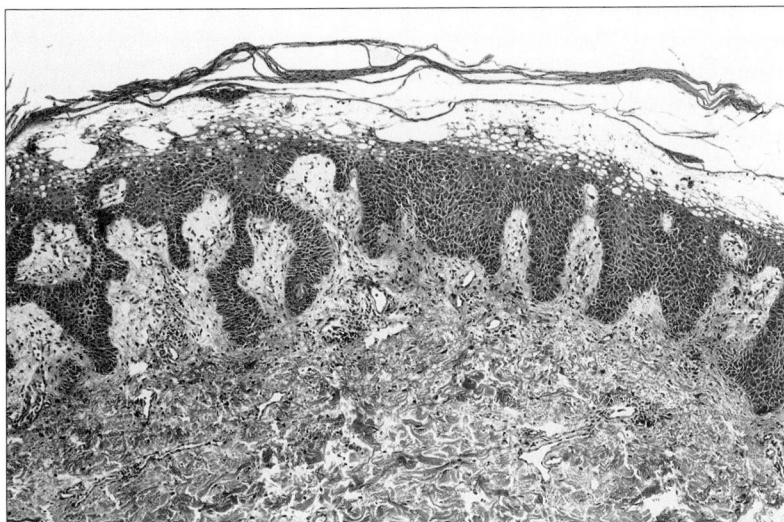

Fig. 12.200
Necrolytic migratory erythema: in this more advanced case, there is very extensive vacuolation with vesiculation.

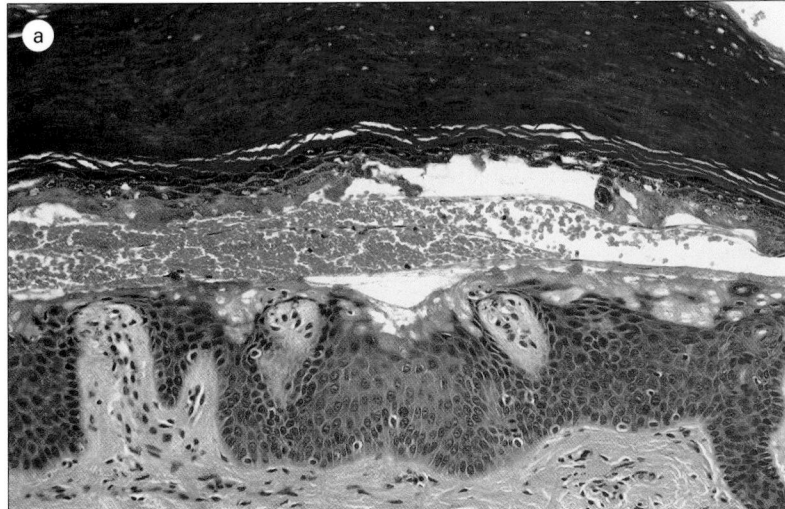

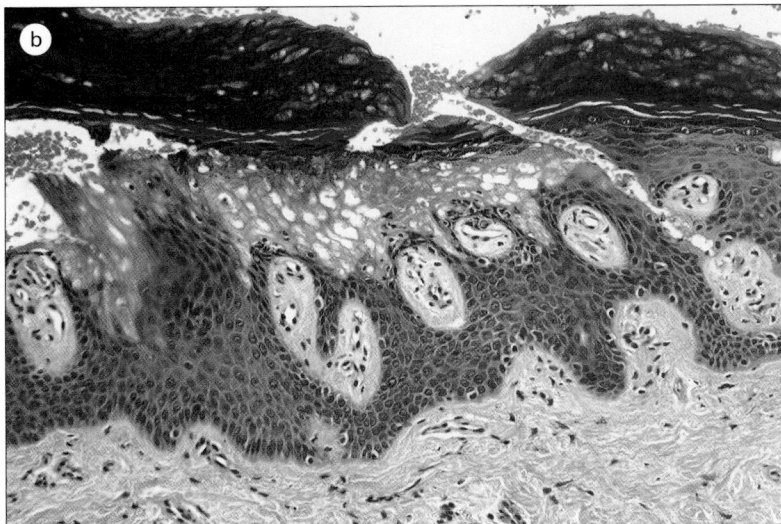

Fig. 12.201
(a, b) Necrolytic migratory erythema: acral lesion showing a well-developed subcorneal blister.

also show similar histological features. The histology of necrolytic acral erythema is that of necrolytic migratory erythema. This condition is, however, associated with hepatitis C infection and clinically tends to be restricted to the dorsum of the feet.[32]

If subcorneal pustules are evident, impetigo, dermatophyte infection, pustular psoriasis, subcorneal pustular dermatosis and pemphigus foliaceus enter the differential diagnosis. Multiple biopsies are sometimes necessary before the correct diagnosis can be established.

References

1. McGavren, M.H., Unger, R.H., Recant, L. et al (1966) A glucagon-secreting alpha-cell carcinoma of the pancreas. *N Engl J Med*, **274**, 1408–1413.
2. Prinz, R.A., Dorsch, T.R., Lawrence, A.M. (1981) Clinical aspects of glucagon-producing islet cell tumors. *Am J Gastroenterol*, **76**, 125–131.
3. Edney, J.A., Hofman, S., Thompson, J.S. et al (1990) Glucagonoma syndrome is an underdiagnosed clinical entity. *Am J Surg*, **160**, 625–629.
4. Ditty, J.F., Lang, P.G. (1982) Cutaneous and oral changes as the only manifestations of the glucagonoma syndrome. *South Med J*, **75**, 222–243.
5. Braverman, I. (1982) Commentary: migratory necrolytic erythema. *Arch Dermatol*, **118**, 796–798.
6. Miller, S.J. (1989) Nutritional deficiency and the skin. *J Am Acad Dermatol*, **21**, 1–30.
7. Wermers, R.A., Fatourechi, V., Wynne, A.G. et al (1996) The glucanoma syndrome. Clinical and pathologic features in 21 patients. *Medicine*, **75**, 53–63.
8. Soga, J., Yakuwa, Y. (1998) Glucagonoma/diabetico-dermogenic syndrome (DDS): a statistical evaluation of 407 reported cases. *J Hepatobiliary Pancreat Surg*, **5**, 312–319.
9. Roggli, V.L., Judge, D.M., McGavran, M.H. (1979) Duodenal glucagonoma: a case report. *Hum Pathol*, **10**, 350–353.
10. Gleeson, M.H., Bloom, S.R., Polak, J.M. et al (1971) Endocrine tumour in kidney affecting small bowel structure, motility and absorptive function. *Gut*, **12**, 773–782.
11. Hunstein, W., Trumper, L.H., Dummer, R. et al (1988) Glucagonoma syndrome and bronchial carcinoma. *Ann Intern Med*, **109**, 920–921.
12. Mallinson, C.N., Bloom, S.R., Warin, A.P. et al (1974) A glucagonoma syndrome. *Lancet*, **2**, 1–5.
13. Van Hecke, E., Geerts, M-L., Kint, A. et al (1991) Glucagonoma syndrome. *Curr Probl Dermatol*, **20**, 24–33.
14. Stacpoole, P.W. (1981) The glucagonoma syndrome: clinical features, diagnosis and treatment. *Endocrinol Rev*, **2**, 347–361.
15. Boden, G., Owen, O.E. (1977) Familial hyperglucagonemia: an autosomal dominant disorder. *N Engl J Med*, **296**, 534–538.
16. Masri-Fridling, G.D., Turner, M.L.C. (1992) Necrolytic migratory erythema without glucagonoma. *J Am Acad Dermatol*, **27**, 486.
17. Kasper, C.S., McMurry, K. (1991) Necrolytic migratory erythema without glucagonoma versus canine superficial necrolytic dermatitis: is hepatic impairment a clue to pathogenesis? *J Am Acad Dermatol*, **25**, 534–541.
18. Marinkovich, M.P., Botella, R., Datloff, J. et al (1995) Necrolytic migratory erythema without glucagonoma in patients with liver disease. *J Am Acad Dermatol*, **32**, 604–609.
19. Blackford, S., Wright, S., Roberts, D.L. (1991) Necrolytic migratory erythema without glucagonoma: the role of dietary essential fatty acids. *Br J Dermatol*, **125**, 460–462.
20. Mullans, E.A., Cohen, P.R. (1998) Iatrogenic necrolytic migratory erythema: a case report and review of nonglucagonoma-associated necrolytic migratory erythema. *J Am Acad Dermatol*, **38**, 866–873.
21. Sinclair, S.A., Reynolds, N.J. (1997) Necrolytic migratory erythema and zinc deficiency. *Br J Dermatol*, **136**, 783–785.

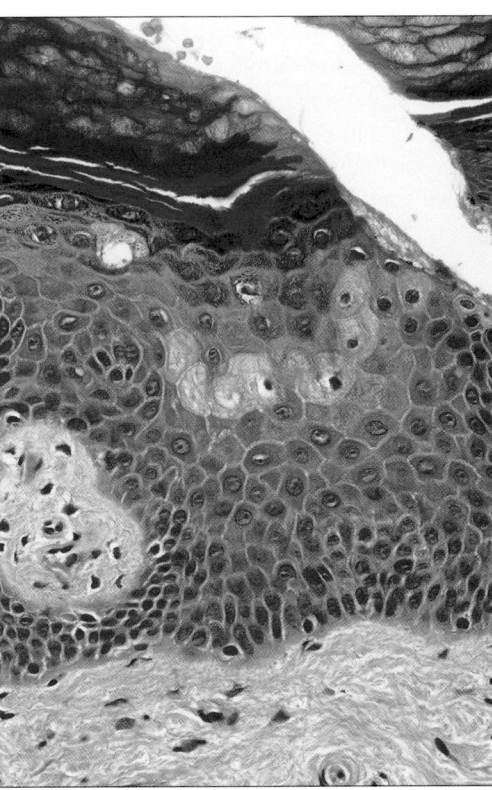

Fig. 12.202
Necrolytic migratory erythema: the adjacent epidermis shows striking cytoplasmic pallor.

22. Goodenberger, D.M., Lawley, T.J., Strober, W. et al (1979) Necrolytic migratory erythema without glucagonoma: report of two cases. *Arch Dermatol*, **115**, 1429–1432.
23. Thivolet, J. (1981) Necrolytic migratory erythema without glucagonoma. *Arch Dermatol*, **117**, 4.
24. Peterson, L.L., Shaw, J.C., Acott, K.M. et al (1984) Glucagonoma syndrome: in vitro evidence that glucagon increases epidermal arachidonic acid. *J Am Acad Dermatol*, **11**, 468–473.
25. Kasper, C.S. (1992) Necrolytic migratory erythema: unresolved problems in diagnosis and pathogenesis. Case report and literature review. *Cutis*, **49**, 120–128.
26. Franchimont, C., Pierard, G.E., Luyckx, A.S. et al (1982) Angioplastic necrolytic migratory erythema. Unique association of necrolytic migratory erythema, extensive angioplasia, and high molecular weight glucagon-like polypeptide. *Am J Dermatopathol*, **4**, 485–495.
27. Hunt, S.J., Narus, V.T., Abell, E. (1991) Necrolytic migratory erythema: dyskeratotic dermatitis, a clue to early diagnosis. *J Am Acad Dermatol*, **24**, 473–477.
28. Kheir, S., Omura, E., Grizzle, W. et al (1986) Histologic variation in the skin lesions of the glucagonoma syndrome. *Am J Surg Pathol*, **10**, 445–453.
29. Long, C., Laidler, P., Holt, P.J.A. (1993) Suprabasal acantholysis – an unusual feature of necrolytic migratory erythema. *Clin Exp Dermatol*, **18**, 464–467.
30. Vandersteen, P.R., Scheithauer, B.W. (1985) Glucagonoma syndrome. A clinicopathologic, immunocytochemical and ultrastructural study. *J Am Acad Dermatol*, **12**, 1032–1039.
31. Ohyama, K., Kitoh, M., Arao, T. (1982) Ultrastructural studies of necrolytic migratory erythema. *Arch Dermatol*, **118**, 679–682.
32. el Darouti, M., Abu el Ela, M. (1996) Necrolytic acral erythema: a cutaneous marker of viral hepatitis C. *Int J Dermatol*, **35**, 252–256.

Bullosis diabeticorum

Clinical features

There are numerous cutaneous manifestations of diabetes mellitus. These include vascular complications such as peripheral gangrene, especially affecting the foot, and infective lesions including candidiasis and dermatophytosis. Other dermatological features include necrobiosis lipoidica diabeticorum, disseminated granuloma annulare, acanthosis nigricans, eruptive xanthomata, scleredema, diabetic dermopathy (shin spots), waxy skin and bullous lesions.[1–3]

Bullosis diabeticorum (bullous eruption of diabetes mellitus) is rare and usually presents as spontaneous blisters affecting the periphery. Lesions, which are sometimes mildly painful or associated with a burning sensation, are found most often on the feet and lower legs although the hands may also be affected.[4–8] The blisters, which are often recurrent, commonly heal in a few weeks and are not associated with scarring.

Pathogenesis and histological features

The cause of blistering in diabetic patients is unknown, but theories of a vascular or neurological mechanism have been favored in the literature. The occasional finding of epidermal infarction overlying the blister cavity favors the former in at least some patients.[4] The discovery that diabetic patients have a diminished threshold for suction-induced blisters may have pathogenetic significance.[9] Others have suggested an abnormality of calcium and magnesium metabolism as a consequence of diabetic nephropathy.[10] Despite lesions being predominantly acral in distribution, trauma does not seem to be generally implicated. In all likelihood the cause is probably multifactorial.

The reported histopathological features have been variable and include subcorneal, suprabasal and subepidermal vesiculation, sometimes associated with spongiosis (*Figs 12.203, 12.204*).[10–12] Some of the discrepancy may be due at least in part to variable ages of the lesions, biopsies with re-epithelialization resulting in an apparent intraepidermal location. Electron microscopic studies in two cases have shown that the plane of separation is through the lamina lucida in the subepidermal lesions.[4,10] Absence of hemidesmosomes and anchoring filaments have also been described.[10]

Immunofluorescence studies are almost invariably negative, although one report described IgM and C3 around the superficial vasculature in uninvolved skin.[13]

References

1. Huntley, A.C. (1982) The cutaneous manifestations of diabetes mellitus. *J Am Acad Dermatol*, **7**, 427–455.
2. Gouterman, I.H., Sibrack, L.A. (1980) Cutaneous manifestations of diabetes. *Cutis*, **25**, 45–54.
3. Stawiski, M.A., Voorhees, J.J. (1976) Cutaneous signs of diabetes mellitus. *Cutis*, **18**, 415–421.
4. Toonstra, J. (1985) Bullosis diabeticorum: report of a case with a review of the literature. *J Am Acad Dermatol*, **13**, 799–805.
5. Oursler, J.R., Goldblum, O.M. (1991) Blistering eruption in a diabetic. *Arch Dermatol*, **127**, 247–251.
6. Collet, J.T., Tooonstra, J. (1985) Bullosis diabeticorum: a case with lesions restricted to the hands. *Diabetes Care*, **8**, 177–179.
7. Basarab, T., Munn, S.E., McGrath, J. et al (1995) Bullosis diabeticorum. A case report and literature review. *Clin Exp Dermatol*, **20**, 218–220.
8. Lipsky, B.A., Baker, P.D., Ahroni, J.H. (2000) Diabetic bullae: 12 cases of a purportedly rare cutaneous disorder. *Int J Dermatol*, **39**, 196–200.
9. Berstein, J.E., Levine, L.E., Medenica, M.M. et al (1983) Reduced threshold to suction-induced blister formation in insulin-dependent diabetics. *J Am Acad Dermatol*, **8**, 790–791.
10. Bernstein, J.E., Medenica, M., Soltani, K. et al (1979) Bullous eruption of diabetes mellitus. *Arch Dermatol*, **115**, 324–325.
11. Kurwa, A., Roberts, P., Whitehead, R. (1971) Concurrence of bullous and atrophic skin lesions in diabetes mellitus. *Arch Dermatol*, **103**, 670–675.
12. Cantwell, A.R., Martz, W. (1967) Idiopathic bullae in diabetics. *Arch Dermatol*, **96**, 42–44.
13. James, W.D., Odom, R.B., Goette, D.K. (1980) Bullous eruption of diabetes mellitus: a case report with positive immunofluorescence microscopy findings. *Arch Dermatol*, **116**, 1191–1192.

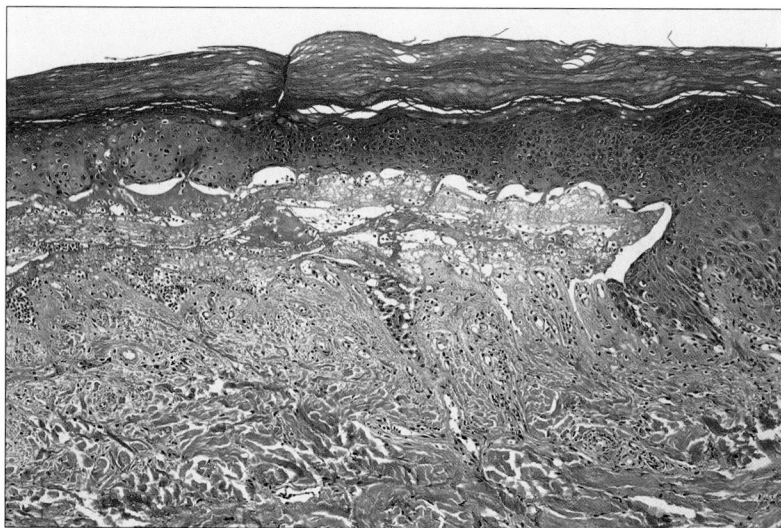

Fig. 12.203
Bullous eruption of diabetes: this example from the finger tip shows a subepidermal vesicle.

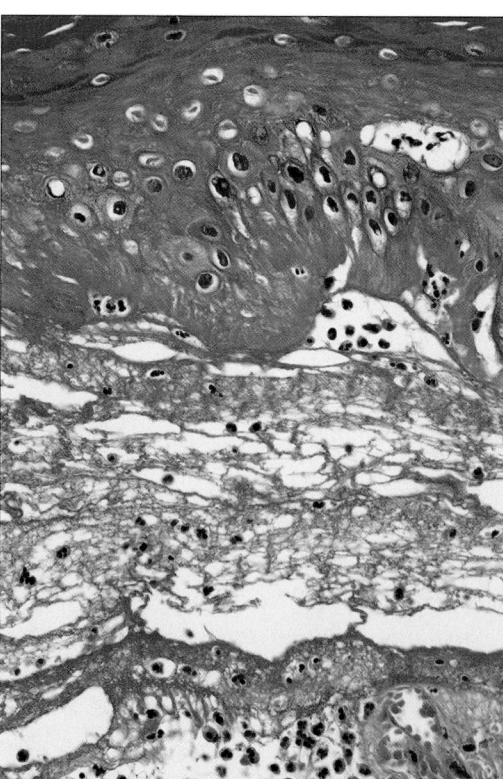

Fig. 12.204
Bullous eruption of diabetes: in this field the epidermis shows the changes of infarction. Note the intense cytoplasmic eosinophilia and absence of nuclei.

Cutaneous adverse reactions to drugs

13

ADVERSE DRUG REACTIONS –
INTRODUCTION 623
Type A drug reactions 624
Type B drug reactions 624
Type C drug reactions 625

ADVERSE DRUG REACTIONS – CLINICAL
MANIFESTATIONS 626

Exanthematous reactions 626

Urticarial reactions, angioedema and
anaphylaxis 629

Serum sickness/serum sickness-like drug
reactions 630

Phototoxic and photoallergic reactions 630

Anticonvulsant hypersensitivity
syndrome 633

Lichenoid drug reactions 635

Fixed drug eruptions 636

Erythema multiforme and Stevens–Johnson
syndrome 638

Toxic epidermal necrolysis 638

Drug-induced hyperpigmentation 638

Vasculitic drug reactions 642

Purpuric drug reactions 643

Granulomatous drug reactions 644

Drug-induced erythema nodosum 645

Drug-induced alopecia 645

Drug-induced lupus erythematosus 645

Bullous drug reactions 646
Drug-induced linear IgA disease 646
Drug-induced bullous pemphigoid 648
Drug-induced epidermolysis bullosa
acquisita 648
Drug-induced pemphigus 648
Drug-induced pseudoporphyria 649

Psoriasiform drug reactions 649

Pityriasiform drug reactions 651

Pustular drug reactions 651

Ichthyosiform drug reactions 652

Drug-induced pseudolymphoma 652

Specific drug reactions 655
Arsenic 655
Iododerma 656
Bromoderma 657
Warfarin 658
Heparin 659
Penicillamine 660
Gold 661
Silver 661
Mercury 662
Bismuth 663
Lithium 663
Barbiturates and coma blisters 664

Chemotherapeutic agents 664
Chemotherapy-induced acral erythema 667

Chemotherapy-associated eccrine gland
reactions 667
Neutrophil eccrine hidradenitis 667
Eccrine squamous syringometaplasia 669

Adverse reactions to cytokine therapy 669

Cutaneous reaction of lymphocyte
recovery 671

Dental amalgam tattoos 671

Adverse drug reactions – introduction

Adverse drug reactions are defined as noxious, unintended and undesired effects of drugs used for prevention, diagnosis or treatment of disease.[1,2] In the light of the ever-increasing number of compounds available for therapeutic purposes it should come as no surprise that such reactions are extremely common. The incidence statistics vary considerably from report to report depending upon the method by which the data are derived and the nature of the population under study.[3] Estimates however range from 2 to 7% of hospital inpatients.[4–8] Although most reactions are mild, they are sometimes severe and a source of considerable morbidity and occasional mortality.[6,7]

The diagnosis of an adverse drug reaction is frequently problematical, the clinical appearances often being similar to, if not identical with, a number of primary dermatoses and infectious conditions (particularly viral exanthems) and, in the context of transplantation patients, graft-versus-host disease (GVHD). The histological diagnosis can also be extremely difficult, as in many cases there is considerable overlapage The problem is exacerbated in the immunologically compromised patient. Frequently, the diagnostic difficulties are worsened by the multitude of drugs and/or chemotherapeutic agents prescribed. The problem is further compounded by the multiplicity of different eruptions that any one particular drug may induce. Contrariwise, a given clinical appearance may be caused by a large number of unrelated drugs.[9]

The prevalence of agents responsible for adverse drug reactions reflects the prescribing tendencies for any given population as much as the relative risks ascribed to any particular drug.[10] It should come as no surprise, therefore, that – in a hospital environment – antibiotics, non-steroidal anti-inflammatory agents (NSAIDs) and psychotropic drugs are commonly reported as being the most frequently incriminated.[8] In a recent hospital survey, penicillin and sulfonamides accounted for over 80% of all adverse drug reactions.[8] Experience in general practice has been much less often documented but in a survey published from the Netherlands, sulfonamide–trimethoprim combinations, fluorquinolones and penicillin were found to be the most common antibacterials causing drug-related eruptions.[3] In the series of approximately 150,000 patients, 1% developed a reaction.

Adverse drug reactions are mostly non-immunologically mediated. They therefore develop either as a result of an unwanted but known property of the drug (and hence are entirely predictable) or else develop as a consequence of drug intolerance/idiosyncrasy (and are completely unpredictable).[5,11–14] The former are by far the more common, accounting for approximately 80% of all adverse drug reactions. Much less often adverse drug reactions represent a manifestation of an immunological phenomenon, so-called allergic drug reactions.[5,15] Although in theory the above subdivisions are sharply defined, in many patients the underlying pathogenetic mechanisms are far from clear.[12]

Adverse drug reactions are particularly encountered in a number of population groups, for example the elderly, females, patients with Sjögren's syndrome and those suffering from the effects of immune deficiency including patients receiving immunosuppressive therapy and those suffering from the acquired immunodeficiency syndrome (AIDS).[5]

Adverse drug reactions can be divided into three categories: type A, type B and type C.[1,11,15]

Type A drug reactions

Type A reactions, which are predictable and are related to the pharmacological actions or metabolism of the drug, include:[1]
- side-effects
- drug toxicity
- drug interactions.

Side-effects

Side-effects, which are common to almost all drugs, represent unwanted pharmacological actions, for example methotrexate, cyclophosphamide and nitrosourea administration commonly results in anagen alopecia by inducing Bax protein-mediated apoptosis.[16–20] Treatment with gold may be associated with cutaneous pigmentation (chrysiasis) and penicillamine may be associated with the development of skin laxity and fragility.[21–24]

Drug toxicity

Drug toxicity develops as a consequence of the gradual accumulation of a drug or its metabolite (e.g. minocycline or amiodarone deposition with resultant abnormal pigmentation).[14,25–28] Delayed toxicity may take months to many years before expression (e.g. arsenical keratoses).[29–32]

Drug interactions

Drug interactions develop when one drug alters the pharmacological efficacy of another that is given concurrently.[11,12,33,34] The effect may enhance or diminish the effect of the drug with resultant toxicity or loss of therapeutic value.[12,13] Drug interactions are thought to arise when one drug affects clearance of the other as a consequence of a number of mechanisms including:[33]
- alteration in the rate of absorption resulting in diminished drug levels
- alteration in the renal excretion resulting in inappropriately high drug levels
- plasma protein or tissue drug binding site competition resulting in displacement and consequent inappropriately high drug levels
- alterations in hepatic cytochrome P-450-mediated drug metabolism.

The last is believed to be of particular importance and includes both increased enzyme synthesis with excessive drug degradation and diminished circulating or tissue levels and inhibition of drug breakdown with increased circulating and tissue levels.[33,35]

Drug interactions are of particular importance in the elderly, the immunosuppressed and in those patients receiving multiple medications.[33]

Type B drug reactions

Type B reactions are uncommon and unpredictable. They do not have an allergic pathogenesis and include:[1]
- idiosyncratic drug reactions
- exacerbation of a pre-existing condition
- pseudoallergic drug reactions.

Idiosyncratic drug reactions

Idiosyncratic reactions (drug intolerance) develop as a result of genetic or metabolic influences. They may represent the effects of abnormal or altered hepatic drug metabolism, for example a lupus erythematosus-like condition is a very rare complication of hydralazine therapy in the average population but the risk is greatly increased in patients who metabolize the drug slowly.[36] Drug-induced lupus erythematosus may also be caused by procainamide, chlorpromazine, isoniazid, methyldopa, penicillamine, quinidine and sulfasalazine.[36,37] Cefaclor-induced serum sickness-like eruptions and the antiepileptic hypersensitivity syndrome are also believed to result from reactive intermediate metabolic products.[38,39]

Exacerbation of a pre-existing condition

This is a not uncommon problem; for example lithium, beta-blockers, antimalarial drugs, NSAIDs and tetracycline may precipitate, aggravate or induce a psoriatic eruption.[40–43]

Pseudoallergic drug reactions

Pseudoallergic reactions result from the non-immunologically mediated release of effector substances such as histamine from tissue-bound mast cells or circulating basophils with resultant urticarial reactions and angioneurotic edema.[13] In more seriously affected patients, anaphylaxis may result. The complement system can also be activated by similar non-immune mechanisms and there is evidence that perturbation of arachidonic acid metabolism may be involved in some cases.[12,16] Drugs which have been incriminated in such pseudoallergic reactions include radiocontrast media, NSAIDs, acetyl salicylic acid, opium derivatives, codeine, curare, d-tubocurare, polymyxin B and angiotensin converting enzyme (ACE) inhibitors.[12–14,44–48]

Type C drug reactions

Type C reactions are rare, immunologically mediated and develop as a consequence of previous exposure to the drug with resultant allergy.[1] The majority of drugs are of low molecular weight (less than 1000 Daltons) and therefore on their own are incapable of eliciting an immune response. By functioning as haptens and forming conjugates with carrier plasma proteins or cell membrane constituents they develop immunogenic potential.[11,16] The ability of the majority of drugs to cause an immune response is, therefore, dependent on its ability to bind to circulating or tissue protein.[49] A number of drugs are particularly liable to induce allergic reactions, including antibiotics, anticonvulsants, chemotherapeutic agents, heparin, insulin, protamine and biological response modifiers such as interferons and growth factors.[1] A variety of mechanisms may be involved in cutaneous drug-induced hypersensitivity reactions including:[11]
- IgE mediated type 1 reactions
- immune complex associated type 3 reactions
- type 4 delayed hypersensitivity reactions.

IgE-mediated type 1 cutaneous reactions

In type 1 reactions, the release of histamine and other chemical mediators from tissue-fixed mast cells results in increased vascular permeability with the subsequent development of edema in the dermis or deeper tissues.[5,16] Immediate reactions which develop within an hour or less of drug exposure present as urticaria, angioedema or anaphylaxis whereas accelerated reactions which develop from 1 to 72 hours following the administration of the drug are usually urticarial in nature.[16] Urticaria following treatment with penicillin is a typical type 1 reaction. Other antibiotics, antisera and gammaglobulin are also common offenders.[11]

The most common cause of anaphylaxis is penicillin.[50] Other important causes include foods, stings, anesthetics, muscle relaxants, latex, contrast material, antibiotics and allergenic extracts.[50-52] In addition to histamine, anaphylaxis is mediated through a number of substances including prostaglandin D2, leukotriene C4, interleukin (IL)-4 and IL-13 and tumor necrosis factor alpha (TNF-α).[49]

Immune complex-associated type 3 reactions

Type 3 reactions are expressed as urticaria, the Arthus reaction, serum sickness and leukocytoclastic (allergic) vasculitis.[11] The disease manifests a week or more after exposure to the drug by which time sufficient circulating antibody has been generated to result in immune complexes of an appropriate size to avoid phagocytosis. Their deposition in the tissues or within blood vessel walls is accompanied by complement fixation and resultant acute inflammatory reaction.

Delayed hypersensitivity type 4 reactions

Delayed hypersensitivity reactions are T-lymphocyte mediated and exemplified in acute allergic contact dermatitis.[11,16] Cytotoxic T-cell-mediated reactions are also of importance in many other adverse allergic drug reactions including exanthematous/morbilliform, bullous and interface variants.[53-56]

References

1. Gruchalla, R.S. (2003) Allergic disorders. 10. Drug allergy. *J Allergy Clin Immunol*, 111 (Suppl. 2), 548–559.
2. World Health Organization (1966) International drug monitoring: the role of the hospital. Geneva: WHO.
3. Van der Linde, P.D., van der Lei, J., Vlug, A.E. et al (1998) Skin reactions to antibacterial agents in general practice. *J Clin Epidemiol*, 51, 703–708.
4. Bates, D.W., Cullen, D.J., Laird, N. et al (1995) Incidence of adverse drug events and potential adverse drug events. ADE Prevention Study Groupage *J Am Acad Dermatol*, 274, 29–34.
5. Breathnach, S. (1995) Mechanisms of drug eruptions: Part 1. *Australas J Dermatol*, 36, 121–127.
6. Arndt, K.A., Jick, H. (1976) Rates of cutaneous reactions to drugs. A report from the Boston Collaborative Drug Surveillance Program. *J Am Med Assoc*, 235, 918–922.
7. Bigby, M., Jick, S., Jick, H. et al (1986) Drug-induced cutaneous reactions. A report from the Boston Collaborative Drug Surveillance Program on 15438 consecutive inpatients, 1975–1982. *JAMA*, 256, 3358–3363.
8. Hunziker, Th., Künzi, U-P., Braunschweig, S. et al (1997) Comprehensive hospital drug monitoring (CHDM): adverse skin reactions, a 20-year survey. *Allergy*, 52, 388–393.
9. Alanko, K., Stubb, S., Kauppinen, K. (1989) Cutaneous drug reactions: clinical types and causative agents. *Acta Derm Venereol*, 69, 223–226.
10. Kauppinen, K., Stubb, S. (1984) Drug eruptions: causative agents and clinical types. *Acta Derm Venereol*, 64, 320–324.
11. Breathnach, S.M., Hintner, H. (1992) Classification and mechanisms of drug reactions. In: Adverse reactions and the skin. Oxford: Blackwell Scientific, pp 14–38.
12. Wintroub, B., Stern, R. (1985) Cutaneous drug reactions: pathogenesis and clinical classification. *J Am Acad Dermatol*, 13, 167–179.
13. Alanko, K., Hannuksela, M. (1998) Mechanisms of drug reactions. In: Kauppinen, K., Alanko, K., Hannuksela, M., Maibach, H. (eds) Skin reactions to drugs. Boca Raton: CRC Press, pp 17–24.
14. Roujeau, J.C., Stern, R.S. (1994) Severe adverse cutaneous reactions to drugs. *N Engl J Med*, 10, 1272–1285.
15. Kauppinen, K., Kariniemim, A-L. (1998) Clinical manifestations and histological characteristics. In: Kauppinen, K., Alanko, K., Hannuksela, M., Maibach, H. (eds) Skin reactions to drugs. Boca Raton: CRC Press, pp 25–50.
16. Sehgal, V.N., Jain, S., Bhattacharya, S.N. (1993) Cutaneous drug reactions. *J Eur Acad Dermatol Venereol*, 2, 281–295.
17. Schilli, M.D., Paus, R., Menrad, A. (1998) Reduction of intrafollicular apoptosis in chemotherapy-induced alopecia by topical calcitriol-analogs. *J Invest Dermatol*, 111, 598–604.
18. Yoshizawa, K., Nambu, H., Yamamoto, D. et al (2000) Time-specific occurrence of alopecia in neonatal C57BL mice treated with N-methyl-N-nitrosourea and the therapeutic efficacy of tacrolimus hydrate. *Pathol Int*, 50, 175–184.
19. Mori, O., Matsuo, K., Hashimoto, T. (2000) Anticancer drugs induce apoptosis in mouse hair follicles. *Kurume Med J*, 47, 193–197.
20. Shirai, A., Tsunoda, H., Tamaoki, T. et al (2001) Topical application of cyclosporine A induces rapid-remodeling of damaged anagen hair follicles produced in cyclophosphamide administered mice. *J Dermatol Sci*, 27, 7–13.
21. Smith, R.W., Cawley, M.I.D. (1997) Chrysiasis. *Br J Rheumatol*, 36, 3–5.
22. Fleming, C.J., Salisbury, E.L.C., Kirwan, P. et al (1996) Chrysiasis after low-dose gold and UV light exposure. *J Am Acad Dermatol*, 34, 349–351.
23. Dalziel, K.L., Burge, S.M., Frith, P.A. et al (1990) Elastic fiber damage by low dose D-penicillamine. *Br J Dermatol*, 123, 305–312.
24. Buckley, C., Sankey, E.A., Harris, D. et al (1991) Progressive skin laxity secondary to penicillamine treatment. *Clin Exp Dermatol*, 16, 310–311.
25. Okada, N., Sato, S., Sasou, T. (1993) Characterization of pigmented granules in minocycline-induced cutaneous pigmentation: observations using fluorescent microscopy and high performance chromatography. *Br J Dermatol*, 129, 403–407.
26. Basler, R.S. (1985) Minocycline-related hyperpigmentation. *Arch Dermatol*, 121, 606–608.
27. Ferguson, J., Addo, H.A., Jones, S. et al (1985) A study of cutaneous photosensitivity induced by amiodarone. *Br J Dermatol*, 113, 537–549.
28. Trimble, J.W., Mendelson, D.S., Fetter, B.F. et al (1983) Cutaneous pigmentation secondary to amiodarone therapy. *Arch Dermatol*, 119, 914–918.
29. Rahman, M.M., Chowdhury, U.K., Mukherjee, S.C. et al (2001) Chronic arsenic toxicity in Bangladesh and West Bengal, India – a review and commentary. *J Toxicol Clin Toxicol*, 39, 683–700.
30. Hall, A.H. (2002) Chronic arsenic poisoning: a review. *Toxicol Lett*, 128, 69–72.
31. Alam, M.G., Allinson, G., Stagnitti, F. et al (2002) Arsenic contamination in Bangladesh groundwater: a major environmental and social disaster. *Int J Environ Health Res*, 12, 235–253.
32. Brown, K.G., Ross, G.L. (2002) Arsenic, drinking water, and health: a position paper of the American Council on Science and Health. *Regul Toxicol Pharmacol*, 36, 162–174.
33. Aria, N., Kauffman, C.L. (2003) Current therapy: important drug interactions and reactions in dermatology. *Dermatol Clin*, 21, 207–215.
34. Gupta, A.K., Katz, H.I., Shear, N.H. (1999) Drug interactions with itraconazole, fluconazole, and terbinafine and their management. *J Am Acad Dermatol*, 41, 237–249.
35. Singer, M.I., Shapiro, L.E., Shear, N.H. (1997) Cytochrome P-4503A: interactions with dermatologic therapies. *J Am Acad Dermatol*, 37, 765–771.
36. Price, E.J., Venables, P.J. (1995) Drug-induced lupus. *Drug Saf*, 12, 283–290.
37. Miyasaka, N. (1996) Drug-induced lupus. *Intern Med*, 35, 527–528.
38. Kearns, G.L., Wheeler, G.J., Childress, S.H. et al (1994) Serum sickness reactions to cefaclor: role of hepatic metabolism and individual susceptibility. *J Pediatriatr*, 125, 805–811.
39. Vittorio, C.C., Muglia, J.J. (1995) Anticonvulsant hypersensitivity syndrome. *Arch Intern Med*, 155, 2285–2290.
40. Abel, E.A., Dicicco, L.M., Orenberg, E.K. et al (1986) Drugs in exacerbation of psoriasis. *J Am Acad Dermatol*, 15, 1007–1022.
41. Abel, E.A. (1992) Diagnosis of drug-induced psoriasis. *Semin Dermatol*, 11, 269–274.
42. Wolff, R., Ruocco, V. (1999) Triggered psoriasis. *Adv Exp Med Biol*, 455, 221–225.
43. Tsankov, N., Angelova, I., Kazandjieva, J. (2000) Drug-induced psoriasis. Recognition and management. *Am J Clin Dermatol*, 1, 159–165.
44. Deswarte, R. (1984) Drug allergy – problems and strategies. *J Allergy Clin Immunol*, 74, 209–217.
45. Lasser, E.G. (1968) Basic mechanisms of contrast media reactions. *Radiology*, 91, 63–65.
46. Schonfeld, M.R. (1960) Acute allergic reactions to morphine, codeine, meperidine hydrochloride and opium alkaloids. *N Y State J Med*, 60, 2591–2593.
47. Arroyaye, C.M., Bhatt, K.N., Crown, N.R. (1976) Activation of the alternative pathway of the complement system by radiocontrast media. *J Immunol*, 117, 1866–1869.
48. Soter, N.A. (1991) Acute and chronic urticaria and angioedema. *J Am Acad Dermatol*, 25, 146–154.
49. Sheppard, G.M. (2003) Hypersensitivity reactions to drugs: evaluation and management. *Mt Sinai J Med*, 70, 113–125.
50. Neugut, A., Ghatak, A., Miller, R. (2001) Anaphylaxis in the United States: an investigation into its epidemiology. *Arch Intern Med*, 161, 15–21.
51. Laxenaire, M. (1993) Epidemiology of anesthetic anaphylactoid reactions: fourth multicenter survey. *Ann Fr Anesth Reanim*, 18, 796–809.
52. Lenier-Peterson, P., Hansen, D., Andersen, M. et al (1996) Drug-induced fatal anaphylactic shock in Denmark 1968–1990. *Ugeskr Laeger*, 158, 3316–3318.
53. Pumphrey, R. (2000) Lessons for management of anaphylaxis from a study of fatal reactions. *Clin Exp Allergy*, 30, 1144–1150.
54. Yawalkar, N., Pichler, W.J. (2001) Immunohistology of drug-induced exanthema: clues to pathogenesis. *Curr Opin Allergy Clin Immunol*, 1, 229–303.
55. Neukomm, C.B., Yawalkar, N., Helbling, A. et al (2001) T-cell reactions to drugs in distinct clinical manifestations of drug allergy. *J Investig Allergol Clin Immunol*, 11, 275–284.
56. Pichler, W.J. (2002) T cells in drug allergy. *Curr Allergy Asthma Rep*, 2, 9–15.

Adverse drug reactions – clinical manifestations

Although the range of drugs that may result in adverse drug reactions is extensive, the variety of clinical responses encountered is fairly limited. Many drugs may cause more than one clinical response and any given reaction pattern may result from a wide range of drugs. There are, however, a number of clinicopathological responses that are fairly unique to a particular drug and these are dealt with individually, later in this chapter.[1-8]

Adverse drug reactions may therefore present with a considerable number of clinical manifestations as outlined in *Table 13.1*.[1,2]

References

1. Kauppinen, K., Kariniemi, A-L. (1998) Clinical manifestations and histological characteristics. In: Kauppinen, K., Alanko, K., Hannuksela, M., Maibach, H. (eds) Skin reactions to drugs. Boca Raton: CRC Press, pp 25–50.
2. Breathnach, S.M., Hintner, H. (1992) Types of clinical reaction. In: Adverse drug reactions and the skin. Oxford: Blackwell Scientific, pp 41–133.
3. Rubianes, E.L., Martin, R.F., Picó, M. et al (1990) Cutaneous drug reactions. *Bol Assoc Med P Rico*, 82, 434–443.
4. Raviglione, M.C., Pablos-Méndez, A., Battan, R. (1990) Clinical features and management of severe dermatological reactions to drugs. *Drug Saf*, 5, 39–64.
5. Alanko, K., Stubbs, S., Kauppinen, K. (1989) Cutaneous drug reactions: clinical types and causative agents. A five year survey of in-patients. *Acta Derm Venereol*, 69, 223–226.
6. Kalish, R.S. (1991) Drug eruptions: a review of clinical and immunological features. *Adv Dermatol*, 6, 221–237.

Table 13.1
Clinical manifestations of adverse drug reactions

- Exanthematous reactions
- Urticaria, angioedema and anaphylaxis
- Serum sickness
- Phototoxic/photoallergic eruptions
- Hypersensitivity syndrome
- Lichenoid drug reactions
- Fixed drug eruptions
- Erythema multiforme
- Stevens–Johnson syndrome/toxic epidermal necrolysis
- Pigmentary abnormalities
- Vasculitis
- Purpura
- Granulomatous drug reactions
- Erythema nodosum
- Drug-induced alopecia
- Lupus erythematosus-like drug reactions
- Bullous drug reactions
- Psoriasiform drug reactions
- Pityriasis rosea-like eruptions
- Pustular drug reactions
- Ichthyosiform drug reactions
- Pseudolymphomatous drug reactions
- Eczematous drug reactions

7. Sehgal, V.N., Jain, S., Bhattacharya, S.N. (1993) Cutaneous drug reactions. *J Eur Acad Dermatol Venereol*, 2, 281–295.
8. Crowson, A.N., Magro, C.M. (1999) Recent advances in the pathology of cutaneous drug reactions. *Dermatol Clin*, 17, 537–560.

Exanthematous reactions

Clinical features

Exanthematous (morbilliform, maculopapular) reactions are the most frequently encountered adverse drug reaction and mimic a variety of infective conditions including scarlet fever, measles and rubella (*Figs 13.1, 13.2*).[1-3] Patients present with erythematous macules and papules that with progression may become confluent or even acquire gyrate/polycyclic features. Pruritus, low-grade fever and eosinophilia are sometimes present.[2] The eruption is often symmetrical and usually presents on the trunk and extremities or sites of pressure and trauma.[1] The palms and soles are sometimes affected but the mucous membranes are not usually involved.

Exanthematous eruptions most commonly develop within 1–2 weeks of starting the drug.[1] Sometimes, however, the eruption is delayed and may even present after the treatment has ceased.[1,4] In more seriously affected patients the eruption can progress to erythroderma (exfoliative dermatitis) in which the erythema becomes generalized and is often accompanied by scaling.[5] Resolution of exanthematous drug reactions is characterized by exfoliation and sometimes is followed by postinflammatory hyperpigmentation.[1] Penicillin, sulfonamides, ampicillin, amoxicillin, phenylbutazone, isoniazid, barbiturates, phenytoin, carbamazepine, benzodiazepines, gold and trimethoprim are especially incriminated.[1,6-8] Patients who suffer from infectious mononucleosis are particularly at

risk of developing an exanthematous reaction following therapy with ampicillin or amoxicillin.[9]

Pathogenesis and histological features

The pathogenesis of exanthematous drug reactions is not fully understood, although a cytotoxic T-cell-mediated reaction is likely in the majority of cases (see immunohistochemistry).

The histological features are often subtle. Although the epidermis may appear normal, focal parakeratosis is commonly present. The characteristic changes include lymphocytic exocytosis with mild spongiosis, typically accompanied by basal cell liquefactive degeneration and one or two dyskeratotic keratinocytes (*Figs 13.3–13.9*).[10,11] The dermis shows a perivascular infiltrate of lymphocytes and histiocytes with variable

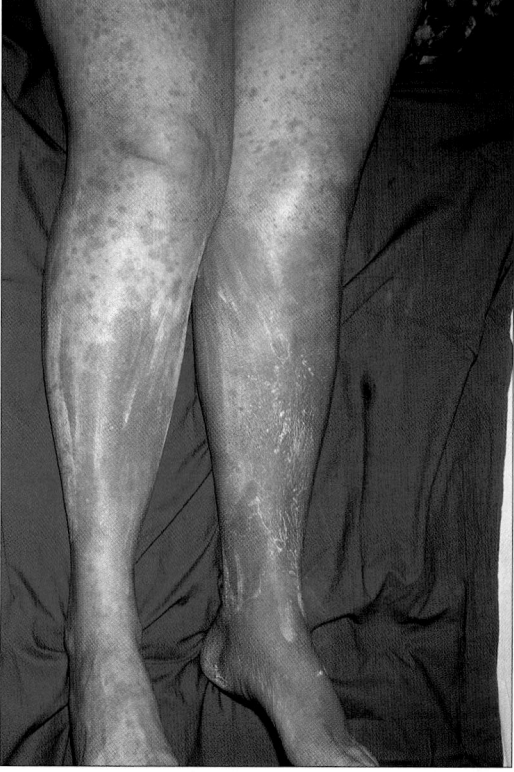

Fig. 13.1
Exanthematous drug reaction: typical erythematous maculopapular eruption on the lower extremities due to ampicillin. By courtesy of the Institute of Dermatology, London, UK.

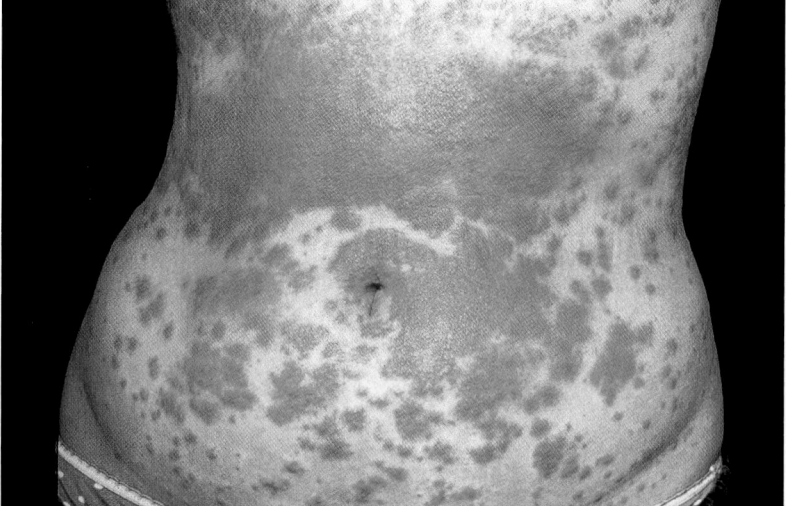

Fig. 13.2
Exanthematous drug reaction: more extensive lesions on the abdomen associated with amoxicillin therapy. By courtesy of the Institute of Dermatology, London, UK.

numbers of eosinophils (*Fig. 13.10*). Eosinophils – although often emphasized in the literature as an important feature of drug reactions – can, in our experience, sometimes be very scanty or even absent. Sometimes marked edema is seen, particularly if an urticarial element is clinically evident. Red cell extravasation may also be a feature in those lesions that include a purpuric component.

By immunohistochemistry, the lymphocytes are largely CD3+ T-cells with a predominance of CD4+ cells in the superficial perivascular infiltrate.[12] Lymphocytes at the epidermodermal junction and within the epidermis typically consist of approximately equal numbers of CD4+ and CD8+ forms.[12–17] These latter cells regularly express human leukocyte antigen (HLA)-DR and a subpopulation also expresses CD25.[17] There is an admixture of T-helper Th1 and Th2 cells.[16] Occasionally, however, the infiltrate is almost entirely composed of the CD4+ lymphocytes and contrariwise, in human immunodeficiency virus (HIV) positive patients, the infiltrate may consist of CD8+ cells alone.[12,15] CD1a+ dendritic cells and CD68+ histiocytes are also present.[16] CD56+ natural killer (NK) cells may be identified.[17] Cytotoxic pathways mediated by perforin and granzyme B have been shown to be of particular importance in exanthematous drug reactions.[14,16,17] Fas/Fas-L cytotoxic mechanisms are not thought to be of relevance.[12]

The features of drug-induced erythroderma are rather non-specific and include parakeratosis and psoriasiform hyperplasia, sometimes

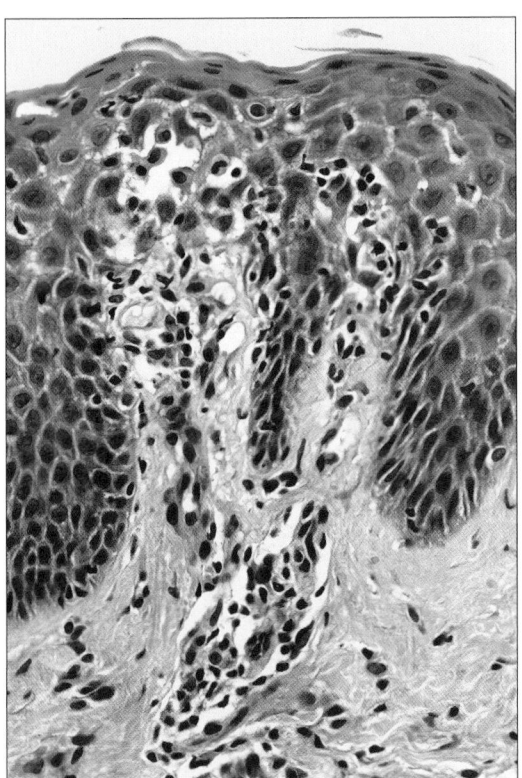

Fig. 13.3
Exanthematous drug reaction: early lesion due to penicillin showing slight interface change, spongiosis and lymphocytic exocytosis. There is a superficial perivascular lymphocytic infiltrate, and one or two plasma cells are present.

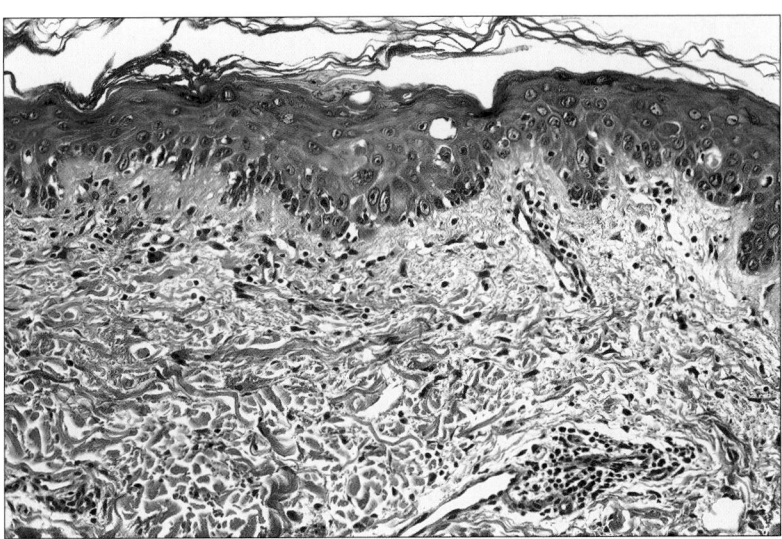

Fig. 13.5
Exanthematous drug reaction: this eruption followed treatment with ceftazidime. There is focal parakeratosis, dyskeratosis, and interface change. There is also a hint of dysmaturation. Note the enlarged and mildly pleomorphic nuclei.

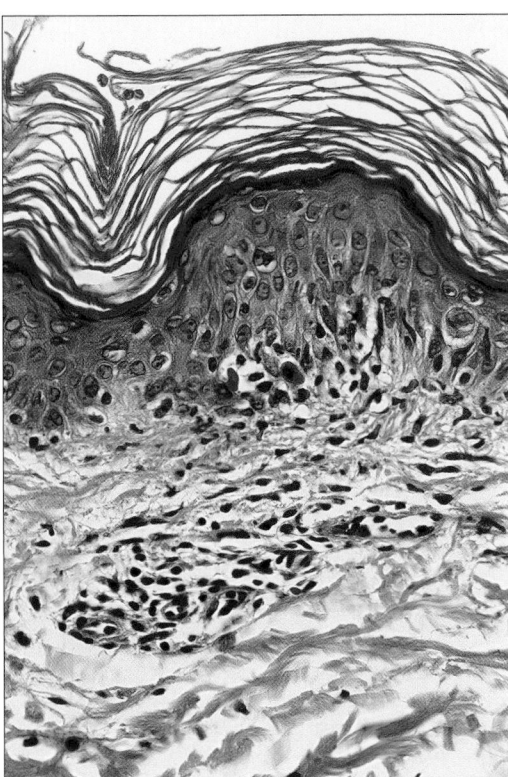

Fig. 13.4
Exanthematous drug reaction: in this example due to carbamazepine therapy, there is spongiosis, dyskeratosis and interface change associated with lymphocytic exocytosis.

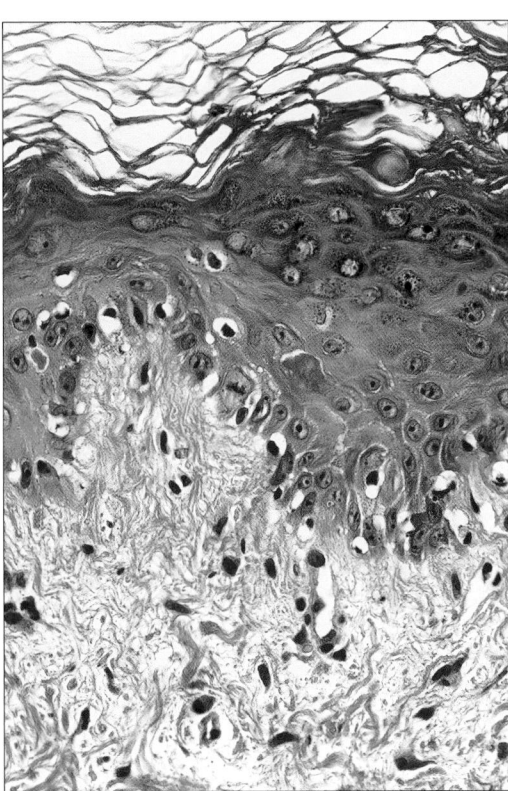

Fig. 13.6
Exanthematous drug reaction: close-up view of *Fig. 13.5* showing interface change and dyskeratosis.

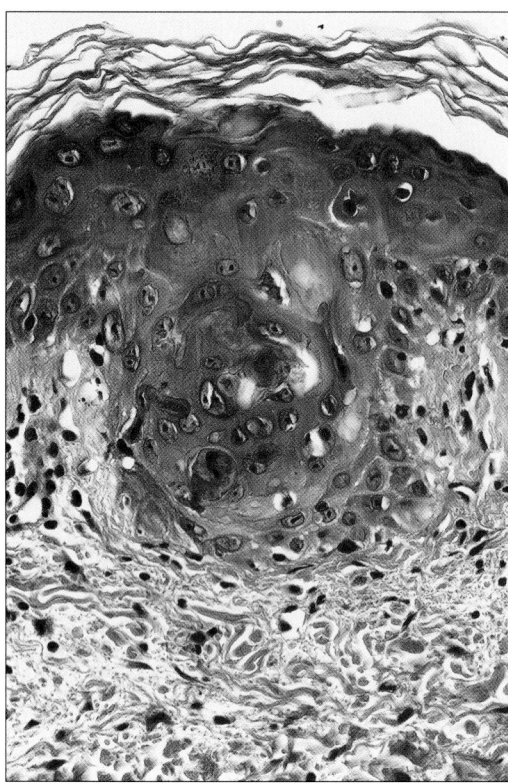

Fig. 13.7
Exanthematous drug reaction: close-up view of *Fig. 13.5* showing dyskeratosis and disorderly maturation.

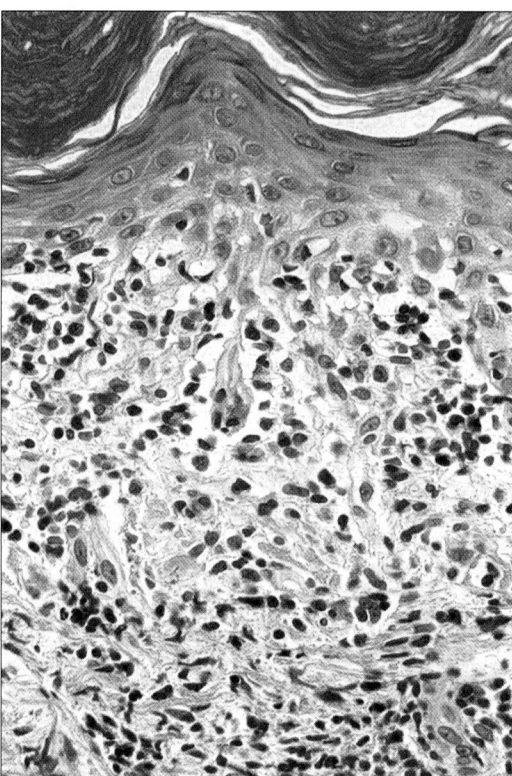

Fig. 13.9
Exanthematous drug reaction: close-up view of *Fig. 13.8*.

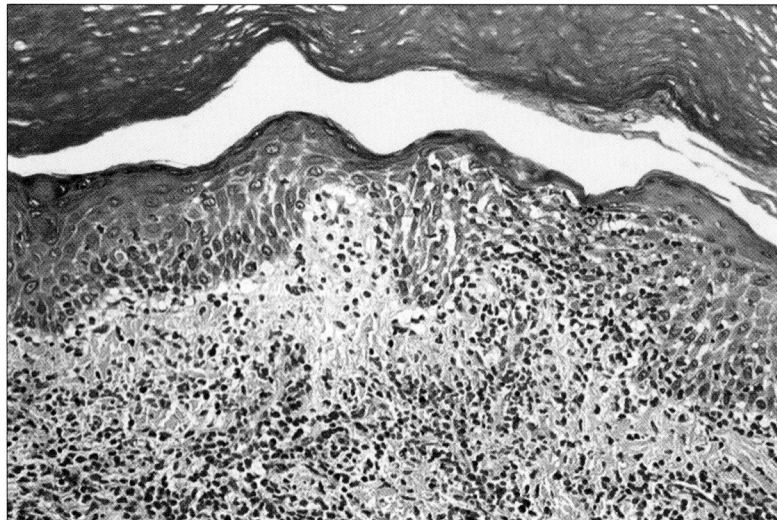

Fig. 13.8
Exanthematous drug reaction: this patient developed a maculopapular eruption on the palms due to sulfasalazine therapy. There is extensive spongiosis with interface change and marked red cell extravasation.

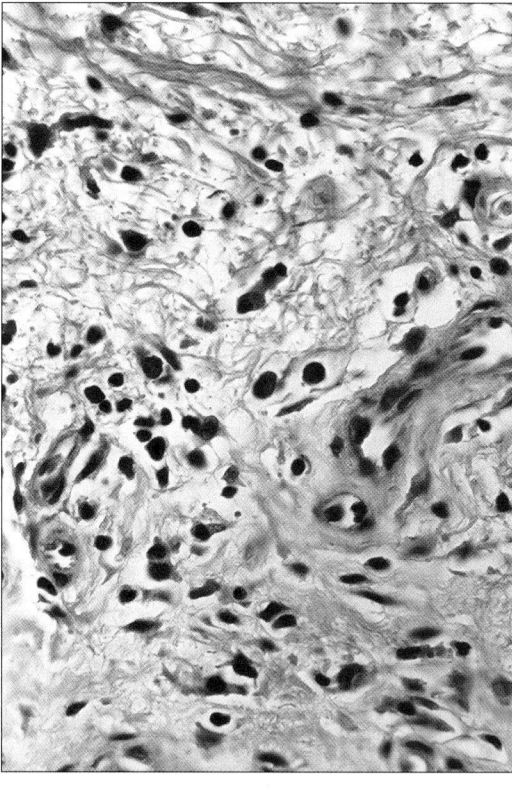

Fig. 13.10
Exanthematous drug reaction: close-up view of *Fig. 13.8*. The eruption had an urticarial element; note the marked edema and eosinophils.

accompanied by mild spongiosis. Eosinophils may be identified within the dermal chronic inflammatory cell infiltrate.

Differential diagnosis

Exanthematous adverse drug reactions are a frequent feature in transplantation patients who are usually taking multiple medications and, therefore, must be distinguished from acute GVHD. In reality, it is difficult if not impossible to make this distinction histologically although the presence of eosinophils may point towards a drug reaction. A viral exanthem also commonly enters the differential diagnosis – the histological findings are often indistinguishable although the presence of eosinophils would again point towards a drug reaction.

References

1. Breathnach, S.M., Hintner, H. (1992) Types of clinical reaction. In: Adverse drug reactions and the skin. Oxford: Blackwell Scientific, pp 41–133.
2. Rubianes, E.L., Martin, R.F., Picó, M. et al (1990) Cutaneous drug reactions. *Bol Assoc Med P Rico*, **82**, 434–443.
3. Bork, M.K. (1988) Cutaneous side effects of drugs. Philadelphia: Saunders.
4. Wintroub, B., Stern, R. (1985) Cutaneous drug reactions: pathogenesis and clinical classification. *J Am Acad Dermatol*, **13**, 167–179.
5. Raviglione, M.C., Pablos-Méndez, A., Battan, R. (1990) Clinical features and management of severe dermatological reactions to drugs. *Drug Saf*, **5**, 39–64.
6. Kauppinen, K., Kariniemi, A-L. (1998) Clinical manifestations and histological characteristics. In: Kauppinen, K., Alanko, K., Hannuksela, M., Maibach, H. (eds) Skin reactions to drugs. Boca Raton: CRC Press, pp 25–50.
7. Sehgal, V.N., Jain, S., Bhattacharya, S.N. (1993) Cutaneous drug reactions. *J Eur Acad Dermatol Venereol*, **2**, 281–295.

8. Breathnach, S.M., Hintner, H. (1992) Classification and mechanisms of drug reactions. In: Adverse drug reactions and the skin. Oxford: Blackwell Scientific, pp 14–38.
9. Porter, J., Jick, H. (1980) Amoxicillin and ampicillin rashes equally likely. *Lancet*, 1, 1037–1038.
10. Fellner, M.J., Prutkin, L. (1970) Morbilliform eruptions caused by penicillin: a study by electron microscopy and immunologic tests. *J Invest Dermatol*, 55, 390–395.
11. Crowson, A.N., Magro, C.M. (1999) Recent advances in the pathology of cutaneous drug reactions. *Dermatol Clin*, 17, 537–560.
12. Pichler, W.J., Yawalkar, N., Britschgi, M. et al (2002) Cellular and molecular pathophysiology of cutaneous drug reactions. *Am J Clin Dermatol*, 3, 229–238.

13. Hari, Y., Frutig, K., Hurni, M. et al (2001) T cell involvement in cutaneous drug eruptions. *Clin Exp Allergy*, 31, 1398–1403.
14. Yawalkar, N., Egli, F., Hari, Y. et al (2000) Infiltration of cytotoxic T cells in drug-induced cutaneous eruptions. *Clin Exp Allergy*, 30, 847–855.
15. Carr, A., Vasak, E., Munro, V. et al (1994) Immunohistological assessment of cutaneous drug hypersensitivity in patients with HIV infection. *Clin Exp Immunol*, 97, 260–265.
16. Yawalkar, N., Pichler, W.J. (2001) Immunohistology of drug-induced exanthema: clues to pathogenesis. *Curr Opin Allergy Clin Immunol*, 1, 299–303.
17. Schnyder, B., Frutig, K., Mauri-Hellweg, D. et al (1998) T-cell mediated cytotoxicity against keratinocytes in sulfamethoxazole-induced skin reaction. *Clin Exp Allergy*, 28, 1412–1417.

Urticarial reactions, angioedema and anaphylaxis

Clinical features

Urticaria is the second most common adverse drug reaction.[1] It is characterized by the presence of pruritic, erythematous and edematous wheals. If accompanied by marked edema involving the deeper dermis and subcutaneous fat or if the submucosal layers are affected, the condition of angioedema results.[2–4] Urticaria may also be a manifestation of serum sickness and anaphylaxis.

Urticarial reactions may result from the use of a large number of drugs, with aspirin, penicillin, ACE inhibitors and blood products being particularly incriminated.[5,6] Drugs, which directly stimulate mast cell release of vasoactive substances such as histamine and thereby cause urticaria, include opiates, curare, vancomycin and polymyxin B.[3,7,8] Radiocontrast media may have a similar effect.[3] Urticarial reactions that complicate the use of aspirin and NSAIDs are thought to sometimes be a result of abnormal arachidonic acid metabolism.[3]

Pathogenesis and histological features

The pathogenesis of urticarial drug reactions includes IgE-mediated type 1 reactions, immune complex mechanisms and pseudoallergic phenomena (non IgE-mediated).[5,9,10]

Histologically, urticaria is characterized by dermal edema and vascular dilatation accompanied by a perivascular infiltrate consisting of lymphocytes and eosinophils. Mast cell degranulation may often be present.[3] Vasculitis is not a feature.

Angioedema is characterized by edema extending into the deeper dermis and subcutaneous fat.

References

1. Breathnach, S.M., Hintner, H. (1992) Types of clinical reaction. In: Adverse drug reactions and the skin. Oxford: Blackwell Scientific, pp 41–133.
2. Kaplan, A.P. (1984) Drug-induced skin disease. *J Allergy Clin Immunol*, 74, 573–579.
3. Soter, N.A. (1991) Acute and chronic urticaria and angioedema. *J Am Acad Dermatol*, 25, 146–154.
4. Ebo, D.G., Stevens, W.J. (1997) Angioedema of ACE inhibitors. *Allergy*, 52, 354–355.
5. Wintroub, B., Stern, R. (1985) Cutaneous drug reactions: pathogenesis and clinical classification. *J Am Acad Dermatol*, 13, 167–179.
6. Beltrani, V.S. (1998) Cutaneous manifestations of adverse drug reactions. *Immunol Allergy Clin North Am*, 18, 867–895.
7. Wolverton, S.E. (1998) Update on cutaneous drug reactions. *Adv Dermatol*, 13, 65–72.
8. Del Rosso, J.Q. (2002) Skin manifestations of drug reactions. *Curr Allergy Asthma Rep*, 2, 282–287.
9. Breathnach, S. (1995) Mechanisms of drug eruptions: Part 1. *Australas J Dermatol*, 36, 121–127.
10. Rubianes, E.L., Martin, R.F., Picó, M. et al (1990) Cutaneous drug reactions. *Bol Assoc Med P Rico*, 82, 434–443.

Serum sickness/serum sickness-like drug reactions

Clinical features

Serum sickness, which represents an immune complex-mediated type 3 reaction, usually develops within 1–3 weeks after taking the serum or vaccine.[1–8] It presents with an erythematous maculopapular or urticarial response or with palpable purpura variably accompanied by fever, arthralgia, myalgia, arthritis, lymphadenopathy, glomerulonephritis, myocarditis and neuritis.[1–4] The cutaneous manifestations often commence on the sides of the fingers, toes and hands before becoming more generalized.[2] A wide range of drugs has been implicated in the development of serum sickness-like drug reactions including phenytoin, phenylbutazone and carbamazepine although in the more recent literature, cefaclor has featured most prominently along with a number of other antibiotics such as cefprozil, ciprofloxacin, minocycline, penicillin V, amoxicillin, flucloxacillin and co-trimoxazole.[6,9–19]

Pathogenesis and histological features

Serum sickness is thought to represent an immune complex-mediated type 3 reaction although the possibility of direct toxicity against vessel wall, autoimmunity and cell-mediated cytotoxicity have been proposed as alternative pathogenetic mechanisms.[2] Direct immunofluorescence reveals immunoglobulin and C3 in relation to blood vessel walls.[6]

The histological features are those of leukocytoclastic vasculitis (Fig. 13.11).[20]

References

1. Rubianes, E.L., Martin, R.F., Picó, M. et al (1990) Cutaneous drug reactions. *Bol Assoc Med P Rico*, 82, 434–443.
2. Roujeau, J.C., Stern, R.S. (1994) Severe adverse cutaneous reactions to drugs. *N Engl J Med*, 10, 1272–1285.
3. Patterson, R., Anderson, J. (1982) Allergic reactions to drugs and biologic agents. *JAMA*, 248, 2637–2645.
4. Dipiro, J., Stafford, C.T. (1995) Allergic and pseudoallergic drug reactions. In: Dipiro, J.T., Talbert, R.L., Hayes, P.E. et al (eds) Pharmacotherapy: a pathophysiologic approach. Norwalk, CT: Appleton & Lange, pp 1279–1281.
5. Beringer, P.M., Middleton, R.K. (1995) Anaphylaxis and drug allergies. In: Young, L.Y., Koda-Kimble, M.A. (eds) Applied therapeutics: the clinical use of drugs. Vancouver, WA: Applied Therapeutics, pp 6/7–6/10.
6. Del Rosso, J.Q. (2002) Skin manifestations of drug reactions. *Curr Allergy Asthma Rep*, 2, 282–287.
7. Knowles, S., Shapiro, L., Shear, N.H. (2000) Drug eruptions. *Curr Prob Dermatol*, 12, 58–62.
8. Arkachaisri, T. (2002) Serum sickness and hepatitis B vaccine including review of the literature. *J Med Assoc Thai*, 85 (Suppl. 2), S607–S612.
9. Vial, T., Pont, J., Pham, E. (1992) Cefaclor-associated serum sickness-like disease: eight cases and review of the literature. *Ann Pharmacother*, 26, 910–914.
10. Martin, J., Abbott, G. (1995) Serum sickness-like illness and antimicrobials in children. *N Z Med J*, 108, 123–124.
11. Kearns, G.L. Wheeler, J.G., Rieder, M.J. et al (1998) Serum sickness-like reaction to cefaclor: lack of cross reactivity with loracarbef. *Clin Pharmacol Ther*, 63, 686–693.
12. Joubert, G.I., Hadad, K., Matsui, D. et al (1999) Selection of treatment of cefaclor-associated urticarial, serum sickness-like reactions and erythema multiforme by emergency pediatricians: lack of uniform standard of care. *Can J Clin Pharmacol*, 6, 197–201.
13. Yerushalmi, J., Zvulunov, A., Halevy, S. (2002) Serum sickness-like reactions. *Cutis*, 69, 395–397.
14. Tatum, A.J., Ditto, A.M., Patterson, R. (2001) Severe serum sickness-like reaction to oral penicillin drugs: three case reports. *Ann Allergy Asthma Immunol*, 86, 330–334.
15. Lowery, N., Kearns, G., Young, R. (1994) Serum sickness-like reactions associated with cefprozil therapy. *J Pediatriatr*, 125, 325–328.
16. Sánchez, G., Vila, L., Pajarón, M. et al (2001) Skin manifestations of phenylbutazone-induced serum sickness-like reactions. *J Investig Allergol Clin Immunol*, 10, 170–172.
17. Harel, L., Amir, J. (1996) Serum sickness-like reaction associated with minocycline therapy in adolescents. *Ann Pharmacother*, 30, 481–483.
18. Knowles, S.R., Shapiro, L., Shear, N.H. (1996) Serious adverse reactions induced by minocycline. Report of 13 cases and review of the literature. *Arch Dermatol*, 132, 934–939.
19. Hoefnagel, J.J., van Leeuwen, R.L., Mattie, H. et al (1997) Side-effects of minocycline in the treatment of acne vulgaris. *Ned Tijdschr Geneeskd*, 141, 1424–1427.
20. Anderson, J.M., Tiede, J.J. (1997) Serum sickness associated with 6-mercaptopurine in a patient with Crohn's disease. *Pharmacotherapy*, 17, 173–176.

Fig. 13.11
(**a**, **b**) Serum sickness: there is a florid leukocytoclastic vasculitis.

Phototoxic and photoallergic reactions

Clinical features

Photosensitization is a process whereby 'a reaction to non-ionizing radiation occurs as a consequence of the introduction of a radiation-absorbing reagent (the sensitizer), which induces another substance (the substrate) to undergo chemical change'.[1–5] There are two basic mechanisms: phototoxic (by far the more common) and photoallergic. However, these are not necessarily mutually exclusive and clinically are not always distinguishable.[6–29] While an enormous range of drugs has been implicated in photosensitivity reactions, NSAIDS, phenothiazines, amiodarone, antibiotics and antifungal agents such as griseofulvin appear to be of particular importance.[29]

Phototoxic photosensitivity which does not involve an immunological mechanism occurs as a direct consequence of cellular damage induced by the reaction between ultraviolet (UV) or visible light and the in vivo bound sensitizer.[1] Both UVB and UVA can produce phototoxic reactions although the former is of greater importance. Two types are recognized: photodynamic and non-photodynamic, the former requiring the presence of oxygen while the latter does not.[5]

- Photodynamic reactions result in singlet oxygen or superoxide anions which cause injury to cellular constituents such as cell membranes, cytoplasmic proteins and nucleic acids.[5]
- Non-photodynamic reactions damage DNA or RNA directly.[5]

Many drug reactions are photodynamic, whereas psoralen represents a typical non-photodynamic reaction. Phototoxic reactions do not depend on prior exposure to the drug and will affect all patients of the same skin type provided that sufficient bound drug is available for reaction with the appropriate radiation.[1] It usually develops within the first 24 hours of exposure.

The clinical appearances of acute phototoxic reactions mimic severe sunburn and include erythema, edema and blistering with subsequent desquamation and postinflammatory hyperpigmentation (*Figs 13.12, 13.13*).[5,6] Typically, only exposed skin is affected. Phototoxicity has also been associated with onycholysis, and use of antimalarials may be complicated by ocular damage including corneal opacity, cataract and permanent retinopathy with blindness.[20,24,30]

Chronic phototoxicity presents with poikilodermatous features including variable hyper- and hypopigmentation, epidermal atrophy and telangiectasia. It is an important feature of the porphyrias and the inherited photodermatoses such as xeroderma pigmentosum, Rothmund–Thomson syndrome and Bloom's syndrome. It rarely results from drug treatment but may follow long-term therapy with psoralen and UVA (PUVA therapy) when there is also an increased incidence of actinic keratosis, basal cell carcinoma, squamous cell carcinoma and, more rarely, melanoma.[5,31–33] Pseudoporphyria – which represents a phototoxic reaction variant – is discussed on page 649.[5] Phototoxic lichenoid reactions are described on page 635.

Drugs that are particularly incriminated in acute phototoxic reactions include thiazide diuretics, sulfonamides, tetracycline antibiotics, NSAIDs (including naproxen, diclofenac and ketoprofen), phenothiazines (parti-

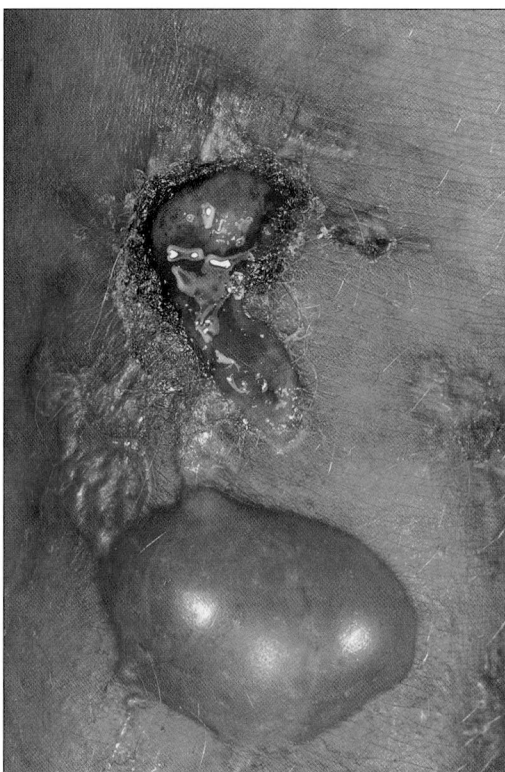

Fig. 13.12
Phototoxic drug reaction: in this example there are well-developed blisters arising on an erythematous base.

cularly chlorpromazine), amiodarone, tars and psoralens.[5–12,18,19,22,23,28] Phototoxicity has also been described with use of St John's wort and following photodynamic therapy.[21,25] Porphyrins are potent phototoxic sensitizers.[5] In this instance, the damage particularly affects the dermal constituents including the vasculature, leaving the epidermis relatively unaffected (see *Figs 12.126, 12.127*). Photoallergic photosensitivity which is immunologically mediated represents either an immediate type 1 solar urticarial reaction or a delayed papular, vesicular or eczematous response.[5] The delayed responses represent lymphocyte-mediated delayed hypersensitivity type 4 reactions and are of particular importance in the context of drug-related photoallergy.[5] By definition, both require previous exposure to the drug or chemical.[1,5] Only a proportion of patients taking the drug will develop a reaction. Photoallergic reactions are usually induced by UVA but not UVB or visible light.[1] The clinical appearances are variable and include eczematous and lichenoid reactions (*Figs 13.14–13.16*).[13] Unlike phototoxic reactions, unexposed skin may also be affected in addition to exposed skin.[6] The majority of photoallergic reactions are induced by the application of topical medicaments and chemicals (contact photoallergy) including antihistamines,

local anesthetics, chlorpromazine, hydrocortisone sunscreens containing *p*-aminobenzoic acid and halogenated phenolic compounds in soaps and fragrances (e.g. 6-methylcoumarin and musk ambrette).[1,6,14–16] Photoallergy can also follow systemic administration of drugs including sulfonamides, griseofulvin, phenothiazines, tetracyclines, NSAIDs, chloroquine and thiazides.[7,17] Diagnosis is best confirmed by a photopatch test.

Phytophotodermatitis represents a phototoxic drug reaction which develops from contact with plants containing furanocoumarins.[34–36] Patients generally develop erythema followed by postinflammatory hyperpigmentation although rarely blisters may develop (*Figs 13.17, 13.18*).[34] Members of the Umbelliferae, Rutaceae and Moraceae families are particularly implicated.[35,36]

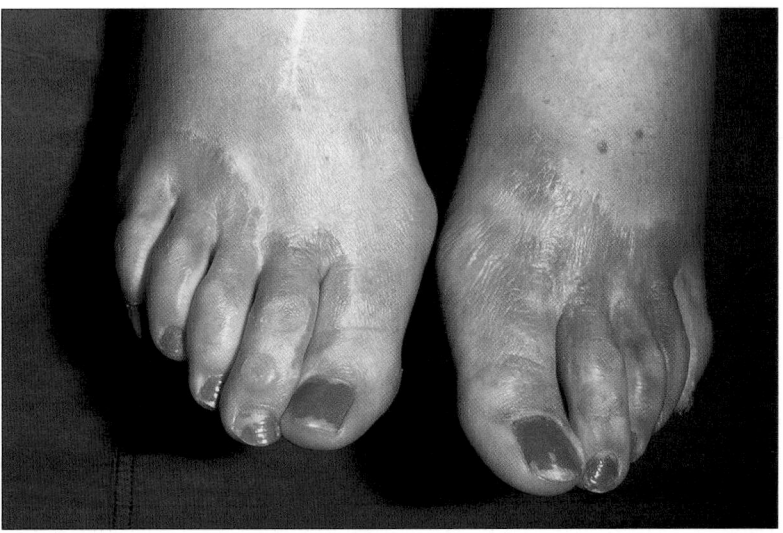

Fig. 13.15
Photoallergic drug reaction: close-up view of a different patient. By courtesy of the Institute of Dermatology, London, UK.

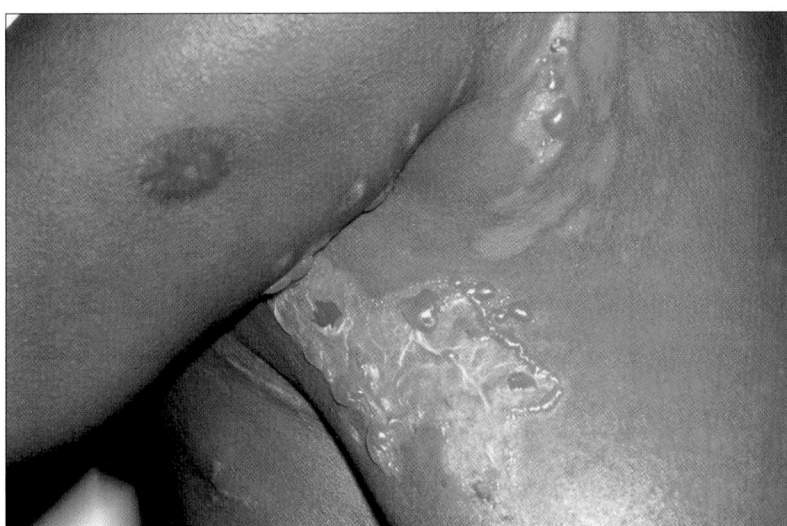

Fig. 13.13
Phototoxic drug reaction: the lesions in this patient followed PUVA therapy. By courtesy of the Institute of Dermatology, London, UK.

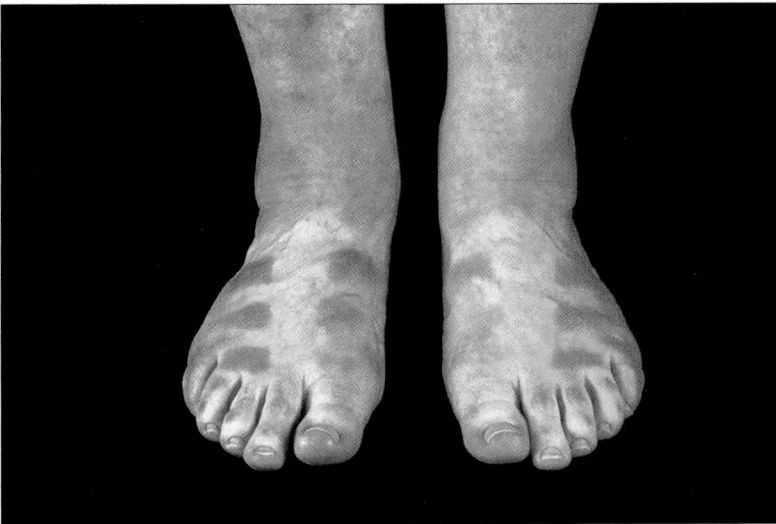

Fig. 13.14
Photoallergic drug reaction: note the obvious sparing of covered skin. By courtesy of the Institute of Dermatology, London, UK.

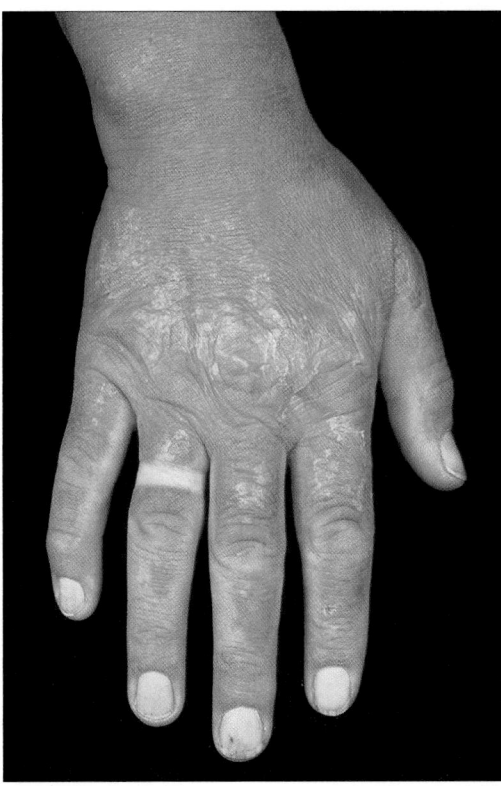

Fig. 13.16
Photoallergic drug reaction: this example resulted from treatment with tetracycline. By courtesy of the Institute of Dermatology, London, UK.

Histological features

The histological appearances of acute phototoxic reactions include conspicuous apoptotic keratinocytes (sunburn cells) which in severe cases may affect the entire epidermis, with variable neutrophil exocytosis, dermal edema and a perivascular lymphohistiocytic infiltrate with small numbers of neutrophils and eosinophils (*Fig. 13.19*).[37]

Chronic lesions are characterized by hyperkeratosis, hypergranulosis, variable acanthosis and epidermal atrophy, increased melanin pigmentation, melanocyte hyperplasia and pigmentary incontinence.[37] Elastosis and telangiectatic vessels may be conspicuous and in severely affected patients stellate atypical myofibroblasts can be a feature. Epidermal disorganization and dyskeratosis may also be present.[5]

The histological appearances of urticarial photoallergic reactions include vascular dilatation, edema and a lymphocytic infiltrate with eosinophils. Delayed reactions are characterized by spongiosis (often with vesiculation, lymphocytic and eosinophil exocytosis), accompanied by papillary dermal edema and an upper dermal lymphohistiocytic infiltrate with variable numbers of eosinophils.[37]

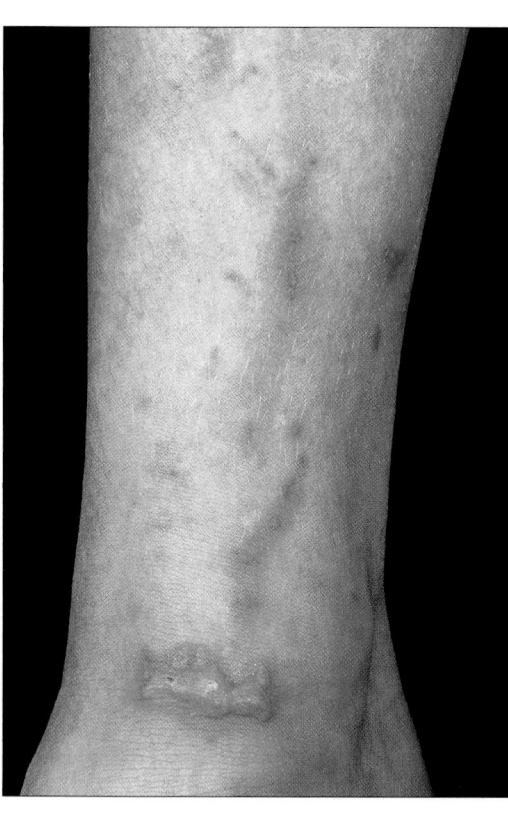

Fig. 13.17
Phytophotodermatitis: this variant represents an allergic reaction to a plant chemical. Linear lesions on the limbs are characteristic and usually follow gardening. By courtesy of the Institute of Dermatology, London, UK.

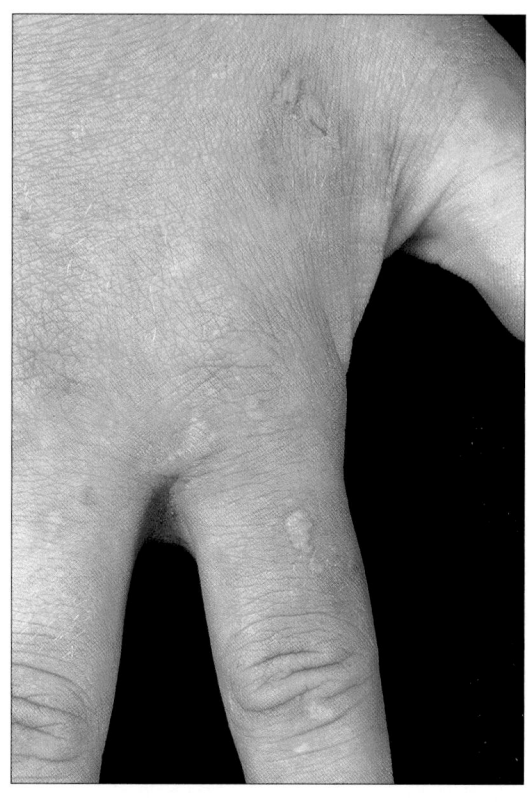

Fig. 13.18
Phytophotodermatitis: the lesions typically result from plants containing 5-methoxypsoralen. By courtesy of the Institute of Dermatology, London, UK.

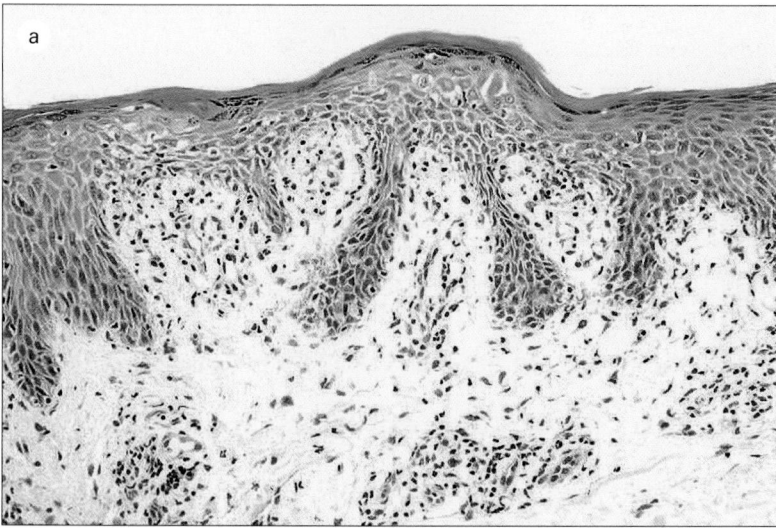

Fig. 13.19
(**a**, **b**) Phototoxic drug reaction: there is hyperkeratosis, hypergranulosis, mild intercellular edema and apoptosis (sunburn cells). A light perivascular lymphohistiocytic infiltrate is present in the superficial dermis.

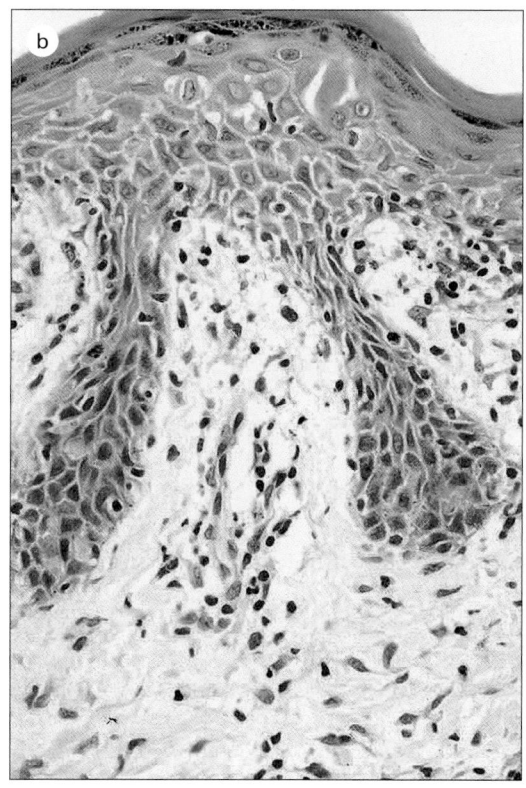

References

1. González, E., González, S. (1996) Drug photosensitivity, idiopathic photodermatoses, and sunscreens. *J Am Acad Dermatol*, **35**, 871–885.
2. Spikes, J.D. (1977) Photosensitization. In: Smith, K.C. (ed.) The science of photobiology. New York: Plenum, pp 87–110.
3. Moore, D.E. (1998) Mechanisms of photosensitization by phototoxic drugs. *Mutat Res*, **422**, 165–173.
4. Moore, D.E. (2002) Drug-induced cutaneous photosensitivity: incidence, mechanism, prevention and management. *Drug Saf*, **25**, 345–372.
5. Epstein, J.H. (1999) Phototoxicity and photoallergy. *Semin Cutan Med Surg*, **18**, 274–284.
6. Breathnach, S.M., Hintner, H. (1992) Types of clinical reaction. In: Adverse drug reactions and the skin. Oxford: Blackwell Scientific, pp 41–133.
7. Raviglione, M.C., Pablos-Méndez, A., Battan, R. (1990) Clinical features and management of severe dermatological reactions to drugs. *Drug Saf*, **5**, 39–64.
8. Bjellerup, M., Ljunggrenm, B. (1987) Double blind cross-over studies on phototoxicity to three tetracycline derivatives in human volunteers. *Photodermatology*, **4**, 281–287.
9. Ljunggren, M., Bjellerup, M., Moller, N. (1983) Experimental studies on the mechanism of benoxaprofen photoreactions. *Arch Dermatol Res*, **275**, 318–323.
10. Epstein, S. (1968) Chlorpromazine photosensitivity: phototoxic and photoallergic reactions. *Arch Dermatol*, **98**, 354–363.
11. Fitzpatrick, J.E. (1992) New histopathologic findings in drug eruptions. *Dermatol Clin*, **10**, 19–36.
12. Ferguson, J., Johnson, B.E. (1989) Retinoid associated phototoxicity and photosensitivity. *Pharmacol Ther*, **40**, 123–135.
13. Wintroub, B., Stern, R. (1985) Cutaneous drug reactions: pathogenesis and clinical classification. *J Am Acad Dermatol*, **13**, 167–179.
14. Smith, S.Z., Epstein, J.H. (1977) Photocontact dermatitis to halogenated salicylanilides and related compounds. *Arch Dermatol*, **113**, 1372–1374.
15. Raugi, G.J., Storrs, J., Larsen, W.G. (1979) Photoallergic contact dermatitis to men's perfumes. *Contact Derm*, **5**, 251–260.
16. Wojnarowska, F., Calnan, C.D. (1986) Contact and photocontact allergy to musk ambrette. *Br J Dermatol*, **114**, 667–675.
17. Ljunggren, B., Bjellerup, M. (1986) Systemic drug photosensitivity *Photodermatology*, **3**, 26–35.
18. Arata, J., Horio, T., Soejima, R. et al (1998) Photosensitivity reactions caused by lomefloxacin hydrochloride: a multicenter survey. *Antimicrob Agents Chemother*, **42**, 3141–3145.
19. Oliveira, H.S., Gonealo, M., Figueiredo, A.C. (2000) Photosensitivity to lomefloxacin. A clinical and photobiological study. *Photodermatol Photoimmunol Photomed*, **16**, 116–120.
20. Young, C.K., Prendiville, J., Peacock, D.L. et al (2000) An unusual presentation of doxycycline-induced photosensitivity. *Pediatrics*, **106**, E13.
21. Lane-Brown, M.M. (2000) Photosensitivity associated with herbal preparations of St John's wort (hypericum perforatum). *Med J Aust*, **172**, 302.
22. Bagheri, H., Lhiaubet, V., Montastruc, J.L. et al (2000) Photosensitivity to ketoprofen: mechanisms and pharmacoepidemiological data. *Drug Saf*, **22**, 339–349.
23. Vousden, M., Ferguson, J., Richards, J. et al (1999) Evaluation of phototoxic potential of gemifloxacin in healthy volunteers compared with ciprofloxacin. *Chemotherapy*, **45**, 512–520.
24. Motten, A.G., Martínez, L.J., Holt, N. et al (1999) Photophysical studies on antimalarial drugs. *Photochem Photobiol*, **69**, 282–287.
25. Wolfsen, H.C., Ng, C.S. (2002) Cutaneous consequences of photodynamic therapy. *Cutis*, **69**, 140–142.
26. Ferguson, J., Dawe, R. (1997) Phototoxicity in quinolones: comparison of ciprofloxacin and grepafloxacin. *J Antimicrob Chemother*, **40** (Suppl. A), 93–98.
27. Bosca, F., Miranda, M.A. (1998) Photosensitizing drugs containing benzophenone chromophore. *J Photochem Photobiol B*, **43**, 1–26.
28. McNeely, W., Goa, K.L. (1998) 5-Methoxypsoralen. A review of its effects in psoriasis and vitiligo. *Drugs*, **56**, 667–690.
29. Vassileva, S.G., Mateev, G., Parish, L.C. (1998) Antimicrobial photosensitive reactions. *Arch Intern Med*, **158**, 1993–2000.
30. Baron, R., Juhlin, L. (1987) Drug induced photo-onycholysis. *J Am Acad Dermatol*, **17**, 1012–1016.
31. Proby, C.M., du Peloux Menagé, H., McGregor, J.M. et al (1993) p53 immunoreactivity in cutaneous PUVA tumors is similar to that in other non-melanoma skin neoplasms. *J Cutan Pathol*, **20**, 435–441.
32. Stern, R.B., Laird, N. (1994) The carcinogenic risk of treatments for severe psoriasis. *Cancer*, **73**, 2759–2764.
33. Stern, R.S., Nichols, K.T., Vakeva, L.H. (1997) Malignant melanoma in patients treated with methoxsalen (psoralen) and ultraviolet A radiation (PUVA). *N Engl J Med*, **336**, 1041–1045.
34. Wagner, A.M., Wu, J.J., Hansen, R.C. et al (2002) Bullous phytophotodermatitis associated with high natural concentrations of furanocoumarins in limes. *Am J Contact Dermat*, **13**, 10–14.
35. Mantle, D., Gok, M.A., Lennard, T.W. (2001) Adverse and beneficial effects of plant extracts on skin and skin disorders. *Adverse Drug React Toxicol Rev*, **20**, 89–103.
36. Bowers, A.G. (1999) Phytophotodermatitis. *Am J Contact Dermat*, **10**, 89–93.
37. Crowson, A.N., Magro, C.M. (1999) Recent advances in the pathology of cutaneous drug eruptions. *Dermatol Clin*, **17**, 537–560.

Anticonvulsant hypersensitivity syndrome

Adverse drug reactions to phenytoin – which include erythematous maculopapular lesions, erythroderma, acneiform lesions, hypo- and hyperpigmentation, vasculitis, erythema multiforme and toxic epidermal necrolysis – affect up to 19% of patients taking this drug.[1-6] Pseudolymphomatous drug reactions may also occur and these are discussed on page 652.

A potentially fatal hypersensitivity syndrome develops in approximately 1 in 3000 patients receiving phenytoin.[5,6] This is defined by a triad of pyrexia, exanthematous skin rash and evidence of systemic involvement.[6] Administration of other antiepileptics including phenobarbital, carbamazepine, primidone and lamotrigine may result in an identical condition.[7-10] It can also be caused by a variety of additional medications including allopurinol, azathioprine, dapsone, minocycline, sulfonamides and terbinafine.[11-15]

The syndrome has been predominantly described in black patients. There is no sex predilection.[4] Children may be affected.[16-18] Clinical features include pyrexia, a maculopapular or erythrodermatous eruption, facial or periorbital edema, strawberry tongue, tender lymphadenopathy, myositis and hepatitis associated with leukocytosis and eosinophilia (*Figs 13.20, 13.21*).[4,5] Less often the cutaneous manifestations include localized or generalized follicular pustules (toxic pustuloderma), erythema multiforme and toxic epidermal necrolysis.[4,6,19,20] In patients with the pustular variant, lesions present on the scalp before becoming

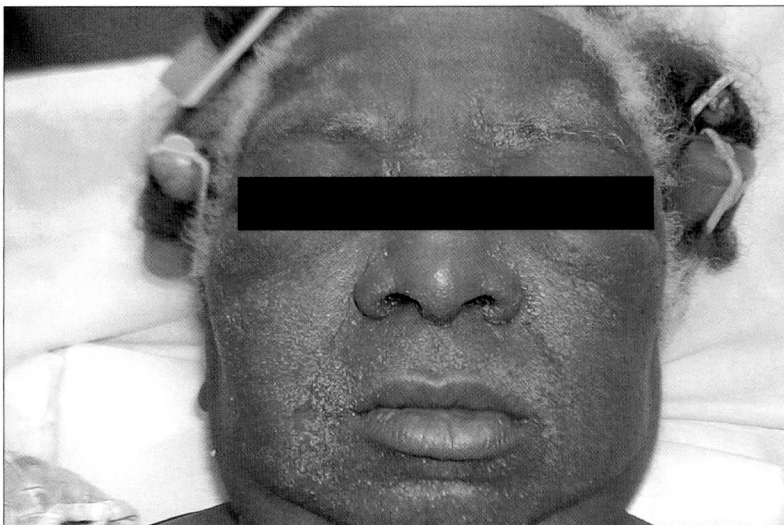

Fig. 13.20
Anticonvulsant hypersensitivity syndrome: there is striking facial edema with periorbital accentuation. By courtesy of C.C. Kim, MD, Department of Dermatology, Harvard Medical School, Boston, USA.

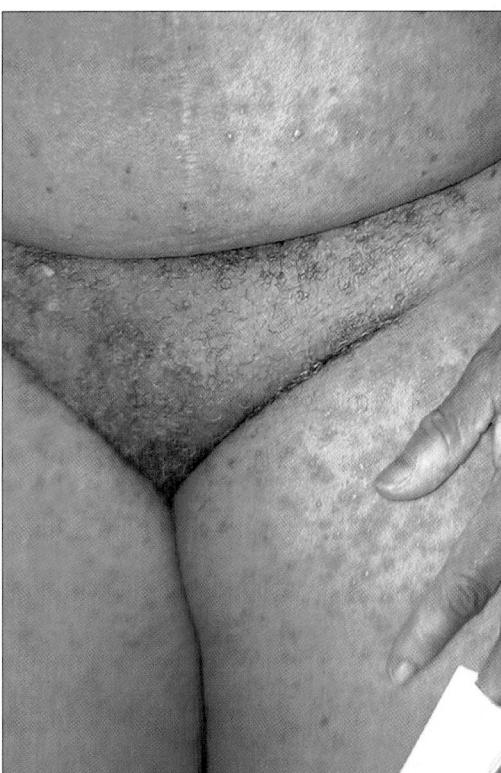

Fig. 13.21
Anticonvulsant hypersensitivity syndrome: there is a maculopapular eruption and pustules are present. By courtesy of C.C. Kim, MD, Department of Dermatology, Harvard Medical School, Boston, USA.

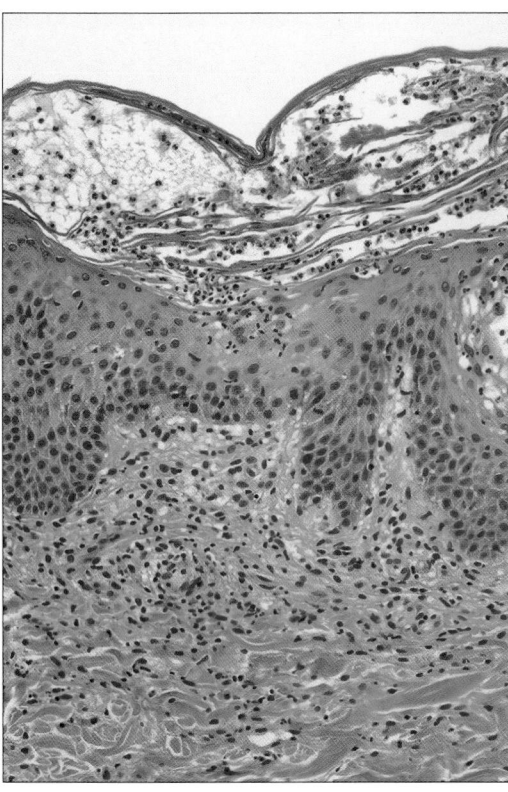

Fig. 13.22
Anticonvulsant hypersensitivity syndrome: this example shows a subcorneal pustule.

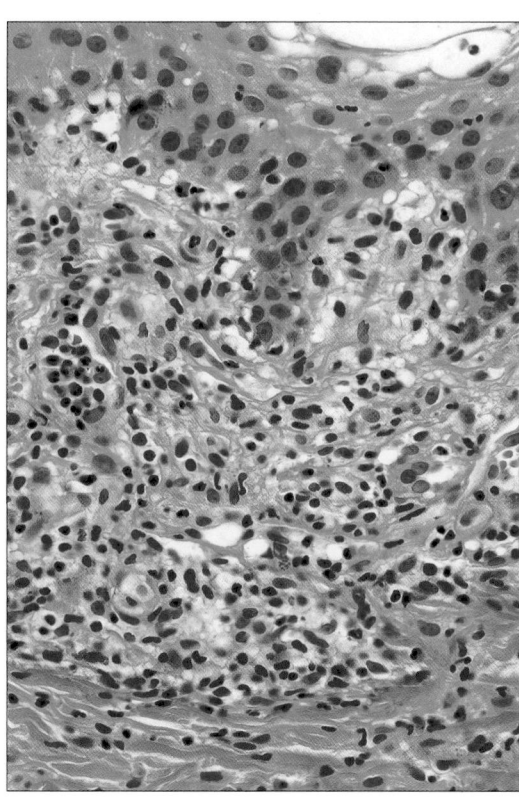

Fig. 13.23
Anticonvulsant hypersensitivity syndrome: the underlying dermis shows a superficial dermal perivascular lymphiohistiocytic infiltrate with scattered eosinophils.

generalized.[7,20,21] Conjunctivitis and/or pharyngitis may also be present.[2] Renal, pulmonary (interstitial pneumonitis) and hematological (atypical lymphocytosis) involvement sometimes occur.[5] The prognosis of this syndrome is variable.[22,23] The majority of patients recover but in those with hepatitis, the mortality is of the order of 20%.[5,24]

Pathogenesis and histological features

The precise etiology of this syndrome is uncertain but it is thought to result from an inability to detoxify arene oxide anticonvulsant metabolites due to absence, possibly genetically determined, of specific hydrolases.[18,24] Recently, the condition has (at least in some cases) been associated with reactivation of human herpesvirus 6 and cytomegalovirus.[25–28]

The histological features of the exanthem vary from spongiotic dermatitis to those of erythema multiforme or toxic epidermal necrolysis. Pustular lesions are characterized by a subcorneal pustule associated with follicular infundibular dilatation (*Figs 13.22, 13.23*).[7]

References

1. Herbert, A.A., Ralston, J.P. (2001) Cutaneous reactions to anticonvulsant medications. *J Clin Psychiatry*, **62** (Suppl. 14), 22–26.
2. Vittorio, C., Muglia, J. (1995) Anticonvulsant hypersensitivity syndrome. *Arch Intern Med*, **155**, 2285–2290.
3. Flowers, F.P., Araujo, O.E., Hamm, K.A. (1987) Phenytoin hypersensitivity syndrome: clinical communications. *Emerg Med*, **5**, 103–108.
4. Silverman, A.K., Fairley, J., Wong, R.C. (1988) Cutaneous and immunologic reactions to phenytoin. *J Am Acad Dermatol*, **18**, 721–741.
5. Conger, L.A., Grabski, W.J. (1996) Dilantin hypersensitivity reaction. *Cutis*, **57**, 223–226.

6. Schlienger, R.G., Shear, N.H. (1998) Antiepileptic drug hypersensitivity syndrome. *Epilepsia*, **39** (Suppl. 7), S3–S7.
7. Kleier, R.S., Breneman, D.L., Boiko, S. (1991) Generalized pustulation as a manifestation of the anticonvulsant hypersensitivity syndrome. *Arch Dermatol*, **127**, 1361–1364.
8. Shear, N.H., Spielberg, S.P. (1998) Anticonvulsant hypersensitivity syndrome: in vitro assessment of risk. *J Clin Invest*, **82**, 1826–1832.
9. Handfield-Jones, S.E., Jenkins, R.E., Whitaker, S.J. et al (1993) The anticonvulsant hypersensitivity syndrome. *Br J Dermatol*, **129**, 175–177.
10. Savich, R.D., Traisman, H.S. (1986) Phenobarbital hypersensitivity reaction. *Ill Med J Orig Commun*, **169**, 232–234.
11. Arellano, F., Sacristán, J.A. (1993) Allopurinol hypersensitivity syndrome: a review. *Ann Pharmacother*, **19**, 337–343.
12. Knowles, S.R., Gupta, A.K., Shear, N.H. et al (1995) Azathioprine hypersensitivity-like reactions – a case report and review of the literature. *Clin Exp Dermatol*, **20**, 353–356.
13. Prussick, R., Shear, N.H. (1996) Dapsone hypersensitivity syndrome. *J Am Acad Dermatol*, **35**, 346–349.
14. Knowles, S.R., Shapiro, L., Shear, N.H. (1996) Serious adverse drug reactions induced by minocycline. Report of 13 patients and review of the literature. *Arch Dermatol*, **132**, 934–939.
15. Gupta, A.K., Kopstein, J.B., Shear, N.H. (1997) Hypersensitivity reaction to terbinafine. *J Am Acad Dermatol*, **36**, 1018–1019.
16. Bessmertny, O., Hatton, R.C., González-Peralta, R.P. (2001) Antiepileptic hypersensitivity syndrome in children. *Ann Pharmacother*, **35**, 533–538.
17. Kaur, S., Sarkar, R., Thami, G.P. et al (2002) Anticonvulsant hypersensitivity syndrome. *Pediatr Dermatol*, **19**, 142–145.
18. Verrotti, A., Trotta, D., Salladini, C. et al (2002) Anticonvulsant hypersensitivity syndrome in children: incidence, prevention and management. *CNS Drugs*, **16**, 197–205.
19. Del Rosso, J.Q. (2002) Skin manifestations of drug reactions. *Curr Allergy Asthma Rep*, **2**, 282–287.
20. Staughton, R.C., Harper, J.I., Rowland-Payne, C.M.E. et al (1984) Toxic pustuloderma: a new entity? *J R Soc Med*, **77** (Suppl.), 6–8.
21. Stanley, J., Fallon-Pellicci, V. (1978) Phenytoin hypersensitivity reaction. *Arch Dermatol*, **114**, 1350–1353.
22. Gungor, E., Alli, N., Comoglu, S. et al (2001) Phenytoin hypersensitivity syndrome. *Neurol Sci*, **22**, 261–265.
23. Bessmertny, O., Pham, T. (2002) Antiepileptic hypersensitivity syndrome: clinicians beware and be aware. *Curr Allergy Asthma Rep*, **2**, 34–39.
24. Romero Maldonado, N., Sendra Tello, J., Rabosa García-Baquero, E. et al (2002) Anticonvulsant hypersensitivity syndrome with fatal outcome. *Eur J Dermatol*, **12**, 503–505.
25. Descamps, V., Bouscarat, F., Laglenne, S. et al (1997) Human herpesvirus 6 infection associated with anticonvulsant hypersensitivity syndrome and reactive hemophagocytic syndrome. *Br J Dermatol*, **137**, 605–608.
26. Conilleau, V., Dompmartin, A., Verneuil, L. et al (1999) Hypersensitivity syndrome due to 2 anticonvulsant drugs. *Contact Dermatitis*, **41**, 141–144.
27. Descamps, V., Valance, A., Edlinger, C. et al (2001) Association of human herpesvirus 6 infection with drug reaction with eosinophilia and systemic symptoms. *Arch Dermatol*, **123**, 301–304.
28. Aihara, M., Sugita, Y., Takahashi, S. et al (2001) Anticonvulsant hypersensitivity syndrome associated with reactivation of cytomegalovirus. *Br J Dermatol*, **144**, 1231–1234.

Lichenoid drug reactions

Clinical features

Lichenoid drug reactions are clinically similar to lichen planus although lesions are often larger, Wickham's striae are usually not apparent and mucosal involvement is commonly absent.[1–4] In contrast to typical lichen planus, where lesions are particularly found on the flexural surfaces of the forearms, the legs and the genitalia, in lichenoid drug reactions the trunk and extremities are more often affected (*Figs 13.24–13.26*).[4,5] The eruption may sometimes be photodistributed and predominantly affect the hands and forearms although other sun-exposed sites can also be involved.[4,6,7] The latent period between starting the drug and the onset of the eruption is often long, being measured in terms of months or even years rather than the 1 or 2 weeks as is the case in most drug reactions.[4]

Atypical features including eczematous and psoriasiform lesions are sometimes seen and bullous or ulcerative variants are occasionally encountered.[3,4,8] Postinflammatory hyperpigmentation may be very marked and is often persistent. Scarring alopecia is sometimes present and some patients may develop anhidrosis.[4]

Although the list of drugs capable of causing a lichenoid reaction is long, those that are particularly implicated include gold, antimalarials such as quinine and quinidine, penicillamine, captopril, various beta-blockers (e.g. propranolol), lithium, the thiazide diuretics furosemide (frusemide) and spironolactone, and ethambutol.[4,7–19]

Contact with *p*-phenylenediamine by workers in the photographic color developing process may also result in a cutaneous lichenoid reaction. This is of two types:
- Continuous exposure to small amounts results in the appearance of typical lichen planus.
- If exposed to a single large dose, the features are those of a lichenoid contact dermatitis.[4]

Other causes of a contact lichenoid eruption include dental restorative materials, musk ambrette, nickel and gold.[4]

Captopril and cinnarizine may cause lichen planus pemphigoides-like eruptions (see bullous drug reactions below).[20,21]

Histological features

The histological features are frequently indistinguishable from typical lichen planus although focal parakeratosis and spongiosis are sometimes present and interface change may be patchy (*Figs 13.27–13.29*). The epidermis is often thinner and hypergranulosis less marked.[15] Cytoid bodies may be found in the upper granular cell layer or even in the stratum corneum.[5,7] Sometimes eosinophils and occasionally plasma cells are found in the dermal infiltrate.[5] Focal interruption of the granular cell layer, exocytosis of lymphoid cells into the upper epidermis and a perivascular infiltrate in the deeper dermis are said to be additional helpful diagnostic pointers.[7] Photodistributed lichenoid drug reactions are said to more closely resemble idiopathic lichen planus than non-photodistributed variants.[5]

References

1. Seghal, V.N., Jain, S., Bhattacharya, S.N. (1993) Cutaneous drug reactions. *J Eur Acad Dermatol Venereol*, 2, 281–295.
2. Rubianes, E.L., Martin, R.F., Pico, M. et al (1990) Cutaneous drug reactions. *Bol Assoc Med P Rico*, 82, 434–443.
3. Almeyda, J., Levantine, A. (1971) Drug reactions XVI. Lichenoid drug reactions. *Br J Dermatol*, 85, 604–607.
4. Halevy, S., Shai, A. (1993) Lichenoid drug eruptions. *J Am Acad Dermatol*, 29, 249–255.
5. West, A.J., Berger, T.G., Leboit, P.E. (1990) A comparative histopathologic study of photodistributed and non-photodistributed lichenoid drug reactions. *J Am Acad Dermatol*, 23, 689–693.
6. Bonnetblanc, J.M., Bernard, P., Catazano, G. et al (1987) Eruptions lichénoïdes photoinduites aux quinidiniques. *Ann Dermatol Venereol*, 114, 957–961.

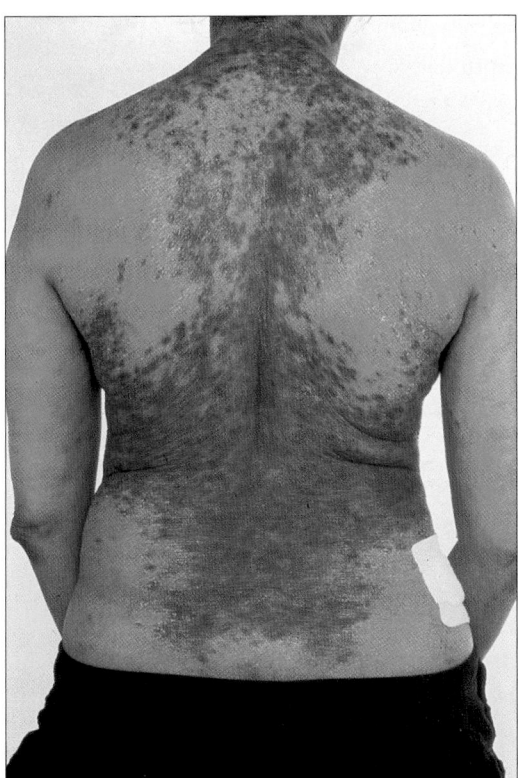

Fig. 13.24
Lichenoid drug reaction: in this patient the eruption followed treatment with gold. Very extensive lesions are seen on the trunk, a characteristic site. By courtesy of the Institute of Dermatology, London, UK.

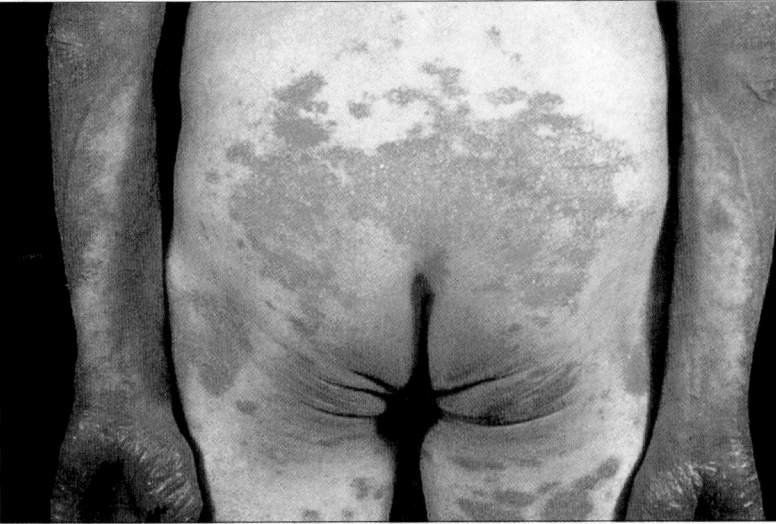

Fig. 13.25
Lichenoid drug reaction: these lesions followed treatment with a beta-blocker. By courtesy of the Institute of Dermatology, London, UK.

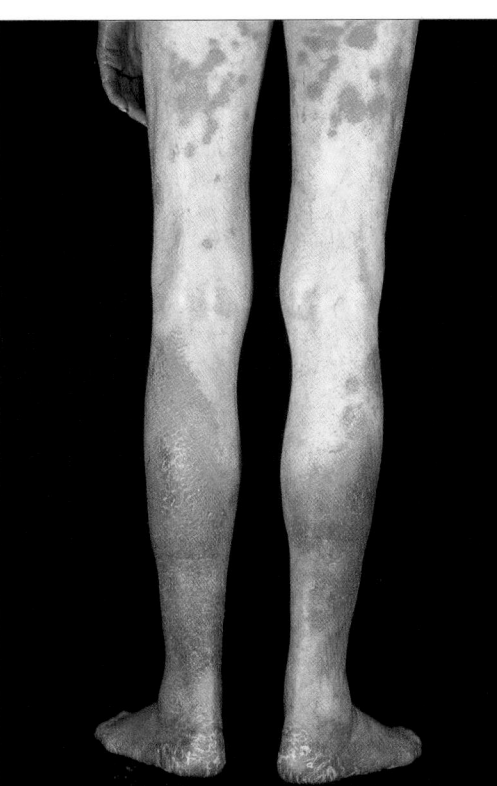

Fig. 13.26
Lichenoid drug reaction: same patient as shown in *Fig. 13.25*. By courtesy of the Institute of Dermatology, London, UK.

7. Van den Hante, J., Antoine, J.L., Lapachelle, J.M. (1989) Histopathological discriminant criteria between lichenoid drug eruption and idiopathic lichen planus: retrospective study of selected samples. *Dermatologica*, **179**, 10–13.
8. Massa, M.C., Jason, S.M., Gradini, R. et al (1991) Lichenoid drug eruption secondary to propranolol. *Cutis*, **48**, 41–43.
9. Hofman, C., Burg, G., Jung, C. (1986) Cutaneous side-effects of gold therapy: clinical and histologic results. *J Rheumatol*, **45**, 100–106.
10. Glenert, U. (1984) Drug stomatitis due to gold therapy. *Oral Surg Oral Med Oral Pathol*, **58**, 52–56.
11. Lazarova, A.Z., Tsankov, N.K., Stoimenov, A.P. (1992) Lichenoide eruptionen nach goldtherapie. Bericht uber zwei falle. *Hautarzt*, **43**, 514–516.
12. Bauer, F. (1981) Quinacrine hydrochloride drug eruption (tropical lichenoid dermatitis.) *J Am Acad Dermatol*, **4**, 239–248.
13. Maltz, B.L., Becker, L.E. (1980) Quinidine induced lichen planus. *Int J Dermatol*, **19**, 96–97.
14. Reinhardt, L.A., Wilkin, J.K., Kirkendall, W.M. (1983) Lichenoid drug reaction produced by captopril. *Cutis*, **31**, 98–99.
15. Wong, S.S., Long, C.C., Holt, P.J.A. (1992) Lichenoid eruption induced by low dose captopril. *Acta Derm Venereol*, **72**, 358–359.
16. Phillips, W.G., Vaughan-Jones, S., Jenkins, R., Breathnach, S.M. (1994) Captopril-induced lichenoid eruption. *Clin Exp Dermatol*, **19**, 317–320.
17. Van Hecke, E., Kint, A., Temmerman, L. (1981) A lichenoid drug reaction induced by penicillamine. *Arch Dermatol*, **117**, 676–677.
18. Halevy, S., Grunwald, M.H., Feuerman, E.J. et al (1986) Lichenoid eruption to hydrothiazide. Diagnostic aid of macrophage migration inhibition factor (MIF) test. *Ann Allergy*, **56**, 402–405.
19. Grossman, M.E., Warren, K., Mady, A. et al (1995) Lichenoid eruption associated with ethambutol. *J Am Acad Dermatol*, **33**, 675–676.
20. Flageul, B., Foldes, C., Wallach, D. et al (1986) Captopril-induced lichen planus pemphigoides with pemphigus-like features: a case report. *Dermatologica*, **173**, 248–255.
21. Miyagawa, S., Ohi, H., Muramatsu, T. et al (1985) Lichen planus pemphigoides-like lesions induced by cinnarizine. *Br J Dermatol*, **112**, 607–613.

Fixed drug eruptions

Clinical features

Fixed drug eruptions present as one or more circumscribed erythematous to violaceous or brown plaques that show a predilection for the extremities including the hands, feet and external genitalia (*Figs 13.30, 13.31*).[1–8] The mucous membranes may also be affected, either alone or in association with cutaneous manifestations.[3] Lesions – which may be pruritic or present with a burning sensation – typically recur at the same site on rechallenge with the offending drug. They usually develop within 30 minutes to 8 hours after taking the drug.[3] Vesiculation and blistering are common. Resolution is typically marked by postinflammatory hyperpigmentation varying from brown to brown–violet or even black.[6]

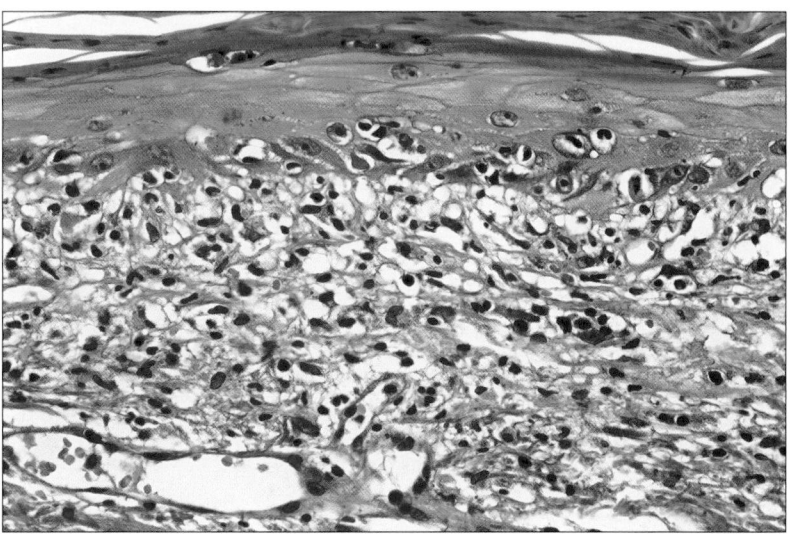

Fig. 13.29
Lichenoid drug reaction: close-up view of *Fig. 13.27*. Note the pigmentary incontinence.

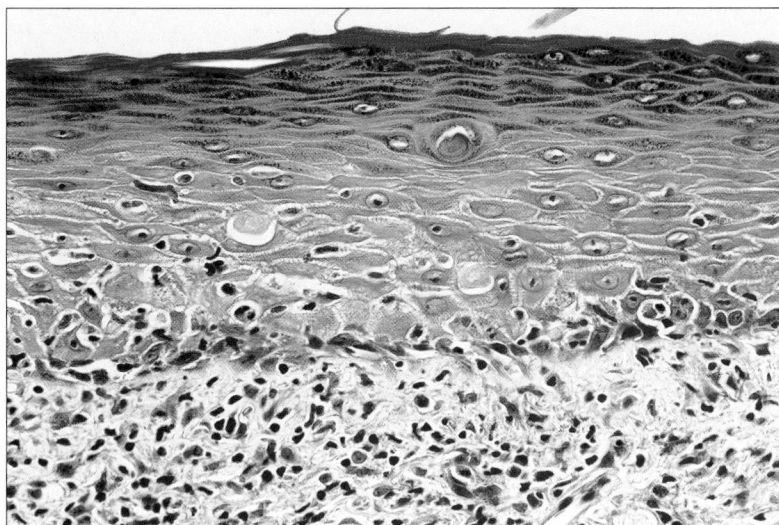

Fig. 13.27
Lichenoid drug reaction: there is hyperkeratosis, hypergranulosis and dyskeratosis with mild interface change. Note also the presence of slight spongiosis, lymphocytic exocytosis and occasional eosinophils.

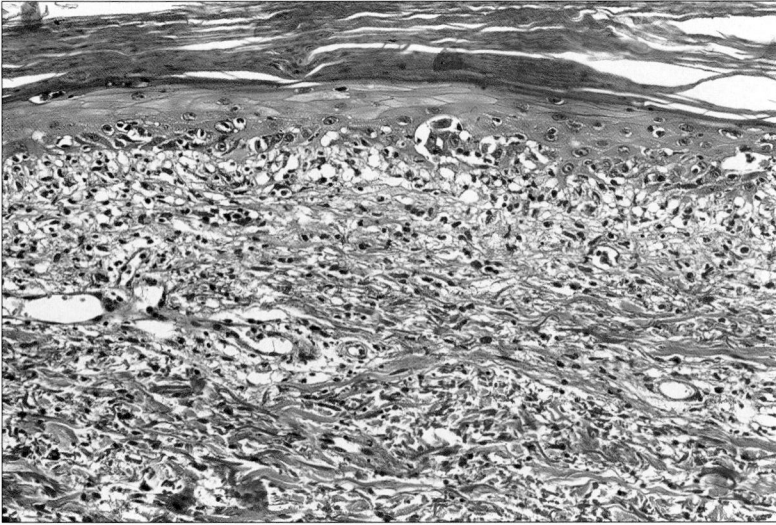

Fig 13.28
Lichenoid drug reaction: more extensive lesion due to treatment with propranolol. There is parakeratosis, widespread interface change and conspicuous apoptosis.

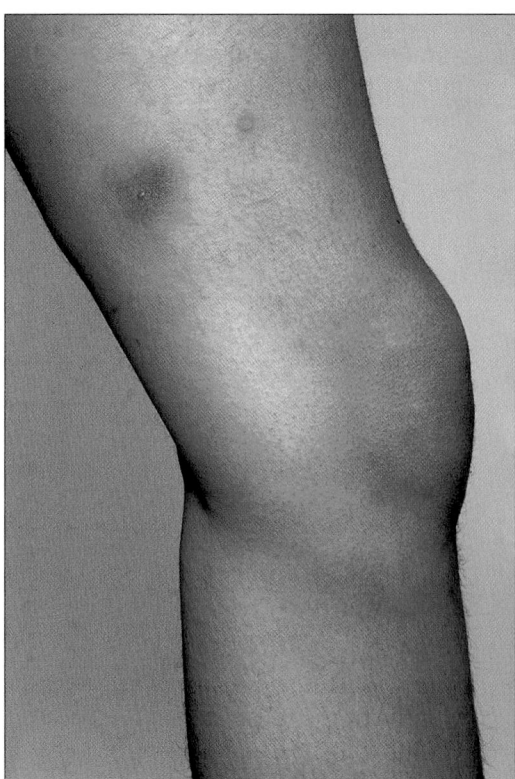

Fig. 13.30
Fixed drug eruption: typical localized brown plaque with a small central blister. By courtesy of the Institute of Dermatology, London, UK.

Occasionally the eruption is generalized and resembles toxic epidermal necrolysis.[9] Although the number of drugs that are capable of eliciting a fixed reaction is very large, those that are said to be more commonly incriminated include barbiturates, phenylbutazone, ibuprofen, acetyl salicylic acid, sulfonamides, trimethoprim–sulfamethoxazole, tetracyclines, dapsone, phenolphthalein and quinine.[2,3,6]

Pathogenesis and histological features

Fixed drug eruption is quite unique owing to the precise localization of the eruption and its recurrence at the same site on rechallenge. To understand this process initial research was directed towards identifying the site of cutaneous memory. Autotransplantation experiments in which normal skin was grafted to a previously affected site and vice versa, followed by rechallenge with the causative drug produced conflicting results. Some workers found that following challenge, grafted normal skin was unaffected, whereas transplanted previously affected skin developed erythema and became symptomatic.[10] Others, however, experienced quite the opposite results.[11]

The results of immunofluorescence studies have been equally conflicting. Thus, while some authors have documented in vivo bound immunoglobulin and complement in the intercellular region of the epidermis or at its basement membrane, the majority of investigations have been negative.[12,13]

It seems unlikely, therefore, that humoral immunity has a significant part to play in the pathogenesis of fixed drug eruption. Current research has been directed more towards understanding and eliciting the role of cellular immunity. On initial exposure, the drug appears to bind to the epidermal keratinocytes (thereby functioning as a hapten) following which it is presented by Langerhans' cells to lymphocytes either within the dermis or else in local lymph nodes. The result is the production of an effector CD8+ lymphocyte population, which on returning to the epidermis produces various cytokines including interferon-gamma (IFN-γ) and TNF-α which result in epidermal necrosis.[14,15] Keratinocyte death is believed to be mediated by both cytolytic pathways (e.g. perforin, granzyme A and granzyme B) and FAS-mediated apoptosis.[14,15]

Although the precise mechanism by which memory in fixed drug eruption is achieved is incompletely understood, there is now considerable evidence to suggest that an intraepidermal effector-memory CD8+ T-cell population residing in the epidermis after the initial drug reaction is of particular importance.[13–18] Such cells are defined

immunohistochemically by expression of CD45RA, CD11a and CD11b and absence of CD27, CD28 and CD62L.[18] It has been demonstrated that they remain in a state of activation (CD69+) in the unchallenged state and, following exposure to the drug, rapidly upregulate IFN-γ expression, soon followed by epidermal necrosis.[18]

Histologically, the acute fixed drug eruption is characterized by marked basal cell hydropic degeneration, with lymphocyte tagging along the epidermodermal junction and individual keratinocyte necrosis (*Figs 13.32, 13.33*).[19] Marked pigmentary incontinence is typical. In more advanced lesions subepidermal vesiculation may be a feature. An infiltrate of lymphocytes, histiocytes and neutrophil polymorphs is evident in the upper dermis. Eosinophils may sometimes be prominent (*Fig. 13.34*). In biopsies of late lesions, pigmentary incontinence may be the sole histological finding.

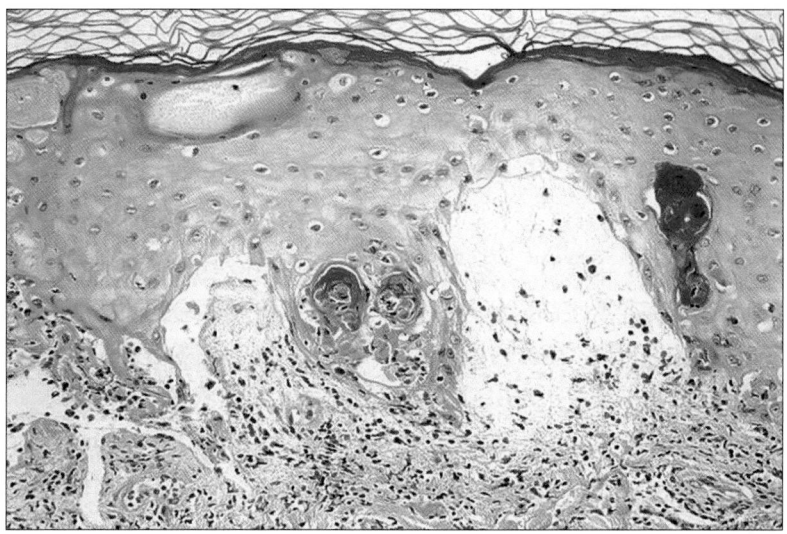

Fig. 13.32
Fixed drug eruption: in this example, in addition to apoptosis, there is subepidermal blistering.

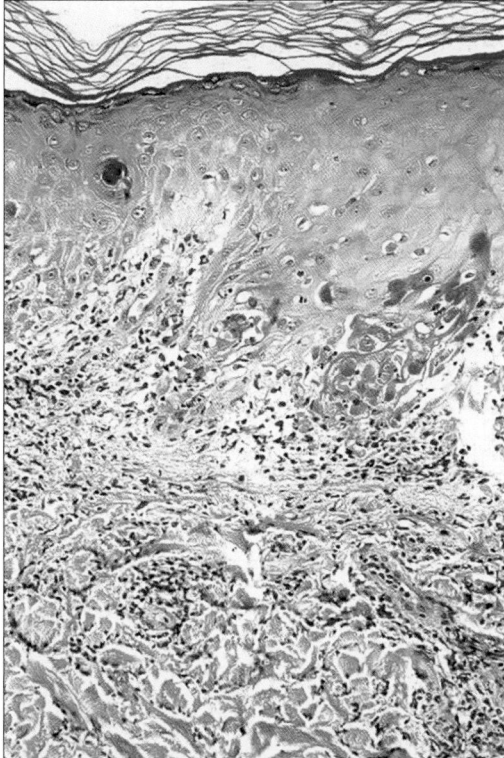

Fig. 13.33
Fixed drug eruption: edge of lesion shown in *Fig. 13.31*. Note the widespread apoptosis.

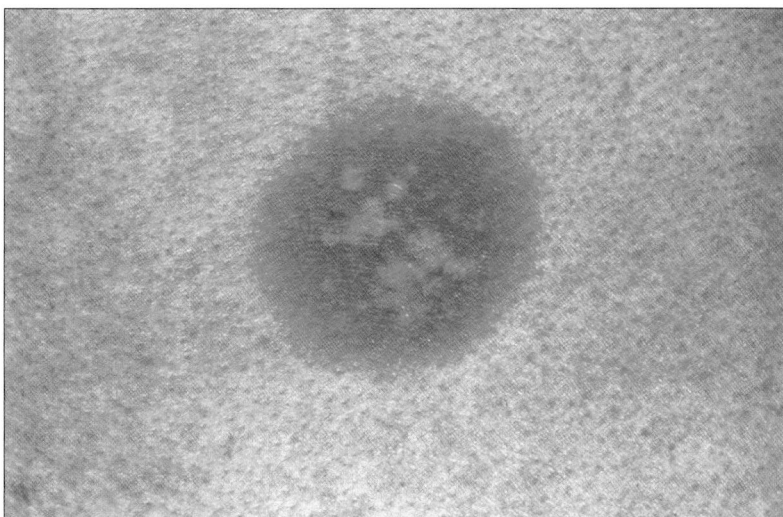

Fig. 13.31
Fixed drug eruption: early, sharply delineated erythematous lesion. By courtesy of the Institute of Dermatology, London, UK.

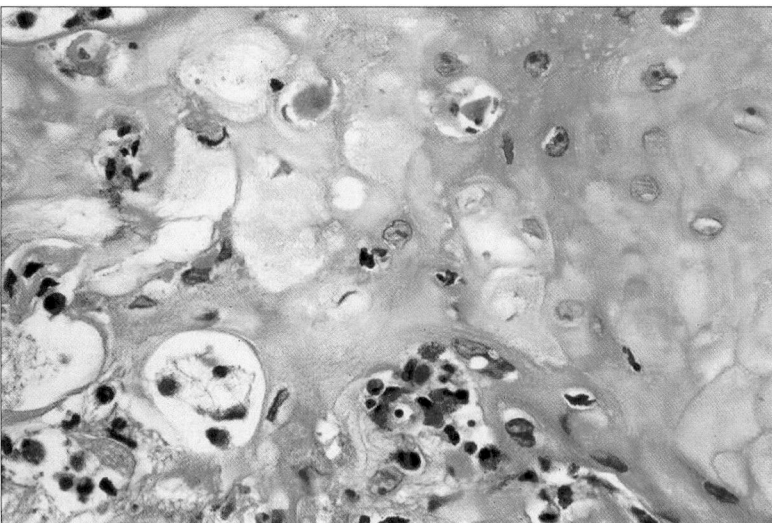

Fig. 13.34
Fixed drug eruption: high power view showing conspicuous eosinophils.

References

1. Wintroub, B., Stern, R. (1985) Cutaneous drug reactions: pathogenesis and clinical classification. *J Am Acad Dermatol*, **13**, 167–179.
2. Kauppinen, K., Kariniemi, A.-L. (1998) Clinical manifestations and histological characteristics. In: Kauppinen, K., Alanko, K., Hannuksela, M., Maibach, H. (eds) Skin reactions to drugs. Boca Raton: CRC Press, pp 25–50.
3. Breathnach, S.M., Hintner, H. (1992) Types of clinical reaction. In: Adverse drug reactions and the skin. Oxford: Blackwell Scientific, pp 41–133.
4. Rubianes, E.L., Martín, R.F., Picó, M. et al (1990) Cutaneous drug reactions. *Bol Assoc Med P Rico*, **82**, 434–443.
5. Raviglione, M.C., Pablos-Mendez, A., Battan, R. (1990) Clinical features and management of severe dermatological reactions to drugs. *Drug Saf*, **5**, 39–64.
6. Sehgal, V.N., Gamgwani, O.P. (1987) Fixed drug eruption. Current concepts. *Int J Dermatol*, **26**, 67–74.
7. Gaffoor, P.M.A., George, W.M. (1990) Fixed drug eruptions occurring on the male genitalia. *Cutis*, **45**, 242–244.
8. Korkij, W., Soltani, K. (1984) Fixed drug eruption. A brief review. *Arch Dermatol*, **120**, 520–524.
9. Baird, B., De Willez, R. (1988) Widespread bullous fixed drug eruption mimicking toxic epidermal necrolysis. *Int J Dermatol*, **27**, 170–174.
10. Naegeli, O., de Quervain, F., Stalder, W. (1930) Nachweis des cellularen sitzes der allergie beim fixen antipyren exanthem. *Klin Wochenschr*, **9**, 924–928.
11. Wise, F., Sulzberger, M.B. (1933) Drug eruptions: fixed phenolphthalein eruptions. *Arch Dermatol Syph*, **27**, 549.
12. Shelley, W.B., Schlappner, O.L.A., Heiss, H.B. (1972) Demonstration of intercellular immunofluorescence and epidermal hysteresis in bullous fixed drug reaction due to phenolphthalein. *Br J Dermatol*, **86**, 118–125.
13. Hindsen, M., Christensen, O.B., Gruic, V. et al (1987) Fixed drug eruption: an immunohistochemical investigation of the acute and healing phase. *Br J Dermatol*, **116**, 3513–3560.
14. Smoller, B.R., Luster, A.D., Krane, J.F. et al (1991) Fixed drug eruptions: evidence for a cytokine-mediated process. *J Cutan Pathol*, **18**, 13–19.
15. Shiohara, T., Moriya, N. (1997) Epidermal T-cells: their functional role and disease relevance for dermatologists. *J Invest Dermatol*, **109**, 271–275.
16. Komatsu, T., Moriya, N., Shiohara, T. (1996) T cell receptor (TCR) repertoire and function of human epidermal T-cells: restricted TCR V α-V β genes are utilized by T cells residing in the lesional epidermis in fixed drug eruption. *Clin Exp Immunol*, **104**, 343–350.
17. Shiohara, T., Moriya, N., Nagashima, M. (1998) Review: the lichenoid tissue reaction. A new concept of the pathogenesis. *Int J Dermatol*, **27**, 365–374.
18. Mizukawa, Y., Yamakazi, Y., Teraki, Y. et al (2002) Direct evidence for interferon-γ production by effector-memory-type intraepidermal T cells residing at an effector site of immunopathology in fixed drug eruption. *Am J Pathol*, **161**, 1337–1347.
19. Crowson, A.N., Magro, C.M. (1999) Recent advances in the pathology of cutaneous drug eruptions. *Dermatol Clin*, **17**, 537–560.

Erythema multiforme and Stevens–Johnson syndrome

These conditions are discussed on pages 237 and 240.

Toxic epidermal necrolysis

This condition is discussed on page 240.

Drug-induced hyperpigmentation

Clinical features

Cutaneous hyperpigmentation is a relatively frequent complication of drug therapy and may result from increased melanin synthesis or else from deposition of the drug or its metabolite within the skin.[1–5] Heavy metals can also result in skin pigmentation.[4] Most often, however, it results from postinflammatory hyperpigmentation.[3]

Long-term treatment with minocycline – as for example in patients with severe acne or rosacea – may result in usually reversible (types I and II) cutaneous pigmentation.[6–13] Three clinical variants of cutaneous minocycline pigmentation are generally recognized (*Figs 13.35–13.37*):[14]

*   *Type I pigmentation* is characterized by blue–black macules localized to areas of scarring and inflammation (e.g. facial acne scars).
*   *Type II pigmentation* (the commonest variant) presents as blue–black, brown or slate-gray pigmentation on the shins, ankles and arms.
*   *Type III pigmentation* presents with generalized muddy-brown pigmentation which may be exacerbated on sunlight-exposed regions.

A fourth variant affecting the lips and possibly representing a fixed drug eruption has been described.[15]

Nail pigmentation most often presents as a persistent slate-gray coloration of the proximal nail bed.[14] Additional features include longitudinal melanonychia, diffuse nail pigmentation and photo-onycholysis.[14]

Minocycline also sometimes involves the teeth (causing a green–gray or blue–gray coloration) predominantly affecting the middle and occasionally the incisal thirds of the crown.[16] Lesions of the oral mucosa are rare although pigmentation has been described on the buccal mucosa, gingiva, tongue and lips.[17–21] The bones underlying the oral cavity (black bone disease) represent the single site most commonly affected by minocycline pigmentation.[22] This is best visualized by inspecting the maxillary and mandibular anterior alveolar mucosa.[14] The hard palate and lingual alveolar bone are also commonly affected.[14]

The conjunctiva, sclera, thyroid, aorta and endocardium may also be involved in minocycline pigmentation.[23–27]

Many other tetracyclines including methacycline and tetracycline hydrochloride have also been associated with cutaneous pigmentation.[28,29]

Amiodarone, which is used primarily in the treatment of cardiac arrhythmias, is associated with a phototoxic/photosensitivity reaction in up to 50% of patients.[30–36] In addition, cutaneous golden-brown to slate-gray or blue/violaceous pigmentation predominantly affecting the exposed surfaces including the face (particularly the cheeks and the forehead) and the backs of the hands may develop, especially in those patients

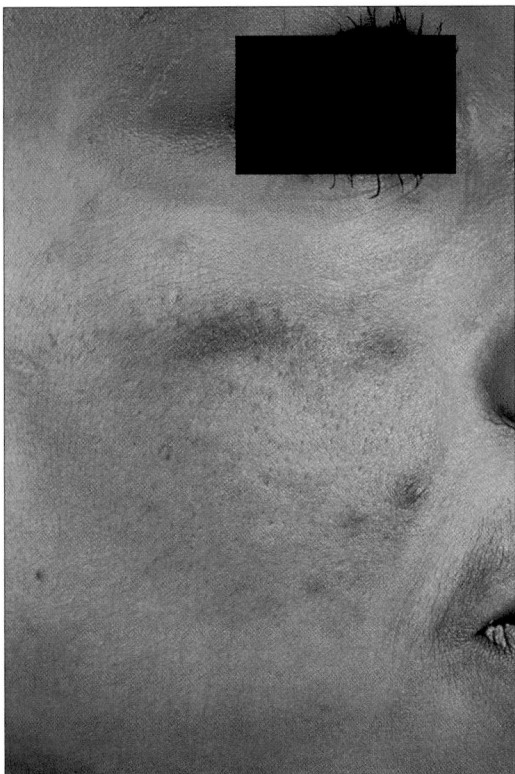

Fig. 13.35
Minocycline pigmentation: extensive lesions involving the cheek and periorbital region. By courtesy of the Institute of Dermatology, London, UK.

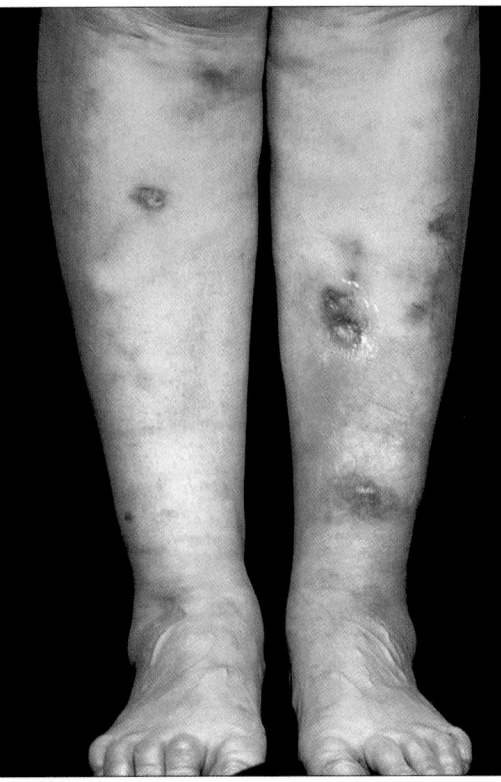

Fig. 13.36
Minocycline pigmentation: these blue–black lesions have developed in a patient with pyoderma gangrenosum. By courtesy of the Institute of Dermatology, London, UK.

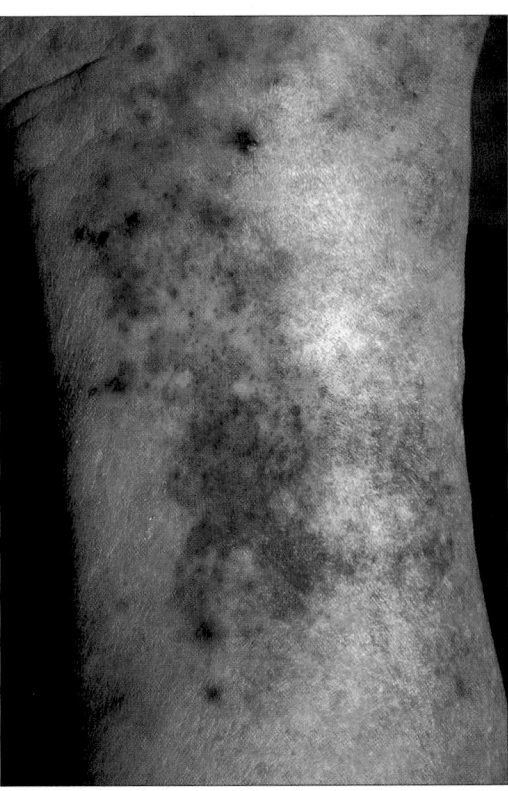

Fig. 13.37
Minocycline pigmentation; typical pigmentation affecting the shin. By courtesy of the Institute of Dermatology, London, UK.

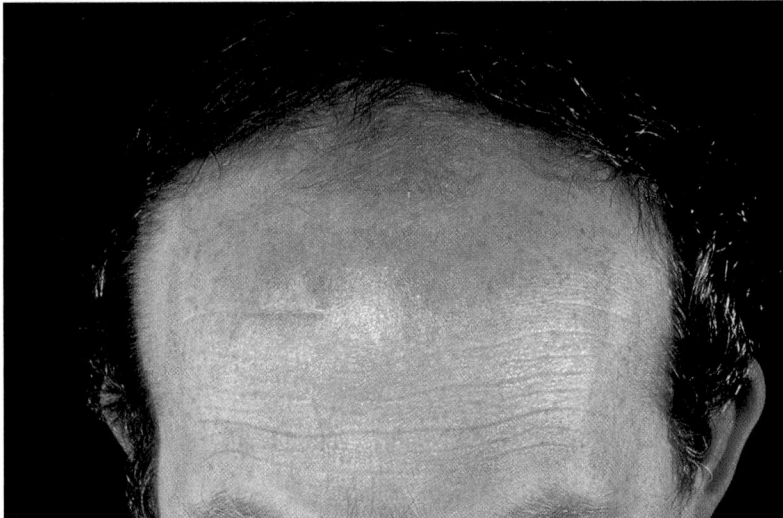

Fig. 13.38
Amiodarone pigmentation: note the slate-gray discoloration on the forehead, a characteristic site. By courtesy of the Institute of Dermatology, London, UK.

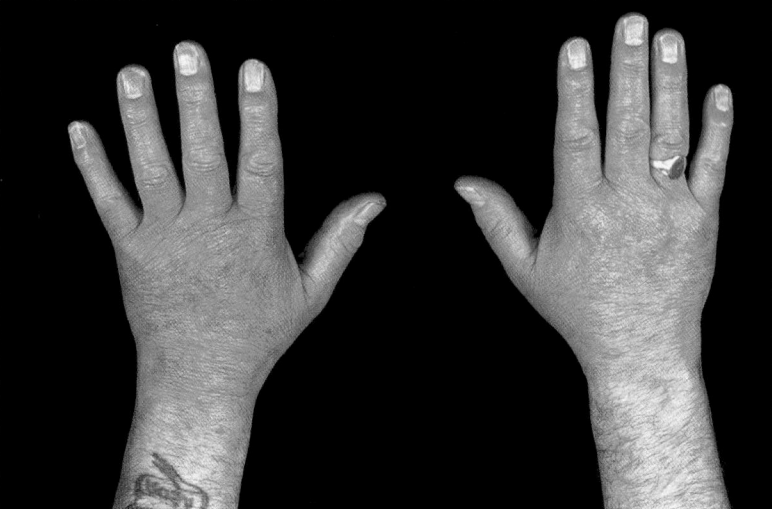

Fig. 13.39
Amiodarone pigmentation: sun-exposed skin is typically affected. By courtesy of the Institute of Dermatology, London, UK.

receiving high doses over a protracted period of time (*Figs 13.38, 13.39*).[30] Pigmentation is also sometimes seen in the sclera and cornea.[33]

Antimalarials also result in abnormal skin pigmentation.[37–40] Mepacrine most typically produces a yellow coloration although localized blue–black mucocutaneous lesions have also been described (*Figs 13.40, 13.41*).[40] Chloroquine and hydroxychloroquine may cause a yellow–brown to gray pigmentation.[2,37–39] Sun-exposed skin is predominantly affected.

In addition to causing photosensitivity and contact dermatitis, chlorpromazine therapy (particularly when protracted and in high doses) can result in cutaneous pigmentation, especially on sun-exposed skin.[2,41–44] The face, the backs of the hands and the neck are therefore most often affected. Patients may initially present with a golden-brown, tanned appearance while others develop a slate-gray, bluish or purple appearance. The cornea and lens of the eye may also sometimes be involved.[2]

Long-term treatment with imipramine may result in photodistributed hyperpigmentation affecting the face, neck, 'V' of chest, arms and hands (*Fig. 13.42*).[45,46] The coloration varies from golden-brown to blue-gray or slate-gray. The irises may also darken.

Photodistributed blue-gray pigmentation has been documented following treatment with desipramine.[47]

Heavy metals including gold, silver and mercury can all result in cutaneous pigmentation (see below).

Pathogenesis and histological features

The histological features of minocycline pigmentation are variable.[7,10,11,14] In types I and II variants, golden-brown to brown–black granules are found predominantly within macrophages distributed mainly around the vasculature and sweat gland coils (*Fig. 13.43*). The

pigment, which fluoresces yellow under ultraviolet light, stains positively with both Masson–Fontana and Perl's Prussian blue reactions in type II variants (*Figs 13.44, 13.45*).[11] The pigment is periodic acid–Schiff (PAS) negative. In contrast, in type I patients, the pigment only stains with Perl's reaction. It is believed to represent minocycline or its breakdown product chelated with hemosiderin, ferritin or iron.[7] Calcium, sulfur and chlorine are also present but melanin is absent.[11] Melanocytes and the epidermis show no increase in melanin pigmentation in types I and II variants. Type III hyperpigmentation, however, is characterized by an increase in epidermal basal cell melanin pigmentation (*Fig. 13.46*).[6] The Perl's stain is negative.

Histologically, amiodarone pigmentation is characterized by the presence of macrophages containing PAS-positive, yellow–brown lipofuscin-like granules predominantly located in a perivascular distribution (*Figs 13.47, 13.48*).[30] Melanin pigmentation of the epidermis is not increased; indeed its absence in involved skin has recently been documented.[36] By electron microscopy the granules are located within lysosomes.[31,35] Lamellar myelin bodies may also be

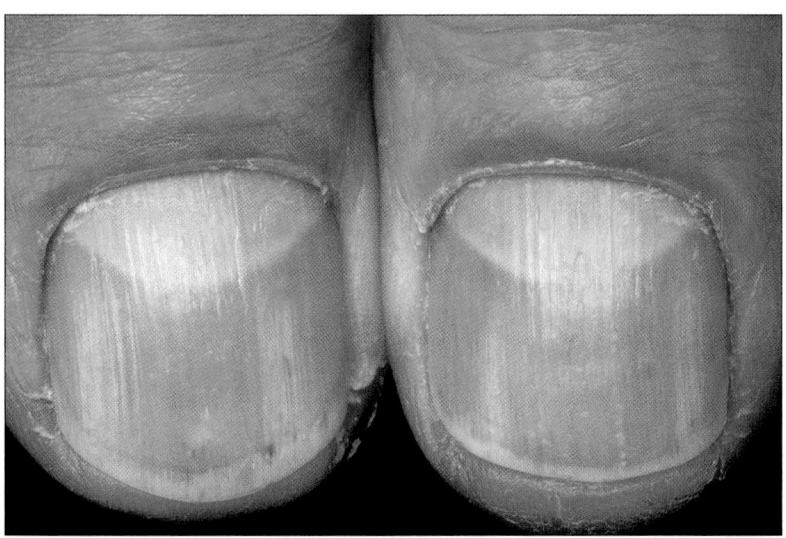

Fig. 13.40
Mepacrine pigmentation: a yellow discoloration is characteristic. By courtesy of the Institute of Dermatology, London, UK.

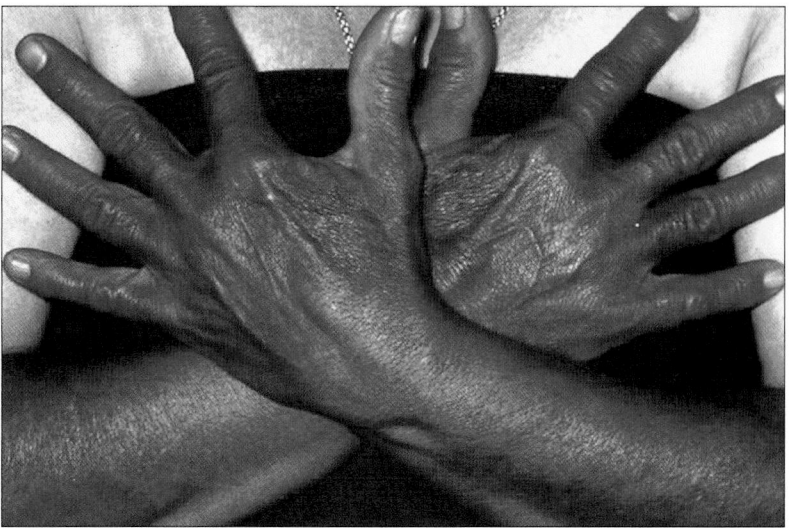

Fig. 13.42
Imipramine pigmentation: note the intense brown pigment of the hands and forearms in comparison with the chest. By courtesy of L. Cohen, MD, Cohen Dermatopathology, Massachusetts, USA.

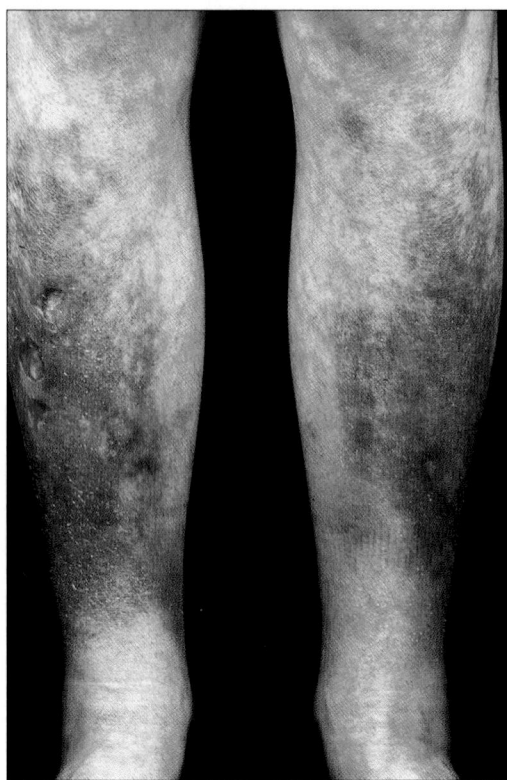

Fig. 13.41
Mepacrine pigmentation: in this patient the drug resulted in black lesions. By courtesy of the Institute of Dermatology, London, UK.

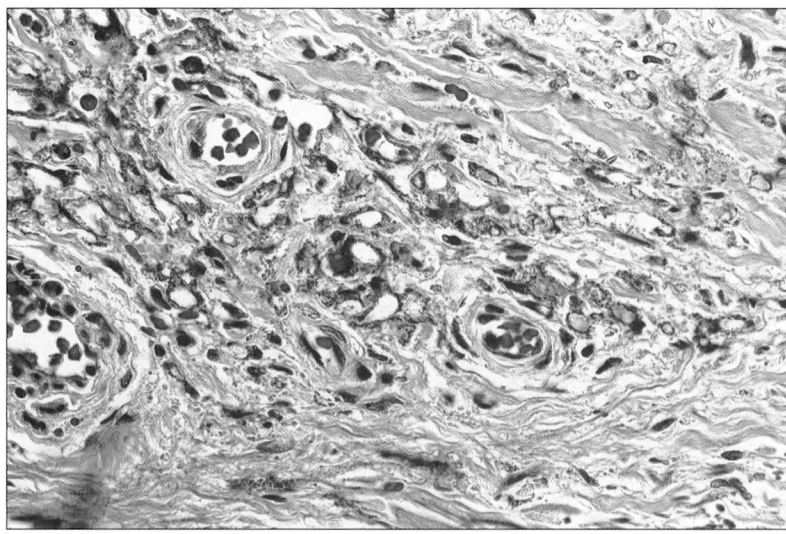

Fig. 13.43
Minocycline pigmentation: note the presence of perivascular granular brown pigment.

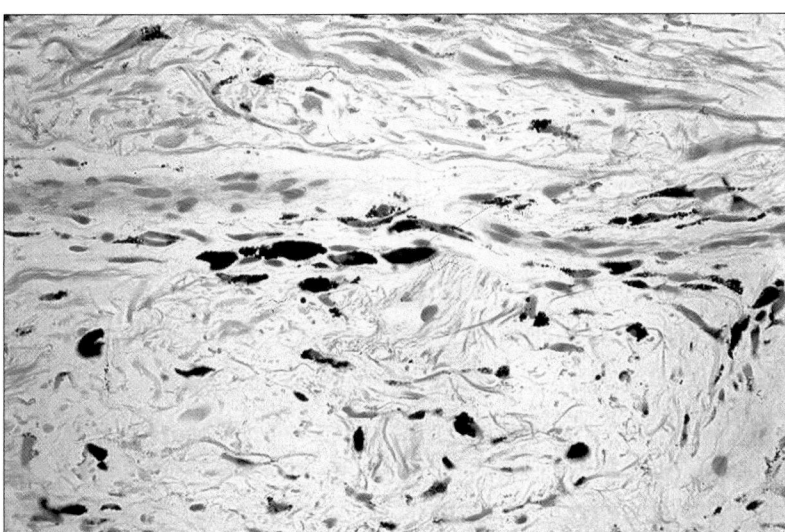

Fig. 13.44
Minocycline pigmentation: the pigment stains positively with Masson–Fontana.

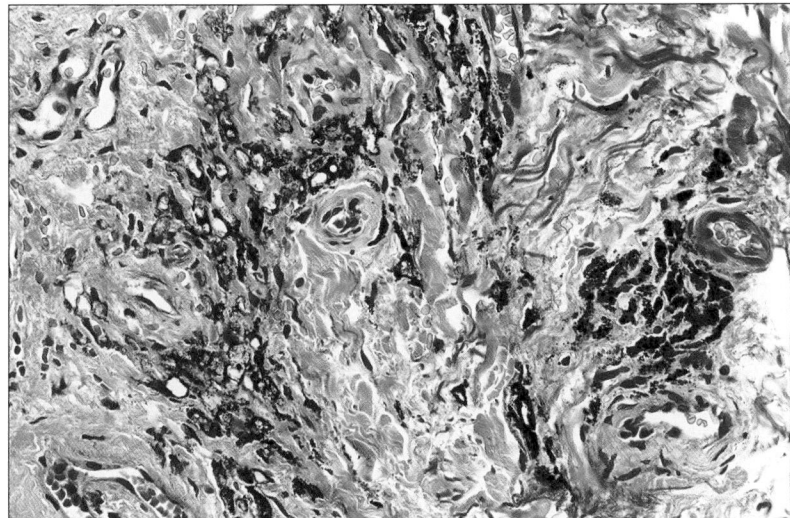

Fig. 13.45
Minocycline pigmentation: the pigment also stains with Prussian blue.

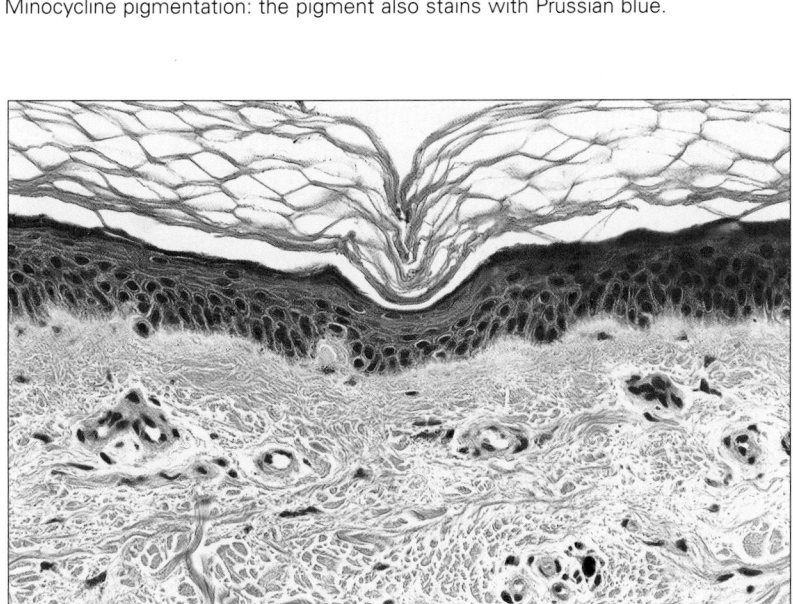

Fig. 13.46
Minocycline pigmentation: the type 3 variant is characterized by epidermal basal keratinocyte hyperpigmentation.

identified.[23] Similar inclusions may be found in the hepatocytes, Kupffer cells, pulmonary macrophages and neutrophil polymorphs.

In mepacrine pigmentation, yellow–brown pigment is found within the cytoplasm of histiocytes throughout the dermis.[40] The pigment is weakly positive with the Perl's Prussian blue reaction for iron and is Masson–Fontana negative.[40]

Histologically, chlorpromazine hyperpigmentation is characterized by the presence of golden-brown macrophage-bound granules surrounding the superficial vasculature. The granules are positive with the Masson–Fontana reaction but do not stain with Perl's Prussian blue.[44] Ultrastructurally, the pigment is lysosome bound and may be found in endothelial cells, fibroblasts, Schwann and smooth muscle cells in addition to macrophages.[41,42] Increased melanin also contributes to the cutaneous pigmentation.[41]

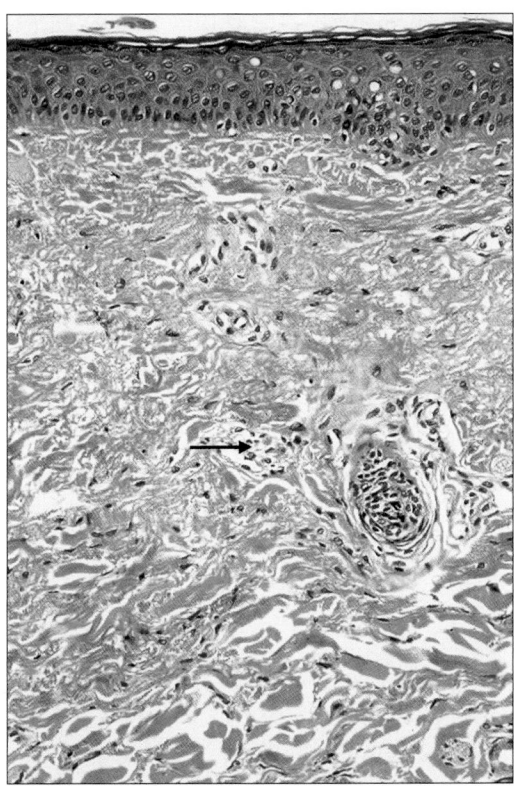

Fig. 13.47
Amiodarone pigmentation: pigmented macrophages are present in a perivascular distribution (arrowed).

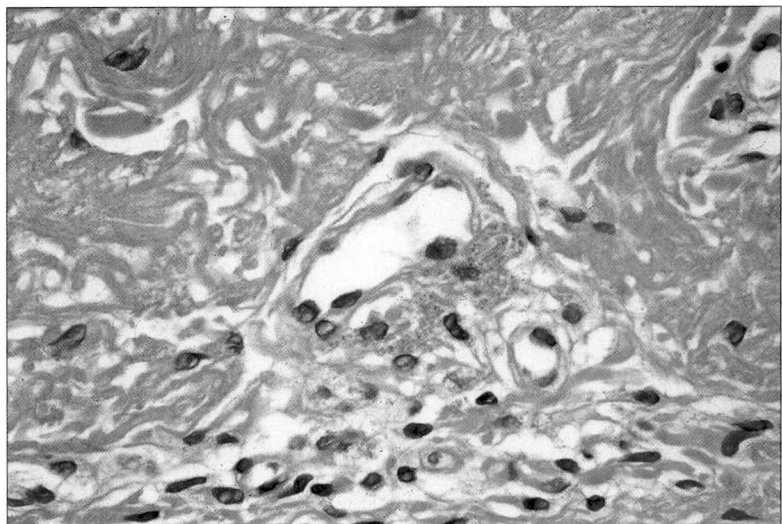

Fig. 13.48
Amiodarone pigmentation: close-up view.

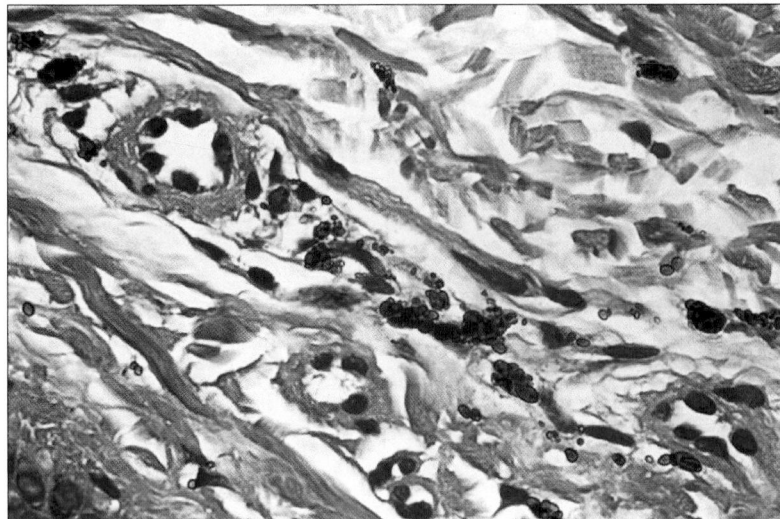

Fig. 13.49
Imipramine pigmentation: typical golden-brown granules. Note that the Prussian blue reaction is negative. By courtesy of L. Cohen, MD, Cohen Dermatopathology, Massachusetts, USA.

Histologically, imipramine hyperpigmentation is characterized by Masson–Fontana positive golden-brown granules within the upper dermis, lying both free and within macrophages (*Fig. 13.49*).[45,46] Perl's Prussian blue is negative. Ultrastructurally, histiocytes contain melanosomes in addition to lysosomal-bound electron-dense granules.[45] Desipramine pigmentation is similar.[47]

References

1. Lerner, E.A., Sober, A.J. (1988) Chemical and pharmacologic agents that cause hyperpigmentation or hypopigmentation of the skin. *Dermatol Clin*, 6, 327–336.
2. Ferguson, J., Frain-Bell, W. (1989) Pigmentary disorders and systemic drug therapy. *Clin Dermatol*, 7, 44–54.
3. Breathnach, S.M., Hintner, H. (1992) Types of clinical reaction. In: Adverse drug reactions and the skin. Oxford: Blackwell Scientific, pp 41–133.
4. Granstein, R.D., Sober, A.J. (1981) Drug and heavy metal-induced hyperpigmentation. *J Am Acad Dermatol*, 5, 1–18.
5. Levantine, A., Almeyda, J. (1973) Drug induced changes in pigmentation. *Br J Dermatol*, 89, 105–112.
6. Simons, J.J., Morales, A. (1980) Minocycline and generalized cutaneous pigmentation. *J Am Acad Dermatol*, 3, 244–247.
7. Fenske, N.A., Millns, J.L. (1980) Cutaneous pigmentation due to minocycline hydrochloride. *J Am Acad Dermatol*, 3, 308–311.
8. McGrae, J.D. Jr, Zelickson, A.S. (1980) Skin pigmentation secondary to minocycline therapy. *Arch Dermatol*, 116, 1262–1265.
9. Basler, R.S.W. (1985) Minocycline-related hyperpigmentation. *Arch Dermatol*, 121, 606–608.
10. Argenyi, Z., Finelli, L. (1987) Minocycline-related cutaneous pigmentation as demonstrated by light microscopy, electron microscopy and X-ray energy spectroscopy. *J Cutan Pathol*, 14, 176–180.
11. Okada, N., Sato, S., Sasou, T. (1993) Characterization of pigmented granules in minocycline-induced
12. cutaneous pigmentation: observations using fluorescent microscopy and high performance chromatography. *Br J Dermatol*, 129, 403–407.
12. Dwyer, C.M., Cuddihy, A.M., Kerr, R.E. et al (1993) Skin pigmentation due to minocycline treatment of facial dermatoses. *Br J Dermatol*, 129, 158–162.
13. Pepine, M., Flowers, F.P., Ramos-Caro, F.A. (1993) Extensive cutaneous hyperpigmentation caused by minocycline. *J Am Acad Dermatol*, 28, 292–295.
14. Eisen, D., Hakim, M.D. (1998) Minocycline-induced pigmentation: incidence, prevention and management. *Drug Saf*, 18, 431–440.
15. Chu, P., Van, S. (1994) Minocycline pigmentation localized to the lips: an unusual fixed drug reaction? *J Am Acad Dermatol*, 30, 802–803.
16. Cheek, C.C., Heymann, H.O. (1999) Dental and oral discolorations associated with minocycline and other tetracycline analogs. *J Esthet Dent*, 11, 43–48.
17. Cockings, J.M., Savage, N.W. (1998) Minocycline and oral pigmentation. *Aust Dent J*, 43, 14–16.
18. Westbury, L.W., Najera, A. (1997) Minocycline-induced intraoral pharmacogenic pigmentation: case reports and review of the literature. *J Periodontol*, 68, 314–316.
19. Meyerson, M.A., Cohen, P.R., Hymes, S.R. (1995) Lingual hyperpigmentation associated with minocycline therapy. *Oral Surg Oral Med Oral Pathol Oral Radiol Endod*, 79, 180–184.
20. Katz, J., Barak, S., Shemer, J. et al (1995) Black tongue associated with minocycline therapy. *Arch Dermatol*, 131, 620.
21. Tanzi, E.L. (2000) Minocycline-induced hyperpigmentation of the tongue. *Arch Dermatol*, 136, 427–428.
22. Odell, E.W., Hodgson, S.P., Haskell, R. (1995) Oral presentation of minocycline-induced black bone disease. *Oral Surg Oral Med Oral Pathol Oral Radiol Endod*, 79, 459–461.
23. Sabroe, R.A., Archer, C.B., Harlow, D. et al (1996) Minocycline-induced discoloration of the sclerae. *Br J Dermatol*, 135, 314–316.
24. Fraunfelder, F.T., Randall, J.A. (1997) Minocycline-induced scleral pigmentation. *Ophthalmology*, 104, 936–938.
25. Enochs, W.S., Nilges, M.J., Swartz, H.M. (1993) The minocycline-induced thyroid pigment and several synthetic models: identification and characterization by electron paramagnetic resonance imaging. *J Pharmacol Exp Ther*, 266, 1164–1176.
26. Butler, J., Marks, R., Sutherland, R. (1985) Cutaneous and cardiac valvular pigmentation with minocycline. *Clin Exp Dermatol*, 10, 432–437.
27. Sant' Ambrogio, S., Connelly, J., DiMaio, J. (1999) Minocycline pigmentation of heart valves. *Cardiovasc Pathol*, 8, 329–332.
28. Moller, H., Rausing, A. (1980) Methacycline hyperpigmentation: a five year follow-up. *Acta Derm Venereol*, 60, 495–501.
29. Hendricks, A. (1980) Yellow lunulae with fluorescence after tetracycline therapy. *Arch Dermatol*, 116, 438–440.
30. Trimble, J.W., Mendelson, D.S., Fetter, B.F. et al (1983) Cutaneous pigmentation secondary to amiodarone therapy. *Arch Dermatol*, 119, 914–918.
31. Holt, D.W., Adams, P.C., Campbell, R.W.F. et al (1984) Amiodarone and its desethyl-metabolite: tissue distribution and ultrastructural changes in amiodarone treated patients. *Br J Clin Pharmacol*, 17, 195–196.
32. Ferguson, J., Addo, H.A., Jones, S. et al (1985) A study of cutaneous photosensitivity induced by amiodarone. *Br J Dermatol*, 113, 537–549.
33. Bahadir, S., Apaydin, R., Cobanoilu, U. et al (2000) Amiodarone pigmentation, eye and thyroid alterations. *J Eur Acad Dermatol Venereol*, 14, 194–195.
34. Zachary, C.B., Slater, D.N., Holt, D.W. et al (1984) The pathogenesis of amiodarone-induced pigmentation and photosensitivity. *Br J Dermatol*, 110, 451–456.
35. Waitzer, S., Butany, J., From, L. et al (1987) Cutaneous ultrastructural changes and photosensitivity associated with amiodarone therapy. *J Am Acad Dermatol*, 16, 779–787.
36. Hass, N., Schadendorf, D. (2001) Hypomelanosis due to block of melanosomal maturation in amiodarone-induced hyperpigmentation. *Arch Dermatol*, 137, 513–514.
37. Doll, J.L.C., Kreane, J.A. (1959) Disturbances of pigmentation with chloroquine. *BMJ*, I, 1387–1389.
38. Sams, W.M., Epstein, J.H. (1965) The affinity of melanin for chloroquine. *J Invest Dermatol*, 45, 482–488.
39. Tuffanelli, D., Abraham, R.K., Dubois, E.J. (1963) Pigmentation from antimalarial therapy. Its possible relationship to the ocular lesions. *Arch Dermatol*, 88, 419–426.
40. Leigh, I.M., Kennedy, C.T.C., Ramsey, J.D. et al (1979) Mepacrine pigmentation in systemic lupus erythematosus. New data from an ultrastructural, biochemical and analytical electron microscopic investigation. *Br J Dermatol*, 101, 147–153.
41. Hashimoto, K., Weiner, W., Albert, J. et al (1966) An electron microscopic study of chlorpromazine pigmentation. *J Invest Dermatol*, 47, 296–306.
42. Zelickson, A.S. (1965) Skin pigmentation and chlorpromazine. *JAMA*, 194, 200–202.
43. Bloom, D., Krishnan, B., Thavundayil, J.X. et al (1993) Resolution of chlorpromazine-induced cutaneous pigmentation following substitution with levomepromazine or other neuroleptics. *Acta Psychiatr Scand*, 87, 223–224.
44. Benning, T.L., MacCormack, K.M., Ingram, P. et al (1988) Microprobe analysis of chlorpromazine pigmentation. *Arch Dermatol*, 124, 1541–1544.
45. Hashimoto, K., Joselow, S.A., Tye, M.J. (1991) Imipramine hyperpigmentation: a slate-gray discoloration caused by long-term imipramine administration. *J Am Acad Dermatol*, 25, 357–361.
46. Ming, M.E., Bhawan, J., Stefanato, C.M. et al (1999) Imipramine-induced hyperpigmentation: four cases and a review of the literature. *J Am Acad Dermatol*, 40, 159–166.
47. Narurkar, V., Smoller, B.R., Hu, C-H. et al (1993) Desipramine-induced blue-gray photosensitive pigmentation. *Arch Dermatol*, 129, 474–476.

Vasculitic drug reactions

Adverse drug reactions are a common cause of vasculitis.[1,2] An immune complex mechanism most probably represents the pathogenesis in the majority of cases. A wide range of drugs has been implicated, mostly in single case reports. These include anti-infective agents, cancer chemotherapeutic agents and adjuvants, NSAIDs, psychoactive and cardiovascular drugs, diuretics, anticoagulants, beta-adrenergic receptor agonists and anticonvulsants.[2] The more important agents include trimethoprim, penicillin, sulfonamides, NSAIDs and aspirin.[3] More recently implicated drugs include cimetidine, clarithromycin, coumadin, furosemide (frusemide), hydralazine, ibuprofen, iodides, phenacetin, phenothiazines, procainamide, rifampin and streptokinase.[4–13] This topic is discussed in greater detail on page 709.

Granulomatous vasculitis has been described following treatment with chlorothiazide, allopurinol, phenytoin and carbamazepine.[4,14–16]

References

1. Sams, M.W. (1989) Hypersensitivity angiitis. *J Invest Dermatol*, 93, 78S–81S.
2. Jain, K.K. (1993) Drug-induced cutaneous vasculitis. *Adverse Drug React Toxicol Rev*, 12, 263–276.
3. Hunziker, T., Kunzi, U-P., Braunschweig, S. et al (1997) Comprehensive hospital drug monitoring (CHDM): adverse skin reactions, a 20-year survey. *Allergy*, 52, 388–393.
4. Calabrese, L.H. (1990) Cutaneous vasculitis, hypersensitivity vasculitis, erythema nodosum, and pyoderma gangrenosum. *Curr Opin Rheumatol*, 2, 66–69.
5. Peacock, A., Weatherall, D. (1981) Hydralazine-induced necrotizing vasculitis. *BMJ*, 282, 1121–1122.
6. Hendricks, W.M., Ader, R.S. (1977) Furosemide-induced cutaneous necrotizing vasculitis. *Arch Dermatol*, 113, 375–376.
7. Mitchell, G.G., Magnusson, A.R., Weiler, J.M. (1983) Cimetidine-induced cutaneous vasculitis. *Am J Med*, 75, 875–876.
8. Tanay, A., Yust, I., Brenner, S. et al (1982) Dermal vasculitis due to coumadin hypersensitivity. *Dermatologica*, 165, 178–185.
9. Davidson, K.A., Ringpfeil, F., Lee, J.B. (2001) Ibuprofen-induced bullous leucocytoclastic vasculitis. *Cutis*, 67, 303–307.
10. Davidson, J.R., Bush, R.K., Grogan, E.W. et al (1988) Immunology of a serum sickness/vasculitis reaction to streptokinase used for acute myocardial infarction. *Clin Exp Rheumatol*, 6, 381–384.
11. Gavura, S.R., Nusinowitz, S. (1998) Leukocytoclastic vasculitis associated with clarithromycin. *Ann Pharmacother*, 32, 543–545.
12. Iredale, J.P., Sankaran, R., Wathen, C.G. (1989) Cutaneous vasculitis associated with rifampin therapy. *Chest*, 96, 215–216.

13. Peters, F., Maessen-Visch, B., Kho, L. (1996) Leukocytoclastic vasculitis induced by a nonsteroidal antiinflammatory drug. *J Rheumatol*, **23**, 2008–2009.

14. Eechout, E., Willemsen, M., Deconinck, A. et al (1987) Granulomatous vasculitis as a complication of potassium iodide treatment for Sweet's syndrome. *Acta Derm Venereol*, **67**, 362–364.

15. Imai, H., Nakamoto, Y., Hirokowa, M. et al (1989) Carbamazepine-induced granulomatous necrotizing angiitis with acute renal failure. *Nephron*, **51**, 405–408.

16. Gaffey, C.M., Chun, B., Harvey, J.C.D. et al (1986) Phenytoin-induced systemic granulomatous vasculitis. *Arch Path Lab Med*, **110**, 131–135.

Purpuric drug reactions

Clinical features

Purpura may be a manifestation of an adverse drug reaction. Causes include NSAIDs, diuretics, meprobamate, zomepirac sodium, ampicillin and pseudoephedrine.[1,2]

Histological features

The histological features are those of red cell extravasation in the absence of changes of vasculitis (*Figs 13.50, 13.51*).

References

1. Ratnam, K.V., Su, W.P.D., Peters, M.S. (1991) Purpura simplex (inflammatory purpura without vasculitis): a clinicopathologic study of 174 cases. *J Am Acad Dermatol*, **25**, 642–647.

2. Díaz-Jara, M., Tornero, P., Barrio, M.D. (2002) Pigmented purpuric dermatosis due to pseudoephedrine. *Contact Dermatitis*, **46**, 300–301.

Granulomatous drug reactions

Clinical features

Interstitial granulomatous drug reactions are very rare and have been described following use of a number of drugs including calcium channel blockers, ACE inhibitors, beta-blockers, lipid-lowering agents, diuretics, NSAIDs, antihistamines, anticonvulsants and antidepressants.[1] In addition to drugs, this reaction pattern may be related to a variety of systemic illnesses including rheumatoid arthritis, hepatobiliary disease, diabetes mellitus, Crohn's disease and chronic infections such as hepatitis C, herpes simplex/varicella zoster, Epstein–Barr virus (EBV) and HIV.[2]

Patients present with erythematous to violaceous, non-pruritic irregular and sometimes annular plaques predominantly affecting the inner arms, inner thighs and the groins.[1]

Histological features

Histologically, the eruption is characterized by an interstitial infiltrate composed of lymphocytes, histiocytes, eosinophils, plasma cells and

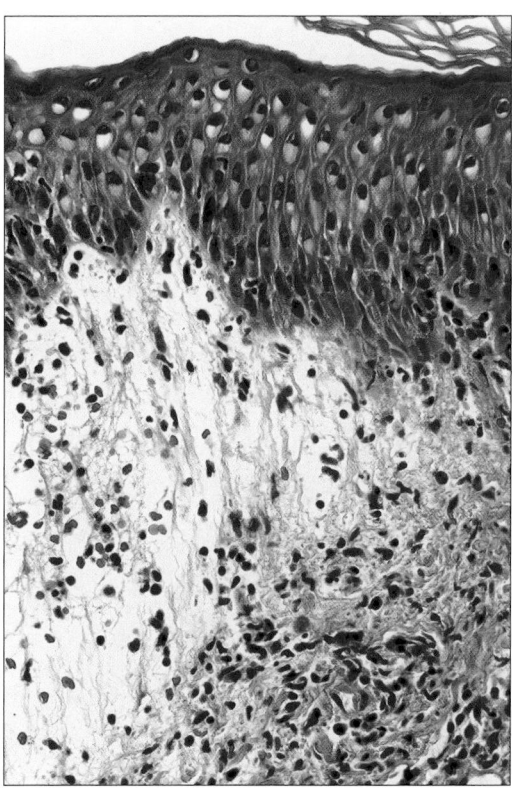

Fig. 13.51
Purpuric drug reaction: there is red cell extravasation. Occasional eosinophils are evident.

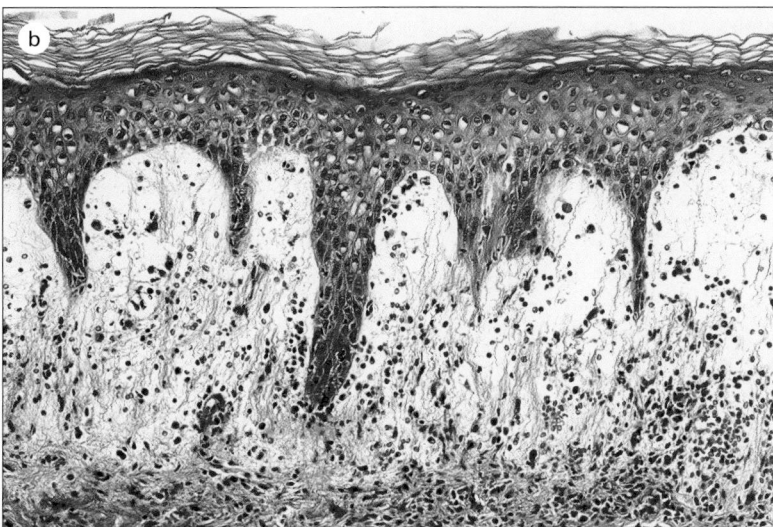

Fig. 13.50
(a, b) Purpuric drug reaction: this example also had an urticarial component. Note the massive edema of the papillary dermis.

multinucleate giant cells, sometimes associated with increased dermal mucin and showing more than a superficial resemblance to interstitial granuloma annulare (*Figs 13.52–13.54*). Fragmentation of collagen fibers and elastic tissue is commonly evident and phagocytosis of connective tissue debris by giant cells is typically seen (*Figs 13.55, 13.56*). Discrete granulomata may also be identified and granulomatous vasculitis has been documented.[2] Flame figures and Churg–Strauss-like granulomata have also been described.[3,4] Atypical lymphocytes with hyperchromatic, irregular and variably enlarged nuclei showing epidermotropism are present in up to 50% of cases.[1] The changes of interface dermatitis sometimes with an associated lichenoid infiltrate are found in the majority of cases.[1]

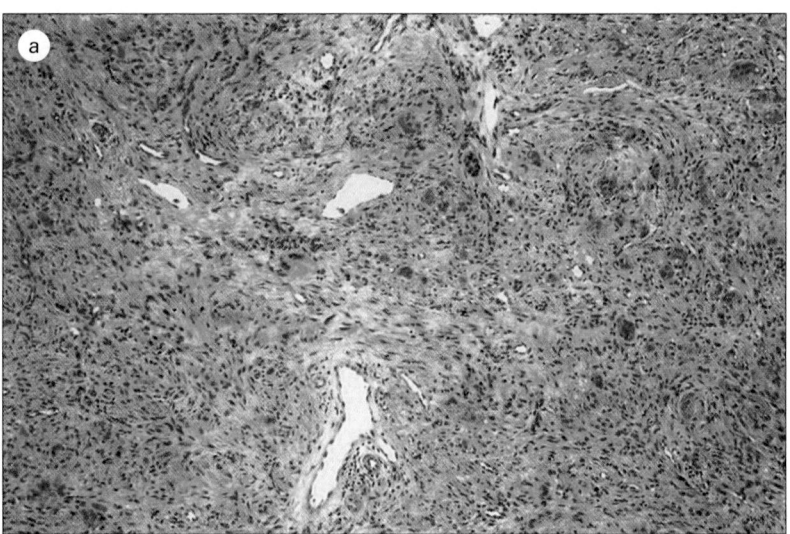

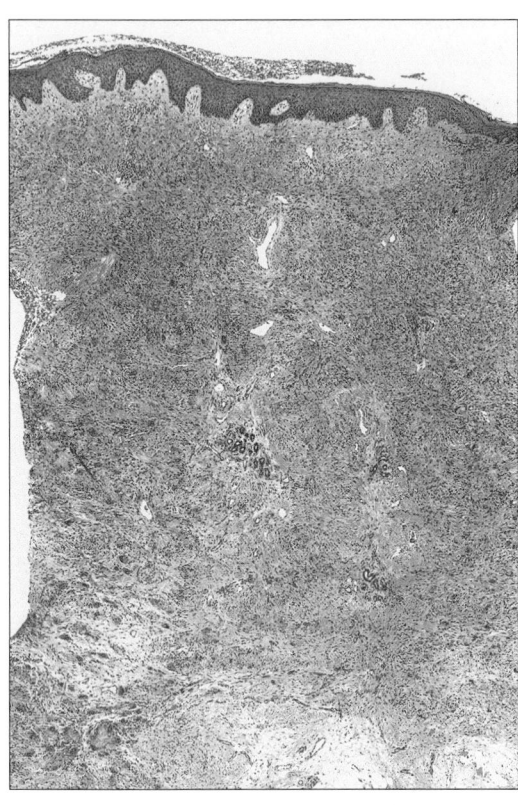

Fig. 13.52
Granulomatous drug reaction: there is a marked infiltrate involving the full thickness of the dermis.

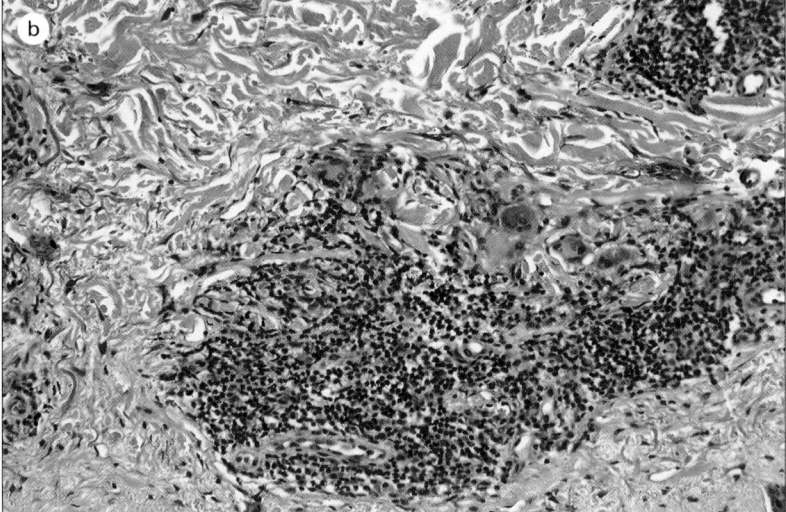

Fig. 13.54
(a, b) Granulomatous drug reaction: the infiltrate consists of lymphocytes, histiocytes and conspicuous multinucleate giant cells.

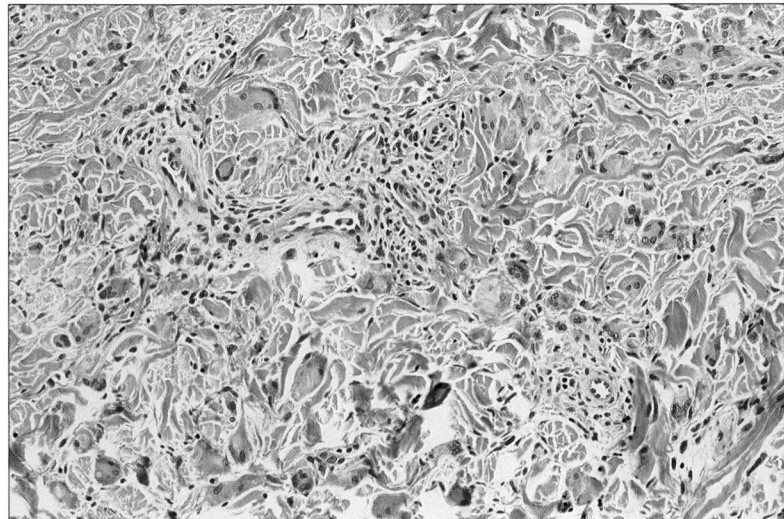

Fig. 13.53
Granulomatous drug reaction: in this example there is an obvious interstitial distribution reminiscent of granuloma annulare.

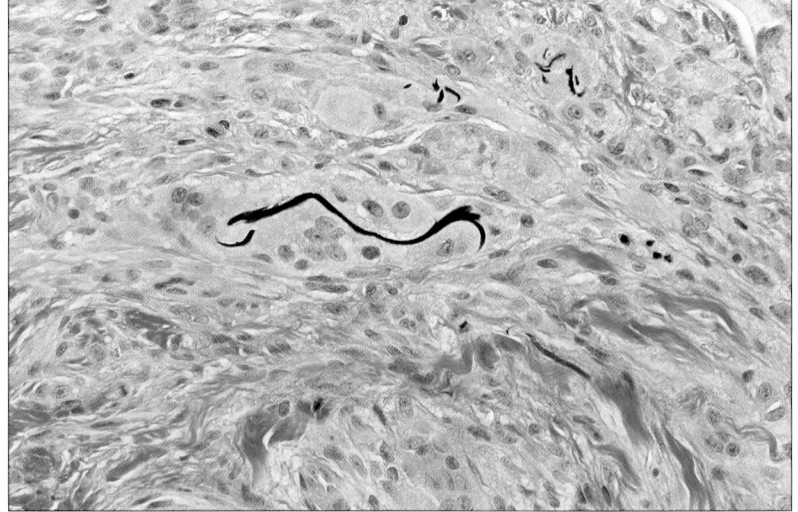

Fig. 13.55
Granulomatous drug reaction: there is extensive elastophagocytosis (elastic van Gieson).

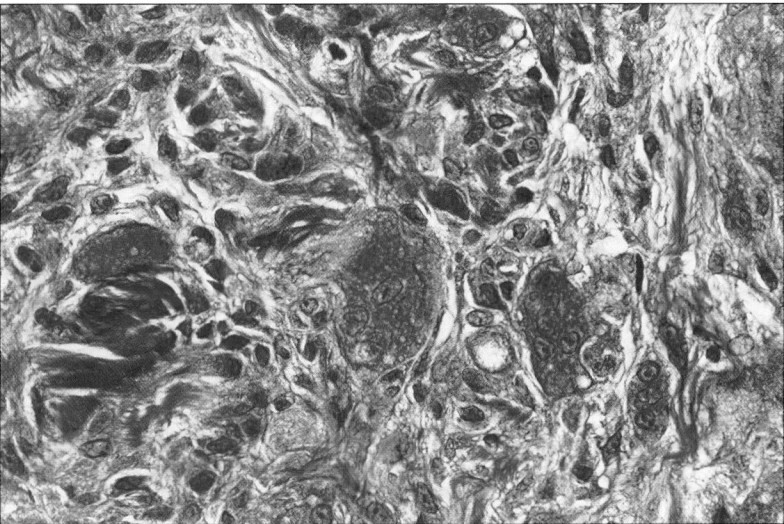

Fig. 13.56
Granulomatous drug reaction: phagocytosis of collagen may also be seen (Masson's trichrome).

Differential diagnosis

Interstitial granulomatous drug reactions must be distinguished from granuloma annulare and systemic disease-associated lesions as described above. Granuloma annulare is not usually associated with the changes of interface dermatitis and necrobiosis is not a feature of granulomatous drug reactions. Systemic disease-associated granulomatous dermatitis is usually associated with vasculitic and/or thrombotic phenomena.[4] In those cases where significant lymphoid atypia is present, cutaneous T-cell lymphoma enters the differential diagnosis. When elastophagocytosis is marked, granulomatous slack skin may be an important diagnostic consideration.

References

1. Magro, C.M., Crowson, A.N., Schapiro, B.L. (1998) The interstitial granulomatous drug reaction: a distinctive clinical and pathological entity. *J Cutan Pathol*, **25**, 72–78.
2. Magro, C.M., Crowson, A.N. (2000) Lichenoid and granulomatous dermatitis. *Int J Dermatol*, **39**, 126–133.
3. Perrin, C., Lacour, J.P., Castanet, J. et al (2001) Interstitial granulomatous drug reaction with a histologic pattern of interstitial granulomatous dermatitis. *Am J Dermatopathol*, **23**, 295–298.
4. Goerttler, E., Kutzner, H., Peter, H.H. et al (1999) Methotrexate-induced papular eruption in patients with rheumatic diseases: a distinctive adverse cutaneous reaction produced by methotrexate in patients with collagen vascular disease. *J Am Acad Dermatol*, **40**, 702–707.

Drug-induced erythema nodosum

This topic is discussed on page 343.

Drug-induced alopecia

Drug-induced alopecia is usually reversible, predominantly non-scarring and affects females more often than males.[1–4]

Anagen effluvium, in which hair growth stops due to cessation of mitotic activity, is a common feature of anticancer therapy and often develops within days or a few weeks of starting the drug.[1] The scalp and beard areas, which contain a high percentage of anagen follicles, are particularly affected. It especially complicates combination chemotherapy and is likely to be severe.[4] Although all anticancer drugs may be associated with some degree of alopecia, particular offenders include bleomycin, cyclophosphamide, dactinomycin, daunorubicin, doxorubicin, 5-fluorouracil, ifosfamide and vindesine.[1] There is some variation in drug effect. Some cause alopecia in all individuals whereas others affect only a minority of patients.[4]

Telogen effluvium, in which hairs are transformed into the telogen phase, develops several months after commencing the therapy.[1] Anticoagulants, including heparin and warfarin and dextran sulfate, result in telogen effluvium in up to 50% of patients.[2,4–10] Other important causes include antithyroid drugs such as iodine, thiouracil and carbimazole, oral contraceptives, lithium, interferons and retinoids.[4,11,12]

References

1. Pillans, P.I., Woods, D.J. (1995) Drug-associated alopecia. *Int J Dermatol*, **34**, 149–158.
2. Blankenship, M.L. (1983) Drugs and alopecia. *Australas J Dermatol*, **24**, 100–104.
3. Brodin, M.B. (1987) Drug-related alopecia. *Dermatol Clin*, **5**, 571–579.
4. Tosti, A., Misciali, C., Piraccini, B.M. et al (1994) Drug-induced hair loss and hair growth. Incidence, management and avoidance. *Drug Saf*, **10**, 310–317.
5. Bick, R.L., Frenkel, E.P. (1999) Clinical aspects of heparin-induced thrombocytopenia and thrombosis and other side-effects of heparin therapy. *Clin Appl Thromb Hemost*, **53** (Suppl. 1), S7–15.
6. Barnes, C., Deidun, D., Hynes, K. et al (2000) Alopecia and dalteparin: a previously unreported association. *Blood*, **96**, 1618–1619.
7. Apsner, R., Horl, W.H., Sunder-Plassmann, G. (2001) Dalteparin-induced alopecia in hemodialysis patients: reversal by anticoagulation. *Blood*, **97**, 2914–2915.
8. Nagao, T., Ibayashi, S., Fujii, K. et al (1995) Treatment of warfarin-induced hair loss with ubidecarenone. *Lancet*, **348**, 1104–1105.
9. Umlas, J., Harken, D.E. (1998) Warfarin-induced alopecia. *Cutis*, **42**, 63–64.
10. Flexner, C., Barditch-Crovo, P.A., Kornhauser, D.M. et al (1991) Pharmokinetics, toxicity, and activity of intravenous dextran sulfate in human deficiency virus infection. *Antimicrob Agents Chemother*, **35**, 2544–2550.
11. Papadopoulos, S., Harden, R.M. (1966) Hair loss in patients treated with carbimazole. *BMJ*, **17**, 1502–1503.
12. van den Bemt, P.M., Brodie-Meijer, C.C., Krijnen, R.M. et al (1999) Drug-induced alopecia. *Ned Tijdschr Geneeskd*, **143**, 990–994.

Drug-induced lupus erythematosus

Clinical features

Drug-induced systemic lupus erythematosus was first described as a complication of hydralazine.[1–7] It has also been reported in association with procainamide, quinidine, sulfasalazine, chlorpromazine, penicillamine, methyldopa, carbamazepine, acebutalol, isoniazid, captopril, propylthiouracil and minocycline.[2] With the exceptions of hydralazine and procainamide (high risk) and quinidine (medium risk), the other associations are low risk.[2] Laboratory investigations reveal anti-Ro, anti-La and antinuclear antibodies (ANA) in the majority of cases.[1] Subacute cutaneous lupus erythematosus-like features have been described following treatment with terbinafine.[8–10]

Clinical manifestations are atypical in that cutaneous lesions including malar erythema, discoid lesions, photosensitivity, oral ulceration and alopecia are rare.[2]

Diagnostic criteria have been defined as follows:[2]

- Continuous treatment with the suspected drug for 1 month or longer
- Common presenting symptoms include arthralgias/arthritis, myositis, serositis, malaise and fever

- Antihistone antibodies common, particularly IgG anti-([H2A-H2B]-DNA)
- Most importantly, clinical improvement within days or weeks after stopping the suspected drug.

Histological features

The histological features of cutaneous lesions are indistinguishable from those seen in the idiopathic forms (see p. 792).[11]

References

1. Del Rosso, J.Q. (2002) Skin manifestations of drug reactions. *Curr Allergy Asthma Rep*, **2**, 282–287.
2. Rubin, R.L. (1999) Etiology and mechanisms of drug-induced lupus. *Curr Opin Rheumatol*, **11**, 357–363.
3. Reed, B.R., Huff, J.C., Jones, S.K. et al (1985) Subacute cutaneous lupus erythematosus associated with hydrochlorothiazide therapy. *Ann Intern Med*, **103**, 49–51.
4. Gough, A., Chapman, S., Wagstaff, K. et al (1996) Minocycline induced autoimmune hepatitis and systemic lupus-like syndrome. *BMJ*, **312**, 169–172.
5. Schlienger, R.G., Bircher, A.J., Meier, C.R. (2000) Minocycline-induced lupus. A systematic review. *Dermatology*, **200**, 223–231.
6. Jain, K.K. (1991) Systemic lupus erythematosus (SLE)-like syndromes associated with carbamazepine therapy. *Drug Saf*, **6**, 350–360.
7. Tsankov, N.K., Lazarova, A.Z., Vasileva, S.G. et al (1990) Lupus erythematosus-like eruption due to D-penicillamine in progressive systemic sclerosis. *Int J Dermatol*, **29**, 571–574.
8. Gupta, A.K., Lynde, C.W., Lauzon, G.J. et al (1998) Cutaneous adverse effects associated with terbinafine therapy: 10 case reports and a review of the literature. *Br J Dermatol*, **138**, 529–532.
9. Bonssmann, G., Schiller, M., Liger, T.A. et al (2001) Terbinafine-induced subacute lupus erythematosus. *J Am Acad Dermatol*, **44**, 925–931.
10. Callen, J.P., Hughes, A.P., Kulp-Shorten, C. (2001) Subacute cutaneous lupus erythematosus induced or exacerbated by terbinafine. *Arch Dermatol*, **137**, 1196–1198.
11. Crowson, A.N., Magro, C.M. (1999) Recent advances in the pathology of cutaneous drug eruptions. *Dermatol Clin*, **17**, 537–560.

Bullous drug reactions

Blisters may develop within the setting of an adverse drug reaction either as a consequence of severe spongiosis or marked interface change (as may be a feature of a fixed drug eruption) or else they may reflect drug-related autoimmune bullous disorders (*Fig. 13.57*). In this section, only the last are discussed. These include drug-induced linear IgA disease, bullous pemphigoid, cicatricial pemphigoid, epidermolysis bullosa acquisita, pemphigus variants and drug-induced pseudoporphyria. Many alleged drug reactions are single case reports, particularly in patients taking multiple medications. It is often difficult to determine which associations are therefore coincidental and which are genuine. In occasional reports, recrudescence following unwitting re-exposure to the offending agent has been documented.

The precise mechanism of drug-induced blistering is unknown although multiple factors have been suggested:[1]

- Direct toxicity to basement membrane constituents or intercellular junctions with resultant autoantibody production
- The drug may function as a hapten
- The drug may be antigenically similar to a basement membrane or intercellular junction constituent
- Perturbation of the immune system with inappropriate production of anti-basement membrane antibodies
- Drug-induced abnormality of cell membrane calcium metabolism.

Reference

1. Shachar, E., Bialy-Golan, A., Srebrnik, A. et al (1998) 'Two-step' drug-induced bullous pemphigoid. *Int J Dermatol*, **37**, 934–938.

Drug-induced linear IgA disease

Drug-induced linear IgA disease is most often associated with intravenous therapy with vancomycin.[1–7] Similar eruptions, however, have also been described following treatment with trimethoprim-sulfamethoxazole, penicillin, phenytoin, somatostatin, lithium, amiodarone, captopril, cefamandole, ceftriaxone, cyclosporin, IL-2, penicillin, vigabatrin and diclophenac.[2,8–15] Cutaneous manifestations of vancomycin-induced linear IgA disease include pruritic, erythematous, urticarial, targetoid and bullous lesions with a predilection for the trunk, extremities, palms and soles (*Fig. 13.58*).[1] Mucosal involvement is present in up to 40% of cases (*Fig. 13.59*).[2] Laryngeal involvement has been documented.[15]

Pathogenesis and histological features

By definition, linear IgA deposition along the basement membrane region is present in all cases (*Fig. 13.60*). C3 is seen in approximately 20% of

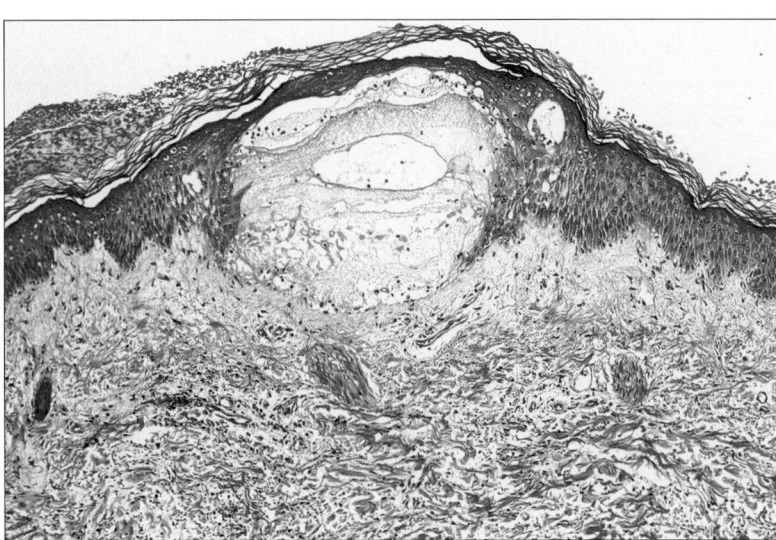

Fig. 13.57
Bullous drug reaction: this subepidermal blister arose against a background of an exanthematous drug reaction.

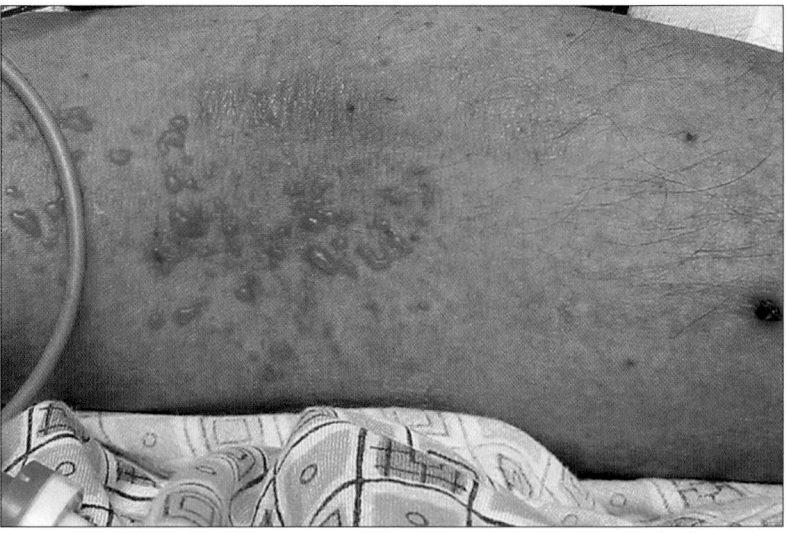

Fig. 13.58
Drug-induced linear IgA disease: these blisters developed following treatment with vancomycin. By courtesy of B.A. Solky, MD, Department of Dermatology, Harvard Medical School, Boston, USA.

cases.[7] Linear IgG may very exceptionally be present although distinction from drug-induced bullous pemphigoid can then be problematical.[3,12] Such cases may in fact represent examples of drug-induced IgA-mediated bullous pemphigoid.[16] Circulating IgA anti-basement membrane zone antibodies are found in 25% of cases.[1] Split skin studies predominantly localize to the floor (dermal aspect) of the blister cavity.[1,2] By immuno-electron microscopy, the results are heterogeneous, IgA having been detected within the lamina lucida, lamina densa and in the sub-lamina densa.[13–15] Western immunoblotting has detected a number of antigens including a 230 kD antigen (bullous pemphigoid antigen 1), a 97 kD antigen (an anchoring filament protein) and also a 250 kD antigen corresponding to type VII collagen.[14,15]

Histologically, a neutrophil-rich subepidermal blister is seen in the majority of cases but sometimes eosinophils can be conspicuous (*Figs 13.61, 13.62*).[2]

References

1. Baden, L.A., Apovian, C., Imber, M.J. et al (1988) Vancomycin-induced linear IgA bullous dermatosis. *Arch Dermatol*, **124**, 1186–1188.
2. Kuechle, M.K., Stegemeir, E., Maynard, B. et al (1994) Drug-induced linear IgA bullous dermatosis: report of six cases and review of the literature. *J Am Acad Dermatol*, 30, 187–192.
3. Whitworth, J.M., Thomas, I., Peltz, S.A. et al (1996) Vancomycin-induced linear IgA-induced linear IgA bullous dermatosis (LABD). *J Am Acad Dermatol*, **34**, 890–891.
4. Bernstein, E.F., Schuster, M. (1998) Linear IgA bullous dermatosis associated with vancomycin. *Ann Intern Med*, **129**, 508–509.
5. Nousari, H.C., Kimyai-Asadi, A., Caeiro, J.P. et al (1999) Clinical, demographic, and immunohistologic features of vancomycin-induced linear IgA bullous disease of the skin. Report of two cases and review of the literature. *Medicine (Baltimore)*, **78**, 1–8.
6. Danielsen, A.G., Thomsen, K. (1999) Vancomycin-induced linear IgA bullous disease. *Br J Dermatol*, **141**, 756–757.
7. Wiadrowski, T.P., Reid, C.M. (2001) Drug-induced linear IgA disease following antibiotics. *Australas J Dermatol*, **42**, 196–199.
8. Tranvan, A., Pezen, D.S., Medenica, M. et al (1996) Interleukin-2 associated linear IgA bullous dermatosis. *J Am Acad Dermatol*, **35**, 865–867.
9. McWhirter, J.D., Hashimoto, K., Fayne, S. et al (1987) Linear IgA bullous dermatosis related to lithium carbonate. *Arch Dermatol*, **123**, 1120–1122.
10. Primka, E.J., Liranzo, M.O., Bergfeld, W.F. et al (1994) Amiodarone-induced linear IgA disease. *J Am Acad Dermatol*, **31**, 809–811.
11. Yawalkar, N., Reimers, A., Hari, Y. et al (1999) Drug-induced linear IgA bullous dermatosis associated with ceftriaxone- and metronidazole-specific T-cells. *Dermatology*, **199**, 25–30.

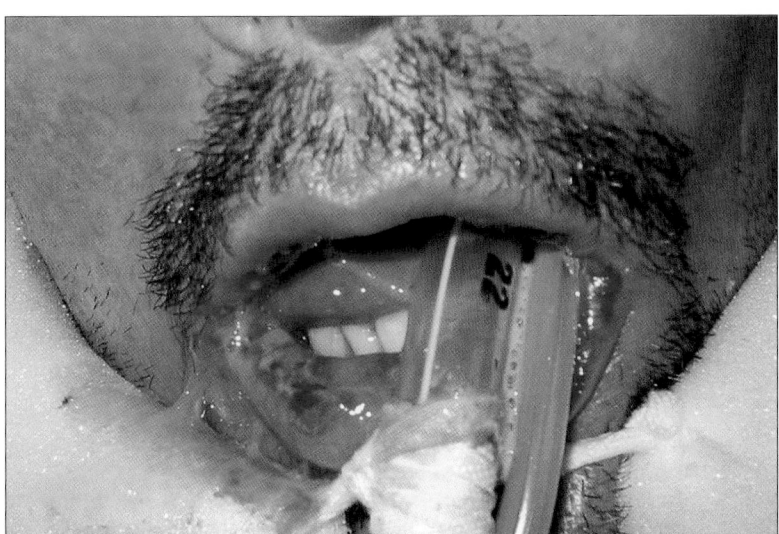

Fig. 13.59
Drug-induced linear IgA disease: oral lesions were also present. By courtesy of B.A. Solky, MD, Department of Dermatology, Harvard Medical School, Boston, USA.

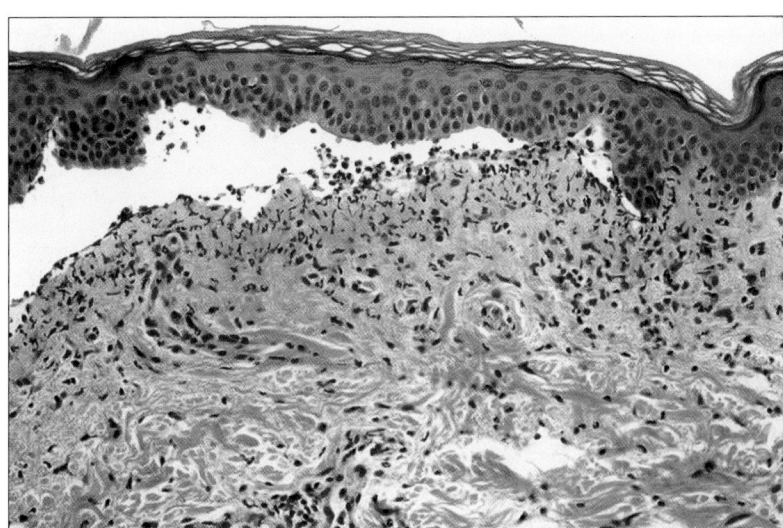

Fig. 13.61
Vancomycin-induced linear IgA disease: this case showed a neutrophil-rich subepidermal blister.

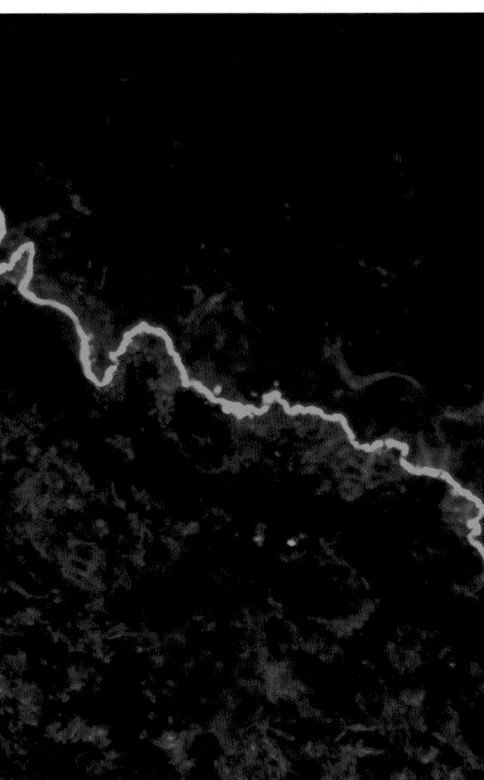

Fig. 13.60
Vancomycin-induced linear IgA disease: immunofluorescence showed strong basement membrane deposition of IgA.

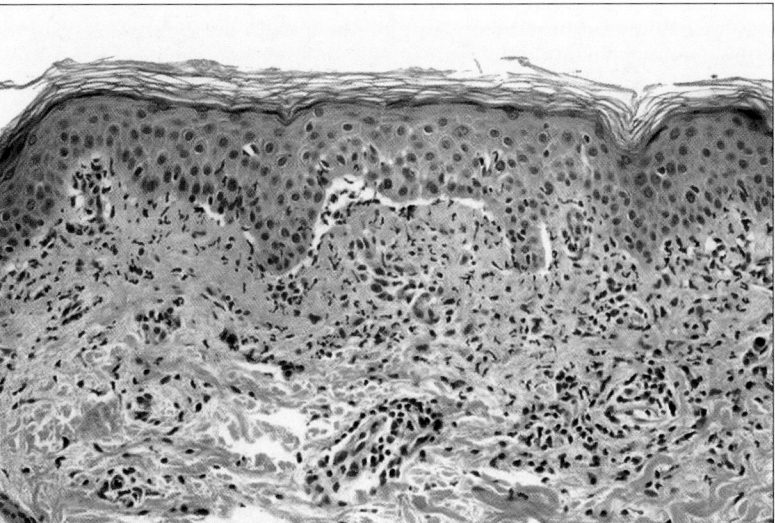

Fig. 13.62
Vancomycin-induced linear IgA disease: the adjacent skin showed neutrophil dermal papillary microabscesses.

12. Acostamadiedo, J.M., Perniciaro, C., Rogers, R.S. 3rd (1998) Phenytoin-induced linear IgA bullous disease. *J Am Acad Dermatol*, **38**, 352–356.
13. Paul, C., Wolkenstein, P., Prost, C. et al (1997) Drug-induced linear IgA disease: target antigens are heterogeneous. *Br J Dermatol*, **136**, 406–411.
14. Wakelin, S.H., Allen, J., Zhou, S. et al (1998) Drug-induced linear IgA disease with antibodies to collagen VII. *Br J Dermatol*, **138**, 310–314.
15. Espagne, E., Prost, C., Chosidow, O. et al (1990) Dermatoses à IgA linéaire médicamenteuses: a propos de trios cas. *Ann Dermatol Venereol*, **117**, 898–899.
16. Smith, E.P., Taylor, T.B., Meyer, L.J. et al (1993) Antigen identification in drug-induced bullous pemphigoid. *J Am Acad Dermatol*, **29**, 879–892.

Drug-induced bullous pemphigoid

Clinical features

A variety of drugs including captopril, ciprofloxacin, chloroquine, furosemide (frusemide), ibuprofen, mefenamic acid, nifedipine, penicillamine, penicillins, phenacetin, sulfasalazine and spironolactone have been incriminated in cases of alleged drug-induced bullous and cicatricial pemphigoid.[1–13] Of these, antirheumatics, cardiovascular drugs and antimicrobial drugs are the most important.[6] Penicillamine is among the most commonly incriminated (cicatricial more than bullous) usually in the context of rheumatoid arthritis patients.[6,14–16] Furosemide (frusemide) is believed to be an important cause of drug-induced bullous pemphigoid although recently this has been challenged, the author suggesting that diagnoses of pseudoporphyria or epidermolysis bullosa acquisita may be more appropriate in many reported cases.[6,17] The ACE inhibitors, captopril and enalapril have both been associated with immunologically proven bullous pemphigoid.[2,8] The penicillins including amoxicillin and procaine penicillin G are the most frequently implicated antibiotics.[6]

Clinically, drug-induced bullous pemphigoid is similar to idiopathic disease although the lesions are often polymorphic, mimicking other drug-induced bullous dermatoses such as erythema multiforme, eczematous dermatitis and porphyria cutanea tarda.[6] In drug-induced disease, mucous membranes are often involved, thereby blurring the distinction between bullous and cicatricial variants. In some patients there appears to be overlap between bullous pemphigoid and pemphigus vulgaris.[6]

Histological features

Drug-induced variants are characterized by the presence of linear deposits of IgG and C3 along the basement membrane region on direct immunofluorescence.[7,8] By indirect immunofluorescence, the antibodies bind to the epidermal side (roof) of split skin.[2,5,6] Western immunoblotting has demonstrated that the antibodies react with both the 230 kD and 180 kD bullous pemphigoid antigens.[2,3]

Histologically, drug-induced variants are similar to typical bullous pemphigoid, being characterized by an eosinophil-rich subepidermal blister.

References

1. Shachar, E., Bialy-Golan, A., Srebrnik, A. et al (1998) 'Two-step' drug-induced bullous pemphigoid. *Int J Dermatol*, **37**, 934–938.
2. Smith, E.P., Taylor, T.B., Meyer, L.J. et al (1993) Antigen identification in drug-induced bullous pemphigoid. *J Am Acad Dermatol*, **29**, 879–892.
3. Fellner, M.J. (1993) Drug-induced bullous pemphigoid. *Clin Dermatol*, **11**, 515–520.
4. Ruocco, V., Sacerdoti, G. (1991) Pemphigus and bullous pemphigoid due to drugs. *Int J Dermatol*, **30**, 307–312.
5. Bastuji-Garin, S., Joly, P., Picard-Dahan, C. et al (1996) Drugs associated with bullous pemphigoid: a case controlled study. *Arch Dermatol*, **132**, 272–276.
6. Vassileva, S. (1998) Drug-induced pemphigoid: bullous and cicatricial. *Clin Dermatol*, **16**, 379–387.
7. Pompeova, L. (1981) Bulozni pemphigoid vyvolany uzivanim Brufenu. *Cesk Dermatol (Prague)*, **56**, 256–258.
8. Mallet, L., Cooper, J.W., Thomas, J. (1989) Bullous pemphigoid associated with captopril. *DCIP*, **23**, 63.
9. Kimyai-Asadi, A., Usman, A., Nousari, H.C. (2000) Ciprofloxacin-induced bullous pemphigoid. *J Am Acad Dermatol*, **42**, 847.
10. Millard, T.P., Smith, H.R., Black, M.M. et al (1999) Bullous pemphigoid developing during systemic therapy with chloroquine. *Clin Exp Dermatol*, **24**, 263–265.
11. Shepherd, A.N., Ferguson, J., Bewick, M. et al (1986) Mefenamic acid-induced bullous pemphigoid. *Postgrad Med J*, **62**, 67–68.
12. Kashihara, M., Danno, K., Miyachi, Y. et al (1984) Bullous pemphigoid-like lesions induced by phenacetin: report of a case and an immunopathologic study. *Arch Dermatol*, **120**, 1196–1199.
13. Grange, F., Scrivener, Y., Koessler, A. et al (1997) Spironolactone-induced pemphigoid. *Ann Dermatol Venereol*, **124**, 700–702.
14. Marti-Huguet, T., Quintana, M., Cabiro, I. et al (1989) Cicatricial pemphigoid associated with D-penicillamine treatment. *Arch Ophthalmol*, **107**, 1115.

15. Yamaguchi, R., Oryu, F., Hidano, A. (1989) A case of bullous pemphigoid induced by tiobutarit (D-penicillamine analogue). *J Dermatol*, **16**, 308–311.
16. Bialy-Golan, A., Brenner, S. (1996) Penicillamine-induced bullous dermatoses. *J Am Acad Dermatol*, **35**, 732–742.
17. Heydenreich, G., Pindborg, T., Schmidt, H. (1977) Bullous dermatosis among patients with chronic renal failure on high-dose frusemide. *Acta Med Scand*, **202**, 61–64.

Drug-induced epidermolysis bullosa acquisita

Drug-induced epidermolysis bullosa acquisita has been described following treatment with granulocyte–macrophage colony stimulating factor (GM-CSF) and in a patient receiving vancomycin and gentamicin therapy.[1,2] In both patients, the blisters were subepidermal and eosinophil rich; direct immunofluorescence disclosed linear IgA and IgG deposits at the basement membrane region. Split skin indirect immunofluorescence in the former patient labeled the floor of the blister cavity and by immunoelectron microscopy the deposits were localized to the lamina densa and the sub-lamina densa region.[1] In the latter patient, IgG antibodies against type VII collagen were recognized by an enzyme-linked immunosorbent assay (ELISA).[2]

A significant number of cases of vancomycin-induced linear IgA disease are characterized by antibodies which label the floor of split skin on indirect immunofluorescence. It has been suggested that many of these might represent further examples of drug-induced epidermolysis bullosa acquisita.[2] An epidermolysis bullosa acquisita-like blistering dermatosis has been described with penicillamine therapy but this has not been confirmed with immunofluorescent or molecular data.[3]

References

1. Ward, J.C., Gitlin, J.B., Garry, D.J. et al (1992) Epidermolysis bullosa acquisita induced by GM-CSF: a role for eosinophils in treatment-related toxicity. *Br J Haematol*, **81**, 27–32.
2. Delbaldo, C., Chen, M., Friedli, A. et al (2002) Drug-induced epidermolysis bullosa acquisita with antibodies to type VII collagen. *J Am Acad Dermatol*, **46** (Suppl.), 161–164.
3. Bialy-Golan, A., Brenner, S. (1996) Penicillamine-induced bullous dermatoses. *J Am Acad Dermatol*, **35**, 732–742.

Drug-induced pemphigus

Clinical features

Pemphigus may be related to a wide range of drugs, either directly as a causative factor or indirectly as a precipitating or triggering factor.[1–14] The range of drugs is quite wide but many belong to the thiol group of compounds (characterized by the presence of an –SH group) including penicillamine, captopril, bucillamine and thioronine.[1,4] Thiol-induced acantholysis is mediated by both immune and direct biochemical mechanisms.[5] Penicillamine most often induces pemphigus in the setting of rheumatoid arthritis.[6] Although foliaceus is most commonly encountered, vulgaris, erythematosus and herpetiform variants may also be found.[2,6–8] Other drugs that contain sulfur, and which can also form –SH groups, include gold compounds, penicillins, rifampicin and cephalosporins.[4]

Clinically, drug-induced pemphigus can resemble vulgaris, foliaceus and erythematosus variants, the first being nowadays most often encountered.[4] In the older literature, foliaceus variants were more typical but with a change in prescribing habits to non-thiol related drugs, vulgaris-type cases have become the more frequently seen.[4]

Pathogenesis and histological features

Histologically, drug-induced and idiopathic variants are indistinguishable.[15] Intercellular IgG and circulating antibodies are variable in drug-induced pemphigus although in a recent series of 10 patients, all had positive direct immunofluorescence and 80% had circulating antibodies.[4] Such antibodies may recognize desmoglein 3 and/or 1.[1,16]

References

1. Ruocco, V., Sacerdoti, G. (1991) Pemphigus and bullous pemphigoid due to drugs. *Int J Dermatol*, **30**, 307–312.
2. Brenner, S., Wolf, R., Ruocco, V. (1993) Drug-induced pemphigus: 1. A survey. *Clin Dermatol*, **11**, 501–505.
3. Brenner, S., Bialy-Golan, A., Anhalt, G.J. (1997) Recognition of pemphigus antigens in drug-induced pemphigus vulgaris and foliaceus. *J Am Acad Dermatol*, **36**, 919–923.
4. Brenner, S., Bialy-Golan, A., Ruocco, V. (1998) Drug-induced pemphigus. *Clin Dermatol*, **16**, 393–397.
5. Wolf, R., Tamir, A., Brenner, S. (1991) Drug-induced versus drug-triggered pemphigus. *Dermatologica*, **182**, 207–210.
6. Bialy-Golan, A., Brenner, S. (1996) Penicillamine-induced bullous dermatoses. *J Am Acad Dermatol*, **35**, 732–742.
7. Santa-Cruz, D., Prioleau, P.G., Marcus, M.D. et al (1981) Pemphigus-like lesions induced by D-penicillamine. *Am J Dermatopathol*, **3**, 85–92.
8. Marsden, R.A., Dawber, R.P.R., Millard, P.R. et al (1977) Herpetiform pemphigus induced by penicillamine. *Br J Dermatol*, **97**, 451–452.
9. Kishimoto, K., Iwatsuki, K., Akiba, H. et al (2001) Subcorneal pustular dermatosis – type IgA pemphigus induced by thiol drugs. *Eur J Dermatol*, **11**, 41–44.
10. Goldberg, I., Kashman, Y., Brenner, S. (1999) The induction of pemphigus by phenol drugs. *Int J Dermatol*, **38**, 888–892.
11. Matz, H., Bialy-Golan, A., Brenner, S. (1997) Diclofenac: a new trigger of pemphigus vulgaris? *Dermatology*, **195**, 48–49.
12. Anadolu, R.Y., Birol, A., Bostanci, S. et al (2002) A case of pemphigus possibly triggered by quinolones. *J Eur Acad Dermatol Venereol*, **16**, 152–153.
13. Ogata, K., Nakajima, H., Ikeda, M. et al (2001) Drug-induced pemphigus foliaceus with features of pemphigus vulgaris. *Br J Dermatol*, **144**, 421–422.
14. Ramseur, W.L., Richards, F., Duggan, D.B. (1989) A fatal case of pemphigus vulgaris in association with beta interferon and interleukin-2 therapy. *Cancer*, **63**, 2005–2007.
15. Korman, N.J., Eyre, R.W., Zone, J. et al (1991) Drug-induced pemphigus: autoantibodies directed against the pemphigus antigen complexes are present in penicillamine and captopril induced pemphigus. *J Invest Dermatol*, **96**, 273–276.
16. Landau, M., Brenner, S. (1997) Histopathologic findings in drug-induced pemphigus. *Am J Dermatopathol*, **19**, 411–414.

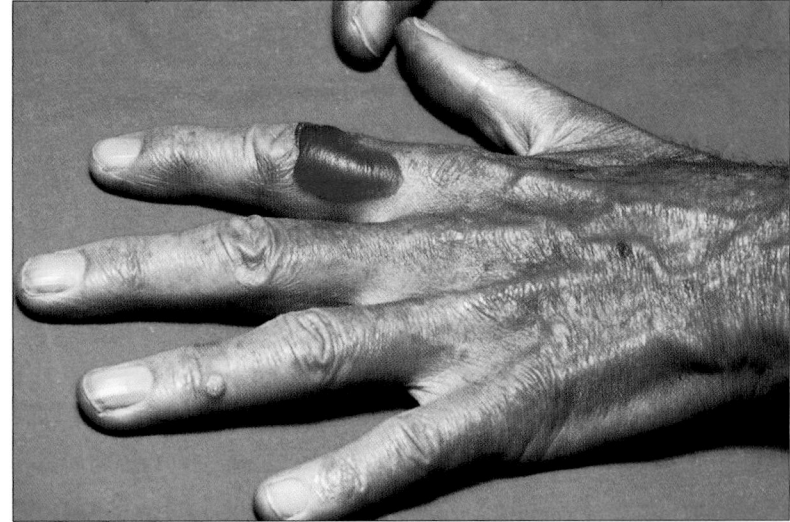

Fig. 13.63

Pseudoporphyria: trauma-induced blisters on the backs of the hands and fingers are characteristic. By courtesy of the Institute of Dermatology, London, UK.

Drug-induced pseudoporphyria

Clinical features

Pseudoporphyria is a rare blistering disease which clinically and histologically mimics porphyria but which develops in the setting of normal porphyrin metabolism (*Fig. 13.63*). There are a number of causes including drugs, chronic renal failure usually in the setting of dialysis, excessive sun-exposure and UVA. It has also been described following excessive use of sunbeds.[1–13] The most common medications have included diuretics such as furosemide (frusemide) and NSAIDs, particularly naproxen. Other drugs include isotretinoin and the oral contraceptive. This topic is also discussed on page 586.

Pathogenesis and histological features

The pathogenesis of pseudoporphyria is unknown but it may (at least in some patients) represent a phototoxic photosensitivity reaction.[12]

Histologically, pseudoporphyria is characterized by a subepidermal cell-free blister typically with preservation of the dermal papillae (festooning).

By immunofluorescence, immunoglobulin (most commonly IgG) is present at the epidermodermal junction and also outlining the superficial dermal vasculature.

References

1. Howard, A.M., Dowling, J., Varigos, G. (1985) Pseudoporphyria due to naproxen. *Lancet*, **1**, 819–820.
2. Murphy, G.M., Wright, J., Nicholls, D.S. et al (1989) Sunbed induced pseudoporphyria. *Br J Dermatol*, **120**, 555–562.
3. Riordan, C.A., Anstey, A., Wojnarowska, F. (1993) Isotretinoin-associated pseudoporphyria. *Clin Exp Dermatol*, **18**, 69–71.
4. Creemers, M.C., Chang, A., Franssen, M.J. et al (1995) Pseudoporphyria due to naproxen. A cluster of 3 cases. *Scand J Rheumatol*, **24**, 185–187.
5. Breier, F., Feldmann, R., Pelzl, M. et al (1998) Pseudoporphyria cutanea tarda induced by furosemide in a patient undergoing peritoneal dialysis. *Dermatology*, **197**, 271–273.
6. Al-Khenaizan, S., Schechter, J.F., Sasseville, D. (1999) Pseudoporphyria induced by proprionic acid derivatives. *J Cutan Med Surg*, **3**, 162–166.
7. Checketts, S.R., Morgan, G.J. Jr (1999) Two cases of nabumetone induced pseudoporphyria. *J Rheumatol*, **26**, 2703–2705.
8. De Silva, B., Banney, L., Uttley, W. et al (2000) Pseudoporphyria and non-steroidal antiinflammatory agents in children with juvenile idiopathic arthritis. *Pediatr Dermatol*, **17**, 480–483.
9. Green, J.J., Manders, S.M. (2001) Pseudoporphyria. *J Am Acad Dermatol*, **44**, 100–108.
10. Schambacher, C.F., Vanness, E.R., Daoud, M.S. et al (2001) Pseudoporphyria: a clinical and biochemical study of 20 patients. *Mayo Clin Proc*, **76**, 488–492.
11. O'Donoghue, N.B., Higgins, E.M. (2002) Naproxen-induced pseudoporphyria. *Clin Exp Dermatol*, **27**, 339–340.
12. La Duca, J.R., Bowman, P.H., Gaspari, A.A. (2002) Nonsteroidal antiinflammatory drug-induced pseudoporphyria: a case series. *J Cutan Med Surg*, **6**, 320–326.
13. Silver, E.A., Silver, A.H., Silver, D.S. et al (2003) Pseudoporphyria induced by oral contraceptive pills. *Arch Dermatol*, **139**, 227–228.

Psoriasiform drug reactions

Clinical features

Psoriasis and psoriasiform dermatoses can be caused by a number of drugs including lithium, beta-blockers, NSAIDs, synthetic antimalarials and tetracycline.[1–5] Drug-induced disease may present in a variety of ways including:[1,2]

- exacerbation of pre-existing psoriasis
- induction of new lesions in uninvolved psoriatic skin
- precipitation of psoriasis de novo
- resistance to treatment.

Lithium-induced psoriasis varies from exacerbation of pre-existing psoriasis to development of new disease.[2] Manifestations vary from plaque disease through to generalized pustular psoriasis, palmoplantar pustulosis, scalp psoriasis and psoriatic erythroderma.[2,6–8] Latency varies from 1 week to years or more.[2]

Beta-blockers (e.g. propranolol, oxprenolol, pindolol, alprenolol and the now discontinued practolol), antimalarials (e.g. chloroquine and hydroxychloroquine) and NSAIDs (e.g. indometacin, phenylbutazone, oxyphenylbutazone and ibuprofen) can also induce psoriasiform eruptions or result in exacerbations and flares.[1,2,9–15]

A large number of other drugs have been linked with exacerbation of psoriasis or development of new disease although many of these are represented by case reports only. These include the antifungal agent terbinafine, antibiotics such as penicillin and tetracycline, digoxin, amiodarone, IFN-α and recombinant IFN-γ.[2,16–24]

Histological features

The histological features overlap lichen simplex chronicus and psoriasis. Occasionally, they are indistinguishable from psoriasis vulgaris (*Figs 13.64–13.66*).

References

1. Abel, E.A., Di Cicco, L.M., Orenberg, E.K. et al (1986) Drugs in exacerbation of psoriasis. *J Am Acad Dermatol*, **15**, 1007–1022.
2. Abel, E.A. (1992) Diagnosis of drug-induced psoriasis. *Semin Dermatol*, **11**, 269–274.
3. Tsankov, N., Kazandjieva, J., Drenovska, K. (1998) Drugs in exacerbation and provocation of psoriasis. *Clin Dermatol*, **16**, 333–351.
4. Wolf, R., Ruocco, V. (1999) Triggered psoriasis. *Adv Exp Med Biol*, **455**, 221–225.
5. Tsankov, N., Angelova, I, Kazandjieva, J. (2000) Drug-induced psoriasis. Recognition and management. *Am J Clin Dermatol*, **1**, 159–165.
6. Heng, M.C.Y. (1982) Cutaneous manifestations of lithium toxicity. *Br J Dermatol*, **106**, 107–109.
7. Gupta, A.K., Knowles, S.A., Gupta, M.A. et al (1995) Lithium therapy associated with hidradenitis suppurativa: case report and review of side-effects of lithium. *J Am Acad Dermatol*, **32**, 382–386.
8. Skoven, I., Thormann, J. (1979) Lithium compound treatment and psoriasis. *Arch Dermatol*, **115**, 1185–1187.
9. Halevy, S., Feuerman, E.J. (1979) Psoriasiform eruption induced by propranolol. *Cutis*, **24**, 95–98.
10. Hodl, S. (1983) Side-effects of beta-receptor blockaders on the skin. *Z Hautkr*, **58**, 17–28.
11. Hu, C.H., Miller, C.M., Peppercorn, R. et al (1985) Generalized pustular psoriasis provoked by propranolol. *Arch Dermatol*, **121**, 1326–1327.
12. Gold, M.H., Holy, A.K., Roenigk, H.H. (1988) Beta blocking drugs and psoriasis: a review of cutaneous side-effects and retrospective analysis of their effects on psoriasis. *J Am Acad Dermatol*, **19**, 837–841.
13. Steinkraus, V., Mensing, V. (1992) Psoriasis and beta-blockade. *Hautarzt*, **43**, 179–183.
14. Tanenbaum, L., Tuffanelli, D.L. (1980) Antimalarial agents: chloroquine, hydroxychloroquine and quinacrine. *Arch Dermatol*, **116**, 587–591.
15. Vine, J.E., Hymes, S.A., Warner, N.B. et al (1996) Pustular psoriasis induced by hydroxychloroquine: a case report and review of the literature. *J Dermatol*, **23**, 357–361.
16. Fierlbeck, G., Rassner, G., Müller, C. (1990) Psoriasis induced at the injection site of recombinant interferon gamma. *Arch Dermatol*, **126**, 351–355.
17. Gupta, A.K., Sibbaid, R.G., Knowles, S.R. et al (1997) Terbinafine therapy may be associated with the development of psoriasis de novo or its exacerbation: four case reports and a review of drug-induced psoriasis. *J Am Acad Dermatol*, **36**, 858–862.
18. Gupta, A.K., Lynde, C.W., Lauzon, G.J. et al (1998) Cutaneous adverse effects associated with terbinafine therapy: 10 case reports and a review of the literature. *Br J Dermatol*, **138**, 529–532.
19. Brenard, R. (1997) Practical management of patients treated with α interferon. *Acta Gastro-Enterol Belg*, **60**, 211–213.
20. Yamamoto, T., Minatohara, K. (1997) Minocycline-induced acute generalized exanthematous pustulosis in a patient with generalized pustular psoriasis showing elevated level of sELAM-1. *Acta Derm Venereol*, **77**, 168–169.
21. Bergner, T., Przybilla, B. (1990) Psoriasis and tetracyclines. *J Am Acad Dermatol*, **23**, 770–771.
22. Tsankov, N.K., Vassileva, S.V., Lazarova, A.Z. et al (1988) Onset of psoriasis coincident with tetracycline therapy. *Australas J Dermatol*, **29**, 111–112.
23. Katz, M., Seidenbaum, M., Weinrauch, L. (1987) Penicillin-induced generalized pustular psoriasis. *J Am Acad Dermatol*, **17**, 918–920.
24. Muir, A.D. (1982) Amiodarone and psoriasis. *N Z Med J*, **13**, 711.

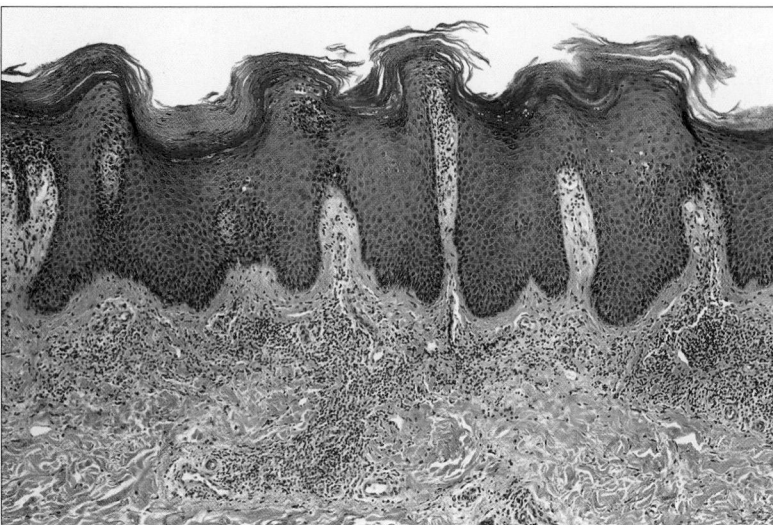

Fig. 13.64
Psoriasiform drug eruption: there is confluent parakeratosis with elongated, broadened and partially fused rete ridges.

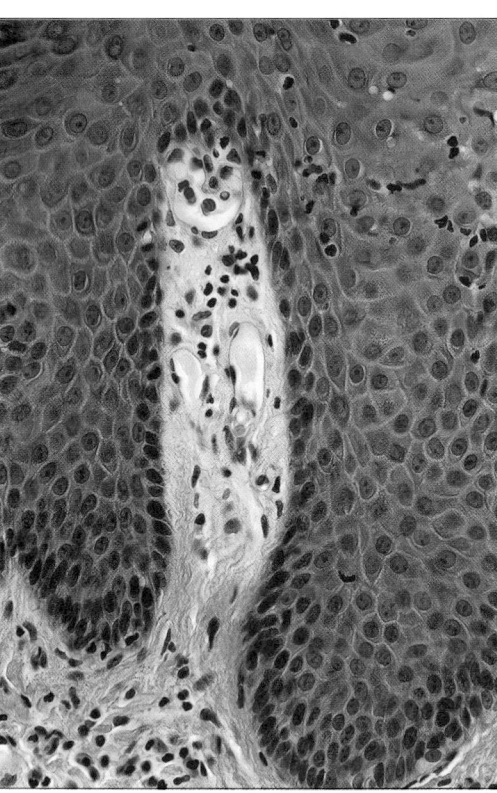

Fig. 13.65
Psoriasiform drug reaction: the capillaries in the dermal papillae are tortuous and dilated.

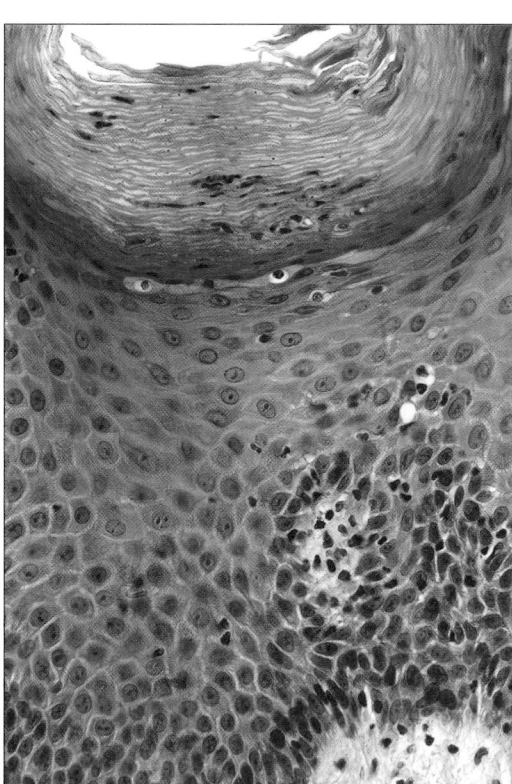

Fig. 13.66
Psoriasiform drug reaction: neutrophils are present in the stratum corneum.

Pityriasiform drug reactions

Clinical features

Pityriasiform drug reactions may be particularly caused by captopril and gold.[1-3] Less often, terbinafine, omeprazole, benflurex, arsenicals, bismuth compounds, isotretinoin, naproxen, acetaminophen, barbiturates and bacille Calmette–Guérin (BCG) therapy have been implicated.[4-8] Patients present with small erythematous lesions accompanied by a peripheral scale, which may follow Langer's lines giving rise to the typical 'fir tree' appearance. The trunk and extremities are predominantly affected.

Histological features

Histologically, pityriasiform drug reactions are typically characterized by patchy parakeratosis, focal spongiosis with lymphocytic exocytosis and a superficial perivascular lymphocytic infiltrate, sometimes associated with red cell extravasation (*Fig. 13.67*).[3,5] On occasions, however, clinically typical pityriasiform drug eruptions may be characterized by a more psoriasiform histology.[8]

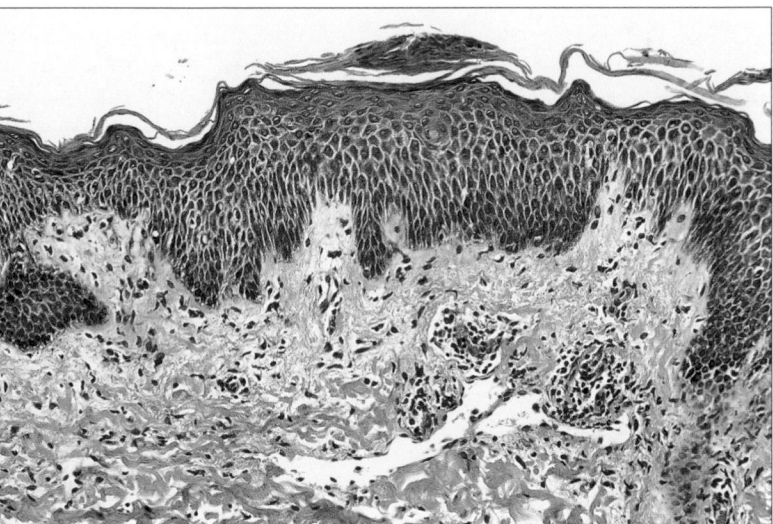

Fig. 13.67
Pityriasiform drug reaction: there is a focal parakeratotic scale associated with acanthosis and spongiosis.

References

1. Ghersetich, I., Rindi, L., Teofoli, P. et al (1990) Pityriasis rosea-like eruption caused by captopril. *G Ital Dermatol Venereol*, **125**, 457–459.
2. Wilkin, J.K., Kirkendall, W.M. (1982) Pityriasis rosea-like rash from captopril. *Arch Dermatol*, **118**, 186–187.
3. Wilkinson, S.M., Smith, A.G., Davis, M.J. et al (1992) Pityriasis rosea and discoid eczema: dose related reactions to treatment with gold. *Ann Rheum Dis*, **51**, 881–884.
4. Loche, F., Thouvenin, M.D., Bazex, J. (2000) Pityriasis-rosea-like eruption due to benflurex. *Dermatology*, **201**, 75.
5. Buckley, C. (1996) Pityriasis rosea-like eruption in a patient receiving omeprazole. *Br J Dermatol*, **135**, 660–661.
6. Honl, B.A., Keeling, J.H., Lewis, C.W. et al (1996) A pityriasis rosea-like eruption secondary to bacillus Calmette–Guérin therapy for bladder cancer. *Cutis*, **57**, 447–450.
7. Yosipovitch, G., Kuperman, O., Livni, E. et al (1993) Pityriasis rosea-like eruption after anti-inflammatory and antipyretic medication. *Harefuah*, **124**, 198–200.
8. Helfman, R.J., Brickman, M., Fahy, J. (1984) Isotretinoin dermatitis simulating acute pityriasis rosea. *Cutis*, **33**, 297–300.

Pustular drug reactions

Clinical features

Drug-induced pustules are a manifestation of acneiform reactions due to corticosteroids, anabolic steroids, oral contraceptives, isoniazid, haloperidol and lithium therapy (*Fig. 13.68*).[1] In addition they are a particular feature of the halogenodermas (see below).

Pustules are also the main feature of acute generalized exanthematous pustulosis (toxic pustuloderma) (*Fig. 13.69*). This rare condition is characterized by the sudden onset of numerous small, non-follicular pustules arising against a background of pruritic or burning edematous erythroderma.[2-10] The eruption often starts on the face or in the intertriginous regions but soon becomes generalized.[3] The mucous membranes are affected in only a minority of patients.[3] Facial edema, purpura, vesicles, blisters and erythema multiforme-like lesions have also been described.[3,4] Pyrexia is usually present. Although in the majority of patients there is no history of significant previous skin disease, in some there is a background of psoriasis.[3] The eruption usually resolves rapidly

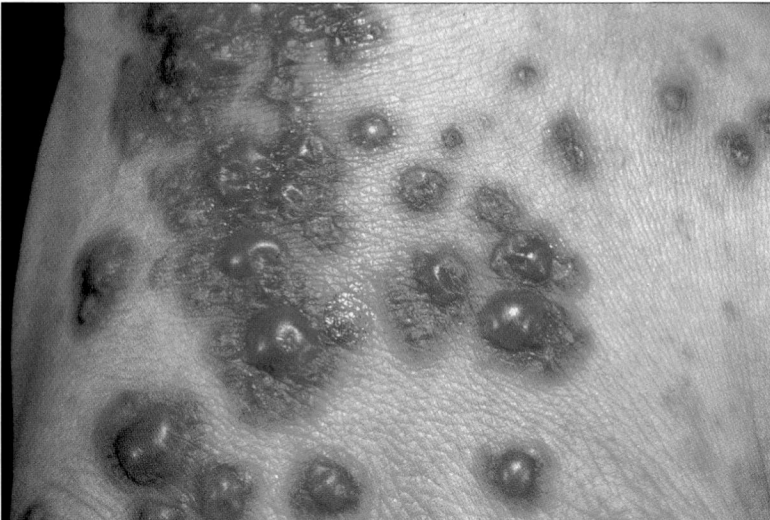

Fig. 13.68
Pustular drug reaction: numerous pustules are present on an erythematous background. By courtesy of the Institute of Dermatology, London, UK.

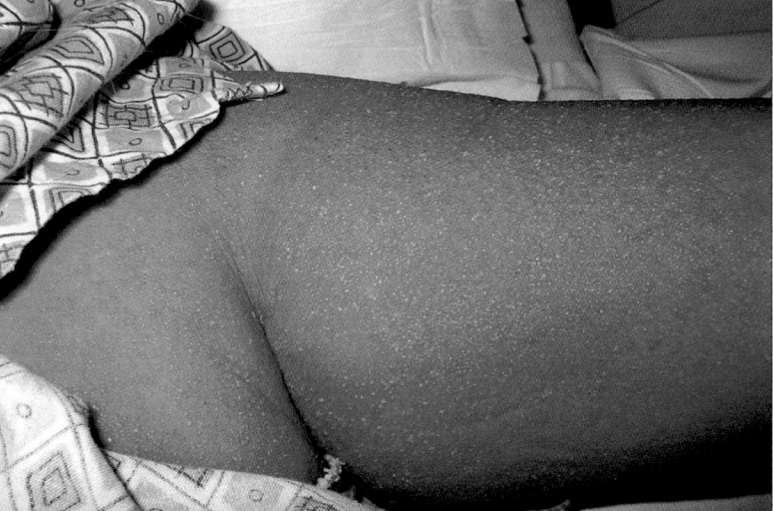

Fig. 13.69
Acute generalized exanthematous pustulosis: tiny pustules are evident. There is intense erythema. By courtesy of B.A. Solky, MD, Department of Dermatology, Harvard Medical School, Boston, USA.

and is often followed by widespread desquamation.[7] Laboratory investigations often reveal a peripheral leukocytosis with high neutrophil levels and sometimes an eosinophilia is also present.[3,7]

While this disorder may occur as a feature of mercury toxicity or follow a viral infection (particularly enteroviruses), in the majority of cases it represents an adverse drug reaction.[3] In most patients, the eruption has followed antibiotic therapy including penicillin, amoxicillin, ampicillin, metronidazole, trimethoprim and erythromycin.[3,7] Analgesics (e.g. acetaminophen), antiepileptics (e.g. carbamazepine), antidiabetics (e.g. carbutamide) and many other drugs have also been implicated.[3,9–12] The condition often develops very rapidly following the administration of the drug – sometimes in only a matter of hours.[3,5]

Histological features

The pustules are present in a subcorneal and/or intraepidermal location and sometimes may contain a few acantholytic keratinocytes in addition to large numbers of neutrophils (*Fig. 13.70*).[3,7] A background of spongiosis is usually evident. The dermal papillae are often edematous and occasionally subepidermal vesiculation is a feature. A perivascular infiltrate of lymphocytes and histiocytes with conspicuous neutrophils and variable numbers of eosinophils is usually present in the superficial dermis. Leukocytoclastic vasculitis may also be a feature in a significant proportion of cases.[3,7,9]

Differential diagnosis

The differential diagnosis includes pustular psoriasis, subcorneal pustular dermatosis, pustular necrotizing angiitis and acute generalized pustular bacterid.[13,14]

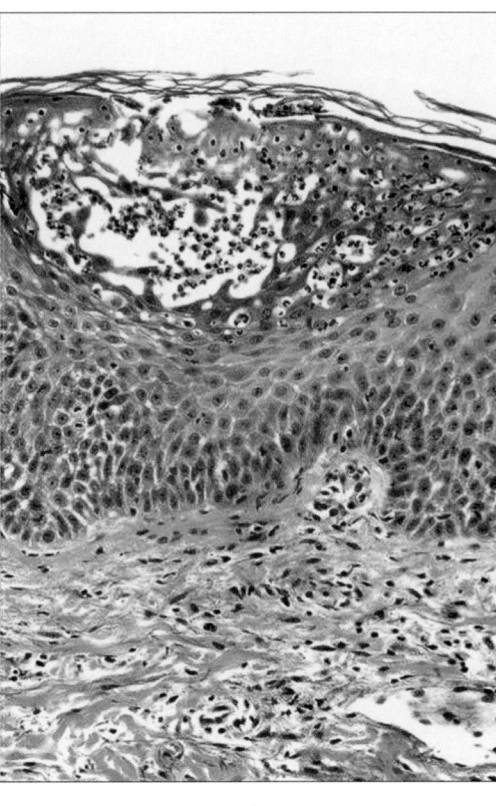

Fig. 13.70
Acute generalized exanthematous pustulosis: there is a superficial neutrophil-rich pustule with adjacent spongiosis.

References

1. Breathnach, S.M., Hintner, H. (1992) Types of clinical reactions. In: Adverse drug reactions and the skin. Oxford: Blackwell Scientific, pp 93–95.
2. Beylot, C., Bioulac, P., Doutre, M.S. (1980) Pustuloses exanthématiques aigües généralisées: a propos de 4 cas. *Ann Dermatol Venereol*, **107**, 37–48.
3. Roujeau, J.C., Biolac-Sage, P., Bourseau, C. et al (1991) Acute generalized exanthematous pustulosis, analysis of 63 cases. *Arch Dermatol*, **127**, 1333–1338.
4. Moreau, A., Dompmartin, A., Castel, B. et al (1995) Drug-induced acute generalized exanthematous pustulosis with positive patch tests. *Int J Dermatol*, **34**, 263–266.
5. Sawhney, R.A., Dubin, D.B., Otley, C.C. et al (1996) Generalized exanthematous pustulosis induced by medications. *Int J Dermatol*, **35**, 826–827.
6. Staughton, R.C.D., Rowland-Payne, C.M.E., Harper, J.I. et al (1984) Toxic pustuloderma: a new entity? *J R Soc Med*, **77** (Suppl. 44), 6–8.
7. Burrows, N.P., Russell-Jones, R. (1993) Pustular drug eruptions: histological spectrum. *Histopathology*, **22**, 569–573.
8. Bissonnette, R., Tousignant, J., Allaire, G. (1992), Drug-induced toxic pustuloderma. *Int J Dermatol*, **31**, 172–174.
9. Rustin, M.H.A., Robinson, T.W.E., Dowd, P.M. (1990) Toxic pustuloderma: a self limiting eruption. *Br J Dermatol*, **123**, 119–124.
10. Feind-Koopmans, A., van der Valk, P.G.M., Steijlen, P.M. et al (1996) Toxic pustuloderma associated with clemastine therapy. *Clin Exp Dermatol*, **21**, 293–295.
11. Yu, R.C.H., Chu, A.C. (1993) Allopurinol induced pustuloderma. *J Dermatol*, **128**, 95–98.
12. Darvay, A., Basarab, T., Russell-Jones, R. (1997) Thalidomide-induced toxic pustuloderma. *Clin Exp Dermatol*, **22**, 297–299.
13. Diaz, L.A., Provost, T.T., Tomasi, T.B. (1973) Pustular necrotizing angiitis. *Arch Dermatol*, **108**, 114–118.
14. Tan, R.S.H. (1974) Acute generalized pustular bacterid: an unusual manifestation of leukocytoclastic vasculitis. *Br J Dermatol*, **91**, 209–215.

Ichthyosiform drug reactions

Clinical features

Exceptionally, acquired ichthyosis following lipid-lowering agents (including triparanol and diazacholesterol) and kava consumption has been documented.[1,2] The clinical features may resemble either ichthyosis vulgaris or lamellar ichthyosis (see *Fig. 2.65*).

Histological features

In ichthyosis vulgaris-like drug-induced variants, there is mild hyperkeratosis associated with a diminished to absent granular cell layer. A mild superficial perivascular lymphohistiocytic infiltrate with occasional eosinophils may also be present.

In the lamellar ichthyosis-like variant, there is marked hyperkeratosis, mild acanthosis and a normal or thickened granular cell layer.

References

1. Proksch, E. (1995) Antilipemic drug-induced skin manifestations. *Hautarzt*, **46**, 76–80.
2. Ruze, P. (1990) Kava-induced dermopathy – a niacin deficiency? *Lancet*, **335**, 1442–1445.

Drug-induced pseudolymphoma

Clinical features

Drug-induced pseudolymphoma includes pseudolymphomatous reactions to systemically administered medications (lymphomatoid drug eruption) and the much less frequently encountered contact variant associated with locally administered agents (lymphomatoid contact dermatitis).[1–3]

Lymphomatoid drug eruptions are generally of a T-cell type although B-cell lymphomatoid drug eruptions are also recognized. T-cell variants are divided into anticonvulsant-related and non-anticonvulsant-related variants.[2]

Anticonvulsant-related T-cell lymphomatoid drug eruption typically develops within weeks or a few months of commencing drug treatment. Patients present with pyrexia, lymphadenopathy and an eruption of

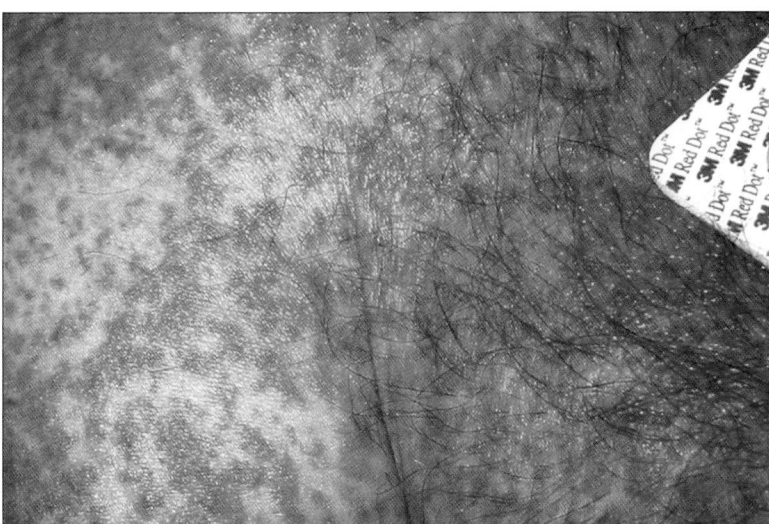

Fig. 13.71
Drug-induced pseudolymphoma: this patient developed a maculopapular eruption following treatment with phenytoin.

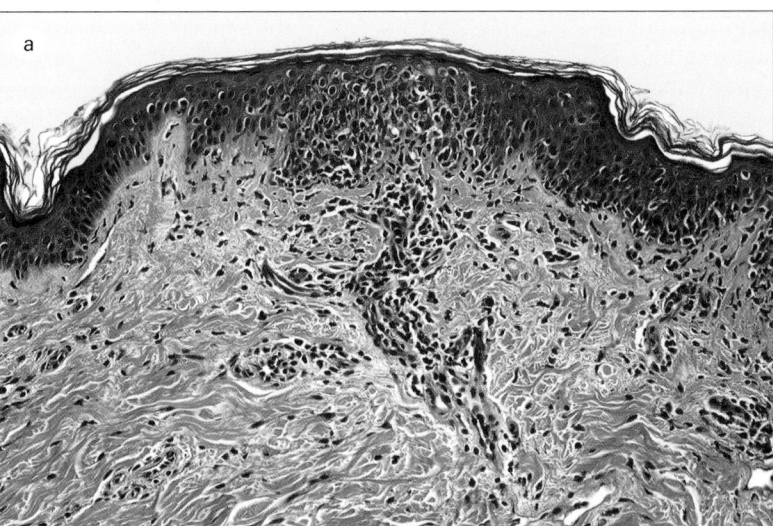

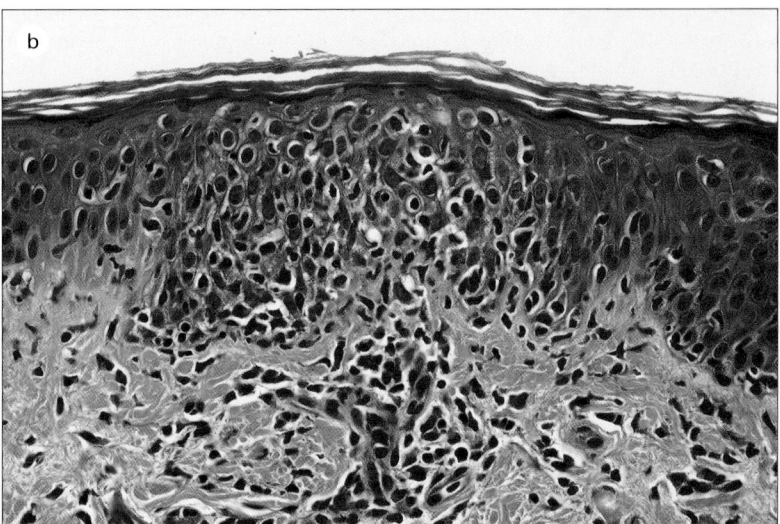

Fig. 13.72
(a, b) Phenytoin-induced pseudolymphoma: there is an atypical superficial perivascular lymphocytic infiltrate. Note the marked epidermotropism. The histological features are suggestive of mycosis fungoides.

single or generalized lesions comprising erythematous, morbilliform maculopapules, plaques, nodules or tumors often associated with leukocytosis, circulating Sézary cells, eosinophilia, hepatosplenomegaly and variable liver dysfunction (*Fig. 13.71*).[2,4–15] Vesicles and purpuric lesions have also been described.[14] Sézary syndrome-like features may rarely be seen.[16] A number of anticonvulsants have been implicated including phenytoin, primidone, mephenytoin, carbamazepine, phenobarbital and trimethadione.[2]

Non-anticonvulsant-related pseudolymphomatous reactions present similarly with single lesions or multiple papules, plaques and nodules and have been described in association with a wide range of drugs including antihypertensive agents, antidepressants, tranquilizers, beta-blockers, calcium channel blockers, diuretics, NSAIDs and antibiotics.[2,17–21] In addition, Sézary syndrome-like features have also been documented.[22]

Lymphomatoid contact dermatitis is much less common and represents usually a T-cell reaction to a contact allergen that histologically shows features reminiscent of mycosis fungoides.[2,23–30] Patients present with pruritic, localized to generalized scaly papules and plaques.[2] A number of antigens have been incriminated including matchbox striking surface antigens, ethylenediamine dihydrochloride, isopropyl-diphenylenediamine, phosphorus, nickel, cobalt naphthenate and *para*-phenylenediamine.

B-cell lymphomatoid drug reaction is rare but has been described in association with fluoxetine hydrochloride and amitriptyline hydrochloride.[2,20,21] Patients present with solitary nodules, multiple infiltrative plaques or multiple papules.

B-cell lymphomatoid contact reactions may be seen with gold and nickel earrings. Patients present with one or more firm, erythematous nodules at the site of piercing.[31–33]

Pathogenesis and histological features

Drug-induced T-cell pseudolymphoma most often presents as a dense superficial perivascular or band-like infiltrate composed of lymphocytes, histiocytes and atypical lymphoid cells with irregular, enlarged and hyperchromatic nuclei (*Figs 13.72–13.74*).[34] Cerebriform variants may be seen and there is often associated epidermotropism. Pautrier-like microabscesses reminiscent of mycosis fungoides, however, are only occasionally identified. Eosinophils are frequently evident and often the epidermis shows significant spongiosis. Giant cells, collections of histiocytes and epithelioid granulomata may also be evident. Dense

nodular and tumor-like variants more suggestive of pleomorphic T-cell lymphoma may also be encountered (*Figs 13.75–13.77*). A follicular mucinosis-like variant has rarely been described.[21]

By immunohistochemistry, the infiltrate consists of CD3+ T-cells. CD4+ cells most often outnumber CD8+ forms and CD20+ B-cells are either extremely sparse or absent. A CD8+ variant has, however, been recently described following treatment with gemcitabine.[35] CD30 expression with resultant confusion with an anaplastic large cell lymphoma has exceptionally been described.[11,35]

Reported T-cell receptor gene rearrangement studies have disclosed a clonal population in only a small minority of patients.[5,6,12,14]

Lymphomatoid contact dermatitis most often is reminiscent of mycosis fungoides and is characterized by a superficial dermal band-like infiltrate composed of atypical lymphocytes and histiocytes with variable lymphocyte epidermotropism. The epidermis is typically acanthotic and spongiosis may sometimes be present.

Immunohistochemical analysis has been reported in a small number of cases. The atypical lymphocytes usually express CD3 and CD4 with no loss of CD5 and CD7. A CD8 predominant variant has been documented.[28]

In the limited number of cases in which T-cell receptor (TCR) gene rearrangements have been documented, two have disclosed a polyclonal pattern while one has displayed a weak monoclonal band.[25,28,30]

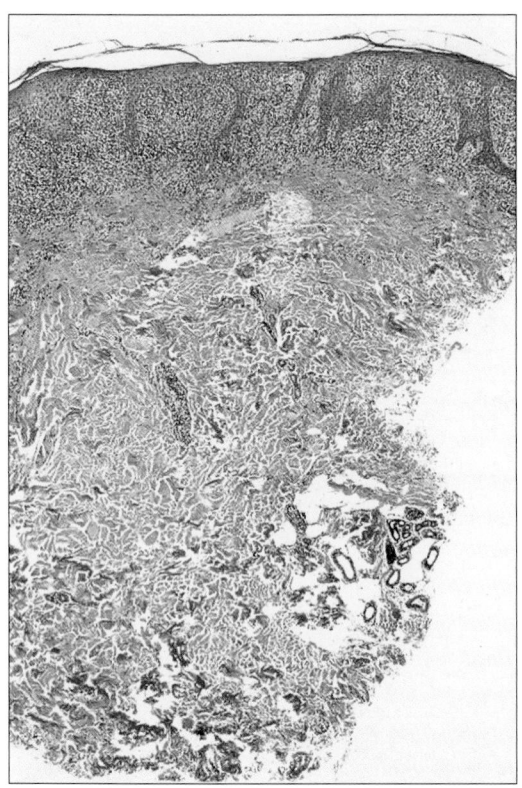

Fig. 13.73
Carbamazepine-induced
pseudolymphoma: in this
example, there is a
dense band-like upper
dermal lymphocytic
infiltrate.

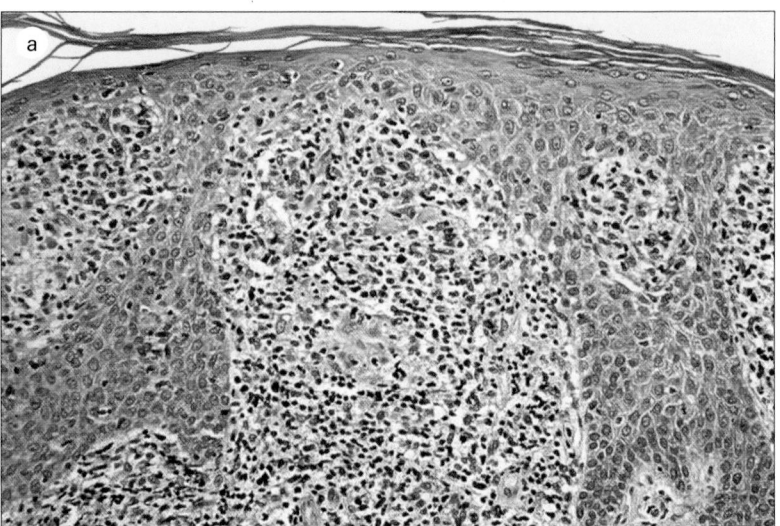

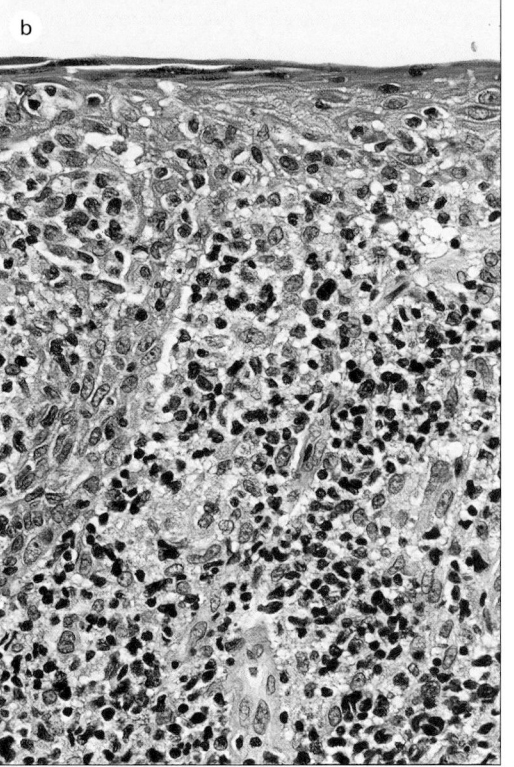

Fig. 13.74
(a, b) Carbamazepine-
induced
pseudolymphoma: there
is marked lymphocytic
atypia. Cerebriform cells
are present. The features
are very suggestive of
plaque stage mycosis
fungoides. Diagnosis
depends upon careful
clinicopathological
correlation.

Fig. 13.75
Drug-induced
pseudolymphoma: this
very dense dermal
infiltrate developed
following treatment with
an antidepressant.
Multiple cutaneous
nodules were present.

confirming the presence of poorly developed follicles. Kappa and lambda immunohistochemistry invariably show no evidence of light chain restriction.

Differential diagnosis

Distinction between cutaneous lymphoma and a drug-induced pseudo-lymphoma can be exceedingly difficult. The histological overlap and rare instances of a T-cell receptor gene rearrangement necessitate close clinicopathological correlation. If cutaneous pseudolymphoma is suspected, the most effective way to make the distinction is withdrawal of the suspected drug. It is exceedingly important that correlation always be undertaken in any case of an unanticipated lymphoma in order that reactive conditions do not receive inappropriate lymphoma treatment.

B-cell lymphomatoid drug reactions are characterized by a nodular or diffuse pandermal infiltrate, often accompanied by extension into the subcutaneous fat. The infiltrate consists of an admixture of lymphocytes and histiocytes with variable numbers of plasma cells and eosinophils. Mitoses are sometimes numerous. Blasts are often present and lymphoid follicles with germinal centers may be evident.

By immunohistochemistry, the majority of the lymphocytes are CD20+ B-cells although a subpopulation of CD3+ T-cells is also present. Identification of CD21+ follicular dendritic cells may be helpful in

References

1. Del Rosso, J.Q. (2002) Skin manifestations of drug reactions. *Curr Allergy Asthma Rep*, **2**, 282–287.
2. Phoysangam, T., Breneman, D.L., Mutasim, D.F. (1998) Cutaneous pseudolymphomas. *J Am Acad Dermatol*, **38**, 877–895.

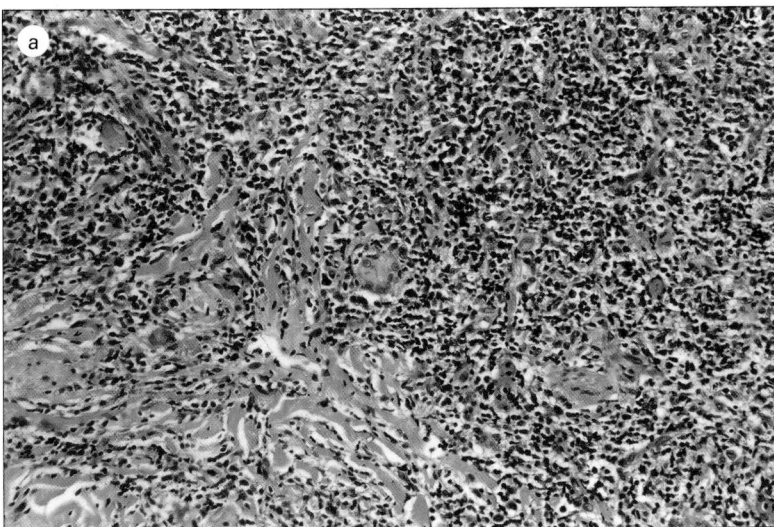

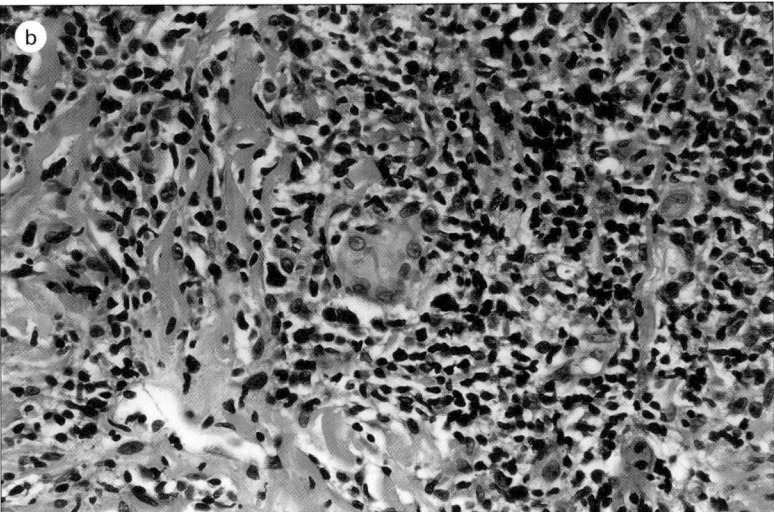

Fig. 13.76

(a, b) Drug-induced pseudolymphoma: scattered multinucleated giant cells are evident.

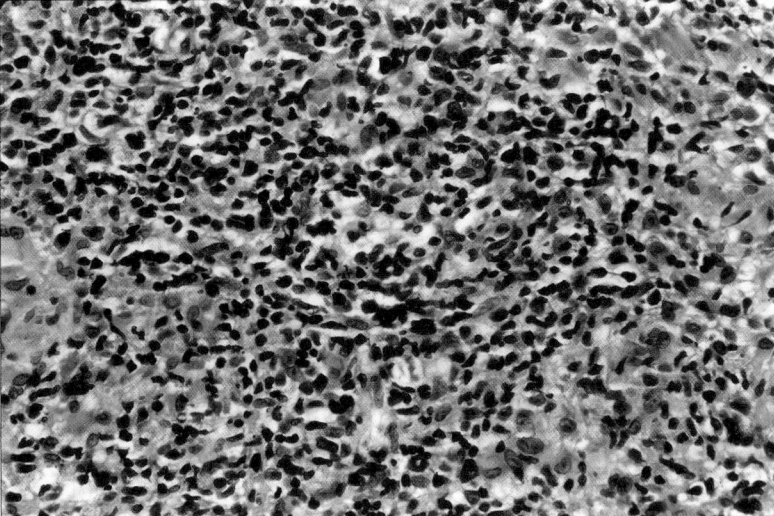

Fig. 13.77

Drug-induced pseudolymphoma: there is marked lymphocytic atypia. The nodules melted away following withdrawal of the antidepressant.

3. Gilliam, A.C., Wood, G.S. (2000) Cutaneous lymphoid hyperplasias. *Semin Cutan Med Surg*, **19**, 133–141.
4. Wolf, R., Kahane, E., Sandbank, M. (1985) Mycosis fungoides-like lesions associated with phenytoin therapy. *Arch Dermatol*, **121**, 1181–1182.
5. Harris, D.W., Osterle, L., Buckley, C. et al (1992) Phenytoin-induced pseudolymphoma. A report of a case and review of the literature. *Br J Dermatol*, **127**, 403–406.
6. Braddock, S.W., Harrington, D., Vose, J. (1992) Generalized nodular cutaneous pseudolymphoma associated with phenytoin therapy. Use of T-cell receptor gene re-arrangement in diagnosis and clinical review of reactions to phenytoin. *J Am Acad Dermatol*, **27**, 337–340.
7. Welykyj, S., Gradini, R., Nakao, J. et al (1990) Carbamazepine-induced eruption histologically mimicking mycosis fungoides. *J Cutan Pathol*, **17**, 111–116.
8. Rijlaarsdam, U., Scheffer, E., Meijer, J. et al (1991) Mycosis fungoides-like lesions associated with phenytoin and carbamazepine therapy. *J Am Acad Dermatol*, **24**, 216–220.
9. De Vriese, S.P., Philippe, J., Van Renterghem, D.M. et al (1995) Carbamazepine hypersensitivity syndrome: report of 4 cases and review of the literature. *Medicine (Baltimore)*, **74**, 144–151.
10. Miranda-Romero, A., Pérez-Olivia, N., Aragoneses, H. et al (2001) Carbamazepine hypersensitivity syndrome mimicking mycosis fungoides. *Cutis*, **67**, 47–51.
11. Nathan, D.L., Belsito, D.V. (1998) Carbamazepine-induced pseudolymphoma with CD-30 positive cells. *J Am Acad Dermatol*, **38**, 806–809.
12. Saeki, H., Etoh, T., Toda, K. et al (1999) Pseudolymphoma syndrome caused by carbamazepine. *J Dermatol*, **26**, 329–331.
13. Cogrel, O., Beylot-Barry, M., Vergier, B. et al (2001) Sodium valproate-induced cutaneous pseudolymphoma followed by recurrence with carbamazepine. *Br J Dermatol*, **144**, 1235–1238.
14. Brady, S.P., Magro, C.M., Diáz-Cano, S.J. et al (1999) Analysis of clonality of atypical cutaneous lymphoid infiltrates associated with drug therapy by PCR/DGGE. *Hum Pathol*, **30**, 130–136.
15. D'Incan, M., Mouillet, M.L., Roger, H. et al (1998) Cutaneous pseudolymphoma caused by carbamazepine. *Ann Dermatol Venereol*, **125**, 52–55.
16. D'Incan, M., Souteyrand, P., Bignon, Y.J. et al (1992) Hydantoin-induced cutaneous pseudolymphoma with clinical, pathologic, and immunologic features of Sézary syndrome. *Arch Dermatol*, **128**, 1371–1374.
17. Gupta, A.K., Cooper, K.D., Ellis, C.N. et al (1990) Lymphocytic infiltrates of the skin in association with cyclosporine therapy. *J Am Acad Dermatol*, **23**, 1137–1141.
18. Rijlaarsdam, U., Scheffer, E., Meijer, C.J.L.M. et al (1992) Cutaneous pseudo-T-cell lymphomas: a clinicopathologic study of 20 patients. *Cancer*, **69**, 717–724.
19. Henderson, C.A., Shanmy, H.K. (1990) Atenolol-induced pseudolymphoma. *Clin Exp Dermatol*, **15**, 119–120.
20. Crowson, A.N., Magro, C.M. (1995) Antidepressant therapy. A possible cause of atypical cutaneous lymphoid hyperplasia. *Arch Dermatol*, **131**, 925–929.
21. Magro, C.M., Crowson, A.N. (1995) Drugs with antihistaminic properties as a cause of atypical cutaneous lymphoid hyperplasia. *J Am Acad Dermatol*, **32**, 419–428.
22. Souteyrand, P., d'Incan, M. (1990) Drug-induced mycosis fungoides-like lesions. *Curr Probl Dermatol*, **19**, 176–182.
23. Orbaneja, J.G., Diez, L.I., Lozano, J.L. et al (1976) Lymphomatoid contact dermatitis: a syndrome produced by epicutaneous hypersensitivity with clinical features and a histopathologic picture similar to that of mycosis fungoides. *Contact Dermatitis*, **2**, 139–143.
24. Ayala, F., Balato, N., Nappa, P. et al (1987) Lymphomatoid contact dermatitis. *Contact Dermatitis*, **17**, 311–313.
25. Danese, P., Bertazzoni, M.G. (1995) Lymphomatoid contact dermatitis due to nickel. *Contact Dermatitis*, **33**, 268–269.
26. Houck, H.E., Wirth, F.A., Kauffman, C.L. (1997) Lymphomatoid contact dermatitis caused by nickel. *Am J Contact Dermat*, **8**, 175–176.
27. Wall, L.M. (1982) Lymphomatoid contact dermatitis due to ethylenediamine dihydrochloride. *Contact Dermatitis*, **8**, 51–54.
28. Calzavara-Pinton, P., Capezzera, R., Zane, C. et al (2002) Lymphomatoid allergic contact dermatitis from para-phenylenediamine. *Contact Dermatitis*, **47**, 173–174.
29. Schena, D., Rosina, P., Chiergato, C. et al (1995) Lymphomatoid-like contact dermatitis from cobalt naphthenate. *Contact Dermatitis*, **33**, 197–198.
30. Marliere, V., Beylot-Barry, M., Doutre, M.S. et al (1998) Lymphomatoid contact dermatitis caused by isopropyl-diphenylenediamine: two cases. *J Allergy Clin Immunol*, **102**, 152–153.
31. Zemtsov, A., Cameron, G.S., Montalvo-Lugo, V. (1997) Nickel-induced lymphocytoma: lymphocytoma cutis of the earlobe. *Contact Dermatitis*, **36**, 266.
32. Fleming, C., Burden, D., Fallowfield, M. et al (1997) Lymphomatoid contact reaction to gold earrings. *Contact Dermatitis*, **37**, 298–299.
33. Park, Y.M., Kang, H., Kim, H.O. et al (1999) Lymphomatoid eosinophilic reaction to gold earrings. *Contact Dermatitis*, **40**, 216–217.
34. Rijlaarsdam, U., Willemze, R. (1991) Cutaneous pseudo-T-cell lymphomas. *Semin Diagn Pathol*, **8**, 102–110.
35. Marucci, G., Sgarbanti, E., Maestri, A. et al (2001) Gemcitabine-associated CD8+ CD30+ pseudo-lymphoma. *Br J Dermatol*, **145**, 650–652.

Specific drug reactions

Arsenic

Clinical features

Arsenic exposure can be encountered under a variety of circumstances.[1–5] It may be a constituent of proprietary medicines and is an active component of pesticides and herbicides.[3] Fowler's solution – once used in the treatment of psoriasis and other dermatological disorders – contained 1% potassium arsenate.[1,3] Arsenic may also contaminate water supplies and for many years (as a consequence of its use as an insecticide) was an ingredient in cigarette tobacco.[2,4] High levels of arsenic occur in the mining and smelting industries.[3]

Exposure to arsenic may give rise to an acute arsenical dermatitis although more commonly patients are seen with long-term sequelae.[2–5] The former presents with a diffuse erythematous papular or pustular/

bullous dermatosis that can progress to exfoliative dermatitis.[5] Transverse white nail striations may also be a feature.[5] Chronic complications of arsenic exposure include pigmentary disturbances and a variety of cutaneous tumors. Patients are also at increased risk of internal malignancies.[1]

Characteristic of arsenicism is the 'rain drops on a dusty road' appearance in which patients develop hyperpigmented macules containing small foci of hypopigmentation and areas of darker pigmentation.[6–8] While any part of the body may be affected, lesions are often more conspicuous on the trunk and in heavily pigmented regions such as the areola and the flexural creases.[3] The cutaneous pigmentary changes are especially seen in Oriental populations.[3]

Palmar and plantar keratoses are common and present 2 years or more after exposure.[5] After many years they may be associated with malignant transformation.[7]

Skin tumors are usually a late manifestation, are often multiple and are particularly found on non-sun-exposed sites. Bowen's disease, squamous cell carcinoma and superficial basal cell carcinoma may all develop.[1,2]

Patients with evidence of arsenic exposure should be investigated for evidence of visceral malignancies, in particular, carcinoma of the lung, bladder and possibly kidney.[9,10] There are occasional reports documenting an association between arsenic and hepatic angiosarcoma[11,12] (see also p. 1198).

Histological features

The cutaneous hyperpigmentation occurs as a result of increased melanin synthesis with excess pigment being present at all levels of the epidermis.[3] There is no evidence of melanocytic proliferation.

The skin cancers arising as a result of arsenic exposure show no particular distinguishing features and are described elsewhere (see p. 1201).

References

1. Bates, M.N., Smith, A.H., Hopenhayn-Rich, C. (1992) Arsenic ingestion and internal cancers: a review. *Am J Epidemiol*, 335, 462–476.
2. Wong, S.S., Tan, K.C., Goh, C.L. (1998) Cutaneous manifestations of chronic arsenicism: review of seventeen cases. *J Am Acad Dermatol*, 38, 179–185.
3. Maloney, M.E. (1996) Arsenic in dermatology. *Dermatol Surg*, 22, 301–304.
4. Person, J.R. (1996) Bowen's disease and arsenism from tobacco smoke: an association? *Cutis*, 58, 65–66.
5. Parish, W.R., Burnett, J.W. (1987) Arsenic exposure: the cutaneous manifestations. *Cutis*, 40, 401–402.
6. Shannon, R.L. (1989) Arsenic-induced skin toxicity. *Hum Toxicol*, 8, 99–104.
7. Yeh, S. (1973) Skin cancer in chronic arsenicism. *Hum Pathol*, 4, 469–485.
8. Yeh, S., How, S.W., Lin, C.S. (1968) Arsenical cancer of skin: histologic study with special reference to Bowen's disease. *Cancer*, 21, 312–339.
9. Jarup, L., Pershagen, G. (1991) Arsenic exposure, smoking, and lung cancer in smelter workers: a case-control study. *Am J Epidemiol*, 134, 545–551.
10. Cuzick, J., Sasieni, P., Evans, S. (1992) Ingested arsenic, keratoses and bladder cancer. *Am J Epidemiol*, 136, 417–421.
11. Roat, J.W., Wald, A., Mendelow, H. et al (1982) Hepatic angiosarcoma associated with short-term arsenic ingestion. *Am J Med*, 73, 933–936.
12. Kasper, M.L., Schonfield, L., Strom, R.L. et al (1984) Hepatic angiosarcoma and bronchioloalveolar carcinoma induced by Fowler's solution. *JAMA*, 252, 3407–3408.

Iododerma

Clinical features

Potassium iodide may be encountered under a variety of circumstances. It is often included in expectorants/bronchodilators and is also used in the treatment of thyroid disease and as a radiocontrast medium.

Adverse reactions are very rare.[1–6] Most often they present as acneiform papulo/pustular lesions which usually affect the face, neck and back.[3] Erythematous, urticarial, vesiculobullous and a pustular psoriasis-like eruption have also been described.[1,6] Lesions affecting the lower limbs may be petechial, hemorrhagic or resemble erythema nodosum.[1,2] Nodular and ulcerated vegetative plaques constitute the more extreme form of iododerma. This latter variant typically affects the face,

shoulders, trunk and extremities and presents as 1–7 cm disfiguring, crusted, erythematous lesions, sometimes with central umbilication (*Figs 13.78, 13.79*).[3] Healing may be complicated with considerable scarring.

Iododerma is commonly associated with systemic diseases including multiple myeloma, polyarteritis nodosa, lymphoma and glomerulonephritis.[3,6,7] Impaired renal function is thought to be an important predisposing factor.

Pathogenesis and histological features

Although delayed hypersensitivity is believed to represent the underlying pathogenesis, the precise mechanism is unknown. Acute lesions are characterized by an intense dermal neutrophil polymorph infiltrate. With chronicity, pseudoepitheliomatous hyperplasia is often present and ulceration is common. Neutrophil microabscesses may be seen both

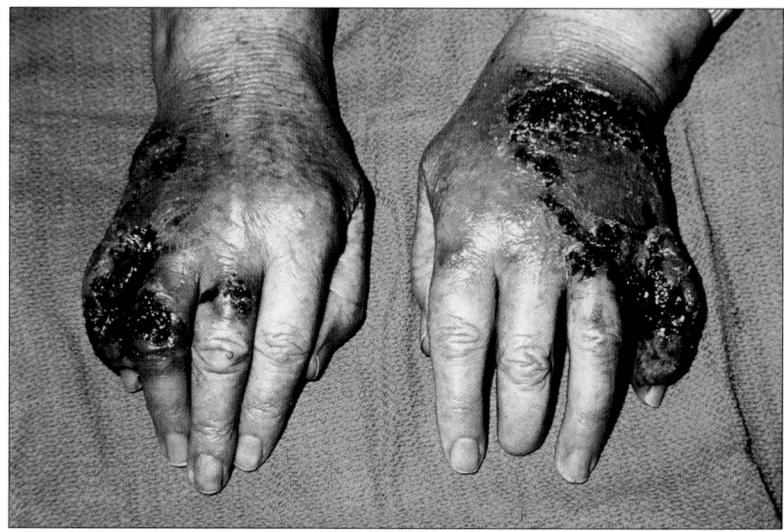

Fig. 13.78
Iododerma: ulcerated vegetative plaques are present on the backs of the hands and fingers. By courtesy of the Institute of Dermatology, London, UK.

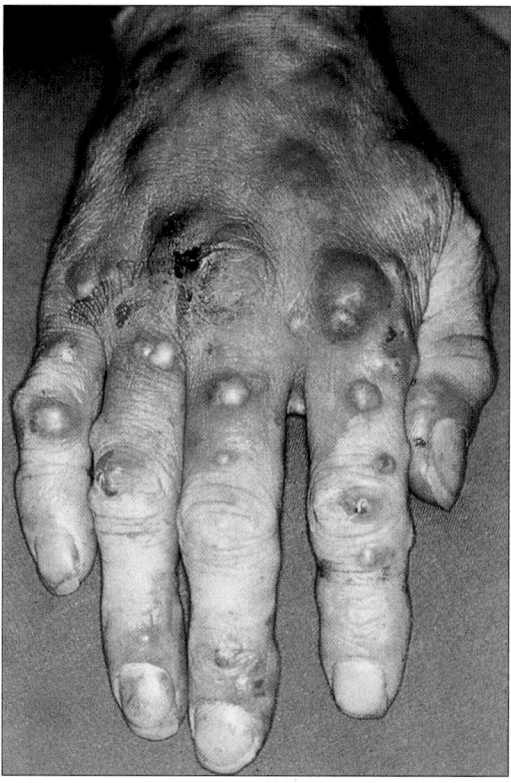

Fig. 13.79
Iododerma: in this patient, nodules are conspicuous. Superimposed pustules are evident. By courtesy of the Institute of Dermatology, London, UK.

in the epidermis and within the dermis; in some cases, there is focal leukocytoclastic vasculitis.[3,4]

Differential diagnosis

Histologically, the nodular lesions of iododerma may be easily mistaken for an infective process such as blastomycosis or an atypical mycobacterial condition, particularly if the clinical information is not available. The presence of occasional eosinophils within the infiltrate accompanied by epidermal degeneration in association with the abscesses may result in confusion with pemphigus vegetans. In early lesions, when the epidermis may be of normal thickness, the features can sometimes be mistaken for Sweet's syndrome and pyoderma gangrenosum may have to be excluded.

References

1. O'Brien, T.J. (1987) Iodic eruptions. *Australas J Dermatol*, **28**, 119–122.
2. Alpay, K., Kurkcuoglu, N. (1996) Iododerma: an unusual side-effect of iodide ingestion. *Pediatr Dermatol*, **13**, 51–53.
3. Soria, C., Allegue, F., España, A. et al (1990) Vegetating iododerma with underlying systemic diseases: report of three cases. *J Am Acad Dermatol*, **22**, 418–442.
4. Noonan, M.P., Williams, C.M., Elgart, M.L. (1994) Fungating pustular plaques in a patient with Graves' disease. *Arch Dermatol*, **130**, 786–787, 789–790.
5. Vaillant, L., Pengloan, J., Blanchier, D.G. et al (1990) Iododerma and acute respiratory distress with leukocytoclastic vasculitis following the intravenous injection of contrast medium. *Clin Exp Dermatol*, **15**, 232–233.
6. Boudoulas, O., Siegle, R.J., Grimwood, R.E. (1987) Iododerma occurring after orally administered iopanoic acid. *Arch Dermatol*, **123**, 387–388.
7. Belaïch, S., Crick, B., Schwartz, C. et al (1985) Iodides végétantes après lymphographie. *Ann Dermatol Venereol*, **112**, 699–700.

Bromoderma

Clinical features

Methyl bromide has been used in the pharmaceutical, film and dye industry in addition to its role as a pesticide and disinfectant.[1–5] It has also been incorporated into sedative syrups and expectorants for both adults and infants. Although occupational exposure has usually been associated with severe respiratory effects including pulmonary edema, very occasional reports of skin contact have also been documented.[3,4] Patients present with sharply circumscribed erythematous lesions associated with vesicles and bullae.[4] The intertriginous regions and sites of mechanical pressure are predominantly affected. Ingested bromide may give rise to hyperpigmentation, urticarial lesions, acneiform/pustular lesions (acne bromica), vegetative and often ulcerated plaques (vegetant bromoderma, tuberous bromoderma), necrotizing panniculitis and pyoderma gangrenosum-like ulcers (*Fig. 13.80*).[6–10] Vegetant bromoderma most often presents on the face, scalp and legs and predominantly affects infants.[6] It is commonly mistaken clinically for an infective condition. A case which complicated bromine secretion in breast milk has been documented.[11]

Histological features

The cutaneous lesions that develop following acute exposure to methyl bromide are characterized by spongiosis, keratinocyte necrosis, papillary dermal edema and subepidermal blister formation.[4] A perivascular mixed inflammatory cell infiltrate consisting of neutrophils, eosinophils and smaller numbers of lymphocytes and histiocytes is present in the superficial dermis.

In the vegetating lesions, there is striking pseudoepitheliomatous hyperplasia with intraepidermal and dermal abscesses accompanied by an intense neutrophil, eosinophil and lymphohistiocytic infiltrate in the underlying dermis.

In urticarial lesions, papillary dermal edema is accompanied by a neutrophil and eosinophil-rich infiltrate.[4]

Differential diagnosis

Vegetating lesions may be easily confused with deep fungal and atypical mycobacterial infections. Pemphigus vegetans also enters the differential diagnosis. The diagnosis may be most easily reached by careful clinicopathological correlation with particular reference to a history of 'over the counter' medications.[10]

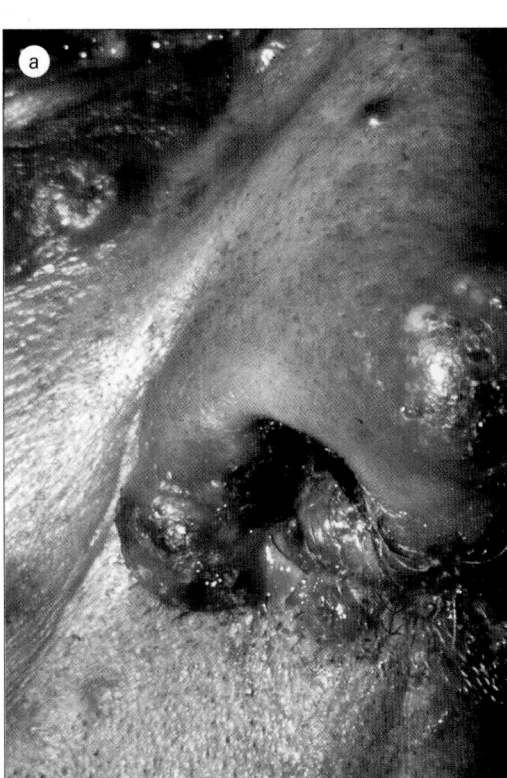
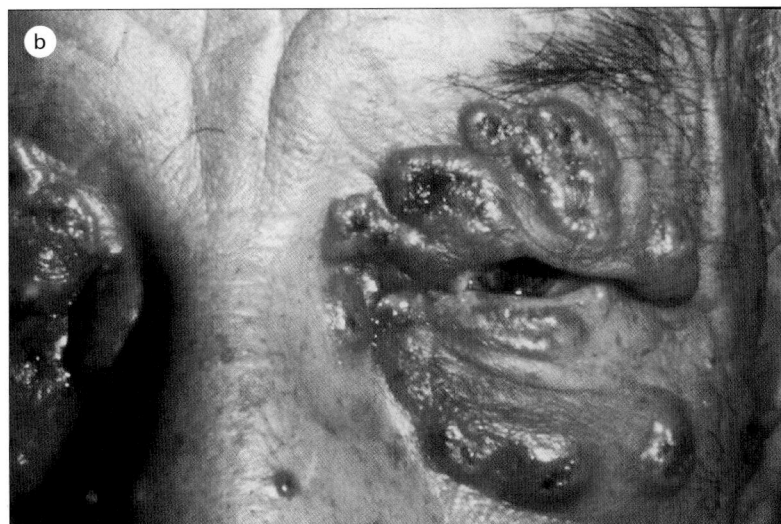

Fig. 13.80
(a, b) Bromoderma: vegetant plaques and nodules are seen around the nose and the eyes. Ulceration is present. By courtesy of the late M. Beare, MD, Royal Victoria Hospital, Belfast, N. Ireland.

References

1. Carney, M.W.P. (1971) Five cases of bromism. *Lancet*, ii, 523–524.
2. Roosels, D., Van den Oever, R., Lahaye, D. (1981) Dangerous concentrations of methyl bromide used as a fumigant in Belgium greenhouses. *Int Arch Occup Environ Health*, **48**, 243–250.
3. Heise, H., Moller, A. (1976) Bericht uber eine dermale intoxication mit methylbromid. *Dermatol Monatsschr*, **162**, 837–840.
4. Hezeman-Boer, M., Toonstra, J., Muelenbelf, J. et al (1988) Skin lesions due to exposure to methyl bromide. *Arch Dermatol*, **124**, 917–921.
5. Burnett, J.W. (1989) Iodides and bromides. *Cutis*, **43**, 130.
6. Bel, S., Bartralot, R., García, D. et al (2001) Vegetant bromoderma in an infant. *Pediatr Dermatol*, **18**, 336–338.
7. Diener, W., Kruse, R., Berg, P. (1993) Halogen-induced panniculitis caused by potassium bromide. *Monatsschr Kinderheilkd*, **141**, 705–707.
8. Pfeifle, J., Grieben, U., Bork, K. (1992) Bromoderma tuberosum caused by anticonvulsive treatment with potassium bromide. *Hautarzt*, **43**, 792–794.
9. David, M., Ingber, A., Sandbank, M. et al (1983) Bromoderma caused by carbromalhydroxyzine hydrochloride. *Biomed Pharmacother*, **37**, 298–300.
10. Smith, S.Z., Scheen, S.R. (1978) Bromoderma. *Arch Dermatol*, **114**, 458–459.
11. Occela, C., Nemlka, O., Schiazza, L. et al (1982) Neonatal tuberous bromoderma caused by maternal milk. *Ital Dermatol*, **117**, 109–112.

Warfarin

Warfarin (Coumadin) may be associated with a number of adverse reactions including hemorrhage, alopecia, urticaria, maculopapular eruptions, dermatitis, purple toe syndrome and cutaneous necrosis.[1–6] The last, with a prevalence of only 0.01–0.1%, is of particular importance because of its associated severe morbidity and significant mortality.[5]

Clinical features

Warfarin necrosis most often develops between the third and sixth days after starting anticoagulation therapy. It may initially present with paresthesia but is soon followed by the development of a painful, well-circumscribed, edematous and erythematous plaque resembling peau d'orange with associated purpura.[1,5] Large blood-filled blisters that rapidly break down, accompanied by progressive necrosis of the underlying dermis and subcutaneous fat, are later sequelae (*Fig. 13.81*). Tissue destruction is often considerable and the resultant scarring is typically very disfiguring. Very occasionally the onset of this condition is delayed for weeks or months although in most instances this probably reflects an interrupted therapeutic regimen.[7,8]

The condition, which shows a striking predilection for obese females (85%), predominantly affects the breasts, buttocks and thighs.[2] The reason for the female predominance is unknown. In males, the thighs and buttocks are also affected and sometimes the penis is involved. Occasionally, lesions are seen on the hands. Warfarin necrosis does not affect the deeper soft tissues nor are the internal viscera affected.

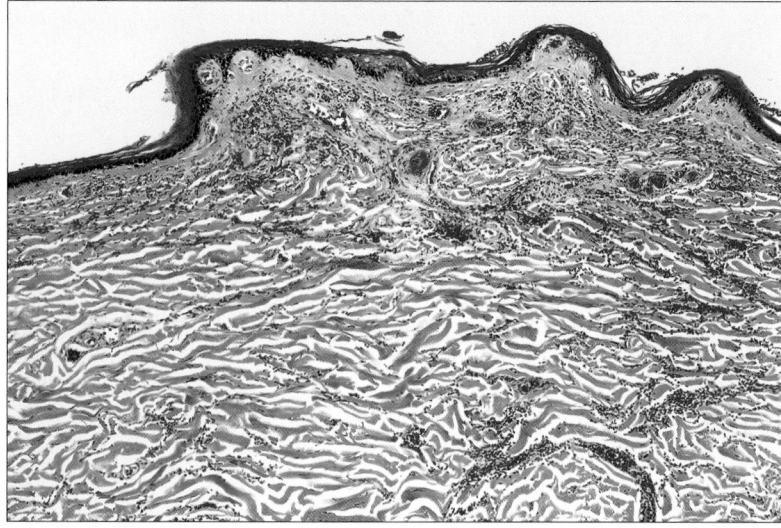

Fig. 13.81
Warfarin necrosis: there are numerous thrombosed vessels throughout the dermis associated with red cell extravasation.

Patients almost invariably have received anticoagulation for thrombophlebitis (deep venous thrombosis) and/or pulmonary embolism. Patients who receive warfarin for outpatient treatment of cardiovascular disorders such as atrial fibrillation only very exceptionally develop this condition.[5]

Pathogenesis and histological features

Cutaneous necrosis only very rarely complicates therapy with warfarin. Although hypersensitivity reactions and direct toxicity have been postulated as etiological factors, an imbalance in the ratio of naturally occurring procoagulative and anticoagulative factors is currently thought to be of paramount importance.[5] In addition to depressing the vitamin K-dependent clotting Factors II, VII, IX and X, warfarin also reduces the levels of naturally occurring anticoagulants including protein C, protein S and antithrombin III. In particular, it first affects protein S, which has an extremely short half-life and, as a consequence, until the anticoagulative effect comes into play with depressed levels of coagulating factors, the patient is paradoxically at increased risk of thrombosis. Why this should so rarely result in skin necrosis is uncertain.

Congenital protein C deficiency may be an important additional predisposing factor in some patients. This is a relatively common autosomal dominant condition that affects between 1:200 and 1:300 of the population. Protein C is activated by thrombin under the influence of the co-factor thrombomodulin.[5] The activated form inactivates Factors VIIIa and Va, which, in turn, inhibit conversion of Factor X to Factor Xa and prothrombin to thrombin with resultant inhibition of coagulation.[5] Protein C deficiency is, therefore, associated with a thrombotic tendency.[9] Approximately 30% of patients who develop warfarin necrosis have an underlying protein C deficiency.[2] Warfarin therapy, therefore, appears to tip the balance in an already protein C-deficient patient. The proposed mechanism, however, by no means offers an explanation in the majority of cases.

Acquired or congenital deficiency of protein S may also be of importance in a small number of cases.[10–13] Protein S is a vitamin K-dependent co-factor for activated protein C.[5] Acquired protein S deficiency may be encountered in patients with renal failure or antiphospholipid syndrome, or who are undergoing hemodialysis.[14,15]

An episode of thrombophlebitis and/or pulmonary embolism leading to the warfarin therapy seems to be of major etiological importance.[1,2] It has been proposed that the vascular inflammatory changes may play a role in precipitating the thrombotic tendency by such mechanisms as reduction in endothelial cell thrombomodulin levels, protein S inactivation and decreased fibrinolytic activity.[1–4] Protein C or protein S deficiency (inherited or developing as a consequence of warfarin therapy) may then represent an additional predisposing factor. Other conditions that may predispose to the development of warfarin necrosis include reduced antithrombin III levels, lupus anticoagulant syndrome, Factor V Leiden and prothrombin gene mutation.[16–18]

Histologically, warfarin-associated skin necrosis is characterized by fibrin thrombi developing in the small veins and venules of the dermis and subcutaneous fat, accompanied by widespread erythrocyte extravasation (*Fig. 13.82*). In more advanced lesions, subepidermal blood-filled blisters are seen. If old lesions are biopsied, the changes of infarction are superimposed; however, vasculitis is not a feature in this condition. Arteries are not affected.

Differential diagnosis

Identical histological features may be seen in a number of conditions including antiphospholipid antibodies, protein C and S deficiencies in the absence of warfarin therapy and disseminated intravascular coagulation (DIC). Cryoglobulinemia and cryofibrinogenemia may also have to be

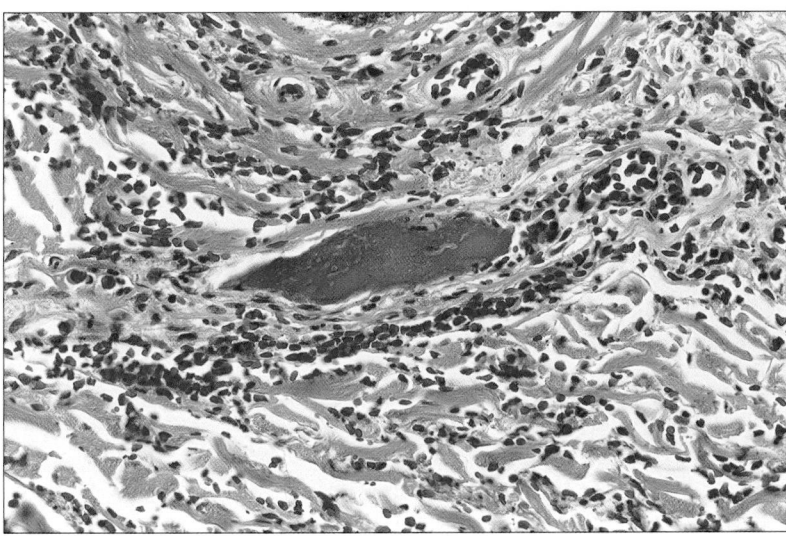

Fig. 13.82
Warfarin necrosis: high power view of *Fig. 13.81.*

excluded. Calciphylaxis can be excluded by the absence of vascular calcification. The diagnosis ultimately depends upon adequate clinicopathological correlation.

References

1. Comps, C.C. (1993) Coumadin-induced skin necrosis: incidence, mechanisms, management and avoidance. *Drug Saf*, **8**, 128–135.
2. Broekmans, A.W., Bertina, R., Loeliger, F.A. et al (1983) Protein C and the development of skin necrosis during anticoagulant therapy. *Thromb Haemost*, **49**, 251.
3. Cole, M.A., Minidee, P.K., Wolma, F.J. (1988) Coumadin necrosis – a review of the literature. *Surgery*, **103**, 271–277.
4. Miura, Y., Ardenghy, M., Ramasastry, S. et al (1996) Coumadin necrosis of the skin: report of four patients. *Ann Plast Surg*, **37**, 332–337.
5. Chan, Y.C., Valenti, D., Mansfield, A.O. et al (2000) Warfarin induced skin necrosis. *Br J Surg*, **87**, 266–272.
6. Comp, P.C., Elrod, J.P., Karzenski, S. (1990) Warfarin-induced skin necrosis. *Semin Thromb Hemost*, **16**, 293–298.
7. Goldberg, S.L., Orthner, C.L., Yalisove, B.L. et al (1991) Skin necrosis following prolonged administration of coumarin in a patient with inherited protein S deficiency. *Am J Hematol*, **38**, 64–66.
8. Essex, D.W., Wynn, S.S., Jin, D.K. (1998) Late-onset warfarin-induced skin necrosis: case report and review of the literature. *Am J Hematol*, **57**, 233–237.
9. Sallah, S., Thomas, D., Roberts, H. (1997) Warfarin and heparin-induced skin necrosis and the purple toe syndrome: infrequent complications of anticoagulant therapy. *Thromb Haemost*, **78**, 785–790.
10. Friedman, K.D., Houston, J.G., Montgomery, R.R. et al (1990) Coumadin-induced skin necrosis in a patient with protein S deficiency. *Blood*, **68** (Suppl. 1), 333 abs.
11. Grimaudo, V.M., Gueissaz, G., Hauert, J. (1989) Necrosis of skin induced by coumadin in a patient deficient in protein S. *BMJ*, **298**, 233–234.
12. Sallah, S., Abdallah, J.M., Gagnon, G.A. (1998) Recurrent warfarin-induced skin necrosis in kindreds with protein S deficiency. *Haemostasis*, **28**, 25–30.
13. Gailani, D., Reese, E.P. Jr (1999) Anticoagulant-induced skin necrosis in a patient with hereditary deficiency of protein S. *Am J Hematol*, **60**, 231–236.
14. Kant, K.S., Glueck, H.J., Coots, M.C. et al (1992) Protein S deficiency and skin necrosis associated with continuous ambulatory peritoneal dialysis. *Am J Kidney Dis*, **19**, 264–271.
15. Wattiaux, M.J., Herve, R., Robert, A. et al (1994) Coumarin-induced skin necrosis associated with acquired protein S deficiency and antiphospholipid antibody syndrome. *Arthritis Rheum*, **37**, 1096–1100.
16. Freeman, B., Schmieg, R.E., McGrath, S. et al (2000) Factor V Leiden mutation in a patient with warfarin-associated skin necrosis. *Surgery*, **127**, 595–596.
17. Yang, Y., Algazy, K.M. (1999) Warfarin-induced skin necrosis in a patient with a mutation of the prothrombin gene. *N Engl J Med*, **340**, 735.
18. Zimbelman, J., Lefkowitz, J., Schaffer, C. et al (2000) Unusual complications of warfarin therapy: skin necrosis and priapism. *J Pediatr*, **137**, 266–267.

Heparin

Adverse side-effects of heparin include hemorrhage, urticaria, anaphylaxis, macular erythema and alopecia.[1,2] Of greater significance, patients may develop thrombocytopenia, paradoxical thrombosis and skin necrosis – heparin-induced thrombocytopenia syndrome (HIT syndrome).[1–3]

Clinical features

Urticarial reactions are exceptionally rare. Delayed hypersensitivity-mediated macular erythema shows a striking female predominance and presents at the injection site.[2] Rarely, blisters may develop and exceptionally the erythema becomes generalized.[4]

HIT syndrome – in addition to definitional thrombocytopenia – is characterized by thrombosis (venous more often than arterial) which account for the high morbidity and potential mortality.[3] Venous thrombosis results in deep venous lesions in the lower legs in up to 50% of patients and of these 25% may develop pulmonary embolism.[3] Additional complications include warfarin-induced limb gangrene, adrenal hemorrhage and DIC.[3] Arterial thrombosis may affect the aorta and ileofemoral arteries, resulting in peripheral gangrene, myocardial infarction or stroke.[3]

Cutaneous necrosis develops in 10–20% of patients with the HIT syndrome.[3,5] The injection site is predominantly involved but more distant areas of the skin (particularly the thighs, abdomen and buttocks) may also be affected in a minority of patients.[1,2,6–15] Initial lesions are painful or burning erythematous plaques soon followed by the development of ulceration and tissue necrosis.[2] The condition shows a predilection for middle-aged females and the obese.[2,6]

Thrombocytopenia and thromboembolism are potentially life-threatening complications.

Histological features

The heparin-induced thrombocytopenia syndrome results from the development of platelet activating HIT/PF4 antibodies induced in response to a platelet factor 4–heparin complex.[1,13,14] The resulting immune complexes bind to platelet Fc receptors and induce platelet activation. In addition, the antibody reacts with surface endothelial cell platelet factor 4-inducing endothelial cell injury and thrombosis.[14] Only a minority of patients with HIT antibodies develops skin necrosis, and it is postulated therefore that additional prothrombotic factors such as protein C or S deficiency are necessary for the development of thrombosis and its sequelae.[1] Adverse side-effects are more common and often more severe in patients receiving unfractionated as opposed to low molecular weight heparin.[15]

The histological features of the macular erythema are those of spongiotic dermatitis. Within the superficial dermis is a perivascular lymphohistiocytic infiltrate with variable numbers of eosinophils. The lymphocytes are predominantly of the T-helper subclass.[16]

Heparin-induced cutaneous necrosis is characterized by widespread superficial small vessel (capillary and venule) thrombi accompanied by hemorrhage and necrosis.[7,8] The changes of leukocytoclastic vasculitis may sometimes be present.[2]

References

1. Denton, M.D., Mauiyyedi, S., Bazari, H. (2001) Heparin-induced skin necrosis in a patient with end-stage renal failure and functional protein S deficiency. *Am J Nephrol*, **121**, 289–293.
2. Wütschert, R., Piletta, P., Bounameaux, H. (1999) Adverse skin reactions to low molecular weight heparins: frequency, management and prevention. *Drug Saf*, **20**, 515–525.
3. Warkentin, T. (1999) Heparin-induced thrombocytopenia: a clinicopathologic syndrome. *Thromb Haemost*, **82**, 439–447.
4. Garijo, A., Arranz, F. (1996) Type IV hypersensitivity to subcutaneous heparin: a new case. *J Investig Allergol Clin Immunol*, **6**, 388–391.
5. Warkentin, T.E. (1996) Heparin induced skin lesions. *Br J Haematol*, **92**, 494–497.
6. Tuneu, A., Moreno, A., De Moragas, J.M. (1985) Cutaneous reactions secondary to heparin injections. *J Am Acad Dermatol*, **12**, 1072–1077.
7. Rongioletti, F., Pisani, S., Ciaccio, M. et al (1989) Skin necrosis due to intravenous heparin. *Dermatologica*, **178**, 47–50.
8. Yates, P., Jones, S. (1993) Heparin skin necrosis: an important indicator of potentially fatal heparin sensitivity. *Clin Exp Dermatol*, **18**, 138–141.
9. Sallah, S., Thomas, D.P., Roberts, H.R. (1997) Warfarin and heparin-induced skin necrosis and the purple toe syndrome: infrequent complications of anticoagulant treatment. *Thromb Haemost*, **78**, 758–790.
10. Warkentin, T.E. (1997) Heparin-induced thrombocytopenia, heparin-induced skin lesions, and arterial thrombosis. *Thromb Haemost*, **77** (Suppl.), 562.
11. Carroza, P., Gabutti, L., Gilliet, F. et al (1997) Heparin-induced systemic inflammatory response syndrome with progressive skin necrosis in hemodialysis. *Nephrol Dial Transplant*, **12**, 2424–2427.
12. Humphreys, J.E., Kaplan, D.M., Bolton, W.K. (1991) Heparin skin necrosis: delayed occurrence in a patient on hemodialysis. *Am J Kidney Dis*, **17**, 233–236.
13. Amiral, J., Bridey, F., Dreyfus, M. et al (1992) Platelet factor 4 complexed to heparin is the target for antibodies generated in heparin-induced thrombocytopenia. *Thromb Haemost*, **68**, 95–96.
14. Viscentin, G.P. (1999) Heparin-induced thrombocytopenia: molecular pathogenesis. *Thromb Haemost*, **82**, 448–456.
15. Füreder, W., Kyrle, P.A., Gisslinger, H. et al (1998) Low-molecular-weight heparin-induced skin necrosis. *Ann Hematol*, **77**, 127–130.
16. Klein, G.F., Kofler, H., Wolf, H. et al (1989) Eczema-like, erythematous, infiltrated plaques: a common side-effect of subcutaneous heparin therapy. *J Am Acad Dermatol*, **21**, 703–707.

Penicillamine

Clinical features

Penicillamine therapy may be associated with a broad spectrum of adverse reactions including, exanthematous eruptions, urticaria, lichenoid reactions, papulosquamous dermatoses, alopecia, hypertrichosis, nail changes, dermatomyositis, systemic lupus erythematosus, pemphigus vulgaris, pemphigus foliaceus, pemphigus erythematosus and cicatricial pemphigoid.[1–8] The autoimmune blistering dermatoses complicating penicillamine therapy are not dose dependent and are seen particularly in patients with other immunologically mediated diseases including rheumatoid arthritis and systemic sclerosis.[8] Pemphigus is by far the most common bullous disorder associated with penicillamine, pemphigus foliaceus being the most frequent variant encountered.[8] Herpetiform pemphigus has also rarely been described as complicating use of penicillamine.[9,10] Bullous pemphigoid following penicillamine treatment is exceptional.[11] A relationship with cicatricial pemphigoid has been better documented.[7]

Additional manifestations – particularly seen in patients taking high doses in the treatment of Wilson's disease and cystinuria – include penicillamine dermopathy, elastosis perforans serpiginosa, skin fragility with hemorrhages and milia formation on the extensor surfaces, wrinkling and anetoderma-like changes, cutis laxa and pseudoxanthoma elasticum-like appearances.[12–15] Patients on long-term therapy may therefore present with small yellow papules resembling a plucked-chicken appearance or disfiguring loose folds of skin particularly affecting the flexures.[14,15]

Histological features

Penicillamine acts by impairing cross-linking in newly formed collagen and elastic fibers.[12] In patients showing chronic dermal damage, the histological features are characteristic. Increased numbers of abnormally formed elastic fibers are present in the reticular dermis (*Fig. 13.83*). These are thickened and have an irregular serrated appearance on cross-section. When viewed in a longitudinal plane, the fibers show conspicuous lateral projections (*Fig. 13.84*).

In addition to cutaneous involvement, evidence of similar elastic tissue damage has been documented in the joint capsules, lungs, intestine and large elastic arteries.[12]

References

1. Levy, R.S., Fisher, M., Alter, J.N. (1983) Penicillamine: review and cutaneous manifestations. *J Am Acad Dermatol*, 8, 548–558.
2. Van Hecke, E., Kint, A., Temmerman, L. (1981) A lichenoid drug reaction induced by penicillamine. *Arch Dermatol*, 117, 676–677.
3. Carroll, G.J., Will, R.K., Peter, J.B. et al (1987) Penicillamine induced polymyositis and dermatomyositis. *J Rheumatol*, 14, 995–1001.
4. From, E., Fredrickson, P. (1976) Pemphigus vulgaris following D-penicillamine. *Dermatologica*, 152, 358–362.
5. Marsden, R.A., Ryan, T.J., Vanhegan, R.I. et al (1976) Pemphigus foliaceus induced by penicillamine. *BMJ*, ii, 1423–1424.
6. Amian, M.L., Ahmed, A.R. (1984) Pemphigus erythematosus. *J Am Acad Dermatol*, 10, 215–222.
7. Shuttleworth, D., Graham-Brown, R.A.C., Hutchinson, P.E. et al (1985) Cicatricial pemphigoid in D-penicillamine treated patients with rheumatoid arthritis: report of three cases. *Clin Exp Dermatol*, 10, 392–397.
8. Bialy-Golan, A., Brenner, S. (1996) Penicillamine-induced bullous dermatoses. *J Am Acad Dermatol*, 35, 732–742.
9. Marsden, R.A., Dawber, R.P.R., Millard, P.R. et al (1977) Herpetiform pemphigus induced by penicillamine. *Br J Dermatol*, 97, 451–452.
10. Morioka, S., Ogawa, H. (1980) Herpetiform pemphigus-like skin lesions induced by penicillamine. *J Dermatol (Tokyo)*, 7, 425–429.
11. Brown, M.D., Dubin, H.V. (1987) Penicillamine-induced bullous pemphigoid-like eruption. *Arch Dermatol*, 123, 119–120.
12. Dalziel, K.L., Burge, S.M., Frith, P.A. et al (1990) Elastic fiber damage by low dose D-penicillamine. *Br J Dermatol*, 123, 305–312.
13. Buckley, C., Sankey, E.A., Harris, D. et al (1991) Progressive skin laxity secondary to penicillamine treatment. *Clin Exp Dermatol*, 16, 310–311.
14. Narron, G.H., Zec, N., Neves, R.I. et al (1992) Penicillamine-induced pseudoxanthoma elasticum-like skin changes requiring rhytidectomy. *Ann Plast Surg*, 29, 367–370.
15. Bolognia, J.L., Braverman, I. (1992) Pseudoxanthoma-elasticum-like skin changes induced by penicillamine. *Clin Lab Invest*, 184, 12–18.

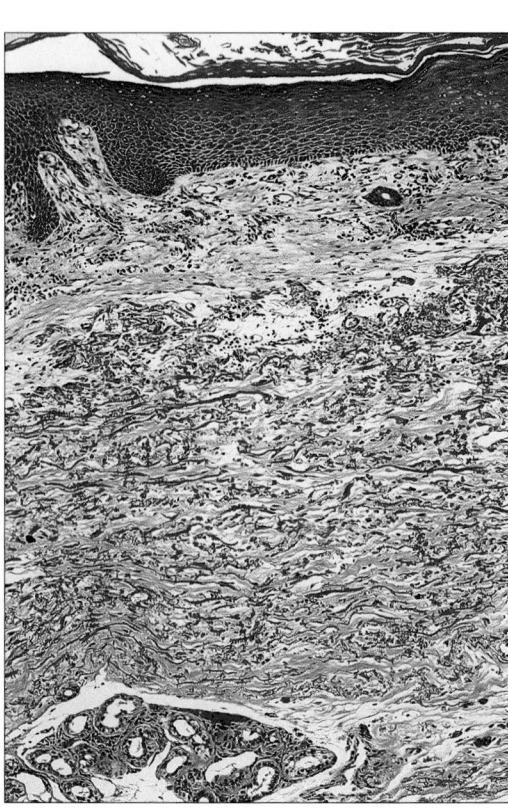

Fig. 13.83
Penicillamine dermopathy: there are thickened, intensely eosinophilic elastic fibers throughout the reticular dermis.

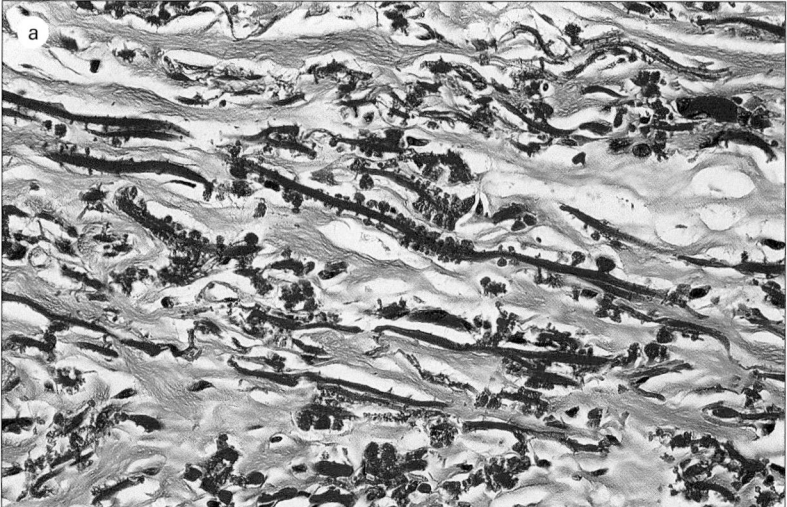

Fig. 13.84
(a, b) Penicillamine dermopathy: the serrated appearance is characteristic.
(b) Elastic tissue stain.

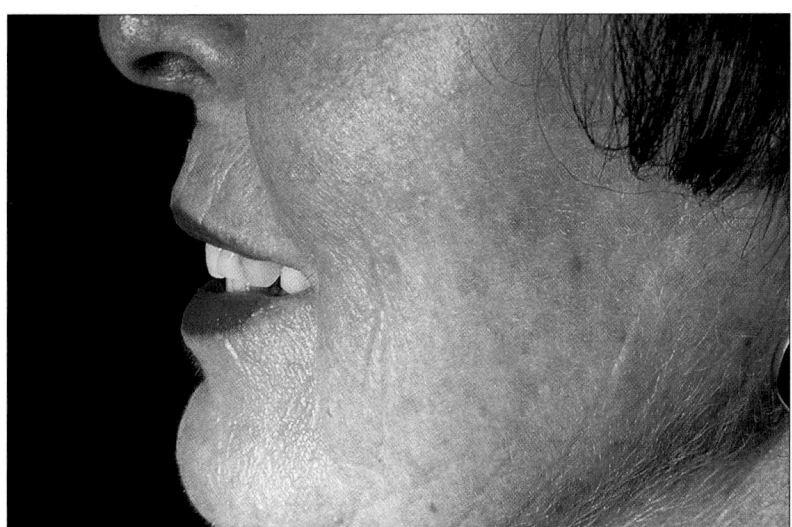

Fig. 13.85
Chrysiasis: multiple foci of blue discoloration are present on the cheek. By courtesy of J. Kerner, MD, Department of Dermatology, Harvard Medical School, Boston, USA.

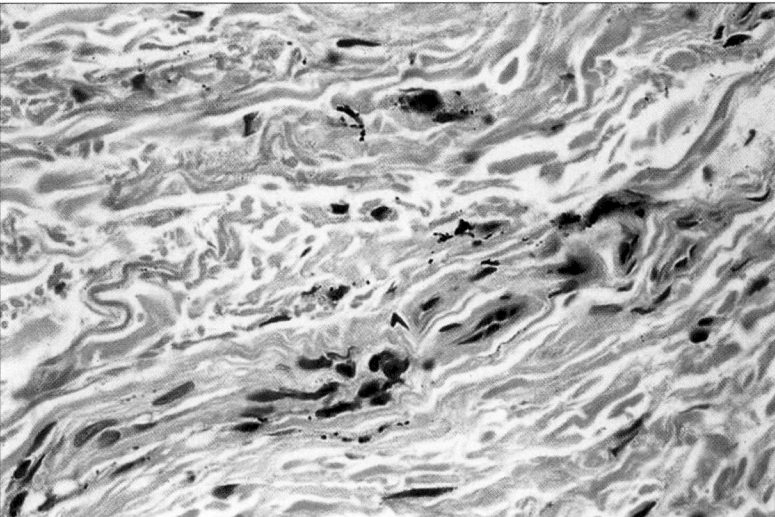

Fig. 13.86
Chrysiasis: there are fine black granules both within macrophages and lying free around the superficial vasculature. By courtesy of S. Lyle, MD, Beth Israel Deaconess Medical Center, Boston, USA.

Gold

Clinical features

Gold therapy may result in eczematous, lichenoid, pityriasiform and psoriasiform dermatoses and stomatitis.

Cutaneous pigmentation which results from parenteral treatment with gold salts is known as chrysiasis (auriasis, chrysoderma, hautaurosis).[1–5] It is a photodependent, irreversible condition most often documented following gold therapy in patients with rheumatoid arthritis.[2,3] Patients are at risk once a threshold of 50 mg/kg of gold is reached.[1] Coloration varies from mauve/blue to blue to slate-gray.[2] The sun-exposed skin of the face is particularly affected but in severe cases lesions may be seen on the neck, front of chest and backs of the forearms and hands (*Fig. 13.85*).[2] In bald patients, scalp involvement is sometimes apparent. Pigmentation has also been described in the sclera and buccal mucosa.[2]

Pathogenesis and histological features

The pathogenesis of chrysiasis is uncertain. It is most probably related to an effect of UV radiation on tissue-bound gold particles. Support for this hypothesis is the observation that skin lesions can be induced by UVB irradiation of sunlight-protected skin.[6] Similarly, typical skin lesions followed Q-switched ruby laser treatment in a patient with psoriatic arthritis receiving gold therapy.[7]

Chrysiasis is characterized by deposits of small black macrophage-bound particles surrounding the vessels in the deeper reticular dermis and around the sweat gland coils (*Fig. 13.86*).[2] Perl's Prussian blue (hemosiderin) and Masson–Fontana staining for melanin are negative. The gold particles show orange–red birefringence with cross-polarized light.[8] There is no inflammatory response. Epidermal melanin pigmentation usually appears normal.[2]

By electron microscopy the gold appears as granular, particulate and filamentous material, sometimes showing a star-like morphology within phagolysosomes (aurosomes). The diagnosis can be confirmed by electron/X-ray probe microanalysis.[2,4,9–11]

Differential diagnosis

Gold pigment must be distinguished from silver deposits (argyria), mercury and tattoo pigment.[5,7] Silver pigment is predominantly deposited in relation to basement membranes, particularly of the sweat glands. It does not show orange–red birefringence with cross-polarized light.[7] Mercury particles are large (up to 340 μm in diameter) and brown–black in color. Tattoo usually consists of a variety of different pigments of varying colors. Clinical history should readily establish the diagnosis in the majority of cases.

References

1. Granstein, R.D., Sober, A.J. (1981) Drug- and heavy metal-induced hyperpigmentation. *J Am Acad Dermatol*, 5, 1–18.
2. Smith, R.W., Leppard, B., Barnett, N.L. et al (1995) Chrysiasis revisited: a clinical and pathological study. *Br J Dermatol*, 133, 671–678.
3. Smith, R.W., Cawley, M.I.D. (1997) Chrysiasis. *Br J Rheumatol*, 36, 3–5.
4. Fleming, C.J., Salisbury, E.L.C., Kirwan, P. et al (1996) Chrysiasis after low-dose gold and UV light exposure. *J Am Acad Dermatol*, 34, 349–351.
5. Miller, M.L., Harford, R.R., Yeager, J.K. et al (1997) A case of chrysiasis. *Cutis*, 59, 256–258.
6. Koch, A.G. (1938) Zur kenntnis der chrysiasis. *Arch Dermatol Syphilol*, 178, 323–330.
7. Trotter, M.J., Tron, V.A., Hollingdale, J. et al (1995) Localized chrysiasis induced by laser therapy. *Arch Dermatol*, 131, 1411–1414.
8. Al-Talib, R.K., Wright, D.H., Theaker, J.M. (1994) Orange–red birefringence of gold particles in paraffin wax embedded sections: an aid to the diagnosis of chrysiasis. *Histopathology*, 24, 176–178.
9. Culora, G.A., Barnett, N., Theaker, J.M. (1995) Artifacts in electron microscopy: ultrastructural features of chrysiasis. *J Pathol*, 176, 421–425.
10. Benn, H-P., von Gaudecker, B., Czank, M. et al (1990) Crystalline and amorphous gold in chrysiasis. *Arch Dermatol Res*, 282, 172–178.
11. Bonet, M., Olive, A., Maymo, J. et al (1990) Chrysiasis in rheumatoid arthritis. *Clin Rheumatol*, 9, 254–255.

Silver

Clinical features

Generalized tissue accumulation of silver (argyria) follows dietary, medicinal and industrial exposure to silver compounds.[1–8] Occupational exposure may be encountered in silver mining and smelting, electroplating and in the photographic industries.[3] Silver deposits are found in the skin and mucous membranes in addition to internal viscera, particularly liver, spleen, adrenals, muscle and brain (*Fig. 13.87*).[1] Argyria initially presents in the gingivae as a slate-blue line due to deposition of metallic silver and silver sulfide.[1–3] Cutaneous manifestations, which follow a sun-exposed distribution, affect the face, neck and backs of hands.[6] The nails may also be involved. Ocular involvement presents as a bluish-gray to brownish-black coloration.

Localized argyria has been documented due to silver earrings, orthodontic surgery, acupuncture and silver polishing.[9–15] In the absence of clinical information, a diagnosis of blue nevus may mistakenly be made.[10]

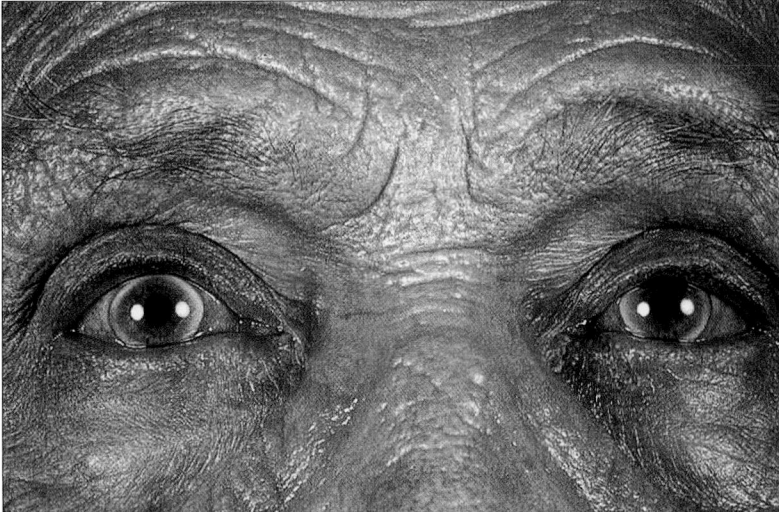

Fig. 13.87
Argyria: there is striking slate-blue pigmentation; the eyes are also affected. By courtesy of the Institute of Dermatology, London, UK.

Histological features

Argyria results from deposition of metallic silver and silver sulfide. In addition, pigmentation is intensified by sunlight due to silver reduction analogous to photographic processing.[6] There is also increased epidermal melanin synthesis.

The silver granules are found in association with the vascular and adnexal basement membranes and adjacent to dermal elastic fibers (*Fig. 13.88*).[2] They measure less than 1.0 μm in diameter and appear brown–black in hematoxylin and eosin stained sections.[6] Ultra-structurally, the silver granules may be membrane bound within macrophage lysosomes or else lie freely in the dermis.[8] The diagnosis can be confirmed by X-ray microanalysis.[6,8]

References

1. Fung, M.C., Bowen, D.L. (1996) Silver products for medical indications. *Clin Toxicol*, **34**, 119–126.
2. Granstein, R.D., Sober, A.J. (1981) Drug- and heavy metal-induced hyperpigmentation. *J Am Acad Dermatol*, **5**, 1–18.
3. Greene, R.M., Su, W.P.D. (1987) Argyria. *Am Fam Physician*, **36**, 151–154.
4. US Department of Health and Human Services (1990) Toxicology profile for silver. Atlanta, GA: Agency for Toxic Substances and Disease Registry, DHHS No TP-90-24.
5. Gulbranson, S.H., Hud, J.A., Hansen, R.C. (2000) Argyria following the use of dietary supplements containing colloidal silver protein. *Cutis*, **66**, 373–374.
6. Sue, Y-M., Lee, Y-Y., Wang, M-C. et al (2001) Generalized argyria in two chronic hemodialysis patients. *Am J Kidney Dis*, **137**, 1048–1051.
7. Hanada, K., Hashimoto, I., Kon, A. et al (1998) Silver in sugar particles and systemic argyria. *Lancet*, **351**, 960.
8. Bleehen, S.S., Gould, D.J., Harrington, C.I. et al (1981) Occupational argyria; light and electron microscopic studies and X-ray microanalysis. *Br J Dermatol*, **104**, 19–26.
9. Shall, L., Stevens, A., Millard, L.G. (1990) An unusual case of acquired localized argyria. *Br J Dermatol*, **123**, 403–407.
10. Rongioletti, F., Robert, E., Buffa, P. et al (1992) Blue nevi-like dotted occupational argyria. *J Am Acad Dermatol*, **27**, 1015–1016.
11. Morton, C.A., Fallowfield, M., Kemmett, D. (1996) Localized argyria caused by silver earrings. *Br J Dermatol*, **135**, 484–485.
12. Sugden, P., Azad, S., Erdmann, M. (2001) Argyria caused by an earring. *Br J Plast Surg*, **54**, 252–253.
13. Kapur, N., Landon, G., Yu, R.C. (2001) Localized argyria in an antique restorer. *Br J Dermatol*, **144**, 191–192.
14. Tanita, Y., Kato, T., Hanada, K. et al (1985) Blue macules of localized argyria caused by implanted acupuncture needles. *Arch Dermatol*, **121**, 1550–1552.
15. Kirchoff, D.A. (1971) Localized argyria after a surgical endodontic procedure. *Oral Surg*, **32**, 613–617.

Mercury

Clinical features

Mercury exposure is encountered under a variety of circumstances.[1–3] It occurs in three different forms: metallic mercury, inorganic mercury and organic mercury.[1]

- *Metallic mercury*, which is a liquid at room temperature, is present in vapor from heating amalgam and paints and in mercury thermometers.[4]

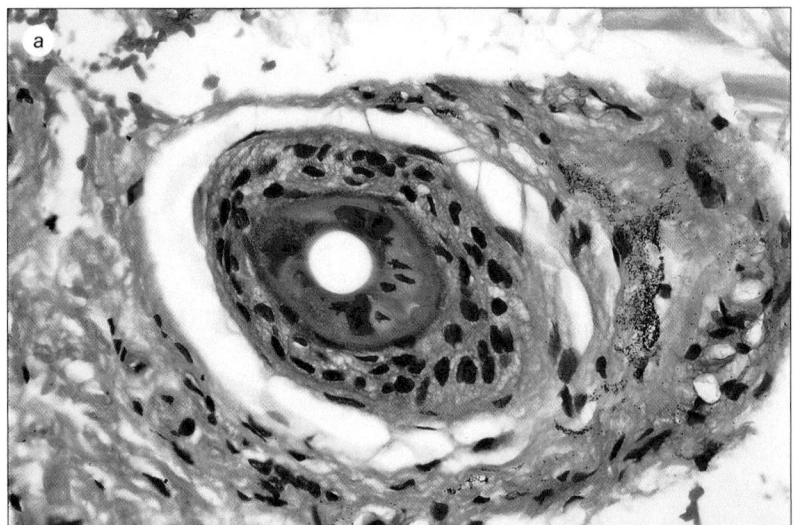

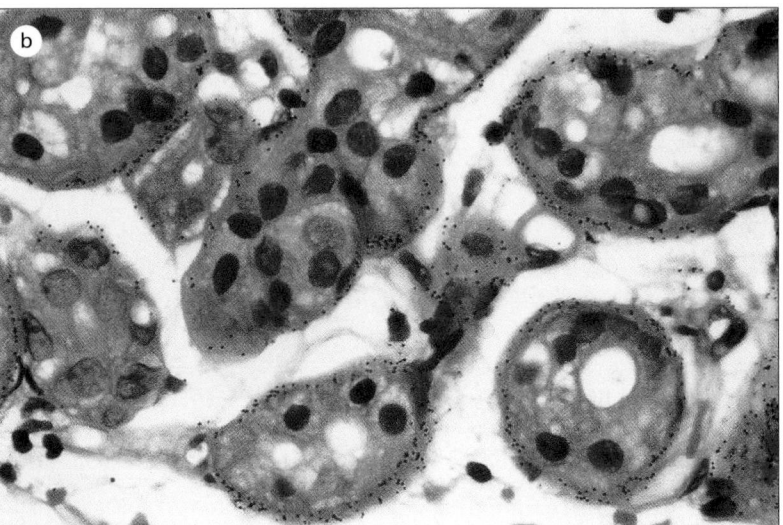

Fig. 13.88
Argyria: (a) note the fine silver granules outlining the basement membrane of the sweat gland epithelium; (b) in this example, the hair follicles are also affected.

- *Inorganic mercurial salts* may be present in laxatives, pesticides, antiseptics and germicides.[1,5]
- *Organomercurials* are used as industrial antifungal agents.[4]

Dermatological reactions to metallic mercury include mercury granuloma and mercury exanthem (acute generalized exanthematous pustulosis). Mercury granuloma follows penetrating skin wounds as for example might result from a broken thermometer, attempted homicide or suicide. Patients present with a flesh-colored to red or hyperpigmented nodule at the site of implantation.[6–9] Membranous fat necrosis following subcutaneous mercury injection has also been documented.[10] Mercury exanthem follows exposure to metallic mercury (as may follow breaking a thermometer) in a previously sensitized patient.[11–18] The eruption presents as a vivid erythema, which particularly affects the flexural sites of the body. An inverted V-shaped erythema affecting the upper anteromedial aspects of both thighs is characteristic.[11,15] Sterile pustules commonly develop and in some patients, a purpuric element develops. Pyrexia and peripheral leukocytosis are typically present. The dermatosis resolves by desquamation.

Topical mercury cream has been used as a skin-bleaching agent.[6] Continuous and protracted use results in slate-gray pigmentation particularly affecting the flexures. The eyelids, nasolabial folds and neck creases are sites of predilection.[19,20]

Parenteral use of mercury results in pigmentation of the gingivae.[20] A lichenoid drug reaction has been documented following acute mercury poisoning.[21]

Dental workers are at risk of allergic contact dermatitis from exposure to mercury or mercury salts.[22]

Mercury may also be associated with palmar/plantar peeling in children (pink disease, acrodynia, erythredema), palmar/plantar hyperkeratosis and acanthosis nigricans-like skin lesions.[23] Pink disease is rarely encountered nowadays due to control of mercury in medications and in the environment.[24–26] The condition is still very occasionally seen and may be a problem in developing countries. It presents in infants and young children following chronic mercury exposure, for example in diaper powders, laxatives, paint, fluorescent light bulbs or other household sources.[1] It is characterized by the development of characteristic painful swelling and pink coloration of the tip of the nose, fingers and toes.[1,10] As the condition resolves, the palms and soles show intense sweating and the skin peels.[1] Sterility in males is a potential long-term sequel.[25]

Lichenoid and granulomatous inflammatory reactions may complicate use of mercuric sulfide (cinnabar) to provide the red color in tattoos.[27–29] Pseudolymphomatous reactions to mercury have also been documented.[30,31]

Amalgam tattoo reactions are discussed on page 671.

Histological features

Mercury pigment is brown–black, round and opaque and measures up to 340 µm in diameter.[5–7,32] The granules may be found within macrophages in addition to extracellular dermal deposition. They are particularly localized around the superficial vasculature and also in association with the connective tissue elements.[32]

Mercury granulomata are characterized by local necrosis associated with free mercury globules surrounded by an intense foreign body granulomatous reaction with associated lymphocytes, histiocytes, plasma cells and varying numbers of eosinophils.[6,7,9] Ulceration is common and the epidermis may show pseudoepitheliomatous hyperplasia.

Mercury exanthem is characterized by subcorneal and/or intraepidermal pustules which may sometimes contain a few acantholytic keratinocytes in addition to large numbers of neutrophils.[12] A background of spongiosis is usually evident. The dermal papillae are often edematous and occasionally subepidermal vesiculation is a feature. A perivascular infiltrate of lymphocytes and histiocytes with conspicuous neutrophils and variable numbers of eosinophils is present in the superficial dermis. Leukocytoclastic vasculitis may also be a feature in a significant proportion of cases.[12]

Cutaneous pigmentation following chronic local exposure to mercury is characterized by increased melanin pigment in the epidermis accompanied by mercury granules in the papillary dermis.[20] Iron stains are negative.[1]

Pink disease is characterized by sweat gland hyperplasia and a non-specific dermal inflammatory cell infiltrate.[1]

References

1. Boyd, A.S., Seger, D., Vannucci, S. et al (2000) Mercury exposure and cutaneous disease. *J Am Acad Dermatol*, 43, 81–90.
2. Gerstner, H.B., Huff, J.E. (1977) Clinical toxicology of mercury. *J Toxicol Environ Health*, 2, 491–526.
3. Graeme, K.A., Pollack, C.V. (1998) Heavy metal toxicity, part 1: arsenic and mercury. *J Emerg Med*, 16, 45–56.
4. Souza, E.M., Cintra, M.L., Melo, V.G. et al (2000) Subcutaneous injection of elemental mercury with distant skin lesions. *J Toxicol Clin Toxicol*, 38, 441–443.
5. Wands, J.R., Weiss, S.W., Yardley, J.H. et al (1974) Chronic inorganic mercury poisoning due to laxative abuse: a clinical and ultrastructural study. *Am J Med*, 57, 92–101.
6. Lupton, G.P., Kao, G.F., Johnson, F.B. et al (1985) Cutaneous mercury granuloma. A clinicopathologic study and review of the literature. *J Am Acad Dermatol*, 12, 296–303.
7. Sau, P., Solivan, G., Johnson, F.B. (1991) Cutaneous reaction from a broken thermometer. *J Am Acad Dermatol*, 25, 915–919.
8. Netscher, D.T. (1995) Subcutaneous mercury granulomas. *J Hand Surg (Am)*, 20, 516–517.
9. Bradberry, S.M., Feldman, M.A., Braithwaite, R.A. (1996) Elemental mercury-induced skin granulomas: a case report and review of the literature. *J Toxicol Clin Toxicol*, 34, 209–216.
10. Ramdial, P.K., Jogessar, V., Dada, M.A. (1999) Membranous fat necrosis due to subcutaneous elemental mercury injections. *Am J Forensic Med Pathol*, 20, 369–373.
11. Nakayama, H., Niki, F., Shono, M. et al (1983) Mercury exanthem. *Contact Dermatitis*, 9, 411–417.
12. Roujeau, J.C., Bioulac-Sage, P., Bourseau, C. et al (1991) Acute generalized exanthematous pustulosis. Analysis of 63 cases. *Arch Dermatol*, 127, 1333–1338.
13. Vena, G.A., Foti, C., Grandolfo, M. et al (1994) Mercury exanthem. *Contact Dermatitis*, 31, 214–216.
14. Koch, P., Nickolaus, G. (1996) Allergic contact dermatitis and mercury exanthem due to mercury chloride in plastic boots. *Contact Dermatitis*, 34, 405–409.
15. Zimmer, J., Grange, F., Straub, P. et al (1997) Mercury erythema after accidental exposure to mercury vapor. *Ann Med Interne (Paris)*, 148, 317–320.
16. Barrazza, V., Meunier, P., Escande, J.P. (1998) Acute contact dermatitis and exanthematous pustulosis due to mercury. *Contact Dermatitis*, 38, 361.
17. McGivern, B., Pemberton, M., Theaker, E.D. et al (2000) Delayed and immediate hypersensitivity reactions associated with use of amalgam. *Br Dental J*, 188, 73–76.
18. Baitschgi, M., Pichler, W.J. (2002) Acute generalized exanthematous pustulosis, a clue to neutrophil-mediated inflammatory processes orchestrated by T-cells. *Curr Opin Allergy Clin Immunol*, 2, 325–331.
19. Lamar, L.M., Bliss, B.O. (1966) Localized pigmentation of the skin due to topical mercury. *Arch Dermatol*, 93, 450–453.
20. Granstein, R.D., Sober, A.J. (1981) Drug- and heavy metal-induced hyperpigmentation. *J Am Acad Dermatol*, 5, 1–18.
21. Schrallhammer-Benkler, K., Ring, J., Przybilla, B. et al (1992) Acute mercury intoxication and lichenoid drug reaction followed by mercury contact allergy and development of antinuclear antibodies. *Acta Derm Venereol*, 72, 294–296.
22. Kanerva, L., Lahtinen, A., Toikkanen, J. et al (1999) Increase in occupational skin disease of dental personnel. *Contact Dermatitis*, 40, 104–108.
23. Dinehart, S.M., Dillard, R., Raimer, S.S. et al (1988) Cutaneous manifestations of acrodynia (pink disease). *Arch Dermatol*, 124, 107–109.
24. Tunnesen, W.W. Jr, McMahon, K.J., Baser, M. (1987) Acrodynia: exposure to mercury from fluorescent light bulbs. *Pediatrics*, 79, 786–789.
25. Dally, A. (1997) The rise and fall of pink disease. *Soc Hist Med*, 10, 291–304.
26. Horowitz, Y., Greenberg, D., Ling, G. et al (2002) Acrodynia: a case report of two siblings. *Arch Dis Child*, 86, 453.
27. Taaffe, A., Knight, A.G., Marks, R. (1978) Lichenoid tattoo hypersensitivity. *BMJ*, 1, 616–618.
28. Bagley, M.P., Schwartz, R.A., Lambert, W.C. (1987) Hyperplastic reaction developing within a tattoo. Granulomatous tattoo reaction, probably to mercuric sulfide (cinnabar). *Arch Dermatol*, 123, 1557, 1560–1561.
29. Sowden, J.M., Byrne, J.P., Smith, A.G. et al (1991) Red tattoo reactions: x-ray microanalysis and patch test studies. *Br J Dermatol*, 124, 576–580.
30. Zinberg, M., Heilman, E., Glickman, F. (1982) Cutaneous pseudolymphoma resulting from a tattoo. *J Dermatol Surg Oncol*, 8, 955–958.
31. Rijlaarsdam, J.U., Bruynzeel, D.P., Vos, W. et al (1988) Immunohistochemical studies of lymphadenosis benigna cutis occurring in a tattoo. *Am J Dermatopathol*, 10, 518–523.
32. Burge, K.M., Winkelmann, R.K. (1970) Mercury pigmentation: an electron microscopic study. *Arch Dermatol*, 102, 51–61.

Bismuth

Clinical features

Bismuth may be used for a variety of gastrointestinal complaints including gastritis and peptic ulceration.[1–3] Adverse cutaneous reactions include erythroderma, exanthemata, purpuric eruptions, stomatitis and urticaria.[2,3] In addition, generalized pigmentation may follow prolonged parenteral and oral use. Patients develop a generalized blue–gray pigmentation, which also affects the conjunctivae and oral mucosa.[1] A blue–black line at the gingival margin is pathognomonic.[1]

Histological features

Bismuth appears as small dark granules in the dermis and within the sweat gland basement membranes.[3] Transfollicular elimination has been documented.[2]

References

1. Granstein, R.D., Sober, A.J. (1981) Drug- and heavy metal-induced hyperpigmentation. *J Am Acad Dermatol*, 5, 1–18.
2. Ruiz-Maldonado, R., Contreras-Ruiz, J., Sierra-Santoyo, A. et al (1997) Black granules on the skin after bismuth subsalicylate ingestion. *J Am Acad Dermatol*, 37, 489–490.
3. Zala, L., Hunziker, T., Braathen, L.R. (1993) Pigmentation following long-term bismuth therapy for pneumatosis cystoids intestinalis. *Dermatology*, 187, 288–289.

Lithium

Clinical features

Lithium therapy is known to precipitate or aggravate psoriasis, in particular pustular lesions.[1–5] In addition, it has been associated with a large number of cutaneous adverse affects including maculopapular eruptions, seborrheic dermatitis, exfoliative dermatitis, atypical acneiform lesions (predominantly affecting the forearms and legs), pustular eruptions, hidradenitis suppurativa, keratosis pilaris-like lesions, palmoplantar hyperkeratosis, bullous disorders, and hair, nail and mucosal changes.[6–9] Exacerbation and the development of Darier's disease has also rarely been documented.[10]

References

1. Skoven, I., Thormann, J. (1976) Lithium compound treatment and psoriasis. *Arch Dermatol*, **115**, 1185.
2. Sasaki, T., Saito, S., Aihara, M. et al (1989) Exacerbation of psoriasis during lithium treatment. *J Dermatol*, **16**, 59–63.
3. Wolf, R., Ruocco, V. (1999) Triggered psoriasis. *Adv Exp Med Biol*, **455**, 15–19.
4. Chan, H.L., Wing, Y-K., Su, R. et al (2000) A control study of the cutaneous side-effects of chronic lithium therapy. *J Affect Disord*, **57**, 107–113.
5. Heng, M.C.Y. (1982) Cutaneous manifestations of lithium toxicity. *Br J Dermatol*, **106**, 107–109.
6. Albrecht, G. (1985) Unerwunschte wirkungen von lithium an der haut. *Der Hautarzt*, **36**, 77–82.
7. Rifkin, A., Kurtin, S.B., Quitkin, F. et al (1973) Lithium-induced folliculitis. *Am J Psychiatry*, **130**, 1018–1019.
8. Wakelin, S.H., Lipscombe, T., Orton, D.I. et al (1996) Lithium-induced follicular hyperkeratosis. *Clin Exp Dermatol*, **21**, 296–298.
9. Gupta, A.K., Knowles, S.R., Gupta, M.A. et al (1995) Lithium therapy associated with hidradenitis suppurativa: case report and review of the dermatologic side-effects of lithium. *J Am Acad Dermatol*, **32**, 382–386.
10. Rubin, M.B. (1995) Lithium-induced Darier's disease. *J Am Acad Dermatol*, **32**, 674–675.

Barbiturates and coma blisters

Clinical features

Barbiturates may be associated with a wide range of adverse drug reactions including erythema multiforme, toxic epidermal necrolysis, hypersensitivity syndrome and pseudolymphoma.[1,2]

In company with many other sedative drugs including chlorpromazine, imipramine and meprobamate, barbiturates, particularly when taken in overdose, may result in blisters (coma blisters), related especially to sites of trauma.[3–8]

Pathogenesis and histological features

These lesions most probably develop as a result of focal persistent hypoxia and ischemia due to chronic localized pressure. They may develop in a comatose patient whatever the cause. There is some evidence to suggest that a direct toxic effect may be of importance in some patients at least, since similar blisters have complicated localized barbiturate extravasation.

Histologically, the blisters are subepidermal in location and are often accompanied by infarction of the overlying epidermis. Sweat gland necrosis is also often present.

References

1. Swart, E., Lochner, J.D. (1992) Skin conditions in epileptics. *Clin Exp Dermatol*, **17**, 169–172.
2. Schlienger, R.G., Shear, N.H. (1998) Antiepileptic drug hypersensitivity syndrome. *Epilepsia*, **39**, (Suppl.), S3–S7.
3. Pinkus, N.B. (1971) Skin eruptions in drug-induced coma. *Med J Aust*, **2**, 886–888.
4. Arndt, K.A., Mihm, M.C., Parrish, J.A. (1973) Bullae: a cutaneous sign of neurologic diseases. *J Invest Dermatol*, **66**, 312–320.
5. Leavell, U.W. (1969) Sweat gland necrosis in barbiturate poisoning. *Arch Dermatol*, **100**, 218–221.
6. Mandy, S., Ackerman, A.B. (1970) Characteristic traumatic skin lesions in drug-induced coma. *JAMA*, **213**, 253–256.
7. Haroun, M., Jakubovic, H.R., Nethercott, J.R. (1987) Localized subepidermal bullae after intravenous phenobarbital. *Cutis*, **39**, 233–234.
8. Dunn, C., Held, J.L., Spitz, J. et al (1990) Coma blisters: report and review. *Cutis*, **45**, 423–426.

Chemotherapeutic agents

Clinical features

The rapid rate of epidermal and mucosal turnover results in a high degree of susceptibility to the effects of chemotherapeutic agents. Among the most commonly encountered adverse responses are stomatitis, alopecia and pigmentary changes.[1–6]

Stomatitis is very common and initially presents as burning erythema, soon followed by the development of extremely painful erosions and ulcers.[2] Drugs that are commonly implicated include cyclophosphamide, methotrexate, bleomycin, cytarabine, doxorubicin, daunorubicin, dactinomycin, 5-fluorouracil, IL-2, hydroxyurea and mercaptopurine.[4,6] Secondary infection, as for example with herpes simplex virus or *Candida albicans*, is an important complication.

Proliferating hair follicles are also highly susceptible to chemotherapeutic agents and as a consequence anagen effluvium (in which there is loss of much of the body hair) is a common and distressing complication.[6] This is reversible once treatment is completed although interestingly, subsequent regrowth of hair may be accompanied by a change in color or texture.[1] Concomitant premature catagen and telogen effluvium can result in total baldness.[2] Drugs that are most often implicated include bleomycin, cyclophosphamide, daunorubicin, docetaxel, doxorubicin, etoposide, ifosfamide, mechlorethamine, methotrexate, mitoxantrone and paclitaxel.[1]

Nail changes, including pale transverse ridges (Beau's lines) which develop as a result of mitosis inhibition with consequent temporary growth arrest, may result from therapy with bleomycin, cyclophosphamide and doxorubicin.[4] Onycholysis can follow treatment with docetaxel, fluorouracil and mitoxantrone.[6] Transverse striate leukonychia (Mees' lines) which result from periodic disruption of nail plate keratinization classically have been described in association with arsenic poisoning.[7] Similar lesions have been documented with a number of agents including cyclosporin and daunorubicin.[8,9]

Maculopapular eruptions may be caused by a number of chemotherapeutic drugs including azathioprine, 5-fluorouracil, chlorambucil, melphalan and hydroxyurea.[5] These are frequently a source of clinical diagnostic difficulty as infectious diseases – including viral exanthemas and, in patients who have undergone transplantation, acute GVHD – are often within the differential diagnosis.

Cutaneous hyperpigmentation is a common complication of chemotherapeutic agents and often affects the hair, nails and mucosae in addition to the skin.[1–7,10–12] Hypopigmentation is much less commonly seen.[4] The mechanism whereby melanocytes are stimulated to increase melanin synthesis is unknown. Alkylating agents including busulfan, cyclophosphamide, ifosfamide, hydroxyurea, 5-fluorouracil, and methotrexate are among the most often implicated agents.[4,13,14] Nail changes (including diffuse pigmentation, longitudinal and transverse banding or streaks) are particularly seen with cyclophosphamide, daunorubicin, doxorubicin, 5-fluorouracil and hydroxyurea.[2,7] Cyclophosphamide also causes hyperpigmentation of the palms and fingers.[12] Immediate or delayed tanning following sun exposure is a frequent complication of therapy with 5-fluorouracil. More rarely, patients may develop linear erythema, later complicated by pigmentation around an injection site, so-called serpentine supravenous hyperpigmentation.[6,15,16] Similar lesions have followed treatment with actinomycin and nitrosourea.[17,18] Hair pigmentation can result from tamoxifen therapy.[1,19]

Bleomycin therapy is commonly associated with cutaneous pigmentation affecting between 30 and 60% of patients.[2,20] In particular, pathognomonic linear flagellate streaks may develop on the skin of the trunk and proximal extremities.[21–28] It has been suggested that these lesions develop as a consequence of trauma-induced vasodilatation with resultant local increased concentration of bleomycin. An early inflammatory phase, as a consequence of scratching, has occasionally been documented, suggesting that the pigmentation occurs as a consequence of postinflammatory changes. A similar problem of patterned hyperpigmentation has been documented following treatment with thio-TEPA (triethylene thiophosphoramide). Localized occlusion during treatment (as for example with adhesive bandages) may be associated with retention of thio-TEPA-rich sweat and subsequent reversible hyperpigmentation confined to the occluded surfaces.[29,30] Transverse banding of hair shafts following therapy with methotrexate – the so-called 'flag sign' – has also been documented.[31]

Chemotherapeutic agents may also interact with radiation therapy to give rise to a variety of unusual manifestations including photosensitivity, radiation enhancement, radiation recall and reactivation.

Photosensitivity may be induced by treatment with dacarbazine, 5-fluorouracil, hydroxyurea and vinblastine.[6]

Radiation enhancement, which may be a feature of both dactino-mycin and doxorubicin therapy, develops as a result of impaired repair of radiation-induced sublethal cellular damage.[2,4] As a consequence the effects of radiation therapy are amplified. Clinical manifestations include increased erythema, hyperpigmentation, erosions, blistering and necrosis at the site of radiation therapy.[32] Radiation enhancement has also been encountered following therapy with adriamycin, bleomycin, cisplatin, 5-fluorouracil, hydroxyurea and methotrexate.[4,6]

Radiation recall presents as erythema, vesiculation and desquamation at the site of previous irradiation and may develop months or even years after the treatment has been completed.[2] The mechanism is unknown. Dactinomycin is particularly incriminated.[2] A similar response has also been reported following therapy with adriamycin, bleomycin, cytarabine, doxorubicin, etoposide, 5-fluorouracil, hydroxyurea, melphalan, methotrexate, tamoxifen and vinblastine.[6,33] More recently, radiation recall reactions have been described following treatment with paclitaxel, gemcitabine, docetaxel, IFN-α2b, dacarbazine, aciclovir and capecitabine.[34–41]

Reactivation of ultraviolet light-induced erythema has been described as a complication of methotrexate and suramin therapy.[6,42] Manifestations include vesiculation in addition to erythema.

Inflammatory changes affecting pre-existing actinic keratoses and seborrheic keratoses have been described following treatment with cisplatin, cytarabine, dacarbazine, dactinomycin, doxorubicin, 5-fluorouracil, 6-thioguanine and vincristine.[3,4] The affected keratoses become pruritic and develop erythema. It has been suggested that such changes are analogous to radiation recall phenomena.[3]

Hypersensitivity reactions (including urticaria, angioedema, serum sickness, anaphylaxis, generalized dermatitis and fixed drug eruption) are uncommon complications of chemotherapy. Although a wide range of agents may occasionally result in these responses, L-asparaginase, intravenous melphalan and cisplatin have been particularly incriminated.[2,43,44] Cyclophosphamide, daunorubicin, doxorubicin, methotrexate and procarbazine have also been implicated.[44] Dacarbazine and procarbazine may cause fixed drug reactions.[1] Immune complex-mediated reactions including vasculitis and some cases of erythema multiforme or toxic epidermal necrolysis may rarely be a result of treatment with hydroxyurea and mechlorethamine.[4] Contact dermatitis is an uncommon but important complication of topical mechlorethamine (mustard) therapy.[45]

An interstitial granulomatous maculopapular eruption following usage of low-dose methotrexate in the treatment of collagen vascular diseases including lupus erythematosus and rheumatoid arthritis has been described.[46] The buttocks and limbs are commonly affected.

Histological features

Interface dermatitis represents the most frequently encountered histological appearance in chemotherapy adverse drug reactions (*Figs 13.89–13.91*).[47–50] In addition to the epidermis, both follicular and

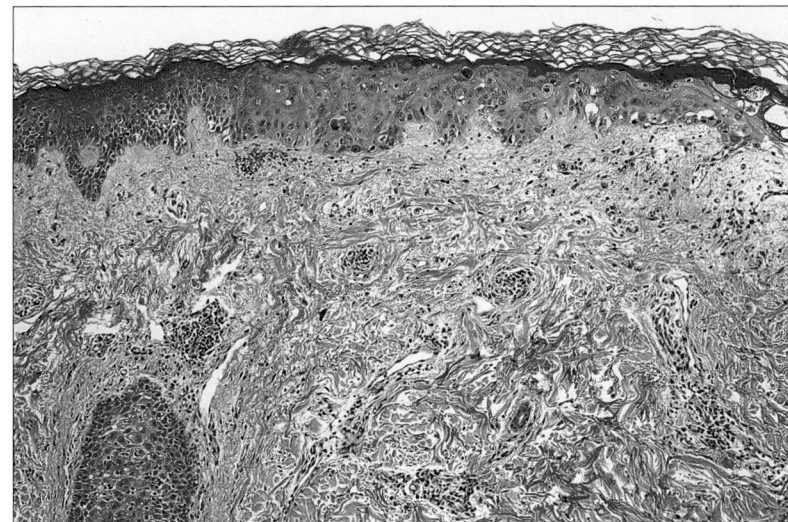

Fig. 13.89
Chemotherapy-related drug reaction: there are interface changes with basal cell hydropic degeneration and apoptosis.

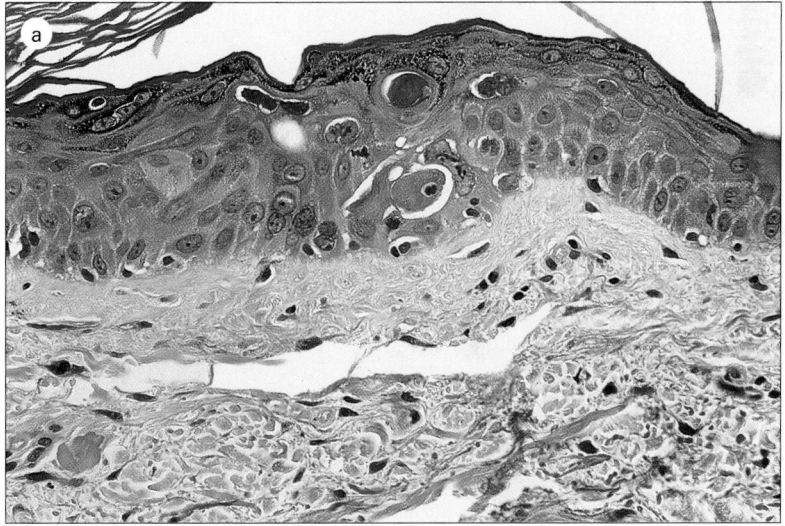

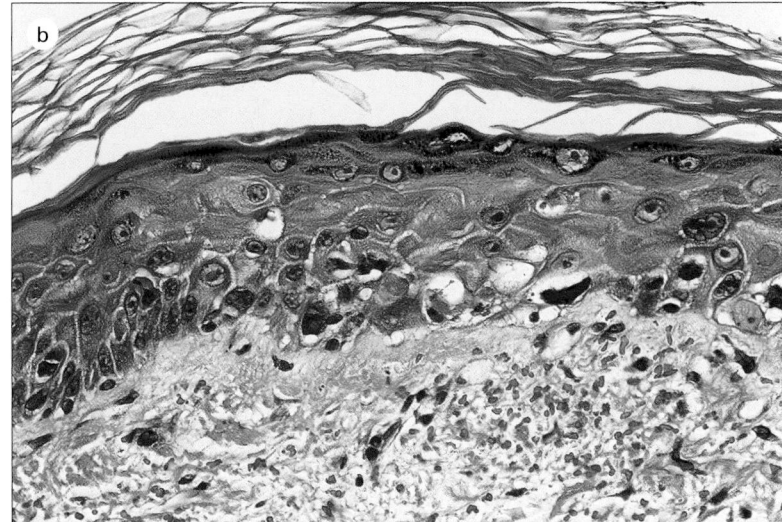

Fig. 13.90
(a, b) Chemotherapy-related drug reaction: there is striking dyskeratosis and abnormal maturation. The latter is a common feature of chemotherapy reactions.

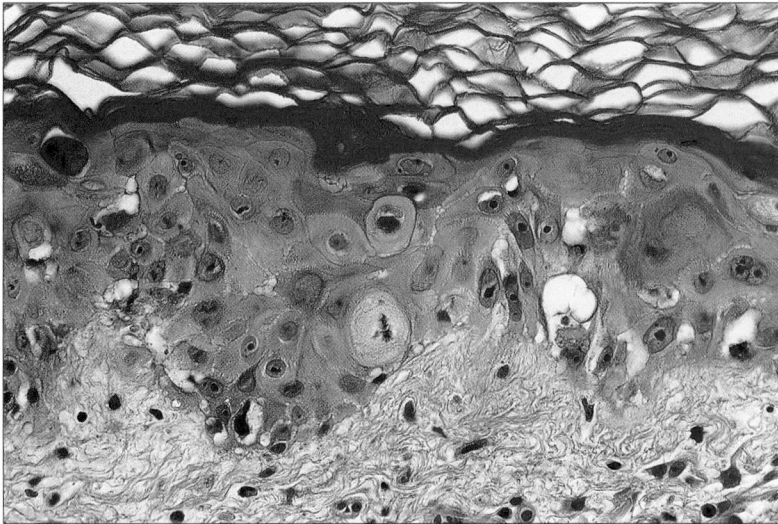

Fig. 13.91
Chemotherapy-related drug reaction: close-up view.

sweat gland/duct epithelium may be affected. Appearances are variable, ranging from lichen planus-like changes (including hyperkeratosis, hypergranulosis, acanthosis, basal cell hydropic degeneration and apoptosis) through to lupus erythematosus-like reactions in which the epidermis is markedly atrophic. The combination of interface changes with severe maturation arrest is pathognomonic of chemotherapy-related reactions. It is particularly a feature of patients receiving long-term chemotherapy, high dose chemotherapy and multiagent chemotherapy. In addition to impaired maturation, the epidermis appears disorganized and individual keratinocytes are enlarged with pleomorphic nuclei containing conspicuous nucleoli. These changes are particularly seen as complications of therapy with bleomycin, busulfan and hydroxyurea. Squamous metaplasia of the dermal sweat ducts may be seen in patients receiving methotrexate therapy.[50]

Etoposide, a podophyllin derivative, in addition to causing maturation abnormalities, can cause metaphase arrest with the production of characteristic fragmented nuclear chromatin resulting in so-called 'starburst cells'.[51]

The hyperpigmentation complicating busulfan therapy predominantly affects the basal layer of the epidermis but also may extend throughout the full thickness and is often accompanied by pigmentary incontinence due to melanocyte toxicity.[52] Similarly, bleomycin-induced hyperpigmentation is characterized by epidermal hyperpigmentation and pigmentary incontinence.[53] Melanocytes are present in normal numbers. The early inflammatory phase is characterized by a superficial perivascular infiltrate of lymphocytes, histiocytes, occasional neutrophils, plasma cells and eosinophils. Some authors, however, have described basal cell pigmentation in the absence of pigmentary incontinence.[24,54] Lymphocytic vasculitis has also been reported.[25]

Thio-TEPA-induced pigmentation is similarly characterized by melanin pigment within all layers of the epidermis including the stratum corneum accompanied by basal cell hydropic degeneration and pigmentary incontinence.[29] A mild perivascular lymphohistiocytic infiltrate is present in the superficial dermis. The melanocyte concentration is normal.

Radiation recall is characterized by epidermal atrophy, basal cell hydropic degeneration and superficial dermal vascular ectasia.

In addition to anagen alopecia and interface changes, pustular folliculitis and allergic contact dermatitis (5-fluorouracil) may be a feature of chemotherapy-associated adverse reactions, particularly with dactinomycin and 5-fluorouracil.[55,56]

Hypersensitivity reactions including urticaria, angioedema and maculopapular eruptions are histologically no different from other drug-induced lesions (see above).

Dermal sclerosis may be a feature of bleomycin and docetaxel therapy.[57]

Extravasation of chemotherapeutic agents including cisplatin, dactinomycin, daunorubicin, doxorubicin, etoposide, idarubicin, mechlorethamine, mithramycin, paclitaxel, vinblastine and vincristine may result in chemical cellulitis and tissue necrosis.[1]

Spongiotic dermatitis is rarely seen as a complication of systemic chemotherapy but has been described following treatment with methotrexate, 5-fluorouracil and dacarbazine.[48,49] It is much more commonly encountered following the topical administration of chemotherapeutic agents including 5-fluorouracil and mechlorethamine.

The interstitial granulomatous reaction associated with low dose methotrexate therapy is characterized by a largely histiocytic interstitial infiltrate with small numbers of neutrophils.[46] Vasculitis is not a feature. The histiocytes may surround neutrophil aggregates, and histiocytes forming a palisade around collagen fibers is a characteristic feature.[46]

References

1. Alley, E., Green, R., Schuchter, L. (2002) Cutaneous toxicities of cancer therapy. *Curr Opin Oncol*, **14**, 212–216.
2. Bronner, A.K., Hood, A.F. (1983) Cutaneous complications of chemotherapeutic agents. *J Am Acad Dermatol*, **9**, 645–663.
3. Kerker, B.J., Hood, A.F. (1989) Chemotherapy-induced cutaneous reactions. *Semin Dermatol*, **8**, 173–181.
4. Hood, A.F. (1986) Cutaneous side-effects of cancer chemotherapy. *Med Clin North Am*, **70**, 187–209.
5. Rapini, R.P. (1991) Cytotoxic drugs in the treatment of skin disease. *Int J Dermatol*, **30**, 313–322.
6. Koppel, R.A., Boh, E.E. (2001) Cutaneous reactions to chemotherapeutic agents. *Am J Med Sci*, **321**, 327–335.
7. Seavolt, M.B., Sarro, R.A., Levin, K. et al (2002) Mees' lines in a patient following acute arsenic intoxication. *Int J Dermatol*, **41**, 399–401.
8. Siragusa, M., Alberti, A., Schepis, C. (1999) Mees' lines due to cyclosporin. *Br J Dermatol*, **140**, 1198–1199.
9. Shelley, W.B., Humphrey, G.B. (1997) Transverse leukonychia (Mees' lines) due to daunorubicin chemotherapy. *Pediatr Dermatol*, **14**, 144–145.
10. Adam, B.A., Ismail, R., Sivansan, S. (1980) Busulfan hyperpigmentation: light and electron microscopic studies. *J Dermatol (Tokyo)*, **7**, 405–411.
11. Flaxman, B.A., Sosis, A.C., Van Scott, E.J. (1973) Changes in melanosome distribution in Caucasoid skin following topical application of nitrogen mustard. *J Invest Dermatol*, **60**, 321–326.
12. Romankiewicz, J.A. (1974) Cyclophosphamide and pigmentation. *Am J Hosp Pharm*, **31**, 1074–1075.
13. Bandini, G., Belardinelli, A., Rosti, G. et al (1994) Toxicity of high-dose busulphan and cyclophosphamide as conditioning therapy for allogeneic bone marrow transplantation in adults with haematological malignancies. *Bone Marrow Transplant*, **13**, 577–581.
14. Teresi, M.E., Murry, D.J., Cornelius, A.S. (1993) Ifosfamide-induced hyperpigmentation. *Cancer*, **71**, 2873–2875.
15. Hrushesky, W.J. (1980) Unusual pigmentary changes associated with 5-fluorouracil therapy. *Cutis*, **26**, 181–182.
16. Allen, B.J., Parker, D., Wright, A.L. (1995) Reticulate pigmentation due to 5-fluorouracil. *Int J Dermatol*, **34**, 219–220.
17. Claudy, A.L., Levigne, V., Boucheron, S. (1992) Serpentine supravenous hyperpigmentation induced by nitrosourea fotemustine. *Dermatology*, **184**, 70–72.
18. Marcoux, D., Anex, R., Russo, P. (2000) Persistent serpentine supravenous hyperpigmented eruption as an adverse reaction to chemotherapy combining actinomycin and vincristine. *J Am Acad Dermatol*, **43**, 540–546.
19. Hampson, J.P., Donnelly, A., Lewis-Jones, M.S. et al (1995) Tamoxifen-induced hair color change. *Br J Dermatol*, **132**, 483–484.
20. Cohen, I.S., Mosher, M.B., O'Keefe, E.J. et al (1973) Cutaneous toxicity of bleomycin therapy. *Arch Dermatol*, **107**, 553–555.
21. Guillet, G., Guillet, M-H., de Meaux, H. et al (1986) Cutaneous pigmented stripes and bleomycin therapy. *Arch Dermatol*, **122**, 381–382.
22. Miori, L., Vignini, M., Rabbiosi, G. (1990) Flagellate dermatitis after bleomycin: a histological and immunohistochemical study. *Am J Dermatopathol*, **12**, 598–602.
23. Wright, A.L., Bleehen, S.S., Champion, A.E. (1990) Reticulate pigmentation due to bleomycin: light- and electron-microscopic studies. *Dermatologica*, **180**, 225–227.
24. Vicente, M.A., Iranzo, P., Azon, A. et al (1990) Flagellated pigmentation caused by bleomycin. Presentation of 2 cases. *Med Cutan Ibero Lat Am*, **18**, 148–150.
25. Duhra, P., Ilchyshyn, A., Das, R.N. (1991) Bleomycin-induced flagellate erythema. *Clin Exp Dermatol*, **16**, 216–217.
26. Spendini, P., Bergonzi, C., Morandi, S. (2000) Cutaneous flagellate pigmentation by bleomycin. *Haematologica*, **85**, 870.
27. Nigro, M.G., Hsu, S. (2001) Bleomycin-induced flagellate pigmentation. *Cutis*, **68**, 285–286.
28. vonHilsheimer, G.E., Norton, S.A. (2002) Delayed bleomycin-induced hyperpigmentation and pressure on the skin. *J Am Acad Dermatol*, **46**, 642–643.
29. Horn, T.D., Beverley, R.A., Egorin, M.J. et al (1989) Observations and proposed mechanism of N, N1, N11-triethylenethiophosphoramide (thio-TEPA)-induced hyperpigmentation. *Arch Dermatol*, **125**, 524–527.
30. Singal, R., Tunnessen, W.W. Jr, Wiley, J.M. et al (1991) Discrete pigmentation after chemotherapy. *Pediatr Dermatol*, **8**, 231–235.
31. Wheeland, R.G., Burgdorf, W.H.C., Humphrey, G.B. (1983) The flag sign of chemotherapy. *Cancer*, **51**, 1356–1358.
32. Greco, F.A., Brereton, H.D., Kent, H. et al (1976) Adriamycin and enhanced radiation reaction in normal esophagus and skin. *Ann Intern Med*, **85**, 294–298.
33. Donaldson, S.S., Glick, J.M., Wilbur, J.R. (1974) Adriamycin activating a recall phenomenon after radiation therapy. *Ann Intern Med*, **81**, 407–408.
34. Shenkier, T., Gelman, K. (1994) Pacitaxel and radiation-recall dermatitis. *J Clin Oncol*, **12**, 439.
35. Fogarty, G., Ball, D., Rischin, D. (2001) Radiation recall reaction following gemcitabine. *Lung Cancer*, **33**, 299–302.
36. Jeter, M.D., Janne, P.A., Brooks, S. et al (2002) Gemcitabine-induced radiation recall. *Int J Radiat Oncol Biol Phys*, **53**, 394–400.
37. Giesel, B.U., Kutz, G.G., Thiel, H.J. (2001) Recall dermatitis caused by re-exposure to docetaxel following irradiation of the brain. Case report and review of the literature. *Strahlenther Onkol*, **177**, 487–493.

38. Thomas, R., Stea, B. (2002) Radiation recall dermatitis from high-dose interferon alfa-2b. *J Clin Oncol*, **20**, 355–357.
39. Kennedy, R.D., McAleer, J.J. (2001) Radiation recall dermatitis in a patient treated with dacarbazine. *Clin Oncol (R Coll Radiol)*, **13**, 470–472.
40. Carrasco, L., Pastor, M.A., Izquierdo, M.J. et al (2002) Drug eruption secondary to aciclovir with recall phenomenon in a dermatome previously affected by herpes zoster. *Clin Exp Dermatol*, **27**, 132–134.
41. Ortmann, E., Hohenberg, G. (2002) Treatment side-effects. Case 1. Radiation recall phenomenon after administration of capecitabine. *J Clin Oncol*, **20**, 3029–3030.
42. Armstrong, R.B., Poh-Fitzpatrick, M.B. (1982) Methotrexate and ultraviolet radiation. *Arch Dermatol*, **118**, 177–178.
43. Killander, D., Dohlwitz, A., Engstedt, L. et al (1976) Hypersensitive reactions and antibody formation during L-asparaginase treatment of children and adults with acute leukemia. *Cancer*, **37**, 220–228.
44. Weiss, R.B., Bruno, S. (1981) Hypersensitivity reactions to cancer chemotherapeutic agents. *Ann Intern Med*, **94**, 66–72.
45. Van Scott, E.J., Winters, P.L. (1970) Responses of mycosis fungoides to intensive external treatment with nitrogen mustard. *Arch Dermatol*, **102**, 507–514.
46. Goerttler, E., Kutzner, H., Peter, H.H. et al (1999) Methotrexate-induced papular eruption in patients with rheumatic diseases: a distinctive adverse cutaneous reaction produced by methotrexate in patients with collagen vascular diseases. *J Am Acad Dermatol*, **40**, 702–707.
47. Fitzpatrick, J.E., Hood, A.F. (1988) Histopathologic reactions to chemotherapeutic agents. *Adv Dermatol*, **3**, 161–182.
48. Fitzpatrick, J.E. (1992) The cutaneous histopathology of chemotherapeutic reactions. *J Cutan Pathol*, **20**, 1–14.
49. Fitzpatrick, J.E. (1992) New histopathologic findings in drug eruptions. *Dermatol Clin*, **10**, 19–36.
50. Crowson, A.N., Magro, C.M. (1999) Recent advances in the pathology of cutaneous drug eruptions. *Dermatol Clin*, **17**, 537–560.
51. Yokel, B.K., Friedman, K.J., Farmer, E.R. et al (1987) Cutaneous pathology following etoposide therapy. *J Cutan Pathol*, **14**, 326–330.
52. Hymes, S.R., Simonton, S.C., Farmer, E.R. et al (1985) Cutaneous busulfan effect in patients receiving bone-marrow transplantation. *J Cutan Pathol*, **12**, 125–129.
53. Werner, Y., Tornberg, B. (1976) Cutaneous side-effects of bleomycin chemotherapy. *Acta Derm Venereol*, **56**, 155–158.
54. Fernández-Obregón, A.C., Hogan, K.P., Bibro, M.K. (1985) Flagellate hyperpigmentation from intrapleural bleomycin. *J Am Acad Dermatol*, **13**, 464–468.
55. Goette, D.K., Odom, R.B., Owens, R. (1977) Allergic contact dermatitis from topical fluorouracil. *Arch Dermatol*, **113**, 196–198.
56. Sevadjian, C.M. (1985) Pustular contact hypersensitivity to fluorouracil with rosacea-like sequelae. *Arch Dermatol*, **121**, 240–242.
57. Battafarano, D.F., Zimmerman, G.C., Older, S.A. et al (1995) Docetaxel (taxotere) associated scleroderma-like changes of the lower extremities. *Cancer*, **76**, 110–115.

Chemotherapy-induced acral erythema

Clinical features

Chemotherapy-induced acral erythema (acral erythema, hand–foot syndrome, palmoplantar erythrodysesthesia syndrome, toxic erythema of the palms and soles) in which the patient presents with circumscribed, extremely painful and tender erythematous macules on the palms, finger tips and soles has been described following treatment with 5-fluorouracil, cyclophosphamide, cytarabine, daunorubicin, doxorubicin and vincristine.[1–11] Etoposide, mercaptopurine, methotrexate and vinblastine have also been incriminated. Patients subsequently develop blisters and healing is associated with desquamation.

Histological features

The histological features include basal cell liquefactive degeneration, keratinocyte necrosis and mild spongiosis.[1–3,12] There is papillary dermal edema, vascular dilatation and a mild superficial perivascular lympho-histiocytic infiltrate. Features of syringosquamous metaplasia and eccrine neutrophilic hidradenitis have also been exceptionally documented.[13,14]

In one case, immunohistochemistry of the dermal lymphocytes disclosed a CD3+, CD16+, CD56+, leukocyte function antigen-1 positive phenotype suggestive of natural killer T-cells.[15] In this patient, the eccrine ducts expressed HLA-DR and intercellular adhesion molecule-1 (ICAM-1).[15]

Differential diagnosis

The features are indistinguishable from graft-versus-host disease. Distinction is dependent upon clinicopathological correlation.

References

1. Burgdorf, W.H.C., Gilmore, W.A., Garick, R.G. (1982) Peculiar acral erythema secondary to high-dose chemotherapy for acute myelogenous leukemia. *Ann Intern Med*, **97**, 61–62.
2. Lokich, J.J., Moore, C. (1984) Chemotherapy associated palmar–plantar erythrodysesthesia syndrome. *Ann Intern Med*, **101**, 798–800.
3. Crider, M.K., Jansen, J., Norins, A.L. et al (1986) Chemotherapy-induced acral erythema in patients receiving bone marrow transplantation. *Arch Dermatol*, **122**, 1023–1027.
4. Cohen, P.R. (1993) Acral erythema: a clinical review. *Cutis*, **51**, 175–179.
5. De Argila, D., Domínguez, J.D., Iglesias, L. (1996) Taxol-induced acral erythema. *Dermatology*, **192**, 377–378.
6. Demircay, Z., Gurbuz, O., Alpdogan, T.B. et al (1997) Chemotherapy-induced acral erythema in leukemic patients: a report of 15 cases. *Int J Dermatol*, **36**, 593–598.
7. Vakalis, D., Ioannides, D., Lazaridou, E. (1998) Acral erythema induced by chemotherapy with cisplatin. *Br J Dermatol*, **139**, 750–751.
8. Millot, F., Auriol, F., Brecheteau, P. et al (1998) Acral erythema in children receiving high-dose methotrexate. *Pediatr Dermatol*, **16**, 398–400.
9. Soker, M., Akdeniz, S., Devecioglu, C. et al (2001) Chemotherapy-induced bullous acral erythema in a subject with B-cell lymphoma. *J Eur Acad Dermatol Venereol*, **15**, 490–491.
10. Morrell, D.S., Chalgren, E., Eaden, M. et al (2002) Bullous acral erythema secondary to high-dose methotrexate. *J Pediatriatr Hematol Oncol*, **24**, 240.
11. Takeuchi, M., Tanizawa, A., Fukomoto, Y. (2001) Skin toxicity associated with bolus infusion of low dose cytarabine. *Rinsho Ketsueki*, **42**, 216–217.
12. Fitzpatrick, J.E. (1992) The cutaneous histopathology of chemotherapeutic reactions. *J Cutan Pathol*, **20**, 1–14.
13. Eich, D., Scharffetter-Kochanek, K., Eich, H.T. et al (2002) Acral erythrodysesthesia syndrome caused by intravenous infusion of docetaxel in breast cancer. *Am J Clin Oncol*, **25**, 599–602.
14. Rongioletti, F., Rebora, A. (1992) Eccrine squamous syringometaplasia in chemotherapy-induced acral erythema. *J Am Acad Dermatol*, **26**, 284.
15. Tsuruta, D., Mochida, K., Hamada, T. et al (2000) Chemotherapy-induced acral erythema: report of a case and immunohistochemical findings. *Clin Exp Dermatol*, **25**, 386–388.

Chemotherapy-associated eccrine gland reactions

Although there is some histological overlap between neutrophil eccrine hidradenitis and eccrine syringosquamous metaplasia, more often they present independently of one another and as such they are considered separately.

Neutrophil eccrine hidradenitis

Clinical features

This rare eccrine gland reaction was initially reported in a patient receiving induction chemotherapy including doxorubicin and cytarabine in the treatment of acute myelogenous leukemia.[1] Subsequently a similar eruption was described in patients with a number of other malignancies such as Hodgkin's lymphoma, non-Hodgkin's lymphoma, breast carcinoma, Wilms' tumor, osteosarcoma and testicular tumors including embryonal carcinoma and teratoma.[2–7] Further cases developing in association with acute myelogenous leukemia have also been documented.[8,9] It was soon appreciated that additional chemotherapeutic agents including bleomycin, chlorambucil, daunorubicin, dactinomycin, vincristine, lomustine, mitoxantrone, thioguanine, *cis*-platinum, vinblastine, topotecan, cyclophosphamide and 5-fluorouracil might be responsible although cytarabine has been most commonly implicated.[10] Recently a case following the use of GM-CSF has been reported.[11] It should be noted, however, that neutrophilic eccrine hidradenitis has also been described as a prodromal manifestation of acute myelogenous leukemia in the absence of chemotherapy.[12] The condition has been described in HIV-positive patients receiving zidovudine and as a complication of treatment with acetaminophen.[13–16]

Clinically, patients (who are commonly febrile) develop a polymorphous eruption consisting of variably asymptomatic or tender erythematous to violaceous macules, papules, plaques, nodules and pustules which most often presents within 1 or 2 weeks of starting chemotherapy.[4] Lesions may be very numerous and although there does not appear to be a site predilection, the trunk and upper limbs are most often affected.[5] Neutrophilic eccrine hidradenitis may also present with periorbital edema, and ear involvement seen as bilateral tender erythema has been documented.[17,18] The lesions desquamate and usually heal spontaneously within 1–3 weeks.[4] Postinflammatory hyperpigmentation and scarring are not usually features. Recurrence following the reintroduction of chemotherapy has been documented.[1,8] Clinically, an infectious condition, leukemia cutis, bullous pyoderma, atypical pyoderma gangrenosum or Sweet's disease is most often suspected.[8]

Pathogenesis and histological features

The pathogenesis of this condition is unknown but it has been proposed that the drug may be concentrated in the sweat glands, thereby exerting a direct toxic effect on the secretory epithelial cells.[1,2] Alternatively, it has been suggested that the condition represents part of the spectrum of acute neutrophilic dermatoses which also includes Sweet's syndrome and pyoderma gangrenosum.[4] Presentation as a prodromal manifestation of leukemia before the introduction of chemotherapy and its development in an otherwise healthy person as a probable complication of prolonged pressure suggests that the etiology is likely to be multifactorial.[12,16]

The most significant histological features are seen in the deeper reticular dermis and subcutaneous fat where a dense neutrophil polymorph infiltrate surrounds the eccrine secretory coils (Fig. 13.92). The coiled and straight dermal ducts are typically unaffected. Leukocytoclasis is sometimes evident.[4,19] The glandular epithelium shows neutrophil infiltration, nuclear pyknosis, cytoplasmic eosinophilia or vacuolation and often appears sloughed off into the lumen of the gland.[7] In occasional patients syringosquamous metaplasia may additionally be present; rarely, necrosis of the eccrine gland is seen in the absence of significant inflammation.[8,17,20,21] The periadnexal fibroadipose tissue stroma typically shows mucinous degeneration and a variable infiltrate of neutrophils, lymphocytes, histiocytes and eosinophils.[8] Recently, it has been shown that the apocrine glands may be affected in addition to the eccrine glands.[22] There is no evidence of vasculitis.

Differential diagnosis

Idiopathic plantar hidradenitis (idiopathic recurrent palmoplantar hidradenitis in children, neutrophilic eccrine hidradenitis in children) is a recently described rare dermatosis in which tender, painful, erythematous papules, plaques and nodules, 0.5–3.0 cm in diameter, develop on the soles of the feet of children.[23–27] Less often, concomitant palmar involvement has been documented.[24] Recurrences are not uncommon. The condition shows a predilection for females (2:1).[23] Incidence shows some seasonal variation, lesions developing most often in spring and autumn. Adults may also rarely be affected.[28] Although trauma does not appear to be an etiological factor, chronic pressure is probably of importance. Prolonged immersion in hot bath water preceded the development of lesions in a number of cases. Pyrexia is not usually present and the patients are otherwise well. The condition usually clears spontaneously.

In contrast to eccrine neutrophilic hidradenitis, the changes are centered on the coiled duct and proximal straight duct, the secretory apparatus usually being spared or only minimally affected.[23] The condition is characterized by an intense neutrophil infiltrate surrounding and involving the ductal epithelium associated with epithelial degenerative changes and necrosis. Abscess formation may also be a feature. Eccrine syringosquamous metaplasia is not seen.

Rarely neutrophilic eccrine hidradenitis may represent a primary infectious process, for example Serratio spp. and Enterobacter cloacae.[29–30]

References

1. Harrist, T.J., Fine, J.D., Berman, R.S. et al (1982) Neutrophilic eccrine hidradenitis: a distinctive type of neutrophilic dermatosis associated with myelogenous leukemia and chemotherapy. Arch Dermatol, 118, 263–266.
2. Beutner, K.R., Packman, C.H., Markowitch, W. (1986) Neutrophilic eccrine hidradenitis associated with Hodgkin's disease and chemotherapy. A case report. Arch Dermatol, 122, 809–811.
3. Fitzpatrick, J.E., Bennison, S.D., Reed, O.M. et al (1987) Neutrophilic eccrine hidradenitis associated with induction chemotherapy. J Cutan Pathol, 14, 272–278.
4. Bailey, D.L., Barron, D., Lucky, A.W. (1989) Neutrophilic eccrine hidradenitis: a case report and review of the literature. Pediatr Dermatol, 6, 33–38.
5. Vion, B., Alvero, H. (1991) Neutrophilic eccrine hidradenitis. Dermatologica, 183, 70–72.
6. Shear, N.H., Knowles, S.R., Shapiro, L. et al (1996) Dapsone in prevention of recurrent neutrophilic eccrine hidradenitis. J Am Acad Dermatol, 35, 819–822.
7. Moisson, Y.F., Aractingi, S., Pinquier, L. et al (1992) Hidradénite eccrine neutrophilique. Ann Dermatol Venereol, 119, 605–611.
8. Flynn, T.C., Harrist, T.J., Murphy, G.F. et al (1984) Neutrophilic eccrine hidradenitis: a distinctive rash associated with cytarabine therapy and acute leukemia. J Am Acad Dermatol, 11, 584–590.
9. Katsanis, E., Luke, K-H., Hsu, E. et al (1987) Neutrophilic eccrine hidradenitis in acute myelomonocytic leukemia. Am J Pediatr Hematol, 9, 204–208.
10. Marini, M., Wright, D., Ropolo, M. (2002) Neutrophilic eccrine hidradenitis secondary to topotecan. J Dermatolog Treat, 13, 35–37.
11. Bachmeyer, C., Chiabi, P., Aractingi, S. (1998) Neutrophilic eccrine hidradenitis induced by granulocyte colony-stimulating factor. Br J Dermatol, 139, 340–341.
12. Pierson, J.C., Helm, T.N., Taylor, J.S. et al (1993) Neutrophilic eccrine hidradenitis heralding the onset of acute myelogenous leukemia. Arch Dermatol, 129, 791–792.
13. Smith, K.J., Skelton, H.G. III, James, W.D. et al (1990) Neutrophilic eccrine hidradenitis in HIV-infected patients. J Am Acad Dermatol, 23, 945–947.
14. Krischer, J., Rotschmann, O., Roten, S.V. et al (1998) Neutrophilic eccrine hidradenitis in a patient with AIDS. J Dermatol, 25, 199–200.
15. Bachmeyer, C., Reygagne, P., Aractingi, S. (2000) Recurrent neutrophilic eccrine hidradenitis in an HIV-1 infected patient. Dermatology, 200, 328–330.
16. Kuttner, B., Kurban, R. (1988) Neutrophilic eccrine hidradenitis in the absence of an underlying malignancy. Cutis, 41, 403–405.

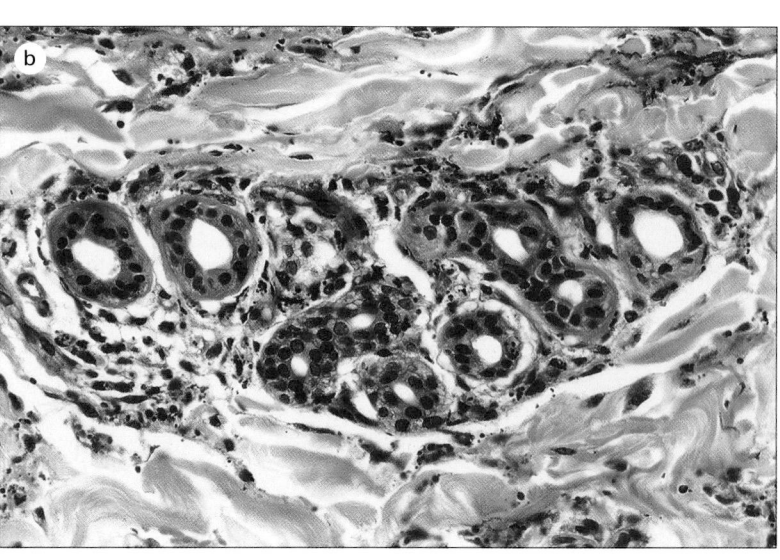

Fig. 13.92
(a, b) Neutrophil eccrine hidradenitis: there is a neutrophil infiltrate surrounding the eccrine gland. Note the sparing of the duct.

17. Bardenstein, D., Haluschak, J., Gerson, S. et al (1994) Neutrophilic eccrine hidradenitis simulating orbital cellulitis. *Arch Ophthalmol*, **112**, 1460–1463.
18. Ostlere, L.S., Wells, J., Stevens, H.P. et al (1993) Neutrophilic eccrine hidradenitis with an unusual presentation. *Br J Dermatol*, **128**, 696–698.
19. Fitzpatrick, J.E. (1992) The cutaneous histopathology of chemotherapeutic reactions. *J Cutan Pathol*, **20**, 1–14.
20. Hurt, M.A., Halvorson, R.D., Petr, C. Jr et al (1990) Eccrine squamous syringometaplasia: a cutaneous sweat gland reaction in the spectrum of 'chemotherapy-associated eccrine hidradenitis' and 'neutrophilic eccrine hidradenitis'. *Arch Dermatol*, **126**, 73–77.
21. Greenbaum, B.H., Heymann, W.R., Reid, C.S. et al (1988) Chemotherapy-associated eccrine hidradenitis: neutrophilic eccrine hidradenitis re-evaluated: the role of neutrophilic infiltration. *Med Pediatr Oncol*, **16**, 351–355.
22. Brehler, R., Reimann, S., Bonsmann, G. et al (1997) Neutrophilic hidradenitis induced by chemotherapy involves the eccrine and apocrine glands. *Am J Dermatopathol*, **19**, 73–78.
23. Stahr, B.J., Cooper, P.H., Caputo, R.V. (1994) Idiopathic plantar hidradenitis: a neutrophilic eccrine hidradenitis occurring primarily in children. *J Cutan Pathol*, **21**, 289–296.
24. Rabinowitz, L.G., Cintra, M.L., Hoof, A.F. et al (1995) Recurrent palmoplantar hidradenitis in children. *Arch Dermatol*, **131**, 817–820.
25. Simon, M., Cremer, H., von den Driesch, P. (1998) Idiopathic recurrent palmoplantar hidradenitis in children. Report of 22 cases. *Arch Dermatol*, **134**, 76–79.
26. Dráke, M., Sánchez-Burson, J.M., Dona-Naranjo, M.A. et al (2000) Juvenile neutrophilic eccrine hidradenitis: a vasculitis-like plantar dermatosis. *Clin Rheumatol*, **19**, 481–483.
27. Erro-Vincent, T., Souillet, A.L., Fouilhoux, A. et al (2001) Eccrine neutrophilic hidradenitis: idiopathic plantar form in children. *Arch Pediatr*, **8**, 290–293.
28. Manganoni, A.M., Facchetti, F., Gavazzoni, R. et al (1994) Neutrophilic eccrine hidradenitis in a healthy woman. *Dermatology*, **189**, 211–212.
29. Moreno, A., Barnadas, M.A., Ravella, A. et al (1985) Infectious eccrine hidradenitis in a patient undergoing hemodialysis. *Arch Dermatol*, **121**, 1106–1107.
30. Allegue, F., Rocamora, A., Martín-González, M. et al (1990) Infectious eccrine hidradenitis. *J Am Acad Dermatol*, **22**, 1119–1120.

Eccrine squamous syringometaplasia

Clinical features

Eccrine squamous syringometaplasia (syringosquamous metaplasia) is a histologically distinctive eruption that may rarely develop following chemotherapy.[1–3] Patients present with erythematous papules often in a generalized distribution following the administration of a number of chemotherapeutic agents including bleomycin, cytarabine, daunorubicin, doxorubicin and *cis*-platinum. Pustules and vesicles are sometimes seen. Presentation as acral erythema has also been documented.[4]

Histological features

The changes primarily affect the upper portion of the eccrine duct and consist of squamous metaplasia associated with apoptosis of the lining epithelium (*Fig. 13.93*).[1] Periductal edema and fibrosis may also be seen. A perivascular infiltrate consisting of lymphocytes and occasionally neutrophils is present in the surrounding dermis.

Differential diagnosis

Eccrine squamous syringometaplasia may occur in a wide variety of settings. It may be found adjacent to cutaneous ulcers, following severe burns, as a feature in panniculitis, linear scleroderma and pyoderma gangrenosum, in recall phenomenon, in association with tumors including squamous cell carcinoma and keratoacanthoma and in infections including herpes virus, cytomegalovirus and human immunodeficiency virus.[5–11] It has also been described as a complication of benoxaprofen therapy.[12]

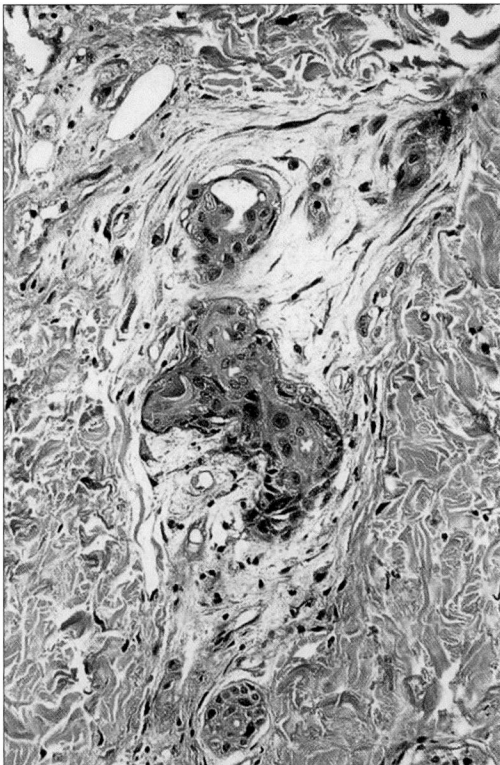

Fig. 13.93
Eccrine squamous syringometaplasia: the eccrine duct shows striking squamous metaplasia and apoptosis. This example developed in a patient receiving cytarabine.

References

1. Bhawan, J., Malhotra, R. (1990) Syringosquamous metaplasia. A distinctive eruption in patients receiving chemotherapy. *Am J Dermatopathol*, **16**, 1–6.
2. Hurt, M.A., Halvorson, R.D., Petr, C. Jr et al (1990) Eccrine squamous syringometaplasia: a cutaneous sweat gland reaction in the spectrum of 'chemotherapy-associated eccrine hidradenitis' and 'neutrophilic eccrine hidradenitis'. *Arch Dermatol*, **126**, 73–77.
3. Valks, R., Fraga, J., Porras-Luque, J. et al (1997) Chemotherapy-induced eccrine squamous syringometaplasia. A distinctive eruption in patients receiving hematopoietic progenitor cells. *Arch Dermatol*, **133**, 873–878.
4. Rongioletti, F., Ballestero, A., Bogliolo, F. et al (1991) Necrotizing eccrine squamous syringometaplasia presenting as acral erythema. *J Cutan Pathol*, **18**, 453–456.
5. Sommer, B., Hagedorn, M., Wood, F. et al (1998) Eccrine squamous syringometaplasia in the skin of children after burns. *J Cutan Pathol*, **25**, 56–58.
6. Sakai, H., Satoh, K., Manabe, A. et al (2002) Eccrine squamous syringometaplasia and syringomatous hyperplasia in association with linear scleroderma. *Dermatology*, **204**, 136–138.
7. Muñoz, E., Valks, R., Fernández-Herrera, J. et al (1997) Herpetic syringitis associated with eccrine squamous syringometaplasia in HIV-positive patients. *J Cutan Pathol*, **24**, 425–428.
8. Dauden, E., Porras, J.L., Buezo, G.F. et al (2000) Eccrine squamous syringometaplasia and cytomegalovirus. *Am J Dermatopathol*, **22**, 559–561.
9. Metcalf, J.S., Maize, J.C. (1990) Syringometaplasia in lobular panniculitis and pyoderma gangrenosum. *Am J Dermatopathol*, **12**, 141–149.
10. Serrano, T., Sáez, A., Moreno, A. (1993) Eccrine squamous syringometaplasia. A prospective clinicopathologic study. *J Cutan Pathol*, **20**, 61–65.
11. Rios-Buceta, L., Peñas, P.F., Dauden-Tello, E. et al (1995) Recall phenomenon with the unusual presence of eccrine squamous syringometaplasia. *Br J Dermatol*, **133**, 630–632.
12. Lerner, T.H., Barr, R.J., Dolezal, J.F. et al (1987) Syringomatous hyperplasia and eccrine squamous syringometaplasia associated with benoxaprofen therapy. *Arch Dermatol*, **123**, 1202–1204.

Adverse reactions to cytokine therapy

Clinical features

A very wide range of adverse reactions to the large number of recombinant cytokines available as therapeutic agents have been described.[1] These are very comprehensively documented in the review article of Asnis and Gaspari.[2] The majority of these agents have to a greater or lesser extent been associated with local injection site reactions (painful or pruritic erythematous wheals).[2] Only a limited number of cytokines, which may be associated with more specific dermatological manifestations, are included in this section.

Granulocyte colony-stimulating factor (G-CSF, filgrastim; a glycoprotein that stimulates proliferation and differentiation of neutrophils) therapy has been documented as causing a number of dermatological conditions including bullous pyoderma gangrenosum, folliculitis, leukocytoclastic vasculitis and Sweet's syndrome.[2–9] G-CSF and GM-CSF have also been incriminated in exacerbation of pre-existent leukocytoclastic vasculitis, psoriasis, a generalized erythematous eruption, erythematous plaques and a localized lichenoid reaction.[10–15]

A number of adverse reactions have been described following treatment with GM-CSF (a growth factor which stimulates proliferation and differentiation of neutrophils, monocytes and eosinophils) including localized angioedema, facial flushing, and generalized erythematous, maculopapular, exfoliative, urticarial, pruritic and pustular cutaneous reactions.[2,16–19] Localized pustular and vasculitic reactions and generalized folliculitis, epidermolysis bullosa acquisita and alopecia have also followed treatment with GM-CSF.[2,7,18–21]

The use of IFN-α may be followed by localized erythema and less often skin necrosis. It is followed by the development of alopecia in up to 10% of patients.[22] Psoriasis, pyoderma gangrenosum, localized granulomatous and suppurative lesions, ulcers, vasculitis, systemic lupus erythematosus, eosinophilic fasciitis, eczematous lesions, photosensitivity and paraneoplastic pemphigus have also complicated its use.[2,23–29]

Single case reports have documented instances of fatal pemphigus vulgaris and allergic facial contact dermatitis following treatment with IFN-β.[30,31] Erythematous plaques, cutaneous ulceration, necrosis, a vasculitis-like eruption and sclerodermiform lesions have also been documented.[32–35]

INF-γ may induce psoriatic plaques at the injection site and its use has been shown to induce erythema nodosum leprosum in patients with leprosy.[36,37]

IL-2, which is produced by activated T-lymphocytes, stimulates the production of a number of cytokines including IFN-γ, tumor necrosis factor and GM-CSF in addition to inducing differentiation of an activated killer cell population which has a cytotoxic effect on tumor cells.[38,39] Dermatological complications of recombinant IL-2 (r IL-2) therapy include a desquamating, diffuse erythematous macular eruption, pruritus, purpura, telogen effluvium, mucositis with aphthous ulcers and glossitis.[2,38] Toxic epidermal necrolysis-like blistering dermatoses, pemphigus vulgaris, linear IgA disease, vitiligo and erythema nodosum have also been reported.[2,29,40–44] IL-2 therapy may be associated with exacerbation of psoriasis.[45,46]

Pruritus, facial edema and a transient acantholytic dermatosis-like eruption affecting the chest, back and proximal extremities have been described following treatment with IL-4 and there is a case report describing the development of vitiligo in association with recombinant IL-4 therapy.[47,48]

Histological features

Histologically, the erythematous lesions associated with G-CSF show epidermal acanthosis, parakeratosis, eosinophilic spongiosis with abscess formation and interface changes.[14] The lichenoid eruption is characterized by hyperkeratosis, dyskeratosis and interface change accompanied by a lymphocytic infiltrate.[15] An atypical dermal histiocytic infiltrate characterized by nuclear pleomorphism and mitotic activity has recently been documented.[49]

The erythematous maculopapular eruption associated with GM-CSF is characterized by edema and a superficial perivascular and interstitial inflammatory cell infiltrate composed of T-helper lymphocytes, histiocytes, eosinophils and conspicuous neutrophils accompanied by epidermal spongiosis and lymphocyte/neutrophil exocytosis.[16–18] Focal dyskeratosis may also be a feature.[16]

Histologically, IL-2 skin reactions are characterized by interface vacuolar degeneration with rare necrotic keratinocytes accompanied by lymphocyte exocytosis and focal spongiosis.[38,46] Papillary dermal edema is present with a superficial perivascular lymphohistiocytic infiltrate. Rarely, epidermal necrosis may be extensive.[38]

The infiltrate consists predominantly of CD3+/CD4+/CD25–/HLA-DR+ T-helper cells with a small subpopulation of CD8+ lymphocytes. Endothelial cells and keratinocytes express ICAM-1.[38]

Histologically, the transient acantholytic dermatosis-like eruption associated with IL-4 therapy is characterized by acantholysis and suprabasal cleft formation with dyskeratosis, spongiosis and a superficial perivascular lymphohistiocytic infiltrate with rare eosinophils.[47] Immunofluorescence studies have not been performed.

References

1. Luger, T.A., Schwarz, T. (1991) Therapeutic use of cytokines in dermatology. *J Am Acad Dermatol*, **24**, 915–926.
2. Asnis, L.A., Gaspari, A.A. (1995) Cutaneous reactions to recombinant cytokine therapy. *J Am Acad Dermatol*, **33**, 393–410.
3. Park, J.W., Mehrotra, B., Barnett, B.O. et al (1992) The Sweet syndrome during therapy with granulocyte colony-stimulating factor. *Ann Intern Med*, **116**, 996–998.
4. Ross, H.J., Moy, L.A., Kaplan, R. et al (1991) Bullous pyoderma gangrenosum after granulocyte colony-stimulating factor treatment. *Cancer*, **68**, 441–443.
5. Ostlere, L.S., Harris, D., Prentice, H.G. et al (1992) Widespread folliculitis induced by human granulocyte-colony-stimulating factor therapy. *Br J Dermatol*, **127**, 193–194.
6. Welte, K., Zeilder, C., Reiter, A. et al (1990) Differential effects of granulocyte–macrophage colony stimulating factor and granulocyte colony stimulating factor in children with severe congenital neutropenia. *Blood*, **75**, 1056–1063.
7. Wodzinski, M.A., Hampton, K.K., Reilly, J.T. (1991) Differential effect of G-CSF and GM-CSF in acquired chronic neutropenia. *Br J Haematol*, **77**, 249–250.
8. Jain, K.K. (1994) Cutaneous vasculitis associated with granulocyte colony-stimulating factor. *J Am Acad Dermatol*, **31**, 213–215.
9. Frampton, J.E., Lee, C.R., Faulds, D. (1994) Filgastrin: a review of its pharmacological properties and therapeutic efficacy in neutropenia. *Drugs*, **48**, 731–760.
10. Dreicer, R., Schiller, J., Carbone, P. (1989) Granulocyte–macrophage colony-stimulating factor and vasculitis (letter). *Ann Intern Med*, **111**, 91–92.
11. Glaspy, J.A., Baldwin, G.C., Robertson, P.A. et al (1988) Therapy for neutropenia in hairy cell leukemia with recombinant human granulocyte colony stimulating factor. *Ann Intern Med*, **109**, 789–795.
12. Negrin, R.S., Haenber, D.H., Nagler, A. et al (1989) Treatment of myelodysplastic syndrome with recombinant human granulocyte colony-stimulating factor. *Ann Intern Med*, **110**, 976–984.
13. Glass, L.F., Fotopoulos, T., Messina, J.L. (1994) A generalized cutaneous reaction induced by granulocyte colony-stimulating factor. *J Am Acad Dermatol*, **34**, 455–459.
14. Samlaska, C.P., Noyes, D.K. (1993) Localized cutaneous reactions to granulocyte colony-stimulating factor. *Arch Dermatol*, **129**, 645–646.
15. Viallard, A.M., Lavenue, A., Balme, B. et al (1999) Lichenoid cutaneous drug reaction at injection sites of granulocyte-colony stimulating factor (Filgastrim). *Dermatology*, **198**, 301–303.
16. Horn, T.D., Burke, P.J., Karp, J.E. et al (1991) Intravenous administration of recombinant human granulocyte–macrophage colony-stimulating factor causes a cutaneous eruption. *Arch Dermatol*, **127**, 49–52.
17. Mehregan, D.R., Fransway, A.F., Edmonson, J.E. et al (1992) Cutaneous reactions to granulocyte–macrophage colony-stimulating factor. *Arch Dermatol*, **128**, 1055–1059.
18. Steger, C.G., Locker, G., Rainer, H. et al (1992) Cutaneous reactions to GM-CSF in inflammatory breast cancer (letter). *N Engl J Med*, **327**, 286.
19. Scott, G.A. (1995) Report of three cases of cutaneous reactions to granulocyte–macrophage colony-stimulating factor and a review of the literature. *Am J Dermatopathol*, **17**, 107–114.
20. Passweg, J., Buser, U., Tichelli, A. et al (1991) Pustular eruption at the site of subcutaneous injection of recombinant human granulocyte–macrophage colony-stimulating factor. *Ann Hematol*, **63**, 326–327.
21. Ward, J.C., Gitlin, J.B., Garry, D.J. et al (1992) Epidermolysis bullosa acquisita induced by GM-CSF: a role for eosinophils in treatment-related toxicity. *Br J Haematol*, **81**, 27–32.
22. Jones, G.J., Itri, L.M. (1986) Safety and tolerance of recombinant interferon α-2a (Roferon®-A) in cancer patients. *Cancer*, **57**, 1709–1715.
23. Quesada, J.R., Gutterman, J.U. (1986) Psoriasis and alpha-interferon. *Lancet*, **1**, 1466–1468.
24. Tolaymat, A., Leventhal, B., Sakarcan, A. et al (1992) Systemic lupus erythematosus in a child receiving long-term interferon therapy. *J Pediatr*, **120**, 429–432.
25. Dereure, O., Raison-Peyron, N., Larrey, D. et al (2002) Diffuse inflammatory lesions in patients treated with interferon alfa and ribavirin for hepatitis C: a series of 20 patients. *Br J Dermatol*, **147**, 1142–1146.
26. Sanders, S., Busam, K., Tahan, S.R. et al (2002) Granulomatous and suppurative dermatitis at interferon alfa injection sites: report of 2 cases. *J Am Acad Dermatol*, **46**, 611–616.
27. Berger, L., Descamps, V., Marck, Y. et al (2000) Alpha interferon-induced eczema in atopic patients infected by hepatitis C virus: 4 case reports. *Ann Dermatol Venereol*, **127**, 51–55.
28. Fortuno, Y., Marcoval, J., Gallego, I. et al (1999) Skin reactions to interferon alpha in a series of 92 patients with multiple sclerosis. *Med Clin (Barc)*, **113**, 447–448.
29. Heinzerling, L., Dummer, R., Wildberger, H. et al (2000) Cutaneous ulceration after injection of polyethylene-glycol-modified interferon alpha associated with visual disturbances in a melanoma patient. *Dermatology*, **201**, 154–157.
30. Ramseur, W.L., Richards, F., Duggan, D.B. (1989) A fatal case of pemphigus vulgaris in association with beta interferon and interleukin-2 therapy. *Cancer*, **63**, 2005–2007.
31. Pigatto, P.D., Bigardi, A., Legori, A. et al (1991) Allergic contact dermatitis from beta-interferon in eyedrops. *Contact Dermatitis*, **25**, 199–200.
32. Garcia-F-Villalta, M., Daudén, E., Sánchez, J. et al (2001) Local reactions associated with subcutaneous injections of both β-interferon 1a and 1b. *Acta Derm Venereol*, **81**, 152.
33. Gaines, A.R., Varricchio, F. (1998) Interferon beta-1b injection site reactions. *Mult Scler*, **4**, 70–73.
34. Cohen, B.A., Greenberger, P.A., Saini, S. (1998) Delayed occurrence of a severe cutaneous reaction in a multiple sclerosis patient taking interferon beta-1b. *Allergy Asthma Proc*, **19**, 85–88.
35. Elgart, G.W., Sheremata, W., Ahn, Y.S. (1997) Cutaneous reactions to recombinant human interferon beta-1b: the clinical and histologic spectrum. *J Am Acad Dermatol*, **39**, 807–808.
36. Fierlbeck, G., Rassner, G., Müller, C. (1990) Psoriasis induced at the injection site of recombinant interferon gamma. *Arch Dermatol*, **126**, 351–355.
37. Sampaio, E.P., Moreira, A.L., Sarno, E.N. et al (1992) Prolonged treatment with recombinant interferon gamma induces erythema nodosum leprosum in lepromatous leprosy patients. *J Exp Med*, **175**, 1729–1737.
38. Wolkenstein, P., Chosidow, O., Wechsler, J. et al (1993) Cutaneous side-effects associated with interleukin 2 administration for metastatic melanoma. *J Am Acad Dermatol*, **28**, 66–70.
39. Grimm, E.A., Mazumder, A., Zhang, H.Z. et al (1982) The lymphokine-activated cell phenomenon: lysis of NK-resistant fresh solid tumor cells by IL-2 activated autologous human peripheral blood lymphocytes. *J Exp Med*, **155**, 1823–1841.
40. Wiener, J.S., Tucker, J.A., Walther, P.J. (1992) Interleukin-2-induced dermatotoxicity resembling toxic epidermal necrolysis. *South Med J*, **85**, 656–659.
41. Weinstein, A., Bujak, D., Mittelman, A. et al (1987) Erythema nodosum in a patient with renal cell carcinoma treated with interleukin 2 and lymphokine-activated killer cells. *JAMA*, **258**, 3120–3121.
42. Prussick, R., Plott, R.T., Stanley, J.R. (1994) Recurrence of pemphigus vulgaris associated with interleukin 2 therapy. *Arch Dermatol*, **130**, 890–893.
43. Guillaume, J.C., Escudier, B., Espagne, E. et al (1990) Dermatose bulleuse avec depots lineares d'IgA le long de la membrane basale au cours d'un traitment par l'interferon gamma et l'interleukine-2. *Ann Dermatol Venereol*, **117**, 899–902.
44. Staunton, M.R., Scully, M.C., LeBoit, P.E. et al (1991) Life-threatening bullous skin eruptions during interleukin-2 therapy. *J Natl Cancer Inst*, **83**, 56–57.
45. Lee, R.E., Gaspari, A.A., Lotze, M.T. et al (1988) Interleukin-2 and psoriasis. *Arch Dermatol*, **124**, 1811–1815.
46. Gaspari, A.A., Lotze, M.T., Rosenberg, S.A. et al (1987) Dermatologic changes associated with interleukin-2 administration. *JAMA*, **258**, 1624–1629.
47. Mahler, S.J., De Villez, R.L., Pulitzer, D.R. (1993) Transient acantholytic dermatosis induced by recombinant interleukin 4. *J Am Acad Dermatol*, **29**, 206–209.
48. Weiss, G.R., Fehrenkamp, S.H., Tokaz, L.K. et al (1996) Vitiligo and Graves' disease following treatment of malignant melanoma with human recombinant interleukin 4. *Dermatology*, **192**, 283–285.
49. Fariña, M.C., Requena, L., Dómine, M. et al (1998) Histopathology of cutaneous reaction to granulocyte colony-stimulating factor: another pseudomalignancy. *J Cutan Pathol*, **25**, 559–562.

Cutaneous reaction of lymphocyte recovery

Clinical features

This unusual condition follows return of lymphocytes to the general circulation and skin after induction or augmentation chemotherapy in leukemia patients.[1,2] It has been described most often following combined cytarabine and daunorubicin treatment and also following treatment with amsacrine, etoposide, interferon, cyclophosphamide and vincristine.[3] Patients present with a pruritic, erythematous maculo-papapular eruption associated with pyrexia.[1] The eruption resolves with desquamation.[2]

Histological features

The histological features include mild spongiosis with lymphocyte exocytosis associated with interface change, keratinocyte atypia with impaired maturation (chemotherapy effect) and minimal dyskeratosis.[1,2] There is vascular dilatation and a perivascular lymphocytic infiltrate is present in the superficial dermis. Eosinophils are absent.[2] Exceptionally, epidermal lymphocyte infiltration may be very marked so as to mimic mycosis fungoides.[4]

The infiltrate is composed of CD3+/CD4+ T-helper cells with a smaller subpopulation of CD8+ cells.[2] The lymphocytes may also express CD25.[4] Epidermal Langerhans' cells are reduced in number and there is minimal to absent keratinocyte HLA-DR and ICAM-1 expression.[2,4]

Nuclear pleomorphism with hyperchromatism and expression of CD30, CD25 and HLA-DR has been described in the eruption of lymphocyte recovery in patients who have also received human recombinant cytokines including GM-CSF and IL-3.[5]

Differential diagnosis

The features are indistinguishable from exanthematous drug reactions, viral infections and acute graft-versus-host disease.[6]

References

1. Horn, T.D., Redd, J.V., Karp, J.E. et al (1989) Cutaneous eruptions of lymphocyte recovery. *Arch Dermatol*, 125, 1512–1517.
2. Horn, T.D. (1994) Acute cutaneous eruptions after marrow ablation: roses by other names? *J Cutan Pathol*, 21, 385–392.
3. Fitzpatrick, J.E. (1992) New histopathologic findings in drug eruptions. *Dermatol Clin*, 10, 19–36.
4. Gibney, M.D., Penneys, N.S., Nelson-Adesokan, P. (1995) Cutaneous eruption of lymphocyte recovery mimicking mycosis fungoides in a patient with acute myelocytic leukemia. *J Cutan Pathol*, 22, 472–475.
5. Horn, T., Lehmkuhle, M.A., Gore, S. et al (1996) Systemic cytokine administration alters the histology of the eruption of lymphocyte recovery. *J Cutan Pathol*, 23, 242–246.
6. Bauer, D.J., Hood, A.F., Horn, T.D. (1993) Histologic comparison of autologous graft-vs-host reaction and cutaneous eruption of lymphocyte recovery. *Arch Dermatol*, 129, 855–858.

Dental amalgam tattoos

Clinical features

Dental amalgam tattoos develop following the accidental implantation of dental amalgam (mercury and silver) into the soft tissue of the mouth following a dental procedure. Lesions, which are most commonly found on the buccal, gingival and alveolar mucosa, measure from 0.10 to 1.5 cm and present as flat gray to blue-gray or slate-colored lesions.[1]

Histological features

Amalgam tattoos, which consist of mercury and silver, sometimes accompanied by tin, present as fine to globular, brown to black deposits lying free or within macrophages and also deposited on the elastic tissue fibers and blood vessels within the lamina propria.[2–4]

References

1. Owens, B.M., Johnson, W.W., Schuman, N.J. (1992) Oral amalgam pigmentations (tattoos): a retrospective study. *Quintessence*, 23, 805–810.
2. Forsell, M., Larsson, B., Ljungqvist, A. et al (1998) Mercury content in amalgam tattoos and its relation to local tissue reactions. *Eur J Oral Sci*, 106, 582–587.
3. Mohr, W., Gorz, E. (2001) Association of silver granules with elastic fibers in amalgam reaction of mouth mucosa. *HNO*, 49, 454–457.
4. Lau, J.C., Jackson-Boeters, L., Daley, T.D. et al (2001) Metallothionin in human gingival amalgam tattoos. *Arch Oral Biol*, 46, 1015–1020.

Neutrophilic and eosinophilic dermatoses

14

Pyoderma gangrenosum   673

Acute febrile neutrophilic dermatosis   679

Neutrophilic dermatoses associated with gastrointestinal and hepatobiliary disease   683

Rheumatoid neutrophilic dermatitis   684

Behçet's disease   685

Arthropod and arachnid bite reactions   689

Seabather's eruption and coelenterate stings   690

Erythema marginatum rheumaticum   691

Still's disease   691

Urticaria   692

Hypereosinophilic syndrome   696

Eosinophilic cellulitis   697

Papular dermatitis associated with HIV/AIDS   700

HIV-associated eosinophilic folliculitis   700

Eosinophilic pustular folliculitis   700

Incontinentia pigmenti   702

Toxic erythema of the neonate   705

Hidranenitis suppurativa   705

Pyoderma gangrenosum

Clinical features

Pyoderma gangrenosum is an uncommon disease of obscure etiology.[1–9] It appears to be somewhat more common in women and, although it may occur at any age, most patients are in their fourth or fifth decade.[4] Presentation in children is uncommon[10–16] and familial cases are rare.[17–19] The disease may also present in pregnancy and in this setting it is associated with an underlying disease in about 50% of the cases.[20–23] Large, necrotic ulcers, often 10 cm or more in diameter, characterize the disease (*Fig. 14.1*). Lesions may arise from acneiform pustules or on a background of erythematous nodules. Typically, the ulcers have undermined edges and red–purple borders (*Fig. 14.2*). They may be solitary or multiple, and occur most often on the lower limbs, although other sites such as the trunk, face, arms and buttocks are sometimes affected (*Fig. 14.3*).[24,25] Rare sites of involvement include the oropharyngeal region, hand, eyelid, eye, vulva, penis, scrotum and the cervix.[26–37] The ulcers are painful and tender, and may persist for months or years. Complications usually result from the site of the lesion and include cranial osteolysis and nasal perforation.[15,38] Recurrent attacks are not uncommon.[2] Cribriform scarring often follows healing. Systemic involvement in pyoderma gangrenosum has rarely been documented and includes the lungs, liver, bone, joints, pancreas and heart.[39–43]

Occasionally bullous variants are encountered.[4,44–49] One large study found that bullous lesions are more common on the upper extremities and they seem to be more frequent in association with hematological

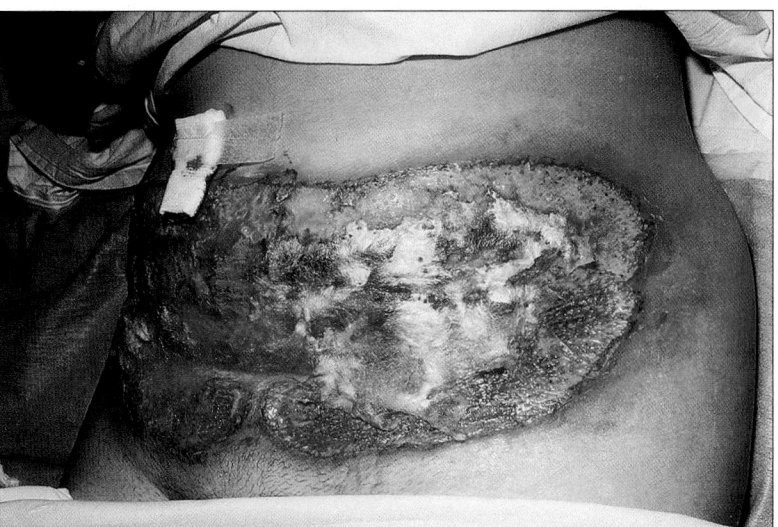

Fig. 14.1
Pyoderma gangrenosum: this unusually severe example is associated with very extensive tissue destruction resembling necrotizing fasciitis. By courtesy of R.A. Marsden, MD, St George's Hospital, London, UK.

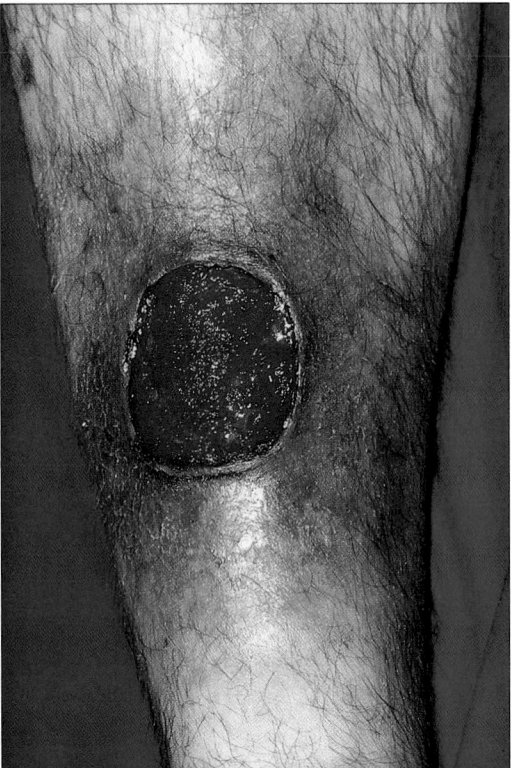

Fig. 14.2
Pyoderma gangrenosum: this shows an area of ulceration with a typical undermined purplish border. By courtesy of R.A. Marsden, MD, St George's Hospital, London, UK.

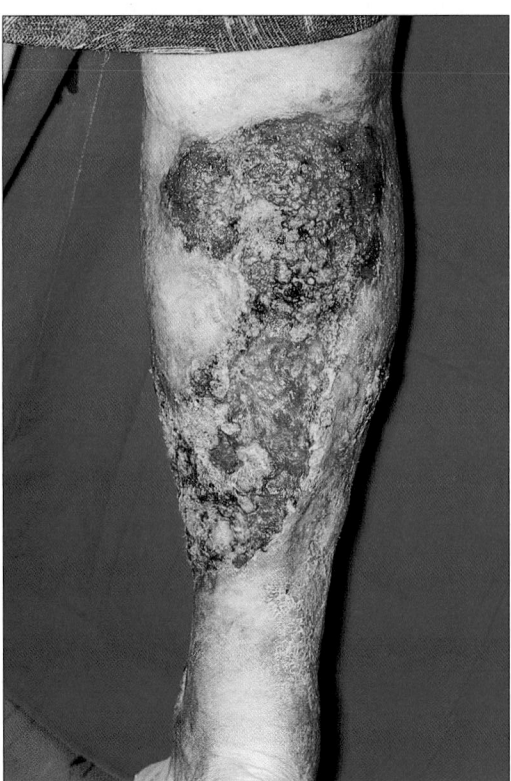

Fig. 14.3
Pyoderma gangrenosum: an extensive lesion with marked crusting and undermining in the proximal and medial margins. By courtesy of R.A. Marsden, MD, St George's Hospital, London, UK.

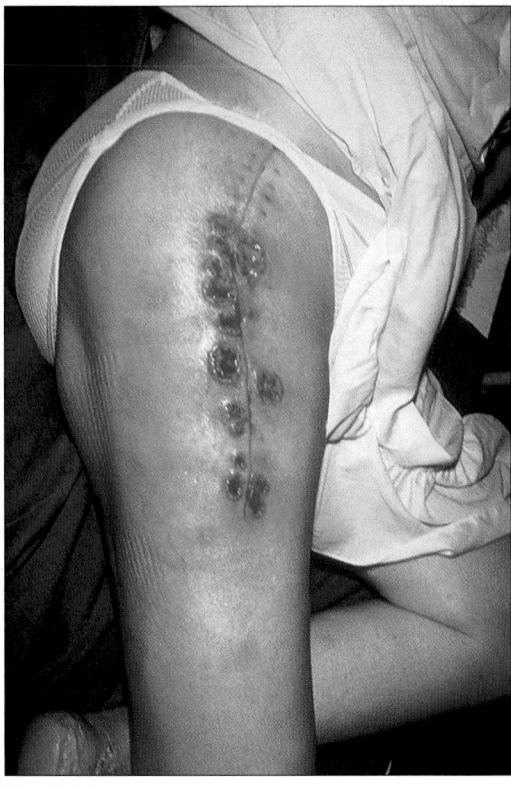

Fig. 14.4
Pyoderma gangrenosum: multiple early lesions at the site of previous surgery. By courtesy of R.A. Marsden, MD, St George's Hospital, London, UK.

Table 14.1
Conditions associated with pyoderma gangrenosum

• Inflammatory bowel disease: both ulcerative colitis and Crohn's disease[2,4]	• SAPHO syndrome (synovitis, acne, pustulosis, hyperostosis, osteitis)[94,95]
• Arthritis (either seronegative or rheumatoid arthritis), ankylosing spondylitis and osteoarthrosis[4,69–71]	• *Chlamydia pneumoniae*[96]
• Monoclonal gammopathy (most often IgA); usually benign but may lead to multiple myeloma[2,46,69]	• Tuberculosis[97]
• Hypogammaglobulinemia	• Psoriasis[98]
• Myeloid leukemia[46,48,72,73]	• Acne fulminans, acne conglobata and hidradenitis suppurativa[99–101]
• Hepatitis[74–77]	• Bullous systemic lupus erythematosus[102]
• Behçet's disease[78]	• Lupus anticoagulant[103]
• Sarcoidosis[79]	• Diverticular disease[104]
• Vasculitis, including Takayasu's disease, erythema elevatum diutinum and Wegener's granulomatosis[80–84]	• Fanconi's anemia[105]
• Antineutrophil cytoplasmic antibodies[85–87]	• Allergic contact dermatitis from rubber[106]
• Cryoglobulinemia[6]	• Paroxysmal nocturnal hemoglobulinuria[107]
• Acquired ichthyosis[88]	• C7 deficiency[108]
• Essential thrombocythemia[89]	• Chronic renal failure[109]
• Polycythemia rubra vera[71]	• Kartagener's syndrome[110]
• Human immunodeficiency virus infection[90–92]	• Cogan's syndrome (interstitial keratitis and vestibuloauditory dysfunction)[111]
• Osteomyelitis[10,93]	• Hypertrophic osteoarthropathy[112]
	• Gastric carcinoma[113]
	• Subcorneal pustular dermatosis[114, 115]

malignancy.[4] Such lesions are sometimes designated atypical pyoderma gangrenosum.[4,45]

A particularly interesting feature seen in as many as 50% of cases is the development of lesions at the sites of trauma (pathergy).[4,50] Lesions may occur at sites of surgery and have been reported after cholecystectomy, breast reduction, splenectomy, hysterectomy, following aortic valve replacement, at the site of a fasciocutaneous flap and in an amputation stump (*Fig. 14.4*).[51–59] They also occur at sites of rather trivial trauma such as injection, blood-drawing or acupuncture.[4,60] Presentation has even been documented at the site of a spider bite.[61]

Occasional reports have implicated drugs including alpha2b interferon (IFN-α2b), isotretinoin, sulpiride and propylthiouracil in the

etiology of the disease.[62–65] In a single case report, pyoderma gangrenosum developed after combination therapy with cytosine arabinoside, aclarubicin and granulocyte colony-stimulating factor for myelodysplastic syndrome.[66] A granulomatous and suppurative dermatitis that may mimic pyoderma gangrenosum has been documented at the site of interferon-alpha (IFN-α) injections.[67]

Of particular importance is the known association of pyoderma gangrenosum with a variety of conditions[4,68] (in up to 50% of patients[2]) as outlined in *Table 14.1*. Of these associations, inflammatory bowel disease (both Crohn's disease and ulcerative colitis) and arthritis are the most well-established. In one study, 27% of patients had associated inflammatory bowel disease and 20% of patients had arthritis.[4] In this same study, 27% of patients with superficial 'atypical' pyoderma gangrenosum had an associated hematological disorder.[4] In another large study, idiopathic pyoderma gangrenosum and that associated with chronic inflammatory bowel disease were found to be more common in females, whereas pyoderma gangrenosum associated with hematological malignancy was more common in males.[5] Many of the other rare associations mentioned in *Table 14.1* are likely to be fortuitous. In any event, a diagnosis of pyoderma gangrenosum should always prompt an evaluation for underlying disease associations.

The disease may also occur in association with other neutrophilic dermatoses including Sweet's syndrome.[116,117]

Pyoderma gangrenosum is one of the components of a recently described autosomal dominant syndrome known as PAPA (pyogenic sterile arthritis, pyoderma gangrenosum and acne).[118] This syndrome has been mapped to chromosome 15q.[119]

Para- and peristomal involvement in patients with ileostomy or colonostomy for inflammatory bowel disease is a well-recognized phenomenon.[4,120–122] In a large series, 13% of patients had peristomal pyoderma.[4] Both Crohn's disease and ulcerative colitis are associated with this complication.[4] It should be noted that peristomal pyoderma gangrenosum has been seen in the absence of inflammatory bowel disease.[120,121] It has been documented in patients with ostomy for gastrointestinal carcinoma and diverticular disease.[120,121] Pyoderma gangrenosum may also occur at urostomy sites following cystectomy for bladder carcinoma.[121]

Superficial granulomatous pyoderma is believed to represent a superficial and rare variant of pyoderma gangrenosum.[3,123–127] Patients develop single or sometimes multiple superficial ulcerated lesions with vegetative borders (for this reason, this variant is sometimes referred to as 'vegetative variant of pyoderma gangrenosum') as a consequence of trauma, frequently surgical (*Fig. 14.5*). Pain is an occasional feature. The ulcers have a cleaner base than those seen in classical pyoderma. Lesions are most commonly found on the trunk and upper extremities and heal with cribriform scarring (*Fig. 14.6*). Draining sinuses are occasionally evident. Often there is no evidence of underlying systemic disease. Superficial granulomatous pyoderma is more likely to follow a chronic course compared with classic pyoderma gangrenosum.[128]

So-called 'malignant pyoderma' is a controversial designation, which we believe should be avoided. Some authors have used the term to describe a variant of pyoderma gangrenosum predominantly affecting the head and neck.[129–131] Recently, however, it has been postulated that at least some cases of so-called malignant pyoderma more likely represent cutaneous Wegener's granulomatosis.[132]

One study found that over 50% of patients with pyoderma gangrenosum required long-term therapy to control their disease.[5] The disease may be fatal in some cases, particularly if diagnosis is delayed.[6,113] In another study, 2 of the 21 patients reported died of pyoderma gangrenosum secondary to pulmonary involvement.[6]

Pathogenesis and histological features

The precise pathogenesis of pyoderma gangrenosum is uncertain. The current state of knowledge suggests that it is due to immune dysfunction and/or that it develops on a vasculitic basis.[73,74,133–135] A variety of immunological abnormalities have been described in patients with pyoderma gangrenosum, including absent delayed hypersensitivity reactions to common antigens such as mycobacteria and *Candida albicans*, defective neutrophil chemotaxis, impaired neutrophil phagocytosis and diminished lymphokine (migration inhibition factor) production.[73,74,134] Overexpression of interleukin-8, a potent chemotactic polypeptide for neutrophils, has been reported in lesions of pyoderma gangrenosum and may be an important factor in the causation of the

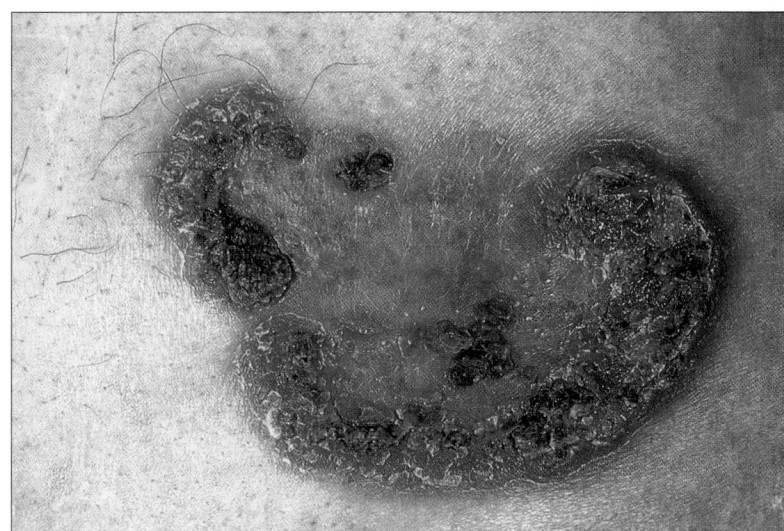

Fig. 14.5
Superficial granulomatous pyoderma: crusted superficial lesion with a cribiform appearance. By courtesy of the Institute of Dermatology, London, UK.

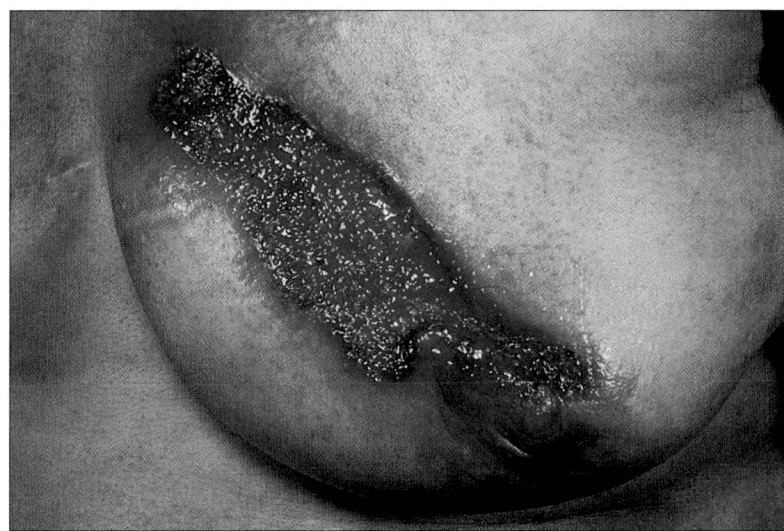

Fig. 14.6
Superficial granulomatous pyoderma: this field shows extensive ulceration of the breast. By courtesy of R.K. Winkelmann, MD, Mayo Clinic, Scottsdale, Arizona, USA.

disease.[136] Other studies have demonstrated aberrant neutrophil trafficking and metabolic integrin β2-CR3 and -CR4 oscillations in lesions from patients with pyoderma gangrenosum.[137,138]

The results of immunofluorescence examinations in large series of patients have revealed both immunoglobulins (usually IgM) and complement in blood vessel walls in the dermis of the leading edge of the ulcer.[139,140] Another study, however, has failed to substantiate this finding.[2] There is no evidence to support an infective pathogenesis.[141]

In general, the histopathology of pyoderma gangrenosum is that of non-specific ulceration with abscess formation (*Fig. 14.7*). The adjacent dermis shows acute and chronic inflammation. Early lesions may present with subcorneal pustulation (*Fig. 14.8*). Although the histological features of both leukocytoclastic and lymphocyte-mediated vasculitis have been described, it is our experience that any vasculitis seen is usually located within the floor of the ulcer or the immediate adjacent tissues and is, therefore, more likely to be a consequence, rather than a cause, of the lesion (*Fig. 14.9*).[1,142]

Giant cells appear to be a common feature of pyoderma gangrenosum in patients with Crohn's disease.[7] In one study, they were present in 6 of

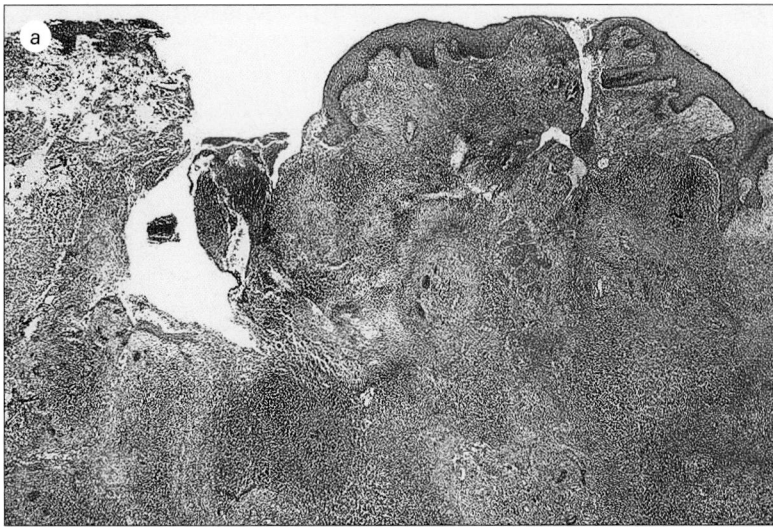

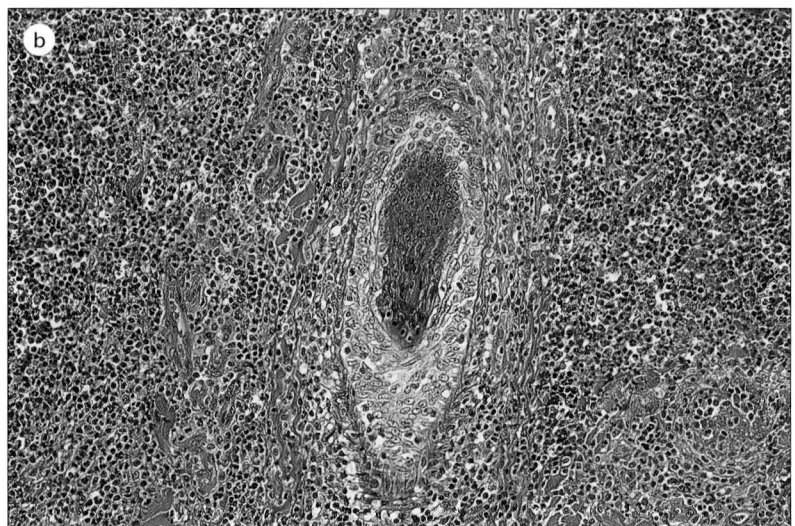

Fig. 14.7
(a, b) Pyoderma gangrenosum: in this biopsy from the edge of an ulcer, there are massive intradermal inflammatory changes, with abscess formation.

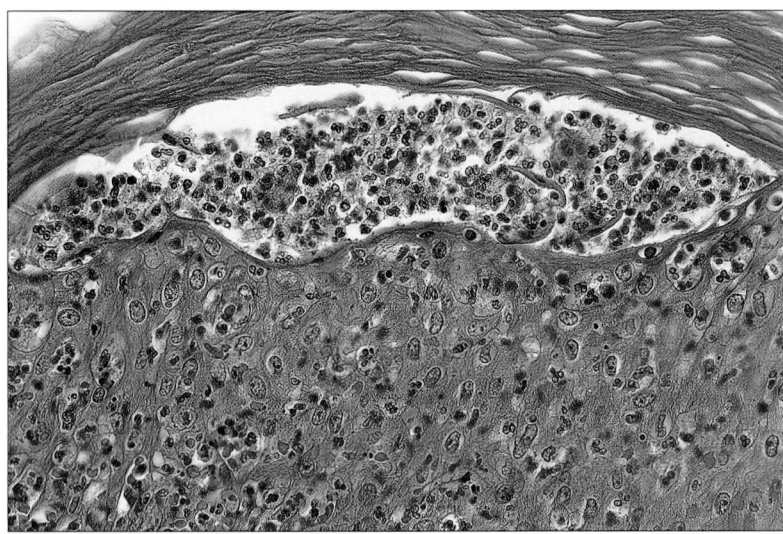

Fig. 14.8
Pyoderma gangrenosum: early acneiform lesion showing a subcorneal pustule.

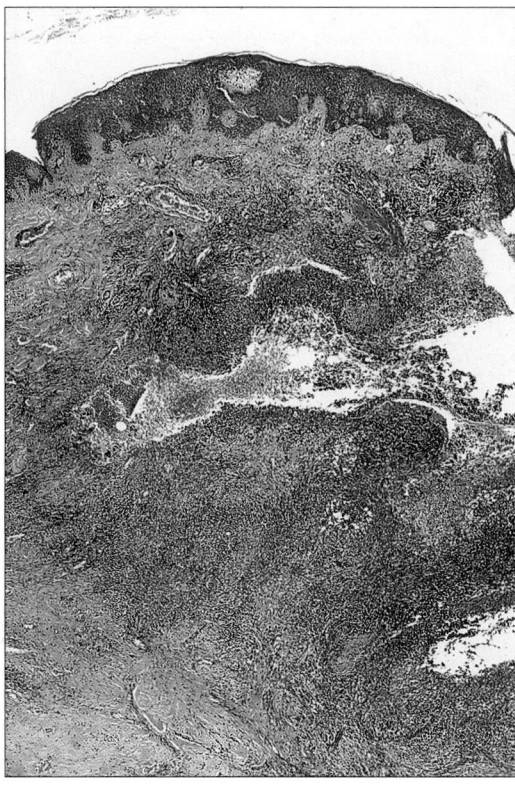

Fig. 14.10
Superficial granulomatous pyoderma: low power view showing an undermining ulcer.

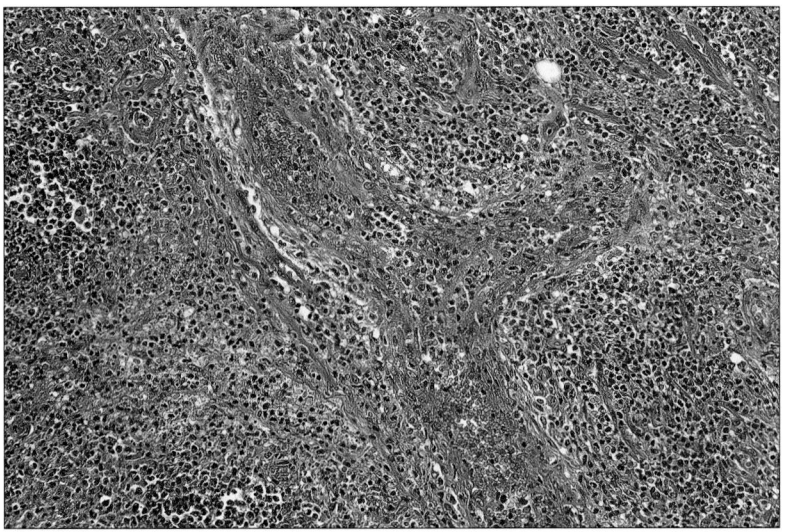

Fig. 14.9
Pyoderma gangrenosum: acute necrotizing vasculitis. It is likely that any active inflammation of the blood vessel walls is a result of the surrounding inflammation rather than its cause.

13 patients with associated inflammatory bowel disease; of these, 5 had Crohn's disease and 1 had underlying ulcerative colitis.[7] Giant cells were not found in any biopsies from 22 patients without associated inflammatory bowel disease.

Superficial granulomatous pyoderma is characterized by a zoned inflammatory infiltrate in the superficial dermis.[3] Focal and sterile abscesses are surrounded by a zone of granulomatous inflammation bordered by a rim of lymphocytes and plasma cells (*Figs 14.10, 14.11*).[3] Hemorrhage is often present and eosinophils may be evident. Any vasculitic change is thought to be secondary (*Fig. 14.12*). The adjacent tissues may show scarring. Acanthosis and pseudoepitheliomatous hyperplasia are often present. Foreign material including starch, sutures, vegetable matter, wood and hair has been identified in a large proportion of these cases.[3] It should be noted that not all cases of pyoderma gangrenosum with granulomatous inflammation are limited to the

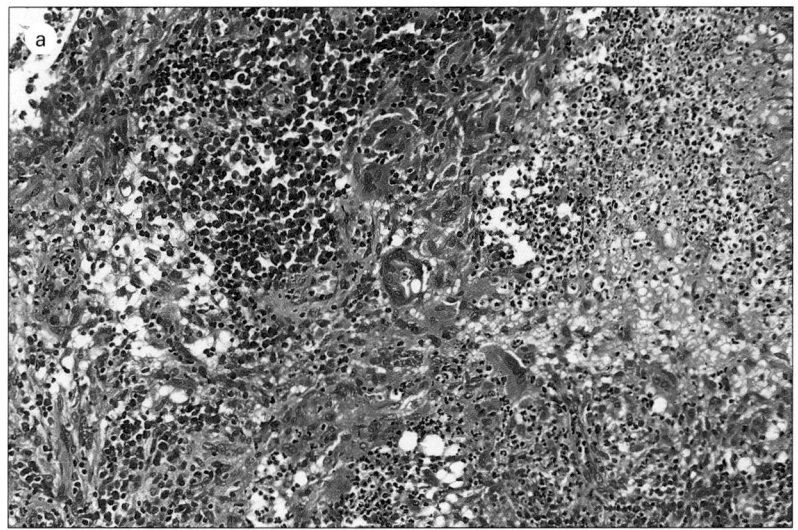

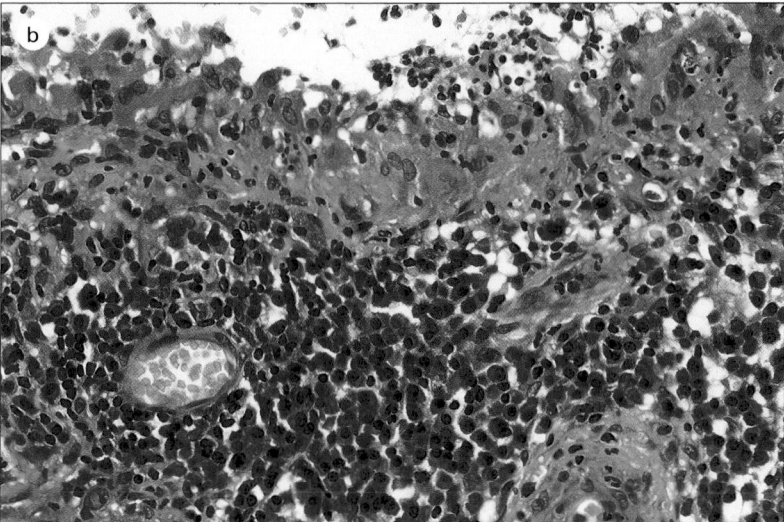

Fig. 14.11
(a, b) Superficial granulomatous pyoderma: the zoned inflammatory reaction is clearly seen. Note the conspicuous giant cells and plasma cells.

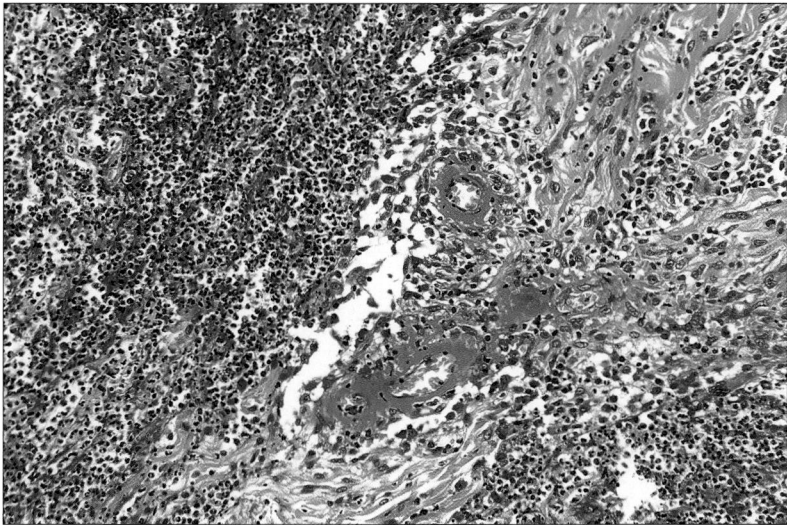

Fig. 14.12
Superficial granulomatous pyoderma: as with classic pyoderma gangrenosum, the presence of acute vasculitis is likely to be secondary. By courtesy of R.K. Winkelmann, MD, Mayo Clinic, Scottsdale, Arizona, USA.

superficial dermis. Some cases show involvement of the deep dermis and even subcutaneous tissue.

Differential diagnosis

The histopathological findings in pyoderma gangrenosum are non-specific. Since surgery is used to manage some of the disorders considered in the histological and clinical differential diagnosis – but is contra-indicated in the case of pyoderma gangrenosum itself – early and accurate diagnosis is critical. Surgery, which tends to exacerbate the disease, is generally contraindicated in pyoderma cases because of the pathergic response. The mainstay of treatment is medical management, such as corticosteroid therapy. Unfortunately, patients with pyoderma are often misdiagnosed early in the course of their disease and are sometimes recognized only after multiple unsuccessful (and damaging) surgeries have been performed. In one study, an average of five physicians had examined the patient before a correct diagnosis was rendered.[24] To avoid this error, obtaining accurate clinical information on wounds and debridement specimens is essential.

Culture is required to exclude infection (bacterial, mycobacterial, fungal). Necrotizing fasciitis tends to affect deeper fascial and sub-cutaneous tissue, while pyoderma is centered in the dermis (albeit some spillover into the subcutis may be seen). Usually sheets of bacteria are evident in untreated necrotizing fasciitis.

Sweet's syndrome is generally not associated with ulceration and shows more prominent karyorrhexis relative to the number of neutro-phils. Bite reactions, particularly resulting from the brown recluse or other spiders, may show similar histological features. Clinical information is necessary to distinguish pyoderma from many other forms of ulcer such as those due to trauma.

Although some authors have noted lymphocytic or neutrophilic vasculitis in lesions of pyoderma gangrenosum, this finding, in our experience, is limited to areas adjacent to the ulcer and likely represents a secondary finding.[5] Indeed, it has been our experience that 'secondary' vasculitis is frequently present at the border of ulcers of many different etiologies in patients without any genuine underlying 'primary' vasculitic process. Evaluation for vasculitis as a cause of ulceration therefore depends upon examination of blood vessels in areas of dermis and subcutaneous tissue away from the ulcer.

It cannot be overemphasized how important accurate clinical information is in establishing the correct diagnosis. Failing to recognize this disease early in its course can be disastrous for the patient.

References

1. Powell, F.C., Schroeter, A.L., Su, W.P.D. et al (1985) Pyoderma gangrenosum: a review of 86 patients. *QJM*, 55, 173–186.
2. Prystowsky, J.H., Kahn, S.N., Lazarus, G.S. (1989) Present status of pyoderma gangrenosum: a review of 21 cases. *Arch Dermatol*, 125, 57–64.
3. Quimby, S.R., Gibson, L., Winkelmann, R.K. (1989) Superficial granulomatous pyoderma: clinicopathological spectrum. *Mayo Clin Proc*, 64, 37–43.
4. Bennett, M.L., Jackson, J.M., Jorizzo, J.L. et al (2000) Pyoderma gangrenosum. A comparison of typical and atypical forms with an emphasis on time to remission. Case review of 86 patients from 2 institutions. *Medicine*, 79, 37–46.
5. Von den Dreisch, P. (1997) Pyoderma gangrenosum: a report of 44 patients with follow-up. *Br J Dermatol*, 137, 1000–1005.
6. Mlika, R.B., Riahi, I., Fenniche, S. et al (2002) Pyoderma gangrenosum: a report of 21 cases. *Int J Dermatol*, 41, 65–68.
7. Sanders, S., Tahan, S.R., Kwan, T. et al (2001) Giant cells in pyoderma gangrenosum. *J Cutan Pathol*, 28, 97–100.
8. Wines, N., Wines, M., Ryman W. (2001) Understanding pyoderma gangrenosum. *MedGenMed*, 27, 6.
9. Powell, F.C., Collins, S. (2000) Pyoderma gangrenosum. *Clin Dermatol*, 18, 283–293.
10. Omidi, C.J., Siegfried, E.C. (1998) Chronic recurrent osteomyelitis preceding pyoderma gangrenosum and occult ulcerative colitis in a pediatric patient. *Pediatr Dermatol*, 15, 435–438.
11. Dourmishev, A.L., Miteva, I., Schwartz, R.A. (1996) Pyoderma gangrenosum in childhood. *Cutis*, 58, 257–262.
12. Jacobs, J.C., Gaffrey, J.A., Marboe, C.C. (1993) Pyoderma gangrenosum in children. *J Am Acad Dermatol*, 29, 509–510.
13. Sood, J., Singh, M., Chatuvedi, P. (1992) Infantile pyoderma gangrenosum. *Australas J Dermatol*, 33, 43–44.
14. Glass, A.T., Bancila, E., Milgraum, S. (1991) Pyoderma gangrenosum in infancy: the youngest reported patient. *J Am Acad Dermatol*, 25, 109–110.
15. Samlaska, C.P., Smith, R.A., Myers, J.B. et al (1995) Pyoderma gangrenosum and cranial osteolysis: case report and review of the paediatric literature. *Br J Dermatol*, 133, 972–977.
16. Bedlow, A.J., Davies, E.G., Moss, A.L. et al (1998) Pyoderma gangrenosum in a child with congenital partial deficiency of leucocyte adherence glycoproteins. *Br J Dermatol*, 139, 1064–1067.

17. al-Rimawi, H.S., Abuekteish, F.M., Daoud, A.S. et al (1996) Familial pyoderma gangrenosum presenting in childhood. *Eur J Pediatr*, **155**, 759–762.
18. Alberts, J.H., Sams, H.H., Miller, J.L. et al (2002) Familial ulcerative pyoderma gangrenosum. *Cutis*, **69**, 427–430.
19. Khandpur, S., Mehta, S., Reddy, B.S. (2001) Pyoderma gangrenosum in two siblings: a familial predisposition. *Pediatr Dermatol*, **18**, 308–312.
20. Sassolas, B., Le Ru, Y., Plantin, P. et al (2000) Pyoderma gangrenosum with pathergic phenomenon in pregnancy. *Br J Dermatol*, **142**, 827–828.
21. Freedman, A.M., Phelps, R.G., Lebwohl, M. (1997) Pyoderma gangrenosum associated with anticardiolipin antibodies in a pregnant patient. *Int J Dermatol*, **36**, 205–207.
22. Aytekin, S., Tarlan, N., Kalkanli, N. et al (2002) Pyoderma gangrenosum in pregnancy. *J Eur Acad Dermatol Venereol*, **16**, 546–548.
23. Tsanadis, G.D., Chouliara, S.T., Voulgari, P.V. et al (2002) Outcome of pregnancy in a patient with relapsing polychondritis and pyoderma gangrenosum. *Clin Rheumatol*, **21**, 538.
24. Huish, S.B., de La Paz, E.M., Ellis, P.R. et al (2001) Pyoderma gangrenosum of the hand: a case series and review of the literature. *Am J Hand Surg*, **26**, 679–685.
25. Setterfield, J.F., Shirlaw, P.J., Challacombe, S.J. et al (2001) Pyoderma gangrenosum associated with severe oropharyngeal involvement and IgA paraproteinaemia. *Br J Dermatol*, **144**, 393–396.
26. Kashefsky, H., Callahan, E., Ruder, U.C. et al (1999) Pyoderma gangrenosum involving the foot. *J Am Podiatr Med Assoc*, **89**, 137–140.
27. Miserocchi, E., Modorati, G., Foster, C.S. et al (2002) Ocular and extracutaneous involvement in pyoderma gangrenosum. *Ophthalmology*, **109**, 1941–1943.
28. Sidwell, R.U., Patel, N.N., Francis, N. et al (2001) Pyoderma gangrenosum of the eyelid and acute rhinosinusitis. *Clin Exp Dermatol*, **26**, 680–682.
29. Valmadre, S., Gee, A., Dalrymple, C. (2002) Pyoderma gangrenosum of the vulva. *Aust N Z J Obstet Gynaecol*, **42**, 548–549.
30. Sau, M., Hill, N.C. (2001) Pyoderma gangrenosum of the vulva. *BJOG*, **108**, 1197–1198.
31. Borum, M.L., Cannava, M., Myrie-Williams, C. (1998) Refractory, disfiguring vulvar pyoderma gangrenosum and Crohn's disease. *Dig Dis Sci*, **43**, 720–722.
32. Lebbe, C., Moulonguet-Michau, I., Perrin, P. et al (1992) Steroid-responsive pyoderma gangrenosum with vulvar and pulmonary involvement. *J Am Acad Dermatol*, **27**, 623–625.
33. Gungor, E., Karakayali, G., Alli, N. et al (1999) Penile pyoderma gangrenosum. *J Eur Acad Dermatol Venereol*, **12**, 59–62.
34. Farrell, A.M., Black, M.M., Bracka, A. et al (1998) Pyoderma gangrenosum of the penis. *Br J Dermatol*, **138**, 337–340.
35. Shah, M., Lewis, F.M., Harrington, C.I. (1996) Scrotal pyoderma gangrenosum associated with dermatomyositis. *Clin Exp Dermatol*, **21**, 151–153.
36. Albertazzi, P., Di Micco, R. (2000) Pyoderma gangrenosum of the cervix. *Obstet Gynecol*, **96**, 825–826.
37. Matsumara, T., Sato-Matsumara, K.C., Ota, M. et al (1999) Two cases of pyoderma gangrenosum complicated with nasal septal perforation. *Br J Dermatol*, **141**, 1133–1135.
38. Vadillo, M., Jucgla, A., Podzamczer, D. et al (1999) Pyoderma gangrenosum with liver, spleen and bone involvement in a patient with chronic myelomonocytic leukaemia. *Br J Dermatol*, **141**, 541–543.
39. Urano, S., Kodama, H., Kato, K. et al (1995) Pyoderma gangrenosum with systemic involvement. *J Dermatol*, **22**, 515–519.
40. Ochiai, T., Hara, H., Shimojima, H. et al (2002) Articular and pancreatic involvement in pyoderma gangrenosum associated with myelodysplastic syndrome. *Dermatology*, **205**, 70–72.
41. Kasuga, I., Yanagisawa, N., Takeo, C. et al (1997) Multiple pulmonary nodules in association with pyoderma gangrenosum. *Respir Med*, **91**, 493–495.
42. Marie, I., Levesque, H., Joly, P. et al (2001) Neutrophilic myositis as an extracutaneous manifestation of neutrophilic dermatosis. *J Am Acad Dermatol*, **44**, 137–139.
43. Hastier, P., Caroli-Bosc, F.X., Bartel, H.R. et al (1996) Pyoderma gangrenosum with hepatopancreatic manifestations in a patient with rheumatoid arthritis. *Dig Dis Sci*, **41**, 594–597.
44. Koester, G., Tarnower, A., Levisohn, D. et al (1993) Bullous pyoderma gangrenosum. *J Am Acad Dermatol*, **29**, 875–878.
45. Hay, C.R.M., Messenger, A.G., Cotton, D.W.K. et al (1987) Atypical bullous pyoderma gangrenosum associated with myeloid malignancies. *J Clin Pathol*, **40**, 387–392.
46. Horton, J.J., Trounce, J.R., MacDonald, D.M. (1984) Bullous pyoderma gangrenosum and multiple myeloma. *Br J Dermatol*, **110**, 227–230.
47. Perry, H.O., Winkelmann, R.K. (1972) Bullous pyoderma gangrenosum and leukemia. *Arch Dermatol*, **106**, 901–905.
48. Rogalski, C., Paasch, U., Glander, H.J. et al (2003) Bullous pyoderma gangrenosum complicated by disseminated intravascular coagulation with subsequent myelodysplastic syndrome (chronic myelomonocytic leukemia). *J Dermatol*, **30**, 59–63.
49. Torok, L., Kirschner, A., Gurzo, M. et al (2000) Bullous pyoderma gangrenosum as a manifestation of leukemia cutis. *Eur J Dermatol*, **10**, 463–465.
50. Rosina, P., Cunego, S., Franz, C.Z. et al (2002) Pathergic pyoderma gangrenosum in a venous ulcer. *Int J Dermatol*, **41**, 166–167.
51. Borlu, M., Utas, S. (2000) Pyoderma gangrenosum after cholecystectomy. *J Eur Acad Dermatol Venereol*, **15**, 185–186.
52. Gudi, V.S., Julian, C., Bowers, P.W. (2000) Pyoderma gangrenosum complicating bilateral mammoplasty. *Br J Plast Surg*, **53**, 440–441.
53. Lifchez, S.D., Larson, D.L. (2002) Pyoderma gangrenosum after reduction mammoplasty in an otherwise healthy patient. *Ann Plast Surg*, **49**, 410–413.
54. Patel, P., Topilow, A. (2002) Images in clinical medicine. Atypical pyoderma gangrenosum in a splenectomy excision. *N Engl J Med*, **347**, 1419.
55. Rothenburger, M., Tjan, T.D., Schimd, C. et al (2001) Pyoderma gangrenosum after aortic valve replacement. *Ann Thorac Surg*, **71**, 349–351.
56. Keohane, S.G., Graham-Brown, R.A. (1995) Pyoderma gangrenosum complicating hysterectomy for fibroids. *Clin Exp Dermatol*, **20**, 490–491.
57. Jain, A., Nanchahal, J., Bunker, C. (2000) Pyoderma gangrenosum occurring in a lower limb fasciocutaneous flap – a lesson to learn. *Br J Plast Surg*, **53**, 437–440.
58. Umezawa, Y., Oyake, S., Oh-i, T. et al (2000) A case of pyoderma gangrenosum on the stump of an amputated right leg. *J Dermatol*, **27**, 529–532.
59. Swinson, B.D., Morrison, C.M., Sinclair, J.S. (2002) Pyoderma gangrenosum – a complication of breast biopsy. *Ulster Med J*, **71**, 66–67.
60. Castro-Durán, J., Martín-Armada, M., Jiménez-Alonso, J. (2000) Pyoderma gangrenosum induced by acupuncture in a patient with ulcerative colitis. *Arch Intern Med*, **160**, 2394.
61. Mohsen, A.H., Mckendrick, M.W. (2001) Pyoderma gangrenosum complicating a spider bite. *J Infect*, **43**, 255–256.
62. Montoto, S., Bosch, F., Estrach, T. et al (1998) Pyoderma gangrenosum triggered by alpha2b-interferon in a patient with chronic granulocytic leukemia. *Leuk Lymphoma*, **30**, 199–202.
63. Gangaram, H.B., Tan, L.P., Gan, A.T. et al (1997) Pyoderma gangrenosum following treatment with isotretinoin. *Br J Dermatol*, **136**, 636–637.
64. Srebrnik, A., Shachar, E., Brenner, S. (2001) Suspected induction of a pyoderma gangrenosum-like eruption due to sulpiride treatment. *Cutis*, **67**, 253–256.
65. Darben, T., Savige, J., Prentice, R. et al (1999) Pyoderma gangrenosum with secondary pyarthrosis following propylthiouracil. *Australas J Dermatol*, **40**, 144–146.
66. Takagi, S., Ohsaka, A., Taguchi, H. et al (1998) Pyoderma gangrenosum following cytosine arabinoside, aclarubicin and granulocyte colony-stimulating factor combination therapy in myelodysplastic syndrome. *Intern Med*, **37**, 316–319.
67. Sanders, S., Busam, K., Tahan, S.R. et al (2002) Granulomatous and suppurative dermatitis at interferon alfa injection sites: report of 2 cases. *J Am Acad Dermatol*, **46**, 611–616.
68. Hickman, J.G., Lazarus, G.S. (1980) Pyoderma gangrenosum: a reappraisal of associated systemic diseases. *Br J Dermatol*, **102**, 235–237.
69. Holt, P.J.A., Davies, M.G., Saunders, K.C. et al (1980) Pyoderma gangrenosum: clinical and laboratory findings in 15 patients with special reference to polyarthritis. *Medicine (Baltimore)*, **59**, 114–133.
70. Lazarus, G.S., Goldsmith, L.A., Rocklin, R.E. et al (1972) Pyoderma gangrenosum, altered delayed hypersensitivity and polyarthritis. *Arch Dermatol*, **105**, 46–51.
71. Ko, C.B., Walton, S., Wyatt, E.H. (1992) Pyoderma gangrenosum: associations revisited. *Int J Dermatol*, **31**, 574–577.
72. Shore, R.N. (1976) Pyoderma gangrenosum, defective neutrophil chemotaxis and leukemia. *Arch Dermatol*, **11**, 1792–1793.
73. Caughman, W., Ster, R., Haynes, H. (1983) Neutrophilic dermatosis of myeloproliferative disorders: atypical forms of pyoderma gangrenosum and Sweet's syndrome associated with myeloproliferative disorders. *J Am Acad Dermatol*, **9**, 751–758.
74. Sampson, J.A., Harris, O.D., van Deth, A.G. (1982) Pyoderma gangrenosum and chronic active hepatitis. *Australas J Dermatol*, **23**, 93–96.
75. Green, L.K., Hebert, A.A., Jorizzo, J.L. et al (1985) Pyoderma gangrenosum and chronic persistent hepatitis. *J Am Acad Dermatol*, **13**, 892–897.
76. Keane, F.M., MacFarlane, C.S., Munn, S.E. et al (1998) Pyoderma gangrenosum and hepatitis C virus infection. *Br J Dermatol*, **139**, 924–925.
77. Smith, J.B., Shenefelt, P.D., Soto, O. et al (1996) Pyoderma gangrenosum in a patient with cryoglobulinemia and hepatitis C successfully treated with interferon alfa. *J Am Acad Dermatol*, **34**, 901–903.
78. Munro, C.S., Cox, N.H. (1988) Pyoderma gangrenosum associated with Behçet's syndrome. *Clin Exp Dermatol*, **13**, 408–410.
79. Banerjee, P., Holden, C.A. (2002) Sarcoidosis presenting with pyoderma gangrenosum. *Br J Dermatol*, **146**, 155–171.
80. Hidano, A., Watanabe, K. (1981) Pyoderma gangrenosum and cardio-vasculopathies, particularly Takayasu's arteritis. Review of the Japanese literature. *Ann Dermatol Venereol*, **108**, 13–21.
81. Fearfield, L.A., Ross, J.R., Farrell, A.M. et al (1999) Pyoderma gangrenosum associated with Takayasu's arteritis responding to cyclosporin. *Br J Dermatol*, **141**, 339–343.
82. Wayte, J.A., Rogers, S., Powell, F.C. (1995) Pyoderma gangrenosum, erythema elevatum diutinum and IgA monoclonal gammopathy. *Australas J Dermatol*, **36**, 21–23.
83. Planaguma, M., Puig, L., Alomar, A. et al (1992) Pyoderma gangrenosum in association with erythema elevatum diutinum. *Cutis*, **49**, 201–206.
84. Le Hello, C., Bonte, I., Mora, J.J. et al (2002) Pyoderma gangrenosum associated with Wegener's granulomatosis: partial response to mycophenolate mofetil. *Rheumatology (Oxford)*, **41**, 236–237.
85. Papi, M., Didona, B., Chinni, L.M. et al (1997) Koebner phenomenon in an ANCA-positive patient with pyoderma gangrenosum. *J Dermatol*, **24**, 583–586.
86. Irvine, A.D., Bruce, I.N., Walsh, M. et al (1996) Dermatological presentation of disease associated with antineutrophil cytoplasmic antibodies: a report of two contrasting cases and a review of the literature. *Br J Dermatol*, **134**, 924–928.
87. Hoffman, M.D. (2001) Pyoderma gangrenosum associated with c-ANCA (h-lamp-2). *Int J Dermatol*, **40**, 135–137.
88. Roger, D., Aldigier, J.C., Peyronnet, P. et al (1993) Acquired ichthyosis and pyoderma gangrenosum in a patient with systemic lupus erythematosus. *Clin Exp Dermatol*, **18**, 268–270.
89. King, K.W., Murray, A. (2000) Pyoderma gangrenosum in a patient with essential thrombocythemia. *J Cutan Med Surg*, **4**, 107–109.
90. Clark, H.H., Cohen, P.R. (1995) Pyoderma gangrenosum in an HIV-infected patient. *J Am Acad Dermatol*, **32**, 912–914.
91. Paller, A.S., Sahn, E.E., Garen, P.D. et al (1990) Pyoderma gangrenosum in pediatric acquired immunodeficiency syndrome. *J Pediatr*, **117**, 63–66.
92. Kreuter, A., Gambichler, T., Hoffmann, K. et al (2002) Association of HIV infection, pyoderma gangrenosum and psoriasis. *Acta Derm Venereol*, **82**, 150–152.
93. Williamson, D., Sibbald, R.G. (2002) Chronic recurrent multifocal osteomyelitis: a rare osteomyelitis with pyoderma gangrenosum in adults. *Br J Dermatol*, **147**, 611–613.
94. Claudepierre, P., Clerc, D., Cariou, D. et al (1996) SAPHO syndrome and pyoderna gangrenosum: is it fortuitous? *J Rheumatol*, **23**, 400–402.
95. Beretta-Piccoli, B.C., Sauvain, M.J., Gal, I. et al (2000) Synovitis, acne, pustulosis, hyperostosis, osteitis (SAPHO) syndrome in childhood: a report of ten cases and review of the literature. *Eur J Pediatr*, **159**, 594–601.
96. Vannucci, S.A., Mitchell, W.M., Stratton, C.W. et al (2000) Pyoderma gangrenosum and Chlamydia pneumoniae infection in a diabetic man: pathogenic role or coincidence? *J Am Acad Dermatol*, **42**, 295–297.
97. Kim, N.Y., Choi, J.Y., Lee, K.H. et al (1994) Pyoderma gangrenosum in a patient with colonic tuberculosis. *Am J Gastroenterol*, **89**, 1257–1259.
98. Phan, J.C., Hargadon, A.P., Salpeter, S.R. (1996) Association between pyoderma gangrenosum and psoriasis. *Lancet*, **348**, 547.
99. Kurokawa, S., Tokura, Y., Nham, N.X. et al (1996) Acne fulminans coexisting with pyoderma gangrenosum-like eruptions and posterior scleritis. *J Dermatol*, **23**, 37–41.
100. Vèlez, A., Alcalá, J., Fernández-Roldán, J.C. (1995) Pyoderma gangrenosum associated with acne conglobata. *Clin Exp Dermatol*, **20**, 496–498.
101. Shenefelt, P.D. (1996) Pyoderma gangrenosum associated with cystic acne and hidradenitis suppurativa controlled by adding minocycline and sulfasalazine to the treatment regimen. *Cutis*, **57**, 315–319.
102. Sakamoto, T., Hashimoto, T., Furukawa, F. (2002) Pyoderma gangrenosum in a patient with bullous systemic lupus erythematosus. *Eur J Dermatol*, **12**, 485–487.
103. Selva, A., Ordi, J., Roca, M. et al (1994) Pyoderma-gangrenosum-like ulcers associated with lupus anticoagulant. *Dermatology*, **189**, 182–184.
104. Kurgansky, D., Foxwell, M.M. Jr (1993) Pyoderma gangrenosum as a cutaneous manifestation of diverticular disease. *South Med J*, **86**, 581–584.
105. Serrano, J., Rojas, R., Sánchez, J. et al (1998) Pyoderma gangrenosum associated with Fanconi's anemia. *Dermatology*, **196**, 370–371.
106. Lenane, P., McKenna, D., Murphy, G.M. (1998) Pyoderma gangrenosum secondary to allergic contact dermatitis from rubber. *Contact Dermatitis*, **38**, 238.
107. Matsubara, K., Isoda, K., Maeda, Y. et al (2002) Pyoderma gangrenosum associated with paroxysmal nocturnal hemoglobulinuria and monoclonal gammopathy. *J Dermatol*, **29**, 86–90.
108. Friduss, S.R., Sadoff, W.I., Hern, A.E. et al (1992) Fatal pyoderma gangrenosum in association with C7 deficiency. *J Am Acad Dermatol*, **27**, 356–359.
109. Goto, M., Okamoto, O., Fujiwara, S. et al (2002) Vegetative pyoderma gangrenosum in chronic renal failure. *Br J Dermatol*, **146**, 141–143.
110. Vázquez, J., Fernández-Redondo, V., Sánchez-Aguilar, D. et al (1993) Cutaneous manifestations in Kartagener's syndrome: folliculitis, nummular eczema and pyoderma gangrenosum. *Dermatology*, **186**, 269–271.
111. Boulinguez, S., Bernard, P., Bedane, C. et al (1998) Pyoderma gangrenosum complicating Cogan's syndrome. *Clin Exp Dermatol*, **23**, 286–289.
112. Han, M.H., Koh, G.J., Koh, J.K. et al (2000) Hypertrophic osteoarthropathy associated with pyoderma gangrenosum. *Br J Dermatol*, **142**, 562–564.
113. Gallo, R., Parodi, A., Rebora, A. (1995) Pyoderma gangrenosum in a patient with gastric carcinoma. *Int J Dermatol*, **34**, 713–714.
114. Stone, M.S., Lyckholm, L.J. (1996) Pyoderma gangrenosum and subcorneal pustular dermatosis: clues underlying immunoglobulin A myeloma. *Am J Med*, **100**, 663–664.
115. Chave, T.A., Hutchinson, P.E. (2001) Pyoderma gangrenosum, subcorneal pustular dermatosis, IgA paraproteinaemia and IgG antiepithelial antibodies. *Br J Dermatol*, **145**, 852–854.
116. Salmon, P., Rademaker, M., Edwards, L. (1998) A continuum of neutrophilic disease occurring in a patient with ulcerative colitis. *Australas J Dermatol*, **39**, 116–118.
117. Benton, E.C., Rutherford, D., Hunter, J.A. (1985) Sweet's syndrome and pyoderma gangrenosum associated with ulcerative colitis. *Acta Derm Venereol*, **65**, 77–80.
118. Lindor, N.M., Arsenault, T.M., Solomon, H. et al (1997) A new autosomal dominant disorder of pyogenic sterile arthritis, pyoderma gangrenosum, and acne: PAPA syndrome. *Mayo Clin Proc*, **72**, 611–615.
119. Yeon, H.B., Lindor, N.M., Seidman, J.G. et al (2000) Pyogenic arthritis, pyoderma gangrenosum and acne syndrome maps to chromosome 15q. *Am J Hum Genet*, **66**, 1443–1448.
120. Hughes, A.P., Jackson, J., Callen, J.P. (2000) Clinical features and treatment of peristomal pyoderma gangrenosum. *JAMA*, **284**, 1546–1548.

121. Lyon, C.C., Smith, A.J., Beck, M.H. et al (2000) Parastomal pyoderma gangrenosum: clinical features and management. *J Am Acad Dermatol*, **42**, 992–1002.
122. Mancini, G.J., Floyd, L., Solla, J.A. (2002) Parastomal pyoderma gangrenosum: a case report and literature review. *Am Surg*, **68**, 824–826.
123. Wilson-Jones, E., Winkelmann, R.K. (1988) Superficial granulomatous pyoderma: a localized vegetative form of pyoderma gangrenosum. *J Am Acad Dermatol*, **18**, 511–521.
124. Lichter, M.D., Welykyj, S.E., Gradini, R. et al (1991) Superficial granulomatous pyoderma. *Int J Dermatol*, **30**, 418–421.
125. Winkelmann, R.K., Wilson-Jones, E., Gibson, L.E. et al (1989) Histopathologic features of superficial granulomatous pyoderma. *J Dermatol*, **16**, 127–132.
126. Heredero, M., Yus, E.S., Gómez-Calcerrado, M.R. et al (1998) Superficial granulomatous pyoderma. *Dermatology*, **196**, 358–360.
127. Miralles, J., Matarredonna, J., Ruiz, J.A. et al (2000) Superficial granulomatous pyoderma. *Cutis*, **66**, 217–219.
128. Thami, G.P., Kaur, S., Punia, R.S. et al (2002) Superficial granulomatous pyoderma: an idiopathic granulomatous cutaneous ulceration. *J Eur Acad Dermatol Venereol*, **16**, 159–161.
129. Malkinson, F.D. (1987) Pyoderma gangrenosum versus malignant pyoderma. *Arch Dermatol*, **123**, 333–337.
130. Dicken, C.H. (1985) Malignant pyoderma. *J Am Acad Dermatol*, **13**, 1021–1025.
131. Novice, F.M., Hacker, P., Unger, W.P. et al (1987) Malignant pyoderma. *Int J Dermatol*, **26**, 42–44.
132. Gibson, L.E., Daoud, M.S., Muller, S.A. et al (1997) Malignant pyoderma revisited. *Mayo Clin Proc*, **72**, 734–736.
133. Haim, S., Friedman-Birnbaum, R. (1976) Pyoderma gangrenosum in immunosuppressed patients. *Dermatologica*, **153**, 44–48.
134. Norris, D.A., Weston, W.L., Thorne, G. et al (1978) Pyoderma gangrenosum: abnormal monocyte function corrected in vitro with hydrocortisone. *Arch Dermatol*, **114**, 906–911.
135. Schroeter, A.L. (1980) The vasculitis of pyoderma gangrenosum: a dermatopathologic and histopathologic study. *Arch Dermatol*, **116** (Suppl.), 1388.
136. Oka, M., Berking, C., Nesbit, M. et al (2000) Interleukin-8 overexpression is present in pyoderma gangrenosum ulcers and leads to ulcer formation in human skin xenografts. *Lab Invest*, **80**, 595–604.
137. Adachi, Y., Kindzelskii, A.L., Cookingham, G. et al (1998) Aberrant neutrophil trafficking and metabolic oscillations in severe pyoderma gangrenosum. *J Invest Dermatol*, **111**, 259–268.
138. Shaya, S., Kindzelskii, A.L., Minor, J. et al (1998) Aberrant integrin (CR4; alpha (x) beta2; CD11c/CD18) oscillations on neutrophils in a mild form of pyoderma gangrenosum. *J Invest Dermatol*, **111**, 154–158.
139. Powell, F.C., Schroeter, A.L., Perry, H.O., Su, W.P. (1983) Direct immunofluorescence in pyoderma gangrenosum. *Br J Dermatol*, **108**, 287–293.
140. Su, W.P.D., Schroeter, A.L., Perry, H.O. et al (1986) Histopathologic and immunopathologic study of pyoderma gangrenosum. *J Cutan Pathol*, **13**, 323–330.
141. Schwaegerle, S.M., Bergfeld, W.F., Senitzer, D. et al (1988) Pyoderma gangrenosum: a review. *J Am Acad Dermatol*, **18**, 559–568.
142. Park, H.J., Kim, Y.C., Cinn, Y.W. et al (2000) Granulomatous pyoderma gangrenosum: two unusual cases showing necrotizing granulomatous inflammation. *Clin Exp Dermatol*, **25**, 617–620.

Acute febrile neutrophilic dermatosis

Clinical features

Acute febrile neutrophilic dermatosis (Sweet's syndrome) is an uncommon disease of unknown etiology and pathogenesis.[1–9] It is associated with a marked female predilection (5:1) and most patients affected are in their third through sixth decades. It may, however, occasionally be seen in children and a few cases presenting in infancy have been documented.[10–18] Patients present with variable numbers of asymmetrically distributed, frequently bilateral, circumscribed, tender and painful red plaques or nodules, particularly on the face, neck, upper and lower limbs (*Figs 14.13–14.15*). Occasionally, the lesions may become bullous or pustular.[19] The plaques vary from about 1 to 4 cm in diameter and typically heal without scarring. Recurrences develop in approximately one-third of patients and postinflammatory hyperpigmentation is sometimes seen.[20,21] Pathergy and koebnerization are occasional features and necrosis with ulceration may rarely be encountered.[7,22] Sweet's syndrome may present with lesions mimicking palmoplantar pustulosis and sometimes erythema nodosum-like lesions are present.[19,23,24] A Sweet's syndrome-like eruption has been described in association with exposure to light.[25]

Sweet's syndrome often follows an upper respiratory tract infection. In some cases it is a complication of drug treatment, for example carbamazepine, furosemide (frusemide), hydralazine, co-trimoxazole, minocycline, trimethoprim–sulfamethoxazole, granulocyte colony-stimulating factor (G-CSF), oral contraceptives, all-trans retinoic acid, isotretinoin, nitrofurantoin, diazepam, clozapine and celecoxib.[19,26–41] The temporal relationship with administration, development of symptoms, and resolution with withdrawal of the offending drug establishes the cause in drug-induced cases.[26] The disease has also been reported after chemotherapy in patients with acute myeloid leukemia.[42]

Patients may also have conjunctivitis, episcleritis, iritis, polyneuropathy, oral involvement (superficial ulcers) and arthralgias.[19,43–46] The larger joints are usually affected and involvement tends to be migratory.[5] Patients with concurrent Sweet's syndrome and erythema nodosum have been described and it is possible that these two disorders share common pathogenetic mechanisms.[47] Dyssynchronous and synchronous Sweet's syndrome and erythema nodosum may occur.[48,49]

Sweet's syndrome is of particular importance since 10–40% of cases are associated with hematological malignancy including leukemia (monocytic or myelomonocytic), myelodysplasia, lymphoma and

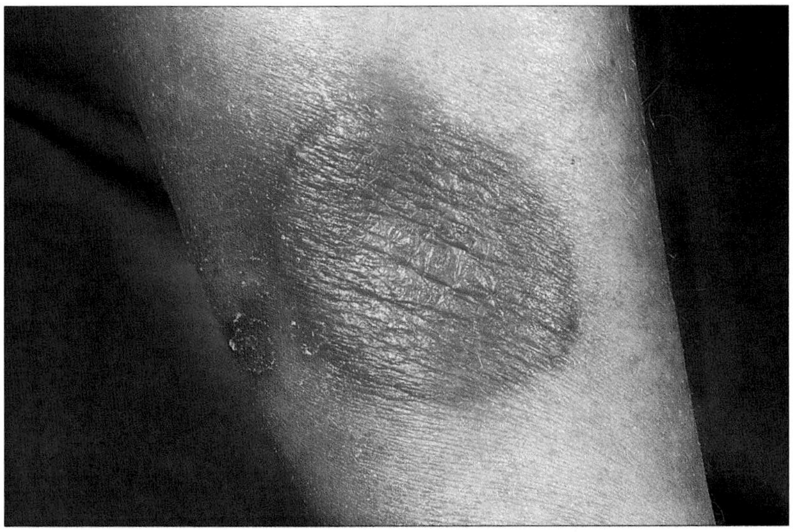

Fig. 14.13
Sweet's syndrome: an erythematous plaque on the forearm. By courtesy of R.A. Marsden, MD, St George's Hospital, London, UK.

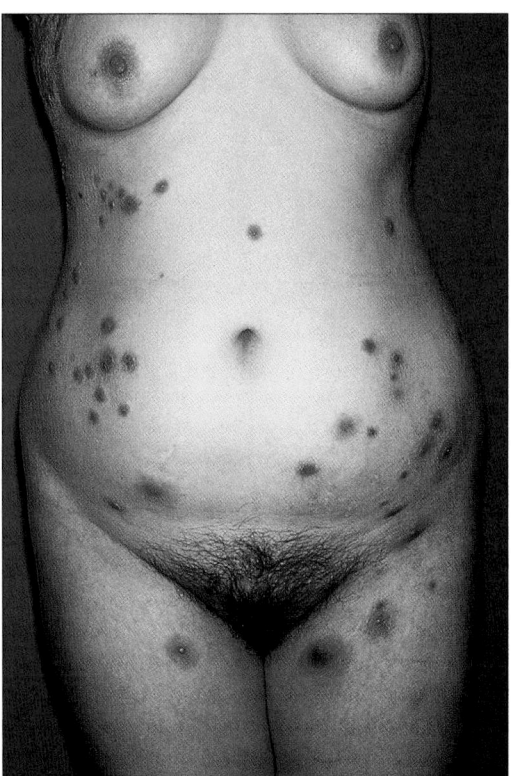

Fig. 14.14
Sweet's syndrome: characteristic edematous red plaques (some showing ulceration and pustulation) are widely distributed on the trunk and proximal limbs. By courtesy of R.A. Marsden, MD, St George's Hospital, London, UK.

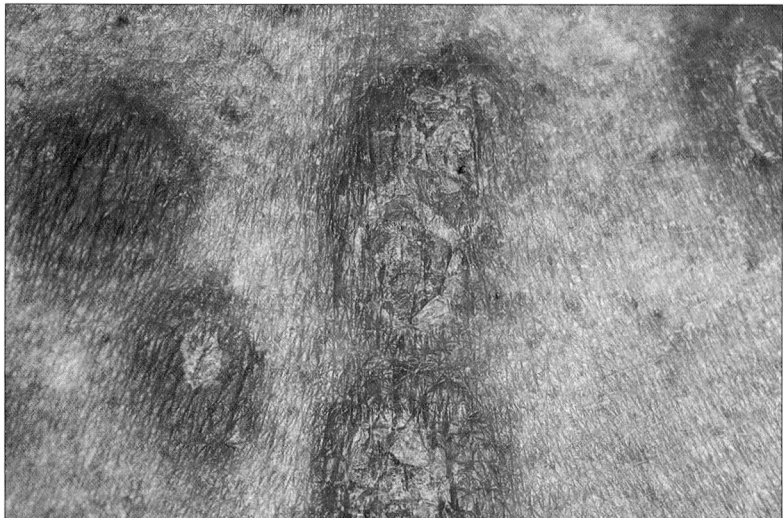

Fig. 14.15
Sweet's syndrome: close-up view of typical plaques. By courtesy of the Institute of Dermatology, London, UK.

Table 14.2
Conditions associated with Sweet's syndrome

Common associations	Rare associations
Inflammatory bowel disease (including ulcerative colitis and Crohn's disease)[64]	Behçet's disease[73]
Sarcoidosis[65,66]	Subacute cutaneous lupus erythematosus[74]
Sjögren's syndrome[67]	Dermatomyositis[75]
Tuberculosis[68]	Relapsing polychondritis[76]
Scrofuloderma[69]	Generalized granuloma annulare[77]
Non-tuberculous mycobacterial infection[70]	Prothrombin gene (G20210A) mutation[78]
Hepatitis B[71]	Bacille Calmette–Guérin (BCG) vaccination[79]
Polycythemia rubra vera[72]	Pigmented villonodular synovitis[80]
	Encephalitis[81]
	Infection with *Francisella tularensis, Chlamydia pneumoniae, Salmonella enteritidis, Helicobacter pylori, Pasteurella multocida, apnocytophaga canimorsus* and human immunodeficiency virus[82–89]
	Bronchiolitis obliterans[90]
	Thyroiditis[91]
	Chronic granulomatous disease[92]
	Surgery[93]

multiple myeloma.[50–58] The development of the disease may herald a relapse of leukemia.[59] Sweet's syndrome has also been reported in patients with monoclonal gammopathy and myelodysplasia in the absence of frank leukemia or lymphoma.[60] The clinical lesions of Sweet's syndrome are said to be more severe in patients with underlying hematological disease.[56] An association with urticaria pigmentosa has also been documented.[7]

Solid tumors (including testicular, bladder, gastrointestinal, breast, lung, ovarian and prostatic malignancies) may also be associated with Sweet's syndrome in up to 7% of patients.[7,19,21,49–53,56,60–62] Association with oral squamous cell carcinoma has been reported,[22] as has a rare association following treatment of herpes simplex in a patient with metastatic breast carcinoma.[63] Sweet's syndrome has also been described in association with a number of other conditions, as outlined in *Table 14.2*.

Systemic involvement may be a feature of Sweet's syndrome with lesions described in the lung, kidney, central nervous system, vagina, liver, gastrointestinal tract and skeletal muscle.[7,54,94–98] An exceptional case with gingival hyperplasia and myositis in the absence of cutaneous involvement has been documented.[99] Associated features include pyrexia, neutrophilia and a raised erythrocyte sedimentation rate (ESR). In one study, six of seven patients had antineutrophil cytoplasmic antibodies (ANCA).[100] Other studies, however, have not found an association between Sweet's syndrome and ANCA.[7]

Pathogenesis and histological features

The etiology of Sweet's syndrome is unknown; however, the disease most probably represents an unusual hypersensitivity reaction. The occasional presence of immune complexes in blood vessel walls may have pathogenetic significance.[19] It has been suggested that neutrophils are activated by interleukin (IL)-1 and that Sweet's syndrome represents a cytokine-mediated inflammatory reaction to a wide variety of different antigens including bacteria, viruses, drugs and malignancies.[101–103] Demonstration of elevated serum IL-1α, IL-1β, IL-2 and interferon-gamma (IFN-γ) but not IL-4 suggests that type 1 (but not type 2) helper T-cells (Th) play a role in the pathogenesis of the disease.[104]

One recent study demonstrated clonality in the skin infiltrate of a patient with Sweet's syndrome and acute myelogenous leukemia undergoing treatment with G-CSF.[105] The authors concluded that Sweet's syndrome in patients with myelogenous leukemia may result from therapy-induced differentiation of neoplastic cells.[105] Clearly, more study of this interesting phenomenon is necessary.

Histologically, the epidermis in Sweet's syndrome is usually unaffected although occasionally slight spongiosis may be present; rarely, vesiculation and spongiform pustules have been described.[19] Necrotic keratinocytes are also sometimes evident.[19] The cardinal feature, however, is an intense neutrophil polymorph infiltrate within the reticular dermis (*Fig. 14.16*).[3,106] This may be diffuse or perivascular in distribution and often surrounds the sweat ducts. Typically, leukocytoclasis is marked (*Fig. 14.17*). Admixed with the neutrophil polymorphs are variable numbers of eosinophils, lymphocytes and histiocytes. Ingestion of nuclear debris by histiocytes is sometimes a conspicuous feature. A histiocyte-rich stage in the evolution of Sweet's syndrome has been described although this observation has not gained wide acceptance.[19,107]

Often the papillary dermis shows very marked edema, which sometimes results in subepidermal vesiculation (*Fig. 14.18*). Rarely, the presence of dermal papillary neutrophil microabscesses may cause diagnostic confusion with dermatitis herpetiformis (*Fig. 14.19*).[106] In Sweet's syndrome the blood vessels are dilated and may show endothelial swelling but changes of frank vasculitis are absent. Purpura, however, is sometimes evident.[108] Immunofluorescence examination of skin biopsies in Sweet's syndrome is usually negative for immunoreactants in the walls of the vasculature. Recently, a case associated with leukocytoclastic neutrophilic lobular panniculitis has been reported.[109]

In some cases, an inflammatory infiltrate is noted within subcutaneous tissue. This infiltrate may be composed of lymphocytes and histiocytes and, less commonly, neutrophils.[106] Sweet's syndrome has also been associated with an erythema nodosum-like panniculitis.[110]

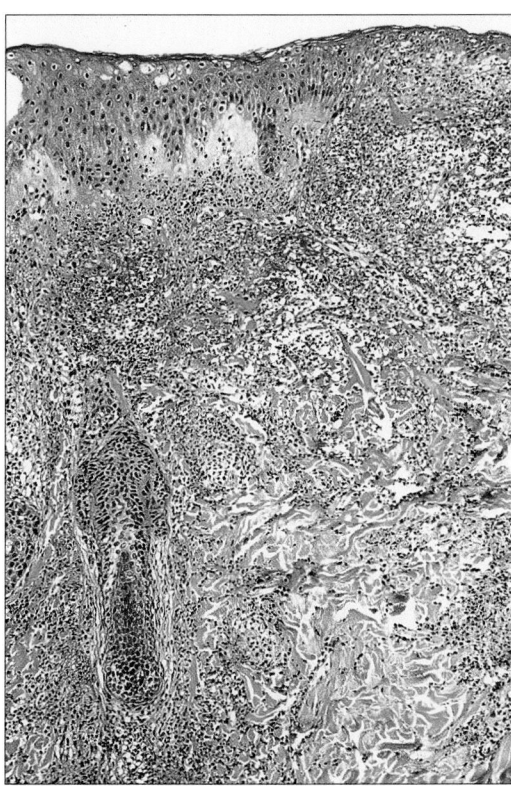

Fig. 14.16
Sweet's syndrome: an intense inflammatory cell infiltrate is present in the dermis.

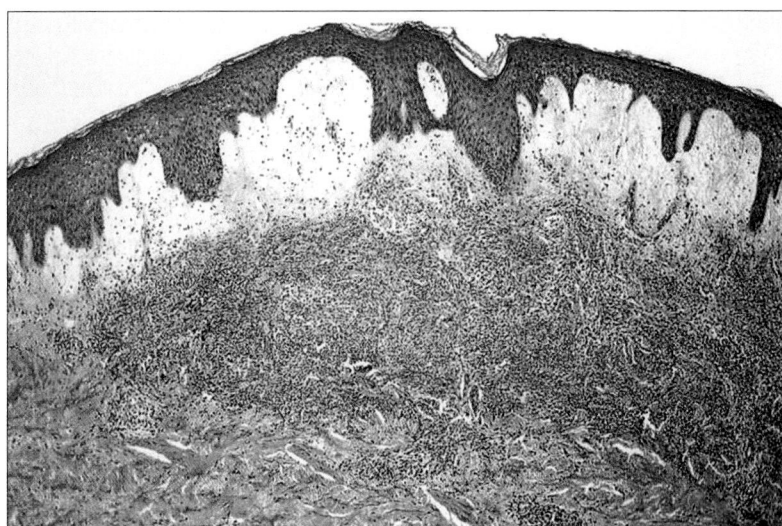

Fig. 14.18
Sweet's syndrome: marked papillary dermal edema is commonly present and sometimes this is associated with subepidermal vesiculation.

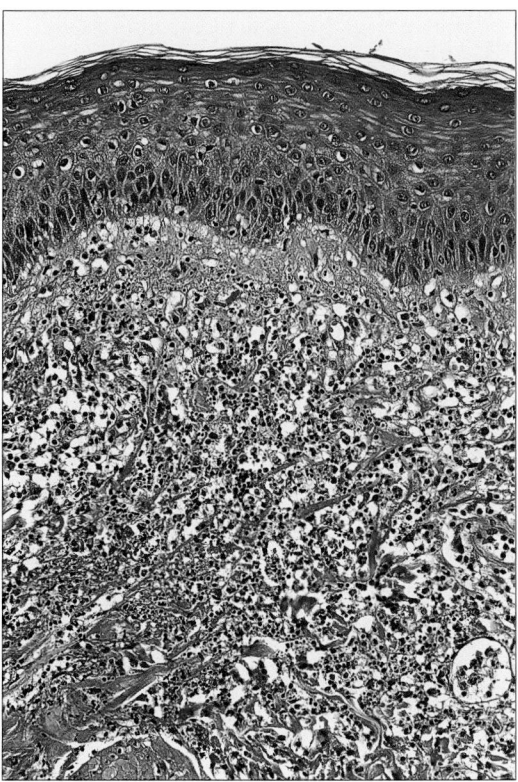

Fig. 14.17
Sweet's syndrome: the infiltrate consists largely of neutrophils. There is edema and marked leukocytoclasis.

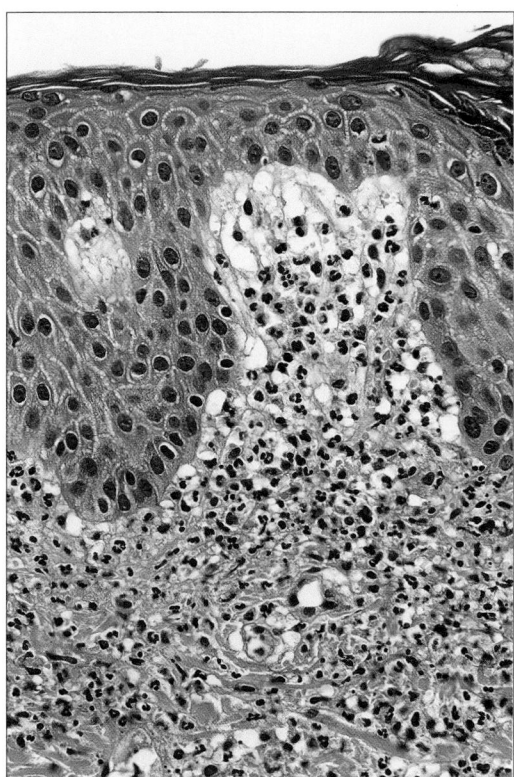

Fig. 14.19
Sweet's syndrome: the occasional presence of dermal papillary neutrophil microabscesses can result in confusion with dermatitis herpetiformis.

Differential diagnosis

The presence of fibrinoid vascular change distinguishes necrotizing vasculidities such as leukocytoclastic vasculitis, erythema elevatum diutinum and granuloma faciale from Sweet's syndrome. In granuloma faciale, fibrinoid necrosis may be minimal but eosinophils tend to be prominent. Late lesions of erythema elevatum diutinum and granuloma faciale show fibrosis, a feature not seen in Sweet's syndrome. Clinically, the presence of characteristic ulcers helps distinguish pyoderma gangrenosum from Sweet's syndrome. Also, pyoderma gangrenosum does not usually show the extent of karyorrhexis that is a typical feature of Sweet's syndrome. A Gram stain and periodic acid–Schiff (PAS) or culture may be necessary to exclude infection. Distinction from some other forms of neutrophilic dermatosis including bowel bypass syndrome may be a definitional issue since the clinical setting determines the terminology applied.[7] Behçet's disease may also be associated with lesions similar to those seen in Sweet's syndrome. Clinical correlation should ensure the correct diagnosis.

References

1. Sweet, R.D. (1964) An acute febrile neutrophilic dermatosis. *Br J Dermatol*, **76**, 349–356.
2. Sweet, R.D. (1979) Acute febrile neutrophilic dermatosis – 1978. *Br J Dermatol*, **100**, 93–99.
3. Going, J.J., Going, S.M., Myskow, M.W. et al (1987) Sweet's syndrome: histological and immunohisto-chemical study of 15 cases. *J Clin Pathol*, **40**, 175–179.
4. Gunawardena, D.A., Gunawardena, K.A., Ratnayaka, R.M.R.S. et al (1975) The clinical spectrum of Sweet's syndrome (acute febrile neutrophilic dermatosis) – a report of eighteen cases. *Br J Dermatol*, **92**, 363–373.
5. Storer, J.S., Nesbitt, L.T., Galen, W.K. et al (1983) Review. Sweet's syndrome. *Int J Dermatol*, **22**, 8–12.

6. Fett, D.L., Gibson, L.E., Su, W.P. (1995) Sweet's syndrome: systemic signs and symptoms and associated disorders. *Mayo Clin Proc*, **70**, 234–240.
7. von den Dreiesch, P. (1994) Sweet's syndrome (acute febrile neutrophilic dermatosis). *J Am Acad Dermatol*, **31**, 535–556.
8. Van Rooijen, M.M., Brand, C.U., Braathen, L.R. (1998) Acute febrile neutrophilic dermatosis (Sweet's syndrome). Review of the cases diagnosed at Dermatologic Clinic of Berne from 1994 to 1997. *Dermatology*, **197**, 299.
9. Su, W.P., Fett, D.L., Gibson, L.E. et al (1995) Sweet syndrome: acute neutrophilic dermatosis. *Semin Dermatol*, **14**, 173–178.
10. Boatman, B.W., Taylor, R.C., Klein, L.E. et al (1994) Sweet's syndrome in children. *South Med J*, **87**, 193–196.
11. Prasad, P.V., Ambujam, S., Priya, K. et al (2002) Sweet's syndrome in an infant – report of a rare case. *Int J Dermatol*, **41**, 928–930.
12. Kourtis, A.P. (2002) Sweet syndrome in infants. *Clin Pediatr (Phila)*, **41**, 175–177.
13. Elliott, S.P., Mallory, S.B. (1999) Sweet syndrome: an unusual presentation of chronic granulomatous disease in a child. *Pediatr Infect Dis J*, **18**, 568–570.
14. Guia, J.M., Frias, J., Castro, F.J. et al (1999) Cardiovascular involvement in a boy with Sweet's syndrome. *Pediatr Cardiol*, **20**, 295–297.
15. Lipp, K.E., Shenefelt, P.D., Nelson, R.P. Jr et al (1999) Persistent Sweet's syndrome occurring in a child with a primary immunodeficiency. *J Am Acad Dermatol*, **40**, 838–841.
16. Tuerlinckx, D., Bodart, E., Despontin, K. et al (1999) Sweet's syndrome with arthritis in an 8-month-old boy. *J Rheumatol*, **26**, 440–442.
17. Schneider, D.T., Schuppe, H.C., Schwamborn, D. et al (1998) Acute febrile neutrophilic dermatosis (Sweet syndrome) as initial presentation in a child with acute myeologenous leukemia. *Med Pediatr Oncol*, **31**, 178–181.
18. Howard, R., Tsuchiya, A. (1998) Adult skin disease in the pediatric patient. *Dermatol Clin*, **16**, 593–608.
19. Sitjas, D., Puig, L., Cuatrecasas, M., de Moragas, J.M. (1993) Acute febrile neutrophilic dermatosis (Sweet's syndrome). *Int J Dermatol*, **32**, 261–268.
20. Kemmett, D., Hunter, J.A. (1990) Sweet's syndrome: a clinicopathologic review of twenty-nine cases. *J Am Acad Dermatol*, **23**, 503–507.
21. Cohen, P.R., Kurzrock, R. (1987) Sweet's syndrome and malignancy. *Am J Med*, **82**, 1220–1226.
22. Tavadia, S.M., Smith, G., Herd, R.M. et al (1999) Sweet's syndrome associated with oral squamous cell carcinoma and exhibiting the Koebner phenomenon. *Br J Dermatol*, **141**, 169–170.
23. Sommer, S., Wilkinson, S.M., Merchant, W.J. et al (2000) Sweet's syndrome presenting as palmoplantar pustulosis. *J Am Acad Dermatol*, **42**, 332–334.
24. Gambichler, T., Menzel, S., Herde, M. et al (2000) Sweet's syndrome with eruption of pustulosis palmaris. *J Eur Acad Dermatol Venereol*, **14**, 327–329.
25. Bessis, D., Dereure, O., Peyron, J.L. et al (2001) Photoinduced Sweet syndrome. *Arch Dermatol*, **137**, 1106–1108.
26. Walker, D.C., Cohen, P.R. (1996) Trimethoprim–sulfamethoxazole-associated acute febrile neutrophilic dermatosis: case report and review of drug-induced Sweet's syndrome. *J Am Acad Dermatol*, **34**, 918–923.
27. Gilmour, E., Chambers, R.J., Rowlands, D.J. (1995) Drug-induced Sweet's syndrome (acute febrile neutrophilic dermatosis) associated with hydralazine. *Br J Dermatol*, **133**, 490–491.
28. Arbetter, K.R., Hubbard, K.W., Markovic, S.N. (1999) Case of granulocyte colony-stimulating factor-induced Sweet's syndrome. *Am J Hematol*, **61**, 126–129.
29. Hasegawa, M., Sato, S., Nakada, M. et al (1998) Sweet's syndrome associated with granulocyte colony-stimulating factor. *Eur J Dermatol*, **8**, 503–505.
30. Khan Durani, B., Jappe, U. (2002) Drug-induced Sweet's syndrome in acne caused by different tetracyclines: case report and review of the literature. *Br J Dermatol*, **147**, 558–562.
31. Saez, M., García-Bustinduy, M., Noda, A. et al (2002) Sweet's syndrome induced by oral contraceptive. *Dermatology*, **204**, 84.
32. Hatake, K., Uwai, M., Ohtsuki, T. et al (1997) Rare but important adverse effects of all-trans retinoic acid in acute promyelocytic leukemia and their management. *Int J Hematol*, **66**, 13–19.
33. Park, C.J., Bae, Y.D., Choi, J.Y. et al (2001) Sweet's syndrome during the treatment of acute promyelocytic leukemia with all-trans retinoic acid. *Korean J Intern Med*, **16**, 218–221.
34. Arun, B., Berberian, B., Azumi, N. et al (1998) Sweet's syndrome during treatment with all-trans retinoic acid in a patient with acute promyelocytic leukemia. *Leuk Lymphoma*, **31**, 613–615.
35. Takada, S., Matumoto, K., Sakura, T. et al (1999) Sweet's syndrome followed by retinoic acid syndrome during the treatment of acute promyelocytic leukemia with all-trans retinoic acid. *Int J Hematol*, **70**, 26–29.
36. Astudillo, L., Loche, F., Reynish, W. et al (2002) Sweet's syndrome associated with retinoic acid syndrome in a patient with promyelocytic leukemia. *Ann Hematol*, **81**, 111–114.
37. Gyorfy, A., Kovacs, T., Szegedi, I. et al (2003) Sweet syndrome associated with 13-cis-retinoic acid (isotretinoin) therapy. *Med Pediatr Oncol*, **40**, 135–136.
38. Retief, C.R., Malkinson, F.D. (1999) Nitrofurantoin-associated Sweet's syndrome. *Cutis*, **63**, 177–179.
39. Guimera, F.J., García-Bustinduy, M., Noda, A. et al (2000) Diazepam-associated Sweet's syndrome. *Int J Dermatol*, **39**, 795–798.
40. Schonfeldt-Lecuona, C., Connemann, B.J. (2002) Sweet's syndrome and polyserositis with clozapine. *Am J Psychiatry*, **159**, 1947.
41. Fye, K.H., Crowley, E., Berger, T.G. et al (2001) Celecoxib-induced Sweet's syndrome. *J Am Acad Dermatol*, **45**, 300–302.
42. Conesa, V., Morales, A., Majado, M.J. et al (1998) Post-chemotherapy Sweet's syndrome in three patients with AML. *Am J Hematol*, **57**, 179.
43. Nicolaides, A., Packles, M.R., Schutzer, P.J. et al (2000) Iritis associated with Sweet's syndrome. *Clin Exp Dermatol*, **25**, 352–353.
44. Chen, T.C., Goldstein, D.A., Tessler, H.H. et al (1998) Scleritis associated with acute febrile neutrophilic dermatosis (Sweet's syndrome). *Br J Ophthalmol*, **82**, 328–329.
45. Kto, T., Kunikata, N., Taira, H. et al (2002) Acute febrile neutrophilic dermatosis (Sweet's syndrome) with nodular episcleritis and polyneuropathy. *Int J Dermatol*, **41**, 107–109.
46. Notani, K., Kobayashi, S., Kondoh, K. et al (2000) A case of Sweet's syndrome (acute febrile neutrophilic dermatosis) with palatal ulceration. *Oral Surg Oral Med Oral Pathol Oral Radiol Endod*, **89**, 477–479.
47. Cohen, P.R., Holder, W.R., Rapini, R.P. (1992) Concurrent Sweet's syndrome and erythema nodosum: a report, world literature review and mechanisms of pathogenesis. *J Rheumatol*, **19**, 814–820.
48. Nishie, W., Kimura, T., Kanagawa, M. (2002) Sweet's syndrome evolved from recurrent erythema nodosum in a patient with myelodysplastic syndrome. *J Dermatol*, **29**, 91–95.
49. Waltz, K.M., Long, D., Marks, J.G. Jr et al (1999) Sweet's syndrome and erythema nodosum: the simultaneous occurrence of 2 reactive dermatoses. *Arch Dermatol*, **135**, 62–66.
50. Caughman, W., Stern, R., Haynes, H. (1983) Neutrophilic dermatosis of myeloproliferative disorders. *J Am Acad Dermatol*, **9**, 751–758.
51. Klock, J.C., Oken, R.L. (1976) Febrile neutrophilic dermatosis in acute myelogenous leukemia. *Cancer*, **37**, 922–927.
52. Clemmensen, O.J., Menné, T., Brandrup, F. et al (1989) Acute febrile neutrophilic dermatosis – a marker of malignancy? *Acta Derm Venereol*, **69**, 52–58.
53. Su, W.P.D., Liu, H.N.H. (1986) Diagnostic criteria for Sweet's syndrome. *Cutis*, **37**, 167–174.
54. Lazarus, A.A., McMillan, M., Miramadi, A. (1986) Pulmonary involvement in Sweet's syndrome (acute febrile neutrophilic dermatosis). Preleukemic and leukemic phases of acute myelogenous leukemia. *Chest*, **90**, 922–924.
55. Cohen, P.R., Talpaz, M., Kurzrock, R. (1988) Malignancy-associated Sweet's syndrome: review of the world literature. *J Clin Oncol*, **6**, 1887–1897.
56. Chan, H.L., Lee, Y.S., Kuo, T.T. (1994) Sweet's syndrome: clinicopathologic study of eleven cases. *Int J Dermatol*, **33**, 425–432.
57. Gille, J., Spieth, K., Kaufmann, R. (2002) Sweet's syndrome as initial presentation of diffuse large B-cell lymphoma. *J Am Acad Dermatol*, **46**, S11–13.
58. Aubin, F., Dufour, M.P., Angonin, R. et al (1998) Sweet's syndrome associated with cutaneous T cell lymphoma. *Eur J Dermatol*, **8**, 178–179.
59. Levy, R.M., Junkins-Hopkins, J.M., Turchi, J.J. et al (2002) Sweet syndrome as the presenting symptom of relapsed hairy cell leukemia. *Arch Dermatol*, **138**, 1551–1554.
60. Bourke, J.F., Keohane, S., Long, C.C. et al (1997) Sweet's syndrome and malignancy. *Br J Dermatol*, **137**, 609–617.
61. Cohen, P.R., Holder, W.R., Tucker, S.B. et al (1993) Sweet syndrome in patients with solid tumors. *Cancer*, **72**, 2723–2731.
62. Inomata, N., Sasaki, T., Nakajima, H. (1999) Sweet's syndrome with gastric cancer. *J Am Acad Dermatol*, **41**, 1033–1034.
63. Coskun, U., Gunel, N., Senol, E. et al (2002) A case of Sweet's syndrome developed after the treatment of herpes simplex infection in a metastatic breast cancer patient. *J Cutan Pathol*, **29**, 301–304.
64. Rappaport, A., Shaked, M., Landau, M. et al (2001) Sweet's syndrome in association with Crohn's disease: report of a case and review of the literature. *Dis Colon Rectum*, **44**, 1526–1529.
65. Cuende Quintana, E., Gómez de Mendarozqueta, M., Gorospe Arrazuria, M.A. et al (1996) Concurrent Sweet's syndrome and Lofgren's syndrome. *J Rheumatol*, **23**, 1995–1998.
66. Stuveling, E.M., Fedder, G., Bruns, H.M. et al (2001) The association of Sweet's syndrome with sarcoidosis. *Neth J Med*, **59**, 31–34.
67. Osawa, H., Yamabe, H., Seino, S. et al (1997) A case of Sjögren's syndrome associated with Sweet's syndrome. *Clin Rheumatol*, **16**, 101–105.
68. Singh, R.K. (2002) Acute febrile neutrophilic dermatosis following tuberculous infection. *J Assoc Physicians India*, **50**, 1322–1323.
69. Mahaisavariya, P., Chaiprasert, A., Manonukul, J. et al (2002) Scrofuloderma and Sweet's syndrome. *Int J Dermatol*, **41**, 28–31.
70. Choonhakarn, C., Chetchotisakd, P., Jirattanapochai, K. et al (1998) Sweet's syndrome associated with non-tuberculous mycobacterial infection: a report of five cases. *Br J Dermatol*, **139**, 107–110.
71. Tan, E., Yosipovitch, G., Giam, Y.C. et al (2000) Bullous Sweet's syndrome associated with acute hepatitis B infection: a new association. *Br J Dermatol*, **143**, 914–916.
72. Wong, G.A., Guerin, D.M., Parslew, R. (2000) Sweet's syndrome and polycythaemia rubra vera. *Clin Exp Dermatol*, **25**, 296–298.
73. Mizoguchi, M., Chikakane, K., Goh, K. et al (1987) Acute febrile neutrophilic dermatosis in Behçet's disease. *Br J Dermatol*, **116**, 727–734.
74. Goette, D.K. (1985) Sweet's syndrome in subacute cutaneous lupus erythematosus. *Arch Dermatol*, **121**, 789–791.
75. Yoo, W.H., Moon, S.K., Park, T.S. et al (1999) A case of Sweet's syndrome in a patient with dermatomyositis. *Korean J Intern Med*, **14**, 78–81.
76. Fujimoto, N., Tajima, S., Ishibashi, A. et al (1998) Acute febrile neutrophilic dermatosis (Sweet's syndrome) in a patient with relapsing polychondritis. *Br J Dermatol*, **139**, 930–931.
77. Antony, F., Holden, C.A. (2001) Sweet's syndrome in association with generalized granuloma annulare in a patient with previous breast carcinoma. *Clin Exp Dermatol*, **26**, 668–670.
78. Tursen, U., Bocekli, E., Kaya, T.I. et al (2002) Sweet's syndrome in a woman with a prothrombin gene (G20210A) mutation. *Int J Dermatol*, **41**, 596–597.
79. Carpentier, O., Piette, F., Delaporte, E. (2002) Sweet's syndrome after BCG vaccination. *Acta Derm Venereol*, **82**, 221.
80. Gosheger, G., Hillmann, A., Ozaki, T. et al (2002) Sweet's syndrome associated with pigmented villonodular synovitis. *Acta Orthop Belg*, **68**, 68–71.
81. Noda, K., Okuma, Y., Fukae, J. et al (2001) Sweet's syndrome associated with encephalitis. *J Neurol Sci*, **188**, 95–97.
82. Ruiz, A.I., González, A., Miranda, A. et al (2001) Sweet's syndrome associated with Francisella tularensis infection. *Int J Dermatol*, **40**, 791–793.
83. Rubegni, P., Marano, M.R., De Aloe, G. et al (2001) Sweet's syndrome and Chlamydia pneumoniae infection. *J Am Acad Dermatol*, **44**, 862–864.
84. Flórez, A., Sánchez-Aguilar, D., Roson, E. et al (1999) Sweet's syndrome associated with Salmonella enteritidis infection. *Clin Exp Dermatol*, **24**, 239–240.
85. Kurkcuoglu, N., Aksoy, F. (1997) Sweet's syndrome associated with Helicobacter pylori infection. *J Am Acad Dermatol*, **37**, 123–124.
86. Boivin, S., Segard, M., Piette, F. et al (2000) Sweet syndrome associated with Pasteurella multocida bronchitis. *Arch Intern Med*, **160**, 1869.
87. Bang, B., Zachariae, C. (2001) Capnocytophaga canimorsus sepsis causing Sweet's syndrome. *Acta Derm Venereol*, **81**, 73–74.
88. Brady, R.C., Morris, J., Connelly, B.L. et al (1999) Sweet's syndrome as the initial manifestation of pediatric human immunodeficiency virus infection. *Pediatrics*, **104**, 1142–1144.
89. Bevilacqua, S., Hermans, P., van Laethem, Y. et al (1999) Sweet's syndrome in an HIV-infected patient. *AIDS*, **13**, 728–79.
90. Longo, M.I., Pico, M., Bueno, C. et al (2001) Sweet's syndrome and bronchiolitis organizing pneumonia. *Am J Med*, **111**, 80–81.
91. Kalmus, Y., Kovatz, S., Shilo, L. et al (2000) Sweet's syndrome and subacute thyroiditis. *Postgrad Med J*, **76**, 229–230.
92. Lyon, C.C., Griffiths, C.E. (1999) Chronic granulomatous disease and acute neutrophilic dermatosis. *Clin Exp Dermatol*, **24**, 368–371.
93. Propst, D.A., Bossons, C.R., Sutterlin, C.E. 3rd (1998) Sweet's syndrome associated with spinal surgical intervention. A case report. *Spine*, **23**, 1708–1710.
94. Vignon-Pennamen, M.D. (2000) The extracutaneous involvement in the neutrophilic dermatoses. *Clin Dermatol*, **18**, 339–347.
95. Matta, M., Malak, J., Tabet, E. et al (1973) Sweet's syndrome: systemic associations. *Cutis*, **12**, 561–565.
96. Delke, I., Veridiano, N.P., Tancer, M.L. et al (1981) Sweet's syndrome with involvement of the female genital tract. *Obstet Gynecol*, **58**, 394–396.
97. McDermott, M.B., Corbally, M.T., O'Marcaigh, A.S. (2001) Extracutaneous Sweet syndrome involving the gastrointestinal tract in a patient with Fanconi anemia. *J Pediatr Hematol Oncol*, **23**, 59–62.
98. Marie, I., Levesque, H., Joly, P. et al (2001) Neutrophilic myositis as an extracutaneous manifestation of neutrophilic dermatosis. *J Am Acad Dermatol*, **44**, 137–139.
99. Melinkeri, S.R., Gupta, R.K., Dabadghao, S. (2002) A Sweet-like syndrome manifesting as ginigival hyperplasia and myositis without cutaneous involvement. *Ann Hematol*, **81**, 397–398.
100. Kemmett, D., Harrison, D.J., Hunter, J.A. (1991) Antibodies to neutrophil cytoplasmic antigens: serologic marker for Sweet's syndrome. *J Am Acad Dermatol*, **24**, 967–969.
101. Going, J.J. (1987) Is the pathogenesis of Sweet's syndrome mediated by interleukin-1? *Br J Dermatol*, **116**, 282.
102. Dreisch, P., Von den Gomez, R.S., Kiesewetter, F. et al (1989) Sweet's syndrome: clinical spectrum and associated conditions. *Cutis*, **44**, 193–200.
103. Bourke, J.F., Jones, J.L., Fletcher, A. et al (1996) An immunohistochemical study of the dermal infiltrate and epidermal staining for interleukin 1 in 12 cases of Sweet's syndrome. *Br J Dermatol*, **134**, 705–709.
104. Giasuddin, A.S., El-Orfi, A.H., Ziu, M.M. et al (1998) Sweet's syndrome: is the pathogenesis mediated by helper T-cell type 1 cytokines. *J Am Acad Dermatol*, **39**, 940–943.
105. Magro, C.M., De Moaes, E., Bruns, F. (2001) Sweet's syndrome in the setting of CD34-positive acute myelogenous leukemia treated with granulocyte colony stimulating factor: evidence for a clonal neutrophilic dermatosis. *J Cutan Pathol*, **28**, 90–96.
106. Jordaan, H.F. (1989) Acute febrile neutrophilic dermatosis. A histopathological study of 37 patients and a review of the literature. *Am J Dermatopathol*, **11**, 99–111.
107. Delabie, J., De Wolf-Peeters, C., Morren, M. et al (1991) Histiocytes in Sweet's syndrome. *Br J Dermatol*, **124**, 348–353.
108. Smolle, J., Kresbach, H. (1990) Acute febrile neutrophilic dermatosis (Sweet syndrome). A retrospective clinical and histological analysis. *Hautarzt*, **41**, 549–556.
109. Cullity, J., Maguire, B., Gebauer, K. (1991) Sweet's panniculitis. *Australas J Dermatol*, **32**, 61–64.
110. Blaustein, A., Moreno, A., Nuguera, J. et al (1985) Septal granulomatous panniculitis in Sweet's syndrome. *Arch Dermatol*, **121**, 785–788.

Neutrophilic dermatoses associated with gastrointestinal and hepatobiliary disease

Clinical features

Pyoderma gangrenosum, the most common neutrophilic dermatosis affecting patients with gastrointestinal disease (particularly ulcerative colitis), is discussed on page 673. The spectrum of lesions described in this section share many histological (and likely pathogenetic) features with pyoderma gangrenosum but lack the characteristic progressive ulceration. Neutrophilic dermatoses associated with gastrointestinal disease are probably best regarded as a continuum, with pyoderma gangrenosum representing an extreme end of the spectrum.

A syndrome of arthritis and pustular skin lesions has been described in patients with inflammatory bowel disease and liver disease, and also in patients who have undergone jejunoileal bypass or Billroth II surgery for morbid obesity.[1-4] Up to 20% of patients with jejunoileal bypass develop this syndrome.[4,5] It may also be associated with peptic ulceration and diverticular disease.

The skin lesions may be papular or vesicular, or form large necrotic lesions resembling pyoderma gangrenosum. They are usually found on the trunk or extremities. Oral lesions have also been described.[2] Associated panniculitis, which may resemble erythema nodosum, is a feature in some patients. Cutaneous manifestations often recur with exacerbation of the associated gastrointestinal disease.[4] Some patients have an elevated ESR.[4] The disease occasionally responds to antibiotic or steroid therapy.

A recurring vesiculopustular eruption may be seen in patients with hepatobiliary disease.[6] The lesions – which can be pruritic and sometimes heal with an atrophic scar – often present on the extremities. In some patients the eruption represents a necrotizing folliculitis.[6] Occasionally, the cutaneous lesions precede a diagnosis of hepatobiliary disease.

Of interest, patients with Crohn's disease complicated by disseminated abscesses (involving the spleen, lymph nodes, liver, pancreas and brain) have recently been described.[7] In some of these, the abscesses preceded the diagnosis of Crohn's disease. Histologically, a granulomatous element was also commonly present. Successful treatment with immunosuppressive therapy suggests that such lesions may represent an unusual extraintestinal manifestation of Crohn's disease.[7]

Pathogenesis and histological features

The presence of circulating immune complexes in occasional patients has led some authors to postulate a pathogenic role.[8,9] It is thought that bacterial overgrowth may play a role in the development of such circulating immune complexes.[4]

The histopathological findings, which are non-specific, are those of a neutrophilic dermatosis. The lesions show variable dermal edema and necrosis associated with a perivascular and interstitial neutrophilic infiltrate. Variable numbers of lymphocytes and histiocytes may also be present. Abundant karyorrhexis gives rise to a histological pattern similar to acute febrile neutrophilic dermatosis (Sweet's syndrome) (*Fig. 14.20*). Leukocytoclastic vasculitis and a pustular vasculitis have also been documented.[10,11] The inflammation is often limited to the dermis but in some patients may be seen to involve the subcutaneous fat, resulting in erythema nodosum or an erythema nodosum-like panniculitis.

The small number of cases described in patients with hepatobiliary disease showed bullae associated with a dermal neutrophilic infiltrate, sometimes accompanied by eccrine hidradenitis or folliculitis.[6]

Differential diagnosis

The main differential diagnoses include infection, Sweet's syndrome, pyoderma gangrenosum and rheumatoid neutrophilic dermatitis. Clinical history is essential to distinguish these conditions.

The literature relating to bowel-associated dermatosis–arthritis and Sweet's syndromes is often confusing and it seems likely that some

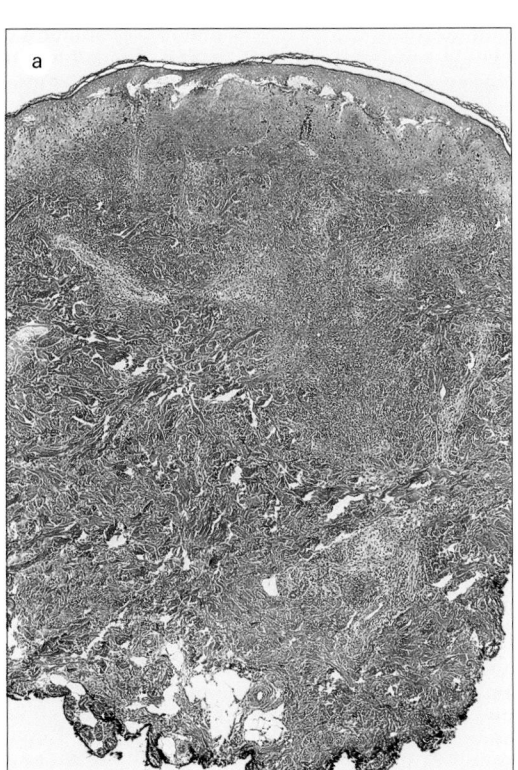

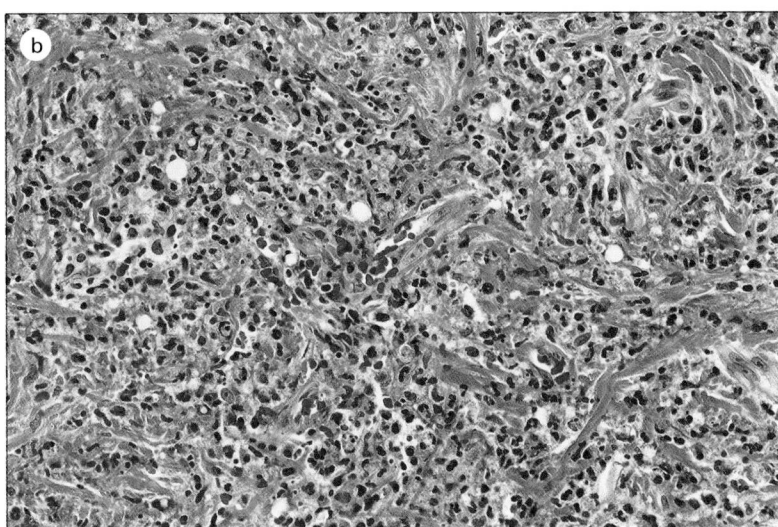

Fig. 14.20
(a, b) Neutrophilic dermatosis associated with gastrointestinal disease: there is an intense dermal neutrophilic infiltrate indistinguishable from Sweet's syndrome.

patients who have been reported as the former would actually have been better classified as the latter. Contrariwise, occasional patients who presented with features more typical of bowel-associated dermatosis–arthritis syndrome have in fact been reported as Sweet's syndrome.[12,13] In many patients such a distinction is semantic. In others, however, the clinical lesions are quite inconsistent with Sweet's syndrome and in these patients a designation of bowel-associated dermatosis–arthritis syndrome is more appropriate.

Pyoderma gangrenosum is another neutrophilic dermatosis which patients with gastrointestinal disease are at risk of developing. Clinically, it may be distinguished by the progressive expansile nature of the cutaneous ulcers.[4] Since the biopsy findings may be similar, clinical correlation is essential to distinguish this condition from bowel-associated dermatosis–arthritis syndrome.

It is likely, given the histological and clinical spectrum encountered in the neutrophilic dermatoses associated with gastrointestinal and hepatobiliary disease, that they result from similar or shared pathogenetic mechanisms. Clearly, more research may clarify their precise pathogenesis and contribute to a more satisfactory classification system.

References

1. Goldman, J.A., Casey, H.L., Davidson, E.D. et al (1979) Vasculitis associated with intestinal bypass surgery. *Arch Dermatol*, **115**, 725–727.
2. Kennedy, C. (1981) The spectrum of inflammatory skin lesions following jejunoileal bypass in the treatment of morbid obesity. *Br J Dermatol*, **105**, 425–436.
3. O'Loughlin, S., Perry, H.O. (1978) A diffuse pustular eruption associated with ulcerative colitis. *Arch Dermatol*, **114**, 1061–1064.
4. Jorizzo, J.L., Apisarnthanarax, P., Supert, P. et al (1983) Bowel bypass syndrome without bypass: bowel-associated dermatosis arthritis syndrome. *Arch Intern Med*, **143**, 457–461.
5. Gregory, B., Ho, V.C. (1992) Cutaneous manifestations of gastrointestinal disorders. *J Am Acad Dermatol*, **26**, 371–383.
6. Magro, C.M., Crowson, A.N. (1997) A distinctive vesiculopustular eruption associated with hepatobiliary disease. *Int J Dermatol*, **36**, 837–844.
7. Andre, M., Aumaitre, O., Papo, T. et al (1998) Disseminated aseptic abscesses associated with Crohn's disease: a new entity? *Dig Dis Sci*, **43**, 420–428.
8. Geary, R.J., Long, L.L., Mutasim, D.F. (1999) Bowel bypass syndrome without bowel bypass. *Cutis*, **63**, 17–20.
9. Jorizzo, J.L., Schmalstieg, F.C., Dinehart, S.M. et al (1984) Bowel-associated dermatosis–arthritis syndrome. Immune complex-mediated vessel damage and increased neutrophil migration. *Arch Intern Med*, **144**, 738–740.
10. Delaney, T.A., Clay, C.D., Randell, P.L. (1989) The bowel-associated dermatosis–arthritis syndrome. *Australas J Dermatol*, **30**, 23–27.
11. McNeely, M.C., Jorizzo, J.L., Solomon, A.R. Jr et al (1986) Primary idiopathic cutaneous pustular vasculitis. *J Am Acad Dermatol*, **14**, 939–944.
12. Callen, J.P. (1985) Acute febrile neutrophilic dermatosis (Sweet's syndrome) and the related conditions of 'bowel bypass' syndrome and bullous pyoderma gangrenosum. *Dermatol Clin*, **3**, 153–163.
13. Bechtel, M.A., Callen, J.P. (1981) Acute febrile neutrophilic dermatosis. Sweet's syndrome. *Arch Dermatol*, **117**, 664–666.

Rheumatoid neutrophilic dermatitis

Clinical features

Rheumatoid neutrophilic dermatitis is an uncommon eruption seen in patients with rheumatoid arthritis. It presents most often as papules, nodules and plaques on the extensor surfaces of the extremities, neck and trunk that in some patients clinically resembles urticaria.[1–6] The lesions, which may ulcerate are often pruritic or painful and sometimes show an annular configuration.[2,7] The disease is uncommon as evidenced by documentation in just 2 of 142 patients with rheumatoid arthritis seeking medical attention for skin disorders in an academic clinic in Japan.[3] The presence of rheumatoid neutrophilic dermatitis correlates with the severity of a patient's joint disease.[3]

Typically, lesions last for up to several weeks.[1] In some patients, the condition resolves spontaneously without treatment, in others it responds to steroid, dapsone or sulphamethoxypyridamine therapy.[1,4,7]

Patients with seronegative arthritis but with cutaneous findings similar to rheumatoid neutrophilic dermatitis have recently been reported.[8,9]

Recently, Magro and Crowson have described sterile neutrophilic folliculitis associated with a Sweet's syndrome-like histology in a setting of systemic disease including rheumatoid arthritis, Crohn's disease, connective tissue disease, hepatitis, Behçet's disease, atopy, hematological dyscrasia, and mycobacterial infection.[10] A similar folliculocentric acute inflammatory process has also been documented in patients with ulcerative colitis.[11,12] It would seem probable that these reports reflect a similar condition or spectrum of disease that likely shares common histopathogenic mechanisms.

Pathogenesis and histological features

The pathogenesis of rheumatoid neutrophilic dermatitis is not understood but some authors have suggested that it may represent an immune-complex-mediated disease.[2,4]

Histologically, it is characterized by a dermal neutrophilic infiltrate with variable karyorrhexis (*Fig. 14.21*). In some cases, however, karyorrhexis is minimal or absent. Variable numbers of histiocytes, plasma cells and eosinophils may be present; abscess formation is sometimes a feature.[1,2,4] Occasionally, the inflammatory infiltrate extends into subcutaneous adipose tissue.[2,6] The overlying epidermis may show spongiosis and intraepidermal vesiculation.[4]

Differential diagnosis

Infection must be considered in the differential diagnosis of rheumatoid neutrophilic dermatitis, particularly given that patients are often at risk of infection as a result of immunosuppressive therapy. Furthermore, the cutaneous eruption may be treated with steroid therapy and, therefore, failure to diagnose an infective process could have disastrous consequences. Gram, AFB/acid fast and silver stains for microorganisms should be routinely performed and the diagnosis made only after infection has been excluded. We have encountered several patients with rheumatoid arthritis on steroid therapy who developed pustular infiltrates associated with *Mycobacterium chelonei* infection.

Pyoderma gangrenosum may show similar, if not identical, features but differs by progressive ulceration. It should be remembered that patients with rheumatoid arthritis may also develop pyoderma gangrenosum.[3] Clinical correlation is necessary to distinguish these entities. Pyoderma gangrenosum may form part of a continuum that may eventually prove to share pathogenetic mechanisms. To those who hold this view, the documentation of a patient with typical features of both pyoderma gangrenosum and rheumatoid neutrophilic dermatitis may not be surprising.[13]

Some authors have pointed out that rheumatoid neutrophilic dermatitis might be classified as a variant of Sweet's syndrome.[1] Certainly, the biopsy findings may be very similar. The lack of fever and the general malaise that accompany Sweet's syndrome are distinguishing clinical findings. The presence of gastrointestinal disease distinguishes rheumatoid neutrophilic dermatitis from bowel-associated dermatosis–arthritis syndrome. As with pyoderma gangrenosum, one might consider Sweet's syndrome and rheumatoid neutrophilic dermatitis to form a spectrum of disease.[1]

Patients with rheumatoid arthritis may sometimes develop lesions that show histological overlap with rheumatoid neutrophilic dermatitis but which can be distinguished by the presence of a palisading necrobiotic and granulomatous component. This spectrum, which also includes interstitial granulomatous dermatitis encountered in a setting of systemic disease (including rheumatoid arthritis), is discussed on page 320. Patients, predominantly adults, present with papules and nodules which particularly affect the extremities or trunk; these are often distributed in a linear pattern.[14,15] The presence of necrobiosis associated with a histio-

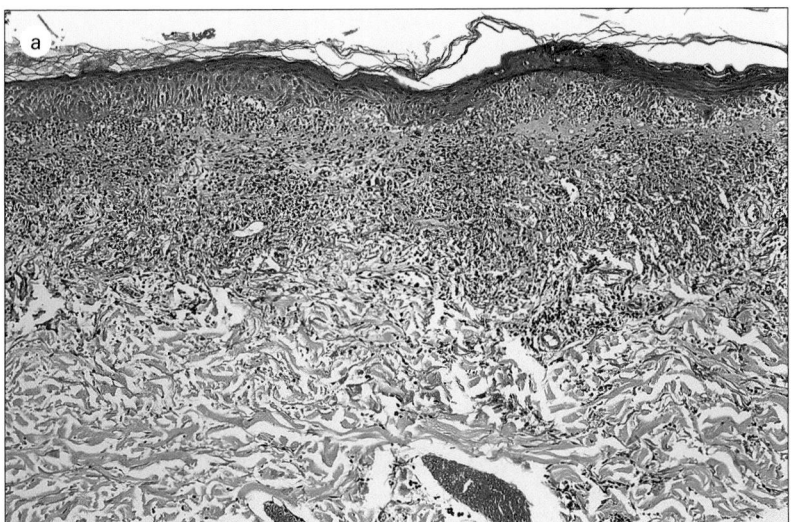
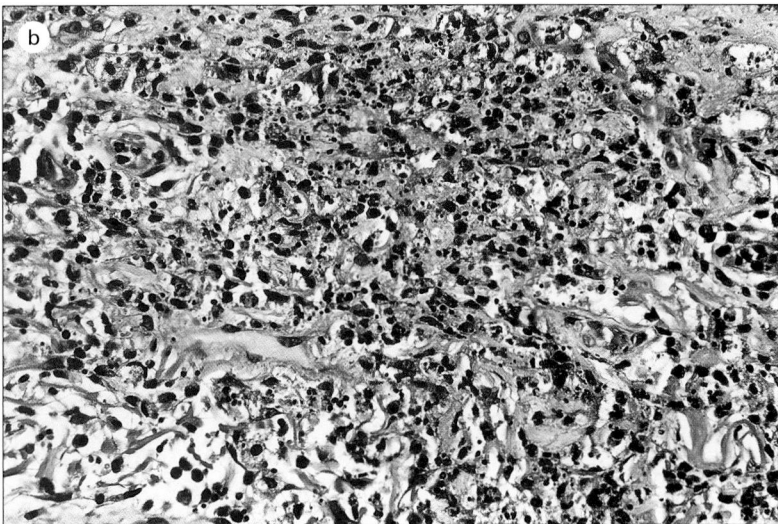

Fig. 14.21
(a, b) Rheumatoid neutrophilic dermatitis: there is an intense upper dermal neutrophilic infiltrate with conspicuous karyorrhexis. By courtesy of J. Cohen, MD, Dermatopathology Laboratory, Tucson, USA.

cytic response reminiscent of granuloma annulare or necrobiosis lipoidica in addition to acute inflammation and variable karyorrhexis, helps distinguish these lesions from typical rheumatoid neutrophilic dermatitis.

Lesions in which the neutrophilic infiltrate is associated with dermal papillary abscess formation may be mistaken for dermatitis herpetiformis, linear IgA disease and bullous lupus erythematosus. Immunofluorescence staining may be necessary in difficult cases.

The presence of vascular necrosis and fibrinoid change distinguishes rheumatoid neutrophilic dermatitis from vasculitis. It must be emphasized that a careful search for evidence of vasculitis is not simply an academic exercise, since patients with rheumatoid arthritis are also at risk of developing vasculitis. In fact, patients with rheumatoid arthritis may present with lesions histologically showing extravascular palisading granulomas, diffuse neutrophilic infiltrates or vasculitis (neutrophilic, lymphocytic or granulomatous). The different patterns may overlap and classification should be based on the dominant histological pattern.

References

1. Mashek, H.A., Pham, C.T., Helm, T.N. (1997) Rheumatoid neutrophilic dermatitis. *Arch Dermatol*, **133**, 757–760.
2. Hirota, T.K., Keough, G.C., David-Bajar, K. et al (1997) Rheumatoid neutrophilic dermatitis. *Cutis*, **60**, 203–205.
3. Yamamoto, T., Ohkubo, H., Nishioka, K. (1995) Skin manifestations associated with rheumatoid arthritis. *J Dermatol*, **22**, 324–329.
4. Lowe, L., Kornfeld, B., Clayman, J. et al (1992) Rheumatoid neutrophilic dermatitis. *J Cutan Pathol*, **19**, 48–53.
5. Sánchez, J.L., Cruz, A. (1990) Rheumatoid neutrophilic dermatitis. *J Am Acad Dermatol*, **22**, 922–925.
6. Scherbenske, J.M., Benson, P.M., Lupton, G.P. et al (1989) Rheumatoid neutrophilic dermatitis. *Arch Dermatol*, **125**, 1105–1108.
7. Hughes, J.R., Erhardt, C.C., Clement, M. (1995) Neutrophilic dermatosis in association with rheumatoid arthritis. *Clin Exp Dermatol*, **20**, 168–170.
8. Brown, T.S., Fearneyhough, P.K., Burruss, J.B. et al (2001) Rheumatoid neutrophilic dermatitis in a woman with seronegative rheumatoid arthritis. *J Am Acad Dermatol*, **45**, 596–600.
9. Gay-Crosier, F., Dayer, J.M., Chavaz, P. et al (2000) Rheumatoid neutrophilic dermatitis/Sweet's syndrome in a patient with seronegative rheumatoid arthritis. *Dermatology*, **201**, 185–187.
10. Magro, C.M., Crowson, A.N. (1998) Sterile neutrophilic folliculitis with perifollicular vasculopathy: a distinctive cutaneous reaction reflecting systemic disease. *J Cutan Pathol*, **25**, 215–221.
11. O'Loughlin, S., Perry, H.O. (1978) A diffuse pustular eruption associated with ulcerative colitis. *Arch Dermatol*, **114**, 1061–1064.
12. Geary, R.J., Long, L.L., Mutasim, D.F. (1999) Bowel bypass syndrome without bowel bypass. *Cutis*, **63**, 17–20.
13. Macaya, A., Servitje, O., Jucgla, A. et al (2000) Rheumatoid neutrophilic dermatitis associated with pyoderma gangrenosum. *Br J Dermatol*, **142**, 1234–1264.
14. Chu, P., Connolly, K., LeBoit, P.E. (1994) The histopathologic spectrum of palisaded neutrophilic and granulomatous dermatitis. *Arch Dermatol*, **130**, 1278–1283.
15. Sangueza, O.P., Caudell, M.D., Mengesha, Y.M. et al (2002) Palisaded neutrophilic granulomatous dermatitis in rheumatoid arthritis. *J Am Acad Dermatol*, **47**, 251–257.

Behçet's disease

Clinical features

Behçet's disease is often manifest as a vasculitis and therefore this complex disorder is also discussed on page 743.

Behçet's disease is a rare condition which was originally described as a combination of recurrent oral and genital ulceration with associated uveitis. However, it is now known to represent a systemic illness with lesions involving the joints and central nervous, vascular, respiratory, gastrointestinal and urogenital systems, in addition to mucous membranes and the integument (*Table 14.3*).[1–7] Although it is encountered worldwide, it shows a high incidence in Japan, Southeast Asia, the Middle East, Turkey and other countries bordering the Mediterranean. Behçet's disease shows a male predominance and most commonly presents in young adults with a peak incidence (of onset) in the third decade. The International Study Group established diagnostic criteria for Behçet's disease in 1990 that is summarized in *Table 14.4*.[4] It should be borne in mind that these criteria are somewhat controversial.[8]

Recurrent oral ulceration is an invariable feature of this condition. The ulcers measure up to 1 cm across and develop anywhere in the oral cavity, pharynx and even the larynx (*Fig. 14.22*).[9] They are exquisitely painful, and usually regress spontaneously within 14 days although they sometimes persist for much longer. A yellow, necrotic crust typically covers the ulcer floor.

Cutaneous lesions are common, recurrent and comprise a wide variety of manifestations including erythema nodosum-like lesions, usually on the lower extremities (*Fig. 14.23*).[10,11] Patients may also develop acneiform papules and pustules, furuncles, pyoderma and thrombophlebitis. In one very large study, papulopustular lesions (followed by erythema nodosum-like lesions) were the most commonly encountered

Table 14.3
Frequency of organ involvement in Behçet's disease

Sign or symptom	Percentage incidence
Oral ulcers	90–100
Genital ulcers	64–88
Ocular lesions	27–90
Cutaneous lesions	48–88
Joint manifestations	18–64
Neurologic features	10–29
Intestinal manifestations	0–59
Thrombophlebitis	10–37

Reproduced with permission from Abersfield. S.J. and Kurban, A.K. (1988) *Journal of the American Academy of Dermatology*, **19**, 767–779. Copyright © 1998 The American Academy of Dermatology.

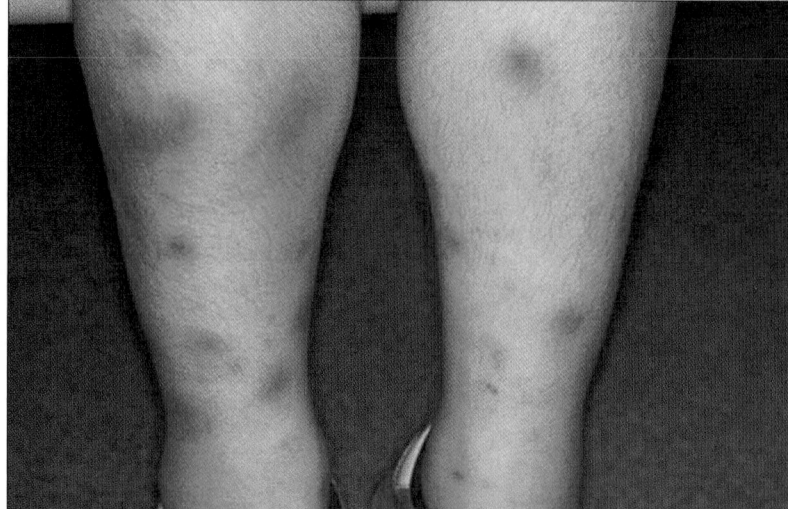

Fig. 14.23
Behçet's disease: erythema nodosum-like lesions. By courtesy of S-B Woo, MD. Brigham and Women's Hospital and Harvard Medical School, Boston, USA.

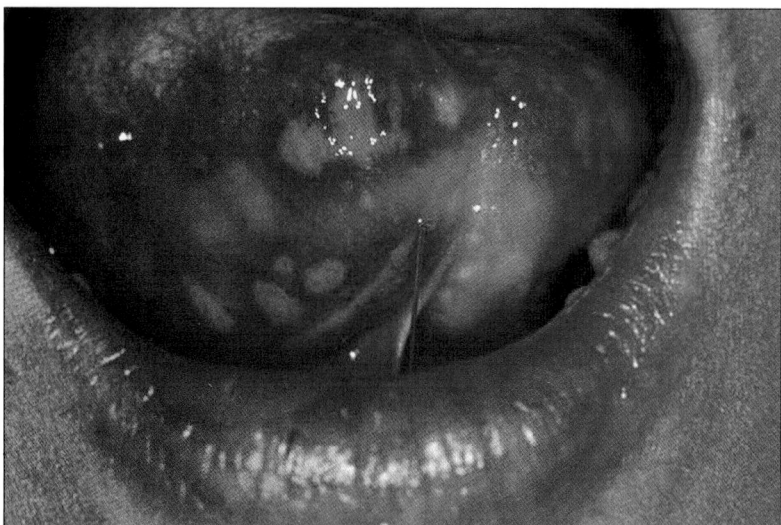

Fig. 14.22
Behçet's disease: multiple superficial ulcers are present. By courtesy of S-B Woo, MD. Brigham and Women's Hospital and Harvard Medical School, Boston, USA.

skin manifestation.[7] Typical of Behçet's disease and an important diagnostic clue is the development of sterile pustules at sites of mild skin trauma such as injection sites (pathergy) (*Fig. 14.24*).[12,13] Patients have also been described manifesting Sweet's syndrome-like features.[14] Genital lesions, similar in appearance to those of the oral mucosa, occur on the scrotum, penis, vagina and vulva (*Figs 14.25, 14.26*).[7]

Ocular lesions are important because if left untreated they may progress to cataracts and blindness. Almost any part of the ocular apparatus can be affected, but bilateral inflammation of the anterior segment (anterior uveitis), posterior uveitis with hypopyon and vitritis are said to be pathognomonic.[15] Conjunctivitis, corneal ulceration, choroiditis and retinal vessel involvement (arterial and venous vasculitis) may be additional features.

Joint involvement is not uncommon and usually affects the knees, ankles, elbows and wrists.[16] The affected joints are swollen, red, tender and painful. Aspiration reveals clear synovial fluid with only a few neutrophils. It is of particular interest that despite many years of arthritic symptoms, joint deformities do not develop.

Vascular changes in Behçet's disease are an important cause of both morbidity and mortality.[17] Thrombophlebitis is common and may affect both superficial and deep veins of the limbs. Superior and inferior vena caval obstruction are not uncommon complications. Vasculitis may affect virtually any artery and the development of an aneurysm with subsequent rupture is an important cause of death.

Respiratory lesions present as dyspnea, cough, pleuritic chest pain and hemoptysis.[18] The last, due to pulmonary artery–bronchial fistula formation, is an important cause of death. Lung involvement occurs in up to 5% of patients.[18]

Intestinal involvement particularly affects the ileocecal region; ulcers may be complicated by perforation, presenting as an intra-abdominal emergency necessitating surgical intervention.

Table 14.4
Behçet's disease: diagnostic criteria

Feature	Manifestation
Recurrent oral ulceration	Minor aphthous, major aphthous or herpetiform ulceration observed by physician or patient, which recurred at least three times in one 12-month period
Plus two of:	
Recurrent genital ulceration	Aphthous ulceration or scarring, observed by physician or patient
Eye lesions	Anterior uveitis, posterior uveitis or cells in vitreous on slit lamp examination *or* Retinal vasculitis observed by ophthalmologist
Skin lesions	Erythema nodosum observed by physician or patient, pseudofolliculitis or papulopustular lesions; or acneiform nodules observed by patient not on corticosteroid treatment
Positive pathergy test	Read by physician at 24–48 hours

Findings applicable only in absence of other clinical explanations. Reproduced with permission from the International Study Group for Behçet's Disease (1990) *Lancet*, **335**, 1078–1080.

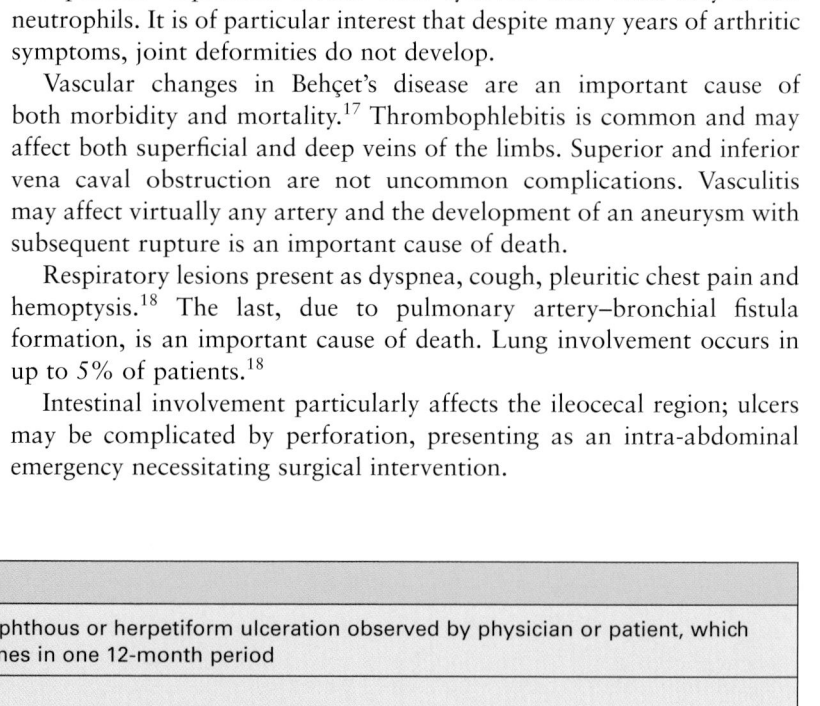

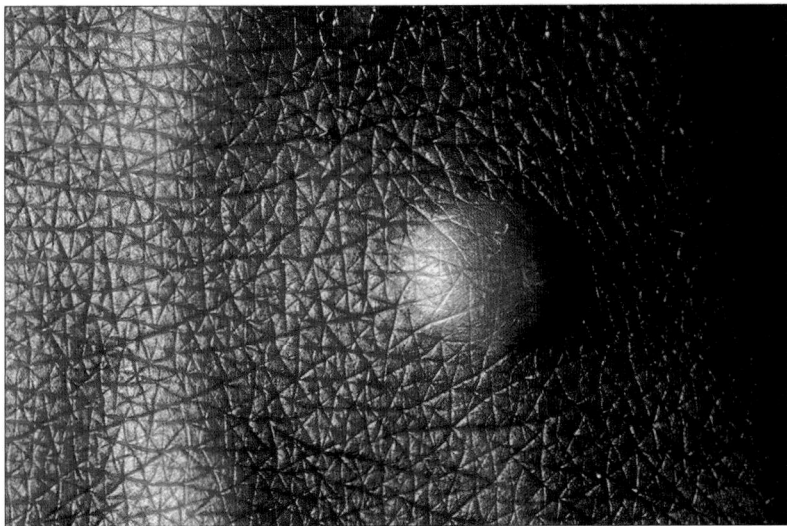

Fig. 14.24
Behçet's disease: this pustule developed at the site of a previous venipuncture. Reproduced with permission from du Vivier, A. (2002) Atlas of clinical dermatology, 3rd edn. Edinburgh: Churchill Livingstone.

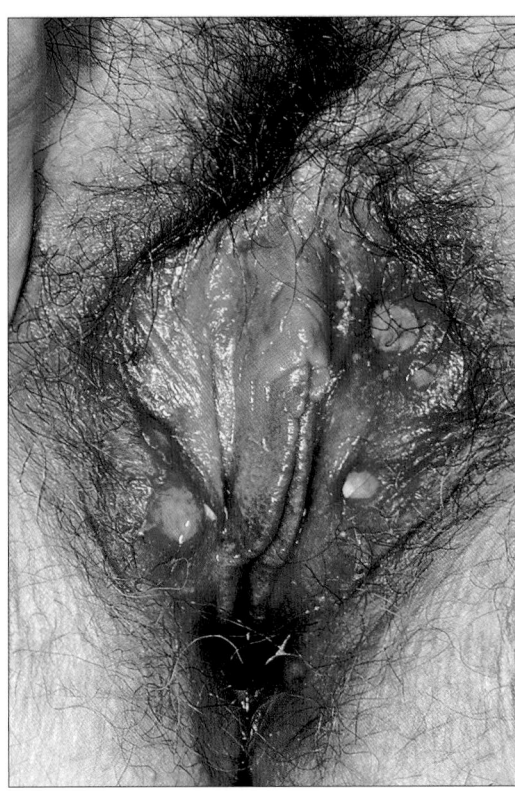

Fig. 14.26
Behçet's disease: multiple superficial vulval ulcers are present. Reproduced with permission from du Vivier, A. (2002) Atlas of clinical dermatology, 3rd edn. Edinburgh: Churchill Livingstone.

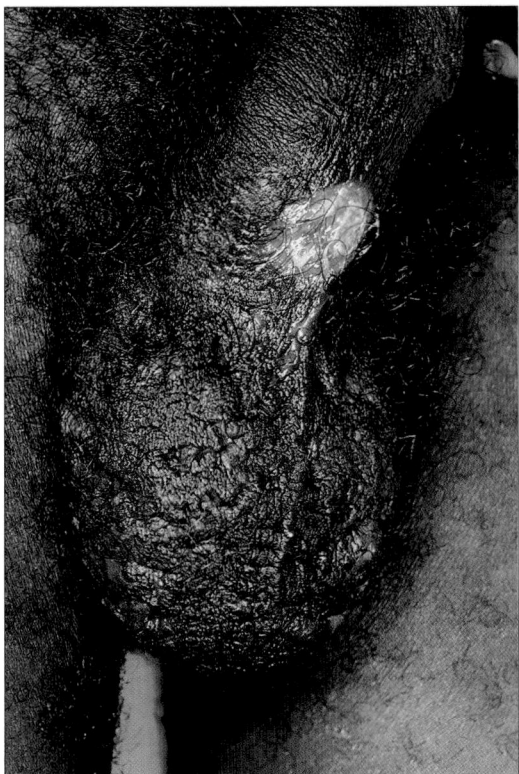

Fig. 14.25
Behçet's disease: there is a large ulcer at the root of the penis. Reproduced with permission from du Vivier, A. (2002) Atlas of clinical dermatology, 3rd edn. Edinburgh: Churchill Livingstone.

Nervous system changes, which are associated with a poor prognosis, occur in up to 25% of patients.[17] Lesions may develop anywhere in the central and peripheral components and, therefore, virtually any neurological sign or symptom may be seen, including sensory losses, strokes, and spinal cord, cranial and peripheral nerve lesions.

A study of relative organ system involvement has led to a subclassification of a spectrum of Behçet's disease.[19,20] The mortality of Behçet's disease is, however, surprisingly low, of the order of 2–4%.

Pathogenesis and histological features

The pathogenesis of Behçet's disease is poorly understood. Data and theories regarding the pathogenesis of Behçet's disease are presented on page 743.

The diagnosis of Behçet's disease is essentially clinical. The histological features are in themselves largely non-specific and include both lymphocytic and necrotizing vasculitis of the superficial postcapillary venules with associated fibrinoid necrosis (see *Fig. 15.86*).[20–23] In one study, nearly 50% of patients had evidence of vasculitis.[24] Often, however, such vasculitic change appears to be a consequence, rather than a cause, of the associated dermal or mucosal inflammatory changes.[22] Endothelial swelling may be a feature and there is often an associated lymphocytic perivascular infiltrate although sometimes neutrophils are abundant.

Additional histological features include a diffuse dermal neutrophilic infiltrate with or without abscess formation, corresponding clinically to the pustular lesions, acute folliculitis and acneiform pustular changes (*Figs 14.27, 14.28*). The erythema nodosum-like lesions correspond to necrotizing vasculitis of the subcutaneous vessels, usually associated with thrombosis. Septal and lobular panniculitis have also been described.[9] Superficial thrombophlebitis is present in up to 30% of patients (see *Fig. 15.88*).[19] Erythema multiforme-like lesions show the features of the classical lesion (see p. 238). The pathergic lesions have been reported as showing leukocytoclastic vasculitis or Sweet's syndrome-like features.[12] Oral lesions and genital ulcers show non-specific ulceration, accompanied in some instances by leukocytoclastic or lymphocytic vasculitis (*Figs 14.29, 14.30*).

Pulmonary involvement is characterized by pulmonary artery vasculitis, sometimes also affecting the veins and capillaries.[18] Thrombosis, infarction, hemorrhage and the development of aneurysm are important sequelae. The inflammation is usually transmural and may be linked with damage to the associated elastic tissue. Older destructive vascular lesions are characterized by fibrous scarring.

Early stage cerebral lesions are characterized by a perivenular lymphocytic infiltrate. In more advanced lesions there is extensive demyelination resembling multiple sclerosis.[17]

Differential diagnosis

Given the myriad non-specific histological manifestations that Behçet's disease may produce, it comes as no surprise that the differential

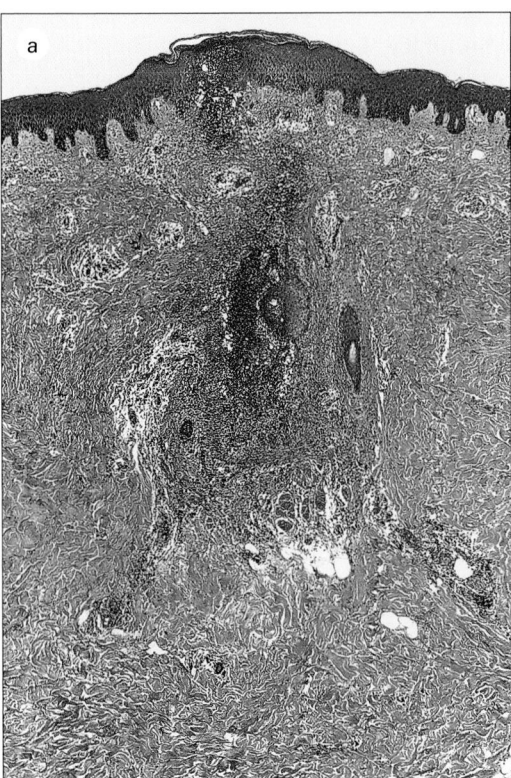

Fig. 14.27
(a, b) Behçet's disease: suppurative folliculitis.

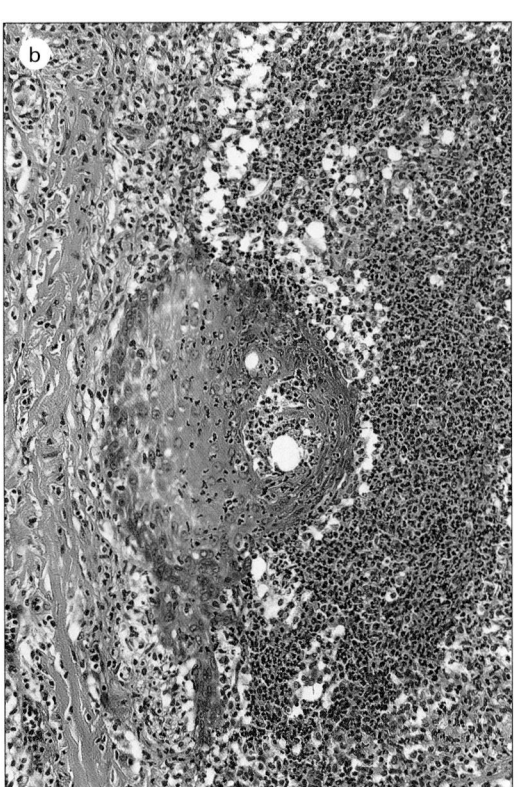

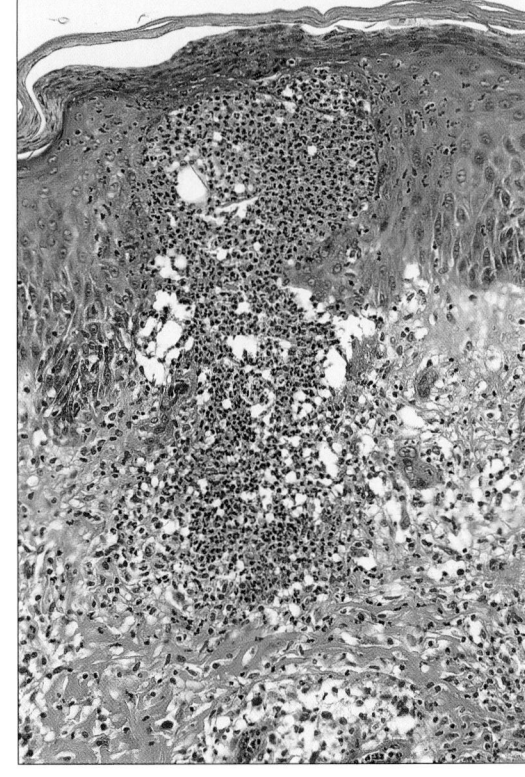

Fig. 14.28
Behçet's disease: subcorneal pustules present as acneiform lesions.

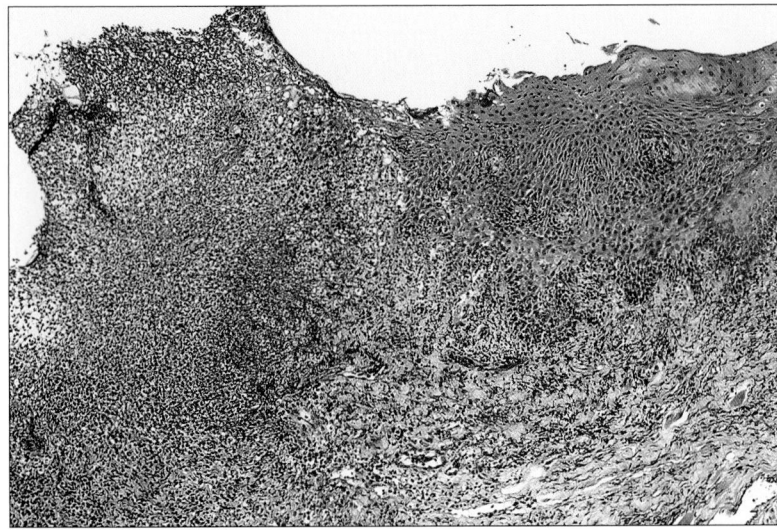

Fig. 14.29
Behçet's disease: oral ulceration. The features are non-specific.

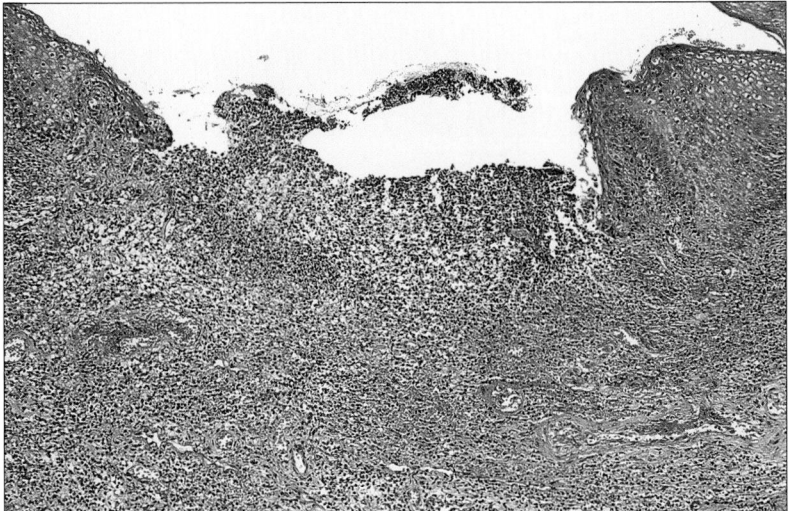

Fig. 14.30
Behçet's disease: vulval ulcer. The features are non-specific.

diagnosis is usually broad. The authors of one large study stated that clinical data are most important in establishing a diagnosis and suggest that the role of biopsy is only to confirm the clinical impression.[7] Other authors propose that biopsy is critical to evaluate for vessel-based pathology as clinical distinction from pustular (non-vascular) lesions may not be possible.[8]

The differential diagnosis includes other causes of folliculitis, infection, erythema nodosum, connective tissue disease, neutrophilic and lymphocytic vasculitis, and neutrophilic dermatoses such as Sweet's syndrome and pyoderma gangrenosum.

References

1. Chajeck, T., Fainaru, M. (1975) Behçet's disease: report of 41 cases and a review of the literature. *Medicine*, 54, 179–195.
2. Hombal, S.M., Ahmed, A.R. (1986) Behçet's disease. In: Thiers, B.H., Dobson, R.L. (eds) Pathogenesis of skin disease. New York: Churchill Livingstone, pp 257–265.
3. Helm, T.N., Camisa, C., Allen, C. et al (1991) Clinical features of Behçet's disease. *Oral Surg Oral Med Oral Pathol*, 72, 30–34.
4. International Study Group for Behçet's Disease (1990) Criteria for diagnosis of Behçet's disease. *Lancet*, 335, 1078–1080.
5. Jorizzo, J.L., Rogers, R.S. (1990) Behçet's disease: an update based on the International Conference held in Rochester, Minnesota, September, 14th and 15th 1989. *J Am Acad Dermatol*, 23, 738–741.
6. Shimizu, T., Ehrlich, G.E., Inaba, G. (1979) Behçet's disease (Behçet's syndrome). *Semin Arthritis Rheum*, 8, 223–260.
7. Balabanova, M., Calmia, K.T., Perniciaro, C. (1999) A study of the cutaneous manifestations of Behçet's disease from the United States. *J Am Acad Dermatol*, 41, 540–545.

8. Jorizzo, J.L., Abernathy, J.L., White, W.L. et al (1995) Mucocutaneous criteria for the diagnosis of Behçets disease: an analysis of clinicopathologic data from multiple centers. *J Am Acad Dermatol*, **32**, 968–976.
9. Chajek, T., Fainaru, M. (1980) Behçet's disease. In: Parker, C.W. (ed.) Clinical immunology. Philadelphia: W.B. Saunders, p 667.
10. Tokjoro, Y., Seto, T., Abe, Y. et al (1977) Skin lesions in Behçet's disease. *Int J Dermatol*, **16**, 227–243.
11. Chun, S.I., Su, W.P.D., Lee, S. et al (1989) Erythema nodosum-like lesions in Behçets syndrome: a histopathologic study of 30 cases. *J Cutan Pathol*, **16**, 259–265.
12. Jorizzo, J.L., Solomon, A.R., Canallo, T. (1985) Behçet's syndrome: immunopathologic and histopathologic assessment of pathergy lesions is useful in diagnosis and follow-up. *Arch Pathol Lab Med*, **109**, 747–751.
13. Sobel, J.D., Haim, S., Shafrir, A. et al (1973) Cutaneous hyperactivity in Behçet's disease. *Dermatologica*, **146**, 350–356.
14. Cho, K.H., Shin, K.S., Sohn, S.J. et al (1989) Behçet's disease with Sweet's syndrome-like presentation – a report of six cases. *Clin Exp Dermatol*, **14**, 20–24.
15. Masuda, K., Inaba, G., Mizushima, H. et al (1975) A nationwide survey of Behçet's disease in Japan. *Jpn J Ophthalmol*, **19**, 278–285.
16. Yurdakul, S., Yazici, H., Tüzün, Y. et al (1983) The arthritis of Behçet's disease: a prospective study. *Ann Rheum Dis*, **42**, 505–515.
17. O'Duffy, J.D. (1990) Vasculitis in Behçet's disease. *Rheum Dis Clin North Am*, **16**, 423–431.
18. Raz, I., Okon, E., Chajek-Shaul, T. (1989) Pulmonary manifestations in Behçet's syndrome. *Chest*, **95**, 585–589.
19. Arbesfield, S.J., Kurban, A.K. (1988) Behçet's disease: new perspectives on an enigmatic syndrome. *J Am Acad Dermatol*, **19**, 767–779.
20. Lehner, T., Barnes, C.G. (1979) Criteria for diagnosis and classification of Behçet's disease. In: Lehner, T., Barnes, C.G. (eds) Behçet's syndrome, clinical and immunological features. New York: Academic Press.
21. Eglin, R.P., Lehner, T., Subak-Sharpe, J.H. (1982) Detection of RNA complementary to herpes simplex virus in mononuclear cells from patients with Behçet's syndrome and recurrent oral ulcers. *Lancet*, **2**, 1356–1358.
22. Chun, S.I., Su, W.P.D., Lee, S. (1990) Histopathologic study of cutaneous lesions in Behçet's syndrome. *J Dermatol*, **17**, 333–341.
23. Jorizzo, J.L. (1986) Behçet's disease: an update based on the 1985 conference in London. *Arch Dermatol*, **122**, 556–558.
24. Chen, K., Kawahara, Y., Miyakawa, S. et al (1997) Cutaneous vasculitis in Behçet's disease: a clinical and histopathologic study of 20 patients. *J Am Acad Dermatol*, **36**, 689–696.

Arthropod and arachnid bite reactions

Clinical features

The vast majority of insect bites pose little more than a minor annoyance. The reaction that results from a given bite depends on the type of offending insect and the patient's immune response. The clinical response to a bite may vary from a trivial erythematous papule to a large nodule associated with marked pruritus and ulceration. Vesicles may sometimes be seen in severe reactions. Careful inspection will often reveal a punctum at the site where insect mouth parts entered skin.

While arthropod bites are rarely of clinical importance, reactions following the bite of certain arachnids may lead to a more serious clinical lesion. Many different species of spiders may bite humans, and reactions to the most significant and well-described – the brown recluse and the black widow – are detailed.[1-3]

Brown recluse spider

The brown recluse spider (*Loxosceles reclusa*) bite begins as a painful bluish macule, papule or nodule, often with a bruise-like appearance. A central punctum is commonly observed. The lesion is often trivial. However, in some patients, blistering and ulceration, often progressing to a large necrotic lesion, is a feature.[4] Chronic ulceration mimicking pyoderma gangrenosum may rarely ensue.[5] The brown recluse is most commonly encountered in Midwest, south–central, and southeastern United States and is easily identified by a violin-shaped marking on the cephalothorax that gives it its vernacular name of 'fiddleback' spider. Sphingomyelinase-D in the venom of the brown recluse spider is thought to be responsible for the extensive necrosis that results in some patients. Spider bites may be associated with morbilliform rash, malaise, fever, nausea, hemoglobinuria, arthralgias and vomiting.[4,6,7] More serious complications (e.g. renal failure, shock, disseminated intravascular coagulation and intravascular hemolysis) have also been described.[6,8]

Widow spiders

The five species of widow spiders found in the United States, including the notorious black widow (*Latrodectus mactans*), are most commonly encountered in the southern states. Compared with the brown recluse, bites by widow spiders are much less commonly encountered by health care providers. The bite often shows a targetoid appearance with a pale center surrounded by an outer erythematous rim.[9] A bite from a black widow spider is commonly associated with severe pain in the vicinity of the bite as well as systemic symptoms such as general malaise, abdominal pain, nausea, headache and muscle spasms.[4,6,9] Occasionally, patients die as a result of a widow spider bite.[8,10]

Hobo spider

Recently, the Hobo spider (*Tegenaria agrestis*) has been implicated as a cause of significant bite reactions in the Pacific Northwest.[11]

Histological features

Just as there is a spectrum of clinical response to an insect bite, the histopathological features also vary. The typical arthropod bite reaction, such as follows a mosquito bite, is characterized by a wedge-shaped polymorphic inflammatory infiltrate composed of lymphocytes, histiocytes, eosinophils and sometimes neutrophils (*Fig. 14.31*). Spongiosis (occasionally with vesicle formation) and variable dermal edema are also seen. Ulceration with scale-crust commonly forms in excoriated lesions. In some cases, insect mouth parts are identified in the center of the lesion. In our experience, this is particularly common in biopsies of tick bites.

As with arthropod bite reactions, the histological sequelae from arachnid bite are variable. Compared with arthropod bites, arachnid bite reactions are typically associated with more extensive necrosis and suppurative inflammation. Necrosis may extend to involve subcutaneous adipose tissue and muscle.[4] Variable numbers of eosinophils and lymphocytes are present and marked dermal edema is often a feature.[4] Secondary vasculitis, involving vessels within the lesion or in the immediate surrounding tissue, may be a feature in some cases. Injection of brown recluse spider venom into rabbits results in 'mummified' coagulation necrosis, a mixed inflammatory cell infiltrate and vasculitis.[12]

Differential diagnosis

The histological findings in biopsies of insect bites, short of identifying mouth parts in the specimen, are non-specific. The main differential diagnosis includes hypersensitivity reactions. The characteristic wedge shape of the infiltrate is an important clue to the diagnosis. The presence of large atypical lymphocytes helps distinguish lymphomatoid papulosis from an arthropod bite reaction. Bite reactions with a dense eosinophil-rich infiltrate may be indistinguishable from Wells' syndrome. The occasional presence of flame figures heightens the similarity. Clinical correlation may be necessary to distinguish these two conditions.

The histological findings associated with arachnid bite are also non-specific. Arachnid bites must be distinguished from pyoderma gangrenosum, factitial disease, primary vasculitis, and infection including cellulitis and necrotizing fasciitis.

References

1. Forks, T.P. (2000) Brown recluse spider bites. *J Am Board Fam Prac*, **13**, 415–423.
2. King, L.E. (1987) Spider bites. *Arch Dermatol*, **123**, 41–43.
3. Wong, R.C., Hughes, S.E., Voorhees, J.J. (1987) Spider bites. *Arch Dermatol,* **123**, 98–104.
4. Anderson, P.C. (1997) Spider bites in the United States. *Dermatol Clin*, **15**, 307–311.
5. Rees, R.S., Fields, J.P., King, L.E. Jr (1985) Do brown recluse spider bites produce pyoderma gangrenosum? *South Med J*, **78**, 283–287.
6. Carbonaro, P.A., Janniger, C.K., Schwartz, R.A. (1995) Spider bite reactions. *Cutis*, **56**, 256–259.
7. Sams, H.H., Hearth, S.B., Long, L.L. et al (2001) Nineteen documented cases of *Loxosceles reclusa* envenomation. *J Am Acad Dermatol*, **44**, 603–608.
8. Williams, S.T., Khare, V.K., Johnston, G.A. et al (1995) Severe intravascular hemolysis associated with brown recluse spider envenomation. *Am J Clin Pathol*, **104**, 463–467.

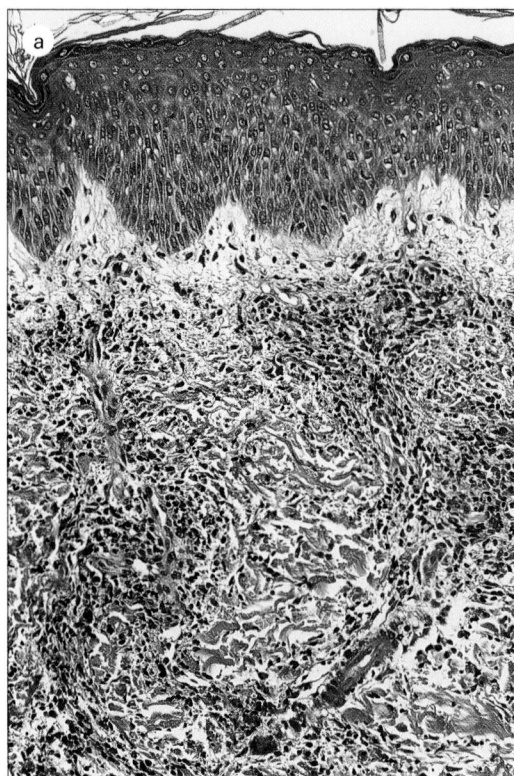

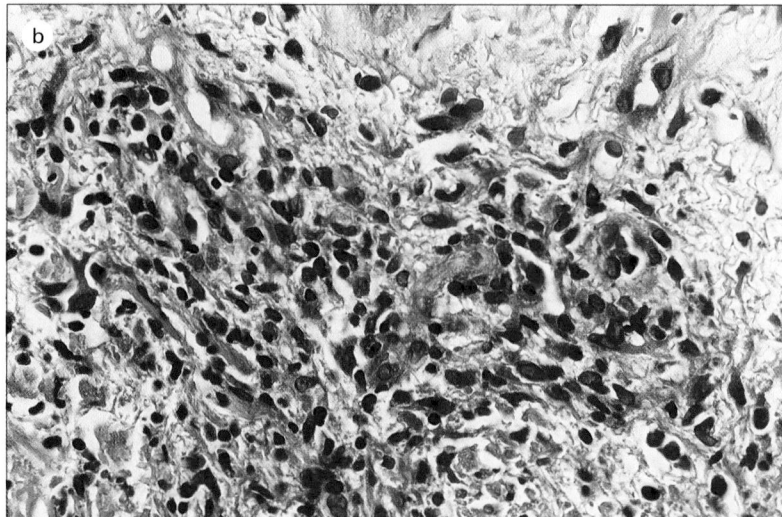

Fig. 14.31
(a, b) Arthropod bite reaction: there is a heavy perivascular and interstitial infiltrate with conspicuous eosinophils.

9.   Clark, R.F., Wethern-Kestner, S., Vance, M.V. et al (1992) Clinical presentation and treatment of black widow envenomation: a review of 163 cases. *Ann Emerg Med*, **21**, 782–787.
10. Wilson, D.C., King, L.E. (1990) Spiders and spider bites. *Dermatol Clin*, **8**, 277–286.
11. Morbidity and Mortality Report (1996) Necrotic arachnidism – Pacific Northwest, 1988–1996. *MMMR*, **45**, 433–436.
12. Elston, D.M., Eggers, J.S., Schmidt, W.E. et al (2000) Histological findings after brown recluse spider envenomation. *Am J Dermatopathol*, **22**, 242–246.

Seabather's eruption and coelenterate stings

Clinical features

Seabather's eruption, sometimes referred to as 'sea lice', is attributed stings from larval forms of coelenterates, often the thimble jellyfish (*Linuche unguiculata*).[1–4] Typically, patients develop a papular eruption in areas covered by the bathing suit, often accentuated where the suit is tight fitting, such as the waistline. The eruption is usually pruritic and may cause a burning sensation. Patients sometimes experience systemic symptoms such as malaise, fever, nausea, diarrhea and vomiting.

Reactions to coelenterates such as jellyfish vary from minor irritation to fatal reactions following stings by highly venomous species such as the 'box jellyfish' (*Chironex fleckeri* and *Chiropsalmus quadrigatus*).[5] Jellyfish stings are often erythematous and show a 'whiplash-like' appearance.[5]

Histological features

Biopsy of papules of seabather's eruption shows a non-specific perivascular inflammatory infiltrate composed of variable numbers of lymphocytes, eosinophils and neutrophils.[2] Apparently, epidermal changes are not usually a feature.[2]

Only few authors have reported the histological findings following reaction to coelenterate stings. Non-specific perivascular inflammation with lymphocytes and variable numbers of eosinophils appear to be characteristic. Some cases show dense, sheet-like aggregates of lympho-

cytes and histiocytes.[6] Variable dermal edema may be an additional feature. Spongiosis and vesicle formation are also sometimes seen.[6–8] One fatal case showed only vascular congestion without significant inflammation, a histological picture that likely reflects the fact that the patient died only 40 minutes after envenomation.[5] Only occasionally are nematocyst capsules and tubes identified.[5,8]

Differential diagnosis

The histological differential diagnosis of reactions to coelenterates includes other hypersensitivity reactions. Short of finding nematocysts, the diagnosis requires clinical correlation.

References

1.   Ubillos, S.S., Vuong, D., Sinnot, J.T. et al (1995) Seabather's eruption. *Southern Med J*, **88**, 1163–1165.
2.   Wong, D.E., Meinkin, T.L., Rosen, L.B. et al (1994) Seabather's eruption. Clinical, histologic and immunologic features. *J Am Acad Dermatol*, **30**, 399–406.
3.   Tomchik, R.S., Russell, M.T., Szmant, A.M. et al (1993) Clinical perspectives on seabather's eruption, also known as 'sea lice'. *JAMA*, **269**, 1669–1672.
4.   Freudenthal, A.R., Joseph, P.R. (1993) Seabather's eruption. *N Engl J Med*, **329**, 542–544.
5.   Strutton, G., Lumley, J. (1988) Cutaneous light microscopic and ultrastructural changes in a fatal case of jellyfish envenomation. *J Cutan Pathol*, **15**, 1249–1255.
6.   Reed, K.M., Bronstein, B.R., Baden, H.P. (1984) Delayed and persistent cutaneous reactions to coelenterates. *J Am Acad Dermatol*, **10**, 462–466.
7.   Pierard, G.E., Letot, B., Pierard-Franchimont, C. (1990) Histologic study of delayed reactions to coelenterates. *J Am Acad Dermatol*, **22**, 599–601.
8.   Letot, B., Pierard-Franchimont, C., Pierard, G.E. (1990) Acute reactions to coelenterates. *Dermatologica*, **180**, 224–227.

Erythema marginatum rheumaticum

Clinical features

Once a common disease, it was thought that, with the effective antibiotic treatment of the causative infection, rheumatic fever would become of historical interest only. However, there has been a resurgence of the condition over the past few decades.[1-4]

Rheumatic fever is an immunologically mediated disease that follows an infection with group A beta-hemolytic streptococcus. The infection causes pharyngitis and carditis. Additional features include polyarthritis, a neurological movement disorder known as Sydenham's chorea, and subcutaneous nodules. Carditis, characterized by a valvular disease, is a major cause of morbidity and mortality.

Erythema marginatum rheumaticum is the designation given to the distinctive annular or polycyclic eruption of rheumatic fever. The lesions are non-pruritic, multiple, flat, erythematous maculopapules, which change and spread over hours, and are often recurrent. The trunk and proximal extremities are most frequently affected.[2] The hands and face may also be involved.[4] By definition, erythema marginatum rheumaticum is associated with rheumatic fever, but only occurs in 1–18% of patients.[1] Some studies have failed to identify significant human leukocyte antigen (HLA) associations.[3,5] However, there are conflicting reports of certain HLA subtypes and the disease.[6]

The subcutaneous nodules of rheumatic fever are discussed in detail on page 317.

Pathogenesis and histological features

The pathogenesis of rheumatic fever is incompletely understood. It appears likely that it results from a hypersensitivity reaction triggered by streptococcal infection. Specifically, patients develop autoantibodies that cross-react with streptococcal antigen.[7] For example, autoantibodies cross-react with cardiac muscle, causing carditis. Mice immunized with the streptococcal M protein develop myocarditis.[7]

Variable numbers of neutrophils (sometimes associated with leukocytoclasis) and mononuclear cells are present in the infiltrate.[5,8] Importantly, however, there is no evidence of vasculitis. Dermal papillary neutrophil microabscesses have occasionally been described.[5]

It has been reported that rare cases are devoid of neutrophils and the infiltrate is instead composed of lymphocytes and histiocytes.[9]

Differential diagnosis

The biopsy findings in erythema marginatum are non-specific. Similar histological features may be seen in patients with Still's disease and acute lupus erythematosus. Careful search for vascular damage is necessary to exclude leukocytoclastic vasculitis. Special stains and culture to rule out an infectious etiology may sometimes be required. Urticaria can demonstrate perivascular neutrophils but additionally it shows significant dermal edema, and interstitial inflammation, including eosinophils and neutrophils.

References

1. Stollerman, G.H. (1997) Changing streptococci and prospects for the global eradication of rheumatic fever. *Perspect Biol Med*, 40, 165–189.
2. Hurley, H.J., Hurley, J.P. (1984) The gyrate erythemas. *Semin Dermatol*, 3, 327–335.
3. Leirisalo, M., Kovuranta, P., Laitenen, O. (1980) Rheumatic fever and its sequels in children. A follow-up study with HLA analysis. *J Rheumatol*, 7, 506–514.
4. White, J.W. (1985) Gyrate erythema. *Dermatol Clin*, 3, 129–139.
5. Bywaters, E.G.L. (1987) Skin manifestations of rheumatic disease. In: Fitzpatrick, T.B., Eisen, A.Z., Wolff, K. (eds) Dermatology in general medicine. New York: McGraw Hill, pp 1859–1863.
6. Gibofsky, A., Kerwar, S., Zabriskie, J.B. (1998) Rheumatic fever. The relationships between host, microbe, and genetics. *Rheum Dis Clin North Am*, 24, 237–259.
7. Cunningham, M.W. (2000) Pathogenesis of group A streptococcal infections. *Clin Microbiol Rev*, 13, 470–511.
8. Troyer, C., Grossman, M., Silvers, D.N. (1983) Erythema marginatum in rheumatic fever: early diagnosis by skin biopsy. *J Am Acad Dermatol*, 8, 724–728.
9. Sahn, E.E., Maize, J.C., Silver, R.M. (1989) Erythema marginatum: an unusual histopathologic manifestation. *J Am Acad Dermatol*, 21, 145–147.

Still's disease

Clinical features

Juvenile rheumatoid arthritis (Still's disease) is a heterogeneous group of disorders that share in common an inflammatory arthritis with many features similar to rheumatoid arthritis in adults. Juvenile rheumatoid arthritis patients, however, are seronegative for rheumatoid factor. There are marked differences in prevalence from region to region. Whites in Europe, the United States and Australia (4 per 1000) have the highest prevalence.[1,2] One study has suggested that the incidence of the disease is decreasing.[3] This same study also documented incidence peaks suggesting a cyclical pattern.[3] Other studies have suggested seasonal variation in certain regions such as the Canadian prairies.[4] However, such seasonal onset has not been apparent in other areas of Canada, in Denmark or in Japan.[4-7]

Juvenile rheumatoid arthritis is classified into three variants: pauciarticular, polyarticular and systemic onset.

- The *pauciarticular* (oligoarticular) form is characterized by arthritis involving up to a maximum of four joints. Systemic manifestations are uncommon. Uveitis, however, is frequently present.
- The *polyarticular* form is manifest by symmetrical arthritis typically involving the knees, wrists and ankles. Fever and hepatosplenomegaly are sometimes present.
- The *systemic-onset* form is a severe variant in which lymphadenopathy, fever and rash precede development of polyarteritis which most often affects the knees, ankles and wrists.[8]

Additional features may include hepatosplenomegaly and effusions. In general, the term Still's disease is restricted to this form of juvenile rheumatoid arthritis; however, some authors use it for any of the variants. The majority of patients with the systemic form have the characteristic rash in contrast to the pauci- and polyarticular variants in which only 20–40% are affected.[8]

The rash of Still's disease is evanescent, and is characterized by a faint erythematous (salmon-colored), sometimes pruritic, macular eruption involving the trunk, extremities, head and neck.[8-10] Often, there is an association between onset of rash and febrile episodes, particularly in the late afternoon or evening.[8,10] The rash is typically present for only a short period of time, usually a matter of a few hours; however, some lesions persist for more than 24 hours.[8,10] The rash characteristically reappears without regard for its former distribution.[10] Macules are often only a few millimeters in size but often become confluent to form larger lesions. Central pallor is sometimes a feature of the latter.[9] The eruption – which may persist for weeks to years – tends to localize to areas of mild trauma and pressure.[8,10]

Laboratory abnormalities include elevated ESR and C-reactive protein. Serum immunoglobulins may also be elevated. Patients sometimes have leukocytosis, anemia and thrombocytosis. Occasional patients have rheumatoid factor and some authors consider this to be *bona fide* juvenile rheumatoid arthritis. Antinuclear antibodies are commonly found in patients with pauci- and polyarticular variants of the disease.[7] In contrast, antinuclear antibody is usually not present in the systemic-onset form.

It is very difficult to predict the outcome of this disease in the individual patient. Approximately 50% of patients experience symptoms into adulthood. Progression of juvenile rheumatoid arthritis to systemic lupus erythematosus (SLE) has been documented.[11]

Still's disease is not limited to the pediatric population. The disease has also been documented in adults, albeit rarely.[12]

Pathogenesis and histological features

The pathogenesis of juvenile rheumatoid arthritis is poorly understood. It would seem likely, however, that the various subtypes have different etiologies. Thus IL-2 mRNA is detected more often in pauciarticular juvenile rheumatoid arthritis than in the polyarticular form.[13] IFN-γ mRNA may be detected in 33% of systemic-onset juvenile rheumatoid arthritis in contrast to 85% in the other forms.[13]

Data suggesting that the incidence of the disease is decreasing with cyclical peaks raise the possibility that environmental factors may play a role in the pathogenesis.[3] The demonstration of T-cell oligoclonal expansions within synovial tissue suggests that an antigen or group of antigens may trigger the disease.[14] The nature of such triggering factors, however, has not yet been identified.

The prevalence of autoimmune disease is increased in relatives of patients with juvenile rheumatoid arthritis compared with control subjects, suggesting that shared susceptibility genes may be of importance in the pathogenesis of juvenile rheumatoid arthritis and other autoimmune diseases.[15]

The influence of various HLA alleles and their association with juvenile rheumatoid arthritis has been an area of considerable interest and has yielded a complex picture of the relationship between certain HLA alleles and risk of disease. HLA-A2, DR8, DR5 and DPB1*0201 are associated with increased risk of pauciarticular disease early in life.[16] While B27 and DR4 may be protective in the early years, these alleles seem confer increased risk of disease later in life.[16]

CD4 reactive T-lymphocytes are the predominant cell type in inflamed synovium.[17] As with other autoimmune disorders, production of predominantly Th1 cytokines (IFN-γ and IFN-β) has been observed in the synovium of patients with juvenile rheumatoid arthritis.[17]

The biopsy findings are non-specific and variable. There is often a perivascular neutrophilic infiltrate.[9] In some cases, mononuclear cells are the predominant cell type.[8,10]

Differential diagnosis

The histological findings, as indicated above, are variable and non-specific. Clinical correlation is necessary to establish the diagnosis. The differential diagnosis includes infection, and culture and stains for organisms should be performed when necessary. The absence of fibrinoid change and necrosis of vessel walls helps to distinguish the lesions from leukocytoclastic vasculitis.

References

1. Manners, P.J., Diepeveen, D.A. (1996) Prevalence of juvenile chronic arthritis in a population of 12-year-old children in urban Australia. *Pediatrics*, **98**, 84–90.
2. Oen, K. (2000) Comparative epidemiology of the rheumatic diseases in children. *Curr Opin Rheumatol*, **12**, 410–414.
3. Peterson, L.S., Mason, T., Nelson, A.M. et al (1996) Juvenile rheumatoid arthritis in Rochester, Minnesota 1960–1993. Is the epidemiology changing? *Arthritis Rheum*, **39**, 1385–1390.
4. Feldman, B.M., Birdi, N., Boone, J.E. et al (1996) Seasonal onset of systemic onset juvenile rheumatoid arthritis. *J Pediatr*, **129**, 513–528.
5. Neilsen, H.E., Dorup, J., Herlin, T. et al (1999) Epidemiology of juvenile rheumatoid chronic arthritis: risk dependent on sibship, parental income, and housing. *J Rheumatol*, **26**, 1600–1605.
6. Uziel, Y., Pomeranz, A., Brik, R. et al (1999) Seasonal variation in systemic onset juvenile rheumatoid arthritis in Israel. *J Rheumatol*, **26**, 1187–1189.
7. Falcini, F., Cimaz, R. (2000) Juvenile rheumatoid arthritis. *Curr Opin Rheumatol*, **12**, 415–419.
8. Calabro, J.J. (1977) Other extraarticular manifestations of juvenile rheumatoid arthritis. *Arthritis Rheum*, **20**, 237–240.
9. Sibbit, W., Williams, R. (1982) Cutaneous manifestations of rheumatoid arthritis. *Int J Dermatol*, **21**, 563–572.
10. Isdale, I.C., Bywaters, E.G.L. (1956) The rash of rheumatoid arthritis and Still's disease. *QJM*, **99**, 377–387.
11. Ragsdale, C.G., Petty, R.E., Cassidy, J.T. et al (1980) The clinical progression of apparent juvenile rheumatoid arthritis to systemic lupus erythematosus. *J Rheumatol*, **7**, 50–55.
12. Larson, E.B. (1984) Adult Still's disease. Evolution of a clinical syndrome and diagnosis, treatment, and follow-up of 17 patients. *Medicine (Baltimore)*, **63**, 82–91.
13. Murray, K.J., Grom, A.A., Thompson, S.D. et al (1998) Contrasting cytokine profiles in the synovium of different forms of juvenile rheumatoid arthritis and juvenile spondyloarthropathy: prominence of interleukin-4 in restricted disease. *J Rheumatol*, **25**, 1388–1398.
14. Thompson, S.D., Murray, K.J., Grom, A.A. et al (1998) Comparative sequence analysis of the human T cell beta chain in juvenile rheumatoid arthritis and juvenile spondyloarthropathies: evidence for antigenic selection of the T cells of the synovium. *Arthritis Rheum*, **41**, 482–497.
15. Prahalad, S., Shear, E.S., Thompson, S.D. et al (2002) Increased prevalence of familial autoimmunity in simplex and multiplex families with juvenile rheumatoid arthritis. *Arthritis Rheum*, **46**, 1851–1856.
16. Murray, K.J., Moroldo, M.B., Donnelly, P. et al (1999) Age-specific effects of juvenile rheumatoid arthritis-associated HLA alleles. *Arthritis Rheum*, **42**, 1843–1853.
17. Grom, A.A., Hirsch, R. (2000) T-cell and T-cell receptor abnormalities in the immunopathogenesis of juvenile rheumatoid arthritis. *Curr Opin Rheumatol*, **12**, 420–424.

Urticaria

Clinical features

Urticaria is an extremely common group of disorders that share common clinical and histological features.[1] As will be seen later, urticaria has many different etiologies but, more often than not, the cause remains unknown and the disease is then classified as idiopathic. In some patients, more than one stimulus may elicit symptoms.[2] The clinical common denominator in urticaria is the development of 'hives' or 'wheals' – raised edematous lesions – which are often surrounded by a zone of erythema and are commonly pruritic (*Figs 14.32–14.34*).[3,4] Dermatographism – pressure such as scratching resulting in linear urticarial lesions – is a common symptom. Urticaria may develop in only seconds. Lesions usually resolve in less than a few hours. By definition, lesions in patients with chronic urticaria, however, persist over a period of greater than 6 weeks.[4,5] In addition, individual lesions in patients with chronic urticaria often last longer – up to 36 hours.[3]

Given that urticaria is best viewed not as a single disease but as a group of related disorders, it comes as no surprise that the natural history of urticaria is highly variable. Resolution is seen in 50% of patients within a few years of onset; however, in some patients the disease persists for decades.[4] The severity of symptoms is also variable.

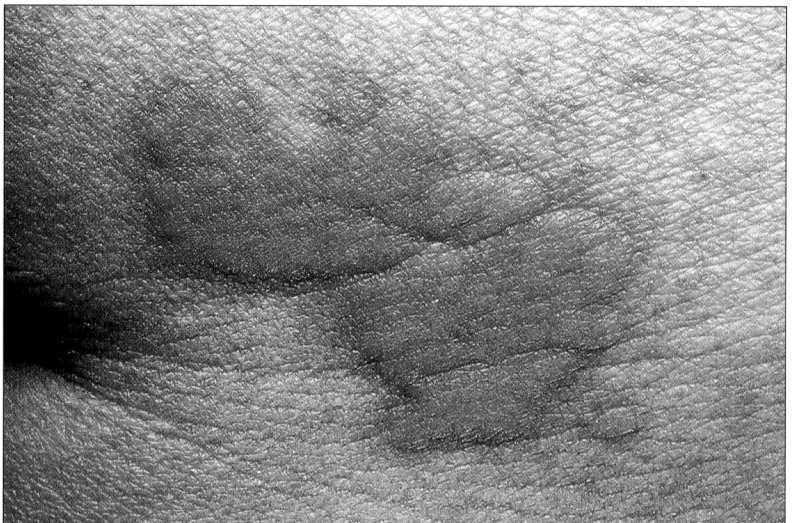

Fig. 14.32
Urticaria: a typical wheal (hive). Note the edema and erythema. By courtesy of the Institute of Dermatology, London, UK.

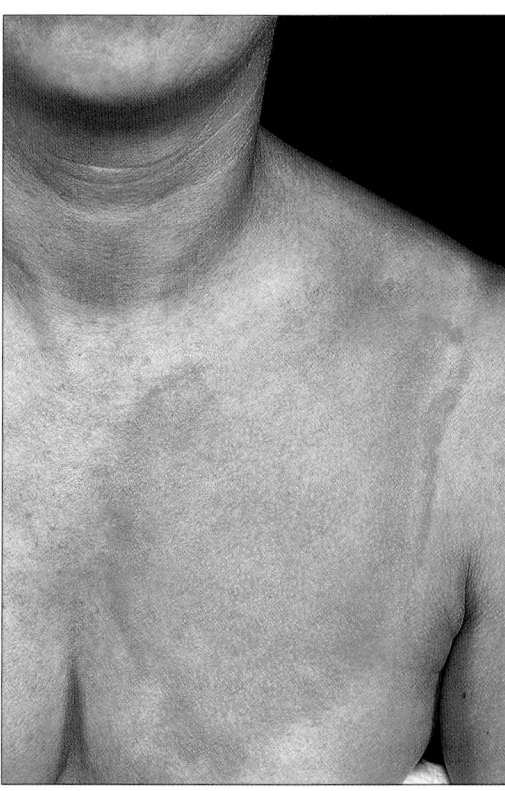

Fig. 14.33
Urticaria: in this patient, the erythematous border is well demonstrated. By courtesy of the Institute of Dermatology, London, UK.

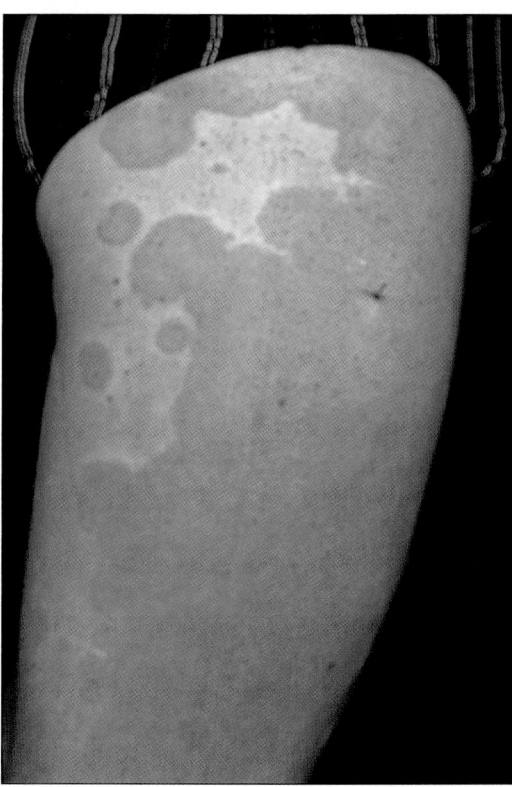

Fig. 14.34
Urticaria: in this extreme example there is intense erythema. By courtesy of the Institute of Dermatology, London, UK.

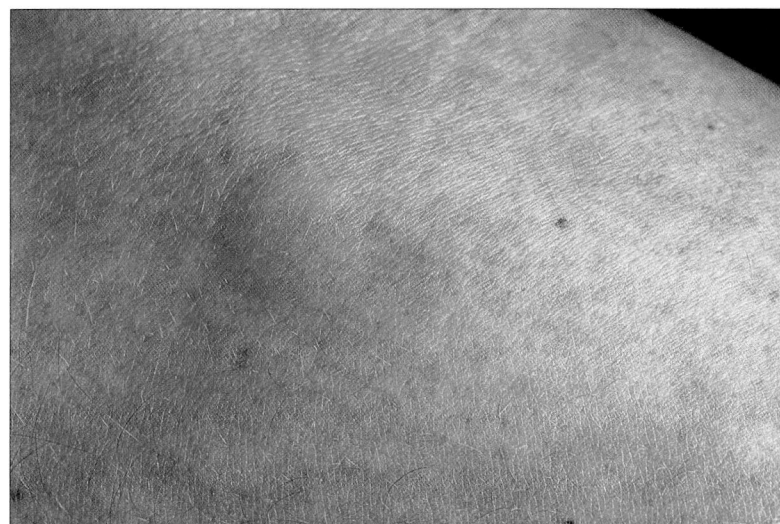

Fig. 14.35
Solar urticaria: in this patient, urticaria developed after exposure to sunlight. By courtesy of the Institute of Dermatology, London, UK.

For many patients, the disease is a minor annoyance; for others, however, severe reactions may be associated with life-threatening anaphylaxis.

Physical causes of urticaria include sunlight, cold, heat, pressure and vibration.

Solar urticaria

Solar urticaria is characterized by development of wheals and pruritus at sites exposed to light (*Fig. 14.35*). A sensitizing agent, such as a drug, may be necessary.[6] In some patients lesions even arise in areas covered by light clothing.[7] 'Fixed solar urticaria' is a designation given to a rare form of urticaria seen in patients who develop lesions at the same sites with repeated light exposure.[8] Solar urticaria has also been described following exposure to infrared radiation.[9]

Aquagenic urticaria

'Aquagenic urticaria' is a bizarre variant in which patients develop lesions following exposure to water (regardless of temperature).[10] Thankfully, patients do not develop symptoms from drinking water.[4,11] Application of petrolatum ointment prior to water exposure prevents lesion development.[10] It has been postulated that a water-soluble epidermal antigen may be responsible for such symptoms, since aqueous extracts of callus cause symptoms in patients' skin but not in that of controls.[12]

Cold urticaria

Placing an ice cube on the skin of patients may elicit a wheal – a condition designated 'cold urticaria'.[4,13] Some patients, however, develop symptoms only after generalized cooling of the body.[4] Occasionally drinking cold liquids or bathing in cold water elicits symptoms.[4] The condition may be associated with other types of physical urticaria. Very rarely, there is associated cryoglobulinemia and in some cases the condition follows a viral infection or drug ingestion.[13,14]

Familial cold syndrome (familial cold autoinflammatory syndrome) is an autosomal dominant condition characterized by urticaria, fever, arthralgias, arthritis, conjunctivitis and leukocytosis following exposure to cold.[15–17] Recently, patients with this syndrome have been shown to have mutations on chromosome 1q44.[18,19] Patients with familial cold syndrome develop symptoms with a decrease in body temperature but do not develop wheals at the site of an ice cube applied to skin. Mutations in this same region of chromosome 1q44 have also been discovered in patients with Muckle–Wells syndrome, a disorder that is also associated with urticaria in addition to amyloidosis, arthritis and sensorineural deafness.[19]

Urticaria induced by heat has rarely been documented.[20,21]

Delayed pressure urticaria

Patients with 'delayed pressure urticaria' develop lesions at sites of pressure, such as areas of tight clothing.[4] This form of urticaria is seen in 40% of patients with chronic urticaria (see below).[4,22,23]

Cholinergic urticaria

Cholinergic urticaria – one of the most common subtypes of urticaria – is thought to result from release of cholinergic substances by nerves.[24,25] Evidence in support of this theory includes the observation that wheals may be elicited by the injection of cholinergic compounds, and injection of anticholinergic agents blocks wheal formation.[24] Furthermore, wheals do not develop in skin innervated by nerves injected with local anesthetic and application of scopolamine to skin prevents aquagenic urticaria.[11,24] Common causes of cholinergic urticaria include increase in body temperature (e.g. following a hot bath or shower), emotional stress, exercise or consumption of spicy food (*Fig. 14.36*).[4,24] Familial cases of cholinergic urticaria have been reported.[26]

Contact urticaria

Contact urticaria may be divided into two main subtypes: allergic and irritant.[4]

- *Allergic contact urticaria* is a hypersensitivity reaction following exposure to an allergen such as chemicals, foods, latex, plants, fruits and vegetables, and animal-derived antigens.[27,28] Not surprisingly, this form of urticaria often occurs in patients with a history of atopy.[27]
- *Irritant contact urticaria* is a non-immunologically mediated form of urticaria secondary to a wide variety of substances found in cosmetics, food and medications.[27]

Urticarial angioedema

Patients with urticaria often develop angioedema characterized by edematous swelling of the lips, eyelids and tissues of the oropharynx.[4,29,30] Two main subtypes of angioedema are recognized: hereditary and non-hereditary (acquired).

- *Hereditary angioedema* is rare, autosomal dominantly inherited, and due to C1-esterase inhibitor deficiency.
- *Acquired angioedema* may be caused by drug reactions, allergic reactions, reaction to physical agents, hypereosinophilia, and acquired (non-hereditary) C1-esterase deficiency.[30] An idiopathic variant is also recognized.

Physical urticaria, secondary to vibration, cold and sunlight, as well as contact (type I) hypersensitivity reaction and cholinergic urticaria may be associated with angioedema.[30]

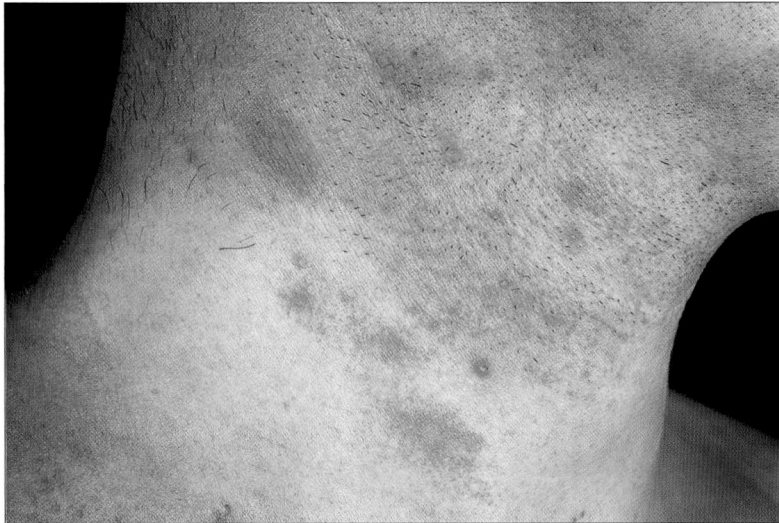

Fig. 14.36
Cholinergic urticaria: in this variant, urticaria follows heat, emotional stress or a spicy meal. By courtesy of the Institute of Dermatology, London, UK.

Urticarial vasculitis

Urticarial vasculitis is an uncommon condition, which combines clinical features of chronic urticaria and histological findings of leukocytoclastic venulitis.[31–33] A type III hypersensitivity reaction (caused by antibody–antigen complexes) appears to be the underlying etiology in a subset of patients.[34,35] In many patients, however, no underlying cause is discovered.

Urticarial vasculitis is associated with a female predominance (2:1) and is most often seen in young to middle-aged adults. Urticarial lesions tend to last 24–72 hours and may be associated with pruritus, a burning sensation or pain.[36] The frequency of attacks varies from daily to monthly.

The spectrum of illness ranges from mild symptoms to a serious systemic illness.[37] In addition to urticarial skin lesions, patients may also have angioedema, gastrointestinal symptoms and evidence of renal involvement. Necrotic skin lesions are not usually seen. Other systemic manifestations/associations include joint pain, stiffness and swelling; however, frank arthritis is extremely rare. Some patients have proteinuria and hematuria. Rarely, renal biopsy reveals the features of focal or diffuse proliferative glomerulonephritis. Crescentic glomerulonephritis, mesangial and membranous nephropathy may be seen in some patients.[37–39] The ESR is frequently raised.

Rarely, urticarial vasculitis has been documented in association with malignancy, a relationship that may be coincidental.[37,40,41]

Hypocomplementemia is seen in many patients and the presence of this sign correlates with systemic involvement and a high prevalence of autoantibodies to endothelial cells.[34,37,42–44] Patients with Schnitzler's syndrome have urticarial vasculitis and monoclonal IgM gammopathy.[45–50] Hepatosplenomegaly, elevated ESR, elevated white blood cell count, fever and joint pain are characteristic features.[46–48] Occasional patients have an associated lymphoproliferative disorder.[45]

Urticarial vasculitis (especially the hypocomplementemic variant) is often associated with or precedes development of a variety of systemic diseases, including myeloma, hepatitis B and C, SLE, arthritis, interstitial lung disease, pericarditis, mixed connective tissue disease, inflammatory bowel disease, serum sickness, polyarteritis nodosa, Wegener's granulomatosis, viral infections, Sjögren's syndrome, cryoglobulinemia, polycythemia rubra vera, reaction to drugs, and as a response to sunlight.[37,42,43,51–58] Urticarial vasculitis has also been documented in association with pregnancy, exercise and cocaine use.[59–61] Methotrexate has been reported to aggravate the disease.[62]

Ocular disease (including uveitis, scleritis, conjunctivitis or episcleritis) is a very common feature.[37] Patients with hypocomplementemia appear to be at risk of developing more severe disease.[51] Some believe that hypocomplementemic urticarial vasculitis represents a form of SLE;[63] other investigators, however, have shown no significant difference in the association with lupus in patients with normocomplementemic compared with hypocomplementemic urticarial vasculitis and refute this view.[37] Obviously, a diagnosis of urticarial vasculitis in any patient should initiate an evaluation for underlying disease.

Drug-induced urticaria

Drug-induced urticaria is fairly common. It is seen in 0.16% of medical inpatients and in 9% of cases of chronic urticaria or angioedema seen in dermatology outpatient departments.[64,65] The drugs most commonly implicated are sulfonamides, penicillins and non-steroidal anti-inflammatory medications.[64] Aspirin may induce acute urticaria, worsen chronic urticaria or act as a co-factor to induce anaphylaxis.[66] Other less common drug associations include antipsychotics, alendronate, recombinant IFN-β, cetirizine, bleomycin and IL-3.[67–72]

Urticarial associations

Urticaria has also been documented in association with autoimmune progesterone dermatitis, dermatophytosis, candidiasis, parasites (anisakiasis), consumption of tonic water, nicotine, alcohol consumption and hepatitis B vaccination.[73–79]

Pathogenesis and histological features

As has been stated above, urticaria is probably best viewed as a group of disorders sharing common clinical and histological features. The pathogenesis of some forms of urticaria (e.g. allergic contact urticaria) is well understood; however, the precise pathogenesis of many causes of urticaria is obscure.[80] Mast cell degranulation appears to be a common denominator in the pathway of most types of urticaria.[81]

Release of histamine following a hypersensitivity reaction after exposure to an allergen is the basis for allergic contact urticaria.[29] In sensitized patients, an allergen binds to IgE on mast cells causing degranulation and the release of histamine, eosinophil chemotactic factor, prostaglandin, leukotrienes, platelet activating factor and enzymes.[27,80–83] Similarly, IgE-mediated mast cell degranulation also underlies the pathogenesis of allergic contact urticaria in which direct contact with allergens on skin bind to the surface IgE on mast cells causing release of histamine and other inflammatory mediators. Auto-antibodies against the IgE high-affinity receptor (FcεRI) or to IgE itself are present in about 30% of patients with chronic urticaria, designated autoimmune urticaria, a type II hypersensitivity reaction.[80,84–87] Patients with physical urticaria or with connective tissue or autoimmune bullous disease may also have anti-FcεRI. However, in the latter group of patients, the autoantibodies are non-functional (non-histamine releasing), whereas in chronic urticaria, the antibodies are functional (histamine-releasing).[87] A type III hypersensitivity reaction, caused by circulating antigen–antibody immune complexes, underlies a form of urticaria associated with serum sickness.

A role for *H. pylori* in the causation of chronic urticaria has been suggested but other studies have challenged this theory.[88–92]

The pathogenesis of irritant contact urticaria is not well-understood but evidence suggests that degranulation of mast cells due to direct, non-immunologically mediated contact causes release of vasogenic mediators.[27,81] Similarly, it is thought that the physical urticarias (heat, cold, pressure, vibration, water) also result from the direct effect on mast cells in susceptible individuals.[83]

Some investigators have suggested that solar urticaria results from a type I hypersensitivity reaction to a photoinduced antigen eliciting IgE-mediated mast cell degranulation.[7] An intriguing study has shown that most (77%) patients develop an urticarial reaction when challenged with autologous serum that has been irradiated using the same spectrum of light that induces lesions in each particular patient.[93] Furthermore, patients with 'fixed' urticaria develop lesions at the same specific sites that are affected by light exposure following injection with irradiated plasma.[10] Consistent with these observations, some patients with severe solar urticaria may be effectively treated by plasma exchange.[94,95]

A type III hypersensitivity reaction (caused by antibody–antigen complexes) appears to be the underlying etiology in some patients with urticarial vasculitis; however, no underlying cause is discovered in many patients.[35,37]

The biopsy findings in urticaria are non-specific. Dermal edema may be mild or severe and its presence is confirmed by separation of dermal reticular collagen fibers. An often sparse dermal perivascular and interstitial mixed inflammatory infiltrate composed of variable numbers of lymphocytes, neutrophils and eosinophils is present (*Fig. 14.37*). Of interest, mast cells – which play such an important role in the pathogenesis of urticaria – do not appear to be increased in number except in

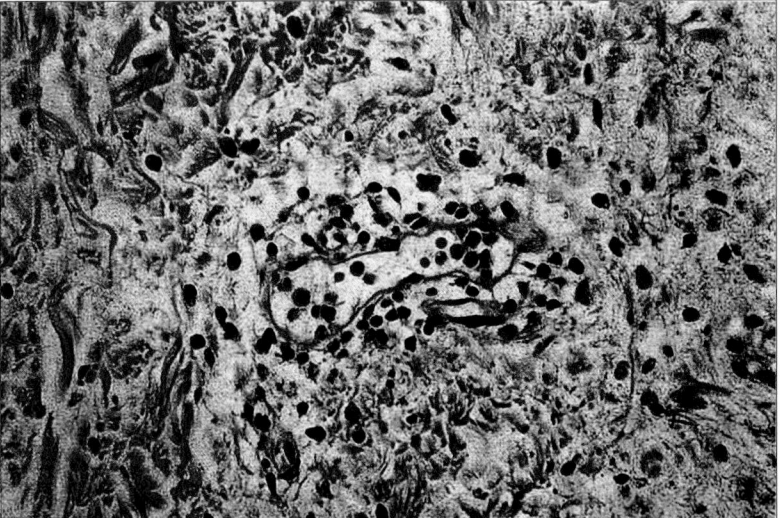

Fig. 14.37
Urticaria: there is edema and a perivascular lymphocytic infiltrate with scattered eosinophils.

chronic urticaria.[86,96] Usually more inflammatory cells are seen in lesions of chronic urticaria compared to those of acute urticaria.[96]

Urticarial vasculitis combines histological features of urticaria with superimposed vascular damage. The vasculitis affects the superficial vascular plexus and shows features of a leukocytoclastic subtype; however, compared with typical leukocytoclastic vasculitis (see p. 000), the histological findings tend to be subtle and are easily overlooked. Mild or focal fibrinoid change apparent on only a few sections associated with few neutrophils and sparse karyorrhexis is typical. Some authors have shown that endothelial necrosis is unusual.[35] Occasionally, impressive necrotizing vasculitis (features of typical leukocytoclastic vasculitis) may be seen. In summary, urticarial vasculitis appears as a continuum, ranging from urticaria with very mild vascular injury to frank necrotizing vasculitis.[97]

Differential diagnosis

The diagnosis requires careful clinical correlation. The biopsy findings are often very subtle: the dermal edema and sparse inflammatory infiltrate may be easily overlooked. A definitive diagnosis may require testing for response to particular antigens. Other forms of hypersensitivity reaction such as arthropod bite and drug eruption may show similar features and require clinical correlation to distinguish them from urticaria. Clinical correlation is necessary to distinguish urticarial vasculitis from other forms of leukocytoclastic vasculitis. Although urticarial vasculitis is often associated with subtle low-grade vascular injury, this pattern should not be relied upon in the distinction from other forms of vasculitis. In short, the pathologist's role in diagnosis is to confirm the presence of vasculitis.

References

1. Zuberbier, T., Greaves, M.W., Juhlin, L. et al (2001) Definiton, classification, and routine diagnosis of urticaria: a consensus report. *J Invest Dermatol Symp Proc*, **6**, 123–127.
2. Sánz de Galdeano, C., Gardeazábal, J., Oleaga, H.M. et al (1994) Solar urticaria and cold urticaria in the same patient. *Br J Dermatol*, **131**, 143–145.
3. Kaplan, A.P. (2002) Chronic urticaria and angioedema. *N Engl J Med*, **346**, 175–179.
4. Black, A.K. (2000) The clinical presentations of urticaria. *Hosp Med*, **61**, 456–461.
5. Grattan, C.E., Sabroe, R.A., Greaves, M.W. (2002) Chronic urticaria. *J Am Acad Dermatol*, **46**, 645–657.
6. Kurumaji, Y., Shono, M. (1994) Drug-induced urticaria due to repirinast. *Dermatology*, **188**, 117–121.
7. Gardeazábal, J., González-Pérez, R., Bilbao, I. et al (1998) Solar urticaria enhanced through clothing. *Photodermatol Photoimmunol Photomed*, **14**, 164–166.
8. Reinauer, S., Leenutahong, V., Holzle, E. (1993) Fixed solar urticaria. *J Am Acad Dermatol*, **29**, 161–165.
9. Mekkes, J.R., de Vries, H.J., Kammeyer, A. (2003) Solar urticaria induced by infrared radiation. *Clin Exp Dermatol*, **28**, 222–223.
10. Sibbald, R.G., Kobza Black, A., Eady, R.A. et al (1981) Aquagenic urticaria: evidence of a cholinergic and histaminergic basis. *Br J Dermatol*, **105**, 297–302.
11. Panconesci, E., Lotti, T. (1987) Aquagenic urticaria. *Clin Dermatol*, **5**, 49–51.

12. Czarnetzki, B.M., Breetholt, H.K., Traupe, H. (1986) Evidence that water acts as a barrier for an epidermal antigen in aquagenic urticaria. *J Am Acad Dermatol*, **15**, 623–627.
13. Claudy, A. (2001) Cold urticaria. *J Investig Dermatol Symp Proc*, **6**, 141–142.
14. Doeglas, H.M.G., Rijnten, W.J., Shroder, F.P. et al (1986) Cold urticaria and virus infections: a clinical and serological study in 39 patients. *Br J Dermatol*, **114**, 311–318.
15. Hoffman, H.M., Wanderer, A.A., Broide, D.H. (2001) Familial cold autoinflammatory syndrome: phenotype and genotype of an autosomal dominant periodic fever. *J Allergy Clin Immunol*, **108**, 615–620.
16. Ormerod, A.D., Smart, L., Reid, T.M. et al (1993) Familial cold urticaria of a family and response to stanozolol. *Arch Dermatol*, **129**, 343–346.
17. Zip, C.M., Ross, J.B., Greaves, M.W. et al (1993) Familial cold urticaria. *Clin Exp Dermatol*, **18**, 338–341.
18. Hoffman, H.M., Wright, F.A., Broide, D.H. et al (2000) Identification of a locus on chromosome 1q44 for familial cold urticaria. *Am J Hum Genet*, **66**, 1693–1698.
19. Hoffman, H.M., Meuller, J.L., Broide, D.H. et al (2001) Mutation of a new gene encoding a putative pyrin-like protein causes familial cold autoinflammatory syndrome and Muckle–Wells syndrome. *Nat Genet*, **29**, 301–305.
20. Baba, T., Nomura, K., Hanada, K. et al (1998) Immediate-type heat urticaria: report of a case and study of plasma histamine release. *Br J Dermatol*, **138**, 326–328.
21. Chang, A., Zic, J.A. (1999) Localized heat urticaria. *J Am Acad Dermatol*, **41**, 354–356.
22. Barlow, R.J., Warburton, F., Watson, K. et al (1993) Diagnosis and incidence of delayed pressure urticaria in patients with chronic urticaria. *J Am Acad Dermatol*, **29**, 954–958.
23. Kobza Black, A. (2001) Delayed pressure urticaria. *J Invest Dermatol Symp Proc*, **6**, 148–149.
24. Hirschmann, J.V., Lawlor, F., English, J.S.C. et al (1987) Cholinergic urticaria – a clinical and histologic study. *Arch Dermatol*, **123**, 462–467.
25. Black, A.K. (2001) Unusual urticarias. *J Dermatol*, **28**, 632–634.
26. Onn, A., Levo, Y., Kivity, S. (1996) Familial cholinergic urticaria. *J Allergy Clin Immunol*, **98**, 847–849.
27. Powell, J., Powell, S. (2000) Mechanisms underlying urticaria. *Hosp Med*, **61**, 470–474.
28. Jaeger, D., Kleinhans, D., Czuppon, A.B. et al (1992) Latex-specific proteins causing immediate-type cutaneous, nasal, bronchial, and systemic reactions. *J Allergy Clin Immunol*, **89**, 759–768.
29. Wakelin, S.H. (2001) Contact urticaria. *Clin Exp Dermatol*, **26**, 132–136.
30. Greaves, M.W., Lawlor, F. (1991) Angioedema: manifestations and management. *J Am Acad Dermatol*, **25**, 155–165.
31. Soter, N.A., Austen, K.F., Gigli, I. (1974) Urticaria and arthralgias as manifestations of necrotizing angiitis (vasculitis). *J Invest Dermatol*, **63**, 485–490.
32. Aboobaker, J., Greaves, M.W. (1986) Urticarial vasculitis. *Clin Exp Dermatol*, **11**, 436–444.
33. Monroe, E.W. (1981) Urticarial vasculitis: an updated review. *J Am Acad Dermatol*, **5**, 88–95.
34. Sánchez, N.P., Winkelman, R.K., Schroeter, A.L. et al (1982) The clinical and histopathologic spectrums of urticarial vasculitis: study of forty cases. *J Am Acad Dermatol*, **7**, 599–605.
35. Jones, R.R., Eady, R.A.J. (1984) Endothelial cell pathology as a marker for urticarial vasculitis: a light microscopic study. *Br J Dermatol*, **110**, 139–149.
36. Kobza Black, A., Lawlor, F., Greaves, M.W. (1996) Consensus meeting on the definition of physical urticarias and urticarial vasculitis. *Clin Exp Dermatol*, **21**, 424–426.
37. Mehregan, D.R., Hall, M.J., Gibson, L.E. (1992) Urticarial vasculitis: a histopathologic and clinical review of 72 cases. *J Am Acad Dermatol*, **26**, 441–448.
38. Messiaen, T., Van Damme, B., Kuypers, D. et al (2000) Crescentic glomerulonephritis complicating the course of a hypocomplementemic urticarial vasculitis. *Clin Nephrol*, **54**, 409–412.
39. Kobayshi, S., Nagase, M., Hidaki, S. et al (1994) Membranous nephropathy associated with hypocomplementemic urticarial vasculitis: report of 2 cases and a review of the literature. *Nephron*, **66**, 1–7.
40. Lewis, J.E. (1990) Urticarial vasculitis occurring in association with visceral malignancy. *Acta Derm Venereol*, **70**, 345–347.
41. Wilson, D., McCluggage, W.G., Wright, G.D. (2002) Urticarial vasculitis: a paraneoplastic presentation of B-cell non-Hodgkin's lymphoma. *Rheumatology (Oxford)*, **41**, 476–477.
42. Asherson, R.A., D'Cruz, D., Stephens, C.J. et al (1991) Urticarial vasculitis in a connective tissue disease clinic: patterns, presentations and treatment. *Semin Arthritis Rheum*, **20**, 285–296.
43. D'Cruz, D.P., Wisnieski, J.J., Asherson, R. et al (1995) Autoantibodies in systemic lupus erythematosus and urticarial vasculitis. *J Rheumatol*, **22**, 1669–1673.
44. Wisnieski, J.J., Baer, A.N., Christensen, J. et al (1995) Hypocomplementemic urticarial vasculitis syndrome. Clinical and serologic findings in 18 patients. *Medicine*, **74**, 24–41.
45. Lim, W., Shumak, K.H., Reis, M. et al (2002) Malignant evolution of Schnitzler's syndrome – chronic urticaria and IgM monoclonal gammopathy: report of a new case and review of the literature. *Leuk Lymphoma*, **43**, 181–186.
46. Lipsker, D., Veran, Y., Grunenberger, F. et al (2001) The Schnitzler syndrome. Four new cases and review of the literature. *Medicine*, **80**, 37–44.
47. Puddu, P., Cianchini, G., Giardelli, C.R. et al (1997) Schnitzler's syndrome: report of a new case and a review of the literature. *Clin Exp Rheumatol*, **15**, 91–95.
48. Baty, V., Hoen, B., Hudziak, H. et al (1995) Schnitzler's syndrome: two case reports and review of the literature. *Mayo Clin Proc*, **70**, 570–572.
49. Janier, M., Bonvalet, D., Blanc, M.F. et al (1989) Chronic urticaria and macroglobulinemia (Schnitzler's syndrome): report of two cases. *J Am Acad Dermatol*, **20**, 206–211.
50. Borradori, L., Rybojad, M., Puissant, A. et al (1990) Urticarial vasculitis associated with a monoclonal IgM gammopathy: Schnitzler's syndrome. *Br J Dermatol*, **123**, 113–118.
51. Wisnieski, J.J. (2000) Urticarial vasculitis. *Curr Opin Rheumatol*, **12**, 24–31.
52. Hamid, S., Cruz, P.D. Jr, Lee, W.M. (1998) Urticarial vasculitis caused by hepatitis C virus infection: response to interferon alfa therapy. *J Am Acad Dermatol*, **39**, 278–280.
53. Chen, H.J., Bloch, K.J. (2001) Hypocomplementemic urticarial vasculitis, Jaccoud's arthropathy, valvular heart disease, and reversible tracheal stenosis. A surfeit of syndromes. *J Rheumatol*, **28**, 383–386.
54. Farell, A.M., Sabroe, R.A., Bunker, C.B. (1996) Urticarial vasculitis associated with polycythemia rubra vera. *Clin Exp Dermatol*, **21**, 302–304.
55. Kuniyuki, S., Katoh, H. (1996) Urticarial vasculitis with papular lesions in a patient with type C hepatitis and cryoglobulinemia. *J Dermatol*, **23**, 279–283.
56. Lin, R.Y., Caren, C.B., Menikoff, H. (1995) Hypocomplementemic urticarial vasculitis, interstitial lung disease and hepatitis C. *Br J Dermatol*, **132**, 821–823.
57. DeAmicis, T., Mofid, M.Z., Cohen, B. et al (2002) Hypocomplementemic urticarial vasculitis: report of a 12-year-old girl with systemic lupus erythematosus. *J Am Acad Dermatol*, **47**, S273–274.
58. Babajanians, A., Chung-Park, M., Wisnieski, J.J. (1991) Recurrent pericarditis and cardiac tamponade in a patient with hypocomplementemic urticarial vasculitis syndrome. *J Rheumatol*, **18**, 752–755.
59. Kwon, C.W., Lee, C.W., Kim, Y.T. et al (1993) Urticarial vasculitis developing on the striae distensae during pregnancy. *Int J Dermatol*, **32**, 751–752.
60. Kano, Y., Orihara, M., Shiohara, T. (1998) Cellular and molecular dynamics in exercise-induced urticarial vasculitis lesions. *Arch Dermatol*, **134**, 62–67.
61. Hofbauer, G.F.L., Hafner, J., Trüeb, R.M. (1999) Urticarial vasculitis following cocaine use. *Br J Dermatol*, **141**, 600–601.
62. Borcea, A., Greaves, M.W. (2000) Methotrexate-induced exacerbation of urticarial vasculitis: an unusual adverse reaction. *Br J Dermatol*, **143**, 203–204.
63. Davis, M.D., Daoud, M.S., Kirby, B. et al (1998) Clinicopathologic correlation of hypocomplementemic and normocomplementemic urticarial vasculitis. *J Am Acad Dermatol*, **38**, 899–905.
64. Shipley, D., Ormerod, A.D. (2001) Drug-induced urticaria. Recognition and treatment. *Am J Clin Dermatol*, **2**, 151–158.
65. Greaves, M.W., Hussein, S.H. (2002) Drug-induced urticaria and angioedema: pathomechanisms and frequencies in a developing country and in developed countries. *Int Arch Allergy Immunol*, **128**, 1–7.
66. Grattan, C.E. (2003) Aspirin sensitivity and urticaria. *Clin Exp Dermatol*, **28**, 123–127.
67. Warnock, J.K., Morris, D.W. (2002) Adverse cutaneous reactions to antipsychotics. *Am J Clin Dermatol*, **3**, 629–636.
68. Kontoleon, P., Ilias, I., Stavropoulos, P.G. et al (2000) Urticaria after administration of alendronate. *Acta Derm Venereol*, **80**, 398.
69. Mazzeo, L., Ricardi, L., Fazio, M.C. et al (2003) Severe urticaria due to recombinant interferon beta-1a. *Br J Dermatol*, **148**, 172.
70. Tella, R., Gaig, P., Bartra, J. et al (2002) Urticaria to cetirizine. *J Investig Allergol Clin Immunol*, **12**, 136–137.
71. Rubeiz, N.G., Salem, Z., Dibbs, R., Kibbi, A.G. (1999) Bleomycin-induced urticarial flagellate drug hypersensitivity reaction. *Int J Dermatol*, **38**, 140–141.
72. Bridges, A.G., Helm, T.N., Bergfeld, W.F. et al (1996) Interleukin-3-induced urticaria-like eruption. *J Am Acad Dermatol*, **34**, 1076–1078.
73. Snyder, J.L., Krishnaswamy, G. (2003) Autoimmune progesterone dermatitis and its manifestations as anaphylaxis: a case report and literature review. *Ann Allergy Asthma Immunol*, **90**, 469–477.
74. Méndez, J., Sánchez, A., Martínez, J.C. (2002) Urticaria associated with dermatophytosis. *Allergol Immunopathol (Madr)*, **30**, 344–345.
75. Daschner, A., Alonso-Gomez, A., Caballero, T. et al (1998) Gastric anisakiasis: an underestimated cause of acute urticaria and angio-oedema? *Br J Dermatol*, **139**, 822–828.
76. González, R., Merchán, R., Crespo, J.F., Rodriguez, J. (2002) Allergic urticaria from tonic water. *Allergy*, **57**, 52.
77. Lee, I.W., Ahn, S.K., Choi, E.H. et al (1998) Urticarial reaction following the inhalation of nicotine in tobacco smoke. *Br J Dermatol*, **138**, 486–488.
78. Emonet, S., Hogendijk, S., Voegeli, J. et al (1998) Ethanol-induced urticaria: elevated tryptase levels after double-blind, placebo-controlled challenge. *Dermatology*, **197**, 181–182.
79. Barbaud, A., Trechot, P., Reichert-Penetrat, S. et al (1998) Allergic mechanisms and urticaria/angioedema after hepatitis B immunization. *Br J Dermatol*, **139**, 925–926.
80. Oliver, J.M., Kepley, C.L., Ortega, E. et al (2000) Immunologically mediated signaling in basophils and mast cells: finding therapeutic targets for allergic diseases in the human FcεR signaling pathway. *Immunopharmacology*, **48**, 269–281.
81. Hide, M., Francis, D.M., Grattan, C.E.H. et al (1993) Autoantibodies against the high affinity IgE receptor as a cause of histamine release in chronic urticaria. *N Engl J Med*, **328**, 1559–1604.
82. Kinet, J-P. (1999) The high-affinity IgE receptor (Fc epsilon RI): from physiology to pathology. *Annu Rev Immunol*, **17**, 931–972.
83. Kwong, K.Y., Maalouf, N., Jones, C.A. (1998) Urticaria and angioedema: pathophysiology, diagnosis, and treatment. *Pediatr Ann*, **27**, 719–724.
84. Greaves, M.W. (1995) Chronic urticaria. *N Engl J Med*, **332**, 1767–1772.
85. Feibiger, E., Maurer, D., Holub, H. et al (1995) Serum IgG autoantibodies directed against the alpha chain of FCαRC: a selective marker and pathogenetic factor for a distinct subset of chronic urticaria patients. *J Clin Invest*, **96**, 2606–2612.
86. Smith, C.H., Kepley, C., Schwartz, L.B. et al (1995) Mast cell numbers and phenotype in chronic idiopathic urticaria. *J Allergy Clin Immunol*, **96**, 360–364.
87. Greaves, M.W. (2002) Pathophysiology of chronic urticaria. *Int Arch Allergy Immunol*, **127**, 3–9.
88. Tebbe, B., Geilen, C.C., Schulzke, J-D et al (1996) *Helicobacter pylori* infection and chronic urticaria. *J Am Acad Dermatol*, **34**, 685–686.
89. Hizal, M., Tüzün, B., Wolf, R. et al (2000) The relationship between *Helicobacter pylori* IgG antibody and autologous serum test in chronic urticaria. *Int J Dermatol*, **39**, 443–445.
90. Radenhausen, M., Schulzke, J-D., Geilen, C.C. et al (2000) Frequent presence of *Helicobacter pylori* in chronic urticaria. *Acta Derm Venereol*, **80**, 48–49.
91. Wustlich, S., Brehler, R., Luger, T.A. et al (1999) *Helicobacter pylori* as a possible bacterial focus of chronic urticaria. *Dermatology*, **198**, 130–132.
92. Daudén, E., Jiménez-Alonso, I., García-Diíez, A. (2000) *Helicobacter pylori* and idiopathic chronic urticaria. *Int J Dermatol*, **39**, 446–452.
93. Uetsu, N., Miyauchi-Hashimoto, H., Okamoto, H. et al (2000) The clinical and photobiological characteristics of solar urticaria in 40 patients. *Br J Dermatol*, **142**, 32–38.
94. Bissonnette, R., Buskard, N., McLean, D.I. et al (1999) Treatment of refractory solar urticaria with plasma exchange. *J Cutan Med Surg*, **3**, 236–238.
95. Leenutaphong, V., Holzle, E., Plewig, G. et al (1991) Plasmapheresis in solar urticaria. *Dermatologica*, **182**, 35–38.
96. Stewart, G.E. 2nd (2002) Histopathology of chronic urticaria. *Clin Rev Allergy Immunol*, **23**, 195–200.
97. Jones, R.R., Bhogal, B., Dash, A. et al (1983) Urticaria and vasculitis: a continuum of histological and immunopathological changes. *Br J Dermatol*, **108**, 695–703.

Hypereosinophilic syndrome

Clinical features

The hypereosinophilic syndrome is defined as an idiopathic condition characterized by persistent eosinophilia (more than 1.5×10^9/L) for at least 6 months and with involvement of one or more organs.[1–3] The diagnosis should be made only after other causes of eosinophilia, particularly parasitic infections, are excluded. The heart, lungs, central and peripheral nervous system, liver and skin are commonly affected. The disease, which may sometimes prove fatal, usually presents in adults.

Cutaneous lesions are seen in up to 53% of patients and usually consist of either pruritic papules and nodules or urticaria and angioedema.[4] Rarely, skin lesions may represent an initial manifestation of the disease and in this setting, annular erythema and erythroderma have been reported.[5–8] Oral and genital erosions are quite characteristic and may be the first manifestation of the disease.[9,10] Other rare cutaneous manifestations include livedo reticularis, cutaneous infarction, deep vein thrombosis, blisters, aquagenic pruritus, erythema gyratum repens and Wells' syndrome.[11–17] Hypereosinophilic syndrome has been reported in association with lymphomatoid papulosis, T-cell lymphoma, systemic mast cell disease, SLE and HIV infection.[18-23]

Pathogenesis and histological features

The etiology is unknown. It has been recently suggested that hypereosinophilic syndrome represents a heterogeneous group of diseases in which there is usually an underlying hematological disorder either in myeloid or lymphoid cells.[24] Recently, elevated serum levels of IL-10 and soluble IL-2 receptor have been documented.[25] IL-2 stimulates release of eosinophilic cationic protein from eosinophils that contain IL-2 receptor (CD25) and this results in tissue damage.

The histological findings vary according to the type of lesion biopsied. Urticarial and papular lesions show a superficial and deep perivascular and interstitial mixed inflammatory cell infiltrate with variable numbers of eosinophils and scattered lymphocytes, histiocytes and occasional plasma cells. Rare flame figures may be present. Dermal edema is seen particularly in urticarial lesions. Eosinophils are not always prominent and the findings may be entirely non-specific. Microthrombi are present in some cases and may correlate with severity of the disease.[11,26]

References

1. Chusid, M.J., Dale, D.C., West, B.C. et al (1975) The hypereosinophilic syndrome: analysis of fourteen cases with review of the literature. *Medicine (Baltimore)*, 54, 1–27.
2. Leiferman, K.M. (1995) Hypereosinophilic syndrome. *Semin Dermatol*, 14, 122–128.
3. Weller, P.F. (1996) The idiopathic hypereosinophilic syndrome. *Arch Dermatol*, 132, 583–585.
4. Kazmierowski, J.A., Chusid, M.J., Parrillo, J.E. et al (1978) Dermatologic manifestations of the hypereosinophilic syndrome. *Arch Dermatol*, 114, 531–535.
5. van den Hoogenband, H.M. (1982) Skin lesions as the first manifestation of the hypereosinophilic syndrome. *Clin Exp Dermatol*, 7, 267–271.
6. Shelley, W.B., Shelley, E.D. (1985) Erythema annulare centrifugum as the presenting sign of the hypereosinophilic syndrome: observations on therapy. *Cutis*, 35, 53–55.
7. Lee, M.L., Fischer, G., Gow, E. (1988) Hypereosinophilic syndrome presenting with erythroderma. *Australas J Dermatol*, 29, 95–101.
8. Launay, D., Catteau, B., Dubost-Brama, A. et al (2002) A four-year history of pruriginous erythroderma leading to the diagnosis of idiopathic hypereosinophilic syndrome. *Acta Derm Venereol*, 82, 376–378.
9. Leiferman, K.M., O'Duffy, J.D., Perry, H.O. et al (1982) Recurrent incapacitating mucosal ulcerations. A prodrome of hypereosinophilic syndrome. *JAMA*, 247, 1018–1020.
10. Aractingi, S., Janin, A., Zini, J.M. et al (1996) Specific cutaneous erosions in hypereosinophilic syndrome. Evidence for eosinophil protein deposition. *Arch Dermatol*, 132, 535–541.
11. Fitzpatrick, J.E., Johnson, C., Simon, P. et al (1987) Cutaneous microthrombi: a histologic clue to the diagnosis of hypereosinophilic syndrome. *Am J Dermatopathol*, 9, 419–422.
12. Narayan, S., Ezugbah, F., Standen, G.R. et al (2003) Idiopathic hypereosinophilic syndrome associated with cutaneous infarction and deep venous thrombosis. *Br J Dermatol*, 148, 817–820.
13. Parker, C.J. (1988) Hypereosinophilic syndrome with cutaneous blisters and bowel necrosis. *Australas J Dermatol*, 29, 103–106.
14. Newton, J.A., Singh, A.K., Greaves, M.W. et al (1990) Aquagenic pruritus associated with the idiopathic hypereosinophilic syndrome. *Br J Dermatol*, 122, 103–106.
15. Morita, A., Sakakibara, N., Tsuji, T. (1994) Erythema gyratum repens associated with hypereosinophilic syndrome. *J Dermatol*, 21, 612–614.
16. Bogerieder, T., Griese, D.P., Schiffner, R. et al (1997) Wells' syndrome associated with idiopathic hypereosinophilic syndrome. *Br J Dermatol*, 137, 978–982.
17. Tsuji, Y., Kawashima, T., Yokota, K. et al (2002) Wells' syndrome as a manifestation of hypereosinophilic syndrome. *Br J Dermatol*, 147, 811–812.
18. Whittaker, S.J., Jones, R.R., Spry, C.J. (1988) Lymphomatoid papulosis and its relationship to 'idiopathic' hypereosinophilic syndrome. *J Am Acad Dermatol*, 18, 339–344.
19. Aractingi, S., Bachmeyer, C., Pautier, P. et al (2002) Necrotic cutaneous lesions induced by hypereosinophilic syndrome secondary to a T-cell lymphoma. *J Am Acad Dermatol*, 46, S133–136.
20. McElroy, E.A. Jr, Phyliky, R.L., Li, C.Y. (1998) Systemic mast cell disease associated with the hypereosinophilic syndrome. *Mayo Clin Proc*, 73, 47–50.
21. Lee, H-J., Yi, J-Y., Kim, T-Y. et al (1997) Hypereosinophilic syndrome associated with systemic lupus erythematosus. *Int J Dermatol*, 36, 152–153.
22. May, L.P., Kelly, J., Sánchez, M. (1990) Hypereosinophilic syndrome with unusual cutaneous manifestations in two men with HIV infection. *J Am Acad Dermatol*, 23, 202–204.
23. Morgan, M.B., Viloria, J., Morgan, J.D. et al (1994) Human immunodeficiency virus infection and hypereosinophilic syndrome. An increasingly recognized association. *J Fla Med Assoc*, 81, 401–402.
24. Roufosse, F., Cogan, E., Goldman, M. (2003) The hypereosinophilic syndrome revisited. *Annu Rev Med*, 54, 169–184.
25. Kanbe, N., Kurosawa, M., Igarashi, N. et al (1998) Idiopathic hypereosinophilic syndrome associated with elevated plasma levels of interleukin-10 and soluble interelukin-2 receptor. *Br J Dermatol*, 139, 916–918.
26. Kim, H.S., Chun, Y.S., Chang, S.N., Park, W.H. (2001) Hypereosinophilic syndrome: correlation between clinical severity and cutaneous microthrombi. *Int J Dermatol*, 40, 330–332.

Eosinophilic cellulitis

Clinical features

Eosinophilic cellulitis (Wells' syndrome) is an uncommon disorder, characterized by recurrent erythematous and edematous plaques.[1-3] It occurs with an equal sex ratio and there is a large age range, with a mean age of 37 years.[4] It is sometimes also encountered in children and rare cases have been documented in neonates.[4-7] It appears that those cases occurring in childhood may be particularly severe. Scalp involvement, with alopecia and scarring is a feature in some patients.[4,5]

The disease particularly affects the extremities and trunk. Although it presents most commonly as well-defined (cellulitis-like) annular erythematous plaques, which are edematous and firm, a wide variety of clinical appearances have been described including blistering, nodular, papulovesicular eruptions and itchy excoriated inflammatory papules (*Fig. 14.38*).[4,8] The plaques, which cause pain and pruritus in some patients, typically heal without scarring.[4] Eosinophilic cellulitis has been associated with urticaria.[9] With progression, the lesions sometimes adopt a greenish hue (*Fig. 14.39*). Clinically, the lesion may occasionally be mistaken for an infective process.[10] The disease tends to be episodic, with remissions and relapses, which may last from months to years.

Large bullae are seen in rare patients.[11] An unusual pattern of involvement following Blaschko's lines has been reported and it has been proposed that this form may represent cutaneous mosaicism.[12]

Rarely, eosinophilic cellulitis is associated with a malignant neoplasm. Cases accompanied by squamous cell carcinoma of the lung and non-Hodgkin's lymphoma have been described.[13,14] Associations with HIV, hypereosinophilic syndrome, tetanus vaccine and varicella infection have occasionally been documented.[15-18]

Rare familial cases have been described.[19,20] In one family, the disease showed an autosomal dominant pattern of inheritance and was associated with mental retardation and dysmorphic body habitus.[19] In another family, the lesions were first noted during infancy.[21]

Pathogenesis and histological features

The pathogenesis is unknown and may simply represent an eosinophil-rich inflammatory reaction to a variety of insults. The only consistent association appears to be a peripheral eosinophilia, manifested either as an elevated total eosinophil count or as an increased percentage of eosinophils. Clinical activity appears to correlate with increased eosinophil cation protein and IL-5 levels in the peripheral blood in addition to blood and bone marrow eosinophilia.[19,20]

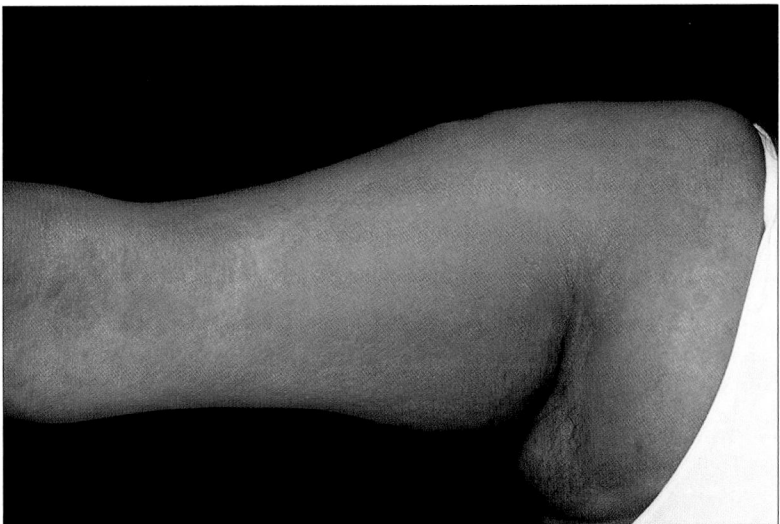

Fig. 14.38
Eosinophilic cellulitis: there is a large erythematous swollen plaque with adjacent papules. The limbs are commonly affected. By courtesy of the Institute of Dermatology, London, UK.

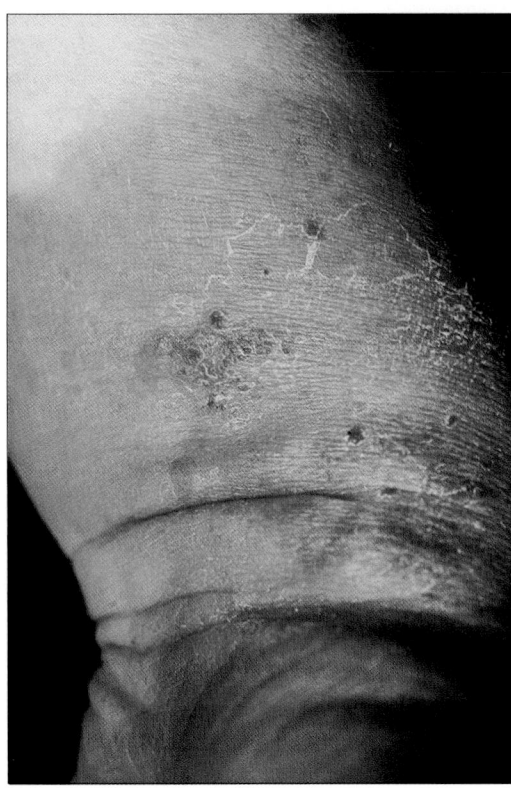

Fig. 14.39
Eosinophilic cellulitis: note the scaling and characteristic green discoloration. By courtesy of the late N.P. Smith, MD, Institute of Dermatology, London, UK.

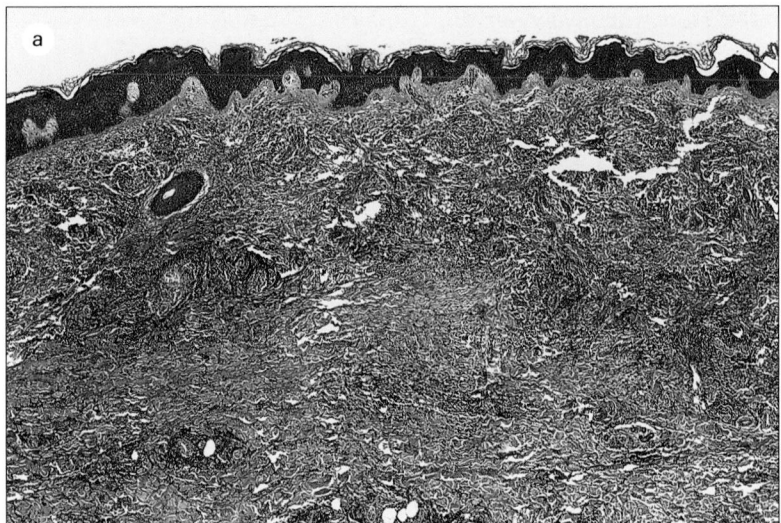

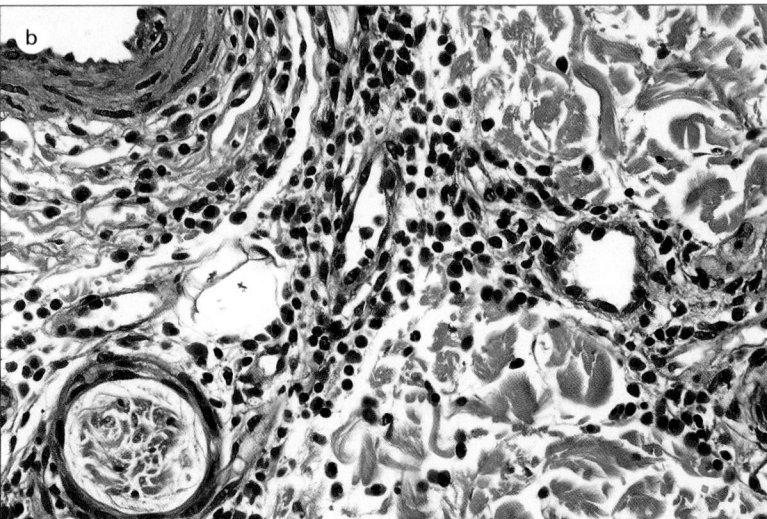

Fig. 14.40
(a, b) Eosinophilic cellulitis: there is a heavy dermal chronic inflammatory cell infiltrate composed of lymphocytes and histiocytes with conspicuous eosinophils.

An elevated ESR may occasionally be present. It is possible that some patients represent the benign end of the spectrum of the hypereosinophilic syndrome.

Histologically, early lesions of eosinophilic cellulitis are characterized by a diffuse and heavy infiltrate of eosinophils in the dermis: this occurs either in the superficial dermis, as a band-like infiltrate, or in the deep dermis with extension into the underlying subcutaneous tissue, fascia and muscle (*Fig. 14.40*).[2,22] In addition, lymphocytes and plasma cells may be present. There is sometimes edema of the papillary dermis to such an extent that subepidermal bullae develop (*Fig. 14.41*).[23] The epidermis may be spongiotic and occasionally intraepidermal vesicles are present.[23] Over a period of 1–3 weeks the eosinophils degranulate and degenerate and eosinophilic material and nuclear debris are deposited on collagen fibers to produce 'flame figures' (*Fig. 14.42*).[23,24] Sometimes these are surrounded by histiocytes and multinucleated giant cells (*Fig. 14.43*). There is no evidence of primary collagen degeneration. It is likely that flame figures represent a non-specific eosinophil reaction pattern to a variety of different provoking stimuli.[24] Later, the lesion becomes more granulomatous and giant cells are occasionally prominent. Vasculitis is not usually a feature, although extravasation of red blood cells may sometimes be evident.[23]

Indirect immunofluorescence studies have shown that the flame figures contain extracellular eosinophil granule major basic protein.[24,25] Ultrastructural investigation confirms that the eosinophil granules invest the associated collagen fibers.[26] Direct immunofluorescence has demonstrated immunoglobulins and/or complement in blood vessel walls in a minority of cases.[2,4,10,24]

Differential diagnosis

The histological features of eosinophilic infiltration with 'flame figures', although characteristic of Wells' syndrome, are not pathognomonic. Similar features may be seen in arthropod bite reactions, spider bites, onchocerciasis, drug hypersensitivity reactions, diffuse erythema, tinea, atopic eczema, allergic contact dermatitis, urticarial vasculitis, eosinophilic pustular folliculitis, bullous pemphigoid, herpes gestationis, the hypereosinophilic syndrome and cutaneous mastocytoma.[2,24,27–32]

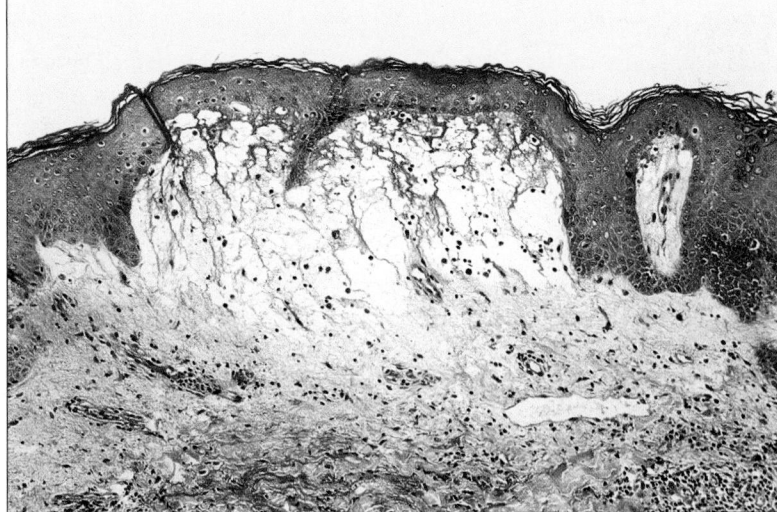

Fig. 14.41
Eosinophilic cellulitis: subepidermal vesiculation as seen here is not uncommon. The blister cavity may contain numerous eosinophils reminiscent of bullous pemphigoid.

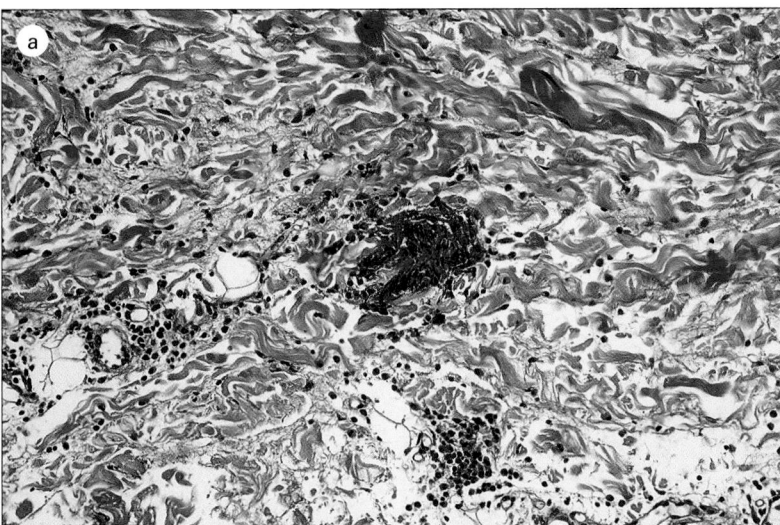

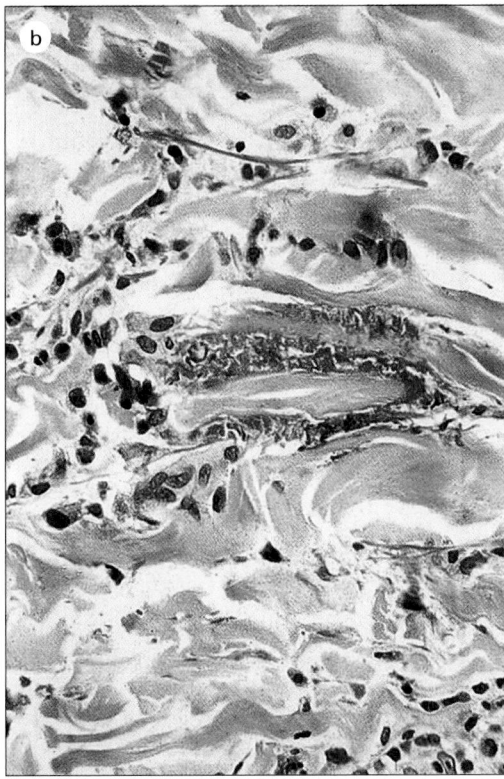

Fig. 14.42
(a, b) Eosinophilic cellulitis: flame figures are typically present.

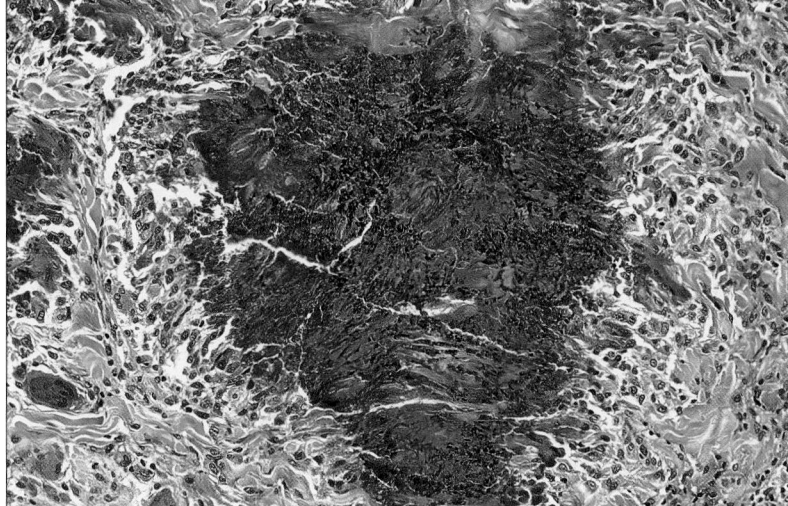

Fig. 14.43
Eosinophilic cellulitis: in this example, a flame figure is surrounded by an intense granulomatous infiltrate.

Prominent flame figures are also seen in eosinophilic ulcer of the oral mucosa.[33–35] It should be emphasized that in regions where parasitic infections are endemic, lesions with the histological appearance of eosinophilic cellulitis have a high likelihood of representing parasitic infection such as giardiasis, toxocariasis and onchocerciasis.[36–38] In eosinophilic fasciitis, diffuse fibrosis of the deep dermis with extension into the fibrous septa of the subcutaneous fat and involvement of the fascia allow for easy distinction from Wells' syndrome.

References

1. Wells, G.C. (1971) Recurrent granulomatous dermatitis with eosinophilia. *Trans St John's Hosp Dermatol Soc*, **57**, 46–56.
2. Wells, G.C., Smith, N.P. (1979) Eosinophilic cellulitis. *Br J Dermatol*, **100**, 101–109.
3. Fisher, G.B., Kenneth, E.G., Cooper, P.H. (1985) Eosinophilic cellulitis (Wells' syndrome). *Int J Dermatol*, **24**, 101–107.
4. Lindskov, R., Illum, N., Weismann, K. et al (1988) Eosinophilic cellulitis: five cases. *Acta Derm Venereol*, **68**, 325–330.
5. Nielson, T., Schmidt, H., Sogaard, H. (1981) Eosinophilic cellulitis (Wells' syndrome) in a child. *Arch Dermatol*, **117**, 427–429.
6. Anderson, C.R., Jenkins, D., Tron, V. et al (1995) Wells' syndrome in childhood: case report and review of the literature. *J Am Acad Dermatol*, **33**, 857–864.
7. Garty, B.Z., Feinmesser, M., Davide, M. et al (1997) Congenital Wells' syndrome. *Pediatr Dermatol*, **14**, 312–315.
8. Newton, J.A., Greaves, M.W. (1988) Eosinophilic cellulitis (Wells' syndrome) with florid histological changes. *Clin Exp Dermatol*, **13**, 318–320.
9. Dijkstra, J.W.E., Bergfeld, W.F., Steck, W.D. et al (1986) Eosinophilic cellulitis associated with urticaria. *J Am Acad Dermatol*, **14**, 32–38.
10. Stierstorfer, M.B., Clendenning, W.E. (1991) Recurrent dermatitis overlying a prosthetic hip. Eosinophilic cellulitis. *Arch Dermatol*, **127**, 1397–1398.
11. Ling, T.C., Antony, F., Holden, C.A. et al (2002) Two cases of bullous eosinophilic cellulitis. *Br J Dermatol*, **146**, 160–161.
12. Sommer, S., Wilkinson, S.M., Merchant, W.J. (1999) Eosinophilic cellulitis following the lines of Blaschko. *Clin Exp Dermatol*, **24**, 449–451.
13. Farrar, C.W., Guerin, D.M., Wilson, N.J. (2001) Eosinophilic cellulitis associated with squamous cell carcinoma of the bronchus. *Br J Dermatol*, **145**, 678–679.
14. Consigny, S., Courville, P., Young, P. et al (2001) Histological and clinical forms of eosinophilic cellulitis. *Ann Dermatol Venereol*, **128**, 213–216.
15. Jones-Caballero, M., Pérez-Santos, S., Bermejo-Martínez, G. et al (2000) Wells' syndrome and human immunodeficiency virus infection. *Br J Dermatol*, **143**, 672–674.
16. Bogenrieder, T., Griese, D.P., Schiffner, R. et al (1997) Wells' syndrome associated with idiopathic hypereosinophilic syndrome. *Br J Dermatol*, **137**, 978–982.
17. Moreno, M., Luelmo, J., Monteagudo, M. et al (1997) Wells' syndrome related to tetanus vaccine. *Int J Dermatol*, **36**, 524–525.
18. Reichel, M., Isseroff, R.R., Vogt, P.J. et al (1991) Wells' syndrome in children: varicella infection as a precipitating event. *Br J Dermatol*, **124**, 187–190.
19. Davis, M.D., Brown, A.C., Blackston, R.D. et al (1998) Familial eosinophilic cellulitis, dysmorphic habitus, and mental retardation. *J Am Acad Dermatol*, **38**, 919–928.
20. España, A., Sanz, M.L., Sola, J. et al (1999) Wells' syndrome (eosinophilic cellulitis): correlation between clinical activity, eosinophil levels, eosinophil cation protein and interleukin-5. *Br J Dermatol*, **140**, 127–130.
21. Kamani, N., Lipsitz, P.J. (1987) Eosinophilic cellulitis in a family. *Pediatr Dermatol*, **4**, 220–224.
22. Spigel, G.T., Winkelmann, R.K. (1979) Wells' syndrome. *J Am Acad Dermatol*, **12**, 161–164.
23. Brehmer-Anderson, E., Kaaman, T., Skog, E. et al (1986) The histopathogenesis of the flame figure in Wells' syndrome based on five cases. *Acta Derm Venereol*, **66**, 213–219.
24. Wood, C., Miller, A.C., Jacobs, A. et al (1986) Eosinophilic infiltration with flame figures. *Am J Dermatopathol*, **8**, 186–193.
25. Peters, M.S., Schroeter, A.L., Gleich, G.J. (1983) Immunofluorescence identification of eosinophil granule major basic protein in the flame figures of Wells' syndrome. *Br J Dermatol*, **109**, 141–148.
26. Stern, J.B., Sobel, H.J., Rotchford, J.P. (1984) Wells' syndrome – is there collagen damage in flame figures? *J Cutan Pathol*, **11**, 501–505.
27. Schorr, W.F., Tauscheck, A.L., Dickson, K.B. et al (1984) Eosinophilic cellulitis (Wells' syndrome): histologic and clinical features in arthropod bite reactions. *J Am Acad Dermatol*, **11**, 1043–1049.
28. Van den Hoogenband, H.M. (1983) Eosinophilic cellulitis as a result of onchocerciasis. *Clin Exp Dermatol*, **8**, 405–408.
29. Andreano, J.M., Kantor, G.R., Bergfeld, W.F. et al (1989) Eosinophilic cellulitis and eosinophilic pustular folliculitis. *J Am Acad Dermatol*, **20**, 34–36.
30. Panizzon, R. (1989) Wells' syndrome (eosinophilic cellulitis): additional cases in the literature. *J Am Acad Dermatol*, **20**, 1136–1137.
31. Seçkin, D., Demirhan, B. (2001) Drugs and Wells' syndrome: a possible casual relationship? *Int J Dermatol*, **40**, 138–140.
32. Hunt, S.J., Santa Cruz, D.J. (1991) Eosinophilic cellulitis: histologic features in a cutaneous mastocytoma. *Dermatologica*, **182**, 132–134.
33. Mezei, M.M., Tron, V.A., Stewart, W.D. et al (1995) Eosinophilic ulcer of the oral mucosa. *J Am Acad Dermatol*, **33**, 734–740.
34. Vélez, A., Alamillos, F.-J., Dean, A. et al (1997) Eosinophilic ulcer of the oral mucosa: report of a recurrent case on the tongue. *Clin Exp Dermatol*, **22**, 154–156.
35. Chung, H-S., Kim, N.S., Kim, Y.B. et al (1998) Eosinophilic ulcer of the oral mucosa. *Int J Dermatol*, **37**, 432.
36. Cannone, D., Dubost-Brama, A., Segard, M. et al (2000) Wells' syndrome associated with recurrent giardiasis. *Br J Dermatol*, **143**, 425–427.
37. Hurni, M.A., Gerbig, A.W., Braathen, L.R. et al (1997) Toxocariasis and Wells' syndrome: a casual relationship? *Dermatology*, **195**, 325–328.
38. Chang, D.K.M., Schloss, E., Jimbow, K. (1997) Wells' syndrome: vesiculobullous presentation and possible role of ectoparasites. *Int J Dermatol*, **36**, 288–291.

Papular dermatitis associated with HIV/AIDS

Clinical features

A pruritic papular dermatitis may be seen in up to 20% of HIV-positive patients.[1–3] Lesions, which measure 2–5 mm, are skin colored and found predominantly on the head, neck and upper trunk.[4,5] It has been suggested that this may represent a hypersensitivity response to insect bites or *Demodex follicularis* infection.[6]

Histological features

Histology reveals a non-specific superficial and deep interstitial infiltrate composed of lymphocytes and eosinophils.[1] Superimposed excoriations or lichen simplex chronicus may also be evident.[1]

Differential diagnosis

The histological features are non-specific and the main differential diagnosis includes hypersensitivity reactions, insect bite reactions and infestations such as scabies. Background inflammatory changes similar to those seen in papular dermatitis associated with HIV infection may be a feature of eosinophilic folliculitis and it is possible that these are related disorders.

References

1. LeBoit, P.E. (1992) Dermatopathologic findings in patients infected with HIV. *Dermatol Clin,* 10, 59–71.
2. James, W.D., Redfield, R.R., Lupton, G.P. et al (1985) A papular eruption associated with human T-cell lymphotrophic virus type III disease. *J Am Acad Dermatol,* 13, 563–566.
3. Boonchai, W., Laohasrisalkul, R., Manonukul, J. et al (1999) Pruritic papular eruption in HIV seropositive patients: a cutaneous marker for immunosuppression. *Int J Dermatol,* 38, 348–350.
4. Warner, L.C., Fisher, B.K. (1986) Cutaneous manifestations of the acquired immunodeficiency syndrome. *Int J Dermatol,* 25, 337–350.
5. Herman, K.L., Jacoby, R.A., Webster, G. (1991) Pathology of HIV-related skin disease. *Clin Dermatol,* 9, 95–110.
6. Ashack, R.J., Frost, M.L., Norins, A.L. (1989) Papular pruritic eruption of Demodex folliculitis in patients with acquired immunodeficiency syndrome. *J Am Acad Dermatol,* 21, 306–307.

HIV-associated eosinophilic folliculitis

Clinical features

This disorder presents as a chronic pruritic dermatosis characterized by discrete smooth-surfaced papules located predominantly on the trunk and proximal extremities.[1] It is said to differ from Ofuji's eosinophilic pustular folliculitis by the presence of discrete, scattered lesions compared to the arcuate plaques of the latter condition, although there is considerable overlap.[2–4] In one study, all patients had raised serum IgE levels.[2]

Pathogenesis and histological features

The pathogenesis of eosinophilic folliculitis is unknown. It has been proposed that it may represent a hypersensitivity reaction to *Demodex follicularis* or fungi.[5] Indeed bacteria, yeast and Demodex are sometimes seen in association with lesions of eosinophilic folliculitis but their role, if any, is unclear. The identification of pityrosporum yeast within some lesions and a clinical response to antifungal therapy has raised the possibility of a pathogenic role for yeast in at least some cases.[6] Similarly, Pseudomonas has been successfully cultured in patients that responded to antibiotic therapy.[7] However, other authors point out that, since these organisms can be seen unassociated with any inflammation, they may represent an incidental finding.[8]

Histologically, HIV-associated eosinophilic folliculitis is characterized by the presence of eosinophils and occasional small eosinophil pustules in the outer root sheath and pilar canal of the hair follicle.[9] A perivascular and interstitial lymphohistiocytic and eosinophil infiltrate involving the superficial and deep dermis is also sometimes present.[1,8]

Eosinophilic folliculitis in HIV patients has been documented in association with follicular mucinosis.[10]

Differential diagnosis

As mentioned above, there is considerable overlap between eosinophilic folliculitis and eosinophilic pustulosis (Ofuji's disease); however, the latter tends to form arcuate plaques. Histologically, well-developed and large eosinophilic pustules in the pilar canals are characteristic of Ofuji's disease but are less common in HIV-associated eosinophilic folliculitis.[11] Fungal infection can also result in a similar histological picture and should be excluded by silver or PAS stains.

References

1. Leboit, P.E. (1992) Dermatopathologic findings in patients infected with HIV. *Dermatol Clin,* 10, 59–71.
2. Rosenthal, D., LeBoit, P.E., Klump, L. et al (1991) Human immunodeficiency virus-associated eosinophilic folliculitis: a unique dermatosis associated with advanced human immunodeficiency virus infection. *Arch Dermatol,* 127, 206–209.
3. Jenkins, D. Jr, Fisher, B.K., Chalvardjian, A. et al (1985) Eosinophilic pustular folliculitis in a patient with AIDS. *Int J Dermatol,* 27, 34–35.
4. Soeprono, F.F., Schinella, R.A. (1986) Eosinophilic pustular folliculitis in patients with acquired immunodeficiency syndrome. Report of three cases. *J Am Acad Dermatol,* 14, 1020–1022.
5. Herman, K.L., Jacoby, R.A., Webster, G. (1991) Pathology of HIV-related skin disease. *Clin Dermatol,* 9, 95–110.
6. Ferrandiz, C., Ribera, M., Barranco, J.C. et al (1992) Eosinophilic pustular folliculitis in patients with acquired immunodeficiency syndrome. *Int J Dermatol,* 31, 193–195.
7. Brenner, S., Wolf, R., Ophir, J. (1994) Eosinophilic pustular folliculitis: a sterile folliculitis of unknown cause. *J Am Acad Dermatol,* 31, 210–212.
8. McCalmont, T.H., Altemus, D., Maurer, T. et al (1995) Eosinophilic folliculitis: the histologic spectrum. *Am J Dermatopathol,* 17, 439–446.
9. Holmes, R.B., Martins, C., Horn, T. (2002) The histopathology of folliculitis in HIV-infected patients. *J Cutan Pathol,* 29, 93–95.
10. Buezo, G.F., Fraga, J., Abajo, P. (1998) HIV-associated eosinophilic folliculitis and follicular mucinosis. *Dermatology,* 197, 178–180.
11. Basarab, T., Jones, R.R. (1996) HIV-associated folliculitis: case report and review of the literature. *Br J Dermatol,* 134, 499–503.

Eosinophilic pustular folliculitis

Clinical features

Eosinophilic pustular folliculitis (Ofuji's disease) is a rare dermatosis seen primarily in Japanese and Chinese, although occasional reports from Europe and the USA are encountered.[1–5] It is a disease that particularly affects the seborrheic regions and, therefore, lesions are predominantly present on the face and back.[6] The extensor surfaces of the upper limbs are also frequently affected. Acral involvement is exceptional.[7] Patients present with crops of occasionally pruritic follicular sterile papulo-pustules measuring 1–2 mm in diameter, grouped to form small plaques, which characteristically spread centrifugally to produce an annular or serpiginous lesion.[1,6] The disease is typically recurrent and spontaneous resolution within months to several years is characteristic.[8,9] Healing is often associated with residual postinflammatory hyperpigmentation.[1] Males are predominantly affected (5:1) and the peak incidence is in the third and fourth decades. Sometimes there is a past or present history of acne vulgaris.

Extensive laboratory investigations reveal leukocytosis with hyper-eosinophilia.[10] Serum IgE levels may be increased.[5,11]

Similar cases have been reported in Caucasians in association with HIV infection.[3,4,12–19] Based on the clinical and histological findings, many authors regard HIV-associated eosinophilic folliculitis as a separate entity (see above).[16,18] Pruritus, which is always present in patients with HIV-associated eosinophilic folliculitis, is seen only in occasional patients with Ofuji's disease.[20]

A small number of childhood cases of eosinophilic pustular folliculitis, including several neonates, have also been reported.[11,21–27] Some authors prefer to categorize these as a separate entity.[5,24] In children, the scalp is particularly involved. There is less of a tendency to affect the seborrheic regions and polycyclic patterns are not evident.[21]

Eosinophilic pustular folliculitis has been described in association with non-Hodgkin's lymphoma, Hodgkin's lymphoma, myelodysplastic syndrome, eosinophilic cellulitis and the nevoid basal cell carcinoma syndrome.[28–34] A case induced by allopurinol and timepidium bromide has also been documented.[35]

Pathogenesis and histological features

The etiology and pathogenesis of eosinophil pustular folliculitis is unknown. The possibility of an inherited or contagious cause for the disease has been raised by the observation of the disease in siblings.[36] However, there is no firm evidence of an infective cause. A variety of immunological abnormalities have been described including raised IgE levels, low immunoglobulin levels and defects of neutrophil motility.[6,24] A pemphigus-like antibody and an anti-basal keratinocyte antibody have also been recorded in patients with this disease.[37,38]

The seborrheic distribution raises a possible role for sebaceous glands in the pathogenesis.[8] A lipid-soluble eosinophil chemotactic factor has been identified from epidermal surface lipids.[39] The association of eosinophil pustular folliculitis with AIDS (if indeed this is the same disease) raises the interesting possibility of a diminished T-helper lymphocyte-mediated pathogenesis.

An increased number of mast cells has been described around hair follicles and sebaceous glands suggesting a role for these cells in the pathogenesis of the disease.[40]

In early lesions, spongiosis of the outer root sheath of the infundibulum with an accompanying eosinophil and mononuclear cell infiltrate is characteristic.[6] As the disease progresses vesiculation and pustulation are seen deep to the stratum corneum, often extending into the sebaceous gland (*Fig. 14.44*). The epithelium is infiltrated by large numbers of eosinophils with an admixture of neutrophils and mononuclear cells. In the superficial dermis there is a perivascular mononuclear and eosinophil infiltrate. Follicular mucinosis may rarely be seen.[41,42]

Differential diagnosis

As mentioned above, there is considerable overlap between eosinophilic folliculitis associated with HIV infection and Ofuji's disease. The latter tends to form arcuate plaques. Histologically, well-developed large eosinophilic pustules in the pilar canals are characteristic of Ofuji's disease but are less common in HIV-associated eosinophilic folliculitis.[43]

Identical histology may be seen in epidermal fungal infections and special stains are essential to exclude this possibility.[40,44–46]

References

1. Ofuji, S., Ogino, A., Horio, T. et al (1970). Eosinophilic pustular folliculitis. *Acta Derm Venereol*, 50, 195–203.
2. Ishibashi, A., Nishiyama, Y., Miyata, C. et al (1974) Eosinophilic pustular folliculitis (Ofuji). *Dermatologica*, 149, 240–247.
3. Holst, R. (1976) Eosinophilic pustular folliculitis. Report of a European case. *Br J Dermatol*, 95, 661–664.
4. Orfanos, C.E., Sterry, W. (1978) Sterile eosinophilic pustulose. *Dermatologica*, 157, 193–205.
5. Tang, M.B., Tan, E., Chua, S.H. (2003) Eosinophilic pustular folliculitis (Ofuji's disease) in Singapore: review of 23 adult cases. *Australas J Dermatol*, 44, 44–47.
6. Ofuji, S. (1987) Eosinophilic pustular folliculitis. *Dermatologica*, 174, 53–56.
7. Tsuboi, H., Wakita, K., Fujimura, T. et al (2003) Acral variant of eosinophilic pustular folliculitis (Ofuji disease). *Clin Exp Dermatol*, 28, 327–328.
8. Blume-Peytavi, U., Chen, W., Djemadji, N. et al (1997) Eosinophilic folliculitis (Ofuji's disease). *J Am Acad Dermatol*, 37, 260–262.
9. Rattana-Apiromyakij, N., Kullavanijaya, P. (2000) Eosinophilic pustular folliculitis: report of seven cases in Thailand. *J Dermatol*, 27, 195–203.
10. Takematsu, H., Nakamura, K., Igarashi, M. et al (1985) Eosinophilic pustular folliculitis: report of two cases and review of the Japanese literature. *Arch Dermatol*, 121, 917–920.
11. Lazarov, A., Wolach, B., Córdoba, M. et al (1996) Eosinophilic pustular folliculitis (Ofuji disease) in a child. *Cutis*, 58, 135–138.
12. Soeprono, F.F., Schinella, R.A. (1986) Eosinophilic pustular folliculitis in patients with acquired immunodeficiency syndrome. *J Am Acad Dermatol*, 14, 1020–1022.
13. Jenkins, D., Fisher, B.K., Chalvardjian, A. et al (1988) Eosinophilic pustular folliculitis in a patient with AIDS. *Int J Dermatol*, 27, 34–35.

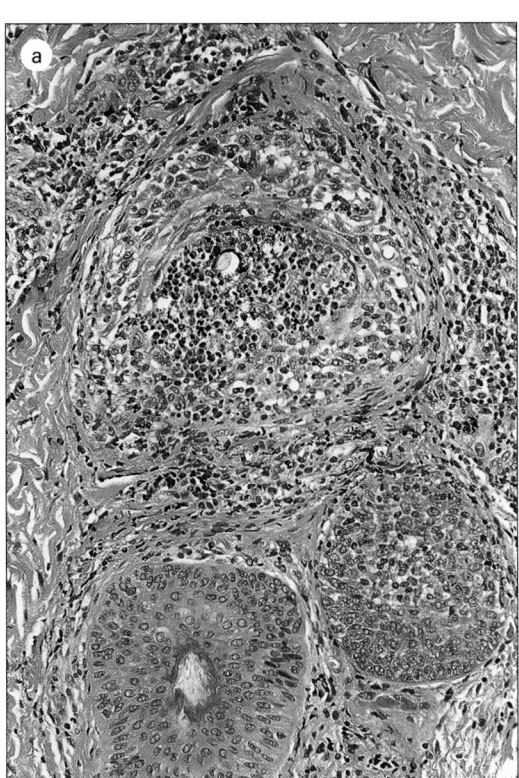
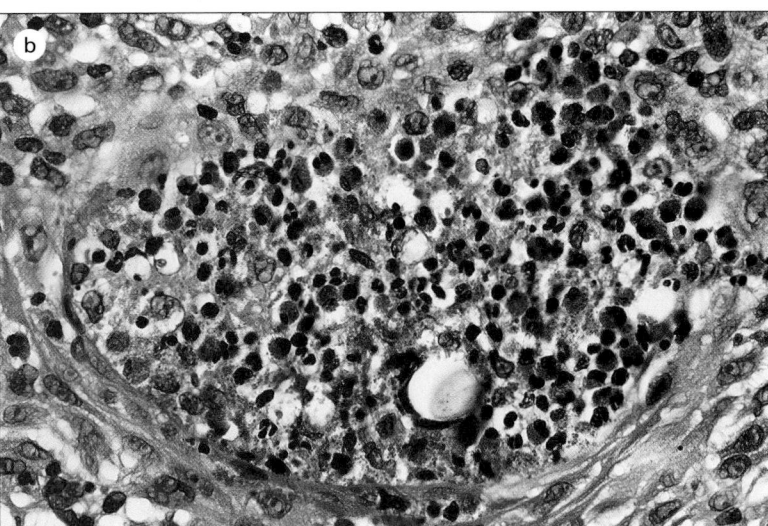

Fig. 14.44
(a, b) Eosinophilic pustular folliculitis: there is spongiosis associated with an eosinophil-rich abscess.

14. Harris, D.W., Ostlere, L., Buckley, C. et al (1992) Eosinophilic pustular folliculitis in an HIV-positive man: response to cetirizine. *Br J Dermatol*, **126**, 392–394.

15. Barranco, J.C., Clotet, B., Lorenzo, J.C. (1992) Eosinophilic pustular folliculitis in patients with acquired immunodeficiency syndrome. *Int J Dermatol*, **31**, 193–195.

16. Rosenthal, D., LeBoit, P.E., Klumpp, L. et al (1991) Human immunodeficiency virus-associated eosinophilic folliculitis. *Arch Dermatol*, **127**, 206–209.

17. Buchness, M.R., Lim, H.W., Soter, N.A. (1991) AIDS-related eosinophilic pustular folliculitis. *J Am Acad Dermatol*, **25**, 866.

18. Hevia, O., Jiménez-Acosta, F., Ceballos, P.I. et al (1991) Pruritic papular eruption of the acquired immunodeficiency syndrome. A clinicopathological study. *J Am Acad Dermatol*, **24**, 231–235.

19. Frentz, G., Niordson, A.M., Thomsen, K. (1989) Eosinophilic pustular dermatosis: an early marker of infection with human immunodeficiency virus? *Br J Dermatol*, **121**, 271–274.

20. Patrone, P., Bragadin, G., Stinco, G. et al (2001) Ofuji's disease: diagnostic and therapeutic problems. A report of 3 cases. *Int J Dermatol*, **40**, 512–515.

21. Moritz, D.L., Elmets, C.A. (1991) Eosinophilic pustular folliculitis. *J Am Acad Dermatol*, **24**, 903–907.

22. Giard, F., Marcoux, D., McCuaig, C. et al (1991) Eosinophilic pustular folliculitis (Ofuji disease) in childhood: a review of four cases. *Pediatr Dermatol*, **8**, 189–193.

23. Lucky, A.W., Esterly, N.B., Heskel, N. et al (1984) Eosinophilic pustular folliculitis in infancy. *Pediatr Dermatol*, **1**, 202–206.

24. Dekio, S., Jidoi, J., Kawasaki, Y. (1989) Eosinophil-infiltrating folliculitis in childhood – report of a case. *J Dermatol*, **16**, 388–391.

25. Taieb, A., Bassan-Andrieu, L., Maleville, J. (1992) Eosinophilic pustulosis of the scalp in childhood. *J Am Acad Dermatol*, **27**, 55–60.

26. Buckely, D.A., Munn, S.E., Higgins, E.M. (2001) Neonatal eosinophilic pustular folliculitis. *Clin Exp Dermatol*, **26**, 251–255.

27. Larralde, M., Morales, S., Muñoz, A.S. et al (1999) Eosinophilic pustular folliculitis in infancy: report of two new cases. *Pediatr Dermatol*, **16**, 118–120.

28. Patrizi, A., Di Lernia, V., Neri, I. et al (1992) Eosinophilic pustular folliculitis (Ofuji's disease) and non-Hodgkin's lymphoma. *Acta Derm Venereol*, **72**, 146–147.

29. Vassallo, C., Ciocca, O., Arcaini, L. et al (2002) Eosinophilic folliculitis occurring in a patient affected by Hodgkin lymphoma. *Int J Dermatol*, **41**, 298–300.

30. Roger, H., Souteyrand, P., Bignon, Y.J. et al (1988) Pustulose folliculaire et éosinophiles révélant un limphone T de haut degré de malignité rapidment fatal. *Ann Dermatol Syphilol*, **115**, 1209–1212.

31. Barkley, A., Shall, L., Millard, L.G. (1989) Simultaneous onset of eosinophilic pustular dermatosis and non-Hodgkin's lymphoma. Abstracts: 1st Congress, European Academy of Dermatology and Venereology, Firenze, p 210.

32. Jang, K.A., Chung, S.T., Choi, J.H. et al (1998) Eosinophilic pustular folliculitis (Ofuji's disease) in myelodysplastic syndrome. *J Dermatol*, **25**, 742–746.

33. Andreano, J.M., Kantor, G.R., Bergfeld, W.F. et al (1989) Eosinophilic cellulitis and eosinophilic pustular folliculitis. *J Am Acad Dermatol*, **20**, 934–936.

34. Kishimoto, S., Yamamoto, M., Nomiyama, T. et al (2001) Eosinophilic pustular folliculitis in association with nevoid basal cell carcinoma syndrome. *Acta Derm Venereol*, **81**, 202–204.

35. Maejima, H., Mukai, H., Hikaru, E. (2002) Eosinophilic pustular follicultis I induced by allopurinol and timepidium bromide. *Acta Derm Venereol*, **82**, 316–317.

36. Dupond, A.S., Aubin, F., Bourezane, Y. et al (1995) Eosinophilic pustular folliculitis in infancy: report of two affected brothers. *Br J Dermatol*, **132**, 296–299.

37. Vakilzadeh, F., Suter, L., Knop, J. et al (1981) Eosinophilic pustulosis with pemphigus-like antibody. *Dermatologica*, **162**, 265–272.

38. Nunzi, E., Parodi, A., Rebora, A. (1985) Ofuji's disease: high circulating titers of IgG and IgM directed to basal cell cytoplasm. *J Am Acad Dermatol*, **12**, 268–273.

39. Takematsu, H., Tagami, H. (1985) Eosinophilic pustular folliculitis. Studies on possible chemotactic factors involved in the formation of pustules. *Br J Dermatol*, **114**, 209–215.

40. Ishiguro, N., Shishido, E., Okamoto, R. et al (2002) Ofuji's disease: a report on 20 patients with clinical and histopathologic analysis. *J Am Acad Dermatol*, **40**, 827–833.

41. Basarab, T., Jones, R.R. (1996) Ofuji's disease with unusual histological features. *Clin Exp Dermatol*, **21**, 67–71.

42. Lee, J.Y., Tsai, Y.M., Sheu, M. (2003) Ofuji's disease with follicular mucinosis and its differential diagnosis from alopecia mucinosa. *J Cutan Pathol*, **30**, 307–313.

43. Basarab, T., Jones, R.R. (1996) HIV-associated folliculitis: case report and review of the literature. *Br J Dermatol*, **134**, 499–503.

44. Kuo, T.T., Chen, S.Y., Chan, H.L. (1986) Tinea infection histologically simulating eosinophilic pustular folliculitis. *J Cutan Pathol*, **13**, 118–122.

45. Haupt, H.M., Stern, J.B., Weber, C.B. (1990) Eosinophilic pustular folliculitis: fungal folliculitis. *J Am Acad Dermatol*, **23**, 1012–1014.

46. Dyall-Smith, D., Mason, G. (1995) Fungal eosinophilic pustular folliculitis. *Australas J Dermatol*, **36**, 37–38.

Incontinentia pigmenti

Clinical features

Incontinentia pigmenti (Bloch–Sulzberger syndrome) is a rare systemic illness with a striking female bias (in excess of 37:1), affected males usually dying in utero.[1,2] It has an X-linked dominant mode of inheritance.[3] Cutaneous manifestations usually present at birth or during the first few weeks of life.[1] There may also be lesions affecting the hair, teeth, nails, eyes, skeleton and the central nervous system in up to 80% of patients.[1,3] The phenotype in females is variable, manifestations being dependent on the effects of mosaicism resulting from X-chromosome lyonization.[4] It has occasionally been described in identical twins.[5] The disease may rarely be transmitted from father to daughter.[6]

Most males with incontinentia pigmenti die in utero and only very rare patients survive. As with females it is associated with the same phenotypic mosaicism. In the majority of cases of male involvement it develops in association with Klinefelter's syndrome.[7] Half chromatid mutation, or more recently an unstable pre-mutation, have been offered as explanations for affected males with a normal karyotype.[8,9]

Typically, the condition has three stages:

- *Stage 1*, comprising erythema and linear vesiculation on the trunk and extremities, is apparent at birth or during the first 2 weeks of life (*Fig. 14.45*).[10] Characteristically, the face is unaffected. Patients usually show associated leukocytosis and eosinophilia. On average, the blistering stage has completely resolved by 4 months.[4]

- *Stage 2*, which is uncommon and usually transitory, consists of hyperkeratotic verrucous papules and plaques most frequently found on the extremities (*Fig. 14.46*). The verrucous lesions develop at sites of previous blistering.[10] They may resemble linear epidermal nevi.[11] This stage (when present) appears during the second to sixth weeks of life and usually resolves completely by 6 months.[4]

- *Stage 3*, which is pathognomonic of incontinentia pigmenti, presents as bizarre reticulated pigmentation, usually between the twelfth and twenty-sixth week after birth. It sometimes occurs de novo. The brown to slate-gray pigmentation appears as splashes, streaks and whorls (sometimes referred to as 'Chinese lettering') on the torso and extremities (*Fig. 14.47*). The nipples are typically hyperpigmented and involvement of the groin and axillae is characteristic.[4] The pigmentation appears to develop independently

of the bullous lesions or verrucous plaques and follows Blaschko's lines.[10,11] Resolution of lesions is associated with atrophy and the pigmentation is usually imperceptible by adulthood.

The only residual changes that may be visible are occasional atrophic, hypopigmented, hairless, reticulated patches and streaks best seen on the lower legs[1,4,12] (these are sometimes referred to as the fourth stage of the disease). Additional cutaneous lesions include mild nail dystrophy (40%), scalp alopecia at the vertex and the woolly hair nevus.[3,4] A whorled scarring alopecia following the lines of Blaschko has been documented.[2]

Painful subungual digital verrucous nodules are occasional late features of incontinentia pigmenti.[12] They are usually multiple, affect the hands more often than the feet and, in addition to nail destruction, they may also be associated with scalloped resorption of the underlying

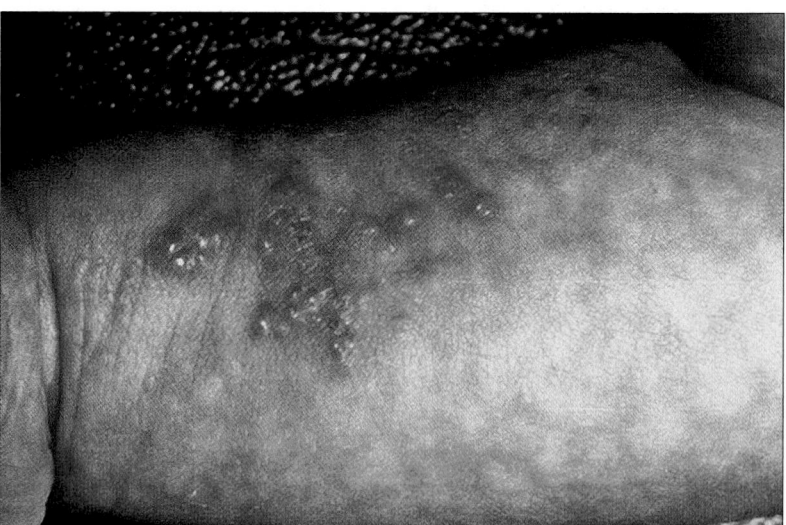

Fig. 14.45
Incontinentia pigmenti: the inflammatory stage is characterized by erythema, linear clusters of intact vesicles, crusts and scaling. By courtesy of D. Atherton, MD, Institute of Dermatology, and Children's Hospital at Great Ormond Street, London, UK.

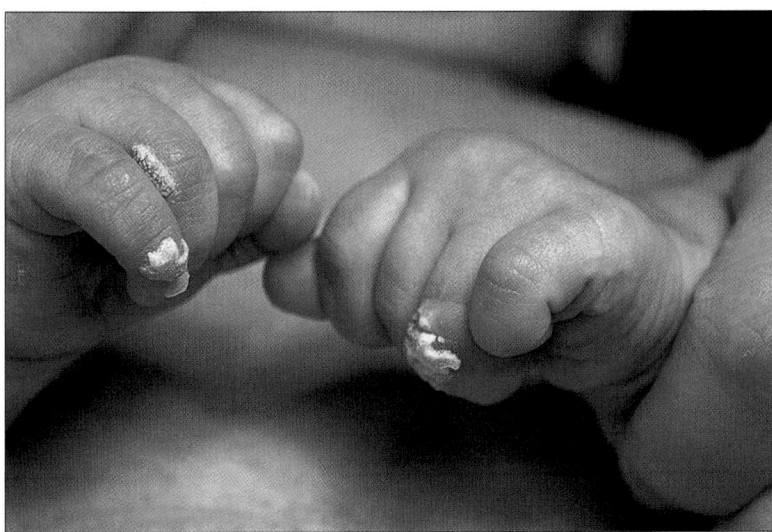

Fig. 14.46
Incontinentia pigmenti: verrucous lesions, seen in the second stage, predominantly affect the extremities. By courtesy of the Institute of Dermatology, London, UK.

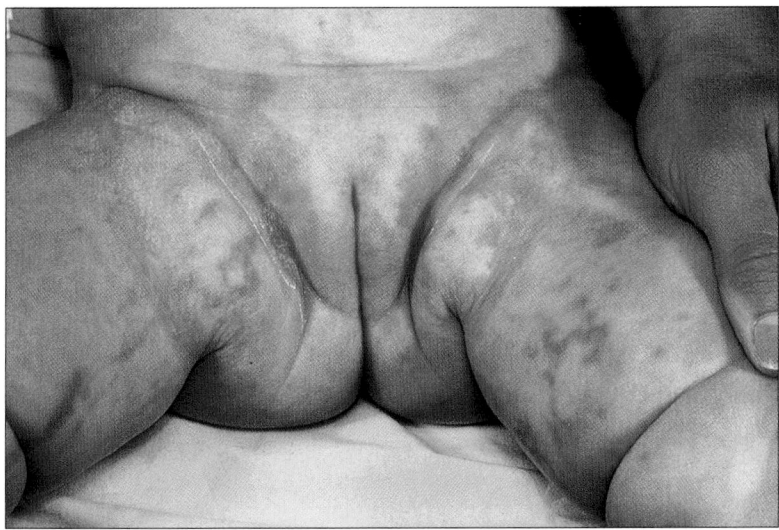

Fig. 14.47
Incontinentia pigmenti: the whorl-like distribution of the pigment is characteristic. By courtesy of R.A. Marsden, MD, St George's Hospital. London, UK.

Table 14.5
General manifestations of incontinentia pigmenti

System	Abnormality
Scalp	Scarring Alopecia of variable severity
Nails	Occasional dystrophy
Teeth	Partial/complete absence Conical (pegged)
Eyes	Strabismus Blindness Cataracts Atrophy of optic nerve
Central nervous system	Spastic paralysis Mental retardation Convulsions

effects including spastic quadriplegia, hemiplegia, slow motor development and psychomotor retardation.[1,22,23] There is some evidence to suggest that incontinentia pigmenti may be associated with chromosomal instability and a slightly increased susceptibility to cancer.[24]

A unique case associated with twenty-nail dystrophy has been described.[25]

Pathogenesis and histological features

Linkage analysis has demonstrated two incontinentia pigmenti loci that reside within the long arm of the X chromosome at Xq11 (IP1) and Xq28 (IP2).[4,26,27] Mutations in the gene for nuclear factor (NF)-kappaB gene modulator (NEMO), which plays a role in inhibiting tumor necrosis factor (TNF)-induced apoptosis, has been shown to be responsible for development of the disease.[28,29] A mouse model has been created by disruption of NEMO, which leads to lethality in males and heterozygous females with skin lesions similar to incontinentia pigmenti.[30] Biopsy of skin lesions of diseased animals shows increased keratinocyte apoptosis, inflammation and pigment incontinence.[30] A relationship between incontinentia pigmenti and the osteopetrosis, lymphedema, anhidrotic ectodermal dysplasia, immunodeficiency (OL-EDA-ID) syndrome has recently been suggested in a patient who presented with the latter syndrome born from a mother with features of incontinentia pigmenti.[31] Both diseases are associated with mutations in the NF-kappaB gene modulator. Male patients with the disease often have less deleterious mutations and present with ectodermal dysplasia and immunodeficiency.[32]

Eotaxin (an NF-kappaB-activated chemokine) is strongly expressed in the suprabasal epidermis of involved skin in patients with the disease.[33] This expression is concomitant with the upper epidermal accumulation of eosinophils, suggesting a pathogenetic role for this chemokine.

Histological examination of lesions in the vesicular stage (stage 1) shows eosinophilic spongiosis (*Fig. 14.48*). Occasionally, aggregates of dyskeratotic cells are evident (*Fig. 14.49*).[3] A chronic inflammatory cell infiltrate with conspicuous eosinophilia may be present within the dermis.

The verrucous lesions (stage 2) show hyperkeratosis, acanthosis, papillomatosis and focal dyskeratosis.[13] The dyskeratotic cells are characteristically arranged in a whorled configuration.

Stage 3 lesions show marked pigmentary incontinence with numerous melanophages in the dermis associated with epidermal basal cell degeneration.

End-stage lesions show epidermal atrophy and there may be loss of the adnexae.[30] Melanocytes appear to be present in normal numbers and ultrastructurally have shown no significant lesion except for one report

phalanx.[13] Spontaneous regression is sometimes a feature. Clinically, these nodules may be mistaken for a wart, subungual fibroma, keratoacanthoma or squamous cell carcinoma.[14]

Dermatoglyphic patterns present in patients and also in non-affected family members have been described.[15]

Some patients develop episodes of late reactivation of the disease in hyperpigmented streaks and this seems to be related to a preceding infection.[16] This suggests that mutated cells persist in the epidermis for a long period of time.

There may be widespread systemic involvement (*Table 14.5*). Dental abnormalities include hypodontia, delayed eruption, impaction and crown malformations such as conical forms and accessory cusps.[4,11,17]

The most characteristic ocular changes are strabismus, microphthalmos, cataract and optic atrophy.[18] Retinal detachment with a fibrovascular retrolental membrane is the commonest intraocular abnormality.[19–21]

Central nervous system involvement may result in encephalopathy, seizures, mental retardation, microcephaly, cerebellar ataxia and motor in which small non-dendritic forms with degenerate melanosomes were described.[5,34]

The subungual verrucous nodules show hyperkeratosis, hypergranulosis, pseudoepitheliomatous hyperplasia and striking dyskeratosis throughout the epidermis.[13,14]

Differential diagnosis

Clinically, incontinentia pigmenti may be confused with hypomelanosis of Ito (incontinentia pigmenti achromians) and the central nervous system involvement in both diseases is similar.[35] The latter, however, is characterized by cutaneous pigmentary changes in the absence of either vesicular or verrucous lesions.

Many conditions may be associated with eosinophilic spongiosis (see Table 5.2, p. 187), but with adequate clinical information none should pose diagnostic problems. Toxic erythema of the neonate can be distinguished histologically from incontinentia pigmenti by the absence of spongiosis in the former condition.

References

1. Carney, R.G. (1976) Incontinentia pigmenti: a world statistical analysis. *Arch Dermatol*, **112**, 535–542.
2. Chan, Y.C., Giam, Y.C. (2001) A retrospective study of incontinentia pigmenti seen at the National Skin Centre, Singapore over a 10-year period. *Ann Acad Med Singapore*, **30**, 409–413.
3. Wiklund, D.A. (1980) Incontinentia pigmenti. A four generations study. *Arch Dermatol*, **116**, 701–703.
4. Landy, S.J., Donnai, D. (1993) Incontinentia pigmenti (Bloch–Sulzberger syndrome). *J Med Genet*, **30**, 53–59.
5. Guerrier, C.J., Wong, C.K. (1974) Ultrastructural evolution of the skin in incontinentia pigmenti (Bloch–Sulzberger). Study of six cases. *Dermatologica*, **149**, 10–22.
6. Emery, M.M., Siegfried, E.C., Stone, M.S. et al (1993) Incontinentia pigmenti: transmission from father to daughter. *J Am Acad Dermatol*, **29**, 368–372.
7. Prendiville, J.S., Gorski, J.L., Stein, C.K. et al (1989) Incontinentia pigmenti in a male infant with Klinefelter syndrome. *J Am Acad Dermatol*, **20**, 937–940.
8. Traupe, H., Vehring, K-H. (1994) Unstable pre-mutation may explain mosaic disease expression of incontinentia pigmenti in males. *Am J Med Genet*, **49**, 397–398.
9. Lenz, W. (1975) Half chromatid mutations may explain incontinentia pigmenti in males. *Am J Hum Genet*, **40**, 332–337.
10. Carney, R.G., Carney, R.G. Jr (1970) Incontinentia pigmenti. *Arch Dermatol*, **102**, 157–162.
11. Wiss, K. (1992) Neurocutaneous disorders: tuberous sclerosis, incontinentia pigmenti, and hypomelanosis of Ito. *Semin Neurol*, **12**, 364–373.
12. Moss, C., Ince, P. (1987) Anhydrotic and achromians lesions in incontinentia pigmenti. *Br J Dermatol*, **116**, 839–850.
13. Mascaró, J.M., Palou, J., Vives, P. (1985) Painful subungual keratotic tumors in incontinentia pigmenti. *J Am Acad Dermatol*, **13**, 913–918.
14. Simmons, D.A., Kegel, M.F., Scher, R.K. et al (1986) Subungual tumors in incontinentia pigmenti. *Arch Dermatol*, **122**, 1431–1434.
15. Tanboga, I., Kargul, B., Ergeneli, S. et al (2001) Clinical findings of incontinentia pigmenti with emphasis on dermatoglyphic findings. *J Clin Pediatr Dent*, **25**, 161–165.
16. Bodak, N., Hadj-Rabia, S., Hamel-Teillac, D. et al (2003) Late recurrence of inflammatory first-stage lesions in incontinentia pigmenti: an unusual phenomenon and a fascinating pathologic mechanism. *Arch Dermatol*, **139**, 201–204.
17. Macey-Dare, L.V., Goodman, J.R. (1999) Incontinentia pigmenti: seven cases with dental manifestations. *Int J Pediatr Dent*, **9**, 293–297.
18. Spallone, A. (1987) Incontinentia pigmenti (Bloch–Sulzberger syndrome): seven case reports from one family. *Br J Ophthalmol*, **71**, 377–379.
19. Heathcote, J.G. (1991) Incontinentia pigmenti (Bloch–Sulzberger syndrome): a case report and review of the ocular pathological features. *Can J Ophthalmol*, **26**, 229–237.
20. Catalano, R.A. (1990) Incontinentia pigmenti. *Am J Ophthalmol*, **110**, 696–700.
21. Rahi, J., Hungerford, J. (1990) Early diagnosis of the retinopathy of incontinentia pigmenti: successful treatment by cryotherapy. *Br J Ophthalmol*, **74**, 377–379.
22. Larsen, R., Ashwal, S., Peckham, N. (1987) Incontinentia pigmenti association with anterior horn cell degeneration. *Neurology*, **37**, 446–450.
23. Shuper, A., Bryan, R.N., Singer, H.S. (1990) Destructive encephalopathy in incontinentia pigmenti: a primary disorder? *Pediatr Neurol*, **6**, 137–140.
24. Roberts, W.M., Jenkins, J.J., Moorhead, E.L. et al (1988) Incontinentia pigmenti, a chromosome instability syndrome, is associated with childhood malignancy. *Cancer*, **62**, 2370–2372.
25. Scardamaglia, L., Howard, A., Sinclair, R. (2003) Twenty-nail dystrophy in a girl with incontinentia pigmenti. *Australas J Dermatol*, **44**, 71–73.
26. Sefiani, A., Abel, L., Heuertz, S. et al (1989) The gene for incontinentia pigmenti is assigned to Xq28. *Genomics*, **4**, 427–429.
27. Hyden-Granskog, C., Salonen, R., von Koskull, H. (1993) Three Finnish incontinentia pigmenti (IP) families with recombinations with the IP locus at Xq28 and Xq11. *Hum Genet*, **91**, 185–189.
28. The International Incontinentia Pigmenti Foundation (2000) Genomic rearrangement in NEMO impairs NF-kappaB activation and is a cause of incontinentia pigmenti. *Nature*, **405**, 466–472.
29. Berlin, A.L., Paller, A.S., Chan, L.S. (2002) Incontinentia pigmenti: a review and update on the molecular basis of pathophysiology. *J Am Acad Dermatol*, **47**, 169–187.
30. Schmidt-Supprian, M., Bloch, W., Courtois, G. et al (2000) NEMO/IKK-gamma-deficient mice model incontinentia pigmenti. *Mol Cell*, **5**, 981–992.
31. Dupuis-Girod, S., Corradini, N., Hadj-Rabia, S. et al (2002) Osteopetrosis, lymphedema, anhidrotic ectodermal dysplasia, immunodeficiency in a boy and incontinentia pigmenti in his mother. *Pediatrics*, **109**, e97.
32. Kenwrick, S., Woffendin, H., Jakins, T. et al (2001) Survival of male patients with incontinentia pigmenti carrying a lethal mutation can be explained by somatic mosaicism or Klinefelter syndrome. *Am J Hum Genet*, **69**, 1210–1217.
33. Jean-Baptiste, S., O'Toole, E.A., Chen, M. et al (2002) Expression of eotaxin, an eosinophil-selective chemokine, parallels eosinophil accumulation in the vesiculobullous stage of incontinentia pigmenti. *Clin Exp Immunol*, **127**, 470–478.
34. Nazzaro, V., Brusasco, A., Gelmetti, C. et al (1990) Hypochromic reticulated streaks in incontinentia pigmenti: an immunohistochemical and ultrastructural study. *Pediatr Dermatol*, **7**, 174–178.
35. Ruggieri, M., Pavone, L. (2000) Hypomelanosis of Ito: clinical syndrome or just phenotype? *J Child Neurol*, **15**, 635–644.

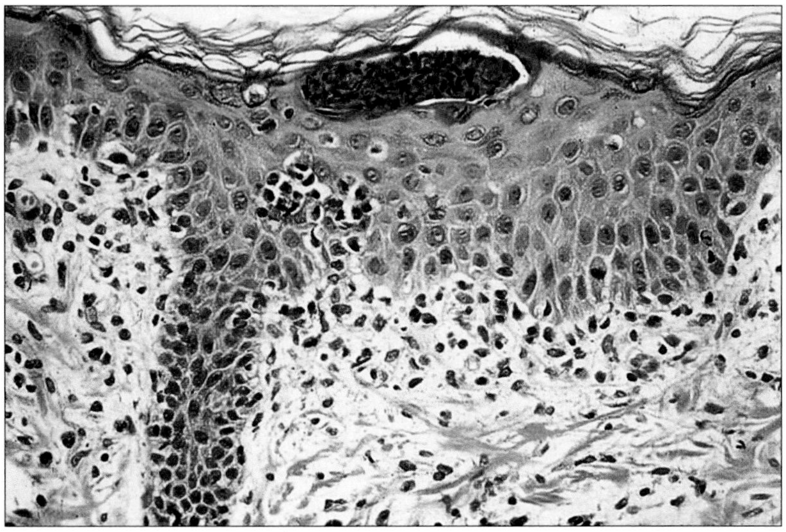

Fig. 14.48
Incontinentia pigmenti: vesicular stage showing a subcorneal eosinophil pustule and intraepidermal eosinophils.

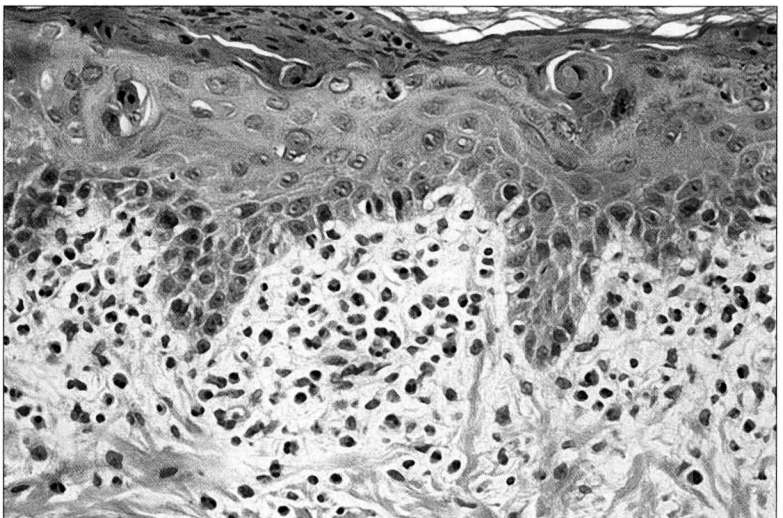

Fig. 14.49
Incontinentia pigmenti: there is dyskeratosis and an upper dermal eosinophil-rich infiltrate.

Toxic erythema of the neonate

Clinical features

Toxic erythema of the neonate (erythema toxicum, erythema toxicum neonatorum) is a very common, self-limiting disorder that presents as an asymptomatic erythematous macular rash usually in the first few days of life. Very rarely, the eruption occurs a week or more after birth.[1] It affects up to 50% of neonates. In survey studies from Japan, Australia, China and India, toxic erythema was found in 40.8%, 34.8%, 33.7% and 20.6% of infants, respectively.[2–5]

It may be associated with papules, and occasionally pustule formation is evident. It most often involves the forehead, face, chest, trunk and extremities.[6] Lesions usually resolve in a few days. Its etiology is obscure.

Histological features

Early erythematous lesions show a somewhat nondescript perivascular inflammatory cell infiltrate with conspicuous eosinophils, which may be seen penetrating the epidermis in close proximity to hair follicles. The pustules are characteristically intrafollicular, may be subcorneal or intraepidermal, and contain large numbers of eosinophils and occasional neutrophils.[7]

Differential diagnosis

Toxic erythema of the neonate must be distinguished from incontinentia pigmenti. The latter, however, is characterized by eosinophilic spongiosis, a feature not seen in toxic erythema. In miliaria rubra the vesicles are related to sweat ducts rather than hair follicles and typically contain mononuclear cells rather than eosinophils.

References

1.   Chang, M.W., Jiang, S.B., Orlow, S.J. (1999) Atypical erythema toxicum neonatorum of delayed onset in a term infant. *Pediatr Dermatol*, 16, 137–141.
2.   Hidano, A., Purwoko, R., Jitsukawa, K. (1986) Statistical survey of skin changes in Japanese neonates. *Pediatr Dermatol*, 3, 140–144.
3.   Rivers, J.K., Frederiksen, P.C., Dibdin, C. (1990) A prevalence study of dermatoses in the Australian neonate. *J Am Acad Dermatol*, 23, 77–81.
4.   Tsai, F.J., Tsai, C.H. (1993) Birthmarks and congenital skin lesions in Chinese newborns. *J Formos Med Assoc*, 92, 838–841.
5.   Nanda, A., Kaur, S., Bhakoo, O.N. et al (1989) Survey of cutaneous lesions in Indian newborns. *Pediatr Dermatol*, 6, 39–42.
6.   Schachner, L., Press, S. (1983) Vesicular, bullous and pustular disorders in infancy and childhood. *Pediatr Clin North Am*, 30, 609–629.
7.   Freeman, R.G., Spiller, R., Knox, J.M. (1960) Histopathology of erythema toxicum neonatorum. *Arch Dermatol*, 82, 586–589.

Hidradenitis suppurativa

Clinical features

Hidradenitis suppurativa is a common disease which is also known as acne inversa and more rarely apocrine acne.[1] Studies from Denmark have found the prevalence to be around 4%.[2,3]

Hidradenitis suppurativa is a chronic relapsing suppurative inflammation of regions where apocrine glands occur, i.e. the axilla, inguinal folds, perineum, genitalia and periareolar region (*Fig. 14.50*).[4,5] It occurs postpubertally in both sexes, but is more common in women.[3] The disease is seen most frequently in young adults, although its first presentation may be in older individuals and even before puberty.[6,7] Initially, there is a firm painful nodule in the groin or axilla. The nodule may involute slowly or else discharge pus through the skin; the discharge of pus is not copious, but is chronic and often foul smelling. In the late stages a complex interconnecting system of sinuses extends deeply into the dermis and subcutaneous fat with extensive dense fibrosis (*Fig. 14.51*).[8]

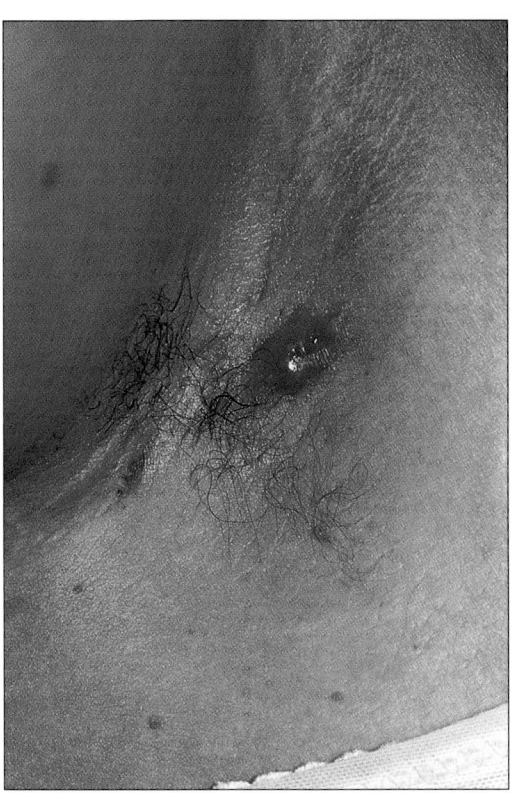

Fig. 14.50
Hidradenitis suppurativa: early lesion presenting as an erythematous nodule discharging clear fluid. The axilla is a commonly affected site. By courtesy of R.A. Marsden, MD, St George's Hospital, London, UK.

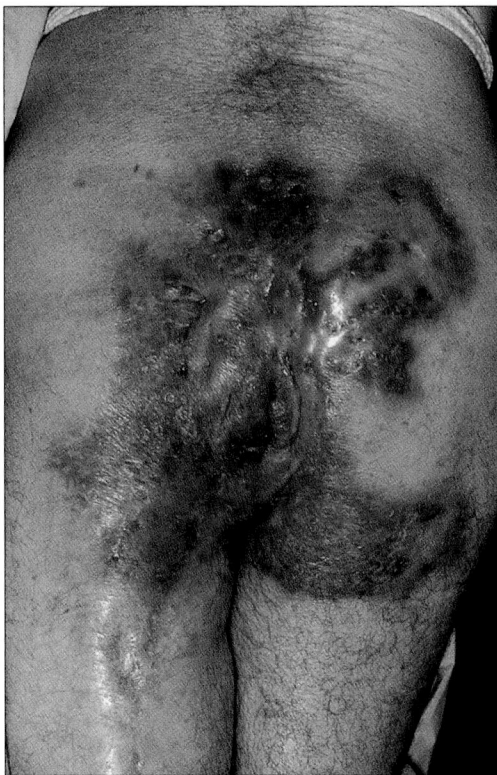

Fig. 14.51
Hidradenitis suppurativa: in this very severe example there is marked scarring and numerous sinuses are present. By courtesy of R.A. Marsden, MD, St George's Hospital, London, UK.

Axillary lesions are more common in women and genitoinguinal lesions are more common in men. Changes may be confined to one region or occur in both, but the axillary region is involved in over 70% of cases.[9] Some reports have attached etiological importance to axillary shaving and the use of deodorants, but this is not generally accepted.[9,10] In women, obesity appears to be a predisposing factor and smoking is closely associated, but it is not clear whether this is a cause or effect.[11] In one study, nearly 90% of German patients were smokers (expected prevalence rate 27%).[12] Whether cessation of smoking improves the course of the disease is unknown.[12] Patients with the hidradenitis suppurativa appear to be at increased risk of developing non-melanoma skin cancer.[13]

The lesions are clearly maintained by bacterial infection as various organisms are often grown. Symptomatic improvement can be achieved with long-term antibiotics. Perineal lesions are often severe and complicated by abscesses, fistulae and draining sinus tracts.[9]

Lesions may also rarely be seen on the malar region of the face and even on the eyelids (glands of Moll), sites with modified apocrine glands.

Hidradenitis suppurativa can be seen in association with conditions which are said to be pathologically similar, namely acne conglobata and dissecting folliculitis of the scalp. These three conditions have been referred to collectively as the 'follicular occlusion triad'.[14] Any one condition, however, may occur separately. Acne conglobata, an extremely severe nodulocystic variant of acne, occurs extensively on the trunk, buttocks and limbs with predilection for males.[15] The disease has been described in association with HIV and following pregnancy.[16,17] Dissecting folliculitis (folliculitis capitis abscedens et suffodiens) is centered on the vertex of the scalp and is characterized by boggy tender lesions that tend to become confluent with formation of draining sinuses and suppuration.[18–21] The disease presents more commonly in black males and it is very rarely familial.[22] Radical surgery is often the only satisfactory means of terminating the process. All the diseases in the follicular occlusion triad can occasionally be complicated by progression of the infective process to cellulitis and septicemia. Squamous carcinoma (including the verrucous variant) is a rare and late additional complication.[23–29] As in Marjolin's ulcer–cancer, the carcinomas are capable of aggressive invasion and metastasis (50%) and are generally associated with a poor prognosis.[9] Such tumors arise most frequently on the buttock and are more often seen in males.[26] Hidradenitis has been shown to be rarely associated with systemic granulomatous lesions, in particular Crohn's disease.[11,30,31] An association with spondylo-arthropathy, Dowling–Degos disease and lithium therapy has also been documented.[32–34]

Treatment of this disease is difficult due to its chronic relapsing nature. Surgery is often used to remove affected areas but the cure rate in some studies is very low.[35] Nevertheless, occasional patients are satisfied with the relief of symptoms, albeit temporary, afforded by surgery.[35] Other studies have shown a low recurrence rate following wide excision.[36,37] Early surgical treatment appears to increase the chance of success.[38]

Pathogenesis and histological features

The pathogenesis of hidradenitis suppurativa is poorly understood.[39–42] It has generally been thought that the earliest lesion is an acute inflammatory process involving the apocrine duct and gland, which extends into the surrounding connective tissue with subsequent abscess and sinus formation (*Fig. 14.52*).[39] Some authors, however, believe that eccrine hidradenitis is more commonly found than apocrine involvement and others think that the primary event is follicular obstruction.[26,41]

The provocation to the initial 'apocrinitis' is believed to be keratin occlusion of the corresponding hair follicle. Certainly, keratin plugging of follicles and sinuses and inflammation in and around the hair follicle are regularly seen.[40] In one study, follicular occlusion was present in all of 118 specimens examined in patients with disease duration that ranged from as little to 1 month to many years.[42] The anatomic distribution of the lesions also supports the concept of an underlying apocrine gland defect. The condition has some similarity to Fox–Fordyce disease, which is more convincingly associated with an inflammatory process of the apocrine duct. Fox–Fordyce disease has the same sex, age incidence and

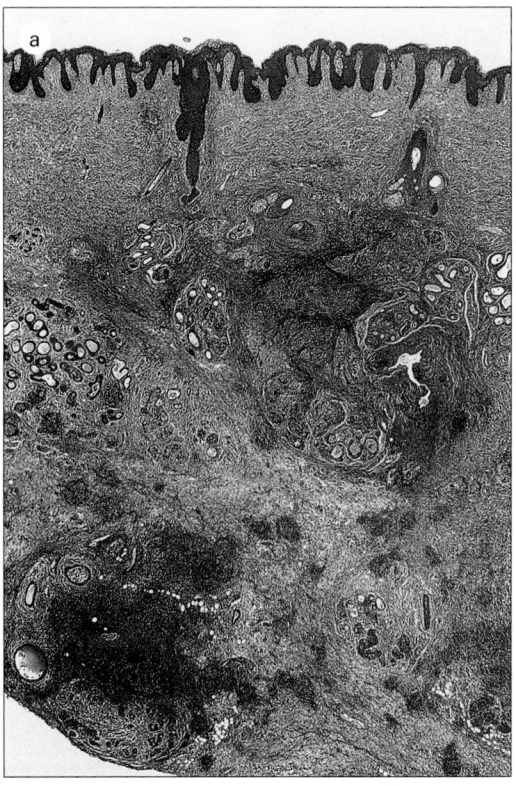

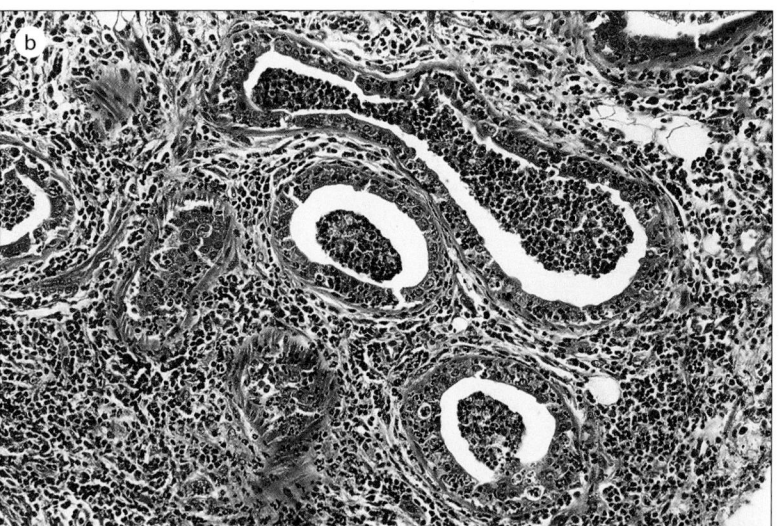

Fig. 14.52
(a, b) Hidradenitis suppurativa: early lesion showing acute inflammation involving the apocrine gland.

anatomic distribution and it too is alleviated by pregnancy. Interestingly, some cases of Fox–Fordyce disease have been reported to progress to hidradenitis suppurativa.

The other members of the follicular occlusion triad – acne conglobata and dissecting folliculitis – are both clearly associated with keratin plugging.

There is no doubt that the main cause of symptoms and chronic disability are the sinuses and fibrosis; these are largely due to the chronic secondary infection, since injection of sterile apocrine sweat into tissues does not induce an inflammatory response.

Organisms that may be found include *Staphylococcus aureus, Streptococcus viridans, Escherichia coli, Proteus mirabilis,* Klebsiella, *Pseudomonas aeruginosa, Streptococcus milleri* and anaerobic organisms. Coagulase-negative *S. aureus* is the most common bacterium isolated from the depth of the lesions.[43] Anaerobic organisms are responsible for the offensive smell, which can be a major problem for the patient. Generally, no immune deficiency can be detected, but there have been occasional reports of a functional neutrophil deficiency.

In considering the pathogenesis of this condition it must also be noted that some cases clearly develop as an autosomal dominantly inherited tendency.[44,45] Others have no suggestion of familial incidence.

The disease has been simulated in 3 of 12 normal volunteers by occlusion of axillary skin with atropine tape following depilation.[46] The latter in itself could be expected to produce some pathology, which is clearly not seen in the normal individual. The absence of lesions in 75% of these volunteers shows at least that there is some variation in susceptibility to developing the disease. This experimental induction of the disease has not been repeated.

In a study of 42 women with hidradenitis suppurativa, the authors noted premenstrual exacerbation of symptoms in two-thirds of patients and over one-third of patients reported menstrual irregularities.[47] In this same study, testosterone and free androgen index were higher compared with control patients.[47] In contrast, another study was not able to correlate hyperandrogenism and development of hidradenitis in women.[5,48] Pregnancy may relieve the symptoms of the disease.

In summary, the precise pathogenesis of hidradenitis suppurativa is not well-understood. It seems likely, however, that while many patients have a tendency to follicular occlusion with resultant acne-like lesions, some individuals show an additional, occasionally inherited, tendency for follicular obstruction to cause, or be associated with, inflammation of the apocrine duct. With the additional occlusive effects of obesity and secondary infection, often by mixed organisms, there is a resultant florid destructive folliculitis centered on, or also involving, the apocrine glands. The secondary bacterial infection perpetuates the chronic inflammatory and scarring nature of the process. A defect in the immune system would be expected to exacerbate this vicious circle, but no consistent abnormality has yet been identified.[49,50] The changes with pregnancy and menstrual cycle can be attributed to the hormonal effects on the apocrine gland and do not appear to be of primary importance.

Biopsies of established hidradenitis suppurativa show sinus tracts with marked suppuration and frank abscess formation, which are lined by a mixture of granulation tissue and squamous epithelium (*Fig. 14.53*). The latter extends from the associated follicular epithelium. These inflammatory sinus tracts usually contain desquamated keratin and sometimes hair shafts, and are surrounded by dense fibrosis.[42] The suppuration may extend into adjacent connective tissue where there may also be a chronic inflammatory infiltrate frequently including histiocytes and giant cells that may be related to keratin fragments. At this stage apocrine glands are conspicuously absent in the scarred and inflamed area, although adjacent apocrine glands often appear quite normal. Although some authors have emphasized the presence of acute inflammation of apocrine glands, in our experience, this is an uncommon

finding in routine surgical specimens. Others have also found primary inflammation of apocrine glands in only a minority of specimens.[41,51]

Differential diagnosis

The main differential diagnoses are primary infection, a response to a ruptured epidermal inclusion cyst, or wounds. Clinical correlation is necessary to establish the correct diagnosis.

References

1. Jansen, I., Altmeyer, P., Plewig, G. (2001) Acne inversa (alias hidradenitis suppurativa). *J Eur Acad Dermatol Venereol*, 15, 532–540.
2. Jemec, G.B. (1988) The symptomatology of hidradenitis suppurativa in women. *Br J Dermatol*, 119, 345–350.
3. Jemec, G.B. (1996) The prevalence of hidradenitis suppurativa and its potential precursor lesions. *J Am Acad Dermatol*, 35, 191–194.
4. Paletta, C., Jurkiewicz, M.J. (1987) Hidradenitis suppurativa. *Clin Plast Surg*, 14, 383–390.
5. Mitchell, K.M., Beck, D.E. (2002) Hidradenitis suppurativa. *Surg Clin North Am*, 82, 1187–1197.
6. Mengesha, Y.M., Holcombe, T.C., Hansen, R.C. (1999) Prepubertal hidradenitis suppurativa: two case reports and review of the literature. *Pediatr Dermatol*, 16, 292–296.
7. Palmer, R.A., Keefe, M. (2001) Early-onset hidradenitis suppurativa. *Clin Exp Dermatol*, 26, 501–503.
8. Kress, D.W., Graham, W.P. III, Davis, T.S. et al (1981) A preliminary report on the use of staphage lysate for treatment of hidradenitis suppurativa. *Ann Plast Surg*, 6, 393–395.
9. Williams, S.T., Busby, R.C., Demuth, R.J. et al (1991) Perineal hidradenitis suppurativa: presentation of two unusual complications and a review. *Ann Plast Surg*, 26, 456–462.
10. Anderson, B.B., Cadogan, C.A., Gangadharam, D. (1982) Hidradenitis suppurativa of the perineum, scrotum and gluteal area: presentation, complications and treatment. *J Natl Med Assoc*, 74, 999–1003.
11. Wiltz, O., Schoetz, D.J., Murray, J.J. et al (1990) Perianal hidradenitis suppurativa: the Lahey Clinic experience. *Dis Colon Rectum*, 33, 731–734.
12. Konig, A., Lehmann, C., Rompel, R. et al (1999) Cigarette smoking as a triggering factor of hidradenitis suppurativa. *Dermatology*, 198, 261–264.
13. Lapins, J., Ye, W., Nyren, O. et al (2001) Incidence of cancer among patients with hidradenitis suppurativa. *Arch Dermatol*, 137, 730–734.
14. Chicarilli, Z.N. (1987) Follicular occlusion triad: hidradenitis suppurativa, acne conglobata, and dissecting cellulitis of the scalp. *Ann Plast Surg*, 18, 230–237.
15. Weinrauch, L., Peled, I., Hacham-Zadeh, S. et al (1981) Surgical treatment of severe acne conglobata. *J Dermatol Surg Oncol*, 7, 492–494.
16. Resnick, S.D., Murrell, D.F., Woosley, J. (1992) Acne conglobata and a generalized lichen spinulosus-like eruption in a man seropositive for human immunodeficiency virus. *J Am Acad Dermatol*, 26, 1013–1014.
17. van Pelt, H.P.A., Juhlin, L. (1999) Acne conglobata after pregnancy. *Acta Derm Venereol*, 79, 169.
18. McMullan, F.H., Zeligman, I. (1956) Perifolliculitis capitis abscedens et suffodiens. *Arch Dermatol*, 73, 256–263.
19. Moyer, D.G., Williams, R.M. (1962) Perifolliculitis capitis abscedens et suffodiens. A report of six cases. *Arch Dermatol*, 85, 378–384.
20. Moschella, S.L., Klein, M.H., Miller, R.J. (1967) Perifolliculitis capitis abscedens et suffodiens. *Arch Dermatol*, 96, 195–197.
21. Shaffer, N., Billick, R.C., Srolovitz, H. (1992) Perifolliculitis capitis abscedens et suffodiens. *Arch Dermatol*, 128, 1329–1331.
22. Bjellerup, M., Wallengren, J. (1990) Familial perifolliculitis capitis abscedens et suffodiens in two brothers successfully treated with isotretinoin. *J Am Acad Dermatol*, 23, 752–753.
23. Curry, S.S., Gaither, D.H., King, L.E. (1981) Squamous cell carcinoma arising in dissecting perifolliculitis of the scalp. A case report and review of secondary squamous cell carcinomas. *J Am Acad Dermatol*, 4, 673–678.
24. Zachary, L.S., Robson, M.C., Rachmaninoff, N. (1987) Squamous cell carcinoma occurring in hidradenitis suppurativa. *Ann Plast Surg*, 18, 71–73.
25. Anstey, A.V., Wilkinson, J.D., Lord, P. (1990) Squamous cell carcinoma complicating hidradenitis suppurativa. *Br J Dermatol*, 123, 527–531.
26. Mendonica, H., Rebelo, C., Fernandes, A. et al (1991) Squamous cell carcinoma arising in hidradenitis suppurativa. *J Dermatol Surg Oncol*, 17, 830–832.
27. Altunay, I.K., Gokdemir, G., Kurt, A. et al (2002) Hidradenitis suppurativa and squamous cell carcinoma. *Dermatol Surg*, 28, 88–90.

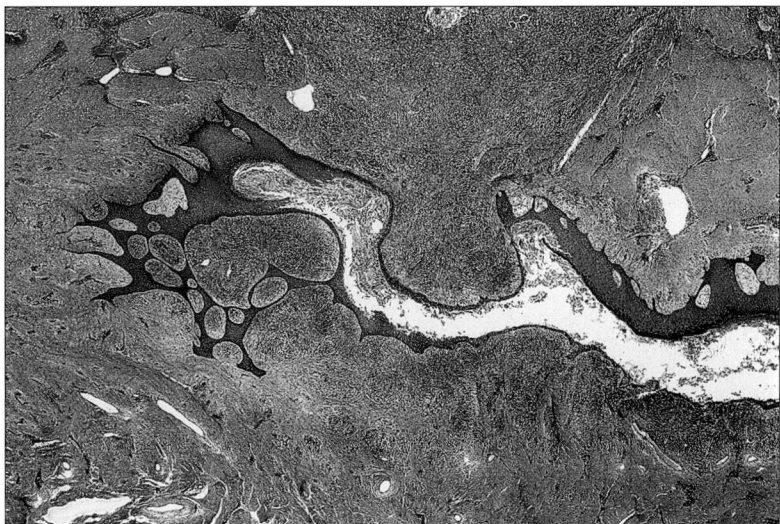

Fig. 14.53
Hidradenitis suppurativa: the sinuses are lined by stratified squamous epithelium and surrounded by fibrosis and inflammation.

28. Manolitsas, T., Blankin, S., Jaworski, R. et al (1999) Vulval squamous cell carcinoma arising in chronic hidradenitis suppurativa. *Gynecol Oncol*, **75**, 285–288.

29. Cosman, B.C., O'Grady, T.C., Pekarske, S. (2000) Verrucous carcinoma arising in hidradenitis suppurativa. *Int J Colorectal Dis*, **15**, 342–346.

30. Attanoos, R.L., Appleton, M.A.C., Hughes, L.E. et al (1993) Granulomatous hidradenitis suppurativa and cutaneous Crohn's disease. *Histopathology*, **23**, 111–115.

31. Ostlere, L.S. Langtry, J.A.A., Mortimer, P.S. et al (1991) Hidradenitis suppurativa in Crohn's disease. *Br J Dermatol*, **125**, 384–386.

32. Leybishkis, B., Fasseas, P., Ryan, K.F. et al (2001) Hidradenitis suppurativa and acne conglobata associated spondyloarthropathy. *Am J Med Sci*, **321**, 195–197.

33. Li, M., Hunt, M.J., Commens, C.A. (1997) Hidradenitis suppurativa, Dowling Degos disease and perianal squamous cell carcinoma. *Australas J Dermatol*, **38**, 209–211.

34. Gupta, A.K., Knowles, S.R., Gupta, M.A. et al (1995) Lithium therapy associated with hidradenitis suppurativa: case report and a review of the dermatologic side effects of lithium. *J Am Acad Dermatol*, **32**, 382–386.

35. Jemec, G.B. (1988) Effect of localized surgical excisions in hidradenitis suppurativa. *J Am Acad Dermatol*, **18**, 1103–1107.

36. Mortimer, P. (2002) Management of hidradenitis suppurativa. *Clin Exp Dermatol*, **27**, 328–337.

37. Rompel, R., Petres, J. (2000) Long-term results of wide surgical excision in 106 patients with hidradenitis suppurativa. *Dermatol Surg*, **26**, 638–643.

38. Endo, Y., Tamura, A., Ishikawa, O. et al (1998) Perianal hidradenitis suppurativa: early surgical treatment gives good results in chronic or recurrent cases. *Br J Dermatol*, **139**, 906–910.

39. Gordon, S.W. (1978) Hidradenitis suppurativa: a closer look. *J Natl Med Assoc*, **70**, 339–343.

40. Boer, J., Weltevreden, E.F. (1996) Hidradenitis suppurativa or acne inversa: a clinicopathological study of early lesions. *Br J Dermatol*, **135**, 721–725.

41. Attanoos, R.L., Appleton, M.A., Douglas-Jones, A.G. (1995) The pathogenesis of hidradenitis suppurativa: a closer look at apocrine and apoeccrine glands. *Br J Dermatol*, **133**, 254–258.

42. Yu, C.C., Cook, M.G. (1990) Hidradenitis suppurativa: a disease of follicular epithelium, rather than apocrine glands. *Br J Dermatol*, **122**, 763–769.

43. Lapins, J., Jarstrand, C., Emtestam, L. (1999) Coagulase-negative staphylococci are the most common bacteria found in cultures from the deep portions of hidradenitis suppurativa lesions as obtained by carbon dioxide laser surgery. *Br J Dermatol*, **140**, 90–95.

44. Fitzsimmons, J.S., Guilbert, P.R., Fitzsimmons, E.M. (1985) Evidence of genetic factors in hidradenitis suppurativa. *Br J Dermatol*, **113**, 1–8.

45. von der Werth, J.M., Williams, H.C., Raeburn, J.A. (2000) The clinical genetics of hidradenitis suppurativa revisited. *Br J Dermatol*, **142**, 947–953.

46. Shelley, W.B., Cahn, M.M. (1955) The pathogenesis of hidradenitis suppurativa in man. *Arch Dermatol Syphilol*, **72**, 562–565.

47. Mortimer, P.S., Dawber, R.P., Gales, M.A. et al (1986) Mediation of hidradenitis suppurativa by androgens. *Br Med J*, **292**, 245–248.

48. Barth, J.H., Layton, A.M., Cunliffe, W.J. (1997) Endocrine factors in pre- and postmenopausal women with hidradenitis suppurativa. *Br J Dermatol*, **134**, 802–803.

49. Dvorak, V.C., Root, R.K., MacGregor, R.R. (1977) Host defense mechanisms in hidradenitis suppurativa. *Arch Dermatol*, **113**, 450–453.

50. Ginder, P.A., Ousley, M., Hinthorn, D. et al (1982) Hidradenitis suppurativa: evidence for a bactericidal defect correctable by cholinergic agonist in vitro and in vivo. *J Clin Immunol*, **2**, 237–241.

51. Jemec, G.B.E., Hansen, U. (1996) Histology of hidradenitis suppurativa. *J Am Acad Dermatol*, **34**, 994–999.

Vascular diseases

15

Introduction 709

Leukocytoclastic vasculitis 709

Henoch–Schönlein purpura 716

Infantile acute hemorrhagic edema 718

Urticarial vasculitis 719

Polyarteritis nodosa and microscopic polyangiitis 720

Wegener's granulomatosis 727

Allergic granulomatosis with angiitis 731

Mucocutaneous lymph node syndrome 735

Granuloma faciale 738

Erythema elevatum diutinum 740

Behçet's disease 743

Thromboangiitis obliterans 747

Temporal arteritis 748

Takayasu's arteritis 751

Infection-related vasculitis 753

Paraneoplastic vasculitis 754

Vasculitis associated with palisaded neutrophilic and granulomatous dermatitis 755

Lymphocytic vasculitis 756

Malignant atrophic papulosis 757

Atrophie blanche 760

Dermatological manifestations of cholesterol crystal embolism 762

Disseminated intravascular coagulation 763

Cryoglobulinemia 764

Antiphospholipid antibody syndrome and Sneddon syndrome 767

Thrombotic thrombocytopenic purpura and hemolytic uremic syndrome 768

Immune thrombocytopenic purpura 770

Factor V Leiden mutation 771

Hypergammaglobulinemic purpura 771

Superficial thrombophlebitis 772

Sclerosing lymphangitis 773

Senile purpura 773

Introduction

Vasculitis and other forms of vascular damage are the subjects of this chapter. Although minimal criteria for the diagnosis of vasculitis may differ among experts, the presence of inflammation and some evidence of vascular damage in the form of vessel wall/endothelial cell necrosis or fibrinoid change fulfill most authorities' criteria for a diagnosis of vasculitis. Some, however, apply the term less restrictively to vascular inflammation associated with non-specific histological features such as extravasated red cells, endothelial swelling, or karyorrhexis but without fibrinoid change or necrosis. When encountering such cases, we prefer to designate them as 'low-grade vascular damage' and include a comment that, although the findings may represent very early vasculitis, they do not meet strict criteria for necrotizing vasculitis. That inflammatory vascular disease is represented by a broad spectrum of histological changes cannot be overemphasized.

The histological features of most forms of vasculitis are not specific for an entity per se. A specific diagnosis requires careful clinical, histological and serological (i.e. presence of antineutrophil antibodies) correlation. The role of the pathologist in evaluating a biopsy is to confirm or deny the presence of vasculitis, and to describe the nature of the inflammatory infiltrate and the type(s) and size(s) of the vessel(s) involved. A histological differential diagnosis is established to guide patient evaluation.

A pathological diagnosis of vasculitis may indicate a primary or secondary disease (i.e. in the setting of connective tissue disease). Secondary forms of vascular disease may manifest as diverse histological patterns. For example, connective tissue diseases may be associated with either a small-vessel leukocytoclastic disease or a large vessel vasculitis. Likewise, different histological patterns may be seen in association with a given primary vasculitis. As an example, Wegener's granulomatosis may be associated with either leukocytoclastic or granulomatous vasculitis.

The myriad schemata for the classification of the vasculitides are a reflection of the complexity of this controversial class of diseases. Over the last decade or so, several new schemes have emerged that attempt to combine both histological and clinical information (*Table 15.1*).[1] Undoubtedly, these classifications will continue to be refined as a more complete understanding of the pathogenesis of these diseases is gained.

Reference

1. Jennette, J.C., Falk, R.J., Andrassy, K. et al (1994) Nomenclature of systemic vasculitis. Proposal of an international consensus conference. *Arthritis Rheum*, 37, 187–192.

Leukocytoclastic vasculitis

Clinical features

Leukocytoclastic vasculitis (allergic vasculitis, hypersensitivity vasculitis, leukocytoclastic angiitis) is the commonest form of vasculitis.[1-6] Leuko-

Table 15.1

Types and definitions of vasculitis adopted by the Chapel Hill Consensus Conference on the Nomenclature of Systemic Vasculitis*

Type of vasculitis	Essential components/non-essential components
Large vessel vasculitis	
Giant cell (temporal) arteritis	Granulomatous arteritis of the aorta and its major branches, with a predilection for the extracranial branches of the carotid artery. *Often involves the temporal artery. Usually occurs in patients older than 50 and often is associated with polymyalgia rheumatica*
Takayasu arteritis	Granulomatous inflammation of the aorta and its major branches. *Usually occurs in patients younger than 50*
Medium-sized vessel vasculitis	
Polyarteritis nodosa[†] (classic polyarteritis nodosa)	Necrotizing inflammation of medium-sized or small arteries without glomerulonephritis or vasculitis in arterioles, capillaries, or venules.
Kawasaki disease	Arteritis involving large, medium-sized and small arteries, and associated with mucocutaneous lymph node syndrome. *Coronary arteries are often involved; aorta and veins may be involved. Usually occurs in children*
Small vessel vasculitis	
Cutaneous leukocytoclastic angiitis	Isolated cutaneous leukocytoclastic angiitis without systemic vasculitis or glomerulonephritis
Henoch–Schönlein purpura	Vasculitis, with IgA-dominant immune deposits, affecting small vessels (i.e. capillaries, venules or arterioles). *Typically involves skin, gut, and glomeruli, and is associated with arthralgias or arthritis*
Microscopic polyangiitis[†] (microscopic polyarteritis)[‡]	Necrotizing vasculitis, with few or no immune deposits, affecting small vessels (i.e. capillaries, venules or arterioles). *Necrotizing arteritis involving small and medium-sized arteries may be present. Necrotizing glomerulonephritis is very common. Pulmonary capillaritis often occurs.*
Wegener's granulomatosis[‡]	Granulomatous inflammation involving the respiratory tract, and necrotizing vasculitis affecting small to medium-sized vessels (e.g. capillaries, venules, arterioles and arteries). *Necrotizing glomerulonephritis is common*
Churg–Strauss syndrome[‡]	Eosinophil-rich and granulomatous inflammation involving the respiratory tract, and necrotizing vasculitis affecting small to medium-sized vessels, and associated with asthma and eosinophilia
Essential cryoglobulinemic vasculitis	Vasculitis, with cryoglobulin immune deposits, affecting small vessels (i.e. capillaries, venules or arterioles), and associated with cryoglobulins in serum. *Skin and glomeruli are often involved*

Reproduced with permission from Jennette, J.C. et al. 1994 *Seminars in Diagnostic Pathology*, **18**, 3–13.
* Large vessel refers to the aorta and the largest branches directed toward major body regions (e.g. to the extremities and the head and neck); medium-sized vessel refers to the main visceral arteries (e.g. renal, hepatic, coronary, and mesenteric arteries); small vessel refers to venules, capillaries, arterioles, and the intraparenchymal distal arterial radicals that connect with arterioles. Some small and large vessel vasculitides may involve medium-sized arteries, but large and medium-sized vessel vasculitides do not involve vessels smaller than arteries. Essential components are represented by normal type; italicized type represents usual, but not essential, components.
[†] Preferred term.
[‡] Strongly associated with antineutrophil cytoplasmic autoantibodies.

cytoclastic vasculitis is not a disease entity but represents a vascular reaction pattern due to circulating immune complexes that may be caused by a number of underlying disorders. The antigens possibly involved are summarized in *Table 15.2*.[1–7] Although the condition may be limited to the skin, it is important to recognize that it may also be associated with systemic manifestations involving the joints, kidneys, and gastrointestinal system in between 20 and 50% of patients.[5,8] The disease occurs equally in men and women, and may present in any age group.

Skin lesions are typically polymorphic, but palpable purpura (non-blanching erythematous papules) is the commonest manifestation (*Fig. 15.1*). Urticarial, bullous or vesicular, ulceroinfarctive, nodular, pustular, livedoid and annular lesions may also be encountered (*Figs 15.2–15.8*).[9–13] The lesions measure from 1 mm to several centimeters in diameter. Occasionally, annular erythema multiforme-like lesions occur (*Fig. 15.9*). The lower legs are affected most often, but lesions may be present at a wide variety of sites, including the buttocks, arms, feet, ankles, trunk and face, particularly in more seriously affected patients (*Figs 15.10, 15.11*). Lesions may be present in the skin of dependent areas of bedridden patients, such as the back and buttocks. A frequent accompaniment is edema of the lower legs or ankles (*Fig. 15.12*). Patients may experience a single occurrence or develop frequent recurrences over months or years. The eruption often occurs in episodes, each lasting 1–4 weeks, at irregular intervals. Lesions usually heal completely, although on occasions atrophic scars and hyperpigmentation may occur. Rarely, leukocytoclastic vasculitis may show erythema gyratum repens gross morphology.[14]

Although occasional cases are asymptomatic, patients not uncommonly complain of pruritus or burning; less frequently, pain is a feature. Additional features, which are sometimes present, include abdominal pain and gastrointestinal bleeding, joint pains with associated erythema and swelling, and evidence of renal involvement.[15] In severe cases, the

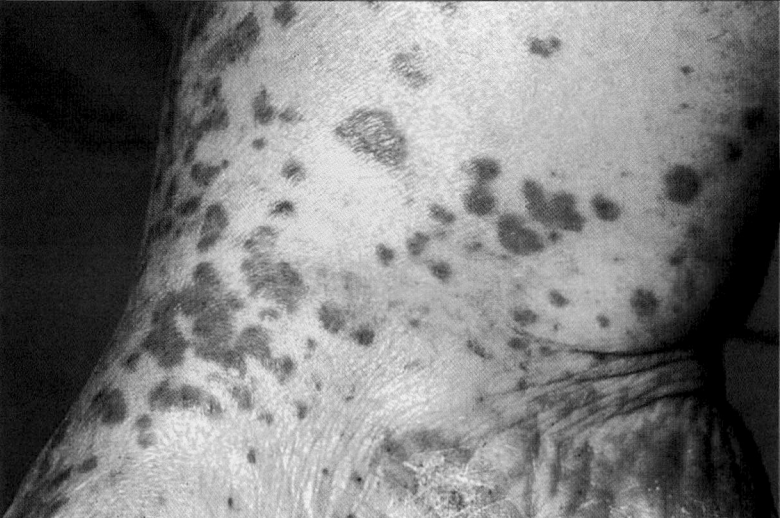

Fig. 15.1
Leukocytoclastic vasculitis: typical erythematous maculopapular lesions are present on the medial aspect of the ankle. By courtesy of R.A. Marsden, MD, St George's Hospital, London, UK.

features resemble acute glomerulonephritis and the nephrotic syndrome may even supervene. Rarely, patients have respiratory involvement (nodular or diffuse infiltrative lesions on X-ray examination), and very exceptionally the central or peripheral nervous system is affected, causing symptoms such as headache, diplopia and dysphagia.

In one study, drug therapy, often following an upper respiratory tract infection, was the inciting event in 45% of patients.[16] Numerous drugs have been implicated as a trigger including non-steroidal anti-inflammatory drugs (aspirin, ibuprofen, naproxen, phenylbutazone), phenytoin, quinidine, amiodarone, potassium iodide, allopurinol, sulfonamides, griseofulvin, penicillin, erythromycin, clindamycin, oxacillin, vancomycin, ofloxacin, clarithromycin, furosemide (frusemide), thiazides, cimetidine, omeprazole, gabapentin, orlistat, zidovudine, indinavir, efavirenz, lisinopril, sotalol, insulin, retinoids, propylthiouracil, thiouracil, mefloquine, methotrexate, azathioprine, sirolimus, granulocyte colony-stimulating factor, haloperidol, cytarabine, gold and disulfiram.[2,17–52] Levamisole has been described as producing a vasculitis localized to the ears in children.[53,54] A localized form of leukocytoclastic vasculitis may occur at the site of interferon alpha injection.[55,56]

Collagen vascular disease (most often rheumatoid arthritis and lupus erythematosus) is commonly associated with leukocytoclastic vasculitis,[2,57] and in one study it was found in 21% of patients.[2] The occurrence of leukocytoclastic vasculitis in a patient with dermatomyositis raises the possibility of associated malignancy.[58]

Infection is also commonly associated with leukocytoclastic vasculitis (see p. 753), with bacterial, fungal and viral infection all being impli-

Table 15.2
Possible causes of allergic vasculitis

- **Infection**
  - bacterial: *Streptococcus*
  - mycobacterial: *Mycobacterium tuberculosis*
  - viral: hepatitis, influenza
  - cytomegalovirus
  - HIV infection
  - leprosy

- Drugs
  - aspirin, phenacetin, sulfonamides, penicillin, iodides, phenothiazines

- Chemicals
  - insecticides, weed killers, petroleum products

- Foreign proteins
  - serum sickness
  - hyposensitization antigens

- Associated diseases
  - autoimmune diseases: systemic lupus erythematosus, inflammatory bowel disease
  - hemolytic anemia
  - Hodgkin's lymphoma, carcinoma
  - rheumatoid arthritis
  - mixed connective tissue disease
  - dermatomyositis
  - relapsing polychondritis
  - Sjögren's syndrome
  - Henoch–Schönlein purpura
  - cryoglobulinemia
  - polyarteritis nodosa
  - Wegener's granulomatosis
  - Churg–Strauss disease
  - granuloma faciale
  - erythema elevatum diutinum
  - Waldenström's hypergammaglobulinemia
  - sarcoidosis

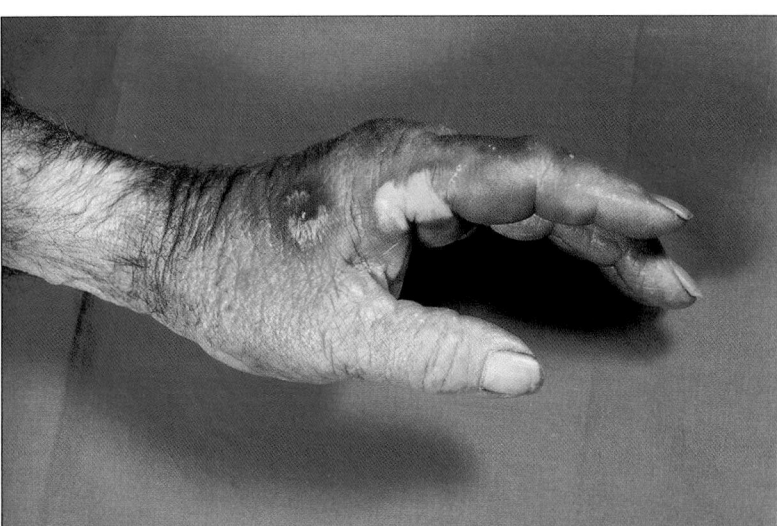

Fig. 15.3
Leukocytoclastic vasculitis: in this patient an extensive purpuric eruption showing central necrosis is evident. By courtesy of R.A. Marsden, MD, St George's Hospital, London, UK.

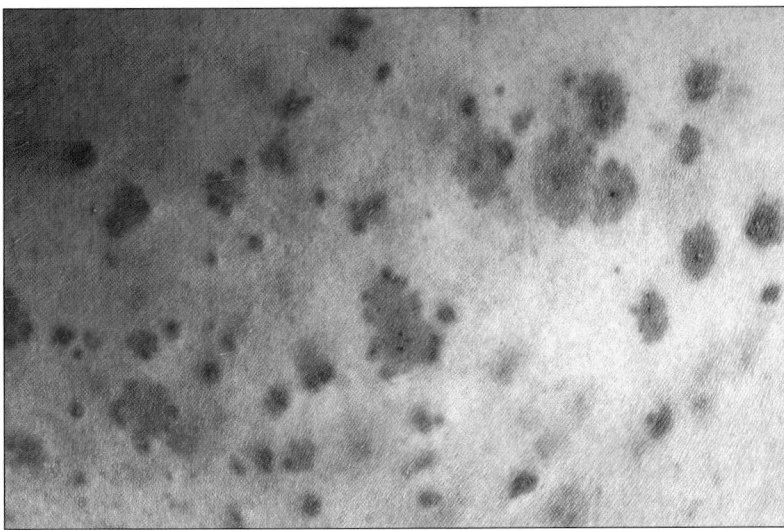

Fig. 15.2
Leukocytoclastic vasculitis: close-up view showing small erythematous lesions. By courtesy of the Institute of Dermatology, London, UK.

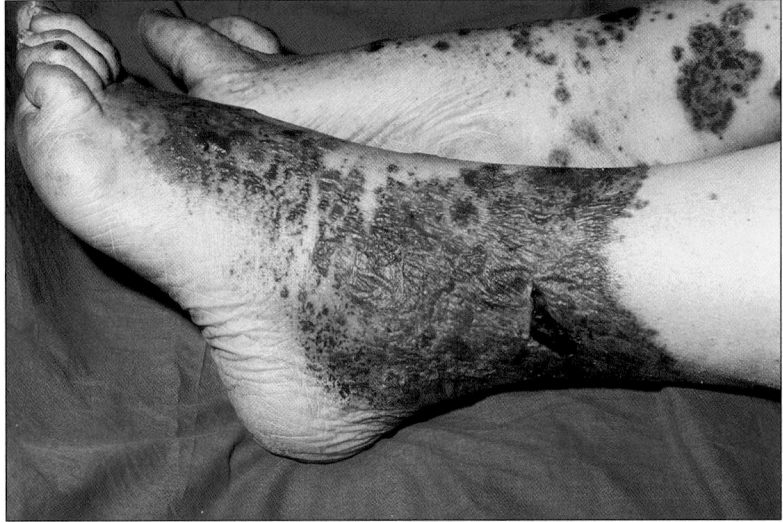

Fig. 15.4
Leukocytoclastic vasculitis: here confluent purpura with ulceration is present. By courtesy of R.A. Marsden, MD, St George's Hospital, London, UK.

cated.[59] Associated bacterial infections include streptococci, *Klebsiella pneumoniae*, *Mycobacterium tuberculosis* and *Mycoplasma pneumoniae*.[60–62] Systemic cat-scratch disease has been documented presenting as leukocytoclastic vasculitis.[63] Hepatitis C infection is a particularly frequent association. It should be noted that hepatitis C is also often associated with cryoglobulins (see section on cryoglobulinemia).[64,65]

Inflammatory bowel disease, both ulcerative colitis and Crohn's disease, may be associated with leukocytoclastic vasculitis.[66,67] Further rare associations include sarcoidosis, α_1-antitrypsin deficiency, cystic fibrosis and the Wiskott–Aldrich syndrome.[11,68,69]

Leukocytoclastic vasculitis rarely represents a paraneoplastic manifestation of an underlying malignancy, especially leukemia and lymphoma (see p. 754).[70] Hairy cell leukemia is particularly often associated with leukocytoclastic vasculitis but other forms of vasculitis may also be seen. In one study of 42 patients with hairy cell leukemia and vasculitis, 21 had leukocytoclastic vasculitis and 17 had polyarteritis nodosa.[71] In addition, four patients had direct infiltration of vessel walls by leukemic cells (see also section on paraneoplastic vasculitis). Although uncommon, leukocytoclastic vasculitis may also be seen in patients with a variety of solid tumors including non-small cell carcinoma of lung, and adenocarcinoma of breast, colon, prostate and kidney (see p. 754).[72,73]

Leukocytoclastic vasculitis can be a manifestation of human immunodeficiency virus (HIV) infection.[74] Unusual associations of leukocytoclastic vasculitis include the use of a nicotine patch, drug additives, sodium benzoate, protein A column pheresis, prolonged exercise and as a complication of an infected hip prosthesis.[75–80]

Laboratory investigation may reveal an elevated erythrocyte sedimentation rate (ESR), proteinuria or hematuria. In some idiopathic cases and those associated with systemic disease (e.g. rheumatoid arthritis, systemic lupus erythematosus (SLE) and Sjögren's syndrome), hypocomplementemia is sometimes evident.[5] Urinalysis may reveal proteinuria or hematuria. Cryoglobulins have been found in up to 25% of patients.[2] Perinuclear staining antineutrophil antibodies are present in about 20% of patients.[2,81]

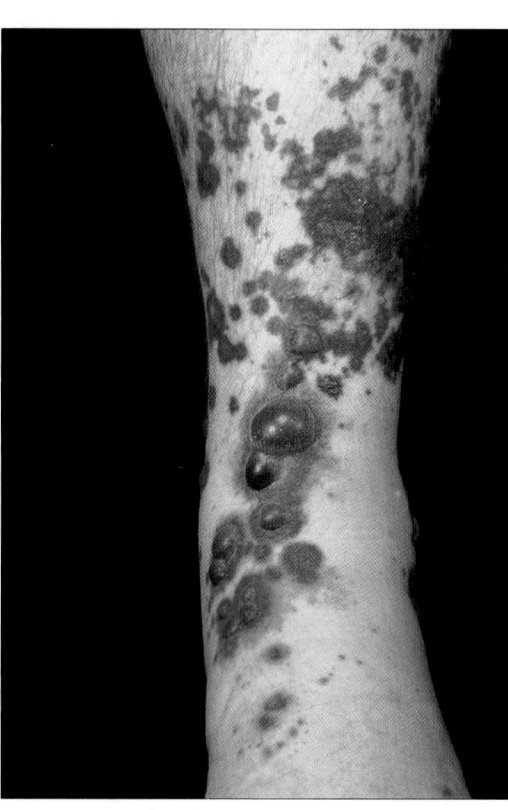

Fig. 15.5
Leukocytoclastic vasculitis: this patient presented with bullous lesions which developed as a consequence of thrombosis with epidermal infarction. By courtesy of the Institute of Dermatology, London, UK.

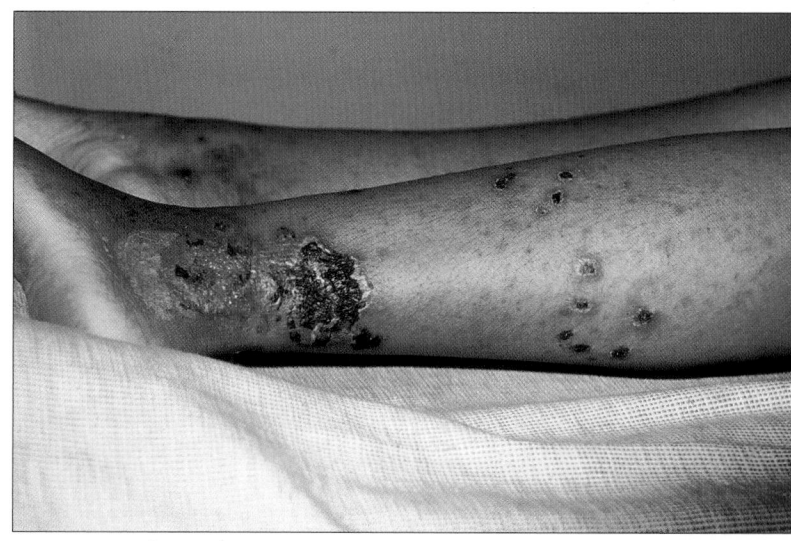

Fig. 15.7
Leukocytoclastic vasculitis: in this patient, there are extensive ulceroinfarctive lesions. By courtesy of the Institute of Dermatology, London, UK.

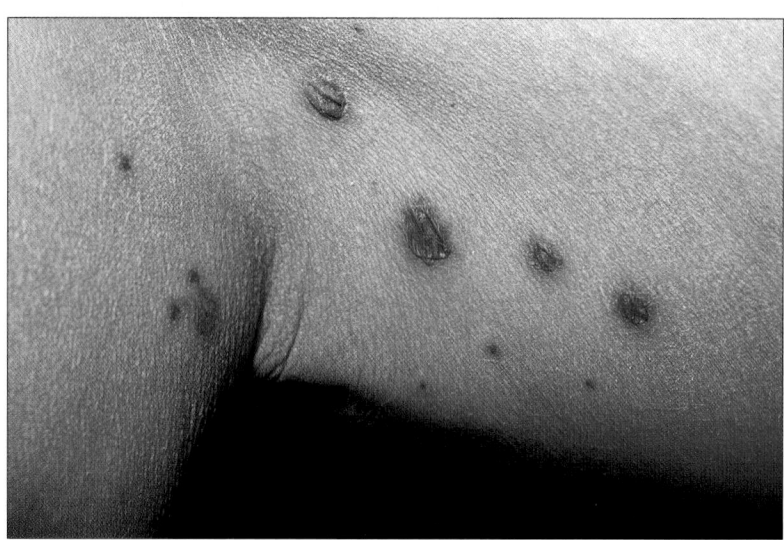

Fig. 15.6
Leukocytoclastic vasculitis: Nodular lesions. By courtesy of the Institute of Dermatology, London, UK.

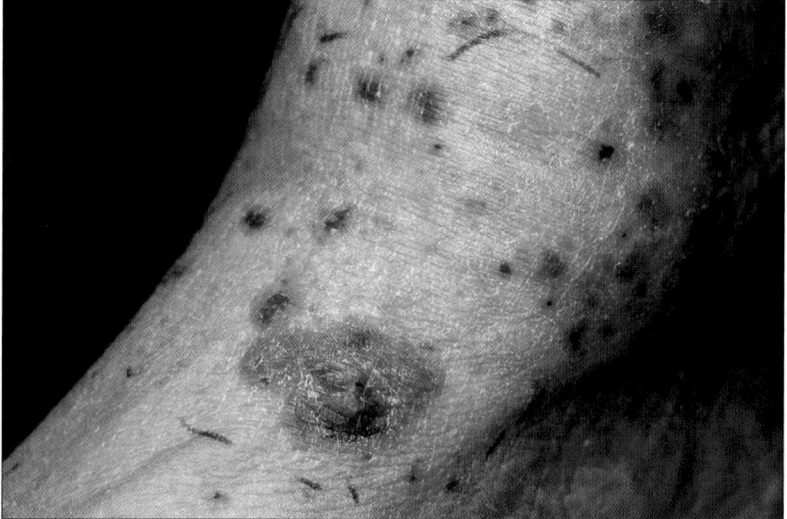

Fig. 15.8
Leukocytoclastic vasculitis: close-up view of a hemorrhagic blister. By courtesy of the Institute of Dermatology, London, UK.

Leukocytoclastic vasculitis is associated with a variable outcome, ranging from a mild, self-limiting illness through to a serious, potentially fatal (due particularly to renal involvement) disorder.[15] About 1.9% of patients die of systemic disease.[2] Most patients have a benign outcome. An acute clinical course is seen in approximately 50% of patients.[2] A chronic course or one characterized by relapses and remissions is seen in some patients.[2] In one study of patients with hypersensitivity vasculitis, 54 did not require therapy, 26 were treated with non-steroidal anti-inflammatory medications, and 14 required immunosuppressive agents, most often corticosteroids.[16]

Specific syndromes associated with leukocytoclastic vasculitis, such as urticarial vasculitis and Henoch–Schönlein purpura, are discussed under separate headings in this chapter.

Pathogenesis and histological features

Leukocytoclastic vasculitis is an immune complex-mediated disorder similar to the classic Arthus reaction.[82] Immune complexes are deposited in the walls of small blood vessels.[5] This is associated with activation of the complement cascade and the production of C5a (a neutrophil polymorph chemotactant). The resultant polymorph influx is associated with release of lysosomal enzymes, including elastases and collagenases, resulting in blood vessel wall damage, fibrin deposition and the release of red blood cells (purpura) into the perivenular connective tissue. Thrombosis may ensue and, in particularly severe examples, epidermal ischemic damage results. Lesions are particularly seen on the lower legs because of hydrostasis and blood vessel flow sludging.[5]

Evidence for an immune complex-mediated pathogenesis is convincing.[1] Patients have been clinically proven to have high levels of circulating immune complexes, and these are shown to correlate with vasculitic lesions. Immunoglobulin and complement can be identified in vitro, by immunofluorescence or immunoperoxidase techniques, and in biopsies from blood vessel wall lesions less than 24 hours old (*Fig. 15.13*).[83] Immune complexes can be identified ultrastructurally as clumps of electron-dense material, usually within the basement membrane between endothelial cells and pericytes of postcapillary venules. Examination of apparently uninvolved skin from patients with

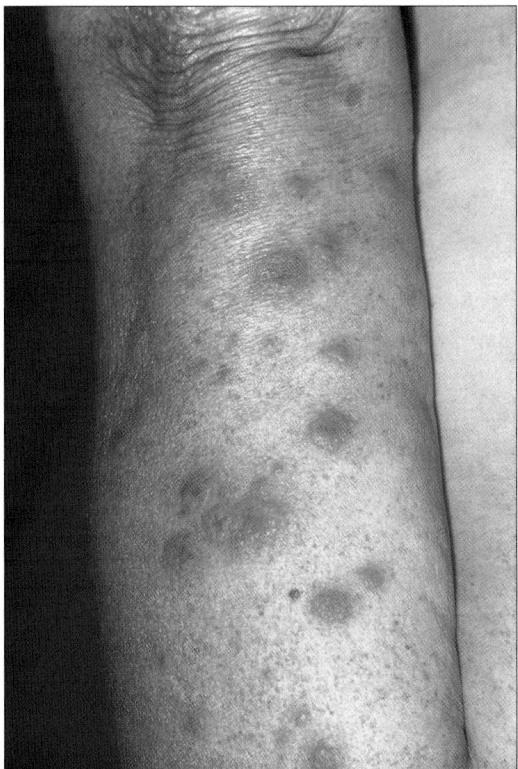

Fig. 15.9
Leukocytoclastic vasculitis: these urticarial lesions on the back of the arm resemble those of erythema multiforme. By courtesy of R.A. Marsden, MD, St George's Hospital, London, UK.

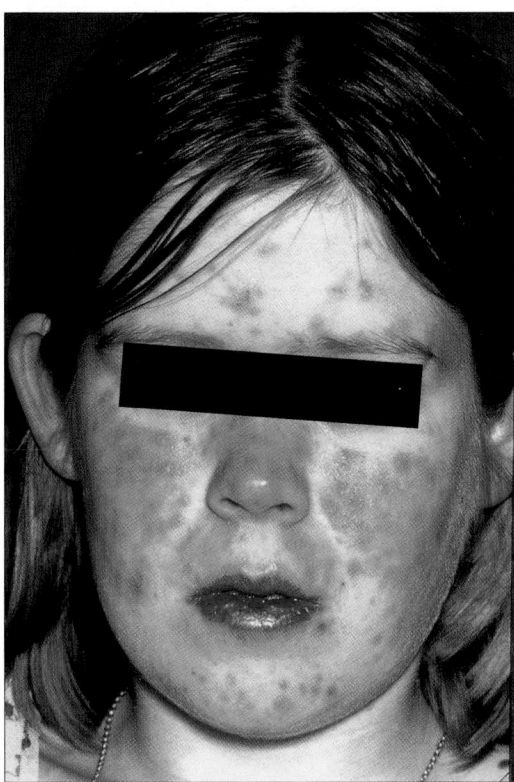

Fig. 15.10
Leukocytoclastic vasculitis: lesions may be widely disseminated in severely affected patients. By courtesy of R.A. Marsden, MD, St George's Hospital, London, UK.

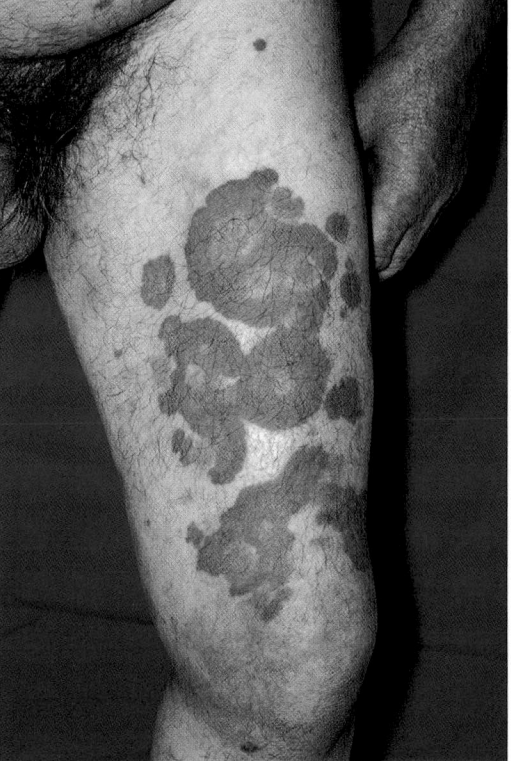

Fig. 15.11
Leukocytoclastic vasculitis: this patient has serological evidence of systemic lupus erythematosus.

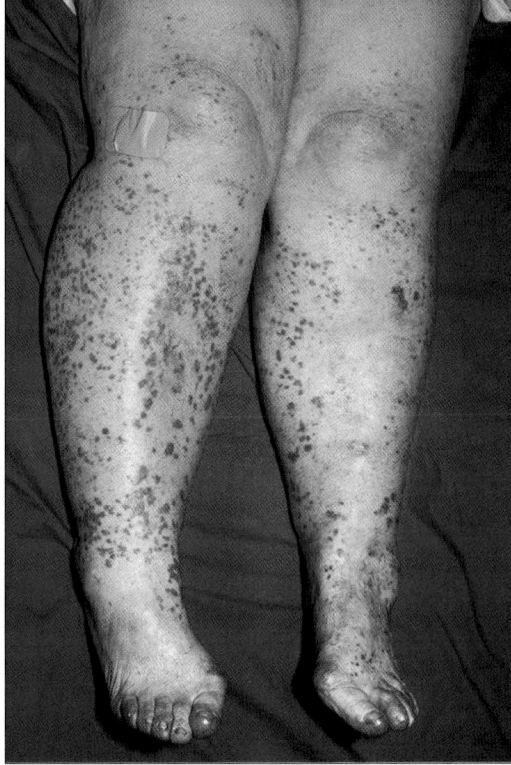

Fig. 15.12
Leukocytoclastic vasculitis: in addition to the typical maculopapular eruption there is marked swelling of the legs. By courtesy of R.A. Marsden, MD, St George's Hospital, London, UK.

leukocytoclastic vasculitis sometimes shows immunoglobulin and complement within the walls of dermal blood vessels. If histamine is injected into uninvolved skin 3–4 hours previously, all the features of leukocytoclastic vasculitis are evident at biopsy, including neutrophil degeneration; this suggests that the immunoreactants are a cause rather than a consequence of the vasculitis.[1]

The findings of immunofluorescence studies vary according to the age of the lesion. Immunoglobulins have been described in up to 81% of patients.[84] In early lesions, C3 and IgM predominate, in fully developed lesions there is predominance of fibrinogen and IgG and in late lesions fibrinogen and C3 are detected.[84]

Some authors, noting that early lesions may contain abundant CD3+, CD4+ and CD1a+ cells, have suggested that cell-mediated immune mechanisms may also play a role in the pathogenesis of leukocytoclastic vasculitis.[84] Consistent with this hypothesis is the demonstration of Langerhans' cells in the late phase of vasculitis.[85] Expression of 72 kD heat shock protein and the presence of gamma/delta T-cells in patients with vasculitis associated with infection has led one group of authors to postulate that the cell-mediated immune response plays an important role in that subset.[86]

In leukocytoclastic vasculitis, it is the postcapillary venule and the capillary loops (and not the arteriole) which are primarily affected, usually within the superficial dermis (*Fig. 15.14*). In severe cases, particularly those associated with malignancy or connective tissue disease, the inflammatory changes may extend into the vasculature of the deep reticular dermis or even the subcutaneous fat (*Fig. 15.15*).[87] The histological features are similar irrespective of the underlying etiology.

The histological features of leukocytoclastic vasculitis are those of fibrinoid necrosis associated with endothelial cell swelling and infiltration of the blood vessel walls by neutrophils and conspicuous nuclear dust (*Fig. 15.16*).[2,88,89] Variable numbers of mononuclear cells and eosinophils may be seen. In early lesions, nuclear dust is associated with a perivascular neutrophilic infiltrate but multiple tissue sections may be needed to identify fibrinoid vascular changes. The former features, even without unequivocal fibrinoid change, are suggestive of an evolving leukocytoclastic vasculitis.

Intravascular thrombi and ischemic necrosis of the overlying epidermis (often with bullae formation) may sometimes be seen (*Figs 15.17–15.19*). Occasionally, one may encounter intradermal or subepidermal pustules.

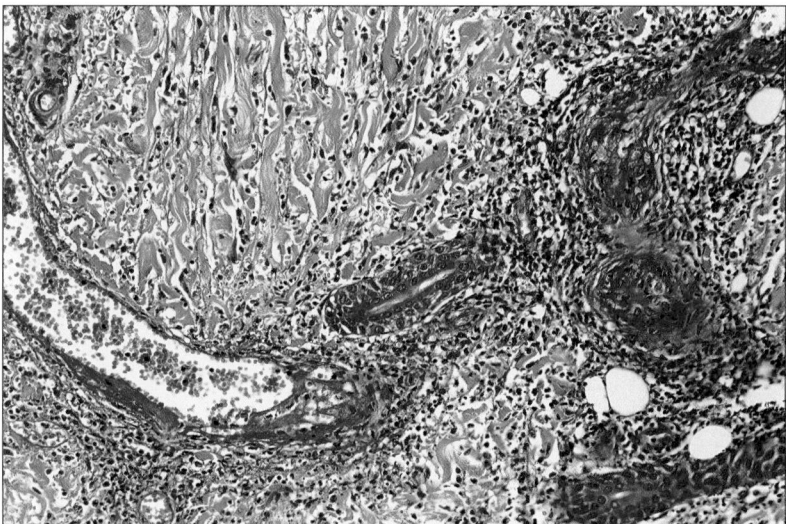

Fig. 15.14
Leukocytoclastic vasculitis: the blood vessels show florid fibrinoid necrosis and intense inflammation.

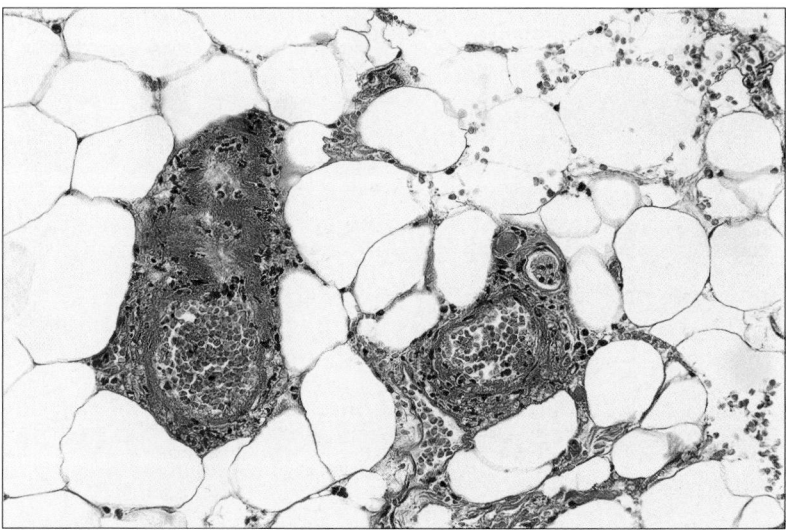

Fig. 15.15
Leukocytoclastic vasculitis: the vessels of the superficial subcutaneous fat are not uncommonly involved.

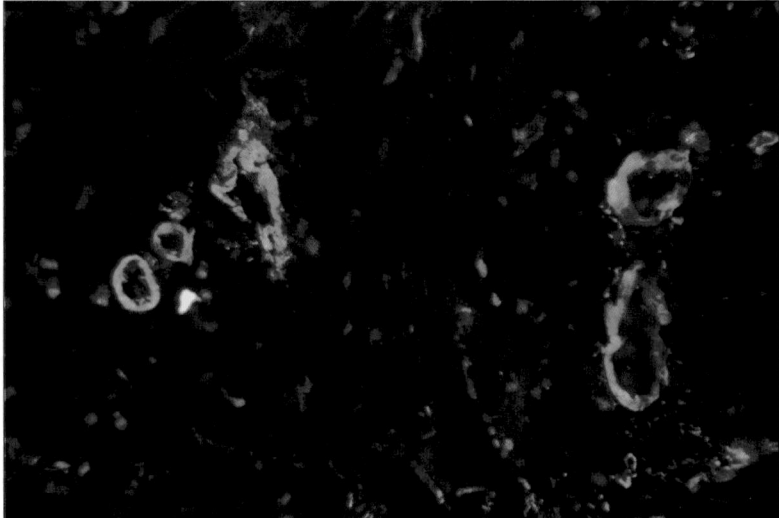

Fig. 15.13
Leukocytoclastic vasculitis: IgM is present in the blood vessel walls (direct immunofluorescence). By courtesy of B. Bhogal, FIMLS, Institute of Dermatology, London, UK.

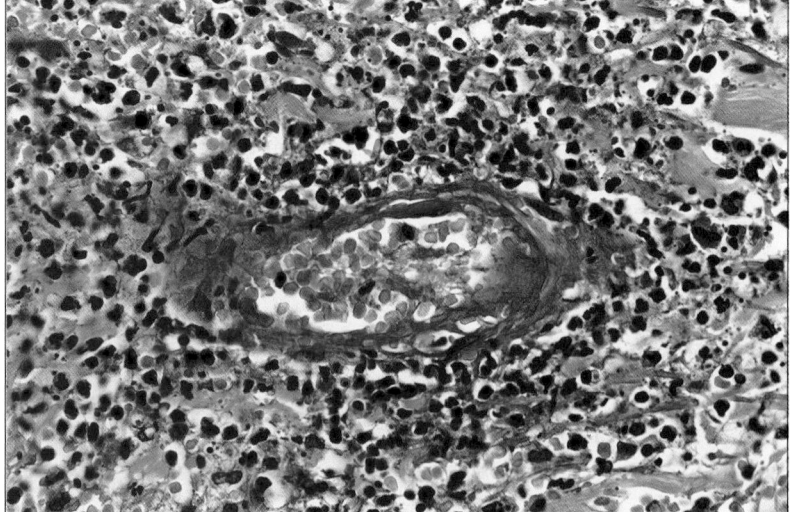

Fig. 15.16
Leukocytoclastic vasculitis: high power view showing fibrinoid necrosis and a mixed inflammatory cell infiltrate composed of neutrophils, eosinophils and lymphocytes. There is marked leukocytoclasis (karyorrhexis, nuclear dust).

In patients with associated hypocomplementemia, neutrophils are the predominant cells with far fewer lymphocytes; patients who are normocomplementemic may show lymphocyte predominance. In the surrounding connective tissue, red cell extravasation, edema and an inflammatory neutrophil infiltrate associated with karyorrhexis (leukocytoclasis) are typically present (*Fig. 15.20*).

The severity of the histopathological changes in the cutaneous lesions of leukocytoclastic vasculitis does not predict extracutaneous involvement.[90]

Differential diagnosis

The diagnosis of leukocytoclastic vasculitis is relatively straightforward. It is critical to understand that leukocytoclastic vasculitis is not a disease *sui generis*. Rather, leukocytoclastic vasculitis represents a reaction pattern due to circulating immune complexes that may be caused by myriad underlying disorders. Furthermore, leukocytoclastic vasculitis is frequently encountered in association with other forms of vasculitis. For example, leukocytoclastic vasculitis is much more commonly encountered in patients with Wegener's granulomatosis than granulomatous vasculitis. Therefore, a biopsy showing leukocytoclastic vasculitis does not exclude diseases that may be associated with other forms of vasculitis. Sometimes leukocytoclastic vasculitis may coexist with a large-vessel vasculitis. An inadequate biopsy that does not include deep dermis and subcutaneous tissue containing large vessels may produce misleading results. The presence of leukocytoclastic vasculitis in a superficial biopsy does not exclude an associated large-vessel vasculitis. The report of a superficial biopsy from a patient suspected of having large-vessel vasculitis should comment on the lack of larger vessels for evaluation.

Sweet's syndrome may resemble leukocytoclastic vasculitis; however, the presence of a diffuse (rather than predominantly perivascular) neutrophilic infiltrate without fibrinoid vascular change or necrosis favors the former condition.

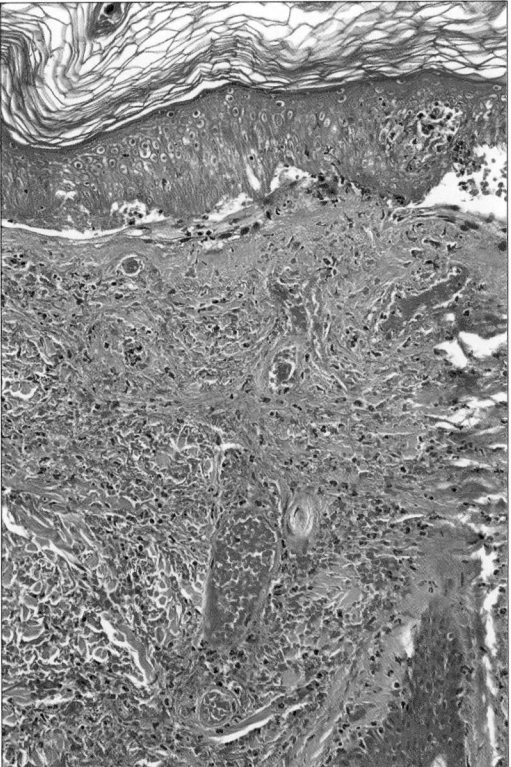

Fig. 15.19
Leukocytoclastic vasculitis: vascular thrombosis is accompanied by epidermal infarction. Note the cytoplasmic eosinophilia and loss of nuclei.

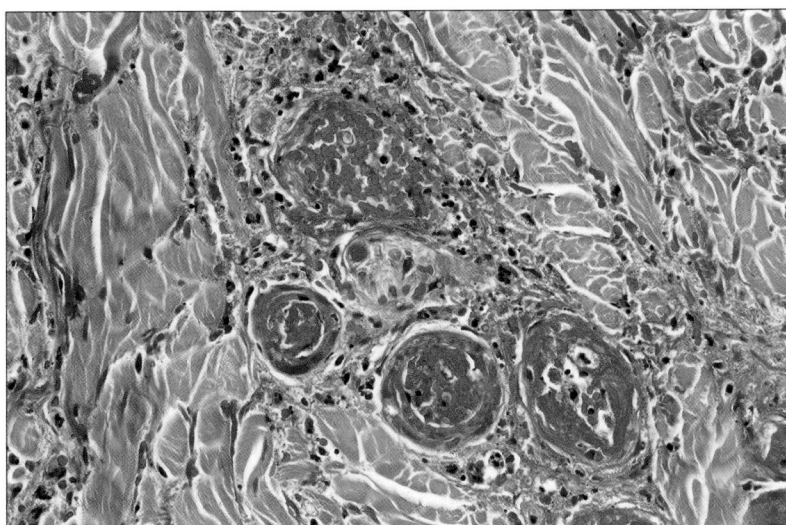

Fig. 15.17
Leukocytoclastic vasculitis: vascular thrombosis as seen in this field is not uncommon.

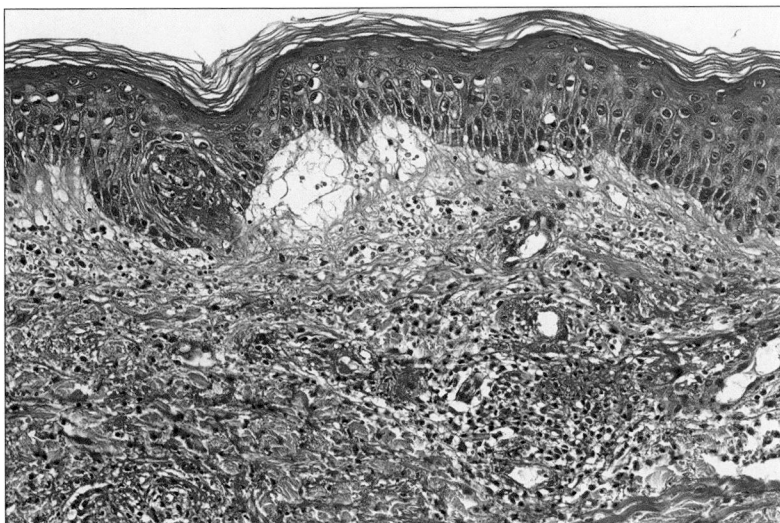

Fig. 15.18
Leukocytoclastic vasculitis: in this example, there is incipient subepidermal vesiculation.

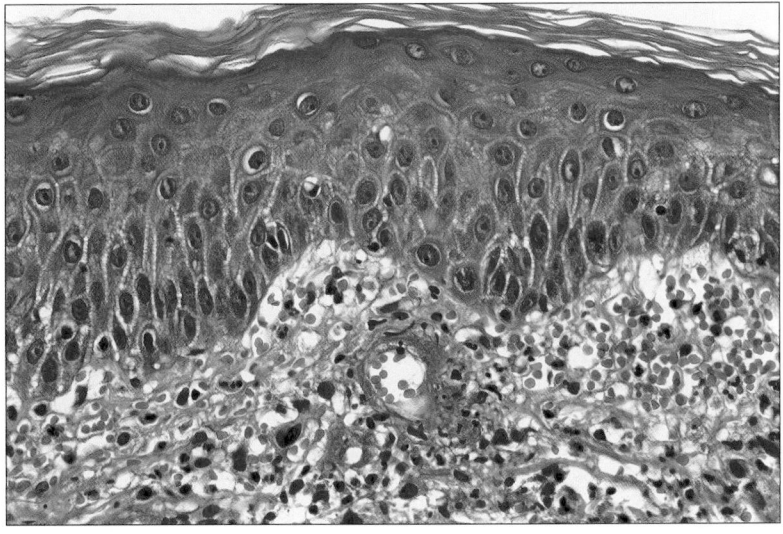

Fig. 15.20
Leukocytoclastic vasculitis: note the marked red cell extravasation.

References

1. Braverman, I.M., Yen, A. (1975) Demonstration of immune complexes in spontaneous and histamine-induced lesions and in normal skin of patients with leucocytoclastic vasculitis. *J Invest Dermatol*, **64**, 105–112.
2. Ekenstam, E.A., Callen, J.P. (1984) Cutaneous leukocytoclastic vasculitis. Clinical and laboratory features of 82 patients seen in private practice. *Arch Dermatol*, **120**, 484–489.
3. Mackel, S.E., Jordan, R.E. (1982) Leucocytoclastic vasculitis: a cutaneous expression of immune complex disease. *Arch Dermatol*, **118**, 296–301.
4. Sams, W.M. (1986) Vasculitis. In: Thiers, B.H., Dobson, R.L. (eds) Pathogenesis of skin disease. New York: Churchill Livingstone, pp 205–218.
5. Sams, W.M. (1989) Hypersensitivity angiitis. *J Invest Dermatol*, **93** (Suppl.), 78–81.
6. Fiorentino, D.F. (2003) Cutaneous vasculitis. *J Am Acad Dermatol*, **48**, 311–340.
7. Blanco, R., Martínez-Taboada, V.M., Valverde-Rodríguez, V. et al (1998) Cutaneous vasculitis in children and adults: associated diseases and etiologic factors in 303 patients. *Medicine*, **77**, 403–418.
8. Sais, G., Vidaller, A., Jucgla, A. et al (1998) Prognostic factors in leukocytoclastic vasculitis: a clinicopathologic study of 160 patients. *Arch Dermatol*, **134**, 309–315.
9. Hafeez, Z.H. (1998) Unusual presentations of cutaneous vasculitis. *Int J Dermatol*, **37**, 687–690.
10. Kelly, F.I., Cook, M.G., Marsden, R.A. (1993) Annular vasculitis associated with pregnancy. *Br J Dermatol*, **129**, 599–601.
11. Brandford, W.A., Farr, P.A., Porter, D.I. (1982) Annular vasculitis of the head and neck in a patient with sarcoidosis. *Br J Dermatol*, **106**, 713–716.
12. Nousari, H.C., Kimyai-Asadi, A., Stone, J.H. (2000) Annular leukocytoclastic vasculitis associated with monoclonal gammopathy of unknown significance. *J Am Acad Dermatol*, **43**, 955–957.
13. Cribier, B., Cuny, J.F., Schubert, B. et al (1996) Recurrent annular erythema with purpura: a new variant of leukocytoclastic vasculitis responsive to dapsone. *Br J Dermatol*, **135**, 972–975.
14. Piqué, E., Palacios, S., Santana, Z. (2002) Leukocytoclastic vasculitis presenting as an erythema repens-like eruption on a patient with systemic lupus erythematosus. *J Am Acad Dermatol*, **47**, S254–S256.
15. Heng, M.C.Y. (1985) Henoch–Schönlein purpura. *Br J Dermatol*, **112**, 235–240.
16. Martínez-Toboada, V.M., Blanco, R., García-Fuentes, M. et al (1997) Clinical features and outcome of 95 patients with hypersensitivity vasculitis. *Am J Med*, **102**, 186–191.
17. Calabrese, L.H., Duna, G.F. (1996) Drug-induced vasculitis. *Curr Opin Rheumatol*, **8**, 34–40.
18. Stern, R.S., Rigby, M. (1984) An expanded profile of cutaneous reactions to non-steroidal anti-inflammatory drugs: reports to a specialty-based system for spontaneous reporting of adverse reactions to drugs. *JAMA*, **252**, 1433–1437.
19. Mullick, F.G., McAllister, H.A. Jr, Wagner, B.M. et al (1979) Drug related vasculitis. Clinicopathologic correlations in 30 patients. *Hum Pathol*, **10**, 313–325.
20. Davidson, K.A., Ringpfeil, F., Lee, J.B. (2001) Ibuprofen-induced bullous leukocytoclastic vasculitis. *Cutis*, **67**, 303–307.
21. Schapira, D., Balbir-Gurman, A., Nahir, A.M. (2000) Naproxen-induced leukocytoclastic vasculitis. *Clin Rheumatol*, **19**, 242–244.
22. Dootson, G., Byatt, C. (1994) Amiodarone-induced vasculitis and a review of the cutaneous side effects of amiodarone. *Clin Exp Dermatol*, **19**, 422–424.
23. Lambert, W.C., Kolber, L.R., Proper, S.A. (1982) Leukocytoclastic angiitis induced by clindamycin. *Cutis*, **30**, 615–619.
24. Markman, M., Lim, H.W., Bluestein, H.G. (1986) Vancomycin-induced vasculitis. *South Med J*, **79**, 382–383.
25. Koutkila, P., Mylokanis, E., Rounds, S. et al (2001) Cutaneous leukocytoclastic vasculitis associated with oxacillin. *Diagn Microbiol Infect Dis*, **39**, 191–194.
26. Huminer, D., Cohen, J.D., Majadla, R. et al (1989) Hypersensitivity vasculitis due to ofloxacin. *BMJ*, **299**, 303.
27. Gavura, S.R., Nusinowitz, S. (1998) Leukocytoclastic vascultis associated with clarithromycin. *Ann Pharmacother*, **32**, 543–545.
28. Hendricks, W.M., Ader, R.S. (1977) Furosemide-induced cutaneous necrotizing vasculitis. *Arch Dermatol*, **113**, 375.
29. Mitchell, G.G., Magnusson, A.R., Weiler, J.M. (1983) Cimetidine-induced cutaneous vasculitis. *Am J Med*, **75**, 875–876.
30. Odeh, M., Lurie, M., Oliven, A. (2002) Cutaneous leukocytoclastic vasculitis associated with omeprazole. *Postgrad Med*, **78**, 114–115.
31. Poon, D.Y., Law, N.M. (2003) A case of cutaneous leukocytoclastic vasculitis associated with gabapentin. *Singapore Med J*, **44**, 42–44.
32. González-Gay, M.A., García-Porrua, C., Lueiro, M. et al (2002) Orlistat-induced cutaneous leukocytoclastic vasculitis. *Arthritis Rheum*, **47**, 567.
33. Torres, R.A., Lin, R.Y., Lee, M. et al (1992) Zidovudine-induced leukocytoclastic vasculitis. *Arch Intern Med*, **152**, 850–851.
34. Rachline, A., Lariven, S., Descamps, V. et al (2000) Leucocytoclastic vasculitis and indinavir. *Br J Dermatol*, **143**, 1112–1113.
35. Domingo, P., Barceló, M. (2002) Efavirenz-induced leukocytoclastic vasculitis. *Arch Intern Med*, **162**, 355–356.
36. Barlow, R.J., Schulz, E.J. (1988) Lisinopril-induced vasculitis. *Clin Exp Dermatol*, **13**, 117–120.
37. Rustmann, W.C., Carpenter, M.T., Harmon, C. et al (1998) Leukocytoclastic vascultis associated with sotalol therapy. *J Am Acad Dermatol*, **38**, 111–112.
38. Mandrup-Poulsen, T., Molvig, J., Pildal, J. et al (2002) Leukocytoclastic vasculitis induced by subcutaneous injection of human insulin in a patient with type I diabetes and essential thrombocytemia. *Diabetes Care*, **25**, 242–243.
39. Dwyer, J.M., Kenicer, K., Thompson, B.T. et al (1989) Adverse reactions: vasculitis and retinoids. *Lancet*, **2**, 494–496.
40. Cox, N.H., Dunn, L.K., Williams, J. (1985) Cutaneous vasculitis associated with long-term thiouracil therapy. *Clin Exp Dermatol*, **10**, 292–295.
41. Casis, F.C., Pérez, J.B. (2000) Leukocytoclastic vasculitis: a rare manifestation of propylthiouracil allergy. *Endocr Pract*, **6**, 329–332.
42. Chastain, M.A., Russo, G.G., Boh, E.E. et al (1999) Propylthiouracil hypersensitivity: report of two patients with vasculitis and review of the literature. *J Am Acad Dermatol*, **41**, 757–764.
43. Scerri, L., Pace, J.L. (1993) Mefloquine-associated cutaneous vasculitis. *Int J Dermatol*, **32**, 517–518.
44. Smith, H.R., Croft, A.M., Black, M.M. (1999) Dermatological adverse effects with the antimalarial drug mefloquine: a review of 74 published case reports. *Clin Exp Dermatol*, **24**, 249–254.
45. Simonart, T., Durez, P., Margaux, J. et al (1997) Cutaneous necrotizing vasculitis after low dose methotrexate therapy for rheumatoid arthritis: a possible manifestation of methotrexate hypersensitivity. *Clin Rheumatol*, **16**, 623–625.
46. Halevy, S., Giryes, H., Avinoach, I. et al (1998) Leukocytoclastic vasculitis induced by low-dose methotrexate: in vitro evidence for an immunologic mechanism. *J Eur Acad Dermatol Venereol*, **10**, 81–85.
47. Beckett, C.G., Hill, P., Hine, K.R. (1996) Leukocytoclastic vasculitis in a patient with azathioprine hypersensitivity. *Postgrad Med*, **72**, 437–438.
48. Hardinger, K.L., Cornelius, L.A., Trulock, E.P. 3rd et al (2002) Sirolimus-induced leukocytoclastic vasculitis. *Transplantation*, **74**, 739–743.
49. Jain, K.K. (1994) Cutaneous vasculitis associated with granulocyte colony-stimulating factor. *J Am Acad Dermatol*, **31**, 213–215.
50. Lee, A-Y. (1999) A case of leukocytoclastic vasculitis associated with haloperidol. *Clin Exp Dermatol*, **24**, 430.
51. Ahmed, I., Chen, K-R., Nakayama, H. et al (1998) Cytosine arabinoside-induced vasculitis. *Mayo Clin Proc*, **73**, 239–242.
52. Sánchez, N.P., van Hale, H.M., Su, W.P.D. (1985) Clinical and histopathologic spectrum of necrotizing vasculitis. Report of findings in 101 cases. *Arch Dermatol*, **121**, 220–224.
53. Menni, S., Pistritto, G., Gianotti, R. et al (1997) Ear lobe bilateral necrosis by levamisole-induced occlusive vasculitis in a pediatric patient. *Pediatr Dermatol*, **14**, 477–479.
54. Rongioletti, F., Ghio, L., Ginevri, F. et al (1999) Purpura of the ears: a distinctive vasculopathy with circulating autoantibodies complicating long-term treatment with levamisole in children. *Br J Dermatol*, **140**, 948–951.
55. Christian, M.M., Diven, D.G., Sánchez, R.L. et al (1997) Injection site vasculitis in a patient receiving interferon alfa for chronic hepatitis C. *J Am Acad Dermatol*, **37**, 118–120.
56. Krainick, U., Kantarjian, H., Broussard, S. et al (1998) Local cutaneous necrotizing lesions associated with interferon injections. *J Interferon Cytokine Res*, **18**, 823–827.
57. Sánchez-Pérez, J., Peñas, P.F., Ríos-Buceta, L. et al (1996) Leukocytoclastic vasculitis in subacute cutaneous lupus erythematosus: clinicopathologic study of three cases and review of the literature. *Dermatology*, **193**, 230–235.
58. Hunger, R.E., Durr, C., Brand, C.U. (2001) Cutaneous leukocytoclastic vasculitis in dermatomyositis suggests malignancy. *Dermatology*, **202**, 123–126.
59. García-Porrua, C., González-Gay, M.A. (1999) Bacterial infection presenting as cutaneous vasculitis in adults. *Clin Exp Rheumatol*, **17**, 471–473.
60. Lum, P.N., Woo, P.C., Wong, S.S. et al (2000) Leukocytoclastic vasculitis complicating Klebsiella pneumoniae bacteremia. *Diagn Microbiol Infect Dis*, **37**, 275–277.
61. Mínguez, P., Pintor, E., Buron, R. et al (2000) Pulmonary tuberculosis presenting with cutaneous leukocytoclastic vasculitis. *Infection*, **28**, 55–57.
62. Millikan, L.E., Flynn, T.C. (1999) Infectious etiologies of cutaneous vasculitis. *Clin Dermatol*, **17**, 509–514.
63. Hashkes, P.J., Trabulsi, A., Passo, M.H. (1996) Systemic cat-scratch disease presenting as leukocytoclastic vasculitis. *Pediatr Infect Dis J*, **15**, 93–95.
64. Schirren, C.A., Zachoval, R., Schirren, C.G. et al (1995) A role for chronic hepatitis C virus infection in a patient with cutaneous vasculitis, cryoglobulinemia, and chronic liver disease. Effective therapy with interferon-alpha. *Dig Dis Sci*, **40**, 1221–1225.
65. Daoud, M.S., Gibson, L.E., Daoud, S. et al (1995) Chronic hepatitis C and skin diseases: a review. *Mayo Clin Proc*, **70**, 559–564.
66. Zlatanic, J., Fleisher, M., Sasson, M. et al (1996) Crohn's disease and acute leukocytoclastic vasculitis of the skin. *Am J Gastroenterol*, **93**, 2410–2413.
67. Iannone, F., Scioscia, C., Musio, A. et al (2003) Leucocytoclastic vasculitis as onset symptom of ulcerative colitis. *Ann Rheum Dis*, **62**, 785–786.
68. Dowd, S.K., Rodgers, G.C., Callen, J.P. (1995) Effective treatment with α1-protease inhibitor of chronic cutaneous vasculitis associated with α1-antitrypsin deficiency. *J Am Acad Dermatol*, **33**, 913–916.
69. Resnick, A.H., Esterly, N.B. (1985) Vasculitis in children. *Int J Dermatol*, **24**, 139–146.
70. Greer, J.M., Longley, S., Edwards, N.L. et al (1988) Vasculitis associated with malignancy: experience with 13 patients and literature review. *Medicine*, **67**, 220–230.
71. Hasler, P., Kistler, H., Gerber, H. (1995) Vasculitides in hairy cell leukemia. *Semin Arthritis Rheum*, **25**, 134–142.
72. Kurzrock, R., Cohen, P.R., Markowitz, A. (1994) Clinical manifestations of vasculitis in a patient with solid tumors. A case report and review of the literature. *Arch Intern Med*, **14**, 334–340.
73. Lacour, J.P., Castanet, J., Perrin, C. et al (1993) Cutaneous leukocytoclastic vasculitis and renal cancer: 2 cases. *Am J Med*, **94**, 104–108.
74. Calabrese, L.H. (1991) Vasculitis and infection with the human immunodeficiency virus. *Rheum Dis Clin North Am*, **14**, 131–147.
75. Van der Klauw, M.M., van Hillo, B., van den Berg, W.H. et al (1996) Vasculitis attributed to the nicotine patch (Nicotinell). *Br J Dermatol*, **134**, 361–364.
76. Lowry, M.D., Hudson, C. E., Callen, J.P. (1994) Leukocytoclastic vasculitis caused by drug additives. *J Am Acad Dermatol*, **30**, 854–855.
77. Vogt, T., Landthaler, M., Stolz, W. (1999) Sodium benzoate-induced acute leukocytoclastic vasculitis with unusual clinical appearance. *Arch Dermatol*, **135**, 726–727.
78. Bourelly, P.E., Grossman, M.E. (1999) Leukocytoclastic vasculitis following staphylococcal protein A column immunoadsorption therapy for idiopathic thrombocytopenic purpura. *Cutis*, **64**, 250–252.
79. Prins, M., Veraart, J.C., Vermeulen, A.H. et al (1996) Leukocytoclastic vasculitis induced by prolonged exercise. *Br J Dermatol*, **134**, 915–918.
80. Dapic, T., Delimar, D., Korzinek, K. (2000) Leukocytoclastic vasculitis as a complication of infected hip prosthesis. *Int Orthoped*, **24**, 299–300.
81. Daoud, M.S., Gibson, L.E., Specks, U. (1999) Cutaneous leukocytoclastic vasculitis with positive antineutrophil cytoplasmic antibodies. *Acta Derm Venereol*, **79**, 328–329.
82. Claudy, A. (1998) Pathogenesis of leukocytoclastic vasculitis. *Eur J Dermatol*, **8**, 75–79.
83. Schroeter, A.L., Copeman, P.W.M., Hordon, R.E. et al (1971) Immunofluorescence of cutaneous vasculitis associated with systemic disease. *Arch Dermatol*, **104**, 254–259.
84. Ghersetich, I., Lotti, T. (1995) Cellular steps in the pathogenesis of cutaneous necrotizing vasculitis. *Int J Angiol*, **14**, 107–112.
85. Romagnoli, P., Ghersetich, I., Lotti, T. (1995) Langerhans cells and vasculitis. *Int J. Angiol*, **14**, 113–118.
86. Campanile, G., Comacchi, C., Ghersetich, I. et al (1995) Gamma/delta T lymphocytes in cutaneous necrotizing vasculitis. *Int Angiol*, **14**, 119–124.
87. Churg, J., Churg, A. (1989) Idiopathic vasculitis and secondary vasculitis: a review. *Mod Pathol*, **2**, 144–160.
88. Sams, W.M. (1980) Necrotizing vasculitis. *J Am Acad Dermatol*, **3**, 1–13.
89. Magro, C.M., Crowson, A.N. (2001) The cutaneous neutrophilic vascular injury syndromes: a review. *Semin Diagn Pathol*, **18**, 47–58.
90. Cribier, B., Couilliet, D., Meyer, P. et al (1999) The severity of histopathologic changes of leukocytoclastic vasculitis not predictive of extracutaneous involvement. *Am J Dermatopathol*, **21**, 532–536.

Henoch–Schönlein purpura

Clinical features

Henoch–Schönlein purpura is a syndrome characterized by abdominal pain, joint symptoms and palpable purpura secondary to leukocytoclastic vasculitis, and caused by circulating IgA immune complexes. The disease typically involves children (males more often than females), although adults may also be affected.[1–4] Occurrence during pregnancy has only rarely been documented.[5] In a large study of children with Henoch–Schönlein purpura, 92% of patients were less than 10 years of age.[6]

Henoch–Schönlein purpura often complicates an upper respiratory tract infection and is characterized by a seasonal incidence with a peak in winter.[1] Clustering of cases has been described and led one group of authors to postulate that person-to-person spread of an infectious agent plays a role in the pathogenesis of this syndrome.[7] Although it may follow a streptococcal throat infection, it sometimes develops after a wide variety of other infective conditions including amebiasis, chickenpox, hepatitis, HIV, yersiniosis, and infection by *Toxocara canis*, *Helicobacter pylori*, *Pseudomonas aeruginosa*, *Staphylococcus aureus*, *Escherichia coli* and erythrovirus (formerly parvovirus) B19.[8–13] Additional causative agents have included adverse reactions to drugs such as ampicillin, penicillin, erythromycin and clarithromycin.[14,15] An association with cocaine inhalation has also been described.[16] In one study, drug therapy may have been a precipitating cause in 26% of patients.[17]

As noted above, classic Henoch–Schönlein purpura is characterized by a triad of purpura, abdominal pain and arthralgia. The cutaneous clinical findings are those of leukocytoclastic vasculitis. Cutaneous lesions comprise palpable purpura predominantly affecting the lower limbs, thighs and buttocks (*Fig. 15.21*).[1] Targetoid lesions are often present.[18] Hemorrhagic bullae are rare.[19,20] Subcutaneous nodules have also been documented.[21] A prodrome of itchy urticaria is sometimes described.[2] Children often have edema, particularly of the feet and lower legs although it may be more widespread.

In one large study, arthritis was seen in 82% of patients and was the presenting feature in 24%.[6] Joint involvement consists of migratory arthralgia predominantly affecting the large joints of the lower limbs. In one study, 37% also had involvement of the upper extremities, with the hand and wrist being more often affected than the elbow.[6]

Intestinal involvement with resultant purpura or hemorrhage leads to abdominal pain and gastrointestinal bleeding. Abdominal pain was seen in 63% of patients in one study of 100 consecutive children presenting with Henoch–Schönlein purpura.[6] Gastrointestinal disease develops as a consequence of acute vasculitis. Bleeding may be either occult or in the form of bloody or melanotic stools.[6] Intussusception is an occasional complication.[22,23] Abdominal pain was the presenting complaint in 19% of patients in one study.[6] Endoscopy may reveal hemorrhage, ulceration, and erosions.[24] IgA is often noted in capillaries of the gastrointestinal tract but frank necrotizing vasculitis was not seen in any patients in two series.[24,25] Rarely, gastrointestinal involvement with minimal skin lesions may be encountered.[26]

Renal symptoms are variable and include microscopic hematuria, acute nephritic syndrome, nephrotic syndrome and acute or chronic renal failure. The pathological features seen on renal biopsy range from mild focal glomerulonephritis to necrotizing or proliferative glomerulonephritis.[1,6] In a consecutive series of 100 pediatric patients, a single patient required transplantation.[6] Patients older than 7 years are at increased risk of renal involvement.[27]

Orchitis is an uncommon, but recognized, complication of Henoch–Schönlein purpura.[6]

Neurological involvement may be manifested by headaches, seizures, mental status changes and, less frequently, ataxia and peripheral neuropathy.[28]

Low serum C3, leukopenia and thrombocytopenia are rare findings.[29]

Henoch–Schönlein purpura in children is generally associated with a good prognosis with less than 2% suffering long-term morbidity.[30,31] However, patients do occasionally die from renal failure, gastrointestinal infarction or respiratory involvement. In contrast to pediatric patients, adults are thought to have a worse prognosis. However, one study found that, although older patients had more severe symptoms, including more frequent renal involvement, prognosis was equally good in young and older patients.[32] In another study, complete recovery was seen in 67% of adults after a median follow-up period of 36 months.[10] In a further series, a third of patients suffered at least one recurrence of symptoms, usually within a few months of initial presentation.[6]

Solid tumors including breast cancer and hematological malignancy may be associated with Henoch–Schönlein purpura.[33–36] One study found that nearly a third of adults with Henoch–Schönlein purpura had an associated tumor.[33] For this reason, the authors concluded that physicians should suspect an underlying malignancy in older patients (especially males of 40 years or more) with Henoch–Schönlein purpura.[34]

Pulmonary hemorrhage is a rare complication that may prove fatal.[37,38]

Pathogenesis and histological features

An incomplete picture of the pathogenesis of Henoch–Schönlein purpura has emerged. As noted above, it seems a wide variety of infective agents may trigger this disease. Henoch–Schönlein purpura is associated with IgA deposition in blood vessel walls, both in the dermis and in the renal glomerulus (mesangium). IgA1 is the major IgA subclass found in the cutaneous blood vessels.[39] Fibrinogen and C3 are also usually present. Raised levels of serum IgA and IgE are present in some, but not all, patients.[6] IgA antineutrophil cytoplasmic antibodies (ANCA) and IgA anticardiolipin antibodies have also been documented.[40,41] There is evidence that patients have an increased number of IgA-type B-cells.[42]

The finding of IgA deposition by immunofluorescence is not equivalent to a diagnosis of Henoch–Schönlein purpura. A vasculitis with the presence of IgA deposition in patients lacking other typical features

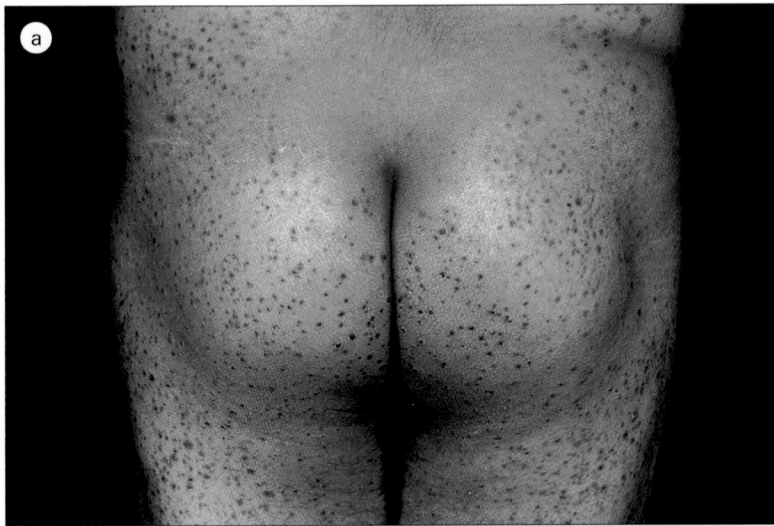

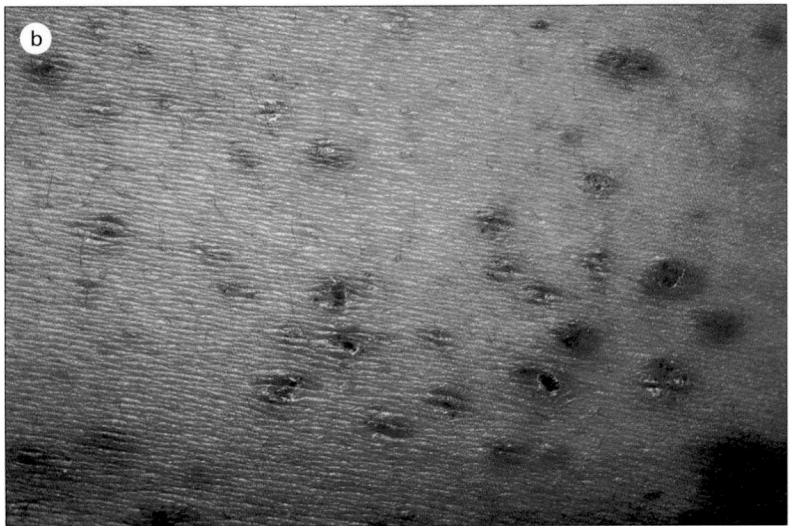

Fig. 15.21
(a, b) Henoch–Schönlein purpura: palpable purpura in the classical distribution on the buttocks and thighs. By courtesy of the Institute of Dermatology, London, UK.

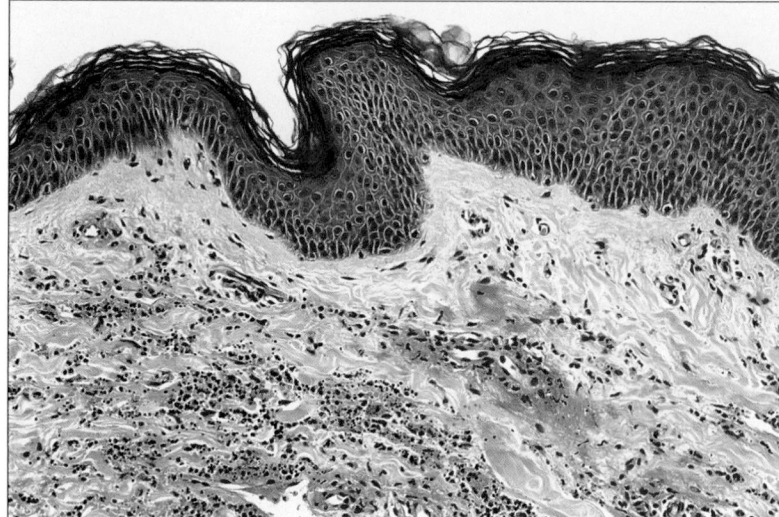

Fig. 15.22
Henoch–Schönlein purpura: this small venule shows striking fibrinoid necrosis. There is considerable red cell extravasation.

of Henoch–Schönlein purpura has been described in association with cancer, Wegener's granulomatosis and inflammatory bowel disease.[43]

The observation of an association between DRB1*01 and DRB1*11 and Henoch–Schönlein purpura suggests a genetic susceptibility in some patients.[44] Other authors have suggested that DQA1*0301 and C4 deletion may also represent risk factors for IgA nephropathy as well as Henoch–Schönlein nephritis.[45]

Biopsies of cutaneous lesions show features of typical leukocytoclastic vasculitis (*Fig. 15.22*).

Differential diagnosis

The histological differential diagnosis includes other forms of leukocytoclastic vasculitis. Since IgA deposition can be seen in the blood vessel walls of patients with leukocytoclastic vasculitis but without evidence of Henoch–Schönlein purpura, this finding is not diagnostic in isolation.[46] In one study, only 24% of patients with vascular IgA deposition had Henoch–Schönlein purpura.[46] Careful clinical correlation is necessary to establish this diagnosis.

References

1. Mills, J.A., Michel, B.A., Bloch, D.A. et al (1990) The American College of Rheumatology 1990 criteria for the classification of Henoch–Schönlein purpura. *Arthritis Rheum*, 33, 1114–1121.
2. Duquesnoy, B. (1991) Henoch–Schönlein purpura. *Clin Rheumatol*, 5, 253–261.
3. Patrignelli, R., Sheikh, S.H., Shaw-Stiffel, T.A. (1995) Henoch–Schönlein purpura. A multisystem disease also seen in adults. *Postgrad Med*, 97, 123–124.
4. Tancrede-Bohin, E., Ochonisky, S., Vignon-Pennamen, M.D. et al (1997) Schönlein–Henoch purpura in adult patients. *Arch Dermatol*, 133, 438–442.
5. Feldmann, R., Rieger, W., Sator, P.G. et al (2002) Schönlein–Henoch purpura during pregnancy with successful outcome for mother and newborn. *BMC Dermatol*, 2, 1.
6. Saulsbuy, F.T. (1999) Henoch–Schönlein purpura in children. Report of 100 patients and review of the literature. *Medicine*, 78, 395–409.
7. Farley, T.A., Gillespie, S., Rasoulpour, M. et al (1989) Epidemiology of a cluster of Henoch–Schönlein purpura. *Am J Dis Child*, 143, 798–803.
8. Reinauer, S., Megahed, M., Goerz, G. et al (1995) Henoch–Schönlein purpura associated with gastric Helicobacter pylori infection. *J Am Acad Dermatol*, 33, 876–879.
9. Saulsbury, F.T. (1998) Hemorrhagic bullous lesions in Henoch–Schönlein purpura. *Pediatr Dermatol*, 15, 357–359.
10. Cioc, A.M., Sedmak, D.D., Nuovo, G.J. et al (2002) Parvovirus B19 associated adult Henoch–Schönlein purpura. *J Cutan Pathol*, 29, 602–607.
11. Egan, C.A., O'Reilly, M.A., Meadows, K.P. et al (2000) Relapsing Henoch–Schönlein purpura associated with Pseudomonas aeruginosa pyelonephritis. *J Am Acad Dermatol*, 42, 381–383.
12. Hamidou, M.A., Gueglio, B., Cassagneau, E. et al (1999) Henoch–Schönlein purpura associated with Toxocara canis infection. *J Rheumatol*, 26, 443–445.
13. Cioc, A.M., Sedmak, D.D., Nuovo, G.J. et al (2002) Parvovirus B19 associated adult Henoch–Schönlein purpura. *J Cutan Pathol*, 29, 602–607.
14. Goldberg, E.I., Shoji, T., Sapadin, A.N. (1999) Henoch–Schönlein purpura induced by clarithromycin. *Int J Dermatol*, 38, 706–708.
15. Borras-Blasco, J., Enríquez, R., Amoros, F. et al (2003) Henoch–Schönlein purpura associated with clarithromycin. Case report and review of literature. *Int J Clin Pharmacol Ther*, 41, 213–216.
16. Chevalier, X., Rostoker, G., Larget-Piet, B. et al (1995) Schönlein–Henoch purpura with necrotizing vasculitis after cocaine snorting. *Clin Nephrol*, 43, 348–349.
17. Demircin, G., Oner, A., Erdogan, O. et al (1998) Henoch Schönlein purpura and amebiasis. *Acta Paediatr Jpn*, 40, 489–491.
18. García-Porrua, C., Gonzalez-Gay, M.A. (1999) Comparative clinical and epidemiological study of hypersensitivity vasculitis versus Henoch–Schönlein purpura in adults. *Semin Arthritis Rheum*, 28, 404–412.
19. Raimer, S.S., Sánchez, R.L. (1992) Vasculitis in children. *Semin Dermatol*, 11, 48–56.
20. Wananukul, S., Pongprasit, P., Korkij, W. (1995) Henoch–Schönlein purpura presenting a hemorrhagic vesicles and bullae: case report and literature review. *Pediatr Dermatol*, 12, 314–317.
21. Robson, W.L., Leung, A.K. (2000) Subcutaneous nodules in Henoch–Schönlein purpura. *Pediatr Nephrol*, 14, 493–494.
22. Cream, J.J., Grumpel, J.M., Peachey, R.D.G. (1970) Schönlein–Henoch purpura in the adult: a study of 77 adults with anaphylactoid or Schönlein–Henoch purpura. *QJM (NS)*, 39, 461–466.
23. Cull, D.L., Rosario, V., Lally, K.P. et al (1990) Surgical implications of Henoch–Schönlein purpura. *J Pediatr Surg*, 25, 741–743.
24. Kato, S., Shibuya, H., Naganuma, H. et al (1992) Gastrointestinal endoscopy in Henoch–Schönlein purpura. *Eur J Pediatr*, 151, 482–484.
25. Kato, S., Ebina, K., Naganuma, H. et al (1996) Intestinal IgA deposition in Henoch–Schönlein purpura with severe gastro-intestinal manifestations. *Eur J Pediatr*, 155, 91–95.
26. Chesler, L., Hwang, L., Patton, W. et al (2000) Henoch–Schönlein purpura with severe jejunitis and minimal skin lesions. *J Pediatr Gastroenterol Nutr*, 30, 92–95.
27. Kaku, Y., Nohara, K., Honda, S. (1998) Renal involvement in Henoch–Schönlein purpura: a multivariate analysis of prognostic factors. *Kidney Int*, 53, 1755–1759.
28. Bulun, A., Topaloglu, R., Duzova, A. et al (2001) Ataxia and peripheral neuropathy: rare manifestations in Henoch–Schönlein purpura. *Pediatr Nephrol*, 16, 1139–1141.
29. Krause, I., Garty, B.Z., Davidovits, M. et al (1999) Low serum C3, leukopenia, and thrombocytopenia: unusual features of Henoch–Schönlein purpura. *Eur J Pediatr*, 158, 906–909.
30. Robson, W.L., Leung, A.K. (1994) Henoch–Schönlein purpura. *Adv Pediatr*, 41, 163–194.
31. Szer, I.S. (1994) Henoch–Schönlein purpura. *Curr Opin Rheumatol*, 6, 25–31.
32. Blanco, R., Martínez-Taboada, V.M., Rodríguez-Valverde, V. et al (1997) Henoch–Schönlein purpura in adulthood and childhood: two different expressions of the same syndrome. *Arthritis Rheum*, 40, 859–864.
33. Hayem, G., Gómez, M.J., Grossin, M. et al (1997) Systemic vasculitis and epithelioma. A report of three case and review of the literature. *Rev Rhum Engl Ed*, 64, 816–824.
34. Pertuiset, E., Liote, F., Launay-Russ, E. et al (2000) Adult Henoch–Schönlein purpura associated with malignancy. *Semin Arthritis Rheum*, 29, 360–367.
35. Blanco, R., Gónzalez-Gay, M.A., Ibañez, D. et al (1997) Henoch–Schönlein purpura as a clinical presentation of small cell lung cancer. *Clin Exp Rheumatol*, 15, 545–547.
36. Maestri, A., Malacarne, P., Santini, A. (1995) Henoch–Schönlein syndrome associated with breast cancer. A case report. *Angiology*, 46, 625–627.
37. Vats, K.R., Vats, A., Kim, Y. et al (1999) Henoch–Schönlein purpura and pulmonary hemorrhage: a report and literature review. *Pediatr Nephrol*, 13, 530–534.
38. Paller, A.S., Kelly, K., Sethi, R. (1997) Pulmonary hemorrhage: an often fatal complication of Henoch–Schönlein purpura. *Pediatr Dermatol*, 14, 299–302.
39. Egan, C.A., Taylor, T.B., Meyer, L.J. et al (1999) IgA1 is the major IgA subclass in cutaneous blood vessels in Henoch–Schönlein purpura. *Br J Dermatol*, 141, 859–862.
40. Burrows, N.P., Lockwood, C.M. (1995) Antineutrophil cytoplasmic antibodies and their relevance to the dermatologist. *Br J Dermatol*, 132, 173–181.
41. Burden, A.D., Gibson, I.W., Rodger, R.S.C. et al (1994) IgA anticardiolipin antibodies associated with Henoch–Schönlein purpura. *J Am Acad Dermatol*, 31, 857–860.
42. Knight, J.F. (1990) The rheumatic poison: a survey of some published investigations of the immunopathogenesis of Henoch–Schönlein purpura. *Pediatr Nephrol*, 4, 533–541.
43. Magro, C.M., Crowson, A.N. (1999) A clinical and histologic study of 37 cases of immunoglobulin A-associated vasculitis. *Am J Dermatopathol*, 21, 234–240.
44. Amoroso, A., Berrino, M., Canale, L. et al (1997) Immunogenetics of Henoch–Schönlein disease. *Eur J Immunogenet*, 24, 323–333.
45. Jin, D.K., Kohsaka, T., Koo, J.W. et al (1996) Complement 4 locus II gene deletion and DQA1*0301 gene: genetic risk factors for IgA nephropathy and Henoch–Schönlein nephritis. *Nephron*, 73, 390–395.
46. Helander, S.D., DeCastro, F.R., Gibson, L.E. (1995) Henoch–Schönlein purpura. Clinicopathologic correlation of cutaneous vascular IgA deposits and the relationship to leukocytoclastic vasculitis. *Acta Derm Venereol*, 75, 125–129.

Infantile acute hemorrhagic edema

Clinical features

Infantile hemorrhagic edema is a form of leukocytoclastic vasculitis that is mostly seen in newborns but has also been described in toddlers under 3 years of age and occasionally in older children.[1–9] Usually, the disease is limited to the skin. It frequently follows vaccination or infection including otitis, upper respiratory tract infection or conjunctivitis.[1] An association with cytomegalovirus infection has been documented.[10] Since many children have received antibiotics for infection prior to development of lesions, a subset may represent a reaction to medication.[1] This disease has a peak incidence in the winter months.

Skin lesions are widely distributed, and often involve the head and neck, and limbs. They present as purpuric lesions that often have a rosette or targetoid configuration.[2,3] The cheeks and ears seem to be sites of predilection.[3] Resolution within a few weeks is typical and recurrences are not reported.[1]

An elevated ESR and leukocytosis are usually present.

Pathogenesis and histological features

The pathogenesis of infantile hemorrhagic edema is unknown; however, it is likely that the disease is immune-mediated. Biopsy shows features of leukocytoclastic vasculitis with variable fibrinoid necrosis.[3]

Differential diagnosis

Some authors consider infantile hemorrhagic edema to be a variant of Henoch–Schönlein purpura. Others, however, do not agree, arguing that the absence of perivascular IgA on immunofluorescence staining, absence of systemic involvement in most patients, and the benign clinical course do not support this view.[3,11] However, a very interesting hypothesis possibly linking the two diseases has been postulated.[12] Goraya and Kaur note that, since the IgA immune system in infants is immature, if acute hemorrhagic edema were related to Henoch–Schönlein purpura, the patient would be incapable of mounting an IgA-mediated immune response and this would explain the lack of IgA on immunofluorescence studies in the majority of patients.[12] Clearly, further study of this disorder is necessary to elucidate its pathogenesis and to clarify its nosological position in the classification of leukocytoclastic vasculitis.

References

1. Paradisi, M., Annessi, G., Corrado, A. (2001) Infantile acute hemorrhagic edema of the skin. *Cutis*, **68**, 127–129.
2. Millard, T., Harris, A., MacDonald, D. (1999) Acute hemorrhagic edema. *J Am Acad Dermatol*, **41**, 837–839.
3. Legrain, V., Lejean, S., Taieb, A. et al (1991) Infantile acute hemorrhagic edema of the skin: study of ten cases. *J Am Acad Dermatol*, **24**, 17–22.
4. Tomac, N., Saraclar, Y., Turktas, I. et al (1996) Acute haemorrhagic oedema of infancy: a case report. *Clin Exp Dermatol*, **21**, 217–219.
5. Gonggryp, L.A., Todd, G. (1998) Acute hemorrhagic edema of childhood. *Pediatr Dermatol*, **15**, 91–96.
6. Long, D., Helm, K.F. (1998) Acute hemorrhagic edema of infancy: Finkelstein's disease. *Cutis*, **61**, 283–284.
7. Crowe, M.A., Jonas, P.P. (1998) Acute hemorrhagic edema of infancy. *Cutis*, **62**, 65–66.
8. Fujimura, T., Funayama, M., Tagami, H. (2001) Acute hemorrhagic edema in a four-year-old Japanese child. *J Dermatol*, **28**, 279–281.
9. Caksen, H., Odabas, D., Kosem, M. et al (2002) Report of eight infants with acute infantile hemorrhagic edema and review of the literature. *J Dermatol*, **29**, 290–295.
10. Kuroda, K., Yabunami, H., Hisanaga, Y. (2002) Acute haemorrhagic oedema of infancy associated with cytomegalovirus infection. *Br J Dermatol*, **147**, 1254–1257.
11. Saraclar, Y., Tinaztepe, K., Adalioglu, G. et al (1990) Acute hemmorhagic edema of infancy (AHEI) – a variant of Henoch–Schönlein purpura or a distinct clinical entity? *J Allergy Clin Immunol*, **86**, 473–483.
12. Goraya, J.S., Kaur, S. (2002) Acute infantile hemorrhagic edema and Henoch–Schönlein purpura: is IgA the missing link? *J Am Acad Dermatol*, **47**, 801.

Urticarial vasculitis

Clinical features

Urticaria and urticarial vasculitis are also discussed in Chapters 7 and 14. In this chapter only urticarial vasculitis is considered.

Urticarial vasculitis is an uncommon condition characterized clinically by urticaria and histologically by leukocytoclastic venulitis.[1-5] In addition to urticarial skin lesions, patients may also experience angioedema, arthralgia, gastrointestinal symptoms and evidence of renal involvement. Urticarial vasculitis encompasses a spectrum of illness with some patients experiencing only mild symptoms while others develop serious systemic involvement.[6]

Urticarial vasculitis is most often seen in the third to fifth decades and shows a female predominance. The cutaneous lesions are urticarial in appearance, consisting of edematous, raised, erythematous plaques associated with non-blanchable purpura (*Figs 15.23, 15.24*). However, in contrast to uncomplicated urticaria, cutaneous lesions in the setting of urticarial vasculitis often last 24–72 hours.[7] Patients commonly complain of pruritus, burning or pain. The frequency of cutaneous symptoms varies considerably, from daily to monthly.

Joint pain, stiffness and swelling, particularly of the hands, elbows, feet, ankles and knees, are seen; however, frank arthritis is extremely rare. Hypocomplementemia, which correlates with systemic involvement, is a feature in many patients.[4,6,8] Proteinuria and hematuria may also be seen. Rarely, patients develop focal or diffuse proliferative glomerulonephritis. Crescentic glomerulonephritis, mesangial glomerulonephritis and membranous nephropathy have also been documented.[6,9,10] Gastrointestinal symptoms may include abdominal pain, nausea, vomiting and diarrhea.

The ESR is raised in many patients with hypocomplementemia. There may also be depression of the early classical pathway components C1q, C4 and C2. Patients with hypocomplementemic urticarial vasculitis have a high prevalence of autoantibodies to endothelial cells.[11,12]

Schnitzler's syndrome is a term that has been applied to patients with urticarial vasculitis and monoclonal IgM gammopathy.[13-18] Hepatosplenomegaly, elevated ESR and white blood cell count, fever and joint pain are characteristic features.[14-16] An underlying lymphoproliferative disorder is present in some patients.[13]

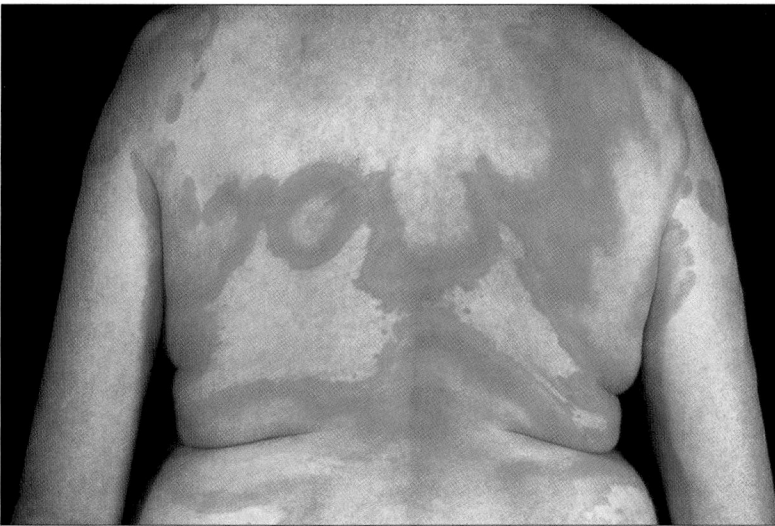

Fig. 15.23
Urticarial vasculitis: this very large lesion has developed a bizarre outline due to central clearing. By courtesy of the Institute of Dermatology, London, UK.

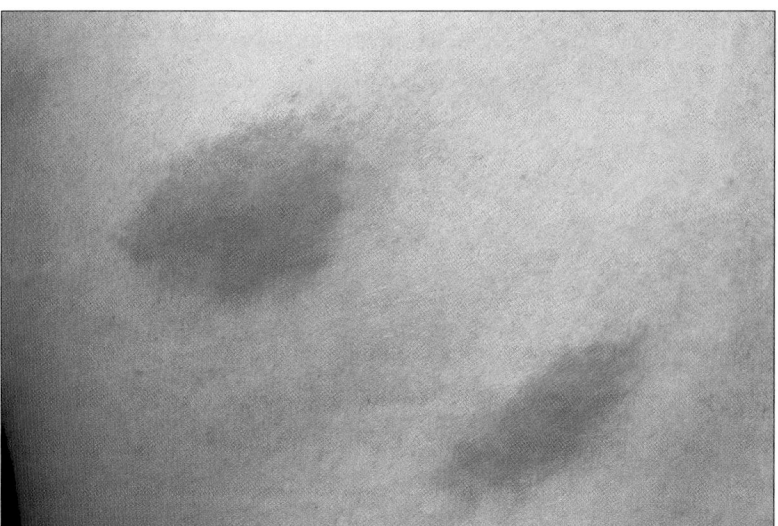

Fig. 15.24
Urticarial vasculitis: close-up view. By courtesy of the Institute of Dermatology, London, UK.

Importantly, urticarial vasculitis (especially the hypocomplementemic variant) is often associated with, or heralds the onset of, a variety of systemic diseases, including SLE, arthritis, interstitial lung disease, pericarditis, mixed connective tissue disease, hepatitis, inflammatory bowel disease, serum sickness, polyarteritis nodosa and Wegener's granulomatosis, viral infection, Sjögren's syndrome, cryoglobulinemia, polycythemia rubra vera, reaction to drugs (including cocaine and diltiazem), and as a response to sunlight.[6,9,19-27] The condition may be exacerbated by methotrexate.[28] In one study, more than 50% of patients had uveitis, scleritis, conjunctivitis or episcleritis.[6] It appears that patients with hypocomplementemia have more severe disease.[19] Some authors have postulated that hypocomplementemic urticarial vasculitis represents a subset of SLE. Others, however, have failed to confirm this observation.[6,29]

Urticarial vasculitis has been documented in association with malignancy.[6,30] Given the rarity of this association, this may well be coincidental.

Clearly, however, a diagnosis of urticarial vasculitis should nevertheless always initiate an evaluation for possible underlying disease. Urticarial vasculitis usually has a benign outcome.[6]

Pathogenesis and histological features

In many patients no underlying cause is discovered. In others, antibody–antigen complexes (a type III hypersensitivity reaction) is implicated.[4,5]

The vasculitis affects the superficial vascular plexus and is characterized by a leukocytoclastic pattern (*Fig. 15.25*). Extravasation of red blood cells is evidence of vascular damage. A background of dermal edema may be seen. Often, the histological features are subtle and are easily overlooked, with only focal fibrinoid vascular change, few neutrophils and sparse karyorrhexis. In our experience, the vasculitis is usually low-grade or subtle in nature; however, more impressive necrotizing vasculitis is seen in some patients. Others have shown that endothelial necrosis is unusual.[5]

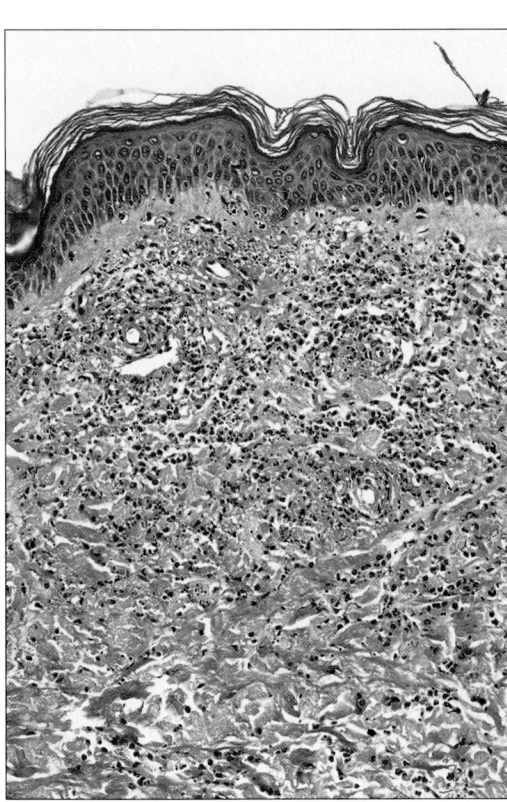

Fig. 15.25
Urticarial vasculitis: the changes are unusually florid in this example. See also *Figs 7.56–7.59*.

In summary, urticarial vasculitis may show a spectrum of histological changes ranging from urticaria with very mild vascular injury to frank necrotizing vasculitis.[31]

Differential diagnosis

Clinical correlation is necessary to distinguish urticarial vasculitis from other forms of leukocytoclastic vasculitis. Although urticarial vasculitis is often associated with subtle low-grade vascular injury, this feature should not be relied upon in its distinction from other forms of vasculitis. In short, the pathologist's role in diagnosis is to confirm the presence of vasculitis.

References

1. Soter, N.A., Austen, K.F., Gigli, I. (1974) Urticaria and arthralgias as manifestations of necrotizing angiitis (vasculitis). *J Invest Dermatol*, **63**, 485–490.
2. Aboobaker, J., Greaves, M.W. (1986) Urticarial vasculitis. *Clin Exp Dermatol*, **11**, 436–444.
3. Monroe, E.W. (1981) Urticarial vasculitis: an updated review. *J Am Acad Dermatol*, **5**, 88–95.
4. Sánchez, N.P., Winkelman, R.K., Schroeter, A.L. et al (1982) The clinical and histopathologic spectrums of urticarial vasculitis: study of forty cases. *J Am Acad Dermatol*, **7**, 599–605.
5. Jones, R.R., Eady, R.A.J. (1984) Endothelial cell pathology as a marker for urticarial vasculitis: a light microscopic study. *Br J Dermatol*, **110**, 139–149.
6. Mehregan, D.R., Hall, M.J., Gibson, L.E. (1992) Urticarial vasculitis: a histopathologic and clinical review of 72 cases. *J Am Acad Dermatol*, **26**, 441–448.
7. Kobza Black, A., Lawlor, F., Greaves, M.W. (1996) Consensus meeting on the definition of physical urticarias and urticarial vasculitis. *Clin Exp Dermatol*, **21**, 424–426.
8. Asherson, R.A., D'Cruz, D., Stephens, C.J. et al (1991) Urticarial vasculitis in a connective tissue disease clinic: patterns, presentations and treatment. *Semin Arthritis Rheum*, **20**, 285–296.
9. Messiaen, T., Van Damme, B., Kuypers, D. et al (2000) Crescentic glomerulonephritis complicating the course of a hypocomplementemic urticarial vasculitis. *Clin Nephrol*, **54**, 409–412.
10. Kobayshi, S., Nagase, M., Hidaki, S. et al (1994) Membranous nephropathy associated with hypocomplementemic urticarial vasculitis: report of 2 cases and a review of the literature. *Nephron*, **66**, 1–7.
11. D'Cruz, D.P., Wisnieski, J.J., Asherson, R. et al (1995) Autoantibodies in systemic lupus erythematosus and urticarial vasculitis. *J Rheumatol*, **22**, 1669–1673.
12. Wisnieski, J.J., Baer, A.N., Christensen, J. et al (1995) Hypocomplementemic urticarial vasculitis syndrome. Clinical and serologic findings in 18 patients. *Medicine*, **74**, 24–41.
13. Lim, W., Shumak, K.H., Reis, M. et al (2002) Malignant evolution of Schnitzler's syndrome – chronic urticaria and IgM monoclonal gammopathy: report of a new case and review of the literature. *Leuk Lymphoma*, **43**, 181–186.
14. Lipsker, D., Veran, Y., Grunenberger, F. et al (2001) The Schnitzler syndrome. Four new cases and review of the literature. *Medicine*, **80**, 37–44.
15. Puddu, P., Cianchini, G., Giardelli, C.R. et al (1997) Schnitzler's syndrome: report of a new case and a review of the literature. *Clin Exp Rheumatol*, **15**, 91–95.
16. Baty, V., Hoen, B., Hudziak, H. et al (1995) Schnitzler's syndrome: two case reports and review of the literature. *Mayo Clin Proc*, **70**, 570–572.
17. Janier, M., Bonvalet, D., Blanc, M.F. et al (1989) Chronic urticaria and macroglobulinemia (Schnitzler's syndrome): report of two cases. *J Am Acad Dermatol*, **20**, 206–211.
18. Borradori, L., Rybojad, M., Puissant, A. et al (1990) Urticarial vasculitis associated with a monoclonal IgM gammopathy: Schnitzler's syndrome. *Br J Dermatol*, **123**, 113–118.
19. Wisnieski, J.J. (2000) Urticarial vasculitis. *Curr Opin Rheumatol*, **12**, 24–31.
20. Hamid, S., Cruz, P.D. Jr, Lee, W.M. (1998) Urticarial vasculitis caused by hepatitis C virus infection: response to interferon alfa therapy. *J Am Acad Dermatol*, **39**, 278–280.
21. Chen, H.J., Bloch, K.J. (2001) Hypocomplementemic urticarial vasculitis, Jaccoud's arthropathy, valvular heart disease, and reversible tracheal stenosis. A surfeit of syndromes. *J Rheumatol*, **28**, 383–386.
22. Farell, A.M., Sabroe, R.A., Bunker, C.B. (1996) Urticarial vasculitis associated with polycythemia rubra vera. *Clin Exp Dermatol*, **21**, 302–304.
23. Kuniyuki, S., Katoh, H. (1996) Urticarial vasculitis with papular lesions in a patient with type C hepatitis and cryoglobulinemia. *J Dermatol*, **23**, 279–283.
24. Lin, R.Y., Caren, C.B., Menikoff, H. (1995) Hypocomplementemic urticarial vasculitis, interstitial lung disease and hepatitis C. *Br J Dermatol*, **132**, 821–823.
25. Babajanians, A., Chung-Park, M., Wisnieski, J.J. (1991) Recurrent pericarditis and cardiac tamponade in a patient with hypocomplementemic urticarial vasculitis syndrome. *J Rheumatol*, **18**, 752–755.
26. Hofbauer, G.F.L., Hafner, J., Trüeb, R.M. (1999) Urticarial vasculitis following cocaine use. *Br J Dermatol*, **141**, 600–601.
27. Wittal, R.A., Fischer, G.O., Georgouras, K.E. et al (1992) Skin reactions to diltiazem. *Australas J Dermatol*, **33**, 11–18.
28. Borcea, A., Greaves, M.W. (2000) Methotrexate-induced exacerbation of urticarial vasculitis: an unusual adverse reaction. *Br J Dermatol*, **143**, 203–204.
29. Davis, M.D., Daoud, M.S., Kirby, B. et al (1998) Clinicopathologic correlation of hypocomplementemic and normocomplementemic urticarial vasculitis. *J Am Acad Dermatol*, **38**, 899–905.
30. Lewis, J.E. (1990) Urticarial vasculitis occurring in association with visceral malignancy. *Acta Derm Venereol*, **70**, 345–347.
31. Jones, R.R., Bhogal, B., Dash, A. et al (1983) Urticaria and vasculitis: a continuum of histological and immunopathological changes. *Br J Dermatol*, **108**, 695–703.

Polyarteritis nodosa and microscopic polyangiitis

Classical polyarteritis nodosa (Kussmaul–Maier disease) is a rare systemic vasculitis involving medium-sized and small arteries.[1] Some view the disorder not as a disease *sui generis* but, less restrictively, as a syndrome with many triggering causes and disease associations. Classic polyarteritis nodosa overlaps both clinically and histologically with microscopic polyangiitis (microscopic polyarteritis nodosa, microscopic polyarteritis). Distinction between these entities may be difficult and criteria for their distinction are controversial. Nevertheless, they seem to represent distinctive syndromes that warrant separate classification to facilitate appropriate treatment.[2] In order to maintain a usable working classification we – while admitting they are separate diseases – prefer to describe them in the same section to facilitate comparisons between them.

Clinical features

Classical polyarteritis nodosa

Classical polyarteritis nodosa is a multisystem disease with protean clinical manifestations (*Table 15.3*).[1,3–5] It should be noted that the 1990 criteria from the American College of Rheumatology do not distinguish polyarteritis nodosa from microscopic polyarteritis. However, in the more recent Chapel Hill nomenclature this discrimination is made (see *Table 15.1*). Polyarteritis nodosa is associated with significant morbidity and mortality even when treated with corticosteroids. With therapy, survival is in the range of 75–80%.[1] Although a wide age group may be affected, patients are most often in their fifth or sixth decade. There is a male predilection (4:1). Patients commonly present with constitutional symptoms including weight loss, pyrexia and anorexia.[1]

Cutaneous lesions are common.[6–8] Palpable purpuric lesions and foci of ulceration, particularly involving the lower limbs, are most often found (*Figs 15.26–15.28*). Livedo reticularis is also a common cutaneous manifestation (*Fig. 15.29*). Cutaneous nodules may also be seen. A maculopapular rash, vesiculation and pustular lesions are occasional features (*Figs 15.30–15.33*).

Joint involvement (arthralgias and arthritis) is often present; arthritis is usually asymmetrical and particularly affects the lower limbs. Non-specific muscle pain and weakness are additional features. Muscle wasting is commonly found.

Both peripheral and central nervous system involvement are often encountered. The former presents as sensory neuropathies (numbness or paresthesias), motor neuropathies (wrist or foot drop) and combined sensorimotor lesions (mononeuritis multiplex and polyneuropathy). Central nervous system involvement may present as confusion, disorientation or delirium. Eye involvement is a rare feature of polyarteritis nodosa.[9] Complications include choroidal infarction, ischemic optic neuropathy, retinal artery occlusion, episcleritis, ulcerative keratitis, uveitis and orbital pseudotumor.[9–11]

Involvement of the kidney is very common and is of major importance because its sequelae – renal failure and hypertension – are among the commonest causes of death in this disease. Patients on occasion have episodes of loin pain due to renal infarction. Hypertension is often present in patients with classical polyarteritis nodosa and in occasional patients it may enter the malignant phase. Urinalysis for proteinuria, hematuria and red cell casts, and serum creatinine estimations are, therefore, mandatory early investigations.

Gastrointestinal involvement is also an important cause of morbidity and mortality.[12] Symptoms include nausea, vomiting and abdominal pain. Serious complications include gastrointestinal hemorrhage, perforation and infarction, the last being a not uncommon cause of death. Involvement of the hepatobiliary tract may also be seen.[13,14] Involvement of the gallbladder and pancreas has also been reported and may be discovered as an incidental finding or patients can present with symptoms of acute cholecystitis.[15,16]

Cardiac manifestations include pericarditis, arrhythmias and myocardial infarction due to coronary artery involvement (*Fig. 15.34*). Although it is often stated that polyarteritis nodosa does not involve the lung, in exceptional cases pulmonary involvement is seen and patients occasionally complain of asthma, hemoptysis and effusions. Although clinical involvement of the lungs is rare, autopsy evaluation has shown that arteritis affecting the bronchial arteries is not uncommon, being seen in 70% in one small series.[17]

Orchitis, usually unilateral is a characteristic feature of polyarteritis nodosa.[18–20] Patients may present with symptoms of acute orchitis or features that suggest a testicular neoplasm.[18,20]

Laboratory investigations often reveal anemia, leukocytosis and a raised ESR. Low-titer rheumatoid factor and antinuclear antibody are sometimes features and, in occasional patients, a cryoglobulin is identified. Diminished serum complement levels may also be detected. ANCAs are uncommonly seen in patients with classic polyarteritis nodosa. One group with extensive experience estimates that less than 5% of patients with the classic form of the disease have ANCAs.[21] Others have found a somewhat higher frequency. Nevertheless, this is in contrast to microscopic polyangiitis, a form of vasculitis that is usually associated with ANCAs (see below).

In younger patients, polyarteritis nodosa in children may present in two forms: the infantile variant, which may be related to Kawasaki

Table 15.3

1990 criteria for the classification of polyarteritis nodosa (traditional format)*

Criterion	Definition
Weight loss ≥ 4 kg	Loss of 4 kg or more of body weight since illness began not due to dieting or other factors
Livedo reticularis	Mottled reticular pattern over the skin of portions of the extremities or torso
Testicular pain or tenderness	Pain or tenderness of the testicles not due to infection, trauma or other causes
Myalgias, weakness, or leg tenderness	Diffuse myalgias (excluding shoulder and hip girdle) or weakness of muscles or tenderness of leg muscles
Mononeuropathy or polyneuropathy	Development of mononeuropathy, multiple mononeuropathies or polyneuropathy
Diastolic BP > 90 mmHg	Development of hypertension with the diastolic BP higher than 90 mmHg
Elevated BUN or creatinine	Elevation of BUN > 40 mg/dL or creatinine > 1.5 mg/dL not due to dehydration or obstruction
Hepatitis B virus	Presence of hepatitis B surface antigen or antibody in serum
Arteriographic abnormality	Arteriogram showing aneurysms or occlusions of the vesical arteries not due to arteriosclerosis, fibromuscular dysplasia, or other non-inflammatory causes
Biopsy of small or medium-sized artery containing PMN	Histological changes showing the presence of granylocytes or granulocytes and mononuclear leukocytes in the artery wall

*For classification purposes, a patient shall be said to have polyarteritis nodosa if at least three of these 10 criteria are present.
The presence of any three or more criteria yields a sensitivity of 82.2% and a specificity of 86.6%.
BP, blood pressure; BUN, blood urea nitrogen; PMN, polymorphonuclear neutrophils.
Reproduced with permission from Lightfoot, D.W. (1991) *Current Opinion in Rheumatology*, **3**, 3–7.

syndrome, and a childhood form, which is similar to adult polyarteritis nodosa (see also section on Kawasaki syndrome).[22]

Cutaneous polyarteritis nodosa

In addition to classical polyarteritis nodosa, 'localized (cutaneous) polyarteritis nodosa' has also been described. This is a relatively benign variant in which patients develop cutaneous lesions, often over very prolonged periods, but serious visceral involvement is, by definition, never a feature. In one study, none of 79 patients with cutaneous polyarteritis nodosa who were followed for an average of 6.9 years developed systemic vasculitis.[23] It may occur at any age and shows no sex predilection.

Patients have recurrent episodes of tender, painful nodules, particularly on the lower legs, although these may sometimes be quite widespread. Individual lesions vary from 2 mm to 2 cm in diameter. Early lesions are pink or red, while more established nodules may have a purplish coloration. Patients may also manifest livedo reticularis, usually on the lower legs and often related to groups of nodules. Other complications include ulceration and, rarely, gangrene. Patients sometimes experience myalgias and peripheral nerves may be affected, but there is never any evidence of more widespread visceral involvement.

Immunofluorescence often reveals IgM and/or complement in the walls of cutaneous arteries, suggesting a possible immune complex pathogenesis.[24] Rare reports of infants of mothers with cutaneous

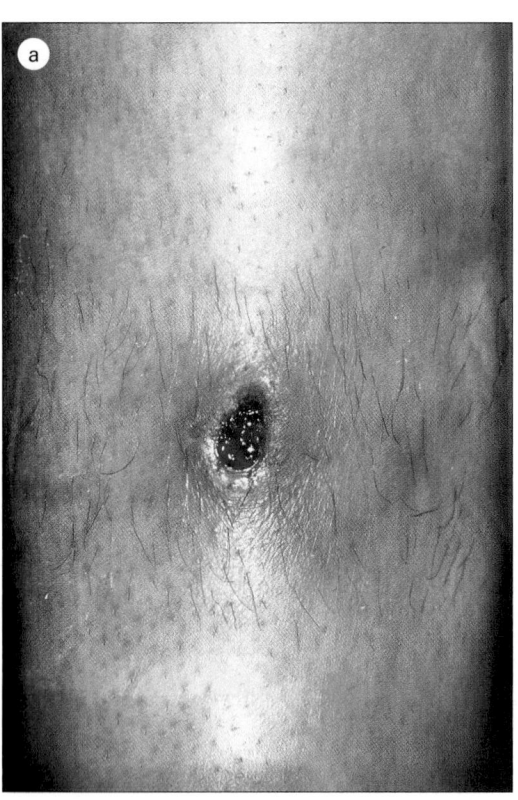
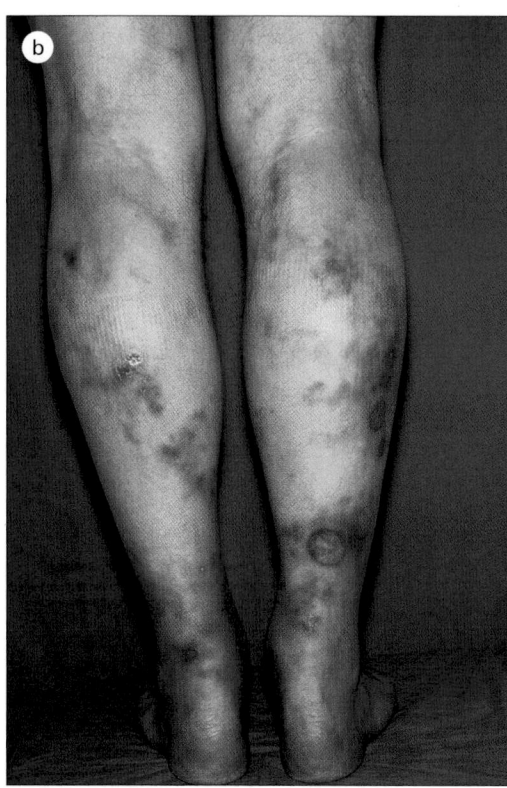
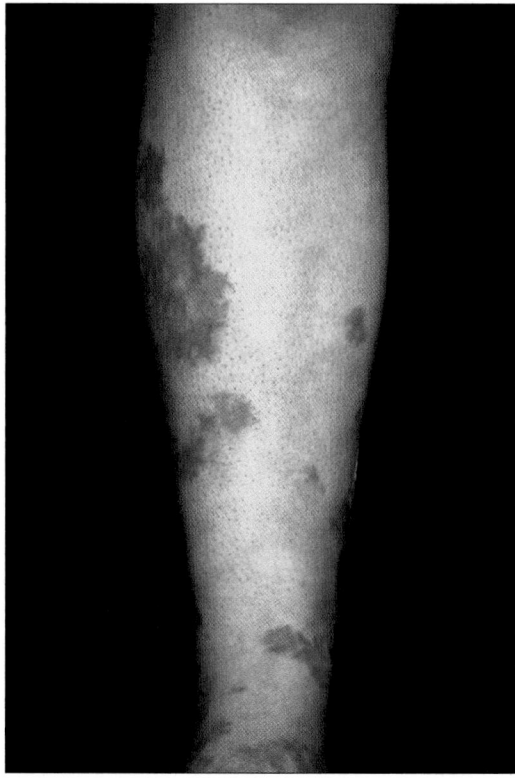

Fig. 15.26
Polyarteritis nodosa: (a) a sharply defined ulcer with an indurated purplish border on the shin; (b) multiple ulcers, nodules and foci of livedo reticularis. By courtesy of R.A. Marsden, MD, St George's Hospital, London, UK.

Fig. 15.27
Polyarteritis nodosa: this patient presented with large hemorrhagic lesions on the legs. By courtesy of the Institute of Dermatology, London, UK.

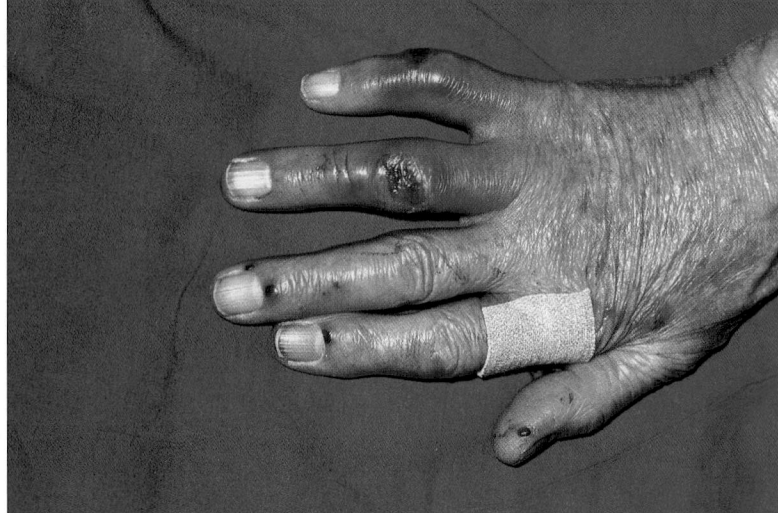
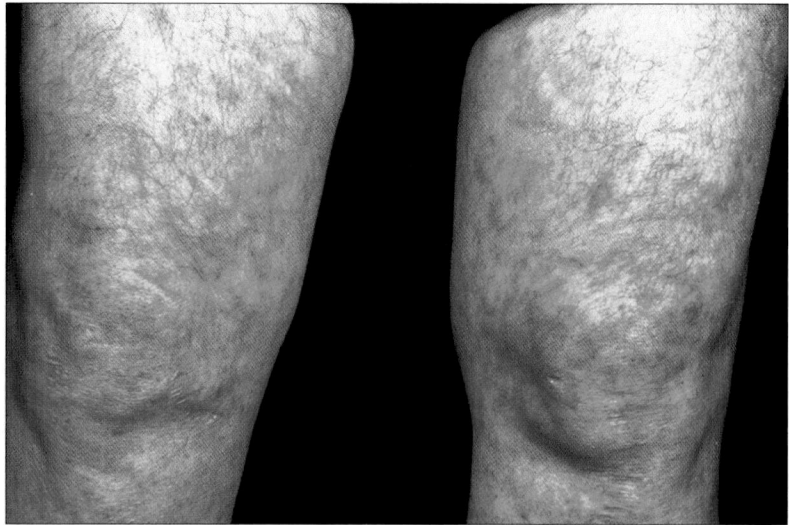

Fig. 15.28
Polyarteritis nodosa: epidermal infarction has resulted in these digital ulcers. By courtesy of R.A. Marsden, MD, St George's Hospital, London, UK.

Fig. 15.29
Polyarteritis nodosa: this patient shows florid livedo reticularis. By courtesy of the Institute of Dermatology, London, UK.

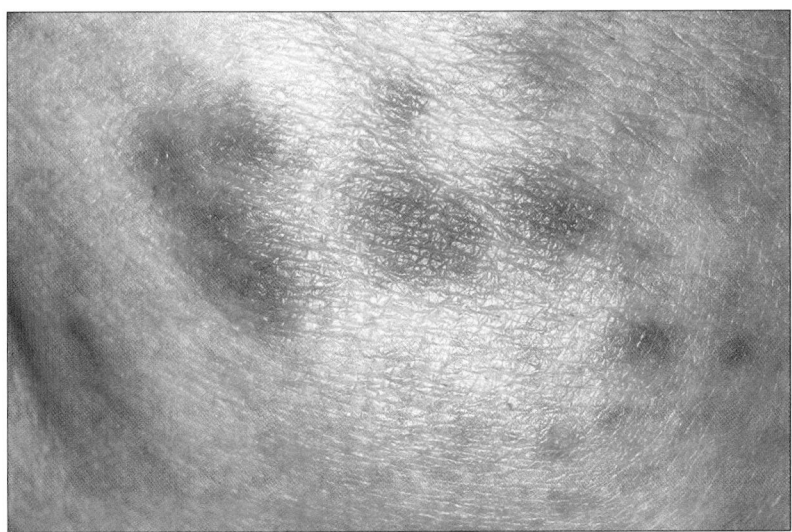

Fig. 15.30
Polyarteritis nodosa: erythematous macules are occasionally seen. By courtesy of the Institute of Dermatology, London, UK.

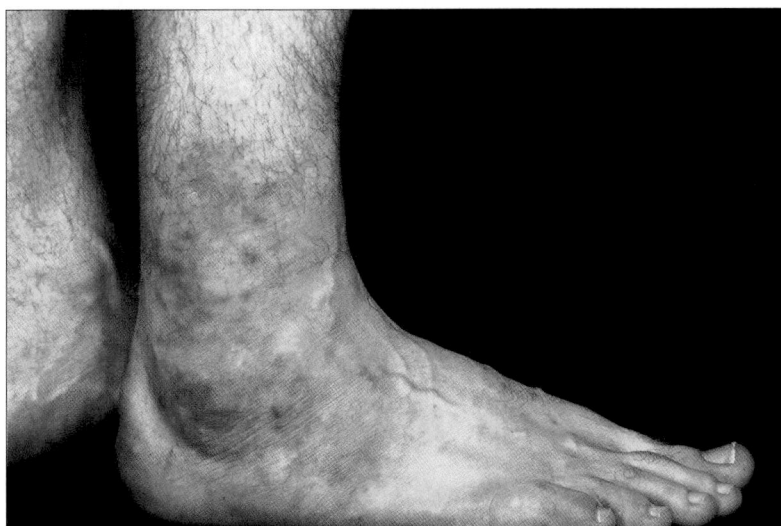

Fig. 15.31
Polyarteritis nodosa: erythematous papules are present around this patient's ankles. By courtesy of the Institute of Dermatology, London, UK.

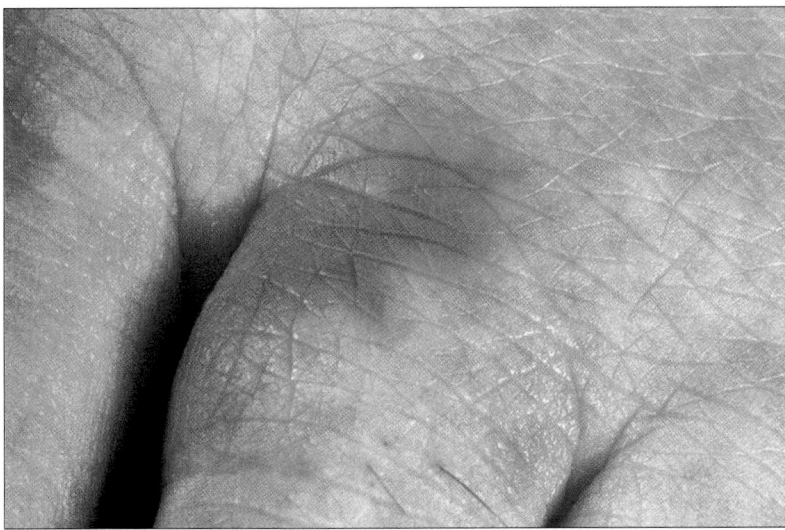

Fig. 15.32
Polyarteritis nodosa: this patient presented with acral erythematous lesions. By courtesy of the Institute of Dermatology, London, UK.

polyarteritis developing the disease and experiencing subsequent resolution are suggestive of a pathogenic circulating factor.[25]

Microscopic polyangiitis

Microscopic polyangiitis (microscopic polyarteritis) is a more recently described entity, which involves the skin in a significant proportion of patients.[2,26–28] Its definition, and relationship to classic polyarteritis nodosa, is somewhat controversial. The disease essentially consists of small vessel vasculitis in association with glomerulonephritis. In contrast, renal involvement in classic polyarteritis is a vascular nephropathy. Lung capillaritis is sometimes seen in patients with microscopic polyangiitis. By way of distinction, classic polyarteritis nodosa is very rarely associated with clinical manifestations of pulmonary involvement (although

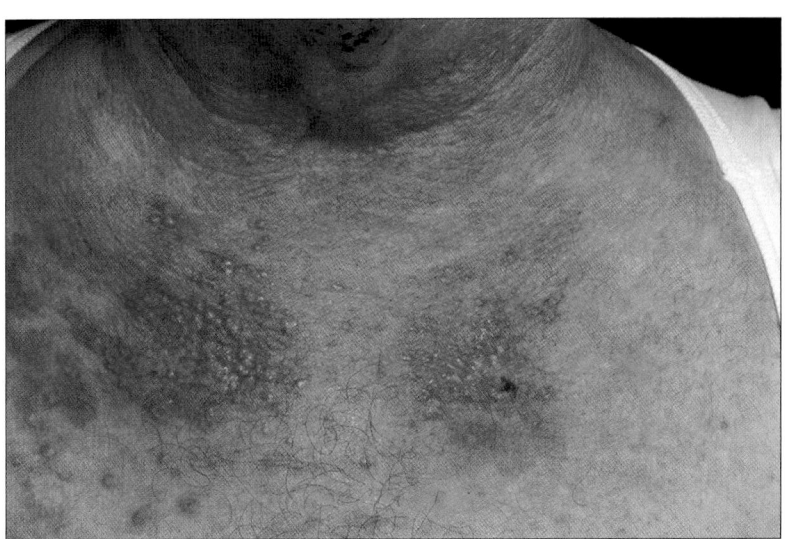

Fig. 15.33
Polyarteritis nodosa: in some patients, an intense neutrophil infiltrate results in pustular lesions as seen in this patient. By courtesy of the Institute of Dermatology, London, UK.

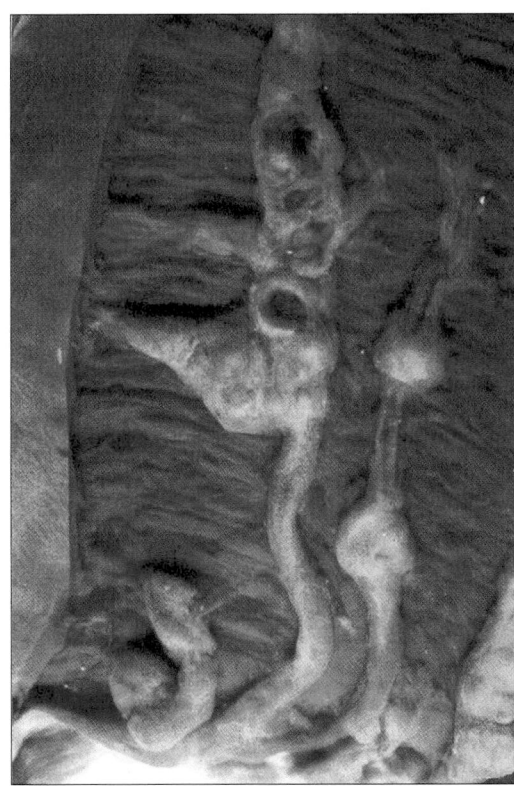

Fig. 15.34
Polyarteritis nodosa: coronary arteries showing conspicuous aneurysmal dilatation are now very rarely seen (museum specimen). By courtesy of the Department of Pathology, St Thomas' Hospital, London, UK.

pathological involvement of large vessels may be more common than suspected: see above) and this clinical difference is helpful in distinguishing these entities.[21] However, since many patients with either disease have neither pulmonary nor renal involvement, precise classification can be difficult.[21] Microscopic polyangiitis is a diagnosis of exclusion; other conditions that may manifest similar renal features include Wegener's granulomatosis, rapidly progressive glomerulonephritis, Churg–Strauss syndrome, SLE, classical polyarteritis nodosa and Henoch–Schönlein purpura.[15]

Microscopic polyangiitis is usually associated with positive neutrophil cytoplasmic antibodies, typically of the antimyeloperoxidase (perinuclear-antineutrophil cytoplasmic antibody, p-ANCA) subtype (*Fig. 15.35*).[28] Since most (but not all) patients with classic polyarteritis nodosa do not have ANCAs, this finding is useful in distinguishing these conditions.

Microscopic polyangiitis is a disease of particular importance owing to its high morbidity and mortality, with a 5-year survival of only approximately 65%.[26]

Patients often present with non-specific constitutional symptoms including non-specific malaise, fever and myalgia. There may be a past history of sore throat or a flu-like illness, which obviously raises the possibility of an iatrogenic pathogenesis for the subsequent vasculitic process.[26] Renal involvement may manifest as microscopic hematuria, proteinuria or acute renal failure. Hypertension is present in a large proportion of patients. Pulmonary lesions present as hemoptysis and intrapulmonary hemorrhage, which may prove fatal.

Dermatological signs, which are found in approximately 40% of patients, include purpura, splinter hemorrhages and leg ulceration.[27] Cutaneous nodules and livedo do not appear to be features of this disease due to absence of involvement of larger vessels. Other manifestations such as nervous system lesions, gastrointestinal bleeding with pain, and diarrhea, are sometimes evident.

Laboratory findings in microscopic polyarteritis include a raised ESR, normochromic normocytic anemia, leukocytosis with neutrophilia and thrombocytosis, raised C-reactive protein and raised α-1 and α-2 globulins. Rheumatoid factor and immune complexes are present in less than 50% of patients.[26] Anti-DNA antibodies are not a feature. Cutaneous immunofluorescence is usually negative.

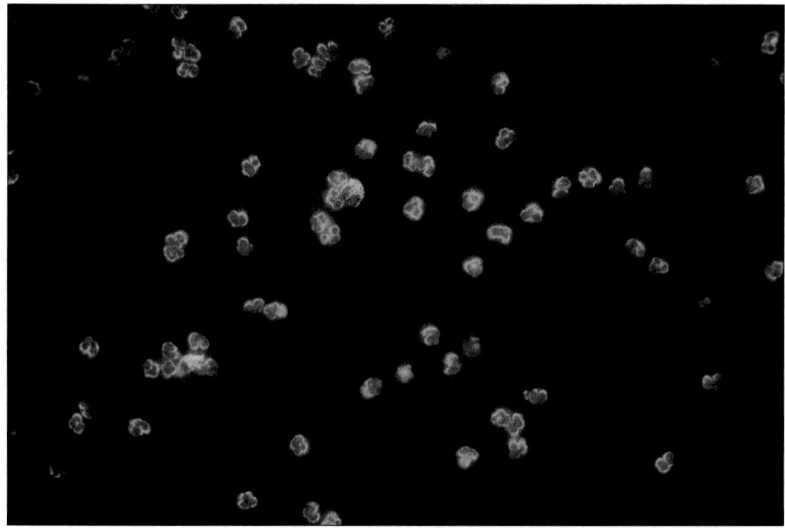

Fig. 15.35
Microscopic polyarteritis: p-ANCA. By courtesy of G. Swana, MD, St Thomas' Hospital, London, UK.

Pathogenesis and histological features

Polyarteritis nodosa

The pathogenesis of polyarteritis nodosa is poorly understood. Classic polyarteritis nodosa has been suggested to be immune-complex mediated, on the basis of serum immune-complex levels, immunofluorescence investigations and ultrastructural studies. However, in many patients immune complexes cannot be demonstrated and their role in the development of this disease is controversial. Important suspect antigens include hepatitis B virus (HBV) surface antigens and cryoglobulins.[29–32] It has been shown that a significant number of patients with polyarteritis nodosa have circulating HBV antigen.[8,32] Furthermore, circulating immune complexes containing HBV antigen and immunoglobulin have been characterized in occasional patients.[8] HBV surface antigen has also been identified within affected vessels in a small number of patients.[8] A decrease in HBV-associated cases of polyarteritis nodosa in France has been reported and it has been suggested that this phenomenon is the result of vaccination programs.[33] Human immunodeficiency viral infection has also been reported in cases of polyarteritis nodosa or a polyarteritis nodosa-like syndrome.[34–39]

Evidence of hepatitis C viral infection has been documented in some patients. In one study, 20% of patients had antibodies against hepatitis C virus.[39,40] Erythrovirus (parvovirus) infection has been associated with polyarteritis nodosa in occasional cases.[41,42]

In childhood polyarteritis nodosa, there appears to be a striking association with group A streptococci.[43]

Although there is some evidence to suggest a role for immune complexes generated during infection, such a relationship cannot be demonstrated in many cases. Therefore, the pathogenesis of classic polyarteritis nodosa is unclear in many patients.

As with other ANCA-associated vasculitides, the presence of ANCAs (usually p-ANCAs) in most patients with microscopic polyangiitis suggests that these antibodies may play a pathogenic role. In contrast, ANCAs are not usually seen in patients with classic polyarteritis nodosa. Additionally, again in contrast to classic polyarteritis nodosa, immune complexes are not thought to play a role in the pathogenesis of microscopic polyarteritis nodosa. The presence of ANCAs suggests a shared pathogenic relationship with other ANCA-associated vasculitides (i.e. Wegener's granulomatosis, Churg–Strauss syndrome). HIV infection has been documented in patients with microscopic polyangiitis.[35]

The histological features of the cutaneous lesions in both the classic and localized variants of classic polyarteritis nodosa are similar and changes are variable.[26,44] In some instances, the changes are indistinguishable from leukocytoclastic vasculitis involving the superficial dermal vessels (*Fig. 15.36*). More characteristic, however, is the finding of necrotizing vasculitis involving the muscular arteries of the deep dermis or subcutaneous fat; these are the changes that are also seen in the internal viscera, often associated with infarction (*Fig. 15.37*). Although the whole circumference and thickness of the vessel wall is often affected, sometimes the changes are focal. Typically in polyarteritis nodosa, the vascular changes are discontinuous, with uninvolved skip lesions between affected segments (*Fig. 15.38*).

The acute changes, those of fibrinoid necrosis, involve the muscle coat and often destroy the internal elastic lamina; this is often best appreciated by the use of a stain for elastic tissue (*Fig. 15.39*). Associated with the necrosis is an inflammatory cell infiltrate of neutrophils, eosinophils and mononuclear cells. Leukocytoclasis is sometimes an additional feature. Thrombosis is common and may be complicated by ischemic necrosis of the surface epithelium. Healing lesions are associated with fibroblastic proliferation and eventual fibrous scarring. Endarteritis is often evident and any disruption of the internal elastic lamina is permanent. A characteristic feature often present in wedge biopsies that contain multiple vessels is the presence of lesions at varying stages of evolution. Deep, surgical incisional biopsies are essential for the diagnosis of cutaneous involvement in polyarteritis nodosa. A punch biopsy will often not sample larger vessels that are typically affected. Furthermore, the diagnosis is subject to sampling error due to the multifocal nature of the disease. Aneurysm formation may sometimes be appreciated microscopically.[1]

Internal visceral involvement is based upon the effects of necrotizing arteritis. Interestingly, nodular swellings (aneurysms) are much more obvious. The effects depend upon the relative interplay of infarction and hemorrhage. Renal involvement in classical polyarteritis nodosa is predominantly due to large vessel vasculitis, with resultant thrombosis

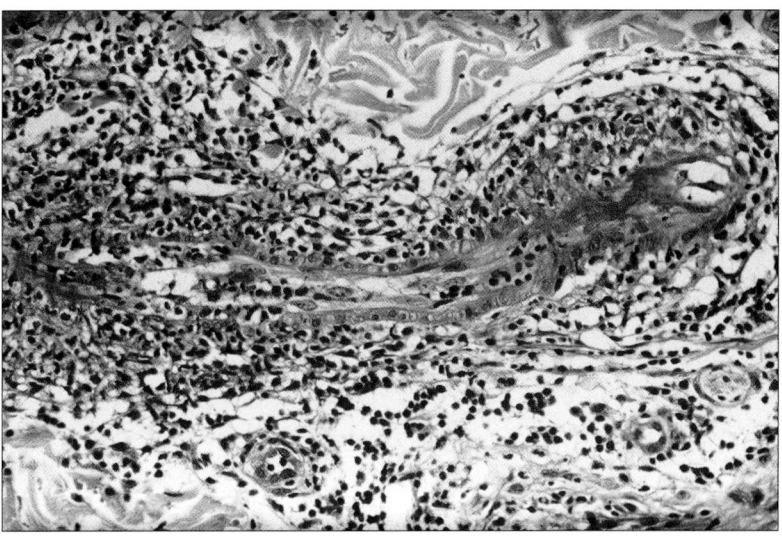

Fig. 15.38
Polyarteritis nodosa: while fibrinoid necrosis involves both lateral extremities of this vascular segment, the middle portion is relatively unaffected.

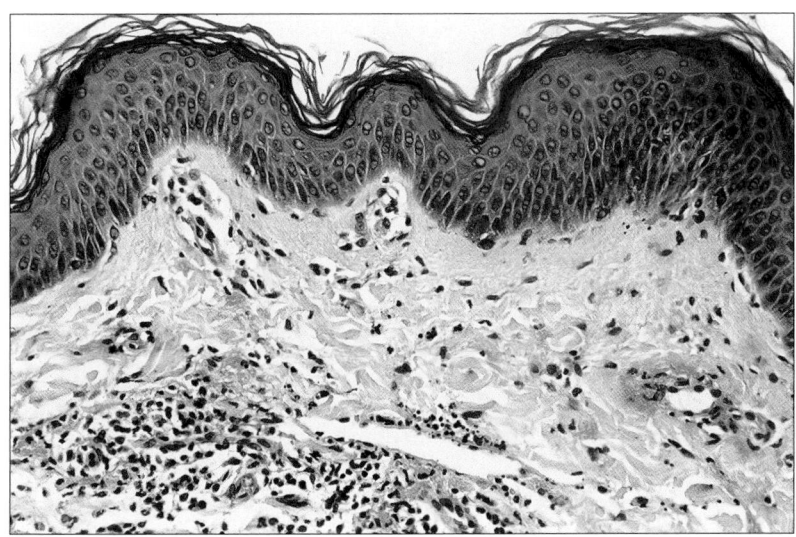

Fig. 15.36
Polyarteritis nodosa: in this case the features are those of a superficial leukocytoclastic vasculitis. It is important to remember that this histological lesion may represent a serious systemic disease.

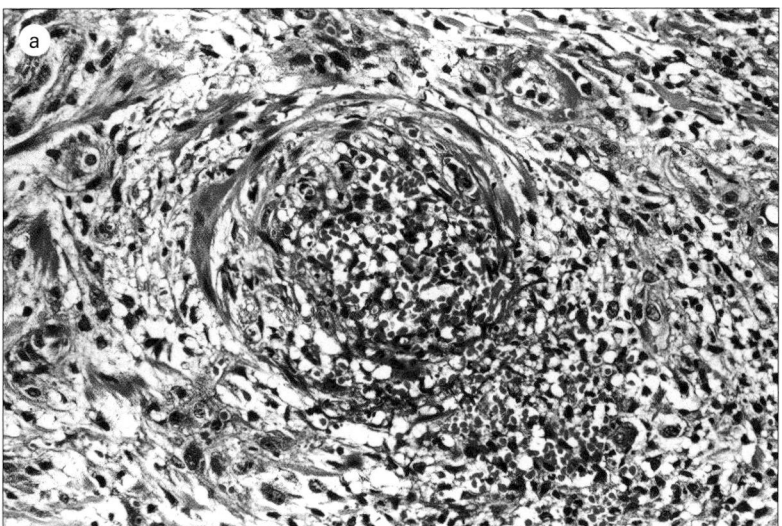

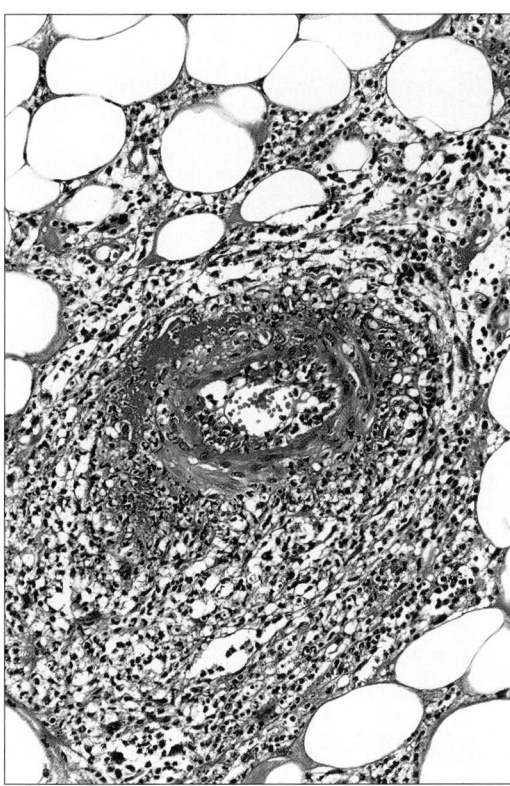

Fig. 15.37
Polyarteritis nodosa: necrotizing arteritis is seen within the subcutaneous fat.

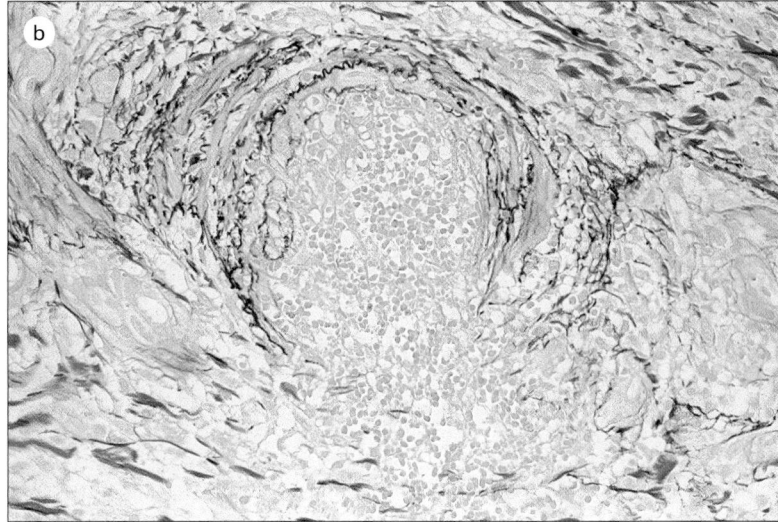

Fig. 15.39
Polyarteritis nodosa: (a) there is marked red cell extravasation; (b) elastic–van Gieson staining shows disruption of the internal elastic lamina.

and infarction, coupled with the effects of hypertension (*Fig. 15.40*).[45] Patients may also manifest focal, segmental proliferative or necrotizing glomerulonephritis similar to that seen in patients with microscopic polyarteritis nodosa (*Fig. 15.41*).

Microscopic polyangiitis

Microscopic polyangiitis (microscopic polyarteritis) is characterized by small vessel vasculitis, which may predominantly affect the muscular arteriole, capillaries and venules (*Fig. 15.42*).[2,28] Given the spectrum of vessel types involved and the absence of arteriolar involvement in some patients, the term 'microscopic polyangiitis' is preferred by some authors.[2,46] The absence of involvement of capillaries and venules in classic polyarteritis nodosa is a major point of distinction from microscopic polyarteritis nodosa. Necrotizing vasculitis with fibrinoid necrosis and variable numbers of neutrophils and monocytes is seen. In early lesions, neutrophils associated with karyorrhexis predominate, while lymphocytes and histiocytes dominate the infiltrate in older lesions. In some patients, acute lesions are indistinguishable from leukocytoclastic vasculitis.

Renal lesions include focal segmental necrotizing glomerulonephritis (often with crescents), vasculitis, interstitial inflammation and tubular atrophy. Large vessel disease, visceral infarction and granulomatous inflammation are not features.

Differential diagnosis

Since other vasculitides may show similar histological features, particularly in cases with only small vessel involvement (leukocytoclastic vasculitis pattern), the biopsy findings must never be used in isolation to determine a patient's diagnosis. Only after careful clinical, serological and histological correlation can a definitive diagnosis be rendered. Criteria are admittedly definitional and as we learn more about this disease (or group of diseases), criteria are likely to change. Careful clinical investigation is required to evaluate for underlying causes/disease associations.

As noted above, distinction between classic polyarteritis nodosa and polyangiitis is based on the size of vessels involved, spectrum and type of organ involvement and presence of ANCAs. Microscopic polyangiitis may also be confused with Wegener's granulomatosis and Churg–Strauss syndrome. The presence of granulomatous inflammation in the lung favors the first of the last two conditions. The presence of blood eosinophilia and asthma favors a diagnosis of Churg–Strauss syndrome. As can be seen, microscopic polyangiitis is approached as a diagnosis of exclusion. In fact, with clinical follow-up, a patient's diagnosis may be revised. For example, patients that appear to fit criteria for microscopic polyangiitis may eventually develop manifestations that allow for classification as Wegener's granulomatosis.[2] Diagnostic criteria are likely to change as we understand more about these disorders.

References

1. Bonsib, S.M. (2001) Polyarteritis nodosa. *Semin Diagn Pathol*, **18**, 14–23.
2. Jennette, J.C., Thomas, D.B., Falk, R.J. (2001) Microscopic polyangiitis (microscopic polyarteritis). *Semin Diagn Pathol*, **18**, 3–13.
3. Cohen, R.D., Conn, D.L., Ilstrup, D.M. (1980) Clinical features, prognosis and response to treatment in polyarteritis. *Mayo Clin Proc*, **55**, 146–155.
4. Lightfoot, R.W. Jr (1991) Churg–Strauss syndrome and polyarteritis nodosa. *Curr Opin Rheumatol*, **3**, 3–7.
5. Lightfoot, R.W. Jr, Michel, B.A., Bloch, D.A. et al (1990) The American College of Rheumatology 1990 criteria for the classification of polyarteritis nodosa. *Arthritis Rheum*, **33**, 1088–1093.
6. Borrie, P. (1972) Cutaneous polyarteritis nodosa. *Br J Dermatol*, **87**, 87–95.
7. Díaz-Perez, J.L., Winkelmann, R.K. (1974) Cutaneous periarteritis nodosa. *Arch Dermatol*, **110**, 407–414.
8. Lawley, T.J., Kubota, Y. (1990) Vasculitis. *Immunodermatology*, **8**, 681–687.
9. Hsu, C.T., Kerrison, J.B., Miller, N.R. et al (2001) Choroidal infarction, anterior ischemic optic neuropathy, and central retinal artery occlusion from polyarteritis nodosa. *Retina*, **21**, 348–351.
10. Yamamoto, S., Takeuchi, S. (2000) Episcleritis as the primary manifestation in a patient with polyarteritis nodosa. *Jpn J Ophthalmol*, **44**, 151–153.

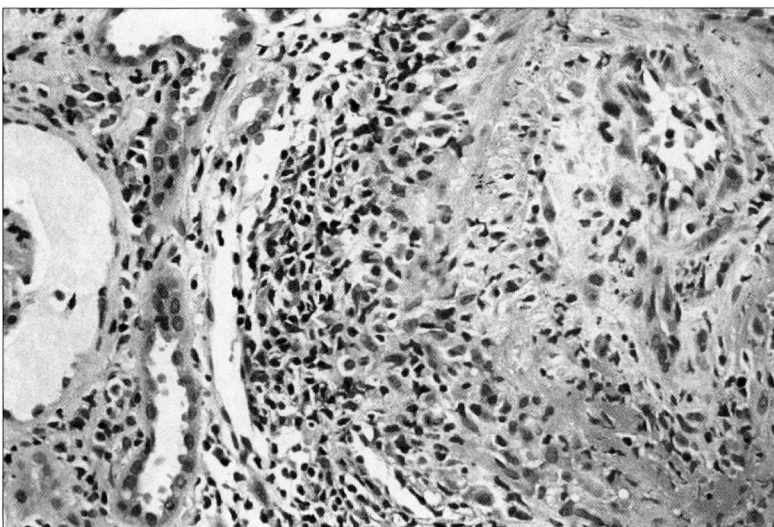

Fig. 15.40
Polyarteritis nodosa: in this kidney section an arcuate artery shows necrotizing vasculitis and fibrointimal thickening. The inflammatory cell infiltrate contains conspicuous eosinophils.

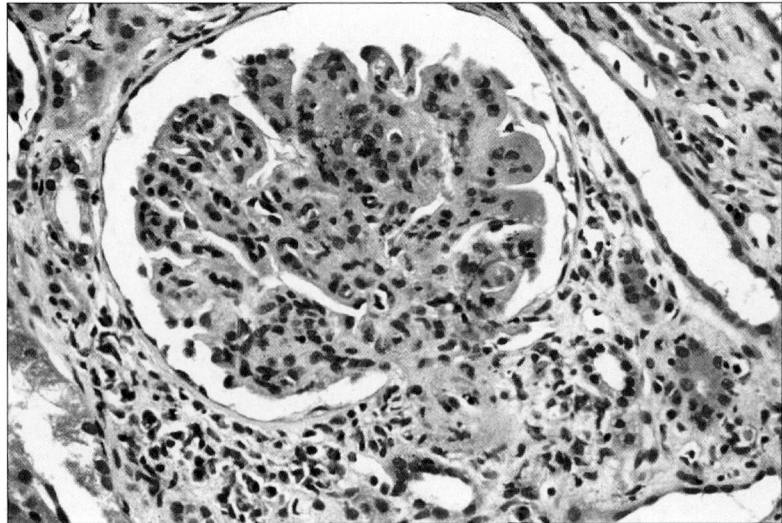

Fig. 15.41
Polyarteritis nodosa: segmental necrotizing glomerulonephritis.

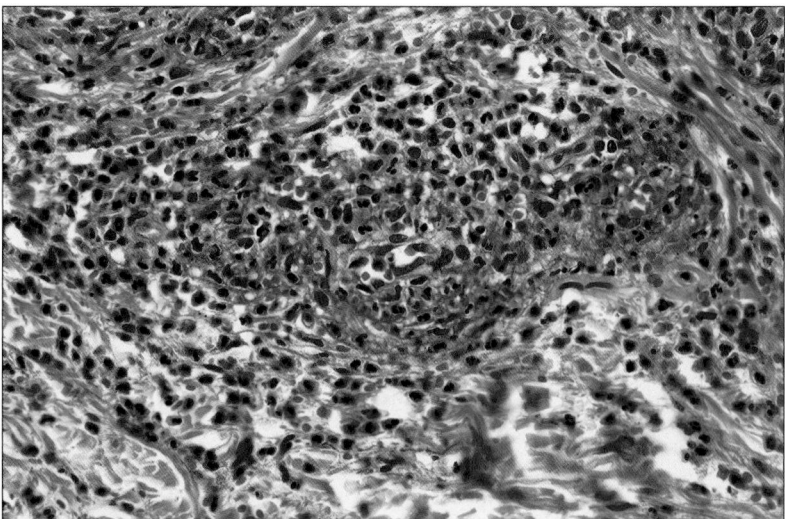

Fig. 15.42
Microscopic polyarteritis nodosa: acute necrotizing vasculitis of a small muscular arteriole is evident. Numerous eosinophils are present.

11. Akova, Y.A., Jabbur, N.S., Foster, C.S. (1993) Ocular presentation of polyarteritis nodosa. Clinical course and management with steroid and cytotoxic therapy. *Ophthalmology*, **100**, 1775–1781.
12. Guillevin, L., Lhote, F., Gallais, V. et al (1995) Gastrointestinal tract involvement in polyarteritis nodosa and Churg–Strauss syndrome. *Ann Med Interne*, **146**, 260–267.
13. Parangi, S., Oz, M.C., Blume, R.S. et al (1991) Hepatobiliary complications of polyarteritis nodosa. *Arch Surg*, **126**, 909–912.
14. Nakazawa, K., Itoh, N., Duan, H.J. et al (1992) Polyarteritis nodosa with atrophy of the left hepatic lobe. *Acta Pathol Jpn*, **42**, 662–666.
15. Ito, M., Sano, K., Inaba, H. et al (1991) Localized necrotizing arteritis. A report of two cases involving the gallbladder and pancreas. *Arch Pathol Lab Med*, **115**, 780–783.
16. Blidi, M., Quang, T.N., Cassan, P. et al (1996) Acute cholecystitis in periarteritis nodosa: 8 cases. *Ann Med Interne*, **147**, 304–312.
17. Matsumoto, T., Homma, S., Okada, M. et al (1993) The lung in polyarteritis nodosa: a pathologic study of 10 cases. *Hum Pathol*, **24**, 717–724.
18. Teichman, J.M., Mattrey, R.F., Demby, A.M. et al (1993) Polyarteritis nodosa presenting as acute orchitis. *J Urol*, **149**, 1139–1140.
19. Guillevin, L., Lhote, F., Jarrouse, B. et al (1992) Polyarteritis nodosa related to hepatitis B virus. A retrospective study of 66 patients. *Ann Med Interne*, **143**, 63–74.
20. Warfield, A.T., Lee, S.J., Phillips, S.M. et al (1994) Isolated testicular vasculitis mimicking a testicular neoplasm. *J Clin Pathol*, **47**, 1121–1123.
21. Guillevin, L. (2001) Polyarteritis nodosa and microscopic polyangiitis. In: Ball, G.V., Bridges, S.L. (eds) *Vasculitis*. New York: Oxford University Press.
22. Ettlinger, R.E., Nelson, A.M., Burke, E.C. et al (1979) Polyarteritis nodosa in childhood. *Arthritis Rheum*, **22**, 820–825.
23. Daoud, M.S., Hutton, K.P., Gibson, L.E. (1997) Cutaneous periarteritis nodosa: a clinicopathologic study of 79 cases. *Br J Dermatol*, **36**, 706–713.
24. Díaz-Perez, J.L., Schroeter, A.L., Winkelmann, R.K. (1980) Cutaneous periarteritis nodosa: immunofluorescence studies. *Arch Dermatol*, **116**, 56–58.
25. Stone, M.S., Olson, R.R., Weismann, D.N. et al (1993) Cutaneous vasculitis in the newborn of a mother with cutaneous polyarteritis nodosa. *J Am Acad Dermatol*, **28**, 101–105.
26. Savage, C.O.S., Winearls, C.G., Evans, D.J. et al (1985) Microscopic polyarteritis, presentation, pathology and prognosis. *QJM*, **56**, 467–483.
27. Rodgers, H., Guthrie, J.A., Brownjohn, A.M. et al (1989) Microscopic polyarteritis: clinical features and treatment. *Postgrad Med J*, **65**, 515–518.
28. Homas, P.B., David-Bajar, K.M., Fitzpatrick, J.E. et al (1992) Microscopic polyarteritis: report of a case with cutaneous involvement and antimyeloperoxidase antibodies. *Arch Dermatol*, **128**, 1223–1228.
29. Duffy, J., Lidsky, M.D., Sharp, J.T. (1976) Polyarthritis, polyarthritis, and hepatitis B. *Medicine*, **55**, 19.
30. Drueke, T., Barbanel, C., Jungers, P. et al (1980) Hepatitis B antigen associated periarteritis nodosa in patients undergoing long-term hemodialysis. *Am J Med*, **68**, 86–90.
31. Sergent, J.S., Locksgin, M.D., Christin, C.L. et al (1976) Vasculitis with hepatitis B antigenemia: long-term observations in nine patients. *Medicine*, **55**, 1–18.
32. Guillivan, L., Lhote, F., Cohen, P. et al (1995) Polyarteritis nodosa related to hepatitis B virus. A prospective study with long-term observation in 41 patients. *Medicine*, **74**, 238–253.
33. Trepo, C., Guillevin, L. (2001) Polyarteritis nodosa and extrahepatic manifestations of HBV infection: the case against autoimmune intervention in pathogenesis. *J Autoimmun*, **16**, 269–274.
34. Chetty, R. (2001) Vasculitides associated with HIV infection. *J Clin Pathol*, **54**, 275–278.
35. Gisselbrecht, M., Cohen, P., Lortholary, O. et al (1998) Human immunodeficiency virus-related vasculitis. Clinical presentation and therapeutic approach to eight cases. *Ann Med Interne*, **149**, 398–405.
36. Font, C., Miró, O., Pedrol, E. et al (1996) Polyarteritis nodosa in human immunodeficiency virus infection: report of four cases and review of the literature. *Br J Rheumatol*, **35**, 796–799.
37. Libman, B.S., Quismorio, F.P., Stimmler, M.M. (1995) Polyarteritis nodosa-like vasculitis in human immunodeficiency virus infection. *J Rheumatol*, **22**, 351–355.
38. Gherardi, R., Belec, L., Mhiri, C. et al (1993) The spectrum of vasculitis in human immunodeficiency virus-infected patients. A clinicopathologic evaluation. *Arthritis Rheum*, **36**, 1164–1174.
39. Valeriono-Marcet, J., Ravichandron, L., Kerr, L.D. (1990) HIV associated systemic necrotizing vasculitis. *J Rheumatol*, **17**, 1091–1093.
40. Carson, C.W., Conn, D.L., Czaja, A.J. et al (1993) Frequency and significance of antibodies to hepatitis C virus in polyarteritis nodosa. *J Rheumatol*, **20**, 304–309.
41. Finkel, T.H., Torok, T.J., Ferguson, P.J. et al (1994) Chronic parvovirus B19 infection and systemic necrotizing vasculitis. *Lancet*, **21**, 1255–1258.
42. Crowson, A.N., Magro, C.M., Dawood, M.R. (2000) A causal role for parvovirus B19 infection in adult dermatomyositis and other autoimmune syndromes. *J Cutan Pathol*, **27**, 505–515.
43. Fink, C.W. (1991) The role of the streptococcus in poststreptococcal reactive arthritis and childhood polyarteritis nodosa. *J Rheumatol*, **18** (Suppl. 29), 14–20.
44. Moskowitz, R.W., Baggenstoss, A.H., Slocumb, C.H. (1963) Histopathologic classification of periarteritis nodosa: a study of 56 cases confirmed at necropsy. *Mayo Clin Proc*, **38**, 345–357.
45. Heptinstall, R.H. (1983) Polyarteritis nodosa. In: Heptinstall, R.H. (ed.) *Pathology of the kidney*, 3rd edn. Boston: Little, Brown, pp 293–813.
46. Jennette, J.C., Falk, R.J., Andrassy, K. et al (1994) Nomenclature of systemic vasculitis. Proposal of an international consensus conference. *Arthritis Rheum*, **37**, 187–192.

Wegener's granulomatosis

Clinical features

Wegener's granulomatosis is a multisystem vascular disease associated with high morbidity and mortality.[1,2] Before the introduction of cyclophosphamide therapy it was associated with a dismal prognosis. Mean survival was of the order of 5 months following diagnosis and approximately 80% of patients died within 1 year, most as a consequence of renal involvement.

Although it may present in a wide variety of age groups, from infancy to the elderly, it is the middle-aged that are predominantly affected, with a peak incidence in the fourth decade.[1-4] There is a slight predilection for males (3:2). In one large study, 97% of patients were Caucasians.[5]

Wegener's granulomatosis comprises a triad of characteristics:

- Necrotizing, destructive, granulomatous lesions in the upper respiratory tract (nose, nasal sinuses, nasopharynx and larynx) and/or in the lower respiratory tract (trachea, bronchi or lungs). Frequently, both are present. Similar lesions may also be found in virtually any organ in the body.
- A generalized focal vasculitis occurring in a wide variety of sites, but particularly affecting the lungs.
- Glomerulonephritis.[6,7]

Early in disease, when patients may not have developed the full clinical triad, definitive diagnosis may be difficult or impossible (see *Table 15.4*). The most common presenting symptoms relate to involvement of the nose and nasal sinuses, and include severe and often purulent nasal discharge or evidence of sinusitis with pain and discharge. Clinical examination may reveal mucosal ulceration, perforated septum, paranasal sinusitis or a saddle-nose deformity. Serous or purulent otitis media is occasionally a presenting feature. Middle and inner ear involvement is also a common manifestation of disease.[8-10]

Pulmonary lesions are invariably present and patients may have cough, chest pain or hemoptysis. Radiological examination frequently reveals solitary or more commonly multiple nodular opacities, which are often bilateral, may be diffuse or sharply delineated, and are typically transient. Cavitation is frequently a feature. Lesions may present as large nodules that are clinically and radiologically suspicious for malignancy.

Renal involvement is common and urinalysis typically reveals hematuria (often microscopic), proteinuria and red cell casts.

Joint involvement may present as arthralgia or, less commonly, frank arthritis.

Table 15.4

1990 criteria for the classification of Wegener's granulomatosis (traditional format)*

Criterion	Definition
Nasal or oral inflammation	Development of painful or painless oral ulcers or purulent or bloody nasal discharge
Abnormal chest radiograph	Chest radiograph showing the presence of nodules, fixed infiltrates or cavities
Urinary sediment	Microhematuria (> 5 red blood cells per high power field) or red cell casts in urine sediment
Granulomatous inflammation on biopsy	Histological changes showing granulomatous inflammation within the wall of an artery or in the perivascular or extravascular area (artery or arteriole)

*For purposes of classification, a patient shall be said to have Wegener's granulomatosis if at least two of these four criteria are present. The presence of any two or more criteria yields a sensitivity of 88.2% and a specificity of 92.0%
Reproduced with permission from Leavitt, R.Y. (1990) *Arthritis and Rheumatism*, **33**, 1101–1107.

In one large series, 34% of patients developed neurological involvement.[11] Peripheral neuropathy was seen in 16%.[11] Central nervous system lesions are not uncommon and occur either as a consequence of direct extension through the base of the skull from sinus involvement or as a result of meningeal or intracerebral necrotizing granulomata. Patients may experience myelopathy or neuropathy.[12] Vasculitis involving intracerebral vessels can also result in cerebral lesions. Patients develop cranioneuropathy, cerebrovascular accidents or seizures.[11] Involvement of the vasa nervora may give rise to mononeuritis multiplex.

Ocular lesions result in a variety of complications including conjunctivitis, granulomatous keratitis, sclerouveitis and orbital pseudotumor. Proptosis is sometimes a feature.[13] Involvement of the temporal artery results in features (i.e. vision loss, jaw claudication) similar to those seen in temporal arteritis.[14]

Cutaneous manifestations are common, occurring in about 14–50% of patients.[15–18] Several different types of skin lesion may be encountered, including vasculitic lesions with purpura, bruising and nodule formation (*Figs 15.43–15.45*). Pyoderma gangrenosum-like lesions with necrosis

and ulceration that have a predilection for the lower limbs are also sometimes encountered. The presence of skin lesions appears to correlate with disease activity. Oral ulceration is common.[18,19]

In addition to the organ-specific features noted above, patients also often have a variety of constitutional symptoms, including anorexia, weight loss, fever and general malaise.

Two limited forms of Wegener's granulomatosis are recognized: pathergic granulomatosis and limited pulmonary granulomatosis.[20–22]

- *Pathergic granulomatosis* is of particular importance because mucosal and cutaneous lesions may predominate and persist for very long periods of time before intractable renal failure develops. In the absence of evidence of pulmonary and renal involvement, there may be a delay in establishing the diagnosis and administration of appropriate chemotherapy, with resultant increased morbidity and mortality. Patients with this variant are at particular risk of facial mutilation; sites especially involved include the nose, nasopharynx, sinuses and middle ears (*Fig. 15.46*).
- In *limited pulmonary granulomatosis* patients have respiratory

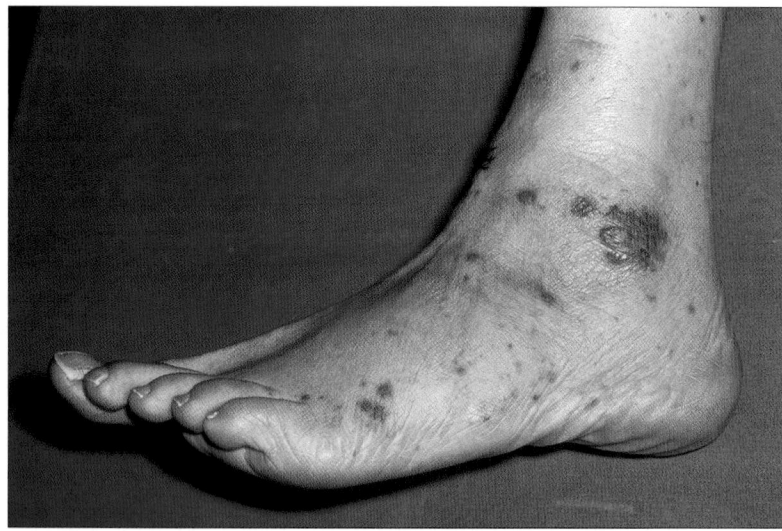

Fig. 15.43
Wegener's granulomatosis: multiple purpuric macules and papules. By courtesy of D. McGibbon, MD, St Thomas' Hospital, London, UK.

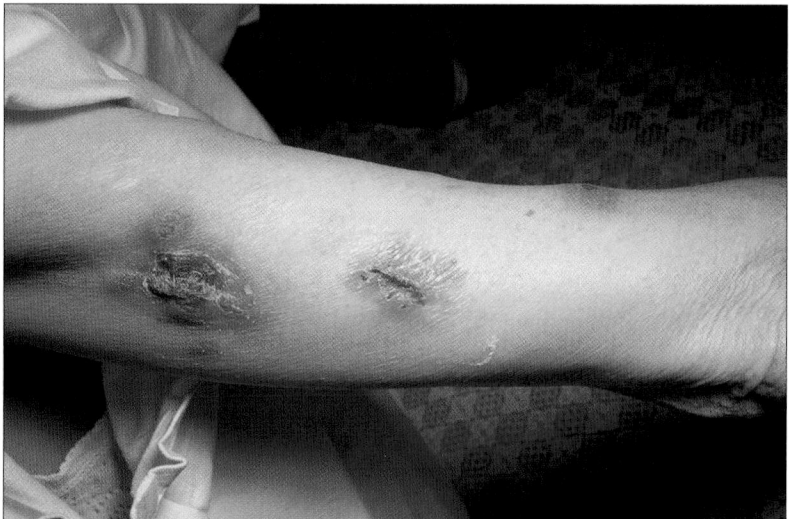

Fig. 15.45
Wegener's granulomatosis: this patient has ulcerating plaques and nodules. By courtesy of the Institute of Dermatology, London, UK.

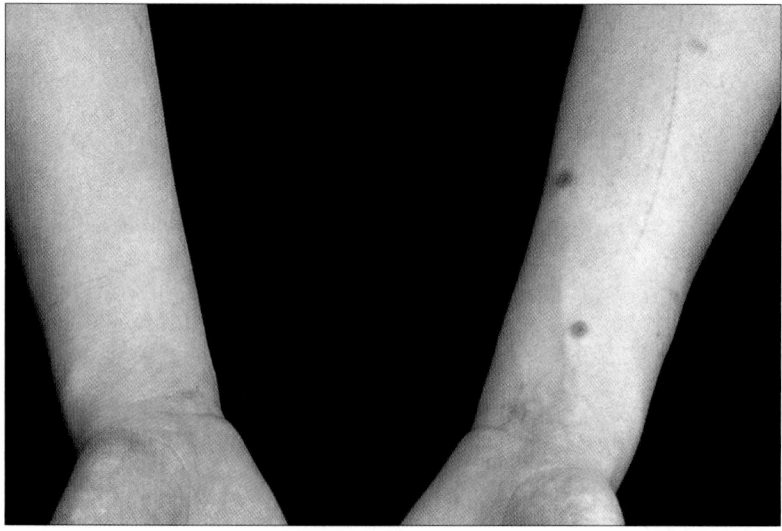

Fig. 15.44
Wegener's granulomatosis: cutaneous nodules as seen in this patient are a not uncommon manifestation. By courtesy of the Institute of Dermatology, London, UK.

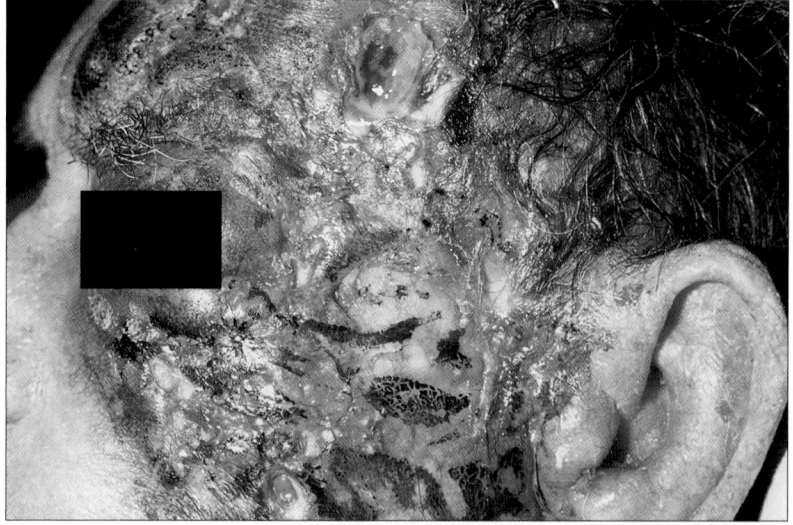

Fig. 15.46
Pathergic granulomatosis: gross necrosis and ulceration has resulted in very disfiguring tissue damage.

symptoms with associated fever and weight loss. Radiologically, multiple bilateral discrete nodular infiltrates and thin-walled cavitating lesions are seen, usually in the lower lobes. No evidence for renal involvement is present. Patients with this variant appear to have a somewhat better prognosis than those with classical (generalized) Wegener's granulomatosis.

A further development is the proposed purely granulomatous Wegener's granulomatosis (PGWG), in which it has been suggested that the presence of extravascular granulomata (particularly affecting the ears, nose, throat, orbit or lung) in association with a positive serum cytoplasmic-antineutrophil cytoplasmic antibody (c-ANCA) represents the earliest stage in the evolution of Wegener's granulomatosis.[23] Such a concept, if proven viable, should result in diagnosis at a stage before the development of more serious multisystem disease and, hence, earlier treatment.

The vast majority of patients with Wegener's granulomatosis have ANCA detected in their sera; rising titers have been shown to correlate with disease activity and are a valuable method of predicting relapse.[2,24] Typically, the indirect immunofluorescence shows a cytoplasmic pattern of staining (c-ANCA) (*Fig. 15.47*).[1] ANCAs have also been detected in patients with Takayasu's arteritis, Churg–Strauss syndrome, Kawasaki's arteritis, microscopic polyangiitis and idiopathic crescentic glomerulonephritis.[24–26]

Pathogenesis and histological features

This rare disease is thought to represent a hypersensitivity reaction to an as yet unidentified allergen. Response to immunosuppressive therapy is consistent with this hypothesis. The presence of ANCAs in most patients with Wegener's granulomatosis and the correlation of circulating levels of ANCAs with disease activity suggest a role in the pathogenesis of this disease. Additionally, although immune complexes have not been demonstrated, disease activity is ameliorated with plasma exchange. Thus, there is compelling anecdotal evidence suggesting ANCAs are central to pathogenesis, most likely through activation of neutrophils, lymphocytes and macrophages.[27] However, the precise role of ANCAs is not yet fully understood.[27]

It is postulated that exposure to an antigen (or antigens) may trigger ANCAs that have pathophysiological effects leading to tissue destruction.[28] Infectious agents have received some attention as potentially playing a role in the pathogenesis of Wegener's granulomatosis. It is interesting to note that relapses of the disease may follow infection.[27] In some patients, a complete or partial remission is achieved with antibiotic treatment combined with immunosuppressive agents.[27,29] Trimethoprim–sulfamethoxazole has also been used to reduce the frequency of relapses in Wegener's patients.[30] Patients who are chronic nasal carriers of *Staphylococcus aureus* seem to have a higher relapse rate compared with non-carriers.[31] Despite considerable research to establish a possible relationship between Wegener's granulomatosis and infection, a categoric role in the disease is elusive.[32]

In addition to infectious agents, a search for putative roles for physical agents in the environment has similarly been undertaken. Perhaps most attention has focused on silicon compounds.[33–35] One case-control study showed that exposure to silicon-containing compounds conferred a seven-fold risk for the development of Wegener's granulomatosis.[34] It has been postulated that silica-induced apoptosis of inflammatory cells may release lysosomal enzymes that stimulate ANCAs.[27,33]

Pulmonary lesions are characterized by necrotizing granulomatous inflammation that may bear more than a superficial resemblance to the caseation of pulmonary tuberculosis (*Fig. 15.48*).[36] The similarity is increased by the presence of large numbers of Langhans' giant cells at the periphery of the necrotic focus (*Fig. 15.49*). In addition, the features of an active angiitis are present; this may involve both arteries and veins and frequently has a granulomatous component (*Fig. 15.50*). The adjacent parenchyma is chronically inflamed and often shows severe, diffuse, interstitial fibrosis.

Early renal lesions are characterized by focal segmental glomerulonephritis. In more advanced cases the glomerulitis becomes generalized, with fibrinoid necrosis and widespread epithelial crescent formation.[37] The renal interstitial tissue may contain necrotizing granulomata and vasculitis is sometimes a feature. Immunofluorescence occasionally reveals granular deposits of immunoglobulin and complement along the glomerular capillary walls. This is taken as evidence for possible immune complex involvement. Similar granulomata and evidence of vasculitis have been described in all organ systems of the body, but are particularly often seen in the spleen.

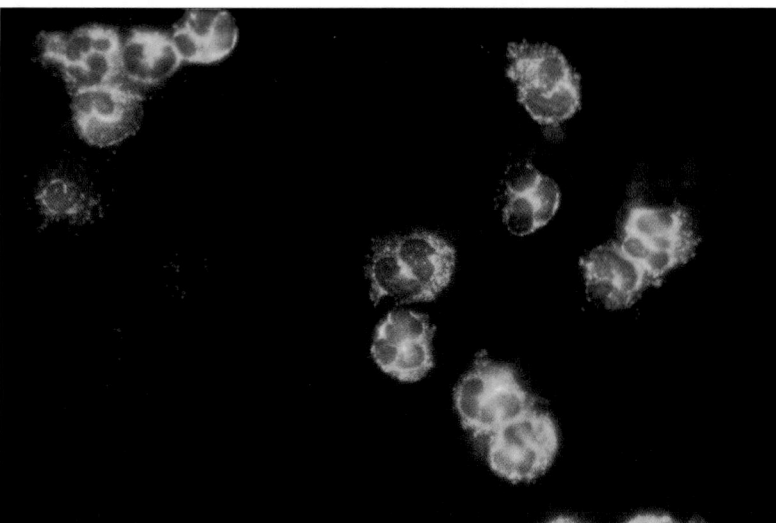

Fig. 15.47
Wegener's granulomatosis: c-ANCA. By courtesy of G. Swana, MD, St Thomas' Hospital, London, UK.

Fig. 15.48
Wegener's granulomatosis: this postmortem lung specimen shows consolidation and numerous abscesses. By courtesy of B. Corrin, MD, Brompton Hospital, London, UK.

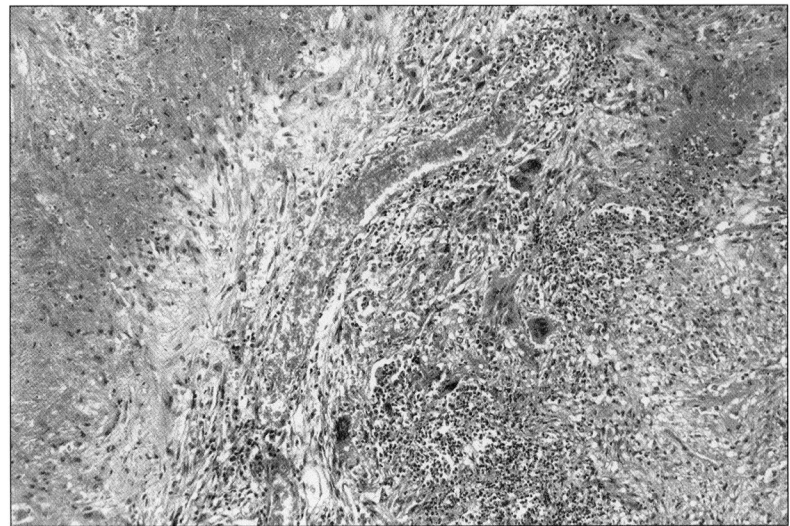

Fig. 15.49
Wegener's granulomatosis: this lung section shows extensive necrosis associated with a granulomatous infiltrate containing Langhans' giant cells. These appearances resemble pulmonary tuberculosis.

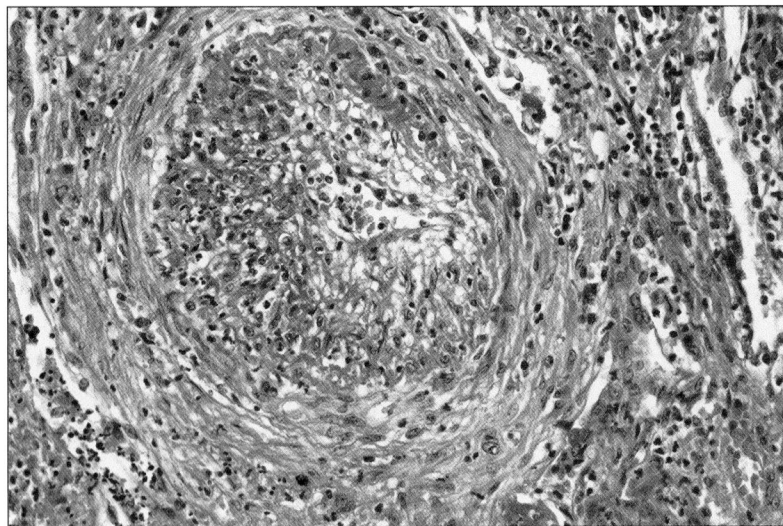

Fig. 15.50
Wegener's granulomatosis: a branch of the pulmonary artery shows necrotizing arteritis with fibrointimal thickening.

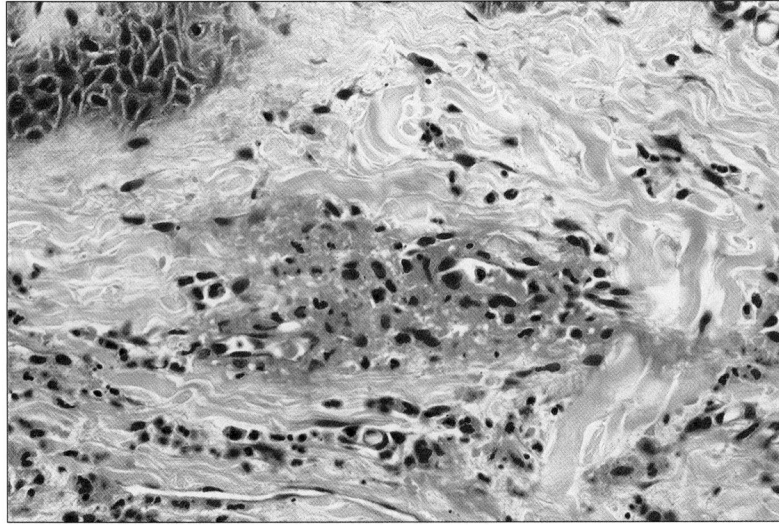

Fig. 15.51
Wegener's granulomatosis: leukocytoclastic vasculitis as shown in this field is the most often encountered cutaneous lesion.

Cutaneous lesions may reveal a variety of features including necrotizing vasculitis, in which small or medium-sized dermal vessels display fibrinoid necrosis, a neutrophil polymorphonuclear infiltrate and nuclear dust (*Figs 15.51–15.54*). In one series, 80% of biopsies from patients with cutaneous lesions (of 244 patients in this series, 14% had cutaneous lesions) showed leukocytoclastic vasculitis.[17] In another study, nearly a third showed leukocytoclastic vasculitis and another third showed non-specific chronic inflammation.[38] In this study, nearly 50% of patients had entirely non-specific findings. Extravasated red blood cells are invariably present.[15,16] In severe cases, the epidermis may show ischemic necrosis. Bone fide granulomatous vasculitis of skin appears to be a very rare feature. In fact, one study failed to demonstrate granulomatous vasculitis in 75 skin biopsies from 46 patients.[38] In other patients, there may be granulomatous infiltration of the dermis, which may be related to foci of collagen necrosis and sometimes resembles the

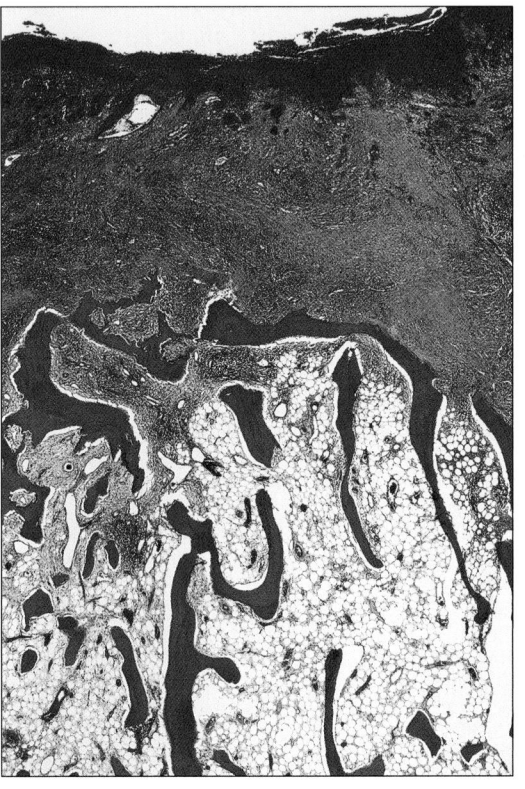

Fig. 15.52
Wegener's granulomatosis: this specimen from a gangrenous toe shows a deep ulcer extending down to the underlying bone.

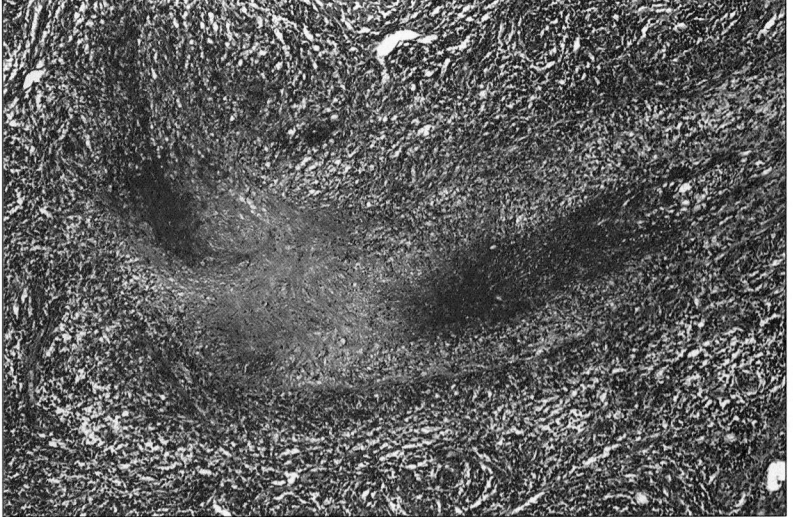

Fig. 15.53
Wegener's granulomatosis: there is necrotizing inflammation involving a muscular artery.

Churg–Strauss granuloma. In some cases, extensive geographic zones of necrosis are present, associated with a mixed inflammatory cell infiltrate including variable numbers of histiocytes, giant cells, lymphocytes, eosinophils and plasma cells. Erythema nodosum and granuloma annulare-like lesions may also be encountered.[38]

Differential diagnosis

As mentioned above, early in disease when patients may not have developed the full clinical triad, definitive diagnosis may be impossible.

In those instances where a granulomatous dermal infiltrate occurs in the absence of vasculitis, a host of conditions enters the differential diagnosis including sarcoidosis and infections, particularly mycobacterial and fungal. Granulomatous vasculitis may also be seen in association with lymphoproliferative diseases including lymphoma, angioimmunoblastic lymphadenopathy and leukemia.[39]

Microscopic polyangiitis can be confused with Wegener's granulomatosis. The presence of granulomatous inflammation in the lung would favor the latter. Microscopic polyangiitis is approached as a diagnosis of exclusion. In fact, a diagnosis may be revised as the pattern of clinical involvement changes. For example, patients that appear to fit criteria for microscopic polyangiitis may eventually develop manifestation allowing for classification as Wegener's granulomatosis.[40]

When granulomata and/or allergic vasculitis are the only features, it may not be possible to histologically distinguish Wegener's granulomatosis from the Churg–Strauss syndrome. A high eosinophil content, however, is somewhat suggestive of the latter condition but certainly not diagnostic, as this finding may sometimes be seen in Wegener's granulomatosis.[38] Therefore, distinction of Wegener's granulomatosis from other forms of granulomatous inflammation and leukocytoclastic and granulomatous vasculitis requires careful clinicopathological and serological correlation.

References

1. Gross, W.L., Schnabel, A., Reinhold-Keller, E. (2002) Wegener's granulomatosis: clinical aspects. In: Ball, G.V., Bridges, S.L. (eds) Vasculitis. New York: Oxford University Press.
2. Eunhee, S.Y., Colby, T.V. (2001) Wegener's granulomatosis. *Semin Diagn Pathol*, **18**, 34–46.
3. Stein, S.L., Miller, L.C., Konnikov, N. (1998) Wegener's granulomatosis: case report and literature review. *Pediatr Dermatol*, **15**, 352–356.
4. Chyu, J.Y.H., Hagstrom, W.J., Soltani, K. et al (1984) Wegener's granulomatosis in childhood: cutaneous manifestations as the presenting signs. *J Am Acad Dermatol*, **10**, 341–346.
5. Hoffman, G.S., Kerr, G.S., Leavitt, R.Y. et al (1992) Wegener granulomatosis: and analysis of 158 patients. *Ann Intern Med*, **15**, 488–498.
6. Fauci, A.S., Wolff, S.M. (1973) Wegener's granulomatosis: studies in eighteen patients and a review of the literature. *Medicine (Baltimore)*, **52**, 535–561.
7. Wolf, S.M., Fauci, A.S., Horn, R.G. et al (1974) Wegener's granulomatosis. *Ann Intern Med*, **81**, 513–525.
8. Kempf, H.G. (1989) Ear involvement in Wegener's granulomatosis. *Clin Otolaryngol*, **14**, 451–456.
9. Kempf, H.G. (1990) Clinical picture and immunology of Wegener's granulomatosis. *Rev Laryngol Otol Rhinol (Bord)*, **111**, 67–69.
10. Kempf, H.G., Bootz, F., Berg, P.A. (1992) Wegener's granulomatosis: otologic and clinico-immunologic aspects. *Laryngorhinootologie*, **71**, 26–30.
11. Nishino, H., Rubino, F.A., DeRemee, R.A. et al (1993) Neurological involvement in Wegener's granulomatosis: an analysis of 324 consecutive cases at the Mayo Clinic. *Ann Neurol*, **33**, 4–9.
12. Nishino, H., Rubino, F.A., Parisi, J.E. (1993) The spectrum of neurologic involvement in Wegener's granulomatosis. *Neurology*, **43**, 1334–1337.
13. Harman, L.E., Margo, C.E. (1998) Wegener's granulomatosis. *Surv Ophthalmol*, **42**, 458–480.
14. Nishino, H.M., DeRemee, R.A., Rubino, F.A. et al (1993) Wegener's granulomatosis associated with vasculitis of the temporal artery: report of 5 cases. *Mayo Clin Proc*, **68**, 115–121.
15. Hu, C.H., O'Loughlin, S., Winkelmann, R.K. (1977) Cutaneous manifestations of Wegener's granulomatosis. *Arch Dermatol*, **113**, 175–182.
16. Reed, W.B., Jenson, A.K., Konwaler, B.E. (1963) The cutaneous manifestations in Wegener's granulomatosis. *Acta Derm Venereol*, **43**, 250–264.
17. Doud, M.S., Gibson, L.E., DeRemee, R.A. et al (1994) Cutaneous Wegener's granulomatosis: clinical, histologic and immunopathologic features of thirty patients. *J Am Acad Dermatol*, **31**, 605–612.
18. Frances, C., Du, L.T., Piette, J.C. et al (1994) Wegener's granulomatosis. Dermatological manifestations in 75 cases with clinicopathological correlation. *Arch Dermatol*, **130**, 861–867.
19. Patten, S.F., Tomecki, K.J. (1993) Wegener's granulomatosis: cutaneous involvement and oral mucosal disease. *J Am Acad Dermatol*, **28**, 710–718.
20. Fienberg, R. (1981) The protracted superficial phenomenon in pathergic (Wegener's) granulomatosis. *Hum Pathol*, **12**, 458–467.
21. Carrington, C.B., Liebow, A.A. (1966) Limited forms of angiitis and granulomatosis of Wegener's type. *Am J Med*, **41**, 497–527.
22. Cassan, S.M., Coles, D.T., Harrison, E.G. Jr (1970) The concept of limited forms of Wegener's granulomatosis. *Am J Med*, **49**, 366–379.
23. Boudes, P. (1990) Purely granulomatous Wegener's granulomatosis: a new concept for an old disease. *Semin Arthritis Rheum*, **19**, 365–370.
24. Field, M. (1991) Antineutrophil cytoplasmic antibodies (ANCA): their role in diagnosis and pathogenesis of vasculitis. *Br J Rheumatol*, **30**, 229–231.
25. Jennette, J.C., Falk, R.J. (1992) Disease associations and pathogenic role of antineutrophil cytoplasmic antibodies in vasculitis. *Curr Opin Rheumatol*, **4**, 9–15.
26. Jennette, J.C., Falk, R.J. (1990) Antineutrophil cytoplasmic autoantibodies and associated diseases: a review. *Am J Kidney Dis*, **XV**, 517–529.
27. Gross, W.L., Csernok, E., Trabandt, A. (2002) Wegener's granulomatosis: pathogenesis. In: Ball, G.V., Bridges, S.L. (eds) Vasculitis. New York: Oxford University Press.
28. Jennette, J.C., Falk, R.J. (1994) Pathogenic role of anti-neutrophil cytoplasmic antibodies. *Lab Invest*, **70**, 135–137.
29. Reinhold-Keller, E., De Groot, K., Rudert, H. et al (1996) Response to trimethoprim/sulfamethoxazole in Wegener's granulomatosis depends on the phase of the disease. *QJM*, **89**, 15–23.
30. Stegemann, C.A., Tervaert, J.W., de Jong, P.E. et al (1996) Trimethoprim/sulfamethoxazole (co-trimoxazole) for the prevention of relapses of Wegener's granulomatosis. Dutch Co-Trimoxazole Wegener Study Group. *N Engl J Med*, **335**, 16–20.
31. Stegemann, C.A., Tervaert, J.W., Manson, W.L. et al (1994) Association of chronic nasal carriage of Staphylococcus aureus and higher relapse rates in Wegener granulomatosis. *Ann Intern Med*, **120**, 12–17.
32. George, J., Levy, Y., Kallenberg, C.G. et al (1997) Infections and Wegener's granulomatosis – a cause and effect relationship? *QJM*, **90**, 367–373.
33. Tervaert, J.W., Stegeman, C.A., Kallenberg, C.G. (1998) Silicon exposure and vasculitis. *Curr Opin Rheumatol*, **10**, 12–17.
34. Nuyts, G.D., van Vlem, E., De Vos, A. et al (1995) Wegener granulomatosis is associated to exposure to silicon compounds: a case control study. *Nephrol Dial Transplant*, **10**, 1162–1165.
35. Duna, G.F., Cotch, M.F., Galperin, C. et al (1998) Wegener's granulomatosis: role of environmental exposures. *Clin Exp Rheumatol*, **16**, 669–674.
36. Godman, G.C., Churg, J. (1954) Wegener's granulomatosis: pathology and review of the literature. *Arch Pathol*, **58**, 533–553.
37. Heptinstall, R.H. (1983) Wegener's syndrome. In: Heptinstall, R.H. (ed.) Pathology of the kidney, 3rd edn. Boston: Little, Brown, pp 813–816.
38. Barksdale, S.K., Hallahan, C.W., Kerr, G.S. et al (1995) Cutaneous pathology in Wegener's granulomatosis. A clinicopathologic study of 75 biopsies in 46 patients. *Am J Surg Pathol*, **19**, 161–172.
39. Gibson, L.E., Winkelmann, R.K. (1986) Cutaneous granulomatous vasculitis: its relationship to systemic disease. *J Am Acad Dermatol*, **14**, 492–501.
40. Jennette, J.C., Thomas, D.B., Falk, R.J. (2001) Microscopic polyangiitis (microscopic polyarteritis). *Semin Diagn Pathol*, **18**, 3–13.

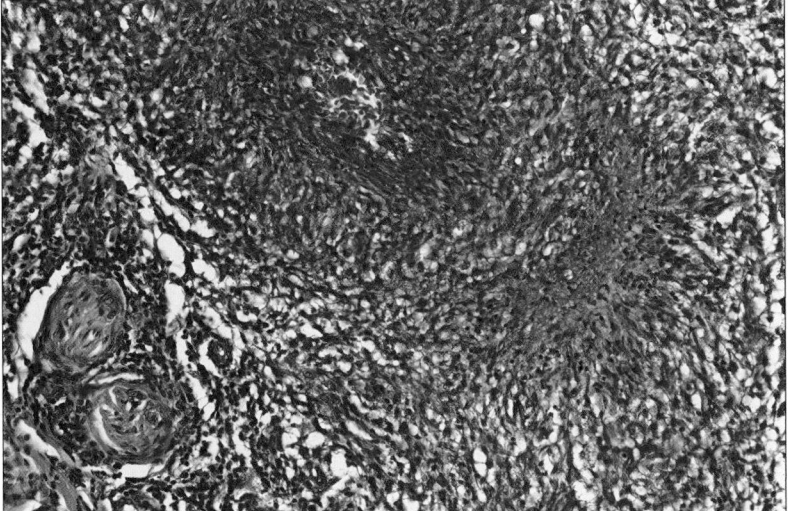

Fig. 15.54
Wegener's granulomatosis: an ill-defined granulomatous infiltrate surrounds this vessel.

Allergic granulomatosis with angiitis

Clinical features

Allergic granulomatosis with angiitis (Churg–Strauss syndrome) is a very rare disease that combines the features of asthma, fever, multisystem necrotizing vasculitis, extravascular granulomata and hypereosinophilia.[1,2] Although there is clinical overlap, it can be distinguished from polyarteritis nodosa and Wegener's granulomatosis (*Table 15.5*). The criteria published by the Chapel Hill Consensus conference differ somewhat.[3] In this scheme, Churg–Strauss syndrome is defined as 'eosinophil-rich and granulomatous inflammation involving the respiratory tract, and necrotizing vasculitis affecting small to medium-sized arteries, and associated with asthma and eosinophilia'.[3] Given differences in classification criteria, it comes as no surprise that inconsistencies between these classification schemes exist.[4,5] One study found good concordance between classification schemes for the diagnosis of Wegener's granulomatosis but not Churg–Strauss syndrome.[4] As we gain further understanding of this disease, refinement of diagnostic criteria is likely.

Churg–Strauss syndrome may present in a wide range of age groups, but most patients are adults, those in the third and fourth decades being most commonly affected. The disease has a slight male predominance.[6–9] Presentation in children is very rare.[10,11]

Asthma and necrotizing vasculitis are invariably present. Asthma often precedes the onset of vasculitis, sometimes by many years, or these features may develop simultaneously. In one large study, asthma preceded definitive diagnosis in 94% of patients.[1] Asthma may be associated with transient pulmonary infiltrates (Loeffler's syndrome) or there may be full-blown chronic eosinophilic pneumonitis.[6] There is some evidence to suggest that patients in whom vasculitis occurs rapidly after presentation of asthma have a particularly poor prognosis. It has been suggested that, in some patients, treatment for allergic rhinitis with steroids suppresses the full-blown syndrome.[12,13] Recently, an association between treatment of asthma with antileukotrienes and development of Churg–Strauss syndrome has been suggested.[2,14] The association is controversial and what role, if any, antileukotrienes play in development of disease in these patients is unclear. However, it has also been proposed that it is the withdrawal of the steroids and not the administration of antileukotrienes that leads to disease.[2] Further investigation is required to resolve this controversy.

Common manifestations of upper respiratory tract involvement include allergic rhinitis (which may be associated with polyp formation and sinusitis) and hay fever. A family history of atopy and allergic reactions to inhaled antigens and drugs is often present.

Chest radiography frequently confirms the presence of pulmonary involvement, which may take a variety of forms including transient patchy infiltrates, discrete non-cavitating nodular masses, or diffuse interstitial disease. On CT scan, pulmonary infiltrates may take the form of opacification, nodules, or bronchial wall and interlobular septal thickening.[15] Bronchoalveolar lavage reveals alveolar eosinophilia.[1] Some patients develop an eosinophil-rich pleural effusion.[1]

In addition to pulmonary lesions, systemic involvement most commonly affects the heart, nervous system, gut and kidneys.[6] Cardiac lesions may be a cause of dysrhythmia or sudden death. Cardiac manifestations also include ventricular insufficiency, global cardiac insufficiency and endomyocarditis.[1,16] Pericardial effusion was seen in 23% of patients in one study.[1] Complications relating to cardiac involvement are the most common cause of death in patients with Churg–Strauss syndrome. Nearly 40% of deaths are due to cardiac involvement.[1]

Neurological manifestations are common, particularly mononeuritis multiplex and symmetric polyneuropathy.[17,18] In one large study, 72% of patients developed mononeuritis multiplex.[1] Intracerebral hemorrhage or infarction may also develop.[17] Ischemic optic and bilateral trigeminal neuropathy are rare complications.[18] Myalgia is an occasional feature.

Evidence of gastrointestinal involvement, such as nausea, bleeding, vomiting and abdominal pain, is often found. In one study, one-third of patients experienced gastrointestinal symptoms, usually abdominal pain.[1] Diffuse bowel ischemia is an uncommon but serious complication.[1]

Renal disease in Churg–Strauss syndrome is usually manifest as glomerulonephritis, most often a focal segmental glomerulonephritis.[1] Patients with renal involvement may show hematuria, proteinuria, and increased creatinine.[1] Renal infarction appears to be a rare complication.[1]

Rheumatological involvement in the form of polyarthralgia and constitutional symptoms, including fever, anemia and weight loss, is common.[1]

Amyloidosis is a rare complication.[19,20] Exceptionally, Churg–Strauss syndrome may present with temporal non-giant cell arteritis.[21] Involvement of the breast occurs exceptionally as eosinophilic mastitis.[22] A limited form of the disease has been described.[23,24]

Cutaneous lesions are seen in 40–70% of patients and include petechiae, purpura, papules, vesicles, facial erythema, urticaria and ulceration.[25–30] Cutaneous infarction and bullae are less common manifestations.[28] Livedo reticularis involving the lower limbs is occasionally a feature. Patients may also develop tender nodules, which particularly affect the extensor aspects of the arms, legs, hands and feet (*Fig. 15.55*). The sacrum, buttocks and scalp may also be involved. The cutaneous lesions tend to appear in crops with spontaneous relapses and remissions.

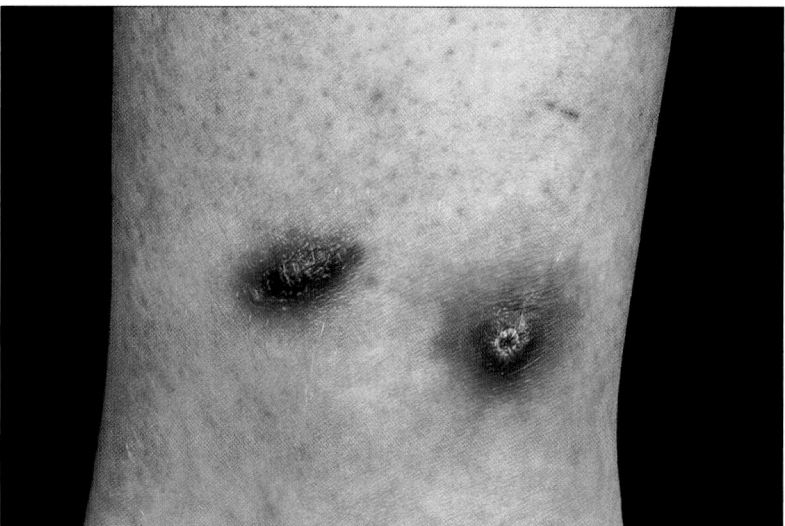

Fig. 15.55
Churg–Strauss syndrome: this patient presented with painful nodules on the limbs. By courtesy of the Institute of Dermatology, London, UK.

Table 15.5
1990 criteria for the classification of Churg–Strauss syndrome (traditional format)*

Criterion	No. of CSS patients (*n* = 20)	Sensitivity (%)	No. of control patients (*n* = 787)	Specificity (%)
Asthma	19	100	782	96.3
Eosinophilia > 10%	20	95	708	96.6
Neuropathy (mono or poly)	20	75	781	79.8
Pulmonary infiltrates, non-fixed	20	40	736	92.4
Parasanal sinus abnormality	14	85.7	366	79.3
Extravascular eosinophils	16	81.3	385	84.4

*For classification purposes, a patient shall be said to have Churg–Strauss syndrome (CSS) if at least four of these six criteria are positive. The presence of any four or more of the six criteria yields a sensitivity of 85% and a specificity of 99.7%.
Reproduced with permission from Masi, A.T. (1990) *Arthritis and Rheumatism*, **33**, 1094–1100.

Churg–Strauss syndrome has been seen in association with HIV infection, hepatitis B, Wells' syndrome and bronchopulmonary candidiasis.[31–34] The disease has also been described in association with drugs including fluticasone and cocaine.[35,36]

Laboratory investigation usually reveals leukocytosis and a raised ESR in association with peripheral blood eosinophilia.[28] Blood eosinophilia often decreases with treatment but some authors stress that such a response should not be taken as evidence that disease activity is under control.[37] ANCAs are demonstrated in many patients (see below).

Pathogenesis and histological features

The etiology and pathogenesis of Churg–Strauss syndrome is poorly understood. The presence of perinuclear-antineutrophil cytoplasmic antibodies (p-ANCA) in many patients is of considerable interest.[38–41] In one study, 67% of patients had ANCAs.[42] The ANCAs seen in patients with Churg–Strauss syndrome usually target myeloperoxidase. However, the various types of ANCA are non-specific, being present in a spectrum of disease.[43] In one small series, it was suggested that patients with ANCAs have a higher risk of developing renal disease.[44] ANCAs may activate neutrophils, causing degranulation and vascular injury.[45] T-lymphocytes may also be stimulated, leading to endothelial cell injury.[45] As with other ANCA-associated vasculitides, it is suspected that ANCAs play a role in the pathogenesis of Churg–Strauss syndrome; however, the precise mechanism, particularly triggering factors, is not yet known. Persistence of ANCAs with therapy may be of limited value in making treatment decisions.[46] One group has found that, although there is poor correlation between ANCA titer and disease activity, disappearance of ANCA may reflect absent disease activity.[47]

Pulmonary lesions comprise variably sized (up to 1.5 cm) nodules, ranging from only a few lesions to hundreds which may coalesce. Histologically, they are composed of granulomata with central necrosis and surrounding epithelioid histiocytes with occasional giant cells. Large numbers of eosinophils with an admixture of lymphocytes, neutrophils, plasma cells and histiocytes infiltrate the adjacent lung parenchyma. Vasculitis involving small arteries and sometimes veins is also present.

Cutaneous lesions are variable. A common feature is the so-called 'Churg–Strauss (extravascular) granuloma'. Early lesions are characterized by focal collagen degeneration in association with a variable and mixed inflammatory cell infiltrate comprising neutrophils, lymphocytes and histiocytes (*Figs 15.56–15.58*). Eosinophils may be sparse or numerous. Leukocytoclasis is often a feature. In more advanced examples the granuloma is more mature in appearance, consisting of a central zone of collagen necrosis surrounded by a peripheral palisade of epithelioid and giant cells (*Fig. 15.59*). In some examples, the features are those of a rather diffuse and ill-defined granulomatous inflammatory process without obvious collagen degeneration. Commonly, features of necrotizing vasculitis are evident: fibrinoid necrosis accompanied by an eosinophilic and neutrophilic infiltrate with leukocytoclasis involving

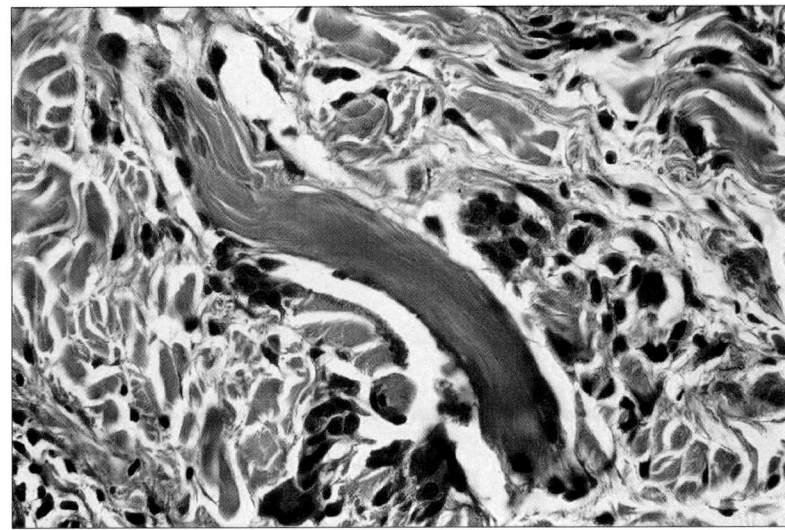

Fig. 15.57
Churg–Strauss syndrome: high power view showing small numbers of surrounding histiocytes.

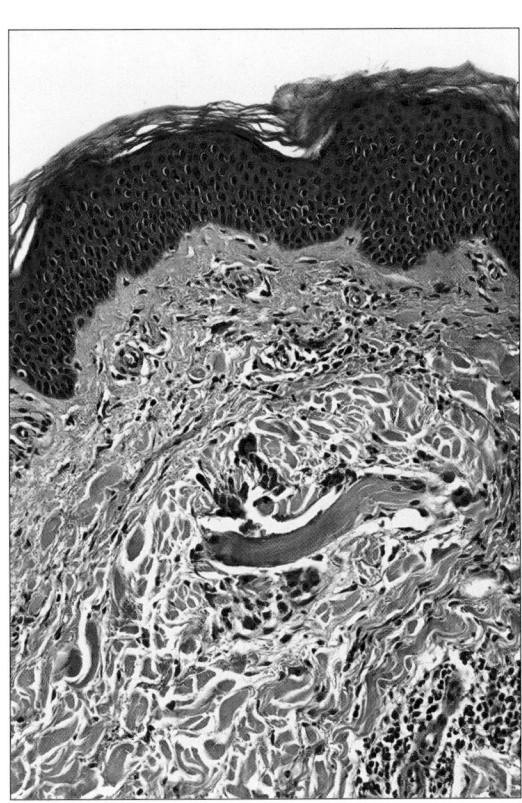

Fig. 15.56
Churg–Strauss syndrome: this early lesion shows a swollen collagen fiber in the superficial dermis.

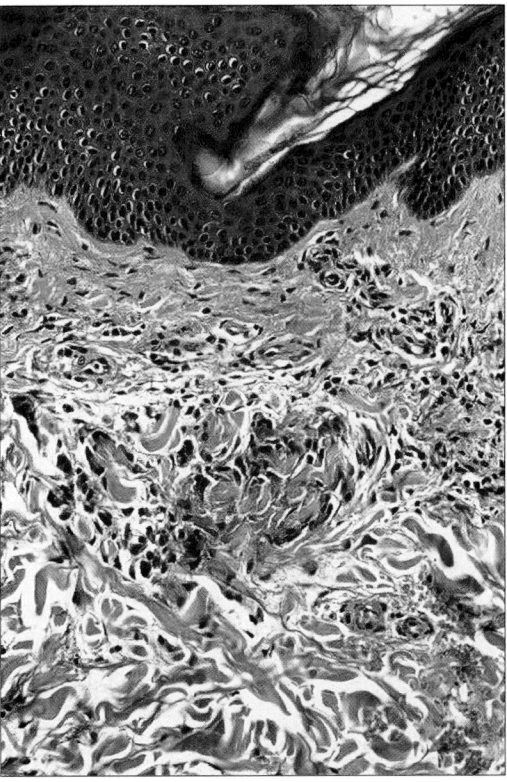

Fig. 15.58
Churg–Strauss syndrome: in this example there is a more obvious granulomatous infiltrate.

the more superficial small blood vessels (*Fig. 15.60*). There may be epidermal ischemic necrosis. In one study, 16 of 37 biopsies (taken from 29 patients) showed leukocytoclastic vasculitis.[27] Occasionally, the arteries of the dermis and subcutaneous fat show changes similar to polyarteritis nodosa.[28] Additionally, acute and chronic panniculitis with eosinophils has been described.[28]

Differential diagnosis

The histological features encountered in skin biopsies of patients with Churg–Strauss syndrome are not diagnostic. Careful clinicopathological and serological evaluation is necessary to establish a definitive diagnosis. Although Churg–Strauss syndrome, polyarteritis nodosa and Wegener's granulomatosis show both clinical and histological overlap, research

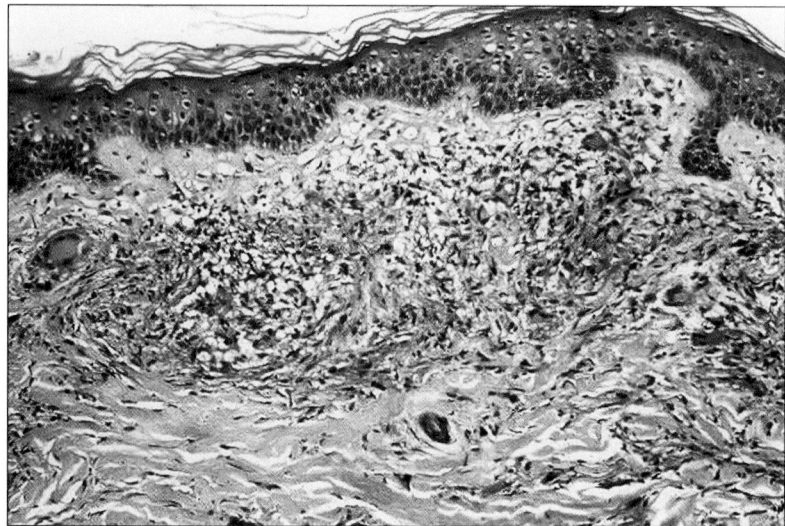

Fig. 15.59
Churg–Strauss syndrome: this florid example shows a granulomatous infiltrate containing prominent giant cells. By courtesy of E. Wilson Jones, MD, Institute of Dermatology, London, UK.

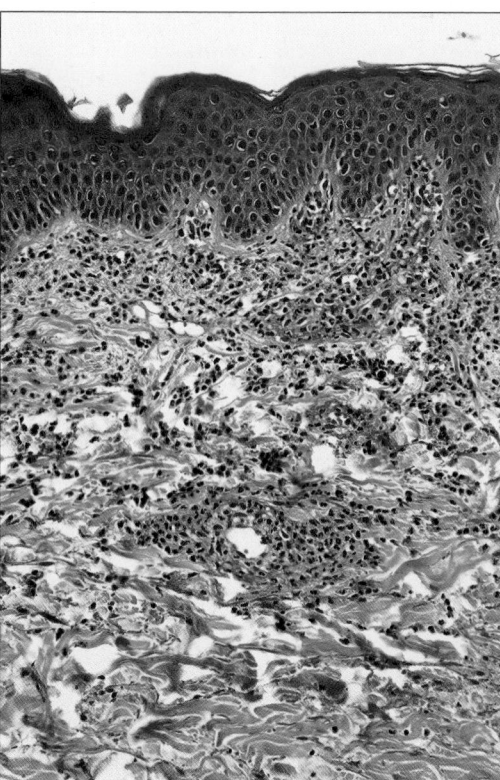

Fig. 15.60
Churg–Strauss syndrome: the features of small vessel leukocytoclastic vasculitis are evident.

over the last several decades leaves no doubt that they represent distinctive entities. Nonetheless, they form a spectrum of disease with similar pathogenesis although there are sufficient differences to justify their separate classification.

- Asthma may be seen in both polyarteritis nodosa and Churg–Strauss syndrome, but characteristically polyarteritis affects medium-sized and small arteries, while Churg–Strauss syndrome typically affects small arteries and veins.
- The neutrophil dominates the inflammatory cell infiltrate in polyarteritis nodosa, whereas in Churg–Strauss syndrome it is the eosinophil.
- Necrotizing extravascular granulomata are not a feature of polyarteritis nodosa.
- Patients with Wegener's granulomatosis present with ulceroproliferative lesions of the upper respiratory tract, chest pain and hemoptysis rather than asthma.
- Marked eosinophilia is uncommon in Wegener's granulomatosis.

Churg–Strauss granulomata may be seen in Wegener's granulomatosis; however, the necrosis is more often of the tuberculocoagulative type. Granulomatous vasculitis is not a feature of Churg–Strauss syndrome.

It must be stressed that Churg–Straus granulomata should not be taken as pathognomonic for Churg–Strauss syndrome (see p. 320). Churg–Strauss granulomata, or nearly identical lesions, have been described in the setting of other systemic disease including rheumatoid arthritis, lupus erythematosus, other forms of vasculitis (Wegener's granulomatosis, polyarteritis nodosa, Takayasu's arteritis), lymphoproliferative disorders, Crohn's disease and ulcerative colitis, bacterial endocarditis, and hepatitis.[28,48–52]

References

1. Guillevin, L., Cohen, P., Gayraud, M. et al (1999) Churg–Strauss syndrome: clinical study and long-term follow-up of 96 patients. *Medicine (Baltimore)*, **78**, 26–37.
2. Noth, I., Strek, M.E., Leff, A.R. (2003) Churg–Strauss syndrome. *Lancet*, **361**, 587–594.
3. Jennette, J.C., Falk, R.J., Andrassy, K. et al (1994) Nomenclature of systemic vasculitis. Proposal of an international consensus conference. *Arthritis Rheum*, **37**, 187–192.
4. Bruce, I.N., Bell, A.L. (1997) A comparison of two nomenclature systems for primary systemic vasculitis. *Br J Rheumatol*, **36**, 453–458.
5. Watts, R.A., Scott, D.G. (1997) Classification and epidemiology of the vasculitides. *Baillieres Clin Rheumatol*, **11**, 191–217.
6. Schwartz, R.A., Churg, J. (1992) Churg–Strauss syndrome. *Br J Dermatol*, **127**, 199–204.
7. Churg, J., Strauss, L. (1951) Allergic granulomatosis, allergic angiitis and periarteritis nodosa. *Am J Pathol*, **27**, 277–301.
8. Chumbley, L.C., Harrison, E.G. Jr, Deremee, R.A. (1977) Allergic granulomatosis and angiitis (Churg–Strauss syndrome): report and analysis of 30 cases. *Mayo Clin Proc*, **52**, 477–484.
9. Lanham, J.G., Elkon, K.B., Pusey, C.D. et al (1984). Systemic vasculitis with asthma and eosinophilia: a clinical approach to the Churg–Strauss syndrome. *Medicine*, **63**, 65–81.
10. Wang, S.J., Yang, Y.H., Lin, Y.T. et al (2000) Childhood Churg–Strauss syndrome: report of a case. *J Microbiol Immunol Infect*, **33**, 263–266.
11. Mpofu, C., Bakalinova, D., Kazi, M.A. et al (1995) Churg–Strauss syndrome in childhood. *Ann Trop Paediatr*, **15**, 341–344.
12. Churg, A., Brallas, M., Cronin, S.R. et al (1995) Formes frustes of Churg–Strauss syndrome. *Chest*, **108**, 320–323.
13. Churg, A. (2001) Recent advances in the diagnosis of Churg–Strauss syndrome. *Mod Pathol*, **14**, 1284–1293.
14. Tang., M.B., Yosipovitch, G. (2003) Acute Churg–Strauss syndrome in an asthmatic patient receiving montelukast therapy. *Arch Dermatol*, **139**, 715–718.
15. Worthy, S.A., Muller, N.L., Hansell, D.M. et al (1998) Churg–Strauss syndrome: the spectrum of pulmonary CT findings in 17 patients. *Am J Roentgenol*, **170**, 297–300.
16. Ramakrishna, G., Connolly, H.M., Tazelaar, H.D. et al (2000) Churg–Strauss syndrome complicated by eosinophilic endomyocarditis. *Mayo Clin Proc*, **75**, 631–635.
17. Sehgal, M., Swanson, J.W., DeRemee, R.A. et al (1995) Neurologic manifestations of Churg–Strauss syndrome. *Mayo Clin Proc*, **70**, 337–341.
18. Hattori, N., Ichimura, M., Nagamatsu, M. et al (1999) Clinicopathological features of Churg–Strauss syndrome-associated neuropathy. *Brain*, **122**, 427–439.
19. Sale, S., Patterson, R. (1981) Recurrent Churg–Strauss vasculitis. With exophthalmos, hearing loss, nasal obstruction, amyloid deposits, hyperimmunoglobulinemia E, and circulating immune complexes. *Arch Intern Med*, **141**, 1363–1365.
20. Meisler, D.M., Stock, E.L., Wertz, R.D. et al (1981) Conjunctival inflammation and amyloidosis in allergic granulomatosis and angiitis (Churg–Strauss syndrome). *Am J Ophthalmol*, **91**, 216–219.
21. Endo, T., Kasuta, Y., Kimura, Y. et al (2000) A variant form of Churg–Strauss syndrome: initial non-giant cell arteritis followed by asthma – is this a distinct clinicopathologic entity? *Hum Pathol*, **31**, 1169–1171.
22. Villalba-Nuno, V., Sabate, J.M., Gómez, A. et al (2002) Churg–Strauss syndrome involving the breast: a rare case of eosinophilic mastitis. *Eur Radiol*, **12**, 646–649.
23. Nissim, F., Von der Valde, J., Czernobilsky, B. (1982) A limited form of Churg–Strauss syndrome: ocular and cutaneous manifestations. *Arch Pathol Lab Med*, **106**, 305–307.
24. Khan, N.A., Shenoy, P.K., McClymont, L. et al (1996) Exophthalmos and facial swelling: a case of limited Churg–Strauss syndrome. *J Laryngol Otol*, **110**, 578–582.
25. Strauss, L., Churg, J., Zak, F. (1951) Cutaneous lesions of allergic granulomatosis: a histopathologic study. *J Invest Dermatol*, **17**, 349–359.
26. Dicken, C.H., Winkelmann, R.K. (1978) The Churg–Strauss granuloma: cutaneous, necrotizing, palisading granuloma in vasculitis syndromes. *Arch Pathol Lab Med*, **102**, 576–580.
27. Crotty, C.P., Deremee, R.A., Wilkelmann, R.K. (1981) Cutaneous clinicopathologic correlation of allergic granulomatosis. *J Am Acad Dermatol*, **5**, 571–581.

28. Davis, M.D., Daoud, M.S., McEvoy, M.T. et al (1997) Cutaneous manifestations of Churg–Strauss syndrome: a clinicopathologic correlation. *J Am Acad Dermatol*, **37**, 199–233.
29. Tiacuilo-Parra, A., Soto-Ortiz, J.A., Guevara-Gutiérrez, E. (2003) Churg–Strauss syndrome manifested by urticarial plaques. *Int J Dermatol*, **42**, 386–388.
30. Abe-Matsuura, Y., Fujimoto, W., Arata, J. (1995) Allergic granulomatosis (Churg–Strauss) associated with cutaneous manifestations: report of two cases. *J Dermatol*, **22**, 46–51.
31. Cooper, L.M., Patterson, J.A.K. (1989) Allergic granulomatosis and angiitis of Churg–Strauss. Case report in a patient with antibodies to human immunodeficiency virus and hepatitis B virus. *Int J Dermatol*, **28**, 597–599.
32. Lee, S-C., Shin, S-S., Lee, J-B. et al (2000) Wells syndrome associated with Churg–Strauss syndrome. *J Am Acad Dermatol*, **43**, 556–557.
33. Schuttelaar, M.L., Jonkman, M.F. (2003) Bullous eosinophilic cellulitis (Well's syndrome) associated with Churg–Strauss syndrome. *J Eur Acad Dermatol Venereol*, **17**, 91–93.
34. Matsumoto, H., Niimi, A., Suzuki, K. et al (2000) Allergic granulomatous angiitis (Churg–Strauss syndrome associated with allergic bronchopulmonary candidiasis. *Respiration*, **67**, 577–579.
35. English, J. 3rd, Greer, K.E., McCrone, S.A. et al (2003) Fluticasone-associated cutaneous allergic granulomatous vasculitis. *J Drugs Dermatol*, **2**, 326–329.
36. Orriols, R., Muñoz, X., Ferrer, J. et al (1996) Cocaine-induced Churg–Strauss vasculitis. *Eur Respir J*, **9**, 175–177.
37. Stone, J.H., Calabrese, L., Hoffman, G.S. et al (2001) Vasculitis. A collection of pearls and myths. *Rheum Dis Clin North Am*, **27**, 677–728.
38. Manger, B.J., Krapf, F.E., Gramatzki, M. et al (1985) IgE-containing circulating immune complexes in Churg–Strauss vasculitis. *Scand J Immunol*, **21**, 369–373.
39. Cohen Tervaert, J.W., Limburg, P.C., Elema, J.D. et al (1991) Detection of auto-antibodies against myeloid lysosomal enzymes: a useful adjunct to classification of patients with biopsy-proven necrotizing arteritis. *Am J Med*, **91**, 59–66.
40. Hagen, E.C., Daha, M.R., Hermans, J. et al (1998) Diagnostic value of standardized assays for anti-neutrophil cytoplasmic antibodies in idiopathic systemic vasculitis. *Kidney Int*, **53**, 743–753.
41. Diri, E., Buscemi, D.M., Nugent, K.M. (2003) Churg–Strauss syndrome: diagnostic difficulties and pathogenesis. *Am J Med Sci*, **325**, 101–105.
42. Guillevin, L., Visser, H., Noel, L.H. et al (1993) Antineutrophil cytoplasm antibodies in systemic polyarteritis nodosa with and without hepatitis B virus infection and Churg–Strauss syndrome – 62 patients. *J Rheumatol*, **20**, 1345–1349.
43. Lesavre, P. (1996) The diagnostic and prognostic significance of ANCA. *Ren Fail*, **18**, 803–812.
44. Yoshihara, K., Arimura, Y., Kobayashi, O. et al (1998) Clinical study on five myeloperoxidase specific anti-neutrophil cytoplasmic antibody (MPO-ANCA) positive Churg–Strauss syndrome cases. *Ryumachi*, **38**, 696–704.
45. Tomer, Y., Lider, O., Gilburd, B. et al (1997) Anti-neutrophil cytoplasmic antibody-enriched IgG induces adhesion to human T lymphocytes to extracellular matrix proteins. *Clin Immunol Immunopathol*, **83**, 245–253.
46. Cohen, P., Guillevin, L., Baril, L. et al (1995) Persistence of antineutrophil cytoplasmic antibodies (ANCA) in asymptomatic patients with systemic polyarteritis nodosa or Churg–Strauss syndrome: follow-up of 53 patients. *Clin Exp Rheumatol*, **13**, 193–198.
47. Geffriaud-Ricouard, C., Noel, L.H., Chauveau, D. et al (1993) Clinical spectrum associated with ANCA of defined antigen specificities in 98 selected patients. *Clin Nephrol*, **39**, 125–136.
48. Perniciaro, C.V., Winkelmann, R.K., Hunder, G.G. (1987) Cutaneous manifestations of Takayasu's arteritis. *J Am Acad Dermatol*, **17**, 998–1005.
49. Finan, M.C., Winkelmann, R.K. (1983) The cutaneous extravascular necrotizing granuloma (Churg–Strauss granuloma) and systemic disease: a review of 27 cases. *Medicine*, **62**, 142–158.
50. Chu, P., Connolly, K., LeBoit, P.E. (1994) The histopathologic spectrum of palisaded neutrophilic and granulomatous dermatitis. *Arch Dermatol*, **130**, 1278–1283.
51. Wilmoth, G.J., Perniciaro, C. (1996) Cutaneous extravascular necrotizing granuloma (Winkelman granuloma): confirmation of the association with systemic disease. *J Am Acad Dermatol*, **34**, 753–759.
52. Calonje, J.E., Greaves, M.W. (1993) Cutaneous extravascular necrotizing granuloma (Churg–Strauss) as a paraneoplastic manifestation of non-Hodgkin lymphoma. *J R Soc Med*, **86**, 549–550.

Mucocutaneous lymph node syndrome

Mucocutaneous lymph node syndrome (Kawasaki syndrome) is a multisystem disease that predominantly affects infants and young children.[1–5] Although it was first described, and shows a marked preponderance, in Japan, it has been diagnosed worldwide and in all races. Kawasaki syndrome is characterized by both endemic and epidemic variants.[4] The incidence among Japanese children is 16–150/100,000/ year whereas in white children the incidence is 6–10/100,000/year.[4] The incidence of reported disease in the United States is rising but has been attributed to increased physician awareness.[6] The syndrome shows a male predominance and occurs most frequently in children aged 6–18 months.[7] Adults are only rarely affected.[8–10] Kawasaki syndrome is thought to have an infectious etiology on the basis of symptoms of fever and exanthem, age distribution, seasonality (peaks in winter and spring) and occurrence of community-wide epidemics.[11]

Clinical features

The diagnostic features of Kawasaki syndrome are summarized in *Table 15.6* and include:

- a spiking fever unresponsive to antibiotic therapy
- an erythematous polymorphic cutaneous eruption (*Fig. 15.61*)
- erythema, edema and induration of the extremities followed by cutaneous desquamation of the tips of the fingers and toes (*Fig. 15.62*)
- oropharyngeal mucosal changes including edema, erythema and fissuring of the lips, erythema of the cheeks and a strawberry (scarletiform) tongue (*Figs 15.63, 15.64*)
- bilateral, non-exudative conjunctivitis
- non-suppurative cervical lymphadenopathy.

In an appropriate clinical context, children are now judged to have Kawasaki syndrome if they show a high fever plus four of the signs described above.[4,12] More recently, this has been amended to include coronary artery aneurysm plus three of the above features.[4]

The cutaneous findings are variable and include erythematous, macular, maculopapular (morbilliform), urticarial, erythema multiforme-like (targetoid) and erythema marginatum-like lesions.[2] A vesiculopustular eruption has also been reported.[13] The skin lesions show a propensity for the trunk and extremities, but may be more generalized.

Table 15.6
Kawasaki syndrome: diagnostic guidelines

• Fever lasting ≥ 5 days plus
• Polymorphous rash
• Bilaterial conjunctival injection
• At least one of the following changes of the mucosal membranes: – erythema or fissuring of the lips – strawberry tongue – diffuse injection of oral and pharyngeal mucosa
• Acute non-purulent cervical lymphadenopathy (at least one node ≥ 1.5 cm)
• At least one of the following changes of the peripheral extremities: – erythema of palms and soles – indurative edema of hands and feet – membranous desquamation from fingertips
Fever plus four of the above criteria must be present for a secure diagnosis; other illness that can present with similar clinical findings must be excluded Reproduced with permission from Wortman, D.W. (1992) *Seminars in Dermatology*, **11**, 37–47.

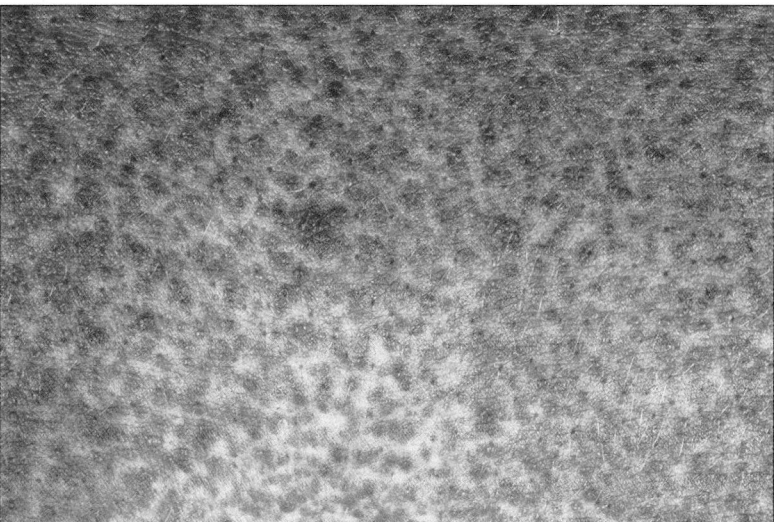

Fig. 15.61
Kawasaki syndrome: erythematous macular eruption. By courtesy of W.G. Phillips, MD, Institute of Dermatology, London, UK.

A diffuse, erythematous macular or plaque-like eruption involving the perineum is said to be characteristic.[5] This may be pruritic or painful and typically desquamates.

Cervical lymphadenopathy affects 50–75% of patients and may be unilateral or bilateral and involves one or a group of nodes.

Cardiovascular involvement is characteristic and is the most important cause of morbidity and mortality.[2] Some 50% of patients show evidence of myocarditis, which may progress to congestive cardiac failure. Pericardial effusion (subclinical) is not uncommon. Of particular significance is the development of coronary artery ectasia or aneurysm, a feature that develops in 15–25% of patients, which may be complicated by coronary artery ischemia, thrombosis and infarction. In 2% of patients, it proves fatal.[10] In a very large follow-up study of 594 patients, the incidence of coronary artery aneurysm was 25%.[14] Angiographic evidence of regression was seen in 55% of patients.[14] There is an inverse relationship between the size of the aneurysm and the likelihood of resolution: large aneurysms, especially giant aneurysms (defined as greater than 8.0 mm), tend to persist, or become obstructed or stenotic.[15]

Gastrointestinal involvement presents as abdominal pain, vomiting and diarrhea. Liver lesions may result in abnormal liver function tests and, less often, jaundice. Pancreatitis and hydrops of the gallbladder are seen in approximately 10% of patients.[2]

Neurological symptoms develop in about 30% of patients and include features of aseptic meningitis, seizures and transient paralyses.[2] Arthralgias and arthritis may be present in up to 30–40%, although chronicity is not a feature. Renal involvement may manifest as sterile pyuria, hematuria and infarction.

The features of adult Kawasaki syndrome are essentially those described above and are illustrated in *Figure 15.65*. Coronary artery aneurysm, however, appears to be a less common complication.[8] It is

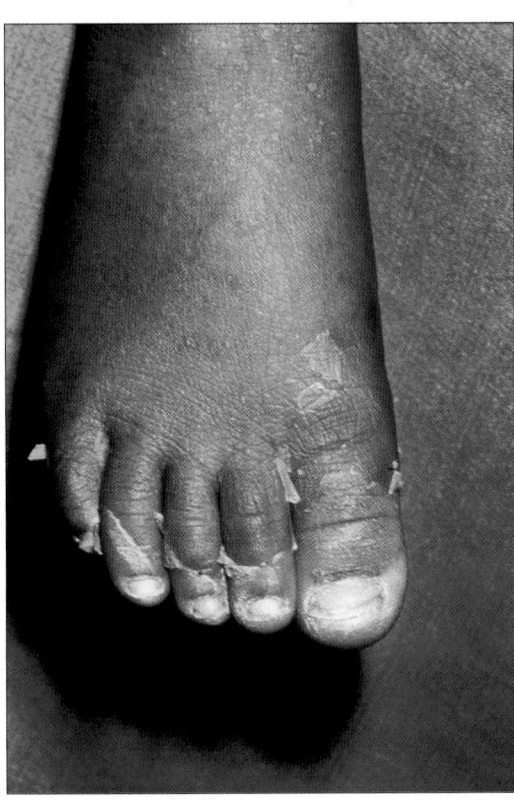

Fig. 15.62
Kawasaki syndrome: desquamation of the skin of the toes is a characteristic finding. By courtesy of J. Ross, MD, Lewisham Hospital, London, UK.

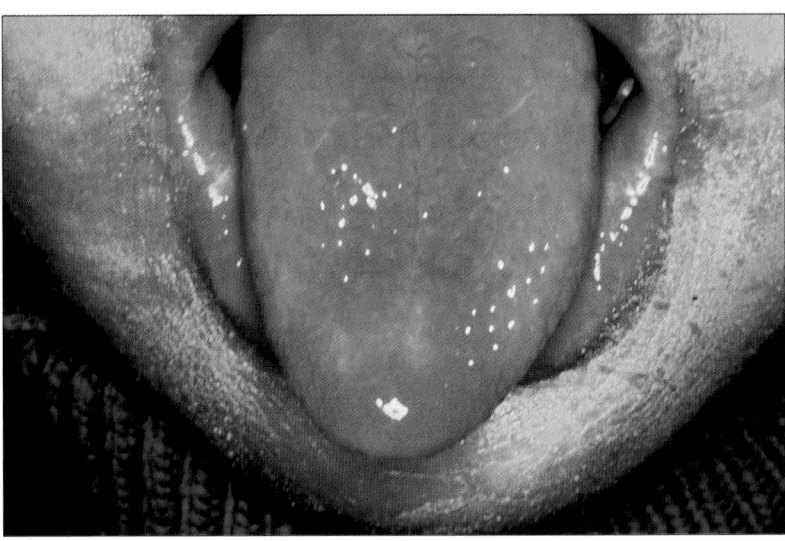

Fig. 15.64
Kawasaki syndrome: the tongue shows intense erythema. By courtesy of J. Ross, MD, Lewisham Hospital, London, UK.

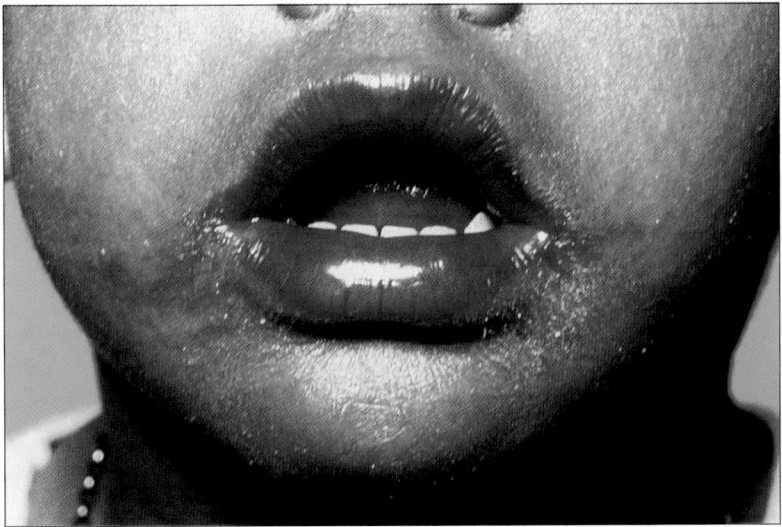

Fig. 15.63
Kawasaki syndrome: the lips are erythematous and swollen. Angular cheilitis is evident. By courtesy of J. Ross, MD, Lewisham Hospital, London, UK.

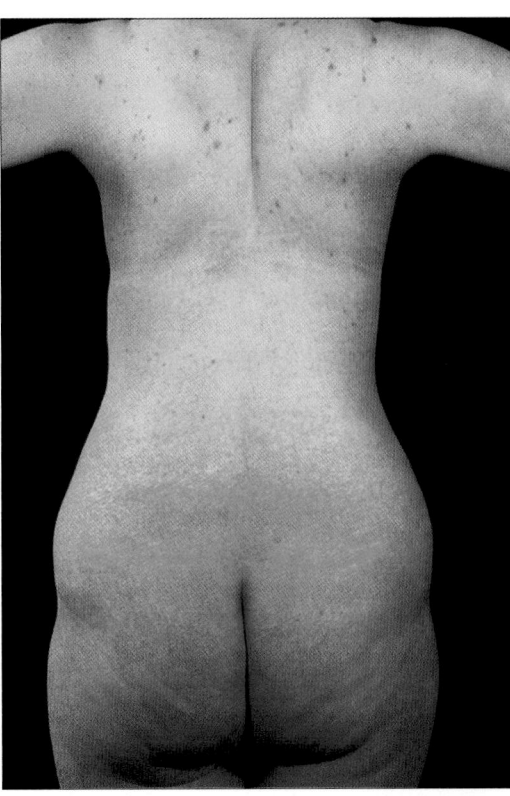

Fig. 15.65
Kawasaki syndrome: disease in an adult is very rare. In this patient the erythema particularly affects the buttocks and thighs. By courtesy of W.G. Phillips, MD, Institute of Dermatology, London, UK.

important to differentiate this entity from staphylococcal toxic shock syndrome.[16]

Occasionally, patients develop a relapse, which may occur years after initial disease and resolution.[17]

Pathogenesis and histological features

The etiology of this disease is unknown. Recent evidence points to an immunoregulatory defect of T-cells stimulated by superantigen-producing strains of *Streptococcus pyogenes* and *Staphylococcus aureus*.[16,18,19] Superantigens are a class of microbial antigens that are thought to be capable of stimulating a large number of naive T-cells in a non-specific manner by binding to histocompatibility antigens on antigen-presenting cells leading to T-cell activation. Superantigens have been postulated to play a role in the pathogenesis of a number of skin diseases in addition to Kawasaki syndrome, such as atopic dermatitis, psoriasis and toxic shock syndrome. However, in one study, superantigen-producing bacteria were found in 56% of cultures (taken from throat, rectum and groin) from patients with Kawasaki syndrome compared with 35% of controls with positive culture.[20] These differences did not achieve statistical significance. Another study found strains of streptococci and staphylococci in the jejunum of patients with Kawasaki syndrome but not in controls.[21] These same authors, in a follow-up study, found V beta 2+ T-cells selectively increased in small bowel mucosa of Kawasaki patients compared with control subjects.[22] Clearly, further research is necessary to elucidate the precise pathogenesis of Kawasaki disease.

Other infectious agents that have been implicated in the pathogenesis of Kawasaki disease include retroviruses, rickettsiae, spirochetes and *Propionibacterium acnes*.[5,23] Additionally favored hypotheses include exposure to house mites and recently cleaned or shampooed carpet, living in close proximity to open water or complicating a recent respiratory illness.[11] It is possible that Kawasaki syndrome represents a vasculitic disorder developing as a consequence of multiple infectious agents.

Of interest, there is a growing body of literature reporting Kawasaki disease, or a Kawasaki-like syndrome, in patients infected with the human immunodeficiency virus.[24–26]

The histopathological features of cutaneous lesions in Kawasaki disease are often non-specific and comprise severe edema of the papillary dermis accompanied by vascular dilatation, endothelial cell swelling and degeneration associated with a superficial perivascular mononuclear infiltrate.[5] Immunopathological studies have shown the infiltrate is usually composed of CD4+ T-lymphocytes and macrophages.[27] Occasionally, however, the features of a leukocytoclastic vasculitis are evident (*Fig. 15.66*). The epidermis may show mild basal cell degeneration.[5] Vesiculopustular lesions develop on the basis of subcorneal spongiform pustulation.[7]

Systemic lesions are characterized by necrotizing vasculitis.[16,28,29] Aneurysm with mural thrombus formation may be evident in advanced lesions.

Lymph node manifestations include vasculitis, focal necrosis and infarction.

Differential diagnosis

The mucocutaneous manifestations of Kawasaki disease show considerable overlap with those seen in the toxic shock syndrome, which is not surprising, given that they appear to share a similar pathogenesis. Palmoplantar erythema, cutaneous desquamation, conjunctivitis and pharyngitis are therefore common to both.[30] The toxic shock syndrome (which is due to a staphylococcal exotoxin complicating constant tampon use in menstruating females) is, however, not associated with systemic vascular involvement. Histologically, it is characterized by a mild, superficial, perivascular lymphocytic infiltrate associated with edema of the papillary dermis and no evidence of vasculitis.[31]

References

1. Kawasaki, T., Kosaki, F., Okawa, S. et al (1974) A new infantile acute febrile mucocutaneous lymph node syndrome (MLNS) prevailing in Japan. *Pediatrics*, 54, 271–276.
2. Leung, D.Y.M. (1990) New developments in Kawasaki disease. *Curr Opin Rheumatol*, 3, 46–55.
3. Melish, M.E., Hicks, R.V. (1990) Kawasaki syndrome: clinical features, pathophysiology, etiology, and therapy. *J Rheumatol*, 17 (Suppl.), 2–10.
4. Wortman, D.W. (1992) Kawasaki syndrome. *Semin Dermatol*, 11, 37–47.
5. Esterly, N.B., Wortmann, D.W. (1990) Kawasaki syndrome. *Australas J Dermatol*, 31, 61–71.
6. Taubert, K.A., Rowley, A.H., Shulman, S.T. (1994) Seven-year national survey of Kawasaki disease and acute rheumatic fever. *Pediatr Infect Dis J*, 13, 704–708.
7. Raimer, S.S., Sánchez, R.L. (1992) Vasculitis in children. *Semin Dermatol*, 11, 48–59.
8. Phillips, W.G., Marsden, J.R. (1993) Adult Kawasaki syndrome. *Br J Dermatol*, 129, 330–333.
9. Thompson, A.C., Lamey, P.J. (1990) Kawasaki syndrome in an adult. *J Laryngol Otol*, 104, 37–38.
10. Tomiyama, J., Hasegawa, Y., Kumagai, Y. et al (1991) Acute febrile mucocutaneous lymph node syndrome (Kawasaki disease) in adults: case report and review of the literature. *Jpn J Med*, 30, 285–289.
11. Ranch, A.M. (1987) Kawasaki syndrome. Review of new epidemiological and laboratory developments. *Pediatr Infect Dis J*, 6, 1016–1021.
12. Management of Kawasaki syndrome: a consensus statement prepared by North American participants of the Third International Kawasaki Disease Symposium, Tokyo, Japan, December 1988. (1989) *Pediatr Infect Dis J*, 8, 663–667.
13. Kimura, T., Miyazawa, H., Wantanabe, K. et al (1988) Small pustules in Kawasaki disease: a clinicopathologic study of four patients. *Am J Dermatopathol*, 10, 218–233.
14. Kato, H., Sugimura, T., Akagi, T. et al (1996) Long-term consequences of Kawasaki disease. A 10- to 21-year follow-up study of 594 patients. *Circulation*, 15, 1379–1385.
15. Nakano, H., Ueda, K., Saito, A. et al (1985) Repeated quantitative angiograms in coronary artery aneurysm in Kawasaki disease. *Am J Cardiol*, 56, 846–851.
16. Abe, J., Kotzin, B.L., Jujo, K. et al (1992) Selective expansion of T-cells expressing T-cell receptor variable regions V beta 2 and V beta 8 in Kawasaki disease. *Proc Natl Acad Sci USA*, 89, 4066–4070.
17. Dimakakos, P., Bredakis, J., Papageorgiou, A. et al (1996) A case of relapsing Kawasaki disease and review of the literature. *Vasa*, 25, 317–326.
18. Leung, D.Y.M., Meissner, H.C., Fulton, D.R. (1993) Toxic shock syndrome-secreting Staphylococcus aureus in Kawasaki syndrome. *Lancet*, 342, 1385–1388.
19. Rider, L.G., Mendelman, P.M., French, J. et al (1991) Group A streptococcal infection and Kawasaki syndrome. *Lancet*, 337, 1100–1101.
20. Leung, D.Y., Meissner, H.C., Shulman, S.T. et al (2002) Prevalence of superantigen-secreting bacteria in patients with Kawasaki syndrome. *J Pediatr*, 140, 742–746.
21. Yamashiro, Y., Nagata, S., Ohtsuka, Y. et al (1996) Microbiologic studies on the small intestine in Kawasaki disease. *Pediatr Res*, 39, 622–624.
22. Yamashiro, Y., Nagata, S., Oguchi, S. et al (1996) Selective increase on V beta 2+ T cells in the small intestinal mucosa in Kawasaki disease. *Pediatr Res*, 39, 264–266.
23. Michels, T.C. (1986) Mucocutaneous lymph node syndrome in adults: differentiation from toxic shock syndrome. *Am J Med*, 80, 724–728.
24. Johnson, R.M., Little, J.R., Storch, G.A. (2001) Kawasaki-like syndrome associated with human immunodeficiency virus infection. *Clin Infect Dis*, 32, 1628–1634.
25. Blanchard, J.N., Powell, H.C., Freeman, W.R. et al (2003) Recurrent Kawasaki disease-like syndrome in a patient with acquired immunodeficiency virus. *Clin Infect Dis*, 36, 105–111.
26. Wolf, C.V., Wolf, J.R., Parker, J.S. (1995) Kawasaki's disease in a man with the human immunodeficiency virus. *Am J Ophthamol*, 120, 117–118.
27. Sato, N., Sagawa, K., Sasaguri, Y. et al (1993) Immunopathology of cytokine detection in the skin lesions of patients with Kawasaki disease. *J Pediatr*, 122, 198–203.
28. Cuttica, R.J. (1990) Kawasaki disease and vasculopathies. *Curr Opin Rheum*, 2, 809–816.
29. Tanaka, N., Naoe, S., Masuda, H. et al (1986) Pathological study of sequelae of Kawasaki disease (MCLS) with special reference to the heart and coronary arterial lesions. *Acta Pathol Jpn*, 36, 1513–1527.
30. Lie, J.T. (1989) Systemic and isolated vasculitis. In: Rosen, P.P., Fechner, R.E. (eds) Pathology annual 1989, Part I. Norwalk, Connecticut: Appleton and Lange, pp 25–114.
31. Findlay, R.F., Odom, R.B. (1982) Toxic shock syndrome. *Int J Dermatol*, 21, 117–121.

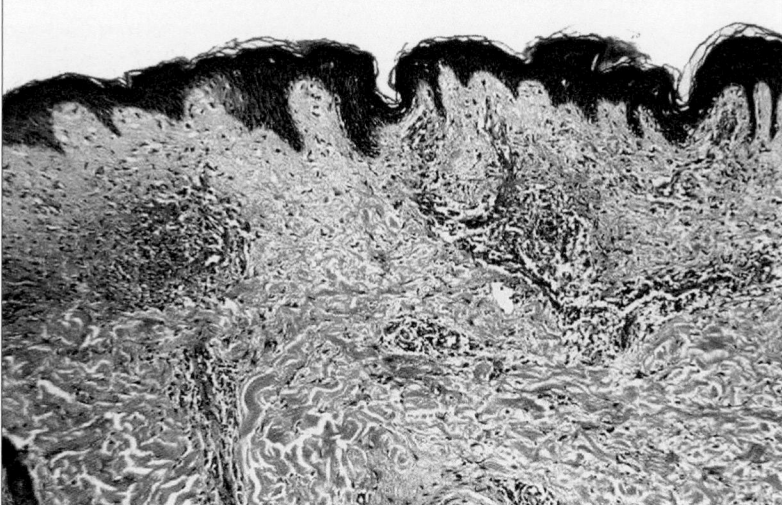

Fig. 15.66
Kawasaki syndrome: in this example the features of severe, acute leukocytoclastic vasculitis are present in the superficial dermis. This is an uncommon finding. By courtesy of W.G. Phillips, MD, Institute of Dermatology, London, UK.

Granuloma faciale

Clinical features

Granuloma faciale is a localized form of leukocytoclastic vasculitis of uncertain pathogenesis. Although children may be affected, most cases occur in people who are middle aged or older. There is a predilection for males. Lesions occur most commonly on the face and are single or more often multiple, erythematous or brownish red, soft discrete papules, plaques or nodules up to several centimeters in diameter (*Fig. 15.67*).[1-3] The surface often shows dilated follicles and fine telangiectasia (*Fig. 15.68*). Common sites include the nose, malar prominence, forehead and ear (*Fig. 15.69*). A case simulating rhinophyma has been documented.[4] Extrafacial lesions may occur on the extremities, neck, chest and scalp (*Fig. 15.70*).[5-12] Although often asymptomatic, patients sometimes report symptoms of mild pruritus or stinging. There is no evidence of associated systemic involvement. Granuloma faciale tends to chronicity and is typified by periods of relapse and partial remissions. Treatment is very difficult and recurrences manifest after surgical excision, even at the site of full-thickness grafting.[13]

A histologically similar lesion affecting the mucosa of the upper respiratory tract has been designated 'eosinophilic angiocentric fibrosis'. Concurrent cases of granuloma faciale and eosinophilic angiocentric fibrosis have been described.[14-16] This suggests that the two diseases represent part of the same spectrum.

Granuloma faciale has been documented in a patient with prostate carcinoma.[17] Any relationship with tumors is likely to be coincidental.

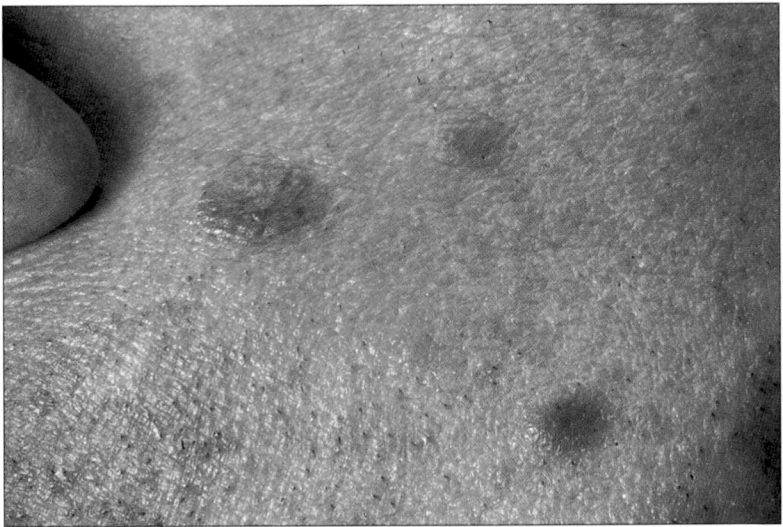

Fig. 15.67
Granuloma faciale: multiple brown nodules. By courtesy of the Institute of Dermatology, London, UK.

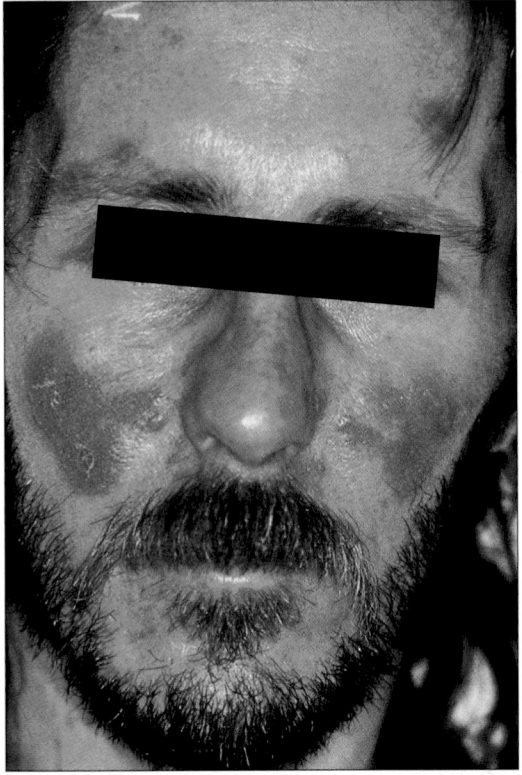

Fig. 15.69
Granuloma faciale: the lesions are frequently multiple. By courtesy of K. Liddell, MD, Eastbourne District Hospital, East Sussex, UK.

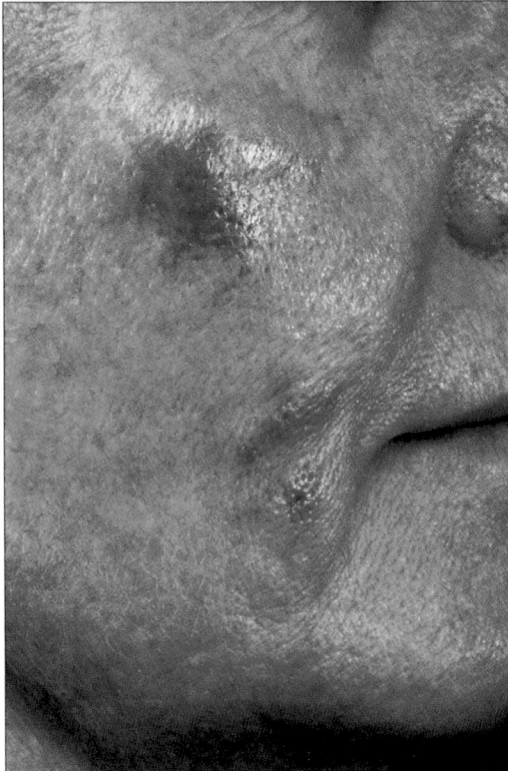

Fig. 15.68
Granuloma faciale: in this example there is associated telangiectasia.

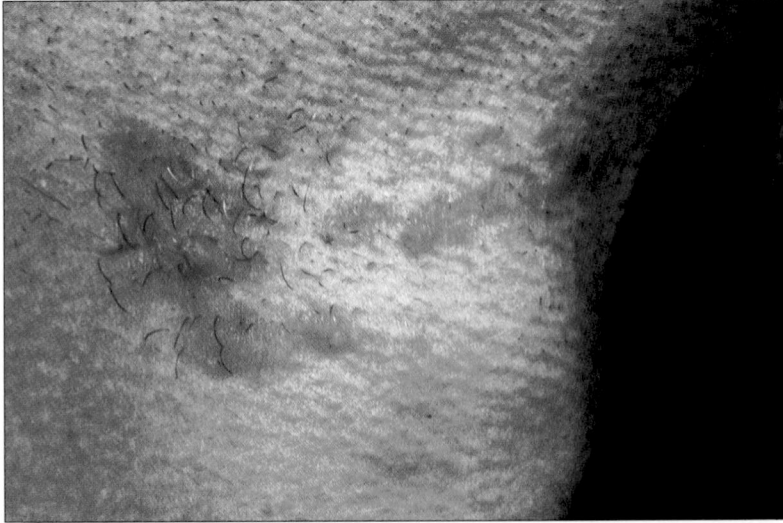

Fig. 15.70
Granuloma faciale: there are multiple lesions on this patient's neck. By courtesy of the Institute of Dermatology, London, UK.

Pathogenesis and histological features

Examination of lesional biopsies by immunofluorescence reveals granular IgG and complement along the epidermal–dermal junction, outlining the hair follicles, and also within the walls of blood vessels; less often IgA and IgM are present, and there is abundant fibrin.[18] Granuloma faciale is, therefore, a chronic vasculitis and may be immune complex mediated. However, some authors consider the above immunofluorescence findings non-specific. Immunohistochemistry shows the presence of abundant eosinophilic cationic protein.[19] T-helper lymphocytes represent the main non-myelocytic cell in the infiltrate and it has been suggested that they play a role in the pathogenesis of the disease, being attracted to the site by gamma-interferon.[20]

Histologically, granuloma faciale is characterized by a dense cellular infiltrate, which often has a nodular outline (*Fig. 15.71*).[21] This infiltrate usually occupies the mid-dermis, although the deep dermis and the subcutaneous fat may be involved; it typically spares the immediate subepidermis and hair follicles, forming a 'Grenz zone' (*Fig. 15.72*). The infiltrate is polymorphic, being composed of large numbers of eosinophils, neutrophils (often displaying leukocytoclasis), and an admixture of plasma cells, mast cells and lymphocytes (*Fig. 15.73*).[22] Red cell extravasation is often present. Blood vessels, which often appear increased in number, are dilated and may show infiltration of their walls by eosinophils with fibrin deposition (*Figs 15.74, 15.75*). Diagnostic features of vasculitis, namely inflammation of vessel walls associated with fibrinoid change, may be difficult to identify in some lesions. In other cases, fibrin is widely distributed in the dermis. Older lesions may show fibrosis and hemosiderin deposition. The microscopic picture in late stages overlaps with that seen in erythema elevatum diutinum.

An ultrastructural study of a case of granuloma faciale has shown that the cytoplasmic granules in the eosinophils display alterations and Langerhans' cells are absent.[23]

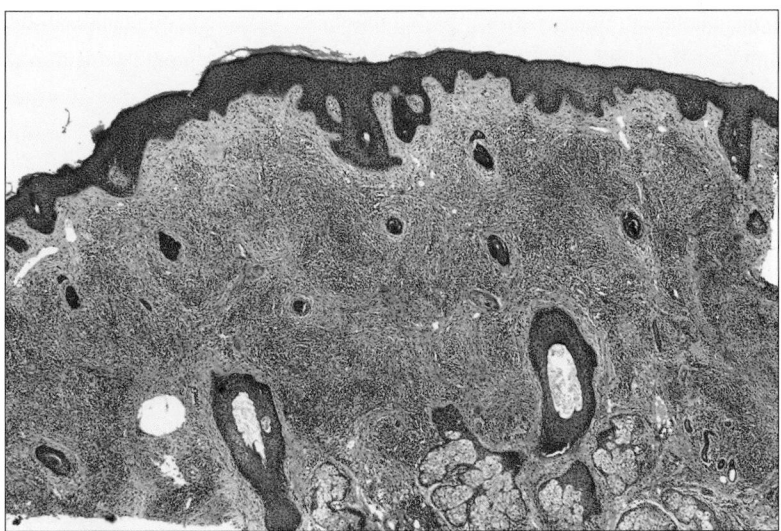

Fig. 15.71
Granuloma faciale: a dense inflammatory cell infiltrate is present in the dermis. Note the conspicuously spared Grenz zone.

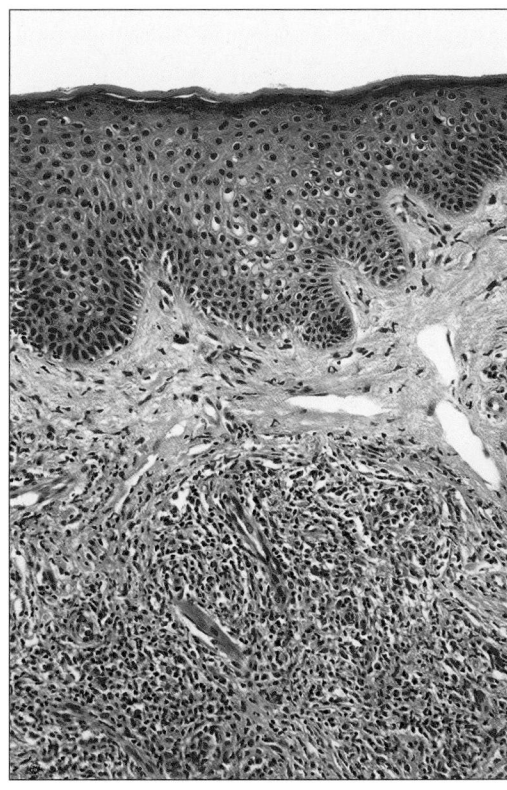

Fig. 15.72
Granuloma faciale: close-up view of Grenz zone.

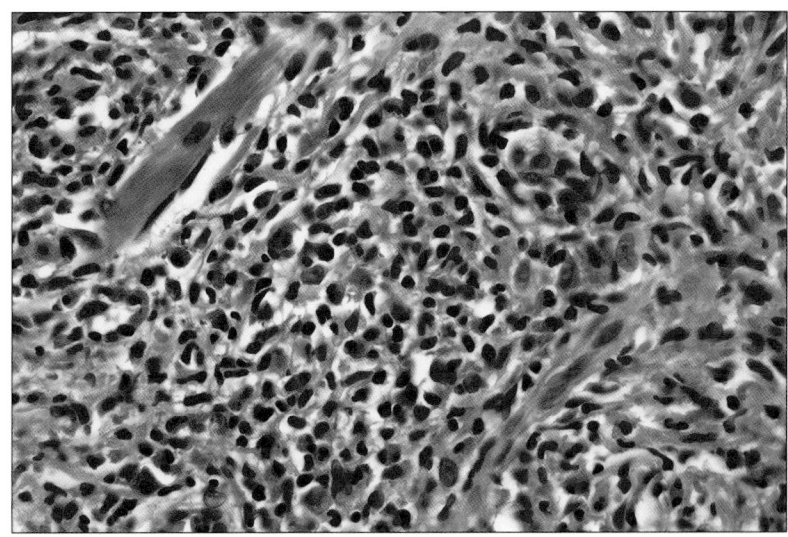

Fig. 15.73
Granuloma faciale: the infiltrate contains large numbers of eosinophils as well as lymphocytes, histiocytes and occasional polymorphs and plasma cells.

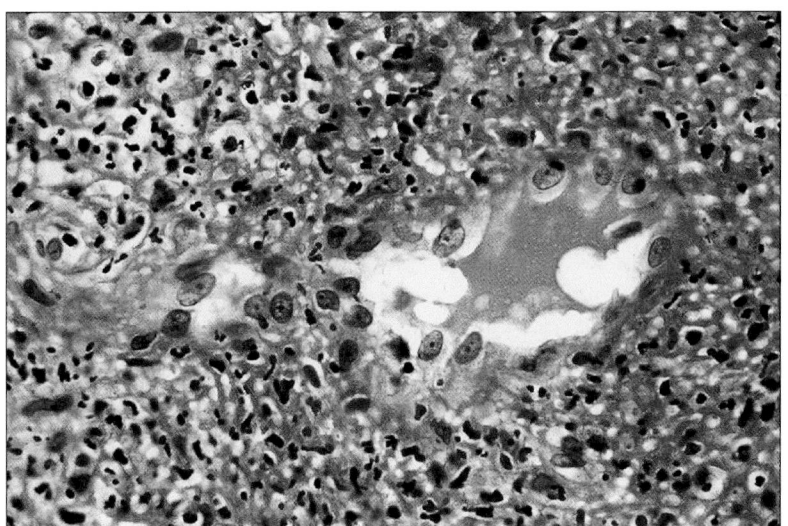

Fig. 15.74
Granuloma faciale: this dilated blood vessel shows marked endothelial swelling, fibrin deposition and disruption of its wall.

Differential diagnosis

The morphological features of granuloma faciale are distinctive. The presence of a mixed infiltrate with a Grenz zone distinguishes granuloma faciale from neutrophilic dermatoses and leukocytoclastic vasculitis. Erythema elevatum diutinum, another form of localized vasculitis, tends to be located on the extensor surfaces of the extremities and shows more sclerosis, more neutrophils and fewer eosinophils. The presence of large numbers of eosinophils may raise the possibility of a Langerhans' cell proliferative disorder; however, the presence of only scattered Langerhans' cells and a Grenz zone (Langerhans' cell proliferative disorders tend to be epidermotropic) with significant numbers of neutrophils favors granuloma faciale. The Grenz zone also helps to distinguish granuloma faciale from hypersensitivity reactions such as to an arthropod bite. Angiolymphoid hyperplasia with eosinophilia (epithelioid hemangioma) is distinguished by the presence of highly unusual thick-walled blood vessels with prominent endothelial cells. An exceptional case of infection by *Trichophyton rubrum* with histology mimicking that of granuloma faciale has been documented.[24]

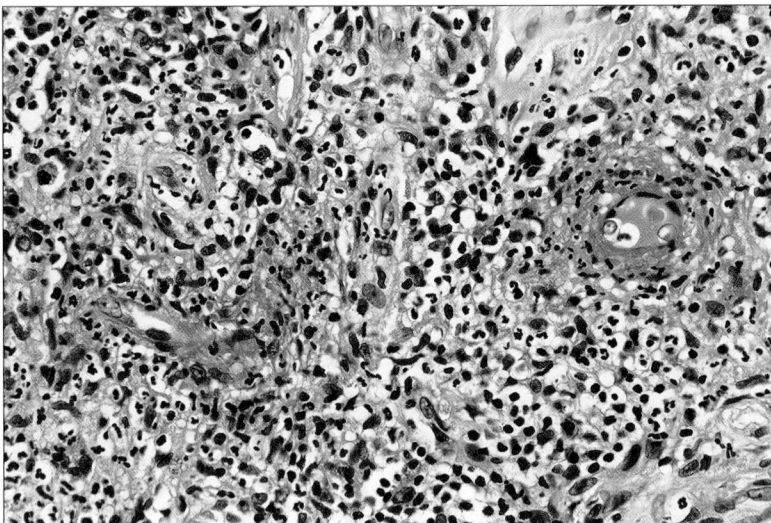

Fig. 15.75
Granuloma faciale: in this example there is florid vasculitis.

Histological features identical to those of granuloma faciale may be seen in patients presenting with a solitary lesion (papule, nodule or plaque) that does not have the clinical appearance or location typical of the disease. The histological picture in these cases has been described as chronic fibrosing vasculitis. As there is also histological overlap with erythema elevatum diutinum, it has been suggested that the microscopic appearances represent a non-specific inflammatory reaction pattern.[25] Therefore, establishing a diagnosis of granuloma faciale requires close clinicopathological correlation.

References

1. Pedace, F.J., Perry, H.O. (1966) Granuloma faciale: a clinical and histopathologic review. *Arch Dermatol*, **94**, 387–395.
2. Black, C.I. (1977) Granuloma faciale. *Cutis*, **20**, 66–68.
3. Buchner, S.A., Koch, B., Itin, P. et al (1988) Facial granuloma. On the clinico-histologic extent of variations of findings in 5 patients. *Hautarzt*, **39**, 217–222.
4. Gómez-de la Fuente, E., del Río, R., Rodríguez, M. et al (2000) Granuloma faciale mimicking rhinophyma: response to clofazimine. *Acta Derm Venereol*, **80**, 144.
5. Konohana, A. (1994) Extrafacial granuloma faciale. *J Dermatol*, **21**, 680–682.
6. Okun, M.R., Bauman, L., Minor, D. (1965) Granuloma faciale with lesions on the hands and face. *Arch Dermatol*, **92**, 78–80.
7. Roustan, G., Sanchez Yus, E., Salas, C. et al (1999) Granuloma faciale with extrafacial lesions. *Dermatology*, **198**, 79–82.
8. Rusin, L.J., Dubin, H.V., Taylor, W.B. (1976) Disseminated granuloma faciale. *Arch Dermatol*, **112**, 1575–1577.
9. Sears, J.K., Gitter, D.G., Stone, M.S. (1991) Extrafacial granuloma faciale. *Arch Dermatol*, **127**, 742–743.
10. Kavanagh, G.M., McLaren, K.M., Hunter, J.A. (1996) Extensive extrafacial granuloma faciale of the scalp. *Br J Dermatol*, **134**, 595–596.
11. Castaño, E., Segurado, A., Iglesias, L. et al (1997) Granuloma faciale entirely in an extrafacial location. *Br J Dermatol*, **136**, 978–979.
12. Inanir, I., Alvur, Y. (2001) Granuloma faciale with extrafacial lesions. *Br J Dermatol*, **145**, 360–362.
13. Phillips, D.K., Hymes, S.R. (1994) Recurrent facial plaques following full-thickness grafting. Granuloma faciale. *Arch Dermatol*, **130**, 1433–1434.
14. Burns, B.V., Roberts, P.F., De Carpentier, J. et al (2001) Eosinophilic angiocentric fibrosis affecting the nasal cavity: a mucosal variant of the skin lesion granuloma faciale. *J Laryngol Otol*, **115**, 223–226.
15. Thompson, L.D., Heffner, D.K. (2001) Sinonasal tract eosinophilic angiocentric fibrosis. A report of three cases. *Am J Clin Pathol*, **115**, 243–248.
16. Roberts, P.F., McCann, B.G. (1997) Eosinophilic angiocentric fibrosis of the upper respiratory tract: a mucosal variant of granuloma faciale? A report of three cases. *Histopathology*, **121**, 1217–1225.
17. Roussaki-Schulze, A., Klimi, E., Zafiriou, E. et al (2002) Granuloma faciale associated with adenocarcinoma of the prostate. *Int J Dermatol*, **41**, 901–903.
18. Nieboer, C., Kalsbeek, G.L. (1978) Immunofluorescence studies in granuloma eosinophilicum faciale. *J Cutan Pathol*, **5**, 68–75.
19. Selvaag, E., Roald, B. (2000) Immunohistochemical findings in granuloma faciale. The role of eosinophilic granulocytes. *J Eur Acad Dermatol Venereol*, **14**, 517–518.
20. Smoller, B.R., Bortz, J. (1993) Immunophenotypic analysis suggests that granuloma faciale is a gamma-interferon-mediated process. *J Cutan Pathol*, **20**, 442–446.
21. LeBoit, P.E. (2002) Granuloma faciale: a diagnosis deserving of dignity. *Am J Dermatopathol*, **24**, 440–443.
22. Crowson, A.N., Mihm, M.C. Jr, Magro, C.M. (2003) Cutaneous vasculitis: a review. *J Cutan Pathol*, **30**, 161–173.
23. Vicente Ortega, V., Sánchez-Pedreno, P., Rodríguez Vicente, J. (1998) Granuloma faciale: an ultrastructural study. *Ultrastruct Pathol*, **22**, 135–140.
24. Frankel, D.H., Soltani, K., Medenica, M.M. et al (1988) Tinea of the face caused by Trichophyton rubrum with histologic changes of granuloma faciale. *J Am Acad Dermatol*, **18**, 403–406.
25. Carlson, J.A., LeBoit, P.E. (1997) Localized chronic fibrosing vasculitis of the skin: an inflammatory reaction that occurs in settings other than erythema elevatum diutinum and granuloma faciale. *Am J Surg Pathol*, **21**, 698–705.

Erythema elevatum diutinum

Clinical features

This uncommon disease represents a localized variant of leukocytoclastic vasculitis.[1–3] Although it may occur in any age group, patients are usually in their third to fifth decade. Incidence is equal in men and women. Patients present with papules and nodules measuring up to about 1 cm in diameter; they may also develop round or oval, indurated, elevated plaques 5–6 cm in diameter. Lesions may be red or purple, although some have a yellowish tinge, which may be confused with a xanthomatous process. Bullous lesions are occasionally present.[1] The disease is characteristically persistent and the distribution of the lesions often symmetrical. Large nodules resembling keloids or tumor are sometimes found.[4,5]

Lesions are located particularly in relation to the extensor surfaces of the joints and are, therefore, seen on the backs of the hands and fingers, wrists, elbows, knees, ankles and toes (*Figs 15.76, 15.77*). The buttocks may also be affected, but the trunk is usually spared. Although lesions are often asymptomatic, some patients complain of itching and pain, and symptoms are frequently made worse in a cold environment. Patients

sometimes also have arthralgia. Eye involvement includes keratolysis and ulcerative keratitis with positive rheumatoid factor.[6,7] Although the disease is chronic and progressive, resolution usually occurs by 5–10 years. The disease characteristically responds to dapsone.

Systemic involvement does not usually occur but pulmonary infiltrates have exceptionally been documented.[8]

An association with paraproteinemia is frequently present, often of the IgA subtype.[1,9,10] Hyperimmunoglobulinemia D syndrome is a further rare association.[11] An underlying myelodysplastic syndrome or a hematological malignancy (e.g. multiple myeloma, B cell lymphoma and chronic lymphocytic leukemia) has been found in some patients.[1,12–15] Often, the skin lesions precede development of the hematological disorder.[1] In one study, an average of 7.8 years separated onset of skin lesions and development of a myeloproliferative disorder.[1,16]

Inflammatory bowel disease – both Crohn's disease and ulcerative colitis – has also been associated with erythema elevatum diutinum.[17–19] Interestingly, in one patient with Crohn's disease, skin lesions seemed to appear during exacerbation of bowel symptoms.[17] In another patient with ulcerative colitis, onset of erythema elevatum diutinum lesions coincided with presentation of bowel disease and skin lesions resolved following colectomy.[18] Erythema elevatum diutinum has also been reported in association with celiac disease.[20,21] In one patient with celiac disease, skin lesions resolved with the introduction of a gluten-free diet.[21]

Rheumatoid arthritis has been described in conjunction with erythema elevatum diutinum.[22–24] Other reported associations include Wegener's granulomatosis, relapsing polychondritis and pyoderma gangrenosum.[25–28] Erythema elevatum diutinum is also seen in patients with HIV infection.[29–34] In HIV-infected patients, lesions may mimic Kaposi's sarcoma.[29] Extensive acro-osteolysis has been described in a single case.[35] The exceptional association with pityriasis rubra pilaris and mosquito bites is probably coincidental.[36]

A condition described as "neutrophilic dermatosis of the dorsal hands" is likely to be part of the spectrum of erythema elevatum diutinum.[37]

Pathogenesis and histological features

Erythema elevatum diutinum is possibly immune complex mediated. Both a streptococcal antigen and *E. coli* have been implicated.[2,38] As mentioned above, the disease has also been recorded in association with cryoglobulin IgA, monoclonal or biclonal gammopathy, multiple myeloma, hairy cell leukemia and polycythemia rubra vera.[1,39–41] In early lesions, there is increased expression of the beta (2)-integrins CR3 and LFA-1 and this diminishes in older lesions.[42] Peripheral blood neutrophils show increased migration in response to interleukin-8 (IL-8) and decreased responsiveness to the bacterial peptide analogue N-formyl-methionyl-leucyl-phenylalanine. These findings suggest that in erythema elevatum diutinum the recruitment of neutrophils occurs as a result of activation of cytokines such as IL-8.[42] Immune complexes and bacterial peptides sustain the persistent local inflammatory response.[42]

Biopsy of early lesions reveals typical features of leukocytoclastic vasculitis (*Fig. 15.78*).[1,43] The epidermis may show acanthosis and parakeratosis. Fibrinoid necrosis and infiltration of the superficial vessels by neutrophil polymorphs are present. The perivenular connective tissue contains abundant fibrin and a dense inflammatory cell infiltrate of

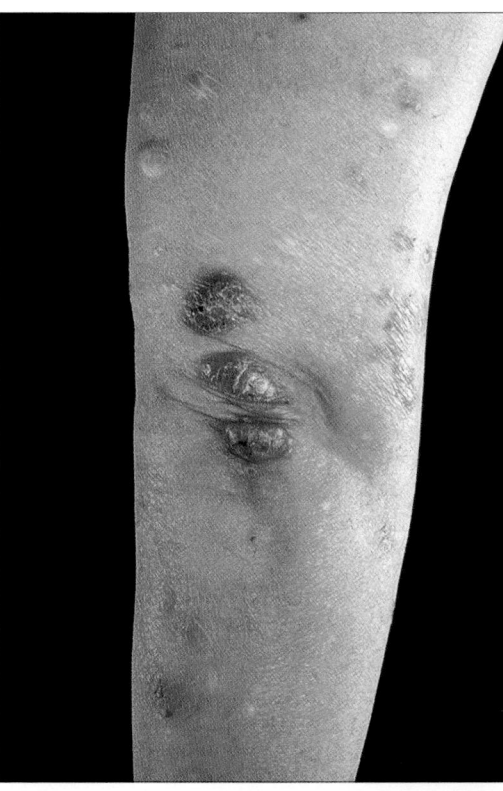

Fig. 15.76
Erythema elevatum diutinum: the tuberose, erythematous nodules present on the elbow clinically resemble xanthomata. By courtesy of the Institute of Dermatology, London, UK.

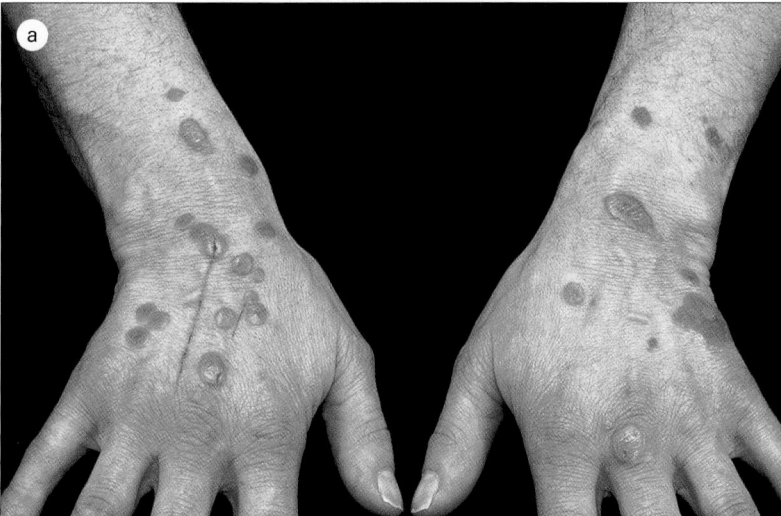

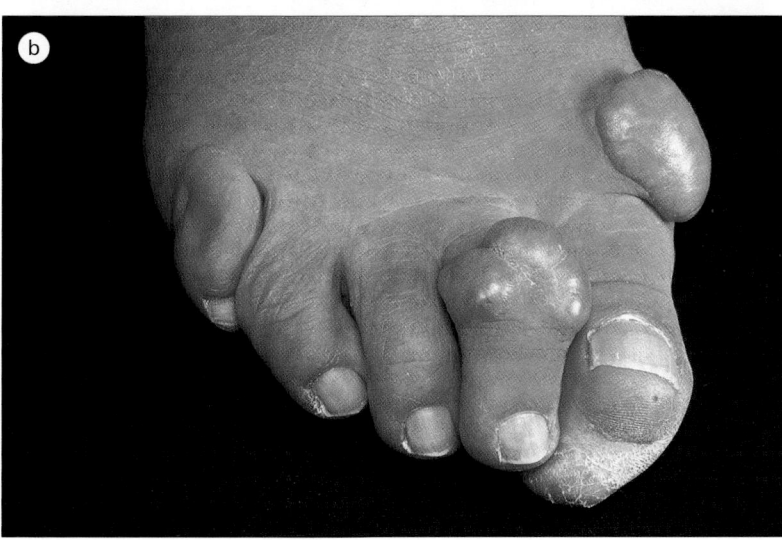

Fig. 15.77
Erythema elevatum diutinum: the hands (a) and feet (b) are commonly affected. By courtesy of the Institute of Dermatology, London, UK.

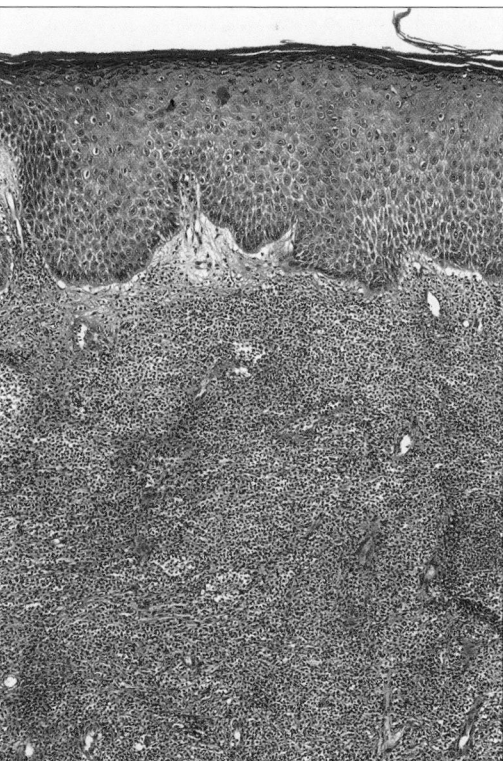

Fig. 15.78
Erythema elevatum diutinum: early lesion showing leukocytoclastic vasculitis in a background of a Sweet's syndrome-like neutrophil infiltrate.

neutrophils, histiocytes, lymphocytes and eosinophils. Leukocytoclasis is usually evident.

Older lesions are characterized by the development of granulation tissue and fibrous scarring, although even then, foci of neutrophilic vasculitis may be found after examination of multiple sections (*Fig. 15.79*). In 'burnt out' lesions, vasculitis may not be present. Granulation tissue and dense scarring mark the site of the previous acute inflammatory process. In older lesions the scarring often shows a storiform pattern (*Fig. 15.80*). Interstitial lipid deposition described in the past as extracellular cholesterolosis is uncommon.

In ocular lesions, leukocytoclastic vasculitis with focal granulomatous inflammation has been described.[7]

Rare histopathological features described include palisaded necrotizing granuloma and pyogenic granuloma-like features.[36]

Differential diagnosis

Erythema elevatum diutinum typically involves the dermis and must, therefore, be distinguished from granuloma faciale. Granuloma faciale usually shows an eosinophil predominance whereas in erythema elevatum diutinum neutrophils are much more numerous. However, the histological features of late lesions in both entities often overlap and similar appearances are found in chronic fibrosing vasculitis. The latter represents a non-specific reaction pattern that is occasionally seen in solitary lesions from patients who have no clinical features of either granuloma faciale or erythema elevatum diutinum.[44] Distinction from Sweet's syndrome is afforded by the presence of neutrophilic vasculitis. Older sclerotic lesions, particularly when they present as mass lesions, may be mistaken for a neoplastic process or dermatofibroma.[5] The presence of a leukocytoclastic vasculitis and neutrophilic infiltrate with karyorrhexis favors erythema elevatum diutinum.

References

1. Yiannias, J.A., El-Azhary, R.A., Gibson, L.E. (1992) Erythema elevatum diutinum: a clinical and histopathologic study of 13 patients. *J Am Acad Dermatol*, **26**, 38–44.
2. Katz, S.I., Gallin, J.L., Hertz, K.C. et al (1977) Erythema elevatum diutinum: skin and systemic manifestations, immunologic studies and successful treatment with dapsone. *Medicine*, **56**, 443–455.
3. Gibson, L.E., el-Azhary, R.A. (2000) Erythema elevatum diutinum. *Clin Dermatol*, **18**, 295–299.
4. Krishnan, R.S., Hwang, L.Y., Tschen, J.A. et al (2001) Erythema elevatum diutinum mimicking extensive keloids. *Cutis*, **67**, 381–385.
5. Shanks, J.H., Banerjee, S.S., Bishop, P.W. et al (1997) Nodular erythema elevatum diutinum mimicking cutaneous neoplasms. *Histopathology*, **31**, 91–96.
6. Takiwaki, H., Kubo, Y., Tsuda, H. et al (1998) Peripheral ulcerative keratitis associated with erythema elevatum diutinum and a positive rheumatoid factor: a report of three cases. *Br J Dermatol*, **138**, 893–897.
7. Casanova, F.H., Meirelles, R.L., Tojar, M. et al (2001) Autoimmune keratolysis in a patient with leukocytoclastic vasculitis: unusual erythema elevatum diutinum with granulomatous pattern. *Cornea*, **20**, 329–332.
8. Creus, L., Salleras, M., Sola, M.A. et al (1997) Erythema elevatum diutinum associated with pulmonary infiltrates. *Br J Dermatol*, **137**, 652–653.
9. Rovel-Guitera, P., Diemert, M.C., Charuel, J.L. et al (2000) IgA antineutrophil cytoplasmic antibodies in cutaneous vasculitis. *Br J Dermatol*, **143**, 99–103.
10. Chowdury, M.M., Inaloz, H.S., Motley, R.J. et al (2002) Erythema elevatum diutinum and IgA paraproteinaemia: a 'preclinical iceberg'. *Int J Dermatol*, **41**, 368–370.
11. Miyagawa, S., Kitamura, W., Morita, K. et al (1993) Association of hyperimmunoglobulinaemia D syndrome with erythema elevatum diutinum. *Br J Dermatol*, **128**, 572–574.
12. Queipo de Llano, M., Yebra, M., Cabrera, R. et al (1992) Myelodysplastic syndrome in association with erythema elevatum diutinum. *J Rheumatol*, **19**, 1005–1006.
13. Gerbig, A.W., Zala, L., Hunziker, T. (1997) Erythema elevatum diutinum. A rare dermatosis with a broad spectrum of associated illnesses. *Hautarzt*, **48**, 113–117.
14. Futei, Y., Konohana, I. (2000) A case of erythema elevatum diutinum associated with B-cell lymphoma: a rare distribution involving palms, soles and nails. *Br J Dermatol*, **142**, 116–119.
15. Delaporte, E., Alfandari, S., Fenaux, P. et al (1994) Erythema elevatum diutinum and chronic lymphocytic leukaemia. *Clin Exp Dermatol*, **19**, 188.

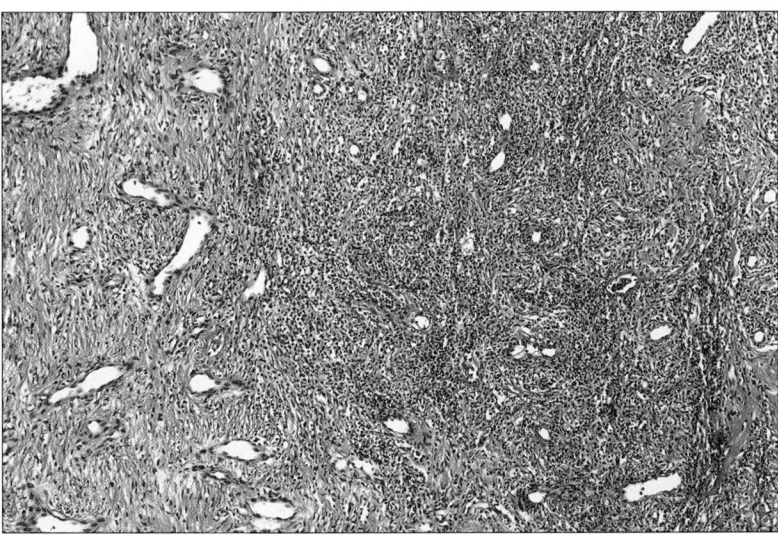

Fig. 15.79
Erythema elevatum diutinum: older lesion showing scar tissue with a vaguely storiform growth pattern.

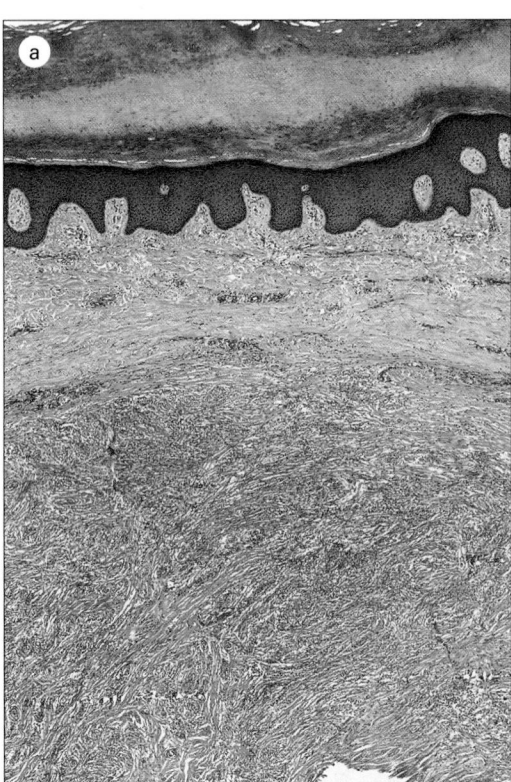

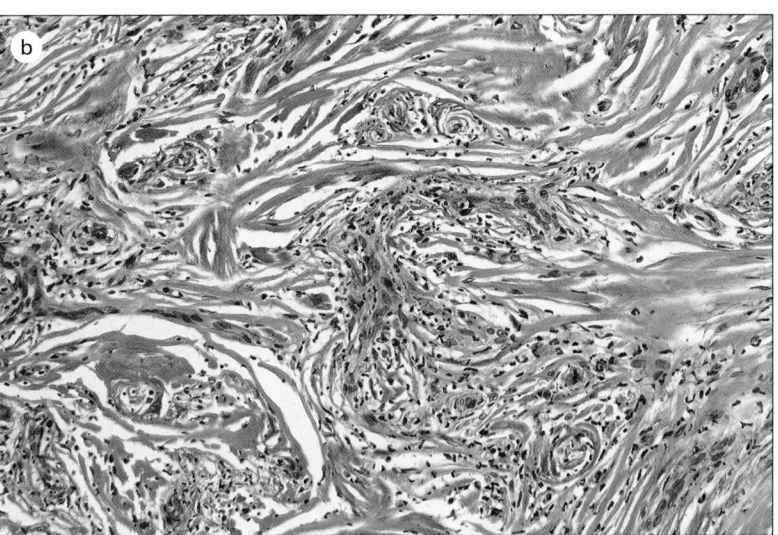

Fig. 15.80
(**a, b**) Erythema elevatum diutinum: this example was clinically thought to represent a keloid. There is a circumscribed dermal nodule composed of spindle cells in a hyalinized stroma. Focally perivascular nuclear debris is evident and there are scattered eosinophils.

16. Chow, R.K., Benny, W.B., Coupe, R.L. et al (1996) Erythema elevatum diutinum associated with IgA paraproteinemia successfully controlled with intermittent plasma exchange. *Arch Dermatol*, **132**, 1360–1364.
17. Elsner, J., Kiehl, P., Kapp, A. et al (1996) Erythema elevatum diutinum in Crohn's disease. *Hautarzt*, **47**, 701–704.
18. Buahene, K., Hudson, M., Mowat, A. et al (1991) Erythema elevatum diutinum – and unusual association with ulcerative colitis. *Clin Exp Dermatol*, **16**, 204–206.
19. Walker, K.D., Badame, A.J. (1990) Erythema elevatum diutinum in a patient with Crohn's disease. *J Am Acad Dermatol*, **22**, 948–952.
20. Tasanen, K., Raudasoja, R., Kallioinen, M. et al (1997) Erythema elevatum diutinum in association with coeliac disease. *Br J Dermatol*, **136**, 624–627.
21. Rodríguez-Serna, M., Fortea, J.M., Pérez, A. et al (1993) Erythema elevatum diutinum associated with celiac disease: response to a gluten-free diet. *Pediatr Dermatol*, **10**, 125–128.
22. Chen, K.R., Toyohara, A., Suzuki, A. et al (2002) Clinical and histopathological spectrum of cutaneous vasculitis in rheumatoid arthritis. *Br J Dermatol*, **147**, 905–913.
23. Nakajima, H., Ikeda, M., Yamamoto, Y. et al (1999) Erythema elevatum diutinum complicated by rheumatoid arthritis. *J Dermatol*, **26**, 452–456.
24. Collier, P.M., Neill, S.M., Branfoot, A.C. et al (1990) Erythema elevatum diutinum – a solitary lesion in a patient with rheumatoid arthritis. *Clin Exp Dermatol*, **15**, 394–395.
25. Kavanagh, G.M., Colaco, C.B., Bradfield, J.W. et al (1993) Erythema elevatum diutinum associated with Wegener's granulomatosis and IgA paraproteinemia. *J Am Acad Dermatol*, **28**, 846–849.
26. Delgado, J., Gómez-Cerezo, J., Siguenza, M. et al (2001) Relapsing polychondritis and erythema elevatum diutinum: an unusual association refractory to dapsone. *J Rheumatol*, **28**, 634–635.
27. Wayte, J.A., Rogers, S., Powell, F.C. (1995) Pyoderma gangrenosum, erythema elevatum diutinum and IgA monoclonal gammopathy. *Australas J Dermatol*, **36**, 21–23.
28. Planaguma, M., Puig, L., Alomar, A. et al (1992) Pyoderma gangrenosum in association with erythema elevatum diutinum: report of two cases. *Cutis*, **49**, 201–206.
29. Requena, L., Sánchez Yus, E., Martín, L. et al (1991) Erythema elevatum diutinum in a patient with acquired immunodeficiency syndrome. Another clinical simulator of Kaposi's sarcoma. *Arch Dermatol*, **127**, 1819–1822.
30. Dronda, F., Gónzalez-López, A., Lecona, M. et al (1996) Erythema elevatum diutinum in human immunodeficiency virus-infected patients: report of a case and review of the literature. *Clin Exp Dermatol*, **21**, 222–225.
31. LeBoit, P.E., Cockerell, C.J. (1993) Nodular lesions of erythema elevatum diutinum in patients infected with the human immunodeficiency virus. *J Am Acad Dermatol*, **28**, 919–922.
32. Muratori, S., Carrera, C., Gorani, A. et al (1999) Erythema elevatum diutinum and HIV infection: a report of five cases. *Br J Dermatol*, **141**, 335–338.
33. Fakheri, A., Gupta, S.M., White, S.M. et al (2001) Erythema elevatum diutinum in a patient with human immunodeficiency syndrome. *Cutis*, **68**, 41–42.
34. Martin, J.L., Dronda, F., Cháves, F. (2001) Erythema elevatum diutinum, a clinical entity to be considered in patients infected with HIV-1. *Clin Exp Dermatol*, **26**, 725–726.
35. Ellabban, A., Schumacher, H.R. Jr (1997) Erythema elevatum diutinum with extensive acro-osteolysis. *J Rheumatol*, **24**, 1203–1205.
36. Sangueza, O.P., Pilcher, B., Martin Sangueza, J. (1997) Erythema elevatum diutinum: a clinicopathological study of eight cases. *Am J Dermatopathol*, **19**, 214–222.
37. Ayoub, N., Tomb, R. (2003) Neutrophilic dermatosis of the dorsal hands: a variant of erythema elevatum diutinum? *Arch Dermatol*, **139**, 102.
38. Cream, J.J., Levene, G.M., Calnan, C.D. (1971) Erythema elevatum diutinum: an unusual reaction to streptococcal antigen and response to dapsone. *Br J Dermatol*, **84**, 393–399.
39. Morrison, J.G.L., Hull, P.R., Fourie, E. (1977) Erythema elevatum diutinum, cryoglobulinemia, and fixed urticaria on cooling. *Br J Dermatol*, **97**, 99–104.
40. Dorsey, J.K., Penick, G.D. (1982) The association of hairy cell leukemia with unusual immunologic disorder. *Arch Intern Med*, **142**, 902–903.
41. Statham, B.N., Greenwood, R., Tring, F.C. (1983) Erythema elevatum diutinum – a report of two unusual patients. *Clin Exp Dermatol*, **8**, 549–552.
42. Grabbe, J., Haas, N., Moller, A. et al (2000) Erythema elevatum diutinum – evidence for disease-dependent leucocyte alterations and response to dapsone. *Br J Dermatol*, **143**, 415–420.
43. Leboit, P.E., Yen, T.S.B., Wintroub, B. (1986) The evolution of lesions in erythema elevatum diutinum. *Am J Dermatopathol*, **8**, 392–402.
44. Carlson, J.A., LeBoit, P.E. (1997) Localized chronic fibrosing vasculitis of the skin: an inflammatory reaction that occurs in settings other than erythema elevatum diutinum and granuloma faciale. *Am J Surg Pathol*, **21**, 698–705.

Behçet's disease

Clinical features

This rare disease was originally described as a combination of recurrent oral and genital ulceration associated with uveitis. However, it is now known to represent a systemic illness with lesions involving the joints and central nervous, vascular, respiratory, gastrointestinal and urogenital systems, in addition to mucous membranes and integument (*Table 15.7*).[1-7] Although it is seen worldwide, it shows a high incidence in Japan, Southeast Asia, the Middle East, Turkey, and some countries bordering the Mediterranean. Behçet's disease shows a male predominance and most commonly presents in young adults with a peak incidence of onset in the third decade. Children may also be affected with an approximately equal sex incidence.[8] One study has suggested that the disease is less aggressive in children.[9] Some data appear to indicate that males have a higher mortality rate.[10]

The International Study Group established diagnostic criteria for Behçet's disease in 1990 and these are summarized in *Table 15.8*.[4] It should be kept in mind that these criteria are somewhat controversial.[11] More research is necessary before we can fully understand this complex disease.

Recurrent oral ulceration is an invariable feature. Some patients have a long history of oral ulceration before developing other features that allow for a definitive diagnosis of Behçet's disease. Ulcers typically measure up to 1 cm across but may be larger. They may develop anywhere in the oral cavity, in the pharynx, and even in the larynx (*Fig. 15.81*).[12] They are exquisitely painful, and usually regress spontaneously within 14 days although they can persist for much longer. A yellow, necrotic crust covers the ulcer floor. Some patients develop ulcerations in a herpetiform configuration.[13] Patients with larger ulcerations tend to have greater severity of oral disease with more frequent relapses.[13]

Cutaneous lesions are common, recurrent and comprise a wide variety of manifestations including erythema nodosum-like lesions, usually on the lower extremities.[14,15] Patients may also develop acneiform papules

Table 15.7

Behçet's disease: frequency of organ involvement

Sign or symptom	Incidence (%)
Oral ulcers	90–100
Genital ulcers	64–88
Ocular lesions	27–90
Cutaneous lesions	48–88
Joint manifestations	18–64
Neurological features	10–29
Intestinal manifestations	0–59
Thrombophlebitis	10–37

Reproduced with permission from Arbesfield, S.J. and Kurban, A.K. (1988) *Journal of the American Academy of Dermatology*, **19**, 767–779. Copyright ©The American Academy of Dermatology, Inc.

Table 15.8

Behçet's disease: diagnostic criteria*

Criterion	Definition
Recurrent oral ulceration	Minor aphthous, major aphthous, or herpetiform ulceration observed by physician or patient, and recurrent at least three times in one 12-month period
Plus two of:	
Recurrent genital ulceration	Aphthous ulceration or scarring, observed by physician or patient
Eye lesions	Anterior uveitis, posterior uveitis or cells in vitreous on slit lamp examination; *or* Retinal vasculitis observed by ophthalmologist
Skin lesions	Erythema nodosum observed by physician or patient, pseudofolliculitis or papulopustular lesions; or acneiform nodules observed by physician, patient not on corticosteroid treatment
Positive pathergy test	Read by physician at 24–48 hours

* Findings applicable only in the absence of other clinical explanations.
Reprinted with permission from Elsevier (International Study Group for Behçet's Disease (1990) *Lancet*, **335**, 1078–1080).

and pustules, furuncles, pyoderma and thrombophlebitis (*Fig. 15.82*). In one very large study, papulopustular lesions (followed by erythema nodosum-like lesions) were the most commonly encountered skin manifestation.[7] Patients have also been described manifesting Sweet's syndrome-like features.[16]

Typical of Behçet's disease, and an important diagnostic clue, is development of sterile pustules at sites of mild skin trauma such as injection sites (pathergic response) (*Fig. 15.83*).[17,18] Paradoxically, some authors have found that wound healing after 4 mm punch biopsy does not seem to differ compared with control subjects.[19]

Genital lesions, similar in appearance to those of the oral mucosa, occur on the scrotum, penis, vagina and vulva (*Figs 15.84, 15.85*).[7]

Ocular lesions are important because if left untreated they may progress to cataracts and blindness. Bilateral involvement is seen in the majority of patients. Almost any part of the eye may be affected and bilateral inflammation of the anterior segment (anterior uveitis), posterior uveitis with hypopyon and vitritis are said to be pathognomonic.[20] Conjunctivitis, corneal ulceration, choroiditis and retinal vessel involvement (arterial and venous vasculitis) may be additional features.

Joint involvement is not uncommon and usually affects the knees, ankles, elbows and wrists.[21] A mono- or oligoarticular pattern of involvement is typical. The affected joints are swollen, red, tender and painful. It is of interest that despite many years of arthritic symptoms, joint deformities do not develop.

Vascular disease in Behçet's disease may take the form of both thrombo-occlusive disease and frank vasculitis. Vascular involvement is an important cause of both morbidity and mortality and is seen in approximately one-third of patients.[22,23] Males appear to be at an increased risk.[23] Thrombophlebitis is common and may affect both superficial and deep veins of the limbs. Superior and inferior vena caval obstruction are not uncommon complications. A particularly perilous form of vascular involvement is hepatic vein occlusion (Budd–Chiari syndrome), which is associated with a high mortality.[24] Pulmonary artery aneurysm occurs in approximately 1% of patients and is associated with a 50% mortality rate.[25]

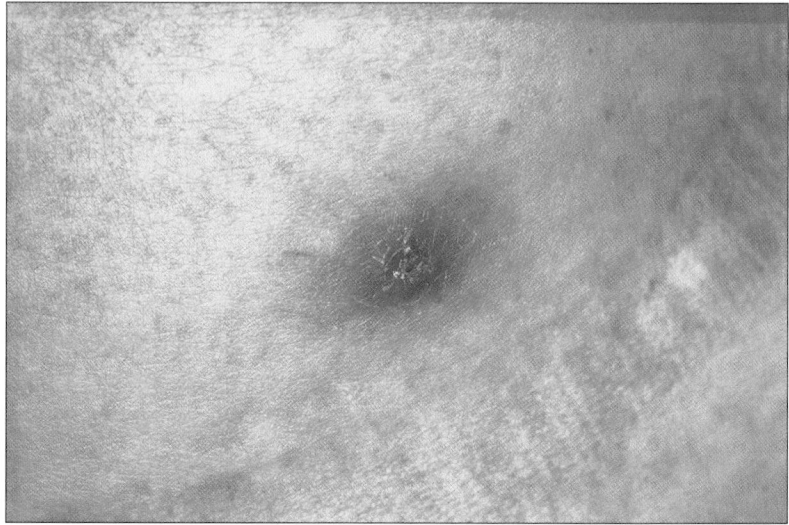

Fig. 15.83
Behçet's disease: this ruptured pustule developed at the site of a previous venipuncture. Such a positive provocation test is virtually pathognomonic for Behçet's disease. By courtesy of D.A.H. Yates, MD, St Thomas' Hospital, London, UK.

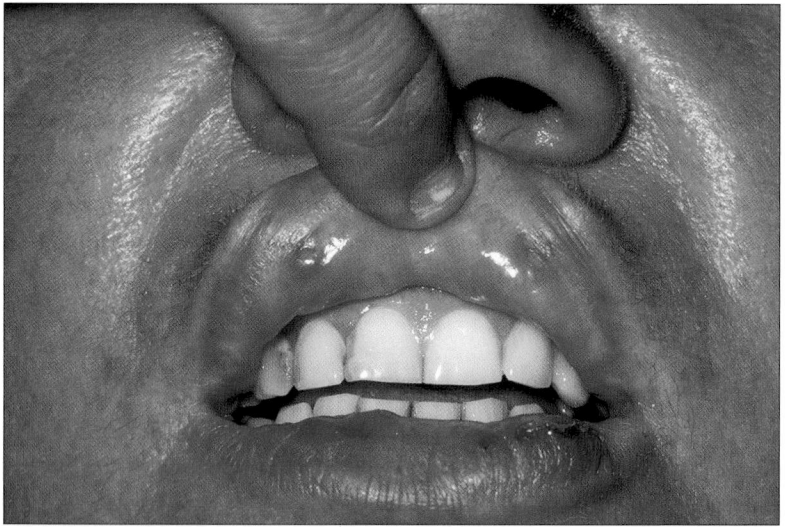

Fig. 15.81
Behçet's disease: superficial ulcers are present on the inner aspect of both lips. By courtesy of R.A. Marsden, MD, St George's Hospital, London, UK.

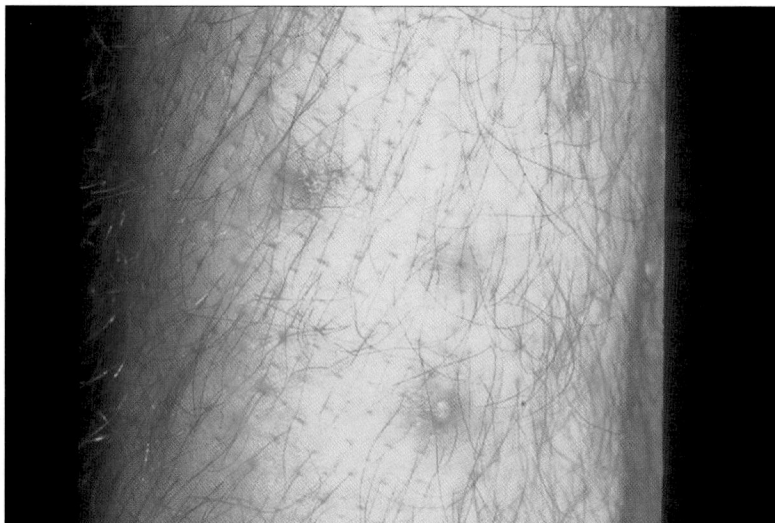

Fig. 15.82
Behçet's disease: typical pustules on the lower leg. By courtesy of R.A. Marsden, MD, St George's Hospital, London, UK.

Fig. 15.84
Behçet's disease: there is a typical scrotal ulcer with central slough. By courtesy of D.A.H. Yates, MD, St Thomas' Hospital, London, UK.

The inflammation may affect virtually any artery and the development of an aneurysm with subsequent rupture is an important cause of death.

Respiratory involvement presents as dyspnea, cough, pleuritic chest pain and hemoptysis.[26] The last, due to pulmonary artery–bronchial fistula formation, is an important cause of death. Lung involvement occurs in up to 5% of patients.[26]

Intestinal involvement particularly affects the ileocecal region; ulcers may be complicated by perforation, presenting as an intra-abdominal emergency necessitating surgical intervention.[27] Esophageal involvement in the form of ulcers and erosion, stenosis or esophagitis is uncommon.[28]

Involvement of the nervous system, which is associated with a poor prognosis, occurs in up to 25% of patients.[22] Lesions may develop anywhere in the central and peripheral components and, therefore, virtually any neurological sign or symptom may be seen, including sensory losses, strokes, and spinal cord, cranial and peripheral nerve lesions. Dural sinus thrombosis is a well-recognized complication.[29]

Kidney involvement has been documented in up to 55% of patients and manifestations include amyloidosis, glomerulonephritis, interstitial nephritis and vasculitis.[30]

A study of relative organ system involvement has led to a subclassification of a spectrum of Behçet's disease.[31,32] The mortality of Behçet's disease is, however, surprisingly low, of the order of 2–4%.

Pathogenesis and histological features

The precise etiology and pathogenesis is unknown. Recent interest has focused on the possibility of an altered immune response in patients with Behçet's disease. It has been suggested that heat shock proteins may play an important role in its pathogenesis.[33,34] Heat shock proteins reactive in Behçet's patients induce uveitis in rats.[34] Oligoclonal expansion of T-cells in some patients with Behçet's disease has been documented.[35] In one study, serum IL-12 and peripheral Th1 lymphocyte levels correlated with disease activity.[36]

Complement components C3 and C9 have been identified in blood vessel walls in oral biopsies.[32] Increased interleukin levels associated with increased B-cell activity have also been described.[37] Of possible importance in the pathogenesis is the frequent presence of high levels of circulating immune complexes and the common detection of immunoglobulins (particularly IgM) and complement in blood vessel walls.[38–40] Behçet's disease is associated with human leukocyte antigen (HLA)-B5, -B12, -B27 and particularly with HLA-BW51.[22] Anticardiolipin antibodies have been described.[22]

Despite the accumulation of considerable immunological and genetic data, the underlying antigen or other stimulus that drives these changes, and is ultimately responsible for the disease, remains elusive.

The histological features are in themselves largely non-specific.[32,37,41,42] The diagnosis of Behçet's disease is essentially clinical. The pathological features that may be detected include both lymphocytic and necrotizing vasculitis affecting the superficial postcapillary venules with associated fibrinoid necrosis (*Fig. 15.86*).[41] In one study, nearly 50% of patients had evidence of vasculitis.[43] Often, however, such vasculitic changes appear to be a consequence, rather than a cause, of the associated dermal or mucosal inflammatory changes.[42] Endothelial swelling may be a feature and there is often an associated lymphocytic perivascular infiltrate although sometimes neutrophils are abundant.[44] Venulitis and phlebitis were the most common forms of vasculitis seen in one series of patients.[11] In this study phlebitis/venulitis was seen in 48% of patients while leukocytoclastic vasculitis and lymphocytic vasculitis were seen in 17% and 31% of patients, respectively.[43]

Non-specific features include a diffuse neutrophil polymorph dermal infiltrate with or without abscess formation, corresponding clinically to pustular lesions, acute folliculitis and acneiform folliculocentric pustular changes (*Fig. 15.87*).[11,45,46] Biopsy after needle trauma in one study

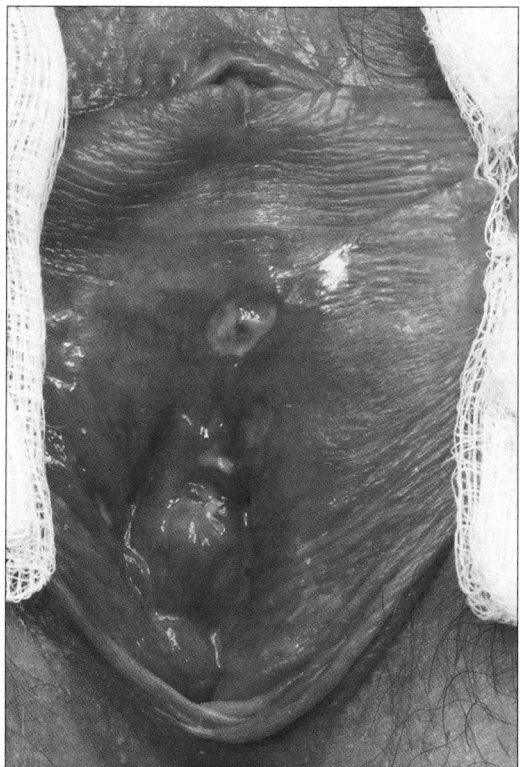

Fig. 15.85
Behçet's disease: multiple superficial vulval ulcers are present. By courtesy of R.A. Marsden, MD, St George's Hospital, London, UK.

Fig. 15.86
Behçet's disease: this field shows a superficial vulval ulcer with an intense neutrophilic infiltrate and changes of acute vasculitis.

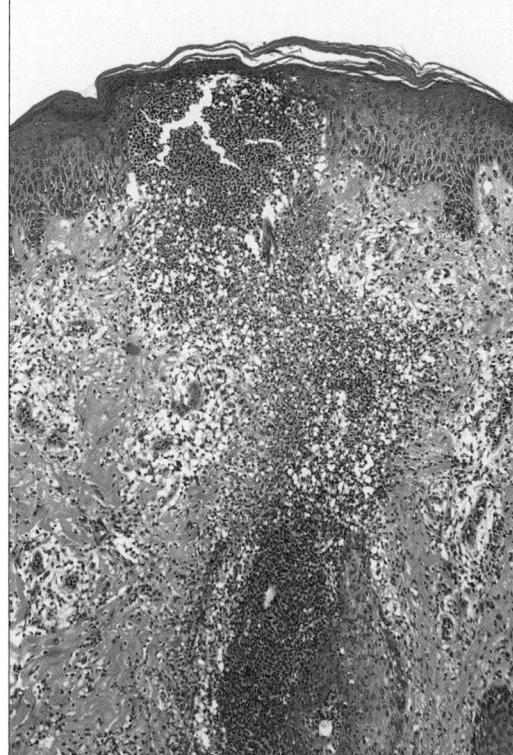

Fig. 15.87
Behçet's disease: there is florid suppurative acute folliculitis.

showed a neutrophilic infiltrate with intraepidermal pustules. Vasculitis was not seen in pathergic lesions in this study.[47] Other authors have found that the pathergic lesions may show leukocytoclastic vasculitis or Sweet's syndrome-like features.[17]

The erythema nodosum-like lesions correspond to necrotizing vasculitis of the subcutaneous vessels, usually associated with thrombosis. Septal and lobular panniculitis have also been described.[12] Superficial thrombophlebitis is present in up to 30% of patients (*Fig. 15.88*).[31] Oral lesions and genital ulcers show non-specific ulceration, accompanied in some instances by leukocytoclastic or lymphocytic vasculitis.

Pulmonary involvement is characterized by pulmonary artery vasculitis, sometimes also affecting the veins and capillaries.[26] Thrombosis, infarction, hemorrhage and the development of aneurysm are important sequelae. The inflammation is usually transmural and may be associated with damage to the associated elastic tissue. Older destructive vascular lesions are characterized by fibrous scarring.

Cerebral lesions in the early stage are characterized by a perivenular lymphocytic infiltrate. In the more advanced lesions there is extensive demyelination resembling multiple sclerosis.[22]

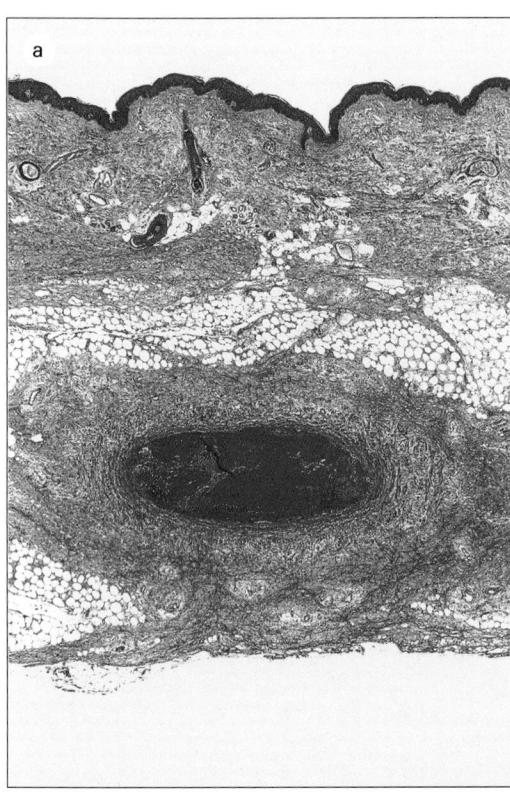

Fig. 15.88

(a, b) Behçet's disease: this section shows thrombophlebitis involving a vein in the subcutaneous fat. The vessel is infiltrated by large numbers of lymphocytes.

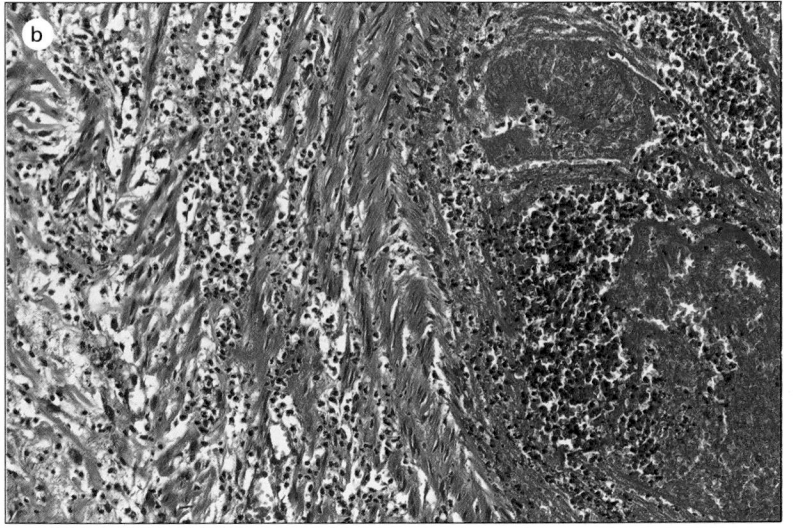

Differential diagnosis

Given the myriad non-specific histological manifestations that Behçet's disease may produce, it comes as no surprise that the histological differential diagnosis is usually broad. The authors of one large study stated that clinical data are most important in establishing a diagnosis and suggest that the role of biopsy is to confirm the clinical impression.[7] Other authors propose that biopsy is critical to evaluate for vessel-based pathology as clinical distinction from pustular (non-vascular) lesions may be important.[11] It is likely that the criteria for diagnosis of Behçet's disease will continue to be refined.

The differential diagnosis includes other causes of folliculitis, infection, erythema nodosum, connective tissue disease, neutrophilic and lymphocytic vasculitis, and neutrophilic dermatoses. There are no pathognomonic histological changes. Both clinical and pathological data must be considered before arriving at a final diagnosis.[7]

References

1. Chajeck, T., Fainaru, M. (1975) Behçet's disease: report of 41 cases and a review of the literature. *Medicine*, 54, 179–195.
2. Hombal, S.M., Ahmed, A.R. (1986) Behçet's disease. In: Thiers, B.H., Dobson, R.L. (eds) Pathogenesis of skin disease. New York: Churchill Livingstone, pp 257–265.
3. Helm, T.N., Camisa, C., Allen, C. et al (1991) Clinical features of Behçet's disease. *Oral Surg Oral Med Oral Pathol*, 72, 30–34.
4. International Study Group for Behçet's Disease (1990) Criteria for diagnosis of Behçet's disease. *Lancet*, 335, 1078–1080.
5. Jorizzo, J.L., Rogers, R.S. (1990) Behçet's disease: an update based on the International Conference held in Rochester, Minnesota, September, 14th and 15th 1989. *J Am Acad Dermatol*, 23, 738–741.
6. Shimizu, T., Ehrlich, G.E., Inaba, G. (1979) Behçet's disease (Behçet's syndrome). *Semin Arthritis Rheum*, 8, 223–260.
7. Balabanova, M., Calmia, K.T., Perniciaro, C. et al (1999) A study of the cutaneous manifestations of Behçet's disease in patients from the United States. *J Am Acad Dermatol*, 41, 540–545.
8. Kone-Paut, I., Yurdakul, S., Bahabri, S.A. et al (1999) Clinical features of Behçet's disease in children: an international collaborative study of 86 cases. *J Pediatr*, 132, 721–725.
9. Krause, I., Uziel, Y., Guedj, D. et al (1999) Childhood Behçet's disease in children: clinical features and comparison with adult-onset disease. *Rheumatology*, 38, 457–462.
10. Yazici, H., Basaran, G., Hamuryudan, V. et al (1996) The ten-year mortality in Behçet's syndrome. *Br J Rheumatol*, 35, 139–141.
11. Jorizzo, J.L., Abernathy, J.L., White, W.L. et al (1995) Mucocutaneous criteria for the diagnosis of Behçet's disease: an analysis of clinicopathologic data from multiple international centers. *J Am Acad Dermatol*, 32, 968–976.
12. Chajek, T., Fainaru, M. (1980) Behçet's disease. In: Parker, C.W. (ed.) Clinical immunology. Philadelphia: Saunders, p 667.
13. Krause, I., Rosen, Y., Kaplan, I. et al (1999) Recurrent aphthous stomatitis in Behçet's disease: clinical features and correlation with systemic disease expression and severity. *J Oral Pathol Med*, 28, 193–196.
14. Tokjoro, Y., Seto, T., Abe, Y. et al (1977) Skin lesions in Behçet's disease. *Int J Dermatol*, 16, 227–243.
15. Chun, S.I., Su, W.P.D., Lee, S. et al (1989) Erythema nodosum-like lesions in Behçet's syndrome: a histopathologic study of 30 cases. *J Cutan Pathol*, 16, 259–265.
16. Cho, K.H., Shin, K.S., Sohn, S.J. et al (1989) Behçet's disease with Sweet's syndrome-like presentation – a report of six cases. *Clin Exp Dermatol*, 14, 20–24.
17. Jorizzo, J.L., Solomon, A.R., Canallo, T. (1985) Behçet's syndrome: immunopathologic and histopathologic assessment of pathergy lesions is useful in diagnosis and follow-up. *Arch Pathol Lab Med*, 109, 747–751.
18. Sobel, J.D., Haim, S., Shafrir, A. et al (1973) Cutaneous hyperactivity in Behçet's disease. *Dermatologica*, 146, 350–356.
19. Mat, M.C., Nasarbaghi, M., Tuzun, Y. et al (1998) Wound healing in Behçet's disease. *Int J Dermatol*, 37, 120–123.
20. Masuda, K., Inaba, G., Mizushima, H. et al (1975) A nationwide survey of Behçet's disease in Japan. *Jpn J Ophthalmol*, 19, 278–285.
21. Yurdakul, S., Yazici, H., Tüzün, Y. et al (1983) The arthritis of Behçet's disease: a prospective study. *Ann Rheum Dis*, 42, 505–515.
22. O'Duffy, J.D. (1990) Vasculitis in Behçet's disease. *Rheum Dis Clin North Am*, 16, 423–431.
23. Koc, Y., Gullu, I., Akpek, G. et al (1992) Vascular involvement in Behçet's disease. *J Rheumatol*, 19, 402–410.
24. Saatci, I., Ozmen, M., Balkanci, F. et al (1993) Behçet's syndrome in the etiology of Budd–Chiari syndrome. *Angiology*, 44, 392–398.
25. Hamuryudan, V., Yurdakul, S., Numan, F. et al (1994) Pulmonary arterial aneurysms in Behçet's syndrome: a report of 24 cases. *Br J Rheumatol*, 33, 48–51.
26. Raz, I., Okon, E., Chajek-Shaul, T. (1989) Pulmonary manifestations in Behçet's syndrome. *Chest*, 95, 585–589.
27. Kasahara, Y., Tankaka, S., Nishino, M. et al (1981) Intestinal involvement in Behçet's disease: review of 136 surgical cases in the Japanese literature. *Dis Colon Rectum*, 24, 103–106.
28. Mori, S., Yoshihira, A., Kawamura, H. et al (1983) Esophageal involvement in Behçet's disease. *Am J Gastroenterol*, 78, 548–553.
29. Farah, S., Al-Shubaili, A., Montaser, A. et al (1998) Behçet's syndrome: a report of 41 cases with emphasis on neurological manifestations. *J Neurol Neurosurg Psychiatry*, 64, 382–384.
30. Akpolat, T., Akkoyunlu, M., Akpolat, I. et al (2002) Renal Behçet's disease: a cumulative analysis. *Semin Arthritis Rheum*, 31, 317–337.
31. Arbesfield, S.J., Kurban, A.K. (1988) Behçet's disease: new perspectives on an enigmatic syndrome. *J Am Acad Dermatol*, 19, 767–779.
32. Lehner, T., Barnes, C.G. (1979) Criteria for diagnosis and classification of Behçet's disease. In: Lehner, T., Barnes, C.G. (eds) Behçet's syndrome, clinical and immunological features. New York: Academic Press.
33. Kaneko, S., Suzuki, N., Yamashitka, N. et al (1997) Characterization of T cells specific for an epitope of human 60-kD heat shock protein in patients with Behçet's disease in Japan. *Clin Exp Immunol*, 108, 204–212.
34. Stanford, M.R., Kasp, E., Whiston, R. et al (1994) Heat shock protein peptides reactive in patients with Behçet's syndrome are uveitogenic in Lewis rats. *Clin Exp Immunol*, 97, 226–231.
35. Direskeneli, H., Eksioglu-Demiralp, E., Kibaroglu, A. et al (1999) Oligoclonal T cell expression in patients with Behçet's disease. *Clin Exp Immunol*, 117, 166–170.
36. Fassanito, M.A., Dammacco, R., Cafforio, R. et al (1999) Th1 polarization of the immune response in Behçet's disease: a putative pathogenetic role of interleukin-12. *Arthritis Rheum*, 42, 1967–1974.
37. Jorizzo, J.L. (1986) Behçet's disease: an update based on the 1985 conference in London. *Arch Dermatol*, 122, 556–558.

38. Sakane, T. (1989) Significance of immune abnormalities in the pathophysiology of Behçet's disease. Presented at the Fifth International Conference on Behçet's Disease, Rochester, Minnesota, pp 14–15.
39. Williams, B.D., Lehner, T. (1977) Immune complexes in Behçet's syndrome and recurrent oral ulceration. *BMJ*, 1, 1376–1377.
40. Levinsky, R.J., Lehner, T. (1978) Circulatory soluble immune complexes in recurrent oral ulceration and Behçet's syndrome. *Clin Exp Immunol*, 32, 193–198.
41. Eglin, R.P., Lehner, T., Subak-Sharpe, J.H. (1982) Detection of RNA complementary to herpes simplex virus in mononuclear cells from patients with Behçet's syndrome and recurrent oral ulcers. *Lancet*, 2, 1356–1358.
42. Chun, S.I., Su, W.P.D., Lee, S. (1990) Histopathologic study of cutaneous lesions in Behçet's syndrome. *J Dermatol*, 17, 333–341.

43. Chen, K., Kawahara, Y., Miyakawa, S. et al (1997) Cutaneous vasculitis in Behçet's disease: a clinical and histopathologic study of 20 patients. *J Am Acad Dermatol*, 36, 689–696.
44. Magro, C.M., Crowson, A.N. (1995) Cutaneous manifestations of Behçet's disease. *Int J Dermatol*, 34, 159–165.
45. Magro, C.M., Crowson, A.N. (1998) Sterile neutrophilic folliculitis with perifollicular vasculopathy: a distinctive cutaneous reaction pattern reflecting systemic disease. *J Cutan Pathol*, 25, 215–221.
46. Ergun, T., Gurbuz, O., Dogusoy, G. et al (1998) Histopathologic features of the spontaneous pustular lesions of Behçet's syndrome. *Int J Dermatol*, 37, 194–196.
47. Ergun, T., Gurbuz, O., Harvell, J. et al (1998) The histopathology of pathergy: a chronologic study of skin hyperreactivity in Behçet's disease. *Int J Dermatol*, 37, 929–933.

Thromboangiitis obliterans

Clinical features

Thromboangiitis obliterans (Buerger's disease) is most often seen in young adults and is much more common in males than in females.[1] However, the ratio of men to women is shifting with the disease becoming more common in women.[2] In one large study, 23% of patients were female.[2] In addition, the disease is seen more frequently in older patients.[2] Buerger's disease occurs almost exclusively in smokers. Although most patients are considered 'heavy' smokers, some smoke less than a pack of cigarettes a day.[3] In fact, some authors view a history of smoking a necessary criterion for diagnosis. In one study from Japan, non-smokers with Buerger's disease were more likely to be women.[4] In Bangladesh, smoking bidis (a hand-rolled, additive-free, unprocessed form of tobacco) is particularly associated with Buerger's disease.[5]

The worldwide incidence of Buerger's disease differs dramatically from region to region. For example, the incidence is 50-fold greater in Nepal compared with North America.[6] This disease has its highest prevalence in Eastern Europe, the Middle East and Asia. Patients most often present with painful cyanotic lesions of the extremities, especially the fingers or toes, which may ulcerate and become gangrenous (*Fig. 15.89*). Sensitivity to cold is a common complaint.

Resolution of disease usually follows cessation of smoking.[7,8] Patients who continue to smoke suffer autoamputation of digits and distal extremities. In one study, only 2% of patients who quit smoking had amputations. In contrast, 42% of those that continued to smoke required amputation.[2]

In most patients, the disease is limited to the extremities; however, some patients develop visceral involvement,[9–12] and this may prove fatal.[9] The vessels of the brain, intestine, heart, kidney and lung may therefore be affected.[13,14] Occasional patients have involvement of multiple organs.[15]

Pathogenesis and histological features

The pathogenesis of Buerger's disease is poorly understood. Clearly, the strong association with smoking suggests that this habit plays an important role in eliciting thrombosis and resultant ischemia.[16] It is unclear if tobacco products are toxic to endothelial cells or elicit immune reactions that damage vessels. Of interest, the disease may be seen in patients who use smokeless tobacco.[17] Antiendothelial antibodies are elevated in a subset of patients with Buerger's disease.[18] Furthermore, disease activity correlates with antiendothelial cell antibody titers.[18] Response to acetylcholine, an endothelium-dependent vasodilator, is diminished in 'non-diseased' extremities of Buerger's patients compared with control subjects.[19] IgG, IgM and IgA are present along the internal elastic lamina.[20]

Lesions are characterized by thrombosis of small or medium-sized arteries and, less commonly, veins associated with a variable inflammatory infiltrate composed of a mixture of neutrophils, lymphocytes, eosinophils, histiocytes and giant cells.[16,21] Immunohistochemical studies have confirmed the heterogeneous nature of the infiltrate. T-cells, B-cells, macrophages and dendritic cells may all be present.[20] A characteristic finding is the presence of a microabscess associated with an intraluminal thrombus. Inflammatory cells may be seen in all layers of the vessel wall (*Fig. 15.90*). Preservation of the internal elastic lamina is a characteristic feature.[16]

As lesions age, thrombi become organized and are replaced by fibrosis, and eventually the vessel is recanalized (*Fig. 15.91*). A definitive diagnosis based on biopsy findings is not possible during the later stages of organization.

Differential diagnosis

The histopathological features are probably not specific for Buerger's disease and differential diagnosis includes other thrombotic vasculopathies. Clinical correlation is advised before rendering a definitive diagnosis. Preservation of the internal elastic lamina is a characteristic feature and is said to help in distinction from other vasculitides.[16,22]

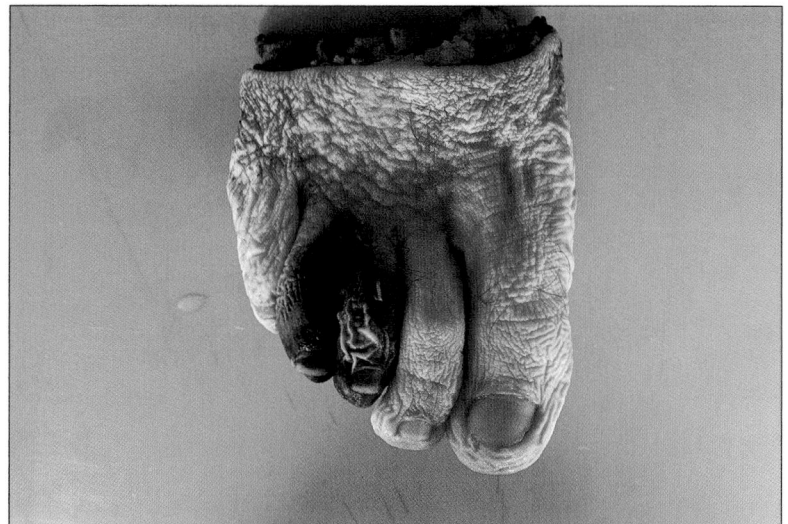

Fig. 15.89
Buerger's disease: digital gangrene is present in this amputation specimen.

References

1. Lie, J.T. (1987) Thromboangiitis obliterans (Buerger's disease) in women. *Medicine*, 66, 65–72.
2. Olin, J.W., Young, J.R., Graor, R.A. et al (1990) The changing clinical spectrum of thromboangiitis obliterans (Buerger's disease). *Circulation*, 82, 3–8.
3. Stone, J.H., Calabrese, L.H., Hoffman, G.S. et al (2001) Vasculitis. A collection of pearls and myths. *Rheum Dis Clin North Am*, 27, 677–728.
4. Sasaki, S., Sakuma, M., Kunihara, T. et al (1999) Current trends in thromboangiitis obliterans (Buerger's disease) in women. *Am J Surg*, 177, 316–320.
5. Rashman, M., Chowdhury, A.S., Fukui, T. et al (2000) Association of thromboangiitis obliterans with cigarette and bidi smoking in Bangladesh: a case control study. *Int J Epidemiol*, 29, 266–270.
6. Fleshman, K. (1998) Buerger's disease in Nepal. *Trop Doct*, 28, 203–206.
7. Buerger, L. (1998) Thromboangiitis obliterans: a study of the vascular lesions leading to presenile spontaneous gangrene. *Am J Med Sci*, 136, 567–580.
8. Joyce, J.W. (1990) Buerger's disease (thromboangiitis obliterans). *Rheum Dis Clin North Am*, 16, 463–470.
9. Lie, J.T. (1998) Visceral intestinal Buerger's disease. *Int J Cardiol*, 66, 249–256.
10. Deitch, E.A., Sikkema, W.W. (1981) Intestinal manifestation of Buerger's disease: case report and literature review. *Am Surg*, 47, 326–328.
11. Hassoun, Z., Lacrosse, M., De Ronde, T. (2001) Intestinal involvement in Buerger's disease. *J Clin Gastroenterol*, 32, 85–89.
12. Iwai, T. (1998) Buerger's disease with intestinal involvement. *Int J Cardiol*, 66, 257–263.
13. Becit, N., Unlu, Y., Kocak, H. et al (2002) Involvement of the coronary artery in a patient with thromboangiitis obliterans: a case report. *Heart Vessels*, 16, 201–203.
14. Bischof, F., Kuntz, R., Melms, A. et al (1999) Cerebral vein thrombosis in a case with thromboangiitis obliterans. *Cerebrovasc Dis*, 9, 295–297.

15. Harten, P., Muller-Huelsbeck, S., Regensburger, D. et al (1996) Multiple organ manifestations of thromboangiitis obliterans (Buerger's disease): a case report. *Angiology*, 47, 419–425.
16. Olin, J.W. (2000) Thromboangiitis obliterans (Buerger's disease). *N Engl J Med*, 343, 864–869.
17. Lie, J.T. (1988) Thromboangiitis obliterans (Buerger's disease) and smokeless tobacco. *Arthritis Rheum*, 31, 812–813.
18. Eichhorn, J., Sima, D., Lindchau, C. et al (1998) Antiendothelial cell antibodies in thromboangiitis obliterans. *Am J Med Sci*, 315, 17–23.
19. Makita, S., Nakamura, M., Murakami, H. et al (1996) Impaired endothelium-dependent vasorelaxation in peripheral vasculature of patients with thromboangiitis obliterans (Buerger's disease). *Circulation*, 94, 211–215.
20. Kobayashi, M., Ito, M., Nakagawa, A. et al (1999) Immunohistochemical analysis of arterial wall cellular infiltration in Buerger's disease (endarteritis obliterans). *J Vasc Surg*, 29, 451–458.
21. Shionoya, S. (1975) Pathology of Buerger's disease, clinico-pathico-angiographic correlation. *Pathol Microbiol*, 43, 163–166.
22. Kurata, A., Franke, F.E., Machinami, R. et al (2000) Thromboangiitis obliterans: classic and new morphologic features. *Virchows Arch*, 436, 59–67.

Temporal arteritis

Clinical features

Temporal arteritis (giant cell arteritis) is a disease of the elderly that shows a marked female predominance (3:1).[1] It is a generalized vasculitis that predominantly affects large and medium-sized arteries.[2] It is mainly seen in Caucasians and its etiology is unknown.[2]

Five of the American College of Rheumatology 1990 criteria are outlined in *Table 15.9*.[1] Classically, the temporal arteries are primarily affected, but giant cell arteritis may also affect the occipital or facial arteries and, in fact, has the potential to involve virtually any medium-sized or large vessel, including the aorta and its branches.[2] Patients with giant cell arteritis present with pyrexia, severe headache and throbbing scalp pain. Clinical examination may reveal scalp tenderness and the skin overlying the affected vessel may be erythematous, edematous or appear bruised.[3] Palpation often reveals a cord-like and nodular vessel. Pulsation may be diminished or absent.

Visual disturbance due to involvement of the ophthalmic or retinal vessels is an important complication and sometimes results in blindness. Lesions of the central nervous system may result in stroke, subarachnoid hemorrhage or mental confusion, and aural involvement can result in deafness. In one large study, neurological problems were present in nearly one-third of patients.[4] Peripheral neuropathic syndromes are evident in 14% of patients.[3] Often the associated lymph nodes are enlarged and tender. Symptoms of polymyalgia rheumatica (i.e. stiffness, weakness, aching and pain in the muscles of the neck, limb girdles and upper limbs) are extremely common, occurring in up to 75% of patients.[5] Laboratory investigations typically reveal mild anemia, neutrophilia and a very high ESR. Elevated levels of von Willebrand factor are characteristic.[6]

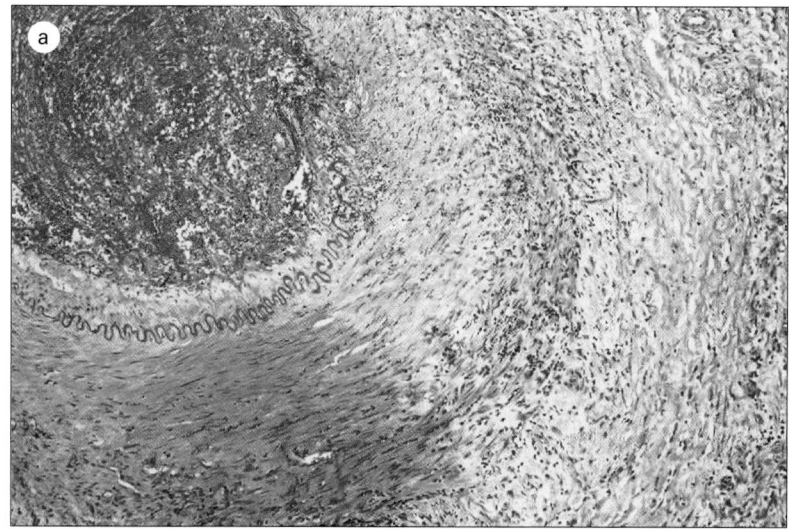
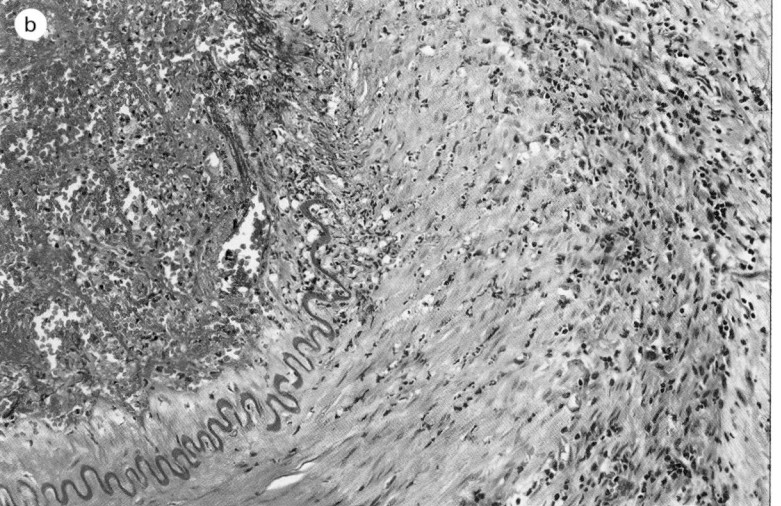

Fig. 15.90
(a, b) Buerger's disease: this acute lesion shows pan-mural inflammation with abscess formation and thrombosis.

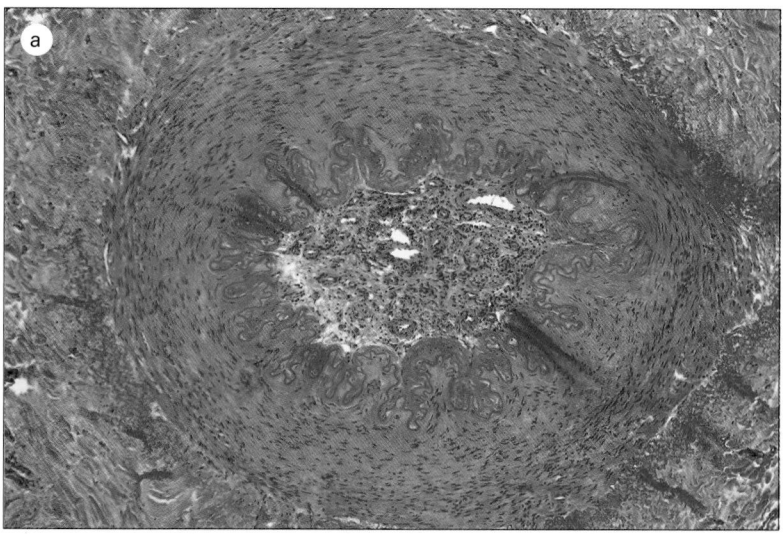
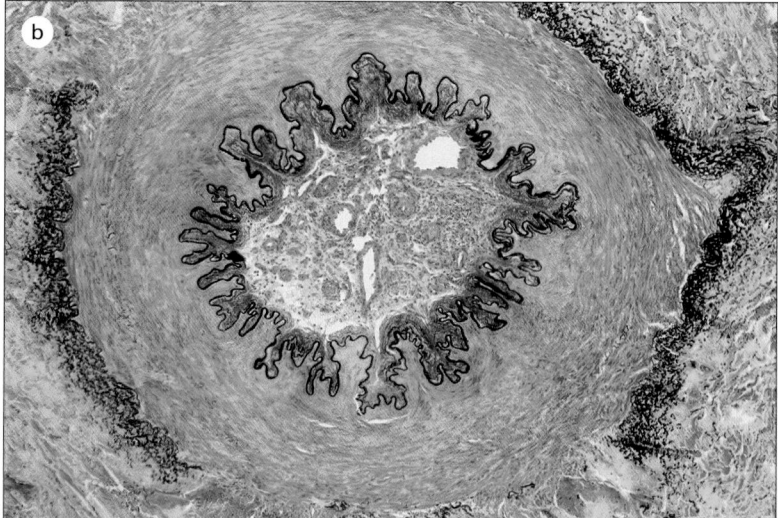

Fig. 15.91
(a, b) Buerger's disease: old lesion showing luminal obliteration and recanalization. Note the intact elastic lamina.

Cutaneous lesions other than those mentioned above are uncommon, presumably reflecting the vast collateral circulation of the integument.[7,8] Patients may occasionally manifest ulcers (sometimes quite widespread), massive necrosis, bullae and gangrene (*Fig. 15.92*). Involvement of the lingual artery can cause glossitis or gangrene of the tongue. Masticatory claudication is an additional feature.

Rare patients with disseminated visceral arteritis with giant cell arteritis-like histological features have been described.[9] The heart, lungs, kidneys, stomach, pancreas and liver may be involved.[9] It is debatable what terminology should be applied to such rare and unusual cases.

Life expectancy does not seem to be adversely affected by having temporal arteritis.[10]

The vast majority of patients have an elevated ESR.[11] C-reactive protein is also typically elevated.[11] Elevated levels of anticardiolipin antibodies are frequently present.[12-15] Some studies suggest that the presence of anticardiolipin antibodies correlates with more severe

Table 15.9

1990 criteria for the classification of giant cell (temporal) arteritis (traditional format)*

Criterion	Definition
Age at disease onset ≥ 50 years	Development of symptoms or findings beginning at age 50 or older
New headache	New onset of or new type of localized pain in the head
Temporal artery abnormality	Temporal artery tenderness to palpation or decreased pulsation, unrelated to arteriosclerosis of cervical arteries
Elevated ESR	ESR ≥ 50 mm/hour by the Westergren method
Abnormal artery biopsy	Biopsy specimen with artery showing vasculitis characterized by a predominance of mononuclear cell infiltration or granulomatous inflammation, usually with multinucleated giant cells

*For purposes of classification, a patient shall be said to have giant cell (temporal) arteritis if at least three of these five criteria are present. The presence of any three or more criteria yields a sensitivity of 93.5% and a specificity of 91.2%. Reproduced with permission from Hunder, G.G. (1990) *Arthritis and Rheumatism*, **33**, 1122–1128.

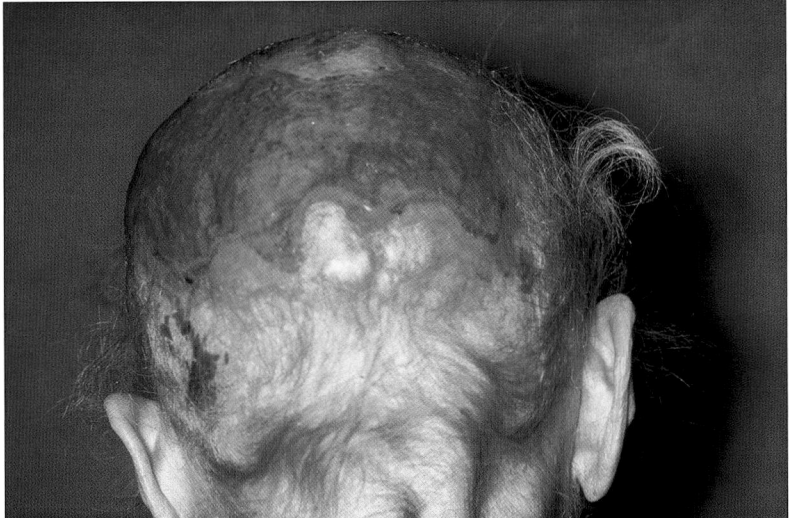

Fig. 15.92
Giant cell arteritis: severe ischemic necrosis with ulceration has destroyed most of this patient's scalp. By courtesy of D. McGibbon, MD, St Thomas' Hospital, London, UK.

vascular damage.[14,15] In most patients, anticardiolipin antibody titers return to normal range with steroid therapy.[13]

Pathogenesis and histological features

The pathogenesis of temporal arteritis is poorly understood. Although an immunological mechanism has been suggested, it has not been proven. Evidence of familial aggregation and an increased incidence of the HLA-DR4 antigen have raised the possibility of a genetic influence.[2] However, consistent reproducible HLA associations have not been demonstrated in all populations.

It has been suggested that giant cell arteritis is an autoimmune disease perhaps directed, at least in part, against the vascular elastic lamina.[2] T-cells in the infiltrate are predominantly of the helper subclass and expression of HLA-DR has been recorded, thereby suggesting that they are activated.[2] The lymphocytes have been shown to respond to antibodies against transferrin and IL-2 receptors.[16] Proliferation of mononuclear cells following incubation in cultures containing elastin-derived peptides is increased compared with control subjects.[17] This finding suggests elastin-derived peptides are the targets of T-cells in giant cell arteritis.[17] Disease activity has been shown to correlate with plasma concentrations of IL-6.[18]

The demonstration by some authors of a fluctuating cyclical pattern of incidence has raised the possibility of an infectious agent or other triggering factor playing a significant pathogenetic role.[19-21] A study from the Mayo Clinic showed a variation in incidence with peak periods occurring approximately every 7 years.[19] Similarly, a study from Denmark demonstrated marked variation in the incidence of temporal arteritis with five peak periods.[21] Of these, there appeared to be association with two epidemics of *Mycoplasma pneumoniae* infection, two possibly related to erythrovirus (parvovirus) B19 epidemics and one peak that may have been related to an epidemic of *Chlamydia pneumoniae*.[21] Another study showed a three-fold increased likelihood of infection in patients with temporal arteritis compared with control subjects.[22] An association between temporal arteritis and antibodies to parainfluenza type 1 has been demonstrated.[23,24] Despite these observations, the precise triggering factors and the pathogenesis of temporal arteritis remain unclear.

The lesions of giant cell arteritis are typically focal in distribution; therefore, the vessel should be carefully palpated to find an obviously affected segment before a biopsy is undertaken. Even then, false negatives are not uncommon (see below). The lesion is granulomatous in nature and may affect only part or the whole circumference of the vessel wall (*Fig. 15.93*).[25] The infiltrate, which particularly affects the intima and media, is composed of lymphocytes, plasma cells, histiocytes and variable numbers of giant cells of both foreign body and Langhans' type (*Fig. 15.94*). Giant cells may sometimes be relatively sparse and multiple levels may have to be examined before they are identified. On some occasions, they are absent. Typical of giant cell arteritis is damage to the internal elastic lamina, which appears swollen and fragmented, and portions may be identified within the cytoplasm of giant cells (*Fig. 15.95*).[3]

A second, less common form consists of a pan-arteritis composed of lymphocytes, macrophages, neutrophils and eosinophils but giant cells are not present. Varying degrees of vessel wall necrosis are evident and the vessel is often thrombosed.

In the late stages of the disease, fibrous scarring takes place and a reconstituted, often multilayered, internal elastic lamina may be identified. In cases of doubt an elastic tissue stain can prove invaluable. The thrombus may on occasions be recanalized.

It is crucial to note that patients with classic symptoms of temporal arteritis may have a negative biopsy, most likely due to the multifocal nature of the arteritis and sampling bias. In one study, 44% of patients who were regarded as having clinical manifestations of temporal arteritis, which improved with steroid treatment, had negative biopsies.[26] Therefore, a negative biopsy does not necessarily exclude this disease. Given the consequences of delayed or no treatment, it is often necessary to treat selected patients even without definitive biopsy diagnosis. One study found that patients with temporal arteritis who have constitutional symptoms or an abnormal temporal artery detected by physical examination are more likely to have a positive biopsy.[27] Doppler flow studies may be used to improve the sensitivity of biopsy.[28] Given the multifocal nature of giant cell arteritis, the diagnostic yield, not surprisingly, is likely improved with longer artery length obtained by biopsy and increased number of sections examined.[29]

Differential diagnosis

The histological findings are identical to those seen in some patients with Takayasu's disease, another form of giant cell arteritis. Careful clinical correlation is required to distinguish these conditions and since overlap exists, many cases are not easily subclassified. Some authors consider these diseases form part of a continuum of giant cell vasculitis, with patient age being an important discriminator: patients under age 40 are more likely to have Takayasu's arteritis; those over 50 are more likely to have temporal arteritis.

It should be noted that fragmentation of the internal elastic lamina may result from either age-related changes or atherosclerosis and these conditions may be difficult to distinguish from healed arteritis. The presence of medial scarring is suggestive of temporal arteritis. The extent of destruction, particularly confluent loss of the internal elastic lamina, is said to correlate with probability of healed arteritis.[5]

References

1. Hunder, G.G., Bloch, D.A., Michel, B.A. et al (1990) The American College of Rheumatology 1990 criteria for the classification of giant cell arteritis. *Arthritis Rheum*, 33, 1122–1128.
2. Bengtsson, B.A., Andersson, R. (1991) Giant cell and Takayasu's arteritis. *Curr Opin Rheumatol*, 3, 15–22.
3. Hunder, G.G. (1990) Giant cell (temporal) arteritis. *Rheum Dis Clin North Am*, 16, 399–409.
4. Caselli, R.H., Hunder, G.G., Whisnant, J.P. (1988) Neurologic disease in biopsy-proven giant cell (temporal) arteritis. *Neurology*, 38, 352–359.
5. Weidner, N. (2001) Giant cell arteritis. *Semin Diagn Pathol*, 18, 24–33.

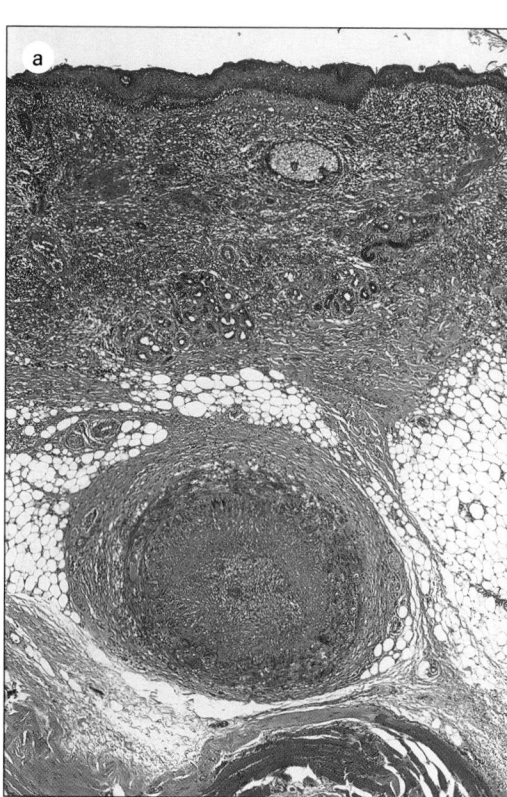

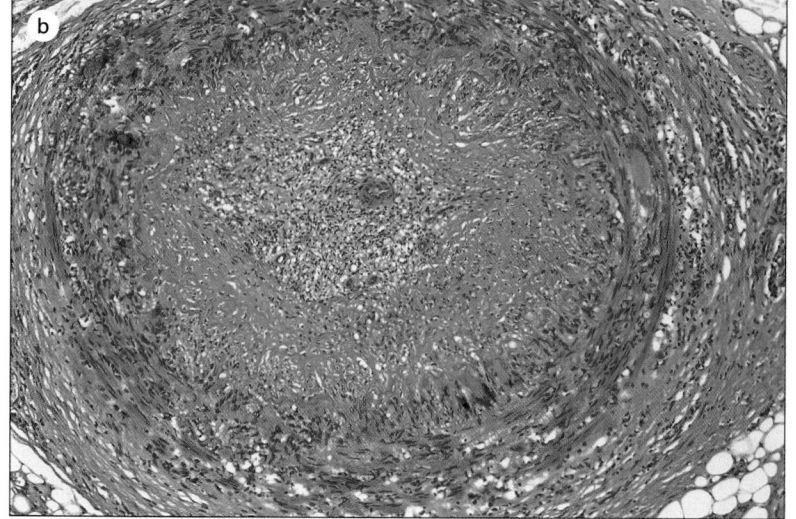

Fig. 15.93
(a, b) Giant cell arteritis: this scalp biopsy showed multiple affected vessels. By courtesy of P.A. Burton, MD, Southmead Hospital, Bristol, UK.

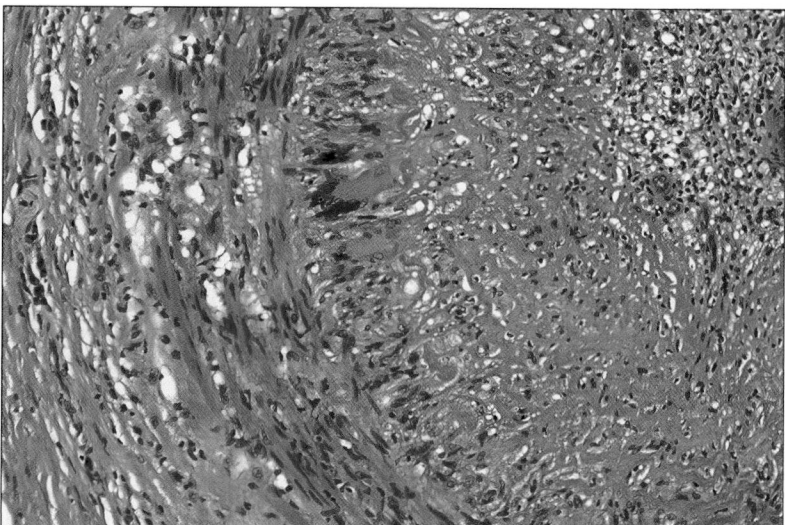

Fig. 15.94
Giant cell arteritis: the intima and media are infiltrated by a dense chronic inflammatory cell infiltrate containing conspicuous Langhans' giant cells. By courtesy of P.A. Burton, MD, Southmead Hospital, Bristol, UK.

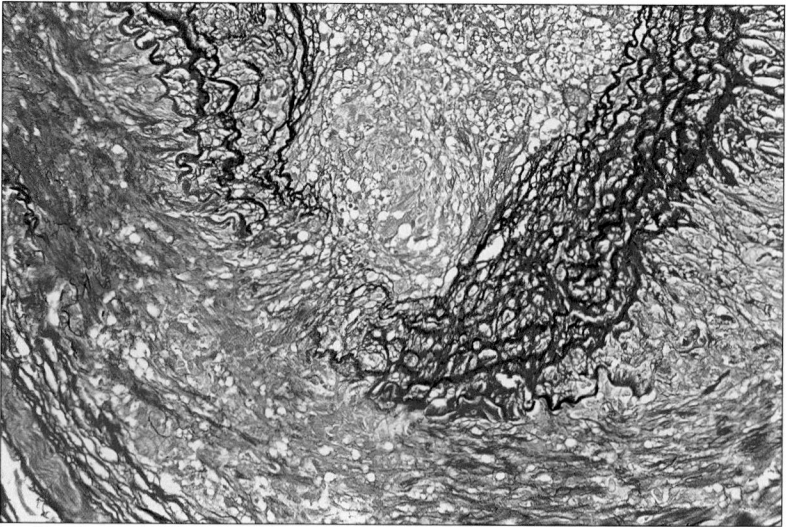

Fig. 15.95
Giant cell arteritis: there is fragmentation of the internal elastic lamina. By courtesy of P.A. Burton, MD, Southmead Hospital, Bristol, UK.

6. Nordborg, E., Andersson, R., Tengborn, L. et al (1991) Von Willebrand factor antigen and plasminogen activator inhibitor in giant cell arteritis. *Ann Rheum Dis*, 50, 316–320.
7. Hitch, J.M. (1970) Dermatologic manifestations of giant-cell (temporal, cranial) arteritis. *Arch Dermatol*, 101, 409–415.
8. Kinmont, P.D.C., McCallum, D.I. (1964) Skin manifestations of temporal arteritis. *Br J Dermatol*, 76, 299–308.
9. Lie, J.T. (1978) Disseminated visceral giant cell arteritis: histopathologic description and differentiation from other granulomatous vasculitides. *Am J Clin Pathol*, 69, 299–305.
10. Matteson, E.L., Gold, K.N., Bloch, D.A. et al (1996) Long-term survival of patients with giant cell arteritis in the American College of Rheumatology giant cell arteritis classification report. *Am J Med*, 100, 193–196.
11. Mykleburst, G., Gran, J.T. (1996) A prospective study of 287 patients with polymyalgia rheumatica and temporal arteritis: clinical and laboratory manifestations at the onset of disease and at the time of diagnosis. *Br J Rheumatol*, 35, 1161–1168.
12. Duhaut, P., Derruyer, M., Pinede, L. et al (1998) Anticardiolipin antibodies and giant cell arteritis: a prospective multicenter case study. *Arthritis Rheum*, 41, 701–709.
13. Kerleau, J.M., Levesque, H., Delpech, A. et al (1994) Prevalence and evolution of anticardiolipin antibodies during corticosteroid therapy. A prospective study of 20 cases. *Br J Rheumatol*, 33, 648–650.
14. Espinoza, L.R., Jara, L.J., Silveira, L.H. et al (1991) Anticardiolipin antibodies in polymyalgia rheumatica–giant cell arteritis: association with severe vascular complications. *Am J Med*, 90, 474–478.
15. Chakravarty, K., Pountain, G., Merry, P. et al (1996) A longitudinal study of anticardiolipin antibody in polymyalgia rheumatica and giant cell arteritis. *J Rheumatol*, 22, 1694–1697.
16. Andersson, R., Jonsson, R., Tarkowski, A. et al (1987) T-cell subsets and expression of immunological activation markers in the arteries of patients with giant cell arteritis. *Ann Rheum Dis*, 46, 915–923.
17. Gillot, J.M., Masy, E., Davril, M. et al (1997) Elastase derived peptides: putative targets in giant cell arteritis. *J Rheumatol*, 24, 677–682.
18. Roche, N.E., Fulbright, J.W., Wagner, A.D. et al (1993) Correlation of interleukin-6 production and disease activity in polymyalgia rheumatica and giant cell arteritis. *Arthritis Rheum*, 36, 1286–1294.
19. Salvarani, C., Gabriel, S.E., O'Fallon, W.M. et al (1995) The incidence of giant cell arteritis in Olmsted County, Minnesota: apparent fluctuations in a cyclic pattern. *Ann Intern Med*, 123, 192–194.
20. Petursdottir, V., Johansson, H., Nordborg, E. et al (1999) The epidemiology of biopsy-positive giant cell arteritis: special reference to cyclic fluctuation. *Rheumatology*, 38, 1208–1212.
21. Elling, P., Olsson, A.T., Elling, H. (1996) Synchronous variations of the incidence of temporal arteritis and polymyalgia rheumatica in different regions of Denmark; association with epidemics of Mycoplasma infection. *J Rheumatol*, 23, 112–119.
22. Russo, M.G., Waxman, J., Abdoh, A.A. et al (1995) Correlation between infection and the onset of giant cell (temporal) arteritis syndrome. A trigger mechanism. *Arthritis Rheum*, 38, 374–380.
23. Duhaut, P., Bosshard, S., Dumontet, C. (2000) Giant cell arteritis and polymyalgia rheumatica: role of viral infections. *Clin Exp Rheumatol*, 18, 22–23.
24. Duhaut, P., Bosshard, S., Calvet, A. et al (1999) Giant cell arteritis, polymyalgia rheumatica, and viral hypotheses: a multicenter, prospective case-control study. *J Rheumatol*, 26, 361–369.
25. Kinmont, P.D.C., McCallum, D.I. (1965) The aetiology, pathology and course of giant-cell arteritis. *Br J Dermatol*, 77, 193–202.
26. Allsop, C.J., Gallagher, P.J. (1981) Temporal artery biopsy in giant-cell arteritis. A reappraisal. *Am J Surg Pathol*, 5, 317–323.
27. Gonzalez-Gay, M.A., Garcia-Porrua, C., Llorca, J. et al (2001) Biopsy-negative giant cell arteritis: clinical spectrum and predictive factors for positive artery biopsy. *Semin Arthritis Rheum*, 30, 249–256.
28. Ponge, T., Barrier, J.H., Grolleau, J.Y. et al (1988) The efficacy of selective unilateral temporal artery biopsy versus bilateral biopsies for diagnosis of temporal arteritis. *J Rheumatol*, 15, 997–1000.
29. Nordborg, E., Norborg, C. (1995) The influence of sectional interval on the reliability of temporal artery biopsy in polymyalgia rheumatica. *Clin Rheumatol*, 14, 330–334.

Takayasu's arteritis

Clinical features

Takayasu's arteritis (pulseless disease, giant cell arteritis) is a rare granulomatous disease that predominantly affects the aorta and its major branches and results in vascular stenoses with bruits and diminished or absent pulses (hence the term 'pulseless disease').[1,2] Aneurysm formation may be an additional feature. It predominantly affects females (7:1), most often involves the upper limbs, and usually presents in the second or third decade. Although most patients are young adults, the disease is also seen in children.[3,4] It is rare in Europe and the United States, occurring more often in Japan, China, Korea, Southeast Asia, India and Mexico.[2] It appears to have two stages:
1. an acute systemic illness characterized by fever, malaise, arthralgias, myalgias and ocular lesions including uveitis and episcleritis
2. a chronic stage of large vessel involvement.[5]

Current diagnostic criteria are shown in *Table 15.10*. In addition to the obligatory criterion, the presence of two major criteria, one major plus two or more minor, or four or more minor criteria, is associated with a high probability of Takayasu's arteritis.[6]

Cutaneous manifestations have been described in up to 50% of patients and include Raynaud's syndrome (due to large vessel involvement), acute inflammatory nodules and erythema nodosum-like features (particularly in Europe and North America), pyoderma gangrenosum-like lesions (especially in the Japanese), pseudoerythema induratum, superficial phlebitis, tuberculid eruptions and purpura (*Fig. 15.96*).[5,7,8] Patients may present with cutaneous necrotizing vasculitis.[8]

Cases have been reported describing an overlap between Takayasu's arteritis and polyarteritis nodosa.[6] Rare patients with a lupus-like malar flush and an urticarial reaction with livedo reticularis have been documented.[7] Renal artery involvement with stenosis causes severe hypertension secondary to renin secretion. Stroke due to severe hypertension is a serious complication in some patients.

Pathogenesis and histological features

The etiology and pathogenesis of Takayasu's arteritis is poorly understood. Occasionally, other diseases are seen in association with Takayasu's arteritis including tuberculosis, inflammatory bowel disease, polymyositis, sarcoidosis and rheumatoid arthritis.[1,5,9–11] Co-expression with polyarteritis nodosa raises the possibility of an autoimmune phenomenon.[12]

The diagnosis is usually made by clinical and radiological correlation; however, in some cases tissue is examined by the pathologist. The histological features are variable and include granulomatous vasculitis indistinguishable from giant cell arteritis, leukocytoclastic vasculitis, lymphocytic vasculitis and polyarteritis nodosa-like features (*Figs 15.97, 15.98*).[5–7,12,13]

Septal and lobular panniculitis with granulomatous vasculitis may be the underlying histology of erythematous nodules and erythema nodosum-like lesions.[7] Features of Churg–Strauss granulomata have also been reported.[5]

Differential diagnosis

As can be seen from the above discussion, several different patterns of vasculitis may be encountered in Takayasu's arteritis. Furthermore, the histological findings seen in this disease may be identical to other forms of vasculitis. Therefore, careful clinical and radiological correlation is necessary to establish the correct diagnosis.

Table 15.10
Takayasu's arteritis: diagnostic criteria

• Obligatory criterion   – age < 40 years

• Major criteria
  – left mid subclavian artery lesion
  – right mid subclavian artery lesion

• Minor criteria
  – high ESR
  – carotid artery tenderness
  – hypertension
  – aortic regurgitation or annuloaortic ectasia
  – pulmonary artery lesion
  – left mid common carotid lesion
  – distal brachiocephalic trunk lesion
  – descending thoracic aorta lesion
  – abdominal aorta lesion

Reproduced with permission from Bentsson, B.A. and Anderson, T. (1991) *Current Opinion in Rheumatology*, **3**, 15–22.

References

1. Lupi-Herrera, E., Sánchez-Torres, G., Marcushamer, J. et al (1977) Takayasu's arteritis: clinical study of 107 cases. *Am Heart J*, 93, 94–103.
2. Hall, S., Barr, W., Lie, J.T. et al (1985) Takayasu arteritis: a study of 32 North American patients. *Medicine (Baltimore)*, 64, 89–99.
3. Hong, C.Y., Yun, Y.S., Choi, J.Y. et al (1992) Takayasu arteritis in Korean children: clinical report of seventy cases. *Heart Vessels*, 7, 91–96.

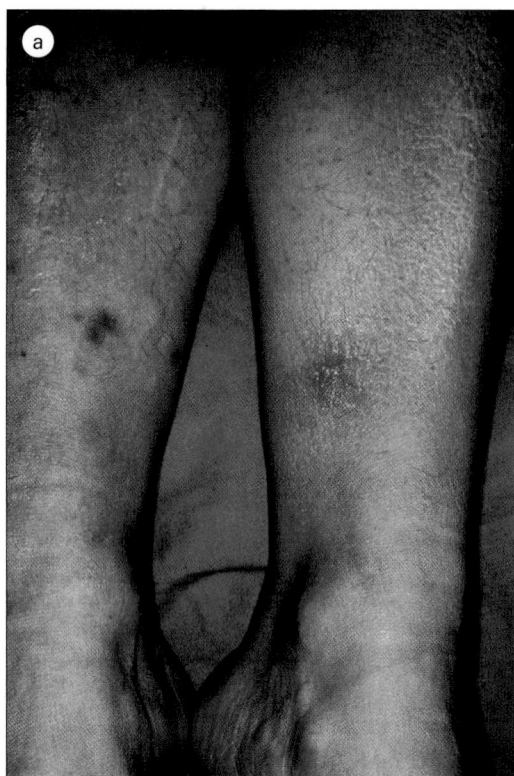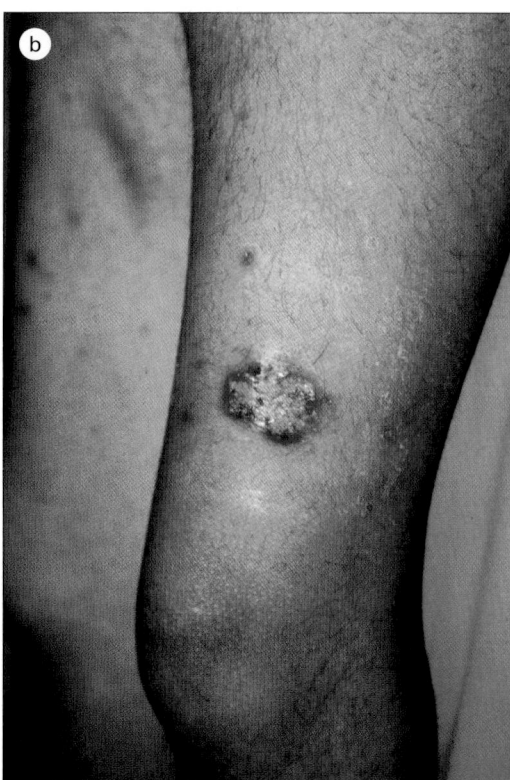

Fig. 15.96
Takayasu's arteritis: (a) this patient presented with multiple lesions as seen here on the lower legs; (b) a large ulcerated inflammatory nodule is present on the left thigh. By courtesy of P. Godeau, MD, and C. Francès, MD, Groupe Hospitalier, Pitié-Salpêtrière, Paris, France.

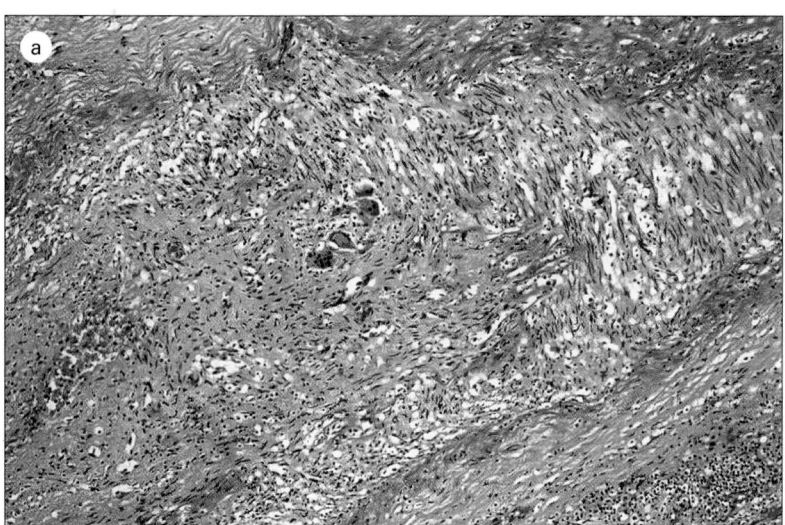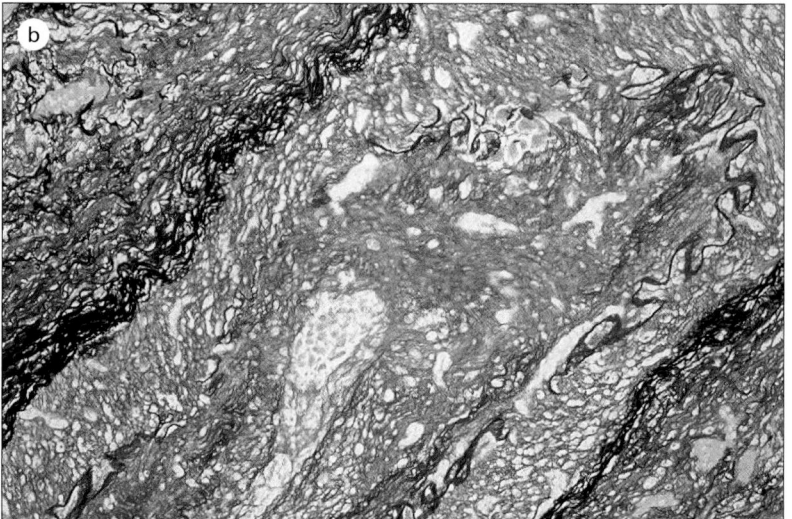

Fig. 15.97
(a, b) Takayasu's arteritis: this occluded artery was present with a thickened septum of the subcutaneous fat from the thigh of a young woman.

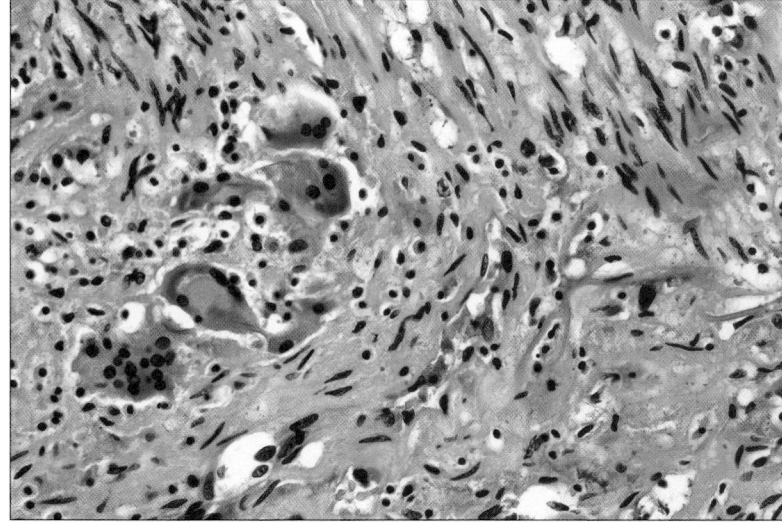

Fig. 15.98
Takayasu's arteritis: high power view showing granulomatous inflammation. The features are indistinguishable from giant cell arteritis.

4. Sharma, B.K., Sagar, S., Singh, A.P. et al (1992) Takayasu arteritis in India. *Heart Vessels*, **7**, 37–43.
5. Perniciaro, C.V., Winkelmann, R.K., Hunder, G.G. (1987) Cutaneous manifestations of Takayasu's arteritis. *J Am Acad Dermatol*, **17**, 998–1005.
6. Bengtsson, B-A., Andersson, R. (1991) Giant cell and Takayasu's arteritis. *Curr Opin Rheumatol*, **3**, 15–22.
7. Frances, C., Boisnic, S., Blétry, O. et al (1990) Cutaneous manifestations of Takayasu arteritis. *Dermatologica*, **181**, 266–272.
8. Skaria, A.M., Ruffieux, P., Piletta, P. et al (2000) Takayasu arteritis and cutaneous necrotizing vasculitis. *Dermatology*, **200**, 139–143.
9. Sharma, B.K., Jain, S., Sagar, S. (1996) Systemic manifestations of Takayasu arteritis: the expanding spectrum. *Int J Cardiol*, **54**, 149–154.
10. Schapiro, J.M., Shiptzer, S., Pinhas, J. et al (1994) Sarcoidosis as the initial manifestation of Takayasu arteritis. *J Med*, **25**, 121–128.
11. Ishii, U., Aoki, N., Nakayama, H. et al (2002) Ulcerative colitis associated with Takayasu's disease in two patients who received proctocolectomy. *J Gastroenterol*, **37**, 297–302.
12. Cajigas, J.C., Amigo, M.C., Pineda, C. et al (1987) Association between Takayasu's arteritis and cutaneous polyarteritis nodosa. *Am J Med*, **82**, 382–384.
13. Moussa, A.R.M., Marafie, A.A., Dajani, A. (1985) Cutaneous necrotizing vasculitis complicating Takayasu arteritis with a review of cutaneous manifestations. *J Rheumatol*, **12**, 607–610.

Infection-related vasculitis

Infection must be considered in the evaluation of many forms of vasculitis, particularly leukocytoclastic vasculitis. Infective vasculitis may be caused by a wide variety of agents including bacteria, fungi, protozoa, viruses, spirochetes and rickettsiae (*Table 15.11*). The relationship between particular microorganisms and vascular lesions is covered under the specific infection in Chapter 17. In general terms, vessel wall damage may occur as a consequence of direct microbial toxic damage or else develop as a complication of an immunologically mediated injury (*Table 15.12*).[1]

Bacterial arteritis may develop as a result of embolization from valvular lesions in patients with infective endocarditis. Although many different organisms are of etiological importance in the latter condition, staphylococcal and streptococcal infections remain the most important.[2] It may also occur by direct spread from an adjacent septic focus, by lymphatic spread, or represent a manifestation of underlying bacteremia or septicemia. There also appears to be a significant relationship between group A streptococci and childhood polyarteritis nodosa, both cutaneous and generalized.[3] In addition, Kawasaki syndrome has been reported in association with group A streptococci, possibly as a result of superantigen stimulation (see discussion of Kawasaki disease, p. 735).[4] Gonococcal bacteremia due to *Neisseria gonorrhea* is another important cause of vasculitis. *Neisseria meningitidis* infection may result in vasculitis associated with considerable morbidity and mortality.

The histological features of small vessel involvement are variable and depend to some extent on the nature of the causative organism. Suppurative features are most likely to be due to staphylococcal, streptococcal, Pseudomonas or Klebsiella infection.[2] A Gram stain is advisable in all suspected cases.

Obviously, in the context of immunosuppressed patients, the range of bacteria and fungi that may be implicated is very broad. In cases of suspected cutaneous infective vasculitis, especially in immunosuppressed patients, a detailed clinical history is essential and the judicious use of special stains is highly advisable.

Candidiasis, aspergillosis, cryptococcosis and mucormycosis are of special importance. *Mycobacterium tuberculosis* is also sometimes a cause of vascular damage. It tends to affect veins rather than arteries.[2] The features are usually those of a granulomatous thrombophlebitis, usually in the absence of caseation necrosis, although sometimes this may be a feature. Occasionally, however, arteries are primarily affected (*Fig. 15.99*). Erythema induratum is discussed on page 366.

Lepra bacilli are very commonly seen in endothelial and vascular smooth muscle cells in lepromatous leprosy. Vasculitis in the setting of leprosy (erythema nodosum leprosum) is a common cause of vasculitis in regions of the world where this disease is endemic (see discussion in Chapter 17).

Vascular lesions in the skin may be seen in a variety of rickettsial infections including epidemic typhus, scrub typhus and Rocky Mountain

Table 15.11
Infections known to be associated with clinically defined vasculitis

Vasculitic syndrome	Infective agent

Leukocytoclastic vasculitis (including Henoch–Schönlein purpura)	Bacterial
	   Streptococcus
	   Staphylococcus
	   Salmonella
	   Yersinia
	   Mycobacterium
	Viral
	   varicella-zoster
	   hepatitis B
	   cytomegalovirus
	   influenza

Polyarteritis nodosa	Bacterial
	   Streptococcus
	Viral
	   hepatitis A, B, C
	   human immunodeficiency virus
	   cytomegalovirus
	   human T-cell leukemia
	   erythrovirus

Isolated granulomatous vasculitis of the central nervous system	*Treponema pallidum*
	Mycobacterium tuberculosis
	Fungal
	   Coccidioides
	   Actinomyces
	   Cryptococcus
	   Histoplasma
	   Nocardia
	   Aspergillus
	Borrelia burgorferi (Lyme)
	Varicella-zoster

Kawasaki disease	Bacterial
	   Streptococcus
	   Salmonella
	   Yersinia
	   Mycoplasma
	Viral
	   parainfluenza
	   rotavirus

Reproduced with permission from Mader, R. and Keystone, E.C. (1992) *Current Opinion in Rheumatology*, **4**, 35–38.

Table 15.12
Mechanisms for infection-associated vasculitis

• Direct microbial toxicity
  – direct endothelial infection
  – effect of microbial toxins

• Immune mediated
  – humoral: soluble immune complexes; in situ complex formation
  – cellular: cytotoxic cell reaction (T-cell, NK cell, other); polyclonal T- or B-cell response; monoclonal T- or B-cell response

NK, natural killer. Reproduced with permission from Calabrese, L.H. (1991) *Rheumatic Disease Clinics of North America*, **17**, 131–147.

spotted fever.[2,5] The histological features include endothelial swelling and a mixed inflammatory cell infiltrate of T-lymphocytes, macrophages and occasionally neutrophils.[2] Thrombosis may sometimes be present.

Small vessel vasculitis may be seen in all three stages of syphilis. The features vary from a non-specific lymphocytic inflammation through to necrotizing granulomatous angiitis.[6–8] *Treponema pallidum*, however, is very rarely identified.[2] Cutaneous vasculitis may be an occasional feature of Lyme disease.[2]

The best known viral association with vasculitis is hepatitis B, which has been described in association with polyarteritis nodosa, leukocytoclastic vasculitis and mixed cryoglobulinemia.[1,9,10] Evidence of HBV infection is found in approximately 35% of all patients with polyarteritis.[1]

Human immunodeficiency virus (HIV) may be present in a very wide spectrum of vasculitic lesions including polyarteritis nodosa, Churg–Strauss syndrome, leukocytoclastic vasculitis, Henoch–Schönlein purpura, lymphomatoid granulomatosis and primary angiitis of the central nervous system.[11,12] Whether these represent a direct effect of HIV, or are a consequence of coexisting viral infections known to cause vasculitis (e.g. cytomegalovirus, HBV or Epstein–Barr virus), is unknown.[10] The identification of HIV within endothelial cells adds some support to the former possibility.[13]

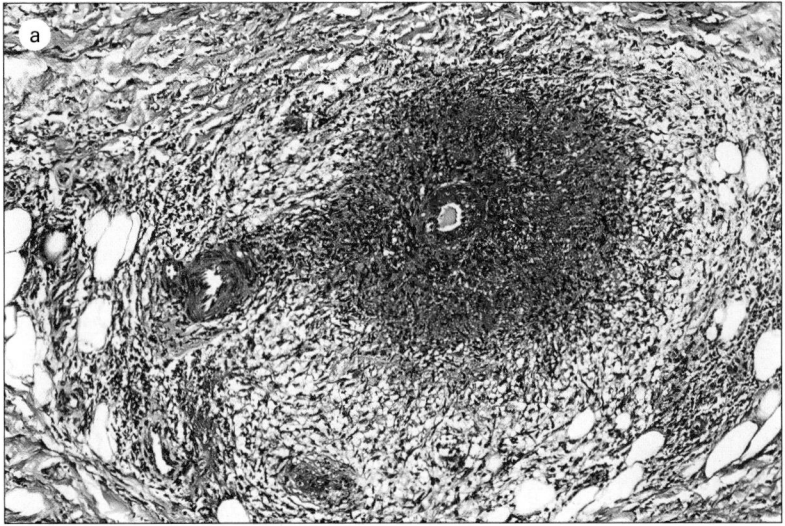

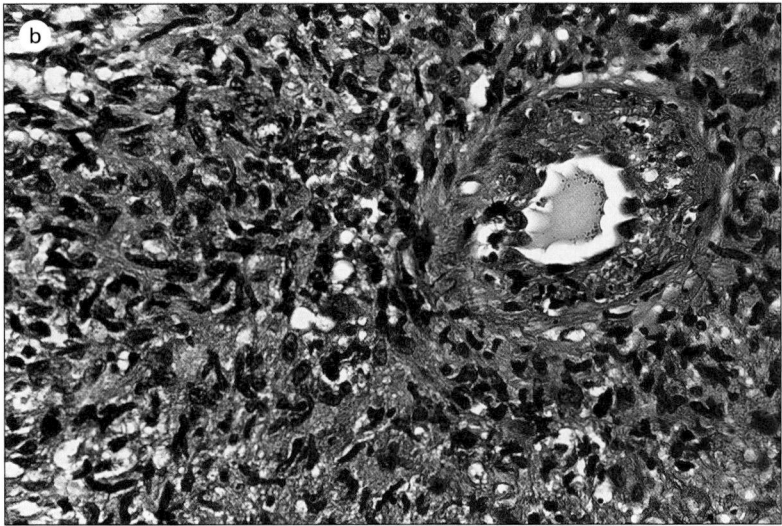

Fig. 15.99
(a, b) Tuberculous vasculitis: this patient with miliary tuberculosis presented with ischemic cutaneous lesions. Note the granulomatous inflammation.

References

1. Mader, R., Keystone, E.C. (1992) Infections that cause vasculitis. *Curr Opin Rheumatol*, **4**, 35–38.
2. Lie, T.J. (1991) Infection related vasculitis. In: Churg, A., Churg, J. (eds) Systemic vasculitides. New York: Igaku-Shoin, pp 243–256.
3. Fink, C.W. (1991) The role of the streptococcus in poststreptococcal reactive arthritis and childhood polyarteritis nodosa. *J Rheumatol*, **18** (Suppl.), 14–20.
4. Rider, L.G., Mendelman, P.M., French, J. et al (1991) Group A streptococcal infection and Kawasaki syndrome. *Lancet*, **337**, 1100–1101.
5. Walker, D.H. (1988) Diagnosis of rickettsial diseases. *Pathol Annu*, **23** (Part 2), 69–96.
6. Kahn, L.B., Gordon, W. (1971) Sarcoid-like granulomas in secondary syphilis. *Arch Pathol*, **92**, 334–337.
7. Jackman, J.D. Jr, Randolf, J.D. (1989) Cardiovascular syphilis. *Am J Med*, **87**, 425–433.
8. McNeely, M.C., Jorizzo, J.L., Solomon, A.R. Jr et al (1986) Cutaneous secondary syphilis: preliminary immunohistopathologic support for a role in immune complexes in lesion pathogenesis. *J Am Acad Dermatol*, **14**, 564–571.
9. Marcellin, P., Calmus, Y., Takahashi, H. et al (1991) Latent hepatitis B virus (HBV) infection in systemic necrotizing vasculitis. *Clin Exp Rheumatol*, **9**, 23–28.
10. Sergent, J.S. (1980) Vasculitides associated with viral infections. *Clin Rheum Dis*, **6**, 339–350.
11. Calabrese, L.H. (1991) Vasculitis and infection with the human immunodeficiency virus. *Rheum Dis Clin North Am*, **17**, 131–147.
12. Kaye, B.R. (1989) Rheumatologic manifestations of infection with human immunodeficiency virus (HIV). *Ann Intern Med*, **111**, 158–167.
13. Wiley, C.A., Schrier, R.D., Nelson, J.A. et al (1986) Cellular localization of human immunodeficiency virus infection within the brains of acquired immune deficiency syndrome patients. *Proc Natl Acad Sci USA*, **83**, 7089–7093.

Paraneoplastic vasculitis

Clinical features

Occasionally, cutaneous vasculitis may represent a marker of an underlying systemic malignancy (*Table 15.13*).[1–11] Although there have been reports of an association with solid tumors, this relationship is tenuous (with the possible exception of squamous carcinoma of the bronchus): such cases may at least sometimes represent nothing more than coincidence.[1,4,6] Vasculitis has nevertheless been reported in patients with carcinoma of the kidney, breast, ovary, lung, nasopharynx, stomach, small bowel, colon and prostate. Leukocytoclastic vasculitis is the most common pattern of vasculitis associated with malignancy but large vessel vasculitis may also be seen. Of interest, vasculitis may be present at the time of initial diagnosis and herald the onset of relapse.[4] Solid tumors and hematological malignancy may be associated with Henoch–Schönlein purpura.[7,10,11] One study found that nearly a third of adults with Henoch–Schönlein purpura had an associated malignancy.[10] For this reason, the authors concluded that physicians should suspect underlying malignancy in older patients (especially men of more than 40 years) with Henoch–Schönlein purpura.[10]

In contrast to some solid tumors, there does appear to be a genuine relationship between cutaneous vasculitis and hematological and lymphoreticular neoplasms including hairy cell leukemia, acute and

Table 15.13
Vasculopathic syndromes associated with malignancy

• Migratory superficial thrombophlebitis
• Deep venous thrombosis
• Non-bacterial thrombotic endocarditis
• Anticardiolipin antibody syndrome
• Embolic features associated with atrial myxoma
• Raynaud's phenomenon
• Erythema nodosum
• Hyperviscosity syndrome
• Cryoglobulinemia
• Lambda light-chain vasculopathy
• Cutaneous vasculitis
• Systemic vasculitis

Reproduced with permission from Mertz, L.E. and Conn, D.L. (1992) *Current Opinion in Rheumatology*, **9**, 39–46.

chronic myeloid leukemia, multiple myeloma and non-Hodgkin's lymphoma.[1]

In general, patients present with the features of leukocytoclastic vasculitis, and occasionally arthralgia or arthritis may also be evident. Cutaneous manifestations include maculopapular eruptions, purpura, urticaria, peripheral ulcers and gangrene.[12] Although vasculitis is seen in patients with a spectrum of hematological malignancies, hairy cell leukemia is particularly associated with leukocytoclastic vasculitis and a polyarteritis nodosa-like picture, including systemic lesions.[4–6] In one study of 42 patients with hairy cell leukemia and vasculitis, 21 also had leukocytoclastic vasculitis and 17 had polyarteritis nodosa.[4] In addition, four patients had direct infiltration of vessel walls by leukemic cells. Hodgkin's lymphoma has occasionally been linked to erythema nodosum, and myelodysplasia has been found in conjunction with leukocytoclastic vasculitis.[13,14] Multiple myeloma is particularly associated with non-thrombocytopenic purpura.[15] It has recently been documented that lymphocytic vasculitis is a relatively common form of paraneoplastic vasculitis associated with lymphoproliferative disorders.[16]

It is important to note that these vasculitic phenomena may antedate the clinical manifestations of the underlying malignancy. Therefore, patients with an unexplained vasculitic rash should be investigated with this in mind.[2] In hairy cell leukemia, vasculitis often follows splenectomy.[5,12]

Pathogenesis and histological features

The pathogenesis of paraneoplastic vasculitis has not been well studied, but may include immune complexes, cross-reacting antigens and direct tumor (leukemic blast) infiltration of blood vessel walls.

Leukocytoclastic, polyarteritis nodosa-like and lymphocytic forms of paraneoplastic vasculitis have all been described and show histological features similar to their non-paraneoplastic counterparts.[16]

Recently, cases of vasculitis in the setting of myelomonocytic or monocytic leukemia cutis have been described in which the vascular injury was mediated by leukemic blasts.[17] The term 'leukemic vasculitis' has been proposed for this form of vasculitis.[17] In these cases, the vasculitis ranged from mild microvascular injury to frank necrotizing vasculitis.[17,18] The former was characterized by low-grade vascular injury with endothelial cell swelling and focal fibrin deposition. Frank necrotizing vasculitis shows infiltration of the vessel wall by neoplastic cells associated with necrosis and fibrin deposition in a pattern that resembles polyarteritis nodosa. Hairy cell leukemia may also show infiltration of vessel walls by leukemic cells.[4,5]

References

1. Greer, J.M., Longley, S., Edwards, N.L. et al (1988) Vasculitis associated with malignancy. Experience with 13 patients and literature review. *Medicine*, **67**, 220–230.
2. Sánchez-Guerrero, J., Gutiérrez-Ureña, S., Vidaller, A. et al (1990) Vasculitis and a paraneoplastic syndrome. Report of 11 cases and review of the literature. *J Rheumatol*, **17**, 1458–1462.
3. Longley, S., Caldwell, J.R., Panush, R.S. (1986) Paraneoplastic vasculitis: unique syndrome of cutaneous angiitis and arthritis associated with myeloproliferative disorder. *Am J Med*, **80**, 1027–1030.
4. Kurzrock, R., Cohen, P.R., Markowitz, A. (1994) Clinical manifestations of vasculitis in a patient with solid tumors. A case report and review of the literature. *Arch Intern Med*, **14**, 334–340.
5. Hasler, P., Kistler, H., Gerber, H. (1995) Vasculitides in hairy cell leukemia. *Semin Arthritis Rheum*, **25**, 134–142.
6. Lacour, J.P., Castanet, J., Perrin, C. et al (1993) Cutaneous leukocytoclastic vasculitis and renal cancer: 2 cases. *Am J Med*, **94**, 104–108.
7. Hayem, G., Gomez, M.J., Grossin, M. et al (1997) Systemic vasculitis and epithelioma. A report of three case and review of the literature. *Rev Rhum Engl Ed*, **64**, 816–824.
8. Stashower, M.E., Rennie, T.A., Turiansky, G.W. et al (1999) Ovarian cancer presenting as leukocytoclastic vasculitis. *J Am Acad Dermatol*, **40**, 287–289.
9. Miyachi, H., Akizuki, M., Yamagata, H. et al (1987) Hypertrophic osteoarthropathy, cutaneous vasculitis, and mixed-type cryoglobulinemia in a patient with nasopharyngeal carcinoma. *Arthritis Rheum*, **30**, 825–829.
10. Pertuiset, E., Liote, F., Launay-Russ, E. et al (2000) Adult Henoch–Schönlein purpura associated with malignancy. *Semin Arthritis Rheum*, **29**, 360–367.
11. Blanco, R., Gonzalez-Gay, M.A., Ibanez, D. et al (1997) Henoch–Schönlein purpura as a clinical presentation of small cell lung cancer. *Clin Exp Rheumatol*, **15**, 545–547.
12. Mertz, L.E., Conn, D.L. (1992) Vasculitis associated with malignancy. *Curr Opin Rheumatol*, **4**, 39–46.
13. Taillan, B., Ferrari, E., Fuzibet, J.G. et al (1990) Erythema nodosum and Hodgkin's disease. *Clin Rheumatol*, **9**, 397–398.
14. Castro, M., Conn, D.L., Su, W.P.D. et al (1991) Rheumatic manifestations in myelodysplastic syndromes. *J Rheumatol*, **18**, 721–727.
15. Kois, J.M., Sexton, M., Lookingbill, D.P. (1991) Cutaneous manifestations of multiple myeloma. *Arch Dermatol*, **127**, 69–74.
16. Pavlidis, N.A., Louvas, G., Tsokos, M. et al (1995) Cutaneous lymphocytic vasculopathy in lymphoproliferative disorders: a paraneoplastic lymphocytic vasculitis of the skin. *Leuk Lymphoma*, **16**, 477–482.
17. Jones, D., Dorfman, D.M., Barnhill, R.L. et al (1997) Leukemic vasculitis: a feature of leukemia cutis in some patients. *Am J Clin Pathol*, **107**, 637–642.
18. Paydas, S., Zorludemir, S. (2000) Leukemia and leukemic vasculitis. *Br J Dermatol*, **143**, 773–779.

Vasculitis associated with palisaded neutrophilic and granulomatous dermatitis

Clinical features

Occasionally, granuloma annulare-, necrobiosis lipoidica- and rheumatoid nodule-like lesions associated with vasculitis are encountered.[1,2] This group of disorders, which is almost always associated with systemic disease, is also discussed in Chapter 8. A number of different terms have been applied including palisaded neutrophilic and granulomatous dermatitis (of immune complex disease), interstitial granulomatous dermatitis with arthritis, rheumatoid papules, superficial ulcerating rheumatoid necrobiosis, cutaneous extravascular necrotizing granuloma and Churg–Strauss granuloma.[1–6] Many types of underlying systemic disease have been reported in association with these lesions, including rheumatoid arthritis, lupus erythematosus, Sjögren's syndrome, thyroiditis, Raynaud's syndrome, hepatitis, inflammatory bowel disease, lymphoproliferative disorders, myelodysplastic syndrome, vasculitis (Wegener's, Churg–Strauss, Takayasu's arteritis, periarteritis nodosa), hemolytic uremic syndrome, thrombotic thrombocytopenic purpura, mixed cryoglobulinemia, drug reactions, carcinoma, diabetes mellitus and infection (streptococcal, HIV, Epstein–Barr virus, erythrovirus).[1–4]

The lesions are usually papules and nodules, or plaques with a predilection for the extremities or trunk in an adult.[2,6] Often, they are arranged in a linear pattern, which may be confluent linear bands or cords that are said to have a 'rope-like' quality.

Pathogenesis and histological features

The pathogenesis of palisaded neutrophilic and granulomatous dermatitis likely depends on the associated/underlying disease. An autoimmune-mediated vasculitis probably plays an important role in at least a subset of cases.

As noted above, this is not a single disease but rather a group of disorders showing a broad spectrum of histology sharing the common denominator of a prominent neutrophilic infiltrate with or without vasculitis in a background of palisading granulomatous inflammation. When present, vasculitis usually shows the features of leukocytoclastic vasculitis.

Differential diagnosis

The precise terminology that is preferred by the dermatopathologist is probably not important. More significant than the nosological nuances is rendering a report that alerts the clinician to the possibility that the patient may have underlying systemic disease and when such lesions are encountered appropriate clinical evaluation is necessary.

References

1.   Finan, M.C., Winkelmann, R.K. (1983) The cutaneous extravascular necrotizing granuloma (Churg–Strauss granuloma) and systemic disease: a review of 27 cases. *Medicine*, **62**, 142–158.

2.   Chu, P., Connolly, K., LeBoit, P.E. (1994) The histopathologic spectrum of palisaded neutrophilic and granulomatous dermatitis. *Arch Dermatol*, **130**, 1278–1283.
3.   Harpster, E.F., Mauro, T., Barr, R.J. (1989) Linear granuloma annulare. *J Am Acad Dermatol*, **21**, 1138–1141.
4.   Magro, C.M., Crowson, A.N., Regauer, S. (1996) Granuloma annulare and necrobiosis lipoidica tissue reactions as a manifestation of systemic disease. *Hum Pathol*, **27**, 50–56.
5.   Wilmoth, G.J., Perniciaro, C. (1996) Cutaneous extravascular necrotizing granuloma (Winkelmann granuloma): confirmation of the association with systemic disease. *J Am Acad Dermatol*, **34**, 753–759.
6.   Aloi, F., Tomasini, C., Pippione, M. (1999) Interstitial granulomatous dermatitis with plaques. *Am J Dermatopathol*, **21**, 320–323.

Lymphocytic vasculitis

Lymphocytic vasculitis may be diagnosed in cases in which a perivascular lymphocytic infiltrate is associated with vascular damage (*Fig. 15.100*). In many cases the vascular changes are subtle and minimal, including only endothelial swelling and extravasated blood cells and sometimes focal fibrin deposition. Not surprisingly, the concept of lymphocytic vasculitis is somewhat controversial.[1–4] This category of vasculitis has been embraced by some authors and rejected by others. To a large extent, this controversy is the result of a lack of precisely defined criteria for diagnosis. Kossard has defined lymphocytic vasculitis as an overlapping spectrum of changes varying from angiodestruction to endovasculitis and including a pattern defined as lichenoid lymphocytic vasculitis.[5]

One can argue that the term 'vasculitis' should not be applied to lesions with minimal vascular damage. Regardless of terminology, it is important for the pathologist to render a report that distinguishes cases of low-grade vascular injury associated with a lymphocytic infiltrate from frank necrotizing vasculitis. Furthermore, it is important to distinguish lymphocytic from neutrophilic vasculitides.

In cases with low-grade vascular injury, we often apply the term low-grade lymphocytic vasculitis and mention in our report that frank necrotizing vasculitis is not present to avoid any ambiguity. If one uses strict criteria – requiring vascular necrosis or significant fibrinoid change for a diagnosis of vasculitis – frank necrotizing lymphocytic vasculitis is an uncommon condition. The differential diagnosis of lymphocytic vasculitis is broad and many entities associated with a perivascular lymphocytic infiltrate may, on occasion, cause vascular changes that warrant a diagnosis of non-necrotizing lymphocytic vasculitis (*Table 15.14*). Entities that exceptionally show features of lymphocytic vasculitis are discussed in their appropriate chapters. Diseases commonly associated with lymphocytic vasculitis include Degos' disease, perniosis, Behçet's disease, livedo vasculitis and Kawasaki syndrome. Other rare associations of lymphocytic vasculitis include leukemia and the tumor necrosis factor receptor-associated periodic syndrome. The latter is a periodic fever syndrome associated with a skin eruption presenting with macules and plaques in early life. It results from mutations in the TNFRSFIA, the gene encoding the tumor necrosis factor receptor.[6,7]

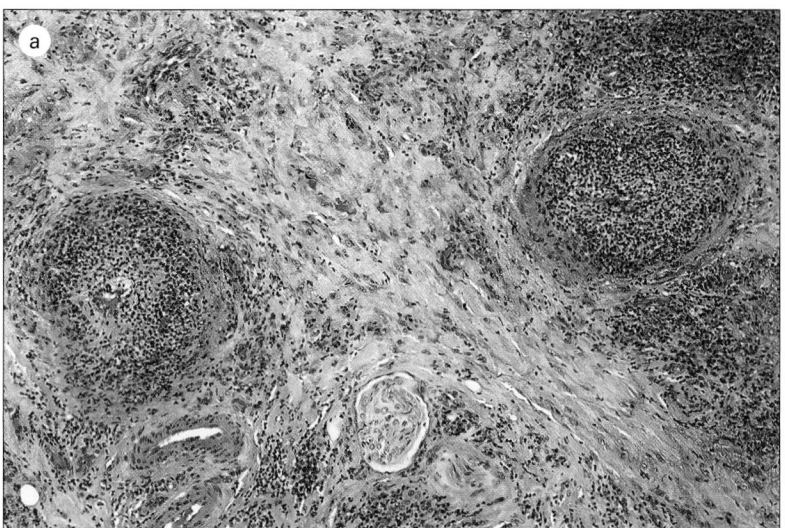

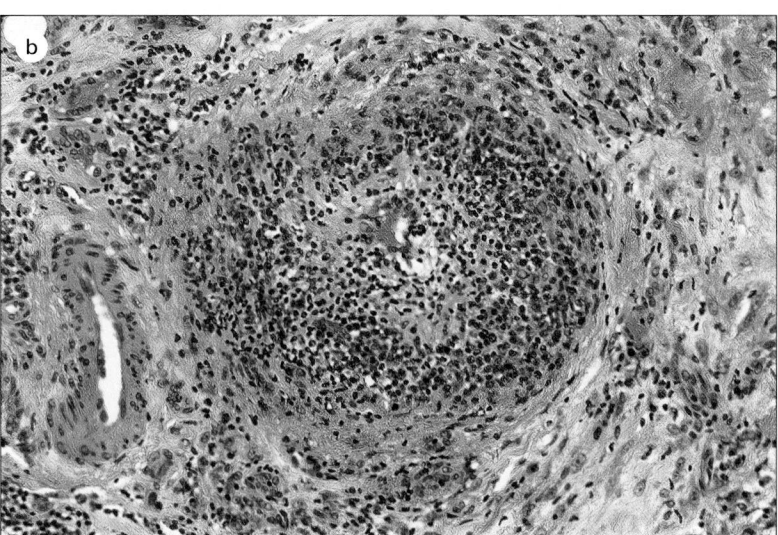

Fig. 15.100
(a, b) Lymphocytic vasculitis: there is mural fibrinoid necrosis accompanied by a dense lymphocytic infiltrate. These images come from a patient with very severe perniosis.

Table 15.14
Causes of lymphocytic vasculitis

• Behçet's disease
• Connective tissue disease
• Degos' disease
• Drug eruptions
• 'Gyrate erythemas' (e.g. erythema annulare centrifugum)
• Infection (especially viral and rickettsial)
• Insect bite reactions
• Kawasaki syndrome
• Livedo vasculitis/atrophie blanche
• Lymphomatoid papulosis
• Perniosis (chilblains)
• Pityriasis lichenoides
• Pigmented purpuric dermatoses
• Polymorphic eruption of pregnancy
• Polymorphous light eruption
• Prurigo of pregnancy

References

1. Massa, M.C., Su, W.P.D. (1984) Lymphocytic vasculitis: is it a special clinicopathologic entity? *J Cutan Pathol*, **11**, 132–139.
2. Carlson, J.A., Mihm, M.C. Jr, LeBoit, P.E. (1996) Cutaneous lymphocytic vasculitis: a definition, a review, and a proposal for classification. *Semin Diagn Pathol*, **13**, 72–90.
3. LeBoit, P.E. (2000) A vessel runs through it. *Am J Dermatopathol*, **22**, 285–287.
4. LeBoit, P.E. (2002) Vasculitis: the true and the near true. *Am J Dermatopathol*, **24**, 267–269.
5. Kossard, S. (2000) Defining lymphocytic vasculitis. *Australas J Dermatol*, **41**, 149–155.
6. Pavlidis, N.A., Klouvas, G., Tsokos, M. et al (1995) Cutaneous lymphocytic vasculopathy in lymphoproliferative disorders – a paraneoplastic lymphocytic vasculitis of the skin. *Leuk Lymphoma*, **16**, 477–482.
7. Toro, J.R., Aksentijevich, I., Hull, K. et al (2000) Tumor necrosis factor receptor-associated periodic syndrome. A novel syndrome with cutaneous manifestations. *Arch Dermatol*, **136**, 1487–1494.

Malignant atrophic papulosis

Clinical features

Malignant atrophic papulosis (lethal intestinocutaneous syndrome, Degos' disease) is a rare disorder affecting multiple systems and usually associated with a poor prognosis.[1–4] It is of unknown etiology, shows a male predominance (3:1) and usually affects the young and middle aged. The mean age at presentation is 33 years; however, a wide age range at diagnosis (from infancy to 67 years) has been described.[5,6] Occasional instances of familial involvement have been recorded.[7–9] Presentation during pregnancy may rarely occur.[10]

The cutaneous lesions are distinctive, although similar lesions may be a manifestation of other diseases such as SLE, systemic sclerosis, rheumatoid arthritis, and Crohn's disease.[11–16] Recently, it has been proposed that malignant atrophic papulosis represents a reaction pattern mainly seen in lupus erythematosus and not a specific disease per se.[17] Lesions, which may be quite numerous, appear in crops, initially as pinkish or yellow–gray papules up to 5 mm in diameter and showing a predilection for the trunk and proximal extremities. Characteristically, the palms, soles, face and scalp are spared. The papules are usually asymptomatic and do not ulcerate or scar. With progression they develop a characteristic appearance: discrete small patches composed of a central zone with a depressed white, porcelain-like appearance and a fine scale, surrounded by a narrow red or violaceous rim associated with fine telangiectasia (*Fig. 15.101*). On rare occasions, similar lesions may be found on the buccal and genital mucosa. Penile ulceration has rarely been documented.[18] Sometimes avascular conjunctival pale patches are seen.[19]

Intestinal manifestations are variable. While any segment of the intestinal system from the oral cavity to the anus may be involved, it is predominantly the small intestine that is affected.[13] Some patients are asymptomatic; others may complain of indigestion, diarrhea, constipation or abdominal distension and pain. Laparoscopy usually reveals characteristic subserosal white, yellow or pinkish plaques, typically slightly depressed and several centimeters in diameter. Of great importance, patients may develop small intestinal perforation with resultant peritonitis. Fistulae involving the small bowel may develop as a complication.[20] Rarely, intestinal involvement precedes the cutaneous features.[21] Acute small bowel perforation may be the first manifestation of the disease.[22] In addition, intestinal lesions may sometimes develop many years after an initial cutaneous presentation.

The condition may involve both the peripheral and central nervous system and occasionally such lesions dominate the clinical features.[23–25] Symptoms are variable and may be multiple due to various sites being affected. For example, hemi- and quadriplegias, sensory losses and cranial nerve lesions may all be encountered.[26]

Malignant atrophic papulosis is a truly systemic illness in most patients. At autopsy, lesions may be found in a variety of sites including the heart, lungs, kidneys, bladder and liver.[27–30]

Although malignant atrophic papulosis is usually associated with a poor prognosis and high mortality, there does appear to be a subgroup of patients in whom the cutaneous features are the sole manifestation and evolution is benign.[10,31–33] Intestinal involvement appears to correlate particularly with a poor outlook.

Malignant atrophic papulosis has been reported in a patient with acquired immunodeficiency syndrome.[34]

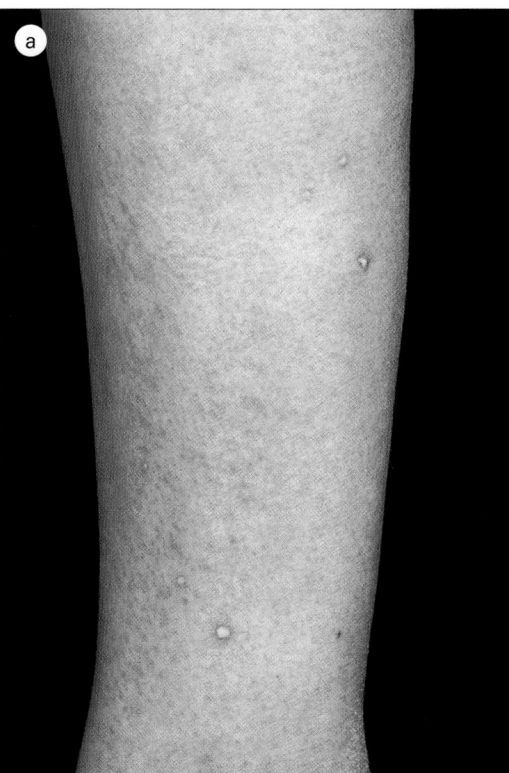

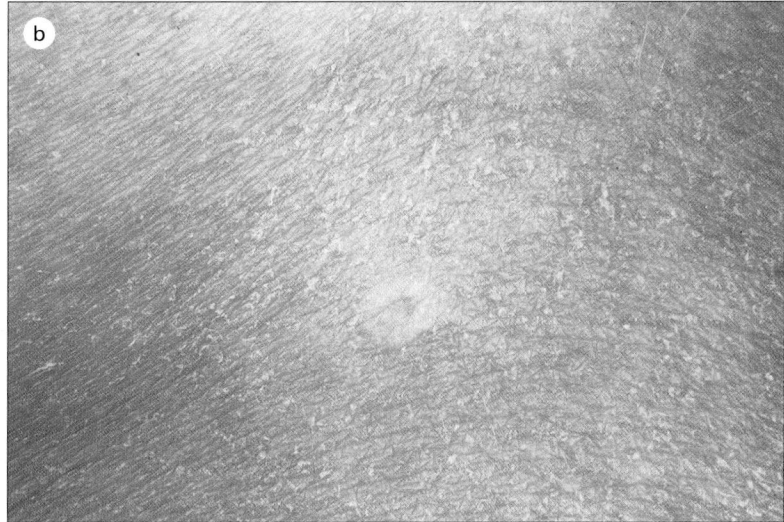

15.101

(a, b) Degos' disease: note the typical small papules with depressed centers and fine white scaling. By courtesy of the Institute of Dermatology, London, UK.

Pathogenesis and histological features

The precise etiology is unknown, although viral, genetic, autoimmune mechanisms and fibrinolysis have all been implicated.[35] Since lesions are sometimes not associated with significant inflammation, it is debatable whether classification as a true vasculitis is appropriate. The pathogenesis is that of vascular thrombosis, the essential pathology of the lesions being that of infarction.[1] A focal fibrinolytic defect within the center of the infarcted lesions and alterations of fibrinolysis and platelet function have been described, but these are not consistent findings.[1,36,37] It has been proposed that endothelial swelling and proliferation with secondary thrombosis is the primary pathogenesis.[1] Consistent with this hypothesis is the documentation of a patient with malignant atrophic papulosis associated with elevated anticardiolipin antibodies.[38] Others, however, have not been able to corroborate this finding.[39]

In most cases, the cause of the initial endothelial vascular insult is unknown, but a mononuclear vasculitis may play a role in the pathogenesis.[4] Most authors regard the mucin deposition described below as a secondary event developing as a consequence of dermal ischemia.

The established cutaneous lesion has a characteristic appearance.[40,41] The overlying epidermis is hyperkeratotic and atrophic. Immediately subjacent to this is a wedge-shaped zone of dermal infarction with the base parallel to the surface epithelium: it is typically pale in color, relatively acellular and associated with mucin deposition (*Figs 15.102, 15.103*).[42] The latter is metachromatic with toluidine blue and demonstrates hyaluronidase-sensitive alcian blue staining. Older lesions are frequently ulcerated (*Fig. 15.104*). Often, the vessels adjacent and deep to the infarct show a perivascular lymphocytic infiltrate. Usually, but not invariably, an endovasculitis can be demonstrated in the blood vessels at the apex of the lesion: this consists of endothelial cell hyperplasia, sometimes complicated by thrombosis (*Fig. 15.105*). The internal elastic lamina, media and serosa are usually not involved. A panniculitis mimicking lupus erythematosus profundus has been described.[43]

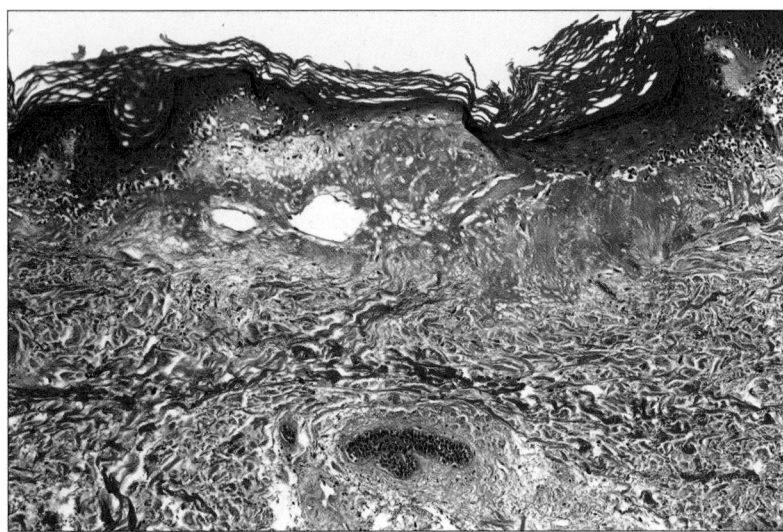

Fig. 15.102
Degos' disease: there is hyperkeratosis and epidermal atrophy associated with a zone of dermal infarction. Note the ectatic vessels.

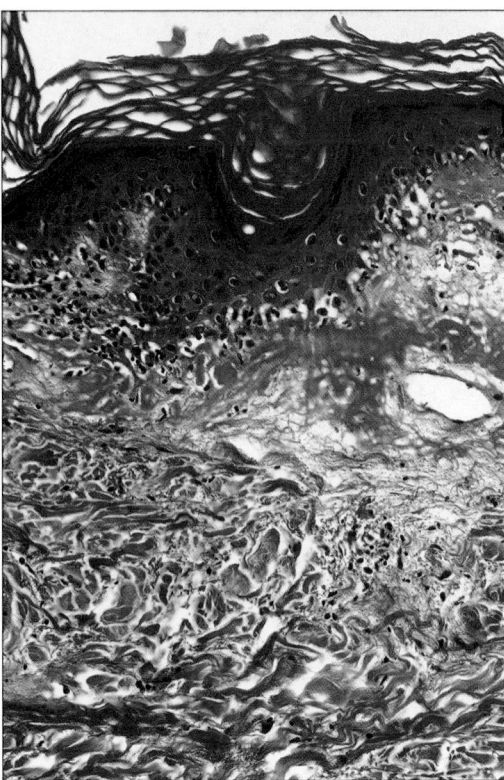

Fig. 15.103
Degos' disease: mucin deposition is present at the edge of the lesion where the epidermis shows basal cell hydropic degeneration.

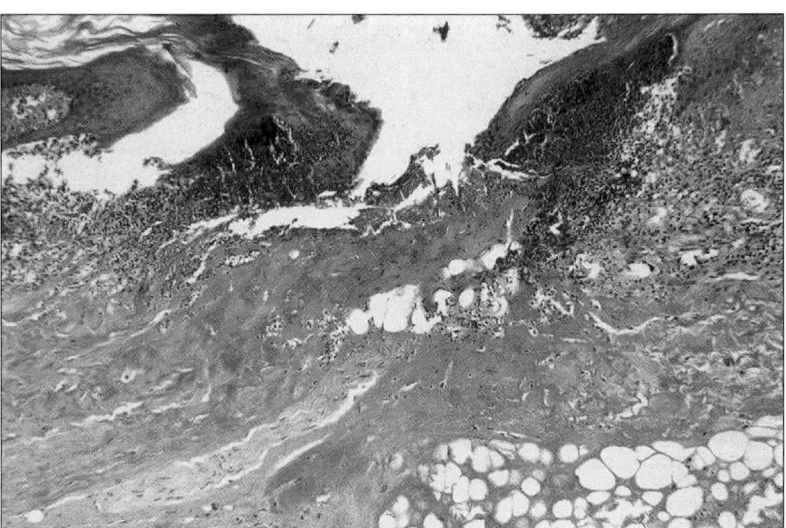

Fig. 15.104
Degos' disease: in this older lesion there is ulceration overlying the infarcted dermis. By courtesy of C.J.J. Mulder, MD, Rijnstate Hospital, Arnhem, The Netherlands.

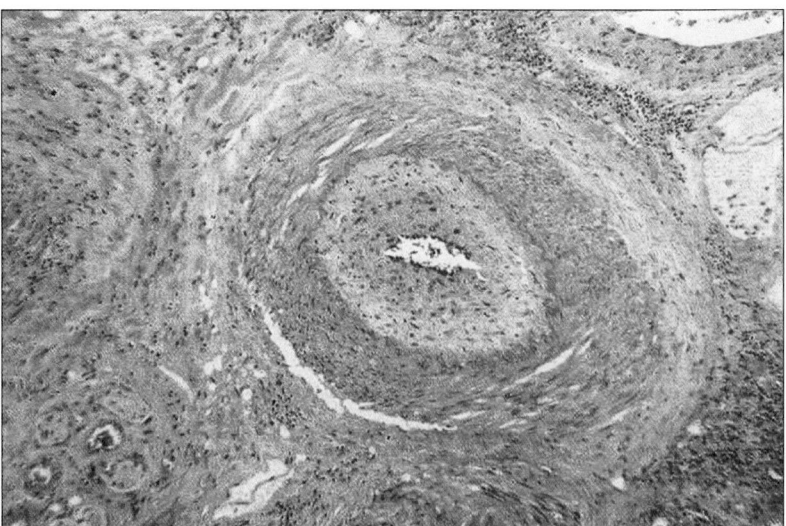

Fig. 15.105
Degos' disease: deep to the infarct shown in *Fig. 15.104*, the arteries show very marked intimal thickening with considerable diminution in the diameter of the lumen. By courtesy of C.J.J. Mulder, MD, Rijnstate Hospital, Arnhem, The Netherlands.

Microscopic examination of the bowel lesions reveals transmural intestinal inflammation with ulceration and hemorrhage. The latter may involve the small and large intestines including the rectum (*Figs 15.106–15.109*). Vascular changes have included gross intimal thickening with consequent severe diminution in the lumen diameter, thrombosis and acute vasculitis.[44]

Differential diagnosis

As mentioned above, the cutaneous findings are distinctive and diagnosis should be relatively straightforward. However, it should be kept in mind that although the cutaneous lesions of malignant atrophic papulosis are distinctive, similar lesions have been described in patients with other diseases such as SLE, systemic sclerosis, rheumatoid arthritis, dermatomyositis and Crohn's disease.[11–16,45] A search for underlying or associated disorders is therefore advised.

References

1. Magrinat, G., Kerwin, K.S., Gabriel, D.A. (1989) The clinical manifestations of Degos' syndrome. *Arch Pathol Lab Med*, **113**, 354–362.
2. Degos, R. (1979) Malignant atrophic papulosis. *Br J Dermatol*, **100**, 21–35.
3. Metz, J., Amschler, A., Henke, M. (1980) Morbus Degos (papulosis atrophicans maligna). *Hautarzt*, **31**, 108–110.
4. Su, W.P.D., Schroeter, A.L., Lee, D.A. et al (1985) Clinical and histologic findings in Degos' syndrome (malignant atrophic papulosis). *Cutis*, **35**, 131–142.
5. Torrelo, A., Sevilla, J., Medeiro, J.G. et al (2002) Malignant atrophic papulosis in an infant. *Br J Dermatol*, **146**, 916–918.
6. Barabino, A., Pesce, F., Gatti, R. et al (1990) An atypical paediatric case of malignant atrophic papulosis (Kohlmeier–Degos disease). *Eur J Pediatr*, **149**, 457–458.
7. Kisch, L.S., Bruynzeel, D.P. (1984) Six cases of malignant atrophic papulosis (Degos' disease) occurring in one family. *Br J Dermatol*, **111**, 469–471.
8. Newton, J.A., Black, M.M. (1984) Familial malignant atrophic papulosis. *Clin Exp Dermatol*, **9**, 298–299.
9. Katz, S.K., Mudd, L.J., Roenigk, H.H. Jr (1997) Malignant atrophic papulosis (Degos' disease) involving three generations of a family. *J Am Acad Dermatol*, **37**, 480–484.
10. Bogenrieder, T., Kuske, M., Landthaler, M. et al (2002) Benign Degos' disease during pregnancy and followed for 10 years. *Acta Derm Venereol*, **82**, 284–287.
11. Black, M.M., Hudson, P.M. (1976) Atrophie blanche lesions closely resembling malignant atrophic papulosis (Degos' disease) in systemic lupus erythematosus. *Br J Dermatol*, **95**, 649–652.
12. Doutre, M.S., Beylot, C., Bioulac, P. et al (1987) Skin lesion resembling malignant strophic papulosis in lupus erythematosus. *Dermatologica*, **175**, 45–46.
13. Dubin, H.V., Stawiski, M.A. (1974) Systemic lupus erythematosus resembling malignant atrophic papulosis. *Arch Intern Med*, **134**, 321–323.
14. Durie, B.G., Stroud, J.D., Kahn, J.A. (1969) Progressive systemic sclerosis with malignant atrophic papulosis. *Arch Dermatol*, **100**, 575–581.
15. Demitsu, T., Kakurai, M., Murata, S. et al (1997) Degos' disease with rheumatoid arthritis. *J Dermatol*, **24**, 488–490.
16. Castanet, J., Lacour, J.P., Perrin, C. et al (1995) Cutaneous vasculitis with lesions mimicking Degos' disease and revealing Crohn's disease. *Acta Derm Venereol*, **75**, 408–409.
17. Ball, E., Newburger, A., Ackerman, A.B. (2003) Degos' disease: a distinctive pattern of disease, chiefly of lupus erythematosus, and not a specific disease. *Am J Dermatopathol*, **25**, 308–320.
18. Thomson, K.F., Highet, A.S. (2000) Penile ulceration in fatal malignant atrophic papulosis (Degos' disease). *Br J Dermatol*, **143**, 1320–1322.
19. Lee, D.A., Su, W.P., Liesegang, T.J. (1984) Ophthalmic changes of Degos' disease (malignant atrophic papulosis). *Ophthalmology*, **91**, 295–299.

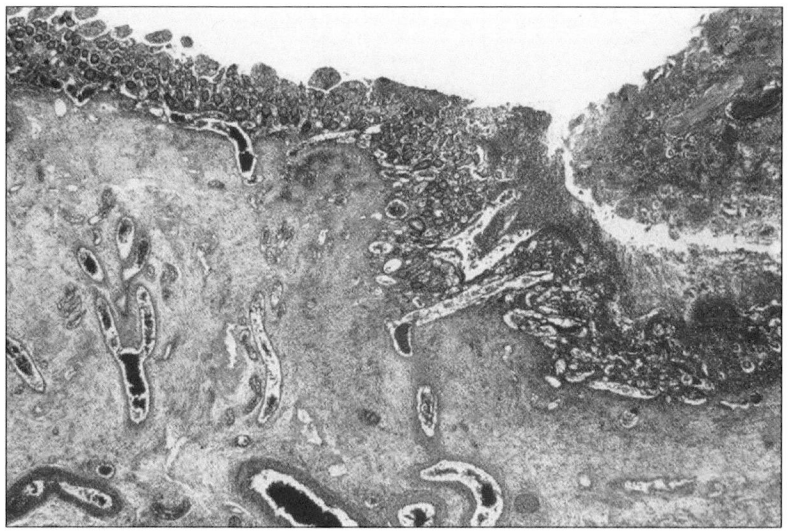

Fig. 15.107
Degos' disease: histological section of jejunum shown in *Fig. 15.106*. Note the acute inflammation and ulceration. By courtesy of C.J.J. Mulder, MD, Rijnstate Hospital, Arnhem, The Netherlands.

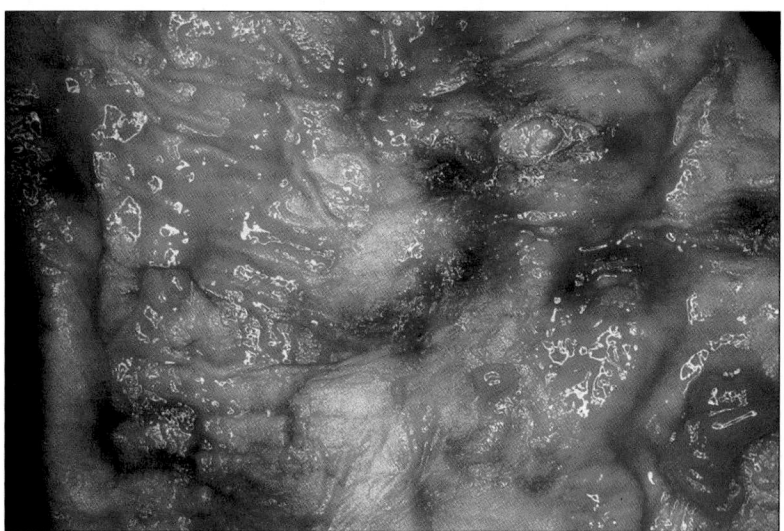

Fig. 15.108
Degos' disease: section of rectum showing focal congestion and ulceration. By courtesy of C.J.J. Mulder, MD, Rijnstate Hospital, Arnhem, The Netherlands.

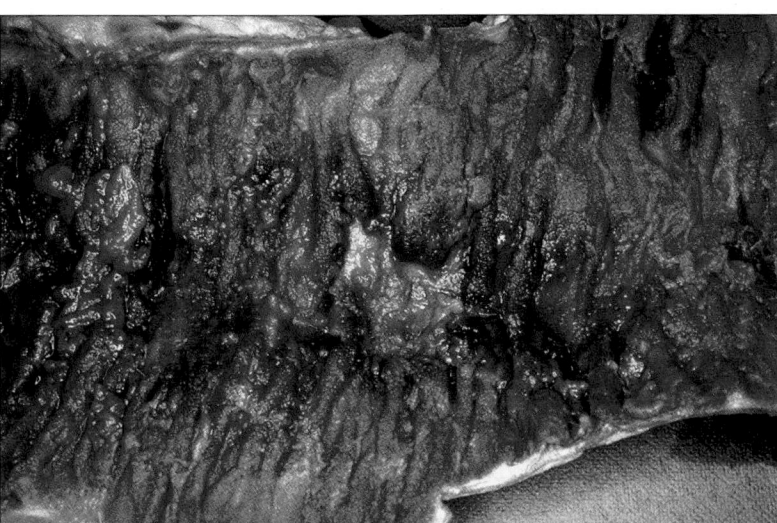

Fig. 15.106
Degos' disease: section of jejunum showing ulceration of the mucosa with surrounding intense congestion. By courtesy of C.J.J. Mulder, MD, Rijnstate Hospital, Arnhem, The Netherlands.

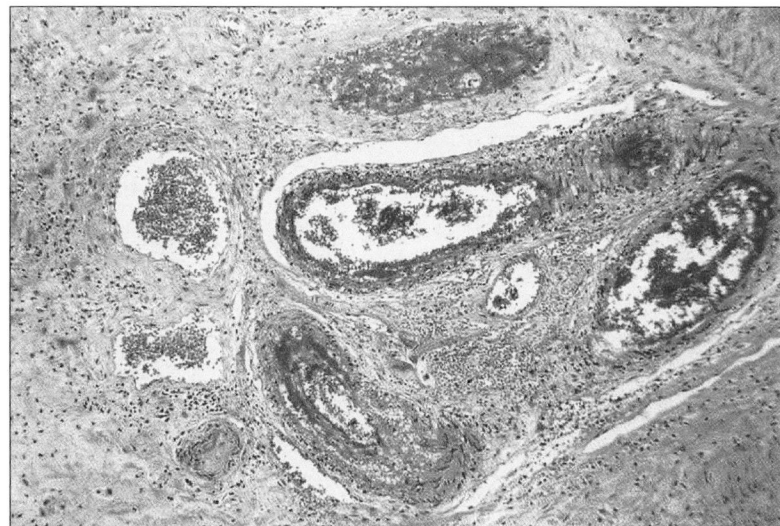

Fig. 15.109
Degos' syndrome: histological section of the submucosa of the rectum. There is acute vasculitis with thrombosis. By courtesy of C.J.J. Mulder, MD, Rijnstate Hospital, Arnhem, The Netherlands.

20. Atchabahian, A., Laisne, M.J., Riche, F. et al (1996) Small bowel fistulae in Degos' disease: a case report and literature review. *Am J Gastroenterol*, **91**, 2208–2221.
21. Fruhwirth, J., Mischinger, H.J., Werkgartner, G. et al (1997) Kohlmeier–Degos's disease with primary intestinal manifestation. *Scand J Gastroenterol*, **32**, 1066–1070.
22. González Valverde, F.M., Menárguez Pina, F., Ruiz, J.A. et al (2003) Presentation of Degos syndrome as acute small-bowel perforation. *Arch Surg*, **138**, 57–58.
23. Label, L.S., Tandan, R., Albers, J.W. (1983) Myelomalacia and hypoglycorrhachia in malignant atrophic papulosis. *Neurology*, **33**, 936–939.
24. Melski, J.W., Murphy, J.F., Putman, C.E. (1980) Progressive neurologic disorder and abdominal pain in an eighteen year old woman (case records of the Massachusetts General Hospital). *N Engl J Med*, **303**, 1103–1111.
25. Burrow, J.N., Blumbergs, P.C., Iyer, P.V. et al (1991) Kohlmeier–Degos disease: a multisystem vasculopathy with progressive cerebral infarction. *Aust N Z J Med*, **21**, 49–51.
26. Leslie, T.A., Goldsmith, P.C., Thompson, A.J. et al (1993) Degos disease and spastic paraplegia. *Clin Exp Dermatol*, **18**, 344–346.
27. McLoud, T.C., Munechika, H., Shaw, R. et al (1978) Calcific constrictive pericarditis in Degos' disease. *South Med J*, **71**, 609–611.
28. Pierce, R.N., Smith, G.J. (1978) Intrathoracic manifestations of Degos' disease (malignant atrophic papulosis). *Chest*, **73**, 79–84.
29. Snow, J.L., Muller, S.A. (1995) Degos syndrome: malignant atrophic papulosis. *Semin Dermatol*, **14**, 99–105.
30. Mauad, T., De Fatima Lopes Calvo Tiberio, I., Baba, E. et al (1996) Malignant atrophic papulosis (Degos' disease) with extensive cardiopulmonary involvement. *Histopathology*, **28**, 84–86.
31. Plantin, P., Labouche, F., Sassolas, B. et al (1989) Degos' disease: a 10 year follow-up of a patient without visceral involvement. *J Am Acad Dermatol*, **21**, 136–137.
32. Mensing, C., Mensing, H. (2002) Degos atrophic malignant papulosis. Not always malignant! *Hautartz*, **53**, 42–46.
33. Ojeda Cuchillero, R.M., Sánchez Regana, M., Umbert Millet, P. (2003) Benign cutaneous Degos' disease. *Clin Exp Dermatol*, **28**, 145–147.
34. Requena, L., Farina, C., Barat, A. (1998) Degos disease in a patient with acquired immunodeficiency syndrome. *J Am Acad Dermatol*, **38**, 852–856.
35. Molenaar, W.M., Rosman, J.B., Donker, A.J. et al (1987) The pathology and pathogenesis of malignant atrophic papulosis (Dego's disease). A case study with reference to other vascular disorders. *Pathol Res Pract*, **182**, 98–106.
36. Black, M.M. (1976) Malignant atrophic papulosis (Degos' disease). *Int J Dermatol*, **15**, 405–411.
37. Vázquez-Doval, F.J., Ruiz de Erenchun, F., Paramo, J.A. et al (1993) Malignant atrophic papulosis. A report of two cases with fibrinolysis and platelet function. *Clin Exp Dermatol*, **18**, 441–444.
38. Englert, H.J., Hawkes, C.H., Boey, M.L. et al (1984) Degos' disease: association with anticardiolipin antibodies and the lupus anticoagulant. *BMJ*, **289**, 576.
39. Assier, H., Chosidow, O., Piette, J.C. et al (1995) Absence of antiphospholipid and anti-endothelial cell antibodies in malignant atrophic papulosis: a study of 15 cases. *J Am Acad Dermatol*, **33**, 831–833.
40. Muller, S.A., Landry, M. (1976) Malignant atrophic papulosis (Degos' disease): a report of two cases with clinical and histological studies. *Arch Dermatol*, **112**, 357–363.
41. Soter, N.A., Murphy, G.F., Mihm, M.C. (1982) Lymphocytes and necrosis of the cutaneous microvasculature in malignant atrophic papulosis: a refined microscope study. *J Am Acad Dermatol*, **7**, 620–630.
42. Feuerman, E.J., Dollberg, L., Salvador, O. (1970) Malignant atrophic papulosis with mucin in the dermis. A clinical and pathological study, including autopsy. *Arch Pathol*, **90**, 310–315.
43. Grilli, R., Soriano, M.L., Izquierdo, M.J. et al (1999) Panniculitis mimicking lupus erythematosus profundus: a new histopathologic finding in malignant atrophic papulosis (Degos disease). *Am J Dermatopathol*, **21**, 365–368.
44. Casparie, M.K., Meyer, J.W.R., van Hystee, B.E.W. et al (1991) Endoscopic and histopathologic features of Degos' disease. *Endoscopy*, **23**, 231–233.
45. Tsao, H., Busam, K., Barnhill, R.L. et al (1997) Lesions resembling malignant atrophic papulosis in a patient with dermatomyositis. *J Am Acad Dermatol*, **36**, 317–319.

Atrophie blanche

Clinical features

Atrophie blanche (livedo vasculitis, livedoid vasculitis, segmental hyalinizing vasculitis) is a common dermatosis that usually occurs in the elderly, particularly females.[1–3] In its fully established state it consists of one or more irregular, smooth, atrophic plaques surrounded by a hyperpigmented border and telangiectases (*Figs 15.110, 15.111*). Ulcerative lesions of two types may precede it:

- small (1–5 mm diameter), very painful erythematous purpuric areas that ulcerate and heal slowly
- chronic large areas of ulceration up to 5 cm in diameter, which, after a long period of time, heal to form extensive areas of atrophic plaque.

Atrophie blanche shows a seasonal variation, typically worsening in the summer months. Lesions recur at periodic intervals and are predominantly located on the lower legs, ankles and the dorsal surfaces of the feet. Occasionally, however, they may be found around the forearms, fingers and hands.[3] The disease is often associated with signs of venous stasis.

Atrophie blanche has been reported in association with lupus erythematosus and antiphospholipid syndrome.[4,5] One study found 17% of lupus patients were affected.[5] This study also noted that the pattern of cutaneous lesions was somewhat unusual with involvement of the knees, elbows, fingers, soles and the back.[5] This same study suggested that patients with lupus erythematosus that have atrophie blanche are at an increased risk of developing lupus central nervous system involvement.[5]

Pathogenesis and histological features

The pathogenesis of atrophie blanche is not well understood but it appears that ischemia may be the end result. Although increased hydrostatic pressure certainly contributes to the development of this condition, the finding of both immunoglobulin (usually IgM, less often IgG and IgA) and complement within the blood vessel walls raises the possibility of an immunological pathogenesis.[6] Atrophie blanche has been associated with a localized defect of tissue plasminogen activator.[3] The location of the lesions certainly suggests that trauma may also play some role in development of lesions. Recently, patients with atrophie blanche and disorders of coagulation such as Factor V Leiden mutation, raised anticardiolipin antibodies, protein C deficiency and raised levels of

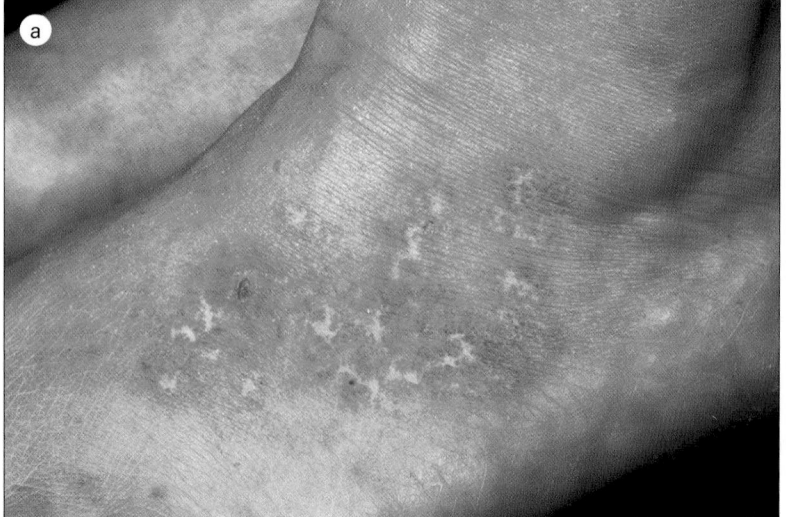
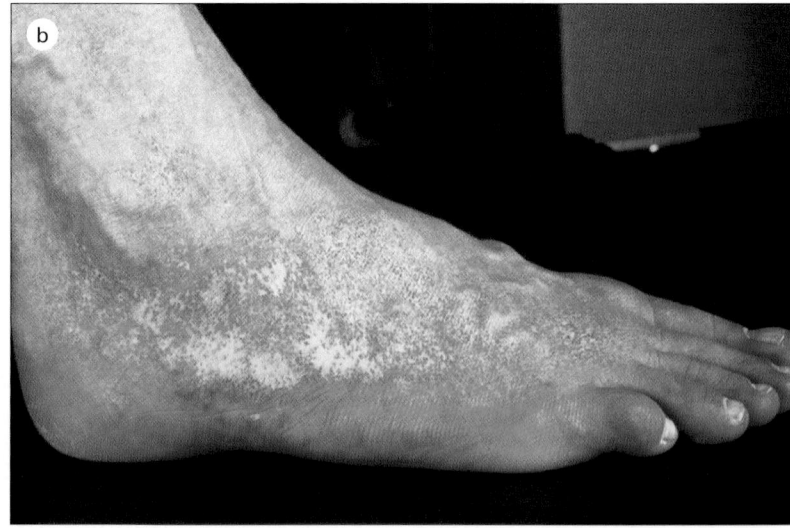

Fig. 15.110
Atrophie blanche: (**a**) there is ulceration with erythema and scaling; (**b**) this example shows marked hyperpigmentation with scarring and atrophy around the ankle and extending onto the dorsum of the foot. By courtesy of the Institute of Dermatology, London, UK.

fibrinopeptide A have been described, suggesting that, at least in some patients, an underlying coagulopathy is the basis of disorder.[7-10]

Early and ulcerative lesions are characterized by the presence of increased numbers of dermal vessels containing fibrin within their walls in addition to intraluminal fibrinoid plugs (*Figs 15.112–15.114*). The latter are typically diastase-resistant and periodic acid–Schiff (PAS) positive, and can also be highlighted by use of the phosphotungstic acid–hematoxylin stain (*Fig. 15.115*). Inflammatory destruction of blood vessels is, however, not a feature and therefore this disorder is not a true vasculitis. Variable degrees of red cell extravasation are evident and hemosiderin pigment is often present. A perivascular lymphohistiocytic infiltrate of varying intensity is usually found and dermal mast cells are often increased in number. Ulcerative lesions show infarction of the superficial dermis and epidermis. In the fully established atrophic plaque, in addition to the vascular changes, the epidermis is atrophic and the dermis shows dense scleroderma-like scarring.

Differential diagnosis

The histological features in the appropriate clinical setting are diagnostic of atrophie blanche. Coagulopathies are associated with intraluminal

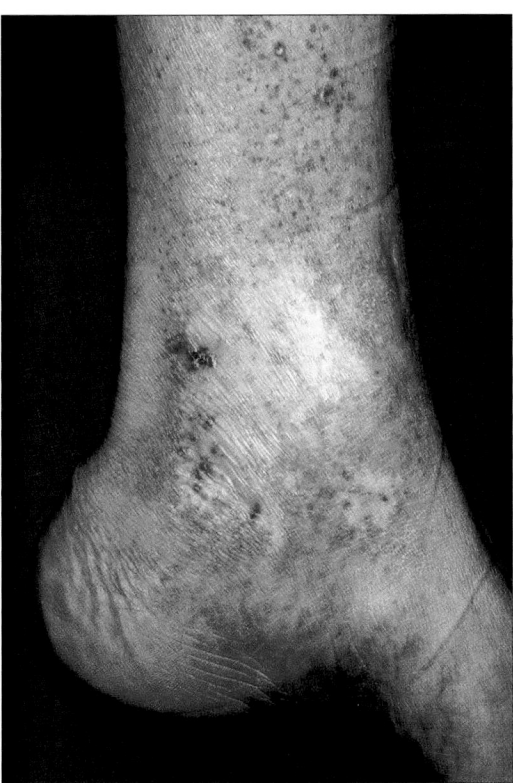

Fig. 15.111
Atrophie blanche: an extensive ivory white area of scarring overlies the medial malleolus. By courtesy of R.A. Marsden, St George's Hospital, London, UK.

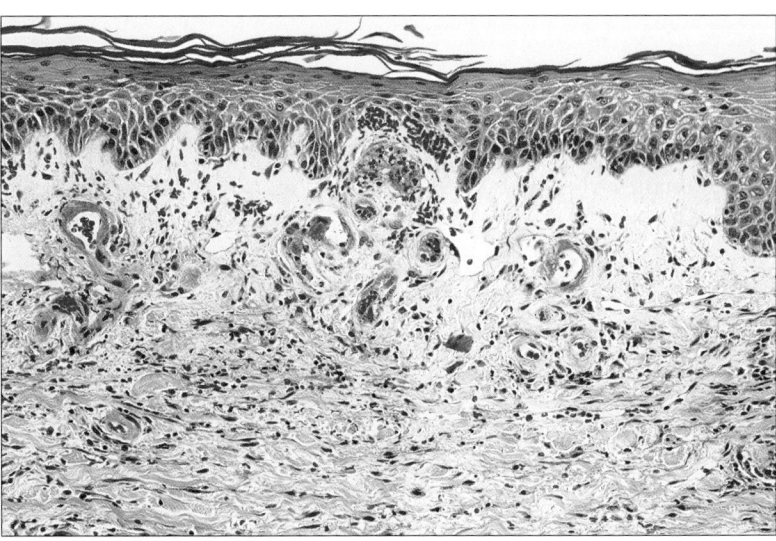

Fig. 15.112
Atrophie blanche: the vessels in the papillary dermis are increased in number and show mural fibrin deposition. There is underlying scarring.

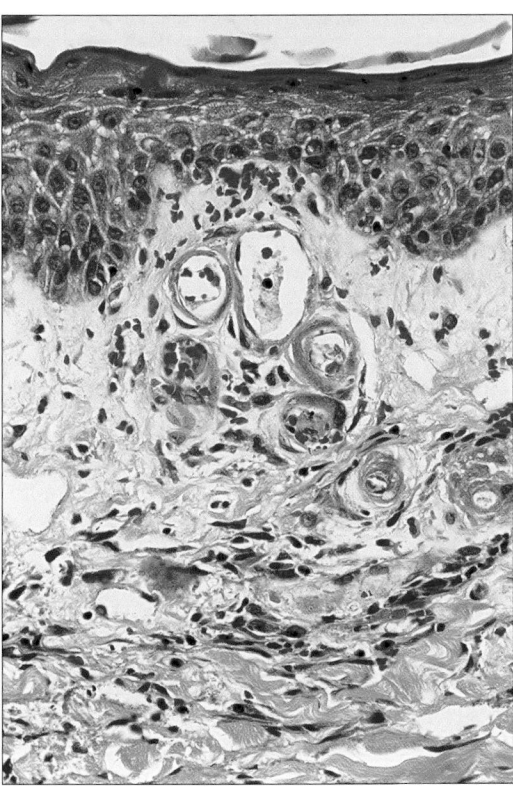

Fig. 15.113
Atrophie blanche: high power view of vessels.

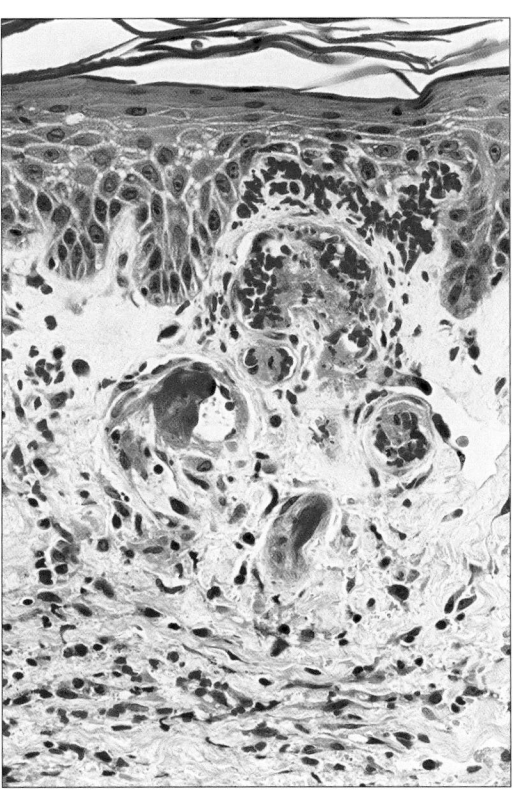

Fig. 15.114
Atrophie blanche: occluded vessels are present. There is marked red blood cell extravasation.

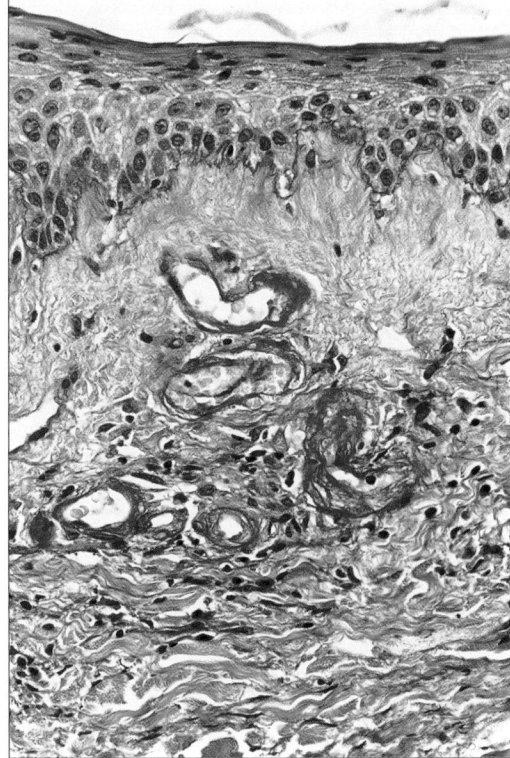

Fig. 15.115
Atrophie blanche: the vessel walls are strongly PAS positive, diastase resistant.

fibrinoid plugs but not extensive fibrinoid change of the vessel wall. Atrophie blanche shows some of the features seen in stasis dermatitis such as clustering of vessels in the superficial dermis; however, uncomplicated stasis does not show fibrinoid change.

References

1. Milstone, L.M., Braverman, I.M., Lucky, P. et al (1983) Classification and therapy of atrophie blanche. *Arch Dermatol*, **119**, 963–969.
2. Schroeter, A.L., Diaz-Perez, J.L., Winkelmann, R.K. et al (1975) Livedo vasculitis (the vasculitis of atrophie blanche). *Arch Dermatol*, **111**, 188–193.
3. Gibson, L.E., Su, W.P.D. (1990) Cutaneous vasculitis. *Rheum Dis Clin North Am*, **16**, 309–324.
4. Gibson, S.E., Su, W.P., Pittelkow, M.R. (1997) Antiphospholipid syndrome and the skin. *J Am Acad Dermatol*, **36**, 970–982.
5. Yasue, T. (1986) Livedoid vasculitis and central nervous system involvement in systemic lupus erythematosus. *Arch Dermatol*, **122**, 66–70.
6. Stiefler, R.E., Bergfeld, W.F. (1982) Atrophie blanche. *Int J Dermatol*, **2**, 1–7.
7. Calamia, K.T., Balabanova, M., Perniciaro, C. et al (2002) Livedo (livedoid) vasculitis and the factor V Leiden mutation: additional evidence for abnormal coagulation. *J Am Acad Dermatol*, **46**, 133–137.
8. Boyvat, A., Kundakci, N., Babikir, M.O. et al (2000) Livedoid vasculitis associated with heterozygous protein C deficiency. *Br J Dermatol*, **143**, 840–842.
9. Acland, K.M., Darvay, A., Wakelin, S.H. et al (1999) Livedoid vasculitis: a manifestation of the antiphospholipid syndrome. *Br J Dermatol*, **140**, 131–135.
10. McCalmont, C.S., McCalmont, T.H., Jorizzo, J.L. et al (1992) Livedo vasculitis: vasculitis or thrombotic angiopathy? *Clin Exp Dermatol*, **17**, 4–8.

Dermatological manifestations of cholesterol crystal embolism

Clinical features

Cholesterol crystal embolism is a disease of the elderly and typically occurs in males (4:1), thereby reflecting the demographics of atherosclerosis.[1,2] Cholesterol embolism may occur spontaneously or complicate trauma to the aorta.[1] It may be seen following warfarin therapy.[3] Systemic symptoms due to infarction are variable and depend upon the organ embolized. Necrotizing vasculitis has been described following cholesterol crystal embolization.[4] Multisystem involvement may result in an initial diagnosis of vasculitis.

Patients commonly manifest pyrexia, myalgia and a sudden onset of systemic hypertension. An increased ESR, blood eosinophilia and raised serum creatinine are additional features. Cutaneous manifestations are common and include:

- livedo reticularis, often bilateral, affecting the feet and legs and sometimes extending up to involve the trunk[5]
- gangrene of the toes (*Fig. 15.116*)
- cyanosis
- purple toes
- cutaneous ulceration
- nodules on the legs, thighs, feet and toes
- purpuric lesions on the legs and feet.

The cutaneous lesions of cholesterol crystal embolism may, therefore, mimic many other vascular lesions and biopsy is essential for diagnosis. Mortality is very high due to cardiac and central nervous system involvement.

Pathogenesis and histological features

Cholesterol emboli are found in the small to large arteries and arterioles of the deep dermis or subcutaneous fat (*Fig. 15.117*). Diagnosis depends upon the identification of typical biconvex cleft- or needle-shaped empty spaces (representing evanescent cholesterol crystals dissolved during tissue processing) often associated with atheromatous debris or luminal thrombosis. It is essential, therefore, that deep biopsies are taken. Multiple levels should also be examined because emboli tend to be patchily distributed and are often difficult to detect. The skin supplied by the occluded vessel may be infarcted (*Fig. 15.118*).

References

1. Falanga, V., Fine, M.J., Kapoor, W.N. (1986) The cutaneous manifestations of cholesterol crystal embolization. *Arch Dermatol*, **112**, 1194–1198.
2. Cappiello, R.A., Espinoza, L.R., Adelman, H. et al (1989) Cholesterol embolism: a pseudovasculitic syndrome. *Semin Arthritis Rheum*, **18**, 240–246.
3. Hyman, B., Landas, S., Ashman, R. et al (1987) Warfarin-related purple toes syndrome and cholesterol microembolization. *Am J Med*, **82**, 1233–1237.
4. Remy, P., Jacquot, C., Dochy, D. et al (1987) Cholesterol atheroembolic renal disease with necrotizing glomerulonephritis. *Am J Nephrol*, **7**, 164–165.
5. Pennington, M., Yeager, J., Skelton, H. et al (2002) Cholesterol embolism syndrome: cutaneous histopathologic features and the variable onset of symptoms in patients with different risk factors. *Br J Dermatol*, **146**, 511–517.

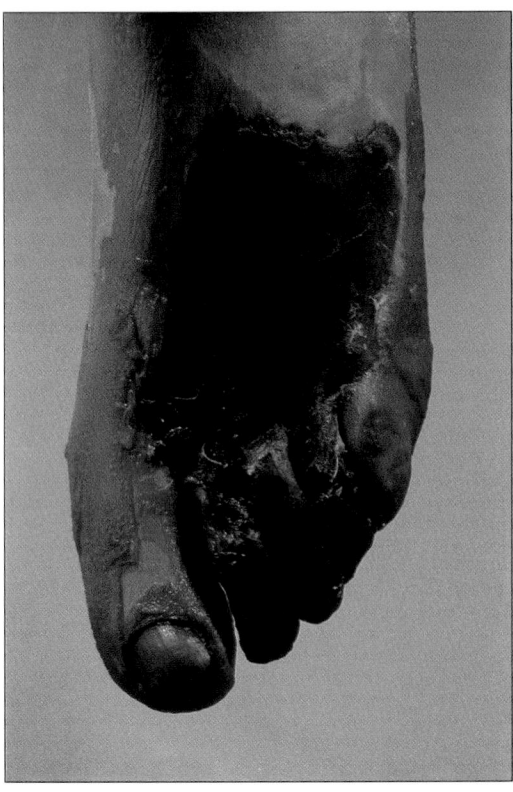

Fig. 15.116
Cholesterol embolism: there is extensive infarction of the toes of this elderly male patient.

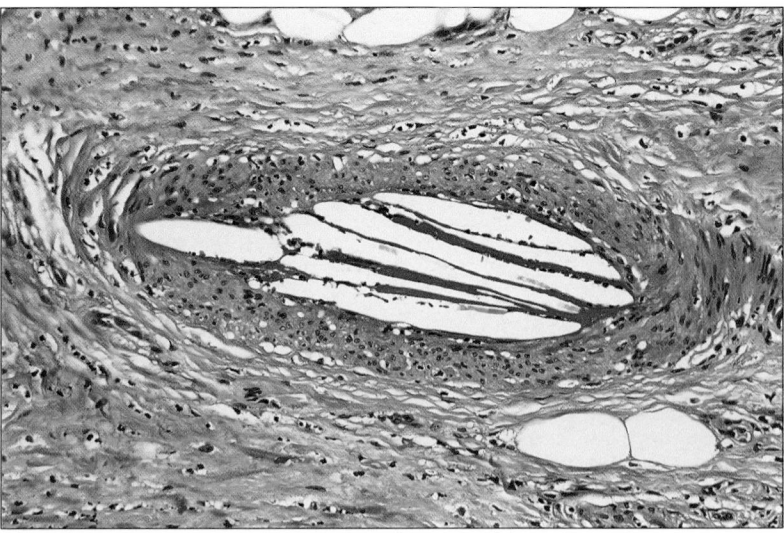

Fig. 15.117
Cholesterol emboli: typical adherent and organized embolus containing cholesterol clefts within a subcutaneous artery. This patient subsequently died from a ruptured atheromatous aortic aneurysm.

Disseminated intravascular coagulation

Clinical features

Disseminated intravascular coagulation (DIC) is a consumptive coagulopathy that is associated with a wide variety of underlying disorders, many of them life threatening. DIC is not uncommonly seen in very ill patients and may be acute, subacute or chronic. Purpura fulminans is a term that has been applied to infection-associated DIC in children. More recently, some authors have applied the term less restrictively to a severe form of DIC associated with high morbidity and mortality.[1,2] Purpura fulminans is characterized by an acute syndrome of rapidly progressive and extensive hemorrhagic skin necrosis associated with dermal vascular thrombosis and vascular collapse due to DIC.[3,4] A common presentation is symmetrical purpura of the fingers and toes.

DIC is commonly associated with complications of pregnancy and delivery such as abruptio placentae, sepsis and amniotic fluid embolism. A wide variety of infections including bacterial sepsis, meningococcemia and fungal infections may also be associated. Massive trauma, heat stroke, shock, snakebite, poisoning and burns may cause DIC. Malignant neoplasms (including carcinoma of the stomach, breast, colon, small cell carcinoma of the lung, brain and pancreas) and hematological malignancies have also been associated with DIC.[5–8]

Purpura fulminans occurs predominantly in children and has an equal incidence in males and females. It develops as a complication of a prodromal infectious illness, most commonly meningococcemia, scarlet fever, viral upper respiratory tract infection, chickenpox, rubella and other exanthemata.[9] The disease shows some seasonal variation, being more common in winter and spring. Children develop large confluent ecchymoses, which particularly affect the buttocks, legs and feet, and commonly appear on the upper limbs and abdomen (*Fig. 15.119*). The ecchymoses frequently become necrotic, and blood-filled blisters are often found. On occasions the limbs may become gangrenous (*Fig. 15.120*). Fever and hypotension accompany the cutaneous lesions.

Hematological studies reveal thrombocytopenia, anemia and often a leukocytosis. The prothrombin and bleeding times are prolonged. Fibrinogen levels are low and fibrin–fibrinogen degradation products elevated.

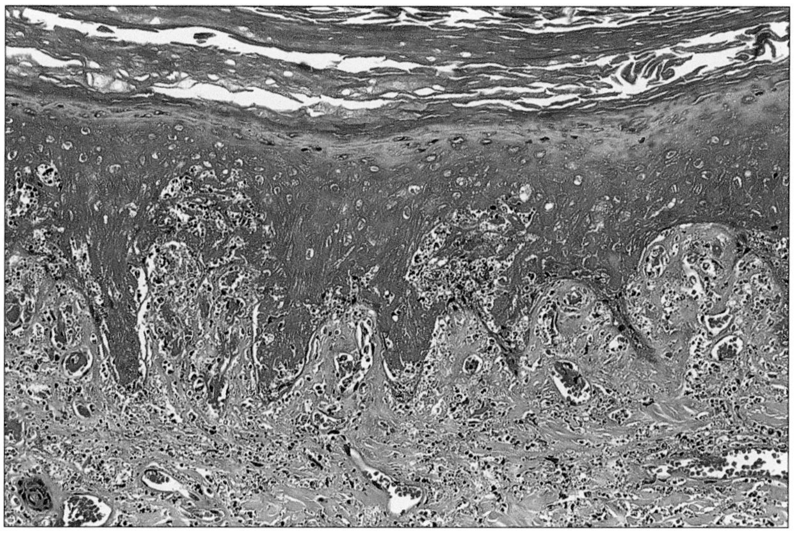

Pathogenesis and histological features

As stated above, DIC is not a disease *sui generis* but represents a coagulopathy resulting from a large number of disorders. These conditions trigger DIC either by causing direct injury to endothelial cells, which causes platelet aggregation, or by increasing circulating procoagulant factors, often tissue factor. The consequences are thrombosis, fibrinolysis leading to depletion of fibrin, clotting factors and platelets, vascular occlusion, tissue ischemia and hemorrhage. Clotting factors may be

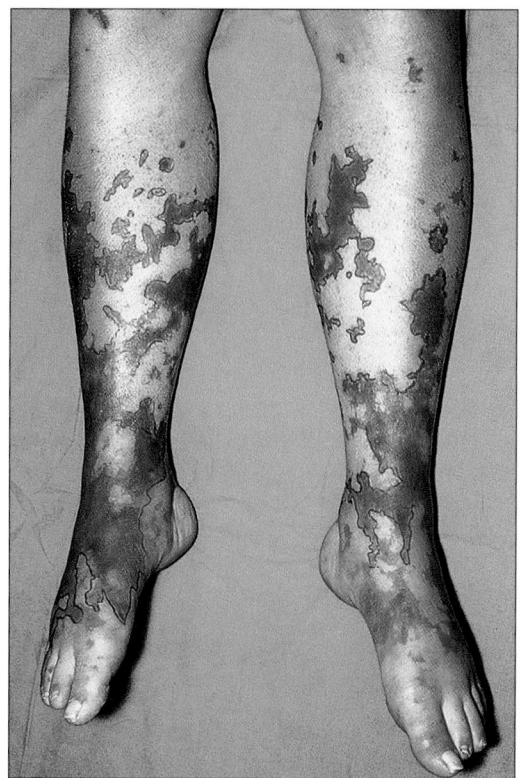

Fig. 15.119
Purpura fulminans: bilateral extensive ecchymoses are present on this child's legs. By courtesy of D. McGibbon, MD, St Thomas' Hospital, London, UK.

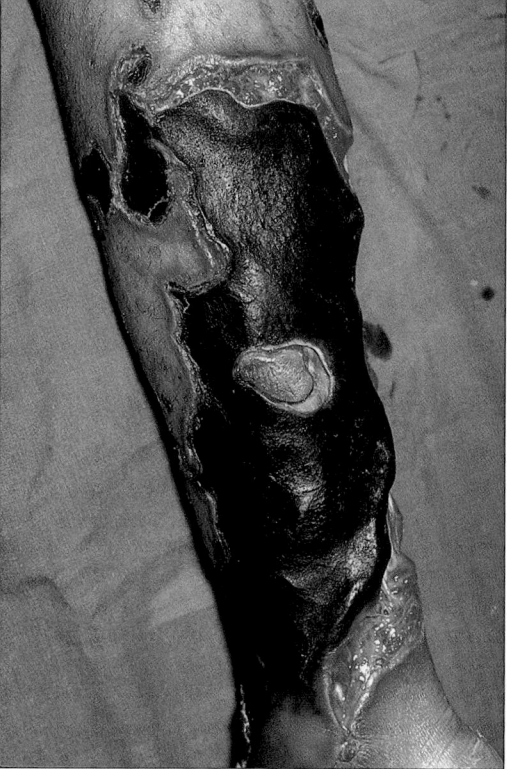

Fig. 15.120
Purpura fulminans: there is complete gangrene of the skin. By courtesy of D. McGibbon, MD, St Thomas' Hospital, London, UK.

Fig. 15.118
Cholesterol embolism: section of the skin from the gangrenous foot shown in *Fig. 15.116* shows complete infarction. Note the epidermis, which shows eosinophilic coagulative necrosis.

consumed at a rate that exceeds the ability of the liver for synthesis. The coagulopathy, in turn, causes a hemolytic anemia by damaging red blood cells.

Purpura fulminans may sometimes be a manifestation of hereditary protein C deficiency, protein S deficiency, coumarin therapy and antiphospholipid antibodies.[3]

Biopsy of skin lesions in patients with DIC are characterized by fibrin, platelet or mixed thrombi in the capillaries and venules, particularly of the skin, but also commonly affecting the internal viscera including the kidneys, bowel, bladder and brain.[3] The number of vessels containing thrombi ranges from scattered to nearly all vessels being involved. Variable numbers of extravasated red blood cells are seen. In patients with purpura fulminans, the thrombi are associated with diffuse and extensive hemorrhage. Early lesions usually show few or no perivascular inflammatory cells. Older lesions are often characterized by epidermal necrosis and subepidermal blood-filled bullae (*Figs 15.121, 15.122*). A mild perivascular inflammatory cell infiltrate of lymphocytes and polymorphs may be present. Infective DIC or purpura fulminans may show features of a leukocytoclastic vasculitis. Immunofluorescence studies for immunoglobulins and complement are uniformly negative.

Differential diagnosis

The differential diagnosis includes other causes of coagulopathy or leukocytoclastic vasculitis. Serological evaluation for disorders of coagulation is required to support the diagnosis. Finally, since successful treatment is both supportive and aimed at the underlying disorder, patients must be evaluated to determine the underlying causes of the DIC.

References

1. Robboy, S.J., Mihm, M.C., Colman, R.W. et al (1973) The skin in disseminated intravascular coagulation: prospective analysis of thirty six cases. *Br J Dermatol*, **88**, 221–229.
2. Spicer, T.E. (1976) Purpura fulminans. *Am J Med*, **61**, 566–571.
3. Adcock, D.M., Hicks, M.J. (1990) Dermatopathology of skin necrosis associated with purpura fulminans. *Semin Thromb Hemost*, **16**, 283–292.
4. Salman, S.M., Kibbi, A.G. (2002) Vascular reactions in children. *Clin Dermatol*, **20**, 11–15.
5. Gordon, L.I., Kwann, H.C. (1999) Thrombotic microangiopathy manifesting as thrombotic thrombocytopenic purpura/hemolyitic uremic syndrome in the cancer patient. *Semin Thromb Hemost*, **25**, 217–221.
6. Origuchi, N., Kimura, W., Muto, T. et al (1998) Pancreatic mucin-producing adenocarcinoma associated with a pancreatic stone. *Surg Today*, **28**, 1261–1265.
7. Sawaya, R.E., Ligon, B.L. (1994) Thrombotic complications associated with brain tumors. *J Neurooncol*, **22**, 173–181.
8. Matsueda, K., Yamamoto, H., Doi, I. (1998) An autopsy case of granulocytic sarcoma of the porta hepatis causing obstructive jaundice. *J Gastroenterol*, **33**, 428–433.
9. Childers, B.J., Cobanov, B. (2003) Acute infectious purpura fulminans: a 15-year retrospective review of 28 consecutive cases. *Am Surg*, **69**, 86–90.

Cryoglobulinemia

Cryoglobulins are immunoglobulins that precipitate at low temperatures (4°C) and which redissolve on warming (*Fig. 15.123*). Typically, the greater their concentration, the higher the temperature at which they precipitate. This has obvious clinical implications, particularly for plasmapheresis therapy.

Cryoglobulins may be subdivided into three classes:[1]
- *Type I* cryoglobulin is composed solely of monoclonal immunoglobulin (either kappa or lamda) and is usually, though not invariably, associated with a variety of lymphoproliferative disorders, including multiple myeloma, Waldenström's macroglobulinemia, chronic lymphocytic leukemia and lymphocytic lymphoma.
- *Type II* (mixed) cryoglobulin is composed of monoclonal (usually IgM) immunoglobulin reacting against polyclonal IgG.
- *Type III* (polyclonal) cryoglobulin is composed of polyclonal immunoglobulins (usually IgG and IgM).

The last two subtypes (mixed cryoglobulins) function as immune complexes and clinical manifestations are therefore due, at least in part, to allergic vasculitis. Mixed cryoglobulinemia may be clinically subdivided into two forms:
- *Essential mixed cryoglobulinemia*, in which most patients are infected with the hepatitis C virus. Hepatitis B virus has been also described in association with essential mixed cryoglobulinemia.[2]
- *Secondary mixed cryoglobulinemia*, which develops as a complication of a variety of conditions, including connective tissue diseases such as SLE, lymphoreticular neoplasms or infective disease processes (e.g. infective endocarditis and glandular fever).[3]

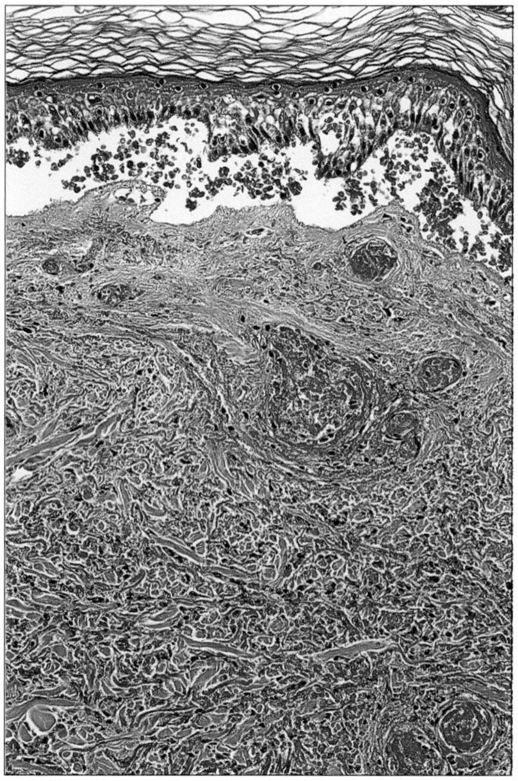

Fig. 15.121
Purpura fulminans: there is epidermal infarction, subepidermal blister formation and occluded vessels.

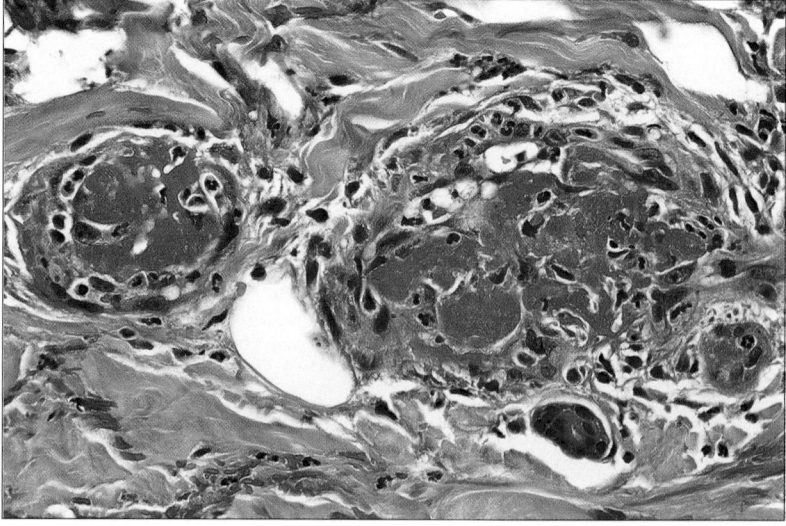

Fig. 15.122
Purpura fulminans: numerous small thrombi are seen in the superficial vessels. Mild secondary inflammatory changes are present.

Clinical features

The eponym 'Meltzer's triad' has been applied to the combined features of purpura, arthralgia and weakness that are often present.[2] Cutaneous manifestations are common to all classes of cryoglobulinemia and are often the presenting complaint.[1,2,4] Purpura is the most frequent initial sign.

Type I cryoglobulinemia is usually characterized by purpuric lesions including inflammatory macules and papules on the extremities, accompanied by foci of ulceration (*Fig. 15.124*).[5] Additional features may include livedo reticularis, Raynaud's phenomenon, scarring and infarction, which particularly affects the digits, ears and nose.[5] Renal lesions are uncommon, but some patients may manifest hematuria, proteinuria (occasionally amounting to the nephrotic syndrome) and, rarely, anuria.[6]

Mixed cryoglobulinemia is characterized by joint involvement (arthralgia and arthritis), Raynaud's phenomenon, fever, purpura, weakness, renal involvement, hepatosplenomegaly and generalized vasculitis. Cutaneous manifestations include palpable purpura, inflammatory macules and papules, necrotizing vasculitis, crural ulcers and, occasionally, cold urticaria.[5,7] Additional rare manifestations have included follicular pustular purpura, erythema multiforme and necrobiotic xanthogranuloma.[5,8,9] Renal involvement may be identified by proteinuria, hematuria and red cell casts. Patients may also have polyneuropathies. Prognosis is variable. Renal involvement, which occurs in 50% of cases, is associated with high morbidity and mortality.

Given the frequent association of hepatitis virus infection with cryoglobulinemia, it comes as no surprise that some patients develop hepatocellular carcinoma.[10,11]

Pathogenesis and histological features

In keeping with an immune complex-mediated pathogenesis, hypocomplementemia is the rule. The cryoprecipitate is composed of polyclonal IgG with either monoclonal or polyclonal IgM and is associated with rheumatoid factor properties.[12] In some patients, hepatitis B virus surface antigen or antihepatitis B antibodies may be identified in either the serum or the cryoprecipitate, suggesting a possible causal relationship. Both hepatitis C and hepatitis B viruses have been reported in cases of mixed cryoglobulinemia.[13–15] Since most patients with essential mixed cryoglobulinemia are infected with the hepatitis C virus, it appears likely that this represents the cause of this form of the disease and consequently this aspect has received much investigative attention. Hepatitis C virus and hepatitis C virus antigen–antibody complexes have been demonstrated in cryoprecipitates.[16] Hepatitis C viral RNA is detected by polymerase chain reaction (PCR) in peripheral blood monocytes of 81–90% of patients with mixed cryoglobulinemia.[17,18] Hepatitis C genome has also been demonstrated in the bone marrow cells of patients with mixed cryoglobulinemia.[19] Interestingly, the E2 envelope protein of the hepatitis C virus binds to CD81, which is present on B-lymphocytes.[20] What role this interaction plays in the pathogenesis of cryoglobulinemia is poorly understood.[20]

Other infective agents may also be associated with cryoglobulinemia including protozoa, fungi, bacteria, chlamydia and rickettsiae. Cryoglobulinemia has been reported in patients infected with the HIV virus.[21–25] However, in HIV patients with circulating cryoglobulins, the clinical symptoms usually associated with cryoglobulinemia are often lacking.[21] Another study has shown that in HIV-infected patients the presence of cryoglobulins is significantly associated with increased

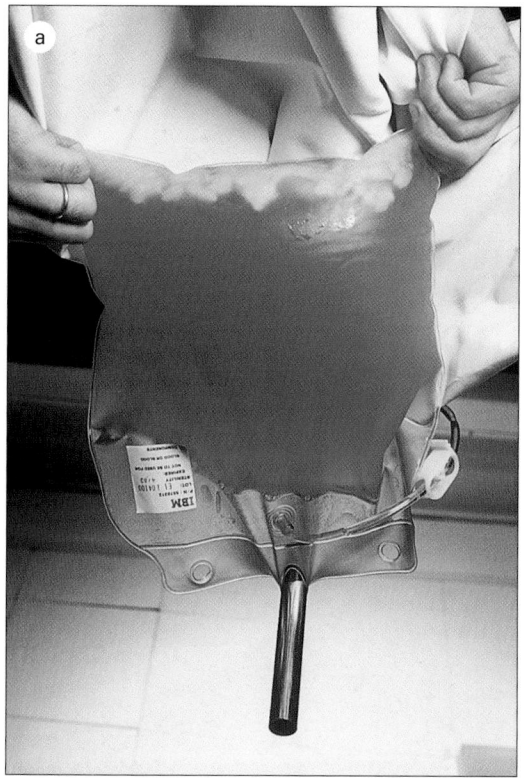
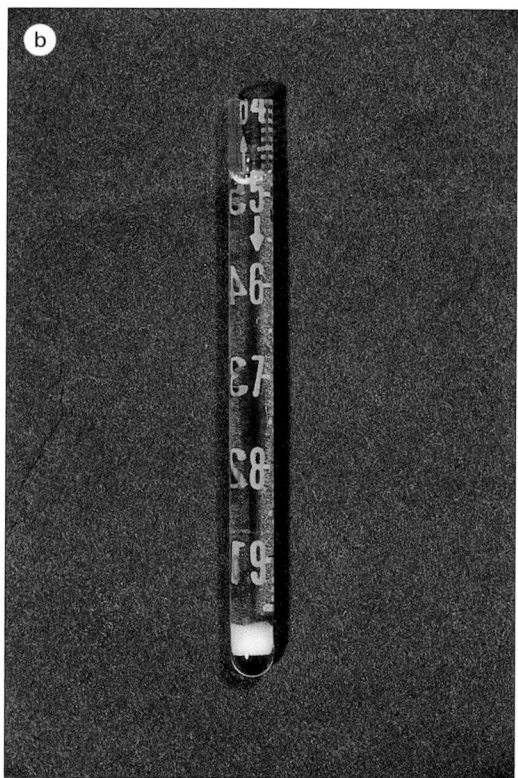

Fig. 15.123
Cryoglobulinemia: (a) there is a large quantity of precipitated cryoglobulin in this plasmapheresis specimen; (b) a cryoprecipitate. By courtesy of N. Slater, MD, St Thomas' Hospital, London, UK.

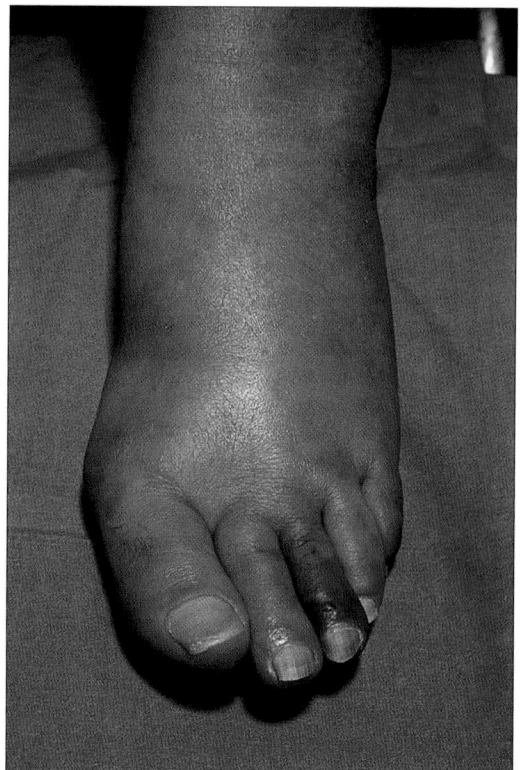

Fig. 15.124
Cryoglobulinemia: there is purplish discoloration of the third toe. By courtesy of N. Slater, MD, St Thomas' Hospital, London, UK.

mortality and risk of developing neoplasia (including B-cell lympho-proliferative disorders).[22] Interestingly, disappearance of the symptoms of cryoglobulinemia following infection with the HIV-1 virus has also been reported. The authors of this report speculate on a significant role for CD4+ T-cells in the pathogenesis of cryoglobulinemia in a subset of patients.[26]

The histological features of monoclonal cryoglobulinemia are those of vascular dilatation, endothelial swelling and plugging of vascular lumina by hyaline material, which is diastase-resistant, PAS positive (*Fig. 15.125*). Intravascular rouleaux formation may also be a feature.[5] On occasion, monoclonal cryoglobulinemia may be associated with leukocytoclastic vasculitis.[5]

In addition to occasional intracapillary hyaline thrombi, patients with severe renal involvement may manifest features of membranoprolifera-tive glomerulonephritis.

Mixed cryoglobulinemia is associated with immune complex-mediated acute leukocytoclastic vasculitis. The cryoglobulins precipitate in small vessels at low temperature and the resultant complement activation ensures the changes of acute vasculitis. Immunofluorescence is positive for IgG, IgM and complement (*Fig. 15.126*). Occasionally, intravascular hyaline thrombi may be seen in early lesions. Red cell extravasation is often a feature.

In biopsies from acute cases, the renal glomeruli may show intra-capillary thrombi. Other renal manifestations include membranoproli-ferative glomerulonephritis and vasculitis.

Differential diagnosis

The histological differential diagnosis of monoclonal cryoglobulinemia includes other causes of thrombotic vasculopathy, for example DIC, thrombotic thrombocytopenic purpura, protein C deficiency and warfarin (coumadin) necrosis. Although subtle histological clues may suggest cryoglobulinemia, such as the waxy hyaline texture of the casts, definitive diagnosis is based on serological testing for cryoglobulins. The differential diagnosis of mixed cryoglobulinemia includes other causes of leukocytoclastic vasculitis.

References

1. Brouet, J.C., Clauvel, J.P., Danon, F. et al (1974) Biologic and clinical significance of cryoglobulins: a report of 86 cases. *Am J Med*, **57**, 775–788.
2. Lie, J.T. (1991) Infection related vasculitis. In: Churg, A., Churg, J. (eds) Systemic vasculitides. New York: Igaku-Shoin, pp 243–256.
3. Monti, G., Galli, M., Invernizzi, F. et al (1995) Cryoglobulinemias: a multicentre study of early clinical and laboratory manifestations of primary and secondary disease. *QJM*, **88**, 115–126.
4. Ellis, F.A. (1964) The cutaneous manifestations of cryoglobulinaemia. *Arch Dermatol*, **89**, 690–697.
5. Cohen, S.J., Pittelkow, M.R., Daniel Su, W.P. (1991) Cutaneous manifestations of cryoglobulinaemia: clinical and histopathologic study of seventy-two patients. *J Am Acad Dermatol*, **25**, 21–27.
6. Heptinstall, R.H. (1983) Cryoglobulins. In: Heptinstall, R.H. (ed.) Pathology of the kidney, 3rd edn. Boston: Little, Brown, pp 1041–1050.
7. Koda, H., Kanaide, A., Asahi, M. et al (1978) Essential IgG cryoglobulinemia with purpura and cold urticaria. *Arch Dermatol*, **114**, 784–786.
8. Nir, M.A., Pick, A.I., Schreibman, S. et al (1974) Mixed IgG–IgM cryoglobulinemia with follicular pustular purpura. *Arch Dermatol*, **109**, 539–542.
9. Huff, J.C., Weston, W.L., Carr, R.I. (1980). Mixed cryoglobulinemia, 125 IClq binding and skin immunofluorescence in erythema multiforme. *J Invest Dermatol*, **74**, 375–377.
10. Ramos-Casals, M., Trejo, O., Gracia-Carrasco, M. et al (2000) Mixed cryoglobulinemia: new concepts. *Lupus*, **9**, 83–91.
11. Donada, C., Crucitti, A., Donadon, V. et al (1998) Systemic manifestations and liver disease in patients with chronic hepatitis C and type II or III mixed cryoglobulinemia. *J Viral Hepat*, **5**, 179–185.
12. Meltzer, M., Franklin, E.C., Elias, K. et al (1966) Cryoglobulinemia – a clinical and laboratory study. II. Cryoglobulins with rheumatoid factor activity. *Am J Med*, **40**, 837–856.
13. Durand, J.M., Lefevre, P., Harle, J.R. et al (1991) Cutaneous vasculitis and cryoglobulinaemia type II associated with hepatitis C infection. *Lancet*, **337**, 449–500.
14. Bambara, L.M., Biasi, D., Carameaschi, S. et al (1991) Cryoglobulinemia and hepatitis C virus (HCV) infection. *Clin Exp Rheumatol*, **9**, 96–97.
15. Gorevic, P.D., Kassab, H.J., Levo, Y. et al (1980) Mixed cryoglobulinemia: clinical aspects and long-term follow-up of 40 patients. *Am J Med*, **69**, 287–308.
16. Agnello, V., Chung, R.T., Kaplan, L.M. (1992) A role for hepatitis C virus infection in type II cryoglobulinemia. *N Engl J Med*, **19**, 1490–1495.
17. Ferri, C., Monti, M., La Civata, L. et al (1993) Infection of peripheral blood mononuclear cells by hepatitis C virus in mixed cryoglobulinemia. *Blood*, **82**, 3701–3704.

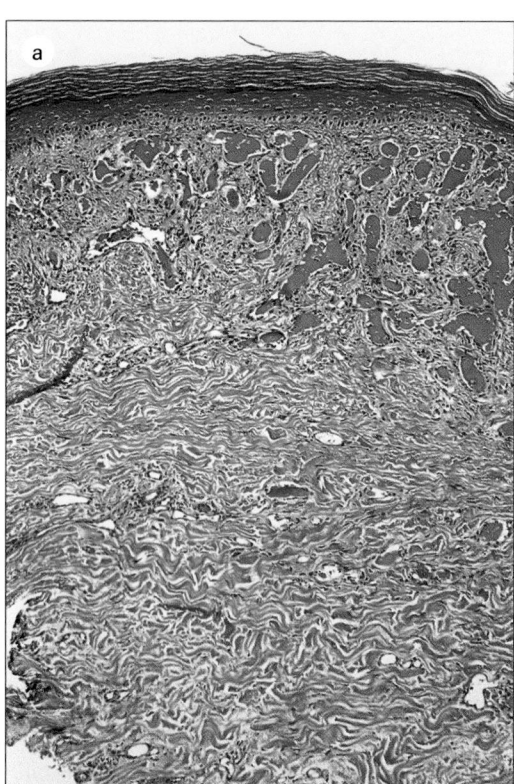

Fig. 15.125
(a, b) Monoclonal cryoglobulinemia: these dilated vessels contain intensely eosinophilic proteinaceous casts. By courtesy of S. Poole, MD, Beth Israel Deaconess Medical Center, Boston, USA.

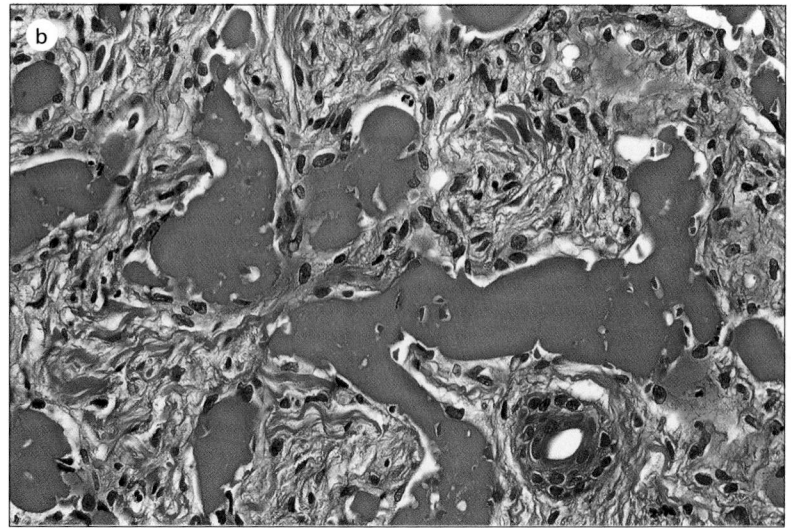

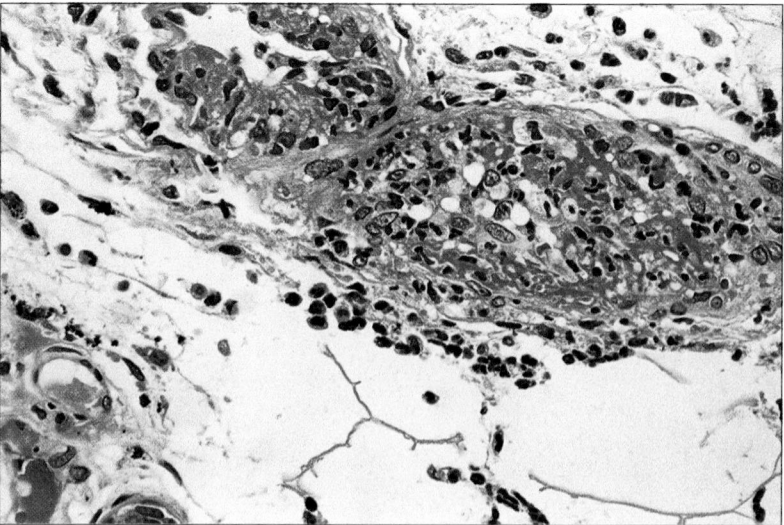

Fig. 15.126
Mixed cryoglobulinemia: in this example the features of acute leukocytoclastic vasculitis are evident.

18. De Maddalena, C., Zehender, G., Bianchi Bosiso, A. et al (1995) HCV-RNA detection using different PRC methods in sera, cryoglobulins, and peripheral blood mononuclear cells of patients with mixed cryoglobulinemia. *Clin Exp Rheumatol*, **13**, S119–S122.
19. Zehender, G., de Maddalena, C., Monti, G. et al (1995) HCV genotypes in bone marrow and peripheral blood mononuclear cells of patients with mixed cryoglobulinemia. *Clin Exp Rheumatol*, **13**, S87–S90.
20. Pileri, P., Uematsu, Y., Campagnoli, S. et al (1998) Binding of hepatitis C virus to CD81. *Science*, **282**, 938–941.
21. Fabris, P., Tositti, G., Giordani, M.T. et al (2003) Prevalence and clinical significance of circulating cryoglobulins in HIV-positive patients with and without co-infection with hepatitis C virus. *J Med Virol*, **69**, 339–343.
22. Kordossis, T., Sipsas, N.V., Kontos, A. et al (2001) Mixed cryoglobulinemia is associated with increased risk for death, or neoplasia in HIV-1 infection. *Eur J Clin Invest*, **31**, 1078–1082.
23. Dimitrakopoulos, A.N., Kordossis, T., Hatzakis, A. et al (1999) Mixed cryoglobulinemia in HIV-1 infection: the role of HIV-1. *Ann Intern Med*, **130**, 226–230.
24. Cohen, P., Roulot, D., Ferriere, F. et al (1997) Prevalence of cryoglobulins and hepatitis C virus infection in HIV-infected patients. *Clin Exp Rheumatol*, **15**, 523–527.
25. Gherardi, R., Belec, L., Mhiri, C. et al (1993) The spectrum of vasculitis in human immunodeficiency virus-infected patients. A clinicopathologic evaluation. *Arthritis Rheum*, **36**, 1164–1174.
26. Antinori, S., Galimberti, L., Rusconi, S. et al (1995) Disappearance of cryoglobulins and remission of symptoms in a patient with HCV-associated type II cryoglobulinemia after HIV-1 infection. *Clin Exp Rheumatol*, **13**, S157–S159.

Antiphospholipid antibody syndrome and Sneddon syndrome

Clinical features

The circulating anticoagulant known as the antiphospholipid antibody is associated with paradoxical thrombosis, spontaneous abortion, premature labor, intrauterine death, labile hypertension, cutaneous necrosis, gangrene, ecchymoses, purpura, leg ulcers, atrophie blanche, livedo reticularis and false positive syphilis serology – the lupus anticoagulant syndrome.[1-6] The last, also known more accurately as the antiphospholipid syndrome because not all patients have associated SLE, is due to the presence of circulating antiphospholipid antibodies, which inhibit coagulation in vitro, and are associated with a greatly increased risk of thrombotic phenomena affecting both arteries and veins. In addition to the 'lupus anticoagulant', another important type of antiphospholipid antibody is the anticardiolipin antibody, named for its ability to bind cardiolipin.

Although this syndrome is most often encountered in young adult women, it has been documented in children as well as the elderly. This demographic pattern is certainly a reflection of the association with lupus erythematosus, which shows a marked predilection for young women (*Table 15.15*).

Cutaneous involvement is often the first manifestation of disease. Patients develop necrosis of skin, which, in some cases, may be widespread and severe.[7] In addition to disfiguring necrosis, these patients suffer pain and are at risk of superimposed infection.[8] Livedo reticularis is due to thrombotic involvement of arterioles and arteries.

Systemic involvement includes deep venous thrombosis, often complicated by pulmonary embolism, renal infarcts, cerebral vascular occlusion with resultant strokes, transient ischemic attacks, multi-infarct dementia, myocardial infarction and gangrene.[3] The term 'catastrophic antiphospholipid syndrome' is applied to patients who develop complications resulting from multiorgan involvement.[8,9] The prognosis for this pernicious form of the disease is poor: in one study, 60% of patients died.[9]

The association of cutaneous thrombotic lesions, hypertension and cerebrovascular disease is sometimes referred to as Sneddon's

Table 15.15

Preliminary criteria for the classification of the antiphospholipid syndrome*

Clinical criteria[†]

1. Vascular thrombosis: One or more clinical episodes of arterial, venous or small vessel thrombosis, in any tissue or organ. Thrombosis must be confirmed by imaging or Doppler studies or histopathology, with the exception of superficial venous thrombosis. For histopathological confirmation, thrombosis should be present without significant evidence of inflammation in the vessel wall.
2. Pregnancy morbidity:
   (a) One or more unexplained deaths of a morphologically normal fetus at or beyond the 10th week of gestation, with normal fetal morphology documented by ultrasound or by direct examination of the fetus, or
   (b) One or more premature births of a morphologically normal neonate at or before the 34th week of gestation because of severe pre-eclampsia or eclampsia, or severe placental insufficiency, or
   (c) Three or more unexplained consecutive spontaneous abortions before the 10th week of gestation, with maternal anatomic or hormonal abnormalities and paternal and maternal chromosomal causes excluded.
   In studies of populations of patients who have more than one type of pregnancy morbidity, investigators are strongly encouraged to stratify groups of subjects according to (a), (b) or (c) above.

Laboratory criteria

1. Anticardiolipin antibody of IgG and/or IgM isotype in blood, present in medium or high titer, on two or more occasions, at least 6 weeks apart, measured by a standardized enzyme-linked immunosorbent assay for β_2-glycoprotein I-independent anticardiolipin antibodies.
2. Lupus anticoagulant present in plasma, on two or more occasions, at least 6 weeks apart, detected according to the guidelines of the International Society on Thrombosis and Hemostasis (Scientific Subcommittee on Lupus Anticoagulants/Phospholipid-Dependent Antibodies), in the following steps:
   (a) Prolonged phospholipid-dependent coagulation demonstrated on a screening test, e.g. activated partial thromboplastin time, kaolin clotting time, dilute Russell's viper venom time, dilute prothrombin time, Textarin time.
   (b) Failure to correct the prolonged coagulation time on the screening test by mixing with normal platelet-poor plasma.
   (c) Shortening or correction of the prolonged coagulation time on the screening test by the addition of excess phospholipid.
   (d) Exclusion of other coagulopathies, e.g. Factor VIII inhibitor or heparin, as appropriate.

Definite antiphospholipid antibody syndrome is considered to be present if at least one of the clinical criteria and one of the laboratory criteria are met.

* No exclusions other than those contained within the above criteria are needed. However, because of the likelihood that thrombosis may be multifactorial in patients with the antiphospholipid antibody syndrome, the workshop participants recommend that: (a) patient populations being studied should be assessed for other contributing causes of thrombosis, and (b) such populations should be stratified according to identifiable or probable risk factors (e.g. age or comorbidities). Specific limits were not placed on the interval between the clinical event and the positive laboratory findings. However, it was the view of many at the workshop that: (a) information about such intervals should be assessed when relevant, and (b) the relatively strict definition of laboratory criteria (including the requirement that results again be positive on repeat tests performed at least 6 weeks after the initial test) would help to exclude antiphospholipid antibody positivity that represents an epiphenomenon to the clinical events.

[†]These criteria were mainly developed by Branch and Silver.

Reproduced with permission from Wilson, W.A. (2001) *Rheumatic Diseases Clinics of North America*, **27**, 499–505.

syndrome.[3,10] Not all patients with Sneddon's syndrome have anti-phospholipid antibodies – the prevalence in various publications has ranged from 0 to 85%.[10]

In addition to lupus erythematosus, the antiphospholipid syndrome has also been documented in association with other autoimmune diseases including rheumatoid arthritis, hemolytic anemia, thrombocytopenic purpura and ulcerative colitis.[11] It may also complicate treatment with a number of drugs including phenothiazines and procainamide, or develop during viral illnesses, and can present with an underlying lymphoma.[11]

There is a growing body of literature documenting systemic vasculitis in patients with antiphospholipid and anticardiolipin antibodies including Takayasu's arteritis, temporal arteritis, polyarteritis nodosa and Wegener's granulomatosis.[12–17] A patient with Degos' disease and anticardiolipin antibodies has also been described.[18]

Carcinomas arising in lung, ovary, gastrointestinal tract and kidney have been reported in association with antiphospholipid syndrome.[19–24]

The antiphospholipid antibody syndrome has been reported in patients infected with the human immunodeficiency virus.[25–27] Some HIV-infected patients have antiphospholipid antibodies without clinical features of the antiphospholipid syndrome.[25]

Pathogenesis and histological features

Antibodies (IgM or IgG) that are reactive with phospholipids clearly play a role in the pathogenesis of the antiphospholipid antibody syndrome; however, the precise pathogenesis is not well understood. Theories include inhibition of protein C (a natural vitamin K-dependent anticoagulant) function and a suppressive effect on endothelial cell prostacyclin.[28] Endothelial cell injury and platelet activation may also play a role. The role of beta-2 glycoprotein, a glycoprotein with antithrombotic properties, has been investigated. Some antiphospholipid antibodies bind to beta-2 glycoprotein 1, which may lead to inhibition of Factor XII and platelet activation and also decrease prothrombinase activity.

Patients with the antiphospholipid antibody are predisposed to thrombosis and have prolonged partial thromboplastin and kaolin clotting times; however, it is important to note that not all patients with the antiphospholipid antibody develop thrombosis. In one study, 28% of lupus patients with antiphospholipid antibodies had no evidence of antiphospholipid antibody syndrome.[29]

Biopsy shows features of a thrombotic vasculopathy, i.e. vascular occlusion of arterioles and arteries with a fibrinoid plug, which may be associated with variable numbers of intraluminal inflammatory cells. Generally, there is minimal or no inflammation of the blood vessel wall or surrounding tissue. Marked dermal necrosis is sometimes a feature. It should be noted that false negative biopsies may occur.[10] Therefore, a negative biopsy does not exclude underlying disease.

Differential diagnosis

The biopsy findings are non-specific and the differential diagnosis of antiphospholipid antibody syndrome includes other forms of thrombotic vasculopathy. Serological studies are required to evaluate for antiphospholipid and anticardiolipin antibodies as well as to evaluate for underlying associated disorders.

References

1. Hughes, G.R.V. (1984) Autoantibodies in lupus and its variants: experience in 1000 patients. *BMJ*, **289**, 339–342.
2. Asherson, R.A., Mayou, S.C., Merry, P. et al (1989) The spectrum of livedo reticularis and anticardiolipin antibodies. *Br J Dermatol*, **120**, 215–221.
3. Grattan, C.E.H., Burton, J.L. (1991) Antiphospholipid syndrome and cutaneous vasoocclusive disorders. *Semin Dermatol*, **10**, 152–159.
4. Gibson, G.E., Su, W.P., Pittelkow, M.R. (1997) Antiphospholipid syndrome and the skin. *J Am Acad Dermatol*, **36**, 970–982.
5. Wilson, W.A., Gharavi, A.E., Koike, T. et al (1999) International consensus statement on preliminary classification criteria for definite antiphospholipid syndrome. *Arthritis Rheum*, **42**, 1309–1311.
6. Wilson, W.A. (2001) Classification criteria for antiphospholipid antibody syndrome. *Rheum Dis Clin*, **27**, 499–505.
7. Creamer, D., Hunt, B.J., Black, M.M. (2000) Widespread cutaneous necrosis occurring in association with the antiphospholipid syndrome. *Br J Dermatol*, **142**, 1199–1203.
8. Asherson, R.A., Cervera, R., Piette, J.C. et al (1998) Catastrophic antiphospholipid syndrome. Clinical and laboratory features of 50 patients. *Medicine*, **77**, 195–207.
9. Asherson, R.A., Piette, J.C. (1996) The catastrophic antiphospholipid syndrome 1996: acute mutiorgan failure associated with antiphospholipid antibodies: a review of 31 patients. *Lupus*, **5**, 414–417.
10. Frances, C., Papo, T., Wechsler, B. et al (1999) Sneddon syndrome with or without antiphospholipid antibodies. A comparative study of 46 patients. *Medicine*, **78**, 209–219.
11. Smith, K.J., Skelton, H.G., James, W.D. et al (1990) Cutaneous histopathologic findings in 'antiphospholipid syndrome'. *Arch Dermatol*, **126**, 1176–1183.
12. Yokoi, K., Hosoi, E., Akaike, M. et al (1996) Takayasu's arteritis with antiphospholipid antibodies: report of two cases. *Angiology*, **47**, 315–319.
13. Dasgupta, B., Almond, M.K., Tanqueray, A. (1997) Polyarteritis nodosa and the antiphospholipid antibody syndrome. *Br J Rheumatol*, **36**, 1210–1212.
14. Norden, D.K., Ostrov, B.E., Shafritz, A.B. et al (1995) Vasculitis associated with antiphospholipid syndrome. *Semin Arthritis Rheum*, **24**, 273–281.
15. McHugh, N.J., James, I.E., Plant, G.T. (1990) Anticardiolipin and antineutrophil antibodies in giant cell arteritis. *J Rheumatol*, **17**, 916–922.
16. Duhaut, P., Berruryer, M., Pinede, L. et al (1998) Anticardiolipin antibodies and giant cell arteritis: a prospective, multicenter case-control study. *Arthritis Rheum*, **41**, 701–709.
17. Bleil, L., Manger, B., Winkler, T.H. et al (1991) The role of antineutrophil cytoplasm antibodies, anticardiolipin antibodies, von Willebrand factor antigen, and fibronectin for the diagnosis of systemic vasculitis. *J Rheumatol*, **18**, 1199–1206.
18. Englert, H.J., Hawkes, C.H., Boey, M.L. et al (1984) Degos' disease: association with anticardiolipin antibodies and the lupus anticoagulant. *BMJ*, **289**, 576.
19. Yamamoto, T., Ito, M., Nagata, S. et al (2000) Catastrophic exacerbation of antiphospholipid syndrome after lung adenocarcinoma. *J Rheumatol*, **27**, 2035–2037.
20. Katsuoka, H., Mimori, Y., Kohriyama, T. et al (2000) An autopsy case of catastrophic antiphospholipid antibody syndrome presenting with recurrent multiple cerebral infarction associated with lung cancer. *No To Shinkei*, **52**, 64–69.
21. Jullien, V., Heudier, P., Carre, Y. et al (1999) Bronchopulmonary cancer, antiphospholipid syndrome and coagulation disorders. *Rev Med Interne*, **20**, 696–700.
22. Samadian, S., Estcourt, L. (1999) Recurrent thrombo-embolic episodes: the association of cholangiocarcinoma with antiphospholipid syndrome. *Postgrad Med J*, **75**, 45–46.
23. Ruffati, A., Aversa, S., Del Ross, T. et al (1995) Antiphospholipid antibody syndrome associated with ovarian cancer. A new paraneoplastic syndrome. *J Rheumatol*, **98**, 2162–2163.
24. Carella, F., Fetoni, V., Pollo, B. et al (1992) Sneddon's syndrome and renal carcinoma. *Funct Neurol*, **7**, 395–400.
25. de Larranaga, G.F., Forastiero, R.R., Carreras, L.O. et al (1999) Different types of antiphospholipid antibodies in AIDS: a comparison with syphilis and the antiphospholipid syndrome. *Thromb Res*, **96**, 19–25.
26. Soweid, A.M., Hajjar, R.R., Hewan-Lowe, K.O. et al (1995) Skin necrosis indicating antiphospholipid antibody syndrome in patient with AIDS. *South Med J*, **88**, 786–788.
27. Leder, A.N., Flansbaum, B., Zandman-Goddard, G. et al (2001) Antiphospholipid antibody syndrome induced by HIV. *Lupus*, **10**, 370–374.
28. Lockshin, M.D. (1991) Antiphospholipid antibody and antiphospholipid antibody syndrome. *Curr Opin Rheumatol*, **3**, 797–802.
29. Guerin, J., Smith, O., White, B. et al (1998) Antibodies to prothrombin in antiphospholipid antibody syndrome and inflammatory disorders. *Br J Haematol*, **102**, 896–902.

Thrombotic thrombocytopenic purpura and hemolytic uremic syndrome

Clinical features

Thrombotic thrombocytopenic purpura (TTP) and hemolytic uremic syndrome (HUS) are related disorders that are due to non-immune thrombocytopenia.[1–4] TTP is a very rare disease of unknown etiology associated with high morbidity and mortality.[5,6] It shows a predilection for females (2.5:1) and tends to affect younger age groups, with a peak incidence in the third decade. In its fully developed form it consists of thrombocytopenic purpura, microangiopathic hemolytic anemia, neurological symptoms, renal involvement and fever.

Hemolytic uremic syndrome is similar to TTP with the exceptions of severe renal involvement and milder CNS symptomatology.[7] However, precise classification into one or the other category is sometimes difficult and, therefore, these related disorders are discussed together.[8,9] Hemolytic uremic syndrome is often seen in patients with infectious colitis.[10,11]

The most common presenting symptoms are transient and usually recurrent neurological complaints including headaches, confusion, pareses, dysphasia and aphasia. Renal involvement includes hematuria, proteinuria and occasionally acute renal failure. Cardiac involvement is important and may precipitate left ventricular failure with resultant pulmonary congestion and edema. The hemorrhagic tendency is manifest predominantly in the skin as petechiae, purpura and ecchymoses, but hemorrhage may also be seen in the retina, conjunctiva and mucous membranes, including those of the gastrointestinal tract (*Fig. 15.127*).

TTP/HUS may be associated with connective tissue disease (especially lupus erythematosus), contraceptive use, neoplasia, chemotherapy, adverse drug reaction, bone marrow transplantation and antiphospholipid antibodies.[4,7,12–17]

Although most patients develop TTP for no apparent reason, it occasionally complicates drug therapy with, for example, penicillin or sulfonamides, or sometimes develops after an upper respiratory tract infection. Quite a high proportion of patients with TTP are pregnant, but the significance of this is uncertain. Rare cases may be associated with lupus erythematosus.

Familial cases of TTP/HUS, with both autosomal dominant and recessive patterns of inheritance, have been described.[7]

Laboratory investigations reveal gross thrombocytopenia and normochromic, normocytic anemia. Examination of peripheral blood smears commonly demonstrates fragmented and misshapen red blood cells, typically schistocytes and helmet cells. Coagulation studies are usually normal or minimally disturbed with occasionally elevated fibrinogen–fibrin degradation products. The Coombs' test is consistently negative.

Pathogenesis and histological features

The pathogenesis of TTP/HUS is poorly understood. It appears that platelet activating substances result in thrombus formation without activation of the coagulation cascade (hence the normal coagulation studies). Direct endothelial injury may also play a role in this group of disorders.

TTP has been shown to be associated with deficiency of von Willebrand factor-cleaving protease.[18–20] Familial cases of TTP appear to be due to a constitutional absence of this enzyme.[18] In some cases,

antibodies to von Willebrand factor-cleaving protease have been demonstrated.[21]

HUS is often seen in patients with colitis associated with verotoxin-producing *E. coli*.[1] In one study, 80% of patients with HUS had positive *E. coli* O157 lipopolysaccharide antibody titers.[10] Investigators have shown that verotoxin enhances platelet adhesion and thrombogenesis using a microvascular endothelial cell line.[22] A minority of patients with HUS have been shown to have mutation in the gene coding for factor H, an alternative complement pathway regulatory protein.[23]

The histological features of thrombotic thrombocytopenic purpura are those of hyaline intravascular thrombi composed of aggregates of platelets in addition to a variable amount of fibrin (*Figs 15.128, 15.129*).[24] They are associated with extravasated red blood cells, but there is no evidence of vasculitis. There may be foci of necrosis, but true

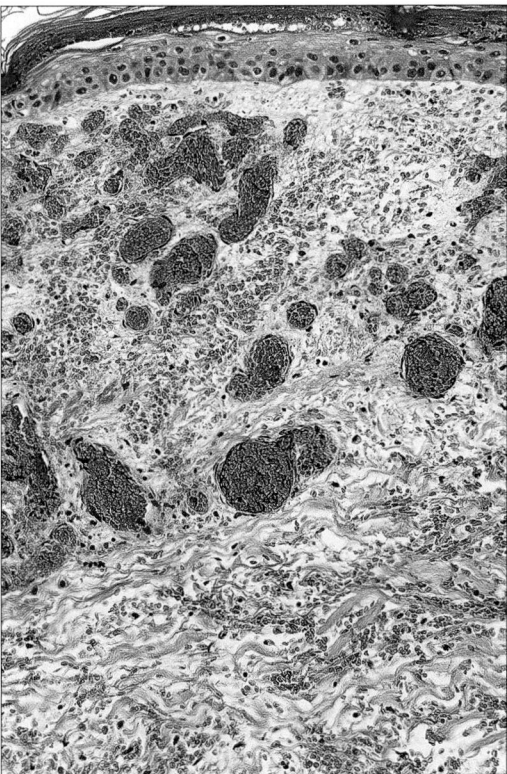

Fig. 15.128
Thrombotic thrombocytopenic purpura: microthrombi are present and there is extensive purpura.

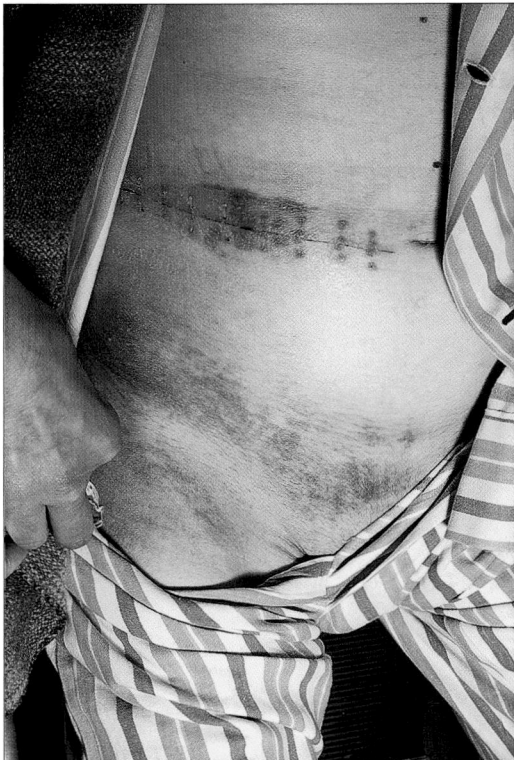

Fig. 15.127
Thrombotic thrombocytopenic purpura: sheeted ecchymoses are present in the groin. By courtesy of N. Slater, MD, St Thomas' Hospital, London, UK.

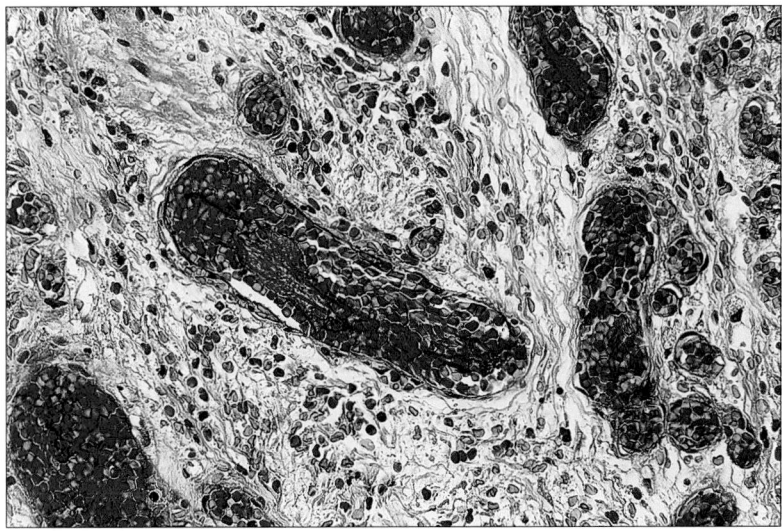

Fig. 15.129
Thrombotic thrombocytopenic purpura: the occlusions contain abundant fibrin (Martius scarlet blue).

infarcts are uncommon. At autopsy the organs most severely involved include the pancreas, adrenal glands, heart, brain and kidney.

Differential diagnosis

Distinction from other thrombotic vasculopathies requires clinicopathological correlation. In contrast to disseminated intravascular coagulation, coagulation studies (prothrombin time, partial thromboplastin time) tend to be normal in patients with TTP/HUS.

References

1. Moake, J.L. (2002) Thrombotic microangiopathies. *N Engl J Med*, 347, 589–600.
2. Halevy, D., Radhakrishnan, J., Markowitz, G. et al (2002) Thrombotic microangiopathies. *Crit Care Clin*, 18, 309–320.
3. Moake, J.L. (2002) Thrombotic thrombocytopenic purpura: The systemic clumping 'plague'. *Annu Rev Med*, 53, 75–88.
4. Elliot, M.A., Nichols, W.L. (2001) Thrombotic thrombocytopenic purpura and hemolytic uremic syndrome. *Mayo Clin Proc*, 76, 1154–1162.
5. Myers, T.J., Wakem, C.J., Ball, E.D. et al (1980) Thrombotic thrombocytopenic purpura: combined treatment with plasmapheresis and anti-platelet agents. *Ann Intern Med*, 92, 149–155.
6. Ridolfi, R.L., Bell, W.R. (1981) Thrombotic thrombocytopenic purpura: report of 25 cases and review of the literature. *Medicine*, 60, 413–428.
7. Ruggenenti, P., Noris, M., Remuzzi, G. (2001) Thrombotic microangiopathy, hemolytic uremic syndrome, and thrombotic thrombocytopenic purpura. *Kidney Int*, 60, 831–846.
8. Liu, J., Hutzler, M., Li, C. et al (2001) Thrombotic thrombocytopenic purpura (TTP) and hemolytic uremic syndrome: the new thinking. *J Thrombosis Thrombolysis*, 11, 261–272.
9. Raife, T., Montgomery, R. (2001) New aspects in the pathogenesis and treatment of thrombotic thrombocytopenic purpura and hemolytic uremic syndrome. *Rev Exp Clin Hematol*, 5, 236–261.
10. Banatvala, N., Griffin, P.M., Greene, K.D. et al (2001) The United States national prospective hemolytic uremic syndrome study: microbiologic, serologic, clinical, and epidemiologic findings. *J Infect Dis*, 183, 1063–1070.
11. Slutsker, L., Ries, A.A., Greene, K.D. et al (1997) Escherichia coli O157:H7 diarrhea in the United States: clinical and epidemiological features. *Ann Intern Med*, 126, 505–513.
12. Trent, K., Neustater, B.R., Lottenberg, R. (1997) Chronic relapsing thrombotic thrombocytopenic purpura and antiphospholipid antibodies: a report of two cases. *Am J Hematol*, 54, 155–159.
13. Gherman, R.B., Tramont, J., Connito, D.J. (1999) Postpartum hemolytic uremic syndrome associated with lupus anticoagulant. A case report. *J Reprod Med*, 44, 471–474.
14. Kniaz, D., Eisenberg, G.M., Elrad, H. et al (1992) Postpartum hemolytic uremic syndrome associated with antiphospholipid antibodies. A case report and review of the literature. *Am J Nephrol*, 12, 126–133.
15. Kwaan, H.C., Gordon, L.I. (2001) Thrombotic microangiopathy in the cancer patient. *Acta Haematol*, 106, 52–56.
16. Kelton, J.G. (2002) Thrombotic thrombocytopenic purpura and hemolytic uremic syndrome: will recent insight into pathogenesis translate in to better treatment? *Transfusion*, 42, 388–392.
17. Gordon, L.I., Kwaan, H.C. (1999) Thrombotic microangiopathy manifesting as thrombotic thrombocytopenic purpura/hemolytic uremic syndrome in a cancer patient. *Semin Thromb Hemost*, 25, 217–221.
18. Farlan, M., Robles, R., Galbusera, M. et al (1998) Von Willebrand factor-cleaving protease in thrombotic thrombocytopenic purpura and the hemolytic-uremic syndrome. *N Engl J Med*, 26, 1578–1584.
19. Bianchi, V., Robles, R., Alberio, L. et al (2002) Von Willebrand factor-cleaving protease (ADAMTS13) in thrombocytopenic disorders: a severely deficient activity is specific for thrombotic thrombocytopenic purpura. *Blood*, 100, 710–713.
20. Furlan, M., Robles, R., Solenthaler, M. et al (1997) Deficient activity of von Willebrand factor-cleaving protease in chronic relapsing thrombotic thrombocytopenic purpura. *Blood*, 89, 3097–3103.
21. Tsai, H.M., Lian, E.C. (1998) Antibodies to von Willebrand factor-cleaving protease in acute thrombotic thrombocytopenic purpura. *N Engl J Med*, 339, 1585–1594.
22. Morigi, M., Galbusera, M., Binda, E. et al (2001) Verotoxin-1 up-regulation of adhesive molecules renders microvascular endothelial cells thrombogenic at high shear stress. *Blood*, 98, 1828–1835.
23. Richards, A., Goodship, J.A., Goodship, T.H.J. (2002) The genetics and pathogenesis of haemolytic uraemic syndrome and thrombotic thrombocytopenic purpura. *Curr Opin Nephrol Hypertens*, 11, 431–435.
24. Berkowitz, L.R., Dalldorf, F.G., Blatt, P.M. (1979) Thrombotic thrombocytopenic purpura: a pathology review. *J Am Acad Dermatol*, 241, 1709–1715.

Immune thrombocytopenic purpura

Clinical features

Immune thrombocytopenic purpura (idiopathic thrombocytopenic purpura, ITP) is a rare disease, of which two forms – acute and chronic – are recognized:

- *Acute ITP* is a disorder that characteristically affects children following a viral illness.[1] Patients present with petechiae, purpura and bleeding. Most cases are self-limiting with the majority of patients recovering within weeks to months.[2] A rare but serious complication is intracranial hemorrhage.
- *Chronic ITP* is so designated when the disorder persists for 6 months or longer.[2] The chronic form tends to affect adults and is associated with connective tissue diseases such as lupus erythematosus or lymphoproliferative disorders.

Thrombocytopenic purpura has also been described in patients with thyroid disorders, including Graves' disease and Hashimoto's thyroiditis.[3,4] The condition may occur in association with multiple concurrent autoimmune diseases such as Graves' disease, diabetes mellitus, Hashimoto's disease, pernicious anemia and systemic sclerosis.[5] Some patients have had associated antiphospholipid antibody syndrome.[6–8] Patients infected with the human immunodeficiency virus may also develop immune thrombocytopenia.[9,10]

The chronic form shows a predilection for women, and presents with a tendency to bruise easily following mild trauma and bleeding (*Fig. 15.130*). In severely affected patients, lesions may develop in the mucous membranes of the respiratory, genitourinary and gastrointestinal systems in addition to the integument.

Laboratory examination reveals thrombocytopenia and a prolonged bleeding time. Partial thromboplastin time and prothrombin time are not affected.

Pathogenesis and histological features

ITP is an autoimmune disease caused by IgG antiplatelet antibodies, which lead to destruction of platelets.[11–13] Molecular mimicry between HIV glycoproteins (GP120/160) and membrane antigens (i.e. glycoprotein GPIIb/IIIa) on platelets may play a role in the development of thrombocytopenia in occasional HIV-infected patients.[11,13–15]

The cutaneous (and other) lesions are characterized by perivascular hemorrhage; there is no evidence of vasculitis (*Fig. 15.131*). Bone marrow examination reveals increased numbers of rather immature megakaryocytes. The spleen is congested and shows reactive follicular hyperplasia and sometimes conspicuous megakaryocytes.

Differential diagnosis

Biopsy findings are entirely non-specific. Serological and clinical correlation is necessary to arrive at a diagnosis.

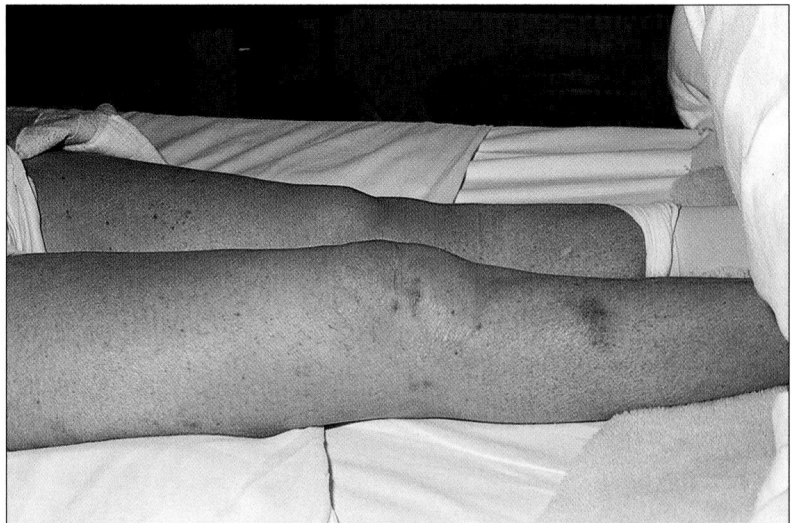

Fig. 15.130
Idiopathic thrombocytopenic purpura: these legs show purpura, petechiae and bruising. By courtesy of N. Slater, MD, St Thomas' Hospital, London, UK.

References

1. Buchanan, G.R. (2001) Idiopathic thrombocytopenic purpura in childhood. *Pediatr Ann*, **30**, 527–533.
2. Di Paola, J.A., Buchman, G.R. (2002) Immune thrombocytopenic purpura. *Pediatr Clin North Am*, **49**, 911–928.
3. Bizzaro, N. (1992) Familial association of autoimmune thrombocytopenia and hyperthyroidism. *Am J Hematol*, **39**, 294–298.
4. Yamaguchi, K., Ookubo, Y., Matsuda, H. et al (1987) Idiopathic thrombocytopenic purpura subsequent to Graves' disease and insulin-dependent diabetes. *Diabetes Res Clin Pract*, **3**, 233–237.
5. Sheehan, N.J., Stanton-King, K. (1993) Polyimmunity in a young woman. *Br J Rheumatol*, **32**, 254–256.
6. Diz-Kucukkaya, R., Hacihanefioglu, A., Yenerel, M. et al (2001) Antiphospholipid antibodies and antiphospholipid antibody syndrome in patients presenting with immune thrombocytopenic purpura: a prospective cohort study. *Blood*, **15**, 1760–1764.
7. Galindo, M., Khamashta, M.A., Hughes, G.R. (1999) Splenectomy for refractory thrombocytopenia in the antiphospholipid antibody syndrome. *Rheumatology*, **38**, 848–853.
8. Hakim, A.J., Machin, S.J., Isenberg, D.A. (1998) Autoimmune thrombocytopenia in primary antiphospholipid antibody syndrome and systemic lupus erythematosus: the response to splenectomy. *Semin Arthritis Rheum*, **28**, 20–25.
9. Louache, F., Vainchenker, W. (1994) Thrombocytopenia in HIV infection. *Curr Opin Hematol*, **1**, 369–372.
10. Yospur, L.S., Sun, N.C., Figuero, P. et al (1996) Concurrent thrombotic thrombocytopenic purpura and immune thrombocytopenic purpura in an HIV-positive patient: case report and review of the literature. *Am J Hematol*, **51**, 73–78.
11. McFarland, J. (2002) Pathophysiology of platelet destruction in immune (idiopathic) thrombocytopenic purpura. *Blood Rev*, **16**, 1–2.
12. Nugent, D.J. (2002) Childhood immune thrombocytopenic purpura. *Blood Rev*, **16**, 27–29.
13. Beardsley, D.S. (2002) Pathophysiology of immune thrombocytopenic purpura. *Blood Rev*, **16**, 13–14.
14. Bettaieb, A., Fromont, P., Louache, F. et al (1992) Presence of cross-reactive antibody between human immunodeficiency virus (HIV) and platelet glycoproteins HIV-related immune thrombocytopenic purpura. *Blood*, **80**, 162–169.
15. Bettaieb, A., Oksenhendler, E., Duedari, N. et al (1996) Cross-reactive antibodies between HIV-gp120 and platelet gpIIIa (CD61) in HIV-related immune thrombocytopenic purpura. *Clin Exp Immunol*, **103**, 19–23.

Factor V (Leiden) mutation

Mutation of Factor V Leiden is the most common inherited condition predisposing to thrombosis.[1] The mutation is associated with a prothrombotic state caused by Factor V resistance to inactivation by protein C. It can be identified by PCR. Patients with this mutation are at particular risk of deep venous thrombosis and may also develop pulmonary embolism, stroke and peripheral vascular disease.[2] Women with recurrent miscarriage have an increased incidence of this condition.[3,4] Among patients with no known explanation for deep venous thrombosis, Factor V Leiden mutation is a common cause. Patients may also develop skin ulcers.

Biopsy of skin lesions shows features of thrombotic vasculopathy. IgM and C3 deposition has been demonstrated by immunofluorescence staining.[5]

Fig. 15.131
Idiopathic thrombocytopenic purpura: there is hemorrhage but no evidence of vasculitis is seen.

References

1. Ridker, P.M., Hennekens, C.H., Lindpaintner, K. et al (1995) Mutation in the gene coding for factor V and the risk of myocardial infarction, stroke, and venous thrombosis in apparently healthy men. *N Engl J Med*, **332**, 912–917.
2. Price, D.T., Ridker, P.M. (1997) Factor V Leiden mutation and the risks of thromboembolic disease. *Ann Intern Med*, **127**, 895–903.
3. Finan, R.R., Tamim, H., Ameen, G. et al (2002) Prevalence of factor V G1691A (factor V-Leiden) and prothrombin G20210A gene mutations in a recurrent miscarriage population. *Am J Hematol*, **71**, 300–305.
4. Ridker, P.M., Miletich, J.P., Buring, J.E. et al (1998) Factor V Leiden mutation as a risk factor for recurrent pregnancy loss. *Ann Intern Med*, **128**, 1000–1003.
5. Biedermann, T., Flaig, M.J., Sander, C.A. (2000) Livedoid vasculopathy in a patient with factor V mutation (Leiden). *J Cutan Pathol*, **27**, 410–412.

Hypergammaglobulinemic purpura

Clinical features

Hypergammaglobulinemic purpura (of Waldenström) is a rare disorder that shows a marked female predilection and tends to affect the young and middle aged.[1] Patients present with recurrent, symmetrical crops of purpura, particularly affecting the lower limbs although the arms and abdomen may also be involved (*Fig. 15.132*).[2] Wearing tight-fitting garments, heat and strenuous exercise may provoke lesions. Frequency of attacks is highly variable, ranging from several times a week to as infrequent as a single episode per year.[3,4]

The clinical findings are those of petechiae measuring from pinhead size up to several millimeters. Various symptoms may be experienced, including tingling, itching, burning and pain. The petechiae resolve over the course of a few days to leave hyperpigmented macules. The purpuric attacks are recurrent and tend to great chronicity. Ecchymoses are not a feature.[1]

Laboratory investigations usually reveal a raised ESR, mild anemia and leukopenia, and polyclonal hypergammaglobulinemia (usually IgG, but sometimes IgM or IgA). Antinuclear antibodies, anti-Ro, anti-La, and rheumatoid factor are present in many patients.[1,3,5,6] Platelet levels, coagulation studies and bone marrow examination are typically normal. Cryoglobulinemia is an occasional feature. There are no known HLA associations and family history is negative.[1] Lymphadenopathy and splenomegaly are sometimes a feature.[1]

It is important to note that hypergammaglobulinemic purpura may be classified into two categories: idiopathic (Waldenström; not to be confused with Waldenström's macroglobulinemia) and secondary. In the latter group, patients may have a wide variety of conditions, including SLE, polymyositis, Hashimoto's thyroiditis, Sjögren's syndrome,

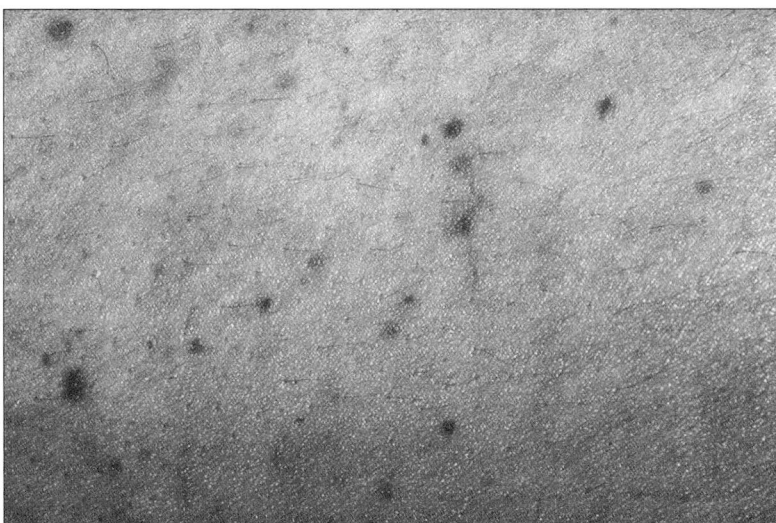

Fig. 15.132
Hypergammaglobulinemic purpura: scattered, tiny, purpuric lesions. By courtesy of J. Newton-Bishop, MD, St Thomas' Hospital, London, UK.

rheumatoid arthritis, hepatitis, chronic lymphocytic leukemia, monoclonal gammopathies and sarcoidosis.[1] The purpura may precede the associated illness for many years. Patients with this disorder, therefore, merit a careful and prolonged follow-up.

Pathogenesis and histological features

Direct immunofluorescence examination of skin lesions reveals IgM and C3 in blood vessel walls.[7] Circulating immune complexes, with both IgG and IgM, have also been demonstrated in patients with this disorder.[8] It is likely, therefore, that hypergammaglobulinemic purpura is another variant of immune complex-mediated vasculitis, namely, a type III hypersensitivity reaction. The precise etiology, however, remains poorly understood.

Histopathological examination of the purpuric lesions usually reveals the typical features of acute leukocytoclastic vasculitis with red cell extravasation.[9] Occasionally, however, lymphocytic perivasculitis is all that is evident.

Differential diagnosis

The histological changes are not specific and other causes of leuko-cytoclastic vasculitis must be considered.

References

1. Finder, K.A., McCullough, M.L., Dixon, S.L. et al (1990) Hypergammaglobulinemic purpura of Waldenström. *J Am Acad Dermatol*, **23**, 669–676.
2. Car, R.D., Heisel, E.B. (1966) Purpura hyperglobulinemia. *Arch Dermatol*, **94**, 536–541.
3. Malaviya, A.N., Kaushik, P., Budhiraja, S. et al (2000) Hypergammaglobulinemic purpura of Waldenstrom: report of 3 cases with a short review. *Clin Exp Rheumatol*, **18**, 518–522.
4. Senecal, J.L., Chartier, S., Rothfield, N. (1995) Hypergammaglobulinemic purpura in systemic autoimmune rheumatic diseases: predictive value of anti-Ro(SSA) and anti-La(SSB) antibodies and treatment with indomethacin and hydroxychloroquine. *J Rheumatol*, **22**, 868–875.
5. Miyagawa, S., Fukumoto, T., Kananuchi, M. et al (1996) Hypergammaglobulinaemic purpura of Waldenstrom and Ro/SSA antibodies. *Br J Dermatol*, **134**, 919–923.
6. Capra, J.D., Winchester, R.J., Kunkel, H.G. (1971) Hypergammaglobulinemic purpura. Studies on the unusual antiglobulins characteristic of the sera of these patients. *Medicine*, **50**, 125–138.
7. Perks, W.H., Green, F., Gleeson, M.H. (1974) A case of purpura hyperglobulinaemia of Waldenström: studies of skin immunofluorescence. *Br J Dermatol*, **91**, 563–568.
8. Olmstead, A.D., Zone, J.L., LaSalle, B., Krueger, G.G. (1980) Immune complexes in the pathogenesis of hypergammaglobulinemic purpura. *J Am Acad Dermatol*, **3**, 174–179.
9. Hudson, C.P., Callen, J.P. (1984) Cutaneous leucocytoclastic vasculitis with hyperglobulinemia and splenomegaly: a variant of hyperglobulinemic purpura of Waldenström. *Arch Dermatol*, **120**, 1224–1226.

Superficial thrombophlebitis

Clinical features

Superficial thrombophlebitis is a common disease presenting as painful, erythematous, thickened areas with a cord-like morphology. Most cases involve the lower limbs, particularly below the knees, and there is a predilection for females. Multifocal segmental disease is frequent and recurrent episodes are often seen. The disease is usually associated with hypercoagulable states. Predisposing factors are numerous and include varicose veins, pregnancy, the use of oral contraceptives (particularly those with a higher concentration of estrogen), cancer (mainly pancreatic, gastric, cholangiocarcinoma or leukemia), Behçet's disease, Factor V (Leiden) mutation, essential thrombocythemia, anticardiolipin antibodies, and deficiencies of protein C, protein S, Factor XII, antithrombin III and heparin co-factor 2C.[1–16] Superficial thrombophlebitis developing in association with secondary syphilis has been documented.[17] Superficial suppurative thrombophlebitis occurs mainly in children and it is caused by a wide variety of microorganisms, mainly bacteria (both aerobic and anaerobic) and, less commonly, fungi.[18–22] The most common bacteria isolated include *S. aureus*, *E. coli* and *P. aeruginosa*.[18,19] Candida is by far the most common fungus associated with the disease.

Superficial thrombophlebitis may be associated with deep vein thrombosis but the risk of this happening appears to be small unless there are additional risk factors.[23,24] The chance of a patient with superficial thrombophlebitis developing pulmonary embolism is low, but it has been documented and the risk appears to be greater in patients with disease affecting the thigh.[25–27]

Histological features

Superficial thrombophlebitis typically involves veins located in the superficial subcutaneous tissue. Early lesions are characterized by an infiltrate predominantly composed of neutrophils obscuring the vessel walls. The neutrophils are progressively replaced by lymphocytes, histiocytes and occasional giant cells. An organizing thrombus is initially present and this is followed by recanalization and fibrosis. The infiltrate tends to remain localized and there is very little involvement of the surrounding subcutaneous tissue. Arteries are not affected.

References

1. Guex, J.J. (1996) Thrombotic complications of varicose veins. A literature review of the role of superficial vein thrombosis. *Dermatol Surg*, **22**, 378–382.
2. Unno, N., Mitsuoka, H., Uchiyama, T. et al (2002) Superficial thrombophlebitis of the lower limbs in patients with varicose veins. *Surg Today*, **32**, 397–401.
3. Vessey, M.P. (1970) Thrombosis and the pill. *Prescr J*, **10**, 1–7.
4. McColl, M.D., Ramsay, J.E., Tait, R.C. et al (1998) Superficial vein thrombosis: incidence in association with pregnancy and prevalence of thrombophilic defects. *Thromb Haemost*, **79**, 741–742.
5. Martins, E.B., Fleming, K.A. Garrido, M.C. et al (1994) Superficial thrombophlebitis, dysplasia and cholangiocarcinoma in primary sclerosing cholangitis. *Gastroenterology*, **107**, 537–542.
6. Bilgrami, S., Greenberg, B.R., Weinstein, R.E. et al (1995) Recurrent venous thrombosis as the presenting manifestation of acute lymphocytic leukemia: leukemic cell procoagulant activity is not responsible for the hypercoagulable state. *Med Pediatr Oncol*, **24**, 40–45.
7. Samlaska, C.P., James, W.D. (1990) Superficial thrombophlebitis II. Secondary hypercoagulable states. *J Am Acad Dermatol*, **23**, 1–18.
8. Sagdic, K., Ozer, Z.G., Saba, D. et al (1996) Venous lesions in Behçet's disease. *Eur J Vasc Endovasc Surg*, **11**, 437–440.
9. Rintelen, C., Mannhalter, C., Ireland, H. et al (1996) Oral contraceptives enhance the risk of clinical manifestation of venous thrombosis at a younger age in females homozygous for factor V Leiden. *Br J Haematol*, **93**, 487–490.
10. de Moerloose, P., Wutschert, R., Heinzmann, M. et al (1998) Superficial vein thrombosis of lower limbs: influence of factor V Leiden, factor II G20210A and overweight. *Thromb Haemost*, **80**, 239–241.
11. Itin, P.H., Winkelmann, R.K. (1991) Cutaneous manifestations of patients with essential thrombocythemia. *J Am Acad Dermatol*, **24**, 59–63.
12. de Godoy, J.M., Batigalia, F., Braile, D.M. (2001) Superficial thrombophlebitis and anticardiolipin antibodies – report of association. *Angiology*, **52**, 127–129.
13. Fiehn, C., Pezzutto, A., Hunstein, W. (1994) Superficial migratory thrombophlebitis in a patient with reversible protein C deficiency and anticardiolipin antibodies. *Ann Rheum Dis*, **53**, 843–844.
14. Samlaska, C.P., James, W.D., Simel, D.L. (1990) Superficial migratory thrombophlebitis and factor XII deficiency. *J Am Acad Dermatol*, **22**, 939–943.
15. Samlaska, C.P., James, W.D. (1990) Superficial thrombophlebitis I. Primary hypercoagulable states. *J Am Acad Dermatol*, **22**, 975–989.
16. de Godoy, J.M., Braile, D.M. (2003) Protein S deficiency in repetitive superficial thrombophlebitis. *Clin Appl Thromb Hemost*, **9**, 61–62.
17. Demitsu, T., Yamada, T., Usui, K. et al (1996) Superficial thrombophlebitis in a patient with secondary syphilis. *Int J Dermatol*, **35**, 821–824.
18. Khan, E.A., Correa, A.G., Baker, C.J. (1997) Suppurative thrombophlebitis in children: a ten year experience. *Pediatr Infect Dis J*, **16**, 63–67.
19. Brook, I., Frazier, E.H. (1996) Aerobic and anaerobic microbiology of superficial suppurative thrombophlebitis. *Arch Surg*, **131**, 95–97.
20. Brook, I. (1998) Superficial suppurative thrombophlebitis in children caused by anaerobic bacteria. *J Pediatr Surg*, **33**, 1279–1282.
21. Salamon, S.A., Prag, J. (2001) A case of superficial septic thrombophlebitis in a varicose vein caused by Salmonella panama. *Clin Microbiol Infect*, **7**, 34–36.
22. Murray, C.K., Beckius, M.L., McAllister, K. (2003) Fusarium proliferatum superficial suppurative thrombophlebitis. *Mil Med*, **168**, 426–427.
23. Bounameaux, H., Reber-Wasem, M.A. (1997) Superficial thrombophlebitis and deep vein thrombosis. A controversial assocation. *Arch Intern Med*, **157**, 1822–1824.
24. Chengelis, D.L., Bendick, P.J., Glover, J.L. et al (1996) Progression of superficial venous thrombosis and deep vein thrombosis. *J Vasc Surg*, **24**, 745–749.
25. Kesteven, P., Robinson, B. (2001) Superficial thrombophlebitis followed by pulmonary embolism. *J R Soc Med*, **94**, 186–187.
26. Schonauer, V., Kyrle, P.A., Weltermann, A. et al (2003) Superficial thrombophlebitis and risk of recurrence of venous thromboembolism. *J Vasc Surg*, **37**, 834–838.
27. Verlato, F., Zucchetta, P., Prandoni, P. et al (1999) An unexpectedly high rate of pulmonary embolism in patients with superficial thrombophlebitis of the thigh. *J Vasc Surg*, **30**, 1113–1115.

Sclerosing lymphangitis

Clinical features

Sclerosing lymphangitis (Mondor's disease) is probably a misnomer as it likely represents a variant of superficial thrombophlebitis that most commonly affects the genitalia, chest wall or breasts. Women with large pendulous breasts seem to be particularly predisposed.[1] In these cases, and in others, trauma likely plays a significant role in development. Some authors have reported an association with breast carcinoma.[2] Intravenous drug abuse may be an occasional cause.[3] Sickle cell disease and protein S deficiency are rare associations.[4,5] Patients present with sometimes painful linear cord-like lesions. Typically, lesions are a few centimeters in length but sometimes may be much larger. The overlying skin is erythematous without color change. The disorder is self-limiting and usually resolves in a few weeks.[6] Rarely, persistent disease requires surgical intervention.[7]

Histological features

The pathology is characterized by organizing thrombus with variable inflammation.

References

1. Bejanga, B.I. (1992) Mondor's disease: analysis of 30 cases. *J R Coll Surg Edinb*, **37**, 322–324.
2. Catania, S., Zurrida, S., Veronesi, P. et al (1992) Mondor's disease and breast cancer. *Cancer*, **69**, 2267–2270.
3. Cooper, R.A. (1990) Mondor's disease secondary to intravenous drug abuse. *Arch Surg*, **125**, 807–808.
4. Nachmann, M.M., Jaffe, J.S., Ginsberg, P.C. et al (2003) Sickle cell episode manifesting as superficial thrombophlebitis of the penis. *J Am Osteopath Assoc*, **103**, 102–104.
5. de Godoy, J.M., Godoy, M.F., Batigalia, F. et al (2002) The association of Mondor's disease with protein S deficiency: case report and review of literature. *J Thromb Thrombolysis*, **13**, 187–189.
6. Mayor, M., Buron, I., de Mora, J.C. et al (2000) Mondor's disease. *Int J Dermatol*, **39**, 922–925.
7. Broaddus, S.B., Leadbetter, G.W. (1982) Surgical management of persistent, symptomatic nonvenereal sclerosing lymphangitis of the penis. *J Urol*, **127**, 987–988.

Senile purpura

Clinical features

Senile purpura affects the extensor surfaces of the forearms, hands and lower legs of the elderly.[1,2] Corticosteroid therapy (topical or systemic) contributes to its development in some patients. Lesions are persistent, lasting 1–3 weeks, and consist of asymptomatic purpuric macules up to several centimeters in diameter, in a background of actinically damaged or atrophic skin (*Fig. 15.133*). Senile purpura develops because of damage to the connective tissue of the dermis, which fails to support the vasculature, rendering it more susceptible to mild trauma.

Histological features

The lesions are characterized by red cell extravastion unassociated with any significant inflammatory cell reaction. There is usually marked solar elastosis.

References

1. Feinstein, R.J., Halprin, K.M., Penneys, N.S. et al (1973) Senile purpura. *Arch Dermatol*, **108**, 229–232.
2. Tattersall, R.N., Seville, R. (1950) Senile purpura. *QJM*, **74**, 151–159.

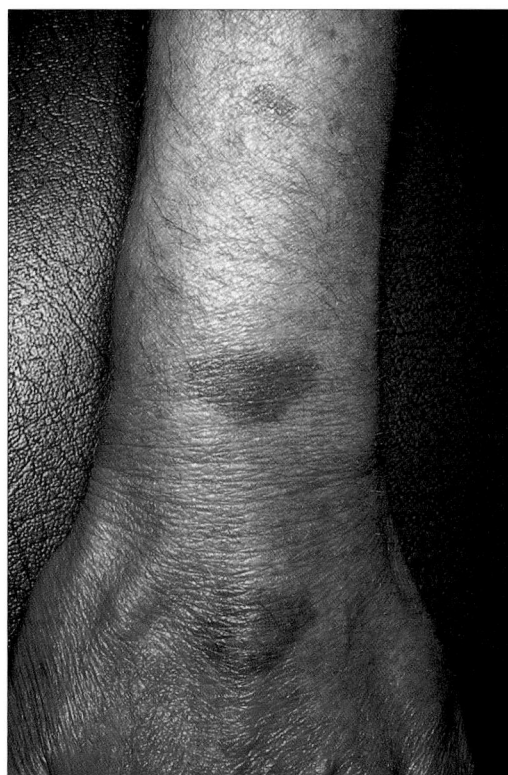

Fig. 15.133
Senile purpura: trauma-induced deep purple ecchymoses on sun-damaged skin. By courtesy of J. Newton-Bishop, MD, St Thomas' Hospital, London, UK.

Idiopathic connective tissue disorders

16

Lupus erythematosus   775

Systemic sclerosis   804

Localized scleroderma   815

Atrophoderma of Pasini and Pierini   821

Eosinophilic fasciitis   822

Lichen sclerosus et atrophicus   825

Polymyositis/dermatomyositis   825

Mixed connective tissue disease   832

Relapsing polychondritis   833

Lupus erythematosus

Lupus erythematosus is a complex disorder associated with numerous clinical signs and symptoms and a wide range of laboratory abnormalities. It shows a spectrum of varying prognosis, ranging from a benign, solely cutaneous variant (localized discoid) through to a potentially fatal systemic illness.[1-4] The range of subtypes is shown in *Table 16.1*.

Although the precise etiology is unknown, it is thought that interplay of genetic factors, autoantibodies, immune complexes, hormones and other factors is responsible for the development of the illness. There is evidence suggesting that the incidence of the systemic variant is increasing, but due to earlier diagnosis and more effective therapy, the mortality rate has significantly diminished and the 10-year overall survival rate in adults now exceeds 90%.[5] The presence of renal and/or neurological involvement, however, remains a poor prognostic indicator.[6]

Pediatric systemic lupus erythematosus (SLE) is an aggressive illness with considerable mortality, largely due to the incidence of renal disease. Even with corticosteroid and immunosuppressive therapy the death rate is as high as 15%.[7]

Clinical features

Discoid lupus erythematosus

Discoid lupus erythematosus (DLE), the commonest form, is subdivided into localized and generalized variants. This is of prognostic importance because only about 1% of patients with localized DLE develop systemic disease, but approximately 5% of those with the generalized form (in

Table 16.1
Lupus erythematosus: subtypes

• Discoid lupus erythematosus (localized)
• Discoid lupus erythematosus (generalized)
• Verrucous lupus erythematosus
• Chilblain lupus erythematosus
• Chronic granulomatous disease with discoid lupus erythematosus-like dermatosis
• Lupus erythematosus–erythema multiforme syndrome
• Subacute cutaneous lupus erythematosus
• Lupus erythematosus profundus
• Systemic lupus erythematosus
• Drug-induced lupus erythematosus
• C_2 deficiency lupus erythematosus-like syndrome
• Neonatal lupus erythematosus

particular those with persistent anemia, leukopenia, thrombocytopenia, false-positive Wassermann reaction and high titer antinuclear factor) develop full-blown SLE.[6,8–10] Discoid lesions develop in up to 20% of patients with systemic lupus.[11] Periungual telangiectasia, sclerodactyly and the presence of Raynaud's phenomenon may also signify potential disease progression.[10] Patients with DLE should not be made unduly worried about the risk of developing systemic involvement, which is not high.

Discoid lupus erythematosus is very persistent and affects twice as many females as males. Although any age group may be involved, it is most common in the third, fourth and fifth decades, with a peak incidence in people in their late thirties.[12] Presentation in childhood is rare.[13–16] Lesions typically arise on sun-exposed sites and patients frequently experience photosensitivity; there may be spring and summer exacerbation.[5] In the localized form, the head and neck are usually affected, but in the generalized variant, lesions may also be present on the dorsal aspect of the arms, hands and fingers and on the 'V' of the neck. Non-exposed sites, including the trunk, upper limbs and the palms and soles, are also commonly involved.[17]

Facial plaques occur most often on the cheeks (*Fig. 16.1*). Other sites affected include the bridge of the nose, the ears, the neck and the scalp (*Figs 16.2–16.5*). The associated scarring of the scalp is followed by permanent alopecia (*Figs 16.6–16.8*). Scalp involvement, which is more

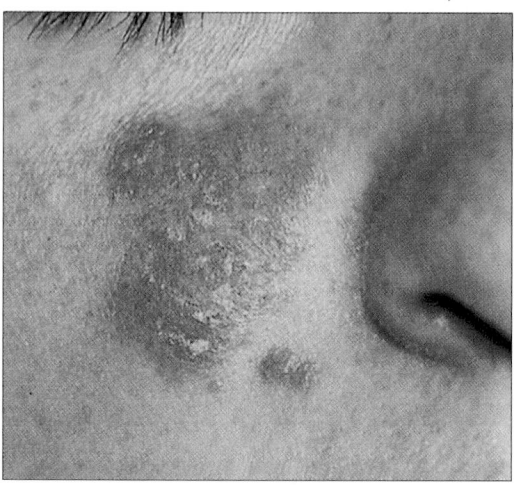

Fig. 16.1
Discoid lupus erythematosus: a typical plaque is present on the cheek of a female. Note the erythema and scale. This is a characteristic site. By courtesy of R.A. Marsden, MD, St George's Hospital, London, UK.

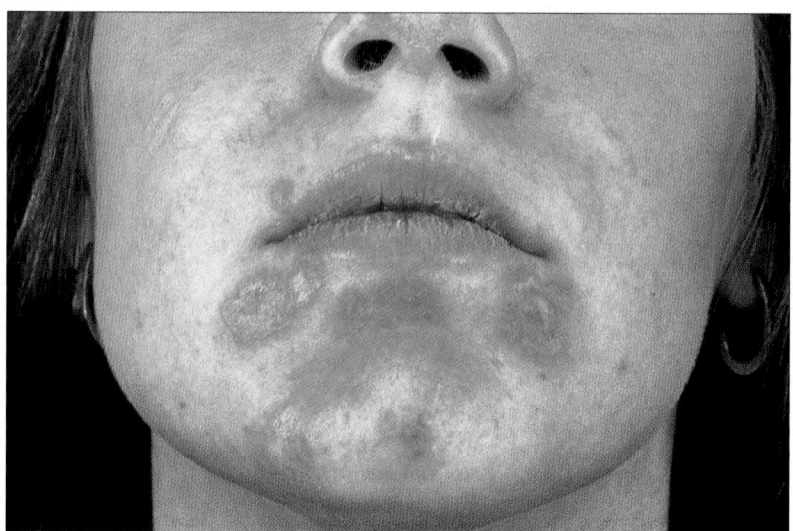

Fig. 16.2
Discoid lupus erythematosus: there are erythematous scaly plaques on the chin and nasolabial regions. By courtesy of the Institute of Dermatology, London, UK.

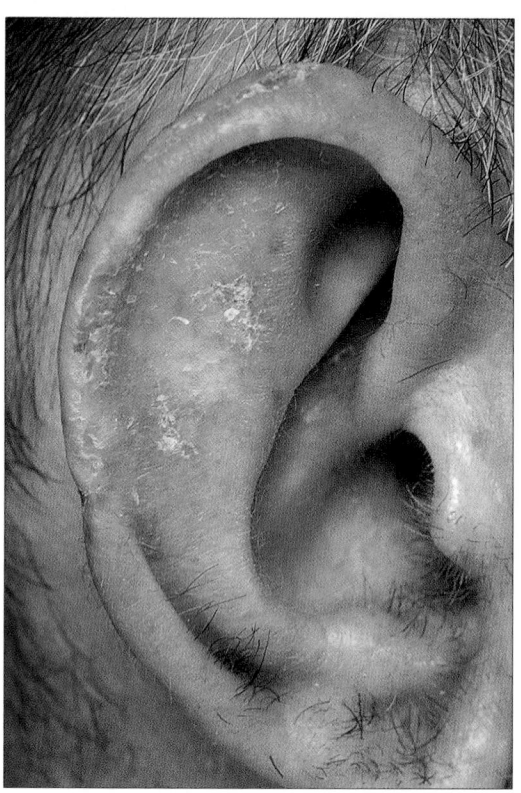

Fig. 16.3
Discoid lupus erythematosus: there is scaling and scarring on the ear lobe, a commonly affected site. By courtesy of the Institute of Dermatology, London, UK.

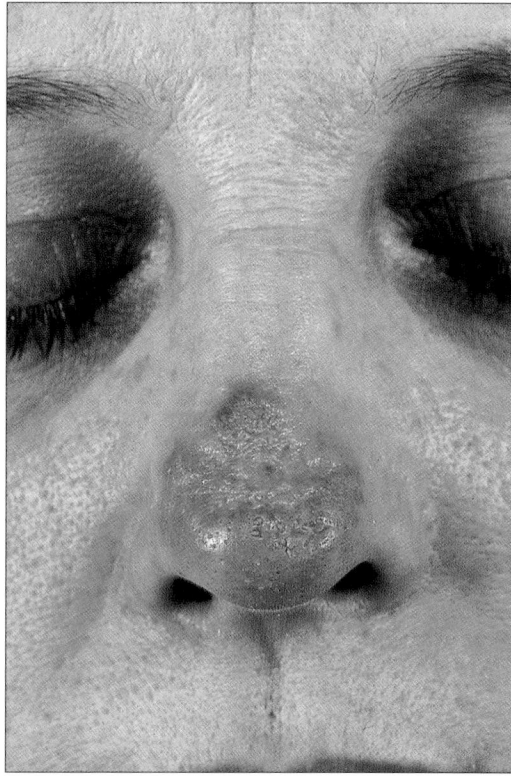

Fig. 16.4
Discoid lupus erythematosus: this severely affected patient shows healed ulceration with marked scarring and disfigurement. By courtesy of the Institute of Dermatology, London, UK.

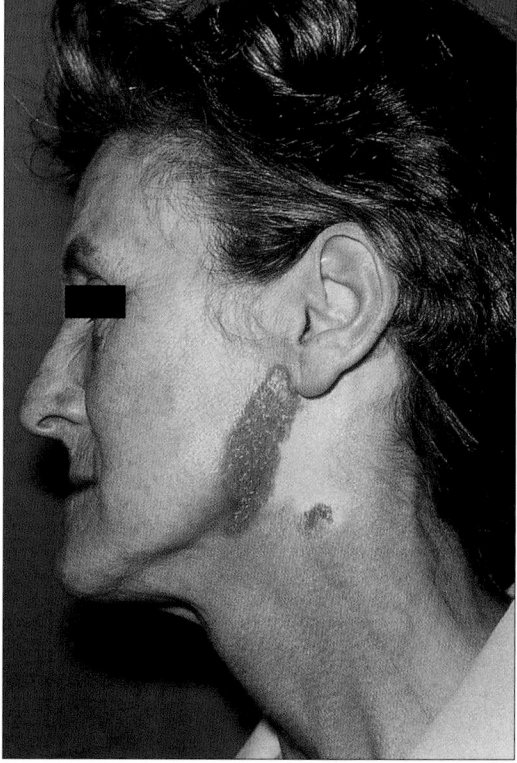

Fig. 16.5
Discoid lupus erythematosus: in this chronic lesion there is marked scarring. By courtesy of R.A. Marsden, MD, St George's Hospital, London, UK.

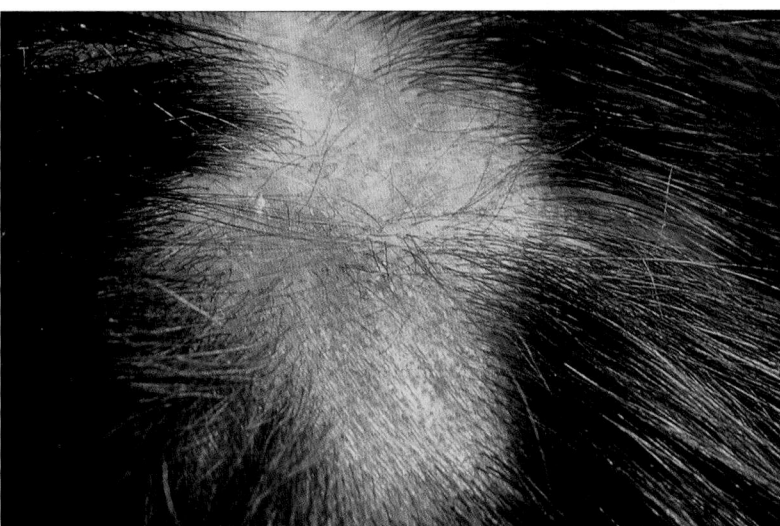

Fig. 16.6
Discoid lupus erythematosus: erythematous lesion with scaling. The scalp is commonly affected. By courtesy of the Institute of Dermatology, London, UK.

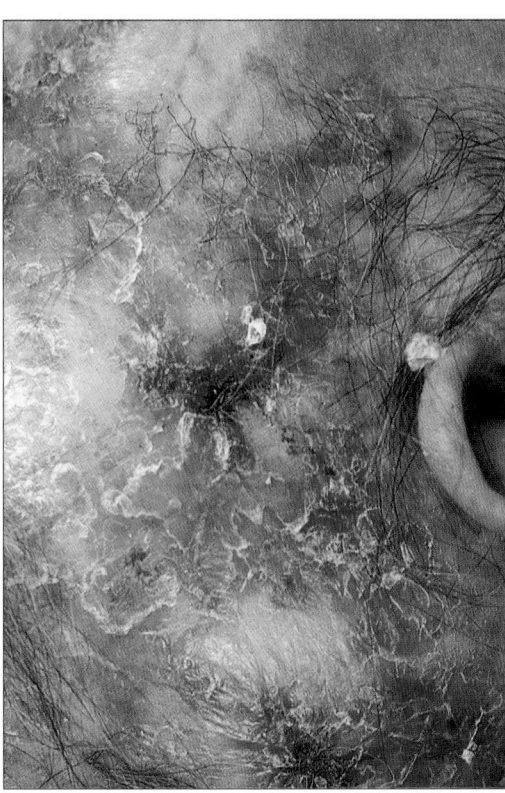

Fig. 16.8
Discoid lupus erythematosus: there is alopecia with very marked scarring. By courtesy of the Institute of Dermatology, London, UK.

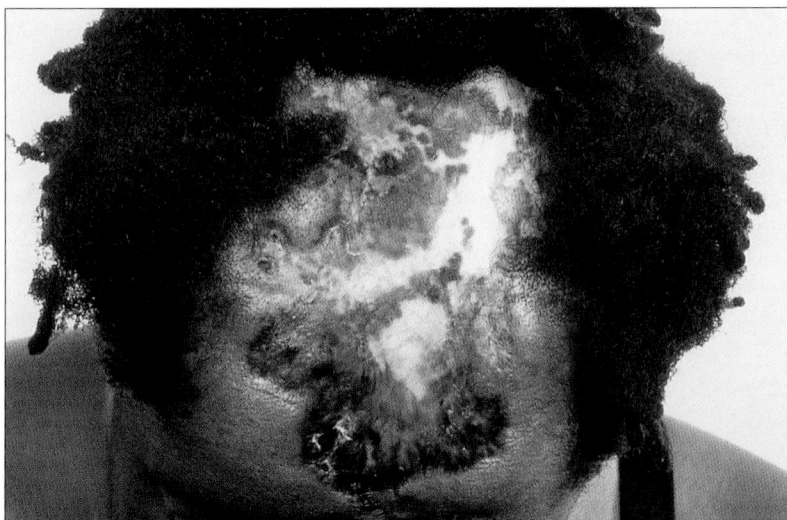

Fig. 16.7
Discoid lupus erythematosus: hair loss is permanent. By courtesy of the Institute of Dermatology, London, UK.

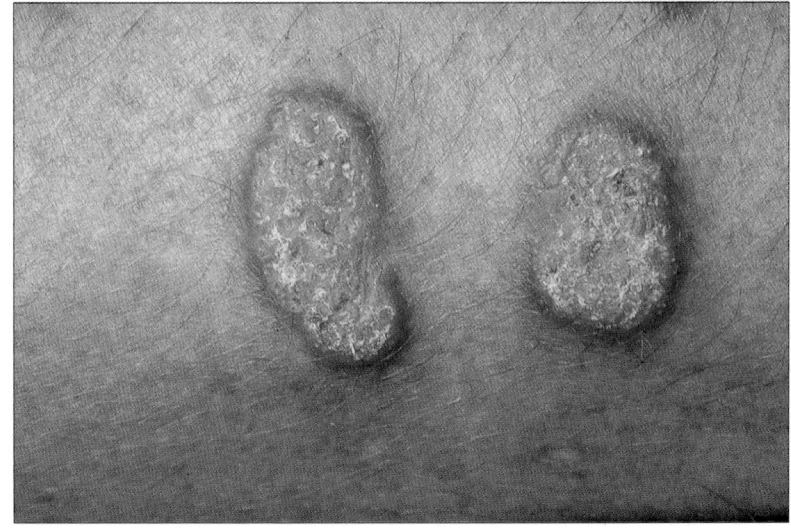

Fig. 16.9
Discoid lupus erythematosus: close-up view of scale. Note the erythematous border. By courtesy of the Institute of Dermatology, London, UK.

common in those patients whose disease started when they were young, is chronic, and correlates with longstanding severe disease.[18]

Early lesions appear edematous and erythematous. An established plaque of DLE, which may measure up to 10.0 cm across, is usually covered with an adherent scale accompanied by epidermal atrophy, follicular dilatation and plugging (*Figs 16.9, 16.10*).[5,17] If the scale is removed the horny plugs are often seen attached to its undersurface ('carpet tacks' sign). Telangiectasia is a common finding and lesions heal with scarring, which is often marked. In dark- or black-skinned individuals the plaque may be hypo- or hyperpigmented and this may be particularly disfiguring (*Figs 16.11, 16.12*).[17]

Oral involvement occurs in 20–25% of patients with DLE, with the vermilion border of the lower lip, alveolar processes, labial and buccal mucosae being particularly affected (*Figs 16.13, 16.14*).[19–23] Chronic lesions are typically erythematous and atrophic with a scalloped white keratotic border and adjacent telangiectasia.[20] Erosions and ulcers may be additional features.[12] Lesions are sometimes indistinguishable from atrophic lichen planus. Involvement of the tongue manifests as erythema,

fissuring and atrophy of the papillae.[21] Chronic lupus cheilitis is associated with cicatricial scarring and an increased risk of squamous carcinoma.[20] Perianal mucosal involvement has occasionally been documented.[21]

Discoid lupus erythematosus has been described in association with osteopoikilosis, α_1-antitrypsin deficiency and polyarteritis nodosa.[24–26]

Verrucous (hypertrophic) discoid lupus erythematosus

Verrucous (hypertrophic) DLE presents as warty, hyperkeratotic papules and plaques with a predilection for the face, scalp, mucous membranes of the lips and upper limbs (*Figs 16.15, 16.16*).[5,27] It affects approximately 2% of patients with chronic discoid disease.[12] Sometimes the palms and soles are affected and occasionally the nails (*Figs 16.17, 16.18*). Rare manifestations include nodular keratoacanthoma-like, squamous cell carcinoma-like and hypertrophic lichen planus-like lesions on the arms and hands (*Fig. 16.19*).[28] A variant with associated necrosis of the subcutaneous tissue is known as lupus erythematosus hypertrophicus et profundus.[29]

Systemic symptoms are usually absent in patients with localized DLE.[30] In the generalized form in which cutaneous plaques may be quite widespread, a small percentage may have Raynaud's phenomenon

and arthralgia (*Figs 16.20, 16.21*). Laboratory abnormalities are more common in the generalized than in the localized variant.[30] Anemia is not seen in localized DLE, but is sometimes a feature of the generalized variant. Leukopenia, a raised erythrocyte sedimentation rate (ESR) and hypergammaglobulinemia can occur in both.[8] Antinuclear factor (diffuse pattern), a positive Wassermann reaction and rheumatoid factor may also be features.[8] Anti-double-stranded DNA (dsDNA) antibodies are detected in a minority of patients with disseminated DLE, and these patients frequently transform to the systemic disease; occasionally antibodies to single-stranded DNA (ssDNA) are present. Urinalysis and renal function tests are normal.

Cutaneous squamous cell carcinoma and less often basal cell carcinoma may arise in patients with chronic lesions including the hypertrophic variant.[17,19,31–33] Squamous cell carcinoma occurs predominantly in males, particularly affects the scalp and is sometimes associated with early metastases.[6,34]

Lupus erythematosus tumidus

Lupus erythematosus tumidus is a distinctive subset of cutaneous lupus clinically presenting mainly in patients with DLE and rarely in patients with SLE. It is characterized by erythematous papules, plaques or even nodules with an urticarial appearance arising mainly on sun-exposed skin of the face, neck and trunk. Scarring does not occur. This variant of lupus is discussed in more detail on p. 613.

Chilblain lupus erythematosus

Chilblain lupus erythematosus, which accounts for approximately 11% of DLE cases, develops almost exclusively in females during the winter months.[35] Patients present with itchy, painful, papuloerythematous or blue–purple plaques and nodules on the fingers, heels and soles of the feet; the hands, calves, knees, knuckles, elbows, nose and ears are less often affected (*Fig. 16.22*).[6] Hyperkeratotic fissured lesions and ulcers are sometimes also present.[36] Although patients usually develop chilblains many years after the typical discoid rash, lesions may develop

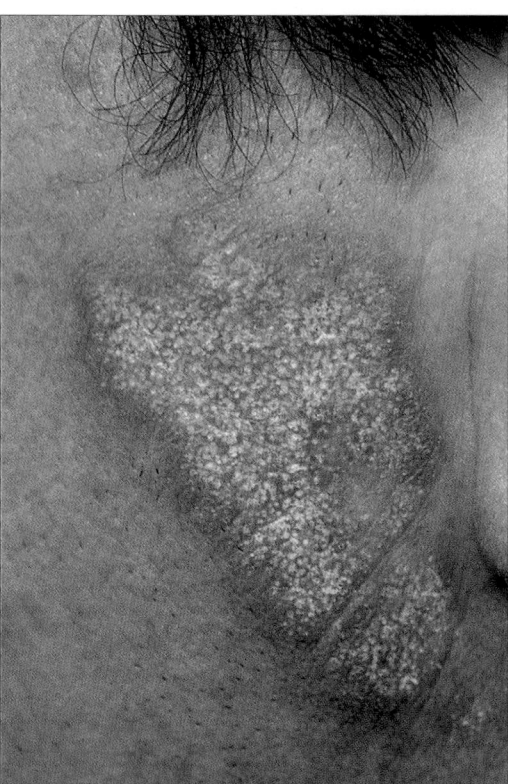

Fig. 16.10
Discoid lupus erythematosus: close-up view showing follicular plugging. By courtesy of the Institute of Dermatology, London, UK.

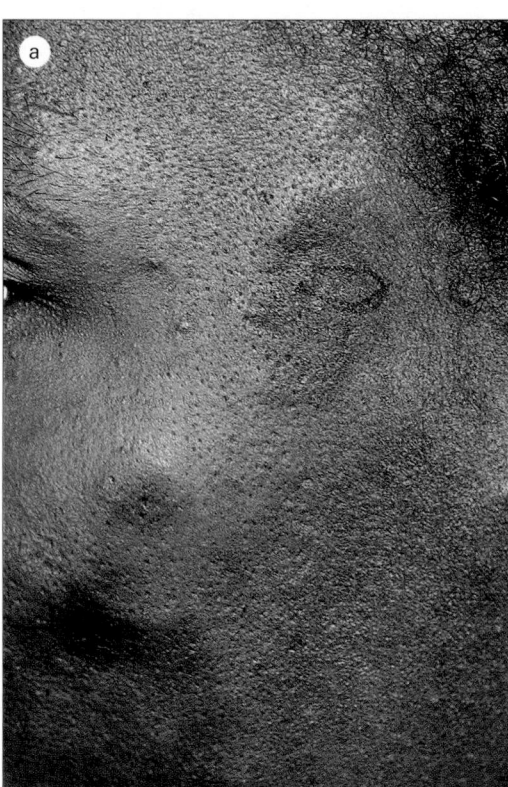

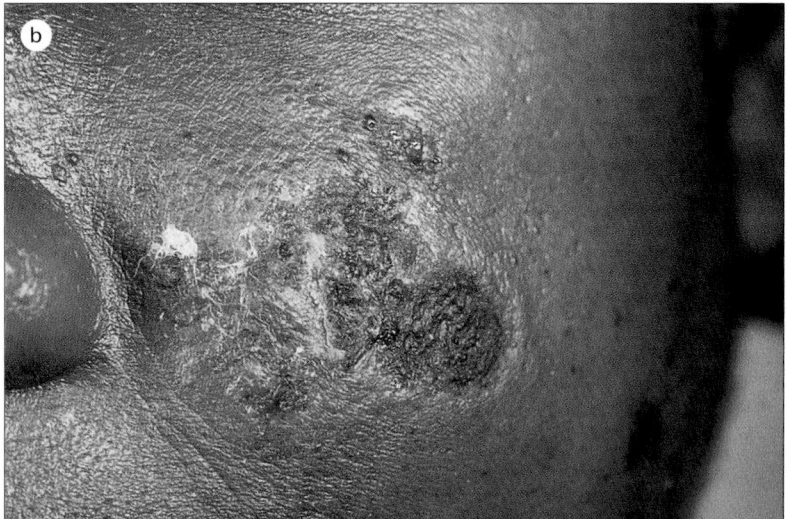

Fig. 16.11
(a, b) Discoid lupus erythematosus: foci of hyperpigmentation can be very disfiguring in dark-skinned patients. By courtesy of the Institute of Dermatology, London, UK.

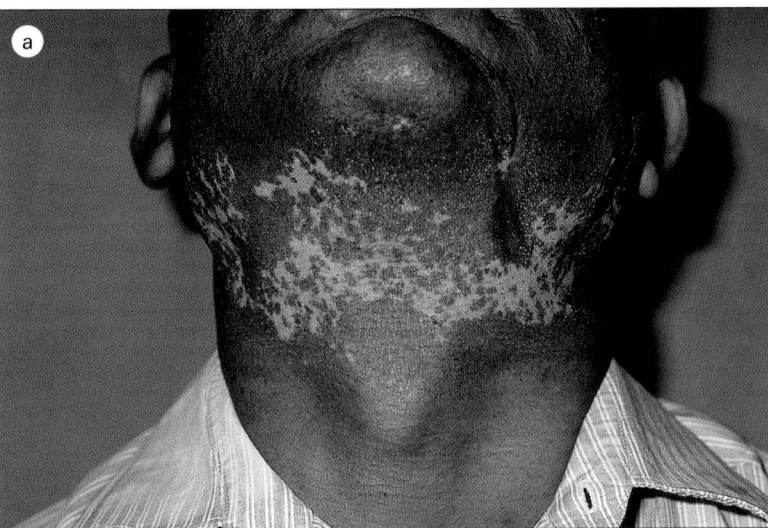

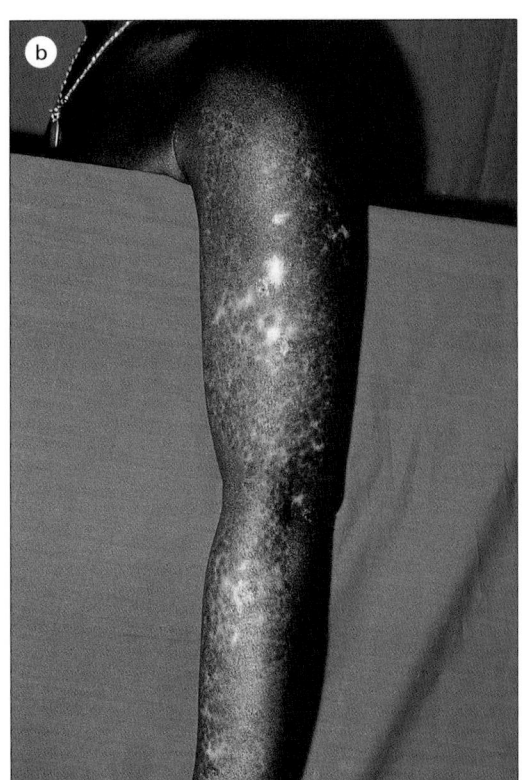

Fig. 16.12
(a, b) Discoid lupus erythematosus: marked hypopigmentation may be a distressing complication. By courtesy of R.A. Marsden, MD, St George's Hospital, London, UK.

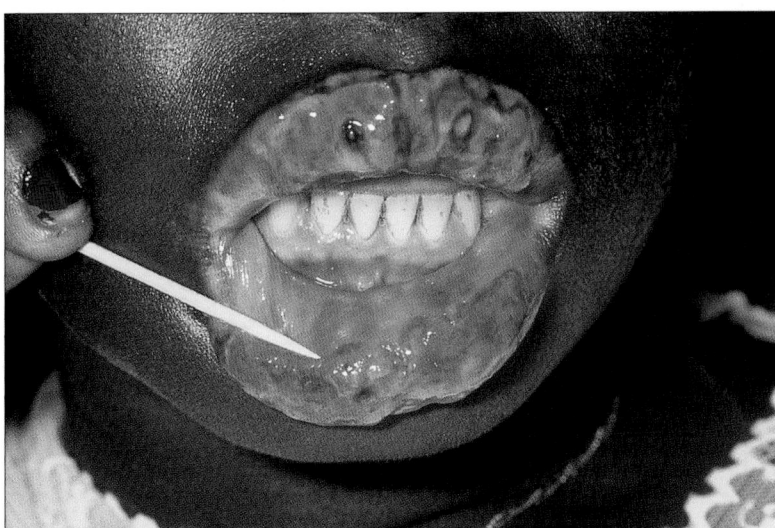

Fig. 16.13
Discoid lupus erythematosus: there is gross ulcerative cheilitis. The upper lip has been stained with gentian violet. By courtesy of R.A. Marsden, MD, St George's Hospital, London, UK.

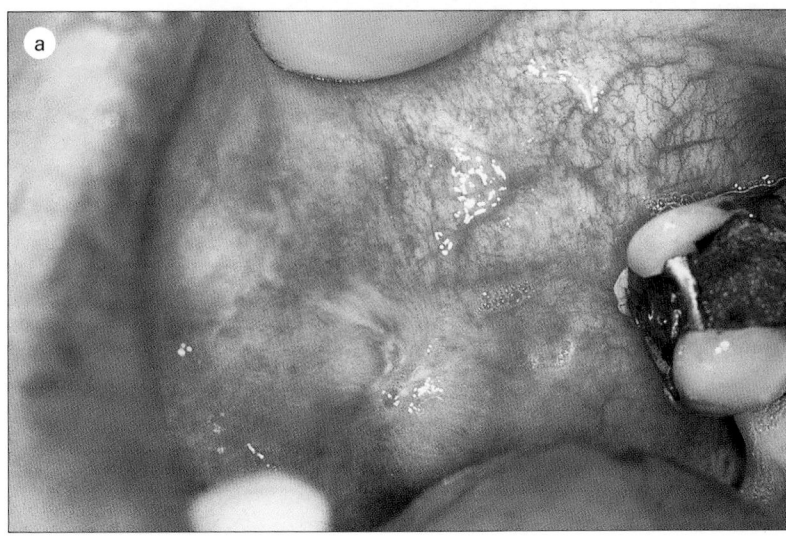

Fig. 16.14
(a, b) Discoid lupus erythematosus: typical scarred lesion on the buccal mucosa. Oral involvement is sometimes difficult to distinguish from lichen planus. (a) By courtesy of R.A. Marsden, St George's Hospital, London, UK; (b) by courtesy of the Institute of Dermatology, London, UK.

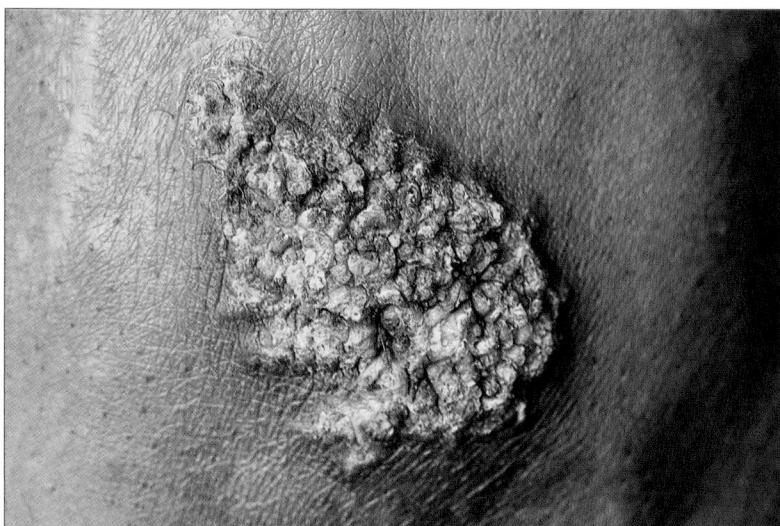

Fig. 16.15
Verrucous discoid lupus erythematosus: this lesion has a very warty appearance.
By courtesy of the Institute of Dermatology, London, UK.

Fig. 16.16
Verrucous discoid lupus erythematosus: extensive disfiguring warty plaque
involving the upper lip and angle of mouth. By courtesy of J. Newton Bishop, MD,
St James's University Hospital, Leeds, UK.

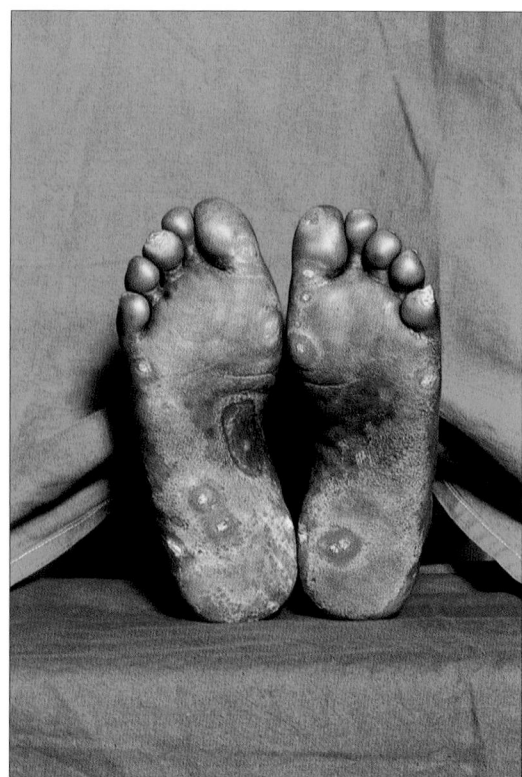

Fig. 16.17
Verrucous discoid lupus
erythematosus: note the
gross hyperkeratosis. By
courtesy of J. Newton
Bishop, MD, St James's
University Hospital,
Leeds, UK.

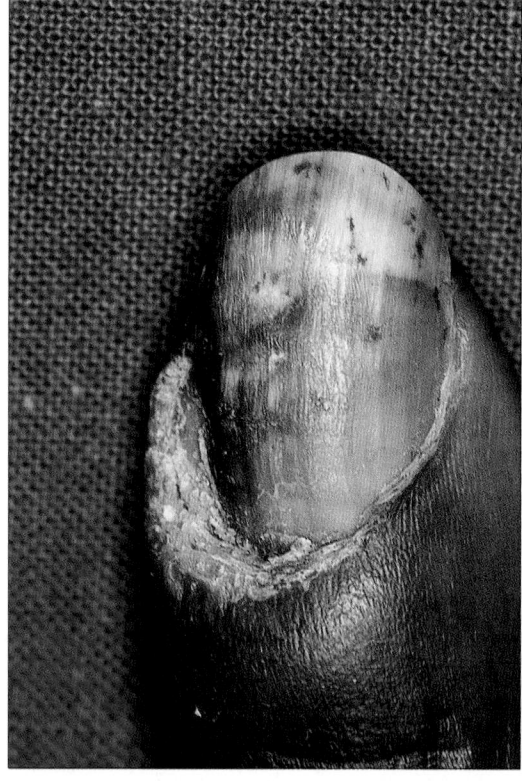

Fig. 16.18
Verrucous discoid lupus
erythematosus: note the
hypertrophic cuticle,
pitting and onycholysis.
By courtesy of J.
Newton Bishop, MD,
St James's University
Hospital, Leeds, UK.

simultaneously and sometimes the chilblains are the sole manifestation.[36] Some patients with chilblain lupus erythematosus have an associated cryofibrinogenemia or cold agglutinin.[6] About 15% of patients develop SLE, particularly those who develop discoid and perniotic lesions simultaneously and those with DLE–erythema multiforme-like syndrome in addition to perniosis.[6,35]

Lupus erythematosus–erythema multiforme-like syndrome

The lupus erythematosus–erythema multiforme-like syndrome (Rowell's syndrome) is rare.[37–43] Patients, mostly females, develop recurrent episodes of annular lesions on the limbs and, to a lesser extent, on the face, neck, chest and mouth, in addition to the features of any variant of lupus erythematosus.[6,37] Early lesions are erythematous papules, which become annular and may vesiculate at the edge. The condition usually heals without scarring, but in severe disease bullae may develop, become necrotic and ulcerate. Patients with this variant also have erythrocyanosis, chilblains and Raynaud's phenomenon. Their serum contains speckled antinuclear factor, rheumatoid factor and anti-La antibody.[6,8,37,38] In rare cases anti-La and rheumatoid factor are negative.[44] Association with antiphospholipid syndrome has exceptionally been documented.[45]

Lupus erythematosus profundus

Lupus erythematosus profundus (panniculitis) is another uncommon variant that may develop in association with either DLE or SLE. This is covered in detail on page 379.

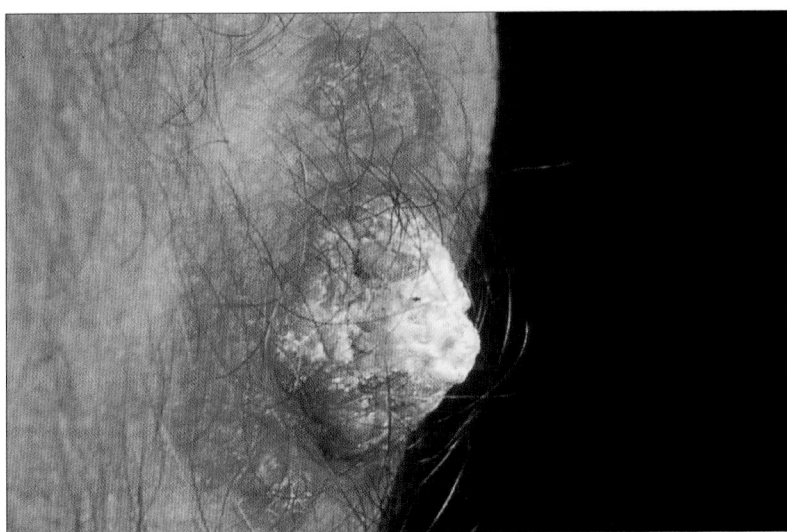

Fig. 16.19
Verrucous discoid lupus erythematosus: this example resembles a keratoacanthoma. By courtesy of the Institute of Dermatology, London, UK.

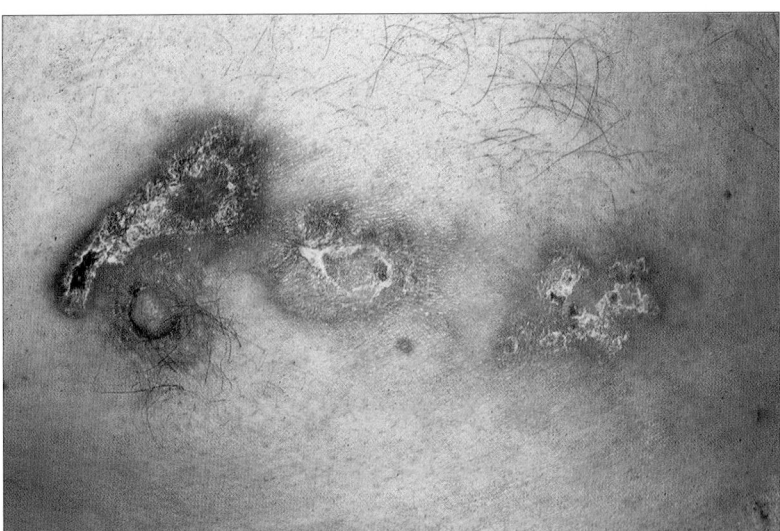

Fig. 16.21
Generalized discoid lupus erythematosus: in this patient, the chest is severely affected. By courtesy of the Institute of Dermatology, London, UK.

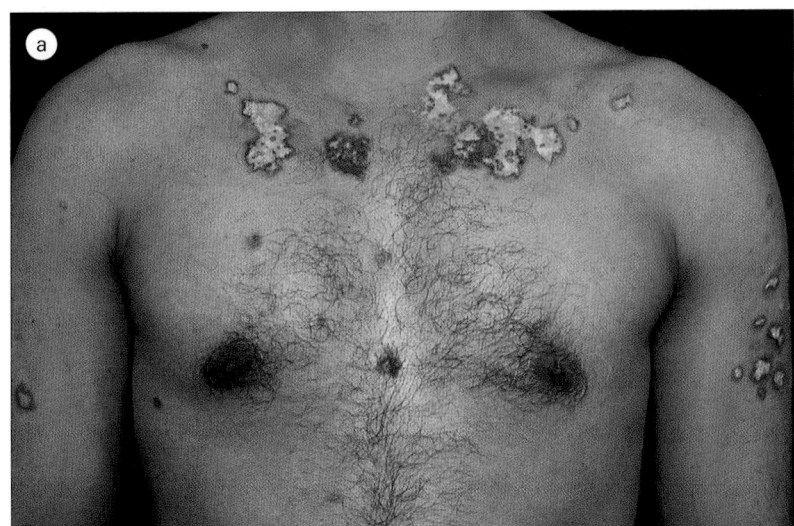

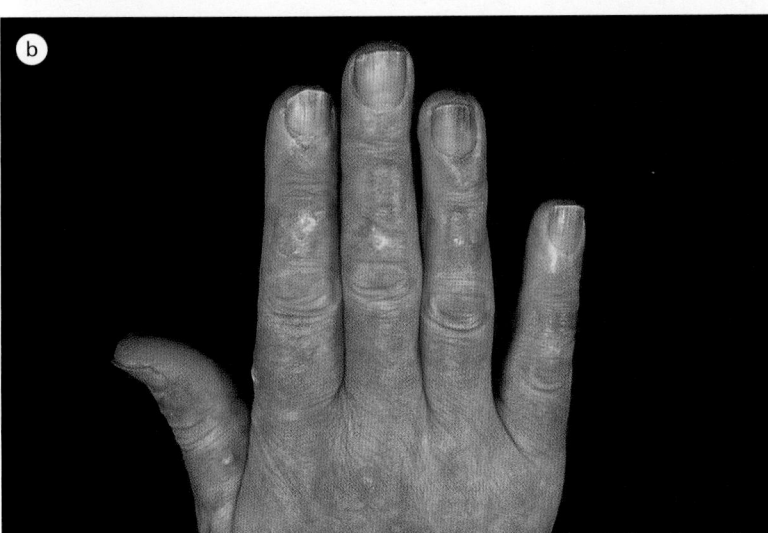

Fig. 16.20
(a, b) Generalized discoid lupus erythematosus: in this variant lesions are widespread and may involve the chest, shoulders and upper limbs. Note the extensive erythema and scaling. By courtesy of R.A. Marsden, St George's Hospital, London, UK.

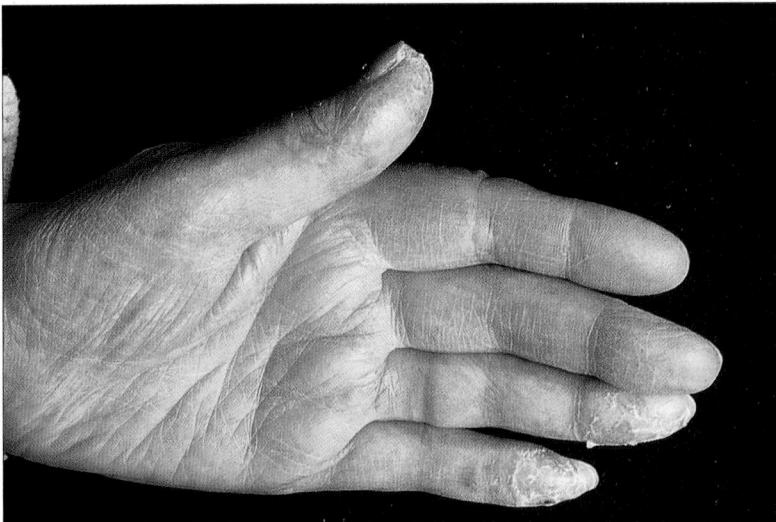

Fig. 16.22
Chilblain lupus erythematosus: resolving perniosis involving the tips of the thumb and ring and little fingers. By courtesy of R.A. Marsden, St George's Hospital, London, UK.

DLE and chronic granulomatous disease

Occasionally a DLE-like dermatosis develops in female carriers of X-linked chronic granulomatous disease.[46–48] Mothers of affected children may occasionally show similar lesions, presenting with bluish-red, infiltrated, scaly papules on the face and hands, sometimes associated with photosensitivity.[47] Additional features include recurrent aphthous-like ulcerative stomatitis and perniosis.

X-linked chronic granulomatous disease is inherited as a recessive trait, and patients (usually boys) have severe and recurrent infections due to defective neutrophil bactericidal activity. Heterozygous female carriers display a partial defect, indicated by diminished nitroblue tetrazolium reductions, but are usually free from infections. An autosomal recessive variant in which discoid lupus-like lesions may occur has also been documented.[49]

Subacute cutaneous lupus erythematosus-like lesions and lupus tumidus may also occur.[50, 51]

Discoid lupus erythematosus has also been described in non-X-linked hyper-IgM syndrome.[52]

Subacute cutaneous lupus erythematosus

Subacute cutaneous lupus erythematosus (SCLE) accounts for 5–10% of patients with lupus erythematosus.[53–55] Approximately 50% have SLE as defined by the revised American Rheumatology Association diagnostic criteria (see below).[56] Females are affected more often than males (2.3:1) and the mean age at presentation is about 40 years.[57] This variant of lupus occurs very rarely in children.[58,59]

The eruption, which is often widely distributed, consists of symmetrical, non-scarring and non-indurated erythematosquamous lesions (Fig. 16.23). Pruritus is very rare.[60] Lesions may become papulosquamous (psoriasiform) or annular, the latter coalescing to produce polycyclic and gyrate configurations (Fig. 16.24).[54,61] In some patients both patterns are evident. Photosensitivity is of major importance and lesions are therefore typically seen on the face, neck, upper part of back and chest, shoulders, extensor aspect of the arms, backs of hands and fingers (Figs 16.25, 16.26).[53,54,62]

The absence of follicular plugging, adherent scale and dermal atrophy helps to distinguish the subacute lesion from the discoid variant.[54]

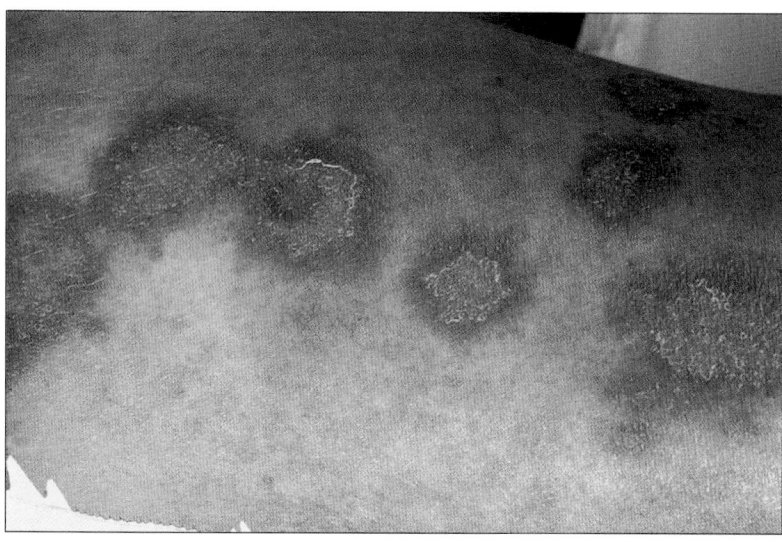

Fig. 16.23
Subacute cutaneous lupus erythematosus: annular lesions with delicate scale. By courtesy of C. Stephens, MD, Poole Hospital, Poole, UK.

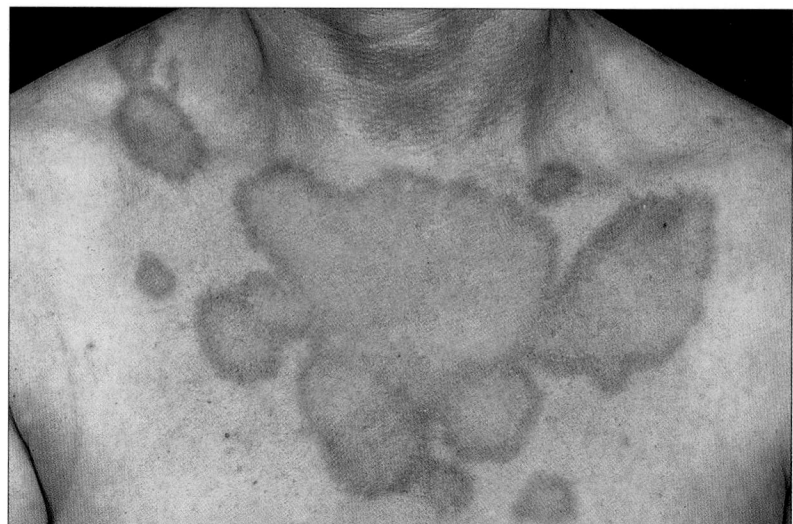

Fig. 16.24
Subacute cutaneous lupus erythematosus: coalescence of annular lesions has resulted in this bizarre eruption. By courtesy of the Institute of Dermatology, London, UK.

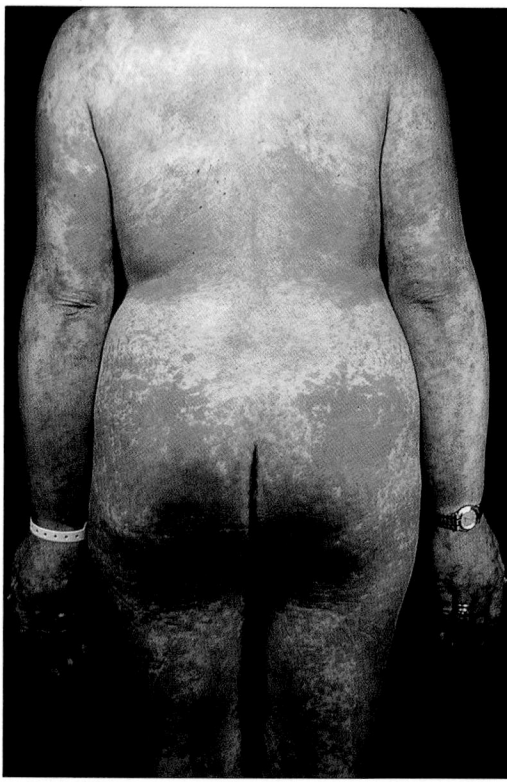

Fig. 16.25
Subacute cutaneous lupus erythematosus: in this patient there is very extensive involvement. By courtesy of the Institute of Dermatology, London, UK.

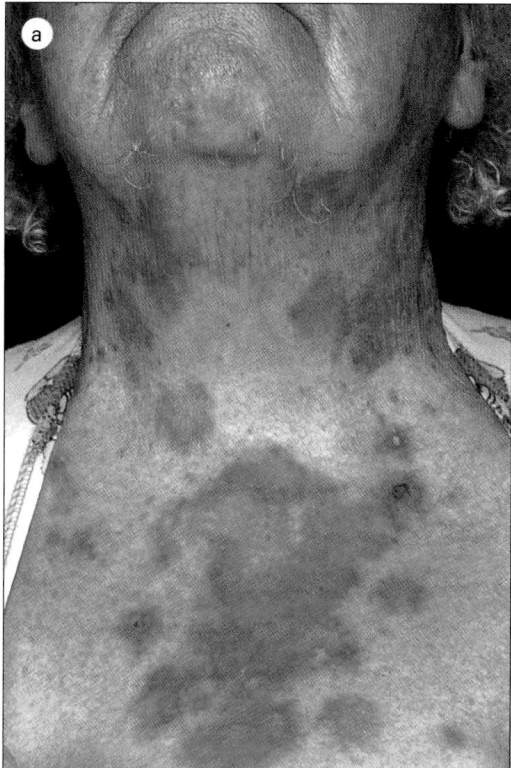
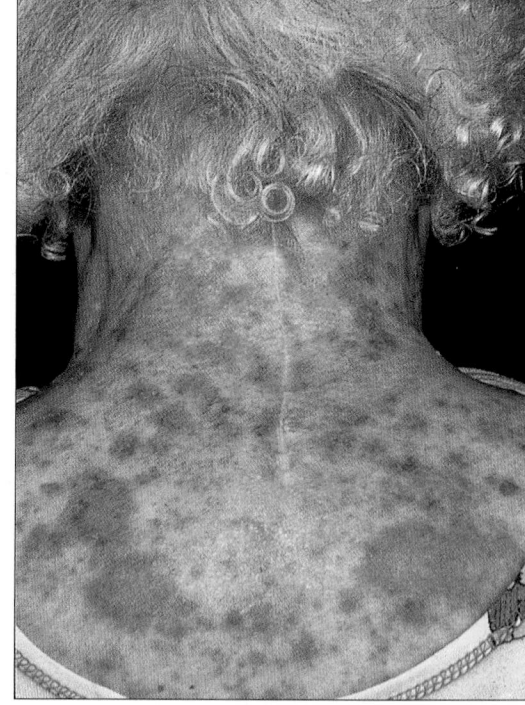

Fig. 16.26
(a, b) Subacute cutaneous lupus erythematosus: close-up views of the patient shown in Fig. 16.25. The lesions are intensely erythematous. The distribution suggests a photosensitive dermatosis. By courtesy of the Institute of Dermatology, London, UK.

Crusting and vesiculation are sometimes evident on the active border of the annular lesions.[57] Pityriasiform and erythema multiforme-like lesions have also been described, as has occasional chronic leukoderma.[54] Exceptionally, the disease may present as generalized poikiloderma.[63] In addition, 15–30% of patients develop features of typical DLE, usually located on the scalp or face.[1,54,56,64] The malar erythema of SLE is also sometimes evident (15%). Subtle hypopigmentation, telangiectasia, non-scarring alopecia, livedo reticularis, Raynaud's phenomenon and mucous membrane ulcers are additional features.[54,57] Dystrophic calcification is exceptional.[65] Cutaneous leukocytoclastic vasculitis is seen in a minority of patients and appears to be self-limited and not associated with a worsened prognosis.[66]

Patients with SCLE have an increased incidence of human leukocyte antigen (HLA)-DR3 (75%) and HLA-B8 and there is a significant association with inherited homozygous C2 and C4 deficiency.[54,56,67–70] HLA-DR2 is also present at a higher frequency, particularly in those with papulosquamous rather than annular skin lesions.[71] Antinuclear antibodies are found in approximately 50% of patients, while anti-Ro (SS-A) antibodies are present in approximately 65%, particularly those with annular polycyclic lesions.[6,55,58,61,70] Anti-La (SS-B) antibodies are also often evident.[5]

The course of SCLE tends to be relatively benign, but systemic manifestations are quite common and may be severe.[72] Severe extracutaneous disease appears to be more common in men with papulosquamous SCLE.[72] The type of cutaneous lesion, however, has not always been proven to correlate with the severity of the extracutaneous manifestations.[73] Renal disease has been reported to be uncommon but a recent study found its frequency to be as similar and equally severe as in SLE.[57,74] Rarely, patients develop other more serious manifestations of SLE.[56]

Patients with SCLE have an increased incidence of both rheumatoid arthritis and Sjögren's syndrome.[55,75,76] Those with SCLE and Sjögren's syndrome have high titers of anti-Ro antibodies, a high incidence of cutaneous vasculitis and an increased risk of severe neuropsychiatric and pulmonary involvement.[77] SCLE has been documented in association with radiotherapy and hepatocellular and lung carcinoma.[78–81] An exceptional association with inclusion body myositis has also been documented.[82] Association with lichen planus is exceptional.[83] Clinically and histologically identical cases have been documented following therapy with hydrochlorothiazide, griseofulvin, antihistamines, terbinafine, calcium channel blockers, nifedipine, angiotensin-converting enzyme (ACE) inhibitors, interferon and phenytoin.[84–95]

Systemic lupus erythematosus

In addition to the variable cutaneous manifestations, lesions may be found in virtually any organ or system in the body in SLE.[96–98] The guidelines of the American Rheumatology Association are valuable in establishing the diagnosis: any patient who has experienced four or more of the criteria, either serially or concurrently, is considered to have SLE (*Table 16.2*).[100] The condition is characterized by a marked female predominance (9:1) and usually presents in the third, fourth and fifth decades. There is a high incidence among Afro-Caribbeans, with a maximum prevalence of 1/150 females in Jamaica. In the United States the incidence is approximately 1/100.[5]

Cutaneous involvement occurs in 75–88% of patients.[62] Lesions are highly polymorphic and may mimic many other dermatoses (*Table 16.3*). The 'butterfly rash' is typical and is a slightly scaly, sometimes edematous, erythema that is particularly distributed on the bridge of the nose and on the cheeks (*Fig. 16.27*). Photosensitivity is common, affecting

Table 16.2
Systemic lupus erythematosus: diagnostic guidelines of the American Rheumatology Association

Criterion	Definition
Malar rash	Fixed erythema, flat or raised, over malar eminences tending to spare nasolabial folds
Discoid rash	Erythematous, raised patches with adherent keratotic scaling and follicular plugging; atrophic scarring may occur in old lesions
Photosensitivity	Skin rash as result of unusual reaction to sunlight (observed by physician or recounted by patient)
Oral ulcers	Oral or nasopharyngeal ulceration, usually painless, observed by physician
Arthritis	Non-erosive arthritis involving two or more peripheral joints, characterized by tenderness, swelling or effusion
Serositis	Pleurisy (convincing history of pleuritic pain or rub heard by physician or evidence of pleural effusion) Pericarditis (confirmed by ECG or rub or evidence of pericardial effusion)
Renal disorder	Persistent proteinuria (> 0.5 g/day or > 3 if quantification is not performed) Cellular casts (may be RBC, hemoglobin, granular, tubular, or mixed)
Neurological disorder	Seizures (in absence of offending drugs or known metabolic derangements, e.g. uremia ketoacidosis or electrolyte imbalance) Psychosis (in absence of offending drugs or known metabolic derangements, e.g. uremia ketoacidosis or electrolyte imbalance)
Hematological disorder	Hemolytic anemia with reticulocytosis Leukopenia (< 4000/mm^3 on two or more occasions) Lymphopenia (< 1500/mm^3 on two or more occasions) Thrombocytopenia (< 1500/mm^3 in absence of offending drug therapy)
Immunological disorder	Positive LE cell preparation Anti-DNA (antibody to native DNA in abnormal titer) Anti-SM (presence of antibody to SM nuclear antigen) False positive serologic test result for syphilis known to be positive for at least 6 months and confirmed by *Treponema pallidum* immobilization or fluorescent treponemal antibody absorption test
Antinuclear antibody	Abnormal ANA titer by immunofluorescence or equivalent assay at any time and in absence of drugs known to be associated with drug-induced lupus syndrome

ANA, antinuclear antibody; LE, lupus erythematosus; RBC, red blood cell. Reproduced with permission from Tan, E.M. et al (1982) *Arthritis and Rheumatism*, **25**, 1271–1277.

Table 16.3
Systemic lupus erythematosus: cutaneous manifestations

• Malar erythema (butterfly rash)
• Inflammatory periorbital edema
• Mucous membrane lesions
• Oral and nasopharyngeal ulceration
• Alopecia – fractured frontal hair – scarring and non-scarring hair loss
• Raynaud's disease with or without skin changes
• Cutaneous vasculitis – urticarial lesions – palpable purpura – digital nodules – cutaneous infarcts – leg ulcers – peripheral grangrene – thrombophlebitis – livedo reticularis – periungual erythema and telangiectasia – hemorrhagic bullous lesions
• So-called bullous SLE
• Lichen planus-like lesions
• Perniotic lesions
• Lupus profundus
• Chilblain lesions
• Sjögren's syndrome
• Calcinosis cutis
• Rheumatoid nodules
• Pigmentary changes

Reproduced from Moschella, S.L. (1989) *Journal of Dermatology*, **16**, 417–428, with permission from Blackwell Publishing Ltd.

more than 50% of patients, and erythematous or violaceous maculo-papular eruptions may develop, particularly in white patients, at other light-exposed areas such as the 'V' of the neck and the forearms.[62] Sensitivity is towards both ultraviolet (UV) A and UVB light. Approximately 15% of patients, particularly Afro-Caribbeans, have lesions similar to those of DLE, apparently associated with a less severe disease and a lower frequency of renal involvement.[3,10,62,96] SCLE-like features are present in 10–15% of patients.[100] It has been suggested that patients with SLE and SCLE-lesions have a more favorable prognosis.[101]

Alopecia is important, occurring in about 20% of patients, and may be scarring or non-scarring. The non-scarring lesions, which are more common, often constitute a fairly diffuse hair loss occurring as a non-specific response to stress (telogen effluvium).[62] Fractured frontal hairs are characteristic.[17]

Raynaud's phenomenon occurs in 10–40% of patients.[62] Purpura and ecchymoses are common and may be partly due to corticosteroid therapy, but thrombocytopenia and immune complex-mediated vasculitis also play a role in the pathogenesis. Vasculitis, which occurs in up to 30% of patients, may also result in infarcts, ulcers, digital nodules, scars and gangrene (*Figs 16.28–16.30*).[62] Livedo reticularis that particularly affects the arms and thighs and periarticular sites may be a presenting feature in up to 10% of patients, and the changes of atrophie blanche have been documented occasionally (livedoid vasculitis) (*Fig. 16.31*).[62] Livedo reticularis is often a feature of the anticardiolipin syndrome and presenting lesions identical to those seen in Degos' disease (malignant atrophic papulosis) have been described occasionally.[102,103] Vasculitic features correlate with renal and central nervous system involvement.[62] Urticaria is frequently found.[104]

Erythromelalgia, a burning sensation accompanied by erythema following exposure to heat, has also been noted.[19] Localized and diffuse hyperpigmentation and urticarial lesions, including urticarial vasculitis, are less commonly found. Digital manifestations in addition to infarction and ulceration include periungual and knuckle erythema, nail fold telangiectases, cuticular lesions and splinter hemorrhages. Telangiectases may also be seen on the fingertips and palms.[61] Some patients develop

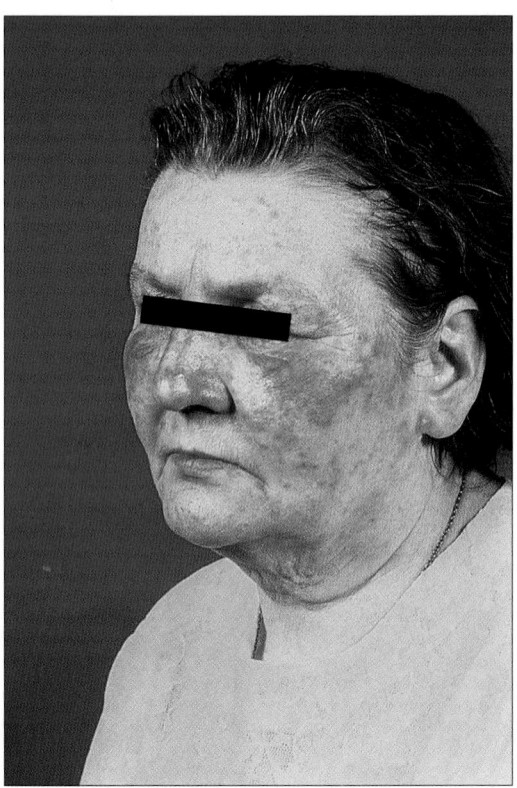

Fig. 16.27
Systemic lupus erythematosus: characteristic 'butterfly erythema' on the cheeks and nose. By courtesy of R.A. Marsden, MD, St George's Hospital, London, UK.

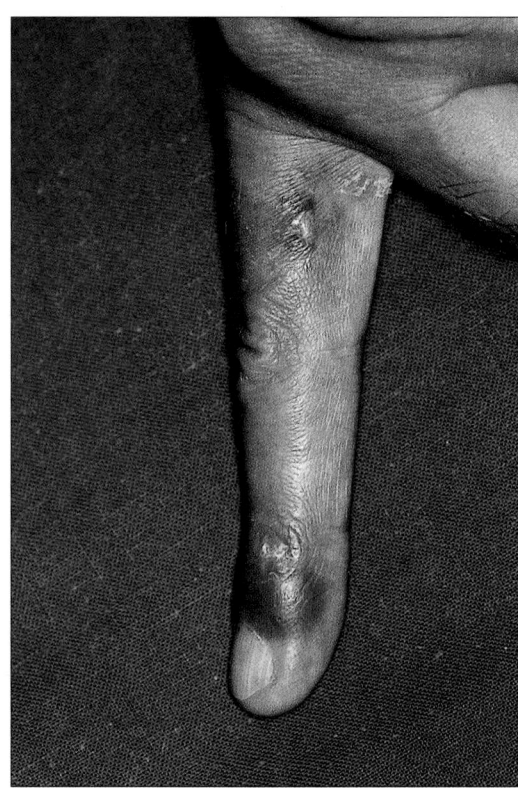

Fig. 16.28
Systemic lupus erythematosus: erythematous vasculitic lesion on the fingertip. By courtesy of M.M. Black, MD, St Thomas' Hospital, London, UK.

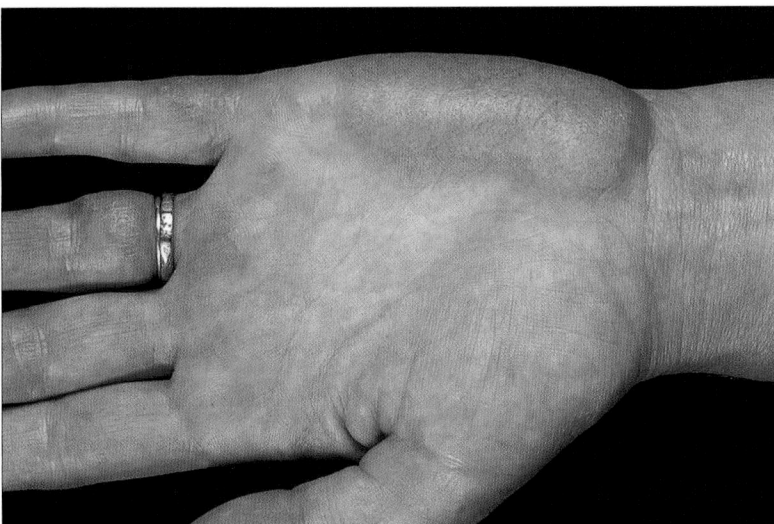

Fig. 16.29
Systemic lupus erythematosus: involvement of the palms is rare and may be vasculitic. By courtesy of the Institute of Dermatology, London, UK.

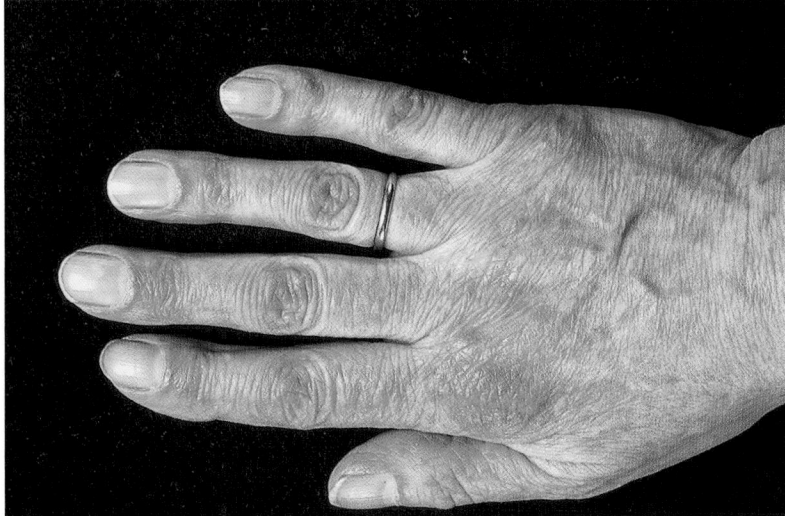

Fig. 16.30
Systemic lupus erythematosus: erythematous nodules are present on the back of the hand and on the fingers. By courtesy of the Institute of Dermatology, London, UK.

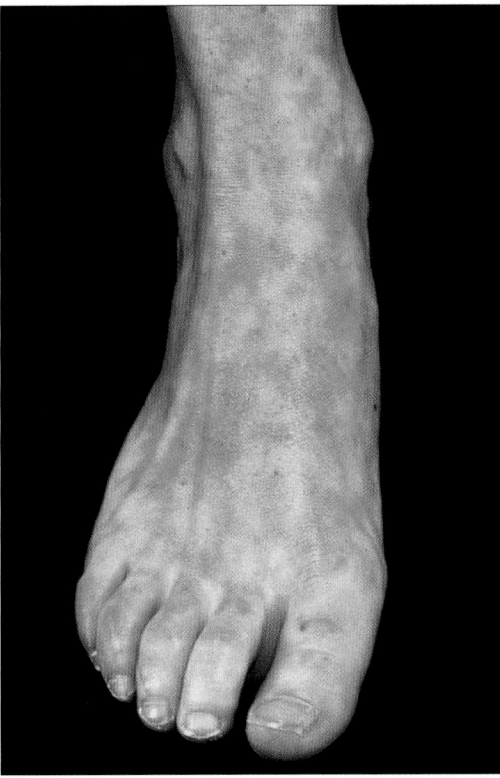

Fig. 16.31
Systemic lupus erythematosus: livedo reticularis develops as a consequence of relative ischemia in the watershed zones. There are numerous causes, particularly connective tissue disease. These features are common to many connective tissue diseases. By courtesy of the Institute of Dermatology, London, UK.

red lunulae.[105,106] The associated erythema multiforme-like and perniotic lesions are described above. Involvement of the mucous membranes occurs in about 10% of patients: painless ulceration is most common, but other features include erythema, petechiae, erosions and hemorrhage. The central part of the hard palate, lips and buccal mucosa are particularly affected.[22,103,107]

Additional lesions that are occasionally seen include rheumatoid-like nodules, dermal mucinosis, bullous variants, thrombotic thrombocytopenic purpura, mixed cryoglobulinemia and soft tissue calcifications.[5,17,108,109] Vesicles and bullae in SLE may complicate extreme basal cell hydropic degeneration, represent co-expression of an autoimmune bullous dermatosis, or signify a specific dermatitis herpetiformis-like eruption (bullous dermatosis of SLE, which is considered in detail on page 128). There is a recognized association with porphyria cutanea tarda.[110]

Approximately 5–10% of patients with SLE are antinuclear antibody negative. This seems to correlate with a specific subtype. Patients are usually HLA-DR3 positive and have Sjögren's syndrome and an increased incidence of pulmonary involvement, psychiatric manifestations, cutaneous vasculitis and hypergammaglobulinemic purpura.[5]

Non-specific symptoms are common and include chronic tiredness, weight loss, fever, malaise and weakness. Arthralgia and myalgia occur in 90% of patients. The myalgia may be disabling, but objective muscle weakness is rare.[111] Similarly, although arthralgia may be marked there is usually little clinical evidence of joint damage. Effusions are common.[96] Approximately 25% of patients have frank arthritis, either a migratory polyarthritis or a chronic progressive polyarthritis with deformity. Patients sometimes develop avascular bone necrosis due either to the primary disease or to steroid therapy.[96,111] Very rarely, involvement of the tendons is associated with the development of contractures.

Lesions of the cardiovascular system manifest as cardiomegaly, pericarditis, pericardial effusion and/or endocarditis (Libman–Sacks valvulitis).[112] In SLE, the mitral valve is predominantly affected, but patients with the lupus anticoagulant syndrome appear to have a particular risk of developing aortic valve disease.[112,113] Conduction defects and congestive cardiac failure are additional features.

Respiratory involvement may present as pleurisy, with or without effusion, bacterial pneumonia or, very rarely, lupus pneumonitis.[111]

Involvement of the central nervous system is an important cause of morbidity and mortality.[96,111] It may affect up to 40% of patients.[6] Encephalitis, meningitis, vasculitis and coagulation defects give rise to a wide range of clinical manifestations, including convulsions, hemiplegias, chorea and psychoses.[17] Convulsions and coma are an indication of severe involvement and portend a grave outcome. Peripheral neuritis affects up to 12% of patients; ocular lesions, including conjunctivitis, fundal hemorrhages and cotton wool exudates, occur in 25%.[17]

Renal manifestations develop in approximately 45% of patients, and progressive renal involvement is an important cause of morbidity and mortality (nephrotic syndrome and lupus glomerulonephritis). Evidence of active renal disease includes the presence in the urine of more than five red blood cells/high power field.[111] Proteinuria of greater than 1 g/24 hours, oval fat bodies, granular, hyaline and red blood cell casts may also be detected.[17]

Generalized lymphadenopathy is present in about 50% of the patients, hepatomegaly in 20% and splenomegaly in 10%.

Gastrointestinal manifestations are uncommon; the most important is esophageal involvement leading to loss of peristalsis and dilatation reminiscent of that seen in scleroderma.[111]

Laboratory investigation commonly reveals anemia, leukopenia, lymphopenia, thrombocytopenia and a raised ESR. False positive reactions to reagin and treponemal tests for syphilis are common, 10–20% of patients are positive for the Coombs' test and rheumatoid factor, and 10–50% have circulating anticoagulants.[96]

While lupus erythematosus (LE) cell preparation used to be the basic screening test for SLE, it has now been superseded by testing for antinuclear factor. This and other autoantibodies will be discussed further under pathogenesis. Serum complement levels are often low in patients with active disease (CH_{50} and C3); estimations of C3 levels are of particular value in following disease activity.[5,17]

SLE is characterized by relapses, with remissions of variable duration sometimes lasting a decade or more. There is still, however, significant mortality. Causes of death include nephritis, infections and central nervous system involvement.

An association between SLE and inherited complement deficiency, involving the early components of the classic pathway including C1r, C1s, C4 and C2, has been described.[114] This deficiency of C2 is inherited in an autosomal recessive fashion; up to 60% of homozygotes develop lupus erythematosus characterized by an erythematous, papulosquamous, SCLE-like photosensitive dermatosis, a low incidence of renal involvement and arthralgia. Additional features may include urticarial vasculitis, malar erythema and nail fold abnormalities.[68] Discoid lesions are sometimes evident, and recently a patient with C2 and C4 deficiency and LE panniculitis has been documented.[12,115] Patients are, however, often (but not invariably) negative for antinuclear factor and manifest a negative lupus band test on unaffected skin. There is an association with HLA-DR2, and over 60% of patients possess anti-Ro antibodies.[53]

Numerous drugs have been implicated in the induction of SLE. These drugs include isoniazid, hydralazine, procainamide, rifampicin, quinidine, penicillamine, terbinafine, carbamazepine, valpromide, amiodarone, atenolol, sulfonamides, methimazole, COL-3, hydrochlorothiazide, minocycline, spironolactone, captopril, methyldopa, gold salts, penicillin, streptomycin, phenylbutazone, reserpine, griseofulvin, clonidine, oral contraceptives, captopril, interleukin (IL)-2, hydroxyurea, clobazam, clozapine, ciprofloxacin, para-amino salicylic acid, yohimbine, infliximab, anti-tumor necrosis factor alpha (TNF-α) and etanercept.[116–155]

Transient skin and serological manifestations of SLE have been documented in two children with *Trichophyton mentagrophytes* infection.[155] The disease has also been linked to hepatitis B vaccination and with exposure to insecticides.[156–158]

Sjögren's syndrome coexists in approximately 10–20% of patients with SLE.[62] SLE has also been described in association with scleroderma, morphea, rheumatoid arthritis, eosinophilic fasciitis, dermatomyositis, lichen sclerosus, pemphigus (including pemphigus vulgaris, foliaceous and paraneoplastic pemphigus), hypergammaglobulinemia of Waldenström, dermatitis herpetiformis, ulcerative colitis, alopecia areata, autoimmune thyroiditis, myasthenia gravis, acanthosis nigricans, Sweet's syndrome, porphyria, gout, sarcoidosis, psoriasis, lichen planus and cutaneous T-cell lymphoma. It is likely that many of these associations are chance associations except for those diseases with an autoimmune basis.[110,159–183]

Neonatal lupus erythematosus

Neonatal lupus erythematosus is very rare, occurring in approximately 1 in 20,000 live births.[184] It associated with maternal anti-Ro (SS-A) antibodies (95%) and/or anti-La (SS-B) antibodies.[185,186] It most commonly presents in female infants.[184–186] Anti-U1-ribonucleoprotein

(RNP) antibodies may also be present.[187–191] Anticardiolipin antibodies have been described in a single case.[192] Transplacental transfer of the anti-Ro and anti-La antibodies results in a SCLE-like eruption consisting of erythematous annular scaly plaques that particularly affect the periorbital region ('owl-eye' or 'eye-mask') and scalp, and to a lesser extent, the trunk and extremities (*Figs 16.32, 16.33*).[5] These cutaneous lesions often appear after exposure to ultraviolet light. Crusted lesions and cutis marmorata telangiectasia congenita are additional features in some cases.[193] Exceptionally, discoid lesions, panniculitis (lupus profundus), erosions and alopecia may also occur.[194,195] Atrophy and scarring are very rare but residual hypopigmentation and telangiectasia are present in about 25% of patients.[196] Babies in subsequent pregnancies may present manifestations of the disease.[197,198]

Neonatal lupus erythematosus is often associated with complete heart block, and sometimes liver disease (cholestatic hepatitis) and thrombocytopenia are also evident.[185] The mortality associated with cardiac involvement is around 19%.[197] Severe hematological and liver involvement without evidence of cutaneous or cardiac involvement has

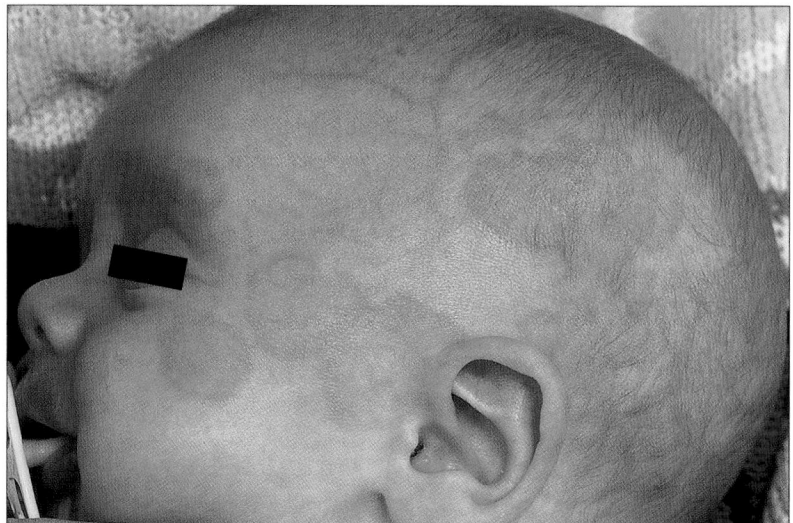

Fig. 16.32
Neonatal lupus erythematosus: note the presence of erythematous, slightly scaly plaques on the cheeks, forehead and scalp. By courtesy of the Institute of Dermatology, London, UK.

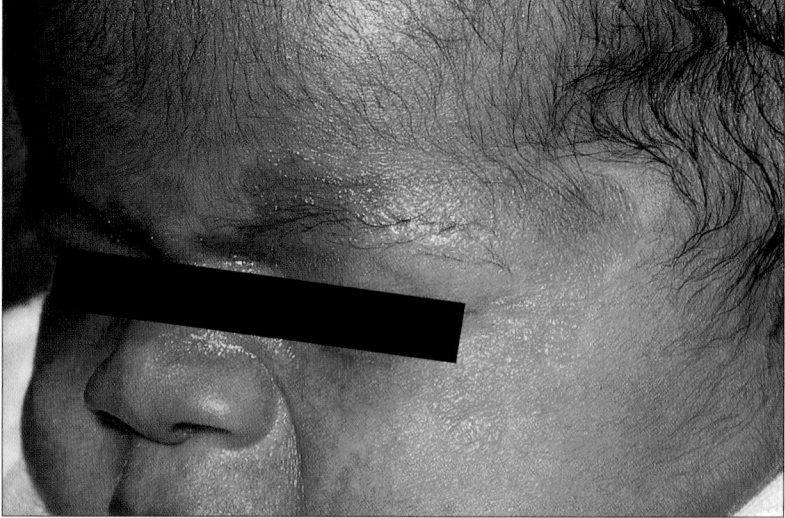

Fig. 16.33
Neonatal lupus erythematosus: in this child there is intense erythema affecting the cheeks and nose and around the eyes.

exceptionally been reported.[199] By 6 months of age the cutaneous, but not the cardiac manifestations usually fade.

The disease also occurs in identical and non-identical twins.[200] A single case has been described in association with Turner's syndrome.[201]

Neonates who survive until infancy have a fairly good prognosis, but there is an overall mortality of about 10% due to heart disease.[185] Mothers of affected infants are commonly asymptomatic initially but they may have systemic lupus, Sjögren's syndrome, leukocytoclastic vasculitis or an overlap syndrome.[202]

A number of mothers who present with no symptoms, often subsequently develop evidence of connective tissue disease, particularly systemic lupus (in about 20% of cases) and Sjögren's syndrome.[185]

Pathogenesis and histological features

Despite enormous research efforts, the precise etiology and pathogenesis are unknown, but the condition is certainly multifactorial.[203] Lupus erythematosus is characterized by B-cell hyperactivity in association with defective suppressor T-cell function. Patients develop a wide range of autoantibodies, many of which result in immune complexes with resultant systemic manifestations including vasculitis and glomerulonephritis. In addition to immunological factors, familial, genetic and hormonal influences play a part. It is believed that in lupus erythematosus there is a genetic predisposition; sex-associated and environmental factors are necessary to promote the development of the disease.

Autoantibodies are important in the diagnosis of lupus erythematosus and have a significant role in its pathogenesis, either by direct cytotoxic effects (such as the lymphopenia induced by antilymphocyte antibodies) or by immune complex deposition. Up until the 1960s the presence of LE cells in a patient's blood was regarded as pathognomonic for lupus erythematosus (*Fig. 16.34*). This was changed, however, by the discovery of antinuclear factor (antinuclear antibody) with direct immunofluorescent techniques. Antinuclear antibody is present in the serum of 90–95% of patients with SLE, in 30% of patients with localized DLE and in 50% of patients with generalized DLE. It should also be noted that 10% of the normal population have antinuclear antibody in the serum, albeit at low concentration. Antinuclear antibody has at least four subtypes:

- A homogeneous or diffuse pattern is most commonly seen (*Fig. 16.35*).
- Speckled fluorescence representing an antibody to saline-soluble nuclear protein is present in patients with the lupus erythematosus–erythema multiforme syndrome (*Fig. 16.36*).
- The nucleolar pattern (representing antinucleolar RNA antibody) is occasionally evident in lupus erythematosus, though it is more common in systemic sclerosis.
- The peripheral (outline) staining pattern reflects high titer anti-DNA antibody and is a marker of active systemic disease.[6,17]

Patients with lupus erythematosus develop antibodies to a variety of nuclear and cytoplasmic antigens; these autoantibodies, both singly and in combination, have varying associations, which may allow a prediction of (to some extent, at least) the course of the disease in individual patients (*Table 16.4*).

Antibodies to native (double-stranded) DNA (nDNA) are pathognomonic for idiopathic (classic) SLE (*Fig. 16.37*).[6,17] They are rarely seen in the drug-induced variant and are only very occasionally present in patients with DLE.[2] The presence of anti-nDNA antibody in association with hypocomplementemia is indicative of active disease and is often accompanied by severe renal involvement.

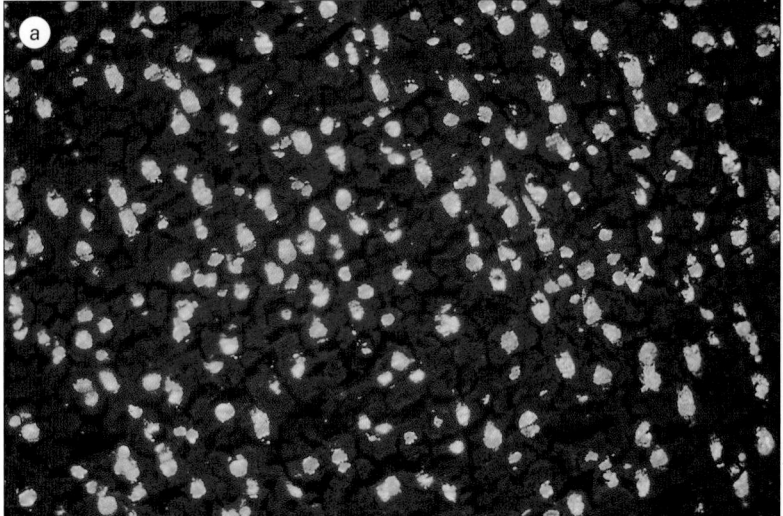

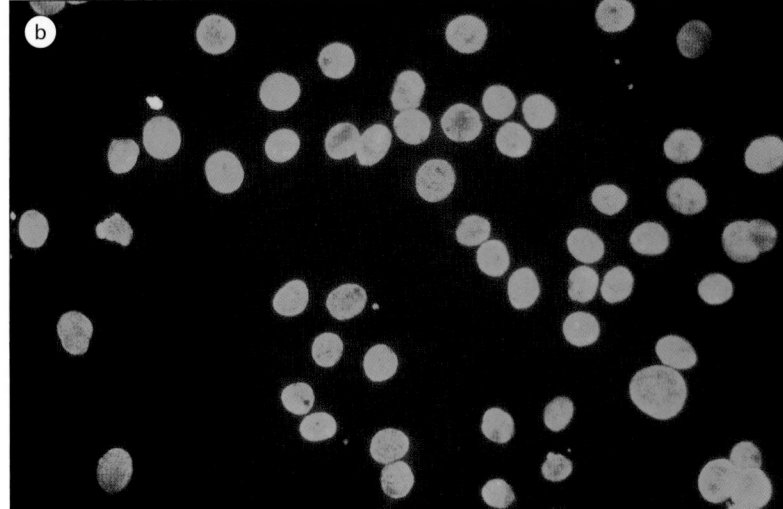

Fig. 16.35
(a, b) Systemic lupus erythematosus: homogeneous antinuclear antibody in rat liver. By courtesy of G. Swana, MD, St Thomas' Hospital, London, UK.

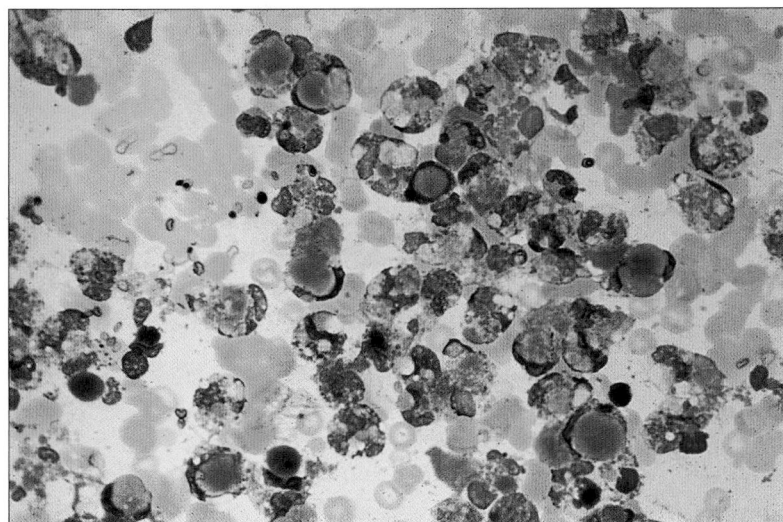

Fig. 16.34
Systemic lupus erythematosus: LE cells. The patient's serum is incubated with normal neutrophils. Note the ingested nuclear debris. By courtesy of N. Slater, MD, St Thomas' Hospital, London, UK.

Table 16.4
Systemic lupus erythematosus: antibodies

Antigen	Antibody	Significance	Comment
Nuclear constituents	Anti-native DNA	Highly specific for SLE associated with hypocomplementemia and glomerulonephritis	Found in NZB/NZW model
	Anti-histone	30% of SLE patients	Found in high titer in drug-induced lupus-like disease
	Anti-single stranded DNA	90% of SLE patients, associated with glomerulonephritis	May be detected in ANF-negative SLE patients
Small nuclear ribonuclear protein	Sm	Highly specific for SLE 15% of SLE patients	
	$_n$RNP	May occur in SLE but also present in MCTD and PSS	May be associated with low incidence of renal disease
	La (SS-B)	Found in 10% of SLE	
Small cytoplasmic ribonuclear protein	Ro (SS-A)	Found in 25% of SLE patients Found in SCLE Found in 50% of complement-deficient LE-like syndromes Found in all neonatal lupus	May be detected in ANF-negative SLE

ANF, antinuclear factor; LE, lupus erythematosus; MCTD, mixed connective tissue disease; PSS, progressive systemic sclerosis; SCLE, subacute cutaneous lupus erythematosus; SLE, systemic lupus erythematosus.

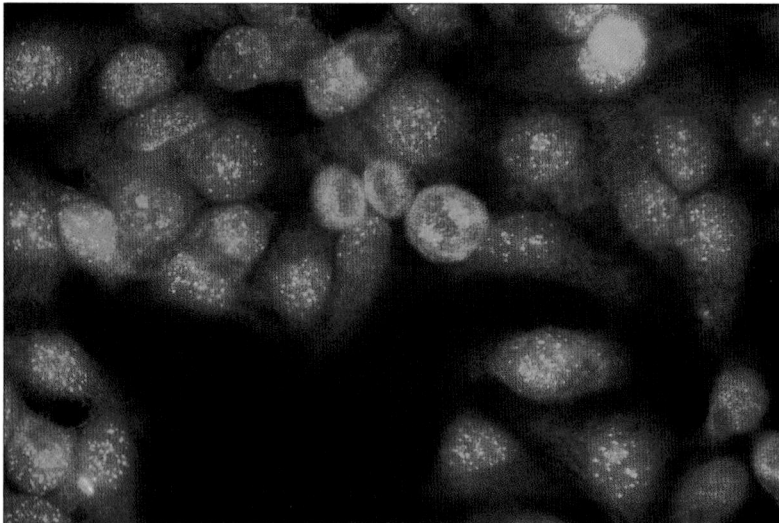

Fig. 16.36
Systemic lupus erythematosus: speckled antinuclear antibody – HEP II. By courtesy of G. Swana, MD, St Thomas' Hospital, London, UK.

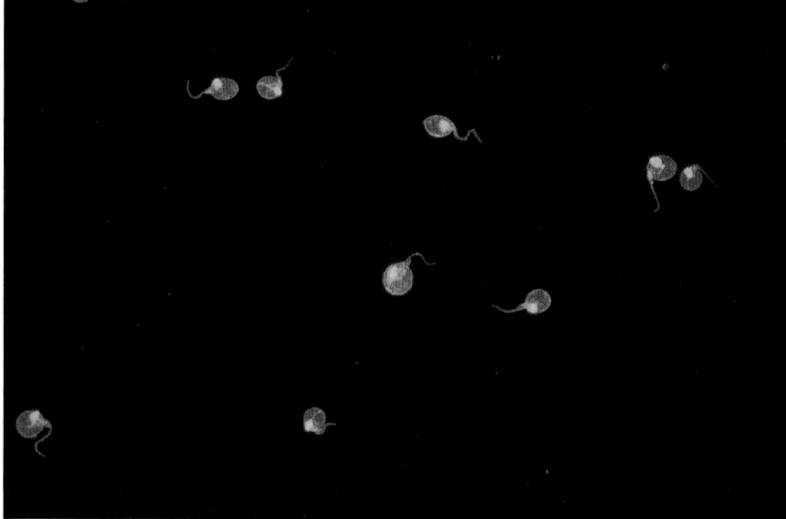

Fig. 16.37
Systemic lupus erythematosus: anti-dsDNA (Crithidia luciliae). By courtesy of G. Swana, MD, St Thomas' Hospital, London, UK.

Antihistone antibodies may be found in approximately 30% of patients with idiopathic SLE, but are particularly associated with the drug-induced variant.[204] The latter is caused by a wide variety of drugs, including hydralazine, procainamide hydrochloride, phenytoin and isoniazid.[14,205,206] Symptoms develop in up to 20% of patients taking procainamide and antinuclear antibodies are present in 50%.[206] Procainamide-induced SLE-like syndrome is characterized by the presence of leukocyte-specific antinuclear antibody.[206] Clinical features include malaise, pneumonitis with pleural effusion, arthralgia, arthritis and serositis; renal, central nervous system and cutaneous lesions are less common and are usually mild. Although antinuclear antibodies are often present, anti-DNA antibodies are not formed in most cases of drug-induced lupus.[111] Drug-induced lupus usually, but not invariably, remits on withdrawal of the drug.[206]

Antibodies to ssDNA occur in 90% of patients with classical SLE and in approximately 20% of patients with disseminated DLE, and may also be found in other connective tissue diseases.[10] Their presence in disseminated DLE correlates with an increased risk of developing SLE.[10] Patients with SLE who are negative for antinuclear antibody may have anti-ssDNA antibodies in their serum.[6]

Antibodies to the soluble nuclear antigen Sm are highly specific for SLE.[204] They may also be found in a group of patients with good prognosis who are positive for antinuclear factor, but anti-nDNA-negative, and who have mild non-progressive glomerulonephritis, hypocomplementemia, mild central nervous system involvement and conspicuous cutaneous eruptions.

Antibodies to ribonucleoprotein are detected in 23% of patients with SLE, but are much more commonly associated with mixed connective tissue disease: they may also be found in patients with progressive systemic sclerosis.[204]

Anti-La (SS-B) antibodies are detected in the serum of 10% of patients with SLE. Anti-La antibodies, which are often present in Sjögren's syndrome, are almost invariably accompanied by anti-Ro (SS-A) antibodies.[204] The latter are particularly associated with SCLE, complement-deficient lupus erythematosus, circulating IgG or IgM anticoagulant and neonatal lupus erythematosus.

The circulating anticoagulant (antiphospholipid or lupus anticoagulant) is associated with paradoxical thrombosis, spontaneous abortion, premature labor, intrauterine death, labile hypertension, cutaneous necrosis, gangrene, ecchymoses, purpura, leg ulcers, atrophie blanche,

Table 16.5

Diagnostic criteria for the antiphospholipid syndrome

Group	Criteria

I. Clinical conditions	Thrombosis
	  venous:
	    recurrent deep vein thrombosis
	    axillary
	    retinal vein
	  arterial:
	    cerebrovascular accident
	    retinal artery
	    coronary
	  other:
	    pulmonary hypertension
	    livedo reticularis
	    neurological syndromes – transient ischemic
	    attack; progressive dementia (repeated
	    cerebrovascular stroke)
	Recurrent fetal loss
	Thrombocytopenia

II. Laboratory	Positive anticardiolipin antibody assay; isotype IgG or IgM Positive lupus anticoagulant test
III. Other clinical conditions	Hemolytic anemia/positive direct Coombs' test Migraine Endocardial/valvular lesions Transient visual loss Chorea

At least one finding from each of groups I and II must be present to constitute a diagnosis.
Group III represent features occasionally present in these patients.
*Laboratory tests should be positive on two occasions 2 months apart.
Modified from ASCP check sample (TH 88-6), American Society of Clinical Pathologists, 1989; with permission.

livedo reticularis and false positive syphilis serology – the lupus anticoagulant syndrome (*Table 16.5*).[204,207–218] The lupus anticoagulant syndrome is more accurately known as the antiphospholipid syndrome because not all patients have associated SLE. It is due to the presence of circulating antiphospholipid antibodies which inhibit coagulation in vitro, but more importantly are associated with a greatly increased risk of thrombotic phenomena affecting both arteries and veins (*Fig. 16.38*). About 50% of patients with SLE present with antiphospholipid antibodies but only half of these will develop manifestations of the disease.[219] Presentation in the skin may also be with papules and nodules or lesions resembling pyoderma gangrenosum.[220,221] Interestingly, patients with antiphospholipid antibodies and SLE appear to be more at risk of developing anetoderma.[222–224] The incidence, however, is not high. Rarely patients develop reactive angioendotheliomatosis.[225,226] Systemic involvement includes deep venous thrombosis often complicated by pulmonary embolism, arterial occlusion with resultant strokes, transient ischemic attacks, multi-infarct dementia, myocardial infarction and gangrene.[204]

The association of cutaneous thrombotic lesions, livedo racemosa, hypertension and cerebrovascular disease is known as Sneddon's syndrome.[208,227–231] This presents mainly in young females and is exceptional in children.[232] Antiphospholipid antibodies are present in around 41% of patients.[233]

How antiphospholipid antibody induces thrombosis is unknown. Theories of inhibition of protein C (a natural vitamin K-dependent anticoagulant) function and a suppressive effect on endothelial cell prostacyclin have not yet been substantiated.[234]

The antiphospholipid syndrome has also been documented in other autoimmune diseases including rheumatoid arthritis, hemolytic anemia, thrombocytopenic purpura, ulcerative colitis, Factor V Leiden mutation and mesothelioma.[235,236] It may also complicate treatment with a number of drugs including phenothiazines and procainamide, develop during viral illnesses including acquired immunodeficiency syndrome (AIDS), and can present with an underlying lymphoma.[237,238]

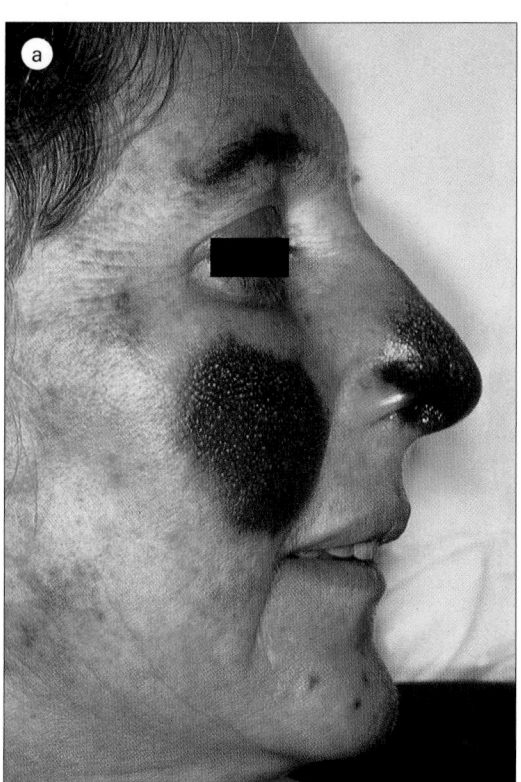
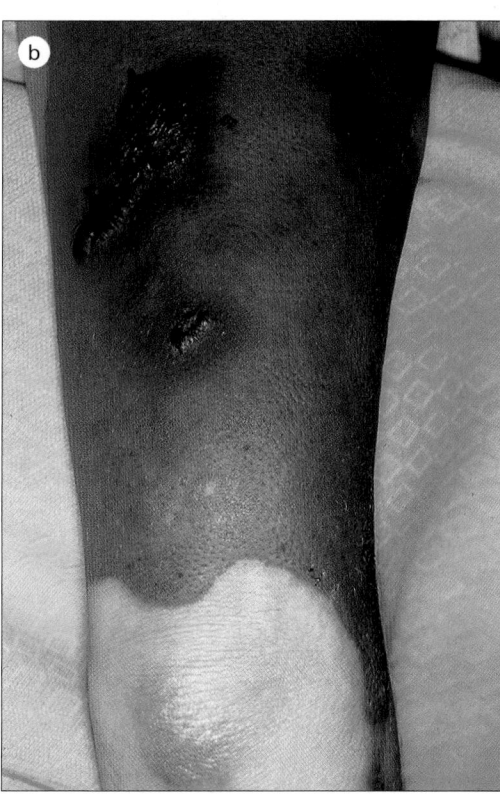

Fig. 16.38
Lupus anticoagulant syndrome: extensive gangrene with ulceration affecting (a) the nose and cheek, and (b) the leg. By courtesy of C. Stephens, MD, Poole Hospital, Poole, UK.

Anti-Ro antibodies have been shown to bind to the epidermis in neonatal and subacute lupus erythematosus, and to the conducting system and myocardium in neonatal lupus erythematosus.[185] They also bind to keratinocytes in vitro and have been shown to react with the epidermis when infused into human-skin-grafted mice.[239,240] This – combined with the disappearance of the cutaneous manifestations as maternal IgG is removed from the circulation – suggests that in neonatal lupus erythematosus, anti-Ro antibodies are of major pathogenetic significance. Ro antigens are present in the nuclei and cytoplasm of keratinocytes and it has been demonstrated that UVB is capable of translocating these antigens to the surface of cultured keratinocytes. Anti-Ro antibodies in the sera bind to the antigens in keratinocytes and appear to be important in inducing antibody-dependent keratinocyte damage.[241]

Immune complexes have been shown to be important in the pathogenesis of both vasculitis and glomerulonephritis in SLE; their presence may be inferred by the detection of immunoglobulin and complement in blood vessel walls in skin biopsies (*Fig. 16.39*). High concentrations of anti-nDNA, anti-ssDNA and anti-Ro (SS-A) antibodies have been detected in the renal cortex of patients with lupus glomerulonephritis.

The finding of large numbers of T-lymphocytes and macrophages with minimal or no B-cells in the dermal infiltrate of skin lesions suggests that cell-mediated immunity may be particularly important in the pathogenesis of lesions at this site.[241,243] Both delayed hypersensitivity and antibody-dependent cellular cytotoxicity mechanisms have been proposed.[237]

There is a striking female predominance in SLE, suggesting that female sex hormones are of pathogenetic significance.[17] Interestingly, in the experimental model of SLE in rabbits, females have a much more serious form of glomerulonephritis than do their male counterparts and this difference can be negated by castration or the administration of male sex hormones.[237]

There is without question a genetic predisposition to the development of SLE.[244] There are many examples of familial incidence, and immunoglobulin abnormalities have often been documented in asymptomatic relatives; indeed, as many as seven members in a single family have been recorded.[111] Lupus erythematosus has also been reported in identical twins.[111] HLA typing has revealed an increased incidence of HLA-A1, HLA-B8, HLA-B15, HLA-DR2 and HLA-DR3 in SLE.[12] It has been suggested that expression of the disease may be inherited as an autosomal dominant trait. HLA-DR4 is associated with hydralazine-induced lupus erythematosus. The frequencies of HLA-DRw6 and HLA-B8 are increased in DLE.[12] It has recently been demonstrated that patients with polymorphic light eruption and HLA-DRB1*0301 have a higher risk of developing either subacute or discoid lupus erythematosus.[245,246] The familial clustering of polymorphic light eruption in relatives of persons with lupus erythematosus suggests that these diseases may share a similar pathogenesis.[247]

SCLE has been demonstrated to be associated with the TNF-308A allele.[248,249] Transcription of TNF-α appears to be photoregulated in subacute lupus.[249] Triggering mechanisms in lupus erythematosus include UV light (both naturally occurring and artificial), drugs and, possibly, viruses. Sunlight commonly worsens the cutaneous manifestations and may exacerbate systemic disease.[111,250,251] Antibodies to UV DNA have been identified in patients with SLE.[252] These may be important in the pathogenesis of the photosensitivity-induced lesions. Lesions are typically worse in spring and summer, and cutaneous lesions can be induced artificially by UV irradiation. Dysregulation of apoptosis has been suggested as an important mechanism in the pathogenesis of lupus erythematosus. A reduction of bcl-2 expression in epidermal basal cells is associated with overexpression of FAS antigen and this appears to correlate with the extent of apoptosis in the epidermis.[253]

Despite early enthusiasm for a viral etiology for lupus erythematosus, the results of extensive research have not provided convincing evidence. For many years paramyxovirus-like inclusions within the cytoplasm of endothelial cells were thought to represent evidence of a viral cause.[254] They are now known to represent a non-specific membranous byproduct (tubuloreticular body) of organelle degeneration (*Fig. 16.40*). An association with parvovirus (erythrovirus) B19 has been suggested.[255] Two experimental virus-induced animal models – Aleutian mink disease and New Zealand black–white hybrid mouse disease – have been described.[17]

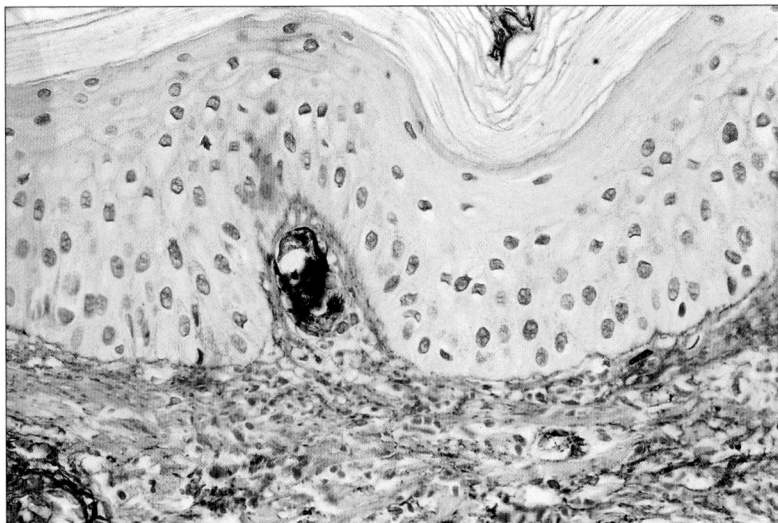

Fig. 16.39
Systemic lupus erythematosus: immunoperoxidase reaction demonstrating IgG within a blood vessel wall.

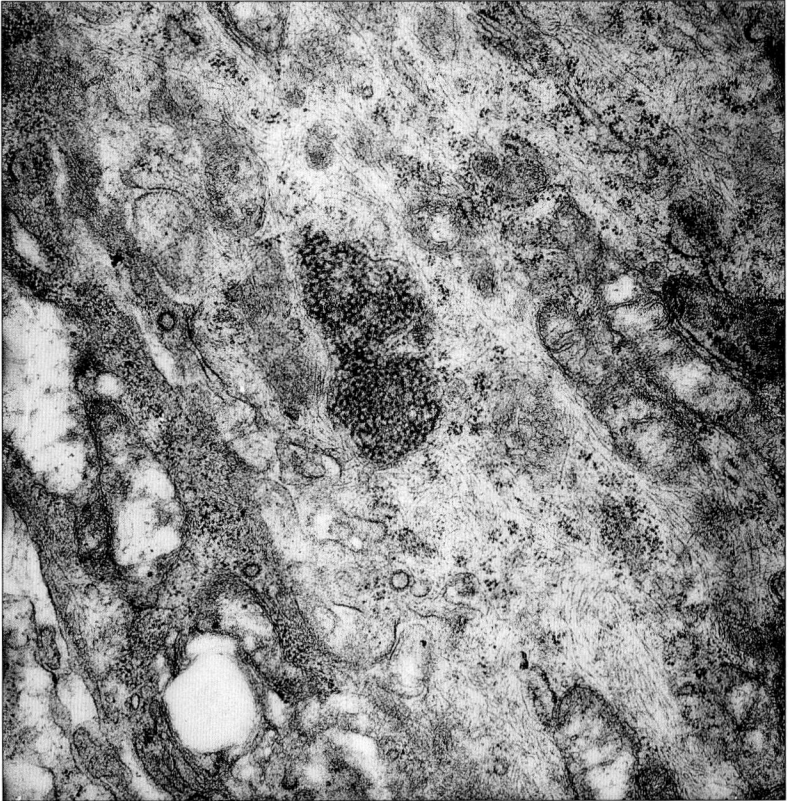

Fig. 16.40
Systemic lupus erythematosus: electron microscopy of an endothelial cell. In the center is a typical tubuloreticular body.

Recent investigations have shown that the latter is associated with a primary stem cell defect. Bone marrow grafts can therefore transfer the disease to previously irradiated normal recipients and induce tolerance defects.[256] Bone marrow cultures produce B-cells with an increased capacity for antibody synthesis.[249] Murine lupus shows a striking similarity to its human counterpart.

The lupus band test is particularly important in the diagnosis of lupus erythematosus. It is also, to a lesser extent, of some value in assessing prognosis. By either immunofluorescence or immunoperoxidase techniques, the presence of immunoglobulin and complement is sought at the epidermodermal junction (*Fig. 16.41*). IgM is most commonly identified, although IgG, IgA and C3 are also frequently present.[257] IgG deposits appear to be the most specific for lupus erythematosus. Other factors that may be identified include properdin, C1q and C4.[262] Deposition of the membrane attack complex (MAC) has also been shown to be a relatively sensitive and specific marker of cutaneous lupus erythematosus.[259,260] Although deposits are usually homogeneous, granular and thready (reticular) patterns are also recognized.[257] Homogeneous bands are typical of chronic lesions, granular bands are seen in uninvolved skin and thready deposits are usually a feature of early lesions.[260]

Ultrastructurally, the immunoreactants are present in the sub-basal lamina connective tissue and intimately associated with reduplicated lamina densa (*Fig. 16.42*).[12] The immunoglobulin deposition does not necessarily correlate with the clinical or histological presence of cutaneous lesions and is therefore unlikely to be of pathogenetic significance.

The lupus band test is positive in involved skin in approximately 50–94% of patients with SLE, 60–80% of those with the discoid variant, 60% of patients with SCLE and 50% of infants with neonatal lupus erythematosus.[257,260–264] Lesional mucosa also shows immunoreactant deposition and this can be of particular value in patients where histological distinction from lichen planus proves impossible.[21] It may also be positive in uninvolved skin in up to 67% of patients with systemic disease.[263] The prevalence of a positive test in uninvolved skin depends upon the site, with the highest incidence in skin from the shoulder (70%). Sun-exposed skin, such as the dorsal aspect of the forearms, is more frequently positive (60–70%) than non-sun-exposed skin (50–60%). However, the observation that 20% of specimens of sun-exposed normal skin from healthy young adults show a positive lupus band test indicates that non-sun-exposed skin is the substrate of choice.[265]

Positivity also depends upon the duration of the disease (lesions less than 3 months old are often negative) and the effect of previous steroid therapy.[266] Much less often, positive immunofluorescence is seen in the uninvolved skin of patients with DLE.[267] The results must, however, be taken in the context of the clinical information. A positive IgM lupus band test may be seen in unrelated conditions such as solar keratosis, polymorphous light eruption, rosacea, lymphocytic infiltrate and dermatomyositis, and as a consequence of UV radiation.[260,263] These latter conditions are usually associated with C3 deposition or a single immunoglobulin class, particularly IgM, in contrast to the multiple immunoglobulin subclasses found in lupus erythematosus.[260] In non-lupus conditions the lupus band is usually fainter and patchy.[267] With such a significant false positive rate, it is stressed that the results of a lupus band test must be interpreted with considerable caution and always in the context of the clinical information and histological features.

A characteristic particulate dust-like deposition of immunoglobulin (predominantly IgG) affecting the basal cells of the epidermis has been described in patients with SCLE.[240,268] Sometimes suprabasal epidermis, adnexal epithelium and the dermal cellular infiltrate show similar fluorescence.[262,268] This pattern of deposition correlates with the presence of Ro antibodies.[263] It is also occasionally evident in SLE. In some cases speckled nuclear staining of keratinocytes for IgG is seen in connective tissue diseases.[269] In the setting of SLE, this finding appears to be associated with a lower incidence of renal disease.[269]

The histopathological features of the various subsets of lupus erythematosus (with the exceptions of lupus erythematosus profundus and bullous dermatosis of SLE) show considerable overlap and their distinction by microscopic techniques is often difficult.[270,271]

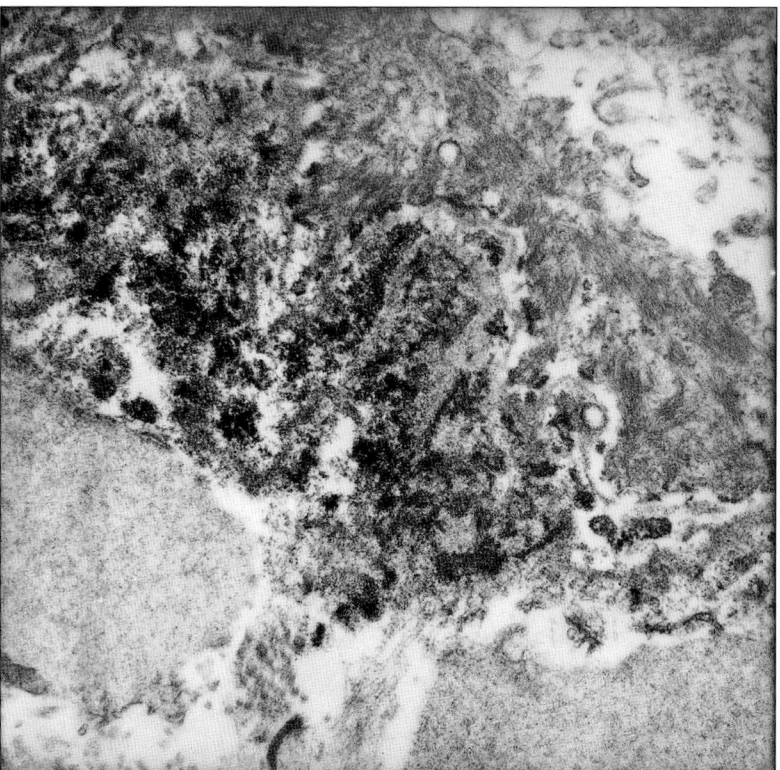

Fig. 16.42
Lupus band test: immunoelectron microscopy (frozen section) showing IgM deposition below the lamina densa.

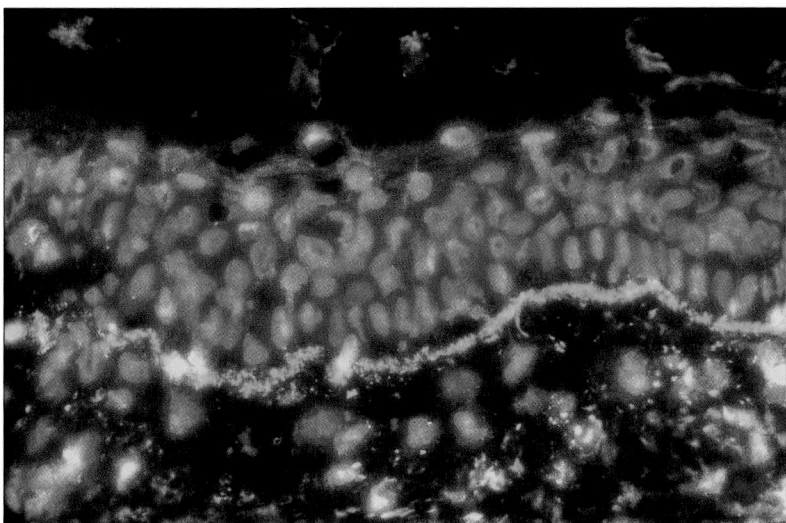

Fig. 16.41
Systemic lupus erythematosus: positive band test (IgG). By courtesy of the Department of Immunofluorescence, Institute of Dermatology, London, UK.

Discoid lupus erythematosus

Discoid lupus erythematosus displays variable features, depending upon the stage of the disease.[12,264,265] The active lesion is characterized by hyperkeratosis and follicular dilatation with keratin plugging; occasionally focal parakeratosis is present (*Figs 16.43, 16.44*). The epidermis is usually atrophic and rather flattened, although sometimes there is acanthosis (*Fig. 16.45*). The most significant features seen at the epidermodermal junction are:

- liquefactive degeneration of the basal layer of the epidermis (*Fig. 16.46*)
- basement membrane thickening (*Fig. 16.47*), which may be accentuated by use of the periodic acid–Schiff (PAS) reaction.

These two features may additionally affect follicular epithelium, and basement membrane thickening of the dermal blood vessels is also sometimes evident (*Fig. 16.48*). Liquefactive degeneration of the basal layer of the epidermis is often accompanied by pigmentary incontinence (*Fig. 16.49*). In some instances the epidermal changes are accompanied by cytoid body formation, but this is not usually as conspicuous as in lichen planus (*Fig. 16.50*). Amyloid formation may occasionally be seen.

The papillary dermis is edematous, and telangiectatic vessels are often present (*Fig. 16.51*). Focal extravasations of red blood cells are sometimes seen (*Fig. 16.52*). Characteristic of DLE is a perivascular and periappendageal chronic inflammatory cell infiltrate of lymphocytes and variable numbers of histiocytes (*Fig. 16.53*). The most common cells are the T-lymphocytes, both helper and suppressor cells.[243,244] Neutrophil polymorphs and plasma cells are not usually evident. However, the presence of neutrophils and leukocytoclasia has been described in the lupus-like lesions of a patient with a lupus-like dermatosis with X-linked chronic granulomatous disease.[48]

CD4+ cells predominate in DLE skin lesions.[243] The majority of these T-lymphocytes are Ia+, indicating an activated state. Occasional CD4+

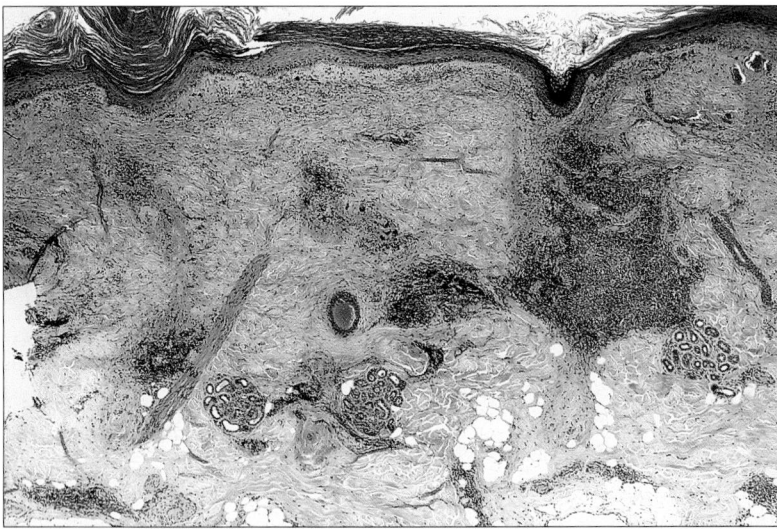

Fig. 16.43
Discoid lupus erythematosus: this scanning view shows hyperkeratosis, a somewhat flattened epidermis and a perivascular and periadnexal chronic inflammatory cell infiltrate.

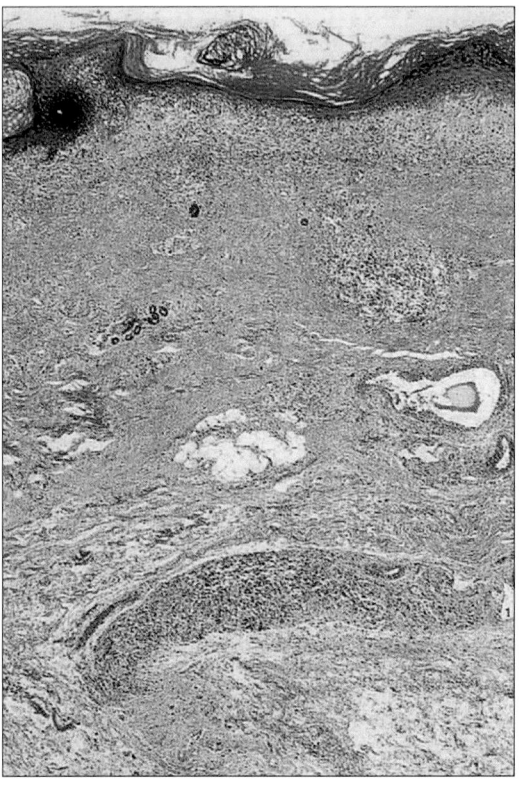

Fig. 16.45
Discoid lupus erythematosus: there is hyperkeratosis and atrophy of the epidermis.

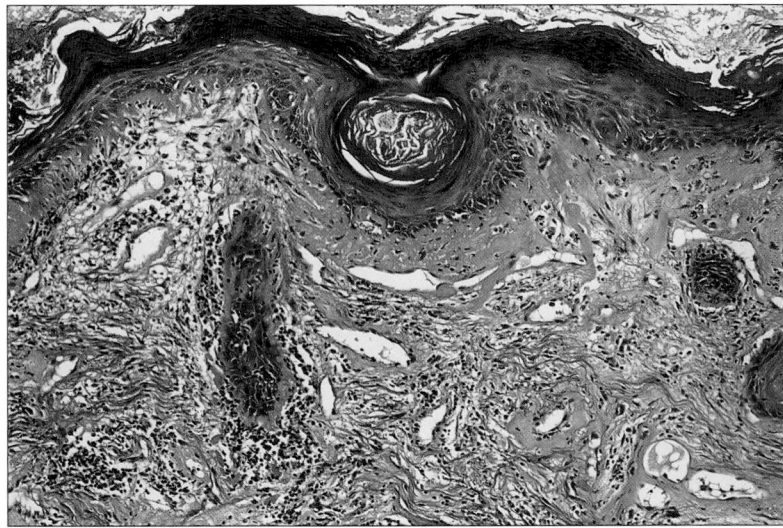

Fig. 16.44
Discoid lupus erythematosus: in this view there is striking follicular plugging.

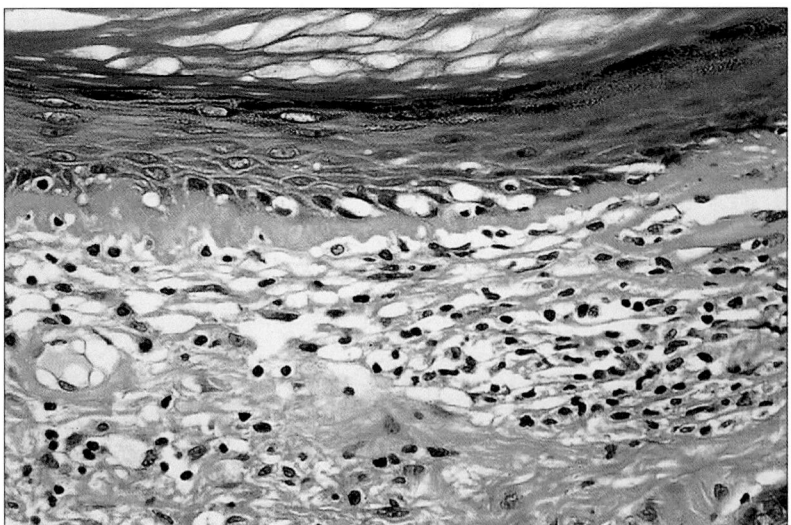

Fig. 16.46
Discoid lupus erythematosus: in this view there is hyperkeratosis, epidermal atrophy and basal cell hydropic degeneration.

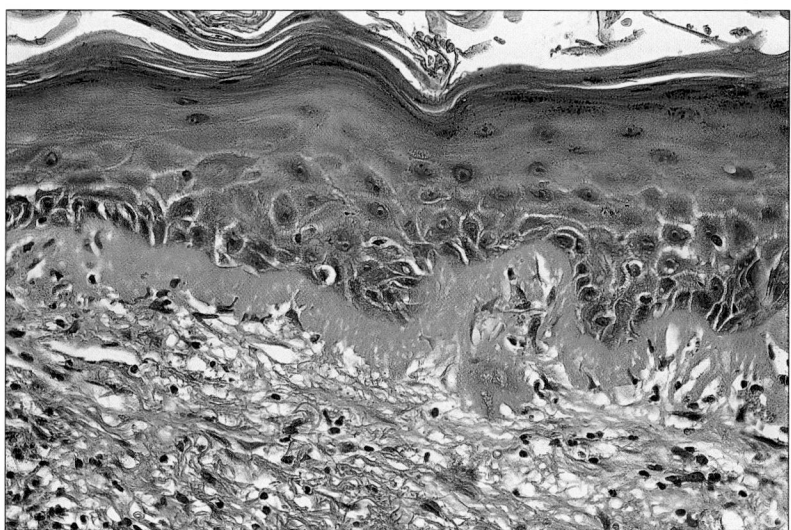

Fig. 16.47
Discoid lupus erythematosus: note the very marked thickening of the basement membrane.

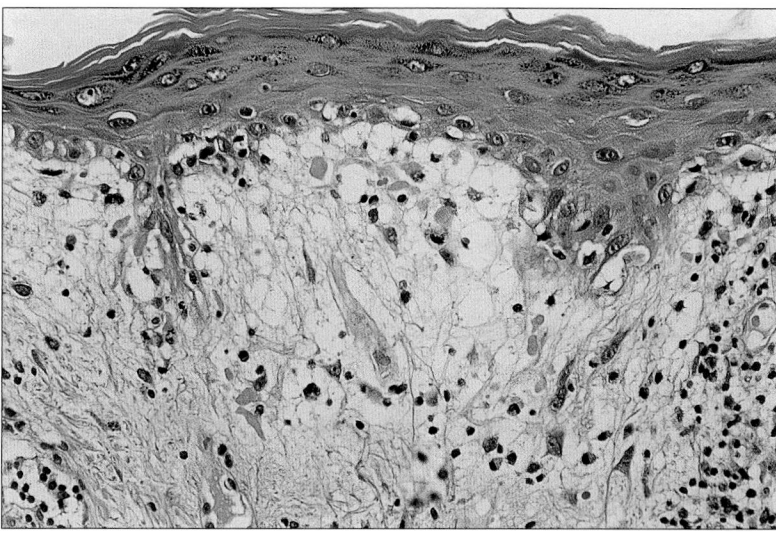

Fig. 16.50
Discoid lupus erythematosus: several cytoid bodies are present in the papillary dermis. Note the hydropic degeneration.

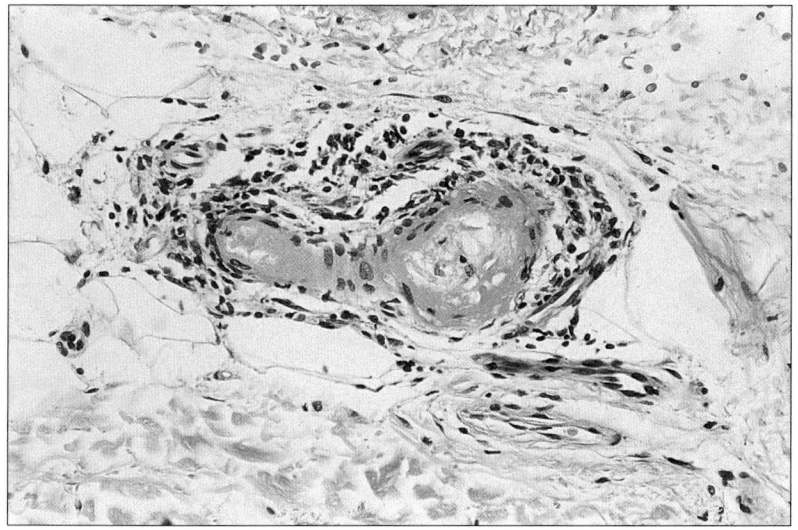

Fig. 16.48
Discoid lupus erythematosus: this arteriole shows marked hyalinization. Ischemic ulceration was present in the adjacent skin.

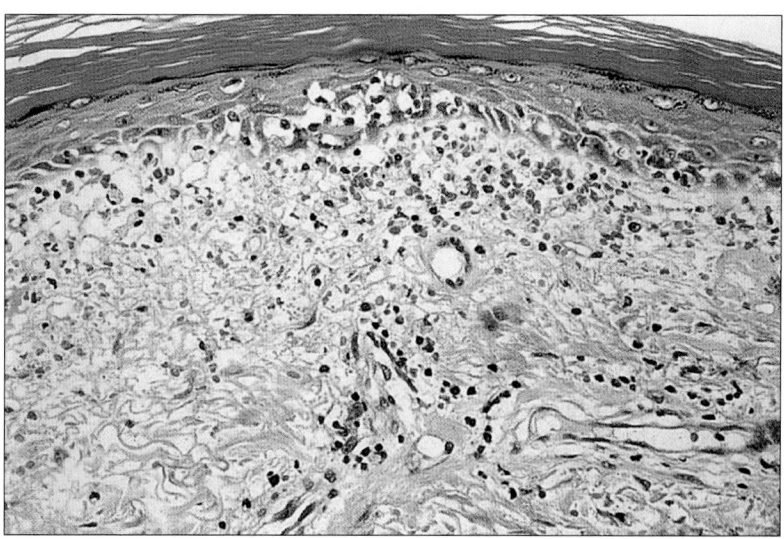

Fig. 16.51
Discoid lupus erythematosus: note the telangiectatic vessels in the superficial dermis.

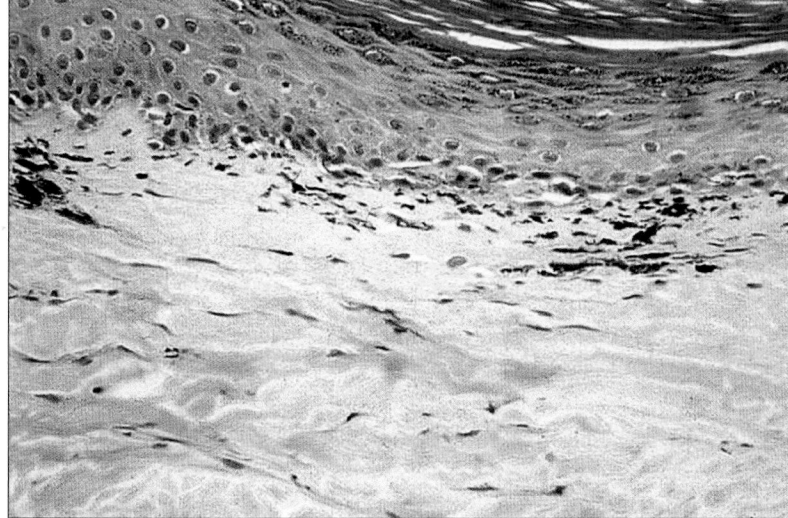

Fig. 16.49
Discoid lupus erythematosus: note the extensive pigmentary incontinence.

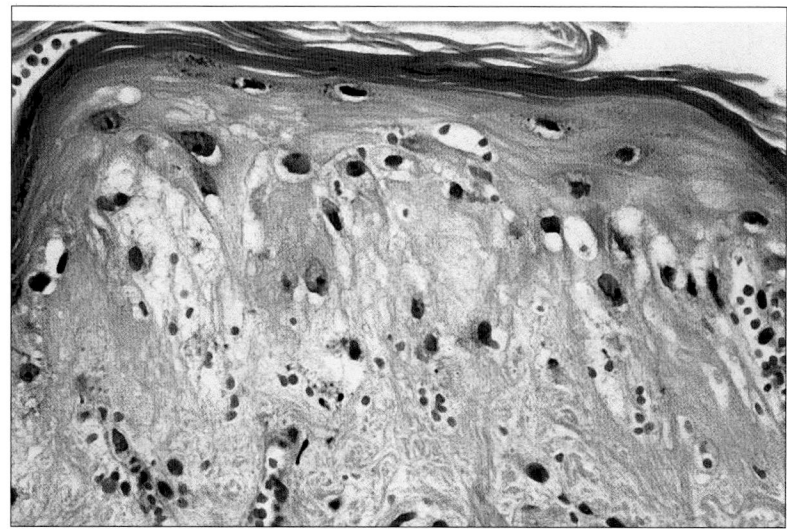

Fig. 16.52
Discoid lupus erythematosus: in addition to hyperkeratosis and epidermal atrophy there is quite marked purpura.

cells are present in the epidermis closely related to foci of basal keratinocyte damage.[243] Epidermal Langerhans' cells are usually reduced in number.[242] B-lymphocytes are generally present in only small numbers. The infiltrate is typically sparse in the papillary dermis, but focal dense aggregates are characteristically found in the reticular dermis and may sometimes extend into the subcutaneous fat.

An increase in glycosaminoglycans (acid mucopolysaccharides) in the reticular dermis is a common feature of the acute lesion; in tumid lupus this is very marked (*Figs 16.54, 16.55*). Very rarely dermal calcification has been documented (*Fig. 16.56*).[272] Very occasionally 'fibrinoid' change of the dermal collagen is present (*Fig. 16.57*).

In the healing lesion of DLE there is hyperkeratosis and the epidermis may be atrophic or, more commonly, slightly thickened. The basement membrane region is characteristically markedly thickened. The dermis is fibrosed, sometimes to a degree that resembles lichen sclerosus (*Fig. 16.58*). In hair-bearing sites, particularly the scalp, there may be very marked follicular plugging with associated chronic inflammation, and in advanced disease there is often complete loss of the pilosebaceous

structures with replacement by collagenous fibrous strands (*Fig. 16.59*).[271] Sebaceous gland atrophy or loss occurs early in scalp involvement and the chronic inflammatory changes are centered at the level of the mid-follicle.[18] It has been suggested that this may represent a focus of follicular stem cells and therefore chronic inflammation at this site could readily result in permanent hair loss.

Rarely DLE may present as a dense superficial and deep perivascular and periappendageal infiltrate in the absence of significant epidermal changes: distinction from lymphocytic infiltrate of Jessner and polymorphous light eruption is, therefore, histologically impossible.[271]

In hypertrophic lesions there is marked hyperkeratosis, hypergranulosis and irregular acanthosis with papillomatosis in addition to the features of basal cell damage.[12] Cytoid bodies are often conspicuous in the lower epidermis.[271] Amyloid deposition has been reported as a frequent finding.[273] The features are commonly histologically indistinguishable from hypertrophic lichen planus. The presence of intraepidermal elastic fibers has been reported in hypertrophic lupus erythematosus.[28] This is not a feature of lichen planus. Resolving or evolving keratoacanthoma may sometimes be mimicked.[28]

Mucous membrane lesions are frequently difficult to distinguish from lichen planus.[20,21,271] They are characterized by hyperkeratosis, often accompanied by parakeratosis. The epithelium may be atrophic or

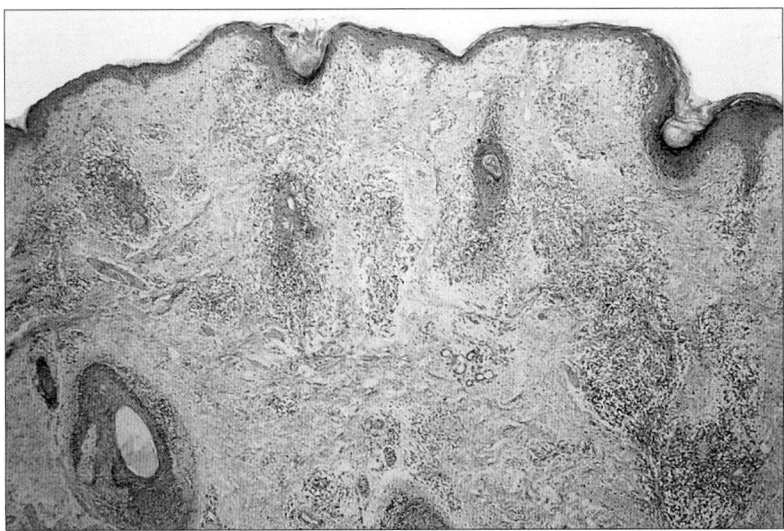

Fig. 16.53
Discoid lupus erythematosus: blood vessels and hair follicles are surrounded by a characteristic heavy lymphohistiocytic infiltrate.

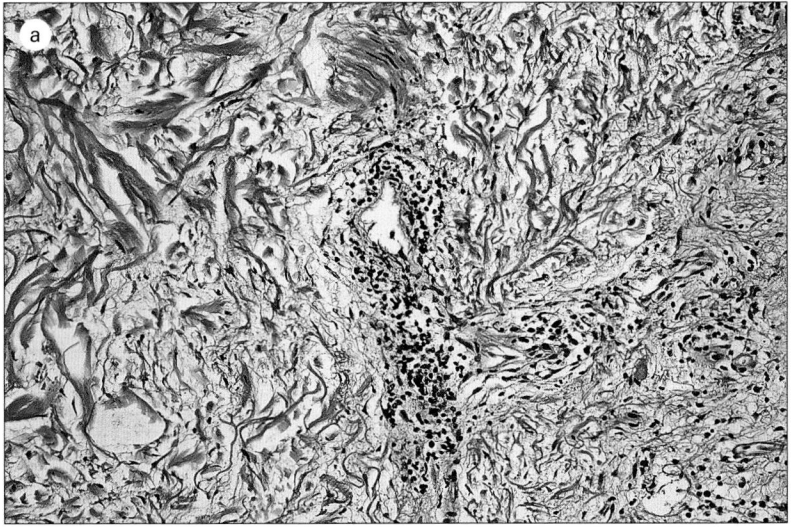

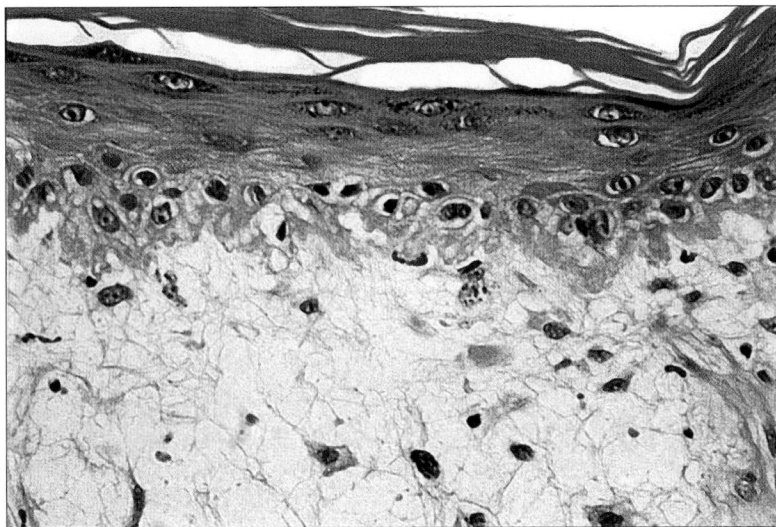

Fig. 16.54
Discoid lupus erythematosus: stromal mucin deposition, as seen in this field, is not uncommon.

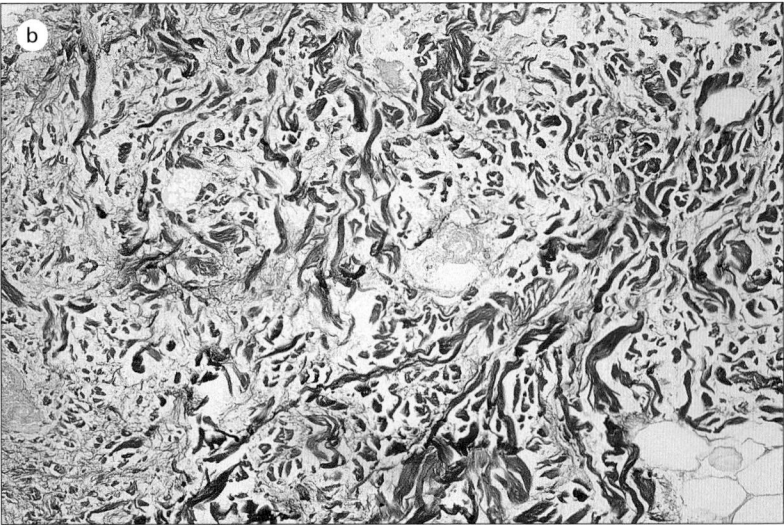

Fig. 16.55
Tumid discoid lupus erythematosus: (a) in this rare variant, there is very marked mucin deposition; (b) the mucin stains with alcian blue, pH 2.5. By courtesy of J. Cohen, MD, Dermatopathology Laboratory, Tucson, USA.

acanthotic. Hydropic degeneration of basal keratinocytes, sometimes associated with cytoid body formation, accompanies a dense lympho-histiocytic infiltrate in which plasma cells are often numerous. The presence of a deep perivascular chronic inflammatory cell infiltrate favors the diagnosis of DLE.[272] Direct immunofluorescence is, however, frequently necessary to establish the diagnosis.[20,21]

Lupus erythematosus profundus

The histological features of lupus erythematosus profundus are considered on page 379.

Subacute cutaneous lupus erythematosus

Although the histological features of SCLE show considerable overlap with those of DLE, there are diagnostic pointers.[55,274,275] In SCLE, the hyperkeratosis tends to be mild, atrophy is more marked and the epidermal ridge pattern is often effaced (*Fig. 16.60*).[275] Parakeratosis may sometimes be a feature. Basement membrane thickening is minimal or absent, and hair follicles are often unaffected or show only slight keratin plugging.[274,275] In DLE, the inflammatory cell infiltrate is denser, occupies the papillary and reticular dermis, and often shows peri-follicular accentuation. In SCLE, lymphocytic exocytosis may be

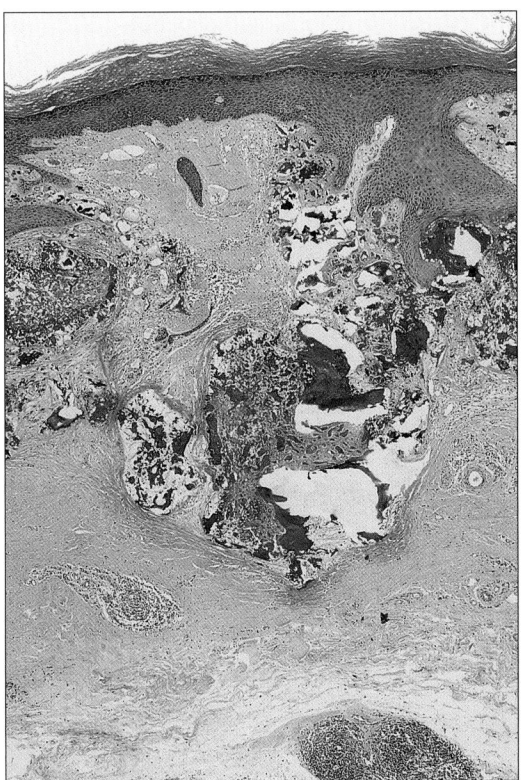

Fig. 16.56
Discoid lupus erythematosus: calcification is a rare feature. In this example, there is striking transepidermal elimination.

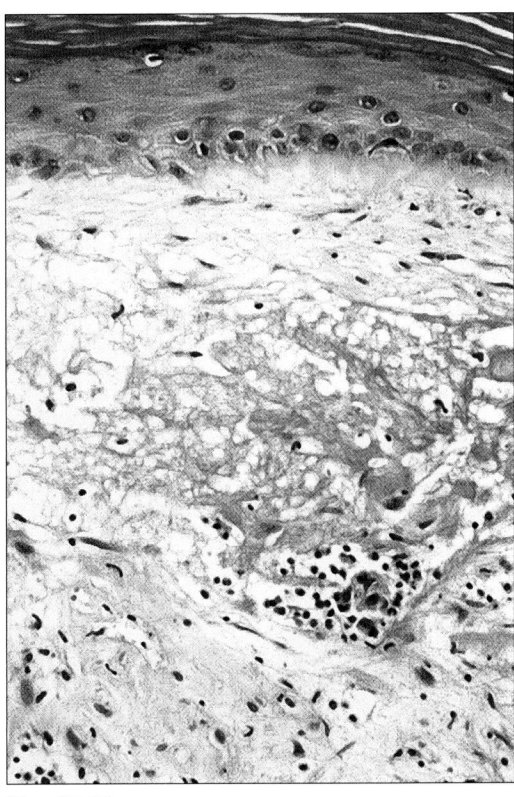

Fig. 16.57
Discoid lupus erythematosus: note the presence of fibrinoid necrosis. This is more usually a feature of the systemic variant.

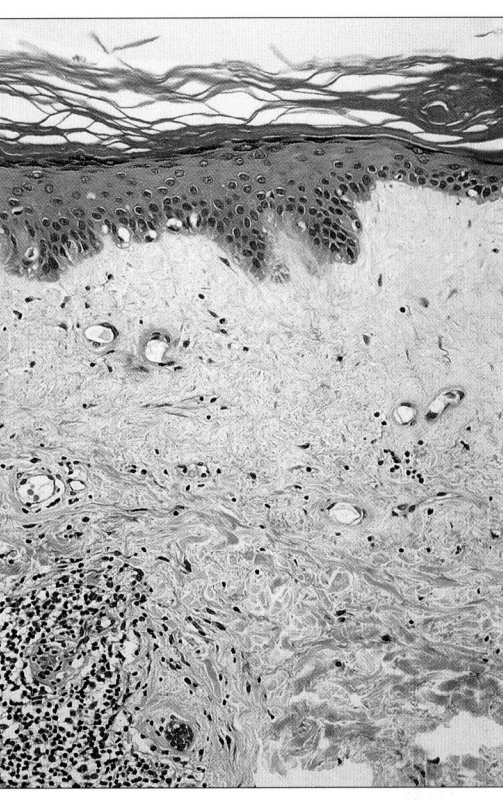

Fig. 16.58
Discoid lupus erythematosus: in this example, the presence of superficial dermal sclerosis is reminiscent of lichen sclerosus.

Fig. 16.59
Discoid lupus erythematosus: note the complete absence of hair follicles in this scalp specimen.

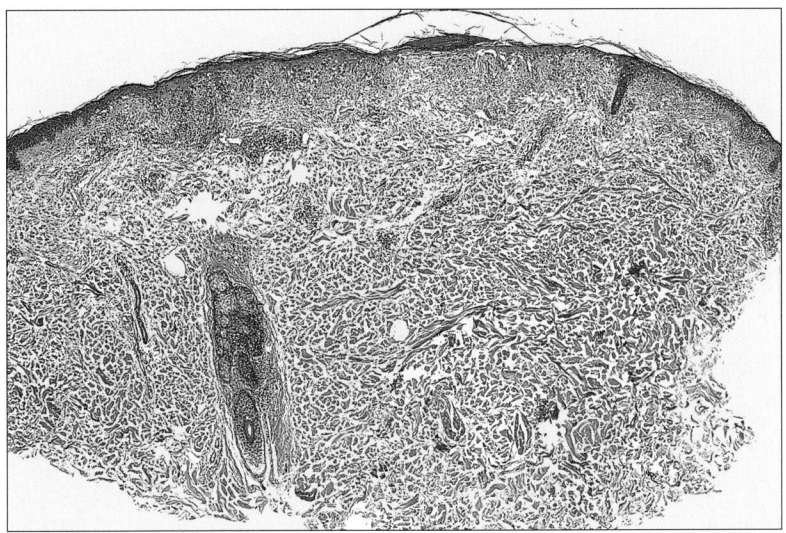

Fig. 16.60
Subacute cutaneous lupus erythematosus: low power view showing slight hyperkeratosis and focal parakeratosis. A perivascular and band-like chronic inflammatory cell infiltrate is present.

conspicuous and satellite cell necrosis is not uncommon (*Fig. 16.61*).[275] Liquefactive degeneration of the basal layer of the epidermis is usually present although often it is only mild (*Figs 16.62, 16.63*). Sometimes, however, it is sufficiently marked that subepidermal vesiculation results.[54,57] Homogenization of the papillary dermal collagen is occasionally seen.[275] Colloid body formation and pigmentary incontinence are often inconspicuous, but sometimes they are a major feature.[57] The inflammatory cell infiltrate is typically mild, superficially located and perivascular in distribution. In some examples, however, it presents as a lichenoid band.[57,61,275]

The histopathological features in cutaneous lesions of patients without SCLE and antibodies to SS-A (Ro) are very similar to those seen in lesions of patients with SCLE.[276] These patients often have different clinical diseases including Sjögren's syndrome and rheumatoid arthritis.

Systemic lupus erythematosus

The histological features of SLE are variable. The changes in early lesions, which may be very mild and subtle, often comprise only slight epidermal basal cell liquefactive degeneration, papillary dermal edema and a mild chronic inflammatory cell infiltrate and are seen, for example, in malar erythema (*Fig. 16.64*).[62,259] On other occasions the appearances are similar to those of SCLE.

The histology of SLE is not uncommonly indistinguishable from that of the discoid variant (*Fig. 16.65*). Fibrinoid degeneration of the dermal collagen is, however, more common in SLE than in DLE. Dermal mucin deposition is often seen between collagen bundles. In most cases, this feature is subtle but mucin deposition may be very prominent.[277] A thick basal membrane is more commonly seen in lesions of DLE. As with DLE, the commonest cell type is the T-lymphocyte, but which subset predominates is uncertain. Both CD4+ and CD4+ subset preponderance have been documented.[242,243] It may be that differences in the age of the lesion, effects of treatment and antibody specificity can account for this apparent anomaly. CD4+ lymphocytes are present in large numbers in the epidermis at sites of basal keratinocyte hydropic degeneration.[242]

The histopathological features of the cutaneous lesions of the antiphospholipid syndrome comprise both venous and arterial thrombosis in the absence of any evidence of vasculitis (*Figs 16.66, 16.67*). In early

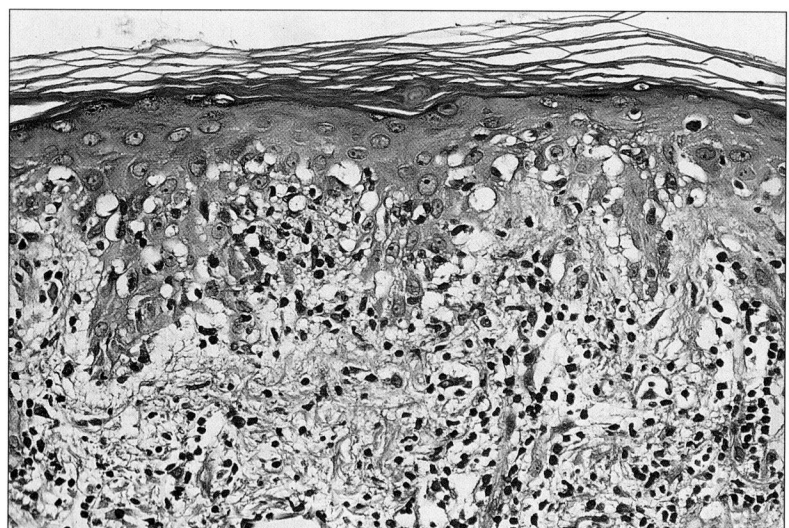

Fig. 16.61
Subacute cutaneous lupus erythematosus: in this example, in addition to basal cell hydropic degeneration, there is intercellular edema of the epidermis with lymphocytic exocytosis.

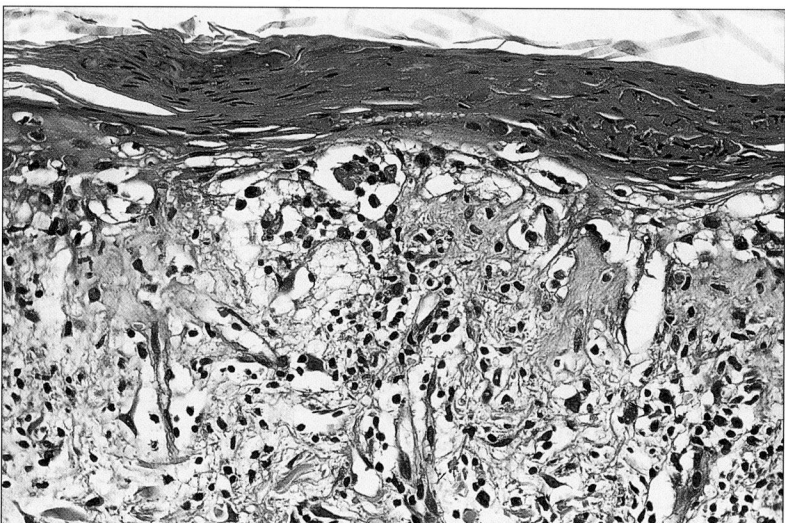

Fig. 16.63
Subacute cutaneous lupus erythematosus: there is marked basal cell hydropic degeneration. Only a patchy chronic inflammatory cell infiltrate is present.

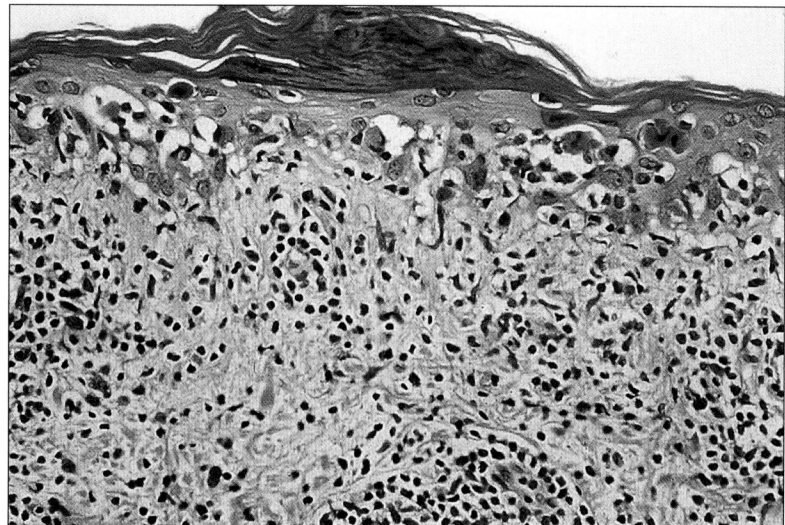

Fig. 16.62
Subacute cutaneous lupus erythematosus: note the presence of numerous cytoid bodies and focal satellite cell necrosis.

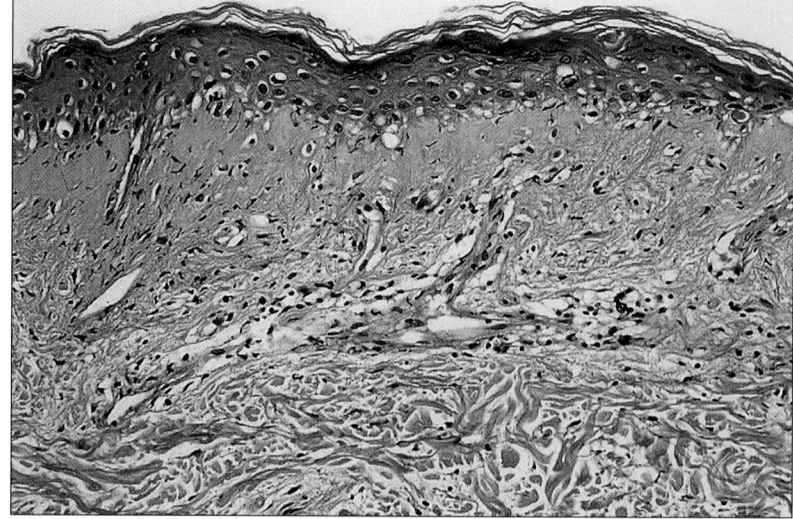

Fig. 16.64
Systemic lupus erythematosus: although the changes may be identical to the discoid or subacute variants sometimes the features are mild, as in this case. There is focal basal cell hydropic degeneration and telangiectasia.

lesions endothelial cell damage may be marked and erythrocyte extravasation is common. Older lesions are characterized by marked vascular proliferation commonly in a lobular distribution accompanied by hemosiderosis (*Fig. 16.68*). Hobnail reactive endothelial cells and eosinophilic hyaline globules are sometimes evident.[237] A lymphocytic infiltrate accompanied by variable numbers of plasma cells is often seen.[237,278,279] In some patients the clinical and histological features of Degos' disease and anetoderma have been documented.[279]

Renal lesions may be detected in 70–80% of patients. The histological features are subdivided into five types, according to the WHO classification:[280]

- In *type I* no abnormality can be detected by light, immunofluorescent or electron microscopy.

- In *type II* lesions (mesangial lupus glomerulonephritis) there are increases in both the mesangial matrix and mesangial cells; immunofluorescence reveals mesangial deposition of IgG and complement and mesangial electron-dense deposits may be detected by electron microscopy (*Fig. 16.69*). Mesangial lupus glomerulonephritis is the mildest form of glomerular lesion and is present in about 10% of patients with renal involvement.

- *Type III* lesions (focal segmental proliferative glomerulonephritis) are found in about 30% of patients. In this variant only scattered glomeruli are affected (focal) and usually only a portion of the tuft is involved (segmental). Lesions may be proliferative and necrotizing (*Fig. 16.70*). Involved glomeruli show mesangial and endothelial proliferation, polymorph infiltration, fibrin deposition and

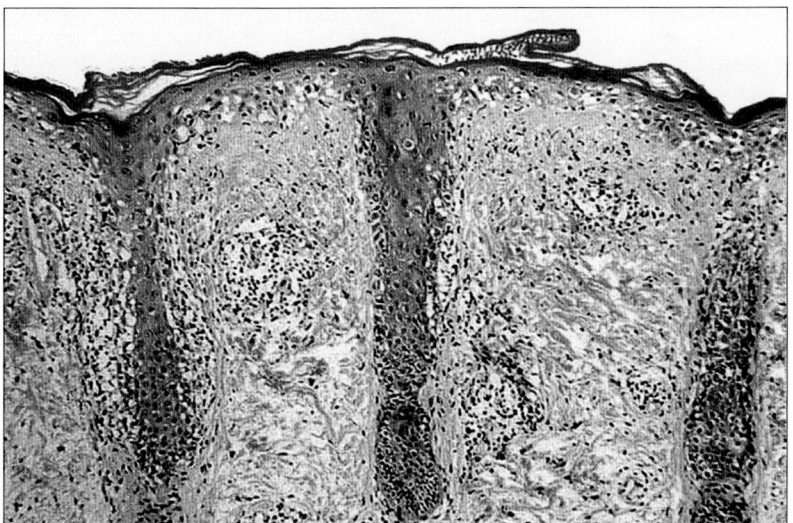

Fig. 16.65
Systemic lupus erythematosus: in this example the features resemble the discoid variant. Note the hyperkeratosis, epidermal atrophy, follicular involvement and gross basal cell hydropic degeneration. A perivascular and perifollicular chronic inflammatory cell infiltrate is present.

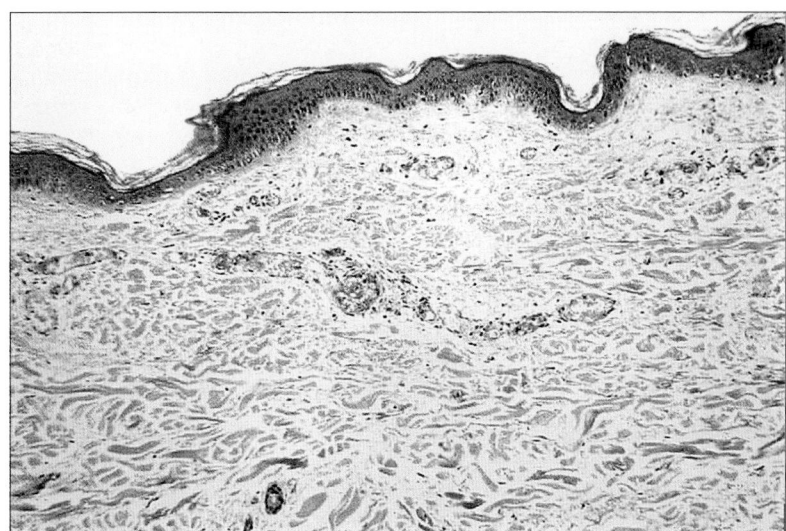

Fig. 16.66
Lupus anticoagulant syndrome: low power view from a specimen of skin adjacent to an area of infarction. The superficial blood vessels are occluded by small thrombi.

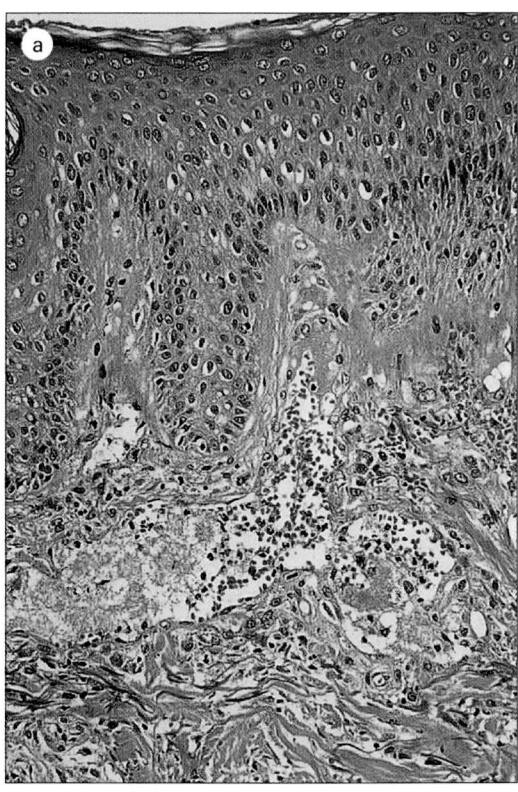
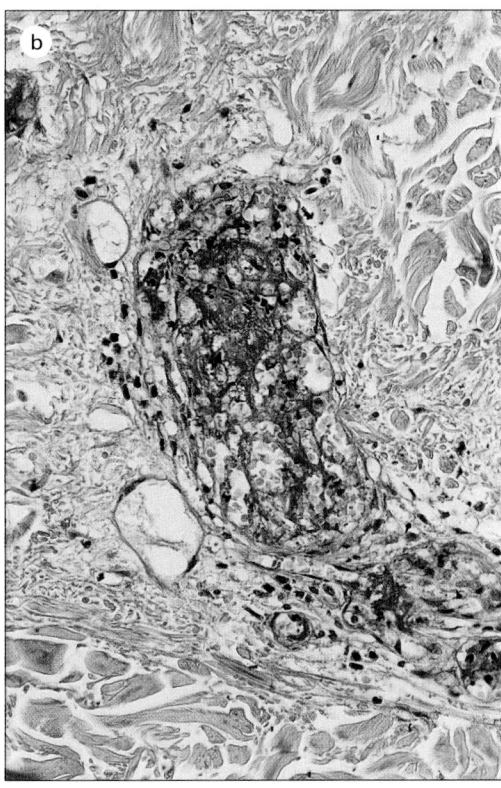

Fig. 16.67
Lupus anticoagulant syndrome: (a) close-up view of occluded vessel – note the absence of inflammatory changes; (b) the presence of fibrin is confirmed in this phosphotungstic acid–hematoxylin stained section.

karyorrhexis; occasionally hematoxylin bodies are evident. Hematoxylin bodies are regarded as the histological hallmark of SLE. They are round-to-oval structures, which stain purple/red–pink/blue with hematoxylin and eosin (*Fig. 16.71*). They stain positively with the Feulgen reaction and are von Kossa negative. Hematoxylin bodies are thought to be the in vivo counterpart of the LE cell phenomenon. Although frequently sought they are often very difficult to find. Electron microscopy typically reveals mesangial and subendothelial electron-dense (immune complex) deposits (*Fig. 16.72*). Clinically, patients present with hematuria and proteinuria, although a proportion may develop chronic renal failure or progress to type IV lesions.

- *Type IV* lesions (diffuse proliferative glomerulonephritis) occur in about 50% of patients with SLE who have the nephritic/nephrotic syndrome or hypertension. Almost all glomeruli are affected and, in addition to mesangial and endothelial proliferation, the epithelial cells may participate, with the formation of crescents (*Fig. 16.73*). Careful examination of the periphery of the glomerular tuft often reveals regularly thickened capillaries – 'wire-loop' lesions, thought to be specific for SLE (*Fig. 16.74*).

- *Type V* (lupus membranous glomerulonephritis) is found in about 10% of patients with SLE and presents as proteinuria or the nephrotic syndrome. Histologically, there is uniform thickening of the glomerular capillaries without any significant inflammatory cell infiltration (*Fig. 16.75*). Ultrastructurally, the electron-dense deposits are found subepithelially.

In addition to glomerular lesions, patients with renal involvement may manifest acute necrotizing vasculitis.

The heart is involved in about 50% of patients with SLE. Acute lesions of fibrinoid degeneration and hematoxylin bodies may be seen in the pericardium, but it is more common to find obliteration of the pericardial sac by fibrous, sometimes gelatinous, adhesions. Fibrinoid necrosis of the myocardial collagen is usually found in the connective tissue septa and occasionally also affects the associated arteries. Libman–Sacks endocarditis is the best-known cardiac manifestation of SLE and is believed to occur in 30–60% of the patients who come to

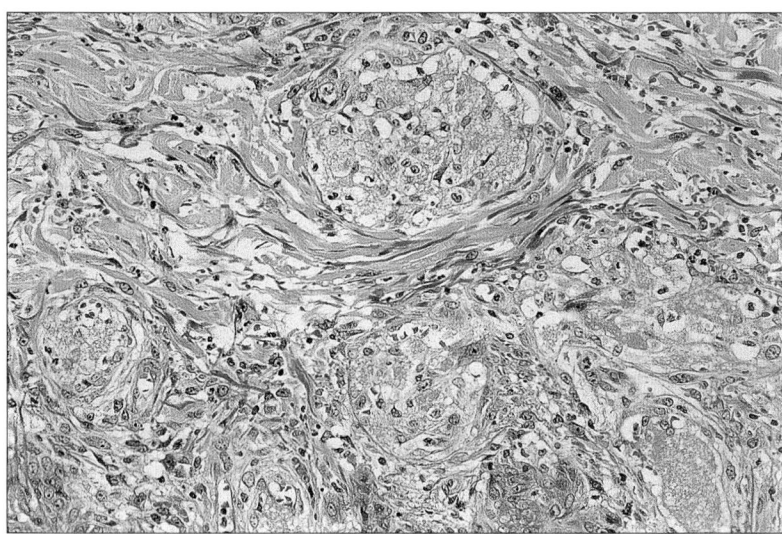

Fig. 16.68
Lupus anticoagulant syndrome: in this more advanced lesion there is nodular vascular proliferation with thrombi.

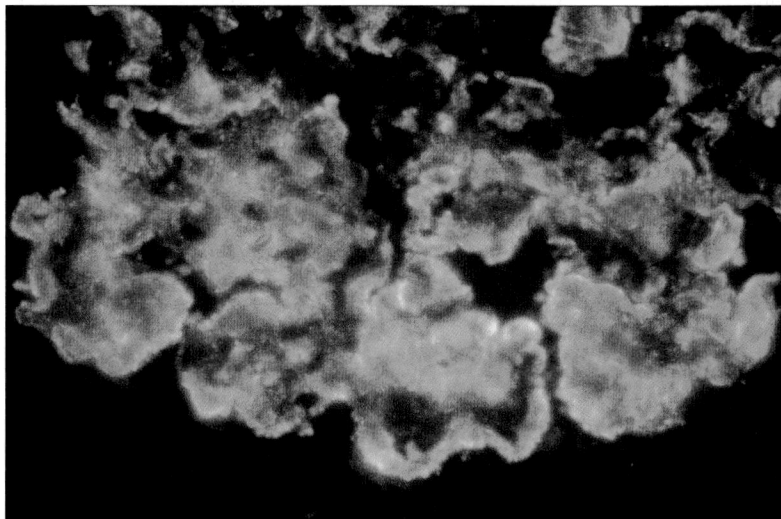

Fig. 16.69
Lupus glomerulonephritis: marked immunofluorescence is seen in the basement membrane region and mesangium. By courtesy of D.R. Davies, MD, Radcliffe Infirmary NHS Trust, Oxford, UK.

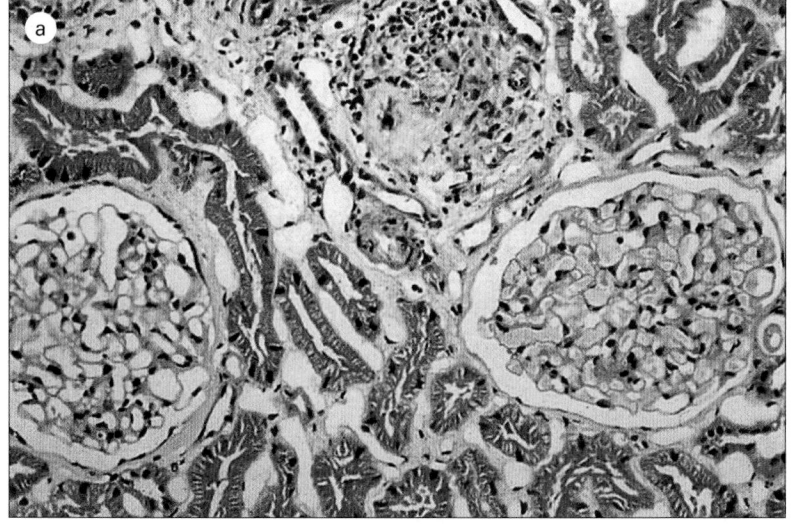

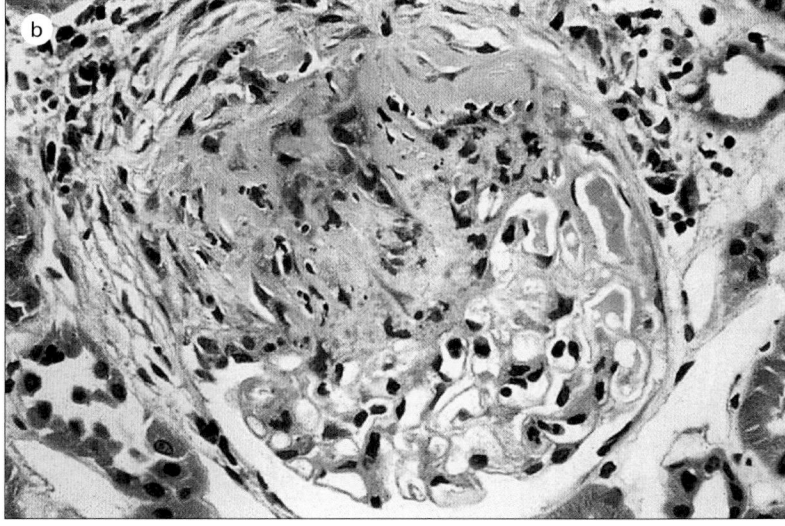

Fig. 16.70
Focal segmental proliferative lupus glomerulonephritis: (**a**) two normal (lower) and one abnormal glomeruli are present; (**b**) the lower half of the glomerulus is normal, the upper half shows a necrotizing and proliferative lesion with adhesion to Bowman's capsule.

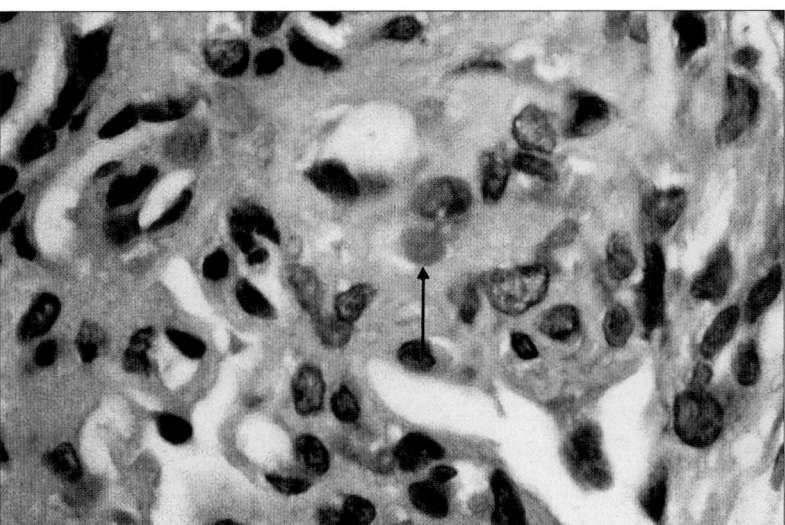

Fig. 16.71
Systemic lupus erythematosus: in the center of the field is a characteristic purplish hematoxylin body. By courtesy of D.R. Davies, MD, Radcliffe Infirmary NHS Trust, Oxford, UK.

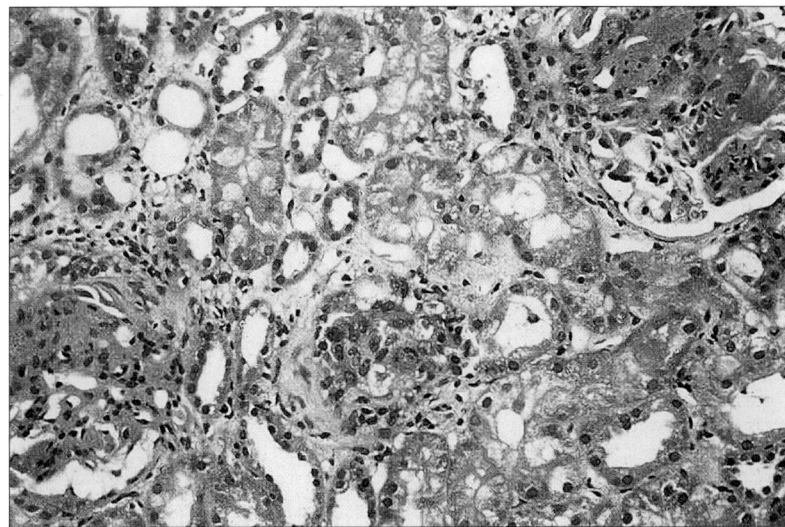

Fig. 16.73
Diffuse proliferative lupus glomerulonephritis: in this field there is global proliferation with fibrinoid necrosis in the lower left glomerulus.

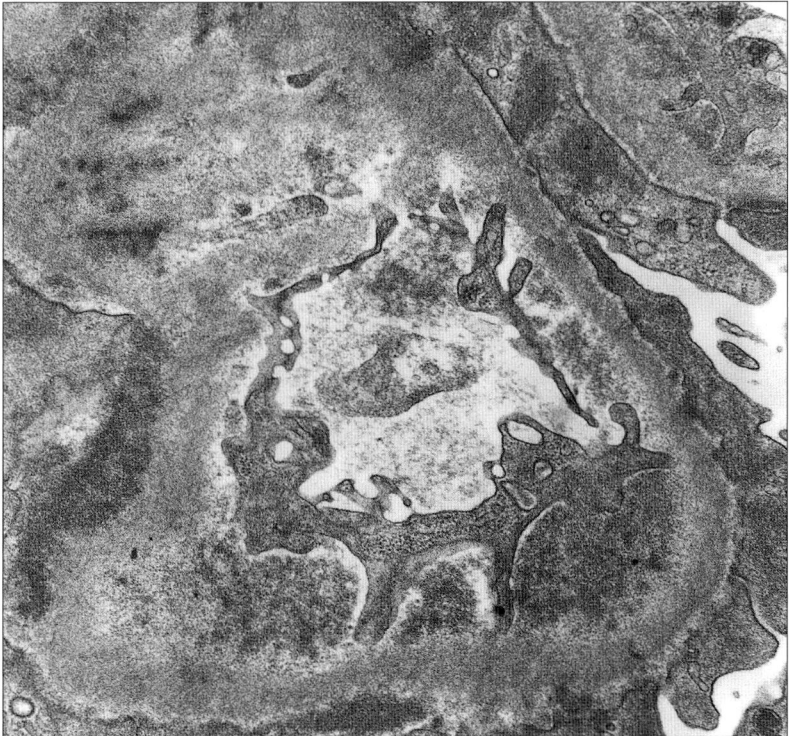

Fig. 16.72
Systemic lupus erythematosus: dense deposits are present, one either side of the basement membrane. By courtesy of J.R. Tighe, MD (retired), St Thomas' Hospital, London, UK.

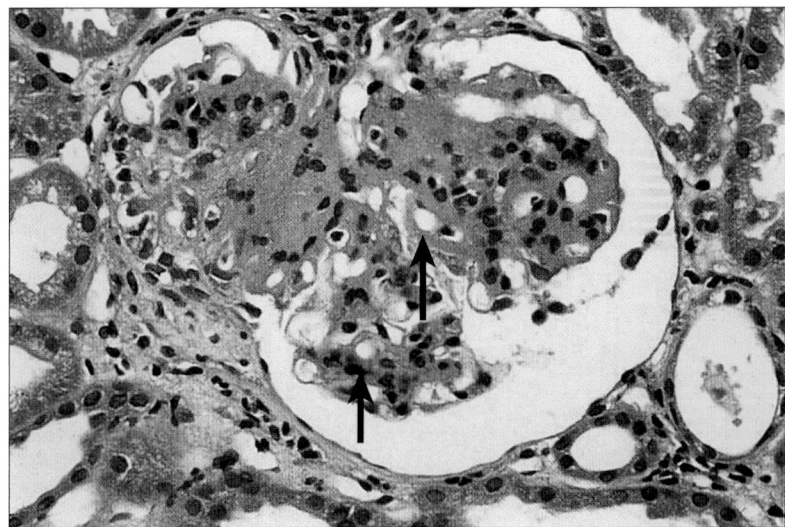

Fig. 16.74
Lupus wire-loop lesion: there is hypercellularity of mesangial and endothelial cells on the left side with obliteration of capillary lumina. On the left side epithelial proliferation has led to occlusion of Bowman's space. Glomerulosclerosis is present. Two capillary loops are arrowed.

autopsy.[113] Small granular vegetations have been found on the surfaces of all valves, although the mitral and tricuspid are most often affected (*Fig. 16.76*). The vegetations may spread to involve the chordae tendinae and adjacent endocardium (*Fig. 16.77*). Histologically they consist of fibrin overlying degenerate collagen, with an associated chronic inflammatory cell infiltrate. Infective endocarditis is an occasional, but important complication. Increased quantities of glycosaminoglycans are usually evident and sometimes hematoxylin bodies are present.

The histological lesions of pulmonary involvement include interstitial pneumonitis, fibrosing alveolitis and infarction. Direct immuno-fluorescent examination of lung biopsies may reveal the presence of both immunoglobulin and complement.

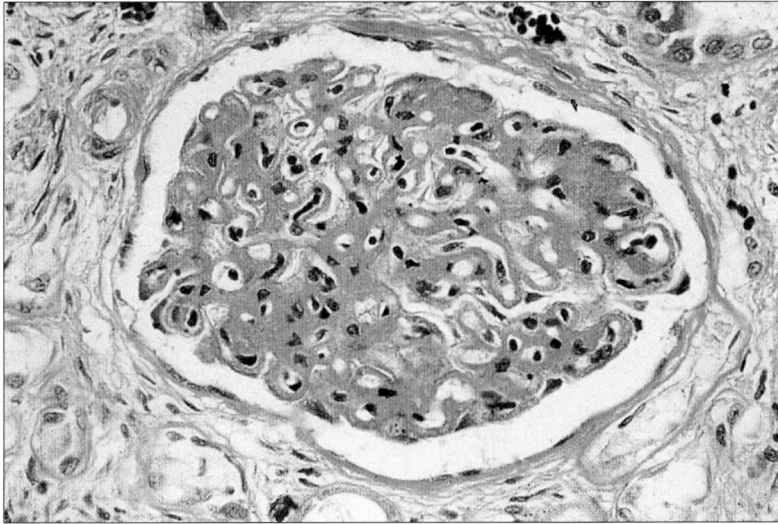

Fig. 16.75
Lupus membranous glomerulonephritis: note the uniform thickening of all glomerular capillary walls (Masson's trichrome).

Lymph nodes often show reactive hyperplasia; occasionally there are striking pathological features, which may be confused with a lymphomatous infiltrate. These changes consist of a necrotizing lymphadenitis with prominent hematoxylin bodies. Surviving follicles show reactive hyperplasia and conspicuous plasma cells and immunoblasts. The thymus may show prominent germinal center formation, with an increase in the size and number of Hassall's corpuscles. Perisplenitis ('sugar icing') of the splenic capsule is common and a characteristic histological finding is concentric fibrosis ('onion skinning') of the adventitia of the central (penicillary) arteries of the malpighian corpuscles.

Joint manifestations include fibrinoid degeneration within the synovium, rheumatoid features and arteritis.

A variety of lesions may be seen in the liver, including fatty change, focal hepatocyte necroses and evidence of vasculitis.

Central nervous system manifestations have an ischemic pathogenesis, most probably on an immune complex-mediated vasculitic basis. There is some evidence to incriminate an antineuronal autoantibody.

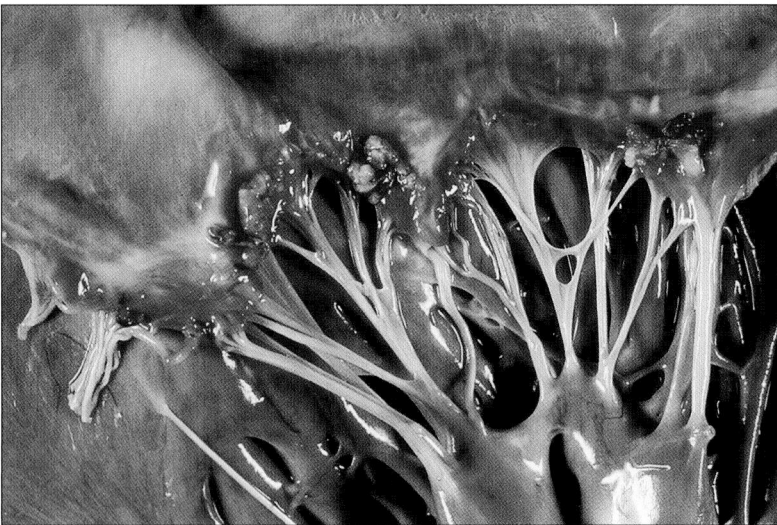

Fig. 16.76
Libman–Sacks endocarditis: note the small yellow, glistening vegetations on the cusps of the mitral valve. By courtesy of C. Fletcher, MD, Brigham and Women's Hospital and Harvard Medical School, Boston, USA.

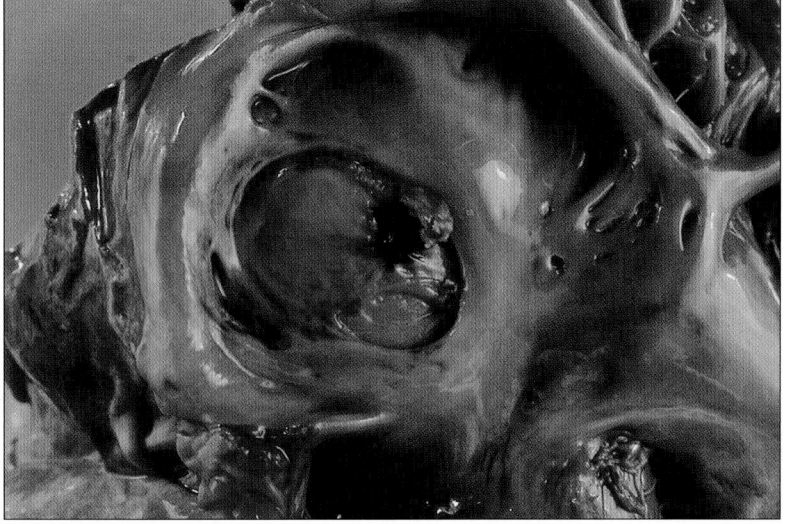

Fig. 16.77
Libman–Sacks endocarditis: note the small vegetation on the edge of the foramen ovale. By courtesy of D.R. Davies, MD, Radcliffe Infirmary NHS Trust, Oxford, UK.

The cardiac pathology of neonatal lupus erythematosus comprises fibrosis and calcification of the atrioventricular node and to a lesser extent the sinoatrial node.[281] Focal lymphocytic myocarditis and endocardial fibroelastosis may also be evident.[185]

Neonatal lupus erythematosus

The histological features and immunofluorescence pattern of the cutaneous lesions in neonatal disease are similar to those seen in SCLE.[111,282] The most frequently documented findings include hydropic degeneration of basal keratinocytes, dermal edema and a superficial lymphohistiocytic chronic inflammatory cell infiltrate.[255]

Differential diagnosis

Lupus erythematosus must be distinguished from other dermatoses that manifest basal cell liquefactive degeneration, particularly lichen planus and poikiloderma. Lupus erythematosus lacks the wedge-shaped hypergranulosis and sawtooth acanthosis of lichen planus. The inflammatory cell infiltrate is typically periappendageal, rather than adopting a band-like distribution. Occasionally hypertrophic lupus erythematosus shows considerable overlap with lichen planus; in such instances a positive lupus band test resolves the problem.

Poikiloderma, whether congenital or associated with dermatomyositis (and rarely SLE) or as a manifestation of mycosis fungoides, is characterized by epidermal atrophy and marked basal cell liquefactive degeneration associated with pigmentary incontinence. A patchy lymphohistiocytic infiltrate is evident in the upper dermis. Papillary dermal edema and telangiectases are typically present. Although there is obviously histological overlap, the very different clinical manifestations should obviate any diagnostic difficulties. The presence of atypical lymphocytes will clearly distinguish the variant associated with mycosis fungoides.

The histological features of lupus erythematosus are sometimes difficult to distinguish from polymorphic light eruption, particularly when the latter is associated with a positive band test (see above). Polymorphic light eruption, which is the most common photodermatosis, usually presents in young people, particularly females, as recurrent, erythematous papules, vesicles and/or plaques following exposure to ultraviolet light (*Figs 16.78, 16.79*).[283] Lesions, which develop after a latent period of hours to days, commonly subside completely within days and heal without sequelae.[275] Histologically, superficial dermal edema and a mild to moderate superficial and deep perivascular lymphohistiocytic infiltrate are often seen.[283] In early lesions helper–inducer T-lymphocytes predominate and increased numbers of dermal Langerhans' cells are present.[284] With chronicity cytotoxic–suppressor T-cells become more conspicuous. Basal cell hydropic degeneration is usually absent and epidermal atrophy is not a feature.

References

1. Gilliam, J.N., Sontheimer, R.D. (1981) Distinctive cutaneous subsets in the spectrum of lupus erythematosus. *J Am Acad Dermatol*, **4**, 471–475.
2. Provost, T. (1979) The relationship between discoid lupus erythematosus and systemic lupus erythematosus. A hypothesis. *Am J Dermatopathol*, **1**, 181–184.
3. Prystowsky, S.D., Gilliam, J.N. (1975) Discoid lupus erythematosus as part of a larger disease spectrum. Correlation of clinical features with laboratory findings in lupus erythematosus. *Arch Dermatol*, **111**, 1448–1452.
4. Wechsler, H.L. (1983) Lupus erythematosus. A clinician's coign of vantage. *Arch Dermatol*, **119**, 887–892.
5. Moschella, S.L. (1989) Dermatologic overview of lupus erythematosus and its subsets. *J Dermatol*, **16**, 417–428.
6. Rowell, N.R. (1984) The natural history of lupus erythematosus. *Clin Exp Dermatol*, **9**, 217–231.
7. Buoncopagni, A., Barbano, G.C., Pistoia, V. et al (1991) Childhood systemic lupus erythematosus: a review of 30 cases. *Clin Exp Rheumatol*, **9**, 425–430.
8. Rowell, N.R. (1971) Laboratory abnormalities in the diagnosis and management of lupus erythematosus. *Br J Dermatol*, **84**, 210–216.
9. Millard, L.E., Rowell, N.R. (1979) Abnormal laboratory test results and their relationship to prognosis in discoid lupus erythematosus. A long-term follow-up study of 92 patients. *Arch Dermatol*, **115**, 1055–1058.
10. Callen, J.P., Fowler, J.F., Kulick, K.B. (1985) Serologic and clinical features of patients with discoid lupus erythematosus: relationship of antibodies to single-stranded deoxyribonucleic acid and of other antinuclear antibody subsets to clinical manifestations. *J Am Acad Dermatol*, **13**, 748–755.

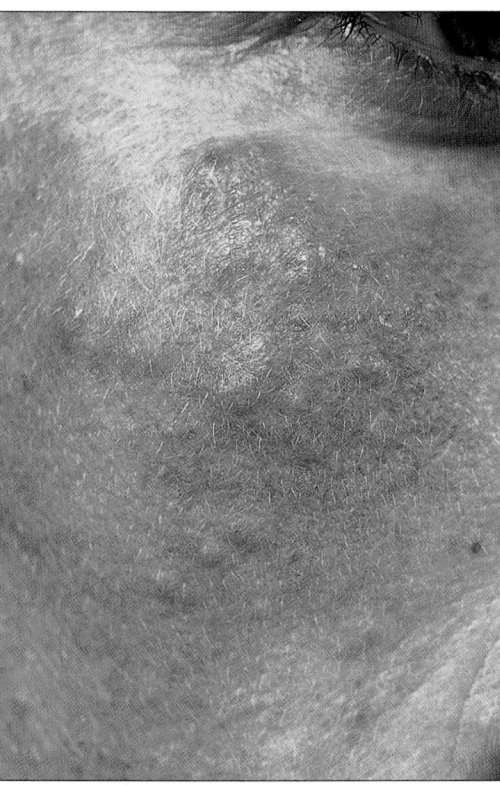

Fig. 16.78
Polymorphic light eruption: patients present with erythematous papules and vesicles on sun-exposed skin. By courtesy of the Institute of Dermatology, London, UK.

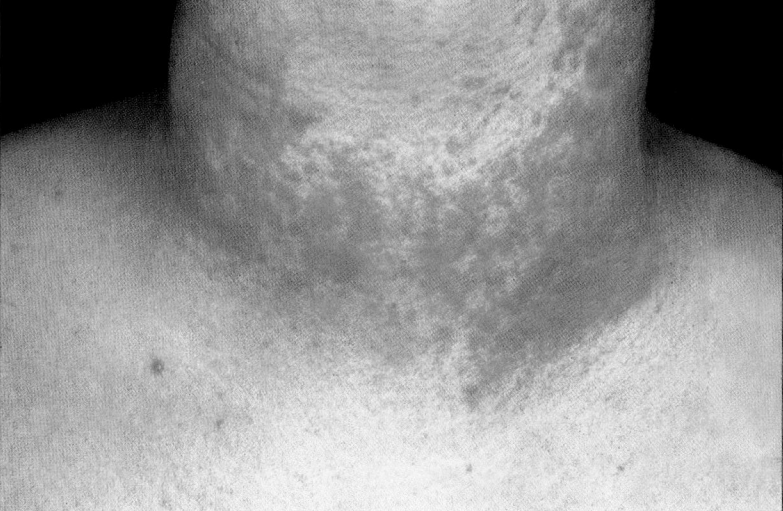

Fig. 16.79
Polymorphic light eruption: the eruption is typically symmetrical and is usually pruritic. By courtesy of the Institute of Dermatology, London, UK.

11. Provost, T.T. (1994) The relationship between discoid and systemic lupus erythematosus. *Arch Dermatol*, **130**, 1308–1310.
12. Hymes, S.R., Jordon, R.E. (1989) Chronic cutaneous lupus erythematosus. *Med Clin North Am*, **73**, 1055–1071.
13. van Giesel, D., de Waard-van der Spek, F.B., Orange, A.P. (2002) Childhood discoid lupus erythematosus: report of five new cases and review of the literature. *J Eur Acad Dermatol Venereol*, **16**, 143–147.
14. George, P.M., Tunnessen, W.W. Jr (1993) Childhood discoid lupus erythematosus. *Arch Dermatol*, **129**, 613–617.
15. McMullen, E.A., Armstrong, K.D.B., Bingham, E.A. et al (1998) Childhood discoid lupus erythematosus: a report of two cases. *Pediatr Dermatol*, **15**, 439–442.
16. Magaña, M., Vázquez, R. (2000) Discoid lupus erythematosus in childhood. *Pediatr Dermatol*, **17**, 241–242.
17. Tuffanelli, D.L. (1981) Lupus erythematosus. *J Am Acad Dermatol*, **4**, 127–142.
18. Wilson, C.L., Burge, S.M., Dean, D., Dawber, R.P.R. (1992) Scarring alopecia in discoid lupus erythematosus. *Br J Dermatol*, **126**, 307–314.
19. De Berker, D., Dissaneyeka, M., Burge, S. (1992) The sequelae of chronic cutaneous lupus erythematosus. *Lupus*, **1**, 181–186.
20. Burge, S.M., Frith, P.A., Juniper, R.P. et al (1989) Mucosal involvement in systemic and chronic cutaneous lupus erythematosus. *Br J Dermatol*, **121**, 727–741.
21. Roundtree, J., Weigand, D., Burgdorf, W. (1982) Lupus erythematosus with oral and perianal mucous membrane involvement. *Arch Dermatol*, **118**, 55–56.
22. Coulson, I.H., Marsden, R.A. (1986) Lupus erythematosus cheilitis. *Clin Exp Dermatol*, **11**, 309–313.
23. Shklar, G., McCarthy, P.L. (1978) Histopathology of oral lesions of discoid lupus erythematosus. A review of 25 cases. *Arch Dermatol*, **114**, 1031–1035.
24. Bicer, A., Tursen, U., Ozer, C. et al (2002) Coexistence of osteopoikilosis and discoid lupus erythematosus: a case report. *Clin Rheumatol*, **21**, 405–407.
25. Pérez Suárez, M., Justo Murades, I., De Teresa Romero, G. et al (2002) Alpha 1-antitrypsin deficiency in a female with discoid lupus erythematosus. *J Eur Acad Dermatol Venereol*, **16**, 295–296.
26. Letellier, E., Lomghurst, H., Díaz-Cano, S.J. et al (2001) Polyarteritis nodosa developing after discoid lupus erythematosus. *Clin Exp Rheumatol*, **19**, 738–739.
27. Rubenstein, D.J., Huntley, A.C. (1986) Keratotic lupus erythematosus: treatment with isotretinoin. *J Am Acad Dermatol*, **14**, 910–914.
28. Santa-Cruz, D.J., Uitto, J., Elsen, A.Z. et al (1983) Verrucous lupus erythematosus: ultrastructural studies on a distinct variant of chronic discoid lupus erythematosus. *Br J Dermatol*, **98**, 507–520.
29. Otani, A. (1977) Lupus erythematosus hypertrophicus et profundus. *Br J Dermatol*, **96**, 75–78.
30. O'Louglin, S., Schroeter, A.L., Jordon, R.E. (1978) A study of lupus erythematosus with particular reference to generalised discoid lupus. *Br J Dermatol*, **99**, 1–11.
31. Sulica, V.I., Kao, G.F. (1988) Squamous cell carcinoma of the scalp arising in lesions of discoid lupus erythematosus. *Am J Dermatopathol*, **10**, 137–141.
32. Sherman, R.N., Lee, C.W., Flynn, K.J. (1993) Cutaneous squamous cell carcinoma in black patients with chronic discoid lupus erythematosus. *Int J Dermatol*, **32**, 677–679.
33. Miyagawa, S., Minowa, R., Yamashina, Y. et al (1996) Development of squamous cell carcinoma in chronic lupus erythematosus: a report of two patients with anti-Ro/SSA antibodies. *Lupus*, **5**, 630–632.
34. Millard, L.G., Barker, D.J. (1978) Development of squamous cell carcinoma in chronic discoid lupus erythematosus. *Clin Exp Dermatol*, **3**, 161–166.
35. Millard, L.G., Rowell, N.R. (1978) Chilblain lupus erythematosus (Hutchinson). A clinical and laboratory study of 17 patients. *Br J Dermatol*, **98**, 497–506.
36. Doutre, M.S., Beylot, C., Beylot, J. et al (1992) Chillblain lupus erythematosus: report of 15 cases. *Dermatology*, **184**, 26–28.
37. Rowell, N.R., Beck, S.J., Anderson, J.R. (1963) Lupus erythematosus and erythema multiforme-like lesions. *Arch Dermatol*, **88**, 176–180.
38. Parodi, A., Drago, E.F., Varaldo, G. et al (1989) Rowell's syndrome. Report of a case. *J Am Acad Dermatol*, **21**, 374–377.
39. Fiallo, P., Tagliapietra, A-G., Santoro, G. et al (1995) Rowell's syndrome. *Int J Dermatol*, **34**, 635–636.
40. Fitzgerald, E.A., Purcell, S.M., Kantor, G.R. (1996) Rowell's syndrome: report of a case. *J Am Acad Dermatol*, **35**, 801–803.
41. Zeitouni, N.C., Funaro, D., Cloutier, R.A. et al (2000) Redefining Rowell's syndrome. *Br J Dermatol*, **142**, 343–346.
42. Shteyngarts, A.R., Warner, M.R., Camisa, C. (1999) Lupus erythematosus associated with erythema multiforme: does Rowell's syndrome exist? *J Am Acad Dermatol*, **40**, 773–777.
43. Child, F.J., Kapur, N., Creamer, D. et al (1999) Rowell's syndrome. *Clin Exp Dermatol*, **24**, 74–77.
44. Roustan, G., Salas, C., Barbadillo, C. et al (2000) Lupus erythematosus with an erythema multiforme-like eruption. *Eur J Dermatol*, **10**, 459–462.
45. Marzano, A.V., Berti, E., Gasparini, G. et al (1999) Lupus erythematosus with antiphospholipid syndrome and erythema multiforme-like lesions. *Br J Dermatol*, **141**, 720–724.
46. Nelson, C.E., Dahl, M.V., Goltz, R.W. (1977) Arcuate dermal erythema in a carrier of chronic granulomatous disease. *Arch Dermatol*, **113**, 798–800.
47. Brandrup, F., Koch, C., Petri, M. et al (1981) Discoid lupus erythematosus-like lesions and stomatitis in female carriers of X-linked chronic granulomatous disease. *Br J Dermatol*, **104**, 495–505.
48. Ortiz-Romero, P.L., Corell-Almuzara, A., López-Estebaranz, J.L. et al (1997) Lupus like lesions in a patient with X-linked chronic granulomatous disease and recombinant X chromosome. *Dermatology*, **195**, 280–283.
49. Stalder, J.F., Dreno, B., Bureau, B. et al (1986) Discoid lupus erythematosus-like lesions in an autosomal form of chronic granulomatous disease. *Br J Dermatol*, **114**, 251–254.
50. Córdoba-Guijarro, S., Feal, C., Dauden, E. et al (2000) Lupus erythematosus-like lesions in a carrier of X-linked chronic granulomatous disease. *J Eur Acad Dermatol Venereol*, **14**, 409–411.
51. Rupec, R.A., Petropoulou, T., Belohradsky, B.H. et al (2000) Lupus erythematosus tumidus and chronic discoid lupus erythematosus in carriers of X-linked chronic granulomatous disease. *Eur J Dermatol*, **10**, 184–189.
52. Wolpert, K.A., Webster, A.D., Whittaker, S.J. (1998) Discoid lupus erythematosus associated with a primary immunodeficiency syndrome showing features of non X-linked hyper-IgM syndrome. *Br J Dermatol*, **138**, 1053–1057.
53. Sontheimer, R.D., Thomas, J.R., Gilliam, J.N. (1979) Subacute cutaneous lupus erythematosus. A cutaneous marker for a distinct lupus erythematosus subset. *Arch Dermatol*, **115**, 1409–1415.
54. Sontheimer, R.D. (1989) Subacute cutaneous lupus erythematosus: a decade's perspective. *Med Clin North Am*, **73**, 1073–1090.
55. Parodi, A., Caproni, M., Cardinali, C. et al (2000) Clinical, histological and immunopathological features of 58 patients with subacute cutaneous lupus erythematosus. A review by the Italian group of immuno-dermatology. *Dermatology*, **200**, 6–10.
56. Callen, J.P., Klein, J. (1988) Subacute cutaneous lupus erythematosus. Clinical, serologic, immunogenetic and therapeutic considerations in seventy-two patients. *Arthritis Rheum*, **31**, 1007–1013.
57. Herrero, C., Bielsa, I., Font, J. et al (1988) Subacute cutaneous lupus erythematosus: clinicopathologic findings in thirteen cases. *J Am Acad Dermatol*, **19**, 1057–1062.
58. Amato, L., Coronella, G., Berti, S. et al (2003) Subacute cutaneous lupus erythematosus in childhood. *Pediatr Dermatol*, **20**, 31–34.
59. Ciconte, A., Mills, A.E., Shipley, A. et al (2002) Subacute cutaneous lupus erythematosus presenting in a child. *Australas J Dermatol*, **43**, 62–64.
60. Tsutsui, K., Imai, T., Hatta, N. et al (1996) Widespread pruritic plaques in a patient with subacute cutaneous lupus erythematosus and hypocomplementemia: response to dapsone therapy. *J Am Acad Dermatol*, **35**, 313–315.
61. David-Bajar, K.M., Bennion, S.D., De Spain, J.D. et al (1992) Clinical, histologic and immunofluorescence distinctions between subacute cutaneous lupus erythematosus and discoid lupus erythematosus. *J Invest Dermatol*, **99**, 251–257.
62. Watson, R. (1989) Cutaneous lesions in systemic lupus erythematosus. *Med Clin North Am*, **73**, 1091–1111.
63. Pramatarov, K., Vassileva, S., Miteva, L. (2000) Subacute cutaneous lupus erythematosus presenting with generalized poikiloderma. *J Am Acad Dermatol*, **42**, 286–288.
64. Sontheimer, R.D. (1985) Clinical significance of subacute cutaneous lupus erythematosus skin lesions. *J Dermatol*, **12**, 205–212.
65. Marzano, A.V., Kolesnikova, L.V., Gasparini, G. et al (1999) Dystrophic calcinosis cutis in subacute lupus. *Dermatology*, **198**, 90–92.
66. Sánchez-Pérez, J., Peñas, P.F., Ríos-Buceta, L. et al (1996) Leukocytoclastic vasculitis in subacute cutaneous lupus erythematosus: clinicopathologic study of three cases and review of the literature. *Dermatology*, **193**, 230–235.
67. Sontheimer, R.D., Stastny, P., Gilliam, J.N. (1981) Human histocompatibility antigen associations in subacute cutaneous lupus erythematosus. *J Clin Invest*, **67**, 312–316.
68. Callen, J.P., Hodge, S.J., Kulick, K.B. et al (1987) Subacute cutaneous lupus erythematosus in multiple members of a family with C2 deficiency. *Arch Dermatol*, **123**, 66–70.
69. Sontheimer, R.D., Maddison, P.J., Reichlin, M. et al (1982) Serologic and HLA associations in subacute cutaneous lupus erythematosus, a clinical subset of lupus erythematosus. *Ann Intern Med*, **97**, 664–671.
70. Buckley, D., Barnes, L. (1995) Childhood subacute cutaneous lupus erythematosus associated with homozygous complement 2 deficiency. *Pediatr Dermatol*, **12**, 327–330.
71. Johansson-Stephansson, E., Koskimies, S., Partanen, J. et al (1989) Subacute cutaneous lupus erythematosus. Genetic markers and clinical and immunological findings in patients. *Arch Dermatol*, **125**, 791–796.
72. Cohen, M.R., Crosby, D. (1994) Systemic disease in subacute cutaneous lupus erythematosus: a controlled comparison with systemic lupus erythematosus. *J Rheumatol*, **21**, 1665–1669.
73. Watanabe, T., Tsuchida, T. (1995) Classification of lupus erythematosus based upon cutaneous manifestations. Dermatological, systemic and laboratory findings in 191 patients. *Dermatology*, **190**, 277–283.
74. Black, D.R., Hornung, C.A., Schneider, P.D. et al (2002) Frequency and severity of systemic disease in patients with subacute cutaneous lupus erythematosus. *Arch Dermatol*, **138**, 1175–1178.

75. Cohen, S., Stastny, P., Sontheimer, R.D. (1986) Concurrence of subacute cutaneous lupus erythematosus and rheumatoid arthritis. *Arthritis Rheum*, **29**, 421–425.

76. Pantoja, L., González-López, M.A., Bouso, M. et al (2002) Subacute cutaneous lupus erythematosus in a patient with rheumatoid arthritis. *Scand J Rheumatol*, **31**, 377–379.

77. Provost, T.T., Talal, N., Harley, J.B. et al (1988) The relationship between anti-Ro (SS-A) antibody positive Sjögren's syndrome and anti-Ro (SS-A) antibody-positive lupus erythematosus. *Arch Dermatol*, **124**, 63–71.

78. Balanova, M.B., Botev, I.N., Michailova, J.I. (1997) Subacute cutaneous lupus erythematosus induced by radiation therapy. *Br J Dermatol*, **137**, 648–649.

79. Ho, C., Shumack, S.P., Morris, D. (2001) Subacute cutaneous lupus erythematosus associated with hepatocellular carcinoma. *Australas J Dermatol*, **42**, 110–113.

80. Brenner, S., Golan, H., Gat, A. et al (1997) Paraneoplastic subacute cutaneous lupus erythematosus: report of a case associated with cancer of the lung. *Dermatology*, **194**, 172–174.

81. Dawn, G., Wainwright, N.J. (2002) Association between subacute cutaneous lupus erythematosus and epidermoid carcinoma of the lung: a paraneoplastic phenomenon? *Clin Exp Dermatol*, **27**, 717–718.

82. Wenzel, J., Uerlich, M., Gerdsen, R. et al (2001) Association of inclusion body myositis with subacute cutaneous lupus erythematosus. *Rheumatol Int*, **21**, 75–77.

83. Grabbe, S., Kolde, G. (1995) Coexisting lichen planus and subacute cutaneous lupus erythematosus. *Clin Exp Dermatol*, **20**, 249–254.

84. Reed, B.R., Huff, J.C., Jones, S.K. et al (1985) Subacute cutaneous lupus erythematosus associated with hydrochlorothiazide therapy. *Ann Intern Med*, **103**, 49–51.

85. Darken, M., McBurney, E.I. (1988) Subacute cutaneous lupus erythematosus-like drug eruption due to combination diuretic hydrochlorothiazide and triamterene. *J Am Acad Dermatol*, **18**, 38–42.

86. Parodi, A., Romagnoli, M., Rebora, A. (1989) Subacute cutaneous lupus erythematosus-like eruption caused by hydrochlorothiazide. *Photodermatology*, **6**, 100–102.

87. Miyagama, S., Okuchi, T., Shiomi, Y. et al (1989) Subacute cutaneous lupus erythematosus lesions precipitated by griseofulvin. *J Am Acad Dermatol*, **21**, 343–346.

88. Crowson, A.N., Magro, C.M. (1999) Lichenoid and subacute cutaneous lupus erythematosus-like dermatitis associated with antihistamine therapy. *J Cutan Pathol*, **26**, 95–100.

89. Crowson, A.N., Magro, C.M. (1997) Subacute cutaneous lupus erythematosus arising in the setting of calcium channel blocker therapy. *Hum Pathol*, **28**, 67–73.

90. Brooke, R., Coulson, I.H., Al-Dawoud, A. (1998) Terbinafine-induced subacute cutaneous lupus erythematosus. *Br J Dermatol*, **139**, 1132–1133.

91. Callen, J.P., Hughes, A.P., Kulp-Shorten, C. (2001) Subacute cutaneous lupus erythematosus induced or exacerbated by terbinafine: a report of 5 cases. *Arch Dermatol*, **137**, 1196–1198.

92. Gubinelli, E., Cocuroccia, B., Girolomoni, G. (2003) Subacute cutaneous lupus erythematosus induced by nifedipine. *J Cutan Med Surg*, 2003.

93. Callen, J.P. (2003) How frequently are drugs associated with the development or exacerbation of subacute cutaneous lupus? *Arch Dermatol*, **139**, 89–90.

94. Srivastava, M., Rencic, A., Diglio, G. et al (2003) Drug-induced Ro/SSA-positive cutaneous lupus erythematosus. *Arch Dermatol*, **139**, 45–49.

95. Ross, S., Ormerod, A.D., Roberts, C. et al (2002) Subacute cutaneous lupus erythematosus associated with phenytoin. *Clin Exp Dermatol*, **27**, 474–476.

96. Hochberg, M.C., Boyd, R.E., Ahearn, J.M. et al (1985) Systemic lupus erythematosus: a review of clinicolaboratory features and immunogenetic markers in 150 patients with emphasis on demographic subsets. *Medicine (Baltimore)*, **64**, 285–295.

97. Dubois, E.L., Tuffanelli, D.L. (1964) Clinical manifestations of systemic lupus erythematosus. Computer analysis of 520 cases. *JAMA*, **189**, 104–119.

98. Estes, D., Christian, C.L. (1971) The natural history of systemic lupus erythematosus by prospective analysis. *Medicine (Baltimore)*, **10**, 85–95.

99. Tan, E.M., Cohen, A.S., Fries, J.F. et al (1982) The 1982 revised criteria for the classification of systemic lupus erythematosus. *Arthritis Rheum*, **25**, 1271–1277.

100. Gilliam, J.N., Sontheimer, R.D. (1981) Skin manifestations of SLE. *Clin Rheum Dis*, **8**, 207–218.

101. López-Longo, F.J., Monteagudo, I., González, C.M. et al (1997) Systemic lupus erythematosus: clinical expression and anti-Ro/SS – a response in patients with and without lesions of subacute lupus erythematosus. *Lupus*, **6**, 32–39.

102. Hughes, G.R.V., Harris, E.N., Ghavavi, A.E. (1986) The anti-cardiolipin syndrome. *J Rheumatol*, **13**, 486–489.

103. Jonsson, R., Heyden, G., Westberg, N.G. et al (1984) Oral mucosal lesions in systemic lupus erythematosus: a clinical, histopathological and immunopathological study. *J Rheumatol*, **11**, 38–42.

104. Yell, J.A., Mbuagbaw, J., Burge, S.M. (1996) Cutaneous manifestations of systemic lupus erythematosus. *Br J Dermatol*, **135**, 355–362.

105. Wollina, U., Barta, U., Uhlemann, C. et al (1999) Lupus erythematosus-associated red lunula. *J Am Acad Dermatol*, **41**, 419–421.

106. Garcia-Patos, V., Bartralot, R., Ordi, J. et al (1997) Systemic lupus erythematosus presenting with red lunulae. *J Am Acad Dermatol*, **36**, 834–836.

107. Urman, J.D., Lowenstein, M.B., Abeles, M. (1978) Oral mucosal ulceration in systemic lupus erythematosus. *Arthritis Rheum*, **21**, 58–61.

108. Fowler, J.F Jr, Callen, J.P. (1984) Cutaneous mucinosis associated with lupus erythematosus. *J Rheumatol*, **11**, 380–383.

109. Quismorio, F.P., Dubois, E.L., Chandor, S.B. (1975) Soft tissue calcification in systemic lupus erythematosus. *Arch Dermatol*, **111**, 352–356.

110. Cram, D.L., Epstein, J.H., Tuffanelli, D.L. (1973) Lupus erythematosus and porphyria. Coexistence in seven patients. *Arch Dermatol*, **108**, 779–784.

111. Tuffanelli, D.L. (1972) Lupus erythematosus. *Arch Dermatol*, **106**, 553–566.

112. Chartash, E.K., Lans, D.M., Paget, S.A. et al (1989) Aortic insufficiency and mitral regurgitation in patients with systemic lupus erythematosus and the antiphospholipid syndrome. *Am J Med*, **86**, 407–412.

113. Asherson, R.A., Lubbe, W.F. (1988) Cerebral and valve lesions in SLE: association with anti-phospholipid antibodies. *J Rheumatol*, **15**, 539–543.

114. Provost, T.T., Arnett, F.C., Reichlin, M. (1983) Homozygous C2 deficiency lupus erythematosus and anti-Ro (SSA) antibodies. *Arthritis Rheum*, **26**, 1279–1282.

115. Taieb, A., Hehunstre, J-P., Goetz, J. et al (1986) Lupus erythematosus panniculitis with partial genetic deficiency of C2 and C4 in a child. *Arch Dermatol*, **122**, 576–582.

116. Siddiqui, M.A., Khan, I.A. (2002) Isoniazid-induced lupus erythematosus presenting with cardiac tamponade. *Am J Ther*, **9**, 163–165.

117. Peterson, L.L. (1984) Hydralazine-induced systemic lupus erythematosus presenting as pyoderma gangrenosum-like ulcers. *J Am Acad Dermatol*, **10**, 379–384.

118. Ullman, S., Wiik, A., Kobayasi, T. et al (1974) Drug-induced lupus erythematosus syndrome. *Acta Derm Venereol*, **54**, 387–390.

119. Berning, S.E., Iseman, M.D. (1997) Rifamycin-induced lupus syndrome. *Lancet*, **349**, 1521–1522.

120. Patel, G.K., Anstey, A.V. (2001) Rifampicin-induced lupus erythematosus. *Clin Exp Dermatol*, **26**, 260–262.

121. Lavie, C.J., Biundo, J., Quinet, R.J. et al (1985) Systemic lupus erythematosus (SLE) induced by quinidine. *Arch Intern Med*, **145**, 446–448.

122. Cohen, M.G., Kevat, S., Prowse, M.V. et al (1988) Two distinct quinidine-induced rheumatic syndromes. *Ann Intern Med*, **108**, 369–371.

123. Thorvaldsen, J. (1981) Penicillamine-induced lupus-like reaction in rheumatoid arthritis and vasculitis. *Dermatologica*, **162**, 277–280.

124. Holmes, S., Kemmett, D. (1998) Exacerbation of systemic lupus erythematosus by terbinafine. *Br J Dermatol*, **139**, 1133.

125. Murphy, M., Barnes, L. (1998) Terbinafine-induced lupus erythematosus. *Br J Dermatol*, **138**, 708–709.

126. Reiffers-Mettelock, J., Hentges, F., Humbel, R-L. (1997) Syndrome resembling systemic lupus erythematosus induced by carbamazepine. *Dermatology*, **195**, 306–307.

127. Bonnet, F., Morlat, P., De Witte, S. et al (2003) Lupus-like syndrome and vasculitis induced by valpromide. *J Rheumatol*, **30**, 208–209.

128. Kundu, A.K. (2003) Amiodarone-induced systemic lupus erythematosus. *J Assoc Physicians India*, **51**, 216–217.

129. McGuiness, M., Frye, R.A., Deng, J-S. (1997) Atenolol-induced lupus erythematosus. *J Am Acad Dermatol*, **37**, 298–299.

130. Gouet, D., Marechaud, R., Aucouturier, P. et al (1986) Atenolol induced systemic lupus erythematosus syndrome. *J Rheumatol*, **13**, 446–447.

131. Adams, J.D. (1978) Drug induced lupus erythematosus – a case report. *Australas J Dermatol*, **19**, 31–32.

132. Kawachi, Y., Nukaga, H., Hoshino, M. et al (1995) ANCA-associated vasculitis and lupus-like syndrome caused by methimazole. *Clin Exp Dermatol*, **20**, 345–347.

133. Ghate, J.V., Turner, M.L., Rudek, M.A. et al (2001) Drug-induced lupus associated with COL-3. Report of 3 cases. *Arch Dermatol*, **137**, 471–474.

134. Goodrich, A.L., Kohn, S.R. (1993) Hydrochlorothiazide-induced lupus erythematosus: a new variant. *J Am Acad Dermatol*, **28**, 1001–1002.

135. Rich, M.W., Eckman, J.M. (1995) Can hydrochlorothiazide cause lupus? *J Rheumatol*, **22**, 1001.

136. Gordon, P.M., White, M.I., Herriot, R. et al (1995) Minocycline-associated lupus erythematosus. *Br J Dermatol*, **132**, 120–121.

137. Crosson, J., Stillman, M.T. (1997) Minocycline-related lupus erythematosus with associated liver disease. *J Am Acad Dermatol*, **36**, 867–868.

138. Schlienger, R.G., Bircher, A.J., Meier, C.R. (2000) Minocycline-induced lupus. A systematic review. *Dermatology*, **200**, 223–231.

139. Tubach, F., Kaplan, G., Berenbaum, F. (1999) Highly positive dsDNA antibodies in minocycline-induced lupus. *Clin Exp Rheumatol*, **17**, 124–125.

140. Porter, D., Harrison, A. (2003) Minocycline-induced lupus: a case series. *N Z Med J*, **116**, U384.

141. Udin, M.S., Lynfield, Y.L., Grosberg, S.J. et al (1979) Cutaneous reaction to spironolactone resembling lupus erythematosus. *Cutis*, **24**, 198–200.

142. Pramatarov, K.D. (1998) Drug-induced lupus erythematosus. *Clin Dermatol*, **16**, 367–377.

143. Farid, N., Anderson, J. (1971) SLE-like reaction to phenylbutazone therapy. *Lancet*, **1**, 1022–1023.

144. Kay, D.R., Bole, G.G., Ledger, W.J. (1969) The use of oral contraceptives and the occurrence of antinuclear antibodies and LE cells in women with early rheumatic disease. *Arthritis Rheum*, **12**, 306.

145. Alexander, S. (1962) Lupus erythematosus in two patients after griseofulvin treatment of *Trichophyton rubrum* infection. *Br J Dermatol*, **74**, 72–74.

146. Sieber, C., Grimm, E., Follath, F. (1990) Captopril and systemic lupus erythematosus. *BMJ*, **310**, 669.

147. Layton, A.M., Cotterill, J.A., Tomlisson, L.W. (1994) Hydroxyurea-induced lupus erythematosus. *Br J Dermatol*, **130**, 687–688.

148. Caramashi, P., Biasi, D., Carletto, A. et al (1995) Clobazam-induced lupus erythematosus. *Clin Rheumatol*, **14**, 116.

149. Wickert, W.A., Campbell, N.R., Martin, L. (1994) Acute severe adverse clozapine reaction resembling systemic lupus erythematosus. *Postgrad Med*, **70**, 940–941.

150. Mysler, E., Paget, S.A., Kimberly, R. (1994) Ciprofloxacin reactions mimicking lupus flares. *Arthritis Rheum*, **37**, 1112–1113.

151. Sandler, B., Aronson, P. (1993) Yohimbine-induced cutaneous drug eruption, progressive renal failure, and lupus-like syndrome. *Urology*, **41**, 343–345.

152. Favalli, E.G., Sinigaglia, L., Varenna, M. et al (2002) Drug-induced lupus following treatment with infliximab in rheumatoid arthritis. *Lupus*, **11**, 753–755.

153. Debandt, M., Vittecoq, O., Descamps, V. et al (2003) Anti-TNF-alpha-induced systemic lupus syndrome. *Clin Rheumatol*, **22**, 56–61.

154. Lepore, L., Marchetti, F., Facchini, S. et al (2003) Drug-induced systemic lupus erythematosus associated with etanercept therapy in a child with juvenile idiopathic arthritis. *Clin Exp Rheumatol*, **21**, 276–277.

155. Boralevi, F., Leaute-Labreze, C., Roul, S. et al (2003) Lupus-erythematosus-like eruption induced by *Trichophyton mentagrophytes* infection. *Dermatology*, **206**, 303–306.

156. Mamoux, V., Dumont, C. (1994) Lupus erythematoue et vaccination contre hepatite B. *Arch Pediatr*, **3**, 307.

157. Beer, K.R., Lorincz, A.L., Medenica, M.M et al (1994) Insecticide-induced lupus erythematosus. *Int J Dermatol*, **33**, 860–862.

158. Curtis, C.F. (1996) Insecticide-induced lupus erythematosus. *Int J Dermatol*, **35**, 74–75.

159. Pope, J.E. (2002) Scleroderma overlap syndromes. *Curr Opin Rheumatol*, **14**, 704–710.

160. Mok, C.C., Cheung, J.C., Yee, Y.K. et al (2001) Unusual overlap of systemic lupus erythematosus and diffuse scleroderma. *Clin Exp Rheumatol*, **19**, 113–114.

161. Majeed, M., Al-Mayouf, S.M., Al-Sabban, E. et al (2000) Coexistent linear scleroderma and juvenile systemic lupus erythematosus. *Pediatr Dermatol*, **17**, 456–459.

162. Wu, K.H., Dai, Y.S., Tsai, M.J. et al (2000) Lichen sclerosus et atrophicus, bullous morphea and systemic lupus erythematosus: a case report. *J Microbiol Immunol Infect*, **33**, 53–56.

163. Gallardo, F., Vadillo, M., Mitjavila, F. et al (1998) Systemic lupus erythematous after eosinophilic fasciitis: a case report. *J Am Acad Dermatol*, **39**, 283–285.

164. Baffoni, L., Frisoni, M., Maccaferri, M. et al (1995) Systemic lupus erythematosus and eosinophilic fasciitis: an unusual association. *Clin Rheumatol*, **14**, 591–592.

165. Marinovic, B., Basta-Juzbasic, A., Bukuic-Mokos, Z. et al (2003) Coexistence of pemphigus herpetiformis and systemic lupus erythematosus. *J Eur Acad Dermatol Venereol*, **17**, 316–319.

166. Hidalgo-Tenorio, C., Sabio-Sánchez, J.M., Tercador-Sánchez, J. et al (2001) Pemphigus vulgaris and systemic lupus erythematosus in a 46-year-old man. *Lupus*, **10**, 824–826.

167. Chan, H.L. (1999) Pemphigus vulgaris associated with systemic lupus erythematosus. *Int J Dermatol*, **38**, 48–49.

168. Mascaró, J.M. Jr, Ferrando, J., Sole, M.T. et al (1999) Paraneoplastic pemphigus: a case of long-term survival associated with systemic lupus erythematosus and polymyositis. *Dermatology*, **199**, 63–66.

169. Ng, P.P., Ng, S.K., Chng, H.H. (1998) Pemphigus foliaceous and oral lichen planus in a patient with systemic lupus erythematosus and thymoma. *Clin Exp Dermatol*, **23**, 181–184.

170. Habib, G.S., Stimmer, M.M., Quismorio, F.P. Jr (1995) Hypergammaglobulinemic purpura of Waldenstrom associated with systemic lupus erythematosus: report of a case and review of the literature. *Lupus*, **4**, 19–22.

171. Thomas, J.R. III, Su, W.P.D. (1983) Concurrence of lupus erythematosus and dermatitis herpetiformis. A report of nine cases. *Arch Dermatol*, **119**, 740–745.

172. Stevens, H.P., Ostlere, L.S., Rustin, M.H.A. (1994) Systemic lupus erythematosus in association with ulcerative colitis: related autoimmune diseases. *Br J Dermatol*, **130**, 385–389.

173. Werth, V.P., White, W.L., Sánchez, M.R. et al (1992) Incidence of alopecia areata in lupus erythematosus. *Arch Dermatol*, **128**, 368–371.

174. Van der Meer-Roosen, C.H., Maes, E.P.J., Faber, W.R. (1979) Cutaneous lupus erythematosus and autoimmune thyroiditis. *Br J Dermatol*, **101**, 91–92.

175. Cruz, P.D. Jr, Coldiron, B.M., Sontheimer, R.D. (1987) Concurrent features of cutaneous lupus erythematosus and pemphigus erythematosus following myasthenia and thymoma. *J Am Acad Dermatol*, **16**, 472–480.

176. Filiotov, A., Vaiopoulos, G., Capsimali, V. et al (2002) Acute intermittent porphyria and systemic lupus erythematosus: report of a case and review of the literature. *Lupus*, **11**, 190–192.

177. Gibson, G.E., McEvoy, M.T. (1998) Coexistence of lupus erythematosus and porphyria cutanea tarda in fifteen patients. *J Am Acad Dermatol*, **38**, 569–573.

178. Sinha, A., Dixon, N., O'Sullivan, M.M. et al (1999) Porphyria cutanea tarda in a patient with systemic lupus erythematosus. *Rheumatology (Oxford)*, **38**, 1166–1168.

179. Clemmensen, O., Thomsen, K. (1982) Porphyria cutanea tarda and systemic lupus erythematosus. *Arch Dermatol*, **118**, 160–162.

180. McMillen, M.A., Cunningham, M.E., Schoen, R. et al (1994) Gout in patients with systemic lupus erythematosus. *Br J Rheumatol*, **33**, 595–596.

181. Hays, S.B., Camisa, C., Luzar, M.J. (1984) The coexistence of systemic lupus erythematosus and psoriasis. *J Am Acad Dermatol*, **10**, 619–622.

182. Begum, S., Li, C., Wedderburn, L.R. et al (2002) Concurrence of sarcoidosis and systemic lupus erythematosus in three patients. *Clin Exp Rheumatol*, **20**, 549–552.

183. McBurney, E.I., Hickham, P.R., Garry, R.F. et al (1998) Lupus erythematosus-like features in patients with cutaneous T-cell lymphoma. *Int J Dermatol*, **37**, 579–585.

184. Lee, L.A. (1993) Neonatal lupus erythematosus. *J Invest Dermatol*, **100**, 9S–13S.

185. Lee, L.A., Weston, W.L. (1988) Neonatal lupus erythematosus. *Semin Dermatol*, **7**, 66–72.

186. Weston, W.L., Harmon, C., Peebles, C. et al (1982) A serological marker for neonatal lupus erythematosus. *Br J Dermatol*, **107**, 377–382.
187. Lee, L.A., Weston, W.L. (1997) Cutaneous lupus erythematosus during the neonatal and childhood periods. *Lupus*, **6**, 132–138.
188. Lee, L.A., Frank, M.B., McCubbin, V.R. et al (1994) Autoantibodies of neonatal lupus erythematosus. *J Invest Dermatol*, **102**, 963–966.
189. Provost, T.T., Watson, R., Gammon, W.R. et al (1987) The neonatal lupus syndrome with U_1RNP (nRNP) antibodies. *N Engl J Med*, **316**, 1135–1138.
190. Sheth, A.P., Esterly, N.B., Ratoosh, S.I. et al (1995) U_1RNP positive neonatal lupus erythematosus: association with anti-la antibodies? *Br J Dermatol*, **132**, 520–526.
191. Dugan, E.M., Tunnessen, W.W., Honig, P.J. et al (1992) U1RNP antibody-positive neonatal lupus. *Arch Dermatol*, **128**, 1490–1494.
192. Katayama, I., Kondo, S., Kawana, S. et al (1989) Neonatal lupus erythematosus with a high anticardiolipin antibody titer. *J Am Acad Dermatol*, **21**, 490–492.
193. Weston, W.L., Morelli, J.G., Lee, L.A. (1999) The clinical spectrum of anti-Ro-positive cutaneous neonatal lupus erythematosus. *J Am Acad Dermatol*, **40**, 675–681.
194. Nitta, Y. (1997) Lupus erythematosus profundus associated with neonatal lupus erythematosus. *Br J Dermatol*, **136**, 112–114.
195. Crowley, E., Frieden, I.J. (1998) Neonatal lupus erythematosus: an unusual congenital presentation with cutaneous atrophy, erosions, alopecia, and pancytopenia. *Pediatr Dermatol*, **15**, 38–42.
196. Neiman, A.R., Lee, L.A., Weston, W.L. et al (2000) Cutaneous manifestations of neonatal lupus without heart block: characteristics of mothers and children enrolled in a national registry. *J Pediatr*, **137**, 674–680.
197. Buyon, J.P., Hiebert, R., Copel, J. et al (1998) Autoimmune-associated congenital heart block: demographics, mortality, morbidity and recurrence rates obtained from a national neonatal lupus registry. *J Am Coll Cardiol*, **31**, 1658–1666.
198. Gawkrodger, D.J., Beveridge, G.W. (1984) Neonatal lupus erythematosus in four successive siblings born to a mother with discoid lupus erythematosus. *Br J Dermatol*, **111**, 683–687.
199. Selander, B., Cedergren, S., Domanski, H. (1998) A case of severe neonatal lupus erythematosus without cardiac or cutaneous involvement. *Acta Paediatr*, **87**, 105–107.
200. Shimosegawa, M., Akasaka, T., Matsuta, M. (1997) Neonatal lupus erythematosus occurring in identical twins. *J Dermatol*, **24**, 578–582.
201. Ruas, E., Moreno, A., Tellechea, O. et al (1996) Neonatal lupus erythematosus in an infant with Turner syndrome. *Pediatr Dermatol*, **13**, 298–302.
202. Borrego, L., Rodríguez, J., Soler, E. et al (1997) Neonatal lupus erythematosus related to maternal leukocytoclastic vasculitis. *Pediatr Dermatol*, **14**, 221–225.
203. Watson, R., Hamilton, R., Provost, T.T. (1986) Systemic lupus erythematosus. In: Thiers, B.H., Dobson, R.L. (eds) Pathogenesis of skin disease. Edinburgh: Churchill Livingstone, pp 219–232.
204. Hughes, G.R.V. (1984) Autoantibodies in lupus and its variants: experience in 1000 patients. *BMJ*, **289**, 339–342.
205. Dubois, E.L. (1969) Procainamide induction of a systemic lupus erythematosus-like syndrome. Presentation of six cases, review of the literature and analysis and follow-up of reported cases. *Medicine (Baltimore)*, **48**, 217–228.
206. Gorsulowsky, D.C., Bank, P.W., Goldberg, A.D. et al (1985) Antinuclear antibodies as indicators for the procainamide-induced systemic lupus erythematosus-like syndrome and its clinical presentations. *J Am Acad Dermatol*, **12**, 245–253.
207. Asherson, R.A., Mayou, S.C., Merry, P. et al (1989) The spectrum of livedo reticularis and anticardiolipin antibodies. *Br J Dermatol*, **120**, 215–221.
208. Grattan, C.E.H., Burton, J.L. (1991) Antiphospholipid syndrome and cutaneous vasoocclusive disorders. *Semin Dermatol*, **10**, 152–159.
209. Acland, K.M., Darvay, A., Wakelin, S.H. et al (1999) Livedoid vasculitis: a manifestation of the antiphospholipid syndrome? *Br J Dermatol*, **140**, 131–135.
210. Goldberg, D.P., Lewis, V.L. Jr, Koenig, W.J. (1995) Antiphospholipid antibody syndrome: a new cause of non-healing ulcers. *Plast Reconstr Surg*, **95**, 837–841.
211. Sharkey, M.P., Daryanani, I.I., Gillett, M.B. et al (2002) Localized cutaneous necrosis associated with the antiphospholipid syndrome. *Australas J Dermatol*, **43**, 218–220.
212. Fehr, T., Cathomas, G., Weber, C. et al (2001) Foetal loss, liver necrosis and acute lupus erythematosus in a patient with antiphospholipid antibody syndrome. *Lupus*, **10**, 576–579.
213. Gantcheva, M. (1998) Dermatologic aspects of antiphospholipid syndrome. *Int J Dermatol*, **37**, 173–180.
214. Lockshin, M.D. (1997) Antiphospholipid antibody. Babies, blood clots and biology. *JAMA*, **277**, 1549–1551.
215. Gibson, G.E., Su, W.P., Pittelkow, M.R. (1997) Antiphospholipid syndrome and the skin. *J Am Acad Dermatol*, **36**, 970–982.
216. Nahass, G.T. (1997) Antiphospholipid antibodies and the antiphospholipid antibody syndrome. *J Am Acad Dermatol*, **36**, 149–168.
217. Abernethy, M.L., McGuinn, J.L., Callen, J.P. (1995) Widespread cutaneous necrosis as the initial manifestation of the antiphospholipid antibody syndrome. *J Rheumatol*, **22**, 1380–1383.
218. Creamer, D., Hunt, B.J., Black, M.M. (2000) Widespread cutaneous necrosis occurring in association with the antiphospholipid syndrome: report of two cases. *Br J Dermatol*, **142**, 1199–1203.
219. Love, P.E., Santoro, S.A. (1990) Antiphospholipid antibodies. Anticardiolipin and the lupus anticoagulant in systemic lupus erythematosus (SLE) and in non-SLE disorders: prevalence and clinical significance. *Ann Intern Med*, **112**, 682–698.
220. Ishikawa, O., Takahashi, A., Tamura, A. et al (1999) Cutaneous papules and nodules in the diagnosis of the antiphospholipid syndrome. *Br J Dermatol*, **140**, 725–729.
221. Schlesinger, I.H., Farber, G.A. (1995) Cutaneous ulceration resembling pyoderma gangrenosum in the primary antiphospholipid syndrome: a report of two additional cases and review of the literature. *J La State Med Soc*, **147**, 357–361.
222. Stephansson, E.A., Niemi, K.M. (1995) Antiphospholipid antibodies and anetoderma: are they associated? *Dermatology*, **191**, 204–209.
223. Disdier, P., Christides, C., Andrac-Meyer, L. et al (1996) Anetoderma during antiphospholipid syndrome. *Ann Dermatol Venereol*, **123**, 800–803.
224. Romani, J., Pérez, F., Llobet, M. et al (2000) Anetoderma associated with antiphospholipid antibodies: case report and review of the literature. *J Eur Acad Dermatol Venereol*, **15**, 175–178.
225. Creamer, D., Black, M.M., Calonje, E. (2000) Reactive angioendotheliomatosis in association with the antiphospholipid syndrome. *J Am Acad Dermatol*, **42**, 903–906.
226. Thai, K.E., Barrett, W., Kossard, S. (2003) Reactive angioendotheliomatosis in the setting of the antiphospholipid syndrome. *Australas J Dermatol*, **44**, 151–155.
227. Alegre, V.A., Winkelmann, R.K., Gastineau, D.A. (1990) Cutaneous thrombosis, cerebrovascular thrombosis and lupus anticoagulant – the Sneddon syndrome. Report of 10 cases. *Int J Dermatol*, **29**, 45–49.
228. Daoud, M.S., Wilmoth, G.J., Su, W.P. et al (1995) Sneddon syndrome. *Semin Dermatol*, **14**, 166–172.
228. Frances, C., Papo, T., Wechsler, B. et al (1999) Sneddon syndrome with or without antiphospholipid antibodies. A comparative study in 46 patients. *Medicine (Baltimore)*, **78**, 209–219.
230. Baleva, M., Boyanovsky, B., Nikolov, K. et al (1999) High levels of IgA anticardiolipin antibodies in patients with systemic lupus erythematosus, Henoch–Schoenlein puprpura, Sneddon's syndrome and recurrent pregnancy loss. *Thromb Haemost*, **82**, 1774–1775.
231. Gantcheva, M., Tsankov, N. (1999) Livedo reticularis and cerebrovascular accident (Sneddon's syndrome) as a clinical expression of antiphospholipid syndrome. *J Eur Acad Dermatol Venereol*, **12**, 157–160.
232. Gottlober, P., Bezold, G., Schaer, A. et al (2000) Sneddon's syndrome in a child. *Br J Dermatol*, **142**, 374–376.
233. Frances, C., Piette, J.C. (2000) The mystery of Sneddon syndrome: relationship with antiphospholipid syndrome and systemic lupus erythematosus. *J Autoimmun*, **15**, 139–143.
234. Lockshin, M.D. (1991) Antiphospholipid antibody and antiphospholipid antibody syndrome. *Curr Opin Rheumatol*, **3**, 797–802.
235. Combemale, P., Amiral, J., Estival, J.L. et al (2002) Cutaneous necrosis revealing the coexistence of antiphospholipid syndrome with acquired protein C deficiency, factor V Leiden and hyperhomocysteinemia. *Eur J Dermatol*, **12**, 278–282.
236. Tucker, S.C., Coulson, I.H., Salman, W. et al (1998) Mesothelioma-associated antiphospholipid syndrome presenting with cutaneous infarction and neuropathy. *Br J Dermatol*, **138**, 1092–1094.
237. Smith, K.J., Skelton, H.G., James, W.D. et al (1990) Cutaneous histopathologic findings in 'antiphospholipid syndrome'. *Arch Dermatol*, **126**, 1176–1183.
238. Soweid, A.M., Hajjar, R.R., Hewan-Lowe, K.O. et al (1995) Skin necrosis indicating antiphospholipid syndrome in patients with AIDS. *South Med J*, **88**, 786–788.
239. David-Bajar, K.M. (1993) Subacute cutaneous lupus erythematosus. *J Invest Dermatol*, **100**, 2S–8S.
240. Lee, L.A., Gaither, K.K., Coulter, S.N. et al (1989) Pattern of cutaneous immunoglobulin G deposition in subacute cutaneous lupus erythematosus is reproduced by infusing purified anti-Ro (SSA) autoantibodies in human skin-grafted mice. *J Clin Invest*, **83**, 1556–1562.
241. Furukawa, F. (1999) Antinuclear antibody–keratinocyte interactions in photosensitive cutaneous lupus erythematosus. *Histol Histopathol*, **14**, 627–633.
242. Andrews, B.S., Schenk, A., Barr, R. et al (1986) Immunopathology of cutaneous human lupus erythematosus defined by murine monoclonal antibodies. *J Am Acad Dermatol*, **15**, 474–481.
243. Kohchiyama, A., Oka, D., Ueki, H. (1985) T cell subsets in lesions of systemic and discoid lupus erythematosus. *J Cutan Pathol*, **12**, 493–499.
244. Millard, L.G., Rowell, N.R., Rajah, S.M. (1977) Histocompatibility antigens in discoid and systemic lupus erythematosus. *Br J Dermatol*, **96**, 139–144.
245. Millard, T.P., Kondeatis, E., Vaughan, R.W. et al (2001) Polymorphic light eruption and the HLA DRB1*0301 extended haplotype are independent risk factors for cutaneous lupus erythematosus. *Lupus*, **10**, 473–479.
246. Millard, T.P., McGregor, J.M. (2001) Molecular genetics of cutaneous lupus erythematosus. *Clin Exp Dermatol*, **26**, 184–191.
247. Millard, T.P., Lewis, C.M., Khamashta, M.A. et al (2001) Familial clustering of polymorphic light eruption in relatives of patients with lupus erythematosus: evidence of a shared pathogenesis. *Br J Dermatol*, **144**, 334–338.
248. Millard, T.P., Kondeatis, E., Cox, A. et al (2001) A candidate gene analysis of three related photosensitivity disorders: cutaneous lupus erythematosus, polymorphic light eruption and actinic prurigo. *Br J Dermatol*, **145**, 229–236.
249. Werth, V.P., Zhang, W., Dortzbach, K. et al (2000) Association of promoter polymorphism of tumor necrosis factor-alpha with subacute cutaneous lupus erythematosus and distinct photoregulation of transcription. *J Invest Dermatol*, **115**, 726–730.
250. Zamansky, G.B. (1985) Sunlight-induced pathogenesis in systemic lupus erythematosus. *J Invest Dermatol*, **85**, 179–180.
251. Lehmann, P., Holzle, E., Kind, P. et al (1990) Experimental reproduction of skin lesions in lupus erythematosus by UVA and UVB radiation. *J Am Acad Dermatol*, **22**, 181–187.
252. Davis, P. (1977) Antibodies to UV DNA and photosensitivity. *Br J Dermatol*, **97**, 197–200.
253. Baima, B., Sticherling, M. (2001) Apoptosis in different cutaneous manifestations of lupus erythematosus. *Br J Dermatol*, **144**, 958–966.
254. Haustein, U-F. (1973) Tubular structures in affected and normal skin in chronic discoid and systemic lupus erythematosus: electron microscopic studies. *Br J Dermatol*, **89**, 1–13.
255. Crowson, A.N., Magro, C. (2001) The cutaneous pathology of lupus erythematosus: a review. *J Cutan Pathol*, **28**, 1–23.
256. Steinberg, A.D. (1992) Concepts of pathogenesis of systemic lupus erythematosus. *Clin Immunol Immunopathol*, **63**, 19–22.
257. Sugai, S.A., Gerbase, A.B., Cernea, S.S. et al (1992) Cutaneous lupus erythematosus: direct immunofluorescence and epidermal basal membrane study. *Int J Dermatol*, **31**, 260–264.
258. Biesecker, G., Lavin, L., Ziskind, M. et al (1982) Cutaneous localisation of the membrane attack complex in discoid and systemic lupus erythematosus. *N Eng J Med*, **306**, 264–270.
259. Helm, K.F., Peters, M.S. (1993) Deposition of membrane attack complex in cutaneous lesions of lupus erythematosus. *J Am Acad Dermatol*, **28**, 687–691.
260. Dahl, M.V. (1983) Usefulness of direct immunofluorescence in patients with lupus erythematosus. *Arch Dermatol*, **119**, 1010–1017.
261. Nieboer, C. (1987) The reliability of immunofluorescence and histopathology in the diagnosis of discoid lupus erythematosus and lichen planus. *Br J Dermatol*, **116**, 189–198.
262. Valeski, J.E., Kumar, V.J., Forman, A.B. et al (1992) A characteristic cutaneous direct immunofluorescent pattern associated with Ro (SS-A) antibodies in subacute cutaneous lupus erythematosus. *J Am Acad Dermatol*, **27**, 194–198.
263. Gruschwitz, M., Keller, J., Hornstein, O.P. (1988) Deposits of immunoglobulins at the dermo-epidermal junction in chronic light-exposed skin: what is the value of the lupus band test? *Clin Exp Dermatol*, **13**, 303–308.
264. Maynard, B., Leiferman, K.M., Peters, M.S. (1991) Neonatal lupus erythematosus syndrome. *J Cutan Pathol*, **18**, 333–338.
265. Fabré, V.C., Lear, S., Reichlin, M. et al (1991) Twenty percent of biopsy specimens from sun-exposed skin of normal young adults demonstrated positive immunofluorescence. *Arch Dermatol*, **127**, 1006–1011.
266. Blaszczyk, M., Dahl, M.V. (1983) Usefulness of direct immunofluorescence in patients with lupus erythematosus. *Arch Dermatol*, **119**, 1010–1017.
267. Wojnarowska, F., Bhogal, B., Black, M.M. (1986) The significance of an IgM band at the dermo-epidermal junction. *J Cutan Pathol*, **13**, 359–362.
268. Nieboer, C., Tak-Diamand, Z., Van Leeuwen-Wallau, H.E. (1988) Dust-like particles: a specific direct immunofluorescence pattern in subacute cutaneous lupus erythematosus. *Br J Dermatol*, **18**, 725–734.
269. Bukilica, M.N., Andrejevic, S.B., Bonaci-Nikolic, B.M. et al (2002) Speckled antinuclear antibodies in keratinocytes – what does it mean? *Clin Exp Rheumatol*, **20**, 499–504.
270. Clark, W.H., Reed, R.J., Mihm, M.C. (1973) Lupus erythematosus. Histopathology of cutaneous lesions. *Hum Pathol*, **4**, 157–163.
271. Hood, A.F., Farmer, E.R. (1985) Histopathology of cutaneous lupus erythematosus. *Clin Dermatol*, **3**, 36–48.
272. Ueki, H., Takei, Y., Nakagama, S. (1980) Cutaneous calcinosis in localized discoid lupus erythematosus. *Arch Dermatol*, **116**, 196–197.
273. Khan, M.A., Maruno, M., Khaskhely, N.M. et al (2002) Amyloid deposition is frequently observed in skin lesions of hypertrophic lupus erythematosus. *J Dermatol*, **29**, 633–637.
274. Bangert, J.L., Freeman, R.G., Sontheimer, R.D. et al (1984) Subacute cutaneous lupus erythematosus and discoid lupus erythematosus. Comparative histopathologic findings. *Arch Dermatol*, **120**, 332–337.
275. Murphy, J.K., Stephens, C., Hartley, T. et al (1991) Subacute cutaneous lupus erythematosus – the annular variant. A histological and ultrastructural study of five cases. *Histopathology*, **19**, 329–336.
276. Magro, C.M., Crowson, A.N. (1999) The cutaneous pathology associated with seropositivity for antibodies to SSA (Ro): a clinicopathologic study of 23 adult patients without subacute cutaneous lupus erythematosus. *Am J Dermatopathol*, **21**, 129–137.
277. Rongioletti, F., Rebora, A. (1986) Papular and nodular mucinosis associated with systemic lupus erythematosus. *Br J Dermatol*, **115**, 631–636.
278. Alegre, V.A., Winkelmann, R.K. (1988) Histopathologic and immunofluorescence study of skin lesions associated with circulating lupus anticoagulant. *J Am Acad Dermatol*, **19**, 117–124.
279. Stephansson, E., Niemi, K-M., Jouhikainen, T. et al (1991) Lupus anticoagulant and the skin. A longterm follow-up study of SLE patients with special reference to histopathological findings. *Acta Derm Venereol*, **71**, 416–422.
280. Silva, F.G. (1983) The nephropathies of systemic lupus erythematosus. In: Rosen, S. (ed.) Contemporary issues in surgical pathology. Vol. 1, Pathology of glomerular diseases. New York: Churchill Livingstone.
281. Ho, S.Y., Esscher, E., Anderson, R.H. et al (1986) Anatomy of congenital complete heart block and relation to maternal anti-Ro antibodies. *Am J Cardiol*, **58**, 291–294.
282. David, K.M., Bennion, S.D., De Spain, J.D. et al (1992) The clinical, histologic, and immunofluorescent distinctions between subacute cutaneous lupus erythematosus and discoid lupus erythematosus. *J Invest Dermatol*, **99**, 251–257.
283. Norris, P.G., Hawk, J.L.M. (1990) The acute idiopathic photodermatoses. *Semin Dermatol*, **9**, 32–38.
284. Norris, P.G., Morris, J., McGibbon, D.M. et al (1989) Polymorphic light eruption: an immunopathological study of evolving lesions. *Br J Dermatol*, **120**, 171–183.

Systemic sclerosis

Clinical features

Progressive systemic sclerosis includes two major variants:[1-5]

- In the more serious diffuse form patients have widespread cutaneous lesions proximal to the metacarpo- and metatarsophalangeal joints (proximal scleroderma) in addition to involvement of the internal viscera, particularly the kidneys, lungs, heart, esophagus and intestinal tract. The illness often has an acute onset with fatigue, weight loss, arthralgia and carpal tunnel syndrome. Tendon friction rubs are characteristic. Anti-Scl-70 (anti-DNA topoisomerase) and RNA polymerase III antibodies are often present and the outlook is generally poor.

- The other major variant is associated with limited peripheral cutaneous sclerosis and an absence of severe systemic disease except for esophageal involvement, small intestinal malabsorption and pulmonary hypertension; it usually has a better prognosis.[2,6] This form is associated with an anticentromere antibody.

Systemic sclerosis has also occasionally been recorded in the absence of cutaneous manifestation (sine scleroderma variant) and overlap syndromes have been described.[7,8] Limited scleroderma also includes the CREST (calcinosis, Raynaud's phenomenon, esophageal dysfunction, sclerodactyly, telangiectasis) syndrome (Thibierge–Weissenbach syndrome, acrosclerosis) where cutaneous disease expression is restricted to the fingers and toes (sclerodactyly) and face (see below).[9] Other generalized variants include sclerodermatomyositis, mixed connective tissue disease and the chemically induced scleroderma-like syndromes.

Because of the variety of systems that can be affected in systemic sclerosis, patients may be primarily under the care of dermatologists, rheumatologists, nephrologists or other specialists, and this results in difficulties in determining the exact incidence of the disease; it is estimated to be in the order of 20 new cases/million of the population/year.[10] In a large series, the diffuse and limited forms were equally common.[11] About 10% were classified as overlap syndromes. The disease occurs more frequently in families and it is regarded as the strongest risk factor identified for this condition.[12] However, the absolute risk for each family member is low.[12] Systemic sclerosis is associated with a marked female predominance (3–4:1); although any age group may be affected, patients most often present in their fourth, fifth and sixth decades.[13,14] Young black females constitute a definite subset with a particularly high risk. Occasional familial instances, usually in children, have also been documented.[10] Systemic sclerosis has a high overall mortality, 5-year survival rates varying from 34 to 73%.[1] It has been demonstrated that improvement of skin thickening is associated with improved survival.[15,16] Older patients and males generally fare worst.

Limited cutaneous systemic sclerosis

In the limited variant, the cutaneous manifestations, which often initially affect the hands, include early edematous, sclerotic and late atrophic stages.[1] The edema is characteristically non-pitting, bilateral and symmetrical. The fingers are commonly described as having a sausage-like appearance (*Fig. 16.80*). The face, forearms, feet and legs are sometimes affected. As the edema subsides the skin becomes thickened and tight and is bound down to the subcutaneous tissues. Typically, the fingers become tapered and, due to ischemia, show pulp atrophy and absorption of the terminal phalanges, with the fingertips often not protruding beyond the free margin of the nails (*Figs 16.81, 16.82*). The latter may show longitudinal ridging and brittleness or be shed. The affected skin has a very characteristic appearance, being shiny, smooth and rather waxy. Patients often have markedly diminished mobility of

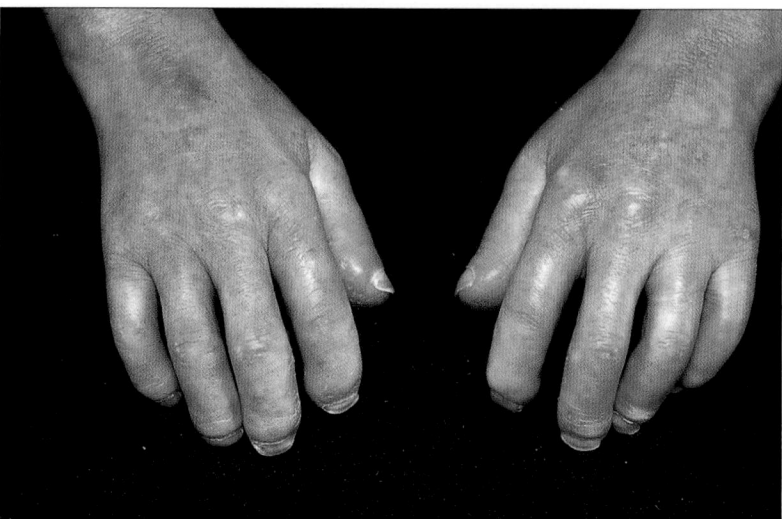

Fig. 16.80
Systemic sclerosis: early stage showing characteristic swollen, sausage-shaped fingers. By courtesy of the Institute of Dermatology, London, UK.

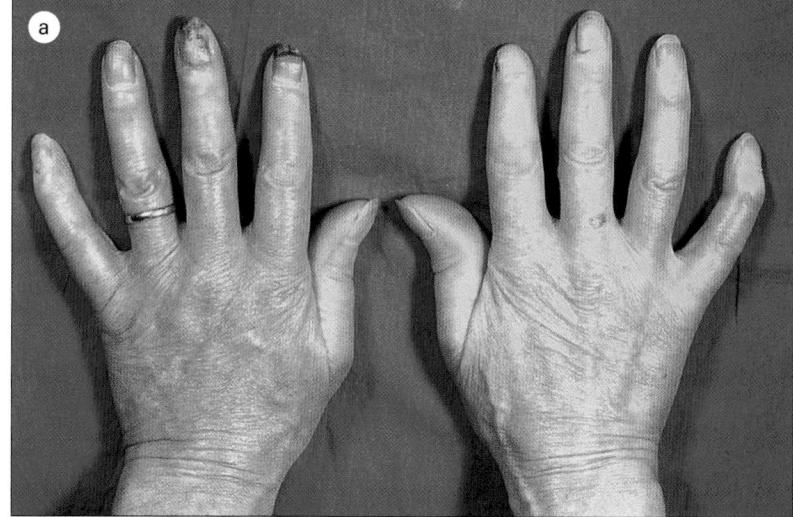

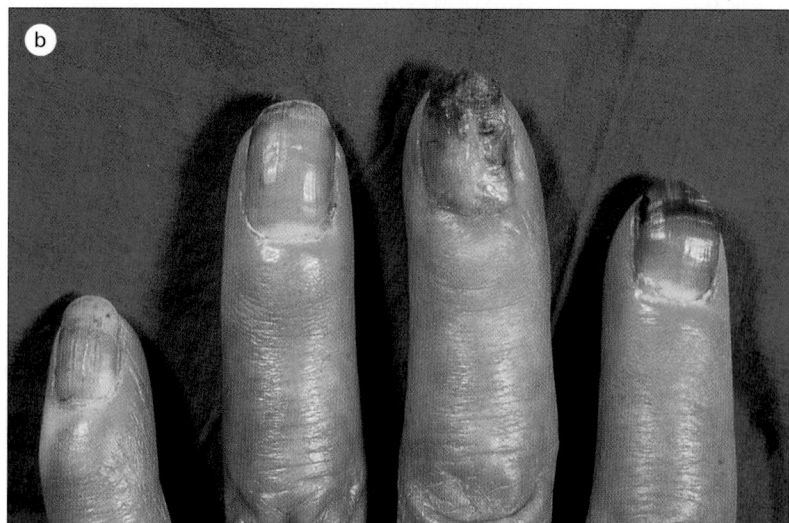

Fig. 16.81
Systemic sclerosis: (a) the fingers are erythematous and shiny and the skin appears slightly bound down; (b) the fingertips are tapered. By courtesy of R.A. Marsden, MD, St George's Hospital, London, UK.

their hands and feet, and flexion contractures are common (*Fig. 16.83*). In advanced disease, many patients acquire a dramatically rigid expressionless face with beaked nose, thinned lips, and perioral furrowing and wrinkling, with an inability to open the mouth fully (*Figs 16.84, 16.85*).[17] Tightness of the lower eyelids may also be noticed and the forehead may appear smooth and free of creases.[2] Ulceration is a common complication, particularly where taut skin is stretched over bony prominences susceptible to trauma (*Fig. 16.86*).

Vascular changes are common and include peripheral gangrene, digital autoamputation and Raynaud's phenomenon.[17] The last occurs so frequently (in both limited and diffuse forms) that it is often taught that a patient who has it must be presumed to have systemic sclerosis, until proven otherwise. In limited cutaneous systemic sclerosis, Raynaud's phenomenon may precede the onset of cutaneous lesions by many years in a large proportion of patients.[10] A useful diagnostic feature of systemic sclerosis is loss of many of the nail fold capillaries and dilatation of the remainder.

The cutaneous changes in CREST syndrome are located predominantly distal to the metacarpophalangeal joints, although the dorsum of the hand and mouth can sometimes also be affected. The inflammatory stage is quite persistent in the CREST syndrome.

Raynaud's phenomenon, either alone or with swollen puffy fingers, is by far the most common mode of presentation and telangiectases tend to be much more numerous (often numbering hundreds) than in patients with diffuse systemic sclerosis. They particularly affect the fingers and hands, face, tongue and mucous membranes (*Figs 16.87–16.89*). The telangiectasias seen in this variant of scleroderma may be difficult to distinguish from those seen in hereditary hemorrhagic telangiectasia.[18] The esophageal dysfunction is identical to that seen in the diffuse variant, but it tends to be more severe and affects the majority of patients.

The value of the designation 'CREST syndrome' has, however, diminished considerably since the discovery that many patients with limited cutaneous disease fail to fulfill all of its criteria and the observation that 'CREST' manifestations may be seen in many patients

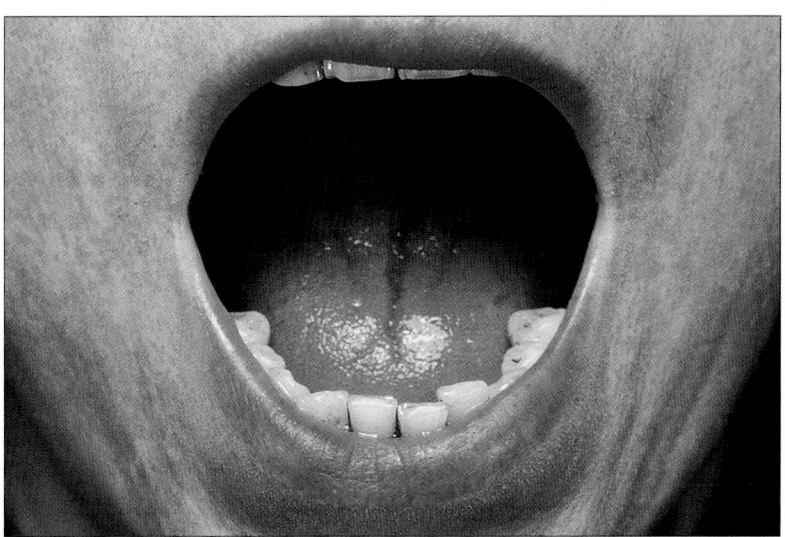

Fig. 16.84
Systemic sclerosis: there is perioral scarring with atrophy. By courtesy of the Institute of Dermatology, London, UK.

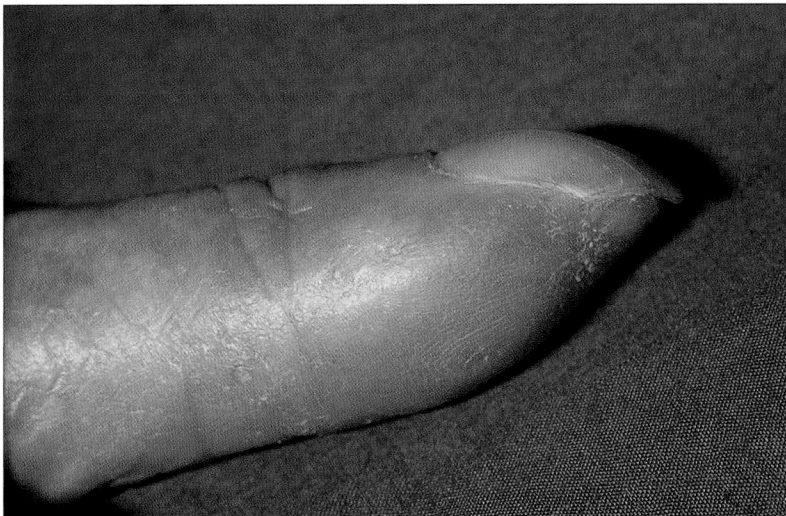

Fig. 16.82
Systemic sclerosis: note the marked atrophy of the fingertip. By courtesy of R.A. Marsden, MD, St George's Hospital, London, UK.

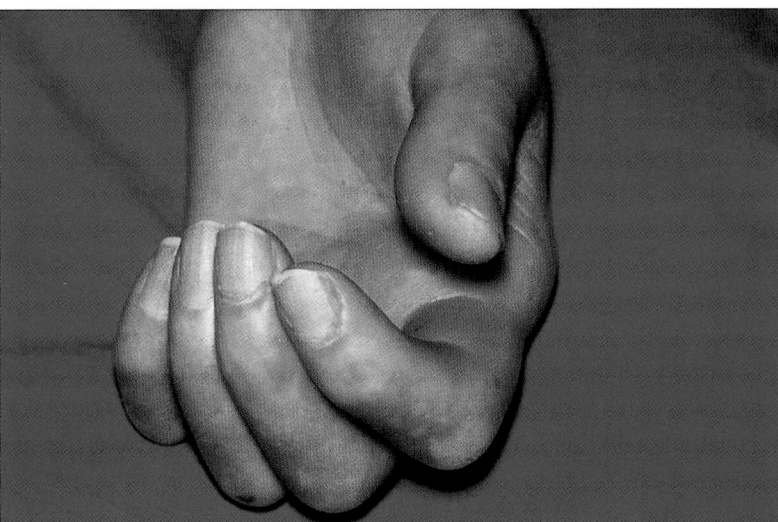

Fig. 16.83
Systemic sclerosis: note the flexion contractures. The skin is bound down and appears atrophic. There is periungual erythema. By courtesy of R.A. Marsden, MD, St George's Hospital, London, UK.

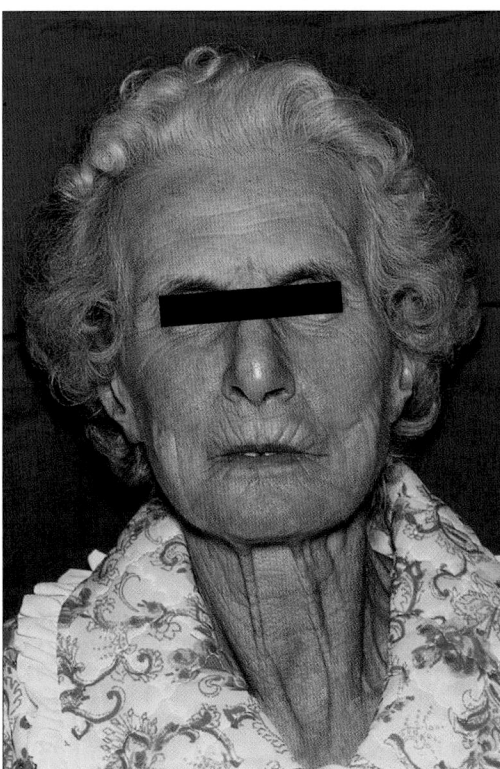

Fig. 16.85
Systemic sclerosis: note the thinned lips and characteristic radiating furrows. By courtesy of R.A. Marsden, MD, St George's Hospital, London, UK.

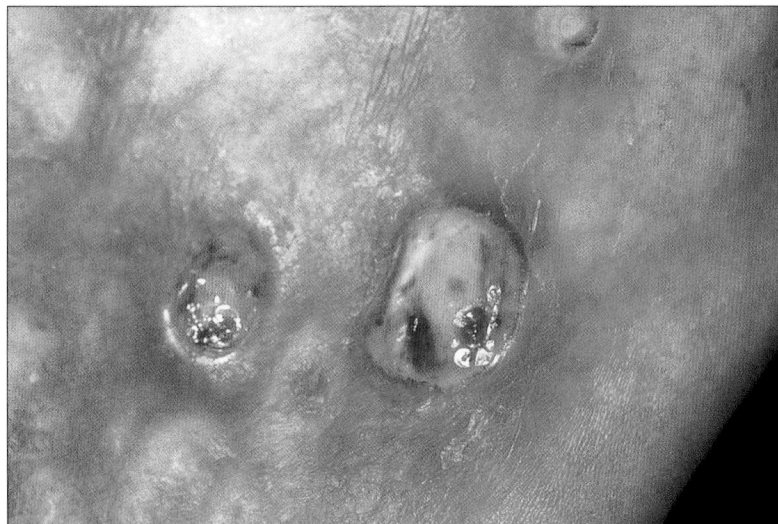

Fig. 16.86
Systemic sclerosis: ulceration is a particularly distressing complication. By courtesy of the Institute of Dermatology, London, UK.

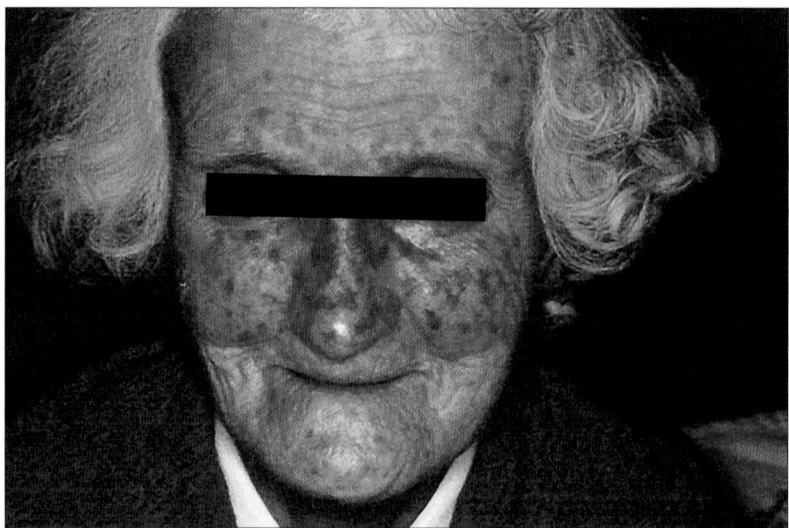

Fig. 16.89
Systemic sclerosis: extensive telangiectasia as seen in this patient is more often a feature of the limited variant. By courtesy of S. Parker, MD, West Middlesex Hospital, London, UK.

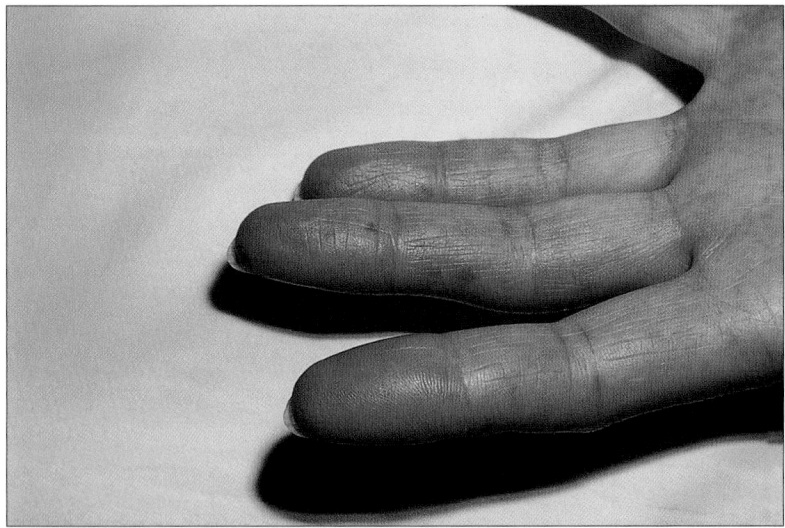

Fig. 16.87
Systemic sclerosis: telangiectasia as seen on these fingers is a common finding. By courtesy of S. Parker, MD, West Middlesex Hospital, London, UK.

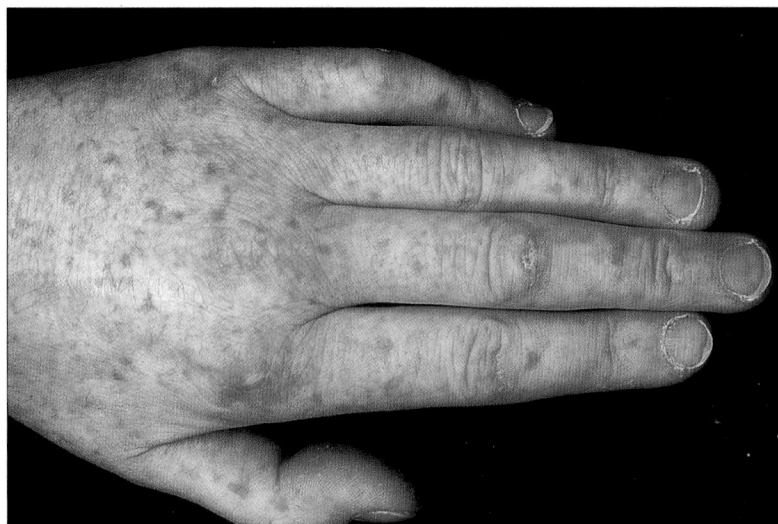

Fig. 16.88
Systemic sclerosis: numerous telangiectases are present. The hand is a commonly affected site. By courtesy of the Institute of Dermatology, London, UK.

with diffuse disease.[8] For example, there is a variant consisting of digital necrosis, Raynaud's phenomenon and anticentromere antibodies without sclerodactyly.[19] The term should probably be abandoned and all patients with limited distal disease classified as a single subtype. However, considering the frequency with which CREST syndrome appears in the current literature, this is unlikely to happen, at least in the foreseeable future. It was originally thought that the limited variant was associated with a relatively benign outcome, but it is now known that if patients are followed for sufficient time a significant proportion will develop severe pulmonary hypertension with its sequelae. There is also an increased risk of Sjögren's syndrome and biliary cirrhosis.[1,20] It has been suggested that patients with coexistent primary biliary cirrhosis have a distinctive subset of the disease, which tends to be milder and with better prognosis.[21]

Hyperpigmentation, from light brown to dark bronze reminiscent of Addison's disease, is a frequent manifestation and is often associated with the presence of small foci of hypopigmentation, giving a characteristic 'salt and pepper' appearance. The pigmentary changes particularly affect the backs of the hands and forearms, and the upper part of the chest and back. Sometimes the degree of accompanying hypopigmentation is so marked that it resembles vitiligo.[22]

The cutaneous changes are often associated with the development of calcinosis cutis, particularly in females.[2] It is dystrophic in type and is due to hydroxyapatite crystal deposition. Patients have no abnormalities of calcium and phosphorus metabolism and their serum alkaline phosphatase levels are normal. The sites of calcium deposition particularly include the metacarpophalangeal joints of the thumbs and the fingertips, although the extensor aspect of the forearms, the buttocks, the olecranon bursae and the prepatellar region may also be affected (*Figs 16.90, 16.91*). The deposits are often exceedingly painful and commonly associated with ulceration and leakage of white granular calcified debris. The combination of phalangeal reabsorption and calcinosis cutis is said to be pathognomonic of systemic sclerosis.[23]

Systemic sclerosis is sometimes associated with an erythema nodosum-like panniculitis syndrome and patients may also develop livedo reticularis and atrophie blanche affecting the lower limbs.[24]

CREST has been documented in association with familial lichen sclerosus, chronic myelogenous leukemia, idiopathic myelofibrosis and porphyria cutanea tarda.[25–27]

Diffuse systemic sclerosis

In diffuse (progressive) systemic sclerosis, cutaneous lesions are particularly common on the proximal extremities, thorax and abdomen. The course tends to be progressive and often there is a more severe superficial vascular involvement.[2] Skin thickening affecting the trunk indicates a poor prognosis and correlates with extensive systemic involvement (*Fig. 16.92*).[10] Although the cutaneous features cause considerable distress, the systemic manifestations are more important in terms of severe morbidity and potential mortality. The early investigation of a patient with systemic sclerosis should establish baseline values of respiratory, cardiac and renal function so that progress may be accurately monitored.

Clinical involvement of the lung is common and an important cause of morbidity and mortality. It is thought to occur to a greater or lesser extent in most patients.[28] There are three major forms: interstitial pneumonitis, bronchiolitis and pulmonary vascular disease.[28]

- *Pulmonary interstitial involvement* results in shortness of breath on exertion and a non-productive cough. Dyspnea is a feature in almost 60% of unselected patients with diffuse scleroderma.[29] Symptoms tend to be particularly evident in patients who have associated Sjögren's syndrome.[28] Interstitial lung disease is the commonest

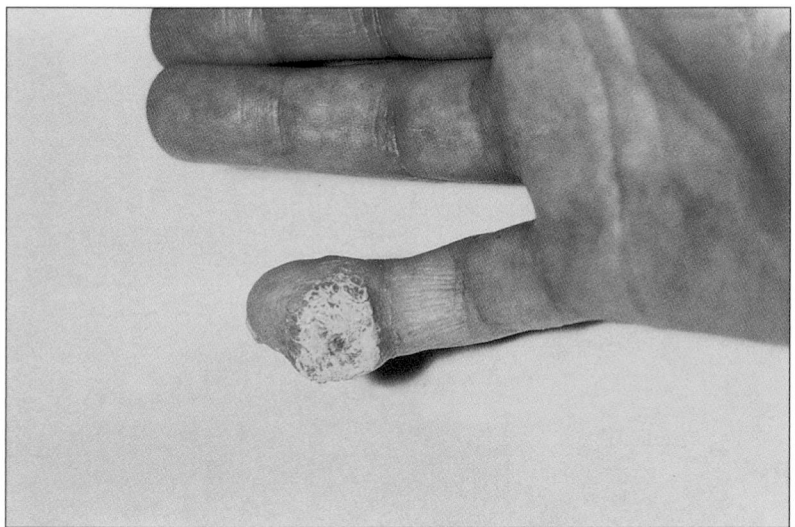

Fig. 16.90
Systemic sclerosis: there is a large calcified nodule on the fingertip. By courtesy of R.A. Marsden, MD, St George's Hospital, London, UK.

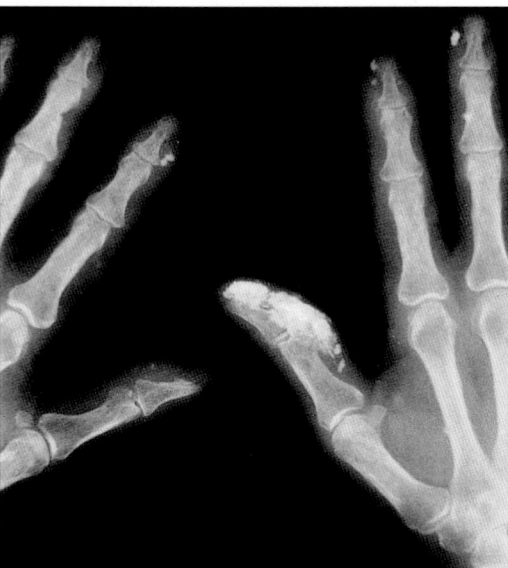

Fig. 16.91
Systemic sclerosis: radiograph demonstrating a more widespread example. By courtesy of R.A. Marsden, MD, St George's Hospital, London, UK.

cause of death in systemic sclerosis. There is evidence suggesting an increased risk of pulmonary fibrosis in patients with the haplotype HLA-DR3/-DRw52A and anti-Scl-70 antibody.[30,31]

- *Bronchiolitis* is evident in approximately 13–25% of patients, but this is usually asymptomatic.[28]
- *Pulmonary hypertension*, which may be a primary manifestation of systemic sclerosis or develop secondary to interstitial fibrosis, is more common in patients with the limited form of the disease.[32] A study has found that the postmenopausal state with or without the presence of HLA-B35 is the main risk factor for the development of pulmonary hypertension.[33] Pulmonary radiographs typically show bilateral basal fibrosis, either as diffuse mottling or linear infiltrates; cyst formation ('honeycomb lung') is a not uncommon feature.

Cardiac, renal, peripheral nervous, gastrointestinal and skeletal systems are also involved:

- *Cardiac involvement* may present as dyspnea on exertion, paroxysmal nocturnal dyspnea, pericarditis, pericardial effusion, congestive heart failure, arrhythmias or, occasionally, atypical angina.[34] Significant cardiac abnormalities including pericarditis and effusion are common pathological findings, being present in more than 50% of cases at autopsy.[35] Usually, however, they are asymptomatic. Occasionally, severe acute pericarditis may develop and rare instances of fatal cardiac tamponade have been documented.[34] Large pericardial effusions correlate with acute renal failure and are a bad prognostic indicator.[35] Patchy myocardial scarring is common and when severe is associated with a poor outlook.[36] It occurs independently of coronary artery disease and has been described in up to 70% of patients in postmortem series.[34] The major coronary arteries are patent and normal (unless there is coexistent atherosclerosis), but the small vessels and arterioles may undergo endothelial and intimal proliferative changes with scarring, resulting in an increased risk of arrhythmia and the consequent sudden death of the patient.
- *Renal involvement* presenting as 'scleroderma renal crisis' is an extremely important complication with high mortality and occurs in approximately 10% of patients with systemic sclerosis.[37] The use of ACE inhibitors has, however, significantly diminished the mortality. It is defined as 'the new onset of accelerated arterial hypertension and/or rapidly progressive oliguric renal failure'.[37] Patients develop headache and blurred vision. Seizures are sometimes a feature. The

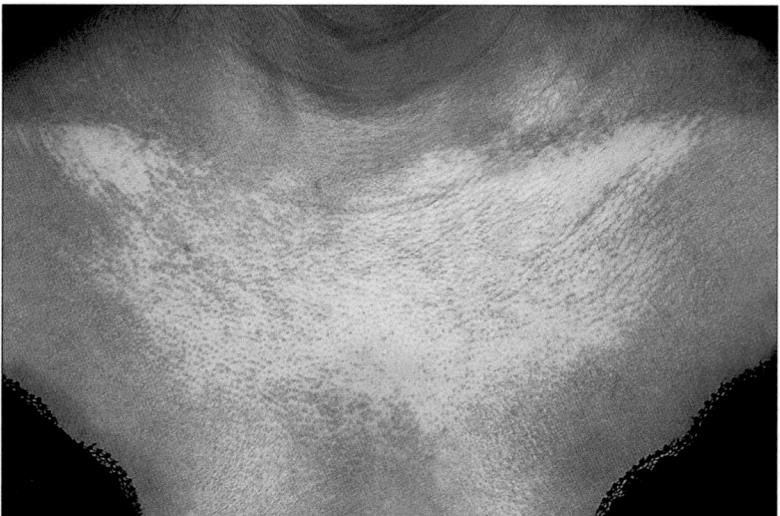

Fig. 16.92
Systemic sclerosis: severe involvement of the trunk as seen in this patient is associated with a poor prognosis. By courtesy of the Institute of Dermatology, London, UK.

renal failure is commonly asymptomatic and detectable only from abnormal renal function tests including proteinuria, microscopic hematuria with casts, raised creatinine levels and hyperreninemia.[37] Microangiopathic hemolytic anemia is sometimes present, particularly in normotensive patients.[38]

- *Peripheral neuropathy* may lead to neuropathic ulceration.[39] Intrauterine fetal death has been described in pregnant women with the disease.[40] Papular and nodular mucinosis has been documented as a presenting sign of systemic sclerosis.[41]

- Clinically relevant *gastrointestinal lesions* occur in up to 50% of patients with systemic sclerosis.[42] Widening of the periodontal space, determined radiographically, is characteristic. Patients frequently have symptoms relating to esophageal involvement including heartburn, dysphagia and regurgitation. Gastrointestinal reflux is common and patients can develop esophagitis, hemorrhage, stricture, Barrett's esophagus (gastric metaplasia) and aspiration.[42] Radiographs may show esophageal dilatation and abnormalities of peristalsis. Systemic sclerosis often involves the small intestine, symptoms ranging from epigastric pain, nausea and vomiting, through to the effects of pseudo-obstruction; a malabsorptive state due to stasis is an important complication. Colonic lesions may result in diarrhea or constipation. Saccular diverticula along the mesenteric border of the colon are characteristic; they sometimes also affect the small bowel.[42]

- *Osteoarticular involvement*, presenting with arthralgia or frank arthritis is seen in the majority of patients.[43] Joint lesions are usually mild and affect the wrists, hands, knees and ankles, although a more serious rheumatoid arthritis-like variant has been documented.[44] Osteoarthrosis and psoriatic arthropathy-like manifestations have also been described.[43] It is important in patients with significant joint manifestations that overlap syndromes and mixed connective tissue disease are excluded. Contractures and ankyloses resulting in immobility are important complications and osteoporosis is common due to a combination of immobilization and ischemia.

The diagnosis of systemic sclerosis may be readily apparent, but early disease, particularly the diffuse form, may clinically mimic a variety of other diseases, for example, scleredema of Buschke. Late graft-versus-host disease (GVHD) and chronic lesions of porphyria cutanea tarda are typically sclerodermatous.[45] The American Rheumatology Association has guidelines for classification, of which the major criterion is proximal scleroderma (*Table 16.6*).[46] Minor criteria are:

- sclerodactyly
- digital pitting scars on the fingertips or loss of substance of the distal fingerpad
- bilateral basal pulmonary fibrosis.

Table 16.6

American Rheumatology Association (ARA) guidelines for the classification of scleroderma*

1. Proximal scleroderma is a single major criterion: sensitivity is 91% and specificity is more than 90%.
2. Sclerodactyly, digital pitting scars of the fingertips or loss of substance of the finger pad, and bibasilar pulmonary fibrosis contribute further minor criteria in the absence of proximal scleroderma.
3. The major or two more minor criteria are present in 97% of definite systemic sclerosis patients, but in only 2% of comparison patients with systemic lupus erythematosus, polymyositis–dermatomyositis or Raynaud's disease.

* Preliminary clinical criteria for systemic sclerosis exclude localized scleroderma and pseudodermatous disorders. Reproduced with permission from Masi, A.T. et al and the ARA Subcommittee for scleroderma (1980) *Arthritis and Rheumatism*, **23**, 581–590.

If patients have either the major or two of the minor criteria there is 97% sensitivity for definite systemic sclerosis and 98% specificity. These criteria have gained wide popularity, but have the disadvantage of excluding at least 10% of cases where, despite a concrete diagnosis of systemic sclerosis, neither major nor minor criteria can be fulfilled. Unclassifiable and overlap syndromes are also excluded. Other classifications have included two, three and even four subtypes based upon the extent of cutaneous sclerosis (*Table 16.7*).[47] Limited cutaneous systemic sclerosis may therefore involve the hands, feet, forearms and face, or skin lesions can be absent, whereas in diffuse disease the trunk skin is also involved. In a comparison of classification by two subtypes (diffuse and limited) or three subtypes (diffuse, intermediate and limited), the latter correlated best with antibody specificity and survival.[48]

A number of chemical-induced scleroderma-like syndromes have been described:

- Workers in the vinyl chloride polymerization industry may develop Raynaud's phenomenon, acral osteolysis, dermal thickening of the skin of the arms, hands, face and trunk, and pulmonary and hepatic fibrosis.[49–51] Examination of the capillaries of the nail folds reveals abnormalities similar to those seen in systemic sclerosis.

- Bleomycin therapy may also be associated with sclerodermiform infiltrated plaques and nodules that particularly affect the hands.[52] Patients may develop hyperpigmentation, peripheral gangrene and pulmonary fibrosis.

- A high incidence of systemic sclerosis is found in those who work in coalmines or who have excessive exposure to silica for other reasons.[53]

- A generalized morphea-like variant with Raynaud's phenomenon, esophageal dysfunction and pulmonary fibrosis has been described following chronic exposure to industrial solvents.[54]

- A variety of autoimmune diseases have been documented following the use of silicone breast implants. Systemic sclerosis appears to be the most common.[55]

- Toxic oil and eosinophilia myalgia syndromes are discussed in the section on eosinophilic fasciitis.

Pathogenesis and histological features

The etiology and precise pathogenesis are unknown. A complete understanding must take into account vascular changes and abnormalities of collagen deposition and distribution, in addition to the significance of the inflammatory cells that characterize the early stages and their role in the control of fibroblast growth and function.[56] Systemic sclerosis has stimulated an enormous research effort, which has resulted in an increased awareness of the multiplicity of factors that may be involved, either singly or in concert, and has also greatly increased our knowledge of the basic processes involved in the mechanisms of collagen synthesis and scarring. The two main areas of investigation have revolved around:

- primary blood vessel endothelial cell damage and its sequelae
- abnormalities of collagen and its synthesis.[57,58]

Inherent to both are the possible initiating and moderating roles of cell-mediated and humoral immunity.

It has long been recognized that many of the features of systemic sclerosis may have an ischemic basis.[59] Alterations have been described in capillaries, venules and arteries and it has been suggested that the initial injury involves capillary endothelial cells.[60] The cause of this is unknown, although a circulating specific cytotoxic substance reactive for endothelial cells has been identified.[60,61] It has been suggested that this may represent a protease.[62] Interestingly, specimens of early lesions and uninvolved skin have shown ultrastructural evidence of endothelial cell damage combined with decreased uptake of tritiated adenosine and

Table 16.7
Classifications of systemic sclerosis

Subsets of systemic sclerosis (SSc)	
Diffuse cutaneous SSc*	Onset of Raynaud's phenomenon within 1 year of onset of skin changes (puffy or hidebound)
	Truncal and acral skin involvement
	Presence of tendon friction rubs
	Early and significant incidence of interstitial lung disease, oliguric renal failure, diffuse gastrointestinal disease and myocardial involvement
	Absence of anticentromere antibodies
	Nail fold capillary dilatation and capillary destruction[†]
	Antitopoisomerase antibodies (20–60% of patients)
Limited cutaneous SSc	Raynaud's for years (occasionally decades)
	Skin involvement limited to hands, face, feet and forearms (acral) or absent
	A significance late incidence of pulmonary hypertension, with or without interstitial lung disease, trigeminal neuralgia, skin calcifications, telangiectasia
	A high incidence of anticentromere antibody
	Dilated nail fold capillary loops, usually without capillary dropout

Subsetting of SSc by early cutaneous involvement[‡]	
Digital	Finger or toes, minimal non-extremity involvements allowed: eyelid, neck and axillary changes
Proximal extremity	Proximal extremity or face, but not trunk
Truncal	Thorax or abdomen

Systemic sclerosis subsets according to skin sclerosis extent

ssSSc   lcSSc   icSSc   dcSSc

ssSSc = sine scleroderma systemic sclerosis
lcSSc = limited cutaneous systemic sclerosis
icSSc = intermediate cutaneous systemic sclerosis
dcSSc = diffuse cutaneous systemic sclerosis

☐ sclerotic skin
☐ uninvolved skin

Skin sclerosis extent in four SSc subsets. LcSSc patients may present minimal sclerotic lesion at eyelids, neck and axillae

* Experienced observers note some patients with dcSSc who do not develop organ insufficiency and suggest the term chronic dcSSc for these patients.
[†] Nail fold capillary dilatation and destruction may also be seen in patients with dermatomyositis, overlap syndromes and undifferentiated connective tissue disease. These syndromes may be considered as part of the spectrum of scleroderma-associated disorders.
[‡] The subject is defined within 1 year from presentation.
Top panel reproduced with permission from Leroy, E.C. et al (1988) *Journal of Rheumatology*, **15**, 202–205; middle and lower panels reproduced with permission from Valentini, R. (1994) *Clinics in Dermatology*, **12**, 217–223.

diminished stores of immunodetectable von Willebrand factor, suggesting that the vascular changes may well initiate the connective tissue damage seen in this disease.[63]

Although immunoreactants (IgG and complement) have been detected in the walls of renal glomerular capillaries by immunofluorescent techniques, they have not been found in the cutaneous vasculature.[63,64] If Raynaud's phenomenon is induced in patients with systemic sclerosis, there is a concomitant reduction in both renal and pulmonary blood flow implying a circulating factor, as yet unidentified.

The dermal capillaries show a variety of ultrastructural changes. The earliest finding is separation of the endothelial cells; this may result in fluid leakage and therefore be responsible, at least in part, for the edema that characterizes the early stages.[1] Evidence of more severe damage is manifest by the presence of endothelial cell vacuolation, increased numbers of intermediate filaments, reduction in pinocytotic vesicles and Weibel–Palade bodies, and abnormal endothelial surface cytoplasmic blebs.[63]

Evidence of endothelial cell injury can be monitored clinically by estimating plasma von Willebrand factor levels.[58] Elevated levels of supranormal von Willebrand factor multimers are typically seen in systemic sclerosis and may have pathogenetic significance as they are known to bind to subendothelial tissues causing platelet aggregation and adhesion with resultant vascular proliferation and thrombosis.[58,65] ACE levels have been shown to be reduced in systemic sclerosis and this may also be of value in assessing the presence of endothelial cell damage.[58]

Increased levels of the endothelial cell-derived peptide, endothelin, which causes vasoconstriction, have been identified.[55] Endothelin also has fibroblast mitogenic activity and stimulates the synthesis of collagen.[66]

The end stage appears as complete destruction of the capillary wall; the nuclei are granular and homogeneous, cell membranes are disrupted and cytoplasmic contents are found in the capillary lumen and extravascular spaces. Endothelial cell uptake of tritiated adenosine has been shown to be reduced.[63] Basement membrane thickening and reduplication is often present and perivascular fibrosis is a common late accompaniment. The end result of vascular damage can be demonstrated most easily by nail fold capillaroscopy. It is likely that the dilatation of the residual vessels represents a compensatory measure. Increased proliferation of the endothelial cells in these residual vessels has been confirmed by tritiated thymidine uptake studies.[56]

Arterioles are also involved in the vasodestructive phenomenon, characterized by vessel wall thickening due to a combination of smooth muscle hyperplasia, fibrosis and the deposition of excessive glyco-saminoglycans. Arteries show very marked intimal thickening, which is particularly well seen in the renal arcuate vessels and is often referred to as 'onion skinning' due to the concentric lamination. It develops as a consequence of myxoid change, cellular proliferation and fibrosis.

Most of the inflammatory cells in the skin of patients with systemic sclerosis are CD4+ T-cells.

A number of cytokines have been linked to the pathogenesis of systemic sclerosis. Transforming growth factor beta (TGF-β) and IL-4 increase fibroblast proliferation and collagen synthesis and may be important in the induction of fibrosis in this disease. IL-17 is a cytokine secreted by T-cells that activates and induces proliferation of fibroblasts and activation of endothelial cells. This cytokine has been demonstrated to be increased in the skin and blood of affected patients, particularly in the early stages of the disease. It activates fibroblasts to secrete the proinflammatory cytokines IL-6 and -8 and to increase surface expression of intercellular adhesion molecule-1 (ICAM-1).[67–69] IL-17 also activates endothelial cells to secrete IL-6 and -1 and to express ICAM-1 and vascular cell adhesion molecule-1 (VCAM-1). IL-6 is also capable of inducing proliferation of fibroblasts and collagen synthesis. The combined effects of IL-17 and other cytokines induced by it lead to damage to the microcirculation and to fibrosis in the skin and internal organs. Recently, it has been suggested that connective tissue growth factor, the production of which is induced by TGF-β, may play an important role in the pathogenesis of fibrosis.[70]

The fibroblasts in systemic sclerosis are capable of assembling microfibrils but these are unstable (probably due to an inherent defect of fibrillin 1, the extracellular matrix protein) and this may also play a role in the pathogenesis of the disease.[71] Interestingly, duplication in the fibrillin-1 gene has been implicated as the cause of tight skin,[1] which is an animal model of systemic sclerosis.[71] Antibodies against fibrillin are raised in the sera of patients with systemic sclerosis. Although this appears to be highly disease specific, it varies amongst ethnic groups. Native Americans and Japanese patients have a high frequency of anti-fibrillin-1 antibodies.[72]

Male cells have been found in multiple organs in women with systemic sclerosis but not in healthy women.[73] The migration of fetal cells into maternal circulation and their survival in different organs is known as microchimerism. It is still not clear what role if any, microchimerism plays in the pathogenesis of systemic sclerosis.

The predominant histological feature of systemic sclerosis is scarring. Intensive investigations have confirmed the presence of increased quantities of collagen, but as yet the precise pathogenetic mechanism(s) remain uncertain. Increased proline hydroxylase activity and increased uptake of labeled proline, both indicators of active collagen synthesis, have been demonstrated in patients with systemic sclerosis.[74] There is typically an elevated level of reducible aldimine cross-links, a feature of newly synthesized collagen.[75] Raised serum concentration of the N-terminal propeptide of type III collagen and increased urinary excretion of hydroxyproline have also been documented.[58]

Cultures of fibroblasts from patients with systemic sclerosis synthesize more collagen than do those from normal controls.[76] Although diminished levels of tissue collagenase have been reported, other workers have not confirmed this finding and its significance is therefore uncertain.[77] The amino acid composition of the collagen fibers is normal.

Electron microscopy of evolving lesions has revealed the presence of immature collagen fibrils, characterized by a narrow caliber (30 nm), immature banding pattern and double-stranded beaded filaments.[1] In the more mature lesion the collagen fibers approach normal thickness (100 nm), but their distribution is highly disorganized. Luse bodies are sometimes a feature.

Histological examination of active lesions often reveals increased numbers of fibroblasts. It has been shown that fibroblasts from the lower dermis synthesize more collagen than do those derived from the upper dermis, suggesting two different populations in systemic sclerosis.[78] The fibrosis, which is due to the deposition of types I, III, V and VI collagen, is accompanied by excessive fibronectin.[58,79]

Recently, abundant type VII collagen has also been demonstrated within the dermis of involved skin accompanied by elevated expression of TGF-β.[79] The latter is known to upregulate the activity of the type VII collagen gene. This finding is of potential importance as type VII collagen distribution is normally restricted to the anchoring fibrils at the epidermodermal junction. Increased expression of types I and III collagen mRNA has been demonstrated in cultured fibroblasts from patients with scleroderma.[80,81] Systemic sclerosis is characterized by a normal concentration of collagen per unit weight. In contrast, however, there is a greatly increased collagen content per unit surface area.[82]

Collagen synthesis has a negative feedback control. Therefore, following cleavage of the amino terminal of the procollagen molecule by the amino terminal peptidase, the released amino terminal inhibits collagen formation. It has been shown by immunoelectron microscopic

techniques that there is retention of the amino peptide at the site of the collagen fibril.[1]

In addition to increased quantities of collagen, the skin of early lesions of systemic sclerosis contains excessive quantities of glycosaminoglycans, notably dermatan sulfate and chondroitin 4- and 6-sulfate.[83] There is some evidence to show that the increase in glycosaminoglycans may be due, at least in part, to diminished degradation; their presence is associated with water binding in vivo and presumably is therefore also responsible for edema.

Systemic sclerosis is associated with abnormalities of both humoral and cellular immunity.[84] In contrast to SLE, anti-DNA antibodies are not usually present. Almost all patients, however, do possess antinuclear antibodies; these may be speckled, homogeneous, or nucleolar in type (*Fig. 16.93*). The last are found in 7–46% of patients, but are not specific, being found in a number of other connective tissue diseases.[8] They form a heterogeneous group reacting against a variety of antigens including U3-RNP (fibrillarin), RNA polymerase I, Th ribonucleoprotein and PM-Scl and have some prognostic significance and subtype specificity (*Table 16.8*).[8,10]

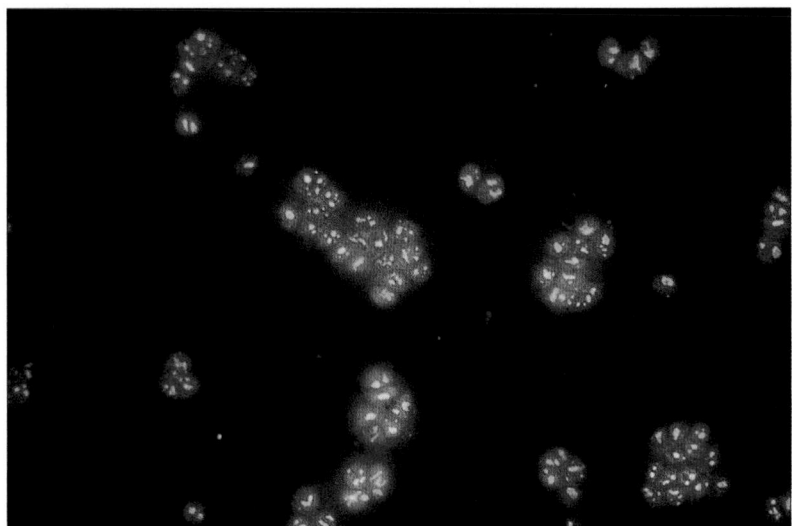

Fig. 16.93
Systemic sclerosis: antinucleolar antibody (HEP II). By courtesy of G. Swana, MD, St Thomas' Hospital, London, UK.

Table 16.8
Systemic sclerosis: main autoantibody specificities giving a nucleolar pattern of fluorescence

Antigen	Frequency in SSc (%)	Clinical associations
Fibrillarin (U3–RNP)	8	Men with more lung and heart, less joint involvement; dcSSc with telangiectasia
RNA polymerase I	4	DcSSc with high frequency of internal and musculoskeletal involvements and shorter disease duration at presentation
Th	4	LcSSc with reduced survival; pulmonary hypertension, small bowel involvement
PM-Scl	3	LcSSc in overlap with myositis; higher frequency of renal involvement

dcSSc, diffuse cutaneous SSc; lcSSc, limited cutaneous SSc; SSc, systemic sclerosis. Reproduced with permission from Valentini, R. (1994) *Clinics in Dermatology*, **12**, 217–223.

There are a number of subsets of antinuclear antibodies, which also have clinical predictive value:[8,85–87]

- *Anticentromere antibody* (which is almost specific for systemic sclerosis) is particularly common in the limited cutaneous variant.[88] It is usually found in patients with less severe disease and a more favorable outcome.[8] Calcinosis and telangiectasia may be conspicuous, but interstitial pulmonary fibrosis is less likely.
- *Scl-70 antibody* (anti-DNA topoisomerase) is found in 20–60% of patients with systemic sclerosis, particularly the diffuse variant.[89] It is also highly specific.[8,90] Scl-70 antibody correlates with severe systemic involvement including pulmonary interstitial fibrosis and a poor prognosis.
- *Anticentriole antibody* occurs in both the limited and diffuse forms.

Although these antibodies are of great diagnostic importance they do not appear to have any pathogenetic significance.

The presence of Ro (SS-A) and La (SS-B) antibodies suggests the coexistence of Sjögren's syndrome.[1]

Antibodies to types I and IV collagen have been described, but it is not clear whether they represent primary pathogenetic agents or are secondary phenomena.[91] More recently, antiendothelial cell antibodies have been documented in scleroderma.[92] Circulating immune complexes have been reported, but are not a constant feature, and their significance, if any, is unknown.[63,93]

Various T-cell abnormalities have been reported, most of which point towards a diminished concentration of circulating T-lymphocytes, particularly of the suppressor subset.[58] An increased T-helper:suppressor ratio has been described.[94]

Investigations have recently been directed towards the role of cytokines in the development of the fibrosis in systemic sclerosis. Evidence suggests that they are major regulators of fibroblast function and collagen synthesis. It has been proposed that in systemic sclerosis there is excessive fibroblast stimulatory activity, due, for example, to fibroblast chemotactic factors including fibronectin, collagen fragments, platelet-derived growth factor, epidermal growth factor and C5a.[1] Fibroblast growth stimulating factors, including IL-1, -2 and -3, TGF-β and platelet-derived growth factor, are also of major importance.[58,95,96]

As yet no consistent strong class I or II major histocompatibility (MHC) antigen associations have been discovered in systemic sclerosis.[10,97] There are, however, significant HLA associations with individual autoantibodies. Therefore PM-Scl antibody correlates with HLA-DR3 and Scl-70 antibody with HLA-DR5.[30,98]

A useful working hypothesis for the pathophysiology of systemic sclerosis, suggested by Fleischmajer and Lebwohl, is shown in *Figure 16.94*.[99] It is proposed that following vascular injury, possibly caused by an autoimmune mechanism, exposure of type IV collagen or other substances leads to the recruitment of both B- and T-lymphocytes in addition to monocytes and mast cells. Excess T-helper cells stimulate the production of autoantibodies by B-cells, whereas the activated T-cells, macrophages and mast cells secrete a variety of cytokines, which in turn promote collagenosis.

Histologically, the edema of the early stage produces a picture that is indistinguishable from scleredema of Buschke.[100,101] In an established lesion the epidermis sometimes appears normal or there may be loss of the ridge pattern. There is often increased pigmentation of the basal cells, and melanophages are common in the superficial dermis. The characteristic change is that of thickening of the dermis by broad elongated swollen collagen bundles that often appear orientated parallel to the surface epithelium (*Figs 16.95, 16.96*). The individual fiber borders are frequently indistinct, giving the collagen a rather homogenous appearance. The elastic fibers are usually unaffected.

The fibrosis characteristically involves the subcutis and therefore fat cells are usually incorporated into the dermis.[102] Atrophic skin appendages, particularly eccrine sweat glands, are a common feature.

The arteries, especially the digital vessels, typically show endothelial cell swelling, intimal thickening and medial hypertrophy. Later they may become hyalinized (*Fig. 16.97*). In early lesions, endothelium-associated platelets are significantly increased in number.[63] Fibrin deposition is sometimes present and occasionally complete occlusion results in digital ulceration and gangrene. With chronicity there is a progressive reduction

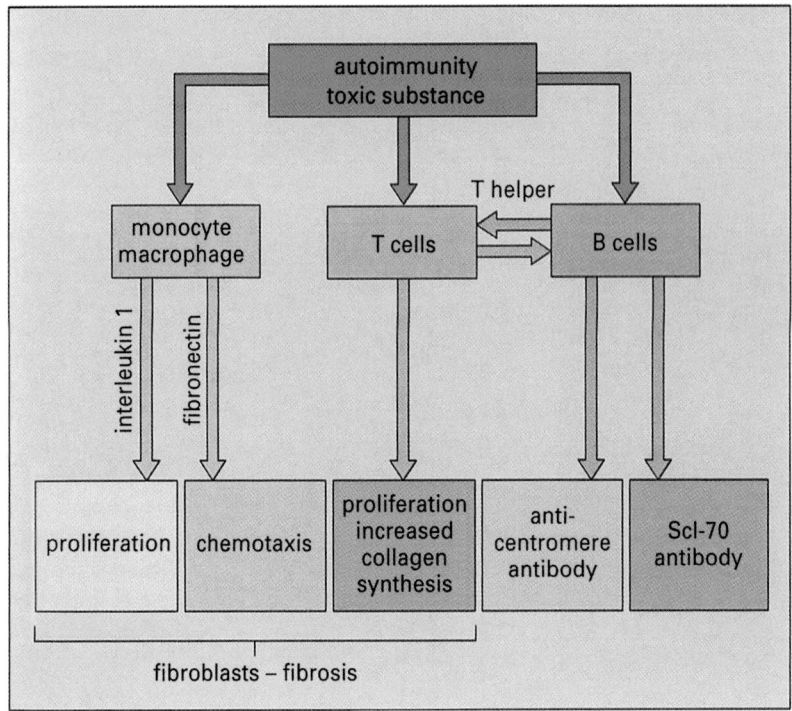

Fig. 16.94
The pathophysiology of systemic sclerosis. After Fleischmajer, R. and Lebwohl, M. (1986) Scleroderma. In: Thiers, B.H., Dobson, R.L. (eds) Pathogenesis of skin disease. Edinburgh: Churchill Livingstone, pp 233–247.

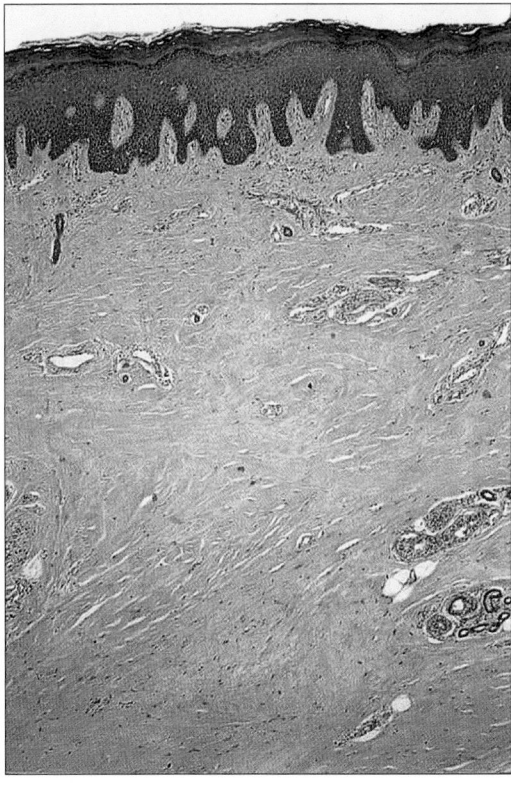

Fig. 16.95
Systemic sclerosis: scanning view of acral skin showing dermal fibrosis. The specimen was a foot amputation performed because of severe vascular involvement.

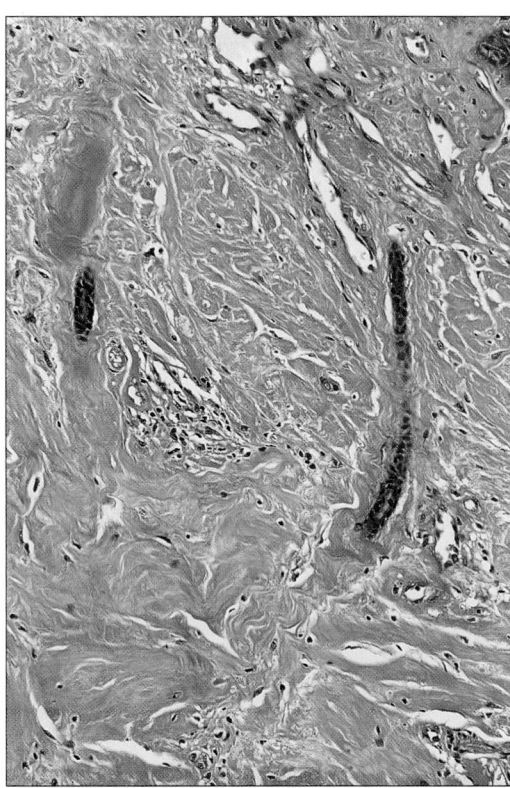

Fig. 16.96
Systemic sclerosis: the dermis is homogenized. Note the compressed eccrine ducts.

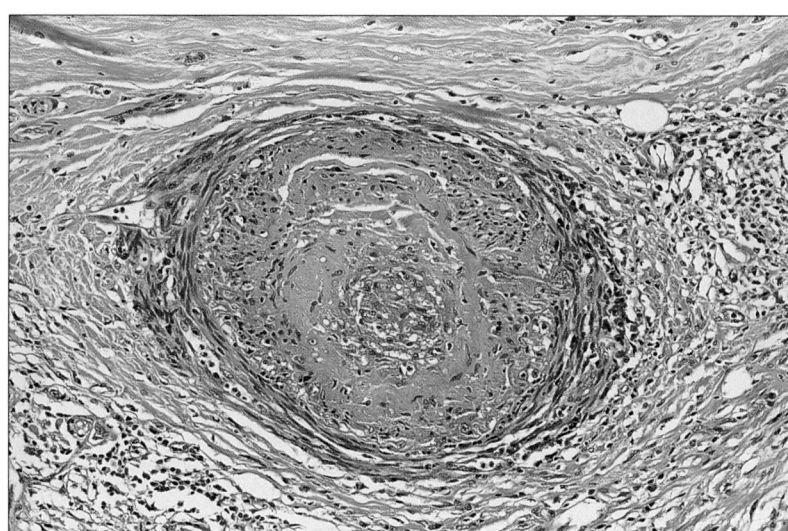

Fig. 16.97
Systemic sclerosis: severe vascular involvement characterized by intimal fibrosis and obliteration of the lumen. Note the surrounding chronic inflammation and scarring.

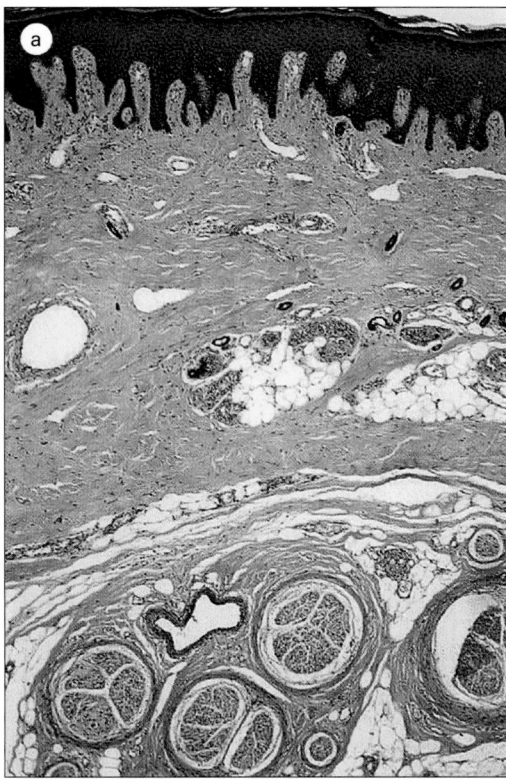

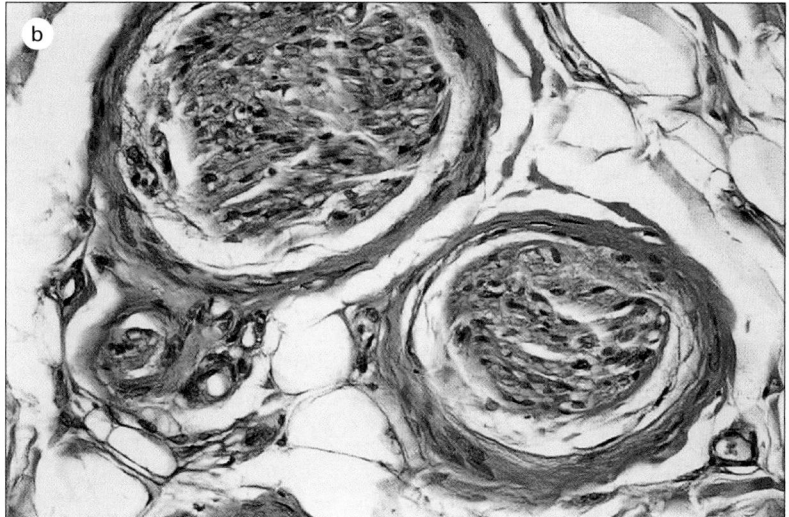

Fig. 16.98
(a, b) Systemic sclerosis: there is dramatic perineural fibrosis.

in the number of vessels, particularly in the more superficial dermis.[63] Perineural fibrosis is sometimes a feature and calcification is not uncommon (*Fig. 16.98*).

In early lesions there may be a chronic inflammatory cell infiltrate comprising lymphocytes, histiocytes and a few plasma cells around blood vessels and at the interface between the dermis and the subcutaneous fat.[1,103] T-helper cells predominate and increased numbers of dermal Langerhans' cells have been described.[63] Mast cells, usually activated, are often present in increased numbers.[104]

It is usually not possible to distinguish localized scleroderma (morphea) from systemic sclerosis on histological grounds, although the epidermis is usually normal in the localized form and vascular changes are less severe. In contrast, the inflammatory cell infiltrate is often heavier in the localized variant and commonly affects the reticular dermis.[103]

Examination of skeletal muscle may reveal focal scarring and a chronic inflammatory cell infiltrate (*Fig. 16.99*).[105] Features of muscle degeneration (vacuolation, homogenization with eosinophilia and loss of cross-striations) and regeneration (basophilia and sarcolemmal nuclear proliferation) similar to that seen in dermatomyositis may also be present. In the sclerotic phase there is atrophy and fibrosis.

Macroscopic examination of the kidney often reveals multiple infarcts, foci of hemorrhage and, occasionally, the features of renal cortical necrosis.[40] The histological appearances are similar to those of malignant hypertension and are characterized by the presence of fibrinoid necrosis, which particularly affects the interlobular and arcuate arteries, and ischemic glomerulosclerosis; an inflammatory cell infiltrate is not a feature (Fig. 16.100).[106] Characteristic of systemic sclerosis is the presence of edema and mucoid change in the initima of the interlobular arteries. There is also increased cellularity, giving rise to a characteristic 'onion skin' appearance with reduction in the lumen of the vessel (Fig. 16.101).

The histological features of sclerodermatous interstitial pneumonitis are indistinguishable from those seen in idiopathic fibrosing alveolitis (Fig. 16.102). Early stages are characterized by intra-alveolar edema with reactive pneumocytes and a variable infiltrate of macrophages, lymphocytes and occasional neutrophils.[30,107] Interstitial accumulations of lymphocytes and plasma cells are evident, sometimes associated with focal lymphoid hyperplasia; in older lesions, these are accompanied by the deposition of glycosaminoglycan-rich new collagen. End-stage disease is characterized by the development of variably sized cysts lined by metaplastic bronchiolar epithelium and containing abundant collagen and hyperplastic smooth muscle in their walls.[108]

The features of pulmonary hypertension are commonly present, particularly in patients with the CREST variant. Muscular arterioles are predominantly affected, although in late stages venules may also be involved, and show medial muscular hypertrophy and concentric myxoid-rich new collagen deposition in the intima with variable reduction in the diameter of the lumen.[108] In late stages, muscular atrophy and medial elastosis may be evident. Focal lymphocytic/plasma cell endovasculitis has been documented, suggesting a possible autoimmune pathogenesis.[108] Pulmonary hypertension correlates with the presence of anticentromere antibody.

Bronchiolitis predominantly affects the terminal and respiratory bronchioles. In addition to chronic inflammation, bronchiolar squamous metaplasia and variable scarring with luminal constriction may be seen.[108]

The most important gastrointestinal lesion is atrophy with fibrosis of the esophageal smooth muscle; similar changes may also develop in the small and large intestines. Vascular myointimal proliferation with luminal narrowing is also usually evident.[42] Reflux esophagitis may show

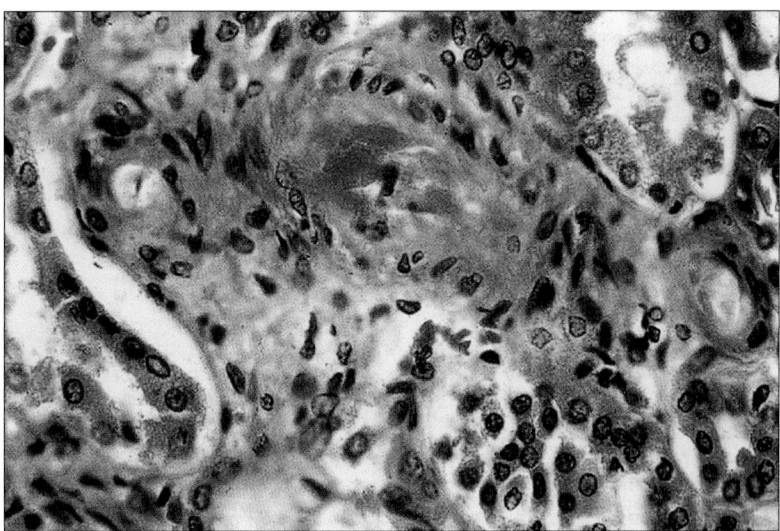

Fig. 16.100
Systemic sclerosis: kidney involvement showing arteriolar fibrinoid necrosis.

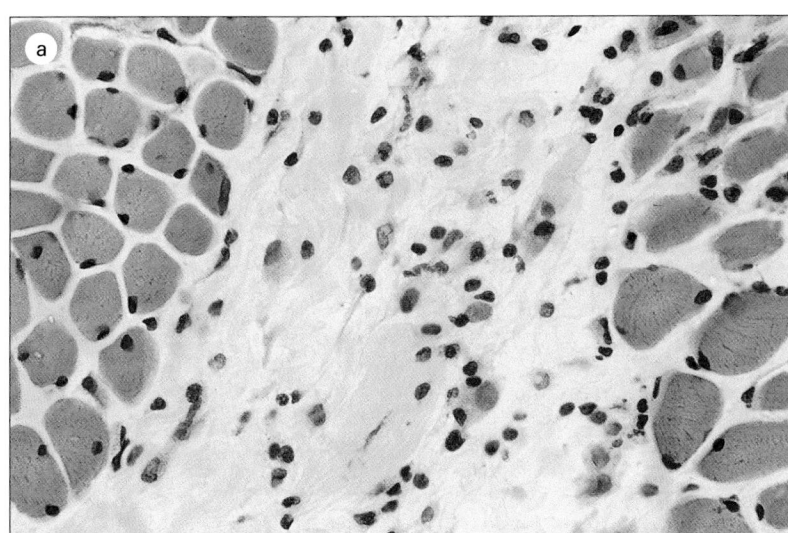

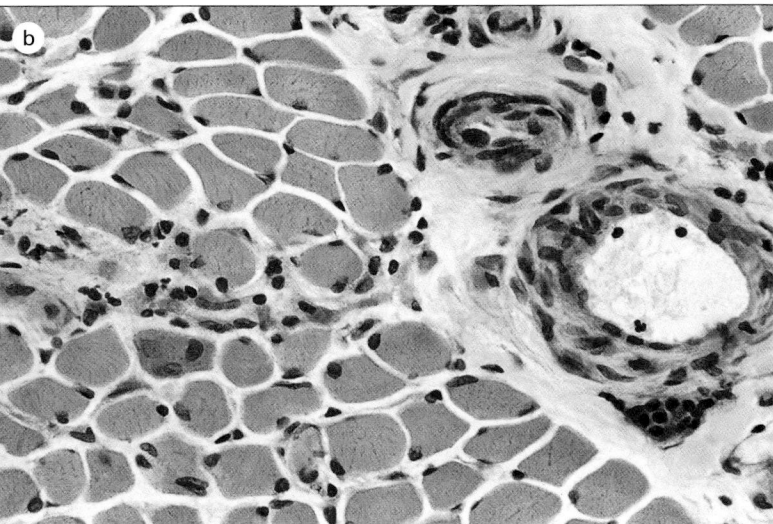

Fig. 16.99
(a, b) Systemic sclerosis: myositis characterized by a lymphohistiocytic infiltrate and focal skeletal muscle regeneration. Note the cytoplasmic basophilia.

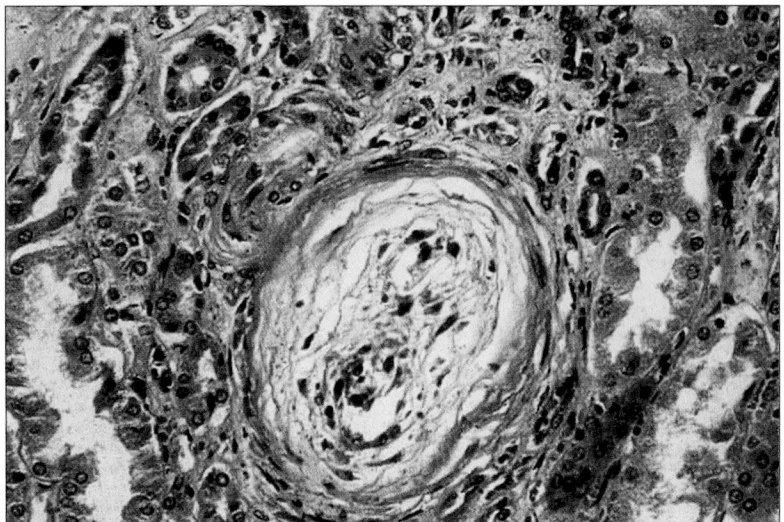

Fig. 16.101
Systemic sclerosis: kidney involvement showing excessive glycosaminoglycans and increased cellularity resulting in a characteristic 'onion skin' appearance.

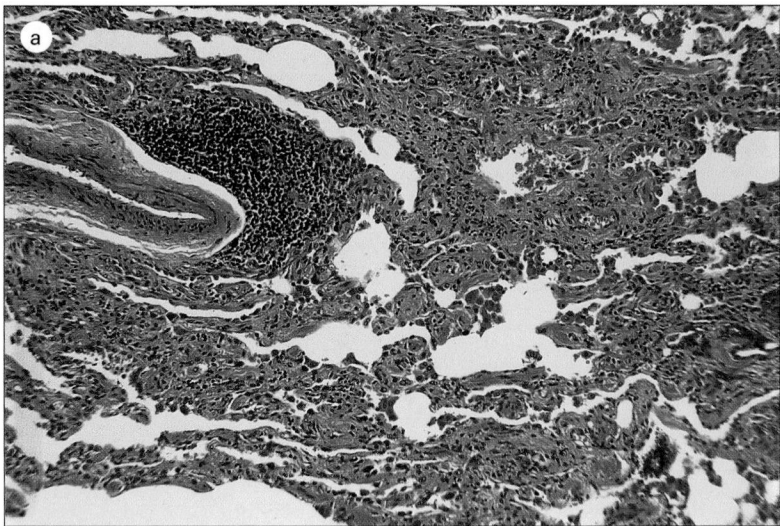
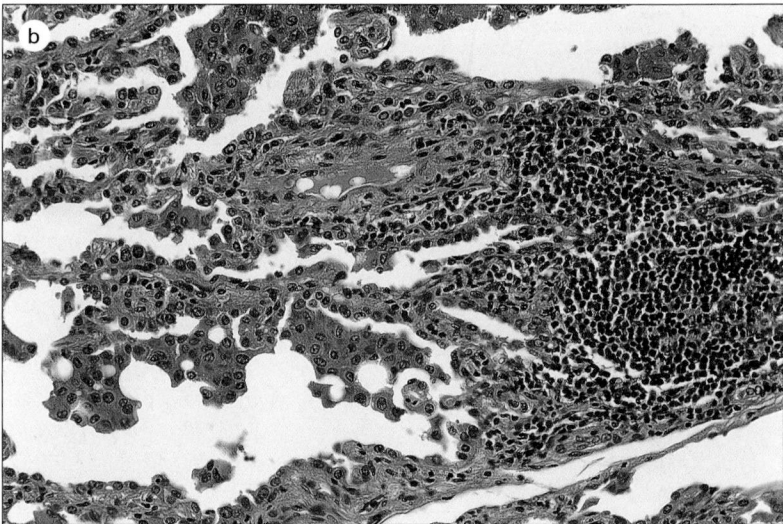

Fig. 16.102
(a, b) Systemic sclerosis: interstitial pneumonitis characterized by a heavy lymphocytic infiltrate and interstitial fibrosis.

erosions and areas of ulceration in addition to chronic inflammatory changes. In contrast to conventional diverticulae, those of systemic sclerosis are composed of all layers of the bowel wall.

Early myocardial changes are characterized by necrosis of muscle fibers accompanied by a chronic inflammatory cell and histiocytic infiltrate.[38] Subsequent fibrosis affects the right and left ventricles with equal frequency.[37] The major coronary arteries appear normal in systemic sclerosis, but arteriolar, endothelial and intimal proliferation accompanied by mural scarring is common.[109]

In active lesions, synovial biopsies show a heavy surface fibrin deposit.[43] There is adjacent chronic synovitis with an admixture of lymphocytes and plasma cells. Lymphoid follicles with germinal center formation as seen in rheumatoid arthritis are not a feature. With chronicity, synovial scarring supervenes.

References

1. Leroy, E.C., Black, C., Fleischmajer, R. et al (1988) Scleroderma (systemic sclerosis): classification, subsets and pathogenesis. *J Rheumatol*, **15**, 202–205.
2. Goodfield, M.J.D. (1994) The skin in systemic sclerosis. *Clin Dermatol*, **12**, 229–236.
3. Rodnan, G.P. (1979) Progressive systemic sclerosis: clinical features and pathogenesis of cutaneous involvement. *Clin Rheum Dis*, **5**, 49–79.
4. Siegel, R.C. (1977) Scleroderma. *Med Clin North Am*, **61**, 283–297.
5. Tuffanelli, D.L., Winkelmann, R.K. (1961) Systemic scleroderma: a clinical study of 727 cases. *Arch Dermatol*, **84**, 49–61.
6. Salerni, R., Rodnan, G.P., Leon, D.F. et al (1977) Pulmonary hypertension in the CREST syndrome variant of progressive systemic sclerosis (scleroderma). *Ann Intern Med*, **86**, 394–399.
7. Masi, A.T., Medsger, T.A. Jr, Rodnan, G.P. (1979) Methods and preliminary results of the scleroderma criteria cooperative study of the American Rheumatism Association. *Clin Rheum Dis*, **5**, 27–48.
8. Valentini, G. (1994) Classification of systemic sclerosis. *Clin Dermatol*, **12**, 207–216.
9. Rodnan, G.P., Medsger, T.A. Jr, Buckingham, R.B. (1975) Progressive systemic sclerosis – CREST syndrome: observations on natural history and late complications in 90 patients. *Arthritis Rheum*, **18** (Abstract), 423.
10. Medsger, T.A. (1994) Epidemiology of systemic sclerosis. *Clin Dermatol*, **12**, 207–216.
11. Medsger, T.A. Jr (1993) Systemic sclerosis (scleroderma), localized forms of scleroderma and calcinosis. In: McCarty, D.J., Koopman, W.J. (eds) Arthritis and allied conditions, 12th edn. Philadelphia: Lea & Febiger, pp 1253–1292.
12. Arnett, F.C., Cho, M., Chatterjee, S. et al (2001) Familial occurrence frequencies and relative risks for systemic sclerosis (scleroderma) in three United States cohorts. *Arthritis Rheum*, **44**, 1359–1362.
13. Steen, V.D., Conte, C., Santoro, D. et al (1988) Twenty-year incidence survey of systemic sclerosis (scleroderma). *Arthritis Rheum*, **31**, S57, A117.
14. Silman, A.J. (1991) Mortality from scleroderma in England and Wales. *Ann Rheum Dis*, **50**, 95–96.
15. Steen, V.D., Medsger, T.A. Jr (2001) Improvement in skin thickening in systemic sclerosis associated with improved survival. *Arthritis Rheum*, **44**, 2828–2835.
16. Clements, P.J., Hurwitz, E.L., Wong, W.K. et al (2000) Skin thickness score as a predictor and correlate of outcome in systemic sclerosis. High-dose versus low-dose penicillamine trial. *Arthritis Rheum*, **43**, 2445–2454.
17. Asboe-Hansen, G. (1987) Scleroderma. *J Am Acad Dermatol*, **17**, 102–108.
18. Lee, J.B., Ben-Aviv, D., Covello, S.P. (2001) The diagnostic quandary of hereditary haemorrhagic telangiectasia vs. CREST syndrome. *Br J Dermatol*, **145**, 646–649.
19. Sachsenberger-Studer, E.M., Prins, C., Saurat, J-H. et al (2000) Raynaud's phenomenon, anticentromere antibodies, and digital necrosis without sclerodactyly: an entity independent of scleroderma? *J Am Acad Dermatol*, **43**, 631–634.
20. Kouraklis, G., Glivavou, A., Karatzas, G. (2002) Primary biliary cirrhosis accompanied by CREST syndrome. *South Med J*, **95**, 1058–1059.
21. Tojo, J., Ohira, H., Suzuki, T. et al (2002) Clinicolaboratory characteristics of patients with primary biliary cirrhosis associated with CREST symptoms. *Hepatol Res*, **22**, 187–195.
22. Sánchez, J.L., Vázquez, M., Sánchez, N.P. (1983) Vitiligo-like macules in systemic scleroderma. *Arch Dermatol*, **119**, 129–133.
23. Yune, Y.H., Vix, V.A., Klatte, E.C. (1971) Early fingertip changes in scleroderma. *JAMA*, **215**, 1113–1116.
24. Thomas, J.R., Winkelmann, R.K. (1983) Vascular ulcers in scleroderma. *Arch Dermatol*, **119**, 803–807.
25. Fitzgerald, E.A., Connelly, C.S., Purcell, S.M. et al (1996) Familial lichen sclerosus et atrophicus in association with CREST syndrome: a case report. *Br J Dermatol*, **134**, 1144–1146.
26. Wooten, M.D., Scott, J.W., Miller, A.M. et al (1998) Chronic myelogenous leukemia and porphyria cutanea tarda in a patient with limited systemic sclerosis. *South Med J*, **91**, 493–495.
27. Lee, S.C., Yun, S.J., Lee, J.B. et al (2001) A case of porphyria cutanea tarda in association with idiopathic myelofibrosis and CREST syndrome. *Br J Dermatol*, **144**, 182–185.
28. Breit, S.N., Thornton, S.C., Penny, R. (1994) Lung involvement in scleroderma. *Clin Dermatol*, **12**, 243–252.
29. Breit, S.N., Cairns, D., Szentirmay, A. et al (1989) The presence of Sjögren's syndrome is a major determinant of the pattern of interstitial lung disease in scleroderma and other connective tissue diseases. *J Rheumatol*, **16**, 1043–1049.
30. Steen, V.D., Powell, D.L., Medsger, T.A. (1988) Clinical correlations and prognosis based on serum autoantibodies in patients with systemic sclerosis. *Arthritis Rheum*, **31**, 196–203.
31. Briggs, D.C., Vaughan, R.W., Welsh, K.I. et al (1991) Immunogenetic prediction of pulmonary fibrosis in systemic sclerosis. *Lancet*, **338**, 661–662.
32. Steen, V.D., Graham, G., Conte, C. et al (1992) Isolated diffusing capacity reduction in systemic sclerosis. *Arthritis Rheum*, **35**, 765–770.
33. Scorza, R., Caronni, M., Bazzi, S. et al (2002) Post-menopause is the main risk factor for developing isolated pulmonary hypertension in systemic sclerosis. *Ann N Y Acad Sci*, **966**, 238–246.
34. Clements, P.J., Furst, D.E. (1994) Heart involvement in systemic sclerosis. *Clin Dermatol*, **12**, 267–275.
35. Janosik, D.L., Osborn, T.G., Moore, T.L. et al (1989) Heart disease in systemic sclerosis. *Semin Arthritis Rheum*, **19**, 191–200.
36. Follansbee, W.P., Miller, T.R., Curtiss, E.I. et al (1990) A controlled clinicopathologic study of myocardial fibrosis in systemic sclerosis (scleroderma). *J Rheumatol*, **17**, 656–662.
37. Steen, V.D. (1994) Renal involvement in systemic sclerosis. *Clin Dermatol*, **12**, 253–258.
38. Helfrich, D.J., Banner, B., Steen, V.D. et al (1989) Renal failure in normotensive patients with systemic sclerosis. *Arthritis Rheum*, **32**, 1128–1134.
39. Sant, S.M., Murphy, G.M. (1994) Neurotropic ulceration in systemic sclerosis. *Clin Exp Dermatol*, **19**, 65–66.
40. Doss, B.J., Jacques, S.M., Mayes, M.D. et al (1998) Maternal scleroderma: placental findings and perinatal outcome. *Hum Pathol*, **28**, 1524–1530.
41. van Zander, J., Shaw, J.C. (2002) Papular and nodular mucinosis as a presenting sign of progressive systemic sclerosis. *J Am Acad Dermatol*, **46**, 304–306.
42. Kahan, A., Menkés, C-J. (1994) Gastrointestinal involvement in systemic sclerosis. *Clin Dermatol*, **12**, 259–265.
43. Schumacher, H.R. (1984) Joint and periarticular involvement in systemic sclerosis. *Clin Dermatol*, **12**, 277–282.
44. Rabinowitz, J.G., Twersky, J., Guttadauria, M. (1974) Similar bone manifestations of scleroderma and rheumatoid arthritis. *Am J Roentgenol Radium Ther Nucl Med*, **121**, 35–44.
45. Simon, N., Berko, G.Y., Schneider, I. (1977) Hepato-erythropoietic porphyria presenting as scleroderma and acrosclerosis in a sibling pair. *Br J Dermatol*, **96**, 663–668.
46. Masi, A.T. et al and the ARA Subcommittee for scleroderma (1980) Preliminary criteria for the classification of systemic sclerosis (scleroderma). *Arthritis Rheum*, **23**, 581–590.
47. Giordano, M., Valentini, G., Migliaresi, S. et al (1986) Different antibody patterns and different prognoses in patients with scleroderma with various extent of skin sclerosis. *J Rheumatol*, **13**, 911–916.
48. Ferri, C., Bernini, L., Cecchetti, R. et al (1991) Cutaneous and serologic subsets of systemic sclerosis. *J Rheumatol*, **18**, 1826–1832.
49. Walker, A. (1975) Occupational acro-osteolysis. *Proc R Soc Med*, **68**, 343–344.
50. Maricq, H.R. (1985) Vinyl chloride disease. In: Black, C.M., Myers, A.R. (eds) Systemic sclerosis (scleroderma). New York: Gower, pp 105–113.
51. Veltman, G., Lange, C.E., Juhe, S. et al (1975) Clinical manifestations and course of vinyl chloride disease. *Ann N Y Acad Sci*, **246**, 6–17.
52. Cohen, I.S., Mosher, N.B., O'Keefe, E.J. et al (1973) Cutaneous toxicity of bleomycin therapy. *Arch Dermatol*, **107**, 553–555.
53. Rustin, M.H.A., Bull, H.A., Ziegler, V. et al (1989) Silica exposure and silica associated systemic sclerosis. *Br J Dermatol*, **121** (Suppl. 34), 29.
54. Yamakage, A., Ishihawa, H. (1982) Generalised morphoea-like scleroderma occurring in people exposed to organic solvents. *Dermatologica*, **165**, 186–193.
55. Press, R.I., Peebles, C.L., Kumagay, Y. et al (1992) Antinuclear autoantibodies in women with silicone breast implants. *Lancet*, **340**, 1304–1307.
56. Fleischmajer, R., Perlish, J.S., Duncan, M. (1983) Scleroderma: a model for fibrosis. *Arch Dermatol*, **119**, 957–962.
57. Jayson, M.I.V. (1984) Systemic sclerosis: a collagen or a microvascular disease? *BMJ*, **288**, 1855–1857.
58. Matucci-Cerinic, M., Pignone, A., Biagini, M. et al (1994) Markers of disease activity in systemic sclerosis. *Clin Dermatol*, **12**, 291–297.
59. Fleischmajer, R., Perlish, J.S. (1980) Capillary alterations in scleroderma. *J Am Acad Dermatol*, **2**, 161–170.
60. Kahaleh, M.B., Sherer, G.K., Leroy, E.C. (1979) Endothelial injury in scleroderma. *J Exp Med*, **149**, 1326–1335.

61. Cohen, S., Johnson, A.R., Hurd, E. (1983) Cytotoxicity of sera from patients with scleroderma: effects on human endothelial cells and fibroblasts in culture. *Arthritis Rheum*, **26**, 170–178.
62. Kahaleh, M.B., Leroy, E.C. (1983) Endothelial injury in scleroderma: a protease mechanism. *J Lab Clin Med*, **101**, 553–560.
63. Prescott, R.J., Freemont, A.J., Jones, C.J.P. et al (1992) Sequential dermal microvascular and perivascular changes in the development of scleroderma. *J Pathol*, **166**, 255–263.
64. Winkelmann, R.K., Carapeto, F.J., Jordon, R.E. (1977) Direct immunofluorescence in the diagnosis of scleroderma syndromes. *Br J Dermatol*, **96**, 231–238.
65. Mannucci, P.M., Lombardi, R., Lattuada, A. et al (1987) Supranormal von Willebrand factor multimers in scleroderma. *Blood*, **73**, 1586–1591.
66. Kahaleh, M.B. (1991) Endothelin, an endothelial dependent vasoconstrictor in scleroderma. Enhanced production and profibrotic action. *Arthritis Rheum*, **34**, 978–983.
67. Kadono, T., Kikuchi, K., Ihn, H. et al (1988) Increased production of interleukin 6 and 8 in scleroderma fibroblasts. *J Rheumatol*, **25**, 296–301.
68. Roberts, A.B., Sporn, M.B., Assoian, R.K. et al (1986) Transforming growth factor type B: rapid induction of fibrosis and angiogenesis in vivo and stimulation of collagen formation in vitro. *Proc Natl Acad Sci USA*, **83**, 4167–4171.
69. Kurasawa, K., Hirose, K., Sano, H. et al (2000) Increased interleukin-17 production in patients with systemic sclerosis. *Arthritis Rheum*, **43**, 2455–2463.
70. Leask, A., Holmes, A., Abraham, D.J. (2002) Connective tissue growth factor: a new and important player in the pathogenesis of fibrosis. *Curr Rheumatol Rep*, **4**, 136–142.
71. Wallis, D.D., Tan, F.K., Kielty, C.M. et al (2001) Abnormalities in fibrillin 1-containing microfibrils in dermal fibroblast cultures from patients with sytemic sclerosis (scleroderma). *Arthritis Rheum*, **44**, 1855–1864.
72. Tan, F.K., Arnett, F.C., Antohi, S. et al (1999) Autoantibodies to the extracellular matrix microfibrillar protein, fibrillin-1, in patients with scleroderma and other connective tissue diseases. *J Immunol*, **163**, 1066–1072.
73. Kirby, L., Johnson, J., Lee, N. et al (2001) Fetal cell microchimerism in tissue from multiple sites in women with systemic sclerosis. *Arthritis Rheum*, **44**, 1848–1854.
74. Kawaguchi, Y., Kitani, A., Hara, M. et al (1992) Cytokine regulation of prolyl 4-hydroxylase production in skin fibroblast cultures from patients with systemic sclerosis. *J Rheumatol*, **19**, 1195–1201.
75. Herbert, C.M., Linberg, V.A., Jayson, M.I.V. et al (1974) Biosynthesis and maturation of skin collagen in scleroderma and effect of D-penicillamine. *Lancet*, **1**, 187–192.
76. Leroy, E.C. (1982) Pathogenesis of scleroderma (systemic sclerosis). *J Invest Dermatol*, **79** (Suppl. 1), S84–S87.
77. Uitto, J., Bauer, E.A., Eisen, A.Z. (1979) Scleroderma: increased biosynthesis of triple helical type I and type III procollagens associated with unaltered expression of collagenase by skin fibroblasts in culture. *J Clin Invest*, **64**, 921–930.
78. Fleischmajer, R., Perlish, J.S., Krieg, T. et al (1981) Variability in collagen and fibronectin synthesis by scleroderma fibroblasts in primary culture. *J Invest Dermatol*, **76**, 400–403.
79. Rudnicka, L., Varga, J., Christiano, A.M. et al (1994) Elevated expression of type VII collagen in the skin of patients with systemic sclerosis. *J Clin Invest*, **93**, 1709–1715.
80. Scharffetter, K., Lankat-Buttgereit, B., Krieg, T. (1988) Localisation of collagen mRNA in normal and scleroderma skin by *in situ* hybridisation. *Eur J Clin Invest*, **18**, 9–17.
81. Kähäri, V-M., Sandberg, M., Kalimo, H. et al (1988) Identification of fibroblasts responsible for increased collagen production in localised scleroderma by *in situ* hybridization. *J Invest Dermatol*, **90**, 664–670.
82. Rodnan, G.P., Lipinski, E., Luksick, J. (1979) Skin collagen content in progressive systemic sclerosis (scleroderma) and localized scleroderma. *Arthritis Rheum*, **22**, 130–140.
83. Buckingham, R.B., Prince, R.K., Rodnan, G.P. (1983) Progressive systemic sclerosis dermal fibroblasts synthesize increased amounts of glycosaminoglycans. *J Lab Clin Med*, **101**, 659–669.
84. Catoggio, L.J., Bernstein, P.M., Black, C.M. et al (1983) Serological markers in progressive systemic sclerosis: clinical correlations. *Ann Rheum Dis*, **42**, 23–27.
85. Tan, E.M., Rodnan, G.P., Garcia, I. et al (1980) Diversity of antinuclear antibodies in progressive systemic sclerosis: anti-centromere antibody and its relationship to CREST syndrome. *Arthritis Rheum*, **23**, 617–625.
86. Shero, J.H., Bordwell, B., Rothfield, N.F. et al (1986) High titers of autoantibodies to topoisomerase 1 (Scl-70) in sera from scleroderma patients. *Science*, **231**, 737–740.
87. Chen, Z.Y., Fedrick, J.A., Pandey, J.P. et al (1985) Anticentromere antibody and immunoglobulin allotypes in scleroderma. *Arch Dermatol*, **121**, 339–344.
88. Chorzelski, T.P., Jablonska, S., Beuner, E.H. et al (1985) Anticentromere antibody: an immunological marker of a subset of systemic sclerosis. *Br J Dermatol*, **113**, 381–389.
89. Dovas, A.S., Achten, M., Tan, E.M. (1979) Identification of a nuclear protein (Scl-70) as a unique target of human anti-nuclear antibodies in scleroderma. *J Biol Chem*, **254**, 10514–10522.
90. Vázquez-Abad, D., Rothfield, N.F. (1995) Autoantibodies in systemic sclerosis. *Int Rev Immunol*, **12**, 145–157.
91. Mackel, A.M., De Lustro, F., Harper, F.E. et al (1982) Antibodies to collagen in scleroderma. *Arthritis Rheum*, **25**, 522–531.
92. Editorial (1991) Antibodies to endothelial cells. *Lancet*, **337**, 649–650.
93. Seibold, J.R., Medsger, T.A. Jr, Winkelstein, A. (1982) Immune complexes in progressive systemic sclerosis (scleroderma). *Arthritis Rheum*, **25**, 1167–1173.
94. Whiteside, T.L., Kumagai, Y., Roumm, A.D. et al (1983) Suppressor cell function and T lymphocyte sub-populations in peripheral blood of patients with progressive systemic sclerosis. *Arthritis Rheum*, **7**, 841–847.
95. Schmidt, J.A., Mizel, S.B., Cohen, D. et al (1982) Interleukin 1: a potential regulator of fibroblast proliferation. *J Immunol*, **128**, 2177–2182.
96. Gay, S., Jones, R.E. Jr, Huang, C.Q. et al (1989) Immunohistologic demonstration of PDGF and cis-oncogene expression in scleroderma. *J Invest Dermatol*, **92**, 301–303.
97. Black, C., Briggs, D., Welsh, K. (1992) The immunogenetic background of scleroderma – an overview. *Clin Exp Dermatol*, **17**, 73–78.
98. Oddis, C.V., Okano, Y., Rudert, W.A. et al (1992) Serum autoantibody to the nuclear antigen PN-Scl. Clinical and immunogenetic associations. *Arthritis Rheum*, **35**, 1211–1217.
99. Fleischmajer, R., Lebwohl, M. (1986) Scleroderma. In: Thiers, B.H., Dobson, R.L. (eds) Pathogenesis of skin disease. Edinburgh: Churchill Livingstone, pp 233–247.
100. O'Leary, P.A., Montgomery, H., Ragsdale, W.E. (1957) Dermato-histopathology of various forms of scleroderma. *Arch Dermatol*, **75**, 78–87.
101. Krieg, T., Meurer, M. (1988) Systemic scleroderma. Clinical and pathophysiologic aspects. *J Am Acad Dermatol*, **18**, 457–481.
102. Fleischmajer, R., Damiano, V., Nedwich, A. (1972) Alteration of subcutaneous tissue in systemic scleroderma. *Arch Dermatol*, **105**, 59–66.
103. Fleischmajer, R., Perlish, J.S., Reeves, J.R.T. (1977) Cellular infiltrates in scleroderma skin. *Arthritis Rheum*, **20**, 975–984.
104. Claman, H.N. (1989) On scleroderma: mast cells, endothelial cells and fibroblasts. *JAMA*, **262**, 1206–1209.
105. Medsger, T.A., Rodnan, G.P., Moossy, J. (1968) Skeletal muscle involvement in progressive systemic sclerosis. *Arthritis Rheum*, **11**, 554–568.
106. Kahaleh, M.B., Leroy, E.C. (1979) Progressive systemic sclerosis: kidney involvement. *Clin Rheum Dis*, **5**, 167–184.
107. Harrison, N.K., Myers, A.R., Corrin, B. et al (1991) Structural features of interstitial lung disease in systemic sclerosis. *Am Rev Resp Dis*, **144**, 706–713.
108. Yousem, S.A. (1990) The pulmonary pathological manifestations of the CREST syndrome. *Hum Pathol*, **21**, 467–474.
109. D'Angelo, W.A., Fries, J.F., Masi, A.T. et al (1969) Pathologic observations in systemic sclerosis/scleroderma. *Am J Med*, **46**, 428–440.

Localized scleroderma

Localized scleroderma (morphea) constitutes a group of diseases characterized by thickening or sclerosis of the dermis with loss of subcutaneous fat, sometimes with involvement of the underlying skeletal muscle.[1-6] There is predilection for children and young adults, and females are more frequently affected.[7-9] A congenital case has been documented.[10] It is not usually associated with severe systemic symptoms or Raynaud's phenomenon, is often self-limited and in general has a good prognosis, although the linear variant in particular may be very disabling and often disfiguring, especially in children.[2] The linear and deep variants may be associated with arthralgias, synovitis, uveitis and joint contractures.[11] A large study of patients with morphea has found mild internal involvement consisting of abnormal lower sphincter pressure and peristaltic failure in the esophagus and slightly impaired carbon monoxide diffusion in the lung in up to 19% of patients.[12] These abnormalities do not result in clinical symptoms and do not affect prognosis adversely. A rare case has been documented in which morphea induced severe extrapulmonary thoracic restriction.[13] Although the plaques and, to a lesser extent, the linear lesions often improve with time, the contractures and hemiatrophy are permanent.[3] Imaging studies frequently reveal muscle atrophy and leg length discrepancy.[14] Localized scleroderma may occur after trauma, radiotherapy and silicone implants.[15-18] It has also been described in association with bromocriptine therapy.[19]

The precise relationship between localized scleroderma and systemic sclerosis is uncertain. Because of clinical and pathological overlap, some authors believe that the two conditions represent extreme ends of a spectrum of connective tissue damage in a manner similar to the relationship between discoid and systemic lupus erythematosus. Indeed,

patients rarely have both morphea and progressive systemic sclerosis (the former usually preceding the latter); this phenomenon occurs so infrequently, however, that most believe that the relationship is purely coincidental.[2] Alternatively, the features of these two disorders may merely represent a common manifestation of tissue damage caused by quite different mechanisms, analogous to the wide range of pathogenetic factors which may result in the histological appearance of allergic vasculitis.

Clinical features

Localized scleroderma includes a variety of conditions, which may arise independently, but which frequently occur together:

- Plaque-form (the most common variant)
- Bullous morphea
- Guttate lesions
- Linear morphea including facial hemiatrophy
- Generalized morphea
- Subcutaneous scleroderma (morphea profunda)
- Disabling pansclerotic morphea of children.[2,20-22]

Plaque-form and linear morphea

Plaque-form and linear morphea are more common in females (3:1) and, in contrast to progressive systemic sclerosis, often occur in childhood.[1] Linear morphea develops before the end of the first decade in up to 20% of patients and by the fourth decade in up to 75%. Localized plaques occur a little later in life, although 75% of patients are between 20 and 50 years of age at presentation.

Morphea usually develops slowly and the onset may manifest as erythema and edema. An established lesion is typically circumscribed, ivory or white in color, and densely sclerotic (*Fig. 16.103*).[2] A characteristic feature is the presence of a violaceous border, an indicator of disease activity (*Figs 16.104, 16.105*).[2] As the lesion subsides, atrophy, loss of hair and sebaceous glands and variable hypo- and hyperpigmentation become evident (*Fig. 16.106*).[20] Vesicles, bullae, purpura and telangiectasia may rarely be present, particularly in the generalized variant.[1,23] Tense bullae, due to subepidermal edema, are a rare manifestation that has been described in morphea, including the profunda variant.[24] They are thought to develop as a consequence of both trauma and lymphatic obstruction. The latter is suggested by the finding of lymphatic dilatation in 77% of biopsies from patients with this variant of morphea.[25] It has also been suggested that this type of morphea may be related to release of major basic protein from eosinophils.[25]

The plaque form of morphea usually consists of multiple, round or oval, sometimes pruritic, 2–15 cm diameter lesions, which are usually bilateral and asymmetrical in distribution (*Fig. 16.107*). Lesions occur (in decreasing order of frequency) on the thorax and neck, the lower

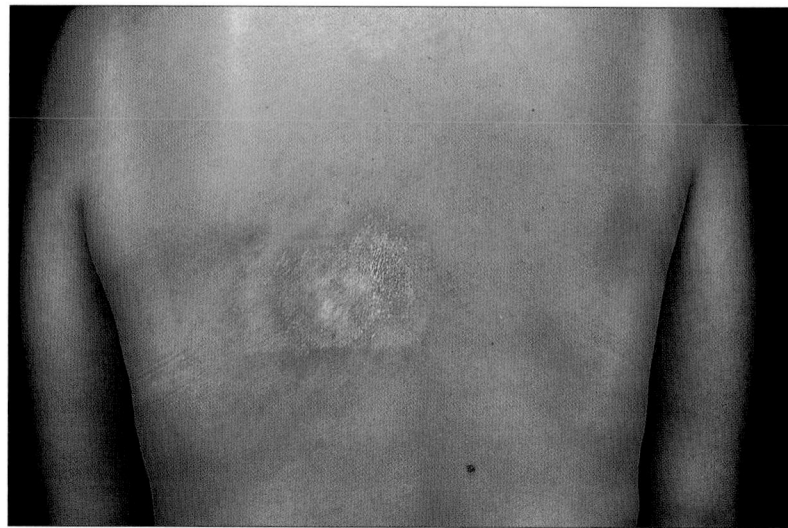

Fig. 16.105
Morphea: the thorax is a very commonly affected site. By courtesy of the Institute of Dermatology, London, UK.

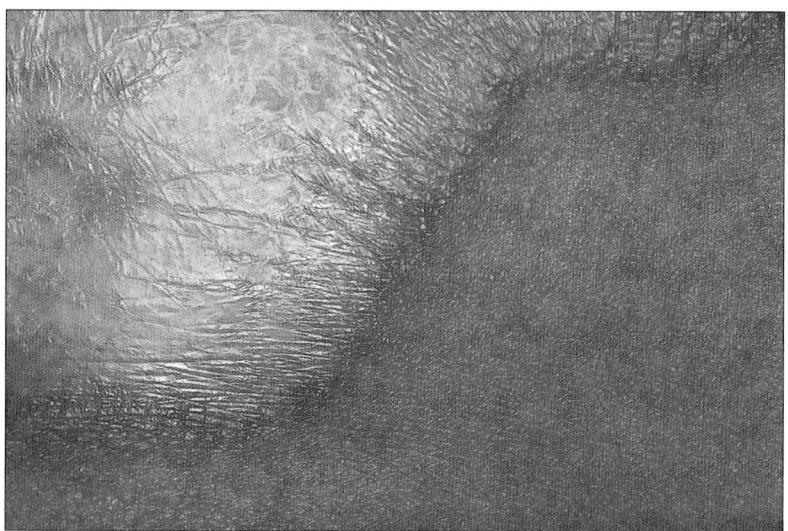

Fig. 16.103
Morphea: characteristic white sclerotic plaque. By courtesy of the Institute of Dermatology, London, UK.

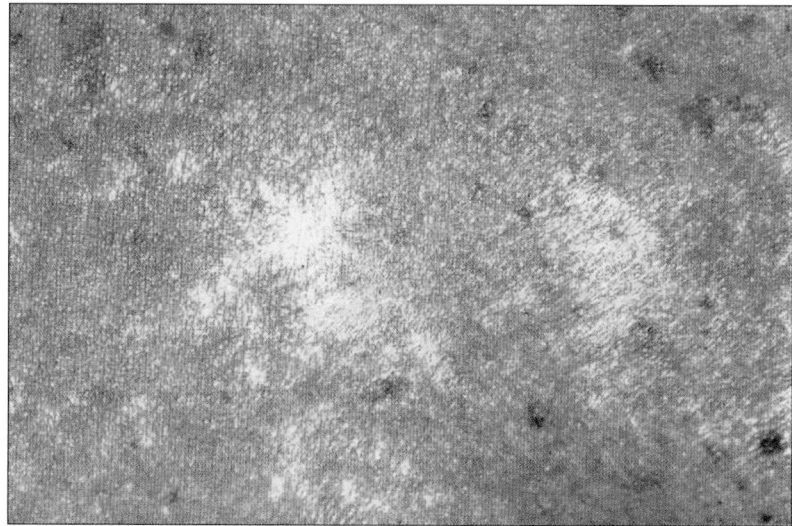

Fig. 16.106
Morphea: atrophic lesions showing variable hypo- and hyperpigmentation. By courtesy of R.A. Marsden, MD, St George's Hospital, London, UK.

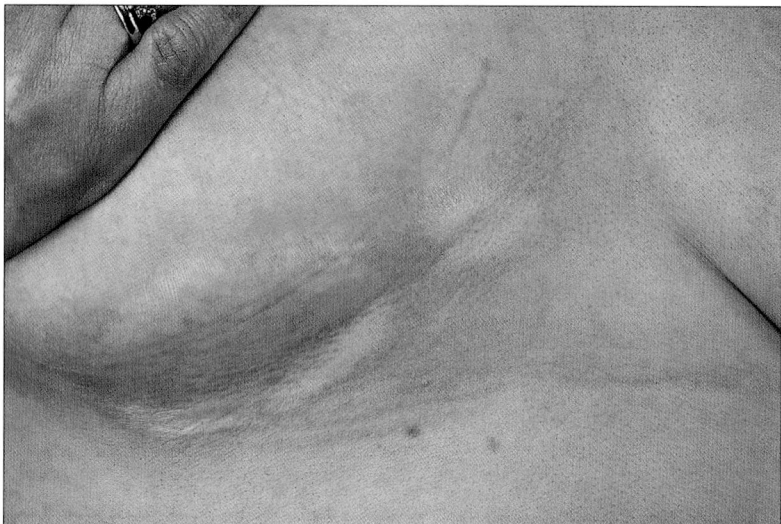

Fig. 16.104
Morphea: in this example the violaceous border is apparent. By courtesy of the Institute of Dermatology, London, UK.

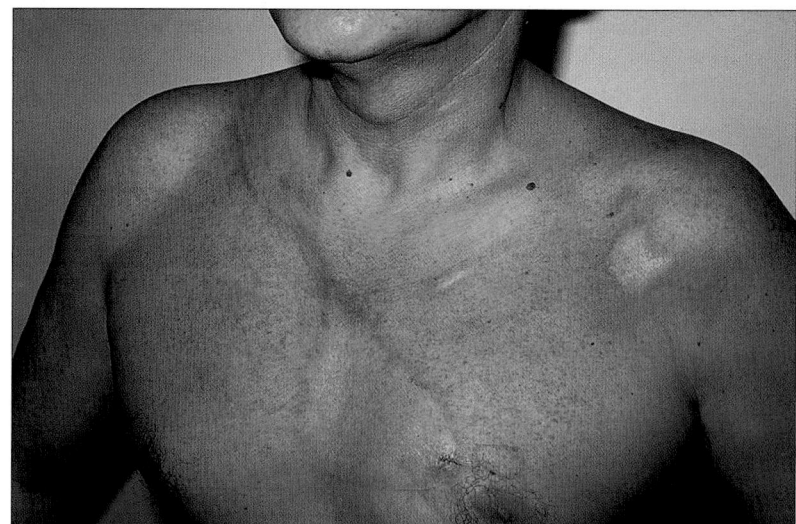

Fig. 16.107
Morphea: multiple asymmetrical lesions are present. Note the characteristic en coup de sabre. By courtesy of D. McGibbon, MD, St Thomas' Hospital, London, UK.

extremities, the upper extremities and the face; the axillae, umbilical region, perineum and perianal area are usually spared (*Fig. 16.108*).

The so-called linear atrophoderma of Moulin, which presents with band-like lesions following Blaschko's lines, is likely to represent a variant of linear morphea.[26]

Linear morphea is usually solitary and unilateral in distribution. Lesions are found (in decreasing order of frequency) on the lower limbs, the upper limbs, the frontoparietal region (e.g. en coup de sabre) and the anterior thorax (*Fig. 16.109*). Linear lesions may involve both the upper and lower extremities simultaneously and on occasion plaque-type morphea is also present.[2] Although the clinical appearances of linear scleroderma are very similar to those of the plaque form, lesions tend to show more pigmentary change and the violaceous border is less conspicuous. Linear morphea may affect the underlying skeletal muscle and even bone, giving rise to contractures and deformities. Calcification of skeletal muscle may exceptionally occur.[27] An association with melorheostosis has been described.[28,29] Cases presenting with hypertrichosis are also documented.[29-31] Occasionally it follows Blaschko's lines.[32,33]

Frontoparietal linear morphea presents as a densely sclerotic plaque extending from the eyebrow onto the scalp and may be associated with alopecia. Involvement of the cheek, nose and upper lip has also been documented.[20] Progression of the lesion results in the development of a groove and hence the term 'en coup de sabre' (*Fig. 16.110*). Gingival recession has occasionally been documented.[34] Familial occurrence is exceptional and bilateral lesions are rare.[35-37] A further complication, particularly in children, is the development of facial hemiatrophy (Romberg's disease) (*Fig. 16.111*).[2] Exceptionally, central nervous system

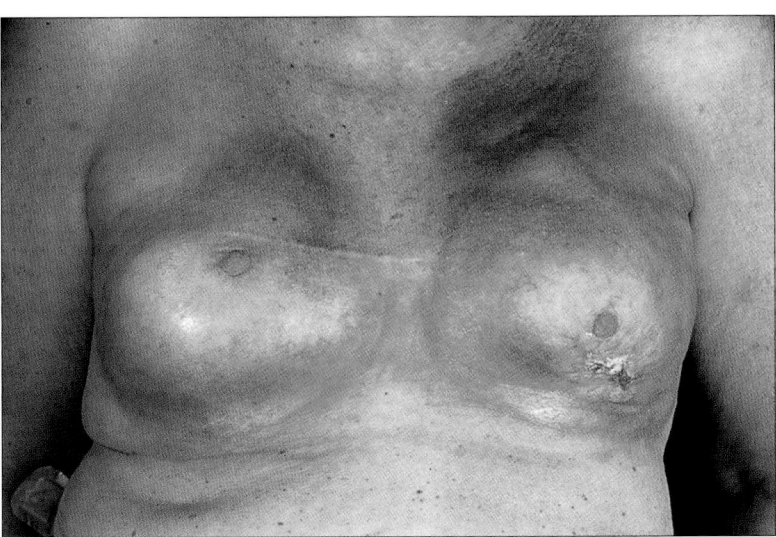

Fig. 16.108
Morphea: extensive lesions can be very disfiguring, as in this patient showing bilateral breast involvement. By courtesy of the Institute of Dermatology, London, UK.

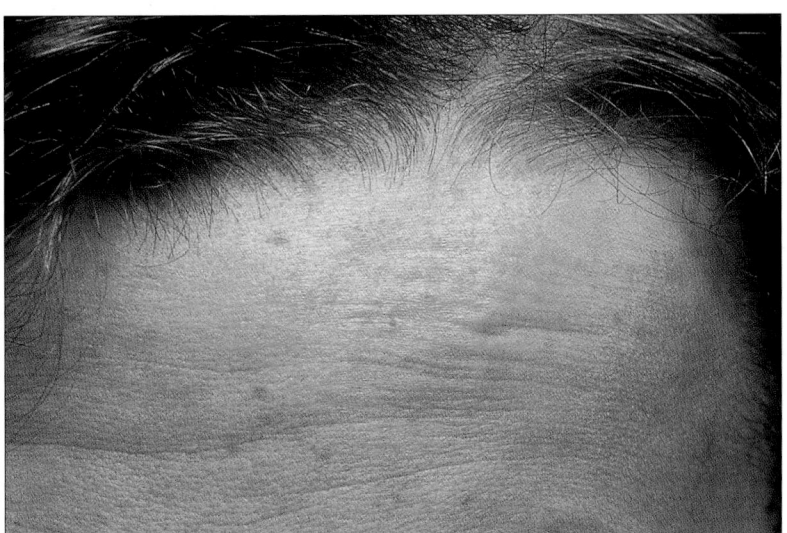

Fig. 16.110
Linear morphea: en coup de sabre. By courtesy of the Institute of Dermatology, London, UK.

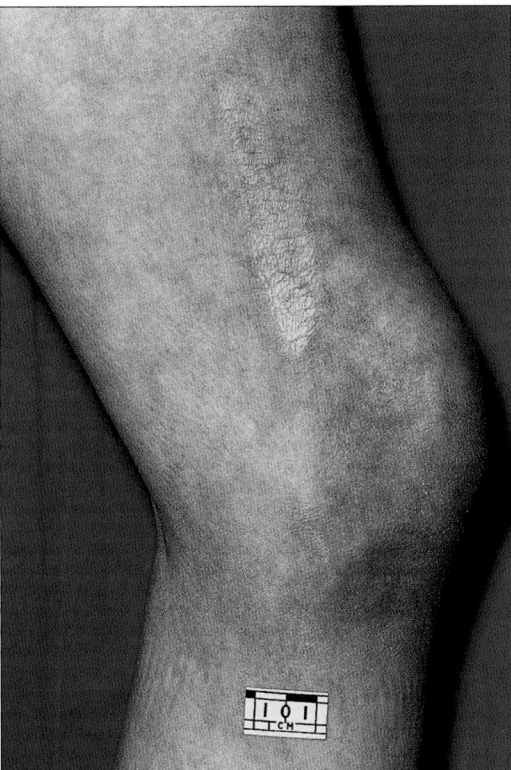

Fig. 16.109
Linear morphea: atrophic lesion on the thigh. By courtesy of R.A. Marsden, MD, St George's Hospital, London, UK.

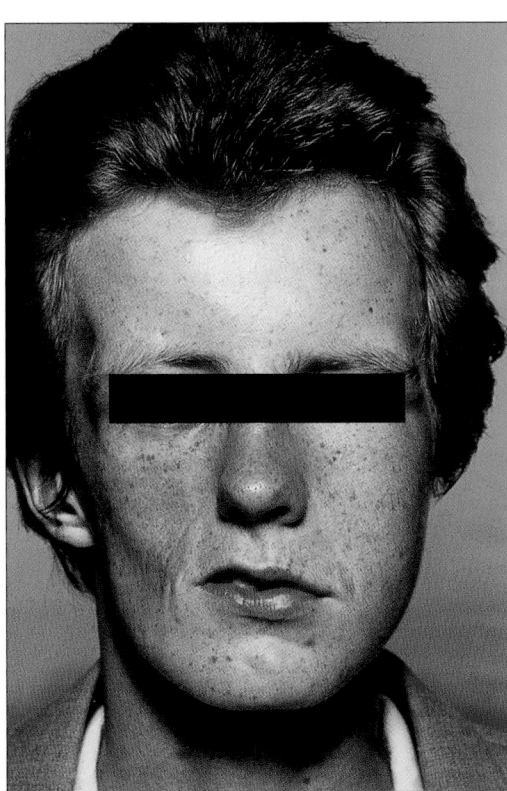

Fig. 16.111
Linear morphea: severe facial hemiatrophy. By courtesy of D. McGibbon, MD, St Thomas' Hospital, London, UK.

involvement may occur.[38] Linear morphea has also been described in association with hereditary deficiency of C2.[39]

Guttate morphea

In guttate morphea lesions are multiple, small (2–10 mm), non-indurated and yellowish-white, and are limited by a delicate lilac border.[1,20] Typically there is no hyperkeratosis or follicular plugging. Coalescence of lesions to form plaques is not uncommon. Guttate morphea most commonly presents on the upper back and shoulders, but the lower back, chest and abdomen may also be affected.[1] There is much clinical (and histological) overlap between the lesions of guttate morphea and lichen sclerosus and it is worthy of note that the two disorders are frequently seen together.[2,40]

Generalized morphea

Generalized morphea, which most commonly affects the trunk and abdomen, is characterized by widespread large lesions resembling plaque-type morphea.[1,41] These may merge and in many patients almost the entire skin surface is involved. Extension to the subcutaneous fat and muscle sometimes results in severe contractures and disabling and disfiguring deformities (*Fig. 16.112*). Generalized morphea may occasionally prove fatal, for example, due to pneumonia. Rarely systemic involvement supervenes.[2] An association with porphyria cutanea tarda has been described.[42] Occurrence with Felty's syndrome and after antitetanus vaccination has also been reported.[43,44] A case of unilateral generalized morphea has been documented.[45] A patient with this form of the disease developed multiple acral adult myofibromas.[46]

Subcutaneous scleroderma

Subcutaneous scleroderma (morphea profunda, nodular scleroderma, keloidal scleroderma) presents clinically as nodular or keloid-like lesions.[20,24,47,48] The abdomen, sacral region and the extremities are affected most commonly.[2]

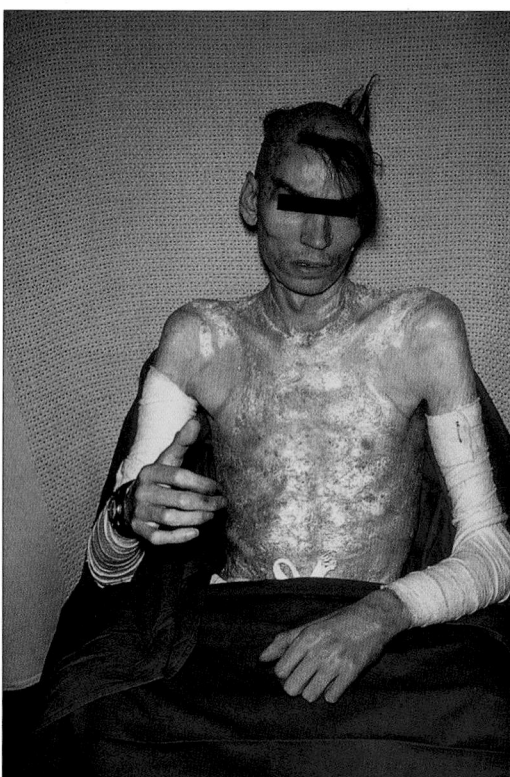

Fig. 16.112
Generalized morphea: a very advanced extreme example showing almost complete involvement of the skin, hair loss and contractures. By courtesy of R.A. Marsden, MD, St George's Hospital, London, UK.

Disabling pansclerotic morphea of children

Disabling pansclerotic morphea of children is a particularly aggressive and mutilating variant, and involves fascia, muscle and bone in addition to the deep dermis and subcutaneous fat. It usually affects the scalp, face, trunk and extremities.[1,49,50] Patients may also have arthralgias, contractures that particularly affect the extensor surfaces of the extremities and osteoporosis.[20,49] This exceedingly severe variant of localized scleroderma is unremitting and permanent, and is fortunately very rare. Some patients have had abnormal respiratory function tests and diminished esophageal motility suggesting overlap with systemic sclerosis.[49] Blood eosinophilia is also seen.[49] A rare complication of squamous cell carcinoma has been documented.[51,52] A further exceptional association is that of hypogammaglobulinemia.[53]

Associated conditions

Localized scleroderma has been associated with a variety of conditions including arthralgia, carpal tunnel syndrome, unilateral Raynaud's phenomenon, intermittent abdominal pain and spina bifida.[20,21] Concurrent lichen planus, often in the company of lichen sclerosus, has also been documented.[1] Other associations include vitiligo, alopecia areata, granuloma annulare, lupus anticoagulant, DLE, SCLE, SLE, xanthomatosis, elastosis perforans serpiginosa, B-cell lymphoma, sarcoidosis, necrotizing vasculitis and necrobiotic xanthogranuloma.[1,2,54–67]

Pathogenesis and histological features

The etiology and pathogenesis of localized scleroderma are unknown. Theories of causation have included trauma, hormonal influences and familial aspects.[20,68,69] Thus localized scleroderma may present or worsen during pregnancy, the menarche or the menopause. The condition has also been described following chickenpox and measles.[1,70] An infectious etiology has received some support with the identification by immunohistochemistry, silver stains and polymerase chain reaction (PCR) of *Borrelia burgdorferi* in biopsies of lesional skin combined with the presence of elevated antibody levels.[71–76] Lymphoproliferative responses to this organism have also been reported in patients with morphea.[77] Most studies, however, have cast doubt on the association between morphea and *B. burgdorferi*.[78–86] It has also been shown that false positive tests for *B. burgdorferi* with indirect immunofluorescence and even enzyme-linked immunosorbent assay (ELISA) are not uncommon.[87] It is therefore more likely that *B. burgorferi* is not etiologically linked to localized morphea. A further possibility is that only certain subspecies of Borrelia are capable of inducing the disease.[88,89] However, this theory has not been substantiated by different studies from the same country.[89]

The occasional simultaneous occurrence of localized scleroderma and systemic sclerosis has led some authors to postulate a shared pathogenetic mechanism.[21,90] In both conditions increased serum levels of procollagen type I carboxyterminal propeptide have been reported.[91] Similarly, the presence of localized scleroderma in both discoid and systemic lupus erythematosus and dermatomyositis has been cited as additional evidence for an immunological basis.[1,92–94] It is also of interest that the clinical appearances and histology of late GVHD are very similar to those of scleroderma (see p. 254).

Antinuclear antibodies may be detected in approximately 70% of patients with morphea.[95] Homogeneous, nucleolar and speckled patterns have all been recognized, but the first is the most common variant.[96] Rheumatoid factor, anti-dsDNA, anticentromere and anti-Scl-70 antibodies have also been documented but are rare.[41] Anti-ssDNA antibodies are present in 38–75% of patients, are frequently of the IgM subclass, and are found more often in linear and generalized morphea than in the plaque form.[41,97] Antihistone antibodies have been reported in up to 50% of cases.[99] Most antibodies are more commonly seen in patients with active or widespread disease.[94] Antinuclear antibodies are frequent in children with localized scleroderma and often have specificity for denatured DNA and for high mobility group proteins.[99] Increased serum levels of ICAM-1 have also been reported, particularly in patients with prominent involvement.[100] Peripheral eosinophilia is sometimes a feature, particularly in the pansclerotic morpheic variant.[1,49]

Direct immunofluorescence studies have demonstrated immuno-globulin (usually IgM) and complement at the basement membrane region and around the dermal vasculature in about 35% of patients.[1] Generalized morphea is more often positive than the plaque and linear variants.

Immunohistochemical studies of established lesions reveal increase in the number of Factor XIIIa+ cells and decrease in the number of CD34+ cells.[101,102]

The histological features of localized scleroderma involve both the dermis and subcutaneous fat; a deep incisional biopsy is therefore indicated if scleroderma is suspected.[41,97] Biopsies from early lesions often show very subtle histological findings and are often non-specific. The histological diagnosis may be more difficult to establish in biopsies of lesions from guttate morphea as the changes tend to be more focal and superficial. In an established indurated plaque, the epidermis is usually normal or occasionally flattened. Mucin deposition is not usually a feature but may be occasionally present. The papillary dermis either appears unaffected or shows a rather homogenized change (*Fig. 16.113*). The most striking features are seen in the reticular dermis, where the collagen bundles are swollen, intensely eosinophilic, and orientated parallel to the surface (*Figs 16.114–16.116*). There is also involvement of the septa of the subcutaneous fat; this is associated with atrophy of the adipocytes and subsequent fibrosis, resulting in an apparent increase in thickness of the dermis.[1] Hair follicles and sebaceous glands may be atrophic or absent and the eccrine ducts often appear compressed within the densely sclerotic dermis. Due to fibrous replacement of the sub-cutaneous fat, the eccrine glands appear to be situated abnormally high within the dermis rather than at the dermosubcuticular interface. In rare cases only the superficial reticular dermis is affected.[103]

An important feature of localized scleroderma, especially in the early stages, is a dense, chronic inflammatory cell infiltrate of lymphocytes, histiocytes and plasma cells; some authors believe this to be the initial feature (*Fig. 16.117*).[41] The infiltrate may surround blood vessels and appendages and tends to be particularly conspicuous in the dermis in addition to the subcutaneous fat (*Fig. 16.118*). In the linear and generalized variants in particular, the inflammatory changes may affect the underlying skeletal muscle.

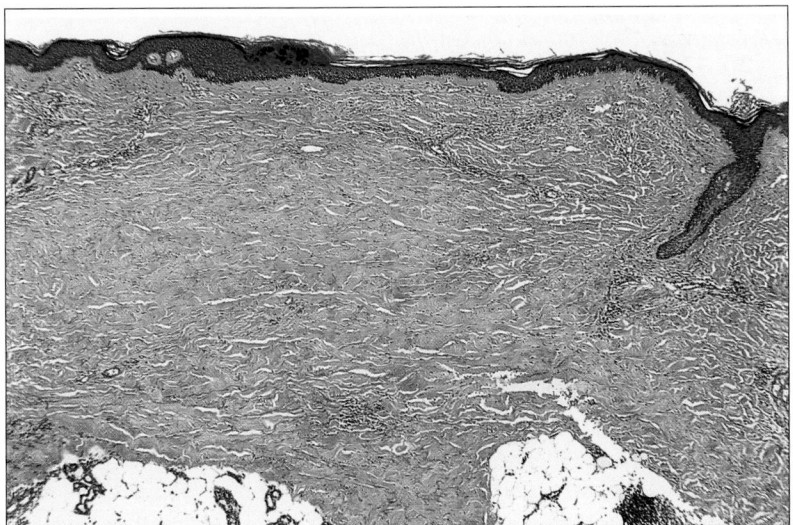

Fig. 16.113
Morphea: the dermis is thickened by dense collagen bundles. Note the perivascular infiltrate.

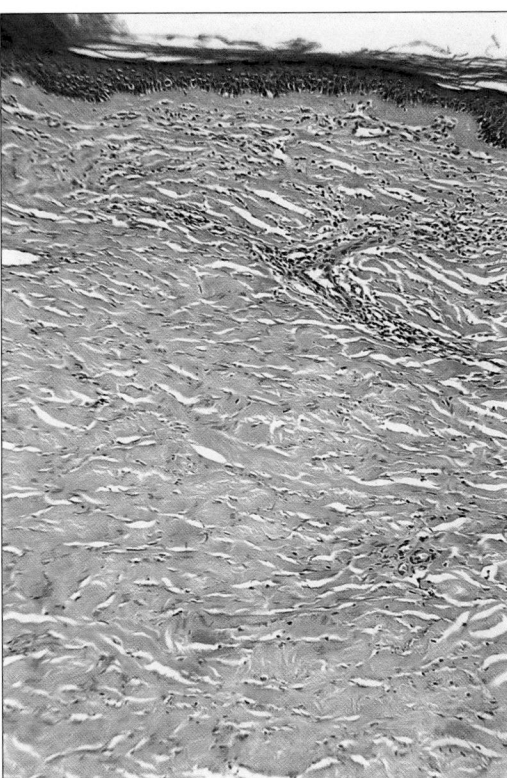

Fig. 16.114
Morphea: the collagen fibers are eosinophilic and swollen.

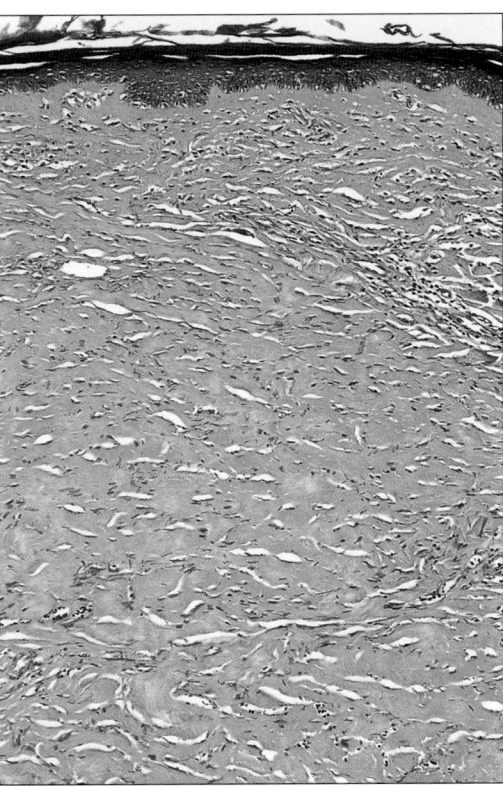

Fig. 16.115
Morphea: the changes are highlighted with this Masson's trichrome stained section. In this example, the papillary dermis is involved.

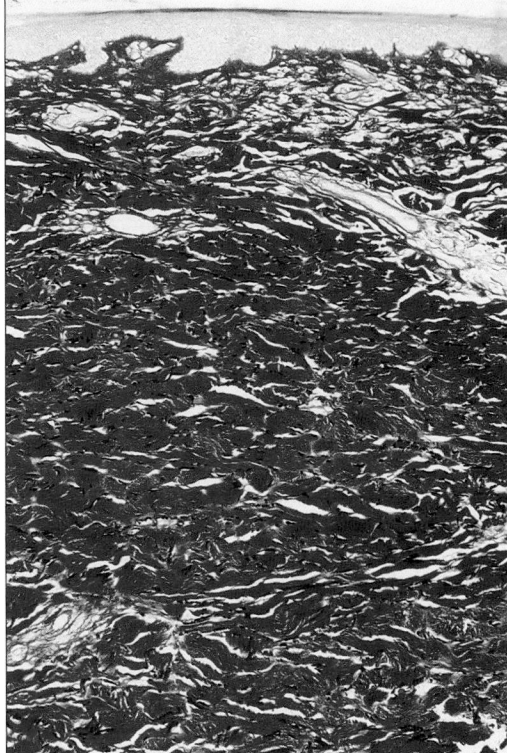

Fig. 16.116
Morphea: this is a chronic lesion. There is loss of elastic tissue (van Gieson).

In the late stages, dermal sclerosis is still evident, but the dermis appears thinned due to concomitant atrophy.[2] Vascular changes similar to those described for systemic sclerosis may be evident and consist of thickening of the walls of small blood vessels. Vasculitis is not a feature.

Calcinosis cutis is occasionally seen and neuritis similar to that seen in indeterminate leprosy has also been documented.[104,105]

In lesions of deep morphea the infiltrate is much more prominent and located predominantly in the junction between the dermis and subcutaneous tissue with extension into the subcutaneous tissue. The infiltrate and the sclerotic collagen have a more nodular distribution.

In bullous morphea several patterns have been described.[25,106,107] The most common pattern is that of prominent superficial edema with prominent lymphatic dilatation.[25] A further pattern is one identical to that seen in lichen sclerosus.[107] It is worth remembering that auto-

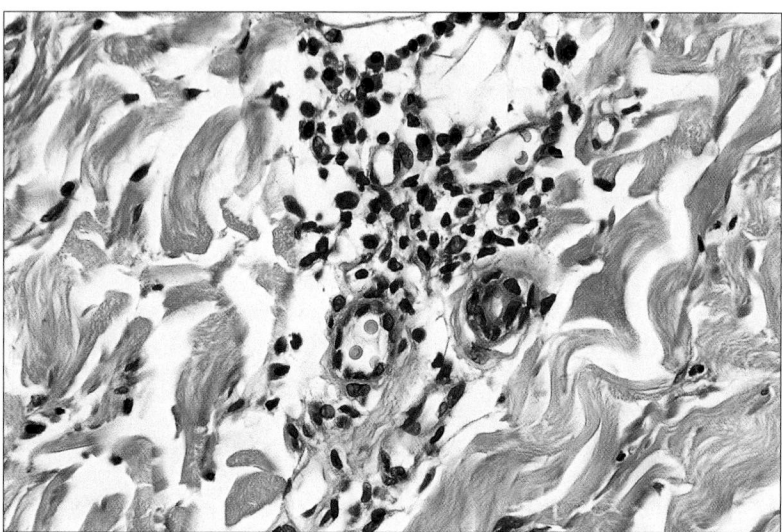

Fig. 16.117
Morphea: a perivascular chronic inflammatory cell infiltrate is usually present, particularly in early lesions.

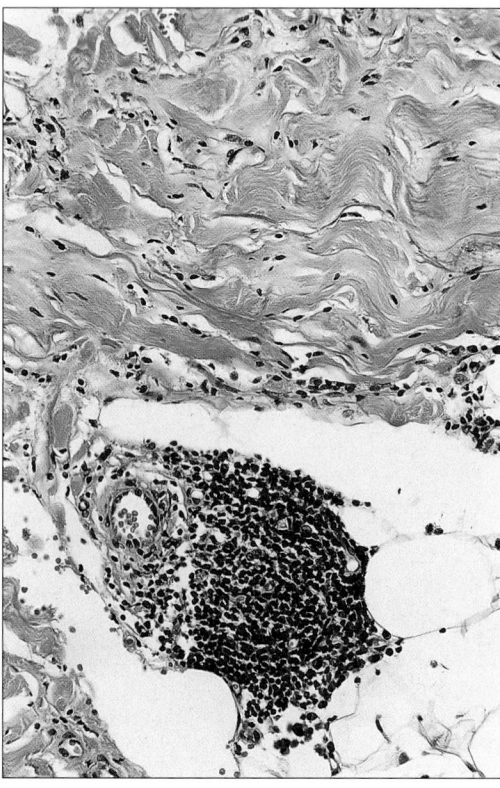

Fig. 16.118
Morphea: the infiltrate often involves the subcutaneous fat.

immune blistering diseases such as epidermolysis bullosa acquisita may occur concomitantly with morphea, and immunofluorescence may be indicated in cases in which a subepidermal blister is present.[106]

In addition to the features described above, generalized morphea and disabling pansclerotic morphea of childhood may show a lymphocytic and hyaline panniculitis with lymphoid follicle formation reminiscent of lupus profundus.[41,49] Eccrine squamous syringometaplasia and syringomatous hyperplasia have been described in linear scleroderma.[108]

Differential diagnosis

The lesions of localized scleroderma may be histologically indistinguishable from those of systemic sclerosis, but the inflammatory cell infiltrate tends to be more pronounced in the former, at least in the early stages. Also, involvement of the papillary dermis may be a feature in some cases of localized scleroderma.[109]

Other diseases that enter the differential diagnosis include late porphyria cutanea tarda and chronic GVHD. Adequate clinical information will resolve most diagnostic dilemmas, but where doubt exists, the presence of PAS-positive thickened dermal vessels is indicative of porphyria, whereas epidermal lichenoid features with cytoid body formation strongly support the diagnosis of chronic GVHD.

The relationship between localized scleroderma, particularly the guttate variety, and lichen sclerosus has been the source of considerable controversy. However, basal cell liquefactive degeneration with a lichenoid inflammatory cell infiltrate is not a feature of morphea, and sclerosis of the reticular dermis and subcutaneous fat with atrophy or loss of appendage structures is not a feature of lichen sclerosus.[40]

Marked dermal sclerosis may also be a feature of atrophie blanche and chronic radiation dermatitis. Vascular changes, including thromboses, purpura and hemosiderosis, however, are conspicuous in the former, while bizarre fibroblasts, elastosis and endarteritis obliterans are characteristic of the latter.

Phenylketonuria has also been reported to show sclerodermatous features.[2]

Histological distinction between morphea and late lesions of acrodermatitis enteropathica may be difficult and occasionally impossible.[110] Close clinicopathological correlation allows distinction between both entities.

References

1. Winkelmann, R.K. (1985) Localized cutaneous scleroderma. *Semin Dermatol*, **4**, 90–103.
2. Jablonska, S., Rodnan, G.P. (1979) Localized forms of scleroderma. *Clin Rheum Dis*, **5**, 215–241.
3. Jablonska, S. (1994) Classification of scleroderma. *Clin Dermatol*, **12**, 225–228.
4. Kim, L.H., Kom, J.H. (2003) Update in systemic sclerosis. *Arthritis Rheum*, **49**, 605–613.
5. Tufanelli, D.L. (1998) Localized scleroderma. *Semin Cutan Med Surg*, **17**, 27–33.
6. Peterson, L.S., Nelson, A.M., Su, W.P. (1995) Classification of morphea (localized scleroderma). *Mayo Clin Proc*, **70**, 1068–1076.
7. Eubanks, L.E., McBurney, E.I., Galen, W., Reed, R. (1996) Linear scleroderma in children. *Int J Dermatol*, **35**, 330–336.
8. Vierra, E., Cunningham, B.B. (1999) Morphea and localized scleroderma in children. *Semin Cutan Med Surg*, **18**, 210–225.
9. Krafchik, B.R. (1999) Localized morphea in children. *Adv Exp Med Biol*, **455**, 49–54.
10. Barba, A., Rosina, P., Chieregato, C. et al (1999) Morphoea in a newborn boy. *Br J Dermatol*, **140**, 365–366.
11. Peterson, L.S., Nelson, A.M., Su, W.P. et al (1997) The epidemiology of morphea (localized scleroderma) in Olmsted County 1960–1993. *J Rheumatol*, **24**, 73–80.
12. Dehen, L., Roujeau, J.C., Cosnes, A. et al (1994) Internal involvement in localized scleroderma. *Medicine (Baltimore)*, **73**, 241–245.
13. Aguayo, S.M., Richardson, C.L., Roman, J. (1993) Severe extrapulmonary thoracic restriction caused by morphea, a form of localized scleroderma. *Chest*, **104**, 1304–1305.
14. Liu, P., Uziel, Y., Chuang, S. et al. (1994) Localized scleroderma: imaging features. *Pediatr Radiol*, **24**, 207–209.
15. Yamanaka, C.T., Gibbs, N.F. (1999) Trauma-induced linear scleroderma. *Cutis*, **63**, 29–32.
16. Gollob, M.H., Dekoven, J.G., Bell, M.J. et al (1998) Postradiation morphea. *J Rheumatol*, **25**, 2267–2269.
17. Schaffer, J.V., Carroll, C., Dvoretsky, I. et al (2000) Postirradiation morphea of the breast: presentation of two cases and review of the literature. *Dermatology*, **200**, 67–71.
18. Granel, B., Serratrice, J., Gaudy, C. et al (2001) Localized morphea after silicone-gel-filled breast implant. *Dermatology*, **202**, 143–144.
19. Leshin, B., Piette, W.W., Caplan, R.M. (1989) Morphea after bromocriptine therapy. *Int J Dermatol*, **28**, 177–179.
20. Ghersetich, I., Teofoli, P., Benci, M. et al (1994) Localized scleroderma. *Clin Dermatol*, **12**, 229–236.
21. Christianson, H.B., Dorsey, C.S., O'Leary, P.A., Kierland, R.R. (1965) Localized scleroderma: a clinical study of two hundred and thirty-five cases. *Arch Dermatology*, **74**, 629–639.
22. Tuffanelli, D., Winkelmann, R.K. (1955) Systemic scleroderma. *Arch Dermatol*, **84**, 359–371.

23. Garb, J., Sims, G. (1959) Scleroderma with bullous lesions. *Dermatologica*, **119**, 341.
24. Su, W.P.D., Person, J.R. (1981) Morphea profunda. *Am J Dermatopathol*, **3**, 251–260.
25. Daoud, M.S., Su, W.P., Leiferman, K.M. et al (1994) Bullous morphea: clinical, pathologic, and immunopathologic evaluation of thirteen cases. *J Am Acad Dermatol*, **30**, 937–943.
26. Rompel, R., Mischke, A.L., Langner, C. et al (2000) Linear atrophoderma of Moulin. *Eur J Dermatol*, **10**, 611–613.
27. Jinnin, M., Ihn, H., Asano, Y. et al (2002) A case of linear scleroderma with muscle calcification. *Br J Dermatol*, **146**, 1084–1086.
28. Wagers, L.T., Young, A.W. Jr, Ryan, S.F. (1972) Linear melorheostotic scleroderma. *Br J Dermatol*, **86**, 297–301.
29. Miyachi, Y., Horio, T., Yamada, A. et al (1979) Linear melorheostotic scleroderma with hypertrichosis. *Arch Dermatol*, **115**, 1233–1234.
30. Fimiani, M., Rubegni, P., de Aloe, G. et al (1999) Linear melorheostotic scleroderma with hypertrichosis sine melorheostosis. *Br J Dermatol*, **141**, 771–772.
31. Juhn, B-J., Cho, Y-H., Lee, M-H. (2000) Linear scleroderma associated with hypertrichosis in the absence of melorheostosis. *Acta Derm Venereol*, **80**, 62–63.
32. Soma, Y., Fujimoto, M. (1998) Frontoparietal scleroderma (en coup de sabre) following Blaschko's lines. *J Am Acad Dermatol*, **38**, 366–368.
33. McKenna, D.B., Benton, E.C. (1999) A tri-linear pattern of scleroderma 'en coup de sabre' following Blaschko's lines. *Clin Exp Dermatol*, **24**, 467–468.
34. Baxter, A.M., Roberts, A., Shaw, L. et al (2001) Localized scleroderma in a 12-year-old girl presenting as gingival recession. A case report and literature review. *Dent Update*, **28**, 458–462.
35. Patrizi, A., Marzaduri, S., Marini, R. (2000) A familial case of scleroderma en coup de sabre. *Acta Derm Venereol*, **80**, 237.
36. Dilley, J.J., Perry, H.O. (1968) Bilateral linear scleroderma en coup de sabre. *Arch Dermatol*, **97**, 688–689.
37. Rai, R., Handa, S., Gupta, S. et al (2000) Bilateral en coup de sabre – a rare entity. *Pediatr Dermatol*, **17**, 22–24.
38. Higashi, Y., Kanekura, T., Fukumaru, K. et al (2000) Scleroderma en coup de sabre with central nervous system involvement. *J Dermatol*, **27**, 486–488.
39. Hulsmans, R.F.H.J., Asghar, S.S., Siddiqui, A.H. et al (1986) Hereditary deficiency of C2 in association with linear scleroderma 'en coup de sabre'. *Arch Dermatol*, **122**, 76–79.
40. Patterson, J.A.K., Ackermann, A.B. (1984) Lichen sclerosus et atrophicus is not related to morphea: a clinical and histologic study of 24 patients in whom both conditions were reputed to be present simultaneously. *Am J Dermatopathol*, **6**, 323–335.
41. Fleischmajer, R., Nedwich, A. (1972) Generalised morphea 1. Histology of the dermis and subcutaneous tissue. *Arch Dermatol*, **106**, 509–514.
42. Stevens, H.P., Ostlere, L.S., Black, C.M. et al (1993) Generalized morphoea secondary to porphyria cutanea tarda. *Br J Dermatol*, **129**, 455–457.
43. Robertson, L.P., Davies, M.G., Hickling, P. (2000) Generalized morphea in a patient with Felty's syndrome. *J Eur Acad Dermatol Venereol*, **14**, 191–193.
44. Drago, F., Rampini, P., Lugani, C. et al (1998) Generalized morphoea after antitetanus vaccination. *Clin Exp Dermatol*, **23**, 142.
45. Nagai, Y., Hattori, T., Ishikawa, O. (2002) Unilateral generalized morphea in childhood. *J Dermatol*, **29**, 435–438.
46. English, J.C. 3rd, Derdeyn, A.S., Smith, P.D. et al (2002) Adult acral cutaneous myofibromas in a patient with generalized morphea. *J Am Acad Dermatol*, **46**, 953–956.
47. James, W.D., Berger, T.G., Butler, D.F. et al (1984) Nodular (keloidal) scleroderma. *J Am Acad Dermatol*, **11**, 1111–1114.
48. Pérez-Wilson, J., Pujol, R.M., Alejo, M. et al (1992) Nodular (keloidal) scleroderma. *Int J Dermatol*, **31**, 422–423.
49. Díaz-Pérez, J.L., Connolly, S.M., Winkelmann, R.K. (1980) Disabling pan-sclerotic morphoea of children. *Arch Dermatol*, **116**, 169–173.
50. Wollina, U., Looks, A., Uhlemann, C. et al (1999) Pansclerotic morphea of childhood – follow-up over 6 years. *Pediatr Dermatol*, **16**, 245–247.
51. Parodi, P.C., Riberti, C., Draganic Stinco, D. et al (2001) Squamous cell carcinoma arising in a patient with long-standing pansclerotic morphoea. *Br J Dermatol*, **144**, 417–419.
52. Wollina, U., Buslau, M., Weyers, W. (2002) Squamous cell carcinoma in pansclerotic morphea of childhood. *Pediatr Dermatol*, **19**, 151–154.
53. Devidayal Singh, S., Kumar, L., Radotra, B.D. (2002) Disabling pansclerotic morphoea of childhood and hypogammaglobulinemia: a curious association. *Rheumatol Int*, **21**, 158–160.
54. Ben-Amital, D., Hodak, E., Lapidoth, M. et al (1999) Coexisting morphoea and granuloma annulare – are the conditions related? *Clin Exp Dermatol*, **24**, 86–89.
55. Freeman, W.E., Lesher, J.L. Jr, Smith, J.G. Jr (1988) Connective tissue disease associated with sclerodermoid features, early abortion, and circulating anticoagulant. *J Am Acad Dermatol*, **19**, 932–936.
56. Mackel, S.E., Kozin, F., Ryan, L.M. et al (1979) Concurrent linear scleroderma and systemic lupus erythematosus: a report of two cases. *J Invest Dermatol*, **73**, 368–372.
57. Mitchell, A.J., Rusin, L.J., Díaz, L.A. (1980) Circumscribed scleroderma with immunologic evidence of systemic lupus erythematosus. *Arch Dermatol*, **116**, 69–73.
58. Umbert, P., Winkelmann, R.K. (1978) Concurrent localized scleroderma and discoid lupus erythematosus. Cutaneous 'mixed' or 'overlap' syndrome. *Arch Dermatol*, **114**, 1473–1478.
59. Rao, B.K., Coldiron, B., Freeman, R.G. et al (1990) Subacute cutaneous lupus erythematosus lesions progressing to morphea. *J Am Acad Dermatol*, **23**, 1019–1022.
60. Reed, J.R., De Luca, N., McIntyre, A.S. et al (2000) Localized morphoea, xanthomatosis and primary biliary cirrhosis. *Br J Dermatol*, **143**, 652–653.
61. Barr, R.J., Siegel, J.M., Graham, J.H. (1980) Elastosis perforans serpiginosa associated with morphea. An example of 'perforating morphea'. *J Am Acad Dermatol*, **3**, 19–22.
62. Ishikawa, O., Akimoto, S., Iijima, C. et al (1997) Morphoea associated with B-cell lymphoma. *Br J Dermatol*, **136**, 294–295.
63. Sawamura, D., Yaguchi, T., Hashimoto, I. et al (1998) Coexistence of generalized morphea with histological changes in lichen sclerosus et atrophicus and lichen planus. *J Dermatol*, **25**, 409–411.
64. Melato, M., Gorji, N., Rizzardi, C. et al (2000) Associated localization of morphea and lichen planus of the lip in a patient with vitiligo. *Minerva Stomatol*, **49**, 549–554.
65. Biasi, D., Caramaschi, P., Carletto, A. et al (1998) Localized scleroderma associated with sarcoidosis. *Clin Exp Rheumatol*, **16**, 761–762.
66. Morita, A., Tsuji, T. (2001) Necrotizing vasculitis in a patient with generalized morphea. *J Am Acad Dermatol*, **45**, S215–217.
67. Chandra, S., Finklestein, E., Gill, D. (2002) Necrobiotic xanthogranuloma occurring within linear morphoea. *Australas J Dermatol*, **43**, 52–54.
68. Jablonska, S. (1975) Scleroderma and pseudoscleroderma, 2nd edn. Warsaw: Polish Medical Publications.
69. Hoesly, J.M., Mertz, L.E., Winkelmann, R.K. (1987) Localized scleroderma (morphea) and antibody to *Borrelia burgdorferi*. *J Am Acad Dermatol*, **17**, 455–459.
70. Sing, J., Beck, G.A. (1975) Morphoea following chicken pox. *Br J Dermatol*, **93**, 43–44.
71. Aberer, E., Kollegger, H., Kristoferistch, W. et al (1988) Neuroborreliosis in morphea and lichen sclerosus et atrophicus. *J Am Acad Dermatol*, **19**, 820–825.
72. Aberer, E., Stanek, G. (1987) Histological evidence of spirochetal origin of morphea and lichen sclerosus et atrophicus. *Am J Dermatopathol*, **9**, 374–379.
73. Schempp, C., Bocklage, H., Lange, R. et al (1993) Further evidence for *Borrelia burgdorferi* infection in morphea and lichen sclerosus et atrophicus confirmed by DNA amplification. *J Invest Dermatol*, **100**, 717–720.
74. Buechner, S.A., Winkelmann, R.K., Lautenschlager, S. et al (1993) Localized scleroderma associated with *Borrelia burgdorferi* infection. *J Am Acad Dermatol*, **29**, 190–196.
75. Breier, F.H., Aberer, E., Stanek, G. et al (1999) Isolation of *Borrelia afzelli* from circumscribed scleroderma. *Br J Dermatol*, **140**, 925–930.
76. Özkan, _., Atabey, N., Fetil, E. et al (2000) Evidence for *Borrelia burgdorferi* in morphea and lichen sclerosus. *Int J Dermatol*, **39**, 278–283.
77. Breier, F., Klade, H., Stanek, G. et al (1996) Lymphoproliferative responses to *Borrelia burgdorferi* in circumscribed scleroderma. *Br J Dermatol*, **134**, 285–291.
78. Aberer, E., Neumann, R., Stanek, G. (1985) Is localised scleroderma a *Borrelia* infection? *Lancet*, **2** (Letter), 273.
79. Ross, S.A., Sanchez, J.L., Taboas, J.O. (1990) Spirochetal forms in the dermal lesions of morphea and lichen sclerosus et atrophicus. *Am J Dermatopathol*, **12**, 357–362.
80. Lecerf, V., Bagot, M., Revuz, J. et al (1989) *Borrelia burgdorferi* and localized scleroderma. *Arch Dermatol*, **125**, 297.
81. Meis, J.F., Koopman, R., van Bergen, B. et al (1993) No evidence for a relation between *Borrelia burgdorferi* infection and old lesions of localized scleroderma (morphea). *Arch Dermatol*, **129**, 386–387.
82. DeVito, J.R., Merogi, A.J., Vo, T. et al (1996) Role of *Borrelia burgdorferi* in the pathogenesis of morphea/scleroderma and lichen sclerosus et atrophicus: a PCR study of thirty-five cases. *J Cutan Pathol*, **23**, 350–358.
83. Dillon, W.I., Saed, G.M., Fivenson, D.P. (1995) *Borrelia burgdorferi* DNA is undetectable by polymerase chain reaction in skin lesions of morphea, scleroderma, or lichen sclerosus et atrophicus of patients from North America. *J Am Acad Dermatol*, **33**, 617–620.
84. Raguin, G., Boisnic, S., Souteyrand, P. et al (1992) No evidence for a spirochaetal origin of localized scleroderma. *Br J Dermatol*, **127**, 218–220.
85. Wienecke, R., Schlupen, E-M., Zochling, N. et al (1995) No evidence for *Borrelia burgdorferi*-specific DNA in lesions of localized scleroderma. *J Invest Dermatol*, **104**, 23–26.
86. Goodlad, J.R., Davidson, M.M., Gordon, P. et al (2002) Morphoea and *Borrelia burgdorferi*: results from the Scottish Highlands in the context of the world literature. *Mol Pathol*, **55**, 374–378.
87. Tuffanelli, D.L., Tuffanelli, L.R., Hoke, A. (1993) False-positive Lyme antibody test in morphea. *J Am Acad Dermatol*, **28**, 112–113.
88. Weide, B., Schittek, B., Klyscz, T. et al (2000) Morphoea is neither associated with features of *Borrelia burgdorferi* infection, nor is this agent detectable in lesional skin by polymerase chain reaction. *Br J Dermatol*, **143**, 780–785.
89. Weide, B., Walz, T., Garbe, C. (2000) Is morphoea caused by *Borrelia burgdorferi*? A review. *Br J Dermatol*, **142**, 636–644.
90. Curtis, A.C., Jansen, T.G. (1958) The prognosis of localized scleroderma. *Arch Dermatol*, **78**, 749–756.
91. Kikuchi, K., Sato, S., Kadono, T. et al (1994) Serum concentration of procollagen type I carboxyterminal propeptide in localized scleroderma. *Arch Dermatol*, **130**, 1269–1272.
92. Dubois, E.L., Chandor, S., Friou, G.J. et al (1971) Progressive systemic sclerosis (PSS) and localized scleroderma (morphea) with positive LE test and unusual systemic manifestations compatible with systemic lupus erythematosus (SLE). *Medicine (Baltimore)*, **50**, 199–222.
93. Takehara, K., Moroi, Y., Nakabayashi, Y. et al (1983) Antinuclear antibodies in localized scleroderma. *Arthritis Rheum*, **26**, 612–616.
94. Falanga, V., Medsger, T.A., Reichlin, M. (1987) Anti-nuclear antibodies and anti-single-stranded DNA antibodies in morphea and generalized morphea. *Arch Dermatol*, **123**, 350–353.
95. Ruffati, A., Peserico, A., Rondinone, R. et al (1991) Prevalence and characteristics of anti-single-stranded DNA antibodies in localized scleroderma. *Arch Dermatol*, **127**, 1180–1183.
96. Falanga, V., Medsger, T.A., Reichlin, M. (1985) High titers of antibodies to single-stranded DNA in linear scleroderma. *Arch Dermatol*, **121**, 345–347.
97. Fleischmajer, R., Perlish, J.S., Reeves, J.R.T. (1977) Cellular infiltrates in scleroderma skin. *Arthritis Rheum*, **20**, 975–984.
98. Sato, S., Fujimoto, M., Ihn, H. et al (1994) Clinical characteristics associated with antihistone antibodies in patients with localized scleroderma. *J Am Acad Dermatol*, **31**, 567–571.
99. Rosenberg, A.M., Uziel, Y., Krafchik, B.R. et al (1995) Antinuclear antibodies in children with localized scleroderma. *J Rheumatol*, **22**, 2337–2343.
100. Ihn, H., Fujimoto, M., Sato, S. et al (1994) Increased levels of circulating intercellular adhesion molecule-1 in patients with localized scleroderma. *J Am Acad Dermatol*, **31**, 591–595.
101. Skobieranda, K., Helm, K.F. (1995) Decreased expression of the human progenitor cell antigen (CD34) in morphea. *Am J Dermatopathol*, **17**, 471–475.
102. Gilmour, T.K., Wilkinson, B., Breit, S.N. et al (2000) Analysis of dendritic cell populations using a revised histological staging of morphoea. *Br J Dermatol*, **143**, 1183–1192.
103. McNiff, J.M., Glusac, E.J., Lazova, R.Z. et al (1999) Morphea limited to the superficial reticular dermis: an underrecognized histologic phenomenon. *Am J Dermatopathol*, **21**, 315–319.
104. Yamamoto, A., Morita, A., Shintani, Y. et al (2002) Localized linear scleroderma with cutaneous calcinosis. *J Dermatol*, **29**, 112–114.
105. Jayakumar, J., Aschhoff, M., Job, C.K. (1997) A case of morphoea with dermal neuritis as in indeterminate leprosy. *Indian J Lepr*, **69**, 407–409.
106. Rencic, A., Goyal, S., Mofid, M. et al (2002) Bullous lesions in scleroderma. *Int J Dermatol*, **41**, 335–339.
107. Trattner, A., David, M., Sandbank, M. (1994) Bullous morphea: a distinct entity? *Am J Dermatopathol*, **16**, 414–417.
108. Sakai, H., Satoh, K., Manabe, A. et al (2002) Eccrine syringometaplasia and syringomatous hyperplasia in association with linear scleroderma. *Dermatology*, **204**, 136–138.
109. Torres, J.E., Sánchez, J.L. (1998) Histopathologic differentiation between localized and systemic scleroderma. *Am J Dermatopathol*, **20**, 242–245.
110. Aberer, E., Klade, H., Hobisch, G.A. (1991) A clinical, histological, and immunohistochemical comparison of acrodermatitis chronica atrophicans and morphea. *Am J Dermatopathol*, **13**, 334–341.

Atrophoderma of Pasini and Pierini

Clinical features

Atrophoderma is a rare, primary dermal atrophic process of uncertain nature. Since its first description by Pasini in 1923 there has been controversy as to whether it represents a distinct entity sui generis or whether it is a variant of localized scleroderma (morphea).[1–3] It presents usually in the second or third decade with a mean age of onset of 30 years and shows a predilection for females (10:2).[4]

The typical lesion is a gray–brown or violaceous, atrophic, round to oval, depressed macule with a 'cliff-drop' border (*Fig. 16.119*).[3] The distribution is usually bilateral and symmetrical and the lower back is the most commonly affected site.[4] Lesions may also be found on the chest, arms and abdomen. The legs are infrequently involved. A case with a zosteriform distribution has been documented.[5]

Atrophoderma of Pasini and Pierini may coexist with lichen sclerosis and morphea, and progression to systemic sclerosis has been documented.[5–9] In contrast to localized scleroderma, it lacks the violaceous border, is primarily atrophic rather than indurated, and tends to great chronicity, lesions often being present for decades rather than resolving after a few years, as is often a feature of morphea.[3]

An entity described as atrophoderma elastolytica discreta clinically simulates atrophoderma of Pasini and Pierini but the histopathological changes are those of anetoderma.[10]

Pathogenesis and histological features

It is still controversial whether this disease represents a variant of morphea. A large study of 139 patients suggested that the disease represents an atrophic abortive variant of morphea in which the sclerotic

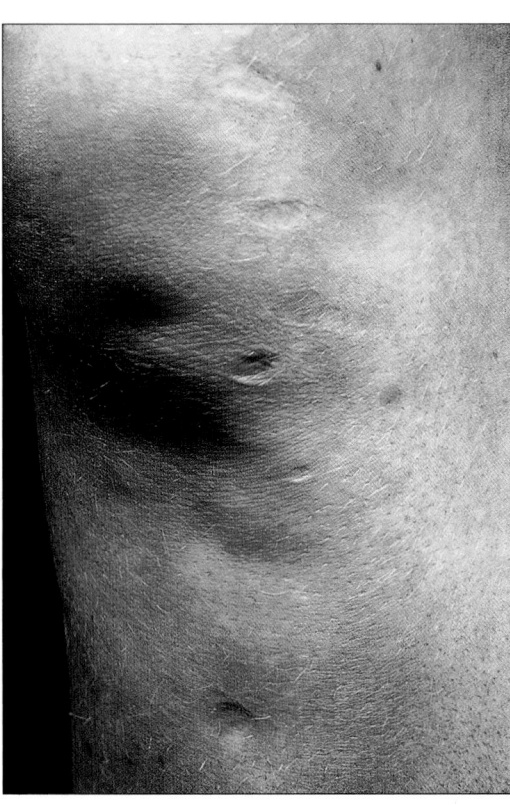

Fig. 16.119
Atrophoderma: lesions present as depressed atrophic plaques with a typical cliff-drop border. By courtesy of the Institute of Dermatology, London, UK.

phase fails to develop.[11] A study of lesional skin of two patients showed a decrease in the total amount of disaccharide and a normal or decreased amount of DeltaDi-4S(DS), the main disaccharide unit of dermatan sulfate.[12] This is in contrast with findings in patients with morphea in which there is increase in the total amount of disaccharide and increase in DeltaDi-4S(DS). This finding suggests that the two diseases are different. However, a further study of lesional and normal skin revealed an increase in the amount of dermatan sulfate in lesional skin as is a feature of morphea.[13] The identification in the serum of antibodies to *Borrelia burgdorferi* in 20–53% of patients, combined with occasional reports of culture of the organism from lesional material, raises the possibility of a causal relationship.[4]

Histologically, atrophoderma often shows very subtle features. The epidermis may be atrophic or normal and is often hyperpigmented. Within the superficial dermis is a perivascular and interstitial chronic inflammatory cell infiltrate consisting of lymphocytes and histiocytes. The lymphocytes are T-cells and the helper–inducer subset predominates.[14,15] Rarely plasma cells may be conspicuous. In early lesions the collagen bundles are homogenized and swollen but, with progression, sclerosis often supervenes in the deeper reticular dermis.[5] The appendage structures are usually normal. The elastic fibers commonly show no change, but diminution and fragmentation have been documented.[4] The late stages of atrophoderma are indistinguishable from localized scleroderma.

References

1. Winkelmann, R.K. (1985) Localized cutaneous scleroderma. *Semin Dermatol*, **4**, 90–103.
2. Jablonska, S., Szczepanski, A. (1975) Atrophoderma Pasini–Pierini. In: Jablonska, S. (ed.) Scleroderma and pseudoscleroderma. Warsaw: Polish Medical Publishers, pp 521–536.
3. Stoner, M.C., Dixon, S.L. (1990) Atrophoderma of Pasini, Pierini. *Arch Dermatol*, **126**, 1641–1644.
4. Buechner, S.A., Rufli, T. (1994) Atrophoderma of Pasini and Pierini: clinical and histopathologic findings and antibodies to *Borrelia burgdorferi* in thirty-four patients. *J Am Acad Dermatol*, **30**, 441–446.
5. Wakelin, S.H., James, M.P. (1995) Zosteriform atrophoderma of Pasini and Pierini. *Clin Exp Dermatol*, **20**, 244–246.
6. Heymann, W.R. (1994) Coexistent lichen sclerosus et atrophicus and atrophoderma of Pasini and Pierini. *Int J Dermatol*, **33**, 133–134.
7. Bisaccia, E.P., Scarborough, D.A., Lowney, E.D. (1982) Atrophoderma of Pasini and Pierini and systemic scleroderma. *Arch Dermatol*, **118**, 1–2.
8. Murphy, P.K., Hymes, S.R., Fenske, N.A. (1990) Concomitant unilateral idiopathic atrophoderma of Pasini and Pierini (IAPP) and morphea. Observations supporting IAPP as a variant of morphea. *Int J Dermatol*, **29**, 281–283.
9. Jablonska, S., Blaszczyk, M. (1999) Scleroderma overlap syndromes. *Adv Exp Med Biol*, **455**, 85–92.
10. Carrington, P.R., Altick, J.A., Sanusi, I.D. (1996) Atrophoderma elastolytica discreta. *Am J Dermatopathol*, **18**, 12–17.
11. Kencka, D., Blaszczyk, M., Jablonska, S. (1995) Atrophoderma Pasini–Pierini is a primary atrophic abortive morphea. *Dermatology*, **190**, 203–206.
12. Yokoyama, Y., Akimoto, S., Ishikawa, O. (2000) Disaccharide analysis of skin glycosaminoglycans in atrophoderma of Pasini and Pierini. *Clin Exp Dermatol*, **25**, 436–440.
13. Tajima, S., Sakuraoka, K. (1995) A case of atrophoderma of Pasini and Pierini: analysis of glycosaminoglycan of the lesional skin. *J Dermatol*, **22**, 767–769.
14. Kernohan, N.M., Stankler, L., Sewell, H.F. (1992) Atrophoderma of Pasini and Pierini: an immunopathologic case study. *Am J Clin Pathol*, **97**, 63–68.
15. Berman, A., Berman, G.D., Winkelmann, R.K. (1988) Atrophoderma (Pasini–Pierini). Findings on direct immunofluorescent, monoclonal antibody, and ultrastructural studies. *Int J Dermatol*, **27**, 487–490.

Eosinophilic fasciitis

Clinical features

The precise nosological status of eosinophilic fasciitis (Schulman's syndrome) is uncertain: some authors regard it as a variant of morphea (morphea profunda) but others consider it an entity in its own right.[1–4] For the purpose of this text it is classified separately.

Eosinophilic fasciitis occurs equally in males and females, and most patients are in their third to sixth decades.[1] Pediatric disease has, however, also been documented.[5] White Caucasians are predominantly affected.[6]

The clinical features of painful, tender swelling, stiffness and sclerodermiform induration affect (in decreasing order of frequency) the forearms, upper arms and lower legs, thighs, hands, trunk, neck and feet.[1,6] The face and fingers are only rarely affected. Localized

involvement of a limb has rarely been documented.[7] Early cutaneous manifestations include pitting edema, peau d'orange or a cobblestone appearance.[1,8] At least 50% of patients relate the onset of their illness to an episode of strenuous physical activity.[9–11] Patients have a variety of non-specific features including malaise, weakness, fever and weight loss.[1] Raynaud's phenomenon is typically absent and the nail fold capillaries are normal – points of distinction from systemic sclerosis.[12] Pediatric disease commonly progresses to sclerodermiform cutaneous scarring.[5,10,13] Blood eosinophilia and hypergammaglobulinemia have been reported.[4,14] Hypogammaglobulinemia is exceptional.[15]

Extracutaneous involvement is becoming increasingly recognized.[16] Patients may develop arthralgia and synovitis. Inflammatory arthritis (predominantly involving the hands, wrists and knees) and carpal tunnel syndrome occur in about 25% of patients.[1,10,12,13,19] Contractures develop in up to 75% of patients and particularly affect the shoulders, elbows, wrists, hands and knees.[6,17] Subclinical myositis is common.[1] Posterior ischemic optic neuropathy has also been described.[18]

Clinically significant systemic features are rare, but have included esophageal dysmotility, pericardial and pleural effusions and lung and kidney involvement.[1,20,21]

A number of other associations have recently been documented including aplastic anemia, thrombocytopenia, hemolytic anemia, monoclonal gammopathy, leukemia, lymphoma, multiple myeloma, combined immunodeficiency, Hashimoto's disease, SLE, myelodysplasia, acquired ichthyosis, vitiligo-like changes and peripheral neuropathy.[1,9,22–35] The association with serious hematological abnormalities has led to the suggestion that all patients with the disease should have a bone marrow examination to exclude myelodysplasia.[36] An exceptional familial case in association with breast cancer has been documented.[37]

Laboratory investigations reveal a raised ESR, peripheral blood eosinophilia and hypergammaglobulinemia (usually IgG).[9] Antinuclear antibodies (speckled and homogeneous), rheumatoid factor and, rarely, anti-nDNA antibodies may be present.[6,10] Serum aldolase levels appear to be a useful indicator of disease activity.[38]

Characteristically, eosinophilic fasciitis responds well to corticosteroid therapy – a diagnostic pointer. Spontaneous resolution occurs in some patients.

Progression to scleroderma and coexistence with lesions of localized morphea may sometimes occur.[5,39–42]

Pathogenesis and histological features

The etiology and pathogenesis of eosinophilic fasciitis are unknown. The clinical findings of hypergammaglobulinemia, occasional antinuclear antibodies and positive immunofluorescence suggests a humoral immune mechanism.[1] Even in those instances when eosinophilic fasciitis has followed strenuous physical activity, it is unlikely that trauma, on its own, is responsible. There are occasional reports of possible drug toxicity following, for example, antituberculous therapy, phenytoin, subcutaneous heparin and fosinopril, and an eosinophilic fasciitis-like picture sometimes constitutes part of the eosinophilia–myalgia syndrome (see below).[12,43,44] The disease has also followed exposure to trichloroethylene, radiotherapy, subcutaneous injection of phytonadione and after the initiation of dialysis.[45–48]

Borrelia burgdorferi has been associated with some cases of eosinophilic fasciitis (*Fig. 16.120*).[49,50]

In some patients, elevation of serum IL-2, -5 and -10, interferon gamma (IFN-γ) and leukemia inhibitory factor has been documented.[51] The increase in IL-5 and -10 possibly leads to eosinophilia and immune globulin overexpression.[51] Eosinophils have been shown to stimulate DNA synthesis and matrix production in dermal fibroblasts, leading to increased collagen deposition.[52]

Immunofluorescence has revealed deposition of IgM at the dermoepidermal junction, immunoglobulin and complement around blood vessels in the deep dermis and IgG and complement in the deep fascia and skeletal muscle.[6,10,53]

The pathology of eosinophilic fasciitis predominantly affects the deep subcutaneous fat and fascia and therefore a substantial incisional biopsy is necessary for diagnosis. The epidermis, papillary dermis and superficial adnexal structures are usually unaffected.[6] A mild chronic inflammatory cell infiltrate consisting of lymphocytes, plasma cells, histiocytes and variable numbers of eosinophils may be present in the deeper reticular dermis, which is also often fibrosed with atrophy of sweat glands.[53] Occasionally the dermal changes are indistinguishable from morphea.[10]

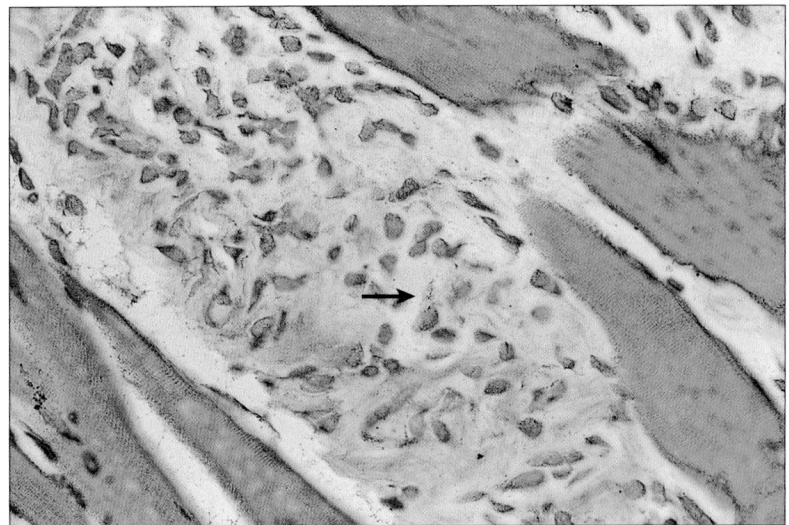

Fig. 16.120
Eosinophilic fasciitis: a spirochete is present in the center of the field (Dieterle stain) (arrowed).

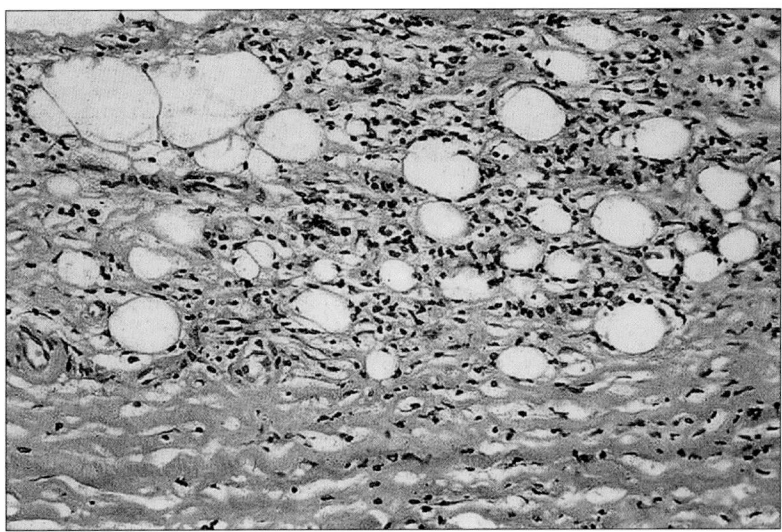

Fig. 16.121
Eosinophilic fasciitis: chronic inflammatory changes extend into the overlying subcutaneous fat.

The most dramatic changes are found in the superficial fascia, which is markedly thickened, fibrosed and sclerotic, and in the acute stages may show focal fibrinoid necrosis and/or myxoid degenerative changes due to excessive glycosaminoglycan deposition.[1,53] A chronic inflammatory cell infiltrate is present within the fascia in both a diffuse distribution and centered around blood vessels (*Fig. 16.121*).[40] Primary vascular lesions, however, are not a feature. Tissue eosinophilia is focal and often transitory. Its absence in no way precludes the diagnosis. Lymphoid follicles, sometimes with germinal centers, are also occasionally evident.[53] The inflammatory changes usually extend into the septae of the subcutaneous fat and fibrosis may result in fat entrapment (*Fig. 16.122*).[9] There may also be superficial infiltration by inflammatory cells into the underlying skeletal muscle, which occasionally shows focal necrosis, degeneration and foci of regeneration (*Fig. 16.123*).[1,53,54]

Differential diagnosis

While there is obvious overlap with morphea, the diffuse nature of the induration clinically, the high peripheral eosinophilia and history of preceding strenuous exercise, combined with the usually less severe dermal changes and preservation of the skin appendages on histology, commonly serve to distinguish the two disorders.

Sclerodermoid and eosinophilic fasciitis-like syndromes have been described as features of the toxic oil and L-tryptophan-related eosinophilia–myalgia syndromes.[55-60]

- The *toxic oil syndrome* arose as a consequence of contaminated rapeseed oil and presented in Spain in 1981.[60,61] Patients developed myopathy, peripheral neuropathy and arthralgia in addition to morphea-like skin induration affecting the face, trunk and extremities.[60] Xerostomia was common and Raynaud's phenomenon was not infrequent.

- The *eosinophilia–myalgia syndrome* is due to contaminated (Peak E) commercial L-tryptophan. Patients develop a wide variety of clinical and laboratory abnormalities involving the skin, muscles, nerves, fascia and lungs.[57] Acute cutaneous involvement is most commonly seen as a non-specific erythematous macular eruption affecting the trunk and extremities.[57] Chronic lesions include edema of the extremities followed by the development of sclerodermiform and/or eosinophilic fasciitis-like features.[55]

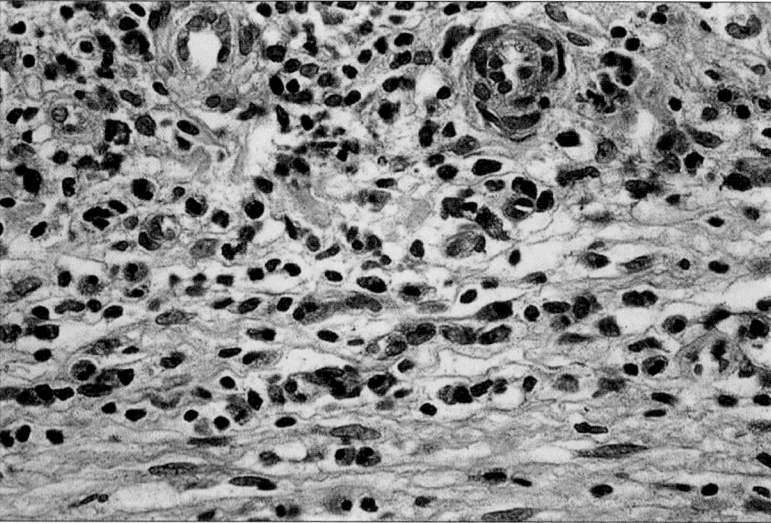

Fig. 16.122
Eosinophilic fasciitis: the infiltrate consists of lymphocytes, occasional plasma cells and, in this case, large numbers of eosinophils.

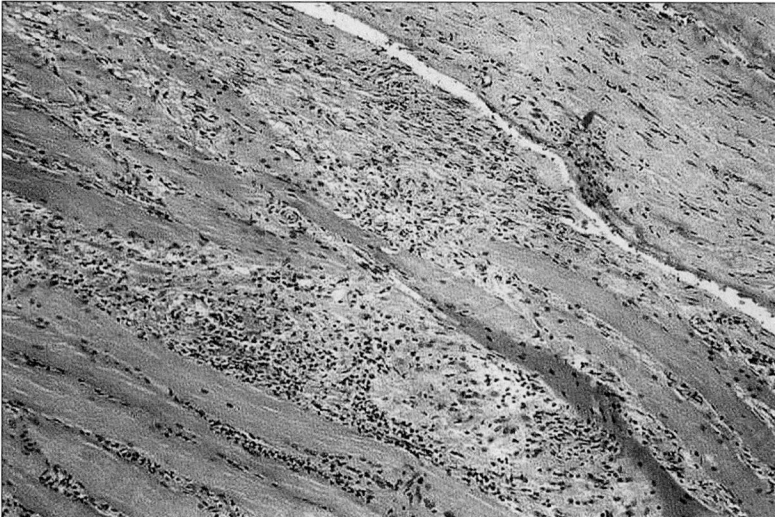

Fig. 16.123
Eosinophilic fasciitis: the inflammatory process not uncommonly involves the adjacent skeletal muscle.

Variable histological features have been documented, presumably reflecting different stages of evolution. In some patients the most conspicuous changes have included fibrosis involving the papillary dermis, periappendageal connective tissue sheath and subcutaneous fat.[56] An inflammatory cell infiltrate composed of lymphocytes, histiocytes, plasma cells and variable numbers of eosinophils is present in the dermis, subcutaneous fat and fascia.[57,58] Mast cells are sometimes conspicuous.[58] Late stages are characterized by hyaline sclerosis involving the dermis through to the subcutaneous fat.[58] Additional features that have been documented include dermal edema with lymphangiectasia and heavy mucin deposition in both the dermis and fascia.[56] The histological features overlap between morphea/systemic sclerosis and eosinophilic fasciitis.

References

1. Doyle, J.A., Ginsburg, W.W. (1989) Eosinophilic fasciitis. *Med Clin North Am*, **73**, 1157–1166.
2. Winkelmann, R.K. (1985) Localized cutaneous scleroderma. *Semin Dermatol*, **4**, 90–103.
3. Rodnan, G.P., Di Bartolomeo, A.G., Medsger, T.A. Jr (1975) Eosinophilic fasciitis: report of six cases of a newly recognised scleroderma-like syndrome. *Clin Res*, **23**, 443.
4. Fleischmajer, R., Jacotot, A.B., Shore, S., Binnick, S.A. (1978) Scleroderma, eosinophilia and diffuse fasciitis. *Arch Dermatol*, **114**, 1320–1325.
5. Farrington, M.L., Haas, J.E., Nazar-Stewart, V. et al (1993) Eosinophilic fasciitis in children frequently progresses to scleroderma-like cutaneous fibrosis. *J Rheumatol*, **20**, 128–132.
6. Moore, T.L., Zuckner, J. (1980) Eosinophilic fasciitis. *Semin Arthritis Rheum*, **9**, 228–235.
7. Lupton, G.P., Goette, D.K. (1979) Localized eosinophilic fasciitis. *Arch Dermatol*, **115**, 85–87.
8. Costenbader, K.H., Kieval, R.I., Anderson, R.J. (2001) Eosinophilic fasciitis presenting as pitting edema of the extremities. *Am J Med*, **111**, 318–320.
9. Shulman, L.E. (1974) Diffuse fasciitis with hypergammaglobulinaemia and eosinophilia: a new syndrome? *J Rheumatol*, **I** (Suppl. 1), 46.
10. Michet, C.J., Doyle, J.A., Ginsburg, W.W. (1981) Eosinophilic fasciitis: a report of 15 cases. *Mayo Clin Proc*, **56**, 27–34.
11. Shewmake, W., Lopez, D.A., McGlamory, C. (1978) The Shulman syndrome. *Arch Dermatol*, **114**, 556–559.
12. Maddison, P.J. (1991) Mixed connective tissue disease, overlap syndromes, and eosinophilic fasciitis. *Ann Rheum Dis*, **50**, 887–893.
13. Lakhanpal, S., Ginsburg, W.W., Michet, C.J. et al (1988) Eosinophilic fasciitis: clinical spectrum and therapeutic response in 52 cases. *Semin Arthritis Rheum*, **17**, 221–231.
14. Falanga, V., Medsger, T.A. Jr (1987) Frequency, levels, and significance of blood eosinophilia in systemic sclerosis, localized scleroderma, and eosinophilic fasciitis. *J Am Acad Dermatol*, **17**, 648–656.
15. Ormerod, R.D., Grieve, J.H.K., Rennie, J.A.N. et al (1984) Eosinophilic fasciitis – a case with hypogammaglobulinaemia. *Clin Exp Dermatol*, **9**, 416–418.
16. Doyle, J.A. (1984) Eosinophilic fasciitis. Extracutaneous manifestations and associations. *Cutis*, **34**, 359–364.
17. Huppke, P., Wilken, B., Brockmann, K. et al (2002) Eosinophilic fasciitis leading to painless contractures. *Eur J Pediatr*, **161**, 528–530.
18. Paul, B., McElvanney, A.M., Agarwal, S. et al (2002) Two rare causes of posterior ischaemic optic neuropathy: eosinophilic fasciitis and Wegener's granulomatosis. *Br J Ophthalmol*, **86**, 1066–1068.
19. McGrory, B.J., Schmidt, I.U., Wolod, L.E. et al (1998) Carpal tunnel syndrome associated with eosinophilic fasciitis. *Orthopedics*, **21**, 368–370.
20. Killen, J.W., Swift, G.L., White, R.J. (2000) Eosinophilic fasciitis with pulmonary and pleural involvement. *Postgrad Med*, **76**, 36–37.
21. Kirschtein, M., Helmchen, U., Jensen, R. et al (1999) Kidney involvement in a 17-year-old boy with eosinophilic fasciitis. *Clin Nephrol*, **52**, 183–187.
22. Garcia, V.P., de Quiros, J.F., Caminal, L. (1998) Autoimmune hemolytic anemia associated with eosinophilic fasciitis. *J Rheumatol*, **25**, 1864–1865.
23. Goldner, B., Furie, R. (1994) Eosinophilic fasciitis associated with a monoclonal immunoglobulin. *Clin Exp Rheumatol*, **12**, 574.
24. Chan, L.S., Hanson, C.A., Cooper, K.D. (1991) Concurrent eosinophilic fasciitis and cutaneous T-cell lymphoma. *Br J Dermatol*, **127**, 862–865.
25. Masuoka, H., Kikuchi, K., Takahashi, S. et al (1998) Eosinophilic fasciitis associated with low-grade T-cell lymphoma. *Br J Dermatol*, **138**, 928–930.
26. Khanna, D., Verity, A., Grossman, J.M. (2002) Eosinophilic fasciitis with multiple myeloma: a new haematological association. *Ann Rheum Dis*, **61**, 1111–1112.
27. Di Gioacchino, M., Masci, S., Paolini, F. et al (2002) Common variable immunodeficiency and eosinophilic fasciitis. *Br J Dermatol*, **12**, 73–74.
28. Mougeot-Martin, M. (1999) Eosinophilic-fasciitis following idiopathic thrombocytopenic purpura, autoimmune hemolytic anemia and Hashimoto's disease. *Dermatology*, **199**, 382.
29. Gallardo, F., Vadillo, M., Mitjavila, F. et al (1998) Systemic lupus erythematosus after eosinophilic fasciitis: a case report. *J Am Acad Dermatol*, **39**, 283–285.
30. Baffoni, L., Frisoni, M., Maccaferri, M. et al (1995) Systemic lupus erythematosus and eosinophilic fasciitis: an unusual association. *Clin Rheumatol*, **14**, 591–592.
31. Fleming, C.J., Clarke, P., Kemmett, D. (1997) Eosinophilic fasciitis with myelodysplasia responsive to treatment with cyclosporin. *Br J Dermatol*, **136**, 297–298.
32. Farrell, A.M., Ross, J.S., Bunker, C.B. (1999) Eosinophilic fasciitis associated with autoimmune thyroid disease and myelodysplasia treated with pulsed methylprednisolone and antihistamines. *Br J Dermatol*, **140**, 1185–1187.
33. de la Cruz-Alvarez, J., Allegue, F., Oliver, J. (1996) Acquired ichthyosis associated with eosinophilic fasciitis. *J Am Acad Dermatol*, **34**, 1079–1080.
34. Stork, J., Nemcova, D., Hoza, J. et al (1996) Eosinophilic fasciitis in an adolescent girl with lymphadenopathy and vitiligo-like and linear scleroderma-like changes. A case report. *Clin Exp Rheumatol*, **14**, 337–341.
35. Moriguchi, M., Terai, C., Kuroki, S. et al (1998) Eosinophilic fasciitis complicated with peripheral polyneuropathy. *Intern Med*, **37**, 417–420.
36. Brito-Babapulle, F. (1997) Patients with eosinophilic fasciitis should have a bone marrow examination to identify myelodysplasia. *Br J Dermatol*, **137**, 316–317.
37. Watts, R.A., Merry, P. (1994) Familial eosinophilic fasciitis and breast cancer. *Br J Rheumatol*, **33**, 93–94.
38. Fujimoto, M., Sato, S., Ihn, H. et al (1995) Serum aldolase level is a useful indicator of disease activity in eosinophilic fasciitis. *J Rheumatol*, **22**, 563–565.
39. Coyle, E., Chapman, R.S. (1980) Eosinophilic fasciitis (Shulman syndrome) in association with morphoea and systemic sclerosis. *Acta Derm Venereol*, **60**, 181–182.
40. Frayha, R.A., Atiyah, F., Karam, P. et al (1985) Eosinophilic fasciitis terminating as progressive systemic sclerosis. *Dermatologica*, **171**, 291–294.
41. Castanet, J., Lacour, J.P., Perrin, C. et al (1994) Association of eosinophilic fasciitis, multiple morphea and antiphospholipid antibody. *Dermatology*, **189**, 304–307.

42. Hulshof, M.M., Boom, B.W., Dijkmans, B.A. (1992) Multiple plaques of morphea developing in a patient with eosinophilic fasciitis. *Arch Dermatol*, **128**, 1128–1129.
43. Cantini, F., Salvarini, C., Olivieri, I. et al (1998) Possible association between eosinophilic fasciitis and subcutaneous heparin use. *J Rheumatol*, **25**, 383–385.
44. Biasi, D., Caramaschi, P., Carletto, A. et al (1997) Scleroderma and eosinophilic fasciitis in patients using fosinopril. *J Rheumatol*, **24**, 1242.
45. Hayashi, N., Igarashi, A., Matsuyama, T. et al (2000) Eosinophilic fasciitis following exposure to trichloroethylene: successful treatment with cyclosporin. *Br J Dermatol*, **42**, 830–832.
46. Desruelles, F., Lacour, J-P., Chevallier, P. et al (2000) Radiation myo-fasciitis. *Acta Derm Venereol*, **80**, 310–311.
47. Janin-Mercier, A., Mosser, C., Souteyrand, P. et al (1985) Subcutaneous sclerosis with fasciitis and eosinophilia after phytonadione injections. *Arch Dermatol*, **121**, 1421–1423.
48. Florell, S.R., Egan, C.A., Gregory, M.C. et al (2001) Eosinophilic fasciitis occurring four weeks after the onset of dialysis in a renal failure patient. *J Cutan Med Surg*, **5**, 33–36.
49. Granter, S.R., Barnhill, R.L., Hewins, M.E. et al (1994) Identification of *Borrelia burgdorferi* in diffuse fasciitis with peripheral eosinophilia: borrelial fasciitis. *JAMA*, **272**, 1283–1285.
50. Hashimoto, Y., Takahashi, H., Matsuo, S. et al (1996) Polymerase chain reaction of *Borrelia burgdorferi* flagellin gene in Shulman syndrome. *Dermatology*, **192**, 136–139.
51. Viallard, J.F., Taupin, J.L., Ranchin, V. et al (2001) Analysis of leukemia inhibitory factor, type 1 and type 2 cytokine production in patients with eosinophilic fasciitis. *J Rheumatol*, **28**, 75–80.
52. Birkland, T.P., Cheavens, M.D., Pincus, S.H. (1994) Human eosinophils stimulate DNA synthesis and matrix production in dermal fibroblasts. *Arch Dermatol Res*, **286**, 312–318.
53. Barnes, L., Rodnan, G.P., Medsger, T.A. Jr et al (1979) Eosinophilic fasciitis. A pathologic study of twenty cases. *Am J Pathol*, **96**, 493–517.
54. Kent, L.T., Cramer, S.F., Moskowitz, R.W. (1981) Eosinophilic fasciitis. Clinical, laboratory and microscopic considerations. *Arthritis Rheum*, **24**, 677–683.
55. DeSpain, J.D., Swinford, R.W. (1992) Collagen vascular disease. *Dermatol Clin*, **10**, 1–18.
56. Kaufman, L.D. (1991) The eosinophilia–myalgia syndrome and related disorders. *Recenti Progressi in Medicina*, **82**, 286–290.
57. Kaufman, L.D., Seidman, R.J., Phillips, M.E. et al (1990) Cutaneous manifestations of the L-tryptophan associated eosinophilia–myalgia syndrome: a spectrum of sclerodermatous skin disease. *J Am Acad Dermatol*, **23**, 1063–1069.
58. Winkelmann, R.K., Connolly, S.M., Quimby, S.R. et al (1991) Histopathologic features of the L-tryptophan-related eosinophilia–myalgia (fasciitis) syndrome. *Mayo Clin Proc*, **66**, 457–463.
59. Umbert, I., Winkelmann, R.K., Wegener, L. (1993) Comparison of the pathology of fascia in eosinophilic myalgia syndrome patients and idiopathic eosinophilic fasciitis. *Dermatology*, **186**, 18–22.
60. Toxic Epidemic Syndrome Study Group (1982) Toxic epidemic syndrome, Spain, 1981. *Lancet*, **2**, 697–702.
61. Posada de la Paz, M., Philen, R.M., Borda, A.I. (2001) Toxic oil syndrome: the perspective after 20 years. *Epidemiol Rev*, **23**, 231–247.

Lichen sclerosus et atrophicus

This disease is discussed on page 483.

Polymyositis/dermatomyositis

Clinical features

Polymyositis is a rare inflammatory disorder of muscle, the etiology of which is unknown.[1,2] If certain cutaneous lesions are also present, the term 'dermatomyositis' is applied. The overall incidence is approximately five new hospital cases/million of the population/year.[1] As many diseases may include features of muscle weakness and elevated muscle enzyme activities, strict criteria must be applied to the diagnosis of these two diseases (*Table 16.9*). Either of these conditions may be confidently diagnosed if a patient fulfills the first four criteria (polymyositis) or three of the four plus the typical rash (dermatomyositis).[3,4]

Five variants of the disease are recognized (*Table 16.10*). With respect to type V, dermatomyositis most commonly coexists with scleroderma (sclerodermatomyositis), but it may also develop in association with SLE, rheumatoid arthritis and Sjögren's syndrome.[4] To diagnose an overlap syndrome the appropriate diagnostic criteria must be fulfilled for each disease and not just a few common manifestations. Overlap syndromes occur more frequently in polymyositis than in dermatomyositis and show a marked female predominance (9:1).[5,6]

Dermatomyositis not uncommonly presents solely with cutaneous manifestations. The quoted frequency of this type of presentation is variable and it is not that rare for the skin eruption to precede the onset of muscle involvement by more than 2 years.[7,8] The proposed concept of amyopathic dermatomyositis or dermatomyositis sine myositis has been the source of much controversy.[9–14] In addition to a prolonged follow-up, adequate electromyographic studies and muscle biopsy are mandatory before accepting that the patient has only cutaneous lesions.[14] Only 5% or less of cases of dermatomyositis can be classified as the amyopathic variant after long-term follow-up.[13] For the diagnosis of amyopathic dermatomyositis to be made, it has been suggested that there should be absence of clinical or laboratory signs of muscle disease for at least 2 years after the onset of skin disease.[15] The clinical cutaneous signs of amyopathic dermatomyositis are identical to those seen in classic dermatomyositis.

Dermatomyositis/polymyositis is associated with severe morbidity and high mortality, the latter particularly reflecting cardiac and pulmonary involvement.

The cutaneous features are usually quite distinctive.[16] Commonly, the patient presents with periorbital edema and a reddish-violet discoloration, often termed heliotrope erythema (heliotrope flower) (*Figs 16.124, 16.125*). The upper eyelids are most often affected and the eruption is typically symmetrical.[17] This is usually associated with a lupus-like erythema, which involves the rest of the face and spreads to the neck, upper trunk and extensor surfaces of the limbs and dorsal aspects of the hands and fingers (*Fig. 16.126*). It is associated with a slight scale.

Other cutaneous features include erythematous papules over the metacarpophalangeal joints (Gottron's sign), periungual erythema, telangiectasia and splinter hemorrhages (*Figs 16.127, 16.128*). Gottron's papules are typically found on the knuckles, but knees, elbows and malleoli may also be affected.[18] The toes are characteristically spared. The nail fold capillaries may be enlarged, dilated and distorted. Avascular areas are also often present.[16] Cuticular overgrowth is sometimes evident, and occasionally there is a cutaneous vasculitis presenting

Table 16.9

Diagnostic criteria for polymyositis/dermatomyositis

• Symmetrical weakness of proximal limb muscles and anterior neck flexors plus esophageal and respiratory muscle involvement
• Positive muscle biopsy features
• Elevated skeletal muscle enzymes
• Appropriate electromyographic features
• A typical rash
After Bohan, A. and Peter, J.B. (1975) Parts 1 and 2. *New England Journal of Medicine*, **292**, 344–347, 403–407.

Table 16.10

Variants of polymyositis

Type	Variant
I	Polymyositis
II	Dermatomyositis
III	Type I or II plus malignancy
IV	Childhood polymyositis or dermatomyositis
V	Overlap syndromes
After Bohan, A. and Peter, J.B. (1975) Parts 1 and 2. *New England Journal of Medicine*, **292**, 344–347, 403–407.	

as digital ulceration, periungual infarcts and mouth ulcers, though more often in the childhood variant.[16] With time the skin may become more atrophic and show the features of poikiloderma, which particularly affects the extensor surfaces and upper back, but may be more widespread (*Fig. 16.129*).[5,6] Scalp involvement, which presents with scaling and erythema, is not uncommon and is frequently pruritic.[16] Photosensitivity has occasionally been reported.[5,17] Other rare or unusual features include gingival telangiectases, follicular papules resembling pityriasis rubra pilaris, erythroderma, lesions resembling malignant atrophic papulosis (Degos' disease), a vesicobullous rash, a pustular eruption, localized mucinosis and panniculitis.[18–30] Some patients present with a centripetal flagellate erythema affecting the trunk and proximal extremities.[31] Subepidermal blistering may occur and this has been linked to internal malignancy.[23,32] A rare case with acute onset vesiculobullous

lesions and massive mucosal necrosis of the intestine has been documented.[33] Bullous pemphigoid may also rarely be associated with dermatomyositis.[34]

Symmetrical proximal (limb girdle) muscle weakness is the most common presenting feature of polymyositis.[5] The legs are almost always the initial site of involvement. The patient experiences difficulty in getting out of a chair, walking up the stairs, combing his hair or raising his head from a pillow. Interestingly, the facial muscles are almost never involved.[35] Although the muscles may be painful, this is not usually severe, and tenderness is often not present. Muscle atrophy develops later in the course of the disease when fibrosis and troublesome contractures may supervene.

Esophageal involvement manifests as dysphagia, which correlates with the presence of an associated malignancy.[4] Symptoms may also

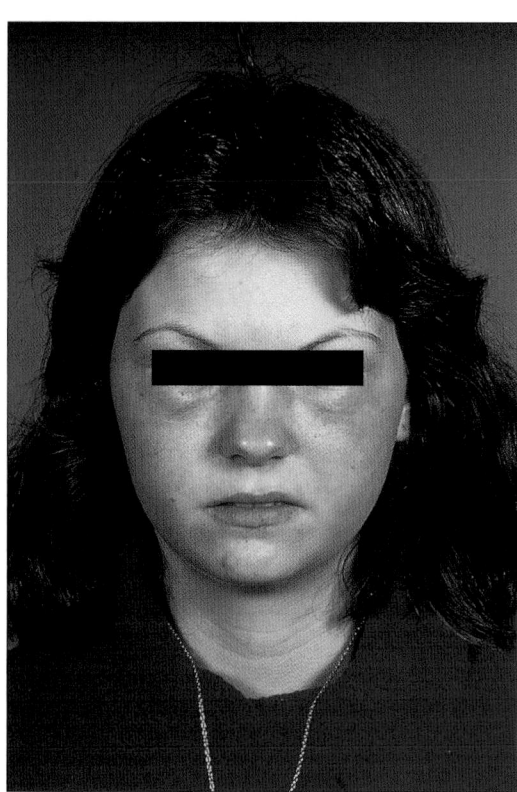

Fig. 16.124
Dermatomyositis: note the characteristic red–mauve discoloration around the eyes. There is also spread onto the cheeks. By courtesy of R.A. Marsden, MD, St George's Hospital, London, UK.

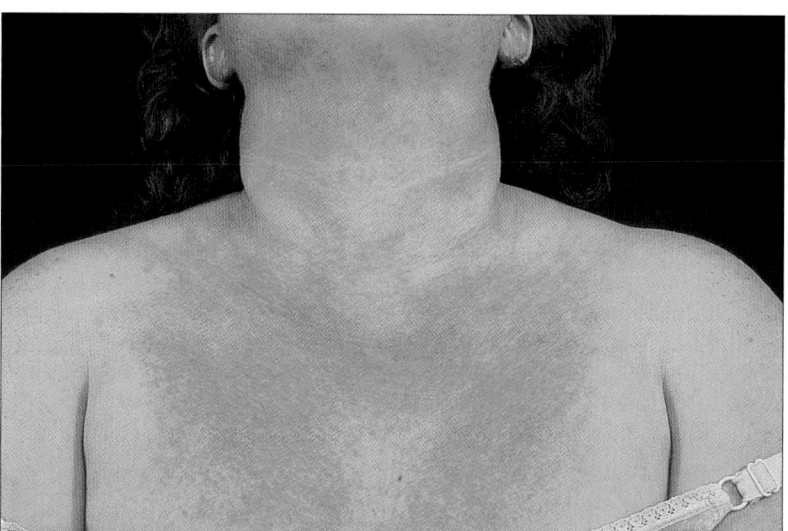

Fig. 16.126
Dermatomyositis: note the erythema and slight scale on this patient's chest. By courtesy of the Institute of Dermatology, London, UK.

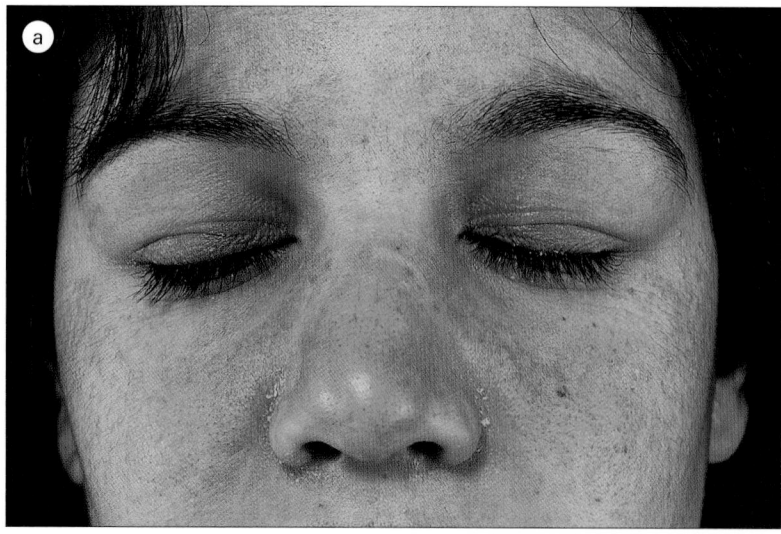

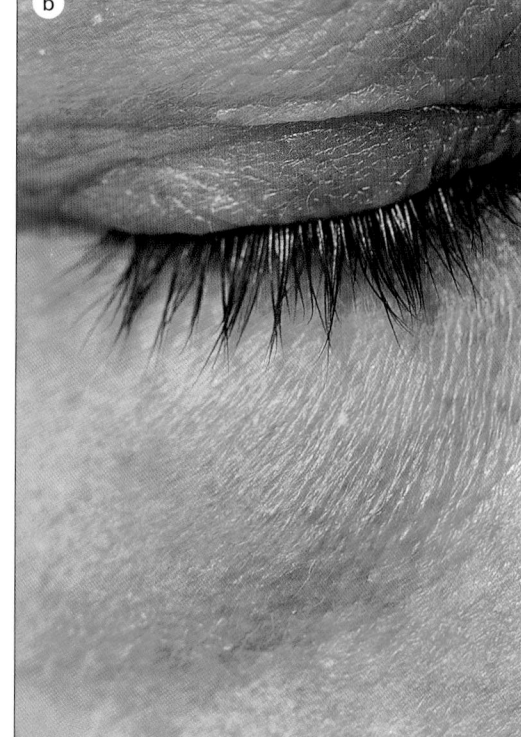

Fig. 16.125
(**a, b**) Dermatomyositis: the upper eyelids are particularly affected. By courtesy of the Institute of Dermatology, London, UK.

indicate pre-esophageal involvement due to cricopharyngeal striated muscle weakness.[5] Sequelae include nasal regurgitation and aspiration pneumonitis, the latter being associated with a high mortality. A change in voice is a not uncommon manifestation.

Electromyographic features in polymyositis/dermatomyositis are said to be pathognomonic and include the triad of short, low amplitude, polyphasic potentials, increased spontaneous activity including fibrillation potentials with positive sharp waves at rest, irritability and bizarre high frequency repetitive discharges.[35,36]

The serum usually contains raised levels of creatine kinase, aldolase, lactate dehydrogenase and transaminases; as not all these may be elevated in any one patient it is usually recommended that all are estimated routinely.[5] Sequential muscle enzyme studies are particularly useful for monitoring progress and response to treatment.

Involvement of cardiac muscle is not uncommon and patients may have tachycardia, electrocardiographic abnormalities (e.g. bundle branch block), congestive heart failure and cardiomegaly.[37]

Pulmonary involvement, as determined by the radiological changes of interstitial fibrosis and/or clinical evidence of impaired respiratory function, may occur in as many as 40% of patients with polymyositis/dermatomyositis.[5] An important recently described association is that between the anti-Jo-1 antibody, pulmonary fibrosis and dermatomyo-

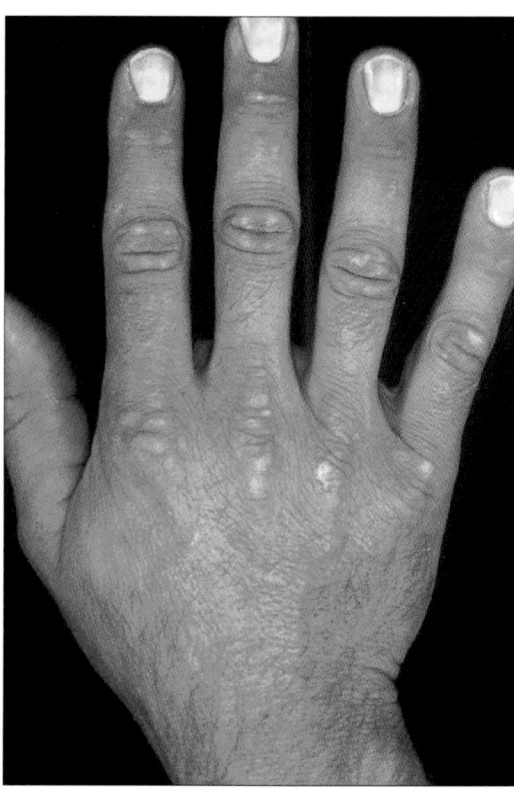

Fig. 16.127
Dermatomyositis: characteristic purple papules on the knuckles (Gottron's sign). By courtesy of the Institute of Dermatology, London, UK.

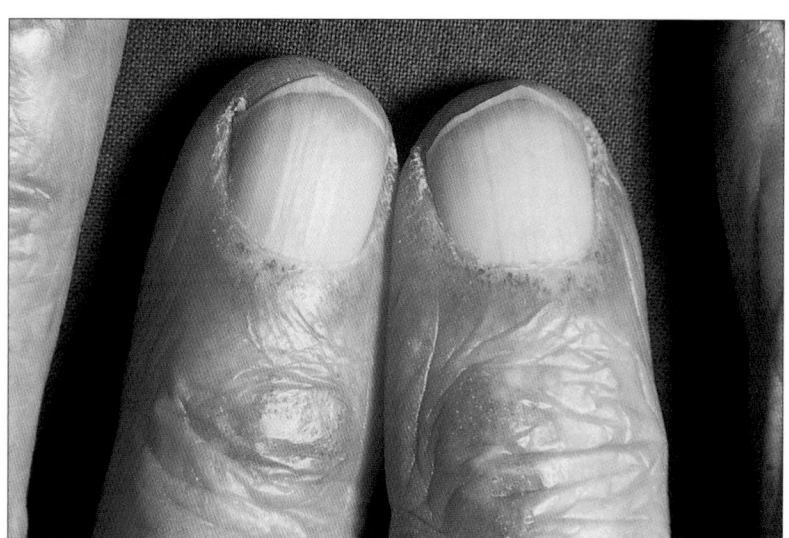

Fig. 16.128
Dermatomyositis: Gottron's papules, periungual erythema and telangiectatic capillary loops. By courtesy of the Department of Medical Illustration, The Radcliffe Infirmary, Oxford, UK.

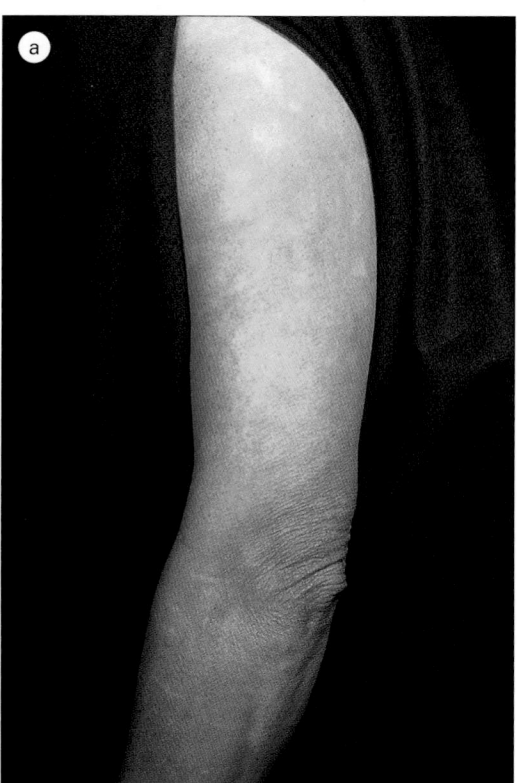

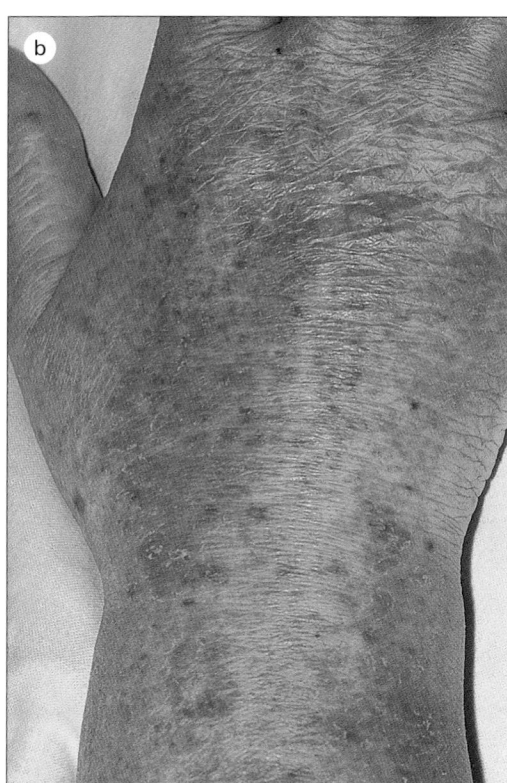

Fig. 16.129
Dermatomyositis: in this patient with longstanding disease, atrophy and variable pigmentary changes (poikiloderma) are present on (a) the extensor aspect of the arm and (b) the dorsum of the hand. By courtesy of the Institute of Dermatology, London, UK.

sitis.[38–42] More than 50% of patients with anti-Jo-1 antibody have interstitial lung disease.[36] Patients with this variant are not at risk of an increased incidence of internal malignancy. Additional features of this variant may include Raynaud's phenomenon, arthritis and tenosynovitis. Spread to the thoracic muscles may result in severe respiratory difficulties; terminal bronchopneumonia is therefore an important cause of death.[43]

Cutaneous vasculitis is characteristic of the childhood variant, which may involve the viscera; it has also been described in adult patients and may be associated with an increased risk of malignancy. Digital ulcers, periungual infarcts and oral ulcers are associated manifestations.[5] Calcification of the skin, soft tissues and muscle is rare except in the childhood variant where it may be widespread and of help diagnostically.[44]

Arthralgia is not uncommon, but frank arthritis is rare except in the overlap group of patients.[4]

Laboratory investigations may reveal non-specific findings of a raised ESR, hypergammaglobulinemia and a false positive Wassermann reaction. Antinuclear factor may be found in a small percentage of patients with polymyositis/dermatomyositis. Anti-RNP and -SM antibodies are only seen in 'overlap' patients. In addition to anti-Jo-1 antibody, additional newly described antibodies include PM-1, Ku, Mi-1, -2 and -3 and Pa-1.[45] The significance of these (except anti-Jo-1) is uncertain.[46]

Often stressed in polymyositis/dermatomyositis is the association with an increased risk of developing malignancy.[47] Although there has been a great range in reported incidences from small studies, varying from 15 to 60% of cases, recent investigations have suggested that the risk is less.[36,48–53] Among the reported associations, breast, stomach and ovarian tumors are most often cited. Patients should have a very thorough physical examination combined with routine laboratory investigations, chest x-ray, CT scan of the abdomen and pelvis and (in female patients) mammography. Underlying malignancy should be suspected in patients who do not respond to therapy or those who develop frequent episodes of myositis.[49,54] A recent study suggests that patients requiring more extensive search for malignancy should include those with constitutional symptoms, with rapid onset of dermatomyositis or polymyositis, without Raynaud's phenomenon, with a high ESR and with a very high creatine kinase level.[53]

There appears to be an increased risk of thyroid disease, particularly hypothyroidism, especially in patients with interstitial lung disease.[36] Juvenile dermatomyositis, which has an annual incidence of about one new case/million of the population/year, shows a female predominance (2:1) and presents most often in the first decade.[44] In addition to the features described above there is a high incidence of vasculopathic manifestations including gastrointestinal ulceration with hemorrhage, which may be fatal.[1] Multiorgan involvement is common. The condition is often preceded by an infection.[55] The prognosis is usually good with up to 70% of children making a full recovery.[55] In severely affected patients, widespread cutaneous involvement may be complicated by extensive scarring and diffuse calcification.[56]

Scleroderma/polymyositis overlap (sclerodermatomyositis) is the most common overlap syndrome. Although the myositis component is usually identical to that seen in dermatomyositis/polymyositis, the heliotrope erythema and Gottron's papules are usually absent.[57] The sclerodermatous cutaneous manifestations tend to be restricted to the peripheries. This overlap syndrome is associated with the Ku antibody and a case has been reported in association with Graves' disease and thrombocytopenic purpura.[58]

Pathogenesis and histological features

While the etiology and pathogenesis of polymyositis/dermatomyositis are unknown, it has been proposed that environmental factors (e.g. drugs, toxins or viruses) acting in association with a genetic predisposition result in a primarily immune-mediated disorder.[36] There is evidence to suggest that both humoral and cell-mediated components are important.

Antinuclear factor is commonly present. Antimyosin and antimyoglobin antibodies have been described, but their significance is uncertain. It is not clear whether they precede or follow the onset of the myositis, and their presence does not explain the cutaneous manifestations. However, antimyosin antibodies accompany any inflammatory myositis and are therefore probably a consequence of muscle necrosis.

A further set of antibodies directed against nuclear antigens have been described in 35–40% of patients with dermatomyositis/polymyositis:[60]

- PM-1 (PM-Scl) antibody correlates closely with polymyositis and polymyositis/scleroderma overlap.
- Ku antibody is a marker for sclerodermatomyositis.
- PA-1 antibody correlates with polymyositis, arthritis and fibrosing alveolitis.
- Mi-2 correlates with dermatomyositis.[5,36,60]

The presence of antibodies to the RNP antigens, U1 and U2, although not specific, are certainly highly suggestive of dermatomyositis/systemic sclerosis overlap syndrome.[57,61,62] Anti-signal recognition particle (SRP) antibodies are uncommon, but are usually associated with severe disease.[58] Although these antinuclear autoantibodies are of diagnostic value, they have not yet been shown to be of pathogenetic significance.

Dermatomyositis and polymyositis may develop in patients with other known autoimmune disorders, including autoimmune thyroid disease and insulin-dependent diabetes mellitus.[36]

The precise role of humoral immunity in dermatomyositis is unclear, but it is thought to be particularly related to the capillary loss and ischemic damage.[59]

Cell-mediated immunity is important in the development of experimental models of polymyositis. Lymphocytes taken from animals with allergic myositis (based upon sequential injections of heterologous muscle with Freund's adjuvant) prove cytotoxic to skeletal muscle fibers in culture and may undergo lymphoblastic transformation. Parallels do exist in the human disease, but whether these represent initiating factors or develop as a consequence of muscle damage is unknown.[1] A variety of cellular immune abnormalities have been documented, including the presence of activated mononuclear cells within skeletal muscle, abnormal trafficking of mononuclears to skeletal muscle, decreased autologous mixed lymphocyte responses, and mitotic and proliferative responses to autologous muscle.[36,63,64]

There is some evidence to suggest an inherited predisposition with an increased incidence of HLA-B8 and HLA-DR3 in both dermatomyositis and polymyositis, particularly in patients who have anti-Jo-1 antibodies.[36,65] There are rare instances of familial disease.[36]

A number of animal experimental models have shed some light on the possible pathogenesis of human myositis.[36] Injection of muscle extracts into a number of animals results in a mild, non-persistent myositis.[36]

A number of viruses – including Coxsackie B virus, simian acquired immunodeficiency retrovirus and murine encephalomyocarditis virus – have been shown to induce a chronic myositis-like disease. Virus strain and host genetic factors appear to be of particular importance.[36] Although uncertain, it has been suggested that some cases of dermatomyositis, particularly the juvenile variant, may represent an abnormal immunological response to a viral infection.[43] Picornaviruses, including the coxsackievirus group, have been particularly implicated.[1] The anti-Jo-1 antibody (an anti-aminoacyl-tRNA synthetase) reacts with histidyl-transfer RNA synthetase.[59] This enzyme has been shown to be capable of interacting with the RNA of a number of picornaviruses in addition to its normal substrate tRNA.[36] It has been suggested that the development of the autoantibody may occur as a consequence of this aberrant interaction.[36]

It is interesting to note that an illness similar to dermatomyositis may be induced by a number of infectious organisms including leishmania, parvovirus (erythrovirus) B19 and toxoplasma and as an adverse reaction to a number of drugs (e.g. hydroxyurea, cyclophosphamide and etoposide).[66–76]

Direct immunofluorescence of lesional skin reveals granular deposits of immunoglobulin (IgG, IgA and IgM) and complement at the dermoepidermal junction in about 35% of patients.[77,78] Site selection is of importance, positivity being most frequent with nail bed biopsies.[77] A more recent study has demonstrated C5b–9 deposition in blood vessel walls and along the dermoepidermal junction in conjunction with a negative lupus band test.[79,80] This finding has high specificity (93.5%) and sensitivity (78.5%). Epidermal keratinocytes may also be positive for C5b–9 and IgG.[80] The finding of C5b–9 in the wall of small blood vessels suggests that a complement-mediated microvascular injury may be of some importance in the pathogenesis of dermatomyositis.

The pathogenesis of childhood dermatomyositis has a predominantly ischemic basis (see below).[55]

The cutaneous findings are variable. The erythematous eruption shows slight hyperkeratosis and epidermal atrophy, with effacement of the ridge pattern (*Fig. 16.130*).[55] Basal cell liquefactive degeneration is typical and cytoid bodies are sometimes present (*Fig. 16.131*). Basement membrane thickening is occasionally prominent. There is upper dermal edema and melanophages may be evident. Rarely, the edema results in subepidermal vesiculation.[81] A light chronic inflammatory cell infiltrate is usually present (*Fig. 16.132*). It is commonly restricted to the superficial dermis and is not associated with the cutaneous adnexae. The infiltrate consists of activated T-lymphocytes and macrophages with occasional dermal Langerhans' cells.[82] Helper T-cells predominate. In some instances the presence of marked hyperkeratosis, follicular plugging, dermal edema and increased quantities of basement membrane-like material results in considerable histological overlap with lupus erythematosus.

Increased quantities of alcian blue-positive glycosaminoglycans are frequently present within the dermis.[81] Sometimes there are foci of calcification and panniculitis is occasionally evident.

The poikilodermatous lesions show hyperkeratosis, mild epidermal atrophy with loss of the epidermal ridge pattern, and basal cell liquefactive degeneration.[55] Additional features may include marked pigmentary incontinence, cytoid body formation and a patchy lymphocytic inflammatory cell infiltrate. The dermis is edematous, often contains increased mucin, and characteristically shows conspicuous dilated vascular channels. Nuclear atypia of the infiltrate as seen in poikilodermatous mycosis fungoides is not a feature.

Gottron's papules are characterized by hyperkeratosis, mild papillomatosis, acanthosis or, less often, epidermal atrophy and the features of an interface dermatitis as described above (*Fig. 16.133*).[83]

The histology of the centripetal flagellate erythema shows the changes of interface dermatitis.[31]

Ultrastructural studies contribute little to our understanding of dermatomyositis. Tubuloreticular inclusions as described in SLE have been described in endothelial cell and pericyte cytoplasm, but their significance is uncertain.[84]

In the juvenile variant, the cutaneous features are similar to those described above with the proviso that fibrosis is sometimes evident, calcification is more common and occlusive vascular disease (as characterized by fibrous intimal proliferation with fibrin thrombi) is often present.[55,56]

Skeletal muscle changes include both degenerative and regenerative features in addition to a focal chronic inflammatory cell infiltrate (*Figs 16.134, 16.135*).[55] The latter is composed predominantly of lymphocytes, but histiocytes, eosinophils and plasma cells may also be

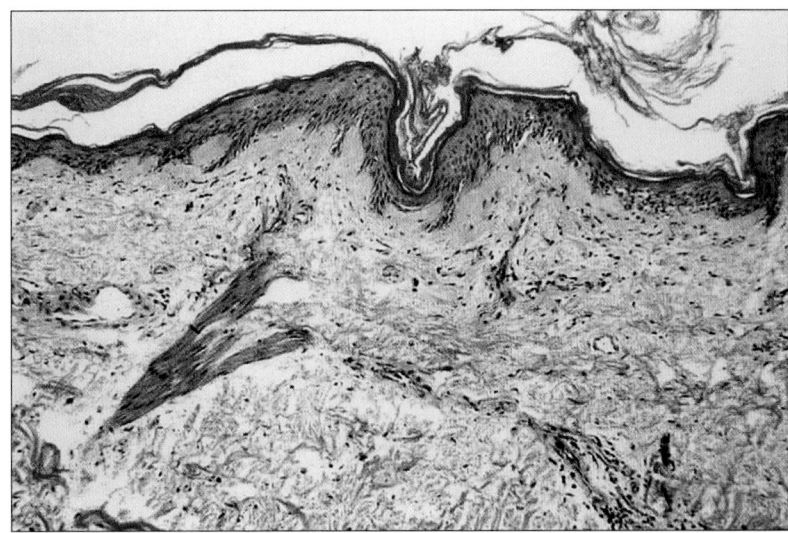

Fig. 16.130
Dermatomyositis: there is hyperkeratosis and epidermal atrophy. Note the mild telangiectasia.

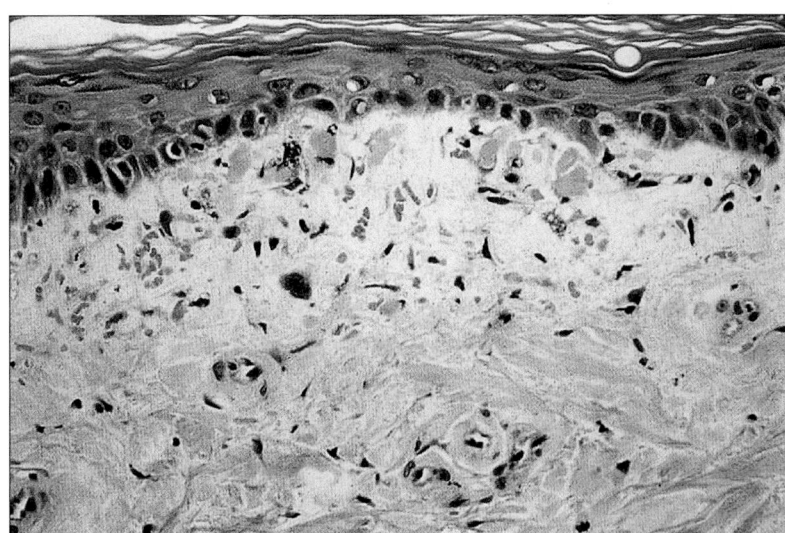

Fig. 16.131
Dermatomyositis: there is atrophy with effacement of the ridge pattern. In this example cytoid bodies are conspicuous. Note the pigmentary incontinence.

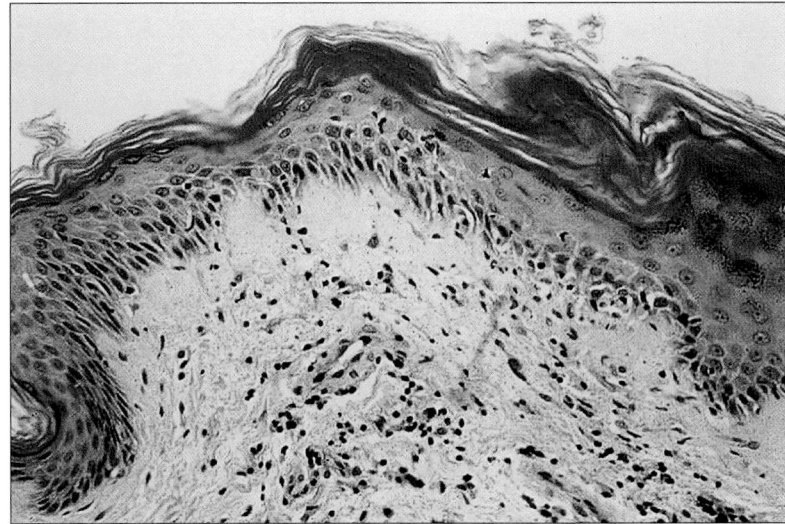

Fig. 16.132
Dermatomyositis: focal, mild basal cell hydropic degeneration is seen on the right. A chronic inflammatory cell infiltrate is present.

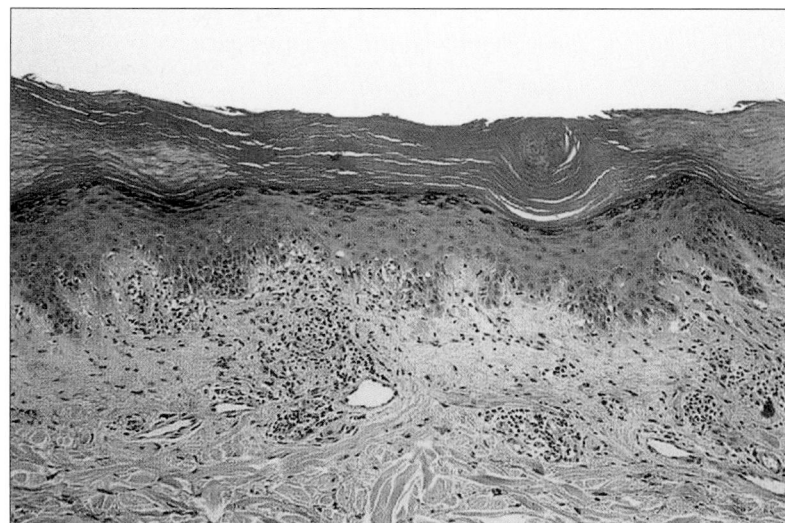

Fig. 16.133
Gottron's papule: hyperkeratosis, hypergranulosis and irregular acanthosis simulating lichen planus. Cytoid bodies are present in the superficial dermis and a perivascular chronic inflammatory cell infiltrate is evident. By courtesy of D. McGibbon, MD, St Thomas' Hospital, London, UK.

evident.[85] The lymphocytes consist of substantial numbers of B-cells, particularly in association with blood vessels, in addition to T-cells, which are predominantly found in and around the altered muscle fibers.[86] As in cutaneous lesions, T-helper cells predominate. Up to 25% of muscle biopsies may, however, show no evidence of inflammation.[4] The degenerative fibers are swollen and intensely eosinophilic and may show loss of striations (*Fig. 16.136*). Some fibers are vacuolated, but others appear granular or fragmented (*Fig. 16.137*). Proliferation and centralization of muscle nuclei is common, as is sarcoplasmic basophilia – features of regeneration (*Fig. 16.138*).

If material from a longstanding 'burnt out' lesion is biopsied, the muscle fibers are atrophic and there is endomysial fibrosis. Perifascicular atrophy – the presence of one or two rows of atrophic fibers at the edge of a fascicle – is said to be characteristic of dermatomyositis.[87] The muscle pathology in dermatomyositis and polymyositis is said to differ.[36] In dermatomyositis the inflammatory cell infiltrate tends to be septal or perivascular whereas in polymyositis it is intrafascicular. Muscle necrosis in dermatomyositis tends to involve small groups of fibers, while in polymyositis the affected fibers tend to be single and sparse.

Denervation neuropathic features are also occasionally present, presumably due to involvement by the inflammatory process of small

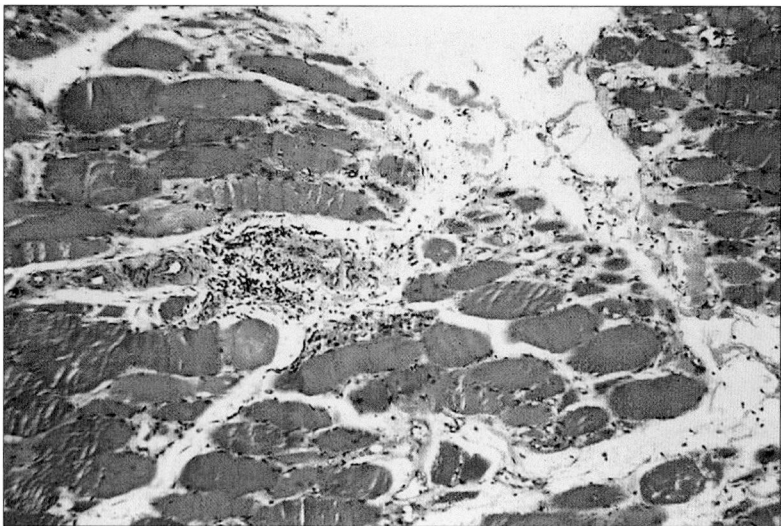

Fig. 16.134
Dermatomyositis: note the perivascular chronic inflammatory cell infiltrate.

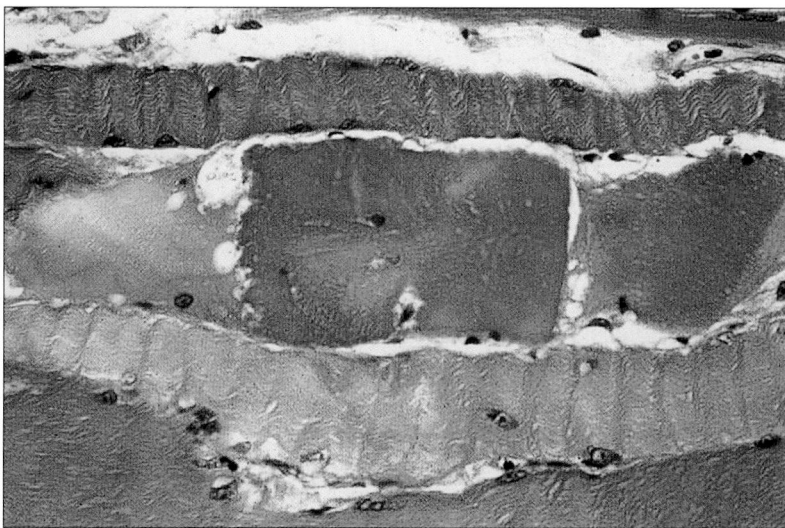

Fig. 16.136
Dermatomyositis: the central fiber is intensely swollen, eosinophilic and fragmented; there is a loss of striations.

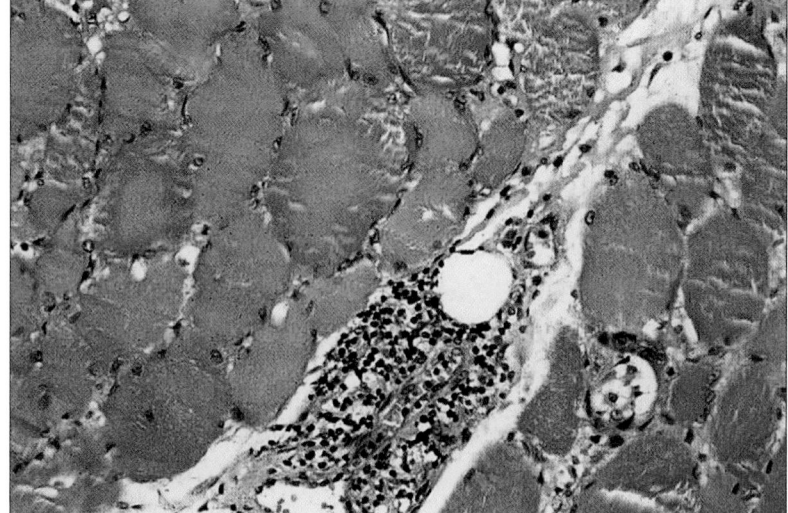

Fig. 16.135
Dermatomyositis: the infiltrate consists predominantly of lymphocytes.

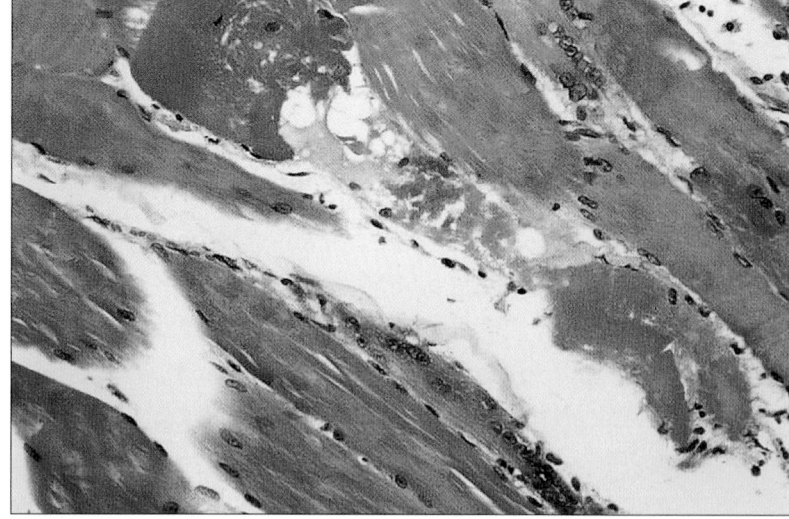

Fig. 16.137
Dermatomyositis: the fiber in the upper midfield is swollen, eosinophilic, vacuolated and in places granular; beneath is a regenerating basophilic cell.

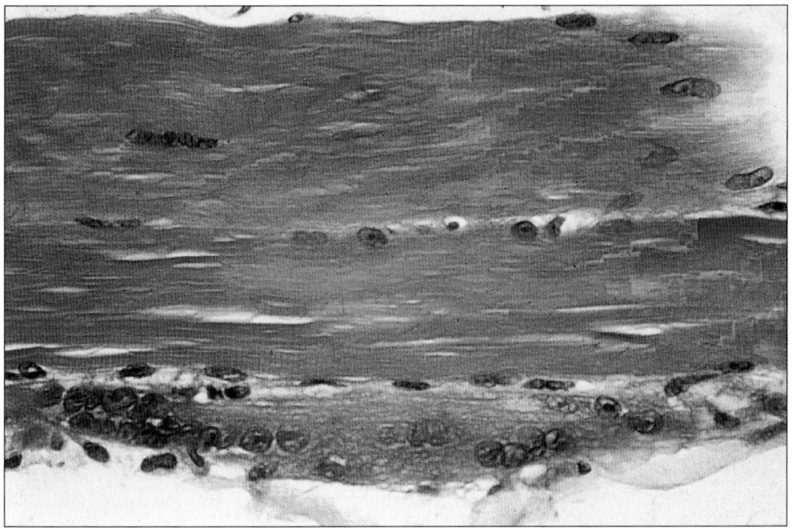

Fig. 16.138
Dermatomyositis: the lower fiber is basophilic and shows excessive nuclei – features of regeneration. Note the centralization of nuclei in the upper fiber.

intramuscular nerve fibers.[55] Steroid atrophy of type II muscle fibers may be seen in biopsies from treated patients.

In childhood dermatomyositis, vascular changes affecting the capillaries, venules and arterioles are common.[88] The inflammatory component, which is usually quite sparse, consists of lymphocytes, monocytes and plasma cells centered predominantly on the vasculature in the perifascicular connective tissue.[89] Muscle changes are variable and range from perifascicular atrophy in milder disease through to focal necroses and infarction in the more seriously affected patients, in whom fibrosis may also be a feature.[89] The vascular lesions include endothelial cell swelling and necrosis with or without occlusion, non-necrotizing lymphocytic vasculitis and loss of the peripheral fascicular capillary bed.[89]

Immunofluorescence of muscle biopsies in childhood dermatomyositis commonly shows vascular intramural IgM and C3.[89]

References

1. Olson, J.C. (1992) Juvenile dermatomyositis. *Semin Dermatol*, **11**, 57–64.
2. Bohan, A., Peter, J.B. (1975) Polymyositis and dermatomyositis. Part 1. *N Eng J Med*, **292**, 344–347.
3. Bohan, A., Peter, J.B. (1975) Polymyositis and dermatomyositis. Part 2. *N Eng J Med*, **292**, 403–407.
4. Bohan, A., Peter, J.B., Bowman, R.L. et al (1977) A computer-assisted analysis of 153 patients with polymyositis and dermatomyositis. *Medicine (Baltimore)*, **56**, 255–286.
5. Caro, I. (1989) Dermatomyositis as a systemic disease. *Med Clin North Am*, **73**, 1181–1192.
6. Callen, J.P. (1985) Dermatomyositis – an update. *Semin Dermatol*, **4**, 114–125.
7. Rockerbie, N.R., Woo, T.Y., Callen, J.P. et al (1989) Cutaneous changes of dermatomyositis precede muscle weakness. *J Am Acad Dermatol*, **20**, 629–632.
8. Kagen, L.J. (1995) Amyopathic dermatomyositis. *Arch Dermatol*, **131**, 1458–1459.
9. Euwer, R.L., Sontheimer, R.D. (1991) Amyopathic dermatomyositis (dermatomyositis siné myositis): presentation of six new cases and review of the literature. *J Am Acad Dermatol*, **24**, 959–966.
10. Caproni, M., Salvatore, E., Bernacchi, E. et al (1998) Amyopathic dermatomyositis: report of three cases. *Br J Dermatol*, **139**, 1116–1118.
11. Erel, A., Toros, P., Tokcaer, A.B. et al (2000) Amyopathic dermatomyositis. *Int J Dermatol*, **39**, 771–773.
12. Caproni, M., Cardinali, C., Parodi, A. et al (2002) Amyopathic dermatomyositis: a review by the Italian Group of Immunodermatology. *Arch Dermatol*, **138**, 23–27.
13. El-Azhary, R.A., Pakzad, S.Y. (2002) Amyopathic dermatomyositis: retrospective review of 37 cases. *J Am Acad Dermatol*, **46**, 560–565.
14. Stonecipher, M.R., Jorizzo, J.L., White, W.L. et al (1993) Cutaneous changes of dermatomyositis in patients with normal muscle enzymes: dermatomyositis sine myositis? *J Am Acad Dermatol*, **28**, 951–956.
15. Hess Schimd, M., Trüeb, M.R. (1997) Juvenile amyopathic dermatomyositis. *Br J Dermatol*, **136**, 431–433.
16. Caro, I. (1988) A dermatologist's view of dermatomyositis. *Clin Dermatol*, **6**, 9–14.
17. Cheong, W-K., Hughes, G.R.V., Norris, P.G. et al (1994) Cutaneous photosensitivity in dermatomyositis. *Br J Dermatol*, **131**, 205–208.
18. Ghali, F.E., Stein, L.D., Fine, J-D. (1999) Gingival telangiectases. An underappreciated physical sign of juvenile dermatomyositis. *Arch Dermatol*, **135**, 1370–1374.
19. Requena, L., Grilli, R., Soriano, L. et al (1997) Dermatomyositis with a pityriasis rubra pilaris-like eruption: a little-known distinctive cutaneous manifestation of dermatomyositis. *Br J Dermatol*, **17**, 37–40.
20. Lupton, J.R., Figueroa, P., Berberian, B.J. et al (2000) An unusual presentation of dermatomyositis: the type Wong variant revisited. *J Am Acad Dermatol*, **43**, 908–912.
21. Nousari, H.C., Kimyai-Asadi, A., Spegman, D.J. (1998) Paraneoplastic dermatomyositis presenting as erythroderma. *J Am Acad Dermatol*, **39**, 653–654.
22. Tsao, H., Busam, K., Barnhill, R.L. et al (1997) Lesions resembling malignant atrophic papulosis in a patient with dermatomyositis. *J Am Acad Dermatol*, **36**, 317–319.
23. McCollough, M.L., Cockerell, C.J. (1998) Vesiculo-bullous dermatomyositis. *Am J Dermatopathol*, **20**, 170–174.
24. Jara, M., Amérigo, J., Duce, S. et al (1997) Dermatomyositis and flagellate erythema. *Clin Exp Dermatol*, **21**, 440–441.
25. Bachmeyer, C., Blum, L., Danne, O. et al (1998) Isolated flagellate eruption in dermatomyositis. *Dermatology*, **197**, 92–93.
26. Lister, R.K., Cooper, E.S., Paige, D.G. (2000) Papules and pustules of the elbows and knees: an uncommon clinical sign of dermatomyositis in Oriental children. *Pediatr Dermatol*, **17**, 37–40.
27. Kaufmann, R., Greiner, D., Schmidt, P. et al (1998) Dermatomyositis presenting as plaque-like mucinosis. *Br J Dermatol*, **138**, 889–892.
28. del Pozo, J., Almagro, M., Martínez, W. et al (2001) Dermatomyositis and mucinosis. *Int J Dermatol*, **40**, 120–124.
29. Molnár, K., Kemény, L., Korom, I. et al (1998) Panniculitis in dermatomyositis: report of two cases. *Br J Dermatol*, **139**, 161–163.
30. Chao, Y-Y., Yang, L-J. (2000) Dermatomyositis presenting as panniculitis. *Int J Dermatol*, **39**, 141–144.
31. Nousari, H.C., Ha, V.T., Laman, S.D. et al (1999) 'Centripetal flagellate erythema': a cutaneous manifestation associated with dermatomyositis. *J Rheumatol*, **26**, 692–695.
32. Kubo, M., Sato, S., Kitahara, H. et al (1996) Vesicle formation in dermatomyositis associated with gynecologic malignancies. *J Am Acad Dermatol*, **34**, 391–394.
33. Fujimoto, M., Murakami, T., Murata, S. et al (2002) Acute onset vesiculo-bullous dermatomyositis associated with massive mucosal necrosis of the intestines. *Clin Exp Dermatol*, **27**, 718–720.
34. Glover, M., Leigh, I. (1992) Dermatomyositis pemphigoides: a case with coexistent dermatomyositis and bullous pemphigoid. *J Am Acad Dermatol*, **27**, 849–852.
35. Greenlee, R. Jr (1988) The neurologist's approach to polymyositis. *Clin Dermatol*, **6**, 23–35.
36. Plotz, P.H., Dalakas, M., Leff, R.L. et al (1989) Current concepts in the idiopathic inflammatory myopathies: polymyositis, dermatomyositis and related disorders. *Ann Intern Med*, **111**, 143–157.
37. Askari, A.D., Heuttner, T.L. (1982) Cardiac abnormalities in polymyositis/dermatomyositis. *Semin Arthritis Rheum*, **12**, 208–219.
38. Yoshida, S., Akizuki, M., Mimori, T. et al (1983) The precipitating antibody to an acidic nuclear antigen protein, the Jo-1, in connective tissue diseases: a marker for a subset of polymyositis with interstitial pulmonary fibrosis. *Arthritis Rheum*, **26**, 604–611.
39. Bernstein, R.M., Morgan, S.H., Chapman, J. et al (1984) Anti-Jo-1 antibody: a marker for myositis with interstitial lung disease. *BMJ*, **289**, 151–152.
40. Nishikai, M., Reichlin, M. (1980) Heterogeneity of precipitating antibodies in polymyositis and dermatomyositis: characterization of the Jo-1 antibody system. *Arthritis Rheum*, **23**, 881–888.
41. Phillips, T.J., Leigh, I.M., Wright, J. (1987) Dermatomyositis and pulmonary fibrosis associated with anti-Jo-1 antibody. *J Am Acad Dermatol*, **17**, 381–382.
42. Douglas, W.W., Tazelaar, H.D., Hartman, T.E. (2001) Polymyositis–dermatomyositis-associated interstitial lung disease. *Am J Respir Crit Care Med*, **164**, 1182–1185.
43. Dickey, B.F., Myers, A.R. (1984) Pulmonary disease in polymyositis/dermatomyositis. *Semin Arthritis Rheum*, **14**, 60–76.
44. Norins, A.L. (1989) Juvenile dermatomyositis. *Med Clin North Am*, **73**, 1193–1209.
45. Nishikai, M., Reichlin, M. (1980) Purification and characterization of a nuclear non-histone basic protien (Mi-1) which reacts with anti-immunoglobulin sera and the sera of patients with dermatomyositis. *Mol Immunol*, **17**, 1129–1141.
46. Cari, I. (1986) Dermatomyositis. In: Thiers, B.H., Dobson, R.L. (eds) Pathogenesis of skin disease. Edinburgh: Churchill Livingstone, pp 244–256.
47. Callen, J.P. (1982) The value of malignant evaluation in patients with dermatomyositis. *J Am Acad Dermatol*, **6**, 253–259.
48. Sigurgeirsson, B., Lindelof, B., Edhag, O. et al (1992) Risk of cancer in patients with dermatomyositis or polymyositis: a population-based study. *N Engl J Med*, **326**, 363–367.
49. Cox, N.H., Lawrence, C.M., Langtry, J.A.A. et al (1990) Dermatomyositis. Disease associations and an evaluation of screening investigations for malignancy. *Arch Dermatol*, **126**, 61–65.
50. Manchul, L.A., Jin, A., Pritchard, K.I. et al (1985) The frequency of malignant neoplasms in patients with polymyositis–dermatomyositis. *Arch Intern Med*, **145**, 1835–1839.
51. Bernard, P., Bonnetblanc, J-M. (1993) Dermatomyositis and malignancy. *J Invest Dermatol*, **100**, 128S–132S.
52. Lakhanpal, S., Bunch, T.W., Ilstrup, D.M. et al (1986) Polymyositis–dermatomyositis and malignant lesions: does an association exist? *Mayo Clin Proc*, **61**, 645–653.
53. Sparsa, A., Liozon, E., Herrmann, F. et al (2002) Routine vs extensive malignancy search for adult dermatomyositis and polymyositis: a study of 40 patients. *Arch Dermatol*, **138**, 885–890.
54. Wakata, N., Kurihara, T., Saita, E. et al (2002) Polymyositis and dermatomyositis associated with malignancy: a 30 year retrospective study. *Int J Dermatol*, **41**, 729–734.
55. Kasper, C.S., White, C.L., Freeman, R.G. (1988) Pathology and immunopathology of polymyositis and dermatomyositis. *Clin Dermatol*, **6**, 64–75.
56. Bowyer, S.L., Clark, R.A., Ragsdale, C.G. et al (1986) Juvenile dermatomyositis: histologic findings and pathogenetic hypothesis for the associated skin change. *J Rheumatol*, **13**, 753–759.
57. Mimori, T. (1987) Scleroderma–polymyositis overlap syndrome: clinical and serological aspects. *Int J Dermatol*, **26**, 419–425.
58. Kamei, N., Yamane, K., Yamashitz, Y. et al (2002) Anti-ku antibody-positive scleroderma–dermatomyositis overlapping syndrome developing Graves' disease and immune thrombocytopenic puprpura. *Intern Med*, **44**, 1199–1203.
59. Targoff, I.N. (1993) Humoral immunity in polymyositis/dermatomyositis. *J Invest Dermatol*, **100**, 116S–123S.
60. Mimori, T., Akizuki, M., Yamagata, H. et al (1981) Characterization of a high molecular weight acidic nuclear protein recognized by autoantibodies in the sera from a patient with polymyositis–scleroderma overlap. *J Clin Invest*, **68**, 611–620.
61. Craft, J.E., Mimori, T., Downs, J. (1986) Autoantigenic epitopes of the U-series snRNPs. *Clin Res*, **34** (Abstract), 616.
62. Reichlin, M., Maddison, P.J., Targoff, I. et al (1984) Antibodies to a nuclear/nucleolar antigen in patients with polymyositis overlap syndromes. *J Clin Immunol*, **4**, 40–44.
63. Miller, F.W., Read, E.J., Carrasquillo, J.A. et al (1988) Abnormal lymphocyte trafficking to muscle in patients with idiopathic inflammatory myopathy. *Arthritis Rheum*, **31**, S60, B4.
64. Cronin, M.E., Plotz, P.H., Miller, F.W. (1988) Abnormalities of the immune system in the idiopathic inflammatory myopathies. *In Vivo*, **2**, 25–30.
65. Friedman, J.M., Pachman, L.M., Maryjowski, M.L. et al (1983) Immunogenetic studies of juvenile dermatomyositis: HLA-DR antigen frequencies. *Arthritis Rheum*, **26**, 214–216.
66. Daudén, E., Peñas, P.F., Rios, L. et al (1996) Leishmaniasis presenting as a dermatomyositis-like eruption in AIDS. *J Am Acad Dermatol*, **35**, 316–319.
67. Crowson, A.N., Magro, C.M., Dawood, M.R. (2000) A causal role for parvovirus B19 infection in adult dermatomyositis and other autoimmune syndromes. *J Cutan Pathol*, **27**, 505–515.
68. Magro, C.M., Dawood, M.R., Crowson, A.N. (2001) The cutaneous manifestations of human parvovirus. *Hum Pathol*, **31**, 488–497.
69. Senet, P., Aractinig, S., Porneuf, M. et al (1995) Hydroxyurea-induced dermatomyositis-like eruption. *Br J Dermatol*, **133**, 455–459.
70. Suehiro, M., Kishimoto, S., Wakabayashi, T. et al (1998) Hydroxyurea dermopathy with a dermatomyositis-like eruption and a large leg ulcer. *Br J Dermatol*, **139**, 748–749.
71. Varma, S., Lanigan, S.W. (1999) Dermatomyositis-like eruption and leg ulceration caused by hydroxyurea in a patient with psoriasis. *Clin Exp Dermatol*, **24**, 164–166.
72. Daoud, M.S., Gibson, L.E., Pittelkow, M. (2000) Hydroxyurea dermatopathy: a unique lichenoid eruption complicating long-term therapy with hydroxyurea. *J Am Acad Dermatol*, **36**, 178–182.
73. Vassallo, C., Passamonti, S., Merante, S. et al (2001) Muco-cutaneous changes during long-term therapy with hydroxyurea in chronic myeloid leukaemia. *Clin Exp Dermatol*, **26**, 141–148.
74. Kirby, B., Gibson, L.E., Rogers, S. et al (2000) Dermatomyositis-like eruption and leg ulceration caused by hydroxyurea in a patient with psoriasis. *Clin Exp Dermatol*, **25**, 256.
75. Oskay, T., Kuthuay, L., Ozylikan, O. (2002) Dermatomyositis-like eruption after long-term hydroxyurea therapy for polycythemia vera. *Eur J Dermatol*, **12**, 586–588.
76. Ruiz-Genaro, D.P., Sánz-Sánchez, T., Bartolomé-González, B. et al (2002) Dermatomyositis-like reaction induced by chemotherapeutical agents. *Int J Dermatol*, **41**, 885–887.

77. Chen, Z., Maize, J.C., Silver, R.M. et al (1985) Direct and indirect immunofluorescent findings in dermatomyositis. *J Cutan Pathol*, **12**, 18–27.
78. Winkelmann, R., Jordan, R.G., de Morogas, J.M. (1972) Immunofluorescent studies of dermatomyositis. *Dermatologica*, **145**, 42–47.
79. Magro, C.M., Crowson, A.N. (1997) The immunofluorescence profile of dermatomyositis: a comparative study with lupus erythematosus. *J Cutan Pathol*, **24**, 543–552.
80. Kissel, J.T., Mendell, J.R., Rammohan, K.W. (1986) Microvascular deposition of complement membrane attack complex in dermatomyositis. *N Engl J Med*, **314**, 329–334.
81. Janis, J.F., Winkelmann, R.K. (1968) Histopathology of the skin in dermatomyositis: a histopathologic study of 55 cases. *Arch Dermatol*, **97**, 640–650.
82. Hausmann, G., Herrero, C., Cid, M.C. et al (1991) Immunopathologic study of skin lesions in dermatomyositis. *J Am Acad Dermatol*, **25**, 225–230.
83. Hanno, R., Callen, J.P. (1985) Histopathology of Gottron's papules. *J Cutan Pathol*, **12**, 389–394.
84. Hashimoto, K., Robinson, L., Velayos, E. et al (1971) Dermatomyositis: electron microscopic, immunologic, and tissue culture studies of paramyxovirus-like inclusions. *Arch Dermatol*, **103**, 120–135.
85. Whitaker, J.N. (1982) Inflammatory myopathy: a review of etiologic and pathogenetic factors. *Muscle Nerve*, **5**, 573–592.
86. Engel, A.G., Arahata, K. (1986) Mononuclear cells in myopathies: quantitation of functionally distinct subsets, recognition of antigen-specific cell-mediated cytotoxicity in some diseases, and implications for the pathogenesis of the different inflammatory myopathies. *Human Pathol*, **17**, 704–721.
87. Peiffer, J., Bahr, M. (1987) Anomalies in perifascicular muscle fibers as a differential-diagnostic criterion: I. Perifascicular atrophy in inflammatory myopathies. *Clin Neuropathol*, **6**, 123–132.
88. Banker, B.Q. (1975) Dermatomyositis of childhood: ultrastructural alterations of muscle and intramuscular blood vessels. *J Neuropathol Exp Neurol*, **34**, 46–75.
89. Crowe, W.E., Bove, K.E., Levinson, J.E. et al (1982) Clinical and pathogenetic implications of histopathology in childhood polydermatomyositis. *Arthritis Rheum*, **25**, 126–139.

Mixed connective tissue disease

Clinical features

As originally defined by Sharp et al, mixed connective tissue disease (MCTD) represents a clinical condition in which patients have an overlap of signs and symptoms of systemic sclerosis, systemic lupus erythematosus and polymyositis/dermatomyositis.[1,2]

Although the concept of mixed connective tissue disease as a distinctive entity separated from other connective tissue diseases has been controversial, the disease has characteristic and reproducible clinical and serological features.[3,4] Some patients present with manifestations that are not entirely diagnostic and may progress over time to develop typical features of MCTD or other connective tissue diseases, particularly SLE. These patients are designated as having an unclassified or undifferentiated connective tissue disease.[5]

MCTD is characterized by a marked female predominance (16:1) and shows no racial predilection.[6,7] Presentation is usually in the second and third decades, but children may also be affected.[1,8] Clinical features include arthralgias and non-deforming arthritis, swollen hands with tapered or sausage-shaped fingers, Raynaud's phenomenon, abnormal esophageal motility, myositis, lymphadenopathy, fever, hepatomegaly, serositis and splenomegaly.[1] Patients were initially thought not to show features of renal, pulmonary or neuropsychiatric involvement or vasculitis. In addition, their sera invariably contained high titers of antibody to a saline extractable nuclear antigen (ENA), U1-RNP and speckled antinuclear antibody. Precipitating antibody to SM soluble nuclear antigen was absent. The disease responded to corticosteroid therapy and had a favorable outcome.

In the light of data from subsequent experience, the above, rather simplistic, overview has had to be modified.[6,9] Although a variety of diagnostic criteria have been proposed, that of Alarcón-Segovia and Cardiel has been chosen, largely because of its simplicity.[10] They suggest that if the criteria used are restricted to certain key clinical manifestations then MCTD may be accurately diagnosed (*Table 16.11*).[7]

Table 16.11
Diagnostic criteria for mixed connective tissue disease

• Serologic   – high anti-RNP titer (> 1:1600 by hemagglutination or an equivalent by another method)

• Clinical
  – edema of the hands
  – synovitis
  – myositis (biopsy proven or elevated CPK)
  – Raynaud's phenomenon (two or three phases)
  – acrosclerosis

• Diagnosis of MCTD requires   – positive serology plus three or more of the clinical criteria

CPK, creatinine phosphokinase; MCTD, mixed connective tissue disease; RNP, ribonucleoprotein. Reproduced with permission from Alarcón-Segovia, D. (1994) *Clinics in Dermatology*, **12**, 309–316.

Essential to the diagnosis is the presence of high titer anti-ENA antibodies (anti-U1-RNP). Anti-ENA antibodies are also present in the sera of patients with SLE. In MCTD, however, the antibody–antigen interaction is sensitive to ribonuclease and trypsin and resistant to deoxyribonuclease, the antigen in fact being ribonucleoprotein (U1-RNP).[11] In SLE, the antibody activity is resistant to ribonuclease and deoxyribonuclease, but sensitive to trypsin, and the antigen is SM. Anti-ENA antibodies are not seen in systemic sclerosis or dermatomyositis. Patients with MCTD do not usually develop antibodies to native DNA.[12] The presence of anti-Ro (SS-A) antibodies appears to identify a subgroup of patients frequently presenting with malar rash and photosensitivity.[13]

In addition to hand and finger changes and Raynaud's phenomenon, patients may develop alopecia, areas of hypo- and hyperpigmentation, and sclerodermiform nail fold capillaropathy. Cutaneous lesions of DLE, SCLE and SLE also occur.[14] Occasionally, the cutaneous lesions of dermatomyositis are evident. Livedoid vasculitis with ulcers has also been documented and was associated with poor prognosis in the single patient described.[15] Other less common manifestations include alopecia and oral ulcers.[16] Sicca symptoms are present in up to one-third of patients.[17]

Systemic features that are more commonly documented in MCTD include deforming polyarthritis, which particularly affects the hands and feet (often in association with rheumatoid factor), juxta-articular and peritendinous nodules, and calcification involving the forearms, wrists, hands and feet.[6,18] A distinctive mutilating arthropathy giving rise to a 'main en lorgnette' appearance is said to be characteristic.[11]

It is now known that if patients are followed for a sufficiently long period there is a much greater risk of visceral lesions than was previously realized.[14] The majority develop asymptomatic respiratory involvement. Pulmonary hypertension with a poor prognosis is, however, not rare.[19,20] Up to 10% of patients develop renal disease (albeit usually mild) and a significant proportion of patients develop neuropsychiatric and cerebral manifestations, including trigeminal neuropathy and migrainous headaches.[21] The mixed nature of the clinical manifestations later becomes less obvious with evolution towards a single disease process, usually systemic sclerosis. It is generally considered that, although mortality is low in MCTD, there is a much greater morbidity due to internal involvement than was originally appreciated.

Pathogenesis and histological features

The etiology and pathogenesis of MCTD are unknown. MCTD has, however, apparently followed vinyl chloride exposure.[21] Immunoglobulin (Gm) allotype association and an increased frequency of HLA-DR4 in patients with polyarthritis have been documented.[11,22] Patients are frequently lymphopenic with diminished circulating T-cells and increased B-cells.[11]

The histological features of the varying cutaneous manifestations have been described in the appropriate sections (*Fig. 16.139*). Biopsies from

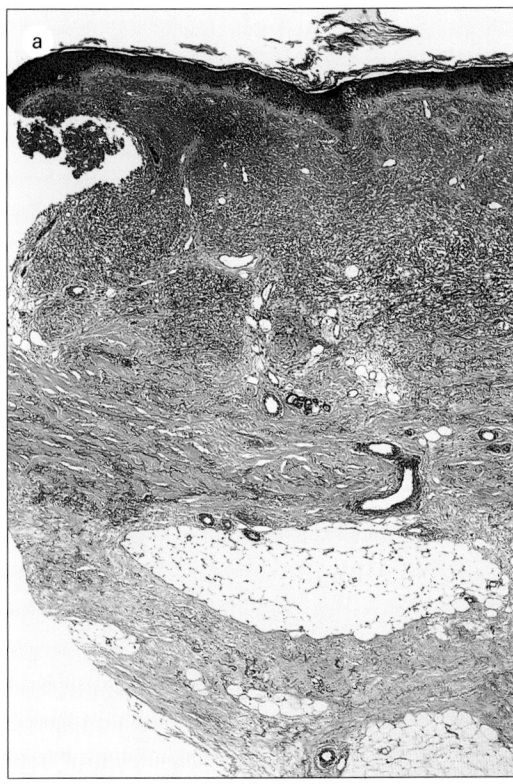
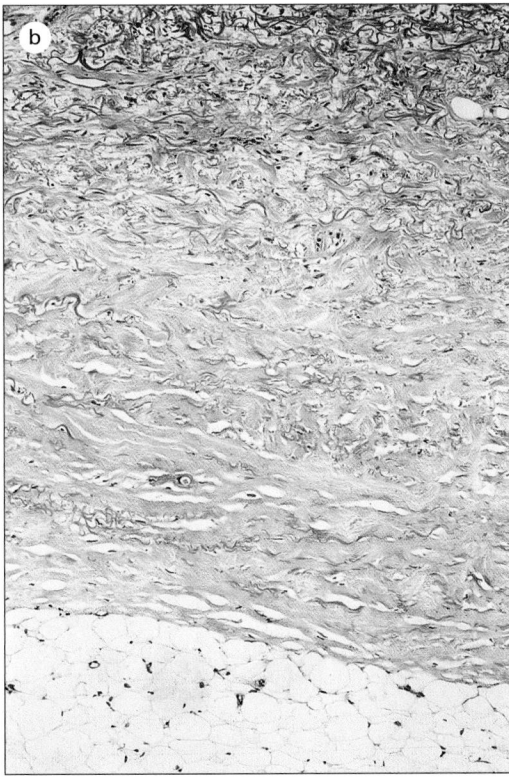

Fig. 16.139
(a, b) Mixed connective tissue disease: morphea-like features. There is dense dermal sclerosis with extension into the subcutaneous fat.

cutaneous lesions with no typical features may show histological features similar to those of subacute lupus.[23]

Direct immunofluorescence may reveal epithelial speckled nuclear positivity, presumably representing in vivo binding of anti-U1-RNP antibodies.[24]

References

1. Sharp, G.C., Irvin, W.S., Tan, E.M. et al (1972) Mixed connective tissue disease – an apparently distinct rheumatic disease syndrome associated with a specific antibody to an extractable nuclear antigen (ENA). *Am J Med*, **52**, 148–159.
2. Sharp, G.C., Anderson, P.C. (1980) Current concepts in the classification of connective tissue diseases. Overlap syndromes and mixed connective tissue disease. *J Am Acad Dermatol*, **2**, 269–279.
3. Maddison, P.J. (2000) Mixed connective tissue disease: overlap syndromes. *Baillieres Best Pract Res Clin Rheumatol*, **14**, 111–124.
4. Sharp, G.C. (2002) MCTD: a concept which stood the test of time. *Lupus*, **11**, 333–339.
5. Alarcón, G.S. (2000) Unclassified or undifferentiated connective tissue disease. *Baillieres Best Pract Res Clin Rheumatol*, **14**, 125–137.
6. Maddison, P.J. (1991) Mixed connective tissue disease, overlap syndromes and eosinophilic fasciitis. *Ann Rheum Dis*, **50**, 887–893.
7. Alarcón-Segovia, D. (1994) Mixed connective tissue disease and overlap syndromes. *Clin Dermatol*, **12**, 309–316.
8. Yang, Y.H., Tsai, M.J., Lin, S.C. et al (2000) Childhood mixed connective tissue disease. *J Formos Med Assoc*, **99**, 158–161.
9. Niemelstein, S.H., Brody, S., McShane, D. et al (1980) Mixed connective tissue disease: a subsequent evaluation of the original 25 patients. *Medicine (Baltimore)*, **59**, 239–248.
10. Alarcón-Segovia, D., Cardiel, M.M. (1989) Comparison between 3 diagnostic criteria for mixed connective tissue disease. Study of 593 patients. *J Rheumatol*, **16**, 328–334.
11. Alarcón-Segovia, D., Uribe-Uribe, O. (1979) Mutilans-like arthropathy in mixed connective tissue disease. *Arthritis Rheum*, **22**, 1013–1018.
12. Bennett, R.M., O'Connell, D.J. (1980) Mixed connective tissue disease: a clinicopathologic study of 20 cases. *Semin Arthritis Rheum*, **10**, 25–51.
13. Setty, Y.N., Pittman, C.B., Mahale, A.S. et al (2002) Sicca symptoms and anti-SSA/Ro antibodies are common in mixed connective tissue disease. *J Rheumatol*, **29**, 487–489.
14. Black, C. (1981) Mixed connective tissue disease. *Br J Dermatol*, **104**, 713–719.
15. Oh, Y.B., Jun, J.B., Kim, C.K. et al (2000) Mixed connective tissue disease associated with skin defects of livedoid vasculitis. *Clin Rheumatol*, **19**, 381–384.
16. Nedumaran, Rajendran, C.P., Porkodi, R., Parthiban, R. (2001) Mixed connective tissue disease – clinical and immunological profile. *J Assoc Physicians India*, **49**, 412–414.
17. Setty, Y.N., Pittman, C.B., Mahale, A.S. et al (2002) Sicca symptoms and anti-SSA/Ro antibodies are common in mixed connective tissue disease. *J Rheumatol*, **29**, 487–489.
18. Lazaro, M.A., Morteo, O.G. (1989) Clinical and serologic characteristics of patients with overlap syndrome: is mixed connective tissue disease a distinct entity? *Medicine (Baltimore)*, **68**, 281–289.
19. Alpert, M.A., Goldberg, S.H., Singsen, B.H. et al (1983) Cardiovascular manifestations of mixed connective tissue disease in adults. *Circulation*, **68**, 1182–1193.
20. Hoffman, R.W., Greidinger, E.L. (2000) Mixed connective tissue disease. *Curr Opin Rheumatol*, **12**, 386–390.
21. Kahn, M-K.A., Bovogeois, P., Aeschlimann, A. et al (1989) Mixed connective tissue disease after exposure to polyvinyl chloride. *J Rheumatol*, **16**, 533–535.
22. Black, C.M., Maddison, P.J., Welsh, K.I. et al (1988) HLA and immunoglobulin allotypes in mixed connective tissue disease. *Arthritis Rheum*, **31**, 131–135.
23. Magro, C.M., Crowson, A.N., Regauer, S. (1997) Mixed connective tissue disease. A clinical, histologic and immunofluorescence study of eight cases. *Am J Dermatopathol*, **19**, 206–213.
24. Gilliam, J.N., Prystowsky, S.D. (1977) Mixed connective tissue disease syndrome. Cutaneous manifestations of patients with epidermal nuclear staining and high titer serum antibody to ribonuclease sensitive extractable nuclear antigen. *Arch Dermatol*, **113**, 583–587.

Relapsing polychondritis

Clinical features

Relapsing polychondritis is a rare disorder characterized by recurrent episodes of inflammation of cartilaginous tissue throughout the body and its subsequent degeneration and replacement by fibrous tissue (*Fig. 16.140*).[1,2] The ears (93%), nose (56%), larynx and trachea (30%) are predominantly affected.[3–7] Skin manifestations are the presenting features in approximately 50% of cases.[6] There is a slight male predominance and the median age at diagnosis in one large study was 46.6 years.[8] Presentation in children is exceptional.[9] Clinical criteria for diagnosis have been established. Three of these, together with biopsy confirmation of chondritis, are required for diagnosis[5] (*Table 16.12*).

Although it particularly affects Caucasians, cases have been recorded in Asians, blacks, Hispanics and the Japanese.[3] The sex incidence is equal. Most patients present in the fourth decade.[4] There is no evidence of a hereditary predisposition.[6] Clinical signs may be subtle and can resemble those seen in Behçet's disease or inflammatory bowel disease; the diagnosis is often difficult.[2,10] Familial cases are exceptional.[11]

Auricular chondritis is the commonest lesion and is frequently bilateral.[3] Patients present with painful, tender, erythematous, sometimes blue–black and swollen ears.[6] Chronicity leads to distortion and flabbiness. Arthritis (seronegative) particularly affects the sternoclavicular, costochondral and sternomanubrial joints.[3] One or more joints may be affected and lesions are often migratory.[6] Painful nasal chondritis may result in epistaxis, and saddle nose is an occasional complication. Nasal involvement is seen in over 50% of patients.[8] Oral aphthosis was present in 11% of patients in a large series.[2] In 6% of patients, oral and genital aphthae were seen.[2] When the disease initially presents, inflammation of a single site may be confused with erysipelas.[12]

Ocular lesions include conjunctivitis, corneal ulceration, iridocyclitis, proptosis, cataract, chorioretinitis, scleromalacia perforans, scleritis, retinal detachment, blindness, edema of the eyelids and muscle palsies.[3,6,8,13,14] Aseptic meningitis is a rare complication.[15]

Respiratory lesions may affect the larynx, trachea and major bronchi with obstructive symptoms, stenosis, collapse and bronchopneumonia.[3,7,8] Exceptionally, airway involvement may be the only manifestation of the disease.[16] Cardiovascular lesions include valvular incompetence, conduction defects, cystic medial necrosis of the aorta, vasculitis and pericarditis.[3,8,17] Involvement of the heart valves occurs in up to 10% of patients and systemic vasculitis, reminiscent of polyarteritis nodosa, has been described.[18] Ear involvement includes external ear chondritis, otitis media, vertigo and deafness.[19]

Dermatological manifestations have included leukocytoclastic vasculitis, cutaneous polyarteritis nodosa, erythema elevatum diutinum, livedo reticularis, alopecia, retarded nail growth, erythematous nodules, erythema nodosum, thrombosis, pyoderma gangrenosum-like lesions, Sweet's syndrome, postinflammatory hyperpigmentation and psoriasis.[2,3,6,20–25] Exceptional associations with normolipemic plane xanthomatosis and with panniculitis showing septal and lobular involvement accompanied by vasculitis have been documented.[26,27]

Significant disease associations that may be present in up to 30% of patients include leukocytoclastic vasculitis, systemic vasculitis (Takayasu and temporal arteritis, Wegener's granulomatosis), Hashimoto's thyroiditis, arthritis, Sjögren's syndrome, dermatomyositis, MCTD, SLE, inflammatory bowel disease and myeloproliferative disorders.[2,6,19,28–31]

An increased ESR and anemia are the commonest significant laboratory manifestations. Increased urinary glycosaminoglycans have also been documented.[32]

Relapsing polychondritis has a significant mortality. The 5-year survival rate is approximately 74%.[19] Infection, respiratory failure, systemic vasculitis, large vessel aneurysm rupture and renal failure are the commonest causes of death.[1,19]

A number of patients have been reported to have myelodysplastic syndrome associated with relapsing polychondritis.[33–36] This is of interest since myelodysplastic syndrome is known to be associated with autoimmune disease.[37,38] In a large study of 200 patients, 11% had myelodysplastic syndrome.[2]

Relapsing polychondritis has been associated with the luteinizing hormone–releasing hormone (LH–RH) analogue goserelin. As the disease may worsen during pregnancy and during chorionic gonadotropin therapy, it is suggested that hormones may be a precipitating factor.[39]

Pathogenesis and histological features

The precise etiology of relapsing polychondritis is poorly understood. Several studies have suggested an immunological mechanism.[6] The association with autoimmune diseases in many patients lends support to this thesis. Antibodies (predominantly IgG) to type II collagen, which accounts for over 50% of the proteins in cartilage, have been detected in a proportion of patients in titers of 1:10–1:320.[24,28,40,41] The antibodies are directed against both native and denatured protein.[28] Using ELISA, one study showed that 50% of patients have antibodies against type II collagen.[42] In this same study, 4% of control subjects and 15% of rheumatoid arthritis patients also had antibodies in their sera. Those patients who have the autoantibody show evidence of active disease, whereas those studied without it are either in remission or being treated.[28] Rats immunized with type II collagen develop auricular chondritis. Cartilage from these same animals had positive immunofluorescence for IgG and C3.[43] In a single patient, T-cell clones were found to be specific for the collagen II peptide 261–273.[44]

An association between the disease and HLA-DR4 has been reported but there is no predominance of any DR4 subtype.[45]

Anti-fetal cartilage antibodies have been detected by indirect immunofluorescence studies.[41] Documentation of transplacental transfer of these antibodies with neonatal involvement suggests that they are of pathogenetic significance. One group of authors suggested that matrilin-1, a cartilage matrix protein, is the target of autoreactivity.[47] Another group found autoantibodies to matrilin-1 in 13% of patients and antibody titers correlated with symptomatology.[48] Rats immunized with matrilin-1 develop nasorespiratory abnormalities (but not ear or joint changes).[49] Cartilage oligometric matrix protein has also been suggested as a potential autoantigen.[50]

Circulating immune complexes have also been demonstrated in relapsing polychondritis, together with deposits of immunoglobulin and complement in inflamed cartilage, adding further support to a possible immune mechanism in this disease.[3,25,28] Granular deposits of immunoglobulin and complement (C3) have been described at the chondrofibrous junction in two patients.[50] The presence of antineutrophil

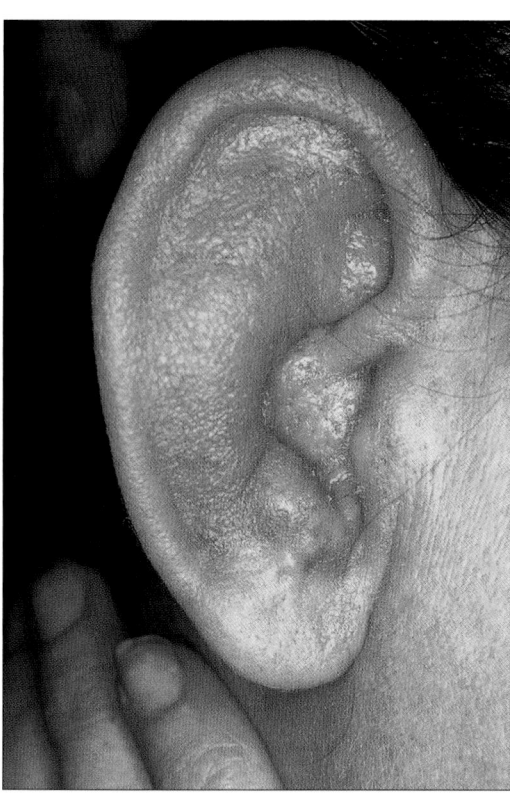

Fig. 16.140
Relapsing polychondritis: the ear shows considerable erythema and swelling. By courtesy of R.A. Marsden, MD, St George's Hospital, London, UK.

Table 16.12
Diagnostic criteria for relapsing polychondritis

• Recurrent articular chondritis
• Cochlear and vestibular damage
• Ocular involvement
• Nasal involvement
• Tracheal/pharyngeal involvement
• Non-erosive polyarthritis

cytoplasmic antibody (ANCA) has been reported.[51] Elevated serum levels of macrophage migration inhibitory factor have also been documented.[52]

There is some evidence suggesting that cell-mediated immunity may also be of importance in the pathogenesis. Patients display positive lymphoblast transformation and macrophage migration inhibition to cartilage glycosaminoglycans.[1] Responses correlate with episodes of disease activity.

Histological examination of the skin is unremarkable. The dermis contains a mild focal lymphohistiocytic infiltrate. Examination of the fibrocartilaginous tissues, however, shows degenerative and inflammatory changes affecting the marginal chondrocytes, with loss of basophilia and poor alcian blue staining of the cartilaginous tissue (*Figs 16.141, 16.142*).

The inflammatory cell infiltrate, which includes lymphocytes, plasma cells, histiocytes and occasional polymorphs, infiltrates the degenerate cartilage. Eventually, there is replacement by granulation and fibrous tissue.[3] Atypical lymphoid infiltrates mimicking a lymphoma have rarely been described.[53]

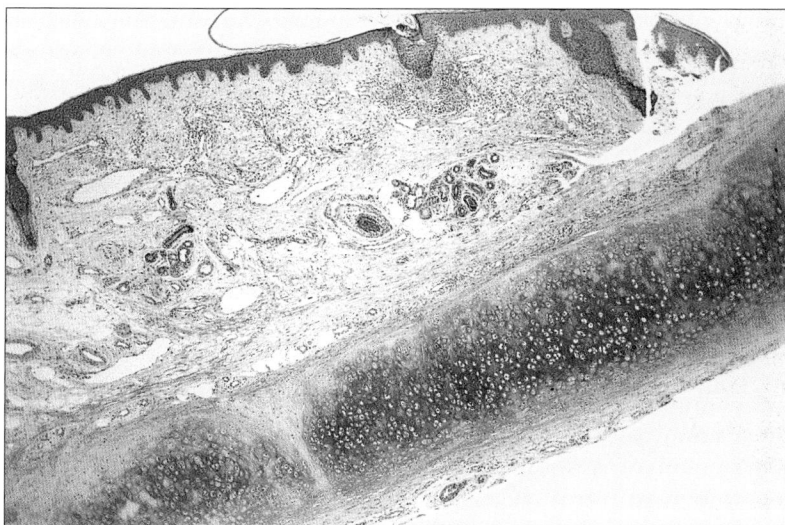

Fig. 16.141
Relapsing polychondritis: in this early lesion, the degenerate cartilage shows intense eosinophilia.

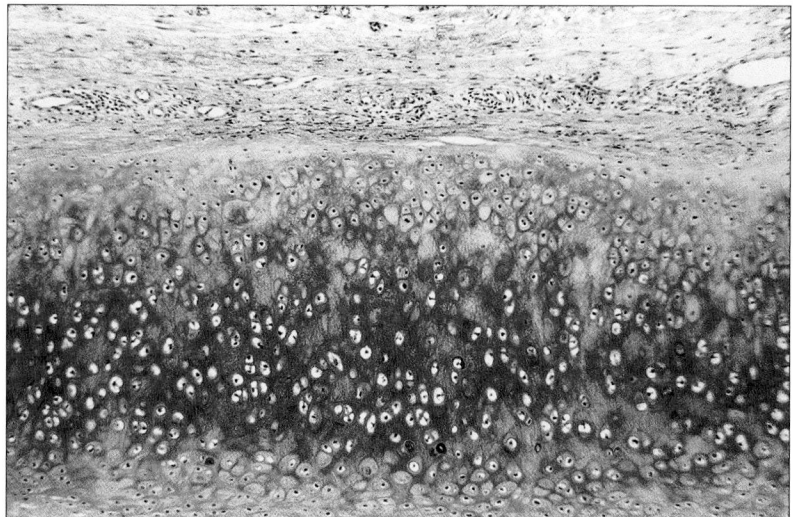

Fig. 16.142
Relapsing polychondritis: a mild chronic inflammatory cell infiltrate is present in the perichondrium.

Differential diagnosis

Chondrodermatitis nodularis helicis differs by the presence of characteristic layering of fibrin, granulation tissue, and cartilage with degenerative changes. Clinically, chondrodermatitis helicis presents as a focal, punched-out ulcer. This differs from the diffuse involvement of the ear seen in relapsing polychondritis.

References

1. Letko, E., Zafirakis, P., Baltatzis, S. et al (2002) Relapsing polychondritis: a clinical review. *Semin Arthritis Rheum*, 31, 384–395.
2. Frances, C., El Rassi, R., Laporte, J.L. et al (2001) Dermatologic manifestations of relapsing polychondritis. A study of 200 cases at a single center. *Medicine (Baltimore)*, 80, 173–179.
3. Cohen, P.R., Rapini, R.P. (1986) Relapsing polychondritis. *Int J Dermatol*, 25, 280–285.
4. Arkin, C.R., Masi, A.T. (1975) Relapsing polychondritis: review of current status and case report. *Semin Arthritis Rheum*, 5, 41–62.
5. McAdam, L.P.O., Hanlan, M.A., Bluestone, R. (1976) Relapsing polychondritis. Prospective study of 23 patients and a review of the literature. *Medicine (Baltimore)*, 55, 193–215.
6. White, J.W. (1985) Relapsing polychondritis. *South Med J*, 78, 448–451.
7. Burlew, B.P., Lippton, H., Klinestiver, D. et al (1992) Relapsing polychondritis: new pulmonary manifestations. *J Louisiana State Med Soc*, 144, 58–62.
8. Zeuner, M., Straub, R.H., Rauh, G.G. et al (1997) Relapsing polychondritis: clinical and immunogenetic analysis of 62 patients. *J Rheumatol*, 24, 96–101.
9. Soto-Romero, I., Fustes-Morales, A.J., De Leon-Bojorge, B. et al (2002) Relapsing polychondritis: a pediatric case. *Pediatr Dermatol*, 19, 60–63.
10. Trentham, D.E., Le, C.H. (1998) Relapsing polychondritis. *Ann Intern Med*, 129, 114–122.
11. Arundell, F.W., Haserick, J.R. (1960) Familial chronic atrophic polychondritis. *Arch Dermatol*, 82, 439–441.
12. Khan, A.J., Lynfield, Y., Baldwin, H. (1994) Relapsing polychondritis: case report and review of the literature. *Cutis*, 54, 98–100.
13. Bhagat, N., Green, R.L., Feldon, S.E. et al (2001) Exudative retinal detachment in relapsing polychondritis: case report and literature review. *Ophthamology*, 108, 1156–1159.
14. Chow, M.T., Anderson, S.F. (2000) Relapsing polychondritis. *Optom Vision Sci*, 77, 286–292.
15. Berg, A.M., Kaszica, J., Hopkins, P. et al (1996) Relapsing polychondritis and aseptic meningitis. *J Rheumatol*, 23, 567–569.
16. Ozbay, B., Dilek, F.H., Yalcinkaya, I. et al (1998) Relapsing polychondritis. *Respiration*, 65, 206–207.
17. Barretto, S.N., Oliveira, G.H., Michet, C.J. Jr et al (2002) Multiple cardiovascular complications in a patient with relapsing polychondritis. *Mayo Clin Proc*, 77, 971–974.
18. Lie, J.T. (1989) Systemic and isolated vasculitis: a rational approach to classification and pathologic diagnosis. In: Pathology annual. Norwalk, CT: Appleton & Lange, Vol. 24, pp 25–114.
19. Rauh, G., Kamilli, I., Gresser, U. et al (1993) Relapsing polychondritis presenting as cutaneous polyarteritis nodosa. *Clin Invest*, 71, 305–309.
20. Delgado, J., Gómez-Cerezo, J., Siguenza, M. et al (2001) Relapsing polychondritis and erythema elevatum diutinum: an unusual association refractory to dapsone. *J Rheumatol*, 28, 634–635.
21. Fujimoto, N., Tajima, S., Ishibashi, A. et al (1998) Acute febrile neutrophilic dermatosis, Sweet's syndrome in a patient with relapsing polychondritis. *Br J Dermatol*, 139, 930–931.
22. Michet, C.J., McKenna, C.H., Luthra, H.S. et al (1986) Relapsing polychondritis. Survival and predictive role of early disease manifestations. *Ann Intern Med*, 104, 74–78.
23. Hedfors, E., Hammar, H., Theorell, H. (1982) Relapsing polychondritis. Presentation of 4 cases. *Dermatologica*, 164, 47–53.
24. Ebringer, R., Rook, G., Swana, G.T. et al (1981) Autoantibodies to cartilage and type II collagen in relapsing polychondritis and other rheumatic diseases. *Ann Rheum Dis*, 40, 473–479.
25. Borbujo, J., Balsa, A., Aguado, P. et al (1989) Relapsing polychondritis associated with psoriasis vulgaris. *J Am Acad Dermatol*, 20, 130–131.
26. Yoshimura, T., Aiba, S., Tadaki, H. et al (1994) Generalized normolipemic plane xanthomatosis associated with relapsing polychondritis. *Acta Derm Venereol*, 74, 221–223.
27. Disdier, P., Andrac, L., Swiader, L. et al (1996) Cutaneous panniculitis and relapsing polychondritis: two cases. *Dermatology*, 193, 266–268.
28. Foidart, J.M., Abe, S., Martin, G.R. et al (1978) Antibodies to type 2 collagen in relapsing polychondritis. *N Engl J Med*, 299, 1203–1207.
28. Balsa, A., Espinosa, A., Cuesta, M. et al (1995) Joint symptoms in relapsing polychondritis. *Clin Exp Rheumatol*, 13, 425–430.
30. Yamazaki, K., Suga, T., Hirata, K. (2001) Large vessel arteritis in relapsing polychondritis. *J Laryngol Otol*, 115, 836–838.
31. Harisdangkul, V., Johnson, W.W. (1994) Association between relapsing polychondritis and systemic lupus erythematosus. *South Med J*, 87, 753–757.
32. Passos, C.O., Onofre, G.R., Martins, R.C. et al (2002) Composition of urinary glycosaminoglycans in a patient with relapsing polychondritis. *Clin Biochem*, 35, 377–381.
33. Hebbar, M., Brouillard, M., Wattel, E. et al (1995) Association of myelodysplastic syndrome and relapsing polychondritis: further evidence. *Leukemia*, 9, 731–733.
34. Banerjee, S.S., Morris, D.P., Rothera, M.P. et al (2001) Relapsing polychondritis associated with monoclonal gammopathy in a patient with myelodysplastic syndrome. *J Laryngol Otol*, 115, 482–484.
35. Manganelli, P., Delsante, G., Bianchi, G. et al (2001) Remitting seronegative symmetrical synovitis with pitting edema in a patient with myelodysplastic syndrome and relapsing polychondritis. *Clin Rheumatol*, 20, 132–135.
36. Myers, G., Gould, J., Dolan, G. (2000) Relapsing polychondritis and myelodysplasia: a report of two cases and review of the current literature. *Clin Lab Haematol*, 22, 45–48.
37. Diebold, L., Rauh, G., Jager, K. et al (1995) Bone marrow pathology in relapsing polychondritis: high frequency of myelodysplastic syndromes. *Br J Haematol*, 89, 820–830.
38. Enright, H., Miller, W. (1997) Autoimmune phenomena in patients with myelodysplastic syndromes. *Leuk Lymphoma*, 24, 483–489.
39. Labarthe, M.P., Bayle-Lebey, P., Bazex, J. (1997) Cutaneous manifestations of relapsing polychondritis in a patient receiving goserelin for carcinoma of the prostate. *Dermatology*, 195, 391–394.
40. Foidart, J.M., Katz, S.I. (1979) Relapsing polychondritis: subtle clues to diagnosis by immunopathology. *Am J Dermatopathol*, 1, 257–259.
41. Meyer, O., Cyna, J., Dryll, A. et al (1981) Relapsing polychondritis – pathogenic role of anti-native collagen type II antibodies: a case report with immunological and pathological studies. *J Rheumatol*, 8, 820–824.
42. Terato, K., Shimozuru, Y., Katayama, K. et al (1990) Specificity of antibodies to type II collagen in rheumatoid arthritis. *Arthritis Rheum*, 33, 1493–1500.
43. Cremer, M.A., Pitcock, J.A., Stuart, J.M. et al (1981) Auricular chondritis in rats. An experimental model of relapsing polychondritis induced with type II collagen. *J Exp Med*, 154, 535–540.
44. Buckner, J.H., van Landerghen, M., Kwok, W.W. et al (2002) Identification of type II collagen peptide 261–273-specific T cell clones in a patient with relapsing polychondritis. *Arthritis Rheum*, 46, 238–244.
45. Lang, B., Rothenfusser, A., Lanchbury, J.R. et al (1993) Susceptibility to relapsing polychondritis is associated with HLA-DR4. *Arthritis Rheum*, 36, 660–664.
46. Buckner, J.H., Wu, J.J., Reife, R.A. et al (2000) Autoreactivity against matrilin-1 in a patient with relapsing polychondritis. *Arthritis Rheum*, 43, 939–943.
47. Hansson, A.S., Heinegard, D., Piette, J.C. et al (2001) The occurrence of autoantibodies to matrilin 1 reflects a tissue-specific response to cartilage of the respiratory tract in patients with relapsing polychondritis. *Arthritis Rheum*, 44, 2402–2412.

48. Hansson, A.S., Heinegard, D., Holmdahl, R. (1999) A new animal model for relapsing polychondritis, induced by cartilage matrix protein (matrilin-1). *J Clin Invest*, **104**, 589–598.

49. Hansson, A.S., Holmdahl, R. (2002) Cartilage-specific autoimmunity in animal models and clinical aspects in patients – focus on relapsing polychondritis. *Arthritis Res*, **4**, 296–301.

50. Valenzuela, R., Cooperrider, P.A., Gogate, P. et al (1980) Relapsing polychondritis – immunomicroscopic findings in cartilage of ear biopsy specimens. *Hum Pathol*, **11**, 19–22.

51. Papo, T., Piette, J-C., Le Thi Huong, D. et al (1993) Antineutrophil cytoplasmic antibodies in polychondritis. *Ann Rheumatol Dis*, **52**, 384–385.

52. Ohwatari, R., Fukuda, S., Iwabuchi, K. et al (2001) Serum level of macrophage inhibitory factor as a useful parameter of clinical course in patients with Wegener's granulomatosis and relapsing polychondritis. *Ann Otol Rhinol Laryngol*, **110**, 1035–1040.

53. Magro, C.M., Crowson, A.N., Harrist, T.J. (1997) Atypical lymphoid infiltrates arising in cutaneous lesions of connective tissue disease. *Am J Dermatopathol*, **19**, 446–455.

Infectious diseases of the skin

Wayne Grayson, Eduardo Calonje and Phillip H McKee

17

VIRAL INFECTIONS   838

Common wart   838

Plantar warts   841

Plane warts   843

Condyloma acuminatum   844

Bowenoid papulosis   847

Epidermodysplasia verruciformis   847

Herpes simplex virus infections   850

Varicella and herpes zoster   855

Cytomegalovirus infections   858

Exanthem subitum   860

Diseases caused by orthopox viruses   860

Milker's nodule   862

Ecthyma contagiosum   862

Molluscum contagiosum   864

Hand, foot and mouth disease   867

Viral hemorrhagic fevers   868

BACTERIAL INFECTIONS   869

Impetigo   869

Staphylococcal scalded skin syndrome   872

Erysipelas and cellulitis   875

Necrotizing fasciitis   876

Infective folliculitis   878

Folliculitis keloidalis nuchae   880

Pseudofolliculitis   880

Meningococcal septicemia   881

Gonorrhea   881

Plague   881

Cutaneous anthrax   882

Brucellosis   884

DISEASES CAUSED BY *BARTONELLA* SPECIES   884

Cat scratch disease   884

Trench fever   885

Bartonellosis   886

Bacillary angiomatosis   887

Lyme disease   889

Venereal syphilis   891

ENDEMIC (NON-VENEREAL) TREPONEMATOSES   891

Endemic syphilis   892

Yaws   893

Pinta   894

Lymphogranuloma venereum   894

Granuloma inguinale (donovanosis)   894

Chancroid   894

Tuberculosis   894

Tuberculids   902

Non-tuberculous environmental mycobacterial infections   904

Leprosy   910

Rhinoscleroma   918

Nocardiosis   919

Botryomycosis   921

Malakoplakia   922

Actinomycosis   923

Erythrasma   924

Trichomycosis   925

Pitted keratolysis   926

Cutaneous diphtheria   927

Sago palm disease   927

Tularemia   927

Rickettsial infections   928

PROTOZOAL INFECTIONS   929

Leishmaniasis   929

Amebiasis cutis   934

Cutaneous acanthamebiasis   935

ALGAL INFECTION   936

Protothecosis   936

FUNGAL INFECTIONS   938

Tinea capitis   **938**

Infections caused by *Microsporum audouinii* and *Microsporum canis*   938

Kerion   939

Endothrix infections   940

Black piedra   940

White piedra   941

Favus   941

Tinea corporis   942

Tinea pedis and tinea cruris   943

Nodular granulomatous perifolliculitis   944

Tinea versicolor   945

Pityrosporum folliculitis   947

Tinea nigra   947

Candidiasis   947

Aspergillosis, fusarium and pseudallescheria   951

Blastomycosis   953

Paracoccidioidomycosis   957

Coccidioidomycosis   958

Cryptococcosis   960

Zygomycosis   963

Chromoblastomycosis   965

Mycetoma   967

Phaeohyphomycosis   968

Alternariosis   971

Histoplasmosis   971

Penicilliosis   974

Sporotrichosis   974

Lobomycosis   976

Rhinosporidiosis   978

ARTHROPOD INFESTATIONS   980

Scabies   980

Tungiasis   981

NEMATODE INFESTATION   982

Onchocerciasis   982

Cutaneous larva migrans   984

TREMATODE INFESTATION   985

Schistosomiasis   985

CESTODE INFESTATION   986

Cysticercosis   986

CUTANEOUS LESIONS IN AIDS   986

Non-infective dermatosis   987

Cutaneous infections   989

Neoplasia   991

Viral infections

Common wart

The common wart (verruca vulgaris) is caused by infection with human papilloma virus (HPV) (*Fig. 17.1*). The HPVs are DNA viruses of the papovavirus family. The number of known HPV genotypes currently stands at more than 100, classified according to the extent of their DNA homology (DNA hybridization) (*Table 17.1*).[1-4] In order for a HPV type to be regarded as 'new', sequences in selected genomic regions must exhibit more than 10% divergence compared to any of the known HPV types.[4] Monoclonal antibodies to intact viruses have been produced and can demonstrate individual types of HPV; antibodies to viral components are only group specific (*Fig. 17.2*). In recent years, advances in molecular pathology have resulted in improved and more specific methods of HPV detection, including in situ polymerase chain reaction (PCR) and non-isotopic in situ hybridization (NISH).[5]

Papilloma viruses, which are small, non-enveloped and show icosahedral symmetry, contain circular double-stranded DNA composed of approximately 8000 base pairs.[6,7] The viral particle, which has a diameter of approximately 55 nm, contains 72 capsomeres.[6,8] The HPV genome is divided into three functional regions: a late region, an early

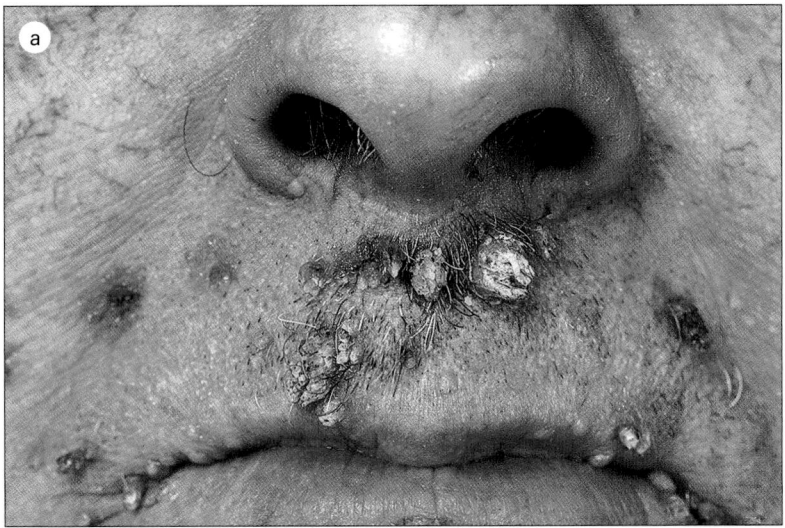

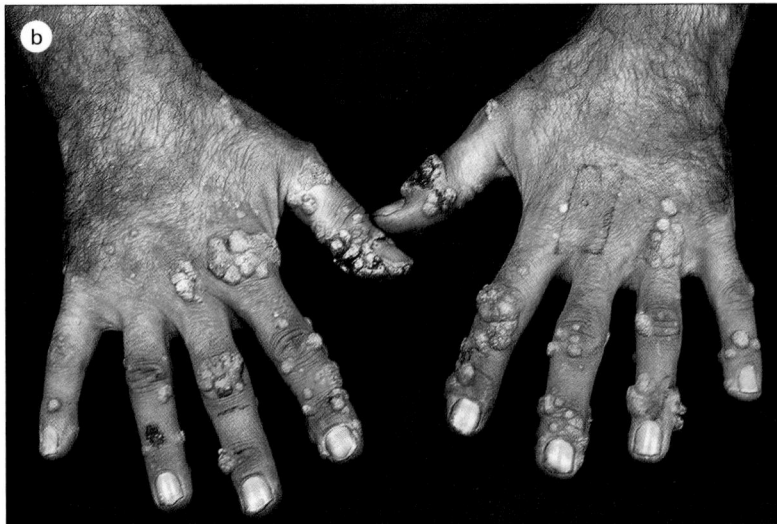

Fig. 17.1
Viral warts: **(a)** these are exceedingly common and may affect any site; **(b)** lesions are frequently multiple. By courtesy of the Institute of Dermatology, London, UK.

Table 17.1
Variants of human wart virus infection

HPV type	Associated clinical lesions
1	Deep plantar warts, common warts
2	Common warts, flat warts
3	Flat warts
4	Common warts, plantar warts
5	Epidermodysplasia verruciformis (EV)
6	Genital warts, laryngeal papilloma
7	Butcher warts
8	EV
9	EV, keratoacanthomas
10	Flat warts
11	Laryngeal papillomas, genital warts
12	EV
13	Focal epithelial hyperplasia
14, 15	EV
16	Genital warts, bowenoid papulosis, cervical dysplasia, cervical carcinoma, digitial, squamous cell carcinoma, non-genital Bowen's disease
17	EV
18	Genital warts, bowenoid papulosis, cervical dysplasia, cervical carcinoma
19–25	EV, keratoacanthomas
26–29	Common warts, flat warts
30	Laryngeal carcinoma, genital warts
31–32	Genital warts, bowenoid papulosis, cervical dysplasia, cervical carcinoma
33	Cervical carcinoma
34	Bowenoid papulosis, Bowen's disease
35	Cervical dysplasia, cervical carcinoma
36	EV
37	EV, keratoacanthomas
38	EV
39	Bowenoid papulosis, cervical carcinoma
41	Flat warts
42	Genital warts, bowenoid papulosis, cervical dysplasia, cervical carcinoma
43, 44	Genital warts, laryngeal papillomas
46, 47	EV
48	Bowenoid papulosis, Bowen's disease
49, 50	EV
51–54	Genital warts, bowenoid papulosis, cervical dysplasia, cervical carcinoma
55	Genital warts, laryngeal papillomas

Reproduced with permission from Melton, J.L. and Rasmussen, J.E. (1991) *Dermatologic Clinics*, 9, 219–233.

region and a non-coding 1000 base pair upstream regulatory region (URR). The URR is located immediately upstream of the E6 open reading frame (ORF) and contains sequences regulating expression of all ORFs, including promoter elements and transcriptional enhancer sequences. In excess of 20 messenger RNAs are expressed, usually in a differentiation-specific and cell-specific manner.[4] Genes in the early region (E1, E2, E4, E5, E6, E7) are responsible for transcription, replication and cellular transformation. The E4 ORF is highly expressed in differentiated HPV-infected epithelial cells. Some forms of E4 encode a protein capable of disrupting the cytokeratin network, resulting in the phenomenon of koilocytosis.[4] The E4 ORF represents a region of maximal divergence between different HPV types.[9] Each viral genotype is most often detected in lesions at specific anatomical sites or shows distinct histological characteristics.[1,10–12]

HPV infection in man may result in a variety of lesions including verruca vulgaris, filiform warts, verruca plana, plantar warts, anogenital warts and bowenoid papulosis.[6] Mucosal lesions include oral warts and condylomata, focal epithelial hyperplasia or Heck's disease (see p. 432), nasal and conjunctival papillomas, laryngeal papillomatosis and cervical lesions.[4,6] In addition to its role in cervical cancer, HPV is increasingly recognized as an important cause of a number of neoplasms including Bowen's disease and malignant lesions of the anus, external genitalia and elsewhere.[1] Of equal importance is the recognition that HPV infection may be asymptomatic or result in a carrier status.

Clinical features

Common warts are caused by HPV types 1, 2, 4, 7 and 26–29.[6] In immunosuppressed patients, HPV subtypes 75, 76 and 77 may be pathogenetic.[13] Rarely, HPV subtypes associated with genital warts such as 6 and 11 have been found in common warts in children.[14] Warts are very common lesions, particularly in children.[15] Adults are also frequently affected. In a survey of 2180 adults, 3.5% had warts.[16] Butchers and slaughterhouse workers have an increased risk.[17,18]

Common warts may occur anywhere on the skin and in people of any age, but are most common on the backs of the hands and the fingers and on the knees of young children, where they appear as firm keratotic papules 1–10 mm across (*Figs 17.3, 17.4*).[15] Koebnerization is common (hence kissing lesions on fingers).[6] In other sites they may appear more filiform and less firm (*Fig. 17.5*).[3] The latter are particularly seen on the lips, nostrils and eyelids.[3] Warts may also present as a cutaneous horn.

They persist for a few months up to several years and often regress spontaneously, particularly in children.

Chronically immunosuppressed patients (e.g. following renal transplantation) often have a large number of warts (*Fig. 17.6*).[19–21] Chronicity is associated with increasing numbers of lesions. Epidermodysplasia verruciformis-like lesions due to HPV-5 have also been described in HIV-positive patients and following renal transplantation.[22] Numerous warts may be seen in other immunosuppressed patients (e.g. with lymphoma, leukemia, Hodgkin's lymphoma and HIV infection).[6,23–25] In patients with AIDS, warts may regress following highly active antiretroviral therapy (HAART).[26]

Pathogenesis and histological features

In situ hybridization studies of HPV lesions have shown that viral DNA synthesis in the epidermis occurs in the superficial prickle cell layer and full virus assembly with capsid production occurs in the granular cell layer.[6] HPV DNA has been demonstrated in apparently normal skin up to 15 mm from a virus-associated lesion.[27] The requirement for growth in very well-differentiated epithelia may explain the difficulty of culturing HPV and why host destruction of the lesions may be protracted.

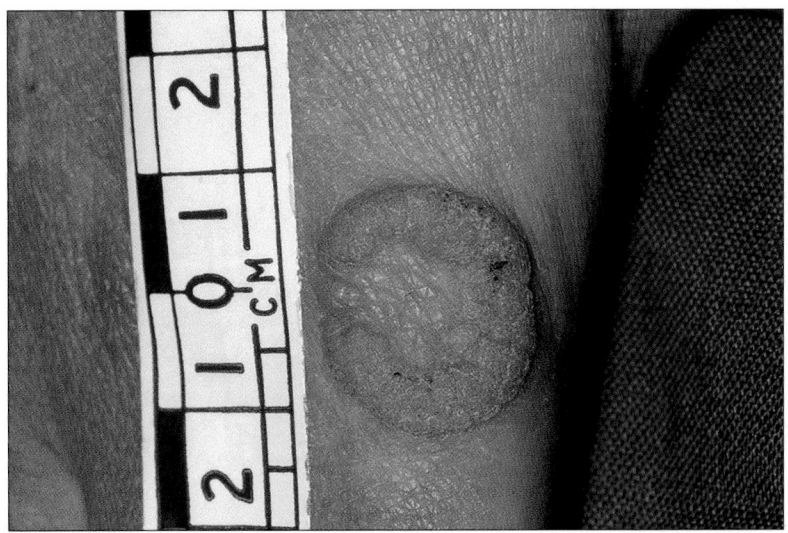

Fig. 17.3
Verruca vulgaris: there is a raised, discrete scaly plaque on the dorsal aspect of the hand. By courtesy of R.A. Marsden, MD, St George's Hospital, London, UK.

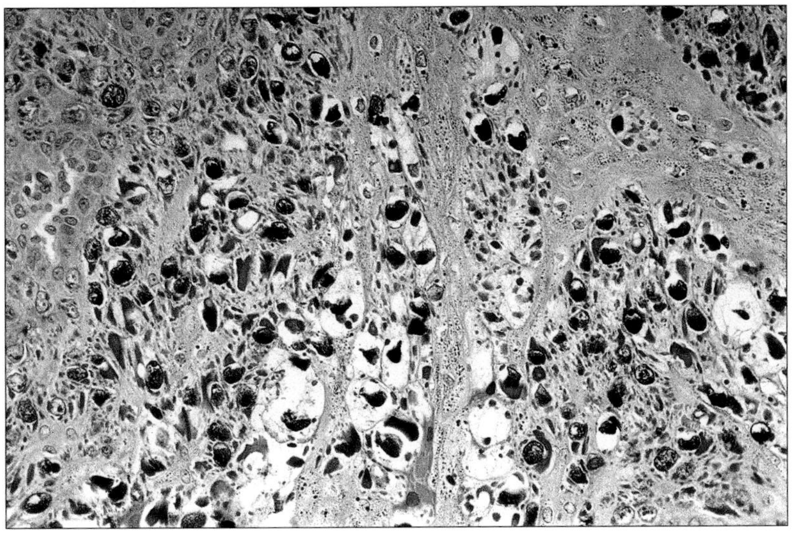

Fig. 17.2
Verruca vulgaris: note the positive labeling of the nuclei in this section stained with a peroxidase-labeled antiserum to papilloma virus.

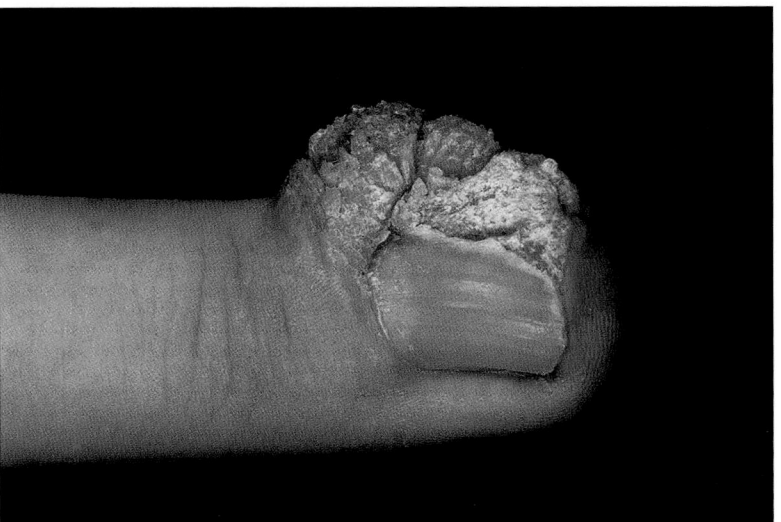

Fig. 17.4
Verruca vulgaris: verrucae are most commonly seen on the hands and fingers. By courtesy of the Institute of Dermatology, London, UK.

Immune mechanisms are presumed to be less effective against organisms or altered cells that are situated superficially with no direct blood supply.

Regression of HPV lesions is usually spontaneous, but the onset of the change may not occur for several years.[28] Cell-mediated immunity seems to be important in effecting the regression since lymphocytes are seen infiltrating the wart epithelium at this stage. Other features of regression include liquefactive basal cell degeneration, epidermal degeneration and vascular thrombosis.[28,29]

Following regression of the wart(s), an individual is usually immune to further HPV infection. Patients with a deficiency in cell-mediated immunity – whether primary or acquired, iatrogenic or virally induced (AIDS) – are particularly susceptible to the development of warts, which do not tend to involute spontaneously and can be a particularly refractory therapeutic problem.

Transmission of HPV is by inoculation of infected desquamated cells through close contact at points of minor trauma; hence common warts are seen most often on the hands. Periungual warts are particularly associated with nail biting and plantar warts are especially related to prolonged immersion in water.[16]

Common warts show filiform acanthosis with vertical tiers of parakeratosis over the tips of the exophytic component (*Fig. 17.7*). There is also marked orthokeratosis. A downward extension of the acanthosis produces a curvilinear deep margin and curved distortion of the adjacent rete ridges in the uninvolved epidermis. There is a prominent granular cell layer within which are enlarged clumps of irregular basophilic keratohyalin (*Fig. 17.8*).[3] These are seen best in the concavities between the papillomatotic epithelial papillae. Large cells with prominent vacuolated cytoplasm and a small pyknotic nucleus are seen in the upper layers of the epidermis (koilocytes) (*Fig. 17.9*). Koilocytes are, however, more frequently observed in genital warts (see below). Connective tissue and tortuous small blood vessels may invade the filiform projections (*Fig. 17.10*). In some cases, involvement of the superficial portion of the hair follicles by HPV results in focal changes identical to a trichilemmoma or an inverted follicular keratosis.[30] However, not all of these lesions are induced by HPV as has been suggested.[31]

Ordinary common warts are only exceptionally associated with in situ or invasive squamous cell carcinoma.[32,33] HPV-16 has been associated

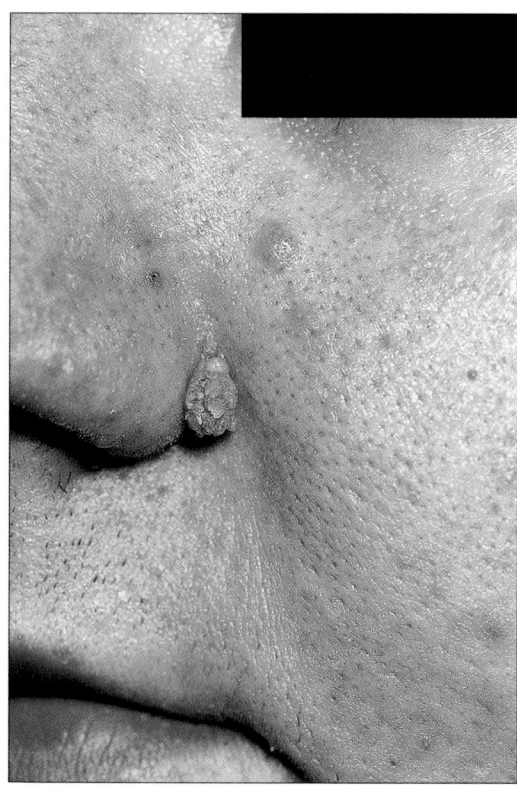

Fig. 17.5
Filiform wart: this variant occurs most often on the face and around the axillae. By courtesy of R.A. Marsden, MD, St George's Hospital, London, UK.

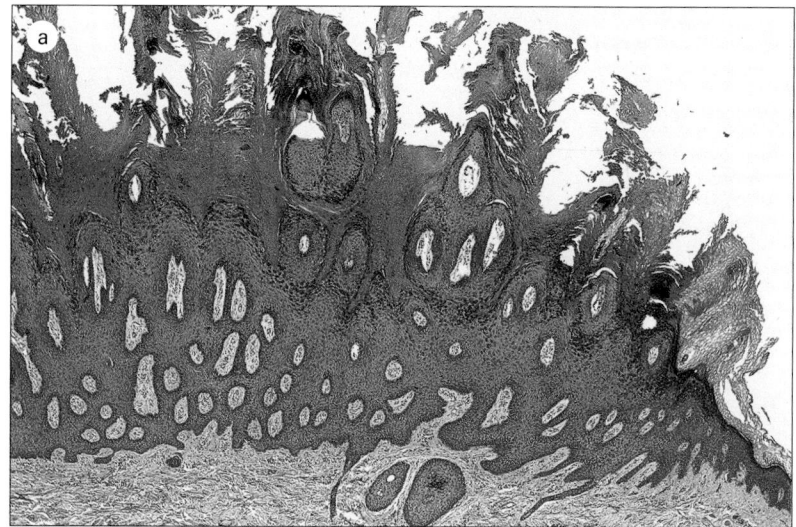

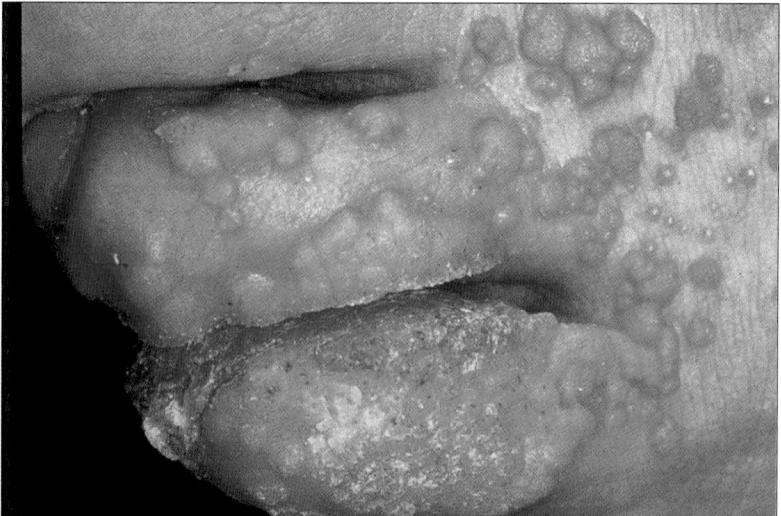

Fig. 17.6
Verruca vulgaris: presentation with such large numbers of lesions raises the possibility of immunosuppression. By courtesy of the Institute of Dermatology, London, UK.

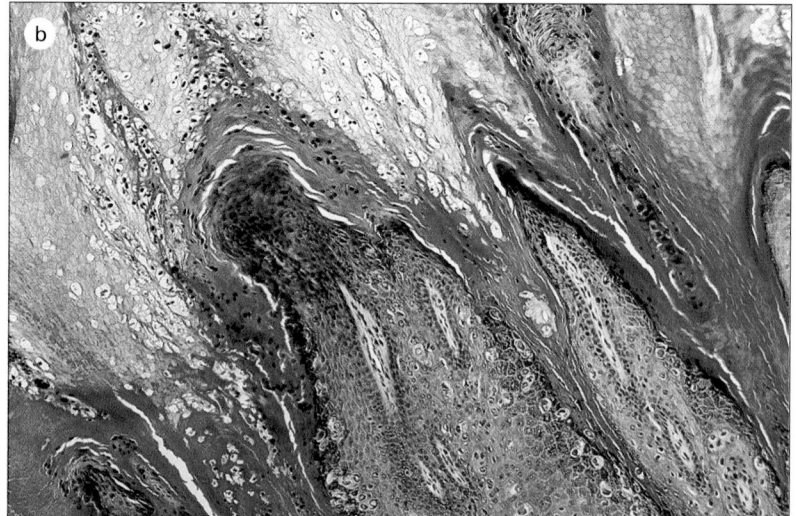

Fig. 17.7
Verruca vulgaris: (**a**) note the hyperkeratosis and papillomatosis; (**b**) there is often marked parakeratosis typically arranged as a vertical tier.

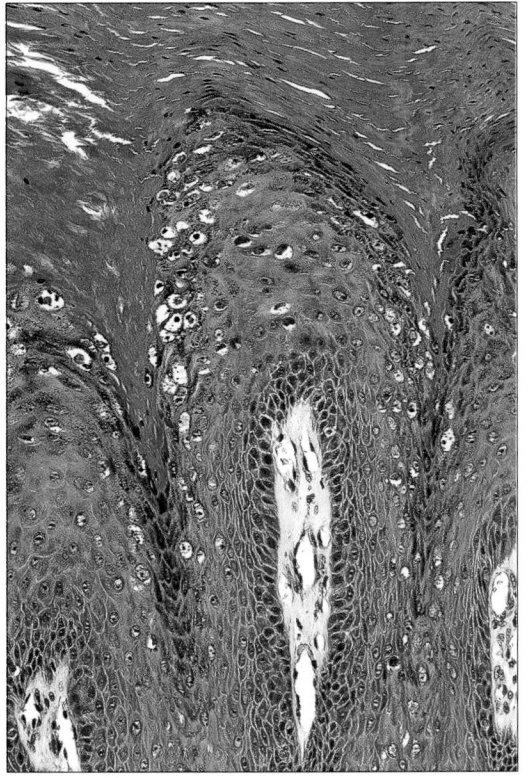

Fig. 17.8
Verruca vulgaris: large vacuolated cells with enlarged and irregular keratohyalin granules are characteristic. Note the intranuclear inclusions.

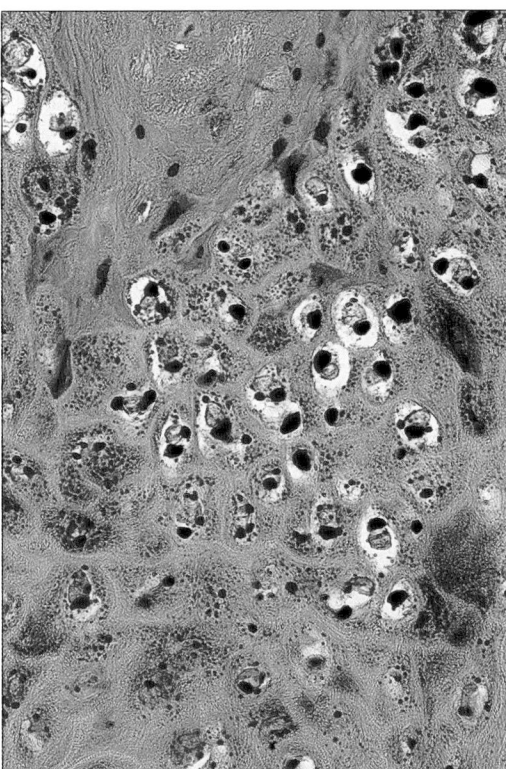

Fig. 17.9
Verruca vulgaris: high power view of koilocytes.

Fig. 17.10
Verruca vulgaris: the core of the papillary projection contains conspicuous dilated capillary loops.

with periungual Bowen's disease and squamous carcinoma.[34-36] The role of HPV in cutaneous neoplasia is discussed further in Chapter 22.

References

1. Siegel, J.F., Mellinger, B.C. (1992) Human papillomavirus in the male patient. *Urol Clin North Am*, **19**, 83–91.
2. Shah, K.V., Gissman, L. (1989) Papaviruses. In: Schmidt, N.J., Emmons, R.W. (eds) Diagnostic procedures for viral, rickettsial and chlamydial infections, 6th edn. Washington DC: Alpha Publications, pp 1067–1102.
3. Melton, J.L., Rasmussen, J.E. (1991) Clinical manifestations of human papilloma-virus infection in non-genital sites. *Derm Clin*, **9**, 219–233.
4. Stoler, M.H. (2000) Human papilloma viruses and cervical neoplasia: A model for carcinogenesis. *Int J Gynecol Pathol*, **19**, 16–28.
5. Poljak, M., Seme, K., Gale, N. (1998) Detection of human papillomaviruses in tissue specimens. *Adv Anat Pathol*, **5**, 216–234.
6. Cobb, M.W. (1990) Human papilloma virus infection. *J Am Acad Dermatol*, **22**, 547–566.
7. Shah, K.V. (1992) Biology of genital tract human papillomaviruses. *Urol Clin North Am*, **19**, 63–69.
8. Clark, D.P. (1987) Condyloma acuminatum. *Derm Clin*, **5**, 779–788.
9. Doorbar, J., Ely, S., Sterling, J. et al (1991) Specific interaction between HPV-16 E1–E4 and cytokeratins results in collapse of the epithelial cell intermediate filament network. *Nature*, **352**, 824–827.
10. Beckman, A.M., Daling, J.R., Sherman, K.J. et al (1989) Human papilloma virus infection and anal cancer. *Int J Cancer*, **43**, 1042–1049.
11. Lutzner, M.A. (1983) The human papillomavirus. *Arch Dermatol*, **119**, 631–635.
12. Cheah, P.L., Looi, L.M. (1998) Biology and pathological associations of the human papillomaviruses: a review. *Malays J Pathol*, **20**, 1–10.
13. Majewski, S., Jablonska, S. (1997) Human papilloma virus-associated tumors of the skin and mucosa. *J Am Acad Dermatol*, **36**, 659–685.
14. Payne, D.A., Sánchez, R., Tyring, S.K. (1997) Cutaneous verruca with genital human papillomavirus in a 2-year-old girl. *Am J Dermatopathol*, **19**, 258–260.
15. Kilkenny, M., Merlin, K., Young, R. et al (1998) The prevalence of common skin conditions in Australian school students: I. Common, plane and plantar viral warts. *Br J Dermatol*, **138**, 840–845.
16. Beutner, K.R., Becker, T.M., Stone, K.M. (1991) Epidemiology of human papillomavirus infections. *Derm Clin*, **9**, 211–218.
17. Finkel, M., Finkel, D. (1984) Warts among meat handlers. *Arch Dermatol*, **120**, 1314–1317.
18. Keefe, M., Al-Ghamdi, A., Coggon, D. et al (1994) Cutaneous warts in butchers. *Br J Dermatol*, **130**, 9–14.
19. Koranda, F.C., Dehmel, E.M., Kahn, G. et al (1974) Cutaneous complications in immunosuppressed renal homograft recipients. *JAMA*, **229**, 419–424.
20. Dyall-Smith, D., Trowell, H., Dyall-Smith, M.L. (1991) Benign human papilloma virus infection in renal transplant recipients. *Int J Dermatol*, **30**, 785–789.
21. Iraji, F., Kiani, A., Shahidi, S. et al (2002) Histopathology of skin lesions with warty appearance in renal allograft recipients. *Am J Dermatopathol*, **24**, 324–325.
22. Barr, B.B.B., Benton, E.C., McLaren, K. et al (1989) Human papilloma virus infection and skin cancer in renal allograft recipients. *Lancet*, **I**, 124–129.
23. Milburn, P.B., Brandsma, J.L., Goldsman, C.I. et al (1988) Disseminated warts and evolving squamous cell carcinoma in a patient with acquired immunodeficiency syndrome. *J Am Acad Dermatol*, **19**, 401–405.
24. Kang, S., Fitzpatrick, T.B. (1994) Debilitating verruca vulgaris in a patient infected with human immunodeficiency virus. *Arch Dermatol*, **130**, 294–296.
25. Chopra, K.F., Tyring, S.K. (1997) The impact of the human immunodeficiency virus on the human papillomavirus epidemic. *Arch Dermatol*, **133**, 629–633.
26. Spach, D.H., Colven, R. (1999) Resolution of recalcitrant hand warts in an HIV-infected patient treated with potent antiretroviral therapy. *J Am Acad Dermatol*, **40**, 818–821.
27. Lancaster, W.D., Jense, N.A.B. (1991) Human papilloma virus infection and neoplasia. *Derm Clin*, **9**, 371–376.
28. Berman, A., Winkelman, R.K. (1980) Involuting common warts. *J Am Acad Dermatol*, **3**, 356–362.
29. Kossard, S., Xenias, S.J., Palestine, R.F. et al (1980) Inflammatory changes in verruca vulgaris. *J Cutan Pathol*, **7**, 217–221.
30. Kimura, S., Komatsu, T., Ohyama, K. (1982) Common and plantar warts with trichilemmal keratinization-like keratinizing process: a possible existence of pseudo-trichilemmal keratinization. *J Cutan Pathol*, **9**, 391–395.
31. Phillips, M.E., Ackerman, A.B. (1982) 'Benign' and 'malignant' neoplasms associated with verrucae vulgaris. *Am J Dermatopathol*, **4**, 61–84.
32. Goette, D.K. (1980) Carcinoma in situ in verruca vulgaris. *Int J Dermatol*, **19**, 98–101.
33. Inaba, Y., Egawa, K., Yoshimura, K. et al (1993) Demonstration of human papillomavirus type I DNA in a wart with bowenoid histologic changes. *Am J Dermatopathol*, **15**, 172–175.
34. Moy, R.L., Eliezri, Y.D., Nuovo, G.J. et al (1989) Human papilloma virus type 16 in periungual squamous cell carcinoma. *JAMA*, **261**, 2669–2673.
35. Sau, P., McMarlin, S.L., Sperling, L.C. et al (1994) Bowen's disease of the nail bed and periungual area. A clinicopathological analysis of seven cases. *Arch Dermatol*, **130**, 204–209.
36. Ashinoff, R., Li, J.J., Jacobson, M. et al (1991) Detection of human papillomavirus DNA in squamous cell carcinoma of the nail bed and finger determined by polymerase chain reaction. *Arch Dermatol*, **127**, 1813–1818.

Plantar warts

Clinical features

Plantar warts occur on the sole of the foot; they are only slightly elevated and appear as a horny plug surrounded by a ring of hyperkeratotic skin (*Fig. 17.11*). Often they are covered with black dots representing thrombosed capillaries (*Fig. 17.12*).[1] They are most common in children and are frequently seen over pressure points. Most plantar warts are caused by HPV-1 and are painful; however, HPV-4 may produce a confluent or mosaic pattern of similar small warts ('mosaic plantar warts') and these are painless (*Fig. 17.13*).[2,3] They may also be seen on the palms and in the periungual region. There have been reports from Japan of unusual plantar warts produced by HPV-60 (see p. 1203).[4,5]

The lesions may be nodular, ridged or pigmented. A cystic variant has also been described.[4–9] The cystic variant has the features of an epidermoid cyst and may rarely be multiple (see p. 1667).[10] Most are associated with HPV-60 but an association with HPV-57 has also been reported.[11–13] Epidermoid cysts induced by HPV may also be seen outside acral locations.[14,15] Pigmented warts are caused by HPV-4, 60 or 65.[16] Pigmented warts may contain fibrillar intracytoplasmic inclusion bodies.[17] A case of a large plantar wart caused by HPV-66 has been documented.[18] A further subtype of HPV associated with palmoplantar warts is HPV-63.[7]

Plantar warts usually regress within a few months in children, but may persist longer in adults. Rarely chronic plantar warts may be associated with the development of verrucous carcinoma (carcinoma cuniculatum) (see Ch. 22).[19,20]

Histological features

Plantar warts are almost entirely endophytic, with a central parakeratotic plug surrounded by multiple deep extensions of acanthotic epidermis (*Fig. 17.14*). The depth and complexity of these downgrowths have been likened to an anthill, giving rise to the term 'myrmecia'. Vacuolation is more prominent in the plantar wart and, in the active growing phase, large eosinophilic (and to a lesser extent basophilic) cytoplasmic inclusions are present, which represent disordered growth of giant keratohyalin granules (*Fig. 17.15*). The large eosinophilic cytoplasmic inclusions are usually seen in infections caused by HPV-1 and to a lesser extent in those caused by HPV-60 and 65.[7] In warts induced by HPV-4, the infected keratinocytes show prominent cytoplasmic vacuolar change with almost no keratohyalin granules. Intranuclear inclusions may also be evident (*Fig. 17.16*). HPV can be demonstrated in the nuclei of these cells by electron microscopy (*Fig. 17.17*). Melanin granules are discernible within the cytoplasm of HPV-60-induced pigmented plantar warts.

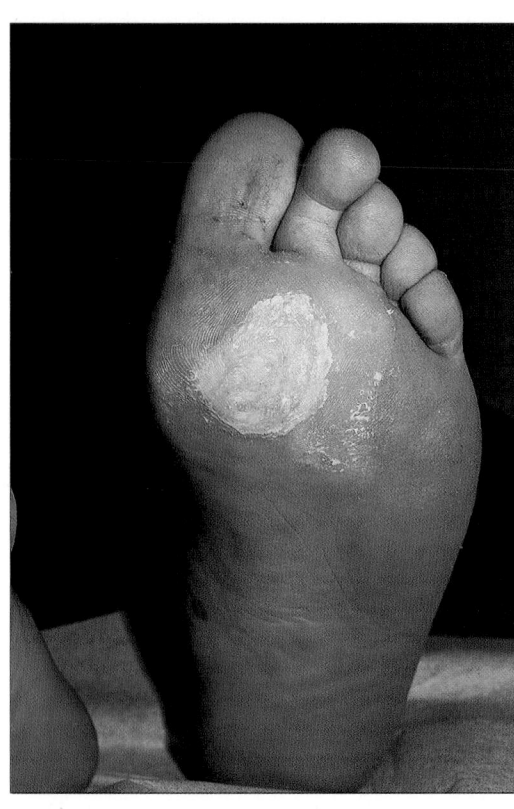

Fig. 17.11
Plantar wart: the lesion is flat and shows very marked hyperkeratosis. By courtesy of R.A. Marsden, MD, St George's Hospital, London, UK.

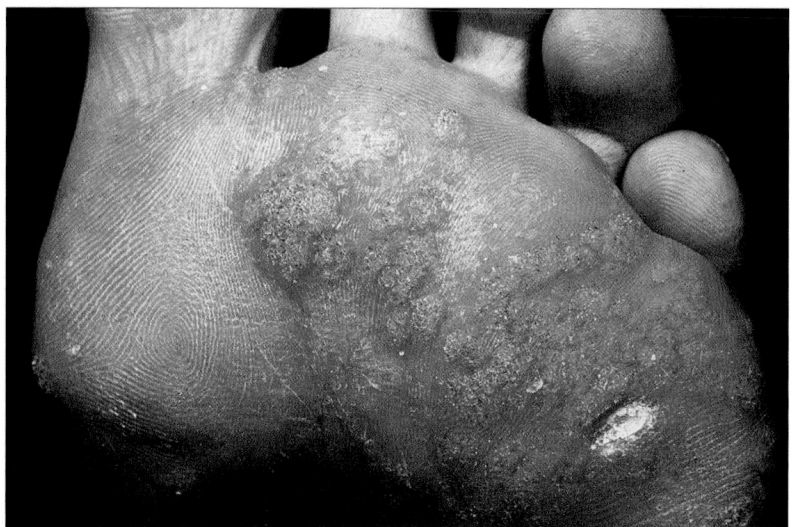

Fig. 17.13
Mosaic warts: here there is a large number of small warts. They are particularly resistant to therapy. By courtesy of the Institute of Dermatology, London, UK.

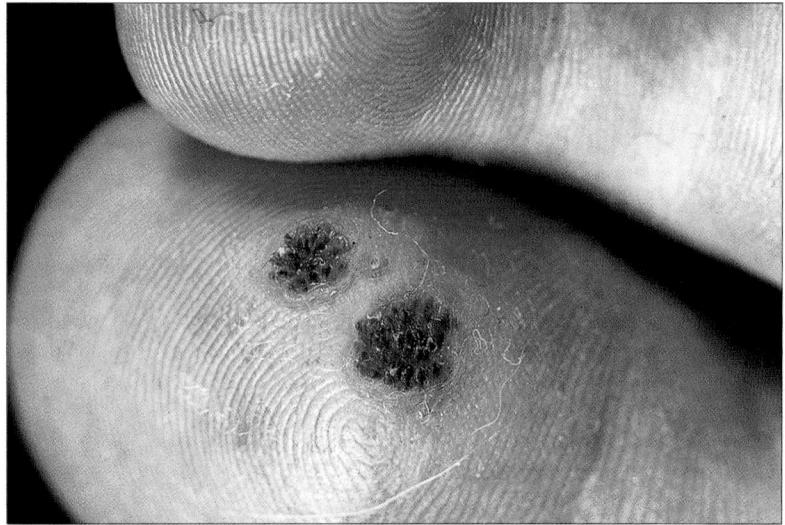

Fig. 17.12
Plantar wart: vascular thromboses as seen in these two lesions are common manifestations of involution. By courtesy of R.A. Marsden, MD, St George's Hospital, London, UK.

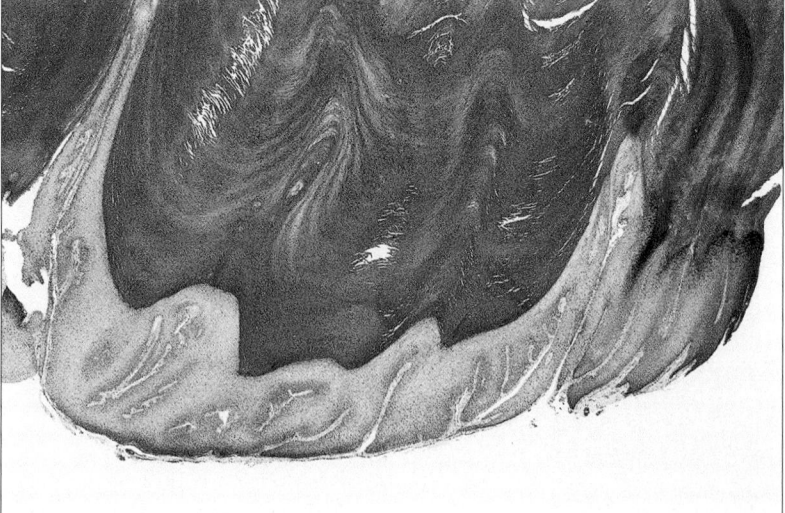

Fig. 17.14
Plantar wart: typical depressed, crateriform lesion containing a parakeratotic plug.

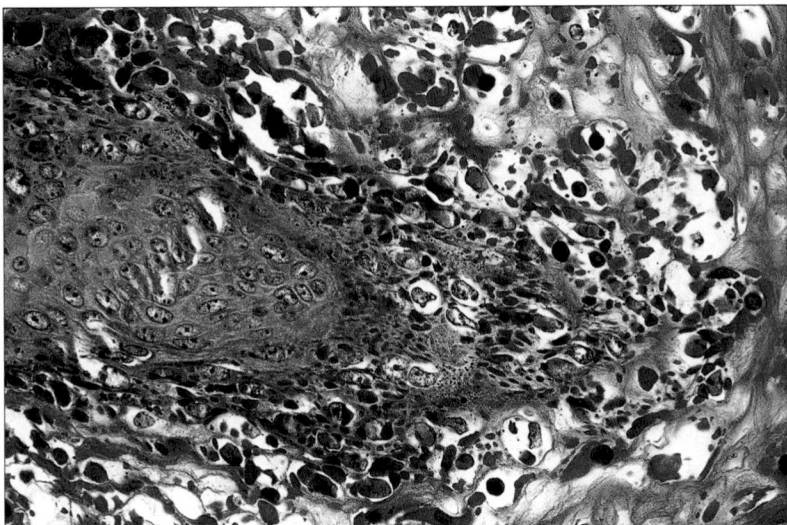

Fig. 17.15
Plantar wart: these eosinophilic keratohyalin granules are characteristic.

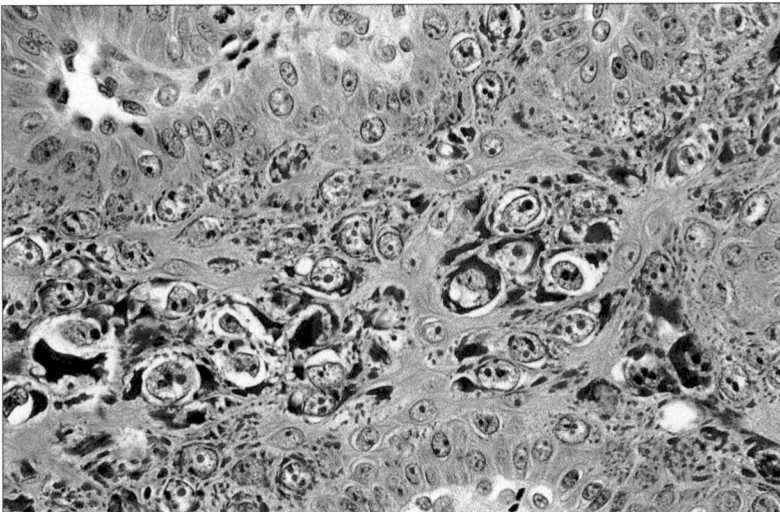

Fig. 17.16
Plantar wart: note the conspicuous intranuclear eosinophilic inclusions.

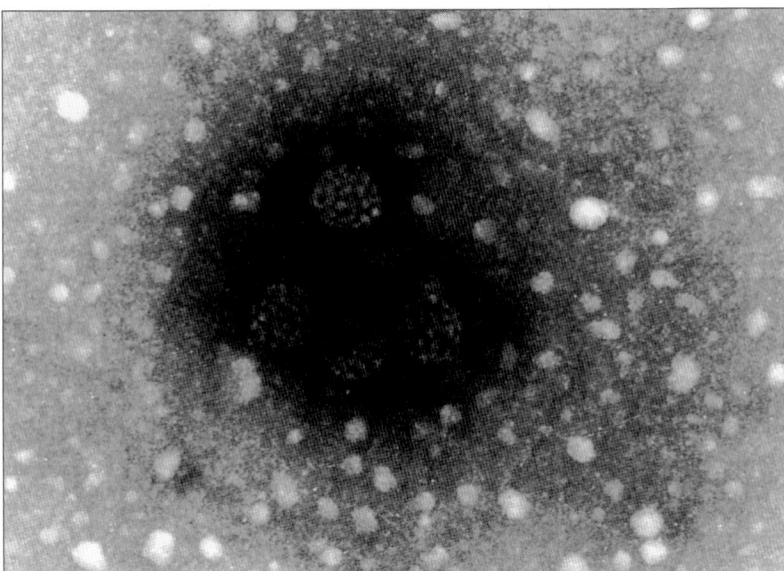

Fig. 17.17
Plantar wart: this honeycomb arrangement of HPV is characteristic. By courtesy of I. Chrystie, FIMLS, St Thomas' Hospital, London, UK.

Regressive changes are the same as those described in common warts and consist of thrombosis of superficial blood vessels, necrosis and a mixed inflammatory cell infiltrate.[21]

References

1. Cobb, M.W. (1990) Human papilloma virus infection. *J Am Acad Dermatol*, **22**, 547–566.
2. Jablonska, S. (1984) Wart viruses: human papilloma viruses. *Semin Dermatol*, **3**, 120–129.
3. Melton, J.L., Rasmussen, J.E. (1991) Clinical manifestations of human papillomavirus infection in nongenital sites. *Derm Clin*, **9**, 219–233.
4. Kashima, M., Adachi, M., Honda, M. et al (1994) A case of peculiar plantar warts. Human papillomavirus type 60 infection. *Arch Dermatol*, **130**, 1418–1420.
5. Egawa, K., Kasai, S., Hattori, N. et al (1998) A case of human-papillomavirus-type-60-induced wart with clinical appearance of both pigmented and ridged warts. *Dermatology*, **197**, 268–270.
6. Ashida, M., Ueda, M., Kunisada, M. et al (2002) Protean manifestations of human papillomavirus type 60 infection on the extremities. *Br J Dermatol*, **146**, 885–890.
7. Egawa, K. (1994) New types of human papilloma viruses and intracytoplasmic inclusion bodies: a classification of inclusion warts according to clinical features, histology and associated HPV types. *Br J Dermatol*, **130**, 158–166.
8. Kato, N., Ueno, H. (1992) Two cases of plantar epidermal cyst associated with human papillomavirus. *Clin Exp Dermatol*, **17**, 252–256.
9. Egawa, K., Honda, Y., Inaba, Y. et al (1994) Multiple plantar epidermoid cysts harboring carcinoembryonic antigen and human papillomavirus DNA sequences. *J Am Acad Dermatol*, **30**, 494–496.
10. Yokogawa, M., Egawa, K., Dabanaka, K. et al (2002) Multiple palmar epidermoid cysts. *Dermatology*, **205**, 398–400.
11. Kawase, M., Honda, M., Niimura, M. (1994) Detection of human papillomavirus type 60 in plantar cystic verruca plantaris by the in situ hybridization method using digoxigenin labeled probes. *J Dermatol*, **21**, 709–715.
12. Kitasato, H., Egawa, K., Honda, Y. et al (1998) A putative human papillomavirus type 57 new subtype isolated from plantar epidermoid cysts without intracytoplasmic inclusion bodies. *J Gen Virol*, **79**, 1977–1981.
13. Kashima, M., Takahama, H., Baba, T. et al (2003) Detection of human papillomavirus type 57 in the tissue of plantar epidermoid cyst. *Dermatology*, **207**, 185–187.
14. Elston, D.M., Parker, L.U., Tuthill, R.J. (1993) Epidermoid cyst of the scalp containing human papillomavirus. *J Cutan Pathol*, **20**, 184–186.
15. Lee, S., Lee, W., Chung, S. et al (2003) Detection of human papillomavirus 60 in epidermal cysts at nonpalmoplantar location. *Am J Dermatopathol*, **25**, 243–247.
16. Egawa, K., Honda, Y., Inaba, Y. et al (1998) Pigmented viral warts: a clinical and histopathological study including human papillomavirus typing. *Br J Dermatol*, **138**, 381–389.
17. Hagari, Y., Yamada, N., Mihara, N. (2003) Pigmented wart showing fibrillar intracytoplasmic inclusion bodies. *Br J Dermatol*, **148**, 187–188.
18. Davis, M.D.P., Gostout, B.S., McGovern, R.M. et al (2000) Large plantar wart caused by human papillomavirus-66 and resolution by topical cidofovir therapy. *J Am Acad Dermatol*, **43**, 340–343.
19. McKee, P.H., Wilkinson, J.D., Black, M.M. et al (1981) Carcinoma (epithelioma) cuniculatum: a clinicopathologic study of nineteen cases and review of the literature. *Histopathology*, **5**, 425–436.
20. McKee, P.H., Wilkinson, J.D., Corbett, M.F. et al (1981) Carcinoma cuniculatum: a case metastasizing to skin and lymph nodes. *Clin Exp Dermatol*, **6**, 613–618.
21. Berman, A., Domnitz, J.M., Winkelmann, R.K. (1982) Plantar warts recently turned black. Clinical and histopathologic findings. *Arch Dermatol*, **118**, 47–51.

Plane warts

Clinical features

Plane warts, usually caused by HPV-2, 3 or 10, are flat, smooth and a few millimeters in diameter with typically little change in color from the adjacent skin, although they may appear gray–yellow or pale brown (*Fig. 17.18*).[1,2] HPV-5 is rarely implicated in HIV-infected patients.[3] Plane warts may also result from HPV types 26–29 and 41 infection.[4] They affect the face, backs of the hands and the shins. There may be only a few present, but occasionally they are very numerous and become confluent in areas of scratching (koebnerization).[5] Plane warts are common in children and may be seen in women, but are not usually found in males after puberty except in association with HIV infection. They may regress spontaneously after a few weeks or months, or may persist for years. Signs of regression include pruritus, an erythematous, edematous appearance, depigmented haloes and an eruption of multiple tiny plane warts.[2,5,6]

Histological features

Plane warts are acanthotic and show orthokeratosis with an open pattern reminiscent of 'chicken wire' ('basket weave' hyperkeratosis). Parakeratosis is not a feature and there is little papillary configuration to the acanthosis (*Fig. 17.19*). Keratinocytes of the upper part of the stratum spinosum show striking cytoplasmic vacuolation with margination of the keratohyalin granules and tonofilaments.[4] Regression is characterized by keratinocyte necrosis (apoptosis), individual cell keratinization, parakeratosis, lymphocytic exocytosis with spongiosis and a superficial

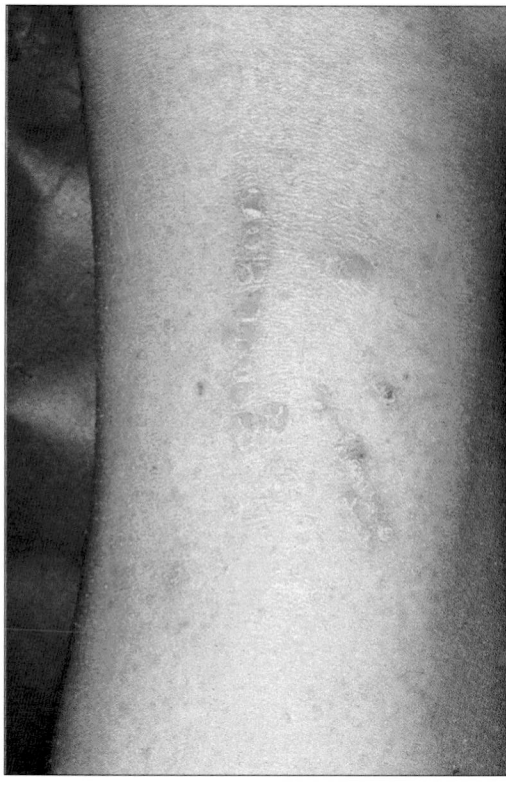

Fig. 17.18
Plane wart: note the typical flat, flesh-colored papules, which have extended in a linear distribution due to scratching (Koebner phenomenon). By courtesy of R.A. Marsden, MD, St George's Hospital, London, UK.

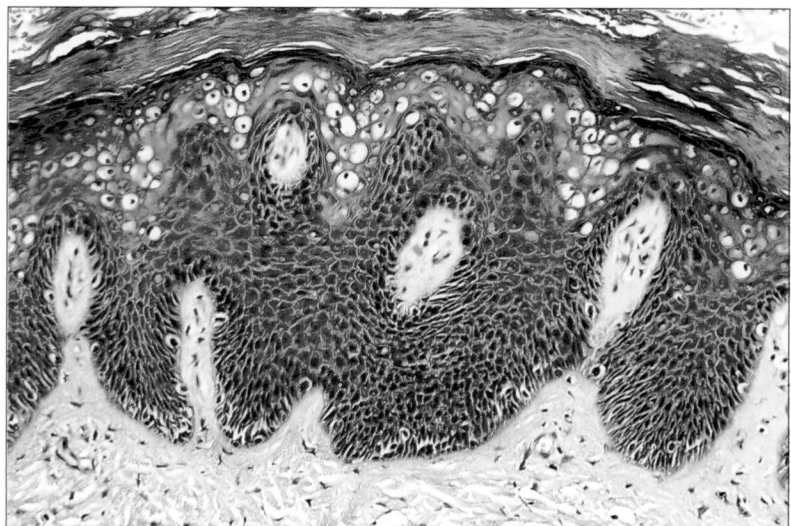

Fig. 17.19
Plane wart: there is hyperkeratosis and slight regular acanthosis; papillomatosis is only mild. Note the prominent cytoplasmic vacuolation.

perivascular chronic inflammatory cell infiltrate.[2,7–9] Extravasation of erythrocytes may be a feature and edema of the papillary dermis is frequently present.[10]

References

1.   Jablonska, S. (1984) Wart viruses: human papilloma viruses. *Semin Dermatol*, 3, 120–129.
2.   Cobb, M.W. (1990) Human papilloma virus infection. *J Am Acad Dermatol*, 22, 547–566.
3.   Prose, N.S., von Knebel-Doeberitz, C., Miller, S. et al (1990) Widespread flat warts associated with human papillomavirus type 5: a cutaneous manifestation of human immunodeficiency virus infection. *J Am Acad Dermatol*, 23, 978–981.
4.   Melton, J.L., Rasmussen, J.E. (1991) Clinical manifestations of human papilloma virus infection in non-genital sites. *Derm Clin*, 9, 219–233.
5.   Berman, A. (1977) Depigmented haloes associated with involution of flat warts. *Br J Dermatol*, 97, 263–265.
6.   Berman, A., Berman, J.E. (1978) Efflorescence of new warts: a sign of onset of involution in flat warts. *Br J Dermatol*, 99, 179–182.
7.   Weedon, D., Robertson, I. (1978) Regressing plane warts – an ultrastructural study. *Australas J Dermatol*, 19, 65–68.
8.   Tagami, H., Ogino, A., Takigawa, M. et al (1974) Regression of plane warts following spontaneous inflammation. A histopathological study. *Br J Dermatol*, 90, 147–154.
9.   Tagami, H., Takigawa, M., Ogino, A. et al (1977) Spontaneous regression of plane warts after inflammation: clinical and histologic studies in 25 cases. *Arch Dermatol*, 113, 1209–1213.
10. Berman, A., Winkelmann, R.K. (1977) Flat warts undergoing involution. *Arch Dermatol*, 113, 1219–1221.

Condyloma acuminatum

Clinical features

Condylomata acuminata are particularly caused by HPV types 2, 6, 11, 16, 18, 30–33, 35, 39, 41–45, 51–56 and 59 and develop as a consequence of the trauma accompanying sexual intercourse.[1–11] HPV-6 and 11 alone account for more than 90% of these lesions, with HPV-6 present in about two-thirds of cases and the remaining one-third caused by HPV-11.[3,4] The incubation period is variable (usually between 2 and 3 months).[12] Condylomata acuminata occur on the glans penis and prepuce or shaft as soft, fleshy, sometimes filiform plaques and may extend into the meatus (*Figs 17.20, 17.21*). On the shaft they are less exophytic. Vulval lesions may be bulky and macerated, and may extend into the introitus (*Fig. 17.22*). Similar fleshy and filiform soft masses may occur perianally, more often in males (*Figs 17.23, 17.24*). Anal squamous carcinoma has also been shown to contain HPV-6, 16 and 18 in a significant proportion of cases (*Fig. 17.25*).[5] The rate of local recurrence is about 30%.[13] The lesions are uncommon in children (when they may be a sign of sexual abuse) and are seen most often in young adults (second and third decades), frequently in association with other genital infections.[3,7,14] Childhood condylomata regress spontaneously in more than 50% of cases.[15]

It is important to note that a significant proportion of genital HPV infections are asymptomatic.[2,16] The female partners of male patients with condyloma acuminata have been shown to have an increased risk of cervical HPV infection and intraepithelial neoplasia (SIL/CIN).[17]

Cervical neoplasia associated with pre-existent condylomata acuminata has also been related to a background of immunosuppression, at least in some patients.[18] The worldwide HPV prevalence in cervical carcinomas is reported to be 99.7%.[19] HPV-16, 18, 31–33, 35, 39, 42 and 51–54 are most commonly associated with cancers of the cervix, vulva and penis.[6,7,20,21]

A large, exuberant and locally destructive variant of condyloma (Buschke–Löwenstein tumor) may rarely be encountered (*Fig. 17.26*).[22,23] This is associated with HPV types 6, 11 or 16. It is likely that this giant

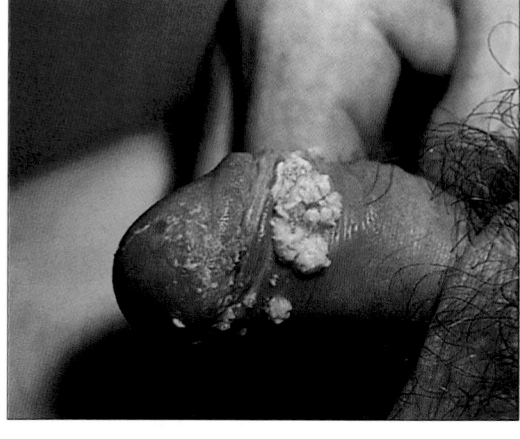

Fig. 17.20
Condyloma acuminatum: note the typical filiform appearance. By courtesy of the Department of Genitourinary Medicine, St Thomas' Hospital, London, UK.

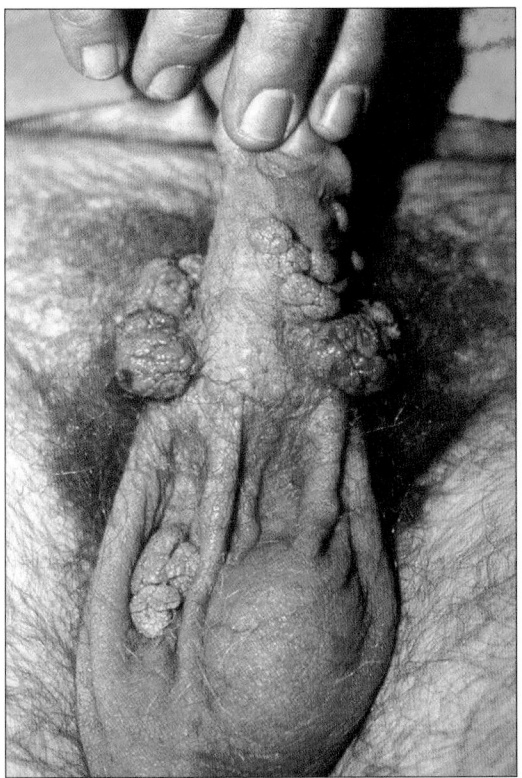

Fig. 17.21
Condyloma acuminatum: there are multiple lesions on the shaft of the penis and scrotum. By courtesy of the Department of Genitourinary Medicine, St Thomas' Hospital, London, UK.

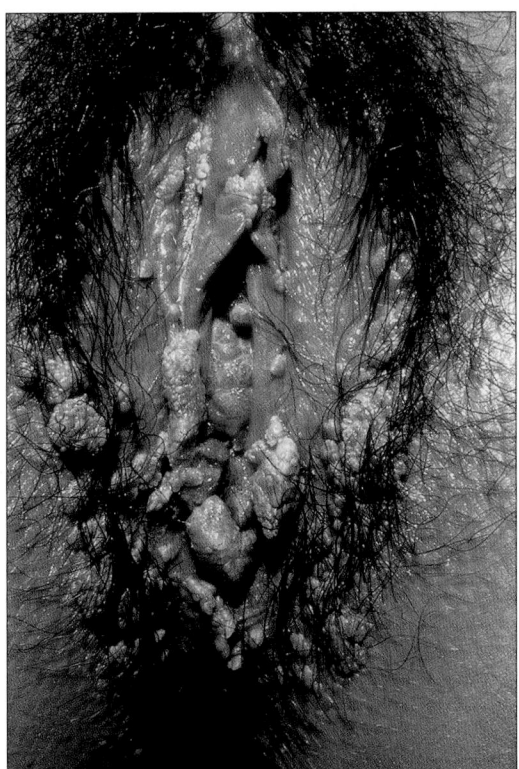

Fig. 17.22
Condyloma acuminatum: in this patient there is very widespread involvement of the vulva and perineum. This patient is likely to have cervical HPV infection. By courtesy of R.A. Marsden, MD, St George's Hospital London, UK.

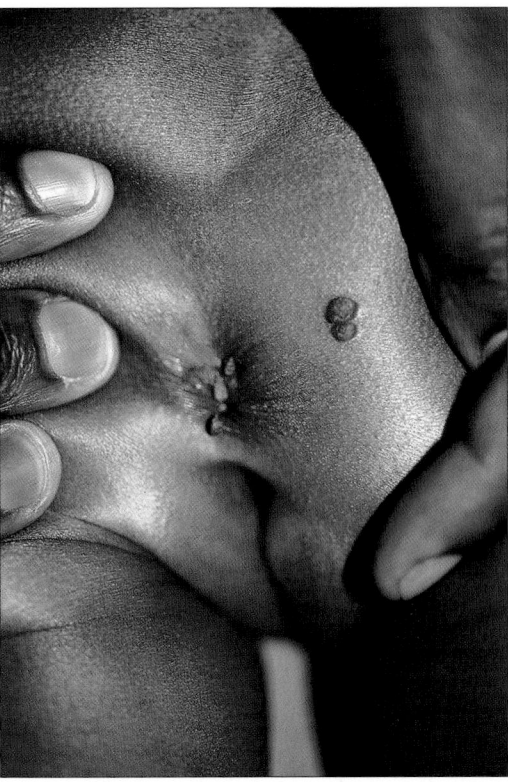

Fig. 17.23
Condyloma acuminatum: multiple perianal lesions are present. By courtesy of N.C. Dlova, MD, Nelson R. Mandela School of Medicine, University of KwaZulu-Natal, South Africa.

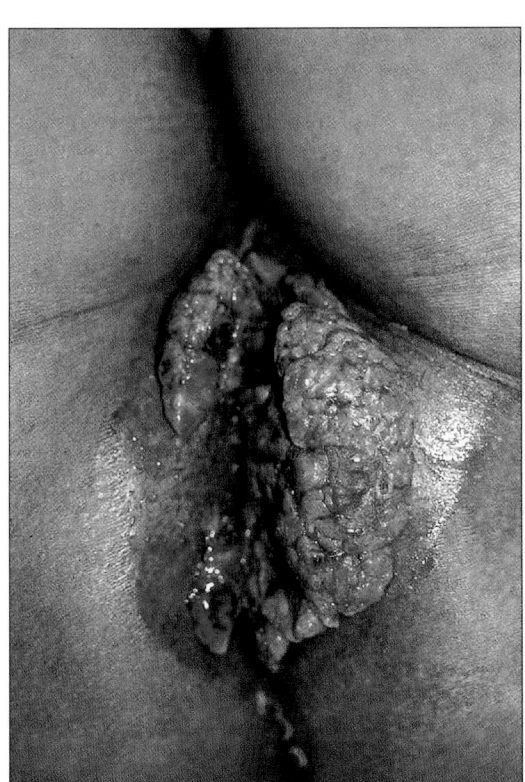

Fig. 17.24
Condyloma acuminatum: there is very extensive involvement of the perineum. By courtesy of N.C. Dlova, MD, Nelson R. Mandela School of Medicine, University of KwaZulu-Natal, South Africa.

variant represents a variant of verrucous carcinoma but the issue has been controversial[22–25] (see Ch. 22). Juvenile laryngeal papillomas containing HPV-6 and 11 can be seen in children born to mothers with condylomata acuminata.[2] They may show malignant progression if irradiated.

Malignant transformation of condyloma acuminatum is uncommon but it is seen more often than in other lesions associated with HPV except for epidermodysplasia verruciformis.

Histological features

Condylomata acuminata are characterized by marked acanthosis with a solid or trabecular pattern and a broad rounded exophytic growth (*Fig. 17.27*). There is a sharp, fairly regular, deep margin. The surface of the lesion is hyperkeratotic and parakeratotic. Superficial vacuolated keratinocytes (koilocytes) are characteristic (*Fig. 17.28*) and coarse keratohyaline granules may be present. The vacuolated epithelium is often most marked in the declivities. Condylomata that are treated with podophyllin prior to removal demonstrate marked epidermal pallor and increased mitoses and necrotic keratinocytes in the lower half of the epidermis.[26] These changes may lead to a misdiagnosis of malignancy. Giant condyloma acuminatum (anogenital verrucous carcinoma, Buschke–Löwenstein tumor) occurs most frequently on the genitalia, and is larger and more cauliflower-like.[22–24] It shows some tendency to endophytic growth, but without any suggestion of frank infiltration. It can recur locally, but metastasizes very rarely (see p. 1218). Anal condylomata may develop bowenoid features and occasionally invasive tumor supervenes.[5,6]

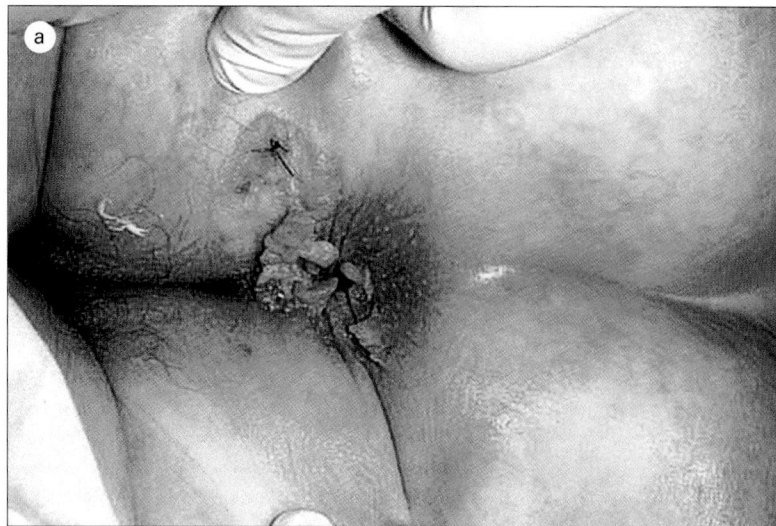

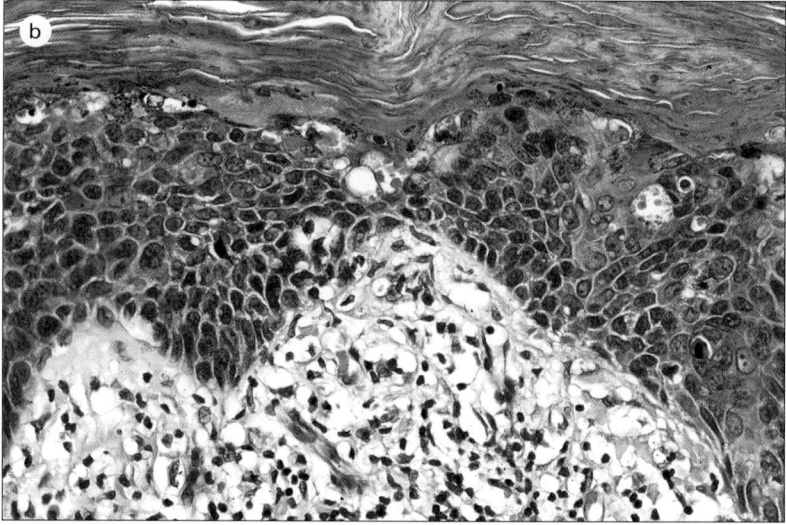

Fig. 17.25
(a, b) Condyloma acuminatum: in addition to multiple condylomata, there was histological evidence of in situ squamous cell carcinoma. By courtesy of P. Ngheim, MD, Dana Farber Cancer Institute and Harvard Medical School, Boston, USA.

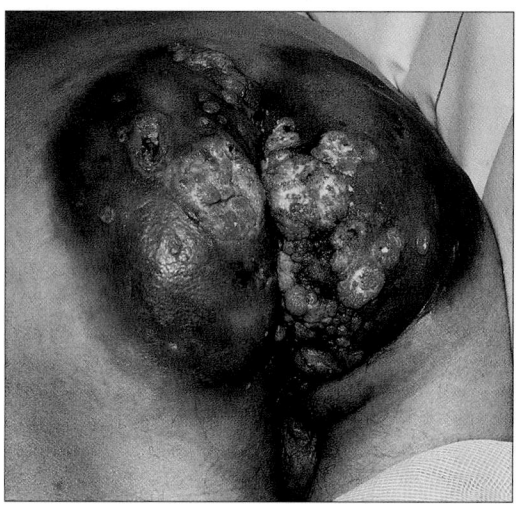

Fig. 17.26
Buschke–Löwenstein tumor: there is massive infiltration of the buttocks and perineum with numerous sinuses. HPV type 6 was identified by DNA in situ hybridization and Southern blot analysis. By courtesy of A. Grassegger, MD, University of Innsbruk, Austria.

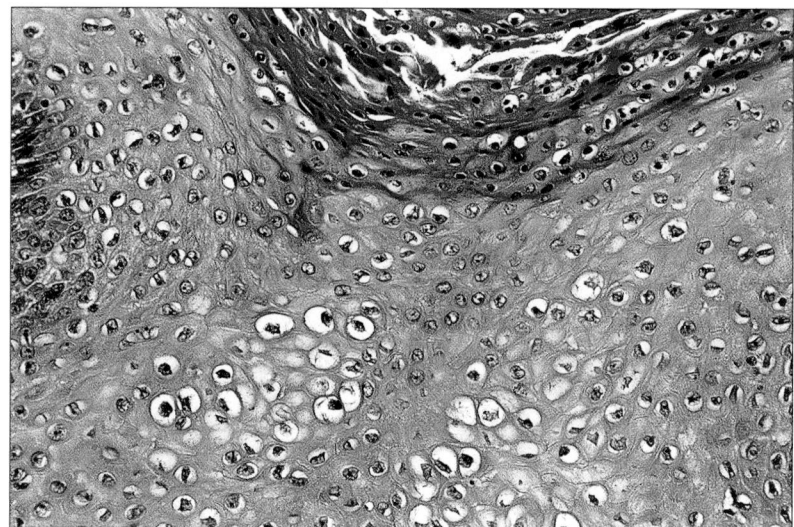

Fig. 17.28
Condyloma acuminatum: note the parakeratosis and vacuolation of the superficial keratinocytes.

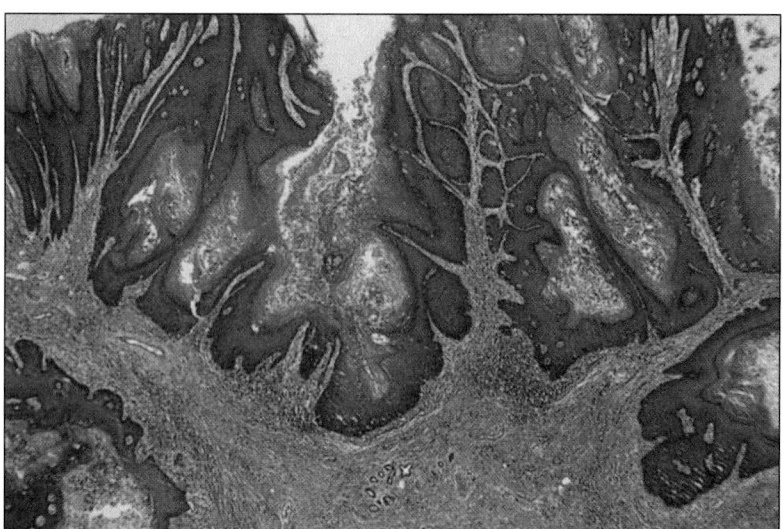

Fig. 17.27
Condyloma acuminatum: note the keratotic acanthotic epidermis with rounded lateral borders. Koilocytes are present in the declivities of the papillomatous epithelium.

References

1. Jablonska, S. (1984) Wart viruses: human papilloma viruses. *Semin Dermatol*, 3, 120–129.
2. Shah, K.V. (1992) Biology of genital tract human papillomaviruses. *Urol Clin North Am*, 19, 63–69.
3. Clark, D. (1987) Condyloma acuminatum. *Derm Clin*, 5, 779–788.
4. Wilbur, D.C., Reichman, R.C., Stoler, M.H. (1988) Detection of infection by human papillomavirus in genital condylomata: a comparison study using immunocytochemistry and in situ nucleic acid hybridization. *Am J Clin Pathol*, 89, 505–510.
5. Gal, A.A., Meyer, P.R., Taylor, C.R. (1987) Papillomavirus antigens in anorectal condyloma and carcinoma in homosexual men. *JAMA*, 257, 337–340.
6. Beckman, A.M., Daling, J.R., Sherman, K.J. et al (1989) Human papilloma virus infection and anal cancer. *Int J Cancer*, 431, 1042–1049.
7. Cobb, M.W. (1990) Human papilloma virus infection. *J Am Acad Dermatol*, 22, 547–566.
8. Rock, B., Shah, K.V., Farmer, E.R. (1992) A morphologic, pathologic and virologic study of anogenital warts in men. *Arch Dermatol*, 127, 495–500.
9. Obalek, S., Misiewicz, J., Jablonska, S. et al (1993) Childhood condyloma acuminatum: association with genital and cutaneous human papillomaviruses. *Pediatr Dermatol*, 10, 101–106.
10. Obalek, S., Jablonska, S., Favre, M. et al (1990) Condylomata acuminata in children: frequent association with human papillomaviruses responsible for cutaneous warts. *J Am Acad Dermatol*, 23, 205–213.
11. Brown, T.J., Yen-Moore, A., Tyring, S.K. (1999) An overview of sexually transmitted diseases. Part II. *J Am Acad Dermatol*, 41, 661–677.
12. Grussendorf-Conen, E-I. (1985) Condylomata acuminata. *Clin Dermatol*, 3, 97–103.
13. Chuang, T-Y., Perry, H.O., Kurland, L.T. et al (1984) Condyloma acuminatum in Rochester, Min, 1950–1978. I. Epidemiology and clinical features. *Arch Dermatol*, 120, 469–475.
14. Herman-Giddens, M.E., Gutman, L.T., Berson, N.L. (1988) Association of co-existing vaginal infections and multiple abusers in female children with genital warts. *Sex Transm Dis*, 15, 63–67.
15. Allen, A.L., Siegfried, E.C. (1998) The natural history of condyloma in children. *J Am Acad Dermatol*, 39, 951–955.
16. Siegel, J.F., Mellinger, B.C. (1992) Human papillomavirus in the male patient. *Urol Clin North Am*, 19, 83–91.
17. Campion, M.J., Singer, A., Clarkson, P.K. et al (1985) Increased risk of cervical neoplasia in consorts of men with penile condylomata acuminata. *Lancet*, 1, 943–946.

18. Krebs, H.B., Schneider, V., Hurt, W.G. et al (1986) Genital condylomas in immunosuppressed women: a therapeutic challenge. *South Med J*, 79, 183–187.

19. Walboomers, J.M., Jacobs, M.V., Manos, M.M. et al (1999) Human papilloma virus is a necessary cause of invasive cervical cancer worldwide. *J Pathol*, 189, 12–19.

20. McCance, D.J., Kalache, A., Ashdown, K. et al (1986) Human papilloma viruses types 16 and 18 in carcinoma of the penis from Brazil. *Int J Cancer*, 37, 55–59.

21. Stoler, M.H. (2000) Human papilloma viruses and cervical neoplasia: a model for carcinogenesis. *Int J Gynecol Pathol*, 19, 16–28.

22. Bogomoletz, W.V., Potet, F., Molas, G. (1985) Condylomata acuminata, giant condyloma acuminatum, (Buschke–Löwenstein tumor) and verrucous squamous carcinoma of the perianal and anorectal region: a continuous precancerous spectrum? *Histopathology*, 9, 1155–1169.

23. Wells, M., Robertson, S., Lewis, F. et al (1988) Squamous carcinoma arising in a giant peri-anal condyloma associated with human papillomavirus types 6 and 11. *Histopathology*, 12, 319–329.

24. Grasseger, A., Höpfl, R., Hussl, H. et al (1994) Buschke–Löwenstein tumor infiltrating pelvic organs. *Br J Dermatol*, 130, 221–225.

25. Anadolu, R., Boyvat, A., Çalikoğlu, E. et al (1999) Buschke–Löwenstein tumour is not a low-grade carcinoma but a giant verruca. *Acta Derm Venereol*, 79, 253–254.

26. Wade, T.R., Ackerman, A.B. (1984) The effects of resin of podophyllin on condyloma acuminatum. *Am J Dermatopathol*, 6, 109–122.

Bowenoid papulosis

Clinical features

Bowenoid papulosis (koilocytosis with intraepithelial neoplasia) is a clinicopathological entity that bears marked histological similarity to koilocytosis, SIL/CIN and Bowen's disease. Clinically it is quite different from genital Bowen's disease in that multiple small papules develop over a short time scale in young people. Prognosis is uncertain; many patients do not show evidence of progression, but a small proportion may develop invasive tumor and on occasions this may have metastatic potential. It is usually associated with HPV-16 or 18, but occasionally HPV types 31–35, 39, 42, 49 and 51–54 are detected.[1–6] Although uncommon, some cases may be associated with mixed infection by different HPV types.[6,7]

Bowenoid papulosis most often presents as multiple reddish-brown, sometimes lichenoid, discrete papules, but occasionally these become a confluent plaque. Papules, on average 4 mm in diameter, are found on the penis, vulva, perianal region and perineum. Extragenital sites of occurrence include the face, neck and fingers.[8–10] It manifests in young, sexually active adults in contrast to true Bowen's disease, which occurs in an older age group. Genital Bowen's disease is, however, also often associated with HPV-16 (see p. 519).[11] The occurrence in childhood should raise suspicion of sexual abuse.[3] Genital bowenoid papulosis has been associated with periungual bowenoid dysplasia.[12]

Spontaneous regression is uncommon.[13] As progression to frank carcinoma in bowenoid papulosis is rare, these lesions are best managed conservatively. However, bowenoid papulosis may be resistant to treatment and may be characterized by a prolonged course in immunosuppressed patients.[2] Bowenoid papulosis has also been associated with oral warts and lingual carcinoma.[4] It has recently been shown that patients with bowenoid papulosis and HPV infection may be primarily immunosuppressed due to diminished T-helper cell levels (non-HIV-associated).[2,11] The condition may also occur in organ transplant recipients.[14] Penile bowenoid papulosis is associated with a high risk of the consort developing cervical dysplasia[15,16] (see also p. 519).

Histological features

The lesion of bowenoid papulosis (see also pp. 519 and 1192) consists of a well-circumscribed area of acanthosis, producing a raised plaque or dome, which is hyperkeratotic and sometimes shows superficial epithelial vacuolation.[17,18] The keratinocytes may show nuclear hyperchromatism and pleomorphism. There is variable dyskeratosis.

These histological features of atypia, associated with numerous mitoses, including atypical forms, are similar to those of true Bowen's disease. The distinction rests in the circumscribed elevated plaque-like pattern, the age of the patient and the size and multiplicity of lesions.

HPV may be identified in bowenoid papulosis by immunoperoxidase techniques.[19] Female patients and consorts should regularly have cervical smears.

References

1. Gross, G., Hagedorn, M., Ikenberg, H. et al (1985) Bowenoid papulosis. Presence of human papilloma virus (HPV) structural antigens and of HPV 16-related DNA sequences. *Arch Dermatol*, 121, 858–863.

2. Feldman, S.B., Sexfon, M., Glenn, J.D. et al (1989) Immunosuppression in men with bowenoid papulosis. *Arch Dermatol*, 125, 651–654.

3. Halasz, C., Silvers, D., Crum, C.P. (1986) Bowenoid papulosis in a three-year-old girl. *J Am Acad Dermatol*, 14, 326–330.

4. Lookingbill, D.P., Kreider, J.W., Howett, M.K. et al (1987) Human papillomavirus type 16 in Bowenoid papulosis, intraoral papillomas and squamous cell carcinoma of the tongue. *Arch Dermatol*, 123, 363–368.

5. Clarke, D.P. (1987) Condyloma acuminatum. *Derm Clin*, 5, 779–788.

6. Park, K.C., Kim, K.H., Youn, S.W. et al (1998) Heterogeneity of human papillomavirus DNA in a patient with Bowenoid papulosis that progressed to squamous cell carcinoma. *Br J Dermatol*, 139, 1087–1091.

7. Pala, S., Poleva, I., Vocatura, A. (2000) The presence of HPV types 6/11, 16/18, 31/33/51 in Bowenoid papulosis demonstrated by DNA in situ hybridization. *Int J STD AIDS*, 11, 823–824.

8. Olhoffer, I.H., Davidson, D., Longley, J. et al (1999) Facial bowenoid papulosis secondary to human papillomavirus type 16. *Br J Dermatol*, 140, 761–762.

9. Johnson, T.M., Saluja, A., Fader, D. et al (1999) Isolated extragenital bowenoid papulosis of the neck. *J Am Acad Dermatol*, 41, 867–870.

10. Purnell, D., Ilchyshyn, A., Jenkins, D. et al (2001) Isolated human papillomavirus 18-positive extragenital bowenoid papulosis and idiopathic CD4+ lymphocytopenia. *Br J Dermatol*, 144, 619–621.

11. Ikenberg, H., Gissman, L., Gross, G. et al (1983) HPV type-16 related DNA in genital Bowen's disease and Bowenoid papulosis. *Int J Cancer*, 32, 563–569.

12. Rudlinger, R., Grob, R., Yu, Y.X. et al (1989) Human papillomavirus 35-positive Bowenoid papulosis of the anogenital area and concurrent human papillomavirus 35-positive verruca with Bowenoid dysplasia of the periungual area. *Arch Dermatol*, 125, 655–659.

13. Patterson, J.W., Kao, G.F., Graham, J.H. et al (1986) Bowenoid papulosis: a clinicopathological study with ultrastructural observations. *Cancer*, 57, 823–836.

14. Euvrard, S., Kanitakis, J., Chardonnet, Y. et al (1997) External anogenital lesions in organ transplant recipients. A clinicopathologic and virologic assessment. *Arch Dermatol*, 133, 175–178.

15. Obalek, S., Jablonska, S., Baudenon, S. et al (1986) Bowenoid papulosis of the male and female genitalia: risk of cervical neoplasia. *J Am Acad Dermatol*, 14, 433–444.

16. Cobb, M.W. (1990) Human papillomavirus infection. *J Am Acad Dermatol*, 22, 547–566.

17. Wade, T.R., Kopf, A.W., Ackerman, A.B. (1978) Bowenoid papulosis of the penis. *Cancer*, 42, 1890–1903.

18. Kimura, S. (1982) Bowenoid papulosis of genitalia. *Int J Dermatol*, 21, 432–436.

19. Guillet, G.Y., Braun, L., Masse, R. et al (1984) Bowenoid papulosis. Demonstration of human papillomavirus (HPV) with anti-HPV immune serum. *Arch Dermatol*, 120, 514–516.

Epidermodysplasia verruciformis

Clinical features

Epidermodysplasia verruciformis (EV) is a rare inherited condition. Affected individuals present with a wide range of HPV subtypes including 3, 5, 8–10, 12, 14, 15, 17, 19–25, 28, 29, 36–38, 46, 47, 49, 50, 51 and 59.[1–3] The more common flat warts, caused by HPV-3 and HPV-10, may also occur in these patients but have an extensive distribution pattern; they may form plaques and may be persistent.[4] These are seen most often on the arms, legs, face and the dorsum of the hands (*Figs 17.29, 17.30, 17.31*).[2] The specific EV subtypes of HPV cause reddish, or pigmented or depigmented, scaly flat macular plane warts, mainly on the trunk, but also on the face, neck and arms.[2] Clinically they resemble pityriasis versicolor (*Fig. 17.32*). Dark-skinned patients may present with seborrheic keratosis-like changes.[5] Spiny hyperkeratosis of the fingers is a rare manifestation.[6]

Susceptibility to EV is usually inherited in an autosomal recessive manner although X-linked recessive inheritance has been reported from one family.[7] The lesions persist throughout life, and after some years (usually more than 20) they may show nuclear atypia resembling Bowen's disease, and frank carcinoma sometimes develops. Basal cell carcinoma can also occur.[8] The tumors develop particularly on sun-exposed skin

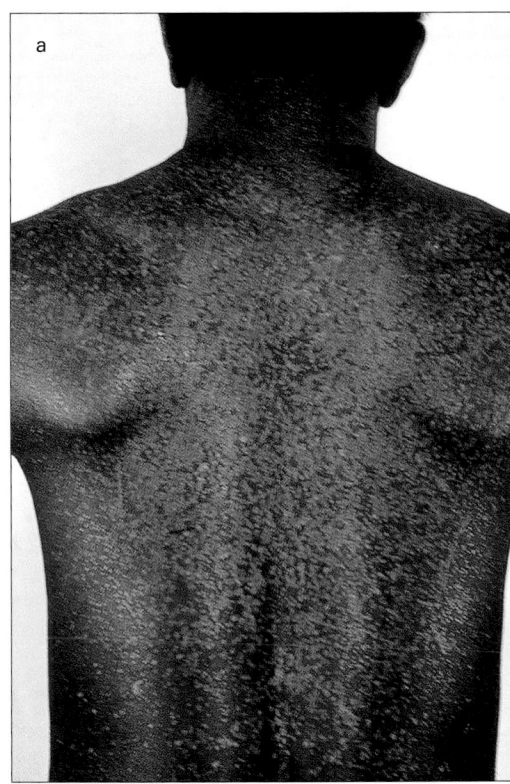

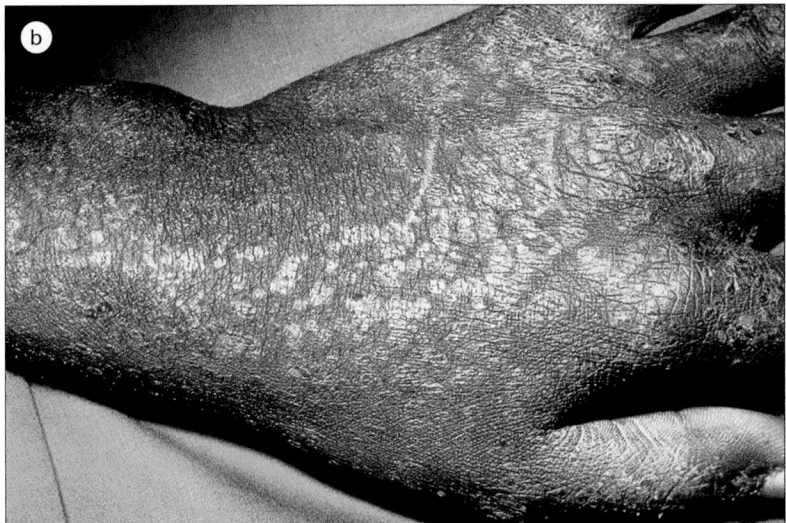

Fig. 17.29
Epidermodysplasia verruciformis: **(a)** innumerable small flat warts are present; **(b)** the dorsum of the hand is a commonly affected site. By courtesy of the Institute of Dermatology, London, UK.

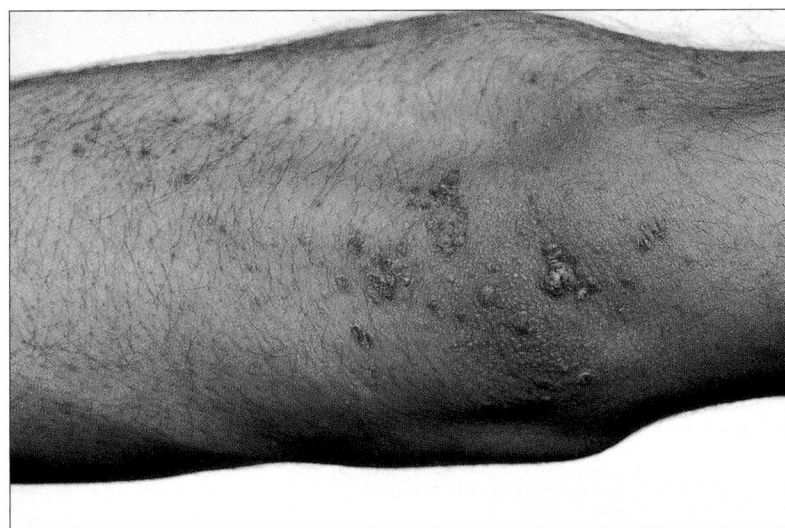

Fig. 17.30
Epidermodysplasia verruciformis: these plane warts are due to HPV-3 and HPV-10 infection. By courtesy of M.M. Black, MD, Institute of Dermatology, London, UK.

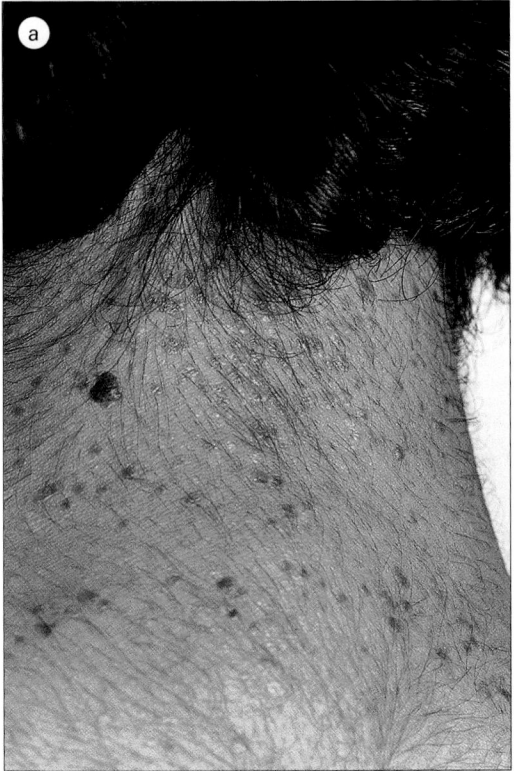

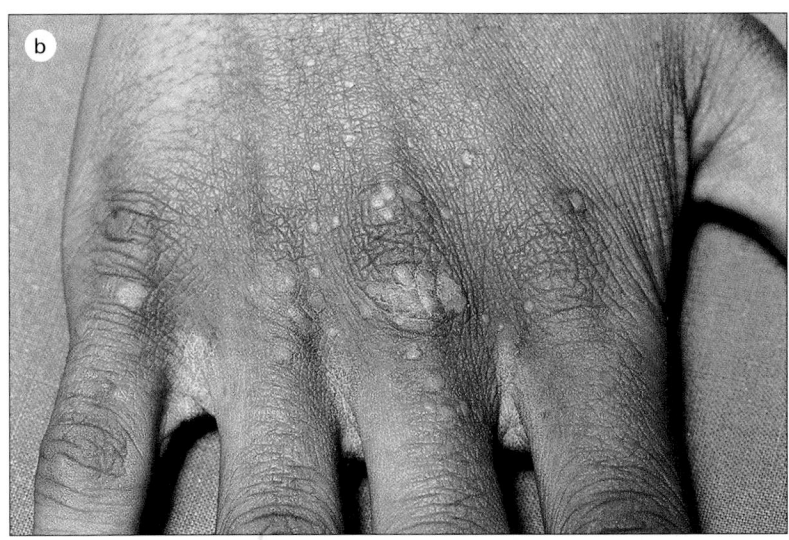

Fig. 17.31
Epidermodysplasia verruciformis: note the numerous flat warts on **(a)** the neck and **(b)** the dorsum of the hand. By courtesy of M.M. Black, MD, Institute of Dermatology, London, UK.

and are most often associated with HPV-5 or 8.[2,9] Patients who develop invasive squamous carcinoma in association with EV do so at a younger age than those who develop similar tumors not in association with EV (27 years compared with 67 years).[9] Such tumors, which are often multiple, are usually associated with a good prognosis unless they are treated with radiotherapy when they may be associated with metastatic disease, which has a high mortality.[1] EV-like disease has been reported in patients with a background of immunosuppression in such conditions as systemic lupus erythematosus, Hodgkin's lymphoma and HIV infection and in patients following renal transplantation.[10,11] An EV-like eruption has been documented in association with idiopathic CD4 lymphopenia.[12]

EV therefore represents an unusual condition in which HPV infection, inherited predisposition (possibly a defect in cell-mediated immunity) and exposure to the sun all play a part (co-carcinogens).[8]

Pathogenesis and histological features

The full pathogenesis of epidermodysplasia verruciformis is not yet clear. The EV-related HPV may be present in the general population, but the characteristic lesions only occur in predisposed individuals

(*Fig. 17.33*).[8,13,14] A putative susceptibility locus for EV has been mapped to the long arm of chromosome 17 (17q25).[15,16] Of interest is the fact that EV was recently reported in a patient with neurofibromatosis type I, another condition linked to chromosome 17.[17] A second susceptibility locus has been mapped to chromosome region 2p21–24.[16]

Patients often manifest impaired cell-mediated immune functions including diminished dinitrochlorobenzene (DNCB) sensitization and poor mitogen-induced blast transformation accompanied by varying degrees of cutaneous anergy.[18,19] There appears to be a specific abnormal T-cell response to HPV-infected keratinocytes.[19] The immune defect most often associated is a reduction in the number and function of T-helper cells, but patients with EV do not show general immunodeficiency or susceptibility to other infections.[14] EV is not usually seen in patients with iatrogenic immunosuppression. Humoral immunity is characteristically normal. EV has been described in association with severe immunodeficiency, lymphoma and disseminated molluscum contagiosum infection.[20] EV has also been reported in a patient with malignant thymoma.[21] EV-associated HPVs have been detected in the amniotic fluid, placenta and cervical scrapes of a pregnant patient with EV, thereby suggesting that vertical transmission of EV HPVs may play a role.[22]

Histologically EV is characterized by hyperkeratosis, hypergranulosis and acanthosis (*Figs 17.34, 17.35*).[1] The keratinocytes are vacuolated and show a striking blue–gray pallor on staining with hematoxylin and

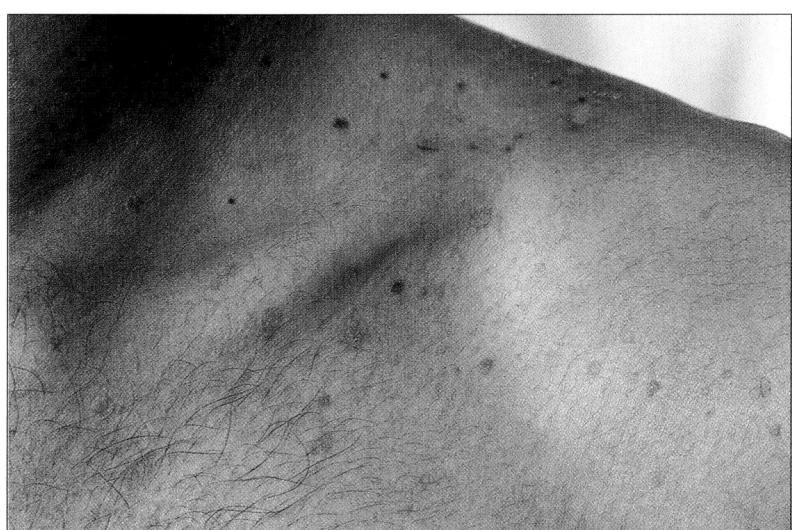

Fig. 17.32
Epidermodysplasia verruciformis: these scaly macules on the chest and axilla resemble pityriasis versicolor. From the same patient as *Fig. 17.31*.

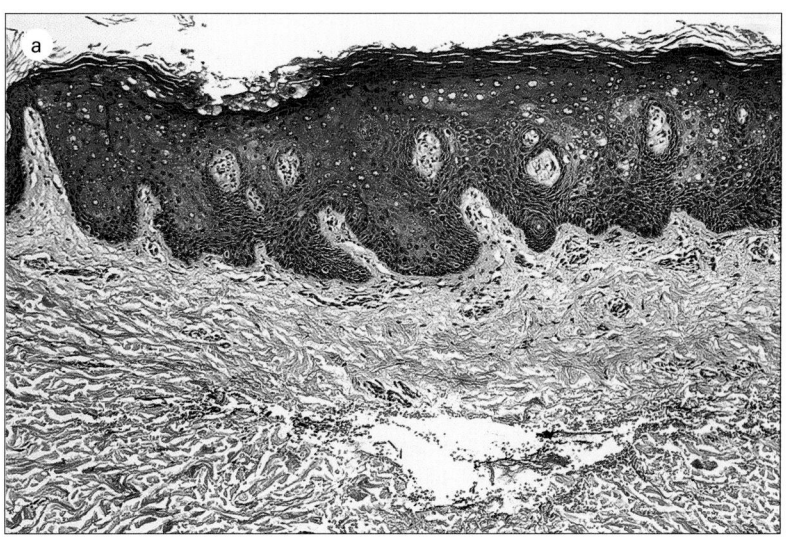

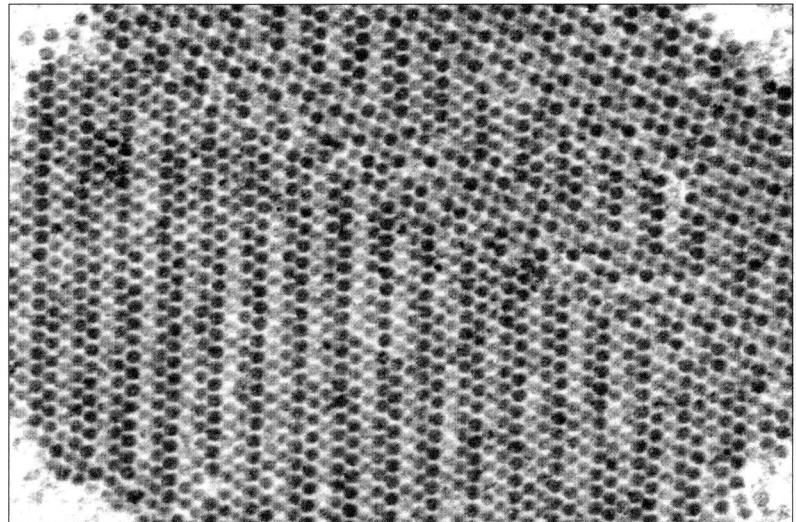

Fig. 17.33
Epidermodysplasia verruciformis: electron micrograph showing the characteristic lattice structure.

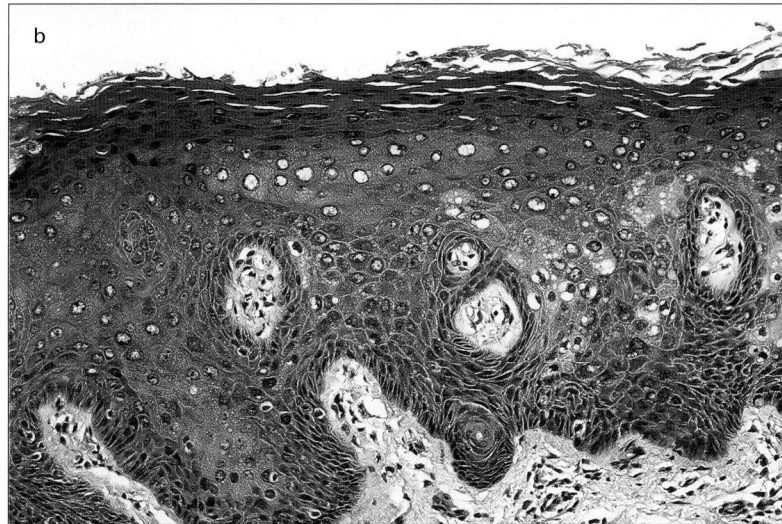

Fig. 17.34
Epidermodysplasia verruciformis: (**a**) there is hyperkeratosis and acanthosis; (**b**) note the characteristic, swollen, paler-staining cells showing nuclear vacuolation.

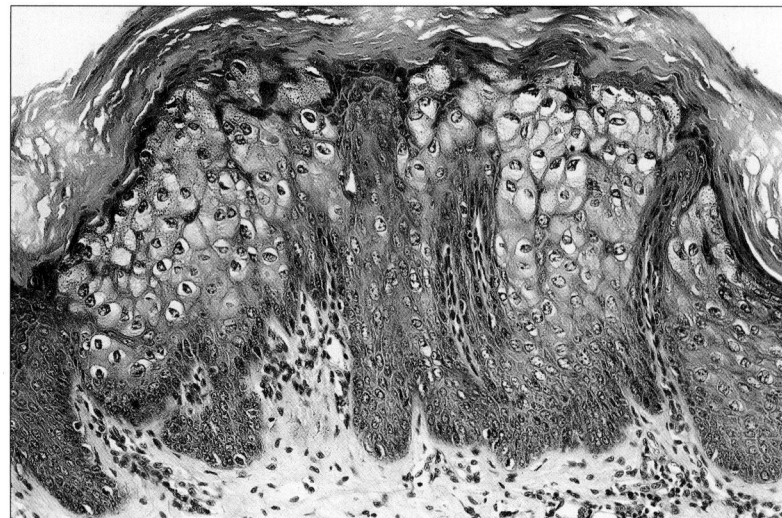

Fig. 17.35
Epidermodysplasia verruciformis: this specimen is from a small plane wart-like lesion.

eosin. They are arranged in clusters or columns, the pallor being most conspicuous in the superficial granular cell layer. As the lesions progress to atypicality, the nuclei of the keratinocytes become larger and hyperchromatic, and cellular maturation is more disorderly. The dysplastic changes may also affect appendigeal epithelium, particularly that of sweat ducts. The atypia eventually amounts to carcinoma in situ and in 30–50% of patients the lesions progress to invasive carcinoma. Cutaneous neoplasia in EV is largely associated with HPV-5 and 8. Most carcinomas are squamous in type, but some show features reminiscent of sweat gland differentiation. The sweat ducts may show markedly disordered growth and atypia. These stages in the progression to frank carcinoma only occur on sun-exposed skin. In contrast to cervical cancer where the viral genome is integrated into the host DNA, in EV it remains extrachromosomal.

Differential diagnosis

Swollen keratinocytes, as described above as a diagnostic feature of EV, have been recorded as a manifestation of immunosuppression, particularly HIV infection.[23]

References

1. Cobb, M.W. (1990) Human papilloma virus infection. *J Am Acad Dermatol*, **22**, 547–566.
2. Melton, J.L., Rasmussen, J.E. (1991) Clinical manifestations of human papilloma virus infection in nongenital sites. *Derm Clin*, **9**, 219–233.
3. Majewski, S., Jablonska, S. (1997) Human papillomavirus-associated tumors of the skin and mucosa. *J Am Acad Dermatol*, **36**, 659–685.
4. Jablonska, S., Orth, G. (1985) Epidermodysplasia verruciformis. *Clin Dermatol*, **3**, 83–96.
5. Jacyk, W.K., de Villiers, E.M. (1993) Epidermodysplasia verruciformis in Africans. *Int J Dermatol*, **32**, 806–810.
6. Caputo, R., Cavicchini, S., Brezzi, A. et al (1995) Spiny hyperkeratosis as an unusual sign of epidermodysplasia verruciformis. *J Am Acad Dermatol*, **32**, 523–524.
7. Androphy, E.J., Dvoretezky, I., Lowry, D.R. (1985) X-linked inheritance of epidermodysplasia verruciformis. Genetic and virologic studies of a kindred. *Arch Dermatol*, **121**, 864–868.
8. Pfister, H. (1987) Human papillomaviruses and impaired immunity vs epidermodysplasia verruciformis. *Arch Dermatol*, **123**, 1469–1470.
9. Kaspar, T.A., Wagner, R.F., Jablonska, S. et al (1991) Prognosis and treatment of advanced squamous cell carcinoma secondary to epidermodysplasia verruciformis: a worldwide analysis of 11 patients. *J Dermatol Surg Oncol*, **17**, 237–240.
10. Berger, T.G., Sawchuk, W.S., Leonardi, C. et al (1991) Epidermodysplasia verruciformis-associated papillomavirus infection complicating human immunodeficiency virus disease. *Br J Dermatol*, **124**, 79–83.
11. Morrison, C., Eliezri, Y., Magro, C. et al (2002) The histologic spectrum of epidermodysplasia verruciformis in transplant and AIDS patients. *J Cutan Pathol*, **29**, 480–489.
12. Tobin, E., Rohwedder, A., Holland, S.M. et al (2003) Recurrent 'sterile' verrucous cyst abscesses and epidermodysplasia verruciformis-like eruption associated idiopathic CD4 lymphopenia. *Br J Dermatol*, **149**, 627–633.
13. Glinski, W., Obalek, S., Jablonska, S. et al (1981) T-cell defect in patients with epidermodysplasia verruciformis due to human papillomavirus type 3 and 5. *Dermatologica*, **162**, 141–147.
14. Majewski, S., Skopinska-Rozewska, E., Jablonska, S. et al (1986) Partial defects of cell-mediated immunity in patients with epidermodysplasia verruciformis. *J Am Acad Dermatol*, **15**, 966–973.
15. Rámoz, N., Rueda, L.A., Bouadjar, B. et al (1999) A susceptibility locus for epidermodysplasia verruciformis, an abnormal predisposition to infection with oncogenic human papillomavirus type 5, maps to chromosome 17qter in a region containing a psoriasis locus. *J Invest Dermatol*, **112**, 259–263.
16. Rámoz, N., Taieb, A., Rueda, L.A. et al (2000) Evidence for a nonallelic heterogeneity of epidermodysplasia verruciformis with two susceptibility loci mapped to chromosome regions 2p21–p24 and 17q25. *J Invest Dermatol*, **114**, 1148–1153.
17. Alpsoy, E., Ciftcioglu, M.A., Keser, I. et al (2002) Epidermodysplasia verruciformis with neurofibromatosis type 1: coincidental association or model for understanding mechanism of the disease. *Br J Dermatol*, **146**, 503–507.
18. Ostrow, R.S., Manias, D., Mitchell, A.J. et al (1987) Epidermodysplasia verruciformis: a case associated with primary lymphatic dysplasia, depressed cell-mediated immunity, and Bowen's disease containing human papillomavirus 16 DNA. *Arch Dermatol*, **123**, 1511–1516.
19. Prawer, S.E., Pass, F., Vance, J.C. et al (1977) Depressed immune function in epidermodysplasia verruciformis. *Arch Dermatol*, **113**, 495–499.
20. Slawsky, L.D., Gilson, R.T., Hockley, A.J. et al (1992) Epidermodysplasia verruciformis associated with severe immunodeficiency, lymphoma and disseminated molluscum contagiosum. *J Am Acad Dermatol*, **27**, 448–450.
21. Jacyk, W.K., Hazelhurst, J.A., Dreyer, L. et al (1993) Epidermodysplasia verruciformis and malignant thymoma. *Clin Exp Dermatol*, **18**, 89–91.
22. Favre, M., Majewski, S., de Jesus, N. et al (1998) A possible vertical transmission of human papillomavirus genotypes associated with epidermodysplasia verruciformis. *J Invest Dermatol*, **111**, 333–336.
23. Penneys, N.S., Friend, A., Zhu, W-Y. et al (1992) Swollen keratinocytes: a histologic marker of unusual human papilloma virus-type infection and immunosuppression. *J Cutan Pathol*, **19**, 217–220.

Herpes simplex virus infections

Herpes simplex virus (HSV) has two subtypes: HSV-1 and HSV-2.[1–3]

There is considerable homology between the two genomes, about 50% of sequences being highly conserved.[4] Humans are the natural hosts for HSV-1 and HSV-2 and therefore also represent the viral reservoir.[5] Herpes viruses are double-stranded DNA viruses with a complex capsid and glycoprotein envelope (*Fig. 17.36*).

Clinical features

HSV-1 usually causes herpes labialis (90%), whereas HSV-2 most often causes herpes genitalis. Although HSV-2 previously accounted for approximately 90% of herpes genitalis cases, recent epidemiological evidence reflects an increase in the proportion of cases attributable to HSV-1 (22–29%) and a diminished number of HSV-2 positive cases (68–71%).[6,7] In some European cohort studies, HSV-1 infection has been a more common cause of genital herpes than HSV-2 infection. This trend may be attributable to the practice of oral sex.[6] Both HSV-1 and HSV-2 are transmitted through mucosal surfaces or traumatized skin by exposure to contaminated secretions.[5,8–10]

A first-episode infection – i.e. in someone who is seronegative (first-episode primary infection) or who has serum antibodies to the heterolo-

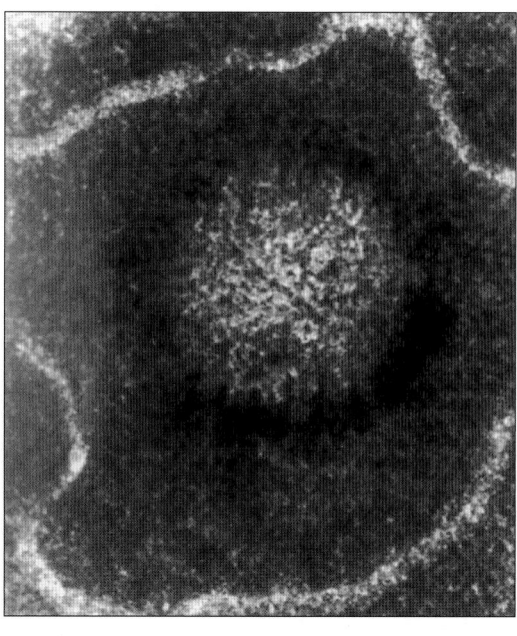

Fig. 17.36
Herpes virus: all members of the herpes virus group have identical ultrastructural morphology. Note the outer membrane surrounding the virus core. The herpes virus is an icosahedron with 162 capsomeres on its surface. By courtesy of I. Chrystie, FIMLS, St Thomas' Hospital, London, UK.

gous HSV type (first-episode, non-primary infection) – may be associated with constitutional symptoms of fever and malaise.[11] These symptoms are often worse in women with genital herpes, perhaps because of the wider area of epithelium involved and the greater viral load. The lesions may be found in the mouth, pharynx, lips, penis, vulva, vagina or cervix (*Figs 17.37–17.41*). HSV infections are also being seen more frequently in perianal and anorectal sites. Involvement of a finger in the form of a herpetic whitlow is most often seen in dental practitioners (*Fig. 17.42*). Primary HSV-1 infection, however, is asymptomatic in about 90% of patients, and primary HSV-2 in about 75%.[12] It is important to remember that infection is for life.

At the original inoculation site there is no detectable change for 3–5 days. The lesions that develop vary with site, but all are associated with the development of small grouped vesicles, often on an erythematous base. On mucosal surfaces the vesicles rupture early and are superseded by grayish-yellow plaques or ulcers. In skin, grouped vesicles are seen on an erythematous base and then evolve into grouped pustules, which rupture and result in a crusted ulcer.[13,14] The lesions are typically painful and sting or itch. The distribution of the lesions is characteristically wider than the initial site of inoculation, involving the area of innerva-tion by the sensory nerve to that site. Occasionally a separate area of lesions may develop away from the initial inoculation site, after transmission along a different branch of the same nerve. These initial cutaneous lesions only develop after involvement of the nerve and the ganglion and subsequent return of the virus to the epithelium.[5] The lesions may then extend peripherally to involve adjacent skin or mucosa. This first episode of infection lasts for around 15 days. The epithelial lesions then resolve completely, but the virus persists, i.e. it becomes latent within the ganglia of the corresponding sensory nerve.[15]

Recurrent HSV lesions are usually less florid than the first infection and are not usually associated with general symptoms. They may be precipitated by sunlight, fever, menstruation, pregnancy, HIV infection, emotional stress or local trauma.[12] The incidence of recurrent orofacial herpes varies from 16 to 45%, while that of recurrent genital herpetic infection varies from about 50 to 65% of patients.[5] Repeated recurrence is usual with genital HSV-2 and common with orofacial HSV-1, but with gradually decreasing frequency. 'Reinfection' with the heterologous type resembles a less severe first-episode primary infection.

Antibodies to HSV-1 are found in about 70–90% of adults, suggesting very wide contact with the virus, with a subclinical infection or an unrecognized oropharyngitis in childhood.[10] Antibodies to HSV-2 are present in about 15–45% of the population. Although HSV-1 occurs most commonly above the waist and HSV-2 below, these are preferential rather than obligatory sites. It has been noted that 10–15% of first-episode genital herpes is associated with pharyngeal lesions, emphasizing not only the frequency of orogenital contact, but that both viruses can affect either orofacial or genital epithelia.

Occasionally a first-episode primary infection in an atopic patient may result in extensive vesicular crops, so-called Kaposi's varicelliform eruption (eczema herpeticum) (*Figs 17.43, 17.44*).[12] These lesions pustulate, ulcerate and crust, as in the usual herpetic infection, but involve more or less the whole skin surface. Systemic symptoms may be severe, with fever and dehydration. The condition may occasionally prove fatal. Recurrent attacks may occur, but they are usually short and less severe. This manifestation of herpetic infection may also complicate Darier's disease, pemphigus foliaceous and other dermatoses. Histori-

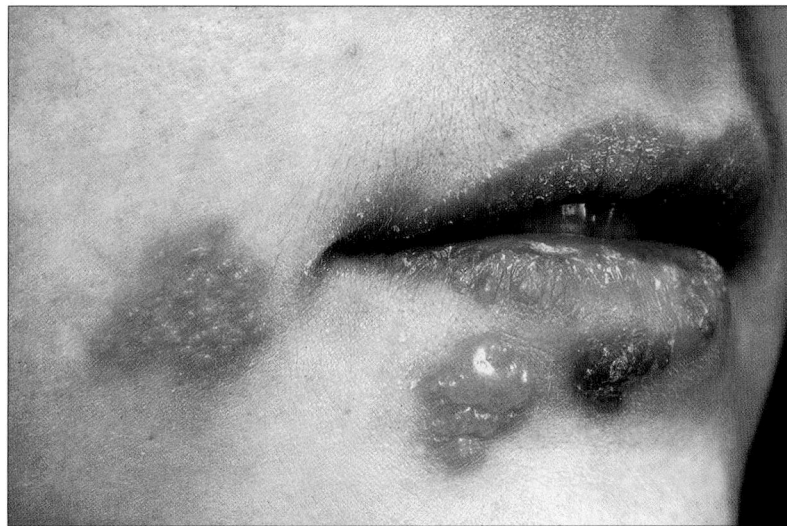

Fig. 17.37
Herpes simplex 1: primary infection showing grouped vesicles on an erythematous base. By courtesy of R.A. Marsden, MD, St George's Hospital, London, UK.

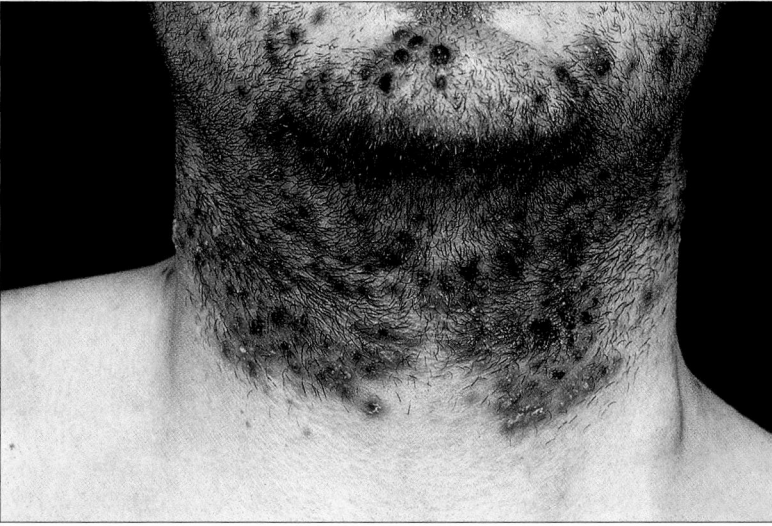

Fig. 17.38
Herpes simplex: this patient shows a particularly severe infection. By courtesy of the Institute of Dermatology, London, UK.

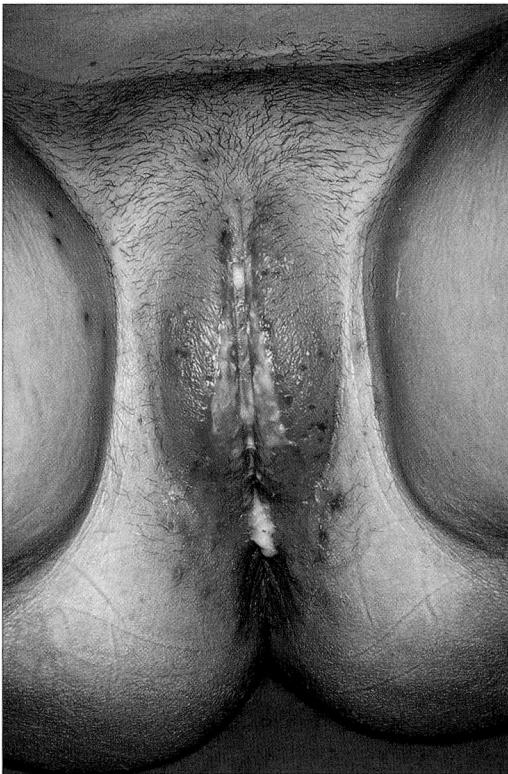

Fig. 17.39
Herpes simplex 2: vulval involvement showing erythema and crusted vesicles. By courtesy of R.A. Marsden, St George's Hospital, London, UK.

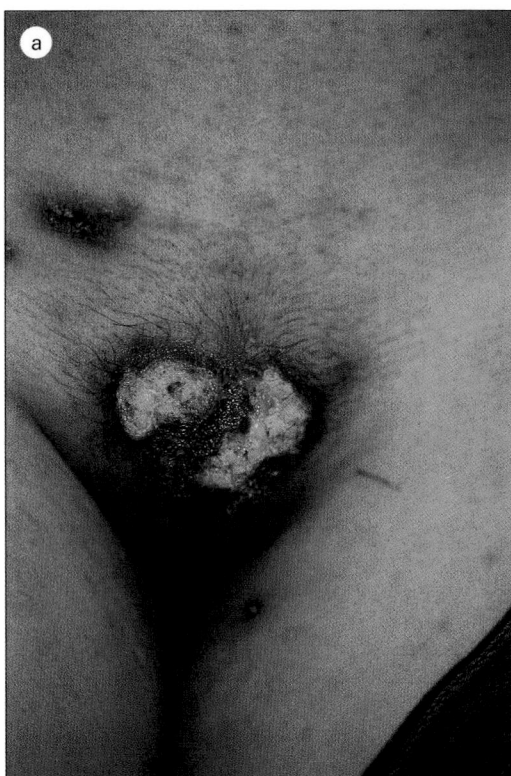

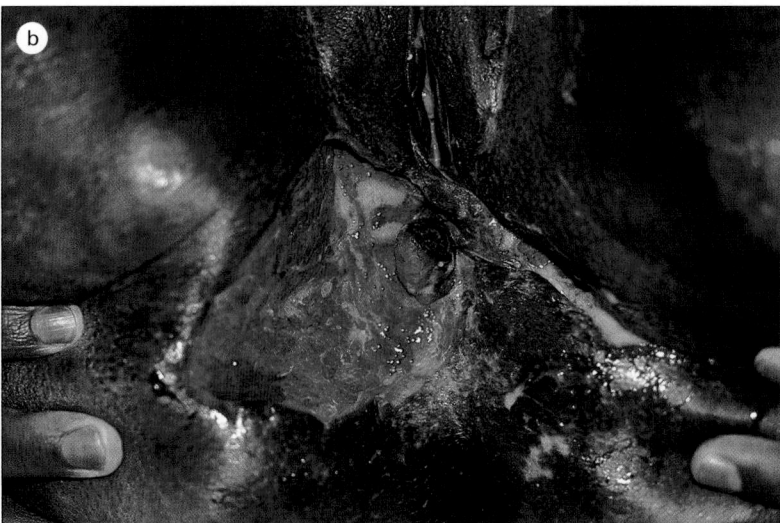

Fig. 17.40
Herpes simplex 2: (a) lesions are often painful or burning; (b) in this patient there is very severe ulceration. By courtesy of N.C. Dlova, MD, Nelson R. Mandela School of Medicine, University of KwaZulu-Natal, South Africa.

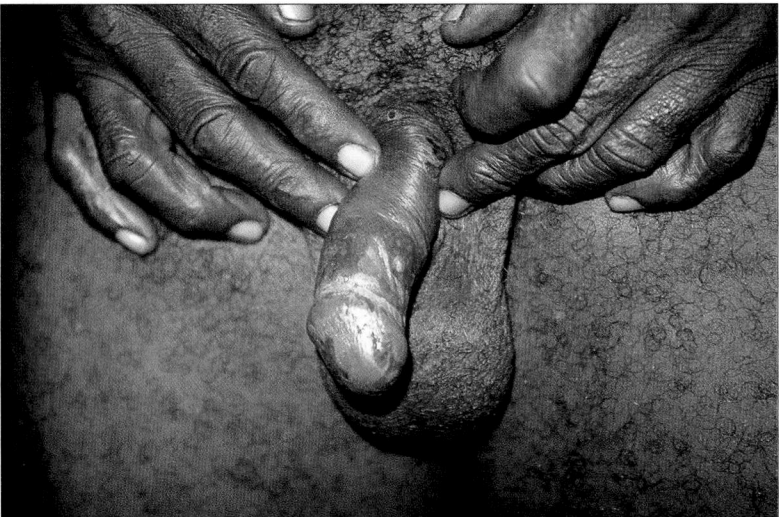

Fig. 17.41
Herpes simplex 2: there is intense erythema and multiple ulcers are present on both the glans and the shaft. By courtesy of C. Furlonge, MD, Port of Spain, Trinidad.

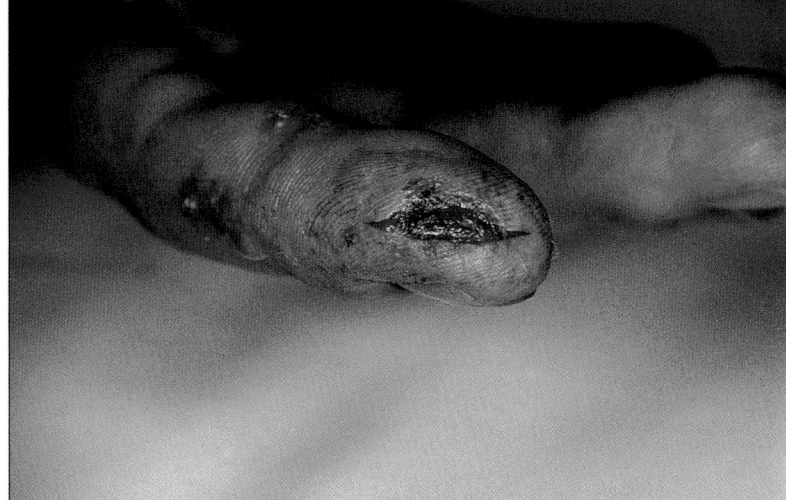

Fig. 17.42
Herpetic whitlow: intact vesicles may be seen on the proximal phalanx. The medical and dental professions are at particular risk from this mode of spread. By courtesy of R.A. Marsden, MD, St George's Hospital, London, UK.

cally, a similar clinical picture was occasionally caused by vaccinia virus (eczema vaccinatum) as a complication of vaccination against smallpox. Histologically, the lesions of Kaposi's varicelliform eruption are the same as those of the more localized form of herpetic infection. Disseminated disease may be seen in the immunosuppressed (*Fig. 17.45*).

Congenital infection is rare, but neonatal herpes simplex infection may be seen in 10% of babies born to women with an active herpetic lesion after the thirty-second week of pregnancy.[16] Congenital HSV infection forms part of the TORCH complex (see also p. 859).[17] Lesions in congenital herpes infection can be extensively bullous, with severe erythroderma and loss of body fluid through exudation. The reported mortality rate in infants with disseminated infection is approximately 57%.[18] Neonatal infections usually present as a relatively mild oropharyngitis and many are probably undiagnosed.

Pathogenesis and histological features

The double-stranded DNA of herpes virus is enclosed in an icosahedral protein shell (capsid) which in turn is invested by a complex envelope of lipid and glycoproteins. The latter are important in the attachment and penetration of cells. The complete virus measures about 150–1200 nm in diameter.[12] Viral replication occurs within the nucleus where a basophilic Feulgen-positive inclusion body, including viral DNA, may be found as well as an eosinophilic inclusion body, which represents a focal deficiency of viral DNA, a so-called 'scar' of viral infection.[4] Heparan sulfate moieties act as receptors to which HSV-1 and HSV-2 bind.[19,20] HSV-1 encodes a complement-interacting glycoprotein (gC) and an IgG Fc binding glycoprotein (gE). These glycoproteins mediate immune evasion.[21] Glycoproteins C and D (gC and gD) play an important role in

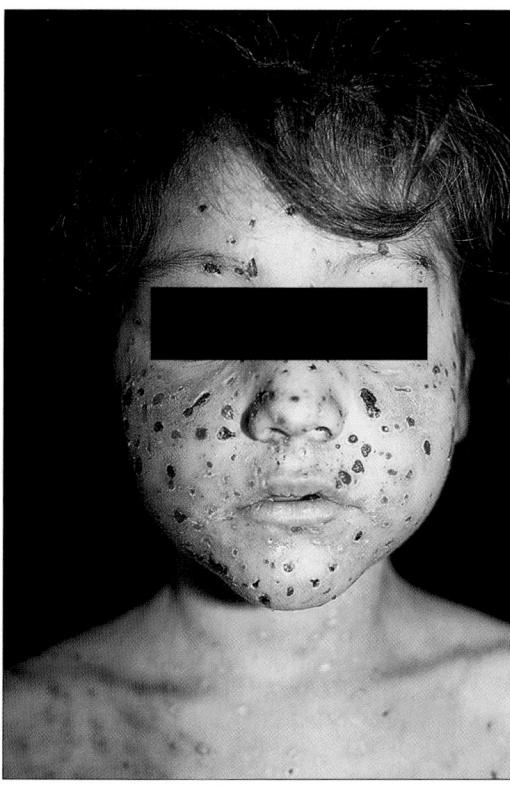

Fig. 17.43
Eczema herpeticum: this variant usually presents in atopic children. By courtesy of J.C. Salas, MD, Azteca, Monterrey, Mexico.

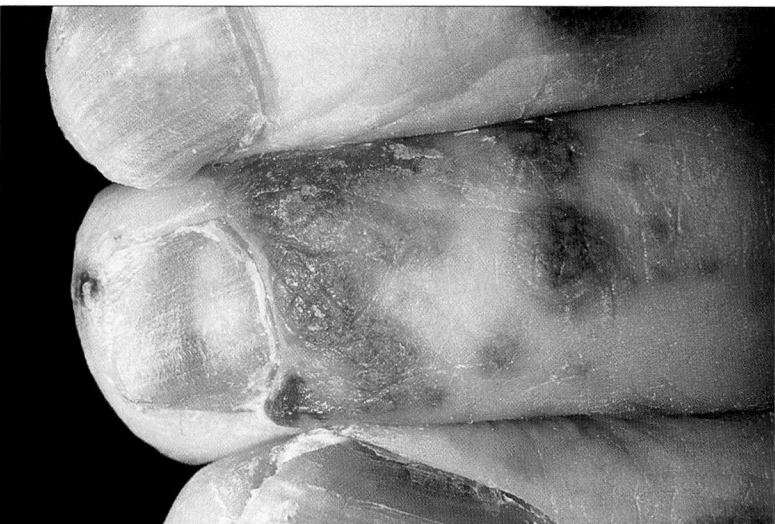

Fig. 17.45
Disseminated herpes infection: widespread lesions may be seen in immunosuppressed patients. By courtesy of the Institute of Dermatology, London, UK.

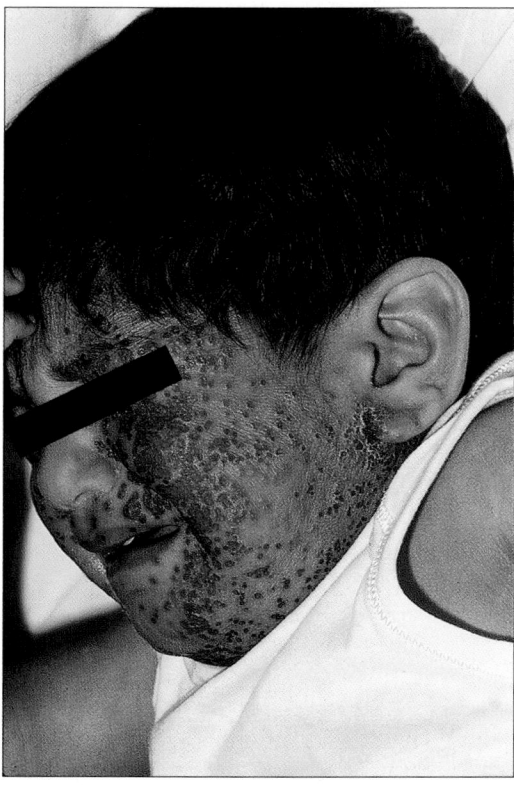

Fig. 17.44
Eczema herpeticum: this can be a very serious condition and affect the whole body. By courtesy of R.A. Marsden, MD, St George's Hospital, London, UK.

the latent periods, which may last for many months or years, is not clear. It may continue as a more or less intact virus, but in virtually suspended animation without cell death, or it may persist as episomes or be incorporated into the cell genome. The exact mechanism of reactivation of the virus is not yet understood.

Although immune defects (particularly of cell-mediated immunity and including HIV infection) are associated with a high incidence of severe and extensive herpetic infections, a state of raised immunity (either humoral or cellular) does not preclude recurrent lesions; indeed, recurrent lesions are usually associated with very high titers of IgG antibody. It is thought that humoral immunity may impede neuronal extension and reduce the likelihood of encephalitis, but cell-mediated immunity is effective in limiting the local cutaneous extension of the lesions and accelerates healing. Low levels of interferon-gamma (IFN-γ) may contribute to reactivation of infections.[23]

Histologically, the early change of HSV infection is increasing edema of the keratinocytes, which progresses to so-called ballooning degeneration.[24] Some adjacent keratinocytes fuse so that they appear large and multinucleate. A number of cells show acantholysis, while others rupture as a result of extreme balloon degeneration (reticular degeneration). The result of acantholysis and balloon degeneration is an irregular intraepidermal vesicle containing groups of keratinocytes, many of which may be multinucleate (*Figs 17.46–17.49*). The nuclei of keratinocytes may contain basophilic and/or pale ground-glass inclusions. As a vesicle expands it involves the full thickness of the epidermis and may not be so clearly intraepidermal. HSV infection of the hair follicle epithelium can result in herpes folliculitis.[25] Involvement of hair follicles is in fact very common in most infections. In cases with very prominent superficial secondary changes, the distinctive findings of the infection are sometimes evident in the infundibular portion of the hair follicle.

The underlying dermis is usually intensely infiltrated by mixed inflammatory cells (*Fig. 17.50*).[24] The infiltrate shows perineural accentuation and occasionally a superficial leukocytoclastic vasculitis is present (*Fig. 17.51*).[24] Dermal nerve twigs may exhibit a perineural inflammatory infiltrate composed of lymphocytes and neutrophils, sometimes associated with intraneural involvement. Schwann cell hypertrophy and frank neuronal necrosis are occasionally encountered.[26]

The features of an ulcerated lesion are not diagnostic unless the epithelial margins retain the characteristic features of intracellular edema, multinucleate epithelial cells and inclusion bodies. The multi-

the attachment of HSV-1 to host cell surface heparan sulfate receptors, whereas glycoprotein B (gB) is responsible for HSV-2 cellular attachment, entry and cell-to-cell spread.[19,20]

The most characteristic feature in the pathogenesis of herpetic infections is the early involvement of sensory nerves within which the virus, without its lipid/glycoprotein envelope, is transported to the ganglia.[22] Further replication (associated with cell lysis) occurs within the ganglia and the complete virus then migrates to the skin around the site of inoculation via the peripheral sensory nerves. This process of viral migration also occurs at times of recurrence. The state of the virus during

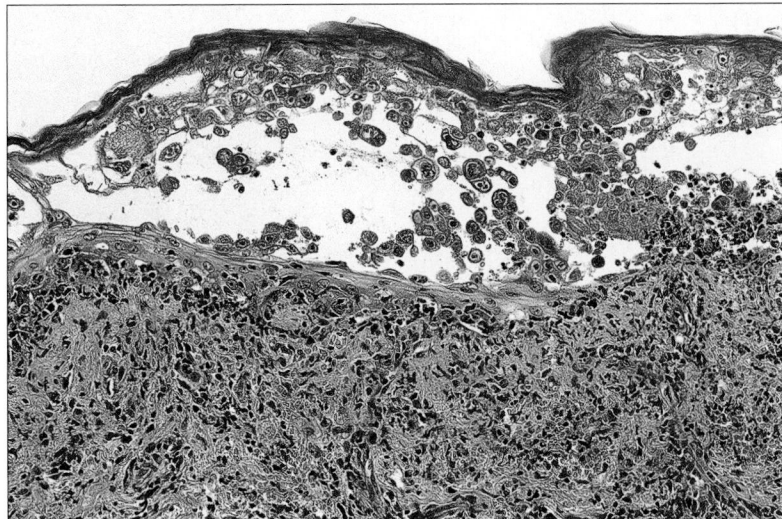

Fig. 17.46
Herpes simplex: intraepidermal vesicle in which the residual keratinocytes show intracellular edema (ballooning degeneration) and acantholysis.

Fig. 17.47
Herpes simplex: scanning view of intact intraepidermal blister.

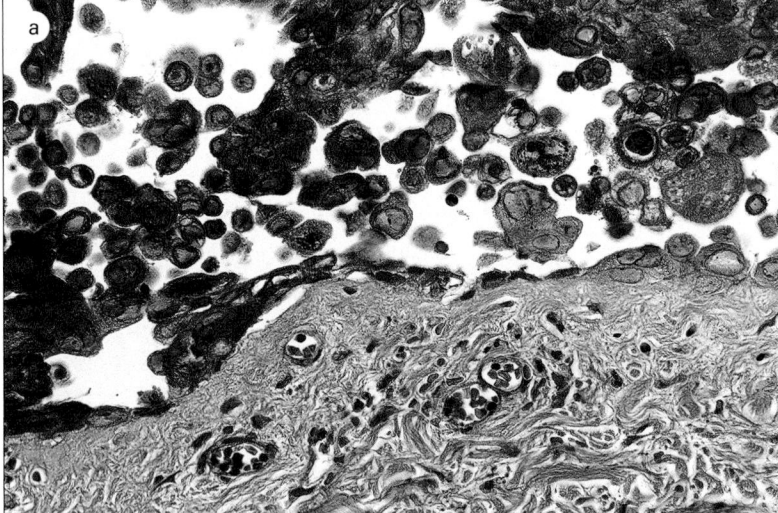

Fig. 17.48
(**a, b**) Herpes simplex: characteristic intranuclear inclusions.

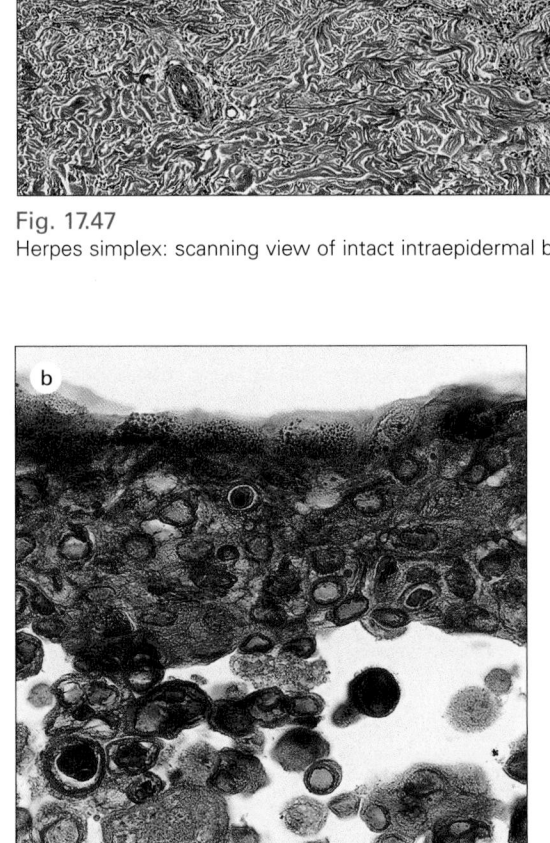

nucleate cells are the diagnostic feature of the Tzanck test, a Giemsa-stained smear of vesicle contents. In the past, laboratory diagnosis of herpes infection was confirmed by growth in tissue culture, electron microscopy, immunofluorescent demonstration of viral-specific protein or viral DNA hybridization.[27] Nowadays, the diagnosis of HSV-1 or HSV-2 infection can also be confirmed by PCR or immunohistochemistry (*Fig. 17.52*).[28,29]

References

1. Wildy, P. (1985) Herpes viruses: a background. *Br Med Bull*, **421**, 339–344.
2. Robinson, T.W.E., Heath, R.B. (1983) Infections with herpes simplex virus. In: Virus diseases and the skin. Edinburgh: Churchill Livingstone, pp 53–73.
3. Dahl, M. (1986) Host defense, herpes, warts and other viruses. In: Clinical immunodermatology, 2nd edn. Chicago: Year Book, pp 158–170.
4. Corey, L., Spear, P.G. (1986) Infections with herpes simplex viruses, Part I. *N Engl J Med*, **314**, 686–691.
5. Chang, T-W. (1983) Herpes simplex virus infection. *Int J Dermatol*, **22**, 1–7.
6. Lafferty, W.E. (2002) The changing epidemiology of HSV-1 and HSV-2 and implications for serological testing. *Herpes*, **9**, 51–55.
7. Lowhagen, G.B., Tunback, P., Bergstrom, T. (2002) Proportion of herpes simplex (HSV) type 1 and type 2 among genital and extragenital HSV isolates. *Acta Derm Venereol*, **82**, 118–120.
8. Vestey, J.P., Norval, M. (1992) Mucocutaneous infections with herpes simplex virus and their management. *Clin Exp Dermatol*, **17**, 221–237.
9. Corey, L., Spear, P.G. (1986) Infections with herpes simplex viruses, Part 2. *N Engl J Med*, **314**, 749–757.
10. Wheeler, C.E. (1988) The herpes simplex problem. *J Am Acad Dermatol*, **18**, 163–168.
11. Corey, L. (1988) First episode, recurrent and asymptomatic herpes simplex infections. *J Am Acad Dermatol*, **18**, 169–172.
12. Fiumara, N.J. (1989) Herpes simplex. *Clin Dermatol*, **7**, 23–26.
13. Snavely, S.R., Liu, C. (1984) Clinical spectrum of herpes simplex virus infections. *Clin Dermatol*, **2**, 8–22.
14. Corey, L., Vontver, L.A., Brown, Z.A. (1984) Genital herpes simplex virus infections: clinical manifestations, course and complications. *Semin Dermatol*, **3**, 89–101.
15. Hill, T.J. (1985) Herpes simplex virus latency. In: Roizman, B. (ed.) The herpes viruses, Vol. 3. New York: Plenum Press, pp 175–240.
16. Meissner, H.C. (1984) Herpes simplex virus infections in the newborn. *Clin Dermatol*, **2**, 23–28.
17. Epps, R.E., Pittelkow, M.R., Su, W.P. (1995) TORCH syndrome. *Semin Dermatol*, **14**, 179–186.
18. Jacobs, R.F. (1998) Neonatal herpes simplex virus infections. *Semin Perinatol*, **22**, 64–71.
19. Liu, J., Shriver, Z., Pope, R.M. et al (2002) Characterization of a heparan sulfate octasaccharide that binds to herpes simplex virus type 1 glycoprotein D. *J Biol Chem*, **277**, 33456–33467.
20. Cheshenko, N., Herold, B.C. (2002) Glycoprotein B plays a predominant role in mediating herpes simplex virus type 2 attachment and is required for entry and cell-to-cell spread. *J Gen Virol*, **83**, 2247–2255.
21. Lubinski, J.M., Jiang, M., Hook, L. et al (2002) Herpes simplex virus type 1 evades the effects of antibody and complement in vivo. *J Virol*, **76**, 9232–9241.
22. Klein, R.J. (1985) Initiation and maintenance of latent herpes simplex virus infections: the paradox of perpetual immobility and continuous movement. *Rev Infect Dis*, **7**, 21–30.

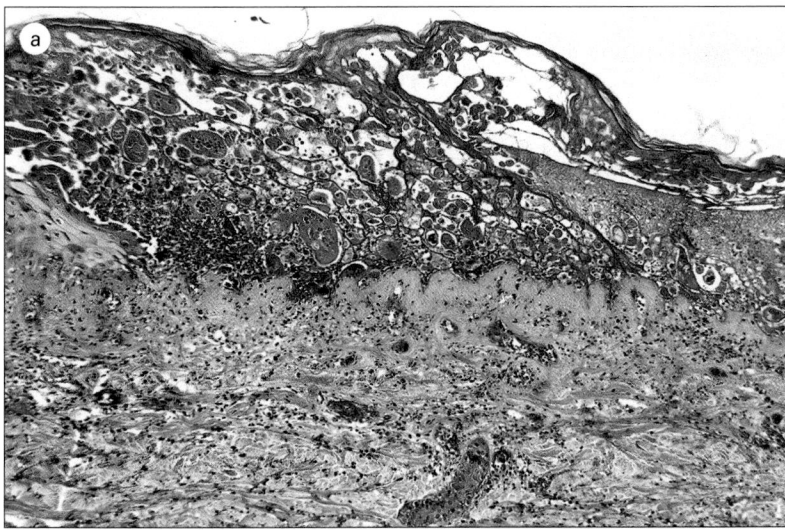
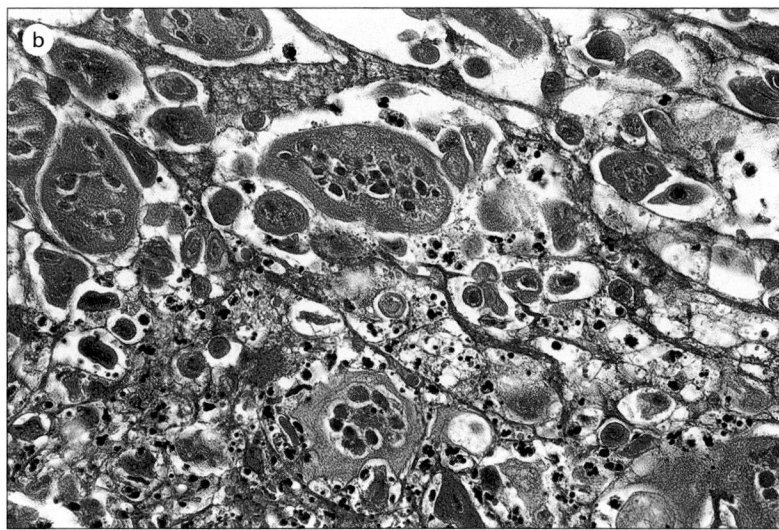

Fig. 17.49
(a, b) Herpes simplex: note the numerous multinucleate giant cells.

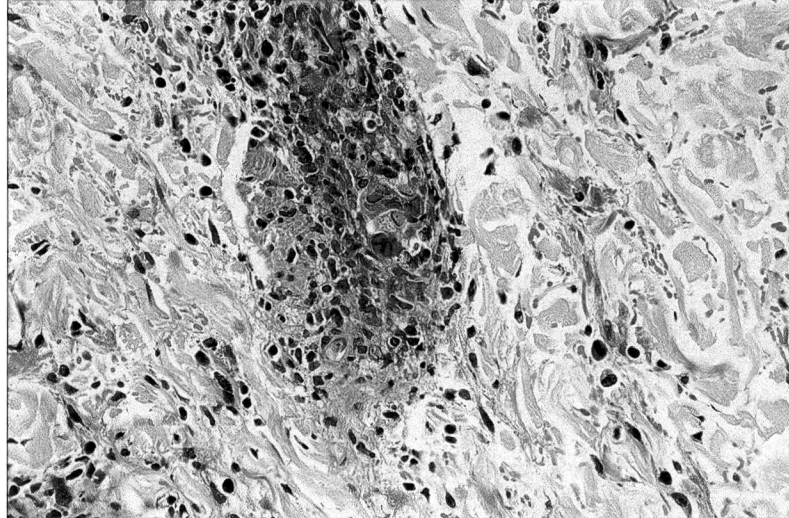

Fig. 17.50
Herpes simplex: there is a dense perivascular chronic inflammatory cell infiltrate. Viral inclusions are present in the endothelial cells.

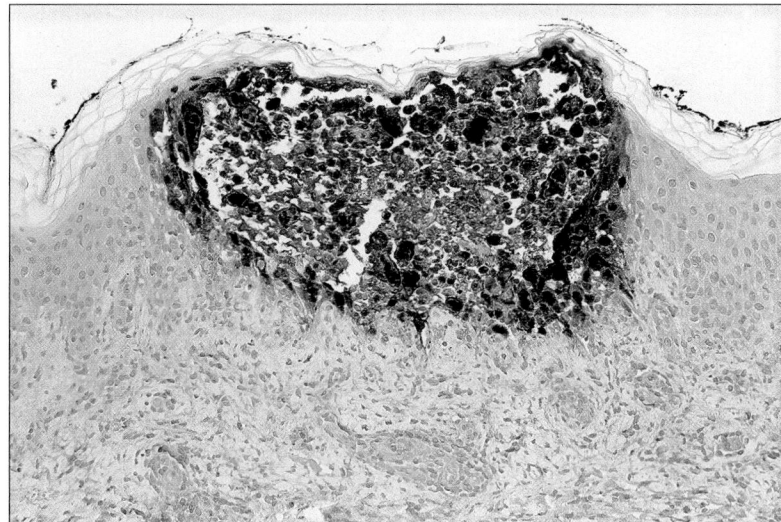

Fig. 17.52
Herpes simplex: positive immunohistochemistry. By courtesy of G. Pinkus, MD, Brigham and Women's Hospital and Harvard Medical School, Boston, USA.

23. McKenna, D.B., Neill, W.A., Norval, M. (2001) Herpes simplex virus specific immune responses in subjects with frequent and infrequent orofacial recrudescences. *Br J Dermatol*, **144**, 459–464.
24. McSorley, J., Shapiro, L., Brownstein, M.H. et al (1974) Herpes simplex and varicella-zoster: comparative histopathology of 77 cases. *Int J Dermatol*, **13**, 69–75.
25. Weinberg, J.M., Mysliwiec, A., Turiansky, G.W. et al (1997) Viral folliculitis. Atypical presentations of herpes simplex, herpes zoster, and molluscum contagiosum. *Arch Dermatol*, **133**, 983–986.
26. Worrell, J.T., Cockerell, C.J. (1997) Histopathology of peripheral nerves in cutaneous herpesvirus infection. *Am J Dermatopathol*, **19**, 133–137.
27. Vestergaard, B.F. (1985) Laboratory diagnosis of herpes viruses. *Scand J Infect Dis*, **47**, 22–32.
28. Lucotte, G., Bathelier, C., Lespiaux, V. et al (1995) Detection and genotyping of herpes simplex virus types 1 and 2 by polymerase chain reaction. *Mol Cell Probes*, **9**, 287–290.
29. Nikkels, A.F., Delvenne, P., Sadzoot-Delvaux, C. et al (1996) Detection of varicella zoster virus and herpes simplex virus in disseminated fatal infections. *J Clin Pathol*, **49**, 243–248.

Varicella and herpes zoster

Clinical features

Varicella-zoster virus (VZV), also referred to as herpes varicella virus, is similar morphologically to HSV, and is the causative agent of varicella and zoster.[1–5]

Varicella, or chickenpox, which is highly contagious, is most often an infection of children and is characterized by a disseminated vesicular eruption in crops. The major route of dissemination is by airborne

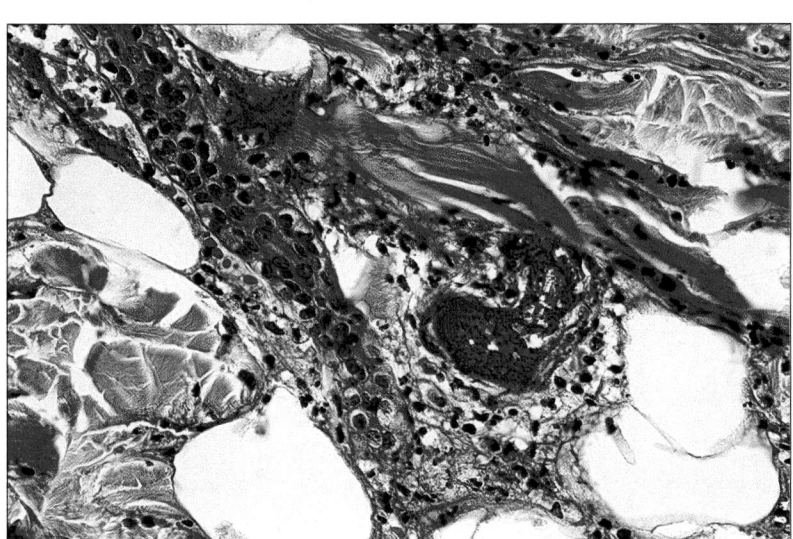

Fig. 17.51
Herpes simplex: this small blood vessel shows intense fibrinoid necrosis.

droplets from the respiratory tract.[3,6] In the immunocompetent, spread via the cutaneous lesions seems to be of little importance. Varicella is endemic in the temperate climates and manifests predominantly in winter and spring.[6]

The incubation period is around 2 weeks and is followed by a rash, which is most pronounced on the trunk. The rash starts as red macules 2–4 mm across, which progress rapidly to fragile vesicles said to resemble 'dew drops on rose petals'; these become pustular and rapidly show crusting (*Fig. 17.53*). Lesions in varying stages are present at any one time. There is often considerable pruritus and the associated scratching may result in secondary infection with *Staphylococcus aureus* or *Streptococcus pyogenes*.[1] Mucosal lesions are frequently also present. Systemic effects in children are mild whereas they are almost invariably severe in adults, neonates and immunocompromised patients.

Complications include pneumonitis, meningitis, encephalitis, myelitis and purpura fulminans. In the last, symmetrical hemorrhagic and necrotic lesions are seen on the legs following typical chickenpox and the condition is associated with disseminated intravascular coagulation. Acquired deficiencies in protein S or protein C have been implicated in the pathogenesis of varicella-associated purpura fulminans.[7,8] Less common complications include orchitis, hepatitis, glomerulonephritis, arthritis, myocarditis and rhabdomyolysis.[6,9,10] Necrotizing fasciitis (see p. 876) is a potentially life-threatening complication of childhood varicella.[11]

Herpes zoster, or shingles, occurs particularly in adults, usually the elderly, and most often presents as a girdle-like vesicular eruption in the thoracic or lumbar region, or with facial lesions as a result of trigeminal nerve involvement (*Figs 17.54, 17.55*).[2,6] It is analogous to a recurrent

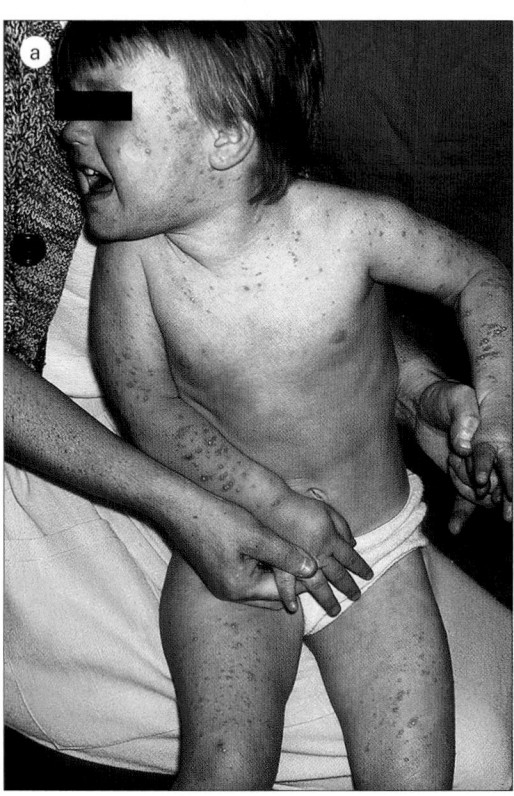

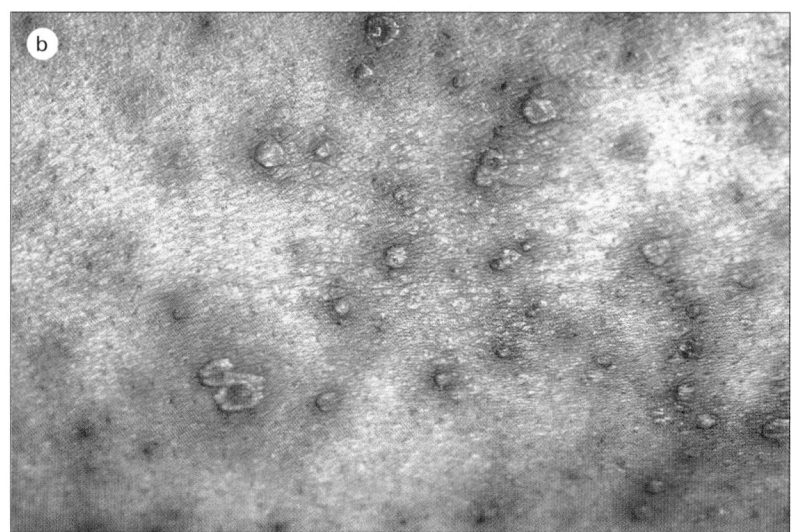

Fig. 17.53
Varicella (chickenpox): (a) note the widespread distribution of vesicles on the face, upper chest, arms and legs; (b) close-up view. (a) By courtesy of R.A. Marsden, MD, St George's Hospital, London, UK; (b) by courtesy of the Institute of Dermatology, London, UK.

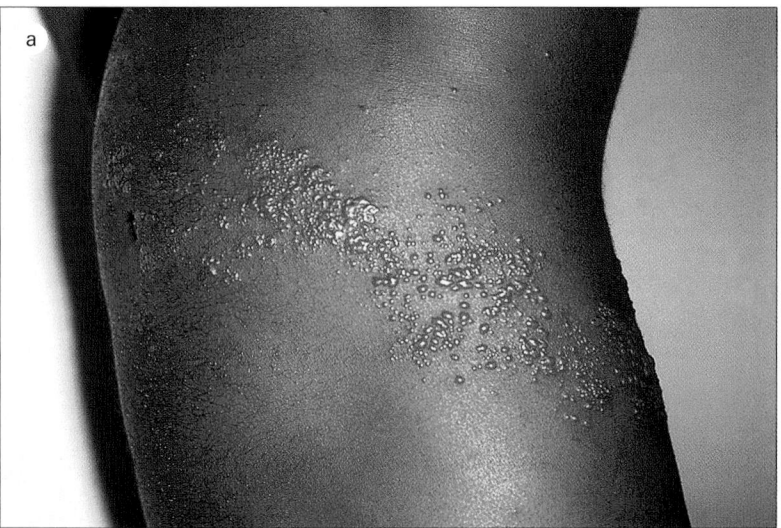

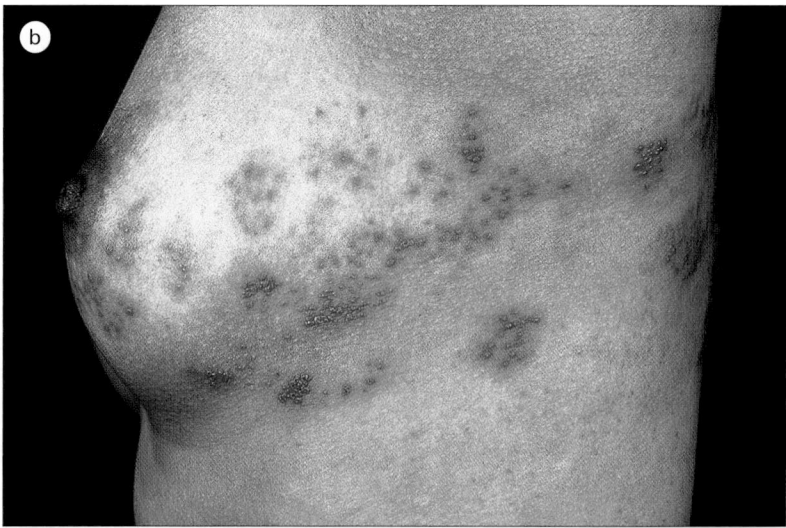

Fig. 17.54
(a, b) Herpes zoster (shingles): intact vesicles in a characteristic dermatomal distribution. (a) By courtesy of C. Furlonge, MD, Port of Spain, Trinidad; (b) by courtesy of the Institute of Dermatology, London, UK.

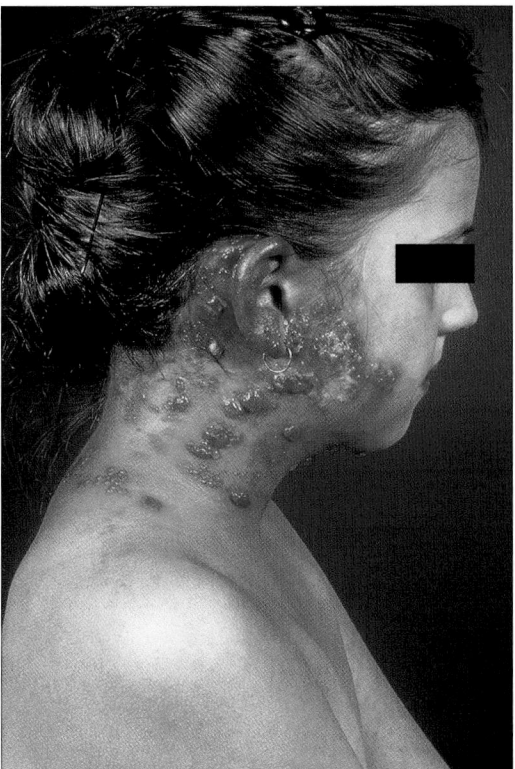

Fig. 17.55
Herpes zoster (shingles): there is intense erythema, intact vesicles and crusted lesions. By courtesy of R.A. Marsden, MD, St George's Hospital, London, UK.

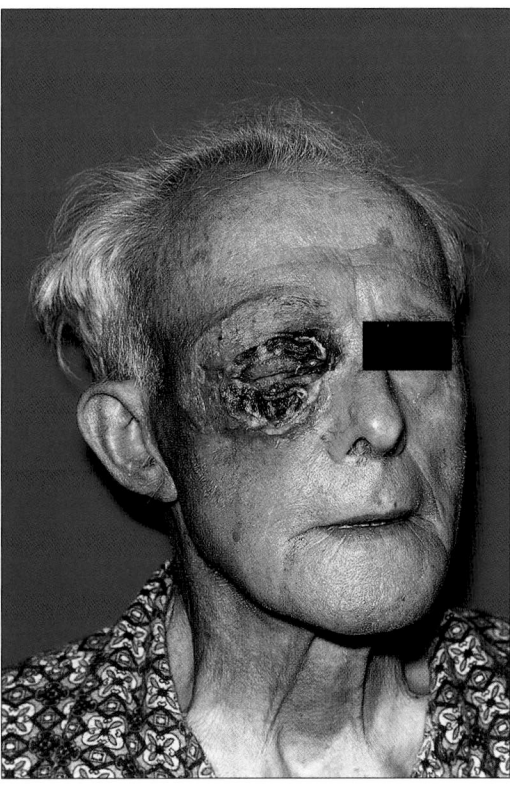

Fig. 17.57
Herpes zoster (shingles): ophthalmic involvement is particularly seen in the elderly. By courtesy of R.A. Marsden, MD, St George's Hospital, London, UK.

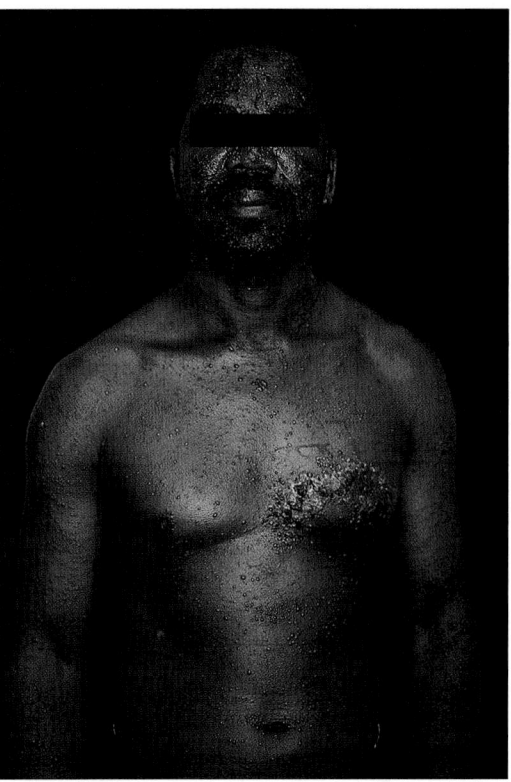

Fig. 17.58
Herpes zoster: disseminated lesions may be seen in immunosuppressed patients. By courtesy of N.C. Dlova, MD, Nelson R. Mandela School of Medicine, University of KwaZulu-Natal, South Africa.

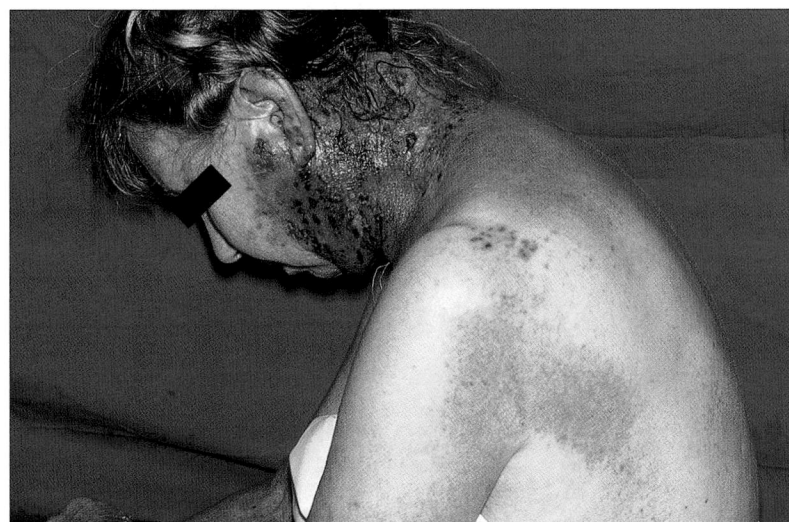

Fig. 17.56
Herpes zoster (shingles): older lesion in which the rash has a hemorrhagic component. By courtesy of R.A. Marsden, MD, St George's Hospital, London, UK.

episode of herpes simplex where the virus remains latent in the ganglia of sensory nerves. It is thought to develop as a consequence of partial immunity.[6] The eruption is preceded by paresthesia or pain in the dermatome supplied by a sensory nerve. This is followed, usually after 2–4 days, by the development of an edematous erythematous plaque on which groups of vesicles arise. As in chickenpox, these rapidly become pustules, which may coalesce to form bullae, occasionally hemorrhagic (*Fig. 17.56*). The areas become crusted and this may very occasionally be followed by scarring and keloid formation. The lesions are usually painful and this may persist for months or years as postherpetic

neuralgia. Involvement of the ophthalmic division of the trigeminal nerve is an important manifestation in the elderly, which may have serious complications (*Fig. 17.57*). Rarely, non-contiguous multidermatomal cutaneous involvement (zoster multiplex) may occur.[12]

Reactivation of latent VZV may be associated with a deficiency in cell-mediated immunity, as immunity to chickenpox per se is normally lifelong. Patients with Hodgkin's lymphoma, non-Hodgkin's lymphoma or systemic lupus erythematosus, and those treated with irradiation or chemotherapy, are particularly at risk and often develop a more serious illness.[6] In more severe cell-mediated immunodeficiency the zoster may become widely disseminated and sometimes proves fatal. Disseminated cutaneous lesions most often present as vesicles, pustules, hemorrhagic bullae, ulcers and black eschars although occasionally patients may develop verrucous, hyperkeratotic lesions (*Fig. 17.58*).[13] Visceral involvement is most often seen in the lung, liver and brain.[6] Cerebral disease most often presents as progressive leukoencephalitis. A non-immune individual may contract chickenpox from a person with herpes zoster. Herpes zoster occurs in 40–50% of patients in the first year following bone marrow transplantation, but the lesions increasingly resemble varicella as the time after transplantation increases. This suggests that T-cells specific for VZV are less well represented as time goes by.

VZV infection in patients with AIDS may present with unusual manifestations, including verrucous skin lesions resembling viral warts and disseminated varicella in the absence of skin lesions.[14–16]

Pathogenesis and histological features

Although inhalation of fomites is the usual route of infection, direct cutaneous inoculation may occur. Initial contact is followed by viremia before the cutaneous lesions develop. The resolution of the lesions is clinically complete, but the virus may remain latent in the ganglia of sensory nerves. IgG, IgM and IgA antibodies develop soon after the vesicles; some IgG antibody is detectable thereafter throughout life, but the other antibodies disappear. It has been noted that cell-mediated immunity is depressed during an episode of chickenpox and for at least the first few days of zoster.

Histologically, the cutaneous lesions of VZV, whether in varicella or zoster form, are generally indistinguishable from those of herpes simplex although it has been suggested that inflammation is more profound in the latter.[17] The intraepidermal blisters associated with intracellular edema and multinucleate epithelial cells with inclusion bodies are characteristic. The dermal infiltrate and fibrinopurulent exudate are seen regularly, but are not diagnostic. There is often more intraepidermal and dermal hemorrhage than in herpes simplex infection.

The wart-like cutaneous lesions encountered in patients with AIDS show hyperkeratosis, verruciform acanthosis and virally induced cyto-pathic alterations, often with minimal or absent cytolysis of the infected epidermal keratinocytes, and little by way of a dermal inflammatory infiltrate.[14,16] Immunosuppressed individuals with VZV infection may have a protracted clinical course in which biopsies may reveal a lichenoid inflammatory reaction pattern rather than cytolysis of keratinocytes.[18]

Biopsies from early herpes zoster lesions may exhibit VZV-infected cells in the hair follicles, suggesting that VZV spreads to an area of skin innervated by myelinated nerves, the latter terminating at the level of the follicular isthmus.[19] Very rarely, VZV infection may manifest with dermal vasculitis in the absence of associated epidermal involvement.[20] A number of cutaneous reactions have been described at the sites of healed herpes zoster scars. These include pseudolymphomatous cutaneous lymphoid hyperplasia, granulomatous vasculitis, granulomatous folliculitis, granuloma annulare, lichen planus, reactive perforating collagenosis, lichen sclerosus and cutaneous Rosai–Dorfman disease.[21,22]

As for HSV, the presence of multinucleate cells may be valuable in the Tzanck test. In shingles, the spinal ganglia may show necrosis with inflammation and intranuclear inclusions are sometimes evident.[23] Otherwise, diagnosis is usually based on clinical criteria, but may be confirmed by electron microscopy, immunofluorescence of blister contents, growth in tissue culture, PCR, in situ hybridization or immunohistochemistry (*Fig. 17.59*). Serological tests are only valuable later, when a rising titer can be demonstrated.

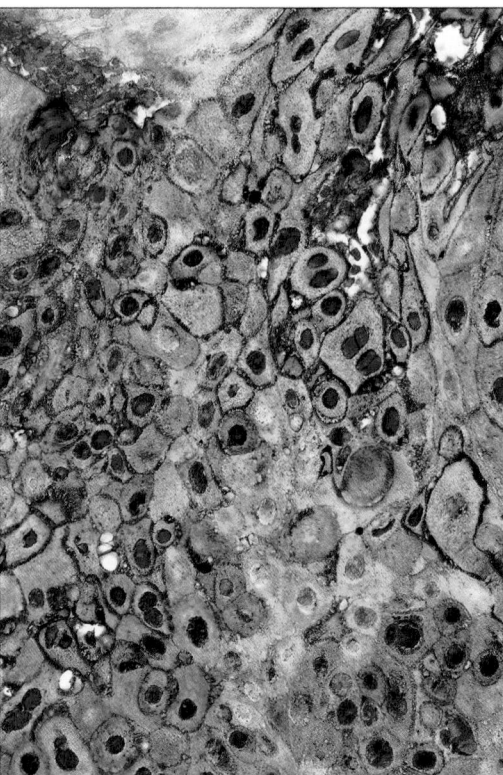

Fig. 17.59
Herpes zoster: positive immunohistochemistry. By courtesy of G. Pinkus, MD, Brigham and Women's Hospital and Harvard Medical School, Boston, USA.

References

1. Burns, W.H., Sarah, R. (1985) Opportunistic viral infections. *Br Med Bull*, **41**, 46–49.
2. Dahl, M. (1986) Host defense, herpes, warts and other viruses. In: Clinical immunodermatology, 2nd edn. Chicago: Year Book, pp 158–170.
3. Robinson, T.W.E., Heath, R.B. (1983) Infections with herpes simplex virus. In: Virus diseases and the skin. Edinburgh: Churchill Livingstone, pp 53–73.
4. Zachariae, H. (1985) Herpes virus infection in man. *Scand J Infect Dis*, **47** (Suppl.), 44–50.
5. Arvin, A.M. (1996) Varicella-zoster virus. *Clin Microbiol Review*, **9**, 361–381.
6. Liesegang, T.J. (1984) The varicella–zoster virus: systemic and ocular features. *J Am Acad Dermatol*, **11**, 165–191.
7. van Ommen, C.H., van Wijnen, M., de Groot, F.G. et al (2002) Postvaricella purpura fulminans caused by acquired protein S deficiency resulting from antiprotein S antibodies: search for the epitopes. *J Pediatr Hematol Oncol*, **24**, 413–416.
8. Canpolat, C., Bakir, M. (2002) A case of purpura fulminans secondary to transient protein C deficiency as a complication of chickenpox infection. *Turk J Pediatr*, **44**, 148–151.
9. Alter, P., Grimm, W., Maisch, B. (2001) Varicella myocarditis in an adult. *Heart*, **85**, E2.
10. al-Langawi, M., al-Marri, M.R., al Soub, H. (2001) Rhabdomyolysis associated with varicella infection. *Int J Clin Pract*, **55**, 484–485.
11. Fustes-Morales, A., Gutiérrez-Castrellon, P., Duran-Mckinster, C. et al (2002) Necrotizing fasciitis: report of 39 pediatric cases. *Arch Dermatol*, **138**, 893–899.
12. Vu, A.Q., Radonich, M.A., Heald, P.W. (1999) Herpes zoster in seven disparate dermatomes (zoster multiplex): report of a case and review of the literature. *J Am Acad Dermatol*, **40** (5 Pt 2), 868–869.
13. McSorley, J., Shapiro, L., Brownstein, M.H. et al (1974) Herpes simplex and varicella-zoster: comparative histopathology of 77 cases. *Int J Dermatol*, **13**, 69–75.
14. Fagan, W.A., Collins, P.C., Pulitzer, D.R. (1996) Verrucous herpes virus infection in human immunodeficiency virus patients. *Arch Pathol Lab Med*, **120**, 956–958.
15. Cohen, J.I., Brunell, P.A., Straus, S.E. et al (1999) Recent advances in varicella-zoster virus infection. *Ann Intern Med*, **130**, 922–932.
16. Nikkels, A.F., Snoeck, R., Rentier, B. et al (1999) Chronic verrucous varicella zoster virus skin lesions: clinical, molecular and therapeutic aspects. *Clin Exp Dermatol*, **24**, 346–353.
17. Ghatak, N.R., Zimmerman, H.M. (1973) Spinal ganglion in herpes zoster. A light and electron microscopic study. *Arch Pathol*, **95**, 411–415.
18. Nikkels, A.F., Sadzoot-Delvaux, C., Rentier, B. et al (1998) Low-productive alpha-herpesviridae infection in chronic lichenoid dermatoses. *Dermatology*, **196**, 442–446.
19. Muraki, R., Iwasaki, T., Sata, T. et al (1996) Hair follicle involvement in herpes zoster: pathway of viral spread from ganglion to skin. *Virchows Arch*, **428**, 275–280.
20. Uhoda, I., Pierard-Franchimont, C., Pierard, G.E. (2000) Varicella-zoster virus vasculitis: a case of recurrent varicella without epidermal involvement. *Dermatology*, **200**, 173–175.
21. Requena, L., Kutzner, H., Escalonilla, P. et al (1998) Cutaneous reactions at sites of herpes zoster scars: an expanded spectrum. *Br J Dermatol*, **138**, 161–168.
22. Lee, H.N., Lee, D.W., Lee, Y.J. et al (2001) Two cases of reactive perforating collagenosis arising at the site of healed herpes zoster. *Int J Dermatol*, **40**, 191–192.
23. Cohen, P.R., Grossman, M.E. (1989) Clinical features of human immunodeficiency virus-associated disseminated herpes zoster virus infection – a review of the literature. *Clin Exp Dermatol*, **14**, 273–276.

Cytomegalovirus infections

Clinical features

The findings of antibody studies suggest that most people have been exposed to cytomegalovirus (CMV).[1] Generally an asymptomatic infection has resulted. CMV infection, however, may result in clinical features under a variety of circumstances. These include neonatal lesions, an infectious mononucleosis-like disease in adults, or a manifestation of disseminated disease in immunocompromised patients.[2,3] Clinical lesions in the skin, however, are distinctly uncommon.

CMV is the most frequently transmitted viral infection in utero.[4] The incidence of reported infection ranges from 0.2 to 2.2% live births.[5] Less

than 10% of affected infants and neonates will actually develop clinical lesions.[4,6] Clinical manifestations have been grouped with other neonatal infections under the rubric 'TORCH syndrome' which includes toxoplasmosis, other infections (e.g. syphilis), rubella, cytomegalovirus and herpes simplex.[6,7]

Affected newborn babies and neonates may develop a wide range of lesions including hepatosplenomegaly, microcephaly, sensorineural deafness, chorioretinitis, pneumonia, direct hyperbilirubinemia, thrombocytopenia with petechiae, purpura and 'blueberry muffin' lesions.[2] The last consist of blue–red or violaceous papules and nodules and represent foci of dermal erythropoiesis.[8] The mortality of this syndrome is of the order of 20–30%.[4] Other childhood manifestations of CMV infections have included scleredema and the Gianotti–Crosti syndrome.[9–12]

Adults, particularly females, most often in the third decade, may develop a heterophil agglutinin negative infectious mononucleosis-like syndrome in which a short-lived rubelliform eruption has been described.[2,13] Patients are also at risk of developing an ampicillin-related allergic dermatosis (cf. infectious mononucleosis).[2,14,15]

CMV infection may also be a feature of immunosuppression.[3,16] Generalized CMV infection is a not uncommon finding at autopsy in AIDS patients. CMV is not infrequently detected in association with toxoplasmosis and *Pneumocystis jiroveci* (formerly *Pneumocystis carinii*) infection, and has also been described in patients with herpes simplex.[17,18]

Cutaneous manifestations have included ulcers on the genitalia, anus, perineum, buttocks and thighs, thrombocytopenia, erythema nodosum, cutaneous vasculitis, hyperpigmented nodules and plaques, lesions resembling prurigo nodularis, erythema multiforme, epidermolysis, urticaria and vesiculobullous lesions.[1,19–29] Cutaneous CMV infection has also been detected in a patient with febrile ulceronecrotic Mucha–Habermann's disease.[30]

Pathogenesis and histological features

In addition to maternally derived infections, there is also some evidence to suggest a venereal mode of spread. In the immunocompromised patient it is uncertain whether CMV infections represent an acquired phenomenon or reactivation of a latent focus. The histological hallmark is the presence of large, often purple-staining intranuclear inclusions surrounded by a clear halo. Smaller, basophilic, periodic acid–Schiff (PAS) positive intracytoplasmic inclusions may also be evident. These have been described within enlarged endothelial cells of dermal blood vessels, sometimes accompanied by the features of leukocytoclastic vasculitis.[14,25] Inclusions may sometimes be identified in dermal fibrocytes, macrophages and eccrine ductal epithelial cells, the last rarely associated with syringosquamous metaplasia.[31,32] They have also been identified within the endothelial cells of blood vessels and histiocytes in the inflammatory bed deep to cutaneous ulcers (*Figs 17.60, 17.61*).[19] Cutaneous nerve involvement (CMV neuritis) has been reported in perineal ulcers.[33]

Vesiculobullous lesions are characterized by spongiosis and reticular degeneration, accompanied by epidermal multinucleate giant cells which

may contain viral inclusion bodies.[17] Diagnosis of CMV infection can be confirmed by immunohistochemistry, in situ hybridization or PCR (*Fig. 17.62*).[34]

References

1. Weigand, D.A., Burgdorf, W.H.C., Tarpay, M.M. (1980) Vasculitis in cytomegalovirus infection. *Arch Dermatol*, **116**, 1174–1176.
2. Lesher, J.L. (1988) Cytomegalovirus infections and the skin. *J Am Acad Dermatol*, **18**, 1333–1338.
3. Drago, F., Aragone, M.G., Lugani, C. et al (2000) Cytomegalovirus infection in normal and immuno-compromised individuals. A review. *Dermatology*, **200**, 189–195.
4. Stagno, S., Whitley, R.J. (1985) Herpes virus infections of pregnancy. *N Engl J Med*, **313**, 1270–1273.
5. Stagno, S., Pass, R.F., Dworsky, M.E. et al (1983) Congenital and perinatal cytomegalovirus infections. *Semin Perinatol*, **7**, 31–42.
6. Fine, J.D., Arndt, K.A. (1985) The TORCH syndrome: a clinical review. *J Am Acad Dermatol*, **12**, 697–706.
7. Epps, R.E., Pittelkow, M.R., Su, W.P. (1995) TORCH syndrome. *Semin Dermatol*, **14**, 179–186.
8. Brough, A.J., Jones, D., Page, R.H. et al (1967) Dermal erythropoiesis in neonatal infants – a manifestation of intrauterine viral disease. *Pediatrics*, **40**, 627–635.
9. Heilbron, B., Saxe, N. (1986) Scleredema in an infant. *Arch Dermatol*, **122**, 1417–1419.
10. Taieb, A., Plantin, P., Du Pasquier, P. et al (1986) Gianotti–Crosti syndrome: a study of 26 cases. *Br J Dermatol*, **115**, 49–59.
11. Berant, M., Naveh, Y., Weissman, I. (1983) Papular acrodermatitis with cytomegalovirus hepatitis. *Arch Dis Child*, **58**, 1024–1025.
12. Baleviciene, G., Maciuleviciene, R., Schwartz, R.A. (2001) Papular acrodermatitis of childhood: the Gianotti–Crosti syndrome. *Cutis*, **67**, 291–294.
13. Jordan, M.C., Rousseau, W.E., Stewart, J.A. et al (1973) Spontaneous cytomegalovirus mononucleosis – clinical and laboratory observations in nine cases. *Ann Intern Med*, **79**, 153–160.
14. Lin, C.S., Penha, P.D., Krishnan, M.N. et al (1981) Cytomegalic inclusion disease of the skin. *Arch Dermatol*, **117**, 282–284.
15. Klemola, E. (1970) Hypersensitivity reactions to ampicillin in cytomegalovirus mononucleosis. *Scand J Infect Dis*, **2**, 29–31.

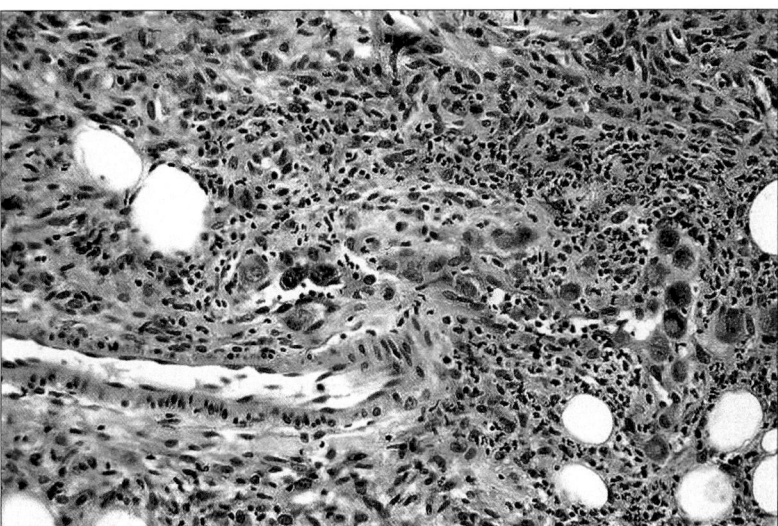

Fig. 17.61
Cytomegalovirus: high power view showing the typical eosinophilic intranuclear inclusions.

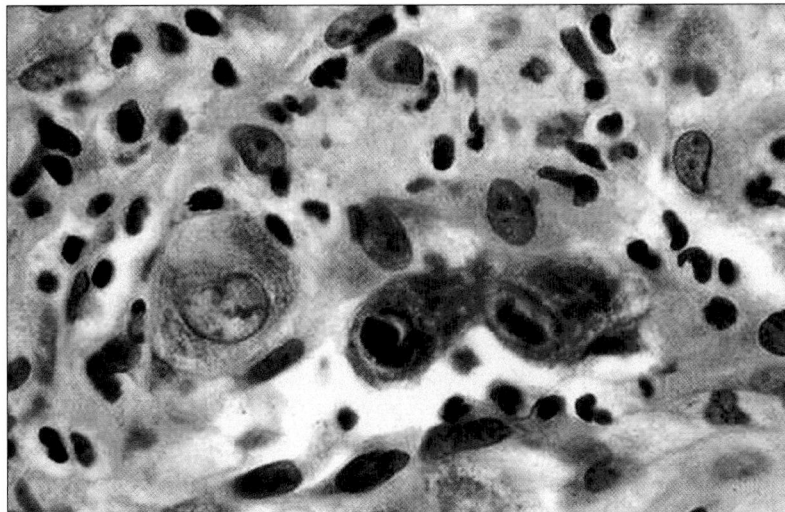

Fig. 17.60
Cytomegalovirus: this is the deep dermis from an immunosuppressed patient. Multiple inclusions are present.

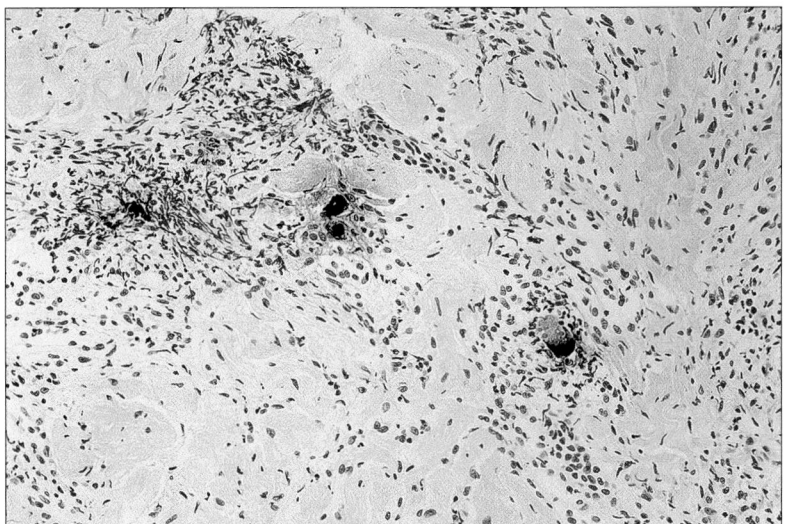

Fig. 17.62
Cytomegalovirus: positive immunohistochemistry. By courtesy of E. Mallon, MD, Charing Cross Hospital, London, UK.

16. Dauden, E., Fernández-Buezo, G., Fraga, J. et al (2001) Mucocutaneous presence of cytomegalovirus associated with human immunodeficiency virus infection: discussion regarding its pathogenetic role. *Arch Dermatol*, 137, 443–448.
17. Bhawan, J., Gellis, S., Ucci, A. et al (1984) Vesiculobullous lesions caused by cytomegalovirus in an immunocompromised adult. *J Am Acad Dermatol*, 11, 743–747.
18. Smith, K.J., Skelton, H.G. 3rd, James, W.D. et al (1991) Concurrent epidermal involvement of cytomegalovirus and herpes simplex virus in two HIV-infected patients. Military Medical Consortium for Applied Retroviral Research (MMCARR). *J Am Acad Dermatol*, 25, 500–506.
19. Pariser, R.J. (1983) Histologically specific skin lesions in disseminated cytomegalovirus infection. *J Am Acad Dermatol*, 9, 937–946.
20. Nakoneczna, I., Kay, S. (1967) Fatal disseminated cytomegalic inclusion disease in an adult presenting with a lesion of the gastrointestinal tract. *Am J Clin Pathol*, 47, 124–128.
21. Walker, J.D., McChesney, T. (1982) Cytomegalovirus infection of the skin. *Am J Dermatopathol*, 4, 263–265.
22. Sahud, M.A., Bachelor, M.M. (1978) Cytomegalovirus-induced thrombocytopenia. *Arch Intern Med*, 138, 1573–1575.
23. Spear, J.B., Kessler, H.A., Dworin, A. et al (1988) Erythema nodosum associated with acute cytomegalovirus mononucleosis in an adult. *Arch Intern Med*, 148, 323–324.
24. Curtis, J.L., Egbert, B.M. (1982) Cutaneous cytomegalovirus vasculitis: an unusual clinical presentation of a common opportunistic pathogen. *Hum Pathol*, 13, 1138–1141.
25. Feldman, P.S., Walker, A.N., Baker, R. (1982) Cutaneous lesions heralding disseminated cytomegalovirus infection. *J Am Acad Dermatol*, 7, 545–548.
26. Chiewchanvit, S., Thamprasert, K., Siriunkgul, S. (1993) Disseminated cutaneous cytomegalic inclusion disease resembling prurigo nodularis in a HIV-infected patient: a case report and literature review. *J Med Assoc Thai*, 76, 581–584.
27. Seishima, M., Oyama, Z., Yamamura, M. (2001) Erythema multiforme associated with cytomegalovirus infection in nonimmunosuppressed patients. *Dermatology*, 203, 299–302.
28. Muller-Stamou, A., Senn, H.J., Emody, G. (1974) Epidermolysis in a case of severe cytomegalovirus infection. *Br Med J*, 3, 609–610.
29. Humphreys, D.M., Meyers, A. (1975) Cytomegalovirus mononucleosis with urticaria. *Postgrad Med J*, 51, 404–406.
30. Tsai, K.S., Hsieh, H.J., Chow, K.C. et al (2001) Detection of cytomegalovirus infection in a patient with febrile ulceronecrotic Mucha–Habermann's disease. *Int J Dermatol*, 40, 694–698.
31. Resnik, K.S., DiLeonardo, M., Maillet, M. (2000) Histopathologic findings in cutaneous cytomegalovirus infection. *Am J Dermatopathol*, 22, 397–407.
32. Chetty, R., Bramdev, A., Govender, D. (1999) Cytomegalovirus-induced syringosquamous metaplasia. *Am J Dermatopathol*, 21, 487–490.
33. Ramdial, P.K., Dlova, N.C., Sydney, C. (2002) Cytomegalovirus neuritis in perineal ulcers. *J Cutan Pathol*, 29, 439–444.
34. Toome, B.K., Bowers, K.E., Scott, G.A. (1991) Diagnosis of cutaneous cytomegalovirus infection: a review and report of a case. *J Am Acad Dermatol*, 24, 860–867.

Exanthem subitum

Clinical features

Exanthem subitum (roseola infantum) is a benign disease of infancy caused by infection with human herpesvirus 6 (HHV-6).[1,2] Usual clinical features include fever and a cutaneous eruption that resembles rubella or measles. A case with vesicular lesions has been reported.[1]

A similar rash has been reported in leukemic patients and bone marrow transplant recipients; a possible link to graft-versus-host disease has also been suggested.[3–5] Other reported clinical associations and cutaneous manifestations of HHV-6 infection include papular-purpuric 'gloves and socks' syndrome, erythema elevatum diutinum, an infectious mononucleosis-like syndrome, the Gianotti–Crosti syndrome and a drug hypersensitivity syndrome.[6–10] HHV-6 DNA has also been detected in lesions of Langerhans' cell histiocytosis.[11]

Histological features

The histopathological findings in exanthem subitum are rather non-specific and include papillary dermal edema and a superficial perivascular mononuclear inflammatory cell infiltrate. Rare cases with a vesicular presentation may show mononuclear inflammatory cell exocytosis into the epidermis, with microscopic intraepidermal spongiotic vesiculation.

Intranuclear inclusions (as seen in herpes simplex virus infection or varicella-zoster virus infection) are absent. Diagnosis may be confirmed by immunofluorescence microscopy, using an antibody to HHV-6.[1]

References

1. Yoshida, M., Fukui, K., Orita, T. et al (1995) Exanthem subitum (roseola infantum) with vesicular lesions. *Br J Dermatol*, 132, 614–616.
2. Yamanishi, K., Okuno, T., Shiraki, K. et al (1988) Identification of human herpesvirus-6 as a causal agent for exanthem subitum. *Lancet*, 1, 1065–1067.
3. Fujita, H., Maruta, A., Tomita, N. et al (1996) Human herpesvirus-6-associated exanthem in a patient with acute lymphocytic leukemia. *Br J Haematol*, 92, 947–949.
4. Yoshikawa, T., Suga, S., Asano, Y. et al (1996) Human herpesvirus-6 infection in bone marrow transplantation. *Blood*, 78, 1381–1384.
5. Appleton, A.L., Sviland, L., Peiris, J.S. et al (1995) Human herpes virus-6 infection in marrow graft recipients: role in graft-versus-host disease. Newcastle upon Tyne Bone Marrow Transplant Group. *Bone Marrow Transplant*, 16, 777–782.
6. Ruzicka, T., Kalka, K., Dierks, K. et al (1998) Papular-purpuric 'gloves and socks' syndrome associated with human herpesvirus 6 infection. *Arch Dermatol*, 134, 242–244.
7. Drago, F., Semino, M., Rampini, P. et al (1999) Erythema elevatum diutinum in a patient with human herpesvirus 6 infection. *Acta Derm Venereol*, 79, 91–92.
8. Sumiyoshi, Y., Kikuchi, M., Ohshima, K., et al (1995) A case of human herpesvirus-6 lymphadenitis with infectious mononucleosis-like syndrome. *Pathol Int*, 45, 947–951.
9. Yasumoto, S., Tsujita, J., Imayama, S. et al (1996) Case report: Gianotti–Crosti syndrome associated with human herpesvirus-6 infection. *J Dermatol*, 23, 499–501.
10. Descamps, V., Valance, V., Edlinger, C. et al (2001) Association of human herpesvirus 6 infection with drug reaction with eosinophilia and systemic symptoms. *Arch Dermatol*, 137, 301–304.
11. Leahy, M.A., Krejci, S.M., Friednash, M. et al (1993) Human herpesvirus 6 is present in lesions of Langerhans cell histiocytosis. *J Invest Dermatol*, 101, 642–645.

Diseases caused by orthopox viruses

Clinical features

The orthopox viruses are DNA in type and cause variola, vaccinia and cowpox.

Variola

Variola, or smallpox, has not been diagnosed endemically since 1977 and until recently appeared to be of historical interest only.[1,2] In recent years, however, there has been renewed interest in smallpox as a potential agent in bioterrorism.[3,4] It was endemic in parts of Africa, South America and Asia, with only occasional cases seen in Europe and North America. Transmission of the virus, which was capable of retaining viability in dried exudate, was by inhalation. The disease was typified after an incubation period of 12 days by a prodromal phase of high fever, headache and vomiting followed 3–4 days later by a transient erythematous and petechial rash. This was in turn followed by the characteristic eruptive lesions (*Fig. 17.63*). These lesions were most common on the face and limbs. They began as papules, which became vesicular and then pustular and crusted. Healing was usually associated with a pitted scar, but mortality varied from 2 to 50%, depending on the severity of the

infection (*Fig. 17.64*). Although death was previously attributed to secondary bacterial sepsis, it has since come to light that mortality was probably the direct result of the cytopathic effects of the smallpox virus itself.[5]

Vaccinia

Vaccinia virus is closely related antigenically to variola virus, but is probably derived from cowpox virus. It was used for immunization against variola and no doubt was effective because of its similar antigenicity. This skin inoculation results in a single vesicle, which becomes pustular and crusts, like variola (*Fig. 17.65*). It also heals similarly, leaving a scar. Since it is accepted that variola has been eradicated in the wild, vaccination is no longer thought necessary except in laboratory workers at special risk.

The vaccination procedure was not without risk. Generalized vaccinia was occasionally seen and the vaccine was responsible for some cases of Kaposi's varicelliform eruption (eczema vaccinatum). Vaccinia necrosum and encephalitis were also rare complications.[6]

Cowpox

Despite the name, the reservoir for cowpox virus is not cattle, but wild animals such as hedgehogs and badgers. Cattle and man are both infected accidentally, although man may acquire the disease from cows. Cats have been identified as an additional source of infection.[7–10] The incubation period after inoculation is usually 5–7 days; a papule then develops, which rapidly becomes pustular. The pustule is surrounded by a zone of erythema and edema. Eschars or necrotic ulcers may occur.[11–13] The lesions are often multiple and can occur on the hands, arms or face (*Figs 17.66, 17.67*).[14] A varicelliform eruption in association with atopy has been reported.[15] Sporotrichoid spread has been documented.[16] Lymphangitis, lymphadenitis and fever are almost invariably present. Healing and recovery occur in 3–4 weeks. A fatal case of a cowpox-like illness has been recorded.[17]

Pathogenesis and histological features

The orthopox viruses are large and have a discrete DNA compartment (nucleoid) and a complex capsid and lipoprotein coat containing characteristic tubular structures. They are brick-shaped and their outer tubular structures are irregularly arranged. The orthopox viruses are all

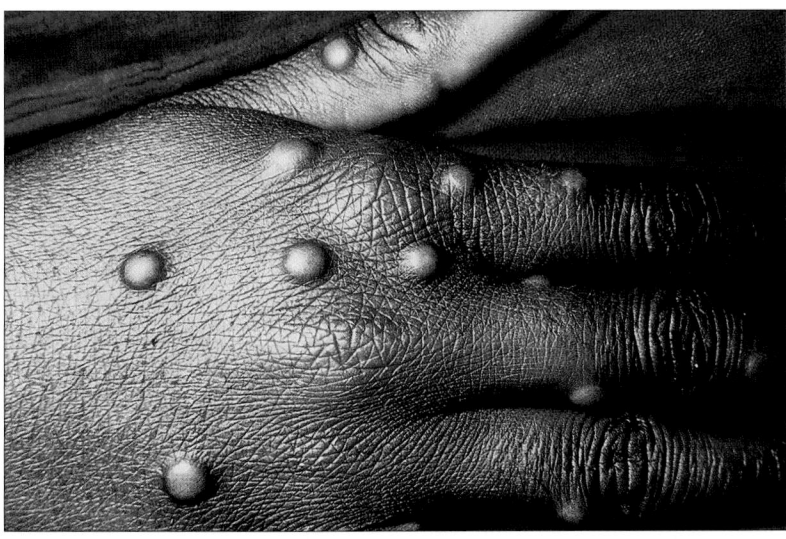

Fig. 17.63
Variola (smallpox): in contrast to those of chickenpox the lesions are larger and less superficial. By courtesy of H.P. Lambert, MD, St George's Hospital, London, UK.

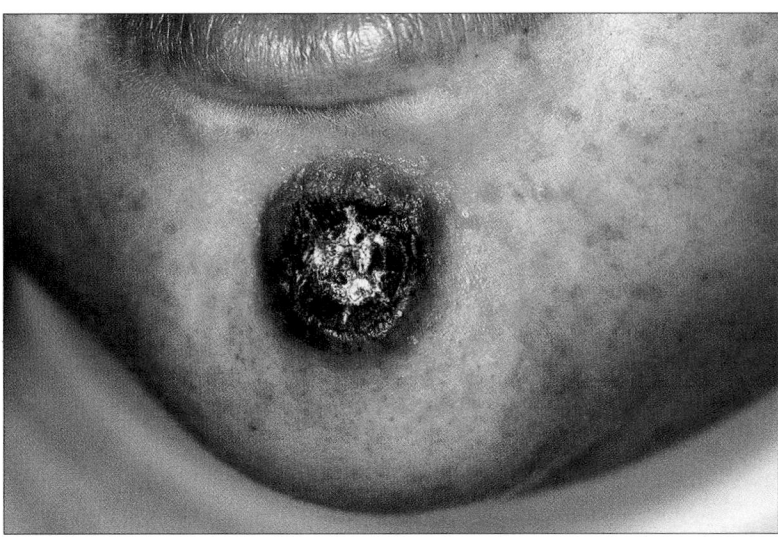

Fig. 17.67
Cowpox: note the edema and surrounding erythema. By courtesy of M.S. Lewis Jones, MD, Wrexham Maelor Hospital, Wrexham, UK.

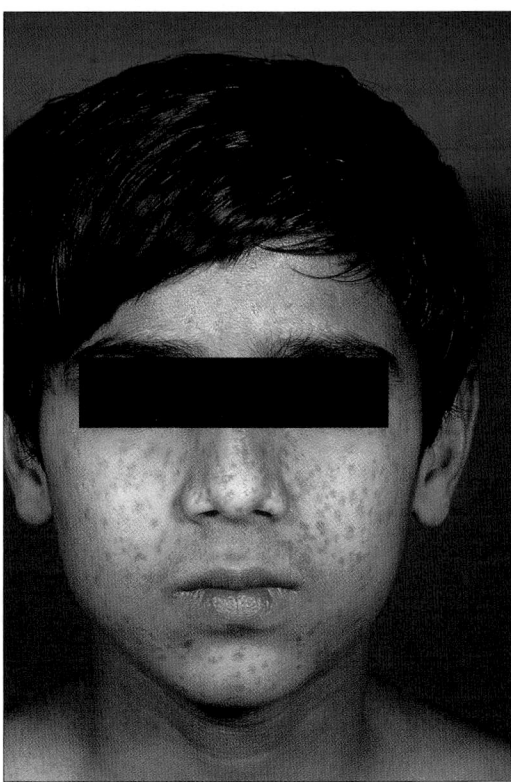

Fig. 17.64
Variola: note the widespread hyperpigmented scars. By courtesy of R.A. Marsden, St George's Hospital, London, UK.

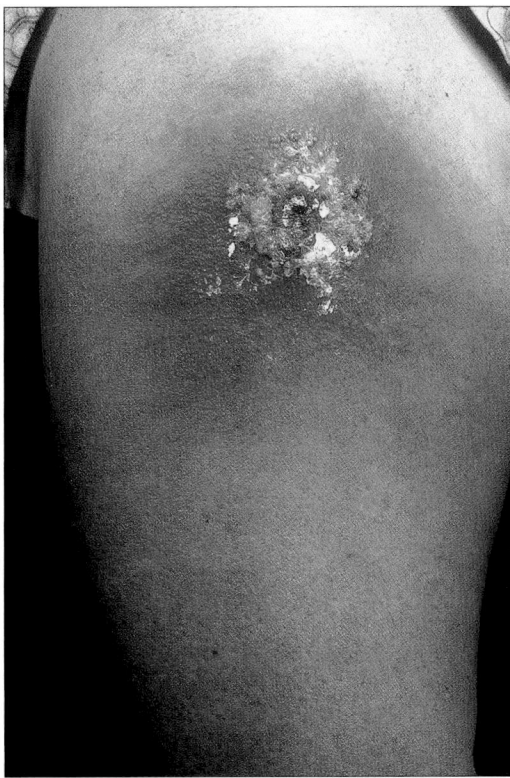

Fig. 17.65
Vaccinia: due to the eradication of smallpox, routine vaccination is no longer performed. Note the eschar, edema and intense erythema. By courtesy of the Institute of Dermatology, London, UK.

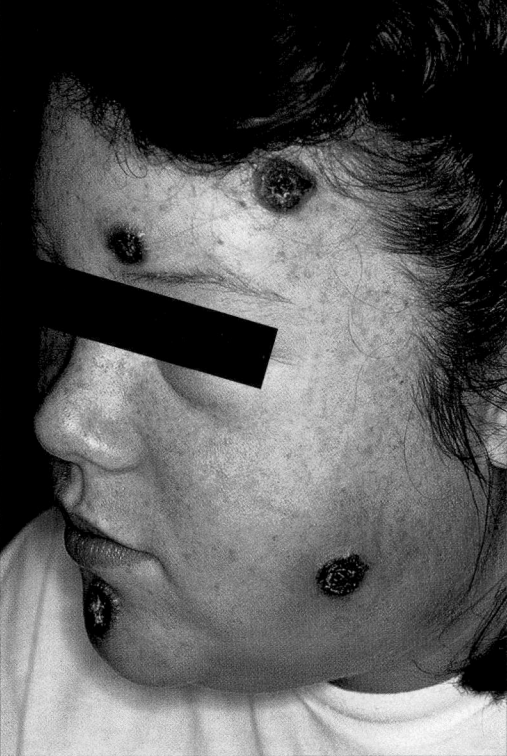

Fig. 17.66
Cowpox: characteristic umbilicated, ulcerated nodules. Lesions are often multiple. By courtesy of M.S. Lewis Jones, MD, Wrexham Maelor Hospital, Wrexham, UK.

transmitted by inoculation except variola, which usually gains entry by inhalation. The viruses are able to resist dehydration outside the host and therefore inhalation or inoculation of dust or inoculation from shared facilities is quite possible, as well as direct inoculation from an active lesion. Recent evidence has shown that these viruses secrete interleukin (IL)-18 binding proteins, resulting in viral dissemination or persistent infection.[18] The vaccinia virus is able to evade the host immune response by impairing the maturation of dendritic cells, with subsequent inhibition of T-cell activation.[19]

After inoculation the viruses proliferate within the keratinocytes and basal cells. This leads to severe intracellular edema with resultant ballooning degeneration and consequent reticular degeneration due to cell rupture, giving rise to multilocular vesicles and subsequent infiltration by polymorphs. In variola and vaccinia there is often extensive epidermal necrosis. Variable degrees of hyperkeratosis and acanthosis are present.

Cytoplasmic eosinophilic inclusion bodies may be seen in the keratinocytes of all three diseases. The small inclusions of variola are called Guarnieri's bodies. They are surrounded by a clear halo and are located close to the nucleus. Similar bodies are seen in vaccinia. Those of cowpox, however, are slightly larger, but are still predominantly seen in the cytoplasm. A dermal chronic inflammatory cell infiltrate consisting of lymphocytes is usually present.

Diagnosis is based upon clinical information, but confirmation can be obtained by electron microscopy, isolation of the viruses in tissue culture or, more recently, with the aid of PCR.[13,20]

References

1. Breman, J.G., Arita, I. (1980) The confirmation and maintenance of smallpox eradication. *N Engl J Med*, 303, 1263–1273.
2. Robinson, T.W.E., Heath, R.B. (1983) Smallpox and other poxvirus infections of man. In: Virus diseases and the skin. Edinburgh: Churchill Livingstone, pp 127–147.
3. Berche, P. (2001) The threat of smallpox and bioterrorism. *Trends Microbiol*, 9, 15–18.
4. Tegnell, A., Wahren, B., Elgh, F. (2002) Smallpox – eradicated, but a growing terror threat. *Clin Microbiol Infect*, 8, 504–509.
5. Martin, D.B. (2002) The cause of death in smallpox: an examination of the pathology record. *Mil Med*, 167, 546–551.
6. Wills, V.L., Boorer, C.J., Foster, H.M. et al (2000) Vaccinia necrosum: a forgotten disease. *Aust N Z J Surg*, 70, 149–150.
7. Casemore, D.P., Emslie, E.S., Whyler, D.K. et al (1987) Cowpox in a child, acquired from a cat. *Clin Exp Dermatol*, 12, 286–287.
8. Baxby, D., Ashton, D.G., Jones, D.M. et al (1982) An outbreak of cowpox in captive cheetahs: virological and epidemiological studies. *J Hygiene (Cambridge)*, 89, 365–372.
9. Lewis-Jones, M.S., Baxby, D., Cefai, C. et al (1993) Cowpox can mimic anthrax. *Br J Dermatol*, 129, 625–627.
10. Stolz, W., Gotz, A., Thomas, P. et al (1996) Characteristic but unfamiliar – the cowpox infection, transmitted by the domestic cat. *Dermatology*, 193, 140–143.
11. Baxby, D., Bennett, M., Getty, B. (1994) Human cowpox 1969–93: a review based on 54 cases. *Br J Dermatol*, 131, 598–607.
12. Stewart, K.J., Telfer, S., Brown, K.J. et al (2000) Cowpox infection: not yet consigned to history. *Br J Plast Surg*, 53, 348–350.
13. Schupp, P., Pfeffer, M., Meyer, H. et al (2001) Cowpox virus in a 12-year-old boy: rapid identification by an orthopoxvirus-specific polymerase chain reaction. *Br J Dermatol*, 145, 146–150.
14. Lawrence, B. (1955) Cowpox in man and its relationship with milker's nodules. *Lancet*, i, 764–766.
15. Blackford, S., Roberts, D.L., Thomas, P.D. (1993) Cowpox infection causing a generalized eruption in a patient with atopic dermatitis. *Br J Dermatol*, 129, 628–629.
16. Motley, R.J., Holt, P.J.A. (1990) Cowpox presenting with sporotrichoid spread: a case report. *Br J Dermatol*, 122, 705–708.
17. Eis-Hübinger, A.M., Gerritzen, A., Schneweis, K.E. et al (1990) Fatal cowpox-like virus infection transmitted by cat. *Lancet*, 336, 880.
18. Smith, V.P., Bryant, N.A., Alcami, A. (2000) Ectromelia, vaccinia and cowpox viruses encode secreted interleukin-18-binding proteins. *J Gen Virol*, 81, 1223–1230.
19. Engelmayer, J., Larsson, M., Subklewe, M. et al (1999) Vaccinia virus inhibits the maturation of human dendritic cells: a novel mechanism of immune evasion. *J Immunol*, 67, 6762–6768.
20. Wienecke, R., Wolff, H., Schaller, M. et al (2000) Cowpox virus infection in an 11-year-old girl. *J Am Acad Dermatol*, 42, 892–894.

Milker's nodule

Clinical features

Milker's nodule (or paravaccinia) is cause by a parapox virus, distinct from that which causes cowpox.[1] It occurs as a localized lesion on the udders of cows and causes little systemic disturbance. It may be recurrent in the same herd. It is acquired by man usually by inoculation, but since the virus is viable in a dried state, indirect fomite infection is possible. Small outbreaks involving several patients have been recorded.[2] The incubation period is around 5 days; some two to five red papules then develop, which gradually become bluish tender nodules.[2] The overlying epidermis is at first tense and shiny, but becomes opaque and gray

(*Fig. 17.68*). The center of the lesion is crusted and slightly depressed. The surrounding skin often shows lymphangitis, but despite this the lesion has the appearance of a tumor and is well circumscribed. There are few systemic symptoms, but there may be an associated short-lived papulovesicular eruption on the upper limbs and occasionally on the legs. The main nodular lesions resolve, without scarring, in 4–6 weeks.

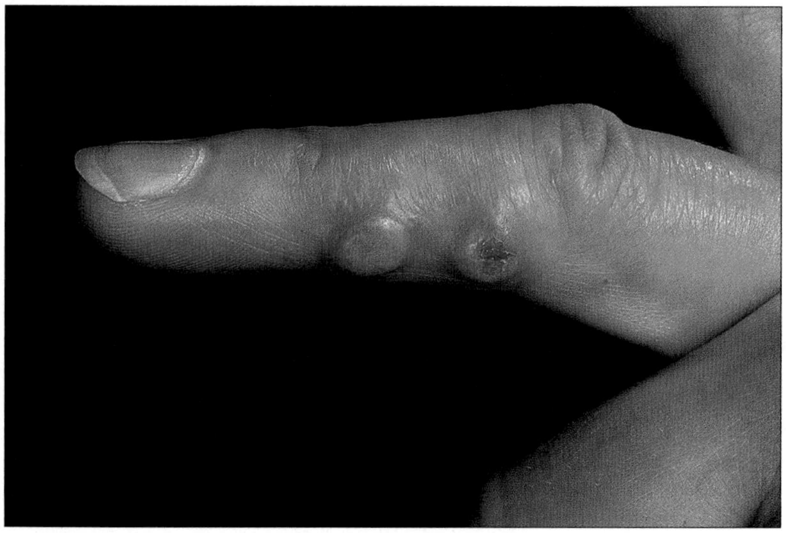

Histological features

Milker's nodule virus measures 260×160 nm and is ellipsoid in shape.[2] It is characterized by spirally arranged tubules. The histological features are indistinguishable from those seen in orf infection (see below).[3,4]

References

1. Leavell, U.W., Phillips, I.A. (1975) Milker's nodules. *Arch Dermatol*, 111, 1307–1311.
2. Hansen, S.K., Mertz, H., Krogdahl, A. et al (1996) Milker's nodule – a report of 15 cases in the county of North Jutland. *Acta Derm Venereol*, 76, 88.
3. Groves, R.W., Wilson Jones, E., MacDonald, D.M. (1991) Human orf and milker's nodule: a clinicopathologic study. *J Am Acad Dermatol*, 25, 706–711.
4. Austin, C., Vuitch, F., Freeman, R. (1987) Milker's nodule and orf. *J Cutan Pathol*, 14, 348.

Fig. 17.68
Milker's nodule: the blister roof has an opaque appearance and there is surrounding erythema. By courtesy of the Institute of Dermatology, London, UK.

Ecthyma contagiosum

Clinical features

Ecthyma contagiosum (orf, contagious pustular dermatosis) is caused by an epitheliotropic DNA parapoxvirus morphologically identical to that causing milker's nodule. The infection is endemic in sheep in which it causes crusted pustules of the lips and perioral area (*Fig. 17.69*).[1–3] This underlies the accurate descriptive term of 'scabby mouth' used by Australian farmers. It is transmitted by inoculation from sheep to sheep, though it is said that the virus can persist in the pastures. It is particularly likely to arise when the pasture is dry and results in minor abrasions of the labial mucosa of the sheep. Transmission to man, most often males and usually sheep-handlers, is usually by direct inoculation from infected lesions, but it may also complicate contact with contaminated objects such as fences and shears.[4] Orf may also be seen in goats.[3,5] In one English study 23% of individuals employed or living on a sheep farm reported having had the condition.[6]

After an incubation period of 5–6 days, the lesion (usually a solitary, small, firm, red–blue papule) develops. It is most common on the hand or forearm (*Figs 17.70, 17.71*).[7] Less commonly, lesions may occur on the facial and perianal regions.[8–10] The papule becomes a flat-topped hemorrhagic blister or pustule, later crusting over its depressed center. By this stage it may be 2–5 cm in diameter. Clinically it may be mistaken for a pyogenic granuloma or keratoacanthoma.[5] The lesions are surrounded by a zone of erythema, which may be associated with itch and tenderness. Lymphangitis, lymphadenitis and mild fever occasionally develop.[1] In addition, some patients develop a transient maculopapular eruption on the trunk or erythema multiforme-like lesions on the limbs.[5,7] The main lesion usually resolves without scarring in 3 weeks. Ocular involvement may be a rare manifestation.[11]

Histological features

The histological features are quite characteristic. The overall appearance of the lesion is that of a symmetrical nodule. There is a parakeratotic crust and acanthosis with thin epidermal strands extending quite deeply into the adjacent dermis.[12] Viral cytopathic changes including cytoplasmic and nuclear vacuolation are usually conspicuous.[13] Reticular degeneration with intraepidermal vesiculation is often evident (*Fig. 17.72*).

If the biopsy is taken from an early lesion, typical 3–5 mm intracytoplasmic eosinophilic inclusions may be seen (*Fig. 17.73*).[13] Sometimes intranuclear inclusions may also be evident.[4] They may be rendered more conspicuous with Lendrum's phloxine tartazine (*Fig. 17.74*). Similar inclusions may also be seen in the cytoplasm of the endothelial cells of the blood vessels among the underlying heavy chronic inflammatory cell infiltrate. The latter comprises lymphocytes and histiocytes although neutrophils and occasional eosinophils may be evident. The dermis is often very edematous, and characteristic of orf (and milker's nodule) is the presence of massive capillary proliferation and dilatation.[8,13] This is attributable to the production of virus-encoded homologues of ovine vascular endothelial growth factor.[3,14] A CD30+ reactive dermal lymphoid infiltrate may occur.[15]

The diagnosis of orf may be confirmed immunocytochemically or by PCR.[16,17] The Tzanck test has also been used as a diagnostic aid.[7] Ultrastructural studies reveal that the orf virus is best visualized in negatively stained preparations (*Fig. 17.75*).[5]

References

1. Leavell, U.W., McNamara, M.J., Muelling, R. et al (1968) Orf. Report of 19 human cases with clinical and pathological observations. *JAMA*, **204**, 657–664.
2. Zimmerman, J.L. (1991) Orf. *JAMA*, **266**, 476.
3. Haig, D.M., Mercer, A.A. (1998) Ovine diseases. Orf. *Vet Res*, **29**, 311–326.
4. Méndez, B., Burnett, J.W. (1989) Orf. *Cutis*, **44**, 286–287.
5. Johannessen, J.V., Krogh, H-K., Solberg, I. et al (1975) Human orf. *J Cutan Pathol*, **2**, 265–283.
6. Paiba, G.A., Thomas, D.R., Morgan, K.L. et al (1999) Orf (contagious pustular dermatitis) in farmworkers: prevalence and risk factors in three areas of England. *Vet Rec*, **145**, 7–11.
7. Bassioukas, K., Orfanidou, A., Stergiopoulou, C.H. et al (1993) Orf. Clinical and epidemiological study. *Australas J Dermatol*, **34**, 119–123.
8. Mayet, A., Sommer, B., Heenan, P. (1997) Rapidly growing cutaneous tumor of the right temple: orf. *Australas J Dermatol*, **38**, 217–219.
9. Bodnar, M.G., Miller, O.F. 3rd, Tyler, W.B. (1999) Facial orf. *J Am Acad Dermatol*, **40**, 815–817.
10. Gurel, M.S., Ozardali, I., Bitiren, M. et al (2002) Giant orf of the nose. *Eur J Dermatol*, **12**, 183–185.
11. Freeman, G., Bron, A.J., Juel-Jensen, B. (1984) Ocular infection with orf virus. *Am J Ophthalmol*, **97**, 601–604.
12. Austin, C., Vuitch, F., Freeman, R. (1987) Milker's nodule and orf. *J Cutan Pathol*, **14**, 348A.
13. Groves, R.W., Wilson Jones, E., MacDonald, D.M. (1991) Human orf and milker's nodule: a clinicopathologic study. *J Am Acad Dermatol*, **25**, 706–711.
14. Savory, L.J., Stacker, S.A., Fleming, S.B. et al (2000) Viral vascular endothelial growth factor plays a critical role in orf virus infection. *J Virol*, **74**, 10699–10706.
15. Rose, C., Starostik, P., Brocker, E.B. (1999) Infection with parapoxvirus induces CD30-positive cutaneous infiltrates in humans. *J Cutan Pathol*, **26**, 520–522.

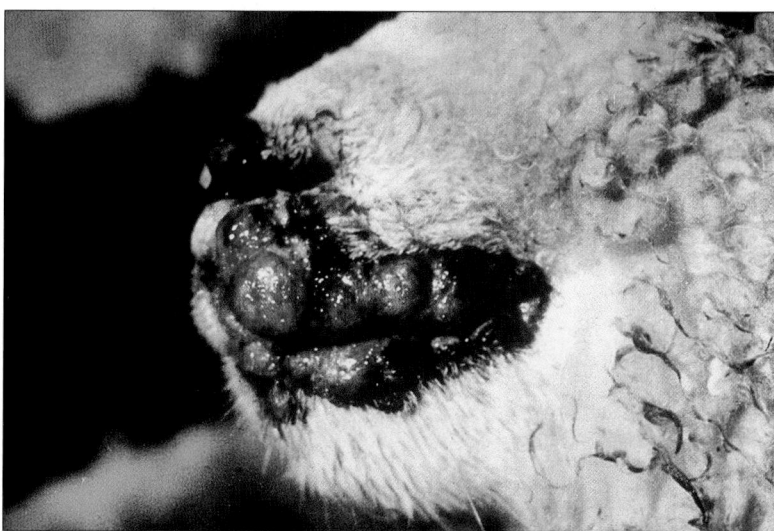

Fig. 17.69
Orf: the scabby mouth. By courtesy of B.J. Leppard, MD, Royal South Hants Hospital, Southampton, UK.

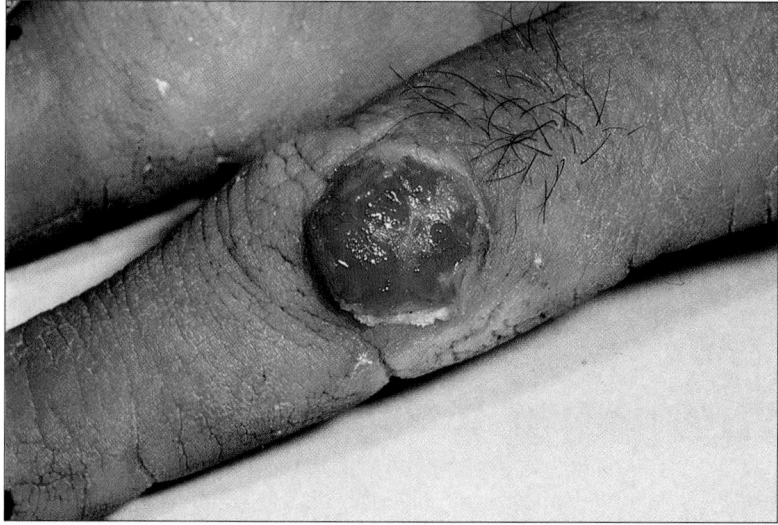

Fig. 17.70
Orf: in this example there is a markedly hemorrhagic component. By courtesy of M.M. Black, MD, Institute of Dermatology, London, UK.

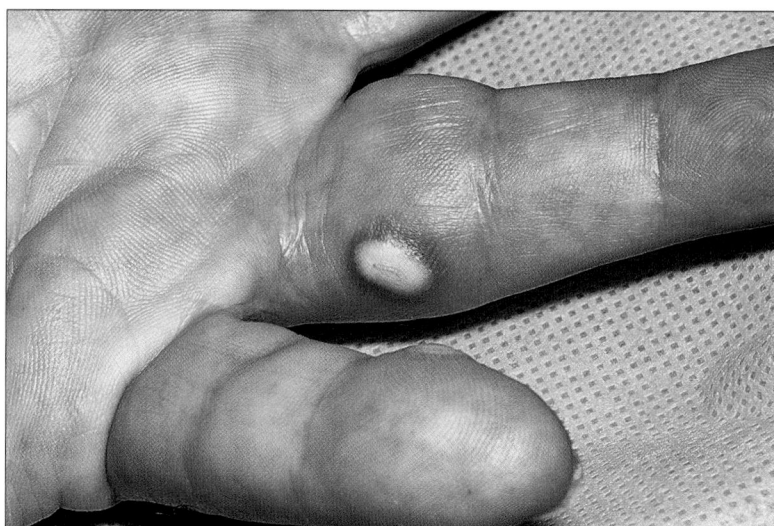

Fig. 17.71
Orf: older lesion with a typical depressed center. By courtesy of A. Qureshi, MD, Harvard Medical School, Boston, USA.

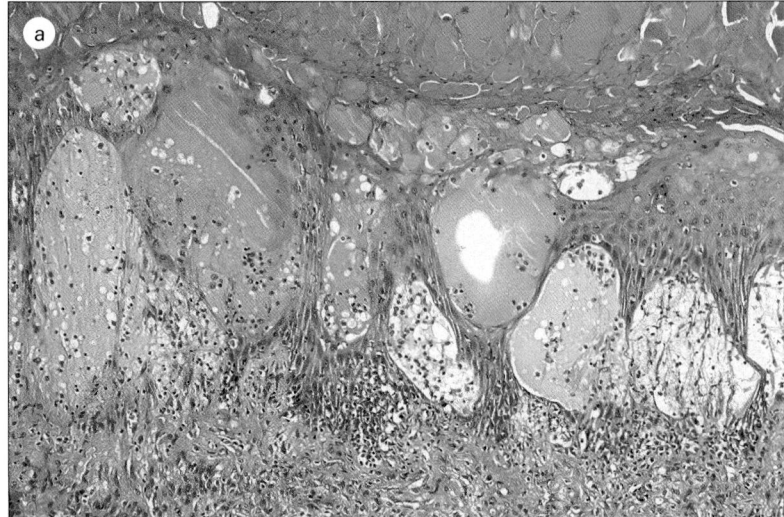

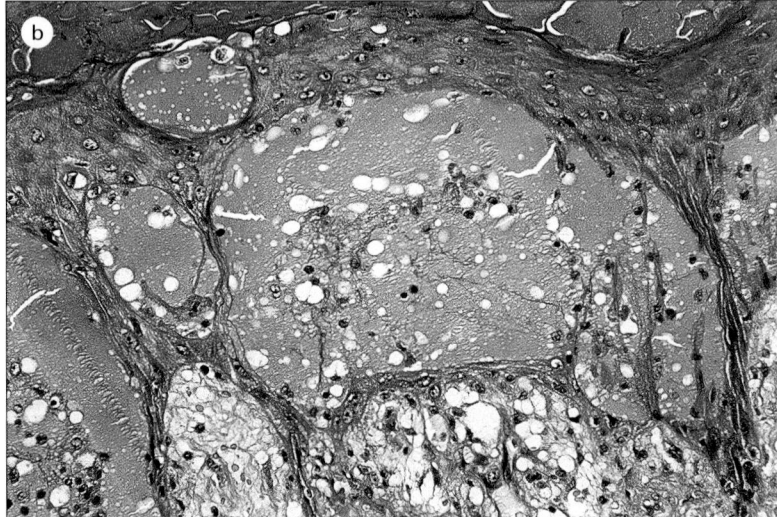

Fig. 17.72
Orf: **(a)** the intraepidermal vesicle is multilocular; **(b)** its walls consist of stretched residual keratinocytes.

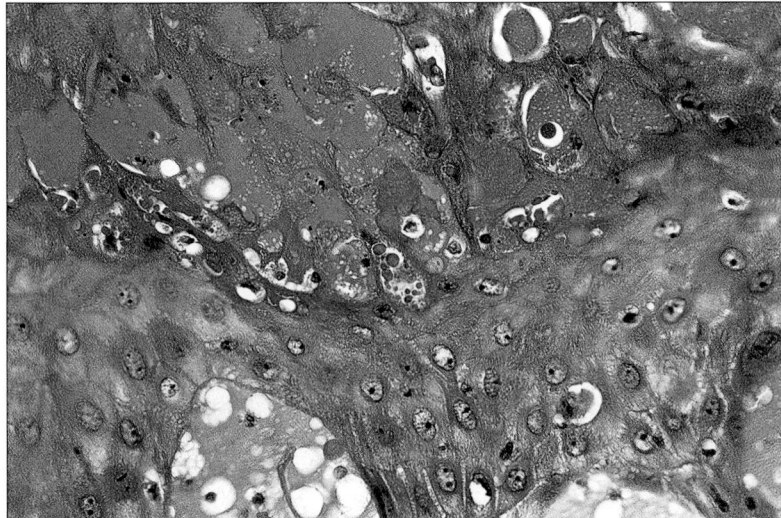

Fig. 17.73
Orf: in the center of the field are two eosinophilic intracytoplasmic inclusions.

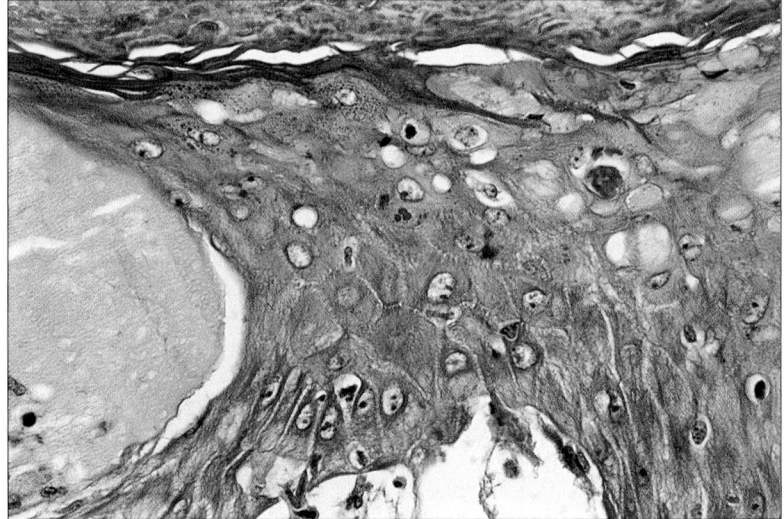

Fig. 17.74
Orf: the inclusions may be highlighted by Lendrum's phloxine tartazine.

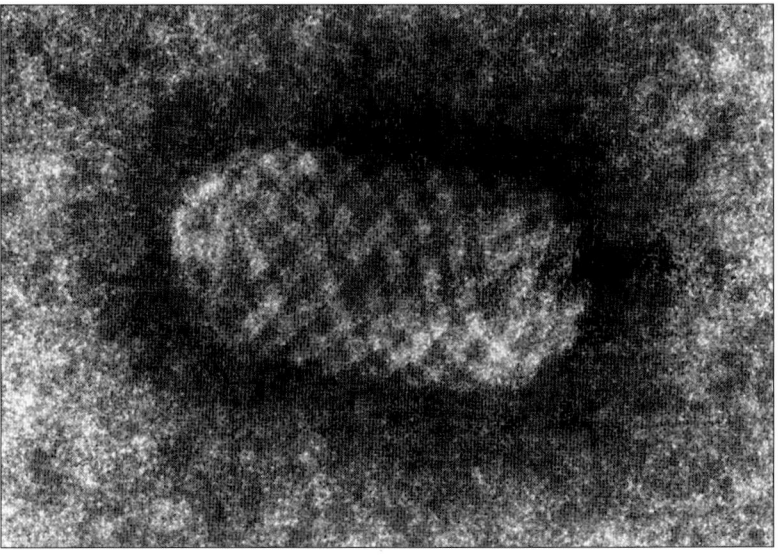

Fig. 17.75
Orf: on electron micrographic examination the parapoxvirus has a cylindrical appearance and a typical criss-crossed internal structure. By courtesy of I. Chrystie, FIMLS, St Thomas' Hospital, London, UK.

16. Groves, R.W., Wilson Jones, E., MacDonald, D.M. (1989) Human orf: morphologic characteristics and immunohistochemical diagnosis. *J Cutan Pathol*, **16**, 305A.
17. Torfason, E.G., Gunadottir, S. (2002) Polymerase chain reaction for laboratory diagnosis of orf virus infections. *J Clin Virol*, **24**, 79–84.

Molluscum contagiosum

Clinical features

Molluscum contagiosum is a self-limiting epidermal papular condition caused by molluscipoxvirus (*Fig. 17.76*).[1] The genome encodes 163 proteins of which 103 are closely related to variola virus.[2] It occurs on the face, trunk and limbs of young children, who are infected by direct cutaneous contact or fomite inoculation, and in young adults on genitalia and surrounding skin after transmission by sexual contact.[3] The palms and soles are usually unaffected.[4] The lesions are particularly common in Fiji and Papua New Guinea where 1 child in 10 has or has had the condition; the peak incidence is in children under 5 years of age.[5,6]

It has been suggested that molluscum contagiosum may be more common in people with atopic dermatitis.[4] In the USA and UK the incidence in adults attending STD clinics is in the range of 1 for every 40–60 cases of gonorrhea. Transmission can also occur between wrestlers, between doctor and patient, and through joint use of equipment and bathing facilities. It has an increased incidence in patients with impaired immunity.[4] In the latter, lesions tend to be more extensive, generalized and persistent.[4] Man is the only host to the virus apart from the chimpanzee and possibly the red kangaroo.

The incubation period ranges from 2 to 7 weeks.[7] Individual lesions are smooth, shiny, pearly, firm, umbilicated papules up to 5 mm across or occasionally larger (*Figs 17.77–17.79*). They are usually quite characteristic in appearance, but may be confused occasionally with a fibrous histiocytoma, intradermal melanocytic nevus, keratoacanthoma, syringoma, basal cell carcinoma, common wart and even cutaneous cryptococcosis. They are often multiple, especially in patients with immune deficiency. Although uncommon, giant lesions may also occur, especially in immunocompromised patients.[8,9] HIV-infected individuals may manifest with exclusive involvement of facial and perioral skin.[10] Symptoms of itching, tenderness and pain are uncommon, but approx-

imately 10% of patients develop an eczematous dermatitis around the molluscum papule. The papule itself may become secondarily infected and then resemble a furuncle. The individual lesion usually persists for 2 months, but sometimes lasts much longer. Since the patient may have numerous lesions at different stages of development, molluscum contagiosum can be present for years in some patients. Pitted scarring sometimes occurs in atopic individuals.[11] Systemic lesions have not been described.[4]

Histological features

In molluscum contagiosum intracellular edema with reticular degeneration and vesiculation are not features in contrast to those caused by the other pox viruses. The characteristic feature is the presence of lobulated, endophytic hyperplasia to produce a circumscribed intradermal pseudo-tumor (*Fig. 17.80*). The keratinocytes contain a very large intracytoplasmic inclusion, which compresses the nucleus against the cell membrane. Although initially eosinophilic in size, they gradually develop

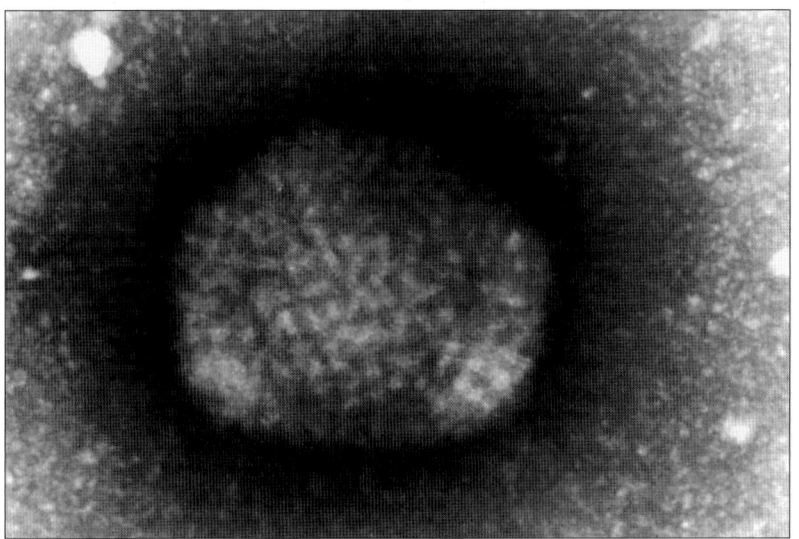

Fig. 17.76
Molluscum contagiosum: electron micrographic examination shows that the molluscum virus body is composed of virions, which are indistinguishable from those in the other poxviruses. By courtesy of I. Chrystie, FIMLS, St Thomas' Hospital, London, UK.

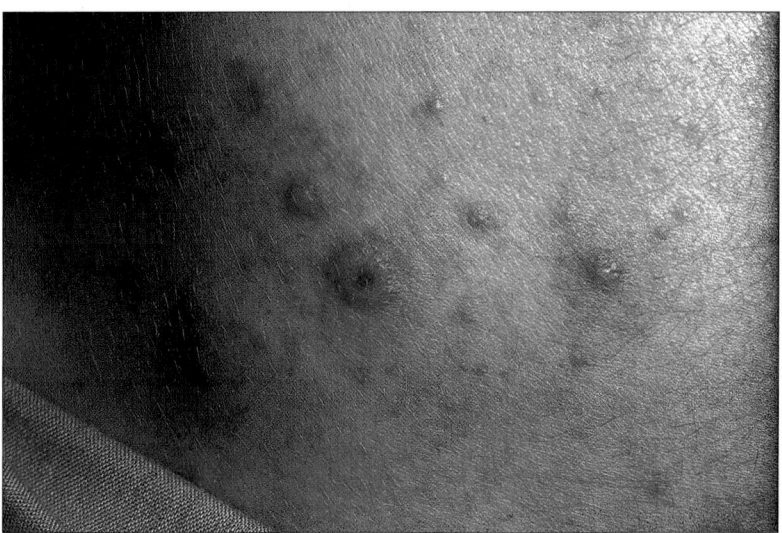

Fig. 17.78
Molluscum contagiosum: central umbilication is a diagnostic clinical marker. By courtesy of the Institute of Dermatology, London, UK.

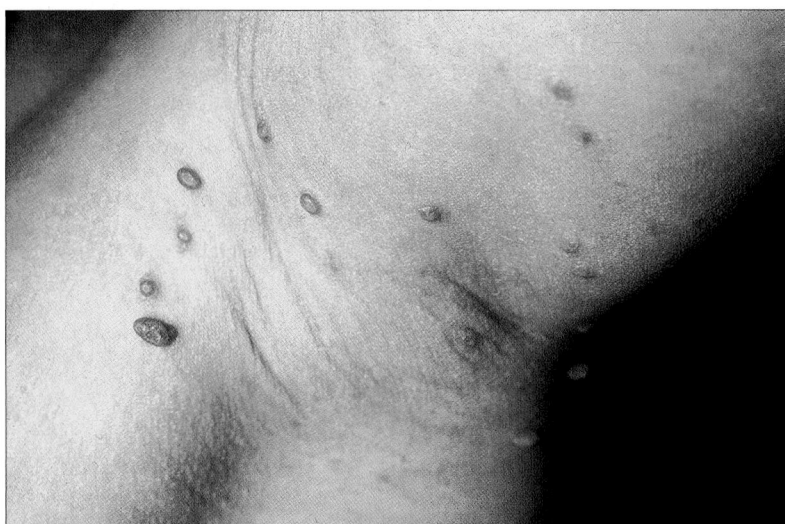

Fig. 17.77
Molluscum contagiosum: multiple lesions in a 2-year-old child. By courtesy of R.A. Marsden, St George's Hospital, London, UK.

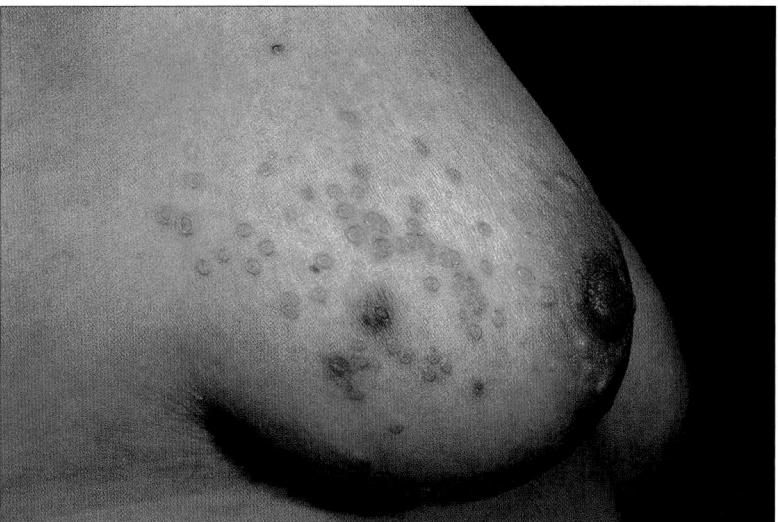

Fig. 17.79
Molluscum contagiosum: this often develops as a result of sexual contact in young adults. By courtesy of R.A. Marsden, St George's Hospital, London, UK.

a marked basophilia (*Fig. 17.81*). Their presence may be rendered more conspicuous by the use of Lendrum's phloxine tartrazine reaction (*Fig. 17.82*).

Usually there is no dermal infiltrate, but when it does occur, allegedly in response to virus or inclusion bodies entering the dermis, the lymphocytic infiltrate is so intense that lymphoma may enter the differential diagnosis if the characteristic inclusion bodies are not obvious (*Figs 17.83, 17.84*). The latter can be useful in quick diagnostic tests in which they can be recognized in a cytological preparation from the surface of the lesion.

The presence of metaplastic bone formation in otherwise typical lesions of molluscum contagiosum has been reported.[9,12] Molluscum contagiosum has also been reported in association with epidermal cysts, melanocytic nevi, sebaceous hyperplasia, soft fibromas, lupus erythematosus and leukemia cutis.[9,13,14]

References

1. Diven, D.G. (2001) An overview of poxviruses. *J Am Acad Dermatol*, **44**, 1–16.
2. Bugert, J.J., Darai, G. (1997) Recent advances in molluscum contagiosum virus research. *Arch Virol Suppl*, **13**, 35–47.
3. Brown, S.T., Nalley, J.F., Kraus, S.J. (1981) Molluscum contagiosum. *Sex Transm Dis*, **8**, 227–234.
4. Hughes, W.T., Parham, D.M. (1991) Molluscum contagiosum in children with cancer or acquired immunodeficiency syndrome. *Pediatr Infect Dis J*, **10**, 152–156.
5. Postlethwaite, R., Watt, J.A., Hawley, T.G. et al (1967) Features of molluscum contagiosum in the north east of Scotland and in Fijian village settlements. *J Hygiene (Cambridge)*, **65**, 281–291.
6. Sturt, R.J., Muller, H.K., Francis, G.D. (1971) Molluscum contagiosum in villages of the West Sepik District of New Guinea. *Med J Aust*, **2**, 751–755.
7. Postlethwaite, R. (1970) Molluscum contagiosum. *Arch Environ Health*, **21**, 432–435.

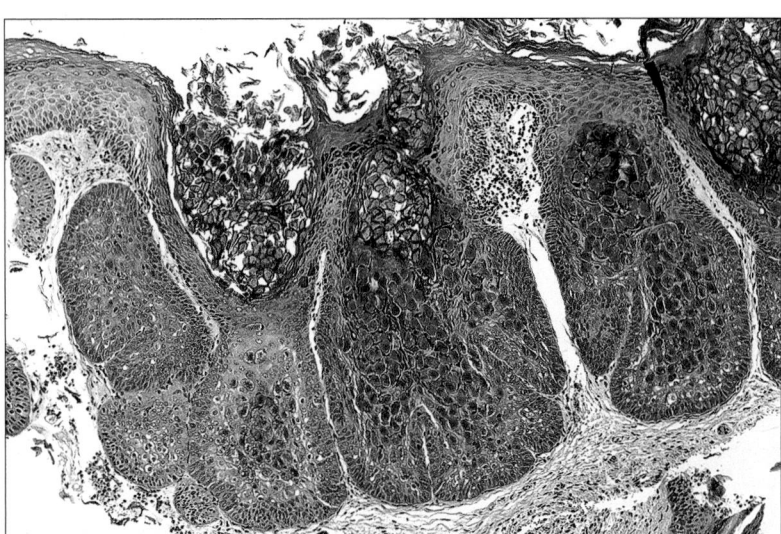

Fig. 17.80
Molluscum contagiosum: characteristic scanning view showing the central umbilication and epidermal hyperplasia.

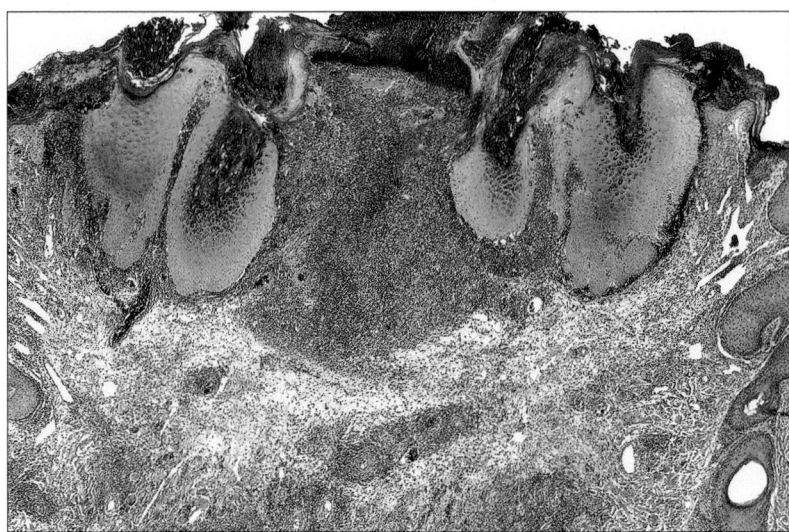

Fig. 17.83
Molluscum contagiosum: rupture of an epidermal nodule has released inclusions into the dermis with a resultant intense chronic inflammatory cell response.

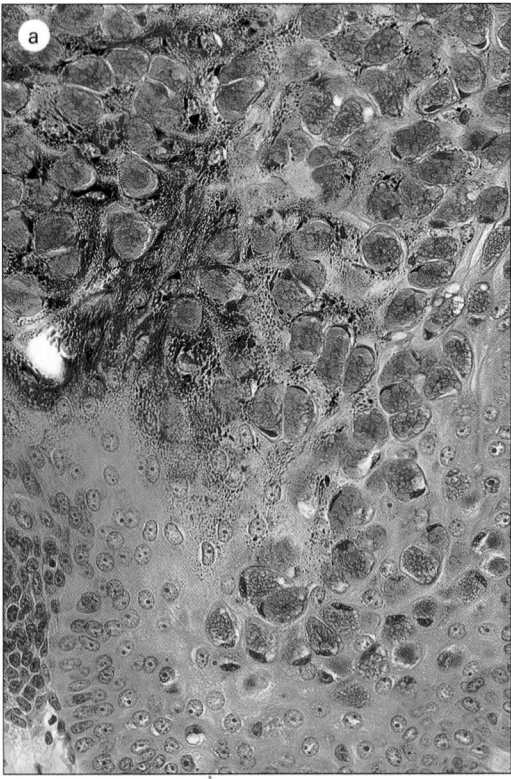
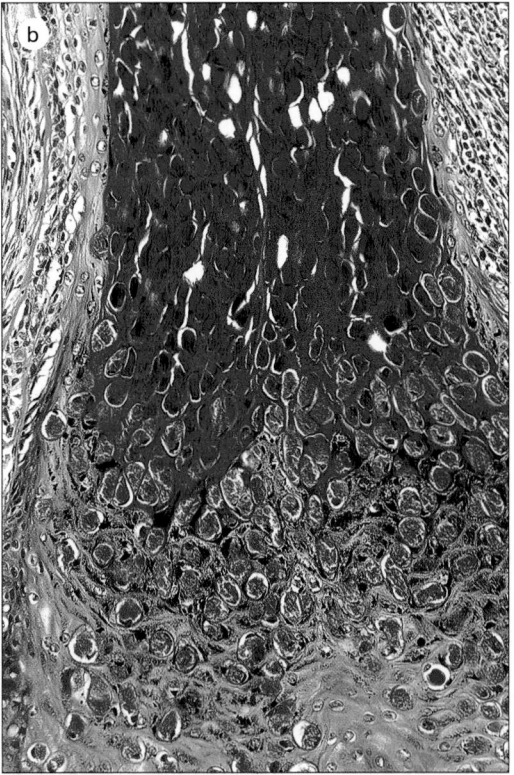
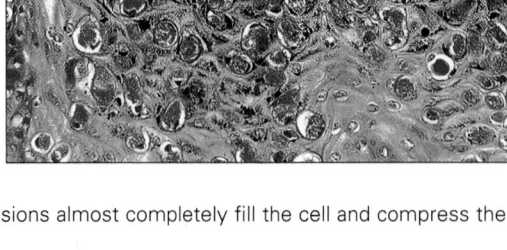

Fig. 17.81
(a, b) Molluscum contagiosum: the intracytoplasmic inclusions almost completely fill the cell and compress the nucleus.

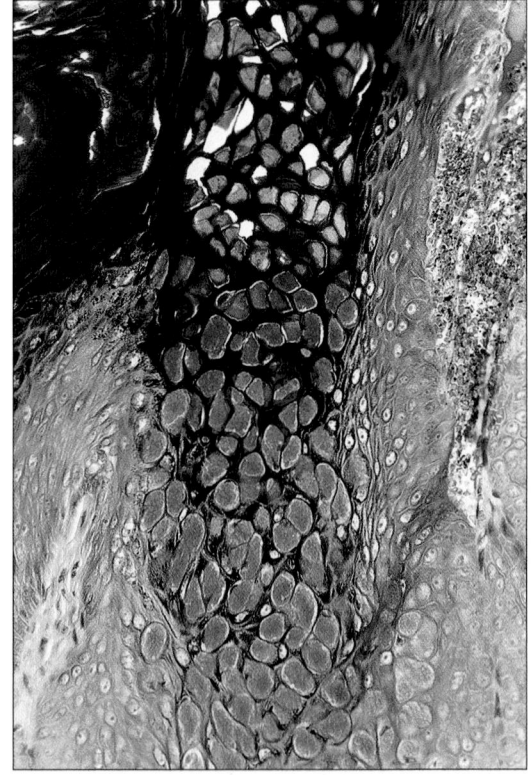

Fig. 17.82
Molluscum contagiosum: note the tinctorial change in this section stained with Lendrum's phloxine tartazine.

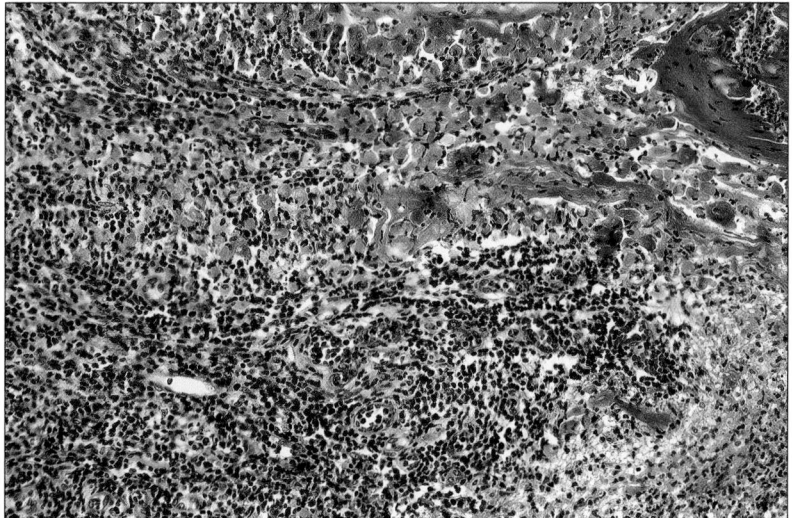

Fig. 17.84
Molluscum contagiosum: there is an intense lymphohistiocytic infiltrate. Numerous infected keratinocytes are present.

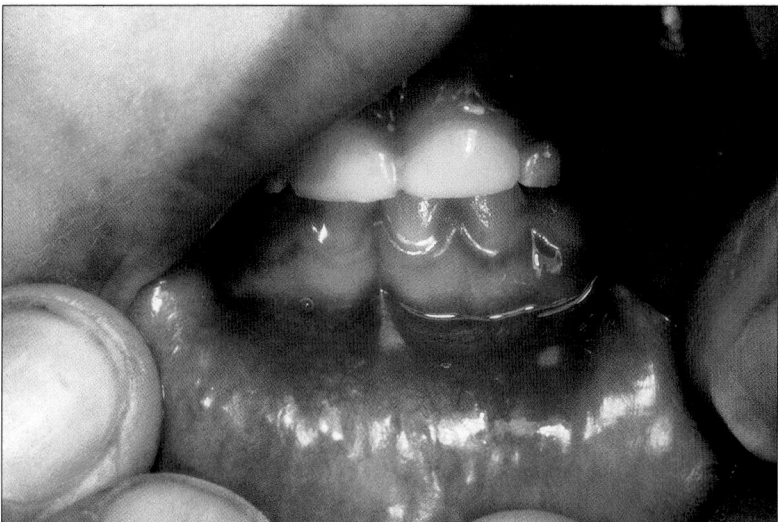

Fig, 17.85
Hand, foot and mouth disease: multiple oral ulcers are present. By courtesy of the Institute of Dermatology, London, UK.

8.   Vozmediano, J.M., Manrique, A., Petraglia, S. et al (1996) Giant molluscum contagiosum in AIDS. *Int J Dermatol*, **35**, 45–47.
9.   Cribier, B., Serivener, Y., Grosshans, E. (2001) Molluscum contagiosum: histologic patterns and associated lesions. A study of 578 cases. *Am J Dermatopathol*, **23**, 99–103.
10. Kolokotronis, A., Antoniades, D., Katsoulides, E. et al (2000) Facial and perioral molluscum contagiosum as a manifestation of HIV infection. *Aust Dent J*, **45**, 49–52.
11. Ghura, H.S., Camp, R.D.R. (2001) Scarring molluscum contagiosum in patients with severe atopic dermatitis: report of two cases. *Br J Dermatol*, **144**, 1094–1095.
12. Naert, F., Lachapelle, J.M. (1989) Multiple lesions of molluscum contagiosum with metaplastic ossification. *Am J Dermatopathol*, **11**, 238–241.
13. Au, W.Y., Lie, A.K., Shek, T.W. (2000) Fulminant molluscum contagiosum infection and concomitant leukemia cutis after bone marrow transplantation for chronic myeloid leukemia. *Br J Dermatol*, **143**, 1097–1098.
14. Charley, M.R., Sontheimer, R.D. (1982) Clearing of subacute cutaneous lupus erythematosus around molluscum contagiosum lesions. *J Am Acad Dermatol*, **6**, 529–533.

Hand, foot and mouth disease

Clinical features

This is a viral illness caused most often by Coxsackie A16 virus and less often by enterovirus 71.[1–7] It usually affects young children, shows seasonal variation (being more common in summer and autumn) and presents as small epidemics. A number of outbreaks have been documented in the East, especially Taiwan.[2,4–7] Children in their first 4 years of life are most susceptible.[5]

Hand, foot and mouth disease has an incubation period of 3–7 days. Following a prodrome of headache, fever, malaise, abdominal pain and sometimes diarrhea, patients develop oral ulcers and blisters most commonly on the inner cheeks and lips, accompanied by small erythematous papules, which soon evolve into grayish vesicles on the soles, palms and ventral surfaces and sides of the fingers and toes (*Figs 17.85–17.88*).[2] Lesions are less commonly found on the perineum, buttocks, trunk and extremities. The eruption is self-limiting. Complications only occur in approximately 6% of cases attributable to Coxsackie A16 virus, notably aseptic meningitis.[4]

Hand, foot and mouth disease due to enterovirus 71 is a more serious illness, with complications occurring in approximately one-third of patients. These include central nervous system lesions predominantly affecting the cerebellum. Encephalitis, aseptic meningitis and a poliomyelitis-like condition can also occur.[2,4] A mortality rate of around 8% has been recorded. Death is usually attributable to cardiopulmonary decompensation and acute pulmonary edema.[4] The mechanism of pulmonary edema is unclear, since it does not appear to be the direct result of viral myocarditis; it has been postulated that increased pulmonary vascular permeability secondary to brainstem lesions or a systemic inflammatory response to encephalitis may play a role.[6,8]

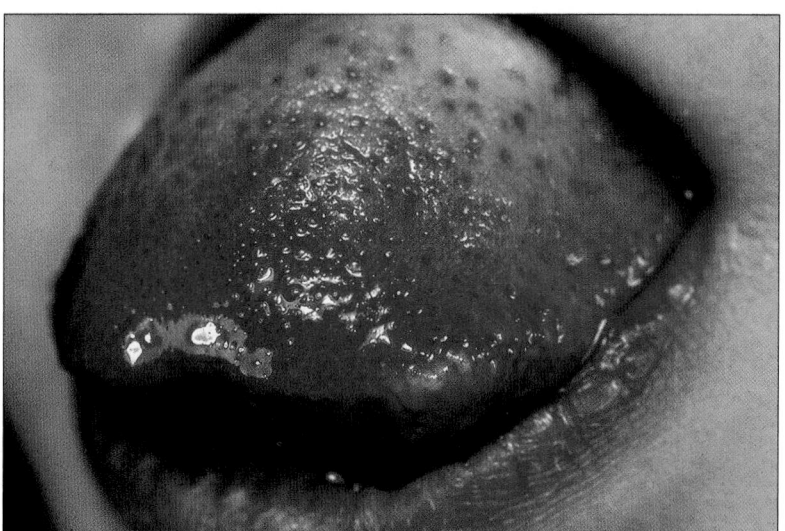

Fig. 17.86
Hand, foot and mouth disease: there are numerous erosions with surrounding erythema. By courtesy of E. Wilson Jones, MD, Institute of Dermatology, London, UK.

Pathogenesis and histological features

This virus is transmitted by direct contact with nasal and pharyngeal secretions, feces and blood. Histologically, the blister is intraepidermal and develops as a consequence of marked inter- and intracellular edema (*Figs 17.89, 17.90*). There may be associated papillary dermal edema. Viral inclusions and giant cells are not a feature. A recent study has shown that enterovirus 71 may induce apoptosis of infected host cells via a virus-encoded protein.[9]

References

1.   Fields, J.P., Mihm, M.C., Hellreich, P.D. et al (1969) Hand, foot and mouth disease. *Arch Dermatol*, **99**, 243–246.
2.   Ishimaru, Y., Nakano, S., Yamaoka, K. et al (1980) Outbreaks of hand, foot and mouth disease by enterovirus 71. *Arch Dis Child*, **55**, 583–588.
3.   Sala, F., Mansi, M., Greppi, F. et al (1989) Hand foot mouth disease: its course in the city of Milan (1980–1986). *G Ital Dermatologica*, **124**, 63–66.
4.   Chang, L.Y., Lin, T.Y., Huang, Y.C. et al (1999) Comparison of enterovirus 71 and coxsackie-virus A16 clinical illnesses during the Taiwan enterovirus outbreak, 1998. *Pediatr Infect Dis J*, **18**, 1092–1096.
5.   Ho, M. (2000) Enterovirus 71: the virus, its infections and outbreaks. *J Microbiol Immunol Infect*, **33**, 205–216.
6.   Chan, L.G., Parashar, U.D., Lye, M.S. et al (2000) Deaths of children during an outbreak of hand, foot and mouth disease in Sarawak, Malaysia: clinical and pathological characteristics of the disease. For the Outbreak Study Group. *Clin Infect Dis*, **31**, 678–683.

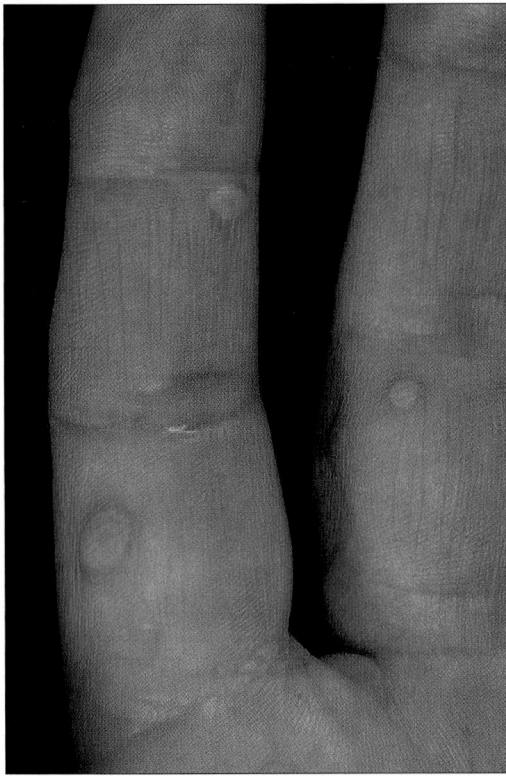

Fig. 17.87
Hand, foot and mouth disease: note the small vesicles with surrounding erythema. By courtesy of E. Wilson Jones, MD, Institute of Dermatology, London, UK.

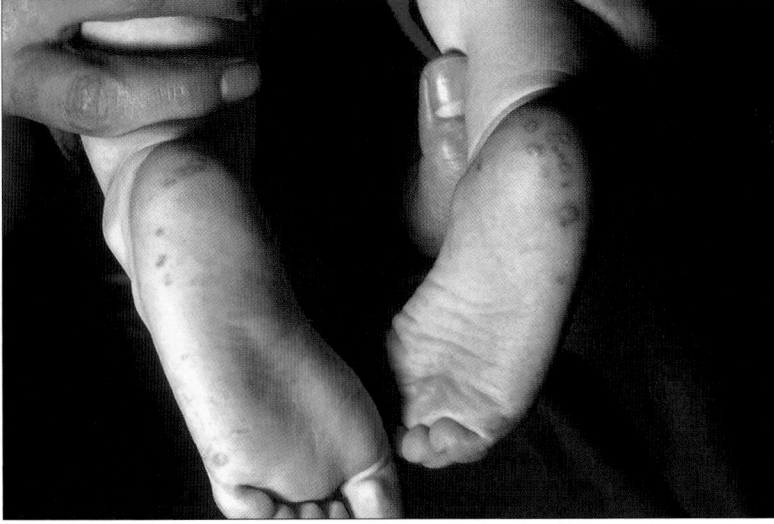

Fig. 17.88
Hand, foot and mouth disease: there are numerous erosions on the sole of the foot. By courtesy of R.A. Marsden, MD, St George's Hospital, London, UK.

7.   Chang, L.Y., King, C.C., Hsu, K.H. et al (2002) Risk factors of enterovirus 71 infection and associated hand, foot, and mouth disease/herpangina in children during an epidemic in Taiwan. *Pediatrics*, **109**, E88.
8.   Wu, J.M., Wang, J.N., Tsai, Y.C. et al (2002) Cardiopulmonary manifestations of fulminant enterovirus 71 infection. *Pediatrics*, **109**, E26.
9.   Kuo, R.L., Kung, S.H., Hsu, Y.Y. et al (2002) Infection with enterovirus 71 or expression of its 2A protease induces apoptotic cell death. *J Gen Virol*, **83**, 1367–1376.

Viral hemorrhagic fevers

Clinical features

The hemorrhagic fever (HF) viruses are a special group of viruses transmitted to humans by arthropods (mosquitos, ticks) or rodents, resulting in systemic illness and a generalized bleeding diathesis.[1-3] The viral etiologic agents may be grouped according to family:

- Flaviviridae, which are responsible for infections such as yellow fever, dengue HF, Omsk HF and Kyasanur Forest disease

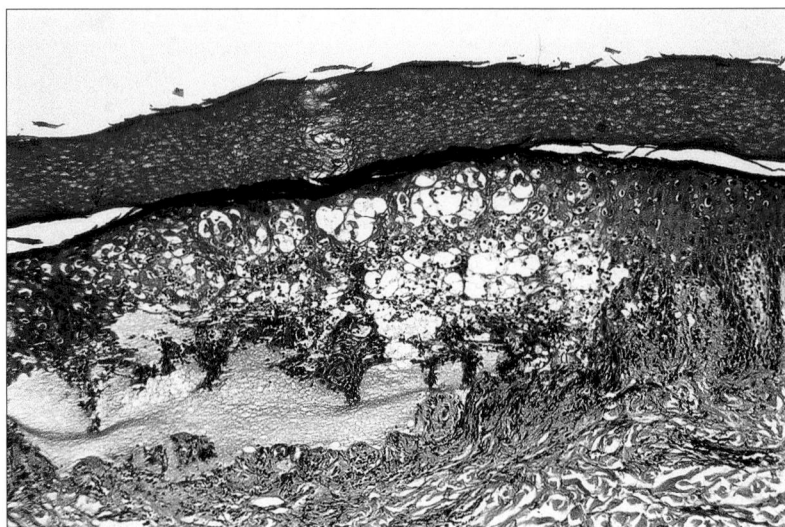

Fig. 17.89
Hand, foot and mouth disease: this low power view of the finger shows gross reticular degeneration with intraepidermal vesiculation. Degenerative changes have resulted in epidermodermal separation. By courtesy of E. Wilson Jones, MD, Institute of Dermatology, London, UK.

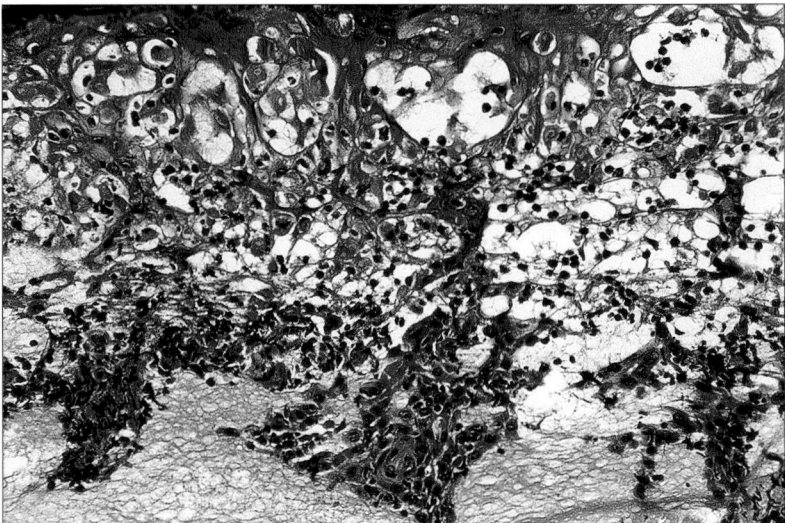

Fig. 17.90
Hand, foot and mouth disease: the epithelium shows necrosis and dyskeratosis. A chronic inflammatory infiltrate is evident. By courtesy of E. Wilson Jones, MD, Institute of Dermatology, London, UK.

- Togaviridae, an example of which is chikungunya fever virus
- Bunyaviridae, which cause Rift Valley fever, Crimean–Congo HF and hantavirus infections (e.g. hantaan)
- Arenaviridae, which are responsible for Argentine HF, Bolivian HF, Lassa fever, etc.
- Filoviridae, which cause Marburg virus disease and Ebola HF.[1,2]

There is marked diversity in the severity of illness and the mortality within this group of diseases; dengue fever, for example, has a mortality of around 5% whereas the purported mortality associated with Ebola HF is 50–90%.[3] Most viral HFs manifest as an acute febrile illness, often with myalgias. Conjunctival injection and periorbital edema may occur.[1,3] A detailed discussion of all of the conditions listed above is not possible, and the reader is referred to reference number 1 for an excellent treatise on the subject. The further discussion here will focus on the potential mucocutaneous manifestations of viral HFs.

A conspicuous, diffuse, non-pruritic maculopapular skin rash is typically encountered in filovirus infections such as Marburg virus disease and Ebola HF. Desquamation may take place during the recovery phase in non-fatal cases.[2] Chikungunya HF is also usually associated with a maculopapular rash. A similar although less prominent eruption may be seen on the trunk and limbs of patients with Rift Valley fever.[2] Omsk HF, Kyasanur Forest disease, Argentine HF and Bolivian HF are associated with a papulovesicular eruption involving the palate.[2]

Thrombocytopenia is a characteristic sequela in the majority of viral HFs and manifests as petechial hemorrhages on the skin and in relation to the mucous membranes. Ecchymoses may develop in severe infections and are usually located over pressure points. There may also be bleeding from venipuncture sites. DIC is known to complicate the clinical course of some infections, especially Rift Valley fever.[1–3] Jaundice is a typical feature of yellow fever but may also be encountered in Rift Valley fever, Crimean–Congo HF and the filoviral HFs.[1,3]

Although Sindbis fever is not strictly one of the viral HFs, this relatively mild, self-limiting togavirus infection may rarely be associated with hemorrhagic skin lesions, and has been included here for the sake of completeness. In usual cases of Sindbis fever the exanthem is papular or vesicular occurring in crops lasting up to 10 days. Lesions tend to be concentrated over the buttocks, legs, palms and soles.[4]

Histological features

The dermatopathological manifestations of this group of infections are poorly documented, largely because of the infectious and hemorrhagic risks associated with biopsy. Cases with a maculopapular eruption show a mild perivascular mononuclear inflammatory cell infiltrate, sometimes accompanied by minor perivascular erythrocytic extravasation.[1,3] Extensive dermal hemorrhage is seen in ecchymotic lesions. Intravascular fibrin-platelet thrombi characterize cases complicated by DIC.

Differential diagnosis

It is important to remember that the HF viruses are not the only infective agents that may be associated with pyrexia and hemorrhage. Other viruses such as smallpox virus and herpes simplex also may produce a hemorrhagic fever picture (e.g. hemorrhagic smallpox). Additional infective agents that may cause a hemorrhagic fever picture are rickettsiae (e.g. *Rickettsia rickettsii*), chlamydiae (e.g. *Chlamydia psittaci*), bacteria (e.g. *Neisseria meningitidis*, *Yersinia pestis*), fungi (e.g. *Aspergillus*), spirochetes (e.g. *Leptospira icterohaemorrhagiae*, *Borrelia recurrentis*) and protozoa (e.g. *Plasmodium falciparum*).[4]

References

1. Isaäcson, M., Hale, M.J. (1995) The viral hemorrhagic fevers. In: Doerr, W., Seifert, G. (eds) Spezielle Pathologische Anatomie, Vol. 8: Tropical pathology, 2nd edn. Berlin: Springer-Verlag, pp 421–473.
2. Zaki, S.R. (2002) Hemorrhagic fevers. *Histopathology*, **41** (Suppl. 2), 53–56.
3. Zaki, S.R., Peters, C.J. (1997) Viral hemorrhagic fevers. In: Connor, D.H., Chandler, F.W., Schwartz, D.A. et al (eds) Pathology of infectious diseases, Vol. I. Stamford: Appleton and Lange, pp 347–364.
4. Monath, T.P. (1991) Viral febrile illnesses. In: Strickland, G.T. (ed.) Hunter's tropical medicine, 7th edn. Philadelphia: Saunders, pp 200–218.

Bacterial infections

Impetigo

The skin has a normal commensal population of bacteria in which *Staphylococcus epidermidis* predominates.[1] Other resident Gram-positive bacteria include *Micrococcus* spp. and *Corynebacterium* spp.[2] The free fatty acids and other lipids derived from the stratum corneum and sebum have an antibacterial role, yet 10–20% of the normal population are cutaneous carriers of *S. aureus* and approximately 10% are pharyngeal carriers of group A β-hemolytic streptococci (*Streptococcus pyogenes*).[1,3] This 'carrier' state may precede infective lesions in the host or may be the origin of infections in others. *S. aureus* and *S. pyogenes* are the most common agents in superficial bacterial infections of the skin, but even organisms of low virulence, such as *S. epidermidis*, can become pathogenic with a sufficiently large inoculum or in an immunocompromised host.[1] *S. aureus* toxin production is also responsible for bullous impetigo, the staphylococcal scalded skin syndrome and the toxic shock syndrome.

Clinical features

Impetigo is the most superficial pyogenic (pyoderma) bacterial skin infection and is highly infectious. It is exceedingly common and occurs most often in childhood, but may be seen in the elderly and in patients with immunodeficiency states (*Fig. 17.94*). It is typically subdivided into non-bullous (simple) impetigo and bullous impetigo and follows the contamination of minor skin abrasions and insect bites by *S. aureus* or *S. pyogenes*.[4–6]

In simple impetigo the lesions present as small superficial vesicles, which rapidly burst and are replaced by a characteristic, adherent thick yellowish dirty crust with a margin of erythema (*Figs 17.91–17.93*). The mouth, nose and extremities are particularly affected. Regional lymphadenopathy is sometimes present. Simple impetigo may occur in endemic or epidemic form and often spreads to involve siblings and schoolmates.[4] It is seen more often in warm, humid conditions.[7] In Europe it is caused by either streptococci or staphylococci with the latter predominant, whereas in North America group A streptococci appear to be much more commonly implicated.[4] Not infrequently the two bacteria appear to coexist.

Streptococcal impetigo may occasionally progress to cellulitis or precede acute glomerulonephritis, erythema nodosum or erythema multiforme.

Bullous impetigo is primarily a staphylococcal-mediated disease, exclusively due to phage group II *S. aureus*.[8] Superficial blisters up to 2 cm across are the initial features (*Fig. 17.95*). The contents are at first clear, but rapidly become cloudy and then develop a thin seropurulent crust; erythema is not marked. The lesions do not usually involve mucosae. There may be mild constitutional symptoms and the lesions resolve in 2–3 weeks.

Ecthyma is probably a variant of impetigo and occurs predominantly on the lower limbs of children, but may occur in adults and at other sites (*Figs 17.96, 17.97*).[9,10] It presents with thick crusting, overlying punched-out ulceration and resultant scarring. *S. pyogenes* is the usual cause. It is more common in tropical climates, where it occurs in all age groups. Minor trauma or scabies infestation may determine the site of the lesions. It is possible that vasculitis and necrosis induced by bacterial toxins determine the different presentation.

Ecthyma gangrenosum is a complication of *Pseudomonas aeruginosa* septicemia that occurs in immunodeficient patients, particularly those with a neutropenia.[11,12] It has also been reported in association with hypogammaglobulinemia.[13] There have been rare reports of ecthyma gangrenosum occurring in the absence of neutropenia or septicemia.[14,15] Lesions, which may be single or multiple, begin as painless erythematous macules that become indurated, bullous or pustular.[12] Annular lesions have been described.[16] They soon become gangrenous and covered by a characteristic gray–black eschar and erythematous halo. Lesions are especially seen on the gluteal and perineal regions and on the limbs.[12] The mortality is high, particularly in those with multiple lesions.

Pathogenesis and histological features

The carrier state or inoculation by a contaminated object is a necessary precondition to superficial infection of the skin. The organisms become attached to the traumatized area, binding strongly to fibronectin and possibly type IV collagen and laminin, which are abundant in the exudate.[1,8] The function of the innate virulence of the organisms and the host defense capability determine the subsequent progress of the infection, but this is facilitated if the bacteria produce coagulase, hyaluronidase or lipases.[1] The form of *S. aureus* responsible for bullous impetigo is of serotype II and mainly of phage type 71 and produces exfoliative toxins A and B; the latter are also involved in the staphylococcal scalded skin syndrome (see below).[17–19]

Impetigo is characterized in early lesions by a split in the epidermis just beneath the stratum granulosum (*Fig. 17.98*). The resultant vesicle becomes filled with neutrophils, Gram-positive cocci and occasional

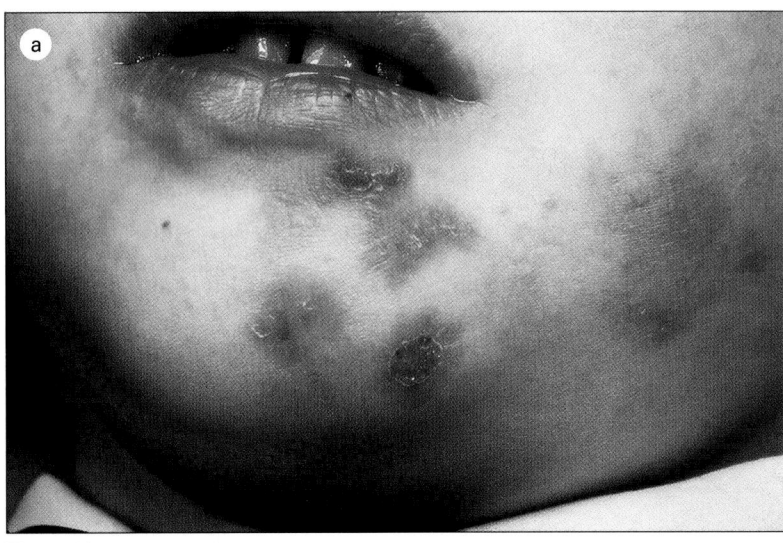
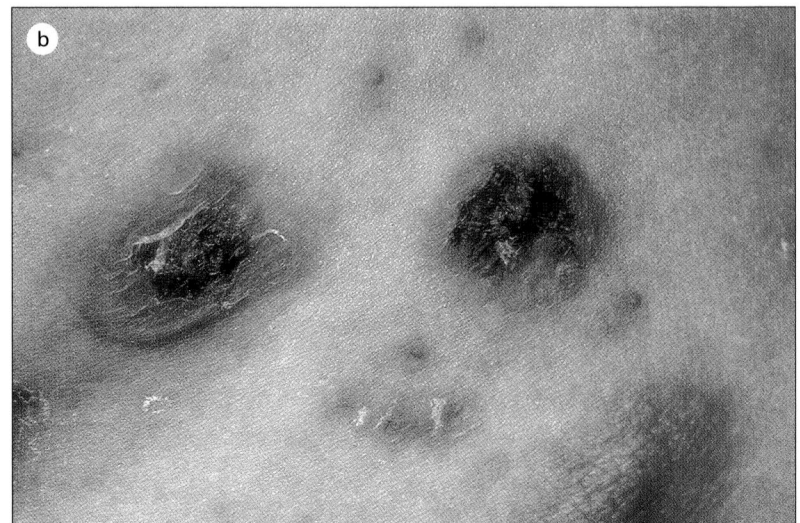

Fig. 17.91
(a, b) Impetigo: note that the vesicles are covered by a golden crust. These perioral lesions are at a characteristic site. By courtesy of R.A. Marsden, MD, St George's Hospital, London, UK.

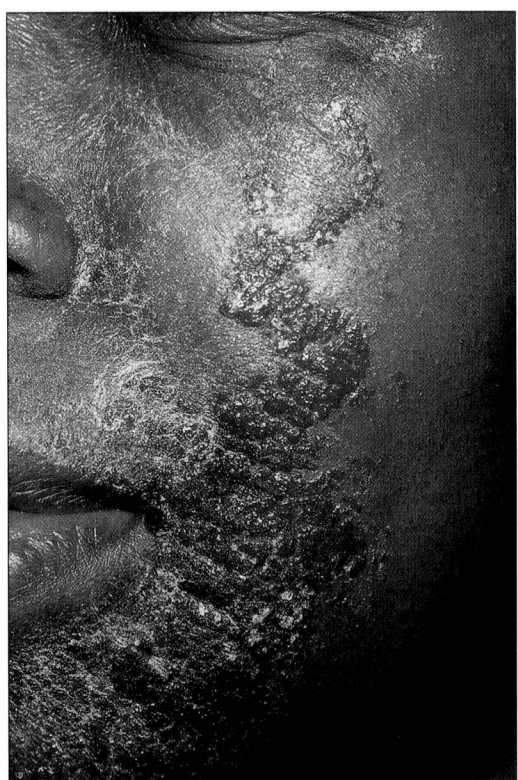

Fig. 17.92
Impetigo: in this patient numerous vesicles are evident. By courtesy of R.A. Marsden, MD, St George's Hospital, London, UK.

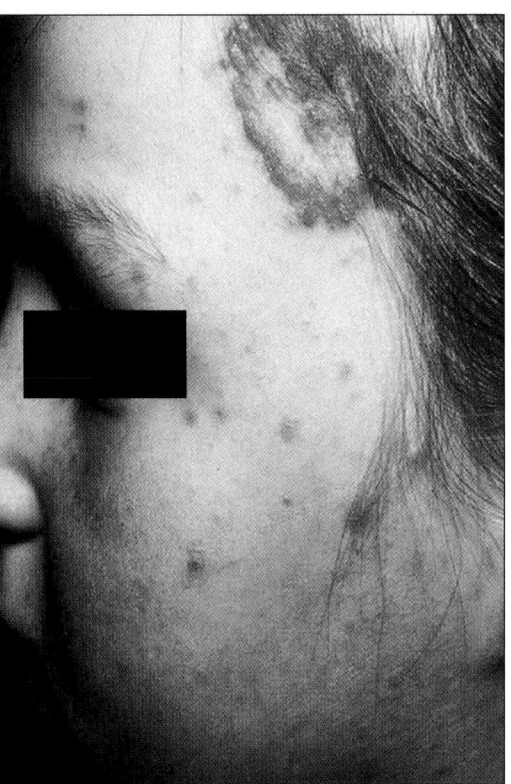

Fig. 17.93
Impetigo: note the crusted healing lesion on the forehead. By courtesy of the Institute of Dermatology, London, UK.

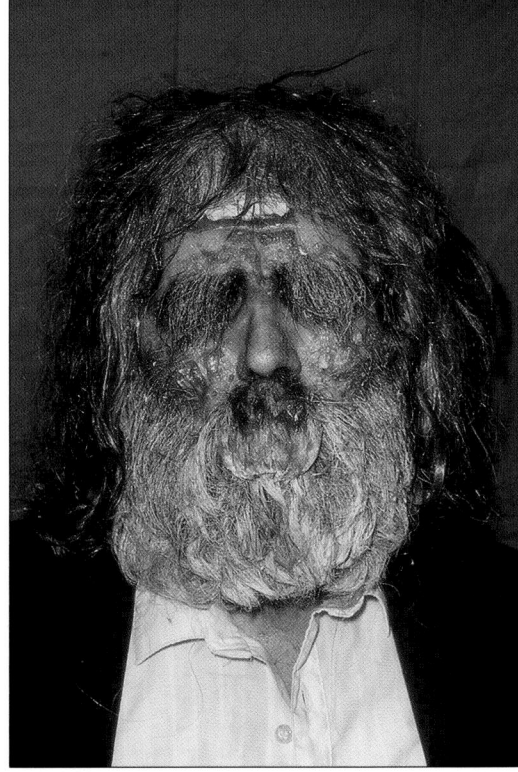

Fig. 17.94
Impetigo: note the crusted lesions on this patient's forehead and cheeks. By courtesy of R.A. Marsden, MD, St George's Hospital, London, UK.

acantholytic cells (*Fig. 17.99*). The underlying dermis contains a mixed neutrophil and lymphocyte infiltrate. Neutrophils may be seen in the spongiotic stratum spinosum beneath the vesicle in the process of migrating from the dermis in a chemotactic response to the causative bacteria. In conditions of impaired neutrophil function impetigo may be common and more extensive.[1]

In echthyma, there is a sharply circumscribed area of ulceration with a heavy neutrophil infiltrate and overlying adherent crust (*Fig. 17.100*).

Ecthyma gangrenosum is characterized by epidermal necrosis with hemorrhage and dermal infarction, usually accompanied by a mixed inflammatory cell infiltrate of lymphocytes, histiocytes and neutrophils.[12]

Less commonly a dearth of inflammatory cells may be noted.[12,20] Gram-negative bacilli may be seen in the dermis and involving the media and adventitia of venules.[12] Vasculitis and thrombosis may be present.

Differential diagnosis

The diagnosis is usually achieved on clinical grounds and supported by culture of the causative organisms. Rarely, a biopsy is necessary.

The lesion may be confused histologically with a superficial variant of pemphigus, particularly as the latter can become secondarily infected and there may be one or two acantholytic cells in impetigo. Antibodies in a

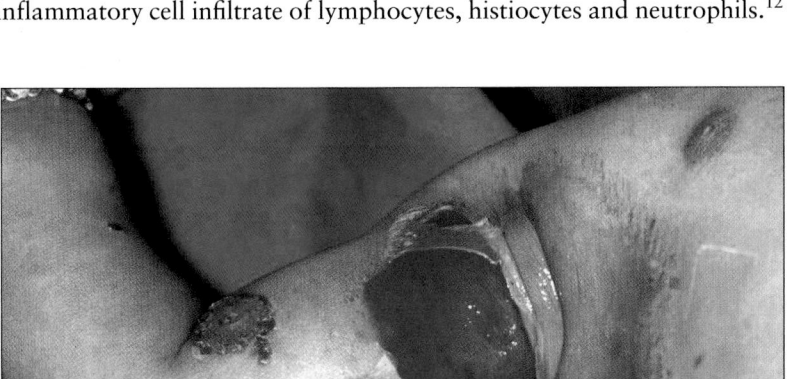

Fig. 17.95
Bullous impetigo: there is a large raw erosion and a healed lesion distally.
By courtesy of the Institute of Dermatology, London, UK.

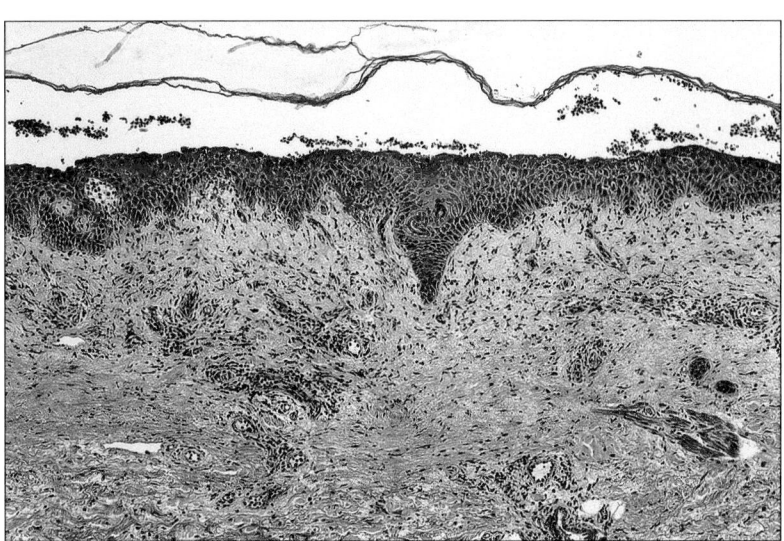

Fig. 17.98
Bullous impetigo: the site of cleavage is immediately below the granular cell layer.

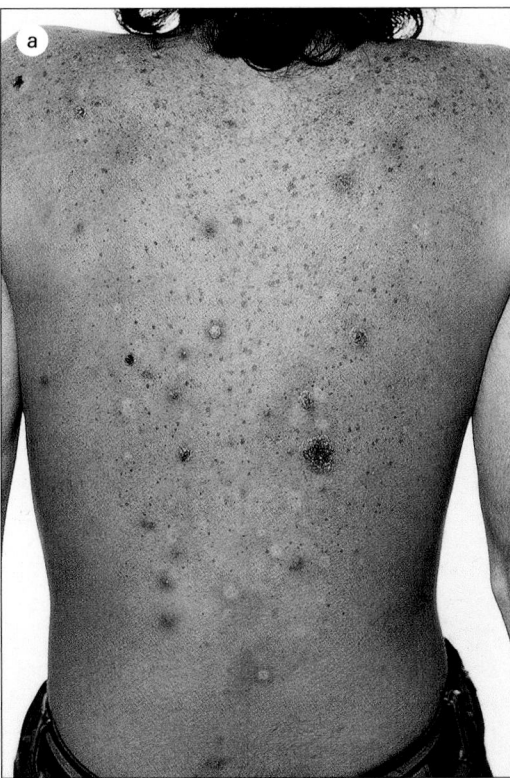
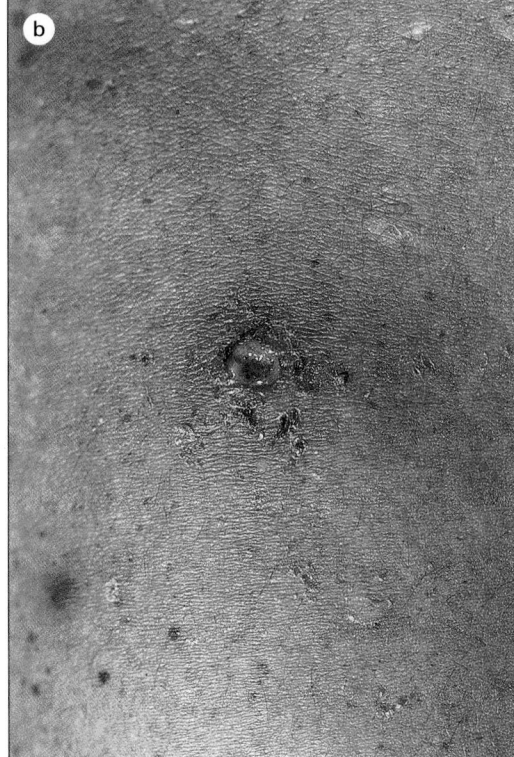

Fig. 17.96
Ecthyma: (a) characteristic lesions in varying stages of evolution; (b) a punched-out ulcer is shown in close-up. By courtesy of M.M. Black, MD, Institute of Dermatology, London, UK.

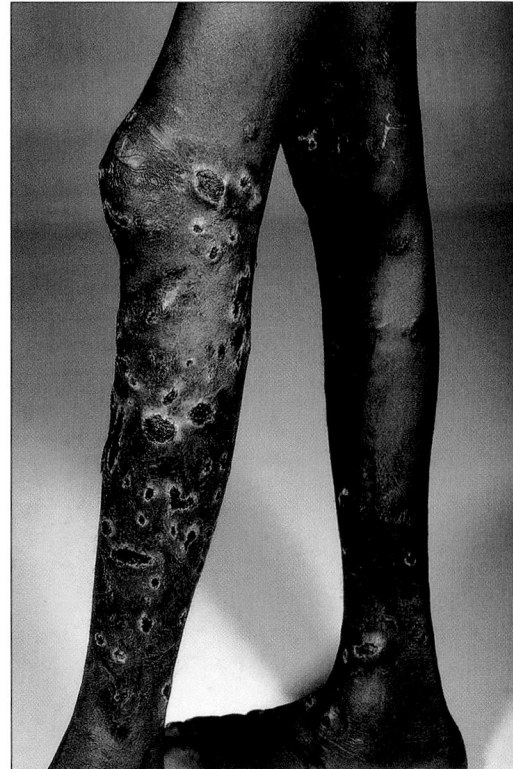

Fig. 17.97
Ecthyma: multiple lesions are present. By courtesy of N.C. Dlova, MD, Nelson R. Mandela School of Medicine, University of KwaZulu-Natal, South Africa.

pemphigus-like pattern may be demonstrated in bullous impetigo and distinction from pemphigus foliaceus may therefore be a problem.[21,22] Generally the presence of numerous neutrophils and the recognition of Gram-positive cocci is sufficiently characteristic to confirm impetigo, as acantholytic cells are very scanty. Distinction from subcorneal pustular dermatosis and pustular psoriasis may be considered histologically, but the lack of acanthosis, although not conclusive, should point towards impetigo.

References

1. Sheagren, J.N. (1985) Staphylococcal infections of the skin and skin structures. *Cutis*, **36**, 2–6.
2. Chiller, K., Selkin, B.A., Murakawa, G.J. (2001) Skin microflora and bacterial infections of the skin. *J Invest Dermatol Symp Proc*, **6**, 170–174.
3. Miller, S.J., Aly, R., Shinefield, H.R. et al (1988) In vitro and in vivo antistaphylococcal activity of human stratum corneum lipids. *Arch Dermatol*, **124**, 209–215.
4. Melish, M.E. (1982) Staphylococci, streptococci and the skin. Review of impetigo and the staphylococcal scalded skin syndrome. *Semin Dermatol*, **1**, 101–109.
5. Barton, L.L., Friedman, A.D. (1987) Impetigo: a reassessment of etiology and therapy. *Pediatr Dermatol*, **4**, 185–188.
6. Lookingbill, D. (1985) Impetigo. *Pediatr Rev*, **7**, 177–181.
7. Finch, R. (1988) Skin and soft tissue infections. *Lancet*, **i**, 164–167.
8. Darmstadt, G.L., Lane, A.T. (1994) Impetigo: an overview. *Pediatr Dermatol*, **11**, 293–303.
9. Findlay, G.H. (1987) The classical infections. In: The dermatology of bacterial infection. Oxford: Blackwell, pp 43–52.
10. Wickboldt, L.G., Fenske, N.A. (1986) Streptococcal and staphylococcal infections of the skin. *Hosp Pract*, **21**, 41–47.
11. Van den Broek, P.J., van den Meer, J.W.K.M., Kunst, M.W. (1979) The pathogenesis of ecthyma gangrenosum. *J Infect*, **1**, 263–267.
12. Greene, S.L., Su, W.P.D., Muller, S.A. (1984) Ecthyma gangrenosum: report of clinical, histopathologic and bacteriologic aspects of eight cases. *J Am Acad Dermatol*, **11**, 781–787.
13. Ng, W., Tan, C.L., Yeow, V. et al (1998) Ecthyma gangrenosum in a patient with hypogammaglobulinemia. *J Infect*, **36**, 331–335.
14. Kim, E.J., Foad, M., Travers, R. (1999) Ecthyma gangrenosum in an AIDS patient with normal neutrophil count. *J Am Acad Dermatol*, **41**, 840–841.
15. Versapuech, J., Leaute-Labreze, C., Thedenat, B. et al (2001) Ecthyma gangrenosum caused by Pseudomonas aeruginosa without septicemia in a neutropenic patient. *Rev Med Interne*, **22**, 877–880.
16. Czechowicz, R.T., Warren, L.J., Moore, L. et al (2001) Pseudomonas aeruginosa infection mimicking erythema annulare centrifugum. *Australas J Dermatol*, **42**, 57–59.
17. Baker, D.H., Dimond, R.L., Wuepper, K.D. (1978) The epidermolytic toxin of Staphylococcus aureus: its failure to bind to cells and its detection in blister fluids of patients with bullous impetigo. *J Invest Dermatol*, **71**, 274–275.
18. Hanakawa, Y., Schechter, N.M., Lin, C. et al (2002) Molecular mechanisms of blister formation in bullous impetigo and staphylococcal scalded skin syndrome. *J Clin Invest*, **110**, 53–60.
19. Amagai, M., Yamaguchi, T., Hanakawa, Y. et al (2002) Staphylococcal exfoliative toxin B specifically cleaves desmoglein 1. *J Invest Dermatol*, **118**, 845–850.
20. Fast, M., Woerner, S., Bowman, W. et al (1979) Ecthyma gangrenosum. *Can Med Assoc J*, **120**, 332–334.
21. Ead, R.D. (1979) Pemphigus-like antibodies: a report of two cases. *Br J Dermatol*, **100**, 723–725.
22. Rapaport, M.J., Ahmad, A.R. (1981) Falsely normal direct immunofluorescent microscopic findings in bullous impetigo. Letter. *Arch Dermatol*, **117**, 524.

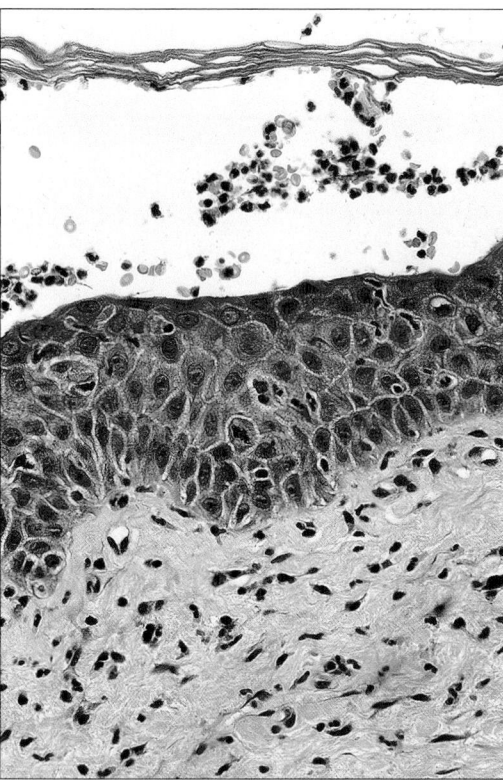

Fig. 17.99
Bullous impetigo: in addition to neutrophils, occasional acantholytic cells may be present causing diagnostic confusion with pemphigus foliaceus.

Staphylococcal scalded skin syndrome

Clinical features

Staphylococcal scalded skin syndrome (SSSS) is so-named because of the presence of staphylococcal toxin and the resemblance of the established lesion to a scald. It may present in epidemic form as well as sporadically.[1–3] It occurs almost entirely in neonates and young children, who develop first a macular scarlatiniform eruption in association with a

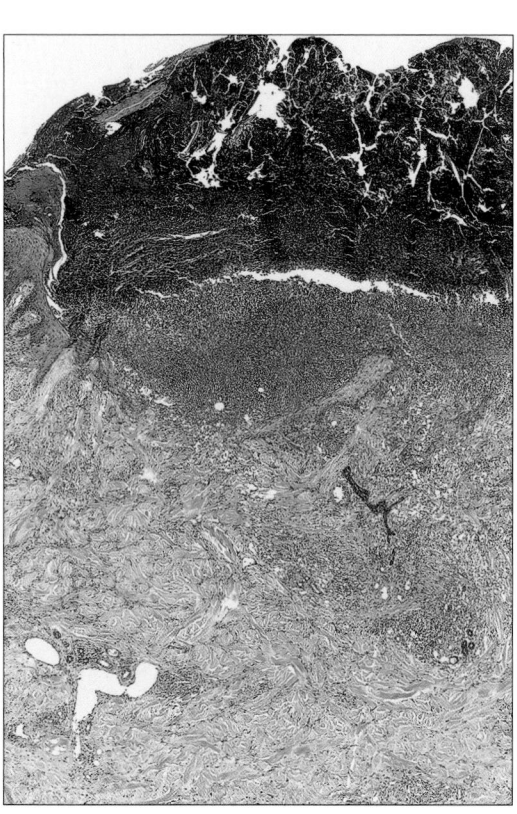

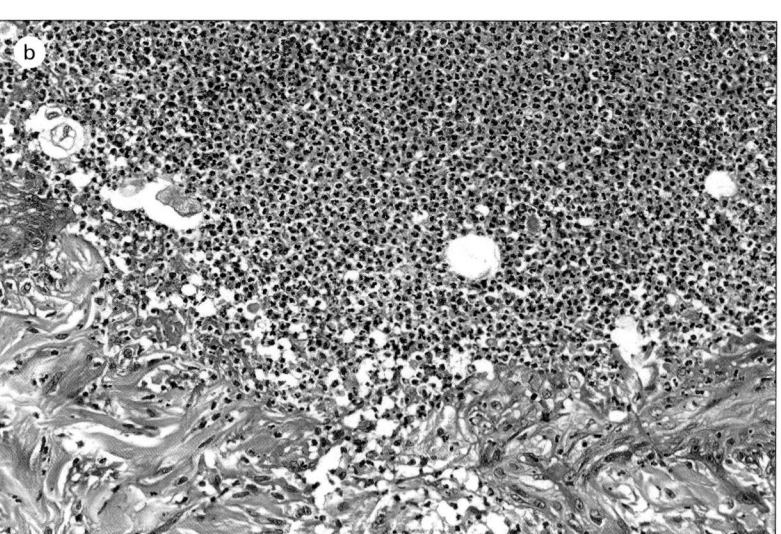

Fig. 17.100
(a, b) Ecthyma: there is a sharply delineated ulcer. Artifact is an important differential diagnosis.

staphylococcal infection. This is often associated with fever, irritability and skin tenderness.[4,5] The eruption then spreads from its usual original sites on the face, axillae and groins to involve large areas of the skin surface. Conjunctivitis is often also present. Mucous membranes, however, are not affected. At the same time the skin becomes edematous and the surface fragile so that it can be sheared off in thin wrinkled sheets, likened to peeling wet wallpaper, leaving a glistening red surface, and the child becomes sick and feverish (*Fig. 17.101*). SSSS is therefore associated with a positive Nikolsky's sign.[6]

Following blistering, desquamation occurs and the skin often returns to normal by 2–3 weeks.[7] Scarring is not usually a feature. The associated source of infection may be an upper respiratory tract infection, conjunctivitis or umbilical sepsis, or it may be more occult, such as in the middle ear, in the pharynx or at the site of minor surgery. The condition is rare at other ages, such as the first day after birth or even at birth, indicating an infection acquired in labor or in utero, or it may be seen in older children.[8] Fewer than 50 adult cases have been reported; although many of these patients were either immunocompromised (including HIV infection) or in renal failure with a possible inability to excrete the toxin, the condition does occur rarely in previously healthy adults or those with relatively minor conditions (*Fig. 17.102*).[9–17]

The disease in neonates (Ritter's disease) is usually self-limiting with rapid resolution of the skin blisters and complete recovery, but there is a mortality of 2–3% due to progression of the staphylococcal infection or the complications of exfoliation. In the adult this rare condition has had a mortality of over 50%.[17] Recovery is facilitated by antistaphylococcal antibiotics and attention to fluid balance.

An abortive form, the scarlatiniform variant (staphylococcal scarlet fever) in which the initial erythroderma evolves into the desquamative phase in the absence of blistering, has been described.[4,5,7] This may be particularly associated with occult bone and joint infections or contaminated wounds.[7]

Pathogenesis and histological features

In SSSS the organism is of group II and usually phage type 71, but phage types 3A, 3B, 3C and 55 have also been found.[4,15] These bacteria all produce an epidermolytic toxin (formerly referred to as exfoliatin) of which there are two antigenic types: exfoliative toxin A (ETA) and exfoliative toxin B (ETB).[18–21] ETA is associated with a chromosomal gene while ETB is plasmid encoded.[4,5,22] They have indistinguishable activity and manifest exquisite pathological sensitivity by inducing blistering only at the level of the superficial epidermis.[19,20] The effect of the toxins is determined by their site of production.

- Toxins produced by the appropriate staphylococcal infection of mucosae or surgical wounds enter the circulation (toxemia) and produce a generalized change in the skin, the SSSS. The intensity is determined by the rapidity with which the toxins are metabolized and excreted renally and by the presence of antibodies against the toxins.[23]
- If the same staphylococcus infects the skin directly, local release of toxin results in bullous impetigo.

Staphylococcal strains also produce toxic shock syndrome toxin (TSST-1) and a variety of enterotoxins (A–E). These are more frequently associated with staphylococcal scarlet fever and the toxic shock syndrome.[19]

The toxin in either SSSS or bullous impetigo causes a split in the epidermis at the level of the granular layer (*Fig. 17.103*). Ultrastructu-

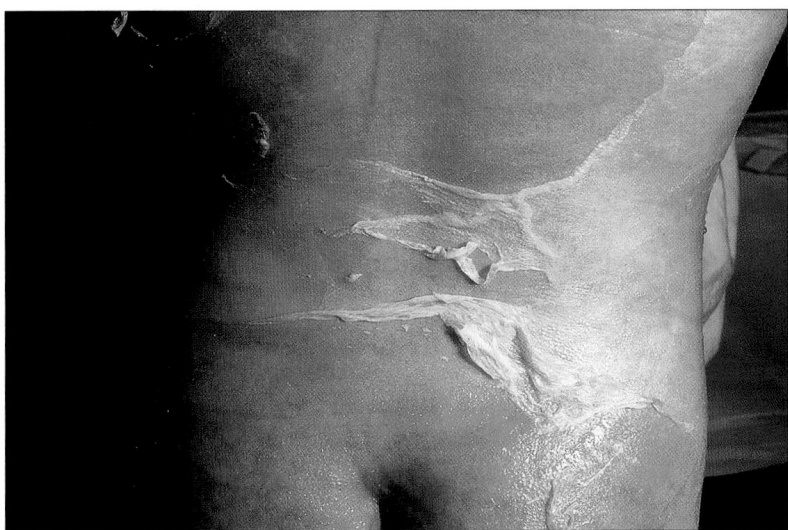

Fig. 17.101
Staphylococcal scalded skin syndrome: note the very extensive blistering. By courtesy of A. du Vivier, MD, King's College Hospital, London, UK.

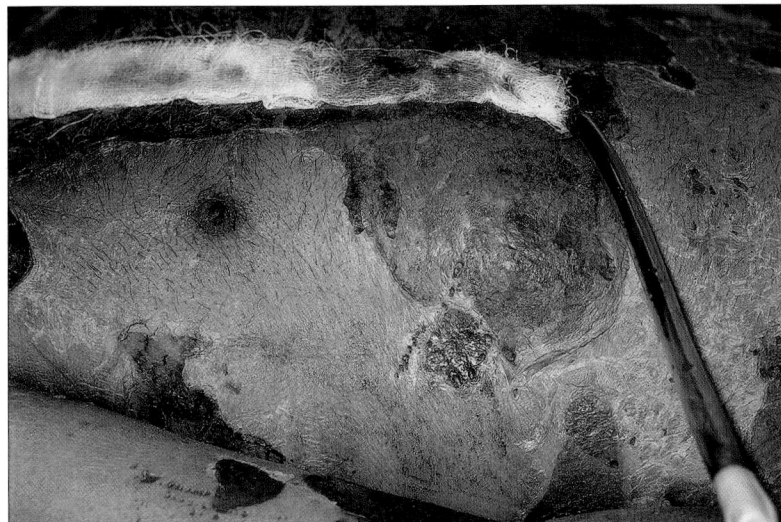

Fig. 17.102
Staphylococcal scalded skin syndrome: note the widespread denuded areas at the edge of which the epithelium is being shed. This case developed in a patient following wound infection after a coronary artery bypass. By courtesy of S. Parker, MD, West Middlesex Hospital, London, UK.

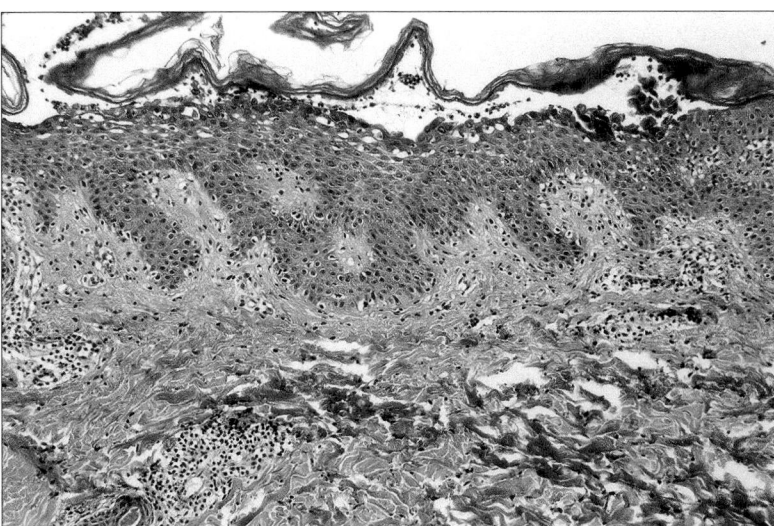

Fig. 17.103
Staphylococcal scalded skin syndrome: vesiculation occurs at the level of the granular cell layer.

rally the level of separation is in the midgranular layer.[24] It is associated with separation of the cell membranes at the desmosomes and the interdesmosomal regions appear less dense.[25] The cells on either side of the cleft appear normal. It has been shown that the epidermolytic toxins (ETA and/or ETB) act as serine proteases and bind desmoglein 1, a desmosomal adhesion molecule.[20,21] The cleavage and subsequent inactivation thereof induces blistering.[21]

Histologically, the clefts through the granular layer of the epidermis in SSSS are associated with only a scanty inflammatory infiltrate in the epidermis or dermis and there may be some dermal edema and dilatation of the superficial vascular plexus. The adjacent epidermis does not show necrosis. Acantholysis is variably present (*Fig. 17.104*).

Differential diagnosis

The main differential diagnosis is from toxic epidermal necrolysis (TEN), a severe variant of erythema multiforme usually due to a drug reaction. This, however, is uncommon in children. In TEN the skin changes are very widespread and mucosal involvement is common, whereas SSSS extends from the face and flexures and does not involve mucosae. The contrasting histology of the two conditions can be used with a frozen section technique to give a rapid diagnosis:[4,6]

- TEN is characterized by a subepidermal blister with a necrotic epidermal roof and a moderately intense lymphocytic infiltrate in the dermis
- SSSS is characterized by separation through the granular cell layer.

Alternatively, a Tzanck smear may be used, which reveals necrotic keratinocytes with inflammatory cells in TEN and viable acantholytic keratinocytes without inflammatory cells in SSSS.

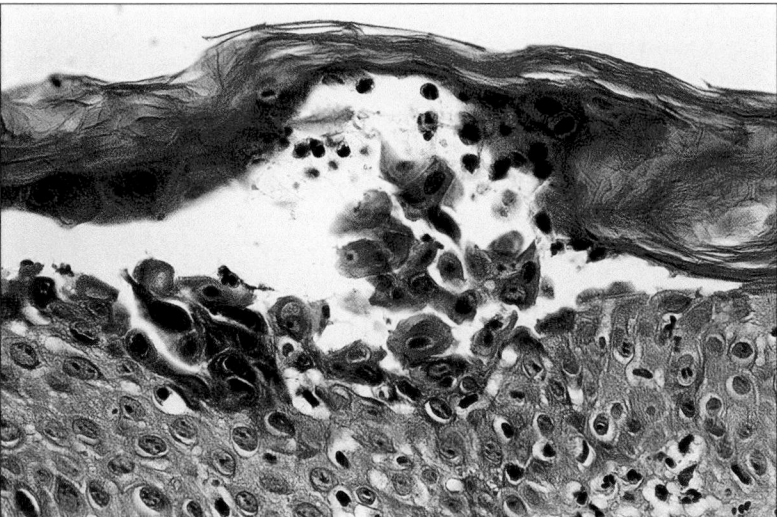

Fig. 17.104
Staphylococcal scalded skin syndrome: there is quite marked acantholysis in this example.

References

1. Lyell, A. (1967) A review of toxic epidermal necrolysis in Britain. *Br J Dermatol*, 79, 662–671.
2. Dowsett, E.G. (1984) The staphylococcal scalded skin syndrome. *J Hosp Infect*, 5, 347–354.
3. Findlay, G.H. (1987) Staphylococcal scalded (peeling) skin syndrome (SSSS) – the staphylococcal 'exfoliatin' syndromes. In: The dermatology of bacterial infections. Oxford: Blackwell, pp 352–355.
4. Resnick, S.D. (1992) Staphylococcal toxin-mediated syndromes in childhood. *Semin Dermatol*, 11, 11–18.
5. Melish, M.E. (1982) Staphylococci, streptococci and the skin. *Semin Dermatol*, 1, 101–109.
6. Amon, R.B., Dimond, R.L. (1975) Toxic epidermal necrolysis. Rapid differentiation between staphylococcal and drug induced disease. *Arch Dermatol*, 111, 1433–1437.
7. Ginsburg, C.M. (1991) Staphylococcal toxin syndromes. *Pediatr Infect Dis J*, 10, 319–321.
8. Loughead, J.L. (1992) Congenital staphylococcal scalded skin syndrome: report of a case. *Pediatr Infect Dis J*, 11, 413–414.
9. Blanc, M-F., Janier, M. (1986) Staphylococcies exfoliantes (SSSS) de l'adulto. *Ann Dermatol Venereol*, 113, 833–843.
10. Beers, B., Wilson, B. (1990) Adult staphylococcal scalded skin syndrome. *Int J Dermatol*, 29, 428–429.
11. Goldberg, N.S., Ahmed, T., Robinson, B. et al (1989) Staphylococcal scalded skin syndrome mimicking acute graft versus host disease in a bone marrow recipient. *Arch Dermatol*, 125, 85–87.
12. Richard, M., Mathieu-Serra, A. (1986) Staphylococcal scalded skin syndrome in a homosexual adult. *J Am Acad Dermatol*, 15, 385–389.
13. Donohue, D., Robinson, B., Goldberg, N.S. (1991) Staphylococcal scalded skin syndrome in a woman with chronic renal failure exposed to human immunodeficiency virus. *Cutis*, 47, 317–318.
14. Cribier, B., Piemont, Y., Grosshans, E. (1994) Staphylococcal scalded skin syndrome in adults. A clinical review illustrated with a new case. *J Am Acad Dermatol*, 30, 319–324.
15. Farrell, A.M., Ross, J.S., Umasankar, S. et al (1996) Staphylococcal scalded skin syndrome in an HIV-1 seropositive man. *Br J Dermatol*, 134, 962–965.
16. Oyake, S., Oh-i, T., Koga, M. (2001) Staphylococcal scalded skin syndrome in a healthy adult. *J Dermatol*, 28, 145–148.
17. Ladhani, S. (2001) Recent developments in staphylococcal scalded skin syndrome. *Clin Microbiol Infect*, 7, 301–307.
18. Lyell, A. (1983) The staphylococcal scalded skin in historical perspective. Emergence of dermopathic strains of Staphylococcal aureus and discovery of epidermolytic toxin. *J Am Acad Dermatol*, 9, 285–294.
19. Lina, G., Gillet, Y., Vandenesch, F. et al (1997) Toxin involvement is staphylococcal scalded skin syndrome. *Clin Infect Dis*, 25, 1369–1373.
20. Hanakawa, Y., Schechter, N.M., Lin, C. et al (2002) Molecular mechanisms of blister formation in bullous impetigo and staphylococcal scalded skin syndrome. *J Clin Invest*, 110, 53–60.
21. Amagai, M., Yamaguchi, T., Hanakawa, Y. et al (2002) Staphylococcal exfoliative toxin B specifically cleaves desmoglein 1. *J Invest Dermatol*, 118, 845–850.
22. Rogolsky, M., Wiley, B.B. (1977) Molecular and serologic differentiation of staphylococcal exfoliative toxin synthesized under chromosomal and plasmid control. *Infect Immunol*, 18, 487–494.
23. Fritsch, P., Elias, P., Varga, J. (1976) The fate of staphylococcal exfoliatin in newborn and adult mice. *Br J Dermatol*, 95, 275–284.
24. Nazzaro, V., Blanchet-Bardon, C., Larrégue, M. et al (1987) Staphylococcal scalded skin syndrome. Uno caso a comparsa precoce con studio ultrasctturale. *G Ital Derm Venereol*, 122, 343–348.
25. McKay, A.C.C., Arbuthnott, J.P., Lyell, A. (1975) Action of staphylococcal epidermolytic toxin on mouse skin: an electron microscopic study. *J Invest Dermatol*, 65, 423–429.

Erysipelas and cellulitis

Clinical features

Erysipelas

Erysipelas is classically a *S. pyogenes* (group A) infection of the skin of the face, characterized by a sharply outlined edematous, erythematous, tender and painful plaque (*Fig. 17.105*). The outer margin is elevated and contrasts with the adjacent normal skin. Towards the edge of the lesion there may be vesicles and hemorrhagic bullae. Other sites commonly affected include the feet and hands. Although *S. pyogenes* is the most common organism, it is not always possible to culture it, and other streptococci (group C or G) or *S. aureus* may occasionally be isolated.[1,2]

The classical presentation of erysipelas is most often on the face, but it has been suggested recently that the features of this condition are changing because it is becoming more common and is predominantly affecting the lower limbs.[3] A seasonal variation in incidence is not uniformly found.

The superficial infection of erysipelas is associated with a fever and malaise. It is similar in its presentation, etiology and associated symptoms to cellulitis, a spreading infection affecting deeper tissues. This lesion is again clearly demarcated, hot, red and painful, but without the elevated margin of erysipelas. An associated lymphangitis and lymphadenitis are common. The lesions may progress to pustulation, ulceration and necrosis; the last may involve underlying fascia and muscle, resulting in necrotizing fasciitis (see p. 876).[4]

Cellulitis

Cellulitis is similar to erysipelas, but tends to involve the deeper tissue and is seen most often on the legs, where it complicates tinea pedis or chronic lymphedema (*Fig. 17.106*).[5] Other potential risk factors include diabetes mellitus, leukemia, post saphenous venectomy and peripheral vascular disease. Patients with dry skin may also be susceptible.[6] Cellulitis is characterized by an expanding area of erythema.[2] Involvement of lymphatics in both erysipelas and cellulitis is characteristic, resulting in the edema which is sometimes associated with vesiculation (*Fig. 17.107*); infective damage to lymphatics in cellulitis may be the reason why this condition can become recurrent.

The term hemorrhagic cellulitis has been applied to an uncommon clinical syndrome caused by Gram-positive or Gram-negative organisms of non-cutaneous origin. Patients manifest with the abrupt onset of painful erythema on the lower extremities, followed by dermal hemorrhage and sloughing of the overlying epidermis.[7] There is usually a satisfactory response to a combination of antibiotics and corticosteroid therapy.

Pathogenesis and histological features

Minor trauma to the skin is important in the development of both erysipelas and cellulitis, but peripheral vascular disease, diabetes, lymphedema and alcohol abuse are additional predisposing factors.

In both erysipelas and cellulitis, *S. pyogenes* is the most common organism and the lesions are initiated by inoculation of minor abrasions or splits in the epidermis.[8] Proliferation of the organisms is associated with the production of enzymes (streptolysins, deoxyribonuclease B, hyaluronidase) which may be detected in rising titers and may therefore be useful diagnostically.[9] These enzymes are also important in facilitating the extension of the bacteria in the skin. Lymphatic involvement with obstruction is common, resulting in edema, and is associated with lymphangitis and lymphadenitis. In the more aggressive forms of cellulitis it is likely that other organisms (certainly *S. aureus* and some anaerobes) may be causative or synergistic.[10] There have been rare reports of severe cellulitis due to organisms such as *S. pneumoniae*, *Haemophilus influenzae* and *Nocardia otitidiscaviarum*.[11–13] In those forms of cellulitis in which necrosis is a more prominent feature bacterial toxins are an important mechanism.

Histologically, the conspicuous features of erysipelas and cellulitis are dermal edema and lymphatic dilatation. There is also a diffuse, heavy neutrophil infiltration with a limited localization around blood vessels. Vascular and lymphatic dilatation and red cell extravasation are variable features. In later stages some lymphocytes and histiocytes are also seen and granulation tissue may be present deep to the zone of subepidermal edema. When clinical vesicles or bullae are noted, there is a corresponding severe papillary edema merging with subepidermal vesiculation.[14]

In hemorrhagic cellulitis the bacterial lipopolysaccharide-induced or bacterial mitogen-induced release of tumor necrosis factor alpha (TNF-α) is thought to result in injury to endothelial cells and epidermal keratinocytes. DNA fragmentation and cell lysis may be the consequence of neutrophil degranulation and anti-DNase activation.[7] Histologically, there is necrosis of epidermal keratinocytes, necrotizing vasculitis affecting dermal blood vessels and large numbers of bacteria.[15]

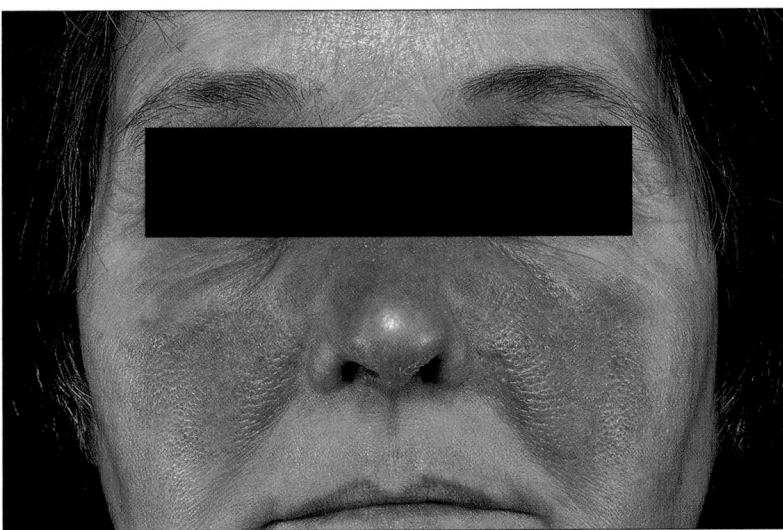

Fig. 17.105
Erysipelas: characteristic sharply demarcated erythematous and edematous plaque. By courtesy of R.A. Marsden, MD, St George's Hospital, London, UK.

References

1. Sheagren, J.N. (1985) Staphylococcal infections of the skin and skin structures. *Cutis*, **36**, 2–6.
2. Hook, E.W. (1987) Acute cellulitis. *Arch Dermatol*, **123**, 460–461.
3. Ronman, M., Suster, S., Schewach-Millet, M. et al (1985) Erysipelas. Changing faces. *Int J Dermatol*, **24**, 169–172.
4. Finch, R. (1988) Skin and soft tissue infections. *Lancet*, i, 164–167.
5. Wickboldt, L.G., Fenske, N.A. (1986) Streptococcal and staphylococcal infections of the skin. *Hosp Pract*, **21**, 41–47.
6. Koutkia, P., Mylonakis, E., Boyce, J. (1999) Cellulitis: evaluation of possible risk factors in hospitalized patients. *Diagn Microbiol Infect Dis*, **34**, 325–327.

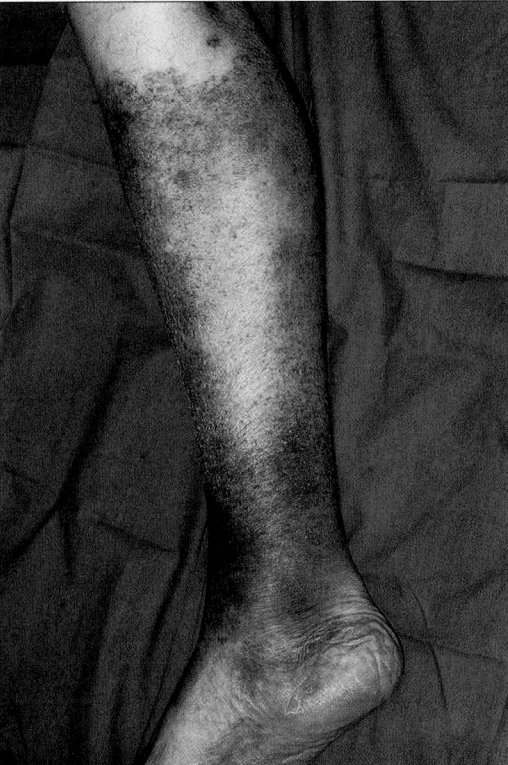

Fig. 17.106
Cellulitis: note the widespread erythema. The lower leg is a characteristic site. By courtesy of R.A. Marsden, MD, St George's Hospital, London, UK.

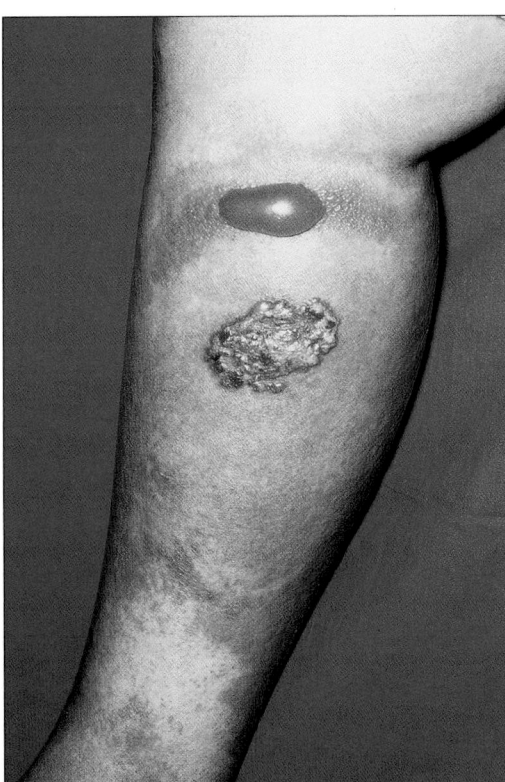

Fig. 17.107
Cellulitis: marked edema has resulted in vesiculation. By courtesy of R.A. Marsden, MD, St George's Hospital, London, UK.

7. Heng, M.C., Khoo, M., Cooperman, A. et al (1994) Hemorrhagic cellulitis: a syndrome associated with tumor necrosis factor-alpha. *Br J Dermatol*, **130**, 65–74.
8. Jorup-Rönström, C. (1986) Epidemiological, bacteriological and complicating features of erysipelas. *Scand J Infect Dis*, **18**, 519–524.
9. Leppard, B.J., Seal, D.V., Colman, G. et al (1985) The value of bacteriology and serology in the diagnosis of cellulitis and erysipelas. *Br J Dermatol*, **112**, 559–567.
10. Guenes, P.M., Brooks, J.S., Huttula, C.S. et al (1994) Staphylococcus aureus cellulitis: an unusual presentation. *Clin Pediatr (Phila)*, **33**, 319–320.
11. Lawlor, M.T., Crowe, H.M., Quintiliani, R. (1992) Cellulitis due to Streptococcus pneumoniae: case report and review. *Clin Infect Dis*, **14**, 247–250.

12. Lev, E.I., Onn, A., Levo, O.Y. et al (1999) Haemophilus influenzae biotype III cellulits in an adult. *Infection*, **27**, 42–43.
13. Clark, N.M., Braun, D.K., Pasternak, A. et al (1995) Primary cutaneous Nocardia otitidiscaviarum infection: case report and review. *Clin Infect Dis*, **20**, 1266–1270.
14. Guberman, D., Gilead, L.T., Zlotogorski, A. et al (1999) Bullous erysipelas: a retrospective study of 26 patients. *J Am Acad Dermatol*, **41** (5 Pt 1), 733–737.
15. Musher, D.M. (1980) Cutaneous and soft tissue manifestations of sepsis due to Gram negative enteric bacilli. *Rev Infect Dis*, **2**, 854–866.

Necrotizing fasciitis

Clinical features

Necrotizing fasciitis (NF) is an uncommon, rapidly progressive and potentially fatal bacterial infection of the subcutaneous soft tissues. In recent years there has been a dramatic resurgence in the number of reported cases.[1] NF may evolve following a surgical procedure (e.g. esthetic liposuction, cesarean section or excision of a skin lesion), minor trauma, seemingly insignificant scratches, in the presence of a chronic wound, or even in apparently intact skin.[2–4] NF occurs predominantly in middle-aged individuals, although the pediatric population may also be affected.[1,5–8] Patients with underlying diabetes mellitus and iatrogenic immunosuppression are particularly susceptible.[5,9–12] NF is a well-recognized complication of childhood varicella.[8] Many reported cases have developed after intramuscular injection of non-steroidal anti-inflammatory drugs.[5,13–15] Rare cases have occurred following the bite of a spider.[16] NF may be a rare complication of fistulating Crohn's disease.[17] Reported mortality ranges from 18 to 53%.[5,8,12] An increased fatality rate may be encountered in the elderly and in those with worsening symptoms and signs within the first 48 hours of hospital admission.[9]

Although group A β-hemolytic streptococci (so-called 'flesh-eating' bacteria) were first recognized as a prime etiological agent, a number of other aerobic and even anaerobic pathogens have been implicated.[1,18,19] It has become increasingly apparent that NF very often is a polymicrobial condition.[19,20] In some series, *Staphylococcus aureus* is the most frequently cultured organism.[19,20] Less often, other streptococci have been identified; these include group B and group G β-hemolytic streptococci, *Streptococcus pneumoniae* and anaerobic streptococci (*Peptostreptococcus* spp.).[14,19,21–23] Other bacteria implicated include marine organisms (*Vibrio vulnificus*, *V. parahaemolyticus*, *Photobacterium damsela*), members of the family Enterobacteriaceae, *Serratia marcescens*, *Pseudomonas* spp., *Clostridium* spp. and *Bacteroides* spp.[6,11,19,24–27] Meleney's postoperative progressive synergistic gangrene (Meleney's gangrene) is synonymous with polymicrobial NF arising as a complication of surgical trauma.[28] The latter condition may be clinically indistinguishable from postsurgical cutaneous amebiasis.[28,29]

The clinical presentation may be fulminant, acute or subacute.[5] NF commences as an ill-defined area of erythema. It is not uncommon for evolving NF to be mistaken for cellulitis or an insignificant wound infection, especially when the hallmark cutaneous necrosis is not established. This may result in a potentially life-threatening delay in diagnosis and aggressive surgical debridement.[30] The clinical features of established NF include severe pain, indurated edema, skin necrosis, cyanosis, bullae, crepitation, muscle weakness and malodorous exudates (*Fig. 17.108*).[15] Patients often have other systemic manifestations of severe sepsis, including hypotension, tachycardia, tachypnea, oliguria and mental confusion.[15,31] In NF caused by streptococcal species, the latter signs are usually attributable to streptococcal toxic shock syndrome.[13] Radiographs may reveal gas in the affected soft tissues.[31] NF occurs mainly on the extremities, although almost any site may be affected, including the abdominal wall, chest wall, eyelids and periorbital region, and the head and neck region.[9,32–35] Periumbilical NF may occur in

newborn infants.[7] The Waterhouse–Friderichsen syndrome is a potential complication of NF.[36]

Fournier's gangrene is a clinical variant of NF which involves the penis, scrotum, perineum and abdominal wall in men and (less often) the vulva in women.[37–39] An obliterative endarteritic process affecting the small branches of the superficial branch of the internal pudendal artery may play a key pathogenetic role.[40] Because of a response to corticosteroids, Fournier's gangrene may be perceived as a localized vasculitis.[41] In addition to the usual risk factors such as diabetes mellitus or immunosuppression, rare associations include vasectomy or unhygienic ritual circumcision.[39] The reported mortality of this polymicrobial synergistic necrotizing infection is in the order of 16–20%.[37,39,42] Extent of infection is a significant predictor of clinical outcome.[42]

Pathogenesis and histological features

NF due to invasive group A β-hemolytic streptococcal infection is associated predominantly with M types 1 and 3, which produce either pyrogenic exotoxin A or B, or both.[18] Tissue invasion is facilitated by CD44-mediated cell signaling with subsequent manipulation of the host cytoskeleton.[43,44] Superantigens and Th1 cytokines appear to play a critical role in severe group A invasive streptococcal infections.[45] Protein S deficiency may be responsible for the necrosis.[46]

Staphylococcus aureus may potentiate the β-hemolytic streptococcal infection in NF.[29]

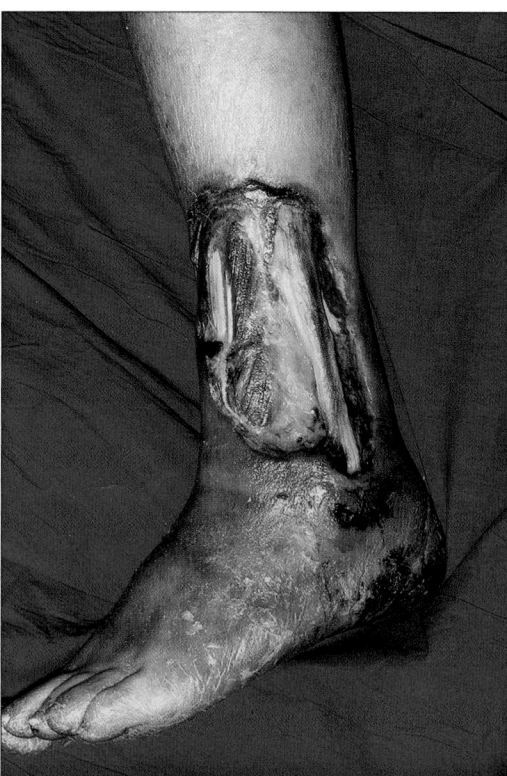

Fig. 17.108
Necrotizing fasciitis: this example has resulted in exposure of muscle and tendons. By courtesy of R.A. Marsden, MD, St George's Hospital, London, UK.

An adequately sized specimen inclusive of subcutaneous soft tissue is essential for diagnosis. The histological appearances are those of a severe necrotizing process with edema, necrosis and inflammation involving skin and subcutaneous tissue, including fascial planes (*Figs 17.109, 17.110*).[47] Deep biopsies or debridement specimens containing underlying skeletal muscle may exhibit concomitant myonecrosis.[1] Vascular thrombosis is encountered at all levels, and secondary vasculitic alterations are not uncommon. Hyaline necrosis of sweat glands has been described.[47] The presence of large numbers of bacteria often results in diffuse basophilia of the tissue on low power examination. A Gram's stain or Brown–Hopps stain confirms the latter (*Fig. 17.111*).

Although the histological picture is sufficiently distinctive to facilitate a diagnosis of NF, microbiological examination (including aerobic and anaerobic tissue culture) is of paramount importance in the identification of the specific infective etiological agent(s). Intraoperative frozen section has a particularly useful role to play, not only in early diagnosis but also in assessing the viability of surgical margins at the time of debridement.[48] PCR detection of streptococcal pyrogenic exotoxin B may be useful in confirming group A streptococcal infection when cultures are negative or unavailable.[49]

Differential diagnosis

Necrotizing cellulitis has a similar etiopathogenesis to NF but shows no extension of the necrotizing inflammatory process into subcutaneous tissue planes. This diagnosis should be made with caution and only when there is a complete absence of subcutaneous involvement in a specimen that is of sufficient depth. NF is invariably associated with necrotizing inflammation of the dermis. Furthermore, necrotizing cellulitis may be a harbinger of impending NF. Tissue autolysis with bacterial overgrowth may closely mimic NF, especially if tissue is obtained from a patient

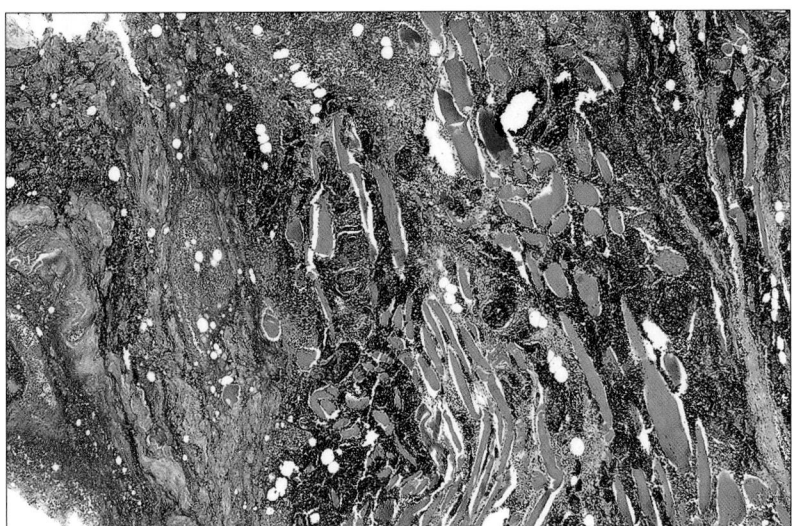

Fig. 17.109
Necrotizing fasciitis: there is intense acute inflammation of the fascia with involvement of the adjacent muscle.

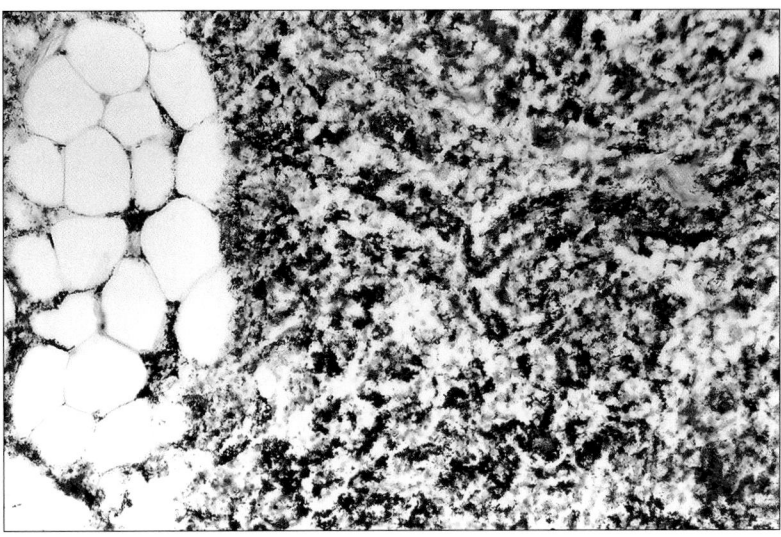

Fig. 17.111
Necrotizing fasciitis: innumerable Gram-positive cocci are present.

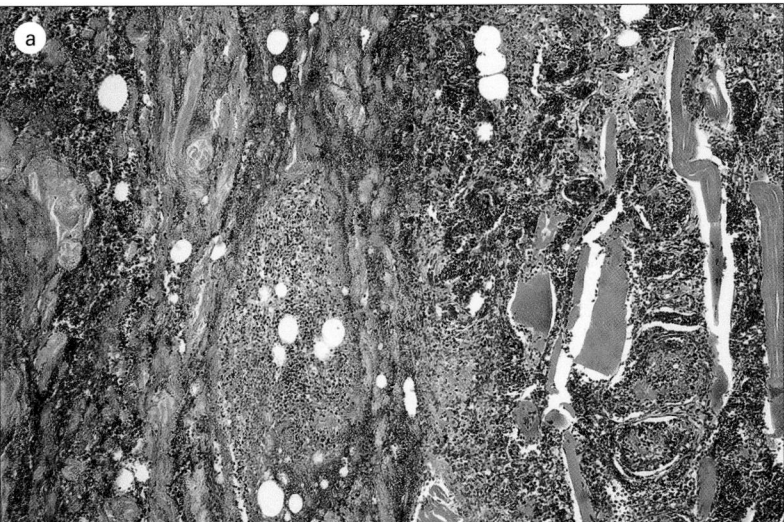

Fig. 17.110
(a, b) Necrotizing fasciitis: there is an almost pure neutrophil infiltrate with necrosis.

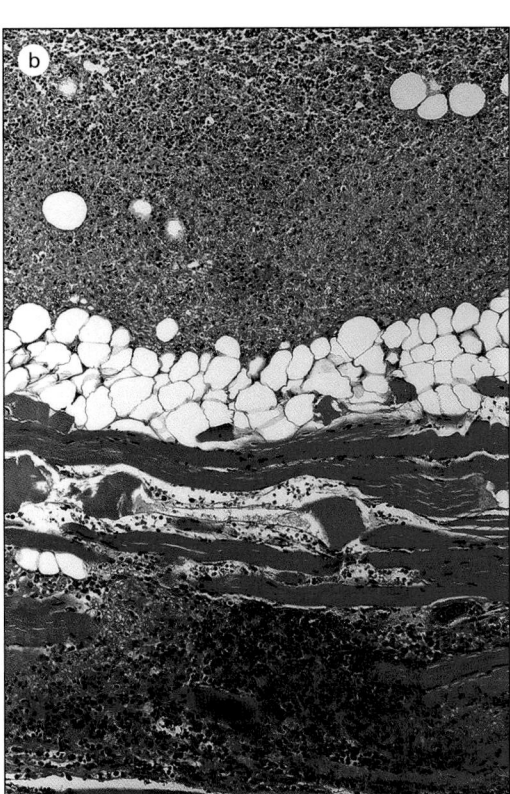

with a relatively minor cutaneous infection and the specimen was not placed in the appropriate formalin fixative prior to submission to the laboratory.

NF is distinguished from pyoderma gangrenosum and Sweet's syndrome by the absence of true tissue necrosis and demonstrable bacterial organisms by culture or appropriate stains in the latter two conditions. Although there is frequent dermal infiltration by polymorphonuclear leukocytes in pyoderma gangrenosum and invariable neutrophilic dermatosis in Sweet's syndrome, the acute inflammatory changes in both conditions are centered on the dermis rather than the subcutis. Vasculitic alterations may occur in both pyoderma gangrenosum and NF but are typically absent in Sweet's syndrome.

References

1. Haywood, C.T., McGeer, A., Low, D.E. (1999) Clinical experience with 20 cases of group A streptococcus necrotizing fasciitis and myonecrosis: 1995 to 1997. *Plast Reconstr Surg*, **103**, 1567–1573.
2. Heitmann, C., Czermak, C., Germann, G. (2000) Rapidly fatal necrotizing fasciitis after aesthetic liposuction. *Aesthetic Plast Surg*, **24**, 344–347.
3. Krowlikowski, A., Gowri, V., Radha, K. (2000) Necrotizing fasciitis of abdominal wall after caesarean section. *Saudi Med J*, **21**, 399–400.
4. Gibbon, K.L., Bewley, A.P. (1999) Acquired necrotizing fasciitis following excision of malignant melanoma. *Br J Dermatol*, **141**, 717–719.
5. Jarrett, P., Rademaker, M., Duffill, M. (1997) The clinical spectrum of necrotizing fasciitis. A review of 15 cases. *Aust N Z Med J*, **27**, 29–34.
6. Brook, I. (1996) Aerobic and anaerobic microbiology of necrotizing fasciitis in children. *Pediatr Dermatol*, **13**, 281–284.
7. Weber, D.M., Freeman, N.V., Elhag, K.M. (2001) Periumbilical necrotizing fasciitis in the newborn. *Eur J Pediatr Surg*, **11**, 86–91.
8. Fustes-Morales, A., Guitierrez-Castrellon, P., Duran-Mckinster, C. et al (2001) Necrotizing fasciitis: report of 39 pediatric cases. *Arch Dermatol*, **138**, 893–899.
9. Hung, C.C., Chang, S.C., Lin, S.F. et al (1996) Clinical manifestations, microbiology and prognosis of 42 patients with necrotizing fasciitis. *J Formos Med Assoc*, **95**, 917–922.
10. Snider, J.M., McNabey, M.K., Perberton, L.B. (1993) Necrotizing fasciitis secondary to discoid lupus erythematosus. *Am Surg*, **59**, 164–167.
11. Huang, J.W., Fang, C.T., Hung, K.Y. et al (1999) Necrotizing fasciitis caused by Serratia marcescens in two patients receiving corticosteroid therapy. *J Formos Med Assoc*, **98**, 851–854.
12. Brandt, M.M., Corpron, C.A., Wahl, W.L. (2000) Necrotizing soft tissue infections: a surgical disease. *Am Surg*, **66**, 970–971.
13. Barnham, M.R., Weightman, N.C., Anderson, A.W. et al (2002) Streptococcal toxic shock syndrome: a description of 14 cases from North Yorkshire, UK. *Clin Microbiol Infect*, **8**, 174–181.
14. Frick, S., Cerny, A. (2001) Necrotizing fasciitis due to Streptococcus pneumoniae after intramuscular injection of nonsteroidal anti-inflammatory drugs: report of 2 cases and review. *Clin Infect Dis*, **33**, 740–744.
15. Roujeau, J.C. (2001) Necrotizing fasciitis. Clinical criteria and risk factors. *Ann Dermatol Venereol*, **128**, 376–381.
16. Majeski, J. (2001) Necrotizing fasciitis developing from a brown recluse spider bite. *Am Surg*, **67**, 188–190.
17. Panter, S.J., Bramble, M.G., Bell, J.R. (2001) Necrotizing fasciitis in Crohn's disease. *Eur J Gastroenterol Hepatol*, **13**, 429–431.
18. Stevens, D.L. (1999) The flesh-eating bacterium: what's next? *J Infect Dis*, **179** (Suppl. 2), S366–S374.
19. Brook, I., Frazier, E.H. (1995) Clinical and microbiological features of necrotizing fasciitis. *J Clin Microbiol*, **33**, 2382–2387.
20. Singh, G., Sinha, S.K., Adhikary, S. et al (1996) Bacteriology of necrotizing infections of soft tissues. *Aust N Z J Surg*, **66**, 747–750.
21. Gardam, M.A., Low, D.E., Saginur, R. et al (1998) Group B streptococcal necrotizing fasciitis and streptococcal toxic shock-like syndrome in adults. *Arch Intern Med*, **158**, 1704–1708.
22. Sharma, M., Khatib, R., Fakih, M. (2002) Clinical characteristics of necrotizing fasciitis caused by group G streptococcus: case report and review of the literature. *Scand J Infect Dis*, **34**, 468–471.
23. Humar, D., Datta, V., Bast, D.J. et al (2002) Streptolysin A and necrotising infections produced by group G streptococcus. *Lancet*, **359**, 124–129.
24. Howard, R.J., Pessa, M.E., Brennaman, B.H. et al (1985) Necrotizing soft tissue infections caused by marine vibrios. *Surgery*, **98**, 126–130.
25. Bisharat, N., Agmon, V., Finketstein, R. et al (1999) Clinical, epidemiological and microbiological features of Vibrio vulnificus biogroup 3 causing outbreaks of wound infection and bacteraemia in Israel. Israel Vibrio Study Group. *Lancet*, **354**, 1421–1424.
26. Barber, G.R., Swygert, J.S. (2000) Necrotizing fasciitis due to Photobacterium damsela in a man lashed by a stingray. *N Engl J Med*, **342**, 824.
27. Liangpunsakul, S., Pursell, K. (2001) Community-acquired necrotizing fasciitis caused by Serratia marcescens: case report and review. *Eur J Clin Microbiol Infect Dis*, **20**, 509–510.
28. Davson, J., Jones, D.M., Turner, L. (1988) Diagnosis of Meleney's synergistic gangrene. *Br J Surg*, **75**, 267–271.
29. Kingston, D., Seal, D.V. (1990) Current hypotheses on synergistic microbial gangrene. *Br J Surg*, **77**, 260–264.
30. Urschel, J.D. (1999) Necrotizing soft tissue infections. *Postgrad Med J*, **75**, 645–649.
31. Wall, D.B., Klein, S.R., Black, S. et al (2000) A simple model to help distinguish necrotizing fasciitis from nonnecrotizing soft tissue infection. *J Am Coll Surg*, **191**, 227–231.
32. Roy, P.K., Patel, S.C., Kataria, Y.P. (2001) Necrotizing fasciitis of abdominal wall in AIDS. *Dig Dis Sci*, **46**, 1139–1142.
33. Safran, D.B., Sullivan, W.G. (2001) Necrotizing fasciitis of the chest wall. *Ann Thorac Surg*, **72**, 1362–1364.
34. Costet-Fighiera, C., Lagier, J., Bastiani-Griffet, F. et al (2002) Necrotizing fasciitis of the eyelids and orbit: a life-threatening ophthalmological emergency. *J Fr Ophthalmol*, **25**, 375–378.
35. Chattar-Cora, D., Tulsyan, N., Cudjoe, E.A. et al (2002) Necrotizing fasciitis of the head and neck: a report of two patients and review. *Head Neck*, **24**, 497–501.
36. Dunstan, S.P. (1999) Reminder – necrotizing fasciitis complicated by Waterhouse–Friderichsen syndrome. *Br J Oral Maxillofac Surg*, **37**, 217–218.
37. Basoglu, M., Gul, O., Yildrigan, I. et al (1997) Fournier's gangrene: review of fifteen cases. *Am Surg*, **63**, 1019–1021.
38. Norton, K.S., Johnson, L.W., Perry, T. et al (2002) Management of Fournier's gangrene: an eleven year retrospective analysis of early recognition, diagnosis, and treatment. *Am Surg*, **68**, 709–713.
39. Eke, N. (2000) Fournier's gangrene: a review of 1726 cases. *Br J Surg*, **87**, 718–728.
40. Negri, S., Petraglia, B., Azzolini, D. (1996) Fournier's gangrene: description of a case. *Pathologica*, **88**, 303–306.
41. Schultz, E.S., Diepgen, T.L., von den Driesch, P. (1995) Systemic corticosteroids are important in the treatment of Fournier's gangrene: a case report. *Br J Dermatol*, **133**, 633–635.
42. Dahm, P., Roland, F.H., Vaslef, S.N. et al (2000) Outcome analysis in patients with primary necrotizing fasciitis of the male genitalia. *Urology*, **56**, 31–36.
43. Cywes, C., Wessels, M.R. (2001) Group A streptococcus tissue invasion by CD44-mediated cell signalling. *Nature*, **414**, 648–652.
44. Dombek, P.E., Cue, D., Sedgewick, J. et al (1999) High-frequency intracellular invasion of epithelial cells by serotype M1 group A streptococci: M1 protein-mediated invasion and cytoskeletal rearrangements. *Mol Microbiol*, **31**, 859–870.
45. Joly, P., Chosidow, O., Gouault-Heilman, M. et al (1993) Protein S deficiency in a patient with necrotizing cellulitis. *Clin Exp Dermatol*, **18**, 305–308.
46. Norrby-Teglund, A., Thulin, P., Gan, B.S. et al (2001) Evidence for superantigen involvement in severe group A streptococcal tissue infections. *J Infect Dis*, **184**, 853–860.
47. Umbert, I.J., Winkelmann, R.K., Oliver, G.F. et al (1989) Necrotizing fasciitis: a clinical, microbiologic, and histopathologic study of 14 patients. *J Am Acad Dermatol*, **20**, 774–781.
48. Stamenkovic, I., Lew, P.D. (1984) Early recognition of potentially fatal necrotizing fasciitis. The use of frozen-section biopsy. *N Engl J Med*, **310**, 1689–1693.
49. Louie, L., Simor, A.E., Louie, M. et al (1998) Diagnosis of group A streptococcal necrotizing fasciitis by using PCR to amplify the streptococcal pyrogenic exotoxin B gene. *J Clin Microbiol*, **36**, 1769–1771.

Infective folliculitis

Clinical features

Infection of hair follicles is probably the commonest form of skin infection. It is usually due to *S. aureus* (impetigo of Bockhart) and although disfiguring is self-limiting.[1–4] Pustular folliculitis usually implies infection of the ostium and upper part of the follicle. It presents as numerous small red and tender pustules, which discharge pus and quickly resolve without scarring (*Fig. 17.112*). Staphylococcal carriers tend to have recurrent infections.[5]

P. aeruginosa has recently been shown to be the cause of epidemics of folliculitis associated with swimming pools, whirlpools or jacuzzis.[6,7] These shared facilities can be infected by *Pseudomonas* if they became alkaline and if the chlorine content drops. Nevertheless, moisture and occlusion are necessary to affect normal skin. For this reason lesions of this type are found only under the area covered by bathing costumes. Other Gram-negative bacteria such as *Klebsiella* spp., *Escherichia coli*, *Enterobacter* spp. and *Proteus* spp. have been implicated in the pathogenesis of folliculitis in patients receiving long-term antibiotic therapy for treatment of acne or rosacea.[8] Extensive folliculitis may be an early manifestation of HIV infection.[1] *Micrococcus* spp., which are considered to be commensal organisms, may be a cause of folliculitis in patients with HIV infection.[9]

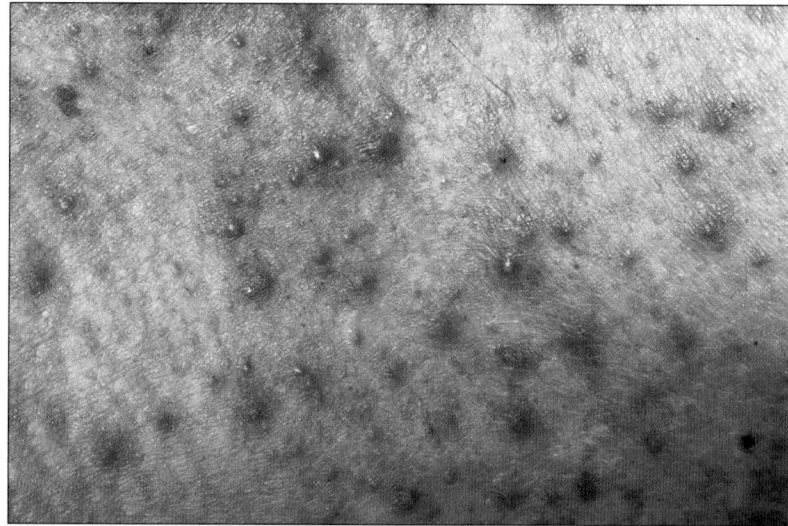

Fig. 17.112
Folliculitis: characteristic small pustules with surrounding erythema. By courtesy of R.A. Marsden, MD, St George's Hospital, London, UK.

A furuncle or boil is a more exuberant form of suppurative folliculitis. It is common in young adults and usually affects the skin of the face, neck, buttocks and axillae (*Figs 17.113–17.115*).[1] Lesions can be up to 2 cm across and the inflammation is not confined within the follicle, but is associated with much surrounding erythema and often systemic symptoms. After discharge of the pustular necrotic core the lesion heals rapidly, but with scarring. A deep folliculitis due to *S. aureus* may affect the beard area; this form is termed sycosis or folliculitis barbae.

A carbuncle is a variant of a furuncle with multiple tracks and routes of discharge. It is most commonly seen in older men and may be associated with systemic symptoms.[1]

Acute paronychia is comparable to a folliculitis in that it is a painful suppurative infection of the nail fold, most commonly caused by *S. aureus*; it heals rapidly on release of the pus (*Fig. 17.116*). A rare scarring alopecia in which *S. aureus* has been implicated is termed folliculitis decalvans.[10] Although the scalp is predominantly affected, lesions may also be found in the axillae and pubic region (*Fig. 17.117*).

Pathogenesis and histological features

Many cases of superficial suppurative folliculitis are associated with *S. aureus*. The infection is not due to a break in the epithelium, but growth occurs with the ostium of the follicle and may progress more deeply around the hair shaft. There is an associated accumulation of neutrophils, forming an abscess associated with spongiosis and infiltration of the adjacent follicular epithelium. The superficial suppurative folliculitis may discharge through the ostium and rapidly resolve. Alternatively it may progress more deeply and rupture through the follicular epithelium; the abscess then extends into perifollicular dermis and surrounds the whole follicle. The follicular epithelium and hair shaft with pus then form the purulent necrotic core of the furuncle or boil. Healing is

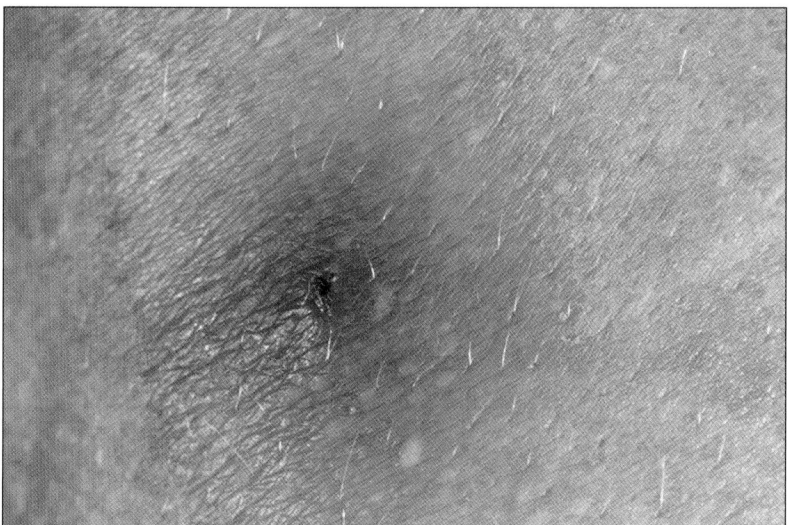

Fig. 17.113
Furuncle: early lesion characterized by edema and erythema. By courtesy of the Institute of Dermatology, London, UK.

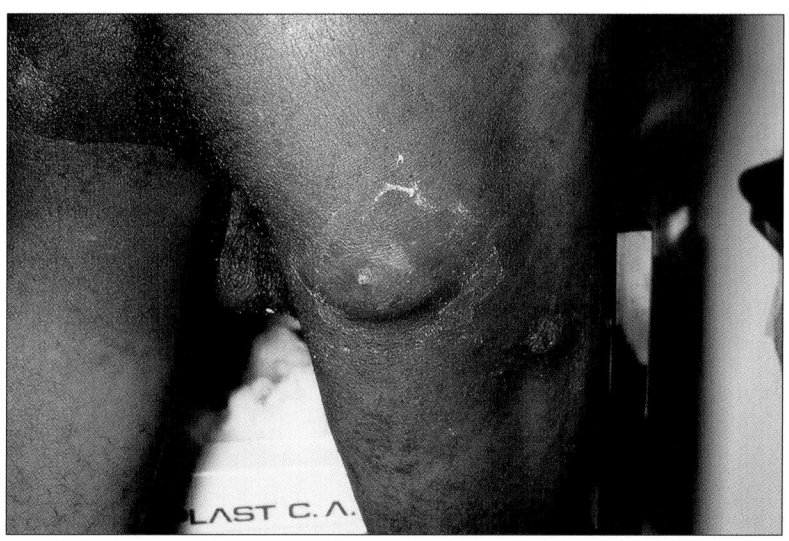

Fig. 17.115
Furuncle: note the large swelling on the thigh. This patient was HIV positive. By courtesy of C. Furlonge, MD, Port of Spain, Trinidad.

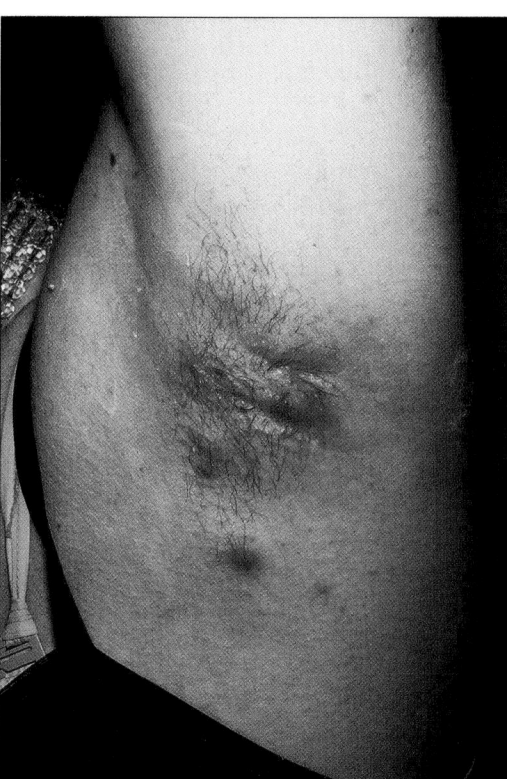

Fig. 17.114
Furuncle: multiple erythematous nodules in the axilla, which is a commonly affected site. The lesions are exquisitely painful. By courtesy of R.A. Marsden, MD, .St George's Hospital, London, UK.

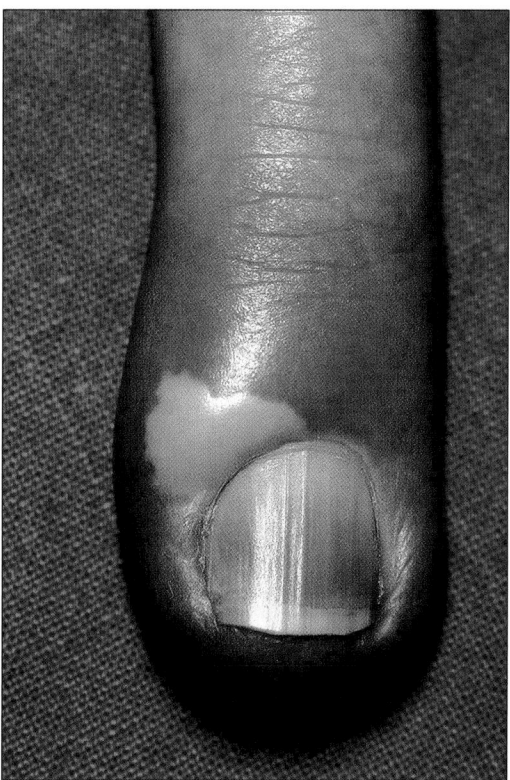

Fig. 17.116
Acute paronychia: pus and erythema are present. By courtesy of E.E. Gluckman, MD, King's College Hospital, London, UK.

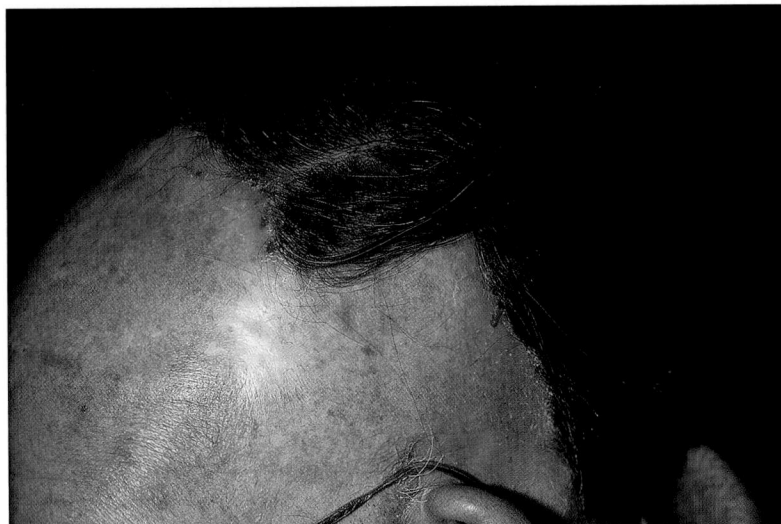

Fig. 17.117
Folliculitis decalvans: there is severe scarring with alopecia. Erosions, crusting and pustules are seen at the hairline. By courtesy of M.M. Black, MD, Institute of Dermatology, London, UK.

preceded by a lymphohistiocytic or even granulomatous phase and is followed by scarring and loss of hair in the involved area. A carbuncle is associated with more persistent suppuration, much more fibrosis and granulation tissue.

Although most of the suppurative forms of folliculitis are due to *S. aureus*, other causal conditions include dermatophytosis, herpes simplex and syphilis; the features of these infections are described under the appropriate headings.

References

1. Finch, R. (1988) Skin and soft tissue infections. *Lancet*, i, 164–167.
2. Roodyn, L. (1960) Epidemiology of staphylococcal infections. *J Hygiene (Cambridge)*, 58, 1–10.
3. Roodyn, L. (1960) Recurrent staphylococcal infections and the duration of the carrier state. *J Hygiene (Cambridge)*, 58, 11–19.
4. Valentine, F.C.O., Hall-Smith, S.P. (1952) Superficial staphylococcal infection. *Lancet*, ii, 351–354.
5. Sheagren, J.N. (1985) Staphylococcal infections of the skin and skin structures. *Cutis*, 36, 2–6.
6. Ratnam, S., Hogan, K., March, S.B. et al (1986) Whirlpool-associated folliculitis caused by Pseudomonas aeruginosa: report of an outbreak and review. *J Clin Microbiol*, 23, 655–659.
7. Zichichi, L., Asta, G., Noto, G. (2000) Pseudomonas aeruginosa folliculitis after shower/bath exposure. *Int J Dermatol*, 39, 270–273.
8. Neubert, U., Jansen, T., Plewig, G. (1999) Bacteriologic and immunologic aspects of Gram-negative folliculitis: a study of 46 patients. *Int J Dermatol*, 38, 270–274.
9. Smith, K.J., Neafie, R., Yeager, J. et al (1999) Micrococcus folliculitis in HIV-1 disease. *Br J Dermatol*, 141, 558–561.
10. Brozena, S.J., Cohen, L.E., Fenska, N.A. (1988) Folliculitis decalvans – response to rifampicin. *Cutis*, 42, 512–516.

Folliculitis keloidalis nuchae

Clinical features

This deep and scarring folliculitis and perifolliculitis (sometimes known as acne keloidalis) occurs on the back of the neck (lower occipital/nuchal region) of postpubertal males. It occurs more commonly in black than in white men and does not appear to develop in females.[1,2] It presents in the early stages with inflamed papules and pustules, but no consistent organisms are found. Patients may complain of itching, burning or pain and advanced lesions may be foul smelling.[1] Each lesion is complicated by dense scarring, producing a keloid-like appearance. Scarring alopecia is a complication.[2] The condition has recently been reported in Caucasian organ transplant recipients on cylosporin therapy[3] (see also p. 1098).

Pathogenesis and histological features

The pathogenesis is unknown. Any bacteria identified probably represent a secondary phenomenon. It is doubtful whether poor hygiene is a factor. There may be an element of pseudofolliculitis (see below) since the condition is common in Afro-Caribbeans and is worsened by close shaving of the neck. The use of pomades and wearing tight collars is said to exacerbate the condition.[1] The term acne keloidalis is a misnomer, as the disorder has nothing to do with acne vulgaris or its variants.

The follicle, which may contain pus extending through the epithelium, is initially surrounded by a lymphocytic and neutrophil infiltrate; later there are large numbers of plasma cells.[4] The perifollicular inflammation is maximal at the level of the isthmus and lower infundibulum.[2,5] The condition is more often seen at a later stage, however, when there is marked fibrosis accompanying free, broken hair shafts, many of which are surrounded by a foreign body giant cell reaction. Hyalinization as seen in a true keloid is only very occasionally a feature. Complete loss of the sebaceous glands is a frequent occurrence.[2,5]

References

1. Dinehart, S.M., Herzberg, A.J., Kerns, B.J. et al (1989) Acne keloidalis: a review. *J Dermatol Surg Oncol*, 15, 642–647.
2. Sperling, L.C., Homoky, C., Pratt, L. et al (2000) Acne keloidalis is a form of primary scarring alopecia. *Arch Dermatol*, 136, 479–484.
3. Azurdia, R.M., Graham, R.M., Weismann, K. et al (2000) Acne keloidalis in Caucasian patients on cyclosporin following organ transplantation. *Br J Dermatol*, 143, 465–467.
4. Cosman, B., Wolff, M. (1972) Acne keloidalis. *Plast Reconstr Surg*, 50, 25–30.
5. Herzberg, A.J., Dinehart, S.M., Kerns, B.J. et al (1990) Acne keloidalis. Transverse microscopy, immunohistochemistry, and electron microscopy. *Am J Dermatopathol*, 12, 109–121.

Pseudofolliculitis

Clinical features

Pseudofolliculitis (pseudofolliculitis barbae) presents with an acneiform papular and pustular eruption on the beard area. Comedones are not a feature. It develops as a consequence of the re-entry of a terminal hair shaft through the epidermis and occurs most often in males with curly hair, but is also seen in women in the pubic region following cosmetic shaving.[1–3] Pseudofolliculitis occurs predominantly in patients of African, African–American and Hispanic origin.[3] The pathogenesis appears to be multifactorial, and seems to relate to the shape of the hair follicle, the hair cuticle and the direction of hair growth.[3] The penetration is facilitated by the sharp ends produced on hairs by shaving and the curliness of the hair bringing the cut end back into contact with the skin surface. Alternatively, the penetration may occur laterally through the superficial part of the follicular infundibulum following partial retraction of the hair after close shaving (see also p. 1124).

Histological features

The process is not a true folliculitis, and is not usually associated with infection. The re-entry of the hair shaft provokes a foreign body granulomatous reaction with accompanying fibrosis. The inflammation is predominantly histiocytic with occasional multinucleate giant cells. Secondary infection may result in superimposed suppuration. Resolution occurs rapidly, with slight scarring, once the hair shaft is removed.

References

1. Smith, J.D., Odom, R.B. (1977) Pseudofolliculitis capitis. *Arch Dermatol*, **113**, 328–329.
2. Alexander, A.M. (1974) Pseudofolliculitis diathesis. *Arch Dermatol*, **109**, 729–730.
3. Perry, P.K., Cook-Bolden, F.E., Rahman, Z. et al (2002) Defining pseudofolliculitis barbae in 2001: a review of the literature and current trends. *J Am Acad Dermatol*, **46** (2 Suppl.), S113–S119.

Meningococcal septicemia

Clinical features

Meningococal septicemia is due to the Gram-positive diplococcus *Neisseria meningitidis*.[1,2] In its acute form this is a very serious condition with a high mortality, which affects children in seasonal epidemics. It is spread via droplet inhalation from upper respiratory tract infections. Children develop widespread purpura that shows a predilection for the trunk and limbs. Ecchymoses may also be a feature. In the more chronic variant, patients present with vasculitis-like lesions, particularly nodules and palpable purpura.

Pathogenesis and histological features

The histological features are essentially those of a leukocytoclastic vasculitis.[3] Superimposed DIC may also be present (see purpura fulminans, p. 763). The hemorrhagic skin lesions and vascular thromboses are attributable to upregulation of tissue factor leading to coagulation, and by inhibition of fibrinolysis by plasminogen activator inhibitor.[4] Impairment of the protein C anticoagulation pathway also plays an important role.[5]

Diplococci may be demonstrable in Gram-stained sections, especially in biopsies obtained from purpuric lesions.[3] Culture or Gram staining of aspirates or biopsies of skin lesions may facilitate early diagnosis.[6]

References

1. Sotto, M.N., Lnager, B., Hoshino-Shimizu, S. et al (1976) Pathogenesis of cutaneous lesions in acute meningococcemia in humans: light, immunofluorescent and electron microscopic studies of skin biopsy specimens. *J Infect Dis*, **133**, 506–514.
2. Hill, W.R., Kinney, T.D. (1947) The cutaneous lesions in acute meningococcemia – a clinical and pathologic study. *JAMA*, **134**, 513–518.
3. Ramesh, V., Mukherjee, A., Chandra, M. et al (1990) Clinical, histopathologic and immunologic features of cutaneous lesions in acute meningococcaemia. *Ind J Med Res*, **91**, 27–32.
4. Brandtzaeg, P., Bjerre, A., Ovstebo, R. et al (2001) Neisseria meningitidis lipopolysaccharides in human pathology. *J Endotoxin Res*, **7**, 401–420.
5. Faust, S.N., Levin, M., Harrison, O.B. et al (2001) Dysfunction of endothelial protein C activation in severe meningococcal sepsis. *N Engl J Med*, **345**, 408–416.
6. van Deuren, M., van Dijke, B.J., Koopman, R.J. et al (1993) Rapid diagnosis of acute meningococcal infections by needle aspiration or biopsy of skin lesions. *BMJ*, **306**, 1229–1232.

Gonorrhea

Clinical features

This common venereal disease is due to infection with the Gram-negative intracellular diplococcus *Neisseria gonorrhoeae*, which especially affects the mucous membranes. In males this results particularly in purulent urethritis, although gonococcal proctitis and oropharyngitis may also be seen. Females most often develop endocervicitis. Urethritis and proctitis can also be features.

Systemic gonococcal infection most commonly affects the skin, but may also result in arthritis and less often endocarditis or meningitis. Patients present with small numbers of erythematous macules that progress to painful papular, petechial or pustular lesions that particularly affect the distal limbs (*Fig. 17.118*).[1] They measure from 1 to 2 mm up to 2 cm in diameter. Rarely, however, patients present with primary cutaneous (genital and extragenital) involvement.[1] Cellulitis, pustules, ulcers and furuncle-like lesions have been documented.[2,3] Pyogenic granuloma-like lesions of the penile shaft have also been described.[4] Primary digital gonorrhea has been recorded.[2]

Pathogenesis and histological features

Disseminated lesions show variable epidermal changes ranging from edema accompanied by a neutrophil infiltrate with purpura, to vesiculation, pustulation and eventually necrosis.[1] In the dermis the histological features are essentially those of a neutrophil-mediated acute vasculitis, often accompanied by thrombosis.[5] Very occasionally Gram-negative diplococci may be identified.

References

1. Buntin, D.M., Rosen, T., Lesher, J.L. et al (1991) Sexually transmitted diseases: bacterial infections. *J Am Acad Dermatol*, **25**, 287–299.
2. Scott, M.J. Jr, Scott, M.J. Sr. (1982) Primary cutaneous Neisseria gonorrhoeae infections. *Arch Dermatol*, **118**, 351–352.
3. Rosen, T. (1982) Unusual presentations of gonorrhea. *J Am Acad Dermatol*, **6**, 369–372.
4. Scott, M.J., Thomsen, J. (1950) Primary cutaneous Neisseria gonorrhoeae infections. *Am J Syphilis*, **34**, 262–264.
5. Shapiro, L., Teisch, J.A., Brownstein, M.H. (1973) Dermatohistopathology of chronic gonococcal sepsis. *Arch Dermatol*, **107**, 403–406.

Plague

Clinical features

Plague is an acute, febrile infectious disease caused by *Yersinia pestis*, a non-motile, bipolar Gram-negative aerobic bacillus.[1–3] The disease has a high incidence in South Africa, Madagascar, the Far East and parts of India. Foci of plague have also been reported from southwestern states of the USA, and in parts of South America.[1,2,4] Rodents act as the reservoir, and the infection is usually transmitted to humans via the bite of a flea; aerosol spread may also occur, leading to pneumonic plague.[1–3] There are three distinct clinicopathological forms of the disease: bubonic plague, primary pneumonic plague and primary septicemic plague.[1,2]

Bubonic plague

Bubonic plague accounts for the vast majority of cases. After a short incubation period of approximately 2–4 days, the disease manifests abruptly with pyrexia, chills, tachycardia and tachypnea, and the formation of a so-called bubo – a painful, pathologically enlarged unilateral group of infected lymph nodes, usually in the groin or axilla (*Fig. 17.119*).[1] Cervical and axillary buboes are more common in children than in adults.[4] Septicemia and secondary pneumonic plague may follow in untreated cases. Minor ('ambulatory') forms of bubonic plague also exist.[1]

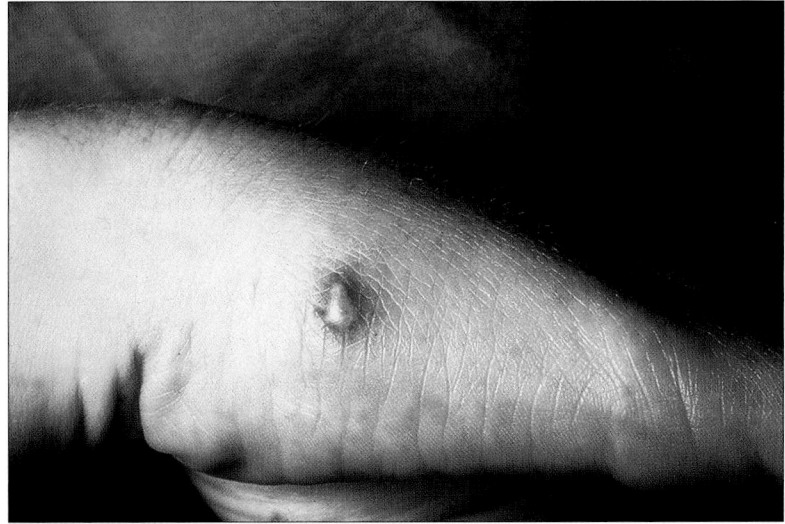

Fig. 17.118
Gonococcemia: pustules are commonly found on the hands and feet. By courtesy of R.N. Thin, MD, St Thomas' Hospital, London, UK.

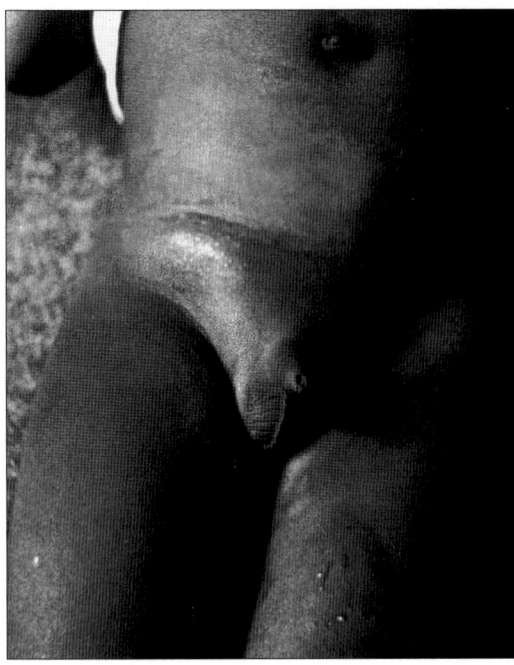

Fig. 17.119
Bubonic plague: note the inguinal lymphadenopathy (bubo). By courtesy of J. Frean, MD, and the late M. Isaäcson, MD, University of Witwatersrand, Johannesburg, South Africa.

Primary pneumonic and primary septicemic plague

Primary pneumonic plague is acquired by inhalation of the organisms, whereas primary septicemic plague tends to occur after the bite of an infected flea on the head and neck region. Untreated, both of these forms of plague carry a mortality of around 90%.[2]

Cutaneous manifestations

Cutaneous manifestations of *Y. pestis* infection are seen predominantly in bubonic plague. A small vesicle, pustule, papule or necrotic lesion may develop at the site of the flea bite. The skin overlying the bubo is erythematous and edematous and may undergo hemorrhage and necrosis, resulting in the formation of fistulae.[1,2] Roseolar, scarlatiniform, vesico-pustular and erythema multiforme-like eruptions may occur elsewhere on the body.[1] Petechial hemorrhages and ecchymoses characterize severe cases. Cutaneous ulceration and necrosis may ensue, hence the term 'black death'.[2]

Histological features

The lymph nodes comprising the buboes show severe acute hemorrhagic lymphadenitis in the presence of large amphophilic or 'ground-glass' aggregates of bacilli. Their characteristic 'safety-pin' appearance is discernible on sections stained with the Gram's or Giemsa methods.[1,2] Extranodal extension results in ulceration of the overlying skin. Subsequent septicemic illness may be complicated by DIC. In the skin the latter manifests with intradermal hemorrhage, thrombotic vascular occlusion and multiple cutaneous infarcts.[2] The diagnosis may be confirmed by microscopy, culture, immunofluorescence, enzyme-linked immunosorbent assay or PCR.[1–4] An immunohistochemical assay has recently been described.[5]

References

1. Canizares, O. (1992) Plague. In: Canizares, O., Harman, R. (eds) Clinical tropical dermatology, 2nd edn. Boston: Blackwell, pp 550–552.
2. Smith, J.H., Reisner, B.S. (1997) Plague. In: Connor, D.H., Chandler, F.W., Schwartz, D.A. et al (eds) Pathology of infectious diseases, Vol. I. Stamford: Appleton and Lange, pp 729–738.
3. Putzker, M., Sauer, H., Sobe, D. (2001) Plague and other human infections caused by Yersinia species. Clin Lab, 47, 453–466.
4. Boisier, P., Rahalison, L., Rasolomaharo, M. et al (2002) Epidemiologic features of four successive annual outbreaks of bubonic plague in Mahajanga, Madagascar. Emerg Infect Dis, 8, 311–316.
5. Guarner, J., Shieh, W.J., Greer, P.W. et al (2002) Immunohistochemical detection of Yersinia pestis in formalin-fixed, paraffin-embedded tissue. Am J Clin Pathol, 117, 205–209.

Cutaneous anthrax

Clinical features

Anthrax is a zoonotic infection caused by *Bacillus anthracis*, an encapsulated, spore-forming Gram-positive bacillus.[1,2] Although the condition is relatively uncommon in humans, epidemic outbreaks still occur in tropical and subtropical regions of the world (including Africa and South America), southern Europe, the Middle East and India.[1,2] Anthrax is very rarely seen in developed countries.[3] Cutaneous anthrax accounts for more than 95% of cases; pulmonary and gastrointestinal forms account for the remainder, and are associated with a high mortality.[1] The condition is usually acquired after contact with infected animals (herbivores) or contaminated animal products. It has also been described in rural Turkish children who were subjected to the ritual smearing of cow's blood on their foreheads.[4] Under ideal conditions, spores may survive in the soil or in animal products for many years.[1] Recently there has been renewed interest in the organism as an agent of bioterrorism.[5]

Cutaneous anthrax occurs after inoculation of *B. anthracis* into abraded skin. An erythematous macule or papule develops after an incubation period of 2–3 weeks. This later evolves into a pruritic vesicle. A characteristic black eschar develops after breakdown of the blister (*Figs 17.120, 17.121*).[1] There is often pronounced edema of the surrounding skin, sometimes accompanied by the formation of bullae.[1] Lymphadenitis is sometimes seen. Septicemia may arise in untreated cases; this carries a mortality of 10–20%.[1,2] A rare form of the disease termed malignant edema presents with severe, rapidly spreading edema, lymphangitis, lymphadenitis and systemic symptoms. Hemorrhagic and necrotic vesicles may evolve in these cases.[1]

Pathogenesis and histological features

B. anthracis is associated with potent virulence factors, namely a poly-D glutamic acid capsule and a plasmid-encoded protein exotoxin consisting of three components: edema factor, protective antigenic factor and lethal factor.[2,6]

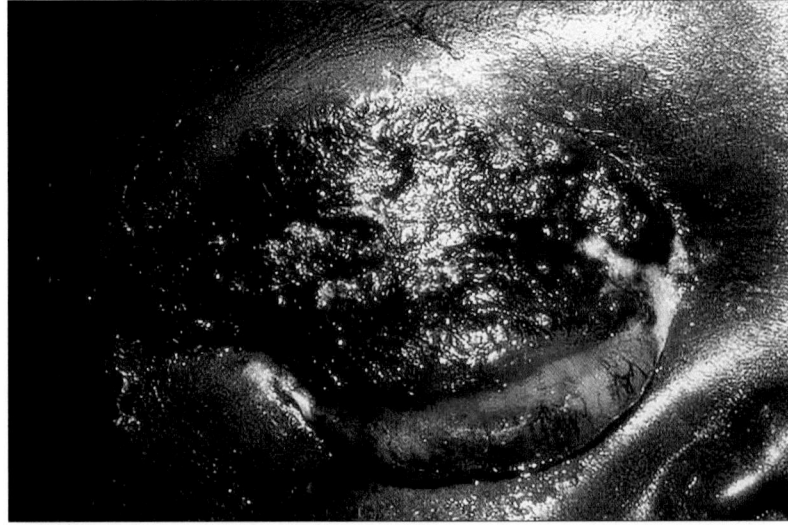

Fig. 17.120
Anthrax: cutaneous disease is the commonest manifestation in humans. This black crusted lesion is typical. By courtesy of J. Frean, MD, and the late M. Isaäcson, MD, University of Witwatersrand, Johannesburg, South Africa.

The histological picture is dominated by massive subepidermal edema (*Fig. 17.122*).[3] Intraepidermal edema results in coalescent intercellular vacuoles.[1] The epidermis is often attenuated. The dermis is expanded by a dense inflammatory infiltrate consisting of large numbers of polymorphonuclear leukocytes, admixed with lymphocytes and histiocytes. The process often extends into subcutaneous fat.[3] Vasodilatation may be prominent. Hemorrhage and fibrin deposition occur in the deep dermis and subcutis (*Fig. 17.123*). Thrombotic vascular occlusion and fibrinoid necrosis of blood vessel walls may be encountered in the deep dermis and subcutaneous fat (*Fig. 17.124*). Gram stain will reveal considerable numbers of large Gram-positive bacilli in the superficial dermis (*Fig. 17.125*).[3] The diagnosis is confirmed by culture. Serological investigations are also available. Immunohistochemical methods of detection may be employed on tissue specimens.[2]

References

1. Canizares, O. (1992) Anthrax. In: Canizares, O., Harman, R. (eds) Clinical tropical dermatology, 2nd edn. Boston: Blackwell, pp 397–406.
2. Jaax, N.K., Fritz, D.L. (1997) Anthrax. In: Connor, D.H., Chandler, F.W., Schwartz, D.A. et al (eds) Pathology of infectious diseases, Vol. I. Stamford: Appleton and Lange, pp 397–406.

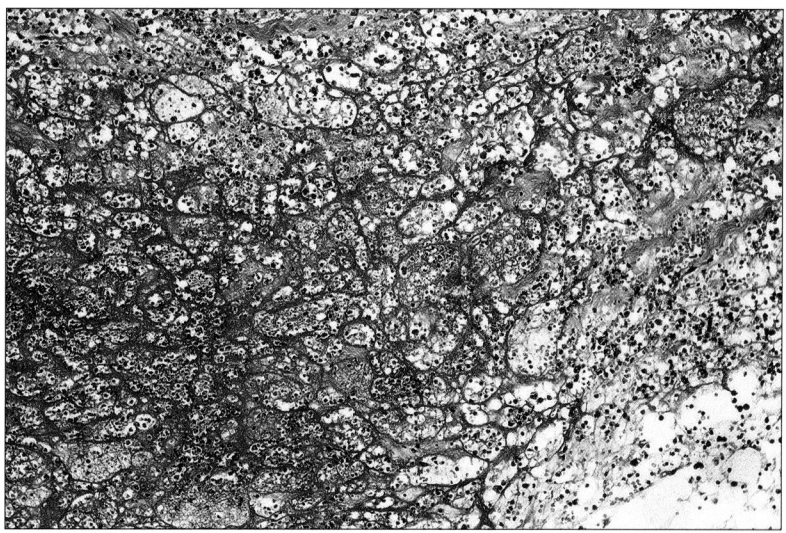

Fig. 17.123
Anthrax: marked fibrin deposition is evident. Reproduced with permisssion from Mallon E, McKee PH. Extraordinary case report: cutaneous anthrax. American Journal of Dermatopathology. 1977; 19: 79-82.

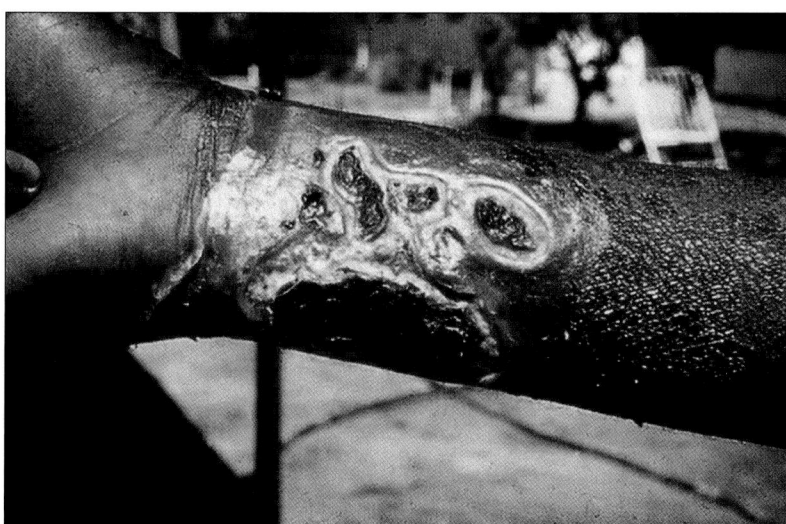

Fig. 17.121
Anthrax: multiple lesions on the forearm. By courtesy of J. Frean, MD, and the late M. Isaäcson, MD, University of Witwatersrand, Johannesburg, South Africa.

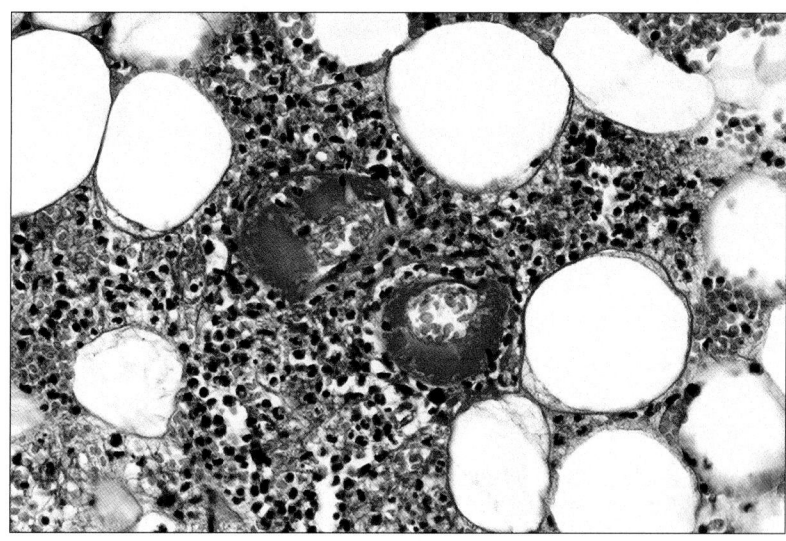

Fig. 17.124
Anthrax: thrombosed vessels are present. Reproduced with permisssion from Mallon E, McKee PH. Extraordinary case report: cutaneous anthrax. American Journal of Dermatopathology. 1977; 19: 79-82.

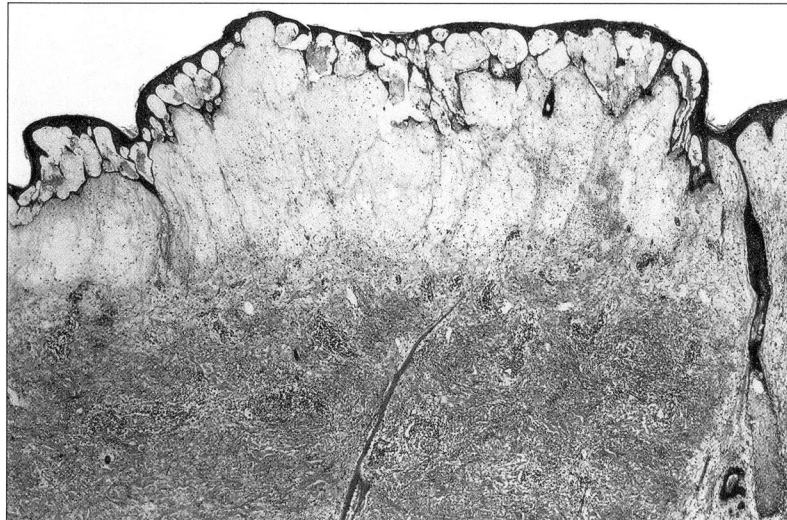

Fig. 17.122
Anthrax: there is massive subepidermal edema with subepidermal vesiculation. Reproduced with permisssion from Mallon E, McKee PH. Extraordinary case report: cutaneous anthrax. American Journal of Dermatopathology. 1977; 19: 79-82.

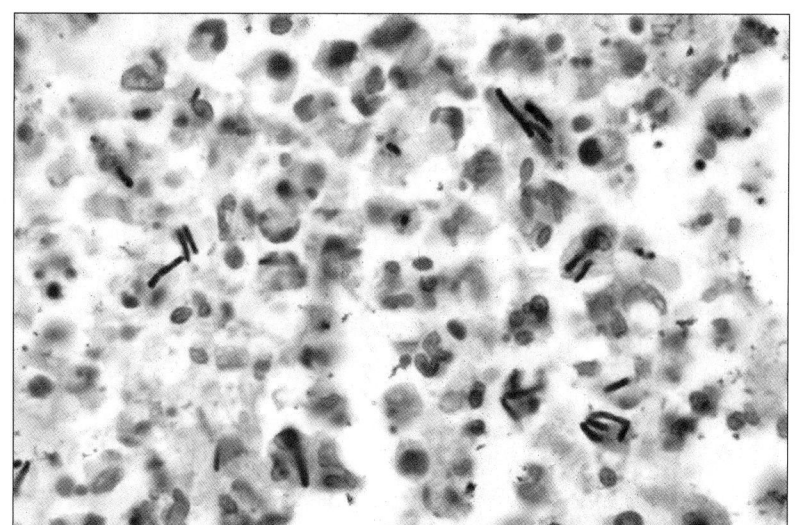

Fig. 17.125
Anthrax: numerous elongated Gram-positive bacilli are present. Reproduced with permisssion from Mallon E, McKee PH. Extraordinary case report: cutaneous anthrax. American Journal of Dermatopathology. 1977; 19: 79-82.

3.   Mallon, E., McKee, P.H. (1997) Extraordinary case report: cutaneous anthrax. *Am J Dermatopathol*, **19**, 79–82.
4.   Ciftci, E., Ince, E., Dogru, U. (2002) Traditions, anthrax, and children. *Pediatr Dermatol*, **19**, 36–38.
5.   Binkley, C.E., Cinti, S., Simeone, D.M. et al (2002) Bacillus anthracis as an agent of bioterrorism: a review emphasizing surgical treatment. *Ann Surg*, **236**, 9–16.
6.   Bhatnagar, R., Batra, S. (2001) Anthrax toxin. *Crit Rev Microbiol*, **27**, 167–200.

Brucellosis

Clinical features

Brucellosis is a zoonotic infection by *Brucella* spp. such as *B. melitensis*, *B. abortus* and *B. suis*.[1] The organism is a Gram-negative bacillus and infection is acquired either by ingesting contaminated, unpasteurized milk/milk products, or by handling infected animal products (contact brucellosis). Human-to-human transmission does not occur. Brucellosis results in either an acute febrile illness or a chronic systemic disease characterized by fever, malaise, sweats, arthralgia, myalgia and/or hepatosplenomegaly.[1,4] The mortality is low and most patients recover within 3 months.[1]

Cutaneous manifestations occur in approximately 6% of cases; however, this figure approached 14% in a recent series from Turkey.[2,3] A number of cutaneous manifestations have been recorded, including a disseminated papulonodular eruption, a diffuse maculopapular rash, erythema nodosum-like subcutaneous nodules, purpura, leukocytoclastic vasculitis, erythema multiforme, urticaria-like papules and plaques, multiple abscesses, cutaneous ulcers and (rarely) livedo reticularis and palmar erythema.[1–6] Contact brucellosis manifests with erythema or pruritus, usually on the forearm or hand. In some cases this may progress to a follicular, vesicular or pustular eruption.[1] A factitious case of brucellosis caused by autoinoculation has been reported; the patient developed bacteremia and ulcerating cutaneous abscesses.[7]

Histological features

The histological features vary according to the type of cutaneous lesion biopsied. Biopsies obtained from the erythematous papular lesions show a perivascular and periadnexal infiltrate of lymphocytes and histiocytes, sometimes accompanied by epithelioid histiocytes and multinucleated giant cells.[2] Erythrocyte extravasation is sometimes seen, and inflammatory cells may infiltrate the overlying epidermis.[4] Erythema nodosum-like nodules are characterized by a perivascular lymphohistiocytic infiltrate centered on the deep dermis and superficial subcutis.[2,5] There is associated vascular endothelial swelling and luminal thrombosis, sometimes with foci of necrosis. Accompanying granulomatous inflammation is not uncommon.[4] Erythema multiforme lesions and leukocytoclastic vasculitic lesions exhibit the usual histological changes associated with these conditions.

The *Brucella* organisms are rarely visualized in histological material. The diagnosis may therefore be confirmed by culture or serology.[1,2,4]

References

1.   Canizares, O. (1992) Brucellosis. In: Canizares, O., Harman, R. (eds) Clinical tropical dermatology, 2nd edn. Boston: Blackwell, pp 556–558.
2.   Berger, T.G., Guill, M.A., Goette, D.K. (1981) Cutaneous lesions in brucellosis. *Arch Dermatol*, **117**, 40–42.
3.   Metin, A., Akdeniz, H., Buzgan, T. et al (2001) Cutaneous findings encountered in brucellosis and review of the literature. *Int J Dermatol*, **40**, 434–438.
4.   Ariza, J., Servitje, O., Pallarés, R. et al (1989) Characteristic cutaneous lesions in patients with brucellosis. *Arch Dermatol*, **125**, 380–383.
5.   Nagalotimath, S.J., Hemashettar, B.M., Patil, C.S. (1985) Subcutaneous nodules in brucellosis. *Indian J Pathol Microbiol*, **28**, 225–228.
6.   Nagore, E., Sánchez-Motilla, J.M., Navarro, V. et al (1999) Leukocytoclastic vasculitis as a cutaneous manifestation of systemic infection caused by Brucella melitensis. *Cutis*, **63**, 25–27.
7.   Martínez Salazar, F., Solera, J., Cebrián, D. et al (1993) Bacteremia and multiple and recurrent skin ulcers due to Brucella melitensis. A new modality of self-induced infection. *Med Clin (Barc)*, **20**, 417–419.

Diseases caused by *Bartonella* species

Cat scratch disease

Clinical features

Cat scratch disease is a not uncommon, usually self-limited illness which, as its name implies, usually follows (after 3–5 days) a scratch or bite by a cat (usually a kitten).[1–9] On rare occasions, it has been reported following a similar injury caused by a dog or even by a monkey.[6] It occurs equally in males and females, most often during the first two decades. Cat scratch disease shows seasonal variation, occurring most often in autumn and winter.[1] The causative agent is *Bartonella henselae* (formerly *Rochalimaea henselae*), a weakly Gram-negative bacillus measuring 1–2 μm in length.[8,9] The condition was first described in 1950, yet the nature of the infective etiological agent remained elusive until recently.[9] In the past, a variety of infectious agents had been suggested as responsible for cat scratch disease, including mycobacteria, *Chlamydia*, herpes-like viruses and, more recently, *Afipia felis*.[8,10] The cat represents the primary reservoir for the bacillus in addition to being its principal vector.[11] Although transmission among cats is via the cat flea, the latter does not appear to play a direct role in transmission to humans.[8,9]

The primary skin lesion – a macule, a papule, a vesicle, a pustule or a nodule – develops most commonly on the arm or hand, followed by the head, leg, conjunctiva, trunk or neck, in decreasing order of frequency. Sometimes more than one member of a family may be affected. The cutaneous lesions measure 1–5 mm or more in diameter and may sometimes resemble an insect bite.[1]

Other rare cutaneous manifestations include a non-pruritic macular or maculopapular rash, erythema nodosum, urticaria, erythema marginatum, erythema annulare and thrombocytopenic purpura. A case with cutaneous lesions resembling those of Sweet's syndrome has been reported.[12] Fever and malaise are occasional symptoms. Less common additional features include headache, nausea, vomiting, arthralgia and splenomegaly.

Patients invariably develop lymphadenopathy in the drainage region, usually within 1–3 weeks of the initial lesion. The enlarged nodes are tender and often persistent, with lymphadenopathy lasting up to 2 months and more. Suppuration is not uncommon. Conjunctival or eyelid lesions may be associated with preauricular lymphadenopathy (Parinaud's syndrome).[13] The only consistently abnormal laboratory function test is a moderately raised erythrocyte sedimentation rate (ESR). Purported cases of disseminated cat scratch disease occurring as a manifestation of the acquired immunodeficiency syndrome (AIDS) probably represent examples of advanced bacillary angiomatosis (see below).[14,15]

Atypical manifestations of cat scratch disease may occur in as many as 25% of cases.[8] These include non-thrombocytopenic purpura and bone, liver, spleen, pulmonary, endocardial and/or neurological involvement, presumably due to bacteremia.[1,8] A vasculitic pathogenesis has also been proposed.[16] Central nervous system lesions have significant morbidity and include coma, encephalitis, convulsions, pareses, cerebellar signs and abnormal tendon jerks.[16] Hepatosplenic infection results in peliosis.[8,9]

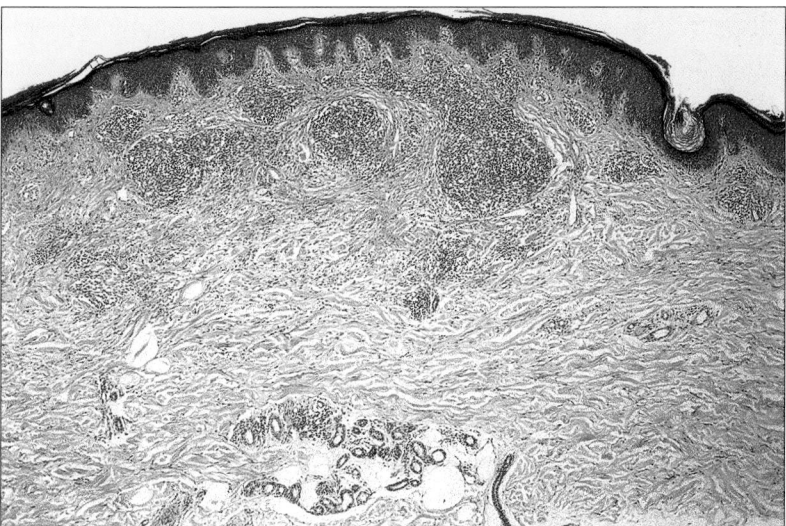

Fig. 17.126
Cat scratch disease: an irregular ill-defined focus of necrobiosis is surrounded by a nodular lymphocytic infiltrate.

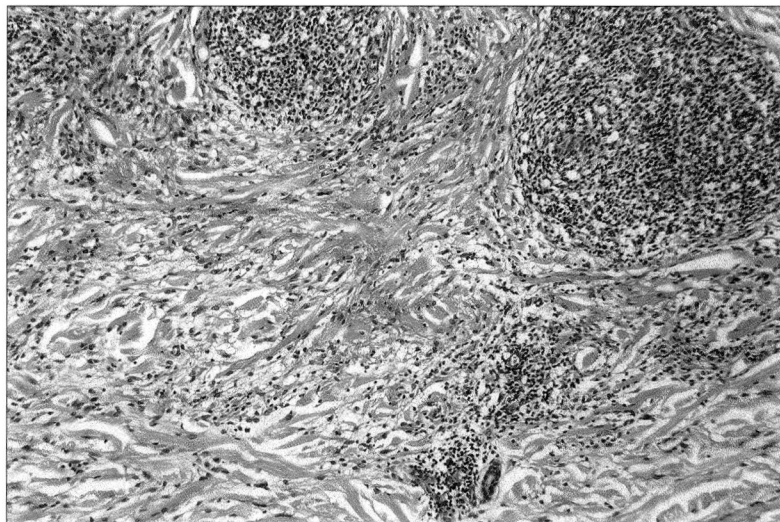

Fig. 17.127
Cat scratch disease: close-up view of the necrobiosis in *Fig. 17.126*.

Histological features

The histopathological features are those of dermal necrobiosis.[17] The necrobiotic foci are round, triangular or stellate and are surrounded by a palisade of histiocytes with occasional multinucleate giant cells (*Figs 17.126, 17.127*). Around the periphery of the histiocytic zone is a lymphocytic infiltrate in which eosinophils may be conspicuous. Nuclear debris may sometimes be prominent. The bacteria may often be identified using the Warthin–Starry reaction or the Brown–Hopps modified Gram stain within histiocytes or lying free.[18–21] Bacteria may also be detected immunocytochemically.[1] In the adjacent dermis the blood vessels are surrounded by an infiltrate consisting of lymphocytes, plasma cells and histiocytes. A granulomatous reaction has been described but this is an uncommon phenomenon.[22]

In early lesions the lymph nodes show subcapsular foci of necrosis associated with a neutrophil polymorph infiltrate. An established lesion is characterized by extensive necrotic lesions often involving the follicular germinal centers and associated with karyorrhexis. A peripheral rim of epithelioid cells and occasional giant cells is characteristic. These features are not in themselves diagnostic because they may be seen in a variety of conditions including lymphogranuloma venereum, yersiniosis and fungal infections.[2]

Previously the diagnosis of cat scratch disease was confirmed by a positive delayed hypersensitivity reaction to the cat scratch disease antigen.[1] Since *B. henselae* is difficult to culture, serology and PCR have been advocated as more reliable diagnostic modalities.[8,9,23]

References

1. Carithers, H.A. (1985) Cat scratch disease. An overview based on a study of 1,200 patients. *Am J Dis Child*, **139**, 1124–1133.
2. Lucus, S.B. (1991) Cat scratch disease. *J Pathol*, **163**, 91–92.
3. Campbell, J.A.H. (1977) Cat scratch disease. *Pathol Ann*, **12**, 277–292.
4. Shinall, E.A. (1990) Cat scratch disease: a review of the literature. *Pediatr Dermatol*, **7**, 11–18.
5. Burnett, J.W. (1991) Cat scratch disease. *Cutis*, **48**, 443–444.
6. Margileth, A.M. (1988) Dermatologic manifestations and update of cat scratch disease. *Pediatr Dermatol*, **5**, 1–9.
7. Margileth, A.M. (1968) Cat scratch disease: non-bacterial regional lymphadenitis. The study of 145 patients and a review of the literature. *Pediatrics*, **42**, 803–818.
8. Windsor, J.J. (2001) Cat-scatch disease: epidemiology, aetiology and treatment. *Br J Biomed Sci*, **58**, 101–110.
9. Chomel, B.B. (2000) Cat-scatch disease. *Rev Sci Tech*, **19**, 136–150.
10. Gerber, M.A., MacAlister, T.J., Ballow, M. et al (1985) The aetiological agent of cat scratch disease. *Lancet*, **1**, 1236–1239.
11. Kirkpatrick, C.E., Glickman, L.T. (1989) Cat-scratch disease and the role of the domestic cat: vector, reservoir, and victim? *Med Hypotheses*, **28**, 145–149.
12. Landau, M., Kletter, Y., Avidor, B. et al (1999) Unusual eruption as symptom of cat scatch disease. *J Am Acad Dermatol*, **41** (5 Pt 2), 833–836.
13. Wear, D.J., Malaty, R.H., Zimmerman, L.E. et al (1985) Cat scratch disease bacilli in the conjunctiva of patients with Parinaud's oculoglandular syndrome. *Ophthalmology*, **92**, 1282–1287.
14. van der Wouw, P.A., Hadderingh, R.J., Reiss, P. et al (1989) Disseminated cat-scratch disease in a patient with AIDS. *AIDS*, **3**, 751–753.
15. Schlossberg, D., Morad, Y., Krouse, T. B. et al (1989) Culture-proven disseminated cat-scratch disease in acquired immunodeficiency syndrome. *Arch Intern Med*, **149**, 1437–1439.
16. Lewis, D.W., Tucker, S.H. (1986) Central nervous system involvement in cat scratch disease. *Pediatrics*, **77**, 714–721.
17. Johnson, W.T., Helwig, E.B. (1969) Cat-scratch disease: histopathologic changes in the skin. *Arch Dermatol*, **100**, 148–154.
18. Wear, D.J., Margileth, A.M., Hadfield, T. L. et al (1983) Cat scratch disease: a bacterial infection. *Science*, **221**, 1403–1405.
19. Miller-Catchpole, R., Variakojis, D., Vardiman, J.W. et al (1986) Cat scratch disease. Identification of bacteria in seven cases of lymphadenitis. *Am J Surg Pathol*, **10**, 276–281.
20. English, C.K., Wear, D.J., Margileth, A.M. et al (1988) Cat scratch disease. Isolation and culture of bacterial agent. *JAMA*, **259**, 1347–1352.
21. Margileth, A.M., Wear, D.J., English, C.K. (1987) Systemic cat scratch disease: report of 23 patients with prolonged or recurrent severe bacterial infection. *J Infect Dis*, **155**, 390–402.
22. Calzavara-Pinton, P.G., Facchetti, F., Carlino, A. et al (1992) Multiple scattered granulomatous skin lesions in cat scatch disease. *Cutis*, **49**, 318–320.
23. Sander, A., Penno, S. (1999) Semiquantitative species-specific detection of Bartonella henselae and Bartonella quintana by PCR-enzyme immunoassay. *J Clin Microbiol*, **37**, 3097–3101.

Trench fever

Clinical features

Although a major epidemic of trench fever was documented during the First World War, more recent outbreaks of this condition have been described among homeless people, in whom there is a high seroprevalence of this bacteremic illness.[1] Outbreaks have also occurred in overpopulated Central African refugee camps.[2] Trench fever is caused by *Bartonella quintana*; human body lice are the known vectors.[1] *B. quintana* may also cause bacillary angiomatosis (see below).

Patients present with non-specific symptoms and signs including headache, malaise, pyrexia, rigors, tachycardia, myalgia, arthralgia and injected conjunctivae. An erythematous macular or papular skin rash may occur. The rash is often seen on the trunk and usually lasts no more than a day or two.[3] The disease is rarely fatal, except in some debilitated patients. Relapsing illness sometimes occurs, and the organism may remain latent in the host for a number of years following the acute infection.[3]

Histological features

The histopathological features in the skin are non-specific. There is a perivascular lymphocytic infiltrate, without evidence of vascular thrombosis.[3] Organisms are not usually demonstrable in routinely stained skin biopsy specimens. Dermal vascular proliferation and neutrophilic infiltration (as seen in bacillary angiomatosis) are not features of trench fever. The diagnosis can be confirmed by serology, culture or PCR.[4]

References

1. Brouqui, P., Lascola, B., Roux, V. et al (1999) Chronic Bartonella quintana bacteremia in homeless patients. *N Engl J Med*, **340**, 184–189.
2. Raoult, D., Ndihokubwayo, J.B., Tissot-Dupont, H. et al (1998) Outbreak of epidemic typhus associated with trench fever in Burundi. *Lancet*, **352**, 353–358.
3. Isaäcson, M., Hale, M.J. (1995) Infections caused by Rickettsiae and rickettsia-like organisms, and bartonellosis. In: Doerr, W., Seifert, G. (eds) Spezielle Pathologische Anatomie, Vol. 8: Tropical pathology, 2nd edn. Berlin: Springer-Verlag, pp 253–289.
4. Sander, A., Penno, S. (1999) Semiquantitative species-specific detection of Bartonella henselae and Bartonella quintana by PCR-enzyme immunoassay. *J Clin Microbiol*, **37**, 3097–3101.

Bartonellosis

Clinical features

Bartonellosis (Carrión's disease) is a biphasic disease caused by *Bartonella bacilliformis*, an organism that is closely related to *B. henselae* and *B. quintana*.[1-3] The initial stage of infection (hematic phase) is referred to as Oroya fever. Patients are acutely ill with pyrexia, rigors, myalgia and a severe hemolytic anemia. The last is attributable to infection of the circulating erythrocytes and can be confirmed with the aid of a blood smear. Later the disease enters an eruptive phase characterized by the evolution of numerous papular, nodular or verrucous vascular skin lesions, referred to as verruga peruana (Peruvian wart, cutaneous verrucous disease).[2,4] These occur predominantly on the face and extremities (*Fig. 17.128*). Atypical cases may present with verrucous skin lesions as the sole manifestation.[2] Most lesions resolve spontaneously.[3]

The condition is endemic in the higher altitude regions of Peru, where it was first decribed in the 19th century. Carrión's disease also occurs in Ecuador and Colombia.[5] Outbreaks have been recorded in non-endemic parts of Peru, with a fatality rate of under 1%.[6] It has also been suggested that the condition may be underreported in some endemic areas due to the existence of mild infection by less virulent strains of *B. bacilliformis*.[2,6] The sand fly, *Lutzomyia* (*Phlebotomus*) *verrucarum* is the suspected vector.[5]

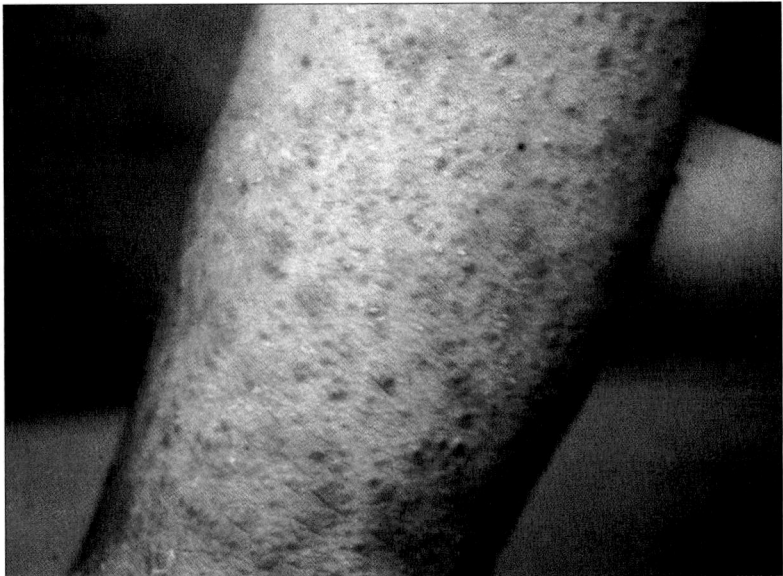

Fig. 17.128
Verruga peruana: widespread papules are present. By courtesy of F. von Lichtenberg, MD, Brigham and Women's Hospital and Harvard Medical School, Boston, USA.

Pathogenesis and histological features

There is infection of endothelial cells and circulating erythrocytes following introduction of *B. bacilliformis* via the bite of the suspected vector. In the cutaneous verruga peruana lesions, organisms are detectable in the extracellular spaces, where they induce angiogenesis by producing putative microbial-encoded or -induced angiogenic factors.[1,7] The dermal angiomatous proliferation appears to occur in concert with the reactivation of latent *B. bacilliformis* organisms.[1]

Histopathological examination of the verrucous lesions reveals an exuberant intradermal capillary proliferation lined by swollen endothelial cells, often accompanied by a neutrophilic infiltrate. Some of the superficial and peripheral vessels may be dilated, whereas deep dermal or subcutaneous nodules tend to have a more compact vascular and endothelial cell proliferation.[3,8] Occasional cases harbor a cytologically atypical endothelial proliferation, resulting in potential confusion with malignant vascular tumors.[9] There is a background mixed inflammatory cell infiltrate of variable intensity comprising neutrophils, histiocytes, lymphocytes and plasma cells. Careful examination of the endothelial cells in early lesions may reveal characteristic intracytoplasmic aggregates of *B. bacilliformis*, referred to as Rocha-Lima inclusions.[3] These may be highlighted with the aid of a Giemsa preparation. Ultrastructurally, the endothelial inclusions represent degraded bacteria and extracellular matrix components contained within cell surface invaginations.[3] Bacteria are conspicuously absent from late lesions.

Differential diagnosis

Verruga peruana should be distinguished from Kaposi's sarcoma, bacillary angiomatosis, pyogenic granuloma and true epithelioid vascular neoplasms (such as epithelioid hemangioma and epithelioid hemangioendothelioma).

References

1. Cáceres-Ríos, H., Rodríguez-Tafur, J., Bravo-Puccio, F. et al (1995) Verruga peruana: an infectious endemic angiomatosis. *Crit Rev Oncog*, **6**, 47–56.
2. Amano, Y., Rumbea, J., Knobloch, J. et al (1997) Bartonellosis in Ecuador: serosurvey and current status of cutaneous verrucous disease. *Am J Trop Med Hyg*, **57**, 174–179.
3. Arias-Stella, J., Lieberman, P.H., Erlandson, R.A. et al (1986) Histology, immunohistochemistry, and ultrastructure of the verruga in Carrion's disease. *Am J Surg Pathol*, **10**, 595–610.
4. Maguina, C., García, P.J., Gotuzzo, E. et al (2001) Bartonellosis (Carrion's disease) in the modern era. *Clin Infect Dis*, **33**, 772–779.
5. Alexander, B. (1995) A review of bartonellosis in Ecuador and Colombia. *Am J Trop Med Hyg*, **52**, 354–359.
6. Kosek, M., Lavarello, R., Gilman, R.H. et al (2000) Natural history of infection with Bartonella bacilliformis in a nonendemic population. *J Infect Dis*, **182**, 865–872.
7. García, F.U., Wojta, J., Broadley, K.N. et al (1990) Bartonella bacilliformis stimulates endothelial cells in vitro and is angiogenic in vivo. *Am J Pathol*, **136**, 1125–1135.
8. Bhutto, A.M., Nonaka, S., Hashiguchi, Y. et al (1994) Histological and electron microscopical features of skin lesions in a patient with bartonellosis (verruga peruana). *J Dermatol*, **21**, 178–184.
9. Arias-Stella, J., Lieberman, P.H., García-Cáceres, U. et al (1987) Verruga peruana mimicking malignant neoplasms. *Am J Dermatopathol*, **9**, 279–285.

Bacillary angiomatosis

Clinical features

Bacillary angiomatosis is a vasoproliferative lesion that may be readily confused with pyogenic granuloma or Kaposi's sarcoma and is seen predominantly (but not exclusively) in the skin.[1-6] Lesions have also been described in the bones, soft tissues, liver, lymph nodes and spleen. Patients may have systemic manifestations including fever, malaise, hepatosplenomegaly and lymphadenopathy.[7] Although it was originally thought to be a disease specific to AIDS, it has also been described in other immunocompromised states, and even in apparently normal individuals.[2,8,9] Patients present with widespread, numerous (sometimes hundreds) of blood-red, smooth-surfaced, superficial papules and skin-colored or dusky subcutaneous nodules (*Figs 17.129, 17.130*).[2] The condition may be caused either by *Bartonella henselae* (the organism responsible for cat scratch disease) or less frequently by *B. quintana* (the cause of trench fever).[8]

Histological features

Histology reveals lobules of capillaries with prominent, often cuboidal vascular endothelial cells, sometimes surrounding ectatic vessels among which are dispersed neutrophil polymorphs showing leukocytoclasis and purplish granules of bacilli, which can be identified best by the Warthin–Starry reaction (*Figs 17.131–17.134*).[5,8] Sometimes solid endothelial cell proliferation is evident.[4] Atypia and mitoses may be present.[4] Superficial lesions have a polypoid configuration and there may be an associated epidermal collarette.[4] Ulceration is seen occasionally.

Although collagen dissection by spindled endothelial cells is encountered at the periphery of some lesions, hemosiderin deposition and hyaline globules as seen in Kaposi's sarcoma are not evident.[10,11]

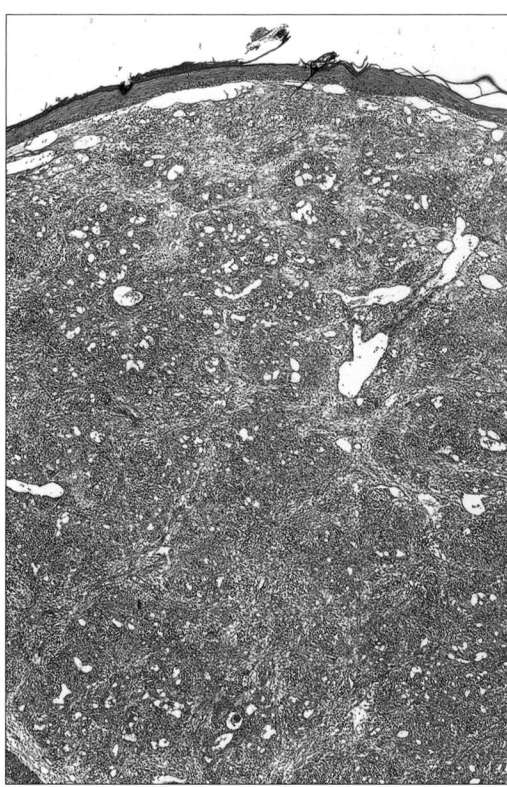

Fig. 17.131
Bacillary angiomatosis: there is a dense nodular capillary proliferative lesion; note the ectatic vessels.

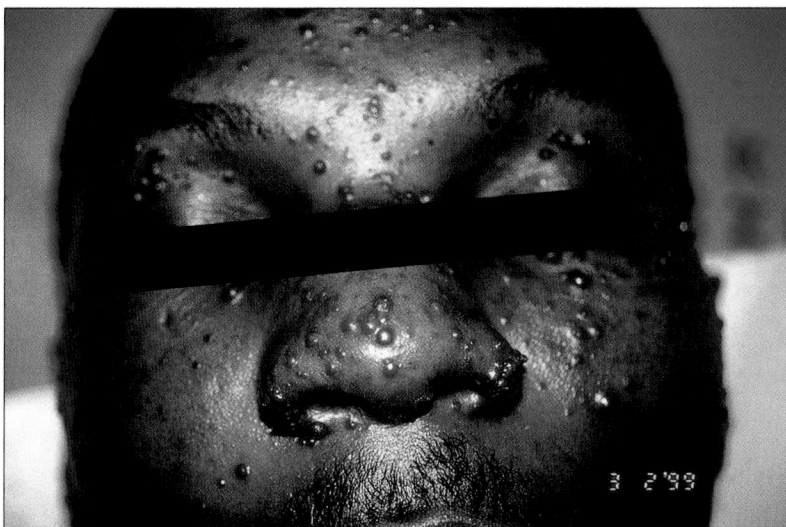

Fig. 17.129
Bacillary angiomatosis: numerous papules and nodules are present. By courtesy of N.C. Dlova, MD, Nelson R. Mandela School of Medicine, University of KwaZulu-Natal, South Africa.

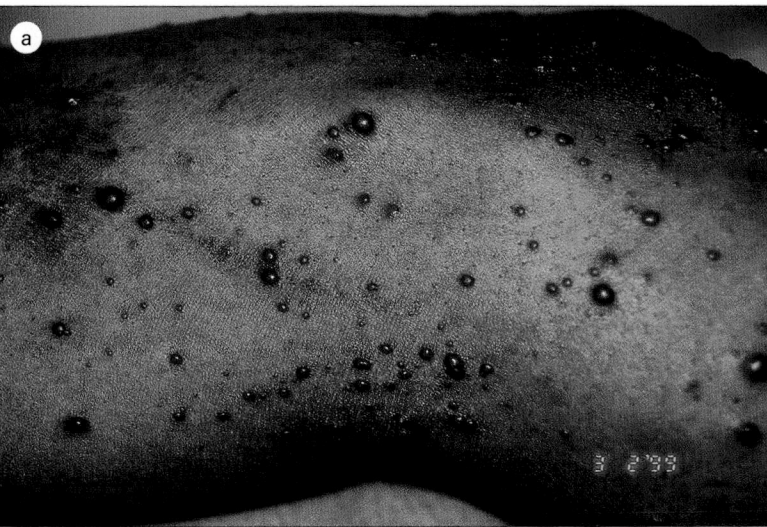

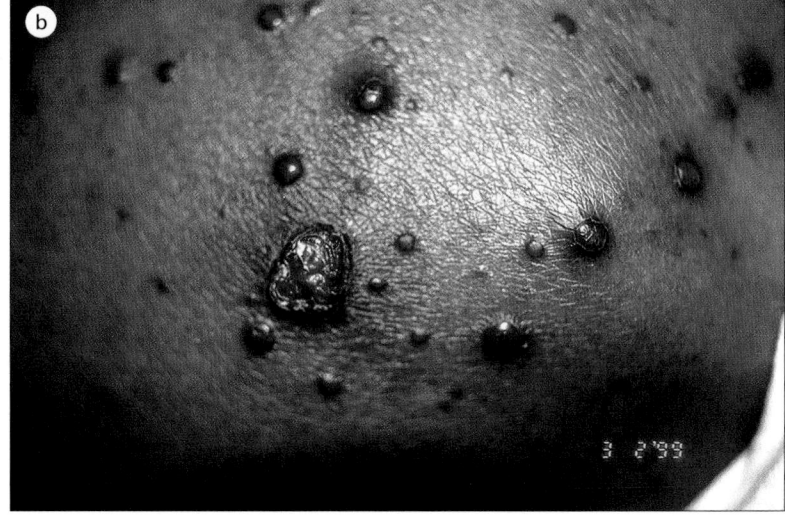

Fig. 17.130
(a, b) Bacillary angiomatosis: the bright red coloration is characteristic. By courtesy of N.C. Dlova, MD, Nelson R. Mandela School of Medicine, University of KwaZulu-Natal, South Africa.

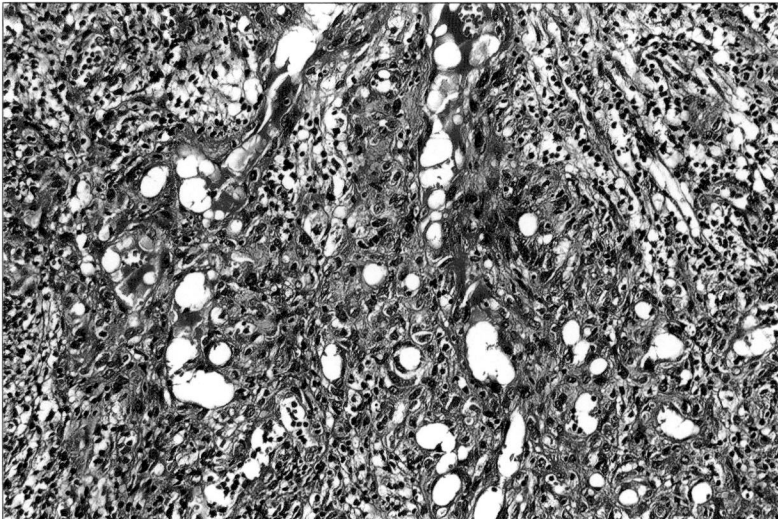

Fig. 17.132
Bacillary angiomatosis: the endothelial cells are swollen. Conspicuous neutrophils are evident.

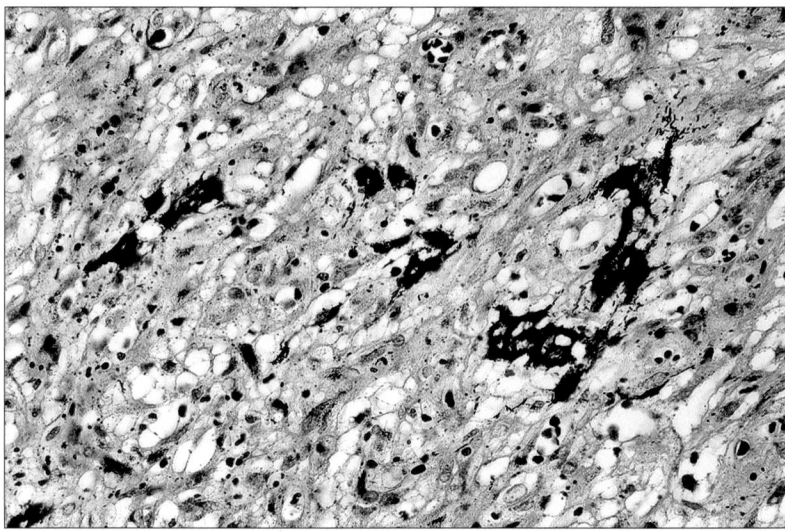

Fig. 17.134
Bacillary angiomatosis: the organisms are easily identified with the Warthin–Starry stain.

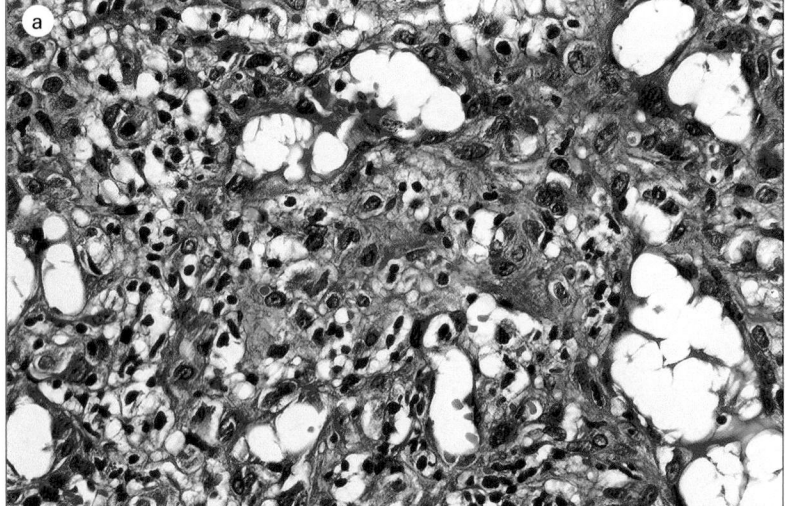

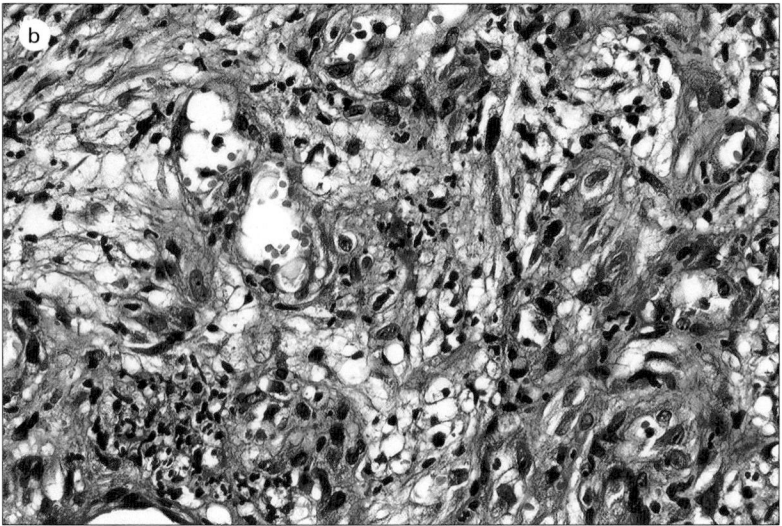

Fig. 17.133
(a, b) Bacillary angiomatosis: lymphocytes and histiocytes are also present. Note the purple colony of bacteria in the center of the field (b).

Late, involuting lesions show extensive fibrosis of the vascularized dermis, and little by way of a polymorphonuclear leukocytic infiltrate with karyorrhexis.[2] Such cases require a high index of suspicion, as the bacteria may be difficult to demonstrate.

The endothelial cells can be labeled with antibodies to Factor VIII-related antigen, *Ulex europaeus* lectin, CD31 and CD34. Histologically, liver and splenic involvement is seen as peliosis.[7] Typical bacteria are, however, also present. Its recognition and distinction from Kaposi's sarcoma and other vasoproliferative lesions is of great importance, particularly as it readily responds to antibiotic therapy.[4]

Ultrastructurally the organisms appear as aggregates of bacilli within the dermis. The bacteria have trilaminar walls.

Differential diagnosis

Bacillary angiomatosis must be distinguished from verruga peruana, pyogenic granuloma, epithelioid hemangioma and Kaposi's sarcoma. Although rare, bacillary angiomatosis and concurrent Kaposi's sarcoma has been described.[12] PCR or immunohistochemistry for detection of HHV-8 is a useful means of differentiating Kaposi's sarcoma from bacillary angiomatosis; the former is invariably associated with HHV-8 whereas the latter has been found to be HHV-8 negative.[13] Furthermore, PCR may be employed to confirm the presence of *Bartonella* spp. in suspected cases of bacillary angiomatosis since these organisms are difficult to culture.[8,14]

References

1. Cockerell, C.J., LeBoit, P.E. (1990) Bacillary angiomatosis: a newly characterized, pseudoneoplastic, infectious, cutaneous vascular disorder. *J Am Acad Dermatol*, **22**, 501–512.
2. LeBoit, P.E. (1991) Bacillary angiomatosis: a systemic opportunistic infection with prominent cutaneous manifestations. *Semin Dermatol*, **10**, 194–198.
3. Relman, D.A., Loutit, J.S., Schmidt, T.M. et al (1990) The agent of bacillary angiomatosis: an approach to the identification of an uncultured pathogen. *N Engl J Med*, **323**, 1573–1580.
4. LeBoit, P.E., Berger, T.G., Egbert, B.M. et al (1989) Bacillary angiomatosis: the histopathology and differential diagnosis of a pseudoneoplastic infection in patients with human immunodeficiency virus disease. *Am J Surg Pathol*, **13**, 909–920.
5. Szaniawski, W.K., Don, P.C., Bitterman, S.R. et al (1990) Epithelioid angiomatosis in patients with AIDS: report of seven cases and a review of the literature. *J Am Acad Dermatol*, **23**, 41–48.
6. Cockerell, C.J., Tierno, P.M., Friedman-Kein, A.E. et al (1991) Clinical, histologic, microbiologic, and biochemical characterisation of the causative agent of bacillary (epithelioid) angiomatosis: a rickettsial illness with features of bartonellosis. *J Invest Dermatol*, **97**, 812–817.
7. LeBoit, P.E. (1992) Dermatopathologic findings in patients infected with HIV. *Dermatol Clin*, **10**, 59–71.
8. Gasquet, S., Maurin, M., Brouqui, P. et al (1998) Bacillary angiomatosis in immunocompromised patients. *AIDS*, **12**, 1793–1803.
9. Tappero, J.W., Koehler, J.E., Berger, T.G. et al (1993) Bacillary angiomatosis and bacillary splenitis in immunocompetent adults. *Ann Intern Med*, **118**, 363–365.
10. Smith, K.J., Skelton, H.G., Angritt, P. (1991) Histopathologic features of HIV-associated skin disease. *Dermatol Clin*, **9**, 551–578.
11. Herman, K.L., Jacoby, R.A., Webster, G. (1991) Pathology of HIV-related skin disease. *Clin Dermatol*, **9**, 95–110.

12. Berger, T.G., Tappero, J.W., Kaymen, A. et al (1989) Bacillary (epithelioid) angiomatosis and concurrent Kaposi's sarcoma in acquired immunodeficiency syndrome. *Arch Dermatol*, **125**, 1543–1547.
13. Nayler, S.J., Allard, U., Taylor, L. et al (1999) HHV-8 (KSHV) is not associated with bacillary angiomatosis. *Mol Pathol*, **52**, 345–348.
14. Sander, A., Penno, S. (1999) Semiquantitative species-specific detection of Bartonella henselae and Bartonella quintana by PCR-enzyme immunoassay. *J Clin Microbiol*, **37**, 3097–3101.

Lyme disease

Clinical features

Lyme disease is a generalized infection due to the spirochete *Borrelia burgdorferi* (*B. burgdorferi sensu lato*), of which there are three pathogenic genospecies in humans: *B. burgdorferi sensu stricto*, *B. garinii* and *B. afzelii*.[1–4] The Centers for Disease Control and Prevention (CDC) recently reported a 40% increase in the annual incidence of this emerging zoonosis in the United States between 2001 and 2002; more than 40,000 cases were documented during this period.[5] This trend has also been observed in parts of the United Kingdom and Europe.[6,7] The disease affects most organ systems of the body.[1,2,8]

Lyme disease has been divided into three stages, I–III:[9]

Stage I

The skin lesion of the primary stage (erythema chronicum migrans) consists initially of a small erythematous papule at the site of an insect bite and expands centrifugally as a flat ring (*Fig. 17.135*). It develops on average 1–3 weeks after the bite.[10] Occasionally target lesions are described.[11] Necrotic lesions are rare.[12] With extension, the macules may develop a bluish or violet hue. If untreated, the ring may spread to a diameter of 50 cm before clearing. Although lesions are usually asymptomatic, patients may complain of pruritus, burning or rarely pain.[13] The lower extremity and trunk are most often affected.

Approximately 50% of patients have secondary lesions, which are smaller. The palms, soles and mucous membranes are usually unaffected.[14] Erythema chronicum migrans may occasionally recur.[13] Other cutaneous manifestations that have been described in the early stage of Lyme disease include granuloma annulare, papular urticaria, and Henoch–Schönlein purpura.[14] Age at presentation is exceedingly variable, ranging from 15 months to 80 years. The sex incidence is equal and lesions present most often from May to September.[14]

Systemic symptoms (due to a spirochetemia), which tend to occur early in the disease, include chills, fever, general malaise and lethargy, arthralgia, myalgia, headache and neck stiffness. Physical examination may reveal lymphadenopathy, splenomegaly, hepatitis and orchitis.[10,15] *B. garinii* and *B. afzelii* are the pathogens most often implicated in cases of Lyme disease reported from Europe, and some authors have described differences in the clinical presentation of erythema chronicum migrans caused by these two organisms.[16,17] Erythemas associated with *B. garinii* tend to evolve more rapidly, are often larger and homogeneous, are more often located on the trunk than the extremities, and are more frequently associated with systemic symptoms when compared with *B. afzelii* erythemas, which are usually annular.[16,17]

Lymphocytoma cutis (borrelial lymphocytoma), a B-cell response, may present in the acute stage and most often affects the lower ear lobes and nipples.[10] It is, however, more often a feature of the third stage of the illness.[15]

Stage II

Stage II disease primarily affects the cardiovascular and nervous system (meningopolyradiculitis).[15,18,19] It may involve both the peripheral and central nervous systems, and tends to present 1–2 months after the primary infection; symptoms include meningism, nerve palsies (especially Bell's palsy) and cerebral symptoms, including personality changes, drowsiness or stupor.[9,20] There have been isolated reports of orbital myositis, neurosensory hearing loss, parkinsonism and spontaneous brain hemorrhage.[21–24] Cardiac involvement presents as myocarditis and conduction defects.[9,18,25]

Stage III

Arthritis, which characterizes the third stage, presents as a recurrent, asymmetrical and oligoarticular process involving the large joints (especially the knee) or as a migratory polyarthritis lasting up to a week in any one particular joint.[15] Cutaneous lesions and peripheral nervous system involvement are also frequently encountered in the third stage. The typical skin lesions of late Lyme disease are acrodermatitis chronica atrophicans, which characteristically presents as a red or violet discoloration of swollen peripheral skin and lymphadenosis benigna cutis.[13,15] Lesions are often bilateral. Patients may also develop sclerodermatous changes. Lichen sclerosus et atrophicus-like lesions have also been described.[9,15] In the late atrophic stages of acrodermatitis chronica atrophicans, the skin may resemble crumpled tissue paper.[26] Nodular or band-like juxta-articular fibrous nodules are not uncommon, and may regress with appropriate antibiotic therapy.[27] Acrodermatitis chronica atrophicans occurs mainly in Europe, where *B. afzelii* is the overwhelmingly predominant etiologic genospecies.[4] *B. afzelii* is not endemic in North America, thereby accounting for the striking geographic distribution of the condition.[4]

There have been rare reports suggesting a possible association between *B. burgdorferi* infection and anetoderma.[28,29] A case with acquired cutis laxa has also been described.[30] The conflicting role of *B. burgdorferi* in the pathogenesis of morphea and lichen sclerosus et atrophicus is discussed elsewhere (see p. 483).[31–33]

Pathogenesis and histological features

Erythema chronicum migrans was first described in association with tick bites; cases were subsequently reported following mosquito bites and thorn pricks, or without preceding trauma.[25] In a proportion of cases an encephalitis was noted and the disease was termed 'tick-borne meningopolyneuritis'. In the 1970s several cases were reported in the United States, and because of a clustering effect near Lyme, Connecticut, the term Lyme disease was coined (these cases had a high proportion of arthritis).[34] The *Ixodes* tick has been known to be the vector for some time, but the actual etiological agent, a spirochete, was only identified in

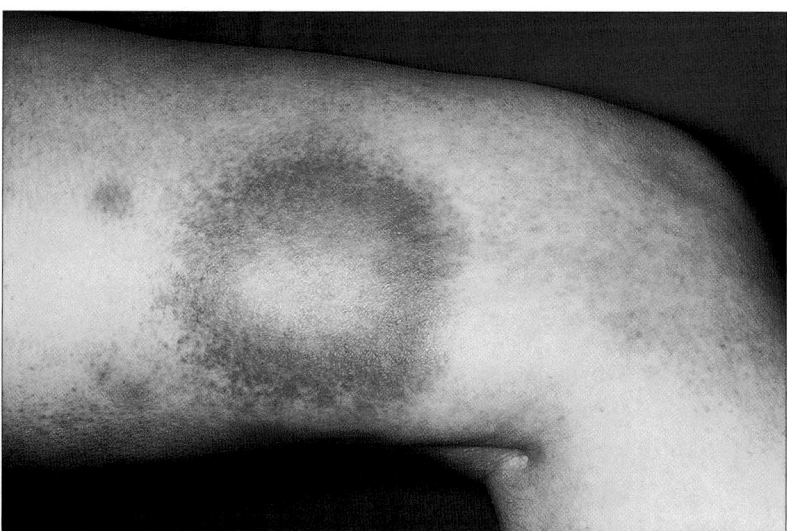

Fig. 17.135
Lyme disease: this annular, erythematous lesion developed (several weeks later) around the site of a tick bite. By courtesy of R.A. Marsden, MD, St George's Hospital, London, UK.

the 1980s after spirochetes were found in *Ixodes dammini* ticks in an endemic disease area.[1,9] In Europe, *Ixodes ricinus* has been incriminated.[15,25] It has a worldwide distribution.[15]

Patients recovering from the disease have been shown to have antibodies to the spirochetes in their serum.[13] Spirochetes have also been identified from biopsy sites, and cultured from or detected by PCR performed on specimens of blood, cerebrospinal fluid, synovial fluid and skin.[3,15,25,35,36]

Borreliae have developed strategies to inactivate host immune defenses via a variety of mechanisms, including recently described complement regulator-acquiring surface proteins (CRASPs), which confer complement resistance.[37,38] Borrelial CRASPs are capable of binding FHL-1/reconectin and factor H, which are two major regulators of the alternative complement pathway.[37,38] The selective upregulation of host matrix metalloproteinase-9 by *B. burgdorferi* in skin lesions of erythema chronicum migrans may play a role in the local spread of the organism and its dissemination to other organs.[39] In the early stage of Lyme disease, *B. burgdorferi* antigens induce a strong host immune response, which is predominated by the production of cytokines such as IFN-γ, TNF-α and transforming growth factor beta 1 (TGF-β_1).[40,41] By contrast, chronic neuroborreliosis is associated with a lack of TNF-α and TGF-β_1 responses.[41]

The central component of the initial lesion shows the typical appearance of an insect bite reaction. Histology reveals a polymorphic inflammatory cell infiltrate including polymorphs, eosinophils, histiocytes, lymphocytes and mast cells.[15] Vascular proliferation and dermal necrosis may additionally be present. A biopsy from the periphery is non-specific, showing a perivascular and interstitial infiltrate of lymphocytes, mast cells and plasma cells in both the superficial and deep dermis (*Figs 17.136, 17.137*). Identification of spirochetes by a silver stain is diagnostic.[42] An immunohistochemical method for demonstrating the etiologic agent has been described.[15] PCR may also be used to detect the organisms in formalin-fixed, paraffin-embedded tissue specimens.[43]

The borrelial lymphocytoma consists of a dense (polyclonal) dermal infiltrate composed of lymphocytes, plasma cells with macrophages and scattered eosinophils. Although it has been suggested that germinal center formation, when present, helps to exclude a cutaneous B-cell lymphoma, this is not necessarily true; cutaneous lymphomas of marginal zone type typically display germinal centers.[13,15,44] The association between *B. burgdorferi* infection and cutaneous B-cell lymphoma is discussed elsewhere (see p. 1454).[44,45]

Acrodermatitis chronica atrophicans is characterized by vascular dilatation in the mid- and upper dermis accompanied by a dense infiltrate of lymphocytes, plasma cells, macrophages and mast cells.[15] Scattered groups of 'vacuoles' may be seen in the dermis; this phenomenon is thought to be attributable to lymphedema.[26] The epidermis, which is usually hyperkeratotic, may be acanthotic or atrophic with loss of ridge pattern.[9] In some patients the appearances are reminiscent of lichen sclerosus et atrophicus or eosinophilic fasciitis.[13,15] Occasionally the histological features may overlap with scleromyxedema.[15] The juxta-articular fibrous nodules are characterized by fibrosis of the superficial subcutaneous tissue, with hyaline collagen bundles encircling clusters of adipocytes.[27] There is an accompanying perivascular and interstitial inflammatory infiltrate comprising lymphocytes and plasma cells.[27] Smaller periarticular fibrous nodules on the fingers show disorganized bundles of thickened dermal collagen.[46]

The triad of meningitis, cranial neuropathy and radiculopathy has been said to be unique for Lyme disease.[15] Central nervous system lesions include cortical, perivascular chronic inflammatory cell infiltrates, mild spongiform changes and gliosis. Plasma cells, however, are said to be absent.[15] The similarity of the late central nervous system changes of Lyme disease and meningovascular syphilis has been stressed.[15] Chronic leptomeningeal inflammation may also be evident. Peripheral nervous system lesions are characterized by nerve and ganglion lymphocyte and occasional plasma cell infiltration.[9,15] Adjacent vessels may show endarteritis obliterans.

Endocardial lesions are characterized by a lymphocytic and plasma cell infiltrate; deep specimens show an interstitial myocarditis.[9] Focal myonecrosis may also be evident.[15]

Histological examination of the synovium may show periadventitial cell onion-skinning proliferation and chronic inflammation.[9,15]

References

1. Burgdorfer, W., Barbour, A.G., Hayes, S.F. (1982) Lyme disease: a tick borne spirochaetosis? *Science*, **216**, 1317–1319.
2. Steere, A.C., Grodziki, R.K., Kornblatt, A.N. (1983) The spirochaetal aetiology of Lyme disease. *N Engl J Med*, **308**, 733–740.
3. Wilske, B. (2002) Microbiological diagnosis of Lyme borreliosis. *Int J Med Microbiol*, **291** (Suppl. 33), 114–119.
4. Picken, R.N., Strle, F., Picken, M.M. et al (1998) Identification of three species of Borrelia burgdorferi sensu lato (B. burgdorferi sensu stricto, B. garinii, and B. afzelii) among isolates from acrodermatitis chronica atrophicans. *J Investig Dermatol*, **110**, 211–214.
5. Centers for Disease Control and Prevention (CDC). (2004) Lyme disease – United States, 2001–2002. *MMWR Morb Mortal Wkly Rep*, 53, 365–369.
6. Smith, R., O'Connell, S., Palmer, S. (2000) Lyme disease surveillance in England and Wales, 1986–1998. *Emerg Infect Dis*, 6, 404–407.

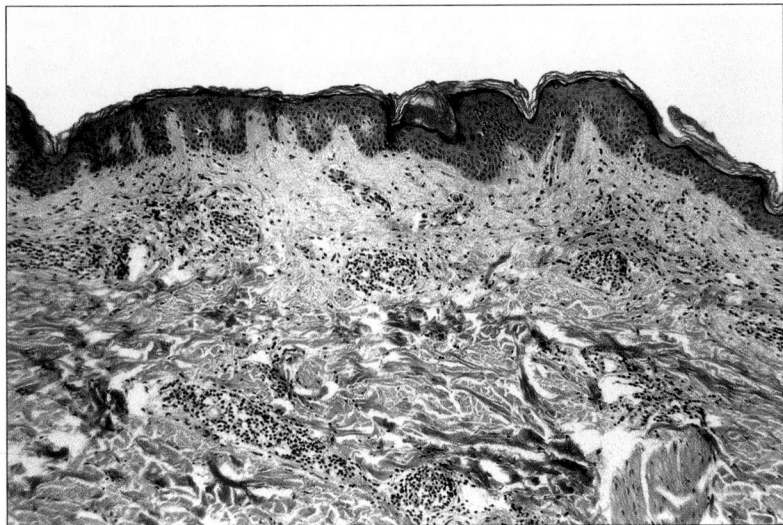

Fig. 17.136
Lyme disease: the epidermis is normal; a chronic inflammatory cell infiltrate surrounds the vessel in both the superficial and deep dermis.

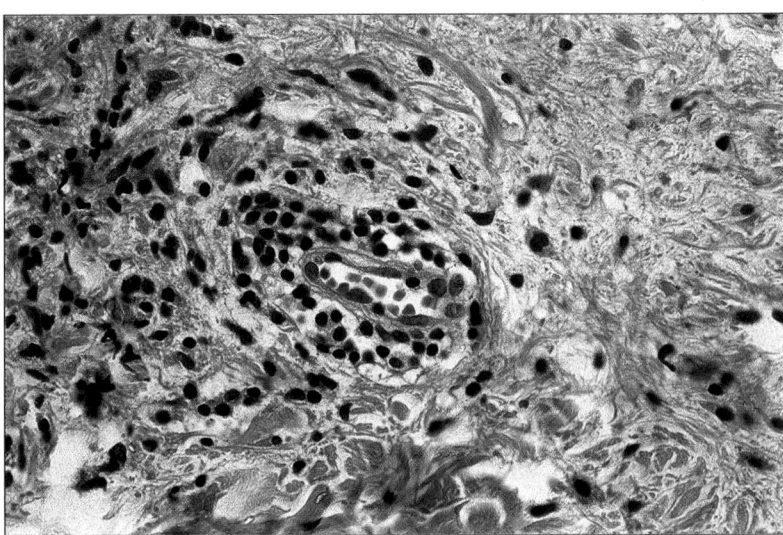

Fig. 17.137
Lyme disease: high power view.

7. Weber, K. (2001) Aspects of Lyme borreliosis in Europe. *Eur J Clin Microbiol Infect Dis*, **20**, 6–13.
8. Mast, W.E., Burrows, W.M. Jr (1976) Erythema chronicum migrans in the United States. *JAMA*, **236**, 859–860.
9. Duray, P.H. (1989) Clinical pathologic correlations of Lyme disease. *Rev Infect Dis*, **11** (Suppl.), 1475–1481.
10. Åsbrink, E. (1991) Cutaneous manifestations of Lyme borreliosis. Clinical definitions and differential diagnosis. *Scand J Infect Dis*, **74** (Suppl.), 44–50.
11. Åsbrink, E., Olsson, I. (1985) Clinical manifestations of erythema chronicum migrans Afzelius in 161 patients: a comparison with Lyme disease. *Acta Derm Venereol*, **65**, 43–52.
12. Osterhoudt, K.C., Zaoutis, T., Zorc, J.J. (2002) Lyme disease masquerading as brown recluse spider bite. *Ann Emerg Med*, **39**, 558–561.
13. Åsbrink, E., Brehmer-Andersson, E., Hovmark, A. (1986) Acrodermatitis chronica atrophicans: a spirochetosis. Clinical and histopathological picture based on 32 patients; course and relationship to erythema chronicum migrans afzelius. *Am J Dermatopathol*, **8**, 209–219.
14. Berger, B.W. (1984) Erythema chronicum migrans of Lyme disease. *Arch Dermatol*, **120**, 1017–1021.
15. Duray, P.H. (1987) The surgical pathology of human Lyme disease: an enlarging picture. *Am J Surg Pathol*, **11** (Suppl.), 47–60.
16. Carlsson, S.A., Granlund, H., Jansson, C., Nyman, D., Wahlberg, P. (2003) Characteristics of erythema migrans in Borrelia afzelii and Borrelia garinii infections. *Scand J Infect Dis*, **35**, 31–33.
17. Logar, M., Ruzic-Sabljic, E., Maraspin, V. et al (2004) Comparison of erythema migrans caused by Borrelia afzelii and Borrelia garinii. *Infection*, **32**, 15–19.
18. Stern, A.C., Batsford, W.P., Weinberg, M. et al (1980) Lyme carditis: cardiac abnormalities of Lyme disease. *Ann Intern Med*, **93**, 8–16.
19. Pachner, A.R., Steere, A.C. (1985) The triad of neurological manifestations of Lyme disease: meningitis, cranial neuritis and radiculoneuritis. *Neurology*, **35**, 47–53.
20. Halperin, J.J. (2004) Nervous system Lyme disease. *Vector Borne Zoonotic Dis*, **2**, 241–247.
21. Carvounis, P.E., Mehta, A.P., Geist, C.E. (2004) Orbital myositis associated with Borrelia burgdorferi (Lyme disease) infection. *Ophthalmology*, **111**, 1023–1028.
22. Iero, I., Elia, A.P., Cosentino, F.I. et al (2004) Isolated monolateral neurosensory hearing loss as a rare sign of neuroborreliosis. *Neurol Sci*, **25**, 30–33.
23. Cassarino, D.S., Quezado, M.M., Ghatak, N.R., Duray, P.H. (2003) Lyme-associated parkinsonism: a neuropathologic case study and review of the literature. *Arch Pathol Lab Med*, **127**, 1204–1206.
24. Seijo Martinez, M., Grandes Ibanez, J., Sanchez Herrero, J., Garcia-Monco, J.C. (2001) Spontaneous brain hemorrhage associated with Lyme borreliosis. *Neurologia*, **16**, 43–45.
25. Hurley, H.J., Hurley, J.P. (1984) The gyrate erythemas. *Semin Dermatol*, **3**, 327–335.
26. Leslie, T.A., Levell, N.J., Cutler, S.J. et al (1994) Acrodermatitis chronica atrophicans: a case report and review of the literature. *Br J Dermatol*, **131**, 687–693.
27. Marsch, W.C.H., Wolter, M., Mayet, A. (1994) Juxta-articular fibrotic nodules in Borrelia infection – ultrastructural details of therapy-induced regression. *Clin Exp Dermatol*, **19**, 394–398.
28. Hofer, T., Goldenberger, D., Itin, P.H. (2003) Anetoderma and borreliosis: is there a pathogenetic relationship? *Eur J Dermatol*, **13**, 399–401.
29. Bauer, J., Leitz, G., Palmedo, G., Hugel, H. (2003) Anetoderma: another facet of Lyme disease? *J Am Acad Dermatol*, **48** (Suppl.), S86–88.
30. Ozkan, S., Fetil, E., Gunes, A.T. et al (1999) Cutis laxa acquisita: is there any association with Borrelia burgdorferi? *Eur J Dermatol*, **9**, 561–564.
31. Weide, B., Walz, T., Garbe, C. (2000) Is morphoea caused by Borrelia burgdorferi? A review. *Br J Dermatol*, **142**, 636–644.
32. Weide, B., Schittek, B., Klyscz, T. et al (2000) Morphoea is neither associated with features of Borrelia burgdorferi infection, nor is the agent detectable in lesional skin by polymerase chain reaction. *Br J Dermatol*, **143**, 636–644.
33. Goodlad, J.R., Davidson, M.M., Gordon, P., Billington, R., Ho-Yen, D.O. (2002) Morphoea and Borrelia burgdorferi: results from the Scottish Highlands in the context of the world literature. *Mol Pathol*, **55**, 374–378.
34. Steere, A.C., Malaivista, S.E., Snydman, D.R. (1977) A cluster of arthritis in children and adults in Lyme, Connecticut (Abstract). *Arthritis Rheum*, **20**, 7–17.
35. Chmielewski, T., Fiett, J., Gniadowski, M., Tylewska-Wierzbanowska, S. (2003) Improvement in the laboratory recognition of Lyme borreliosis with the combination of culture and PCR methods. *Mol Diagn*, **7**, 155–162.
36. Liveris, D., Wang, G., Girao, G. et al (2002) Quantitative detection of Borrelia burgdorferi in 2-millimeter skin samples of erythema chronicum migrans lesions: correlation of results with clinical and laboratory findings. *J Clin Microb*, **40**, 1249–1253.
37. Kraiczy, P., Sherka, C., Kirschfink, M., Zipfel, P.F., Brade, V. (2002) Immune evasion of Borrelia burgdorferi: insufficient killing of the pathogens by complement and antibody. *Int J Med Microbiol*, **291** (Suppl. 33), 141–146.
38. Kraiczy, P., Hellwage, J., Sherka, C. et al (2004) Complement resistance of Borrelia burgdorferi correlates with the expression of BbCRASP-1, a novel linear plasmid-encoded surface protein that interacts with human factor H and FHL-1 and is unrelated to Erp proteins. *J Biol Chem*, **279**, 2421–2429.
39. Zhao, Z., Chang, H., Trevino, R.P. et al (2003) Selective up-regulation of matrix metalloproteinase-9 expression in human erythema migrans skin lesions of acute Lyme disease. *J Infect Dis*, **188**, 1098–1104.
40. Glickstein, L., Moore, B., Bledsoe, T. et al (2003) Inflammatory cytokine production predominates in early Lyme disease in patients with erythema migrans. *Infective Immunol*, **71**, 6051–6053.
41. Widhe, M., Grusell, M., Ekerfelt, C. et al (2002) Cytokines in Lyme borreliosis: lack of early tumour necrosis factor-α and transforming growth factor-β₁ responses are associated with chronic neuroborreliosis. *Immunology*, **107**, 46–55.
42. Berger, B.W. (1989) Dermatologic manifestations of Lyme disease. *Rev Infect Dis*, **11** (Suppl.), 1475–1481.
43. Wienecke, R., Neubert, U., Volkenandt, M. (1993) Molecular detection of Borrelia burgdorferi in formalin-fixed, paraffin-embedded lesions of Lyme disease. *J Cutan Pathol*, **20**, 385–388.
44. Goodlad, J.R., Davidson, M.M., Hollowood, K., Batstone, P., Ho-Yen, D.O. (2000) Borrelia burgdorferi-associated cutaneous marginal zone lymphoma: a clinicopathological study of two cases illustrating the temporal progression of B. burgdorferi-associated B-cell proliferation in the skin. *Histopathology*, **37**, 501–508.
45. Wood, G.S., Kamath, N.V., Guitart, J. et al (2001) Absence of Borrelia burgdorferi DNA in cutaneous B-cell lymphomas from the United States. *J Cutan Pathol*, **28**, 502–507.
46. España, A., Torrelo, A., Guerrero, A. et al (1991) Periarticular fibrous nodules in Lyme borreliosis. *Br J Dermatol*, **125**, 68–70.

Venereal syphilis

This disease is discussed in page 494.

Endemic (non-venereal) treponematoses

Endemic syphilis

Clinical features

Endemic syphilis (Syrian *bejel*) is a form of non-venereal treponematosis caused by *Treponema pallidum* subsp. *endemicum*, an organism nearly identical to *Treponema pallidum* subsp. *pallidum*, the etiological agent of venereal syphilis.[1–3] The condition usually occurs in children living in conditions of poor hygiene and is transmitted by cutaneous inoculation.[1,3–5] Other endemic forms have been associated with shared drinking vessels and other contaminated domestic utensils when some members of the community have oral or labial syphilitic lesions.[1,3,4] The disease still occurs in parts of the Middle East and Africa, especially in rural desert regions.[3,6]

Unlike venereal syphilis, a primary chancre seldom occurs in endemic syphilis; women suckling infected infants may, however, develop primary infections of the nipple.[3] The primary lesions usually involve the oropharynx but are easily overlooked. Early secondary lesions manifest as soft, oval mucous patches with a predilection for the buccal and labial mucosae, sometimes accompanied by angular stomatitis. Mucous patches may also occur in the perianal and genital areas, where they sometimes appear condylomatous. Osteoperiostitis may occur, and generalized lymphadenopathy is common.[3]

The late (tertiary) manifestations develop following a latent period of between 5 and 15 years. The lesions may evolve in the skin, naso-pharynx, bone or joints and are clinically similar to those encountered in late yaws.[3] Articular and osseous involvement is frequently destructive. Cardiovascular involvement may also occur, but the disease does not affect the central nervous system. A further point of distinction from venereal syphilis is the fact that there is no congenital form of endemic syphilis.[3]

Histological features

The histopathology of the primary lesion is poorly documented. The light microscopic features of the secondary lesions are virtually identical to those encountered in venereal syphilis (see Ch. 11).[3,7] Granulomatous dermal inflammation is encountered in the tertiary skin lesions.[7]

References

1. Antal, G.M., Lukehart, S.A., Meheus, A.Z. (2002) The endemic treponematoses. *Microbes Infect*, **4**, 83–94.
2. Centurion-Lara, A., Castro, C., Castillo, R. et al (1998) The flanking region sequences of the 15-kDa lipoprotein gene differentiate pathogenic treponemes. *J Infect Dis*, **177**, 1036–1092.
3. Gonçalves, A.P., Basset, A., Maleville, J. (1992) Tropical treponematoses. In: Canizares, O., Harman, R. (eds) Clinical tropical dermatology, 2nd edn. Boston: Blackwell, pp 129–150.
4. Findlay, G.H. (1987) Treponemal infections. In: The dermatology of bacterial infections. Oxford: Blackwell, pp 106–130.
5. Sehgal, V.N. (1990) Leg ulcers caused by yaws and endemic syphilis. *Clin Dermatol*, **8**, 166–174.
6. Meheus, A.Z., Antal, G.M. (1992) The endemic treponematoses: not yet eradicated. *World Health Stat Q*, **45**, 228–237.
7. Hasselmann, C.M. (1957) Comparative studies on the histopathology of syphilis, yaws and pinta. *Br J Venereol Dis*, **33**, 5–12.

Yaws

Clinical features

Yaws (framboesia tropica) is a tropical disease occurring in people living in poor conditions due to infection by the spirochete *Treponema pallidum* subsp. *pertenue*.[1-4] Although it was thought to have been almost eradicated by the WHO treatment program, it has been recently seen in a number of warm, humid tropical regions including Africa, parts of Asia, Indonesia and Papua New Guinea, Ecuador and Vanuatu.[2,3,5-9] It is not transmitted sexually, but rather by close contact, for example inoculation of skin previously traumatized by insects or scratching.[3,10]

Yaws is most common in children 6–10 years of age, who present with lesions on the feet, legs and buttocks.[11] Clinically it is divided into early and late yaws.[12-14] The initial lesion, known as a 'mother yaw', develops 3–5 weeks after inoculation.[11] It starts as a non-tender papilloma, which ulcerates and is then covered with a yellow crust (*Fig. 17.138*).[11] It resembles a raspberry, hence the alternative designation framboesia (Dutch *framboos*, raspberry). This mother yaw may be surrounded by smaller papillomas, which develop 2–4 months after the initial lesion.[3,10] Lesions in the perineum and natal cleft may become condylomatous.[10] Subsequently these warty lesions may become very widespread ('daughter yaws') (*Fig. 17.139*). Macules, papules and nodules have also been described.[5,11] They eventually resolve to leave a depressed and hyperpigmented scar.[10] The mucous membranes, bones (osteitis and periostitis) and joints may also be affected in early yaws.[11] Palmar and plantar hyperkeratosis, which can be exceedingly painful and may result in walking difficulties (crab yaws), are characteristic.[5,15]

There may be a symptom-free period of 3–5 years before the lesions of late yaws arise. The late lesions, which develop in about 10% of patients, are destructive ulcers and gummatous nodules which affect the skin, bones (e.g. saber tibia) and joints (*Figs 17.140, 17.141*).[3,5,11,12] Cutaneous manifestations of late yaws include palmar and plantar hyperkeratosis (crab yaws), loss of pigment (pintoid yaws) and gummata.[3,12] Pintoid yaws includes hyperkeratosis, contractures, juxta-articular nodules and bony lesions.[3,12] Gummata characteristically involve the long bones, the bones of the hands and feet and typically lead to gross destruction of the face (gangosa).[16] The cardiovascular and nervous systems are said not to be involved, but there is evidence to suggest that ophthalmic and myeloneuropathies may occur in endemic areas.[11,13,17]

Pathogenesis and histological features

The spirochete responsible for yaws is morphologically indistinguishable from *T. pallidum* subsp. *pallidum*.[5] The organism is, however, differentiated from other pathogenic treponemes by unique differences in the genetic sequences flanking the 15-kDa lipoprotein gene.[4]

Early lesions are characteristically parakeratotic, acanthotic and papillomatous. They show focal spongiosis and intraepidermal neutrophils with microabscess formation (*Fig. 17.142*).[5] There is a dense perivascular dermal infiltrate containing numerous plasma cells. The vascular changes in contrast to syphilis are usually insignificant. Treponemes can be seen around the blood vessels, in the tips of the dermal papillae and within the epidermis (*Fig. 17.143*).[15,18-20]

The palmoplantar lesions are characterized by hyperkeratosis, parakeratosis and acanthosis. A mild non-specific chronic inflammatory cell infiltrate is present in the superficial dermis.

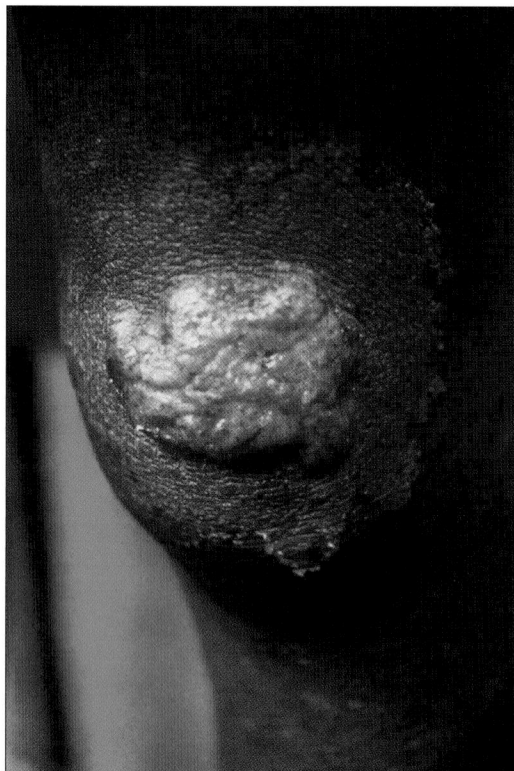

Fig. 17.138
Early yaws: typical framboesiform 'mother yaw'. Note the yellow crust and surrounding hypopigmentation. By courtesy of H.J.H. Engelkens, MD, and E. Stolz, MD, University Hospital, Rotterdam–Dijkzigt and Erasmus University, Rotterdam, The Netherlands.

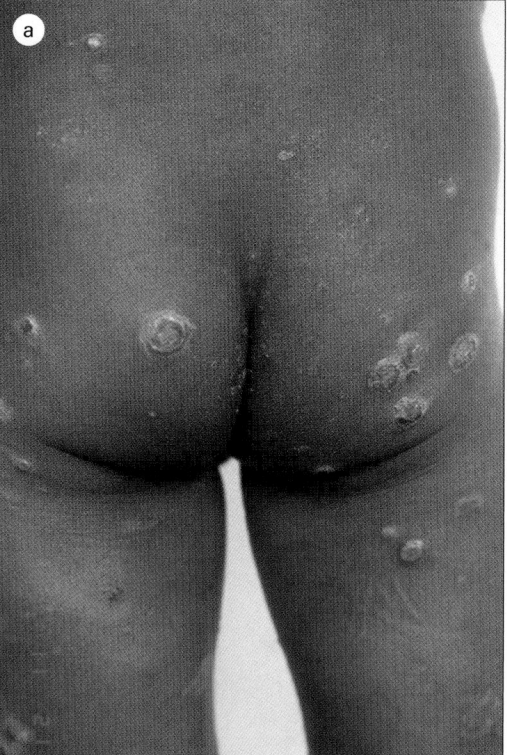
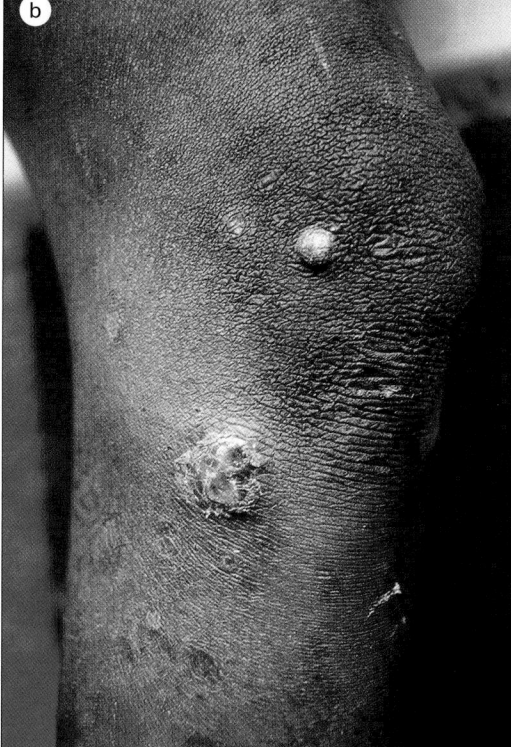

Fig. 17.139
(a, b) Early yaws: multiple smaller 'daughter yaws' may be widely distributed and usually present 2–4 months after the 'mother yaw'. By courtesy of H.J.H. Engelkens, MD, and E. Stolz, MD, University Hospital, Rotterdam–Dijkzigt and Erasmus University, Rotterdam, The Netherlands.

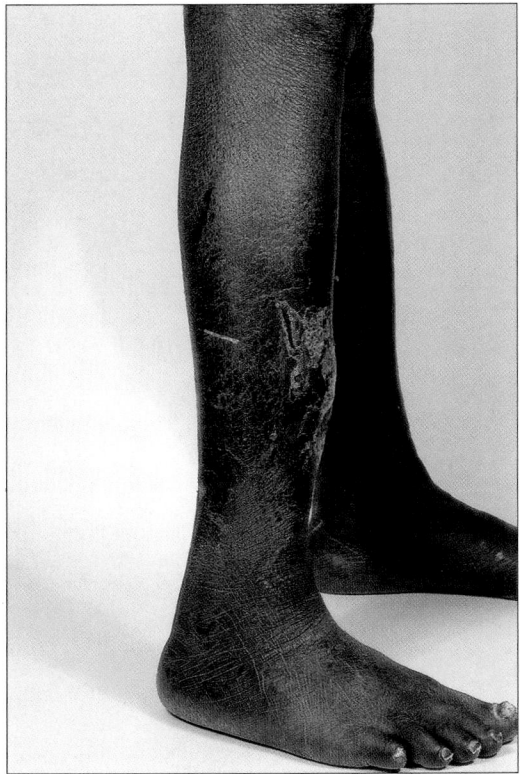

Fig. 17.140
Late yaws: note the bowing of the lower leg with cutaneous ulcerated and crusted lesions in this late stage. By courtesy of R.A. Marsden, MD, St George's Hospital, London, UK.

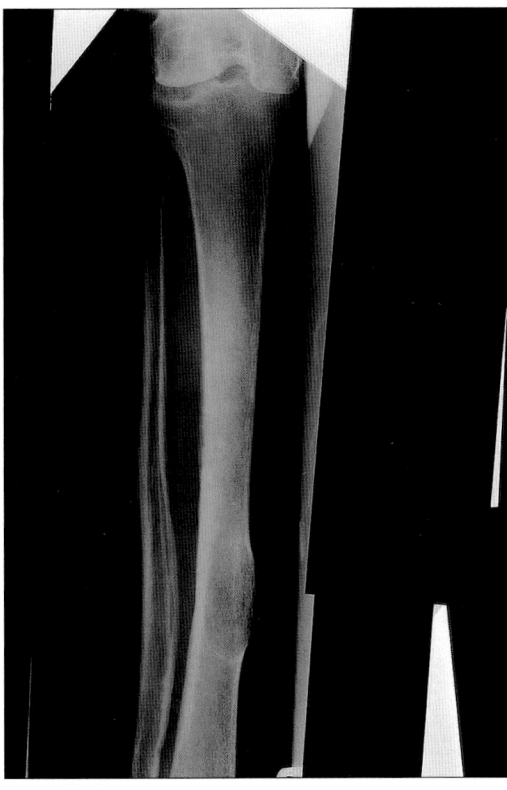

Fig. 17.141
Late yaws: note the cyst with an overlying periosteal reaction. By courtesy of R.A. Marsden, MD, St George's Hospital, London, UK.

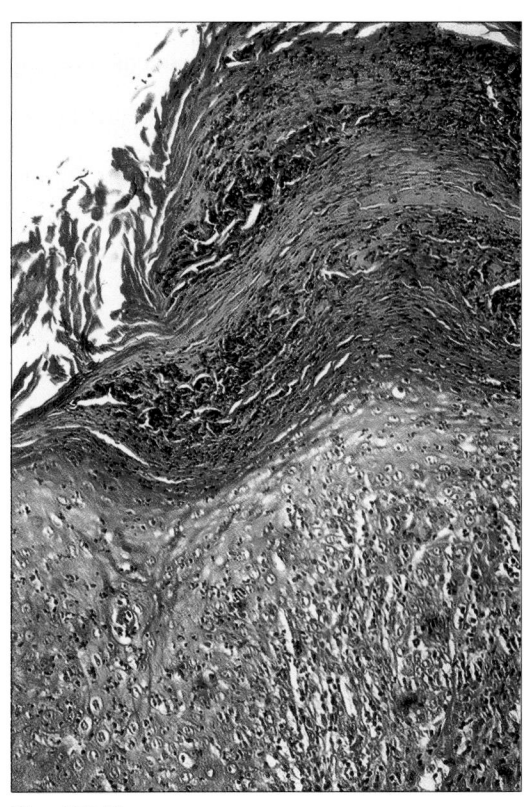

Fig. 17.142
Early yaws: biopsy through an evolving papilloma. There is very marked parakeratosis associated with abundant neutrophil debris. The epidermis shows intense acute inflammation. By courtesy of H.J.H. Engelkens, MD, and E. Stolz, MD, University Hospital, Rotterdam–Dijkzigt and Erasmus University, Rotterdam, The Netherlands.

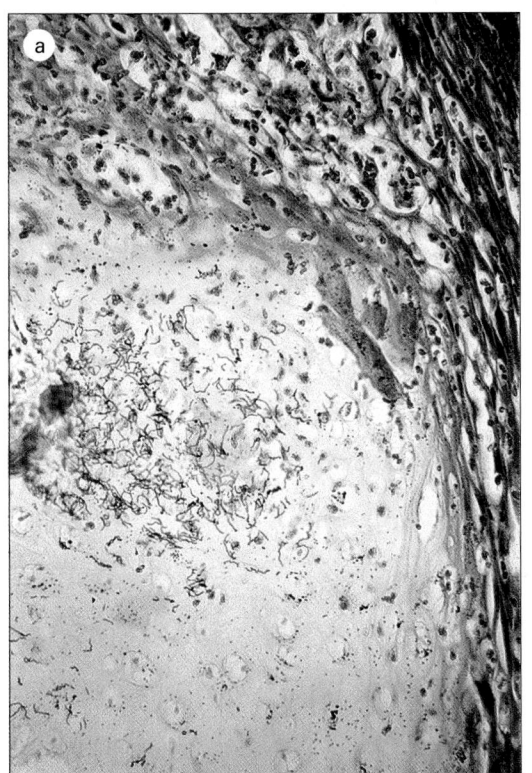

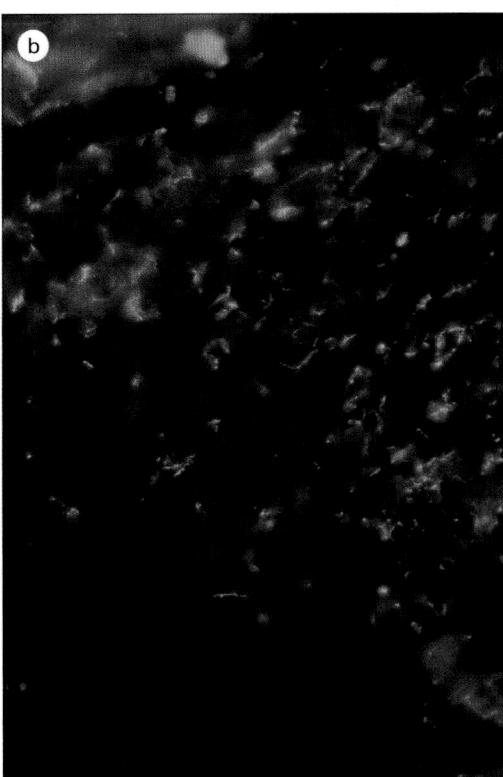

Fig. 17.143
(a, b) Early yaws: same specimen as that shown in *Fig. 17.142*. Note the presence of numerous spirochetes. (a) Warthin–Starry; (b) immunofluorescence. By courtesy of H.J.H. Engelkens, MD, and E. Stolz, MD, University Hospital, Rotterdam–Dijkzigt and Erasmus University, Rotterdam, The Netherlands.

The gummata show central caseation necrosis surrounded by a rim of lymphocytes, plasma cells, histiocytes, epithelioid cells and giant cells.[15] There is associated fibrosis.

References

1. Antal, G.M., Lukehart, S.A., Meheus, A.Z. (2002) The endemic treponematoses. *Microbes Infect,* **4,** 83–94.
2. Walker, S.J., Hay, R.J. (2000) Yaws – a review of the last 50 years. *Int J Dermatol,* **60,** 19–29.
3. Gonçalves, A.P., Basset, A., Maleville, J. (1992) Tropical treponematoses. In: Canizares, O., Harman, R. (eds) Clinical tropical dermatology, 2nd edn. Boston: Blackwell, pp 129–150.
4. Centurion-Lara, A., Castro, C., Castillo, R. et al (1998) The flanking region sequences of the 15-kDa lipoprotein gene differentiate pathogenic treponemes. *J Infect Dis,* **177,** 1036–1092.
5. Engelkens, H.J.H., Judanarso, J., Oranje, A.P. et al (1991) Endemic treponematosis Part 1. Yaws. *Int J Dermatol,* **30,** 77–83.
6. Guerian, R.H., Guzmán, J.R., Calvopina, M. et al (1991) Studies on a focus of yaws in the Santiago Basin, province of Esmeraldas, Ecuador. *Trop Geogr Med,* **43,** 142–147.
7. Harris, M., Nako, D., Hopkins, T. et al (1991) Yaws infection in Tanna, Vanuatu, 1989. *S As J Trop Med Public Health,* **22,** 113–119.
8. Meheus, A.Z., Antal, G.M. (1992) The endemic treponematoses: not yet eradicated. *World Health Stat Q,* **45,** 228–237.
9. Engelkens, H.J., Stolz, E. (1992) A small yaws survey on the island of Sumatra, Indonesia. *Acta Leiden,* **60,** 19–29.
10. Brown, S.G. (1982) Yaws. *Int J Dermatol,* **21,** 220–223.
11. Nagreh, D.S. (1986) Yaws. *Cutis,* **38,** 303–305.
12. Green, C.A., Harman, R.R. (1986) Yaws truly – a survey of patients indexed under 'Yaws' and a review of the clinical and laboratory problems of diagnosis. *Clin Exp Dermatol,* **11,** 41–48.
13. Lawton-Smith, J., David, N.G., Indgin, S. et al (1971) Neuro-ophthalmological study of late yaws and pinta. II The Caracas project. *Br J Vener Dis,* **47,** 226–251.
14. Hackett, C.J. (1957) An international nomenclature of yaws lesions. WHO monograph series, No. 36. Geneva: World Health Organization.
15. Sehgal, V.N. (1990) Leg ulcers caused by yaws and endemic syphilis. *Clin Dermatol,* **8,** 166–174.
16. Elango, S., Palaniappan, S.P. (1989) Nasal manifestations of yaws. *Ear Nose Throat J,* **68,** 870, 873–875.
17. Román, G.C., Román, L.N. (1986) Occurrence of congenital cardiovascular visceral neurologic and neuro-ophthalmologic complications in late yaws: a theme for further research. *Rev Infect Dis,* **8,** 760–770.
18. Engelkens, H.J., Vuzevski, V.D., Judanarso, J. et al (1990) Early yaws: a light microscopic study. *Genitourin Med,* **66,** 264–266.
19. Hasselmann, C.M. (1957) Comparative studies on the histopathology of syphilis, yaws and pinta. *Br J Vener Dis,* **33,** 5–12.
20. Engelkens, H.J., ten Kate, F.J., Judanarso, J. et al (1993) The localisation of treponemes and characterisation of the inflammatory infiltrate in skin biopsies from patients with primary or secondary syphilis, or early infectious yaws. *Genitourin Med,* **69,** 102–107.

Pinta

Clinical features

This is a non-sexually transmitted treponematosis characterized by depigmented skin lesions. It is caused by *Treponema pallidum* subsp. *carateum*, an organism that is very similar to *T. pallidum* subsp. *pallidum*.[1–3] It is confined to remote primitive regions in tropical Central and South America where the inhabitants live in poor hygiene and in close proximity.[4–6] Children are primarily affected and transmission is thought to be by direct cutaneous or mucous membrane contact, possibly via minute abrasions.[4,5]

The lesions present as small scaly erythematous indurated papules and plaques on exposed skin, usually on the hands and feet. These disappear, but recur in a more disseminated form (pintids).[4] Late stages of pinta are characterized by disfiguring hyperpigmentation, achromia, hyperkeratosis and atrophy (*Fig. 17.144*).[7]

Unlike syphilis and yaws there is no evidence of systemic disease.

Histological features

Histologically, the features comprise hyperkeratosis with acanthosis or occasionally epidermal atrophy.[3,7] Lymphocytic exocytosis, basal cell hydropic degeneration and pigmentary incontinence is evident.[3] A perivascular lymphocytic infiltrate is usually seen without endothelial swelling.

References

1. Antal, G.M., Lukehart, S.A., Meheus, A.Z. (2002) The endemic treponematoses. *Microbes Infect,* **4,** 83–94.
2. Centurion-Lara, A., Castro, C., Castillo, R. et al (1998) The flanking region sequences of the 15-kDa lipoprotein gene differentiate pathogenic treponemes. *J Infect Dis,* **177,** 1036–1092.
3. Fohn, M.J., Wignall, F.S., Baker-Zander, S.A. et al (1988) Specificity of antibodies from patients with pinta for antigens of Treponema pallidum subspecies pallidum. *J Infect Dis,* **157,** 32–37.
4. Engelkens, H.J.H., Niemel, P.L.A., van der Sluis, J.J. et al (1991) Endemic treponematoses. part II. Pinta and endemic syphilis. *Int J Dermatol,* **30,** 231–238.
5. Gonçalves, A.P., Basset, A., Maleville, J. (1992) Tropical treponematoses. In: Canizares, O., Harman, R. (eds) Clinical tropical dermatology, 2nd edn. Boston: Blackwell, pp 129–150.
6. Meheus, A.Z., Antal, G.M. (1992) The endemic treponematoses: not yet eradicated. *World Health Stat Q,* **45,** 228–237.
7. Pecher, S.A., Azevedo, E.B. (1987) Aspectos histpatológicos da pinta terciária. *Medicina Cutanea Ibero Latino Americana,* **15,** 239–242.

Lymphogranuloma venereum

This condition is discussed on page 505.

Granuloma inguinale (donovanosis)

This condition is discussed on page 502.

Chancroid

This condition is discussed on page 504.

Tuberculosis

Clinical features

Tuberculous (*Mycobacterium tuberculosis*) infection of the skin, which was once common worldwide, has shown a declining incidence in the latter decades.[1] This was due in part to improved therapy, a reduction in the size of the active reservoir of infection and increased immuno-

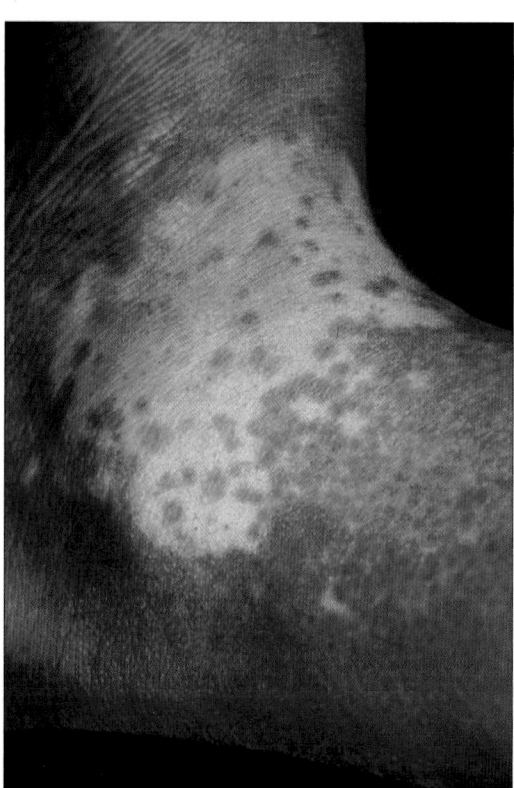

Fig. 17.144
Pinta: this is a late lesion showing characteristic complete loss of pigmentation surrounded by a hyperpigmented border. By courtesy of R. Arenas, MD, and J. Salas, MD, Azteca, Monterrey, Mexico.

resistance to infection. More recently, however, an apparent upward trend in the incidence of cutaneous tuberculosis has been recorded, especially in Asian countries.[2] This is of particular importance because cutaneous lesions can readily simulate other conditions, and may be insidious in onset. The source of infection is sometimes not obvious, and tissue destruction may be very marked.

Mycobacterial infections (tuberculous and atypical) are of increasing importance in the context of acquired immunosuppression, whether due to lymphoma, AIDS or aggressive chemotherapy. Atypical modes of presentation with microorganisms of borderline virulence are becoming of particular significance.[3] Cutaneous tuberculosis has re-emerged in those parts of the world where the incidence of HIV infection and multidrug-resistant tuberculosis is high.[4,5]

In Europe and North America cutaneous infection is still relatively infrequent, due to a reduction in the numbers of infected cases by therapy and immunization programs and to an increased standard of living. Nevertheless, there remains an apparently irreducible number of people with tuberculosis, usually living in circumstances of poor hygiene and nutrition.[6] This is borne out by the number of unsuspected cases of tuberculosis diagnosed at autopsy. Moreover, there exists an important reservoir of infected immigrants, particularly of Asian origin, who often present with cervical lymphadenopathy.

The manifestations of the disease in the skin are influenced by previous infection or immunity and by the route of infection. Because of the virulence and resistance to phagocytosis by *M. tuberculosis*, neutrophils are completely ineffective in dealing with this bacterial infection, whereas macrophages and their derivatives are characteristically seen in the cellular response. These lead on to (giant cell) granuloma formation with or without necrosis and this underlies the varied clinical presentations of this infection.

The majority of cases of cutaneous tuberculosis are a manifestation of systemic involvement.[4] The usual portals of entry of *M. tuberculosis* include the lungs and intestine, but the mucous membranes and skin occasionally show primary involvement.[7] Cutaneous involvement may include papules, nodules, plaques, ulcerative lesions, warty tumors or scarring reactions.[8] Although preferred, it is not always possible to package cutaneous tuberculous lesions neatly into the categories detailed below, and on occasions tuberculous skin disease may be reported as of non-specific type, particularly in this current era of profound immunosuppression. In this account a modified 'Beyt' classification is used.[7,9]

Appropriate classification, when possible, is important because some variants may be associated with systemic lesions and therefore clinical management and prognostic implications are highly variable.[7] Tuberculids in which bacilli are not detectable are now rare in the West, but are still common in developing countries and are considered separately below.

Infections by inoculation (exogenous source)

Tuberculous chancre, which is rare, occurs by direct inoculation of infected material into the skin of a previously uninfected and non-immune patient. The response is analogous to a Ghon complex in the lung.[9] These lesions develop 2–4 weeks after inoculation, which may be through minor trauma to the skin of various sites, such as the face and limbs of children (*Fig. 17.145*). Infection may also follow minor surgery such as ear piercing, tattooing or circumcision. The earliest lesion is a reddish-brown papule, which may rapidly progress to an ulcer with ragged undermined edges. The margins of the lesion become indurated and lymphadenopathy is usually noted at this stage. Satellite papules may be seen around the original lesion and this pattern of spread is termed 'lupoid'. Inoculation tuberculosis from bacille Calmette–Guérin (BCG) injection is a similar phenomenon.[10]

Warty lupus (tuberculosis verrucosa cutis) occurs by inoculation of *M. tuberculosis* into the skin of individuals who have some degree of immunity or may have active infection elsewhere. It is the most common variant seen in India and China (*Fig. 17.146*).[7,11] This lesion occurs classically as 'prosector's warts' in pathologists or autopsy technicians, but may also be seen in butchers dealing with infected cattle (*Fig. 17.147*).[9] Inoculation of the skin by infected sputum, even from the same patient, can cause a similar lesion. Children tend to be affected on the lower limbs or buttocks (*Fig. 17.148*).

The lesion begins as a small indurated nodule with a keratotic warty surface at the site of inoculation and then slowly extends in a serpiginous manner producing an irregular reddish-brown warty plaque. Although much of the lesion is firm, some softer areas may be present from which pus may exude. In some areas the lesion continues to extend, but elsewhere it may show focal involution to leave an atrophic pale scar.

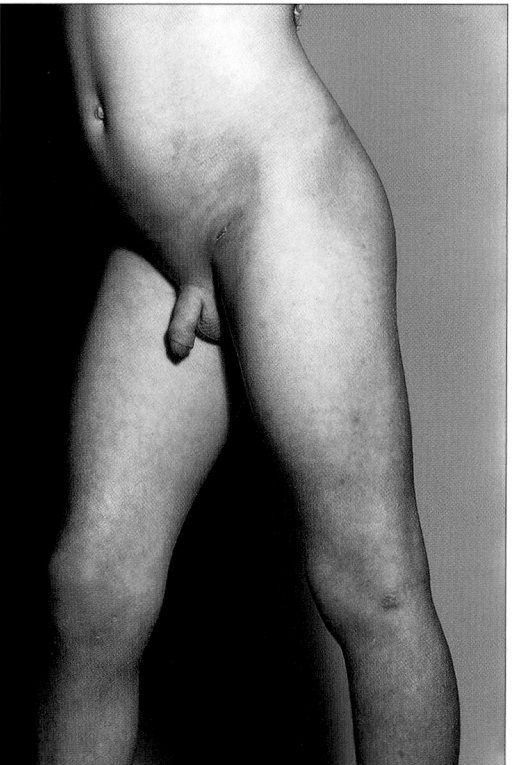

Fig. 17.145
Tuberculous chancre: the cutaneous equivalent of a Ghon complex. Note the healing lesion on the outer aspect of the knee and the ulcerated inguinal nodes from this patient from the 1950s. By courtesy of M.M. Black, MD, Institute of Dermatology, London, UK.

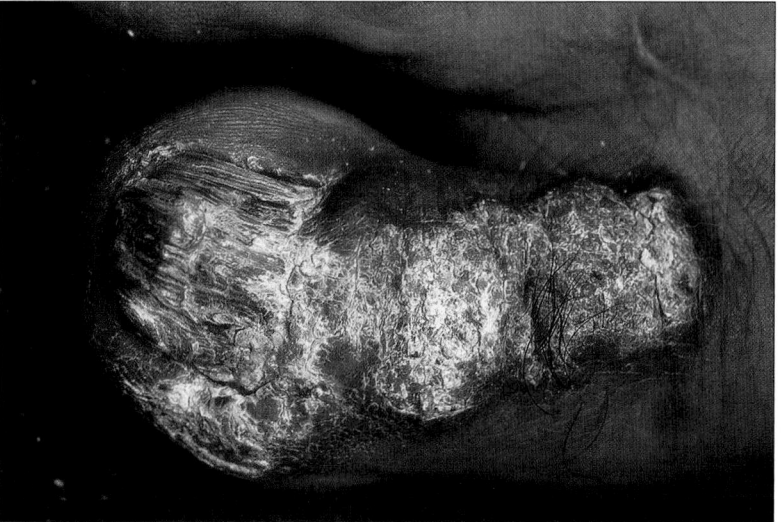

Fig. 17.146
Warty lupus: in this example, there is a grossly hyperkeratotic lesion associated with destruction of the nail. By courtesy of the Institute of Dermatology, London, UK.

The warty component may persist for years, but usually resolves eventually.

Secondary tuberculosis (endogenous source)

Orificial tuberculous ulcers are rare and occur in the skin or mucosa adjacent to an orifice draining an active tuberculous infection. They represent autoinoculation and are most commonly seen around the nose, mouth, genitalia or anus (*Fig. 17.149*). Patients are usually hyperreactive to tuberculin testing. The lesions start as edematous red papules, which ulcerate and develop undermined edges. These ulcers are painful and do not progress or regress.

Scrofuloderma (L. *scrofula*, brood sow; *derma*, skin) is a complication of deep tuberculous infection of lymph node, bone, joint or subcutaneous tissue (*Figs 17.150–17.152*). The lesion is seen as a bluish-red nodule,

which ulcerates and discharges pus or necrotic material.[7] Lesions are commonly seen in the neck, submandibular area or axilla. There is associated scarring, and the combination of scarring and a chronic discharging ulcer may resemble hidradenitis suppurativa. Very rarely, scrofuloderma may arise over the lacrimal system.[12]

Infection by hematogenous spread

Lupus vulgaris may occur following inoculation of bacteria into individuals showing some immunity (see above); more commonly, however, it represents hematogenous or lymphatic spread from a tuberculous focus, which is usually occult. Lesions occur mostly on the face (particularly around the nose), neck and earlobes in the West, and are more common in women (*Figs 17.153, 17.154*).[10] The extremities and buttocks are more commonly involved in the East. The arms and legs may also be affected (*Fig. 17.155*). It is a very chronic disease. This form of cutaneous tuberculosis used to be particularly evident in Northern Europe and is still the most frequently encountered variant in the West.[7] It is a common form of cutaneous tuberculosis in childhood.[13]

Lupus vulgaris occasionally results from direct inoculation and may even occur at the site of BCG inoculation.[14]

Lupus vulgaris is characterized by papules and raised erythematous and sometimes scaly plaques of gelatinous consistency, said with diascopy to resemble apple jelly. These lesions may gradually extend, while involuting with scarring in other areas. There may be adjacent cellulitis or ulceration. Squamous and basal cell carcinoma, melanoma and lymphoma may develop in chronic lupus vulgaris.[15–17] Contractures and lymphedema are late complications. Ocular involvement is an additional serious complication. Lupus vulgaris is a rare cause of alopecia.[18]

Tuberculous gumma represents a metastatic tuberculous subcutaneous abscess derived from infection at another site by a hematogenous route.[7] It is most commonly seen in the malnourished, the immunodeficient or the immunosuppressed.[4,7,19] Clinically it presents as a firm subcutaneous nodule, usually on the arms or legs. The lesion slowly becomes fluctuant and the overlying skin perforates to form a chronic undermined ulcer as seen in scrofuloderma.

Miliary tuberculosis of the skin (tuberculosis cutis miliaris disseminata) occurs in association with generalized miliary tuberculosis and is very rare. It is usually seen in infants and has a poor prognosis. The infection may be seen in mother and child concurrently and then the cutaneous lesions may be scanty and the prognosis less grave.[20] Other

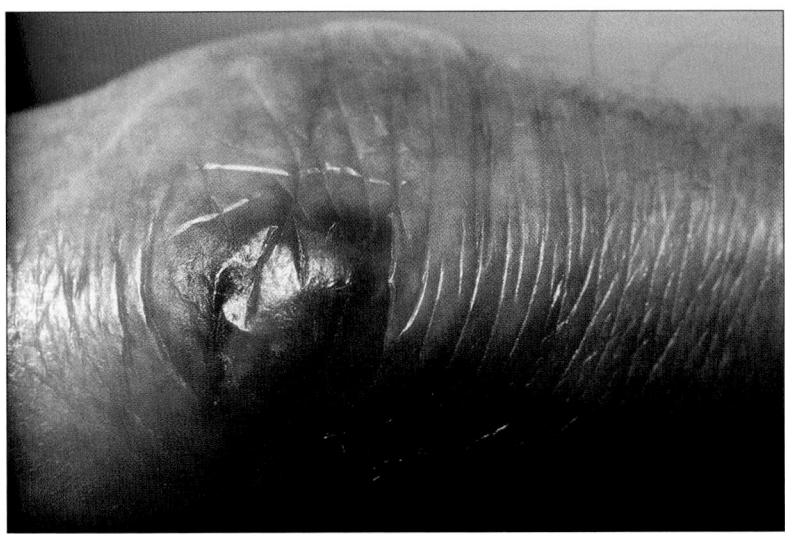

Fig. 17.147
Warty lupus: prosector's wart. This indurated lesion on the finger developed after a pathologist had performed a tuberculous autopsy. By courtesy of R. Vellor, MD, St Thomas' Hospital, London, UK.

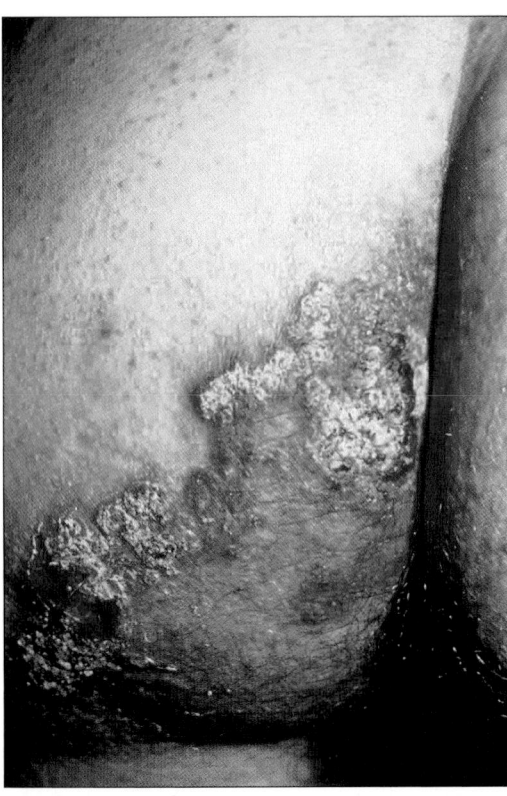

Fig. 17.148
Warty lupus: in children, the buttock is a commonly affected site. By courtesy of the Institute of Dermatology, London, UK.

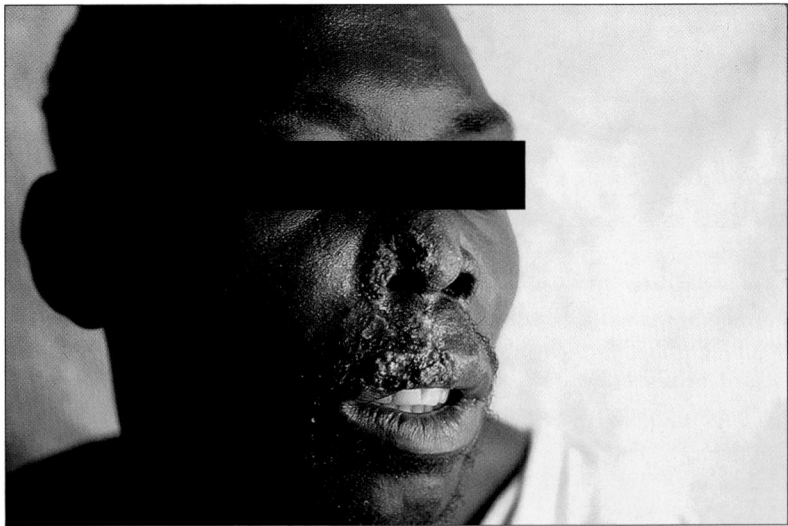

Fig. 17.149
Orificial tuberculosis: widespread ulcerative lesions involving the upper lip and nostril. By courtesy of S. Lucas, MD, St Thomas' Hospital, London, UK.

cases are associated with immunodeficiency and may follow a minor systemic infection such as measles. In these patients there are numerous lesions which are usually centrally crusted papules or pustules, but they may be ulcerative, necrotic, hemorrhagic or vesicular.[7] In recent years there have been a number of reports in patients with AIDS, especially those with multidrug-resistant tuberculosis.[4,5,21–23] The cutaneous lesions can be confused with folliculitis, resulting in delayed diagnosis.[21] The prognosis is poor.[4,23]

Comparison of the variants of cutaneous tuberculosis is made in *Table 17.2*.

Other rare manifestations of cutaneous tuberculosis that have been reported include tuberculous cellulitis and neutrophilic tuberculous panniculitis.[24–26] These uncommon forms of tuberculosis have occurred in patients who were iatrogenically immunosuppressed.

Pathogenesis and histological features

M. tuberculosis, an 'obligate pathogen', is a slender aerobic rod, characterized by a high lipid content. This lipid is responsible for resistance to phagocytosis. It also allows the bacterium to retain basic dyes, even during treatment with strong differentiating agents, and this is the basis of the Ziehl–Neelsen/acid-fast stain (*Fig. 17.156*). Organisms are easily identified in tuberculous chancre, scrofuloderma, orificial lesions and the miliary variant. They may be difficult to find or absent

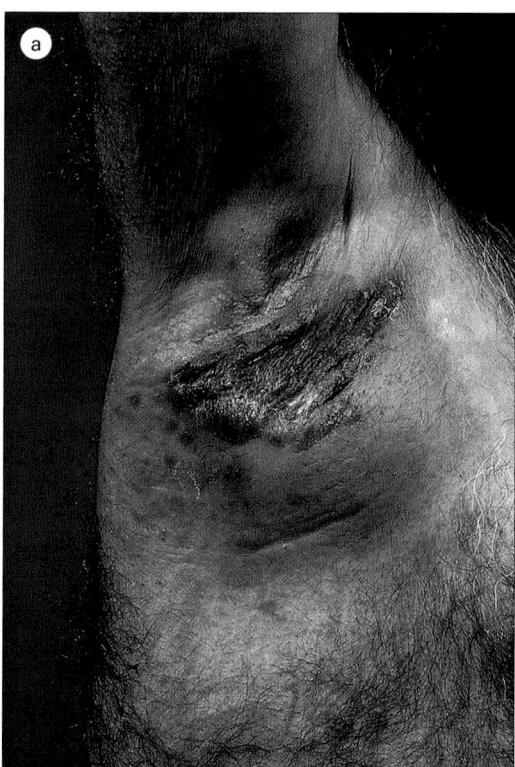

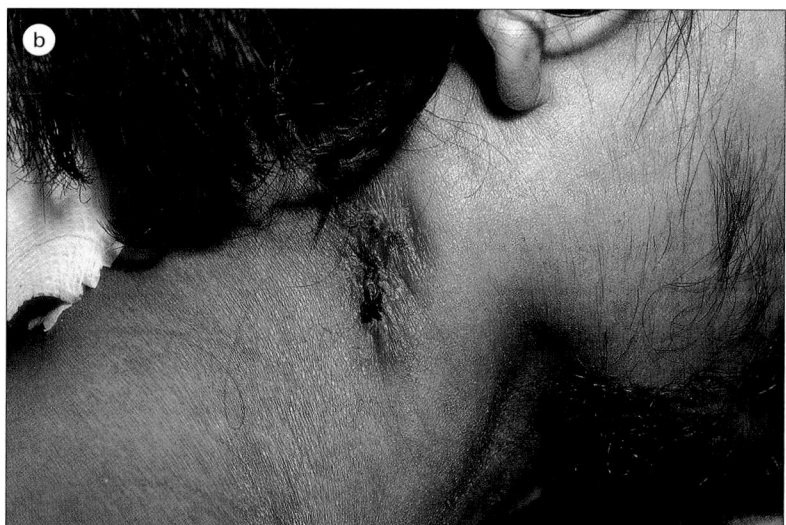

Fig. 17.150
Scrofuloderma: (a) note the marked axillary swelling and scarring with multiple sinuses; (b) in this example there was underlying cervical tuberculous lymphadenopathy. The puckered scarring is characteristic. By courtesy of R.A. Marsden, MD, St George's Hospital, London, UK.

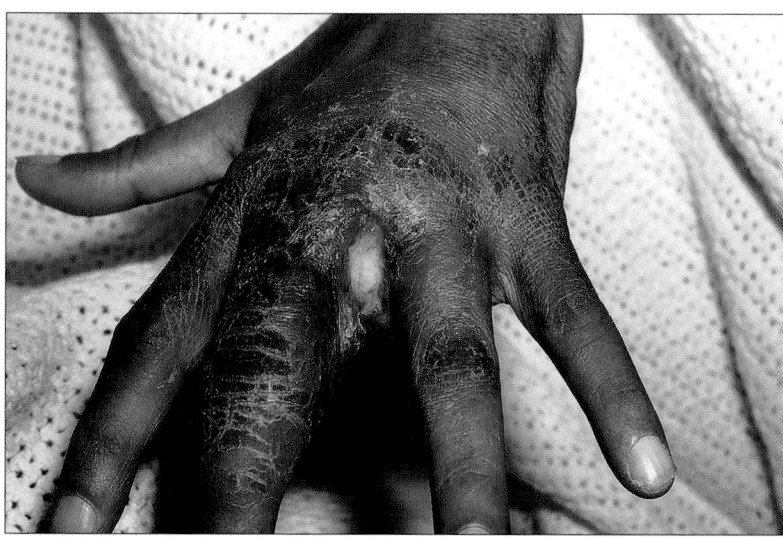

Fig. 17.151
Scrofuloderma: in this case there was underlying tuberculous osteoarticular disease. By courtesy of the Institute of Dermatology, London, UK.

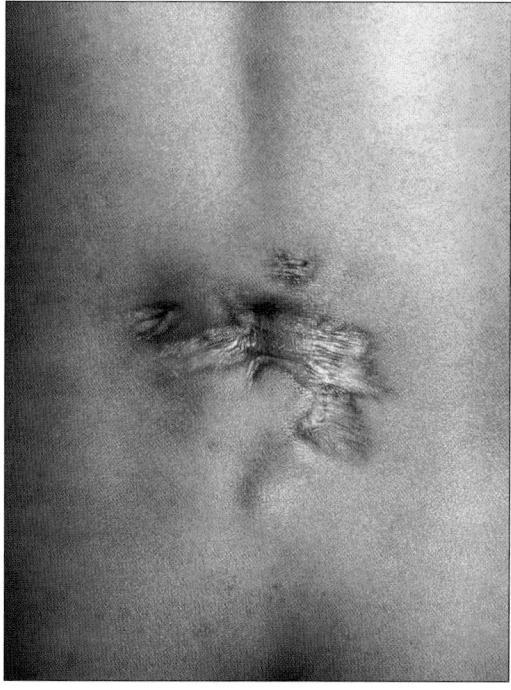

Fig. 17.152
Scrofuloderma: lesions in the midline of the back commonly complicate vertebral tuberculous osteomyelitis. By courtesy of the Institute of Dermatology, London, UK.

in lupus vulgaris, gummata and warty tuberculosis.[7] Mycobacteria are found at water/air interfaces and were so named because of their mold-like growths on the surface of liquid media.[27]

The organism is highly resistant to drying and therefore can retain infectivity by inoculation or contamination of minor wounds.

The reaction to the bacterium depends on:

- the size of the inoculum
- the virulence of the organism
- the immune state of the patient.

In general the cellular response is characterized by epithelioid macrophages, Langhans' giant cells and caseous necrosis, with perivascular lymphocytes in the surrounding tissue (tuberculous granuloma) (*Figs 17.157, 17.158*). Tuberculoid granulomata, as seen for example in sarcoidosis, by definition do not show caseation. The presence of large numbers of bacilli in a lesion implies a non-immune or anergic state, such as in tuberculous chancre or orificial lesions. Caseation is an indication of hypersensitivity and is not a toxic effect of the organisms; it is clear that it is not always beneficial to the host because it is invariably associated with destruction of surrounding tissue.

The recruitment of large numbers of macrophages is mediated by cytokines released by T-lymphocytes. In *M. tuberculosis* infections it appears that various cytokines operate, some of which participate in toxic or necrogenic functions, while others mainly activate macrophages. These responses are graded and the balance between the various components determines the eventual response. It is by no means clear what determines the balance between tissue damage and protective functions.

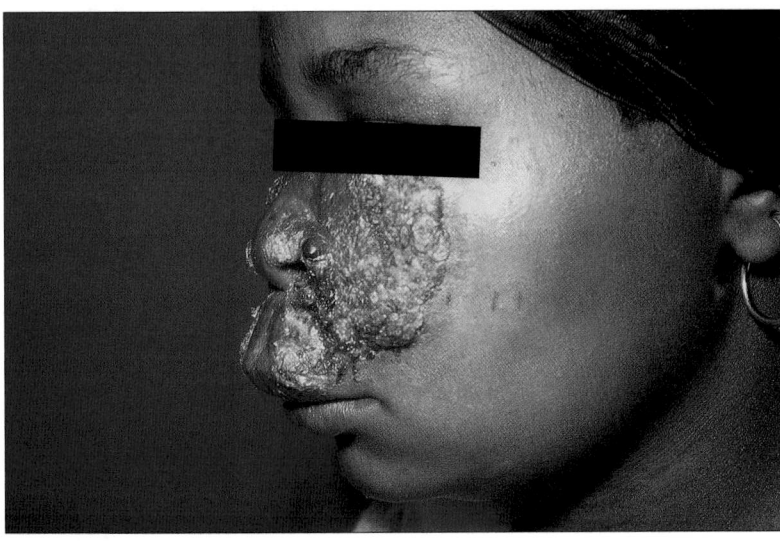

Fig. 17.153
Lupus vulgaris: the nose is a commonly affected site. By courtesy of N.C. Dlova, MD, Nelson R. Mandela School of Medicine, University of KwaZulu-Natal, South Africa.

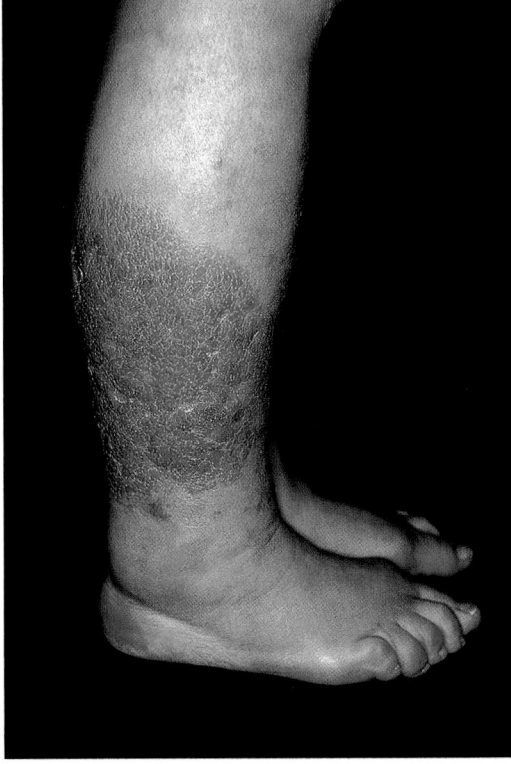

Fig. 17.155
Lupus vulgaris: this is a chronic lesion showing marked scaling, erythema and induration. Squamous cell carcinoma may occasionally supervene. By courtesy of R.A. Marsden, MD, St George's Hospital, London, UK.

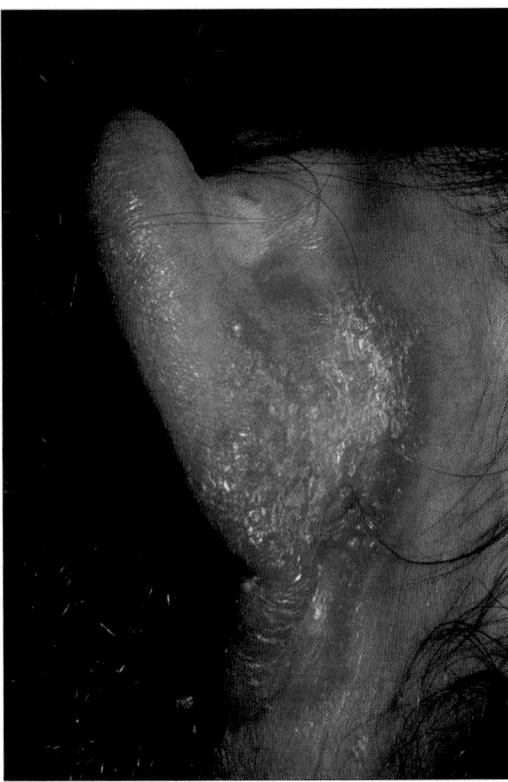

Fig. 17.154
Lupus vulgaris: typical plaque with golden-yellow appearance. By courtesy of R.A. Marsden, MD, St George's Hospital, London, UK.

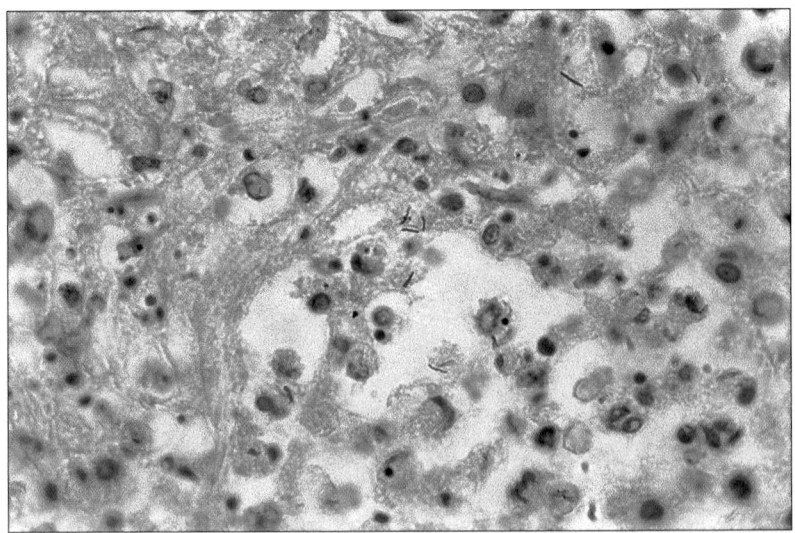

Fig. 17.156
Ziehl–Neelsen stain: in the center of the field is a small collection of red, acid-fast rods (oil immersion).

Table 17.2
Variants of cutaneous tuberculosis

Variant	Route of infection	Association with other TB	Level of infection	Histological features	Presence of bacilli
Tuberculous chancre	Inoculation	None	Dermis	Neutrophil abscess → caseating granuloma, lymphadenopathy	Present
Warty lupus	Inoculation	Previous or current infection	Dermis	Scanty granulomata, papillomatous acanthosis	Absent or very scanty
Orificial ulcers	Autoinoculation	Active infection in associated organs	Submucosa dermis	Mixed inflammation, few granulomata, necrosis	Numerous
Lupus vulgaris	Inoculation and/or hematogenous	Previous or current often occult, infection	Superficial dermis	Variable but prominent granulomata, little caseation	May be seen in deep aspect
Scrofuloderma	Extension from underlying infection	Active infection	Subcutaneous and dermal	Mixed inflammation, granuloma, marked fibrosis	May be seen in deep aspect
Tuberculous gumma	Hematogenous	Systemic infection	Subcutaneous	Much caseation, granulomatous fibrosis	Scanty
Miliary tuberculosis	Hematogenous	Systemic infection	Dermis	Central abscess, with surrounding histiocytic infiltrate	Absent or scanty in benign form; present in aggressive form

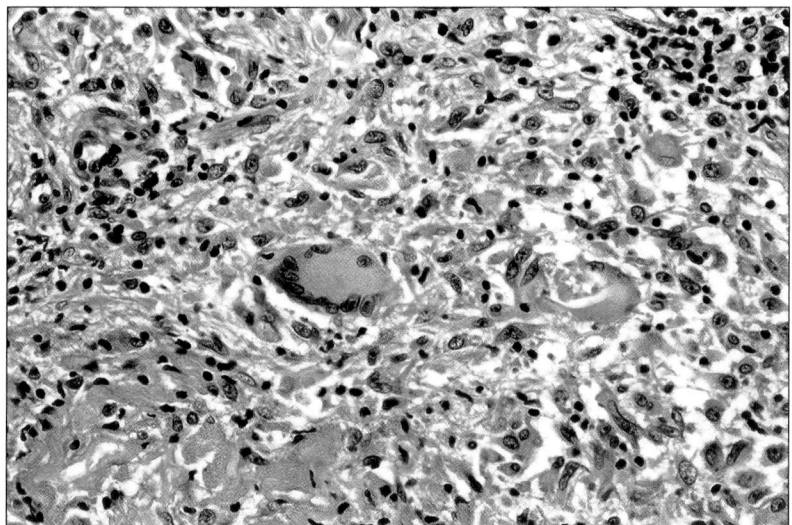

Fig. 17.157
Tuberculosis: characteristic Langhans' giant cell with horseshoe peripheral rim of nuclei.

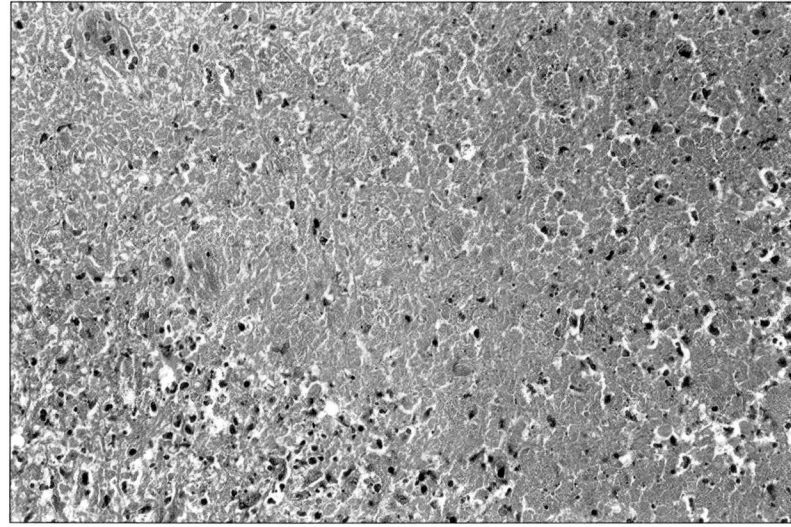

Fig. 17.158
Tuberculosis (caseation necrosis): the cell outlines are not completely lost giving an amorphous granular appearance.

Primary chancre

The primary chancre is characterized by a neutrophilic abscess with numerous bacilli, associated with necrosis leading to ulceration. This is gradually surrounded by histiocytes; after 6 weeks, giant cells (derived by fusion of epithelioid cells) are seen. Central necrosis remains prominent, but diminishes, along with the number of bacilli, as the granulomatous element increases.[7]

Warty lupus

Warty lupus is characterized by acanthotic papillomatosis with marked hyperkeratosis (*Fig. 17.159*). The dermal infiltrate consists mainly of neutrophils and lymphocytes, and abscesses may sometimes be present. Granulomata are present in the deeper dermis and caseation is occasionally a feature (*Fig. 17.160*).[7] Bacilli are found on careful searching.

Orificial lesions

Orificial lesions, in contrast, show extensive necrosis and numerous bacilli. The inflammatory infiltrate is not conspicuously granulomatous and may consist of lymphocytes and neutrophils with few histiocytes.

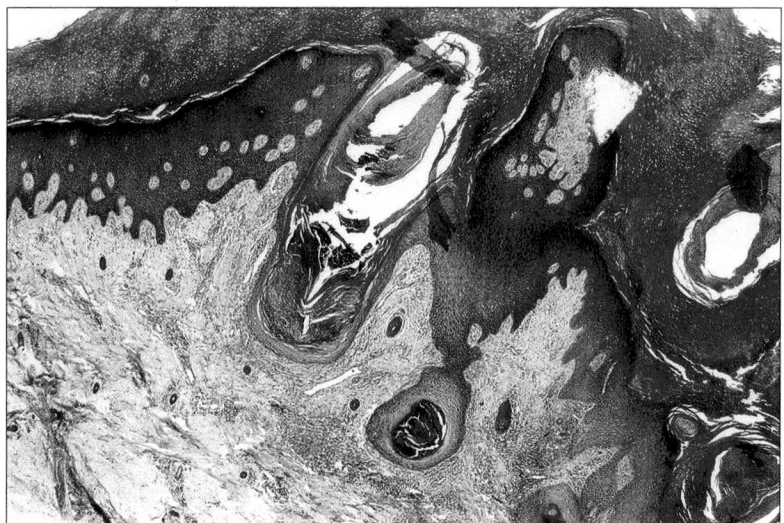

Fig. 17.159
Warty lupus: the epidermis is hyperkeratotic and shows marked irregular acanthosis. An inflammatory cell infiltrate is present in the dermis.

Lupus vulgaris

Lupus vulgaris is more varied in its histological features. It is seen in the superficial dermis, consisting of tubercles, some of which coalesce, with scanty or absent central caseation surrounded by epithelioid histiocytes and multinucleate giant cells (*Figs 17.161, 17.162*). Peripheral lymphocytes are also usually prominent. Bacteria are very infrequent. The overlying epidermis may be ulcerated (in which case there is usually a more mixed inflammatory infiltrate), atrophic or acanthotic. The last may be severe (pseudoepitheliomatous hyperplasia), raising the problem of distinction from invasive squamous carcinoma, especially as such tumors are an important rare complication of lupus vulgaris. This may sometimes be impossible if only superficial specimens are submitted for pathological interpretation. Transepithelial elimination of granulomata has been described.[28]

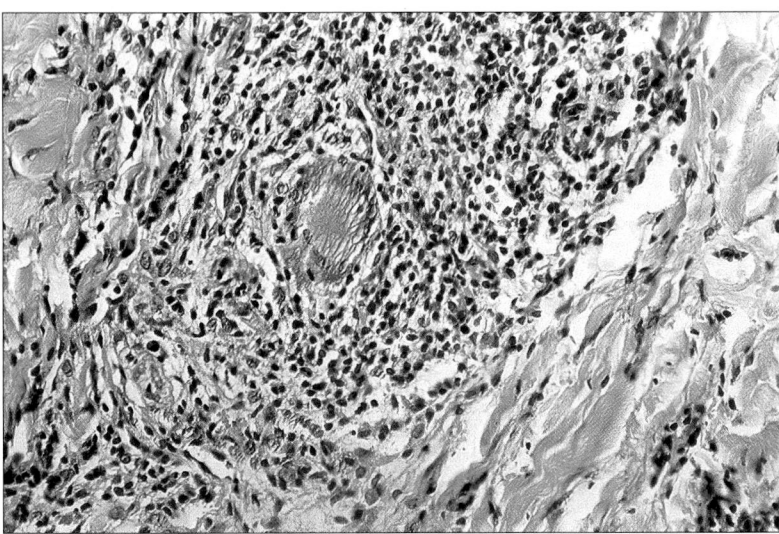

Fig. 17.160
Warty lupus: in addition to neutrophils and lymphocytes, an occasional Langhans' giant cell may be present.

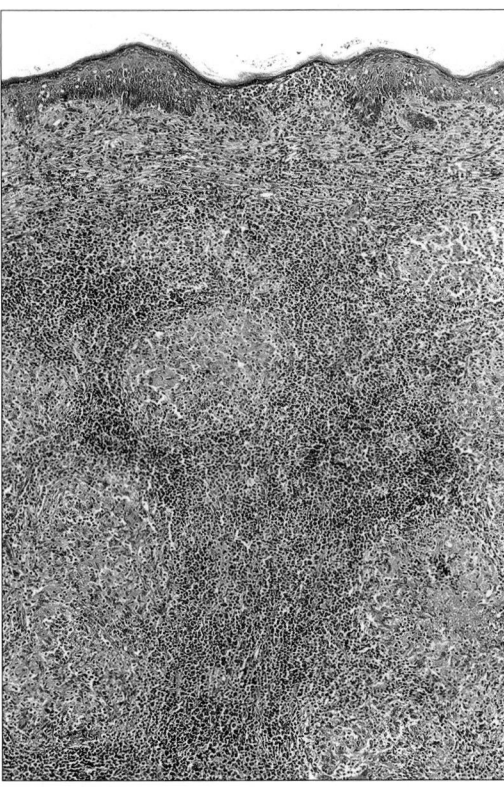

Fig. 17.161
Lupus vulgaris: the infiltrate is located in the superficial dermis.

Lupus vulgaris typically presents around the nose: this location is determined by the presence of large venous channels with stasis of blood flow and relative cold and hypoxia, which impair fibrinolysis and impair host defences. Lupus vulgaris may affect other areas with relatively low temperature.

Miliary tuberculosis

Miliary lesions include a severe form in which numerous central bacilli within a neutrophil abscess are surrounded by histiocytes (*Fig. 17.163*). Vascular thrombi containing microorganisms may be seen.[10] The less aggressive form is similar, but lacks the large numbers of bacteria.

The skin lesions of disseminated miliary tuberculosis (especially those in AIDS patients) are often either devoid of granulomata or exhibit only poorly formed granulomata. Extensive necrosis and abscess formation are often seen. Langhans' giant cells are rare. Special stains reveal numerous acid-fast bacilli.[23]

Scrofuloderma

Scrofuloderma usually appears as an ulcerated dermal abscess with an ill-defined histiocytic component (*Fig. 17.164*). Peripheral granulomata may be present. Marked caseation necrosis, in which bacilli may be numerous, can be seen in the deeper tissues.

Tuberculous gummata

Subcutaneous gummata are associated with marked caseation, but there are few bacilli (*Fig. 17.165*). There is a surrounding granulomatous infiltrate, which may be associated with dermal involvement.

Tuberculous cellulitic lesions are characterized by granulomatous inflammation with giant cells and demonstrable bacilli.[25–27] Panniculitis with vasculitis may occasionally be seen in cutaneous tuberculous lesions.[3] Rare cases of subcutaneous mycobacterial granulomatous arteritis have been documented (see *Fig. 15.99*).[29]

Differential diagnosis

The typical granulomatous and caseating picture is virtually pathognomonic for tuberculous infection, although sarcoidosis can have a similar appearance. Sarcoid, however, can be distinguished by the lack of caseation, but often this is not particularly helpful since necrosis is seen in only a minority of cases of tuberculosis. Necrosis when present in sarcoidosis is rather more fibrinoid than caseating.[3] More helpful is the lack of a surrounding lymphocytic infiltrate and fewer giant cells in

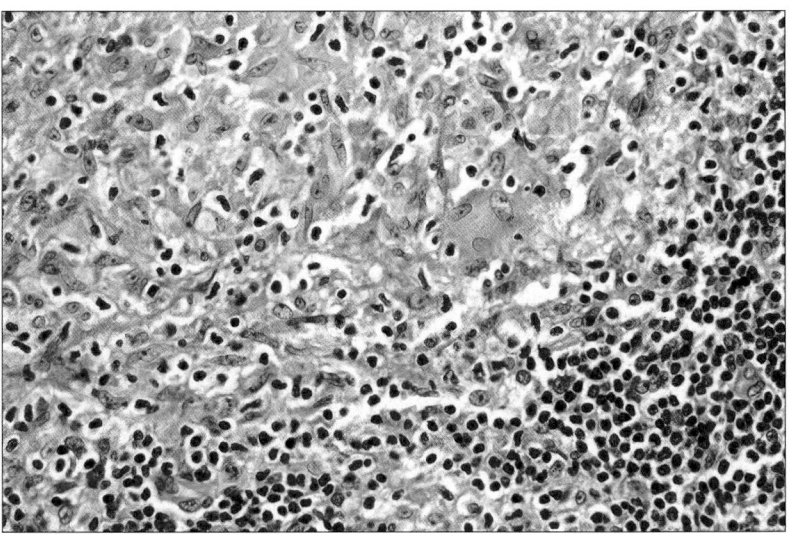

Fig. 17.162
Lupus vulgaris: the granulomata are often surrounded by lymphocytes.

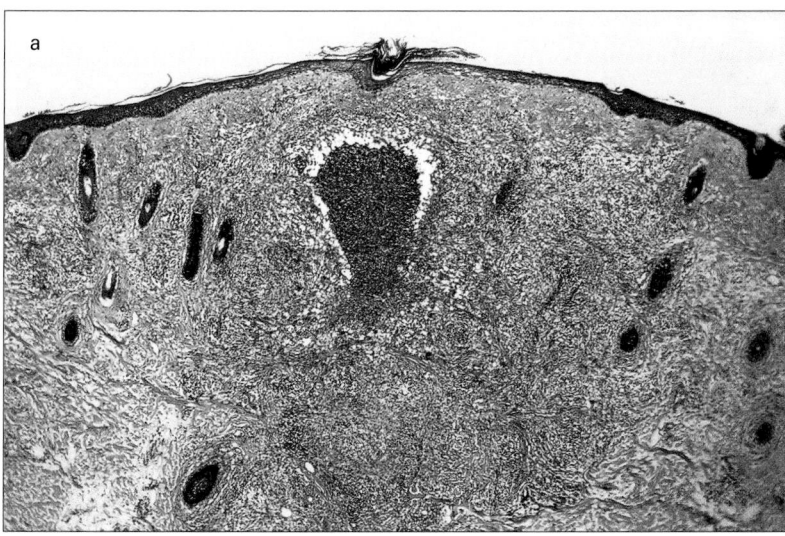

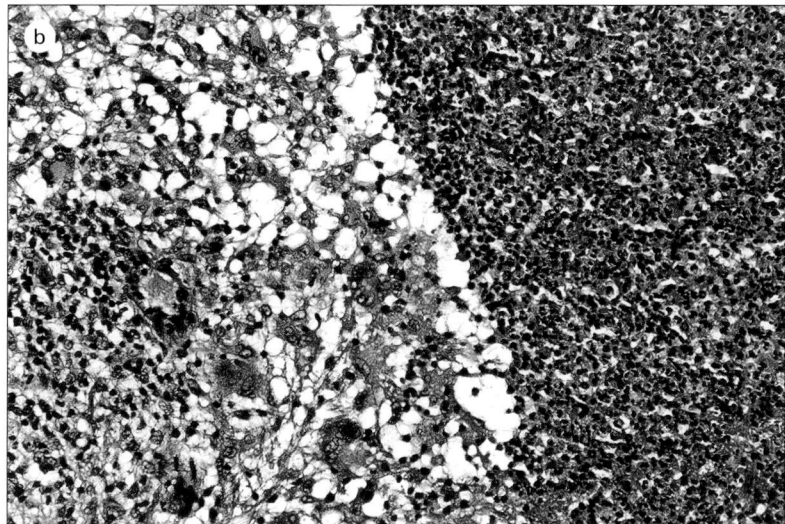

Fig. 17.163
Miliary tuberculosis: (**a**) a neutrophil abscess is present in the mid-dermis; (**b**) it is surrounded by histiocytes. Occasional giant cells are also evident.

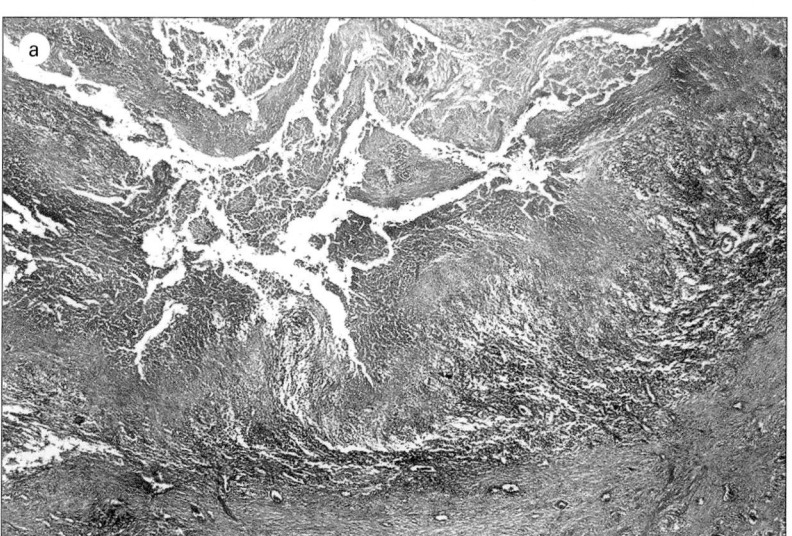

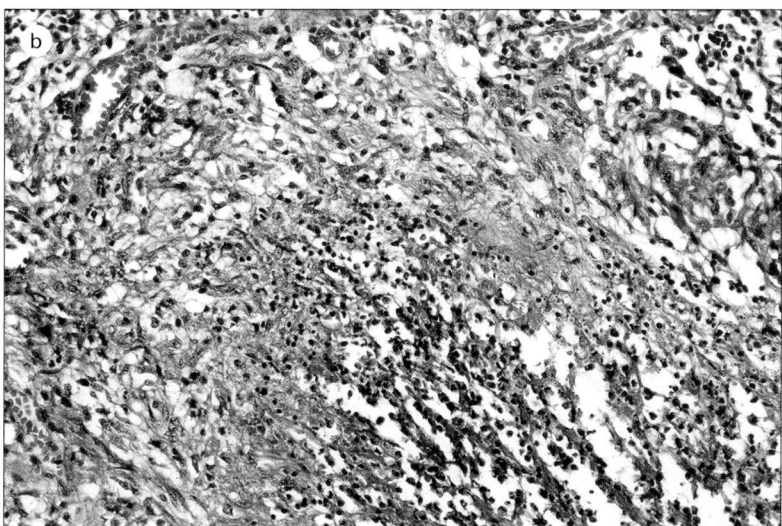

Fig. 17.164
Scrofuloderma: the appearances are rather deceptive, consisting of an abscess surrounded by a predominantly histiocytic infiltrate.

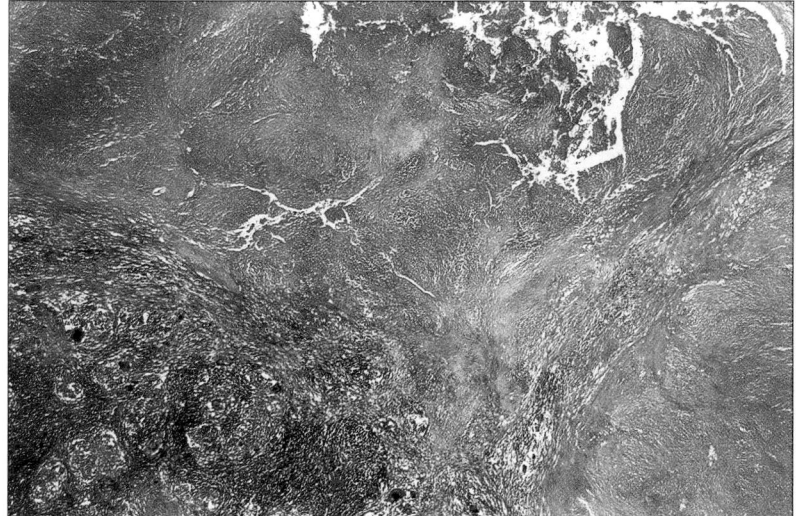

Fig. 17.165
Tuberculous gumma: there is massive caseation surrounded by a well-defined granulomatous infiltrate.

sarcoidosis and a more discrete arrangement of the granulomata (the sarcoidal naked granuloma). Schaumann bodies are characteristic of sarcoidosis, but may occasionally be seen in mycobacterial infections.[3]

In less granulomatous forms of cutaneous tuberculosis a distinction from leprosy must be made. The perineural distribution of the inflammation is a pointer towards leprosy.

Deep fungal infections and leishmaniasis may also be confused with tuberculosis and recognition of the organism is vital. Granulomatous late secondary and tertiary syphilis is distinguished by the vascular changes and numerous plasma cells. Caseation necrosis is typical of acne agminata and may also be seen in foreign body reactions to beryllium and zirconium.[30] It may also be a feature of Wegener's granulomatosis, although this would be distinctly unusual in cutaneous lesions (see p. 727).

Despite these pointers diagnosis may still not be possible. The difficulty is made worse by the frequent failure to demonstrate bacilli even in definite cases of tuberculosis, and the results of culture take 3–4 weeks. Therefore, occasionally, it may be a diagnosis of exclusion, which is confirmed by a therapeutic trial of antituberculous drugs.[7] The shortcomings of these traditional methods have led to increased use of PCR for confirmation of the diagnosis.[4]

References

1. Findlay, G.H. (1987) Lupus, scrofuloderma, etc. In: The dermatology of bacterial infections. Oxford: Blackwell, pp 71–83.
2. Sehgal, V.N., Jain, M.K., Srivastava, G. (1989) Changing pattern of cutaneous tuberculosis. A prospective study. *Int J Dermatol*, 28, 231–236.
3. Santa Cruz, D.J., Strayer, D.S. (1982) The histologic spectrum of the cutaneous mycobacterioses. *Hum Pathol*, 13, 485–495.
4. Barbagallo, J., Tager, P., Ingleton, R. et al (2002) Cutaneous tuberculosis: diagnosis and treatment. *Am J Clin Dermatol*, 3, 319–328.
5. Inwald, D., Nelson, M., Cramp, M. et al (1994) Cutaneous manifestations of mycobacterial infection in patients with AIDS. *Br J Dermatol*, 130, 111–114.
6. Sehgal, V.N., Scrivastava, G., Khurana, V.K. et al (1987) An appraisal of epidemiologic, clinical, bacteriologic, histopathologic and immunologic parameters in cutaneous tuberculosis. *Int J Dermatol*, 26, 521–526.
7. Kakakhel, K., Fritsch, P. (1989) Cutaneous tuberculosis. *Int J Dermatol*, 28, 355–362.
8. Brown, F.S., Anderson, R.H., Burnett, J.W. (1982) Cutaneous tuberculosis. *J Am Acad Dermatol*, 6, 101–106.
9. Beyt, B.E., Ortbals, D.W., Santa Cruz, D.J. et al (1980) Cutaneous mycobacteriosis: analysis of 34 cases with a new classification of disease. *Medicine (Baltimore)*, 60, 95–109.
10. Saxe, N. (1985) Mycobacterial skin infections. *J Cutan Pathol*, 12, 300–312.
11. Dinning, W.J., Marston, S. (1985) Cutaneous and ocular tuberculosis: a review. *J R Soc Med*, 78, 576–581.
12. Tur, E., Brenner, S., Meiron, Y. (1996) Scrofuloderma (tuberculosis colliquativa cutis). *Br J Dermatol*, 134, 350–352.
13. Kumar, B., Rai, R., Kaur, I. et al (2001) Childhood cutaneous tuberculosis: a study over 25 years from northern India. *Int J Dermatol*, 40, 26–32.
14. Kokcam, I., Kose, A., Yekeler, H. et al (2001) Lupus vulgaris in a child following BCG immunization. *Australas J Dermatol*, 42, 275–277.
15. Haim, S., Friedman-Birnbaum, R. (1978) Cutaneous tuberculosis and malignancy. *Cutis*, 21, 643–647.
16. Bowden, J., Paramsothy, Y., Smith, A.G. (1988) Malignant melanoma arising in the scar of lupus vulgaris and response to treatment with topical azelaic acid. *Clin Exp Dermatol*, 13, 353–356.
17. Harrison, P.V., Marks, J.M. (1980) Lupus vulgaris and cutaneous lymphoma. *Clin Exp Dermatol*, 5, 73–77.
18. Miteva, L. (2001) Alopecia: a rare manifestation of lupus vulgaris. *Int J Dermatol*, 40, 659–661.
19. Chen, C.H., Shih, J.F., Wang, L.S. et al (1996) Tuberculous subcutaneous abscess: an analysis of seven cases. *Tuber Lung Dis*, 77, 184–187.
20. McCray, M.K., Esterly, N.B. (1981) Cutaneous eruptions in congenital tuberculosis. *Arch Dermatol*, 117, 460–464.
21. Antinori, S., Galimberti, L., Tadini, G.L. et al (1995) Tuberculosis cutis miliaris diseminata due to multidrug-resistant Mycobacterium tuberculosis AIDS patients. *Eur J Clin Microbiol Infect Dis*, 14, 911–914.
22. Libraty, D.H., Byrd, T.F. (1996) Cutaneous miliary tuberculosis in the AIDS era: case report and review. *Clin Infect Dis*, 23, 706–710.
23. Daikos, G.L., Uttamchandani, R.B., Tuda, C. et al (1998) Disseminated miliary tuberculosis of the skin in patients with AIDS: report of four cases. *Clin Infect Dis*, 27, 205–208.
24. Chin, P.W., Koh, C.K., Wong, K.T. (1999) Cutaneous tuberculosis mimicking cellulitis in an immunosuppressed patient. *Singapore Med J*, 40, 44–45.
25. Lee, N.H., Choi, E.H., Lee, W.S. et al (2000) Tuberculous cellulitis. *Clin Exp Dermatol*, 25, 222–223.
26. Langenberg, A., Egbert, B. (1993) Neutrophilic tuberculous panniculitis in a patient with polymyositis. *J Cutan Pathol*, 20, 177–179.
27. Grange, J.M. (1982) Mycobacteria and the skin. *Int J Dermatol*, 21, 497–503.
28. Goette, D.K., Odom, R.B. (1986) Transepithelial elimination of granulomas in cutaneous tuberculosis and sarcoidosis. *J Am Acad Dermatol*, 14, 126–128.
29. Rodrígues, C.J., de Campos, F.P., Furtado-Mendonca, L.L. et al (1990) Mycobacterial subcutaneous arteritis. *Rev Inst Med Trop Sao Paulo*, 32, 346–350.
30. Neave, H.J., Frank, S.B., Tolmach, J. (1950) Cutaneous granulomas following laceration by fluorescent light bulbs. *Arch Dermatol*, 61, 401–406.

Tuberculids

Clinical features

A tuberculid is a cutaneous immunological reaction to the presence of tuberculosis, which is often occult, elsewhere in the body.[1,2] By definition special stains and cultures for tubercle bacilli from tuberculids are negative. Although tuberculids are rare in Western countries, they are still important conditions in developing countries where tuberculosis is a common disease.[3]

Tuberculids may be papular or nodular and may be separately classified on that basis, but variations and combinations of those features may be seen and are only valid descriptively.

One variety of papular tuberculid is the papulonecrotic tuberculid. This chronic condition presents as recurring crops of flesh-colored, erythematous or darkish red papules, most often on the ears and the limbs and in particular on extensor aspects around the elbows and knees (*Figs 17.166–17.168*).[3–5] Lesions may occur widely or present in isolated sites.[5,6] The papules may become pustular, ulcerate or develop crusts. They are often symmetrically distributed.[7] Genital involvement may occasionally occur.[5] They regress slowly over several weeks, leaving depressed, varioliform scars.[7,8] Usually they occur in young people who otherwise often appear rather well. Occasional cases have been reported to progress to lupus vulgaris.[4]

Lichen scrofulosorum characteristically presents as yellow or brown asymptomatic follicular papules, less than 3 mm across, on the trunk (*Fig. 17.169*).[9] These lesions regress slowly and do not leave scars. This uncommon tuberculous reaction usually occurs in children and young adults.[10,11] The eruption is said to be more frequently associated with tuberculous lymphadenitis (cervical, hilar or mediastinal) or osseous tuberculosis than with pulmonary tuberculosis.[11] The latter observation has not been supported by some recent reports.[10,11]

The only nodular tuberculid that is now generally accepted is

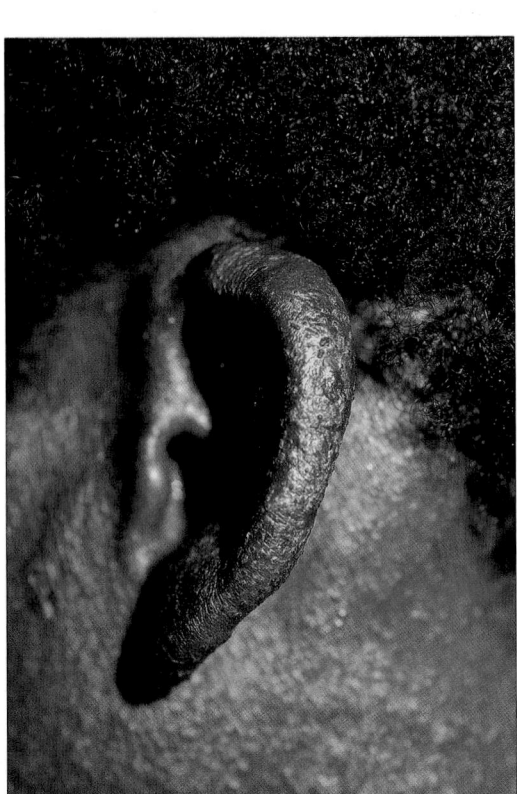

Fig. 17.166
Papulonecrotic tuberculid: widely distributed small purple papules are present on the ear, a commonly affected site. By courtesy of N.C. Dlova, MD, Nelson R. Mandela School of Medicine, University of KwaZulu-Natal, South Africa.

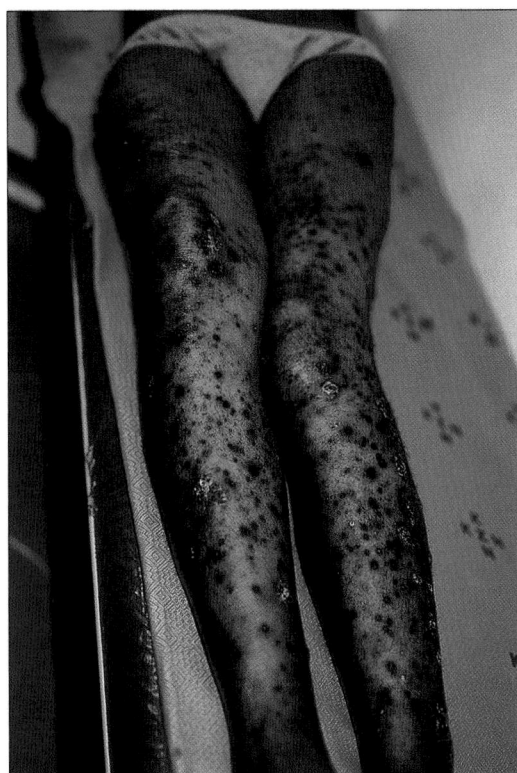

Fig. 17.167
Papulonecrotic tuberculid: innumerable papules are distributed on the dorsal aspect of the legs. Tuberculids imply an active infection elsewhere in the body. By courtesy of N.C. Dlova, MD, Nelson R. Mandela School of Medicine, University of KwaZulu-Natal, South Africa.

erythema induratum (Bazin's disease) (see p. 366). This presents as ill-defined nodules on the calves of women, characteristically those who are obese and have erythrocyanotic skin in this area. The lesion may be worse in cold weather, which raises the problem of distinction from pernio. With progression, the nodules eventually form irregular ulcers, which tend to have bluish undermined edges. Resolution is slow.

More recently, the term nodular tuberculid has been applied to a subset of patients with non-ulcerated nodules on the lower legs and in whom the pathological changes were centered on both the dermis and the subcutaneous fat. It has been proposed that this entity represents a hybrid between papulonecrotic tuberculid and erythema induratum of Bazin.[12] A case of papulonecrotic tuberculid coexistent with erythema induratum has also been reported.[13]

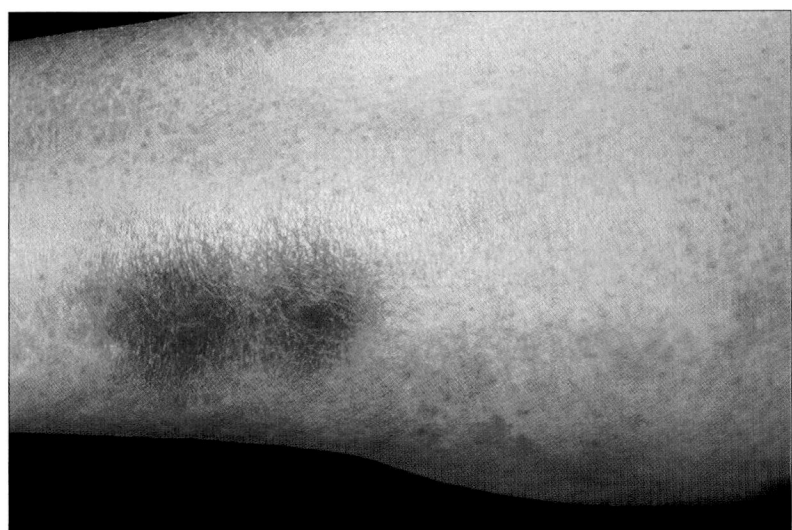

Fig. 17.168
Papulonecrotic tuberculid: in this example the patient has presented with deeper seated erythematous lesions. By courtesy of the Institute of Dermatology, London, UK.

The term nodular granulomatous phlebitis of the skin has been proposed for an additional type of tuberculid which presents as subcutaneous nodules along the course of a leg vein, and shows histological evidence of granulomatous inflammation centered on the wall of the affected vessel.[14] This condition should be distinguished from true tuberculous phlebitis as a consequence of miliary tuberculosis.

Pathogenesis and histological features

All tuberculids are thought to be due to hematogenous dissemination of small numbers of dead bacteria, possibly opsonized. These embolize to produce lesions, particularly in areas of slow circulation. As a result of changes in small dermal vessels (either an Arthus reaction or a lymphohistiocytic vasculitis), degenerative responses develop in the dermal collagen. In the case of papulonecrotic tuberculid, this amounts to frank necrosis. Histologically, the lesions show variable combinations of vasculitis with necrosis, a moderate to intense lymphohistiocytic infiltrate and granulomatous inflammation.

Papulonecrotic tuberculid, when fully developed, shows cutaneous infarction comprising a necrotic epidermis with ulceration and an underlying V-shaped zone of dermal coagulative necrosis accompanied by a dense chronic inflammatory cell infiltrate with scattered giant cells.[3,7,8] Necrosis of hair follicles may occur.[15] On occasions a histiocytic palisade has been described, resulting in features reminiscent of granuloma annulare. Neutrophils are generally inconspicuous. Well-formed granulomata may be present but bacilli cannot be identified. Vasculitis may be present.[4,7] These features may sometimes be histologically confused with pityriasis lichenoides et varioliformis acuta.[6,15]

In lichen scrofulosorum, a granulomatous infiltrate in which Langhans' giant cells are conspicuous is centered around hair follicules and eccrine units (*Fig. 17.170*).[3,10]

Erythema induratum has a less histiocytic infiltrate and is indistinguishable from nodular vasculitis (see p. 366). The presence of both primary vasculitic changes and granulomatous inflammation suggests that type III and type IV hypersensitivity reactions are important in the latter condition.[16]

Although acid-fast organisms are not detectable by special stains, and mycobacterial cultures from these lesions invariably are negative, *M. tuberculosis* DNA has been detected by PCR in a number of cases; this suggests that mycobacterial components are indeed responsible for the pathological manifestations.[8,17,18]

The validity of the concept of the tuberculids rests on the association with underlying tuberculosis, a strong tuberculin reaction and an invariable response to antituberculous drugs.

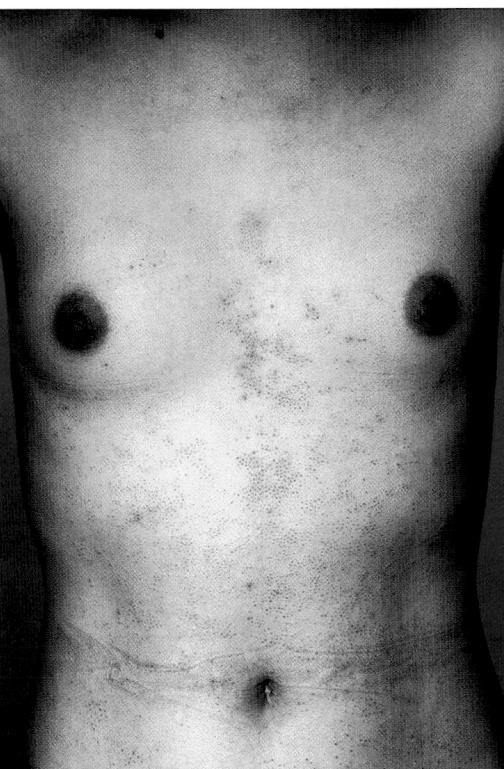

Fig. 17.169
Lichen scrofulosorum: note the numerous tiny papules on the chest and upper abdomen. By courtesy of S. Lucas, MD, St Thomas' Hospital, London, UK.

References

1. Findlay, G.H. (1987) Tuberculides. In: The dermatology of bacterial infections. Oxford: Blackwell, pp 81–83.
2. Findlay, G.H. (1987) Bacterial ides. In: The dermatology of bacterial infections. Oxford: Blackwell, pp 154–156.
3. Saxe, N. (1985) Mycobacterial skin infections. *J Cutan Pathol*, **12**, 300–312.
4. Morrison, J.G.L., Fourie, E.D. (1974) The papulonecrotic tuberculide: from Arthus reaction to lupus vulgaris. *Br J Dermatol*, **91**, 263–270.
5. Israelewicz, S., Dharan, M., Rosenman, D. et al (1985) Papulonecrotic tuberculid of the glans penis. *J Am Acad Dermatol*, **12**, 1104–1106.
6. Ihm, C.W., Suh, J.I. (1987) Papulonecrotic tuberculid – report of a case. *J Dermatol (Tokyo)*, **14**, 63–66.
7. Wilson Jones, E., Winkelmann, R.K. (1986) Papulonecrotic tuberculid: a neglected disease in Western countries. *J Am Acad Dermatol*, **14**, 815–826.
8. Jordaan, H.F., Schneider, J.W., Schaaf, H.S. et al (1996) Papulonecrotic tuberculid in children. A report of eight patients. *Am J Dermatopathol*, **18**, 172–185.
9. Smith, N.P., Ryan, T.J., Sanderson, K.V. et al (1976) Lichen scrofulosorum. A report of four cases. *Br J Dermatol*, **94**, 319–325.
10. Beena, K.R., Ramesh, V., Mukherjee, A. (2000) Lichen scrofulosorum – a series of eight cases. *Dermatology*, **201**, 272–274.
11. Ramdial, P.K., Mosam, A., Pillay, T. et al (2000) Childhood lichen scrofulosorum revisited. *Pediatr Dev Pathol*, **3**, 211–215.
12. Jordaan, H.F., Schneider, J.W., Abdulla, E.A. (2000) Nodular tuberculid: a report of four patients. *Pediatr Dermatol*, **17**, 183–188.
13. Roblin, D., Kelly, R., Wansbrough-Jones, M. et al (1994) Papulonecrotic tuberculide and erythema induratum as presenting manifestations of tuberculosis. *J Infect*, **28**, 193–197.
14. Hara, K., Tsuzuki, T., Tagaki, N. et al (1997) Nodular granulomatous phlebitis of skin: a fourth type of tuberculid. *Histopathology*, **30**, 129–134.

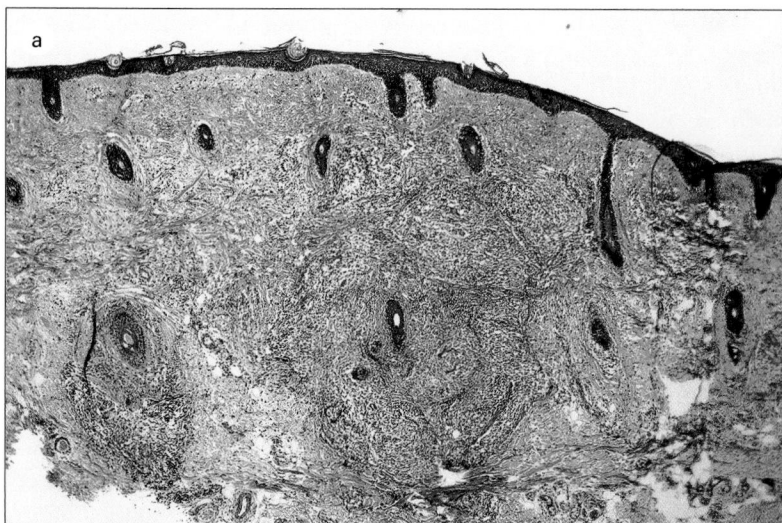
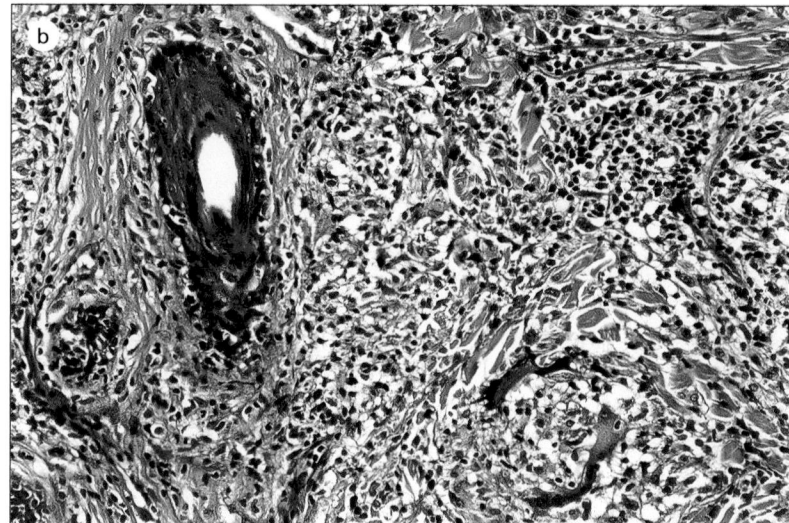

Fig. 17.170
(a, b) Lichen scrofulosorum: note the perifollicular distribution of this well-defined granulomatous infiltrate.

15. Jordaan, H.F., van Niekerk, D.J., Louw, M. (1994) Papulonecrotic tuberculid. A clinical, histological, and immunohistochemical study of 15 patients. *Am J Dermatopathol*, **16**, 474–485.
16. Schneider, J.W., Jordaan, H.F. (1997) The histopathologic spectrum of erythema induratum of Bazin. *Am J Dermatopathol*, **19**, 323–333.
17. Schneider, J.W., Jordaan, H.F., Geiger, D.H. et al (1995) Erythema induratum of Bazin. A clinicopathological study of 20 cases and detection of Mycobacterium tuberculosis DNA in skin lesions by polymerase chain reaction. *Am J Dermatopathol*, **17**, 350–356.
18. Chen, Y.H., Yan, J.J., Chao, S.C. et al (2001) Erythema induratum: a clinicopathologic and polymerase chain reaction study. *J Formos Med Assoc*, **100**, 244–249.

Non-tuberculous environmental mycobacterial infections

Non-tuberculous mycobacteria, which are usually non-pathogenic, are widespread in varied sites throughout the world.[1–3] They inhabit vegetation and water (stagnant, fresh or salty), and are saprophytic in soil, on animals and within animal feces. They are traditionally subdivided according to their growth rate on culture media and by their ability to produce a yellow pigment in culture with and without exposure to light. There are therefore four categories:[4–6]

- Group I organisms are photochromogens, which produce pigment after exposure to light (e.g. *Mycobacterium marinum* and *Mycobacterium kansasii*).
- Group II organisms are the scotochromogens, which produce pigmented colonies whether light is present or not (e.g. *Mycobacterium scrofulaceum* and *Mycobacterium szulgai*).
- Group III organisms are consistently non-pigmented and include *Mycobacterium avium* and *Mycobacterium intracellulare*.
- Group IV organisms are the fast growers and include *Mycobacterium chelonei* and *Mycobacterium fortuitum*.

Exact species identification may also be facilitated by PCR performed on mycobacteria that are grown in liquid media.[7] The environmental mycobacterial infections are becoming of increasing importance in immunocompromised patients, particularly in those with AIDS. Cutaneous infection with these organisms in the immunocompent patient usually follows an episode of trauma and gives rise to a localized lesion often clinically resembling panniculitis.[8,9] In the immunosuppressed, a history of trauma is usually lacking and patients tend to present with multiple subcutaneous nodules, more diffuse inflammation and frequent abscess formation.[8,9] Systemic spread is obviously of particular importance in this latter group. As the features may be atypical, diagnosis is facilitated by a healthy index of suspicion.

Clinical features

Mycobacterium marinum

M. marinum (balnei) is a slow-growing photochromogen, which is associated with injuries in aquatic environments or by fish or equipment, usually under water.[10] The upper limb is the site of infection in more than 90% of cases.[11] Infections have been contracted most often in swimming pools (swimming pool granuloma, fish tank granuloma), usually on the elbows and knees of children, or from aquaria, usually on the hands (*Fig. 17.171*).[12] In some studies inoculation related to fish tank exposure has accounted for more than 80% of cases.[11] The lesions usually present 1 week to 2 months (average 2–3 weeks) after superficial injury and are typically painless inflammatory nodules or plaques.[13] They may ulcerate and discharge yellow fluid and older lesions can be warty (*Fig. 17.172*). Occasionally abscesses are seen. Quite often there is extension along lymphatics, with the development of secondary nodules in a pattern comparable to sporotrichosis (*Fig. 17.173*).[12,14,15] Sporotrichoid spread has also been reported in an HIV-infected patient.[16] Penetrating injuries sometimes result in tenosynovitis. Infection in immunodeficient individuals produces a deeply undermined ulcer; otherwise lesions usually resolve within a few months. In one large retrospective study the mean duration of disease was 19 months.[17]

Mycobacterium fortuitum chelonae

M. fortuitum chelonae comprises a group of rapid-growing organisms found in soil and water and occasionally non-pathogenically in sputum. The organisms are *M. fortuitum*, *M. chelonae* and *M. chelonae* subsp. *abscessus* (*M. abscessus*). Lesions, which are uncommon, usually develop

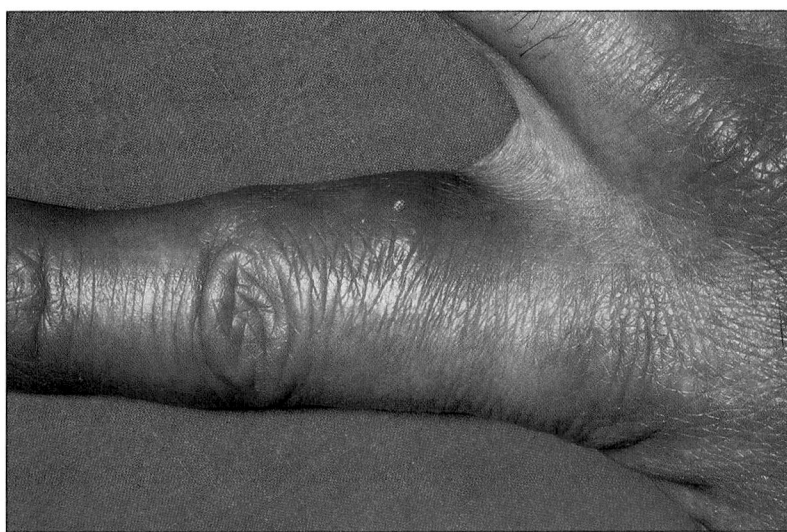

Fig. 17.171
Mycobacterium marinum (balnei): inflammatory nodule on the finger of an aquarium enthusiast. By courtesy of R.A. Marsden, MD, St George's Hospital, London, UK.

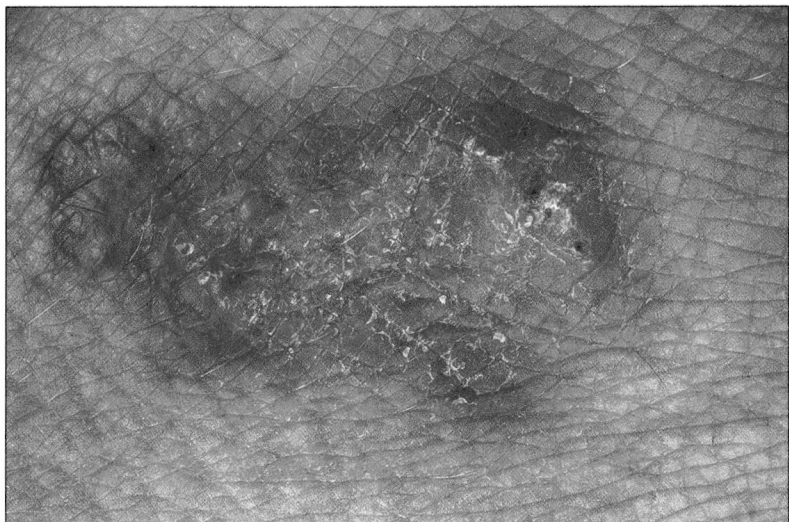

Fig. 17.172
Mycobacterium marinum (balnei): close-up view of an erythematous plaque with scaling. By courtesy of the Institute of Dermatology, London, UK.

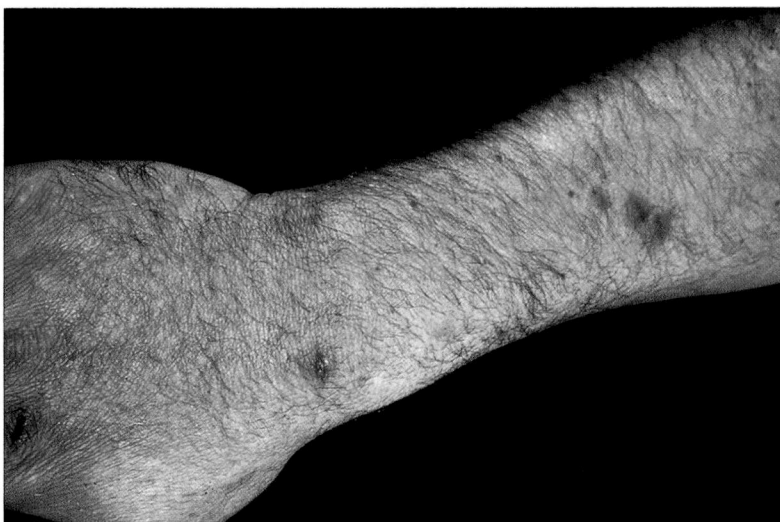

Fig. 17.173
Mycobacterium marinum (balnei): this example demonstrates sporotrichoid spread. By courtesy of the Institute of Dermatology, London, UK.

3–4 weeks after contamination of skin wounds, including surgical incisions, injections, liposuction, liposculpture and even acupuncture.[5,10,18–20] An outbreak of mycobacterial furunculosis due to *M. fortuitum* was acquired via the communal use of footbaths at a nail salon.[21] Disease may present in a disseminated form, often associated with immunosuppression, including AIDS (*Figs 17.174, 17.175*).[9,22] Pulmonary infection with subsequent cutaneous dissemination has also been reported in an apparently immunocompetent patient.[23] The lesions comprise indolent abscesses with fistula formation, purulent discharge and scarring. A sporotrichoid distribution has also been recorded (*Fig. 17.176*).[8,24] Healing is usually delayed for many months, but may be helped by adequate debridement. The *M. chelonae* variant is the more refractory to treatment.

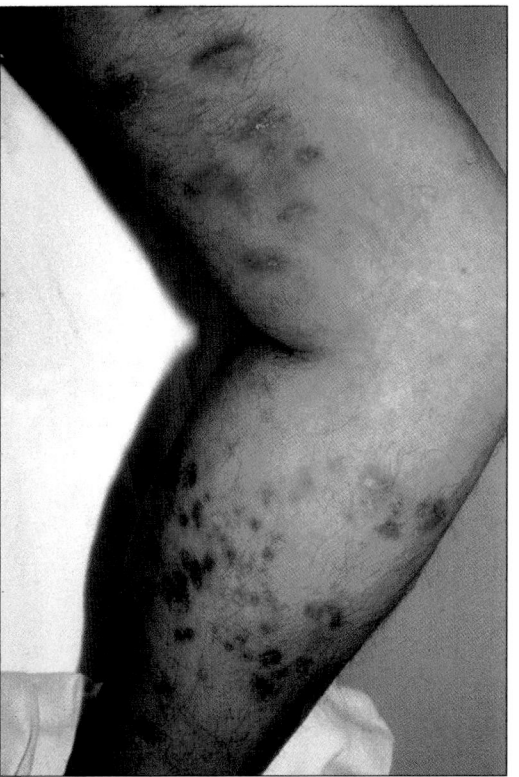

Fig. 17.174
Mycobacterium fortuitum chelonae: numerous abscesses are distributed along this patient's leg. This infection is more often seen in the immunosuppressed. By courtesy of the Institute of Dermatology, London, UK.

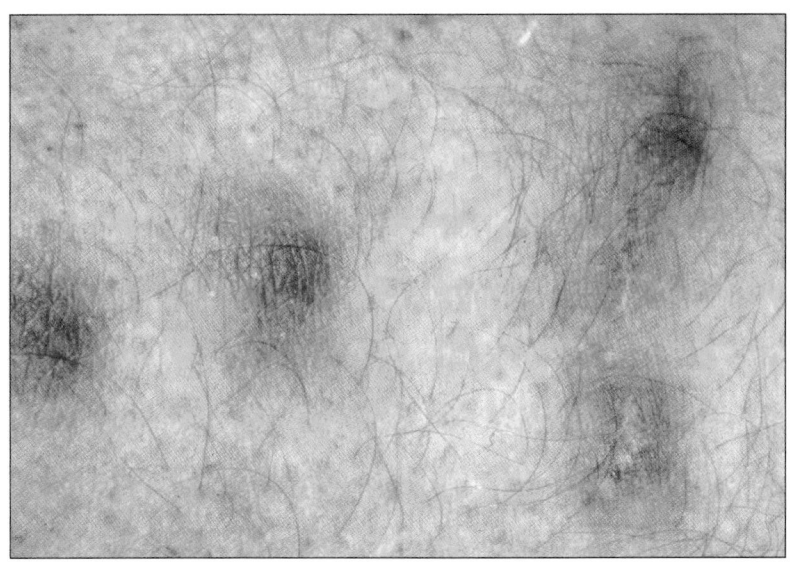

Fig. 17.175
Mycobacterium fortuitum chelonae: close-up view. By courtesy of the Institute of Dermatology, London, UK.

Mycobacterium kansasii

M. kansasii is a slow-growing photochromogen found worldwide in various habitats. This is a disease mainly of the lungs and lymph nodes; it only rarely causes skin lesions and these are most common in the immunosuppressed, when they are usually associated with disseminated disease.[25,26] Iatrogenically immunosuppressed patients and patients with AIDS may, however, also present with primary cutaneous infection.[27,28] Cases of infection by *M. kansasii* are varied in their presentation: they may appear as nodules (which can be verrucous), as crusted ulcers, as papulopustules, as cellulitis or with a spreading infection resembling sporotrichosis.[29,30]

Mycobacterium ulcerans

M. ulcerans infection is a rapidly re-emerging disease, and is currently recognized as the third most common mycobacterial disease in immunocompetent people (after tuberculosis and leprosy).[31] The causative organism is a slow-growing non-chromogen, which is present on lush vegetation in swampy areas sporadically in the tropics.[32–34] It is particularly seen in the tropical wetlands of West and Central Africa (Buruli ulcer), but was characterized in Australia (Bairnsdale ulcer). It has subsequently been recorded in the koala bear in the same region.[35] The condition also occurs in tropical regions of Asia and South America.[34] *M. ulcerans* infection has not been linked to HIV infection.[34]

The lesion develops about 8 weeks after minor trauma or skin abrasions which came into contact with contaminated water, soil or vegetation.[31,36] Consequently, the lesion usually appears on the legs and tends to occur more often in children.[36] The initial erythematous nodule progresses to an indolent ulcer, which may be very large, up to 50 cm across (*Fig. 17.177*). The ulcer is without exudate or surrounding reaction, but extends to involve underlying fascia or fat and typically has an undermined border.[36] There is little or no malaise or fever. After 6–9 months, a granulomatous response develops, which precedes healing. This is usually associated with scarring, which may lead to severe deformity and contractures.[31] The extensive tissue necrosis and ulceration that are hallmarks of the infection are attributable to production of a soluble toxin.[33,37] A non-ulcerative form is recognized with increasing frequency in highly endemic areas.[37] Occasionally severe systemic disease and death may result from secondary infection or tetanus.[31] Rarely squamous cell carcinoma may arise in a chronic Buruli ulcer.[38]

M. ulcerans infection tends to occur in parts of Africa where there is a high prevalence of *Schistosoma haematobium* infection. This observation has led some authors to suggest that schistosomiasis may be a risk factor for the development of Buruli ulcer by driving the host immunological reaction away from a Th1 response and toward a Th2 response.[34]

Mycobacterium avium intracellulare

M. avium intracellulare (MAI) complex is a group of slow-growing non-chromogens, which are present widely in dust, soil and water.[39,40] They are seen most commonly causing a cervical adenitis or disseminated infection in immunocompromised hosts. MAI is one of the commonest causes of bacteremia in AIDS patients and is also frequently isolated from the liver, bone marrow, lung or gastrointestinal tract.[41] Although the skin may be involved as part of disseminated MAI disease, primary cutaneous infection is uncommon.[41] A disseminated varioliform pustular eruption due to MAI has been described in a patient with AIDS.[42] Primary infections may develop in immunocompetent individuals who present with subcutaneous nodules, which subsequently undergo ulceration.[43–45] Isolated lesions such as perineal ulcers or subcutaneous masses may also occur in AIDS patients.[41]

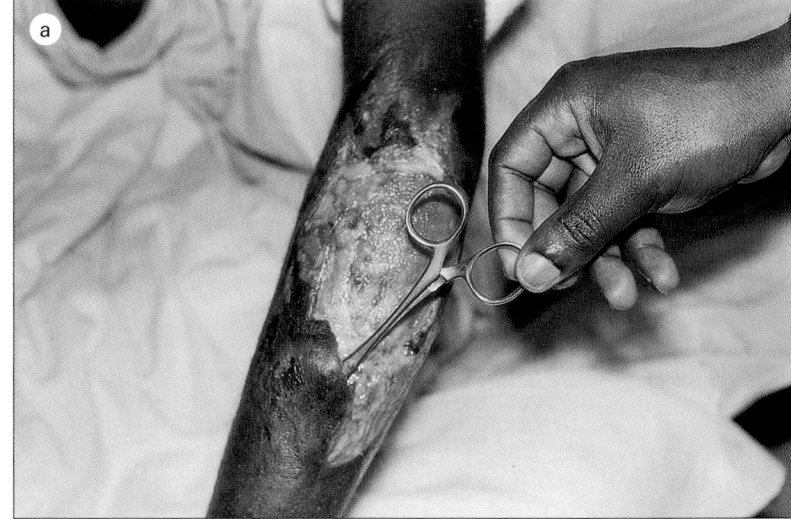

Fig. 17.177
Mycobacterium ulcerans: (a) note the extensive ulceration with undermining of the edge; (b) gross specimen showing opaque necrosis of the central subcutaneous fat. (a) By courtesy of S. Lucas, MD, St Thomas' Hospital, London, UK; (b) by courtesy of the late M. Hutt, MD, St Thomas' Hospital, London, UK.

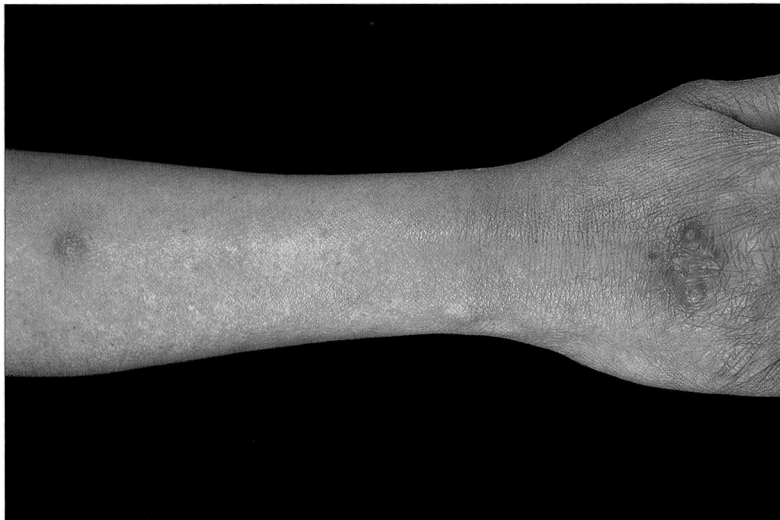

Fig. 17.176
Mycobacterium fortuitum chelonae: note the indurated, nodular, ulcerated lesion on the hand with sporotrichoid spread. By courtesy of S. Lucas, MD, St Thomas' Hospital, London, UK.

Generally, the skin lesions present as a panniculitis, often in relation to affected lymph nodes, or as nodules progressing to abscesses and ulcers (*Fig. 17.178*). Healing is slow, even with appropriate drug therapy, and excision may be necessary.

Other mycobacteria

Other mycobacteria, including *M. scrofulaceum*, *M. gordonae*, *M. simiae* and *M. haemophilum* may rarely cause cutaneous lesions, mostly following inoculation, to produce nodules and abscesses, usually with ulceration and sinus formation.

Histological features

Most of these 'atypical' mycobacteria show early cutaneous necrosis with neutrophil abscess formation. This phase is usually associated with readily demonstrable bacilli. The abscess phase is gradually replaced by granulomatous inflammation and fibrosis, often with sinus formation.

Mycobacterium marinum

M. marinum follows the common histological progression from abscess to granuloma, but few of the broad long bacilli are seen, except in immunocompromised patients (*Fig. 17.179*).[9,46] Caseation is absent, but there may be fibrinoid necrosis. Langhans' cells may be conspicuous or scanty (*Fig. 17.180*). A lymphohistiocytic infiltrate is present in the surrounding dermis. The overlying epidermis is parakeratotic, acanthotic or ulcerated. Pseudoepitheliomatous hyperplasia may occur (*Fig. 17.181*).[9] The sporotrichoid nodules, which are frequently present, are tuberculoid granulomata without the preceding abscess phase. There is often a poor yield of positive isolates from culture specimens, and PCR may be a more useful means of confirming the diagnosis.[17]

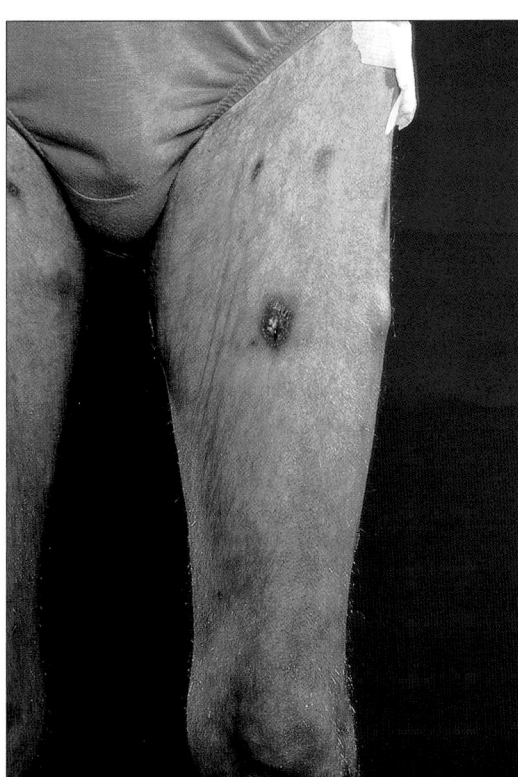

Fig. 17.178
Mycobacterium avium intracellulare: these multiple nodules on the thighs resemble panniculitis. By courtesy of S. Lucas, MD, St Thomas' Hospital, London, UK.

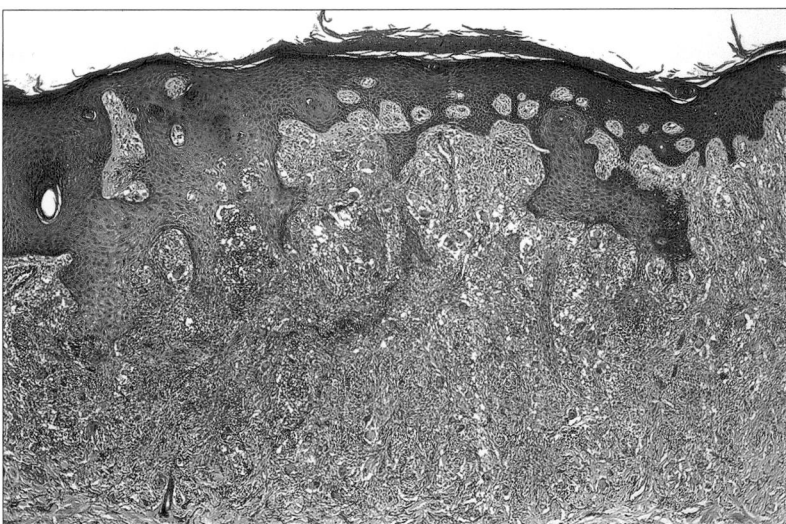

Fig. 17.179
Mycobacterium marinum (balnei): there is hyperkeratosis and very marked acanthosis.

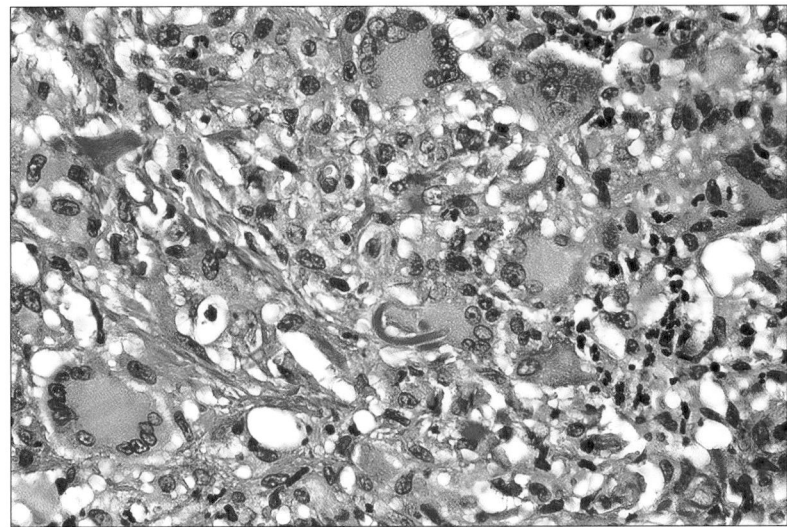

Fig. 17.180
Mycobacterium marinum (balnei): conspicuous Langhans' giant cells are present.

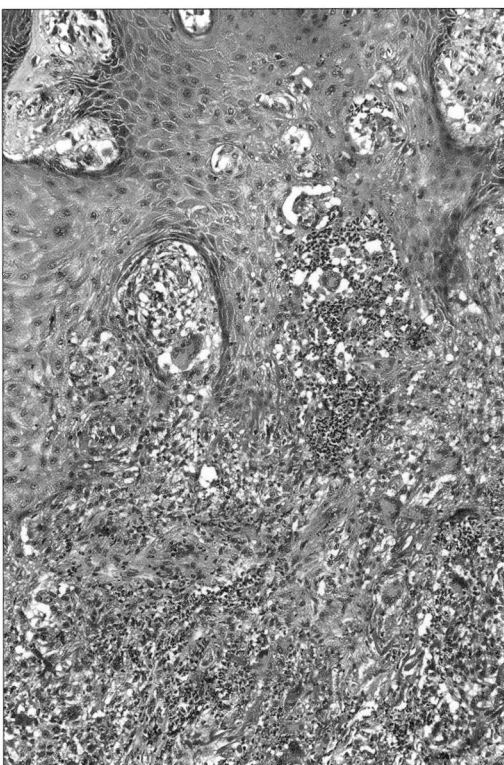

Fig. 17.181
Mycobacterium marinum (balnei): abscess formation and granulomatous inflammation have eroded the overlying epidermis. The features of this condition closely mimic the deep fungal infections.

Mycobacterium fortuitum chelonae

M. fortuitum chelonae infection shows early acute inflammation, which progresses to ill-defined granulomata with occasional necrotic foci. Panniculitis and acute suppurative folliculitis may also be observed (*Fig. 17.182*).[9] Bacilli are easily seen and are present in clusters (*Figs 17.183, 17.184*).[24,47]

Mycobacterium kansasii

M. kansasii infection shows a pattern similar to other non-tuberculous mycobacterial infections. The early mixed inflammation is usually intense before becoming tuberculoid. Abscesses may be present. Bacilli are frequent. *M. kansasii* organisms are larger, broader and more coarsely beaded.[48] Some cases show overlying acanthosis with hyperkeratosis and parakeratosis. The acute lesions seen in immunosuppressed patients typically show an intense neutrophil infiltrate with abscess formation.[26,29]

Mycobacterium ulcerans

M. ulcerans infection is characterized by extensive coagulative necrosis and ulceration with very little inflammatory reaction for a few months (*Fig. 17.185*).[32,36,49] The necrosis is hypothesized to be due to

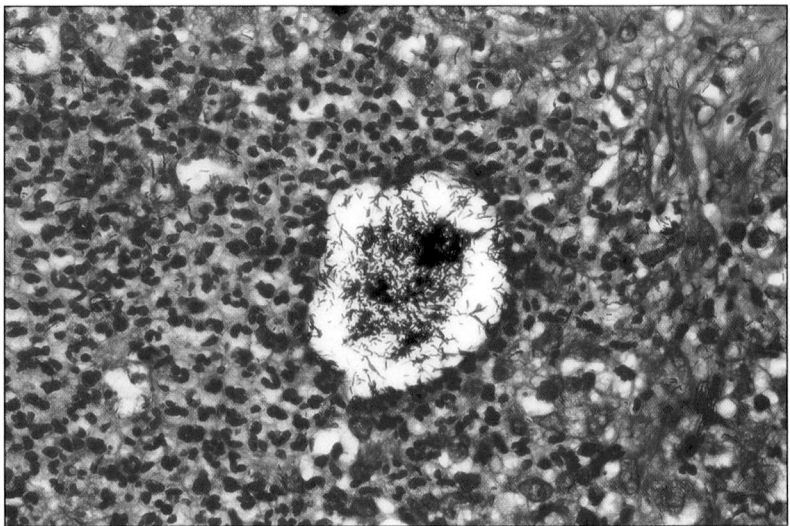

Fig. 17.184
Mycobacterium fortuitum chelonae: the bacilli are strongly acid fast.

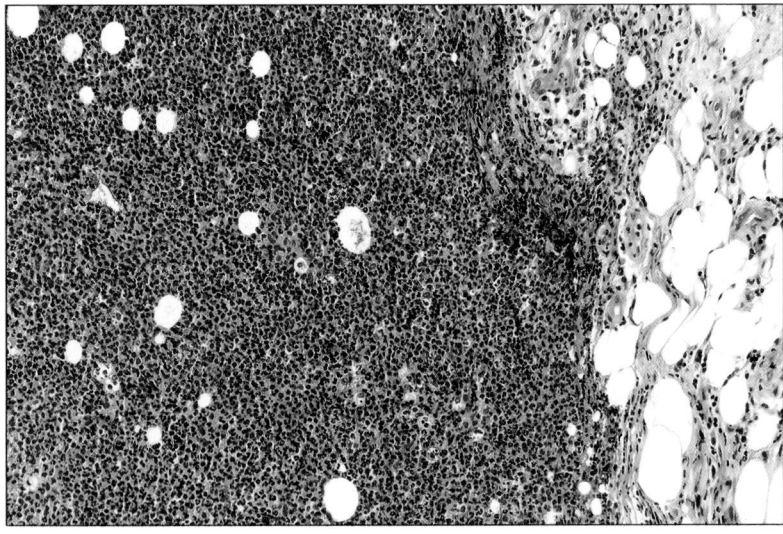

Fig. 17.182
Mycobacterium fortuitum chelonae: this is a predominantly neutrophil-mediated infection.

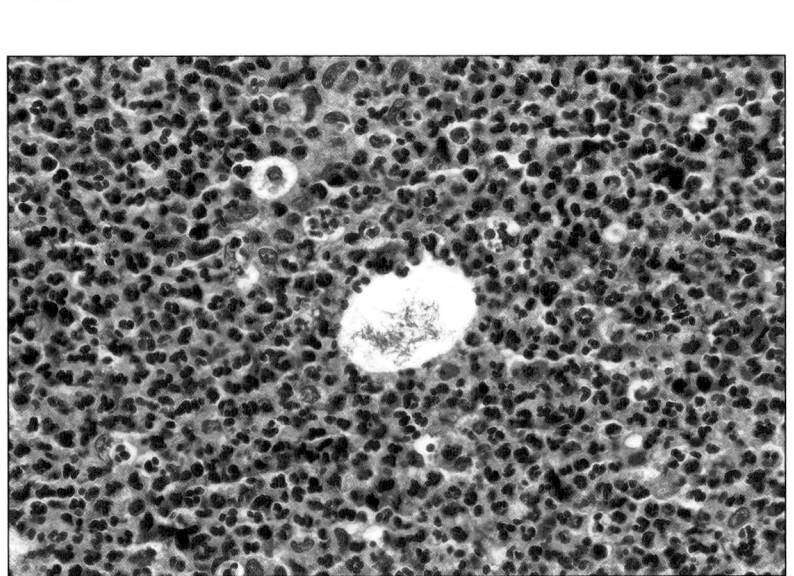

Fig. 17.183
Mycobacterium fortuitum chelonae: aggregates of bacilli are typically visible in the hematoxylin and eosin stained sections.

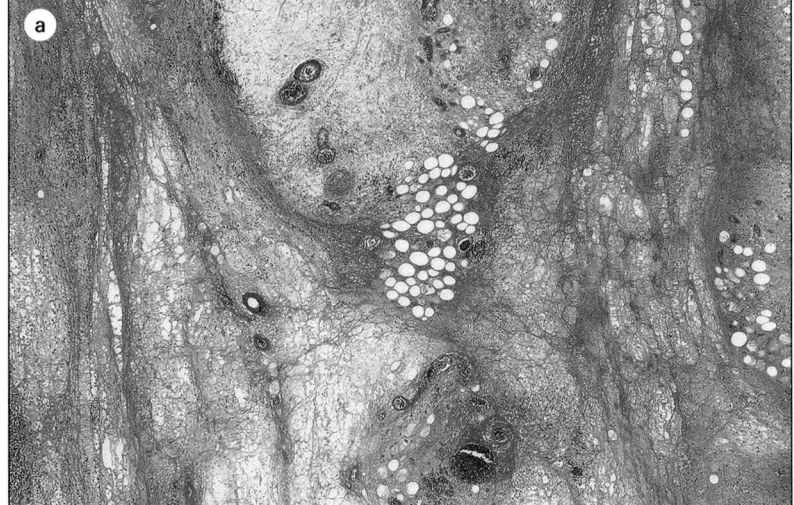

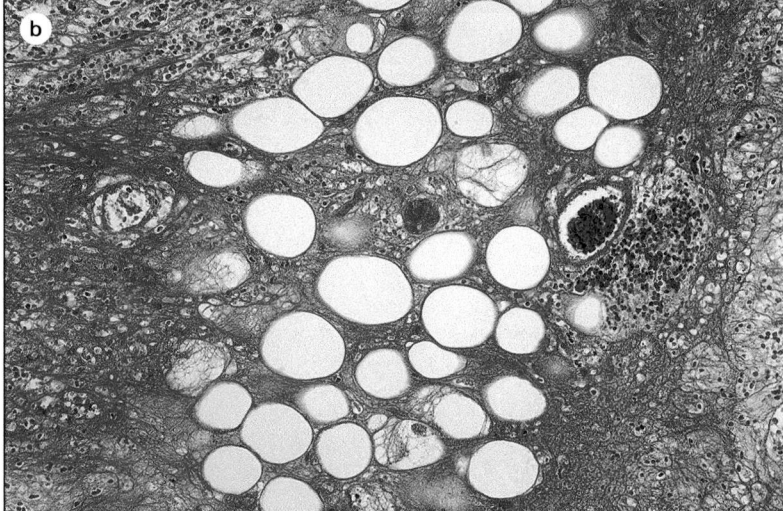

Fig. 17.185
(a, b) *Mycobacterium ulcerans*: there is widespread coagulative necrosis. Note the absence of an inflammatory reaction.

mycolactone, a macrolide toxin.[48] In this anergic stage, bacilli are very numerous and are seen clustering on the collagen of fascia or in fat at the base of the ulcer (*Fig. 17.186*). Leukocytoclastic vasculitis has been described in both the dermis and septae of the subcutaneous fat.[36,50] Focal calcification may be seen. Healing of the ulcer corresponds with progressive positivity of the 'burulin' test and a granulomatous reaction. Mycobacteria are then sparse or absent.[36] Caseation is not a feature. Variable septolobular panniculitis may be present. Resolving lesions may exhibit pseudoepitheliomatous hyperplasia of the epidermis.[51] In the non-ulcerated form there is massive contiguous necrosis of the dermis and subcutaneous tissue.[37] The ulcerated lesions may demonstrate immunoreactivity for phenolic glycolipid-I (PGL-I).[50]

Mycobacterium avium intracellulare

M. avium intracellulare infection sometimes appears to have an early abscess phase before the granulomatous phase, but in other cases the inflammatory infiltrate is more lymphohistiocytic, so that it resembles lepromatous leprosy (*Fig. 17.187*).[39,40] Bacilli are present, but are usually seen intracellularly. Rarely, the infected histiocytes may become large and voluminous and have been referred to as pseudogaucher cells.[52]

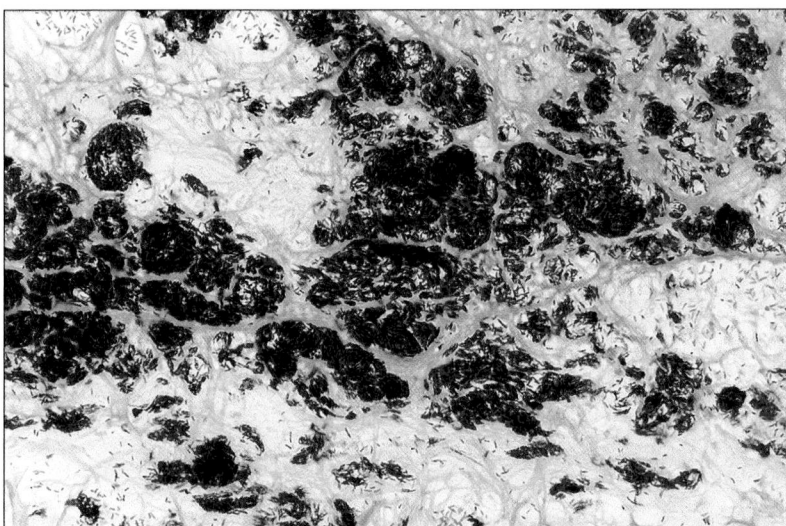

Fig. 17.186
Mycobacterium ulcerans: the lesions contain numerous acid-fast bacilli (Ziehl–Neelsen).

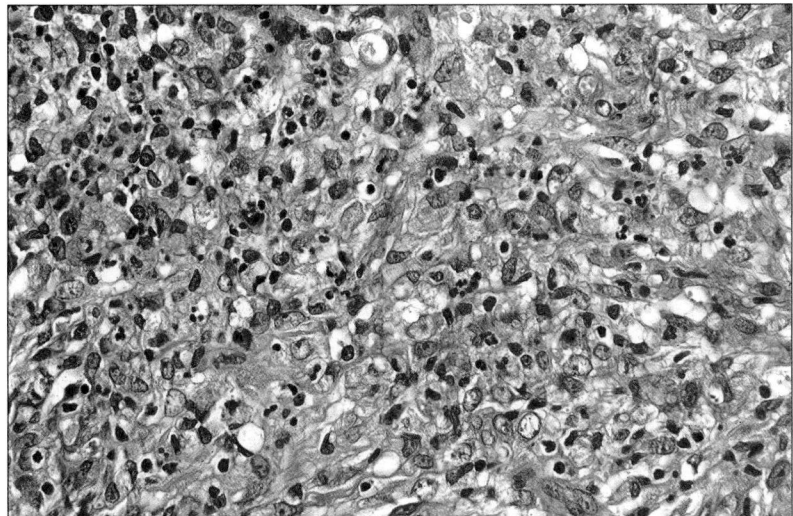

Fig. 17.187
Mycobacterium avium intracellulare: in this variant, the infiltrate typically consists of histiocytes, lymphocytes and neutrophils. Bacteria are often numerous.

Other mycobacteria

M. haemophilum may produce a mixed suppurative and granulomatous reaction in addition to a paucigranulomatous reaction, lichenoid interface dermatitis and lymphocytic vasculitis.[53]

References

1. Saxe, N. (1985) Mycobacterial skin infections. *J Cutan Pathol*, **12**, 300–312.
2. Wolinsky, E. (1979) Nontuberculous mycobacteria and associated diseases. *Am Rev Resp Dis*, **119**, 107–159.
3. Findlay, G.H. (1987) Mycobacterial infections. In: The dermatology of bacterial infections. Oxford: Blackwell, pp 334–345.
4. Runyon, E.H. (1965) Pathogenic mycobacteria. *Adv Tuberc Res*, **14**, 235–287.
5. Hendrick, S.J., Jorizzo, J.L., Newton, R.C. (1986) Giant Mycobacterium fortuitum abscess associated with systemic lupus erythematosus. *Arch Dermatol*, **122**, 695–697.
6. Hautmann, G., Lotti, T. (1994) Atypical mycobacterial infections of the skin. *Dermatol Clin*, **12**, 657–668.
7. Ena, P., Sechi, L.A., Saccabusi, S. et al (2001) Rapid identification of cutaneous infections by nontuberculous mycobacteria by polymerase chain reaction-restriction analysis length polymorphism of the hsp65 gene. *Int J Dermatol*, **40**, 495–499.
8. Murdoch, M.E., Leigh, I.M. (1989) Sporotrichoid spread of cutaneous Mycobacterium chelonei infection. *Clin Exp Dermatol*, **14**, 309–312.
9. Bartralot, R., Pujol, R.M., Garcia-Patos, V. et al (2000) Cutaneous infections due to nontuberculous mycobacteria: histopathological review of 28 cases. Comparative study between lesions observed in immunosuppressed patients and normal hosts. *J Cutan Pathol*, **27**, 124–129.
10. Wallace, R.J. (1987) Recent clinical advances in knowledge of the nonleprous environmental mycobacteria responsible for cutaneous disease. *Arch Dermatol*, **123**, 337–339.
11. Aubry, A., Chosidow, O., Caumes, E. et al (2002) Sixty-three cases of Mycobacterium marinum infection: clinical features, treatment, and antibiotic susceptibility of causative isolates. *Arch Intern Med*, **162**, 1746–1752.
12. Huminer, D., Pitlik, S.D., Block, C. et al (1986) Aquarium-borne Mycobacterium marinum skin infection. *Arch Dermatol*, **122**, 698–703.
13. Jernigan, J.A., Farr, B.M. (2000) Incubation period and sources of exposure for cutaneous Mycobacterium marinum infection: case report and review of the literature. *Clin Infect Dis*, **31**, 439–443.
14. Kern, W., Vanek, E., Jungbluth, H. (1989) Fish breeder granuloma: infection caused by Mycobacterium marinum and other atypical mycobacteria in the human. Analysis of 8 cases and review of the literature. *Med Klin*, **84**, 578–583.
15. Beyt, B.E., Ortbals, D.W., Santa Cruz, D.J. et al (1980) Cutaneous mycobacteriosis: analysis of 34 cases with a new classification of disease. *Medicine (Baltimore)*, **60**, 95–109.
16. Tan, H.H., Chan, R.K. (1999) Atypical mycobacterium infection with sporotrichoid spread in a patient with human immunodeficiency virus. *Ann Acad Med Singapore*, **28**, 846–848.
17. Ang, P., Rattana-Apiromyakij, N., Goh, C.L. (2000) Retrospective study of Mycobacterium marinum skin infections. *Int J Dermatol*, **39**, 343–347.
18. Camargo, D., Saad, C., Ruiz, F. et al (1996) Iatrogenic outbreak of M. chelonae skin abscesses. *Epidemiol Infect*, **117**, 113–119.
19. Murillo, J., Torres, J., Bofill, L. et al (2000) Skin wound infection by rapidly growing mycobacteria: an unexpected complication of liposuction and liposculpture. The Venezuelan Collaborative Infectious and Tropical Diseases Study Group. *Arch Dermatol*, **136**, 1347–1352.
20. Woo, P.C., Leung, K.W., Wong, S.S. et al (2002) Relatively alcohol-resistant mycobacteria are emerging pathogens in patients receiving acupuncture treatment. *J Clin Microbiol*, **40**, 1219–1224.
21. Winthrop, K.L., Abrams, M., Yakrus, M. et al (2002) An outbreak of mycobacterial furunculosis associated with footbaths at a nail salon. *N Engl J Med*, **346**, 1366–1371.
22. Smith, M.B., Schnadig, V.J., Boyars, M.C. et al (2001) Clinical and pathological features of Mycobacterium fortuitum infections. An emerging pathogen in patients with AIDS. *Am J Clin Pathol*, **116**, 225–232.
23. Paul, J., Baigrie, C., Parums, D.V. (1992) Fatal case of disseminated infection with the turtle bacillus Mycobacterium chelonae. *J Clin Pathol*, **45**, 528–530.
24. Endzweig, C.H., Strauss, E., Murphy, F. et al (2001) A case of cutaneous Mycobacterium chelonae abscess infection in a renal transplant patient. *J Cutan Med Surg*, **5**, 28–32.
25. Bolivar, R., Satterwhite, T.K., Floyd, M. (1980) Cutaneous lesions due to Mycobacterium kansasii. *Arch Dermatol*, **116**, 207–208.
26. Stellbrink, H.J., Koperski, K., Albrecht, H. et al (1990) *Mycobacterium kansasii* infection limited to skin and lymph node in a patient with AIDS. *Clin Exp Dermatol*, **15**, 457–458.
27. Stengem, J., Grande, K.K., Hsu, S. (1999) Localized primary cutaneous Mycobacterium kansasii infection in an immunocompromised host. *J Am Acad Dermatol*, **41** (5 Pt 2), 854–856.
28. Curco, N., Pagerols, X., Gomez, L. et al (1996) Mycobacterium kansasii infection limited to the skin in a patient with AIDS. *Br J Dermatol*, **135**, 324–326.
29. Hanke, C.W., Temofeew, R.K., Slama, S.L. (1987) Mycobacterium kansasii infection with multiple cutaneous lesions. *J Am Acad Dermatol*, **16**, 1122–1128.
30. Owens, D.W., McBride, M.E. (1969) Sprotrichoid cutaneous infection with Mycobacterium kansasii. *Arch Dermatol*, **100**, 54–58.
31. van der Werf, T.S., van der Graaf, W.T., Tappero, J.W. et al (1999) Mycobacterium ulcerans infection. *Lancet*, **354**, 1013–1018.
32. Connor, D.H., Lunn, F. (1966) Buruli ulceration. A clinicopathologic study of 38 Ugandans with Mycobacterium ulcerans infection. *Arch Pathol*, **81**, 183–189.
33. Portaels, F., Chemlal, K., Elsen, P. et al (2001) Mycobacterium ulcerans in wild animals. *Rev Sci Tech*, **20**, 252–264.
34. Stienstra, Y., van der Graaf, W.T., te Meerman, G.J. et al (2001) Susceptibility to development of Mycobacterium ulcerans disease: review of possible risk factors. *Trop Med Int Health*, **6**, 554–562.
35. Mitchell, P.J., Jerrett, I.V., Slee, K.J. (1984) Skin ulcers caused by Mycobacterium ulcerans in koalas near Bairnsdale, Australia. *Pathology*, **16**, 256–260.
36. Hayman, J., McQueen, A. (1985) The pathology of Mycobacterium ulcerans infection. *Pathology*, **17**, 594–600.
37. Abalos, F.M., Aguiar, J. Sr, Guedenon, A. et al (2000) Mycobacterium ulcerans infection (Buruli ulcer): a case report of the disseminated nonulcerative form. *Ann Diagn Pathol*, **4**, 386–390.
38. Evans, M.R., Etuaful, S.N., Amofah, G. et al (1999) Squamous cell carcinoma secondary to Buruli ulcer. *Trans R Soc Trop Med Hyg*, **93**, 63–64.
39. Cox, S.K., Strausbaugh, L.J. (1981) Chronic cutaneous infection caused by Mycobacterium intracellulare. *Arch Dermatol*, **117**, 794–796.
40. Wood, C., Nickoloff, B.J., Tode-Taylor, N.R. (1985) Pseudotumor resulting from atypical mycobacterial infection: a histoid variety of Mycobacterium avium–intracellulare complex infection. *Am J Clin Pathol*, **83**, 524–527.
41. Inwald, D., Nelson, M., Cramp, M. et al (1994) Cutaneous manifestations of mycobacterial infections in patients with AIDS. *Br J Dermatol*, **130**, 111–114.
42. Bachelez, H., Ducloy, G., Pinquier, L. et al (1996) Disseminated varioliform pustular eruption due to Mycobacterium avium intracellulare in an HIV-infected patient. *Br J Dermatol*, **134**, 801–803.
43. Tchiki, Y., Hirose, M., Akiyama, T. et al (1997) Skin infection caused by Mycobacterium avium. *Br J Dermatol*, **136**, 260–263.
44. Hide, M., Hondo, T., Yonehara, S. et al (1997) Infection with the Mycobacterium avium-intracellulare with abscess, ulceration and fistula formation. *Br J Dermatol*, **136**, 121–123.
45. Sugita, Y., Ishii, N., Katsuno, M. et al (2000) Familial cluster of cutaneous Mycobacterium avium infection resulting from use of a circulating, constantly heated bath water system. *Br J Dermatol*, **142**, 789–793.

46. Travis, W.D., Travis, L.B., Roberts, G.D. et al (1985) The histopathologic spectrum in Mycobacterium marinum infection. *Arch Pathol Lab Med*, **109**, 1109–1113.
47. Wallace, R.J. Jr, Swenson, J.M., Silcox, V.A. et al (1983) Spectrum of disease due to rapidly growing mycobacteria. *Rev Infect Dis*, **5**, 657–679.
48. Hale, M.J. (2000) Mycobacterial infection: a histopathological chameleon. *Curr Diagn Pathol*, **6**, 93–102.
49. Hayman, J. (1993) Out of Africa: observations on the histopathology of Mycobacterium ulcerans infection. *J Clin Pathol*, **46**, 5–9.

50. Mwanatambwe, M., Fukunishi, Y., Yajima, M. et al (2000) Clinico-histopathological findings in Buruli ulcer. *Nihon Hansenbyo Gakkai Zasshi*, **69**, 93–100.
51. Hayman, J.A., Smith, I.M., Flood, P. (1996) Pseudoepitheliomatous hyperplasia in Mycobacterium ulcerans infection. *Pathology*, **28**, 131–134.
52. Kahn, H., Phelps, R.G. (1999) Pseudogaucher cells in cutaneous Mycobacterium avium intracellulare infection: report of a case. *Am J Dermatopathol*, **21**, 51–54.
53. Busam, K.J., Kiehn, T.E., Salob, S.P. et al (1999) Histologic reactions to cutaneous infections by Mycobacterium haemophilum. *Am J Surg Pathol*, **23**, 1379–1385.

Leprosy

Clinical features

Mycobacterium leprae is the bacillus recognized as causing leprosy, but as yet it can only be cultured in experimental animals, particularly the nine-banded armadillo.[1–3] It is an obligate, intracellular, Gram-positive and weakly acid-fast organism. The disease is found worldwide, due to extensive traveling and migration, but is endemic in the tropics. Over five million patients are under treatment and an estimated 10 million more are untreated.

Although the disease has been recognized for many centuries and its causative organism has been known for over 100 years, many aspects of the pathogenesis remain unclear, and leprosy is still a problem to diagnosticians, epidemiologists and pharmacologists. The complexity of the presentation is related intimately to the varied immunological responses. The incubation period may be as short as 1–2 years, but is usually 3–5 years, and may be 10 years or more. There are two extremes of presentation:
- the tuberculoid form, tuberculoid leprosy (TT)
- the lepromatous form, lepromatous leprosy (LL).

Between these are:
- borderline tuberculoid leprosy (BT)
- borderline lepromatous leprosy (BL)
- borderline leprosy (BB) occupying an intermediate position.

Tuberculoid leprosy

Tuberculoid leprosy (TT) is associated with high resistance to the *Lepra* bacillus, but in the lepromatous form resistance to the *Lepra* bacillus is low.[4]

TT occurs in individuals with good cell-mediated immunity, but low antibody titers to *M. leprae*. It appears as localized, sometimes single, asymmetrical truncal or limb lesions. The lesion is typically an erythematous plaque with raised margins and a flat hypopigmented center (*Fig. 17.188*). Sensory impairment is invariable because of associated involvement of nerves by the bacilli; these nerves may be palpably thickened. Alternatively, the skin lesion may be an erythematous macule, hypopigmented in dark skins. Sometimes the skin is not involved primarily, cutaneous manifestations being seen as a result of minor trauma associated with anesthesia from the neural lesion.

Lepromatous leprosy

Lepromatous leprosy (LL) is a systemic disease that occurs in patients with poor cell-mediated immunity to *M. leprae*, but with higher levels of antibodies. The cutaneous lesions are multiple, symmetrical and may affect the whole skin, giving a sclerodermatous appearance (diffuse or Lucio-type leprosy). The lesions are typically firm and nodular and are concentrated on the face and backs of hands, facial lesions being associated with hair loss round the eyes (*Figs 17.189, 17.190*). The distribution of the lesions is said to be favored by lower skin temperature. The mucosa of the nose is characteristically involved and becomes hyperemic with frequent epistaxes. The nasal cartilages and bone may be affected, and collapse may result in a picture similar to the saddle nose of congenital syphilis. A variety of macules, papules and plaques may be present at one time, characteristically sparing the axillae, groins and perineum. These lesions become anesthetic due to widespread neural involvement with resultant claw hand and foot drop (*Fig. 17.191*).

Borderline leprosy

Lesions in BT, BL and BB manifest in a form intermediate between the polar forms TT and LL (*Figs 17.192–17.194*). The lesions are fewer in number and less symmetrically distributed than in LL and there is less localization and nerve involvement than in TT. There is, however, a continuous spectrum and individual patients may downgrade to more closely resemble LL or upgrade towards the tuberculoid pole.

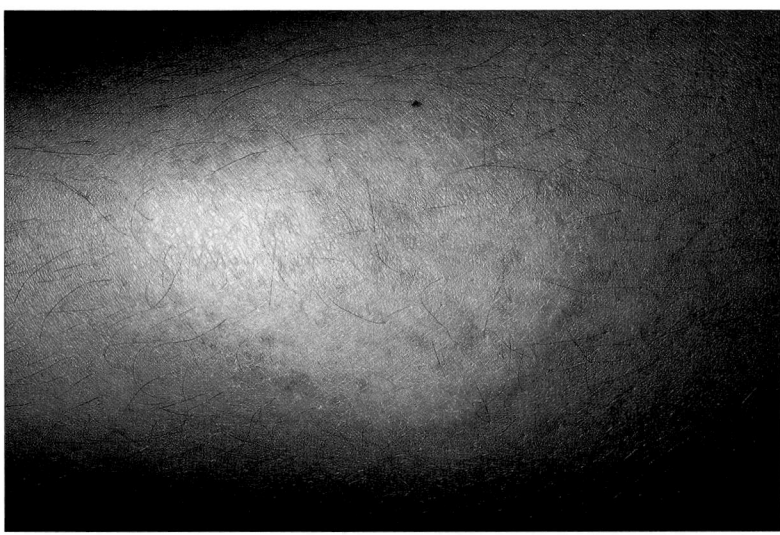

Fig. 17.188
Tuberculoid leprosy: note the hypopigmented center and the raised erythematous border. By courtesy of M.M. Black, MD, St Thomas' Hospital, London, UK.

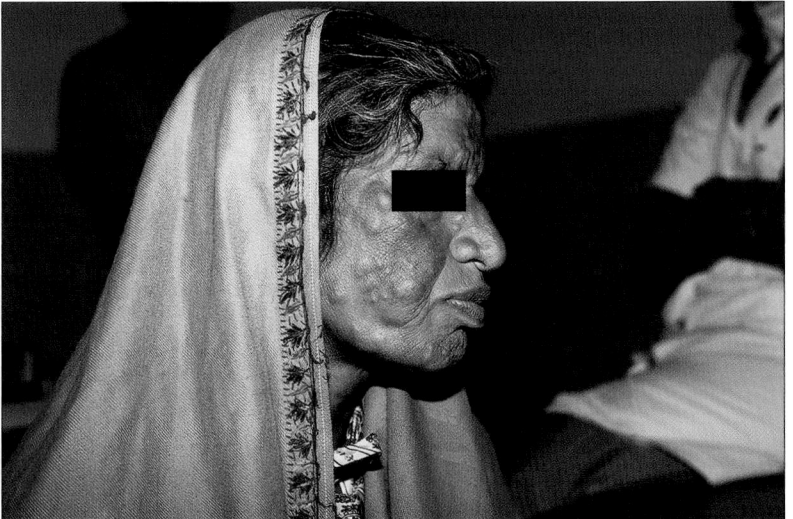

Fig. 17.189
Lepromatous leprosy: numerous nodules are present on the face. By courtesy of S. Lucas, MD, St Thomas' Hospital, London, UK.

Lepra *reactions*

Type I *Lepra* (reversal) reactions, which usually develop in BL patients, are associated with an upgrading to a more resistant tuberculoid pole of the spectrum and the development of a positive Mitsuda (lepromin) reaction.[5,6] Patients therefore have developed an improved immunological reaction. Less often type I reactions may be associated with downgrading. They may be associated with treatment, and consequently are characterized by an accelerated destruction of bacilli. Type I *Lepra* reactions are also associated with pregnancy, stress and intercurrent infections. The upgrading causes marked inflammatory changes within the skin: nerve lesions manifest as nerve swelling and pain; cutaneous lesions may become tender and edematous with an increased cellular infiltrate (*Fig. 17.195*).

Type II reaction, also known as erythema nodosum leprosum (ENL), occurs in LL and BL, usually during treatment. It may also be provoked by physical or mental stress, injury, other infections, vaccinations or pregnancy.[7,8] There appears to be a direct relationship between an increasing bacterial index and the risk of developing ENL. Increasing age, on the other hand, has been found to have an inverse relationship with ENL.[9] The reaction may occur prior to, during or after the introduction of multidrug therapy.[9] The changes of ENL are believed to be due, at least in part, to immune complex deposition in vessels following the release of bacterial antigens in patients who have high levels of antibodies. Both immunoglobulins and complement have been identified in blood vessel walls. Delayed hypersensitivity mechanisms, however, are also thought to have a pathogenetic role. In ENL there are, therefore, increased numbers of T-helper cells and an increased lesional helper:suppressor T-cell ratio is characteristic.[7] The symptoms are nocturnal pains, mainly of the face, thighs and arms. Lesions include tender erythematous or deep purple nodules with fever and painful nerve swelling, swollen joints, myositis, painful fingers, iritis, lymphadenitis,

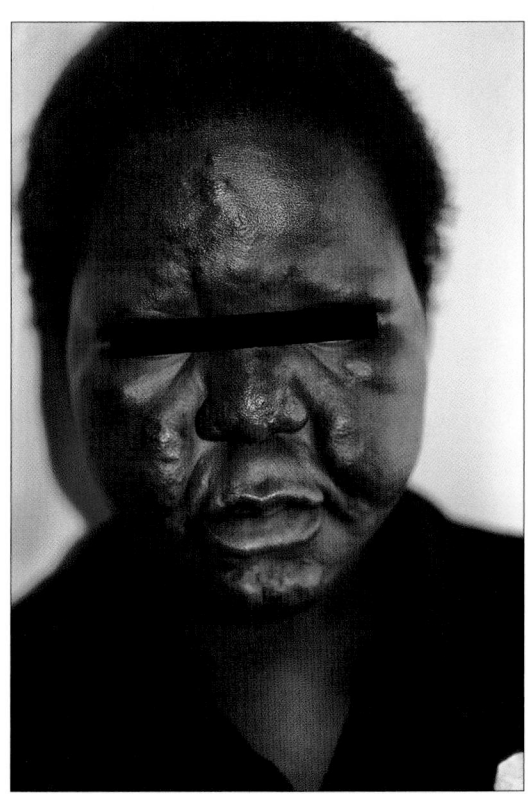

Fig. 17.190
Lepromatous leprosy: note the symmetry and characteristic loss of the eyebrows. By courtesy of N.C. Dlova, MD, Nelson R. Mandela School of Medicine, University of KwaZulu-Natal, South Africa.

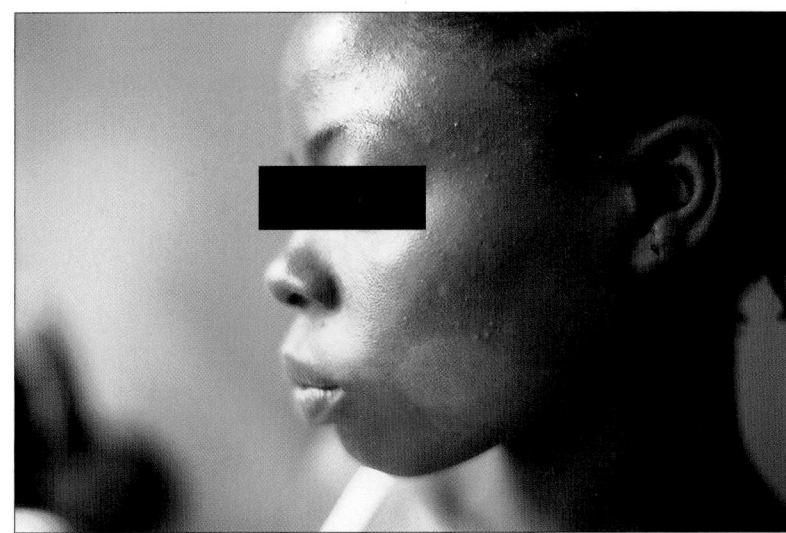

Fig. 17.192
Borderline tuberculoid leprosy: an early hypopigmented macule. By courtesy of S. Lucas, MD, St Thomas' Hospital, London, UK.

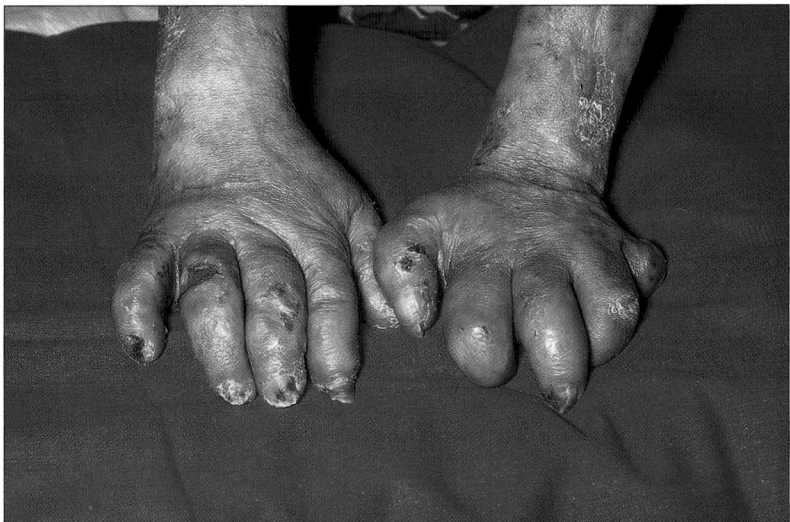

Fig. 17.191
Lepromatous leprosy: these hands show loss of the digits and trauma-related ulcers due to gross nerve damage. By courtesy of S. Lucas, MD, St Thomas' Hospital, London, UK.

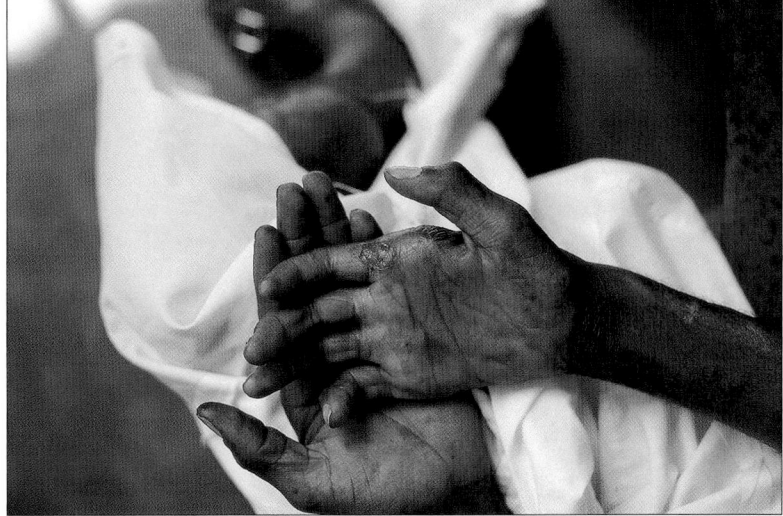

Fig. 17.193
Borderline tuberculoid leprosy: note the ulceration and muscle wasting due to median and ulnar nerve involvement. By courtesy of S. Lucas, MD, St Thomas' Hospital, London, UK.

glomerulonephritis and epididymo-orchitis (*Fig. 17.196*).[7] A case with bullous skin lesions has been reported.[10]

Lucio's phenomenon

Lucio's phenomenon is seen in Mexican and Central American patients who present with untreated, diffuse, non-nodular (pure and primitive diffuse, PPDL) lepromatous leprosy associated with hemorrhagic infarction and epidermal necrosis (*Fig. 17.197*).[7,11] Lesions, which are initially macular, soon break down to become irregular jagged ulcerations, which heal to leave irregular atrophic scars. The extremities are most commonly affected. Lucio's phenomenon is mediated by immune complexes.[11,12] A further rare reaction occurring in patients with LL is the development of numerous histiocytoma-like lesions: the histoid variant (*Fig. 17.198*).[13] Although uncommon, cutaneous and subcu-

taneous nodules and plaques measuring up to 3.5 cm in diameter have been described.[14]

Indeterminate leprosy

Indeterminate leprosy is an early form of leprosy, which often resolves spontaneously.[15] In 25% of patients, however, evolution to one of the determinant types occurs. It appears as poorly defined areas of slight hypopigmentation or erythema, without systemic or neural changes. The condition is only likely to be recognized readily in endemic areas where there is a high awareness of leprosy. It must be carefully distinguished from other dermatoses.

The Mitsuda reaction (intradermal injection of armadillo-derived *Lepra* bacilli) is useful for classification purposes.[4] Tuberculoid patients develop a granulomatous response, lepromatous patients do not (*Fig. 17.199*).[5]

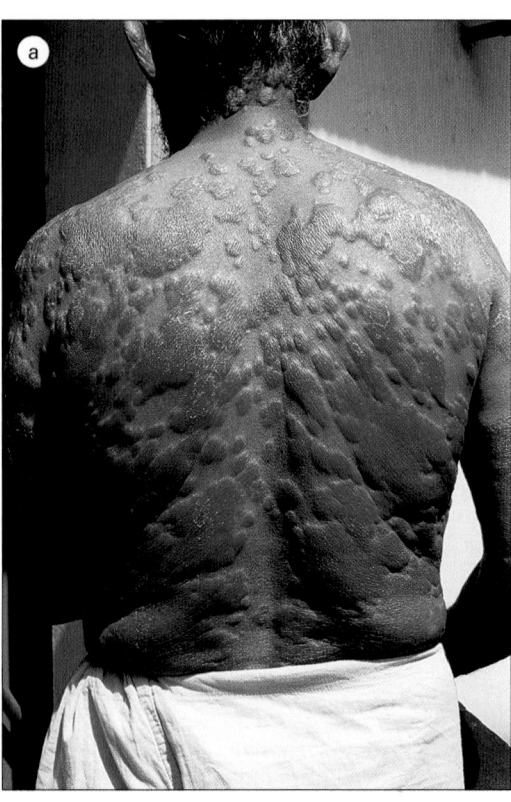

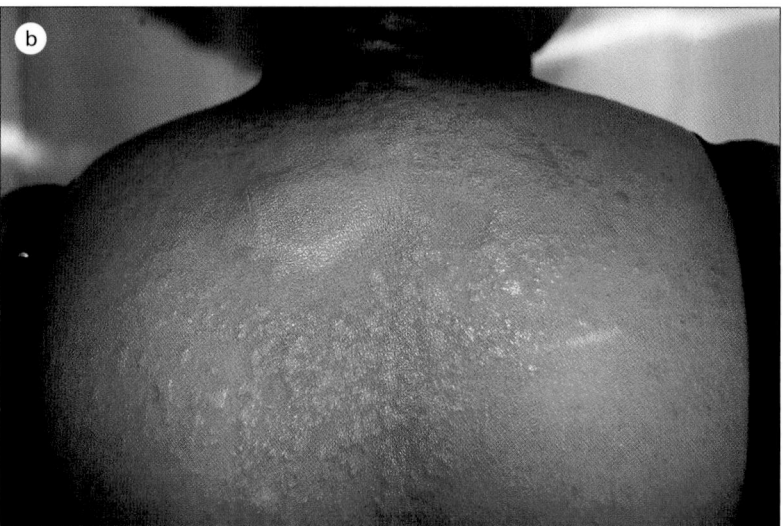

Fig. 17.194
(a, b) Borderline lepromatous leprosy: there are gross infiltrated erythematous plaques with well-defined borders. (a) By courtesy of S. Lucas, MD, Institute of Dermatology, London, UK; (b) by courtesy of N.C. Dlova, MD, Nelson R. Mandela School of Medicine, University of KwaZulu-Natal, South Africa.

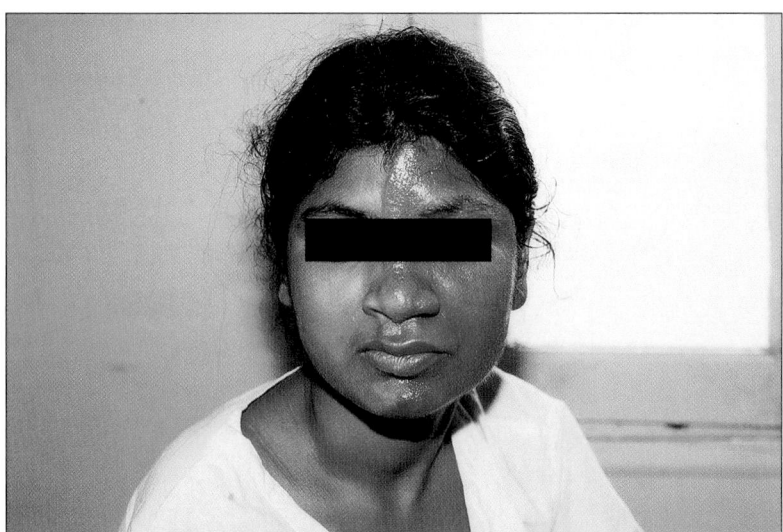

Fig. 17.195
Type I *Lepra* reaction: note the edema and intense erythema in this widespread lesion. By courtesy of S. Lucas, MD, St Thomas' Hospital, London, UK.

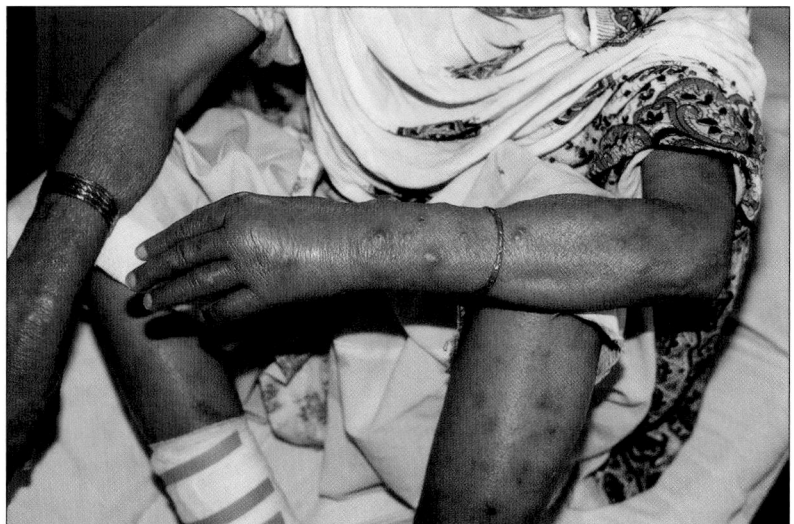

Fig. 17.196
Erythema nodosum leprosum: note the erythematous nodules on the dorsal aspect of the forearms and shins. By courtesy of S. Lucas, MD, St Thomas' Hospital, London, UK.

Although leprosy has been reported in patients infected with HIV, current evidence suggests that *M. leprae* is not an opportunistic pathogen in these individuals.[16–18]

Leprosy patients with chronic cutaneous ulcers (especially plantar lesions) are at increased risk for the development of squamous cell carcinoma.[19]

Pathogenesis and histological features

The varied clinical manifestations of leprosy are the result of a number of factors, including the host's immune response, the mode of infection and certain genetic factors.[20] It was long assumed that transmission of leprosy was by long-term close direct skin contact, but this can be seriously questioned as there is no evidence that infection can occur through intact skin. LL is far more infective than other forms and the nasal mucosa and nasal secretions of patients with LL are heavily infected with bacilli. This is a most important source of infection, but it is not clear that the route of transmission is via the lungs or gastrointestinal tract, even though inhalation of droplets and ingestion of bacilli does occur. Lactating mothers with LL produce high counts of bacilli in milk and yet do not appear to spread leprosy to their babies.

It seems most likely that infection in leprosy occurs by a combination of nasal discharge and digital impregnation of the skin, as bacilli can be carried under the nails and inoculated into the skin by scratching. The responses of those that are infected may be determined by a genetic predisposition, as suggested by associations with human leukocyte antigen (HLA) types (e.g. DR2 and DR3).

In tuberculoid lesions there is an efficient macrophage response, associated with a preponderance of T-helper (CD4+) cells over T-suppressor cells (CD8+) and no antibody production. There is associated elimination of the bacteria, which are therefore difficult to find in tuberculoid lesions. The tuberculoid response is therefore characterized by a persistent or chronic delayed hypersensitivity reaction.[5] In lepromatous lesions T-suppressor cells are more numerous and IL-2 producing cells are scarce, whereas they are 10 times more common in TT. One explanation for the different response suggests that T-helper cells are defective or absent in individuals who develop LL. An alternative theory suggests that T-suppressor cells are activated by the leprosy bacilli in patients of certain HLA-DR types. It is proposed that this represents a response to PGL-I, which is peculiar to the cell envelope of the leprosy bacillus. The T-suppressor cells effect a reduction of T-helper cells reactive to *M. leprae*. In this way the T-suppressor and T-helper theories are not incompatible. The variable immune response to the *Lepra* bacillus is manifest in the wide variety of clinical manifestations in leprosy.[21] Other genetic factors including Lewis factor and natural resistance-associated macrophage protein 1 (NRAMP1) may also play a role.[20]

In LL there is an inability to develop a significant T-cell-mediated delayed hypersensitivity reaction to the leprosy bacillus.[5] The high level of antibodies in LL appear to have no beneficial effect, but are relevant to the development of the immune complex-mediated ENL lesions (see above). Lucio's phenomenon, in which purpura and leg ulcers develop,

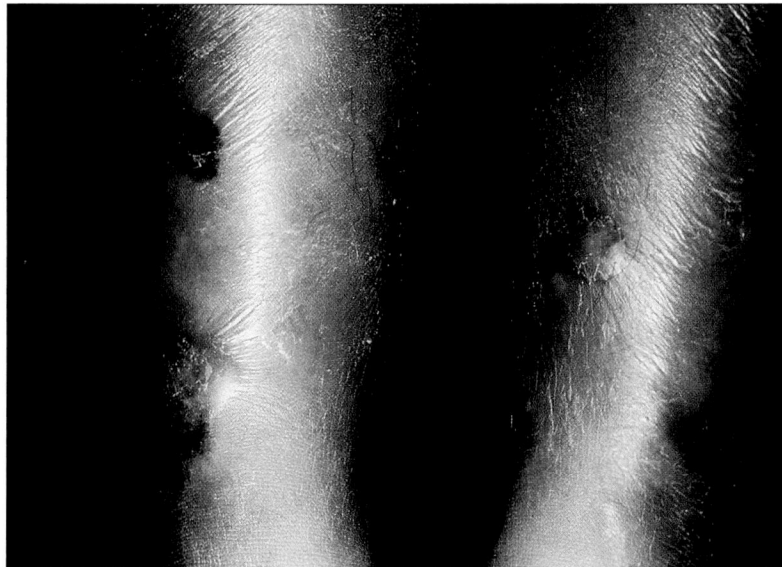

Fig. 17.197
Lucio's phenomenon: note the multiple infarcted cutaneous nodules, which have developed against a background of diffuse lepromatous leprosy. By courtesy of R. Arenas, MD, and J.C. Salas, MD, Monterrey, Mexico.

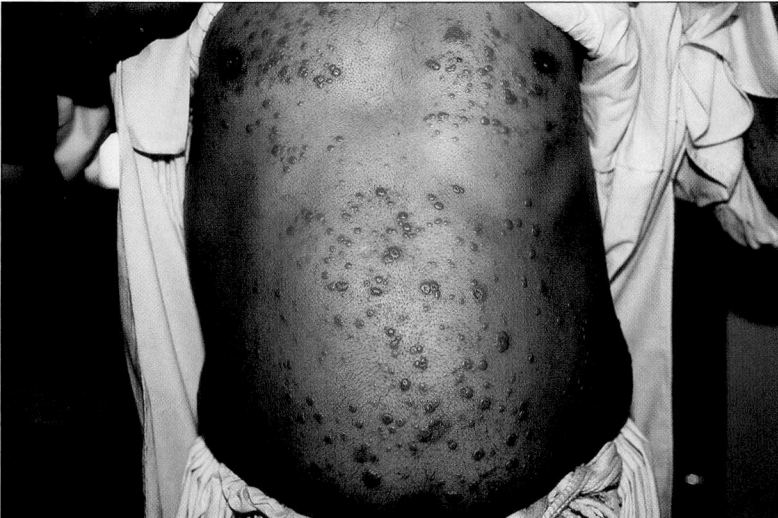

Fig. 17.198
Histoid leprosy: these numerous brown papules and nodules may be histologically mistaken for a 'fibrohistiocytic' tumor if the clinical information is not available. By courtesy of S. Lucas, MD, St Thomas' Hospital, London, UK.

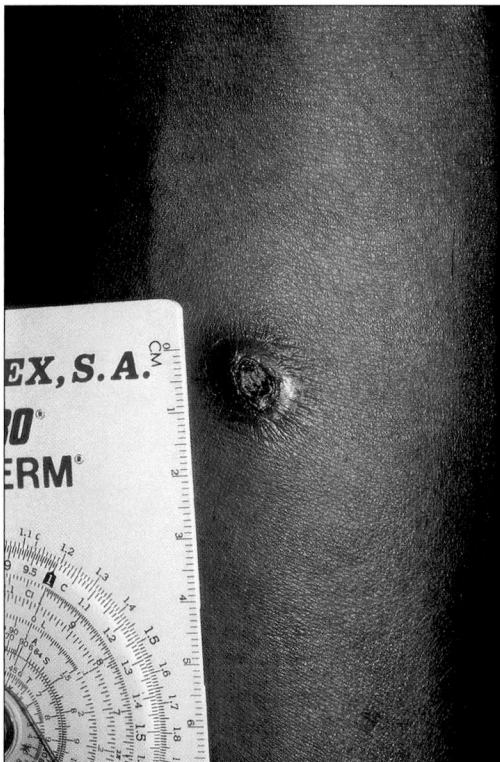

Fig. 17.199
Mitsuda reaction: this is positive in a patient with tuberculoid leprosy. By courtesy of R. Arenas, MD, and J.C. Salas, MD, Monterrey, Mexico.

involves a similar immune complex-mediated mechanism to produce episodes of necrotizing vasculitis in this diffuse type of leprosy. Antiphospholipid antibodies may also play a role.[22]

Histologically, TT is characterized by an epithelioid histiocyte response around small cutaneous nerves (*Figs 17.200–17.202*). It may be entirely confined to the immediate vicinity of nerves in highly immune patients, but it often extends into the adjacent dermis. When there are clinical cutaneous lesions the infiltrate involves the papillary dermis up to the epidermis. In contrast, BT and more lepromatous forms have a preserved Grenz zone in the papillary dermis. Tuberculoid lesions usually contain a number of Langhans' giant cells, but necrosis is not a feature. Bacilli are so scarce in tuberculoid lesions that they are usually not identified; they are present in increasing numbers in variations closer to the lepromatous type of response. Distinguishing TL from other forms of granulomatous infiltrate of the skin is dependent on noting the association with nerves, which often gives the granuloma a serpentine shape. In addition, there are numerous lymphocytes, largely T-helper type, which may infiltrate the nerves in highly immune cases; the lymphoid infiltrate may be intense and extensive.

In LL, as in TL, the macrophage is the most important cell, but it is not arranged in discrete granulomata nor clearly related to nerves. Rather, macrophages are found in poorly circumscribed masses in the dermis with few, if any, lymphocytes (*Figs 17.203, 17.204*). Those lymphocytes that are present are T-suppressor cells. The macrophages are inert and often vacuolated or foamy (*Fig. 17.205*). They may be distended with large groups (or globi) of leprosy bacilli. These give the cytoplasm a grayish tinge on staining with hematoxylin and eosin; the bacilli are revealed more clearly with a modified Ziehl–Neelsen stain (Wade–Fite) (*Fig. 17.206*). The bacteria are present in large numbers of cutaneous nerves and are also seen in that site in the borderline forms of leprosy. Bacilli may also be present in the endothelium and media of small and large vessels, in arrector pili muscles and in the eccrine secretory and ductal cells.[23]

Plasma cells are rarely seen in leprosy. They may, however, be found in subpolar LL, which clinically lies between BL and polar LL (*Figs 17.207–17.209*).

In borderline leprosy perineural fibrosis with a lamellar or 'onion skin' pattern may be seen. Borderline leprosy shows increased

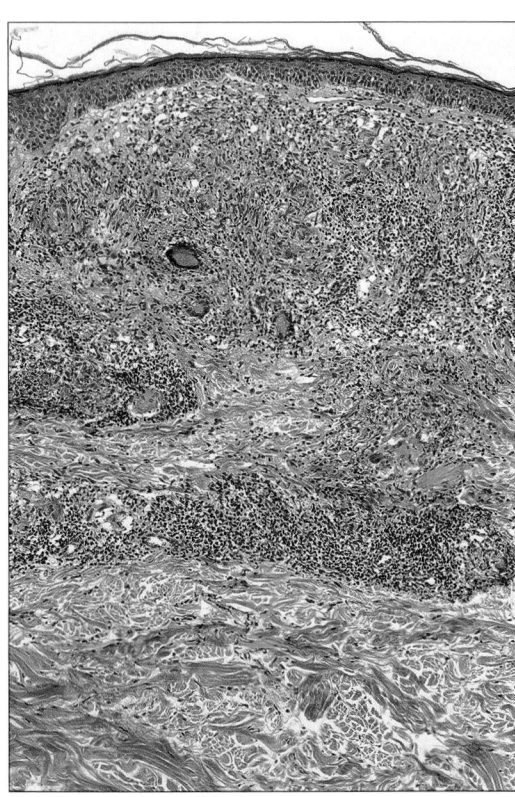

Fig. 17.200
Tuberculoid leprosy: there is extensive infiltration of the dermis and subcutaneous fat by non-caseating granulomata.

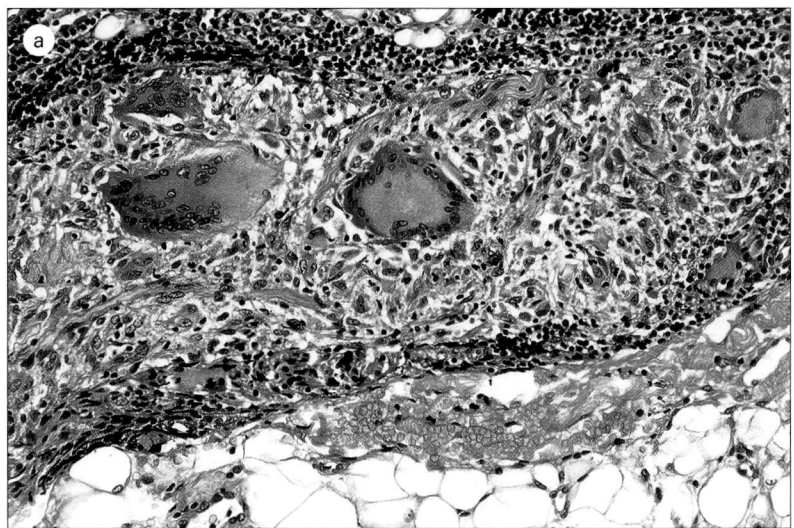

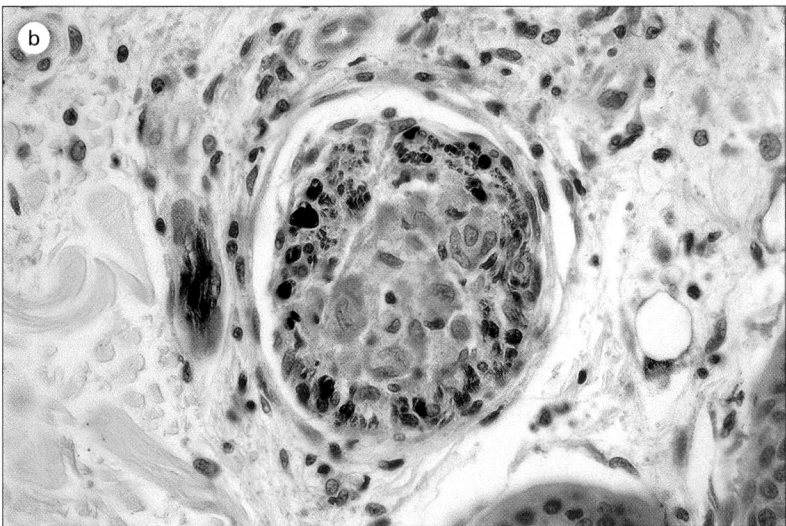

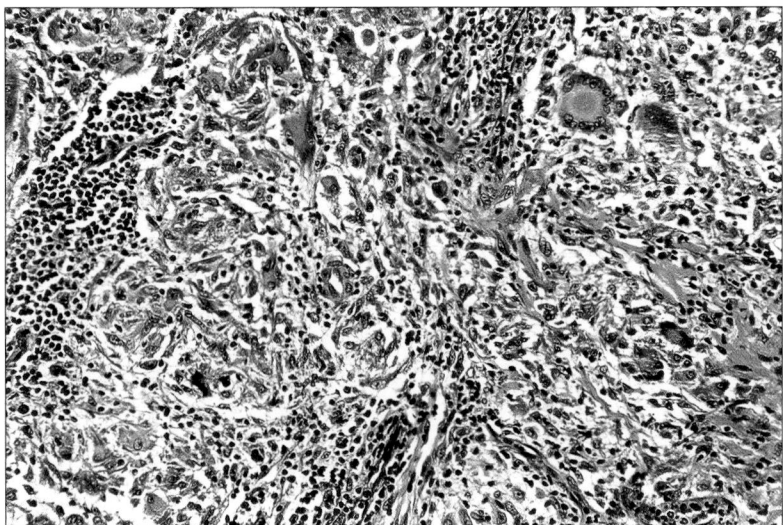

Fig. 17.201
Tuberculoid leprosy: lymphocytes are present in addition to giant cells and granulomata.

Fig. 17.202
Tuberculoid leprosy: (a) this small nerve is almost completely replaced by the granulomatous infiltrate; the residual nerve tissue is arrowed. (b) S-100 protein immunohistochemistry is invaluable in identifying damaged nerves.

circumscription of the granulomatous response, more lymphocytes and more relation to nerves as it approaches the polar tuberculoid form.

Indeterminate leprosy shows only a scanty superficial and deep lymphohistiocytic infiltrate in the dermis, with some tendency to localization around appendages (*Fig. 17.210*). Bacilli are infrequent, but scantily present in nerves (*Fig. 17.211*). Mast cells are increased.[24] S-100 protein immunohistochemistry is a useful means of identifying dermal nerves and foci of nerve damage in skin biopsy specimens.[25]

Histologically, in most instances Lucio's phenomenon is characterized by the features of a leukocytoclastic vasculitis and epidermal

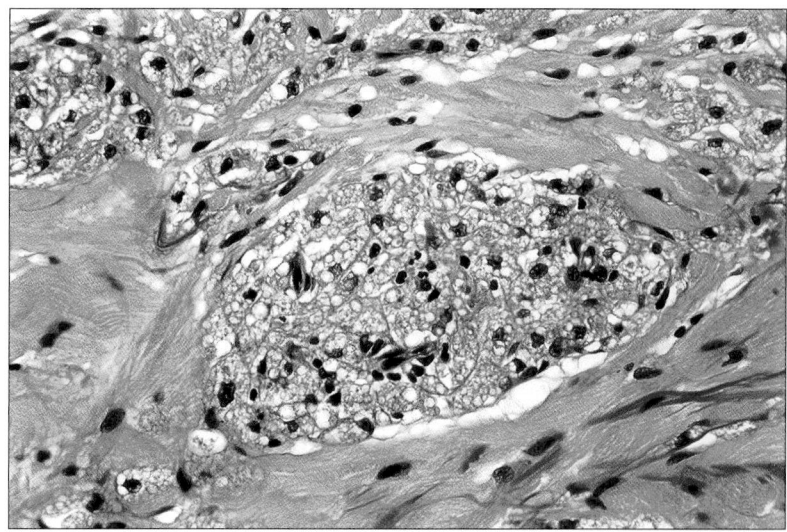

Fig. 17.205
Lepromatous leprosy: the cytoplasm of the histiocytes is bubbly and has a grayish hue.

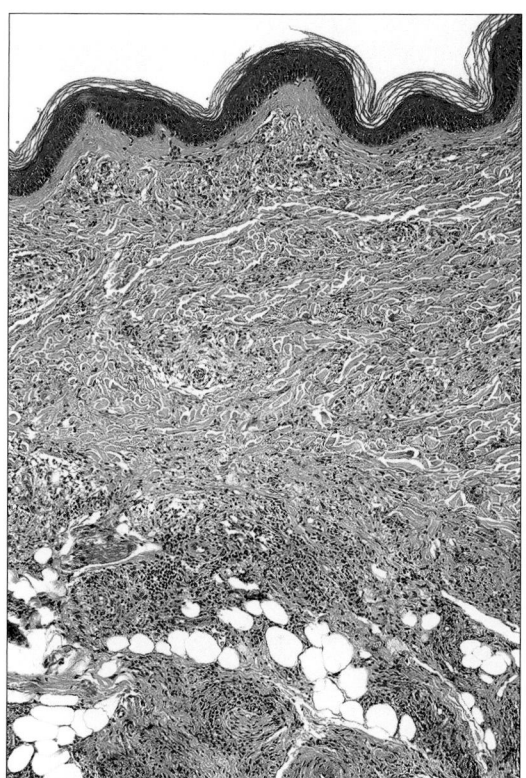

Fig. 17.203
Lepromatous leprosy: there is infiltration of the dermis by large numbers of histiocytes.

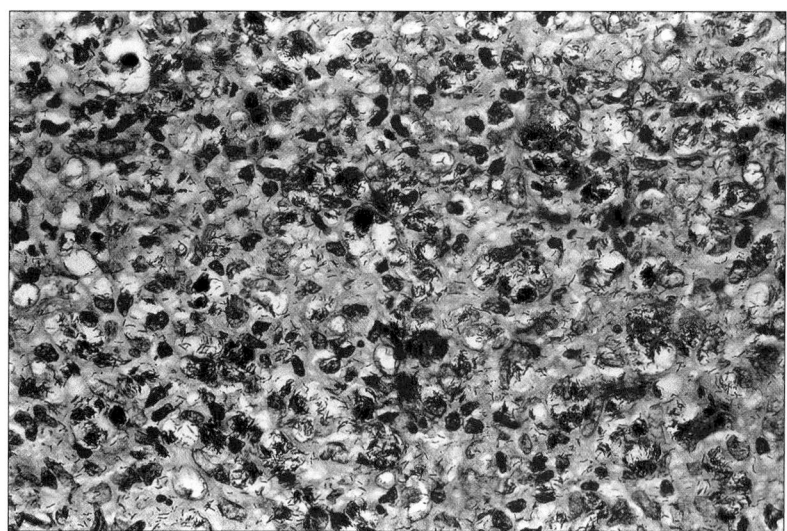

Fig. 17.206
Lepromatous leprosy: large numbers of bacilli are present; note the globi (Wade–Fite).

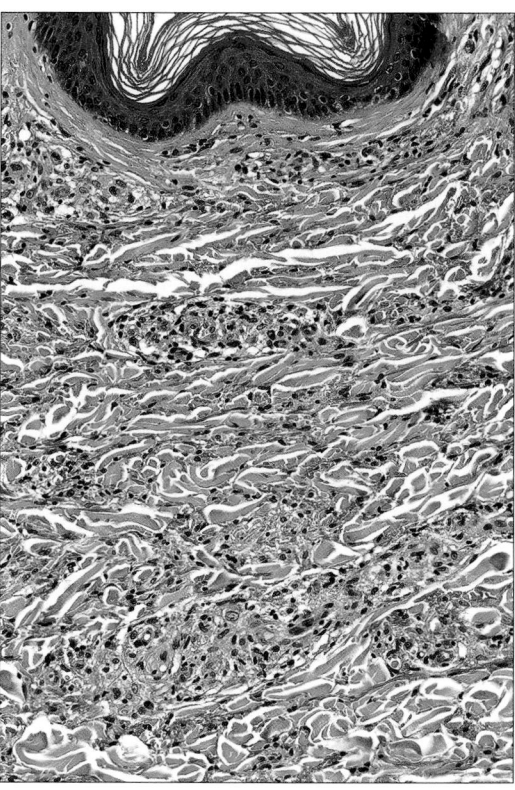

Fig. 17.204
Lepromatous leprosy: a Grenz zone of sparing of the papillary dermis is characteristic.

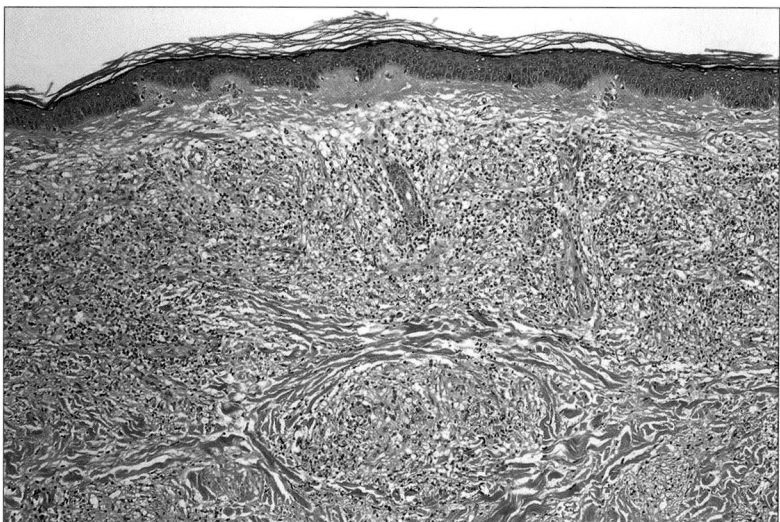

Fig. 17.207
Subpolar lepromatous leprosy: there is a dense dermal infiltrate. A Grenz zone is present.

infarction.[7,11] Severe passive venous congestion of the superficial veins is common.[7] Occasionally, however, some vessels are thrombosed and there is endothelial cell proliferation and swelling.[26] Marked intraendothelial cell bacillary proliferation is characteristic.[7] It has been suggested that this feature is indicative of a very poor immune response facilitating antigen–antibody interaction with consequent acute necrotizing vasculitis. This seems to be rather unlikely (on its own) as similar numbers of leprosy bacilli have been described in the endothelium of 100% of small vessels in untreated polar and subpolar LL.[23]

Histoid leprosy shows a spindle cell proliferative pattern suggestive of fibrous histiocytoma (*Figs 17.212, 17.213*). A storiform pattern may be conspicuous. Careful examination, however, will reveal foci of *Lepra* cells. A Wade–Fite reaction reveals large numbers of bacilli, often arranged in sheaves.

ENL is characterized by an inflammatory cell infiltrate in the dermis and adjacent subcutaneous fat (*Figs 17.214–17.216*). In addition to *Lepra* cells, large numbers of neutrophils are typically present, and there is often an acute vasculitis (*Fig. 17.217*).[27]

References

1. Findlay, G.H. (1987) Leprosy. In: The dermatology of bacterial infections. Oxford: Blackwell, pp 54–71.
2. Sehgal, V.N., Koranne, R.V., Nayyar, M. et al (1980) Application of clinical and histopathological classification of leprosy. *Dermatologica*, **161**, 93–96.
3. Huang, C.L-H. (1980) The transmission of leprosy in man. *Int J Leprosy*, **48**, 309–318.
4. Rea, T.H., Modlin, R.L. (1991) Immunopathology of leprosy skin lesions. *Semin Dermatol*, **10**, 188–193.
5. Rea, T.H., Levan, H.E. (1977) Current concepts in the immunology of leprosy. *Arch Dermatol*, **113**, 345–352.
6. Sehgal, V.N. (1987) Reactions in leprosy. *Int J Dermatol*, **26**, 278–285.
7. Vázquez-Botet, M., Sánchez, J.L. (1987) Erythema nodosum leprosum. *Int J Dermatol*, **26**, 436–437.
8. Saunderson, P., Gebre, S., Byass, P. (2000) Reversal reactions in the skin lesions of AMFES patients: incidence and risk factors. *Lepr Rev*, **71**, 309–317.

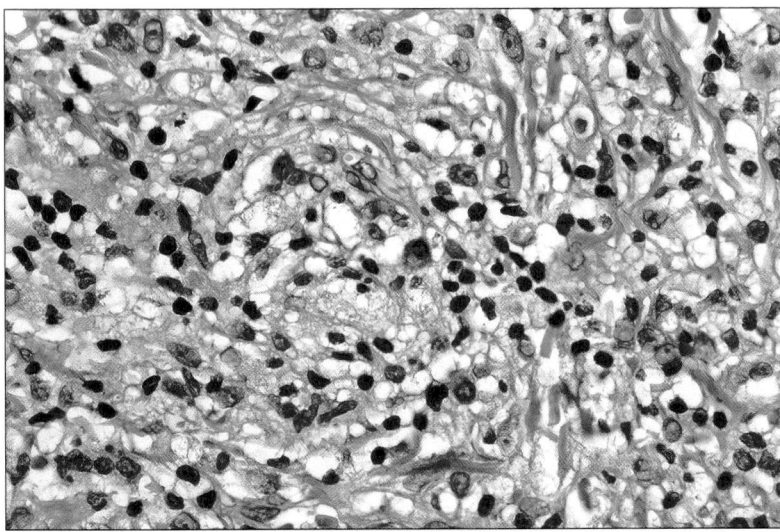

Fig. 17.208
Subpolar lepromatous leprosy: in addition to histiocytes and lymphocytes, there are conspicuous plasma cells.

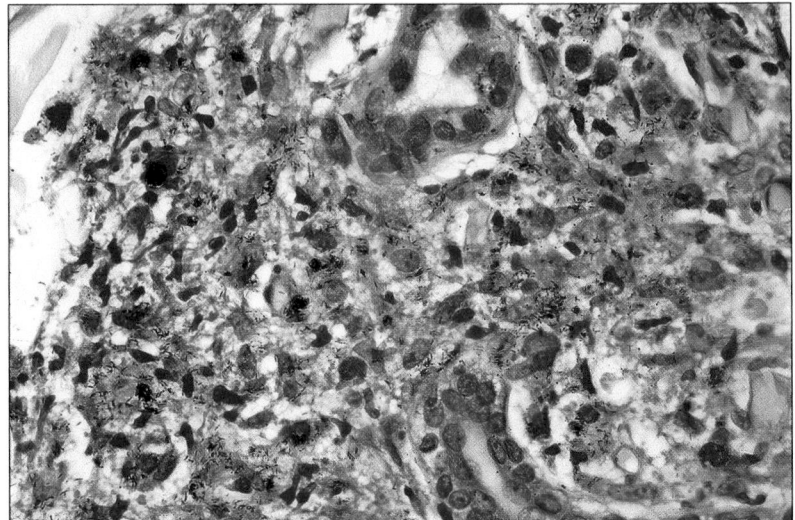

Fig. 17.209
Subpolar lepromatous leprosy: leprosy bacilli are numerous (Wade–Fite).

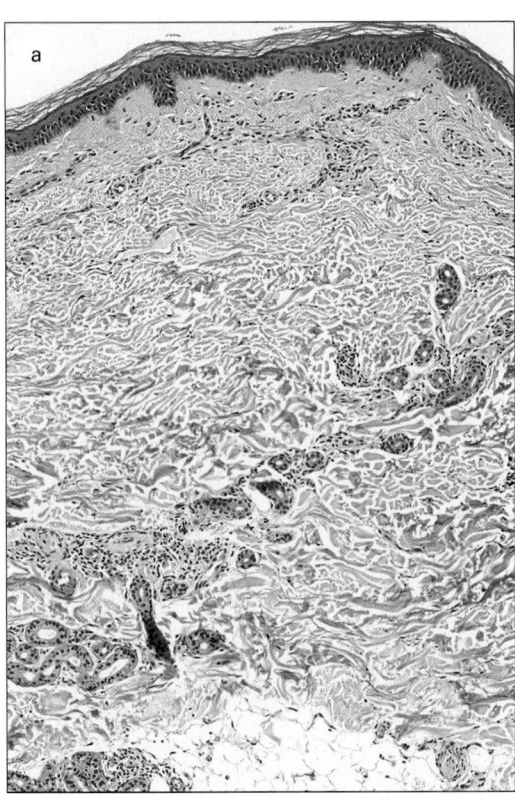

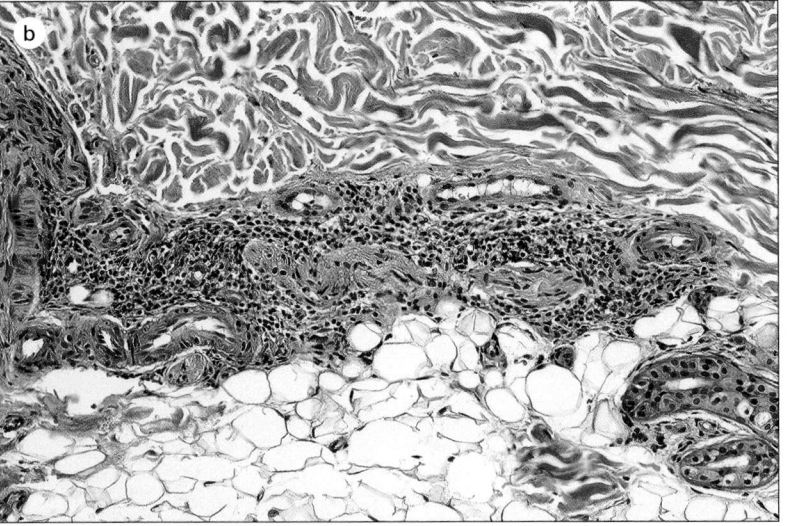

Fig. 17.210
(a, b) Indeterminate leprosy: a perivascular chronic inflammatory cell infiltrate is present in the deep dermis. Diagnosis depends on a high index of suspicion.

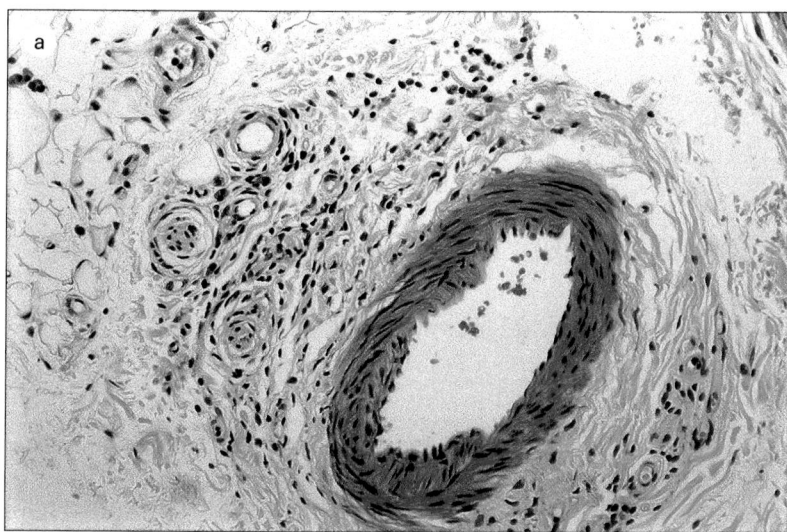

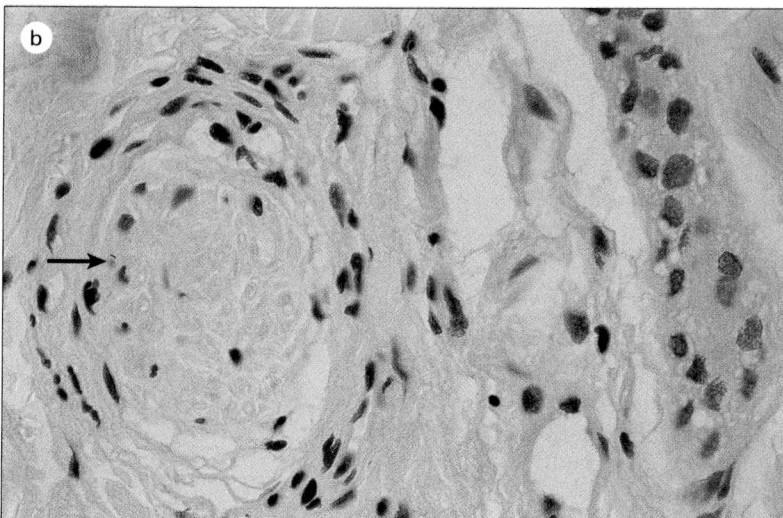

Fig. 17.211
Indeterminate leprosy: **(a)** the inflammation involves the small nerve trunks; **(b)** a Wade–Fite reaction may reveal one or two bacilli (arrowed). By courtesy of S. Lucas, MD, St Thomas' Hospital, London, UK.

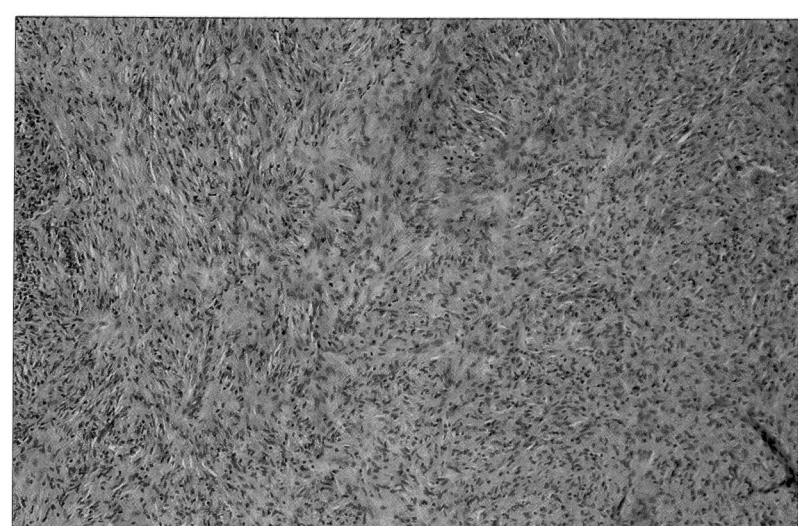

Fig. 17.212
Histoid leprosy: in this field appearances are highly suggestive of a fibrohistiocytic tumor. By courtesy of S. Lucas, MD, St Thomas' Hospital, London, UK.

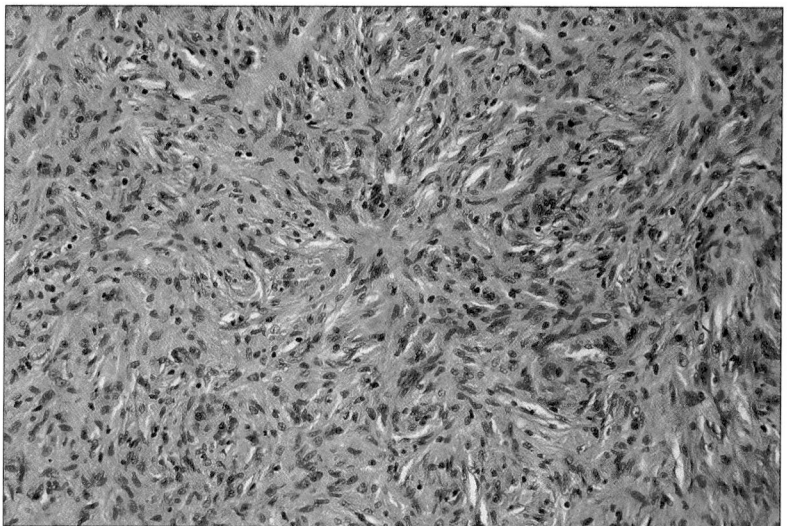

Fig. 17.213
Histoid leprosy: there is a well-developed storiform pattern. By courtesy of S. Lucas, MD, St Thomas' Hospital, London, UK.

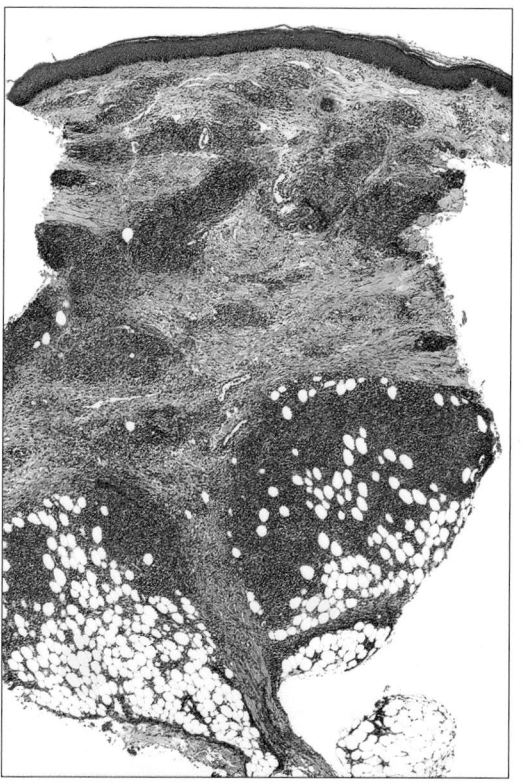

Fig. 17.214
Erythema nodosum leprosum: an intense inflammatory cell infiltrate outlines the dermal vasculature and extends into the subcutaneous fat.

9. Manandhar, R., LeMaster, J.W., Roche, P.W. (1999) Risk factors for erythema nodosum leprosum. *Int J Lepr Other Mycobact Dis*, **67**, 270–278.
10. Sethuraman, G., Jeevan, D., Srinivas, C.R. et al (2002) Bullous erythema nodosum leprosum (bullous type 2 reaction). *Int J Dermatol*, **41**, 362–364.
11. Rea, T.H., Ridley, D.S. (1979) Lucio's phenomenon: a comparative histological study. *Int J Dermatol*, **47**, 161–166.
12. Pursley, T.V., Jacobson, R.R., Apisarnthanarax, P. (1980) Lucio's phenomenon. *Arch Dermatol*, **116**, 201–204.
13. Sehgal, V.N., Srivastava, G. (1985) Histoid leprosy. *Int J Dermatol*, **24**, 286–292.
14. Triscott, J.A., Nappi, O., Ferrara, G. et al (1995) 'Pseudoneoplastic' leprosy. Leprosy revisited. *Am J Dermatopathol*, **17**, 297–302.
15. Brown, S.G. (1985) Indeterminate leprosy. *Int J Dermatol*, **24**, 555–559.
16. Munyao, T.M., Bwayo, J.J., Owili, D.M. et al (1994) Human immunodeficiency virus-1 in leprosy patients attending Kenyatta National Hospital, Nairobi. *East Afr Med J*, **71**, 490–492.
17. Morán, C.A., Nelson, A.M., Tuur, S.M. et al (1995) Leprosy in five human immunodeficiency virus-infected patients. *Mod Pathol*, **8**, 662–664.
18. Sampaio, E.P., Caneshi, J.R., Nery, J.A. et al (1995) Cellular immune response to mycobacterium leprae infection in human immunodeficiency virus-infected individuals. *Infect Immun*, **63**, 1848–1854.
19. Kumaravel, S. (1998) Neoplastic transformation of chronic ulcers in leprosy patients – a retrospective study of 23 consecutive cases. *Indian J Lepr*, **70**, 179–187.
20. Naafs, B., Silva, E., Vilani-Moreno, F. et al (2001) Factors influencing the development of leprosy: an overview. *Int J Lepr Other Mycobact Dis*, **69**, 26–33.
21. Modlin, R.L., Rea, T.H. (1987) Leprosy: new insight into an ancient disease. *J Am Acad Dermatol*, **17**, 1–13.

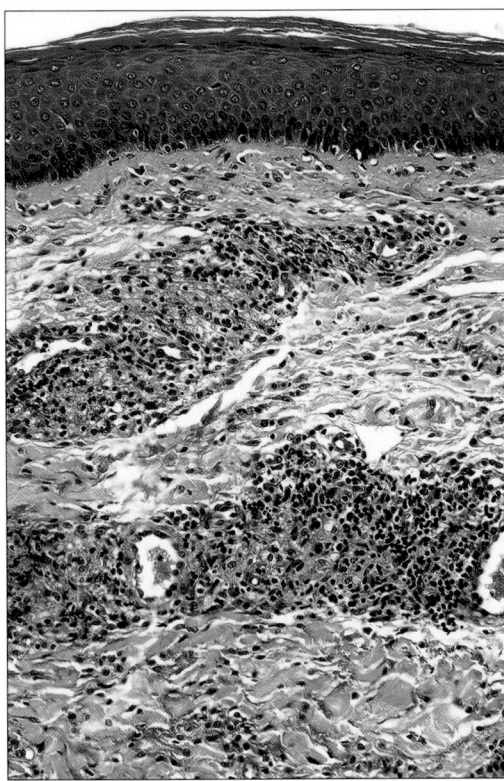

Fig. 17.215
Erythema nodosum leprosum: note the perivascular lymphocyte and histiocyte infiltrate.

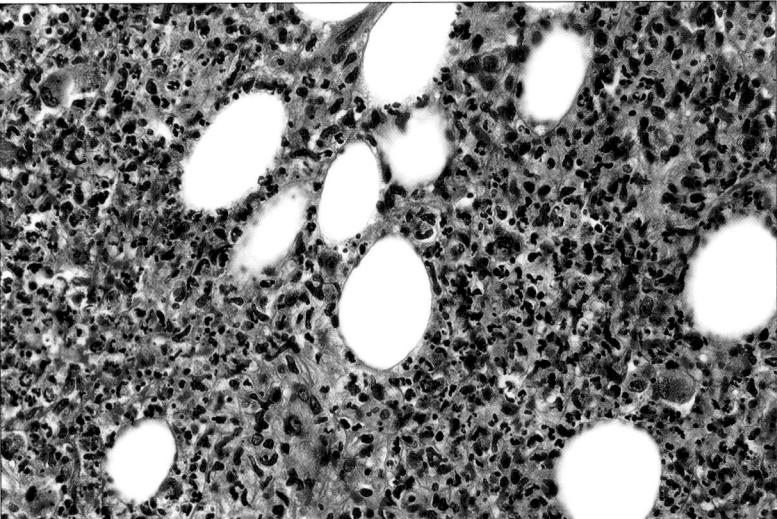

Fig. 17.216
Erythema nodosum leprosum: numerous polymorphs are intermingling with the *Lepra* cells.

22. Elbeialy, A., Strassburger-Lorna, K., Atsumi, T. et al (2000) Antiphospholipid antibodies in leprotic patients: a correlation with disease manifestations. *Clin Exp Rheumatol*, **18**, 492–494.
23. Coruh, G., McDougal, A.C. (1979) Untreated lepromatous leprosy: histopathological findings in cutaneous blood vessels. *Int J Lepr*, **47**, 500–511.
24. Tze-Chun, L., Li-Zung, Y., Gan-Yun, Y. et al (1982) Histology of indeterminate leprosy. *Int J Lepr*, **50**, 172–176.
25. Thomas, M.M., Jacob, M., Chandi, S.M. et al (1999) Role of S-100 staining in differentiating leprosy from other granulomatous diseases of the skin. *Int J Lepr Other Mycobact Dis*, **67**, 1–5.
26. Rea, T.H., Levan, N.E. (1978) Lucio's phenomenon and diffuse non-nodular lepromatous leprosy. *Arch Dermatol*, **114**, 1023–1028.
27. Murphy, G.F., Sánchez, N.P., Flynn, T.C. et al (1986) Erythema nodosum leprosum: nature and extent of the cutaneous microvascular alterations. *J Am Acad Dermatol*, **14**, 59–69.

Rhinoscleroma

Clinical features

Rhinoscleroma is usually seen in adults and is now confined to the tropics, although it was previously common in Eastern Europe.[1,2] It is a severe chronic infection of the upper respiratory tract, especially

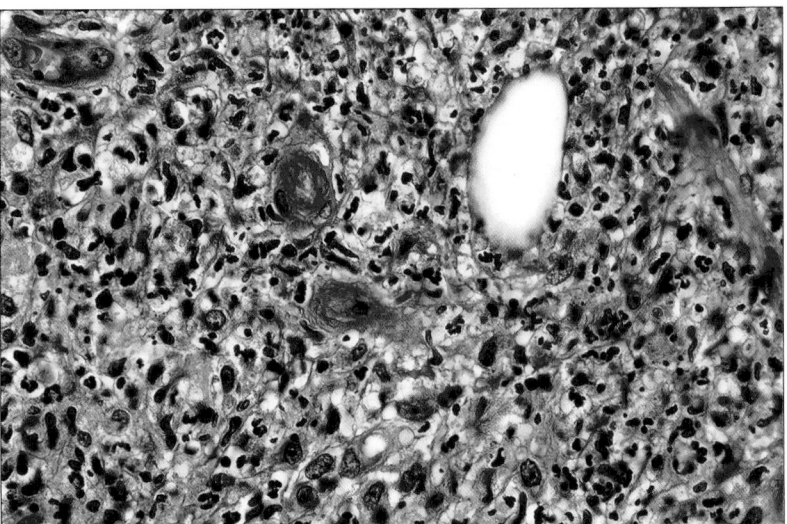

Fig. 17.217
Erythema nodosum leprosum: several small vessels show fibrinoid necrosis. This type II reaction develops on the basis of an immune complex-mediated vasculitis.

the nose. The disease is contracted by direct droplet infection or, more indirectly, by contamination of material that is subsequently inhaled. It has a very long incubation period.

There are three phases to the clinical features of the disease:
- It begins with symptoms suggesting a non-specific rhinitis or coryza with frontal headaches.[2] These symptoms persist for weeks or months, becoming gradually more severe with superimposed epistaxes and difficulty in nasal breathing associated with swollen mucous membranes.
- An infiltrative phase follows during which the nasal septum and base of the nasal fossa become swollen by a reddish waxy induration.[2] This change is painless and the soft palate is anesthetic. Similar involvement of the larynx causes changes in the voice.
- The infiltrative phase merges into a nodular phase during which there is increasing deformity as the nose, upper lips and gums become grossly enlarged and distorted.[2] Involvement of regional lymph nodes is not usual, but has been reported.[3] Nasal obstruction, loss of smell, loss of voice, laryngeal stenosis and increasing difficulty with breathing may follow.[4] Respiratory obstruction may cause death; alternatively the process can persist with some temporary remissions for years. Squamous carcinoma is an occasional late complication.

Contiguous involvement of the soft and hard palate, the upper lip and the maxillary sinuses may occur; the term respiratory scleroma has been proposed for these cases with extranasal extension of the disease.[5]

Pathogenesis and histological features

The causative bacterium *Klebsiella rhinoscleromatis* is a Gram-negative aerobic diplobacillus.[5,6] It is spread during the rhinitis phase of the disease and appears to be confined to close-living groups. There is no animal reservoir.

The incubation period is very long so that presentation is most often in adults. The organism is phagocytosed, but not killed by neutrophils. When the neutrophils rupture the still viable bacteria are phagocytosed by histiocytes, which become greatly distended. These eventually appear vacuolated with an eccentric nucleus (*Fig. 17.218*). Warthin–Starry or Giemsa staining reveals that this vacuole contains bacteria (*Fig. 17.219*). This cell, 10–100 μm in diameter, is termed a Mikulicz cell and, together with Russell bodies (plasma cells grossly distended with proteinaceous product) is characteristic of the disease. As well as these characteristic

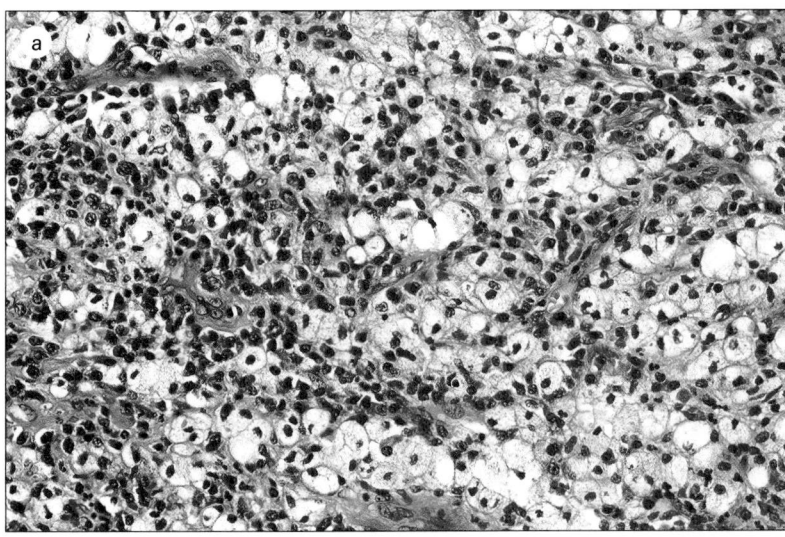

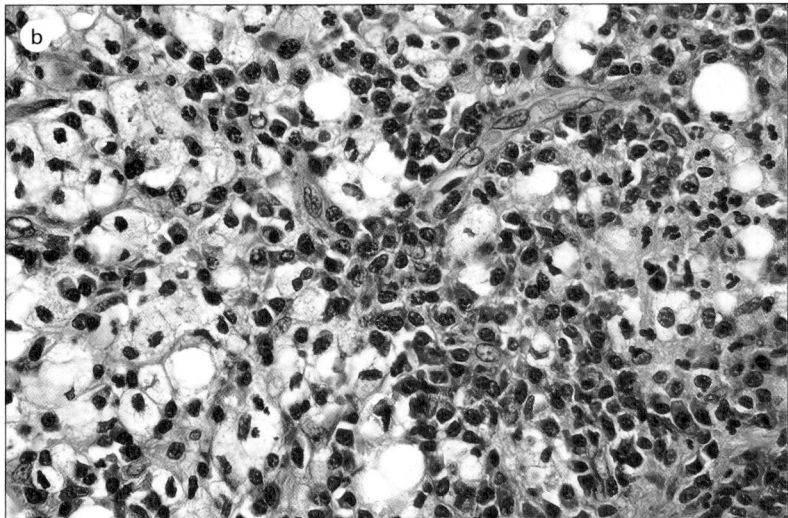

Fig. 17.218
(a, b) Rhinoscleroma: in addition to lymphocytes and numerous plasma cells, foamy macrophages (Mikulicz cells) are present.

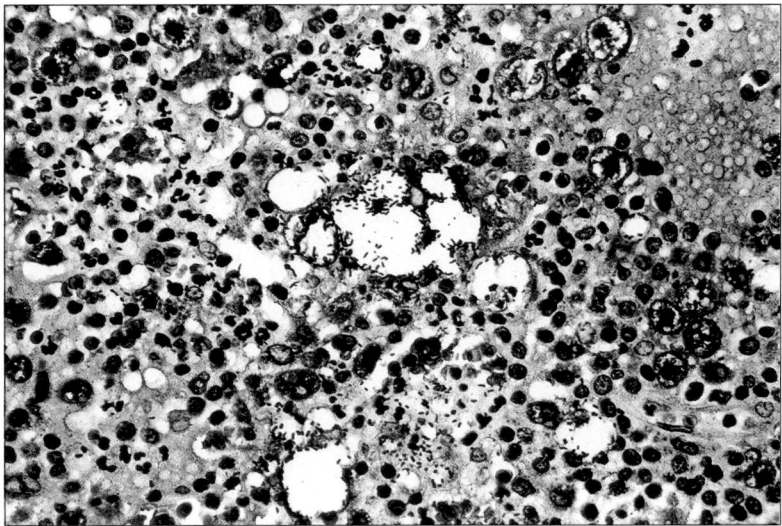

Fig. 17.219
Rhinoscleroma: numerous organisms are revealed by the Warthin–Starry reaction. By courtesy of S. Lucas, MD, Institute of Dermatology, London, UK.

cells there is a dense infiltrate of plasma cells and lymphocytes, which becomes very extensive and eventually causes such gross thickening of the mucosae that the respiratory tract tends to be occluded at several points. The mucosa can be ulcerated or atrophic. Amyloid deposition has been described.[7]

Differential diagnosis

This includes midfacial granulomata, lymphomas, tertiary syphilis, lepromatous leprosy, leishmaniasis and rhinosporidiosis. The histology, as described above, should exclude these clinical alternatives.

References

1. Okoth-Olende, C.A., Bjerregaard, B. (1990) Scleroma in Africa: a review of cases from Kenya. *East Afr Med J*, **67**, 231–236.
2. Tapia, A. (1987) Rhinoscleroma: A naso-oral dermatosis. *Cutis*, **40**, 101–103.
3. Soni, N.K., Chaundri, J.N., Chatterji, P. (1985) Scleromatous lymphadenitis. *Ear Nose Throat J*, **64**, 540–542.
4. Rifai, M. (1989) Laryngotracheal resection for post scleromatous laryngeal stenosis. *J Laryngol Otol*, **103**, 935–958.
5. Sedano, H.O., Carlos, R., Koutlas, I.G. (1996) Respiratory scleroma: a clinicopathologic and ultrastructural study. *Oral Surg Oral Med Oral Pathol Radiol Endod*, **81**, 665–671.
6. Batsakis, J.G., el-Naggar, A.K. (1992) Rhinoscleroma and rhinosporidiosis. *Ann Otol Rhinol Laryngol*, **101**, 879–882.
7. Karchev, T., Kabachiev, P. (1989) Amyloid-like protein in children with rhinoscleroma. *Rhinology*, **27**, 27–36.

Nocardiosis

Clinical features

Nocardia is found in soil and rotting vegetation worldwide and man is only rarely infected.[1–3] Until recently, three main pathogenic species were recognized:

- *Nocardia asteroides*, which is most common in North America
- *Nocardia brasiliensis* in South America
- *Nocardia caviae* in South-East Asia.[2,4]

Other species of *Nocardia* have been associated with infection in humans, including N. *transvalensis*, N. *otididiscaviarum*, N. *nova* and N. *farcinica*.[3,5–11] Infection complicates inhalation or direct inoculation into a wound.[2] Nocardiosis therefore represents a respiratory illness, with or without dissemination (the majority), or a primary cutaneous disease.[1]

N. *asteroides*, N. *caviae* and N. *farcinica* most often affect immunocompromised hosts, causing pulmonary lesions from which systemic dissemination may involve the skin.[2] Predisposing factors include steroid therapy, HIV infection and solid organ transplantation.[3,9–15] Central nervous system involvement is an important cause of morbidity and high mortality.[9,13] Primary cutaneous infection has been reported in an immunocompetent adult following a cat scratch.[16]

N. *brasiliensis* causes primary skin lesions in immunocompetent individuals and can also cause primary pulmonary lesions.[3,17] The cutaneous lesions are varied and usually follow trauma. They include a mycetoma, usually on the limbs, and a sporotrichosis-like pattern (including a cervicofacial variant that occurs in children), i.e. with multiple lesions following the line of lymphatics.[2,18,19] In addition, superficial nodules, ulcers and abscesses, with or without fistulae and pustules, may occur (*Fig. 17.220*).[20,21] Some more trivial infections resemble staphylococcal infections and are usually self-limiting; the deeper infections are progressive and can be destructive without treatment. Dissemination of primary cutaneous nocardiasis is exceptionally uncommon.[22] Infection has been reported after an insect bite.[23] Lymphocutaneous nocardiosis may also be caused by N. *trans-*

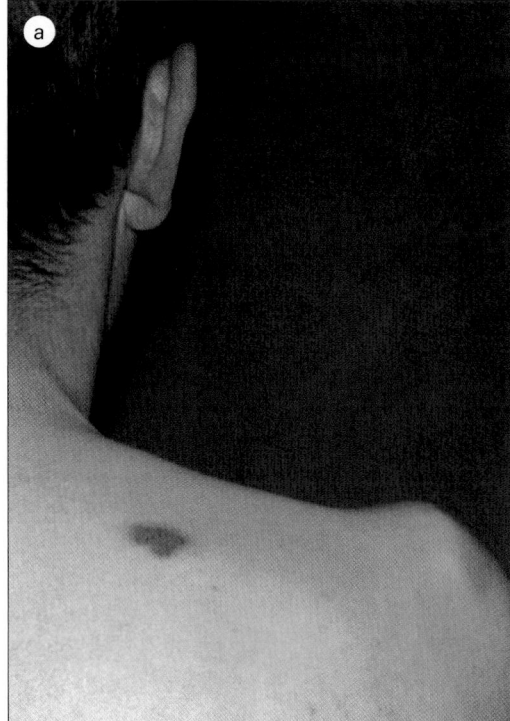

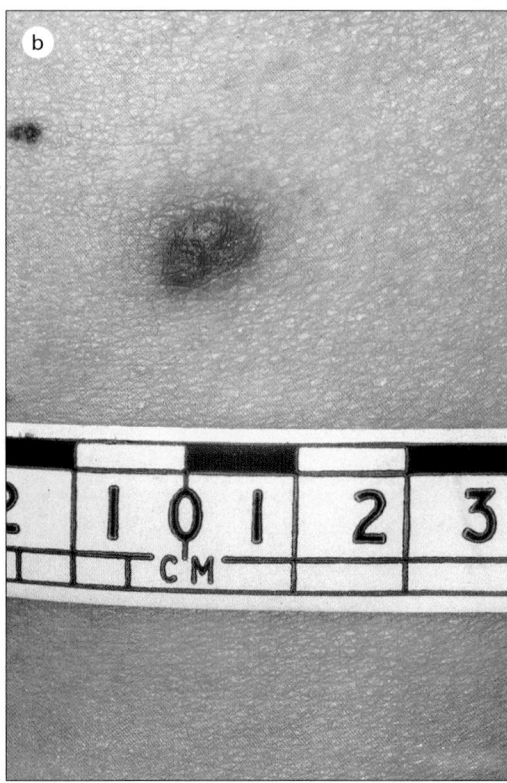

Fig. 17.220
Nocardiosis: (a) this cutaneous nodule developed in an immunocompromised young male; (b) a different lesion is shown in close-up. By courtesy of R.A. Marsden, St George's Hospital, London, UK.

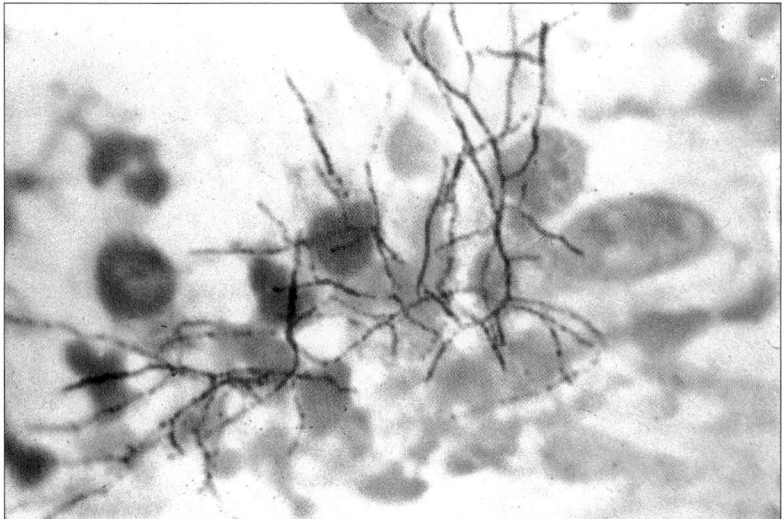

Fig. 17.221
Nocardia: the organisms appear mainly as irregularly staining filaments in this specimen, but a variety of forms, including rods and cocci, is often seen. By courtesy of A.E. Prevost, MD, and H.P. Lambert, MD, St George's Hospital, London, UK.

valensis.[5] Mycetomas due to *N. nova* and *N. otididiscaviarum* have been reported.[6,8]

Pathogenesis and histological features

Nocardia is a Gram-positive, partially acid-fast aerobic beaded rod, which grows with branching filaments in a similar way to *Actinomyces* (Fig. 17.221).[24] Infection by *N. asteroides*, a relatively avirulent organism, is usually by inhalation. *N. brasiliensis* is more virulent and can infect the immunocompetent through inoculation of soil into skin. It is the most commonly identified organism in the sporotrichoid form of nocardiosis.[3,18]

Grains, analogous to the sulfur granules of actinomycosis, can develop in the mycetoma lesions of the immunocompetent. Filamentous growth is a feature of greater virulence or less immunity; methenamine silver is most satisfactory for demonstrating the filaments in tissue sections.

The histological features in the skin are of ulcers, abscesses with pus, necrosis, hemorrhage and fibrosis associated with sinus tracks. The organism is not readily seen with hematoxylin and eosin staining, but can be demonstrated histologically by its weak acid-fastness, distinguishing it from *Actinomyces*. Differential culture may be necessary to distinguish the two, although the presence of sulfur grains is a pointer towards actinomycosis.[25]

References

1. Curry, W.A. (1980) Human nocardiosis. A clinical review with selected case reports. *Arch Intern Med*, **140**, 818–826.
2. Kalb, R.E., Kaplan, M.H., Grossman, M.E. (1985) Cutaneous nocardiosis. Case reports and review. *J Am Acad Dermatol*, **13**, 125–133.
3. Georghiou, P.R., Blacklock, Z.M. (1992) Infection with Nocardia species in Queensland. A review of 102 clinical isolates. *Med J Aust*, **156**, 692–697.
4. Smego, R.A., Gallis, H.A. (1984) The clinical spectrum of Nocardia brasiliensis infection in the United States. *Rev Infect Dis*, **6**, 164–180.
5. Schiff, T.A., Goldman, R., Sanchez, M. et al (1993) Primary lymphocutaneous nocardiosis caused by an unusual species of Nocardia: Nocardia transvalensis. *J Am Acad Dermatol*, **28** (2 Pt 2), 336–340.
6. Saarinen, K.A., Lestringant, G.G., Czechowski, J. et al (2001) Cutaneous nocardiosis of the chest wall and pleura – 10-year consequences of a hand actinomycetoma. *Dermatology*, **202**, 131–133.
7. Mereghetti, L., van der Mee-Marquet, N., Dubost, A.F. et al (1997) Nocardia otididiscaviarum infection of a traumatic skin wound. *Eur J Clin Microbiol Infect Dis*, **16**, 383–384.
8. Shimizu, A., Ishikawa, O., Nagai, Y. et al (2001) Primary cutaneous nocardiosis due to Nocardia nova in a healthy woman. *Br J Dermatol*, **145**, 154–156.
9. Torres, O.H., Domingo, P., Pericas, R. et al (2000) Infection caused by Nocardia farcinica: case report and review. *Eur J Clin Microbiol Infect Dis*, **19**, 205–212.
10. Rinaldi, S., d'Argenio, P., Fiscarelli, E. et al (2000) Fatal disseminated Nocardia farcinica infection in a renal transplant recipient. *Pediatr Nephrol*, **14**, 111–113.
11. Jones, N., Khoosal, M., Louw, M. et al (2000) Nocardial infection as a complication of HIV in South Africa. *J Infect*, **41**, 232–239.
12. Frumkin, A. (1989) Nocardial infections in Israel: a survey. *Isr J Med Sci*, **25**, 324–327.
13. Fontaneda-Lopez, D., Corrales-Rodríguez-de Templeque, M., Fernandez-Ortega, F. et al (1989) Nocardiosis: clinical observations apropos of 9 cases. *Rev Clin Esp*, **185**, 454–458.
14. Chapman, S.W., Wilson, J.P. (1990) Nocardiosis in transplant recipients. *Semin Resp Infect*, **5**, 74–79.
15. Boixeda-de Miguel, P., Espana-Alonso, A., Hermida, J.M. et al (1991) Cutaneous nocardiosis and AIDS. *Rev Clin Esp*, **189**, 395–396.
16. Astudillo, L., Dahan, S., Escourrou, G. et al (2001) Cat scratch responsible for primary cutaneous Nocardia asteroides in an immunocompetent patient. *Br J Dermatol*, **145**, 684–685.
17. Hironaga, M., Mochizuki, T., Watanabe, S. (1990) Acute primary cutaneous nocardiosis. *J Am Acad Dermatol*, **23**, 399–400.
18. Tsuboi, R., Takamori, K., Ogawa, H. et al (1986) Lymphocutaneous nocardiosis caused by Nocardia asteroides. Case report and review of the literature. *Arch Dermatol*, **122**, 1183–1185.
19. Fergie, J.E., Purcell, K. (2001) Nocardiosis in South Texas children. *Pediatr Infect Dis J*, **20**, 711–714.
20. Shapiro, P.E., Grossman, M.E. (1989) Disseminated Nocardia asteroides with pustules. *J Am Acad Dermatol*, **20**, 889–892.

21. Curley, R.K., Hayward, T., Holden, C.A. (1990) Cutaneous abscesses due to systemic nocardiosis – a case report. *Clin Exp Dermatol*, **15**, 459–461.
22. Lakshmi, V., Sundaram, C., Meena, A.K. et al (2002) Primary cutaneous nocardiasis with epidural abscess caused by *Nocardia brasiliensis*: a case report. *Neurol India*, **50**, 90–92.
23. Paredes, B.E., Hunger, R.E., Braathen, L.R. et al (1999) Cutaneous nocardiosis caused by Nocardia brasiliensis after an insect bite. *Dermatology*, **198**, 159–161.
24. Boudoulas, O., Camissa, C. (1985) Nocardia asteroides infection with dissemination to skin and joints. *Arch Dermatol*, **121**, 898–900.
25. Findlay, G.H. (1987) Nocardial infections. In: The dermatology of bacterial infections. Oxford: Blackwell, pp 207–214.

Botryomycosis

Clinical features

Botryomycosis (Gr. *botrys*, bunch of grapes) is also known as bacterial pseudomycosis and is due to a chronic bacterial infection, usually of skin.[1] It has also been described in lung, bone, kidney and liver.[1–4] A case of gingival botryomycosis resembling a pyogenic granuloma has been reported.[5]

In the skin the lesions are chronic suppurative nodules, which may resemble an infected epidermoid cyst, plaques and ulcers. The interconnecting fistulae which develop give it a similarity to acne conglobata and hidradenitis suppurativa, but the sites commonly involved are the hands, feet and head.[1] There may be a history of preceding trauma or the presence of a foreign body. Deeper tissues, including muscle and bone, may become involved. Botryomycosis of the cervicofacial region has also been described in a patient with mandibular chronic osteomyelitis.[2]

The pulmonary involvement has the radiological features of lobar consolidation, sometimes with adjacent osteomyelitis. Involvement of liver, tongue, orbit, bowel and brain has also been described. Cystic fibrosis appears to predispose to some pulmonary cases. Although immunodeficiency has been noted in some cases and the condition has been reported in association with AIDS, most patients who develop botryomycosis have no detectable abnormality of the immune system.[6–9] The cutaneous lesions of botryomycosis in patients with AIDS may, however, present with atypical features; lesions resembling prurigo nodularis and lichen simplex chronicus have been described.[9]

Pathogenesis and histological features

The lesions of botryomycosis include a characteristic granule surrounded by suppuration and the features of a chronic abscess. The granule consists of non-filamentous bacteria in a hyaline matrix, containing IgG and complement C3 (the Splendore–Hoeppli phenomenon), and is a lobulated or 'bunch of grapes-like' structure (*Figs 17.222, 17.223*).[8] The granule is basophilic in the center and eosinophilic at the periphery.[1] It is PAS positive. The bacteria present are not specific to the condition; *S. aureus* is most common, but *Pseudomonas*, *E. coli*, *Proteus* and streptococci may also be found.[1,2,9] Fungi, actinomycetes and *Nocardia* are not causes.

The abscess persists with numerous sinuses and extensive fibrosis, and may extend to involve deep adjacent structures. Rarely, the granules are

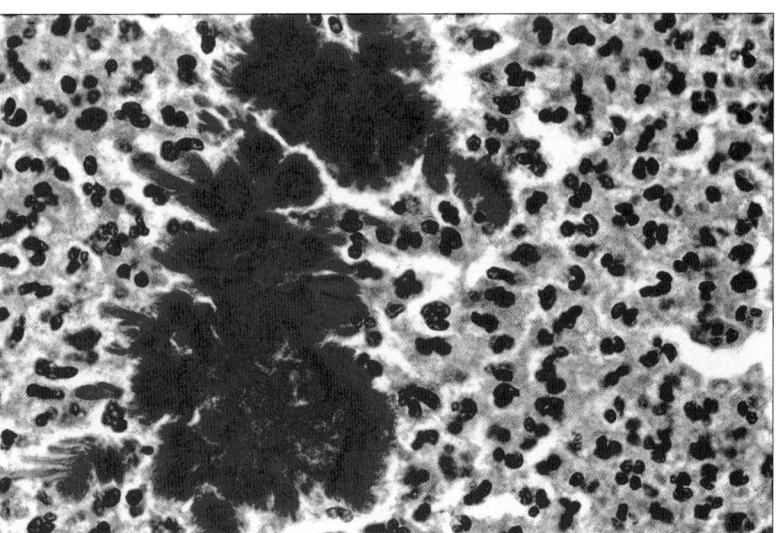

Fig. 17.223
Botryomycosis: note the blue-staining bacteria surrounded by an intensely eosinophilic fibrillary coat (the Splendore–Hoeppli phenomenon). The inflammatory response is characteristically neutrophil mediated. By courtesy of S. Lucas, MD, St Thomas' Hospital, London, UK.

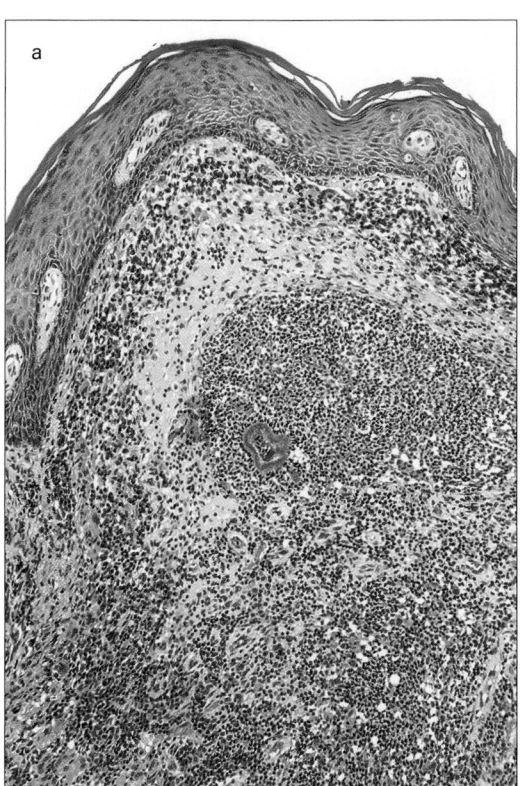

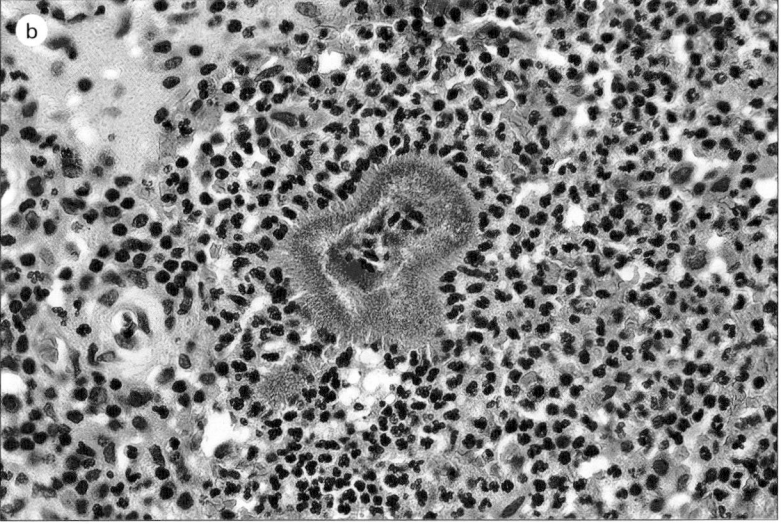

Fig. 17.222
(a, b) Botryomycosis: there is a superficial dermal abscess surrounding a discrete bacterial colony.

eliminated transepithelially.[10] The reasons for the persistence and for granule formation are not fully understood. Although some patients show immunodeficiency, sometimes analogous to the anergy of lepromatous leprosy, this is not so for most cases. The size of the original inoculum appears to be critical – excessive numbers of bacteria produce an overwhelming abscess and cellulitis, too few bacteria are rapidly eliminated by normal inflammatory responses – but an intermediate size of inoculum can produce what may be interpreted as a balance between the bacteria and the inflammatory response, with granule and chronic abscess formation.[1,11] This balance may be attained more easily with less virulent strains.

A foreign body may contribute to the initiation of the lesion, but is not invariable. A local factor may be important, such as some as yet undemonstrated defect in the cutaneous immune mechanisms, diabetes or an underlying dermatosis such as follicular mucinosis.[12] In the pulmonary cases, cystic fibrosis represents that local underlying defect.

References

1. Hacker, P. (1983) Botryomycosis. *Int J Dermatol*, **22**, 455–458.
2. Yencha, M.W., Walker, C.W., Karakla, D.W. et al (2001) Cutaneous botryomycosis of the cervicofacial region. *Head Neck*, **23**, 594–598.
3. Yorukoglu, K., Ozer, E., Sade, M. et al (1998) Renal botryomycosis mimicking renal cell carcinoma. *J Urol*, **159**, 2076.
4. Schlossberg, D., Pandey, M., Reddy, R. (1998) The Splendore–Hoeppli phenomenon in hepatic botryomycosis. *J Clin Pathol*, **51**, 399–400.
5. Rawal, S.Y., Rawal, Y. B. (1998) Intraoral botryomycosis masquerading as a pyogenic granuloma. *Indian J Dental Res*, **9**, 19–22.
6. Brunken, R.C., Lichon-Chao, N., van den Broek, H. (1983) Immunologic abnormalities in botryomycosis. A case report with review of the literature. *J Am Acad Dermatol*, **9**, 428–434.
7. Patterson, J.W., Kitces, E.W., Neafie, R.C. (1987) Cutaneous botryomycosis in a patient with acquired immunodeficiency syndrome. *J Am Acad Dermatol*, **16**, 238–242.
8. Toth, I.R., Kazal, H.L. (1987) Botryomycosis in acquired immuno-deficiency syndrome. *Arch Pathol Lab Med*, **111**, 246–249.
9. Salvemini, J.N., Baldwin, H.E. (1995) Botryomycosis in a patient with acquired immunodeficiency syndrome. *Cutis*, **56**, 158–160.
10. Goette, D.K. (1981) Transepithelial elimination in botryomycosis. *Int J Dermatol*, **20**, 198–200.
11. Findlay, G.H., Vismer, H.F. (1990) Botryomycosis: some African cases. *Int J Dermatol*, **29**, 340–344.
12. Harman, R.R., English, M.P., Halford, M. et al (1980) Botryomycosis: a complication of extensive follicular mucinosis. *Br J Dermatol*, **102**, 215–222.

Malakoplakia

Clinical features

Malakoplakia (soft plaque) most often affects the urinary tract, but it can involve many other organs including the gastrointestinal tract, lymph nodes, genitalia, brain, bone, lungs, retroperitoneum, adrenals and skin.[1–3] The median age at presentation is approximately 53 years, and the disease appears to be twice as common in males as in females.[3] Cutaneous lesions are most common around the genitalia or perineum, but are occasionally seen in other sites.[2,3] Their appearance is variable and includes plaques, ulceration, polyps and sinuses, with surrounding induration, as well as nodules and papules. They may be associated with malakoplakia elsewhere.

Underlying or associated conditions (which are usually linked with immunosuppression) can include carcinoma, rheumatoid arthritis, systemic lupus erythematosus, diabetes mellitus, leukemia, lymphoma and immunosuppression following transplantation.[2,3] However, the condition remains distinctly uncommon in patients with AIDS; this has been ascribed to selective or relative preservation of antimicrobial monocytic function.[4] The skin lesions are non-progressive but are persistent.

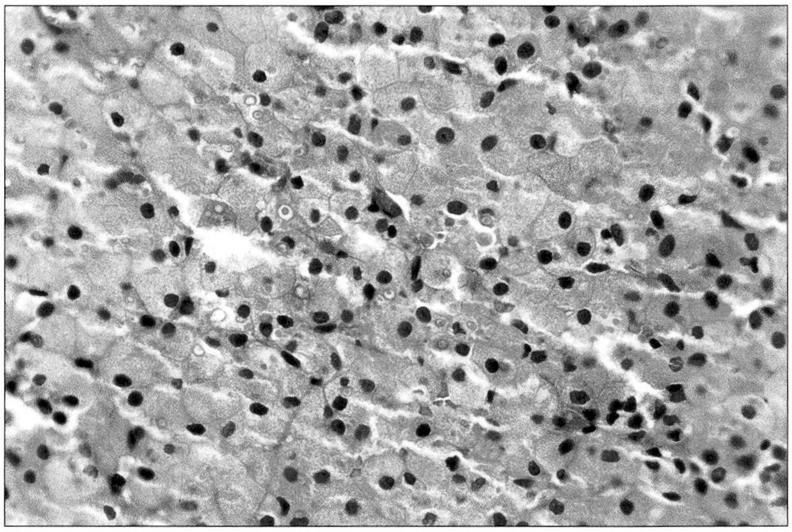

Pathogenesis and histological features

Lesions of malakoplakia are characterized by confluent sheets of histiocytes (von Hansemann cells) with eosinophilic granular cytoplasm and small, usually eccentric nuclei. These cells also contain characteristic cytoplasmic basophilic bodies shown to be calcified with von Kossa staining (*Figs 17.224, 17.225*). These round, sometimes laminated structures are known as Michaelis–Gutmann bodies. Their targetoid pattern is accentuated by staining with periodic acid–Schiff. They may also be positive on staining with Perls' reaction for iron. The Michaelis–Gutmann body is sufficiently distinctive to allow cytological distinction of malakoplakia in a preparation from skin scraping.[5] Immunohistochemistry with an antibody to BCG may highlight the intracytoplasmic bacteria.[6]

The histiocytic infiltrate may be mixed with neutrophils, lymphocytes and plasma cells, with associated granulation tissue. Electron microscopy of malakoplakia shows that the histiocytes contain numerous phago-lysosomes that occasionally contain intact and partly digested bacteria. It has been suggested that phagolysosomes in macrophages accumulate in response to chronic bacterial infection. The infection is not by one specific organism, but the agent is usually *E. coli*.[3] The phagolysosomes

Fig. 17.224
Malakoplakia: the infiltrate consists of histiocytes with eosinophilic granular cytoplasm. Note the pale blue, laminated Michaelis–Gutmann bodies.

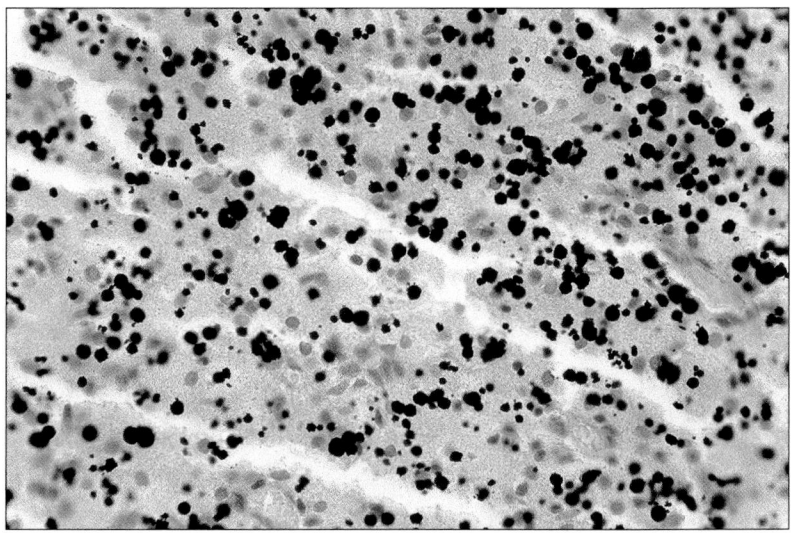

Fig. 17.225
Malakoplakia: use of the von Kossa reaction renders the Michaelis–Gutmann bodies more conspicuous and reveals that they are much more numerous than was apparent in the hematoxylin and eosin stain.

tend to fuse and then calcify; the reason for these changes is not clear, although some cases occur in systemic disease associated with a probable impairment of macrophage function.[1] Other organisms that have been cultured from lesions of malakoplakia include Gram-negative bacilli (*Klebsiella* spp., *Enterobacter* spp., *Proteus* spp., *Pseudomonas* spp.) and Gram-positive cocci, including *Staphylococcus aureus*, *Streptococcus* spp. and enterococci.[3,6]

Differential diagnosis

Malakoplakia should be distinguished from infectious granulomata, histiocytosis and granular cell tumor, and from pseudomalakoplakia,[3,6,7] which refers to an abnormal histiocytic proliferation in a previous surgical site. Although pseudomalakoplakia also comprises sheets of large histiocytes with intracytoplasmic calcific material, this condition is distinguished from true malakoplakia by the lack of concentric lamination of the granules.[6,7]

References

1. McClure, J. (1983) Malakoplakia. *J Pathol*, **140**, 275–330.
2. Palazzo, J.P., Ellison, D.J., García, I.E. et al (1990) Cutaneous malakoplakia simulating relapsing malignant lymphoma. *J Cutan Pathol*, **17**, 171–175.
3. Lowitt, M.H., Kariniemi, A.L., Niemi, K.M. et al (1996) Cutaneous malakoplakia: a report of two cases and review of the literature. *J Am Acad Dermatol*, **34**, 325–332.
4. Barnard, M., Chalvardijian, A. (1998) Cutaneous malakoplakia in a patient with aquired immunodeficiency syndrome (AIDS). *Am J Dermatopathol*, **20**, 185–188.
5. Kumar, P.V., Tabbei, S.Z. (1988) Cutaneous malakoplakia diagnosed by scraping cytology. *Acta Cytol*, **32**, 125–127.
6. Mehregan, D.R., Mehregan, A.H., Mehregan, D.A. (2000) Cutaneous malakoplakia: a report of two cases with the use of anti-BCG for the detection of micro-organisms. *J Am Acad Dermatol*, **43** (2 Pt 2), 351–354.
7. Sina, B., Kauffman, L. (1998) Pseudomalakoplakia (abstract). *J Cutan Pathol*, **25**, 513.

Actinomycosis

Clinical features

Actinomyces israelii is a commensal in the human mouth, along with other organisms including *Actinobacillus actinomycetemcomitans*. *A. israelii* is the usual pathogen but occasionally other species including *A. viscosus*, *A. naeslundii*, *A. odontolyticus*, *A. meyeri*, *A. turicensis* and *A. radingae* are implicated.[1-3] The most common manifestation is cervicofacial actinomycosis, but more grave pulmonary and intestinal infections can occur and, rarely, purely cutaneous lesions.[4] The cervicofacial form is common in farm workers and is associated with poor oral hygiene, usually starting from carious teeth and following dental extractions or oral trauma. The condition is infrequent in children and most common in young men. Respiratory involvement as lung abscess and fistulae may 'point' through the thoracic wall (*Fig. 17.226*). Abdominal lesions include appendiceal and colonic actinomycosis and hepatic involvement and it may complicate the use of intrauterine contraceptive devices, with lesions affecting the internal female genitalia.

The cervicofacial lesion presents as a hard swelling on the lower jaw or occasionally as a plaque-like infiltration of the cheek from the upper jaw (cf. bovine lumpy jaw). These firm thickened areas tend to discharge through sinuses and are associated with scarring and the formation of new nodules (*Fig. 17.227*). Yellow granules measuring up to 2 mm in diameter – the so-called 'sulfur granules' – are occasionally found in the discharging pus. Extensions of some maxillary lesions may reach the orbit and base of the skull. Rarely, direct inoculation of skin may produce a similar chronically discharging abscess with adjacent scarring (*Fig. 17.228*). Alternatively, a mycetoma or chronic discharging abscess mass with multiple sinuses may develop. An uncommon form of the disease is the presence of disseminated cutaneous lesions in the absence of demonstrable extracutaneous infection; this has been reported in a patient with acute leukemia.[5]

Pathogenesis and histological features

The mixture of organisms involved in actinomycosis is not purely accidental but is synergistic. *A. israelii* is a Gram-positive, non-acid-fast, microaerophilic bacterium with filamentous branching hyphae. *A. actinomycetemcomitans* is a Gram-negative coccobacillus, which inhibits growth of fibroblasts and keratinocytes. It is speculated that this, together with its different susceptibility to antibiotics, helps to maintain the actinomycotic lesion.

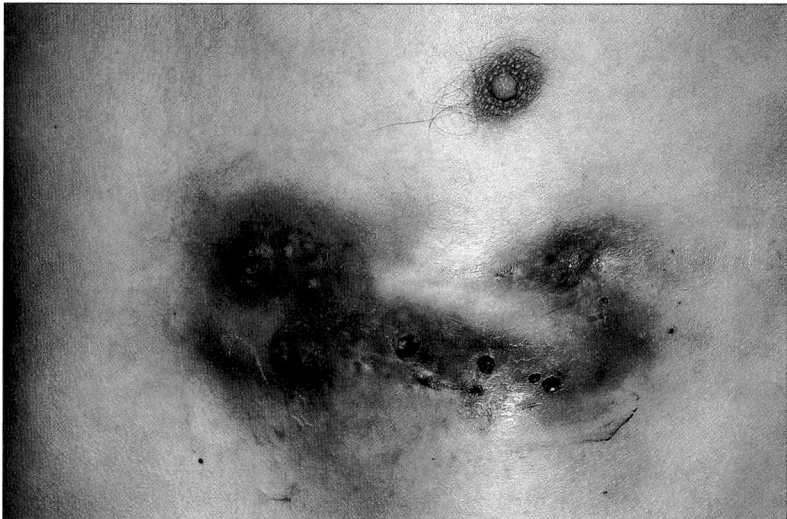

Fig. 17.226
Actinomycosis: extensive intrathoracic disease has resulted in involvement of the anterior chest wall. Numerous sinuses are evident. By courtesy of P. Duhra, MD, Coventry and Warwickshire Hospital, Coventry, UK.

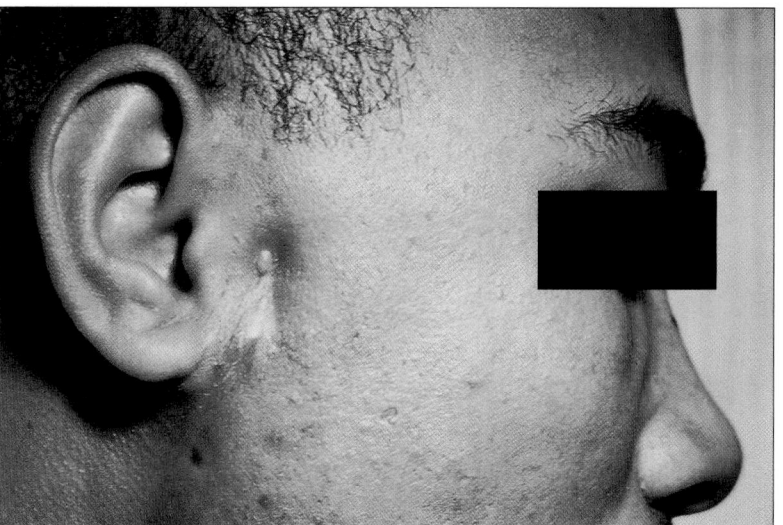

Fig. 17.227
Actinomycosis: infection of the cervicofacial region; note the scarring and dimple at the site of the draining sinus. By courtesy of T.F. Sellers, MD, and H.P. Lambert, MD, St George's Hospital, London, UK.

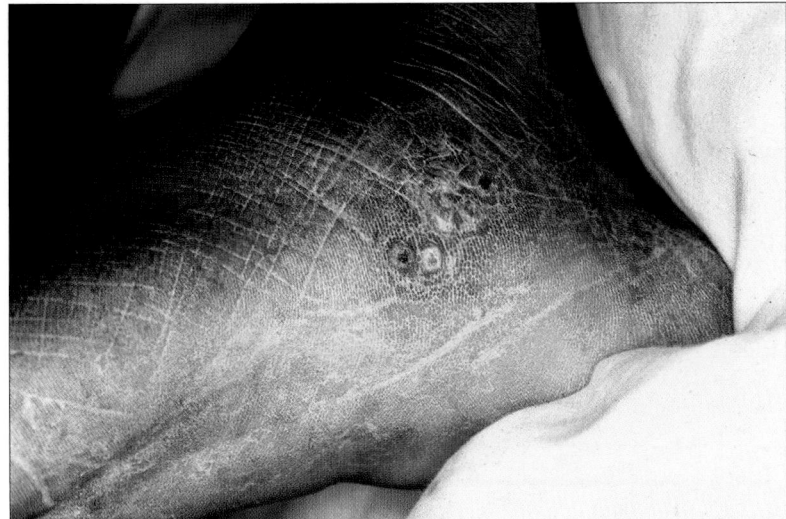

Fig. 17.228
Actinomycosis: multiple sinuses are present about the lateral malleolus.
By courtesy of R. Hay, Institute of Dermatology, London, UK.

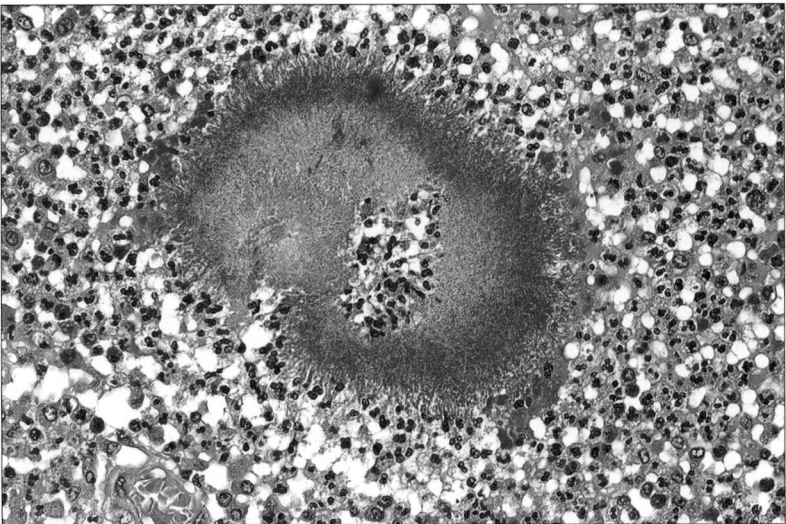

Fig. 17.230
Actinomycosis: high power view.

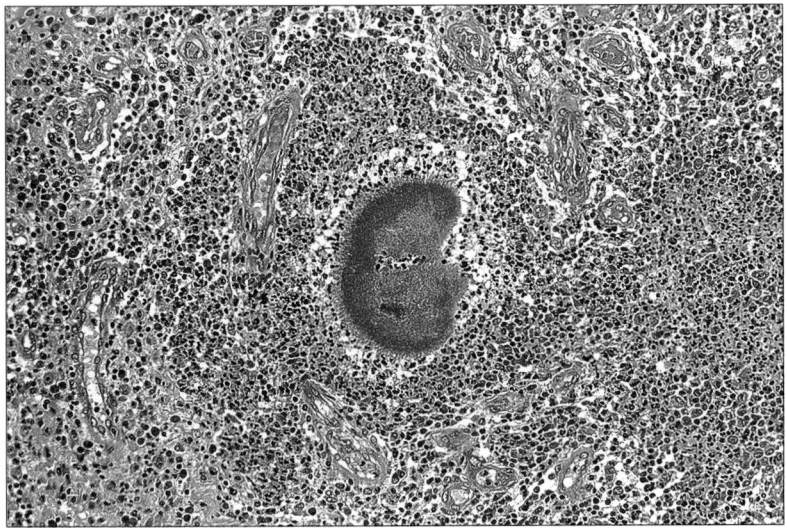

Fig. 17.229
Actinomycosis: a bacterial colony lies in the center of an abscess.

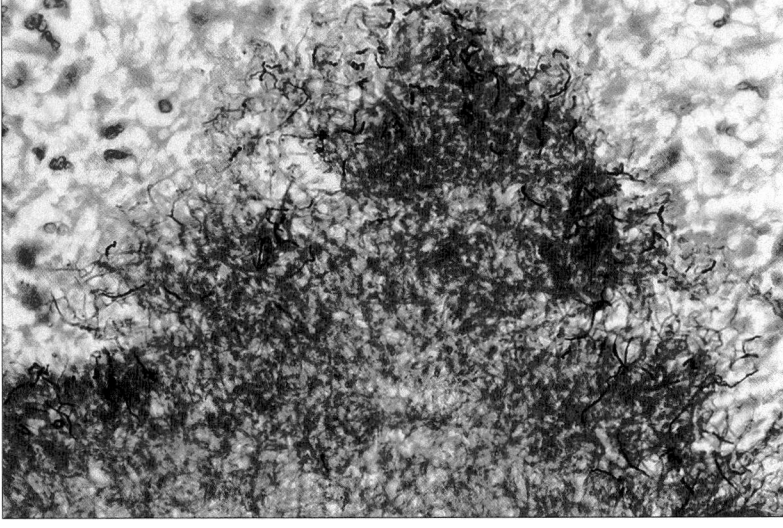

Fig. 17.231
Actinomycosis: Gram-positive bacteria with club-shaped ends are present at the periphery of the granule.

Histologically, the lesions have the features of chronic abscesses and sinuses containing pus and surrounded by fibrosis and a mixed inflammatory infiltrate (*Fig. 17.229*). Locules separated by granulation tissue are present. Sulfur granules of intertwined bacteria are seen, radiating mycelial filaments, often with opaque clubs at their tips (*Figs 17.230, 17.231*).[6]

References

1. Behberhani, M.J., Heeley, J.D., Jordan, H.V. (1983) Comparative histopathology of lesions produced by Actinomyces israelii, A. naeslundii and A. viscosus in mice. *Am J Pathol*, **110**, 267–274.
2. Apotheloz, C., Regamey, C. (1996) Disseminated infection due to Actinomyces meyeri: case report and review. *Clin Infect Dis*, **22**, 621–625.
3. Sabbe, L.J., van der Merwe, D., Schouls, L. et al (1999) Clinical spectrum of infections due to the newly described Actinomyces species A. turicensis, A. radingae, and A. europaeus. *J Clin Microbiol*, **37**, 8–13.
4. Brown, J.R. (1973) Human actinomycosis. A study of 181 subjects. *Hum Pathol*, **4**, 319–330.
5. Takeda, H., Mitsuhashi, Y., Kondo, S. (1998) Cutaneous disseminated actinomycosis in a patient with acute lymphocytic leukemia. *J Dermatol*, **25**, 37–40.
6. Findlay, G.H. (1987) Actinomycosis and actinobacillosis. In: The dermatology of bacterial infections. Oxford: Blackwell, pp 249–253.

Erythrasma

Clinical features

Erythrasma is a bacterial infection caused by *Corynebacterium minutissimum*, a Gram-positive bacillus.[1,2] It characteristically presents as asymptomatic, well-defined scaly red patches on the inguinal and intergluteal skin (*Fig. 17.232*). It has predilection for obese and diabetic patients and it is more common in areas with a humid and hot climate. The clinical diagnosis is easy because of the demonstration of a typical coral-red fluorescence under Wood's light (*Fig. 17.233*).[3] This fluorescence is the result of production of coproporphyrin III by the organism. In exceptional cases fluorescence is not seen.[4] Erythrasma rarely presents as a disciform eruption with an atrophic appearance involving non-intertriginous areas.[5,6] Involvement of the feet (particularly the toewebs) and toenails has also been documented.[7–9] Rarely, lesions on the feet have a vesiculobullous appearance.[10] Nail involvement is characterized by hyperkeratosis and onycholysis. Erythrasma may coexist with a dermatophyte infection.[11] An association with trichomycosis axillaris

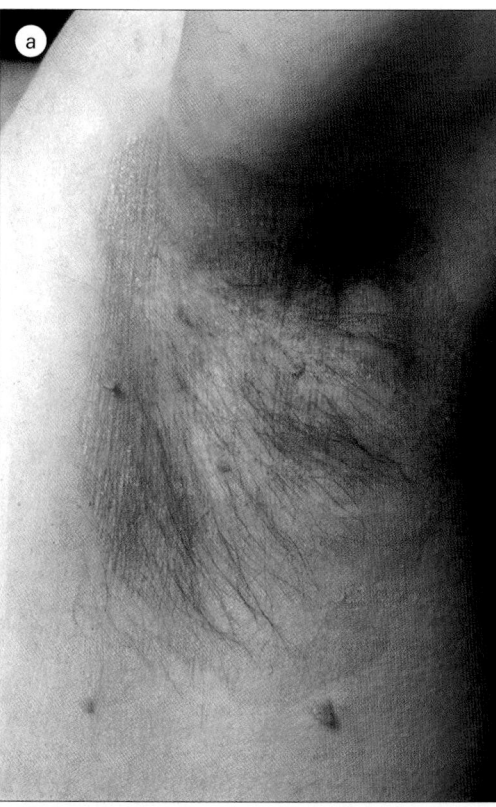

Fig. 17.232
Erythrasma: (a) note the well-demarcated axillary scaly red patch; (b) there is a scaly inguinal patch with associated hyper-pigmentation. By courtesy of the Institute of Dermatology, London, UK.

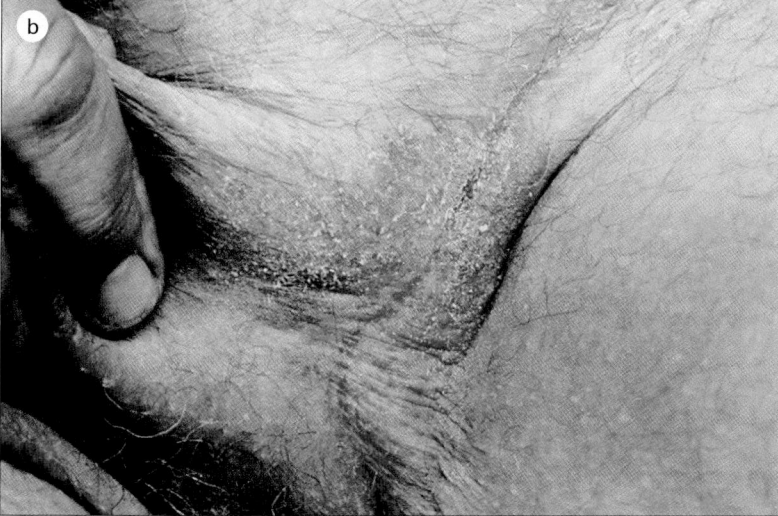

Fig. 17.233
Erythrasma: typical coral-red fluorescence under Wood's light. By courtesy of the Institute of Dermatology, London, UK.

and pitted keratolysis may also occur.[12] A biopsy is only exceptionally performed as the diagnosis is confirmed by the use of Wood's light or scrapings stained by Gram, PAS, Grocott, Giemsa or methylene blue.

Corynebacterium minutissimum has rarely been associated with bacteremia or abscess formation in immunocompetent or immuno-compromised patients.[13–15]

Histological features

A skin biopsy usually appears unremarkable when stained with hematoxylin and eosin except for mild hypergranulosis and occasional superficial perivascular lymphocytes. The special stains mentioned before, particularly Gram, show the presence of bacilli in the stratum corneum.

References

1. Holdiness, M.R. (2003) Erythrasma and common bacterial skin infections. *Am Fam Physician*, **67**, 254.
2. Golledge, C.L., Phillips, G. (1991) Corynebacterium minutissimum infection. *J Infect*, **23**, 73–76.
3. Wigger-Alberti, W., Eisner, P. (1997) Fluorescence with Wood's light. Current applications in dermatologic diagnosis, therapy, follow-up and prevention. *Hautarzt*, **48**, 523–527.
4. Mattox, T.F., Rutgers, J., Yoshimori, R.N. et al (1993) Nonfluorescent erythrasma of the vulva. *Obstet Gynecol*, **81**, 862–864.
5. Tschen, J.A., Ramsdell, W.M. (1983) Disciform erythrasma. *Cutis*, **31**, 541–542.
6. Engber, P.B., Mandel, E.H. (1979) Generalized disciform erythrasma. *Int J Dermatol*, **18**, 633–635.
7. Hodson, S.B., Henslee, T.M., Tachibana, D.K. et al (1988) Interdigital erythrasma. Part I: A review of the literature. *J Am Podiatr Med Assoc*, **78**, 551–558.
8. Henslee, T.M., Tanaka, T.J., Hodson, S.B. et al (1988) Interdigital erythrasma. Part II: An incidence study. *J Am Podiatr Med Assoc*, **78**, 559–562.
9. Negroni, P. (1976) Erythrasma of the nails. *Med Cutan Ibero Lat Am*, **4**, 349–357.
10. Grigoriu, D., Delacretaz, J. (1976) Vesiculo-bullous erythrasma of the feet. *Dermatologica*, **152**, 1–7.
11. Schlappner, O.L., Rosenblum, G.A., Rowden, G. et al (1979) Concomitant erythrasma and dermatophytosis of the groin. *Br J Dermatol*, **100**, 147–151.
12. Shelley, W.B., Shelley, E.D. (1982) Coexistent erythrasma, trichomycosis axillaris, and pitted keratolysis: an overlooked corynebacterium triad. *J Am Acad Dermatol*, **7**, 752–757.
13. Granok, A.B., Benjamin, P., Garrett, L.S. (2002) Corynebacterium minutissimum bacteremia in an immunocompetent host with cellulitis. *Clin Infect Dis*, **35**, e40–42.
14. Rupp, M.E., Stiles, K.G., Tarantolo, S. et al (1998) Central venous catheter-related Corynebacterium minutissimum bacteremia. *Infect Control Hosp Epidemiol*, **19**, 786–789.
15. Bandera, A., Gori, A., Rossi, M.C. et al (2000) A case of costochondral abscess due to Corynebacterium minutissimum in an HIV-infected patient. *J Infect*, **41**, 103–105.

Trichomycosis

Clinical features

Despite the name, trichomycosis is a bacterial infection caused by three different species of corynebacteria.[1,2] The bacteria invade the cuticle of the hair and it has been suggested that they adhere to the hair shaft by producing a cement-like substance.[3] However, this view has been challenged and it is proposed that the material that provides support for the organisms is the apocrine sweat.[4] The disease typically involves the axillary hair and exceptionally may be seen in the pubic hair and scrotum (*Fig. 17.234*).[5–9] The disease is characterized by yellow, red or (more uncommonly) black nodules along the hair shaft. These nodules may be confused with nits. However, the nodules in trichomycosis fluoresce under Wood's light. In black piedra, the nodules are usually black and the disease mainly involves the scalp. Distinction from white piedra may be more difficult as the disease has a wide anatomical distribution and it has been suggested that the latter disease is the result of a synergistic interaction between corynebacteria and *Trichosporon beigelii*, the causative organism of white piedra.[10]

References

1. Freeman, R.G., McBride, M.E., Knox, J.M. (1969) Pathogenesis of trichomycosis axillaris. *Arch Dermatol*, **100**, 90–95.
2. McBride, M.E., Freeman, R.G., Knox, J.M. (1968) The bacteriology of trichomycosis axillaris. *Br J Dermatol*, **80**, 509–513.
3. Shelley, W.B., Miller, M.A. (1984) Electron microscopy, histochemistry, and microbiology of bacterial adhesion in trichomycosis axillaris. *J Am Acad Dermatol*, **10**, 1005–1014.
4. Levit, F. (1988) Trichomycosis axillaris: a different view. *J Am Acad Dermatol*, **18**, 778–779.
5. Levit, F. (1990) Trichomycosis axillaris. *J Am Acad Dermatol*, **22**, 858–859.
6. White, S.W., Smith, J. (1979) Trichomycosis pubis. *Arch Dermatol*, **115**, 444–445.
7. Noble, W.C., Savin, J.A. (1985) Trichomycosis of the scrotal hair. *Arch Dermatol*, **121**, 25.
8. Bargman, H. (1984) Trichomycosis of the scrotal hair. *Arch Dermatol*, **120**, 299.

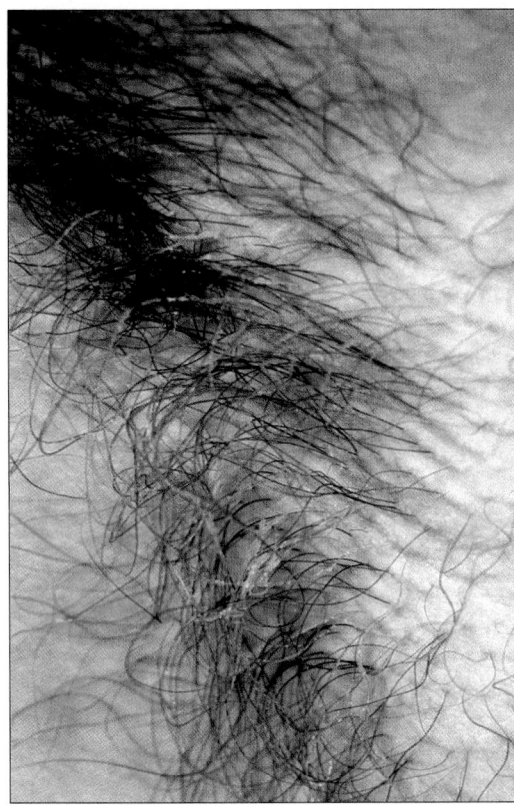

Fig. 17.234
Trichomycosis: this matted appearance of the hair results from the presence of multiple tiny nodules. By courtesy of the Institute of Dermatology, London, UK.

9.   Lestringant, G.G., Qayed, K.I., Fletcher, S. (1991) Is the incidence of trichomycosis of genital hair understimated? *J Am Acad Dermatol*, **24**, 297–298.
10.   Ellner, K.M., McBride, M.E., Kalter, D.C. et al (1990) White piedra: evidence for a synergistic infection. *Br J Dermatol*, **123**, 355–363.

Pitted keratolysis

Clinical features

Pitted keratolysis (keratolysis plantare sulcatum) is an unusual bacterial infection of plantar skin occurring predominantly but not exclusively in humid tropical regions of the world.[1,2] Although the cause of the disease remained elusive for many years, two Gram-positive organisms have been implicated in the pathogenesis of pitted keratolysis: *Dermatophilus congolensis* (accounting for the majority of infections) and *Kytococcus* (*Micrococcus*) *sedentarius*.[1-4] The disease occurs predominantly in young men. Children are rarely affected.[5] Frequent presenting symptoms include hyperhidrosis, malodor or even sliminess of the feet.[2] Soreness and pruritus may also occur. *D. congolensis* causes a variety of dermatidites in domesticated herbivores, and it has been suggested that human infections result from contact with infected animals or contaminated soil.[6]

As indicated by the name, pitted keratolysis is associated with superficial pit-like erosions of the stratum corneum of the plantar skin. These coalesce to form characteristic crateriform defects which are concentrated on the pressure-bearing areas of the foot (*Figs 17.235, 17.236*). The circular crateriform pits measure 0.7–3 mm or more in diameter and appear to be distributed along the plantar furrows.[1,2] Rarely the palms may be involved.[7]

Pathogenesis and histological features

In vitro studies have shown that both *D. congolensis* and *K. sedentarius* produce keratinolytic enzymes, thus accounting for the superficial defects in the stratum corneum.[3,8] The early lesions demonstrate stratum corneum pallor.

Biopsies of the plantar pits show small defects in the upper stratum corneum, the walls being almost vertical in configuration.[1,2] Special stains (Gram, methenamine silver, PAS or Giemsa) are required to visualize the organisms, which comprise both coccoid and filamentous forms.[1,2,4] The coccoid forms tend to be concentrated near the surface of the pit whereas the filamentous forms are present in relation to the deeper portions of the defect.[2,4] The filamentous forms show both branching and septation. The filamentous form of *D. congolensis* is characteristically composed of chains of small coccoid bodies.[1]

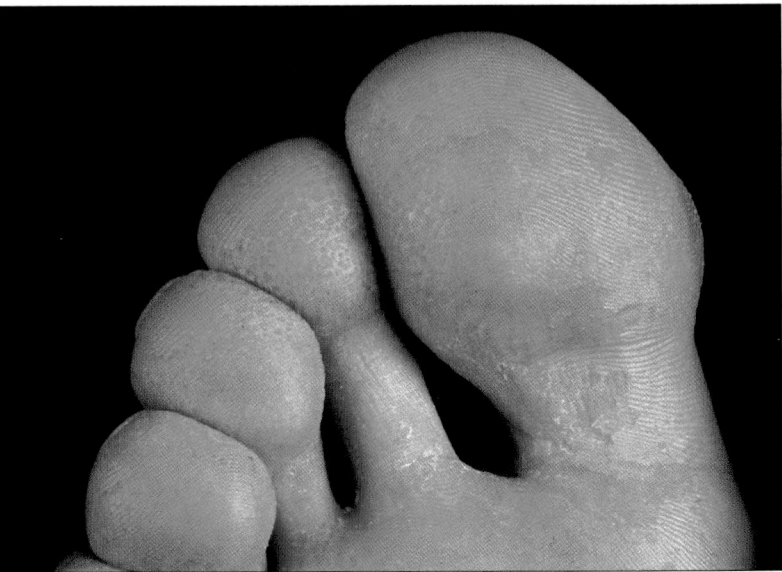

Fig. 17.235
Pitted keratolysis: note the typical scaliness and pit-like areas. By courtesy of the Institute of Dermatology, London, UK.

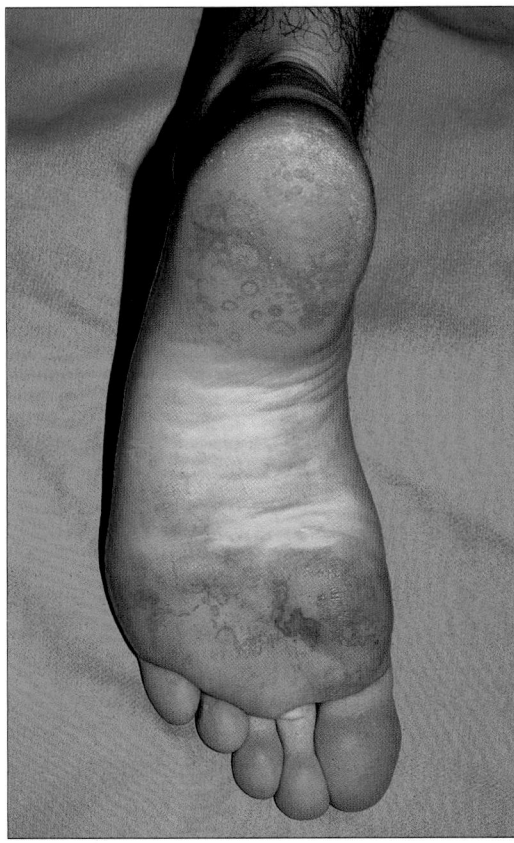

Fig. 17.236
Pitted keratolysis: note the tiny pits on the weight-bearing aspect of the foot. By courtesy of S. Glassman, MD, Division of Dermatology, University of Witwatersrand, Johannesburg, South Africa.

References

1. Lack, E.E., Gallivan, M.V.E. (1997) Pitted keratolysis. In: Connor, D.H., Chandler, F.W., Schwartz, D.A. et al (eds) Pathology of infectious diseases, Vol. I. Stamford: Appleton and Lange, pp 725–728.
2. Takama, H., Tamada, Y., Yano, K. et al (1997) Pitted keratolysis: clinical manifestations in 53 cases. *Br J Dermatol*, **137**, 282–285.
3. Longshaw, C.M., Wright, J.D., Farrell, A.M. et al (2002) Kytococcus sedentarius, the organism associated with pitted keratolysis, produces two keratin-degrading enzymes. *J Appl Microbiol*, **93**, 810–816.
4. Wohlrab, J., Rohrbach, D., Marsch, W.C. (2000) Keratosis sulcata (pitted keratolysis): clinical symptoms with different histological correlates. *Br J Dermatol*, **143**, 1348–1349.
5. Shah, A.S., Kamino, H., Prose, N.S. (1992) Painful, plaque-like, pitted keratolysis occurring in childhood. *Pediatr Dermatol*, **9**, 251–254.
6. Gillum, R.L., Qadri, S.M., Al-Ahdal, M.N. et al (1988) Pitted keratolysis: a manifestation of human dermatophilosis. *Dermatologica*, **177**, 305–308.
7. Lee, H-J., Roh, K-Y., Ha, S-J. et al (1999) Pitted keratolysis of the palm arising after herpes zoster. *Br J Dermatol*, **140**, 974–975.
8. Hanel, H., Kalisch, J., Keil, M. et al (1991) Quantitation of keratinolytic activity from Dermatophilus congolensis. *Med Microbiol Immunol (Berlin)*, **180**, 45–51.

Cutaneous diphtheria

Clinical features

Cutaneous diphtheria is an uncommon condition caused by the Gram-positive bacillus *Corynebacterium diphtheriae*.[1,2] Toxicogenic and non-toxicogenic strains exist. Although cutaneous diphtheria is essentially a tropical condition, increasing tourism to tropical regions and a decline in adult booster vaccination against diphtheria have resulted in numerous cases being reported from developed countries.[2–4] The disease usually results from inoculation of *C. diphtheriae* organisms into pre-existing lesions such as burns, ulcers and eczematous rashes; cutaneous diphtheria may also manifest in apparently normal skin.[1–3] The condition has been reported in intravenous drug users.[5]

The lower legs and feet are sites of predilection but sites such as the face, trunk and even the genitalia may be involved.[1] Initially there is a vesicle or pustule. This later evolves into an ulcer which is often reddish-purple in color, with rolled and undermined borders, and a yellow–gray membrane or dark crust covering its base.[1,3] The ulcers are painful initially but are later hypoanesthetic.[3] Regional lymphadenopathy may occur, and toxicogenic strains may result in systemic complications involving the nervous system or heart.[1]

Histological features

Histological examination of the ulcer reveals a necrotic epidermis and dermis. The dermal base of the ulcer contains necrotic debris, fibrin and an admixture of acute and chronic inflammatory cells.[2] Since the club-shaped and beaded Gram-positive rods are often difficult to visualize in histological material, microbiological examination of swabs from the center of the lesion is required for confirmation of the diagnosis.[1]

Differential diagnosis

Cutaneous infection by *C. ulcerans* may mimic true cutaneous diphtheria both clinically and histologically.[6] The distinction is made by microbiological investigations.

References

1. Adriaans, B. (1992) Cutaneous diphtheria. In: Canizares, O., Harman, R. (eds) Clinical tropical dermatology, 2nd edn. Boston: Blackwell, pp 231–233.
2. Hofler, W. (1991) Cutaneous diphtheria. *Int J Dermatol*, **30**, 845–847.
3. Itin, P.H., Grob, H., Bircher, A.J. et al (1998) Cutaneous diphtheria in returning vacationers – mirror of inappropriate vaccination practice? *Schweiz Rundsch Med Prax*, **87**, 1188–1190.
4. Thomann, U., Gasser, M., Pietrzak, J. et al (1998) Cutaneous diphtheria imported from tropical countries. *Schweiz Med Wochenschr*, **118**, 676–679.
5. Gruner, E., Opravil, M., Altwegg, M. et al (1994) Nontoxicogenic Corynebacterium diphtheriae isolated from intravenous drug users. *Clin Infect Dis*, **18**, 94–96.
6. Wagner, J., Ignatius, R., Voss, S. et al (2002) Infection of the skin caused by Corynebacterium ulcerans and mimicking classical cutaneous diphtheria. *Clin Infect Dis*, **33**, 1598–1600.

Sago palm disease

Clinical features

Sago palm disease is an exceedingly uncommon chronic bacterial infection of the skin which appears to be restricted to a swampy region of Papua New Guinea where there are groves of sago palms.[1–3] The disease was first described in 1973 and is caused by a hitherto unclassifiable Gram-positive bacillus.[1,3] Infection is acquired by traumatic inoculation while handling the palms.[1]

The primary cutaneous lesions manifest only months later and tend to spread contiguously over a prolonged period, ranging from months to years. The limbs, trunk and face are the major sites of predilection.[1–3] The clinical appearances are those of verrucous, hyperkeratotic nodules which are not associated with ulceration or hemorrhage (*Fig. 17.237*).[1] Systemic spread has not been documented thus far.[1] The infection is resistant to treatment.

Histological features

The pathological changes in sago palm disease are centered on the dermis, which is expanded by a relatively circumscribed nodular mass composed of sheets of foamy histiocytes, lymphocytes, plasma cells and fibroblasts.[1,2] The overlying epidermis is hyperkeratotic. The causative bacteria are difficult to identify in routinely stained sections. The Gomori methanamine silver stain reveals large numbers of bacteria which appear to be embedded in amorphous ground substance.[1,2] The bacilli measure approximately 1.8 μm in length and 0.5 μm in width; beading and branching of the organisms may be observed.[1,2] The ultrastructural features are characteristic.[1]

Since the etiological agent has not been cultured successfully, the diagnosis of sago palm disease is based upon the clinicopathological features, supported by electron microscopy.[1]

References

1. Strano, A.J. (1997) Sago palm disease. In: Connor, D.H., Chandler, F.W., Schwartz, D.A. et al (eds) Pathology of infectious diseases, Vol. I. Stamford: Appleton and Lange, pp 801–803.
2. Strano, A.J. (1976) Sago palm disease. In: Bunford, C.H., Connor, D.H. (eds) Pathology of tropical and extraordinary diseases, Vol. 1. Washington: Armed Forces Institute of Pathology, pp 197–198.
3. Wilkey, I.S. (1973) An unusual cutaneous infection from Papua, New Guinea. *Pathology*, **5**, 335.

Tularemia

Clinical features

Tularemia is a zoonotic infection caused by *Francisella tularensis*, a non-motile Gram-negative bacillus.[1,2] The infection is usually acquired via the bite of an arthropod (such as a tick or deerfly) or by handling the carcasses of infected animals, especially rabbits, hares and rodents.[1,2] Tularemia is a disease of the northern hemisphere, with the majority of infections reported from North America, Scandinavia and other parts of Europe.[1–7] The incubation period is approximately 3–6 days.[4]

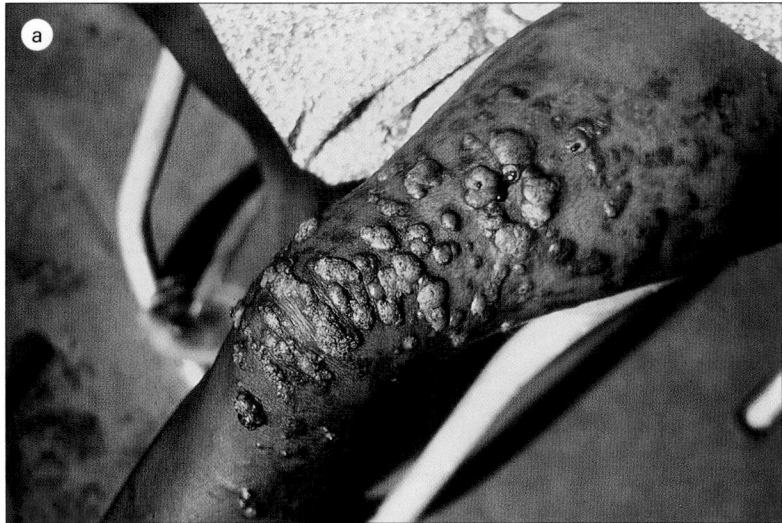
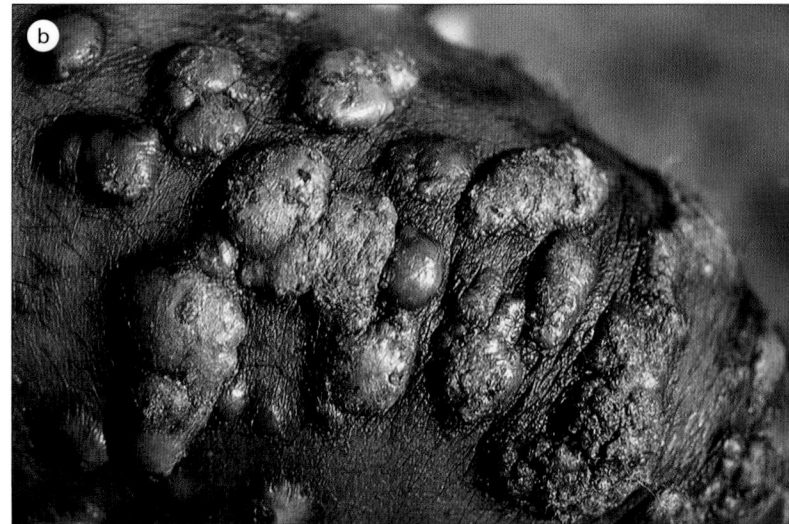

Fig. 17.237
(a, b) Sago palm disease: widely distributed keratotic nodules and plaques are present. By courtesy of E. Wilson Jones, MD, Institute of Dermatology, London, UK.

The most common form of tularemia is the ulceroglandular type, which accounts for up to 80% of infections.[2] Other clinical forms include typhoidal, oculoglandular, oropharyngeal and primary pulmonary tularemia.[2] The ulceroglandular form is characterized by a small, painful erythematous papule at the site of inoculation, usually on an exposed limb. After a few days the papule breaks down to form a punched-out ulcer which may discharge seropurulent material.[1] This is almost invariably associated with lymphangitis and severe, acute painful lymphadenitis of the regional lymph nodes.[1,6] Other potential cutaneous manifestations, which may develop in all of the clinicopathologic forms of tularemia, include macular, papular, vesicular or pustular eruptions, erythema nodosum lesions, and erythema multiforme.[1,5] Associated constitutional symptoms and signs may be pronounced and include fever, chills, headache, weakness, myalgia and coughing.[1,6] Ulceroglandular tularemia generally carries a good prognosis, although death due to septicemia may occur in untreated patients.[2,4] Acute tularemic pneumonia, which is acquired by inhalation of aerosolized organisms, carries a high mortality.[2]

Pathogenesis and histological features

F. tularensis is a highly virulent pathogen; as few as 10 organisms inoculated into the subcutis may initiate infection.[4] The organism is also extremely hazardous to laboratory personnel.

The early papular lesions show non-specific features, including intercellular and intracellular edema of the epidermis, sometimes accompanied by vesiculation.[1] There is also dermal edema, telangiectasia and a mild perivascular infiltrate. Early cutaneous ulcers are characterized by fibrinopurulent exudation and an accompanying infiltrate of lymphocytes and macrophages.[1] Later there is a well-developed zonal pattern of suppurative granulomatous inflammation, a phenomenon that is recapitulated in the affected regional lymph nodes.[2] The central zone contains necrotic material and karyorrhectic debris. An intermediate zone comprising epithelioid histiocytes and giant cells envelops this. An outer mantle containing lymphocytes, histiocytes, plasma cells and extravasated erythrocytes in turn surrounds the latter zone.[1,4]

The diagnosis of tularemia is usually confirmed by serology or culture of the organism.[2] *F. tularensis* is not demonstrable in routinely stained sections, but may be detected in histological material by direct immunofluorescence or PCR.[1,2,7]

References

1. Canizares, O. (1992) Tularemia. In: Canizares, O., Harman, R. (eds) Clinical tropical dermatology, 2nd edn. Boston: Blackwell, pp 259–261.
2. Geyer, S.J., Burkey, A., Chandler, F.W. (1997) Tularemia. In: Connor, D.H., Chandler, F.W., Schwartz, D.A. et al (eds) Pathology of infectious diseases, Vol. I. Stamford: Appleton and Lange, pp 869–873.
3. Young, L.S., Bickness, D.S., Archer, B.G. et al (1969) Tularemia epidemia: Vermont, 1968. Forty-seven cases linked to contact with muskrats. *N Engl J Med*, **280**, 1253–1260.
4. Evans, M.E., Gregory, D.W., Schaffner, W. et al (1985) Tularemia: a 30-year experience with 88 cases. *Medicine (Baltimore)*, **64**, 251–269.
5. Syrjälä, H., Karvonen, J., Salminen, A. (1984) Skin manifestations of tularemia: a study of 88 cases in northern Finland during 16 years (1967–1983). *Acta Derm Venereol*, **64**, 513–516.
6. González Quijada, S., Rubio Díaz, M., Yáñez Ortega, J.L. et al (2002) Tularemia: study of 27 patients. *Med Clin (Barc)*, **119**, 455–457.
7. Johansson, A., Berglund, L., Eriksson, U. et al (2000) Comparative analysis of PCR versus culture for diagnosis of ulceroglandular tularemia. *J Clin Microbiol*, **38**, 22–26.

Rickettsial infections

Clinical features

The rickettsiae are small, obligate intracellular pathogens. Rickettsial infections can be divided into three groups:
- The typhus group, which includes epidemic typhus fever (a louse-borne infection caused by *Rickettsia prowazekii*), the recrudescent form of the latter (Brill–Zinsser disease) and murine (endemic) typhus fever (a tick-borne infection caused by *R. typhi*)
- The spotted fever group, which includes Rocky Mountain spotted fever (a tick-borne infection caused by *R. rickettsii*), other spotted fevers/forms of tick typhus (e.g. boutonneuse fever caused by *R. conorii*, geographically specific strains of *R. conorii* resulting in conditions such as South African tick-bite fever or Indian tick

typhus, Queensland tick typhus caused by *R. australis*, etc.) and rickettsial pox (caused by *R. akari*, and the only infection in this group to be transmitted by a mite)
- Scrub typhus caused by *R. tsutsugamushi* and transmitted by infected chiggers or larval mites of *Leptothrombium* spp.[1]

Coxiella burnetii (the cause of Q fever), *Ehrlichia* spp. (the cause of ehrlichiosis) and *Bartonella* (formerly *Rochalimaea*) spp. (see p. 884) represent a separate group of rickettsia-like organisms and are not discussed here.

Although all of the true rickettsial infections listed above are associated with variable cutaneous manifestations, there is great diversity in the extent of involvement and degree of clinical severity. A detailed discussion of the epidemiological, clinical and pathological characteristics of each entity is beyond the scope of this text; for more information the reader is referred to reference number 1, which provides an outstanding overview of the subject.

Endemic typhus and rickettsial pox are mild infections whereas Rocky Mountain spotted fever is a severe multisystem disease which may involve the central nervous system, kidneys, lungs, heart and liver; gangrene of the extremities and a coagulopathy may also occur.[1,2] Scrub typhus is extremely variable, ranging from an asymptomatic illness to a severe infection with significant mortality if untreated. The earliest symptoms of rickettsial infection are non-specific and include fever, headache, chills and myalgias. Rocky Mountain spotted fever often has additional symptoms of nausea, vomiting and abdominal pain. Lymphadenopathy is encountered in rickettsial pox, tick typhus and scrub typhus.

An eschar characteristically develops at the site of the arthropod bite in the spotted fever group (with the exception of Rocky Mountain spotted fever) and in scrub typhus; eschar formation is not a feature of the typhus fever group.[2] Initially there may be a papule or papulovesicle. After a variable interval a skin rash evolves. In most cases this is macular, eventually becoming maculopapular. Generally, the rash commences on the trunk and spreads to the extremities, frequently involving the palms and soles; the converse is true for Rocky Mountain spotted fever. Vesiculation and scab formation are features of rickettsial pox, and the palms and soles are usually not involved in the latter condition. A petechial or hemorrhagic rash may occur in epidemic typhus fever, Rocky Mountain spotted fever and the other spotted fevers but is not observed in scrub typhus.[1]

Pathogenesis and histological features

A hallmark of the rickettsial infections is the presence of vascular endothelial invasion by the organisms. Following the bite of the vector, the *Rickettsia* organisms adhere to vascular endothelium and later become internalized into the cytoplasm of these cells. Replication occurs, followed by hematogenous dissemination. *R. rickettsii* has the unique capacity to also invade and induce necrosis of vascular smooth muscle cells, thereby accounting for the greater severity of the illness and multiorgan involvement.[1]

Histological examination of the eschar reveals coagulative necrosis of the epidermis and superficial dermis, sometimes accompanied by vasculitic changes and an infiltrate of macrophages at the base. A small vessel lymphocytic vasculitis of variable severity is encountered in biopsies from the maculopapular lesions. This is usually mild in cases of endemic typhus and scrub typhus whereas the dermal vessels in established cases of Rocky Mountain spotted fever show severe involvement, with endothelial hyperplasia and non-occlusive intravascular fibrin-platelet thrombi, focal lymphocytic vasculitis and leukocytoclastic vasculitis.[1,3–5] Dermal erythrocytic extravasation is a feature of the petechial and hemorrhagic lesions. There is epidermal basal layer vacuolar degeneration. Biopsies from the vesicular lesions of rickettsial pox will show an intraepidermal vesicle, sometimes accompanied by a neutrophilic infiltrate at the base or subepidermal edema.[6,7]

In the past the diagnosis was confirmed by the Weil–Felix test. Although this has been superseded by tests employing complement fixation, latex agglutination and immunofluorescence methods, these are generally not capable of yielding a more rapid result. Immunofluorescence studies on frozen skin biopsy material, however, may be a useful and relatively rapid means of confirming the diagnosis of a suspected rickettsial infection. Immunohistochemistry and PCR have also been used with success.[1,2]

References

1. Isaäcson, M., Hale, M.J. (1995) Infections caused by Rickettsiae and rickettsia-like organisms, and bartonellosis. In: Doerr, W., Seifert, G. (eds) Spezielle Pathologische Anatomie, Vol. 8: Tropical pathology, 2nd edn. Berlin: Springer-Verlag, pp 253–289.
2. Walker, D.H., Dumler, J.S. (1997) Rickettsial infections. In: Connor, D.H., Chandler, F.W., Schwartz, D.A. et al (eds) Pathology of infectious diseases, Vol. I. Stamford: Appleton and Lange, pp 789–799.
3. Woodward, T.E., Pedersen, C.E., Oster, C.N. et al (1976) Prompt confirmation of Rocky Mountain spotted fever: identification of Rickettsiae in skin tissues. *J Infect Dis*, 134, 297–301.
4. Bradford, W.D., Hawkins, H.K. (1977) Rocky Mountain spotted fever in childhood. *Am J Dis Child*, 131, 1228–1232.
5. Kao, G.F., Evancho, C.D., Ioffe, O. et al (1997) Cutaneous histopathology of Rocky Mountain spotted fever. *J Cutan Pathol*, 24, 604–610.
6. Dolgopol, V.B. (1948) Histologic changes in rickettsial pox. *Am J Pathol*, 24, 119–133.
7. Brettman, L.R., Lewin, S., Holzman, R.S. et al (1981) Rickettsial pox: report of an outbreak and a contemporary review. *Medicine*, 60, 363–372.

Protozoal infections

Leishmaniasis

Clinical features

Leishmania is an organism related to the trypanosomes.[1–3] The life cycle contains a flagellate phase (promastigote) which occurs in the intestine of its vector, a female *Phlebotomus* sand fly, and a phase in which the flagellum is retracted (amastigote). The latter is the form seen in the human host. Various mammals, including gerbils, rodents, dogs, jackals and foxes, may act as reservoirs of infection.

An estimated 12 million people are affected worldwide, with as many as 2 million new cases occurring annually.[4] Visceral leishmaniasis and to a lesser extent cutaneous leishmaniasis are increasingly recognized as opportunistic diseases in immunocompromised patients, especially those infected with HIV.[4,5]

The various species of *Leishmania* are distinguished on the grounds of biochemical and antigenic differences. Although leishmaniasis tends to be seen in Asia, Africa, the Americas and the Mediterranean countries it is being seen more often in non-endemic countries, particularly among refugees and returning holiday-makers.[6,7] There are eight main types

of cutaneous presentation, with many local geographic and species variations.

In endemic regions a significant number of people appear to have asymptomatic (subclinical) infection, so-called cryptic leishmaniasis.[6]

Cutaneous leishmaniasis

Cutaneous leishmaniasis has many local names, including oriental sore, Baghdad boil, Chiclero's ulcer and Aleppo boil. It is caused by *Leishmania tropica*, *Leishmania major* and *Leishmania aethiopica* and affects men, women and children. Mediterranean cutaneous leishmaniasis is caused predominantly by *Leishmania donovani infantum*.[6]

Lesions occur on any site accessible to biting by the sandfly vector, most commonly the hands, arms and face (*Figs 17.238, 17.239*). They present as an erythematous papule that enlarges over the course of a few weeks into an ulcerated and crusted nodule. Occasionally multiple lesions are seen. Lesions show a tendency to orientation along the skin creases and grossly the ulcers have been compared to a volcano in surface appearance and configuration.[8] Variants may be hypoesthetic, psoriasiform, eczematous, varicelliform, paronychial, chancriform, zosteriform, annular, verrucous or keloidal or present as macrocheilia.[6] Regional lymphadenopathy may be a feature.[9] In the Eastern hemisphere these lesions may be 'wet' or 'dry':

- The wet type has a short incubation period (2 weeks) and occurs in rural areas. It is caused by *L. major* and develops like a suppurative folliculitis which ulcerates, the surrounding edematous, indurated erythema extending gradually to reach a maximum of 6 cm. Small secondary nodules may be seen around this. Slow resolution with cribriform scarring occurs over 3–12 months.
- The dry form is caused by *L. tropica*, has a longer incubation period (2 months) and is mostly seen in urban areas.[10] The initial lesion is a brown nodule and this becomes a plaque up to 2 cm across. It may

ulcerate centrally with a firm crust (*Fig. 17.240*). Resolution occurs with scarring over 12 months or longer.

The American forms are caused predominantly by *L. mexicana* and *L. braziliensis*. Other species implicated recently include *L. amazonensis* and *L. guyanensis*.[11,12] The lesions of *L. mexicana* are usually like those of cutaneous leishmaniasis in the Eastern hemisphere, but some subvariants can cause destructive ulceration of the ear. Most infections with *L. braziliensis* are local and heal without much damage.

Chronic cutaneous leishmaniasis represents persistence (or spread) of an acute lesion for more than 1 year. Lesions are particularly seen on the face as raised erythematous plaques which may resemble erysipelas (*Fig. 17.241*).[6] The erysipeloid lesions are erythematous and infiltrative and are said to occur more frequently in women above the age of 50 years.[13]

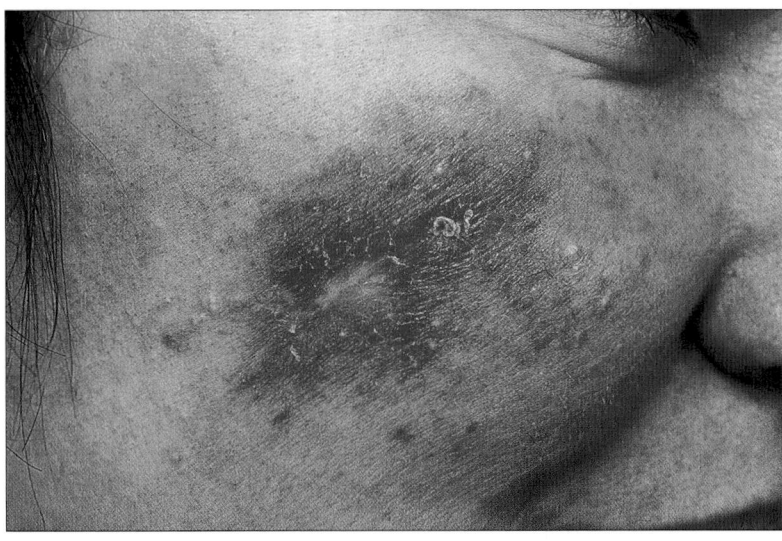

Fig. 17.238
Cutaneous leishmaniasis: there is an extensive erythematous plaque with scaling and central scarring. By courtesy of the Institute of Dermatology, London, UK.

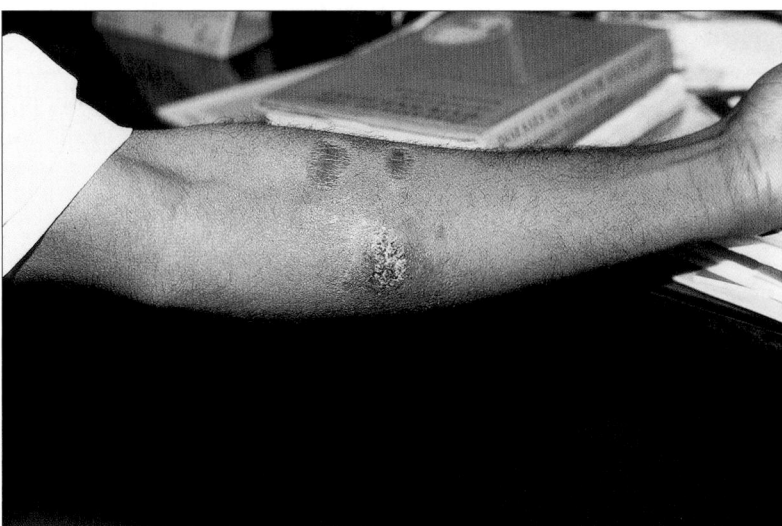

Fig. 17.240
Leishmania tropica: healing lesions with crusting and scarring. By courtesy of S. Lucas, MD, St Thomas' Hospital, London, UK.

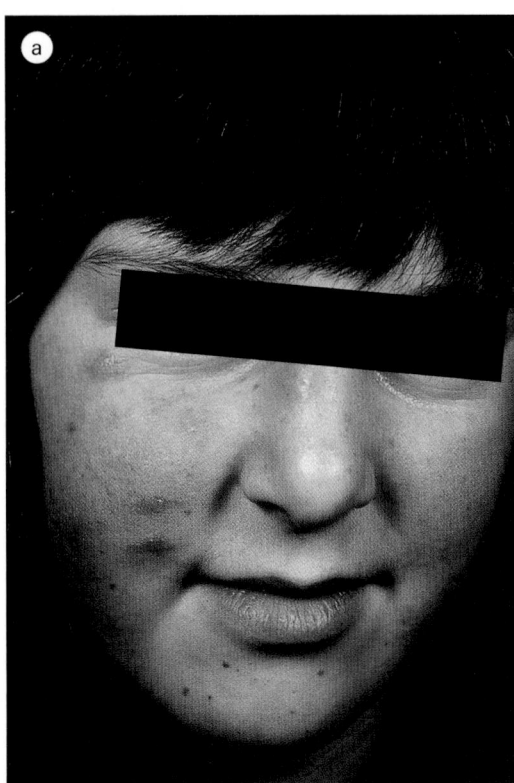

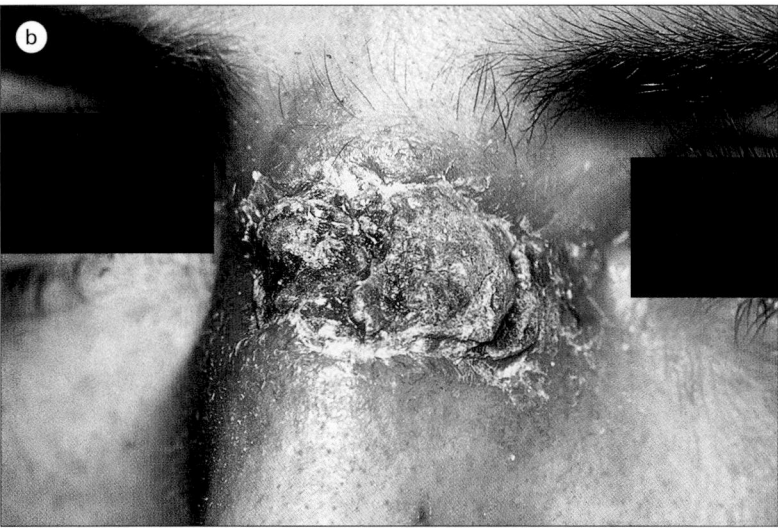

Fig. 17.239
Cutaneous leishmaniasis: (**a**) the face is commonly affected and lesions may be multiple; (**b**) healing lesion with tough, adherent crust. Scarring is usually present. By courtesy of S. Lucas, MD, St Thomas' Hospital, London, UK.

The acute lesions may be followed by a relapsing chronic or lupoid stage (leishmaniasis recidivans or leishmaniasis recidiva cutis) in which brownish papules develop close to the scar of the earlier stages. This occurs in 3–10% of patients.[14] These papules extend to resemble lupus vulgaris; they may develop hypertrophic scars or become verrucous. They are extremely slow to resolve, even under treatment, and may persist for many years. It is thought that a change in local immunity results in reactivation of intracytoplasmic organisms.[14] The leishmanin or Montenegro skin test for cellular immunity to *Leishmania* is strongly positive in nearly all cases. It has been suggested that that leishmaniasis recidivans represents a hypergic form of the disease, but this has been disputed by others.[15] Although this presentation is typically encountered in the Eastern hemisphere leishmaniasis, a small number of cases of leishmaniasis recidiva cutis complicating American leishmaniasis have been reported.[15,16]

Skin infections with *L. braziliensis* are liable to recur as mucosal lesions, known as espundia (in which there is much tissue destruction), sometimes years later. The mucosal lesions occur most often in the nasal septum and mouth and rarely around the eyes, genitalia and anus (*Fig. 17.242*). Patients may also develop 'tapir nose' in which there is considerable damage to the nasal cartilage resulting in a free-hanging nose.[6] The mucosal lesions start as superficial erosions, but become deeply ulcerative and destructive. The Montenegro skin test is almost always positive.

Diffuse cutaneous leishmaniasis, also known as pseudolepromatous leishmaniasis, is caused by variants of *L. mexicana* and *L. aethiopica*. The former occurs in Bolivia, Venezuela, Mexico and Brazil, while the latter is seen predominantly in Ethiopia. It develops as a consequence of an impaired cellular immune response.[14] A study from Egypt showed a significant association between histocompatibility antigens HLA-A11, B5 and B7 and the occurrence of this disease.[17] It begins as a nodule, which grows and becomes surrounded by other similar lesions. This process is repeated until eventually, over many years, most of the skin becomes nodular (*Fig. 17.243*). The nodules do not ulcerate and can closely resemble lepromatous leprosy. Although lesions may develop in the nasal mucosa, these are not destructive like those of the muco-cutaneous form of American leishmaniasis. Response to therapy is slow and relapse is common. The Montenegro test is invariably negative.

L. major and *L. braziliensis panamensis* may develop a sporotrichoid spreading reaction.[4]

Visceral leishmaniasis

Visceral leishmaniasis (kala-azar, black fever) is due to infection by *L. donovani* and occurs widely in South America, Africa, the Mediterranean and Asia. It may be a manifestation of HIV infection.[4,5,18] In patients

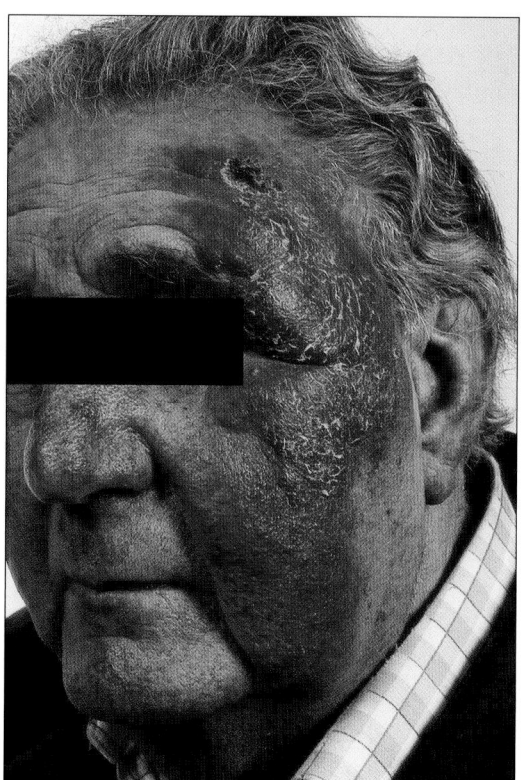

Fig. 17.241
Chronic cutaneous leishmaniasis: there is intense edema, erythema and scaling. By courtesy of S. Lucas, MD, St Thomas' Hospital, London, UK.

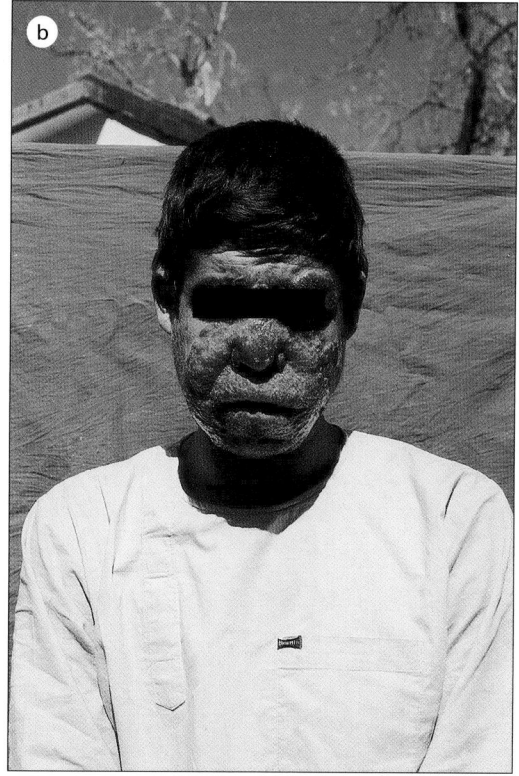

Fig. 17.242
(a, b) Mucocutaneous leishmaniasis: the lesions are destructive and very disfiguring. By courtesy of S. Lucas, MD, St Thomas' Hospital, London, UK.

with AIDS, leishmaniasis may occur in herpes zoster lesions and dermatofibroma cells may be parasitized by the organisms. Nodular cutaneous lesions arising in AIDS-related visceral leishmaniasis may mimic Kaposi's sarcoma clinically.[19] Following inoculation, the organisms multiply in histiocytes; the onset of disease is insidious after 2–4 months. The macrophages of the liver and spleen take up the organisms, resulting in hepatosplenomegaly associated with lymphadenopathy, pancytopenia, irregular and intermittent fever and marked weight loss. In India, patients may develop an earthy-gray pigmentation, particularly on the temples, around the mouth and on the hands and feet.[6]

A small number of patients who recover subsequently develop post kala-azar dermal leishmaniasis.[20] This has been reported from India and East Africa. The lesions start as erythematous or hypopigmented macules (particularly on the face) and become nodular and coalesce so that they closely resemble lepromatous leprosy, but they lack sensation abnormalities. The lesions are persistent, but resolve slowly on treatment.

Pathogenesis and histological features

In all variants of the disease the amastigote form of the parasite multiplies within the histiocytes of the mammalian host. The host response is related to the number of amastigotes and the degree of cellular immunity. Large numbers of amastigotes are associated with an anergic response and many histiocytes without other inflammatory cells. Moderate numbers of amastigotes are usually associated with necrosis, which is an important mechanism for eliminating infection. Smaller numbers are associated with a good epithelioid granulomatous response after the necrosis phase. Some infections are eliminated by an effective granulomatous response without necrosis, while others are associated with focal necrosis and ulceration when organisms are released. In others there is more extensive necrosis. The events following necrosis depend on the rate at which an effective epithelioid granulomatous reaction develops.[21,22] An unusual case of late stage cutaneous leishmaniasis harboring foci of caseous necrosis with no demonstrable organisms has been reported.[23]

Healing is often relatively rapid once necrosis has occurred. In parallel with developing immunity the overlying epidermis shows pseudo-epitheliomatous hyperplasia. Lymphocytes and plasma cells also become more numerous at the periphery of the granuloma. Scarring eventually replaces the granuloma.

Histologically, the acute lesion (oriental sore) is characterized by hyperkeratosis and acanthosis although occasionally epidermal atrophy and parakeratosis are features.[14] Ulceration is frequently seen (*Fig. 17.244*). Liquefactive degeneration of the basal keratinocytes has been described.[14] The epidermis may show pseudoepitheliomatous hyperplasia and intraepidermal neutrophil microabscesses are not infrequent.

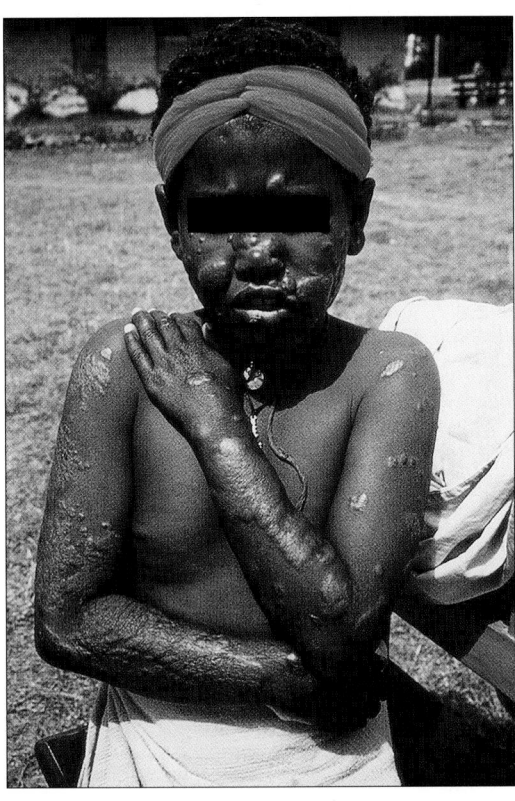

Fig. 17.243
Diffuse cutaneous leishmaniasis: note the widespread lesions, many of which appear keloidal. By courtesy of the late M.S.R. Hutt, MD, St Thomas' Hospital, London, UK.

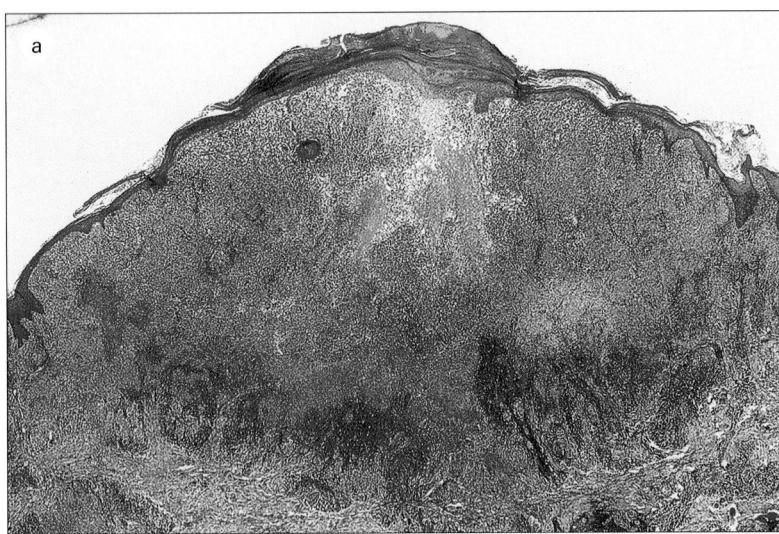

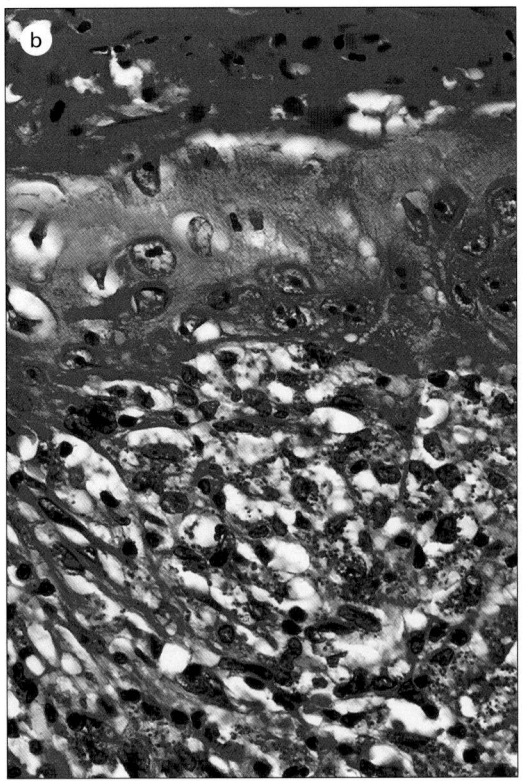

Fig. 17.244
Oriental sore: (a) there is extensive ulceration and the adjacent epithelium is acanthotic, intense inflammation is seen deep to the ulcer bed; (b) numerous amastigotes are present.

The dermis typically contains an intense infiltrate of histiocytes, lymphocytes and plasma cells. Rarely a Grenz zone is evident.[24] Neutrophils and eosinophils are usually sparse.[24] Large numbers of amastigotes are evident and these may be seen within the overlying keratinocytes (*Fig. 17.245*).[14,24] Foci of dermal necrosis may be evident. Vascular changes are usually not seen.[24] Perineural and intraneural chronic inflammatory changes associated with perineural *Leishmania* organisms have been described.[25] The patient was found to be hyperesthetic clinically. In chronic lesions the dermis contains large numbers of small non-caseating granulomata (*Fig. 17.246*). Giant cells tend to be sparse. Leishman bodies are sparse or absent.[14] Necrosis is very rare.[24]

Histologically, mucocutaneous leishmaniasis is extensively necrotic, with many plasma cells, lymphocytes, neutrophils and macrophages, but few organisms. Occasional tuberculoid or suppurative granulomata may be present.[26]

As with lepromatous leprosy, diffuse cutaneous leishmaniasis is characterized histologically by numerous macrophages distended with amastigotes and a lack of granuloma formation. There are few lymphocytes and plasma cells. These features indicate anergy, but not primary immunodeficiency.

The features of post kala-azar dermal leishmaniasis are similar to those of the diffuse cutaneous variety; the overlying epidermis is atrophic, but is not usually ulcerated (*Figs 17.247–17.249*). Nodular lesions show a dense dermal lymphohistiocytic infiltrate. There are a variable number of organisms. Vascular hyalinization is evident, and marked follicular plugging may be observed.[27]

The lupoid form of chronic cutaneous leishmaniasis may be difficult to diagnose because it represents an exaggerated tuberculoid response to very few organisms (and as such closely resembles lupus vulgaris) or perhaps only leishmanial antigen; it is best distinguished from other tuberculoid diseases on the basis of its positive Montenegro skin test.[14] There is no necrosis and plasma cells are sparse.

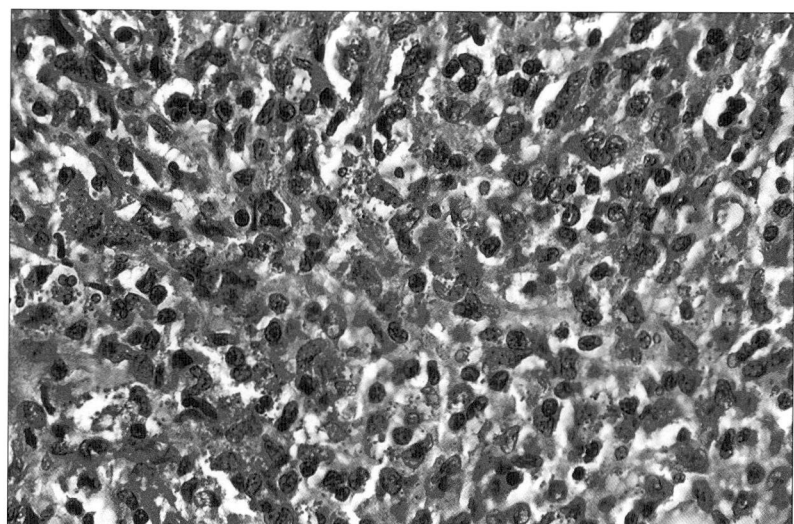

Fig. 17.245
Oriental sore: the infiltrate consists of parasite-laden histiocytes with small numbers of lymphocytes.

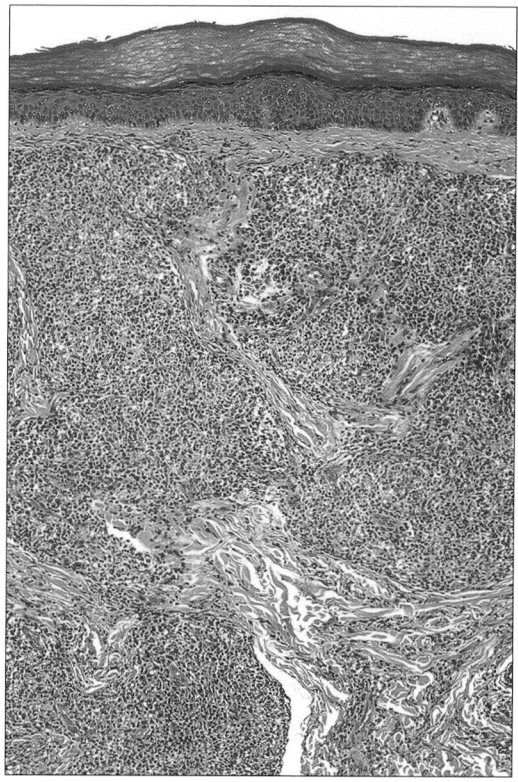

Fig. 17.247
Post kala-azar dermal leishmaniasis: there is a dense dermal nodular infiltrate. The Grenz zone is spared.

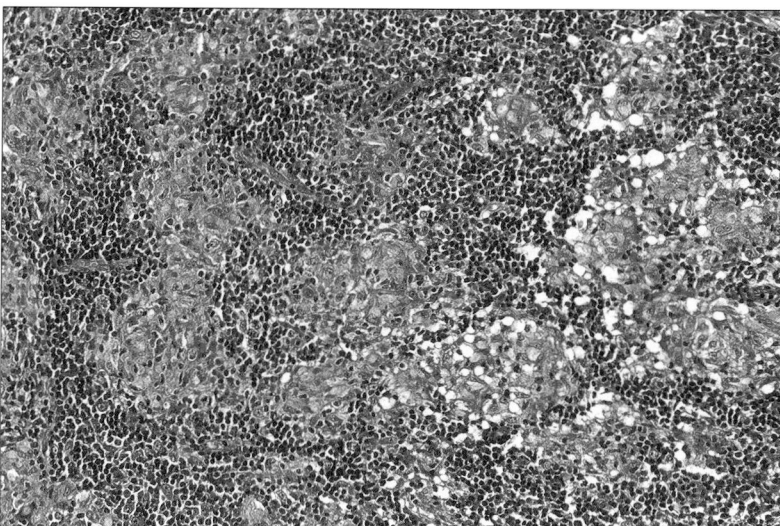

Fig. 17.246
Oriental sore: epithelioid cell granulomata as seen in this field are a feature of chronic lesions.

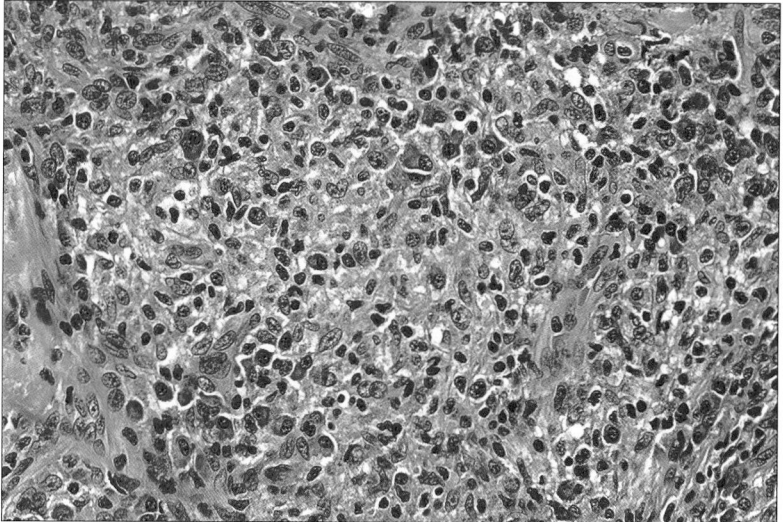

Fig. 17.248
Post kala-azar dermal leishmaniasis: there is a heavy mixed infiltrate of histiocytes, lymphocytes and plasma cells.

In all other forms of cutaneous leishmaniasis the diagnosis is confirmed by the demonstration of amastigotes in a smear or skin section.[28] The organisms are best revealed by Giemsa stain as reddish cytoplasmic round to oval structures measuring from 1.5 × 2.5 μm to 4.5 × 6.8 μm.[6] They appear blue–gray on hematoxylin and eosin staining. A small rod-like similarly stained kinetoplast may be visible (*Fig. 17.250*). Many of the organisms are within macrophages, but some occur extracellularly. They are termed Leishman–Donovan bodies. These features must be distinguished from the similar bodies of histoplasmosis and, to a lesser extent, those of granuloma inguinale and rhinoscleroma. The clinical features will usually be distinctive; skin testing, serology and culture of the organisms will confirm the diagnosis. PCR may be useful in providing a rapid diagnosis with precise species identification.[29,30]

References

1. Connor, D.H., Neafie, R.C. (1976) Cutaneous leishmaniasis. In: Bunford, C.H., Connor, D.H. (eds) Pathology of tropical and extraordinary diseases, Vol. 1. Washington: Armed Forces Institute of Pathology, pp 258–264.
2. Huaman, J.A., Castillo, M.C. (1990) Mucocutaneous leishmaniasis. Histologic classification and anatomoclinical correlations. A propos of 102 cases. *Arch Anat Cytol Pathol*, 38, 135–142.
3. Neafie, R.C., Connor, D.H. (1976) Visceral leishmaniasis. In: Bunford, C.H., Connor, D.H. (eds) Pathology of tropical and extraordinary diseases, Vol. 1. Washington: Armed Forces Institute of Pathology, pp 265–272.
4. Choi, C.M., Lerner, E.A. (2001) Leishmaniasis as an emerging infection. *J Investig Dermatol Symp Proc*, 6, 175–182.
5. Choi, C.M., Lerner, E.A. (2002) Leishmaniasis: recognition and management with a focus on the immunocompromised patient. *Am J Clin Dermatol*, 3, 91–105.
6. Kubba, R., Al-Gindan, Y. (1989) Leishmaniasis. *Dermatol Clin*, 7, 331–351.
7. Hepburn, N.C. (2000) Cutaneous leishmaniasis. *Clin Exp Dermatol*, 25, 363–370.
8. Kubba, R., Al-Gindan, Y., El-Hassan, A.M. et al (1987) Clinical diagnosis of cutaneous leishmaniasis (oriental sore). *J Am Acad Dermatol*, 16, 1183–1189.
9. Al-Gindan, Y., Kubba, R., El-Hassan, A.M. et al (1989) Dissemination in cutaneous leishmaniasis. 3. Lymph node involvement. *Int J Dermatol*, 28, 248–254.
10. Azadeh, B., Samad, A., Ardehali, S. (1985) Histological spectrum of cutaneous leishmaniasis due to Leishmania tropica. *Trans R Soc Trop Med Hyg*, 79, 631–636.
11. Martínez, E., le Pont, F., Torrez, M. et al (1998) A new focus of cutaneous leishmaniasis due to Leishmania amazonensis in a Sub Andean region of Bolivia. *Acta Trop*, 71, 97–106.
12. Romero, G.A., Vinitius de Farias Guerra, M., Gomes Paes, M. et al (2001) Comparison of cutaneous leishmaniasis due to Leishmania (Viannia) braziliensis and L. (V.) guyanensis in Brazil: clinical findings and diagnostic approach. *Clin Infect Dis*, 32, 1304–1312.
13. Salmanpour, R., Handjani, F., Zerehsaz, F. et al (1999) Erysipeloid leishmaniasis: an unusual clinical presentation. *Eur J Dermatol*, 9, 458–459.
14. Nicolis, G.D., Tosca, A.D., Stratigos, J.D. et al (1978) A clinical and histological study of cutaneous leishmaniasis. *Acta Derm Venereol*, 58, 521–525.
15. Bittencourt, A.L., Costa, J.M., Carvalho, E.M. et al (1993) Leishmaniasis recidiva cutis in American cutaneous leishmaniasis. *Int J Dermatol*, 32, 802–805.
16. Oliveira-Neto, M.P., Mattos, M., Souza, C.S. et al (1998) Leishmaniasis recidiva cutis in New World cutaneous leishmaniasis. *Int J Dermatol*, 37, 846–849.
17. El-Mogy, M.H., Abdel-Hamid, I.A., Abdel-Razic, M.M. et al (1993) Histocompatibility antigens in Egyptians with cutaneous leishmaniasis: a preliminary study. *J Dermatol Sci*, 5, 89–91.
18. Berenguer, J., Moreo, S., Cercenado, E. et al (1989) Visceral leishmaniasis in patients infected with human immunodeficiency virus (HIV). *Ann Intern Med*, 111, 129–132.
19. Gonzalez-Beato, M.J., Moyano, B., Sanchez, C. et al (2000) Kaposi's sarcoma-like lesions and other nodules as cutaneous involvement in AIDS-related visceral leishmaniasis. *Br J Dermatol*, 143, 1316–1318.
20. Rees, P.H., Kager, P.A. (1987) Visceral leishmaniasis and post kala-azar dermal leishmaniasis. In: Peters, W., Killick-Kendrick, R. (eds) The leishmaniases in biology and medicine, Vol. 2. London: Academic Press, pp 584–615.
21. Ridley, D.S., Ridley, M.J. (1983) The evolution of the lesion in cutaneous leishmaniasis. *J Pathol*, 141, 83–96.
22. Ridley, D.S., de Magalhaes, A.V., Marsden, P.D. (1989) Histological analysis and the pathogenesis of cutaneous leishmaniasis. *J Pathol*, 159, 293–299.
23. Peltier, E., Wolkenstein, P., Deniau, M. et al (1996) Caseous necrosis in cutaneous leishmaniasis. *J Clin Pathol*, 49, 517–519.
24. Kurban, A.K., Malak, J.A., Farah, F.S. et al (1966) Histopathology of cutaneous leishmaniasis. *Arch Dermatol*, 93, 396–401.
25. Satti, M.B., El Hassan, A.M., Al Gindan, Y. et al (1989) Peripheral neural involvement in cutaneous leishmaniasis. A pathologic study of human and experimental animal lesions. *Int J Dermatol*, 28, 243–247.
26. Price, S.M., Silvers, D.N. (1977) New world leishmaniasis. Serologic aids to diagnosis. *Arch Dermatol*, 113, 1415–1416.
27. Singh, N., Ramesh, V., Arora, V.K. et al (1998) Nodular post-kala-azar dermal leishmaniasis: a distinct histopathological entity. *J Cutan Pathol*, 25, 95–99.
28. Northcutt, A.D., Tschen, J.A. (1991) New ways to demonstrate pathogenic organisms. *Clin Dermatol*, 9, 205–215.
29. Mimori, T., Sasaki, J., Nakata, M. et al (1998) Rapid identification of Leishmania species from formalin-fixed biopsy samples by polymorphism-specific polymerase chain reaction. *Gene*, 210, 179–186.
30. Anders, G., Eisenberger, C.L., Jonas, F. et al (2002) Distinguishing Leishmania tropica and Leishmania major in the Middle East using polymerase chain reaction with kinetoplast DNA-specific primers. *Trans R Soc Trop Med Hyg*, 96 (Suppl. 1), S87–S92.

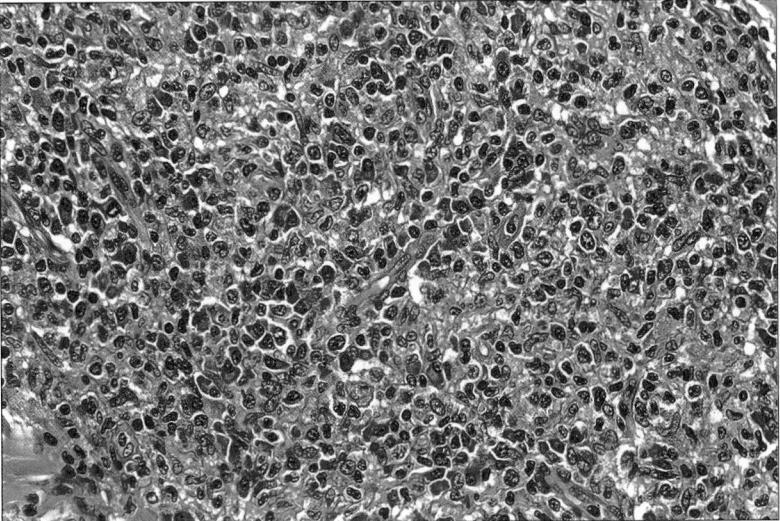

Fig. 17.249
Post kala-azar dermal leishmaniasis: in this example, organisms are no longer visible.

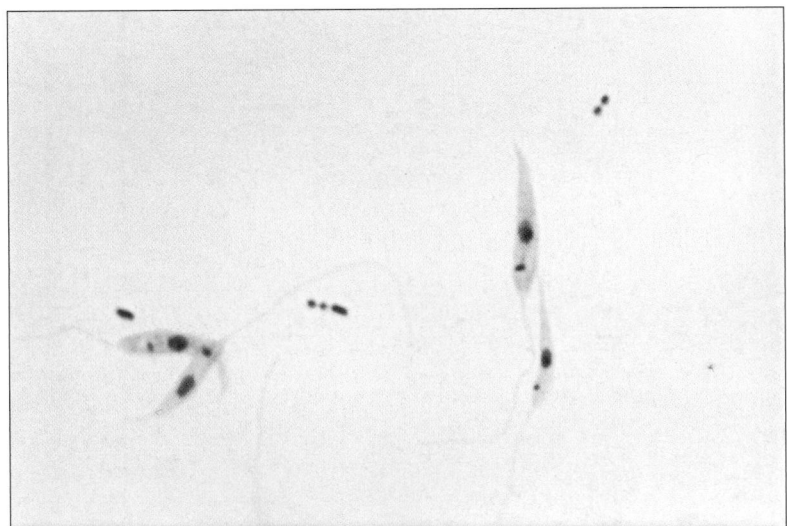

Fig. 17.250
Visceral leishmaniasis: promastigote forms of *Leishmania donovani*; note the anterior kinetoplast and flagellum (the latter is not seen in human infection) (Giemsa stain). By courtesy of H.P. Lambert, MD, and the London School of Hygiene and Tropical Medicine, London, UK.

Amebiasis cutis

Clinical features

Entamoeba histolytica can cause cutaneous lesions, although this is rare.[1,2] These are most commonly seen after surgical treatment of intestinal or hepatic amebiasis, but may also occur by direct extension perianally from the bowel or from hepatic involvement, and by direct inoculation of the skin from other infected lesions. Penile amebiasis may follow anal intercourse.[3] Cutaneous lesions have been recorded on the trunk, buttocks, genitalia and perineum and on the legs.[4,5] Subcutaneous swellings called amebomas have also been described.[6]

The lesions have a central necrotic zone with a purulent exudate, gray slough, an undermined margin and an erythematous halo. The ulcers are irregular but sharply defined. They spread and do not heal spontaneously. They are extremely painful and may be destructive. Occasionally they resemble ulcerating tumors and are associated with surrounding verrucous lesions.

Histological features

The trophozoites of *E. histolytica* are found among the purulent exudate of the ulcer and are seen more clearly with PAS staining (*Fig. 17.251*). They are 12–20 μm in diameter and are distinguished by their tendency

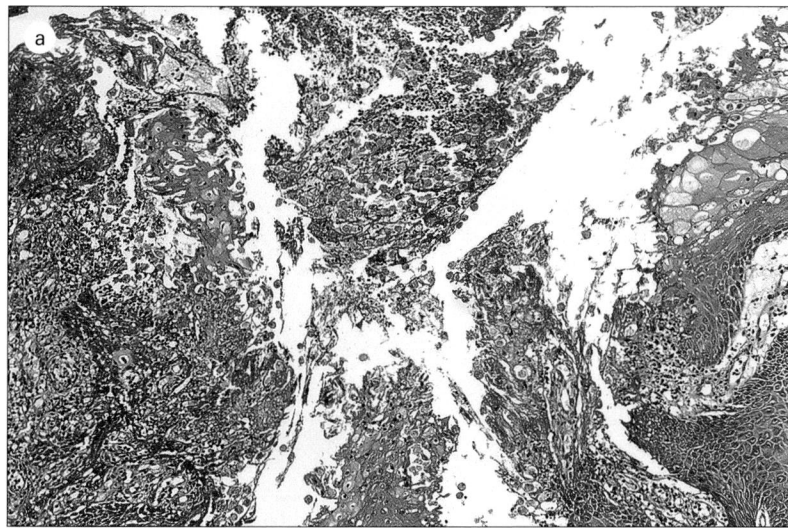

Fig. 17.251
Amebiasis cutis: (a) this biopsy is from a woman with vulval ulceration due to direct spread from the anus; the epithelium is hyperplastic and the lamina propria is chronically inflamed. (b) There are numerous trophozoites present; note the ingested red cells.

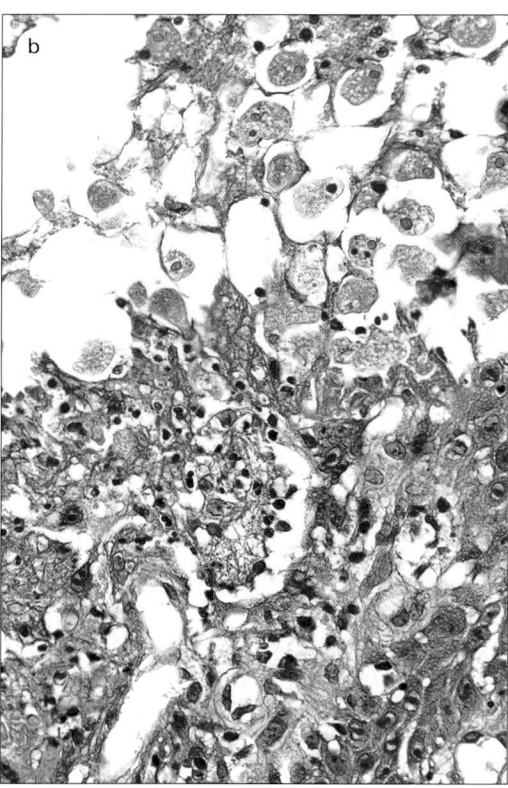

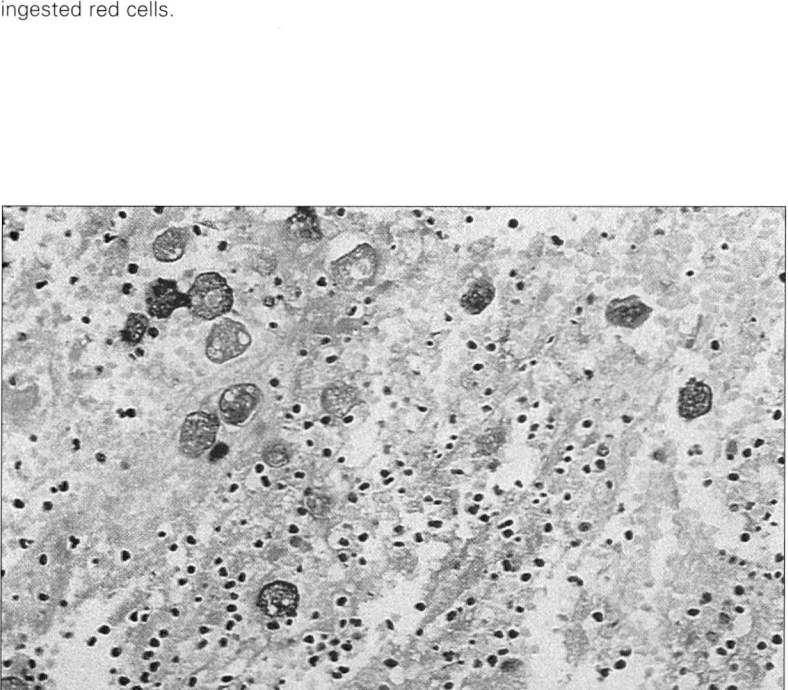

Fig. 17.252
Amebiasis cutis: the trophozoites are strongly periodic acid–Schiff positive.

to phagocytose red cells (*Fig. 17.252*) Trophozoites and cysts are usually found in the patient's feces. The organisms are surrounded by neutrophils, with some lymphocytes and plasma cells. The adjacent epidermis appears acanthotic and this may be marked or pseudoepitheliomatous in verrucous forms.

References

1. Cooke, R. (1986) The colorful people of Papua New Guinea. Some of their habits and some diseases which result from their habits. *Pathol Ann*, **21**, 311–346.
2. Saul, A. (1982) Amoebiasis cutis. *Int J Dermatol*, **21**, 472–475.
3. Hejase, M.J., Bihrle, R., Castillo, G. et al (1996) Amebiasis of the penis. *Urology*, **48**, 151–154.
4. Fujita, W.H., Barr, R.J., Gottschalk, H.R. (1981) Cutaneous amoebiasis. *Arch Dermatol*, **117**, 309–310.
5. Magaña-García, M., Arista-Viveros, A. (1993) Cutaneous amebiasis in children. *Pediatr Dermatol*, **10**, 352–355.
6. El-Zawahry, M., El-Kowy, M. (1973) Amoebiasis cutis. *Int J Dermatol*, **12**, 305–307.

Cutaneous acanthamebiasis

Clinical features

Acathamoeba spp. are free-living amebae that are seldom implicated in human disease with the possible exception of contact lens-associated keratitis.[1] However, in recent years acanthamebiasis has received increasing recognition as an opportunistic pathogen in immuno-compromised hosts, especially those with AIDS.[1–5] Infection results in an often fatal progressive encephalitis, and associated cutaneous lesions are a frequent occurrence.[1,3] The condition has been reported almost exclusively from the United States, although cases have occurred in Korea.[6] Spread to the cental nervous system and skin is from a primary source of infection in the lungs or paranasal sinuses.[2,6] Involvement of the skin may be the presenting manifestation of disseminated infection.[1] Isolated cutaneous disease with chronic, non-healing skin lesions may be the sole manifestation in patients with AIDS.[4]

Acanthamebiasis of the skin presents as multiple deep dermal and subcutaneous nodules, usually on the extremities and face.[3,7] Necrotizing panniculitis may occur.[5] Pustular, ulcerating and purpuric lesions have also been described.[2,3]

Histological features

Cutaneous infection results in severe suppurative inflammation in the dermis with extension into the subcutis, where necrotizing neutrophilic lobular panniculitis, tuberculoid granulomatous inflammation and vasculitis may occur.[1,3,5] The epidermis is usually intact. Purpuric lesions are associated with leukocytoclastic vasculitis.[2] The trophozoites, which tend to concentrate near blood vessels, measure 20–30 μm in diameter (*Fig. 17.253*).[5,6] Recognition of the *Acanthamoeba* trophozoites may be difficult in view of their macrophage-like appearance.[3] PAS and Gomori's methenamine silver stains highlight the amebic cyst walls. Diagnosis is confirmed by culture or immunofluorescence studies.[1]

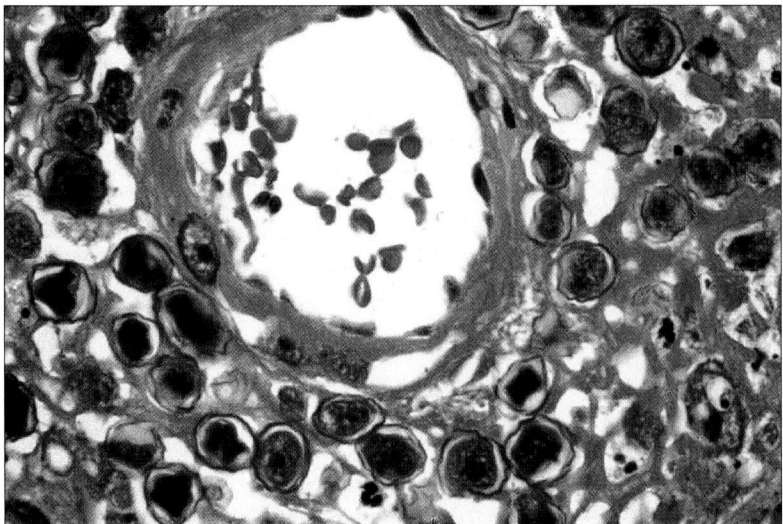

Fig. 17.253
Cutaneous acanthamebiasis: the amebae are large and have a thick cell wall.
By courtesy of K. Culpepper, MD, Brigham and Women's Hospital and Harvard
Medical School, Boston, USA.

References

1. Tan, B., Weldon-Linne, C.M., Rhone, D.P. et al (1993) Acanthamoeba infection presenting as skin lesions in patients with the acquired immunodeficiency syndrome. *Arch Pathol Lab Med*, **117**, 1043–1046.
2. Helton, H.J., Loveless, M., White, C.R. Jr (1993) Cutaneous acanthamoeba infection associated with leukocytoclastic vasculitis in an AIDS patient. *Am J Dermatopathol*, **15**, 146–149.
3. Murakawa, G.J., McCalmont, T., Altman, J. et al (1995) Disseminated acanthamebiasis in patients with AIDS. A report of five cases and a review of the literature. *Arch Dermatol*, **131**, 1291–1296.
4. Torno, M.S. Jr, Bapapour, R., Gurevitch, A. et al (2000) Cutaneous acanthamoebiasis in AIDS. *J Am Acad Dermatol*, **42**, 351–354.
5. Rosenberg, A.S., Morgan, M.B. (2001) Disseminated acanthamoebiasis presenting as lobular panniculitis with necrotizing vasculitis in a patient with AIDS. *J Cutan Pathol*, **28**, 307–313.
6. Im, K., Kim, D.S. (1998) Acanthamoebiasis in Korea: two new cases with clinical cases review. *Yonsei Med J*, **39**, 478–484.

Algal infection

Protothecosis

Clinical features

Protothecosis is a rare condition, representing infection by the achloric alga *Prototheca*, usually *P. wickerhamii*.[1,2] Approximately 80 cases have been reported.[3] The alga is assumed to be inoculated into the skin by minor trauma, presumably from contaminated water or soil. *Prototheca* are ubiquitous, being found in the mucus flux of trees, water stabilization ponds, acid rivers and lakes, and a variety of animals including cows, dogs, cats and deer.[4,5] The disease has been reported worldwide.[6] One recorded case occurred after an arthropod bite.[5]

Protothecosis occurs in both iatrogenically immunosuppressed patients and those with AIDS.[3,5–9] The condition manifests as a papular or eczematoid dermatitis, usually over an extremity.[3,6] The dermatitis form is often extensive and scaly, hypertrophic and resistant to therapy. Vesicular, herpetiform, plaquiform, ulcerative, granulomatous and verrucous variants have been described (*Fig. 17.254*).[1,3,10] Lesions may also resemble pyoderma gangrenosum.[3] Disseminated lesions have been rarely reported.[5,6,11] In immunocompetent patients the infection is most often localized to the olecranon bursa following trauma.[1,6] Localized tenosynovial involvement of the thumb has been reported in an HIV-positive patient.[7]

Histological features

The localized lesions consist of necrotic centers surrounded by granulation and fibrous tissue with a few multinucleate giant cells. The algae are found in the necrotic centers.

In the dermatitis lesions the epidermis is parakeratotic, acanthotic and papillomatous, and there is a mixed infiltrate in the upper dermis, including occasional multinucleate giant cells (*Fig. 17.255*).[1] Organisms (3–15 μm in diameter) can be found at all levels of the epidermis and in the superficial dermis (*Figs 17.256, 17.257*).[6] Infection can also involve the regional lymph nodes. Only basophilic spherical bodies are seen with hematoxylin and eosin staining, while a silver stain or a PAS reaction

reveals spore-like bodies in the epidermis and among the inflammatory infiltrate (*Fig. 17.258*). Sporangia with symmetrically arranged endospores are characteristic; these have been described as morula-like or daisy-like.[3,7,12,13] Identification of the organism depends on culture characteristics. *Prototheca* are distinguished from green algae (*Chlorella*) by the absence of chloroplasts and from *Coccidiodes immitis* by its

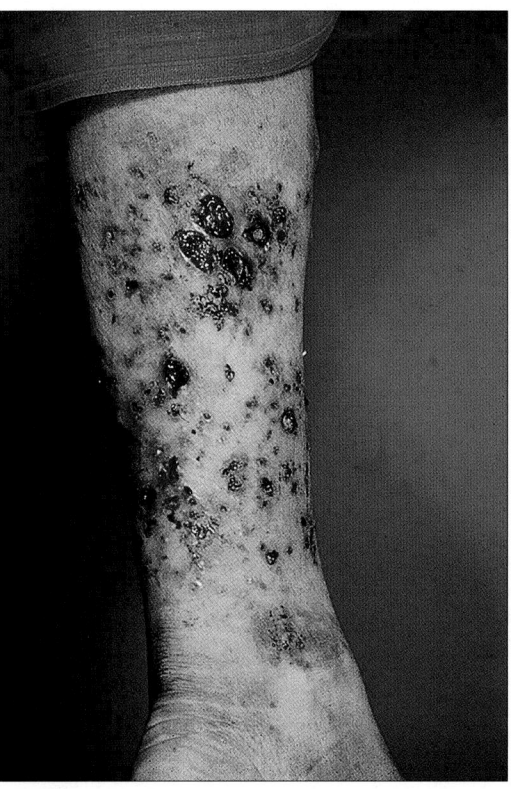

Fig. 17.254
Protothecosis: numerous crusted and ulcerative lesions are present. By courtesy of the Institute of Dermatology, London, UK.

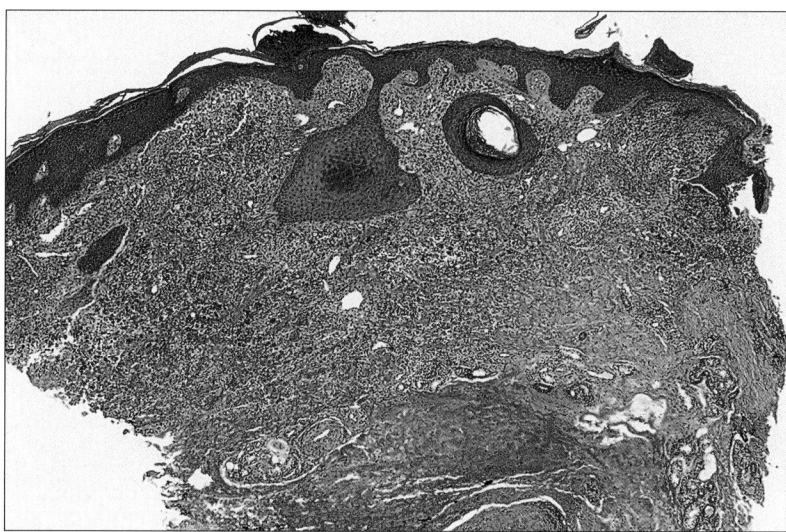

Fig. 17.255
Protothecosis: note the crusting, marked acanthosis and heavy dermal infiltrate.
By courtesy of I. Van den Berghe, AZ, Sint-Jan AV Hospital, Bruges, Belgium.

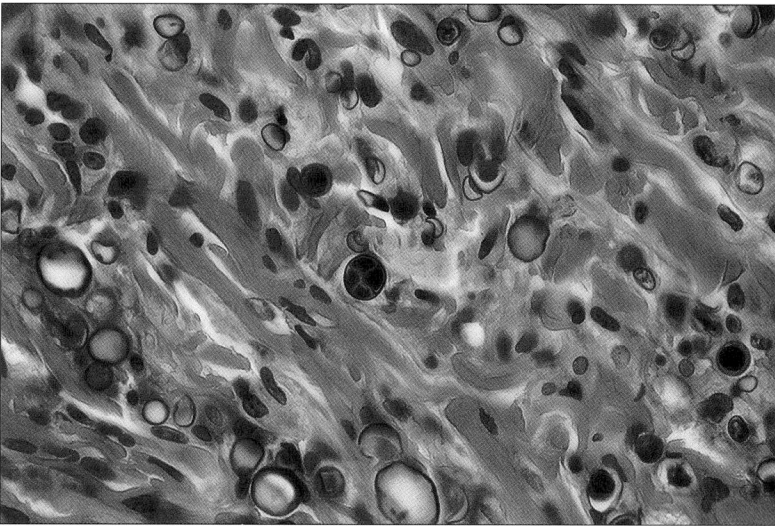

Fig. 17.257
Protothecosis: the internal septation is characteristic. By courtesy of I. Van den
Berghe, AZ, Sint-Jan AV Hospital, Bruges, Belgium.

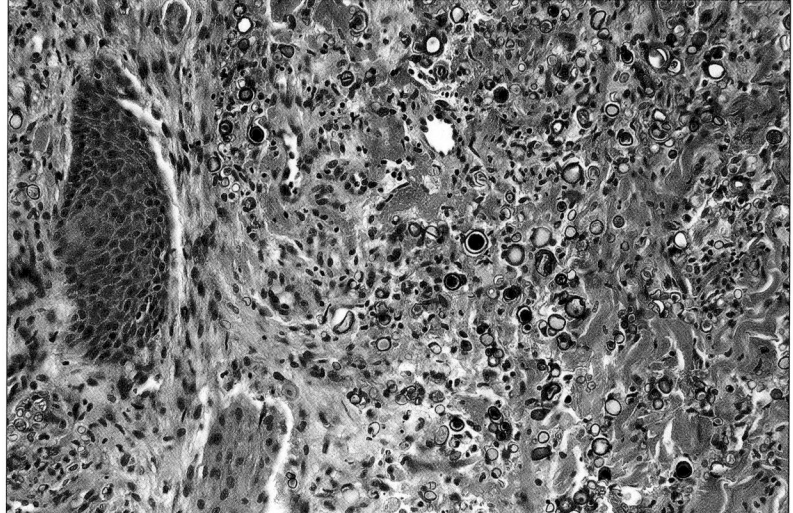

Fig. 17.256
Protothecosis: numerous organisms are present in the dermis. By courtesy of
I. Van den Berghe, AZ, Sint-Jan AV Hospital, Bruges, Belgium.

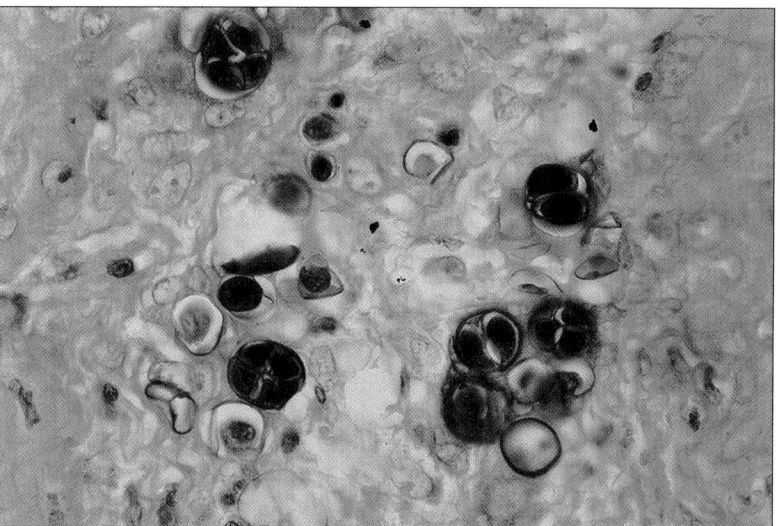

Fig. 17.258
Protothecosis: the organisms have thick cell walls: note the presence of two or
four internal spores (periodic acid–Schiff). By courtesy of the late H. Spencer, MD,
St Thomas' Hospital, London, UK.

smaller size.[12,14] Diagnosis may also be confirmed by direct immunofluorescence.[7]

Bursal lesions show stellate caseating necrosis surrounded by a
palisade of epithelioid cells, Langhans' giant cells, plasma cells and
lymphocytes.[6,7] The organisms are present within the necrotic centers.
Sinus tracts may be evident. There is associated fibrosis.

References

1. Modley, C.E., Burnett, J.W. (1989) Cutaneous algal infections: protothecosis and chlorellosis. *Cutis*, **44**, 23–24.
2. Kuo, T., Hsueh, S., Wu, J-L. et al (1987) Cutaneous protothecosis. A clinicopathologic study. *Arch Pathol Lab Med*, **111**, 737–740.
3. Chao, S.C., Hsu, M.M., Lee, J.Y. (2002) Cutaneous protothecosis: report of five cases. *Br J Dermatol*, **146**, 688–693.
4. Nelson, A.M., Neafie, R.C., Connor, D.H. (1987) Cutaneous protothecosis and chlorellosis, extra-ordinary 'aquatic-borne' algal infections. *Clin Dermatol*, **5**, 76–87.
5. Wirth, F.A., Passalacqua, J.A., Kao, G. (1994) Disseminated cutaneous protothecosis in an immunocompromised host: a case report and literature review. *Cutis*, **63**, 185–188.
6. Cox, G.E., Wilson, J.D., Brown, P. (1974) Protothecosis: a case of disseminated algal infection. *Lancet*, **2**, 379–382.
7. Laeng, R.H., Egger, C., Schaffner, T. et al (1994) Protothecosis in an HIV-positive patient. *Am J Surg Pathol*, **18**, 1261–1264.
8. Piyophirapong, S., Linpiyawan, R., Mahaisavariya, P. et al (2002) Cutaneous protothecosis in an AIDS patient (Letter). *Br J Dermatol*, **146**, 713–715.
9. Woolrich, A., Koestenblatt, E., Don, P. et al (1994) Cutaneous protothecosis and AIDS. *J Am Acad Dermatol*, **31** (5 Pt 2), 920–924.
10. Otoyama, K., Tomizawa, N., Higuchi, I. et al (1989) Cutaneous protothecosis. *J Dermatol*, **16**, 496–499.
11. Venezio, F.R., Lavou, E., Williams, J.E. (1982) Progressive cutaneous protothecosis. *Am J Clin Pathol*, **77**, 485–493.
12. Hirsch, B.C., Johnson, W.C. (1984) Pathology of granulomatous diseases: mixed inflammatory granulomas. *Int J Dermatol*, **23**, 585–597.
13. Connor, D.H., Gibson, D.W., Ziefer, A. (1982) Diagnostic features of three unusual infections: micronemiasis, pheomycotic cyst, and protothecosis. *Monogr Pathol*, **23**, 305–339.
14. Walsh, S.V., Johnson, R.A., Tahan, S.R. (1998) Protothecosis: an unusual cause of chronic subcutaneous and soft tissue infection. *Am J Dermatopathol*, **20**, 379–382.

Fungal infections

Fungal infections include:

- superficial variants involving skin, hair, nails and mucous membranes, for example ringworm (dermatophytosis), and the dermatomycoses (tinea versicolor and candidiasis)
- subcutaneous lesions
- disseminated infection.[1]

Ringworm fungi include three species: *Microsporum*, *Trichophyton* and *Epidermophyton*. *Epidermophyton* invades epidermal keratin while *Microsporum* and *Trichophyton* also affect the hair. Cutaneous ringworm on non-hairy skin presents as slowly enlarging, scaly, erythematous annular lesions with central clearing (*Fig. 17.259*).

Dermatophytes can infect the keratin of the stratum corneum, hair or nail, without extending into deeper parts of the skin. They may also be associated with intradermal spread (Majocci's granuloma). With few exceptions, identification of pathogenic fungi is better served by culture rather than by histological scrutiny.[2,3] Dermatophytes use the soluble non-keratin parts for nutrition and rely on the keratin for protection from serum and the host response.[4,5] The keratin is penetrated by means of putative keratinases. Other virulence factors include elastase and proteinases.[5] *T. rubrum* produces mannan, which suppresses or diminishes the host immune response, presumably by inhibiting critical steps in antigen presentation or processing.[5,6] The epidemiology and pathogenesis of dermatophytosis is complex and beyond the remit of this text. For excellent review articles the reader is referred to references 4, 5 and 6.

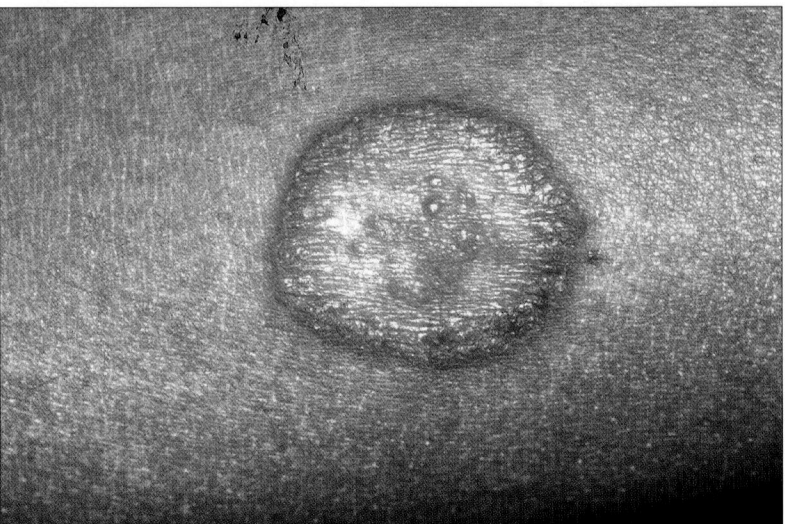

Fig. 17.259
Tinea corporis: note the annular configuration and erythematous margin. By courtesy of M.M. Black, MD, Institute of Dermatology, London, UK.

References

1. Svejgaard, E. (1986) Epidemiology and clinical feaures of dermatomycoses and dermatophytoses. *Acta Derm Venereol*, **121** (Suppl.), 19–26.
2. Googe, P.B., De Coste, S.D., Herold, W.H. et al (1989) Primary cutaneous aspergillosis mimicking dermatophytosis. *Arch Pathol Lab Med*, **113**, 1284–1286.
3. Hernandez, A.D. (1980) An approach to the diagnosis and therapy of dermatophytosis. *Int J Dermatol*, **19**, 540–547.
4. De Vroey, C. (1985) Epidemiology of ringworm (dermatophytosis). *Semin Dermatol*, **4**, 185–200.
5. Weitzman, I., Summerbell, R.C. (1995) The dermatophytes. *Clin Microbiol Rev*, **8**, 240–259.
6. Dahl, M.V., Grando, S.A. (1994) Chronic dermatophytosis: what is special about Trichophyton rubrum? *Adv Dermatol*, **9**, 97–109.

Tinea capitis

Dermatophyte infections of the scalp are characterized by involvement of the hair shaft by pathogenic fungi. The pattern of hair invasion, related to the type of dermatophyte, determines the degree and site of hair damage and the clinical picture. Patients may therefore present with variable features including hair loss with scaling, follicular inflammation, pustulation and kerion formation, often in association with drainage lymphadenopathy. A carrier state is recognized. Infection depends upon contact with spores and follicular trauma. Tinea capitis (scalp ringworm) frequently presents as small epidemics (e.g. in schools). Disease may develop as a consequence of sharing combs or hairbrushes.

Infections caused by *Microsporum audouinii* and *Microsporum canis*

Clinical features

M. audouinii and *M. canis* grow on the outside of the hair shaft, an ectothrix type of hair involvement.[1–3] The lesions are recognized as areas of alopecia, with numerous broken-off dull hairs (*Fig. 17.260*). Some scaling is present, but overt inflammation is not marked. The areas of infection are recognized by fluorescence under Wood's lamp (*Fig. 17.261*). The process commonly affects children, boys much more often than girls. *Microsporum ferrugineum* may also cause this picture.

M. audouinii and *M. canis* were once the most common causes of tinea capitis in North America and Western Europe.[4,5]

Histological features

The fungal arthrospores coat the outside of the hair shaft and the hyphae extend into the hair shaft down to the level of the mid-follicle. The epidermis shows some acanthosis and patchy parakeratosis and there is usually a mixed inflammatory infiltrate in the superficial dermis, more marked with *M. canis*.

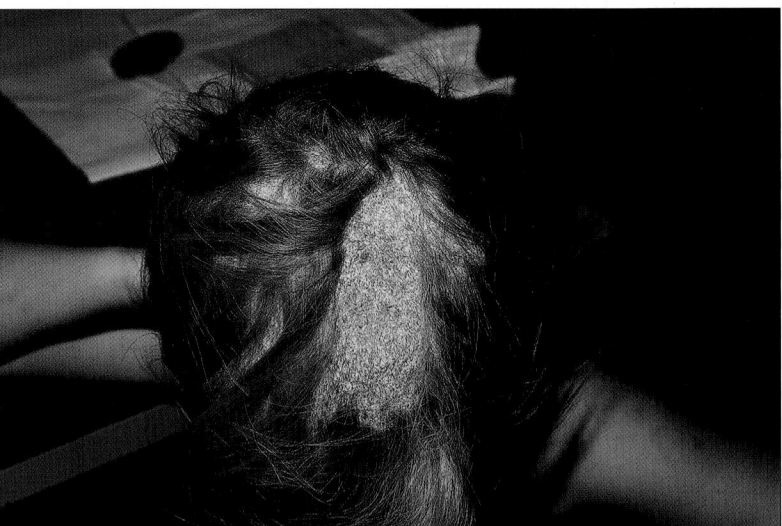

Fig. 17.260
Tinea capitis: there is marked hair loss. In this example scaling and crusting are pronounced. By courtesy of M.M. Black, MD, Institute of Dermatology, London, UK.

References

1. Svejgaard, E. (1986) Epidemiology and clinical features of dermatomycoses and dermatophytoses. *Acta Derm Venereol*, **121** (Suppl.), 19–26.
2. Hebert, A.A. (1988) Tinea capitis. Current concepts. *Arch Dermatol*, **124**, 1554–1557.
3. Ayaya, S.O., Kamar, K.K., Kakai, R. (2001) Aetiology of tinea capitis in school children. *East Afr Med J*, **78**, 531–535.
4. Gupta, A.K., Summerbell, R.C. (2000) Tinea capitis. *Med Mycol*, **38**, 255–287.
5. Elewski, B.E. (2000) Tinea capitis: a current perspective. *J Am Acad Dermatol*, **42**, 1–20.

Kerion

Clinical features

This is a severe, boggy inflammatory form of tinea, most often caused by *Trichophyton verrucosum* or *Trichophyton mentagrophytes*.[1] Kerion is seen as an area of inflamed alopecia in which the broken-off hairs are loose in their follicles and are associated with suppuration (*Figs 17.262, 17.263*). This may be severe enough to discharge via sinuses, with the formation of fibrinopurulent crusts around adjacent hairs. Secondary bacterial infection may play a part. Fluorescence is not a feature. Involvement of the beard area (tinea barbae), which occurs most often in farm workers, invariably affects adult males. The lesions appear as erythematous areas of pustular folliculitis in the beard area and may present as a kerion (*Fig. 17.264*).

Histological features

Trichophyton is a large-spored fungus with an ectothrix pattern of hair involvement. There is much associated pus with abscesses. The epidermis is acanthotic and spongiotic, with parakeratosis and intraepidermal collections of neutrophils (*Figs 17.265, 17.266*). Other *Microsporum* and *Trichophyton* species are frequent causes of kerion.[2,3]

References

1. Powell, F.C., Muller, S.A. (1982) Kerion in the glabrous skin. *J Am Acad Dermatol*, **7**, 490–494.
2. Stephens, C.J.M., Hay, R., Black, M.M. (1989) Fungal kerion – total scalp involvement due to Microsporum canis infection. *Clin Exp Dermatol*, **14**, 442–444.
3. Gupta, G., Burden, A.D., Roberts, D. T. (1999) Acute suppurative ringworm (kerion) caused by Trichophyton rubrum. *Br J Dermatol*, **140**, 369–370.

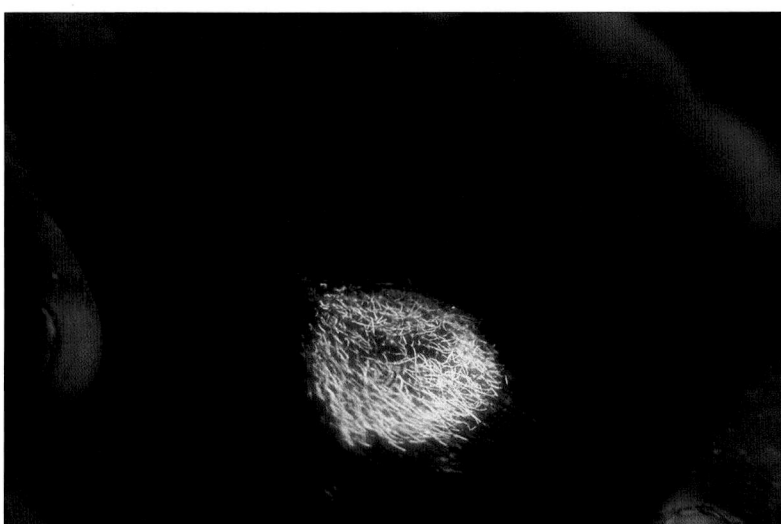

Fig. 17.261
Tinea capitis: note the characteristic fluorescence under Wood's light. By courtesy of M.M. Black, MD, Institute of Dermatology, London, UK.

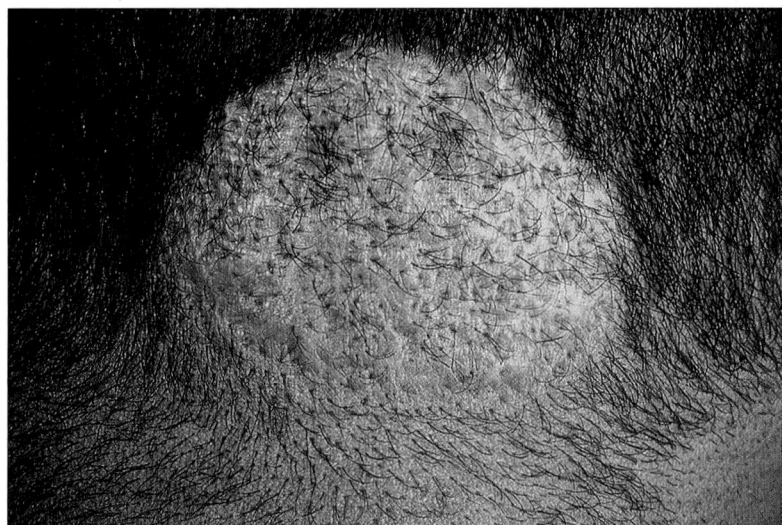

Fig. 17.263
Kerion: there is marked alopecia; dilated follicular ostia are apparent. By courtesy of the Institute of Dermatology, London, UK.

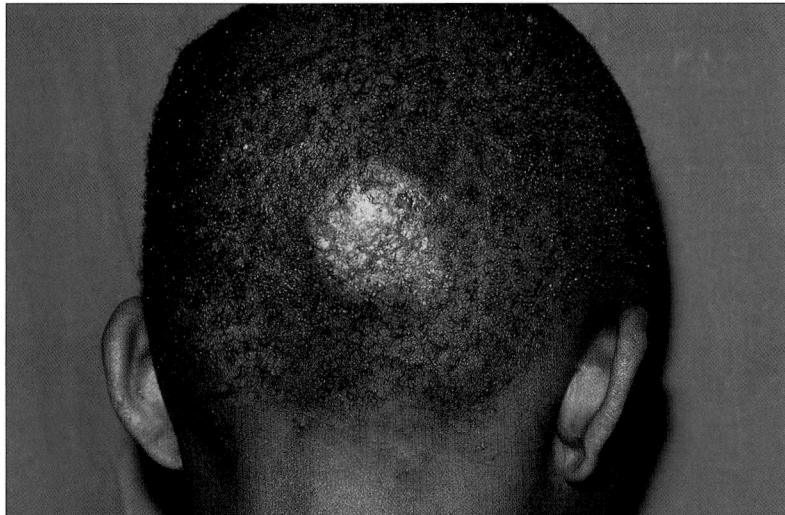

Fig. 17.262
Kerion: in addition to alopecia there is marked erythema and matting of hairs due to purulent exudate. By courtesy of R.A. Marsden, MD, St George's Hospital, London, UK.

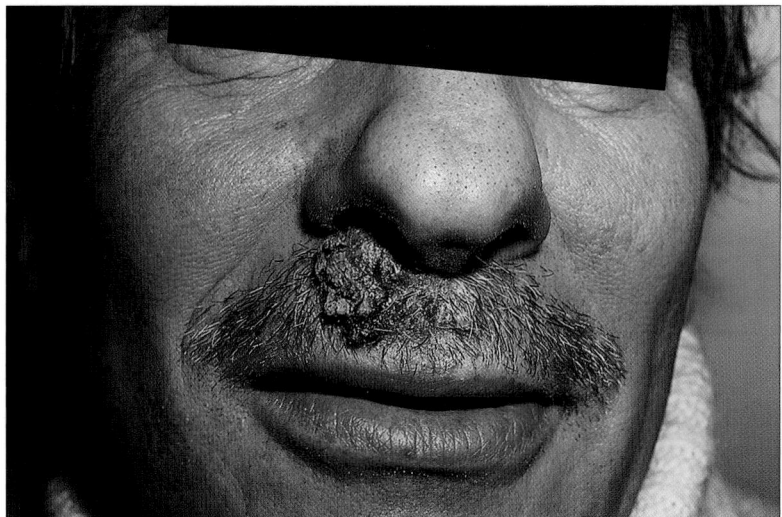

Fig. 17.264
Kerion: in males, dermatophyte infection of the beard area may also present as a kerion. By courtesy of R.A. Marsden, MD, St George's Hospital, London, UK.

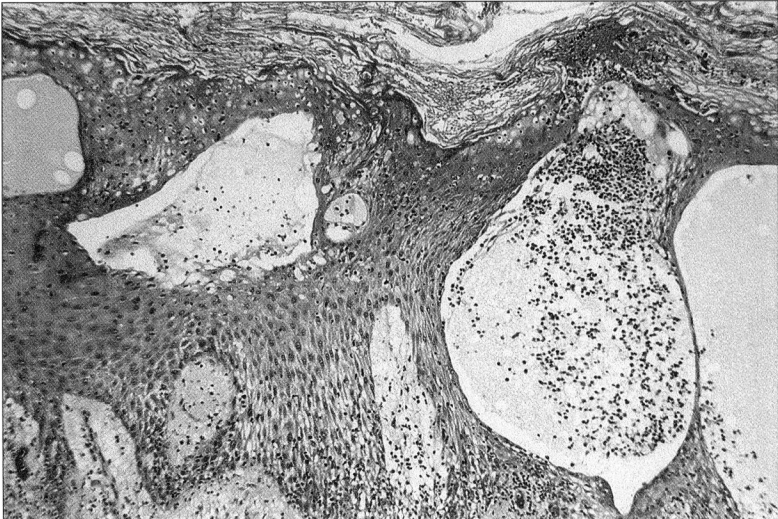

Fig. 17.265
Kerion: there is hyperkeratosis, acanthosis, epidermal edema with acute inflammation and abscess formation.

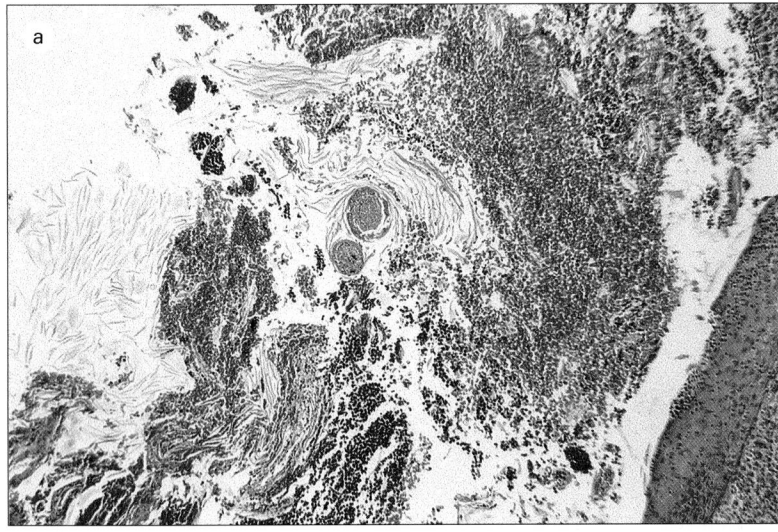

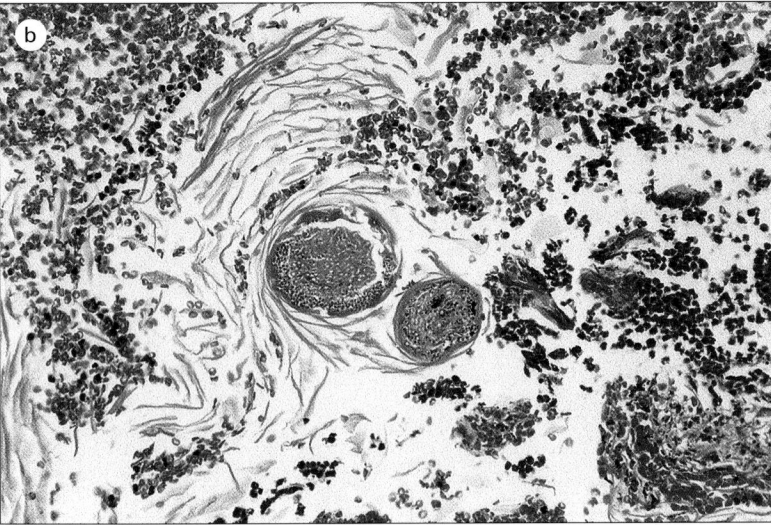

Fig. 17.266
Kerion: (a) crust scrapings from a patient with a typical scalp lesion. In addition to blood, keratinous debris and numerous neutrophils, two hair shafts are present in the center of the field. (b) High power view showing numerous fungal spores coating the outside of the shaft.

Endothrix infections

Clinical features

These infections, most often with *Trichophyton tonsurans* and *Trichophyton violaceum*, usually cause patchy alopecia with little inflammation. *T. tonsurans* is now the most common cause of scalp ringworm in the United States.[1-3] The hair break is at the ostium of the follicle so that broken hairs are seen as dots rather than stumps. The intervening skin usually shows only slight scaling, but occasionally pustules and kerion can develop.[1] Drainage lymphadenopathy may be evident. The hairs do not fluoresce with a Wood's lamp.

Histological features

The hyphae of *T. tonsurans* and *T. violaceum* extend within the hair shaft and produce spores. The epidermis is patchily parakeratotic and there are remnants of infected hair shaft in the dilated keratin-plugged ostia. Perifollicular inflammation is variable in intensity, but often includes histiocytes and multinucleate cells as well as lymphocytes and plasma cells.

References

1. Herbert, A.A. (1988) Tinea capitis – current concepts. *Arch Dermatol*, **124**, 1554–1557.
2. Elewski, B.E. (2000) Tinea capitis: a current perspective. *J Am Acad Dermatol*, **42** (1 Pt 1), 1–20.
3. Gupta, A.K., Summerbell, R.C. (2000) Tinea capitis. *Med Mycol*, **38**, 255–287.

Black piedra

Clinical features

Black piedra (Spanish *piedra*, stone) is caused by an ascomycete, *Piedraia hortae*, and involves almost exclusively the scalp.[1-4] It is characterized by black nodules firmly attatched to the hair shafts (*Fig. 17.267*). The disease mainly occurs in the tropics. Patients of all ages are affected but there is predilection for adults.

Histological features

Microscopic examination reveals numerous asci and ascospores within the black nodules (*Fig. 17.268*). Damage of the hair at the level of the

Fig. 17.267
Black piedra: there are numerous tiny black nodules attached to hair shafts. By courtesy of the late C. Kalter, MD, Walter Reed Medical Center, Washington, USA.

cuticle and cortex is secondary to the keratolytic activity of the organism.[4]

References

1. Adam, B.A., Soo-Hoo, T.S., Chong, K.C. (1977) Black piedra in west Malaysia. *Australas J Dermatol*, **18**, 45–47.
2. Coimbra, C.E. Jr, Santos, R.V. (1989) Black piedra among the Zoro Indians from Amazonia (Brazil). *Mycopathologia*, **107**, 57–60.
3. Gip, L. (1994) Black piedra: the first case treated with terbinafine (Lamisil). *Br J Dermatol*, **130**, 26–28.
4. Figueras, M.J., Guarro, J., Zaror, L. (1996) New findings in black piedra infection. *Br J Dermatol*, **135**, 157–158.

White piedra

Clinical features

White piedra (Spanish *piedra*, stone) – or trichosporosis – is a trichomycosis caused by the saprophyte fungus *Trichosporon beigelii*.[1] However, it has also been suggested that the disease is caused by a synergistic infection of the fungus and *Corynebacteria*.[2–4] The disease has a worldwide distribution but is rare in cold climates.[5–8] It may affect any hair-bearing areas including the scalp, eyebrows, eyelashes, beard area, axillae and genital skin (*Fig. 17.269*).[9] Men are more commonly affected than women and there is a higher incidence in black patients.[1] Nail involvement is exceptional.[10] Typically, white nodules are seen firmly attached to the hair shaft. The condition is asymptomatic but hairs may break as a result of invasion of the cuticle and cortex by the fungus.

Trichosporon beigelii can occasionally cause a disseminated disease in neutropenic immunocompromised patients and in HIV infection.[11–14] In these patients, cutaneous lesions consist of purpuric papules and nodules with necrosis.[14]

Histological features

Microscopic examination of the white nodules under potassium hydroxide (KOH) shows the presence of numerous hyphae and arthrospores.

References

1. Avram, A., Buot, G., Binet, O. et al (1987) Clinical and mycological study of 11 cases of genitopubic trichosporosis nodosa (white piedra). *Ann Dermatol Venereol*, **114**, 819–827.
2. Kalter, D.C., Tschen, J.A., Cernoch, P.L. et al (1986) Genital white piedra: epidemiology, microbiology and therapy. *J Am Acad Dermatol*, **14**, 982–993.

3. Ellner, K.M., McBride, M.E., Kalter, D.C. et al (1990) White piedra: evidence for a synergistic infection. *Br J Dermatol*, **123**, 355–363.
4. Youker, S.R., Andreozzi, R.J., Appelbaum, P.C. et al (2003) White piedra: further evidence for a synergistic infection. *J Am Acad Dermatol*, **49**, 746–749.
5. Benson, P.M., Lapins, N.A., Odom, R.B. (1983) White piedra. *Arch Dermatol*, **119**, 602–604.
6. Kotovirta, M., Stubb, S., Salonen, A. (1975) Trichosporosis (white piedra). A case report from Finland. *Acta Derm Venereol*, **55**, 218–220.
7. Kubec, K., Dvorak, R., Alsaleh, Q.A. (1998) Trichosporosis (white piedra) in Kuwait. *Int J Dermatol*, **37**, 186–187.
8. Peel, M.M., Bodey, A.S., Taylor, C.J. (1981) White piedra in Australia. *Med J Aust*, **1**, 595.
9. Schwinn, A., Ebert, J., Hamm, H. et al (1996) White genital piedra. *Hautarzt*, **47**, 638–641.
10. Elmer, K.B., Elston, D.M., Libow, L.F. (2002) Trichosporon beigelii infection presenting as white piedra onychomycosis in the same patient. *Cutis*, **70**, 209–211.
11. Gold, J.W., Poston, W., Mertelsmann, R. et al (1981) Systemic infection with Trichosporon cutaneum in a patient with acute leukemia: report of a case. *Cancer*, **48**, 2163–2167.
12. Kim, W.G. (2001) A case of disseminated Trichosporon beigelii infection in a patient with myelodysplastic syndrome after chemotherapy. *J Korean Med Sci*, **16**, 505–508.
13. Lascaux, A.S., Bouscarat, F., Descamps, V. et al (1998) Cutaneous manifestations during disseminated trichosporonosis in an AIDS patient. *Ann Dermatol Venereol*, **125**, 111–113.
14. Nahass, G.T., Rosenberg, S.P., Leonardi, C.L. et al (1993) Disseminated infection with Trichosporon beigelii. Report of a case and review of the cutaneous and histologic manifestations. *Arch Dermatol*, **129**, 1020–1203.

Favus

Clinical features

This pattern of tinea capitis is seen in the Middle East, South Africa and Greenland, and sporadically elsewhere. It is characterized by cup-shaped crusts, or scutula, around the ostia of hair follicles.[1,2] The hair penetrates the crust and is not necessarily broken off or shortened. The crusts may become confluent. Permanent and scarring alopecia occurs (*Fig. 17.270*). Removal of the scutula leaves an erythematous oozing base. The hairs show a gray–green fluorescence under Wood's lamp.

Histological features

Favus is caused by *Trichophyton schoenleinii*, which invades the hair and produces air spaces, but arthrospores are not seen.[1] Relatively little damage occurs to the hair shafts. Fungal hyphae and spores are seen in the scutula, which rests on the acanthotic stratum spinosum around the follicular ostia. The underlying dermis shows a mixed inflammatory infiltrate (including giant cells) and marked fibrosis, which sometimes resembles folliculitis keloidalis.

References

1. McGinnis, M.R., Ajello, L., Schell, W.A. (1985) Mycotic diseases: a proposed nomenclature. *Int J Dermatol*, **24**, 9–15.
2. Dvoretzky, I., Fisher, B.K., Movshovitz, M. et al (1980) Favus. *Int J Dermatol*, **19**, 89–93.

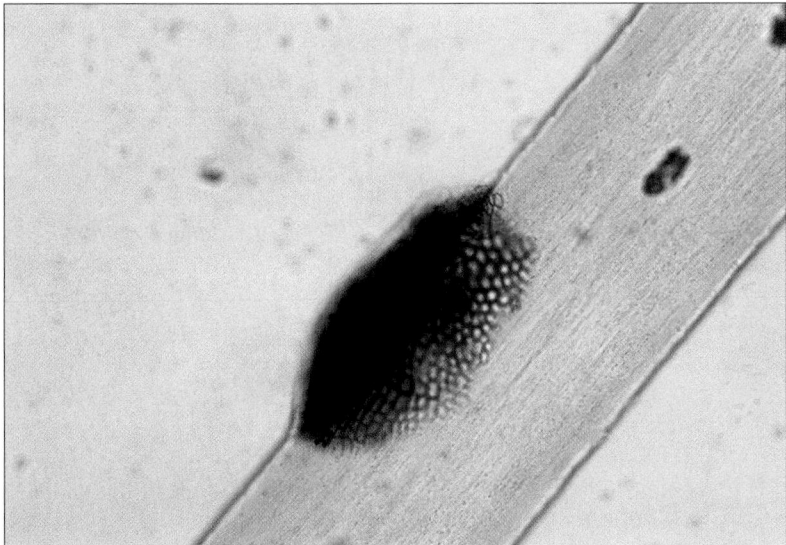

Fig. 17.268
Black piedra: close-up view of a brown nodule firmly attached to the hair shaft. By courtesy of the late C. Kalter, MD, Walter Reed Medical Center, Washington, USA.

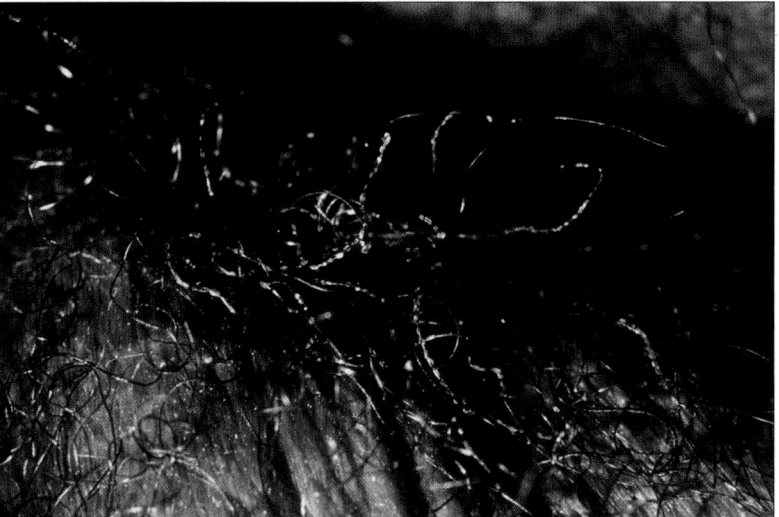

Fig. 17.269
White piedra: numerous tiny white nodules are attached to hair shafts. By courtesy of the Institute of Dermatology, London, UK.

Tinea corporis

Clinical features

This fungal infection of non-hairy skin is seen as expanding erythematous scaly areas with well-defined elevated margins (*Figs 17.271–17.274*).[1] The center may return to normal as the lesion expands. The condition commonly affects children. Spread is by contact with infected lesions.

Tinea gladiatorum is a clinical variant of tinea corporis that occurs among competetive wrestlers. Most outbreaks are caused by *Trichophyton tonsurans* and transmission is via person-to-person contact.[2]

Histological features

The expanding edge of the lesion is characterized by parakeratosis and acanthosis, with some neutrophils among the parakeratotic crust. The causative organisms are very varied and are usually the ones most prevalent in the geographic area. The presence of fungal hyphae in the keratin is easily demonstrated by the PAS reaction. Underlying inflammation is usually mild, but is more severe if there is follicular involvement.

Lesions, which may be single or multiple, present on exposed skin. In cases where inflammation is marked, pustulation may be a feature. Inappropriate treatment with local steroids may modify the clinical appearance and cause further diagnostic confusion (tinea incognito) (*Fig. 17.275*).

References

1. Svejgaard, E. (1986) Epidemiology and clinical features of dermatomycoses and dermatophytoses. *Acta Derm Venereol*, **121** (Suppl.), 19–26.
2. Kohl, T.D., Linsey, M. (2000) Tinea gladiatorum: wrestling's emerging foe. *Sports Med*, **29**, 439–447.

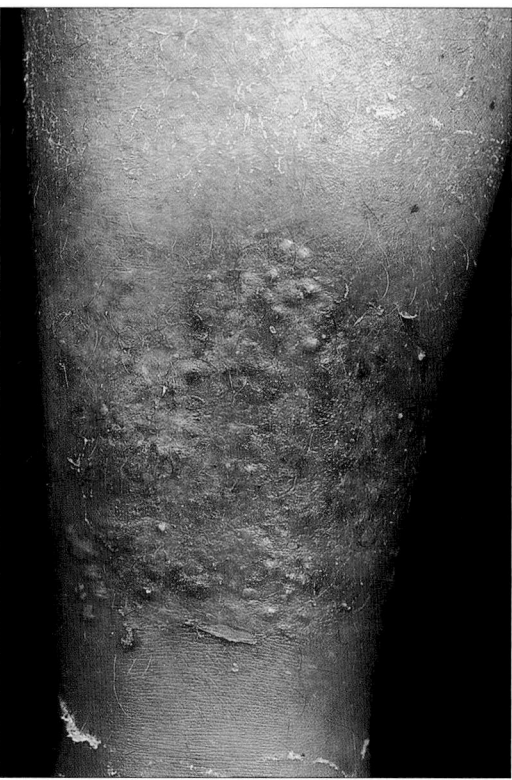

Fig. 17.272
Tinea corporis: in this example there is gross pustulation; note the erythema and induration. By courtesy of R.A. Marsden, MD, St George's Hospital, London, UK.

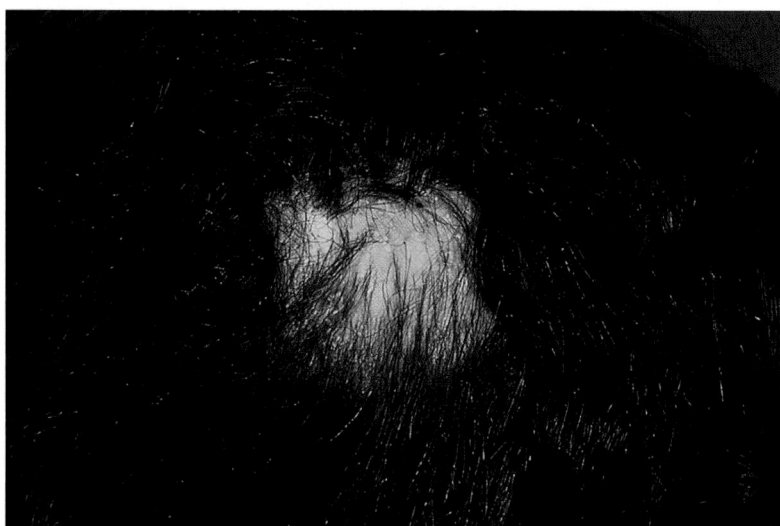

Fig. 17.270
Favus: scarring alopecia due to infection by *Trichophyton schoenleinii*. By courtesy of R.A. Marsden, MD, St George's Hospital, London, UK.

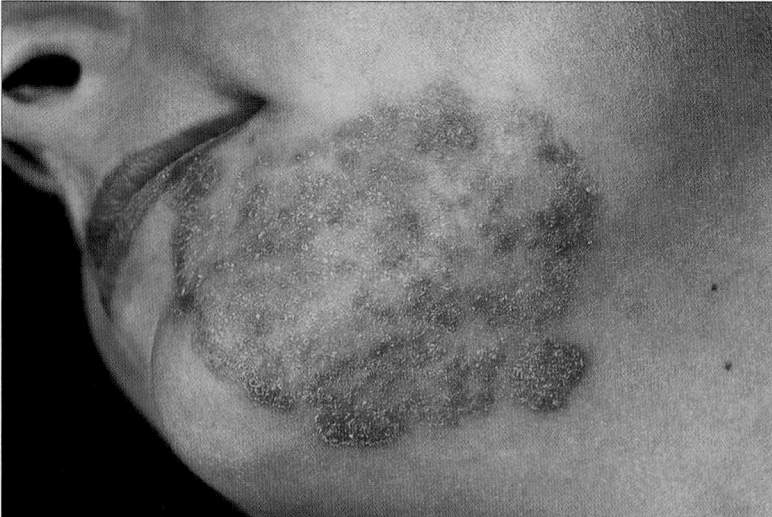

Fig. 17.271
Tinea corporis: note the sharply defined elevated scaly border. By courtesy of R.A. Marsden, MD, St George's Hospital, London, UK.

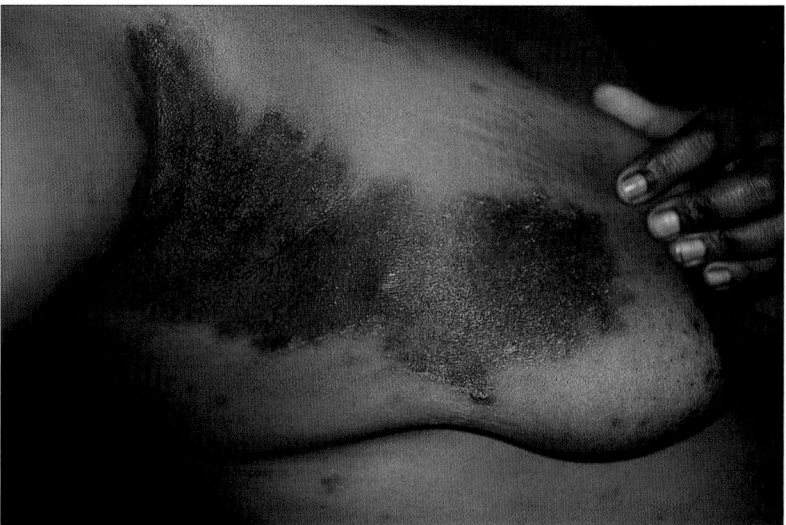

Fig. 17.273
Tinea corporis: in this patient, the infection is associated with severe hyperpigmentation. By courtesy of N.C. Dlova, MD, Nelson R. Mandela School of Medicine, University of KwaZulu-Natal, South Africa.

Tinea pedis and tinea cruris

Clinical features

Tinea pedis

Tinea pedis is usually centered on the interdigital clefts and is the most frequent form of dermatophyte infection, commonly referred to as 'athlete's foot' (*Fig. 17.276*). It is seen as a macerated fissuring area between the toes, which may extend onto the plantar aspect of the foot. The lesions are itchy, worse in hot weather due to sweating, and the smell is also a frequent cause of complaint. Pustular lesions may be seen.[1] Secondary bacterial infection is common. Tinea pedis is a predisposing factor for cellulitis of the lower extremities.

Tinea cruris

Tinea cruris is a very common dermatophyte infection of the groin, more common in men than in women. Isolated penile involvement may occur rarely.[2] It presents as an erythematous plaque, extending crescentically down the thighs (*Fig. 17.277*). Diaper dermatitis is a variant of tinea cruris, seen mainly in infants 7–12 months of age.[3]

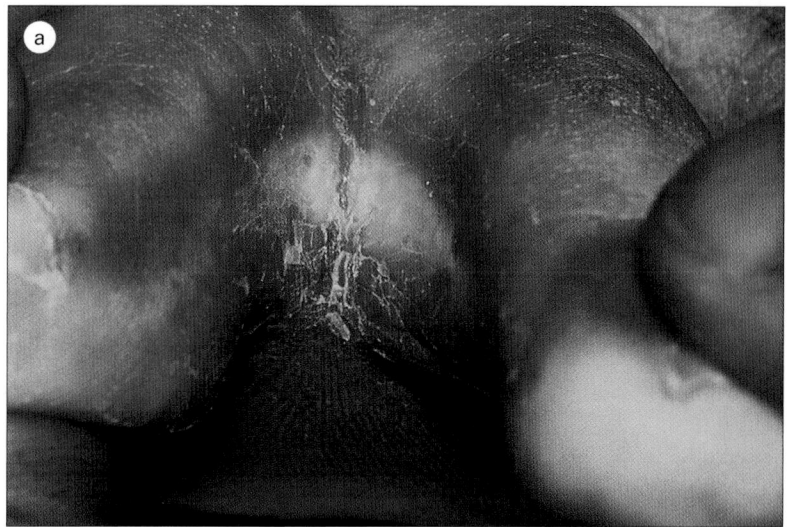

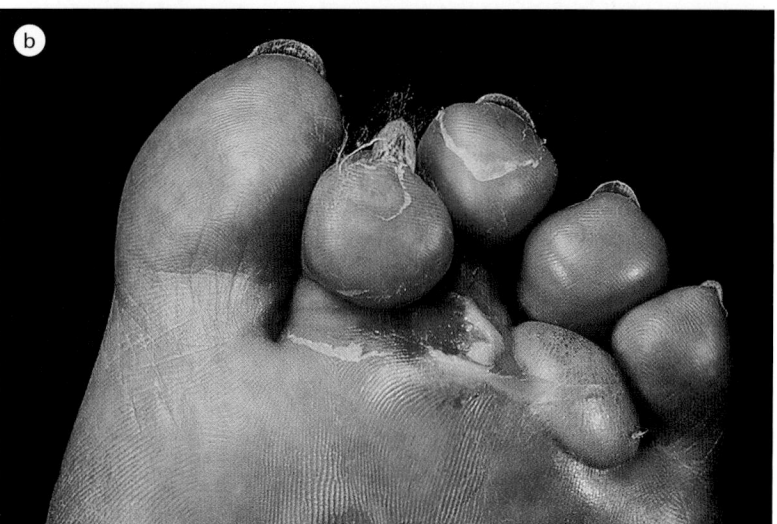

Fig. 17.276
Tinea pedis: **(a)** maceration between the toes; **(b)** severe dermal edema has resulted in this bullous variant. **(a)** By courtesy of A. Du Vivier, MD, King's College Hospital, London, UK; **(b)** by courtesy of the Institute of Dermatology, London, UK.

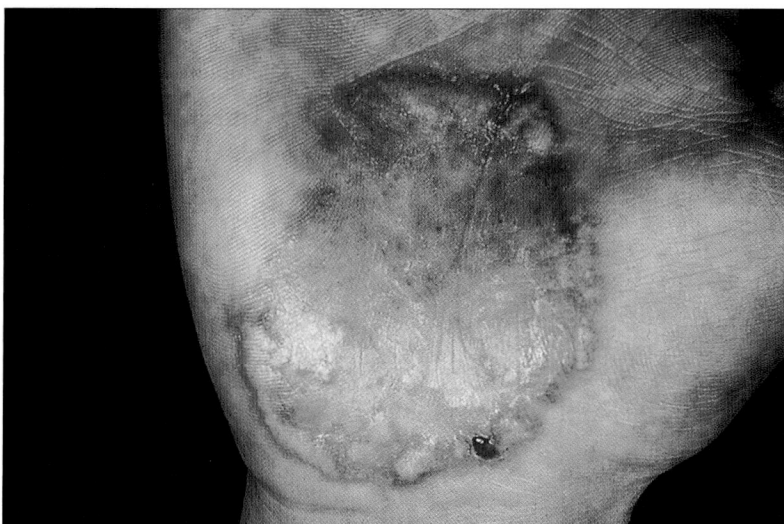

Fig. 17.274
Tinea corporis: this palmar lesion shows an erythematous border, scale and central clearing. By courtesy of the Institute of Dermatology, London, UK.

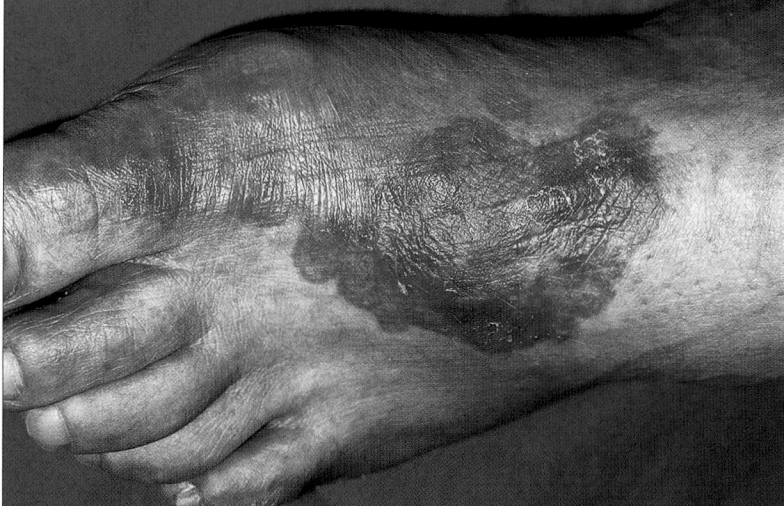

Fig. 17.275
Tinea corporis: steroid therapy may improve the clinical features with resultant masking of the true nature of the eruption (tinea incognito). By courtesy of R.A. Marsden, MD, St George's Hospital, London, UK.

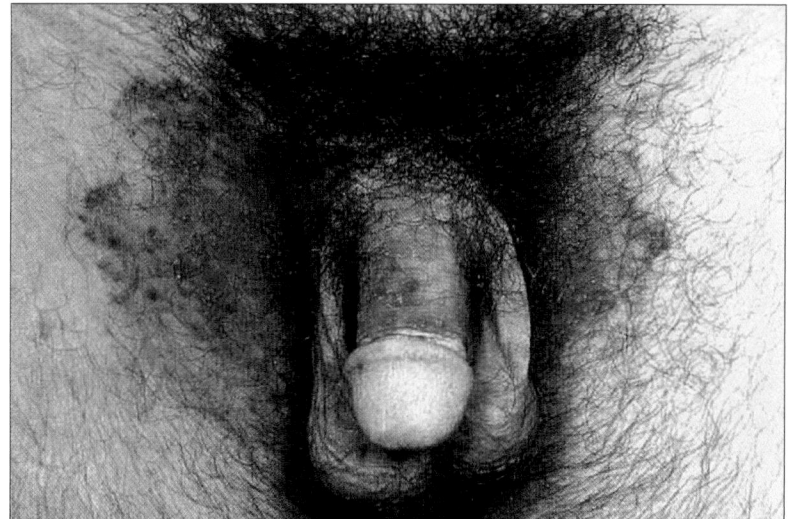

Fig. 17.277
Tinea cruris: this is much more common in males than in females. In this example pustulation is evident. By courtesy of R.A. Marsden, MD, St George's Hospital, London, UK.

Histological features

The warm humid conditions of the groin and the feet predipose to superficial fungal infections. On the feet the organisms are usually *Trichophyton rubrum*, *Trichophyton interdigitale* and *Epidermophyton floccosum*, in order of frequency. In the groin the same organisms are involved, but in reverse order of frequency. Candidal and secondary bacterial infections are often seen. The histology is similar to that of tinea at other sites (*Figs 17.278–17.280*).

References

1.　Hirschmann, J.V., Raugi, G.J. (2000) Pustular tinea pedis. *J Am Acad Dermatol*, **42**, 132–133.
2.　Pielop, J., Rosen, T. (2001) Penile dermatophytosis. *J Am Acad Dermatol*, **44**, 864–867.
3.　Baudraz-Rosselet, F., Ruffieux, P., Mancarella, A. et al (1993) Diaper dermatitis due to Tinea verrucosum. *Pediatr Dermatol*, **10**, 368–369.

Nodular granulomatous perifolliculitis

Clinical features

Nodular granulomatous perifolliculitis (Majocchi's granuloma) represents an uncommon intradermal infection by dermatophytes that are more usually associated with follicular lesions. As a consequence of injury to a hair follicle, fungi (often with keratinous debris) are released into the surrounding tissues where they produce an intense inflammatory response.[1] Clinically, lesions may present as granulomata, cellulitis or plaques (*Fig. 17.281*).[1] In some instances patients may have an associated immunodeficiency state (particularly due to corticosteroid therapy) that predominantly affects delayed hypersensitivity reactions, and may occur following renal transplantation.[1–3]

Histological features

Trichophyton rubrum is the dermatophyte usually involved, but *T. mentagrophytes*, *T. epilans*, *T. tonsurans*, *T. violaceum*, *Microsporum*

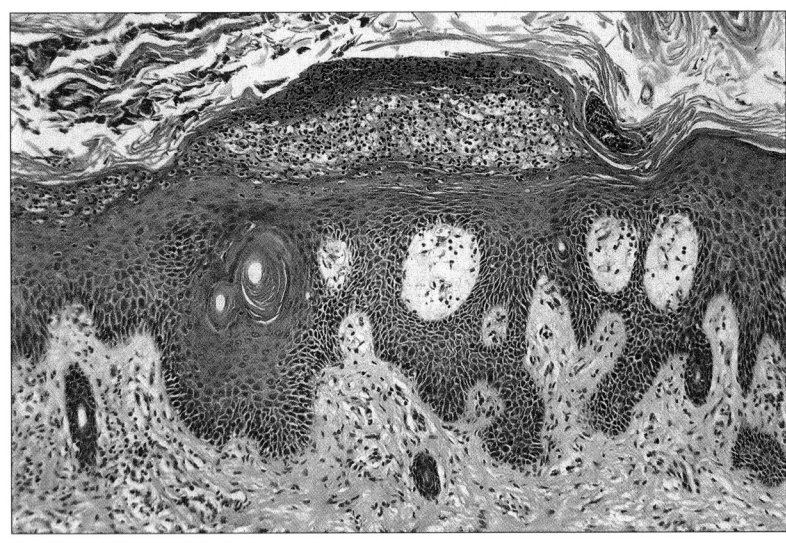

Fig. 17.278
Dermatophyte infection: there is parakeratosis overlying a subcorneal pustule. The epidermis shows psoriasiform hyperplasia.

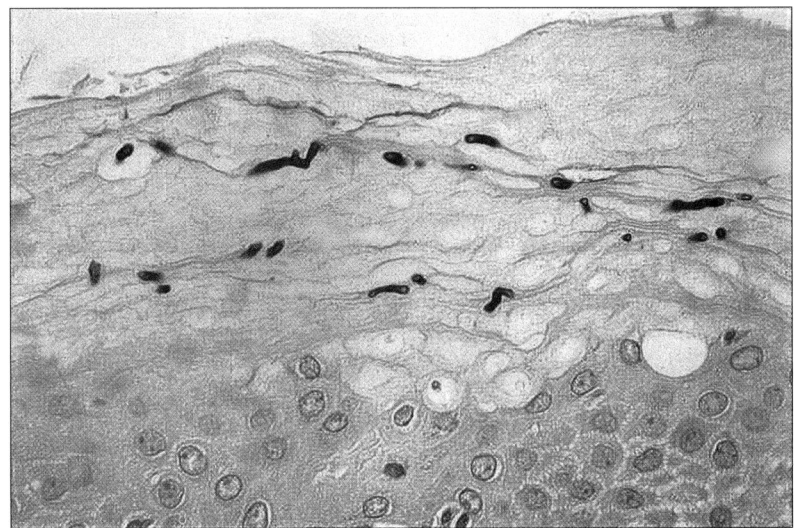

Fig. 17.280
Tinea pedis: periodic acid–Schiff stain of the same region shown in *Fig. 17.279*.

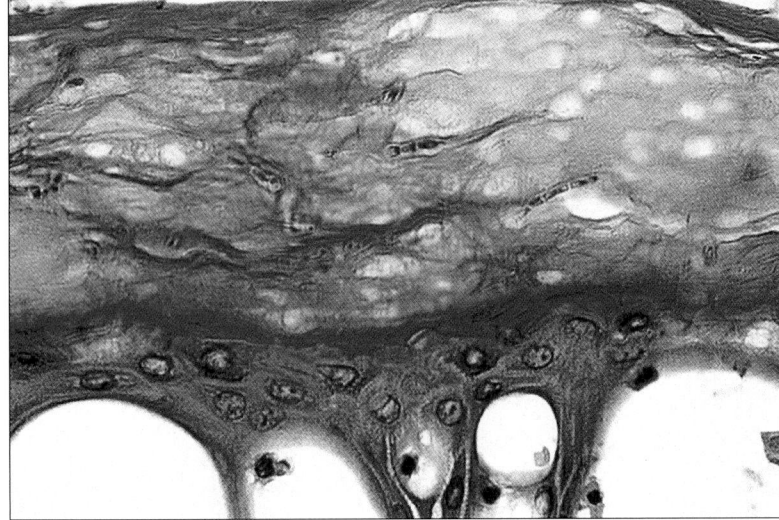

Fig. 17.279
Tinea pedis: fungi are visible in the thick stratum corneum.

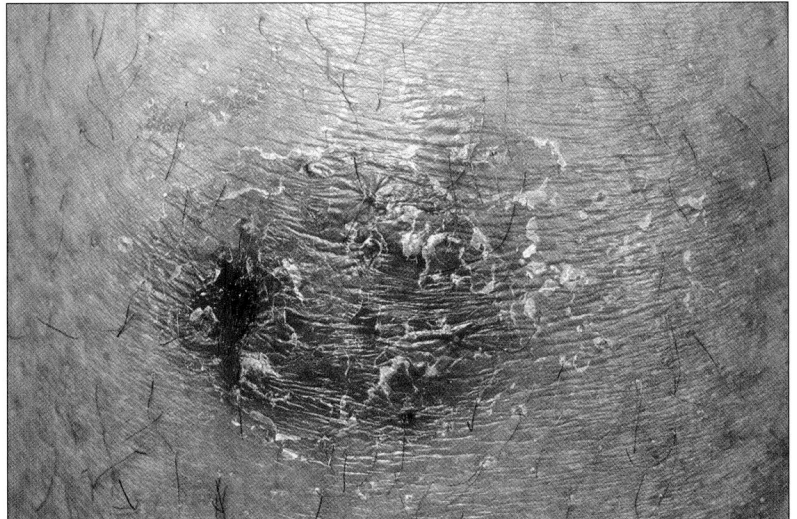

Fig. 17.281
Majocchi's granuloma: there is a crusted granulomatous infiltrated plaque with pustules. By courtesy of the Institute of Dermatology, London, UK.

audouinii, *M. gypseum*, *M. ferrugineum* and *M. canis* have also been incriminated.[1,4,5]

Hyphae and arthrospores are present in the dermis, often showing budding sporulation, intercellular septation, and abnormal and sometimes bizarre forms (*Figs 17.282–17.285*).[1] Granuloma formation as mycetoma may be a feature and the Splendore–Hoeppli phenomenon has been described.[1] There is usually a heavy acute on chronic inflammatory cell infiltrate, often with granulomatous features.

References

1. Smith, K.J., Neafie, R.C., Skelton, H.G. et al (1991) Majocchi's granuloma. *J Cutan Pathol*, **18**, 28–35.
2. Novick, N.L., Tapis, L., Bottone, E.J. (1987) Invasive Trichophyton rubrum infection in an immunocompromised host. *Am J Med*, **82**, 321–325.
3. Tse, K.C., Yeung, C.K., Tang, S. et al (2001) Majocchi's granuloma and posttransplant lymphoproliferative disease in a renal transplant recipient. *Am J Kidney Dis*, **38**, E38.
4. Barston, W.J. (1985) Granuloma and pseudogranuloma of the skin due to Microsporum canis. *Arch Dermatol*, **121**, 895–897.
5. Ravaghi, M. (1976) Superficial and deep granulomatous lesions caused by Trichophyton violaceum. *Cutis*, **17**, 976–977.

Tinea versicolor

Clinical features

Tinea versicolor (pityriasis versicolor), which represents a superficial fungal infection, is a common condition. It has a worldwide distribution but is more common in tropical climates and occurs with a greater frequency in summer months in temperate zones. It presents most often in young adults (20–40 years of age) and there is a slight predilection for females (2:1).[1–3] A papulopustular form may occur in infants.

The condition presents as chronic multiple irregular areas of hypo- or hyperpigmentation usually on the seborrheic areas of the body.[4] Lesions, which are circular and macular, may become confluent. The surface is covered by a fine scale, which may be rendered more prominent by scratching with a fingernail. The color varies from pink to yellow,

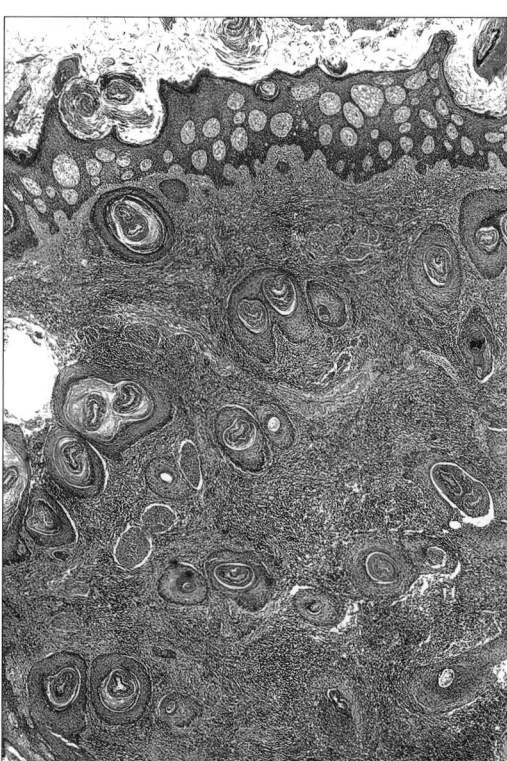
Fig. 17.282
Majocchi's granuloma: this scalp biopsy shows intense dermal inflammation with involvement of numerous hair follicles.

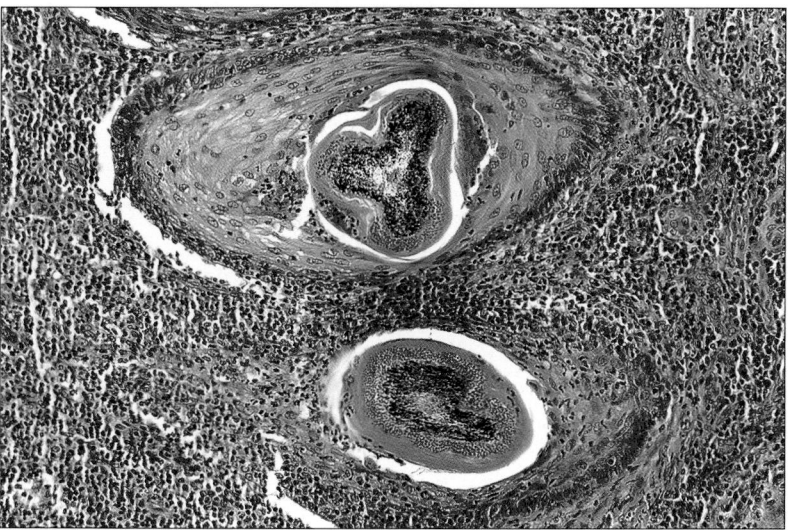
Fig. 17.283
Majocchi's granuloma: the follicles are acutely inflamed and fungi are clearly visible surrounding the shafts.

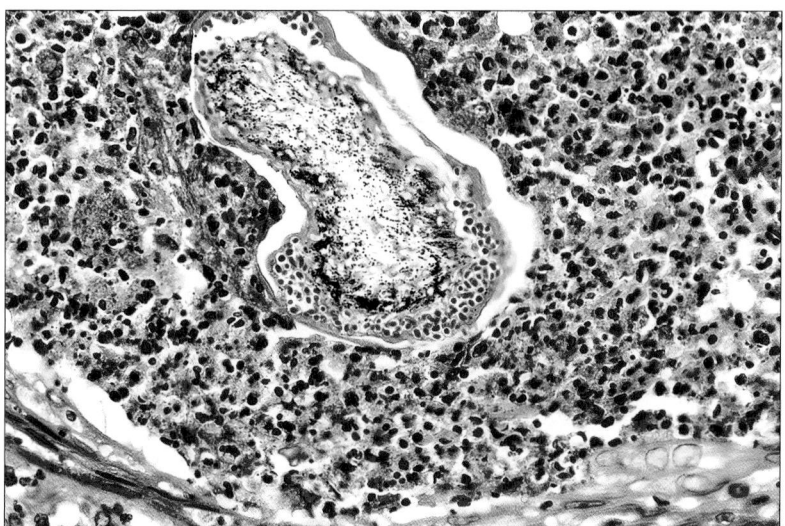
Fig. 17.284
Majocchi's granuloma: close-up view of a free hair shaft with fungi within a dermal abscess.

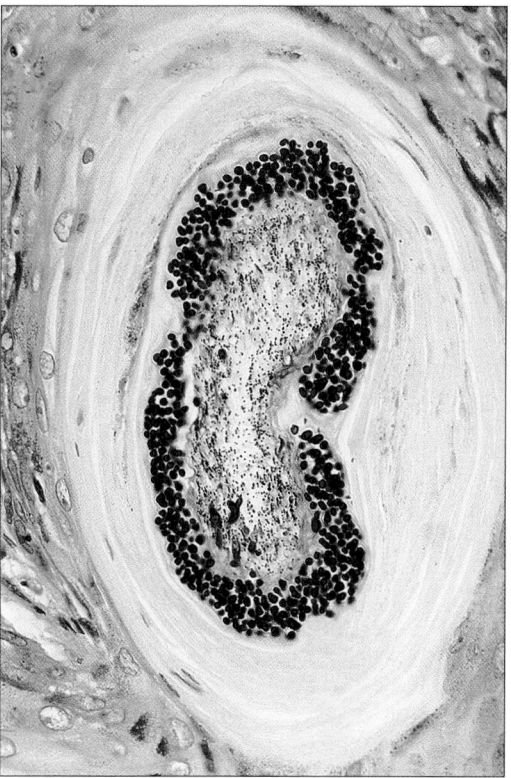
Fig. 17.285
Majocchi's granuloma: the periodic acid–Schiff stain is strikingly positive.

yellow–brown or even dark brown in dark-skinned patients (*Fig. 17.286*). In the fair-skinned, they appear hyperpigmented (brown on white) (*Fig. 17.287*).

The yeast has a 'stunning' effect on melanocytes and eventually produces hypopigmentation of affected skin. Hence in a dark-skinned patient or a fair-skinned individual who has acquired a suntan the lesions look pale relative to normal skin (white or brown). Yellow or yellow–blue fluorescence under a Wood's lamp is characteristic.[1] An erythrasmoid variant characterized by exclusive involvement of the inguinal folds has been described.[5]

Pathogenesis and histological features

Conditions predisposing to the development of tinea versicolor are numerous and include greasy skin, excessive steroids, hyperhidrosis, immunosuppresion (including AIDS), diabetes mellitus, pregnancy and the oral contraceptive.[1]

The lesions are caused by the mycelial phase of the lipophilic yeast *Malassezia globosa* (formerly *Malassezia furfur*, *Pityrosporon orbiculare* or *Pityrosporum ovale*), a very common commensal of hair follicles, where it is seen as basophilic round bodies among the keratin.[4,6–8] It is normally present in the majority of adults and is most commonly found on the chest, upper back and scalp.[2,9]

In lesions of tinea versicolor the mycelial or hyphal forms are seen among the interfollicular keratin.[1] They may be identified more readily by using a PAS reaction or methenamine silver stain.

Histological changes are mild, consisting of mild acanthosis and hyperkeratosis, with focal parakeratosis (*Fig. 17.288*). Occasional degenerate keratinocytes may be evident.[6] The stratum corneum contains round budding yeasts and short septate hyphae, imparting the 'spaghetti and meatballs' appearance. A hypopigmented basal layer is seen in biopsies of pale lesions; in hyperpigmented lesions there is hyperkeratosis, the basal pigmentation is increased, and there is pigmentary incontinence with pigment-laden macrophages in the upper dermis. Greater numbers of spores and hyphae are present in hyperpigmented lesions.[4]

The mechanism for the changes in pigmentation is not clear, although suggestions have included racial factors, light exposure, the inflammatory response, the fungal load, the thickness of the keratin layer and a direct effect of the fungus (dicarboxylic acids) on melanocytes.[4,10–14] Dopa cell counts have been shown to be normal.[4] In hypopigmented lesions there appear to be reduced numbers of smaller melanosomes in both the melanocytes and their neighboring keratinocytes.[4] Mito-

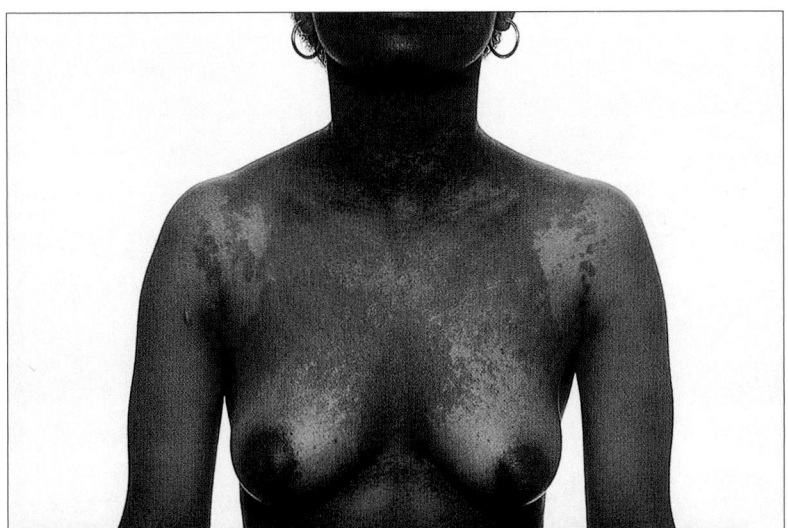

Fig. 17.286
Tinea versicolor: hyperpigmented macules, many of which have coalesced, are present on the chest, which is a commonly affected site. By courtesy of M.M. Black, MD, Institute of Dermatology, London, UK.

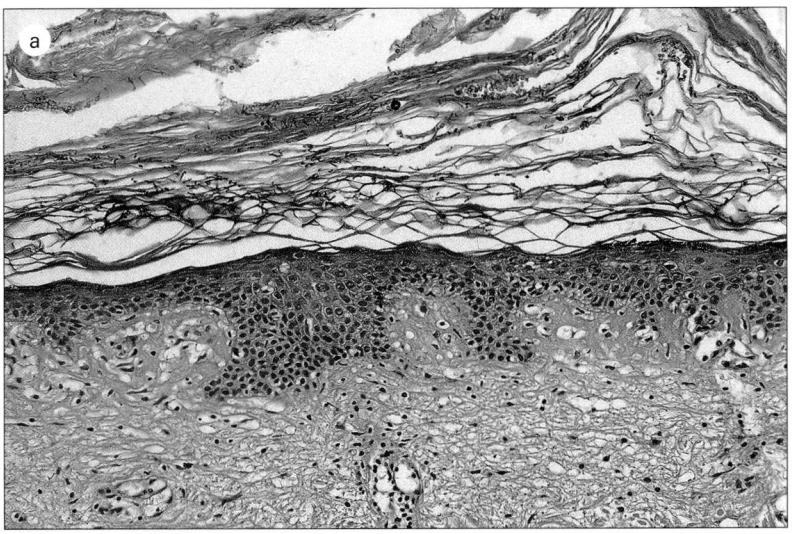

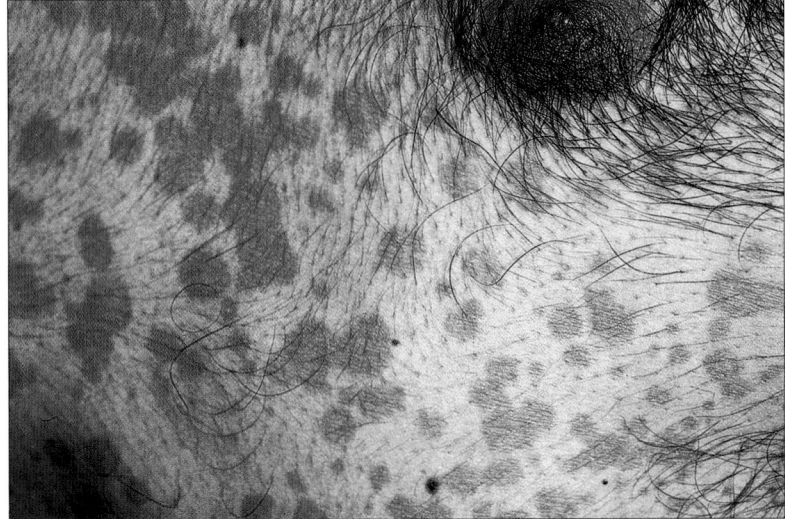

Fig. 17.287
Tinea versicolor: pale brown macules are typically seen in whites. By courtesy of R.A. Marsden, MD, St George's Hospital, London, UK.

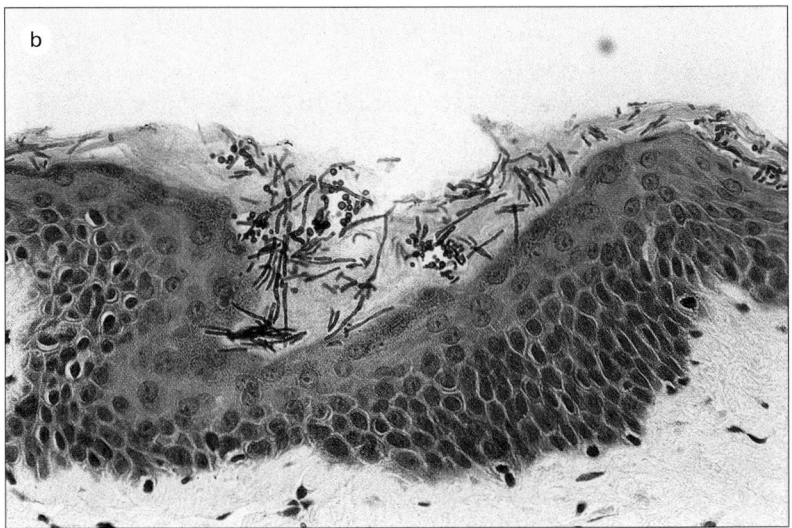

Fig. 17.288
Tinea versicolor: (a) there is hyperkeratosis and small basophilic spores are easily seen; (b) the periodic acid–Schiff reaction reveals numerous hyphae.

chondrial and cytoplasmic vacuolation has also been documented. In the superficial dermis, a slight perivascular chronic inflammatory cell infiltrate consisting of lymphocytes, histiocytes and occasional plasma cells may be evident.

There is also evidence to suggest that infection with the fungus rarely presents as systemic illness and that it is of importance in the pathogenesis of some cases of chronic folliculitis (pityrosporum folliculitis, see below) and seborrheic dermatitis.[2,7–9,15,16]

References

1. Borelli, D., Jacobs, P.H., Nall, L. (1991) Tinea versicolor: epidemiologic, clinical and therapeutic aspects. *J Am Acad Dermatol*, **25**, 300–305.
2. Faergemann, J. (1989) Epidemiology and ecology of pityriasis versicolor. *Curr Top Med Mycol*, **3**, 153–167.
3. Assaf, R.R., Weil, M.L. (1996) The superficial mycoses. *Dermatol Clin*, **14**, 57–67.
4. Galadari, I., El Komy, M., Mousa, A. et al (1992) Tinea versicolor: histologic and ultrastructural investigation of pigmentary changes. *Int J Dermatol*, **31**, 253–256.

5. Gorani, A., Oriani, A., Falconi Klein, E. et al (2001) Case report. Erythrasmoid pityriasis versicolor (Letter). *Mycoses*, **44**, 516–517.
6. Dorn, M., Roehnert, K. (1977) Dimorphism of Pityrosporon orbiculare in a defined culture medium. *J Invest Dermatol*, **69**, 244–248.
7. Crespo Erchiga, V., Ojeda Martos, A., Vera Casano, A. et al (2000) Malassezia globosa as the causative agent of pityriasis versicolor. *Br J Dermatol*, **143**, 799–803.
8. Crespo Erchiga, V., Delgado Florencio, V. (2002) Malassezia species in skin diseases. *Curr Opin Infect Dis*, **15**, 133–142.
9. Schmidt, A. (1997) Malassezia furfur: a fungus belonging to the physiological skin flora and its relevance to skin disorders. *Cutis*, **59**, 21–24.
10. Allen, H.B., Charles, C.R., Johnson, B.L. (1976) Hyperpigmented tinea versicolor. *Arch Dermatol*, **112**, 1110–1112.
11. Dotz, W.I., Hendrikson, D.M., Yu, G.S. et al (1985) Tinea versicolor: a light and electron microscopic study of hyperpigmented skin. *J Am Acad Dermatol*, **12**, 37–40.
12. Karaoui, R., Bou-Resli, M., Al-Zaid, N.S. et al (1981) Ultrastructural studies of hypopigmented skin. *Dermatologica*, **162**, 69–73.
13. El-Gothamy, Z. (1975) Tinea versicolor hypopigmentation, histochemical and therapeutic studies. *Int J Dermatol*, **14**, 510–517.
14. Hattori, M., Ogawa, H., Takamori, K. et al (1984) De (hypo) pigmentation mechanism of affected area of pityriasis versicolor. *J Dermatol*, **11**, 63–66.
15. Redline, R.W., Dahms, B.B. (1981) Malassezia pulmonary vasculitis in an infant on long-term intralipid therapy. *N Engl J Med*, **305**, 1395.
16. Faergemann, J. (1997) Pityrosporum yeasts – what's new? *Mycoses*, **40** (Suppl. 1), 29–32.

Pityrosporum folliculitis

Clinical features

Pityrosporum folliculitis is a form of chronic folliculitis attributed to infection by the yeast phase of *Malassezia globosa* (formerly *Malassezia furfur* or *Pityrosporum ovale*).[1,2] The condition occurs in adults, who present with pruritic pustules centered mainly on the trunk, neck and upper arms (*Fig. 17.289*).[2]

Pathogenesis and histological features

Follicular occlusion may be the pathogenetic event.[3]

Histopathological examination shows distension of occluded hair follicle infundibula by basophilic keratinous debris containing clusters of round budding yeast cells (*Fig. 17.290*).[2] Mycelial forms are characteristically absent. A mild perifollicular mononuclear inflammatory cell infiltrate is usually observed. Intradermal rupture of dilated follicles may incite an intense folliculocentric suppurative inflammatory infiltrate and perifollicular foreign body giant cell reaction. There may be intrafollicular mucin deposition.[4]

References

1. Crespo Erchiga, V., Delgado Florencio, V. (2002) Malassezia species in skin diseases. *Curr Opin Infect Dis*, **15**, 133–142.
2. Faergemann, J. (1997) Pityrosporum yeasts – what's new? *Mycoses*, **40** (Suppl. 1), 29–32.

3. Hill, M.K., Goodfield, M.J.D., Rodgers, F.G. et al (1990) Skin surface electron microscopy in Pityrosporum folliculitis. *Arch Dermatol*, **126**, 181–184.
4. Sina, B., Kauffman, L., Samorodin, C.S. (1995) Intrafollicular mucin posits in Pityrosporum folliculitis. *J Am Acad Dermatol*, **32**, 807–809.

Tinea nigra

Clinical features

Tinea nigra is an uncommon superficial mycosis caused by *Exophiala werneckii* or *Exophiala mansoni*. It occurs mainly in the tropics and presents as a slowly growing, irregular, brown, black or dark green slightly scaly asymptomatic patch.[1–3] The disease involves mainly the palms followed by the soles and is exceptional at other sites. Bilateral involvement may be seen. Clinical confusion with a melanocytic lesion is possible.[4]

Histological features

The epidermis shows the presence of numerous short, segmented hyphae and spores in the superficial aspect of the stratum corneum. The organisms are easily recognized as they stain brown or yellow with hematoxylin and eosin.

References

1. Chadfield, H.W., Campbell, C.K. (1972) A case of tinea nigra in Britain. *Br J Dermatol*, **87**, 505–508.
2. Hughes, J.R., Moore, M.K., Pembroke, A.C. (1993) Tinea nigra palmaris. *Clin Exp Dermatol*, **18**, 481–482.
3. Reid, B.J. (1998) Exophiala werneckii causing tinea nigra in Scotland. *Br J Dermatol*, **139**, 157–158.
4. Babel, D.E., Pelachyk, J.M., Hurley, J.P. (1986) Tinea nigra masquerading as acral lentiginous melanoma. *J Dermatol Surg Oncol*, **12**, 502–504.

Candidiasis

Clinical features

Oral candidiasis appears in several forms:[1–4]

- In neonates it appears as a curd-like pseudomembrane overlying an erythematous base, which may be painful and atrophic.
- In adults, usually males, a chronic hyperplastic form is seen as a plaque with an erythematous margin (*Fig. 17.291*). This must be distinguished from leukoplakia. This hyperplastic plaque-like form also occurs in the chronic mucocutaneous forms of candidiasis and in immunodeficient individuals, including those with AIDS.[5–9]
- Chronic atrophic candidiasis is seen in the elderly, often as a sore red patch associated with dentures. It may be accompanied by angular cheilitis and sometimes extends onto the facial skin as an

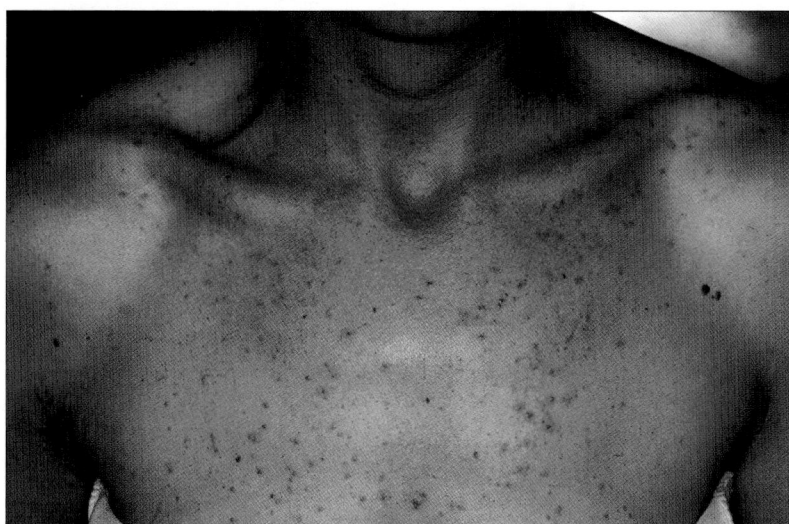

Fig. 17.289
Pityrosporum folliculitis: note the numerous follicular pustules. By courtesy of S. Glassman, MD, University of Witwatersrand, Johannesburg, South Africa.

erythematous granular lesion. Candidal cheilitis may affect the lips of patients with a heavy oral candidal infection (*Fig. 17.292*). Steroid therapy, whether local or systemic, appears to predispose to oral involvement.

Cutaneous candidiasis tends to be confined to skin folds in the obese and to the genital mucous membranes (*Fig. 17.293*). The lesions appear as moist erythematous areas with small pustules at the margins (*Fig. 17.294*).

Vulvovaginitis occurs mainly during pregnancy or as a complication of diabetes mellitus, oral contraceptives or antibiotic therapy.

Candidal balanitis is associated with vaginal infections in the sexual partner: transient papules develop on the glans, become white and pustular, and rupture; they may heal rapidly or persist with exacerbations (*Fig. 17.295*).

Chronic mucocutaneous candidiasis is a persistent and refractory condition, usually starting in the young and often associated with an immunodeficient state. These patients have oral candidiasis, which recurs after therapy and may become hypertrophic. They also have cutaneous candidiasis involving intertriginous areas and the face and hands or in a more widespread distribution. Paronychia and vulvovaginitis or balanitis also occur (*Fig. 17.296*). Chronic mucocutaneous candidiasis is also an important feature of AIDS.[7] Indeed oral candidiasis may represent an early marker of immunosuppression in patients with HIV infection.[8] *Candida* vaginitis is an important early manifestation in female AIDS patients.[7]

Some of these patients have a severe congenital primary defect of cellular immunity, such as hereditary thymic dysplasia or the DiGeorge syndrome, and in these the outlook is poor (*Fig. 17.297*). In other

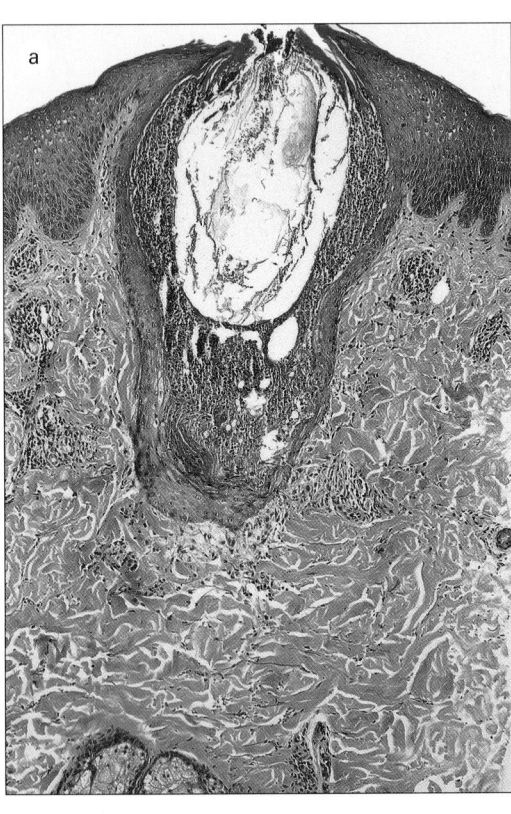
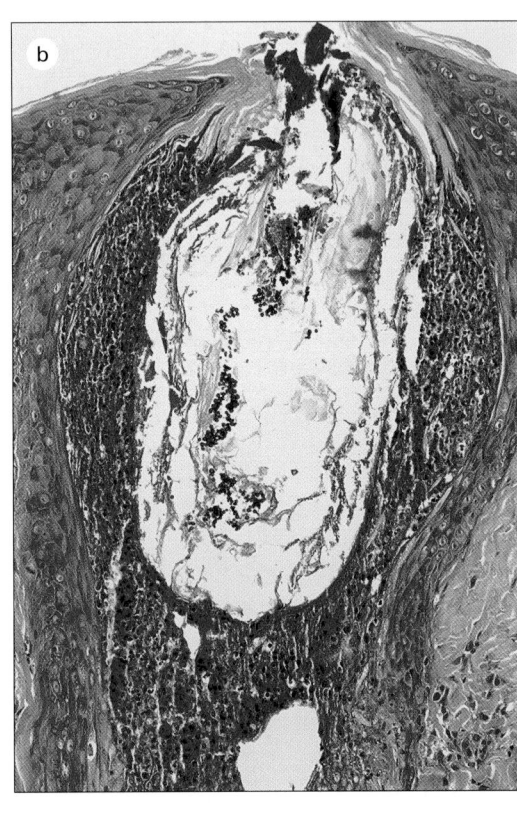

Fig. 17.290
Pityrosporum folliculitis: (a) there is infundibular dilatation with abscess formation; (b) yeast forms are conspicuous in the periodic acid–Schiff stained section.

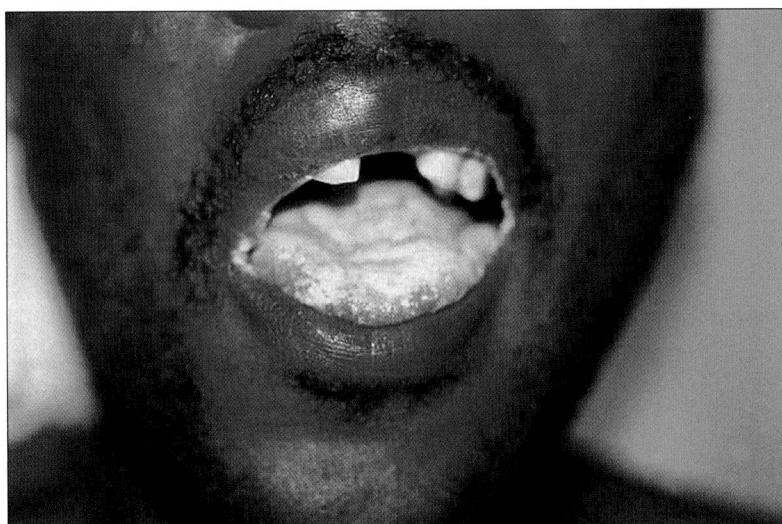

Fig. 17.291
Candida glossitis: the tongue is covered with a white plaque. There is also involvement of the angles of the mouth. By courtesy of N.C. Dlova, MD, Nelson R. Mandela School of Medicine, University of KwaZulu-Natal, South Africa.

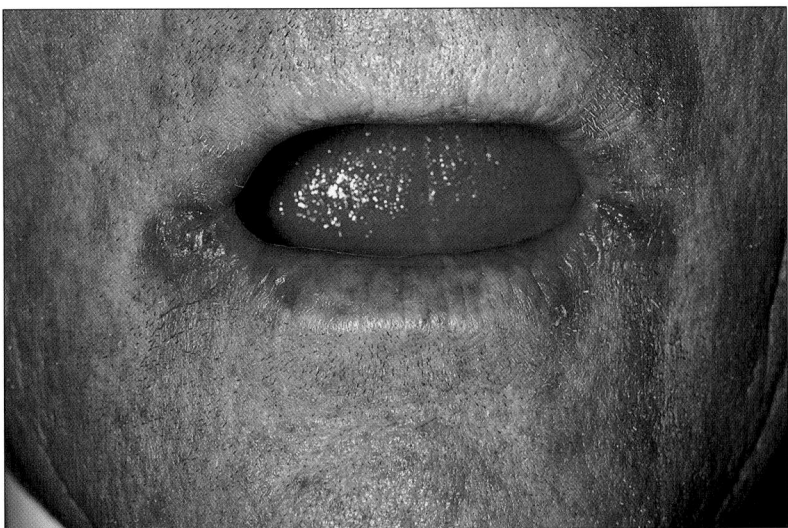

Fig. 17.292
Candidal angular cheilitis: note the erythematous crusted lesions at the angles of the mouth. By courtesy of M.M. Black, MD, Institute of Dermatology, London, UK.

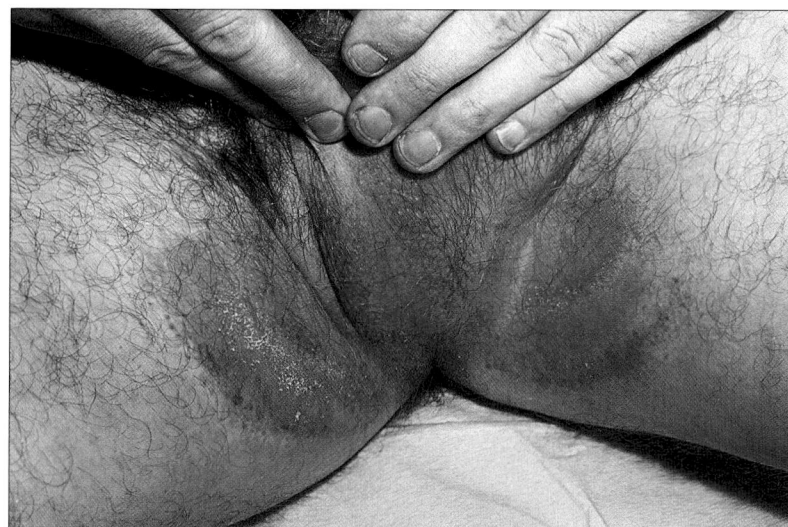

Fig. 17.293
Cutaneous candidiasis: the warm, moist environment of the upper thighs and scrotum predisposes to intertriginous candidiasis. Note the erythema and peripheral pustules. By courtesy of M.M. Black, MD, Institute of Dermatology, London, UK.

patients chronic mucocutaneous candidiasis is the dominant feature, but immune defects cannot be demonstrated. One subtype, which shows autosomal recessive inheritance, is associated with endocrinopathies involving the parathyroids, thyroid, adrenals and diabetes mellitus. The condition may also have a sporadic or autosomal dominant mode of inheritance.[10] A candidate linkage region on chromosome 2p was identified recently in a large family with an autosomal dominant form of this condition.[11] Other disorders that may coexist with chronic mucocutaneous candidiasis include dental enamel dysplasia, vitiligo and alopecia totalis.[12] Recent evidence has shown that patients with this condition may have altered patterns of cytokine production in response to infection by *Candida* organisms.[10]

In patients with AIDS and others who are immunosuppressed, disseminated candidiasis follows hematogenous spread from an underlying gastrointestinal or urinary tract primary focus of infection. Candidemia is associated with a very high mortality rate.[2] Cutaneous lesions include macules, papules, petechiae, hemorrhagic foci, nodules and an ecthyma gangrenosum-like presentation. These are painful, multiple and widely distributed over the body.[2,9] A rare congenital form of disseminated candidiasis has been described in very low birth weight

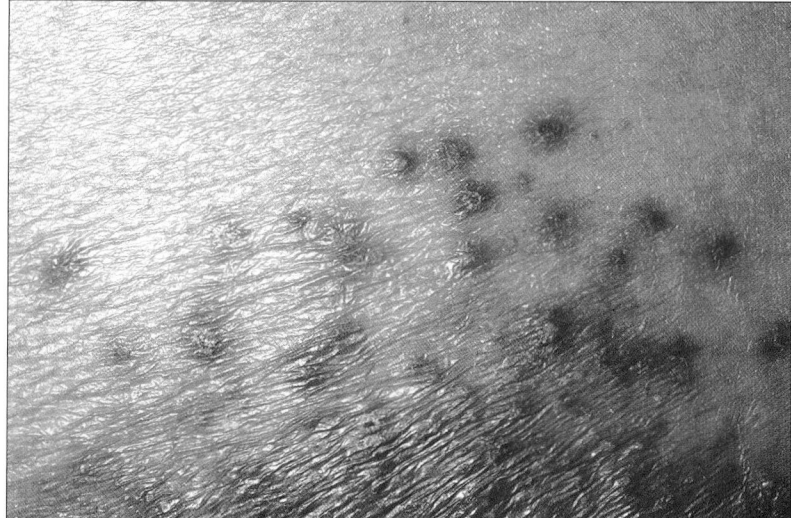

Fig. 17.294
Cutaneous candidiasis: intertriginous involvement may be characterized by the development of pustules as seen in this picture. By courtesy of R.A. Marsden, MD, St George's Hospital, London, UK.

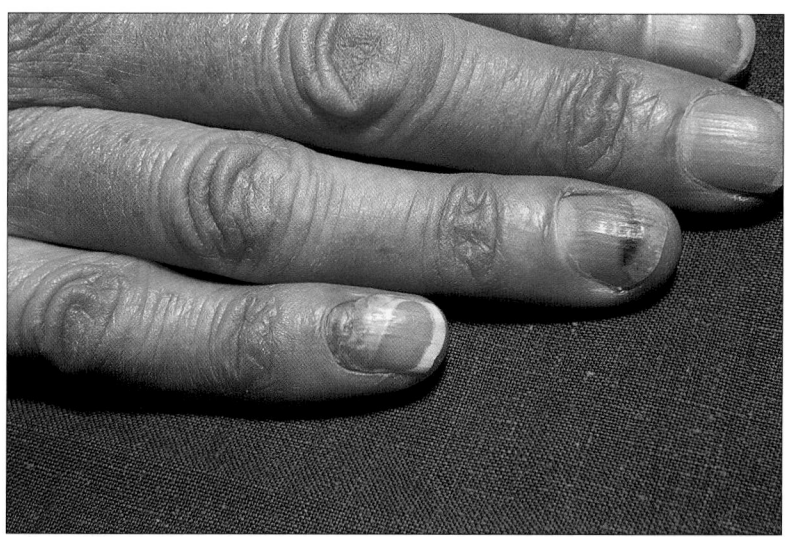

Fig. 17.296
Candida: there is proximal nail dystrophy and onycholysis with pigmentary changes. By courtesy of the Institute of Dermatology, London, UK.

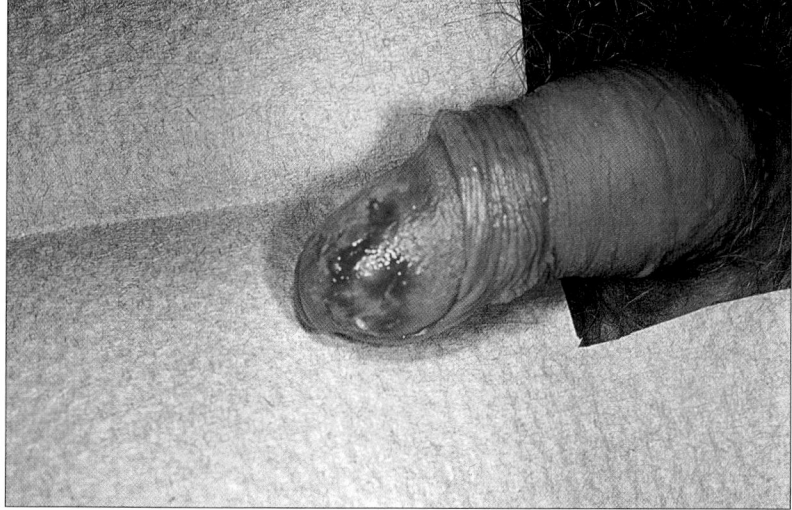

Fig. 17.295
Candidal balanitis: note the erythema with erosion and the small white pustule at the margin of the lesion. By courtesy of C. Furlonge, MD, Port of Spain, Trinidad.

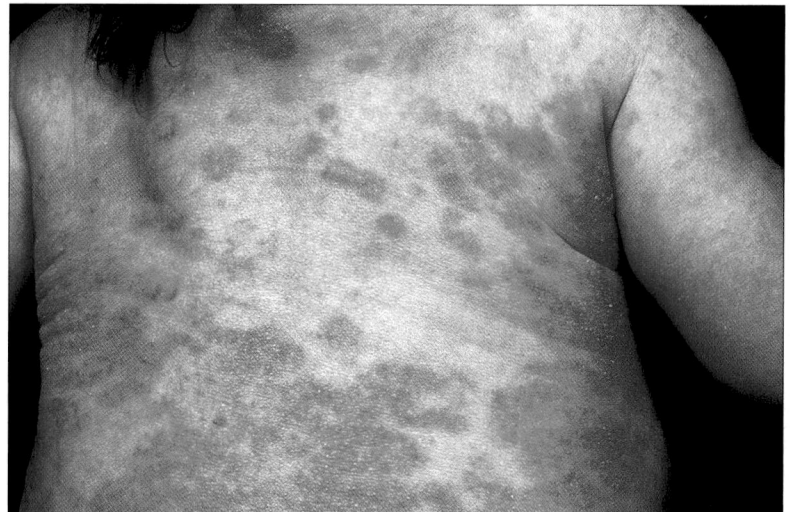

Fig. 17.297
Disseminated candidiasis: disseminated disease in infants may be a sign of immunosuppression such as DiGeorge syndrome. By courtesy of the Institute of Dermatology, London, UK.

infants.[13] Disseminated disease may also be seen in heroin addicts, patients with central venous catheters and those on broad spectrum antibiotics.

Pathogenesis and histological features

Candida is a yeast-like fungus with budding and hyphal forms. There are several species, but *Candida albicans* is by far the most common human pathogen. *Candida glabrata* infections have, however, become increasingly important in recent years, especially in immunosuppressed hosts.[14,15] *Candida dubliniensis* has recently been reported as a cause of oral candidiasis in HIV-infected patients.[16]

Candida albicans has a number of virulence factors that potentiate infection. These factors include adhesins (which facilitate adhesion to epithelial surfaces), aspartyl proteinases (which facilitate penetration of keratinized cells) and phospholipases.[17,18] In addition, the organism utilizes at least two signaling pathways that potentiate its conversion from a yeast form to a hyphal form; the latter is a prerequisite for deeper penetration into keratinized epithelium.[17,19]

Candidal lesions appear similar in varying sites. There is a prominent neutrophil infiltrate of the oral mucosa or epidermis and hyphae can be seen (*Fig. 17.298*). The yeast-like form is often seen in the mouth and does not necessarily indicate pathogenicity. There is often an intense chronic inflammatory infiltrate in the underlying connective tissue, and in chronic hypertrophic forms the epithelium is hyperplastic and hyperkeratotic.

The disseminated lesions are characterized by a fibrinous exudate with both yeast and pseudohyphae forms, sometimes accompanied by the features of a leukocytoclastic vasculitis. In this variant *Candida tropicalis* is of etiological importance.[6] Suppurative folliculitis and perifolliculitis are seen in heroin addicts.[20]

The closely related species *Torulopsis glabrata* differs from *Candida albicans* by the absence of pseudohyphae (*Fig. 17.299*).[21]

References

1. Neilson, H., Daugaard, K., Schiodt, M. (1985) Chronic mucocutaneous candidiasis: a review. *Tandlaegebladet*, **89**, 667–673.
2. Meyer, R.D. (1986) Cutaneous and mucosal manifestations of the deep mycotic infections. *Acta Derm Venereol*, **121** (Suppl.), 57–72.
3. Edwards, J.E. Jr, Lehrer, R.I., Stiehm, E.R. et al (1978) Severe candidal infections – clinical perspective, immune defense mechanisms and current concepts of therapy. *Ann Intern Med*, **89**, 91–106.
4. Reichart, P.A., Samaranayake, L.P., Philipsen, H.P. (2000) Pathology and clinical correlates in oral candidiasis and its variants: a review. *Oral Dis*, **6**, 85–91.
5. Gottlieb, M.S., Groopman, J.E., Weinstein, W.M. et al (1983) The acquired immunodeficiency syndrome. *Ann Intern Med*, **99**, 218–220.
6. Wingard, J.R., Merz, W.G., Saral, R. (1979) Candida tropicalis: a major pathogen in immunocompromised patients. *Ann Intern Med*, **91**, 539–543.
7. Stein, D.K., Sugar, A.M. (1989) Fungal infections in imunocompromised hosts. *Diagn Microbiol Infect Dis*, **12** (Suppl. 4), 221–228.
8. Klein, R.S., Harris, C.A., Small, C.B. et al (1984) Oral candidiasis in high risk patients as the initial manifestation of the acquired immunodeficiency syndrome. *N Engl J Med*, **311**, 354–358.
9. Bodey, G.P., Luna, A.M. (1974) Skin lesions associated with disseminated candidiasis. *JAMA*, **229**, 1466–1468.
10. Lilic, D. (2002) New perspectives on the immunology of chronic mucocutaneous candidiasis. *Curr Opin Infect Dis*, **15**, 143–147.
11. Atkinson, T.P., Schaffer, A.A., Grimbacher, B. et al (1984) An immune defect causing dominant chronic mucocutaneous candidiasis and thyroid disease maps to chromosome 2p in a single family. *Am J Hum Genet*, **69**, 791–803.
12. Kirkpatrick, C.H. (1994) Chronic mucocutaneous candidiasis. *J Am Acad Dermatol*, **31**, S14–S17.
13. Pradeepkumar, V.K., Rajadurai, V.S., Tan, K.W. (1998) Congenital candidiasis: varied presentations. *J Perinatol*, **18**, 311–316.
14. Fidel, P.L. Jr, Vazquez, J.A., Sobel, J.D. (1999) Candida glabrata: review of epidemiology, pathogenesis, and clinical disease with comparison to C. albicans. *Clin Microbiol Rev*, **12**, 80–96.
15. Sobel, J.D. (1998) Vulvovaginitis due to Candida glabrata. An emerging problem. *Mycoses*, **41** (Suppl. 2), 18–22.
16. Schorling, S.R., Kortinga, H.C., Froschb, M. et al (2000) The role of Candida dubliniensis in oral candidiasis in human immunodeficiency virus-infected individuals. *Crit Rev Microbiol*, **26**, 59–68.
17. Odds, F.C. (1994) Pathogenesis of infections. *J Am Acad Dermatol*, **31** (3 Pt 2), S2–S5.
18. Calderone, R.A. (2001) Virulence factors of Candida albicans. *Trends Microbiol*, **9**, 327–335.
19. Calderone, R.A., Suzuki, S., Cannon, R. et al (2000) Candida albicans: adherence, signaling and virulence. *Med Mycol*, **38** (Suppl. 1), 125–137.
20. Podzamczer, D., Ribera, M., Gudiol, F. (1987) Skin abscesses caused by Candida albicans in heroin addicts. *J Am Acad Dermatol*, **16**, 386–387.
21. Chandler, F.W., Ajello, L. (1997) Torulopsis. In: Connor, D.H., Chandler, F.W., Schwartz, D.A. et al (eds) Pathology of infectious diseases. Stamford: Appleton and Lange, pp 1105–1107.

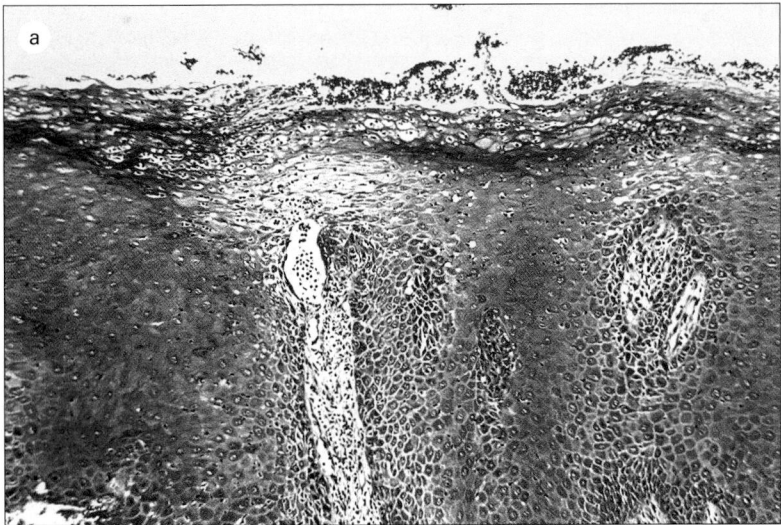

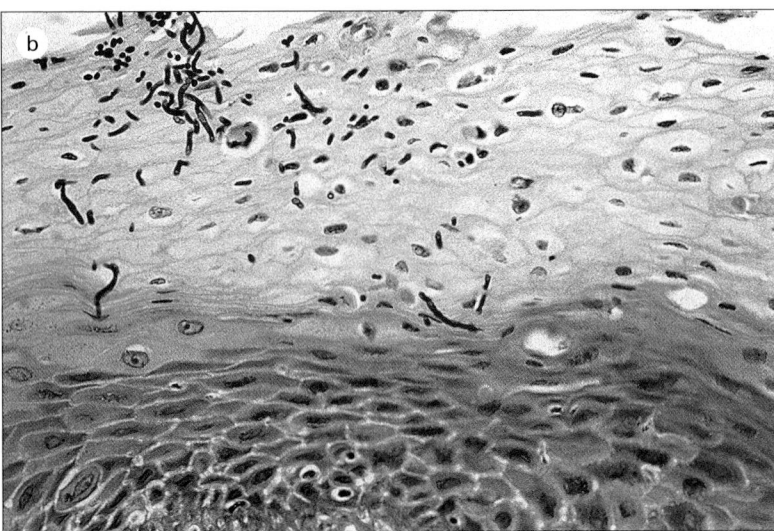

Fig. 17.298
Cutaneous candidiasis: (**a**) there is marked acanthosis and the superficial layers of the epithelium are infiltrated by large numbers of neutrophils; (**b**) there are abundant yeast-like and pseudohyphal forms (periodic acid–Schiff).

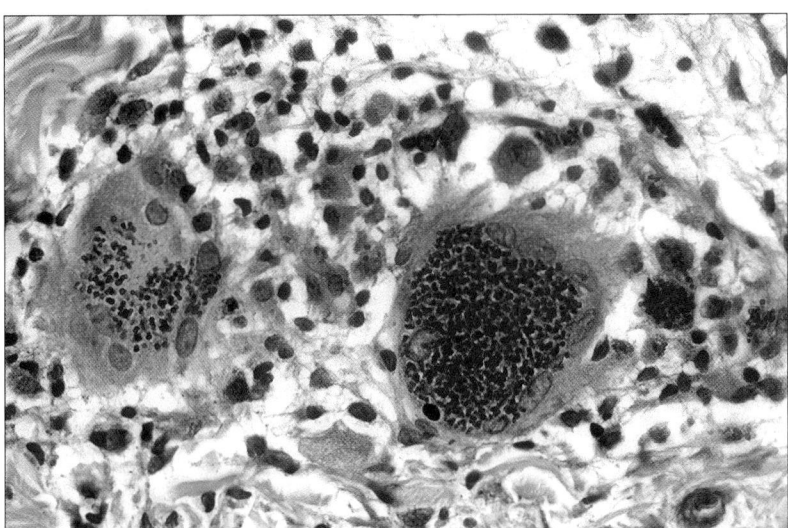

Fig. 17.299
Torulopsis: this yeast form is most probably a variant of *Candida*. An intracytoplasmic location is an uncommon manifestation.

Aspergillosis, Fusarium and Pseudallescheria

Clinical features

Aspergillosis

Species of *Aspergillus* occur worldwide and can cause cutaneous lesions, either by hematogenous spread from a primary infection in an immunosuppressed patient, usually in the lung, or by direct inoculation of the skin.[1-3] Patients with neutropenia are particularly at risk of systemic spread, especially those with hematological malignancies.[3-6] Patients may develop widespread pulmonary infiltrates or infarction, which is soon followed by disseminated vaso-occlusive disease.[7] Systemic lesions are most commonly seen in the gastrointestinal tract, the central nervous system, the liver, kidney, heart and thyroid.[6] Destructive lesions of the palate and nasal septum may occur.[8] In hematogenous spread the lesions develop as small red discrete macules and papules, which may become pustular or necrotic/infarcted (*Fig. 17.300*). Plaques studded with pustules may be seen. Noduloulcerative lesions with central eschar formation and raised borders are sometimes encountered.[8]

Primary aspergillosis of the skin, which usually follows local trauma (e.g. intravenous injection therapy site, cutaneous maceration or burns), appears as a purplish thickened edematous area at the site of inoculation.[9-13] In the immunosuppressed these lesions may ulcerate and develop a black crust (*Fig. 17.301*).[9] Occasional immunosuppressed patients with primary cutaneous aspergillosis have presented with solitary non-ulcerated nodules.[14,15] Skin involvement in disseminated aspergillosis is uncommon, however, being present in only about 4–5% of patients.[4,16]

All lesions of aspergillosis are commoner in the immunosuppressed and the outcome follows the progress of the immune status. In general, however, the infection is often rapidly fatal due to visceral involvement.[9] Patients receiving corticosteroid therapy appear to be particularly susceptible to the development of cutaneous aspergillosis.[3,9]

Fusarium

Fusarium species (plant molds) are of increasing importance, particularly in immunosuppressed patients.[17-21] Patients can present with localized skin or soft tissue lesions, nail involvement, sinus infection or with disseminated disease.[17] Risk factors for localized disease include trauma, burns and foreign bodies.[21] Systemic involvement occurs particularly in hematological malignancy and neutropenia, graft-versus-host disease and corticosteroid therapy.[17,20,21]

Pseudallescheria

Pseudallescheria boydii is also an important cause of infection in the immunosuppressed, especially following solid organ transplantation.[22-25] Patients may also develop localized disease in the skin and subcutaneous fat including mycetoma.[25] Clinical features in a large series of patients following organ transplantation included disseminated disease, skin lesions, lung disease, endophthalmitis, meningitis, brain abscess, mycotic aneurysm and sinusitis.[24] A sporotrichoid presentation has been described.[22]

Pathogenesis and histological features

Aspergilli are found in soil and organic debris so that pulmonary lesions are found in farmers and gardeners (*Fig. 17.302*). It can contaminate grain and affect birds. It is often present in public buildings, including hospitals, due to contamination of air vents and central heating plants by bird droppings. Despite the wide distribution of the fungus, infection usually requires previous immunosuppression, such as in patients receiving corticosteroids or who have lymphoma or leukemia. The host response to the mycelial component of the infection is the neutrophil, whereas the conidia forms are phagocytosed and killed by macrophages. Both lines of cellular response need to be deficient for the infection to become progressive. The production of fungal toxins also assists the establishment of infection.

In the skin the lesions appear as abscesses in the dermis, with central necrosis and pus and surrounded by granulomata. Eosinophils are sometimes numerous.[8] The epidermis may occasionally exhibit pseudo-

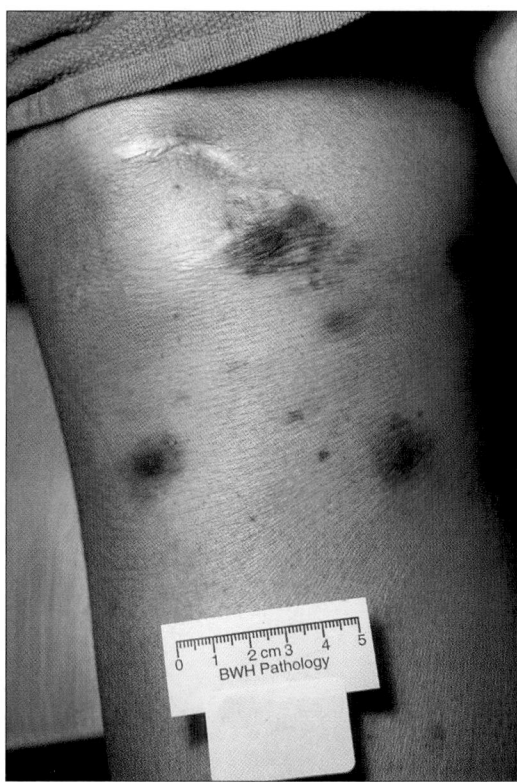

Fig. 17.300
Aspergillosis: this immunosuppressed patient developed multiple purple nodules on the limbs secondary to esophageal candidiasis. By courtesy of A.F. Nascimento, MD, Brigham and Women's Hospital and Harvard Medical School, Boston, USA.

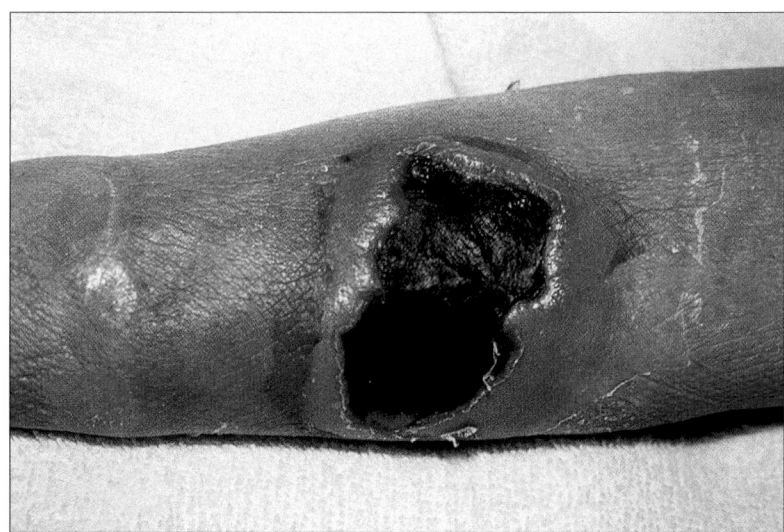

Fig. 17.301
Aspergillosis: there is extensive ulceration with characteristic black crusting. Primary cutaneous aspergillosis most often follows trauma or it may develop in the immunosuppressed. By courtesy of N. Khardori, MD, University of South Illinois, USA.

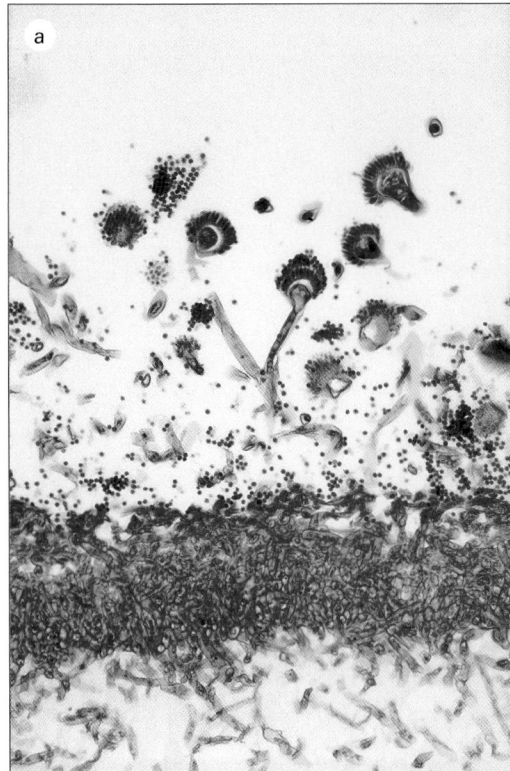

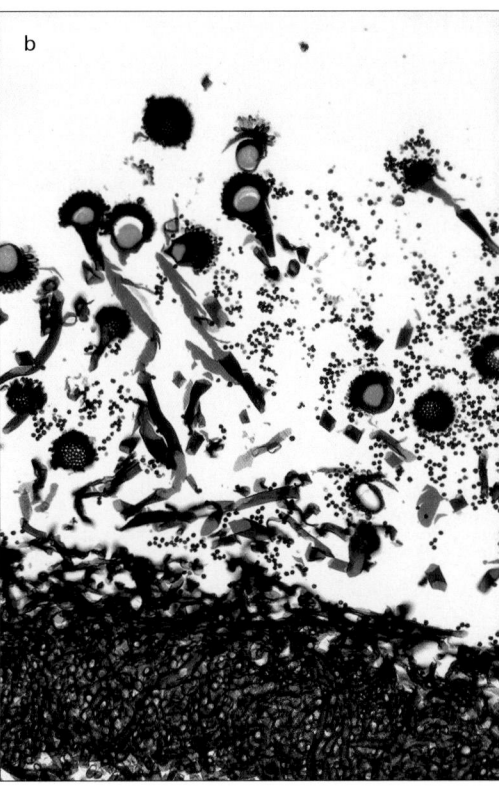

Fig. 17.302
(a, b) Aspergillosis: the fruiting head (aspergillum) as shown in these pictures is formed when the fungus is exposed to air. It is not usually seen in the tissues. **(a)** Periodic acid–Schiff; **(b)** methenamine silver. By courtesy of R. Margolis, MD, St Elizabeth's Medical Center, Boston, USA.

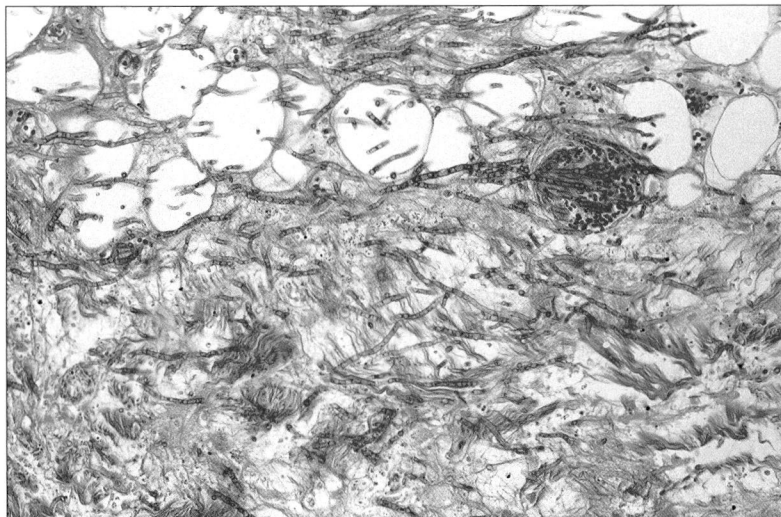

Fig. 17.303
Aspergillosis: this field comes from the patient shown in *Fig. 17.300.* Emanating from the cutaneous vessels are innumerable fungal hyphae.

epitheliomatous hyperplasia.[8,13] The fungal elements, most commonly of *Aspergillus fumigatus*, are found in the necrotic center of the lesion. *Aspergillus flavus*, *Aspergillus niger*, *Aspergillus glaucus* and *Aspergillus versicolor* may also be present.[3,13]

In cases of hematogenous spread, fungal hyphae may be identified within the lumen of thrombosed dermal blood vessels.[17] The fungus is recognized by its uniform septate branching and radiating hyphae (with an arboreal growth pattern), branches being equal in thickness (dichotomous) and at 45° (*Figs 17.303–17.305*). The hyphae are often not seen well with hematoxylin and eosin, but are well demonstrated by a silver stain, such as Gomori's. The fungus must be distinguished from other branching fungal infections, including *Fusarium*, *Pseudallescheria boydii* and zygomycetes. The last often stain well with hematoxylin and eosin and consist of twisted hyphae of variable thickness. Diagnosis usually requires culture of the organism, but the finding of a fruiting

head in tissue is confirmatory. Alternatively, a specific immunofluorescent antibody test can be used.

The most frequently encountered *Fusarium* species include *F. sonai*, *F. oxysporum* and *F. moniliforme.*[21] The histological features vary from granulomatous to suppurative.[27] In patients with disseminated disease, vascular involvement similar to aspergillosis is seen (*Figs 17.306, 17.307*). The fungi present as hyaline, branching septate hyphae measuring 3–8 μm in width.[27] In contrast to aspergilli, the hyphae branch irregularly, varying from acute-angled through to 90°.[27] The distinction, however, ultimately depends on the results of culture.

In immunosuppressed patients, *P. boydii* is most often encountered as a vascular lesion similar to aspergillosis. The hyphae are septate, branching, hyaline and measure 2–5 μm in width.[27] They are indistinguishable from *Aspergillus* species (*Figs 17.308, 17.309*).

References

1. Braude, A.I. (1981) The aspergilli. In: Braude, A.I. (ed.) Medical microbiology and infectious diseases. Philadelphia: Saunders, pp 669–674.
2. Rinaldi, M.G. (1983) Invasive aspergillosis. *Rev Infect Dis*, **5**, 1061–1077.
3. Galimberti, R., Kowalczuk, A., Hidalgo Parra, I. et al (1998) Cutaneous aspergillosis: a report of six cases. *Br J Dermatol*, **139**, 522–526.
4. D'Antonio, D., Pagano, L., Girmenia, C. et al (2000) Cutaneous aspergillosis in patients with hematological malignancies. *Eur J Clin Microbiol Infect Dis*, **19**, 362–365.
5. Nenoff, P., Kliem, C., Mittag, M. et al (2002) Secondary cutaneous aspergillosis due to Aspergillus flavus in an acute myeloid leukemia patient following stem cell transplantation. *Eur J Dermatol*, **12**, 93–98.
6. Stein, D.K., Sugar, A.M. (1989) Fungal infections in the immunocompromised host. *Diagn Microbiol Infect Dis*, **12** (Suppl.), 221–228.
7. Meyer, R.D. (1986) Cutaneous and mucosal manifestations of the deep mycotic infections. *Acta Derm Venereol*, **121** (Suppl.), 57–72.
8. Khatari, M.L., Stefanato, C.M., Benghazeil, M. et al (2000) Cutaneous and paranasal aspergillosis in an immunocompetent patient. *Int J Dermatol*, **39**, 853–856.
9. Khardori, N., Hayat, S., Rolston, K. et al (1989) Cutaneous rhizopus and aspergillus infections in five patients with cancer. *Arch Dermatol*, **125**, 952–956.
10. Roth, J.G., Troy, J.L., Esterly, N.B. (1991) Multiple cutaneous ulcers in the neonate. *Pediatr Dermatol*, **8**, 253–255.
11. Larkin, J.A., Greene, J.N., Sandin, R.L. et al (1996) Primary cutaneous aspergillosis: case report and review of the literature. *Infect Control Hosp Epidemiol*, **17**, 365–366.
12. Stanford, D., Boyle, M., Gillespie, R. (2000) Human immunodeficiency virus-related primary cutaneous aspergillosis. *Australas J Dermatol*, **41**, 112–116.
13. Goel, R., Wallace, M.L. (2001) Pseudoepitheliomatous hyperplasia secondary to cutaneous aspergillosis. *Am J Dermatopathol*, **23**, 224–226.
14. Richards, K.A., Mancini, A.J. (2000) A painful erythematous forearm nodule in a girl with Hodgkin disease: primary cutaneous aspergillosis. *Arch Dermatol*, **136**, 1165–1170.
15. Cornely, O.A., Pels, H., Bethe, U. et al (2001) A novel type of metastatically spreading subcutaneous aspergillosis without epidermal lesions following allogeneic stem cell transplantation. *Bone Marrow Transplant*, **28**, 899–901.
16. Findlay, G., Roux, H., Simson, I. (1971) Skin manifestations in disseminated aspergillosis. *Br J Dermatol*, **85** (Suppl. 7), 94–97.

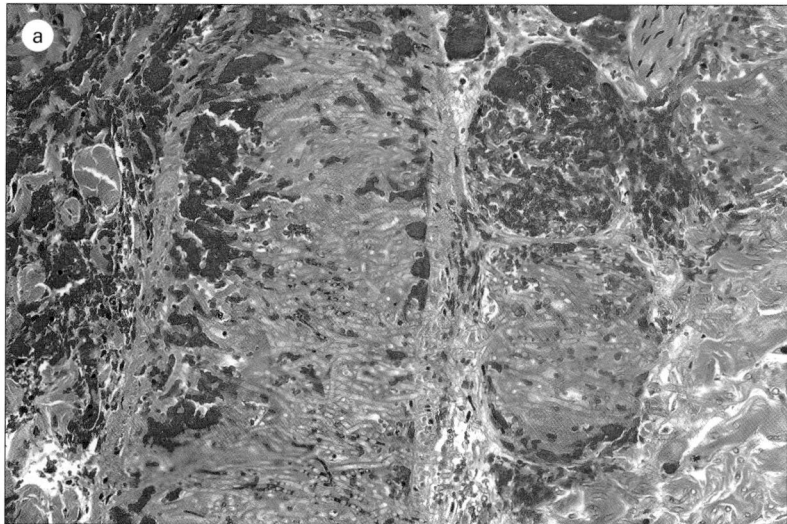

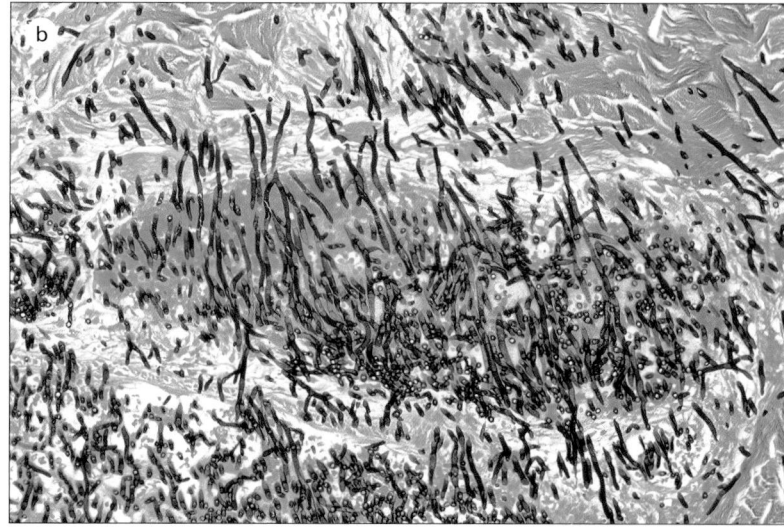

Fig. 17.304
(a, b) Aspergillosis: high power view showing vascular occlusion and fungal hyphae. (b) Methenamine silver stain.

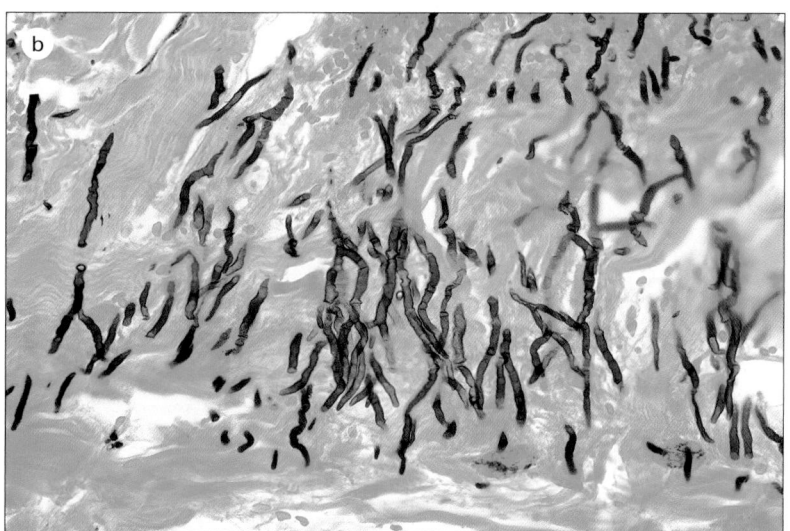

Fig. 17.305
Aspergillosis: (a) low power view showing the arboreal growth pattern; (b) the hyphae are septate and branch at 45° (methenamine silver).

17. Bodey, G.P., Boktour, M., Mays, S. et al (2002) Skin lesions associated with Fusarium infection. *J Am Acad Dermatol*, **47**, 659–666.
18. Cocuroccia, B., Gaido, J., Gubinelli, E. et al (2003) Localized cutaneous hyalohyphomycosis caused by a Fusarium species infection in a renal trasplant. *J Clin Microbiol*, **41**, 905–907.
19. Rodriguez-Villalobos, H., Georgala, A., Beguin, H. et al (2003) Disseminated infection due to Cylindrocarpon (Fusarium) lichenicola in a neutropenic patient with acute leukemia: report of a case and review of the literature. *Eur J Clin Microbiol*, **22**, 62–65.
20. Latenser, B.A. (2003) Fusarium infections in burn patients: a case report and review of the literature. *J Burn Care Rehabil*, **24**, 285–288.
21. Dignani, M.C., Anaissie, E. (2004) Human fusariosis. *Clin Microbiol Infect*, **10**, 67–75.
22. Severo, L.C., Oliveira, F. de M., Londero, A.T. (1997) Subcutaneous scedosporiosis. Report of two cases and review of the literature. *Rev Inst Med Trop Sao Paolo*, **39**, 227–230.
23. Miyamoto, T., Sasaoka, R., Kawaguchi, M. et al (1998) Scedosporium apiospermum skin infection: a case report and review of the literature. *J Am Acad Dermatol*, **39**, 498–500.
24. Castiglioni, B., Sutton, D.A., Rinaldi, M.G. et al (2002) Pseudallescheria boydii (Anamorph Scedosporium apiospermum). Infection in solid organ transplant recipients in a tertiary medical center and review of the literature. *Medicine (Baltimore)*, **81**, 333–348.
25. Chaveiro, M.A., Vieira, R., Cardoso, J. et al (2003) Cutaneous infection due to Scedosporium apiospermum in an immunosuppressed patient. *J Eur Acad Dermatol Venereol*, **17**, 47–49.
26. Watsky, K.L., Eisen, R.N., Bolognia, J.L. (1990) Unilateral cutaneous emboli of aspergillus. *Arch Dermatol*, **126**, 1214–1217.
27. Watts, J.C., Chandler, F.W. (1997) Fusariosis. In: Connor, D.H., Chandler, F.W., Schwartz, D.A. et al (eds) Pathology of infectious diseases, Vol. I. Stamford: Appleton and Lange, pp 999–1001.
28. Schwartz, D.A. (1997) Pseudallescheriasis and scedosporiasis. In: Connor, D.H., Chandler, F.W., Schwartz, D.A. et al (eds) Pathology of infectious diseases. Stamford: Appleton and Lange, pp 1073–1079.

Blastomycosis

Clinical features

Blastomycosis (North American blastomycosis) is caused by *Blastomyces dermatitidis*. The usual habitat of this fungus is not certain, but is probably in wood and bird droppings more often than soil. It was thought to be restricted to North America, as infections were initially confined to the Mississippi basin, the South-East of the USA and Canada, but more recently cases have occurred in South America, Africa, India and Israel.[1,2] It has not yet presented as an endogenous disease in Europe or the Far East. It occurs most often in young to middle-aged adults, and in males more frequently than in females.[3] The infection is most commonly acquired via the lungs.[4] There are three clinical forms of the disease: pulmonary, disseminated and primary cutaneous blastomycosis.

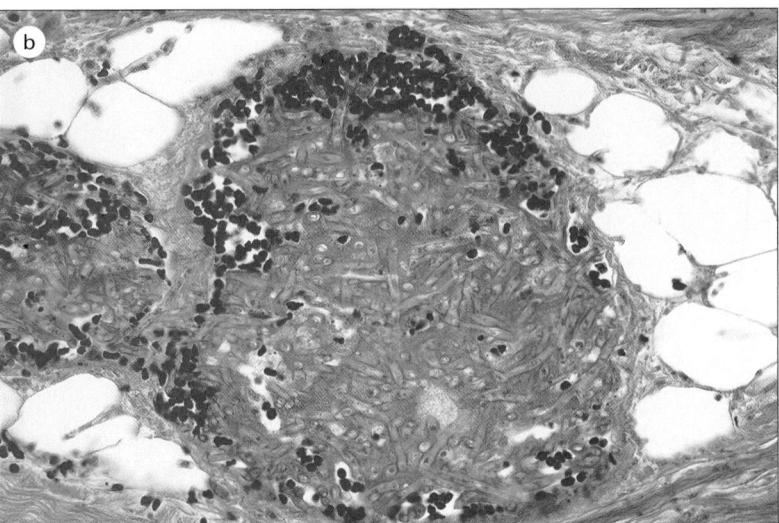

Fig. 17.306
Fusarium spp.: (a) low power view showing epidermal infarction and massive hemorrhage; (b) note the thrombosed vessel containing numerous hyphae. By courtesy of A. Zembowitz, MD, Massachusetts General Hospital, Boston, USA.

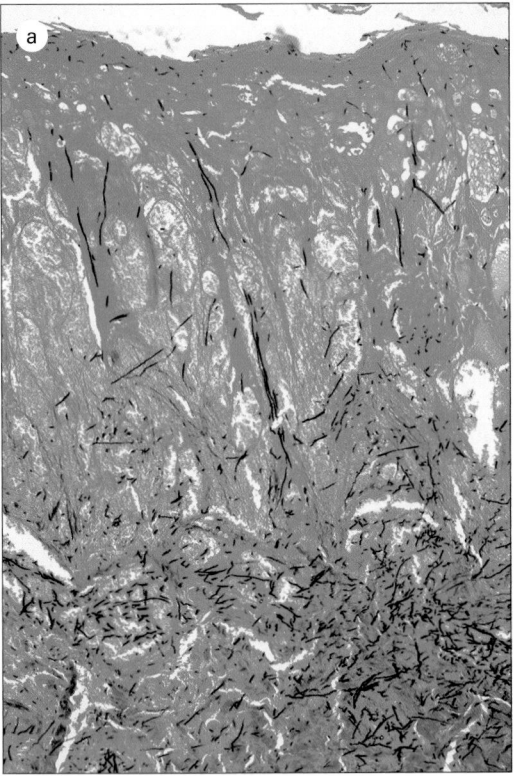

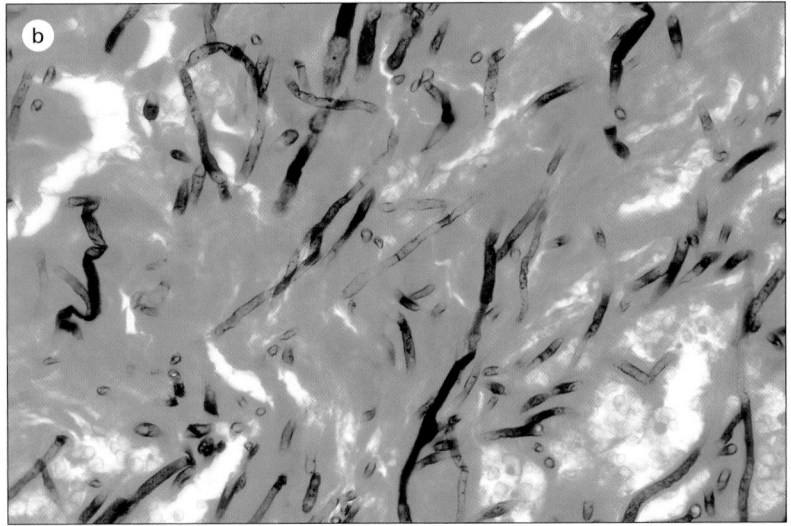

Fig. 17.307
Fusarium spp.: (a) hyphae extend from the deep dermis to the epidermis; (b) note the septa (methenamine silver). By courtesy of A. Zembowitz, MD, Massachusetts General Hospital, Boston, USA.

There is an incubation period of 33–44 days before the onset of respiratory systems, which are usually insidious, but may resemble tuberculosis. Blastomycosis is not uncommonly associated with subclinical infection. In contrast to many of the other deep fungal infections mentioned in this chapter, blastomycosis most often develops in previously healthy hosts.[3] A number of cases have nevertheless been documented in HIV-infected individuals, and although blastomycosis is not regarded as an AIDS-defining infection, a number of clinical differences exist.[5] Central nervous system involvement is said to occur in 46% of patients, i.e. 5–10 times more frequently than in the HIV-negative population. Furthermore, the estimated mortality rate is five times that of non-HIV-infected patients with blastomycosis (54% versus less than 10%).[5]

The skin – in addition to bone, joints, central nervous system and the genitourinary tract (prostatitis and epididymo-orchitis) – is usually involved following dissemination of a pulmonary infection.[6] The lesions may be single or multiple and may affect any part of the body. The skin lesion starts as a papule, but gradually spreads and becomes an ulcerated and crusted, verrucous nodule or ulcerated plaque, with a serpiginous swollen red border (*Fig. 17.310*). This border extends, while the center

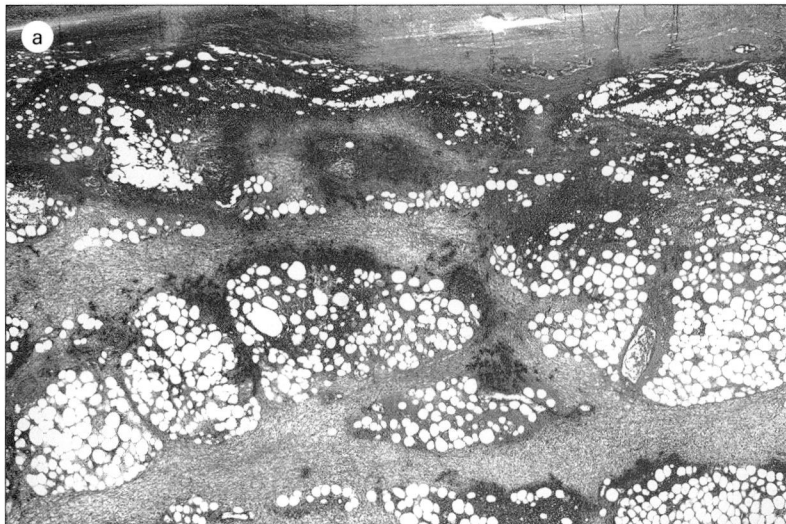

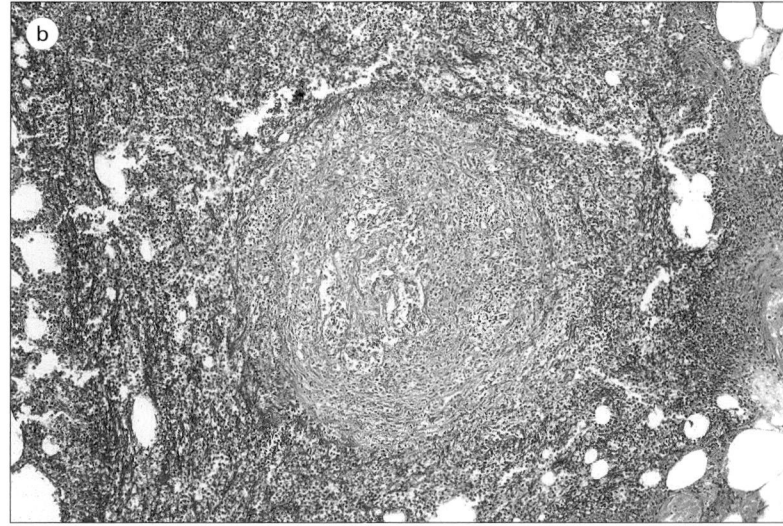

Fig. 17.308
Pseudallescheria boydii: (**a**) low power view showing massive dermal inflammatory changes; (**b**) this field shows an inflamed and thrombosed vessel.

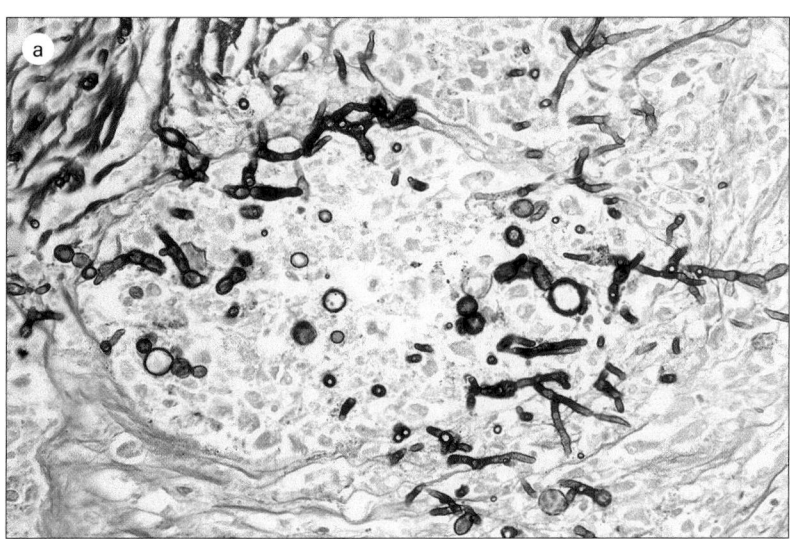

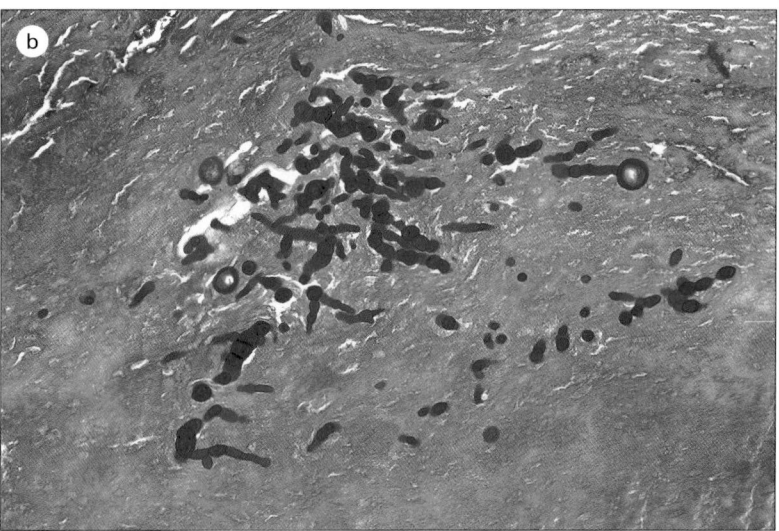

Fig. 17.309
Pseudallescheria boydii: (**a**) silver stain showing hyphae with chlamydoconidia; (**b**) periodic acid–Schiff stain.

may heal with scarring. Exuding pus is present beneath the peripheral crust. Rarely, a widespread pustular eruption may occur.

Occasionally, primary cutaneous blastomycosis occurs 1–2 weeks after inoculation.[7,8] This lesion starts as a pustule, which ulcerates superficially (chancre) and is associated with regional lymphadenitis, lymphadenopathy, and lymphangitic skin nodules, similar to sporotrichosis.

Pathogenesis and histological features

B. dermatitidis is a dimorphic fungus which exists in the yeast phase at 37°C in tissues. It grows as a mycelial form at 25°C. The yeasts are round, usually 8–15 μm, but occasionally up to 30 μm across, and have a refractile thick cell wall (*Fig. 17.311*).[6] They are multinucleate and produce single buds, which have a broad base (*Fig. 17.312*).[6] Infections with large yeast forms measuring 30–35 μm in diameter are an exceedingly uncommon occurrence.[9] The yeast forms of *B. dermatitidis* possess an adhesion-promoting protein termed WI-1 adhesin which is thought to play a crucial pathogenetic role.[10]

The histological features of blastomycosis include, in the early stages, a predominantly neutrophil infiltrate and many organisms are seen.

Subsequently a granulomatous reaction develops in which multinucleate giant cells are numerous and neutrophils are still plentiful. The overlying epidermis shows striking pseudoepitheliomatous hyperplasia, often containing numerous microabscesses (*Figs 17.313, 17.314*).[6] The *Blastomyces* organism is seen within giant cells and also free in the connective tissue. Recognition is facilitated by the use of PAS or methenamine silver stains.

Differential diagnosis

Distinction from other deep cutaneous fungal infections showing similar histological features including chromoblastomycosis, coccidioidomycosis, paracoccidioidomycosis and sporotrichosis rests on the absence of pigment and the presence of a characteristic multinucleate yeast form with single broad-based buds.

References

1. Carman, W.F., Frean, J.A., Crewe-Brown, H.H. et al (1989) Blastomycosis in Africa. *Mycopathologia*, 107, 25–32.
2. Tenenbaum, M.J., Greenspan, J., Kerkering, T.M. (1982) Blastomycosis. *CRC Crit Rev Microbiol*, 9, 139–163.
3. Bradsher, R.W. (1992) Blastomycosis. *Clin Infect Dis*, 14 (Suppl. 1), 82–90.

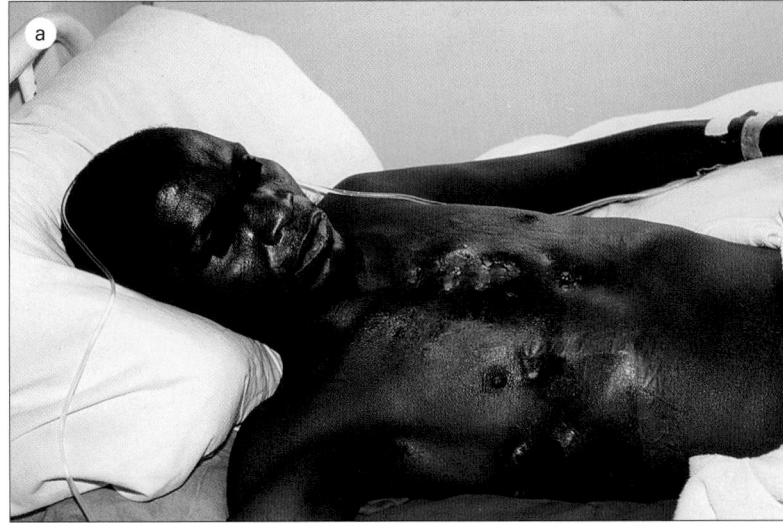

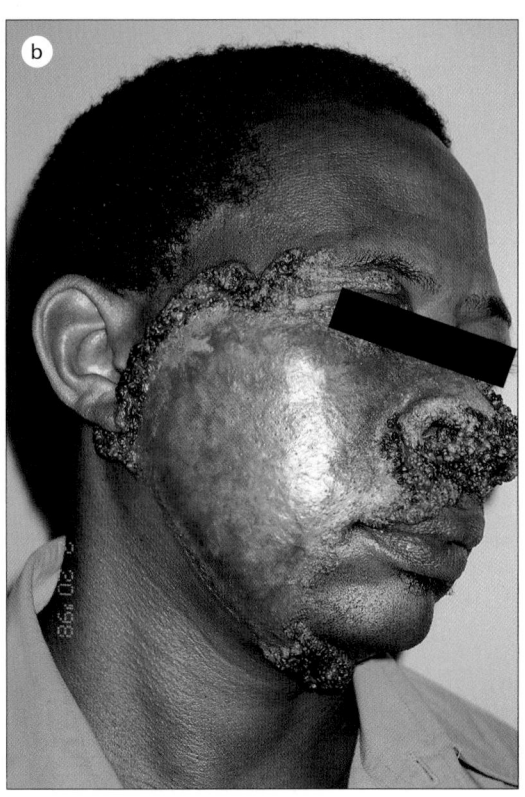

Fig. 17.310
Blastomycosis: **(a)** numerous ulcerated and crusted nodules are visible on the chest; the patient had systemic involvement. **(b)** There is severe facial involvement. Note the sepiginous border. **(a)** By courtesy of W. Weir, MD, Coppetts Wood Hospital, London, UK; **(b)** by courtesy of N.C. Dlova, MD, Nelson R. Mandela School of Medicine, University of KwaZulu-Natal, South Africa.

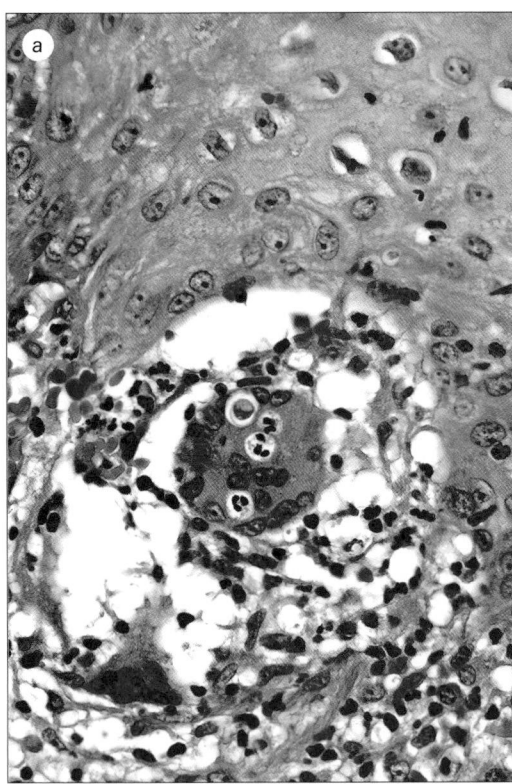

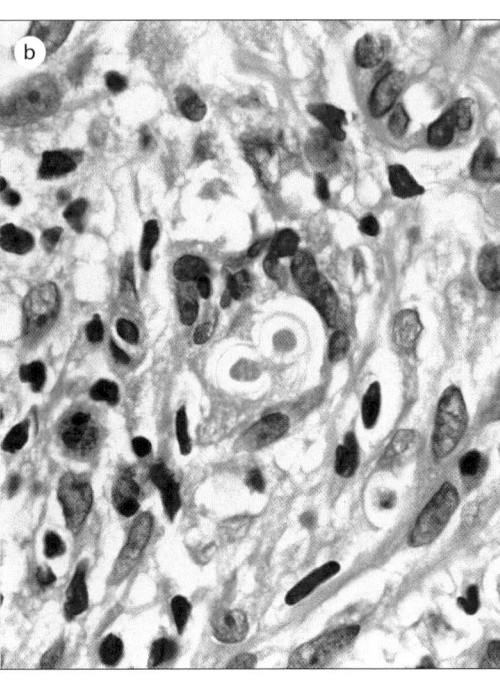

Fig. 17.311
Blastomycosis: **(a)** note the large yeast form with a thick cell wall within the multinucleate giant cell; **(b)** broad-based budding. **(b)** By courtesy of S. Lucas, MD, St Thomas' Hospital, London, UK.

4. Hicks, K., Smith, G.W., Stinson, J.M. (1982) Blastomycosis. *JAMA*, **74**, 87–90.
5. Witzig, R.S., Hoadley, D.J., Greer, D.L. et al (1994) Blastomycosis and human immunodeficiency virus: three new cases and review. *South Med J*, **87**, 715–719.
6. Hirsh, B.C., Johnson, W.C. (1984) Pathology of granulomatous diseases. Mixed inflammatory granuloma. *Int J Dermatol*, **23**, 585–597.
7. Graham, W.R., Callaway, J.L. (1982) Primary inoculation blastomycosis in a veterinarian. *J Am Acad Dermatol*, **7**, 785–786.
8. Gray, N.A., Baddour, L.M. (2002) Cutaneous inoculation blastomycosis. *Clin Infect Dis*, **34**, E44–E49.
9. Hussain, Z., Martin, A., Youngberg, G.A. (2001) Blastomyces dermatitidis with large yeast forms. *Arch Pathol Lab Med*, **125**, 663–664.
10. Klein, B.S. (2000) Molecular basis of pathogenicity in Blastomyces dermatitidis: the importance of adhesion. *Curr Opin Microbiol*, **3**, 339–343.

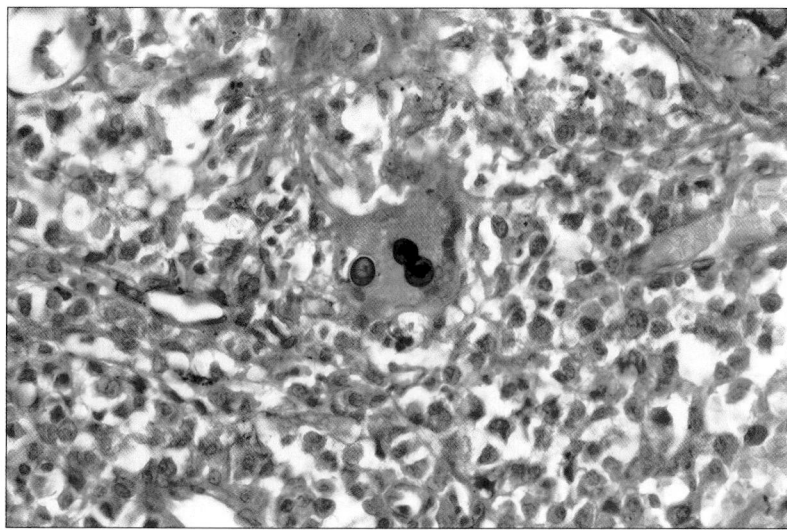

Fig. 17.312
Blastomycosis: close-up view of broad-based budding (methenamine silver).
By courtesy of S. Lucas, MD, Institute of Dermatology, London, UK.

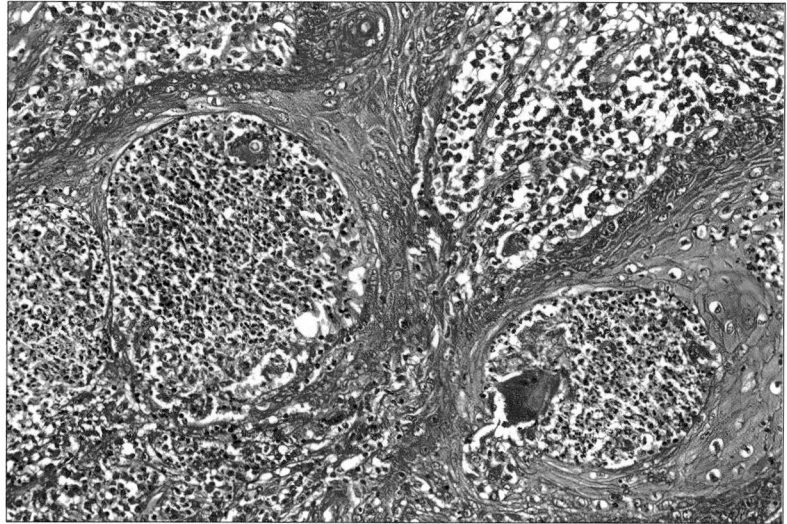

Fig. 17.314
Blastomycosis: intraepidermal and dermal abscesses are typically present.

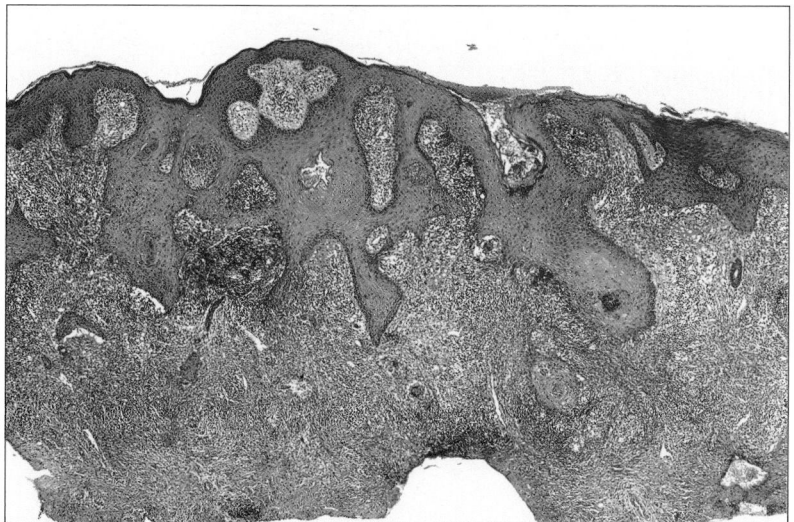

Fig. 17.313
Blastomycosis: there is pseudoepitheliomatous hyperplasia and intense dermal inflammation.

Paracoccidioidomycosis

Clinical features

Paracoccidioidomycosis (South American blastomycosis) is caused by *Paracoccidioides brasiliensis* and occurs in Central and South America, particularly Brazil. It affects males much more commonly than females, usually in rural areas.[1] The natural habitat of the fungus remains an enigma.[2] It is assumed to be contracted by inhalation of conidia from soil contamination. The most common initial presentation is with pulmonary disease, which cavitates in 35% of cases.[3] Involvement of the mucocutaneous junction in the nose and mouth occurs in 60% of patients, whereas other skin sites are affected in only 10%. The most common other site is the face, where lesions may be ulcerative, verrucous or crusted nodules. Primary lesions of the skin are very rare.

Paracoccidioidomycosis is uncommon in patients infected with HIV. A possible explanation for this is the fact that the disease tends to occur only in patients with advanced AIDS who are not receiving trimethoprim–sulfamethoxazole prophylaxis for *Pneumocystis jiroveci*

(formerly *Pneumocystis carinii*) pneumonia, since this drug is also effective against *P. brasiliensis*.[4] The infection carries a 30% mortality in AIDS patients.[4]

Pathogenesis and histological features

The fungus *P. brasiliensis* is morphologically similar to *B. dermatitidis* but *P. brasiliensis* has a thinner cell wall with a double contour appearance and produces multiple, narrow-based buds, said to resemble a 'pilot's wheel' (*Fig. 17.315*).[1] Mycelia from the dimorphic fungus produce conidia, which when inhaled into the lungs transform into pathogenic yeast forms.[5] This transition is inhibited by estrogens, accounting for the higher incidence of infection in males.[5] Although a genetic susceptibility to infection is suspected, no specific HLA antigen association has been confirmed thus far.[5,6]

The histological reaction to the infection in the skin resembles that of blastomycosis in that it is characterized by suppurative and granulomatous inflammation.[7] Neutrophilic abscesses superimposed on pseudoepitheliomatous hyperplasia are seen. Eosinophils may be present in a high proportion of cases. The budding yeast form is seen most often within multinucleate giant cells.

The 'pilot's wheel' appearance is diagnostic; however, if this is not seen, isolation of the organism in vitro is necessary to confirm the diagnosis. Musosal reactions are similar to those seen in the skin.[8] Transepidermal (transepithelial) elimination of the microorganism in association with spongiosis, microvesiculation and microabscesses is commonly present.[8] Scarring is a feature of older lesions.

Differential diagnosis

Distinction from blastomycosis can be difficult, but *P. brasiliensis* does not have the multiple nuclei of *B. dermatitidis* and the budding pattern is quite different. *Cryptococcus* can show a similar variation in yeast size, but has its own characteristic mucicarmine-positive mucinous capsule and produces single buds.

References

1. Hirsh, B.C., Johnson, W.C. (1984) Pathology of granulomatous diseases. Mixed inflammatory granuloma. *Int J Dermatol*, **23**, 585–597.
2. Restrepo, A., McEwen, J.G., Castañeda, E. (2001) The habitat of Paracoccidioides brasiliensis: how far from solving the riddle? *Med Mycol*, **39**, 233–241.
3. Londero, A.T., Ramos, C.D., Lopes, J.O. (1978) Progressive pulmonary paracoccidioidomycosis. *Mycopathologica*, **63**, 53–56.
4. Goldani, L.Z., Sugar, A.M. (1995) Paracoccidioidomycosis and AIDS. *Clin Infect Dis*, **21**, 1275–1281.

5.   Borges-Walmsley, M.I., Chen, D., Shu, X. et al (2002) The pathobiology of Paracoccidioides brasiliensis. *Trends Microbiol*, **10**, 80–87.
6.   Días, M.F., Pereira, A.C., Pereira, A. et al (2000) The role of HLA antigens in the development of paracoccidioidomycosis. *J Eur Acad Dermatol Venereol*, **14**, 166–171.
7.   Meyer, R.D. (1986) Cutaneous and mucosal manifestations of deep mycotic infection. *Acta Derm Venereol*, **121** (Suppl.), 57–72.
8.   Uribe, F., Zuluaga, A.I., Leon, W. et al (1987) Histopathology of cutaneous and mucosal lesions in human paracoccidioidomycosis. *Rev Instit Med Trop Sao Paulo*, **29**, 90–96.

Coccidioidomycosis

Clinical features

Coccidioides immitis, the cause of coccidioidomycosis, is found in its mycelial form in the soil of desert regions of North West America (especially the lower Sonoran life zone) and parts of Mexico, Central and South America.[1] Infection occurs by inhalation of arthrospores in dust and, in view of increased tourism in these areas, is becoming more common. A significant increase in the incidence of this infection has been observed in California since the early 1990s.[2] In those in whom symptoms (usually influenza-like) do develop, coccidioidomycosis is usually a self-limiting disease.[3] Most episodes, however, are asymptomatic.[2,4] It may also develop in the immunosuppressed, including patients with AIDS.[2,5] Symptomatic lung involvement may progress to cavitating, chronic progressive pneumonia and miliary pulmonary disease.[4]

Cutaneous lesions are uncommon and develop almost invariably as a result of the rare dissemination from pulmonary lesions.[6] Dissemination occurs more often in blacks, Filipinos, Hispanics and native Americans and shows a slight male preponderance.[3,7] There is also an increased risk in the immunosuppressed. The lesions include papulonodules, papulopustules, granulomatous plaques and subcutaneous masses (*Figs 17.316, 17.317*).[1] Sinus tracts complicating osteomyelitis may also be seen.[3]

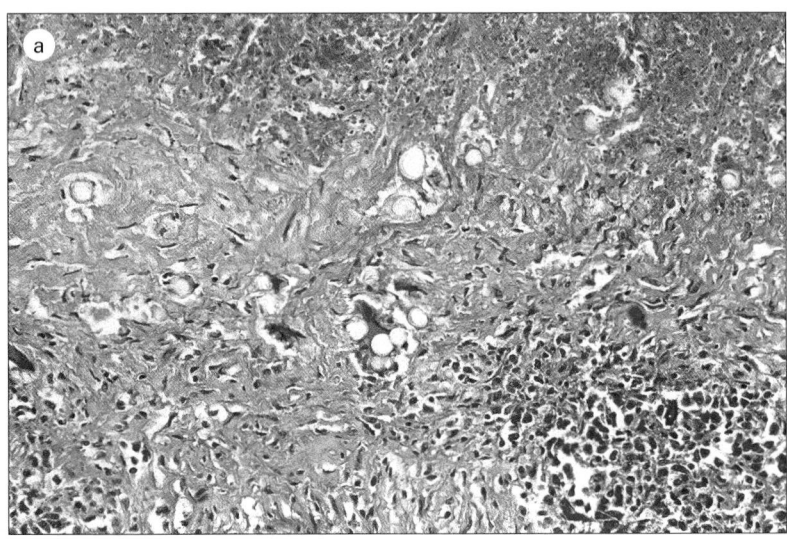

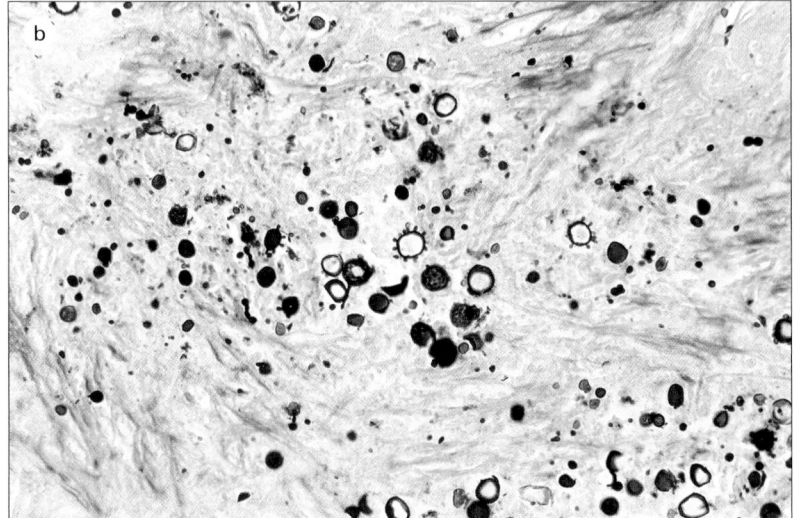

Fig. 17.315
Paracoccidioidomycosis: (a) there is widespread necrosis surrounded by a chronic inflammatory cell infiltrate containing giant cells; (b) typical 'pilot's wheel' budding is evident. By courtesy of W. Roble, MD, Institute of Dermatology, London, UK.

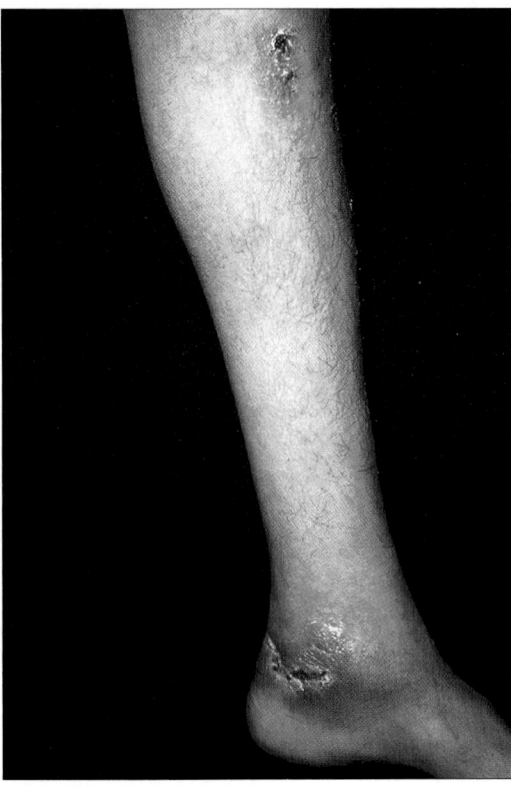

Fig. 17.316
Coccidioidomycosis: ulcerated nodules are present on the knee and ankle. By courtesy of R. Arenas, MD, and J.C. Salas, MD, Monterrey, Mexico.

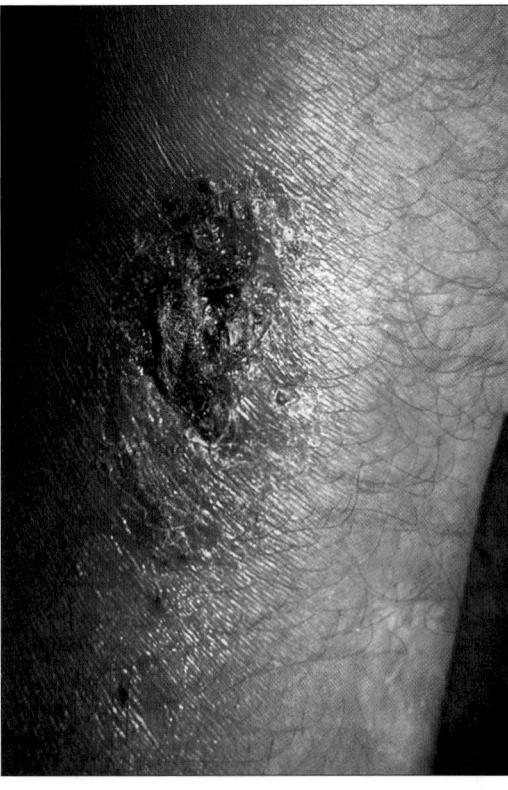

Fig. 17.317
Coccidioidomycosis: there is a crusted plaque on the arm. By courtesy of R. Arenas, MD, and J.C. Salas, MD, Monterrey, Mexico.

Although generally multiple, solitary nodular presentation has been rarely described.[8] The face, in particular the nasolabial fold, is most often affected.[4] Involvement of the face may be indicative of a propensity to develop meningitis.[7]

Disseminated lesions may also affect bone, joints and central nervous system.[4] In the immunosuppressed this may be as a consequence of reactivation of previously quiescent foci.[4] These secondary lesions are sometimes seen in areas of minor trauma, often for example on the face.[9] They appear as verrucous plaques and nodules with crusting and ulceration.[10] Sinus tracts may extend from the primary lung lesion through the chest wall. Hypercalcemia is a rare complication of systemic disease.

The rare primary lesions in the skin occur following inoculation, usually in farmers, laboratory workers, nurses and morticians.[4] These lesions are chancriform and there is regional lymphadenopathy. Sometimes sporotrichoid features are evident. Toxic erythema, erythema nodosum and erythema multiforme may occur as hypersensitivity reactions during systemic infection.[4] The development of erythema nodosum in infected pregnant patients may be a favorable prognostic indicator.[11] The combination of erythema nodosum or erythema multiforme with arthritis and arthralgia is known as 'valley fever'.[3] Systemic eosinophilia may be evident.

Histological features

C. immitis is a dimorphic fungus, which in tissues appears as spherules up to 100 µm in diameter containing endospores (up to 5 µm) that increase in size as the lesions mature (*Figs 17.318, 17.319*). The incubation period ranges from 1 to 4 weeks.[4] Diagnosis may be aided by the coccidioidin or spherulin skin tests.[3] The histology resembles North American blastomycosis in that there is a combination of suppuration with pseudoepitheliomatous hyperplasia and an associated dermal perivascular infiltrate of neutrophils, eosinophils, plasma cells, histiocytes and giant cells (*Fig. 17.320*).[1,9] Eosinophil abscesses may be present and flame figures have been described.[1] Interstitial granulomatous dermatitis has also been reported.[12]

The spherules (sporangia) are seen mixed with this inflammatory infiltrate and occasionally are present in giant cells. They are demonstrated best by methenamine silver techniques. The endospores are PAS positive, but the spherules are negative.[9] The fungi show autofluorescence under ultraviolet light and may be stained with Congo red.[13] They are typically very difficult to find and may often only be demonstrated after examining numerous sections. The spherules increase in size with the formation of numerous endospores. Following rupture into the tissues, each endospore has the capacity to develop into a spherule, therefore repeating the growth cycle in the host.[6]

Differential diagnosis

Diagnosis depends on the demonstration of spherules with endospores.[14] Fragments of spore or immature forms cannot be distinguished from blastomycosis or paracoccidioidomycosis. When spherules and endospores are present rhinosporidiosis should also be considered, although the clinical and histological features are usually different. The spherules and endospores of rhinosporidiosis are much larger than those of coccidioidomycosis. Distinction from tuberculosis verrucosa cutis and halogenoderma may sometimes be necessary.[1] Aggregates of altered red blood cells in myospherulosis may mimic *C. immitis* (*Fig. 17.321*).[15]

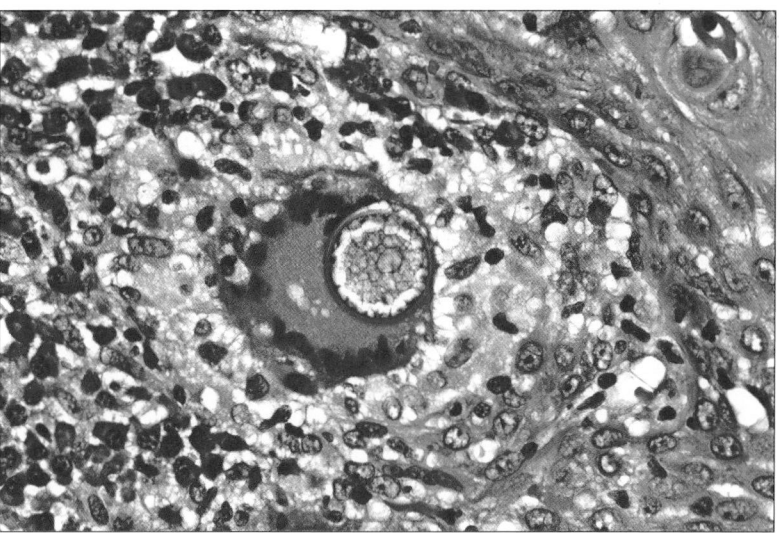

Fig. 17.319
Coccidioidomycosis: high power view of spherule. By courtesy of J. Cohen, MD, Dermatopathology Laboratory, Tucson, USA.

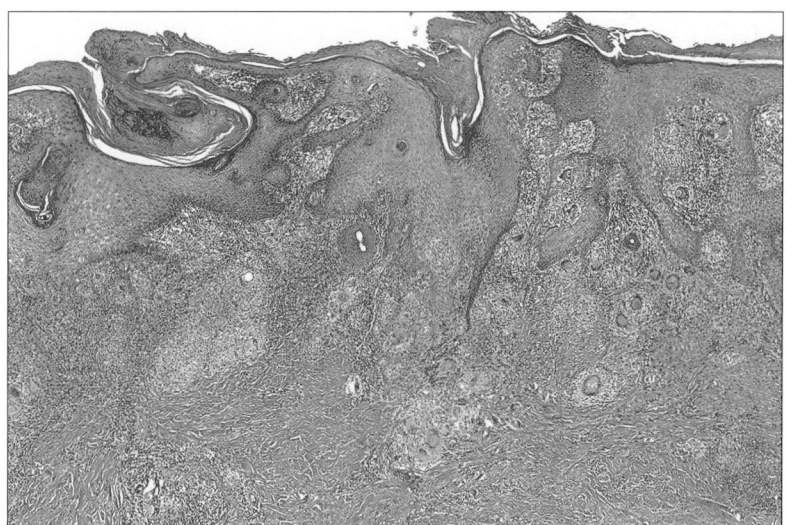

Fig. 17.320
Coccidioidomycosis: the epidermis shows pseudoepitheliomatous hyperplasia. There is intense dermal inflammation with abscesses. By courtesy of J. Cohen, MD, Dermatopathology Laboratory, Tucson, USA.

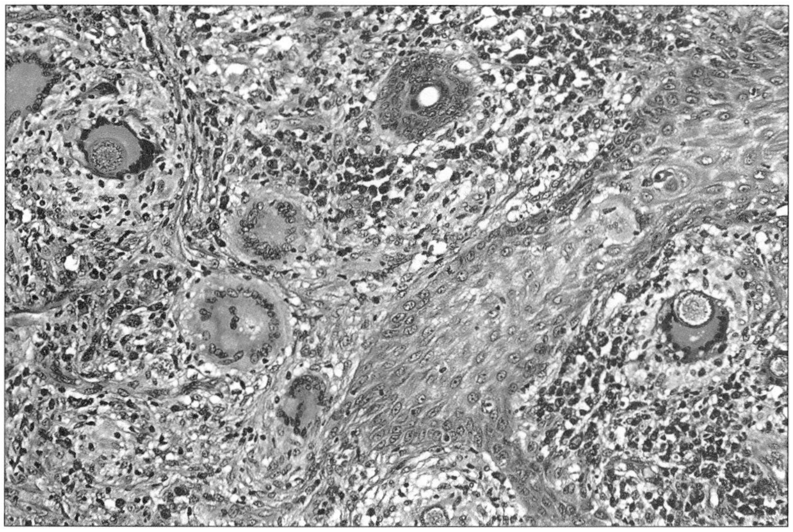

Fig. 17.318
Coccidioidomycosis: numerous giant cells are present within the dermis. A spherule is present in the lower right quadrant. By courtesy of J. Cohen, MD, Dermatopathology Laboratory, Tucson, USA.

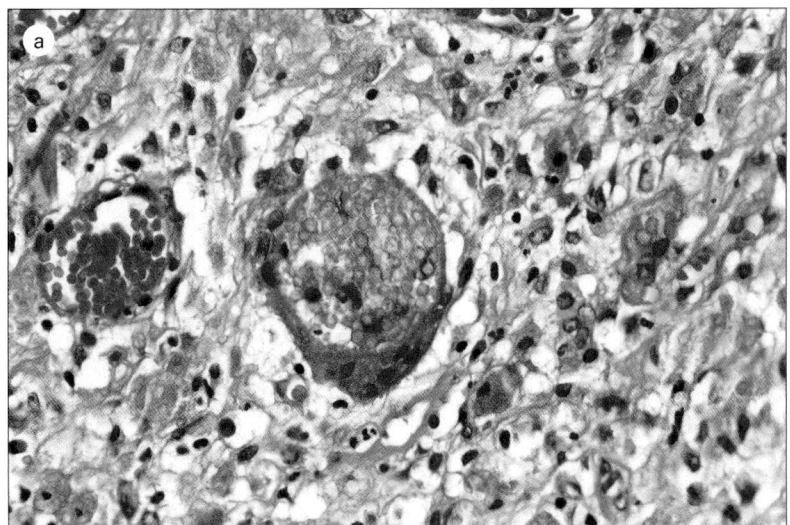
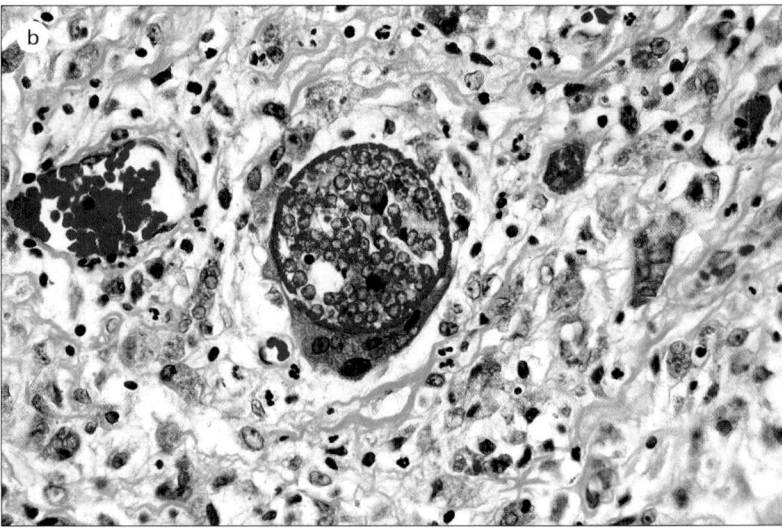

Fig. 17.321
(a, b) Myospherulosis: cutaneous lesions are exceptionally rare. This 'cystic' structure contains altered erythrocytes. The condition was originally recognized following the use of antibiotics – in this example, tetracycline ointment for an ear infection. (b) Masson's trichrome. By courtesy of the late M.S.R. Hutt, MD, St Thomas' Hospital, London, UK.

References

1. Quimby, S.R., Connolly, S.M., Winkelmann, R.K. et al (1992) Clinicopathologic spectrum of specific cutaneous lesions of disseminated coccidioidomycosis. *J Am Acad Dermatol*, **26**, 79–85.
2. Kirkland, T.N., Fierer, J. (1996) Coccidioidomycosis: a reemerging infectious disease. *Emerg Infect Dis*, **2**, 192–199.
3. Bronnimann, D.A., Galgianni, J.N. (1989) Coccidioidomycosis. *Eur J Clin Microbiol Infect Dis*, **8**, 466–473.
4. Hobbs, E. (1989) Coccidioidomycosis. *Dermatol Clin*, **7**, 227–239.
5. Prichard, J.G., Sorotzkin, R.A., James, R.E. 3rd (1987) Cutaneous manifestations of disseminated coccidioidomycosis in the acquired immunodeficiency syndrome. *Cutis*, **39**, 203–205.
6. Jitsukawa, K., Sato, S., Hayashi, Y. et al (1990) Disseminated coccidioidomycosis. *J Dermatol*, **17**, 120–126.
7. Arsura, E.L., Kilgore, W.B., Caldwell, J.W. et al (1998) Association between facial cutaneous coccidioidomycosis and meningitis. *West J Med*, **169**, 13–16.
8. Schwartz, R.A., Lamberts, R.J. (1981) Isolated, nodular, cutaneous coccidioidomycosis. *J Am Acad Dermatol*, **4**, 38–46.
9. Hirsh, B.C., Johnson, W.C. (1984) Pathology of granulomatous diseases. Mixed inflammatory granuloma. *Int J Dermatol*, **23**, 585–597.
10. Pappagianis, D. (1985) The phenomenon of locus minoris restistenciae in coccidioidomycosis. In: Einstein, H.E., Catanzaro, A. (eds), Coccidioidomycosis: Proceedings of the 4th International Conference on Coccidioidomycosis, San Diego, 1984. Washington DC: National Federation of Infectious Diseases, pp 319–329.
11. Arsura, E.L., Kilgore, W.B., Ratnayake, S.N. (1998) Erythema nodosum in pregnant patients with coccidioidomycosis. *Clin Infect Dis*, **27**, 1201–1203.
12. DiCaudao, D.J., Connolly, S.M. (2001) Interstitial granulomatous dermatitis associated with pulmonary coccidioidomycosis. *J Am Acad Dermatol*, **45**, 840–845.
13. Ampel, N.M., Wieden, M.A., Galgiani, J.N. (1989) Coccidioidomycosis: clinical update. *Rev Infect Dis*, **11**, 897–911.
14. Meyer, R.D. (1986) Cutaneous and mucosal manifestations of deep mycotic infection. *Acta Derm Venereol*, **121** (Suppl.), 57–72.
15. Waldman, J.S., Barr, R.J., Espinoza, F.P. et al (1989) Subcutaneous myospherulosis. *J Am Acad Dermatol*, **21**, 400–403.

Cryptococcosis

Clinical features

Cryptococcus neoformans var. *neoformans* causes systemic infections sporadically throughout the world because it is abundant in soil, fruits and pigeon droppings.[1,2] It causes disease in adults and, rarely, in children. The infection often complicates immunosuppression including that due to coticosteroid therapy, neoplastic disease (particularly the terminal phases of Hodgkin's lymphoma) and AIDS.[1,3] Cryptococcosis (torulosis) is the most frequent and potentially lethal mycosis in patients with AIDS.[4]

The portal of entry is usually the lungs and systemic spread to the brain is common. Indeed central nervous system involvement (meningitis and meningoencephalitis) is the major source of morbidity and mortality. Other sites commonly affected in disseminated disease include the skin, bone and prostate.[4] Untreated cryptococcosis, particularly if AIDS related, has a very high mortality.

Secondary cutaneous lesions occur in approximately 10% (6–13%) of cases.[5–7] Skin lesions may also precede evidence of cerebral pathology.[1] Cutaneous manifestations comprise a wide range of lesions including papules, pustules, vesicles, nodules, plaques, cellulitis, ulcers, papable purpura (pseudo-Kaposi) and subcutaneous lesions, which may resemble erythema nodosum (*Fig. 17.322*).[6–9] Herpetiform, keloidal and molluscum contagiosum-like lesions have also been recorded.[7,8,10–12] The head and neck are the most commonly affected sites (*Fig. 17.323*).[13] Ulcerated lesions have a punched-out appearance with gelatinous-looking margins resembling basal cell carcinomas.

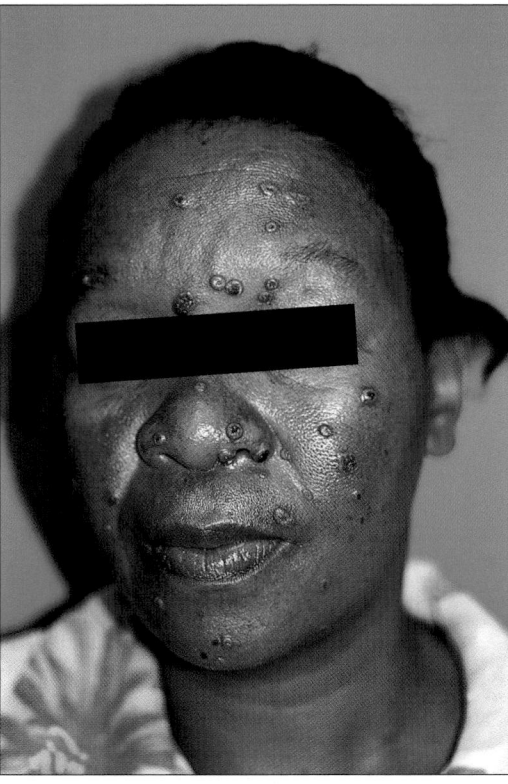

Fig. 17.322
Cryptococcosis: multiple erythematous nodules are present. By courtesy of N.C. Dlova, MD, Nelson R. Mandela School of Medicine, University of KwaZulu-Natal, South Africa.

Lesions developing as a result of primary inoculation of the skin are very rare, but appear to have a good prognosis since the overwhelming majority of these infections have occurred in immunocompetent individuals.[14–18] Inoculation as a consequence of needlestick injury has been reported among health care workers.[15] Features said to be indicative of secondary cutaneous involvement rather than primary disease are deep dermal or subcutaneous inflammation and multifocal skin lesions, especially when present on covered parts of the body.[19]

Humans may also be infected by species of *Cryptococcus* other than *C. neoformans* var. *neoformans*. *C. neoformans* var. *gatti* is endemic in Australia and is associated with two species of Eucalyptus tree.[20,21] Disseminated infection may occur in immunocompromised patients. Primary cryptococcal cellulitis has been reported in an immunocompetent host.[20] *C. laurentii* infection is rare and is usually acquired nosocomially. Patients are often neutropenic and develop fungemia in the presence of an indwelling intravenous catheter.[22] Fewer than 15 cases of systemic *C. albidus* infection have been reported; primary cutaneous infections due to this organism are exceptionally rare.[23]

Pathogenesis and histological features

C. neoformans is a spherical yeast, which measures from 4 to 20 μm in diameter. It is characterized by a mucoid capsule and by reproducing by (narrow-based) budding.[1] There are four serotypes (A–D).[1] In patients with AIDS, serotypes A and D are almost always implicated.[4]

Cell-mediated immunity is of particular importance in the host response and corresponding likelihood of systemic lesions.[1,21] The first line of defense against *C. neoformans* is offered by alveolar macrophages following inhalation of the organisms.[21] Proinflammatory monokines released by these macrophages results in the local recruitment of monocytes and polymorphonuclear leukocytes, offering a second line of defense. The production of lymphokines and specific antibodies constitutes the third tier of defense. IL-12 and IL-18 play a critical role through their action on lymphocyte responses.[21] Patients with low CD4+ T-lymphocyte counts are particularly susceptible to infection.

The mucoid capsule is the characteristic feature in the tissues. It is, however, unencapsulated in nature.[1] It may also be unencapsulated in patients with AIDS.[4] The development of a polysaccharide capsule appears to correlate with its pathogenicity.[24] There may be chains of budding cells in some lesions. Often there is a gelatinous reaction with little inflammation, but in other lesions there is a granulomatous response with necrosis and in some patients there is a suppurative reaction (*Figs 17.324–17.329*).[25–27] In the gelatinous reaction, organisms are very numerous, but in the others the cryptococcus may be more difficult to see and mucicarmine, PAS, alcian blue and methenamine silver stains can be useful (*Figs 17.330–17.332*). Mucicarmine positivity in particular discriminates between cryptococcus and other tissue fungal infections with similar morphology, which are characteristically negative (e.g. histoplasmosis and blastomycosis).[1,28] A unique palisading granulomatous response to chronic cryptococcosis has been described.[29]

Diagnosis is usually very simple and is based on morphological features.[30] In cases of doubt, cryptococcal antigen may be identified in serum or cerebrospinal fluid using the latex agglutination test.[4]

References

1. Hernandez, A.D. (1989) Cutaneous cryptococcosis. *Dermatol Clin*, 7, 269–274.
2. Sarosi, G.A., Siberfarb, P.M., Tosh, F.E. (1971) Cutaneous cryptococcosis: a sentinel of disseminated disease. *Arch Dermatol*, **104**, 1–3.
3. Kovacs, J.A., Kovacs, A.A., Polis, M. et al (1985) Cryptococcosis in the acquired immunodeficiency syndrome. *Ann Intern Med*, **103**, 533–538.

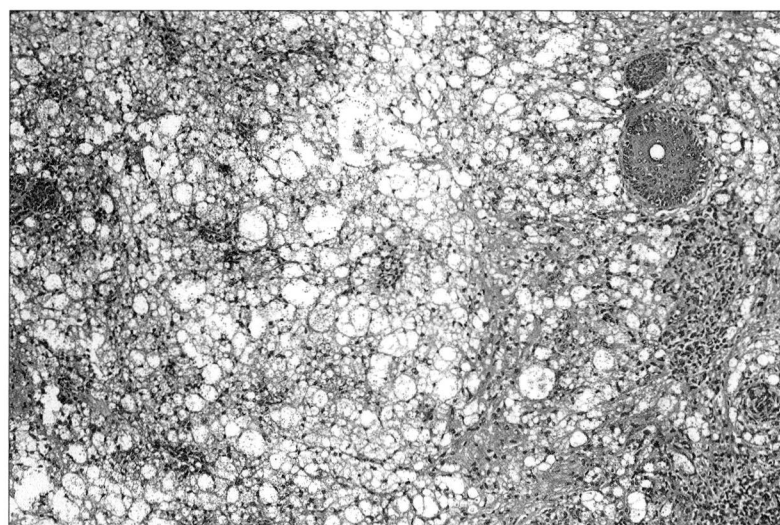

Fig. 17.324
Cryptococcosis: there is an intense mucoid dermal infiltrate.

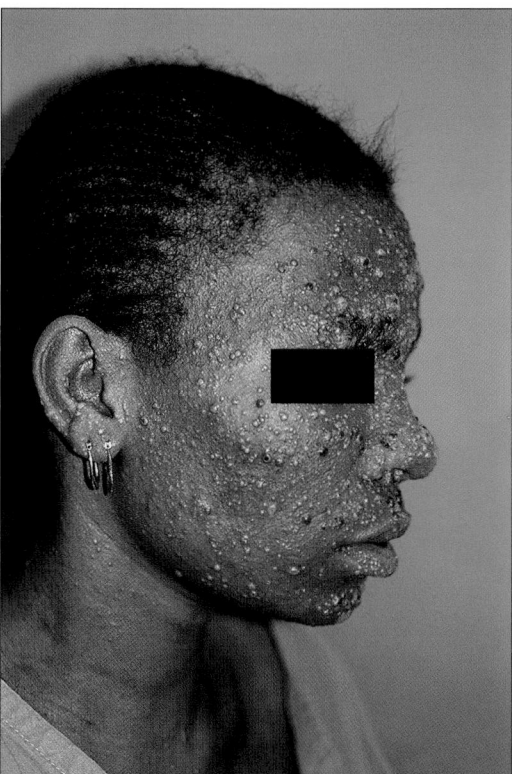

Fig. 17.323
Cryptococcosis: this patient has innumerable facial papules. By courtesy of N.C. Dlova, MD, Nelson R. Mandela School of Medicine, University of KwaZulu-Natal, South Africa.

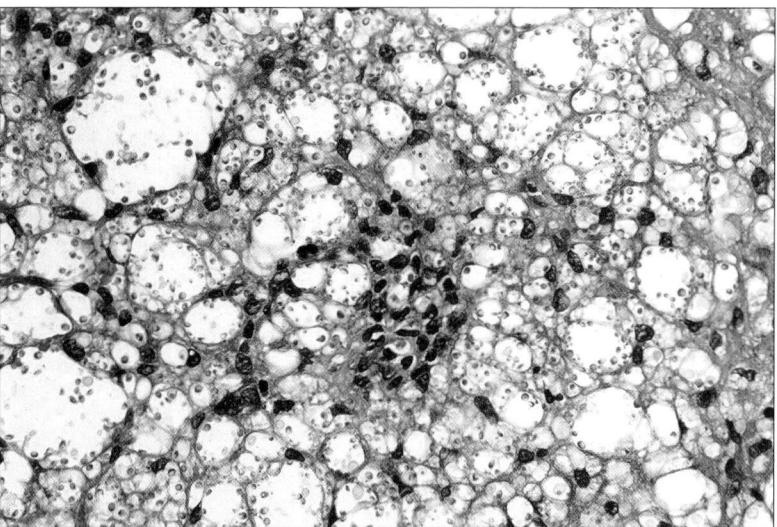

Fig. 17.325
Cryptococcosis: the yeast forms are widely separated by their thick capsules.

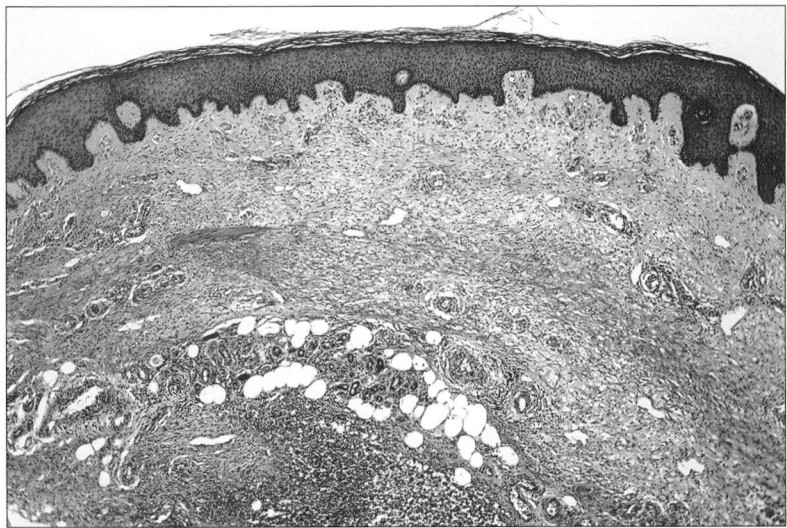

Fig. 17.326
Cryptococcosis: this suppurative variant developed in a patient with lymphoma.

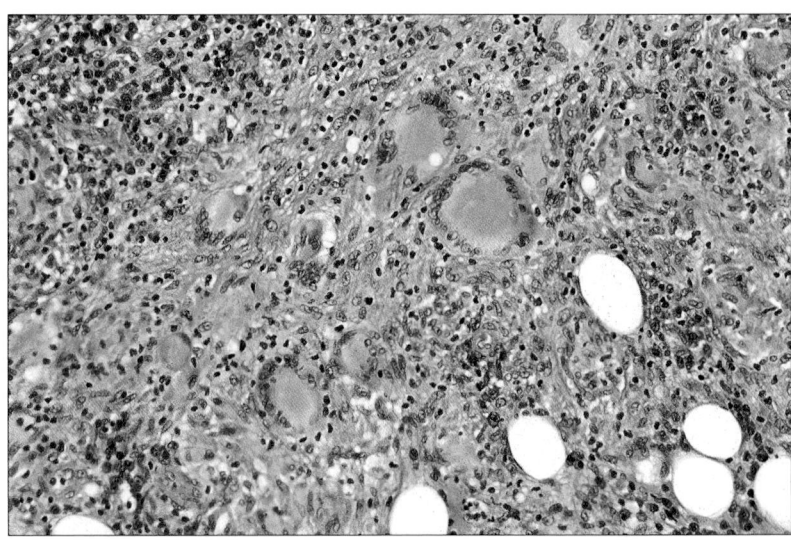

Fig. 17.329
Cryptococcosis: in this example, the inflammatory reaction is granulomatous.

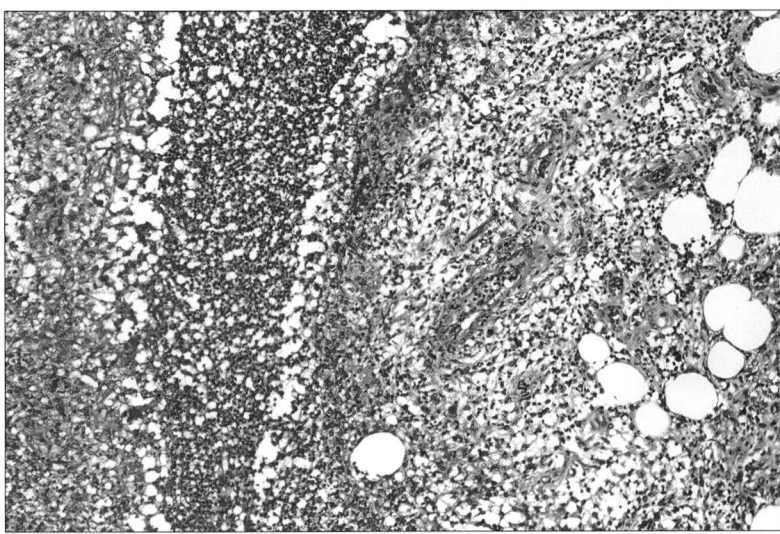

Fig. 17.327
Cryptococcosis: high power view showing a dense neutrophil infiltrate.

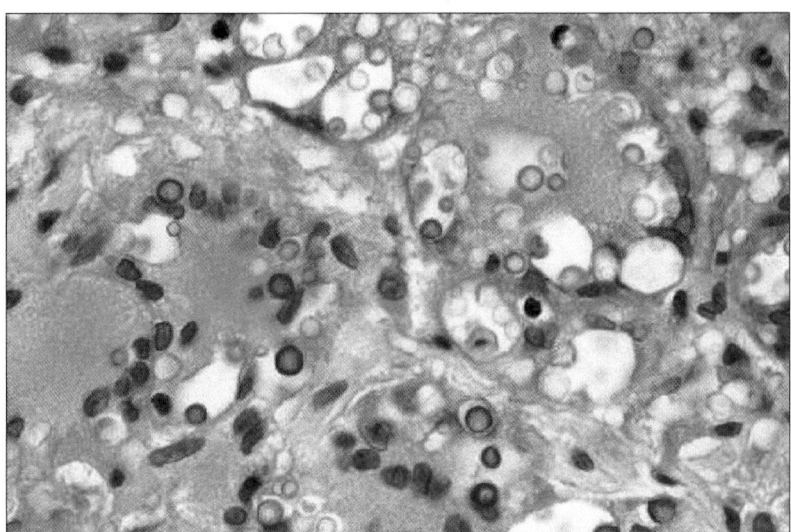

Fig. 17.330
Cryptococcosis: the capsule is clearly demonstrated with the mucicarmine stain.

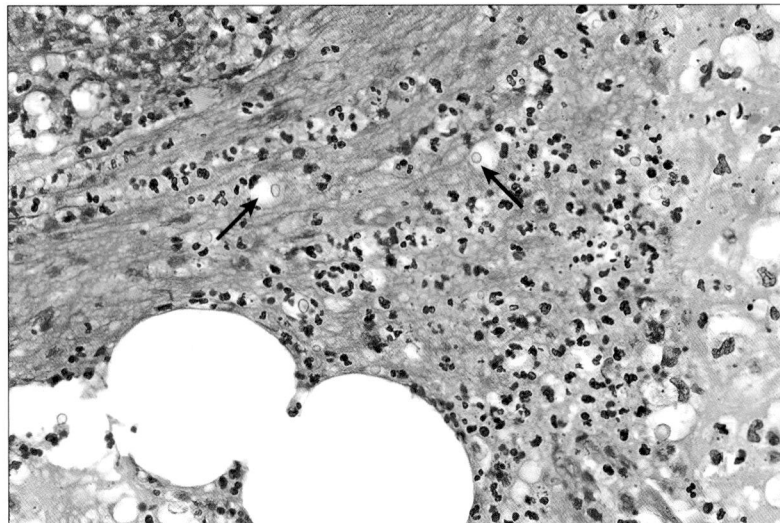

Fig. 17.328
Cryptococcosis: multiple yeasts are present (arrowed); this patient was receiving corticosteroid therapy for systemic lupus erythematosus.

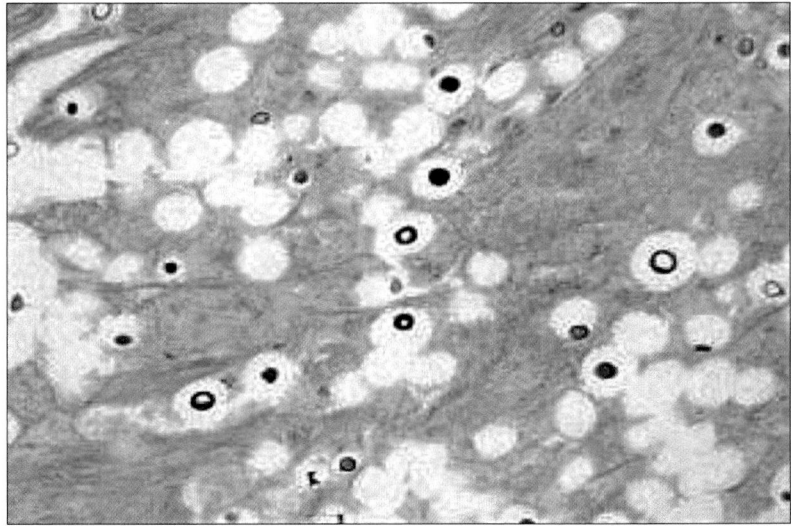

Fig. 17.331
Cryptococcosis: the organisms are positive with methenamine silver.

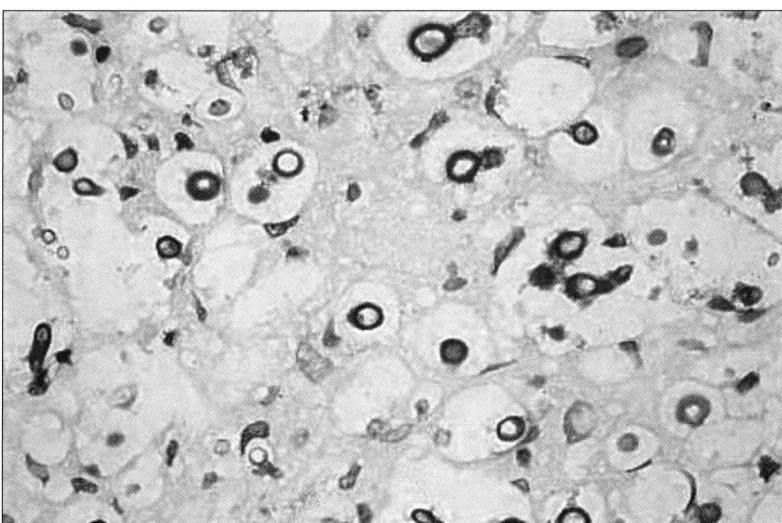

Fig. 17.332
Cryptococcosis: budding yeast forms are present (periodic acid–Schiff).
By courtesy of S. Lucas, MD, St Thomas' Hospital, London, UK.

8. Manfredi, R., Mazzoni, A., Nanetti, A. et al (1996) Morphologic features and clinical significance of skin involvement in patients with AIDS-related cryptococcosis. *Acta Derm Venereol*, **76**, 72–74.
9. Chu, A.C., Hay, R.J., MacDonald, D.M. (1980) Cutaneous cryptococcosis. *Br J Dermatol*, **103**, 95–99.
10. Porges, D.Y., Krueger, J.G. (1992) A novel use of the cryptococcal latex agglutination test for rapid presumptive diagnosis of cutaneous cryptococcosis. *Arch Dermatol*, **128**, 461–463.
11. Yantsos, V.A., Carney, J., Greer, D.L. (1994) Review of the morphological variations in cutaneous cryptococcosis with a new case resembling varicella. *Cutis*, **54**, 343–347.
12. Picon, L., Vaillant, L., Duong, T. et al (1989) Cutaneous cryptococcosis resembling molluscum contagiosum: a first manifestation of AIDS. *Acta Derm Venereol*, **69**, 365–367.
13. Moore, M. (1957) Cryptococcosis with cutaneous manifestations: four cases with a review of published reports. *J Invest Dermatol*, **28**, 159–182.
14. Iacobellis, F.W., Jacobs, M.I., Cohen, R.P. (1979) Primary cutaneous cryptococcosis. *Arch Dermatol*, **115**, 984–985.
15. Casadevall, A., Mukherjee, J., Yuan, R. et al (1994) Management of injuries caused by Cryptococcus neoformans – contaminated needles. *Clin Infect Dis*, **19**, 951–953.
16. Naka, W., Masuda, M., Konohana, A. et al (1995) Primary cutaneous cryptococcosis and Cryptococcus neoformans serotype D. *Clin Exp Dermatol*, **20**, 221–225.
17. Bellosta, M., Gaviglio, M.R., Mosconi, M. et al (1999) Primary cutaneous cryptococcosis in an HIV-negative patient. *Eur J Dermatol*, **9**, 224–226.
18. Revenga, F., Paricio, J.F., Merino, F.J. et al (2002) Primary cutaneous cryptococcosis in an immunocompetent host: case report and review of the literature. *Dermatology*, **204**, 145–149.
19. Ng, W.F., Loo, K.T. (1993) Cutaneous cryptococcosis – primary versus secondary disease. Report of two cases with review of literature. *Am J Dermatopathol*, **15**, 372–377.
20. Hamann, I.D., Gillespie, R.J., Ferguson, J.K. (1997) Primary cryptococcal cellulitis caused by Cryptococcus neoformans var. gatti in an immunocompetent host. *Australas J Dermatol*, **38**, 29–32.
21. Brummer, E. (1998–1999) Human defenses against Cryptococcus neoformans: an update. *Mycopathologia*, **143**, 121–125.
22. Johnson, L.B., Bradley, S.F., Kauffman, C.A. (1998) Fungaemia due to Cryptococcus laurentii and a review of non-neoformans cryptococcaemia. *Mycoses*, **41**, 277–280.
23. Narayan, S., Batta, K., Colloby, P. et al (2000) Cutaneous cryptococcus infection due to C. albidus associated with Sezary syndrome. *Br J Dermatol*, **143**, 632–634.
24. Dykstra, M.A., Friedman, L., Murphy, J.W. (1977) Capsule size of Cryptococcus neoformans. Control and relationship to virulence. *Infect Immun*, **16**, 129–135.
25. Narisawa, Y., Kojima, T., Iriki, A. et al (1989) Tissue changes in cryptococcosis: histologic alteration from gelatinous to suppurative tissue response with asteroid body. *Mycopathologia*, **106**, 113–119.
26. Baker, R.D., Haugen, R.K. (1955) Tissue changes and tissue diagnosis in cryptococcosis. A study of 26 cases. *Am J Clin Pathol*, **25**, 14–24.
27. Hirsh, B.C., Johnson, W.C. (1984) Pathology of granulomatous disease: mixed inflammatory granulomas. *Int J Dermatol*, **23**, 585–597.
28. Gutiérrez, F., Fu, Y.S., Lurie, H.I. (1975) Cryptococcosis histologically resembling histoplasmosis. A light and electron microscopical study. *Arch Pathol*, **99**, 347–352.
29. Leidel, G.D., Metcalf, J.S. (1989) Formation of palisading granulomas in a patient with chronic cutaneous cryptococcosis. *Am J Dermatopathol*, **11**, 560–562.
30. Meyer, R.D. (1986) Cutaneous and mucosal manifestations of the deep mycotic infections. *Acta Derm Venereol*, **121** (Suppl.), 57–72.

4. Sugar, A.M. (1991) Overview: cryptococcosis in the patient with AIDS. *Mycopathologia*, **114**, 153–157.
5. Kozel, T.R., Gotschlich, E.C. (1982) The capsule of Cryptococcus neoformans passively inhibits phagocytosis of the yeast by macrophages. *J Immunol*, **129**, 1675–1680.
6. Schupbach, C.W., Wheeler, C.E., Briggaman, R.A. et al (1976) Cutaneous manifestations of disseminated cryptococcosis. *Arch Dermatol*, **112**, 1734–1740.
7. Murakawa, G.J., Kerschmann, R., Berger, T. (1996) Cutaneous Cryptococcus infection and AIDS. Report of 12 cases and review of the literature. *Arch Dermatol*, **132**, 545–548.

Zygomycosis

Clinical features

The term zygomycosis (formerly phycomycosis) refers to fungal infections caused by members of the class Zygomycetes and encompasses:

- mucormycosis, caused by members of the order Mucorales
- entomophthoromycosis, caused by members of the order Entomophthorales.[1–3]

Mucormycosis

Mucormycosis is usually attributable to species such as *Rhizopus* and *Absidia* (bread molds), which cannot be distinguished in tissues.[4] *Mucor* is less frequently involved.[5] These infections are rare and usually develop in the immunosuppressed or in those with diabetic ketoacidosis.[6–9] Protein–calorie malnutrition, leukemia, liver disease, burns, intravenous drug abuse and, more recently, iron overload with or without desferrioxamine therapy, have also been shown to be of pathogenetic significance.[4,10,11]

The fungi, which are aerobic and saphrophytic on fruit and vegetable matter, are present worldwide; nevertheless infections are uncommon. *Mucor* infection follows spore inhalation and has been characterized into seven syndromes including rhinocerebral, pulmonary, cutaneous, gastrointestinal, central nervous system involvement, disseminated and miscellaneous.[4] Rhinocerebral mucormycosis presents with orbital cellulitis, proptosis and deteriorating mental function.[6] Patients may manifest black necrotic lesions on the palate or nasal mucosae.[6]

Infection of the skin is most often a complication of burns or trauma, but can occur during disseminated infection from a pulmonary source in which instance the lesions closely resemble those of disseminated aspergillosis.[6] The lesions develop as small erythematous macules, which enlarge and ulcerate with profuse offensive purulent discharge. They may resemble a vasculitic process or ecthyma gangrenosum, often with conspicuous black eschar formation.[6,12,13] Lesions with a zosteriform appearance have been described.[14] Nosocomial outbreaks of primary cutaneous zygomycosis have been associated with contaminated elastic bandages.[15] Cutaneous infections have also resulted from spider bites and contaminated intravenous infusion catheter sites.[9] Although cases of cutaneous zygomycosis have been reported in immunocompromised HIV-infected patients, the vast majority have been intravenous drug abusers.[16]

Isolated cutaneous mucormycosis carries an excellent prognosis with adequate treatment. The mortality rate associated with rhinocerebral, pulmonary or disseminated disease, however, is very high (78–100% in some series).[9] Very rarely, visceral dissemination from a primary cutaneous site of infection may occur.[12]

Entomophthoromycosis

Entomophthoromycosis (subcutaneous zygomycosis) encompasses rare infections caused by *Basidiobolus ranarum*, *Basidiobolus haptosporus* (basidiobolomycosis), *Conidiobolus coronatus* and *Conidiobolous incongruus* (conidiobolomycosis).[3,17–21] These organisms are also responsible for cutaneous and nasopharyngeal infections in animals such as horses.[20] Entomophthoromycosis occurs predominantly in tropical regions of Africa, Asia and South America.[3] Unlike mucormycosis, basidiobolomycosis and conidiobolomycosis do not appear to be opportunistic pathogens: infection is usually acquired by inoculation, either through minor trauma or occasionally via an insect bite.[3] Both *B. ranarum* and *C. coronatus* are found in soil and decaying vegetable material.[3,20] *B. ranarum* also occurs in the gut of fish, amphibians, reptiles and bats.[22]

Basidiobolomycosis is seen most frequently in children or adolescents who present with confluent cutaneous and subcutaneous plaques.

Lesions are fluctuant and well demarcated, and occur predominantly on the limbs, trunk or buttocks (*Fig. 17.333*).[3,20] Tumor-like masses may evolve.[3] There is a male predilection. Involvement of the lymph nodes, with lymphedema and elephantiasis has been reported.[23,24] Although rare, primary or secondary visceral involvement may occur.[3,25]

Conidiobolomycosis by contrast is an infection that tends to occur in adults, who manifest with mucocutaneous lesions of the nose with subsequent spread to the paranasal sinuses and rhinofacial subcutaneous tissues.[3] There is erythema and thickening of the nasal skin. Involvement may progress to massive deforming tumefaction of the nose, cheeks and/or lips.[3] The infection may also spread to involve the eyelid and orbit.[3,26] Visceral dissemination is a rare complication.

Histological features

The fungi in mucormycosis are seen as broad (10–20 μm diameter) non-septate hyphae, which branch irregularly at 90°.[4,27] They must be distinguished from *Aspergillus*, which is narrower, septate and shows more regular dichotomous branching. The fungus often invades blood vessels, with resultant vasculitis, causing thrombosis, hemorrhage and infarction.[4] The hyphae are seen well with hematoxylin and eosin, as well as with special stains for fungi (*Fig. 17.334*).[28]

The non-septate fungal hyphae in entomophthoromycosis are not as broad as those encountered in mucormycosis, and have an average diameter of 8–10 μm. An additional point of distinction is the fact that angioinvasion does not tend to occur in entomophthoromycosis.[3] There is extensive granulomatous inflammation with neutrophilic micro-abscesses and large numbers of eosinophilic leukocytes (*Figs 17.335, 17.336*). The hyphae are clearly discernible in hematoxylin and eosin stained sections but can be highlighted with Gomori's methenamine silver, and are frequently associated with the Splendore–Hoeppli phenomenon (*Figs 17.337, 17.338*).[3] Phagocytosed hyphal fragments are sometimes visible within the cytoplasm of giant cells.[20] As with all fungal infections, precise identification of the species responsible for the infection is by fungal culture.

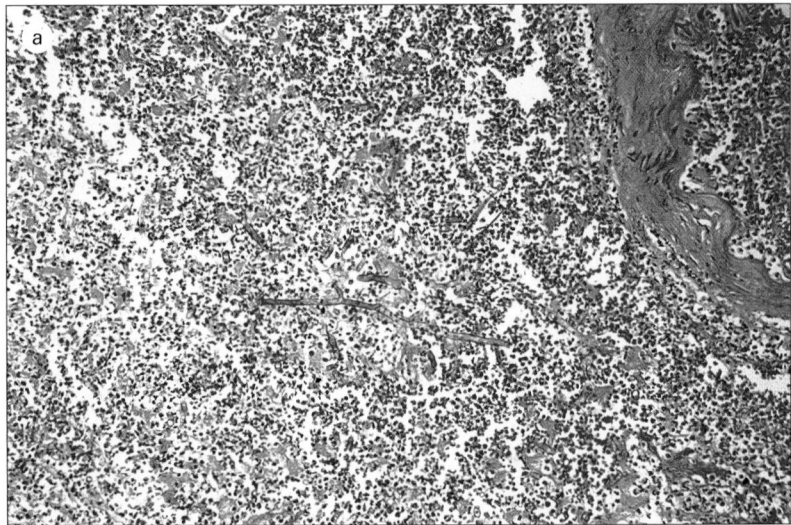

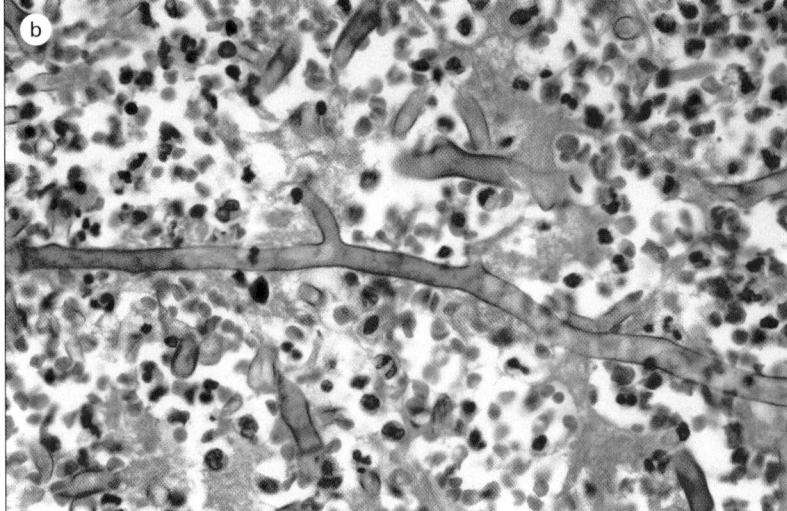

Fig. 17.334
Zygomycosis (mucormycosis): (a) the fungi are recognizable even at this low power magnification; (b) the hyphae are very broad (much more than *Aspergillus*), are non-septate and branch at 90°. By courtesy of R. Hay, MD, Institute of Dermatology, London, UK.

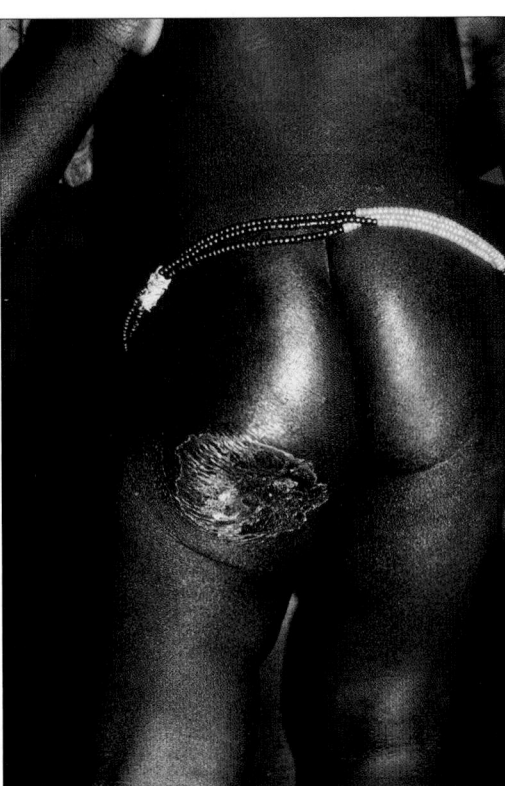

Fig. 17.333
Zygomycosis: there is a large abscess in the left buttock. By courtesy of S. Lucas, MD, St Thomas' Hospital, London, UK.

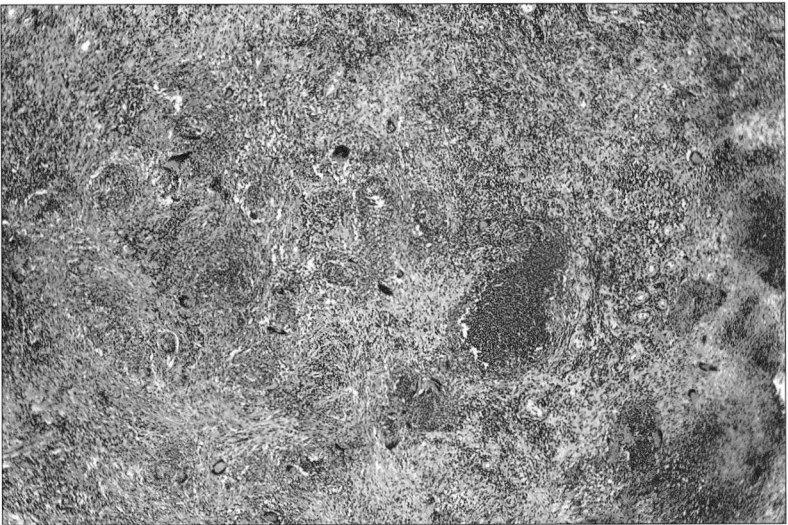

Fig. 17.335
Zygomycosis: within the dermis is a heavy mixed granulomatous and suppurative infiltrate.

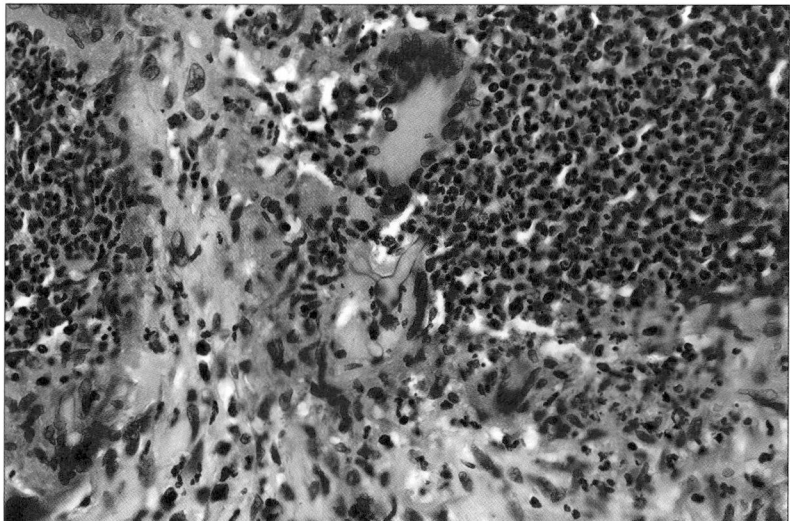

Fig. 17.336
Zygomycosis: a hypha is present in the center of the field.

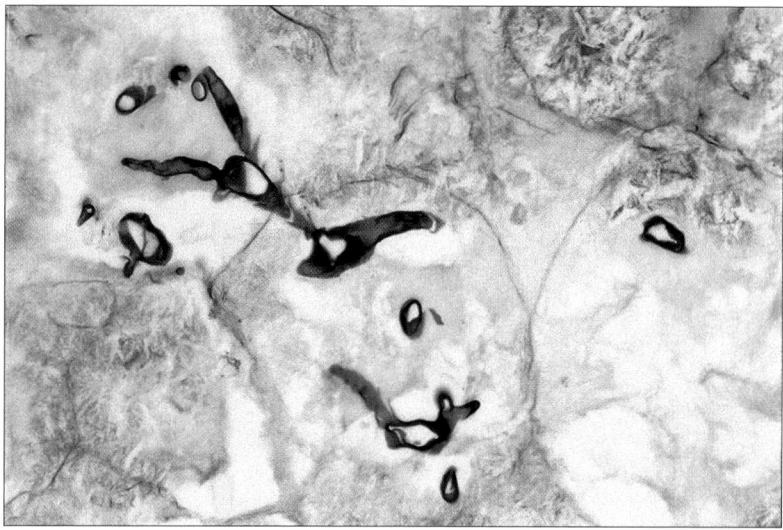

Fig. 17.338
Zygomycosis: the hyphae are irregular and often appear twisted.

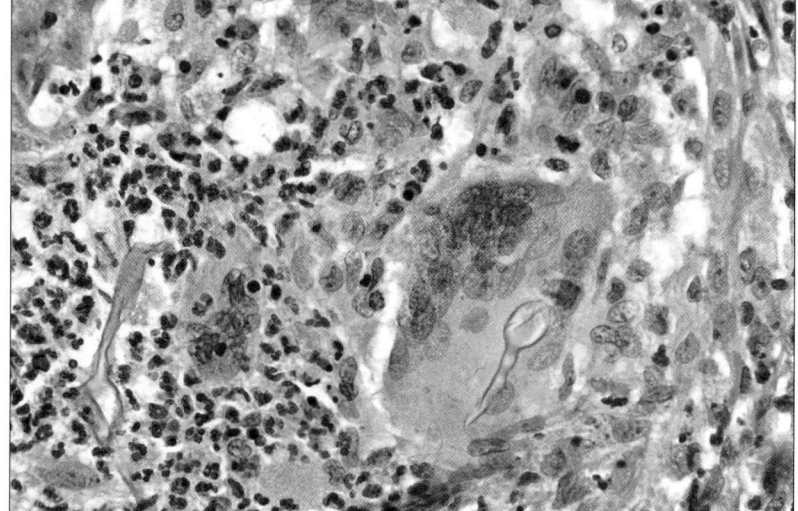

Fig. 17.337
Zygomycosis: the fungi are often clearly visible in hematoxylin and eosin stained sections.

References

1. Odds, F.C., Arai, T., Disalvo, F. et al (1992) Nomenclature of fungal diseases: a report and recommendations from the sub-committee of the International Society for Human and Animal Mycology (ISHAM). *J Med Vet Mycol*, **30**, 1–10.
2. Hocquet, P. (1979) Phycomycoses. *Dermatologica*, **159**, 191–202.
3. Bittencourt, A.L., Londero, A.T. (1995) Tropical mycotic diseases. In: Doerr, W., Seifert, G. (eds) Spezielle Pathologische Anatomie, Vol. 8: Tropical pathology, 2nd edn. Berlin: Springer-Verlag, pp 707–798.
4. Sugar, A.M. (1992) Mucormycosis. *Clin Infect Dis*, **14** (Suppl. 1), 126–129.
5. Lehrer, R.I., Howard, D.H., Sypherd, P.S. (1980) Mucormycosis. *Ann Intern Med*, **93**, 93–108.
6. Meyer, R.D. (1986) Cutaneous and mucosal manifestations of deep mycotic infections. *Acta Derm Venereol*, **121** (Suppl.), 57–72.
7. Meyer, R.D., Rosen, P., Armstrong, D. (1972) Phycomycosis complicating leukaemia and lymphoma. *Ann Intern Med*, **77**, 871–879.
8. Meyer, R.D., Armstrong, D. (1973) Mucormycosis – changing status. *CRC Crit Rev Clin Lab Sci*, **4**, 421–451.
9. Adam, R.D., Hunter, G., DiTomasso, J. et al (1994) Mucormycosis: emerging prominence of cutaneous infections. *Clin Infect Dis*, **19**, 67–76.
10. van Cutsem, J., Boelaert, J.R. (1989) Effects of desferrioxamine, feroxamine and iron on experimental mucormycosis (zygomycosis). *Kidney Int*, **36**, 1061–1068.
11. Abe, F., Inaba, H., Katoh, T. et al (1990) Effects of iron and desferrioxamine on Rhizopus infection. *Mycopathologia*, **110**, 87–91.
12. Wirth, F., Perry, R., Eskenzai, A. et al (1997) Cutaneous mucormycosis with subsequent visceral dissemination in a child with neutropenia: a case report and review of the pediatric literature. *J Am Acad Dermatol*, **36**, 336–341.
13. Chandra, S., Woodgyer, A. (2002) Primary cutaneous zygomycosis due to Mucor circinelloides. *Australas J Dermatol*, **43**, 39–42.
14. Woods, S.G., Elewski, B.E. (1995) Zosteriform zygomycosis. *J Am Acad Dermatol*, **32**, 357–361.
15. Linder, N., Keller, N., Huri, C. et al (1998) Primary cutaneous mucormycosis in a premature infant: case report and review of the literature. *Am J Perinatol*, **15**, 35–38.
16. Gugnani, H.C. (1992) Entomophthoromycosis due to Conidiobolus. *Eur J Epidemiol*, **8**, 391–396.
17. Krishnan, S.G., Sentamilselvi, G., Kamalam, A. et al (1998) Entomophthoromycosis in India – a 4-year study. *Mycosis*, **41**, 55–58.
18. Bittencourt, A.L., Arruda, S.M., de Andrade, J.A. et al (1991) Basidiobolomycosis: a case report. *Pediatr Dermatol*, **8**, 325–328.
19. Sánchez, M.R., Ponge-Wilson, I., Moy, J.A. et al (1994) Zygomycosis and HIV infection. *J Am Acad Dermatol*, **30**, 904–908.
20. Sharma, N.L., Mahajan, V.K., Singh, P. (2003) Orofacial conidiobolomycosis due to Conidiobolus incongruus. *Mycoses*, **46**, 137–140.
21. Gugnani, H.C. (1999) A review of zygomycosis due to Basidiobolus ranarum. *Eur J Epidemiol*, **15**, 923–929.
22. Miller, R.I., Campbell, R.S. (1984) The comparative pathology of equine cutaneous phycomycosis. *Vet Pathol*, **21**, 325–332.
23. Kamalam, A., Thambiah, A.S. (1975) Basidiobolomycosis with lymph node involvement. *Sabouraudia*, **13**, 44–48.
24. Kamalam, A., Thambiah, A.S. (1982) Lymphedema and elephantiasis in basidiobolomycosis. *Mykosen*, **25**, 508–511.
25. Pasha, T.M., Leighton, J.A., Smilack, J.D. et al (1997) Basidiobolomycosis: an unusual fungal infection mimicking inflammatory bowel disease. *Gastroenterology*, **112**, 250–254.
26. al-Hajjar, S., Perfect, J., Hashem, F. et al (1996) Orbitofascial conidiobolomycosis in a child. *Pediatr Infect Dis*, **15**, 1130–1132.
27. Mikat, D.M. (1980) Unusual fungal conditions of the skin. *Int J Dermatol*, **19**, 18–23.
28. Binford, C.H., Dooley, J.R. (1976) Mucormycosis. In: Bunford, C.H., Connor, D.H. (eds) Pathology of tropical and extraordinary diseases, Vol. 2. Washington: Armed Forces Institute of Pathology, pp 564–565.

Chromoblastomycosis

Clinical features

Chromoblastomycosis (chromomycosis) is a term applied to infection with some black (dematiaceous) fungi and is characterized by finding sclerotic pigmented bodies intermediate between a yeast and hyphal form in the tissues. Five main fungal species are associated with chromo-blastomycosis:[1]

- *Cladosporium carrionii*
- *Fonsecaea compacta*
- *Fonsecaea pedrosoi*
- *Phialophora verrucosa*
- *Rhinocladiella aquaspersa*.

Other organisms such as *Exophiala spinifera* or *Aureobasidium pullulans* have rarely been implicated.[2,3] Infections have occurred throughout the world, almost entirely in adult males (more than 90% in some series).[4] The fungi are thought to be present in soil, wood and vegetable debris. Other infections caused by dematiaceous fungi include mycetoma and phaeohyphomycosis.[1,5,6] Chromomycosis is particularly seen in farmers and agricultural workers.[4,7,8]

The infection occurs primarily in skin following trauma. It begins as scaly pink papules, most often on the lower leg or foot. These enlarge slowly to become nodules and then purplish irregular plaques and verrucous nodules (*Fig. 17.339*). Eventually many of these become large papillomatous lesions, which are pruritic. The associated scratching may result in adjacent satellitosis. The condition progress slowly for many years and may end as grossly deforming large tumor masses. Secondary bacterial infection often causes foul smelling discharge, ulceration and lymphadenitis. Involvement of underlying tissues does not occur, although hematogenous spread to the central nervous system has been reported.[9] Secondary (bacterial) regional lymphadenopathy may be evident.[7] Squamous cell carcinoma is a rare complication of chronic disease.[8] There have been rare reports of penile, vulval and nasal chromoblastomycosis. Extracutaneous lesions involving the pleura, ileocecal region, laryngotracheal region and tonsils have also been described.[10]

Pathogenesis and histological features

The most common fungus causing chromoblastomycosis is *F. pedrosoi*.[5,7] The latter organism has been isolated from 90% or more of cases in some series.[8,11] A multinational study has shown that *F. pedrosoi* can be classified into seven mitochondrial DNA types; these appear to correspond to geographic origin.[12]

The sclerotic bodies are round or polyhedral, pigmented, thick-walled fungal cells 5–12 µm in diameter.[5] Despite its name, blast formation does not occur.[1] The sclerotic body is phenotypically midway between a yeast and a hypha and therefore has cross walls in two planes.[1]

The tissue reaction resembles that seen in blastomycosis.[5,13] There is marked epidermal acanthosis, with neutrophil microabscesses (*Figs 17.340, 17.341*). The hyperplasia often becomes pseudoepitheliomatous.[9] The dermis shows abscess formation with necrosis and a surrounding granulomatous and mixed inflammatory infiltrate consisting of neutrophils, eosinophils, lymphocytes and plasma cells. The admixture of neutrophil microabscesses and granulomatous inflammation is described as a mixed (mycotic) granuloma (it is also a feature of blastomycosis, sporotrichosis, phaeohyphomycosis, coccidioidomycosis and paracoccidioidomycosis).[9,13] The sclerotic bodies are seen both

within giant cells and extracellularly (*Figs 17.342, 17.343*). Transepidermal elimination of fungal cells has been described.[14] Dematiaceous hyphae may also be seen in the dermis.[5] Dermal fibrosis is often marked and in many cases the subcutaneous fat is also affected. Classification of the causative organism depends on culture.

References

1. McGinnis, M.R., Hilger, A.E. (1987) Infections caused by black fungi. *Arch Dermatol*, **123**, 1300–1302.
2. Padhye, A.A., Hampton, A.A., Hampton, M.T. et al (1996) Chromoblastomycosis caused by Exophiala spinifera. *Clin Infect Dis*, **22**, 331–335.
3. Redondo-Bellon, P., Idoate, M., Rubio, M. et al (1997) Chromoblastomycosis produced by Aureobasidium pullulans in an immunosuppressed patient (Letter). *Arch Dermatol*, **133**, 663–664.
4. Silva, J.P., de Souza, W., Rozental, S. (1998–1999) Chromoblastomycosis: a retrospective study of 325 cases on Amazonic Region (Brazil). *Mycopathologia*, **143**, 171–175.
5. McGinnis, M.R. (1983) Chromoblastomycosis and phaeohyphomycosis: new concepts, diagnosis and mycology. *J Am Acad Dermatol*, **8**, 1–16.

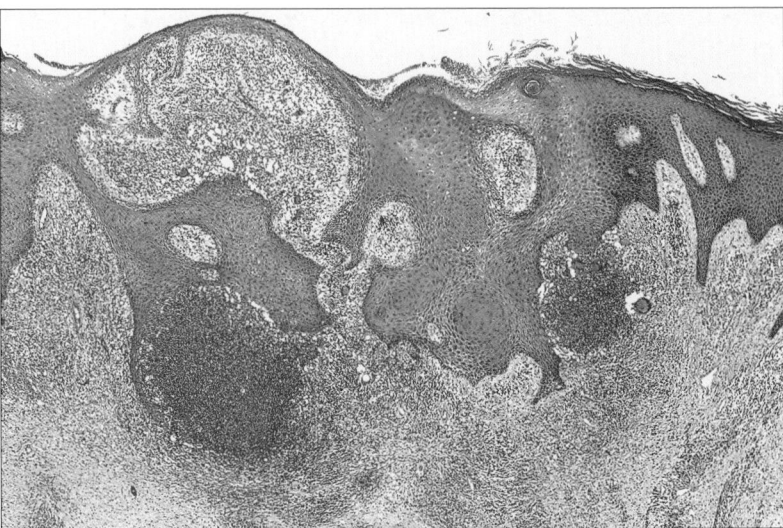

Fig. 17.340
Chromoblastomycosis: the epidermis is hyperkeratotic, crusted and shows very marked acanthosis.

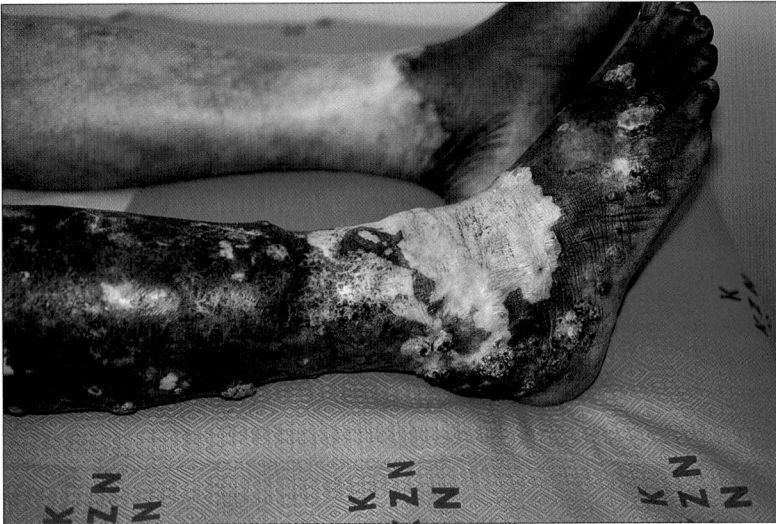

Fig. 17.339
Chromoblastomycosis: there are multiple nodules and disfiguring plaques. By courtesy of N.C. Dlova, MD, Nelson R. Mandela School of Medicine, University of KwaZulu-Natal, South Africa.

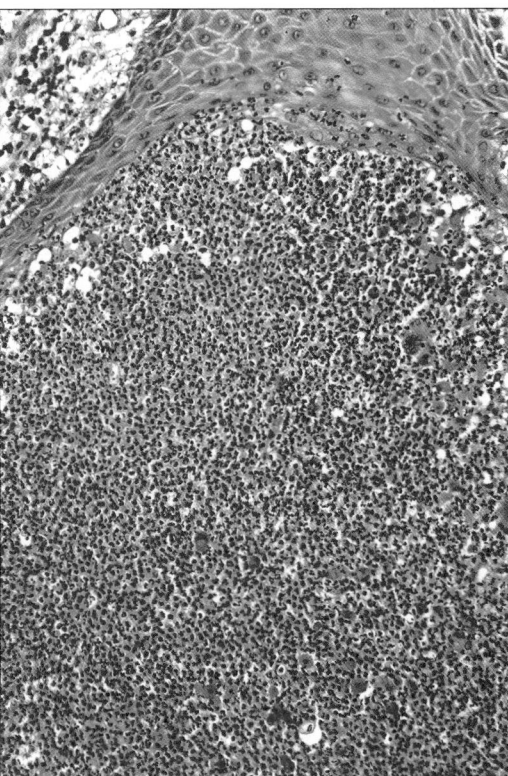

Fig. 17.341
Chromoblastomycosis: abscesses within both the epidermis and dermis are characteristic.

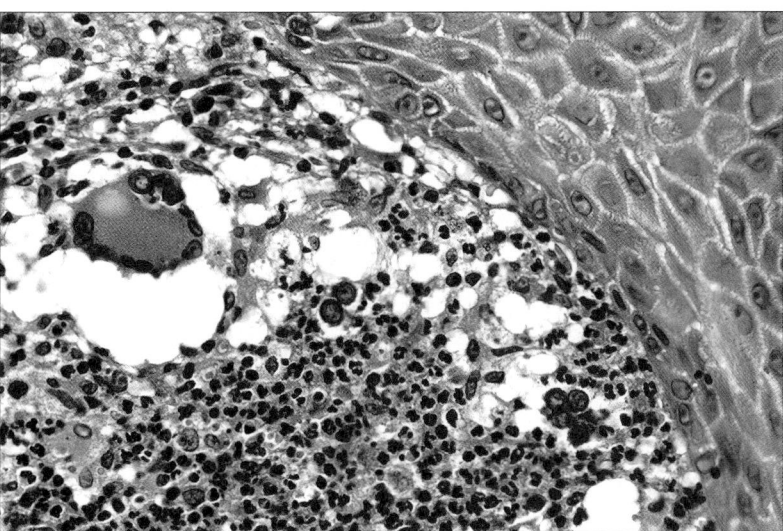

Fig. 17.342
Chromoblastomycosis: pigmented cells within multinucleated giant cells are a characteristic feature.

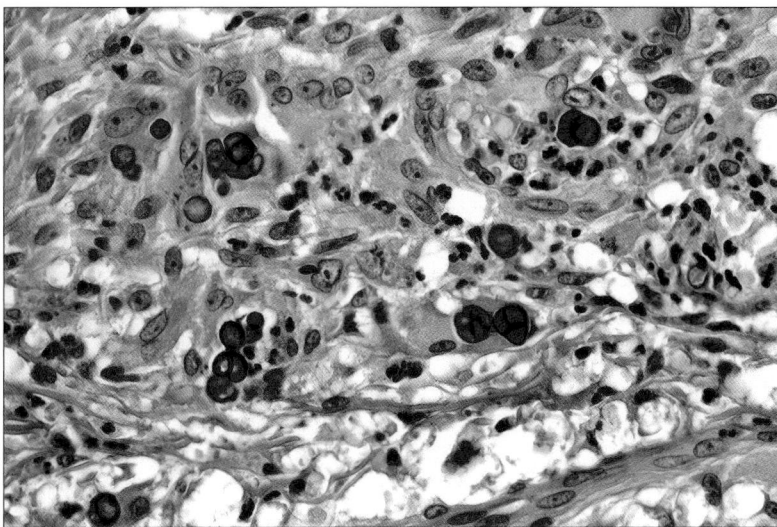

Fig. 17.343
Chromoblastomycosis: the brown-staining (sometimes septate) cells are pathognomonic. Giant cells are also conspicuous in this condition.

6.   Zaias, N. (1978) Chromomycosis. *J Cutan Pathol*, 5, 155–164.
7.   Bansal, A.S., Prabhakar, P. (1989) Chromomycosis: a twenty-year analysis of histologically confirmed cases in Jamaica. *Trop Geograph Med*, **41**, 222–226.
8.   Minotto, R., Bernardi, C.D., Mallmann, L.F. et al (2001) Chromoblastomycosis: a review of 100 cases in the state of Rio Grande do Sul, Brazil. *J Am Acad Dermatol*, **44**, 585–592.
9.   Uribe, J.F., Zuluaga, A.I., Leon, W. et al (1989) Histopathology of chromoblastomycosis. *Mycopathologia*, 105, 1–6.
10. Sharma, N.L., Sharma, R.C., Grover, P.S. et al (1999) Chromoblastomycosis in India. *Int J Dermatol*, 38, 846–851.

11. Bonifaz, A., Carrasco-Gerard, E., Saul, A. (2001) Chromoblastomycosis: clinical and mycologic experience of 51 cases. *Mycoses*, **44**, 1–7.
12. Kawasaki, M., Aoki, M., Ishizaki, H. et al (1999) Molecular epidemiology of Fonsecaea pedrosoi using mitochondrial DNA analysis. *Med Mycol*, 37, 435–440.
13. Hirsh, B.C., Johnson, W.C. (1984) Pathology of graulomatous diseases: mixed inflammatory granulomas. *Int J Dermatol*, **23**, 585–597.
14. Batres, E., Wolf, J.E., Rudolph, A.H. et al (1978) Transepithelial elimination of cutaneous chromomycosis. *Arch Dermatol*, **114**, 1231–1232.

Mycetoma

Clinical features

Mycetoma (Gr. *mykes*, fungus; *oma*, tumor) is a chronically discharging infection of skin and subcutaneous tissue, characterized by multiple sinus tracks and the presence of granules in the exudate.[1–3] It can be caused by bacteria (actinomycetoma) (e.g. *Nocardia*, see above) or (less commonly) by fungi (eumycetoma). Mycetoma is more or less confined to tropical zones. It most commonly occurs on the foot, although other sites can be affected (*Fig. 17.344*).

Repeated inoculation by minor trauma is necessary to produce a lesion, which begins as a papule and enlarges to become a discharging nodule. This process extends to the adjacent skin and the discharging fistulae do not heal (*Fig. 17.345*). The affected area becomes distorted by inflammation and fibrosis, and the underlying bone may become involved. Mycetoma occurs most commonly in 20 to 50-year-olds and shows a marked male preponderance. It relates to repeated occupational trauma. Mycetomas caused by fungi are in general less inflammatory and less deeply invasive than bacterial lesions.

Pathogenesis and histological features

The most common fungal causes of mycetoma include:
- *Madurella mycetomatis*
- *Madurella grisea*
- *Pseudallescheria boydii*
- *Pyrenochaeta romeroi*
- *Leptosphaeria senegalensis*
- *Neotestudina rosatti*.

Bacterial causes include species of *Nocardia*, *Actinomyces* and *Streptomyces*.[1,4] Fungal causes account for only 2% of cases of mycetoma.[2] Of these, *M. mycetomatis* is the most important.[5]

All the organisms produce granules, the configuration and color of which may be helpful in identifying the causative agent (*Figs 17.346–17.349, Table 17.3*).[2] The granules are seen within areas of suppuration and are surrounded by palisaded histiocytes. They consist of an organized compact mass of hyphae, which may be associated with adherent neutrophils or a crystalline matrix.[5,6] Multinucleate giant cells occur beyond this and there is a peripheral region of edematous granulation tissue. The use of special stains is of value in distinguishing actinomycetic from fungal (eumycetic) causes of mycetoma. The latter

Fig. 17.344
Mycetoma: the foot is grossly swollen and misshapen. Numerous draining sinuses are present.

stain positively with PAS and silver stains but are negative with Gram stain (*Fig. 17.350*). A Splendore–Hoeppli phenomenon is sometimes evident (*Fig. 17.351*).

Response to therapy is variable, but the condition is more problematical when deep tissues are involved.

References

1. Magana, M. (1984) Mycetoma. *Int J Dermatol*, 23, 221–236.
2. Magana, M., Magana-Garcia, M. (1989) Mycetoma. *Dermatol Clin*, 7, 203–217.
3. McGinnis, M.R. (1996) Mycetoma. *Dermatol Clin*, 14, 97–104.
4. Boiron, P., Locci, R., Goodfellow, M. et al (1998) Nocardia, nocardiosis and mycetoma. *Med Mycol*, 36 (Suppl. 1), 26–37.
5. McGinnis, M.R., Hilger, A.E. (1987) Infections caused by black fungi. *Arch Dermatol*, 123, 1300–1302.
6. Fahal, A.H., el Toum, E.A., el Hassan, A.M. et al (1995) The host tissue reaction to Madurella mycetomatis: new classification. *J Med Vet Mycol*, 33, 15–17.

Phaeohyphomycosis

Clinical features

Phaeohyphomycetes are a heterogeneous group of pigmented (dematiaceous) fungi with both yeast-like and hyphae-like forms in tissues.[1] The sclerotic bodies of chromoblastomycosis are not seen. There are very large numbers of causative organisms, all of which show pigmented yeast-like cells, pseudohyphae and distorted short or long hyphae in variable proportions.[1,2]

Phaeohyphomycosis can be subdivided into superficial, cutaneous, corneal, subcutaneous and systemic/disseminated forms.[2–4] Keratitis is an additional manifestation.[5]

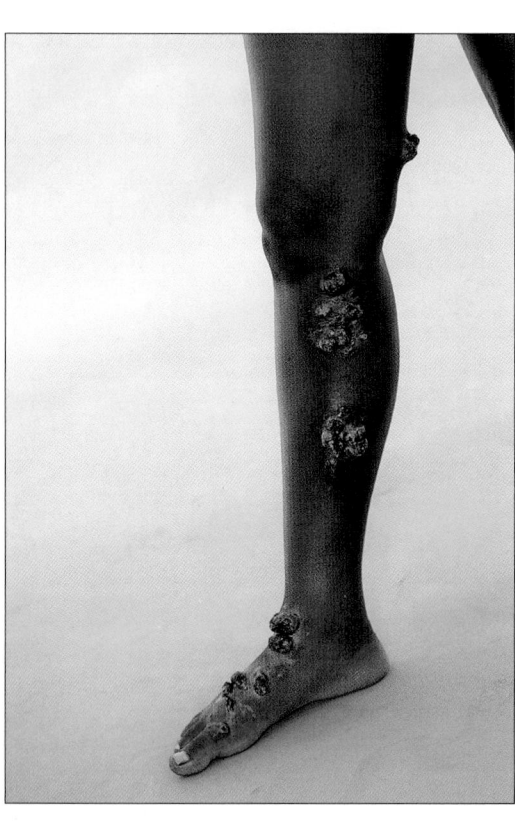

Fig. 17.345
Mycetoma: multiple ulcerated verrucous nodules are present. By courtesy of N.C. Dlova, MD, Nelson R. Mandela School of Medicine, University of KwaZulu-Natal, South Africa.

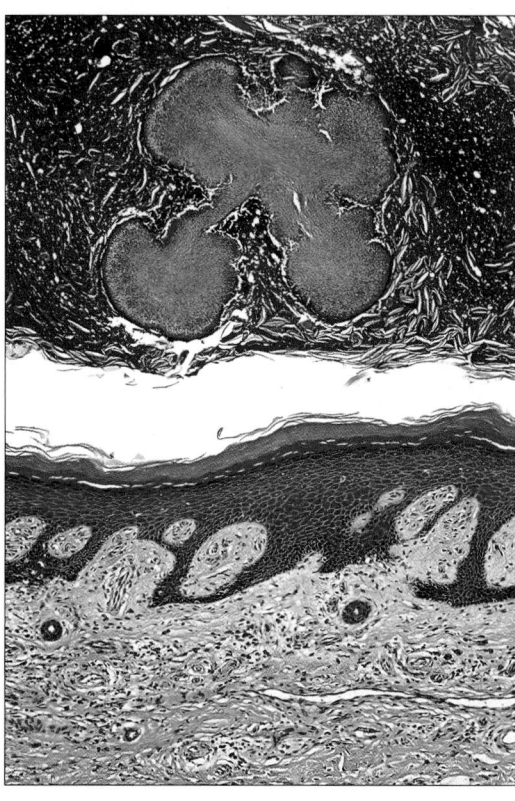

Fig. 17.347
Mycetoma: in this example a colony is present in the overlying crust.

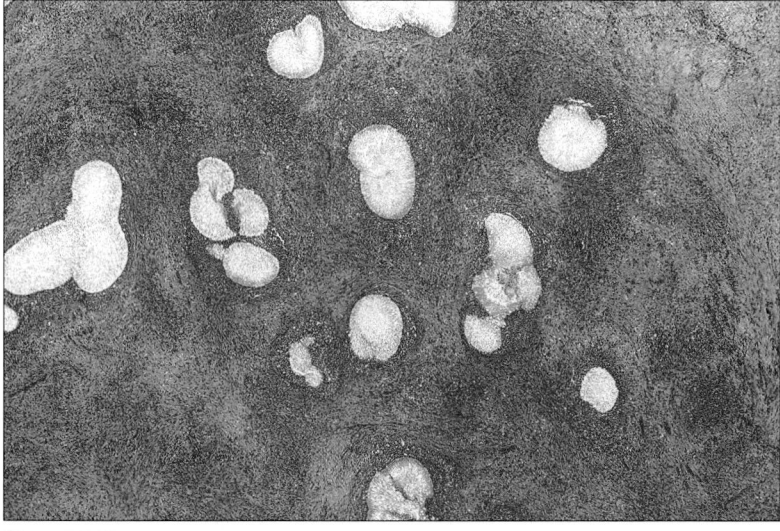

Fig. 17.346
Mycetoma: characteristic granules are present in neutrophil abscesses. There is a peripheral histiocytic/giant cell palisade.

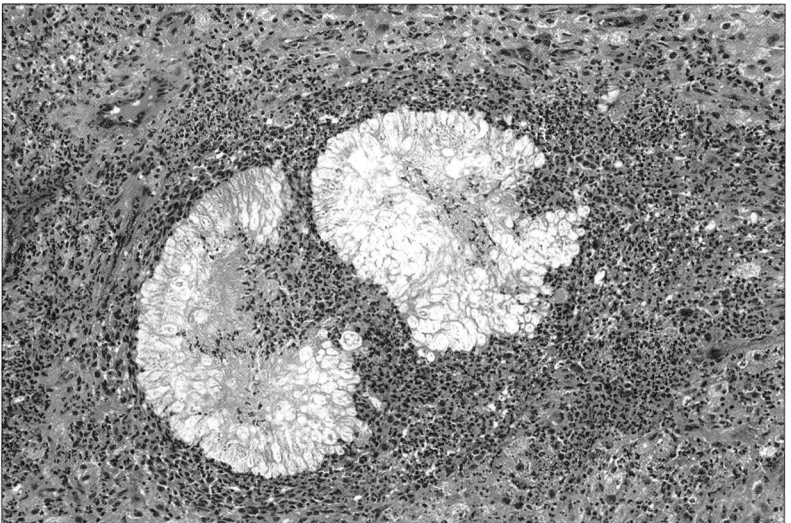

Fig. 17.348
Mycetoma: the internal structure of the granule is clearly visible in this high power view.

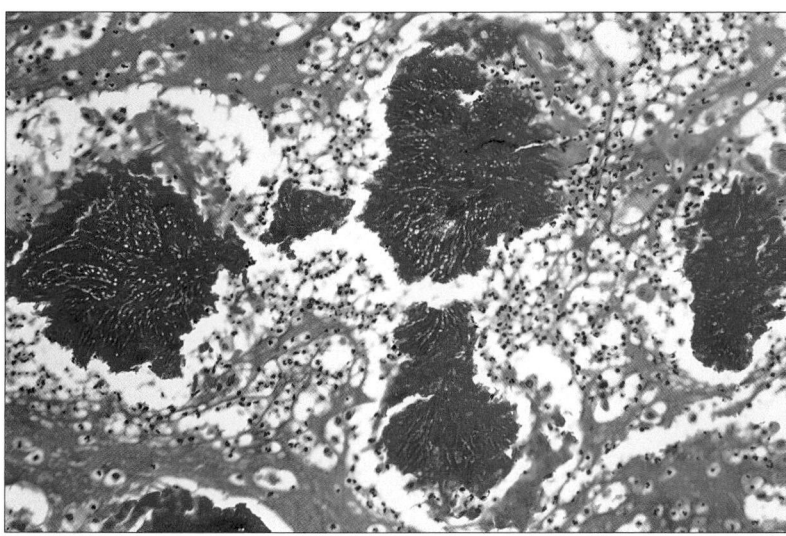

Fig. 17.349
Mycetoma: pigmented granules are characteristic of *Madurella mycetomatis* infection.

Table 17.3
Color of granules in mycetoma

	Maduromycotic (eumycetic)	Actinomycetic
Black	*Madurella mycetomatis* *Madurella grisea* *Pyrenochaeta romeroi* *Phialophora jeanselmei* *Leptosphaeria senegalensis* *Leptosphaeria tompkinsii*	
Yellow or yellowish-white	*Allescheria boydii* *Cephalosporium* sp. *Fusarium* sp. *Neotestudina rosatti* *Actinomadura madurae* *Streptomyces somaliensis*	
Red		*Actinomadura pelletieri*
White or not visible		*Nocardia brasiliensis* *Nocardia caviae* *Nocardia asteroides*

Reproduced with permission from Magaña, M. and Magaña-Garcia, M. (1989) *Dermatologic Clinics*, 7, 203–217.

- Black piedra caused by *Piedraia hortae* is an example of superficial phaeohyphomycosis affecting the hair shaft (see p. 940).[3]
- Cutaneous lesions include macules, papules, plaques, nodules, cystic or verrucous lesions, sometimes with ulceration.[1]
- *Exophila jeanselmei* is the most common cause of subcutaneous phaeohyphomycosis, the patients presenting with solitary discrete asymptomatic well-circumscribed subcutaneous nodules.[2] These usually follow trauma, most often to the limbs.[6–9]

Phaeohyphomycosis may also present in the immunosuppressed, especially those who have received organ transplants.[1,8–10] Nodules often become large (up to several centimeters across) but epidermal involvement is not seen. The necrotic yellow–gray central contents can be aspirated from well-developed lesions.

Disseminated phaeohyphomycosis carries a mortality of almost 80%.[4] The organism most frequently implicated is *Scedosporium prolificans*, and although some patients have been immunocompetent, the majority of infections have occurred in immunocompromised individuals.[4] Endocarditis may occur, particularly in relation to prosthetic cardiac valves.

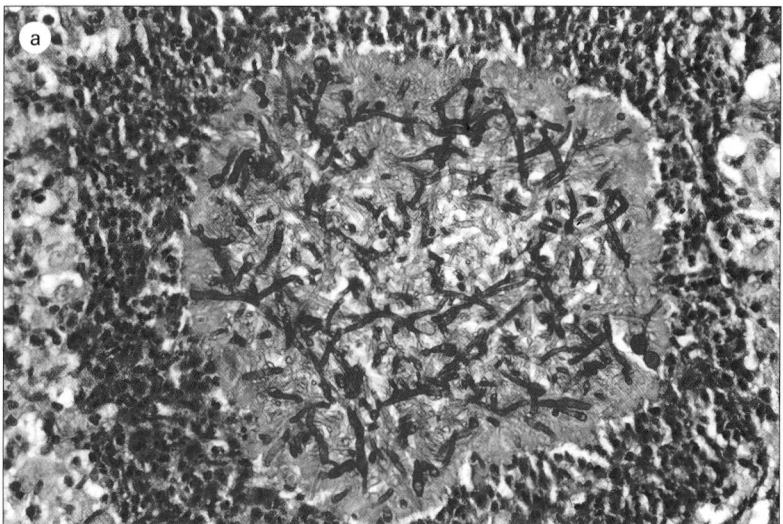

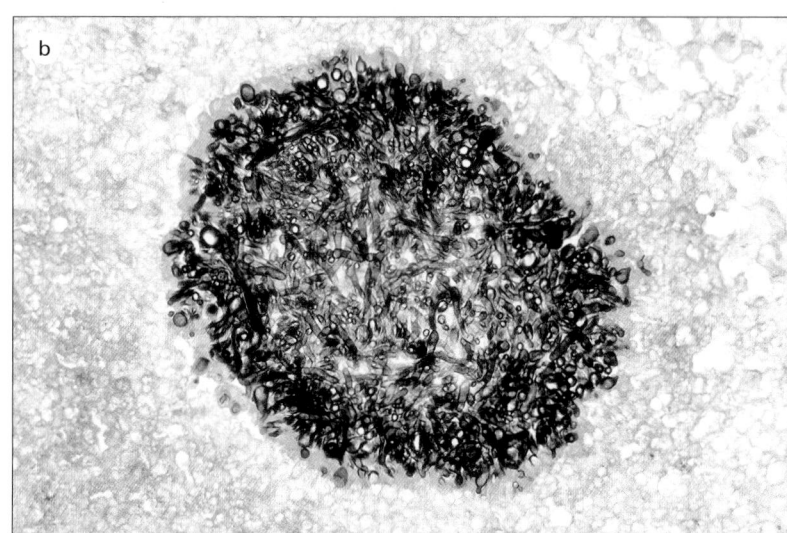

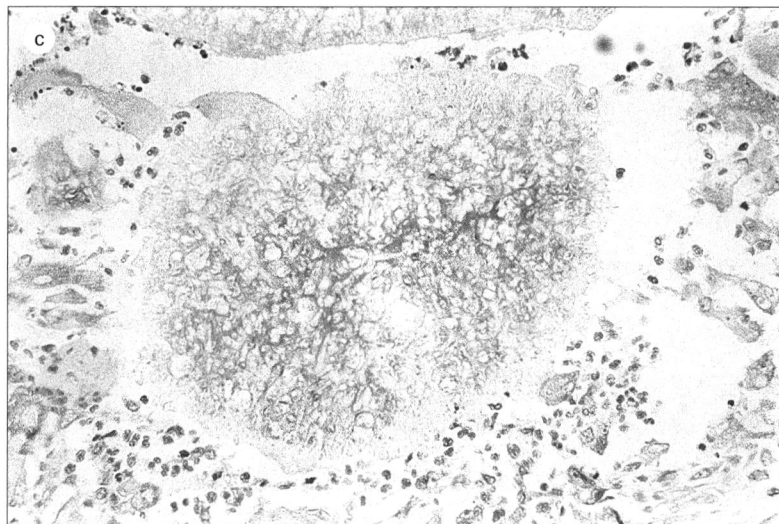

Fig. 17.350
(a–c) Mycetoma: the use of special stains readily confirms the fungal nature of this variant. (a) Periodic acid–Schiff; (b) methenamine silver; (c) Gram.

Pathogenesis and histological features

Phaeohyphomycetes are present in vegetation, soil and decaying organic material.[1] The disease occurs by traumatic implantation. Phaeohyphomycetes are mostly opportunistic pathogens.[10]

E. jeanselmei is seen as yellow–brown/chestnut-brown, irregularly swollen, septate hyphae, which can be branched or unbranched.[2] Yeast-like forms are also seen, sometimes in chains.[1] The organisms occur in the necrotic center of the abscess and in the surrounding cellular infiltrate of epithelioid macrophages, giant cells and neutrophils (*Figs 17.352–17.354*). Sometimes it can be very difficult to find the organisms and special stains can be invaluable (*Fig. 17.355*). A wood splinter may occasionally be present. There is a dense fibrotic reaction around the inflammatory component.[2]

Differential diagnosis

Phaeohyphomycosis is distinguished from chromoblastomycosis by the absence of the pigmented sclerotic bodies seen in tissue sections in the latter condition. It is of interest that the same fungus may cause either condition depending upon the response to the host's internal environment.[1,6]

References

1. Noel, S.B., Greer, D.L., Abadie, S.M. et al (1988) Primary cutaneous phaeohyphomycosis: report of three cases. *J Am Acad Dermatol*, **18**, 1023–1030.
2. McGinnis, M.R. (1983) Chromoblastomycosis and phaeohyphomycosis: new concepts, diagnosis and mycology. *J Am Acad Dermatol*, **8**, 1–16.
3. McGinnis, M.R., Hilger, A.E. (1987) Infections caused by black fungi. *Arch Dermatol*, **123**, 1300–1302.

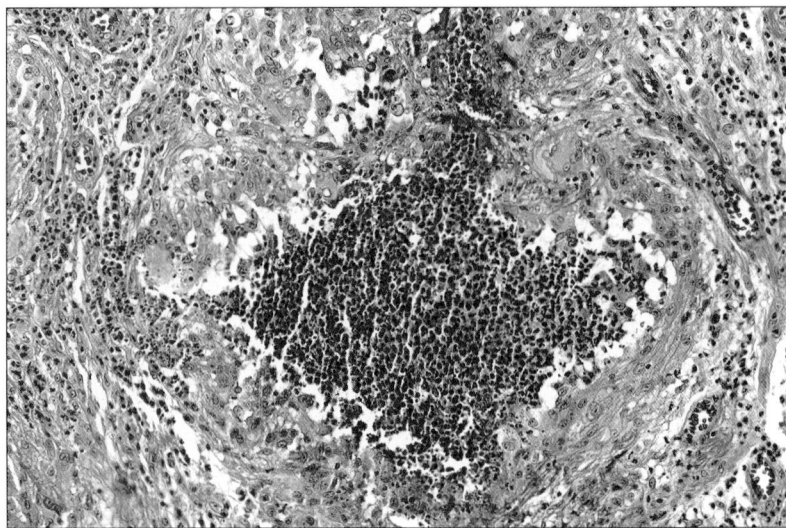

Fig. 17.353
Phaeohyphomycosis: high power view showing mixed suppurative and granulomatous inflammation.

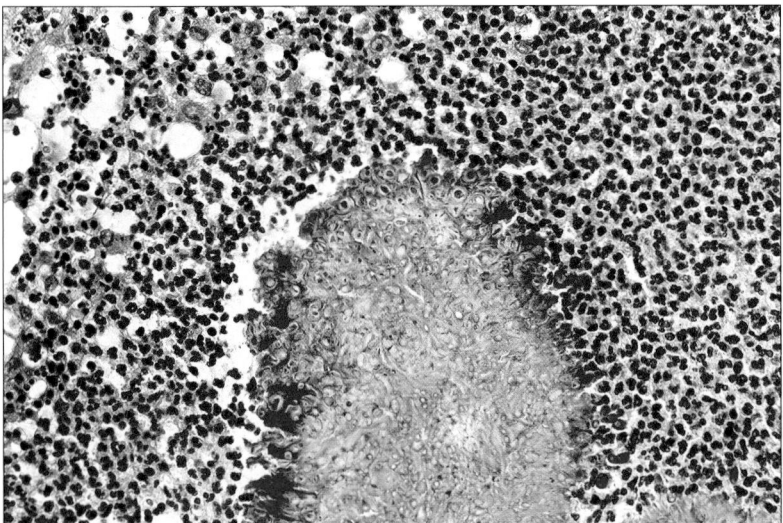

Fig. 17.351
Mycetoma: this fibrin stain highlights the Splendore–Hoeppli phenomenon.

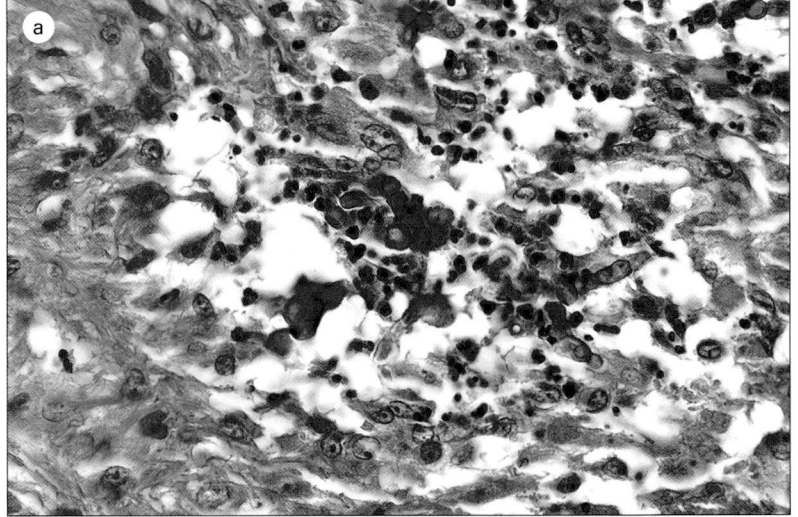

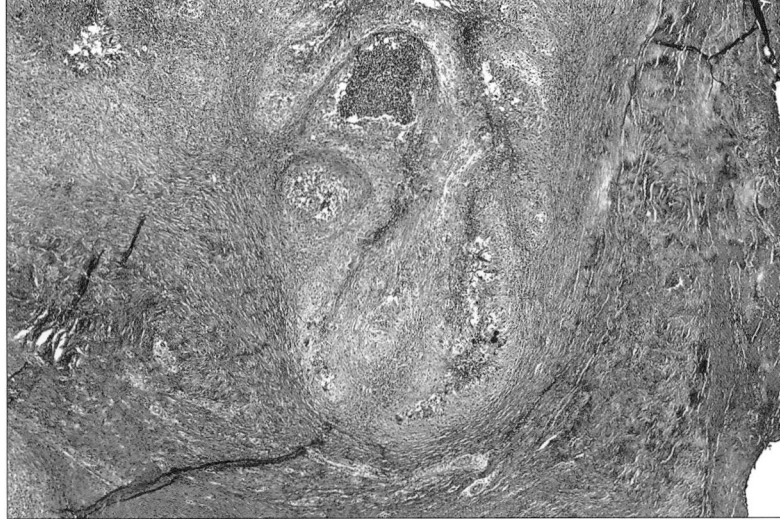

Fig. 17.352
Phaeohyphomycosis: this low power view shows the typical appearance of a deep dermal discrete nodule.

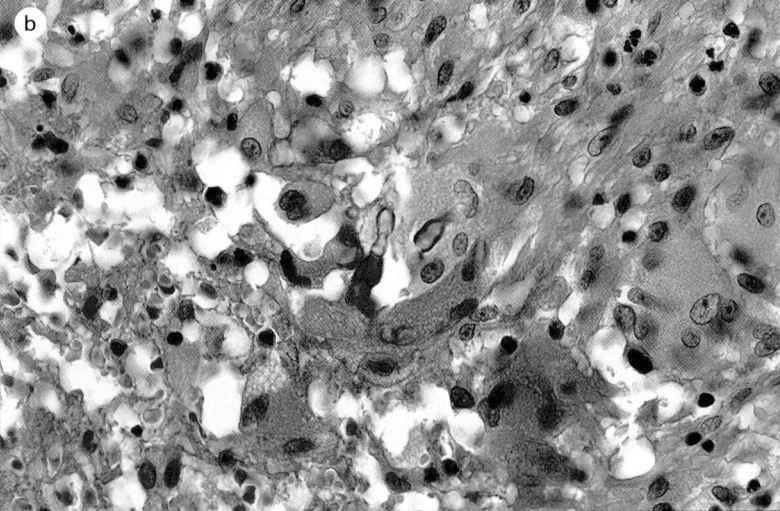

Fig. 17.354
(a, b) Phaeohyphomycosis: pigmented hyphae and yeast forms are present.

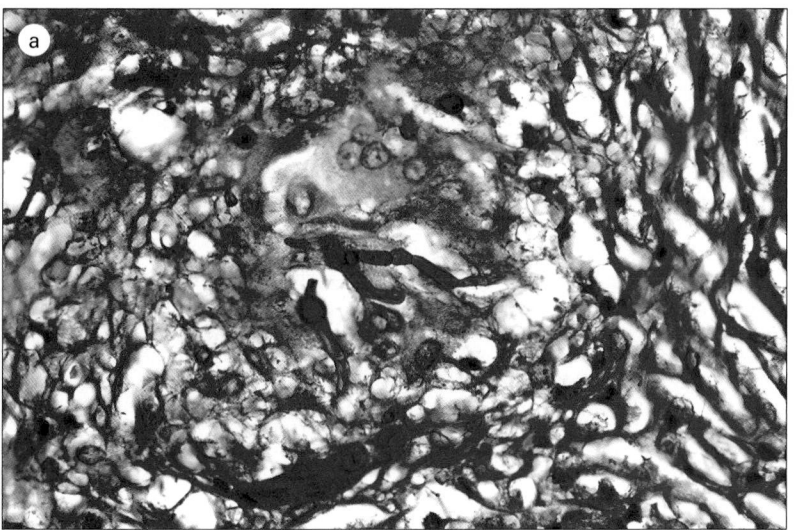
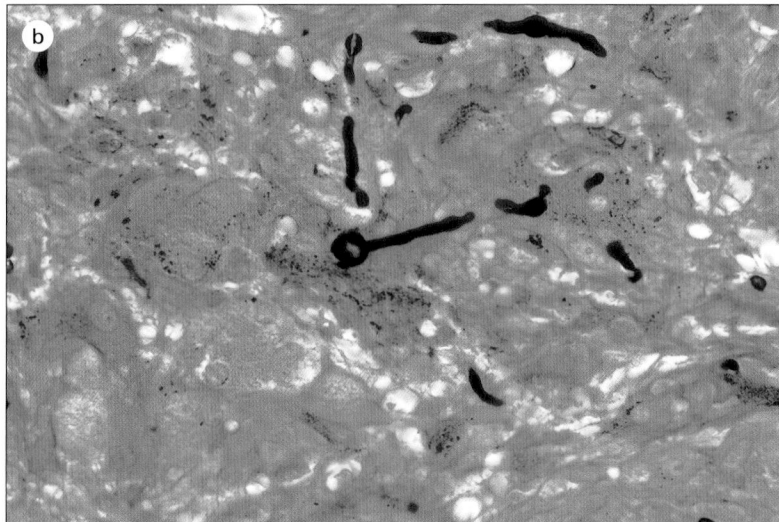

Fig. 17.355
Phaeohyphomycosis: the hyphae can be highlighted with (a) periodic acid–Schiff and (b) silver stains. Note the septa.

4. Revankar, S.G., Patterson, J.E., Sutton, D.A. et al (2002) Disseminated phaeohyphomycosis: review of an emerging mycosis. *Clin Infect Dis*, **34**, 467–476.
5. Forster, R.K., Rebell, G., Wilson, D.A. (1975) Dematiaceous fungal keratitis. Clinical isolates and management. *Br J Ophthalmol*, **59**, 372–376.
6. Ajello, L. (1986) Hyalohyphomycosis and phaeohyphomycosis: two global disease entities of public health importance. *Eur J Epidemiol*, **2**, 243–251.
7. Suzuki, Y., Udagawa, S., Wakita, H. et al (1998) Subcutaneous phaeohyphomycosis caused by Geniculosporium species: a new fungal pathogen. *Br J Dermatol*, **138**, 346–350.

8. Matsui, T., Nishimoto, K., Udagawa, S. et al (1999) Subcutaneous phaeohyphomycosis caused by Phaeoacremonium rubrigenum in an immunosuppressed patient. *Nippon Ishinkin Gakkai Zasshi*, **40**, 99–102.
9. Castro, L.G., da Silva Lacaz, C., Guarro, J. et al (2001) Phaeohyphomycotic cyst caused by Colletotrichum crassipes. *J Clin Microbiol*, **39**, 2321–2324.
10. Ikai, K., Tomono, H., Watanabe, S. (1988) Phaemohyphomycosis caused by Phialophora richardsiae. *J Am Acad Dermatol*, **19**, 478–481.

Alternariosis

Clinical features

Alternaria is a pigmented fungus within the heterogenous phaeohyphomycete group.[1,2] It is associated with inoculation during minor trauma and is often found in immunocompromised hosts.[3]

Patients present with ulcers, erythematous macules and papules, pustules and nodules on exposed skin surfaces, sometimes crusted or verrucous (*Fig. 17.356*).[4] Large ulcerated plaques with pustules may also occur.[5,6] Lesions may be found on the dorsa of the hands, the fingers, elbows, knees, face and dorsa of the feet.[7] A sporotrichoid distribution of skin lesions has been reported.[8] The lesions occasionally regress spontaneously; otherwise, they respond well to antimycotic drugs and leave only slight scars.

Pathogenesis and histological features

Alternaria is found widely in soil and plants and is most often inoculated into skin with wood splinters. In the tissues the fungus is seen as pigmented hyphae and open rounded bodies 5–20 μm in diameter. They may be seen free or in histiocytes or giant cells. There is a dermal inflammatory infiltrate comprised of a mixed neutrophil and granulomatous reaction. A variable number of microabscesses may be present. Epidermal changes are not marked.

References

1. Di Silverio, A., Sacchi, S. (1986) Cutaneous alternariosis: a rare chromohyphomycosis. *Mycopathologia*, **95**, 159–166.
2. Viviani, M.A., Tortorano, A.M., Laria, G. et al (1986) Two new cases of alternariosis with a review of the literature. *Mycopathologia*, **96**, 3–12.
3. Watzig, V., Schmidt, U. (1989) Primary cutaneous granulomatous alternariosis. *Hautarzt*, **40**, 718–720.
4. Pederson, N.B., Mardh, P.A., Hallberg, T. et al (1976) Cutaneous alternariosis. *Br J Dermatol*, **94**, 201–209.
5. Acland, K.M., Hay, R.J., Groves, R. (1998) Cutaneous infection with Alternaria alternata complicating immunosuppression: successful treatment with itraconazole. *Br J Dermatol*, **138**, 354–356.
6. Ioannidou, D.J., Stefanidou, M.P., Maraki, S.G. et al (2000) Cutaneous alternariosis in a patient with idiopathic pulmonary fibrosis. *Int J Dermatol*, **39**, 293–295.
7. Mikat, D.M. (1980) Unusual fungal conditions of the skin. *Int J Dermatol*, **19**, 18–23.
8. Gerdsen, R., Uerlich, M., de Hoog, G.S. et al (2001) Sporotrichoid phaeohyphomycosis due to Alternaria infectoria. *Br J Dermatol*, **145**, 484–486.

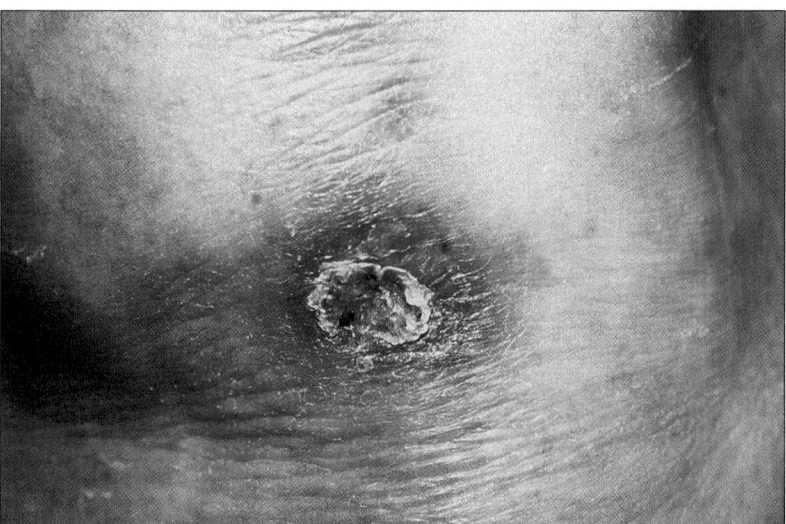

Fig. 17.356
Cutaneous alternariosis: crusted ulcer at the base of the thumb. By courtesy of S.W. Lanigan, MD, Bridgend General Hospital, Bridgend, UK.

Histoplasmosis

Clinical features

Histoplasmosis is caused by two very similar fungi, *Histoplasma capsulatum* var. *capsulatum* (*Histoplasma capsulatum*) and *Histoplasma capsulatum* var. *duboisii*. Despite the morphological similarity, the two species have different geographical distributions and clinical presentations.

Histoplasma capsulatum

H. capsulatum is very common in North America (Ohio and Mississippi river valleys) but is seen worldwide.[1] It is rare in Europe, although cases have occurred there since the advent of the AIDS pandemic.[2] It is present in soil and in poultry and bat droppings and the infection has also been reported following chopping rotten wood.[3] Spore inhalation can cause an acute pulmonary infection (if the inoculum is very large) but it is probable that more often a subclinical infection provokes a positive histoplasmosis skin test.[4]

Chronic pulmonary (cavitatory) histoplasmosis (buckshot calcification) and disseminated disease are also recognized variants.[1,5] Chronic pulmonary histoplasmosis may sometimes mimic secondary tuberculosis. Disseminated histoplasmosis is uncommon, but is an important complication of immunosuppression including AIDS; as a consequence it is being recognized with increasing frequency.[6–10] Lesions are particularly seen in the liver, spleen, lymph nodes and bone marrow.[4] A wide variety of systems may be involved, however, and therefore symptoms and signs are very variable. Fever and weight loss, although non-specific, are common.[10]

Disseminated histoplasmosis may be classified into acute, subacute and chronic forms in diminishing degrees of severity.[5] The acute form usually affects infants while chronic disseminated histoplasmosis is characteristically seen in adults. Patients with AIDS are at particular risk of developing lethal progressive disseminated histoplasmosis.[1] Under such conditions it has been suggested that the disease may sometimes represent reactivation of a quiescent lesion.[4,5] The possibility of patient-to-patient transmission has also been reported.[11] Disseminated histoplasmosis can occasionally be the initial mode of presentation of an HIV infection.[10] Cutaneous involvement is uncommon and is almost always a feature of disseminated (fungemic) disease. It occurs in 4–11% of cases.[5,8,12] Lesions are most common on the arms, face and trunk, but obviously may be encountered elsewhere.[10] Skin lesions present as macules, papules, nodules, pustules, indurated (sometimes ulcerated) plaques, purpura, pyoderma gangrenosum-like lesions, abscesses, furuncles, cellulitis, eczematous eruptions, panniculitis and subcutaneous nodules (*Fig. 17.357*).[4,13–15] Oral ulcers may also be present.[10] An unusual case with vaginal ulcerations as the presenting sign of disseminated infection has been reported.[16] The very rare primary cutaneous lesions (representing local inoculation) present as nodules, ulcers, cellulitis or lymphangitis.[4,17] Diffuse cutaneous hyperpigmentation sometimes reflects an underlying histoplasmosis-related Addison's disease.[10] Erythema nodosum and erythema multiforme are not infrequent hypersensitivity manifestations.[4,18]

Histoplasma capsulatum var. duboisii

H. capsulatum var. *duboisii* usually occurs in equatorial Africa although it has been documented elsewhere.[19,20] Occasional cases have, for example, been encountered in Europe, reflecting the impact of travel and immigration patterns.[2] It has two main forms of presentation:
- Patients may develop a localized chronic form with single lesions in the skin, subcutaneous fat or bone.
- Patients may manifest disseminated disease, which in addition affects lymph nodes and abdominal viscera.[1]

Skin lesions include superficial cutaneous and subcutaneous granulomata and abscesses and osteomyelitis with overlying cutaneous spread (*Fig. 17.358*).[3] The calvarium and long bones are predominantly affected.[3] In contrast to *H. capsulatum*, pulmonary disease is rare.

Pathogenesis and histological features

H. capsulatum is a dimorphic fungus appearing as a mycelium at room temperature, but growing as a yeast at body temperature.[1] Despite its name it is *not* encapsulated. Infection is most commonly transmitted by the inhalation of spores or hyphae of *H. capsulatum*. The hyphal form grows in the soil; the yeast form (2–4 μm in diameter) occurs in the tissues, entirely intracellularly following inhalation of the spores.

The tissue response to infection with *H. capsulatum* parallels that seen with *M. tuberculosis* including primary lesions, reinfection and the development of caseation.[4] Following pulmonary and nodal involvement, susceptible people develop a fungemia, with spread of the organism widely throughout the body. A chronic tuberculoid granulomatous inflammatory response develops. The yeast is present within distended macrophages as a basophilic dot with a surrounding artifactual halo (pseudocapsule) (*Fig. 17.359*). Its features are similar to those of *Leishmania*, but it lacks the kinetoplast. It may be further differentiated by the use of special stains including the PAS reaction and methenamine

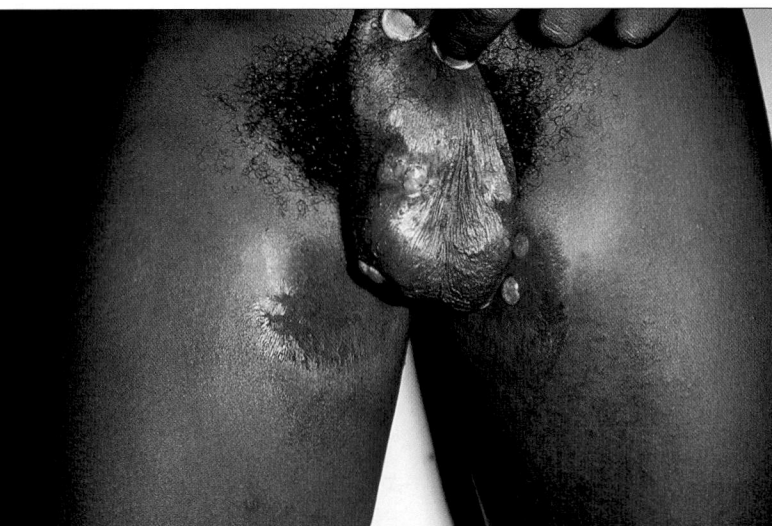

Fig. 17.357
Histoplasma capsulatum: note the ulcerated lesions on the scrotum and thigh. This patient was HIV positive. By courtesy of C. Furlonge, MD, Port of Spain, Trinidad.

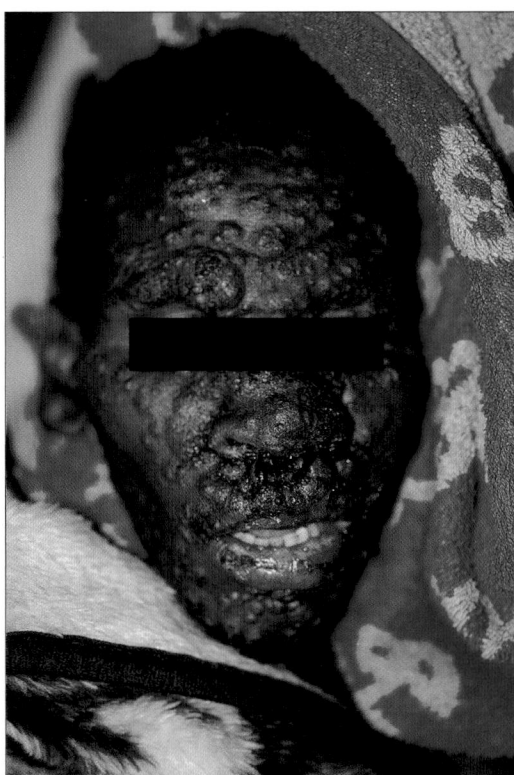

Fig. 17.358
Histoplasma duboisii: there are innumerable disfiguring papules, nodules and plaques. By courtesy of N.C. Dlova, MD, Nelson R. Mandela School of Medicine, University of KwaZulu-Natal, South Africa.

silver (*Fig. 17.360*). Transepidermal elimination of *Histoplasma* has been reported in association with AIDS.[13,21] It should be noted that some AIDS-associated cases lack a granulomatous tissue response and may instead show focal necrosis and a mild perivascular and interstitial infiltrate predominated by polymorphonuclear leukocytes, lymphocytes and some histiocytes. Karyorrhexis may be a prominent feature, resulting in potential confusion with atypical leukocytoclastic vasculitis.[22] Involvement of cutaneous nerves by the organism has also been described in association with AIDS.[23]

   H. capsulatum var. *duboisii* is also seen intracellularly, but usually within multinucleate giant cells (*Figs 17.361–17.363*). It is a large yeast, 7–15 μm in diameter, with characteristically thick cell walls. Narrow-based budding may be seen and short chains are occasionally formed.[1] The early stages are followed by necrosis and then by a granulomatous and fibrous reaction.

Differential diagnosis

H. capsulatum var. *capsulatum* must be differentiated from *Penicillium* species. Macrophages parasitize both organisms. *H. capsulatum* is

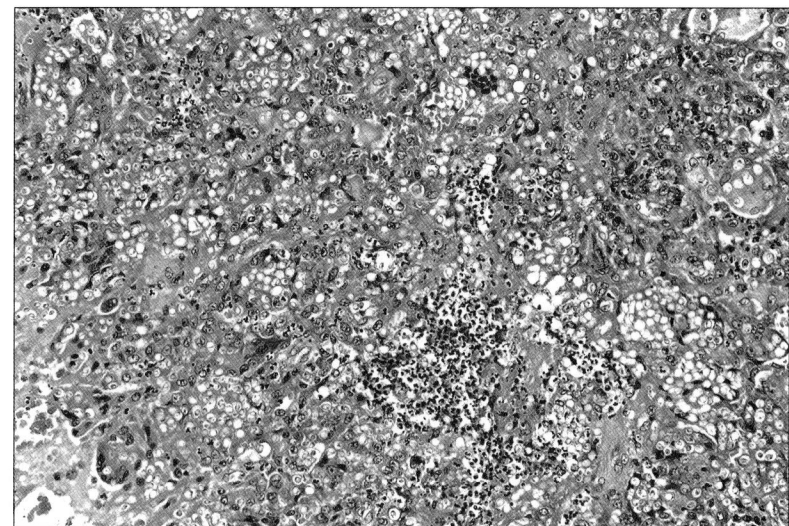

Fig. 17.361
Histoplasma duboisii: a dense granulomatous infiltrate is present in the reticular dermis. The organisms are larger than *Histoplasma capsulatum* and are located within giant cells. By courtesy of S. Lucas, MD, St Thomas' Hospital, London, UK.

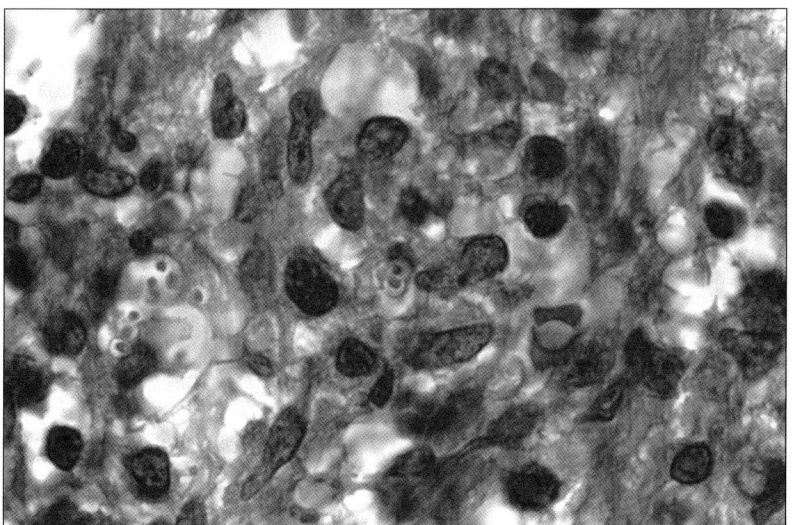

Fig. 17.359
Histoplasma capsulatum: the small yeast forms are intracellular and consist of a small basophilic particle surrounded by a clear halo (a cytoplasmic retraction artifact). By courtesy of R. Carr, MD, Warwick Hospital, Warwick, UK.

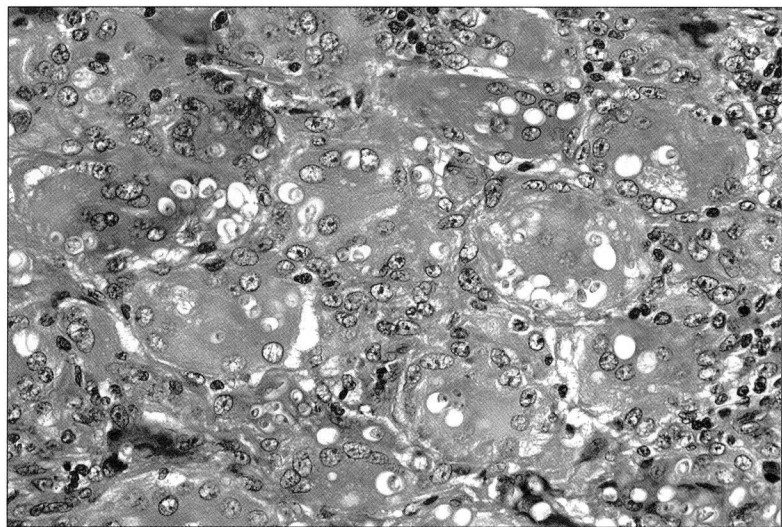

Fig. 17.362
Histoplasma duboisii: the yeast cells have very thick walls and the nuclei are single. This distinguishes *Histoplasma duboisii* from *Blastomyces dermatitidis*, in which nuclei are multiple. By courtesy of S. Lucas, MD, St Thomas' Hospital, London, UK.

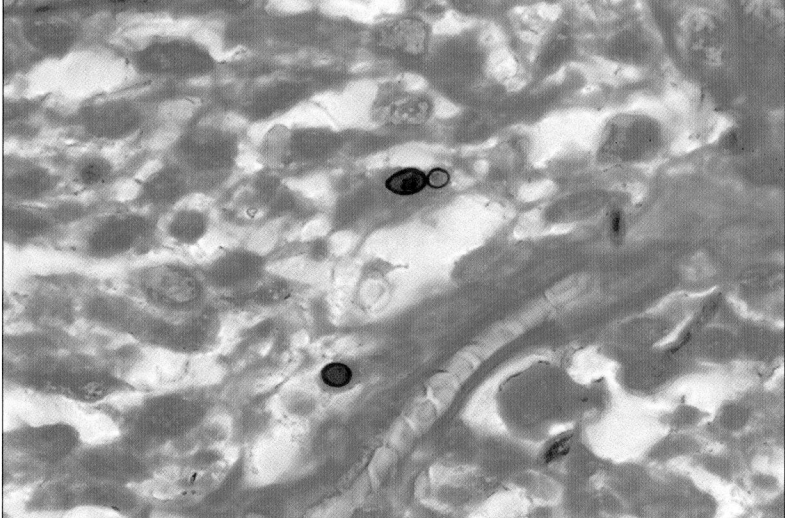

Fig. 17.360
Histoplasma capsulatum: differentiation from leishmaniasis is readily effected by the use of methenamine silver. By courtesy of R. Carr, MD, Warwick Hospital, Warwick, UK.

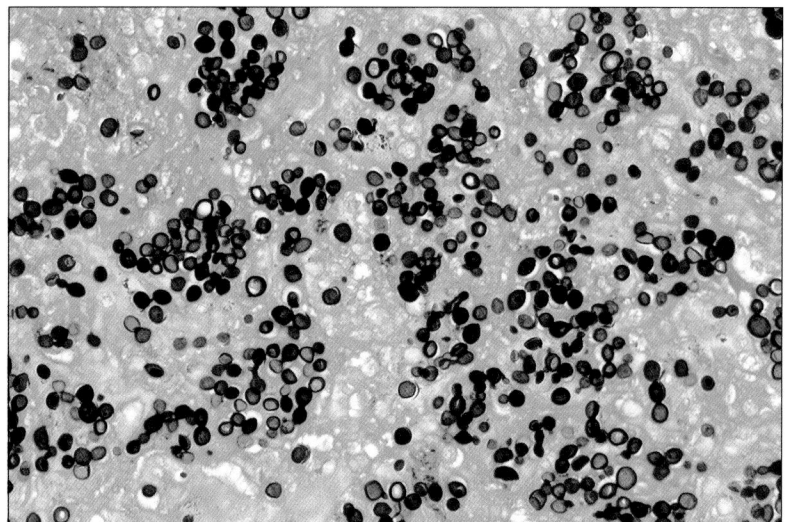

Fig. 17.363
Histoplasma duboisii: the fungi are highlighted with the methenamine silver stain. By courtesy of S. Lucas, MD, St Thomas' Hospital, London, UK.

characterized by narrow-necked budding while *Penicillium* divides by septation.

H. capsulatum var. *duboisii* may be distinguished from *B. dermatitidis* by having single rather than multiple nuclei.

References

1. Davies, S.F. (1990) Histoplasmosis: update, 1989. *Semin Resp Infect*, 5, 93–104.
2. Manfredi, R., Mazzoni, A., Nanetti, A. et al (1994) Histoplasmosis capsulati and duboisii in Europe: the impact of the HIV pandemic, travel and immigration. *Eur J Epidemiol*, 10, 675–681.
3. Pladson, T.R., Stiles, M.A., Kuritsky, J.N. (1984) Pulmonary histoplasmosis. A possible risk in people who cut decayed wood. *Chest*, 86, 435–438.
4. Dijkstra, J.W.E. (1989) Histoplasmosis. *Dermatol Clin*, 7, 251–257.
5. Goodwin, R.A. Jr, Shapiro, J.L., Thurman, G.H. et al (1980) Disseminated histoplasmosis: clinical and pathologic correlations. *Medicin (Baltimore)*, 59, 1–33.
6. Johnson, P.C., Khardori, N., Najjar, A.F. et al (1988) Progressive disseminated histoplasmosis in patients with acquired immunodeficiency syndrome. *Am J Med*, 85, 152–158.
7. Salzman, S.H., Smith, R.L., Aranda, C.P. (1988) Histoplasmosis in patients at risk for the acquired immunodeficiency syndrome in a non-endemic setting. *Chest*, 93, 916–921.
8. Sathapatayavongs, B., Battieger, B.E., Wheat, J. et al (1983) Clinical and laboratory features of disseminated histoplasmosis during two large urban outbreaks. *Medicine (Baltimore)*, 62, 263–270.
9. Graybill, J.R. (1988) Histoplasmosis and AIDS. *J Infect Dis*, 158, 623–626.
10. Cohen, P.R., Bank, D.E., Silvers, D.N. et al (1990). Cutaneous lesions of disseminated histoplasmosis in human immunodeficiency virus-infected patients. *J Am Acad Dermatol*, 23, 422–428.
11. Cohen, P.R., Held, J.L., Grossman, M.E. et al (1991) Disseminated histoplasmosis presenting as an ulcerated verrucous plaque in an HIV-infected man: report of a case possibly involving human to human transmission of histoplasmosis. *Int J Dermatol*, 30, 104–108.
12. Studdard, J., Sneed, W.F., Taylor, M.R. Jr et al (1976) Cutaneous histoplasmosis. *Am Rev Resp Dis*, 113, 689–693.
13. Welykyj, S., von Heimburg, A., Massa, M.C. et al (1991) Cutaneous lesions of histoplasmosis with transepidermal elimination in a patient with acquired immunodeficiency syndrome. *Cutis*, 47, 397–400.
14. Laochumroonvorapong, P., DiCostanzo, D.P., Wu, H. et al (2001) Disseminated histoplasmosis presenting as pyoderma gangrenosum-like lesions in a patient with acquired immunodeficiency syndrome. *Int J Dermatol*, 40, 518–521.
15. Stong, G.C., Raval, H.B., Martin, J.W. et al (1994) Nodular subcutaneous histoplasmosis. A case report with diagnosis by fine needle aspiration biopsy. *Acta Cytol*, 38, 777–781.
16. Smith, M.B., Schnadig, V.Z., Zaharopoulos, P. et al (1997) Disseminated Histoplasma capsulatum infection presenting as genital ulcerations. *Obstet Gynecol*, 89, 842–844.
17. Giessel, M., Rau, J.M. (1980) Primary cutaneous histoplasmosis. *Cutis*, 25, 152–154.
18. Chapman, S.W., Daniel, C.R. 3rd (1994) Cutaneous manifestations of fungal infection. *Infect Dis Clin North Am*, 8, 879–910.
19. Nethercott, J.R., Schachter, R.K., Givan, K.F. et al (1978) Histoplasmosis due to Histoplasma capsulatum var. duboisii in a Canadian immigrant. *Arch Dermatol*, 114, 595–598.
20. Shore, R.N., Waltersdorff, R.L., Edelstein, M.V. et al (1981) African histoplasmosis in the United States. *JAMA*, 245, 734.
21. Mayoral, F., Penneys, N.S. (1985) Disseminated histoplasmosis presenting as a transepidermal elimination disorder in an AIDS victim. *J Am Acad Dermatol*, 13, 842–844.
22. Eidbo, J., Sánchez, R.L., Tschen, J.A. et al (1993) Cutaneous manifestations of histoplasmosis in the acquired immunodeficiency syndrome. *Am J Surg Pathol*, 17, 110–116.
23. Rodríguez, G., Ordoñez, N., Motta, A. (2001) Histoplasma capsulatum var. capsulatum within cutaneous nerves in patients with disseminated histoplasmosis in AIDS. *Br J Dermatol*, 144, 205–207.

Penicilliosis

Clinical features

Penicilliosis is caused by *Penicillium marneffei*.[1–3] The fungus is endemic in countries of South-East Asia, particularly Thailand, and also in the south of China.[4,5] The fungus also occurs in northeastern India.[6] The organism has become an important cause of morbidity and mortality in patients infected with HIV. The great majority of patients with penicilliosis are HIV positive. The disease is systemic with frequent involvement of lungs, spleen, liver, lymph nodes, bone marrow and skin.[3,4] Patients present with fever, weight loss, anemia, cough and skin lesions. The skin lesions consist of papules and nodules that may appear ulcerated or show umbilication. The mortality is high unless systemic treatment is given promptly.

Pathogenesis and histological features

Penicillium marneffei is the only fungus of the *Penicillium* species that is dimorphic. A presumptive diagnosis is usually possible by microscopic examination of touch preparations or tissue obtained by aspiration and stained with Wright.[5,6] Histologically, a granulomatous response is usually minimal or absent. Instead, there is focal necrosis and a predominantly perivascular inflammatory cell infiltrate consisting of scattered neutrophils with nuclear dust, lymphocytes and variable numbers of histiocytes. Organisms are abundant and present in the cytoplasm of histiocytes. Extracellular organisms are also seen. Oval and elongated yeasts are identified on staining with PAS and Grocott. Distinction from leishmaniasis is based on the presence of a kinetoplast in the latter. Distinction from histoplasmosis is based on the fact that *H. capsulatum* displays narrow-necked budding while *P. marneffei* divides by septation.

References

1. Supparatpinyo, K., Chiewchanvit, S., Hirunsri, P. et al (1992) Penicillium marneffei infection in patients infected with human immunodeficiency virus. *Clin Infect Dis*, 14, 871–874.
2. Tsui, W.M., Ma, K.F., Tsang, D.N. (1992) Disseminated Penicillium marneffei infection in HIV infected subject. *Histopathology*, 20, 287–293.
3. Duong, T.A. (1996) Infection due to Penicillium marneffei, an emerging pathogen: review of 155 reported cases. *Clin Infect Dis*, 23, 125–130.
4. Supparatpinyo, K., Khamwan, C., Baosoung, V. et al (1994) Disseminated Penicillium marneffei infection in South-East Asia. *Lancet*, 344, 110–113.
5. Cooper, C.R. Jr, McGinnis, M.R. (1997) Pathology of Penillium marneffei. An emerging immunodeficiency syndrome-related pathogen. *Arch Pathol Lab Med*, 121, 798–804.
6. Ranjana, K.H., Priyokumar, K., Singh, T.J. et al (2002) Disseminated Penicillium marneffei infection and HIV-infected patients in Manipur state, India. *J Infect*, 45, 268–271.

Sporotrichosis

Clinical features

Sporothrix schenckii has a worldwide distribution, growing saprophytically in decaying vegetation and on wood.[1] Most often it represents a localized infection limited to the skin and lymphatics but rarely systemic disease may occur, particularly affecting the skin, bones, joints, meninges and, occasionally, the oropharyngeal region.[2–4] It is inoculated into skin, often by wood splinters, thorns and sphagnum moss. Rare cases have been acquired as a result of ritual tattooing.[5] Man-to-man and animal-to-man transmission has also been reported.[6–9] Infection is often acquired occupationally. The condition is most common in adult males. Children, however, may also be affected.[10] Much less often, in immunosuppressed patients, inhalation, aspiration or ingestion can result in systemic disease.[1] Although most infections are sporadic, outbreaks of the disease have been reported occasionally.[11,12] Spontaneous healing of lesions may occur.

Mitochondrial DNA analysis of isolates from South Africa and Australia has allowed for phylogenetic clustering of *S. schenckii* into two main groups: group A isolates occur predominantly in South Africa; those from Australia belong mainly to group B.[13] The cell wall components of the organism are capable of adhering to extracellular matrix proteins, in particular to fibronectin.[14] This facilitates tissue invasion.

The cutaneous reactions to infection with *S. schenkii* have been divided into three types: lymphocutaneous, localized (fixed) cutaneous and disseminated cutaneous.[1,15]

- In the most common form, lymphocutaneous sporotrichosis, the lesions develop at the site of inoculation (most often on exposed areas), after an incubation period of a few days to several weeks, as a nodule, which ulcerates (*Fig. 17.364*). Lymphatic involvement develops, with asymptomatic secondary nodules arising along the line of lymphatic drainage (*Fig. 17.365*). Regional lymph nodes then become enlarged. Meanwhile the initial lesions expands as a crusted verrucous plaque.

- In the localized (fixed) form the patient presents with pyodermatous erosions, acneiform, nodular, ulcerated or verrucous lesions (*Fig. 17.366*).[1,15–18] This variant may indicate a high degree of immunity.
- Disseminated cutaneous sporotrichosis is exceedingly rare.[19] There have, however, been a growing number of reports of this form of disease in patients with AIDS.[20]

The extracutaneous forms, which include pulmonary and systemic variants, are very rare.[10,21] Visceral involvement may occur in the absence of cutaneous lesions. Primary pulmonary infection and disseminated systemic sporotrotrichosis is seen in the immunosuppressed and occurs most often in alcoholics and patients with pulmonary tuberculosis, sarcoidosis, diabetes mellitus and chronic steroid treatment.[1]

This form of the disease has also been reported in patients with HIV infection.

Pathogenesis and histological features

S. schenckii is a dimorphic fungus, which is filamentous in culture but yeast-like in tissues.[22] The organism is not easily seen with conventional staining and is best demonstrated with methenamine silver or PAS stains. It presents as round to oval bodies, 4–6 μm in diameter, sometimes within giant cells. Occasionally the spores are seen as thin cigar-shaped rods up to 8 μm long; rarely, these may be present in conspicuous numbers.[1,18] They may be present in the center of eosinophilic radiating material, an example of the Splendore–Hoeppli phenomenon (*Fig. 17.367*).[23] This structure probably represents an immunological

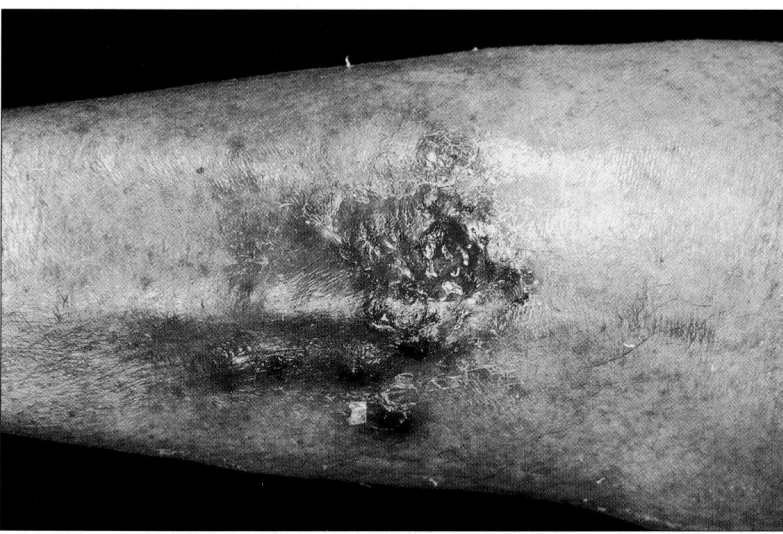

Fig. 17.364
Sporotrichosis: note the multiple nodules with ulceration on the shin, which is a characteristic site. By courtesy of S. Lucas, MD, St Thomas' Hospital, London, UK.

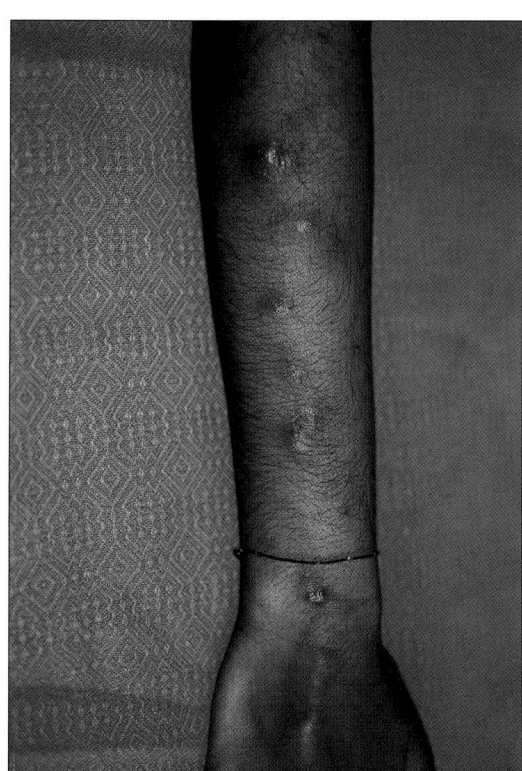

Fig. 17.365
Sporotrichosis: multiple nodules are present along the lymphatic channels draining the primary lesion. By courtesy of N.C. Dlova, MD, Nelson R. Mandela School of Medicine, University of KwaZulu-Natal, South Africa.

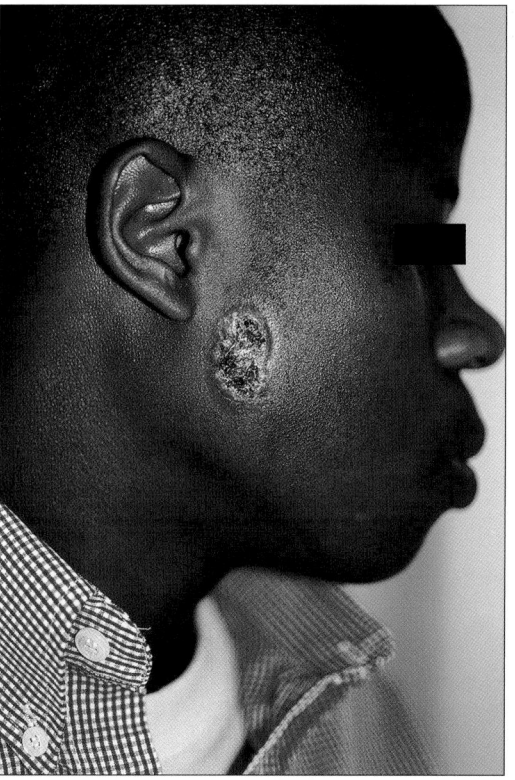

Fig. 17.366
Sporotrichosis: localized variant presenting as an ulcerated plaque. By courtesy of N.C. Dlova, MD, Nelson R. Mandela School of Medicine, University of KwaZulu-Natal, South Africa.

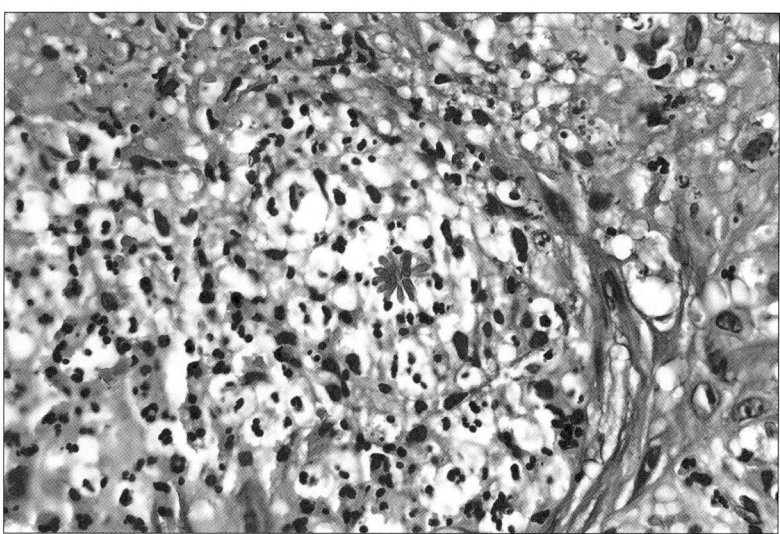

Fig. 17.367
Sporotrichosis: the yeast form is characteristically surrounded by radiating eosinophilic spokes (the Splendore–Hoeppli phenomenon).

reaction between host and fungus. These so-called asteroid bodies are characteristically located within intradermal microabscesses (*Fig. 17.368*).[24] Occasionally hyphae may be identified in PAS stained sections. The mycelial form of the organism (including conidia) may also be observed in the dried-up purulent exudate in chronic ulcerated lesions.[25] Surrounding the giant cells containing the often scanty organisms is an intense granulomatous infiltrate. Lymphocytes, plasma cells and histiocytes are also present. The overlying epidermis shows acanthosis with areas of pseudoepitheliomatous hyperplasia; ulceration is often evident.[26] Neutrophil abscesses are present in both acanthotic epidermis and dermis.

The nodules resulting from lymphatic spread are located in the deep dermis or subcutaneous tissues. They consist of a central necrotic zone with neutrophils, a surrounding zone of epithelioid cells and giant cells, and an outer zone of plasma cells and lymphocytes with fibrosis.[1,23]

Although the tissue reaction is often suggestive of sporotrichosis, confirmation should be sought by isolation and culture of the organism. The organism may also be demonstrated by immunohistochemistry.[27]

References

1. Belknap, B.S. (1989) Sporotrichosis. *Dermatol Clin*, 7, 193–202.
2. Edwards, C., Reuther, W.L. 3rd, Greer, D.L. (2000) Disseminated osteoarticular sporotrichosis: treatment of a patient with acquired immunodeficiency syndrome. *South Med J*, 93, 803–806.
3. Wescott, B.L., Nasser, A., Jarolim, D.R. (1999) Sporothrix meningitis. *Nurse Pract*, 24, 93–94.
4. Aarestrup, F.M., Guerra, R.O., Vieira, B.J. et al (2001) Oral manifestation of sporotrichosis in AIDS patients. *Oral Dis*, 7, 134–136.
5. Choong, K.Y., Roberts, L.J. (1996) Ritual Samoan tattooing and associated sporotrichosis. *Australas J Dermatol*, 37, 50–53.
6. Smith, L.M., Garrett, H.D. (1947) Verrucous sporotrichosis. *Arch Dermatol Syph*, 56, 532–534.
7. Nusbaum, B.P., Gulbas, N., Horwitz, S.N. (1983) Sporotrichosis acquired from a cat. *J Am Acad Dermatol*, 8, 386–391.
8. Fleury, R.N., Taborda, P.R., Gupta, A.K. et al (2001) Zoonotic sporotrichosis. Transmission to humans by infected domestic cat scratching: report of four cases in Sao Paulo, Brazil. *Int J Dermatol*, 40, 318–322.
9. Dunstan, R.W., Langham, R.F., Reimann, K.A. et al (1986) Feline sporotrichosis: a report of five cases with transmission to humans. *J Am Acad Dermatol*, 15, 37–45.
10. Itoh, M., Okamoto, S., Kariya, H. (1986) Survey of 200 cases of sporotrichosis, *Dermatologica*, 172, 209–213.
11. Quintal, D. (2000) Sporotrichosis infection on mines of the Witwatersrand. *J Cutan Med Surg*, 4, 51–54.
12. Coniasl, S., Wilson, P. (1998) Epidemic cutaneous sporotrichosis: report of 16 cases in Queensland due to mouldy hay. *Australas J Dermatol*, 39, 34–37.
13. Ishikazi, H., Kawasaki, M., Aoki, M., Vismer, H., Muir, D. (2000) Mitochondrial DNA analysis of Sporothrix schenkii in South Africa and Australia. *Med Mycol*, 38, 433–436.
14. Lima, O.C., Figueiredo, C.C., Previato, J.O. et al (2001) Involvement of fungal cell wall components in adhesion of Sporothrix schenkii to human fibronectin. *Infect Immunol*, 69, 6874–6880.
15. Rafal, E.S., Rasmussen, J.E. (1991) An unusual presentation of fixed cutaneous sporotrichosis: a case report and review of the literature. *J Am Acad Dermatol*, 25, 928–932.
16. Bullpitt, P., Weedon, D. (1978) Sporotrichosis: a review of 39 cases. *Pathology*, 10, 249–256.
17. Dolezal, J.F. (1981) Blastomycoid sporotrichosis. *J Am Acad Dermatol*, 4, 523–537.
18. Byrd, D.R., El-Azhary, R.A., Gibson, L.E. et al (2001) Sporotrichosis masquerading as pyoderma gangrenosum: case report and review of 19 cases of sporotrichosis. *J Eur Acad Dermatol Venereol*, 15, 581–584.
19. Wilson, D.E., Mann, J.J., Bennett, J.E. et al (1967) Clinical features of extracutaneous sporotrichosis. *Medicine*, 46, 265–279.
20. al-Tawfiq, J.A., Wools, K.K. (1998) Disseminated sporotrichosis and Sporothrix schenkii fungemia as the initial presentation of human immunodeficiency virus infection. *Clin Infect Dis*, 26, 1403–1406.
21. Friedman, S.J., Doyle, J.A. (1983) Extracutaneous sporotrichosis. *Int J Dermatol*, 22, 171–176.
22. Binford, C.H., Dooley, J.R. (1976) Sporotrichosis. In: Bunford, C.H., Connor, D.H. (eds) Pathology of tropical and extraordinary diseases, Vol. 1. Washington: Armed Forces Institute of Pathology, pp 574–577.
23. Hirsh, B.C., Johnson, W.C. (1984) Pathology of granulomatous diseases. Mixed inflammatory granuloma. *Int J Dermatol*, 23, 585–597.
24. Rodriguez, G., Sarmiento, L. (1998) The asteroid bodies of sporotrichosis. *Am J Dermatopathol*, 20, 246–249.
25. Lopes, J.O., Alves, S.H., Benevenga, J.P. et al (1992) Filamentous forms of Sporothrix schenkii in material from human lesions. *J Med Vet Mycol*, 30, 403–406.
26. Urabe, H., Honbo, S. (1986) Sporotrichosis. *Int J Dermatol*, 25, 255–257.
27. Marques, M.E., Coelho, K.I., Sotto, M.N. et al (1992) Comparison between histochemical and immunohistochemical methods for diagnosis of sporotrichosis. *J Clin Pathol*, 45, 1089–1093.

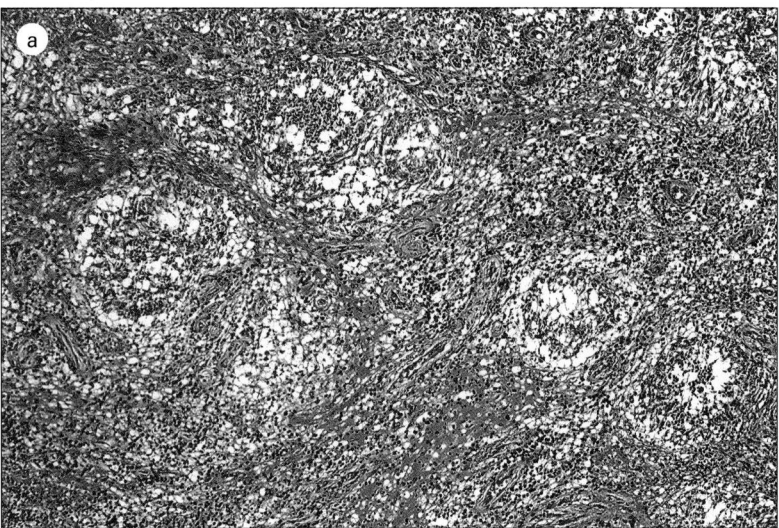

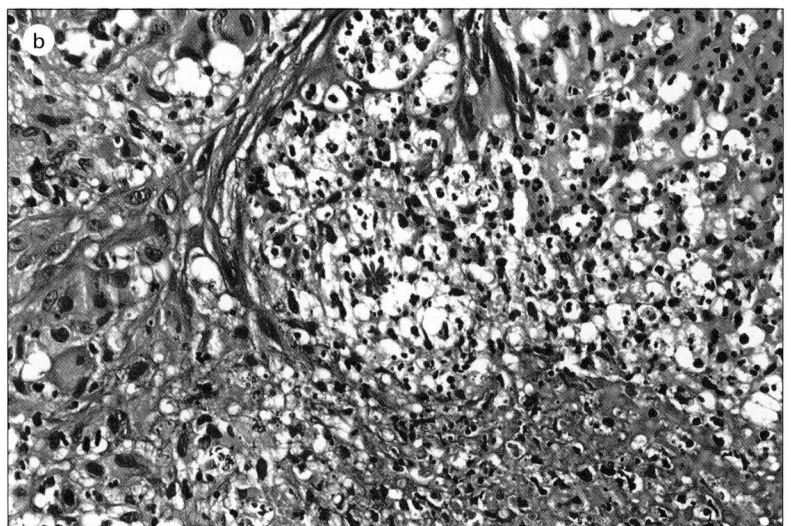

Fig. 17.368
(a, b) Sporotrichosis: multiple dermal abscesses are typically present in this condition.

Lobomycosis

Clinical features

Lobomycosis is a very rare dermatosis caused by the fungus *Lacazia loboi* (formerly *Paracoccidioides loboi* or *Loboa loboi*).[1–4] Although culture is exceedingly difficult, the organism has been successfully inoculated into mice, rats and armadillos.[5] It is confined to tropical forest areas of Central and South America, especially the Amazon basin.[6–8] The first case of lobomycosis in the United States was reported in 2000.[9] The natural habitat of the fungus has not been identified, although infections of dolphins have been reported, suggesting the possibility of a waterborne mechanism.[10] The disease is seen in whites, blacks and native South American Indians, and particularly affects males.[5]

Lesions due to this fungus are mainly confined to the skin.[8] They are extremely insidious in development, following presumed inoculation of the skin, and present characteristically after many years. They occur on exposed skin, often on the face and earlobes, but the arms, chest, legs and buttocks may also be affected (*Figs 17.369, 17.370*). Lesions are associated with keloid-like scarring, hence the disease's previous designation 'keloidal blastomycosis'.[3,6,9] There are usually papular, nodular and verrucous components; some of the nodules may become large and confluent, and ulceration sometimes occurs. Drainage lymph nodes are affected.[11,12] There is no tendency to heal and the infection is resistant to medical therapy, leaving surgical excision as the sole effective treatment. Squamous carcinoma is an occasional long-term complication.[7]

Histological features

The fungus presents in the tissues as characteristic bulbous chains of yeast-like cells, 9–10 μm in diameter, with thick (double) walls and interconnecting tubular structures which later disappear.[12] Budding forms are occasionally present.

The fungus provokes a distinctive reaction.[13] The dermis becomes infiltrated by fungus-containing histiocytes and giant cells, with the latter predominating centrally (*Figs 17.371, 17.372*). Few other inflammatory cells are evident and fibroblasts appear later within the surrounding keloid. The fungi are unstained and seen easily with hematoxylin and eosin staining but PAS and silver stains enhance their recognition (*Fig. 17.373*). In heavily infected lesions, skin appendages and nerves can be destroyed, and therefore the condition can clinically mimic leprosy.

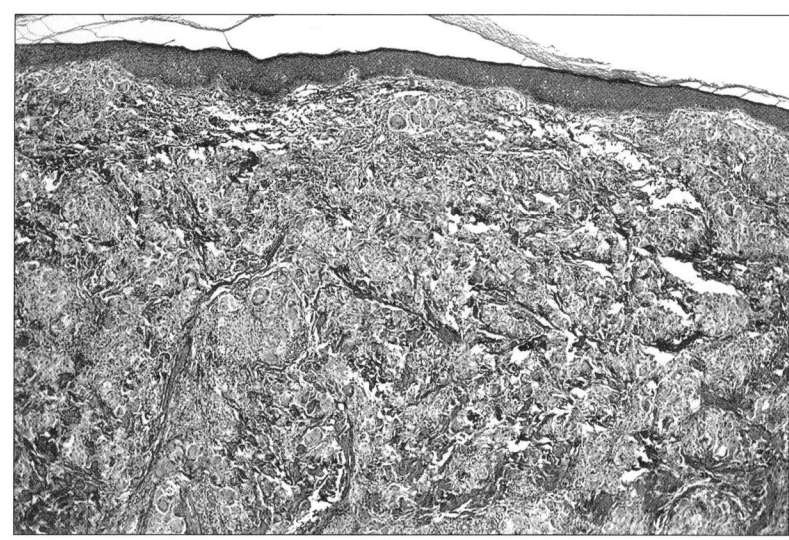

Fig. 17.371
Lobomycosis: there is an extensive granulomatous infiltrate in the dermis; the intervening eosinophilic bundles represent early keloidal scarring.

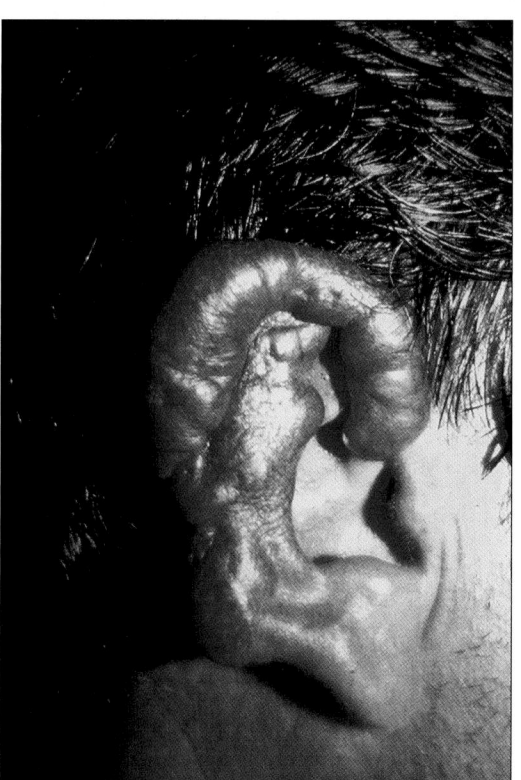

Fig. 17.369
Lobomycosis: the ear is a commonly affected site. By courtesy of S.A. Pecher, MD, Centro Manaus, Amazonas, Brazil.

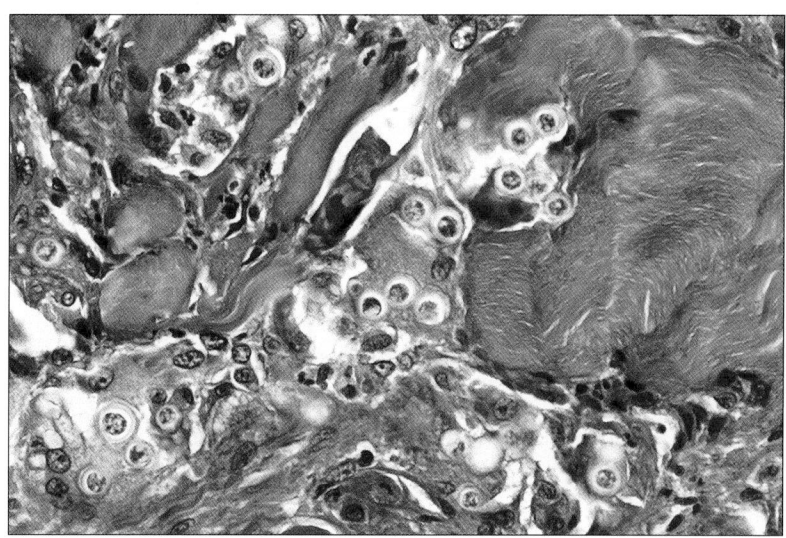

Fig. 17.372
Lobomycosis: the fungi have very thick cell walls and are often arranged in chains.

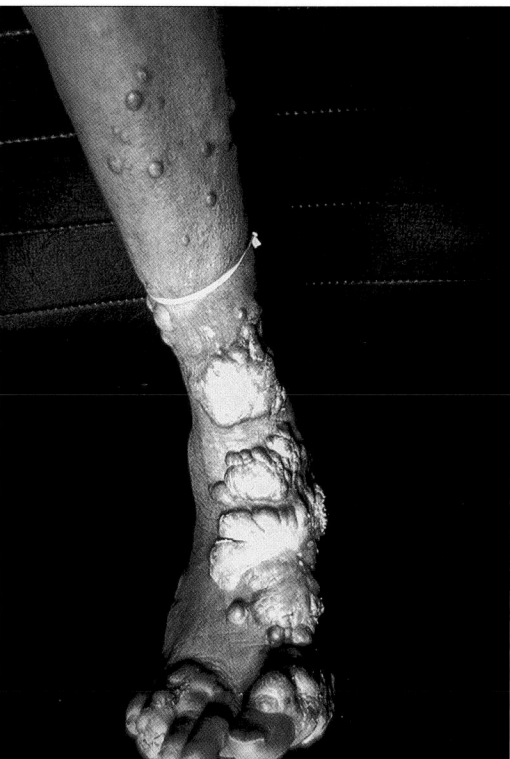

Fig. 17.370
Lobomycosis: note the gross keloidal scarring with considerable disfigurement. By courtesy of S.A. Pecher, MD, Centro Manaus, Amazonas, Brazil.

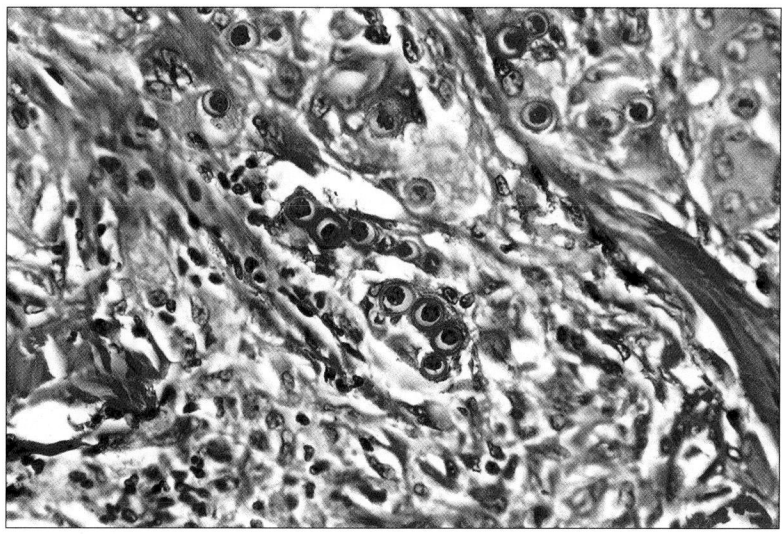

Fig. 17.373
Lobomycosis: there is striking periodic acid–Schiff positivity.

References

1. Taborda, P.R., Taborda, V.A., McGinnis, M.R. (1999) Lacazia loboi gen. nov., comb. nov., the etiologic agent of lobomycosis. *J Clin Microbiol*, 37, 2031–2033.
2. Rodriguez-Toro, G. (1993) Lobomycosis. *Int J Dermatol*, 32, 324–332.
3. Jardim, M.L. (1992) Lobo's disease. In: Canizares, O., Harman, R. (eds) Clinical tropical dermatology, 2nd edn. Boston: Blackwell, pp 69–72.
4. Binford, C.H., Dooley, J.R. (1976) Lobo's disease. In: Bunford, C.H., Connor, D.H. (eds) Pathology of tropical and extraordinary diseases, Vol. 1. Washington: Armed Forces Institute of Pathology, pp 583–584.
5. Fuchs, J., Milbradt, R., Pecher, S.A. (1990) Lobomycosis (keloidal blastomycosis): case reports and overview. *Cutis*, 46, 227–234.
6. Tapia, A., Torres-Calcindo, A., Arosemena, R. (1978) Keloidal blastomycosis (Lobo's disease) in Panama. *Int J Dermatol*, 17, 572–574.
7. Baruzzi, R.G., Rodrigues, D.A., Michalany, N.S. et al (1989) Squamous-cell carcinoma and lobomycosis (Jorge Lobo's disease). *Int J Dermatol*, 28, 183–185.
8. Baruzzi, R.G., Marcopito, L.F., Michalany, N.S. et al (1981) Early diagnosis and prompt treatment by surgery in Jorge Lobo's disease (keloidal blastomycosis). *Mycopathologia*, 74, 51–54.
9. Burns, R.A., Roy, J.S., Woods, C. et al (2000) Report of first human case of lobomycosis in the United States. *J Clin Microbiol*, 38, 1283–1285.
10. Caldwell, D.K., Caldwell, M.C., Woodard, J.C. et al (1975) Lobomycosis as a disease of the Atlantic bottle nosed dolphin. *Am J Trop Med Hyg*, 24, 105–114.
11. Azulay, R.D., Carneiro, J.A., Da Graca, M. et al (1976) Keloidal blastomycosis (Lobo's disease) with lymphatic involvement: a case study. *Int J Dermatol*, 15, 40–42.
12. Jaramillo, D., Cortes, A., Restrepo, A. et al (1976) Lobomycosis. Report of the eight Colombian cases and review of the literature. *J Cutan Pathol*, 3, 180–189.
13. Miranda, J.L. (1981) Lobomycosis. In: Braude, A.I. (ed.) Medical microbiology and infectious diseases. Philadelphia: Saunders, pp 1589–1596.

Rhinosporidiosis

Clinical features

Rhinosporidiosis is an uncommon and somewhat enigmatic disease that until recently was attributed to infection by *Rhinosporidium seeberi*. Infection results in polypoid lesions containing characteristic cyst-like sporangia.[1,2] For many years the organism was considered to be a fungus based on its morphological and staining characteristics.[3,4] The organism was recently cultured for the first time, and molecular analysis has since revealed that it probably belongs to a novel clade of aquatic protistan parasites or cyanobacteria.[2,4–6] The etiological agent has now been renamed *Microcystis aeruginosa*.[5,7,8]

Rhinosporidiosis is found in India and Sri Lanka as a waterborne infection affecting mainly the nasopharynx, and as a dustborne infection affecting equally conjunctiva and nasopharynx in the dry southern states of the USA. Sporadic cases have been reported worldwide.[3] The infection affects men much more commonly than women and presents as hyperplastic polypoid mucosal lesions. Conjunctival involvement is more frequent in females.[9] Lesions in the nose resemble 'allergic' nasal polyps. The same polypoid presentation is seen in the lesions of the conjunctiva. The infection occasionally involves the larynx, trachea and the mucosae of the rectum, urethra and genitalia, where it resembles condylomata.[3,10–12]

Exceptionally rarely, disseminated variants have been recorded.[6,7,13–17] Disseminated disease manifests with widespead cutaneous or sub-cutaneous nodules, soft tissue masses or even osteolytic bone lesions.[13–17] Primary cutaneous lesions are rare, and are described as papules which become verrucous and granulomatous.[2,18] Giant cutaneous lesions have also been described.[19]

Pathogenesis and histological features

The mechanism of infection is unknown. It has been proposed that the organism is present in soil, dust and water and that involvement of the nose and conjunctiva follows rubbing with contaminated fingers.[3] Cutaneous involvement occurs by contiguous extension from a mucosal infection, autoinoculation and rarely through hematogenous dissemination.[14,20]

In tissues the causative agent is characterized by thick-walled (birefringent) endospore-filled sporangia.[21] These are seen in the stroma of the polyps as cysts, 10–200 μm in diameter (*Figs 17.374, 17.375*). The cysts have a thick wall, which remains in a collapsed form after the endospores have been released. Endospores are seen initially at the periphery of the sporangium, but they gradually fill the cyst-like center before rupture occurs. The spores are 7–8 μm in diameter and contain 8–10 eosinophilic globular bodies (*Fig. 17.376*). They mature to form small trophic cysts (*Fig. 17.377*). The lesions are easily identified on hematoxylin and eosin stained sections and can also be demonstrated by PAS and methenamine silver stains. Watery substances stimulate mature sporangia to undergo rupture, with subsequent discharge of the endo-spores. This affinity for wet environments may also explain why infections tend to involve the mucous membranes of human hosts.[6]

The cysts are associated with a stromal mixed neutrophil, histiocyte, plasma cell and lymphocyte infiltrate. The overlying epidermis in skin lesions may show pseudoepitheliomatous hyperplasia, hyperkeratosis and papillomatosis.[3] Foreign body giant cells may be abundant.

References

1. Braude, A.I. (ed.) (1981) Rhinosporidium. In: Medical microbiology and infectious diseases. Philadelphia: Saunders, pp 686–687.
2. Ali, A., Flieder, D., Guiter, G. et al (2001) Rhinosporidiosis: an unusual affliction. *Arch Pathol Lab Med*, 125, 1392–1393.
3. Thianprasit, M., Thagerngpol, K. (1989) Rhinosporidiosis. *Curr Top Med Mycol*, 3, 64–85.
4. Fredricks, D.N., Jolley, J.A., Lepp, P.W. et al (2000) Rhinosporidium seeberi: a human pathogen from a novel group of acquatic protistan parasites. *Emerg Infect Dis*, 6, 273–282.
5. Ahluwalia, K.B. (1999) Culture of the organism that causes rhinosporidiosis. *J Laryngol Otol*, 113, 523–528.
6. Mendoza, L., Herr, R.A., Arseculeratne, S.N. et al (1999) *In vitro* studies on the mechanisms of endospore release by *Rhinosporidium seeberi*. *Mycopathologia*, 148, 9–15.
7. Arseculeratne, S.N. (2001) *Microcystis aeruginosa* as the causative organism of rhinosporidiosis (Letter). *Mycopathologia*, 151, 3–4.
8. Ahluwalia, K.B. (2001) Causative agent of rhinosporidiosis (Letter). *J Clin Microbiol*, 39, 413–415.
9. Rippon, J.W. (1982) Medical mycology: the pathologic fungi and the pathogenic actinomycetes. In: Rhinosporidiosis. Philadelphia, Saunders, pp 325–334.
10. Palaniswani, R., Bhandari, M. (1983) Rhinosporidiosis of the male terminal urethra. *J Urol*, 129, 598–599.
11. Sasidharan, K., Subramonian, P., Moni, V.N. et al (1987) Urethral rhinosporidiosis: analysis of 27 cases. *Br J Urol*, 59, 66–69.
12. Sah, S.P., Singh, R.K., AshokRaj, G. (1999) Urethral rhinosporidiosis: report of a case presenting with a penile growth and urethral fistula. *Trans R Soc Trop Med Hyg*, 93, 298–299.
13. Ho, M.S., Tay, B.K. (1986) Disseminated rhinosporidosis. *Ann Acad Med Singapore*, 15, 80–83.
14. Mahakrisnan, A., Rajasekaram, V., Pandian, P.J. (1981) Disseminated cutaneous rhinosporidiosis treated with dapsone. *Trop Geogr Med*, 33, 189–192.
15. Gokhale, S., Ohri, V.C., Subramanya, H. et al (1997) Subcutaneous and osteolytic rhinosporidiosis. *Indian J Pathol Microbiol*, 40, 95–98.
16. Thappa, D.M., Venkatesan, S., Sirka, C.S. et al (1998) Disseminated cutaneous rhinosporidiosis. *J Dermatol*, 25, 527–532.
17. Angunawela, P., de Tissera, A., Dissanaike, A.S. (1999) Rhinosporidiosis presenting as two soft tissue tumors followed by dissemination. *Pathology*, 31, 57–58.
18. Ghorpade, A., Ramanan, C. (1998) Verrucoid cutaneous rhinosporidiosis. *J Eur Acad Dermatol Venereol*, 10, 269–270.
19. Ramanan, C. (1996) Giant cutaneous rhinosporidiosis. *Int J Dermatol*, 35, 441–442.
20. Agrawal, S., Sharma, K.D., Shrivasat, J.B. (1959) Generalized rhinosporidiosis with visceral involvement. Report of a case. *Arch Dermatol*, 80, 22–26.
21. Binford, C.H., Dooley, J.R. (1976) Rhinosporidiosis. In: Bunford, C.H., Connor, D.H. (eds) Pathology of tropical and extraordinary diseases, Vol. 1. Washington: Armed Forces Institute of Pathology, pp 597–599.

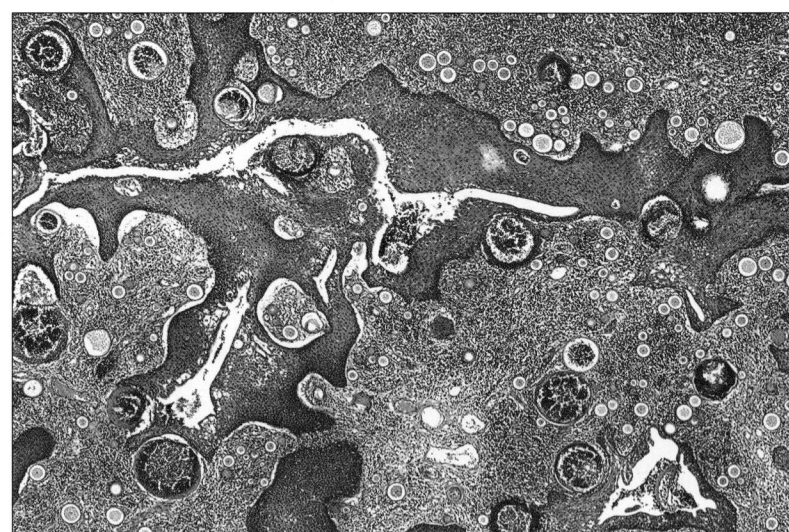

Fig. 17.374
Rhinosporidiosis: this is part of a polypoid nasal lesion. Multiple sporangia containing conspicuous spores are present.

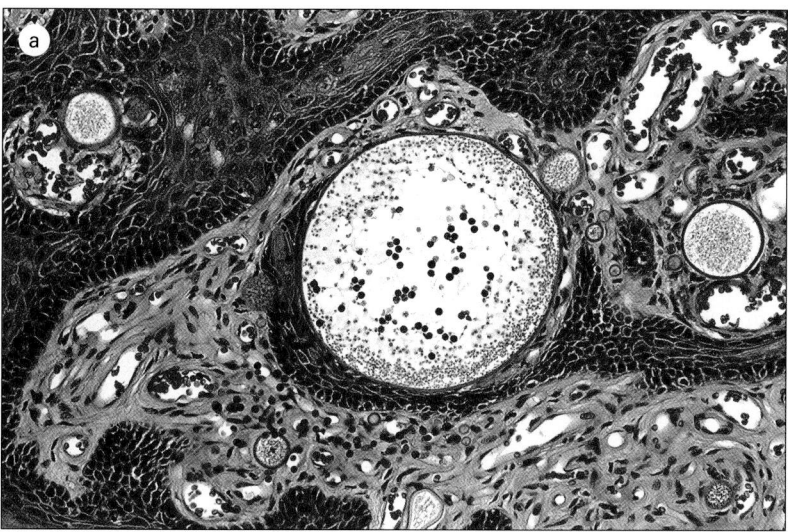 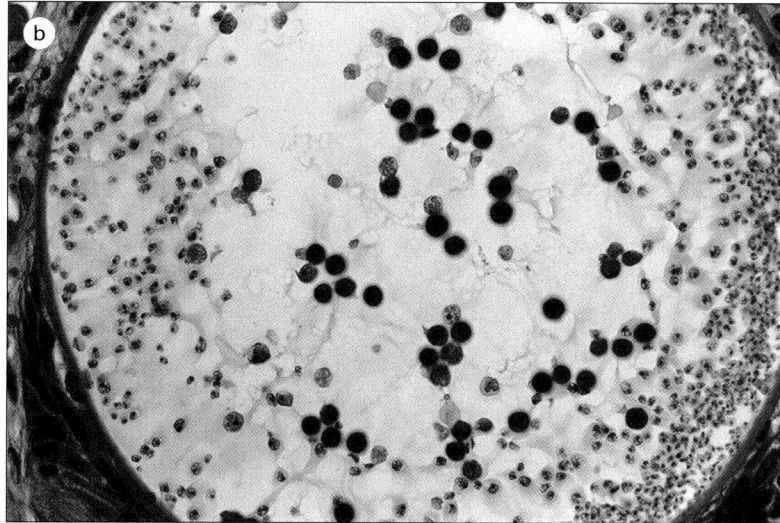

Fig. 17.375
(a, b) Rhinosporidiosis: maturation of the spores is from the periphery to the center of the cyst; note the thick hyaline eosinophilic wall.

Fig. 17.376
Rhinosporidiosis: (a) in this high power field the internal structure of the spores is evident (periodic acid–Schiff); (b) methenamine silver reaction.

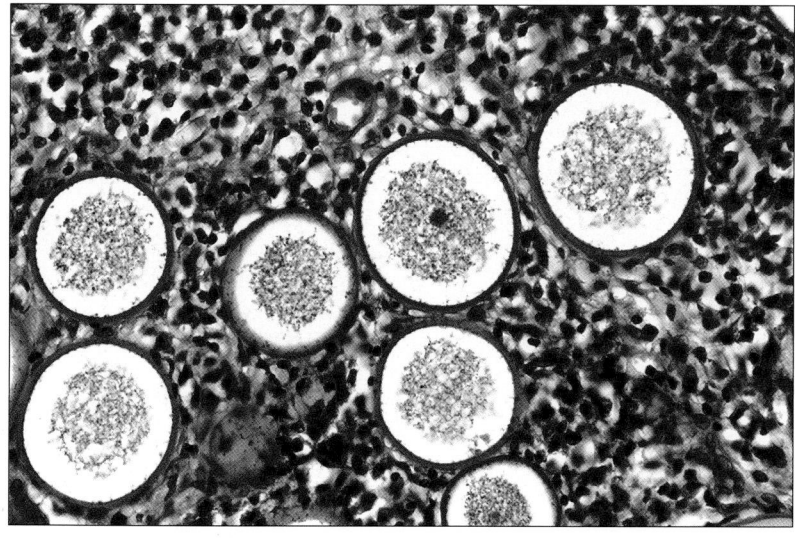

Fig. 17.377
Rhinosporidiosis: individual spores mature to form small trophic cysts.

Arthropod infestations

Scabies

Clinical features

Scabies is caused by the itch mite *Sarcoptes scabiei* (*S. scabiei* var. *hominis*), which penetrates the skin in many areas, but usually below the neck.[1,2] The most commonly affected sites are about the hands and feet (*Fig. 17.378*). Papules and burrows are often found between the fingers or along the sides of the fingers. The soles and sides of the feet are especially affected in children. As a secondary phenomenon (unrelated to burrows) patients develop an intensely pruritic papular generalized eruption, particularly affecting the abdomen, thighs and buttocks.[3] This is often excoriated and may be associated with secondary infection (*Fig. 17.379*). This reaction may be immune complex-mediated or develop as a consequence of a cell-mediated immune reaction. Patients may have raised serum IgE levels.[3] This contagious infection is spread through close personal contact and may be transmitted sexually, resulting in genital scabies.[2]

The uncomplicated lesion is a sinuous burrow up to 1 cm in length and associated with intense itching, particularly at night. A small proportion of patients may go on to develop nodular scabies, which is seen particularly in the axillae, about the genitalia and on the abdomen.[3] These are intensely pruritic and remarkably persistent. Severe keratotic and psoriasiform lesions are seen in physically and mentally debilitated and immunosuppressed (including HIV positive) patients due to massive infestation and is termed hyperkeratotic or Norwegian scabies (*Fig. 17.380*).[4]

Pathogenesis and histological features

Scabies is associated with poor socioeconomic conditions, overcrowding and poor personal hygiene, and may be acquired during sexual contact.

The fertilized female *S. scabiei* mite deposits eggs in the burrows in the epidermis. The larvae emerge in 3–5 days and mature in 10–14 days. The burrows extend at a shallow angle through the stratum corneum and may reach the deeper epidermis. There is acanthosis and hyperkeratosis

and often associated spongiosis with a lymphocytic infiltrate in the epidermis (*Fig. 17.381*). The spongiosis may progress to vesiculation. Eggs, larvae, mites, mite parts and excreta may be identified in the stratum corneum.[5,6] In the dermis there is a superficial perivascular (and sometimes diffuse) infiltrate of lymphocytes and histiocytes, sometimes accompanied by polymorphs and less often eosinophils. The presence of

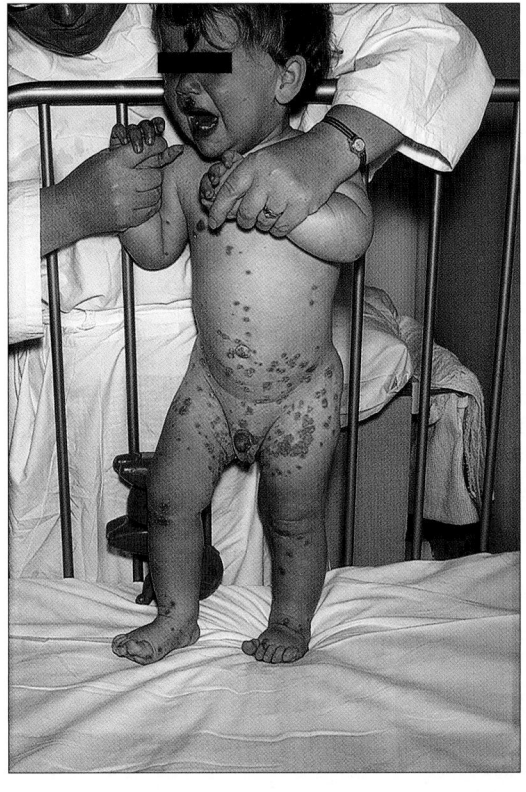

Fig. 17.379
Scabies: this is an intensely itchy condition and therefore secondary infection is a not uncommon complication, as for example in this child with staphylococcal sepsis. By courtesy of M.M. Black, MD, Institute of Dermatology, London, UK.

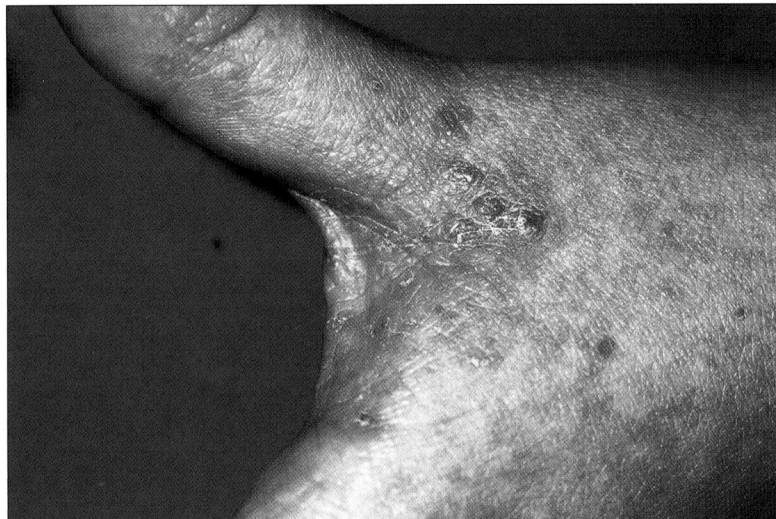

Fig. 17.378
Scabies: the burrows are linear, slightly raised lesions. The most common sites affected include the lateral aspects of the fingers, the web between thumb and first finger, and the wrists. By courtesy of R.A. Marsden, MD, St George's Hospital, London, UK.

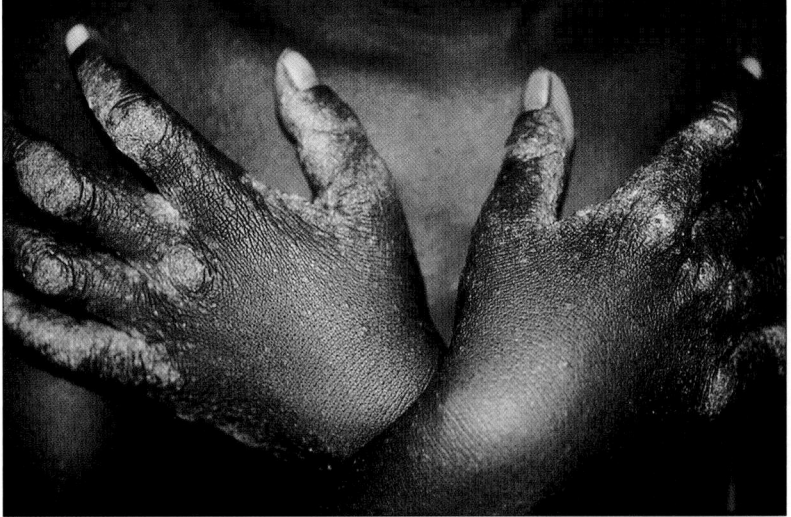

Fig. 17.380
Norwegian scabies: this example (also known as the hyperkeratotic variant) may affect widespread areas of the body, and is associated with severe crusting and a very heavy infestation of mites. It is exceedingly infectious. By courtesy of N.C. Dlova, MD, Nelson R. Mandela School of Medicine, University of KwaZulu-Natal, South Africa.

the last may be associated with the features of acute vasculitis and flame figures.[7] The lymphocytes are predominantly of T-cell lineage.[8]

C3 and Ig may be detected at the epidermodermal junction and within the perivascular region, adding support to the concept of an immune complex-mediated pathogenesis.[8] IgE has been detected in vessel walls and IgA and C3 in the stratum corneum.[9] There have also been reports of eruptions resembling bullous pemphigoid in association with proven scabies.[10,11] In one study these patients were found to have circulating antibodies against BP180 and/or BP230 antigens, indicating that at least a proportion of bullous eruptions in scabetic patients are indeed attributable to bullous pemphigoid.[11] There have been rare reports of Grover's disease in association with *Sarcoptes scabiei* infestation.[12]

In nodular skin lesions, the dermal infiltrate may be very dense and, in addition to histiocytes, plasma cells, eosinophils and lymphocytes, atypical and hyperchromatic cells may be evident, which may suggest a lymphomatous process if the clinical information is not evident.[13] A case of pediatric scabies with conspicuous dermal Langerhans' cell proliferation has also been described.[14]

The papular lesions show mild hyperkeratosis and parakeratosis in association with acanthosis and spongiosis.[3] A perivascular inflammatory cell infiltrate of lymphocytes, histiocytes and sometimes neutrophils may be evident in the superficial dermis. Eosinophils may be absent.[3]

In the hyperkeratotic variant, mites and eggs are numerous, but they are scanty in the other forms. In such cases PCR may be a useful adjunct to the diagnosis.[15]

References

1. Meyers, W.M., Connor, D.H. (1976) Scabies. In: Bunford, C.H., Connor, D.H. (eds) Pathology of tropical and extraordinary diseases, Vol. 1. Washington: Armed Forces Institute of Pathology, pp 615–617.
2. Chouela, E., Abeldano, A., Pellerano, G. et al (2002) Diagnosis and treatment of scabies: a practical guide. *Am J Clin Dermatol*, 3, 9–18.
3. Falk, E.S., Eide, T.J. (1981) Histologic and clinical findings in human scabies. *Int J Dermatol*, 20, 600–605.
4. Schlesinger, I., Oerlich, D.M., Tyring, S.K. (1994) Crusted (Norwegian) scabies in patients with AIDS: the range of clinical presentations. *South Med J*, 87, 352–356.
5. Fernández, N., Torres, A., Ackerman, A.B. (1977) Pathologic findings in human scabies. *Arch Dermatol*, 113, 320–324.
6. Head, E.S., Macdonald, E.M., Ewert, A. et al (1990) Sarcoptes scabiei in histologic sections of skin in human scabies. *Arch Dermatol*, 126, 1475–1477.
7. Seraly, M.P., Schockman, J., Jacoby, R.A. (1991) Flame figures in scabies: a case report. *Arch Dermatol*, 127, 1850–1851.
8. Van Neste, D.J.J. (1988) Human scabies in perspective. *Int J Dermatol*, 27, 10–15.
9. Frenz, G., Keien, N.K., Eriksen, K. (1977) Immunofluorescence studies in scabies. *J Cutan Pathol*, 4, 191–193.
10. Slawsky, L.D., Maroon, M., Tyler, W.B. et al (1996) Association of scabies with a bullous pemphigoid-like eruption. *J Am Acad Dermatol*, 34, 878–879.
11. Konishi, N., Suzuki, K., Tokura, Y. et al (2000) Bullous eruption associated with scabies: evidence for scabetic induction of true bullous pemphigoid. *Acta Derm Venereol*, 80, 281–283.
12. Kaddu, S., Mullegger, R.R., Kerl, H. (2001) Grover's disease associated with Sarcoptes scabiei. *Dermatology*, 202, 252–254.
13. Ploysangam, T., Breneman, D.L., Mutasim, D. F. (1998) Cutaneous pseudolymphomas. *J Am Acad Dermatol*, 38 (6 Pt 1), 877–895.
14. Talanin, N.Y., Smith, S.S., Shelley, E.D. et al (1994) Cutaneous histiocytosis with Langerhans cell features induced by scabies: a case report. *Pediatr Dermatol*, 11, 327–330.
15. Bezold, G., Lange, M., Schiener, R. et al (2001) Hidden scabies: diagnosis by polymerase chain reaction. *Br J Dermatol*, 144, 614–618.

Tungiasis

Clinical features

Tunga penetrans, the sand flea or jigger flea, causes skin lesions in Central and South American, Caribbean, African and Pakistani populations.[1–4] Although increasing urbanization and improved housing has led to a decrease in the overall incidence of the disease, the condition remains highly prevelant in communities living in extreme poverty.[4] *Tunga penetrans* is found most often in dry, warm, shady and sandy soil.[1] The gravid female flea burrows into the skin, most commonly along the edge of the plantar aspect of the feet, interdigitally and under the nails, though many parts of the skin surface may be involved. As the flea enlarges within the epidermis a pruritic, painful white or erythematous papulonodule develops. A black central punctum is characteristic. The gravid flea, which has burrowed deep into the epithelium so that it is flush with the epidermal surface, extrudes eggs and excreta through the remaining epidermal opening. It eventually reaches a size of 1 cm in diameter. The eggs pass through the larval stages to a mature flea capable of jumping 35 cm – 350 times its own length! After laying its eggs the flea dies, the lesion collapses and is sloughed off before healing occurs.

The lesion itself is irritating, but in itself innocuous; however, secondary infections such as cellulitis, tetanus and gangrene are more sinister. Autoamputation of the toes is an additional complication.[1] Organisms most frequently associated with bacterial superinfection include *Staphylococcus aureus* and various enterobacteriaceae; secondary infection by anaerobes such as *Peptostreptococcus* spp. and *Clostridium* spp. may also occur.[5]

Histological features

The bulk of the flea is intraepidermal in location.[6,7] It communicates with the outside through a pore in the stratum corneum via which it defecates, breathes and lays eggs. The proboscis penetrates through the basement membrane into the dermis, which contains a mixed inflammatory infiltrate of lymphocytes, plasma cells and eosinophils (*Figs 17.382, 17.383*). The most consistently identifiable parts of the flea in skin biopsy specimens are the exoskeleton, a hypodermal layer beneath the latter, tracheae and developing eggs; the head is rarely seen.[7]

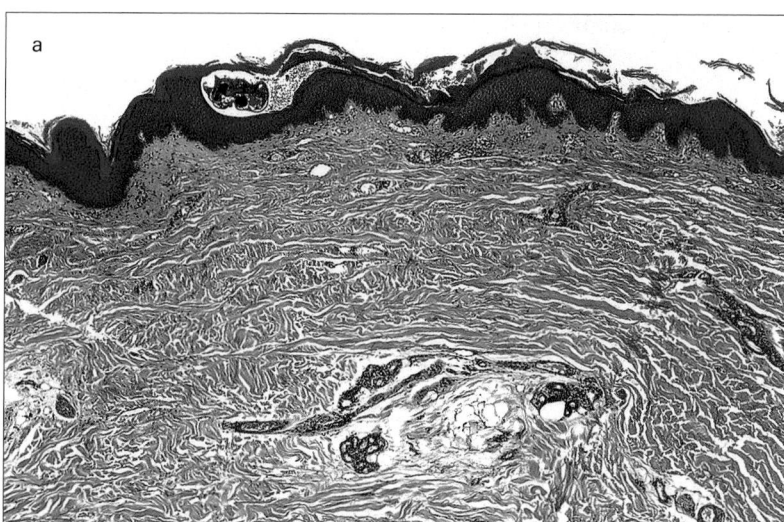

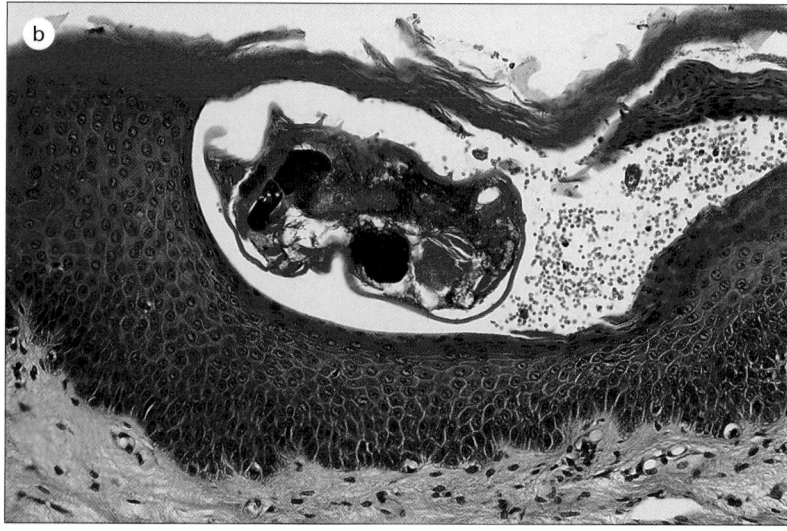

Fig. 17.381

(a, b) Scabies: the mite is located at the junction between the epidermis and the stratum corneum.

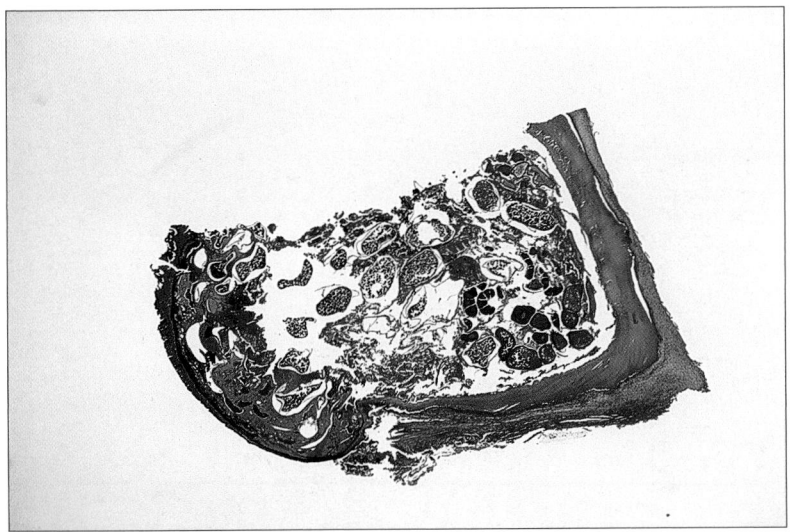

Fig. 17.382
Tungiasis: the flea is surrounded by epidermis except for an ostium in the stratum corneum through which it defecates and lays eggs. Similarly its head penetrates into the dermis to feed from the superficial blood vessels. By courtesy of C.D.M. Fletcher, MD, Brigham and Women's Hospital and Harvard Medical School, Boston, USA.

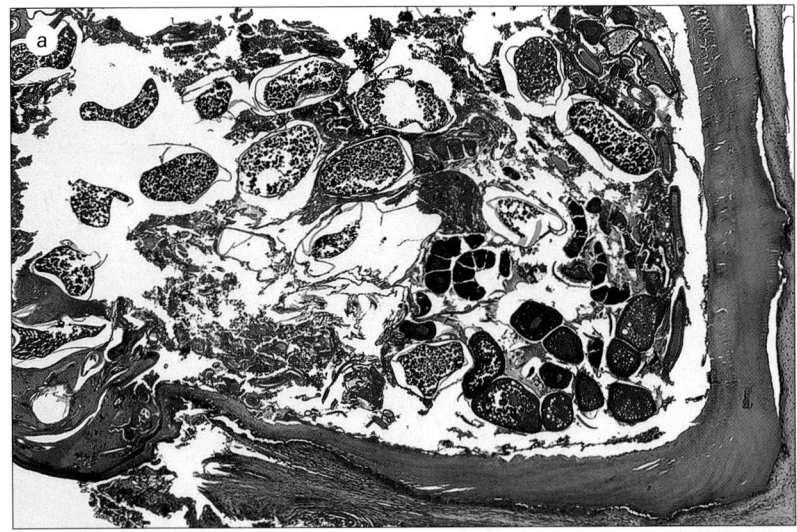

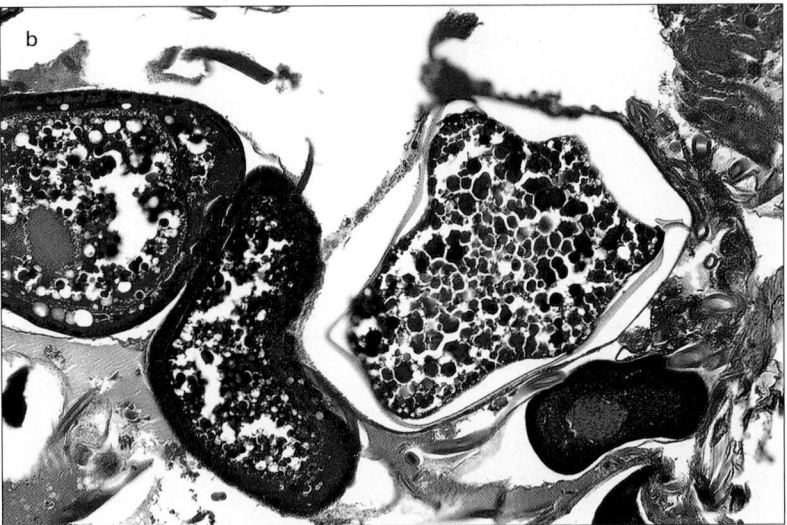

Fig. 17.383
(a, b) Tungiasis: numerous eggs are evident. By courtesy of C.D.M. Fletcher, MD, Brigham and Women's Hospital and Harvard Medical School, Boston, USA.

References

1. Sanusi, I.D., Brown, E.B., Shepard, T.G. et al (1989) Tungiasis: report of one case and review of the 14 cases reported in the United States. *J Am Acad Dermatol*, **20**, 941–944.
2. Wentzell, J.M., Schwartz, B.K., Pesce, J.R. (1986) Tungiasis. *J Am Acad Dermatol*, **15**, 117–119.
3. Heukelbach, J., de Oliveira, F.A., Hesse, G. et al (2001) Tungiasis: a neglected health problem of poor communities. *Trop Med Int Health*, **6**, 267–272.
4. Zalar, G.L., Walther, R.R. (1980) Infestation by Tunga penetrans. *Arch Dermatol*, **116**, 80–81.
5. Feldmeier, H., Heukelbach, J., Eisele, M. et al (2002) Bacterial superinfection in human tungiasis. *Trop Med Int Health*, **7**, 559–564.
6. Connor, D.H. (1976) Tungiasis. In: Bunford, C.H., Connor, D.H. (eds) Pathology of tropical and extraordinary diseases, Vol. 1. Washington: Armed Forces Institute of Pathology, pp 610–614.
7. Smith, M.D., Procop, G.W. (2002) Typical histologic features of Tunga penetrans in skin biopsies. *Arch Pathol Lab Med*, **126**, 714–716.

Nematode infestation

Onchocerciasis

Clinical features

Onchocerciasis (river blindness) is endemic in parts of tropical Africa, the Yemen and Central and South America.[1–5] Most symptoms of onchocerciasis are associated with the microfilarial stage of the filarial nematode *Onchocerca volvulus*. Onchocerciasis particularly affects individuals living close to fast-flowing rivers.[6]

The microfilariae migrate to the skin and other organs, causing itching and macules showing altered pigmentation.[7] Scratching results in excoriation and sometimes secondary infection. Dermal thickening, edema and wrinkling of the skin follow in severe cases. Scaling and depigmentation are termed, respectively, lizard and leopard skin (*Fig. 17.384*). Lymph nodes often become involved, exacerbating the problems of edema. Adult worms exist in dermal nodules, often associated with scar tissue; these nodules are mobile and tender, and are usually seen over bony prominences.

The clinical cutaneous manifestations have been classified into a number of categories including acute papular onchodermatitis, chronic papular onchodermatitis, lichenified onchodermatitis, atrophy and depigmentation (*Figs 17.385–17.388*).[6] The authors also recognized palpable onchocercal nodules, lymphadenopathy, hanging groin and lymphedema. In endemic areas 30% or more of the population may have onchocercal skin lesions; this figure approaches 60% in some hyperendemic communities.[4,5] The varying clinical features are believed to reflect variable host immune reactions to the presence of the microfilariae in the dermis.[8] The migrating microfilariae can enter the eyes and cause river blindness. Ocular lesions, which are a cause of major morbidity, include punctate keratitis, sclerosing keratitis, iritis, chorioretinitis and optic atrophy.[9,10]

Pathogenesis and histological features

O. volvulus is transmitted in its larval form to man in rural areas by the bite of black flies (*Simulium*).[3,11] The larvae develop into adult worms in the deep dermis. Microfilariae are produced by gravid females and these

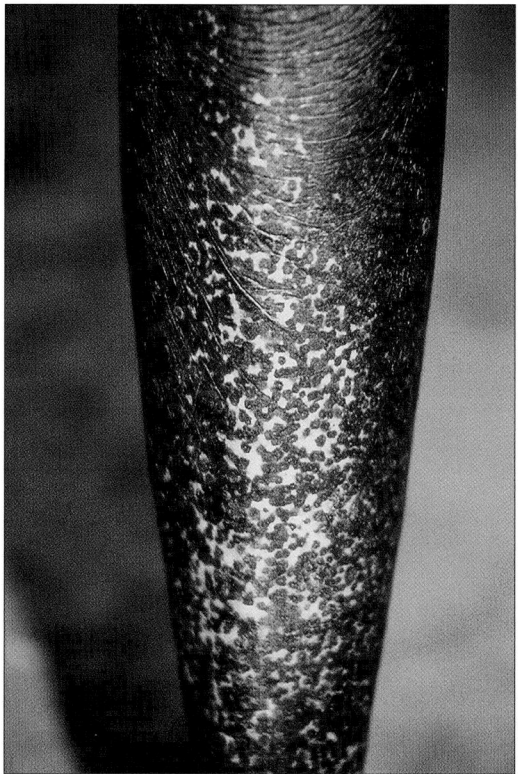

Fig. 17.384
Onchocerciasis: leopard skin. There are numerous depigmented macules. Rarely these are pruritic. By courtesy of M.E. Murdoch, MD, Watford Hospital, Watford, UK.

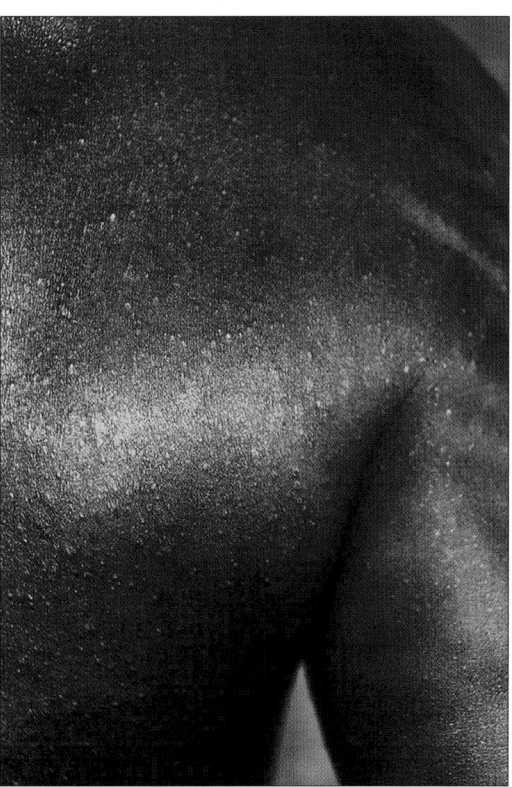

Fig. 17.385
Acute papular onchodermatitis: numerous small papules are present on the back and upper arm. Vesiculation and pustulation may sometimes be present. By courtesy of M.E. Murdoch, MD, Watford Hospital, Watford, UK.

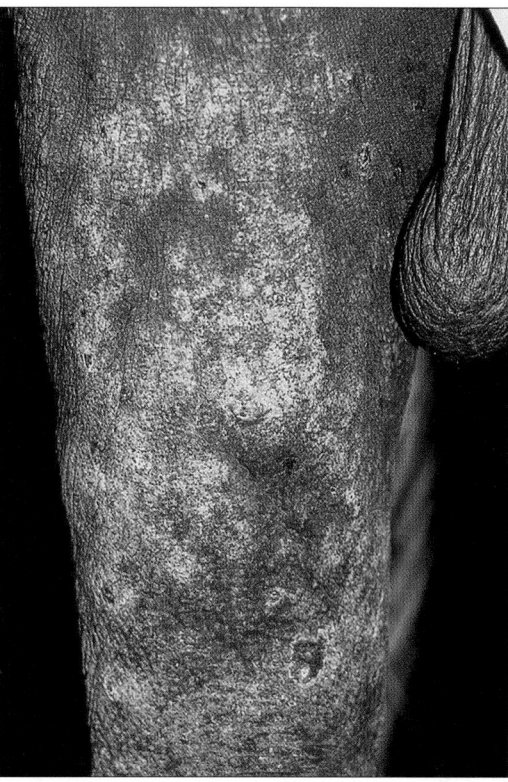

Fig. 17.387
Lichenified onchodermatitis: this variant most often affects teenagers and young adults. There is marked hyperkeratosis associated with confluent plaques. Lymphadenopathy is often a feature. By courtesy of M.E. Murdoch, MD, Watford Hospital, Watford, UK.

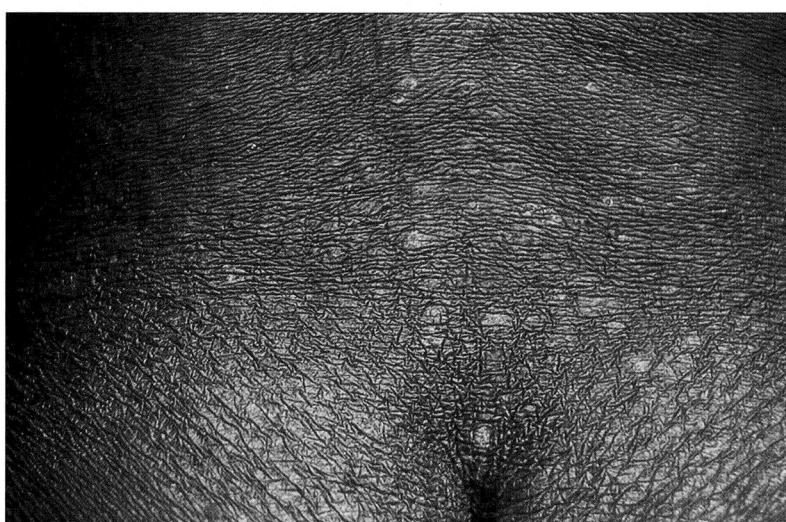

Fig. 17.386
Chronic papular onchodermatitis: numerous flat-topped macules and papules are present on the buttocks. By courtesy of M.E. Murdoch, MD, Watford Hospital, Watford, UK.

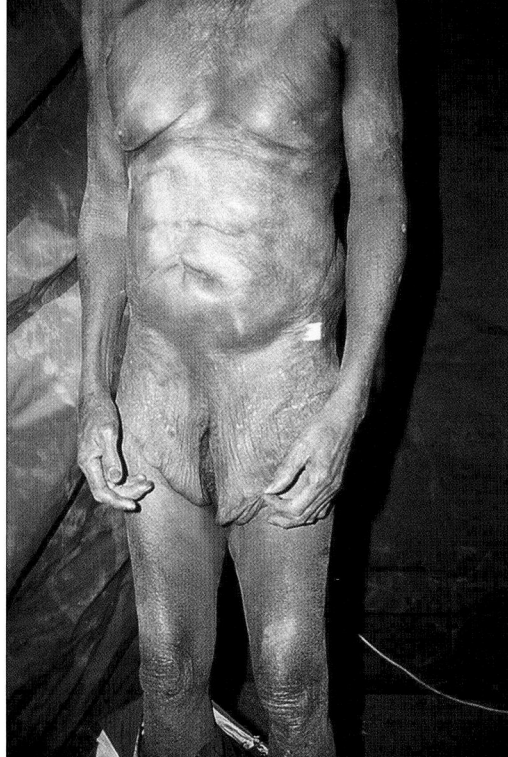

Fig. 17.388
Chronic onchocerciasis: the presence of redundant folds of skin in the inguinal region is a late manifestation (late hanging groin). By courtesy of M.E. Murdoch, MD, Watford Hospital, Watford, UK.

can migrate throughout the host (*Fig. 17.389*). Most are present in the superficial dermis, and may be identified by the histological examination of 'skin snips'. The adult female worm is up to 50 cm in length, with a diameter of up to 0.45 mm, and is found in complex coils in the fixed nodules. The microfilariae are 220–360 × 5–9 μm. The nodules contain several entwined worms within surrounding inflammation, which may be suppurative or granulomatous (*Figs 17.390, 17.391*).

There is extensive fibrosis, often calcification and sometimes ossification. Microfilariae may be seen free within the dermis and also in lymphatics. The skin shows hyperkeratosis and parakeratosis, with acanthosis and melanophages in the dermis, but only a mild lymphocytic and eosinophilic inflammatory infiltrate. Fibrosis becomes prominent, resulting in hyalinization of the papillary dermis. Mucin is prominent

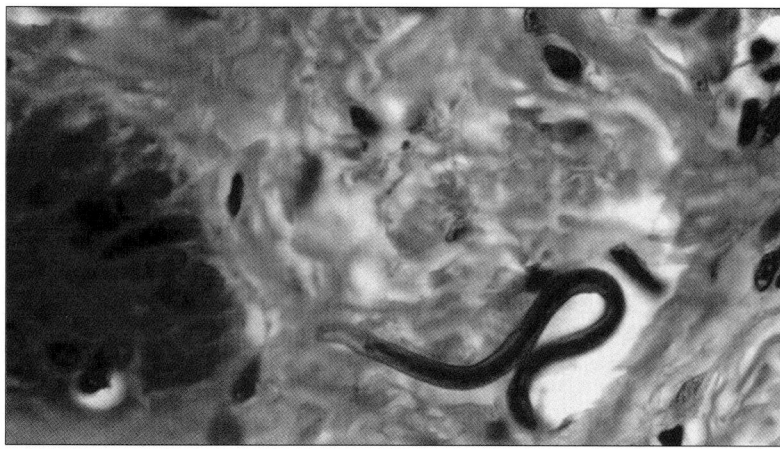

Fig. 17.389
Onchocerciasis: microfilariae in the dermis may elicit a lymphohistiocytic infiltrate and eosinophils may be conspicuous. By courtesy of S. Lucas, MD, St Thomas' Hospital, London, UK.

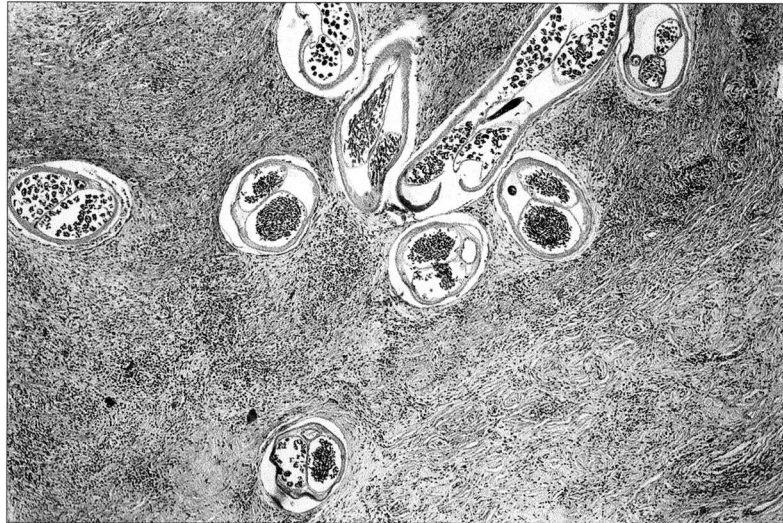

Fig. 17.390
Onchocerciasis: multiple sections of adult worm are evident.

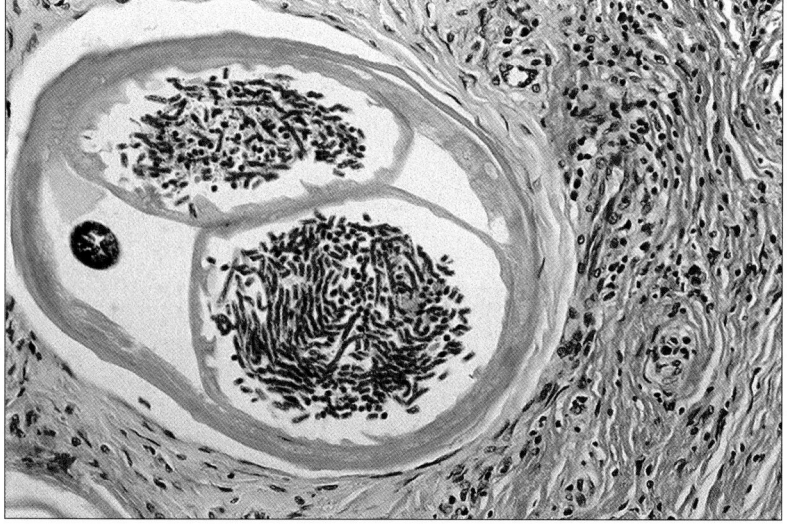

Fig. 17.391
Onchocerciasis: numerous developing microfilariae are evident.

between collagen bundles and foci of fibrinoid change are occasionally seen. Degeneration of microfilariae is foreshadowed by an eosinophilic change with fragmentation of the nuclei; these changes are accompanied by an intense infiltrate of eosinophils. The microfilariae may also be seen with surrounding eosinophils in the epidermis. The number of microfilariae shows an inverse relationship to the level of specific immune complexes.

References

1. Connor, D.H., Neafie, R.C. (1976) Onchocerciasis. In: Bunford, C.H., Connor, D.H. (eds) Pathology of tropical and extraordinary diseases, Vol. 1. Washington: Armed Forces Institute of Pathology, pp 360–372.
2. Hay, R.J., MacKenzie, C.D., Guderian, R. et al (1989) Onchodermatitis – correlation between skin disease and parasitic load in an endemic focus in Ecuador. *Br J Dermatol*, **121**, 187–198.
3. Convit, C., Rassi, E., Harman, R. (1992) Onchocerciasis. In: Canizares, O., Harman, R. (eds) Clinical tropical dermatology, 2nd edn. Boston: Blackwell, pp 344–356.
4. Murdoch, M.E., Asuzu, M.C., Hagan, M. et al (2002) Onchocerciasis: the clinical and epidemiological burden of disease in Africa. *Ann Trop Med*, **96**, 283–296.
5. Vivas-Martinez, S., Basanez, M.G., Botto, C. et al (2000) Amazonian onchocerciasis: parasitological profiles by host-age, sex, and endemicity in southern Venezuela. *Parasitology*, **121** Pt 5, 513–525.
6. Abiose, H., Jones, B. R. (1993) A clinical classification and grading system of the cutaneous changes in onchocerciasis. *Br J Dermatol*, **129**, 260–269.
7. Nwoke, B.E.B. (1990) The socio-economic aspects of human onchocerciasis in Africa: present appraisal. *J Hyg Epidemiol Microbiol Immunol*, **34**, 37–44.
8. Murdoch, M.E., Abiose, A., Hay, R.J. et al (1992) Cutaneous mesoendemic savannah onchocerciasis in Northern Nigeria: a clinico-histopatological correlation study. *Br J Dermatol*, **127** (Suppl.) 80A.
9. Bird, A.C., Anderson, J., Fuglsang, H. (1976) Morphology of posterior segment lesions of the eye in patients with onchocerciasis. *Br J Ophthalmol*, **60**, 2–20.
10. Anderson, J., Fuglsang, H. (1977) Ocular onchocerciasis. *Trop Dis Bull*, **74**, 257–272.
11. Connor, D.H., George, G.H., Gibson, D.W. (1985) Pathologic changes of human onchocerciasis: implications for future research. *Rev Infect Dis*, **7**, 809–819.

Cutaneous larva migrans

Clinical features

Cutaneous larva migrans (creeping eruption) is a distinctive dermatitis resulting from penetration of and migration through the skin by infectious nematode larvae, usually of animal origin.[1,2] The condition is most prevalent in warm, humid tropical regions, especially along the coastline.[1] Returning travelers may present with the disease after visiting endemic areas.[3] The larval forms of *Ancylostoma braziliensis* (the cat and dog hookworm) are the most frequent cause of cutaneous larva migrans.[1,2] Other animal nematodes implicated include *A. caninum* (dog hookworm), *A. tubaeformis* (cat hookworm) and *Uncinaria stenocephala* (European dog hookworm). Larvae of human hookworm species, i.e. *Gnathostoma spinigerum*, *A. duodenale* and *Necator americanus*, may also be associated with cutaneous larva migrans. *Pleodora strongyloides*, a free-living soil nematode, is another potential etiological agent of the disease.[1,2]

Rhabditiform larvae evolve in the soil from eggs passed in the feces of infected hosts. These metamorphose into infectious filariform larvae capable of penetrating human skin upon contact.[1,2] The larvae appear to enter the skin via the ostia of hair follicles or sweat glands, usually on the feet, buttocks or abdomen, in decreasing order of frequency.[1,3] An intensely pruritic erythematous papule or vesicle develops at the site of larval penetration. Follicular papules and pustules are sometimes seen.[4] Migration of the larvae commences 2–4 days later, and is associated with the evolution of a characteristic erythematous, serpiginous tract (*Fig. 17.392*). The larvae may migrate at a rate of 2–5 cm per day.[1,2]

Although the condition is usually self-limiting, with spontaneous resolution over a period of several weeks, secondary bacterial infection introduced by scratching is a relatively frequent complication.[1] Erythema multiforme has been reported in association with cutaneous larva migrans.[5] Löffler's syndrome is a rare complication of the disease.[6]

Histological features

Biopsy specimens obtained from the advancing tract confirm the presence of tunneling larvae. Although this usually takes place at or near the dermoepidermal junction, larvae may also be encountered more

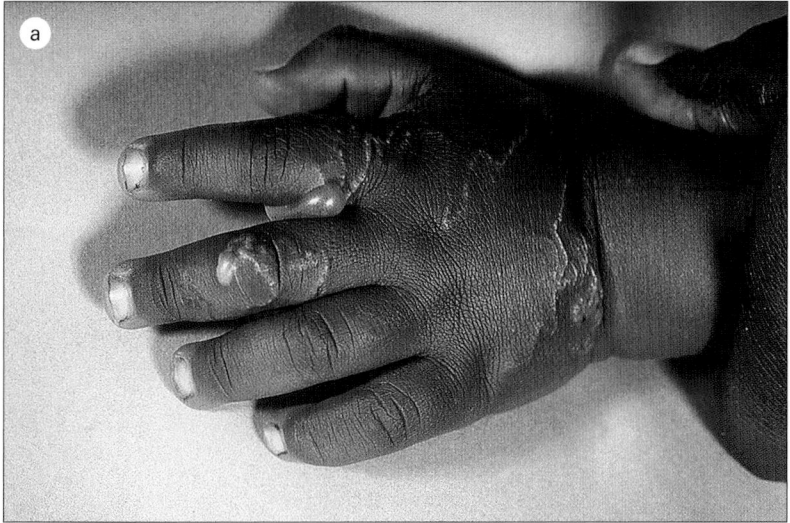
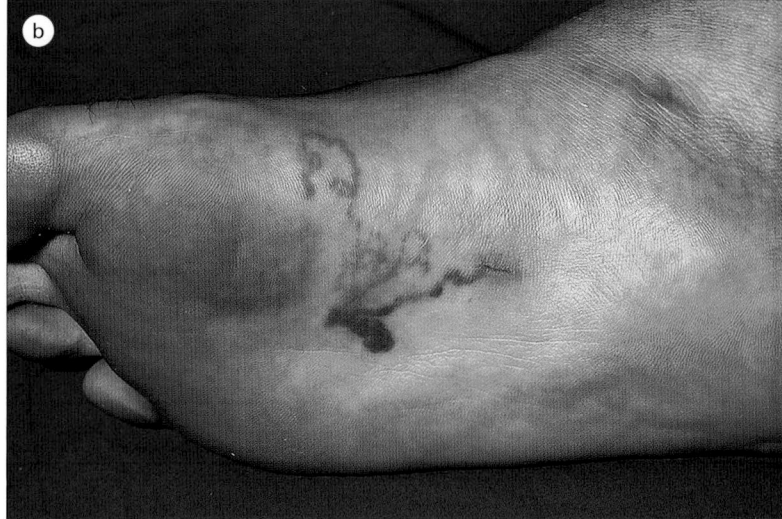

Fig. 17.392
Cutaneous larva migrans: (a) multiple irregular tracts are present; (b) the foot is a commonly affected site. (a) By courtesy of N.C. Dlova, MD, Nelson R. Mandela School of Medicine, University of KwaZulu-Natal, South Africa; (b) by courtesy of R.A. Marsden, MD, St George's Hospital, London, UK.

superficially in the epidermis.[1,2,7] The surrounding epidermis often shows only mild spongiosis, whereas in some cases there is marked intra-epidermal spongiotic vesiculation with exocytosis of neutrophils and eosinophils.[7] The underlying dermis exhibits telangiectasia and a mild mixed inflammatory cell infiltrate containing eosinophilic leukocytes.[1,2,7] Follicular involvement has been reported.[4]

References

1. Canizares, O. (1992) Larva migrans. In: Canizares, O., Harman, R. (eds) Clinical tropical dermatology, 2nd edn. Boston: Blackwell, pp 332–334.
2. Nikolaides, G., Rosen, T. (1997) Cutaneous larva migrans. In: Connor, D.H., Chandler, F.W., Schwartz, D.A. et al (eds) Pathology of infectious diseases, Vol. I. Stamford: Appleton and Lange, pp 1455–1457.
3. Blackwell, V., Vega-Lopez, F. (2001) Cutaneous larva migrans: clinical features and mangement of 44 cases presenting in the returning traveller. *Br J Dermatol*, **145**, 434–437.
4. Caumes, E., Ly, F., Bricaire, F. (2002) Cutaneous larva migrans with folliculitis: report of seven cases and review of the literature. *Br J Dermatol*, **146**, 314–316.
5. Vaughan, T.K., English, J.C. 3rd (1998) Cutaneous larva migrans complicated by erythema multiforme. *Cutis*, **62**, 33–35.
6. Schaub, N.A., Perruchoud, A.P., Buechner, S.A. (2002) Cutaneous larva migrans associated with Löffler's syndrome. *Dermatology*, **205**, 207–209.
7. Balfour, E., Zalka, A., Lazova, R. (2002) Cutaneous larva migrans with parts of the larva in the epidermis. *Cutis*, **69**, 368–370.

Trematode infestation

Schistosomiasis

Clinical features

Schistosoma haematobium and *Schistosoma mansoni* are both found extensively in Africa. *S. mansoni* is also found in the West Indies and in parts of South America. *Schistosoma japonicum* is found in China, Japan and South-East Asia. These trematodes (blood flukes) do not often cause major disease of the skin, but skin lesions do occur at various stages of infestation.[1,2]

Invasion of the human host by the aquatic cercarial stage may be associated with a dermatitis (swimmer's itch, cercarial dermatitis).[3,4] The rash is erythematous, pruritic and urticarial, but eventually resolves to leave a pigmented spot. It is more often associated with invasion of avian species.[3]

The mature worms may be associated non-specifically with erythematous itching macules at the time of release of large numbers of eggs. This probably represents a systemic reaction to antigen liberation. A more severe reaction seen most often with *S. japonicum* is Katayama disease or Yellow River fever. In addition to erythema, macules and pruriginous lesions, patients may also have fever, malaise, chills, sweats, arthralgias, headache, lymphadenopathy, hepatosplenomegaly, diarrhea, bronchitis, pneumonitis and peripheral blood eosinophilia.[3,4]

Specific skin lesions are seen, usually around the genitalia and most often in women, when ova are deposited there. The lesions appear as grouped solid papules, which subsequently become warty and vegetative. Occasionally progression to squamous carcinoma supervenes. Periurethral granulomata due to schistosomes may be associated with thrombosis and necrosis, resulting sometimes in fistulation to the perineum ('watering can perineum').[3] More rarely, entrapped ova can be seen in other areas of skin, but the means of their migration to those sites is not understood. Lymphedema may be a late complication[4] (see also p. 506).

Pathogenesis and histological features

Part of the life cycle of schistosomes takes place in water snails and these release the cercariae, which penetrate the skin, are carried to the lungs and then migrate as schistosomules to the portal vein where they mature into adult male and female worms. Adult females then migrate to the mesenteric plexus (*S. mansoni* and *S. japonicum*) or vesical plexus (*S. haematobium*). Ova are then deposited in the venules and the clinical and pathological sequelae are a direct consequence of the immunological response to their presence.

Eggs are released into the urine or feces where they hatch, releasing miracidia, which enter the snail host. Involvement of the female genital tract is usually due to *S. haematobium* and occurs as a consequence of worms being transported via anastomoses between the vesical and uterovaginal venous plexuses.

Histologically, adult worms may occasionally be seen within the lumina of dilated deep dermal veins and lymphatics. Viable ova may be seen with a recognizable miracidial structure. These are usually located within abscesses containing numerous neutrophils and variable numbers of eosinophils. Poorly formed granulomata with Langhans' giant cells may also be a feature. *S. haematobium* is recognized by its terminal spine. The dead ova typically calcify and provoke a chronic, frequently granulomatous, inflammatory response. The overlying epidermis is usually acanthotic, sometimes to the point of pseudoepitheliomatous hyperplasia, with variable transepidermal elimination of ova.

References

1.   McKee, P.H., Wright, E., Hutt, M.S.R. (1983) Vulval schistosomiasis. *Clin Exp Dermatol*, **8**, 189–194.
2.   Grossetete, G., Diabate, I., Pichard, E. et al (1989) Skin manifestations of bilharziasis. Apropos of 24 case reports in Mali. *Bull Soc Pathol Exotique Ses Filiales*, **82**, 225–232.
3.   Amer, M. (1982) Cutaneous schistosomiasis. *Int J Dermatol*, **21**, 44–46.
4.   Amer, M. (1992) Trematoda. In: Canizares, O., Harman, R. (eds) Clinical tropical dermatology, 2nd edn. Boston: Blackwell, pp 363–371.

Cestode infestation

Cysticercosis

Clinical features

The adult pork tapeworm *Taenia solium* may be present in the small intestine of man (the definitive host). The intermediate host, the pig, ingests the eggs, which develop to the cysticercus stage in muscle and elsewhere and are then infective if eaten by man. If man ingests eggs, however, he can become the host for the cysticercus stage; this occurs most commonly in skin, brain and eye.[1] Cystercerci in the skin present as painless nodules up to 2 cm across (*Fig. 17.393*). The vast majority of patients present with solitary cutaneous nodules. Nodules may also occur in the oral cavity or breast in a small percentage of cases.[2]

Pathogenesis and histological features

The viable cysticercus compresses adjacent dermis without inflammation (*Fig. 17.394*). However, when it begins to degenerate there is an infiltration of neutrophils, histiocytes and eosinophils, which becomes more granulomatous, with giant cells, fibrosis and eventual calcification.

References

1.   Falanga, V., Kapdor, W. (1985) Cerebral cysticercosis: diagnostic value of subcutaneous nodules. *J Am Acad Dermatol*, **12** (2 Pt 1), 304–307.
2.   Amatya, B.M., Kimula, Y. (1999) Cysticercosis in Nepal: a histopathologic study of sixty-two cases. *Am J Surg Pathol*, **23**, 1276–1279.

Cutaneous lesions in AIDS

Immunodeficiency in AIDS is due to depletion of T-helper cells as a result of HIV replication selectively within those cells. HIV is a retrovirus of which two types are recognized:

- HIV-1 is responsible for infections in the USA and Europe
- HIV-2 occurs particularly in West Africa.[1]

The T4 antigen appears to act as a receptor for HIV, as monoclonal antibodies can block its attachment. The result of T-helper cell depletion is a severe defect in cell-mediated immunity, making people with AIDS particularly susceptible to infection, sometimes of more than one etiological type.[2] AIDS is characterized by skin anergy to delayed hypersensitivity testing, a polyclonal rise in IgG and a diminished T4:T8 T-cell ratio.[3] The CD4 (T-helper cell) count is used to assess progression in HIV infection. There is also evidence to suggest that epidermal and mucosal Langerhans' cells may also be infected with HIV.[1,4]

Exposure to HIV may result in:

- an asymptomatic infection
- the chronic lymphadenopathy syndrome
- AIDS-related complex (ARC)
- AIDS.[5]

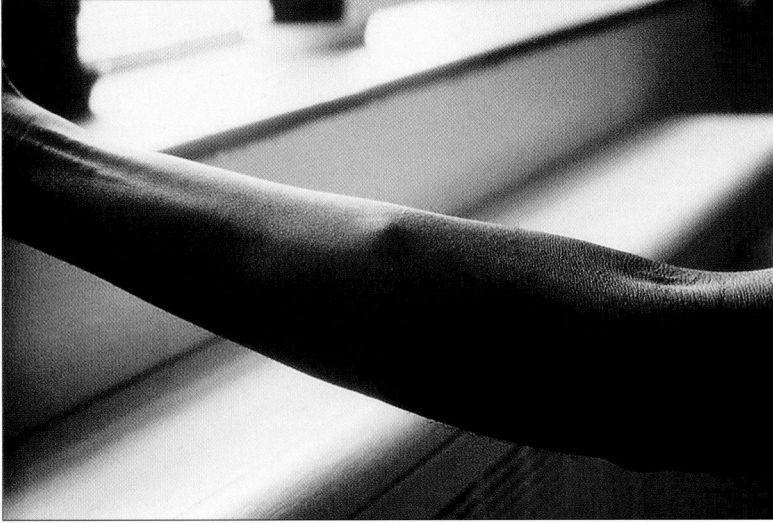

Fig. 17.393
Cysticercosis: a solitary nodule is present on the ventral aspect of the forearm. Cysticercosis develops when humans are harboring the larval (cysticercus) stage of the tapeworm. By courtesy of S. Lucas, MD, St Thomas' Hospital, London, UK.

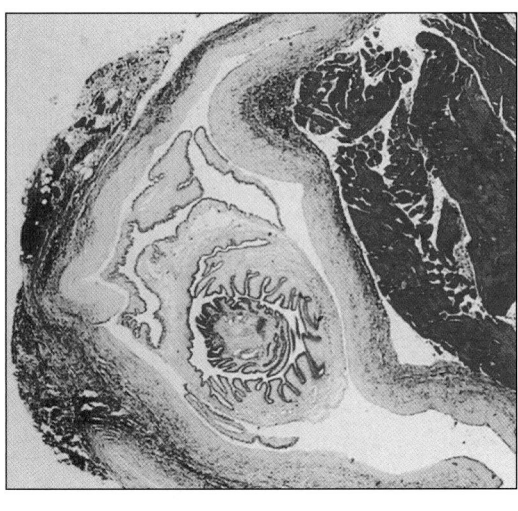

Fig. 17.394
Cysticercosis: the worm lies within a cystic cavity surrounded by a dense fibrous capsule. By courtesy of S. Lucas, MD, St Thomas' Hospital, London, UK.

The chronic lymphadenopathy syndrome consists of a minimum of 3 months of chronic lymphadenopathy at two or more extrainguinal sites occurring without any evidence of underlying infection or drug abuse.[5]

ARC includes malaise, fever, anorexia, chronic diarrhea, weight loss, oral candidiasis, skin eruptions and generalized lymphadenopathy.[5] Opportunistic infections and neoplasia are not present. It has been shown that 5–20% of patients with ARC will develop AIDS within a 3-year period.[5] Useful progression indicators include oral candidiasis, hairy leukoplakia and the presence of hepatitis B infection or syphilis (*Figs 17.395, 17.396*).[6] AIDS is defined clincially as the presence of opportunist infections, Kaposi's sarcoma and B-cell lymphomas.[1]

Skin diseases are among the most common manifestations of HIV infection.[7] The cutaneous responses to HIV can be classified into three types:

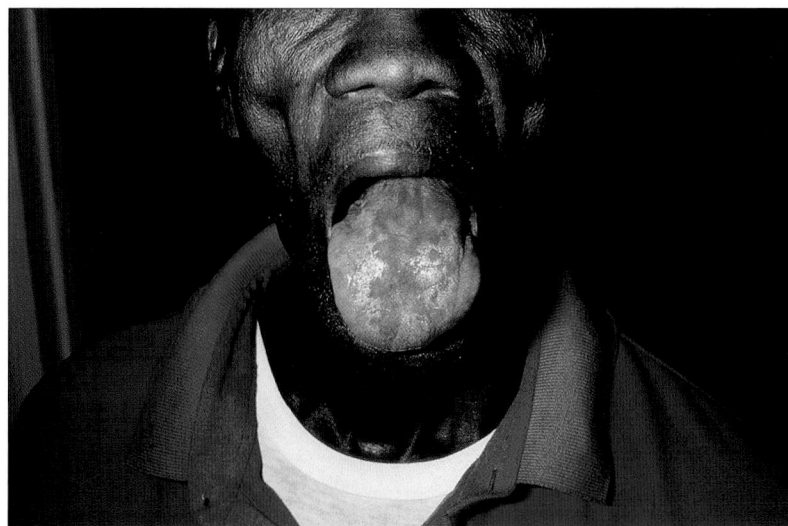

Fig. 17.395
Candidal atrophic glossitis with HIV infection: infection with *Candida* is a very common manifestation. In addition to the oral cavity, intertriginous and nail infections may be present. By courtesy of C. Furlonge, MD, Port of Spain, Trinidad.

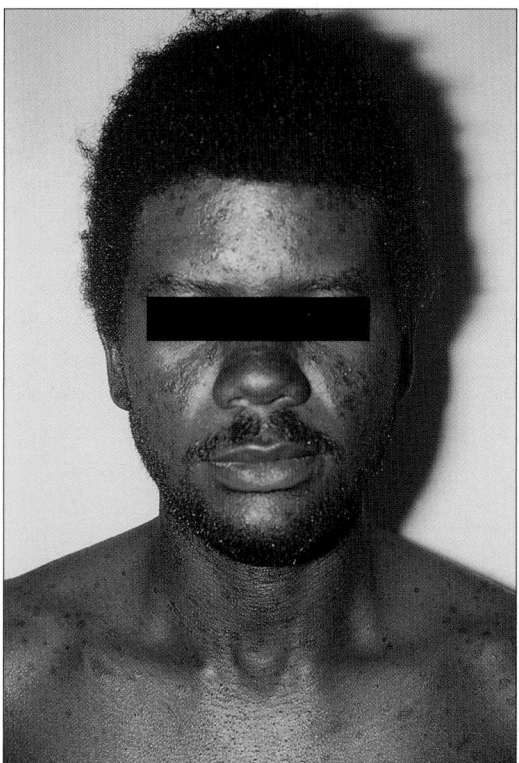

Fig. 17.396
Secondary syphilis with HIV infection: there are numerous pigmented macules on the face, neck and chest. Patients with HIV infection show an increased incidence of syphilis. By courtesy of C. Furlonge, MD, Port of Spain, Trinidad.

- Primary (non-infective) dermatoses that may represent a specific manifestation of HIV infection or a common dermatosis that is present in increased frequency in (and often modified by) AIDS
- Infective dermatoses including fungal, mycobacterial, viral and protozoal disorders
- Neoplasms.

Immunosuppression often results in dermatoses displaying unusual or atypical presentations and an abnormal course.[8,9] Characteristic of HIV infection is a failure to respond to standard treatment and a greater severity of disease than is usually anticipated.[8] Diagnosis therefore depends upon a high index of suspicion. Syphilis in HIV-positive patients, for example, often presents as a papulosquamous eruption showing a psoriasiform histology with spongiotic vesiculation and interface dermatitis. Only the presence of plasma cells in the superficial perivascular infiltrate gives a clue to the correct diagnosis.[10] Patients are also at risk for developing lues maligna, an uncommon and clinically aggressive form of secondary syphilis.[11]

Non-infective dermatosis

HIV exanthem

Patients sometimes display a non-scaly, macular, roseoliform dermatosis that may represent the first sign of seroconversion to HIV positivity.[12,13] The short-lived eruption sometimes mimics infectious mononucleosis or secondary syphilis. Patients may experience prodromal symptoms including fever, sweats, malaise and myalgia.[14] The histological features have included a superficial perivascular lymphohistiocytic infiltrate, purpura, basal cell hydropic degeneration and slight spongiosis.[15] HIV exanthem is said to occur in 10–20% of patients.[16]

Papular dermatitis

A pruritic papular dermatitis (pruritic papular eruption) may be present in up to 20% of HIV-positive patients.[12,17] In some series this figure is higher (in excess of 30%).[18] The eruption has been found to be associated with advanced immunosuppression, with a CD4 count of less than 50 cells per mm^3 in 75% of patients.[19] Lesions, which measure 2–5 mm in diameter and are skin colored, are found predominantly on the head, neck and upper trunk (*Fig. 17.397*).[5,14] It has been suggested that this may represent a hypersensitivity response to insect bites or *Demodex* infection.[20] Histology reveals a superficial and deep interstitial infiltrate composed of lymphocytes and eosinophils.[12] Superimposed excoriations or lichen simplex chronicus may also be evident.[12]

Seborrheic dermatitis-like eruption

This occurs in 46–83% of patients with AIDS.[21,22] It may also be a feature of ARC. It is, therefore, the most common dermatological condition associated with HIV infection.[16] It has been suggested that seborrheic dermatitis may correlate with AIDS dementia.[23] Patients present with erythematous, scaly patches and yellowish crusts on the scalp, face, axillae, chest, inguinal regions and genitalia.[5,24] The eruption may have a sudden onset and be particularly severe. It is sometimes an initial manifestation of AIDS.[5] The severity of the eruption appears to correlate with the clinical state and the T4:T8 ratio.[23] Histologically it is characterized by the typical features of seborrheic dermatitis, i.e. hyperkeratosis, focal parakeratosis (especially related to the edges of the follicular infundibula), acanthosis with elongation of the epidermal ridges (thereby resembling psoriasis), slight spongiosis and a superficial perivascular lymphohistiocytic infiltrate.[12] In addition, however, widespread parakeratosis, marked lymphocytic exocytosis and occasional necrotic keratinocytes may be seen.[12] The dermal infiltrate can include plasma cells and neutrophils showing leukocytoclasia.[12,14] It is always wise to do a PAS reaction to exclude concomitant superficial fungal infection.

Psoriasis

Atypical and severe psoriasis may be a cutaneous feature of AIDS.[14] Although the overall incidence does not appear to exceed that of the general population, HIV-infected patients tend to develop more severe forms of psoriasis.[16] The histological features are identical to those seen in conventional psoriasis with the addition of plasma cells in the superficial dermal infiltrate.

Eosinophilic folliculitis

This presents as a chronic pruritic dermatosis characterized by discrete, smooth-surfaced papules located predominantly on the trunk and proximal extremities (*Fig. 17.398*).[12] It is said to differ from Ofuji's eosinophilic pustular folliculitis by the presence of discrete, scattered lesions compared to the arcuate plaques of the latter condition, although there is considerable overlap.[25–28] It is exceedingly difficult if not impossible to differentiate between eosinophilic folliculitis and suppurative (infective) folliculitis on clinical grounds, and all HIV-positive patients with pruritic follicular lesions should undergo skin biopsy.[29]

Histologically, HIV-associated eosinophilic folliculitis is characterized by the presence of eosinophils and occasional small eosinophil pustules in the outer root sheath or pilar canal of the hair follicle accompanied by a perivascular and interstitial lymphohistiocytic and eosinophil infiltrate in the superficial and deep dermis.[12] Well-developed and large eosinophilic pustules in the pilar canals is characteristic of Ofuji's disease (*Fig. 17.399*).[11] Bacteria and fungi are consistently absent.[27] It has been proposed that this may represent a hypersensitivity reaction to *Demodex folliculorum*; however, the latter organism seems to be present in only a minority of cases.[14,30] It has also been postulated that eosinophilic folliculitis has an autoimmune basis, with either the sebocytes or a consti-

tuent of sebum functioning as the autoantigen.[29] The condition tends to manifest when the CD4 count is less than 250 cells per mm³.[16]

Leukocytoclastic vasculitis

In addition to typical immune complex small vessel vasculitis, patients with AIDS appear to be at an increased risk of developing erythema elevatum diutinum.[8,12,31] The clinical features, however, have been somewhat atypical, the presenting lesions tending to resemble the juxta-articular nodules of syphilis.

Xerosis

Xerosis presenting as a severely pruritic, generalized dry scaly skin syndrome is a common manifestation of HIV infection (*Fig. 17.400*).[22,32] It is associated with diminished sebum and sweat production accompanied by abnormal epidermal lipid release. It may be associated with fissures and eczema craquelé.[5] Xerosis may be the first sign of AIDS.[32] Histology reveals slight hyperkeratosis and parakeratosis with acanthosis and focal spongiosis.[23] There may be a perivascular lymphocytic infiltrate in the superficial dermis. On occasions the features of acquired ichthyosis are evident, i.e. marked hyperkeratosis with diminished granular cell layer.[23]

Drug reactions

HIV-infected patients are at risk for developing drug hypersensitivity reactions for two reasons: first, they are often receiving multiple medications simultaneously, and second, they are more susceptible because of a declining T-helper cell population.[16] The commonly prescribed combination of trimethoprim and sulfamethoxazole is strongly associated with adverse reactions; these may occur at a frequency 10 times that of the HIV-negative population.[16] The antiretroviral drug nevirapine (a non-nucleoside reverse transcriptase inhibitor) is associated

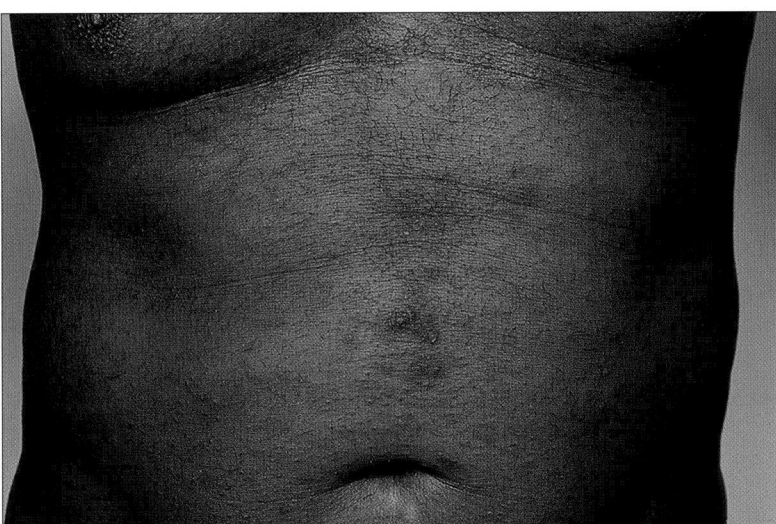

Fig. 17.397
Papular dermatitis: a non-specific, intensely pruritic, papular eruption is a common manifestation of HIV infection. By courtesy of D. McGibbon, MD, St Thomas' Hospital, London, UK.

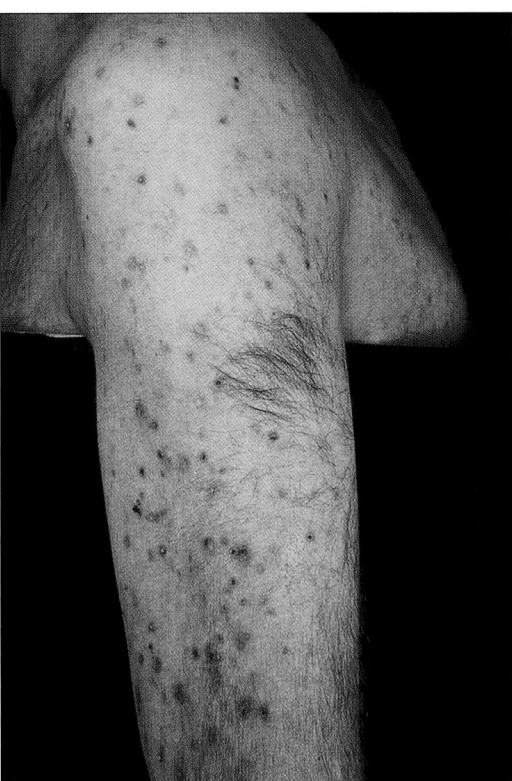

Fig. 17.398
HIV-associated folliculitis: follicular pustules and excoriations are present on the shoulder, arm and back. By courtesy of D. McGibbon, MD, St Thomas' Hospital, London, UK.

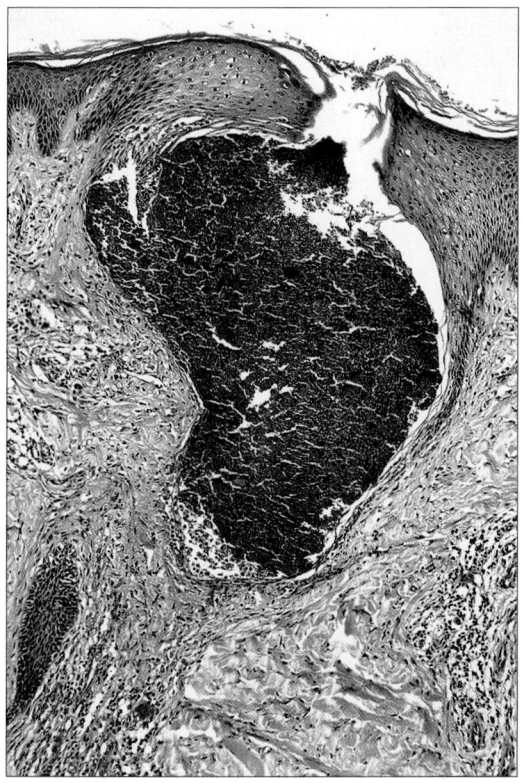

Fig. 17.399
Ofuji's disease: note the eosinophil abscess, which has dilated and obstructed the follicular canal. By courtesy of D. McGibbon, MD, St Thomas' Hospital, London, UK.

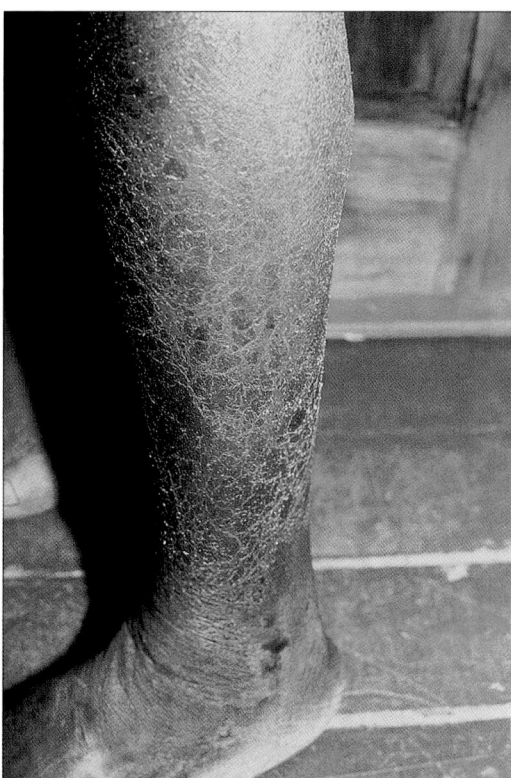

Fig. 17.400
HIV-associated xerosis: marked scaling has resulted in an eczema craquelé-like appearance. Dry skin is a common complaint in patients with HIV infection. By courtesy of C. Furlonge, MD, Port of Spain, Trinidad.

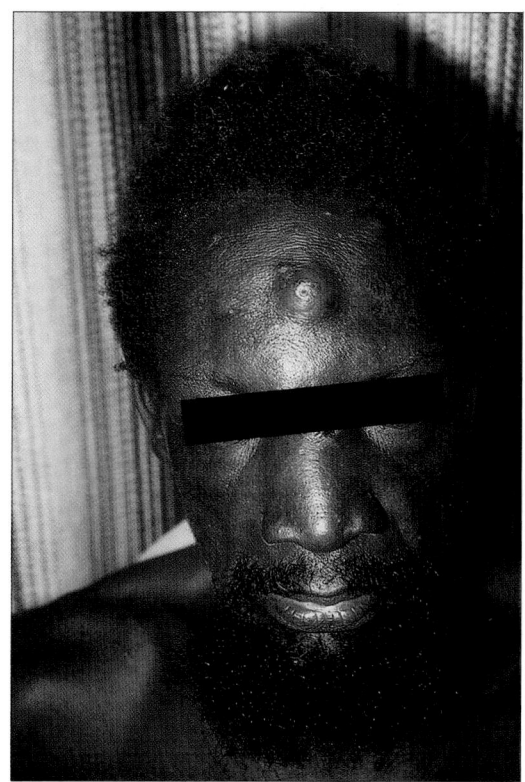

Fig. 17.402
Furunculosis with HIV infection: staphylococcal infections are common in patients with HIV. Angular stomatitis, acute bacterial folliculitis and impetigo may also be seen. By courtesy of C. Furlonge, MD, Port of Spain, Trinidad.

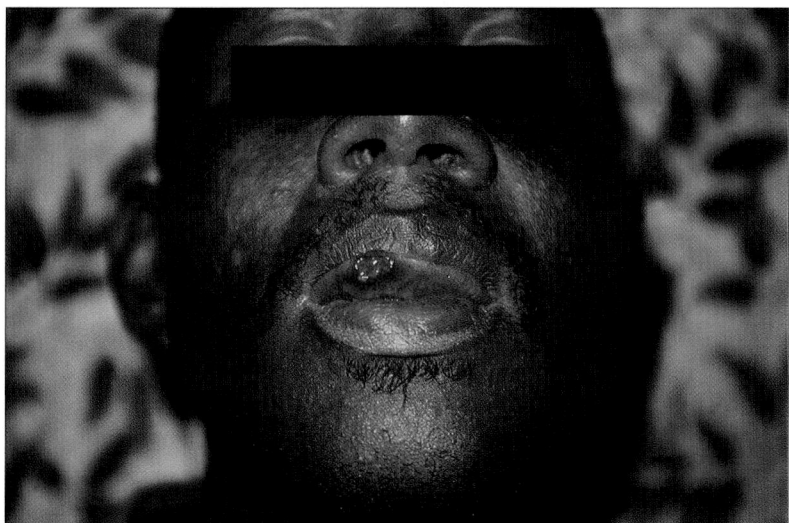

Fig. 17.401
Labial ulceration: non-specific mucosal ulceration is a common feature of HIV infection. Lesions are extremely painful and difficult to treat. By courtesy of C. Furlonge, MD, Port of Spain, Trinidad.

with a particularly high rate of adverse reactions involving the skin (32–48%), including the Stevens–Johnson syndrome.[33] Female patients and individuals with a CD4 count of less than 100 cells per mm[3] are at greater risk for developing a reaction to this drug.[33]

Additional dermatoses

Additional dermatoses that have been described in AIDS patients have included granuloma annulare, photosensitivity, atopic dermatitis, porphyria cutanea tarda, lichenoid reactions, Grover's disease and alopecia.[5,8,34–38] Both alopecia areata and telogen effluvium have been described in AIDS and ARC.[38] A granulomatous, scarring permanent alopecia has also been recorded.[39] Telogen effluvium is characterized by a non-inflammatory diminution in anagen follicles.[8]

Ulcers on both oral and genital mucosae are a particularly distressing feature of HIV infection (*Fig. 17.401*). They are exquisitely painful and difficult to treat.[8]

Cutaneous infections

The cutaneous infections that occur in AIDS can be classified into five types. The infections outlined below are discussed in greater detail earlier in this chapter.

Type 1 infections

Type 1 infections are serious (but common) infections, which are less significant in the immunocompetent. They include those by group A streptococci and *S. aureus*, which may be causative organisms in cellulitis, impetigo, necrotizing folliculitis, furunculosis, pyoderma and erysipelas (*Fig. 17.402*). *S. aureus* is the most common bacterial pathogen in patients with AIDS.[40] It may present as botryomycosis.[10,41] Bacterial folliculitis can also be a feature of HIV infection. It presents as an acneiform eruption affecting the face, back, chest and buttocks or else as a relapsing condition in the axillae.[14] Histologically, bacterial folliculitis is characterized by a purulent exudate within the follicular epithelium accompanied by a surrounding lymphohistiocytic infiltrate.[14] Plasma cells and eosinophils may also be evident.

Bacillary angiomatosis is a vasoproliferative lesion induced by infection with either *Bartonella henselae* or *Bartonella quintana*.[42] Patients with CD4 lymphocyte counts of less than 100 per mm³ are at risk.[43]

Type 2 infections

Type 2 infections are extensive infections which are focal or trivial in the immunocompetent. They include HPV-induced lesions such as verruca vulgaris and condylomata acuminata, cytomegalovirus, molluscum contagiosum, herpes simplex virus, herpes zoster virus and scabies (often presenting as the Norwegian variant) (*Figs 17.403, 17.404*).[44,45] Patients with HIV infection and scabies may also present with an erythematous papulosquamous eruption, with skin scrapings containing numerous mites.

Cytomegalovirus is the most common viral pathogen seen in advanced AIDS, evidence for which is found in 93% of autopsies.[1] It is responsible for retinitis, colitis, pneumonitis, encephalitis and generalized wasting.[1] Skin involvement, however, is very rare.

Warts and associated squamous carcinoma become a severe problem in AIDS and zoster infections have a high incidence. HPV-associated cervical and anal carcinoma in situ are also of importance.[46]

Oral, genital, digital and perianal herpes simplex (reactivation) are very common and severe infections in patients with AIDS (*Figs 17.405, 17.406*).[1] Perianal lesions may present as very extensive, painful, necrotic, non-healing ulcers with a circinate border.[5]

Dermatophyte infections (e.g. tinea pedis, tinea cruris and tinea capitis) and onychomycosis often become very severe and extensive. In patients with AIDS there are often numerous lesions of molluscum

contagiosum affecting the face, although any other skin area may be involved.[47]

Pseudomolluscum contagiosum may be a manifestation of a systemic mycosis (e.g. *C. neoformans*, coccidioidomycosis, *H. capsulatum*).[1,9,48] Oral candidiasis is often a sign of progression of HIV positivity without AIDS symptoms to establishment of the full syndrome. Perlèche and onychomycosis are frequent manifestations of candidiasis in AIDS patients.[10]

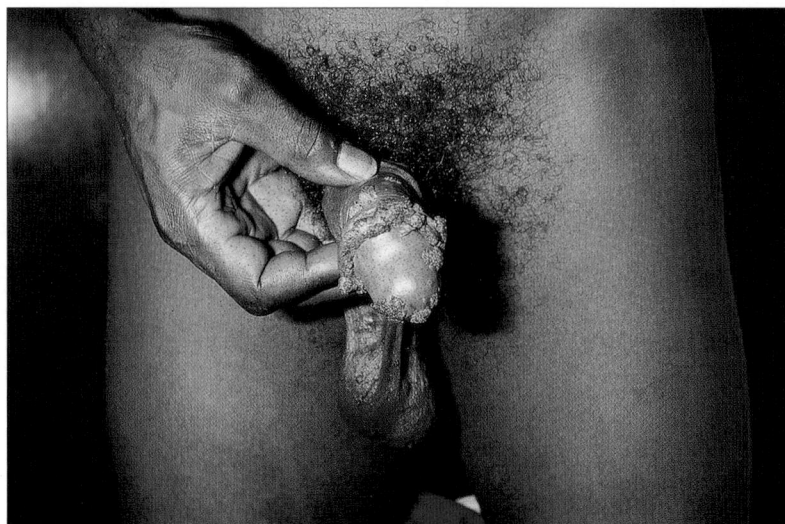

Fig. 17.403
Genital condylomata and HIV infection: genital and perianal warts may sometimes be associated with exuberant growth in this condition. By courtesy of C. Furlonge, MD, Port of Spain, Trinidad.

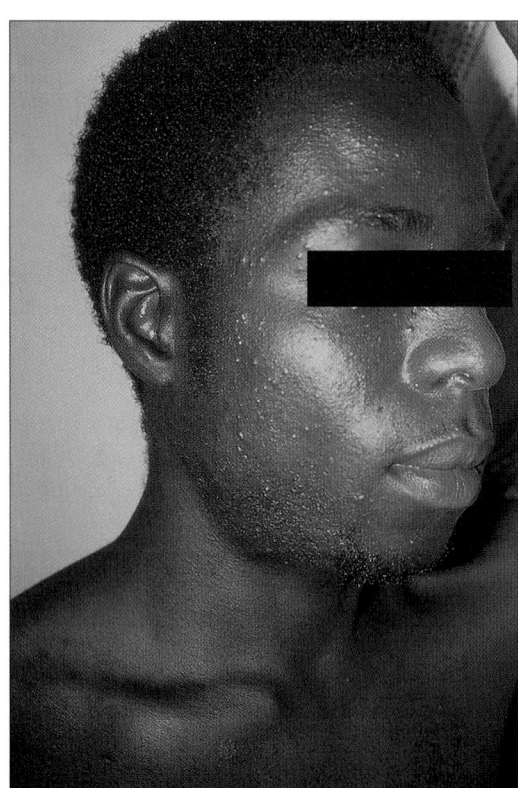

Fig. 17.404
Molluscum contagiosum and HIV infection: this is commonly seen and particularly affects the face. Lesions are typically numerous. By courtesy of C. Furlonge, MD, Port of Spain, Trinidad.

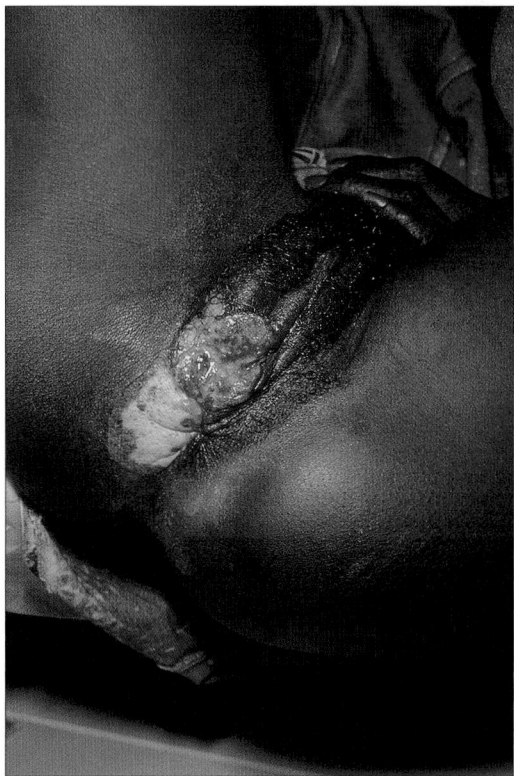

Fig. 17.405
Herpes simplex and HIV infection: there is gross destruction of the vulva with involvement of the thigh. By courtesy of C. Furlonge, MD, Port of Spain, Trinidad.

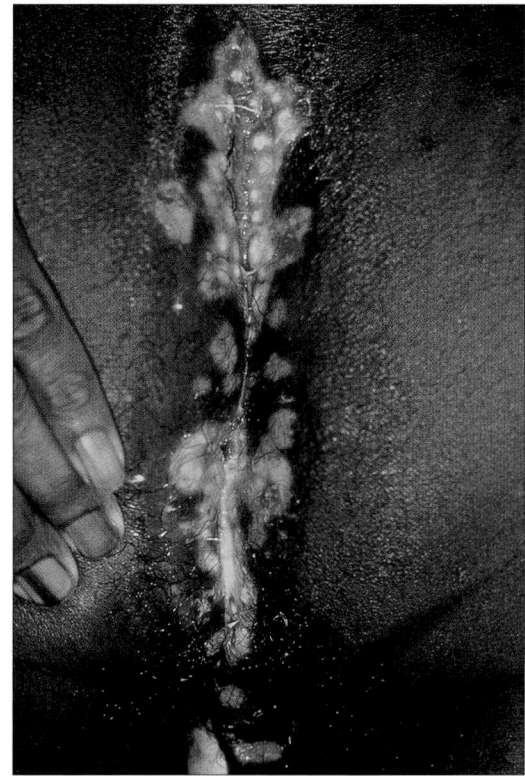

Fig. 17.406
Herpes simplex and HIV infection: severe perianal disease has spread to involve much of the perineum and natal cleft. By courtesy of D. McGibbon, MD, St Thomas' Hospital, London, UK.

Type 3 infections

Type 3 infections are due to opportunistic organisms which do not usually produce disease in the immunocompetent. They include fungal infections (*Alternaria, Aspergillus, Mucor, Cryptococcus, Histoplasma*), *Prototheca* and *Mycobacterium* including the *avium intracellulare* variant (although skin lesions due to this particular organism are rare).[12,49] The latter usually represents disseminated disease.[10]

In patients with AIDS who have *M. tuberculosis* infections, the histological features may vary from non-caseating granulomata to caseating granulomata, to an absence of granulomata.[10] In *M. avium intracellulare* infection the features may be granulomatous, but more commonly consist of a non-granulomatous infiltrate of neutrophils, numerous foamy macrophages, lymphocytes, plasma cells and eosinophils.[10] Organisms are usually very numerous in this reaction. *M. kansasii* infection may result in a spindle cell 'proliferative' lesion reminiscent of the histoid variant of lepromatous leprosy.[50] Obviously the presence of more typical foamy macrophages is a useful diagnostic discriminant.

An interesting and unusual observation has been the identification of *Pneumocystis jiroveci* (formerly *Pneumocystis carinii*) in middle ear infections presenting as polypi within the external auditory meatus.[51] Histologically these lesions show features similar to those seen in the more typical pulmonary lesions.

Type 4 infections

Type 4 infections are metastatic from systemic disease and include *Pseudomonas, Histoplasma, Coccidioides, Blastomycosis, Nocardia, Aspergillus, Cryptococcus, Candida* and *Mucor*.

Type 5 infections

Type 5 infection is peculiar to AIDS patients, and is represented by oral hairy leukoplakia, which is due to Epstein–Barr virus. It is seen as a usually asymptomatic, white, poorly demarcated, raised plaque most often on the lateral border of the tongue (*Fig. 17.407*).[5] The ventral and dorsal surfaces, buccal mucosa, palate and floor of the mouth may also be affected.[14] Although *Candida* is often found in the lesions, they do not respond to anticandidal therapy. There are fine projections of keratin from the surface said to resemble hairs. Alternatively there may be

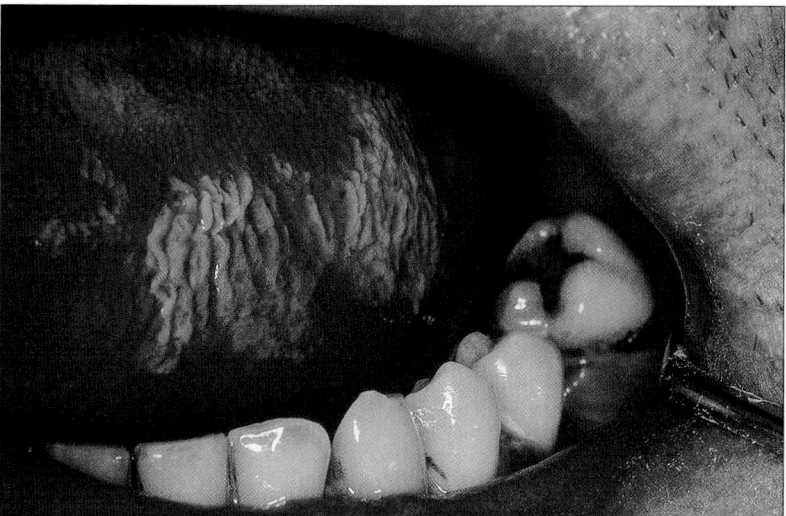

Fig. 17.407
Oral hairy leukoplakia: characteristic delicate linear white lesions on the tongue.
By courtesy of P.R. Morgan, MD, Institute of Dermatology, London, UK.

vertical white lines running across the edge of the tongue. Balloon cells with pyknotic nuclei are seen in the superficial epithelium as well as marked parakeratosis and epithelial hyperplasia.[52] Electron microscopy has revealed both papilloma and herpes-type virus.[53] Epstein–Barr virus replication has been demonstrated within the epithelial cells of hairy leukoplakia[54] (see also p. 430).

Neoplasia

AIDS is also complicated by the development of a number of neoplasms including Kaposi's sarcoma (see p. 1832) and malignant lymphoma (see p. 1450).[12,46,55-58] The latter is predominantly of B-cell type and most often an undifferentiated (large cell) non-Burkitt's variant.[59] It has a poor prognosis. Primary skin involvement is rare. Surprisingly, mycosis fungoides may also develop in patients with AIDS.[12] People with AIDS also have an increased risk of developing both oral and anorectal squamous cell carcinoma.[14,46]

References

1. Dover, J.S., Johnson, R.A. (1991) Cutaneous manifestations of human immunodeficiency virus infection. Part I. *Arch Dermatol*, 127, 1383–1391.
2. Piérard, G.E., Piérard-Franchimont, C., Estrada, J.A. et al (1990) Cutaneous mixed infections in AIDS. *Am J Dermatopathol*, 12, 63–66.
3. Farthing, C.F., Staughton, R.C.D., Rowland Payne, C.M.E. (1985). Skin disease in homosexual patients with acquired immune deficiency syndrome and lesser forms of human T cell leukemia virus (HTLV-III) disease. *Clin Exp Dermatol*, 10, 3–12.
4. Tschachler, E., Groh, V., Popvic, M. et al (1987) Epidermal Langerhans' cells: a target for HTLV-III/LAV infection. *J Invest Dermatol*, 88, 233–237.
5. Warner, L.C., Fisher, B.K. (1986) Cutaneous manifestations of the acquired immunodeficiency syndrome. *Int J Dermatol*, 25, 337–350.
6. Greenspan, D., Greenspan, J.S., Overby, G. et al (1991) Risk factors for rapid progression from hairy leukoplakia to AIDS: a nested case-control study. *J Acquir Immune Defic Synd*, 4, 652–658.
7. Cockerall, C.J. (1991) Human immunodeficiency virus infection and the skin. *Arch Intern Med*, 151, 1295–1303.
8. Cockerell, C.J. (1991) Noninfectious inflammatory skin diseases in HIV-infected individuals. *Dermatol Clin*, 9, 531–541.
9. Penneys, N.S., Hicks, B. (1985) Unusual cutaneous lesions associated with acquired immunodeficiency syndrome. *J Am Acad Dermatol*, 13, 845–852.
10. Smith, K.J., Skelton, H.G., Angritt, P. (1991) Histopathologic features of HIV-associated skin disease. *Dermatol Clin*, 9, 551–578.
11. Don, P.C., Rubinstein, R., Christie, S. (1995) Malignant syphilis (lues maligna) and concurrent infection with HIV. *Int J Dermatol*, 34, 403–407.
12. LeBoit, P.E. (1992) Dermatopathologic findings in patients infected with HIV. *Dermatol Clin*, 10, 59–71.
13. Wantzin, G.R., Lindhardt, B.D., Weismann, K. et al (1986) Acute HTLV-III infection associated with exanthema, diagnosed by seroconversion. *Br J Dermatol*, 115, 601–606.
14. Herman, K.L., Jacoby, R.A., Webster, G. (1991) Pathology of HIV-related skin disease. *Clin Dermatol*, 9, 95–110.
15. Hulsebosch, H.J., Claessen, F.A., van Ginkel, C.J. et al (1990) Human immunodeficiency virus exanthem. *J Am Acad Dermatol*, 23, 483–486.
16. Myskowski, P.L., Ahkami, R. (1996) Dermatologic complications of HIV infection. *Med Clin North Am*, 80, 1415–1435.
17. James, W.D., Redfield, R.R., Lupton, G.P. et al (1985) A papular eruption associated with human T-cell lymphotrophic virus type III disease. *J Am Acad Dermatol*, 13, 563–566.
18. Siviyathorn, A., Srihra, B., Leesanguankul, W. (1995) Prevalence of skin disease in patients infected with human immunodeficiency virus in Bangkok, Thailand. *Ann Acad Med Singapore*, 24, 528–533.
19. Boonchai, W., Laohasrisakul, R., Manonukul, J. et al (1999) Pruritic papular eruption in HIV seropositive patients: a cutaneous marker for immunosuppression. *Int J Dermatol*, 38, 348–350.
20. Ashack, R.J., Frost, M.L., Norins, A.L. (1989) Papular pruritic eruption of Demodex folliculitis in patients with acquired immunodeficiency syndrome. *J Am Acad Dermatol*, 21, 306–307.
21. Mathes, B.M., Douglas, M.C. (1985) Seborrhoeic dermatitis in patients with acquired immunodeficiency syndrome. *J Am Acad Dermatol*, 13, 947–951.
22. Sadick, N.S., McNutt, N.S., Kaplan, M.H. (1990) Papulosquamous dermatoses of AIDS. *J Am Acad Dermatol*, 22, 1270–1277.
23. Eisenstat, B., Wormser, G.P. (1984) Seborrhoeic dermatitis and butterfly rash in AIDS. *N Engl J Med*, 311, 358–364.
24. Soeprono, F.F., Schinella, R.A., Cockerell, C.J. et al (1986) Seborrheic-like dermatitis of acute immunodeficiency syndrome. *J Am Acad Dermatol*, 14, 242.
25. Rosenthal, D., LeBoit, P.E., Klump, L. et al (1991) Human immunodeficiency virus-associated eosinophilic folliculitis: a unique dermatosis associated with advanced human immunodeficiency virus infection. *Arch Dermatol*, 127, 206–209.
26. Jenkins, D. Jr, Fisher, B.K., Chalvardjian, A. et al (1985) Eosinophilic pustular folliculitis in a patient with AIDS. *Int J Dermatol*, 27, 34–35.
27. Seoprono, F.F., Schinella, R.A. (1986) Eosinophilic pustular folliculitis in patients with acquired immunodeficiency syndrome. *J Am Acad Dermatol*, 14, 1020–1022.
28. Soeprono, F.F., Schinella, R.A. (1986) Eosinophilic pustular folliculitis in patients with AIDS: report of 3 cases. *J Am Acad Dermatol*, 14, 1020–1022.
29. Fearfield, L.A., Rowe, A., Francis, N. et al (1999) Itchy folliculitis and human immunodeficiency virus infection: clinicopathological and immunological features, pathogenesis and treatment. *Br J Dermatol*, 141, 3–11.
30. McCalmont, T.H., Altemus, D., Maurer, T. et al (1995) Eosinophilic folliculitis. The histologic spectrum. *Am J Dermatopathol*, 17, 439–446.
31. Chren, M.M., Silverman, R.A., Sorensen, R.U. et al (1989) Leukocytoclastic vasculitis in a patient infected with human immunodeficiency virus. *J Am Acad Dermatol*, 21, 1161–1164.
32. Kaplan, M.H., Sadick, N.S., McNutt, N.S. et al (1987) Dermatologic findings and manifestation of acquired immunodeficiency syndrome (AIDS). *J Am Acad Dermatol*, 16, 485–506.
33. Nelson, A.M. (2002) The pathology induced by modern anti-retroviral therapy against HIV. *Histopathology*, 41 (Suppl. 2), 73–76.
34. Toback, A.C., Longley, J., Cardullo, A.C. et al (1986) Severe chronic photosensitivity in association with acquired immunodeficiency syndrome. *J Am Acad Dermatol*, 15, 1056–1057.

35. Ball, L.M., Harper, J.I. (1987) Atopic eczema in HIV-seropositive hemophiliacs. *Lancet*, **2**, 627–628.
36. Conrad, M.E. (1988) AIDS and porphyria cutanea tarda. *Am J Hematol*, **28**, 207–208.
37. Cockerall, C.J., Friedman-Kien, A.E. (1989) Skin manifestations of HIV infection. *Prim Care*, **16**, 621–644.
38. Schonwetter, R.S., Nelson, E.B. (1986) Alopecia areata and the acquired immunodeficiency syndrome-related complex. *Ann Intern Med*, **104**, 287.
39. Cockerell, C.J. (1990) Cutaneous manifestations of HIV infection other than Kaposi's sarcoma: clinical and histologic aspects. *J Am Acad Dermatol*, **22**, 1260–1269.
40. Aly, R., Bibel, D.J., Conant, M. et al (1990) The cutaneous microbiology of HIV+ patients. Carriage of Staphylococcus aureus and Candida albicans. *J Invest Dermatol*, **94**, 503A.
41. Patterson, J.W., Kitces, E.N., Neafie, R.C. (1987) Cutaneous botryomycosis in a patient with acquired immunodeficiency syndrome. *J Am Acad Dermatol*, **16**, 238–242.
42. Gasquet, S., Maurin, M., Brouqui, P. et al (1998) Bacillary angiomatosis in immunocompromised patients. *AIDS*, **12**, 1793–1803.
43. Tappero, J.W., Perkins, B.A., Wenger, P. et al (1995) Cutaneous manifestations of opportunistic infections in patients infected with human immunodeficiency virus. *Clin Microbiol Rev*, **8**, 440–450.
44. Siegal, F.P., Lopex, C., Hammer, G.S. et al (1981) Severe acquired immunodeficiency in male homosexuals manifested by chronic perianal ulcerative herpes simplex lesions. *N Engl J Med*, **305**, 1439–1442.
45. Horn, T.D., Hood, A.F. (1990) Cytomegalovirus is predictably present in perineal ulcers from immunosuppressed patients. *Arch Dermatol*, **126**, 642–644.
46. Lucas, S. (2002) The changing global clinical pathology of HIV/AIDS. *Histopathology*, **41** (Suppl. 2), 61–68.
47. Lombard, P.C. (1985) Molluscum contagiosum and acquired immunodeficiency syndrome. *Arch Dermatol*, **121**, 834–835.
48. Rico, M.J., Pennys, N.S. (1985) Cutaneous cryptococcosis resembling molluscum contagiosum in a patient with AIDS. *Arch Dermatol*, **121**, 901–902.
49. Kovacs, J.A., Kovacs, A.A., Polis, M. et al (1985) Cryptococcus in patients with the acquired immunodeficiency syndrome. *Ann Intern Med*, **103**, 533–538.
50. Brandwein, M., Choi, H.S., Strauchen, J. et al (1990) Spindle cell reaction to nontuberculous mycobacteriosis in AIDS mimicking a spindle cell neoplasm. *Virch Arch (A)*, **416**, 281–286.
51. Sandler, E.D., Sandler, J.M., LeBoit, P.E. et al (1990) Pneumocystis carinii otitis media in AIDS: a case report and review of the literature regarding extrapulmonary pneumocyststosis. *Otolaryngol Head Neck Surg*, **103**, 817–821.
52. Greenspan, D., Greenspan, J. (1985) Oral viral lesion (hairly leukoplakia associated with acquired immunodeficiency syndrome). *MMWR*, **34**, 549–550.
53. Fowler, C.B., Reed, K.D., Brannon, R.B. (1989) Intranuclear inclusions correlate with ultrastructural detection of herpes-type virions in oral hairy leukoplakia. *Am J Surg Pathol*, **13**, 114–119.
54. Greenspan, J.S., Greenspan, D., Lennette, E.T. et al (1985) Replication of Epstein–Barr virus within the epithelial cells of oral 'hairy' leukoplakia, an AIDS-associated lesion. *N Engl J Med*, **313**, 1564–1571.
55. Groopman, J.E., Sullivan, J.L., Mulder, C. et al (1986) Pathogenesis of B-cell lymphoma in a patient with AIDS. *Blood*, **67**, 612–615.
56. Kaplan, L.D., Abrams, D.I., Feigel, E. et al (1989). AIDS-associated non-Hodgkin's lymphoma in San Francisco. *JAMA*, **261**, 719–724.
57. Pluda, J.M., Yarchoan, R., Jaffe, E.S. et al (1990) Development of non-Hodgkin's lymphoma in a cohort of patients with severe HIV infection on long-term antiretroviral therapy. *Ann Intern Med*, **113**, 276–282.
58. Rabkin, C.S., Biggar, R.J., Horm, J.W. (1991) Increasing incidence of cancers associated with the human immunodeficiency virus epidemic. *Int J Cancer*, **47**, 692–696.
59. Knowles, D.M., Chamulak, G.A., Subar, M. et al (1988). Lymphoid neoplasia associated with the acquired immunodeficiency syndrome (AIDS). *Ann Intern Med*, **108**, 744–753.

5-ARD 5-α-reductase

AA alopecia areata

ACE angiotensin converting enzyme [inhibitor]

AgNORS argyrophilic nucleolar organizer regions

AHNMD associated clonal hematological non-mast cell lineage disease

AIDS acquired immunodeficiency syndrome

AILD angioimmunoblastic lymphadenopathy with dysproteinemia

ALA aminolevulinic acid

ALK activin-like receptor kinase; anaplastic lymphoma kinase

ALM acral lentiginous melanoma

AN acanthosis nigricans

ANA antinuclear antibodies

ANCA antineutrophil cytoplasmic antibodies

API2 apoptosis inhibitor-2

ARC AIDS-related complex

ATF1 activating transcription factor 1

ATLL adult T-cell leukemia/lymphoma

BANS **b**ack, **a**rm, **n**eck and **s**calp [sites]

BB borderline leprosy

BCC basal cell carcinoma

BCG bacille Calmette–Guérin

B-FGF basic fibroblast growth factor

BIDS brittle sulfur-deficient hair, intellectual impairment, decreased fertility and short stature

BL borderline lepromatous leprosy

BLAISE Blaschko linear acquired inflammatory skin eruption

BMP bone morphogenetic protein

BP bullous pemphigoid

BPA bullous pemphigoid antigen

BSAP B-cell-specific activator protein

BSLE bullous systemic lupus erythematosus

BT borderline tuberculoid leprosy

C3NeF C3 nephritic factor

CAD chronic actinic dermatitis

cAMP cyclic adenosine 3′:5′ monophosphate

c-ANCA cytoplasmic-antineutrophil cytoplasmic antibodies

CDC Centers for Disease Control and Prevention

CEA carcinoembryonic antigen

CGRP calcitonin-gene-related polypeptide

CHILD congenital hemidysplasia with ichthyosiform nevus and limb defects [syndrome]

CK cytokeratin

CLA cutaneous lymphocyte antigen

CLL chronic lymphocytic leukemia

CMG capillary morphogenesis protein

CNS central nervous system

CP cicatricial pemphigoid

CRASP complement regulator-acquiring surface protein

CREST calcinosis, Raynaud's phenomenon, esophageal dysfunction, sclerodactyly, telangiectasis [syndrome]

CTCL cutaneous T-cell lymphoma

dcSSc diffuse cutaneous systemic sclerosis

DDEB dominant dystrophic epidermolysis bullosa

DEB dystrophic epidermolysis bullosa

DH dermatitis herpetiformis

DIC disseminated intravascular coagulation

DIMF direct immunofluorescence

DLE discoid lupus erythematosus

DNCB dinitrochlorobenzene

DSAP disseminated superficial actinic porokeratosis

Dsc desmocollin

dsDNA double-stranded DNA

Dsg desmoglein

DSP disseminated superficial porokeratosis

EB epidermolysis bullosa

EBA epidermolysis bullosa acquisita

EBS epidermolysis bullosa simplex

EBS-DM epidermolysis bullosa simplex, Dowling–Meara

EBS-K epidermolysis bullosa simplex, Koebner

EBS-MD epidermolysis bullosa simplex with muscular dystrophy

EBS-WC epidermolysis bullosa simplex, Weber–Cockayne

EBV Epstein–Barr virus

ECE endothelin-converting enzyme

ECM extracellular membrane

EDS Ehlers–Danlos syndrome

EGFR endothelial growth factor receptor

ELAM endothelial leukocyte adhesion molecule

ELISA enzyme-linked immunosorbent assay

EM electron microscopy

EMA epithelial membrane antigen

ENA extractable nuclear antigen

ENL erythema nodosum leprosum

EPPER eosinophilic, polymorphic and pruritic eruption associated with radiotherapy

EPPK epidermolytic palmoplantar keratoderma

EPS extracellular polysaccharide substance

ESR erythrocyte sedimentation rate

ETA exfoliative toxin A

ETB exfoliative toxin B

EV epidermodysplasia verruciformis

EWS Ewing's sarcoma [oncogene]

FACE facial Afro-Caribbean childhood eruption

FADS fetal akinesia deformation sequence

FAMMM familial atypical multiple mole melanoma [syndrome]

FAP familial adenomatous polyposis

FAPA fever, aphthous stomatitis, pharyngitis, adenitis [syndrome]

FHIT fragile histidine triad

FIGURE facial idiopathic granulomata with regressive evolution

FISH fluorescent in situ hybridization

GA granuloma annulare

GABEB generalized atrophic benign epidermolysis bullosa

GCDFP gross cystic disease fluid protein

G-CSF granulocyte-colony stimulating factor

GFAP glial fibrillary acidic protein

GM-CSF granulocyte–macrophage colony stimulating factor

GSE gluten-sensitive enteropathy

GVHD graft-versus-host disease

HA hyperandrogenism

HAART	highly active antiretroviral therapy
HAIR-AN	hyperandrogenism–insulin resistance–acanthosis nigricans [syndrome]
HBV	hepatitis B virus
HDL	high density lipoprotein
HF	hemorrhagic fever
HG	herpes gestationis
HHV	human herpesvirus
HIT	heparin-induced thrombocytopenia [syndrome]
HIV	human immunodeficiency virus
HLA	human leukocyte antigen
HMFG	human milk fat globulin
HNPCC	hereditary non-polyposis colorectal carcinoma
HPF (hpf)	high power fields
HPL	hyperlipoproteinemia
HPV	human papillomavirus
HRF	histamine-releasing factor
HSP	heat shock protein
HSV	herpes simplex virus
HTLV	human T-cell lymphotropic virus
hTR	telomerase RNA
HUS	hemolytic uremic syndrome
IBIDS	ichthyosis and BIDS (*see BIDS above*)
ICAM	intercellular adhesion molecule
ICH	indeterminate cell histiocytosis
IDL	intermediate density lipoproteins
IEN	intraepidermal neutrophilic [IgA dermatosis variant]
IFAP	ichthyosis follicularis–alopecia–photophobia [syndrome]; intermediate filament associated protein
IFN	interferon
Ig	immunoglobulin
IIMF	indirect immunofluorescence
ILVEN	inflammatory linear verrucous epidermal nevus
IMF	immunofluorescence
IP	inducible protein
IR	insulin resistance
ISSVD	International Society for the Study of Vulvovaginal Disease
JEB	junctional epidermolysis bullosa
JEB-H	junctional epidermolysis bullosa, Herlitz
JEB-nH	junctional epidermolysis bullosa, non-Herlitz
JEB-PA	junctional epidermolysis bullosa with pyloric atresia
KID	keratitis–ichthyosis–deafness [syndrome]
KOH	potassium hydroxide
KPAF	keratosis pilaris atrophicans facei
L&H cells	lymphocytic and/or histiocytic Reed–Sternberg cell variants
LAD	linear IgA disease
LATS	long-acting thyroid stimulator
LCA	leukocyte common antigen

LCH	Langerhans' cell histiocytosis
lcSSc	limited cutaneous systemic sclerosis
LDL	low density lipoprotein
LE	lupus erythematosus
LFA	lymphocyte function-associated antigen
LH–RH	luteinizing hormone–releasing hormone
LL	lamina lucida; lepromatous leprosy
LP	lichen planus
LPP	lichen planus pemphigoides
LS	lichen sclerosus
LYVE	lymphatic vessel endothelial [hyaluronan receptor]
MAC	membrane attack complex
MAI	*M. avium intracellulare*
MALT	mucosa-associated lymphoid tissue
MART-1	melanoma antigen recognized by T-cells 1
MBP	myelin basic protein
MC1R	melanocortin-1 receptor [gene]
MCGN	mesangiocapillary glomerulonephritis
MCP	molecule chemoattractant protein
M-CSF	macrophage colony stimulating factor
MCTD	mixed connective tissue disease
MDR	multidrug resistance gene
Mel-CAM	melanoma cell adhesion molecule
MEN	multiple endocrine neoplasia [syndrome]
MFH	malignant fibrous histiocytoma
MGS/ GRO	melanoma growth stimulatory activity
MHC	major histocompatibility complex
miH	minor histocompatibility [antigen]
MITF	microphthalmia transcription factor [gene]
MMP	matrix metalloproteinase
MMR	mismatch repair [gene]
MSA	muscle-specific actin
MSI	microsatellite instability
NADH	nicotine adenine dinucleotide, reduced
nDNA	native [double-stranded] DNA
NEMO	nuclear factor [NF]-kappaB gene modulator
NF	necrotizing fasciitis
NFI	neurofibromatosis type I
NFII	neurofibromatosis type II
NFP	neurofilament protein
NIH	National Institutes of Health
NISH	non-isotopic in situ hybridization
NK	natural killer
NL	necrobiosis lipoidica
NRAMP1	natural resistance-associated macrophage protein 1
NSAIDs	non-steroidal anti-inflammatory drugs
NSE	neuron-specific enolase

OL-EDA-ID	osteopetrosis, lymphedema, anhidrotic ectodermal dysplasia, immunodeficiency [syndrome]
ORF	open reading frame
PAIN	perianal intraepithelial neoplasia
p-ANCA	perinuclear-antineutrophil cytoplasmic antibodies
PAPA	pyogenic sterile arthritis, pyoderma gangrenosum and acne [syndrome]
PAS	periodic acid–Schiff
PBG	porphobilinogen
PCNA	proliferating cell nuclear antigen
PCR	polymerase chain reaction
PDGFB	platelet-derived growth factor B
PECAM	platelet endothelial cell adhesion molecule
PEComa	perivascular epithelioid cell tumor
PGL	phenolic glycolipid
PGP	protein gene product
PGWG	purely granulomatous Wegener's granulomatosis
PI	protease inhibitor
PIBIDS	photosensitivity and IBIDS (*see IBIDS above*)
PILA	papillary intralymphatic angioendothelioma
PLEVA	pityriasis lichenoides et varioliformis acuta
PNET	primitive neuroectodermal tumor
POEMS	polyneuropathy, organomegaly, endocrinopathy, M-protein and skin changes [syndrome]
PPD	purified protein derivative
PPDL	pure and primitive diffuse leprosy
PPK	palmoplantar keratoderma
pRB	retinoblastoma protein
PSS	progressive systemic sclerosis
PTEN	phosphatase and tensin homolog
PUPPP	pruritic urticarial papules and plaques of pregnancy
PUVA	psoralen plus ultraviolet light of A [long] wavelength
r IL-2	recombinant interleukin 2
RBC	red blood cell
RDEB	recessive dystrophic epidermolysis bullosa
RDEB-HS	recessive dystrophic epidermolysis bullosa, Hallopeau–Siemens
RDEB-nHS	recessive dystrophic epidermolysis bullosa, non-Hallopeau–Siemens
RER	rough endoplasmic reticulum
RNP	ribonucleoprotein
RT-PCR	reverse transcription polymerase chain reaction
SA	syphilitic alopecia
SA1	slowly adapting type-1 [mechanoreceptor]
SALE	summertime actinic lichenoid eruption

SALT	skin-associated lymphoid tissue	**SPTL**	subcutaneous panniculitis-like T-cell lymphoma	**tTA**	tetracycline transactivator [transcription factor]
SAPHO	synovitis, acne, pustulosis, hyperostosis, osteitis [syndrome]	**SRP**	signal recognition particle	**TTF-1**	thyroid-transcription factor 1
SCC	squamous cell carcinoma	**ssDNA**	single-stranded DNA	**tTG**	tissue transglutaminase
SCH	squamous cell hyperplasia	**SSSS**	staphylococcal scalded skin syndrome	**TTP**	thrombotic thrombocytopenic purpura
SCID	severe combined immunodeficiency	**STD**	sexually transmitted disease	**URO**	uroporphyrinogen
SCLE	subacute cutaneous lupus erythematosus	**sub-LD**	sub-lamina densa	**URO-D**	uroporphyrinogen decarboxylase
scRNP	small cytoplasmic ribonuclear protein	**TCR**	T-cell receptor	**URR**	upstream regulatory region
		TEN	toxic epidermal necrolysis	**UV**	ultraviolet
SEA	staphylococcal enterotoxin A	**TFIIH**	transcription/DNA repair factor IIH	**UVA**	ultraviolet A
SEB	staphylococcal enterotoxin B	**TGF**	transforming growth factor	**UVB**	ultraviolet B
Shh	*Sonic Hedgehog*	**thio-TEPA**	triethylene thiophosphoramide	**UVL**	ultraviolet light
SIBIDS	osteosclerosis and IBIDS (*see IBIDS above*)	**TIMP**	tissue inhibitor of metalloproteinase	**VCAM**	vascular cell adhesion molecule
SIL	squamous intraepithelial lesion			**VEGF**	vascular endothelial growth factor
SLE	systemic lupus erythematosus	**TNF**	tumor necrosis factor	**VEGFR**	vascular endothelial growth factor receptor
SLL	small lymphocytic lymphoma	**TORCH**	**t**oxoplasmosis, **o**ther infections, **r**ubella, **c**ytomegalovirus and **h**erpes simplex [syndrome]	**VIN**	vulval intraepithelial neoplasia
SMA	smooth muscle actin			**VIP**	vasoactive intestinal peptide
snRNP	small nuclear ribonuclear protein	**TRAPS**	tumor necrosis factor receptor-associated periodic syndrome	**VLDL**	very low density lipoprotein
SPD	subcorneal pustular dermatosis			**VZV**	varicella-zoster virus
SPRRs	small proline rich proteins/cornifins	**TSST**	toxic shock syndrome toxin	**wrfr**	wrinkle free [mouse model]
		TT	tuberculoid leprosy	**XP**	xeroderma pigmentosum

A

5α-reductase type-2
  acne vulgaris, 1118
  androgenetic alopecia, 1070
19-DEJ-1 antibody, junctional epidermolysis bullosa and, 93
AA3 (antibody), junctional epidermolysis bullosa and, 93
ABCC6 gene mutation, 1041
Abdomen, desmoid fibromatosis, 1726
Abscesses
  botryomycosis, 921–922
  Crohn's disease, 683
  see also Eosinophil microabscesses; Neutrophil microabscesses
Acanthamebiasis, 935–936
Acantholysis
  pseudovascular squamous cell carcinoma, 1215
  pustular dermatoses, 213
Acantholytic acanthoma, 169–170
Acantholytic actinic keratoses, 1189, *1191*
Acantholytic dermatitis herpetiformis *see* Pemphigus herpetiformis
Acantholytic dermatoses, 139–170
  with dyskeratosis, 156–170
  of genitocrural area, 166
    Hailey–Hailey disease *vs*, 158
  see also Pemphigus
Acantholytic dyskeratotic epidermal nevus *see* Linear Darier's disease
Acantholytic seborrheic keratosis, acantholytic acanthoma *vs*, 169
Acantholytic solar keratosis, 144
Acantholytic squamous cell carcinoma, 1214–1215
  see also Adenoid squamous cell carcinoma
Acanthoma fissuratum, 1157–1158
Acanthosis
  condyloma acuminatum, 492, *493*, 845, *846*
  congenital bullous ichthyosiform erythroderma, 47
  lichen planus, 223, *224*, 225
  peaked/church spire, 1165
  pseudoepitheliomatous hyperplasia, 1167, *1168*
  psoriasis, 201, *202*
  sawtooth, 223, *224*
  verruciform xanthoma, *549*
Acanthosis nigricans, 615–617
  epidermal nevus similarity, 1155
  oral, 411
Acanthotic seborrheic keratosis, 1159, *1161*
Accessory tragus, 1519
  rhabdomyomatous mesenchymal hamartoma *vs*, 1802
Acne *see* Acne vulgaris; PAPA (pyogenic sterile arthritis, pyoderma gangrenosum and acne)
Acne aestivalis, 1121
Acne agminata, 322–323, 1123
Acne bromica, 657
Acne conglobata, 706, 1117
Acne cosmetica, 1118
Acne fulminans, 1120–1121
Acne inversa (hidradenitis suppurativa), 705–708, 1614
Acne keloidalis, 1117
  see also Folliculitis keloidalis nuchae
Acne keloidalis nuchae, 1116–1117
  dissecting cellulitis of the scalp *vs*, 1097
  see also Folliculitis keloidalis nuchae
Acne necrotica, 1120
Acne necrotica miliaris, 1120
Acne necrotica variioliformis *see* Acne necrotica
Acne vermoulante (atrophoderma vermiculata), 57, 58
Acne vulgaris, 1116–1119
  comedones, 1118, *1119*, 1667–1668
  papular scars, 1047
    papular elastorrhexis *vs*, 1052
Acnitis (acne agminata), 322–323, 1123
Acoustic neurofibromatosis, 1768, 1778–1779
Acquired angioedema, 694
Acquired brachial cutaneous dyschromatosis, 1019

Acquired cutis laxa, 349, 1023, 1039–1040
Acquired diffuse palmoplantar Keratoderma, 60, 68–69
Acquired digital fibrokeratoma, 1721
Acquired elastotic hemangioma, 1822
Acquired generalized lipodystrophy, *375*, 376
  see also Lipoatrophic panniculitis
Acquired ichthyosis, 58, *59*
Acquired immune deficiency syndrome (AIDS) *see* HIV infection
Acquired lipodystrophy, 376–377
Acquired palmoplantar keratoderma and internal malignancy, 68–69
Acquired partial lipodystrophy, *375*, 376
Acquired progressive kinking of hair, 1115, 1520
Acquired progressive lymphangioma, 1845, 1846
Acquired relapsing self-healing Blaschko dermatitis, 233
Acquired reticulated lentigo, 1248, *1249*
Acral erythema, chemotherapeutic agents, 667
Acral fibromyxoma, superficial, 1718
Acral ichthyosiform mucinosis, 604
Acral keratoderma, 62–63
Acral lentiginous melanoma, 1139, 1312, 1318, *1319*
  lentiginous acral nevus *vs*, 1261
  subungual nevus *vs*, 1138–1139
Acral lentigo, 1245
Acral mucinous syringometaplasia *see* Mucinous syringometaplasia
Acral myxoinflammatory fibroblastic sarcoma, 1735
Acral nevus, 1260–1261
Acral persistent papular mucinosis, 609
Acral variants
  dystrophic epidermolysis bullosa, 92
  junctional epidermolysis bullosa, 87
Acroangiodermatitis, 185
  Kaposi's sarcoma *vs*, 185, 1834
Acrochordon
  fibrofolliculoma, 1560
  see also Fibroepithelial polyp
Acrodermatitis chronica atrophicans, 889, 890
  sclerosing panniculitis *vs*, 372
Acrodermatitis continua (Hallopeau), nails, 1132, 1133
Acrodermatitis enteropathica, 617–619
  morphea *vs*, 820
  necrolytic migratory erythema *vs*, 620
  Netherton syndrome *vs*, 51
Acrodermatitis of childhood, papular, 188–190
  see also Gianotti–Crosti syndrome
Acrodermatosis continua (Hallopeau), 199
Acrodynia (pink disease), 663
Acrokeratoderma, marginal papular, 64–65
Acrokeratoelastoidosis of Costa, 64–65
Acrokeratosis paraneoplastica, 211–212
Acrokeratosis verruciformis
  of Hopf, 74
  lesions like, Darier's disease, 159
  stucco keratoses *vs*, 1165
Acromegaly, Carney complex, 1014
Acropustulosis of Hallopeau *see* Acrodermatitis continua (Hallopeau); Acrodermatosis continua (Hallopeau)
Acrosclerosis, 804, 805–806
Acrospiroma, malignant *see* Clear cell hidradenocarcinoma
Acrosyringeal nevus, 1610–1611
Acrosyringium, eccrine sweat gland, 24, *26*
Actin
  inclusion body fibromatosis, 1719
  leiomyosarcoma, *1802*
Actinic comedonal plaque, 1053
Actinic damage, 16, 1202–1203
  bullous ichthyosiform erythroderma *vs*, 47
  inflammation induced by chemotherapeutic agents, 665
Actinic dermatitis, chronic, 1425–1427
  see also Actinic reticuloid
Actinic granuloma, *304*, 312, 313–314, 1053
  atypical facial necrobiosis lipoidica *vs*, 315
Actinic keratosis, 1187–1192

  bowenoid, 1189, *1192*, 1196
  squamous cell carcinoma, 1189–1190, 1199
  see also Solar keratosis
Actinic lentigo, 1246–1248
Actinic lichen nitidus, 227
Actinic nuclear atypia, *1316*
Actinic porokeratosis, disseminated superficial, 75
Actinic reticuloid, 272–273
  see also Chronic actinic dermatitis
Actinobacillus actinomycetemcomitans, 923
Actinomyces israelii, 923
Actinomycosis, 923–924
  nocardiosis *vs*, 920
Activating transcription factor 1, gene fusion, soft tissue melanoma, 1795
Activin-like receptor kinase 1 (ALK1), gene mutations, 1812
Acute adult T-cell leukemia/lymphoma, 1413
Acute cutaneous leishmaniasis, 931
Acute febrile neutrophilic dermatosis *see* Sweet's syndrome
Acute generalized eczematous pustulosis, 651
Acute generalized exanthematous pustulosis, 662, 663
Acute generalized Langerhans' cell histiocytosis, 1458–1459, *1460*, 1461–1462, *1463*, 1464, *1465*, 1466
Acute graft-versus-host disease, 250–251, 253–254
Acute intermittent porphyria, 575, 576
Acute lymphoblastic leukemia, skin involvement, 1489
Acute monoblastic leukemia, histiocytic lymphoma *vs*, 1485
Acute paronychia, 879
Acute vesicular dermatitis of the hands and feet *see* Pompholyx
Adams–Oliver syndrome, 307, 1810
Adamson's fringe, 1065, *1066*
Adenoacanthoma *see* Adenoid squamous cell carcinoma
Adenocarcinoma
  aggressive digital papillary adenocarcinoma *vs*, 1629
  anogenital mammary-like glands, 1595–1596
  ceruminous glands, 1597, 1600
  metastases, 1506–1508
    epithelioid hemangioendothelioma *vs*, 1839
  see also Clear cell hidradenocarcinoma; Eccrine spiradenocarcinoma
Adenocystic carcinoma, 1654–1657
Adenoid and pseudopapillary melanoma, 1340
Adenoid basal cell carcinoma, 1174, *1176*
  adenoid cystic carcinoma *vs*, 1653
Adenoid cystic carcinoma, 1509, 1651–1653
  basaloid squamous cell carcinoma *vs*, 463
  syringoid eccrine carcinoma *vs*, 1647
Adenoid seborrheic keratosis, 1159, *1160*
Adenoid squamous cell carcinoma, 463
  see also Acantholytic squamous cell carcinoma
Adenoma
  anogenital mammary-like glands, 1595–1596
  apocrine, 1594–1595
    ceruminous, 1600
  Bartholin's glands, 530
  minor vestibular glands, 530
  nipple, 1596
  papillary eccrine, 1628–1629
    tubular apocrine adenoma *vs*, 1595
  sebaceous, 1574–1575
    sebaceoma *vs*, 1577
    Torre–Muir syndrome, 1574, 1584
    see also Adenoma sebaceum
  sebocrine, 1587
    see also Apocrine poroma
Adenoma sebaceum, 1030, 1031
  see also Sebaceous adenoma
Adenosquamous carcinoma, 1217–1218
  acantholytic squamous cell carcinoma *vs*, 1215
  basaloid squamous cell carcinoma *vs*, 463
  penis, 528
  see also Mucoepidermoid carcinoma
Adipocytes, 36
  hibernoma, 1694

Adipocytic tumors, 1684–1699
Adipose tissue *see* Subcutaneous fat
Adiposis dolorosa, 1691
Adnexal carcinoma, locally aggressive *see* Microcystic adnexal carcinoma
Adnexal polyp of neonatal skin, 1610
Adnexal structures, basal cell carcinoma with differentiation towards, 1178, *1180*, *1181*
Adolescents, mycosis fungoides, 1377–1378
Adult Blaschkitis, 233
Adult colloid milium, 568–569, 1053
Adult generalized acquired cutis laxa, 1039
Adult hemangiopericytoma, 1851–1852
Adult lipophagic atrophic panniculitis, 379
Adult-onset GM1 gangliosidosis, diffuse angiokeratomata, 552
Adult respiratory distress syndrome, toxic epidermal necrolysis, 241
Adult rhabdomyoma, 1803
Adult T-cell leukemia/lymphoma, 1412–1415
AF-1 (monoclonal antibody), epidermolysis bullosa, 93
AF-2 (monoclonal antibody), epidermolysis bullosa, 93
African Kaposi's sarcoma, 1831
Age-related fibroelastolytic syndrome *see* Pseudoxanthoma elasticum-like papillary dermal elastolysis
Agglomerate keratoacanthoma, 1222
Aggressive angiomyxoma, 534–535
    angiomyofibroblastoma *vs*, 534
Aggressive digital papillary adenocarcinoma, 1629–1630
    papillary eccrine adenoma *vs*, 1629
Aggressive trichoblastoma, 1557
Aging, 1053–1054
    dermatoheliosis, 1053–1054
    pseudoxanthoma elasticum-like papillary dermal elastolysis *vs*, 1048
    see also Actinic keratosis; *entries beginning* Senile...
Agminate acne, 322–323, 1123
Agminate blue nevus, 1301
Agminate xanthogranuloma, 1469
AgNORs (argyrophilic staining of nucleolar organizing regions), melanoma, 1330
AIDS *see* HIV infection
AIDS-related complex, 987
AIDS-related Kaposi's sarcoma, 1831, 1833
AIDS-related psoriasis, 206, 988
AILD (angioimmunoblastic lymphadenopathy with dysproteinemia), 1411–1412
Airway obstruction, plasma cell orificial mucositis, 438
AJCC (American Joint Committee on Cancer), melanoma staging system, 1321
ALA dehydratase deficiency, 575, 576
Alanine:glyoxylate aminotransferase deficiency, 362
Albinism, 998
    actinic skin damage, 16
    oculocutaneous, 998–1001
        squamous cell carcinoma, 999, 1202
    see also Amyloid P component
Albopapuloid lesions, dominant dystrophic epidermolysis bullosa, 89
Albright's disease, 468
    see also McCune-Albright syndrome
Aleppo boil (cutaneous leishmaniasis), 929–931, 932–934
Aleukemic leukemia cutis, 1488
Aleutian mink disease, 790
Algal infection, 936–937
Alibert form, mycosis fungoides, 1360
ALK *see* Anaplastic lymphoma kinase
Alkaptonuria, 592
Allergic contact dermatitis, 175–176
Allergic contact urticaria, 694
Allergic drug reactions, 624–625
Allergic granulomatosis with angiitis *see* Churg–Strauss syndrome
Allergic vasculitis *see* Leukocytoclastic vasculitis
Alopecia, 1068–1103
    anagen alopecia, 624
    androgenetic, 1069–1072
        acquired progressive kinking of the hair, 1115
    classification, 1068–1069
    Cronkhite–Canada syndrome, 1014
    drug-induced, 645, 664
    generalized myxedema, 602
    hidrotic ectodermal dysplasia, 71
    ichthyosis follicularis with alopecia and photophobia, 56
    physical examination, 1062
    porphyria cutanea tarda, 585
    scarring, 880, 1068, 1089–1103
    systemic lupus erythematosus, 784, 1091
    tinea capitis, 938, 939
Alopecia areata, 1073–1079
    alopecia neoplastica *vs*, 1503
    androgenetic alopecia *vs*, 1071
    HIV infection, 989
    pili annulati, 1110
    syphilitic alopecia *vs*, 1078, 1088
    trichotillomania *vs*, 1078, 1081

Alopecia mucinosa, 1387–1390
Alopecia neoplastica, 1503, *1506*, *1507*
Alopecia syphilitica, 496, 1087–1088
    alopecia areata *vs*, 1078, 1088
    trichotillomania *vs*, 1081
Alopecia totalis, 1073, *1074*, *1075*
Alopecia universalis, 1073, *1074*
ALOX12B gene, 43
ALOXE3 gene, congenital ichthyosiform erythroderma, 43
α_1-antitrypsin (marker), melanoma, 1328
α_1-antitrypsin deficiency-associated panniculitis, 349–350
    neutrophilic lobular infiltrate, 369
$\alpha_3\beta_1$ integrin, 6–7
$\alpha_6\beta_4$ integrin, 6
    mutations, 95
α_6 integrin subunit, gene mutations, epidermolysis bullosa, 85
α-galactosidase A deficiency, 551
α-galactosidosis, diffuse angiokeratomata, 552
α-N-acetylgalactosaminidase deficiency, diffuse angiokeratomata, 552
Alstrom syndrome, 615
Alternariosis, 971
Aluminum granuloma, 327–328
Alveolar rhabdomyosarcoma, 1804, *1805*
Alveolar ridge
    benign keratosis, 457–458
    lymphangioma, 396
Alveolar soft part sarcoma, 1864
Amalgam, oral lichen planus, 434
Amalgam tattoo, 465–466, 671
Amastigotes, *Leishmania* spp., 929, 932, 934
Amebiasis cutis, 508, 934–935
Amebomas, 934
Amelanotic blue nevus, 1302–1303
Amelanotic clear cell melanoma, clear cell squamous cell carcinoma *vs*, 1210
Amelanotic lentigo maligna, 1315
Amelanotic lentigo maligna melanoma, 1315
Amelanotic melanoma, 1312, *1320*
    differential diagnosis, 1325–1326
    vulva, 514
Ameloblastoma, peripheral, 424
American Joint Committee on Cancer (AJCC), melanoma staging system, 1321
Aminoacidopathies, acrodermatitis enteropathica, 618
Aminolevulinic acid dehydratase deficiency, 575, 576
Amiodarone, adverse effects, 638–639, 640–641
Amputees, acroangiodermatitis, 185
Amyloid, 553–554
    basal cell carcinoma, 1173–1174
    colloid milium, 567–568
    notalgia paresthetica, 1020
    oral lesions, 427
    Riehl's melanosis, 1020
    see also Amyloid P component
Amyloid A, serum, 559
Amyloid elastosis, 559
Amyloid-K, 562
    colloid milium, 568
Amyloidosis, 553–567
    tumor necrosis factor receptor-associated periodic syndrome, 285
Amyloidosis cutis dyschromica, 564
Amyloid P component, 554
    adult colloid milium, 569
Amyloid rings, 557
Amyopathic dermatomyositis, 825
Anabolic syndrome, congenital generalized lipodystrophy, 375
Anagen, 1065, 1066
Anagen alopecia, 624
Anagen effluvium, 645, 664, 1086
Anaphylaxis, drug reactions, 624, 625
Anaplastic CD30+ large cell lymphoma, 1403
Anaplastic lymphoma kinase (ALK)
    CD30+ lymphoproliferative disorders, 1409
    inflammatory myofibroblastic tumor, 1736
Anaplastic variant of Paget's disease, 1516
ANCA *see* Antineutrophil cytoplasmic antibodies
Anchoring fibrils, 9
    dystrophic epidermolysis bullosa, 96–97
    epidermis, 9
    epidermolysis bullosa acquisita, 126
Anchoring filaments, 8
Ancient nevus, 1255
Ancient schwannoma, 1769, *1770*
    pleomorphic hyalinizing angiectatic tumor *vs*, 1859
Ancylostoma spp., 984
Anderson–Fabry's disease, 1812
    see also Angiokeratoma corporis diffusum
Androgen(s), acne vulgaris, 1118
Androgenetic alopecia, 1069–1072
    acquired progressive kinking of the hair, 1115

Androgen receptors
    androgenetic alopecia, 1070
    Paget's disease, 1516
Anetoderma, 789, 1045–1047
    of prematurity, 1046
Anetoderma-like scars, 1047
Aneurysmal benign fibrous histiocytoma, Kaposi's sarcoma *vs*, 1834
Aneurysmal fibrous histiocytoma, 1747–1748
    Kaposi's sarcoma *vs*, 1834
Angiectatic tumor, pleomorphic hyalinizing, 1859
Angioblastoma of Nakagawa, 1814–1815
Angiocentric fibrosis, eosinophilic, 738
Angiocentric immunoproliferative lesion *see* Lymphomatoid granulomatosis
Angiocentric lymphoma
    NK/T-cell, subcutaneous panniculitic T-cell lymphoma *vs*, 1417
    T-cell
        cytophagic histiocytic panniculitis and, 356
        subcutaneous panniculitic T-cell lymphoma *vs*, 1417
        see also Extranodal NK/T-cell lymphoma, nasal/nasal type
    see also Lymphomatoid granulomatosis
Angioedema
    drug reactions, 625, 629
    orofacial granulomatosis *vs*, 441
    urticarial, 694
Angioendotheliomatosis
    malignant, 1445
    reactive, 1807–1808
        intravascular large B-cell lymphoma *vs*, 1447
Angioendotheliomatosis proliferans systemisata, 1445
Angiofibroma
    cellular, 535–536
    giant cell, 1718
    periungual, 1146
Angiogenesis, melanoma, 1324, 1330
Angioid streaks, retina, 1041, 1042
Angioimmunoblastic lymphadenopathy with dysproteinemia (AILD), 1411–1412
Angioimmunoblastic T-cell lymphoma, 1411–1412
Angiokeratoma, 1812–1813
    verrucous hemangioma *vs*, 1813, 1815
Angiokeratoma circumscriptum, 1812
Angiokeratoma corporis diffusum, 551–555, 1812
    see also Anderson–Fabry's disease
Angioleiomyoma, 1799–1800, 1852
Angiolipoleiomyoma, 1799
Angiolipoma, 1687–1688
Angiolupoid sarcoid, 289
Angiolymphoid hyperplasia with eosinophilia
    granuloma faciale *vs*, 740
    traumatic ulcerative granuloma *vs*, 409
    see also Epithelioid hemangioma
Angioma, 1815
Angioma serpiginosum, 1810–1811
Angiomatoid fibrous histiocytoma, 1754–1755
    aneurysmal fibrous histiocytoma *vs*, 1748
Angiomatoid melanoma, 1342–1343
Angiomatoid Spitz nevus, 1277
Angiomatosis, 1828
Angiomatous nodule, cutaneous epithelioid, 1822–1823
Angiomyofibroblastoma, genital region, 533–534
Angiomyofibroblastoma-like tumor, 533
Angiomyolipoma, 1799
Angiomyxoma
    Carney complex, 1015, 1856
    superficial, 614, 1856–1857
        neurothekeoma *vs*, 1784
    see also Aggressive angiomyxoma
Angioneurotic edema, drug reactions, 624
Angiosarcoma, 1839–1843
    cavernous hemangioma *vs*, 1819
    epithelioid, 1843–1845
        epithelioid sarcoma *vs*, 1862
    intravascular papillary endothelial hyperplasia *vs*, 1806–1807
    Kaposi's sarcoma *vs*, 1834
    lymphangiosarcoma *vs*, 1846
    meningeal heterotopias *vs*, 1788
    retiform hemangioendothelioma *vs*, 1828–1829
    spindle cell hemangioma as variant, 1826
    see also Lymphangiosarcoma
Angiotensin converting enzyme
    sarcoidosis, 293
    systemic sclerosis, 809
Angiotensin converting enzyme inhibitors
    lichen planus pemphigoides, 117
    pemphigus vegetans, 146
Angiotropic large cell lymphoma, 1445–1448
Angiotropic melanoma, 1342–1343, 1348
Anhidrosis, apocrine, Fox–Fordyce disease, 194
Anhidrotic ectodermal dysplasia, sebaceous hyperplasia with, 1566

Animal-type melanoma, 1344–1345
  epithelioid blue nevus *vs*, 1303
  neurocristic hamartoma as, 1304
Ankle-type (lipidized) fibrous histiocytoma, 545, 1750–1751
Ankylosing spondylitis, psoriatic arthritis, 200
Annexin I, 11
Annually recurring acroerythema, 618
Annular elastolytic giant cell granuloma, 312
Annular erythema *see* Erythema annulare centrifugum; Toxic
  erythema
Annular lipoatrophy, 377–384
Annular lipodystrophy, 377–384
  localized lipoatrophy, 377–384
Annular psoriasis, 196, 198
Annulus migrans, 400–403
Anogenital mammary-like glands, 1595–1596
Anogenital region, 473–538
  angiokeratoma of Fordyce, 1812
  bowenoid papulosis, 1192
  Bowen's disease, 519, 1196
  hidradenoma papilliferum, 1592, *1593*
  Paget's disease, 1515, 1516
  see also Anus; Genital lesions
Anogenital 'sweat' glands, 475
Anogenital verrucous carcinoma, 494
Anosacral amyloidosis, 560–561
Antenatal diagnosis *see* Prenatal diagnosis
Anthrax, cutaneous, 882–884
Anti-basement membrane antibodies
  bullous pemphigoid, 105–107
  epidermolysis bullosa acquisita, 126
Antibiotics, Gram-negative folliculitis, 1125
Anticardiolipin antibody, 767
  temporal arteritis, 749
Anticardiolipin syndrome, systemic lupus erythematosus, 784
Anticentriole antibody, systemic sclerosis, 811
Anticentromere antibody, systemic sclerosis, 811
Anticonvulsants
  hypersensitivity syndrome, 633–634
  lymphomatoid drug eruption, 652–655
Anti-ENA antibodies, mixed connective tissue disease, 832
Antifetal cartilage antibodies, relapsing polychondritis, 834
Antigen-presenting cells, Langerhans' cells as, 18
Antigliadin antibodies, dermatitis herpetiformis, 132
Antihistone antibodies, 788
  morphea, 818–819
Anti-Jo-1 antibody, dermatomyositis, 827–828
Anti-La antibodies, 788
  systemic sclerosis, 811
Antileukotrienes, Churg–Strauss syndrome, 732
Antimalarials
  ochronosis, 592, 593
  pigmentation, 639, *640*
Antineutrophil cytoplasmic antibodies
  Churg–Strauss syndrome, 733
  microscopic polyarteritis, 724
  polyarteritis nodosa, 721, 724
  Wegener's granulomatosis, 729
    oral, 442
Antinuclear antibodies
  lupus erythematosus, 787
  morphea, 818–819
  systemic sclerosis, 810
Antinuclear antibody negative SLE, 785
Antinucleolar antibodies, 787, 810
Anti-P105 pemphigoid, 108
Anti-P200 pemphigoid, 108
Anti-P450 pemphigoid, 108
Antiphospholipid antibodies
  anetoderma, 1046
  see also Lupus anticoagulant
Antiphospholipid antibody syndrome, 767–768, 789, 796–797,
  798
  see also Lupus anticoagulant syndrome
Anti-Ro antibodies, 790, 791
  mixed connective tissue disease, 832
  systemic sclerosis, 811
Anti-smooth muscle endomysial antibody, dermatitis
  herpetiformis, 132
Antoni A areas, 1768
Antoni B areas, 1769
Anus
  Bowen's disease, 1194, 1196
  condyloma acuminatum, 845, *846*
  Darier's disease, 160
  verrucous carcinoma, 1218, 1219
Aphthous stomatitis, recurrent, 406–407
Aplasia cutis congenita, 1027–1028
Apocrine acne (hidradenitis suppurativa), 705–708, 1614
Apocrine adenoma, 1594–1595
  ceruminous, 1600
Apocrine anhidrosis, Fox–Fordyce disease, 194

Apocrine chondroid syringoma, 1600–1601
Apocrine cystadenoma, 1588
  median raphe cyst *vs*, 517, 1677
  papillary, 1592
Apocrine glands, 22–24
  hidradenitis suppurativa, 706, 707
Apocrine hamartoma, 1587
Apocrine hidrocystoma, 1587–1590
Apocrine miliaria (Fox–Fordyce disease), 194–195, 706–707
Apocrine nevus, 1587
Apocrine papillary cystadenoma, 1592
Apocrine poroma, 1596–1597
  see also Sebocrine adenoma
Apoeccrine glands, 28
Apolipoprotein E, in amyloid-K, 562
Aponeurotic fibroma, calcifying, 1719–1720
Apoproteins, 539
Apoptosis, keratinocytes, erythema multiforme, 238–239
Apoptotic theory, amyloidosis, 562
Aquagenic urticaria, 693
  scopolamine on, 694
Arachnid bite reactions, 689–690
ARC (AIDS-related complex), 987
Areca (betel) nut *see* Betel nut chewers
Areola
  Montgomery's tubercles, 20, 1565
  sebaceous hyperplasia, 1566
  skin, *3*
Argentaffin reaction, carcinoid tumor, 1512
Argentine hemorrhagic fever, 868, 869
Argyria, 661–662
Argyrophilic staining of nucleolar organizing regions
  (AgNORs), melanoma, 1330
Argyrophil reaction, carcinoid tumor, 1512
Arrector pili muscle, 1064
Arsenic, 655–656, 1198–1199
  Bowen's disease, 1194
  squamous cell carcinoma, 1204
  superficial basal cell carcinoma, 1170
Arsenical keratoses, 624, 1198–1199
Artecoll, foreign body granulomata, 325, *326*
Arteries
  pseudoxanthoma elasticum, 1041, 1042
  radiation damage, 1055
Arterioles, skin, 32–33
Arteriovenous anastomoses, 34
Arteriovenous hemangioma, 1819–1820
Arteriovenous malformation with angiodermatitis *see*
  Acroangiodermatitis
Arteritis
  group A streptococci, 753
  Neisseria spp., 753
  temporal, *710*, 748–751
  see also Microscopic polyarteritis; Polyarteritis nodosa;
    Takayasu's arteritis
Arthritis
  alkaptonuria, 592
  Behçet's disease, 686, 744
  eosinophilic fasciitis, 822
  gout, 590
  Henoch–Schönlein purpura, 717
  interstitial granulomatous dermatitis with, 320
  Lyme disease, 889
  mixed connective tissue disease, 832
  multicentric reticulohistiocytosis, 1482
  psoriatic, 200
  Reiter's syndrome, 477, 479
  relapsing polychondritis, 833–834
Arthrochalasia (Ehlers–Danlos syndrome types VIIA and VIIB),
  1024, 1025, *1026*
Arthropod bite reactions, 689–690
Arthropod infestations, 980–982
Asboe–Hansen sign, pemphigus vulgaris, 141
Ash leaf macules, 1030, *1031*
Ashy dermatosis, 234–236
Asian variant of intravascular large B-cell lymphoma, 1446
Askin tumor, 1793–1795
Aspartylglycosaminuria, diffuse angiokeratomata, 552
Aspergillosis, 951–952, *953*
Aspergillus spp., 952, *953*
Aspirin, urticaria, 694
Asteatotic dermatitis, 177
Asteroid bodies, 294
  actinic granuloma, *314*
  necrobiotic xanthogranuloma, 320
  sporotrichosis, 976
Asthma, Churg–Strauss syndrome, 732
Asymmetric lipomatosis, 1691
Ataxia–telangiectasia, 327
Atherosclerosis, cholesterol crystal embolism, 762
Athlete's foot, 943, 944
Athlete's nodules, 1038

ATLL (adult T-cell leukemia/lymphoma), 1412–1415
Atopic dermatitis, 172–173
Atopy, 173
  pityriasis alba, 1006
ATP2A2 gene mutations
  Darier's disease, 161
  linear Darier's disease, 163
ATP2C1 gene mutations, Hailey–Hailey disease, 157
Atrial myxoma
  Carney complex, 1014, 1015
  skin involvement, 1503
Atrichia, 56
Atrophic actinic keratosis, *1192*
Atrophic benign epidermolysis bullosa, generalized, 85, 86
  see also Junctional epidermolysis bullosa–non-Herlitz
Atrophic Bowen's disease, 1195
Atrophic connective tissue panniculitis, 378
Atrophic dermatofibroma, 1751
Atrophic glossitis, candidiasis, HIV infection, *987*
Atrophic lichen planus, 220
  oral, 433
Atrophic panniculitis, adult lipophagic, 379
Atrophic papulosis, malignant *see* Degos' disease
Atrophie blanche, 760–762
  morphea *vs*, 820
  see also Livedoid vasculitis
Atrophoderma
  follicular, 1186
  linear atrophoderma of Moulin, 817
Atrophoderma elastolytica discreta, 822
Atrophoderma of Pasini and Pierini, 821–822
Atrophoderma reticulata, 57, 58
Atrophoderma vermiculata (vermiculatum), 57, 58
Atropine, for eccrine hidrocystoma, 1614
Atropine tape, hidradenitis suppurativa experiment, 707
Atypical acral nevus, 1260
Atypical adult pityriasis rubra pilaris, 207
Atypical cellular blue nevus, 1308
Atypical cellular neurothekeoma, 1785
Atypical chilblains, 274, 276
Atypical clear cell acanthoma, 1167
Atypical cutaneous lymphoproliferative disorder of HIV
  infection, 1423
Atypical decubital fibroplasia, 1706–1707
Atypical facial necrobiosis lipoidica, 314–315
Atypical fibrous histiocytoma, 1749–1750, 1759
Atypical fibroxanthoma, 1757–1760
  atypical fibrous histiocytoma *vs*, 1750
  reticulohistiocytoma *vs*, 1483
  see also Clear cell atypical fibroxanthoma
Atypical flexural nevus, 512
Atypical genital nevus, 512, 513, *514*
Atypical gingivostomatitis, 487
Atypical hidradenoma, 1633, 1634
Atypical histiocytic granuloma, traumatic ulcerative granuloma
  vs, 409
Atypical histiocytosis, regressing, 1404, 1410, 1484
Atypical lipoma, 1688, 1695–1697
  lipoma *vs*, 1686
Atypical lipomatous tumor, 1699
  of the tongue, 415
Atypical melanocytic nevus of genital type, 512
Atypical mycobacteria, 904–910
Atypical necrobiosis lipoidica, *304*, 305
Atypical pityriasis rosea, 190
Atypical pityriasis rubra pilaris, juvenile, 208
Atypical pyoderma gangrenosum, 674
Atypical pyogenic granuloma *see* Epithelioid hemangioma
Atypical Spitz nevus, 1268, 1269, 1273, 1274, *1275*
Atypical target lesions, 236
Atypical vascular proliferation after radiotherapy, 1847–1848
Auriasis, 661
Auricular chondritis, 833, *834*
Auspitz's sign, 195
Autoamputation, Halloreau–Siemens variant, dystrophic
  epidermolysis bullosa, 90
Autoantibodies
  lupus erythematosus, 787–789
  see also specific antibodies
Autoimmune diseases
  alopecia areata as, 1075
  bullous systemic lupus erythematosus with, 128
  dermatitis herpetiformis, 131
  hair diseases, investigations, 1062
  multicentric reticulohistiocytosis, 1482
  oral lesions, 443–447
  psoriasis and, 204
  sarcoidosis and, 293
  vitiligo, 994
Autoimmune hypothesis, vitiligo, 995–996
Autoimmune progesterone dermatitis, urticaria, 695
Autoimmune urticaria, 695
Autolysis, epidermolysis bullosa *vs*, 127

Autosensitization reaction, 175
Autosomal dominant periodic fever with amyloidosis (TNF receptor-associated periodic syndrome), 285, 756
Autosomal recessive congenital ichthyosis, 42–45

B

Bacillary angiomatosis, 887–889
    AIDS, 990
    epithelioid hemangioma vs, 1825
    lobular capillary hemangioma vs, 1817
Back, skin, 2
Bacteria (infections), 869–872
    arteritis, 753
    folliculitis
        AIDS, 989
        Gram-negative, 1125
    hidradenitis suppurativa, 707
    leukocytoclastic vasculitis, 712
    oral lymphoepithelial cyst vs, 394
    progressive macular hypomelanosis, 1005
    pseudomycosis, 921–922
    superinfection, tungiasis, 981
Baghdad boil, 929–931, 932–934
Bairnsdale ulcer, 906
Balanitis, candidal, 948
Balanitis circumscripta plasmacellularis, 487
Balanitis xerotica obliterans, 483
Balloon cell melanoma, 1338–1339
    sebaceous carcinoma vs, 1338, 1583
Balloon cell nevus, 1265–1266
Ballooning degeneration, keratinocytes
    herpes simplex virus, 853, 854
    orthopox virus infections, 862
Bamboo hair see Trichorrhexis invaginata
Banal nevus see Melanocytic nevus
Bannayan–Riley–Ruvalcaba syndrome, 615, 1528
    Proteus syndrome and, 1154
    see also Ruvalcaba–Myrhe–Smith syndrome
Bannayan–Zonana syndrome see Ruvalcaba–Myrhe–Smith syndrome
BANS sites, melanoma, 1310, 1321
Barbiturates, 664
Barraquer–Simons syndrome (acquired partial lipodystrophy), 375, 376
Bartholin's duct cyst, 517, 518
Bartholin's glands, 475
    benign tumors, 530
    carcinoma, 531
Bartonella spp., diseases, 884–889
    AIDS, 990
Bartonellosis, 886
Bart's syndrome, 1027
Basal cell carcinoma, 1167–1184
    adenoid, 1174, 1176
        adenoid cystic carcinoma vs, 1653
    anogenital region, 531–532
    basaloid follicular hamartoma vs, 1523–1524
    desmoplastic, microcystic adnexal carcinoma vs, 1649
    with differentiation towards adnexal structures, 1178, 1180, 1181
    with eccrine differentiation see Syringoid eccrine carcinoma
    eccrine porocarcinoma vs, 1624
    with follicular differentiation, 1178
        see also basaloid follicular hamartoma
    with matrical differentiation, 1178, 1542
    with myoepithelial differentiation, 1177–1178, 1180
    nail region, 1145
    with neuroid-type nuclear palisading, 1182
    nevoid basal cell carcinoma syndrome, 1173, 1184
    nevus sebaceus and, 1569
    pedunculated, 1171
    porokeratosis, 76
    renal transplantation, 1203
    salivary glands, basaloid squamous cell carcinoma vs, 463
    sebaceoma vs, 1577
    with sebaceous differentiation, 1578–1579
    syringoid eccrine carcinoma vs, 1647
    with thickened basement membrane, 1182
    trichoblastoma vs, 1557
    trichoepithelioma vs, 1547, 1549
    see also Morpheaform basal cell carcinoma
Basal cell epithelioma see Basal cell carcinoma
Basal cells
    cytolysis, epidermolysis bullosa simplex, 93
    epidermis, 2, 3
    hyperpigmentation, mastocytosis, 1493–1494
    liquefactive degeneration (hydropic degeneration)
        Bowen's disease, 1195
        bullous lichen planus, 222
        dermatomyositis, 829
        discoid lupus erythematosus, 792
        subacute cutaneous lupus erythematosus, 796
        see also Interface dermatitis

Basaloid cells, 462
    pilomatrixoma, 1537
    sebaceoma, 1576–1577
    sebaceous adenoma, 1574–1575
Basaloid follicular hamartoma, 1522–1524
    see also Infundibulocystic basal cell carcinoma
Basaloid follicular hamartoma syndrome, 1522
Basaloid proliferation, folliculocentric, 1586
Basaloid squamous cell carcinoma, 462–463
    genital region, 523, 525
Basaloid variant, intraepithelial neoplasia, genital region, 1195
Basement membrane, 3
    blisters, 82
    discoid lupus erythematosus, 792, 793, 794
    erythema gyrata repens, 265–266
    porphyrias, 584
    pseudoporphyria, 588, 589
    ultrastructure, 4–6
Basement membrane antigens, 7–8
    immunoperoxidase mapping, 83–84
    see also Anti-basement membrane antibodies
Basement membrane-like structure
    adenoid cystic carcinoma, 1652
    dermal cylindroma, 1637
Basic fibroblast growth factor, glomangiomas, 1848
Basidiobolomycosis, 963–964
Basket weave hyperkeratosis see Chicken wire appearance
Basosquamous (metatypical) basal cell carcinoma, 1175, 1178
Bathing-trunk congenital nevus
    giant hairy 'bathing-trunk' nevus, 1294–1296
    see also Giant congenital nevus
BAX protein, gene mutations, 1173
Bazex–Dupré–Christol syndrome, 1113, 1186
Bazex syndrome, 211–212
Bazin's disease see Erythema induratum
B-cell(s), lymphomatoid drug eruption, 653, 654
B-cell lymphoma, 1427–1457
    classification, 1358, 1359
B-cell pseudolymphoma, 1454–1457
    primary cutaneous marginal zone B-cell lymphoma vs, 1431
    see also Lymphocytoma cutis
Bcl-2
    melanoma, 1329
    Spitz nevus vs melanoma, 1272
Bcl-2 associated X-protein, gene mutations, 1173
Bean-bag cells, 356
Beau's lines, 664
Becker's melanosis see Becker's nevus
Becker's nevus, 1249–1250
    congenital smooth muscle hamartoma and, 1796
Bednár tumor (pigmented dermatofibrosarcoma protuberans), 1728, 1733
Behçet's disease, 685–689, 743–747
    erythema nodosum-like lesions, 348
    recurrent aphthous stomatitis vs, 407
Bejel, 494, 891
Benign alveolar ridge keratosis, 457–458
Benign autosomal dominant familial periodic fever (TNF receptor-associated periodic syndrome), 285, 756
Benign cephalic histiocytosis, 1472, 1473–1474
Benign familial acanthosis nigricans, 616
Benign familial pemphigus see Hailey–Hailey disease
Benign fibrous histiocytoma, intradermal fasciitis vs, 1705
Benign joint hypermobility syndrome, 1024
Benign lymphangioendothelioma, 1845, 1846
Benign migratory glossitis, 400–403
Benign mucinous metaplasia, genital region, 515–516
Benign mucous membrane pemphigoid, 117
Berardinelli–Seip syndrome, 375
Berlin classification, Ehlers–Danlos syndrome, 1023
Beryllium, 324–325
β-2 glycoprotein, antiphospholipid antibody syndrome, 768
β₄ integrin subunit, gene mutations, epidermolysis bullosa, 85
β-catenin
    pilomatrix carcinoma, 1540
    pilomatrixoma, 1536–1537
    Torre–Muir syndrome, 1585
β-sitosterol, 541
Betel nut chewers, oral lesions, 399, 458
    squamous cell carcinoma, 459
BIDS (syndrome), 1105
Bifurcated hairs see Pili bifurcati
Bile pigment, graft-versus-host disease, 254
Bilharziasis see Schistosomiasis
Bioplastique, foreign body granulomata, 325
Biopsy
    anogenital lesions, 473
    Behçet's disease, 746
    chondrodermatitis nodularis chronica helicis, 338–339
    hair, report, 1066, 1067
    inflammatory diseases of subcutaneous fat, 341
    jejunal, dermatitis herpetiformis, 133
    leukocytoclastic vasculitis, 715

metastases to skin, 1497–1498
    nails, 1129
    scalp, 1062
    sentinel lymph node, melanoma, 1274, 1324–1325
    soft tissue neoplasms, 1684
    see also Frozen section
Biphasic amyloidosis, 559
Bipolar disorder, Darier's disease and, 161
Birbeck granules, 1465
    see also Langerhans' granules
Birt–Hogg–Dubé syndrome, 1559, 1560, 1561–1562
    fibroepithelial polyps, 1708
    mantleoma vs, 1586
Bismuth, 663
Bite fibroma see Fibroma
Bjornstad syndrome, 1113
B–K mole syndrome, 1285
Black bone disease, 638
Black fever, 931–932
Blackheads, 1118, 1667, 1668
Black piedra, 925, 940–941, 969
Blacks
    hair counts, 1068
    pseudofolliculitis, 1125
    squamous cell carcinoma, 1199
    albinism, 1202
Black widow spider, 689
BLAISE (Blaschko linear acquired inflammatory skin eruption) see Lichen striatus
Blaschko linear acquired inflammatory skin eruption see Lichen striatus
Blaschko's lines, 232
    adult Blaschkitis, 233
    lesions following
        bullous ichthyosiform erythroderma variant, 45
        incontinentia pigmenti, 702
        inflammatory linear verrucous epidermal nevus, 210
        keratosis pilaris atrophicans, 58
        lichen striatus, 232
        linear Darier's disease, 163
        nevus depigmentosus, 1004
        pityriasis rosea, 190
        relapsing linear acantholytic dermatosis, 158
        Wells' syndrome, 697
Blastoid mantle cell lymphoma, 1435
Blastomyces dermatitidis, 955
    Histoplasma capsulatum vs, 974
Blastomycosis, 953–957
    paracoccidioidomycosis vs, 957
Blau's syndrome, 288
Bleaching agents, mercury, 662
Bleomycin, 664–665, 666
    scleroderma-like syndrome, 808
Blistering
    amyloidosis, 555
    chronic lymphocytic leukemia, 1437
    coma blisters, 664
    diabetes mellitus, 622
    drug reactions, 646
    porphyrias, 584–585
    see also Bullae; Vesicles
Blistering diseases see Subepidermal blistering diseases
Blistering mechanism, bullous pemphigoid, 108
Bloch–Sulzberger syndrome see Incontinentia pigmenti
Blood transfusion, porokeratosis, 76
Blood vessels
    fibroma of tendon sheath, 1716
    lymphomatoid papulosis, 1402
    myxofibrosarcoma, 1762
    skin blood supply, 32–35
        capillaries, 33, 34
        glomus bodies, 34
        postcapillary venules, 34
    see also specific types
Bloom's syndrome, 247–248
Blotchy mouse, 333
Blueberry muffin lesions, 858–859, 1503
Blue nevus, 469, 1299–1308
    Carney complex, 1014, 1015, 1016
    desmoplastic, 1302
    see also Epithelioid blue nevus; Malignant blue nevus
Blue rubber bleb nevus syndrome, 1818
Blunt trauma
    traumatic panniculitis, 351–353
    see also Trauma
Boils (furuncles), 879–880
Bolivian hemorrhagic fever, 868, 869
Bone
    acute generalized Langerhans' cell histiocytosis, 1459
    focal dermal hypoplasia syndrome, 1029
    Hutchinson–Gilford syndrome, 1054
    Langerhans' cell histiocytosis, 1462
    multifocal chronic Langerhans' cell histiocytosis, 1460

Bone (*cont'd*)
  osseous choristoma, 390
  sarcoidosis, 292
  tumors, 1853
  see also Osseous metaplasia
Bone marrow transplantation
  on atopy, 173
  Chédiak–Higashi syndrome, 1001
  graft-versus-host disease, 250
  herpes zoster, 857
  psoriasis, 201
Bone morphogenetic protein-2, pilomatrixoma, 1537
Borderline leprosy, 910, *911*, *912*, 914–915
Borrelia burgdorferi
  atrophoderma of Pasini and Pierini, 822
  eosinophilic fasciitis, 823
  Lyme disease, 889, *890*
  marginal zone B-cell lymphoma, 1428
  morphea, 818
  pseudolymphoma, 1454
  pseudopélade of Brocq, 1094
Borst–Jadassohn appearance (clonal seborrheic keratosis), 1159,
  1162
Borst–Jadassohn intraepidermal epithelioma, 1165–1166,
  1195–1196
  from hidroacanthoma simplex, 1615
Botryomycosis, 921–922
Bottom-heavy infiltrates, nodal B-cell lymphoma, 1452
Botulinum toxin, for eccrine hidrocystoma, 1614
Bourneville's disease *see* Tuberous sclerosis
Bovine lumpy jaw, 923
Bowel-associated dermatosis–arthritis, 683–684
Bowel bypass panniculitis, neutrophilic lobular infiltrate, 369
Bowenoid actinic keratoses, 1189, *1192*, 1196
Bowenoid papulosis, 519, 520, 847, 1192–1193
  focal epithelial hyperplasia *vs*, 433
  leukoplakia *vs*, 456
Bowenoid plaques, verrucous hyperkeratotic, 1195
Bowenoid porocarcinoma, 1623, *1625*
Bowen's disease, 1193–1198
  bowenoid papulosis *vs*, 847
  genital region, 519, 1196
  hidroacanthoma simplex *vs*, 1616
  nail, 1141–1142
  Paget's disease *vs*, 1516, 1517
  porokeratosis, 76
Box jellyfish, 690
BP180 *see* Bullous pemphigoid 180kD antigen; Bullous
  pemphigoid 180 kD antigen
BPAG2 *see* Bullous pemphigoid 180kD antigen
Brachial cutaneous dyschromatosis, acquired, 1019
Brain *see* Central nervous system
Branchial cyst, *1675*, *1676*
Brazilian pemphigus foliaceus, 148
Breast
  Carney complex, 1014
  cutaneous postirradiation angiosarcoma, 1840
  lupus mastitis, 380
  Montgomery's tubercles, 1565
Breast carcinoma
  eccrine ductal carcinoma *vs*, 1657, 1658
  mammary ductal apocrine carcinoma, 1598
  Paget's disease, 1514–1518
  postirradiation pseudosclerodermatous panniculitis,
    383–384
  skin metastases, 1498, 1499, *1500*, 1501–1503, 1504, 1506,
    1507
Breast-feeding, pemphigoid gestationis, 111
Breast implants, scleroderma-like syndrome, 808
Breslow tumor thickness, 1321
Brick wall, dilapidated, Hailey–Hailey disease, 157
Brill–Zinsser disease, 928
Broad beta disease, 547
Broders' classification, squamous cell carcinoma differentiation,
  1204
Bromoderma, 657–658
Bronchiolitis, systemic sclerosis, 807, 813
Bronchiolitis obliterans, paraneoplastic pemphigus, 153
Bronchogenic cysts, 1674–1675
Brooke–Spiegler syndrome, 1547, 1636–1637
  eccrine spiradenoma, 1640
Brown fat, 36
Brown oculocutaneous albinism, 1000
Brown recluse spider, 689
Brucellosis, 884
Bruch's membrane, calcification, 1042, *1043*
Brünauer–Fuhs–Siemens syndrome, 62–63
Brunsting–Perry pemphigoid, 101
Brunsting–Perry variant
  epidermolysis bullosa acquisita, 124
  localized cicatricial pemphigoid, 119, 121, 122
B symptoms, mantle cell lymphoma, 1435
Bubble hair, 1112–1113

Buboes
  chancroid, 504
  lymphogranuloma venereum, 505
  plague, 881, 882
Bubonic plague, 881, 882
Buccal mucosa, focal non-epidermolytic palmoplantar
    keratoderma with esophageal squamous cell carcinoma,
    68
Buckshot calcification (histoplasmosis), 972
Buckshot scatter, 1315
Budd–Chiari syndrome, Behçet's disease, 744
Buerger's disease, 747–748
Bulb, hair, 1065, *1066*
  absence, *1072*
Bulbourethral glands, female equivalent, 475
Bullae, 81
  morphea, 816, 820
  pyoderma gangrenosum, 673
  solar elastosis, 1053
  see also Blistering
Bullosis diabeticorum, 622
Bullous amyloidosis, 555
Bullous dermatosis
  of childhood, chronic, 134, 135–136
  in end-stage renal failure *see* Pseudoporphyria
  of hemodialysis *see* Pseudoporphyria
  of SLE, 785
  see also Bullous systemic lupus erythematosus
Bullous dermolysis of the newborn, transient, 92, 97
Bullous drug reactions, 646–649
Bullous erythema multiforme, 236
Bullous erythroderma ichthyosiformis congenita of Brocq *see*
    Bullous ichthyosiform erythroderma
Bullous ichthyosiform erythroderma, 45–48
  mosaicism, 1155
Bullous ichthyosis *see* Bullous ichthyosiform erythroderma
Bullous impetigo, 869, *871*, 873–874
Bullous lichen planus, 222, 225
  oral cicatricial pemphigoid *vs*, 444
Bullous mycosis fungoides, 1390–1391
Bullous pemphigoid, 98–111
  cell-rich bullous pemphigoid *vs*, 109
  cicatricial pemphigoid *vs*, 119
  dermatitis herpetiformis *vs*, 133
  drug-induced, 648
  generalized cutaneous pemphigoid, 98–100
  histology, 102–109
  immunoperoxidase antigen mapping, 83, 107
  linear IgA disease *vs*, 109, 136
  no blistering, 101
  pathogenesis, 102–109
  pustular psoriasis with, *204*, *205*
  scabies and, 981
Bullous pemphigoid 108 kD antigen, 108
  NC16A subunit, 108
    lichen planus pemphigoides, 116
Bullous pemphigoid 180 kD antigen, 7
  epidermolysis bullosa, 93
  gene mutations, 85, 95
  mucous membrane pemphigoid, 122
Bullous pemphigoid 230 kD antigen, 7–8, 107–108
Bullous pemphigoid antigen, paraneoplastic pemphigus, 153
Bullous pemphigoid antigen-1, epidermolysis bullosa, 92
Bullous pemphigoid-like epidermolysis bullosa acquisita, 123,
    124–125
Bullous solar elastosis, 1053
Bullous systemic lupus erythematosus, 128–130
  cell-rich bullous pemphigoid *vs*, 109
  see also Bullous dermatosis, of SLE
Burns, Marjolin's ulcer, *1202*, 1204
Burrows, scabies, 980
Buruli ulcer, 906
Buschke–Fischer–Brauer disease *see* Punctate palmoplantar
    keratoderma
Buschke–Löwenstein tumor, 492, 526, 844–845, *846*, 1218
Buschke–Ollendorf syndrome, 1050–1052
  familial cutaneous collagenoma *vs*, 1037
Busulfan, 666
Butterfly rash, SLE, 783, *784*

C

C1-esterase inhibitor deficiency, 694
C2 and C4 complement deficiency
  homozygous, subacute cutaneous lupus erythematosus, 783
  systemic lupus erythematosus, 786
C3 nephritic factor, 376
C5b-9 (complement), dermatomyositis, 829
Cadherins *see* Desmoglein 1; Desmoglein 3
Cadherins-11, 10
Café-au-lait spots, neurofibromatosis, 1768, 1776
Calcification
  calcinosis cutis, 596
  calciphylaxis, 364

connective tissue disorders, 596–597
  dural, nevoid basal cell carcinoma syndrome, 1184
  histoplasmosis, 972
  peripheral odontogenic fibroma, 422–423
  pilomatrixoma, 1537, *1538*
  pseudoxanthoma elasticum, 1042, 1043
  thrombi, sialolithiasis *vs*, 449
  vasculopathy, 597
Calcifying aponeurotic fibroma, 1719–1720
Calcifying epithelioma of Malherbe *see* Pilomatrixoma
Calcifying fibroblastic granuloma *see* Peripheral ossifying
    fibroma
Calcifying fibrous epulis *see* Peripheral ossifying fibroma
Calcifying fibrous pseudotumor, 1713, *1714*
Calcifying fibrous tumor, 1713, *1714*
Calcifying odontogenic cyst, peripheral, 424
Calcifying odontogenic tumor, peripheral, 424
Calcinosis, 595–600
  idiopathic, 510, 595, 596, 597–598
  systemic sclerosis, 806
Calcinosis universalis, 597
Calciphylaxis, 363–365, 597, 598
Calcium, sarcoidosis, 293
Calcium channel blockers, gingival hyperplasia, 426
Calcium oxalate, 362
Calcium pump gene mutation, Hailey–Hailey disease, 139, 157
Calculi, salivary glands, 449
Calculus, cutaneous *see* Subepidermal calcified nodule
Caliber-persistent labial artery, 428
Callus, 74
Calpain 1, ichthyosis fetalis and, 50
Calymmatobacterium granulomatis, 503
Campbell de Morgan spot, 1815
Canal of Nuck, cyst, 519
C-ANCA (cytoplasmic antineutrophil cytoplasmic antibodies),
    Wegener's granulomatosis, 442
Candida spp., 950
Candidiasis, 947–950
  benign migratory glossitis *vs*, 402
  disseminated, 949–950
  hairy leukoplakia with, 430
  HIV infection, 948, 949, *987*, 990
  median rhomboid glossitis, 402–403
  nails, 1129–1130, *1131*
Cannonball distribution of capillaries, tufted angioblastoma,
    1814–1815
Canon's white sponge nevus, 387–388
Capillaries, 33, 34
  acquired elastotic hemangioma, 1822
  angioendotheliomatosis, 1808
  crow's feet appearance
    lipoblastoma, 1693
    myxoid liposarcoma, 1698
  orf, 863
  systemic sclerosis, 809
  tufted angioblastoma, 1814
Capillary hemangioma, 1813–1828
  immature, cellular angiolipoma *vs*, 1687
  lobular, 1815–1818
  see also Pyogenic granuloma
Capillary morphogenesis protein 2, 1723
Carbuncles, 879, 880
Carcinoembryonic antigen (CEA)
  melanoma, 1328
  microcystic adnexal carcinoma, 1648
Carcinoid tumor, 1512
  diazo reaction, 1512, *1513*
Carcinoma
  cervical, human papilloma virus, 844
  metastases
    epithelioid malignant peripheral nerve sheath tumor *vs*,
      1793
    meningeal heterotopias *vs*, 1788
    thyroglossal duct cyst, 1675
  see also specific sites and types
Carcinoma cuniculatum *see* Verrucous carcinoma
Carcinoma en cuirasse, 1502, 1506
Carcinoma erysipelatoides, 1501–1502
Carcinoma-in-situ
  oral, 454
  see also Bowen's disease; Intraepithelial neoplasia
Carcinoma telangiectaticum, 1502, 1506
Carcinosarcoma
  eccrine spiradenoma, 1643
  see also Metaplastic carcinoma
Cardiocutaneous syndrome *see* Multiple lentigines syndrome
Cardiofaciocutaneous syndrome, keratosis pilaris atrophicans,
    58
Cardiomyopathic lentiginosis *see* Multiple lentigines syndrome
Carney complex, 511, 1014–1016, 1303
  angiomyxoma, 1015, 1856
  lentigines, 1014, *1246*, 1856
  psammomatous melanotic schwannoma, 1770

Carotenemia, 602
Carpal tunnel syndrome, amyloidosis, 555, 565
Carpet tacks sign, 777
Carrier states, 869
Carrión's disease, 886
Cartilage
    relapsing polychondritis, 835
    tumors, 1853–1854
Cartilaginous choristoma, 390–391
Cartilaginous exostosis
    osteoma cutis vs, 1853
    see also Osteochondroma
Casal's necklace, 594
Caseation, 898, 899, 901
Castleman's disease, glomeruloid hemangioma, 1808
Catagen, 1065, 1066
Catastrophic antiphospholipid syndrome, 767
Caterpillar bodies, 585
Cathepsin C, palmoplantar keratoderma with periodontopathia,
    70
Cat scratch disease, 884–889
Cavernous hemangioma, 1818–1819
Cavernous lymphangioma, 1845–1846
CD4 cells, HIV infection, 986
CD8+ epidermotropic cytotoxic T-cell lymphoma, primary
    cutaneous, 1420–1421
CD30+ large cell lymphoma, primary cutaneous, 1403–1409
CD30+ lymphoproliferative disorders, 1399–1409
CD30+ T-cells, mycosis fungoides, 1376–1377, 1378
CD34 antigen, acroangiodermatitis, 185–186
CD40, Spitz nevus vs melanoma, 1272, 1329
CD44, melanoma, 1329–1330
    Spitz nevus vs, 1272
CD68 (marker), melanoma, 1328
CD99 antibodies, peripheral primitive neuroectodermal tumor,
    1794
CD146 see Melanoma cell adhesion molecule
CDKN2a gene mutations, 1286
    familial melanoma, 1310
CEA see Carcinoembryonic antigen
Celenterate stings, 690
Celiac disease
    dermatitis herpetiformis, 131
    erythema elevatum diutinum, 741
    linear IgA disease, 136
Cell-mediated immunity
    allergic contact dermatitis, 176
    granuloma annulare, 299–300
    leukocytoclastic vasculitis, 714
    polymyositis, 828
    warts, 840
Cell-poor pemphigoid, 103–104, 105
    differential diagnosis, 110
Cell-rich bullous pemphigoid, differential diagnosis, 109–110
Cellular angiofibroma, 535–536
Cellular angiolipoma, 1687
Cellular blue nevus, 1304–1308
Cellular fibrous histiocytoma, 1746–1747
    dermatofibrosarcoma with myoid nodules vs, 1734
Cellular nerve sheath myxoma, 1783–1784
Cellular neurofibroma
    with atypia, 1774
    pilar leiomyoma vs, 1798
Cellular neurothekeoma, 1783–1785
Cellular schwannoma, 1769–1770
Cellulitis, 874–876
    necrotizing fasciitis vs, 877
Cell-within-a-cell appearance, hereditary benign intraepithelial
    dyskeratosis, 388
Central centrifugal scarring alopecias, 1089, 1099–1103
    acne keloidalis nuchae vs, 1098
Central nervous system
    Behçet's disease, 687, 745, 746
    hand, foot and mouth disease, 867
    incontinentia pigmenti, 703
    intravascular large B-cell lymphoma, 1446
    Lyme disease, 889, 890
    malignant atrophic papulosis, 757
    sarcoidosis, 292
    systemic lupus erythematosus, 785
    tuberous sclerosis, 1031, 1032, 1033
    Wegener's granulomatosis, 728
    xeroderma pigmentosum, 1230
Centrifugal lipoatrophy, 377–384
    see also Localized lipoatrophy
Centripetal flagellate erythema, 826, 829
Centroblasts, centrocytes, primary cutaneous follicular
    lymphoma, 1432
Centrocytic lymphoma, 1435–1436
Centrofacial lentiginosis, 1246
Centrofacial malignant granuloma see Midline destructive disease
Centrofacial papular lymphangiectasis, 580, 587
Cephalic histiocytosis, benign, 1472, 1473–1474

Cephalothoracic progressive lipodystrophy (acquired partial
    lipodystrophy), 375, 376
C-erbB-2 oncogene, sebaceous carcinoma, 1580
Cercarial dermatitis, 985
Cerebriform lymphocytes see Sézary cells
Cerebriform tongue, pemphigus vegetans, 146
Cerebrotendinous xanthomatosis, 541
Ceruminoma see Ceruminous gland tumors
Ceruminous glands, 22
Ceruminous gland tumors, 1600
    adenocarcinoma, 1597, 1600
Cervical thymic cyst, 1675–1676
Cervicofacial actinomycosis, 923
Cervix uteri, carcinoma
    human papilloma virus, 844
    metastases to skin, 1498
Cestodes, cysticercosis, 986
Chancre
    syphilitic, 494, 495, 499–500
    tuberculous, 895, 899
Chancroid, 504–505
Charcot–Leyden crystals, pemphigus vegetans, 146
Checkerboard appearance, proliferative myositis, 1706
Chédiak–Higashi syndrome, 1001
Cheilitis
    candidal, 948
    chronic actinic, 1187
    granulomatous (granulomatosa)
        metastatic Crohn's disease vs, 322
        orofacial granulomatosis, 440–441
Cheilitis glandularis, 452
Cheilitis glandularis apostematosa, 452
Chemicals, industrial
    scleroderma-like syndromes, 808
    squamous cell carcinoma, 1204
Chemotherapeutic agents, 664–669
    acral erythema, 667
    alopecia, 645, 664
    eccrine sweat gland reactions, 667–669
Cherry angioma, 1815
Chest involvement
    sarcoidosis, 291–292
    see also Pulmonary involvement
Cheveux incoiffables, 1108–1109
Chewing gum, plasma cell orificial mucositis, 438
Chickenpox see Varicella
Chicken wire appearance
    plane warts, 843
    see also Crow's feet appearance
Chiclero's ulcer, 929–931, 932–934
Chikungunya fever virus, 868, 869
Chilblain lupus erythematosus, 276, 778–780, 781
Chilblains (perniosis), 274–275, 354
Childhood dermatomyositis, 831
Childhood epidermolysis bullosa acquisita, 124
Childhood fibrous tumor with psammoma bodies, 1713,
    1714
Childhood lichen planus, 222
Childhood linear IgA disease, 134, 135–136
Childhood longitudinal melanonychia, 1137
Childhood pemphigoid, 101, 102, 103
    antigens, 108
Children
    acute generalized Langerhans' cell histiocytosis, 1458–1459
    African Kaposi's sarcoma, 1831
    chronic bullous dermatosis, 134, 135–136
    disabling pansclerotic morphea, 818
    epidermotropic cytotoxic T-cell lymphoma, 1420, 1421
    FACE (facial Afro-Caribbean childhood eruption), 323
    lipophagic panniculitis, 379
    melanoma, 1309, 1353–1355
    metastases to skin, 1498–1499
    mycosis fungoides, 1377–1378
    myofibroma, 1714
    neutrophil eccrine hidradenitis, 668
    papular acrodermatitis, 188–190
        see also Gianotti–Crosti syndrome
    pediatric systemic lupus erythematosus, 775
CHILD syndrome, 1155
Chinese lettering, 702
Chlamydia trachomatis
    lymphogranuloma venereum, 505–506
    Reiter's syndrome and, 479
Chloracne, 1119–1120
    comedones, 1667–1668
Chloroacetate esterase, 1491, 1493
Chloroma, 1488
Chloroquine, pigmentation, 639
Chlorpromazine, pigmentation, 639, 641
Cholestasis, plane xanthomata of, 548
Cholesterol, sex-linked ichthyosis, 40
Cholesterol clefts, trichilemmal cyst, 1672
Cholesterol crystal embolism, 762

Cholinergic urticaria, 694
Chondritis, auricular, 833, 834
Chondroblastic differentiation, melanoma, 1343
Chondrodermatitis nodularis chronica helicis, 338–339
    relapsing polychondritis vs, 835
Chondroid lipoma, 1690
Chondroid metaplasia, calcifying aponeurotic fibroma, 1720
Chondroid syringoma, 1600–1601, 1604
    malignant see Malignant mixed tumor
    ossifying fibromyxoid tumor vs, 1857
    see also Mixed tumor of skin
Chondroitin-6-sulfate proteoglycan, 8
Chondroma
    soft tissue, 1853–1854
        calcifying aponeurotic fibroma vs, 1720
    see also Enchondroma
Chondromyxoid tumor, ectomesenchymal, 471–472
Chondrosarcoma
    extraskeletal mesenchymal, 1855, 1856
    see also Myxoid chondrosarcoma
Choriocarcinoma, 1499, 1509, 1510
Chorionic gonadotropins, relapsing polychondritis, 834
Choristoma
    ganglion cell, 1765
    gastrointestinal, 391–392
    lingual thyroid see Lingual thyroid
    oral, 390–392
Choroid plexus, palmoplantar keratoderma with
    periodontopathia, 69
Chromoblastomycosis, 965–967
    phaeohyphomycosis vs, 970
Chromomycosis see Chromoblastomycosis
Chronic actinic dermatitis, 1425–1427
    see also Actinic reticuloid
Chronic adult T-cell leukemia/lymphoma, 1413
Chronic benign follicular mucinosis, 1388
Chronic bite injury, 399–400
    hairy leukoplakia vs, 399, 431
    leukoedema vs, 398
Chronic bullous dermatosis of childhood, 134, 135–136
Chronic capillaritis, 277–279
Chronic cutaneous leishmaniasis, 930
Chronic erythema nodosum, 344, 347
Chronic fibrosing vasculitis, granuloma faciale, 740
Chronic graft-versus-host disease, 251, 253
    oral lesions, 434
Chronic granulomatous disease, 327
    discoid lupus erythematosus and, 781
Chronic itching papular eruption of the axillae and pubic region
    (Fox–Fordyce disease), 194–195, 706–707
Chronic lymphadenopathy syndrome, HIV infection, 987
Chronic lymphocytic leukemia
    lymphocytic infiltrate of the skin vs, 268
    squamous cell carcinoma with, 1228
Chronic lymphocytic leukemia/small lymphocytic lymphoma,
    1436–1437
Chronic mucocutaneous candidiasis, 947, 948–949
Chronic myeloid leukemia, skin involvement, 1489
Chronic pain syndrome, vestibulitis as, 509
Chronic renal failure, oxalosis, 362
Chronic superficial dermatitis, 261–263, 1360, 1362,
    1373–1374
Chronic telogen effluvium, 1084
Chronic ulcerative stomatitis, 436–437
Chronic vulval purpura, 487
Chronological aging see Aging
Chrysiasis, 661
Chrysoderma, 661
CHS1/LYST gene, 1001
'Church spire' lesions, acrokeratosis verruciformis of Hopf, 74
Churg–Strauss granuloma, 320, 733, 734
Churg–Strauss syndrome, 710, 731–735
    polyarteritis nodosa vs, 731, 734
Chylomicrons, 540, 541, 542
Cicatricial (scarring) alopecia, 880, 1068, 1089–1103
Cicatricial junctional EB, 87
Cicatricial pemphigoid see Mucous membrane pemphigoid
Cicatricial pemphigoid-like epidermolysis bullosa acquisita,
    123–124
Ciliated cyst, cutaneous, 1676
Cinnamon, lichenoid hypersensitivity, 436, 437
Circinate balanitis, 478
Circled and rolled hair, 1116
Circulating anticoagulant see Lupus anticoagulant
Circulating antigen, lichen planus, 225–226
Circulating IgG, pemphigus, 142
Circumscribed neurodermatitis see Lichen simplex chronicus
Circumscribed pityriasis rubra pilaris, 208
Cirsoid aneurysm, 1819–1820
Civatte bodies see Cytoid bodies
c-Kit gene, 13
    mastocytosis, 1491
CLA (cutaneous lymphocyte antigen), 173, 176

Clark's levels, melanoma thickness, 1321–1322
Classical variants
  CD30+ large cell lymphoma, 1405
  epidermolysis bullosa acquisita, 123
Classic (endemic) Kaposi's sarcoma, 1830–1831
Clavus, 74, 75
Clear cell(s)
  epidermis, 3
  Toker cells, 4, 1514
Clear cell acanthoma, 1166–1167
Clear cell actinic keratosis, 1189, *1192*
Clear cell atypical fibroxanthoma
  clear cell squamous cell carcinoma *vs*, 1210
  see also Atypical fibroxanthoma
Clear cell basal cell carcinoma, 1177, *1180*
Clear cell carcinoma, 1509–1510, *1511*
Clear cell eccrine porocarcinoma, 1623, *1624*
Clear cell fibrous histiocytoma, 1751
Clear cell hidradenocarcinoma, 1634–1636
  clear cell squamous cell carcinoma *vs*, 1210
  sebaceous carcinoma *vs*, 1583
  trichilemmal carcinoma *vs*, 1533
Clear cell hidradenoma, 1631, *1632*
  malignant *see* Clear cell hidradenocarcinoma
  see also Hidradenoma
Clear cell melanoma, 1338, *1339*
Clear cell myoepithelioma *see* Hidradenoma
Clear cell papulosis, Paget's disease *vs*, 1517
Clear cell porocarcinoma, trichilemmal carcinoma *vs*, 1533
Clear cell sarcoma, 1795–1796
Clear cell squamous cell carcinoma, 1209–1210
  sebaceous carcinoma *vs*, 1210, 1583
  trichilemmal carcinoma *vs*, 1210, 1533
Clear cell trichoblastoma, 1555
Cliff-drop borders, atrophoderma of Pasini and Pierini, 821, *822*
Climacteric keratoderma, 65–66
Clitoris, 475
CLL/SLL (chronic lymphocytic leukemia/small lymphocytic lymphoma), 1436–1437
Cloacogenic carcinoma, 528–529
Clonal nevus, 1259–1260
Clonal seborrheic keratosis (Borst–Jadassohn appearance), 1159, *1162*
Clonal T-cell gene rearrangements, pigmented purpuric dermatoses, 279
Clonal T-cell populations, chronic superficial dermatitis, 263
Clonidine, cicatricial pemphigoid, 119
Closed comedones, acne vulgaris, 1118
Clouston syndrome, 71
'Cluster of jewels' appearance
  bullous pemphigoid, 99, 100
  childhood pemphigoid, 101
  linear IgA disease, 135
CMG2 (capillary morphogenesis protein 2), 1723
Coal tar, keratoacanthoma, 1223
Coat sleeve appearance, erythema annulare centrifugum, 264
Cobb syndrome, 1809
Coccidioides immitis, 958, 959
  Prototheca spp. *vs*, 936–937
Coccidioidomycosis, 958–960
Cochlea, keratitis–ichthyosis–deafness syndrome, 72–73
Cockade nevus, 1262, *1263*
Cockarde nevus, 1262, *1263*
Cockayne's syndrome, 248–249
Cockayne–Touraine variant, dominant dystrophic epidermolysis bullosa, 89
Coelenterate stings, 690
Cohen syndrome, 616
COL1A1 gene, dermatofibrosarcoma protuberans, 1730
Cold panniculitis, 353–354
  equestrian, 274, 275, 353–354
Cold urticaria, 693
Collagen(s)
  antibodies, relapsing polychondritis, 834
  dermis, 29–31
  diseases, 1023–1038
  dissection, angiosarcoma, *1841*
  hyalinized, sclerosing perineurioma, 1787
  hyalinosis cutis et mucosae, 573
  keloid, 1701
  morphea, 819
  storiform collagenoma, 1711
  synthesis, 29–30
  systemic sclerosis, 810, 811
  transepidermal elimination
    chondrodermatitis nodularis chronica helicis, 338
    necrobiosis lipoidica, 308
    perforating granuloma annulare, 299
    prurigo nodularis, 330
    reactive perforating collagenosis, 328
  type IV, 8
    epidermolysis bullosa, 92
    gene mutations, epidermolysis bullosa, 85

type VII, 9
  dystrophic epidermolysis bullosa, 97
  epidermolysis bullosa acquisita, 123, 126
  see also LH7:2 (monoclonal antibody)
type XVII *see* Bullous pemphigoid 180 kD antigen
Collagenoma, 1037–1038
  eruptive, 1037–1038
    papular elastorrhexis *vs*, 1038, 1052
  shagreen patch as, 1032
  storiform, 1711–1712, 1716
  trichilemmoma like, 1530
Collagenosis, reactive perforating, 328, *329*, 331
  Kyrle's disease *vs*, 336
Collagenosis nuchae *see* Nuchal fibroma
Collagenous and elastotic plaques of the hand, 1053
  see also Degenerative collagenous plaques of the hand; Digital papular calcific elastosis
Collagenous fibroma, 1717
Collagenous vasculopathy, cutaneous, 1812
Collar of Venus, 494
Collision tumors, seborrheic keratosis, 1160
'Collodion baby', 42
Colloid bodies *see* Cytoid bodies
Colloid milium, 567–571
Colon *see* Large intestine
Colostomy, pyoderma gangrenosum, 675
Coma blisters, 664
Combined adnexal tumor *see* Microcystic adnexal carcinoma
Combined immune deficiency, granuloma, 327
Combined myxoid and round cell liposarcoma, 1698
Combined nevus, 1262–1263, 1300
  epithelioid, 1303
  malignant, 1262
Comedonal cyst, 1667–1668
Comedone(s)
  acne vulgaris, 1118, *1119*, 1667–1668
  dilated pore (Winer), 1524
  familial dyskeratotic, 168–169, 1668
    warty dyskeratoma *vs*, 167
  open *see* Whiteheads
Comedone nevus *see* Comedo nevus
Comedo nevus, 1520–1522
  of the palm, 1613
Commensal bacteria, 869
Committed cells, epidermis, 2
Common baldness *see* Androgenetic alopecia
Common blue nevus, 1299–1300
Common fibrous histiocytoma, cellular fibrous histiocytoma *vs*, 1746
Common variable immunodeficiency, 327
Complement activation, bullous systemic lupus erythematosus, 130
Complementation groups, xeroderma pigmentosum, 1229
Complement deficiency
  systemic lupus erythematosus, 786
  urticarial vasculitis, 282
  see also C2 and C4 complement deficiency; Hypocomplementemia
Complement fixation, bullous pemphigoid, 107
Complement regulator-acquiring surface proteins (CRASPs), *Borrelia burgdorferi*, 890
Complex aphthosis, 406
Complex poroma-like adnexal adenoma *see* Apocrine poroma
Composite hemangioendothelioma, 1836
Compound blue nevus, 1301–1302
Compound nevus, 469, 1250, 1251–1252, 1253
Concha amyloidosis, 564
Condyloma acuminatum, 491–494, 844–847
  focal epithelial hyperplasia *vs*, 433
  oral squamous papilloma *vs*, 411
  podophyllin, 493, 845, 1196
Condylomata lata, 494, 498, 500
Confetti lesions, 1030
Congenital abnormalities, pruritic urticarial papules and plaques of pregnancy, 280
Congenital absence of skin, 1027–1028
Congenital dermoid fistula, dermoid cyst *vs*, 1673
Congenital dysplastic angiopathy *see* Acroangiodermatitis
Congenital epulis, 1781–1782
Congenital erythropoietic porphyria, 575, 576–577
Congenital generalized fibromatosis, 1714
Congenital generalized lipodystrophy, 375
Congenital gingival leiomyomatous polyp/hamartoma, congenital granular cell epulis *vs*, 396
Congenital granular cell epulis/tumor, 395–396, 417
Congenital ichthyosiform erythroderma, 38, 43–45
Congenital immunodeficiency syndromes, granulomata, 326–327
Congenital lymphedema, spindle cell hemangioma with, 1826
Congenital neural hamartoma, 1765
Congenital neurovascular hamartoma, 1765
Congenital nevus, 1291–1294
  neonate, 1294–1296
Congenital self-healing histiocytosis, 1467–1468

Congenital self-healing reticulohistiocytosis, 1467–1468
Congenital smooth muscle hamartoma, 1796–1797
Congenital syphilis, 498
Congenital telangiectatic erythema with dwarfism, 247–248
Congenital triangular alopecia *see* Temporal triangular alopecia
Congenital vellus hamartoma, 1519–1520
Congo red, amyloidosis, 553
Conidiobolomycosis, 963, 964
Conjunctiva
  angiokeratoma corporis diffusum, 551
  keratitis–ichthyosis–deafness syndrome, 72
  lamellar ichthyosis, 42
  linear IgA disease, 135
  mucous membrane pemphigoid, 117–118, 120
  rhinosporidiosis, 978
  sarcoidosis, 292
Conjunctivitis
  ligneous, 426–427
  Reiter's syndrome, 477
Connective tissue disorders, 775–836
  calcification, 596–597
  leukocytoclastic vasculitis, 711
  vasculitis, 709
Connective tissue nevus, 1030–1031
  see also Collagenoma
Connective tissue panniculitis, 379
  atrophic, 378
Connective tissue tumors, 1683–1865
Connexin genes
  erythrokeratoderma variabilis, 62
  hidrotic ectodermal dysplasia, 71
  keratitis–ichthyosis–deafness syndrome, 72
  Vohwinkel syndrome, 70
Contact brucellosis, 884
Contact dermatitis, 175–177
  lymphomatoid, 652–655
  mycosis fungoides-like features, 1424
  systemic, 177, 179
Contact lichenoid eruption, substances causing, 635
Contact pemphigus, 155–156
Contact photoallergy, 631
Contact urticaria, 694
  irritant, 694, 695
Contagious pustular dermatosis, 862–864
Contraceptives
  melanoma, 1310
  pemphigoid gestationis, 111
Contractures
  eosinophilic fasciitis, 823
  generalized morphea, 818
  systemic sclerosis, 805
Copper metabolism, elastosis perforans serpiginosa, 333
Coproporphyrin(s), 577
Coproporphyrinogen oxidase deficiency, 579
Corium *see* Dermis
Cornea
  arcus, 547
  Darier's disease, 160
  ichthyosis follicularis with alopecia and photophobia, 56
  keratitis–ichthyosis–deafness syndrome, 72
  sex-linked ichthyosis, 39
  verticillate, angiokeratoma corporis diffusum, 551
Cornelia de Lange syndrome, keratosis pilaris atrophicans, 58
Cornified cell envelope, 11
Cornoid lamellae, 1155
  porokeratosis, 76, 77
Corns (clavus), 74, 75
Cornu cutaneum, 1157
  see also Cutaneous horns
Coronary artery aneurysm, mucocutaneous lymph node syndrome, 736
Coronary artery bypass grafting, vein graft site dermatitis, 188
Corps ronds, 161, 389
Cortex, hair shaft, 1065
Corticosteroids
  cutaneous atrophy, 1054
  panniculitis syndrome, 360–361
  rosacea-like dermatosis, 1123, *1124*
Cortisol, acne vulgaris, 1118
Corymbose papules, 494, 497, 500
Corynebacterium diphtheriae, 927
Corynebacterium minutissimum, 490, 924, 925
Corynebacterium ulcerans, 927
Costello syndrome, 615
Coumadin (warfarin), 658–659
Cowden's syndrome, 1527–1528
  follicular infundibulum tumor associated, 1525
  Proteus syndrome and, 1154
  Ruvalcaba–Myrhe–Smith syndrome as variant, 1013
  storiform collagenoma, 1711
Cowper's glands, female equivalent, 475
Cowpox, 861
Coxsackie A16 virus, hand, foot and mouth disease, 867

Crab yaws, 892
Cradle cap, 173
Cranial fasciitis, 1704
CRASPs (complement regulator-acquiring surface proteins),
    Borrelia burgdorferi, 890
Creeping eruption, 984–985
Cremaster, 474
Creole dyschromia, 1005
CREST syndrome, 804, 805–806
Cricopharyngeus muscle, dermatomyositis, 827
Crimean–Congo hemorrhagic fever, 868, 869
Crohn's disease
    abscesses, 683
    anogenital region, 489–490
    erythema elevatum diutinum, 740
    metastatic, 321–322, 489
        subcutaneous sarcoidosis *vs*, 369
    oral, 441–442
    orofacial granulomatosis *vs*, 441
Cronkhite–Canada syndrome, 1013–1014
Cross syndrome, gingival fibromatosis, 396
Crosti's lymphoma, 1432
Crouzon syndrome, 615
Crow's feet appearance, capillaries
    lipoblastoma, 1693
    myxoid liposarcoma, 1698
Cryoglobulin(s), 764
Cryoglobulinemia, 764–767
    angioendotheliomatosis, 1808
    see also Essential cryoglobulinemic vasculitis
Cryptococcosis, 960–963
    panniculitis, *371*
    paracoccidioidomycosis *vs*, 957
Cryptococcus (spp.), 961
Cryptococcus neoformans var. *neoformans*, 960, 961–963
Crystal storing histiocytosis, 365–366, 1444, *1445*
CSA gene, CSB gene, Cockayne's syndrome, 248
Cumulative toxicity, drugs, 624
Cushing's syndrome, *101*
    Carney complex, 1014
Cutaneous adenocystic carcinoma, 1654–1657
Cutaneous calculus, 597
    see also Subepidermal calcified nodule
Cutaneous ciliated cyst, 1676
Cutaneous collagenous vasculopathy, 1812
Cutaneous epithelioid angiomatous nodule, 1822–1823
Cutaneous extravascular necrotizing granuloma, 320
Cutaneous focal mucinosis, 614
Cutaneous follicle center lymphoma *see* Primary cutaneous
    follicular lymphoma
Cutaneous ganglion cell choristoma, 1765
Cutaneous ganglioneuroma, 1765
Cutaneous horns
    familial dyskeratotic comedones, 168
    see also Cornu cutaneum
Cutaneous hyperpigmentation *see* Hyperpigmentation
Cutaneous larva migrans, 984–985
Cutaneous leiomyosarcoma, 1800
Cutaneous leishmaniasis, 929–931, 932–934
Cutaneous leukocytoclastic angiitis, *710*
Cutaneous lung tissue heterotopia, 1674
Cutaneous lymphadenoma, 1553, 1558–1559
    see also Trichoblastoma, with adamantinoid features
Cutaneous lymphocyte antigen (CLA), 173, 176
Cutaneous lymphoid hyperplasia *see* B-cell pseudolymphoma
Cutaneous macroglobulinosis, 574–575
Cutaneous mastocytosis, 1491
Cutaneous mature cystic teratoma, 1673–1674
Cutaneous memory, 637
Cutaneous meningioma, 1788–1789, *1790*
Cutaneous mucinosis of infancy, 610
Cutaneous Müllerian cyst, 1676
Cutaneous myxoma, 1856
    see also Myxoid cyst
Cutaneous nerve hamartoma, 1765
Cutaneous neurocristic hamartoma *see* Neurocristic hamartoma
Cutaneous nodular elastoidosis with cysts and comedones,
    1053, 1057
Cutaneous nodulosis, 310
Cutaneous oxalosis, 362–363
Cutaneous pemphigus, 142
Cutaneous perineurioma with epithelioid change, epithelioid
    fibrous histiocytoma *vs*, 1749
Cutaneous plasmacytosis, 1443
Cutaneous polyarteritis nodosa, 722–723
Cutaneous pseudosarcomatous polyp, 1709
Cutaneous reaction of lymphocyte recovery, 671
Cutaneous sinus histiocytosis, 1479
Cutaneous T-cell lymphoma, 1358
Cutaneous T-cell pseudolymphoma, 1423–1424
Cuticle
    hair shaft, 1065
        see also Ruffled cuticle
    nail, 1128

Cuticular layer, anagen hair follicle, 1065
Cutis laxa, 1038–1040
    acquired, 349, 1023, 1039–1040
Cutis marmorata telangiectasia congenita, 1810
    neonatal lupus erythematosus, 786
Cutis rhomboidalis nuchae, 1053
Cw6 (HLA antigen), psoriasis, 200
Cyclin D1
    mantle cell lymphoma, 1435
    melanoma, 1329
    nevoid melanoma, *1334*
    Spitz nevus *vs* melanoma, 1272
Cyclophosphamide, 664
Cyclosporin, hyperplastic oral lesions, 426, 427, *428*
CYLD gene mutations, 1547, 1637
Cylindroma, 1547
    dermal, 1636–1639
    malignant, 1639–1640
Cyst(s), 1663–1682
    of canal of Nuck, 519
Cystatin A, 11
Cystatin α, 11
Cysticercosis, 986
Cystic fibrosis, botryomycosis, 921, 922
Cystic hygroma, 1845, 1846
Cystic pilomatrixoma, 1663
Cystic teratoma, cutaneous mature, 1673–1674
Cystic variant plantar warts, 841–842
Cytochrome P-450 enzymes, 624
Cytoid bodies, 223, 225
    amyloidosis, 562
    dermatomyositis, 829
    discoid lupus erythematosus, 792, *793*
    erythema dyschromicum perstans, 235
    lichenoid keratosis, 230
    lichen planus of nails, 1134
Cytokeratins
    keratotic basal cell carcinoma *vs* trichoepithelioma, 1549
    Paget's disease, 1516–1517
    skin metastases, 1504, 1505, 1506
    trichogenic tumors, 1557
Cytokines
    adverse reactions, 669–670
    Sweet's syndrome, 680
Cytolysis, basal cells, epidermolysis bullosa simplex, 93
Cytomegalovirus, 858–860
    HIV infection, 990
    mycosis fungoides, 1365
Cytophagic histiocytic panniculitis, 354, 356
    subcutaneous panniculitic T-cell lymphoma *vs*, 1417
Cytoplasmic antineutrophil cytoplasmic antibodies, Wegener's
    granulomatosis, 442
Cytotoxic drugs *see* Chemotherapeutic agents
Cytotoxic T-cell(s), drug reactions, 625
Cytotoxic T-cell lymphoma, primary cutaneous CD8+
    epidermotropic, 1420–1421
Cytotrophoblast, 1509

D

DAB389 IL-2 treatment, psoriasis, 201
Dabska's tumor *see* Papillary intralymphatic angioendothelioma
Dandruff, 173
Dapsone
    bullous systemic lupus erythematosus, 128
    dermatitis herpetiformis, 131
Darier's disease, 158–163
    acrokeratosis verruciformis of Hopf, 74
    familial dyskeratotic comedones *vs*, 169
    Hailey–Hailey disease *vs*, 156, 157, 158, 162
    nails, 159, *160*, 161, 1135–1136
    oral lesions, 159–160, 389–390
    pemphigus *vs*, 143, 144
    proteins, 11
    transient acantholytic dermatosis *vs*, 162–163, 165
    zosteriform, 1155
        see also Linear Darier's disease
Darier's sign, 1492
Darier–White disease *see* Darier's disease
Dartos muscle, hamartoma, 536, 1799
Daughter yaws, 892
Davis–Colley disease *see* Punctate palmoplantar keratoderma
Deafness, keratitis–ichthyosis–deafness syndrome, 72
De Barsy syndrome, 1038
Decapitation secretion, 22, *23*
    apocrine carcinoma, 1597
    apocrine hidrocystoma, 1588, *1589*
    mixed tumor of skin, *1602*
Decubital fibroplasia, atypical, 1706–1707
Dedifferentiation, atypical lipomatous tumor, 1696, 1697
Deep dermal pyogenic granuloma, 1816
Deep granuloma annulare
    rheumatoid nodules *vs*, 311–312
    see also Subcutaneous granuloma annulare
Deep penetrating nevus, 1281–1282, *1283*, *1284*

Deep variant, erythema annulare centrifugum, 264
Deep vein thrombosis, factor V Leiden mutation, 771
Degenerative collagenous plaques of the hand, 64–65
    see also Collagenous and elastotic plaques of the hand
Degos' disease (malignant atrophic papulosis), 382, *757–760*
    systemic lupus erythematosus, 784
Delayed hypersensitivity
    drug reactions, 625
    granuloma annulare, 299–300
    oral lichen planus, 434
Delayed pressure urticaria, 693
Delleman's syndrome (oculocerebrocutaneous syndrome),
    rhabdomyomatous mesenchymal hamartoma, 1802
Delling, lichen sclerosus, 484
DeltaDi-4S(DS) (dermatan sulfate subunit), atrophoderma of
    Pasini and Pierini, 822
Dematiaceous fungi, 965–967
Demodex folliculorum
    AIDS-related eosinophilic folliculitis and, 988
    rosacea, 1122, 1124
Dendritic cell(s), 13–18
    epidermal, 13–18
    Langerhans' cells, 16–18, 1457
    melanocytes, 13–16
        see also Melanocytes
Dendritic cell neoplasms, 1484–1487
    classification, *1359*
Dendritic cell neurofibroma with pseudorosettes, 1774, *1775*
Dengue hemorrhagic fever, 868
Dennie–Morgan folds, atopic dermatitis, 173
De novo variant, desmoplastic melanoma, 1347
Dental abrasives (dentifrice)
    foreign body gingivitis, 405
    Sanguinaria, 456
Dental lamina cysts of the newborn, 425
Dental sinus, 1680
Denture-associated fibrous hyperplasia, 416–417
    cartilaginous choristoma *vs*, 391
    see also Epulis fissuratum
Denture hyperplasia *see* Denture-associated fibrous hyperplasia
Derbyshire neck *see* Poikiloderma, of Civatte
Dercum's disease, 1691
Dermal cylindroma, 1636–1639
Dermal duct tumor, 1619–1620
Dermal fasciitis, 1702, *1703*, *1704*, *1705*
Dermal fenestration, 611
Dermal lipoma, 1685, *1686*
    storiform collagenoma *vs*, 1711
Dermal liposarcoma, 1699
Dermal melanocytic hamartoma, 1299
Dermal melanocytic lesions, 1297–1308
Dermal microfibril bundles, 9
Dermal myxoma, neurothekeoma *vs*, 1784
Dermal nerve sheath myxoma, 1782–1784
Dermal nevus, 1250, 1252, 1254–1256, *1257*
    melanoma *vs*, 1258
Dermal nevus cells, 1258
Dermal squamomelanocytic tumor, 1355–1356
Dermatan sulfate, atrophoderma of Pasini and Pierini, 822
Dermatitis herpetiformis, 131–134
    cell-rich bullous pemphigoid *vs*, 109
    oral lesions, 446
    pemphigus herpetiformis *vs*, 151
Dermatofibroma, 1742–1752
    atrophic, 1751
    dermatofibrosarcoma protuberans *vs*, 1732
    desmoplastic melanoma *vs*, 1347
    with monster cells (atypical fibrous histiocytoma),
        1749–1750, 1759
    multinucleate cell angiohistiocytoma *vs*, 1742
    pilar leiomyoma *vs*, 1798
    progressive nodular histiocytosis *vs*, 1475
    xanthogranuloma *vs*, 1472
    see also Fibrous histiocytoma
Dermatofibrosarcoma
    with myoid nodules, 1733–1734
    myxoid, 1733
Dermatofibrosarcoma protuberans, 1729–1735
    cellular fibrous histiocytoma *vs*, 1747
    dermatomyofibroma *vs*, 1710
    desmoplastic melanoma *vs*, 1347
    fibrosarcomatous, 1729–1730, 1732–1733
    giant cell fibroblastoma and, 1728, 1730
    lentigo maligna *vs*, 1314
    neurofibroma *vs*, 1775
    perineurioma *vs*, 1787
    spindle cell squamous cell carcinoma *vs*, 1210
Dermatofibrosis lenticularis disseminata, 1050
Dermatographism, 692, 1492
Dermatoheliosis, 1053–1054
Dermatomyofibroma, 1709–1711
    plexiform fibrous histiocytoma *vs*, 1755–1757
Dermatomyositis, 825–832
    calcification, 596

Dermatomyositis panniculitis, 383
Dermatopathia pigmentosa reticularis, 1011
Dermatopathic lymphadenopathy, 1372–1373, *1374*
Dermatophilus congolensis, 926
Dermatophytes, 938
  AIDS, 990
Dermatosis cenicienta, 234–236
Dermatosis papulosa nigra, 1163, *1164*
Dermatosparaxis (Ehlers–Danlos syndrome type VIIC), *1024*,
    1025–1026
Dermis, 28–32
  collagens, 29–31
  elastic tissue, 31
  ground substance, 32
  nail, 1128
  papillary, 28
    discoid lupus erythematosus, 792
Dermographism, 692, 1492
Dermoid, 393–394
Dermoid cyst, 1673
  oral, 392–393
  oral lymphoepithelial cyst *vs*, 394
  sebaceous trichofolliculoma *vs*, 1545
Dermoid fistula, median nasal, *1674*
  sebaceous trichofolliculoma *vs*, 1545–1546
Dermoid tumor, 393–394
Dermolytic pemphigoid *see* Epidermolysis bullosa acquisita
De Sanctis–Cacchione syndrome, 1230
Descemet's membrane, sex-linked ichthyosis, 39
Desipramine, pigmentation, 640
Desmocollin, 10–11
Desmoglein 1 (Dsg1), 10–11
  antibodies, paraneoplastic pemphigus, 153
  pemphigus, 142
  pemphigus foliaceus, 148
  pemphigus herpetiformis, 151
Desmoglein 3 (Dsg3), 10–11
  antibodies, paraneoplastic pemphigus, 153
  pemphigus, 142
  pemphigus herpetiformis, 151
  pemphigus vegetans, 146
Desmoid fibromatosis, 1726–1727
  nuchal fibroma *vs*, 1712
  palmar fibromatosis *vs*, 1725
Desmoplakin, 11
  striate palmoplantar keratoderma, 63
Desmoplakin I, paraneoplastic pemphigus, 153
Desmoplasia, lentigo maligna, 1314
Desmoplastic basal cell carcinoma, microcystic adnexal
    carcinoma *vs*, 1649
Desmoplastic blue nevus, 1302
Desmoplastic fibroblastoma, 1717
Desmoplastic melanocytic nevus (desmoplastic nevus), 1255,
    1271, 1276–1277, *1278*
Desmoplastic melanoma, 1346–1353
  desmoplastic nevus *vs*, 1277
Desmoplastic nevus (desmoplastic Spitz nevus), 1255, 1271,
    1276–1277, *1278*
Desmoplastic squamous cell carcinoma, 1212–1214
Desmoplastic trichilemmoma, 1530–1531
Desmoplastic trichoepithelioma, 1550–1552
  microcystic adnexal carcinoma *vs*, 1649
  syringoma *vs*, 1627
Desmosomes, 3, 5, 6, 10–11
  acantholytic disorders, 139
Desquamation, follicular degeneration syndrome, 1101
Desquamative gingivitis, 102, *103*, 433, 445
  cicatricial pemphigoid, 443
  oral pemphigoid, 117
Diabetes insipidus
  multifocal chronic Langerhans' cell histiocytosis, 1460
  xanthoma disseminatum, 1477
Diabetes mellitus, 622
  acanthosis nigricans, 616
  congenital generalized lipodystrophy, 375
  epidermolysis bullosa acquisita, 124
  necrobiosis lipoidica, 305, 306
  scleredema, 610
Diaper dermatitis, 943
  see also Napkin rash
Diazo reaction, carcinoid tumor, 1512, *1513*
Differentiated VIN, 521, 522–523
Differentiating cells, epidermis, 2
Diffuse basal cell carcinoma, 1170
Diffuse cutaneous leishmaniasis, 931
Diffuse cutaneous mastocytosis, 1493
Diffuse dermal angiomatosis, 1808
Diffuse familial comedones, familial dyskeratotic comedones *vs*,
    169
Diffuse granuloma annulare, 300–301, *302*
Diffuse large B-cell lymphoma, 1441–1443
Diffuse leprosy, 910
Diffuse necrobiosis lipoidica, 308
Diffuse neurofibroma, 1773–1774

dermatomyofibroma *vs*, 1710
  neurofibromatosis type I, 1776, *1777*
Diffuse palmoplantar keratoderma, 60–61, 68–69
Diffuse plane xanthomatosis, 547
Diffuse proliferative glomerulonephritis, systemic lupus
    erythematosus, 798, 799
Diffuse systemic sclerosis, 804, 807–808
  see also Progressive systemic sclerosis
Diffuse tenosynovial giant cell tumor, 1752
Digital fibrokeratoma, acquired, 1721
Digital fibromatosis, infantile, 1718–1719
Digital pacinian neuroma, 1764
Digital papular calcific elastosis, 64–65
  see also Collagenous and elastotic plaques of the hand
Digitate dermatosis (chronic superficial dermatitis), 261–263,
    1360, *1362*, 1373–1374
Dilantin (phenytoin), adverse effects, 633–634
Dilapidated brick wall, Hailey–Hailey disease, 157
Dilated pore (Winer), 1524
Dinitrochlorobenzene, allergic contact dermatitis, 175
Dioxin, punctate palmoplantar keratoderma, 63
Dipeptidyl aminopeptidase I (cathepsin C), palmoplantar
    keratoderma with periodontopathia, 70
Diphtheria, cutaneous, 927
Disabling pansclerotic morphea of children, 818
Discoid dermatitis, 174, *175*
Discoid lupus erythematosus, 775–787, 792–795
  alopecia, 1091–1093
  alopecia areata *vs*, 1078
  chronic granulomatous disease and, 781
  fibrinoid necrosis, 794, *795*
  hair follicle absence, 794, *795*
  Jessner's lymphocytic infiltrate of the skin *vs*, 267, 268
  lichen planopilaris *vs*, 1090, 1093
  lichen planus *vs*, 226
  lupus erythematosus profundus, 379
  oral lesions, 447, 777
  oral lichen planus *vs*, 437
Dissecting cellulitis of the scalp, 1096–1098, 1102
Dissecting folliculitis of the scalp, 706
Disseminated histoplasmosis, 972
Disseminated intravascular coagulation, 763–764
  hemorrhagic fevers, 869
  meningococcal septicemia, 881
  purpura fulminans, 763, 764, 856
Disseminated linear epidermolytic epidermal nevus, 49
Disseminated rosacea, 1121
Disseminated superficial porokeratosis, 75
Distinctive exudative discoid and lichenoid dermatosis, 188
Diverticula, colon, systemic sclerosis, 808
DKC1 gene mutations, dyskeratosis congenita, 249
DNA
  HTLV tax proviral, mycosis fungoides, 1365
  repair abnormality
    hereditary non-polyposis colorectal carcinoma, 1585
    xeroderma pigmentosum, 1228–1229
  see also Native DNA; Single-strand DNA
DNA helicases, 247
DNA repair factor TFIIH, 1105
Dominant dystrophic epidermolysis bullosa, 89
Dominant dystrophic epidermolysis bullosa–pretibial, 91–92
Dominant dystrophic epidermolysis bullosa–transient bullous
    dermolysis of the newborn (transient bullous dermolysis
    of the newborn), 92, 97
Donovan bodies, 503
Donovanosis, 502–504
Dopa reaction, 14
Double-stranded DNA *see* Native DNA
Dowling–Degos disease, 1009–1010
Dowling–Meara variant, epidermolysis bullosa simplex, 86,
    94
Down syndrome
  acanthosis nigricans, 616
  isolated collagenoma with, 1038
Drug hypersensitivity syndrome
  anticonvulsants, 633–634
  cutaneous T-cell pseudolymphoma, 1423–1424
Drug-induced conditions, 623–671
  acanthosis nigricans, 616
  acne vulgaris, 1118
  alopecia, 645, 664
  angioimmunoblastic T-cell lymphoma, 1411
  anticonvulsants *see* Anticonvulsants
  bullous reactions, 646–649
  erythema multiforme, 238
    see also Erythema multiforme
  erythema nodosum, 344
    see also Erythema nodosum
  exanthematous reactions, 626–629
  fixed eruptions, 636–638
  graft-versus-host disease and, 254, 628
  granulomatous reactions, 643–645
  Henoch–Schönlein purpura, 717
  HIV infection, 988–989

hyperpigmentation, 638–647
  minocycline, 468, 638, *639*, 640, *641*
  ichthyosiform reactions, 652
  leukocytoclastic vasculitis, 711
  lichenoid reactions, 634–636
    oral, 434
  lichen planus *vs*, 226
  lipoatrophy, 377–384
  lupus erythematosus *see* Lupus erythematosus, drug-induced
  lymphomatous reactions, 1423–1424
  mycosis fungoides-like lesions, 1360
    see also Drug hypersensitivity syndrome
  pemphigoid, pseudo-ocular cicatricial pemphigoid, 118
  pemphigus, 155, 648–649
  photosensitive reactions *see* Photosensitivity, drug reactions
  pityriasiform reactions, 651
  pityriasis rosea, 191
  pseudolymphoma *see* Pseudolymphoma
  pseudolymphoma syndrome *see* Drug hypersensitivity
      syndrome
  pseudoporphyria, 587, 649
  psoriasiform reactions, 649–650
  psoriasis *vs*, 205
  purpuric reactions, 643
  pustular reactions, 651–652
  pyoderma gangrenosum, 674
  Stevens–Johnson syndrome *see* Stevens–Johnson syndrome
  Sweet's syndrome, 679
  systemic lupus erythematosus, 786, 788
  telogen effluvium, 1084
  toxic epidermal necrolysis, 242
    see also Toxic epidermal necrolysis
  transient acantholytic dermatosis, 164
  type A reactions, 624
  type B reactions, 624
  type C reactions, 624–625
  urticaria, 624, 625, 629, 694
  vasculitic reactions, 642–643
  vitiligo, 995
  see also specific substances
Dry leishmaniasis, 930
Ductal hidrocystoma, 1588
Duhring–Brocq disease *see* Dermatitis herpetiformis
Dunnigan variant familial partial lipodystrophy, 375
Dupuytren's contracture, 1720, 1724–1725
Dusty pigmentation, dysplastic nevus, 1288
Dutcher's bodies
  marginal zone B-cell lymphoma, 1430
  plasmacytoma, 1444
Dylon, amyloidosis, 553
Dysbetalipoproteinemia, familial, 547
Dyschromatosis symmetrica hereditaria, 1012
Dyshidrosiform dermatitis
  dyshidrosiform pemphigoid *vs*, 101
  see also Pompholyx
Dyshidrosiform pemphigoid, 101
Dyshidrotic eczema, 174–175
Dyskeratosis congenita, 249
  oral lesions, 389
Dysplastic cerebellar gangliocytoma, 1527
Dysplastic keratoses, PUVA therapy, 203–204
Dysplastic nevus, 1283–1290, *1291*
  banal nevi *vs*, 1258
  differential diagnosis, 1289
  grading, 1288
  lentiginous acral nevus *vs*, 1261
Dysplastic nevus syndrome, 1283–1290
Dystopia canthorum, 1003
Dystrophic calcinosis cutis, 595, 596–597, 598
Dystrophic epidermolysis bullosa, 84–85, 89–92, 96–97
  immunofluorescent antigen mapping, 92
  see also Recessive dystrophic epidermolysis bullosa
Dystrophic epidermolysis bullosa–inversa, 92
Dystrophic epidermolysis bullosa–minimus, 92
Dystrophic epidermolysis bullosa–pruriginosa, 92

E
Ear
  keratitis–ichthyosis–deafness syndrome, 72–73
  Pneumocystis jiroveci, AIDS, 991
Earlobe
  chondritis, 833, *834*
  chondrodermatitis nodularis chronica helicis, 338
  elastotic nodules, 1053
  epithelioid hemangioma, *1824*
  pseudocyst, 1682
  relapsing polychondritis, 834
  skin, 4
  squamous cell carcinoma, 1199, 1200
Early patch stage, Kaposi's sarcoma, 1831–1832, *1833*
EB *see* Epidermolysis bullosa
EBA antigen, 126
Eberhartinger and Niebauer variant (localized cutaneous
    non-scarring bullous pemphigoid), 101

Ebola hemorrhagic fever, 868, 869
Eburneous (sclerodermatous) metastasis, 1502–1503, *1507*
ECCR genes, xeroderma pigmentosum, 1229
Eccrine acrospiroma *see* Hidradenoma
Eccrine adenoma *see* Papillary eccrine adenoma
Eccrine angiomatous hamartoma, 1611–1613
Eccrine carcinoma, syringoid, 1645–1647
Eccrine centered nevus, 1260
Eccrine chondroid syringoma, 1604
Eccrine duct(s)
   actinic keratosis, 1188, *1189*, *1190*
   prominent involvement, transient acantholytic dermatosis, 195
Eccrine ductal carcinoma, 1657–1658
Eccrine epithelioma
   syringoma *vs*, 1627
   see also Syringoid eccrine carcinoma
Eccrine glands *see* Eccrine sweat glands
Eccrine hidradenitis *see* Neutrophil eccrine hidradenitis
Eccrine hidradenoma *see* Hidradenoma
Eccrine hidrocystoma, 1614–1615
   apocrine hidrocystoma *vs*, 1588
Eccrine nevus, 1609
   porokeratotic, cornoid lamellae, 77
Eccrine porocarcinoma, 1620–1625
   squamous cell carcinoma *vs*, 1208, 1624
   see also Chondroma
Eccrine poroma, 1617–1619
   trichilemmoma *vs*, 1530
Eccrine spiradenocarcinoma, 1642–1645
Eccrine spiradenoma, 1640–1642
   glomus tumor *vs*, 1851
   malignant change, 1643
Eccrine squamous syringometaplasia, 669
Eccrine sweat glands, 24–28
   chemotherapeutic agents, reactions, 667–669
   keratitis–ichthyosis–deafness syndrome, 72
   lichen planus poritis, 1090
   scleredema, 611
Eccrine syringofibroadenoma, 1610–1611
Eclabion, lamellar ichthyosis, *43*
Ecthyma, 869, 871, 872
Ecthyma contagiosum, 862–864
Ecthyma gangrenosum, 869–870, 871
Ectodermal dysplasia
   apocrine hidrocystoma, 1588
   hidrotic, 71
   keratitis–ichthyosis–deafness syndrome, 72
   multiple eccrine syringofibroadenoma with, 1610
   X-linked anhidrotic, 1566
   see also Palmoplantar ectodermal dysplasia
Ectodysplasin, 1566
Ectomesenchymal chondromyxoid tumor, 471–472
Ectopic geographic tongue *see* Geographic stomatitis
Ectopic hidradenoma papilliferum, 1592
Ectopic lingual thyroid *see* Lingual thyroid
Ectopic meningothelial hamartoma, 1788
Ectopic oral tonsils, 394
Ectopic sebaceous glands, 1565–1566
Ectropion, lamellar ichthyosis, 42
Eczema *see* Eczematous dermatitis
Eczema craquelé, 177
Eczema herpeticum, 851–852, *853*
   Darier's disease, 159
Eczematous dermatitis, 171–195
   chemotherapeutic agents, 666
   endogenous dermatitis, 172–175
   exogenous dermatitis, 172, 175–195
   genital region, 476
   pityriasis alba and, 1006
   pityriasis rosea *vs*, 191–192
Eczematous pustulosis, acute generalized, 651
Eczema vaccinatum, 852
   Darier's disease, 159
EDA gene, mutations, 1566
Ehlers–Danlos syndrome, 1023–1026
   isolated collagenoma with, 1038
   type VI, 30
   type VII, 30
Elafin, 11
Elastic microfibrils, 9, 31
Elastic tissue, 31
   diseases, 1038–1059
   elastofibroma, 1707–1708
   elastosis perforans serpiginosa, 333
   transepidermal elimination
      elastosis perforans serpiginosa, 333
      keratoacanthoma, 1224
      perforating pseudoxanthoma elasticum, 337
Elastic tissue nevus, 1050–1052
Elastin, 31
   elastosis perforans serpiginosa, 333
Elastoclasis, actinic granuloma, 313
Elastofibroma, 1707–1708
Elastolysis, generalized *see* Cutis laxa

Elastolytic granulomata, 312–317
Elastoma, 1050–1052
Elastorrhexis, 65
Elastosis
   amyloid, 559
   digital papular calcific, 64–65
   see also Collagenous and elastotic plaques of the hand
Elastosis perforans serpiginosa, *331*, 333–334
   Kyrle's disease *vs*, 334, 336
Elastotic hemangioma, acquired, 1822
Elastotic nodules of the ear, 1053
Elastotic striae (linear focal elastosis), 1049, 1053
Electromyography, dermatomyositis, 827
Electron microscopy, skin metastases, 1505
Elejalde syndrome, 1002
Elephantiasiform neurofibroma, 1776, *1778*
Elephantiasis, beryllium and zirconium, 325
EMA (epithelial membrane antigen), microcystic adnexal
   carcinoma, 1648
Embryonal rhabdomyosarcoma, 1804, *1805*
Emperipolesis, Rosai–Dorfman disease, 1480, *1481*, *1482*
Encephalocele, 1790, 1791
Encephalocraniocutaneous lipomatosis, 1691
Enchondroma, 1151
   subungual, 1152
   see also Chondroma
En coup de sabre, linear morphea, 817
Endarteritis, 33
Endemic Kaposi's sarcoma, 1830–1831
Endemic pemphigus foliaceus, 148
Endemic syphilis (bejel), 494, 891
Endemic treponematoses, 891–894
Endemic typhus fever, 928, 929
Endocarditis *see* Libman-Sacks endocarditis
Endochondral pseudocyst, 1682
Endogenous dermatitis, 172–175
Endoglin gene mutations, 1811–1812
Endometriosis, 516
Endomysial antibody, anti-smooth muscle, dermatitis
   herpetiformis, 132
Endosalpingiosis, 516
Endothelial leukocyte adhesion molecule-1 (ELAM-1),
   polymorphous light eruption, 272
Endothelin, systemic sclerosis, 809
Endothelium, 33
   angiokeratoma corporis diffusum, 552
   angiosarcoma, 1840, *1841*
   cavernous hemangioma, 1818–1819
   hobnail hemangioma, 1821, 1822
   hyperplasia, intravascular papillary, 1806–1807
   immunostains for, 35
   leprosy, 916
   malignant atrophic papulosis, 758
   retiform hemangioendothelioma, 1828
   rickettsial infections, 929
   systemic sclerosis, 808–809
Endothrix infections, 940
ENL (erythema nodosum leprosum), 911, *912*, 916, *917*, *918*
Entactin, 8
Entamoeba histolytica, 508
Enterovirus 71, hand, foot and mouth disease, 867
Entomophthoromycosis, 963–964
Environmental mycobacteria, 904–910
Envoplakin, 11
   paraneoplastic pemphigus, 153
Enzymes
   apocrine glands, 23
   cytochrome P-450, 624
   eccrine poroma, 1618, *1619*
   erysipelas, 875
   leukocytoclastic vasculitis, 713
   membrane-coating granules, 11
EORTC classification, lymphoma, 1358
Eosinophil(s)
   alopecia areata, 1076
   drug reactions *vs* exanthems, 628
   eosinophilic cellulitis, 698
   erythema elevatum diutinum *vs* granuloma faciale, 742
   granuloma annulare, 301
   lichenoid keratosis, 231
   linear IgA disease *vs* bullous pemphigoid, 136
   palisaded neutrophilic and granulomatous dermatitis, 321
   toxic erythema of the neonate, 214
   transient acantholytic dermatosis, 164
   traumatic ulcer
      vs Behçet's disease, 407
      vs Langerhans' cell histiocytosis, 409
   xanthogranuloma *vs* Langerhans' cell histiocytosis, 1471
Eosinophil granuloma (focal chronic Langerhans' cell
   histiocytosis), 1461, 1463, *1465*
Eosinophilia
   epithelioid hemangioma, 1823
   hypereosinophilic syndrome, 696

   see also Angiolymphoid hyperplasia with eosinophilia;
      Epithelioid hemangioma
Eosinophilia–myalgia syndrome, 824
Eosinophilic angiocentric fibrosis, 738
Eosinophilic cellulitis *see* Wells' syndrome
Eosinophilic fasciitis, 822–824
   Wells' syndrome *vs*, 699
Eosinophilic folliculitis, HIV-associated, 700, 988
   eosinophilic pustular folliculitis *vs*, 700, 701, 988
Eosinophilic hyaline globules, Kaposi's sarcoma, 1833, *1835*
Eosinophilic inclusions, inclusion body fibromatosis, 1719
Eosinophilic panniculitis, 370
Eosinophilic, polymorphic and pruritic eruption associated with
   radiotherapy, 285
Eosinophilic pustular folliculitis (Ofuji's disease), 700–702, *989*
   HIV-associated eosinophilic folliculitis *vs*, 700, 701, 988
   of infancy, 215
   transient neonatal pustular melanosis *vs*, 215
Eosinophilic spongiosis, 187–188
   bullous pemphigoid, *105*
   pemphigoid gestationis, 113
Eosinophilic ulcer/granuloma of the tongue, 407, 408–410
Eosinophil microabscesses
   bullous pemphigoid, 103, *105*
   pemphigus vegetans, 146
Eosinophil-rich variant, CD30+ large cell lymphoma, 1407
Eotaxin, incontinentia pigmenti, 703
Ephelides, 1241–1242
   oral melanotic macule *vs*, 468
Epidemic typhus fever, 928
Epidermal cyst *see* Epidermoid cyst
Epidermal dendritic cells, 13–18
Epidermal melanin unit, 15
Epidermal nevus, 1153–1156
   linear Darier's disease *vs*, 163
Epidermal nevus syndrome, 1154, 1568
Epidermal transglutaminases 1 and 3, 11
Epidermis, 1–28
   basal cells, 2, 3
Epidermodermal junction
   discoid lupus erythematosus, 792
   lupus band test, 791
   separation, cell-free epidermolysis bullosa acquisita, 127
Epidermodysplasia verruciformis, 847–850
   lesions like, immunosuppression, 839
   squamous cell carcinoma, 849, 1203
      HPV, 1204
Epidermoid cyst, 1664–1666
   human papilloma virus infection, 842
   oral, 392–393
   oral lymphoepithelial cyst *vs*, 394
   proliferating, 1666–1667
   of the sole, 1667
   see also Milia
Epidermolysis bullosa, 84–98
   aplasia cutis, 1027
   classifications, 84–85
   clinical features, 85–92
   dystrophic *see* Dystrophic epidermolysis bullosa
   hemidesmosomal, 85, 86–87, 95
   see also Junctional epidermolysis bullosa–non-Herlitz
   histology, 92–97
   with late-onset muscular dystrophy, 85, 86
   pathogenesis, 92–97
   with pyloric atresia *see* Pyloric atresia–junctional EB
      syndrome
   recessive dystrophic
      Hallopeau–Siemens variant dystrophic epidermolysis
         bullosa, 89, 90–91, 96, 97
      squamous cell carcinoma, 1204
   see also Junctional epidermolysis bullosa
Epidermolysis bullosa acquisita, 123–128
   bullous systemic lupus erythematosus *vs*, 128, 130
   cell-rich bullous pemphigoid *vs*, *109*
   drug-induced, 648
   immunoperoxidase antigen mapping, *83*
   oral lesions, 446–447
Epidermolysis bullosa atrophicans generalisata gravis, 88
Epidermolysis bullosa generalisata mitis *see* Junctional
   epidermolysis bullosa–non-Herlitz
Epidermolysis bullosa gravis (Hallopeau–Siemens variant
   dystrophic epidermolysis bullosa), 89, 90–91, 96, 97
Epidermolysis bullosa hereditaria letalis, 88
Epidermolysis bullosa mitis, 91
Epidermolysis bullosa simplex, 84–85, 85–87, 93–95
   immunofluorescent antigen mapping, 92
   Ogna variant, 85
Epidermolysis bullosa simplex herpetiformis, 86
   with mottled pigmentation and punctate keratoderma, 86
Epidermolysis bullosa simplex superficialis, 86, 94
Epidermolytic hyperkeratosis, *38*, 1155
   focal, 49–50
   see also Bullous ichthyosiform erythroderma

Epidermolytic palmoplantar keratoderma, 59–60
Epidermolytic (exfoliative) toxins, *Staphylococcus aureus*, 873, 874
Epidermophyton (spp.), 938
Epidermophyton floccosum, 944
Epidermotropic cytotoxic T-cell lymphoma, 1420–1421
Epidermotropic eccrine carcinoma, 1623
Epidermotropic metastatic melanoma, 1345–1346
Epidermotropic metastatic squamous cell carcinoma, 1506
Epidermotropism
    adenocarcinoma metastases, 1506
    mycosis fungoides, 1365–1366
    pagetoid reticulosis, 1394
Epignathus, 393–394
Epilepsy, tuberous sclerosis, 1031
Epiligrin *see* Laminin-5
Epiloia *see* Tuberous sclerosis
Epithelial dysplasia
    with lichenoid inflammatory infiltrate, 456
    oral, 452–457
    smokeless tobacco keratosis, 403
Epithelial hyperplasia, oral focal, 411, 432–433
Epithelial membrane antigen, microcystic adnexal carcinoma, 1648
Epithelial sheath neuroma, 1767
Epithelioid angiomatous nodule, cutaneous, 1822–1823
Epithelioid angiosarcoma, 1843–1845
    epithelioid sarcoma *vs*, 1862
Epithelioid blue nevus, 1303
    Carney complex, 1015, *1016*, 1303
    of genital skin, 514
Epithelioid cell(s)
    cutaneous metaplastic synovial cyst, 1679
    melanoma, 1319–1320
Epithelioid cell nevus
    pigmented, 1275
    see also Hyalinizing spindle and epithelioid cell nevus
Epithelioid cell Spitz nevus, 1270, *1272*
Epithelioid cell tumor, perivascular, 1858–1859
Epithelioid combined nevus, 1303
Epithelioid fibrous histiocytoma, 1748–1749
    desmoplastic nevus *vs*, 1277
Epithelioid glomus tumor, 1848, *1850*
Epithelioid hemangioendothelioma, 1837–1839
    epithelioid sarcoma *vs*, 1862
Epithelioid hemangioma, 1823–1826
    cutaneous epithelioid angiomatous nodule *vs*, 1822
    see also Angiolymphoid hyperplasia with eosinophilia
Epithelioid histiocytoma *see* Epithelioid fibrous histiocytoma
Epithelioid malignant nerve sheath tumor, 1793
    soft tissue melanoma *vs*, 1796
Epithelioid neurofibroma, 1774
Epithelioid sarcoma, 1859–1862
    granuloma annulare *vs*, 302, 1862
    rheumatoid nodules *vs*, 312, 1862
Epithelioid sarcoma-like hemangioendothelioma, 1837
Epithelioid schwannoma, 1771
Epithelioma adenoides cysticum, 1546, *1547*
Epithelioma cuniculatum, 1218
Epithelium
    anogenital region, lesions, 515–532
    oral mucosa, 386–387
Epithelium cuniculatum, 526
Eponychium, 1127–1128
EPPER (eosinophilic, polymorphic and pruritic eruption associated with radiotherapy), 285
Epstein–Barr virus
    hairy leukoplakia, 430, 431
    Lipschutz ulcer, 488
    lymphomatoid granulomatosis, 1438
    mycosis fungoides, 1365
    nasopharyngeal carcinoma *vs* lymphoepithelioma-like carcinoma of skin, 1239
Epulis, 417–418
    fibrous, 418
Epulis fissuratum, 417
    see also Denture-associated fibrous hyperplasia; Granuloma fissuratum
Equestrian cold panniculitis, 274, 275, 353–354
Equine melanoma *see* Animal-type melanoma
Equine melanotic disease, 1344
    see also Animal-type melanoma
Erosive adenomatosis (nipple adenoma), 1596
Erosive lichen planus
    genital, 480
    oral, 433
Eruptive blue nevus, 1301
Eruptive collagenoma, 1037–1038
    papular elastorrhexis *vs*, 1038, 1052
Eruptive histiocytoma, generalized, 1474–1475
Eruptive keratoacanthoma, 1222
Eruptive milia, 1669
Eruptive psoriasis *see* Guttate psoriasis

Eruptive syringoma, 1626
Eruptive vellus hair cysts, 1672
    pachyonychia congenita, 1573
Eruptive xanthomata, 542–544
    Rosai–Dorfman disease *vs*, 1480
Erysipelas, 874, 875–876
Erythema, UV radiation, reactivation by chemotherapeutic agents, 665
Erythema annulare centrifugum, 263–265
    tumid lupus erythematosus *vs*, 274
Erythema areata migrans, 400–403
Erythema chronicum migrans, 889, 890
Erythema circinata, 400–403
Erythema dyschromicum perstans, 234–236
Erythema elevatum diutinum, 740–743
    granuloma faciale *vs*, 740, 742
    Sweet's syndrome *vs*, 680
Erythema gyratum repens, 265–267
Erythema induratum, 366–369
    nodular vasculitis, 366–369
Erythema induratum (Bazin's disease), 366, 903
Erythema marginatum rheumaticum, 691
Erythema multiforme, 236, 237–240
    graft-versus-host disease *vs*, 254
    toxic epidermal necrolysis *vs*, 239, 243–244
    see also Lupus erythematosus–erythema multiforme-like syndrome; Rowell syndrome
Erythema multiforme major, 238
Erythema neonatorum *see* Toxic erythema, of the neonate
Erythema nodosum, 288, 343–348
    coccidioidomycosis, 959
    Sweet's syndrome, 679
Erythema nodosum leprosum (ENL), 911, *912*, 916, *917, 918*
Erythema nodosum-like lesions, Behçet's disease, 348
Erythema nodosum migrans, 343, 344, 345–347
Erythematous oral lichen planus, 433
Erythematous stage mycosis fungoides, 1360
Erythema toxicum *see* Toxic erythema
Erythema toxicum neonatorum *see* Toxic erythema, of the neonate
Erythrasma, 490–491, 924–925
Erythredema, 663
Erythrocytes *see* Red cell extravasation
Erythroderma, 188
    bullous ichthyosiform, 45–48
        mosaicism, 1155
    congenital ichthyosiform, *38*, 43–45
    drug reactions, 626, 627–628
    pityriasis rubra pilaris, 206, *207*
    psoriasis and, 198, *199*
    see also Psoriatic erythroderma
Erythrodermic cutaneous T-cell lymphoma, 1396
Erythrodermic cutaneous T-cell lymphoma not otherwise specified (NOS), 1396
Erythrodermic mycosis fungoides, 1396
Erythrodermic pemphigoid, 98, 99
Erythrokeratoderma progressiva symmetrica, 62
Erythrokeratoderma variabilis, 61–62
Erythroleukoplakia, 452
Erythromelalgia, 784
Erythronychia, 1136
Erythrophagocytosis, 355, 356
Erythroplakia, 453
Erythroplasia of Queyrat, 519, 1194
Erythropoietic porphyrias
    congenital erythropoietic porphyria, 575, 576–577
    erythropoietic protoporphyria, 575, 576, 577–581, 583, *584*
Erythropoietic protoporphyria, 575, 576, 577–581, 583, *584*
Esophagitis dissecans superficialis, 141
Esophagus
    carcinoma, Howell-Evans syndrome, 60, 67–68
    dermatomyositis, 826–827
    Hallopeau–Siemens variant dystrophic epidermolysis bullosa, 90, *91*
    junctional epidermolysis bullosa-Herlitz, 88
    lichen planus, 219, 225
    mucous membrane pemphigoid, 117
    systemic lupus erythematosus, 786
    systemic sclerosis, 805, 808, 813–814
    tumor metastases to skin, 1498
    vulvar leiomyomatosis, 537
Espundia, 931
Essential cryoglobulinemic vasculitis, *710*
    see also Cryoglobulinemia
Esthetic microimplants, foreign body granulomata, 325
17β-Estradiol, acne vulgaris, 1118
Estrogens
    erythrokeratoderma variabilis, 61
    pemphigoid gestationis, 111
Etoposide, starburst cells, 666
Eumelanin, 15
Ewing's sarcoma
    extraosseous, 1793–1795
    neuroendocrine carcinoma *vs, 1237*

Ewing's sarcoma oncogene fusions
    melanoma of soft tissues, 1795
    peripheral primitive neuroectodermal tumor, 1794
Exanthemata, viral infections, 285
Exanthematous drug reactions, 626–629
Exanthematous psoriasis, 198
Exanthematous pustulosis, acute generalized, 662, 663
Exanthem subitum, 860
Excision–repair defects, xeroderma pigmentosum, 1228–1229
Exclamation mark hairs, 1073–1074, *1075*
Exfoliative toxins (epidermolytic toxins), *Staphylococcus aureus*, 873, 874
Exocytosis, 178
    epidermotropism of T-cell lymphoma *vs*, 1366
    lichenoid keratosis, 230
    lichen striatus, *232*
    oral lymphoepithelial cyst, 394
    subacute cutaneous lupus erythematosus, 795–796
Exogenous dermatitis, 172, 175–195
Exogenous ochronosis, 592–594
    sarcoidosis *vs*, 295
Exophiala spp., 947
Exophila jeanselmei, 969–970
Exophytic elastoma, 1052
Exostosis
    cartilaginous
        osteoma cutis *vs*, 1853
        see also Osteochondroma
    subungual, 1150–1151
External auditory meatus, keratitis–ichthyosis–deafness syndrome, 72–73
External fibrous layer, anagen hair follicle, 1065
Extracellular polysaccharide substance, miliaria, 194
Extramedullary hematopoiesis, 1490–1491
    leukemia *vs*, 1489
Extramedullary hematopoietic tumor, 1490–1491
Extranodal NK/T-cell lymphoma, nasal/nasal type, 1418–1420
    see also Angiocentric lymphoma, T-cell
Extraocular sebaceous carcinoma, 1579–1580
Extraosseous Ewing's sarcoma, 1793–1795
Extrarenal rhabdoid tumor, 1864–1865
Extraskeletal mesenchymal chondrosarcoma, 1855, *1856*
Extraskeletal myxoid chondrosarcoma, 1854–1855
Extraskeletal osteosarcoma, 1853
Extravasation, chemotherapeutic agents, 666
Eye *see* Ocular involvement
Eyelid
    breast carcinoma metastases, 1506
    primary signet ring carcinoma, 1659
Eye-mask, neonatal lupus erythematosus, 786

F

Fabry's disease *see* Angiokeratoma corporis diffusum
FACE (facial Afro-Caribbean childhood eruption), 323
Facial hemiatrophy, linear morphea, 817
Facial idiopathic granulomata with regressive evolution (acne agminata), 322–323, 1123
Facial nerve palsy, orofacial granulomatosis, 440
Facies
    leonine, chronic actinic dermatitis, *1426*
    systemic sclerosis, 805
Factitial panniculitis, 351–353
Factor V Leiden mutation, 771
Factor XIIIA (FXIIIA), verruciform xanthoma, 550
Factor XIIIA positive cells, nephrogenic fibrosing dermopathy, 1034, *1036*
Falx cerebri, palmoplantar keratoderma with periodontopathia, 69
Familial adenomatous polyposis coli syndrome
    Torre–Muir syndrome *vs*, 1584
    see also Gardner's syndrome
Familial amyloidotic polyneuropathy, 559
Familial atypical multiple mole melanoma syndrome, 1283–1290
Familial cold autoinflammatory syndrome, 559, 693
Familial cold syndrome, 559, 693
Familial cold urticaria, 559, 693
Familial comedones, 1668
Familial cutaneous collagenoma, 1037
Familial cutis laxa variants, 1038–1039, 1040
Familial cylindromatosis *see* Brooke–Spiegler syndrome
Familial dysbetalipoproteinemia, 547
Familial dyskeratotic comedones, 168–169, 1668
    warty dyskeratoma *vs*, 167
Familial eosinophilic cellulitis, 697
Familial glomangioma, 1848
Familial Hibernian fever (TNF receptor-associated periodic syndrome), 285, 559
Familial lipodystrophy, 375–376
Familial Mediterranean fever, 559
Familial melanoma, 1310
Familial multiple trichoepithelioma, 1546, *1547*

Familial partial lipodystrophy
  associated with mandibuloacral dysplasia, 376
  Dunnigan variant, 375
  Köbberling variant, 376
Familial primary cutaneous amyloidosis, 564
Familial primary self-healing squamous epitheliomata of the
  skin, 1222, *1223*
Familial variants, pityriasis rubra pilaris, 208
Familial white folded dysplasia of mouth, 387–388
Family cancer syndrome, 1584
FAMMM syndrome (dysplastic nevus syndrome), 1283–1290
FAP *see* Familial adenomatous polyposis coli syndrome
FAPA syndrome, 407
Fasciitis ossificans, 1704
Fas-L, Langerhans' cell histiocytosis, 1465
Fat
  deposition in dermis, 1691, *1692*
  see also Subcutaneous fat
Fat necrosis, 341, 360
  α₁-antitrypsin deficiency-associated panniculitis, 349
  erythema induratum, 368
  lipophagic, 341, *342*
  membranous, 373–374
  metastatic, 358
    pancreatic disease, 357
  of the newborn, hypercalcemia, 359–360
  nodular cystic, 351, 352
  traumatic, 351, 352, *353*, *1685*
Fatty acid transport protein 4, mutation, 1036
Fatty infiltration, focal dermal hypoplasia syndrome, 1030
Favre-Racouchot syndrome
  cutaneous nodular elastoidosis with cysts and comedones,
    1053, 1057
  solar comedones, 1668
Favus, 941
FcεRI (IgE high-affinity receptor), antibody *vs*, 695
Febrile ulceronecrotic Mucha–Haberman disease, 255, 257, 258
Female androgenetic alopecia, 1069, 1070
Female pattern androgenetic alopecia, 1069, *1070*
Fergusson-Smith syndrome, 1222, *1223*
Ferritin, hair diseases, 1062
Ferrochelatase gene, 577
Festooning
  bullous pemphigoid, 103, *104*
  pseudoporphyria, 588
Fetal rhabdomyoma, 1803, *1804*
Fetus
  ichthyosis fetalis, 50–51
  pemphigoid gestationis and, 112
Fibrillarin, antibodies, systemic sclerosis, *810*
Fibrillary component, amyloid, 554
Fibrillar zone, 8–9
Fibrillin(s), 31
  systemic sclerosis, 810
Fibrillin-1, 1048
Fibrin, thrombotic thrombocytopenic purpura, 769
Fibrinoid necrosis
  discoid lupus erythematosus, 794, *795*
  systemic sclerosis, kidney, 813
Fibroblast(s)
  cultures, DNA repair study, 1229
  inflammatory myofibroblastic tumor, 1736
  juvenile hyalin fibromatosis, 397
  keratinocytes and, keloid, 1701
  mucinoses, 601
  radiation damage, 1055
Fibroblast growth factor receptor, gene mutation, acanthosis
  nigricans, 615
Fibroblastoma
  desmoplastic, 1717
  see also Giant cell fibroblastoma
Fibroelastolytic papulosis of the neck, 1037
  see also Pseudoxanthoma elasticum-like papillary dermal
    elastolysis
Fibroepithelial polyp, 1708–1709
  see also Acrochordon; Skin tag
Fibroepithelial stromal polyp, 532–533
Fibroepithelioma of Pinkus, 1186–1187
Fibrofolliculoma, 1560–1561
  hair follicle nevus *vs*, 1519
  mantleoma *vs*, 1586
Fibrohistiocytic lipoma, 1695
Fibrohistiocytic tumors, 1741–1760
Fibrokeratoma
  acquired digital, 1721
  subungual, 1146–1147
Fibrolipoma, *1685*, 1692
  oral, 413
Fibrolipomatous hamartoma of nerve, 1693
Fibroma
  calcifying aponeurotic, 1719–1720
  collagenous, 1717
  garlic clove, 1146–1147

giant cell, 414–415
gingival, 418
oral, 413–414, 418
perifollicular, 1559–1560
periungual, 1147
  acquired digital fibrokeratoma *vs*, 1721
pleomorphic, 1709, *1710*
sclerotic *see* Storiform collagenoma
soft *see* Fibroepithelial polyp
subungual, 1147
of tendon sheath, 1716–1717
  desmoplastic fibroblastoma *vs*, 1717
  giant cell tumor *vs*, 1753
  storiform collagenoma *vs*, 1711
trichoblastic, 1552, 1553–1554
  plaque variant, 1553
see also Nuchal fibroma
Fibromatosis
congenital generalized, 1714
desmoplastic fibroblastoma *vs*, 1717
gingival, 396–397
inclusion body, 1718–1719
infantile, 1726
infantile digital, 1718–1719
juvenile hyaline, 397–398, 1722–1723
palmar, 1720, 1724–1725
penile, 1725–1726
plantar, 1725
plexiform fibrous histiocytoma *vs*, 1755–1757
see also Desmoid fibromatosis
Fibromatosis colli, 1713
Fibromyxoid sarcoma, low grade, 1740, *1741*
Fibromyxoid stroma, trichoblastoma, 1554
Fibromyxoid tumor, ossifying, 1857–1858
Fibromyxoma, superficial acral, 1718
Fibro-osseous pseudotumor or florid reactive periostitis, 1704
Fibrosarcoma
adult variant, 1738
desmoid fibromatosis *vs*, 1726
infantile variant, 1738–1739
malignant peripheral nerve sheath tumor *vs*, 1793
Fibrosarcomatous dermatofibrosarcoma protuberans,
  1729–1730, 1732–1733
Fibrosing alopecia in a pattern distribution, 1090
Fibrosis
eosinophilic angiocentric, 738
penile fibromatosis, 1725–1726
submucous, 458–459
systemic sclerosis, 810
Fibrous dysplasia, polyostotic, 1008–1009
Fibrous epulis, 418
Fibrous hamartoma of infancy, 1721–1722, 1728
  plexiform fibrous histiocytoma *vs*, 1757
Fibrous histiocytoma, 545
aneurysmal, 1747–1748
  Kaposi's sarcoma *vs*, 1834
angiomatoid, 1754–1755
  aneurysmal fibrous histiocytoma *vs*, 1748
atypical, 1749–1750, 1759
cellular, 1746–1747
  dermatofibrosarcoma with myoid nodules *vs*, 1734
clear cell, 1751
dermatofibrosarcoma with myoid nodules *vs*, 1734
epithelioid, 1748–1749
  desmoplastic nevus *vs*, 1277
hypopigmented common blue nevus *vs*, 1302
intradermal fasciitis *vs*, 1705
lipidized, 545, 1750–1751
malignant *see* Malignant fibrous histiocytoma
myofibroma *vs*, 1715
palisading cutaneous, 1751
plexiform, 1755–1757
reticulohistiocytoma *vs*, 1483
solitary fibrous tumor *vs*, 1738
storiform collagenoma *vs*, 1711
see also Dermatofibroma
Fibrous hyperplasia, gingival, 418
Fibrous nodule, gingival, 418
Fibrous papule, 1741
Fibrovascular polyp
gingival fibrous nodule, 418
see also Fibroma
Fibroxanthoma *see* Atypical fibroxanthoma; Clear cell atypical
  fibroxanthoma
Figurate papulosquamous vitiligo, 994
FIGURE (facial idiopathic granulomata with regressive
  evolution) *see* Acne agminata
Filaggrin, 12
Filgrastim, 669, 670
Filiform palmoplantar keratoderma, 68–69
Finasteride, androgenetic alopecia, 1070
Fine needle aspiration cytology, skin metastases, 1505–1506
Fingers, systemic sclerosis, 804, 805, 808

Fingertip, skin, 6
Fish tank granuloma, 904, *905*
5α-reductase type-2
  acne vulgaris, 1118
  androgenetic alopecia, 1070
Fixed drug eruptions, 636–638
Fixed solar urticaria, 693
Flagellate streaks, 664
Flag sign, methotrexate, 665
Flaky tail mice, 39
Flame figures
  eosinophilic panniculitis, 370
  Wells' syndrome, 698, 699
Flat atypical target lesions, 236
Flat seborrheic keratosis, *1162*
Fleas (tungiasis), 981, *982*
Flegel's disease *see* Hyperkeratosis lenticularis perstans
Flexural dermatitis, 172–173
Flexural nevus, atypical, 512
FLI-1 protein, peripheral primitive neuroectodermal tumor,
  1794
Floret giant cells, 1689, *1690*
  giant cell fibroblastoma, 1728
Florid cutaneous papillomatosis, 616, 617
Florid papillomatosis (nipple adenoma), 1596
Fluorescence
  erythrasma, 491, 924, *925*
  Microsporon spp., 938, *939*
  porphyrias, 577
  tinea versicolor, 946
  trichomycosis, 925
  Trichophyton schoenleinii, 941
5-Fluorouracil, 664
Focal acantholytic dyskeratosis, 170, 1155
Focal acral kyperkeratosis, 64–65
Focal chronic Langerhans' cell histiocytosis, 1461, 1463, *1465*
Focal dermal hypoplasia, 1692
Focal dermal hypoplasia syndrome, 1028–1030
  apocrine hidrocystomas, 1588
  apocrine nevus, 1587
Focal elastosis, linear, 1049, 1053
Focal epidermolytic hyperkeratosis, 49–50
Focal epithelial hyperplasia, oral, 411, 432–433
Focal non-epidermolytic palmoplantar keratoderma with
  esophageal squamous cell carcinoma (Howell-Evans
  syndrome), 60, 67–68
Focal palmoplantar keratoderma with oral hyperkeratosis,
  66–67
Fogo selvagem, 148
Follicular atrophoderma, 1186
Follicular colonization, marginal zone B-cell lymphoma, 1428
Follicular cyst, 1663–1674
Follicular decalvans, 1099–1103
Follicular degeneration syndrome, 1099–1103
Follicular dendritic cells, histiocytic disorders, 1457
Follicular dendritic cell sarcoma, 1485–1486
Follicular dendritic cell tumor/sarcoma, 1484–1487
Follicular differentiation, mixed tumor of skin, 1602
Follicular hamartoma, basaloid, 1522–1524
  see also Infundibulocystic basal cell carcinoma
Follicular hyperkeratosis *see* Keratosis pilaris
Follicular ichthyosis, 54–55
  with alopecia and photophobia, 56
Follicular infundibulum tumor, 1525–1526
  superficial epithelioma with sebaceous differentiation *vs*, 1578
Follicular keratosis
  inverted, 1159–1160
    see also Irritated seborrheic keratosis
  see also Darier's disease
Follicular lymphoma, primary cutaneous, 1432–1434
  grades 1 to 3, 1432
  primary cutaneous marginal zone B-cell lymphoma *vs*, 1431
Follicular lymphomatoid papulosis, folliculotropic mycosis
  fungoides *vs*, 1386
Follicular mantle, 1586
Follicular mucinosis, 1387–1390
Follicular mycosis fungoides, 1390
  see also Folliculotropic mycosis fungoides
Follicular occlusion triad, 706–707, 1097
Follicular ostium, 1064
Follicular stella (follicular streamer), 1066, *1068*
  androgenetic alopecia, 1070, *1071*
Follicular units, 1063
  counts by race, *1068*
Folliculin, 1561
Folliculitis
  bacterial
    AIDS, 989
    Gram-negative, 1125
  dissecting *see* Dissecting folliculitis of the scalp
  eosinophilic *see* Eosinophilic folliculitis; Eosinophilic pustular
    folliculitis
  Gram-negative, 1125–1126

Folliculitis (*cont'd*)
  infective, 878–880
    eosinophilic folliculitis *vs*, 988
  perforating *see* Perforating folliculitis
  pseudolymphomatous, 1386–1387
  sterile neutrophilic, 479, 684
  tufted *see* Tufted folliculitis
Folliculitis barbae *see* Sycosis
Folliculitis capitis abscedens et suffodiens, 706
Folliculitis decalvans, 879, *880*
  pustules, 1099, *1100*
Folliculitis keloidalis nuchae, 880
  see also Acne keloidalis nuchae
Folliculitis ulerythema reticulata, 57, 58
Folliculitis ulerythematosa, 57, 58
Folliculocentric basaloid proliferation, 1586
Folliculosebaceous–apocrine unit, apocrine poroma, 1596
Folliculosebaceous cystic hamartoma, 1542, 1543–1545
Folliculotropic metastases, 1506
Folliculotropic mycosis fungoides, 1384–1386
  see also Follicular mycosis fungoides
Fonsecaea pedrosoi, 966
'Footprints in the snow', 1093–1094
Fordyce, angiokeratoma of, 1812
Fordyce granules, 391
Fordyce papules, sebaceous adenoma with, 1574
Fordyce spots, 474, 475, 1565
Forearm, skin, 2
Foreign body gingivitis, 405
Foreign body granulomata, 324–326
Foreign body reaction
  chondrodermatitis nodularis chronica helicis, 338
  epidermoid cyst, 1664, *1665*
Foster staging system, ocular pemphigoid, 118
Fournier's gangrene, 876
Fox–Fordyce disease, 194–195, 706–707
Frambesiform syphilids, 494
Framboesia tropica (yaws), 892–894
Francisella tularensis, 927, 928
Freckles *see* Ephelides
Freudenthal funnel, actinic keratosis, 1188
Friction amyloidosis, 561
Frontal fibrosing alopecia, postmenopausal, 1091
Frontoparietal linear morphea, 817
Frozen section
  necrotizing fasciitis, 877
  staphylococcal scalded skin syndrome, 874
Fucosidosis, diffuse angiokeratomata, 552
Fumarate hydratase deficiency, 1797
Functional cells, epidermis, 2
Functional longitudinal melanonychia, 1137
Fungal infections, 938–979
  AIDS, 990
  diffuse palmoplantar keratoderma, 61
  eczematous dermatitis *vs*, 180
  HIV-associated eosinophilic folliculitis, 700
  nails *see* Onychomycosis
  oral, Wegener's granulomatosis *vs*, 443
  pityriasis rotunda *vs*, 54
  Reiter's syndrome *vs*, 479
  see also Malassezia globosa; *specific fungi*
Furanocoumarins, phytophotodermatitis, 631
Furosemide, bullous pemphigoid, 648
Furuncles, 879–880
Fusarium spp., 951, 952, *954*

G

GABEB (generalized atrophic benign epidermolysis bullosa) *see*
  Junctional epidermolysis bullosa–non-Herlitz
Galli-Galli disease, 1009
Gamma-delta cells, recurrent aphthous stomatitis, 407
Gamma-delta T-cell lymphoma, 1422–1423
Ganglion cell choristoma, cutaneous, 1765
Ganglion cyst, acral myxoinflammatory fibroblastic sarcoma,
  1735
Ganglioneuroma, cutaneous, 1765
Ganglion-like giant cells
  ischemic fasciitis, 1707
  proliferative fasciitis, 1705
Gangosa, 892
Gardner fibroma, 1712–1713
Gardner's syndrome, 1664
  cysts, 1667
  desmoid fibromatosis, 1726
  pilomatrixoma, 1536
  see also Familial adenomatous polyposis coli syndrome
Garlic clove fibroma, 1146–1147
Gastric autoimmune disease, dermatitis herpetiformis, 131
Gastrointestinal choristoma, 391–392
Gastrointestinal tract
  Behçet's disease, 745
  Ehlers–Danlos syndrome, 1023
  Henoch–Schönlein purpura, 717

malignant atrophic papulosis, 757
  Peutz–Jeghers syndrome, 1012, 1013
  polyarteritis nodosa, 721
  pseudoxanthoma elasticum, 1041
  systemic sclerosis, 808
GB3 (monoclonal antibody), epidermolysis bullosa, 93
GCDPF-15, hidradenoma, 1631
G-CSF (granulocyte colony-stimulating factor), 669, 670
Gelatinous reaction, cryptococcosis, 961
Generalized adult acquired cutis laxa, 1039
Generalized atrophic benign epidermolysis bullosa, 85, 86
  see also Junctional epidermolysis bullosa–non-Herlitz
Generalized basaloid follicular hamartoma, 1522
Generalized cutaneous pemphigoid, 98–100
Generalized eczematous pustulosis, acute, 651
Generalized elastolysis *see* Cutis laxa
Generalized eruptive histiocytoma, 1474–1475
Generalized essential telangiectasia, 1812
Generalized exanthematous pustulosis, acute, 662, 663
Generalized fibromatosis, congenital, 1714
Generalized gingival hyperplasia, 426–428
Generalized granuloma annulare, 298
Generalized Langerhans' cell histiocytosis, acute, 1458–1459,
  1460, *1461*–1462, *1463*, *1464*, *1465*, *1466*
Generalized lentigines, 1242
Generalized lipodystrophy
  acquired, *375*, 376
    see also Lipoatrophic panniculitis
  congenital, 375
Generalized melanosis associated with metastatic melanoma,
  1020–1021
Generalized morphea, 818
Generalized myxedema, 602–603
Generalized non-Herlitz junctional epidermolysis bullosa *see*
  Junctional epidermolysis bullosa–non-Herlitz
Generalized plane xanthomatosis, 547
Generalized pustular psoriasis, 195–197, 202–203
Genetic damage, UV radiation, 1202–1203
Genital anatomy, 473–475
Genital leiomyoma, 536, 1799
Genital lesions, 475–538
  Behçet's disease, 744, *745*
  Fournier's gangrene, 876
  HIV infection, 990
  lichen planus, 219, *220*
  mucous membrane pemphigoid, 118, 119
  pemphigus vulgaris, 141–142
  verrucous carcinoma, 1218, 1219
  see also Acantholytic dermatoses, of genitocrural area
Genital lichen planus, 480–482
Genital melanosis, 511–512
Genital melanotic macules, 511
Genital melanotic nevus, 512–514
Genital papular acantholytic dyskeratosis, 488
Genital region *see* Anogenital region
Genital ulcer disease, 504–505
Genitoperineal raphe cyst (median raphe cyst), 516–517, 1677,
  1678
Geographic stomatitis, 400–403
Geographic tongue (benign migratory glossitis), 400–403
Ghost cells, pilomatrixoma, 1537
Ghost cell tumor, odontogenic, 424
Gianotti–Crosti syndrome
  cytomegalovirus, 859
  see also Papular acrodermatitis of childhood
Giant basal cell carcinoma, 1171–1172
Giant cell(s)
  ganglion-like
    ischemic fasciitis, 1707
    proliferative fasciitis, 1705
  giant cell fibroblastoma, 1728
  Langhans giant cells, 899
  necrobiotic xanthogranuloma, 319–320
  wreath-like, alveolar rhabdomyosarcoma, 1804
  see also Floret giant cells; Osteoclast-like giant cells; Touton
    giant cells
Giant cell angioblastoma, 1836
Giant cell angiofibroma, 1718
Giant cell arteritis
  temporal arteritis, 710, 748–751
  see also Takayasu's arteritis
Giant cell basal cell carcinoma, 1176–1177, *1179*
Giant cell collagenoma, 1711
Giant cell fibroblastoma, 1727–1729
  dermatofibrosarcoma protuberans and, 1728, 1730
Giant cell fibroma, 414–415
Giant cell granuloma, peripheral, 421–422
  oral, 418
Giant cell malignant fibrous histiocytoma, 1761
Giant cell melanoma, 1320, *1321*
Giant cell tumor of soft tissue, 1754, 1761
Giant cell tumor of tendon sheath, 1752–1754
  acral myxoinflammatory fibroblastic sarcoma, 1735

Giant condyloma acuminatum, 494
Giant condyloma of Buschke–Löwenstein, 526
Giant congenital nevus, 1292
  melanoma from, 1309, 1353
Giant hairy 'bathing-trunk' nevus, 1294–1296
Giant keratoacanthoma, 1221
Giant melanosomes (macromelanosomes), 16, 1001, 1242,
  1244
Giant pilomatrixoma, 1536
Giant rosettes, hyalinizing spindle cell tumor with, 1740, *1741*
Giant solitary/senile sebaceous hyperplasia, 1566
Giant solitary trichoepithelioma, 1553
Giant xanthogranuloma, 1469
Gingival cyst(s), epidermoid cysts *vs*, 392
Gingival cyst of the adult, 425–426
Gingival epithelial hamartoma, odontogenic, 423
  see also Peripheral odontogenic fibroma
Gingival fibroma, 418
Gingival fibromatosis, 396–397
Gingival fibrous hyperplasia, 418
Gingival fibrous nodule, 418
Gingival fibrovascular polyp, 418
Gingival granular cell tumor of neonate, 1781–1782
Gingival hyperplasia, ligneous, 427, *428*
Gingival inflammatory fibrous hyperplasia, 418
Gingival lesions
  benign alveolar ridge keratosis, 457–458
  foreign body gingivitis, 405
  generalized gingival hyperplasia, 426–428
  giant cell fibroma, 414–415
  parulides, 422
    mucoceles *vs*, 448
  peripheral odontogenic fibroma, 422–425
  verruciform xanthoma, 549
  vulvovaginal gingival syndrome, 219, 434, 480, *481*, *482*
  Wegener's granulomatosis, 442
  see also Plasma cell gingivitis; Pyogenic granuloma
Gingival lipoid proteinosis, 427
Gingival nodules, 417–418
Gingivitis
  foreign bodies, 405
  palmoplantar keratoderma with periodontopathia, 69
  strawberry gingivitis, 442
  see also Desquamative gingivitis; Plasma cell gingivitis
Glabrous skin, 1
Glands of Zeis, 20, 1579
Glandular cysts, 1674–1678
  classification, *1663*
Glandular differentiation, adenosquamous carcinoma, 1217
Glans clitoris/glans penis, 474
Glass blowers, oral lesions, 399
Gliadin, dermatitis herpetiformis, 132
Glial heterotopias, 1789–1791
Globi, leprosy bacilli, 914, *915*
Glomangioma, 1848–1849, *1850*
  familial, 1848
Glomangiomatosis, 1850
Glomangiomyoma, 1850
Glomangiopericytoma, 1852
Glomeruloid hemangioma, 1808
Glomerulonephritis, systemic lupus erythematosus, 797–798
Glomulin gene mutations, 1848
Glomus bodies, 34
Glomus cells, 1149, 1848, 1850
Glomus tumor, 1848–1851
  nail region, 1148–1150
  of uncertain malignant potential, 1851
Glucagonoma syndrome, 619
Glucocorticoid-related cutaneous atrophy, 1054
GLUT-1, infantile hemangioendothelioma, 1813
Gluten-sensitive enteropathy *see* Celiac disease
L-Glyceric aciduria, 362
Glycogen
  clear cell acanthoma, 1166
  clear cell hidradenocarcinoma, *1635*
  dermal duct tumor, 1619
  myocardial rhabdomyoma, 1032
  nevus sebaceus, 1569
  see also entries beginning Clear cell...
Glycoproteins, herpes simplex virus, 852–853
Glycosaminoglycans, 32, 600
  dermatomyositis, 829
  discoid lupus erythematosus, 794
  systemic sclerosis, 810
GM-CSF *see* Granulocyte–macrophage colony-stimulating
  factor
Gold, 661
Golf-tee hair, 1107
Goltz syndrome *see* Focal dermal hypoplasia syndrome
Gonorrhea, 881
Gorlin–Goltz syndrome *see* Nevoid basal cell carcinoma
  syndrome
Goserelin, relapsing polychondritis, 834

Gottron's papules, 825, *827*, 829, *830*
Gottron's sign, 825, *827*
Gougerot–Blum variant, pigmented purpuric lichenoid
  dermatitis, 277
Gout, 590–592
Gouty panniculitis, 366
Graft-versus-host disease, 250–255
  acute, 250–251, 253–254
  chronic, 251, 253
    oral lesions, 434
  drug reactions *vs*, 254, 628
  morphea *vs*, 820
  radiation exposure *vs*, 1058
  stages I-IV, 251
  toxic epidermal necrolysis, 242, 250, 254
Graham Little syndrome, 1090
Grains of Darier, 161
Gram-negative folliculitis, 1125–1126
Granular cell basal cell carcinoma, 1178, *1180*
Granular cell epulis/tumor, congenital, 395–396, 417
Granular cell myoblastoma *see* Granular cell tumor
Granular cell neurofibroma, 1774
Granular cell tumor, 1779–1781
  congenital granular cell epulis *vs*, 395
  gingival, neonate, 1781–1782
  hibernoma *vs*, 1695
  oral, 470–471
  primitive polypoid, 470–471, 1782
  verruciform xanthoma *vs*, 550
Granular layer, epidermis, 3, *11*
Granular parakeratosis, 79–80
Granulocyte colony-stimulating factor, 669, 670
Granulocyte–macrophage colony-stimulating factor (GM-CSF),
  669–670
  atopic dermatitis, 173
Granulocytic sarcoma/myeloid sarcoma, 1488
Granuloma
  actinic, *304*, 312, 313–314, 1053
    atypical facial necrobiosis lipoidica *vs*, 315
  aluminum, 327–328
  atypical histiocytic, traumatic ulcerative granuloma *vs*, 409
  congenital immunodeficiency syndromes, 326–327
  elastolytic, 312–317
  epithelioid sarcoma *vs*, 1860
  fish tank, 904, *905*
  foreign body, 324–326
  infantile gluteal, 476
  infective, 324
  injection-site, epithelioid hemangioma *vs*, 1825
  Majocchi's, 938
    see also Nodular granulomatous perifolliculitis
  mercury, 662, 663
  Miescher's, 345
    see also Sarcoidal variant, necrobiosis lipoidica
  peripheral giant cell, 421–422
    oral, 418
  plasma cell *see* Plasma cell granuloma
  pyogenic *see* Pyogenic granuloma
  sarcoidal 'naked', 324–325, 901
  sarcoidosis, 293–295
  traumatic ulcerative, 407, 408–410
  umbilicus, 1681–1682
Granuloma annulare, 297–305
  actinic granuloma *vs*, 314
  deep
    rheumatoid nodules *vs*, 311–312
    see also Subcutaneous granuloma annulare
  epithelioid sarcoma *vs*, 302, 1862
  granulomatous drug reactions *vs*, 645
Granuloma faciale, 738–739
  erythema elevatum diutinum *vs*, 740, 742
  Sweet's syndrome *vs*, 680
Granuloma fissuratum, 1157
  see also Epulis fissuratum
Granuloma gravidarum, 419, 1816
Granuloma inguinale, 502–504
Granuloma multiforme, *304*, 316–317
Granulomatous cheilitis
  metastatic Crohn's disease *vs*, 322
  orofacial granulomatosis, 440–441
Granulomatous drug reactions, 643–645
Granulomatous mycosis fungoides, 1380–1381
  granulomatous slack skin *vs*, 1381, 1383
Granulomatous pigmented purpuric dermatoses, 278
Granulomatous rosacea, 1121, 1122
Granulomatous slack skin, 1381–1383
  granulomatous mycosis fungoides *vs*, 1381, 1383
Granulomatous vasculitis
  differential diagnosis, 731
  drugs causing, 642
Graphite, tattoo, 466
Graves' disease, 603, 604
Gravis variant *see* Junctional epidermolysis bullosa-Herlitz

Grease gun injury, 351
Green algae, *Prototheca* spp. *vs*, 936
Grenz rays, 1055, 1203
Grenz zones, granuloma faciale, 739, 740
Grinspan's syndrome, 434
Griscelli syndrome, 1001–1002
Grönblad–Strandberg syndrome *see* Pseudoxanthoma elasticum
Gross cystic disease fluid protein-15, Paget's disease, 1505
Ground substance, 32
Grover's disease *see* Transient acantholytic dermatosis
Grzybowski syndrome, 1222
GTP-binding protein, 1001
Guarnieri's bodies, 862
Guinea pig esophagus, indirect immunofluorescence, 436–437
Gum-boil *see* Parulis
Gumma
  syphilis, 497, *499*, 501
  tuberculosis, 896, 899, 900, *901*
  yaws, 892, 894
Gunther's disease, 575, 576–577
Guttate hypomelanosis
  idiopathic, 998
  vitiligo *vs*, 996
Guttate morphea, 818, 819
  lichen sclerosus and, 818, 820
Guttate parapsoriasis, 255
Guttate psoriasis, 195, *197*, 202
  pityriasis rosea *vs*, 191
GVHD *see* Graft-versus-host disease
Gyrate erythema *see* Toxic erythema

H

Haarscheibe *see* Hair discs
Haber's syndrome, 1009
Haemophilus ducreyi, 504, *505*
Hailey–Hailey disease, 139, 156–158
  acrokeratosis verruciformis of Hopf, 74
  Darier's disease *vs*, 156, 157, 158, 162
  pemphigus *vs*, 143, 144, 158
  transient acantholytic dermatosis *vs*, 165
Hailey–Hailey-like epidermal nevus, 158
Hair, 1061–1126
  acquired progressive kinking, 1115, 1520
  biopsy report, 1066, *1067*
  growth cycle, 1065–1066
  tinea capitis, 938–941
  trichomycosis, 925
  see also Alopecia
HAIR-AN syndrome, 616
Hair-bearing skin, 1
Hair bulge, 1064
Hair casts, 1116
Hair discs, 35
  trichodiscoma, 1561
Hair-dryer effect, lymphangiomatosis, 1848
Hair follicle(s), 1061
  absence
    discoid lupus erythematosus, 794, *795*
    nevus sebaceus, 1569
  acne agminata, 322
  anatomy, 1062–1068
  eosinophilic pustular folliculitis, 701
  hair growth cycle, 1065–1066, *1067*, *1068*
  herpes simplex virus infection, 853
  hidradenitis suppurativa, 707
  human papilloma virus infection, 840
  lentigo maligna involvement, 1314, *1315*
  mantles, 1586
  nerve supply, 35
  perforating folliculitis, 332
  trichotillomania, 1081
  tumors, 1519–1563
  see also entries beginning Follicul-
Hair follicle nevus, 1519–1520
Hair-growth window technique, 1080–1081
Hair nevus, 1519
Hair-pluck test, 1062
Hair-pull test, 1062
Hair shaft diseases, 1103–1116
  foreign body granulomata, *326*
Hairy cell leukemia, vasculitis, 755
Hairy leukoplakia, 430–431
  AIDS, 991
  chronic bite injury *vs*, 399, 431
  leukoedema *vs*, 399
Hairy pacinian neurofibromas, multiple, 1765
Hallopeau–Besnier variant, mycosis fungoides, 1360
Hallopeau's acrodermatitis continua, 199
  nails, 1132, 1133
Hallopeau–Siemens variant, dystrophic epidermolysis bullosa,
  89, 90–91, 96, 97
Hallopeau variant, pemphigus vegetans, 146
Halogen acne *see* Chloracne

Halogenoderma, pemphigus vegetans *vs*, 147
Halo nevus, 1266–1268
  Spitz nevus with, 1271
Hamartoma
  apocrine, 1587
  basaloid follicular, 1522–1524
    see also Infundibulocystic basal cell carcinoma
  congenital neurovascular, 1765
  connective tissue, 1764–1765
  dartos muscle, 536, 1799
  dermal melanocytic, 1299
  eccrine angiomatous, 1611–1613
  ectopic meningothelial, 1788
  folliculosebaceous cystic, 1542, 1543–1545
  hair follicle nevus, 1519–1520
  neurocristic, 1303–1304
    bathing-trunk nevus as, 1295
  neurofollicular, 1562–1563
  odontogenic gingival epithelial, 423
    see also Peripheral odontogenic fibroma
  rhabdomyomatous mesenchymal, 1802–1803
  sclerosing epithelial *see* Desmoplastic trichoepithelioma
  sebaceous trichofolliculoma, 1545–1546
  smooth muscle, 1796–1802
    congenital, 1796–1797
  trichoepithelioma, 1546–1550
  trichofolliculoma, 1542–1543
  see also Cowden's syndrome; Fibrous hamartoma of infancy;
    Trichodiscoma
Hamartomatous apocrine gland hyperplasia, 1587
Hamilton's 'male pattern', 1069, *1070*
Hand eczema, 174–175
Hand, foot and mouth disease, 867–868
Hand–foot syndrome, 667
Hand–Schüller–Christian disease, 1460–1461, 1462–1463
Hanging groin, onchocerciasis, *983*
Hantaan, 868
Hantavirus infections, 868
Harderoporphyria, 579
Harlequin fetus, 50–51
Harlequin ichthyosis, 50–51
Hartnup disease, 594
Hashimoto–Pritzker disease, 1467–1468
Hashimoto's thyroiditis, reticular erythematous mucinosis, 269
Hautaurosis, 661
Haxthausen's disease, 65–66
Heart
  angiokeratoma corporis diffusum, 551
  Churg–Strauss syndrome, 732
  Lyme disease, 890
  mucocutaneous lymph node syndrome, 736
  Naxos disease, 1114
  neonatal lupus erythematosus, 800
  polyarteritis nodosa, 721
  pseudoxanthoma elasticum, 1041
  relapsing polychondritis, 834
  sarcoidosis, 292
  systemic lupus erythematosus, 798–799
  systemic sclerosis, 807, 814
  tuberous sclerosis, 1032
  see also Atrial myxoma
Heat intolerance, Naegele–Franchescetti–Jadassohn syndrome,
  1010
Heat shock proteins, Behçet's disease, 745
Heck's disease (focal epithelial hyperplasia), oral, 411,
  432–433
Heel, piezogenic pedal papules, 1692
Heerfordt's syndrome (uveoparotid fever), 292
Helicases, DNA, 247
Heliotrope erythema, 825
Helper T-cells, HIV infection, 986
Hemangioblastoma *see* Angiosarcoma
Hemangioendothelioma
  composite, 1836
  epithelioid, 1837–1839
    epithelioid sarcoma *vs*, 1862
  infantile, 1813–1814
  retiform, 1828–1829
    hobnail hemangioma *vs*, 1822
  see also Kaposiform hemangioendothelioma
Hemangioma
  cavernous, 1818–1819
  epithelioid, 1823–1826
    cutaneous epithelioid angiomatous nodule *vs*, 1822
    see also Angiolymphoid hyperplasia with eosinophilia
  glial heterotopias *vs*, 1790
  glomeruloid, 1808
  immature capillary hemangioma, cellular angiolipoma *vs*,
    1687
  spindle cell, 1826–1828
  verrucous, 1815
    angiokeratoma *vs*, 1813, 1815
  see also Capillary hemangioma; Hobnail hemangioma

Hemangiopericytoma
  adult, 1851–1852
  infantile, 1715, 1851
  lipomatous, 1738
Hemangiopericytoma-like pattern, extraskeletal mesenchymal
    chondrosarcoma, 1855, *1856*
Hemangiosarcoma *see* Angiosarcoma
Hematoxylin bodies, systemic lupus erythematosus, 798, *799*
Hemidesmosomal epidermolysis bullosa, 85, 86–87, 95
  see also Junctional epidermolysis bullosa–non-Herlitz
Hemidesmosomes, 5–6, *8*
  junctional epidermolysis bullosa, 95–96
Hemochromatosis gene mutations, 579
Hemodialysis
  pseudoporphyria, 587
  scleromyxedema-like illness, 1033–1035, *1036*
Hemodialysis-associated amyloidosis, 558–559
Hemoglobinopathies, pseudoxanthoma elasticum, 1044–1045
Hemolytic syndromes, pseudoxanthoma elasticum,
    1044–1045
Hemolytic uremic syndrome, 768–769
Hemophagocytic lymphohistiocytosis
  hemophagocytosis syndrome, 1415, 1487–1488
  see also Histiocytic lymphoma
Hemophagocytic syndrome, 354, 355–356
Hemophagocytic T-cell lymphoma, 1415–1418
  see also Histiocytic medullary reticulosis; Malignant
    histiocytosis; Weber–Christian disease
Hemophagocytosis syndrome, 1415, 1487–1488
Hemorrhage, aneurysmal fibrous histiocytoma, 1748
Hemorrhagic cellulitis, 875
Hemorrhagic fevers, 868–869
Hemorrhagic metastases to skin, 1501
Hemosiderin, pigmented purpuric dermatoses, 278
Hemosiderotic fibrohistiocytic lipomatous lesion, 1695
Hemosiderotic fibrous histiocytoma, 1748, *1749*
Henle's layer, 1065
Henoch–Schönlein purpura, *710*, 716–718
  infantile acute hemorrhagic edema and, 719
  malignant disease, 754
Heparin, 659
Heparin-induced thrombocytopenia syndrome, 659
Heparin sulfate, granuloma annulare, 300
Heparin sulfate proteoglycan, 8
Hepatic porphyrias
  acute intermittent porphyria, 575, 576
  aminolevulinic acid dehydratase deficiency, 575, 576
  hepatoerythropoietic porphyria, 575, 576, 582
  hereditary coproporphyria, 575, 576, 579
  porphyria cutanea tarda, 575, 576, 579–581, 584, 585
  variegate porphyria, 575, 576, 582–583
Hepatic vein occlusion, Behçet's disease, 744
Hepatitis B virus
  lichen planus, 222
  papular acrodermatitis of childhood, 189
  polyarteritis nodosa, 724
  vasculitis, 754
Hepatitis C virus
  cryoglobulinemia, 765
  lichen planus, 222
  sarcoidosis, 291
  vasculitis, 712
Hepatoerythropoietic porphyria, 575, 576, 582
Herald patch, pityriasis rosea, 190
Hereditary angioedema, 694
Hereditary benign intraepithelial dyskeratosis, 388
Hereditary coproporphyria, 575, 576, 579
Hereditary hair thinning *see* Androgenetic alopecia
Hereditary hemorrhagic telangiectasia, 1811–1812
Hereditary non-polyposis colorectal carcinoma, 1585
Hereditary oral diseases, 387–398
Heredofamilial amyloidosis, 559
Herlitz variant, junctional epidermolysis bullosa, 88
Hermansky–Pudlak syndrome, 1000
Heroin, pemphigus vegetans, 146
Herpes gestationis, 111
Herpes simplex virus, 850–855
  AIDS, 990
  erythema multiforme, 238
Herpes zoster, 856–857, *858*
Herpetiform blisters, systemic lupus erythematosus *see* Bullous
    systemic lupus erythematosus
Herpetiform pemphigus *see* Pemphigus herpetiformis
Herpetiform ulcers, oral, 406
Heterotopias, 1788–1796
  cutaneous ciliated cyst, 1676
  lung tissue, 1674
Heterotopic brain tissue, 392
HG factor, 114
HHb (human hair keratin) gene mutations, monilethrix, 1111
Hibernian fever, familial (TNF receptor-associated periodic
    syndrome), 285, 756
Hibernoma, 1694–1695

Hidradenitis
  idiopathic plantar, 668
  neutrophil eccrine, 667–669
Hidradenitis suppurativa, 705–708, 1614
Hidradenocarcinoma *see* Clear cell hidradenocarcinoma
Hidradenoma, 1630–1634
  see also Clear cell hidradenoma
Hidradenoma papilliferum, 1592–1593
  see also Papillary hidradenoma
Hidroacanthoma simplex, 1615–1617
  trichilemmoma *vs*, 1530
Hidrocystoma
  apocrine, 1587–1590
  see also Eccrine hidrocystoma
Hidrotic ectodermal dysplasia, 71
High density lipoproteins, 540, *541*
High grade myxoid liposarcoma, 1698
Highly active anti-retroviral therapy (HAART), lipodystrophy, 377
Hip stone, 598
Hirsutoid papillomas, 476
Histamine, leukocytoclastic vasculitis, 714
Histidyl-transfer RNA synthetase, 828
Histiocytes
  malakoplakia, 922
  rhinoscleroma, 918
  xanthoma disseminatum, 1477, *1478*
Histiocytic disorders, 1457–1495
  see also Cytophagic histiocytic panniculitis
Histiocytic granuloma, atypical, traumatic ulcerative granuloma
    vs, 409
Histiocytic lymphoma, 1485
  see also Hemophagocytic T-cell lymphoma
Histiocytic medullary reticulosis, 1484
  see also Hemophagocytic T-cell lymphoma
Histiocytic neoplasms, classification, *1359*
Histiocytic sarcoma, 1484–1487
Histiocytoid carcinoma, eyelid, 1659
Histiocytoid hemangioma, 1823
Histiocytoma
  generalized eruptive, 1474–1475
  see also Fibrous histiocytoma
Histiocytoma cutis *see* Dermatofibroma
Histiocytosis
  benign cephalic, 1472, 1473–1474
  crystal storing, 365–366, 1444, *1445*
Histiocytosis, progressive nodular, 1475
Histiocytosis X
  malignant, 1467
  see also Langerhans' cell histiocytosis
Histoid leprosy, 912, *913*, 916, *917*
Histoplasma capsulatum spp., 971–974
Histoplasmosis, 971–974
HIT (heparin-induced thrombocytopenia) syndrome, 659
HIV (human immunodeficiency virus), 986
HIV-associated eosinophilic folliculitis, 700, 988
  eosinophilic pustular folliculitis *vs*, 700, 701, 988
HIV-associated lipodystrophy, 378
HIV-associated lymphoma, 1450–1451
Hives, 692
HIV exanthem, 987
HIV infection, 986–992
  atypical cutaneous lymphoproliferative disorder of, 1423
  blastomycosis, 954
  candidiasis, 948, 949, 987, 990
  cryoglobulinemia, 765–766
  hairy leukoplakia and, 430
  histoplasmosis, 972, 973
  immune restoration syndrome, 293
  interface dermatitis of, 244
  leishmaniasis, 931–932
  lipodystrophy, 376–377
  mucinoses, 269
  Mycobacterium avium intracellulare, 906–907
  papular dermatitis, 700, 987
  paracoccidioidomycosis, 957
  pemphigus vegetans, 146
  pityriasis rubra pilaris, 208
  sebaceous adenoma, 1574
  seborrheic dermatitis-like eruption, 181–182, 987–988
  syphilis and, 494, 987
  T-cell lymphoma, 1365
  toxic epidermal necrolysis, 242
  vasculitic diseases, 754
  warts, 839
HLA antigens
  alopecia areata, 1075
  cicatricial pemphigoid, 119
  dermatitis herpetiformis, 131
  erythema multiforme, 238
  fogo selvagem, 149
  graft-versus-host disease, 250
  lichen planus, 222
    oral, 434

lichen sclerosus, 484
linear IgA disease, 136
lupus erythematosus, 790
migratory glossitis, 401
mycosis fungoides, 1365
pemphigoid gestationis, 114
pemphigus, 142
pityriasis rosea, 191
psoriasis, 200
Reiter's syndrome, 479
sarcoidosis, 293
Still's disease, 692
subacute cutaneous lupus erythematosus, 783
temporal arteritis, 749
HMB-45 antigen
  dermal nevus, 1258
  melanoma, 1328
    desmoplastic, 1348
  nevoid melanoma *vs* banal nevus, 1332
  Spitz nevus, 1272, 1328
HMLH1 (MMR gene product), 1585
HMSH2 (MMR gene product), 1585, 1586
Hobnail cells, 1821, 1822, 1828, 1829
Hobnail hemangioma, 1820–1822
  vs radiotherapy-induced lesions, 1847
  see also Targetoid hemosiderotic hemangioma
Hobo spider, 689
Hodgkin's cells, 1448, 1449
Hodgkin's lymphoma, 1448–1450
  classification, *1359*, 1448
  traumatic ulcerative granuloma *vs*, 409
Hodgkin's lymphoma-like variant, CD30+ large cell lymphoma,
    1405
Holocrine glands, 20–21
Homogentisate 1,2-dioxygenase deficiency, 592–593
Homozygous C2 and C4 deficiency, subacute cutaneous lupus
    erythematosus, 783
Honeycomb atrophy, 57, 58
Hookworm, cutaneous larva migrans, 984
Hori's nevus, 1299
Horizontal growth phase *see* Radial growth phase
Horn
  familial dyskeratotic comedones, 168
  keratin horn, Bowen's disease, 1196, *1197*
  occipital horn syndrome, 1026, 1038–1039
  see also Cornu cutaneum
Horn cysts, trichoepithelioma, 1547
Hornstein–Knickenberg syndrome, 1559, 1561
Horny layer, 12
Horse-riding, equestrian cold panniculitis, 274, 275, 353–354
Hot comb alopecia, 1099
Howell-Evans syndrome (focal non-epidermolytic palmoplantar
    keratoderma with esophageal squamous cell carcinoma),
    60, 67–68
HTLV (viruses)
  adult T-cell leukemia/lymphoma, 1413
  mycosis fungoides, 1364–1365, 1378
Human erythrocyte glucose transporter, necrobiosis lipoidica,
    306
Human hair keratin gene mutations, monilethrix, 1111
Human herpesvirus-6, 860
  Rosai–Dorfman disease, 1480
Human herpesvirus-7, atypical pityriasis rosea, 190
Human herpesvirus-8
  Kaposi's sarcoma, 1830, *1835*
    latent nuclear antigen-1 monoclonal antibody, 1833–1834
  vascular tumors, 1823
Human milk fat globulin 1, apocrine hidrocystoma *vs* eccrine
    hidrocystoma, 1588
Human papilloma virus, 838–841
  AIDS and, 990
  bowenoid papulosis, 456, 847, 1193
  Bowen's disease, 1194
  condyloma acuminatum, 491–492, 844
  epidermodysplasia verruciformis, 847, 849
  epidermoid cyst, 842, 1667
  focal epithelial hyperplasia, 432
  genital intraepithelial neoplasia, 520
  keratoacanthoma, 1223
  nails, 1131
  oral carcinoma, 460
  plane warts, 843
  plantar warts, 841, 842
  seborrheic keratosis, 1160
  squamous cell carcinoma, 491, 492, 840–841, 1203–1204
    anus, 524
    nail, 1131, 1141, 1142
    penis, 524
  verrucous carcinoma, 1219
  verrucous cyst, 1667
Human T lymphotropic viruses *see* HTLV (viruses)
Huriez syndrome, 60
Hutchinson–Gilford syndrome, 1054–1055

Hutchinson's incisors, 498
Hutchinson's melanotic freckle *see* Lentigo maligna
Hutchinson's melanotic whitlow, 1137, 1139
Hutchinson's sign, 1137, 1139
Huxley's layer, anagen hair follicle, 1065
Hyaline cells, mixed tumor of skin, 1601–1602, *1603*
Hyaline deposits, smokeless tobacco keratosis, 403, 404
Hyaline fibromatosis, juvenile, 397–398, 1722–1723
Hyaline globules, eosinophilic, Kaposi's sarcoma, 1833, *1835*
Hyaline mantle, trichilemmal carcinoma, *1532*
Hyaline nodules, malignant peripheral nerve sheath tumor, 1792
Hyalinization
　lupus erythematosus profundus, 380
　submucous fibrosis, 458
Hyalinizing angiectatic tumor, pleomorphic, 1859
Hyalinizing spindle and epithelioid cell nevus, 1276
　desmoplastic nevus (desmoplastic Spitz nevus), 1255, 1271, 1276–1277, *1278*
Hyalinizing spindle cell tumor with giant rosettes, 1740, *1741*
Hyalinizing vasculitis, segmental *see* Atrophie blanche
Hyalinosis cutis et mucosae, 571–574
　see also Lipoid proteinosis
Hyaluronic acid, 601
Hybrid cyst, 1667
Hybrid epidermoid and apocrine cyst, 1590
Hybrid epidermoid and trichilemmal cyst, 1664, 1667
Hybrid tumor (neurofibroma and schwannoma), 1774
Hybrid tumor (verrucous/squamous cell carcinoma), oral, 465
Hydralazine, 624
Hydroa-like cutaneous T-cell lymphoma, 1421
Hydroa vacciniforme, 1421
Hydroa vacciniforme-like presentation, lymphomatoid papulosis, 1400
Hydrocarbons
　coal tar, keratoacanthoma, 1223
　squamous cell carcinoma, 1204
Hydrocortisone, rosacea-like dermatosis, 1123
Hydropic degeneration (liquefactive degeneration), basal cells
　Bowen's disease, 1195
　bullous lichen planus, 222
　dermatomyositis, 829
　discoid lupus erythematosus, 792
　subacute cutaneous lupus erythematosus, 796
　see also Interface dermatitis
Hydroquinone, ochronosis, 567, 592, 593
Hydroxychloroquine, pigmentation, 639
Hydroxyproline, collagen, 29
Hypercalcemia
　acute ATLL, 1413
　subcutaneous fat necrosis of the newborn, 359–360
Hypereosinophilic syndrome, 696–697
Hypergammaglobulinemic purpura, 771–772
Hyperhidrosis, localized unilateral, 1609
Hyper-IgM syndrome, non-X-linked, discoid lupus erythematosus, 781
Hyperkeratosis
　actinic keratosis, 1187, 1188
　discoid lupus erythematosus, 792
　epidermolytic, *38*, 1155
　　focal, 49–50
　　see also Bullous ichthyosiform erythroderma
　follicular *see* Keratosis pilaris
　oral, focal palmoplantar keratoderma with, 66–67
　yaws, 892
　see also Chicken wire appearance
Hyperkeratosis follicularis et parafollicularis in cutem penetrans *see* Kyrle's disease
Hyperkeratosis lenticularis perstans (Flegel's disease), 78–79
　familial dyskeratotic comedones *vs*, 169
Hyperkeratotic mycosis fungoides, 1393
Hyperkeratotic scabies, 980
Hyperlipidemias, 539–550
　eruptive xanthomata *see* Eruptive xanthomata
　planar xanthomata, 547–549
　tendinous xanthomata, 541, 544–545
　tuberous xanthomata, 541, 545–547
　verruciform xanthoma, 412–413, 549–550
Hypermobility (Ehlers–Danlos syndrome type III), 1024
Hyperpigmentation, 1007–1021
　basal cells, mastocytosis, 1493–1494
　chemotherapeutic agents, 664
　drug-induced, 638–647
　　bleomycin, 664
　　minocycline, 468, 638, *639*, 640, *641*
　　thio-TEPA, 665, 666
　systemic sclerosis, 806
Hyperpigmented mycosis fungoides, 1379–1380
Hyperpyrexia, lamellar ichthyosis, 42
Hypersensitivity
　chemotherapeutic agents, 665
　lichenoid, cinnamon, 436, *437*
　see also Delayed hypersensitivity

Hypersensitivity syndrome
　anticonvulsants, 633–634
　cutaneous T-cell pseudolymphoma, 1423–1424
Hypersensitivity vasculitis *see* Leukocytoclastic vasculitis
Hyperthyroidism, 603, 604
Hypertrichosis, porphyria cutanea tarda, 580, *581*
Hypertrophic discoid lupus erythematosus, 777–778, *780*, *781*
Hypertrophic lichen planus, 221–222, 224
Hypertrophic scar, 1699–1700
Hypoaminoacidemia, necrolytic migratory erythema, 620
Hypocomplementemia
　acquired partial lipodystrophy, 376
　leukocytoclastic vasculitis, 715
　urticarial vasculitis, 694, 720
Hypocomplementemic urticarial vasculitis, 282
Hypodermatitis sclerodermaformis, 372–373
Hypomelanosis of Ito, 1005–1006
　incontinentia pigmenti *vs*, 704, 1005
Hyponychium, 1127, 1128
Hypopigmentation
　postinflammatory, 1007
　　vitiligo *vs*, 996
　systemic sclerosis, 806
Hypopigmented blue nevus, 1302–1303
Hypopigmented mycosis fungoides, 1379–1380
Hypoplasia
　Proteus syndrome, 1058
　see also Focal dermal hypoplasia syndrome
HZIP4 (transmembrane protein), 618

I

Iatrogenic calcinosis cutis, 596
IBIDS (syndrome), 1105
ICAM-1 *see* Intercellular adhesion molecule-1
Ichthyosiform drug reactions, 652
Ichthyosiform erythroderma
　bullous, 45–48
　　mosaicism, 1155
　congenital, *38*, 43–45
Ichthyosiform mucinosis, acral, 604
Ichthyosis, 37–54
　acquired, 58, 59
　erythema gyrata repens, 265
　mycosis fungoides and, 1390
　Sjögren–Larsson syndrome, *38*, 52–54
　systemic diseases with, *39*
　see also Keratosis pilaris
Ichthyosis bullosa of Siemens, 48
Ichthyosis congenita
　autosomal recessive, 42–45
　ichthyosis fetalis, 50–51
Ichthyosis fetalis, 50–51
Ichthyosis follicularis, 54–55
　with alopecia and photophobia, 56
Ichthyosis hystrix, 45, 1153, *1154*
Ichthyosis linearis circumflexa, Netherton syndrome, 51
Ichthyosis nigricans *see* Sex-linked ichthyosis
Ichthyosis vulgaris, 37–39
　keratosis punctata of palmar creases and, 64
Idiopathic angiosarcoma of head and neck, 1839
Idiopathic calcinosis, 510, 595, 596, 597–598
Idiopathic guttate hypomelanosis, 998
Idiopathic lenticular mucocutaneous pigmentation (Laugier–Hunziker syndrome), 467, 511, 1007–1008, 1242, *1243*
Idiopathic lipoatrophy, 374
Idiopathic onychodysplasia *see* Trachyonychia
Idiopathic plantar hidradenitis, 668
Idiopathic recurrent palmoplantar hidradenitis in children, 668
Idiopathic thrombocytopenic purpura, 770
Idiosyncratic drug reactions, 624
Id reaction (autosensitization reaction), 175
IFAP300, epidermis, 6
IFAP syndrome, 56
IgA
　dermatitis herpetiformis, 131
　Henoch–Schönlein purpura, 717–718
IgA herpetiform pemphigus *see* IgA pemphigus
IgA pemphigus, 154–155
　pustular psoriasis *vs*, 205
　subcorneal pustular dermatosis *vs*, 212
IgA pemphigus foliaceus *see* IgA pemphigus
IgA pemphigus vulgaris *see* IgA pemphigus
IgE, urticaria, 695
IgE-mediated type 1 drug reactions, 624–625
IgM storage papules, 574–575
Ileostomy, pyoderma gangrenosum, 675
ILVEN (inflammatory linear verrucous epidermal nevus), 210–211
Imatinib mesylate, dermatofibrosarcoma protuberans, 1730
Imipramine, pigmentation, 640, 642
Immature capillary hemangioma, cellular angiolipoma *vs*, 1687

Immature trichoepithelioma, 1553
Immune complexes
　drug reactions, 625
　granuloma annulare, 299
　leukocytoclastic vasculitis, 713
　polyarteritis nodosa and, 724
　reticular erythematous mucinosis, 269
　rheumatoid nodules, 310–311
Immune restoration syndrome, 293
Immune thrombocytopenic purpura, 770
Immunoblastic CD30+ large cell lymphoma, 1403
Immunoblastic lymphadenopathy, 1411–1412
Immunocytoma, 1358
　primary cutaneous, 1428, 1430
Immunodeficiency (syndromes)
　bowenoid papulosis, 847
　candidiasis, 948–949
　　HIV infection, 948, 949, *987*, 990
　congenital, granulomata, 326–327
　epidermodysplasia verruciformis, 849
　herpes zoster, 857
　immunosuppression-related lymphoproliferative disorders, 1450
　non-tuberculous mycobacteria, 904
Immunoelectron microscopy
　bullous pemphigoid, 107
　mucous membrane pemphigoid, 122
Immunofluorescence
　split skin, 81–83
　studies of localized cutaneous pemphigoid, 107
Immunofluorescent antigen mapping, epidermolysis bullosa, 92
Immunoglobulin A *see* IgA
Immunohistochemistry
　atypical cellular neurothekeoma, 1785
　CD30+ lymphoproliferative disorders, 1408
　melanoma, 1328–1331
　　desmoplastic, 1348–1349
　　differential diagnosis, 1325–1326
　metastases to skin, 1504–1505
　mixed tumor of skin, 1604–1605
　neuroendocrine carcinoma, 1235–1236, *1237*, 1504
　nevoid melanoma *vs* banal nevus, 1332
　Paget's disease, 1516–1517
　Sézary cells, 1397–1398
　spindle cell tumors, 1211
　Spitz nevus, 1272
Immunoperoxidase antigen mapping, 83–84
　bullous pemphigoid, *83*, 107
Immunosuppression
　actinic keratosis, 1188
　lymphomatoid granulomatosis, 1439
　neuroendocrine carcinoma, 1231–1232
　tumors, 1203
　UV radiation, 1203
　warts, 839, 840
Immunosuppression-associated Kaposi's sarcoma, 1831
Immunosuppression-related lymphoproliferative disorders, 1450–1451
Impetigo, 869, 870–872
　of Bockhart, 878
　bullous, 869, *871*, 873–874
　subcorneal pustular dermatosis *vs*, 213
Impetigo herpetiformis, 198
Implantation variant, epidermoid cyst, 1664
Incidental epidermolytic hyperkeratosis, 49–50
Inclusion body fibromatosis, 1718–1719
Incontinence, papuloerosive dermatitis, 476
Incontinentia pigmenti, 702–704
　erythema toxicum neonatorum *vs*, 214
　hypomelanosis of Ito *vs*, 704, 1005
　toxemic erythema of the neonate *vs*, 704, 705
　see also Pigmentary incontinence
Incontinentia pigmenti achromians *see* Hypomelanosis of Ito
Indeterminate cell histiocytoma, 1468
Indeterminate cell histiocytosis, 1468
Indeterminate hairs, 1063
Indeterminate leprosy, 912–913, 915, *916*, *917*
Indian tick typhus, 928
Indirect immunofluorescence guinea pig esophagus, 436–437
　see also Split skin immunofluorescence
Industrial chemicals
　scleroderma-like syndromes, 808
　squamous cell carcinoma, 1204
Infantile acropustulosis, 214
Infantile acute hemorrhagic edema, 718–719
Infantile calcinosis cutis of the heel, 596
Infantile dermatitis, 172–173
Infantile digital fibromatosis, 1718–1719
Infantile familial cutaneous mucinosis, self-healing, 615
Infantile fibromatosis, 1726
Infantile gluteal granuloma, 476
Infantile hemangioendothelioma, 1813–1814
Infantile hemangiopericytoma, 1715, 1851

Infantile hypogammaglobulinemia, X-linked, 327
Infantile myofibromatosis, 1714
    juvenile hyaline fibromatosis vs, 1723
Infantile papular acrodermatitis see Papular acrodermatitis of childhood
Infantile sarcoidosis, 288
Infantile systemic hyalinosis, 397, 1722
Infantile variant, fibrosarcoma, 1738–1739
Infarction, papulonecrotic tuberculid, 903
Infections, 837–992
    AIDS, 989–991
        type 1, 989–990
        type 2, 990
        types 3, 4, 5, 991
        see also HIV infection
    algal, 936–937
    anogenital region, 490–509
    bacteria see Bacteria (infections)
    Darier's disease, 158–159
    dissecting cellulitis of the scalp, 1096, 1097
    eczematous dermatitis, 178
    endothrix, 940
    erythema multiforme, 238
    erythema nodosum, 344
    fungal see Fungal infections
    hair, laboratory tests, 1062
    hantavirus, 868
    Henoch–Schönlein purpura, 717
    hidradenitis suppurativa, 707
    infantile acute hemorrhagic edema, 718
    keratitis–ichthyosis–deafness syndrome, 72
    leukocytoclastic vasculitis, 711–712
    morphea, 818
    Olmsted syndrome, 73
    oral lesions, 430–433
        Wegener's granulomatosis vs, 443
    papular acrodermatitis of childhood, 189
    polyarteritis nodosa, 724
    psoriasis, 200–201
    Reiter's syndrome, 479
    rickettsial, 928–929
        vasculitis, 753–754, 929
    scleredema, 610
    squamous cell carcinoma, 1204
    sterile neutrophilic folliculitis vs, 684
    temporal arteritis, 749
    vasculitis, 753–754
    viral see Viral infections
    Wegener's granulomatosis, 729
Infectious mononucleosis
    drug reactions, 626
    Lipschutz ulcer, 488
    syndrome like, cytomegalovirus, 859
Infective dermatitis, 177
Infective endocarditis, systemic lupus erythematosus, 799
Infective folliculitis, 878–880
    eosinophilic folliculitis vs, 988
Infective granulomata, 324
Infective panniculitis, 371–372
Infiltrating ductal carcinoma of breast, eccrine ductal carcinoma vs, 1657, 1658
Infiltrating glomus tumor, 1850
Infiltrative basal cell carcinoma, 1175, *1177*
Inflammation
    alopecia areata, 1077
    chemotherapeutic agents and actinic damage, 665
    epidermoid cyst, 1664
    intravenous pyogenic granuloma, 1817
    lichenoid keratosis, 230
    lupus erythematosus profundus, 380
    morphea, 819
    nodular prurigo, 184
    psoriasis, 201
    squamous cell carcinoma, 1204, 1205–1206
Inflammatory angiomatous nodule see Epithelioid hemangioma
Inflammatory bowel disease
    epidermolysis bullosa acquisita, 124
    erythema elevatum diutinum, 740–741
    pemphigoid vegetans, 100
Inflammatory carcinoma, 1506, *1508*
Inflammatory cell-rich bullous pemphigoid, differential diagnosis, 109–110
Inflammatory conditions, nails, 1129–1136
Inflammatory diseases of subcutaneous fat, 341–384
    equestrian cold panniculitis, 274, 275, 353–354
Inflammatory fibrosarcoma see Inflammatory myofibroblastic tumor
Inflammatory fibrous hyperplasia
    gingival fibrous nodule, 418
    see also Denture-associated fibrous hyperplasia
Inflammatory linear verrucous epidermal nevus, 210–211
Inflammatory malignant fibrous histiocytoma, 1763
Inflammatory metastases, 1501–1502

Inflammatory myofibroblastic tumor, 1736
    see also Inflammatory pseudotumor
Inflammatory myxohyaline tumor, 1735
Inflammatory papillary hyperplasia see Denture-associated fibrous hyperplasia
Inflammatory pseudotumor, 1457
    see also Inflammatory myofibroblastic tumor; Plasma cell granuloma
Infraorbital folds, atopic dermatitis, 173
Infundibular cyst see Epidermoid cyst
Infundibulocystic basal cell carcinoma, 1178
    see also Basaloid follicular hamartoma
Infundibuloma see Follicular infundibulum tumor
Infundibulum, hair follicle, 1064
Infundibulum tumor, follicular, 1525–1526
    superficial epithelioma with sebaceous differentiation vs, 1578
Inherited basaloid follicular hamartoma, 1522
Inherited cutis laxa, 1038–1039, 1040
Inherited hemolytic syndromes, pseudoxanthoma elasticum and, 1044–1045
Injection-site granuloma, epithelioid hemangioma vs, 1825
Injection-site lipoatrophy, 377
Injection-site panniculitis, 351
Ink spot lentigo, 1248, *1249*
Inner plaque proteins
    plakophilin (band 6), 11
    see also Plakoglobin
Inner root sheath, anagen hair follicle, 1065
Insect bite reactions, 689
    Lyme disease, 890
    persistent, epithelioid hemangioma vs, 1825
In situ porocarcinoma, 1621
In situ squamous cell carcinoma see Bowen's disease
Insulin receptors, localized lipoatrophy, 377
Insulin resistance, acanthosis nigricans, 616
Integrins, 6–7
    subunit mutations, 95
        epidermolysis bullosa, 85
Interactions, drugs, 624
Intercellular adhesion molecule-1 (ICAM-1)
    polymorphous light eruption, 272
    psoriasis, 201
Intercellular IgA dermatosis see IgA pemphigus
Intercellular IgA vesiculopustular dermatosis see IgA pemphigus
Intercellular substance antibody, 142
Interdigitating dendritic cell tumor/sarcoma, 1484–1487
Interface dermatitis, 217
    chemotherapeutic agents, 665–666
    of HIV infection, 244
Interface dermatoses, 217, 236–260
Interferon alpha (IFN-α), 670
    sarcoidosis, 291
Interferon beta (IFN-β), 670
    intravascular papillary endothelial hyperplasia and, 1806
Interferon gamma (IFN-γ), 670
Interleukin(s), graft-versus-host disease, 252–253
Interleukin-1, pemphigus, 142
Interleukin-2, 670
    hypereosinophilic syndrome, 697
    see also DAB389 IL-2 treatment
Interleukin-4, 670
    atopic dermatitis, 173
Interleukin-6, cutaneous plasmacytosis, 1443
Interleukin-8
    pemphigus herpetiformis, 151
    pyoderma gangrenosum, 675
Interleukin-17, systemic sclerosis, 809, 810
Intermediate density lipoproteins, 540, *542*
Intermediate filaments, 5
Intermediate grade lymphocytic lymphoma, 1435–1436
Intermediate variant, neuroendocrine carcinoma, 1233, *1234*
Interstitial dendritic cells, histiocytic disorders, 1457
Interstitial granuloma annulare, 300–301, *302*
Interstitial granulomatous dermatitis
    with arthritis, 320
    see also Palisaded neutrophilic and granulomatous dermatitis
Interstitial granulomatous drug reactions, 643–645
Interstitial pneumonitis, systemic sclerosis, 807, 813
Intertriginous xanthomata, 547
Intertrigo, 173
Intracytoplasmic lumina
    eccrine poroma, 1618
    epithelioid hemangioendothelioma, 1837
Intradermal fasciitis, 1702, *1703*, *1704*, 1705
Intraepidermal epithelioma of Borst–Jadassohn, 1165–1166, 1195–1196
    from hidroacanthoma simplex, 1615
Intraepidermal IgA pustulosis see IgA pemphigus
Intraepidermal neutrophilic dermatosis variant, IgA pemphigus see IgA pemphigus
Intraepidermal neutrophilic IgA dermatosis see IgA pemphigus
Intraepithelial dyskeratosis, hereditary benign, 388

Intraepithelial neoplasia
    genital region, 519–523
        basaloid variant, 1195
    squamous, 455
    see also Bowenoid papulosis
Intramucosal nevus, 469
Intraneural infiltration, melanoma, 1324, *1326*
Intraneural lipoma, 1693
Intraneural perineurioma, 1786, 1787
Intravascular angioleiomyoma, 1800
Intravascular fasciitis, 1705
Intravascular large B-cell lymphoma, 1445–1448
Intravascular lymphoma, 1445–1448
Intravascular lymphomatosis, 1445–1448
Intravascular malignant lymphomatosis, 1445–1448
Intravascular melanocytes, 1256
Intravascular papillary endothelial hyperplasia, 1806–1807
Intravenous atypical vascular proliferation see Epithelioid hemangioma
Intravenous pyogenic granuloma, 1816, 1817, *1818*
Intrinsic atopic dermatitis, 173
Invasive (vertical) growth phase, melanoma, 1313, 1321
Inversa variant, dystrophic epidermolysis bullosa, 92
Inverted follicular keratosis, 1159–1160
    see also Irritated seborrheic keratosis
Inverted type A nevus, 1259–1260
Invisible mycosis fungoides, 1393
Invisible pigmented lichen planus (lichen planus pigmentosus), 221, 224
Involucrin, 11
    inflammatory linear verrucous epidermal nevus, 211
Involutional lipoatrophy, 377–384
    localized lipoatrophy, 377–384
Iododerma, 656–657
Iris lesions, 236, 237
Iris xanthogranuloma, 1469
Iron overload, porphyria cutanea tarda, 580
Irregular Bowen's disease, 1195
Irritant contact dermatitis, 176–177
Irritant contact urticaria, 694, 695
Irritated seborrheic keratosis, 1158, *1163*
    see also Inverted follicular keratosis
Irritation fibroma see Fibroma
Ischemic fasciitis, 1706–1707
Isolated collagenoma, 1038
Isolated linear epidermolytic epidermal nevus, 49
Isolated mucocutaneous melanotic pigmentation, 1012
Isomorphic phenomenon see Koebner's phenomenon
Isthmus, hair follicle, 1064
Itching purpura, 277
Ixodes spp., Lyme disease vectors, 889–890

J

Jackson–Lawler syndrome see Pachyonychia congenita, type 2
Jackson–Sertoli syndrome see Pachyonychia congenita, type 2
Jadassohn effect, seborrheic keratosis, hidroacanthoma simplex vs, 1616
Jadassohn–Lewandowsky syndrome, 66–67
Jadassohn's nevus see Nevus sebaceus
Jadassohn variant, anetoderma, 1045–1047
Jarisch–Herxheimer reaction, 496
Jaundice, hemorrhagic fevers, 869
Jeep disease see Pilonidal sinus
Jejunal biopsy, dermatitis herpetiformis, 133
Jejunoileal bypass, 683
Jellyfish stings, 690
Jessner's lymphocytic infiltrate of the skin see Lymphocytic infiltrate of the skin
Jigger flea, 981, *982*
Joints
    benign hypermobility syndrome, 1024
    systemic sclerosis, 808, 814
Junctional activity, 1250
Junctional epidermolysis bullosa, *84*, *85*, 87–89, 95–96
    acral/minimus, 87
    antibodies, 93
    immunofluorescent antigen mapping, 92
Junctional epidermolysis bullosa-Herlitz, 88
Junctional epidermolysis bullosa inversa, 89
Junctional epidermolysis bullosa-late onset, 89
Junctional epidermolysis bullosa mitis see Junctional epidermolysis bullosa–non-Herlitz
Junctional epidermolysis bullosa–non-Herlitz, 88–89
    see also Generalized atrophic benign epidermolysis bullosa
Junctional epidermolysis bullosa progressiva, 89
Junctional nevus, 469, 1250, 1251, *1253*
    lentiginous, 1242, *1244*, 1252, *1253*
Juvenile aponeurotic fibroma, 1719–1720
Juvenile colloid milium, 567–568
Juvenile cutaneous mucinosis, self-healing, 610
Juvenile dermatomyositis, 828, 829
Juvenile elastoma, 1050, *1051*
    papular elastorrhexis vs, 1052

Juvenile hemangioma, 1813–1814
Juvenile hyaline fibromatosis, 397–398, 1722–1723
Juvenile lentigo, 1242
Juvenile melanoma *see* Spitz nevus
Juvenile pityriasis rubra pilaris, 208
    atypical, 208
Juvenile plantar dermatosis, 192–193
Juvenile rheumatoid arthritis, 691–692
Juvenile spring eruption, 271–272
    ears, 272
Juvenile xanthogranuloma *see* Xanthogranuloma

K

Kala-azar, 931–932
Kalinin *see* Laminin-5
Kallin syndrome, 85
Kamino bodies, 1270, *1274*
    pigmented spindle cell tumor of Reed, 1280
Kanzaki disease, diffuse angiokeratomata, 552
Kaposiform hemangioendothelioma, 1830
    angiolipoma *vs*, 1687
    lymphangiomatosis with, 1830, 1848
    tufted angioblastoma, 1814
Kaposi's sarcoma, 1830–1836
    acroangiodermatitis *vs*, 185, 1834
    bacillary angiomatosis *vs*, 887, 888
    dermatomyofibroma *vs*, 1710
    hobnail hemangioma *vs*, 1822
    kaposiform hemangioendothelioma *vs*, 1830
    lymphangiosarcoma *vs*, 1846
    multinucleate cell angiohistiocytoma *vs*, 1742
    radiotherapy-induced lesions *vs*, 1848
    spindle cell hemangioma, 1827
    tufted angioblastoma *vs*, 1814–1815
Kaposi's varicelliform eruption (eczema herpeticum), 851–852, *853*
    Darier's disease, 159
Kasabach–Merritt syndrome, 1814, 1818
    kaposiform hemangioendothelioma with, 1830
Katayama disease, 506, 985
Kava, acquired ichthyosis, 58
Kawasaki syndrome (mucocutaneous lymph node syndrome), *710*, 735–737
Keloid, 1700–1701
    hypertrophic scar *vs*, 1699
Keloidal basal cell carcinoma, 1182
Keloidal blastomycosis, 976–978
Keloidal scleroderma *see* Subcutaneous scleroderma
Keratin(s), 9–10
    amyloid from, 562
    apocrine hidrocystoma *vs* eccrine hidrocystoma, 1588–1589
    dermatophytes on, 938
    epidermolysis bullosa, 93–95
    melanoma, 1328
    mutations
        bullous ichthyosiform erythroderma, 45–47
        monilethrix, 1111
    steatocystoma *vs* vellus hair cyst, 1672
Keratin 4, gene mutations, oral white sponge nevus, 387
Keratin 5, gene mutations, epidermolysis bullosa, 85
Keratin 9, epidermolytic palmoplantar keratoderma, 59
Keratin 13, gene mutations, oral white sponge nevus, 387
Keratin 14, gene mutations, epidermolysis bullosa, 85
Keratin 17, mutations, steatocystoma, 1573
Keratin horn, Bowen's disease, 1196, *1197*
Keratinization, 12
    nail bed, 1129
    trichoadenoma, 1526
    verrucous carcinoma, 1220
Keratinization disorders, 37–80
    acquired ichthyosis, 58, 59
    acrokeratosis verruciformis *see* Acrokeratosis verruciformis
    acrokeratosis verruciformis of Hopf, 74
    callus, 74
    clavus, 74, 75
    follicular ichthyosis, 54–55
    granular parakeratosis, 79–80
    ichthyosis, 37–54
        see also Ichthyosis
    ichthyosis follicularis with alopecia and photophobia, 56
    keratosis pilaris, 56–58
    keratosis pilaris atrophicans, 56, 57–58
    lichen spinulosus, 55
    Olmsted syndrome, 73
    palmoplantar ectodermal dysplasia, 66–73
    palmoplantar keratoderma, 59–66
        see also Palmoplantar keratoderma
    phrynoderma, 55
    pityriasis rotunda, 54
    porokeratosis, 74–77
        see also Porokeratosis
Keratinized sites, oral mucosa, 385, 386
Keratinizing cysts, classification, *1663*

Keratinizing trichilemmoma, 1528
Keratin layer, epidermis, 3
    cell structure, 11–12
Keratinocytes, 12
    apoptosis, erythema multiforme, 238–239
    epidermodysplasia verruciformis, 849–850
    fibroblasts and, keloid, 1701
    herpes simplex virus, 853, *854*
    Langerhans' cells *vs*, 17
    large cell acanthoma, 1164
    lichen planopilaris, 1090
    orthopox virus infections, 862
    psoriasis, 201
    vacuolated *see* Koilocytes
Keratitis–ichthyosis–deafness (KID) syndrome, *38*, 72–73
Keratoacanthoma, 1221–1227
    verrucous carcinoma *vs*, 465, 1220
        see also Subungual keratoacanthoma
Keratoacanthoma centrifugum marginatum, 1222
Keratoconus, keratitis–ichthyosis–deafness syndrome, 72
Keratocyst, odontogenic
    nevoid basal cell carcinoma syndrome, 1184
    peripheral, 425
Keratoderma
    epidermolysis bullosa simplex herpetiformis with mottled
        pigmentation and punctate keratoderma, 86
        see also Palmoplantar keratoderma
Keratoderma blenorrhagicum, 477, *478*
Keratoderma climactericum, 65–66
Keratoderma hereditarium mutilans, 70–71
Keratoderma palmaris et plantaris, 59
    see also Palmoplantar keratoderma
Keratoelastoidosis marginalis, 1053
    of the hands, 65
Keratohyalin, 12
    plantar warts, 842
    warts, 840, *841*
Keratohyaline granules, 11
    bullous ichthyosiform erythroderma, 47
Keratolysis plantare sulcatum, 926–927
Keratosis
    acantholytic seborrheic, acantholytic acanthoma *vs*, 169
    alveolar ridge, 457–458
    inverted follicular, 1159–1160
        see also Irritated seborrheic keratosis
    lichenoid, 229–231
    mosaic acral, 64–65
    PUVA, 1198
    seborrheic *see* Seborrheic keratosis
    subungual, localized multinucleate distal, 1136
    trichilemmal, 1528
        see also Actinic keratosis; Smokeless tobacco keratosis
Keratosis follicularis *see* Darier's disease
Keratosis follicularis spinulosa decalvans, 57, 58
Keratosis lichenoides chronica, 233–234
Keratosis palmoplantaris striata, 62–63
Keratosis pilaris, 37, 39, 56–58
    elastosis perforans serpiginosa *vs*, 334
    perforating folliculitis *vs*, 332
Keratosis pilaris atrophicans, 56, 57–58
Keratosis pilaris atrophicans facei, 57, 58
Keratosis punctata
    ichthyosis vulgaris with, 37
    of palmar creases, 64
Keratosis punctata palmaris et plantaris *see* Punctate
    palmoplantar keratoderma
Keratotic basal cell carcinoma, 1175, *1178*
    trichoepithelioma *vs*, 1549
Keratotic melanocytic nevus, 1253
Keratotic pits of palmar creases, 64
Keratotic seborrheic keratosis, 1159, *1160*
Kerion, 939, *940*
Ketron–Goodman disease, 1394, 1395
Ketron–Goodman variant, mycosis fungoides, 1368, *1371*
KF-1 (monoclonal antibody), epidermolysis bullosa, 92
Ki-67
    dermal nevus *vs* melanoma, 1258
    melanoma, 1329
    see also MIB-1
Kidney
    Cockayne's syndrome, 248
    diffuse systemic sclerosis, 807–808
    gout, 590
    Henoch–Schönlein purpura, 717
    nephrogenic fibrosing dermopathy, 1033
    polyarteritis nodosa, 721, 725–726
    sarcoidosis, 293
    systemic lupus erythematosus, 785, 797–798, 799
        WHO lesion types, 797–798
    systemic sclerosis, 813
    transplantation, tumors, *1201*, 1203
    tuberous sclerosis, 1032
    tumors

Birt–Hogg–Dubé syndrome, 1561
    clear cell metastases from, 1210
    metastases to skin, 1498, 1499–1500, *1501*
        see also Renal cell carcinoma
    urticarial vasculitis, 282
    Wegener's granulomatosis, 727, 729
        see also headings beginning Renal...
KID syndrome *see* Keratitis–ichthyosis–deafness (KID) syndrome
Kimura's disease, 1825, *1826*
    epithelioid hemangioma and, 1823
Kindler syndrome, actinic keratosis, 1187
Kinking of hair, acquired progressive, 1115, 1520
Kitamura variant, reticulate acropigmentation, 1009
Kit gene
    piebaldism, 1003
    see also c-Kit gene
Klebsiella rhinoscleromatosis, 918
Klippel–Trénaunay syndrome, 1809
    acroangiodermatitis, 185
    spindle cell hemangioma with, 1826
Knife-cut sign, Crohn's disease, 489
Knotted hair, 1115–1116
Knuckle pads, 1038, 1720, *1721*
Köbberling variant familial partial lipodystrophy, 376
Koebner's phenomenon, 200
    keratosis lichenoides chronica, 233
    lichen nitidus, 227
    lichen planus, 218
    lichen striatus and, 231
    plane warts, 843, *844*
    reactive perforating collagenosis, 328
    warts, 839
Koebner variant, epidermolysis bullosa simplex, 86, 94
Koenen tumor *see* Periungual fibroma
Koilocytes, 840, *841*
    condyloma acuminatum, 845
Koilocytic dysplasia, 456
Koilocytosis
    human papilloma virus infection, 839
    myrmecia, 1131
        see also Bowenoid papulosis
Koreans, hair counts, *1068*
KPAF (ulerythema ophryogenes), 57, 58
Ku antibody, 828
Kussmaul–Maier disease *see* Polyarteritis nodosa
Kveim test, 293
Kyasanur Forest disease, 868, 869
Kyphoscoliosis (Ehlers–Danlos syndrome type VI), *1024*, 1025,
    1026
Kyrle's disease, *331*, 335–337
    elastosis perforans serpiginosa *vs*, 334, 336
    familial dyskeratotic comedones *vs*, 169
    hyperkeratosis lenticularis perstans *vs*, 78, 79
    perforating folliculitis *vs*, 332, 337
    reactive perforating collagenosis *vs*, 336
Kytococcus sedentarius, 926

L

Labial artery, caliber-persistent, 428
Labial melanotic macule, 467–468
Labia majora, normal skin, 474
Labia minora, 474
Lacazia loboi, 976
Lactate dehydrogenase
    M subunit deficiency, 618
    pseudocyst of the auricle, 1682
Ladinin, linear IgA disease, 137
LAMB *see* Carney complex
Lamellar bodies, ichthyosis fetalis, 50
Lamellar ichthyosis, *38*, 42–43
Lamina densa, 8
    bullous pemphigoid, 105, *106*
Laminin(s), 8
Laminin-1, 8
    epidermolysis bullosa, 92
Laminin-5, 8
    epidermolysis bullosa, 92
    gene mutations
        epidermolysis bullosa, 85
        junctional epidermolysis bullosa, 96
    see also GB3 (monoclonal antibody)
Laminin-6, 8
L&H cells, 1449
Langerhans' cell(s), 16–18, 1457
Langerhans' cell disease *see* Langerhans' cell histiocytosis
Langerhans' cell granulomatosis *see* Langerhans' cell
    histiocytosis
Langerhans' cell histiocytosis, 1458–1466
    anogenital region, 532
    traumatic ulcerative granuloma *vs*, 409
    xanthogranuloma *vs*, eosinophils, 1471
Langerhans' cell lymphoma, 1467
Langerhans' cell sarcoma, 1467

Langerhans' cell tumor, malignant, 1467
Langerhans' granules, 17–18
  see also Birbeck granules
Langhans giant cells, 899
Large B-cell lymphoma
  diffuse, 1441–1443
  HIV-associated, 1450
  intravascular, 1445–1448
Large cell acanthoma, 1164–1165
Large cell lymphoma, 1437
  primary cutaneous CD30+ large cell lymphoma, 1403–1409
Large cell transformation, mycosis fungoides, 1376–1377, 1378
Large intestine
  carcinoma
    hereditary non-polyposis colorectal carcinoma, 1585
    Torre–Muir syndrome, 1584
  diverticula, systemic sclerosis, 808
  polyps
    perifollicular fibroma with, 1559
    see also Familial adenomatous polyposis coli syndrome
  tumor metastases to skin, 1498, 1506, 1508, 1509
Large plaque parapsoriasis (poikiloderma atrophicans
    vasculare), 1360–1361, 1362, 1369, 1371, 1372
Large T-cell lymphoma, HIV-associated, 1450
Large vessel vasculitis, 710
Larva migrans, cutaneous, 984–985
Larynx
  focal palmoplantar keratoderma with oral hyperkeratosis, 66
  mucous membrane pemphigoid, 117
  papilloma, 845
  plasma cell orificial mucositis, 438
  see also Airway obstruction
Lassa fever, 868
Latent nuclear antigen-1 monoclonal antibody, human
    herpesvirus-8, Kaposi's sarcoma, 1833–1834
Late onset focal dermal elastosis, 1045
Late onset prurigo of pregnancy see Pruritic urticarial papules
    and plaques of pregnancy
Late phase reaction, 173
Laugier–Hunziker syndrome, 467, 511, 1007–1008, 1242,
    1243
Launois–Bensaude multiple symmetric lipomatosis, 1691
Lawrence syndrome see Acquired generalized lipodystrophy
Ledderhose's disease, 1725
Leg, diffuse large B-cell lymphoma, 1441, 1442
Leiomyoma
  genital, 536, 1799
  pilar, 1797–1799
Leiomyomatosis, vulva, 537
Leiomyomatous polyp, congenital granular cell epulis vs, 396
Leiomyosarcoma, 1800–1802
  cellular fibrous histiocytoma vs, 1747
  fibrosarcoma vs, 1738
  genital region, 536–537
Leishman–Donovan bodies, 934
Leishmaniasis, 929–934
Leishmaniasis recidiva cutis, 931
Leishmaniasis recidivans, 931
Leishmanin test, 931
Lendrum's phloxine tartazine
  healed epidermoid cyst, 1666
  molluscum contagiosum, 866
  orf, 863, 864
Lentigines
  Carney complex, 1014, 1246, 1856
  generalized, 1242
  LEOPARD syndrome, 1016, 1017
  UV radiation, 1248
Lentigines profusa, 1242
Lentiginosis profusa syndrome see Multiple lentigines syndrome
Lentiginous acral nevus, dysplastic nevus vs, 1261
Lentiginous junctional nevus, 1242, 1244, 1252, 1253
Lentiginous melanoma see Acral lentiginous melanoma
Lentiginous nevus, speckled, 1262
Lentigo
  acral, 1245
  actinic, 1246–1248
  ink spot, 1248, 1249
  oral melanotic macule vs, 468
  simple (lentigo simplex), 1242, 1243, 1244
    nail, 1138
    oral, 468
  subungual, 1137
Lentigo maligna, 1310–1311, 1313–1315, 1316, 1317
  dysplastic nevus vs, 1289
Lentigo maligna melanoma, 1250, 1309, 1310–1311,
    1313–1315, 1316, 1317
Lentigo senilis, 1246–1248
Leonine appearance, chronic actinic dermatitis, 1426
Leopard skin, onchocerciasis, 983
LEOPARD syndrome, 1016–1017
  see also Multiple lentigines syndrome
Lepra reactions, 911–912

Leprechaunism, acanthosis nigricans, 615
Lepromatous leprosy, 910, 911, 912, 913, 914, 915
  subpolar leprosy, 914, 916
Lepromin reaction (Mitsuda reaction), 911, 912, 913
Leprosy, 910–918
  granuloma multiforme vs, 316, 317
  sarcoidosis vs, 295
  squamous cell carcinoma, 913, 1204
  tuberculosis vs, 901
  vasculitis, 753, 916
Leptomeningeal melanocytosis, 1295
Leser–Trélat sign, 616, 1158–1159
Lethal intestinocutaneous syndrome see Degos' disease
Lethal midline granuloma see Extranodal NK/T-cell lymphoma,
    nasal/nasal type; Midline destructive disease
Letterer–Siwe disease, 1458–1459, 1460, 1461–1462, 1463,
    1464, 1465, 1466
Leu 8 expression, lymphocytic infiltrate of the skin, 268
Leukemia
  acute monoblastic, histiocytic lymphoma vs, 1485
  chronic lymphocytic
    chronic lymphocytic leukemia/small lymphocytic
      lymphoma, 1436–1437
    lymphocytic infiltrate of the skin vs, 268
    squamous cell carcinoma with, 1228
  cutaneous infiltrates, 1488–1490
  neutrophil eccrine hidradenitis, 667, 668
  Sweet's syndrome, 680
  vasculitis, 755
  see also Adult T-cell leukemia/lymphoma
Leukemia cutis, 1488
Leukemic mycosis fungoides, 1396
Leukemic vasculitis, 755
Leukocytoclasis
  dermatitis herpetiformis, 133
  leukocytoclastic vasculitis, 714
Leukocytoclastic angiitis see Leukocytoclastic vasculitis
Leukocytoclastic vasculitis, 283, 284, 709–716
  AIDS, 988
  erythema nodosum vs, 347
  malignant disease, 754, 755
  polyarteritis nodosa, 725
  see also Henoch–Schönlein purpura; Infantile acute
    hemorrhagic edema; Urticarial vasculitis
Leukoderma acquisitum centrifugum see Halo nevus
Leukoedema, 398–399
Leukoedema exfoliativum mucosae oris, 387–388
Leukokeratosis oris, focal palmoplantar keratoderma with oral
    hyperkeratosis, 66
Leukoplakia, 452–457
  benign alveolar ridge keratosis vs, 457
  dyskeratosis congenita, 249
  oral, dyskeratosis congenita, 389
  oral lichen planus, 434
  see also Hairy leukoplakia
L-glyceric aciduria, 362
LH7:2 (monoclonal antibody)
  dystrophic epidermolysis bullosa, 97
  epidermolysis bullosa, 93
L'Hermitte-Duclos disease, 1527
Libman-Sacks endocarditis, systemic lupus erythematosus,
    798–799, 800
  valvulitis, 785
Lichen amyloidosis, 560, 561, 562, 563
Lichen aureus, 279–280
Lichenification, 172, 182
Lichen myxedematosus, 605–608
Lichen nitidus, 227
Lichenoid actinic keratosis, 1189
Lichenoid dermatoses, 217–236
  see also Pigmented purpuric lichenoid dermatitis of Gougerot
    and Blum
Lichenoid drug reactions, 634–636
  oral, 434
Lichenoid dysplasia, 456
  oral, 436
Lichenoid eruption, substances causing, 635
Lichenoid keratosis, 229–231
Lichenoid pityriasis see Pityriasis lichenoides
Lichenoid stomatitis, 433–438
Lichenoid xanthogranuloma, 1469
Lichen planopilaris, 219–220, 223–224, 226, 1089–1091
  alopecia areata vs, 1078
  discoid lupus erythematosus vs, 1090, 1093
  folliculotropic mycosis fungoides vs, 1386
Lichen planoporitis, 224
Lichen planus, 217–227
  bullous, 222, 225
    oral cicatricial pemphigoid vs, 444
  of the eccrine glands, 1090
  erythema dyschromicum perstans and, 236
  genital, 480–482
  graft-versus-host disease vs, 254

intraepithelial neoplasia mimic, 520
lichen nitidus with, 229
lichenoid drug reactions vs, 634, 635
lichenoid keratosis vs, 231
lichen sclerosus vs, 486
lupus erythematosus vs, 800
nails, 219, 220, 1133–1134
oral, 433–438
Lichen planus actinicus, 221, 224
Lichen planus-like keratosis, 229–231
Lichen planus linearis, 222
Lichen planus pemphigoides, 115–117, 222, 227
Lichen planus pigmentosus, 221, 224
Lichen planus poritis, 1090
Lichen planus subtropicus (lichen planus actinicus), 221, 224
Lichen planus vesiculosis, 115
Lichen purpuricus, 279–280
Lichen ruber pemphigoides (lichen planus pemphigoides),
    115–117, 222, 227
Lichen ruber verrucosus et reticularis, 233–234
Lichen sclerosus
  anogenital, 482–487
    differentiated VIN, 522
    lichen planus and, 482
  guttate morphea and, 818, 820
  morphea vs, 820
  submucous fibrosis vs, 458
Lichen scrofulosorum, 902, 903, 904
Lichen simplex chronicus, 172, 182
  anogenital, 477
  benign alveolar ridge keratosis, 457–458
  psoriasis vs, 205
Lichen spinulosus, 55
Lichen striatus, 231–233
  nails, 233, 1135
Ligneous conjunctivitis, 426–427
Ligneous gingival hyperplasia, 427, 428
Limb girdle muscle weakness, 826
Limited cutaneous systemic sclerosis, 804–806, 808
Limited pulmonary granulomatosis, 728–729
Linea alba, 385
  leukoedema, 398
Linear acantholytic dermatosis, relapsing, 158
Linear atrophoderma of Moulin, 817
Linear basal cell carcinoma, 1171
Linear circumflex ichthyosis see Ichthyosis linearis circumflexa
Linear cutaneous neuroma, 1765
Linear Darier's disease, 163
  see also Zosteriform Darier's disease
Linear eccrine syringofibroadenoma, non-familial unilateral, 1610
Linear epidermal nevus, 1154
Linear epidermolytic epidermal nevus, 49
Linear focal elastosis, 1049, 1053
Linear granuloma annulare, 299
Linear IgA disease, 134–138
  cell-rich bullous pemphigoid vs, 109
  drug-induced, 646–648
  oral lesions, 446
Linear IgA disease-like epidermolysis bullosa acquisita, 124
Linear IgG anti-basement membrane antibodies
  bullous pemphigoid, 105–107
  epidermolysis bullosa acquisita, 126
Linear lichen planus see Lichen planus linearis
Linear morphea, 815–818
Linear nevoid basaloid follicular hamartoma, 1522
Linear nevus sebaceus syndrome, 1568
Linear porokeratosis, 75
Linear psoriasis, 195
  inflammatory linear verrucous epidermal nevus vs, 211
Linear unilateral basal cell nevus syndrome, 1185
Linear unilateral basal cell nevus with comedones, 1522
Linear verrucous epidermal nevus, inflammatory, 210–211
Lingual thyroid, 394–395
Lingual thyroid choristoma see Lingual thyroid
Lip
  skin, 3, 4
  squamous cell carcinoma, 1199, 1200
Lipedematous alopecia, 1088
Lipedematous scalp, 1088
Lipid(s), 539
  epidermis, 12
  skin surface, 22
Lipid inclusions, sebaceous carcinoma, 1581
Lipidized fibrous histiocytoma, 545, 1750–1751
Lipid lowering agents, acquired ichthyosis, 58
Lipoatrophic diabetes see Acquired generalized lipodystrophy
Lipoatrophic panniculitis, 378–379
  see also Acquired generalized lipodystrophy
Lipoatrophy
  acanthosis nigricans, 615
  localized, 377–384
Lipoblast(s), 1685
  liposarcoma, 1685, 1698, 1699

Lipoblastoma, 1693–1694
  liposarcoma *vs*, 1699
Lipoblastoma-like tumor of the vulva, 1693
Lipoblastomatosis, 1693
Lipodermatosclerosis, 372–373
Lipodystrophia centrifugalis abdominalis infantilis, 377–384
  see also Localized lipoatrophy
Lipodystrophic diabetes *see* Acquired generalized lipodystrophy
Lipodystrophy, 374–384
  in HIV positive patients, 376–377
  see also Localized lipoatrophy
Lipofibromatosis, 1695
Lipogranuloma, sclerosing, 351, 511
  see also Paraffinoma
Lipogranulomatous panniculitis, 351
Lipoid dermatoarthritis, 1482
Lipoid necrobiosis *see* Necrobiosis lipoidica
Lipoid proteinosis
  gingival, 427
  oral lesions, 427, 571
  see also Hyalinosis cutis et mucosae
Lipoma, 1684–1687
  chondroid, 1690
  dermal, 1685, *1686*
    storiform collagenoma *vs*, 1711
  fibrohistiocytic, 1695
  oral, 415–416
  spindle cell, 1688–1689
  see also Adipocytic tumors; Atypical lipoma
Lipomatosis, 1691
  of nerve, 1693
Lipomatous hemangiopericytoma, 1738
Lipomatous neurofibroma, 1774
Lipomembranous change in chronic panniculitis, 372–373
Lipophagic atrophic panniculitis, adult, 379
Lipophagic fat necrosis, 341, *342*
Lipophagic–granulomatous lipoatrophy, 379
Lipophagic panniculitis, 352
  of childhood, 379
Lipoproteins, 539–540, 541, *542*
Liposarcoma, 1695–1699
  lipoblasts, 1685, *1698*, 1699
  oral, 415
  spindle cell, 1697
Lipoxygenase-3 gene, congenital ichthyosiform erythroderma, 43
12(R)-Lipoxygenase gene, 43
Lipschutz ulcer, 488
Lisch nodules, 1776
Lithium, 663–664
  migratory glossitis, 401
  psoriasis, 649
Livedoid vasculitis
  mixed connective tissue disease, 832
  systemic lupus erythematosus, 784
  see also Atrophie blanche
Livedo reticularis
  polyarteritis nodosa, 722
  systemic lupus erythematosus, 784
Livedo vasculitis *see* Atrophie blanche
Liver disease
  erythropoietic protoporphyria, 578, 585–586
  keratitis–ichthyosis–deafness syndrome, 72
  Langerhans' cell histiocytosis, 1462
  lichen planus, 222
  neutrophilic dermatoses, 683
  porphyria cutanea tarda, 585
Liver spot, 1246–1248
LKB1 gene mutations, 1012–1013
Lobomycosis, 976–978
Lobster claw hand, 1029
Lobular capillary hemangioma, 1815–1818
  see also Pyogenic granuloma
Localized acquired cutaneous pseudoxanthoma elasticum, 1045
Localized basaloid follicular hamartoma, 1522
Localized bullous pemphigoid, 101, *103*
Localized cicatricial pemphigoid, Brunsting–Perry variant, 119,
  121, 122
Localized cutaneous amyloidoses, 559–564
Localized cutaneous non-scarring bullous pemphigoid
  (Eberhartinger and Niebauer variant), 101
Localized cutaneous pemphigoid, 101–102
  immunofluorescence studies, 107
Localized cutis laxa, 1039
Localized EB simplex of the hands and feet, 85–86
Localized granuloma annulare, 297, *300, 301*
Localized lipoatrophy (localized lipodystrophy), 377–384
Localized multinucleate distal subungual keratosis, 1136
Localized myxedema, 603–605
Localized non-scarring bullous pemphigoid, pretibial variant,
  104–105
Localized oral pemphigoid, 102
Localized scleroderma *see* Morphea
Localized unilateral hyperhidrosis, 1609

Locally aggressive adnexal carcinoma *see* Microcystic adnexal
  carcinoma
Locally aggressive fibrous lesions, 1724–1727
Locally invasive cellular blue nevus, 1308
Lochkern, 1685, *1686*
Lofgren's syndrome, 288
Longitudinal erythronychia, 1136
Longitudinal melanonychia, *1129*, 1136, 1137–1138
  see also Laugier–Hunziker syndrome
Loose anagen hair syndrome, 1086–1087
  microscopy, 1104
Loricrin, 12
  gene mutation, 43
  progressive symmetric erythrokeratoderma, 62
Low density lipoproteins, 540, *541, 542*
Low grade fibromyxoid sarcoma, 1740, *1741*
Low grade malignant lesions, connective tissue, 1727–1738
Low grade myofibroblastic sarcoma, 1738
Lucio's phenomenon, 912, 913–914, 915–916
Lucio-type leprosy, 910
Ludwig's 'female pattern', 1069, *1070*
Lues maligna, 987
Lumina, intracytoplasmic
  eccrine poroma, 1618
  epithelioid hemangioendothelioma, 1837
Lung
  tumor metastases from
    clear cell tumor, 1210
    to skin, 1498, *1499, 1502, 1505*
  see also Pulmonary involvement
Lung tissue heterotopia, 1674
Lunula, 1128–1129
Lupoid chronic cutaneous leishmaniasis, 933
Lupoid miliaris, 1121, *1122*
Lupus, warty, 895–896, 899
Lupus anticoagulant, 788–789
  see also Antiphospholipid antibody
Lupus anticoagulant syndrome, 789
  valvular heart disease, 785
  see also Antiphospholipid antibody syndrome
Lupus band test, 791
  discoid lupus erythematosus, 1093
  pemphigus erythematosis, 152
Lupus erythematosus, 775–803
  alopecia, 1091–1093
  atrophie blanche, 760
  chilblain lupus erythematosus, 276
  discoid *see* Discoid lupus erythematosus
  drug-induced, 624, 645
    subacute, 783
  oral lesions, 434, 447
  perniosis and, 274
  polymorphous light eruption and, 271, 272, 274, 800
  reticular erythematous mucinosis *vs*, 270
  systemic *see* Systemic lupus erythematosus
  tumid, 273–274, 778, 794
Lupus erythematosus–erythema multiforme-like syndrome, 780
  see also Rowell syndrome
Lupus erythematosus hypertrophicus et profundus, 778
Lupus erythematosus–lichen planus overlap syndrome, 227
Lupus erythematosus profundus (lupus panniculitis), 379–382,
  780
  alopecia, 1092
Lupus erythematosus tumidus, 273–274, 778, 794
Lupus gyratum repens, subacute, 265
Lupus hair, 1091
Lupus mastitis, 380
Lupus miliaris disseminatus faciei (acne agminata), 322–323,
  1123
Lupus panniculitis *see* Lupus erythematosus profundus
Lupus pernio, 290, *291*
  see also Chilblain lupus erythematosus
Lupus vulgaris, 896, 898, 899, 900
  squamous cell carcinoma and, 900, *1200*
Luse bodies, 810
Lyell's syndrome *see* Toxic epidermal necrolysis
Lyme disease, 889–891
Lymphadenoma
  cutaneous, 1553, 1558–1559
    see also Trichoblastoma, with adamantinoid features
  lymphoepithelioma-like carcinoma of skin *vs*, 1239
Lymphadenopathy
  cat scratch disease, 884, 885
  dermatopathic, 1372–1373, *1374*
  HIV infection, 987
  Hodgkin's lymphoma, 1448
  immunoblastic, 1411–1412
  Rosai–Dorfman disease, 1479, 1480
  sarcoidosis, 291, 292
  systemic lupus erythematosus, 800
  see also Chronic lymphadenopathy syndrome
Lymphadenosis benigna cutis *see* B-cell pseudolymphoma
Lymphangioendothelioma, benign, 1845, 1846

Lymphangioma
  acquired progressive, 1845, 1846
  of the alveolar ridge, 396
  in radiotherapy fields, 1847
Lymphangioma circumscriptum, 1845, 1846
  lymphangioma of the alveolar ridge *vs*, 396
Lymphangiomatosis, 1848
  kaposiform hemangioendothelioma with, 1830, 1848
Lymphangiomatous Kaposi's sarcoma, 1833
Lymphangiomyomatosis, 1032
Lymphangiosarcoma, 1845–1847
  see also Angiosarcoma; Lymphedema-associated
    angiosarcoma
Lymphatics, 34–35
  cellulitis, 874
  melanoma invasion, 1324
  morphea, 816
  tufted angioblastoma, 1814
  see also Papillary intralymphatic angioendothelioma (PILA)
Lymphedema
  atypical lipomatous tumor *vs*, 1699
  congenital, spindle cell hemangioma with, 1826
Lymphedema-associated angiosarcoma, 1840
Lymph nodes
  inflammatory pseudotumor *vs*, 1457
  Langerhans' cell histiocytosis, 1462
  nodal blue nevi, 1300
  sentinel lymph node biopsy, melanoma, 1274, 1324–1325
  sentinel lymph node mapping, neuroendocrine carcinoma,
    1231
  Sézary cells (mycosis cells), 1372, *1375*
  see also Lymphadenopathy
Lymphoblastic lymphoma, peripheral primitive neuroectodermal
  tumor *vs*, 1794
Lymphocutaneous sporotrichosis, 974–975
Lymphocytes
  cerebriform *see* Sézary cells
  halo nevus, 1267
  melanoma infiltration, 1322–1323
  see also Cutaneous reaction of lymphocyte recovery
Lymphocytic infiltrate of the skin, 267–269
  polymorphous light eruption *vs*, 268, 272
  reticular erythematous mucinosis *vs*, 268, 270
  tumid lupus erythematosus *vs*, 274
Lymphocytic lymphoma
  of intermediate grade, 1435–1436
  lymphocytic infiltrate of the skin *vs*, 268
Lymphocytic vasculitis, 756–757
Lymphocytoma cutis, 889, 890
  see also B-cell pseudolymphoma
Lymphoepithelial cyst
  oral, 393–394
  see also Branchial cyst
Lymphoepithelial-like carcinoma of skin, cutaneous
  lymphadenoma *vs*, 1559
Lymphoepithelioma, of skin *see* Cutaneous lymphadenoma
Lymphoepithelioma-like carcinoma, 1238–1240
Lymphogranuloma venereum, 505–506
Lymphohistiocytic variant, CD30+ large cell lymphoma,
  1407
Lymphohistiocytosis, discoid lupus erythematosus, 794
Lymphoma, 1357–1457
  adenocarcinoma metastases to skin *vs*, 1506
  AIDS, 991
  anogenital, 515
  classification, 1357–1359
  cytophagic histiocytic panniculitis and, 354, 356
  drug-induced pseudolymphoma *vs*, 654
  epithelioid hemangioma *vs*, 1825
  histiocytic, 1485
  see also Hemophagocytic T-cell lymphoma
  inflammatory pseudotumor *vs*, 1457
  Langerhans' cell, 1467
  lymphoblastic, peripheral primitive neuroectodermal tumor
    vs, 1794
  lymphocytic
    of intermediate grade, 1435–1436
    lymphocytic infiltrate of the skin *vs*, 268
  lymphoepithelioma-like carcinoma of skin *vs*, 1239
  midline destructive disease, 465
  molluscum contagiosum *vs*, 866
  neuroendocrine carcinoma *vs*, 1236, *1237*
  pityriasis lichenoides, 257
  rhabdomyosarcoma *vs*, 1806
  traumatic ulcerative granuloma *vs*, 409
Lymphomatoid contact dermatitis, 652–655
Lymphomatoid drug eruptions, 652–655
Lymphomatoid granulomatosis, 1438–1441
  grades I to III, 1439
  NK/T-cell lymphoma *vs*, 1420
Lymphomatoid papulosis, 257, 258, 1399–1403
  Hodgkin's lymphoma *vs*, 1449
Lymphomatous ATLL, 1413

Lymphophagocytosis, Rosai–Dorfman disease, 1480
Lysosomes, hyalinosis cutis et mucosae, 573

M

Mac 387 (marker), melanoma, 1328
Macroglobulinosis, cutaneous, 574–575
Macromelanosomes (giant melanosomes), 16, 1001, 1242, *1244*
Macrophages
   histiocytic disorders, 1457
   lepromatous leprosy, 914
Macular amyloid, notalgia paresthetica *vs*, 1020
Macular degeneration, Sjögren–Larsson syndrome, 53
Macular lesions
   hereditary oral, 387–390
   tuberous sclerosis, 1030
Macular primary cutaneous amyloidosis, 559–560, *561*, *562*
Macules with or without blisters, 236
Maculopapular cutaneous mastocytosis, 1492, *1493*, *1494*
Maculopapular drug reactions, 626–629
Maculopapular eruptions
   chemotherapeutic agents, 664
   methotrexate, 665, 666
   sarcoidosis, 288–289
Madarosis, 1092
Madelung's disease, 1691
Madurella mycetomatis, 969
Maffucci's syndrome, 1818
   spindle cell hemangioma with, 1826
Main en lorgnette, 1482
   mixed connective tissue disease, 832
Majocchi's disease, 277
Majocchi's granuloma, 938
   see also Nodular granulomatous perifolliculitis
Malabsorption, phrynoderma, 55
Malakoplakia, 508–509, 922–923
Malassezia globosa (*M. furfur*), 174
   pityrosporum folliculitis, 947
   tinea versicolor, 946
Mal de Meleda, 60
Male pattern androgenetic alopecia, 1069, *1070*
Malignancy
   arsenic exposure, 656
   condyloma acuminatum, 845
   epidermodysplasia verruciformis, 847–849, 850
   in epidermoid cyst, 1664
   Henoch–Schönlein purpura and, 754
   internal
      acanthosis nigricans, 616, 617
      acquired palmoplantar keratoderma and, 68–69
      Birt–Hogg–Dubé syndrome, 1561
      Bowen's disease and, 1194
      bullous pemphigoid and, 99
      dermatomyositis, 828
      erythema gyrata repens, 265
      erythema nodosum, 344
      Henoch–Schönlein purpura, 717
      Leser–Trélat sign, 1158
      multicentric reticulohistiocytosis, 1482
      panniculitis, *342*
      primary signet ring carcinoma of eyelid *vs*, 1659
      Torre–Muir syndrome, 1584
      see also Paraneoplastic disorders
   leukocytoclastic vasculitis and, 754, 755
   leukoplakia, oral lichen planus, 434
   neurofibromatosis type I, 1778
   oral, 459–465
   Peutz–Jeghers syndrome, 1012, 1243–1244
   pilar tumors, 1535
   pilonidal sinus, 1679
   radiation dermatitis, 1055
   seborrheic keratosis, 1160
   Sweet's syndrome, 679–680
   see also Metastases; Second malignancy
Malignant acrospiroma *see* Clear cell hidradenocarcinoma
Malignant angioendotheliomatosis, 1445
Malignant atrophic papulosis *see* Degos' disease
Malignant blue nevus, 1340–1342
   atypical blue nevus *vs*, 1308
   cellular blue nevus *vs*, 1306
Malignant chondroid syringoma *see* Malignant mixed tumor
Malignant clear cell hidradenoma *see* Clear cell hidradenocarcinoma
Malignant combined nevus, 1262
Malignant connective tissue tumors, 1738–1741
Malignant cylindroma, 1639–1640
Malignant eccrine poroma *see* Eccrine porocarcinoma
Malignant eccrine spiradenoma, 1642–1645
Malignant edema, 882
Malignant endolymphatic angioendothelioma (Dabska's tumor) *see* Papillary intralymphatic angioendothelioma
Malignant fibrous histiocytoma, 1761–1763
   inflammatory, 1763
   pleomorphic, 1761

leiomyosarcoma *vs*, 1801
Malignant glomus tumor, 1851
Malignant granular cell tumors, 470
Malignant hemangioendothelioma *see* Angiosarcoma
Malignant hidradenoma papilliferum, 1592
Malignant hidroacanthoma simplex, 1615, *1616*
Malignant histiocytosis, 1484
   see also Hemophagocytic T-cell lymphoma
Malignant histiocytosis X, 1467
Malignant Langerhans' cell tumor, 1467
Malignant mixed tumor, 1605–1607
   extraskeletal myxoid chondrosarcoma *vs*, 1855
Malignant myoepithelioma, 1607–1609
Malignant nerve sheath tumor, 1791–1793
   epithelioid, 1793
      soft tissue melanoma *vs*, 1796
Malignant nodular hidradenoma *see* Clear cell hidradenocarcinoma
Malignant peripheral nerve sheath tumor, 1791–1793
Malignant pilomatrixoma *see* Pilomatrix carcinoma
Malignant pyoderma, 675
Malignant schwannoma, 1791–1793
Malignant soft tissue perineurioma, 1786
Malignant Spitz nevus, 1335
   see also Spitzoid melanoma
Malignant syringoma *see* Microcystic adnexal carcinoma
Malignant transformation
   bathing trunk nevus, 1295
   eccrine spiradenoma, 1643
   neurofibroma *see* Malignant peripheral nerve sheath tumor
Malignant vascular tumors, 1837–1848
Mallorcan acne, 1121
Malpighian corpuscles, onion skinning, 800
Mammary ductal apocrine carcinoma, 1598
Mammary-like glands, anogenital, 1595–1596
Mandibuloacral dysplasia, familial partial lipodystrophy associated with, 376
Mannan, 938
Manta ray cells, giant cell fibroma, 414
Mantle, follicular, 1586
Mantle cell lymphoma, 1435–1436
Mantleoma, 1586–1587
Mantle zone lymphoma, 1435–1436
Mantle zone pattern, 1435
Manual labor, punctate palmoplantar keratoderma, 63
Marburg virus disease, 868–869
Marginal papular acrokeratoderma, 64–65
Marginal zone B-cell lymphoma, primary cutaneous, 1428–1432
Marjolin's ulcer, *1202*, 1204
Marmoreal rash, Rothmund–Thomson syndrome, 246
Marshall's syndrome
   acquired cutis laxa, 349, 1023, 1039–1040
   postinflammatory elastolysis and cutis laxa, 1039, 1040
MART-1 (Melan-A), melanoma, 1328
   desmoplastic, 1348
Masson–Fontana reaction, 14
   melanoma metastases, 1512
Masson's trichrome, follicular units, 1063
Masson's tumor, 1806–1807
Mast cell(s), 1491, 1493, 1494
   neurofibroma, 1772
   spindle cell lipoma, 1688
   urticaria, 695
Mast cell disease *see* Mastocytosis
Mastitis, lupus, 380
Mastocytoma, 1491–1492, *1494*
Mastocytosis, 1491–1495
   classification, *1359*
Matrilin-1, relapsing polychondritis, 834
Matrix epithelium, nail, 1128, 1129
Matrix metalloproteinases
   gingival fibromatosis and, 396
   melanoma, 1330
   tumor invasion, 1203
Mature cystic teratoma, cutaneous, 1673–1674
Mauserung phenomenon, 48
Max Joseph spaces, lichen planus, 223
McCune–Albright syndrome, 1008–1009
MCTC cells, 1491
MCT cells, 1491
Mechanobullous dermatosis, epidermolysis bullosa, 84, 127
Mechanoreceptors, 35
Median nasal dermoid fistula, *1674*
   sebaceous trichofolliculoma *vs*, 1545–1546
Median raphe cyst, 516–517, 1677, *1678*
Median rhomboid glossitis, 402–403
   benign migratory glossitis *vs*, 402
Mediterranean cutaneous leishmaniasis, 929
Medium-sized vessel vasculitis, *710*
Medulla, hair shaft, 1065
Mees' lines, 664
Megakaryocytes, extramedullary hematopoietic tumor, 1490
Meibomian glands, 20, 1579

Meissnerian differentiation, diffuse neurofibroma, 1774
Meissner's corpuscles, 35
Melan-A *see* MART-1
Melanin, 13–16
Melanoacanthoma, 1159, *1161*
   oral, 468–469
Melanoacanthosis, 468–469
Melanocortin-1 receptor, gene mutations, 1000
Melanocytes, 13–16
   intravascular, 1256
   melanocytic nevi, 1252–1253
   mycosis fungoides, 1379
   nail units, 1136
   neurotization, 1255
   postinflammatory hyperpigmentation, 1019
Melanocytic lesions
   dermal, 1297–1308
   oral, 467–470
Melanocytic matricoma, 1541–1542
Melanocytic neoplasm of indeterminate malignant potential (Spitz nevus type), 1274
Melanocytic nevus (banal nevus), 1250–1259
   junctional epidermolysis bullosa–non-Herlitz, 89
   nail, 1138–1139
   nevoid melanoma *vs*, 1331
   oral, 469
Melanoma, 1309–1356
   acral lentiginous *see* Acral lentiginous melanoma
   amelanotic clear cell melanoma, clear cell squamous cell carcinoma *vs*, 1210
   animal-type *see* Animal-type melanoma
   atypical fibroxanthoma *vs*, 1759
   balloon cell, 1338–1339
      sebaceous carcinoma *vs*, 1338, 1583
   banal nevus *vs*, 1256–1257
   children, 1309, 1353–1355
   deep penetrating growth pattern, *1284*
   dermal nevus *vs*, 1258
   desmoplastic, 1346–1353
      desmoplastic nevus *vs*, 1277
      differential diagnosis, 1325–1327
   in dysplastic nevus, *1290*
   dysplastic nevus syndrome, 1283–1290
   epidermoid cyst and, 1664
   epithelioid malignant peripheral nerve sheath tumor *vs*, 1793
   fibroepithelial polyp *vs*, 1708
   genital, 514–515
   genital melanosis, 511
   halo nevus *vs*, 1267, 1268
   with heterologous differentiation, 1140
   immunohistochemistry, 1328–1331
      desmoplastic, 1348–1349
      differential diagnosis, 1325–1326
   interdigitating dendritic cell tumor/sarcoma *vs*, 1485
   leukoderma, 995
   lymphoepithelioma-like carcinoma of skin *vs*, 1239
   malignant combined nevus, 1262
   metastases, 1345–1346, *1498*, *1499*, *1502*, 1512–1513
      epidermotropic, 1345–1346
      generalized melanosis associated, 1020–1021
      to skin, *1498*, *1502*, 1512–1513
   minimal deviation, 1331
      Spitz nevus type, 1274
   nail, 1136–1137, 1139–1141, 1312
   non-cutaneous, 1312
   oral, 469–470
   prognostic indicators, 1320–1325
   proliferation nodule *vs*, 1296
   radial growth phase (in situ) superficial spreading, dysplastic nevus *vs*, 1289
   recurrent nevus *vs*, 1265
   risk from melanocytic nevi, 1250, 1251
   sentinel lymph node biopsy, 1274, 1324–1325
   soft tissue melanoma *vs*, 1795–1796
   of soft tissues, 1795–1796
   spindle cell, leiomyosarcoma *vs*, 1801
   Spitz nevus *vs*, 1269–1270, 1272, 1335
      CD40, 1272, 1329
   subungual nevus *vs*, 1138–1139
   variants, 1331–1345
   vascular invasion, *1326*
   'uncertain', 1343
   veins, 1343
   see also Small cell melanoma
Melanoma cell adhesion molecule, 1330
   melanoma, desmoplastic, 1348
Melanonychia, longitudinal, *1129*, 1136, 1137–1138
   see also Laugier–Hunziker syndrome
Melanonychia striata, 467
   see also Longitudinal melanonychia
Melanophages, 1253
Melanosis
   genital, 511–512

Melanosis (cont'd)
   metastatic melanoma, 1020–1021
   Riehl's, 1019–1020
   transient neonatal pustular, 215
   see also Melanotic pigmentation
Melanosis neviformis Becker see Becker's nevus
Melanosomes, 15–16
   see also Macromelanosomes
Melanotic disease, equine, 1344
   see also Animal-type melanoma
Melanotic macule
   genital, 511
   nail, 1137, 1138
   oral, 467–468
Melanotic nevus, genital, 512–514
Melanotic pigmentation
   isolated mucocutaneous, 1012
   see also Melanosis
Melanotic schwannoma, 1770
   psammomatous, 1014, 1015, 1016, 1770
Melanotrichoblastoma, 1553
Melasma, 1007
Mel-CAM see Melanoma cell adhesion molecule
Meleney's gangrene, 876
Melkersson–Rosenthal syndrome, 440
Meltzer's triad, 765
Membrane attack complex
   dermatitis herpetiformis, 131–132
   lupus erythematosus, 791
Membrane-coating granules, 11
   see also Odland bodies
Membranoproliferative glomerulonephritis, acquired partial
      lipodystrophy, 376
Membranous fat necrosis, 373–374
Memory, cutaneous, 637
MEN see Multiple endocrine neoplasia syndrome
Meningeal heterotopias, 1788–1789, 1790
Meningioma, 1788
   cutaneous, 1788–1789, 1790
Meningocele, 1790
Meningococcal septicemia, 881
Menkes disease, pili torti, 1114
Mental retardation, keratitis–ichthyosis–deafness syndrome, 72
Mepacrine, pigmentation, 639, 640, 641
Mercury
   amalgam tattoo, 465–466, 671
   mercuric sulfide tattoo, 663
   oral lichen planus, 434
   pigmentation with, 661–662
Mercury exanthem, acute generalized, 662, 663
Mercury granuloma, 662, 663
Merkel cell(s), 18–20, 35
Merkel cell carcinoma
   basaloid squamous cell carcinoma vs, 463
   see also Neuroendocrine carcinoma
Mesangial lupus glomerulonephritis, 797
Mesangiocapillary glomerulonephritis, acquired partial
      lipodystrophy, 376
Mesenchymal cells, fibrous hamartoma of infancy, 1721, 1722
Mesenchymal chondrosarcoma, extraskeletal, 1855, 1856
Mesenchymal component, metaplastic carcinoma, 1227–1228
Mesenchymal hamartoma, rhabdomyomatous, 1802–1803
Mesodermal stromal polyp, 532–533
Mesonephric cyst, 518
Mesothelial cyst, 519
Mesothelioma, 1510–1511, 1512
Metabolic studies, hair diseases, 1062
Metaplastic basal cell carcinoma, 1178, 1181
Metaplastic carcinoma, 461–462, 1227–1228
   malignant mixed tumor vs, 1606
   see also Carcinosarcoma
Metaplastic melanoma, 1343–1344
Metaplastic synovial cyst, cutaneous, 1678–1679
Metastases
   adenocarcinoma, 1506–1508
      epithelioid hemangioendothelioma vs, 1839
   to anogenital region, 532
   apocrine carcinoma, 1597
   basal cell carcinoma, 1172
   carcinoma
      epithelioid malignant peripheral nerve sheath tumor vs,
         1793
      meningeal heterotopias vs, 1788
   clear cell tumors, 1210
   dermatofibrosarcoma protuberans, 1729
   desmoplastic melanoma, 1349
   eccrine spiradenocarcinoma, 1642
   epithelioid sarcoma and, 1859, 1862
   extrarenal rhabdoid tumor as, 1865
   melanoma see Melanoma, metastases
   metaplastic carcinoma, 1228
   neuroendocrine carcinoma, 1230, 1231, 1236
   oral carcinoma, 460

sebaceous carcinoma, 1579
to skin, 1497–1514, 1515
Spitz nevus, 1273
squamous cell carcinoma, 1506
   actinic keratosis and, 1188
   oral, 1498, 1499
   rates, 1200–1201, 1206, 1207
   subungual, 1145–1146, 1499
Metastatic calcinosis cutis, 595, 596, 597
Metastatic Crohn's disease, 321–322, 489
   subcutaneous sarcoidosis vs, 369
Metastatic fat necrosis, 358
   pancreatic disease, 357
Metatarsalgia, 1764, 1765
Metatypical basal cell carcinoma, 1175, 1178
Methotrexate
   flag sign, 665
   maculopapular eruption, 665, 666
Methyl bromide, bromoderma, 657–658
Meyerson's nevus, 1268
Meyerson's phenomenon, 1158
Mi-2 antibody, 828
MIB-1
   nevoid melanoma vs banal nevus, 1332, 1334
   Spitz nevus vs melanoma, 1272
   see also Ki-67
Mibelli
   angiokeratoma of, 1812
   porokeratosis of, 75, 77
MIC-2 protein, antibody, peripheral primitive neuroectodermal
      tumor, 1794
Mica scale, 256
Michaelis–Gutmann bodies, 509, 922
Michelin tire appearance, 1691
Microabscesses see Eosinophil microabscesses; Neutrophil
      microabscesses
Microchimerism, systemic sclerosis, 810
Microcomedone, 1667–1668
Microcystic adnexal carcinoma, 1647–1651
   adenosquamous carcinoma vs, 1217
   squamous cell carcinoma vs, 1208
   syringoid eccrine carcinoma vs, 1647
Microcystis aeruginosa, 978
Microfibrils, 9
Microfilariae, onchocerciasis, 982–983, 984
Microinvasive radial growth phase melanoma, 1313
Micronodular basal cell carcinoma, 1174–1175, 1177
Micropapular lesions, sarcoidosis, 289
Microphthalmia transcription factor
   gene mutations, 1004
   melanoma, 1329
   soft tissue melanoma, 1795
Microsatellite(s), melanoma, 1324
Microsatellite instability, 1585
Microscopic polyarteritis, 710, 723–724, 726, 731
   oral, Wegener's granulomatosis vs, 443
   see also Polyarteritis nodosa
Microscopic satellites, melanoma, 1324
Microsomal fatty aldehyde dehydrogenase, Sjögren–Larsson
      syndrome, 53
Microsporum (spp.), 938–939
Microsporum audouinii, 938–939
Microsporum canis, 938–939
Microvenular hemangioma, 1820
Mid-dermal elastolysis, 1048–1049
Midline destructive disease, 465
   Wegener's granulomatosis vs, 443
Midline lethal granuloma see Extranodal NK/T-cell lymphoma,
      nasal/nasal type; Midline destructive disease
Miescher's granuloma, 345
   see also Sarcoidal variant, necrobiosis lipoidica
Migratory panniculitis (erythema nodosum migrans), 343, 344,
      345–347
Mikulicz cells, 918, 919
Milia, 1669–1670
   dystrophic epidermolysis bullosa, 97
Milia en plaque, 1669
Miliaria, 193–194
Miliaria crystallina, 193, 194
Miliaria profunda, 194
Miliaria pustulosa, 193, 194
Miliaria rubra (prickly heat), 193, 194
   erythema toxicum neonatorum vs, 214, 705
Miliary tuberculosis of the skin, 896–897, 899, 900, 901
Milium-like syringoma, 1626, 1627
Milker's nodule, 862
Milk-line nevus, 512
Minimal deviation melanoma, 1331
   Spitz nevus type, 1274
Minimus variants
   dystrophic epidermolysis bullosa, 92
   junctional epidermolysis bullosa, 87
Minocycline, hyperpigmentation, 468, 638, 639, 640, 641

Mitochondrial DNA syndrome-associated poikiloderma,
      245–246
Mitosoid figures, focal epithelial hyperplasia, 432
Mitotic rates, melanoma, 1323
Mitsuda reaction, 911, 912, 913
Mitten lesions (pseudosyndactyly), Hallopeau–Siemens variant
      dystrophic epidermolysis bullosa, 90
Mixed connective tissue disease, 832–833
Mixed cryoglobulinemia, 764, 765
Mixed tumor of skin, 1600–1605
   see also Chondroid syringoma
MMR gene and products, 1585–1586
Moccasin lesion, 1154
Moll's gland(s), 22
   hidradenitis suppurativa, 706
Moll's gland carcinoma, 1597
Moll's gland cysts, 1588
Molluscoid pseudotumors, 1023
Molluscum contagiosum, 864–867
   AIDS, 990
Molluscum sebaceum see Keratoacanthoma
Mondor's disease see Sclerosing lymphangitis
Mongolian blue spot, 1297
Monilethrix, 1110–1112
   pili torti vs, 1113
Moniliform blepharosis (string of beads appearance), 571
Monoblastic leukemia, acute, histiocytic lymphoma vs, 1485
Monoclonal cryoglobulinemia, 764, 765, 766
Monoclonal gammopathy
   IgA pemphigus, 154
   necrobiotic xanthogranuloma, 319
   Schnitzler's syndrome, 282
Monocytoid B-cells, marginal zone B-cell lymphoma, 1428
Mononuclear histiocyte-like cells, traumatic ulcerative
      granuloma, 408
Montenegro skin test, 931
Montgomery's tubercles, 20, 1565
Morbilliform drug reactions, 626–629
Morbus Darier see Darier's disease
Morphea, 815–821
   atrophoderma of Pasini and Pierini vs, 822
   eosinophilic fasciitis vs, 823–824
   systemic sclerosis and, 812, 815, 818
Morpheaform basal cell carcinoma, 1170, 1171, 1175,
      1178
   desmoplastic trichoepithelioma vs, 1552
   microcystic adnexal carcinoma vs, 1649
Morphea profunda, 383
   sclerosing panniculitis vs, 372
   see also Subcutaneous scleroderma
Morsicatio see Chronic bite injury
Morton's neuroma, 1764, 1765
Mosaic acral keratosis, 64–65
Mosaicism
   bullous ichthyosiform erythroderma, 1155
   incontinentia pigmenti, 702
Mosaic plantar warts, 841, 842
Moth-eaten alopecia, 1088
Mother yaw, 892
Mouse model, nevus sebaceus, 1569
MSI (microsatellite instability), 1585
MUC18 see Melanoma cell adhesion molecule
Mucha–Haberman disease (pityriasis lichenoides et
      varioliformis acuta), 192, 255
Mucicarmine, cryptococcosis, 961, 962
Mucin
   cutaneous mucinous carcinoma vs gastrointestinal
      carcinomas, 1657
   dermal, mycosis fungoides, 1393
   follicular mucinosis, 1388
Mucin core proteins, Paget's disease, 1516
Mucinorrhea, 1387
Mucinoses, 269–271, 600–615
   follicular, 1387–1390
   see also Reticular erythematous mucinosis
Mucinous alopecia see Alopecia mucinosa
Mucinous carcinoma, primary, 1654–1657
Mucinous cyst, vestibule, 517
Mucinous eccrine nevus, 1609
Mucinous metaplasia
   benign, genital region, 515–516
   squamous cell carcinoma with, 1215, 1217
   see also Mucinous syringometaplasia
Mucinous nevus, 614
Mucinous syringometaplasia, 1680–1681
   genital region, 516
Muciparous epidermal tumor see Mucinous syringometaplasia
Muckle–Wells syndrome, 559, 693
Mucoblasts, 1148
Mucocele, 447–449
   oral lymphoepithelial cyst vs, 394
Mucocutaneous candidiasis, chronic, 947, 948–949
Mucocutaneous leishmaniasis, 931, 933

Mucocutaneous lymph node syndrome (Kawasaki syndrome), 710, 735–737
Mucoepidermoid carcinoma, 1215, 1217–1218
  necrotizing sialometaplasia *vs*, 450
  see also Adenosquamous carcinoma
Mucoid carcinoma, skin metastases, 1508–1509
Mucoid cyst, penis (median raphe cyst), 516–517, 1677, *1678*
Mucopapillary cyst, 448
Mucopapillary cyst, 448
Mucormycosis, 963
Mucosa
  buccal, focal non-epidermolytic palmoplantar keratoderma
    with esophageal squamous cell carcinoma, 68
  oral *see* Oral mucosa
  see also Mucous membranes
Mucosal melanotic macule, 468–469
Mucosal neuroma, 1764–1765
Mucosal pemphigoid, 102
Mucositis, plasma cell orificial, 438–439, 487
Mucous extravasation/retention phenomenon *see* Mucocele
Mucous membrane pemphigoid (cicatricial pemphigoid),
    117–122
  drug-induced, 648, 660
  oral, 443–444
Mucous membranes
  linear IgA disease, 135
  see also Mucosa
Mulberry's molars, 498
Müllerian cyst, 1676
Multicentric pigmented Bowen's disease *see* Bowenoid papulosis
Multicentric reticulohistiocytosis, 1482
Multidrug resistance protein-6, mutations, 1041
Multifocal basal cell carcinoma (superficial basal cell
    carcinoma), 1170, 1171, 1176, *1179*
Multifocal chronic Langerhans' cell histiocytosis, 1460–1461,
    1462–1463
Multifocal papilloma virus epithelial hyperplasia (focal
    epithelial hyperplasia), oral, 411, 432–433
Multifocal pigmented Bowen's disease, 519
Multi hair, 1109–1110
Multinodular keratoacanthoma, 1222
Multinucleate cell angiohistiocytoma, 1742, *1743*
  oral, 415
Multinucleate distal subungual keratosis, localized, 1136
Multiple eccrine syringofibroadenoma, 1610
Multiple endocrine neoplasia syndrome
  type 2A, amyloidosis, 564
  type 2B, mucosal neuroma, 1764–1765
Multiple familial trichoepithelioma, 1546, *1547*
Multiple hairy pacinian neurofibromas, 1765
Multiple hamartoma disease *see* Cowden's syndrome
Multiple lentigines syndrome, 1245–1246
  see also LEOPARD syndrome
Multiple myeloma *see* Myeloma
Multiple symmetric lipomatosis (Launois–Bensaude), 1691
Multisystem disease, 1460–1461, 1462–1463
  with organ dysfunction (acute generalized Langerhans' cell
    histiocytosis), 1458–1459, 1460, 1461–1462, *1463,
    1464, 1465, 1466*
Munro microabscess, 202
  Netherton syndrome, 52
Murine lupus, 790–791
Murine typhus fever, 928, 929
Muscle
  polymyositis, 826, 829–830
  proliferative myositis, 1706
  systemic sclerosis, 812–813
  see also entries beginning Smooth muscle; *entries beginning*
    Striated muscle
Muscular dystrophy, epidermolysis bullosa with, 85, 86
Mycetoma, 967–968, *969, 970*
Mycobacteria
  infective panniculitis, 371
  metastatic Crohn's disease *vs* infection with, 322
  non-tuberculous, 904–910
  sarcoidosis, 293
Mycobacterium avium intracellulare, 906–907, 909
  AIDS, 991
Mycobacterium fortuitum chelonae, 904–905, 908
Mycobacterium gordonae, 907
Mycobacterium haemophilum, 907, 909
Mycobacterium kansasii, 906, 908
  AIDS, 991
Mycobacterium leprae, 910
Mycobacterium marinum (balnei), 904, *905*, 907
Mycobacterium scrofulaceum, 907
Mycobacterium simiae, 907
Mycobacterium tuberculosis, 897–898
Mycobacterium ulcerans, 906, 908–909
Mycosis cells *see* Sézary cells
Mycosis fungoides, 1359–1393
  adult T-cell leukemia/lymphoma *vs*, 1414
  AIDS, 991, 1365
  amyloidosis, 564

chronic actinic dermatitis *vs*, 1427
chronic superficial dermatitis *vs*, 262, 263
  with dermal mucin, 1393
  erythrodermic, 1396
  granuloma annulare *vs*, 302
  HIV-associated, 1450
  ichthyosis and, 1390
  palmoplantar, 1392–1393
    Ketron–Goodman disease *vs*, 1395
  pigmented purpuric dermatoses *vs*, 279
  pityriasis lichenoides, 257
  poikiloderma, 800
  staging, 1362, *1365*
  transformation, 1376–1377, *1378*
  variants, 1377–1393
Mycosis fungoides d'emblée, 1360, 1376
Mycosis fungoides-like features, contact dermatitis, 1424
Mycosis fungoides palmaris et plantaris *see* Palmoplantar
    mycosis fungoides
Myelodysplastic syndrome, relapsing polychondritis, 834
Myeloid sarcoma (granulocytic sarcoma/myeloid sarcoma),
    1488
Myeloma
  amyloidosis and, 554
  multiple, cutaneous manifestations, 1444–1445
  plane xanthoma, 547
Myeloma-associated systemic amyloidosis, 555–558
Myelomonocytic leukemia cells, 1489
Myocardium
  dermatomyositis, 827
  rhabdomyoma, 1032
  systemic sclerosis, 807, 814
Myoepithelial cells, eccrine sweat glands, 25–26
Myoepithelial differentiation, signet ring cell basal cell
    carcinoma, 1177–1178, *1180*
Myoepithelioma, 1607–1609
  ectomesenchymal chondromyxoid tumor *vs*, 472
  of soft tissue, 1858
Myofibroblast(s)
  calcifying aponeurotic fibroma, 1720
  dermatofibrosarcoma with myoid nodules, 1733, *1734*
  fibrous hamartoma of infancy, 1721, *1722*
  inclusion body fibromatosis, 1719
  inflammatory myofibroblastic tumor, 1736
  plexiform fibrous histiocytoma, *1756*
Myofibroblastic differentiation, dermatomyofibroma,
    1709–1710
Myofibroblastic sarcoma, low grade, 1738
Myofibroblastic tumor, inflammatory, 1736
  see also Inflammatory pseudotumor
Myofibroma, 1713–1716
  fibrous hamartoma of infancy *vs*, 1722
  storiform collagenoma *vs*, 1711
Myofibromatosis, 1713–1716
Myoid nodules, dermatofibrosarcoma with, 1733–1734
Myointima, 537–538
Myolipomas, 1685
Myopericytoma, 1800, 1851–1852
Myosin-Va gene, 1001
Myositis, proliferative, 1706
Myospherulosis, *960*
  coccidioidomycosis *vs*, 959
  see also Spherulocystic disease
Myotonic dystrophy, pilomatrixoma, 1536
Myrmecia
  nails, 1131
  plantar warts, 842
Myxedema
  generalized, 602–603
  localized, 603–605
Myxofibrolipoma, *1686*
Myxofibrosarcoma, 1761–1763
  acral myxoinflammatory fibroblastic sarcoma *vs*, 1736
  low grade fibromyxoid sarcoma *vs*, 1740
  myxoid liposarcoma *vs*, 1699
  superficial angiomyxoma *vs*, 1856–1857
Myxoid chondrosarcoma
  chondroid lipoma *vs*, 1690
  epithelioid hemangioendothelioma *vs*, 1839
  extraskeletal, 1854–1855
  ossifying fibromyxoid tumor *vs*, 1857
Myxoid cyst, 613–614
  nail region, 1148
  superficial angiomyxoma *vs*, 1857
  see also Cutaneous myxoma
Myxoid dermatofibrosarcoma, 1733
Myxoid liposarcoma, 1696, 1697–1698
  chondroid lipoma *vs*, 1690
  extraskeletal myxoid chondrosarcoma *vs*, 1855
  lipoblastoma *vs*, 1694
  myxofibrosarcoma *vs*, 1699
Myxoid malignant fibrous histiocytoma *see* Myxofibrosarcoma
Myxoid melanoma, 1339–1340

Myxoid neurofibroma, 1773
  neurothekeoma *vs*, 1784
Myxoid pseudocyst, nail region, 1148
Myxoinflammatory fibroblastic sarcoma, acral, 1735
Myxoma
  atrial
    Carney complex, 1014, 1015
    skin involvement, 1503
  Carney complex, 1014, 1015
  cutaneous, 1856
    see also Myxoid cyst
  dermal, neurothekeoma *vs*, 1784
  see also Nerve sheath myxoma

N

NADPH steroid dehydrogenase-like protein, gene mutations,
    1155
Naegele–Franchescetti–Jadassohn syndrome, 1010–1011
Nail(s), 1127–1152
  alopecia areata, 1074, *1075*
  anatomy, 1127–1129
  chemotherapeutic agents, 664
  Darier's disease, 159, *160, 161,* 1135–1136
  growth, 1127–1152
  Hailey–Hailey disease, 156
  hidrotic ectodermal dysplasia, 71
  Laugier–Hunziker disease, *1243*
  lichen planus, 219, *220,* 1133–1134
  lichen striatus, 233, 1135
  melanoma, 1136–1137, 1139–1141, 1312
  Naegele–Franchescetti–Jadassohn syndrome, 1010
  paronychia, 879
  pathological specimens, 1129
    onychomycosis, 1130
  pemphigus vulgaris, 141
  psoriasis, 199, 1132–1133
  see also Melanonychia; Melanonychia striata; Pachyonychia
    congenita; Trachyonychia; *entries beginning*
    Periungual...; *entries beginning* Subungual...
Nail folds, 1127–1128
Nail ligaments, 1128
Nail plate, 1129
NAME *see* Carney complex
Nanogen hairs, 1077, 1078
Napkin rash, 476
  see also Diaper dermatitis
Nasal dermoid fistula, median, *1674*
  sebaceous trichofolliculoma *vs*, 1545–1546
Nasal glioma, 1789, *1790, 1791*
Nasal lesions
  granuloma faciale, 738
  leprosy, 910
  lupus vulgaris, 900
  mucous membrane pemphigoid, 117
  NK lymphoma *see* Extranodal NK/T-cell lymphoma,
    nasal/nasal type
  relapsing polychondritis, 834
  rhinoscleroma, 918–919
  rhinosporidiosis, 978
  subcutaneous panniculitic T-cell lymphoma *vs*, 1417
  Wegener's granulomatosis, 727
Nasopharyngeal carcinoma, lymphoepithelioma-like carcinoma
    of skin *vs*, 1239
Nasu-Halola's disease, 373
National Institutes of Health, neurofibromatosis type I,
    diagnostic criteria, 1775
Native DNA, antibodies, 787
  verrucous discoid lupus erythematosus, 778
Natural killer cells, 1418
Naxos disease, 1114
NC16A subunit, bullous pemphigoid 108 kD antigen, 108
  lichen planus pemphigoides, 116
Necrobiosis, cat scratch disease, 885
Necrobiosis lipoidica, 304, 305–310
  atypical facial, 314–315
  necrobiotic xanthogranuloma *vs*, 309, 320
Necrobiotic collagen, transepidermal elimination
  necrobiosis lipoidica, 308
  perforating granuloma annulare, 299
  prurigo nodularis, 330
Necrobiotic xanthogranuloma, 318–320
  necrobiosis lipoidica *vs*, 309, 320
  with paraproteinemia, 318–320
Necrolytic acral erythema, 618, 620–621
Necrolytic migratory erythema, 619–622
Necrosis, epithelioid sarcoma, 1860
Necrotizing cellulitis, necrotizing fasciitis *vs*, 877
Necrotizing fasciitis, 372, 874, 876–878
  pyoderma gangrenosum *vs*, 677, 878
  varicella, 856
Necrotizing granuloma, cutaneous extravascular, 320
Necrotizing lymphocytic folliculitis *see* Acne necrotica
Necrotizing sialometaplasia, 449–450

Neisseria spp., 881
  arteritis, 753
Nekam's disease, 233–234
Nematodes, 982–985
NEMO (nuclear factor κB gene modulator), gene mutations,
  incontinentia pigmenti, 703
Neonate
  adnexal polyp of skin, 1610
  congenital nevus, 1294–1296
  cytomegalovirus, 858–859
  extramedullary hematopoiesis, 1490
  fat necrosis of the newborn, hypercalcemia, 359–360
  gingival granular cell tumor, 1781–1782
  herpes simplex virus, 852
  lupus erythematosus, 786–787, 800
    anti-Ro antibodies, 790
  pemphigus, 142
  restrictive dermopathy, 1036
  sclerema neonatorum, 361–362
  toxemic erythema, 705
    incontinentia pigmenti *vs*, 704, 705
  toxic erythema, 214, 705
    incontinentia pigmenti *vs*, 704, 705
  transient pustular melanosis, 215
Nephrogenic fibrosing dermopathy, 1033–1035, *1036*
Nerve(s)
  lipomatosis, 1693
  Morton's neuroma, 1764, *1765*
  tuberculoid leprosy, 910, 914
Nerve fibers
  herpes simplex virus, 853
  Merkel cells related to, 19
  necrobiosis lipoidica, 305
  neurofibromas, 1773
  nodular prurigo and, 184
  sarcoidosis, 292
Nerve sheath myxoma
  cellular, 1783–1784
  dermal, 1782–1784
  superficial angiomyxoma *vs*, 1856
Nerve sheath tumor *see* Malignant nerve sheath tumor
Nervous system
  skin supply, 35–36
    Meissner's corpuscles, 35
    Pacinian corpuscles, 35
  see also Central nervous system
Netherton syndrome, 51–52, 1106
Neumann variant, pemphigus vegetans, 146
Neural hamartoma, congenital, 1765
Neural transformation, desmoplastic melanoma, 1347, *1351*
Neurilemmoma, 1767–1768
  see also Schwannoma
Neuroblastoma
  metastases to skin, 1498–1499, 1503
    peripheral primitive neuroectodermal tumor *vs*, 1794
  rhabdomyosarcoma *vs*, 1806
Neurocristic hamartoma, 1303–1304
  bathing-trunk nevus as, 1295
Neurocutaneous melanocytosis, 1295
Neuroectodermal melanolysosomal syndrome, 1002
Neuroectodermal tumors, 1763–1764
  see also Primitive neuroectodermal tumor
Neuroendocrine carcinoma, 1230–1238, 1510
  immunohistochemistry, 1235–1236, *1237*, 1504
  lymphoepithelioma-like carcinoma of skin *vs*, 1239
  see also Merkel cell carcinoma; Small cell carcinoma
Neuroendocrine differentiation, primary mucinous carcinoma,
  1655
Neuroepithelioma, peripheral, 1793–1795
Neurofibroma, 1771–1775
  cellular
    with atypia, 1774
    pilar leiomyoma *vs*, 1798
  fibrous hamartoma of infancy *vs*, 1722
  low grade fibromyxoid sarcoma *vs*, 1740
  malignant change *see* Malignant peripheral nerve sheath
    tumor
  multiple hairy pacinian, 1765
  myxoid, 1773
    neurothekeoma *vs*, 1784
  neurofibromatosis type I, 1772, 1773–1774, 1776
  neurofibromatosis type II, 1768
  superficial acral fibromyxoma *vs*, 1718
  traumatic neuroma *vs*, 1763
  see also Diffuse neurofibroma
Neurofibromatosis, 1775–1779
  type I, 1775–1778
    malignant peripheral nerve sheath tumor, 1791–1792
    neurofibromas, 1772, 1773–1774, 1776
    schwannomas, 1767
  type II, 1768, 1778–1779
Neurofibrosarcoma, 1791–1793
Neurofilament protein, desmoplastic melanoma, 1352

Neurofollicular hamartoma, 1562–1563
Neurogenic hypothesis, vitiligo, 995
Neuroid features, nevi, 1292
Neuroma
  epithelial sheath, 1767
  Morton's, 1764, *1765*
  mucosal, 1764–1765
  solitary circumscribed, 1765–1766
  traumatic, 1763–1764
Neuropathia mucinosa cutanea, 614–615
Neuropathy
  Behçet's disease, 745
  dermatomyositis, 830–831
  familial amyloidotic polyneuropathy, 559
  leprosy, 910
  Lyme disease, 889, 890
  notalgia paresthetica, 561, 1020
  polyarteritis nodosa, 721
  temporal arteritis, 748
Neurothekeoma, 1782–1784
Neurotization, melanocytes, 1255
Neurotrophins, alopecia areata, 1075
Neurotropic melanoma, 1346–1353
Neurotropism
  lentigo maligna, 1314
  squamous cell carcinoma, 1206–1207
Neurovascular hamartoma, congenital, 1765
Neutrophil eccrine hidradenitis, 667–669
Neutrophilic dermatoses
  acute febrile *see* Sweet's syndrome
  associated with gastrointestinal and hepatobiliary disease,
    683–684
  of the dorsal hands, 741
Neutrophilic lobular panniculitis associated with rheumatoid
    arthritis, 369
Neutrophil microabscesses
  bullous pemphigoid, 103, 104, *106*
  bullous systemic lupus erythematosus, 129
  dermatitis herpetiformis, 132
  IgA pemphigus, 155
Neutrophil-rich variant, CD30+ large cell lymphoma, 1407
Nevirapine, adverse reactions, 988–989
Nevocytes, 1252
Nevoid basal cell carcinoma syndrome, 1184–1185
  basal cell carcinoma, 1173, 1184
Nevoid basaloid follicular hamartoma, linear, 1522
Nevoid melanoma, 1331–1333, *1334*
  small cell melanoma *vs*, 1333
Nevoid variant, bullous ichthyosiform erythroderma, 45
Nevoxanthoendothelioma *see* Xanthogranuloma
Nevus
  epidermoid cyst with, 1664
  first year of life, 1294–1296
  hair, 1519
  hair follicle, 1519–1520
  immunohistochemistry, 1328–1329
  melanoma from, incidence, 1309
  ossification, 1853
  see also Blue rubber bleb nevus syndrome; *specific types*
Nevus achromicus, 1004–1005
Nevus anemicus, 1004
Nevus comedonicus *see* Comedo nevus
Nevus comedonicus syndrome, 1154, 1520
Nevus depigmentosus, 1004–1005
Nevus elasticus, 1050–1052
Nevus flammeus, 1808–1810
Nevus fuscoceruleus ophthalmomaxillaris *see* Nevus of Ota
Nevus fuscoceruleus zygomaticus, 1299
Nevus lipomatosus superficialis, 1691–1692
Nevus maturation, 1254–1255
Nevus mucinosus, 614
Nevus of Ito, 1298–1299
Nevus of Ota, 1297–1298
Nevus of Ota acquisica, 1299
Nevus sebaceus, 1568–1572
Nevus sebaceus syndrome, linear, 1568
Nevus spilus, 1262
Nevus sudoriferus *see* Eccrine nevus
Nevus unius lateris, 1153
Nevus verrucosus, 1153
Nevus with senescent atypia, 1255
New Zealand black-white hybrid mouse disease, 790–791
Nicein *see* Laminin-5
Nickel sensitivity, 175, *176*
Nicolav and Balus syndrome, 1626
Nicotinic stomatitis, 451
Nifedipine, gingival hyperplasia, 426
Nikolsky's sign
  bullous pemphigoid and, 99
  mucous membrane pemphigoid and, 118
  pemphigus vulgaris, 141
  staphylococcal scalded skin syndrome, 873
  toxic epidermal necrolysis, 241

19-DEJ-1 (monoclonal antibody), epidermolysis bullosa, 93
Nipple adenoma, 1596
Nipple leiomyoma, 1799
NK-cell(s), 1418
NK-cell nasal tumors, subcutaneous panniculitic T-cell
    lymphoma *vs*, 1417
NK/T-cell angiocentric lymphoma, subcutaneous panniculitic
    T-cell lymphoma *vs*, 1417
NK/T-cell lymphoma, 1418–1420
Nocardiosis, 919–921
Nodal B-cell lymphoma, 1451–1454
Nodal blue nevus, 1300
Nodal CD30+ T-cell lymphoma, skin involvement, 1403
Nodular amyloidosis, 564–567
Nodular and papular cutaneous mucinosis of systemic lupus
    erythematosus, 613
Nodular colloid degeneration, 567
Nodular cystic fat necrosis, 351, 352
Nodular elastoidosis with cysts and comedones, 1053, 1057
Nodular fasciitis, 1701–1705
  desmoplastic fibroblastoma *vs*, 1717
Nodular granulomatous perifolliculitis, 944–945
  see also Majocchi's granuloma
Nodular granulomatous phlebitis of the skin, 903
Nodular hidradenoma, malignant *see* Clear cell
    hidradenocarcinoma
Nodular histiocytosis, progressive, 1475
Nodular hyperplasia, Bartholin's glands, 530
Nodular lymphocyte predominant Hodgkin's lymphoma, 1448
Nodular melanoma, 1312, 1319, *1320*
Nodular mucinosis, 613
Nodular pemphigoid *see* Pemphigoid nodularis
Nodular prurigo, 182–184
  necrobiotic collagen, transepidermal elimination, 330
Nodular scabies, 980
Nodular scleroderma *see* Subcutaneous scleroderma
Nodular stage, Kaposi's sarcoma, 1833, *1834*, *1835*
Nodular subepidermal fibrosis *see* Dermatofibroma
Nodular trichoblastoma, 1555
Nodular tuberculids, 902–903
Nodular vasculitis, 366–369
Nodulocystic basal cell carcinoma (nodular basal cell
    carcinoma), 1170, 1173–1174, *1175*, *1176*
Non-epidermolytic palmoplantar keratoderma with oral
    hyperkeratosis, 66–67
Non-familial unilateral linear eccrine syringofibroadenoma,
    1610
Non-Hodgkin's lymphoma, genital region, 515
Non-scarring alopecia, 1068, 1069–1088
Non-tuberculous mycobacteria, 904–910
Non-venereal treponematoses, 891–894
Non-X-linked hyper-IgM syndrome, discoid lupus
    erythematosus, 781
Noonan's syndrome, 1016
  keratosis pilaris atrophicans, 58
North American blastomycosis *see* Blastomycosis
Northerton's syndrome, *38*
Norwegian scabies, 980
Nose
  skin, 2
  see also Nasal lesions
Notalgia paresthetica, 561, 1020
NSDHL (NADPH steroid dehydrogenase-like protein), gene
    mutations, 1155
Nuchal fibrocartilaginous pseudotumor, 1713
Nuchal fibroma, 1712
  elastofibroma *vs*, 1708
  juvenile hyaline fibromatosis *vs*, 1723
Nuchal-type fibroma, 1712
Nuclear atypia, actinic, *1316*
Nuclear dust *see* Leukocytoclasis
Nuclear factor κB gene modulator, gene mutations,
    incontinentia pigmenti, 703
Nuclear molding, neuroendocrine carcinoma, 1232, *1233*
Nucleophosmin-ALK fusion protein, CD30+
    lymphoproliferative disorders, 1408–1409
Nummular eczema, 174, *175*

O

Occipital horn syndrome, 1026, 1038–1039
Ochronosis, 592–594
  exogenous, 592–594
    sarcoidosis *vs*, 295
  from hydroquinone, 567, 592, 593
Ocular involvement
  angiokeratoma corporis diffusum, 551
  Behçet's disease, 686, *743*, 744
  Cockayne's syndrome, 248
  Ehlers–Danlos syndrome, 1023
  focal dermal hypoplasia syndrome, 1029
  hereditary benign intraepithelial dyskeratosis, 388
  herpes zoster, 857
  incontinentia pigmenti, 703

Ocular involvement (*cont'd*)
  lichen planus, 218
  oculocutaneous albinism, 998–999
  onchocerciasis, 982
  polyarteritis nodosa, 721
  Proteus syndrome, 1058
  pseudoxanthoma elasticum, 1041, 1042
  Reiter's syndrome, 477
  relapsing polychondritis, 834
  rosacea, 1122
  sarcoidosis, 292
  Schimmelpenning syndrome, 1154
  toxic epidermal necrolysis, 241
  urticarial vasculitis, 694
  xanthogranuloma, 1469
  xeroderma pigmentosum, 1230
  see also Periocular sebaceous carcinoma
Ocular pemphigoid, 117–118, 120
Ocular sebaceous glands, 1579
Oculocerebrocutaneous syndrome (Delleman's syndrome),
    rhabdomyomatous mesenchymal hamartoma, 1802
Oculocutaneous albinism, 998–1001
  squamous cell carcinoma, 999, 1202
Oculodermal melanosis *see* Nevus of Ota
Odland bodies
  nevoid basal cell carcinoma syndrome, 1185
  see also Membrane-coating granules
Odontogenic cyst, peripheral calcifying, 424
Odontogenic fibroma, peripheral, 422–425
Odontogenic ghost cell tumor, 424
Odontogenic gingival epithelial hamartoma, 423
  see also Peripheral odontogenic fibroma
Odontogenic keratocyst
  nevoid basal cell carcinoma syndrome, 1184
  peripheral, 425
Odontogenic sinus, 1680
Odontogenic tumor, peripheral calcifying, 424
Ofuji's disease *see* Eosinophilic pustular folliculitis
Ogna variant, epidermolysis bullosa simplex, 85
Oil spot sign, 1133
Oligodendrocytes, nasal glioma, *1791*
Olmsted syndrome, 73
Omphalomesenteric duct, 1681
Omsk hemorrhagic fever, 868, 869
Onchocerciasis, 982–984
Oncocytic sialocyst, 447
Onion skinning
  malpighian corpuscles, 800
  systemic sclerosis, 809
    kidney, 813
Onion skin pattern, myopericytoma, 1852
Onychokeratin, 1129
Onychomatricoma, 1147–1148
Onychomycosis, 1129–1131
  psoriasis *vs*, 1133
Open comedones
  acne vulgaris, 1118
  see also Whiteheads
Opioids, panniculitis, 351
Opportunistic infections, AIDS, 991
Oral Crohn's disease, 441–442
Oral florid papillomatosis, 1218
Oral focal acantholytic dyskeratosis *see* Warty dyskeratoma
Oral hairy leukoplakia *see* Hairy leukoplakia
Oral hyperkeratosis, focal palmoplantar keratoderma with, 66–67
Oral lentigo simplex, 468
Oral lesions
  acanthosis nigricans, 615–616, 617
  AIDS, 991
  amyloidosis, 556–557
  Behçet's disease, 685, 743
  chemotherapeutic agents, 664
  Darier's disease, 159–160, 389–390
  discoid lupus erythematosus, 447, 777
  erythema multiforme, 237, *238*
  Hallopeau–Siemens variant dystrophic epidermolysis bullosa,
      90
  lichen planus, 218, *219*, 224–225
  lipoid proteinosis, 427, 571
  melanocytic, 467–470
  papillary, 410–413
    squamous papilloma, 410–411
    verruciform xanthoma, 412–413, 549–550
  pemphigus vulgaris, 140, 445
    Darier's disease *vs*, 389
  pityriasis rosea, 190
  reactive *see* Reactive oral conditions
  Schimmelpenning syndrome, 1154
  sebaceous hyperplasia, 1567
  trichilemmoma, 1527
  tumor-like *see* Tumor-like oral conditions
  ulcerative *see* Ulcerative oral conditions
  vulvovaginal gingival syndrome, 219, 434, 480, *481*, *482*

warty dyskeratoma, 167, 390
  see also Hairy leukoplakia
Oral lymphoepithelial cyst, 393–394
Oral melanoacanthoma, 468–469
Oral melanocytic nevus, 469
Oral melanoma, 469–470
Oral melanotic macule, 467–468
Oral mucosa, 385–472
  bullous pemphigoid, 99, *100*, 104–105
  focal non-epidermolytic palmoplantar keratoderma with
    esophageal squamous cell carcinoma, 68
  see also Oral lesions
Oral mucosal calcified nodule, 597
Oral pemphigoid, 117, *118*, 119–120
  localized, 102
Oral squamous cell carcinoma, 459–461
  metastases to skin, 1498, 1499
Orange–brown pigmentation, pigmented purpuric dermatoses,
    277
Orange–yellow erythema, pityriasis rubra pilaris, 206, *207*
Orchitis
  Henoch–Schönlein purpura, 717
  polyarteritis nodosa, 721
Orf, 862–864
Organic acidemias, acrodermatitis enteropathica, 618
Organoid nevus *see* Nevus sebaceus
Organoid nevus phakomatosis (Schimmelpenning syndrome),
    1154, 1568
Organ transplantation
  graft-versus-host disease, 250
  kidney, tumors, *1201*, *1203*
  lymphoproliferative disorder, *1451*
  porokeratosis, 76
Oriental sore, 929–931, 932–934
Orificial mucositis, plasma cell, 438–439, 487
Orificial tuberculous ulcers, 896, 899
Orofacial granulomatosis, 440–441
Oroya fever, 886
'Orphan Annie' nuclei, thyroid papillary carcinoma, 1508
Orthokeratosis, warts, 840
Orthopox viruses, 860–862
Osler–Weber–Rendu syndrome, 1811–1812
Osseous choristoma, oral, 390
Osseous metaplasia, pilomatrixoma, 1537, *1538*
Ossification, 1853
Ossifying fibroma, peripheral, 420–421
  oral, 418
Ossifying fibromyxoid tumor, 1857–1858
Osteochondroma
  subungual, 1151
  see also Cartilaginous exostosis
Osteoclast-like giant cells
  extraskeletal osteosarcoma, 1853
  giant cell malignant fibrous histiocytoma, 1761
  giant cell tumor of soft tissue, 1754
Osteogenic melanoma, 1343–1344
Osteoma cutis, 1853
Osteomyelitis, squamous cell carcinoma, *1201*
Osteopathia striata, 1029
Osteopoikilosis, 1051
Osteosarcoma
  extraskeletal, 1853
  Rothmund–Thomson syndrome, 246
  soft tissue, 1761
Ota's nevus, 1297–1298
  Sun's nevus, 1299
Otitis externa, multifocal chronic Langerhans' cell histiocytosis,
    1460
Outer root sheath, anagen hair follicle, 1065
Ovary, tumor metastases to skin, 1498
Overlap eccrine ductal tumors, 1618
Overlap Stevens–Johnson syndrome/toxic epidermal necrolysis,
    237
Owl-eye, neonatal lupus erythematosus, 786
Oxalosis, 362–363

P
P16 protein, melanoma and, 1329
P53 (tumor suppressor gene) and product
  basal cell carcinoma and, 1173
  dermal nevus *vs* melanoma, 1258
  oral carcinoma, 460
  sebaceous carcinoma, 1580
  Spitz nevus *vs* melanoma, 1272
  UV signature of mutations, 1173, 1202
PA-1 antibody, 828
Pachyonychia congenita
  oral lesions, 389
  type 2, 67, 1573
  pili torti, 1113
Pachyonychia type I, 66–67
Pacinian corpuscle(s), 35
  hyperplasia, 1764

Pacinian neurofibroma, 1774
Pacinian neuroma, digital, 1764
Pacinian schwannoma, 1770–1771
Pacinioma, sacrococcygeal, 1765
Paget cells, Toker cells *vs*, 4
Pagetoid Bowen's disease, 1196, *1197*
Pagetoid dyskeratosis, 1517
Pagetoid melanoma *see* Superficial spreading melanoma
Pagetoid reticulosis, 1393–1395
  palmoplantar mycosis fungoides *vs*, 1392–1393
Pagetoid Spitz nevus, 1275–1276, *1277*
Pagetoid spread, melanocytes, 1253
Paget's disease, 4, 1514–1518
  apocrine carcinoma, 1597
  gross cystic disease fluid protein-15, 1505
Palisaded encapsulated neuroma, 1765–1766
Palisaded neutrophilic and granulomatous dermatitis, 320–321
  associated with systemic disease, rheumatic fever nodule, 317
  with vasculitis, 312, 755–756
  see also Interstitial granulomatous dermatitis
Palisading, neuroid-type nuclear, basal cell carcinoma with, 1182
Palisading cutaneous fibrous histiocytoma, 1751
Palisading granulomata, *304*
  granuloma annulare, 300
Palm, skin, 7
Palmar fibromatosis, 1720, 1724–1725
Palmoplantar ectodermal dysplasia, 59, 66–73
  acquired palmoplantar keratoderma and internal malignancy,
      68–69
  focal non-epidermolytic palmoplantar keratoderma with
      esophageal squamous cell carcinoma, 67–68
  focal palmoplantar keratoderma with oral hyperkeratosis,
      66–67
  hidrotic ectodermal dysplasia, 71
  keratitis–ichthyosis–deafness syndrome, 72–73
  pachyonychia congenita type II, 67
  type I, 66–67
  type III (Howell-Evans syndrome), 60, 67–68
  type IV, 69–70
  type VII, 70–71
  type X, 71
  type XVI *see* Keratitis–ichthyosis–deafness syndrome
  Vohwinkel syndrome, 70–71
Palmoplantar eczema (hand eczema), 174–175
Palmoplantar erythrodysesthesia syndrome, 667
Palmoplantar keratoderma, 59–66
  diffuse palmoplantar keratoderma, 60–61
  epidermolytic palmoplantar keratoderma, 59–60
  erythrokeratoderma variabilis, 61–62
  focal, with oral hyperkeratosis, 66–67
  focal non-epidermolytic, with esophageal squamous cell
    carcinoma (Howell-Evans syndrome), 60, 67–68
  keratoderma climactericum, 65–66
  keratosis punctata of palmar creases, 64
  marginal papular acrokeratoderma, 64–65
  Naxos disease, 1114
  with periodontopathia, 69–70
  progressive symmetric erythrokeratodermia, 62
  punctate palmoplantar keratoderma, 63
    see also Punctate palmoplantar keratoderma
  Sézary syndrome, 1396
  striate palmoplantar keratoderma, 62–63
Palmoplantar mycosis fungoides, 1392–1393
  Ketron–Goodman disease *vs*, 1395
Palmoplantar pustular psoriasis of Barber, 198, *199*
Palmoplantar pustulosis, nails, 1132
P-ANCA (perinuclear antineutrophil cytoplasmic antibodies),
  Wegener's granulomatosis, 442
Pancreatic panniculitis, 357–359
  neutrophilic lobular infiltrate, 369
Panfolliculoma, 1555
Panniculitis (inflammatory diseases of subcutaneous fat), 341–384
  associated with hemophagocytic syndrome, 354, 356
  cytophagic histiocytic, 354, 356
    subcutaneous panniculitic T-cell lymphoma *vs*, 1417
  equestrian cold, 274, 275, 353–354
  see also Lupus erythematosus profundus
Panniculitis-associated lipoatrophy, 374
PAPA (pyogenic sterile arthritis, pyoderma gangrenosum and
  acne), 675
Paper-tissue scarring, 1023
Papillary carcinomas
  metastases to skin, 1508
    thyroid, 1508, *1509*
  penis, 524
  see also Papillary squamous cell carcinoma
Papillary cystadenoma, mucocele *vs*, 448
Papillary cystadenoma lymphomatosum, mucocele *vs*, 448
Papillary dermal edema, polymorphous light eruption, 272
Papillary dermal elastolysis, pseudoxanthoma elasticum-like,
    1047–1048
  white fibrous papulosis with, 1037, 1048
  see also Fibroelastolytic papulosis of the neck

Papillary dermis, 28
  discoid lupus erythematosus, 792
Papillary eccrine adenoma, 1628–1629
  tubular apocrine adenoma vs, 1595
Papillary endothelial hyperplasia, intravascular, 1806–1807
Papillary hidradenoma
  anogenital region, 529
  see also Hidradenoma papilliferum
Papillary hyperplasia see Denture-associated fibrous hyperplasia
Papillary intralymphatic angioendothelioma (PILA),
  1829–1830
  retiform hemangioendothelioma vs, 1828
Papillary mesenchymal bodies
  trichoblastoma, 1554
  trichoepithelioma, 1547
Papillary oral lesions, 410–413
  squamous papilloma, 410–411
  verruciform xanthoma, 412–413, 549–550
Papillary squamous cell carcinoma, 460
  verrucous carcinoma vs, 465
  well-differentiated, 460, 461, 465
Papillary tubular adenoma see Tubular apocrine adenoma
Papillary well-differentiated squamous cell carcinoma, 460, 461,
  465
Papillomatous melanocytic nevus, 1253
Papillomatous seborrheic keratosis, 1159, 1160
Papillon–Lefèvre syndrome, 69–70
Papular acantholytic dermatosis of vulvocrural area see
  Acantholytic dermatoses, of genitocrural area
Papular acantholytic dyskeratosis, genital, 488
Papular acne scars, 1047
  papular elastorrhexis vs, 1052
Papular acrodermatitis of childhood, 188–190
  see also Gianotti–Crosti syndrome
Papular acrokeratoderma, marginal, 64–65
Papular amyloidosis (lichen amyloidosis), 560, 561, 562, 563
Papular and nodular cutaneous mucinosis of systemic lupus
  erythematosus, 613
Papular angioplasia see Epithelioid hemangioma
Papular calcific elastosis, digital, 64–65
  see also Collagenous and elastic plaques of the hand
Papular dermatitis associated with HIV/AIDS, 700, 987
Papular elastorrhexis, 1052
  eruptive collagenoma vs, 1038, 1052
Papular elastosis (adult colloid milium), 568–569, 1053
Papular granuloma annulare, 299
Papular lymphangiectasis, centrofacial, 580, 587
Papular mucinosis, acral persistent, 609
Papular oral lichen planus, 433
Papular plaque-like blue nevus, 1301
Papular tuberculid (acne agminata), 322–323, 1123
Papular variant, lichen myxedematosus, 605
  see also Cutaneous mucinosis of infancy
Papular xanthoma, 1475–1476
Papules
  amyloidosis, 555–556
  corymbose, 494, 497, 500
  fibrous, 1741
  Fordyce papules, sebaceous adenoma with, 1574
  Gottron's, 825, 827, 829, 830
  piezogenic pedal, 1692
  rheumatoid, 320
Papuloerosive dermatitis
  incontinence, 476
  of Jacquet and Sevestre, 476
Papulonecrotic tuberculid, 902, 903
Paracoccidioidomyces brasiliensis, 957, 958
Paracoccidioidomycosis, 957–958
Paracolloid of the skin, 567
Paraffinoma, 351
  see also Sclerosing lipogranuloma
Parakeratosis
  granular, 79–80
  warts, 840
  yaws, 893
Parameatal cyst (median raphe cyst), 516–517, 1677, 1678
Paraneoplastic disorders, 153
  acquired ichthyosis, 58, 59
  Bazex syndrome, 211–212
  Hodgkin's lymphoma, 1448
  neuroendocrine carcinoma, 1232
  punctate palmoplantar keratoderma as, 63
  vasculitis, 712, 754–755
Paraneoplastic pemphigus, 152–154, 244
  oral lesions, 445
Paraneoplastic vasculitis, 754–755
Parapoxvirus infections, 862–864
Paraproteinemia
  lichen myxedematosus, 607
  necrobiotic xanthogranuloma with, 318–320
  plane xanthoma with, 547
  scleredema, 610, 611
Parapsoriasis en plaques

benign type (chronic superficial dermatitis), 261–263, 1360,
  1362, 1373–1374
premalignant type (poikiloderma atrophicans vasculare),
  1360–1361, 1362, 1369, 1371, 1372
Paravaccinia, 862
Paravestibular tumor, 530
Parinaud's syndrome, 884
Paronychia, acute, 879
Parotid gland
  Darier's disease, 160
  Heerfordt's syndrome, 292
  sebaceous neoplasms, 1580
Partial lipodystrophy
  acquired, 375, 376
  see also Familial partial lipodystrophy
Partial monosomy 18, keratosis pilaris atrophicans, 58
Parulis, 422
  mucocele vs, 448
Pasini and Pierini see Atrophoderma of Pasini and Pierini
Pasini variant, dominant dystrophic epidermolysis bullosa, 89
Patched homolog, mutations, 1173, 1184
Patch-like blue nevus, 1301
Patch stage, Kaposi's sarcoma, 1831–1832, 1833
Patch stage mycosis fungoides, 1360, 1361, 1366–1367, 1368
Patch testing, contact dermatitis, 177
Pathergic granulomatosis, 728
Pathergy
  Behçet's disease, 686, 743, 744, 745–746
  pyoderma gangrenosum, 674, 677
Pathominia mucosae oris see Chronic bite injury
Patterned hyperpigmentation
  bleomycin, 664
  thio-TEPA, 665, 666
Pautrier microabscess, 1366, 1368, 1391
PAX-3 gene mutations, 1004
P component, amyloid, 554
  adult colloid milium, 569
PDFGB gene, dermatofibrosarcoma protuberans, 1730
Peak E commercial L-tryptophan, eosinophilia–myalgia
  syndrome, 824
Pearson's syndrome, 245
Peau de chagrin, 1030–1031, 1032
Peau d'orange, 1502
PEComa (perivascular epithelioid cell tumor), 1858–1859
Pediatric systemic lupus erythematosus, 775
Pedunculated basal cell carcinoma, 1171
Pedunculated lipofibroma, 1691
Pel–Ebstein fever, 1448
Pellagra, 594–595
  necrolytic migratory erythema vs, 620–621
Pemphigoid
  anti-P105, 108
  anti-P200, 108
  anti-P450, 108
  Brunsting–Perry, 101
  cell-poor, 103–104, 105
    differential diagnosis, 110
  childhood, 101, 102, 103
    antigens, 108
  dermolytic see Epidermolysis bullosa acquisita
  dyshidrosiform, 101
  erythrodermic, 98, 99
  generalized cutaneous, 98–100
  localized cutaneous, 101–102
    immunofluorescence studies, 107
  mucosal, 102
  ocular, 117–118, 120
  oral, 117, 118, 119–120
  polymorphic, 100
    see also Vesicular pemphigoid
  prebullous, 104
  pruritic, 99
  vesicular, 100, 104, 105, 106
  see also Bullous pemphigoid; Mucous membrane pemphigoid
Pemphigoid gestationis, 111–115
  pruritic urticarial papules and plaques of pregnancy vs, 281
Pemphigoid nodularis, 100, 102, 104, 106
Pemphigoid vegetans, 100, 102, 104
Pemphigus, 139–156
  contact pemphigus, 155–156
  drug-induced, 155, 648–649
  fogo selvagem, 148
  Hailey–Hailey disease vs, 143, 144, 158
  IgA pemphigus see IgA pemphigus
  impetigo vs, 871–872
  oral, 445
  paraneoplastic, 152–154, 244
    oral lesions, 445
  pemphigus erythematosus see Pemphigus erythematosus
  pemphigus foliaceus, 147–149
  pemphigus herpetiformis see Pemphigus herpetiformis
  pemphigus vegetans see Pemphigus vegetans
  pemphigus vulgaris see Pemphigus vulgaris

pustular psoriasis vs, 205
transient acantholytic dermatosis vs, 143, 144, 165
Pemphigus antibody, 142
Pemphigus erythematosus, 151–152
  sebaceous hyperplasia with, 1566
Pemphigus foliaceus, 147–149
Pemphigus herpetiformis, 151
  penicillamine, 660
Pemphigus vegetans, 145–147
  oral lesions, 445
  pyostomatitis vegetans vs, 147, 406
  Wegener's granulomatosis vs, 443
Pemphigus vulgaris, 140–145
  oral lesions, 140, 445
    Darier's disease vs, 389
  pyostomatitis vegetans vs, 405–406
Pencil-point hairs, 1077
  tapered hairs, 1107
Penicillamine, 660
  cicatricial pemphigoid, 119, 648, 660
  drug-induced pemphigus, 155, 648
  elastosis perforans serpiginosa, 333, 334
  pemphigus erythematosus, 152
  pemphigus foliaceus, 147, 148
  pseudoxanthoma elasticum-like changes, 1043
Penicilliosis, 974
Penicillium (spp.), Histoplasma capsulatum vs, 973–974
Penicillium marneffii, 974
Penile fibromatosis, 1725–1726
Penile pearly papules, 476
Penis, 474, 475
  adenosquamous carcinoma, 528
  apocrine hidrocystoma, 1588
  erythroplasia of Queyrat, 519, 1194
  intraepithelial neoplasia, nomenclature, 519
  median raphe cyst, 1677
  melanoma, 515
  mucoid cyst (median raphe cyst), 516–517, 1677, 1678
  myointimoma, 537–538
  pilonidal sinus, 511
  sclerosing lymphangitis, 488–489, 773
  squamous cell carcinoma, 524
  verrucous carcinoma, 1218, 1219
  see also Balanitis; headings beginning Genital...
Pentazocine abuse, 351–352
Perforating calcific elastosis, 1045
Perforating disorders, 328–337
  elastosis perforans serpiginosa, 331, 333–334
    Kyrle's disease vs, 334, 336
  hyperkeratosis follicularis et parafollicularis in cutem
    penetrans see Kyrle's disease
  perforating pseudoxanthoma elasticum, 337
  reactive perforating collagenosis see Reactive perforating
    collagenosis
Perforating folliculitis, 331–332
  elastosis perforans serpiginosa vs, 334
  familial dyskeratotic comedones vs, 169
  Kyrle's disease vs, 332, 337
Perforating granuloma annulare, 299, 301–302, 303, 304
Perforating lichen striatus, 232
Perforating necrobiosis lipoidica, 308
Perforating pseudoxanthoma elasticum, 337
Perianal lesions see Anogenital region; Anus
Pericarditis, diffuse systemic sclerosis, 807
Pericytes, capillaries, 33
Perifascicular atrophy, dermatomyositis, 830
Perifollicular elastolysis, 1047
Perifollicular fibroma, 1559–1560
Perifolliculitis, nodular granulomatous, 944–945
  see also Majocchi's granuloma
Perifolliculitis capitis abscedens et suffodiens, 1096
Perineural fibrolipoma, 1693
Perineural fibrosis, systemic sclerosis, 812
Perineural lipoma, 1693
Perineural spread
  epithelioid sarcoma, 1860, 1861
  melanoma, 1324
  squamous cell carcinoma, 1206–1207
Perineurioma, 1786–1788
Perinuclear antineutrophil cytoplasmic antibodies, Wegener's
  granulomatosis, 442
Periocular sebaceous carcinoma, 1579, 1581–1582
Periodic fever syndrome, 407
Periodontitis, chronic, 439
Periodontopathia, palmoplantar keratoderma with, 69–70
Perioral dermatitis, 323–324, 1123–1124
Perioral granulomatous dermatitis (perioral dermatitis),
  323–324, 1123–1124
Periosteal fasciitis, 1704
Periostitis, florid reactive, 1704
Peripheral ameloblastoma, 424
Peripheral calcifying odontogenic cyst, 424
Peripheral calcifying odontogenic tumor, 424

Peripheral giant cell granuloma, 421–422
  oral, 418
Peripheral nerve sheath tumor, malignant, 1791–1793
Peripheral neuroepithelioma, 1793–1795
Peripheral odontogenic fibroma, 422–425
Peripheral odontogenic keratocyst, 425
Peripheral ossifying fibroma, 420–421
  oral, 418
Peripheral primitive neuroectodermal tumor, 1793–1795
Peripilar keratin casts, 1116
Periplakin, paraneoplastic pemphigus, 153
Peristomal pyoderma gangrenosum, 675
Periumbilical pseudoxanthoma elasticum, 1045
Periungual angiofibroma, 1146
Periungual fibrokeratoma, 1146–1147
Periungual fibroma, 1147
  acquired digital fibrokeratoma *vs*, 1721
Periungual squamous cell carcinoma, 1199
Periungual warts, 840
Periurethral cyst, 519
Perivascular cell tumors, 1848–1852
Perivascular epithelioid cell tumor, 1858–1859
Perivascular whorling, malignant peripheral nerve sheath tumor, 1792
Perniosis, 274–275, 354
Persistent acantholytic dermatosis *see* Transient acantholytic dermatosis (Grover's disease)
Persistent benign follicular mucinosis, 1388
Persistent erythema multiforme, 237
Persistent insect-bite reaction, epithelioid hemangioma *vs*, 1825
Persistent papular mucinosis, acral, 609
Persistent (chronic) superficial dermatitis, 261–263, 1360, *1362*, 1373–1374
Peruvian wart, 886
Peutz–Jeghers syndrome, 1012–1013, 1243–1245
Peyronie's disease, 1725–1726
Phaeohyphomycosis, 968–971
Phaeomelanin, 15
Phagolysosomes
  congenital self-healing histiocytosis, 1467
  malakoplakia, 922–923
Phakoma, tuberous sclerosis, 1031
Pharynx, mucous membrane pemphigoid, 117
P-Phenylenediamine, lichenoid reaction, 635
Phenylketonuria, morphea *vs*, 820
Phenytoin, adverse effects, 633–634
Phlebitis
  Behçet's disease, 745
  see also Nodular granulomatous phlebitis of the skin; Thrombophlebitis
Phleboliths, sialolithiasis *vs*, 449
Phlebotomus sand fly, leishmaniasis, 929
Photoaging, 1053–1054
Photoallergic photosensitivity, 631
Photochromogens, 904
Photodynamic drug reactions, 630
Photophobia, ichthyosis follicularis with alopecia and, 56
Photosensitivity
  dermatitis *see* Chronic actinic dermatitis
  drug reactions, 630–633
    chemotherapeutic agents, 665
  porphyrias, 575
  subacute cutaneous lupus erythematosus (SCLE), 782
  xeroderma pigmentosum, 1229
  see also Polymorphous light eruption
Phototoxic photosensitivity, 630–631
Phrynoderma, 55
Physical urticaria, angioedema, 694
Phytophotodermatitis, 631, *632*
PIBIDS (syndrome), 1105
Picker's nodule, 183
Piebaldism, 13, 1002–1003
Piedraia hortae, 940–941
Piezogenic pedal papules, 1692
Pigmentary incontinence
  discoid lupus erythematosus, 792, *793*
  melanocytic nevi, 1253
  postinflammatory hyperpigmentation, 1019
  see also Incontinentia pigmenti
Pigmentation (disorders), 993–1021
  arsenicism, 656
  bismuth, 663
  bleomycin, 664–665, 666
  busulfan, 666
  dysplastic nevus, 1288
  epidermolysis bullosa simplex herpetiformis with mottled pigmentation and punctate keratoderma, 86
  gold, 661
  incontinentia pigmenti, 702
  mercury, 661–662
  ochronosis, 592–593
  silver, 661–662
  tinea versicolor, 945–946

see also Hyperpigmentation; Hypopigmentation; *specific substances*
Pigment casts, trichotillomania, 1081
Pigmented basal cell carcinoma, 1171, *1172*, 1175, *1179*
Pigmented dermatofibrosarcoma protuberans, 1728, 1733
Pigmented eccrine poroma, 1618
Pigmented epithelioid cell nevus, 1275
Pigmented follicular cyst, 1664
Pigmented hairy epidermal nevus *see* Becker's nevus
Pigmented hairy epidermal nevus syndrome, 1154, 1249
Pigmented lesions
  anogenital region, 511–515
  nail unit, 1136–1141
  oral, 465–470
Pigmented nail streaks *see* Longitudinal melanonychia
Pigmented neurofibroma, 1774
Pigmented porocarcinoma, 1623, *1625*
Pigmented purpura-like mycosis fungoides, 1392–1393
Pigmented purpuric dermatoses, 277–279
Pigmented purpuric lichenoid dermatitis of Gougerot and Blum, 277
Pigmented seborrheic keratosis, *1161*
Pigmented spindle cell tumor of Reed, 1278–1281, *1282*
Pigmented trichoblastoma, 1555, *1556*
Pigmenting pityriasis alba, 1006
Pilar cyst, 1663
  see also Trichilemmal cyst
Pilar keratosis *see* Keratosis pilaris
Pilar leiomyoma, 1797–1799
Pilar neurocristic hamartoma *see* Neurocristic hamartoma
Pilar pityriasis rubra *see* Pityriasis rubra pilaris
Pilar sheath acanthoma, 1524–1525
Pilar tumors, 1535
  of scalp, 1533–1536
Pili annulati, 1110, *1111*
Pili bifurcati, 1109
  trichoptilosis *vs*, 1108, 1109
Pili canaliculi et trianguli, 1108–1109
Pili incarati *see* Pseudofolliculitis
Pili multigemini, 1109–1110
Pili torti, 1113–1114
  Netherton syndrome, 51
Pilomaticoma *see* Pilomatrixoma
Pilomatrix carcinoma, 1539–1541
  melanocytic matricoma *vs*, 1542
Pilomatrixoma, 1536–1539
  cystic, 1663
  epidermoid cyst with, 1666
  melanocytic matricoma *vs*, 1542
  ossification, 1853
Pilonidal sinus, 1679–1680
  penis, 511
Pilotropic mycosis fungoides *see* Folliculotropic mycosis fungoides
Pilot's wheel appearance, paracoccidioidomycosis, 957, *958*
Pink disease, 663
Pinkus tumor, 1186–1187
Pinna *see* Earlobe
Pinta, 894
Pintoid yaws, 892
Pipe smoking, nicotinic stomatitis, 451
Pipe-stem appearance, erythema annulare centrifugum, 264
Pitted keratolysis, 926–927
Pitting
  nails, 1132
  palms and soles, nevoid basal cell carcinoma syndrome, 1184, *1185*
Pityriasiform drug reactions, 651
Pityriasis alba, 186–187, 1006
Pityriasis circinata, 54
Pityriasis lichenoides, 255–260
  chronic superficial dermatitis *vs*, 263
Pityriasis lichenoides acuta, lymphomatoid papulosis and, 1399
Pityriasis lichenoides chronica, 192, 255
Pityriasis lichenoides et varioliformis acuta, 192, 255
Pityriasis rosea, 190–192
Pityriasis rotunda, 54
Pityriasis rubra pilaris, 206–209
  focal acantholytic dyskeratosis with, 170
  psoriasis *vs*, 204, 208
Pityriasis versicolor, 945–947
Pityrosporum folliculitis, 947, *948*
Pityrosporum ovale see Malassezia globosa
Placenta, antibodies against, pemphigoid gestationis, 114
PLAG1 oncogene, 1693
Plague, 881–882
Plakins, 7–8
Plakoglobin, 11
  pemphigus, 142
Plakophilin (band 6), 11
Planar xanthomata, 547–549
Plane warts, 843–844
  epidermodysplasia verruciformis, 847, *848*

Plane xanthomata of cholestasis, 548
Plantar dermatosis, juvenile, 192–193
Plantar fibromatosis, 1725
Plantar hidradenitis, idiopathic, 668
Plantar warts, 840, 841–843
Plaque, dental, 418
Plaque-form morphea, 815–818
Plaque-like blue nevus, 1301
Plaque-like cutaneous mucinosis, 269
Plaque psoriasis, 195, *196*, *197*, 201–202
  PUVA therapy, 203–204
Plaques
  actinic comedonal, 1053
  sclerodermatous, necrobiosis lipoidica, 305
  verrucous hyperkeratotic bowenoid, 1195
  see also Collagenous and elastotic plaques of the hand; Degenerative collagenous plaques of the hand; Digital papular calcific elastosis; Psoriasiform plaques
Plaque stage, Kaposi's sarcoma, 1832, *1833*, *1834*
Plaque stage mycosis fungoides, 1360, 1361, 1367–1370, *1372*
Plaque variant, trichoblastic fibroma, 1553
Plasma cell(s)
  marginal zone B-cell lymphoma, 1430
  subpolar leprosy, 914
  see also Russell bodies
Plasma cell gingivitis
  foreign body gingivitis *vs*, 405
  oral lichen planus *vs*, 437
Plasma cell gingivostomatitis, 438
Plasma cell granuloma
  oral, 439
  see also Inflammatory pseudotumor
Plasma cell orificial mucositis, 438–439, 487
Plasma cell panniculitis, 382, 383
  Sjögren's syndrome, 381–382
Plasmacytoid cells (hyaline cells), mixed tumor of skin, 1601–1602, *1603*
Plasmacytoid monocytes, lymphocytic infiltrate of the skin, 268
Plasmacytoma, primary cutaneous, 1444–1445
Plasmacytosis, cutaneous, 1443
Plasminogen activator type 2, 11
Plectin, 8
  antibody, bullous pemphigoid, 108
  gene mutations, epidermolysis bullosa, 85
  hemidesmosomal epidermolysis bullosa, 95
Pleomorphic basal cell carcinoma, 1176–1177, *1179*
Pleomorphic CD30+ large cell lymphoma, 1403, 1407
Pleomorphic fibroma, 1709, *1710*
Pleomorphic hyalinizing angiectatic tumor, 1859
Pleomorphic lipoma, 1689, *1690*
Pleomorphic liposarcoma, 1696, 1698, 1699
Pleomorphic malignant fibrous histiocytoma, 1761
  leiomyosarcoma *vs*, 1801
Pleomorphic rhabdomyosarcoma, 1804, *1806*
Pleomorphic sarcomas, 1761
Pleomorphic small/medium-sized T-cell lymphoma, primary cutaneous, 1410–1411
Pleomorphism, leiomyosarcoma, 1801
PLEVA (pityriasis lichenoides et varioliformis acuta), 192, 255
Plexiform fibrohistiocytic tumor, 1755–1757
Plexiform fibrous histiocytoma, 1755–1757
Plexiform malignant peripheral nerve sheath tumor, 1791, 1793
Plexiform neurofibroma, 1773
  neurofibromatosis type I, 1776, *1778*
Plexiform schwannoma, 1769
Plexiform spindle cell nevus, 1281–1282, *1283*, *1284*
Plunging ranula, 447
PM-Scl (antigen), antibodies
  polymyositis, 828
  systemic sclerosis, *810*, 811
Pneumocystis jiroveci, ear, AIDS, 991
Pneumonic plague, primary, 882
Podagra, 590
Podoconiosis, 325
Podophyllin, condyloma acuminatum, 493, 845, 1196
Podophyllin, condyloma acuminatum, 493, 845, 1196
POEMS syndrome, glomeruloid hemangioma, 1808
Poikiloderma, 244–245, 800
  of Civatte (of head and neck), 245, 1053
    acquired brachial cutaneous dyschromatosis and, 1019
  dermatomyositis, 826, *827*, 829
  dyskeratosis congenita, 249
  lichen planus *vs*, 226
  mitochondrial DNA syndrome-associated, 245–246
Poikiloderma atrophicans vasculare, 1360–1361, *1362*, 1369, *1371*, *1372*
Poikiloderma congenitale, 246
Poikiloderma-like cutaneous amyloidosis, 561
Poison ivy, contact dermatitis, *177*
Poliosis, 1030
Polyarteritis *see* Microscopic polyarteritis
Polyarteritis nodosa, *710*, 720–727
  Churg–Strauss syndrome *vs*, 731, 734
  erythema nodosum *vs*, 347

Polydactyly, focal dermal hypoplasia syndrome, 1029
Polydysplastic epidermolysis bullosa (Hallopeau–Siemens
    variant dystrophic epidermolysis bullosa), 89, 90–91, 96,
    97
Polymorphic eruption of pregnancy, 111
    see also Pruritic urticarial papules and plaques of pregnancy
Polymorphic light eruption see Polymorphous light eruption
Polymorphic pemphigoid, 100
    see also Vesicular pemphigoid
Polymorphic reticulosis see Extranodal NK/T-cell lymphoma,
    nasal/nasal type; Midline destructive disease
Polymorphous light eruption, 271–272, 801
    lupus erythematosus and, 271, 272, 274, 800
    lymphocytic infiltrate of the skin vs, 268, 272
    reticular erythematous mucinosis vs, 270, 272
    tumid lupus erythematosus vs, 274
Polymorphous sweat gland carcinoma, 1658
Polymyalgia rheumatica, temporal arteritis, 748
Polymyositis, 825–832
Polyostotic fibrous dysplasia (McCune–Albright syndrome),
    1008–1009
Polyp(s)
    adnexal polyp of neonatal skin, 1610
    fibroepithelial, 1708–1709
        see also Acrochordon; Skin tag
    fibroepithelial stromal, 532–533
    fibrovascular
        gingival fibrous nodule, 418
        see also Fibroma
    large intestine
        perifollicular fibroma with, 1559
        see also Familial adenomatous polyposis coli syndrome
    leiomyomatous, congenital granular cell epulis vs, 396
    Peutz–Jeghers syndrome, 1012, 1013, 1243
    pseudosarcomatous, 1709
    umbilicus, 1681–1682
Polypoid basal cell carcinoma, 1171
Polypoid granular cell tumor, primitive, 470–471, 1782
Polypoid melanoma, 1312
Polytrichia, 1094, 1095, 1098, 1101
    see also Tufted folliculitis
Polyvinylpyrrolidone panniculitis, 351, 352
Pomade acne, 1118
Pompholyx, 172, 175
    hand eczema, 174–175
    see also Dyshidrosiform dermatitis
Ponytails, 1080
Popcorn cells, 1449
Popsicle panniculitis, 353
Porocarcinoma
    eccrine, 1620–1625
        squamous cell carcinoma vs, 1208, 1624
    subungual, 1143
    see also Clear cell porocarcinoma
Poroid hidradenoma, 1631
Porokeratosis, 74–77
    amyloidosis, 564
Porokeratotic eccrine nevus, cornoid lamellae, 77
Porokeratotic eccrine ostial and dermal duct nevus, 1613–1614
Poroma
    apocrine (with divergent or sebaceous differentiation),
        1596–1597
        see also Sebocrine adenoma
    eccrine, 1617–1619
        trichilemmoma vs, 1530
Poromatosis, 1617
Porphyria(s), 575–586
    congenital erythropoietic porphyria, 575, 576–577
    erythropoietic protoporphyria, 575, 576, 577–581, 583, 584
    hepatoerythropoietic porphyria, 575, 576, 582
    hereditary coproporphyria, 575, 576, 579
    porphyria cutanea tarda, 575, 576, 579–581, 584, 585
    variegate porphyria, 575, 576, 582–583
    see also Pseudoporphyria
Porphyria cutanea tarda, 575, 576, 579–581, 584, 585
Porphyrins, phototoxicity, 631
Port wine stain, 1809, 1810
Postcapillary venules, 34
Postinflammatory elastolysis and cutis laxa, 1039, 1040
Postinflammatory hypermelanosis, oral melanotic macule vs,
    467–468
Postinflammatory hyperpigmentation, 1018–1019
Postinflammatory hypopigmentation, 1007
    vitiligo vs, 996
Postinjection lipoatrophy, 377–384
    see also Localized lipoatrophy
Postirradiation angiosarcoma, 1840
Postirradiation pseudosclerodermatous panniculitis, 383–384
Post-kala-azar dermal leishmaniasis, 932, 933
Postmenopausal frontal fibrosing alopecia, 1091
Postoperative spindle-cell nodule, 538
Poststeroid panniculitis syndrome, 360–361
Potassium hydroxide, white piedra, 941

Potassium iodide, iododerma, 656–657
Potassium permanganate reaction, amyloid, 554
Pott's cancer, 1204
Povidone panniculitis, 351, 352
PPD (purified protein derivative), erythema induratum, 366
PPK see Palmoplantar keratoderma
Practolol, cicatricial pemphigoid, 119
PRAD1/CCND1 gene, mantle cell lymphoma, 1435
Prader–Will syndrome, acroangiodermatitis, 185
Prebullous pemphigoid, 104
Pregnancy
    antiphospholipid antibody syndrome, 767
    desmoid fibromatosis, 1726
    fibroepithelial stromal polyp, 532
    granuloma gravidarum, 419, 1816
    melanoma, 1310
    nevi, 1252
    polymorphic eruption of, 111
        see also Pruritic urticarial papules and plaques of
            pregnancy
    pruritic urticarial papules and plaques of (PUPPP), 111, 114,
        280–281
        see also Polymorphic eruption of pregnancy
Pregnancy prurigo, 111, 114, 281–282
Preleukemic ATLL, 1412–1413
Premalignant conditions
    oral, 452–459
        see also Intraepithelial neoplasia
Prematurity, anetoderma of, 1046
Prenatal diagnosis
    bullous ichthyosiform erythroderma, 47
    epidermolysis bullosa, 92
Prepuce, 474
Preradial myxedema, 603
Pressure alopecia, 1079
Pressure-induced lipoatrophy, 374
    see also Semicircular lipoatrophy
Pretibial myxedema, 603–605
Pretibial variant
    dominant dystrophic epidermolysis bullosa, 91–92
    localized non-scarring bullous pemphigoid, 104–105
Prickle(s) see Desmosomes
Prickle cells, 6
    epidermis, 3
Prickly heat (miliaria rubra), 193, 194
    erythema toxicum neonatorum vs, 214, 705
Primary adenoid cystic carcinoma, 1651–1653
Primary biliary cirrhosis
    acanthosis nigricans, 615
    limited cutaneous systemic sclerosis, 806
Primary cutaneous B-cell lymphoma, 1428
Primary cutaneous CD8+ epidermotropic cytotoxic T-cell
    lymphoma, 1420–1421
Primary cutaneous CD30+ large cell lymphoma, 1403–1409
Primary cutaneous follicle center cell lymphoma see Primary
    cutaneous follicular lymphoma
Primary cutaneous follicular lymphoma, 1432–1434
    grades 1 to 3, 1432
    primary cutaneous marginal zone B-cell lymphoma vs, 1431
Primary cutaneous marginal zone B-cell lymphoma, 1428–1432
Primary cutaneous plasmacytoma, 1444–1445
Primary cutaneous pleomorphic small/medium-sized T-cell
    lymphoma, 1410–1411
Primary localized cutaneous amyloidoses, 559–564
Primary mucinous carcinoma, 1654–1657
Primary scarring alopecia, 1068–1069
Primary signet ring carcinoma of eyelid, 1659
Primary systemic amyloidosis, 555–558
Primitive neuroectodermal tumor
    neuroendocrine carcinoma vs, 1237
    peripheral, 1793–1795
    rhabdomyosarcoma vs, 1806
Primitive polypoid granular cell tumor, 470–471, 1782
PRKAR1A gene mutation, 1014
Procainamide, systemic lupus erythematosus, 788
Procollagen, 29, 30
Procollagen type I carboxyterminal propeptide, morphea and
    systemic sclerosis, 818
Profilaggrin, 12
    deficiency, 39
Progeria, 1054–1055
Prognostic indicators
    melanoma, 1320–1325
    mycosis fungoides, 1362
Progressive kinking of hair, acquired, 1115, 1520
Progressive lipodystrophy, 375, 376
Progressive lymphangioma, acquired, 1845, 1846
Progressive macular hypomelanosis, 1005
Progressive nodular histiocytosis, 1475
Progressive papular xanthoma, 1476
Progressive sudanophilic leukoencephalopathy, 373
Progressive symmetric erythrokeratoderma, 62
Progressive systemic sclerosis

submucous fibrosis vs, 458
    see also Diffuse systemic sclerosis
Proliferating cell nuclear antigen, melanoma vs Spitz nevus, 1335
Proliferating epidermoid cyst, 1666–1667
Proliferating pilomatrixoma, 1537
Proliferating trichilemmal cyst, 1533–1536
Proliferation nodule, in congenital nevus, 1296
Proliferative actinic keratosis, 1189, 1190, 1191
Proliferative fasciitis, 1705
Proliferative myositis, 1706
Proliferative verrucous leukoplakia, 453, 455–456
Promontory sign, Kaposi's sarcoma, 185
Propionibacterium acnes, 22
    acne vulgaris, 1118
    progressive macular hypomelanosis, 1005
    sarcoidosis, 293
Prosector's warts, 895, 896
Protein C deficiency, 658
Protein kinase A type 1α regulatory subunit, 1014–1015
Protein S, 658
Proteus syndrome, 1058–1059, 1154–1155, 1528
Protoporphyrin(s), 577
Protoporphyrin oxidase, gene mutations, 583
Prototheosis, 936–937
Proximal nail fold, 1127–1128
Proximal nail groove, 1128, 1129
Proximal scleroderma, 804
Proximal-type epithelioid sarcoma, 1859, 1861
Pruriginous angiodermatitis, 277
Prurigo gestationis, 111, 114, 281–282
Prurigo gravidarum, 111, 114, 281–282
Prurigo nodularis see Nodular prurigo
Prurigo nodule, 183
Prurigo pigmentosa, 1017, 1018
Pruritic papular eruption, AIDS, 700, 987
Pruritic pemphigoid, 99
Pruritic urticarial papules and plaques of pregnancy (PUPPP),
    111, 114, 280–281
    see also Polymorphic eruption of pregnancy
Pruritus gravidarum, 111
Psammomatous bodies
    calcifying fibrous tumor, 1713
    tumor metastases, 1508
Psammomatous melanotic schwannoma, 1014, 1015, 1016,
    1770
Pseudoacanthosis nigricans, 616
Pseudoainhum, 62, 70
Pseudoallergic drug reactions, 624
Pseudoallescheria boydii, 951, 952, 955
Pseudoangiosarcomatous squamous cell carcinoma, 1215–1216
Pseudocapsules
    apocrine hidrocystoma, 1588
    eccrine hidrocystoma, 1614
Pseudocarcinomatous hyperplasia see Pseudoepitheliomatous
    hyperplasia
Pseudocyst
    of the auricle, 1682
    myxoid, nail region, 1148
Pseudoepitheliomatous hyperplasia, 900, 1167, 1168
    blastomycosis, 955
    coccidioidomycosis, 959
    granular cell tumor, 1780
    lymphomatoid papulosis, 1402
    squamous cell carcinoma vs, 1208
Pseudoepitheliomatous, keratotic and micaceous balanitis, 528
Pseudofolliculitis, 880, 1124–1125
Pseudofolliculitis barbae see Pseudofolliculitis
Pseudogaucher cells, 365–366, 909
Pseudoglandular squamous cell carcinoma, 1214
    see also Adenoid squamous cell carcinoma
Pseudojunctional epidermolysis bullosa
    epidermolysis bullosa with muscular dystrophy, 85, 86
    see also Hemidesmosomal epidermolysis bullosa
Pseudo-Kaposi's sarcoma see Acroangiodermatitis
Pseudolepromatous leishmaniasis, 931
Pseudolipomatosis cutis, 1686
Pseudolumina, adenoid cystic carcinoma, 1652
Pseudolymphoma
    B-cell, 1454–1457
        primary cutaneous marginal zone B-cell lymphoma vs, 1431
        see also Lymphocytoma cutis
    Borrelia burgdorferi, 1454
    drug-induced, 652–655
    T-cell
        cutaneous, 1423–1424
        primary cutaneous pleomorphic small/medium-sized T-cell
            lymphoma vs, 1411
        traumatic ulcerative granuloma vs, 409
        see also Atypical histiocytic granuloma
Pseudolymphomatous folliculitis, 1386–1387
Pseudomalakoplakia, 923
Pseudomelanoma, 1263–1265
Pseudomolluscum contagiosum, AIDS, 990

Pseudomonas aeruginosa, infective folliculitis, 878
Pseudomonilethrix, 1112
Pseudomycosis, bacterial, 921–922
Pseudo-nits, 1116
Pseudo-ocular cicatricial pemphigoid (drug-induced pemphigoid), 118
Pseudopélade, 1099–1103
Pseudopélade of Brocq, 220, 224, 1093–1096
  alopecia areata *vs*, 1078
  discoid lupus erythematosus *vs*, 1093
  dissecting cellulitis of the scalp *vs*, 1097
  lichen planopilaris and, 1089, 1090
Pseudopili annulati, 1110
Pseudoporphyria, 586–589
  drug-induced, 649
Pseudopyogenic granuloma *see* Epithelioid hemangioma
Pseudorheumatoid nodule
  of childhood *see* Subcutaneous granuloma annulare
  see also Deep granuloma annulare
Pseudorosettes, dendritic cell neurofibroma with, 1774, *1775*
Pseudosarcoma botryoides, 532–533
Pseudosarcomatous fibrous histiocytoma (atypical fibrous histiocytoma), 1749–1750, 1759
Pseudosarcomatous polyp, cutaneous, 1709
Pseudosclerodermatous panniculitis, postirradiation, 383–384
Pseudo-Sézary syndrome, 1423
Pseudosyndactyly (mitten lesions), Hallopeau–Siemens variant dystrophic epidermolysis bullosa, 90
Pseudotumor
  fibro-osseous, 1704
  inflammatory, 1457
    see also Inflammatory myofibroblastic tumor; Plasma cell granuloma
  molluscoid, 1023
  nuchal fibrocartilaginous, 1713
Pseudovascular clefts, ectopic meningeal hamartoma, *1789*
Pseudovascular melanoma, 1342–1343
Pseudovascular squamous cell carcinoma, 1215–1216
Pseudoxanthoma elasticum, 1041–1044
  inherited hemolytic syndromes and, 1044–1045
  perforating, 337
Pseudoxanthoma elasticum-like papillary dermal elastolysis, 1047–1048
  white fibrous papulosis with, 1037, 1048
  see also Fibroelastolytic papulosis of the neck
Psoralen, 630
Psoralen photochemotherapy *see* PUVA therapy
Psoriasiform Bowen's disease, 1195
Psoriasiform dermatoses, 195–212
  AIDS-related psoriasis, 206, 988
  Bazex syndrome, 211–212
  drug reactions, 649–650
  inflammatory linear verrucous epidermal nevus, 210–211
  pityriasis rubra pilaris, 206–209
    focal acantholytic dyskeratosis with, 170
    psoriasis *vs*, 204, 208
  Reiter's syndrome, 206, 477–480
    benign migratory glossitis, 401
  syphilids, 500
  see also Psoriasis
Psoriasiform napkin rash, 476
Psoriasiform plaques
  ichthyosis follicularis with alopecia and photophobia, 56
  palmoplantar keratoderma with periodontopathia, 69
Psoriasis, 195–206
  AIDS-related, 206, 988
  anogenital region, 477, *478*
  benign migratory glossitis and, 400–401, 402
  drug-induced, 649
  erythema annulare centrifugum *vs*, 265
  inflammatory linear verrucous epidermal nevus *vs*, 211
  nails, 199, 1132–1133
  pityriasis rosea *vs*, 191
  pityriasis rubra pilaris *vs*, 204, 208
  type I, 195, 200
  type II, 195, 200
  see also Pustular psoriasis
Psoriasis inversa, 195
Psoriasis vulgaris *see* Plaque psoriasis
Psoriatic arthritis, 200
Psoriatic erythroderma, 198, *199*, 203, *204*
PTCH1 (*patched* homolog), mutations, 1173, 1184
PTCH gene
  deletion, nevus sebaceus, 1569
  Torre–Muir syndrome, 1585
PTEN (homolog), mutations, 1058–1059, 1154, 1528
PTPN11 gene mutations, 1016
Pulmonary artery aneurysm, Behçet's disease, 744
Pulmonary edema, hand, foot and mouth disease, 867
Pulmonary embolism, warfarin necrosis, 658
Pulmonary granulomatosis, limited, 728–729
Pulmonary hypertension, systemic sclerosis, 807, 813
Pulmonary involvement

acute generalized Langerhans' cell histiocytosis, 1459, *1460*, *1464*
  Behçet's disease, 686, 687, 745, 746
  Birt–Hogg–Dubé syndrome, 1561
  Churg–Strauss syndrome, 732
  dermatomyositis, 827–828
  histoplasmosis, 972
  Langerhans' cell histiocytosis, 1462
  lymphangiomyomatosis, 1032
  lymphomatoid granulomatosis, 1439
  multifocal chronic Langerhans' cell histiocytosis, 1460–1461
  polyarteritis nodosa, 721, 723–724
  sarcoidosis, 291–292
  systemic sclerosis, 807, 813
  Wegener's granulomatosis, 727, 729
  see also Limited pulmonary granulomatosis
Pulseless disease *see* Takayasu's arteritis
Punctate keratosis *see* Keratosis punctata
Punctate palmoplantar keratoderma, 63
  see also Keratosis punctata, of palmar creases
Punctate porokeratosis, 75
Punctate porokeratotic keratoderma, 68–69
PUPPP *see* Pruritic urticarial papules and plaques of pregnancy
Purely granulomatous Wegener's granulomatosis (PGWG), 729
Purified protein derivative (PPD), erythema induratum, 366
Purpura
  amyloidosis, 555
  colloid milium, 567
  drug reactions, 643
  thrombocytopenic
    immune, 770
    thrombotic, 768–769
  see also Henoch–Schönlein purpura
Purpura fulminans, 763, 764, 856
Purpura-like mycosis fungoides, pigmented, 1392–1393
Purpura simplex, 277–279
Purpuric dermatoses, pigmented, 277–279
Purpuric mycosis fungoides, 1392–1393
Pustular dermatoses, 212–215
  infantile acropustulosis, 214
  pustular drug reactions, 651–652
  subcorneal pustular dermatosis, 212–214
    pustular psoriasis *vs*, 205, 213
  toxic erythema of the neonate, 214, 705
    incontinentia pigmenti *vs*, 704, 705
  transient neonatal pustular melanosis, 215
  see also Eosinophilic pustular folliculitis
Pustular drug reactions, 651–652
Pustular folliculitis, 878
  see also Eosinophilic pustular folliculitis
Pustular mycosis fungoides, 1391–1392
Pustular panniculitis, 369
Pustular psoriasis, 195–198, 202–203, *204*
  of Barber, palmoplantar, 198, *199*
  benign migratory glossitis, 400
  differential diagnosis, 205
  subcorneal pustular dermatosis *vs*, 205, 213
Pustular scarring alopecias, 1089
Pustules
  folliculitis decalvans, 1099, *1100*
  spongiform, 202
  subcorneal, 620, 621
Pustuloderma, toxic, 651
Pustulosis palmaris et plantaris, 198, *199*
PUVA keratosis, 1198
PUVA lentigines, 1248
PUVA therapy
  drug reactions, 630
  lichen planus pemphigoides, 117
  on mycosis fungoides, *1369*
  neuroendocrine carcinoma, 1231
  plaque psoriasis, 203–204
  squamous cell carcinoma, 203–204, 1202
Pyloric atresia–junctional EB syndrome, 85, 87
  genetics, 95
Pyoderma *see* Impetigo
Pyoderma faciale, 1124
Pyoderma gangrenosum, 673–679
  conditions associated, 674–675
  necrotizing fasciitis *vs*, 677, 878
  sterile neutrophilic folliculitis *vs*, 684
  Sweet's syndrome *vs*, 677, 680
Pyodermite vegetante, 146
Pyogenic granuloma, 1150
  atypical *see* Epithelioid hemangioma
  intravenous, 1816, 1817, *1818*
  oral, 418, 419–420
  see also Lobular capillary hemangioma
Pyogenic lymphoma, 1407
Pyostomatitis vegetans, 405–406
  Darier's disease *vs*, 389
  pemphigus vegetans *vs*, 147, 406
  Wegener's granulomatosis *vs*, 443

Q
Queensland tick typhus, 928

R
RAB27A gene (for GTP-binding protein), 1001
Rabbit warren appearance, 1218
Radial granuloma *see* Miescher's granuloma
Radial growth phase, melanoma, 1310, 1313
Radial growth phase (in situ) superficial spreading melanoma, dysplastic nevus *vs*, 1289
Radiation damage, 1055–1058
  morphea *vs*, 820
  porokeratosis, 76
  see also Radiotherapy; UV radiation
Radiation enhancement, 665
Radiation recall, 665, 666
Radiotherapy
  atypical vascular proliferation, 1847–1848
  eosinophilic, polymorphic and pruritic eruption associated with, 285
  oral verrucous carcinoma, 464
  postirradiation angiosarcoma, 1840
  postirradiation pseudosclerodermatous panniculitis, 383–384
  squamous cell carcinoma and epidermodysplasia verruciformis, 849
  squamous cell carcinoma from, *1201*
  transient acantholytic dermatosis, 164
  tumors from, 1203
Raimer's bands, 1053
Raindrop seborrheic keratosis, 1158
Raised atypical target lesions, 236
Ramon syndrome, gingival fibromatosis, 396
Ranula *see* Mucocele
RASA1 mutations, 1809
Raynaud's phenomenon, systemic sclerosis, 805
RCAS1 (receptor-binding cancer antigen expressed on SiSo cells), Paget's disease, 1517
Reactive angioendotheliomatosis, 1807–1808
  intravascular large B-cell lymphoma *vs*, 1447
Reactive eccrine syringofibroadenoma, 1610
Reactive follicles, B-cell lymphoma, 1428, 1431
Reactive hemophagocytosis syndrome, 1415, 1487–1488
Reactive oral conditions, 398–406
  benign migratory glossitis, 400–403
  chronic bite injury *see* Chronic bite injury
  foreign body gingivitis, 405
  leukoedema *see* Leukoedema
  pyostomatitis vegetans *see* Pyostomatitis vegetans
  smokeless tobacco keratosis *see* Smokeless tobacco keratosis
Reactive perforating collagenosis, 328, *329*, *331*
  Kyrle's disease *vs*, 336
Reactive periostitis, florid, 1704
Reactive salivary gland disease, 447–449
Reactive tumor-like proliferations, oral, 417
Recessive dystrophic epidermolysis bullosa
  squamous cell carcinoma, 1204
  see also Hallopeau–Siemens variant, dystrophic epidermolysis bullosa
Recessive dystrophic epidermolysis bullosa–non-Hallopeau–Siemens, 91
Recombinant interleukin-2, 670
RecQ helicase proteins, genes, 247
Rectum, lymphogranuloma venereum, 505
Recurrent aphthous stomatitis, 406–407
Recurrent erythema multiforme, 237
Recurrent nevus, 1263–1265
Red cell extravasation
  pigmented purpuric dermatoses, 277
  pityriasis lichenoides, 258
Red oculocutaneous albinism, 1000
Reed–Sternberg cells, 1448, 1449
Refsum's disease, 38
Regressing atypical histiocytosis, 1404, 1410, 1484
Regression
  melanoma, 1323, 1325
  plane warts, 843–844
  plantar warts, 843
  warts, 840
Regressive evolution, facial idiopathic granulomata with (acne agminata), 322–323, 1123
Reiter's syndrome, 206, 477–480
  benign migratory glossitis, 401
Relapsing linear acantholytic dermatosis, 158
Relapsing polychondritis, 833–836
Renal cell carcinoma
  fumarate hydratase deficiency, 1797
  metastases to skin, 1499, *1500*, *1511*
Renal crisis, scleroderma, 807–808
Renal disease, scleromyxedema-like illness of, 1033–1035, *1036*
Renal failure, oxalosis, 362
Renal transplantation, tumors, *1201*, 1203
Respiratory involvement
  Behçet's disease, 686, 745

Respiratory involvement (*cont'd*)
 relapsing polychondritis, 834
 see also Pulmonary involvement
Respiratory scleroma, 918
Restrictive dermopathy, 1036
Reticular degeneration
 herpes simplex virus infection, 853
 orf, 863
Reticular dermatopathia pigmentosa *see* Dermatopathia
 pigmentosa reticularis
Reticular dermis, 28
 morphea, 819
Reticular erythematous mucinosis, 269–271
 lymphocytic infiltrate of the skin *vs*, 268, 270
 polymorphous light eruption *vs*, 270, 272
Reticular lentigo, 1248, *1249*
Reticular livedo *see* Livedo reticularis
Reticular oral lichen planus, 433, 434, 435
Reticular variant, soft tissue perineurioma, 1787
Reticulate acropigmentation of Dohi, 1012
Reticulate acropigmentation of Kitamura, 1009
Reticulated black solar lentigo, 1248, *1249*
Reticulated melanotic macule, 1248, *1249*
Reticulate pigmentary disorder, X-linked, 564
Reticulate pigmented anomaly of the flexures, 1009–1010
Reticulin, angiosarcoma, 1842
Reticulohistiocytoma, 1482–1484
 xanthogranuloma *vs*, 1471–1472, 1483
Reticulohistiocytoma dorsi, 1432
Retiform hemangioendothelioma, 1828–1829
 hobnail hemangioma *vs*, 1822
Retinoblastoma, sebaceous carcinoma with, 1579
Reversal reactions, 911–912
Reverse smoking, nicotinic stomatitis, 451
Rhabdoid (signet ring cell) basal cell carcinoma, 1177–1178, *1180*
Rhabdoid melanoma, 1337–1339
Rhabdoid tumor, 1337
 epithelioid sarcoma *vs*, 1862
 extrarenal, 1864–1865
Rhabdomyoblast(s), 1803, 1804, *1805*
Rhabdomyoblastic differentiation
 malignant Triton tumor, 1793
 melanoma, 1344
Rhabdomyoma, 1803, *1804*
 myocardium, 1032
Rhabdomyomatous mesenchymal hamartoma, 1802–1803
Rhabdomyosarcoma, 1804–1806
 metastases to skin, 1498–1499
 peripheral primitive neuroectodermal tumor *vs*, 1794
Rheumatic fever, 691
Rheumatic fever nodule, 317
 rheumatoid nodule *vs*, 312, 317
Rheumatoid arthritis, neutrophilic lobular panniculitis
 associated with, 369
Rheumatoid neutrophilic dermatitis, 684–685
Rheumatoid nodule, *304*, 310–312
 epithelioid sarcoma *vs*, 312, 1862
 rheumatic fever nodule *vs*, 312, 317
Rheumatoid nodulosis, 310
Rheumatoid papules, 320
Rhinocerebral mucormycosis, 963
Rhinophyma, 1121, 1122, *1123*
Rhinoscleroma, 918–919
Rhinosporidiosis, 978, *979*
 coccidioidomycosis *vs*, 959
Ribonucleoprotein, antibodies, 788
Richter's syndrome *see* Large cell lymphoma
Rickettsial infections, 928–929
 vasculitis, 753–754, 929
Rickettsial pox, 928, 929
Riehl's melanosis, 1019–1020
Rift Valley fever, 868, 869
Riga–Fede disease (traumatic ulcerative granuloma), 407,
 408–410
Riley–Smith syndrome *see* Ruvalcaba–Myrhe–Smith syndrome
Ring chromosomes, dermatofibrosarcoma protuberans, 1730
Ringed hair, 1110, *1111*
Ringworm fungi, 938
Rippled-pattern trichoblastoma (rippled-pattern
 trichomatricoma), 1553, 1555
Ritter's disease, 873
 see also Staphylococcal scalded skin syndrome
River blindness, 982–984
RNA polymerase I, antibodies, systemic sclerosis, 810
RNP antigens, antibodies, 828
Ro antigens, 790
Robinson variant, apocrine hidrocystoma, 1587
Rocha-Lima inclusions, 886
Rocky Mountain spotted fever, 928, 929
Rodent ulcer (ulcerative basal cell carcinoma), 1169, 1176
Romberg's disease, linear morphea, 817
Rombo syndrome, 1186, 1547
Rosacea, 1121–1124

Rosacea fulminans, 1124
Rosacea-like tuberculid of Lewandowsky (granulomatous
 rosacea), 1121, 1122
Rosai–Dorfman disease, 1479–1482
 cytophagic histiocytic panniculitis *vs*, 356
Roseola infantum, 860
Rosette(s) (pseudorosettes), dendritic cell neurofibroma with,
 1774, *1775*
Rosette-like nevus, 1262, *1263*
Rothmann–Makai syndrome, 348
Rothmund–Thomson syndrome, 246–247
Round cell liposarcoma, 1698
Rowell syndrome, 238
 see also Lupus erythematosus–erythema multiforme-like
 syndrome
Rubber sensitivity, 175, *176*
Rubinstein–Taybi syndrome
 keratosis pilaris atrophicans, 58
 pilomatrixomas, 1536
Rud's syndrome, *38*
Ruffled cuticle, 1086
Rupial lesions, 496, 500
Russell bodies, 918, 1444
Rutherford syndrome, gingival fibromatosis, 396
Ruvalcaba–Myrhe–Smith syndrome, 1013
 see also Bannayan–Riley–Ruvalcaba syndrome

S
S-100 protein
 atypical fibroxanthoma, 1758
 granular cell myoblastoma, 470
 melanoma, 1328
Sacrococcygeal paciniomas, 1765
Sacroiliitis, psoriatic arthritis, *200*
Sago-grain-like vesicles, dyshidrosiform dermatitis, 101
Sago palm disease, 927
SALE (summertime actinic lichenoid eruption; lichen planus
 actinicus), 221, 224
Salivary duct cyst *see* Mucocele
Salivary glands
 calculi, 449
 carcinomas, basaloid squamous cell carcinoma *vs*, 463
 Darier's disease, 160
 reactive disease, 447–449
Salmon patch, 1808, 1809
SALT (skin-associated lymphoid tissue), 1428
Salt and pepper appearance, 806
Saltpetre, 1043
Sand flea, 981, *982*
Sanguinaria, dentifrice, 456
Sarcoidal 'naked' granulomata, 324–325, 901
Sarcoidal variant, necrobiosis lipoidica, 308
 see also Miescher's granuloma
Sarcoidosis, 287–296
 erythema induratum *vs*, 368
 granulomatous mycosis fungoides and, 1380
 metastatic Crohn's disease *vs*, 322
 orofacial granulomatosis *vs*, 441
 perioral dermatitis *vs*, 324
 subcutaneous, 369
 tuberculosis *vs*, 900–901
Sarcoma(s)
 pleomorphic, 1761
 skin involvement, 1505, 1684
 see also specific types
Sarcoma botryoides, fibroepithelial stromal polyp *vs*, 533
Sarcoma-like hemangioendothelioma, 1837
Sarcomatoid squamous cell carcinoma, 1759
 genital region, 525
 see also Metaplastic carcinoma
Sarcomatoid variant, CD30+ large cell lymphoma, 1405
Sarcomatous differentiation, eccrine spiradenoma, 1643

skin, 3
 tumor metastases to, 1499–1500, *1501*
Scandinavian snuff, 403, 404
Scar(s)
 acne, 1047, 1052
 basal cell carcinoma, 1169
 desmoplastic melanoma *vs*, 1350
 Ehlers–Danlos syndrome, 1023
 hypertrophic, 1699–1700
 metastases like, 1500
 metastases to, 1501
Scarlet fever, staphylococcal, 873
Scarring alopecia, 880, 1068, 1089–1103
Scedosporium prolificans, 969
Schamberg's disease, 277
Schaumann bodies, 294, 901
Schimmelpenning–Feuerstein–Mims syndrome
 (Schimmelpenning syndrome), 1154, 1568
Schimmelpenning syndrome, 1154, 1568
Schistosoma spp., 985, 986
Schistosomiasis, 506–507, 985–986
 Buruli ulcer and, 906
Schnitzler's syndrome, 282, 694, 719
Schöpf–Schulz–Passarge syndrome, 60
 see also Ectodermal dysplasia
Schöpf syndrome, 1610
Schulman's syndrome *see* Eosinophilic fasciitis
Schwann cells, ganglion cell choristoma, 1765
Schwannoma
 ancient, 1769, *1770*
  pleomorphic hyalinizing angiectatic tumor *vs*, 1859
 Carney complex, 1014, 1015, *1016*
 cellular, 1769–1770
 epithelioid, 1771
 fibrosarcoma *vs*, 1738
 hybrid tumor (neurofibroma and schwannoma), 1774
 malignant, 1791–1793
 melanotic, 1770
  psammomatous, 1014, 1015, *1016*, 1770
 neurofibromatosis type I, 1767
 pacinian, 1770–1771
 plexiform, 1769
 see also Neurilemmoma
Schwannomatosis, 1768
Schweninger–Buzzi variant, anetoderma, 1045–1047
Scl-70 antibody, systemic sclerosis, 811
Scleredema, 610–613
 cytomegalovirus, 859
Sclerema neonatorum, 361–362
Sclerodactyly, 804
 Huriez syndrome, 60
Scleroderma
 calcification, 596
 localized *see* Morphea
 proximal, 804
 scleredema *vs*, 611
 sclerosing panniculitis *vs*, 372
 subcutaneous, 818
  see also Morphea profunda
 submucous fibrosis *vs*, 458
Scleroderma panniculitis, 383
Scleroderma renal crisis, 807–808
Sclerodermatomyositis, 825, 828
Sclerodermatous metastasis, 1502–1503, *1507*
Sclerodermatous plaques, necrobiosis lipoidica, 305
Sclerodermiform features, porphyrias, 580, *581*, 585
Scleromyxedema, 606–608
 nephrogenic fibrosing dermopathy *vs*, 1034
Scleromyxedema-like illness of hemodialysis (of renal disease),
 1033–1035, *1036*
Sclerosing basal cell carcinoma *see* Morpheaform basal cell
 carcinoma
Sclerosing blue nevus, 1302
Sclerosing epithelial hamartoma *see* Desmoplastic
 trichoepithelioma
Sclerosing extramedullary hematopoietic tumor, 1490
Sclerosing fibrosarcoma, 1739–1740
Sclerosing hemangioma *see* Dermatofibroma; Fibrous
 histiocytoma
Sclerosing lipogranuloma, 351, 511
 see also Paraffinoma
Sclerosing liposarcoma, 1697
Sclerosing lymphangitis, 488–489
 of the penis, 488–489, 773
Sclerosing panniculitis, 372–373
Sclerosing perineurioma, 1786, 1787
Sclerosing pyogenic granuloma, 419, *420*
Sclerosing sweat duct carcinoma *see* Microcystic adnexal
 carcinoma
Sclerotic bodies, *Fonsecaea pedrosoi*, 966
Sclerotic fibroma *see* Storiform collagenoma
Scotochromogens, 904
Scratching, atopic dermatitis, 173

Rheumatoid papules, 320
Rhinocerebral mucormycosis, 963

Scalp
 biopsy, 1062
 dermal cylindroma, 1636
 discoid lupus erythematosus, 776–777
 dissecting cellulitis, 1096–1098, 1102
 dissecting folliculitis, 706
 encephalocraniocutaneous lipomatosis, 1691
 lipedematous, 1088
 locally invasive cellular blue nevus, 1308
 pilar tumors, 1533–1536

Scrofuloderma, 896, 897, 899, 900, *901*
Scrotal tongue, pemphigus vegetans, 146
Scrotum, 474
  basal cell carcinoma, 1168
  calcinosis, 510, 598
  exophytic elastoma, 1052
  leiomyoma, 536, 1799
  leiomyosarcoma, 536
  Pott's cancer, 1204
  squamous cell carcinoma, 1201, *1202*
Scrub typhus, 928, 929
Scurvy, 595
Seabather's eruption, 690
Sebaceoma, 1575–1578
Sebaceous adenoma, 1574–1575
  sebaceoma *vs*, 1577
  Torre–Muir syndrome, 1574, 1584
  see also Adenoma sebaceum
Sebaceous and apocrine adenoma *see* Apocrine poroma
Sebaceous carcinoma, 1579–1584
  balloon cell melanoma *vs*, 1338, 1583
  clear cell squamous cell carcinoma *vs*, 1210, 1583
  sebaceoma *vs*, 1577
Sebaceous choristoma and hyperplasia, oral, 391
Sebaceous cyst, steatocystoma as, 1573
Sebaceous differentiation
  mixed tumor of skin, 1602
  tumors with, 1587
    see also specific tumors
  see also under Seborrheic keratosis
Sebaceous epithelioma, 1575, 1578
Sebaceous follicles, 20
  acne vulgaris, 1117
Sebaceous glands, 20–22, 1565–1587
  genital region, hyperplasia, 475–476
  nevus sebaceus, 1569
  ocular, 1579
  scarring alopecia, 1089
Sebaceous hyperplasia, 1566–1578
  sebaceous trichofolliculoma *vs*, 1545
Sebaceous trichofolliculoma, 1545–1546
Sebocrine adenoma, 1587
  see also Apocrine poroma
Sebocystomatosis (steatocystoma multiplex) suppurativum, 1572
Sebomatricoma, 1577, 1578
Sebo-psoriasis, 205
Seborrheic dermatitis, 173–174, 179
  psoriasis *vs*, 205
Seborrheic dermatitis-like eruption of AIDS, 181–182, 987–988
Seborrheic keratosis, 1158–1163
  acantholytic, acantholytic acanthoma *vs*, 169
  Bowen's disease *vs*, 1196
  hidroacanthoma simplex *vs*, 1616
  with sebaceous differentiation
    apocrine poroma *vs*, 1597
    superficial epithelioma with sebaceous differentiation *vs*, 1578
Seborrheic pemphigoid, 100
Sebum, 21–22
  acne vulgaris, 1118
Secondary amyloidosis, 558
Secondary B-cell lymphoma, 1451–1454
Secondary CD30+ T-cell lymphoma, 1403
Secondary localized cutaneous amyloidosis, 564
Secondary (endogenous) tuberculosis, 896
Second malignancy
  melanoma, 1310
  neuroendocrine carcinoma, 1231
Segmental Darier's disease *see* Linear Darier's disease
Segmental glomerulonephritis, systemic lupus erythematosus, 797–798
Segmental hyalinizing vasculitis *see* Atrophie blanche
Segmental neurofibromatosis, 1779
Seip–Lawrence syndrome, 615
Self-destruction theory, vitiligo, 995
Self-healing histiocytosis, congenital, 1467–1468
Self-healing infantile familial cutaneous mucinosis, 615
Self-healing juvenile cutaneous mucinosis, 610
Self-healing squamous epitheliomata of the skin, familial primary, 1222, *1223*
Semicircular lipoatrophy, 377–384
  localized lipoatrophy (localized lipodystrophy), 377–384
Senear–Usher syndrome *see* Pemphigus erythematosus
Senile alopecia, 1082–1083
Senile angioma, 1815
Senile freckle, 1246–1248
Senile keratosis *see* Actinic keratosis
Senile lentigo, 1246–1248
Senile purpura, 773
Senile/solitary sebaceous hyperplasia, giant, 1566
Sentinel lymph node biopsy, melanoma, 1274, 1324–1325
Sentinel lymph node mapping, neuroendocrine carcinoma, 1231

Septal panniculitis, 344–345
Septicemic plague, primary, 882
Sequestrated meningocele, 1788
SERCA2 (calcium pump) *see* ATP2A2 gene mutations
Serpentine supravenous hyperpigmentation, 664
Serum, nail diseases, 1133, 1134
Serum amyloid A, 559
Serum amyloid P component, adult colloid milium, 569
Serum sickness, 629–630
  drug reactions like, 629
Sex hormones
  acne vulgaris, 1118
  androgenetic alopecia, 1069–1070
  lupus erythematosus, 790
  melasma, 1007
  relapsing polychondritis, 834
Sex-linked ichthyosis, 39–41
  ichthyosis vulgaris *vs*, 37
Sex mismatch, graft-versus-host disease, 250
Sexual abuse
  bowenoid papulosis, 847
  childhood pemphigoid *vs*, 101
  condyloma acuminatum, 844
Sexual partners, pemphigoid gestationis and, 111
Sexual precocity, Carney complex, 1014
Sézary cells (mycosis cells), 1366, *1368*, *1374*, *1375*, 1397–1398
  lymph nodes, 1372, *1375*
Sézary syndrome, 1395–1399
  adult T-cell leukemia/lymphoma *vs*, 1414
  chronic actinic dermatitis *vs*, 1427
Shadow cell basal cell carcinoma (basal cell carcinoma with matrical differentiation), 1178, 1542
Shagreen patch, 1030–1031, 1032
Shaving bumps *see* Pseudofolliculitis
Sheep, scabby mouth, 862–863
Shh *see* Sonic Hedgehog
Shingles (herpes zoster), 856–857, 858
Shoulder phenomenon, dysplastic nevi, 1286, 1287
Sialidosis, diffuse angiokeratomata, 552
Sialocyst *see* Mucocele
Sialolithiasis, 449
Sialomucin, cutaneous mucinous carcinoma, 1657
SIBIDS (syndrome), 1105
Signet ring carcinoma, primary, eyelid, 1659
Signet ring cell(s), apocrine carcinoma, 1598
Signet ring cell basal cell carcinoma, 1177–1178, *1180*
Signet ring cell melanoma, 1337
Signet ring metastases, 1508–1509
Signet ring squamous cell carcinoma, 1210
Silica
  scleroderma-like syndrome, 808
  Wegener's granulomatosis, 729
Silicone breast implants, scleroderma-like syndrome, 808
Silicone granulomata, 325
Silver, 661–662
Silver tattoos, 466
Simple lentigo (lentigo simplex), 1242, 1243, *1244*
  nail, 1138
  oral, 468
Simulium nigrimanum, fogo selvagem, 149
Sindbis fever, 869
Sine scleroderma variant, 804
Single-strand DNA, antibodies, 788
  morphea, 818
Single system disease (focal chronic Langerhans' cell histiocytosis), 1461, 1463, *1465*
Sinus histiocytosis
  cutaneous, 1479
  with massive lymphadenopathy *see* Rosai–Dorfman disease
Sinusoidal hemangioma, 1818, *1819*
Sinusoidal spaces, giant cell fibroblastoma, 1728
Sipple syndrome *see* Multiple endocrine neoplasia syndrome
Sister Mary Joseph's nodule, 1499, *1500*
Sjögren–Larsson syndrome, *38*, 52–54
Sjögren's syndrome
  acral ichthyosiform mucinosis, 604
  plasma cell panniculitis, 381–382
  subacute cutaneous lupus erythematosus, 783
Skene's glands, 475
Skin
  congenital absence, 1027–1028
  normal, 1–36
    see also Genital anatomy
Skin-limited amyloidoses, 559–564
Skin tag, 1692
  see also Fibroepithelial polyp
Skull, multifocal chronic Langerhans' cell histiocytosis, 1460
Slow-cycling stem cells, epidermis, 2
SLUG gene, 1003
Sm (soluble nuclear antigen), antibodies, 788
Small cell carcinoma, *1511*
  neuroendocrine carcinoma *vs*, 1236, *1237*

see also Neuroendocrine carcinoma
Small cell melanoma, 1333–1335
  neuroendocrine carcinoma *vs*, 1236, *1237*
Small cell melanoma cells, 1258
Small cell variants
  CD30+ large cell lymphoma, 1407
  neuroendocrine carcinoma, 1233, *1234*
Small lymphocytic lymphoma, 1436–1437
Small/medium-sized T-cell lymphoma, primary cutaneous pleomorphic, 1410–1411
Small plaque parapsoriasis (chronic superficial dermatitis), 261–263, 1360, *1362*, 1373–1374
Smallpox
  hemorrhagic, 869
  variola, 860, *861*, 862
Small proline rich proteins/cornifins (SPRRs), 11
Small vessel vasculitis, *710*
Smoh (*smoothened*), basal cell carcinoma and, 1173
Smokeless tobacco keratosis, 403–404
  chronic bite injury *vs*, 399
  leukoedema *vs*, 399
  submucous fibrosis *vs*, 458
Smoking
  hidradenitis suppurativa, 706
  leukoplakia, 452
    oral lichen planus, 434
  nicotinic stomatitis, 451
  thromboangiitis obliterans, 747
Smoldering ATLL, 1413
Smoothened (transmembrane protein), basal cell carcinoma and, 1173
Smooth muscle, endomysial antibody *vs*, dermatitis herpetiformis, 132
Smooth muscle cells, glomangiomyoma, 1850, *1851*
Smooth muscle differentiation, melanoma, 1344
Smooth muscle hamartoma, 1796–1802
  congenital, 1796–1797
Smooth muscle tumors, 1796–1802
  myofibroma *vs*, 1715
Snail track ulcers, 498
Sneddon's syndrome, 767–768, 789
Sneddon–Wilkinson disease *see* Subcorneal pustular dermatosis
Snuff dipper's keratosis *see* Smokeless tobacco keratosis
NaCl-split skin studies
  bullous pemphigoid, 107
  subepidermal blisters, 81, 83, 107
Soft chancre, 504–505
Soft fibroma *see* Fibroepithelial polyp
Soft plaque, 508–509, 922–923
Soft tissue
  giant cell tumor of, 1754, 1761
  myoepithelioma, 1858
Soft tissue chondroma, 1853–1854
  calcifying aponeurotic fibroma *vs*, 1720
Soft tissue giant cell tumor of low malignant potential (giant cell tumor of soft tissue), 1754, 1761
Soft tissue melanoma, 1795–1796
Soft tissue osteosarcomas, 1761
Soft tissue perineurioma, 1786
  reticular variant, 1787
  see also Perineurioma
Soft tissue tumors, anogenital region, 532–538
Solar comedones, 1668
Solar elastosis, 313, 1053
Solar keratosis
  acantholytic, 144
  see also Actinic keratosis
Solar lentigo, 1246–1248
Solar urticaria, 693, 695
Solehorn, 1128, 1129
Sole of foot
  epidermoid cyst, 1667
  skin, 2
Solid–cystic hidradenoma, 1631
  see also Hidradenoma
Solitary basaloid follicular hamartoma, 1522
Solitary circumscribed neuroma, 1765–1766
Solitary collagenoma, 1038
Solitary eccrine syringofibroadenoma, 1610
Solitary fibrous tumor, 1736–1738
Solitary lichen planus, 229–231
Solitary mycosis fungoides, 1393
Solitary/senile sebaceous hyperplasia, giant, 1566
Solitary trichoepithelioma, 1547
  giant, 1553
Solvents, scleroderma-like syndrome, 808
Sonic Hedgehog
  basal cell carcinoma and, 1173
  basaloid follicular hamartoma, 1523
  Brooke–Spiegler syndrome, 1547
  nevoid basal cell carcinoma syndrome and, 1184
South African tick-bite fever, 928
Spasticity, Sjögren–Larsson syndrome, 53

Specimens
  skin metastases, 1497–1498
  see also Biopsy
Speckled lentiginous nevus, 1262
Spectacle frame acanthoma, 1157–1158
Spheroids, Ehlers–Danlos syndrome, 1023
Spherules, *Coccidioidomyces immitis*, 959
Spherulocystic disease, 1572
  see also Myospherulosis
Spider bite reactions, 689
Spider nevus, 1810
Spiegler–Fendt sarcoid *see* B-cell pseudolymphoma
Spindle and epithelioid cell nevus *see* Spitz nevus
Spindle cell(s)
  angiosarcoma, 1840–1842
  dermatofibroma, 1744
  dermatomyofibroma, 1709–1711
  desmoid fibromatosis, 1726, *1727*
  fibrosarcoma, 1738, *1739*
  giant cell fibroblastoma, 1728
  infantile myofibromatosis, 1714–1715
  Kaposi's sarcoma, 1832, *1835*
  melanoma, 1319, 1320
  metaplastic carcinoma, 461
  neurofibroma, 1772
  neurofollicular hamartoma, 1563
  nodular fasciitis, 1702, *1703*
Spindle cell atypical fibroxanthoma, 1758, *1759, 1760*
Spindle cell carcinoma *see* Metaplastic carcinoma
Spindle cell hemangioendothelioma, 1826–1828
Spindle cell hemangioma, 1826–1828
Spindle cell lipoma, 1688–1689
Spindle cell liposarcoma, 1697
Spindle cell melanoma, leiomyosarcoma *vs*, 1801
Spindle cell nevus
  pigmented spindle cell tumor of Reed *vs*, 1280
  plexiform, 1281–1282, *1283, 1284*
  see also Hyalinizing spindle and epithelioid cell nevus
Spindle cell nodule, postoperative, 538
Spindle cell Spitz nevus, 1270, *1272, 1273*
Spindle cell squamous cell carcinoma, 1210–1212, *1213*
  atypical fibroxanthoma *vs*, 1759
Spindle cell tumor, 1740, *1741*
  of Reed, 1278–1281, *1282*
Spindle cell xanthogranuloma, 1475
SPINK5 gene, Netherton syndrome, 51
Spiradenoma *see* Eccrine spiradenoma
Spirochetes, 499
Spitz nevus, 1268–1275
  desmoplastic, 1255, 1271, 1276–1277, *1278*
  epithelioid fibrous histiocytoma *vs*, 1749
  with halo nevus, 1271
  HMB-45 antigen, 1272, 1328
  melanoma *vs*, 1269–1270, 1272, 1335
    CD40, 1272, 1329
  pagetoid, 1275–1276, *1277*
  xanthogranuloma *vs*, 1472
Spitzoid melanoma, 1268, 1269, 1335–1337
Spitzoid tumor of uncertain biological potential (atypical Spitz nevus), 1268, 1269, 1273, 1274, *1275*
Spitz tumor, 1273–1274
  see also Spitz nevus
Spleen
  capsule, sugar icing, 800
  sarcoidosis, 292
  systemic lupus erythematosus, 800
Splendore–Hoeppli phenomenon, 921, 945
  entomophthoromycosis, 964
  mycetoma, 968, *970*
  sporotrichosis, 975–976
Split ends *see* Trichoptilosis
Split skin immunofluorescence, 81–83
Split skin studies
  bullous pemphigoid, 107
  subepidermal blisters, 81, 83, 107
Spongiform pustules of Kogoj, 202
Spongiosis, 177
  see also Eosinophilic spongiosis
Spongiotic dermatitis *see* Eczematous dermatitis
Spongiotic dermatoses, 171–195
Sporothrix schenkii, 974, 975–976
Sporotrichoid spread
  mycobacterial infections, 904, *906*, 907
  nocardiosis, 919
Sporotrichosis, 974–976
Spotted fevers, 928
Spotted grouped pigmented nevus, 1260
Spreading pigmented actinic keratosis, 1189
SPRRs (small proline rich proteins/cornifins), 11
Spun glass hair, 1108–1109
Squamoid eccrine ductal carcinoma, 1658
Squamomelanocytic tumor, dermal, 1355–1356
Squamous carcinoma showing mucinous metaplasia, 1215, 1217

Squamous cell carcinoma, 1199–1209
  acantholytic, 1214–1215
    see also Adenoid squamous cell carcinoma
  actinic keratosis as risk, 1187–1188
  actinic keratosis *vs*, 1189–1190, 1199
  adenoid, 463
    see also Acantholytic squamous cell carcinoma
  AIDS, 990, 991
  anal, human papilloma virus, 844
  basaloid, 462–463
    genital region, 523, 525
  betel nut alkaloids, 458
  with chronic lymphocytic leukemia, 1228
  clear cell, 1209–1210
    sebaceous carcinoma *vs*, 1210, 1583
    trichilemmal carcinoma *vs*, 1210, 1533
  desmoplastic, 1212–1214
  differential diagnosis, 1207–1208
  differentiation, 1204–1207
  discoid lupus erythematosus, 778
  dyskeratosis congenita, 249
  dystrophic epidermolysis bullosa, 96
    Hallopeau–Siemens variant, 90–91, *96*
  eccrine porocarcinoma *vs*, 1208, 1624
  epidermodysplasia verruciformis and, 849, 1203
    HPV, 1204
  follicular occlusion triad, 706
  genital epithelia, 523–526
  Hailey–Hailey disease, 156
  Howell-Evans syndrome, 60, 67–68
  human papilloma virus, 491, 492, 840–841, 1203–1204
    anal, 844
    nails, 1131, 1141, 1142
    penis, 524
  hypertrophic lichen planus *vs*, 224
  in situ *see* Bowen's disease
  keratitis–ichthyosis–deafness syndrome, 72
  keratoacanthoma *vs*, 1225
  leprosy, 913, 1204
  lichen planus
    oral, 218, *219*
    vulval, 219
  lichen sclerosus, 484, *485*
  lupus vulgaris and, 900, *1200*
  metastases, 1506
    actinic keratosis and, 1188
    oral, 1498, 1499
    rates, 1200–1201, 1206, *1207*
  with mucinous metaplasia, 1215, 1217
  nail
    human papilloma virus, 1131, 1141, 1142
    in situ (Bowen's disease), 1141–1142
    invasive, 1142–1143
  necrotizing sialometaplasia *vs*, 450
  neuroendocrine carcinoma with, 1232, *1233*
  oculocutaneous albinism, 999, 1202
  oral, 459–461
    metastases to skin, 1498, 1499
  in oral hybrid tumor, 465
  papillary, 460
    verrucous carcinoma *vs*, 465
    well-differentiated, *460, 461*, 465
  porokeratosis, 76
  proliferating trichilemmal cyst *vs*, 1536
  pseudovascular, 1215–1216
  PUVA therapy, 203–204, 1202
  sarcomatoid, 1759
    genital region, 525
    see also Metaplastic carcinoma
  Schöpf–Schulz–Passarge syndrome, 60
  smokeless tobacco keratosis, 403–404
  spindle cell, 1210–1212, *1213*
    atypical fibroxanthoma *vs*, 1759
  squamoid eccrine ductal carcinoma *vs*, 1658
  variants, 1209–1228
  vitiligo, 994
  see also Adenosquamous carcinoma; Bowen's disease; Keratoacanthoma; Verrucous carcinoma
Squamous cell hyperplasia, 486
Squamous eddies, 1159, *1163*, 1535
Squamous epithelium, epithelial sheath neuroma, 1767
Squamous intraepithelial neoplasia, 455
Squamous papilloma, oral, 410–411
Squamous syringometaplasia, eccrine, 669
Stacked-penny appearance, 1506, *1507*
  primary signet ring carcinoma of eyelid, 1659
Staphylococcal scalded skin syndrome, 872–874
  subcorneal pustular dermatosis *vs*, 213
  toxic epidermal necrolysis *vs*, 243
Staphylococcus aureus, 869, 870
  carriage, 869
  Darier's disease, 158, 159
  HIV infection, 989

staphylococcal scalded skin syndrome, 873
superantigens, 173
Wegener's granulomatosis, 729
Staphylococcus epidermidis, 22, 869
  miliaria, 194
Starburst cells, etoposide, 666
Stasis-associated sclerosing panniculitis, 372–373
Stasis dermatitis, 185, *186*
Stasis ulcers, basal cell carcinoma and, 1168
Steatocystoma, 1572–1574
  vellus hair cyst, 1672
Steatocystoma multiplex suppurativum, 1572
Steatocystoma simplex, 1572
Stem cells, epidermis, 2
Sterile neutrophilic folliculitis, 479, 684
Steroids
  cutaneous atrophy, 1054
  panniculitis syndrome, 360–361
  rosacea-like dermatosis, 1123, *1124*
Steroid sulfatase deficiency *see* Sex-linked ichthyosis
Stevens–Johnson syndrome, 236, 237, 240–244
  cicatricial pemphigoid, 119
  erythema multiforme *vs*, 239
Stewart–Bluefarb syndrome, acroangiodermatitis, 185
Stewart–Treves syndrome, 1840
Still's disease, 691–692
Stomach cancer, tumor metastases to skin, 1498, *1501*
Stomatitis
  atypical gingivostomatitis, 487
  chemotherapeutic agents, 664
  geographic, 400–403
    benign migratory glossitis, 400–403
  lichenoid, 433–438
  nicotinic, 451
  recurrent aphthous, 406–407
  see also Oral lesions; Pyostomatitis vegetans
Stomatitis areata migrans, 400–403
Stomatitis glandularis *see* Cheilitis glandularis
Stomatitis nicotina, 451
Storiform collagenoma, 1711–1712, 1716
  trichilemmoma like, 1530
Storiform pattern, dermatofibrosarcoma protuberans, 1731
Storiform perineural fibroma, 1786–1788
Stratum corneum *see* Keratin layer
Strawberry gingivitis, 442
Strawberry nevus, 1813–1814
Streptococci, group A
  arteritis, 753
  carriage, 869
  HIV infection, 989
  necrotizing fasciitis, 876
Streptococcus pyogenes, 875
  carriage, 869
Stress, alopecia areata and, 1075
Stretch marks *see* Striae distensae
Striae *see* Wickham's striae
Striae alba, 1049
Striae distensae, 1049–1050
  focal elastosis, *1049*
Striae rubra, 1049, *1050*
Striated muscle hamartoma, 1802–1803
Striated muscle tumors, 1802–1806
  see also specific tumors
Striate palmoplantar keratoderma, 62–63
String of beads appearance, 571
Stromal eosinophilia (traumatic ulcerative granuloma), 407, 408–410
Stromelysin, dermatofibrosarcoma protuberans, 1732
STS gene, sex-linked ichthyosis, 40
Stucco keratoses, 1165
  hyperkeratosis lenticularis perstans *vs*, 78, 79
Sturge–Weber syndrome, 1809
Subacute cutaneous lupus erythematosus (SCLE), 782–783, 790, 795–796
Subacute lupus gyratum repens, 265
Subacute necrotizing sialadenitis, 450
Subacute nodular migratory panniculitis (erythema nodosum migrans), 343, 344, 345–347
Subcorneal pustular dermatosis, 212–214
  pustular psoriasis *vs*, 205, 213
Subcorneal pustular dermatosis variant, IgA pemphigus, 154, 155
  see also IgA pemphigus
Subcorneal pustules, 620, 621
Subcutaneous fat, 36
  inflammatory diseases, 341–384
    equestrian cold panniculitis, 274, 275, 353–354
  neonate, 360, 361
Subcutaneous fat necrosis *see* Fat necrosis
Subcutaneous granuloma annulare, 299, 302, *303, 304*
  see also Deep granuloma annulare
Subcutaneous leiomyosarcoma, 1800–1801
Subcutaneous panniculitic T-cell lymphoma, 356, 1415–1418

Subcutaneous panniculitis-like T-cell lymphoma, 356, 1415–1418
Subcutaneous pyogenic granuloma, 1816
Subcutaneous sarcoidosis, 369
Subcutaneous scleroderma, 818
  see also Morphea profunda
Subcutaneous trichoepithelioma, 1553
Subcutaneous Whipple's disease, 357
Subepidermal blistering diseases, 81–138
  bullous systemic lupus erythematosus, 128–130
    cell-rich bullous pemphigoid *vs*, 109
    see also Bullous dermatosis, of SLE
  dermatitis herpetiformis, 131–134
    cell-rich bullous pemphigoid *vs*, 109
    oral lesions, 446
    pemphigus herpetiformis *vs*, 151
  epidermolysis bullosa *see* Epidermolysis bullosa
  epidermolysis bullosa acquisita *see* Epidermolysis bullosa
    acquisita
  immunoperoxidase antigen mapping, 83–84
    bullous pemphigoid, 83, 107
  lichen planus pemphigoides, 115–117, 222, 227
  linear IgA disease, 134–138
    cell-rich bullous pemphigoid *vs*, 109
    drug-induced, 646–648
    oral lesions, 446
  mucous membrane pemphigoid (cicatricial pemphigoid),
    117–122
    drug-induced, 648, 660
    oral, 443–444
  pemphigoid gestationis, 111–115
    pruritic urticarial papules and plaques of pregnancy *vs*,
    281
  split skin immunofluorescence, 81–83
Subepidermal calcified nodule, 597, 598
  see also Cutaneous calculus
Subepidermal fibrosis, nodular *see* Dermatofibroma
Sublingual varicositis, 428
Submucous fibrosis, 458–459
Subpolar leprosy, 914, 916
Subungual enchondroma, 1152
Subungual exostosis, 1150–1151
Subungual fibrokeratoma, 1146–1147
Subungual fibroma, 1147
Subungual keratoacanthoma, 1222, 1225
  squamous cell carcinoma *vs*, 1142–1143
  verrucous carcinoma *vs*, 1144
Subungual keratosis, localized multinucleate distal, 1136
Subungual lentigo, 1137
Subungual lesions, incontinentia pigmenti, 702–703
Subungual melanoma, 1136–1137, 1139–1141, 1312
Subungual metastases, 1145–1146, 1499
Subungual nevus, 1138–1139
Subungual osteochondroma, 1151
Subungual warty dyskeratoma, 1136
Succinate dehydrogenase
  adenoid cystic carcinoma, 1651
  eccrine poroma, 1618, 1619
Sucquet–Hoyer canals, 34, 1848
Sudanese snuff, 403, 404
Sudoriferous acrosyringeal acantholytic disease, 164, 165, 195
Sudoriferous Grover's disease (sudoriferous acrosyringeal
  acantholytic disease), 164, 165, 195
Sudoriferous hamartoma *see* Eccrine nevus
Sudoriferous nevus *see* Eccrine nevus
Sugar icing, splenic capsule, 800
Sulfamethoxazole, AIDS, adverse reactions, 988
Sulfonamides, toxic epidermal necrolysis, 241, 242
Sulfur granules, 923, 924
Sulzberger–Garbe syndrome, 188
Summertime actinic lichenoid eruption (lichen planus actinicus),
  221, 224
Sunbed lentigines, 1248
Sunburn cells, 632
Sunflower-like configuration, intraepidermal neutrophilic
  dermatosis variant, IgA pemphigus, 154
Sunlight damage, 14, 15, 1053–1054
  acantholytic solar keratosis, 144
  actinic granuloma, 313
  actinic keratosis, 1187, 1188
  actinic lichen nitidus, 227
  actinic porokeratosis, 75
  basal cell carcinoma, 1168, 1173
  epidermodysplasia verruciformis, 847–849, 850
  hands, 65
  lichen planus actinicus, 221, 224
  melanocytic nevi, 1251
  melanoma, 1309–1310
  mid-dermal elastolysis, 1048
  polymorphous light eruption, 271
  porphyrias, 576, 578
  reticular erythematous mucinosis, 269
  squamous cell carcinoma, 1199
    immunosuppression and, 1203

transient acantholytic dermatosis, 164
  xeroderma pigmentosum, 1228–1229
Sun's nevus, 1299
Superantigens, 173, 737
Superficial acral fibromyxoma, 1718
Superficial actinic porokeratosis, disseminated, 75
Superficial angiomyxoma, 614, 1856–1857
  neurothekeoma *vs*, 1784
Superficial basal cell carcinoma, 1170, 1171, 1176, *1179*
Superficial blue nevus with prominent intraepidermal dendritic
  melanocytes, 1301–1302
Superficial dermatitis, chronic, 261–263, 1360, *1362*,
  1373–1374
Superficial epidermolysis bullosa simplex *see* Epidermolysis
  bullosa simplex superficialis
Superficial epithelioma with sebaceous differentiation,
  1578
Superficial esophagitis dissecans *see* Esophagitis dissecans
  superficialis
Superficial granulomatous pyoderma, 675, 676–677
Superficial nevus lipomatosus *see* Nevus lipomatosus
  superficialis
Superficial papillary adenomatosis, 1596
Superficial porokeratosis, disseminated, 75
Superficial scaly dermatitis *see* Chronic superficial dermatitis
Superficial spreading melanoma, 1311–1312, 1315–1318
  dysplastic nevus *vs*, 1289
  Paget's disease *vs*, 1517
  sunlight, 1310
Superficial thrombophlebitis, 772
  erythema nodosum *vs*, 347
Superficial ulcerating rheumatoid necrobiosis, 320
Superficial variant, erythema annulare centrifugum, 264
Superinfection, bacteria, tungiasis, 981
Supine alopecia, 1079
Suppurative thrombophlebitis, 772
Sutton's nevus *see* Halo nevus
Suture granuloma, *326*
Sweat duct carcinoma, sclerosing *see* Microcystic adnexal
  carcinoma
Sweat gland(s)
  in lipomas, 1685
  tumors, 1587–1659
  see also Eccrine sweat glands
Sweat gland carcinoma with syringomatous features *see*
  Microcystic adnexal carcinoma
Sweating, 28
  transient acantholytic dermatosis, 164
Swedish snuff, 403, 404
Sweet's syndrome, 679–682
  α₁-antitrypsin deficiency-associated panniculitis, 349
  bowel-associated dermatosis–arthritis *vs*, 683–684
  cutis laxa, 1040
  leukocytoclastic vasculitis *vs*, 715
  necrotizing fasciitis *vs*, 878
  pyoderma gangrenosum *vs*, 677, 680
  sterile neutrophilic folliculitis *vs*, 684
Swimmer's itch, 985
Swimming pool granuloma, 904
Swiss cheese pattern, paraffinoma, 351
Sycosis, 879
Sycosis barbae *see* Pseudofolliculitis
Symblephara, 118
Symmetrical dyschromatosis of the extremities, 1012
Symplastic glomus tumor, 1850
Synapses, Merkel cells, 19
Syncytiotrophoblast, 1509
Syndactyly, focal dermal hypoplasia syndrome, 1029
Synovial cyst
  cutaneous metaplastic, 1678–1679
  see also Myxoid cyst
Synovial metaplasia, 1855–1856
Synovial sarcoma, 1862–1863
  fibrosarcoma *vs*, 1738
  malignant peripheral nerve sheath tumor *vs*, 1793
Syphilids, 494, 500
Syphilis, 494–502
  alopecia *see* Alopecia syphilitica
  endemic (bejel), 494, 891
  HIV infection, 494, 987
  vasculitis, 754
Syringocystadenocarcinma papilliferum, 1592
  tubular apocrine adenoma with, 1594–1595
Syringocystadenoma papilliferum, 1590–1592
  nevus sebaceus with, 1569, *1571*
Syringofibroadenoma, eccrine, 1610–1611
Syringoid eccrine carcinoma, 1645–1647
  see also Eccrine epithelioma
Syringolymphoid hyperplasia, 1383–1384
Syringoma, 1625–1628
  malignant see Microcystic adnexal carcinoma
  microcystic adnexal carcinoma *vs*, 1649
Syringomatous carcinoma *see* Microcystic adnexal carcinoma

Syringometaplasia
  eccrine squamous, 669
  mucinous, 1680–1681
    genital region, 516
Syringosquamous metaplasia, 669
Syringotropic mycosis fungoides, 1383–1384
Systemic amyloidosis, 555–558
Systemic CD30+ T-cell lymphoma, skin involvement, 1403
Systemic contact dermatitis, 177, 179
Systemic hyalinosis, infantile, 397, 1722
Systemic lupus erythematosus, 783–786, 796–800
  alopecia, 784, 1091
  bullous *see* Bullous systemic lupus erythematosus
  calcification, 596–597
  chilblain lupus erythematosus, 276
  drug-induced, 645, 786, 788
  lupus erythematosus profundus, 379
  oral lesions, 447
  papular and nodular cutaneous mucinosis of, 613
  pediatric, 775
  see also Subacute lupus gyratum repens
Systemic mastocytosis, 1491
  cutaneous involvement, 1493
Systemic plasmacytosis, 1443
Systemic sclerosis, 804–815
  morphea and, 812, 815, 818
  progressive
    submucous fibrosis *vs*, 458
    see also Diffuse systemic sclerosis

T

Tactile corpuscles, Merkel cells as, 20
Tadpole appearance
  rhabdomyoblasts, *1805*
  syringoid eccrine carcinoma, *1646*
  syringoma, *1627*
Taenia solium, 986
Takayasu's arteritis, *710*, 751–753
  temporal arteritis *vs*, 750
Tangier disease, 540
Tanko's nodule, 511
Tapered hairs, 1107
Tapir nose, 931
Tar, keratoacanthoma, 1223
Target blue nevus, 1301
Target lesions, 236, 237
Target-like nevus, 1262, *1263*
Targetoid hemosiderotic hemangioma
  retiform hemangioendothelioma *vs*, 1828
  see also Hobnail hemangioma
Tarsal glands (meibomian glands), 20, 1579
Tattoos
  amalgam, 465–466, 671
  graphite, 466
  mercuric sulfide, 663
  sarcoid granulomata, 290–291
Tax proviral DNA, HTLV, mycosis fungoides, 1365
Tay syndrome, 1105
T-cell(s)
  atopic dermatitis, 173
  clonal populations, chronic superficial dermatitis,
    263
  discoid lupus erythematosus, 792–793
  erythema nodosum leprosum, 911
  fixed drug eruptions, 637
  graft-versus-host disease, 250, 252
  helper cells, HIV infection, 986
  Kawasaki syndrome, 737
  lymphocytic infiltrate of the skin, 267
  lymphomatoid drug eruption, 653
  mycosis fungoides, 1365–1366, 1371
  pemphigus, 142
  pityriasis lichenoides, 257
  psoriasis, 201
  recurrent aphthous stomatitis, 407
  sarcoidosis, 293
  systemic lupus erythematosus, 796–800
  systemic sclerosis, 811
  tuberculoid leprosy, 913
T-cell gene rearrangements, pigmented purpuric dermatoses,
  279
T-cell lymphoma, 1359–1427
  classification, *1359*
    EORTC, 1358
  cytophagic histiocytic panniculitis, 354
  HIV-associated large T-cell lymphoma, 1450
  midline destructive disease, 465
  subcutaneous panniculitic, 356, 1415–1418
  'unspecified' category, 1410
T-cell pseudolymphoma
  cutaneous, 1423–1424
  primary cutaneous pleomorphic small/medium-sized T-cell
    lymphoma *vs*, 1411

T-cell receptors, gene mutations
  granulomatous slack skin, 1382
  mycosis fungoides, 1362, 1371–1372
Tear drop lesions, pemphigoid gestationis, 113
TEC locus, focal non-epidermolytic palmoplantar keratoderma
    with esophageal squamous cell carcinoma, 68
Teeth, 387
  focal dermal hypoplasia syndrome, 1029
  incontinentia pigmenti, 703
  minocycline pigmentation, 638
Telangiectasia
  discoid lupus erythematosus, 792, *793*
  generalized essential, 1812
  systemic sclerosis, 805, *806*
  see also Hereditary hemorrhagic telangiectasia
Telangiectasia macularis eruptiva perstans, *1491, 1493, 1494*
Telangiectatic carcinoma, 1502, 1506
Telogen, 1065, 1066
Telogen effluvium, 645, 1083–1086
  alopecia areata *vs*, 1073, 1078–1079
  androgenetic alopecia *vs*, 1070
  HIV infection, 989
  systemic lupus erythematosus, 784
Telomerase, dyskeratosis congenita, 249
Temporal arteritis, *710*, 748–751
Temporal triangular alopecia, 1072–1073
  alopecia areata *vs*, 1078
Temporary wrinkles, 1053
Tendinous xanthomata, 541, 544–545
Tendon sheath
  giant cell tumor, 1752–1754
    acral myxoinflammatory fibroblastic sarcoma, 1735
  see also Fibroma, of tendon sheath
Teratoid cysts, oral, 392
Teratoma
  cutaneous mature cystic, 1673–1674
  oral, 393–394
Terminal hair(s), 1064
  counts by race, *1068*
Terminal hair follicles, 1063
Testes, sex-linked ichthyosis, 39
Testosterone, female androgenetic alopecia, 1070
Tetracyclines, hyperpigmentation, 638
TFIIH (DNA repair factor), 1105
TGM 1 gene (transglutaminase 1 gene), lamellar ichthyosis, 42
Th (antigen), antibodies, systemic sclerosis, *810*
Thalassemias, pseudoxanthoma elasticum, 1044–1045
Thallium, tapered hairs, 1107
T-helper cells, HIV infection, 986
Thermoregulation, 34
Thibierge-Weissenbach syndrome (CREST syndrome), 804,
    805–806
Thiol drugs, drug-induced pemphigus, 155, 648
Thio-TEPA, patterned hyperpigmentation, 665, 666
Thrombi, calcification, sialolithiasis *vs*, 449
Thromboangiitis obliterans, 747–748
Thrombocytopenia
  hemorrhagic fevers, 869
  HIT syndrome, 659
  idiopathic angiosarcoma of head and neck, 1839
Thrombocytopenic purpura
  immune, 770
  thrombotic, 768–769
Thrombophlebitis
  superficial, 772
    erythema nodosum *vs*, 347
  warfarin necrosis, 658
Thrombosis
  Behçet's disease, 686
  deep vein thrombosis, factor V Leiden mutation, 771
  HIT syndrome, 659
Thrombotic thrombocytopenic purpura, 768–769
Thymic cyst, cervical, 1675–1676
Thymidine, DNA repair study, 1229
Thymoma, pemphigus erythematosis, 152
Thymus, systemic lupus erythematosus, 800
Thyroglossal duct cyst, 1675
Thyroid
  Carney complex, 1014
  function, hair diseases, 1062
  lingual, 394–395
  papillary carcinoma, skin metastases, 1508, *1509*
Thyroiditis, Hashimoto's, reticular erythematous mucinosis, 269
Thyroid stimulating hormone receptor, pretibial myxedema, 604
Thyroid transcription factor, skin metastases, 1504
Tibia, yaws, *893*
Tick-borne neningopolyneuritis, 889
Tick typhus, 928, 929
Timber grain pattern, erythema gyrata repens, 265
Tinea barbae, 939
Tinea capitis, 938–941
  alopecia areata *vs*, 1078
Tinea corporis, 942, *943*

Tinea cruris, 943, 944
Tinea gladiatorum, 942
Tinea incognito, 180, 942, *943*
Tinea nigra, 947
Tinea pedis, 943, 944
Tinea versicolor, 945–947
Tissue-paper scarring, 1023
Tissue transglutaminase antibodies, dermatitis herpetiformis, 132
TNFRSF1A gene mutation, 285
Toad skin, 55
Tobacco
  leukoplakia, 452
  oral cancer, 459
  see also Smokeless tobacco keratosis; Smoking
Tobacco cells, 388
Toenails, Naegele–Franchescetti–Jadassohn syndrome, 1010
Toker cells, 4, 1514
Tombstone pattern, pemphigus, 142, *143*
Tonofilaments, 9
  amyloid from, 562
  Hailey–Hailey disease, 158
  loss in epidermolysis bullosa simplex, 93–94
Tonsils
  cartilaginous rests, 391
  ectopic oral, 394
Toombak (Sudanese snuff), 403, 404
Tophi, 590
TORCH syndrome, 858
Torre–Muir syndrome, 1584–1586
  benign sebaceous lesions, 1577
  keratoacanthoma, 1222
  sebaceous adenoma, 1574, 1584
  sebaceous carcinoma, 1580
Torticollis, fibromatosis colli, 1713
Torulopsis glabrata, 950
Torulosis *see* Cryptococcosis
Touch domes of Pinkus, Merkel cells as, 20
Touton giant cells, 1470–1471
  necrobiotic xanthogranuloma, 319
  xanthoma disseminatum, *1478*
Toxemic rash of pregnancy *see* Pruritic urticarial papules and
    plaques of pregnancy
Toxic epidermal necrolysis, 236, 237, 240–244, 874
  erythema multiforme *vs*, 239, 243–244
  graft-versus-host disease, 242, 250, 254
  overlap with Stevens–Johnson syndrome, 237
Toxic erythema, 263–267
  erythema annulare centrifugum, 263–265
    tumid lupus erythematosus *vs*, 274
  erythema gyrata repens, 265–267
  of the neonate, 214, 705
    incontinentia pigmenti *vs*, 704, 705
  of the palms and soles, 667
  of pregnancy *see* Pruritic urticarial papules and plaques of
    pregnancy
Toxicity, cumulative, 624
Toxic oil syndrome, 824
Toxic pustuloderma, 651
Toxic shock syndrome, Kawasaki syndrome *vs*, 737
Toxins
  anthrax, 882
  Staphylococcus aureus, 873, 874
  verotoxin, hemolytic uremic syndrome, 769
Trabecular carcinoma *see* Neuroendocrine carcinoma
Trabecular pattern, neuroendocrine carcinoma, 1232, *1233*
Trachyonychia, 1134–1135
  alopecia areata, 1074, *1075*, 1078
Traction alopecia, 1079–1080
Transepidermal elimination
  calcium, tumoral calcinosis, *598*
  collagen
    chondrodermatitis nodularis chronica helicis, 338
    necrobiosis lipoidica, 308
    perforating granuloma annulare, 299
    prurigo nodularis, 330
    reactive perforating collagenosis, 328
  elastic fibers
    elastosis perforans serpiginosa, 333
    keratoacanthoma, 1224
    perforating pseudoxanthoma elasticum, 337
  nests, lentiginous acral nevus, 1260
Transfollicular penetration, pseudofolliculitis, 1125
Transforming growth factor β
  keloid, 1701
  nephrogenic fibrosing dermopathy, 1034
  systemic sclerosis, 810
Transglutaminase 1 gene, lamellar ichthyosis, 42
Transient acantholytic dermatosis (Grover's disease), 164–166
  Darier's disease *vs*, 162–163, 165
  pemphigus *vs*, 143, 144, 165
  with prominent eccrine ductal involvement, 195
  scabies and, 981
Transient bullous dermolysis of the newborn, 92, 97

Transient neonatal pustular melanosis, 215
Transit-amplifying cells, epidermis, 2
Transplantation *see* Bone marrow transplantation; Organ
    transplantation
Transverse striate leukonychia, 664
TRAPS (tumor necrosis factor receptor-associated periodic
    syndrome), 285, 756
Trauma
  alopecia *see* Trichotillomania
  chondrodermatitis nodularis chronica helicis, 338
  cutaneous metaplastic synovial cyst, 1678
  epidermoid cyst, 1664
  pyoderma gangrenosum, 674
  reactive perforating collagenosis, 328
  sarcoid granuloma, 290–291
  subungual exostosis, 1151
  warty dyskeratoma, 390
Traumatic fat necrosis, 351, 352, *353, 1685*
Traumatic neuroma, 1763–1764
Traumatic panniculitis, 351–353
Traumatic ulcerative granuloma, 407, 408–410
Traumatic ulcers, recurrent aphthous stomatitis *vs*, 407
Tree bark-like appearance, lichen simplex chronicus, 182
Trematodes *see* Schistosomiasis
Trench fever, 885
Treponema pallidum, 499
Treponematoses
  endemic, 891–894
  see also Syphilis
Triangular alopecia, temporal, 1072–1073
  alopecia areata *vs*, 1078
Trichiasis, mucous membrane pemphigoid, 118
Trichilemmal carcinoma, 1531–1533
  clear cell squamous cell carcinoma *vs*, 1210, 1533
Trichilemmal cyst, 1670–1671, *1672*
  hybrid with epidermoid cyst, 1664, 1667
  proliferating, 1533–1536
  see also Pilar cyst
Trichilemmal keratosis, 1531
Trichilemmoma, 1527–1530
  desmoplastic, 1530–1531
  keratinizing, 1528
Trichoadenoma, 1526
  microcystic adnexal carcinoma *vs*, 1649
Trichoblastic carcinoma, 1553
Trichoblastic fibroma, 1552, 1553–1554
  plaque variant, 1553
Trichoblastoma, 1552–1557
  with adamantinoid features, 1558
    see also Cutaneous lymphadenoma
  nevus sebaceus and, 1569, *1570, 1571*
  sebaceoma *vs*, 1577
Trichoclasis, 1106
Trichodiscoma, 1561–1562
  mantleoma *vs*, 1586
Trichoepithelioma, 1546–1550
  basaloid follicular hamartoma *vs*, 1523
  Brooke–Spiegler syndrome, 1636
  giant solitary, 1553
  trichoblastoma *vs*, 1557
  see also Desmoplastic trichoepithelioma
Trichofolliculoma, 1542–1543
  sebaceous, 1545–1546
Trichogenic trichoblastoma, 1552
Trichogenic tumors
  cytokeratins, 1557
  nomenclature, 1552–1553
Trichogerminoma, 1553, 1555
Trichogram (hair-pluck test), 1062
Trichoids, 1542
Trichomalacia, 1077, 1081
Trichomycosis, 925–926
Trichonodosis, 1115–1116
Trichophyton (spp.), 938
Trichophyton interdigitale, 944
Trichophyton mentagrophytes, 939
Trichophyton rubrum, 944
Trichophyton schoenleinii, 941
Trichophyton tonsurans, 940, 942
Trichophyton verrucosum, 939
Trichophyton violaceum, 940
Trichoptilosis, 1104, 1107–1108
  pili bifurcati *vs*, 1108, 1109
Trichorrhexis invaginata (bamboo hair), 1106–1107
  Netherton syndrome, 51, *52*, 1106
Trichorrhexis nodosa, 1104–1105
Trichoschisis, 1106, *1107*
Trichosporon beigelii, 941
Trichostasis spinulosa, 1110
Trichothiodystrophy, 1105–1106
Trichotillomania, 1079–1082, *1083*
  alopecia areata *vs*, 1078, 1081
  androgenetic alopecia *vs*, 1071

Trichrome vitiligo, 993–994
Trimethoprim, AIDS, adverse reactions, 988
Tripe palms, 615, *616*, 617
Trisomy 9, pilomatrixomas, 1536
Triton tumor, malignant, 1793
Trophozoites
   Acanthameba spp., 935
   Entamoeba histolytica, 934–935
Tropocollagen, 29
Tryptophan
   peak E commercial L-tryptophan, eosinophilia–myalgia
      syndrome, 824
   pellagra, 594
TSC gene mutations, 1031
TTG antibodies (tissue transglutaminase antibodies), dermatitis
   herpetiformis, 132
Tuberculids, 902–904
Tuberculoid leprosy (TT), 910, 913, 914
   Mitsuda reaction, 912
Tuberculosis, 894–904
   AIDS, 991
   differential diagnosis, 900–901
   erythema induratum, 366, 367
   hematogenous, 896–897, 899
   infections by inoculation, 895–896, *899*
   pathogenesis, 897–900
   secondary (endogenous), 896
   syphilis *vs*, 501
   vasculitis, 753
Tuberous bromoderma, 657
Tuberous sclerosis, 1030–1033
   subungual fibroma, 1147
Tuberous xanthomata, 541, 545–547
Tubular apocrine adenoma, 1594–1595
   see also Apocrine adenoma
Tubuloalveolar foci, mixed tumor of skin, 1601
Tubulopapillary hidradenoma *see* Tubular apocrine adenoma
Tubuloreticular bodies, lupus erythematosus, 790
Tubuloreticular structures, reticular erythematous
   mucinosis, 270
Tufted angioblastoma, 1814–1815
Tufted folliculitis, 1089, 1099–1103
   pili multigemini *vs*, 1109
   see also Polytrichia
Tularemia, 927–928
Tumeur d'emblée mycosis fungoides (Vidal Brocq), 1360, 1376
Tumid lupus erythematosus, 273–274, 778, 794
Tumoral calcinosis, 597–598, *600*
Tumor angiogenesis, melanoma, 1324, 1330
Tumor-infiltrating lymphocytes, melanoma, 1322–1323
Tumor-like oral conditions, 413–430
   denture-associated fibrous hyperplasia, 416–417
      cartilaginous choristoma *vs*, 391
      see also Epulis fissuratum
   fibroma, 413–414, 418
      giant cell, 414–415
      gingival, 418
   generalized gingival hyperplasia, 426–428
   giant cell fibroma, 414–415
   gingival cyst of the adult, 425–426
   gingival fibroma, 418
   gingival nodules, 417–418
   lipoma, 415–416
   parulis, 422
      mucocele *vs*, 448
   peripheral giant cell granuloma, 418, 421–422
   peripheral odontogenic fibroma, 422–425
   peripheral ossifying fibroma, 418, 420–421
   pyogenic granuloma, 418, 419–420
   varices, 428–430
Tumor necrosis factor 1, pemphigus, 142
Tumor necrosis factor α, graft-versus-host disease, 252–253
Tumor necrosis factor receptor-associated periodic syndrome,
   285, 756
Tumor stage mycosis fungoides, 1370–1372, *1373*
Tumor suppressor gene p53 *see* P53 (tumor suppressor gene)
Tungiasis, 981, *982*
Tunica dartos labialis, 474
Turban tumor syndrome *see* Brooke–Spiegler syndrome
Turner syndrome, pilomatrixomas, 1536
Twenty-nail dystrophy *see* Trachyonychia
Twin gestation, pruritic urticarial papules and plaques of
   pregnancy (PUPPP), 280
Tylosis, 60–61
Type A nevus cells, 1252
Type B nevus cells, 1254
Type C nevus cells, 1255
Typhus fevers, 928, 929
Tyrosinase, 14
Tyrosinase positive oculocutaneous albinism, 1000
Tzanck test, 854
   staphylococcal scalded skin syndrome, 874

U
Ulcer(s)
   aplasia cutis, 1028
   chondrodermatitis nodularis chronica helicis, 338
   ecthyma, 871, *872*
   HIV infection, 989
   leishmaniasis, 929–930
   of Lipschutz, 488
   Marjolin's, *1202*, 1204
   melanoma staging, 1322
   Mycobacterium ulcerans, 906
   necrobiosis lipoidica, 305
   pyoderma gangrenosum, 673, *674*
   snail track, *498*
   systemic sclerosis, *806*
   tuberculosis, orificial, 896, 899
   tularemia, 928
   varicose dermatitis, 185
   venous stasis, basal cell carcinoma and, 1168
Ulcerative basal cell carcinoma (rodent ulcer), 1169, 1176
Ulcerative colitis, erythema elevatum diutinum, 740
Ulcerative lichen planus, 222
   oral, 433
Ulcerative oral conditions, 406–410
   chronic ulcerative stomatitis, 436–437
   recurrent aphthous stomatitis, 406–407
   traumatic ulcerative granuloma, 407, 408–410
Ulcerative stomatitis, chronic, 436–437
Ulceroglandular tularemia, 928
Ulerythema acneiforme, 57, 58
Ulerythema ophryogenes, 57, 58
Ultraviolet light *see* PUVA therapy; UV radiation
Umbilicus
   granuloma, 1681–1682
   polyp, 1681–1682
   tumor metastases to, 1499, *1500*
   see also Periumbilical pseudoxanthoma elasticum
Uncein, 19-DEJ-1 antibody *vs*, junctional epidermolysis bullosa
   and, 93
'Uncertain' vascular invasion, melanoma, 1343
Uncombable hair syndrome, 1108–1109
Undifferentiated vulvar intraepithelial neoplasia, 522
Unilateral Darier's disease *see* Linear Darier's disease
Unilateral hyperhidrosis, localized, 1609
Unilateral linear basal cell nevus syndrome, 1185
Unilateral linear eccrine syringofibroadenoma
   non-familial, 1610
Unilesional mycosis fungoides, 1393
Unna-Thost palmoplantar keratoderma, 60–61
Urachal sinus or cyst, 1681
Urethroid cyst (median raphe cyst), 516–517, 1677, *1678*
Uric acid, 590
URO-D (uroporphyrinogen decarboxylase), defects, 579
Uroplakin III, Paget's disease, 1517
Uroporphyrin I, *576*
Uroporphyrinogen decarboxylase, defects, 579
URO-synthase gene, 577
Urticaria, 692–696
   drug reactions, 624, 625, 629, 694
   Muckle–Wells syndrome, 559
   pruritic urticarial papules and plaques of pregnancy *vs*, 281
   see also Pruritic urticarial papules and plaques of pregnancy
Urticarial angioedema, 694
Urticarial bullous pemphigoid, 100
Urticarial vasculitis, 282–284, 694, 695, 719–720
Urticaria pigmentosa, 1492, *1493*, *1494*
UVA-induced cutaneous erythema, 1057–1058
Uveitis, sarcoidosis, 292
Uveoparotid fever (Heerfordt's syndrome), 292
UV radiation, 1055, 1057–1058
   acne vulgaris, 1118
   actinic keratosis, 1188
   atypical fibroxanthoma, 1757
   basal cell carcinoma, 1173
   Cockayne's syndrome, 248
   drug reactions, 630
   erythema, reactivation by chemotherapeutic agents, 665
   gold toxicity, 661
   keratoacanthoma, 1223
   lentigines, 1248
   lupus erythematosus, 790
   melanin as protection, 13–14
   melanoma, 1309–1310
   mid-dermal elastolysis, 1048
   molecular biology, 1202–1203
   neuroendocrine carcinoma, 1231
   polymorphous light eruption, 271
   pseudoporphyria, 649
   squamous cell carcinoma, 1202–1203
   xeroderma pigmentosum, 1228–1229
   see also PUVA therapy; Sunlight
UV signature, p53 mutations, 1173, 1202

V
Vaccination, smallpox, 860
   see also Eczema vaccinatum
Vaccines, aluminum granuloma, 327
Vaccinia, 860
Vacuolated keratinocytes *see* Koilocytes
Valley fever, 959
Valvular heart disease
   lupus anticoagulant syndrome, 785
   systemic lupus erythematosus, 799
Vancomycin, linear IgA disease, 646, 647
   epidermolysis bullosa acquisita, 648
Varicella, 855–856, 858
Varicella-zoster virus, 855, 858
   HIV infection, 857
Varices
   oral, 428–430
   see also Venous lakes
Varicose dermatitis, 185, *186*
Varicose veins, spindle cell hemangioma with, 1826
Variegate porphyria, 575, *576*, 582–583
Variola, 860, *861*, *862*, 869
Vascular cell adhesion molecule-1 (VCAM-1)
   polymorphous light eruption, 272
   psoriasis, 201
Vascular channels
   epithelioid hemangioma, 1823–1824
   Kaposi's sarcoma, 1833
   multinucleate cell angiohistiocytoma, 1742
   myopericytoma, 1852
   papillary intralymphatic angioendothelioma, 1829
   in radiotherapy fields, 1847
   spindle cell hemangioma, 1826–1827
Vascular Ehlers–Danlos syndrome (type IV), 1024–1025, *1026*
Vascular endothelial growth factor, melanoma, 1330
Vascular invasion
   melanoma, *1326*
   'uncertain', 1343
   veins, 1343
   tumors metastasizing to skin, 1499
   see also headings beginning Intravascular...
Vascular plexuses, 32–33
Vascular poikiloderma atrophicans *see* Poikiloderma
   atrophicans vasculare
Vascular tumors, 1806–1852
   see also specific tumors
Vasculitis, 709–773
   Behçet's disease, 686
   dermatomyositis, 828
   drug reactions, 642–643
   erythema nodosum, 345
   leprosy, 753, 916
   nodular, 366–369
   palisaded neutrophilic and granulomatous dermatitis with,
      312, 755–756
   pyoderma gangrenosum, 677
   rickettsial infections, 753–754, 929
   sarcoidosis, 292
   sterile neutrophilic folliculitis *vs*, 685
   systemic lupus erythematosus, 784
   urticarial, 282–284, 694, 695, 719–720
   see also Leukocytoclastic vasculitis; Livedoid vasculitis
Vasculopathy
   calcification, 597
   collagenous, 1812
   necrobiosis lipoidica, 306, 308
   necrotizing sialometaplasia, 450
Vegetant bromoderma, 657
Vegetant pemphigus *see* Pemphigus vegetans
Vegetant pyostomatitis *see* Pyostomatitis vegetans
Vegetative variant of pyoderma gangrenosum, 675, 676–677
VEGFR-3
   hobnail hemangioma, 1822
   papillary intralymphatic angioendothelioma, 1829
Veil cells, 34
Vein(s)
   leprosy, 916
   melanoma invasion, 1343
   varicose, spindle cell hemangioma with, 1826
Vein graft site dermatitis, 188
Vellus hair(s), 1063, 1064
   counts by race, *1068*
   retention, trichostasis spinulosa, 1110
Vellus hair cysts, 1671–1673
Vellus hamartoma, 1519–1520
Venous lakes, 1811, *1812*
   see also Varices
Venous stasis
   sclerosing panniculitis, 372
   ulcers, basal cell carcinoma and, 1168

Venules
  Behçet's disease, 745
  microvenular hemangioma, 1820
  postcapillary, 34
Vernix-like covering, keratitis–ichthyosis–deafness syndrome, 72
Verocay bodies, 1768
Verotoxin, hemolytic uremic syndrome, 769
Verruca vulgaris *see* Wart(s)
Verruciform acrokeratosis *see* Acrokeratosis verruciformis
Verruciform epidermodysplasia *see* Epidermodysplasia
    verruciformis
Verruciform xanthoma, 412–413, 549–550
Verrucous carcinoma, 1218–1221
  anogenital, 526–527
    see also Giant condyloma acuminatum
  nail, 1143–1144
    keratoacanthoma *vs*, 1145
    squamous cell carcinoma *vs*, 1143, 1144
  oral, 464–465
  plantar warts, 842
  verruciform xanthoma *vs*, 550
Verrucous compound nevus, *1255*
Verrucous cyst, 1667
Verrucous discoid lupus erythematosus, 777–778, *780, 781*
Verrucous epidermal nevus, inflammatory linear, 210–211
Verrucous hemangioma, 1815
  angiokeratoma *vs*, 1813, 1815
Verrucous hyperkeratotic bowenoid plaques, 1195
Verrucous hyperplasia, oral, 455
Verrucous lesions, incontinentia pigmenti, 702, 703
Verrucous leukoplakia, 452
  proliferative, 453, 455–456
Verrucous mycosis fungoides, 1393
Verrucous nevoid melanoma, 1332
Verrucous nevus *see* Nevus verrucosus
Verrucous trichoadenoma, 1526
Verruga peruana, 886
Vertical growth phase, melanoma, 1313, 1321
Verticillate cornea, angiokeratoma corporis diffusum, 551
Very low density lipoproteins, 540, *541, 542*
Vesicles, 81
  congenital self-healing histiocytosis, 1467
  sago-grain-like, dyshidrosiform dermatitis, 101
  see also Blistering; Bullae
Vesicular pemphigoid, 100, 104, *105, 106*
Vesiculobullous mycosis fungoides, 1390–1391
Vesiculobullous systemic lupus erythematosus *see* Bullous
    systemic lupus erythematosus
Vestibular dysesthesia, 509–510
Vestibular papillomatosis, 476
Vestibule, 475
  adenoma of minor vestibular glands, 530
  mucinous cyst, 517
  skin, *4*
Vestibulitis, 509–510
  as chronic pain syndrome, 509
Villefranche classification, Ehlers–Danlos syndrome, 1023, *1024*
VIN *see* Vulva, intraepithelial neoplasia
Vinyl chloride, scleroderma-like syndrome, 808
Violaceous border, morphea lesion, 816
Viral infections, 838–869
  erythema multiforme, 238
  exanthemata, 285
  hemorrhagic fevers, 868–869
  lupus erythematosus and, 790
  morphea, 818
  mycosis fungoides, 1364–1365
  papular acrodermatitis of childhood, 189
  polymyositis, 828
  see also Wart(s); *specific viruses*
Virus-associated hemophagocytosis syndrome, 1415,
    1487–1488
Visceral leishmaniasis, 931–932
Vitamin A, pityriasis rubra pilaris and, 208
Vitamin deficiencies, phrynoderma, 55
Vitelline duct, 1681
Vitiligo, 993–997
  idiopathic guttate hypomelanosis *vs*, 998
Vitiligo-spasticity syndrome, 995
Vitreous layer, anagen hair follicle, 1065
Vogt–Koyanagi–Harada disease, 997–998
Vohwinkel syndrome, 70–71
Von Hansemann cells, 922
Von Kossa stain
  calcinosis, 598, *599*
  malakoplakia, 922
Von Recklinghausen's neurofibromatosis *see* Neurofibromatosis,
    type I
Von Willebrand factor, systemic sclerosis, 809

Von Willebrand factor-cleaving protease deficiency, 769
Von Zumbusch disease (generalized pustular psoriasis),
    195–197, 202–203
Vorner's disease, 59–60
Vulva
  anatomy, 473, 474
  chronic purpura, 487
  classification of disorders, 473
  cloacogenic carcinoma, 528–529
  intraepithelial neoplasia (VIN), 519, 520, 521
    undifferentiated, 522
  leiomyoma, 536, 1799
  leiomyomatosis, 537
  leiomyosarcoma, 536
  lichen planus, squamous cell carcinoma, 219
  lipoblastoma-like tumor, 1693
  melanoma, 514–515
  nevus, 512
  Paget's disease, 1515
  squamous cell carcinoma, 523
  syringoma, 1626
  vestibular papillomatosis, 476
  see also Vestibule; *headings beginning* Genital...
Vulvitis, Zoon's, 438, 487–488
Vulvodynia *see* Vestibulitis
Vulvovaginal gingival syndrome, 219, 434, 480, *481, 482*
Vulvovaginitis, candidal, 948

W

Waardenburg's syndrome, 1003–1004
Waldenström's hypergammaglobulinemic purpura, 771
Waldenström's macroglobulinemia, cutaneous
    macroglobulinosis, 574–575
Warfarin, 658–659
Wart(s) (verruca vulgaris), 838–841
  AIDS, 990
  nails, 1131–1132
    squamous cell carcinoma and, 1141, 1142–1143
  oral squamous papilloma *vs*, 410–411
  plane *see* Plane warts
  plantar, 840, 841–843
    verruciform xanthoma *vs*, 550
    verrucous carcinoma and, 1219, 1220
Warthin's tumor, mucocele *vs*, 448
Warty carcinoma, penis, 524
Warty dyskeratoma, 166–168
  Darier's disease *vs*, 162
  oral lesions, 167, 390
  subungual, 1136
Warty lupus, 895–896, 899
Watering can perineum, 506–507, 985
'Wear and tear' dermatitis, 176
Weber–Christian disease, 348
  cytophagic histiocytic panniculitis as, 354
  see also Hemophagocytic T-cell lymphoma
Weber–Cockayne variant, epidermolysis bullosa simplex, 85–86
Wegener's granulomatosis, *710*, 727–731
  Churg–Strauss syndrome *vs*, 734
  lymphomatoid granulomatosis *vs*, 1440
  oral lesions, 442–443
  orofacial granulomatosis *vs*, 441
  vasculitis, 709
Weibel–Palade bodies, 33
  angiosarcoma, 1843
Weil–Felix test, 929
Wells' syndrome (eosinophilic cellulitis), 697–699
  arthropod bite reactions *vs*, 689
Werner's syndrome, 1055
Wet leishmaniasis, 930
Wheals (hives), 692
Whipple's disease, 357
Whisker hair, 1115
White fibrous papulosis, 1036–1037
  eruptive collagenoma *vs*, 1038
  pseudoxanthoma elasticum-like papillary dermal elastolysis
    vs, 1037, 1048
Whiteheads
  acne vulgaris, 1118
  see also Open comedones
White piedra, 925, 941
Whites, hair counts, *1068*
White sponge nevus, 387–388
Whitlow, herpetic, 851
WHO classification, lymphoma, 1358
Wickham's striae
  graft-versus-host disease, 251
  lichen planus, 218, 223
    genital, 480
    papular oral, 433

Widow spiders, 689
Wild fire (fogo selvagem), 148
Wilson's disease, acanthosis nigricans, 615
Wire-loop lesions, systemic lupus erythematosus, 798, 799
Wiskott–Aldrich syndrome, 173
Witten and Zak syndrome, 1222
Wnt signaling cascade
  basal cell carcinoma and, 1173
  pilomatrix carcinoma, 1540
  pilomatrixoma, 1536
Wood's light *see* Fluorescence; UV radiation
Woolly hair, 1114–1115
  keratosis pilaris atrophicans, 58
Woolly hair nevus, 1114, 1520
Woringer–Kolopp disease, 1393
World Health Organization classification, lymphoma, 1358
Worm-eaten appearance, 58
Wound healing, nephrogenic fibrosing dermopathy
    similarity, 1034
Wreath-like giant cells, alveolar rhabdomyosarcoma, 1804
Wrinkled tissue appearance, lichen sclerosus, *485*
Wrinkle free mouse, 1036
WRN gene and protein, 1055

X

Xanthelasmata, 547
Xanthogranuloma, 1468–1473
  reticulohistiocytoma *vs*, 1471–1472, 1483
  scalloped cell, 1476
  spindle cell, 1475
  see also Necrobiotic xanthogranuloma
Xanthoma, 539, 540–541
  balloon cell melanoma *vs*, 1338
  eruptive, 542–544
    Rosai–Dorfman disease *vs*, 1480
  intertriginous, 547
  papular, 1475–1476
  planar, 547–549
  progressive papular, 1476
  tendinous, 541, 544–545
  tuberous, 541, 545–547
  verruciform, 412–413, 549–550
  xanthogranuloma *vs*, 1471
Xanthoma cells, 539
  lipidized fibrous histiocytoma, *1751*
  verruciform xanthoma, 412
Xanthoma disseminatum, 1476–1479
  Langerhans' cell histiocytosis *vs*, 1465
  papular xanthoma *vs*, 1476
Xanthoma striatum palmare, 547
Xanthomatosis
  cerebrotendinous, 541
  diffuse plane, 547
Xanthomatous disorders *see* Hyperlipidemias
X chromosome, incontinentia pigmenti, 702, 703
Xeroderma pigmentosum, 1228–1230
  squamous cell carcinoma, 1202
Xerosis, 37
  HIV infection, 988, 989
X-linked anhidrotic ectodermal dysplasia, 1566
X-linked chronic granulomatous disease, 781
X-linked ichthyosis, *38*
  see also Sex-linked ichthyosis
X-linked infantile hypogammaglobulinemia, 327
X-linked reticulate pigmentary disorder, 564
XPB gene mutations, 1105
XPD gene mutations, 1105
XP genes, 1229

Y

Yaws, 892–894
Yellow fever, 868, 869
Yellow mutant, oculocutaneous albinism, 999
Yellow River disease (Katayama disease), 506, 985

Z

Zebra-like pattern, erythema gyrata repens, 265
Zeis, glands of, 20, 1579
Zellballen, trichogerminoma, 1555
Zimmerman–Laband syndrome, gingival fibromatosis, 396
Zinc deficiency, 617–618
Zirconium, 324–325
Zoon's balanitis/vulvitis, 438, 487–488
Zoster, 856–857, 858
Zosteriform Darier's disease, 1155
  see also Linear Darier's disease
Zosteriform metastases, 1501
Zygomycosis, 963–965
  panniculitis, *371*